GW00646336

The Form Book ®

FLAT ANNUAL FOR 2012

THE OFFICIAL FORM BOOK

ALL THE 2011 RETURNS

Complete record of Flat Racing
from 1 January to 31 December 2011

Associated Raceform products

The Form Book, is updated weekly. Subscribers receive a binder, together with all the early racing. Weekly sections and a new index are threaded into the binder to keep it up to date.

The data contained in The Form Book Flat Annual for 2012 is available in paper form or on computer disk. The disk service, Raceform Interactive, contains the same data as Raceform, The Form Book, and operates on any PC within a 'Windows' environment. The database is designed to allow access to the information in a number of different ways, and is extremely quick and easy to use.

Published in 2012 by Raceform Ltd
Compton, Newbury, Berkshire, RG20 6NL

A catalogue record for this book is available from the British Library,

ISBN 978-1-906820-88-6

Printed and bound by CPI Group (UK) Ltd, Croydon, CR0 4YY

Full details of all Raceform services and publications are available from:

Raceform Ltd, Compton, Newbury, Berkshire RG20 6NL
Tel: 01933 304858 • Fax: 01933 270300
Email: rfsubscription@racingpost.co.uk
www.racingpost.com

Cover photo: Frankel (Tom Queally) wins the
Queen Elizabeth II Stakes at Ascot October 2011
© Edward Whitaker/Racing Post

CONTENTS

Editor: Graham Dench

Head of Analysis Team: Ashley Rumney

Race Analysts & Notebook Writers:
Gavin Beech, Dave Bellingham, Mark Brown, Steffan Edwards,
Walter Glynn, Jeremy Grayson, Niall Hannity, David Lawrence,
Richard Lowther, Lee McKenzie, Tim Mitchell,
Dave Moon, Graeme North, Sandra Noble, David Orton,
Ashley Rumney, Anthony Rushmer, Andrew Sheret,
Steve Taylor, David Toft, Ron Wood, Richard Young.

Production: Ashley Rumney

The Official Scale of Weight, Age & Distance (Flat)

The following scale should only be used in conjunction with the Official ratings published in this book. Use of any other scale will introduce errors into calculations. The allowances are expressed as the number of pounds that is deemed the average horse in each group falls short of maturity at different dates and distances.

Dist		Jan		Feb		Mar		Apr		May		Jun		Jul		Aug		Sep		Oct		Nov		Dec	
(fur)	Age	1-15	16-31	1-14	15-28	1-15	16-31	1-15	16-30	1-15	16-31	1-15	16-30	1-15	16-31	1-15	16-31	1-15	16-30	1-15	16-31	1-15	16-30	1-15	16-31
5	2	-	-	-	-	-	47	44	41	38	36	34	32	30	28	26	24	22	20	19	18	17	17	16	16
	3	15	15	14	14	13	12	11	10	9	8	7	6	5	4	3	2	1	1	-	-	-	-	-	-
6	2	-	-	-	-	-	-	-	-	44	41	38	36	33	31	28	26	24	22	21	20	19	18	17	17
	3	16	16	15	15	14	13	12	11	10	9	8	7	6	5	4	3	2	2	1	1	-	-	-	-
7	2	-	-	-	-	-	-	-	-	-	-	-	-	38	35	32	30	27	25	23	22	21	20	19	19
	3	18	18	17	17	16	15	14	13	12	11	10	9	8	7	6	5	4	3	2	2	1	1	-	-
8	2	-	-	-	-	-	-	-	-	-	-	-	-	-	-	37	34	31	28	26	24	23	22	21	20
	3	20	20	19	19	18	17	15	14	13	12	11	10	9	8	7	6	5	4	3	3	2	2	1	1
9	3	22	22	21	21	20	19	17	15	14	13	12	11	10	9	8	7	6	5	4	4	3	3	2	2
	4	1	1	-	-	-	-	-	-	-	-	-	-	-	-	-	-	-	-	-	-	-	-	-	-
10	3	23	23	22	22	21	20	19	17	15	14	13	12	11	10	9	8	7	6	5	5	4	4	3	3
	4	2	2	1	1	-	-	-	-	-	-	-	-	-	-	-	-	-	-	-	-	-	-	-	-
11	3	24	24	23	23	22	21	20	19	17	15	14	13	12	11	10	9	8	7	6	6	5	5	4	4
	4	3	3	2	2	1	1	-	-	-	-	-	-	-	-	-	-	-	-	-	-	-	-	-	-
12	3	25	25	24	24	23	22	21	20	19	17	15	14	13	12	11	10	9	8	7	7	6	6	5	5
	4	4	4	3	3	2	2	1	1	-	-	-	-	-	-	-	-	-	-	-	-	-	-	-	-
13	3	26	26	25	25	24	23	22	21	20	19	17	15	14	13	12	11	10	9	8	8	7	7	6	6
	4	5	5	4	4	3	3	2	1	-	-	-	-	-	-	-	-	-	-	-	-	-	-	-	-
14	3	27	27	26	26	25	24	23	22	21	20	19	17	15	14	13	12	11	10	9	9	8	8	7	7
	4	6	6	5	5	4	4	3	2	1	-	-	-	-	-	-	-	-	-	-	-	-	-	-	-
15	3	28	28	27	27	26	25	24	23	22	21	20	19	17	15	14	13	12	11	10	9	8	8	7	7
	4	6	6	5	5	4	4	3	3	2	1	-	-	-	-	-	-	-	-	-	-	-	-	-	-
16	3	29	29	28	28	27	26	25	24	23	22	21	20	19	17	15	14	13	12	11	10	9	9	8	8
	4	7	7	6	6	5	5	4	4	3	2	1	-	-	-	-	-	-	-	-	-	-	-	-	-
18	3	31	31	30	30	29	28	27	26	25	24	23	22	21	20	18	16	14	13	12	11	10	10	9	9
	4	8	8	7	7	6	6	5	5	4	3	2	1	-	-	-	-	-	-	-	-	-	-	-	-
20	3	33	33	32	32	31	30	29	28	27	26	25	24	23	22	20	18	16	14	13	12	11	11	10	10
	4	9	9	8	8	7	7	6	6	5	4	3	2	1	-	-	-	-	-	-	-	-	-	-	-

The Form Book

Welcome to the 2012 edition of *The Form Book,* comprising the complete year's results from 2011.

Race details contain Racing Post Ratings assessing the merit of each individual performance, speed figures for every horse that clocks a worthwhile time, weight-for-age allowances, stall positions for every race and the starting price percentage, in addition to the traditional features.

Race Focus comments are printed below each race along with official explanations and notebook comments for all British races of Class 3 and above, all two-year-old races and foreign races. The comments provide an analysis of the winning performance and, where applicable, explain possible reasons for improvement or attempt to explain why any horse failed to run to its best. More importantly, our team will also indicate the conditions under which horses are likely to be seen to best advantage.

The official record

THE FORM BOOK records comprehensive race details of every domestic race, every major European Group race and every foreign event in which a British-trained runner participated. In the **NOTEBOOK** section, extended interpretation is provided for all runners worthy of a mention, including all placed horses and all favourites. Generally speaking, the higher the class of race, the greater the number of runners noted.

MEETING BACK REFERENCE NUMBER is the Raceform number of the last meeting run at the track and is shown to the left of the course name. Abandoned meetings are signified by a dagger.

THE GOING, The Official going, shown at the head of each meeting, is recorded as follows: Turf: Hard; Firm; Good to firm; Good; Good to soft; Soft; Heavy. All-Weather: Fast; Standard to fast; Standard; Standard to slow; Slow. There may be variations for non-British meetings

Where appropriate, a note is included indicating track bias and any differences to the official going indicated by race times.

THE WEATHER is shown below to th e date for selected meetings.

THE WIND is given as a strength and direction at the Winning Post, classified as follows:
Strength: gale; v.str; str; fresh; mod; slt; almost nil; nil.
Direction: (half) against; (half) bhd; (half) across from or towards stands.

VISIBILITY is good unless otherwise stated.

RACE NUMBERS for Foreign races carry the suffix 'a' in the race header and in the index.

RACE TITLE is the name of the race as shown in the Racing Calendar.

COMPETITIVE RACING CLASSIFICATIONS are shown on a scale from Class 1 to Class 7. All Pattern races are Class 1.

THE RACE DISTANCE is given for all races, and is accompanied by (s) for races run on straight courses and (r) for courses where there is a round track of comparable distance. On All-Weather courses (F) for Fibresand or (P) for Polytrack indicates the nature of the artificial surface on which the race is run.

OFFICIAL RACE TIME as published in the Racing Calendar is followed in parentheses by the time when the race actually started. This is followed by the race class, age restrictions, handicap restrictions and the official rating of the top weight.

PRIZE MONEY shows penalty values down to sixth place (where applicable).

THE POSITION OF THE STARTING STALLS is shown against each race, in the form of: High (H), Centre (C) or Low (L). If one stands at the start facing towards the finish, the stalls are numbered from left to right. If the stalls are placed adjacent to the left rail they are described as low, if against the right rail they are described as high. Otherwise they are central.

IN THE RACE RESULT, the figures to the far left of each horse (under FORM) show the most recent form figures. The figure in bold is the finishing position in this race as detailed below.

1...40 - finishing positions first to fortieth; **b** - brought down; **c** - carried out; **f** - fell; **p** - pulled up; **r** - refused; **ro** - ran out; **s** - slipped up; **u** - unseated rider; **v** - void race.

THE OFFICIAL DISTANCES between the horses are shown on the left-hand side immediately after their position at the finish.

NUMBER OF DAYS SINCE PREVIOUS RUN is the superscript figure immediately following the horse name and suffix.

PREVIOUS RACEFORM RACE NUMBER is the boxed figure to the right of the horse's name.

THE HORSE'S AGE is shown immediately before the weight carried.

WEIGHTS shown are actual weights carried.

OFFICIAL RATING is the figure in bold type directly after the horse's name in the race result. This figure indicates the Official BHB rating, at entry, after the following adjustments had been made:
(i) Overweight carried by the rider.
(ii) The number of pounds out of the handicap (if applicable).
(iii) Penalties incurred after the publication of the weights.
However, no adjustments have been made for:
(i) Weight-for-age.
(ii) Riders' claims.

HEADGEAR is shown immediately befoe the jockey's name and in parentheses and expressed as: **b** (blinkers); **v** (visor); **h** (hood); **e** (eyeshield); **c** (eyecover); **p** (sheepskin cheekpieces).

THE JOCKEY is shown for every runner followed, in superscript, by apprentice allowances in parentheses.

APPRENTICE ALLOWANCES The holders of apprentice jockeys' licences under the provisions of Rule 60(iii) are permitted to claim the following allowances in Flat races:
7lb until they have won 20 Flat races run under the Rules of any recognised Turf Authority; thereafter 5lb until they have won 50 such Flat races; thereafter 3lb until they have won 95 such Flat races. These allowances can be claimed in the Flat races set out below, with the exception of races confined to apprentice jockeys:
(a) All handicap handicaps other than those Rated stakes which are classified as listed races.
(b) All selling and claiming races.
(b) All weight-for-age races classified 3, 4, 5, 6 and 7.

THE DRAW for places at the start is shown after each jockey's name.

RACING POST RATINGS, which record the level of performance attained in this race for each horse, appear in the end column after each horse. These are the work of handicappers Simon Turner, Sam Walker and Paul Curtis, who head a dedicated team dealing with Flat races for Raceform and sister publication, the *Racing Post*.

THE TRAINER is shown for every runner.

COMMENT-IN-RUNNING is shown for each horse in an abbreviated form. Details of abbreviations appear later in this section.

STARTING PRICES appear below the jockey in the race result. The favourite indicator appears to the right of the Starting Price; 1 for the favourite, 2 for the second-favourite and 3 for third-favourite. Joint favourites share the same number.

RACE TIMES in Great Britain are official times which are electronically recorded and shown to 100th of a second. Figures in parentheses following the time show the number of seconds faster or slower than the Raceform Median Time for the course and distance.

RACEFORM MEDIAN TIMES are compiled from all races run over the course and distance in the preceding five years. Times equal to the median are shown as (0.00). Times under the median are preceded by minus, for instance, 1.8 seconds under the median would be shown (-1.8). Record times are displayed either referring to the juvenile record (1.2 under 2y best) or to the overall record (1.2 under best).

GOING CORRECTION appears against each race to allow for changing conditions of the ground. It is shown to a hundredth of a second and indicates the adjustment per furlong against the median time. The going based on the going correction is shown in parentheses and is recorded in the following stages:
Turf: HD (Hard); F (Firm); GF (Good to firm); G (Good); GS (Good to soft); S (Soft); HVY (Heavy). All-Weather: FST (Fast); SF (Standard to fast); STD (Standard); SS (Standard to slow); SLW (Slow)

WEIGHT-FOR-AGE allowances are given where applicable for mixed-age races.

STARTING PRICE PERCENTAGE follows the going correction and weight-for-age details, and gives the total SP percentage of all runners that competed. It precedes the number of runners taking part in the race.

SELLING DETAILS (where applicable) and details of any claim are given. Friendly claims are not detailed.

SPEED RATINGS appear below the race time and going correction. They are the work of time expert Dave Bellingham and differ from conventional ratings systems in that they are an expression of a horse's ability in terms of lengths-per-mile, as opposed to pounds in weight. They are not directly comparable with BHB and Racing Post ratings.

The ratings take no account of the effect of weight, either historically or on the day, and this component is left completely to the user's discretion. What is shown is a speed rating represented in its purest form, rather than one that has been altered for weight using a mathematical formula that treats all types of horses as if they were the same.

A comparison of the rating achieved with the 'par' figure for the grade of race - the rating that should be achievable by an average winner in that class of race- will both provide an at-a-glance indication of whether or not a race was truly run and also highlight the value of the form from a time perspective.

In theory, if a horse has a best speed figure five points superior to another and both run to their best form in a race over a mile, the first horse should beat the second by five lengths. In a race run over two miles, the margin should be ten lengths and so on.

Before the speed figures can be calculated, it is necessary to establish a set of standard or median times for every distance at every track, and this is done by averaging the times of all winners over a particular trip going back several years. No speed ratings are produced when insufficient races have been run over a distance for a reliable median time to be calculated.

Once a meeting has taken place, a raw unadjusted speed rating is calculated for each winner by calculating how many lengths per mile the winning time was faster or slower than the median for the trip. A difference of 0.2 of a second equals one length. The raw speed ratings of all winners on the card are then compared to the 'par' figure for the class of race. The difference between the 'raw' speed rating and the 'par' figure for each race is then noted, and both the fastest and slowest races are discarded before the rest are averaged to produce the going allowance or track variant. This figure gives an idea as to how much the elements, of which the going is one, have affected the final times of each race.

The figure representing the going allowance is then used to adjust the raw speed figures and produce the final ratings, which represent how fast the winners would have run on a perfectly good surface with no external influences, including the weather. The ratings for beaten horses are worked out by taking the number of lengths they were behind the winner, adjusting that to take into account the distance of the race, and deducting that figure from the winner's rating. The reader is left with a rating which provides an instant impression of the value of a time performance.

The speed 'pars' below act as benchmark with which to compare the speed figures earned by each horse in each race. A horse that has already exceeded the 'par' for the class he is about to run in, is of special interest, especially if he has done it more than once, as are horses that have consistently earned higher figures than their rivals.

Class 1 Group One	117
Class 1 Group Two	115
Class 1 Group Three	113
Class 1 Listed	111
Class 2	109
Class 3	107
Class 4	105
Class 5	103
Class 6	101
Class 7	97

Allowances need to be made for younger horses and for fillies. These allowances are as follows.

MONTH	2yo	3yo
Jan / Feb	n/a	-6
Mar / Apr	-11	-5
May / Jun	-10	-4
Jul / Aug	-9	-3
Sep / Oct	-8	-2
Nov / Dec	-7	-1
Races contested by fillies only		-3

Allowances are cumulative. For example, using a combination of the above pars and allowances, the par figure for the Epsom Oaks would be 110. The Group One par is 117, then deduct 4 because the race is confined to three year olds and run in June, then subtract another 3 because the race is confined to fillies.

TOTE prices include £1 stake. Exacta dividends are shown in parentheses. The Computer Straight Forecast dividend is preceded by the letters CSF, Computer Tricast is preceded by CT and Tote Trio dividend is preceded by the word Trio. Jackpot, Placepot and Quadpot details appear at the end of the meeting to which they refer.

OWNER is followed by the breeder's name and the trainer's location.

STEWARDS' ENQUIRIES are included with the result, and any suspensions and/or fines incurred. Objections by jockeys and officials are included, where relevant.

HISTORICAL FOCUS details occasional points of historical significance.

FOCUS The Focus section has been enhanced to help readers distinguish good races from bad races and reliable form from unreliable form, by drawing together the opinions of handicapper, time expert and paddock watcher and interpreting their views in a punter-friendly manner.

NOTEBOOK horses marked with the diamond symbol are those deemed by our racereaders especially worthy of note in future races.

OFFICIAL EXPLANATIONS, where the horse is deemed to have run well above or below expectations

Abbreviations and their meanings

Paddock comments

attr - attractive
gd bodied - good bodied, well put together
gd sort - well made, above average on looks
h.d.w - has done well, improved in looks
wl grwn - well grown, has filled to its frame
lengthy - longer than average for its height
tall - tall
rangy - lengthy and tall but in proportion.
cl cpld - close coupled
scope - scope for physical development
str - strong, powerful looking
w'like - workmanlike, ordinary in looks
lt-f - light-framed, not much substance
cmpt - compact
neat - smallish, well put together
leggy - long legs compared with body
angular - unfurnished behind the saddle, not filled to frame
unf - unfurnished in the midriff, not filled to frame
narrow - not as wide as side appearance would suggest
small - lacks any physical scope
nt grwn - not grown
lw - looked fit and well
bkwd - backward in condition
t - tubed
swtg - sweating
b (off fore or nr fore) - bandaged in front
b.hind (off or nr) - bandaged behind

At the start

stdd s - jockey purposely reins back the horse
dwlt - missed the break and left for a short time
s.s - slow to start, left longer than a horse that dwelt
s.v.s - started very slowly
s.i.s - started on terms but took time to get going
ref to r - does not jump off, or travels a few yards then stops
rel to r - tries to pull itself up in mid-race
w.r.s - whipped round start

Position in the race

led - in lead on its own

disp ld - upsides the leader
w ldr - almost upsides the leader
w ldrs - in a line of three or more disputing the lead
prom - on the heels of the leaders, in front third of the field
trckd ldr(s) - just in behind the leaders giving impression that it could lead if asked
chsd ldr - horse in second place
chsd clr ldrs - horse heads main body of field behind two clear leaders
chsd ldrs - horse is in the first four or five but making more of an effort to stay close to the pace than if it were tracking the leaders.
clsd - closed
in tch - close enough to have a chance
hdwy - making ground on the leader
gd hdwy - making ground quickly on the leader, could be a deliberate move
sme hdwy - making some ground but no real impact on the race
w.w - waited with
stdy hdwy - gradually making ground
ev ch - upsides the leaders when the race starts in earnest
rr - at the back of main group but not detached
bhd - detached from the main body of runners
hld up - restrained as a deliberate tactical move
nt rcvr - lost all chance after interference, mistake etc.
wknd - stride shortened as it began to tire
lost tch - had been in the main body but a gap appeared as it tired
lost pl - remains in main body of runners but lost several positions quickly

Riding

effrt - short-lived effort
pushed along - received urgings with hands only, jockey not using legs
rdn - received urgings from saddle, including use of whip
hrd rdn - received maximum assistance from the saddle including use of whip
drvn - received forceful urgings, jockey putting in a lot of effort and using whip
hrd drvn - jockey very animated, plenty of kicking, pushing and reminders

Finishing comments

jst failed - closing rapidly on the winner and probably would have led a stride after the line
r.o - jockey's efforts usually involved to produce an increase in pace without finding an appreciable turn of speed
r.o wl - jockey's efforts usually involved to produce an obvious increase in pace without finding an appreciable turn of speed
unable qckn - not visibly tiring but does not possess a sufficient change of pace
one pce - not tiring but does not find a turn of speed, from a position further out than unable qckn
nt r.o. - did not consent to respond to pressure
styd on - going on well towards the end, utilising stamina
nvr able to chal - unable to produce sufficient to reach a challenging position
nvr nr to chal - in the opinion of the racereader, the horse was never in a suitable position to challenge.
nrst fin - nearer to the winner in distance beaten than at any time since the race had begun in earnest
nvr nrr - nearer to the winner position-wise than at any time since the race had begun in earnest
rallied - responded to pressure to come back with a chance having lost its place
no ex - unable to sustain its run
bttr for r - likely to improve for the run and experience
rn green - inclined to wander and falter through inexperience
too much to do - left with too much leeway to make up

Winning comments

v.easily - a great deal in hand
easily - plenty in hand
comf - something in hand, always holding the others
pushed out - kept up to its work with hands and heels without jockey resorting to whip or kicking along and wins fairly comfortably
rdn out - pushed and kicked out to the line, with the whip employed
drvn out - pushed and kicked out to the line, with considerable effort and the whip employed
all out - nothing to spare, could not have found any more
jst hld on - holding on to a rapidly diminishing lead, could not have found any more if passed
unchal - must either make all or a majority of the running and not be challenged from an early stage

Complete list of abbreviations

a - always
abt - about
a.p - always prominent
appr - approaching
awrdd - awarded
b.b.v - broke blood-vessel
b.d - brought down
bdly - badly
bef - before
bhd - behind
bk - back
blkd - baulked
blnd - blundered
bmpd - bumped
bnd - bend
btn- beaten
bttr - better
c - came
ch - chance
chal - challenged
chse - chase
chsd - chased
chsng - chasing
circ - circuit
cl - close
clr - clear
clsd - closed
comf - comfortably
cpld - coupled
crse - course
ct - caught
def - definite
dismntd - dismounted
disp - disputed
dist - distance
div - division
drvn - driven
dwlt - dwelt
edgd - edged
effrt - effort

ent - entering
ev ch - every chance
ex - extra
f - furlong
fin - finished
fnd - found
fnl - final
fr - from
gd - good
gng - going
gp - group
grad - gradually
grnd - ground
hd - head
hdd - headed
hdwy - headway
hld - held
hmpd - hampered
imp - impression
ins - inside
j.b - jumped badly
j.w - jumped well
jnd - joined
jst - just
kpt - kept
l - length
ld - lead
ldr - leader

lft - left
mod - moderate
m - mile
m.n.s - made no show
mde - made
mid div - mid division
mstke - mistake
n.d - never dangerous
n.g.t - not go through
n.m.r - not much room
nk - neck
no ex - no extra
nr - near
nrr - nearer
nrst fin - nearest finish
nt - not
nvr - never
one pce - one pace
out - from finish
outpcd - outpaced
p.u - pulled up
pce - pace
pckd - pecked
pl - place
plcd - placed
plld - pulled
press - pressure
prog - progress

prom - prominent
qckly - quickly
qckn - quicken
r - race
racd - raced
rch - reach
rcvr - recover
rdn - ridden
rdr - rider
reard - reared
ref - refused
rn - ran
rnd - round
r.o - ran on
rr - rear
rspnse - response
rt - right
s - start
sddle - saddle
shkn - shaken
slt - slight
sme - some
sn - soo
spd- speed
st - straight
stmbld - stumbled
stdd - steadied
stdy - steady

strly - strongly
styd - stayed
styng - staying
s. u - slipped up
swtchd - switched
swvd - swerved
tk - took
t.k.h - took keen hold
t.o - tailed off
tch - touch
thrght - throughout
trbld - troubled
trckd - tracked
u.p - under pressure
u.str.p- under strong pressure
w - with
w.r.s - whipped round start
wd - wide
whn - when
wknd - weakened
wl - well
wnr - winner
wnt - went
1/2-wy - halfway

Racing Post Ratings

Racing Post Ratings for each horse are shown in the right hand column, headed RPR, and indicate the actual level of performance attained in that race. The figure in the back index represents the BEST public form that Raceform's Handicappers still believe the horse capable of reproducing.

To use the ratings constructively in determining those horses best-in in future events, the following procedure should be followed:

(i) In races where all runners are the same age and are set to carry the same weight, no calculations are necessary. The horse with the highest rating is best-in.

(ii) In races where all runners are the same age but are set to carry different weights, add one point to the Raceform Rating for every pound less than 10 stone to be carried; deduct one point for every pound more than 10 stone.

For example,

Horse	Age & wt	Adjustment from 10st	Base rating	Adjusted rating
Treclare	3-10-1	-1	78	77
Buchan	3-9-13	+1	80	81
Paper Money	3-9-7	+7	71	78
Archaic	3-8-11	+17	60	77

Therefore Buchan is top-rated (best-in)

(iii) In races concerning horses of different ages the procedure in (ii) should again be followed, but reference must also be made to the Official Scale of Weight-For-Age.

For example,

12 furlongs, July 20th

Horse	Age & wt	Adjustment from 10st	Base rating	Adjusted rating	W-F-A deduct	Final rating
Orpheus	5-10-0	0	90	90	Nil	90
Lemonora	4-9-9	+5	88	88	Nil	88
Tamar	3-9-4	+10	85	95	-12	83
Craigangower	4-8-7	+21	73	94	Nil	94

Therefore Craigangower is top-rated (best-in)

(A 3-y-o is deemed 12lb less mature than a 4-y-o or older horse on 20th July over 12f. Therefore, the deduction of 12 points is necessary.)

The following symbols are used in conjunction with the ratings:

++: almost certain to prove better

+: likely to prove better

d: disappointing (has run well below best recently)

?: form hard to evaluate

t: tentative rating based on race-time rating may prove unreliable

Weight adjusted ratings for every race are published daily in Raceform Private Handicap and our new service Raceform Private handicap ONLINE (www.raceform.co.uk).

For subscription terms please contact the Subscription Department on 01933 304858.

Effect of the draw

(R.H.) denotes right-hand and (L.H.) left-hand courses.

* Draw biases shown below apply to straight-course races unless otherwise stipulated.

** Most races, outside Festival meetings, are now restricted to 20 runners, which means it's now particularly worth looking at the stalls position, as many courses can accommodate more than that number.

ASCOT (R-H) - Following extensive redevelopment there have been some pretty exaggerated draw biases. Watering often seems to be the deciding factor and far too much has been applied on more than one occasion.

STALLS: Usually go up the stands' side (low).

BIASES: One side or other was often favoured last season but the middle can also ride best, and biases remain very hard to predict.

SPLITS: Are common in big-field handicaps and occasionally will occur on soft ground in round-course races, when some head for the outside rail (covered by trees).

AYR (L-H) - Throughout the 90s high numbers were massively favoured in the Gold and Silver Cups but things have become less clear-cut since. Traditionally the centre of the course has ridden slower here but the strip is nothing like the disadvantage it once was.

STALLS: Usually go up the stands' side (high) in sprints, but occasionally go on the other side. It isn't uncommon for jockeys to switch from the far side to race down the centre or even come right across to the stands' rail.

BIASES: There's ultimately not a lot between the two sides in big fields now.

SPLITS: Are becoming more common, having only usually occurred in the Silver and Gold Cups in the past.

BATH (L-H) - The draw is of less importance than the pace at which races are run. In big fields, runners drawn low are often inclined to go off too fast to hold a rail position (the course turns left most of the way, including one major kink) and this can see hold-up horses drawn wide coming through late. Conversely, in smaller fields containing little pace, up front and on the inside is often the place to be.

STALLS: Always go on the inside (low).

SPLITS: Fields almost always stick together, but soft ground can see a split, with the outside rail (high) then favoured.

BEVERLEY (R-H) - A high draw used to be essential on good to soft or faster ground over 5f and also on the round course, particularly in races of 7f100y and 1m100y. However, things were far less clear cut last year, presumably down to watering. The course management experimented with moving stalls to the stands' side over 5f in 2002 (unsuccessfully, as it led to a huge low bias) and haven't done so since.

STALLS: Go on the inside (high) at all distances.

BIASES: High numbers are traditionally best on good to soft or faster ground but watering looked to play a big part last year.

SPLITS: Splits are rare and only likely over 5f on soft ground.

BRIGHTON (L-H) - Much depends on the going and time of year. On good to soft or slower ground runners often head for the outside rail, while in late season it's usually just a case of whichever jockey finds the least cut-up strip of ground. Otherwise, low-drawn prominent-racers tend to hold sway in fast-ground sprints, with double figures always facing an uphill task over 5f59y.

STALLS: Always go on the inside (low) in sprints.

SPLITS: These occur frequently, as jockeys look for a fresh strip on ground that seems to churn up easily.

CARLISLE (R-H) - Runners racing with the pace and hardest against the inside rail (high) do well in big fields on decent ground. This is largely down to the fact that the Flat course and NH course are one and the same, and that those racing nearest the fence are running where the hurdle wings were positioned, while those wider out are on the raced-on surface. On soft ground, the bias swings completely, with runners racing widest (low) and grabbing the stands' rail in the straight favoured at all distances.

STALLS: Normally go on the inside (high) but can go down the middle in sprints (usually on slow ground).

BIASES: High numbers are best in fast-ground sprints, but look to back low numbers on soft/heavy ground.

SPLITS: Rarely will two groups form but, on easy ground, runners often spread out.

CATTERICK (L-H) - When the ground is testing, the stands' rail is definitely the place to be, which suits high numbers in 5f races and high-drawn prominent-racers at all other distances. However, when the ground is good to firm or faster, horses drawn on the inside (low) often hold the edge, and there have been several meetings over the last few seasons in which those racing prominently hardest against the inside rail have dominated (over all distances).

STALLS: Go on the inside (low) at all distances these days (they often used to go on the outer over 5f212y).

BIASES: Low numbers are best in sprints on fast ground (particularly watered firm going) but the stands' rail (high) rides faster under slower conditions.

SPLITS: Are common over 5f on easy ground.

CHEPSTOW (L-H) - High numbers enjoyed a massive advantage in straight-course races in 2000 and the course management duly took steps to eradicate the faster strip, using the same 'earthquake' machine as had been employed at Goodwood in the late 90s. This has led to little in the way of a draw bias since.

STALLS: Always go stands' side (high) on the straight course.

BIASES: Have become hard to predict in recent times.

SPLITS: Are common and jockeys drawn low often head far side.

CHESTER (L-H) - It's well known that low numbers are favoured at all distances here, even in the 2m2f Chester Cup, and the bias is factored into the prices these days. That said sprints (and in particular handicaps) are still playable, as it often pays to stick to a runner drawn 1-3.

STALLS: Go on the inside (low) at all distances bar 1m2f75y and 2m2f117y (same starting point) when they go on the outside. Certain starters ask for the stalls to come off the inside rail slightly in sprints.

BIASES: Low numbers are favoured at all distances. Soft ground seems to accentuate the bias until a few races have been staged, when a higher draw becomes less of a disadvantage as the ground on the inside becomes chewed up.

DONCASTER (L-H) - There's been very little between the two sides since the course reopened. Jockeys now tend to swerve the stands' rail (high) on good or slower ground, instead preferring to head for the centre.

STALLS: Can go either side but tend to go up the stands' side (high) when possible.

BIASES: Runners down the centre are usually worst off. The longer the trip on the straight course the better chance the far side (low) has against the stands' side in big fields.

EPSOM (L-H) - When the going is on the soft side, jockeys tack over to the stands' side for the better ground (this strip rides quicker in such conditions as the course cambers away from the stands' rail). In 5f races, the stalls are invariably placed on the stands' side, so when the going is soft the majority of the runners are on the best ground from the outset. Prominent-racers drawn low in round-course races are able to take the shortest route around Tattenham Corner, and on faster ground have a decisive edge over 6f, 7f and 1m114y. Over 5f, high numbers used to hold quite an advantage, but the bias is not so great on fast going these days.

STALLS: Always go on the outside (high) over 5f and 6f (races over the latter trip start on a chute) and inside (low) at other distances, bar 1m4f10y (centre).

BIASES: Low-drawn prominent racers are favoured at between 6f and 1m114y.

SPLITS: Good to soft ground often leads to a few trying the stands'-side route.

FFOS LAS (L-H) - So far the evidence suggests there is no clear bias in races on the straight track, despite the stalls being placed on the stands' side. On the round course high numbers are slightly favoured.

STALLS Usually go up the stands' side (high)on the straight course.

BIASES High numbers appear to have a slight advantage, particlarly in races beyond a mile.

SPLITS As fields are not often big, splits are rare.

FOLKESTONE (R-H) - Prior to 1998, Folkestone was never thought to have much in the way of a bias, but nowadays the draw is often crucial on the straight course (up to 7f). On very soft ground, the far rail (high) rides faster than the stands' rail. However, on good to soft or faster ground runners tend to stay up the near side now (the ambulance used to go this side of the far rail but now goes the other side of the fence) and those racing on the pace hardest against the fence often enjoy a major advantage.

STALLS: Usually go up the stands' side (low) on the straight track, but occasionally down the centre.

BIASES: High numbers are favoured over 6f and 7f, and also over the minimum trip when 14 or more line up. However, very low numbers have a good record in smaller fields over 5f. Front-runners are well worth considering at all distances.

SPLITS: Often occur.

GOODWOOD (R-H) & (L-H) - The course management took steps to end the major high bias seen in the Stewards' Cup throughout the late 90s by breaking up the ground by machine in 1998. This led to the stands' side (low) dominating the race in 1999 before the far side gradually took over again.

STALLS: Invariably go on the stands' side (low).

BIASES: High numbers are best at between 7f-1m1f and the faster the ground the more pronounced the bias (keep an eye out for the rail on the home turn being moved during Glorious week, usually after the Thursday).

SPLITS: Although fields tend not to break into groups in most sprints, runners often spread out to about two-thirds of the way across in fields of around 20.

HAMILTON (R-H) - Extensive drainage work was carried out in the winter of 2002 in a bid to level up the two sides of the track but, after encouraging early results, the natural bias in favour of high numbers (far side) kicked in again. This can be altered by watering on faster going, though, and low numbers were definitely favoured under such conditions in 2008. Things were less clear cut last year, however, and jockeys more often than not headed for the centre. High numbers are best over 1m65y, thanks to runners encountering a tight right-handed loop soon after the start.

STALLS: It's not uncommon for the ground to become too soft for the use of stalls, but otherwise they go either side.

BIASES: High draws are best in soft/heavy-ground sprints, but the bias becomes middle to high otherwise (often switching to low on watered fast ground). Front-runners do particularly well at all distances.

SPLITS: Rarely happen now.

HAYDOCK (L-H) - High numbers used to enjoy a major advantage in soft-ground sprints and there were signs last year that this bias has returned. Otherwise, runners usually head for the centre these days, the draw rarely making much of a difference.

STALLS: Usually go down the centre in the straight.

KEMPTON All-Weather (R-H) - High numbers are best over 5f and preferable over 6f, while those drawn very low over 7f often have a bit to do. Otherwise, pace of races counts for a lot and this is one of the fairest courses around in that respect.

LEICESTER (R-H) - There was a four-year spell between 1998 and 2001 when the centre-to-far-side strip (middle to high) enjoyed a decisive advantage over the stands' rail, jockeys eventually choosing to avoid the near side. However, that's changed recently, with very low numbers more than holding their own.

STALLS: Invariably go up the stands' side (low).

SPLITS: Still occur occasionally.

LINGFIELD Turf (L-H) - Following a less predictable spell, the stands' rail (high) has taken over again in the past couple of years. The one factor that can have a massive effect on the draw is heavy rainfall on to firm ground. Presumably because of the undulating nature of the track and the fact that the far rail on the straight course is towards the bottom of a slope where it joins the round course, rainfall seems to make the middle and far side ride a deal slower. In these conditions, the top three or four stalls have a massive edge.

STALLS: Go up the stands' side (high) at between 5f and 7f and down the middle over 7f140y.

BIASES: High numbers favoured unless ground is genuinely soft.

SPLITS: It's unusual to see two distinct groups, but runners often fan out centre to stands' side in big fields.

LINGFIELD All-Weather (L-H) - There is little bias over most trips, but it is an advantage to be drawn low over 6f and 1m2f, with both starts being situated very close to the first bend. A low to middle draw is preferable over 5f, even with a safety limit of just ten, though the very inside stall has a poor recent record. No horse managed to win from stall 1 over that trip in 2004, which suggests the ground right against the inside rail is slower than elsewhere.

STALLS: Go against the outside rail (high) over 5f and 1m, but against the inside rail (low) for all other distances.

SPLITS: Fields never split but runners usually come wide off the home turn.

MUSSELBURGH (R-H) - The bias in favour of low numbers over 5f isn't as pronounced as many believe, apart from on soft ground, while the bias in favour of high numbers at 7f and 1m isn't that big.

STALLS: Usually go up the stands' side (low) over 5f nowadays, but they can be rotated.

SPLITS: Look out for runners drawn very high in big-field 5f races on fast ground, as they occasionally go right to the far rail.

NEWBURY (L-H) - There's basically little between the two sides these days, apart from on soft ground, in which case the stands' rail (high) is definitely the place to be. When the ground is testing it's not uncommon to see runners race wide down the back straight and down the side at between 1m3f56y and 2m (particularly over 1m5f61y). In such circumstances, a high draw becomes an advantage.

STALLS: Can go anywhere for straight-course races.

SPLITS: Are pretty rare.

NEWCASTLE (L-H) - It used to be a case of high numbers best at up to and including 7f on good or firmer, and low numbers having the advantage when the ground is good to soft or softer. However, now things depend largely on the positioning of the stands' rail. If the course is at its widest high numbers are almost always best off, while if the rail is further in things are less clear cut.

STALLS: Invariably go on the stands' side (high) and are only switched to the inside under exceptional circumstances.

SPLITS: Two groups are usually formed when 14+ go to post, and often when 8-13 line up.

NEWMARKET July Course (R-H) - The major draw biases seen under the former Clerk of the Course have become a thing of the past and now only the occasional meeting will be affected. The course is permanently divided into two halves by a rail (the Racing Post now carry information regarding which side is to be used) and, as a rule of thumb, the two outside rails (stands' rail when they're on the stands'-side half, far rail when they're on the far-side half) ride faster than the dividing rail.

Stands'-side half - On fast ground (particularly watered) very high numbers are often favoured at up to 1m, when there's a narrow strip hard against the fence that rides quicker. However, on good to soft or slower ground, runners racing in the centre are favoured.

Far-side half - There's rarely much in the draw, apart from on slow ground, when the far side (low) rides faster.

STALLS: Can go either side on either half of the track.

SPLITS: Runners just about tend to form two groups in capacity fields, but are more likely to run to their draw here than at tracks such as Newcastle.

NEWMARKET Rowley Mile (R-H) - Similarly to the July Course, the draw seems to have been evened out since the Clerk of the Course change, although it's still generally a case of the further away from the stands' rail (low) the better.

STALLS: Can go anywhere and are rotated.

BIASES: High numbers have dominated the 2m2f Cesarewitch in recent years, the logic being that those on the inside can be switched off early, while low numbers have to work to get into position before the sole right-handed turn.

SPLIT: It's not unusual for jockeys to come stands' side on slow ground in round-course races.

NOTTINGHAM (L-H) - Biases are far harder to predict now on the both the inner (spring/autumn) and outer (summer) course.

STALLS: Tend to go on the stands' side (high) unless the ground is very soft.

SPLITS: Fields usually split in sprints when 14+ line up.

PONTEFRACT (L-H) - Low numbers have always been considered best here for the same reason as at Chester, in that the course has several distinct left-hand turns with a short home straight, and it's always worth considering low-drawn front-runners on fast going. Drainage work was carried out in the late 90s to try and eradicate the outside-rail bias on slow ground, and this worked immediately afterwards, but during the last few seasons there have been definite signs that it's now riding much faster when it's bottomless.

STALLS: Go on the inside (low) unless the ground is very soft, when they're switched to the outside rail.

SPLITS: Although it's uncommon to see distinct groups, high numbers usually race wide these days on soft/heavy ground.

REDCAR (L-H) - It's not unusual to see big fields throughout the season but the draw rarely makes a difference.

STALLS: Go towards the stands' side (high).

SPLITS: Splits are unusual.

RIPON (R-H) - The draw is often the sole deciding factor in big-field sprints and watering plays a major part. As a general rule, low numbers are best when the ground is good to firm or faster, while the far side is always best on softer going but, ultimately, the best guide these days is the most recent meeting.

STALLS: Go on the stands' side (low) apart from under exceptional circumstances.

BIASES: Front-runners (particularly from high draws over 1m) have an excellent record and any horse trying to make ground from behind and out wide is always facing a tough task.

SPLITS: Fields tend to stay together in races of 12 or fewer, but a split is near guaranteed when 15 or more line up. Look for 'draw' jockeys who might chance going far side in fields of 13-14.

SALISBURY (R-H) - For most of last year those racing against the inside rail (high) on fast ground looked worst off if anything (centre often best), which is the opposite of how things have been in the past. Presumably this was down to watering. On slower ground jockeys invariably head towards the stands' rail (good to soft seems to be the cut-off point) and whoever grabs the fence in front can prove hard to pass.

STALLS: Go on the far side (high) unless the ground is soft, when they're often moved to the near side.

BIASES: Low numbers are always best on soft/heavy ground.

SPLITS: Fields only tend to divide on good to soft ground; otherwise they converge towards either rail, dependent on going.

SANDOWN (R-H) - On the 5f chute, when the going is on the soft side and the stalls are on the far side (high), high numbers enjoy a decisive advantage. On the rare occasions that the stalls are placed on the stands' side, low numbers enjoy a slight advantage when all the runners stay towards the stands' rail, but when a few break off and go to the far side high numbers comfortably hold the upper hand again. High numbers enjoy a decent advantage in double-figure fields over 7f and 1m on good going or faster, but jockeys invariably head for the stands' side on slow ground.

STALLS: Usually go far side (high) over 5f, as the course is more level that side.

SPLITS: It's unusual for runners to split over 5f, with capacity fields rare and jockeys all inclined to head for the far rail.

SOUTHWELL All-Weather (L-H) - Over most trips on the round track it is preferable to be drawn away from the extreme inside or outside. The exceptions are over 6f and 1m3f, which both start close to the first bend (better to be drawn low to middle). At most meetings the centre of the track rides faster than either rail, although that can change in extreme weather when power-harrowing can even out the bias. A low to middle draw is preferable over 5f.

STALLS: Are placed next to the inside rail (low), except over 5f when they go next to the stands' rail (high).

SPLITS: Fields don't split into groups as such, but can fan out and take varied routes once into the home straight. Even in big fields over the straight 5f, the runners basically stick to their draw and race straight from start to finish.

THIRSK (L-H) - This used to be the biggest draw course in the country, back in the days of the old watering system (which was badly affected by the wind) but, while biases still often show up, they're not as predictable as used to be the case. Field sizes, watering and going always have to be taken into account when 12 or more line up (11 or fewer runners and it's rare to see anything bar one group up the stands' rail, with high numbers best). Otherwise, either rail can enjoy the edge on watered fast ground (the one place not to be under any circumstances is down the middle). Low-drawn prominent-racers are well worth considering whatever the distance on the round course.

STALLS: Always go up the stands' side (high).

BIASES: High numbers are best in sprints when 11 or fewer line up, but it's hard to know which side is likely to do best in bigger fields on fast ground. The far (inside) rail is always best on slow going (the softer the ground, the greater the advantage).

SPLITS: Runners invariably stay towards the stands' side in sprints containing 12 or fewer runners (unless the ground is soft) and frequently when 13-14 line up. Any more and it becomes long odds-on two groups.

WARWICK (L-H) - Low numbers are no longer favoured, whatever the ground, and jockeys rarely if ever stick to the inside rail now. Presumably this is down to watering (hold-up runners are not as badly off as they used to be).

STALLS: Always go on the inside (low).

WINDSOR (Fig. 8) - The bias in favour of high numbers on fast ground is nothing like as predictable as it used to be, presumably because of watering. On slower ground, jockeys head centre to far side, and right over to the far rail (low) on genuine soft/heavy.

STALLS: Can be positioned anywhere for sprints.

BIASES: High-drawn prominent-racers are often favoured in fast-ground sprints, and also over 1m67y. On good to soft going, there's rarely much between the two sides, but it's a case of nearer to the far rail (low) the better on bad ground.

SPLITS: Splits only tend to occur on good to soft ground, and even then it's rare to see two defined groups.

WOLVERHAMPTON All-Weather (L-H) - A low draw is a big advantage over 5f20y and 5f216y, and low to middle is preferable over 7f32y. Beyond that it doesn't seem to matter, although it's never a good idea to race too wide on the home bend, as those that do rarely seem to make up the lost ground.

STALLS: Are placed against the outside rail (high) over 7f32y and against the inside (low) at all other distances.

YARMOUTH (L-H) - High numbers enjoyed a major advantage for much of the 90s, but this was put an end to by the course switching from pop-up sprinklers (which were affected by the off-shore breeze) to a Briggs Boom in '99. These days a bias will appear occasionally but it's hard to predict, and runners often head for the centre whatever the going.

STALLS: Go one side or the other.

SPLITS: It's common to see groups form, often including one down the centre, in big fields.

YORK (L-H) - The draw is nothing like as unpredictable in sprints as many believe, although things are never quite as clear cut in September/October as earlier in the season. Essentially, on good or faster ground, the faster strip is to be found centre to far side, which means in capacity fields, the place to be is stall 6-12, while in fields of 12-14 runners drawn low are favoured (the course is only wide enough to house 20 runners). On soft/heavy ground, the stands' side (high) becomes the place to be.

STALLS: Can go anywhere.

BIASES: Prominent-racers drawn down the centre are favoured in fast-ground sprints, but high numbers take over on genuine soft/heavy ground.

SPLITS: Defined groups are rare.

Key to racereaders' initials

WG ....Walter Glynn
RL ....Richard Lowther
LM....................Lee McKenzie
TM ....Tim Mitchell

JN.............Jonathan Neesom
DO ....Darren Owen
SP ....Steve Payne
CR ....Colin Roberts

JR ....Joe Rowntree
AS ....Andrew Sheret
ST ....Steve Taylor
RY ....Richard Young

SOUTHWELL (L-H)

Saturday, January 1

OFFICIAL GOING: Standard

Wind: Light across Weather: Overcast

1 BLUESQ.COM ON YOUR IPHONE APPRENTICE MEDIAN AUCTION MAIDEN STKS 1m 3f (F)

12:15 (12:16) (Class 6) 4-6-Y-0 **£1,535** (£453; £226) **Stalls** Low

Form RPR

/42- **1** **Luck Of The Draw (IRE)**[200] 3055 4-8-8 60 ... RosieJessop(5) 5 80+
(Sir Mark Prescott Bt) *trckd ldr: cl up 1/2-way: led over 4f out: rdn over 2f out: drvn and kpt on wl fnl 2f* **10/11**[1]

2 *1* **Sail Home**[85] 4-8-8 67 ... RossAtkinson 3 70
(Julia Feilden) *trckd ldrs: hdwy over 3f out: chsd wnr wl over 1f out: sn rdn and ev ch ent fnl f: drvn and no ex last 100yds* **13/2**[3]

50- **3** *5* **Donny Briggs**[16] 7896 6-9-2 0 ... MartinLane 1 66
(Tim Easterby) *s.i.s and in rr: hdwy on outer to chse ldrs 1/2-way: rdn along 4f out: outpcd 3f out and wd st: drvn and kpt on fnl 2f: tk 3rd nr fin* **20/1**

23- **4** *7* **Bull Five**[130] 5380 4-8-8 0 ... RyanClark(5) 2 53
(Nick Littmoden) *led: pushed along and hdd over 4f out: rdn over 3f out: drvn over 2f out and grad wknd* **2/1**[2]

000- **5** *15* **Always De One**[32] 7634 4-8-3 40 ... (p) NannaHansen(5) 4 21
(Julia Feilden) *in tch: pushed along 1/2-way: rdn over 3f out: outpcd fnl 2f* **28/1**

450- **6** *54* **Red Valerian Two (IRE)**[67] 7147 4-8-13 47 ... PaulPickard 6 —
(Paul Midgley) *chsd ldrs: rdn along 1/2-way: sn wknd: bhd and eased fnl 2f* **33/1**

2m 29.59s (1.59) **Going Correction** +0.125s/f (Slow)
WFA 4 from 6yo 3lb **6** Ran SP% **110.2**
Speed ratings: **99,98,94,89,78 39**
toteswingers: 1&2 £1.50, 1&3 £2.60, 2&3 £3.20. CSF £7.07 TOTE £1.50 : £1.02, £3.60; EX 6.40.
Owner L A Larratt - Osborne House **Bred** Castlemartin Stud And Skymarc Farm **Trained** Newmarket, Suffolk

FOCUS
Traditionally a weak opener to the year and this renewal looked little different. The pace was just a fair one.

2 HAPPY NEW YEAR FROM BLUE SQUARE H'CAP 5f (F)

12:50 (12:50) (Class 3) (0-95,90) 4-Y-0+ **£4,533** (£1,348; £674; £336) **Stalls** High

Form RPR

222- **1** **Silaah**[4] 7993 7-8-13 85 ... (p) MichaelO'Connell(3) 8 99+
(David Nicholls) *sltly hmpd s: trckd ldrs: effrt whn n.m.r 2f out: led over 1f out: sn rdn and kpt on wl fnl f* **11/4**[1]

003- **2** *1 1/2* **Waveband**[37] 7566 4-9-7 90 ... GrahamGibbons 1 99
(David Barron) *prom on outer: effrt and cl up 1/2-way: rdn and ev ch whn edgd rt over 1f out: drvn and one pce ins fnl f* **9/2**[3]

121- **3** *2 1/2* **Sir Geoffrey (IRE)**[18] 7866 5-9-3 86 ... (b) IanMongan 9 86
(David Nicholls) *wnt lft s: cl up: effrt and edgd lft 2f out: sn rdn and ev ch tl drvn and one pce jst ins fnl f* **3/1**[2]

006- **4** *3* **Luscivious**[25] 7740 7-9-3 89 ... (b) BillyCray(3) 4 78
(David Nicholls) *chsd ldrs: hdwy and cl up 1/2-way: sn rdn and wknd wl over 1f out* **14/1**

015- **5** *hd* **Cape Vale (IRE)**[25] 7740 6-9-0 86 ... MichaelGeran(3) 5 74
(David Nicholls) *wnt rt s: led: rdn along and edgd rt 2f out: hdd & wknd wl over 1f out* **8/1**

634- **6** *2 1/2* **Green Manalishi**[75] 6987 10-9-7 90 ... (p) PhillipMakin 2 69
(Kevin Ryan) *prom: rdn along 2f out: sn drvn and grad wknd* **25/1**

405- **7** *4 1/2* **Duplicity**[21] 7842 4-8-4 76 ... JamesSullivan(3) 7 39
(James Given) *hmpd s: a towards rr* **40/1**

300- **8** *6* **Nickel Silver**[25] 7740 6-9-5 88 ... (p) JoeFanning 6 29
(Bryan Smart) *hmpd s: chsd ldrs: rdn along over 2f out: sn wknd* **12/1**

/10- **9** *8* **Mo Mhuirnin (IRE)**[244] 1727 5-8-12 88 ... GeorgeChaloner(7) 3 —
(Richard Fahey) *s.i.s: a in rr* **8/1**

59.02 secs (-0.68) **Going Correction** +0.05s/f (Slow) **9** Ran SP% **112.7**
Speed ratings (Par 107): **107,104,100,95,95 91,84,74,61**
toteswingers: 1&2 £3.00, 1&3 £2.30, 2&3 £3.60. CSF £14.93 CT £38.09 TOTE £3.60 : £1.70, £1.10, £2.40; EX 22.10 Trifecta £87.70 Pool: £375.97 - 3.17 winning units. .
Owner Mrs Jackie Love & David Nicholls **Bred** Bearstone Stud **Trained** Sessay, N Yorks

FOCUS
A useful handicap, though perhaps not one run at the burning gallop that seemed likely beforehand with the field well bunched to halfway. Even so, plenty came into this in good heart and the form seems likely to prove reliable.

NOTEBOOK
Silaah is in the form of his life right now and followed up his good second in a hot Lingfield handicap the other day with a ready win, reversing recent C&D form with stablemate Sir Geoffrey in the process. Getting a good trail into the race behind the leaders, he wasn't hard ridden to draw clear and probably has a bit more to give in current form. This was his first win at the minimum trip and it possibly suits him slightly better than further these days. (op 10-3 tchd 7-2)
Waveband ran a cracker following her recent Wolverhampton third on debut for this stable, coping as well with the switch to Fibresand and drop to 5f as her pedigree and running style suggested she would. She's in good hands for a sprinter and shouldn't be long going one better. (op 7-2)
Sir Geoffrey (IRE) was readily left behind when the race really began in earnest and that he was, having looked a natural on the surface on his debut here last time out, suggests that the first two put up useful performances. (op 10-3)
Luscivious, having just his second run for his new yard, was again below his best, but he showed enough in plugging on for fourth to think that now he is dropping down the weights his turn might not be far away as his stable get to know him better. (tchd 12-1)
Cape Vale (IRE) wasn't able to dictate as easily as he had when winning at 6f here two runs back and paid for his exertions late on. (op 7-1)
Green Manalishi is a bit long in the tooth to be making his Fibresand debut but he wasn't far away before lack of a recent run and a mark that still looks a bit high given some of his more recent efforts took their toll. (tchd 20-1)
Nickel Silver compromised his chance with a tardy start. (tchd 14-1)
Mo Mhuirnin (IRE) was another soon on the back foot after a slow start. She dropped right away when beaten and probably needed this first run since April badly. (op 10-1)

3 MEMBERSHIP OF SOUTHWELL GOLF CLUB H'CAP 1m 6f (F)

1:25 (1:25) (Class 5) (0-75,69) 4-Y-0+ **£1,910** (£564; £282) **Stalls** Low

Form RPR

223- **1** **Shifting Gold (IRE)**[11] 7957 5-8-12 57 ... (b) AmyRyan(3) 5 65
(Kevin Ryan) *dwlt: sn led: pushed along and hdd 4f out: rdn 3f out: swtchd wd over 2f out and sn drvn: styd on gamely u.p to chal ent fnl f: kpt on gamely to ld last 50yds* **9/2**[3]

321- **2** *1/2* **Stadium Of Light (IRE)**[16] 7896 4-9-7 69 ... BarryMcHugh 4 76
(Brian Ellison) *hld up in rr: niggled along over 4f out: hdwy on inner 3f out: rdn to chse ldr 2f out: styd on to ld appr fnl f: sn drvn: hdd and no ex last 50yds* **5/2**[1]

2/3- **3** *5* **Agglestone Rock**[153] 1012 6-9-10 66 ... RussKennemore 2 66
(Philip Kirby) *t.k.h: prom: led gng wl 4f out: rdn 2f out: hdd appr fnl f and sn wknd* **7/2**[2]

032- **4** *6* **Jasmin Rai**[15] 7909 4-8-6 54 ... CathyGannon 1 46
(Des Donovan) *hld up in tch: hdwy to trck ldng pair bef 1/2-way: pushed along over 4f out: rdn over 3f out and grad wknd* **7/1**

012- **5** *14* **Dart**[33] 7632 7-9-12 68 ... GrahamGibbons 3 40
(John Mackie) *trckd ldrs: effrt 4f out: rdn along over 3f out: sn drvn and wknd* **5/2**[1]

3m 10.05s (1.75) **Going Correction** +0.125s/f (Slow)
WFA 4 from 5yo+ 6lb **5** Ran SP% **110.0**
Speed ratings (Par 103): **100,99,96,93,85**
CSF £15.96 TOTE £4.30 : £2.30, £1.10; EX 13.60.
Owner Hambleton Racing Ltd VIII **Bred** Watership Down Stud **Trained** Hambleton, N Yorks
■ Stewards' Enquiry : Barry McHugh one-day ban: used whip with excessive frequency (Jan 15)

FOCUS
A modest handicap run at a fair pace yet one in which the complexion changed dramatically in the straight.
Dart Official explanation: trainer had no explanation for the poor form shown

4 PAY AND PLAY SOUTHWELL GOLF CLUB H'CAP 6f (F)

1:55 (1:56) (Class 5) (0-75,76) 3-Y-0 **£1,910** (£564; £282) **Stalls** Low

Form RPR

111- **1** **Even Stevens**[15] 7908 3-9-3 73 ... BillyCray(3) 4 78
(David Nicholls) *s.i.s: hdwy 1/2-way: chsd ldrs 2f out: sn rdn and edgd rt: drvn to ld ins fnl f: hld on gamely towards fin* **8/13**[1]

251- **2** *hd* **Shostakovich (IRE)**[5] 7982 3-9-9 76 6ex ... (tp) JamesDoyle 1 80
(Sylvester Kirk) *cl up on inner: led 1/2-way: rdn 2f out: drvn over 1f out: hdd ins fnl f: kpt on wl u.p* **6/1**[2]

120- **3** *1 1/4* **Je Suis Unrockstar**[3] 7997 3-8-13 69 ow1 ... (p) MichaelO'Connell(3) 6 69
(David Nicholls) *chsd ldng pair: hdwy on outer and cl up 1/2-way: rdn to chal 2f out and ev ch tl drvn and one pce ins fnl f* **12/1**

433- **4** *3/4* **Sacrosanctus**[3] 7997 3-9-6 73 ... IanMongan 2 71
(David Nicholls) *led to 1/2-way: cl up: rdn: sltly outpcd and n.m.r 2f out: sn swtchd lft and drvn: kpt on same pce* **13/2**[3]

053- **5** *14* **Lexi's Boy (IRE)**[160] 4402 3-8-9 62 ... CathyGannon 3 15
(Kevin Ryan) *in tch: rdn along 1/2-way: outpcd and bhd fnl 2f* **28/1**

1m 17.22s (0.72) **Going Correction** +0.125s/f (Slow) **5** Ran SP% **100.7**
Speed ratings (Par 97): **100,99,98,97,78**
toteswinger: 1&2 £2.80. CSF £3.61 TOTE £1.40 : £1.10, £1.90; EX 3.10.
Owner Paul J Dixon **Bred** Mrs Yvette Dixon **Trained** Sessay, N Yorks
■ Monsieur Jamie was withdrawn (17/2, broke out of stalls). Deduct 10p in the £ under R4.
■ Stewards' Enquiry : James Doyle three-day ban: used whip with excessive frequency (Jan 15-17)

FOCUS
Quite an interesting nursery despite the late withdrawal of one of the runners, with the first four all coming into the race in top form. The gallop was only a fair one but the result still takes little explaining.

5 NEW YEAR AT SOUTHWELL GOLF CLUB (S) STKS 1m (F)

2:30 (2:30) (Class 6) 3-Y-0 **£1,535** (£453; £226) **Stalls** Low

Form RPR

0- **1** **Double Duchess**[37] 7567 3-8-7 0 ... LiamJones 6 61+
(Paul D'Arcy) *mde all: rdn 2f out: drvn over 1f out: styd on strly and clr ins fnl f* **85/40**[2]

052- **2** *4 1/2* **Ad Vitam (IRE)**[30] 7664 3-8-12 57 ... (t) JamesDoyle 3 56
(Sylvester Kirk) *prom: rdn along and sltly outpcd 1/2-way: hdwy u.p to chse wnr over 1f out: drvn and no imp fnl f* **11/4**[3]

651- **3** *nk* **Boogie Star**[22] 7801 3-8-13 60 ... (p) RyanPowell(5) 1 61
(J S Moore) *hld up towards rr: hdwy on inner wl over 2f out: rdn wl over 1f out: sn drvn and no imp appr fnl f* **2/1**[1]

005- **4** *2 1/2* **Blade Pirate**[21] 7839 3-8-12 45 ... (v1) KirstyMilczarek 2 50
(John Ryan) *trckd ldrs: hdwy and cl up 1/2-way: rdn to chal over 2f out and ev ch tl drvn and wknd over 1f out* **9/1**

000- **5** *5* **Evelyns Diamond**[22] 7801 3-8-5 26 ow1 ... PaulPickard(3) 4 34
(Paul Midgley) *chsd ldrs: rdn along 1/2-way: wknd over 2f out* **33/1**

0- **6** *33* **Ice Angel**[42] 7527 3-8-8 0 ow1 ... RobbieFitzpatrick 5 —
(Derek Shaw) *a in rr: rdn along bef 1/2-way: sn outpcd and bhd* **25/1**

1m 45.78s (2.08) **Going Correction** +0.125s/f (Slow) **6** Ran SP% **108.8**
Speed ratings (Par 95): **94,89,89,86,81 48**
toteswingers: 1&2 £1.50, 1&3 £1.60, 2&3 £1.20. CSF £7.82 TOTE £3.90 : £3.20, £1.30; EX 8.80.The winner was bought in for 10,500gns.
Owner Mrs Jan Harris **Bred** Mrs J Harris **Trained** Newmarket, Suffolk

FOCUS
A weak seller but the winner is unexposed and probably a bit better than this grade. Once again, the pace wasn't strong.

6 PLAY GOLF BEFORE RACING AT SOUTHWELL H'CAP 1m (F)

3:05 (3:06) (Class 3) (0-95,96) 4-Y-0+ **£4,533** (£1,348; £674; £336) **Stalls** Low

Form RPR

400- **1** **Reve De Nuit (USA)**[70] 7100 5-9-2 90 ... JamesDoyle 8 99
(Alan McCabe) *prom: hdwy to ld over 2f out: rdn wl over 1f out: drvn and edgd rt ent fnl f: kpt on gamely* **4/1**[2]

621- **2** *3/4* **Nightjar (USA)**[14] 7935 6-9-4 92 ... PhillipMakin 4 99
(Kevin Ryan) *trckd ldrs: hdwy over 2f out: rdn and ev ch whn n.m.r and swtchd lft ent fnl f: sn drvn and kpt on same pce* **5/1**[3]

142- **3** *3/4* **Lowther**[10] 7970 6-9-3 96 ... (be) SladeO'Hara(5) 6 101
(Alan Bailey) *dwlt: hdwy 1/2-way: chsd ldrs whn n.m.r and swtchd rt wl over 1f out: sn rdn and ev ch tl drvn: n.m.r and one pce wl ins fnl f* **8/1**

353- **4** *3* **Trans Sonic**[14] 7935 8-8-9 86 ... JamesSullivan(3) 2 84
(David O'Meara) *led: rdn along and hdd 3f out: drvn and sltly outpcd wl over 1f out: kpt on u.p fnl f* **8/1**

014- **5** *3/4* **Hidden Glory**[21] 7828 4-8-11 85 ... MickyFenton 1 82
(James Given) *in tch: hdwy on inner over 2f out: rdn and ch over 1f out: sn drvn and kpt on same pce* **10/1**

001- **6** *5* **Webbow (IRE)**[22] 7816 9-9-0 88 ... J-PGuillambert 9 73
(Brian Ellison) *prom on outer: hdwy and cl up 3f out: sn rdn and ch tl drvn and wknd over 1f out* **11/4**[1]

600- **7** *1 1/4* **Thunderstruck**[3] 8009 6-8-11 85 ... (p) BarryMcHugh 5 67
(David Nicholls) *cp: led briefly 3f out: sn rdn and hdd over 2f out: drvn wl over 1f out and grad wknd* **16/1**

404- **8** *4* **Rasselas (IRE)**[85] 6709 4-8-6 **83**.. BillyCray(3) 3 56
(David Nicholls) *a towards rr* **14/1**
613- **9** *4 ½* **Bencoolen (IRE)**[79] 6877 6-8-13 **90**.................... MichaelO'Connell(3) 10 53
(David Nicholls) *j. awkwardly and s.i.s: a in rr* **12/1**
041- **10** *14* **Rugell (ARG)**[96] 6423 6-9-3 **91**.................................. RobbieFitzpatrick 7 22
(Derek Shaw) *nvr bttr than midfield* **25/1**
1m 42.9s (-0.80) **Going Correction** +0.125s/f (Slow) **10** Ran SP% **118.7**
Speed ratings (Par 107): **109,108,107,104,103 98,97,93,89,75**
toteswingers: 1&2 £5.90, 1&3 £8.40, 2&3 £4.10. CSF £24.92 CT £155.10 TOTE £5.80: £2.20, £2.30, £1.70; EX 22.50 Trifecta £286.50 Pool: £704.80 - 1.82 winning units..
Owner Mrs Z Wentworth **Bred** Ecurie Du Haras De Meautry **Trained** Averham Park, Notts
■ Stewards' Enquiry : Phillip Makin caution: used whip down the shoulder in the forehand position

FOCUS
A competitive race run at a fair gallop and given that the first two from the 2010 renewal edged out one at the top of his game, the trio clear of some other course specialists, then this promises to represent solid form.

NOTEBOOK
Reve De Nuit(USA) hasn't often been in the frame since winning this same race last year off a 2lb lower mark, but he'd often run creditably in that time. Gelded since he last ran, he showed a degree of versatility in overcoming a steadier-than-ideal gallop back in trip under a good ride, sent for home early in the straight and seeing his race out strongly to land some good support. He's now 2-3 on this surface but his new rating will ensure he won't get many more opportunities back here. (op 12-1)
Nightjar(USA) had been second in this last year off a 3lb higher mark and once again made a bold bid trying this trip for the first time since. He wasn't making much impression inside the last and for all he clearly stays he is probably best round here given a strongly-run 7f. (op 4-1)
Lowther ran very well considering that he was set a bit more to do than the first two, in so doing putting his only previous run on the surface behind him. He was probably just anchored late on by a recent 4lb rise for chasing home the progressive Final Drive, but his run here suggests he's right back to his best as well as reflecting great credit on that horse. (op 7-1)
Trans Sonic is finding life tough now he's up at this sort of mark but he ran creditably for all he left the impression rallying late that he might have fared better had he set a stronger gallop in front. (tchd 15-2)
Hidden Glory seemed to find the competition back in trip a bit hot having won over as far as 1m3f here at the start of last month. (op 8-1)
Webbow(IRE), a winner here back in 2006, wasn't able to build on his recent win in a rather muddling-looking race at Dundalk on his debut for his new yard, dropping out tamely as if all wasn't well. He's long been a reliable performer in the top handicaps on turf and he should do well in that sphere in 2011 for all that he's an infrequent winner. (op 4-1)
Thunderstruck wasn't discredited turned out quickly again following a long break and two runs in a week will ensure his mark quickly gets downgraded. He should be spot on soon and is worth looking out for in a race where he seems guaranteed an easy lead. (tchd 14-1)

7 BET AT BLUESQ.COM H'CAP 1m (F)
3:40 (3:41) (Class 6) (0-55,55) 4-Y-0+ **£1,535** (£453; £226) **Stalls** Low

Form RPR
530- **1** **Zarius**[19] 7863 4-8-9 **55**.. NannaHansen(7) 1 64
(Chris Wall) *cl up on inner: led after 2f: styd far side home st: rdn wl over 1f out: kpt on wl towards fin* **8/1**
2 *1* **Powerful Presence (IRE)**[82] 6822 5-8-11 **50**............... BarryMcHugh 6 57
(David O'Meara) *hld up in tch: smooth hdwy on outer 3f out: rdn to chal 2f out: drvn and edgd rt over 1f out: ev ch tl kpt on same pce last 100yds* **9/4**[1]
142- **3** *½* **Royal Island (IRE)**[21] 7835 9-8-13 **52**............................ MickyFenton 3 58
(Michael Quinlan) *dwlt: hld up in rr: gd hdwy on outer over 2f out: sn rdn to chse ldng pair: swtchd lft over 1f out: drvn and styd on ins fnl f* **7/2**[2]
433- **4** *2 ¼* **Bring Sweets (IRE)**[15] 7918 4-8-5 **49**.......................... DeanHeslop(5) 5 50
(Brian Ellison) *hld up in tch: hdwy 3f out: rdn 2f out: kpt on appr fnl f: nrst fin* **7/2**[2]
000- **5** *10* **Very Well Red**[16] 7890 8-9-0 **53**................................. WilliamCarson 7 31
(Peter Hiatt) *led 2f: cl up on outer: rdn along over 3f out: drvn over 2f out and sn wknd* **5/1**[3]
000- **6** *4 ½* **Montego Breeze**[123] 5634 5-8-13 **52**....................... RobbieFitzpatrick 4 19
(Derek Shaw) *chsd ldrs: rdn along over 3f out: sn wknd* **14/1**
060- **7** *23* **Yorksters Prince (IRE)**[101] 6287 4-8-13 **52**.............. KirstyMilczarek 2 —
(George Prodromou) *chsd ldrs: rdn along over 3f out: sn wknd* **18/1**
1m 44.14s (0.44) **Going Correction** +0.125s/f (Slow) **7** Ran SP% **114.9**
Speed ratings (Par 101): **102,101,100,98,88 83,60**
toteswingers: 1&2 £3.60, 1&3 £2.90, 2&3 £2.40. CSF £26.69 TOTE £8.00: £4.60, £1.90; EX 35.30.
Owner Mervyn Ayers **Bred** Executive Bloodlines Ltd **Trained** Newmarket, Suffolk
■ Nanna Hansen's first winner in Britain, but she has ridden winners in Denmark.

FOCUS
A weak finale. Again the pace wasn't particularly strong and the winner was able to make all.
T/Plt: £19.00 to a £1 stake. Pool of £45,008.23 - 1,726.61 winning tickets. T/Qpdt: £7.80 to a £1 stake. Pool of £3,287.26 - 311.50 winning tickets. JR

[1]SOUTHWELL (L-H)
Sunday, January 2

OFFICIAL GOING: Standard
Wind: Light, half behind Weather: Fine but overcast and cold

8 BLUESQ.COM ON YOUR IPHONE AMATEUR RIDERS' H'CAP 2m (F)
12:30 (12:31) (Class 6) (0-65,65) 4-Y-0+ **£1,483** (£456; £228) **Stalls** Low

Form RPR
232- **1** **Zed Candy (FR)**[23] 7805 8-10-1 **55**......... MissPernillaHermansson(3) 10 64
(Richard Ford) *hld up in rr: hdwy 9f out: chal over 3f out: led and wnt lft over 2f out: kpt on wl* **11/2**[3]
003- **2** *1 ¾* **Elite Land**[39] 7145 8-10-8 **64**.. MrFMitchell(5) 8 71
(Brian Ellison) *swtchd lft after s: hld up in rr: stdy hdwy 8f out: chsd wnr over 1f out: styd on same pce* **4/1**[1]
004- **3** *2 ½* **Night Orbit**[55] 6621 7-10-3 **57**.................................. MrPCollington(3) 13 61
(Julia Feilden) *in rr: sn drvn along: bhd 8f out: hdwy on outside over 3f out: styd on to take 3rd clsng stages* **12/1**
405- **4** *1 ¼* **Mashdood (USA)**[29] 7695 5-10-9 **60**.............................. MrSWalker 12 62
(Peter Hiatt) *led tl 7f out: led over 3f out: hdd over 2f out: sn hmpd and swtchd rt: one pce* **11/1**
005- **5** *3 ¾* **Silent Lucidity (IRE)**[53] 7398 7-10-1 **52**...............(p) MissSBrotherton 14 50
(Peter Niven) *chsd ldrs: drvn 6f out: outpcd over 3f out: no threat after* **8/1**
232- **6** *11* **Baltimore Patriot (IRE)**[189] 1816 8-9-13 **57**.............. MissEHughes(7) 6 42+
(Barry Brennan) *hld up in mid-div: lost pl 6f out: rdr lost irons 2f out* **14/1**
020- **7** *nk* **Hi Dancer**[34] 7632 8-10-8 **64**........................ MissCharlotteHolmes(5) 7 48
(Ben Haslam) *t.k.h: w ldrs: lost pl over 2f out* **20/1**
000/ **8** *¾* **Sovereign Spirit (IRE)**[395] 7608 9-9-6 **50**.........(t) MissAmyAppleton(7) 1 33
(Chris Gordon) *trckd ldrs: t.k.h: hmpd and stmbld bnd after 2f: lost pl over 4f out* **33/1**
043- **9** *1 ¾* **Sir Boss (IRE)**[46] 7490 6-10-11 **65**........................ MissMMullineaux(3) 3 46
(Michael Mullineaux) *chsd ldrs: led 7f out tl over 3f out: wknd over 2f out* **8/1**
200/ **10** *¾* **Calatagan (IRE)**[48] 6662 12-10-1 **55**...................... MissRJefferson(3) 11 35
(Malcolm Jefferson) *hld up in rr: hdwy after 6f: in tch and drvn over 5f out: rdn over 3f out: sn wknd* **11/1**
455- **11** *21* **Yeomanry**[17] 7896 6-9-10 **52** ow2..................................(p) MrJHodson(5) 4 —
(Ian Williams) *w ldrs: lost pl over 3f out: sn bhd: t.o* **5/1**[2]
006/ **12** *dist* **Carlton Mac**[331] 6177 6-9-6 **48** oh1 ow2.......................... JustinNewman(5) 5 —
(Simon Griffiths) *chsd ldrs: lost pl after 4f: sn bhd: t.o 7f out: virtually p.u: eventually completed* **100/1**
/00- **R** **Aberdeen Park**[12] 7957 9-9-5 **47** oh1 ow1........(v[1]) JonathanEngland(5) 9 —
(David Evans) *ref to r: lft in stalls* **22/1**
3m 49.97s (4.47) **Going Correction** +0.15s/f (Slow)
WFA 4 from 5yo+ 7lb **13** Ran SP% **118.3**
Speed ratings (Par 101): **94,93,91,91,89 83,83,83,82,82 71,—,—**
toteswingers: 1&2 £9.50, 1&3 £12.80, 2&3 £9.50. CSF £26.34 CT £257.42 TOTE £4.50: £1.70, £2.30, £6.10; EX 23.30 Trifecta £74.20 Part won. Pool: £100.40 - 0.60 winning units..
Owner J T S (International) Ltd **Bred** Haras De Saint Pair Du Mont **Trained** Butterton, Staffs
■ Stewards' Enquiry : Miss Pernilla Hermansson two-day ban: careless riding (tbn)
Mr J Hodson three-day ban: weighed in 2lbs heavy (tbn)
Mr S Walker three-day ban: careless riding (tbn)

FOCUS
A modest handicap for amateur riders. The pace didn't seem strong with several pulling hard early but plenty were in trouble a long way out.

9 ENHANCED SP'S AT BLUESQ.COM H'CAP 7f (F)
1:00 (1:00) (Class 5) (0-70,75) 4-Y-0+ **£1,978** (£584; £292) **Stalls** Low

Form RPR
231- **1** **Dubai Hills**[12] 7956 5-9-5 **75**.. AdamCarter(7) 6 102+
(Bryan Smart) *edgd lft after s and led: pushed along and qcknd 3f out: wl clr over 1f out: heavily eased: v easily* **4/6**[1]
532- **2** *8* **The Lock Master (IRE)**[12] 7956 4-9-3 **66**.................... NeilChalmers 4 66
(Michael Appleby) *in rr: hdwy on outside over 3f out: styd on to take 2nd jst ins fnl f* **10/1**
342- **3** *nk* **This Ones For Eddy**[19] 7870 6-8-10 **59**.........................(p) LukeMorris 8 58
(John Balding) *chsd ldrs: hung lft and one pce fnl 2f* **13/2**[2]
100- **4** *1 ¼* **Elusive Warrior (USA)**[52] 7403 8-8-13 **69**...............(p) NoraLooby(7) 7 65
(Alan McCabe) *w wnr: drvn 3f out: one pce* **25/1**
165- **5** *4* **Peter's Gift (IRE)**[12] 7956 5-8-13 **62**...........................(p) PhillipMakin 2 48
(Kevin Ryan) *chsd ldrs: drvn over 4f out: wknd over 1f out* **25/1**
400- **6** *¾* **Headache**[3] 8014 6-9-2 **68**...................................(bt) RobertLButler(3) 3 52
(Brendan W Duke, Ire) *s.i.s: in rr: nvr nr ldrs* **16/1**
003- **7** *1 ¼* **Fault**[12] 7956 5-9-3 **66**...(t) TomQueally 1 46
(Stef Higgins) *chsd ldrs: outpcd 4f out: wknd 2f out* **18/1**
016- **8** *¾* **Sirjosh**[5] 7992 5-8-12 **61**.. CathyGannon 5 39
(Des Donovan) *s.i.s: sn drvn along: lost pl over 4f out: eased fnl f* **7/1**[3]
1m 29.24s (-1.06) **Going Correction** +0.15s/f (Slow) **8** Ran SP% **113.8**
Speed ratings (Par 103): **112,102,102,101,96 95,94,93**
toteswingers: 1&2 £2.60, 1&3 £1.60, 2&3 £4.70. CSF £8.34 CT £24.69 TOTE £1.80: £1.10, £2.70, £1.80; EX 6.20 Trifecta £24.20 Pool: £369.72 - 11.29 winning units..
Owner Mrs F Denniff **Bred** A S Denniff **Trained** Hambleton, N Yorks

FOCUS
A one-horse race and another very impressive performance from the fast-improving winner.
Sirjosh Official explanation: jockey said gelding had no more to give

10 BOOK TICKETS AT SOUTHWELL-RACECOURSE.CO.UK CLAIMING STKS 6f (F)
1:30 (1:31) (Class 6) 3-Y-O **£1,535** (£453; £226) **Stalls** Low

Form RPR
355- **1** **Local Diktator**[16] 7910 3-8-11 54..(t) LukeMorris 5 62
(Ronald Harris) *sn w ldr: rdn 3f out: edgd lft over 1f out: kpt on to ld last 75yds* **12/1**[3]
503- **2** *1 ¼* **Honkers Bonkers**[27] 7722 3-8-10 65................................ JamesDoyle 4 57
(Alan McCabe) *led: qcknd 3f out: edgd rt over 1f out: hdd and no ex wl ins fnl f* **9/4**[2]
214- **3** *2 ½* **Bilko Pak (IRE)**[33] 7636 3-9-2 80....................................... TomQueally 2 55
(James Given) *chsd ldrs: drvn and outpcd 3f out: kpt on one pce* **8/15**[1]
600- **4** *7* **Miss Moneypenni**[104] 6258 3-8-3 59 ow1......................... RyanClark(5) 3 25
(Nick Littmoden) *chsd ldrs on outer: drvn 3f out: wknd 2f out* **33/1**
05-4 **5** *shd* **Blade Pirate**[1] 5 3-8-7 49...(e[1]) KirstyMilczarek 1 23
(John Ryan) *chsd ldrs: drvn and outpcd over 3f out: wknd over 1f out* **28/1**
1m 18.0s (1.50) **Going Correction** +0.15s/f (Slow) **5** Ran SP% **110.1**
Speed ratings (Par 95): **96,94,91,81,81**
CSF £38.83 TOTE £8.50: £2.20, £1.30; EX 49.10.
Owner P Nurcombe **Bred** Mrs D J Hughes **Trained** Earlswood, Monmouths

FOCUS
A two-horse race according to the betting but something of a surprise at the end of a well-run affair.
Bilko Pak(IRE) Official explanation: jockey said colt was unsuited to fibersand

11 STANLEY "JOCK" MAIDEN STKS 1m 4f (F)
2:05 (2:05) (Class 5) 4-Y-0+ **£1,813** (£539; £269; £134) **Stalls** Low

Form RPR
33- **1** **Odin's Raven (IRE)**[24] 7787 6-9-7 55.............................. JimmyQuinn 4 68
(Brian Ellison) *mid-div: wnt 2nd over 4f out: led over 1f out: styd on u.p* **11/2**[3]
432- **2** *2 ¼* **Palawi (IRE)**[50] 6623 4-9-3 75... PhillipMakin 8 64
(John Quinn) *trckd ldr: led 6f out: hdd over 1f out: kpt on same pce* **4/6**[1]
23- **3** *1 ¼* **Eshtyaaq**[236] 2011 4-9-3 0... MartinLane 3 62
(David Evans) *chsd ldrs: styd on one pce fnl 2f* **9/2**[2]
4 *1* **River Dragon (IRE)**[11] 6-9-7 0..................................(p) BarryMcHugh 1 61
(Neville Bycroft) *dwlt: in rr: hdwy over 4f out: one pce fnl 2f* **12/1**
0- **5** *2* **Bullring (FR)**[17] 7896 5-9-4 0.................................. JamesSullivan(3) 7 58?
(Peter Niven) *dwlt: mid-div: hdwy over 7f out: one pce fnl 3f* **100/1**
000- **6** *6* **Sweet Seville (FR)**[11] 7968 7-8-11 42.......................... MarkCoumbe(5) 6 43
(Terry Clement) *led tl 6f out: wknd 2f out* **100/1**
000- **7** *2 ½* **Maybeme**[68] 7147 5-9-2 47.. ChrisCatlin 5 39
(Neville Bycroft) *in rr: bhd and drvn over 5f out: nvr a factor* **40/1**
4- **8** *nk* **Bold Warning**[17] 7896 7-9-7 0....................................... GregFairley 10 44
(Alex Hales) *mid-div: drvn over 5f out: wknd over 2f out* **50/1**

2- **9** *11* **Truly Magnificent (USA)**[22] 7834 4-8-9 0................. RobertLButler(3) 2 21
(Brendan W Duke, Ire) *in rr: sn pushed along: bhd fnl 4f* **25/1**

55- **10** *1 ½* **Cabuchon (GER)**[17] 7887 4-9-3 0.................................... TomQueally 9 24
(Barney Curley) *sn chsng ldrs: lost pl over 2f out* **20/1**

2m 43.69s (2.69) **Going Correction** +0.15s/f (Slow)
WFA 4 from 5yo+ 4lb **10** Ran SP% **116.2**
Speed ratings (Par 103): **97,95,94,94,92 88,87,86,79,78**
toteswingers: 1&2 £1.50, 1&3 £4.20, 2&3 £1.90. CSF £9.22 TOTE £4.90: £1.30, £1.30, £1.02; EX 13.00 Trifecta £30.60 Pool: £447.54 - 10.80 winning units..
Owner Racing Management & Training Ltd **Bred** Newberry Stud Company **Trained** Norton, N Yorks

FOCUS
A modest maiden in which the field were well bunched to the home turn.

12 MEMBERSHIP OF SOUTHWELL GOLF CLUB CLAIMING STKS 1m (F)
2:35 (2:35) (Class 6) 4-Y-0+ **£1,535** (£453; £226) **Stalls** Low

Form RPR

544- **1** **Ours (IRE)**[19] 7867 8-9-9 83..(p) BarryMcHugh 2 83
(John Harris) *s.s: detached in last tl hdwy on wd outside over 2f out: rdn to ld appr fnl f: kpt on wl* **10/3**[2]

212- **2** *1 ½* **Lakeman (IRE)**[17] 7897 5-8-8 65..............................(be) DeanHeslop(5) 4 70
(Brian Ellison) *chsd ldrs: chal over 1f out: kpt on same pce* **4/1**[3]

410- **3** *6* **April Fool**[30] 7679 7-8-13 67..(v) ChrisCatlin 3 56
(Ronald Harris) *led: hdd 3f out: wknd appr fnl f* **5/2**[1]

000- **4** *1 ½* **Raghdaan**[27] 7731 4-8-9 43.. CathyGannon 7 49
(Peter Hiatt) *sn w ldr: led 3f out: hdd appr fnl f: sn wknd* **33/1**

000- **5** *11* **Hard Rock City (USA)**[16] 7906 11-9-0 84......................... NeilFarley(5) 6 33
(Declan Carroll) *mid-div on outer: drvn over 4f out: lost pl over 2f out* **5/1**

004- **6** *1 ¾* **Vogarth**[22] 7832 7-8-7 45..(v) WilliamCarson 5 17
(Michael Chapman) *mid-div: drvn over 4f out: hung lft over 2f out: sn lost pl* **50/1**

510- **7** *11* **Aviso (GER)**[51] 7421 7-9-9 71.. TomQueally 1 8
(Barney Curley) *mid-div: drvn and lost pl over 4f out: bhd whn eased fnl f* **5/1**

1m 44.14s (0.44) **Going Correction** +0.15s/f (Slow) **7** Ran SP% **109.9**
Speed ratings (Par 101): **103,101,95,94,83 81,70**
toteswingers: 1&2 £2.20, 1&3 £2.10, 2&3 £1.90. CSF £15.62 TOTE £2.60: £1.90, £2.10; EX 13.60.
Owner Peter Smith P C Coaches Limited **Bred** David John Brown **Trained** Eastwell, Leics

FOCUS
An uncompetitive claimer run at a strong pace that played very much into the hands of the winner.

13 GOLF BEFORE RACING AT SOUTHWELL H'CAP 6f (F)
3:05 (3:06) (Class 5) (0-70,70) 4-Y-0+ **£1,910** (£564; £282) **Stalls** Low

Form RPR

024- **1** **Sir Louis**[16] 7911 4-8-7 **56**.. BarryMcHugh 3 66+
(Richard Fahey) *trckd ldrs gng wl: led on bit over 2f out: rdn rigtht out* **14/1**

002- **2** *1* **Bel Cantor**[15] 7936 8-8-10 **59**...(p) WilliamCarson 2 66
(Bill Ratcliffe) *chsd ldrs: wnt 2nd over 1f out: styd on same pce fnl 100yds* **7/1**

166- **3** *1 ½* **Takajan (IRE)**[16] 7906 4-8-10 **66**.................................. JamesRogers(7) 4 68
(Mark Brisbourne) *trckd ldrs: effrt on wd outside 2f out: hung lft: kpt on same pce* **17/2**

000- **4** *2 ¾* **Charles Parnell (IRE)**[19] 7870 8-8-4 **60**......................... NoraLooby(7) 10 53+
(Simon Griffiths) *dwlt: in rr: hdwy over 2f out: kpt on: nvr trbld ldrs* **12/1**

213- **5** *shd* **Boy The Bell**[26] 7738 4-8-1 **57**.................................. JosephYoung(7) 6 50
(Michael Mullineaux) *chsd ldrs on outer: edgd lft over 2f out: kpt on one pce fnl f* **11/1**

241- **6** *2 ½* **Prince James**[22] 7841 4-9-4 **70**.................................. JamesSullivan(3) 9 55
(Michael Easterby) *in rr: effrt on outer 3f out: sn outpcd: edgd lft and kpt on appr fnl f* **9/2**[2]

424- **7** *nk* **Memphis Man**[11] 7973 8-8-7 **56** oh2.................................... MartinLane 8 40
(David Evans) *dwlt: in rr: hrd drvn over 2f out: nvr a factor* **16/1**

341- **8** *nse* **Cups Of Storms**[26] 7738 8-9-1 **64**....................................(b) PhillipMakin 1 48
(Roy Brotherton) *led tl over 2f out: wknd over 1f out* **11/[illegible]**[3]

120- **9** *2 ¼* **Desert Strike**[4] 8004 5-9-5 **68**......................................(p) NeilChalmers 7 45
(Alan McCabe) *dwlt: swtchd lft after s: hdwy on ins over 2f out: edgd rt and wknd over 1f out* **4/1**[1]

450- **10** *1* **Errigal Lad**[40] 7537 6-8-8 **57**...(p) LukeMorris 5 31
(John Balding) *w ldrs: rdn 3f out: sn lost pl* **15/2**

1m 16.68s (0.18) **Going Correction** +0.15s/f (Slow) **10** Ran SP% **116.9**
Speed ratings (Par 103): **104,102,100,97,96 93,93,93,90,88**
toteswingers: 1&2 £27.60, 1&3 £22.00, 2&3 £17.90. CSF £108.80 CT £651.09 TOTE £11.60: £2.90, £2.80, £4.30; EX 103.70 Trifecta £252.80 Part won. Pool: £341.69 - 0.50 winning units..
Owner P Ashton **Bred** Brigadier C K Price **Trained** Musley Bank, N Yorks

FOCUS
A fair handicap run at a sound enough tempo, though little got into the race from the rear.

14 PLAY RAINBOW RICHES AT BLUESQ.COM H'CAP 7f (F)
3:40 (3:41) (Class 6) (0-55,55) 4-Y-0+ **£1,535** (£453; £226) **Stalls** Low

Form RPR

066- **1** **Penrod Ballantyne (IRE)**[29] 7706 4-9-0 **53**...................... LukeMorris 7 60
(Mike Hammond) *in rr: effrt over 2f out: hung lft and kpt on on ins to ld last 75yds* **25/1**

042- **2** *½* **Gold Story**[16] 7912 4-8-12 **51**.......................................(be[1]) JimmyQuinn 3 57
(Brian Ellison) *trckd ldrs: led on inner 2f out: hdd and no ex wl ins fnl f* **3/1**[1]

232- **3** *nk* **Itsthursdayalready**[16] 7911 4-9-0 **53**........................... ShaneKelly 4 58
(Mark Brisbourne) *trckd ldrs: chal over 1f out: no ex fnl 50yds* **4/1**[2]

004- **4** *1 ¼* **Downhill Skier (IRE)**[23] 7812 7-9-2 **55**........................ PhillipMakin 8 57
(Mark Brisbourne) *chsd ldrs on outside: hung lft and kpt on same pce appr fnl f* **7/1**

642- **5** *1 ¼* **Norcroft**[3] 8024 9-8-7 **46** oh1..(p) WilliamCarson 1 44
(Christine Dunnett) *chsd ldrs: led over 4f out: sn rdn: hdd 2f out: hung rt and fdd appr fnl f* **11/2**

420- **6** *½* **Kielty's Folly**[6] 7986 7-8-12 **51**................................... GrahamGibbons 10 48
(Brian Baugh) *s.i.s: sn drvn along: kpt on fnl 2f: nvr a factor* **9/2**[3]

060- **7** *shd* **Sweet Possession (USA)**[208] 2840 5-8-11 **53**......... JamesSullivan(3) 6 50
(Pat Eddery) *chsd ldrs: one pce fnl 2f* **10/1**

054- **8** *6* **Baraconti (IRE)**[22] 7833 4-8-8 **47**......................................(p) ChrisCatlin 5 27
(Ruth Carr) *led tl over 4f out: wknd appr fnl f* **20/1**

660- **9** *6* **Sophie's Beau (USA)**[12] 7953 4-8-0 **46**........................ JackDuern(7) 11 10
(Michael Chapman) *s.s: hdwy on wd outside to chse ldrs over 4f out: wknd 2f out* **40/1**

50/- **10** *4 ½* **Sion Hill (IRE)**[384] 7755 10-8-11 **50**...............................(p) BarryMcHugh 9 —
(John Harris) *a towards rr* **50/1**

365- **11** *3 ½* **Captain Bluebird (IRE)**[81] 6847 4-9-0 **53**........................ CathyGannon 2 —
(Des Donovan) *rrd s: in rr: sme hdwy 3f out: sn wknd: eased fnl f* **16/1**

1m 30.93s (0.63) **Going Correction** +0.15s/f (Slow) **11** Ran SP% **119.0**
Speed ratings (Par 101): **102,101,101,99,98 97,97,90,83,78 74**
toteswingers: 1&2 £16.00, 1&3 £18.50, 2&3 £2.10. CSF £97.71 CT £380.76 TOTE £45.10: £10.10, £2.10, £1.10; EX 165.70 Trifecta £392.70 Part won. Pool: £530.70 - 0.01 winning units..
Owner J M T Court **Bred** Scuderia Eurosia Sas **Trained** Abberley, Worcs
■ Mike Hammond's first winner on the Flat.

FOCUS
A very modest handicap but an open one with several in with a chance from a long way out.
Penrod Ballantyne(IRE) Official explanation: trainer said, regarding the apparent improvement in form shown, gelding appeared to benefit from racing on the fibresand surface
T/Plt: £50.80 to a £1 stake. Pool of £47,564.05 - 683.09 winning tickets. T/Qpdt: £35.30 to a £1 stake. Pool of £3,598.06 - 75.30 winning tickets. WG

[8]SOUTHWELL (L-H)
Monday, January 3

OFFICIAL GOING: Standard
Wind: Virtually nil Weather: Overcast

15 BET ON WINNING DISTANCES AT BLUESQ.COM H'CAP 5f (F)
1:05 (1:08) (Class 6) (0-60,60) 4-Y-0+ **£1,535** (£453; £226) **Stalls** High

Form RPR

521- **1** **Residency (IRE)**[13] 7952 5-8-11 57...........................(p) AdamCarter(7) 7 67
(Bryan Smart) *cl up: rdn along wl over 1f out: hdwy to ld ins fnl f: sn edgd lft and kpt on ins fnl f* **5/2**[1]

132- **2** *1 ¼* **Your Gifted (IRE)**[13] 7953 4-9-0 60............................(e) DavidKenny(7) 3 65
(Patrick Morris) *trckd ldrs: hdwy on outer 1/2-way: rdn to ld 1 1/2f out: drvn and hdd ins fnl f: one pce* **4/1**[3]

204- **3** *nk* **Guto**[13] 7953 8-9-5 58.. WilliamCarson 2 62
(Bill Ratcliffe) *cl up: effrt over 2f out: sn rdn and ev ch tl drvn and one pce ent fnl f* **6/1**

601- **4** *2 ½* **Lets Move It**[13] 7953 4-8-13 52......................................(v) PatrickMathers 5 47
(Derek Shaw) *s.i.s: sn rdn along and outpcd in rr: hdwy wl over 1f out: kpt on ins fnl f: nrest at fin* **6/1**

004- **5** *½* **Stolt (IRE)**[21] 7859 7-9-3 59...................................... JamesSullivan(3) 4 52
(Linda Stubbs) *led: pushed along over 2f out: rdn and hdd wl over 1f out: sn drvn and wknd* **3/1**[2]

000- **6** *3 ¾* **Egyptian Lord**[7] 7984 8-8-8 47 oh1 ow1.................(b) RobbieFitzpatrick 1 27
(Peter Grayson) *prom on outer: rdn along after 2f: sn outpcd and bhd* **40/1**

000- **7** *2 ¾* **Steel City Boy (IRE)**[20] 7868 8-9-2 55................................ AdamKirby 6 25
(Derek Shaw) *chsd ldrs: rdn along 2f out: sn drvn and wknd* **12/1**

60.56 secs (0.86) **Going Correction** +0.20s/f (Slow) **7** Ran SP% **112.3**
Speed ratings (Par 101): **101,99,98,94,93 87,83**
toteswingers:1&2:£1.60, 2&3:£3.70, 1&3:£2.80 CSF £12.32 TOTE £4.20: £1.30, £1.20; EX 12.00.
Owner B Smart **Bred** Tally-Ho Stud **Trained** Hambleton, N Yorks
■ Stewards' Enquiry : William Carson one-day ban: used whip with excessive frequency (Jan 17)

FOCUS
A moderate sprint in which several had run against each other recently and two of them dominated the finish. The winner is rated back to his best old form under a claimer.
Stolt(IRE) Official explanation: vet said gelding bled from nose

16 ENHANCED SP'S AT BLUESQ.COM H'CAP 1m 3f (F)
1:40 (1:42) (Class 6) (0-60,58) 4-Y-0+ **£1,535** (£453; £226) **Stalls** Low

Form RPR

404- **1** **Stanley Rigby**[31] 7678 5-8-9 45.. BarryMcHugh 8 55
(Richard Fahey) *prom: hdwy to ld 3f out: rdn 2f out: drvn clr ent fnl f: kpt on* **8/1**

063- **2** *2 ½* **Carnac (IRE)**[13] 7958 5-8-12 48......................................(p) ShaneKelly 7 54
(Alan McCabe) *hld up: hdwy 1/2-way: trckd ldrs 4f out: effrt 3f out: sn rdn: drvn wl over 1f out: kpt on u.p fnl f: tk 2nd nr line* **3/1**[2]

045- **3** *shd* **Tivers Song (USA)**[79] 6921 7-8-6 45.......................(b) JamesSullivan(3) 1 50
(John Harris) *a.p: rdn along to chse wnr over 2f out: drvn over 1f out and kpt on same pce: lost 2nd nr line* **9/1**

041- **4** *1 ¾* **Miereveld**[17] 7909 4-9-5 58..(be) JimmyQuinn 2 60
(Brian Ellison) *trckd ldrs whn n.m.r bnd after 1 1/2f: sn taking t.k.h: hdwy on outer to trck ldrs 1/2-way: rdn along over 4f out: drvn over 2f out and sn one pce* **9/4**[1]

042- **5** *3 ¼* **Ramora (USA)**[7] 7985 5-9-2 57.................................... KylieManser(5) 6 55
(Olivia Maylam) *hld up: hdwy on inner to trck ldrs 4f out: pushed along and sltly outpcd whn n.m.r over 3f out: sn rdn and no imp fr wl over 1f out* **15/2**[3]

606- **6** *9* **Aldaado (IRE)**[16] 7933 5-9-5 55..(be) AdamKirby 4 35
(Paul Midgley) *sn led: rdn along 4f out: hdd 3f out and grad wknd* **8/1**

035- **7** *hd* **Mojeerr**[13] 7958 5-8-4 47 ow2......................................(v) HobieGill(7) 9 27
(Alan McCabe) *chsd ldrs: rdn along over 4f out: wknd 3f out* **18/1**

500- **8** *19* **Spacecraft (IRE)**[23] 7840 4-8-8 47................................ FrannyNorton 5 —
(Christopher Kellett) *a in rr: outpcd and bhd fnl 3f* **25/1**

460- **9** *5* **Northumberland**[18] 7896 5-8-9 45................................. WilliamCarson 3 —
(Michael Chapman) *a towards rr: outpcd and bhd fnl 3f* **20/1**

2m 28.1s (0.10) **Going Correction** +0.125s/f (Slow)
WFA 4 from 5yo+ 3lb **9** Ran SP% **113.6**
Speed ratings (Par 101): **104,102,102,100,98 91,91,77,74**
toteswingers:1&2:£5.50, 2&3:£4.20, 1&3:£13.10 CSF £31.71 CT £221.41 TOTE £6.60: £2.40, £2.10, £4.20; EX 41.60.
Owner Dean Hardman and Stella Kelsall **Bred** F C T Wilson **Trained** Musley Bank, N Yorks

FOCUS
A very moderate handicap with very few in any sort of form. The winner is rated back to his best with the runner-up close to recent form.

17 BLUESQ.COM ON YOUR IPHONE (S) STKS 7f (F)
2:10 (2:13) (Class 6) 4-Y-0+ **£1,535** (£453; £226) **Stalls** Low

Form RPR

510- **1** **Ace Of Spies (IRE)**[4] 8019 6-9-5 70................................. KirstyMilczarek 2 75
(Conor Dore) *cl up: rdn to ld over 2f out: drvn and hdd over 1f out: rallied wl u.p ins fnl f to ld nr fin* **2/1**[2]

550- **2** *nse* **Army Of Stars (IRE)**[74] 7047 5-9-0 73.........................(p) FergusSweeney 3 70
(Jamie Osborne) *cl up on outer: chal 3f out: rdn and slt ld over 1f out: drvn ins fnl f: hdd and nt qckn nr fin* **7/4**[1]

00-4 **3** *1 ¼* **Elusive Warrior (USA)**[1] 9 8-9-5 69............................(p) ShaneKelly 1 71
(Alan McCabe) *led: rdn along and hdd over 2f out: cl up tl drvn and one pce ent fnl f* **9/2**

421- **4** *10* **William Morgan (IRE)**[23] [7832] 4-9-5 60........................ VinceSlattery 4 44
(Alan Juckes) *dwlt: sn rdn along and outpcd in rr: a bhd* **4/1**[3]

1m 31.23s (0.93) **Going Correction** +0.125s/f (Slow) 4 Ran SP% **107.9**
Speed ratings (Par 101): **99,98,97,86**
CSF £5.82 TOTE £3.60; EX 4.20.There was no bid for the winner. Army of Stars was claimed by James Given for £5,000.

Owner Mrs Louise Marsh **Bred** Gainsborough Stud Management Ltd **Trained** Cowbit, Lincs

■ Stewards' Enquiry : Kirsty Milczarek five-day ban: used whip with excessive frequency and without giving mount time to repsond (Jan 17-21)

Fergus Sweeney caution: excessive use of whip

FOCUS
A fair race for this seller despite the small field, with the front three, all above-average for the grade, prducing a three-way battle and a close finish. The winner is rated to the form of his win two starts back.

18 PLACE ONLY BETTING AT BLUESQ.COM H'CAP 1m (F)
2:45 (2:47) (Class 4) (0-85,89) 4-Y-O+ **£3,399** (£1,011; £505; £252) **Stalls** Low

Form RPR

253- **1** **Follow The Flag (IRE)**[13] [7955] 7-9-1 77........................(v) ShaneKelly 3 84
(Alan McCabe) *in rr and outpcd after 1f: wd st: hdwy over 2f out: rdn over 1f out: led ins fnl f: kpt on wl* **8/1**

44-1 **2** *½* **Ours (IRE)**[1] [12] 8-9-13 89 6ex........................(p) BarryMcHugh 6 95
(John Harris) *s.i.s and bhd: hdwy on wd outside over 2f out: rdn wl over 1f out: led briefly ins fnl f: sn hdd and drvn: edgd lft and one pce last 75yds* **8/1**

634- **3** *4* **Elusive Fame (USA)**[13] [7955] 5-8-13 75........................(b) JimmyQuinn 5 72
(Mark Johnston) *trckd ldng pair: smooth hdwy on inner 3f out: led 2f out: rdn clr over 1f out: drvn and hdd ins fnl f: wknd* **7/2**[2]

052- **4** *7* **Snow Bay**[13] [7955] 5-9-4 83........................ MichaelO'Connell(3) 7 64
(David Nicholls) *trckd ldr: cl up 1/2-way: led 3f out: rdn and hdd 2f out: drvn over 1f out and sn wknd* **15/8**[1]

201- **5** *4* **El Dececy (USA)**[7] [7988] 7-9-3 79 6ex........................(p) AdamKirby 2 50
(John Balding) *led: rdn along and hdd 3f out: sn drvn and wknd over 2f out* **4/1**[3]

304- **6** *nse* **Unbreak My Heart (IRE)**[23] [7842] 6-8-13 82......... GeorgeChaloner(7) 4 53
(Richard Fahey) *chsd ldrs: hdwy over 3f out: rdn over 2f out and sn btn* **8/1**

1m 42.78s (-0.92) **Going Correction** +0.125s/f (Slow) 6 Ran SP% **110.3**
Speed ratings (Par 105): **109,108,104,97,93 93**
toteswingers:1&2:£9.70, 2&3:£1.80, 1&3:£4.90 CSF £63.27 TOTE £6.10: £2.10, £4.70; EX 47.40.

Owner S Gillen **Bred** Martin Francis **Trained** Averham Park, Notts

FOCUS
A decent handicap and quite competitive, with several in good recent form. They appeared to go a sound gallop as the first two came from well off the pace, and this may not be form to take too literally.

El Dececy(USA) Official explanation: jockey said gelding had no more to give

19 10% FORECAST BONUS AT BLUESQ.COM FILLIES' H'CAP 7f (F)
3:15 (3:17) (Class 5) (0-70,64) 4-Y-O+ **£2,047** (£604; £302) **Stalls** Low

Form RPR

004- **1** **Amary (IRE)**[13] [7956] 4-9-7 64........................(p) BarryMcHugh 5 71
(John Harris) *cl up: rdn along over 2f out: drvn to chse ldr over 1f out: styd on u.p ins fnl f to ld last 75yds* **9/1**[3]

604- **2** *1* **Positivity**[7] [7986] 5-8-11 54........................(p) JimmyQuinn 4 58
(Bryan Smart) *cl up: led 3f out: rdn over 1f out: drvn ins fnl f: hdd and no ex last 75yds* **3/1**[2]

006- **3** *2* **Noble Attitude**[110] [6098] 5-8-2 45........................ FrannyNorton 3 44
(Richard Guest) *hld up: hdwy on outer 2f out: rdn over 1f out: kpt on ins fnl f: nrest at fin* **22/1**

612- **4** *1 ¾* **Exopuntia**[7] [7986] 5-8-10 56........................ MichaelStainton(3) 1 50
(Julia Feilden) *trckd ldrs: hdwy wl over 2f out: rdn wl over 1f out: drvn and no imp ent fnl f* **4/6**[1]

620- **5** *3 ¼* **Always Dazzling**[119] [5820] 4-9-3 63........................ JamesSullivan(3) 6 48
(Ollie Pears) *cl up on outer: effrt 3f out and ev ch tl rdn wl over 1f out and sn wknd* **9/1**[3]

00-6 **6** *7* **Montego Breeze**[2] [7] 5-8-9 52........................ RobbieFitzpatrick 2 18
(Derek Shaw) *led: rdn along 1/2-way: hdd 3f out: wknd fnl 2f* **25/1**

1m 31.14s (0.84) **Going Correction** +0.125s/f (Slow) 6 Ran SP% **113.2**
Speed ratings (Par 100): **100,98,96,94,90 82**
toteswingers:1&2:£2.90, 2&3:£5.90, 1&3:£9.00 CSF £36.42 TOTE £10.40: £3.20, £1.20; EX 19.30.

Owner Peter Smith P C Coaches Limited **Bred** Marie & Mossy Fahy **Trained** Eastwell, Leics

FOCUS
A modest fillies' handicap and not form to view too positively. The race is rated through the runner-up.

20 PLAY RAINBOW RICHES AT BLUESQ.COM MAIDEN STKS 6f (F)
3:45 (3:48) (Class 5) 3-Y-O+ **£2,047** (£604; £302) **Stalls** Low

Form RPR

1 **El Djebena (IRE)** 3-8-7 0........................ RosieJessop(5) 2 73+
(Sir Mark Prescott Bt) *hld up in tch: hdwy on outer 2f out: rdn ent fnl f: styd on wl to ld nr fin* **15/2**

322- **2** *nk* **Fifth In Line (IRE)**[5] [7999] 3-8-7 68........................ FergusSweeney 4 67
(Jamie Osborne) *led: rdn along wl over 1f out: drvn ins fnl f: hdd and no ex nr fin* **2/1**[2]

3U4- **3** *1 ¾* **Barnet Fair**[5] [7999] 3-8-12 74........................ FrannyNorton 3 66
(Richard Guest) *t.k.h: trckd ldr: effrt 2f out and sn rdn: drvn ent fnl f and kpt on same pce* **11/4**[3]

03- **4** *6* **Speedy Joe**[22] [7843] 3-8-12 0........................ JimmyQuinn 1 47
(Bryan Smart) *trckd ldr on inner: effrt over 2f out: rdn wl over 1f out: drvn and wknd appr fnl f* **7/4**[1]

1m 18.53s (2.03) **Going Correction** +0.125s/f (Slow) 4 Ran SP% **108.1**
Speed ratings (Par 103): **91,90,88,80**
CSF £22.06 TOTE £10.20; EX 14.70.

Owner Ne'Er Do Wells III **Bred** Moyglare Stud Farm Ltd **Trained** Newmarket, Suffolk

FOCUS
A modest maiden but a pleasing success for the racecourse debutant. The other three were closely matched on their limited form.

T/Plt: £1,579.20 to a £1 stake. Pool £39,590.62. 18.30 winning tickets. T/Qpdt: £172.00 to a £1 stake. Pool £3,301.87. 14.20 winning tickets. JR

WOLVERHAMPTON (A.W) (L-H)
Monday, January 3

OFFICIAL GOING: Standard to slow
Wind: Light, behind Weather: Overcast

21 BLUESQ.COM ON YOUR IPHONE APPRENTICE H'CAP 1m 141y(P)
2:00 (2:00) (Class 5) (0-75,75) 4-Y-O+ **£1,813** (£539; £269; £134) **Stalls** Low

Form RPR

433- **1** **Kidlat**[26] [7756] 6-9-0 73........................ NatashaEaton(5) 1 79
(Alan Bailey) *led and sn clr: rdn and hdd over 1f out: rallied to ld wl ins fnl f: r.o* **9/4**[2]

14- **2** *½* **Buaiteoir (FR)**[37] [7600] 5-9-4 75........................ RyanClark(3) 3 80
(Paul D'Arcy) *s.i.s: hld up: hdwy to chse wnr over 2f out: rdn to ld and rdr dropped reins over 1f out: hdd wl ins fnl f* **13/8**[1]

000- **3** *6* **Tuscan King**[12] [7964] 4-8-4 64........................(b) MatthewCosham(5) 4 55
(David Evans) *s.i.s: sn chsng ldrs: rdn over 2f out: edgd lft over 1f out: no ex fnl f* **16/1**

332- **4** *shd* **Nicholas Pocock (IRE)**[21] [7856] 5-8-7 61 oh1........................ DeanHeslop 5 57+
(Brian Ellison) *hld up: nt clr run and outpcd over 2f out: nt rcvr* **7/2**[3]

21- **5** *8* **D'Artagnan (SAF)**[12] [7969] 4-8-7 74........................ RyanPowell(3) 6 47
(Gay Kelleway) *chsd wnr tl rdn and wknd 2f out* **10/1**

100- **6** *30* **Lytham (IRE)**[25] [7778] 10-8-7 61........................ AmyBaker 2 —
(Tony Carroll) *sn wl bhd: t.o* **20/1**

1m 52.82s (2.32) **Going Correction** +0.325s/f (Slow)
WFA 4 from 5yo+ 1lb 6 Ran SP% **110.8**
Speed ratings (Par 103): **102,101,96,96,89 62**
toteswingers: 1&2 £1.60, 1&3 £6.10, 2&3 £4.90 CSF £6.13 TOTE £3.70: £2.00, £1.10; EX 7.80.

Owner John Stocker **Bred** Darley **Trained** Newmarket, Suffolk

FOCUS
Run at a decent pace, this opener contained a couple of progressive sorts, but the form is weakish and the first two probably only ran to their recent marks despite finishing clear.

22 SPONSOR A RACE BY CALLING 01902 390000 (S) STKS 5f 216y(P)
2:35 (2:36) (Class 6) 4-Y-O+ **£1,535** (£453; £226) **Stalls** Low

Form RPR

535- **1** **Apache Ridge (IRE)**[4] [8019] 5-9-7 63........................(p) PhillipMakin 4 61
(Kevin Ryan) *chsd ldrs tl led over 2f out: rdn over 1f out: jst hld on* **11/4**[1]

030- **2** *nk* **Kersivay**[30] [7701] 5-9-7 54........................(b) StevieDonohoe 2 60
(David Evans) *a.p: rdn to chse wnr over 1f out: r.o* **18/1**

040- **3** *6* **Jack O'Lantern**[184] [3680] 4-8-11 67........................(t) JamieSpencer 5 31
(Ian Williams) *hld up: pushed along 1/2-way: hdwy u.p over 1f out: nvr trbld ldrs* **11/4**[1]

360- **4** *1 ¾* **Johannesgray (IRE)**[7] [7984] 4-8-13 69........................ BillyCray(3) 3 30
(David Nicholls) *sn pushed along in rr: hdwy over 1f out: rdn fnl f: nt run on* **4/1**[2]

622- **5** *3 ½* **Equinity**[52] [7425] 5-9-2 54........................(bt) MickyFenton 6 19
(Jeff Pearce) *chsd ldrs tl rdn and wknd over 1f out* **8/1**

423- **6** *1 ¼* **Decider (USA)**[3] [8037] 8-10-8 62........................(p) LukeMorris 1 35
(Ronald Harris) *led: rdn and hdd over 2f out: wknd fnl f* **9/2**[3]

1m 16.42s (1.42) **Going Correction** +0.325s/f (Slow) 6 Ran SP% **107.9**
Speed ratings (Par 101): **103,102,94,92,87 85**
toteswingers: 1&2 £7.00, 1&3 £1.80, 2&3 £7.70 CSF £43.99 TOTE £2.80: £1.20, £17.60; EX 44.00.There was no bid for the winner.

Owner Aidan Heeney **Bred** Allevamento Ficomontanino Srl **Trained** Hambleton, N Yorks

FOCUS
A modest seller but run in the best relative time on the card and it would seem the winner is back to form. There are doubts over the form with the third and fourth not at their best.

23 WOLVERHAMPTON HOSPITALITY - A PLEASURE MAIDEN STKS 1m 141y(P)
3:05 (3:06) (Class 5) 3-Y-O+ **£1,813** (£539; £269; £134) **Stalls** Low

Form RPR

23- **1** **Destiny Of A Diva**[18] [7896] 4-9-7 0........................ GrahamGibbons 1 72
(Reg Hollinshead) *disp ld 3f: rdn to chse ldr over 1f out: styd on u.p to ld wl ins fnl f* **3/1**[2]

053- **2** *¾* **Riot Police (USA)**[39] [7567] 3-8-5 74........................ MartinLane 5 71
(David Simcock) *chsd ldrs: led on bit over 2f out: rdn over 1f out: sn hung rt: hung lft and hdd wl ins fnl f* **4/6**[1]

60- **3** *9* **Rainbows Reach**[113] [6001] 3-8-0 0........................(bt[1]) AndreaAtzeni 6 46
(Gay Kelleway) *chsd ldrs: rdn over 3f out: wkng whn hung lft fr 1f out: wnt 3rd nr fin* **33/1**

422- **4** *1* **Penbryn (USA)**[12] [7969] 4-9-12 66........................(be[1]) J-PGuillambert 3 52
(Nick Littmoden) *led: rdn and hdd over 2f out: wknd fnl f* **8/1**[3]

4- **5** *11* **Diplomatic (IRE)**[12] [7969] 6-9-13 0........................ CathyGannon 2 27
(Michael Squance) *hld up: hdwy 6f out: rdn and wknd 3f out* **9/1**

005- **6** *17* **Jack Jicaro**[21] [7862] 5-9-13 41........................ LukeMorris 4 —
(Nicky Vaughan) *dwlt: a in rr: rdn and wknd over 3f out* **50/1**

1m 53.72s (3.22) **Going Correction** +0.325s/f (Slow)
WFA 3 from 4yo 22lb 4 from 5yo+ 1lb 6 Ran SP% **111.0**
Speed ratings (Par 103): **98,97,89,88,78 63**
toteswingers: 1&2 £1.40, 1&3 £9.40, 2&3 £6.10 CSF £5.23 TOTE £3.40: £2.40, £1.10; EX 7.10.

Owner M A Massarella **Bred** M Massarella **Trained** Upper Longdon, Staffs

FOCUS
A weakish maiden but with little early pace, and the slowest of the four C/D races. The form is taken at face value around the front pair, who pulled well clear.

24 HOTEL & CONFERENCING AT WOLVERHAMPTON CLAIMING STKS 1m 4f 50y(P)
3:35 (3:36) (Class 6) 4-Y-O+ **£1,535** (£453; £226) **Stalls** Low

Form RPR

000- **1** **Munsef**[37] [7594] 9-9-9 95........................ JamieSpencer 5 77
(Ian Williams) *trckd ldrs: rdn and hung lft ins fnl f: styd on to ld nr fin* **13/8**[1]

614- **2** *hd* **Camps Bay (USA)**[5] [8007] 7-9-4 78........................ HayleyTurner 4 71
(Conor Dore) *chsd ldr tl led 2f out: rdn over 1f out: hdd nr fin* **11/4**[2]

103- **3** *4 ½* **Traphalgar (IRE)**[3] [8032] 6-8-13 69........................(vt) StevieDonohoe 1 59
(David Evans) *hld up: hdwy over 4f out: rdn over 1f out: styd on same pce* **12/1**[3]

020- **4** *¾* **Abulharith**[13] [7958] 5-9-0 54........................(p) LukeMorris 3 59
(Ronald Harris) *led: rdn and hdd 2f out: no ex fnl f* **33/1**

2m 46.97s (5.87) **Going Correction** +0.325s/f (Slow) 4 Ran SP% **75.4**
Speed ratings (Par 101): **93,92,89,89**
CSF £2.60 TOTE £1.90; EX 3.10.

Owner Dr Marwan Koukash **Bred** Shadwell Estate Company Limited **Trained** Portway, Worcs

■ Country Road (2/1) was withdrawn on vet's advice. R4 applies to all bets, deduct 30p in the £.

The Form Book, Raceform Ltd, Compton, RG20 6NL

FOCUS
A muddling claimer in which the front pair were not at their best.

25 ENHANCED SP'S AT BLUESQ.COM H'CAP 1m 1f 103y(P)
4:05 (4:06) (Class 5) (0-75,70) 3-Y-O **£1,813** (£539; £269; £134) **Stalls** Low

Form RPR

050- **1** **Memorabilia**[108] 6163 3-8-12 **61**.......................... JoeFanning 3 69
(Mark Johnston) *mde all: rdn over 1f out: styd on wl* **7/2**[3]

144- **2** *1* **Urban Kode (IRE)**[23] 7831 3-8-7 **56** oh3........................ CathyGannon 4 61
(David Evans) *hld up: hdwy 4f out: rdn to chse wnr fnl f: sn ev ch: unable qck towards fin* **3/1**[1]

422- **3** *2 ¼* **Mrs Neat (IRE)**[18] 7888 3-8-7 **56** oh1........................ ChrisCatlin 6 57
(Sylvester Kirk) *hld up: rdn 1/2-way: hdwy over 2f out: styd on u.p: nt rch ldrs* **15/2**

123- **4** *1 ¾* **Imaginary World (IRE)**[26] 7758 3-9-7 **70**........................ JamesDoyle 2 67
(Alan McCabe) *a.p: rdn to chse wnr over 2f out to 1f out: no ex* **10/3**[2]

404- **5** *4* **Roi Du Boeuf (IRE)**[67] 7197 3-8-3 **59**........................ AliceHaynes(7) 7 48
(David Simcock) *hld up: racd keenly: hdwy over 5f out: rdn over 2f out: edgd lft and wknd over 1f out* **6/1**

356- **6** *3* **Polly Holder (IRE)**[23] 7839 3-8-13 **62**........................ LukeMorris 1 44
(Alan Bailey) *chsd ldrs: pushed along over 6f out: rdn over 3f out: sn wknd* **11/1**

254- **7** *7* **Szabo's Destiny**[5] 8001 3-9-5 **68**........................ MickyFenton 5 36
(James Given) *chsd wnr tl rdn over 2f out: wkng whn n.m.r sn after* **10/1**

2m 4.94s (3.24) **Going Correction** +0.325s/f (Slow) 7 Ran SP% **113.8**
Speed ratings (Par 97): **98,97,95,93,90 87,81**
toteswingers: 1&2 £3.80, 1&3 £4.80, 2&3 £3.30 CSF £14.28 TOTE £4.50: £2.70, £1.40; EX 15.80.
Owner Sheikh Hamdan Bin Mohammed Al Maktoum **Bred** Whitley Stud **Trained** Middleham Moor, N Yorks

FOCUS
A modest handicap but the pick of the four C/D times taking into account grade and age. The winner has quickly come down the weights.

26 ENJOY THE PARTY PACK GROUP OFFER H'CAP 1m 141y(P)
4:35 (4:37) (Class 6) (0-60,60) 4-Y-O+ **£1,535** (£453; £226) **Stalls** Low

Form RPR

455- **1** **Wavertree Warrior (IRE)**[140] 5158 9-8-13 **57**........................ RyanClark(5) 11 67
(Nick Littmoden) *hld up: hdwy over 1f out: sn rdn: r.o to ld last strides* **50/1**

201- **2** *nk* **No Complaining (IRE)**[17] 7917 4-9-1 **55**........................ TomQueally 9 65
(Barney Curley) *trckd ldrs: led over 2f out: rdn over 1f out: hdd last strides* **2/1**[1]

041- **3** *2 ½* **Pie Poudre**[21] 7863 4-8-11 **51**........................(p) LukeMorris 8 55
(Roy Brotherton) *hld up: hdwy over 2f out: rdn over 1f out: styd on same pce ins fnl f* **14/1**

214- **4** *½* **Join Up**[29] 7717 5-9-3 **59**........................ RossAtkinson(3) 12 62
(Mark Brisbourne) *a.p: jnd ldr over 2f out: rdn and edgd rt over 1f out: no ex wl ins fnl f* **11/1**

042- **5** *2* **Hector Spectre (IRE)**[51] 7449 5-9-4 **57**........................(p) RobertWinston 4 55
(Nikki Evans) *hld up in tch: rdn over 1f out: no ex ins fnl f* **22/1**

520- **6** *nse* **Know No Fear**[12] 7968 6-9-7 **60**........................(p) RobertHavlin 3 58
(Alastair Lidderdale) *hld up: hdwy over 2f out: rdn over 1f out: styd on* **14/1**

005- **7** *1 ½* **Justcallmehandsome**[32] 7663 9-9-4 **60**........................(be[1]) BillyCray(3) 2 55
(Dominic Ffrench Davis) *hld up: hdwy under presure over 1f out: nt rch ldrs* **20/1**

030- **8** *½* **Ocean Countess (IRE)**[51] 7445 5-8-11 **53**........................ KierenFox(3) 10 47
(Tony Carroll) *s.s: bhd: r.o ins fnl f: nvr nrr* **25/1**

415- **9** *7* **Talent Scout (IRE)**[30] 7706 5-8-11 **57**........................ LukeStrong(7) 6 34
(Tim Walford) *racd keenly: led over 7f out: hdd over 2f out: wknd fnl f* **16/1**

034- **10** *1* **Katmai River (IRE)**[21] 7863 4-9-1 **55**........................(v) SteveDrowne 5 33
[illegible] *[illegible] 2f out: wknd over 1f out* **8/1**[3]

455- **11** *1* **Merrymadcap (IRE)** [illegible] [illegible] [illegible]
(Matthew Salaman) *hld up in tch: rdn over 2f out: sn wknd: hung lft and eased fnl f* **11/2**[2]

116- **12** *6* **Princess Lexi (IRE)**[192] 3390 4-9-0 **54**........................ JamieSpencer 13 18
(Ian Williams) *led: hdd over 7f out: chsd ldrs tl wknd over 1f out: eased fnl f* **12/1**

1m 53.08s (2.58) **Going Correction** +0.325s/f (Slow)
WFA 4 from 5yo+ 1lb 12 Ran SP% **110.0**
Speed ratings (Par 101): **101,100,98,98,96 96,94,94,88,87 86,81**
toteswingers: 1&2 £22.80, 1&3 £44.10, 2&3 £5.20 CSF £122.72 CT £1172.04 TOTE £47.80: £8.70, £1.40, £4.40; EX 189.90 Trifecta £341.50 Part won. Pool: £461.57 - 0.30 winning units..
Owner Wavertree Racing Partnership C **Bred** Liam Queally **Trained** Newmarket, Suffolk

FOCUS
A competitive looking handicap that was run at a good pace. The winner is rated close to the form he was showing this time last year.
Katmai River(IRE) Official explanation: jockey said gelding was never travelling
Princess Lexi(IRE) Official explanation: jockey said filly hung right handed

27 PLAY ROULETTE AT BLUESQ.COM H'CAP 7f 32y(P)
5:05 (5:06) (Class 5) (0-75,74) 3-Y-O **£1,813** (£539; £269; £134) **Stalls** High

Form RPR

452- **1** **Palm Pilot (IRE)**[29] 7718 3-9-3 **70**........................ GeorgeBaker 1 80
(Ed Dunlop) *chsd ldr over 2f: remained handy: shkn up over 1f out: rdn to ld and edge lft wl ins fnl f* **11/4**[2]

013- **2** *½* **Islesman**[34] 7636 3-9-7 **74**........................ JoeFanning 2 83
(Heather Main) *a.p: chsd ldr over 4f out: rdn to ld over 1f out: hdd wl ins fnl f* **8/1**

352- **3** *1 ¾* **Kingscroft (IRE)**[19] 7880 3-9-1 **68**........................ GregFairley 3 72
(Mark Johnston) *led: rdn and hdd over 1f out: ev ch ins fnl f: hung lft and no ex towards fin* **5/4**[1]

613- **4** *2 ¼* **Irie Ute**[25] 7785 3-8-9 **62**........................ JamesDoyle 4 60
(Sylvester Kirk) *hld up in tch: rdn over 1f out: no ex ins fnl f* **7/1**

513- **5** *2 ¼* **Better Self**[17] 7910 3-8-13 **66**........................ StevieDonohoe 5 58
(David Evans) *s.s: hdwy 1/2-way: sn rdn: outpcd fr over 2f out* **11/2**[3]

1m 32.18s (2.58) **Going Correction** +0.325s/f (Slow) 5 Ran SP% **110.1**
Speed ratings (Par 97): **98,97,95,92,90**
CSF £22.42 TOTE £3.40: £1.10, £3.80; EX 20.90.
Owner Cliveden Stud **Bred** Cliveden Stud Ltd **Trained** Newmarket, Suffolk

FOCUS
A small but competitive looking field. The overall time was slow but the form makes sense overall.
T/Plt: £19.80 to a £1 stake. Pool: £53,822.03. 1,982.39 winning tickets. T/Qpdt: £7.00 to a £1 stake. Pool: £4,222.90. 440.80 winning tickets. CR

KEMPTON (A.W) (R-H)
Tuesday, January 4

OFFICIAL GOING: Standard
Wind: virtually nil Weather: rainy drying out

28 GREAT SALE OFFERS DAILY AT WILLIAMHILL.COM MAIDEN STKS 5f (P)
2:30 (2:30) (Class 5) 3-Y-O+ **£2,047** (£604; £302) **Stalls** Low

Form RPR

522- **1** **Quality Art (USA)**[22] 7858 3-8-13 72........................ RyanMoore 3 74+
(Gary Moore) *chsd ldr: effrt and edging rt over 1f out: rdn to chal ent fnl f: led fnl 150yds: rdn out* **2/13**[1]

304- **2** *1 ¼* **Mandy's Hero**[22] 7858 3-8-13 66........................ JamieSpencer 5 69
(Ian Williams) *led: rdn over 1f out: hdd and one pce fnl 150yds* **8/1**[2]

05- **3** *5* **Una Vita Pius (IRE)**[25] 7811 3-8-8 0........................ JamieMackay 6 46
(Patrick Gilligan) *wnt lft s: racd off the pce in midfield: rn green and edgd rt wl over 1f out: hdwy to go modest 3rd jst over 1f out: kpt on but no ch w ldng pair* **50/1**

060- **4** *3 ¼* **Rightcar Dominic**[13] 7960 6-9-7 37........................(b) LeonnaMayor(7) 4 45
(Peter Grayson) *sn wl outpcd in last pair: c wd wl over 1f out: r.o past btn horses fnl f: n.d* **80/1**

U- **5** *1 ¼* **Pickled Pumpkin**[22] 7858 3-8-13 0........................ AdamKirby 8 35
(Olivia Maylam) *pushed lft sn after s and sn wl outpcd in last: edgd lft and kpt on fnl f: n.d* **80/1**

046- **6** *2* **Dancing Again**[27] 7757 5-9-9 42........................(b[1]) SteveDrowne 7 29
(Eric Wheeler) *wnt lft s: racd in midfield: rdn and outpcd 1/2-way: no ch w ldng pair fnl 2f: wknd fnl f* **50/1**

6- **7** *2* **See The Storm**[81] 6899 3-8-13 0........................ StephenCraine 2 20
(Patrick Morris) *chsd ldrs: rdn and outpcd over 2f out: wknd over 1f out* **40/1**

040- **8** *¾* **Gower Sophia**[13] 7960 4-9-9 50........................(p) CathyGannon 9 19
(Ronald Harris) *in tch: rdn and struggling 1/2-way: wl btn fnl 2f* **25/1**[3]

000- **9** *1 ½* **Louie's Lad**[4] 8036 5-10-0 40........................(b[1]) NeilChalmers 1 18
(John Bridger) *racd wl off the pce in midfield: rdn and struggling 1/2-way: wl btn fnl 2f* **66/1**

60.43 secs (-0.07) **Going Correction** +0.10s/f (Slow)
WFA 3 from 4yo+ 15lb 9 Ran SP% **111.9**
Speed ratings (Par 103): **104,102,94,88,86 83,80,79,76**
Tote Swingers: 1&2 £1.20, 1&3 £3.90, 2&3 £5.40 CSF £1.48 TOTE £1.10: £1.02, £1.30, £4.70; EX 1.90.
Owner R A Green **Bred** Farfellow Farms & Darley Stud Management **Trained** Lower Beeding, W Sussex

FOCUS
The front pair drew clear in this weak maiden. The time was fair but the fourth limits the form.
Pickled Pumpkin Official explanation: jockey said colt ran green

29 WILLIAMHILL.COM 15% BONUS ON KEMPTON WINNERS H'CAP 5f (P)
3:00 (3:00) (Class 5) (0-75,80) 4-Y-O+ **£2,388** (£705; £352) **Stalls** Low

Form RPR

321- **1** **Feelin Foxy**[6] 7998 7-9-12 **80** 6ex........................ FrannyNorton 7 88
(James Given) *taken down early: mde all: rdn jst over 1f out: kpt on wl fnl f* **11/2**[3]

130- **2** *1* **Fear Nothing**[6] 8005 4-9-2 **70**........................(v) AdamKirby 5 74
(Ian McInnes) *chsd ldrs: rdn to chse wnr over 1f out: kpt on same pce ins fnl f* **9/1**

500- **3** *nk* **Absa Lutte (IRE)**[6] 8005 8-9-0 **75**........................(t) JosephYoung(7) 3 78
(Michael Mullineaux) *taken down early: dwlt and bustled along early: towards rr: hdwy ent fnl f: kpt on to snatch 3rd last stride* **15/2**

305- **4** *shd* **Elhamri**[8] 7984 7-9-5 **73**........................ HayleyTurner 4 76
(Conor Dore) *chsd wnr tl over 1f out: styd on same pce u.p fnl f* **10/1**

060- **5** *1* **Sherjawy (IRE)**[41] 7556 7-8-11 **65**........................ KirstyMilczarek 6 64
[illegible] *fnl 100yds: nt rch ldrs* [illegible]

320- **6** *shd* **Riflessione**[6] 8004 5-9-2 **70**........................(b) JoeFanning 1 69
(Ronald Harris) *dwlt: sn pushed along and hdwy into midfield: rdn over 1f out: kpt on same pce and hld whn hung rt ins fnl f: eased fnl 50yds* **7/2**[2]

350- **7** *1 ¼* **Lord Of The Reins (IRE)**[6] 8004 7-8-13 **67**........................ JimCrowley 8 61
(James Given) *stdd s: hld up in last pair: rdn and effrt over 1f out: no real hdwy: nvr trbld ldrs* **8/1**

324- **8** *2 ¾* **Love You Louis**[13] 7961 5-9-7 **75**........................ FergusSweeney 2 59
(J R Jenkins) *t.k.h early: chsd ldrs: swtchd to outer over 3f out: drvn and edgd rt over 1f out: wknd ent fnl f* **3/1**[1]

60.27 secs (-0.23) **Going Correction** +0.10s/f (Slow) 8 Ran SP% **110.5**
Speed ratings (Par 103): **105,103,102,102,101 101,99,94**
Tote Swingers: 1&2 £5.70, 1&3 £7.40, 2&3 £14.80 CSF £49.54 CT £353.02 TOTE £4.70: £2.00, £2.50, £2.60; EX 38.70.
Owner Peter Swann **Bred** Bearstone Stud **Trained** Willoughton, Lincs

FOCUS
A competitive sprint handicap. A small personal best for the winner, with the runner-up to form.
Love You Louis Official explanation: jockey said gelding anticipated the start

30 TOP FOOTBALL OFFERS AT WILLIAMHILL.COM H'CAP 1m 2f (P)
3:30 (3:31) (Class 6) (0-60,62) 4-Y-O+ **£1,535** (£453; £226) **Stalls** Low

Form RPR

461- **1** **Rustic Deacon**[7] 7995 4-9-7 **62** 6ex........................ JamieMackay 8 76+
(Willie Musson) *t.k.h: chsd ldng pair tl wnt 2nd over 2f out: rdn to ld over 1f out: r.o wl fnl f: rdn out* **5/4**[1]

064- **2** *¾* **Ice Road Trucker (IRE)**[20] 7874 4-7-13 **47**........(b[1]) NathanAlison(7) 10 55
(Jim Boyle) *led tl over 8f out: rdn to ld ent fnl 3f: hdd over 1f out: kpt on wl u.p ins fnl f* **14/1**

403- **3** *2 ¼* **Forbidden (IRE)**[24] 7825 8-9-4 **57**........................(vt[1]) DaneO'Neill 9 60
(Ian McInnes) *s.i.s: hld up in rr: stdy hdwy fr 6f out: rdn and effrt on outer ent fnl 2f: chal jst over 1f out: wknd fnl 100yds* **12/1**[3]

444- **4** *3 ¼* **Little Meadow (IRE)**[29] 7727 4-8-8 **49**........................ CathyGannon 13 46
(Julia Feilden) *racd in midfield: rdn and effrt on inner over 1f out: kpt on u.p ins fnl f: nvr gng pce to threaten ldrs* **12/1**[3]

000- **5** *½* **Etruscan (IRE)**[7] 7996 6-9-6 **59**........................(p) LiamKeniry 12 55
(Chris Gordon) *in tch: effrt to chse ldrs over 1f out: racd awkwardly u.p and no hdwy ent fnl f: wknd ins fnl f* **33/1**

605- **6** *½* **Hatch A Plan (IRE)**[27] 7760 10-8-9 **48**........................ FrankieMcDonald 4 43
(Mouse Hamilton-Fairley) *chsd ldrs: wnt 3rd over 2f out tl rdn over 1f out: wknd fnl f* **33/1**

212- **7** *hd* **Love In The Park**[18] 7919 6-9-3 **56** .... JackMitchell 2 50+
(Roy Brotherton) *s.i.s: hld up in rr: stl bhd over 2f out: hdwy over 1f out: kpt on fnl f: nvr trbld ldrs* **6/1**[2]

000- **8** *1 1/4* **Vinces**[7] 7996 7-9-2 **60** .... TobyAtkinson(5) 1 52+
(Tim McCarthy) *hld up towards rr: nt clr run over 2f out tl swtchd lft over 1f out: no ch after but kpt on fnl f: nvr able to chal* **25/1**

054- **9** *1 1/2* **Barbirolli**[18] 7921 9-8-7 **46** oh1 .... ChrisCatlin 11 35
(William Stone) *sn niggled along in midfield: rdn and struggling over 3f out: no threat to ldrs fnl 2f* **50/1**

000- **10** *1/2* **Carr Hall (IRE)**[26] 7778 8-8-10 **56** .... GeorgeDowning(7) 7 44+
(Tony Carroll) *stdd s: hld up in last trio: nt clr run and swtchd ins wl over 1f out: nt clr run again and swtchd lft over 1f out: kpt on: nvr able to chal* **33/1**

064- **11** *1 1/2* **Munich (IRE)**[96] 6518 7-9-0 **58** ....(p) RyanPowell(5) 3 43+
(Roger Curtis) *t.k.h early: hld up towards rr: n.m.r and hmpd wl over 1f out: styng on but no threat to ldrs whn nt clr run and squeezed out ent fnl f: n.d* **25/1**

300- **12** *1* **Pedasus (USA)**[7] 7996 5-9-4 **57** .... WilliamCarson 5 40
(Ronald Harris) *bustled along in rr early: a in rr: effrt on outer bnd 2f out: no hdwy: n.d* **25/1**

402- **13** *11* **Vezere (USA)**[7] 7995 4-9-3 **58** .... HayleyTurner 6 19
(Simon Dow) *chsd ldr tl led over 8f out untl rdn and hdd ent fnl 3f: sn struggling: wl btn and eased fr over 1f out* **6/1**[2]

0/0- **14** *1 3/4* **Softly Killing Me**[27] 7759 6-8-7 **46** oh1 .... NeilChalmers 14 —
(Brian Forsey) *chsd ldrs tl 4f out: steadily lost pl: bhd whn n.m.r and hmpd wl over 1f out: sn lost tch* **66/1**

2m 8.42s (0.42) **Going Correction** +0.10s/f (Slow)
WFA 4 from 5yo+ 2lb **14** Ran SP% **118.9**
Speed ratings (Par 101): **102,101,99,97,96 96,96,95,93,93 92,91,82,81**
Tote Swingers: 1&2 £6.40, 1&3 £5.30, 2&3 £13.70 CSF £18.35 CT £156.54 TOTE £2.20: £1.10, £5.00, £3.50; EX 28.10.
Owner Mrs Rita Brown **Bred** P V Jackson **Trained** Newmarket, Suffolk

FOCUS
Although there were 14 runners, this looked a weak handicap. The well-in winner stood out and was value for further.
Vezere(USA) Official explanation: jockey said filly stopped quickly

31 TOP GREYHOUND OFFERS TODAY AT WILLIAMHILL.COM CLAIMING STKS 1m (P)
4:00 (4:02) (Class 6) 4-Y-O+ **£1,535** (£453; £226) **Stalls** Low

Form RPR

440- **1** **Erinjay (IRE)**[251] 1617 5-9-3 76 .... JamieMackay 3 82+
(Michael Wigham) *s.i.s: hld up in tch: hdwy ent fnl 2f: chsd ldr 1f out: swtchd lft ins fnl f: rdn and qcknd to ld fnl 50yds: readily* **5/2**[2]

165- **2** *3/4* **Opus Maximus (IRE)**[23] 7844 6-9-5 77 .... JoeFanning 2 82
(Mark Johnston) *led: rdn ent fnl 2f: kpt on wl tl hdd and no ex fnl 50yds* **4/1**

056- **3** *3/4* **Final Verse**[29] 7724 8-8-12 74 ....(be) LiamKeniry 1 73
(Matthew Salaman) *s.i.s: chsd ldng pair: wnt 2nd over 2f out: rdn and effrt over 1f out: lost 2nd 1f out and styd on same pce fnl f* **15/8**[1]

106- **4** *12* **Cobo Bay**[31] 7688 6-9-5 78 ....(b) RobertWinston 4 53
(Conor Dore) *chsd ldr tl over 2f out: wknd wl over 1f out: wl btn fnl f* **7/2**[3]

5 *16* **Polly's Instinct** 6-8-12 0 .... ChrisCatlin 5 —
(Peter Hiatt) *s.i.s: a bhd: lost tch over 2f out* **50/1**

1m 40.34s (0.54) **Going Correction** +0.10s/f (Slow) **5** Ran SP% **107.5**
Speed ratings (Par 101): **101,100,99,87,71**
CSF £11.91 TOTE £3.20: £1.20, £2.20; EX 11.10.
Owner Seyhan Osman, Michael Wigham **Bred** Bill Benson **Trained** Newmarket, Suffolk

FOCUS
A competitive little claimer in which any one of three could be called the winner inside the final furlong. The winner is rated close to the form of last year's C&D handicap win, but the form is a bit muddling.

32 MOBILE BETTING - VISIT WILLIAMHILL.COM H'CAP 1m 4f (P)
4:30 (4:31) (Class 4) (0-85,85) 4-Y-O+ **£3,561** (£1,059; £529; £264) **Stalls** Centre

Form RPR

000- **1** **Porgy**[87] 6754 6-9-4 **79** .... JamieSpencer 7 87+
(David Simcock) *stdd s and hld up in last pair: plld out and hdwy on outer over 2f out: rdn to ld 1f out: in command fnl 100yds: r.o wl* **7/1**[3]

131- **2** *1 1/4* **Cozy Tiger (USA)**[27] 7765 6-9-0 **75** .... JamieMackay 6 80+
(Willie Musson) *t.k.h: hld up in tch: rdn and effrt ent fnl 2f: nt clr run ent fnl f: swtchd lft and kpt on u.p ins fnl f to go 2nd nr fin: no threat to wnr* **11/4**[1]

2- **3** *nk* **Al Amaan**[28] 7736 6-8-12 **73** .... RyanMoore 4 78
(Gary Moore) *chsd ldr: rdn jst over 1f out: ev ch and edgd lft ent fnl f: nt pce of wnr fnl 150yds: lost 2nd nr fin* **7/2**[2]

460- **4** *hd* **Hatton Flight**[54] 5949 7-9-10 **85** ....(v) DavidProbert 3 89
(Andrew Balding) *t.k.h: hld up in tch: effrt and rdn jst over 2f out: drvn and kpt on ins fnl f: nt pce to trble wnr* **15/2**

430- **5** *1 1/2* **Record Breaker (IRE)**[37] 7612 7-9-9 **84** ....(b) JoeFanning 2 86
(Mark Johnston) *led and set stdy gallop: rdn and qcknd over 2f out: hdd 1f out: no ex ins fnl f* **8/1**

640- **6** *1* **Brouhaha**[40] 7568 7-8-13 **77** .... RossAtkinson(3) 1 77
(Tom Dascombe) *chsd ldrs: rdn and unable qck on inner 2f out: nt clr run over 1f out: swtchd lft ins fnl f: one pce and no imp after* **8/1**

311- **7** *3 1/2* **Kiss A Prince**[28] 7736 5-9-5 **80** ....(b) AdamKirby 8 75
(Dean Ivory) *stdd s: hld up in last pair: rdn and effrt ent fnl 2f: no hdwy: n.d* **7/2**[2]

2m 35.84s (1.34) **Going Correction** +0.10s/f (Slow) **7** Ran SP% **117.6**
Speed ratings (Par 105): **99,98,97,97,96 96,93**
Tote Swingers: 1&2 £4.70, 1&3 £5.30, 2&3 £3.40 CSF £27.74 CT £80.45 TOTE £3.00: £1.10, £1.50; EX 28.50.
Owner Dr Marwan Koukash **Bred** Juddmonte Farms Ltd **Trained** Newmarket, Suffolk

FOCUS
A good handicap run at just a steady pace, and the form is perhaps not the most reliable. The winner did not need to match last year's best.
Kiss A Prince Official explanation: jockey said gelding was unsuited by the slow early pace

33 DOWNLOAD THE RACING POST IPHONE APP! H'CAP 2m (P)
5:00 (5:00) (Class 6) (0-60,60) 4-Y-O+ **£1,535** (£453; £226) **Stalls** Low

Form RPR

046- **1** **Inside Knowledge (USA)**[22] 7861 5-9-1 **49** .... KirstyMilczarek 7 61
(Garry Woodward) *stdd s: hld up in tch in rr: pushed along and gd hdwy on outer over 2f out: led 2f out: pushed along and drew wl clr fnl f: readily* **6/1**[3]

/40- **2** *6* **Black Tor Figarro (IRE)**[5] 8013 6-9-2 **53** .... RobertLButler(3) 1 58
(Brendan W Duke, Ire) *chsd ldrs: rdn to chse ldr wl 3f out: ev ch 2f out: sn drvn and nt pce of wnr over 1f out: no ch w wnr fnl f* **16/1**

/24- **3** *3* **Wester Ross (IRE)**[40] 6855 7-9-9 **57** ....(v[1]) JoeFanning 5 58
(James Eustace) *led: rdn over 3f out: drvn and hdd 2f out: sn btn: no ch but hld on for modest 3rd fnl f* **7/2**[2]

004- **4** *nk* **Rosy Dawn**[20] 7884 6-9-2 **50** .... FrankieMcDonald 3 51
(Luke Dace) *hld up in tch in last trio: hdwy to chse ldrs and rdn ent fnl 2f: sn outpcd: wl hld and duelling for modest 3rd fnl f* **33/1**

064- **5** *10* **Etoile Filante (IRE)**[19] 7887 4-8-6 **47** .... ChrisCatlin 10 36
(Jeremy Gask) *restless in stalls: t.k.h: hld up wl in tch in midfield: rdn and wknd qckly ent fnl 2f* **17/2**

500- **6** *nse* **Bushy Dell (IRE)**[22] 7861 6-8-13 **50** .... AmyBaker(3) 4 39
(Julia Feilden) *in tch in midfield: pushed along and effrt on outer bnd 4f out: wknd jst over 2f out* **12/1**

050- **7** *3/4* **Drummers Drumming (USA)**[20] 7759 5-9-2 **50** ....(t) IanMongan 2 38
(Charlie Morlock) *in tch in midfield: hdwy to chse ldrs 7f out: drvn and wknd over 2f out* **16/1**

005- **8** *15* **Pocket Too**[35] 7634 8-9-5 **53** ....(p) LiamKeniry 8 23
(Matthew Salaman) *chsd ldr tl ent fnl 3f: wknd qckly over 2f out: wl bhd and eased ins fnl f* **8/1**

/12- **9** *29* **Brabazon (IRE)**[31] 7704 8-9-12 **60** ....(bt) SteveDrowne 9 —
(Emmet Michael Butterly, Ire) *hld up in rr: pushed along and detached last over 5f out: lost tch 4f out: t.o fr over 2f out* **15/8**[1]

3m 31.94s (1.84) **Going Correction** +0.10s/f (Slow)
WFA 4 from 5yo+ 7lb **9** Ran SP% **115.3**
Speed ratings (Par 101): **99,96,94,94,89 89,88,81,66**
Tote Swingers: 1&2 £10.70, 1&3 £4.60, 2&3 £9.60 CSF £95.04 CT £386.57 TOTE £9.70: £2.80, £5.70, £1.10; EX 116.70.
Owner Garry Woodward **Bred** Juddmonte Farms Inc **Trained** Maltby, S Yorks

FOCUS
A pretty weak race with the favourite flopping. The winner confirmed the form of his penultimate Wolverhampton run.
Brabazon(IRE) Official explanation: jockey said gelding was never travelling

34 GREAT SALE OFFERS DAILY AT WILLIAMHILL.COM H'CAP 7f (P)
5:30 (5:30) (Class 6) (0-65,63) 4-Y-O+ **£1,535** (£453; £226) **Stalls** Low

Form RPR

003- **1** **Double Carpet (IRE)**[25] 7812 8-8-13 **55** .... KirstyMilczarek 1 63
(Garry Woodward) *mde all: rdn ent fnl 2f: kpt on wl fnl f: rdn out* **8/1**

023- **2** *1* **Musical Script (USA)**[13] 7972 8-9-1 **57** ....(b) DaneO'Neill 2 62
(Mouse Hamilton-Fairley) *hld up in tch: effrt ent fnl 2f: chsd wnr ent fnl f: kpt on but a hld* **11/4**[2]

000- **3** *1 1/2* **Sasheen**[92] 6633 4-9-4 **60** ....(p) StephenCraine 5 61
(Jim Boyle) *chsd ldrs: rdn jst over 2f out: drvn ent fnl f: no ex and btn ins fnl f* **12/1**

510- **4** *1* **Silvee**[4] 8035 4-8-12 **54** .... NeilChalmers 3 53
(John Bridger) *chsd wnr tl ent fnl f: edgd lft u.p and styd on same pce fnl f* **14/1**

014- **5** *3* **Jaldarshaan (IRE)**[19] 7892 4-9-7 **63** .... TravisBlock 7 53
(Bill Ratcliffe) *t.k.h: hld up wl in tch: rdn jst over 2f out: wknd u.p over 1f out* **5/2**[1]

000- **6** *3* **State General (IRE)**[209] 2866 5-8-13 **55** .... FergusSweeney 4 37
(Tony Carroll) *hld up in rr: effrt on inner 2f out: no prog and btn ent fnl f* **16/1**

000- **7** *hd* **Durham Town (IRE)**[13] 7964 4-9-1 **57** .... AdamKirby 6 39
(Dean Ivory) *hld up in last pair: rdn and effrt over 2f out: no prog and wl hld over 1f out* **7/1**[3]

030- **8** *2 1/2* **King's Caprice**[5] 8014 10-9-5 **61** ....(t) SamHitchcott 8 36
(Jimmy Fox) *taken down early: awkward leaving stalls: sn rcvrd and chsng ldrs: wknd u.p over 2f out* **7/1**[3]

1m 26.58s (0.58) **Going Correction** +0.10s/f (Slow) **8** Ran SP% **111.6**
Speed ratings (Par 101): **100,98,97,96,92 89,88,86**
Tote Swingers: 1&2 £3.10, 1&3 £14.80, 2&3 £6.80. totesuper7: Win Not won; Place Not won. CSF £28.84 CT £259.46 TOTE £7.10: £1.70, £2.20, £7.60; EX 24.20.
Owner Garry Woodward **Bred** Dr John Waldron **Trained** Maltby, S Yorks
■ Stewards' Enquiry : Adam Kirby one-day ban: used whip down the shoulder with excessive force (Jan 18)

FOCUS
There wasn't as much early pace on here as anticipated. A modest handicap with the winner basically to form.
Jaldarshaan(IRE) Official explanation: jockey said saddle slipped
Durham Town(IRE) Official explanation: jockey said gelding hung right
T/Plt: £141.50 to a £1 stake. Pool: £52,911.36 - 272.85 winning tickets. T/Qpdt: £37.80 to a £1 stake. Pool: £4,502.92 - 88 winning tickets. SP

15 SOUTHWELL (L-H)
Tuesday, January 4

OFFICIAL GOING: Standard to slow
Wind: Light across Weather: Bright and dry

35 BLUESQ.COM ON YOUR IPHONE CLAIMING STKS 6f (F)
12:40 (12:40) (Class 6) 4-Y-O+ **£1,535** (£453; £226) **Stalls** Low

Form RPR

124- **1** **Bonnie Prince Blue**[17] 7934 8-8-12 78 ....(be) DeanHeslop(5) 6 87
(Brian Ellison) *chsd ldng pair on outer: hdwy over 2f out: rdn to ld over 1f out: clr fnl f: readily* **7/4**[1]

316- **2** *7* **Punching**[14] 7956 7-9-3 72 .... TomQueally 5 65
(Conor Dore) *cl up: led wl over 2f out: rdn wl over 1f out: sn drvn and hdd: kpt on same pce* **4/1**[3]

50-0 **3** *3 3/4* **Errigal Lad**[2] 13 6-8-9 57 ....(p) MartinLane 3 45
(John Balding) *trckd ldrs on inner: hdwy 2f out: sn rdn: kpt on same pce appr fnl f* **22/1**

500- **4** *hd* **Tourist**[21] 7866 6-9-3 79 .... JimmyQuinn 4 52
(Derek Shaw) *trckd ldrs: pushed along wl over 2f out: sn rdn and one pce* **13/2**

512- **5** *1 1/2* **Abbondanza (IRE)**[18] 7906 8-9-4 82 .... BillyCray(3) 1 51
(David Nicholls) *led: rdn along 1/2-way: sn hdd: wknd wl over 1f out* **15/8**[2]

1m 18.5s (2.00) **Going Correction** +0.55s/f (Slow) **5** Ran SP% **108.8**
Speed ratings (Par 101): **108,98,93,93,91**
CSF £8.80 TOTE £2.70: £1.70, £2.00; EX 10.00.
Owner Koo's Racing Club **Bred** George Joseph Hicks **Trained** Norton, N Yorks

The Form Book, Raceform Ltd, Compton, RG20 6NL

FOCUS
The course was power harrowed before racing due to overnight frost and, as such, the going was officially Standard to Slow. This looked an open-looking race but the form cannot be taken literally. The winner is credited with a little improvement on last year's form.
Abbondanza(IRE) Official explanation: trainer's rep had no explanation for the poor form shown

36 SOUTHWELL-RACECOURSE.CO.UK MAIDEN FILLIES' STKS 6f (F)
1:10 (1:10) (Class 5) 3-Y-0+ **£1,910** (£564; £282) **Stalls** Low

Form RPR
5- **1** **Silver Turn**[108] 6182 3-8-8 0 .... MartinLane 5 76+
(Bryan Smart) *dwlt: sn in tch: hdwy on outer 1/2-way: chal 2f out: rdn to ld over 1f out: kpt on* **13/8**[2]

404- **2** *2* **Close To The Edge (IRE)**[20] 7879 3-8-8 65 .... ShaneKelly 2 64
(Alan McCabe) *trckd ldng pair on inner: hdwy to chal 2f out: sn rdn and ev ch whn edgd rt and one pce ent fnl f* **11/2**[3]

022- **3** *3* **Les Verguettes (IRE)**[4] 8030 3-8-8 69 .... MickyFenton 3 54
(Stef Higgins) *sn led: rdn along over 2f out: drvn and hdd over 1f out: sn wknd* **1/1**[1]

545- **4** *3 ¾* **Southwark Newshawk**[14] 7953 4-9-7 43 ....(p) KierenFox(3) 6 46?
(Christine Dunnett) *cl up: rdn along wl over 2f out: wknd wl over 1f out* **50/1**

1m 20.47s (3.97) **Going Correction** +0.55s/f (Slow)
WFA 3 from 4yo 16lb **4** Ran SP% **105.4**
Speed ratings (Par 100): **95,92,88,83**
CSF £9.35 TOTE £2.70; EX 9.10.
Owner Fawzi Abdulla Nass **Bred** F J O' Connor **Trained** Hambleton, N Yorks

FOCUS
A weak and uncompetitive maiden, with the favourite way off her Polytrack form. It has been rated around the runner-up.

37 SOUTHWELL-RACECOURSE.CO.UK (S) H'CAP 7f (F)
1:40 (1:40) (Class 6) (0-60,60) 4-Y-0+ **£1,535** (£453; £226) **Stalls** Low

Form RPR
002- **1** **Feet Of Fury**[54] 7402 5-8-13 **52** .... GrahamGibbons 9 72+
(Ian Williams) *prom: hdwy on outer to ld over 2f out: rdn clr over 1f out: eased towards fin* **5/2**[2]

351- **2** *6* **Olympic Dream**[18] 7911 5-9-0 **56** ....(p) BillyCray(3) 3 58
(Michael Herrington) *in tch: swtchd outside and hdwy 2f out: rdn wl over 1f out: kpt on ins fnl f: no ch w wnr* **9/4**[1]

464- **3** *2 ½* **Toby Tyler**[21] 7870 5-9-7 **60** ....(b[1]) MickyFenton 5 55
(Paul Midgley) *dwlt and in rr: hdwy over 3f out: rdn to chse ldrs wl over 1f out: kpt on ins fnl f: nrst fin* **9/2**[3]

64- **4** *¾* **Mackintosh (IRE)**[19] 7899 5-8-4 **46** oh1 ....(e) JamesSullivan(3) 8 39
(Patrick Morris) *trckd ldrs: hdwy over 2f out: rdn wl over 1f out: sn one pce* **16/1**

000- **5** *5* **Lethal**[49] 7473 8-9-3 **56** .... TomQueally 4 36
(Richard Price) *cl up on inner: rdn along over 2f out: grad wknd* **16/1**

00- **6** *14* **Lord's Seat**[24] 7832 4-8-7 **46** oh1 ....(b[1]) PatrickMathers 2 —
(Alan Berry) *dwlt: a in rr* **50/1**

500- **7** *4 ½* **Craicattack (IRE)**[54] 7403 4-9-5 **58** ....(b[1]) PhillipMakin 7 —
(Sharon Watt) *led: rdn along 1/2-way: hdd wl over 2f out and sn wknd* **20/1**

000- **8** *11* **Diamond Daisy (IRE)**[46] 7501 5-9-1 **54** .... NickyMackay 6 —
(Ann Duffield) *midfield: rdn along 3f out: sn wknd and bhd fnl 3f* **8/1**

420- **9** *5* **Spirit Of Dixie**[14] 7953 4-9-0 **56** ow1 .... MichaelO'Connell(3) 1 —
(David Nicholls) *midfield: rdn along over 3f out: sn wknd and bhd fnl 2f* **25/1**

1m 33.03s (2.73) **Going Correction** +0.55s/f (Slow) **9** Ran SP% **111.0**
Speed ratings (Par 101): **106,99,96,95,89 73,68,56,50**
Tote Swingers: 1&2 £2.10, 1&3 £2.90, 2&3 £3.20 CSF £7.89 CT £21.14 TOTE £3.40: £1.10, £1.10, £1.80; EX 9.10 Trifecta £20.00 Pool: £606.07 - 22.35 winning units..There was no bid for the winner.
Owner Stratford Bards Racing No 2 **Bred** The National Stud **Trained** Portway, Worcs

FOCUS
A weak-looking selling handicap but the winner did it well. The form is rated through the runner-up.

38 10% FORECAST BONUS AT BLUESQ.COM H'CAP 1m (F)
2:10 (2:12) (Class 5) (0-75,79) 4-Y-0+ **£1,878** (£558; £279; £139) **Stalls** Low

Form RPR
001- **1** **Mcconnell (USA)**[49] 7474 6-9-7 **75** ....(b) GeorgeBaker 8 85
(Gary Moore) *trckd ldr: effrt 2f out: rdn over 1f out: drvn to chal ins fnl f: led last 100yds* **5/4**[1]

010- **2** *1 ¼* **Alpha Tauri (USA)**[14] 7952 5-9-7 **75** ....(t) JamesDoyle 9 82
(Frank Sheridan) *led: rdn and qcknd 2f out: jnd and drvn ins fnl f: hdd and no ex last 100yds* **6/1**[3]

041- **3** *hd* **Avonrose**[23] 7844 4-8-13 **72** .... RyanClark(5) 2 79
(Derek Shaw) *trckd ldrs: hdwy over 2f out: rdn to chse ldng pair wl over 1f out: sn drvn and kpt on fnl f* **11/2**[2]

/05- **4** *8* **Revelator (IRE)**[14] 7955 4-8-6 **67** .... HobieGill(7) 6 55
(Alan McCabe) *in rr: pushed along after 3f: hdwy wl over 2f out: sn rdn and kpt on: n.d* **40/1**

540- **5** *5* **Veroon (IRE)**[41] 7548 5-9-6 **74** ....(p) MickyFenton 3 51
(James Given) *dwlt: a towards rr* **10/1**

155- **6** *¾* **General Tufto**[8] 7988 6-9-5 **73** ....(b) MartinLane 1 48
(Charles Smith) *chsd ldrs on inner: rdn along over 3f out: sn no prog* **25/1**

002- **7** *2* **Petomic (IRE)**[127] 5584 6-8-9 **66** ....(e[1]) KierenFox(3) 4 36
(Richard Guest) *chsd ldng pair: rdn along 3f out: drvn 2f out and sn wknd* **7/1**

046- **8** *1* **Buzz Bird**[23] 7845 4-8-12 **66** .... GrahamGibbons 5 34
(David Barron) *a towards rr: rdn along 3f out: nvr a factor* **8/1**

1m 46.82s (3.12) **Going Correction** +0.55s/f (Slow) **8** Ran SP% **113.1**
Speed ratings (Par 103): **106,104,104,96,91 90,88,87**
Tote Swingers: 1&2 £2.60, 1&3 £2.30, 2&3 £5.10 CSF £8.88 CT £30.08 TOTE £2.80: £1.30, £2.00, £1.30; EX 10.70 Trifecta £61.20 Pool: £845.47 - 10.22 winning units..
Owner B Siddle & B D Haynes **Bred** Hall Et Al Farm **Trained** Lower Beeding, W Sussex

FOCUS
An ordinary handicap. The winner is getting closer to his old form and the first three finished clear.

39 PLAY GOLF AT SOUTHWELL GOLF CLUB H'CAP 1m 6f (F)
2:40 (2:40) (Class 6) (0-60,61) 4-Y-0+ **£1,535** (£453; £226) **Stalls** Low

Form RPR
102- **1** **Short Supply (USA)**[14] 7958 5-9-7 **52** .... GrahamGibbons 2 63
(Tim Walford) *mde all: set stdy pce: rdn and qcknd over 2f out: drvn over 1f out: kpt on strly fnl f* **4/1**[3]

041- **2** *2 ¼* **Six Of Clubs**[25] 7805 5-9-0 **48** ....(b) KierenFox(3) 7 56
(Bill Turner) *hld up in tch: hdwy on outer 3f out: rdn to chse wnr wl over 1f out: sn drvn and edgd lft: no imp ins fnl f* **7/4**[1]

050- **3** *8* **Astroleo**[55] 7398 5-9-0 **45** .... JimmyQuinn 1 42
(Mark H Tompkins) *trckd ldng pair on inner: hdwy over 3f out: rdn and ch 2f out: sn drvn and one pce* **9/1**

32-1 **4** *1 ¼* **Zed Candy (FR)**[2] 8 8-10-2 **61** 6ex .... J-PGuillambert 8 56
(Richard Ford) *trckd ldrs: effrt over 3f out: rdn to chse ldrs over 2f out: sn drvn and btn* **5/2**[2]

605/ **5** *¾* **Viscount Rossini**[58] 169 9-9-0 **45** ....(b) TomQueally 6 39
(Steve Gollings) *trckd wnr: rdn along 4f out: drvn 3f out: sn wknd* **13/2**

3m 18.03s (9.73) **Going Correction** +0.55s/f (Slow) **5** Ran SP% **108.3**
Speed ratings (Par 101): **94,92,88,87,87**
CSF £11.06 TOTE £3.60: £1.30, £1.90; EX 9.80 Trifecta £68.40 Pool: £575.39 - 6.22 winning units..
Owner Keith Hanson **Bred** Juddmonte Farms Inc **Trained** Sheriff Hutton, N Yorks

FOCUS
A moderate staying handicap and only the front pair showed their form. Both are on the upgrade.

40 HOSPITALITY AT SOUTHWELL RACECOURSE H'CAP 1m 4f (F)
3:10 (3:10) (Class 5) (0-70,60) 4-Y-0+ **£1,910** (£564; £282) **Stalls** Low

Form RPR
42-1 **1** **Luck Of The Draw (IRE)**[3] 1 4-9-6 **60** .... StevieDonohoe 1 76+
(Sir Mark Prescott Bt) *hld up in rr: smooth hdwy over 3f out: cl up 2f out: sn led on bit: pushed out* **2/5**[1]

455- **2** *2 ¼* **Dunaskin (IRE)**[17] 7933 11-9-2 **55** ....(b) KierenFox(3) 3 61
(Richard Guest) *led: rdn along 3f out: jnd 2f out: sn drvn and hdd: kpt on u.p fnl f but no ch w wnr* **9/2**[2]

000- **3** *10* **Savaronola (USA)**[27] 7765 6-9-10 **60** .... TomQueally 2 50
(Barney Curley) *trckd ldr: rdn along 3f out: sn drvn and outpcd* **10/1**

4 *7* **Sweetest Of Peas (IRE)**[99] 6434 4-9-2 **56** .... PhillipMakin 4 35
(Kevin Ryan) *trckd ldng pair: effrt 4f out: rdn over 3f out: sn wknd* **8/1**[3]

2m 49.81s (8.81) **Going Correction** +0.55s/f (Slow)
WFA 4 from 6yo+ 4lb **4** Ran SP% **109.8**
Speed ratings (Par 103): **92,90,83,79**
CSF £2.65 TOTE £1.30; EX 2.50.
Owner L A Larratt - Osborne House **Bred** Castlemartin Stud And Skymarc Farm **Trained** Newmarket, Suffolk

FOCUS
A weak handicap. The easy winner was well in and against rivals not at their best recently.

41 PLAY MEGAJACKPOTS CLEOPATRA AT BLUESQ.COM H'CAP 6f (F)
3:40 (3:40) (Class 6) (0-60,60) 3-Y-O **£1,535** (£453; £226) **Stalls** Low

Form RPR
022- **1** **Finn's Rainbow**[21] 7864 3-9-7 **60** .... PhillipMakin 5 75
(Kevin Ryan) *prom: effrt to ld wl over 2f out: rdn clr over 1f out: styd on strly* **11/8**[1]

044- **2** *1 ¾* **Rhal (IRE)**[81] 6893 3-9-0 **53** .... MartinLane 4 62
(Bryan Smart) *in tch: wd st: hdwy on outer 2f out: rdn wl over 1f out: styd on to chse wnr ins fnl f: no imp towards fin* **5/1**[3]

006- **3** *1* **Jay Jays Joy**[24] 7831 3-8-9 **48** oh1 ow2 ....(b[1]) GrahamGibbons 1 54
(David Barron) *chsd ldrs on inner: rdn along over 2f out: drvn over 1f out: kpt on ins fnl f* **11/1**

022- **4** *1 ¼* **Rylee Mooch**[5] 8011 3-9-2 **58** ....(e) KierenFox(3) 2 60
(Richard Guest) *led: rdn along 1/2-way: sn hdd and drvn: one pce appr fnl f* **7/2**[2]

565- **5** *hd* **Ridgeway Hawk**[21] 7864 3-8-11 **50** ....(v) RobertHavlin 7 51
(Mark Usher) *dwlt: hdwy and in tch after 2f: rdn to chse ldrs over 2f out: sn drvn and one pce fr over 1f out* **16/1**

002- **6** *3 ¼* **William Wainwright (IRE)**[8] 7982 3-8-8 **47** ....(p) NickyMackay 6 38
(Ann Duffield) *hld up towards rr: hdwy 1/2-way: chsd ldrs over 2f out: sn rdn and grad wknd* **5/1**[3]

000- **7** *5* **Mini Bon Bon**[8] 7983 3-8-13 **52** ....(p) LiamJones 8 27
(Alan Bailey) *a in rr* **40/1**

304- **8** *1 ¼* **Ever Roses**[91] 6658 3-9-1 **54** .... MickyFenton 3 25
(Paul Midgley) *cl up: rdn along 3f out: sn wknd* **40/1**

1m 19.5s (3.00) **Going Correction** +0.55s/f (Slow) **8** Ran SP% **110.0**
Speed ratings (Par 95): **102,99,98,96,96 92,85,83**
Tote Swingers: 1&2 £3.60, 1&3 £5.40, 2&3 £8.90 CSF £8.96 CT £53.18 TOTE £3.20: £1.80, £2.30, £2.40; EX 11.70 Trifecta £65.10 Pool: £892.28 - 10.14 winning units..
Owner F Gillespie **Bred** Stuart McPhee Bloodstock Ltd **Trained** Hambleton, N Yorks
■ Stewards' Enquiry : Kieren Fox three-day ban: used whip with excessive frequency and down the shoulder in the forehand position (Jan 18-20)

FOCUS
A fair 3-y-o handicap run in a good time compared with the other C&D races, and the winner is an improver.
T/Plt: £16.40 to a £1 stake. Pool: £54,146 - 2,398.81 winning tickets. T/Qpdt: £2.20 to a £1 stake. Pool: £4,574 - 1,538.19 winning tickets. JR

DEAUVILLE (R-H)
Monday, January 3

OFFICIAL GOING: Fibresand: standard

42a PRIX DU VAL DE SAIRE (CLAIMER) (5YO+) (JOCKEYS WITHOUT 15 WINS SINCE JAN 1 2010) (FIBRESAND) 1m 1f 110y
2:10 (12:00) 5-Y-0+ **£7,758** (£3,103; £2,327; £1,551; £775)

RPR
1 **Peace Keeper (FR)**[66] 5-9-4 0 .... CharlesBegue 10 68
(U Suter, France) **28/1**

2 *¾* **Escargot (GER)**[122] 5-8-11 0 .... CyrilleStefan 8 60
(Y Fertillet, France) **35/1**

3 *nk* **Bosco (GER)**[13] 5-8-11 0 ....(b) YannickLetondeur 5 59
(C Von Der Recke, Germany) **23/1**

4 *½* **Bold Marc (IRE)**[61] 7306 9-8-13 0 ow2 .... LaurentHuart 15 60
(Mrs K Burke) *racd midfield fr s: proged early in st: r.o wl fnl f* **24/1**

5 *nk* **Class Attraction (IRE)**[12] 7-9-1 0 .... Jean-MichelBreux 13 61
(J E Hammond, France) **2/1**[1]

6 *¾* **The Joe McArdle (GER)**[56] 6-9-1 0 .... MichaelPoirier 2 60
(Alex Fracas, France) **8/1**

7 *snk* **Sadyra (FR)**[7] 5-9-1 0 .... SamuelFargeat 7 60
(Y Fertillet, France) **19/1**

8 *nk* **Same As Gold (FR)**[11] 7-9-2 0 ....(p) CedricGueude 1 60
(D De Waele, France) **41/1**

9 *shd* **Twin Prince (IRE)**[12] 6-8-11 0 .... AnthonyClement 3 55
(E Leenders, France) **43/10**[2]
10 *snk* **Lomirana (FR)**[11] 5-9-1 0 .... (p) YohannBourgois 12 58
(A Spanu, France) **54/1**
0 **Learco (FR)**[12] 10-8-11 0 .... VincentVion 14 —
(Y Fertillet, France) **67/1**
0 **Irish Kelt (IRE)**[7] 8-8-11 0 .... (p) JohannBensimon 6 —
(F-X Belvisi, France) **60/1**
0 **Sina (GER)**[12] 6-8-8 0 .... (p) RomainLeDrenDoleuze 16 —
(H-A Pantall, France) **9/1**
0 **Monserrat (FR)**[64] 5-9-4 0 .... (p) FredericSpanu 4 —
(P Demercastel, France) **11/2**[3]
0 **All Night Blues (IRE)**[113] 5-8-11 0 .... NadegeOuakli 9 —
(Mlle Valerie Boussin, France) **51/1**
0 **Valandraud (FR)**[12] 10-8-11 0 .... RomainBriard 11 —
(Y Fertillet, France) **93/1**

2m 0.40s (120.40) **16** Ran SP% **118.4**
WIN (incl. 1 euro stake): 29.10. PLACES: 9.60, 13.40, 7.70. DF: 481.20. SF: 609.40.
Owner Mme Martina Stadelmann **Bred** Mme Kim Sundgren Lindfors **Trained** France

[28]KEMPTON (A.W) (R-H)

Wednesday, January 5

OFFICIAL GOING: Standard
Wind: Moderate, behind Weather: Very overcast with drizzle

43 GREAT SALE OFFERS DAILY AT WILLIAMHILL.COM MEDIAN AUCTION MAIDEN STKS 6f (P)

4:05 (4:07) (Class 6) 3-Y-O **£1,535** (£453; £226) **Stalls** Low

Form RPR
023- **1** **Kuala Limper (IRE)**[56] 7385 3-9-3 76 .... DaneO'Neill 6 71
(David Elsworth) *trckd ldr: led 2f out: drvn and narrowly hdd over 1f out: styd on wl to ld again last 100yds* **11/10**[1]
620- **2** *¾* **Morermaloke**[99] 6435 3-9-3 71 .... ShaneKelly 7 69
(Brian Meehan) *trckd ldrs: prog 2f out: cajoled into narrow ld over 1f out: hdd and fnd nil last 100yds* **9/4**[2]
- **3** *7* **Liberal Lady** 3-8-12 0 .... SamHitchcott 1 42
(Jimmy Fox) *trckd ldrs: effrt and on terms 2f out: wknd over 1f out* **50/1**
5- **4** *2* **Look Twice**[201] 3156 3-8-12 0 .... JimmyQuinn 3 35
(Alex Hales) *v restless in stalls: in tch: rdn and struggling over 2f out: wnt modest 4th fnl f* **9/1**
5 *7* **Defer** 3-8-12 0 .... JamieSpencer 4 13
(Jeremy Noseda) *s.s: jst in tch in rr to over 2f out: sn wknd u.p* **11/2**[3]
0- **6** *¾* **Fantale**[8] 7990 3-8-12 0 .... MartinLane 5 10
(David Evans) *led to 2f out: wknd v rapidly* **66/1**
7 *2 ¼* **Five Cool Kats (IRE)** 3-9-3 0 .... WilliamCarson 2 —
(Paul Burgoyne) **50/1**

1m 13.37s (0.27) **Going Correction** +0.075s/f (Slow) **7** Ran SP% **109.2**
Speed ratings (Par 95): **101,100,90,88,78 77,74**
Tote Swingers: 1&2 £1.20, 1&3 £7.40, 2&3 £9.60 CSF £3.33 TOTE £1.70: £1.10, £2.70; EX 4.30.
Owner John Dwyer **Bred** Oghill House Stud & Jimmy Hyland **Trained** Newmarket, Suffolk

FOCUS
The first pair drew right away from their rivals in this modest 3-y-o maiden. The form could be rated a little higher on time.
Defer Official explanation: jockey said filly was slowly away
Five Cool Kats(IRE) Official explanation: jockey said gelding was slowly away

44 WILLIAMHILL.COM - ENHANCED SPS ON KEMPTON WINNERS H'CAP 6f (P)

4:35 (4:35) (Class 5) (0-70,69) 3-Y-O **£2,047** (£604; £302) **Stalls** Low

Form RPR
641- **1** **Stirling Bridge**[6] 8011 3-9-4 66 6ex .... (b) SteveDrowne 3 77+
(William Jarvis) *trckd ldr: led over 1f out: nudged along and sn clr: v comf* **4/9**[1]
534- **2** *2 ¼* **Reginald Claude**[35] 7652 3-9-7 69 .... DaneO'Neill 7 71
(Mark Usher) *dropped in fr wd draw and hld up in last pair: prog 2f out: wnt 3rd and swtchd lft over 1f out: styd on to take 2nd ins fnl f* **9/1**[3]
430- **3** *2 ¼* **Fairy Tales**[6] 8011 3-8-7 55 .... NeilChalmers 2 50
(John Bridger) *led to over 1f out: no ch w wnr after: fdd and lost 2nd ins fnl f* **50/1**
611- **4** *4 ½* **Dunmore Boy (IRE)**[18] 7931 3-8-13 68 .... (p) GeorgeChaloner(7) 5 48
(Richard Fahey) *t.k.h: racd wd: in tch: outpcd on wd outside over 2f out: no ch after* **10/1**
536- **5** *½* **Pizzarra**[7] 7997 3-8-10 58 .... FrannyNorton 4 37
(James Given) *hld up in last pair: in tch 2f out: sn wknd* **13/2**[2]
053- **6** *3* **Koha (USA)**[26] 7809 3-8-7 55 .... SamHitchcott 1 24
(Dean Ivory) *t.k.h: cl up on inner: rdn 2f out: hanging and fnd nil: sn wknd* **20/1**

1m 13.45s (0.35) **Going Correction** +0.075s/f (Slow) **6** Ran SP% **108.4**
Speed ratings (Par 97): **100,97,94,88,87 83**
Tote Swingers: 1&2 £1.70, 1&3 £6.00, 2&3 £12.40 CSF £4.73 TOTE £1.50: £1.10, £2.70; EX 4.60.
Owner Dr J Walker **Bred** Mrs W H Gibson-Fleming **Trained** Newmarket, Suffolk

FOCUS
Modest handicap. The well-in winner did not need to match last week's C&D win.

45 TOP FOOTBALL OFFERS TODAY AT WILLIAMHILL.COM CLAIMING STKS 7f (P)

5:05 (5:08) (Class 6) 4-Y-O+ **£1,535** (£453; £226) **Stalls** Low

Form RPR
310- **1** **Caprio (IRE)**[5] 8033 6-9-7 79 .... NickyMackay 5 80
(Jim Boyle) *trckd ldr: shkn up to ld over 1f out: jnd and tried to lunge at rival last strides: jst prevailed* **10/3**[3]
200- **2** *nse* **Jake The Snake (IRE)**[165] 4354 10-9-7 86 .... GeorgeBaker 6 80
(Tony Carroll) *hld up in 6th: c wd bnd 3f out: stdy prog on outer 2f out: clsd on ldrs fnl f: got up last strides: pipped on the nod* **2/1**[1]
245- **3** *1 ¼* **Vhujon (IRE)**[6] 8016 6-9-2 77 .... MartinLane 2 72
(David Evans) *chsd ldng trio: shkn up over 2f out: clsd u.p over 1f out: one pce last 100yds* **9/2**
430- **4** *hd* **Profligate (IRE)**[56] 7389 4-8-9 65 .... SteveDrowne 1 64
(William Jarvis) *led: rdn over 2f out: hdd and one pce over 1f out* **15/2**
314- **5** *½* **Grand Vizier (IRE)**[83] 6864 7-9-0 84 .... HayleyTurner 3 68
(Conor Dore) *s.s: reluctant in last early and reminders: prog under duress over 2f out: kpt on same pce fnl f* **3/1**[2]
640- **6** *2 ¼* **Mororless**[46] 6020 4-8-6 45 .... (p) SamHitchcott 4 54?
(Zoe Davison) *trckd ldng pair: u.p over 2f out: nt qckn over 1f out: wknd fnl f* **100/1**
030- **7** *6* **Takitwo**[237] 2053 8-8-10 48 .... ChrisCatlin 7 41
(Peter Cundell) *chsd ldrs in 5th: pushed along 1/2-way: no prog over 2f out: wknd sn after* **33/1**

1m 26.75s (0.75) **Going Correction** +0.075s/f (Slow) **7** Ran SP% **115.3**
Speed ratings (Par 101): **98,97,96,96,95 93,86**
Tote Swingers: 1&2 £2.80, 2&3 £3.30 CSF £10.64 TOTE £9.00: £5.00, £1.50; EX 12.50.
Owner M Khan X2 **Bred** P Rabbitte **Trained** Epsom, Surrey

FOCUS
There was a cracking, if controversial, finish to this claimer. It was steadily run and the form is muddling.

46 MOBILE BETTING - VISIT WILLIAMHILL.COM CONDITIONS STKS 6f (P)

5:35 (5:36) (Class 4) 4-Y-O+ **£3,399** (£1,011; £505; £252) **Stalls** Low

Form RPR
22-1 **1** **Silaah**[4] 2 7-8-13 85 .... (p) MichaelO'Connell(3) 6 106
(David Nicholls) *sn led: dashed wl clr fr 1/2-way: in n.d after: rdn fnl f tl eased last 50yds* **3/1**[3]
530- **2** *3 ¾* **Brave Prospector**[21] 7875 6-9-7 102 .... (t) JamieSpencer 5 99
(Jane Chapple-Hyam) *t.k.h: sn restrained bhd ldng pair: wnt 2nd over 2f out but wnr already wl clr: kpt on but no real inroads* **9/4**[1]
633- **3** *1* **Five Star Junior (USA)**[8] 7993 5-8-13 92 .... JamesSullivan(3) 3 91
(Linda Stubbs) *t.k.h: hld up in 4th: nt qckn over 2f out: kpt on fr over 1f out to take 3rd fnl f* **8/1**
515- **4** *1* **Piscean (USA)**[8] 7993 6-9-2 97 .... GeorgeBaker 1 88
(Tom Keddy) *t.k.h: hld up in last pair: effrt to go 3rd wl over 1f out but no ch of catching wnr: one pce* **5/2**[2]
141- **5** *3 ¼* **Perfect Act**[6] 8016 6-8-11 81 .... DavidProbert 4 72
(Andrew Balding) *awkward s and slowly away: t.k.h: hld up last: shkn up and no prog over 2f out: no ch after* **6/1**
05-0 **6** *7* **Duplicity**[4] 2 4-9-2 76 .... FrannyNorton 2 55
(James Given) *t.k.h: sn chsd wnr: lost 2nd over 2f out: wknd* **66/1**

1m 11.95s (-1.15) **Going Correction** +0.075s/f (Slow) **6** Ran SP% **111.2**
Speed ratings (Par 105): **110,105,103,102,98 88**
Tote Swingers: 1&2 £2.10, 1&3 £2.60, 2&3 £4.30 CSF £9.98 TOTE £3.30: £2.30, £4.60; EX 11.60.
Owner Mrs Jackie Love & David Nicholls **Bred** Bearstone Stud **Trained** Sessay, N Yorks

FOCUS
This was a good line up for the prize money on offer. It was run at a very messy pace, however, and the winner nicked the race from the front so the form should be treated with caution, even though it did appear a much improved effort.
Perfect Act Official explanation: jockey said mare ran too free

47 DOWNLOAD THE RACING POST IPHONE APP! (S) H'CAP 1m 3f (P)

6:05 (6:05) (Class 6) (0-60,60) 3-Y-O **£1,535** (£453; £226) **Stalls** Low

Form RPR
004- **1** **Blue Cossack (IRE)**[20] 7888 3-8-7 46 oh1 .... DavidProbert 1 51
(Mark Usher) *trckd ldrs: effrt to go 2nd wl over 2f out: rdn to cl on ldr over 1f out: led last 150yds: styd on* **11/2**[3]
325- **2** *2* **Indian Wish (USA)**[26] 7813 3-9-7 60 .... JamieSpencer 9 61
(Michael Quinlan) *awkward s: rapid rcvry to ld after 100yds: racd v wd bk st and in home st: urged along 2f out: hdd and nt qckn last 150yds* **10/3**[2]
550- **3** *2 ¼* **Bathwick Scanno (IRE)**[25] 7839 3-9-2 55 .... CathyGannon 5 52
(David Evans) *led 100yds: chsd ldr: rdn 4f out: lost 2nd 3f out: plugged on u.p fnl 2f* **9/1**
51-3 **4** *nk* **Boogie Star**[4] 5 3-9-2 60 .... (p) RyanPowell(5) 2 56
(J S Moore) *t.k.h: trckd ldrs: moved up to go 2nd briefly 3f out: hanging and nt qckn over 2f out: n.d after: kpt on to press for 3rd nr fin* **9/1**
065- **5** *2 ¼* **Amore Et Labore**[23] 7857 3-9-1 54 .... JamesDoyle 6 46
(Sylvester Kirk) *hld up towards rr: rdn and nt qckn over 2f out: no threat after: plugged on fnl f* **25/1**
000- **6** *1 ½* **Shirocco Vice (IRE)**[37] 7630 3-8-7 46 oh1 .... JimmyQuinn 3 36
(Richard Fahey) *dwlt: towards rr: nt gng wl most of way: reminders and wanting to hang over 2f out: nt persevered w over 1f out: rdn fnl f* **6/1**
000- **7** *2* **Algris**[23] 7857 3-8-11 50 .... (b[1]) StevieDonohoe 4 36
(Sir Mark Prescott Bt) *dwlt: sn chsd ldrs on outer: rdn 4f out: hung bdly lft bnd 3f out: dropped to rr and no ch after* **2/1**[1]
540- **8** *1 ¼* **Senor Sassi (USA)**[26] 7813 3-8-8 47 .... (b[1]) LiamKeniry 8 31
(J S Moore) *hld up in last pair: rdn over 2f out: hanging and fnd nil* **20/1**
000- **9** *3* **I Dreamed A Dream**[189] 3562 3-8-7 46 oh1 .... (p) SamHitchcott 7 24
(Dean Ivory) *mostly last: rdn and no prog over 2f out* **33/1**

2m 25.26s (3.36) **Going Correction** +0.075s/f (Slow) **9** Ran SP% **117.6**
Speed ratings (Par 95): **90,88,86,86,85 83,82,81,79**
Tote Swingers: 1&2 £4.20, 1&3 £6.50, 2&3 £6.40 CSF £24.10 CT £164.68 TOTE £10.40: £2.10, £1.10, £4.20; EX 19.40.The winner was bought in for £4,000.
Owner Reg Brookes & Richard Jurd **Bred** Morgan Ferris **Trained** Upper Lambourn, Berks

FOCUS
This selling handicap was run at an uneven pace and the first pair came clear. A 5lb best from the winner.
Shirocco Vice(IRE) Official explanation: jockey said filly hung left
Senor Sassi(USA) Official explanation: jockey said colt hung right

48 RACING AT SKYSPORTS.COM H'CAP 1m (P)

6:35 (6:36) (Class 5) (0-75,75) 4-Y-O+ **£2,047** (£604; £302) **Stalls** Low

Form RPR
022- **1** **Hip Hip Hooray**[20] 7890 5-8-13 67 .... IanMongan 5 75
(Luke Dace) *trckd ldng trio: clsd fr 2f out: rdn to ld jst over 1f out: hld on wl nr fin* **7/1**[3]
14-2 **2** *nk* **Buaiteoir (FR)**[2] 21 5-9-7 75 .... LiamJones 1 82
(Paul D'Arcy) *stdd s: t.k.h: hld up in last pair: prog over 2f out: pushed along over 1f out: wnt 2nd last 100yds: clsd on wnr fin: post c too sn* **1/1**[1]
021- **3** *1 ¼* **One Oi**[14] 7966 6-8-8 62 .... LiamKeniry 7 66
(David Arbuthnot) *trckd ldr to over 2f out: shkn up and styd prom: tried to chal over 1f out: one pce fnl f* **3/1**[2]
424- **4** *½* **Unlimited**[82] 6903 9-8-5 62 .... KierenFox(3) 6 65
(Tony Carroll) *trckd ldng pair: wnt 2nd on inner over 2f out: rdn to ld briefly over 1f out: fdd fnl f* **20/1**
202- **5** *4* **Abriachan**[14] 7964 4-8-9 63 .... WilliamCarson 3 57
(Michael Quinlan) *hld up in 5th: effrt on inner over 2f out: nt qckn wl over 1f out: no imp after* **12/1**

600- **6** ½ **Tudor Prince (IRE)**[20] 7892 7-8-12 **66**............................ JimmyQuinn 8 59
(Tony Carroll) *led and nt pressed: tried to kick on 3f out: hdd & wknd rapidly over 1f out* **33/1**

326- **7** *shd* **Having A Ball**[20] 7889 7-8-11 **65**............................ ChrisCatlin 2 57
(Peter Cundell) *hld up in 6th: pushed along over 3f out: struggling in last pair over 2f out: no ch after* **10/1**

010- **8** *7* **Dinner Date**[39] 7597 9-9-1 **74**............................(b) RyanClark(5) 4 50
(Tom Keddy) *stdd s: hld up last: struggling 3f out: sn wl bhd* **25/1**

1m 40.31s (0.51) **Going Correction** +0.075s/f (Slow) 8 Ran SP% **115.8**
Speed ratings (Par 103): **100,99,98,97,93 93,93,86**
Tote Swingers: 1&2 £2.10, 1&3 £1.80, 2&3 £2.00 CSF £14.39 CT £26.44 TOTE £7.10: £1.80, £1.30, £1.70; EX 20.60.
Owner M C S D Racing Partnership **Bred** Mrs R S Evans **Trained** Five Oaks, W Sussex

FOCUS
This moderate handicap was another race run at an ordinary pace. The form is rated around the third.

49 SKYSPORTS.COM RACING H'CAP 1m (P)
7:05 (7:05) (Class 5) (0-75,71) 3-Y-O **£2,047** (£604; £302) **Stalls** Low

Form RPR

065- **1** **Sammy Alexander**[37] 7630 3-8-13 **63**............................ MartinLane 2 67
(David Simcock) *hld up in 3rd: shkn up over 2f out and hung fire briefly: rdn and clsd to ld over 1f out: sn in command* **5/1**

144- **2** *1* **Whodathought (IRE)**[54] 7417 3-9-7 **71**............................(b) DaneO'Neill 4 72
(Richard Hannon) *s.i.s: pushed up to ld after 1f: kicked on 3f out: hdd and nt qckn over 1f out* **9/4[2]**

124- **3** *nse* **Sky Diamond (IRE)**[20] 7888 3-8-12 **62**............................ FrannyNorton 3 63
(James Given) *led 1f: chsd ldr: nt qckn and dropped to last 2f out: styd on again fnl f: nrly snatched 2nd* **3/1[3]**

21- **4** 1 ¾ **Swimsuit**[26] 7802 3-9-7 **71**............................ JackMitchell 1 68
(Michael Jarvis) *t.k.h: hld up last: effrt to dispute 2nd 2f out: nt qckn on inner over 1f out: fdd fnl f* **6/4[1]**

1m 41.45s (1.65) **Going Correction** +0.075s/f (Slow) 4 Ran SP% **112.4**
Speed ratings (Par 97): **94,93,92,91**
CSF £16.54 TOTE £9.90; EX 21.10.
Owner Mrs T A Foreman **Bred** Mrs T A Foreman **Trained** Newmarket, Suffolk

FOCUS
A moderate handicap. Despite the small field there was a fair early pace on, but things still developed into something of a dash from the top of the home straight. The form does make a fair bit of sense at face value.
T/Plt: £16.00 to a £1 stake. Pool: £58,297.81 - 2,644.21 winning tickets. T/Qpdt: £9.00 to a £1 stake. Pool: £5,701.30 - 465.60 winning tickets. JN

LINGFIELD (L-H)
Wednesday, January 5

OFFICIAL GOING: Standard
Wind: fresh, behind Weather: bright spells, breezy

50 BLUESQ.COM ON YOUR IPHONE (S) STKS 1m 2f (P)
12:55 (12:55) (Class 6) 4-Y-O+ **£1,535** (£453; £226) **Stalls** Low

Form RPR

124- **1** **Scary Movie (IRE)**[22] 7865 6-9-0 **70**............................ RobertWinston 6 71
(Denis Coakley) *chsd ldrs: hdwy to chse ldr 2f out: ev ch ent fnl 2f: rdn to ld ent fnl f: sn in command: rdn out* **5/2[1]**

241- **2** 3 ½ **Orchard Supreme**[25] 7825 8-9-5 **75**............................(p) J-PGuillambert 7 69
(John Akehurst) *stdd after s: hld up in tch in last trio: rdn 4f out: chsd ldrs ent fnl f: plugged on fnl f to go 2nd towards fin: nt pce to trble wnr* **8/1**

034- **3** *nk* **Aflaam (IRE)**[14] 7966 6-9-0 **62**............................(t) CathyGannon 2 63
(Ronald Harris) *chsd ldr tl led ent fnl 3f: rdn over 2f out: drvn wl over 1f out: hdd ent fnl f: nt pce of wnr ins fnl f: lost 2nd towards fin* **10/1**

336- **4** *3* **Visions Of Johanna (USA)**[160] 4520 6-9-0 **73**............ StevieDonohoe 4 57
(Ian Williams) *hld up wl in tch: chsd ldng trio and rdn jst over 2f out: wknd ent fnl f* **7/2[2]**

000- **5** *6* **Timeteam (IRE)**[30] 7725 5-9-0 **69**............................ TomQueally 8 45
(Gary Moore) *t.k.h: hld up in tch in last trio: rdn and wknd wl over 1f out* **20/1**

03-3 **6** 2 ¾ **Traphalgar (IRE)**[2] 24 6-9-5 **69**............................(vt) GeorgeBaker 9 45
(David Evans) *stdd s: hld up in tch in rr: rdn and btn 2f out: nvr trbld ldrs* **4/1[3]**

254- **7** 3 ¼ **What's Up Doc (IRE)**[156] 3814 10-9-0 **64**............................ DaneO'Neill 3 33
(Lawney Hill) *led tl hdd and rdn ent fnl 3f: wknd jst over 2f out: wl bhd fnl f* **8/1**

054- **8** 1 ½ **Public Image**[8] 7989 5-8-9 **46**............................ MartinLane 1 25
(Jamie Poulton) *chsd ldrs tl wknd u.p over 2f out: wl bhd over 1f out* **100/1**

2m 7.72s (1.12) **Going Correction** +0.25s/f (Slow) 8 Ran SP% **113.1**
Speed ratings (Par 101): **105,102,101,99,94 92,89,88**
Tote Swingers: 1&2 £2.50, 1&3 £4.30, 2&3 £4.80 CSF £22.82 TOTE £3.20: £1.10, £1.50, £1.90; EX 16.20 Trifecta £131.50 Pool: £276.35 - 2.10 winning units..The winner was sold to Ron Harris for 5,000gns.
Owner J G Mountford **Bred** Mrs T Brudenell **Trained** West Ilsley, Berks

FOCUS
Not the worst seller ever run here, but the pace set by early leader What's Up Doc was ordinary. Only the first three showed their form.
Traphalgar(IRE) Official explanation: vets said gelding was found to be lame in front post race

51 TANDRIDGE CLAIMING STKS 1m 2f (P)
1:25 (1:25) (Class 6) 3-Y-O **£1,535** (£453; £226) **Stalls** Low

Form RPR

426- **1** **Paco Belle (IRE)**[79] 6978 3-8-8 **65**............................ SteveDrowne 4 62
(Richard Hannon) *chsd ldr: rdn ent fnl 2f: drvn to ld jst ins fnl f: hld on cl home* **7/2[3]**

322- **2** *nk* **Woop Woop (IRE)**[5] 8031 3-9-2 **62**............................ AdamKirby 1 69
(Stef Higgins) *in tch: rdn and sltly outpcd ent fnl 2f: drvn and rallied over 1f out: chsd wnr fnl 100yds: edgd rt but kpt on wl towards fin: nt quite rch wnr* **9/4[2]**

561- **3** *1* **Danzigs Grandchild (USA)**[35] 7650 3-8-8 **67**............................ RyanPowell(5) 3 64
(J S Moore) *t.k.h: hld up wl in tch: hdwy to press ldr over 2f out: kpt on same pce fnl f* **15/8[1]**

312- **4** *2* **Ivan's A Star (IRE)**[26] 7801 3-8-9 **60**............................(p) LiamKeniry 2 56
(J S Moore) *led: rdn and qcknd jst over 2f out hdd jst ins fnl f: edgd rt u.p and wknd fnl 100yds* **13/2**

56-6 **5** 1 ¾ **Polly Holder (IRE)**[2] 25 3-8-6 **62**............................ CathyGannon 5 50
(Alan Bailey) *hld up in tch in last: rdn and outpcd ent fnl 2f: no imp after* **12/1**

2m 12.0s (5.40) **Going Correction** +0.25s/f (Slow) 5 Ran SP% **108.8**
Speed ratings (Par 95): **88,87,86,85,83**
CSF £11.44 TOTE £7.80: £4.10, £1.10; EX 8.60.
Owner The Calvera Partnership No 2 **Bred** Knockainey Stud **Trained** East Everleigh, Wilts

FOCUS
All five of these were attempting the trip for the first time, but they went no pace until over 2f from home so it wasn't the test of stamina it might have been. The winning time was 4.28 seconds slower than the older horses in the seller. Muddling form, rated around the winner and third.

52 COWDEN MAIDEN STKS 7f (P)
1:55 (1:56) (Class 5) 3-4-Y-O **£1,910** (£564; £282) **Stalls** Low

Form RPR

1 **Satwa Royal** 4-9-13 0............................ GeorgeBaker 4 71+
(Ed Dunlop) *t.k.h: hld up in tch: trckd ldrs 2f out: chsd ldng pair and nt clr run 1f out tl ins fnl f: rdn and ev ch fnl 75yds: led on post* **13/2[3]**

344- **2** *nse* **Al Jaadi**[20] 7889 4-9-8 65............................ DaneO'Neill 7 66
(William Jarvis) *trckd ldrs: rdn to ld over 1f out: drvn ins fnl f: hdd on post* **9/4[2]**

60- **3** 1 ¼ **Ana Emarati (USA)**[14] 7962 3-8-9 0............................ JimCrowley 8 64
(Ed Dunlop) *t.k.h: hld up in tch: hdwy over 3f out: chsd ldrs and rdn over 1f out: kpt on same pce fnl 100yds* **25/1**

\- **4** *1* **Ever The Optimist (IRE)** 3-8-9 0............................ MickyFenton 10 61+
(Stef Higgins) *s.i.s: outpcd in last pair: rdn along over 4f out: clsd and in tch 3f out: hdwy into midfield and swtchd rt ent fnl 2f: swtchd rt again 1f out: r.o wl fnl 100yds: nt rch ldrs* **20/1**

660- **5** 2 ¼ **Lynchpin**[24] 7843 3-8-9 56............................(p) CathyGannon 6 55
(Ronald Harris) *chsd ldr: rdn to ld over 2f out: drvn and hdd over 1f out: wknd ins fnl f* **33/1**

02- **6** 1 ¼ **Sottovoce**[21] 7879 3-8-4 0............................ HayleyTurner 3 46
(Simon Dow) *chsd ldrs: n.m.r and rdn along over 2f out: styd on same pce fr over 1f out* **11/8[1]**

00- **7** 4 ½ **Scarborough Lily**[7] 8001 3-8-4 0............................ MartinLane 5 34
(Edward Vaughan) *s.i.s: bhd: clsd over 3f out: hdwy on outer into midfield over 2f out: lost pl bnd 2f out: no threat to ldrs after* **66/1**

060- **8** *3* **Kyncraighe (IRE)**[50] 7469 3-8-2 55............................(t) KatiaScallan(7) 1 31
(Alastair Lidderdale) *in tch in midfield tl wknd u.p ent fnl 2f: wl btn over 1f out* **80/1**

9 *hd* **Pizzetti (IRE)** 3-8-9 0............................ StevieDonohoe 2 31
(Sir Mark Prescott Bt) *v.s.a: sn outpcd and pushed along in last: n.d* **9/1**

06- **10** *29* **Kassiodor (GER)**[21] 7872 4-9-13 0............................ TomQueally 9 —
(Barney Curley) *bolted to post: led tl over 2f out: sn dropped out: t.o and virtually p.u ins fnl f* **33/1**

1m 26.69s (1.89) **Going Correction** +0.25s/f (Slow)
WFA 3 from 4yo 18lb 10 Ran SP% **113.4**
Speed ratings (Par 103): **99,98,97,96,93 92,87,83,83,50**
Tote Swingers: 1&2 £4.00, 1&3 £4.80, 2&3 £10.50 CSF £19.71 TOTE £12.30: £2.60, £1.02, £8.00; EX 22.10 Trifecta £84.00 Pool: £446.14 - 3.93 winning units..
Owner The Lamprell Partnership **Bred** Mrs Ann Jenkins **Trained** Newmarket, Suffolk

FOCUS
A moderate maiden though the pace was sound. The favourite disappointed and the form is best rated around the second and fifth.

53 DRY HILL H'CAP 1m (P)
2:25 (2:25) (Class 6) (0-60,57) 3-Y-O **£1,535** (£453; £226) **Stalls** High

Form RPR

033- **1** **Aquilifer (IRE)**[20] 7888 3-9-4 **54**............................ ShaneKelly 8 60
(William Jarvis) *t.k.h: hld up in tch: hdwy and racd awkwardly bnd 2f out: sn rdn to chal: led 1f out: racd awkwardly but drvn to assert ins fnl f: rdn out* **2/1[1]**

002- **2** 1 ½ **Investment World (IRE)**[25] 7831 3-8-13 **49**............................ FrannyNorton 5 52+
(Mark Johnston) *stdd after s: t.k.h early: hld up in tch in last: pushed along 2f out: swtchd rt and rdn over 1f out: r.o wl fnl f: wnt 2nd towards fin: no threat to wnr* **9/2[2]**

006- **3** ½ **Titan Diamond (IRE)**[26] 7813 3-8-4 **45**............................ RyanPowell(5) 7 47
(Mark Usher) *in tch on outer: effrt and ev ch 2f out: led over 1f out: sn hdd: no ex fnl 100yds: lost 2nd towards fin* **20/1**

505- **4** *4* **Bathwick Freeze**[163] 4429 3-9-1 **51**............................ StevieDonohoe 3 44
(David Evans) *stdd after s: t.k.h: hld up in tch in last pair: rdn and outpcd ent fnl 2f: rallied ent fnl f: kpt on past btn horses fnl f: nvr trbld ldrs* **8/1**

000- **5** *hd* **Seadream**[26] 7813 3-8-5 **48**............................ RachealKneller(7) 4 40
(Mark Usher) *s.i.s: sn rcvrd and chsd ldrs: pushed along and outpcd over 1f out: rdn and plugged on again ins fnl f* **25/1**

050- **6** ½ **Dances With Words (IRE)**[119] 5865 3-9-7 **57**............ FergusSweeney 6 48
(Rodney Farrant) *t.k.h: chsd ldr tl wl over 1f out: sn wknd: wl hld fnl f* **8/1**

651- **7** 1 ½ **Granny Anne (IRE)**[19] 7910 3-9-6 **56**............................ CathyGannon 1 44
(Alan Bailey) *led and set stdy gallop: qcknd ent fnl 2f: hdd over 1f out: wknd qckly 1f out* **11/2[3]**

1m 43.59s (5.39) **Going Correction** +0.25s/f (Slow) 7 Ran SP% **110.3**
Speed ratings (Par 95): **83,81,81,77,76 76,74**
Tote Swingers: 1&2 £2.10, 1&3 £7.50, 2&3 £3.50 CSF £6.20 CT £57.19 TOTE £2.30: £1.10, £2.50; EX 8.90 Trifecta £108.20 Pool: £419.97 - 2.87 winning units..
Owner John Kelsey-Fry **Bred** Miss L Magnier **Trained** Newmarket, Suffolk

FOCUS
A moderate 3-y-o handicap and, with the early pace slow, a few of these were inclined to pull. The winner has been a gradual improver recently.
Bathwick Freeze Official explanation: jockey said filly hung right throughout

54 10% FORECAST BONUS AT BLUESQ.COM H'CAP 1m 2f (P)
2:55 (2:55) (Class 5) (0-75,75) 4-Y-O+ **£2,047** (£604; £302) **Stalls** Low

Form RPR

13- **1** **Pertuis (IRE)**[32] 7687 5-9-5 **71**............................ ChrisCatlin 5 78
(Harry Dunlop) *chsd ldrs: rdn to ld jst over 1f out: kpt on wl fnl f: rdn out* **10/1**

010- **2** 1 ¼ **Khun John (IRE)**[215] 2723 8-8-10 **62**............................ StevieDonohoe 9 66
(Willie Musson) *stdd after s: sn detached in last and pushed along 9f out: clsd and in tch 4f out: pushed along 2f out: rdn and hdwy 1f out: r.o wl fnl 150yds to go 2nd last strides: nvr gng to rch wnr* **20/1**

33-1 **3** *nk* **Kidlat**[2] 21 6-9-7 **73**............................ GrahamGibbons 4 76
(Alan Bailey) *led: stdd gallop 5f out: drvn and qcknd over 2f out: hdd jst over 1f out: kpt on same pce u.p fnl f: lost 2nd last strides* **11/10[1]**

001- **4** *hd* **Suntrap**[28] 7767 4-9-7 **75**............................(v) ShaneKelly 7 78
(William Knight) *stdd s: t.k.h early: hdwy into midfield 8f out: rdn and effrt to chse ldrs over 1f out: styd on same pce u.p fnl f* **10/1**

023- **5** *nse* **Fonterutoli (IRE)**[21] 7876 4-9-5 **73** RobertHavlin 2 76
(Roger Ingram) *stdd s: hld up in last trio: clsd and in tch 4f out: hdwy to trck ldrs and nt clr run wl over 1f out: sn swtchd lft: rdn to chse ldrs ent fnl f: no imp and onepced after* **9/1**[3]

005- **6** *3 ¼* **Humungous (IRE)**[32] 7688 8-9-4 **70** MickyFenton 6 66
(Charles Egerton) *hld up in last trio: clsd and in tch 4f out: rdn and effrt on outer wl over 1f out: no imp fr over 1f out: nvr trbld ldrs* **16/1**

143- **7** *1 ½* **Commerce**[36] 7638 4-8-13 **67** HayleyTurner 8 60
(Simon Dow) *chsd ldr: rdn over 2f out: btn ent fnl f: wknd fnl 150yds* **4/1**[2]

200- **8** *34* **Free Tussy (ARG)**[29] 7732 7-9-6 **72** (bt) GeorgeBaker 3 —
(Gary Moore) *in tch in midfield: lost pl qckly jst over 2f out: wl bhd and eased ins fnl f: t.o* **11/1**

2m 6.70s (0.10) **Going Correction** +0.25s/f (Slow)
WFA 4 from 5yo+ 2lb **8** Ran SP% **114.8**
Speed ratings (Par 103): **109,108,107,107,107 104,103,76**
Tote Swingers: 1&2 £20.60, 1&3 £2.90, 2&3 £9.30 CSF £180.12 CT £392.36 TOTE £5.40: £1.70, £7.50, £1.10; EX 160.10 Trifecta £438.20 Part won. Pool: £592.22 - 0.74 winning units..
Owner Rupert Hambro **Bred** Killeen Castle Stud **Trained** Lambourn, Berks

FOCUS
A fair handicap and although the early pace was decent, the tempo had steadied after half a mile. It was still the pick of the three C&D times and the form looks sound overall.
Free Tussy(ARG) Official explanation: jockey said gelding was wrong and eases

55 LINGFIELDPARK.CO.UK H'CAP 7f (P)
3:25 (3:25) (Class 5) (0-75,75) 4-Y-0+ **£2,047** (£604; £302) **Stalls** Low

Form RPR

305- **1** **Lastkingofscotland (IRE)**[14] 7971 5-9-4 **72** (b) HayleyTurner 4 78
(Conor Dore) *hld up in tch in rr: hdwy 3f out: rdn and swtchd lft over 1f out: chsd ldrs 1f out: nt clr run on rail and hmpd ins fnl f: gap opened and styd on cl home to go 2nd last stride: fin 2nd: plcd 1st* **5/2**[1]

236- **2** *shd* **Cat Hunter**[25] 7837 4-9-0 **68** CathyGannon 5 74
(Ronald Harris) *in tch: effrt to chse ldrs ent fnl 2f: rdn to chal and carried sltly lft fr 1f out: ev ch and bmpd ins fnl f: led cl home: fin 1st: disqualified and plcd 2nd* **6/1**

500- **3** *shd* **Cuthbert (IRE)**[49] 7488 4-9-1 **69** JoeFanning 7 74
(William Jarvis) *led: rdn ent fnl 2f: edgd lft u.p fr 1f out: kpt on wl tl hdd and lost 2 pls cl home* **7/2**[3]

641- **4** *2* **Highland Harvest**[8] 7992 7-9-2 **70** 6ex IanMongan 6 70
(Jamie Poulton) *chsd ldrs: rdn and sltly outpcd bnd 2f out: hung lft u.p over 1f out: kpt on ins fnl f* **10/3**[2]

003- **5** *¾* **Pytheas (USA)**[181] 3816 4-9-2 **70** (p) RobbieFitzpatrick 1 68
(Michael Attwater) *chsd ldr: ev ch and rdn ent fnl 2f: hung lft and hmpd over 1f out: onepced and btn fnl f* **10/1**

000- **6** *½* **Kai Mook**[102] 6371 4-8-11 **65** (t) FergusSweeney 2 62
(Amy Weaver) *in tch: rdn and outpcd jst over 2f out: kpt on again u.p fnl f: nt pce to rch ldrs* **25/1**

430- **7** *15* **Blakey's Boy**[32] 7688 4-9-7 **75** ChrisCatlin 3 31
(Harry Dunlop) *taken down early: restless in stalls: in tch on outer: rdn and struggling over 2f out: wknd ent fnl 2f* **8/1**

1m 25.7s (0.90) **Going Correction** +0.25s/f (Slow) **7** Ran SP% **112.2**
Speed ratings (Par 103): **103,104,103,101,100 100,82**
Tote Swingers: 1&2 £1.30, 1&3 £3.20, 2&3 £3.40 CSF £17.23 TOTE £3.20: £2.90, £2.10; EX 14.30.
Owner Mrs Jennifer Marsh **Bred** Baronrath Stud **Trained** Cowbit, Lincs
■ Stewards' Enquiry : Cathy Gannon two-day ban; careless riding (19th-20th Jan)
Joe Fanning one-day ban; careless riding (19th Jan)

FOCUS
An ordinary handicap, but as it turned out a rough and controversial race with things getting very tight between the first three inside the final furlong. The promoted winner is rated to his recent best.

56 PLAY MEGAJACKPOTS CLEOPATRA AT BLUESQ.COM APPRENTICE H'CAP 7f (P)
3:55 (3:55) (Class 6) (0-60,60) 4-Y-0+ **£1,535** (£453; £226) **Stalls** Low

Form RPR

553- **1** **Rubenstar (IRE)**[8] 7991 8-9-7 **60** RyanClark 2 69
(Patrick Morris) *hld up off he pce in midfield: wnt 3rd 3f out: rdn and clsd over 1f out: led jst ins fnl f: kpt on wl u.p* **11/4**[1]

203- **2** *1 ½* **Lord Deevert**[8] 7989 6-8-12 **54** MatthewLawson(3) 8 59
(Bill Turner) *reminder after s: sn chsng ldrs: wnt 2nd over 3f out: rdn and clsd over 1f out: led 1f out: sn hdd and styd on same pce after* **8/1**

300- **3** *nk* **Chinese Democracy (USA)**[25] 7824 4-8-13 **55**(v) MatthewCosham(3) 1 59
(David Evans) *stdd after s: hld up wl off the pce towards rr: hdwy into modest 4th over 2f out: clsd and swtchd rt jst ins fnl f: r.o wl: nt rch ldrs* **5/1**[3]

003- **4** *3 ¼* **Resplendent Alpha**[25] 7824 7-9-3 **56** (p) NathanAlison 5 51
(Alastair Lidderdale) *sn wl bhd in rr: rdn and hdwy over 1f out: r.o ins fnl f: nvr able to chal* **13/2**

022- **5** *hd* **Wishformore (IRE)**[7] 8006 4-9-7 **60** (p) RyanPowell 4 55
(J S Moore) *racd off the pce in midfield: rdn along over 3f out: styd on u.p fnl f: nvr rchd ldrs* **8/1**

554- **6** *shd* **Decency (IRE)**[8] 7991 4-8-11 **57** DavidCoyle(7) 9 52
(Harry Dunlop) *mounted on crse: hld up wl bhd: hdwy over 1f out: kpt on ins fnl f: nvr rchd ldrs* **15/2**

30-2 **7** *¾* **Kersivay**[2] 22 5-8-8 **54** (b) KevinLundie(7) 7 47
(David Evans) *led: clr over 4f out: stl clr and rdn over 1f out: wknd and hdd 1f out: fdd fnl f* **7/2**[2]

000- **8** *34* **Chateau Galliard (IRE)**[90] 6696 5-8-0 **46** oh1 (p) JessicaSteven(7) 3 —
(Terry Clement) *chsd ldr tl over 3f out: sn lost pl: t.o fr over 1f out: burst blood vessel* **100/1**

1m 25.63s (0.83) **Going Correction** +0.25s/f (Slow) **8** Ran SP% **113.9**
Speed ratings (Par 101): **105,103,102,99,99 98,98,59**
Tote Swingers: 1&2 £4.20, 1&3 £5.40, 2&3 £8.40 CSF £25.21 CT £104.27 TOTE £1.50: £1.10, £2.70; EX 4.60 Trifecta £116.00 Pool: £589.58 - 3.76 winning units..
Owner L Walsh **Bred** Schwindibode Ag **Trained** Tarporley, Cheshire

FOCUS
A moderate handicap, but run at a strong pace. The winner is rated up a length on his recent form.
Chinese Democracy(USA) Official explanation: jockey said filly hung left
Wishformore(IRE) Official explanation: jockey said filly hung right
Chateau Galliard(IRE) Official explanation: trainer said gelding beld from nose
T/Jkpt: Not won. T/Plt: £26.30 to a £1 stake. Pool: £68,831.47 - 1,909.64 winning tickets. T/Qpdt: £10.00 to a £1 stake. Pool: £5,195.69 - 381.50 winning tickets. SP

35 SOUTHWELL (L-H)
Thursday, January 6

OFFICIAL GOING: Standard
Wind: Virtually nil Weather: Bright and dry

57 BLUESQ.COM ON YOUR IPHONE H'CAP 6f (F)
12:50 (12:50) (Class 6) (0-52,52) 4-Y-0+ **£1,535** (£453; £226) **Stalls** Low

Form RPR

004- **1** **Figaro Flyer (IRE)**[27] 7807 8-8-12 **51** MichaelStainton(3) 11 61
(Jane Chapple-Hyam) *in tch: hdwy 2f out: swtchd rt and rdn to chal over 1f out: drvn to ld and edgd lft ins fnl f: hld on wl* **5/1**[2]

01-4 **2** *nk* **Lets Move It**[3] 15 4-9-2 **52** (v) PatrickMathers 2 61
(Derek Shaw) *midfield: hdwy on inner wl over 2f out: rdn to chse ldrs over 1f out: drvn and kpt on ins fnl f: jst hld* **9/2**[1]

01R- **3** *2 ¼* **Pinball (IRE)**[24] 7859 5-9-2 **52** (b) PhillipMakin 1 54
(Lisa Williamson) *dwlt: sn in tch: hdwy on inner over 2f out: rdn to chse ldr over 1f out: ev ch tl drvn and one pce ins fnl f* **14/1**

0/0- **4** *¾* **Archilini**[146] 5023 6-8-5 **46** oh1 DeanHeslop(5) 12 45
(Matt Sheppard) *dwlt and in rr: wd st: hdwy over 2f out: sn rdn: styd on wl fnl f: nrst fin* **9/1**

000- **5** *½* **Angle Of Attack (IRE)**[48] 7132 6-8-10 **46** oh1 (v) GrahamGibbons 9 44
(Alan Brown) *led: rdn along and hdd over 2f out: drvn over 1f out and kpt on same pce* **11/2**[3]

000- **6** *nk* **Bertbrand**[20] 7906 6-8-10 **46** oh1 (v) KirstyMilczarek 10 43
(Ian McInnes) *cl up: led over 2f out: sn rdn: jnd and drvn over 1f out: hdd & wknd ins fnl f* **16/1**

656- **7** *1* **Itwasonlyakiss (IRE)**[193] 3480 4-9-2 **52** ChrisCatlin 8 46
(J W Hills) *chsd ldrs on outer: prom and wd st: rdn 2f out: drvn and hung rt over 1f out: sn wknd* **9/1**

006- **8** *¾* **Best Known Secret (IRE)**[20] 7911 5-8-11 **47** (b) FrankieMcDonald 4 38
(Chris Bealby) *chsd ldng pair: rdn along wl over 2f out: sn drvn and wknd* **15/2**

400- **9** *nse* **Flow Chart (IRE)**[29] 7764 4-8-10 **46** oh1 (b) RobbieFitzpatrick 7 37
(Peter Grayson) *chsd ldrs: rdn along 1/2-way: sn wknd* **40/1**

500- **10** *2 ¼* **Head To Head (IRE)**[169] 4244 7-8-9 **48** (t) JamesSullivan(3) 13 32
(Alan Brown) *midfield: rdn along 1/2-way: nvr a factor* **20/1**

650- **11** *5* **Frill A Minute**[132] 5482 7-8-10 **46** oh1 (v[1]) BarryMcHugh 6 14
(Lynn Siddall) *a in rr* **80/1**

653- **12** *5* **Rose Bed (IRE)**[10] 7987 4-8-11 **47** oh1 ow1 (b) JackMitchell 5 —
(Michael Quinlan) *a in rr: bhd fnl 2f* **22/1**

13 *8* **Angel Instead (IRE)**[433] 7160 6-8-10 **46** oh1 LukeMorris 3 —
(Mrs K Burke) *a towards rr: outpcd and bhd fnl 2f* **8/1**

1m 19.46s (2.96) **Going Correction** +0.25s/f (Slow) **13** Ran SP% **118.4**
Speed ratings (Par 101): **90,89,86,85,84 84,83,82,82,79 72,65,55**
toteswingers: 1&2 £3.80, 1&3 £10.70, 2&3 £6.20. CSF £26.41 CT £308.24 TOTE £6.30: £2.00, £1.80, £4.70; EX 21.90 Trifecta £42.80 Pool: £210.76 - 3.64 winning units..
Owner P Woodward **Bred** Mohammad Al Qatami **Trained** Dalham, Suffolk
■ Michael Stainton lost his right to claim with this winner.
■ Stewards' Enquiry : Patrick Mathers one-day ban: used whip with excessive frequency (Jan 20)

FOCUS
With little frost overnight, the track wasn't prepared the same way it had been during the recent cold spell and the Fibresand was expected to ride faster as a result, but the winning time in this opener was slow and even though this was a moderate race, that suggests the going was still testing enough.

58 SOUTHWELL-RACECOURSE.CO.UK H'CAP 6f (F)
1:20 (1:20) (Class 5) (0-75,75) 4-Y-0+ **£2,007** (£597; £298; £149) **Stalls** Low

Form RPR

16-2 **1** **Punching**[2] 35 7-9-4 **72** HayleyTurner 3 81
(Conor Dore) *mde all: rdn wl over 1f out: kpt on wl fnl f* **8/1**[3]

060- **2** *1 ¾* **Onceaponatime (IRE)**[15] 7971 6-9-3 **71** LukeMorris 1 74
(Michael Squance) *trckd ldrs: hdwy on inner over 2f out: rdn wl over 1f out: drvn and kpt on ins fnl f: tk 2nd nr line* **17/2**

000- **3** *shd* **Besty**[43] 7554 4-9-0 **73** AdamCarter(5) 4 76
(Bryan Smart) *cl up: rdn 2f out and ev ch tl drvn and one pce ent fnl f: lost 2nd nr line* **10/1**

11- **4** *1* **Benato The Great (IRE)**[25] 7847 5-9-1 **72** MichaelO'Connell(3) 6 72
(David Nicholls) *trckd ldng pair: effrt over 2f out and sn rdn: drvn over 1f out: sn no imp* **1/1**[1]

503- **5** *nk* **Harlech Castle**[20] 7906 6-9-3 **71** (b) StephenCraine 5 70
(Jim Boyle) *towards rr: rdn along 1/2-way: hdwy wl over 1f out: kpt on u.p fnl f: nrst fin* **5/1**[2]

004- **6** *¾* **Masked Dance (IRE)**[20] 7906 4-9-7 **75** (b) PhillipMakin 8 72
(Kevin Ryan) *cl up on outer: rdn along wl over 2f out: drvn over 1f out and sn one pce* **12/1**

005- **7** *2 ¼* **Silver Wind**[19] 7934 6-8-4 **65** (p) HobieGill(7) 7 54
(Alan McCabe) *a in rr* **33/1**

144- **8** *2 ¾* **Perlachy**[23] 7868 7-8-12 **66** (v) KellyHarrison 2 47
(Derek Shaw) *a in rr* **25/1**

1m 17.94s (1.44) **Going Correction** +0.25s/f (Slow) **8** Ran SP% **111.9**
Speed ratings (Par 103): **100,97,97,96,95 94,91,88**
toteswingers: 1&2 £8.40, 1&3 £9.50, 2&3 £15.30. CSF £69.67 CT £679.09 TOTE £5.30: £1.40, £1.60, £3.40; EX 95.80 TRIFECTA Not won..
Owner Liam Breslin **Bred** Cheveley Park Stud Ltd **Trained** Cowbit, Lincs

FOCUS
A fair sprint handicap and the winning time was 1.52 seconds faster than the opener. This was a race where it was a big advantage to race up front.

59 MEMBERSHIP OF SOUTHWELL GOLF CLUB CLAIMING STKS 7f (F)
1:50 (1:51) (Class 6) 3-Y-O **£1,535** (£453; £226) **Stalls** Low

Form RPR

323- **1** **Fred Willetts (IRE)**[20] 7916 3-9-4 **79** (v) MatthewCosham(7) 1 89
(David Evans) *trckd ldng pair: hdwy on outer to chal whn rdr lost whip over 2f out: led wl over 1f out and sn rdn clr: readily* **15/8**[2]

361- **2** *7* **So Is She (IRE)**[16] 7954 3-8-6 **70** CathyGannon 4 51
(Alan Bailey) *trckd ldr: hdwy and cl up 1/2-way: rdn to ld briefly 2f out: sn hdd and one pce* **6/5**[1]

053- **3** *3 ¼* **Bernisdale**[26] 7831 3-8-4 **57** ow2 ChrisCatlin 5 40
(George Moore) *led: rdn along and jnd 3f out: hdd jst over 2f out and sn one pce* **7/2**[3]

1m 31.63s (1.33) **Going Correction** +0.25s/f (Slow) **3** Ran SP% **102.5**
Speed ratings (Par 95): **102,94,90**
CSF £4.14 TOTE £2.30; EX 3.60.
Owner 24 - 7 / Gap Personnel **Bred** Liam Queally **Trained** Pandy, Monmouths

The Form Book, Raceform Ltd, Compton, RG20 6NL

FOCUS
An ordinary small-field claimer.

60 SOUTHWELL-RACECOURSE.CO.UK RATING RELATED MAIDEN STKS — 1m (F)
2:20 (2:20) (Class 6) 3-Y-O+ **£1,535** (£453; £226) **Stalls** Low

Form RPR
003- **1** **Volcanic Ash (USA)**[56] [7412] 3-8-7 56 .... JoeFanning 2 76+
(Mark Johnston) *mde all: pushed clr wl over 1f out: easily* **6/4**[1]
406- **2** *8* **Gordy Bee (USA)**[21] [7895] 5-9-10 62 .... (e) MichaelO'Connell(3) 6 57
(Richard Guest) *chsd wnr: rdn along over 2f out: sn drvn and one pce* **3/1**[2]
52-2 **3** *3/4* **Ad Vitam (IRE)**[5] [5] 3-8-7 57 .... (t) DavidProbert 4 51
(Sylvester Kirk) *chsd ldrs: rdn along over 3f out: drvn and kpt on same pce fnl 2f* **5/1**[3]
400- **4** *7* **Windsor Knights**[38] [7630] 3-8-8 62 ow1 .... (v) GrahamGibbons 1 36
(Alastair Lidderdale) *s.i.s and in rr: hdwy 3f out: sn rdn and nvr a factor* **9/1**
630- **5** *2 1/2* **Willow's Wish**[76] [7057] 3-8-4 50 .... ChrisCatlin 5 26
(George Moore) *dwlt: a towards rr* **25/1**
433- **6** *2 1/2* **Thank You Joy**[34] [7677] 3-7-11 60 .... DannyBrock(7) 8 20
(J R Jenkins) *dwlt: a towards rr* **6/1**
635- **7** *7* **Bigalo's Vera B**[10] [7983] 3-8-4 45 .... DuranFentiman 3 —
(Lawrence Mullaney) *prom: rdn along 3f out: drvn over 2f out and sn wknd* **66/1**

1m 45.69s (1.99) **Going Correction** +0.25s/f (Slow) 7 Ran SP% **111.3**
WFA 3 from 4yo+ 20lb
Speed ratings (Par 101): **100,92,91,84,81 79,72**
toteswingers: 1&2 £2.50, 1&3 £1.70, 2&3 £2.80. CSF £5.75 TOTE £2.10: £1.10, £3.00; EX 7.40 Trifecta £19.80 Pool: £409.83 - 15.26 winning units..
Owner Crone Stud Farms Ltd **Bred** Nardelli Et Al **Trained** Middleham Moor, N Yorks

FOCUS
A poor and uncompetitive maiden and this lot had been beaten 49 times between them previously.

61 VISIT SOUTHWELL H'CAP — 1m (F)
2:50 (2:50) (Class 6) (0-60,64) 4-Y-O+ **£1,535** (£453; £226) **Stalls** Low

Form RPR
2 **1** **Powerful Presence (IRE)**[5] [7] 5-8-11 50 .... JoeFanning 7 67
(David O'Meara) *cl up gng wl: led 2f out: pushed along over 1f out: rdn ins fnl f and kpt on* **2/1**[1]
131- **2** *2 1/4* **Bentley**[10] [7986] 7-9-11 64 6ex .... (p) GrahamGibbons 5 76
(Brian Baugh) *led: rdn and hdd 2f out: drvn over 1f out: kpt on fnl f* **4/1**[3]
303- **3** *3* **Almahaza (IRE)**[10] [7986] 7-9-7 60 .... NeilChalmers 4 65
(Adrian Chamberlain) *in tch: hdwy over 2f out: rdn to chse ldng pair over 1f out: sn drvn and no imp* **7/1**
240- **4** *1 1/2* **On The Cusp (IRE)**[7] [8023] 4-8-8 47 .... KellyHarrison 2 49
(Paddy Butler) *chsd ldrs on inner: rdn along wl over 2f out: sn drvn and one pce* **28/1**
035- **5** *4 1/2* **Chez Vrony**[73] [7122] 5-9-4 57 .... ChrisCatlin 1 48
(Dave Morris) *dwlt and towards rr: hdwy 3f out: rdn over 2f out: n.d* **17/2**
064- **6** *8* **Jingoism (USA)**[28] [7786] 5-8-5 49 .... DeanHeslop(5) 6 22
(Brian Ellison) *cl up: rdn along 1/2-way: sn wknd* **20/1**
32-4 **7** *59* **Nicholas Pocock (IRE)**[3] [21] 5-9-7 60 .... BarryMcHugh 3 —
(Brian Ellison) *hld up towards rr: pushed along over 3f out: sn rdn and wknd qckly: bhd and eased fnl 2f* **11/4**[2]

1m 44.98s (1.28) **Going Correction** +0.25s/f (Slow) 7 Ran SP% **111.2**
Speed ratings (Par 101): **103,100,97,96,91 83,24**
toteswingers: 1&2 £2.00, 1&3 £3.30, 2&3 £3.80. CSF £9.71 TOTE £2.30: £1.20, £1.80; EX 8.70.
Owner Mrs S O'Meara **Bred** Corduff Stud **Trained** Nawton, N Yorks

FOCUS
A moderate handicap, though the winning time was 0.71 seconds faster than the preceding rating related maiden.
Nicholas Pocock (IRE) Official explanation: vet said the gelding finished distressed

62 EXCLUSIVE LIVE SHOWS AT BLUESQ.COM FILLIES' H'CAP — 5f (F)
3:20 (3:20) (Class 5) (0-70,66) 4-Y-O+ **£2,007** (£597; £298; £149) **Stalls** High

Form RPR
052- **1** **Caramelita**[6] [8034] 4-9-4 63 .... StephenCraine 3 72
(J R Jenkins) *trckd ldng pair: smooth hdwy on outer 2f out and sn cl up: rdn and qcknd to ld ins fnl f: sn edgd rt and kpt on* **3/1**[3]
32-2 **2** *2 1/2* **Your Gifted (IRE)**[3] [15] 4-8-12 60 .... (be) JamesSullivan(3) 4 60
(Patrick Morris) *trckd ldng pair: hdwy and cl up 2f out: rdn to ld over 1f out: hdd and one pce ins fnl f* **2/1**[1]
416- **3** *3 1/2* **Fashion Icon (USA)**[23] [7868] 5-9-6 65 .... (b) GrahamGibbons 2 52
(David O'Meara) *slt ld: rdn along 2f out: sn drvn and hdd over 1f out: kpt on one pce* **9/4**[2]
034- **4** *nk* **Hypnosis**[54] [7446] 8-9-7 66 .... PhillipMakin 5 52
(Noel Wilson) *dwlt: sn cl up: rdn along 2f out: sn drvn and one pce* **9/2**

61.62 secs (1.92) **Going Correction** +0.475s/f (Slow) 4 Ran SP% **107.3**
Speed ratings (Par 100): **103,99,93,92**
CSF £9.12 TOTE £2.70; EX 10.00.
Owner La Senoritas **Bred** R B Hill **Trained** Royston, Herts

FOCUS
A modest fillies' sprint and it may be significant that the pair who raced furthest off the stands' rail were running all over the pair who raced closest to it from some way out.

63 PLAY MEGAJACKPOTS AT CLEOPATRA AT BLUESQ.COM APPRENTICE H'CAP — 1m 4f (F)
3:50 (3:50) (Class 6) (0-65,67) 4-Y-O+ **£1,489** (£443; £221; £110) **Stalls** Low

Form RPR
121- **1** **Dontpaytheferryman (USA)**[10] [7985] 6-10-1 67 6ex .... DaleSwift 3 85
(Brian Ellison) *trckd ldng pair: hdwy to ld over 4f out: clr 2f out: v easily* **4/7**[1]
430- **2** *11* **Magic Haze**[203] [3110] 5-9-1 56 .... RyanPowell(3) 1 56
(Sally Hall) *hld up in rr: hdwy over 3f out: wd st and rdn over 2f out: styd on to take 2nd ent fnl f: no ch w wnr* **10/1**
224- **3** *3 1/2* **Yossi (IRE)**[16] [7958] 7-8-8 51 .... (be) SeanPalmer(5) 7 46
(Richard Guest) *in tch: hdwy over 4f out: chsd wnr 3f out: rdn over 2f out and plugged on same pce: lost 2nd ent fnl f* **10/1**
023- **4** *8* **Minortransgression (USA)**[10] [7988] 4-9-4 65 ....(t) MatthewCosham(5) 5 47
(David Evans) *in tch: effrt over 4f out and sn rdn along: wd st and drvn over 2f out: n.d* **9/1**[3]
134- **5** *8* **Kingaroo (IRE)**[33] [7695] 5-9-5 57 .... TobyAtkinson 2 26
(Garry Woodward) *slt ld and set str pce to 1/2-way: rdn along and hdd over 4f out: drvn over 3f out and sn wknd* **8/1**[2]
600- **6** *4* **Sirdave**[167] [4327] 5-9-1 56 .... RyanClark(3) 6 19
(Peter Hiatt) *in tch: hdwy to chse ldrs 5f out: rdn along over 3f out: sn drvn and wknd* **22/1**
0/0- **7** *3* **Novestar (IRE)**[96] [6578] 6-9-7 62 .... (t) AdamCarter(3) 4 20
(Michael Appleby) *cl up: rdn along over 5f out: sn outpcd and bhd fnl 3f* **40/1**

2m 43.75s (2.75) **Going Correction** +0.25s/f (Slow)
WFA 4 from 5yo+ 4lb 7 Ran SP% **109.7**
Speed ratings (Par 101): **100,92,90,85,79 77,75**
toteswingers: 1&2 £2.90, 1&3 £1.70, 2&3 £7.00. totesuper7: WIN: Not won. PLACE: £72.90 - 7 winning units. CSF £6.48 TOTE £1.60: £1.50, £5.60; EX 8.80.
Owner Koo's Racing Club **Bred** Rojan Farms **Trained** Norton, N Yorks

FOCUS
The two established front-runners Novestar and Kingaroo decided to hold their own sprint contest over the first 4f and only succeeded in destroying each other's chances.
T/Plt: £463.40 to a £1 stake. Pool: £55,915.22 - 88.07 winning tickets. T/Qpdt: £35.70 to a £1 stake. Pool: £5,732.87 - 118.70 winning tickets. JR

[21] WOLVERHAMPTON (A.W) (L-H)
Thursday, January 6

OFFICIAL GOING: Standard to slow
Wind: Nil Weather: Overcast

64 BLUESQ.COM ON YOUR IPHONE H'CAP — 5f 20y(P)
4:10 (4:10) (Class 6) (0-55,55) 3-Y-O **£1,706** (£503; £252) **Stalls** Low

Form RPR
024- **1** **Juarla (IRE)**[23] [7864] 3-8-11 50 .... LukeMorris 9 60
(Ronald Harris) *midfield: hdwy 2f out: r.o to ld ins fnl f: kpt on wl towards fin* **13/2**[3]
600- **2** *1* **Go Maggie Go (IRE)**[31] [7722] 3-8-10 49 .... FergusSweeney 3 55
(Kevin Ryan) *w ldr: led over 2f out: rdn and edgd rt fr over 1f out: hdd ins fnl f: nt qckn towards fin* **8/1**
042- **3** *1* **Shutterbug**[35] [7666] 3-9-2 55 .... (t) WilliamCarson 6 57
(Stuart Williams) *chsd ldrs: rdn to take 2nd 2f out tl over 1f out: kpt on u.p ins fnl f but no imp on front 2* **15/8**[1]
000- **4** *nse* **Place And Chips**[129] [5581] 3-9-0 53 .... (t) RichardKingscote 10 55
(Tom Dascombe) *bhd: rdn and hdwy over 1f out: styd on ins fnl f: nt quite pce to chal ldrs* **13/2**[3]
360- **5** *1 3/4* **Miss Toldyaso (IRE)**[8] [7997] 3-8-9 55 .... JamesRogers(7) 12 51
(Michael Quinlan) *hld up: hdwy on wd outside wl over 1f out: styd on ins fnl f: nt pce to rch ldrs* **9/1**
004- **6** *3/4* **Mi Sun Donk**[31] [7722] 3-9-2 55 .... GeorgeBaker 7 48
(Brett Johnson) *midfield: effrt on wd outside 2f out: one pce fr over 1f out: no imp on ldrs* **6/1**[2]
500- **7** *1 1/4* **Look'N'Listen (IRE)**[41] [7577] 3-8-9 48 .... (p) JimmyQuinn 4 37
(Alan Brown) *midfield: rdn and outpcd over 1f out: nvr able to chal* **33/1**
000- **8** *3/4* **Renesmee (IRE)**[24] [7858] 3-8-7 46 oh1 .... (b) RobbieFitzpatrick 8 32
(Peter Grayson) *bhd: rdn and sme hdwy over 1f out: nt pce to trble ldrs* **66/1**
055- **9** *1 1/2* **Ladydolly**[27] [7809] 3-8-7 46 oh1 .... MartinLane 1 27
(Roy Brotherton) *chsd ldrs: rdn over 2f out: wknd ins fnl f* **12/1**
005- **10** *12* **Sea Of Love (IRE)**[33] [7692] 3-8-7 46 oh1 .... CathyGannon 5 —
(Ronald Harris) *chsd ldrs: pushed along over 3f out: wknd 2f out* **20/1**
000- **11** *15* **Hey Mambo**[22] [7871] 3-8-7 46 oh1 .... FrannyNorton 2 —
(Roger Ingram) *led: hdd over 2f out: wknd wl over 1f out* **40/1**

63.70 secs (1.40) **Going Correction** +0.275s/f (Slow) 11 Ran SP% **116.2**
Speed ratings (Par 95): **99,97,95,95,92 91,89,88,86,66 42**
toteswingers: 1&2 £7.90, 1&3 £3.10, 2&3 £4.00. CSF £54.80 CT £138.66 TOTE £6.30: £1.90, £2.90, £1.30; EX 69.90.
Owner Robert & Nina Bailey **Bred** D And Mrs D Veitch **Trained** Earlswood, Monmouths

FOCUS
A weak handicap.
Mi Sun Donk Official explanation: jockey said that the gelding failed to handle the bend
Look'N'Listen(IRE) Official explanation: jockey said that the filly suffered interference in running
Hey Mambo Official explanation: jockey said the filly stopped very quickly

65 ENJOY THE PARTY PACK GROUP OFFER MEDIAN AUCTION MAIDEN STKS — 5f 216y(P)
4:40 (4:40) (Class 6) 3-5-Y-O **£1,569** (£463; £231) **Stalls** Low

Form RPR
045- **1** **Madam Mayem**[156] [4675] 3-8-5 67 .... RichardKingscote 1 65+
(Tom Dascombe) *chsd ldrs: led over 1f out: r.o wl and in command ins fnl f* **1/2**[1]
005- **2** *3* **Libertino (IRE)**[27] [7810] 4-9-12 54 .... GeorgeBaker 5 64
(Tony Carroll) *a.p: rdn over 1f out: chsd wnr thrght fnl f but no imp* **8/1**[2]
445- **3** *6* **Colamandis**[104] [6332] 4-9-7 55 .... PatrickMathers 6 40
(Hugh McWilliams) *led: rdn and hdd over 1f out: sn btn and wl outpcd ins fnl f* **8/1**[2]
40-0 **4** *3/4* **Gower Sophia**[2] [28] 4-9-7 50 .... (p) CathyGannon 3 37
(Ronald Harris) *racd keenly: hld up: hdwy to chse ldrs 4f out: wknd over 2f out* **16/1**
06- **5** *4 1/2* **Inde Country**[24] [7858] 3-8-5 0 .... LukeMorris 4 19
(Nicky Vaughan) *racd keenly: in tch: prom 4f out: rdn and wknd wl over 1f out* **20/1**
44- **6** *2 1/4* **Gorgeous Goblin (IRE)**[23] [7869] 4-9-7 0 .... DaneO'Neill 2 16
(David C Griffiths) *hld up: pushed along over 3f out: lft wl bhd fnl f* **9/1**[3]

1m 17.61s (2.61) **Going Correction** +0.275s/f (Slow)
WFA 3 from 4yo 16lb 6 Ran SP% **109.5**
Speed ratings (Par 101): **93,89,81,80,74 71**
toteswingers: 1&2 £1.70, 1&3 £1.70, 2&3 £4.10. CSF £4.82 TOTE £1.60: £1.60, £3.00; EX 4.10.
Owner Owen Promotions Limited **Bred** Owen Promotions Ltd **Trained** Malpas, Cheshire
■ Stewards' Enquiry : Luke Morris one-day ban: careless riding (20 Jan)

FOCUS
This took little winning.

66 GREAT OFFERS AT WOLVERHAMPTON-RACECOURSE.CO.UK CLASSIFIED CLAIMING STKS — 5f 216y(P)
5:10 (5:11) (Class 5) 3-Y-O **£2,007** (£597; £298; £149) **Stalls** Low

Form RPR
342- **1** **Slatey Hen (IRE)**[8] [8002] 3-7-13 62 .... NathanAlison(7) 3 64
(Paddy Butler) *a.p: chalng whn bmpd ent st wl over 1f out: sn led: kpt on and a doing enough towards fin* **9/2**[2]

436- **2** *nk* **Just For Leo (IRE)**[7] 8011 3-7-9 60....(v) RPWalsh(7) 7 59
(David Evans) *racd keenly: led: wnt rt ent st wl over 1f out: sn hdd: continued to press wnr ins fnl f: a looked hld* **13/2**[3]

22-2 **3** *1 1/4* **Fifth In Line (IRE)**[3] 20 3-8-10 68.... FergusSweeney 2 63
(Jamie Osborne) *prom: outpcd over 2f out: rdn and tried to get on terms w front pair over 1f out: styd on and clsd towards fin* **11/8**[1]

024- **4** *2* **Misty Morn**[10] 7983 3-8-0 57.... JimmyQuinn 5 47+
(Alan Brown) *hld up: rdn over 2f out: sme hdwy over 1f out: nt pce to chal* **9/2**[2]

040- **5** *3/4* **Princess Dayna**[122] 5818 3-8-11 64.... RossAtkinson(3) 6 58
(Tom Dascombe) *racd keenly: prom: rdn to chal briefly over 2f out: wknd over 1f out* **10/1**

360- **6** *3 1/2* **Welsh Dresser (IRE)**[127] 5667 3-8-12 47.... RobbieFitzpatrick 1 45
(Peter Grayson) *a bhd: nvr gng pce to get on terms* **100/1**

330- **7** *3/4* **Jambo Bibi (IRE)**[64] 7301 3-9-0 67.... LukeMorris 4 45
(Bruce Hellier) *hld up in tch: outpcd over 3f out: n.d after* **17/2**

1m 17.39s (2.39) **Going Correction** +0.275s/f (Slow) **7** Ran SP% **112.4**
Speed ratings (Par 97): **95,94,92,90,89 84,83**
toteswingers: 1&2 £3.10, 1&3 £1.90, 2&3 £3.30. CSF £31.98 TOTE £4.00: £2.40, £5.20; EX 30.40.
Owner Rakebackmypoker.com **Bred** Shane Doyle **Trained** East Chiltington, E Sussex
■ Stewards' Enquiry : R P Walsh one-day ban: careless riding (20 Jan) caution: use of whi[p

FOCUS
Quite a competitive little claimer.
Princess Dayna Official explanation: jockey said that the filly hung off the bend

67 WOLVERHAMPTON-RACECOURSE.CO.UK H'CAP 1m 4f 50y(P)
5:40 (5:40) (Class 5) (0-75,73) 4-Y-0+ **£2,007** (£597; £298; £149) **Stalls** Low

Form RPR
120- **1** **Kiama Bay (IRE)**[48] 7504 5-9-8 **69**.... LiamKeniry 1 84
(John Quinn) *chsd ldr to 6f out: regained 2nd over 3f out: led over 1f out: sn hung lft: r.o and in command ins fnl f* **11/4**[2]

213- **2** *2 1/4* **Albertus Pictor**[22] 7884 4-9-8 **73**.... StevieDonohoe 5 84
(Sir Mark Prescott Bt) *led: pushed along over 4f out: rdn whn pressed over 2f out: hdd over 1f out: hld ins fnl f* **11/8**[1]

153- **3** *11* **Bold Adventure**[29] 7765 7-9-2 **63**.... JamieMackay 6 57
(Willie Musson) *trckd ldrs: chsd ldr fr 6f out tl over 3f out: sn outpcd: lft bhd fnl 2f* **3/1**[3]

161- **4** *7* **Straversjoy**[8] 8010 4-9-2 67 6ex....(p) GrahamGibbons 4 50
(Reg Hollinshead) *in rr: clsd 5f out: rdn and outpcd 3f out: lft bhd fnl 2f* **6/1**

2m 43.5s (2.40) **Going Correction** +0.275s/f (Slow) **4** Ran SP% **108.1**
WFA 4 from 5yo+ 4lb
Speed ratings (Par 103): **103,101,94,89**
toteswinger: 1&2 £3.70. CSF £6.93 TOTE £2.50; EX 9.20.
Owner Mrs S Quinn **Bred** Tipper House Stud **Trained** Settrington, N Yorks

FOCUS
Just the four runners following defections and two of them drew clear.
Straversjoy Official explanation: jockey said that the filly ran flat

68 EXCLUSIVE LIVE SHOWS AT BLUESQ.COM H'CAP 2m 119y(P)
6:10 (6:10) (Class 4) (0-85,78) 4-Y-0+ **£3,561** (£1,059; £529; £264) **Stalls** Low

Form RPR
215- **1** **Treacle Tart**[30] 7736 6-9-2 **68**.... GeorgeBaker 4 74
(Peter Charalambous) *hld up: hdwy 3f out: chsd ldr over 2f out: rdn over 1f out: styd on to move upsides fnl 110yds: led post* **13/2**[3]

111- **2** *nse* **Jezza**[24] 7861 5-9-7 **73**.... StevieDonohoe 1 79
(Victor Dartnall) *in tch: led wl over 2f out: rdn over 1f out: jnd fnl 110yds: hdd post* **4/7**[1]

310- **3** *1 1/4* **Admirable Duque (IRE)**[22] 5591 5-9-12 **78**....(p) MartinLane 2 83
(Dominic Ffrench Davis) *in rr: hdwy over 3f out: chsd ldrs over 2f out: rdn over 1f out: styd on ins fnl f: nt quite pce to chal front pair* **20/1**

000- **4** *12* **Blue Nymph**[153] 4785 5-9-11 **77**....(p) LiamKeniry 7 67
(John Quinn) *chsd ldr: led 3f out: hdd wl over 2f out: sn wknd* **12/1**

065- **5** *1 3/4* **Calculating (IRE)**[71] 7181 7-8-13 **70**.... LeeNewnes(5) 6 58
(Mark Usher) *led: pushed along and hdd 3f out: wknd over 2f out* **18/1**

032- **6** *shd* **Houston Dynimo (IRE)**[24] 7861 6-9-1 **70**.... JamesSullivan(3) 3 58
(Nicky Richards) *chsd ldrs tl rdn and wknd 3f out* **11/2**[2]

3m 43.79s (1.99) **Going Correction** +0.275s/f (Slow) **6** Ran SP% **110.1**
Speed ratings (Par 105): **106,105,105,99,98 98**
toteswingers: 1&2 £1.40, 1&3 £5.00, 2&3 £3.20. CSF £10.32 TOTE £3.50: £2.00, £1.10; EX 13.30.
Owner P Charalambous **Bred** Middleton Stud **Trained** Newmarket, Suffolk

FOCUS
This staying handicap didn't work out as many expected.

69 HORIZONS RESTAURANT, THE PLACE TO DINE H'CAP 1m 141y(P)
6:40 (6:41) (Class 7) (0-50,50) 4-Y-0+ **£1,535** (£453; £226) **Stalls** Low

Form RPR
011- **1** **John Potts**[20] 7918 6-9-3 **50**.... KellyHarrison 4 59
(Brian Baugh) *in tch: effrt 2f out: led 1f out: styd on gamely ins fnl f: a looked on top* **5/1**[1]

405- **2** *1/2* **Fortunate Bid (IRE)**[24] 7863 5-9-0 **50**.... JamesSullivan(3) 11 58
(Linda Stubbs) *hld up: hdwy on outer 3f out: led wl over 1f out: hdd 1f out: ev ch thrght fnl f but nt run on* **11/2**[2]

250- **3** *2 1/2* **Corrib (IRE)**[70] 7199 8-9-2 **49**....(p) DavidProbert 8 51
(Bryn Palling) *hld up: hdwy 2f out: rdn over 1f out: styd on ins fnl f: unable to chal front pair* **12/1**

060- **4** *nk* **Crianza**[122] 5820 5-9-1 **48**....(p) GrahamGibbons 12 49
(Nigel Tinkler) *hld up: swtchd rt and hdwy over 2f out: chsd ldrs fnl f: styd on* **28/1**

050- **5** *1/2* **Dane Cottage**[9] 7996 4-9-0 **48**.... CathyGannon 3 48
(David Evans) *hld up: pushed along over 2f out: prog ins fnl f: gng on at fin* **12/1**

0- **6** *1/2* **Sopran Nad (ITY)**[26] 7829 7-8-13 **46**....(t) AndreaAtzeni 13 45
(Stuart Williams) *in tch: chalng 3f out: led briefly wl over 1f out: no ex fnl 100yds* **9/1**[3]

333- **7** *1 3/4* **Al Rayanah**[20] 7917 8-9-3 **50**....(p) KirstyMilczarek 7 45
(George Prodromou) *midfield: hdwy 3f out: chsd ldrs over 2f out: wknd over 1f out* **5/1**[1]

655- **8** *2 3/4* **Dancing Poppy**[9] 7996 4-8-12 **46**.... HayleyTurner 9 35
(Rodney Farrant) *handy: pushed along over 2f out: wknd over 1f out* **14/1**

520- **9** *1 1/4* **Djalalabad (FR)**[15] 7966 7-9-1 **48**....(t) MickyFenton 6 34
(Jeff Pearce) *bhd: hrd at work over 3f out: nvr able to get on terms* **18/1**

200- **10** *3/4* **Hedgerow (IRE)**[33] 7705 4-9-0 **48**....(t) SamHitchcott 5 32
(David Bourton) *midfield: rdn over 2f out: sn outpcd* **22/1**

650- **11** *4 1/2* **The Graig**[24] 7863 7-9-3 **50**....(p) LukeMorris 1 24
(John Holt) *trckd ldrs: pushed along 3f out: wknd 2f out* **20/1**

04- **12** *hd* **Celtic Life (IRE)**[20] 7918 5-8-12 **45**....(vt[1]) DaneO'Neill 2 18
(Amy Weaver) *led: hdd over 6f out: remained prom: rdn over 1f out: wknd and eased ins fnl f* **11/2**[2]

002- **13** *5* **Fitzwarren**[163] 4454 10-8-12 **45**....(tp) JimmyQuinn 10 7
(Alan Brown) *prom: led over 6f out: hdd wl over 1f out: sn wknd* **33/1**

1m 53.34s (2.84) **Going Correction** +0.275s/f (Slow)
WFA 4 from 5yo+ 1lb **13** Ran SP% **116.9**
Speed ratings (Par 97): **98,97,95,95,94 94,92,90,89,88 84,84,79**
toteswingers: 1&2 £6.70, 1&3 £6.70, 2&3 £8.80. CSF £29.40 CT £325.61 TOTE £4.20: £1.40, £3.20, £3.40; EX 26.50.
Owner Miss S M Potts **Bred** Miss S M Potts **Trained** Audley, Staffs

FOCUS
A low-grade handicap.

70 PLAY FREE BINGO AT BLUESQ.COM H'CAP 7f 32y(P)
7:10 (7:11) (Class 7) (0-50,50) 4-Y-0+ **£1,535** (£453; £226) **Stalls** High

Form RPR
064- **1** **Piccolo Express**[76] 7070 5-9-1 **48**.... J-PGuillambert 5 61
(Brian Baugh) *racd keenly: in tch: effrt 2f out: led wl over 1f out: r.o gamely ins fnl f: a doing enough to hold on gamely cl home* **17/2**

30- **2** *hd* **Kanace**[62] 7338 4-9-0 **47**.... StevieDonohoe 12 59+
(Jeff Pearce) *hld up: rdn and hdwy over 1f out: str chal and ev ch ins fnl f: jst hld cl home* **9/1**

056- **3** *3 1/4* **Guildenstern (IRE)**[29] 7761 9-9-3 **50**.... JimmyQuinn 7 54
(Jane Chapple-Hyam) *hld up: hdwy over 1f out: sn chsd ldrs: no imp on front pair ins fnl f* **7/2**[1]

650- **4** *3/4* **Transfixed (IRE)**[26] 7829 4-9-3 **50**....(v) CathyGannon 1 52
(David Evans) *a.p: rdn to chal 2f out: nt qckn over 1f out: no imp on ldrs ins fnl f* **6/1**[2]

643- **5** *1/2* **Suttonia (IRE)**[7] 8024 5-8-13 **46**.... TravisBlock 9 46
(Noel Chance) *midfield: pushed along 3f out: rdn and hdwy over 2f out: styd on same pce ins fnl f* **16/1**

553- **6** *hd* **Cane Cat (IRE)**[21] 7885 4-9-2 **49**....(t) AdamKirby 10 49
(Tony Carroll) *hld up: rdn and hdwy over 1f out: nt clr run and swtchd lft ins fnl f: kpt on but unable to chal* **13/2**[3]

444- **7** *nk* **Carnival Dream**[20] 7917 6-9-2 **49**.... PatrickMathers 11 48
(Hugh McWilliams) *dwlt: hld up in rr: rdn over 1f out: kpt on ins fnl f: nt pce to rch ldrs* **14/1**

005- **8** *3/4* **Polemica (IRE)**[21] 7885 5-9-1 **48**....(bt) HayleyTurner 6 47
(Frank Sheridan) *missed break: hld up in midfield: rdn whn nt clr run ins fnl f: one pce after* **14/1**

500- **9** *1* **Gilderoy**[28] 7783 4-9-0 **47**....(be) MartinLane 3 41
(Dominic Ffrench Davis) *racd keenly: midfield: pushed along and wknd 2f out* **20/1**

006- **10** *3/4* **Daily Double**[7] 8023 5-8-13 **46**....(v) FrannyNorton 2 38
(Martin Bosley) *trckd ldrs: rdn 2f out: sn wknd* **20/1**

665- **11** *2* **Abhainn (IRE)**[36] 7649 5-9-0 **47**.... DavidProbert 4 43+
(Bryn Palling) *led: rdn 2f out: sn hdd: wknd and eased ins fnl f* **6/1**[2]

/50- **12** *15* **See That Girl**[337] 388 5-9-0 **47**.... LukeMorris 8 —
(Martin Bosley) *dwlt: racd keenly in tch: effrt 2f out: wknd over 1f out* **40/1**

1m 32.26s (2.66) **Going Correction** +0.275s/f (Slow) **12** Ran SP% **115.8**
Speed ratings (Par 97): **95,94,91,90,89 89,89,88,87,86 83,66**
toteswingers: 1&2 £24.00, 1&3 £7.40, 2&3 £17.70. CSF £78.71 CT £324.02 TOTE £13.10: £4.30, £4.30, £1.10; EX 155.80.
Owner G B Hignett **Bred** G B Hignett **Trained** Audley, Staffs

FOCUS
A very moderate contest.
Transfixed(IRE) Official explanation: jockey said that the filly hung right-handed throughout
Abhainn(IRE) Official explanation: jockey said the gelding lost its action
T/Plt: £122.80 to a £1 stake. Pool: £73,288.21 - 435.54 winning tickets. T/Qpdt: £60.20 to a £1 stake. Pool: £6,769.60 - 83.20 w. tickets. DO

71-76a (Foreign Racing) See Raceform Int.

50 LINGFIELD (L-H)
Friday, January 7

OFFICIAL GOING: Standard
Wind: Fresh, behind Weather: Cloudy, rain Race 7

77 BLUESQ.COM ON YOUR IPHONE MEDIAN AUCTION MAIDEN STKS 1m (P)
12:40 (12:45) (Class 5) 3-5-Y-0 **£1,910** (£564; £282) **Stalls** High

Form RPR
5- **1** **Elvira Delight (IRE)**[65] 7294 3-8-3 0.... ChrisCatlin 1 56+
(Jeremy Noseda) *cl up on inner: rdn over 2f out: wnt 2nd over 1f out: styd on u.p to ld last 150yds: sn clr* **10/11**[1]

050- **2** *2 1/4* **Soviet Spring (IRE)**[8] 8011 3-8-8 62.... DavidProbert 4 56
(Andrew Balding) *led: set stdy pce early: kicked on over 2f out: looked likely wnr over 1f out: folded rather tamely and hdd last 150yds* **14/1**

0- **3** *1 1/2* **Mountain Myst**[9] 8000 3-8-8 0.... FrannyNorton 2 53
(William Muir) *rn green in last: lost tch 3f out: 5 l bhd adrift 2f out: styd on wl fnl f to take 3rd last strides* **25/1**

33- **4** *1/2* **Links Drive Lady**[10] 7990 3-8-3 0.... NickyMackay 5 46
(Mark Rimmer) *t.k.h early: trckd ldr: rdn over 2f out: nt qckn and lost 2nd over 1f out: fdd and lost 3rd last strides* **2/1**[2]

554- **5** *shd* **Entrance**[38] 7644 3-8-3 65.... CathyGannon 3 46
(Julia Feilden) *hld up in 4th: rdn wl over 2f out bef pce lifted: no imp on ldrs after* **13/2**[3]

1m 40.35s (2.15) **Going Correction** +0.225s/f (Slow) **5** Ran SP% **109.6**
Speed ratings (Par 103): **98,95,94,93,93**
CSF £14.01 TOTE £1.90: £1.10, £5.80; EX 11.10.
Owner Newsells Park Stud **Bred** Lagartijo S L **Trained** Newmarket, Suffolk

FOCUS
A modest maiden run at a steady pace, resulting in a time over four seconds above standard, by far the slowest of the three 1m races.

78 LINGFIELDPARK.CO.UK (S) STKS 1m (P)
1:10 (1:16) (Class 6) 4-Y-0+ **£1,535** (£453; £226) **Stalls** High

Form RPR
000- **1** **Silver Guest**[182] 3855 6-8-13 75.... JamieGoldstein 1 71
(Ralph Smith) *hld up towards rr: smooth prog over 2f out: trckd ldr over 1f out: pushed into ld ins fnl f* **10/1**

The Form Book, Raceform Ltd, Compton, RG20 6NL

206- **2** ¾ **Shared Moment (IRE)**[16] 7966 5-8-8 54.........................(v[1]) ChrisCatlin 7 64
(John Gallagher) *trckd ldng pair: prog on inner to ld 2f out gng strly: rdn over 1f out: hdd and hld ins fnl f* **10/1**

044- **3** 3 **Rich Boy**[30] 7763 4-8-13 58.........................(vt[1]) IanMongan 4 62
(Laura Mongan) *racd wd: hld up in tch: drvn over 2f out: plugged on to take 3rd ins fnl f: n.d* **7/1**[3]

434- **4** ¾ **Goodbye Cash (IRE)**[8] 8019 7-8-11 57.............. AndrewHeffernan(3) 5 61
(Ralph Smith) *rousted along to ld and racd off the rail: rdn and hdd 2f out: grad fdd* **25/1**

323- **5** 6 **Kipchak (IRE)**[16] 7966 6-8-13 64.........................(p) KirstyMilczarek 6 47
(Conor Dore) *unable to ld: pressed ldr to 3f out: u.p and btn after: wknd over 1f out* **1/1**[1]

000- **6** 6 **Desert Dreamer (IRE)**[7] 8033 10-8-13 73.................. StevieDonohoe 3 33
(David Evans) *dwlt: hld up in last pair: lost tch and struggling 3f out: nvr on terms after* **15/2**

110- **7** 20 **So Surreal (IRE)**[68] 7255 4-9-0 66.........................(b) LiamKeniry 2 —
(Gary Moore) *hld up in last pair: rdn and wknd rapidly wl over 2f out: t.o* **6/1**[2]

1m 38.03s (-0.17) **Going Correction** +0.225s/f (Slow) 7 Ran SP% **110.6**
Speed ratings (Par 101): **109,108,105,104,98 92,72**
Tote Swingers: 1&2 £11.90, 1&3 £9.40, 2&3 £8.00 CSF £93.94 TOTE £12.70: £2.90, £7.20; EX 129.70.There was no bid for the winner.
Owner H B & Mrs R H Bulteel **Bred** Timberhill Racing Partnership **Trained** Epsom, Surrey

FOCUS
They went a good pace and this was the quickest of three 1m races on the card.
So Surreal(IRE) Official explanation: jockey said filly was never travelling

79 EDEN BROOK H'CAP 1m 5f (P)
1:40 (1:45) (Class 6) (0-65,66) 4-Y-0+ £1,535 (£453; £226) Stalls Low

Form RPR
2-11 **1** **Luck Of The Draw (IRE)**[3] 40 4-9-6 **66** 6ex............ StevieDonohoe 6 76+
(Sir Mark Prescott Bt) *trckd ldrs: prog to go 2nd wl over 2f out: rdn to ld 1f out: styd on wl* **4/5**[1]

/60- **2** 3 **Jenny Potts**[29] 7778 7-9-5 **65**.............................. TobyAtkinson(5) 3 70+
(Chris Down) *hld up towards rr: gng easily on wd outside over 2f out but stl only 7th: rdn over 1f out: r.o wl to take 2nd last strides: hopeless task* **40/1**

654- **3** nk **Soundbyte**[16] 7967 6-9-5 **60**.............................. AdamKirby 11 65
(John Gallagher) *mostly pressed ldr: drvn ahd 3f out: hdd 1f out: fdd and lost 2nd last strides* **5/1**[2]

020- **4** ½ **Squad**[30] 7765 5-9-7 **62**.............................. JimCrowley 1 66
(Simon Dow) *stdd s: hld up in rr: prog 3f out: drvn into 3rd over 1f out: kpt on same pce after* **13/2**[3]

601- **5** 4 **Active Asset (IRE)**[30] 7760 9-9-0 **55**.............................. SteveDrowne 8 53
(David C Griffiths) *hld up towards rr: prog over 2f out: chsd ldrs over 1f out but nt on terms: no imp after* **16/1**

030- **6** hd **Dawson Creek (IRE)**[23] 7878 7-8-10 **51**.................. CathyGannon 5 49
(Luke Dace) *led: drvn and hdd 3f out: styd chsng ldrs to wl over 1f out: wknd* **33/1**

641- **7** nse **Burnbrake**[100] 6454 6-9-0 **55**.........................(b) JamesMillman 7 52
(Les Hall) *hld up last: shuffled along fnl 2f: kpt on: nvr nr ldrs* **33/1**

460- **8** 9 **It's Dubai Dolly**[82] 6959 5-9-7 **62**.............................. IanMongan 9 46
(Alastair Lidderdale) *plld hrd early: w ldrs: rdn to chal on wd outside 3f out: nt qckn over 2f out: sn wknd: eased* **16/1**

000- **9** ¾ **Fleur De'Lion (IRE)**[30] 7759 5-8-5 **51** oh5.................. RyanPowell(5) 4 34
(Sylvester Kirk) *mostly in midfield on inner: lost pl over 3f out: struggling over 2f out* **66/1**

453- **10** 25 **Hibba (USA)**[79] 7022 4-9-5 **65**.............................. ChrisCatlin 2 10
(Mouse Hamilton-Fairley) *dwlt: sn prom: wknd rapidly over 3f out: wl t.o* **14/1**

2m 48.2s (2.20) **Going Correction** +0.225s/f (Slow)
WFA 4 from 5yo+ 5lb 10 Ran SP% **113.8**
Speed ratings (Par 101): **102,100,99,99,97 97,97,91,91,75**
Tote Swingers: 1&2 £11.30, 1&3 £2.20, 2&3 £26.50 CSF £51.41 CT £111.11 TOTE £1.60: £1.10, £7.10, £1.80; EX 37.30 Trifecta £200.00 Pool: £807.68 - 2.21 winning units.
Owner L A Larratt - Osborne House **Bred** Castlemartin Stud And Skymarc Farm **Trained** Newmarket, Suffolk

FOCUS
A modest handicap and they didn't go particularly fast, resulting in a time nearly four seconds above standard.

80 DORMANSLAND H'CAP 5f (P)
2:10 (2:15) (Class 6) (0-65,67) 4-Y-0+ £1,535 (£453; £226) Stalls High

Form RPR
151- **1** **You'relikemefrank**[7] 8036 5-9-11 **67** 6ex.................(p) GrahamGibbons 3 79+
(John Balding) *trckd ldng pair: wnt 2nd 2f out: led over 1f out: drvn 2 l clr ins fnl f: clung on* **11/4**[1]

611- **2** ½ **Estonia**[7] 8037 4-9-4 **60** 6ex.............................. CathyGannon 1 70
(Michael Squance) *t.k.h: hld up towards rr: prog 1/2-way: drvn to go 2nd jst ins fnl f: clsd on wnr fin* **11/4**[1]

405- **3** 1 **Radiator Rooney (IRE)**[7] 8035 8-8-7 **52**.................. AmyRyan(3) 2 58
(Patrick Morris) *stdd s: hld up in last pair: prog on inner 2f out: rdn and styd on fnl f to take 3rd last strides* **11/1**

665- **4** hd **Jimmy Ryan (IRE)**[108] 6270 10-9-2 **58**.........................(t) J-PGuillambert 6 64
(Tim McCarthy) *trckd ldrs: drvn and nt qckn wl over 1f out: styd on again ins fnl f* **40/1**

042- **5** ¾ **Speak The Truth (IRE)**[7] 8035 5-8-13 **58**............(p) MatthewDavies(3) 4 61
(Jim Boyle) *hld up towards rr: effrt 2f out: rdn and fnd nil over 1f out: kpt on same pce after* **5/1**[2]

004- **6** 1 ¾ **Ten Down**[33] 7721 6-8-9 **51**.............................. AndreaAtzeni 5 48
(Michael Quinn) *led to over 1f out: wknd ins fnl f* **14/1**

00- **7** 1 ¾ **Silver Linnet (IRE)**[55] 7446 4-9-3 **59**.........................(b) AdamKirby 7 49
(Michael Quinlan) *stdd s: hld up in last: wdst of all bnd 2f out: reminder over 1f out and ins fnl f: nvr involved* **15/2**[3]

332- **8** ½ **The Tatling (IRE)**[7] 8036 14-9-7 **63**.................. RussKennemore 9 52
(Milton Bradley) *chsd ldrs on outer: struggling to hold pl 2f out: grad wknd* **8/1**

246- **9** 1 ¼ **Cape Royal**[39] 7628 11-9-6 **62**.........................(bt) LiamKeniry 8 46
(Milton Bradley) *s.i.s: rcvrd to chse ldr: lost 2nd 2f out: sn wknd: eased* **16/1**

58.80 secs **Going Correction** +0.225s/f (Slow) 9 Ran SP% **116.2**
Speed ratings (Par 101): **109,108,106,106,105 102,99,98,96**
Tote Swingers: 1&2 £2.00, 1&3 £6.90, 2&3 £8.40 CSF £9.90 CT £70.33 TOTE £3.10: £1.50, £1.10, £3.30; EX 10.00 Trifecta £58.10 Pool: £745.81 - 9.49 winning units..
Owner Kate Barrett, Paul & David Clarkson **Bred** J R Mitchell **Trained** Scrooby, Notts

FOCUS
A good race for the grade, although the anticipated strong gallop didn't quite materialise.

81 MARRIOTT HOTEL AT LINGFIELD PARK (S) STKS 1m 4f (P)
2:40 (2:50) (Class 6) 4-Y-0+ £1,535 (£453; £226) Stalls Low

Form RPR
600- **1** **Barodine**[8] 7200 8-9-3 48.............................. GeorgeBaker 1 64
(Ron Hodges) *hld up in cl tch: trckd ldr over 2f out: rdn to ld 1f out: styd on wl* **25/1**[3]

044- **2** 2 **Addwaitya**[9] 8003 6-9-3 77.............................. IanMongan 2 62
(Laura Mongan) *hld up bhd ldr: c u.p over 4f out: drvn ahd 3f out but flat out: hdd and no ex 1f out* **1/10**[1]

05-6 **3** 20 **Hatch A Plan (IRE)**[3] 30 10-9-3 48....................(p) FrankieMcDonald 4 30
(Mouse Hamilton-Fairley) *led at slow pce: hdd 3f out: sn dropped out: t.o* **10/1**[2]

2m 40.64s (7.64) **Going Correction** +0.225s/f (Slow) 3 Ran SP% **103.8**
Speed ratings (Par 101): **83,81,68**
CSF £30.34 TOTE £17.80; EX 14.10.There was no bid for the winner.
Owner The Gardens Entertainments Ltd **Bred** Mrs A M Jenkins And E D Kessly **Trained** Charlton Mackrell, Somerset

FOCUS
The pace was slow (time 10.94 seconds outside standard) for this three-runner seller, contested by moderate and/or unreliable types, and the form is worth little.

82 EXCLUSIVE LIVE SHOWS AT BLUESQ.COM H'CAP 1m (P)
3:10 (3:20) (Class 5) (0-75,75) 4-Y-0+ £2,320 (£685; £342) Stalls High

Form RPR
610- **1** **Kilburn**[32] 7724 7-9-5 **73**.............................. SteveDrowne 5 83
(Alastair Lidderdale) *mde virtually all: stretched clr over 2f out: pushed out and wl in command fnl f: eased nr fin* **7/1**

005- **2** 2 ¾ **Charlie Smirke (USA)**[32] 7724 5-9-3 **71**.....................(bt) GeorgeBaker 6 74
(Gary Moore) *hld up disputing 6th: cajoled along and prog 2f out: hanging but r.o to take 2nd last strides* **8/1**

322- **3** hd **Could It Be Magic**[8] 8014 4-8-12 **69**.........................(b) KierenFox(3) 2 71
(Bill Turner) *chsd wnr: drvn and nt qckn 2f out: no imp after: lost 2nd last strides* **11/4**[1]

140- **4** ¾ **Syrian**[32] 7724 4-9-7 **75**.............................. JimCrowley 9 75
(Ian Williams) *s.s: hld up in last pair: drvn and wd bnd 2f out: hd high over 1f out: styd on fnl f: nrst fin* **9/2**[3]

402- **5** ½ **Copperwood**[32] 7724 6-9-1 **69**.............................. FrannyNorton 10 70+
(Michael Blanshard) *hld up disputing 6th: nt clr run fr 2f out to jst over 1f out: pushed along and kpt on: no ch to rcvr* **7/2**[2]

404- **6** 1 ¾ **Ilie Nastase (FR)**[11] 7988 7-9-7 **75**.............................. LiamKeniry 1 70
(Conor Dore) *hld up in midfield: rdn on inner over 2f out: effrt to dispute 3rd briefly over 1f out: sn wknd* **14/1**

025- **7** 1 ¼ **Expensive Problem**[8] 8022 8-9-0 **71**.................. AndrewHeffernan(3) 3 63
(Ralph Smith) *t.k.h: sn restrained into 4th: rdn over 2f out: wknd over 1f out* **8/1**

/60- **8** 1 ¾ **Ensnare**[65] 7306 6-9-4 **72**.............................. StevieDonohoe 7 60
(Jeff Pearce) *hld up in last pair: drvn and wd bnd 2f out: no prog and sn btn* **16/1**

502/ **9** hd **Tiger Dream**[51] 7523 6-9-6 **74**.........................(p) ChrisCatlin 4 62
(Chris Down) *trckd ldr tl wknd fr 2f out* **25/1**

1m 38.41s (0.21) **Going Correction** +0.225s/f (Slow) 9 Ran SP% **118.2**
Speed ratings (Par 103): **107,104,104,103,102 101,99,98,97**
Tote Swingers: 1&2 £11.40, 1&3 £5.20, 2&3 £4.20 CSF £63.02 CT £193.85 TOTE £7.80: £2.40, £3.10, £1.10; EX 54.60 Trifecta £222.00 Pool: £834.20 - 2.78 winning units..
Owner Royal Windsor Racing Club **Bred** Barry Walters **Trained** Eastbury, Berks

FOCUS
The time was 0.38 seconds slower than the earlier seller.
Copperwood Official explanation: jockey said gelding was denied a clear run

83 PLAY FREE BINGO AT BLUESQ.COM APPRENTICE H'CAP 1m 2f (P)
3:40 (3:50) (Class 6) (0-65,65) 4-Y-0+ £1,569 (£463; £231) Stalls Low

Form RPR
015- **1** **Lord Theo**[9] 8008 7-9-7 **65**.............................. RyanClark 2 73
(Nick Littmoden) *t.k.h: hld up in last trio: prog out wd to chse ldr over 2f out: rdn wl over 1f out: grad clsd fnl f: led last stride* **11/4**[1]

462- **2** shd **Catbells (IRE)**[16] 7968 4-8-13 **62**.........................(p) NatashaEaton(3) 4 70
(Alan Bailey) *t.k.h: hld up in last trio: prog 6f out: led 4f out: urged along 2f out: kpt on: hdd last stride* **10/3**[2]

320- **3** 3 **Crystal Gale (IRE)**[22] 7887 4-8-13 **59**.........................(v) JamesRogers 3 61
(William Knight) *t.k.h: trckd ldrs: outpcd over 2f out: drvn and plugged on to dispute 3rd ins fnl f* **6/1**

060- **4** hd **Red Storm Rising**[121] 5869 4-8-8 **57**.......................... LucyKBarry(3) 1 59
(Kevin Morgan) *t.k.h: cl up: outpcd and pushed along over 2f out: plugged on to dispute 3rd ins fnl f* **7/1**

00-0 **5** 2 ½ **Vinces**[3] 30 7-9-2 **60**.............................. NathanAlison 7 57
(Tim McCarthy) *dwlt: t.k.h and sn trckd ldr: led 6f out to 4f out: rdn 3f out: wl hld in 3rd 2f out: fdd fnl f* **16/1**

240- **6** 2 ¾ **Sennybridge**[35] 7685 4-8-10 **59**.............................. HollyHall(3) 5 50
(J W Hills) *t.k.h: hld up last: outpcd and adrift over 3f out: no ch after: kpt on fnl f* **16/1**

022- **7** 7 **Lucky Diva**[21] 7917 4-8-5 **51**.............................. RyanPowell 6 28
(Sylvester Kirk) *led at modest pce for 4f: rdn over 3f out: wknd rapidly over 1f out* **7/2**[3]

2m 10.42s (3.82) **Going Correction** +0.225s/f (Slow)
WFA 4 from 7yo 2lb 7 Ran SP% **110.5**
Speed ratings (Par 101): **93,92,90,90,88 86,80**
Tote Swingers: 1&2 £2.70, 1&3 £3.30, 2&3 £3.50 CSF £11.23 TOTE £3.40: £1.60, £1.20; EX 8.70.
Owner Mrs Karen Graham **Bred** Mike Perkins **Trained** Newmarket, Suffolk

FOCUS
The pace was steady (time over six seconds above standard).

T/Plt: £728.70 to a £1 stake. Pool: £57,809 - 57.91 winning tickets. T/Qpdt: £54.60 to a £1 stake. Pool: £5,837 - 79 winning tickets. JN

[64]WOLVERHAMPTON (A.W) (L-H)

Friday, January 7

OFFICIAL GOING: Standard to slow

Wind: Nil Weather: Misty turning to rain

84 BLUESQ.COM ON YOUR IPHONE CLAIMING STKS 5f 20y(P)

4:10 (4:10) (Class 5) 4-Y-0+ **£2,072** (£616; £308; £153) **Stalls** Low

Form RPR

233- **1** **Sloop Johnb**[11] 7984 5-9-1 72....................(p) BarryMcHugh 2 79
(Richard Fahey) *mde all: rdn over 1f out: r.o* **10/11**[1]

05-4 **2** 2 1/4 **Elhamri**[3] 29 7-9-3 73.................... HayleyTurner 1 73
(Conor Dore) *chsd wnr: rdn over 1f out: styd on same pce ins fnl f* **7/4**[2]

600- **3** 1 **Weet A Surprise**[36] 7665 6-8-12 72....................(v) LukeMorris 5 64
(James Unett) *chsd ldrs: rdn over 1f out: no ex ins fnl f* **13/2**[3]

040- **4** 3/4 **Avonvalley**[7] 8037 4-8-10 62.................... RobbieFitzpatrick 4 60
(Peter Grayson) *s.i.s: hld up: r.o ins fnl f: nvr trbld ldrs* **25/1**

000- **5** 8 **Clifton Bridge**[88] 6799 4-8-6 73....................(b) LeonnaMayor(7) 6 34
(Peter Grayson) *s.i.s: in rr: rdn 1/2-way: sn wknd* **33/1**

62.85 secs (0.55) **Going Correction** +0.25s/f (Slow) **5** Ran SP% **108.9**

Speed ratings (Par 103): **105,101,99,98,85**

CSF £2.65 TOTE £1.30: £1.02, £2.60; EX 2.50.

Owner Jonathan Gill **Bred** Manor Farm Stud (rutland) **Trained** Musley Bank, N Yorks

FOCUS

After snow and an inspection in the morning it was a foggy, damp evening at Dunstall Park and the surface was riding on the slow side.

85 HORIZONS RESTAURANT MEDIAN AUCTION MAIDEN STKS 1m 4f 50y(P)

4:40 (4:41) (Class 6) 4-6-Y-0 **£1,535** (£453; £226) **Stalls** Low

Form RPR

246- **1** **Gearbox (IRE)**[76] 7089 5-9-7 69.................... RobbieFitzpatrick 1 57
(Peter Brookshaw) *trckd ldrs: wnt 2nd 3f out: rdn to ld over 1f out: r.o wl: eased nr fin* **13/8**[1]

643- **2** 3 1/2 **New Den**[16] 7963 4-9-3 58....................(p) NickyMackay 4 51
(Jim Boyle) *led: rdn and hdd over 1f out: no ex ins fnl f* **3/1**[2]

600- **3** 1 1/2 **Oak Leaves**[42] 7570 4-8-12 42.................... DavidProbert 7 44
(Nikki Evans) *chsd ldrs: rdn over 1f out: edgd lft and no ex ins fnl f* **16/1**

4 nk **Gabrielle Da Vinci**[16] 5-9-2 0.................... SamHitchcott 6 44
(David Evans) *s.i.s: hld up: hdwy over 1f out: rdn and hung lft fnl f: styd on same pce* **40/1**

300- **5** 5 **Desert Fairy**[162] 4514 5-9-2 43.................... LukeMorris 2 36
(James Unett) *hld up: hdwy over 2f out: rdn and wknd over 1f out* **8/1**

00/- **6** 3 **Potemkin (USA)**[16] 3303 6-9-0 0....................(t) MatthewCosham(7) 8 36
(David Evans) *hld up: hdwy over 3f out: rdn: hung lft and wknd wl over 1f out* **4/1**[3]

7 3 1/2 **Tobayornottobay**[42] 5-8-11 0.................... AdamCarter(5) 5 25
(Bruce Hellier) *hld up in tch: rdn over 3f out: wknd wl over 1f out* **50/1**

66- **8** 32 **Maitre 'D**[25] 7862 4-9-3 0.................... JimmyQuinn 9 —
(Christopher Kellett) *chsd ldr 9f: wknd over 2f out: t.o* **50/1**

9 57 **Bird Dog** 5-9-7 0.................... WilliamCarson 3 —
(Phil McEntee) *s.s: hld up: drvn along 7f out: wknd 4f out: t.o* **20/1**

2m 47.4s (6.30) **Going Correction** +0.25s/f (Slow)

WFA 4 from 5yo+ 4lb **9** Ran SP% **111.2**

Speed ratings: **89,86,85,85,82 80,77,56,18**

Tote Swingers: 1&2 £1.50, 1&3 £6.40, 2&3 £4.70 CSF £5.96 TOTE £2.50: £1.10, £1.20, £5.90; EX 6.90.

Owner Balios Racing **Bred** P Heffernan **Trained**

FOCUS

A weak maiden run at a sound pace with plenty of deadwood.

86 DINE IN THE HORIZONS RESTAURANT H'CAP 1m 1f 103y(P)

5:10 (5:14) (Class 7) (0-50,53) 4-Y-0+ **£1,535** (£453; £226) **Stalls** Low

Form RPR

501- **1** **Lord Lansing (IRE)**[8] 8018 4-9-5 53 6ex.................... LukeMorris 3 67+
(Mrs K Burke) *hld up: hdwy 1/2-way: led over 1f out: rdn and hung rt ins fnl f: r.o: eased nr fin* **5/2**[1]

233- **2** 2 1/4 **Tres Froide (FR)**[22] 7899 6-9-3 50....................(p) JoeFanning 5 59
(Nigel Tinkler) *hld up in tch: rdn to chse wnr fnl f: no imp* **11/2**[3]

433- **3** 8 **Mr Maximas**[21] 7919 4-9-0 48.................... RichardKingscote 8 40
(Bryn Palling) *chsd ldrs: led over 2f out: rdn and hdd over 1f out: wknd ins fnl f* **13/2**

505- **4** nk **Our Kes (IRE)**[21] 7918 9-9-2 49.................... JimmyQuinn 9 41
(Jane Chapple-Hyam) *hld up: hmpd 7f out: styd on fr over 1f out: nt rch ldrs* **6/1**

300- **5** 1 1/4 **Laura Land**[131] 5564 5-8-9 45.................... RossAtkinson(3) 10 34
(Mark Brisbourne) *prom: rdn over 2f out: wknd fnl f* **33/1**

360- **6** 2 **Rigid**[25] 7863 4-9-2 50.................... HayleyTurner 4 35
(Tony Carroll) *chsd ldrs: rdn over 2f out: wknd over 1f out* **22/1**

33-0 **7** 3/4 **Al Rayanah**[1] 69 8-9-3 50....................(p) KirstyMilczarek 12 33
(George Prodromou) *hld up: rdn over 2f out: nvr on terms* **8/1**

606- **8** 1/2 **Fastinthestraight (IRE)**[32] 7728 4-9-0 48....................(p) DaneO'Neill 2 30
(Jim Boyle) *s.i.s: sn drvn along in rr: n.d* **5/1**[2]

60- **9** 1 1/2 **Duneen Dream (USA)**[168] 4327 6-9-2 49.................... DavidProbert 13 28
(Nikki Evans) *plld hrd: led over 7f out: rdn and hdd over 2f out: wknd fnl f* **16/1**

030- **10** 3/4 **Flyjack (USA)**[21] 7918 4-8-10 47....................(p) PatrickDonaghy(3) 6 27
(Lisa Williamson) *hld up: hmpd 7f out: nt clr run and eased fnl f* **50/1**

000- **11** 2 3/4 **Gems**[218] 2678 4-8-13 47.................... WilliamCarson 7 19
(Peter Hiatt) *led 1f: chsd ldrs: rdn over 3f out: wknd over 2f out* **33/1**

005- **12** 12 **Mouchez**[32] 7727 4-9-1 49.................... SamHitchcott 1 —
(Dean Ivory) *hld up: rdn and wknd 3f out* **25/1**

004- **13** 6 **Briary Mac**[22] 7897 4-8-6 47.................... RichardRowe(7) 11 —
(Peter Pritchard) *prom: chsd ldr 7f out tl rdn over 3f out: wknd over 2f out* **66/1**

2m 4.51s (2.81) **Going Correction** +0.25s/f (Slow)

WFA 4 from 5yo+ 1lb **13** Ran SP% **122.8**

Speed ratings (Par 97): **97,95,87,87,86 84,84,83,82,81 79,68,63**

Tote Swingers: 1&2 £3.40, 1&3 £4.00, 2&3 £6.60 CSF £15.40 CT £84.02 TOTE £3.70: £1.50, £1.30, £2.20; EX 17.00.

Owner Mrs Elaine M Burke **Bred** C J Wall **Trained** Middleham Moor, North Yorks

FOCUS

A low grade 45-53 handicap.

Al Rayanah Official explanation: jockey said mare hung right

Flyjack(USA) Official explanation: jockey said gelding had no more to give

87 10% FORECAST BONUS AT BLUESQ.COM H'CAP 5f 216y(P)

5:40 (5:42) (Class 4) (0-85,85) 4-Y-0+ **£3,464** (£1,030; £515; £257) **Stalls** Low

Form RPR

/03- **1** **Diriculous**[8] 8016 7-9-5 83.................... JoeFanning 4 93
(Robert Mills) *a.p: chsd ldr over 1f out: rdn to ld wl ins fnl f: r.o* **4/1**[3]

31- **2** 3/4 **Methaaly (IRE)**[34] 7702 8-8-6 77....................(be) JosephYoung(7) 5 85
(Michael Mullineaux) *chsd ldr tl led over 2f out: rdn and hdd wl ins fnl f* **6/1**

224- **3** 2 1/4 **Lujeanie**[29] 7782 5-9-5 83....................(p) AdamKirby 3 83
(Dean Ivory) *hld up: hdwy u.p and edgd rt over 1f out: nt trble ldrs* **3/1**[1]

231- **4** 1/2 **Breathless Kiss (USA)**[16] 7961 4-9-4 82....................(b) PhillipMakin 6 81
(Kevin Ryan) *hld up: hdwy over 1f out: sn rdn and edgd lft: no imp fnl f* **7/1**

530- **5** 2 1/2 **Billy Red**[10] 7993 7-9-7 85....................(b) FergusSweeney 1 76
(J R Jenkins) *led: rdn and hdd over 2f out: wknd fnl f* **7/2**[2]

000- **6** 2 1/4 **Northern Dare (IRE)**[27] 7841 7-8-7 71.................... BarryMcHugh 2 55
(Richard Fahey) *chsd ldrs: rdn over 2f out: wknd over 1f out* **11/2**

1m 15.19s (0.19) **Going Correction** +0.25s/f (Slow) **6** Ran SP% **109.4**

Speed ratings (Par 105): **108,107,104,103,100 97**

Tote Swingers: 1&2 £4.60, 1&3 £2.90, 2&3 £2.50 CSF £25.75 TOTE £4.40: £3.50, £1.40; EX 18.60.

Owner Sherwoods Transport Ltd **Bred** Sherwoods Transport Ltd **Trained** Headley, Surrey

FOCUS

A competitive 71-85 sprint handicap but it developed into a two-horse race in the final furlong.

88 HOTEL & CONFERENCING AT WOLVERHAMPTON MEDIAN AUCTION MAIDEN STKS 7f 32y(P)

6:10 (6:11) (Class 6) 3-5-Y-0 **£1,535** (£453; £226) **Stalls** High

Form RPR

42- **1** **Dare It And Smile (USA)**[98] 6521 3-8-5 0.................... MartinLane 3 63+
(David Simcock) *sn trcking ldrs: rdn 2f out: led 1f out: styd on wl: eased nr fin* **4/7**[1]

60- **2** 1 3/4 **Kristollini**[9] 8001 3-8-5 0.................... HayleyTurner 5 56
(William Muir) *led: shkn up over 2f out: rdn and hdd 1f out: styd on same pce* **8/1**[3]

05- **3** 3/4 **Diamond Sunrise (IRE)**[58] 7392 3-8-5 0.................... DuranFentiman 8 54
(Noel Wilson) *hld up: hdwy over 2f out: sn rdn: r.o* **33/1**

0/2- **4** nk **Belles Beau**[350] 267 4-9-9 0.................... GrahamGibbons 2 57
(Reg Hollinshead) *hld up: rdn over 5f out: r.o ins fnl f: nrst fin* **14/1**

004- **5** 3 3/4 **Steel Rain**[36] 7667 3-8-10 43.................... AndreaAtzeni 7 48
(Nikki Evans) *chsd ldr 6f out: rdn and ev ch over 1f out: wknd ins fnl f* **66/1**

6 1/2 **Refusetosurrender (IRE)** 3-8-5 0.................... JimmyQuinn 4 42
(Richard Fahey) *s.i.s: in rr: pushed along 1/2-way: hung lft fnl f: nvr on terms* **7/2**[2]

0- **7** 15 **Depden (IRE)**[17] 7954 3-8-10 0.................... WilliamCarson 1 —
(Richard Price) *pushed along to chse ldr 1f: remained handy tl rdn and wknd over 1f out* **80/1**

1m 32.22s (2.62) **Going Correction** +0.25s/f (Slow)

WFA 3 from 4yo 18lb **7** Ran SP% **109.3**

Speed ratings (Par 101): **95,93,92,91,87 86,69**

Tote Swingers: 1&2 £1.10, 1&3 £4.10, 2&3 £16.10 CSF £5.31 TOTE £1.40: £1.10, £4.10; EX 5.00.

Owner Jaber Abdullah **Bred** Star Pointe Ltd **Trained** Newmarket, Suffolk

■ Stewards' Enquiry : Andrea Atzeni £140 fine; failed to arrive in time to weigh out

FOCUS

A weak maiden.

Kristollini Official explanation: trainer said filly had sustained a loosened shoe

89 SPONSOR A RACE BY CALLING 01902 390000 H'CAP 2m 119y(P)

6:40 (6:40) (Class 5) (0-70,68) 4-Y-0+ **£2,072** (£616; £308; £153) **Stalls** Low

Form RPR

066- **1** **French Hollow**[66] 7284 6-9-4 58.................... BarryMcHugh 6 74+
(Tim Fitzgerald) *hld up: hdwy over 4f out: chsd clr ldr over 3f out: led over 2f out: sn rdn clr: eased wl ins fnl f* **7/2**[3]

023- **2** 11 **Master At Arms**[39] 7632 8-10-0 68.................... AndreaAtzeni 3 68
(Daniel Mark Loughnane, Ire) *hld up: hdwy to chse ldr over 4f out tl rdn over 3f out: outpcd fr over 2f out: wnt 2nd nr fin* **9/4**[1]

623- **3** 1/2 **Carlton Scroop (FR)**[25] 7861 8-10-0 68.................... JimmyQuinn 5 67
(Tony Carroll) *chsd clr ldrs: rdn to go mod 2nd wl over 1f out: no imp: lost 2nd nr fin* **9/2**

601- **4** 6 **Juwireya**[17] 7957 4-9-2 63....................(v) WilliamCarson 1 55
(Peter Hiatt) *led and sn wl clr: rdn and hdd over 2f out: sn wknd* **8/1**

3/2- **5** 1 1/2 **L'Homme De Nuit (GER)**[313] 232 7-10-0 68....................(t) SamHitchcott 2 58
(Jim Best) *s.s: hld up: a bhd* **3/1**[2]

260- **6** 60 **Zefooha (FR)**[55] 6921 7-9-4 58....................(p) GrahamGibbons 4 —
(Tim Walford) *chsd clr ldr 12f: sn wknd: t.o* **14/1**

3m 45.59s (3.79) **Going Correction** +0.25s/f (Slow)

WFA 4 from 6yo+ 7lb **6** Ran SP% **114.0**

Speed ratings (Par 103): **101,95,95,92,92 63**

Tote Swingers: 1&2 £1.30, 1&3 £2.50, 2&3 £2.30 CSF £12.11 TOTE £3.90: £3.50, £1.20; EX 18.80.

Owner T J Fitzgerald **Bred** T J Fitzgerald **Trained** Norton, N Yorks

FOCUS

A modest 63-68 stayers' handicap run at a furious pace and in the end a clear cut and most decisive winner.

Zefooha(FR) Official explanation: jockey said mare had no more to give

90 PLAY RAINBOW RICHES AT BLUESQ.COM H'CAP 1m 141y(P)

7:10 (7:10) (Class 6) (0-65,60) 4-Y-0+ **£1,706** (£503; £252) **Stalls** Low

Form RPR

05-0 **1** **Justcallmehandsome**[4] 26 9-9-7 60....................(be) HayleyTurner 4 72
(Dominic Ffrench Davis) *hld up: hdwy over 2f out: shkn up to ld over 1f out: r.o wl* **9/1**

511- **2** 4 **Zafeen's Pearl**[23] 7874 4-9-6 60.................... SamHitchcott 6 63
(Dean Ivory) *chsd ldr tl led wl over 1f out: sn rdn and hdd: no ex ins fnl f* **5/4**[1]

005- **3** 4 **My Sister**[25] 7856 4-8-8 55.................... RachealKneller(7) 3 49
(Mark Usher) *chsd ldrs: rdn over 1f out: edgd lft and styd on same pce* **12/1**

42-5 **4** 4 **Hector Spectre (IRE)**[4] 26 5-9-4 57....................(p) GrahamGibbons 5 41
(Nikki Evans) *sn drvn along to ld: rdn and hdd wl over 1f out: wknd fnl f* **7/1**[3]

005- **5** *6* **Atacama Sunrise**[21] 7919 5-9-7 **60**.............................. KirstyMilczarek 1 31
(George Prodromou) *chsd ldrs: rdn over 2f out: wknd over 1f out* **25/1**
14-4 **6** *35* **Join Up**[4] 26 5-9-3 **59**.. RossAtkinson(3) 2 —
(Mark Brisbourne) *hld up: rdn over 3f out: wknd over 2f out: eased: t.o* **2/1**[2]

1m 51.85s (1.35) **Going Correction** +0.25s/f (Slow)
WFA 4 from 5yo+ 1lb **6** Ran SP% **111.8**
Speed ratings (Par 101): **104,100,96,93,88 56**
CSF £20.75 TOTE £7.40: £5.70, £1.60; EX 26.20.
Owner Mrs J E Taylor **Bred** Mrs J E Taylor **Trained** Lambourn, Berks
FOCUS
A modest 55-60 handicap and something of a tactical affair.
Justcallmehandsome Official explanation: jockey said gelding ran flat
T/Plt: £10.80 to a £1 stake. Pool: £77,934.72 - 5,233.02 winning tickets. T/Qpdt: £12.40 to a £1 stake. Pool: £8,399.13 - 499.98 winning tickets. CR

[42]DEAUVILLE (R-H)
Friday, January 7
OFFICIAL GOING: Fibresand: standard

91a PRIX DE LA DUNANERIE (CONDITIONS) (4YO) (FIBRESAND) 1m 1f 110y
11:05 (12:00) 4-Y-O **£9,482** (£3,793; £2,844; £1,896; £948)

RPR
1 **Belle Masquee (IRE)**[21] 4-9-1 0..............................(b) RonanThomas 8 82
(D Smaga, France) **21/10**[2]
2 *½* **Green China (FR)**[18] 7951 4-8-7 0.......................... TheoBachelot(8) 11 81
(S Wattel, France) **9/5**[1]
3 *2* **Layline (IRE)**[9] 8009 4-9-4 0.. RobertWinston 5 80
(Gay Kelleway) *racd midfield: pulling freely: rdn early in st: hung lft: hrd rdn fnl f: r.o wl: wnt 3rd cl home* **21/1**
4 *snk* **Queen Of Silence (FR)**[18] 4-8-11 0............................ ThierryJarnet 10 73
(N Leenders, France) **12/1**
5 *hd* **Madushka (FR)**[4] 4-8-8 0.. FabriceVeron 3 70
(Y De Nicolay, France) **25/1**
6 *2* **Saronsla Belle (FR)**[21] 4-8-6 0.................................. MatthieuAutier(5) 1 69
(L Edon, France) **13/1**
7 *2* **Casa Ingrid (FR)**[17] 4-8-11 0............................ Pierre-CharlesBoudot 2 65
(Y De Nicolay, France) **11/2**[3]
8 *5* **Settebellezze (FR)**[119] 5935 4-9-4 0.............................. TonyPiccone 4 62
(J Rossi, France) **16/1**
9 *2½* **Majordome (FR)**[16] 4-8-11 0... FlavienPrat 9 51
(P Van De Poele, France) **41/1**
10 *3* **Mathurino (FR)**[17] 7959 4-8-11 0.............................. ThomasMessina 6 45
(H Billot, France) **71/1**
0 **Talelook Bareliere (FR)** 4-8-8 0............................ Jean-BaptisteHamel 7 —
(Mme C Dufreche, France) **78/1**

2m 2.50s (122.50) **11** Ran SP% **117.5**
WIN (incl. 1 euro stake): 3.10; PLACES: 1.30, 1.20, 3.30; DF: 2.70; SF: 6.00.
Owner J-M Hegesippe & J-J Taieb **Bred** Paget Bloodstock **Trained** Lamorlaye, France

92a PRIX MISS SATAMIXA (LISTED RACE) (4YO+ FILLIES & MARES) (FIBRESAND) 7f 110y
2:10 (12:00) 4-Y-O+ **£22,413** (£8,965; £6,724; £4,482; £2,241)

RPR
1 **Love Queen (IRE)**[18] 7951 4-8-11 0................ Francois-XavierBertras 3 95
(Mlle V Dissaux, France) **102/10**
2 *nk* **Rada Angel (IRE)**[18] 7951 4-9-2 0..............................(b) AlexisBadel 14 99
(Mme M Bollack-Badel, France) **9/2**[2]
3 *¾* **Boise (FR)**[116] 4-8-11 0.. Jean-BernardEyquem 10 92
([illegible], France) **11/1**
4 *hd* **High Ville (FR)**[21] 5-8-11 0.. AntoineHamelin 11 92
(P Chevillard, France) **54/1**
5 *nse* **Baroness (FR)**[30] 4-8-11 0.. JohanVictoire 7 92
(Jean De Roualle, France) **15/2**[3]
6 *½* **Hulcote Rose (IRE)**[21] 7915 4-8-11 0.................................. JamesDoyle 4 90
(Sylvester Kirk) *racd in midfield: picked up wl 1f out towards outside: r.o wl* **15/2**[3]
7 *¾* **Akhmatova**[41] 7591 4-8-11 0.................................. IoritzMendizabal 5 88
(Gerard Butler) *racd towards rr: c wd into st: rdn: short of room: picked up wl whn clr fnl f: fin wl* **14/5**[1]
8 *hd* **Amica (SAF)**[9] 8006 4-8-9 0.. FabriceVeron 12 86
(Gay Kelleway) *racd in midfield: wnt wd into st: rdn 1 1/2f out: no ex fnl f* **37/1**
9 *hd* **Intolerance (FR)**[86] 6857 4-8-11 0.............................. MickaelBarzalona 2 87
(A Fabre, France) **31/1**
10 *¾* **Dam D'Augy (FR)**[29] 7800 6-9-2 0..............................(b) ThierryJarnet 9 91
(Mlle S-V Tarrou, France) **14/1**
0 **Charlotte Point (USA)**[10] 5-8-11 0.............................. ThomasMessina 13 —
(J E Pease, France) **35/1**
0 **Marny (GER)**[15] 6-8-11 0.. RobertWinston 1 —
(H Blume, Germany) **75/1**
0 **American Nizzy (FR)**[30] 4-8-11 0..............................(p) RonanThomas 15 —
(Y De Nicolay, France) **24/1**
0 **Full Steam**[18] 7951 4-8-11 0.................................. Pierre-CharlesBoudot 8 —
(A Fabre, France) **10/1**
0 **Fly Tartare (FR)**[124] 4-8-11 0..............................(p) RemiCampos 6 —
(T Larriviere, France) **32/1**

1m 31.1s (91.10) **15** Ran SP% **118.1**
WIN (incl. 1 euro stake): 11.20. PLACES: 2.80, 2.10, 4.10. DF: 28.50. SF: 63.60.
Owner Gerard Augustin-Normand **Bred** Ecurie Skymarc Farm **Trained** France

NOTEBOOK
Love Queen(IRE) swooped late to win.
Akhmatova looked a little unfortunate as she was denied a clear run at a crucial moment two furlongs from home and only got going when the race was already over.

93a PRIX DE THAON (CLAIMER) (5YO+) (JOCKEYS NOT RIDDEN 15 WINNERS SINCE 1ST JAN 2010) (FIBRESAND) 7f 110y
2:45 (12:00) 5-Y-O+ **£6,465** (£2,586; £1,939; £1,293; £646)

RPR
1 **Dream Land (FR)**[159] 5-9-2 0.................................. YannickLetondeur 4 71
(B Goudot, France) **32/1**
2 *½* **Libretto (GER)**[16] 5-9-2 0.. ASuborics 5 70
(H-W Hiller, Germany) **9/5**[1]
3 *1½* **Eastern Gift**[21] 7920 6-9-2 0.. FredericSpanu 9 66
(Gay Kelleway) *racd towards rr: wnt wd ent st: rdn and picked up wl 1f out: fin wl to go 3rd fnl 100yds* **6/1**[3]
4 *½* **Ciboney Moon (FR)**[16] 8-9-6 0.................................. MichaelPoirier 14 69
(Alex Fracas, France) **63/10**
5 *1* **Carimo (IRE)**[17] 7-8-11 0..............................(b) JohannBensimon 7 58
(P Adda, France) **20/1**
6 *nk* **Peinture Texane (FR)**[38] 5-8-13 0.......................... AnthonyClement 15 59
(F Monnier, France) **10/1**
7 *snk* **Cape Velvet (IRE)**[16] 7-8-8 0.. AntoineHamelin 1 53
(Mme J Bidgood, France) **19/5**[2]
8 *snk* **Shranaski (FR)**[16] 6-9-2 0.. CedricSagot 11 61
(A Sagot, France) **136/1**
9 *½* **Meora (FR)**[51] 5-8-8 0..(b) AllanBonnefoy 12 52
(P Demercastel, France) **77/1**
10 *1½* **Sir Dolois (FR)**[17] 5-9-6 0.. VincentVion 10 60
(A Bonin, France) **21/1**
0 **Swinging Sixties (FR)**[1276] 7-8-13 0.......................... SylvainBellanger 13 —
(L Guilloux, France) **44/1**
0 **Haadeej (USA)**[56] 6-8-11 0.. SoufyaneMoulin 3 —
(C Boutin, France) **71/1**
0 **Diable Des Aigles (FR)**[16] 5-8-13 0 ow2...............(b) YohannBourgois 6 —
(J Lepenant, France) **39/1**
0 **Queenofnerverland (IRE)**[175] 5-8-13 0.............................. CarinaFey 2 —
(T Doumen, France) **73/1**
0 **Kaulbach (GER)**[56] 5-8-11 0.................................. GuillaumeFourrier 16 —
(Mme L Barreaud, France) **142/1**
0 **Dinaday (FR)**[16] 5-8-9 0 ow1.. CedricGueude 8 —
(N Leenders, France) **129/1**

1m 30.6s (90.60) **16** Ran SP% **116.9**
WIN (incl. 1 euro stake): 33.20. PLACES: 6.80, 1.50, 2.40. DF: 37.50. SF: 140.80.
Owner A Ciampi & E Ciampi **Bred** M Parrish **Trained** France

[77]LINGFIELD (L-H)
Saturday, January 8
OFFICIAL GOING: Standard
Wind: Fresh, half behind becoming fresh, across (towards stand) by race 3
Weather: Cloudy

94 FA CUP BETTING AT BLUESQ.COM CLASSIFIED CLAIMING STKS 1m 2f (P)
11:50 (11:50) (Class 6) 4-Y-O+ **£1,535** (£453; £226) **Stalls** Low

Form RPR
312- **1** **Edgeworth (IRE)**[9] 8018 5-8-5 63..................................(p) ChrisCatlin 6 64
(Brendan Powell) *dropped out in rr: pushed along over 3f out: gd hdwy on inner to ld jst ins fnl 2f: drvn out* **9/4**[1]
311- **2** *1¼* **Mighty Clarets (IRE)**[10] 8008 4-8-9 72.................. GeorgeChaloner(7) 7 75
(Richard Fahey) *trckd ldrs: rdn to press wnr over 1f out: one pce ins fnl f: regained 2nd nr fin* **6/1**[3]
000- **3** *½* **Layla's Dancer**[78] 7053 4-8-11 68.. JamieSpencer 3 69
(David Simcock) *hld up in tch: rdn and sltly wd st: styd on ins fnl f* **7/2**[2]
326- **4** *hd* **Dream Of Fortune (IRE)**[10] 8008 7-8-10 68..............(bt) CathyGannon 4 65
(David Evans) *hld up in tch: effrt 2f out: chsd wnr ins fnl f: no ex and lost 2nd nr fin* **9/4**[1]
520- **5** *2¾* **Pinsplitter (USA)**[11] 7995 4-8-3 56.................. AndrewHeffernan(3) 5 58
(Alan McCabe) *led tl jst ins fnl 2f: wknd over 1f out* **33/1**
442- **6** *9* **Lean Machine**[9] 8021 4-8-2 60..(p) LukeMorris 1 42
(Ronald Harris) *t.k.h in 2nd: hrd rdn and wknd 2f out: eased whn no ch ins fnl f* **10/1**

2m [illegible] **Going Correction** [illegible]
WFA 4 from 5yo+ 2lb **6** Ran SP% **110.1**
Speed ratings (Par 101): **101,100,99,99,97 90**
toteswingers:1&2 £2.40, 2&3 £2.10, 1&3 £2.60 CSF £15.55 TOTE £4.30: £3.00, £3.30; EX 16.40.
Owner K Rhatigan **Bred** Yvonne & Gerard Kennedy **Trained** Upper Lambourn, Berks
FOCUS
This looked a decent contest for the grade, but the early pace didn't look that strong.
Lean Machine Official explanation: jockey said colt ran flat

95 FELBRIDGE MAIDEN STKS 1m 2f (P)
12:20 (12:21) (Class 5) 3-Y-O **£1,910** (£564; £282) **Stalls** Low

Form RPR
1 **Hurricane Higgins (IRE)** 3-9-3 .... JoeFanning 10 81+
(Mark Johnston) *prom: wnt 2nd after 3f: led 3f out: rdn clr 1f out: rn green and swvd rt fnl 50yds: comf* **11/8**[1]
463- **2** *4* **Duke Of Florence (IRE)**[31] 7755 3-9-3 68....................(b1) DaneO'Neill 9 72
(Richard Hannon) *dwlt: sn chsng ldrs: wnt 2nd 3f out: nt pce of wnr appr fnl f* **4/1**[3]
5- **3** *3¾* **Heavenly Music (IRE)**[31] 7755 3-8-12 .... LiamKeniry 2 60
(Sylvester Kirk) *chsd ldrs: lost pl 6f out: rdn and styd on fnl 2f* **20/1**
024- **4** *½* **Nothing To Hide (IRE)**[17] 7962 3-9-3 73.............................. JamesDoyle 1 64
(Dominic Ffrench Davis) *prom tl outpcd 2f out* **10/3**[2]
5 *1¼* **Hope It Is (USA)** 3-9-3 .... MartinLane 5 61+
(David Simcock) *dwlt: in rr on outer: sme hdwy 3f out: nvr rchd ldrs* **25/1**
6 *½* **Manifestation** 3-9-3 .... NickyMackay 6 60+
(John Gosden) *rn green: in tch: cajoled along after 2f: unable to chal fnl 3f* **8/1**
7 *5* **Fleeting Storm** 3-8-12 .... TravisBlock 3 45
(Hughie Morrison) *s.i.s: towards rr: sme hdwy on inner ent st: sn wknd* **40/1**
6- **8** *1¼* **Larimar (IRE)**[31] 7755 3-9-3 .... JimCrowley 4 48
(Amanda Perrett) *sn in rr: n.d fnl 3f* **33/1**
0- **9** *6* **Talkin Italian**[80] 7020 3-8-12 .... SteveDrowne 7 31
(Hughie Morrison) *led tl 3f out: wknd over 2f out* **40/1**
10 *9* **Bellaboolou** 3-8-9 ....(t) KierenFox(3) 8 13
(David Pinder) *mid-div: hdwy 5f out: wknd 3f out* **100/1**

2m 8.84s (2.24) **Going Correction** +0.075s/f (Slow) **10** Ran SP% **113.7**
Speed ratings (Par 97): **94,90,87,87,86 86,82,81,76,69**
toteswingers:1&2 £2.50, 2&3 £5.50, 1&3 £5.10 CSF £6.22 TOTE £2.30: £1.10, £2.20, £4.20; EX 7.90 Trifecta £33.40 Pool: £447.36 - 9.89 winning units..
Owner A D Spence **Bred** Paul Nataf **Trained** Middleham Moor, N Yorks

FOCUS
This looked an interesting maiden considering the stables that took part, and it produced a nice prospect. However, the winning time was slower than the 4-y-o+ claimer on the card.

96 HEVER H'CAP 7f (P)
12:50 (12:51) (Class 5) (0-70,70) 4-Y-O+ **£2,047** (£604; £302) **Stalls** Low

Form RPR
355- **1** **The Happy Hammer (IRE)**[9] 8014 5-8-13 **62**.............. WilliamCarson 3 71
(Eugene Stanford) *chsd ldrs: effrt whn nt clr run and swtchd rt over 1f out: r.o to ld fnl strides* **8/1**
612- **2** *nk* **I Confess**[11] 7992 6-9-4 **67**..............................(b) GeorgeBaker 7 75
(David Evans) *led: hrd rdn and hdd ins fnl f: r.o* **4/1**[1]
532- **3** *nk* **Yankee Storm**[8] 8033 6-9-5 **68**..............................(v) JimmyQuinn 2 75
(Hugh Collingridge) *prom: drvn into narrow ld ins fnl f: kpt on: hdd fnl strides* **11/2**[2]
044- **4** *½* **Pilgrim Dancer (IRE)**[11] 7992 4-8-7 **56** oh1..................(v) LukeMorris 4 62
(Patrick Morris) *prom: rdn over 2f out: pressed ldrs ins fnl f: kpt on* **16/1**
323- **5** *½* **Lockantanks**[9] 8014 4-9-6 **69**........................ NeilChalmers 10 74
(Michael Appleby) *t.k.h: cl up: rdn over 2f out: pressed ldrs ins fnl f: nt qckn fnl 100yds* **10/1**
051- **6** *1* **Lisahane Bog**[9] 8014 4-9-7 **70**..............................(be) FergusSweeney 1 72
(Peter Hedger) *dwlt: sn in midfield: drvn along 3f out: hung bdly rt fr over 1f out: styd on ins fnl f* **7/1**[3]
001- **7** *nk* **Buxton**[11] 7991 7-9-4 **67**..............................(t) RobertHavlin 8 68+
(Roger Ingram) *stdd s: hld up in rr: rdn and sme hdwy over 1f out: nt rch ldrs* **12/1**
060- **8** *1* **Dingaan (IRE)**[17] 7971 8-9-5 **68**.............................. RobbieFitzpatrick 11 66
(Peter Grayson) *mid-div: drvn along and no hdwy fr 3f out* **33/1**
23-2 **9** *½* **Musical Script (USA)**[4] 34 8-8-8 **57**..............................(b) ChrisCatlin 5 54
(Mouse Hamilton-Fairley) *t.k.h in midfield: rdn and no hdwy fnl 3f* **16/1**
011- **10** *1 ¾* **Khajaaly (IRE)**[29] 7812 4-9-5 **68**.............................. CathyGannon 9 60
(Julia Feilden) *dwlt: plld hrd towards rr: rdn over 2f out: nvr a factor* **7/1**[3]
054- **11** *½* **Hierarch (IRE)**[69] 7251 4-9-5 **68**.............................. DaneO'Neill 12 59
(David Flood) *towards rr: effrt and hung lft ent st: nvr nr ldrs* **8/1**

1m 25.17s (0.37) **Going Correction** +0.075s/f (Slow) **11** Ran SP% **114.1**
Speed ratings (Par 103): **100,99,99,98,98 97,96,95,94,92 92**
toteswingers:1&2 £8.30, 2&3 £2.70, 1&3 £8.70 CSF £38.74 CT £191.90 TOTE £10.40: £3.30, £1.80, £1.70; EX 48.40 Trifecta £195.60 Pool: £306.74 - 1.16 winning units..
Owner Newmarket Connections Ltd **Bred** Rathbarry Stud **Trained** Newmarket, Suffolk

FOCUS
The pace looked sound throughout, and five horses fought out a good finish in the final furlong.
Lisahane Bog Official explanation: jockey said gelding hung right
Khajaaly(IRE) Official explanation: jockey said gelding reared leaving stalls and was slowly away

97 BLUE SQUARE SPRINT SERIES (ROUND 1) (H'CAP) (QUALIFIER) (DIV I) 6f (P)
1:25 (1:26) (Class 6) (0-65,65) 4-Y-O+ **£2,388** (£705; £352) **Stalls** Low

Form RPR
132- **1** **Rio Royale (IRE)**[39] 7640 5-9-2 **60**..............................(p) JimCrowley 2 67
(Amanda Perrett) *mde all: hld on wl ins fnl f: drvn out* **6/1**[2]
224- **2** *½* **Dancing Welcome**[8] 8035 5-9-4 **62**..............................(b) LiamKeniry 5 67
(Milton Bradley) *mid-div: rdn and r.o fr over 1f out: wnt 2nd fnl 50yds: jst hld* **11/2**[1]
203- **3** *nk* **Norville (IRE)**[8] 8035 4-9-5 **63**..............................(b) CathyGannon 11 67
(David Evans) *pressed wnr tl nt qckn wl ins fnl f* **6/1**[2]
661- **4** *¾* **Nubar Boy**[8] 8035 4-9-5 **63**..............................(v) StevieDonohoe 8 65+
(David Evans) *dropped out s: bhd: gd hdwy fr over 1f out: fin wl* **6/1**[2]
601- **5** *nk* **Athaakeel (IRE)**[9] 8019 5-9-7 **65**..............................(b) LukeMorris 4 66
(Ronald Harris) *in rr of midfield: effrt and wd st: styd on fnl f* **16/1**
144- **6** *1* **Cheery Cat (USA)**[8] 8034 7-8-10 **61**................(v) MatthewCosham[(7)] 10 59
(John Balding) *prom tl no ex ins fnl f* **8/1**[3]
316- **7** *hd* **South African Gold (USA)**[8] 8034 4-9-4 **62**................(p) JackMitchell 6 59
(James Eustace) *chsd ldrs tl no ex ins fnl f* **8/1**[3]
055- **8** *hd* **West Leake (IRE)**[8] 8034 5-8-9 **53**.............................. WilliamCarson 9 50
(Paul Burgoyne) *in tch: rdn to chse ldrs over 1f out: sn wknd* **14/1**
342- **9** *1 ¾* **Wanchai Whisper**[31] 7764 4-9-3 **64**...................... AndrewHeffernan[(3)] 1 55
(Peter Hedger) *towards rr: mod effrt ent st: no imp* **14/1**
006- **10** *½* **Monte Major (IRE)**[18] 7952 10-8-11 **55**..............................(v) PatrickMathers 7 44
(Derek Shaw) *chsd ldrs 3f* **66/1**
000- **11** *2* **White Shift (IRE)**[8] 8034 5-9-1 **62**.......................... MichaelStainton[(3)] 3 45
(Jane Chapple-Hyam) *mid-div tl outpcd fnl 2f* **10/1**
000- **12** *1 ½* **Valentino Swing (IRE)**[9] 8014 8-8-11 **55**...................... NeilChalmers 12 33
(Michael Appleby) *s.s: bhd: mod effrt and wd st: n.d* **33/1**

1m 11.78s (-0.12) **Going Correction** +0.075s/f (Slow) **12** Ran SP% **113.2**
Speed ratings (Par 101): **103,102,101,100,100 99,98,98,96,95 93,91**
toteswingers:1&2 £2.80, 2&3 £6.10, 1&3 £7.20 CSF £37.06 CT £208.29 TOTE £4.00: £1.60, £2.10, £2.20; EX 19.50 Trifecta £115.60 Pool: £165.66 - 1.06 winning units..
Owner Mrs Amanda Perrett **Bred** Glending Bloodstock **Trained** Pulborough, W Sussex

FOCUS
Not a strong contest considering the top two in the weights contested sellers last time.
Valentino Swing(IRE) Official explanation: jockey said gelding lost his action

98 BLUE SQUARE SPRINT SERIES (ROUND 1) (H'CAP) (QUALIFIER) (DIV II) 6f (P)
2:00 (2:02) (Class 6) (0-65,65) 4-Y-O+ **£2,388** (£705; £352) **Stalls** Low

Form RPR
032- **1** **Waterloo Dock**[9] 8019 6-9-4 **62**..............................(v) ChrisCatlin 8 71
(Michael Quinn) *w ldrs: led 2f out: drvn out* **11/1**
210- **2** *½* **Chjimes (IRE)**[8] 8035 7-9-7 **65**..............................(b) HayleyTurner 7 72
(Conor Dore) *mid-div: swtchd outside and hdwy over 1f out: r.o to press wnr fnl 100yds: jst hld* **7/2**[1]
321- **3** *1 ¼* **Loyal Royal (IRE)**[8] 8034 8-9-2 **60**..............................(bt) LiamKeniry 2 63
(Milton Bradley) *chsd ldrs: rdn 2f out: nt qckn ins fnl f* **6/1**[2]
120- **4** *shd* **Bold Ring**[49] 7519 5-8-9 **58**.............................. RosieJessop[(5)] 5 61
(Edward Creighton) *chsd ldrs: rdn 2f out: one pce ins fnl f* **14/1**
064- **5** *½* **Desert Icon (IRE)**[36] 7683 5-8-13 **64**.......................... AliceHaynes[(7)] 9 65+
(David Simcock) *hld up towards rr: r.o fr over 1f out: nrst fin* **13/2**[3]
453- **6** *hd* **Dvinsky (USA)**[38] 7656 10-9-5 **63**..............................(b) JimmyQuinn 11 64
(Jane Chapple-Hyam) *chsd ldrs tl no ex ins fnl f* **11/1**
000- **7** *1 ¼* **Misaro (GER)**[8] 8035 10-9-4 **62**..............................(b) DavidProbert 6 59
(Ronald Harris) *disp ld 4f: wknd 1f out* **12/1**
003- **8** *¾* **Mushy Peas (IRE)**[8] 8034 4-8-7 **51**..............................(v) CathyGannon 4 45
(David Evans) *stmbld s and missed break: bhd: rdn 3f out: sme hdwy over 1f out: nt trble ldrs* **7/2**[1]
310- **9** *2* **Mind The Monarch**[24] 7882 4-8-4 **53**..............................(v) RyanPowell[(5)] 3 41
(Roger Teal) *mid-div: promising hdwy ent st: wknd 1f out* **25/1**
061- **10** *2 ¾* **Mary's Pet**[28] 7827 4-9-4 **62**.............................. J-PGuillambert 1 41
(John Akehurst) *a towards rr* **12/1**
00-0 **11** *1* **Steel City Boy (IRE)**[5] 15 8-8-11 **55**..................(p) PatrickMathers 10 31
(Derek Shaw) *stdd in rr s: a bhd* **50/1**
054- **12** *1 ¼* **Whatyouwoodwishfor (USA)**[199] 3322 5-9-2 **63**.... RobertLButler[(3)] 12 35
(Paddy Butler) *reluctant to load: disp ld on outer of ldng gp tl wknd over 2f out* **40/1**

1m 11.65s (-0.25) **Going Correction** +0.075s/f (Slow) **12** Ran SP% **119.0**
Speed ratings (Par 101): **104,103,101,101,100 100,98,97,95,91 90,88**
toteswingers:1&2 £9.50, 2&3 £3.60, 1&3 £5.10 CSF £48.91 CT £264.80 TOTE £13.30: £2.30, £1.50, £1.80; EX 64.80 Trifecta £66.60 Pool: £284.41 - 3.16 winning units..
Owner M J Quinn **Bred** Norman Court Stud **Trained** Newmarket, Suffolk

FOCUS
The second division of the sprint series qualifier was run in slightly quicker time.
Mushy Peas(IRE) Official explanation: jockey said gelding stumbled leaving stalls

99 HAXTED H'CAP 7f (P)
2:35 (2:35) (Class 3) (0-95,94) 4-Y-O+ **£5,828** (£1,734; £866; £432) **Stalls** Low

Form RPR
064- **1** **Bravo Echo**[49] 7522 5-9-4 **91**.............................. JoeFanning 1 103
(Michael Attwater) *mde all: edgd rt ins fnl f: hld on wl* **13/2**[3]
551- **2** *nk* **Hazzard County (USA)**[9] 8017 7-8-8 **88**...................... LauraPike[(7)] 8 99
(David Simcock) *hld up in rr: gd hdwy over 1f out: clsd on wnr fnl 100yds: jst hld* **13/2**[3]
000- **3** *3* **Alhaban (IRE)**[11] 7993 5-9-0 **87**..............................(t) LukeMorris 11 90
(Ronald Harris) *chsd ldrs: rdn over 2f out: one pce* **16/1**
000- **4** *¾* **Ocean Legend (IRE)**[22] 7915 6-8-5 **81**...................... KierenFox[(3)] 2 82
(Tony Carroll) *mid-div: rdn to chse ldrs over 1f out: styd on same pce* **33/1**
403- **5** *¾* **Mr Macattack**[22] 7915 6-8-11 **84**..............................(t) RichardKingscote 4 83
(Tom Dascombe) *towards rr: rdn and r.o fr over 1f out: nrst fin* **8/1**
034- **6** *nk* **Elna Bright**[35] 7689 6-9-7 **94**.............................. LiamKeniry 12 92
(Brett Johnson) *mid-div: effrt and wd st: styd on fnl f* **11/2**[2]
003- **7** *nk* **Mastership (IRE)**[49] 7529 7-8-7 **80**..............................(v) ChrisCatlin 5 77
(John Quinn) *towards rr: rdn 2f out: styd on ins fnl f: nvr able to chal* **14/1**
200- **8** *½* **Viva Ronaldo (IRE)**[27] 7846 5-8-7 **80** oh2...................... BarryMcHugh 3 76
(Richard Fahey) *prom: hrd rdn over 1f out: wknd ins fnl f* **33/1**
226- **9** *½* **Seek The Fair Land**[21] 7935 5-9-1 **91**................(b) MatthewDavies[(3)] 10 86
(Jim Boyle) *pressed wnr tl wknd 1f out* **9/2**[1]
652- **10** *1 ½* **Avon River**[17] 7965 4-9-0 **87**..............................(b) DaneO'Neill 6 78
(Richard Hannon) *mid-div tl outpcd fnl 2f* **13/2**[3]
4/6- **11** *3 ¼* **Jungle Bay**[17] 7965 4-8-7 **80**.............................. JimmyQuinn 7 62
(Jane Chapple-Hyam) *s.i.s: a towards rr* **66/1**
400- **12** *4 ½* **Rjeef (IRE)**[35] 7689 4-9-1 **88**.............................. MartinLane 9 58
(David Simcock) *dwlt: sn in tch on outer: wknd 2f out* **10/1**

1m 23.25s (-1.55) **Going Correction** +0.075s/f (Slow) **12** Ran SP% **113.7**
Speed ratings (Par 107): **111,110,107,106,105 105,104,104,103,101 98,93**
toteswingers:1&2 £8.60, 2&3 £24.80, 1&3 £26.00 CSF £45.70 CT £653.21 TOTE £7.70: £2.60, £1.80, £7.60; EX 47.50 TRIFECTA Not won..
Owner Canisbay Bloodstock **Bred** Juddmonte Farms Ltd **Trained** Epsom, Surrey

FOCUS
A quality event for some useful AW performers, in which a couple ran a bit better than their final position suggests.

NOTEBOOK
Bravo Echo, just behind Elna Bright on his previous outing, broke smartly and kept finding for pressure to gain success. Having his first outing since late November and more importantly since being gelded, he should be one to be with next time under similar conditions. (op 6-1 tchd 7-1)
Hazzard County(USA) ◆, raised 8lb for winning over 7f at Kempton, is the type that needs things to fall right for him and was given an excellent ride by Laura Pike, even in defeat. This course probably doesn't suit his hold-up style of racing despite the fact that he has a sound record at Lingfield, so a return to Kempton or a visit to Wolverhampton would make him even more interesting next time. (tchd 6-1)
Alhaban(IRE) ◆ showed the benefit of an ease in class with a fine performance. His connections are sure to find him the rights opportunities after this effort.
Ocean Legend(IRE) hadn't run particularly well on his previous two starts (both at Wolverhampton), so this was a bit better.
Mr Macattack ◆ caught the eye here after making good late ground from the rear. He was never going to get seriously involved from so far back and there will be other days for him. (op 7-1 tchd 13-2)
Elna Bright, successful in this contest last year, looked only fairly treated on his winning form and couldn't really quicken inside the final furlong. (tchd 5-1)
Mastership(IRE) ◆ is nicely handicapped but didn't help his cause early by being keen. The way he stayed on suggests he is one to keep on side from now on, especially as he should be straighter for this run after a break. Any easing in the handicap would take him down into the 70s, a mark he is more than capable off. (op 11-1)
Seek The Fair Land, back in blinkers after trying a visor last time, needs to come down the handicap to have an obvious winning chance. Hisd rider reported afterwards that his mount hung right. Official explanation: jockey said gelding hung right (op 11-2)
Avon River raced keenly and didn't get home. His rider reported afterwards that his mount had missed the break. Official explanation: jockey said gelding missed the break (op 8-1)

100 HOLTYE H'CAP 5f (P)
3:10 (3:10) (Class 5) (0-75,72) 3-Y-O **£2,047** (£604; £302) **Stalls** High

Form RPR
120- **1** **Liberty Green (IRE)**[23] 7891 3-9-7 **72**.............................. JamesDoyle 6 76
(Alan McCabe) *mde virtually all: hrd rdn over 1f out: hld on gamely ins fnl f* **7/4**[1]
500- **2** *¾* **Pineapple Pete (IRE)**[10] 7997 3-8-4 **55**..............................(t) ChrisCatlin 1 56
(Paul Cole) *chsd wnr: drvn level over 1f out: nt qckn fnl 75yds* **12/1**
36-2 **3** *nk* **Just For Leo (IRE)**[2] 66 3-8-1 **59**..................(v) MatthewCosham[(7)] 2 59
(David Evans) *chsd ldng pair: rdn over 2f out: kpt on ins fnl f: clsng at fin* **4/1**[2]
201- **4** *1 ½* **Johnny Hancocks (IRE)**[30] 7777 3-9-4 **72**............ JamesSullivan[(3)] 3 67
(Linda Stubbs) *towards rr: effrt and hrd rdn over 1f out: kpt on ins fnl f: nvr able to chal* **13/2**[3]
310- **5** *2 ¼* **Albany Rose (IRE)**[10] 7997 3-9-0 **65**.............................. SteveDrowne 4 52
(Rae Guest) *in rr: effrt and hrd rdn over 1f out: no ex fnl f* **4/1**[2]
200- **6** *3* **Lady Brookie**[154] 4831 3-9-4 **69**.............................. RobbieFitzpatrick 5 45
(Peter Grayson) *s.i.s: sn in tch in 5th: wknd wl over 1f out* **66/1**
305- **7** *½* **Golden Shine**[30] 7777 3-9-0 **65**..............................(p) AdamKirby 7 39
(Alan Bailey) *chsd ldrs tl wd and wknd ent st* **9/1**

59.46 secs (0.66) **Going Correction** +0.075s/f (Slow) **7** Ran SP% **108.9**
Speed ratings (Par 97): **97,95,95,92,89 84,83**
toteswingers:1&2 £5.30, 2&3 £10.50, 1&3 £2.20 CSF £21.98 CT £65.11 TOTE £2.00: £1.10, £6.70; EX 20.70 Trifecta £122.70 Pool of £466.09 - 2.81 winning units..
Owner Mrs Linda Francis **Bred** Martin Francis Ltd **Trained** Averham Park, Notts

FOCUS
Not many of these got into this.

101 PLAY ROULETTE AT BLUESQ.COM H'CAP — 1m (P)
3:40 (3:41) (Class 4) (0-85,90) 3-Y-O — **£3,412** (£1,007; £504) **Stalls** High

Form	Pos	Dist	Horse / Trainer / Comment	Jockey	SP	RPR
61-	**1**		**The Tichborne (IRE)**[11] 7990 3-9-5 **83** (Roger Teal) *w ldr: led 2f out: drvn out*	JackMitchell 5	**13/8**[1]	85
021-	**2**	*1*	**If You Whisper (IRE)**[23] 7893 3-9-0 **78** (Mike Murphy) *hld up in cl last: hdwy to press wnr over 1f out: nt qckn ins fnl f*	MartinLane 1	**10/1**[3]	77
233-	**3**	*1*	**Amwell Pinot**[137] 5392 3-9-12 **90** (Alan Bailey) *hld up in cl 3rd: effrt on inner 2f out: hrd rdn and one pce 1f out*	(p) CathyGannon 2	**5/2**[2]	87
1-	**4**	*3*	**Coral Moon (IRE)**[42] 7603 3-8-13 **77** (Richard Fahey) *set weak tempo: led tl 2f out: sn outpcd*	BarryMcHugh 4	**5/2**[2]	67

1m 41.45s (3.25) **Going Correction** +0.075s/f (Slow) **4** Ran SP% **104.3**
Speed ratings (Par 99): **86,85,84,81**
CSF £13.23 TOTE £1.90; EX 20.60.
Owner Chris Simpson & Mick Waghorn **Bred** Ms Alyson Flower And Chris Simpson **Trained** Ashtead, Surrey

FOCUS
A tight-looking contest, in which a few were both unexposed and making their handicap debuts. The race lost its most experienced runner when Malice Or Mischief was withdrawn after going into the stalls; 8/1, deduct 10p in the £ under R4..
T/Plt: £78.70 to a £1 stake. Pool of £48,405.07 - 448.93 winning tickets. T/Qpdt: £25.50 to a £1 stake. Pool of £4,488.61 - 130.10 winning tickets. LM

57 SOUTHWELL (L-H)
Sunday, January 9

OFFICIAL GOING: Standard
Wind: moderate 1/2 behind Weather: fine but cold

102 10% FORECAST BONUS AT BLUESQ.COM APPRENTICE H'CAP — 5f (F)
1:10 (1:10) (Class 6) (0-55,54) 4-Y-O+ — **£1,535** (£453; £226) **Stalls** High

Form	Pos	Dist	Horse / Trainer / Comment	Jockey	SP	RPR
213-	**1**		**Kheley (IRE)**[19] 7953 5-9-0 **52** (Mark Brisbourne) *chsd ldrs: outpcd over 2f out: hdwy over 1f out: styd on to ld last 100yds*	JamesRogers 1	**11/4**[1]	60
06-	**2**	*½*	**Cheveyo (IRE)**[37] 7676 5-8-0 **45** (Patrick Morris) *chsd ldrs: chal over 1f out: edgd rt and led jst ins fnl f: sn hdd and no ex*	(e[1]) RossCoakley(7) 4	**28/1**	51
1R-3	**3**	*1*	**Pinball (IRE)**[3] 57 5-9-0 **52** (Lisa Williamson) *t.k.h: hdwy to ld over 2f out: edgd rt over 1f out: hdd and hmpd jst ins fnl f: no ex*	(b) AdamCarter 7	**6/1**	55
553/	**4**	*1*	**Valdemar**[573] 2964 5-8-7 **45** (Alan Brown) *chsd ldrs on outside: kpt on same pce appr fnl f*	(v) RyanPowell 2	**20/1**	44
U00-	**5**	*nk*	**Lucky Art (USA)**[47] 7542 5-8-8 **51** (Ruth Carr) *dwlt: t.k.h: sn trcking ldrs: kpt on same pce appr fnl f*	GeorgeChaloner(5) 3	**8/1**	49
320-	**6**	*1*	**Bluebok**[9] 8037 10-8-7 **48** (Milton Bradley) *led tl over 2f out: one pce appr fnl f*	(bt) MatthewCosham(3) 5	**12/1**	42
305-	**7**	*2½*	**The Magic Of Rio**[9] 8037 5-8-3 **46** (David Evans) *racd stands' side: in rr: edgd lft over 1f out: nvr a factor*	RPWalsh(5) 8	**4/1**[2]	31
053-	**8**	*4*	**Thoughtsofstardom**[9] 8036 8-9-2 **54** (Phil McEntee) *chsd ldrs: edgd rt and wknd over 1f out*	RyanClark 6	**5/1**[3]	25
500-	**9**	*4*	**Flaxen Lake**[27] 7859 4-9-0 **52** (Milton Bradley) *racd stands' side: a outpcd and in rr*	(bt) RosieJessop 9	**14/1**	9

60.83 secs (1.13) **Going Correction** +0.275s/f (Slow) **9** Ran SP% **111.3**
Speed ratings (Par 101): **101,100,98,97,96 94,90,84,78**
toteswingers:1&2:£10.60, 1&3:£[illegible], 2&3:£[illegible] CSF £78.90 CT £415.00 TOTE £[illegible]: £1.10, £9.10, £2.30; EX 88.70 Trifecta £222.20 Part won. Pool: £300.35 - 0.10 winning units..
Owner W M Clare **Bred** Matt Gilsenan **Trained** Great Ness, Shropshire

FOCUS
A low-grade apprentice handicap. The principals ended up near the stands' rail.

103 SOUTHWELL-RACECOURSE.CO.UK (S) STKS — 1m 3f (F)
1:40 (1:40) (Class 6) 4-Y-O+ — **£1,535** (£453; £226) **Stalls** Low

Form	Pos	Dist	Horse / Trainer / Comment	Jockey	SP	RPR
132-	**1**		**Castle Myth (USA)**[22] 7932 5-9-2 **62** (Brian Ellison) *chsd ldrs: sn pushed along: swtchd wd over 5f out: wnt cl 2nd 3f out: led 2f out: edgd rt ins fnl f: 1 1/2 l ahd whn eased nr fin*	(be) MatthewCosham(7) 1	**11/8**[1]	67+
55-2	**2**	*½*	**Dunaskin (IRE)**[5] 40 11-9-3 **55** (Richard Guest) *led after 1f: hdd 2f out: kpt on same pce*	(b) MartinLane 3	**2/1**[2]	58
505-	**3**	*4*	**Sir Haydn**[9] 8032 11-8-10 **50** (J R Jenkins) *in rr and sn drvn along: hdwy to chse ldrs after 3f: wknd over 1f out*	DannyBrock(7) 4	**22/1**	51?
0/0-	**4**	*6*	**Holyrood**[8] 5102 5-9-3 **80** (Tim Vaughan) *sn drvn along in last: hdwy to chse ldrs 7f out: lost pl over 2f out*	(vt) ChrisCatlin 5	**7/2**[3]	40
005-	**5**	*17*	**Lava Steps (USA)**[30] 7806 5-9-3 **54** (Paul Midgley) *led 1f: chsd ldrs: reminders 6f out: lost pl over 4f out: sn bhd*	(be[1]) MickyFenton 2	**16/1**	10

2m 30.53s (2.53) **Going Correction** +0.025s/f (Slow) **5** Ran SP% **107.9**
Speed ratings (Par 101): **91,90,87,83,71**
CSF £4.18 TOTE £1.60: £1.10, £2.60; EX 4.20.There was no bid for the winner.
Owner Brian Ellison **Bred** Mr & Mrs Gerald J Stautberg **Trained** Norton, N Yorks

FOCUS
A very ordinary seller run at a brisk initial pace. Not form to treat too positively, but Castle Myth was value for further.

104 HOLD YOUR BIRTHDAY PARTY AT SOUTHWELL H'CAP — 1m 3f (F)
2:15 (2:15) (Class 6) (0-65,75) 4-Y-O+ — **£1,535** (£453; £226) **Stalls** Low

Form	Pos	Dist	Horse / Trainer / Comment	Jockey	SP	RPR
21-1	**1**		**Dontpaytheferryman (USA)**[3] 63 6-9-12 **75** (Brian Ellison) *trckd ldrs: effrt over 4f out: drvn to take cl 2nd over 2f out: led over 1f out: edgd lft: all out*	DaleSwift(5) 4	**2/5**[1]	86+
223-	**2**	*nk*	**Mediterranean Sea (IRE)**[30] 7806 5-9-3 **61** (J R Jenkins) *dwlt: hdwy to chse ldrs after 3f: wnt handy 3rd over 2f out: chal over 1f out: no ex nr fin*	StephenCraine 7	**5/1**[2]	72
260-	**3**	*4½*	**Eseej (USA)**[104] 6427 6-9-5 **63** (Peter Hiatt) *t.k.h: led: reminders over 3f out: hung rt and hdd over 1f out: sn fdd*	WilliamCarson 6	**14/1**	67
004-	**4**	*12*	**Jackie Kiely**[54] 7475 10-8-10 **54** (Roy Brotherton) *hld up in rr: drvn over 5f out: sn hmpd and wl outpcd*	(tp) JackMitchell 1	**8/1**[3]	39+
/00-	**5**	*½*	**Crimson Monarch (USA)**[11] 8010 7-8-11 **55** (Peter Hiatt) *hld up in rr: t.k.h: trcking ldrs over 4f out: lost pl over 2f out*	(b) ChrisCatlin 2	**22/1**	39
/00-	**6**	*22*	**Credential**[102] 6472 9-8-8 **52** oh3 ow1 (John Harris) *chsd ldrs: hung rt and lost pl over 3f out: sn bhd*	RobbieFitzpatrick 5	**50/1**	—
0/0-	**7**	*35*	**Wogan's Sister**[13] 7986 6-8-13 **57** (Paul Midgley) *trckd ldrs: t.k.h: drvn over 4f out: sn lost pl and bhd: t.o and eased 2f out*	MickyFenton 3	**100/1**	—

2m 27.5s (-0.50) **Going Correction** +0.025s/f (Slow) **7** Ran SP% **113.2**
Speed ratings (Par 101): **102,101,98,89,89 73,47**
toteswingers:1&2:£1.40, 1&3:£2.00, 2&3:£2.50 CSF £2.72 TOTE £1.60: £1.10, £1.40; EX 2.80.
Owner Koo's Racing Club **Bred** Rojan Farms **Trained** Norton, N Yorks
■ Stewards' Enquiry : Stephen Craine three-day ban: careless riding (23rd-25th Jan)

FOCUS
This handicap was run in a time around three seconds quicker than the preceding seller. The first two came clear to fight it out.

105 BET AT BLUESQ.COM ON YOUR IPHONE H'CAP — 7f (F)
2:45 (2:46) (Class 4) (0-85,81) 4-Y-O+ — **£2,914** (£867; £433; £216) **Stalls** Low

Form	Pos	Dist	Horse / Trainer / Comment	Jockey	SP	RPR
31-1	**1**		**Dubai Hills**[7] 9 5-9-2 **81** 6ex (Bryan Smart) *swtchd lft after s: w ldr: shkn up to ld over 2f out: wnt clr 1f out: eased towards fin*	AdamCarter(5) 8	**4/7**[1]	101+
436-	**2**	*3*	**Fishforcompliments**[28] 7846 7-8-8 **75** (Richard Fahey) *chsd ldrs: outpcd over 3f out: hdwy on ins over 2f out: edgd rt and chsd wnr over 1f out: styd on same pce*	GeorgeChaloner(7) 2	**14/1**	82
214-	**3**	*1*	**Everymanforhimself (IRE)**[10] 8016 7-9-7 **81** (Kevin Ryan) *hld up in rr: effrt on outside over 2f out: wnt 3rd over 1f out: kpt on same pce*	(b) PhillipMakin 7	**13/2**[2]	85
015-	**4**	*3*	**Slikback Jack (IRE)**[37] 7680 4-9-5 **79** (David Nicholls) *hld up on outer: effrt over 2f out: one pce over 1f out*	IanMongan 6	**16/1**	75
550-	**5**	*½*	**Thunderball**[22] 7935 5-9-0 **77** (David Nicholls) *chsd ldrs: n.m.r and swtchd lft 1f out: one pce*	(b) BillyCray(3) 3	**28/1**	72
34-3	**6**	*1½*	**Elusive Fame (USA)**[6] 18 5-9-1 **75** (Mark Johnston) *mid-div: effrt over 2f out: one pce whn n.m.r 1f out*	(b) JoeFanning 5	**13/2**[2]	66
10-2	**7**	*10*	**Alpha Tauri (USA)**[5] 38 5-9-1 **75** (Frank Sheridan) *mde most: hdd over 2f out: hung bdly lft and lost pl over 1f out*	(t) JamesDoyle 4	**9/1**[3]	39
106-	**8**	*9*	**Fantasy Fighter (IRE)**[106] 6374 6-8-13 **73** (John Quinn) *dwlt: hld up in rr: effrt over 2f out: sn lost pl and bhd*	JimmyQuinn 1	**33/1**	13

1m 28.71s (-1.59) **Going Correction** +0.025s/f (Slow) **8** Ran SP% **119.3**
Speed ratings (Par 105): **110,106,105,102,101 99,88,78**
toteswingers:1&2:£3.10, 1&3:£2.60, 2&3:£9.30 CSF £11.68 CT £34.17 TOTE £1.60: £1.10, £4.20, £1.40; EX 12.70 Trifecta £87.10 Pool: £649.76 - 5.52 winning units..
Owner Mrs F Denniff **Bred** A S Denniff **Trained** Hambleton, N Yorks
■ Stewards' Enquiry : George Chaloner one-day ban: careless riding (23rd Jan)

FOCUS
A decent handicap run at a brisk pace, and less than a second outside the standard. The Bryan Smart stable has now won both runnings of this event, having been on target with Snow Bay 12 months ago.

106 PLAY GOLF BEFORE RACING AT SOUTHWELL H'CAP — 6f (F)
3:20 (3:20) (Class 4) (0-85,85) 3-Y-O — **£2,914** (£867; £433; £216) **Stalls** Low

Form	Pos	Dist	Horse / Trainer / Comment	Jockey	SP	RPR
23-1	**1**		**Fred Willetts (IRE)**[3] 59 3-9-1 **85** 6ex (David Evans) *chsd ldrs: edgd lft and styd on to ld last 150yds*	(v) MatthewCosham(7) 2	**9/1**	92
624-	**2**	*½*	**Il Battista**[57] 7444 3-9-4 **84** (Alan McCabe) *led: edgd lft and hdd jst ins fnl f: hrd rdn and no ex*	(p) AndrewHeffernan(3) 4	**9/2**[3]	90
51-2	**3**	*2¾*	**Shostakovich (IRE)**[8] 4 3-9-1 **78** ([illegible]) *dwlt: in rr: effrt on ins over 2f out: hung lft and wnt n.d 3rd over 1f out: eased towards fin*	(tp) JamesDoyle 3	**7/2**	75
11-1	**4**	*3½*	**Even Stevens**[8] 4 3-8-10 **76** (David Nicholls) *awkward s: sn chsng ldrs: drvn 3f out: hung rt and wknd appr fnl f*	BillyCray(3) 5	**7/4**[1]	62
020-	**5**	*hd*	**Karate (IRE)**[71] 7224 3-8-8 **71** (Mark Johnston) *chsd ldrs: drvn 3f out: wknd over 1f out*	GregFairley 1	**9/2**[3]	56
221-	**6**	*10*	**Its You Again**[35] 7715 3-9-1 **78** (Michael Quinlan) *trckd ldrs on outer: t.k.h: hung lft over 2f out: lost pl and eased over 1f out*	JackMitchell 6	**8/1**	31

1m 16.2s (-0.30) **Going Correction** +0.025s/f (Slow) **6** Ran SP% **116.1**
Speed ratings (Par 99): **103,102,98,94,93 80**
toteswingers:1&2:£6.70, 1&3:£8.00, 2&3:£3.50 CSF £49.77 TOTE £12.30: £4.10, £2.00; EX 53.40.
Owner 24 - 7 / Gap Personnel **Bred** Liam Queally **Trained** Pandy, Monmouths

FOCUS
A competitive little handicap contested by some in-form 3yos.
Shostakovich(IRE) Official explanation: jockey said colt was slow away
Even Stevens Official explanation: jockey said gelding hung right throughout

107 PLAY RAINBOW RICHES AT BLUESQ.COM H'CAP — 6f (F)
3:55 (3:55) (Class 6) (0-55,61) 4-Y-O+ — **£1,535** (£453; £226) **Stalls** Low

Form	Pos	Dist	Horse / Trainer / Comment	Jockey	SP	RPR
32-3	**1**		**Itsthursdayalready**[7] 14 4-9-0 **53** (Mark Brisbourne) *trckd ldrs: effrt on outside over 2f out: r.o to ld last 150yds*	ShaneKelly 3	**6/4**[1]	59
03-1	**2**	*¾*	**Double Carpet (IRE)**[5] 34 8-9-8 **61** 6ex (Garry Woodward) *led tl hdd and no ex ins fnl f*	KirstyMilczarek 2	**9/2**[2]	65
00-6	**3**	*1¼*	**Bertbrand**[3] 57 6-8-7 **46** oh1 (Ian McInnes) *chsd ldrs on outer: styd on same pce fnl f*	(v) GregFairley 10	**9/1**	46
003-	**4**	*5*	**Fiancee (IRE)**[25] 7877 5-8-9 **48** (Roy Brotherton) *w ldrs: wknd fnl f*	(b) JackMitchell 8	**7/1**	32
00-0	**5**	*1¼*	**Flow Chart (IRE)**[3] 57 4-8-7 **47** oh1 ow1 (Peter Grayson) *hmpd s: in rr: sme hdwy over 2f out: nvr nr ldrs*	(b) RobbieFitzpatrick 4	**28/1**	27
005-	**6**	*1¼*	**Fair Bunny**[43] 7605 4-8-13 **52** (Alan Brown) *chsd ldrs: outpcd over 2f out: no threat after*	(p) JimmyQuinn 7	**6/1**[3]	28
006-	**7**	*2¼*	**Brazilian Brush (IRE)**[31] 7784 6-8-7 **46** oh1 (Milton Bradley) *chsd ldrs: wknd over 1f out*	(tp) JoeFanning 6	**8/1**	15
000-	**8**	*20*	**Dubai Legend**[36] 7699 5-9-2 **55** (Noel Wilson) *sn chsng ldrs: reminders on ins over 3f out: lost pl over 1f out: sn bhd and eased: t.o*	(p) DuranFentiman 1	**25/1**	—

006- **9** *15* **Ettrick Mill**[52] [7498] 5-8-7 **46** oh1................................(tp) WilliamCarson 5 —
(Milton Bradley) *in rr: lost pl over 3f out: bhd and eased 1f out: t.o* **40/1**

1m 17.17s (0.67) **Going Correction** +0.025s/f (Slow) **9** Ran SP% **115.8**
Speed ratings (Par 101): **96,95,93,86,85 83,80,53,33**
toteswingers:1&2:£2.10, 1&3:£4.30, 2&3:£9.10 CSF £8.07 CT £44.93 TOTE £2.30: £1.50, £1.30, £2.20; EX 9.10 Trifecta £64.40 Pool: £1,067.30 - 12.25 winning units..
Owner Raymond McNeill **Bred** St Clare Hall Stud **Trained** Great Ness, Shropshire

FOCUS
A weak handicap, run around a second slower than the earlier race for 3yos.
T/Jkpt: £696.20 to a £1 stake. Pool:£16,670.27 - 17.00 winning tickets T/Plt: £36.00 to a £1 stake. Pool:£104,633.32 - 2,118.92 winning tickets T/Qpdt: £12.70 to a £1 stake. Pool:£7,382.10 - 427.94 winning tickets WG

91 DEAUVILLE (R-H)
Saturday, January 8

OFFICIAL GOING: Fibresand: standard

108a PRIX DE LA PERDRIERE (CONDITIONS) (4YO FILLIES) (APPRENTICES) (FIBRESAND) 7f 110y
12:20 (12:00) 4-Y-O **£7,758** (£3,103; £2,327; £1,551; £775)

RPR
1 **Bertie's Best**[18] 4-9-1 0................................ MathieuTavaresDaSilva(5) 1 77
(F Doumen, France) **4/1**[2]
2 *1 ½* **Irish Cat (IRE)**[8] 4-8-13 0................................ AnthonyCaramanolis(7) 8 73
(N Clement, France) **7/10**[1]
3 *2* **Jumooh**[17] 4-8-6 0................................ TheoBachelot(5) 3 59
(F Head, France) **11/2**[3]
4 *1 ½* **Lady Des Biches (FR)**[117] 4-8-6 0.............. AlexandreChampenois(5) 7 55
(J-V Toux, France) **46/1**
5 *1 ½* **Pearl Argyle (FR)**[5] 4-9-1 0.......................... MlleCharleneBaron(5) 5 61
(J Boisnard, France) *broke wl: racd freely in 3rd: rdn early in st: outpcd: dropped bk: picked up again ins fnl f: r.o but wandered lft: causing interference to rival on outside: fin 5th: disqualified and plcd 6th* **18/1**
6 *1 ½* **Let It Rock (IRE)**[8] 4-8-8 0................................ TristanNormand(3) 2 48
(Mrs K Burke) **14/1**
7 *1 ½* **Toccata Jem (FR)** 4-8-8 0................................ WilliamsSaraiva(3) 4 44
(D Sepulchre, France) **15/1**
8 *1 ½* **Coriante (FR)**[242] 4-8-6 0................................ SoufyaneMoulin(5) 9 40
(Mme C Dufreche, France) **36/1**

1m 36.3s (96.30) **8** Ran SP% **117.2**
WIN (incl. 1 euro stake): 5.00. PLACES: 1.10, 1.10, 1.10. DF: 2.80. SF: 8.40.
Owner Robert Jeffcock **Bred** Jenny Hall Bloodstock Ltd **Trained** Bouce, France

NOTEBOOK
Let It Rock(IRE) finished fifth but was demoted a place.

84 WOLVERHAMPTON (A.W) (L-H)
Monday, January 10

OFFICIAL GOING: Standard to slow
Wind: Fresh, behind. Weather: Overcast

109 BLUESQ.COM ON YOUR IPHONE H'CAP 7f 32y(P)
2:05 (2:06) (Class 6) (0-60,60) 3-Y-O **£1,457** (£433; £216; £108) **Stalls** High

Form RPR
000- **1** **City Legend**[11] [8011] 3-9-7 **60**................................(bt) JamesDoyle 7 65
(Alan McCabe) *chsd ldr: rdn to ld over 1f out: styd on* **7/1**
006- **2** *½* **Not So Bright (USA)**[10] [8031] 3-9-2 **55**......................(t) GeorgeBaker 6 59
(Des Donovan) *hld up in tch: rdn over 2f out: chsd wnr ins fnl f: r.o* **3/1**[1]
51-0 **3** *2* **Granny Anne (IRE)**[5] [53] 3-9-3 **56**................................ CathyGannon 10 54+
(Alan Bailey) *hld up: hdwy over 2f out: rdn and hung lft over 1f out: r.o: eased whn hld nr fin* **16/1**
000- **4** *1 ½* **Scommettitrice (IRE)**[31] [7811] 3-9-2 **55**........................ AndreaAtzeni 5 49
(Ronald Harris) *hmpd s: hld up: hdwy 1/2-way: rdn over 1f out: styd on same pce ins fnl f* **25/1**
60-5 **5** *nse* **Lynchpin**[5] [52] 3-9-3 **56**................................(p) LukeMorris 8 50
(Ronald Harris) *chsd ldrs: rdn over 2f out: no ex ins fnl f* **14/1**
50-2 **6** *3* **Soviet Spring (IRE)**[3] [77] 3-9-0 **60**................................ ThomasBrown(7) 1 46
(Andrew Balding) *led: rdn and hdd over 1f out: wknd ins fnl f* **7/2**[2]
300- **7** *hd* **Cathcart Castle**[11] [8011] 3-9-5 **58**................................ SamHitchcott 3 43
(Mick Channon) *hmpd s: sn mid-div: rdn over 2f out: styd on ins fnl f: nt trble ldrs* **5/1**
020- **8** *6* **Boushra**[11] [8011] 3-9-7 **60**................................ LiamKeniry 12 29
(Sylvester Kirk) *hld up: hdwy over 2f out: sn rdn and wknd* **25/1**
362- **9** *½* **Three Scoops**[53] [7497] 3-8-11 **53**................................(t) BillyCray(3) 4 21
(Dominic Ffrench Davis) *hmpd s: a in rr* **9/2**[3]
000- **10** *2 ¼* **Oh What's Occuring**[29] [7843] 3-8-7 **46** oh1........................ ChrisCatlin 9 —
(Terry Clement) *mid-div: rdn 1/2-way: wknd over 2f out* **40/1**
60-6 **11** *3 ¼* **Welsh Dresser (IRE)**[4] [66] 3-8-8 **47**...................... RobbieFitzpatrick 2 —
(Peter Grayson) *free to post: edgd rt s: chsd ldrs: rdn 1/2-way: wknd over 2f out* **50/1**
046- **12** *1 ¾* **Pyrenean**[24] [7910] 3-9-5 **58**................................ MickyFenton 11 —
(James Given) *a in rr* **20/1**

1m 31.83s (2.23) **Going Correction** +0.25s/f (Slow) **12** Ran SP% **124.0**
Speed ratings (Par 95): **97,96,94,92,92 88,88,81,81,78 75,73**
Tote Swingers:1&2:£9.80, 2&3:£28.90, 1&3:£23.60 CSF £28.05 CT £340.72 TOTE £12.80: £3.10, £1.10, £5.40; EX 55.20 Trifecta £316.40 Part won. Pool £427.58 - 0.41 winning units..
Owner Contango Syndicate **Bred** Contango Bloodstock Ltd **Trained** Averham Park, Notts

FOCUS
The going was kept as standard to slow after an opening time almost five second above standard. This didn't look a strong race with only two previous winners in the field and the form is rated slightly negatively.
City Legend Official explanation: trainer said, regarding apparent improvement in form, that the colt had returned from a long break previous outing and appreciated the step up in trip.
Granny Anne(IRE) Official explanation: jockey said saddle slipped
Cathcart Castle Official explanation: jockey said gelding jumped right at start

110 HOTEL & CONFERENCING AT WOLVERHAMPTON MAIDEN STKS 7f 32y(P)
2:35 (2:39) (Class 5) 3-Y-O **£1,942** (£578; £288; £144) **Stalls** High

Form RPR
1 **Dasho** 3-9-3 0................................ HayleyTurner 9 71
(Olivia Maylam) *chsd ldrs: rdn to ld over 1f out: edgd lft ins fnl f: drvn out* **16/1**
4- **2** *½* **Spirit Of Grace**[51] [7530] 3-8-12 0................................ JamesDoyle 6 64
(Alan McCabe) *chsd ldrs: rdn over 1f out: styd on wl* **10/3**[2]
54- **3** *1 ¼* **Monadreen Dancer**[31] [7811] 3-8-12 0................................ ShaneKelly 12 61
(Daniel Mark Loughnane, Ire) *a.p: rdn over 1f out: styd on same pce ins fnl f* **25/1**
05- **4** *½* **Icebuster**[26] [7880] 3-9-3 0................................ JamesMillman 7 65
(Rod Millman) *mid-div: rdn 1/2-way: r.o wl ins fnl f: nt rch ldrs* **25/1**
63- **5** *1 ¼* **Too Many Questions (IRE)**[12] [7999] 3-9-3 0................ CathyGannon 2 61
(David Evans) *led: rdn over 2f out: hdd over 1f out: styd on same pce* **5/2**[1]
40- **6** *nk* **Encore View**[26] [7879] 3-8-12 0................................ LiamKeniry 11 55
(Andrew Balding) *chsd ldrs: rdn over 2f out: styd on same pce appr fnl f* **13/2**
7 *10* **Lakota Ghost (USA)** 3-9-3 0................................ GeorgeBaker 1 33
(Seamus Durack) *s.s: nvr nrr* **10/1**
8 *1* **Avon Light** 3-9-3 0................................ RussKennemore 10 31
(Milton Bradley) *s.i.s: sn pushed along in rr: rdn 1/2-way: wknd 2f out* **66/1**
304- **9** *1 ½* **Lady Mango (IRE)**[11] [8011] 3-8-12 **63**................................ LukeMorris 5 22
(Ronald Harris) *chsd ldrs tl rdn and wknd over 2f out* **9/1**
\- **10** *5* **Westhaven (IRE)** 3-9-3 0................................ RobertWinston 8 13
(David Elsworth) *unruly in stalls: s.s: rn green and outpcd* **4/1**[3]
0- **11** *11* **Renn**[168] [4436] 3-8-12 0................................ RobbieFitzpatrick 4 —
(Peter Grayson) *sn outpcd: t.o* **80/1**
0-6 **12** *25* **Ice Angel**[9] [5] 3-8-12 0................................ PatrickMathers 3 —
(Derek Shaw) *sn outpcd: t.o* **66/1**

1m 30.97s (1.37) **Going Correction** +0.25s/f (Slow) **12** Ran SP% **121.9**
Speed ratings (Par 97): **102,101,100,99,98 97,86,85,83,77 65,36**
Tote Swingers:1&2:£12.10, 2&3:£12.20, 1&3:£24.20 CSF £69.11 TOTE £11.80: £6.10, £1.40, £7.10; EX 96.40 TRIFECTA Not won..
Owner Mrs P A Clark **Bred** Mrs P A Clark **Trained** Epsom, Surrey

FOCUS
An interesting maiden with plenty of newcomers and unexposed runners. The first six all finished in a bit of a heap so the merit of the form is difficult to judge, and the third and the fourth are worries, but the time was relatively good.
Lakota Ghost(USA) Official explanation: jockey said colt was slowly away
Lady Mango(IRE) Official explanation: jockey said filly lost its action
Westhaven(IRE) Official explanation: jockey said colt ran green

111 DINE IN HORIZONS APPRENTICE H'CAP 7f 32y(P)
3:05 (3:06) (Class 6) (0-65,67) 4-Y-O+ **£1,535** (£453; £226) **Stalls** High

Form RPR
53-1 **1** **Rubenstar (IRE)**[5] [56] 8-9-5 **67** 6ex................................ RyanClark(5) 7 79
(Patrick Morris) *hmpd sn after s: hld up: hdwy 2f out: led over 1f out: rdn ins fnl f: jst hld on* **3/1**[2]
012- **2** *nk* **Saddlers Bend (IRE)**[13] [7989] 5-9-4 **61**........................ MatthewDavies 3 75+
(George Baker) *chsd ldrs: lost pl over 2f out: rallied over 1f out: r.o wl u.p: jst failed* **11/4**[1]
000- **3** *1 ½* **El Libertador (USA)**[13] [7992] 5-8-12 **58**..................(p) TobyAtkinson(3) 9 65
(Jeremy Gask) *hld up: hdwy over 2f out: rdn and ev ch over 1f out: styd on same pce ins fnl f* **10/1**
04-4 **4** *2 ¾* **Downhill Skier (IRE)**[8] [14] 7-8-12 **55**................................ KierenFox 4 55
(Mark Brisbourne) *hld up: hdwy u.p over 1f out: r.o: nt rch ldrs* **7/2**[3]
4- **5** *¾* **Little Luxury (IRE)**[26] [7872] 4-9-0 **64**............................ RossCoakley(7) 8 62
(Denis W Cullen, Ire) *chsd ldrs: rdn over 1f out: styd on same pce appr fnl f* **25/1**
000- **6** *1 ½* **Trade Centre**[128] [5766] 6-9-0 **57**................................ RussKennemore 1 51
(Milton Bradley) *chsd ldr tl rdn 3f out: wknd ins fnl f* **14/1**
000- **7** *2* **Spinning Ridge (IRE)**[13] [7991] 6-9-5 **62**......................(b) RossAtkinson 5 50
(Ronald Harris) *s.i.s: hdwy over 5f out: led wl over 2f out: rdn and hdd over 1f out: wknd ins fnl f* **7/1**
005- **8** *2 ¼* **Zeffirelli**[52] [7502] 6-8-10 **58**................................ RyanPowell(5) 2 40
(Michael Quinn) *led: hdd over 4f out: led again 3f out: sn hdd: wknd over 1f out* **16/1**
24-0 **9** *6* **Memphis Man**[8] [13] 8-8-3 **53**................................ KevinLundie(7) 6 19
(David Evans) *s.s: racd keenly: rapid hdwy over 5f out: led over 4f out: hdd 3f out: wknd over 2f out* **25/1**

1m 31.76s (2.16) **Going Correction** +0.25s/f (Slow) **9** Ran SP% **115.7**
Speed ratings (Par 101): **97,96,94,91,90 89,86,84,77**
Tote Swingers:1&2:£2.40, 2&3:£9.40, 1&3:£5.60 CSF £11.73 CT £69.43 TOTE £5.30: £1.60, £1.50, £2.90; EX 10.90 Trifecta £65.80 Pool £375.43 - 4.22 winning units..
Owner L Walsh **Bred** Schwindibode Ag **Trained** Tarporley, Cheshire
■ Stewards' Enquiry : Matthew Davies caution: used whip with excessive frequency.

FOCUS
An open-looking race which became a bit messy. The form is rated around the winner.

112 PARADE RESTAURANT (S) STKS 1m 141y(P)
3:35 (3:35) (Class 6) 4-Y-O+ **£1,535** (£453; £226) **Stalls** Low

Form RPR
010- **1** **Midnight Strider (IRE)**[12] [8008] 5-9-4 **63**.............(t) RichardKingscote 1 69
(Tom Dascombe) *led early: chsd ldr: shkn up over 2f out: rdn to ld ins fnl f f: r.o wl* **5/2**[2]
04-6 **2** *3 ¾* **Unbreak My Heart (IRE)**[7] [18] 6-10-0 **82**................(p) BarryMcHugh 2 70
(Richard Fahey) *stmbld s: sn rcrvd to ld: clr over 6f out: rdn and hung lft over 1f out: hdd and nt qckn ins fnl f* **8/15**[1]
63- **3** *4* **Haveahaarth (IRE)**[19] [7964] 4-8-12 **60**........................ TobyAtkinson(5) 4 51
(Michael Quinlan) *hld up: rdn over 2f out: no imp* **13/2**[3]

1m 52.51s (2.01) **Going Correction** +0.25s/f (Slow)
WFA 4 from 5yo+ 1lb **3** Ran SP% **107.1**
Speed ratings (Par 101): **101,97,94**
CSF £4.37 TOTE £3.00; EX 4.00.There was no bid for the winner. Unbreak My Heart was claimed by P. Butler for £6,000.
Owner Owen Promotions Limited **Bred** Jim McDonald **Trained** Malpas, Cheshire

FOCUS
A weak-looking seller and dubious form, rated around the winner.

113 BLUE SQUARE WISH CRAWLEY TOWN GOOD LUCK FILLIES' H'CAP 5f 216y(P)
4:05 (4:05) (Class 5) (0-70,69) 4-Y-0+ **£2,104** (£626; £312; £156) **Stalls** Low

Form RPR
124- **1** **Dreamacha**[58] 7442 4-8-12 **65**.. RyanClark(5) 4 71+
(Stuart Williams) *trckd ldrs: racd keenly: led over 4f out: rdn over 1f out: r.o* **11/10**[1]
/60- **2** *nk* **Goddess Of Light (IRE)**[30] 7837 4-9-7 **69**........................ ShaneKelly 5 74
(Daniel Mark Loughnane, Ire) *a.p: rdn over 2f out: chsd wnr fnl f: r.o* **14/1**
302- **3** *1 ¼* **Sparking**[38] 7684 4-8-10 **58**.. GrahamGibbons 3 59
(David Barron) *chsd ldrs: rdn over 1f out: styd on* **11/2**[3]
421- **4** *3 ¾* **Kate Skate**[76] 7154 4-9-0 **65**.. KierenFox(3) 2 54
(Gay Kelleway) *trckd ldrs: plld hrd: rdn over 1f out: wknd ins fnl f* **7/1**
40-4 **5** *2* **Avonvalley**[3] 84 4-8-10 **58**....................................... RobbieFitzpatrick 6 41
(Peter Grayson) *s.s: hld up: hdwy over 1f out: wknd ins fnl f* **14/1**
510- **6** *4 ½* **Mrs Mogg**[119] 6026 4-9-3 **65**..................................... RichardKingscote 1 33
(Tom Dascombe) *broke wl: led: hdd over 4f out: rdn over 2f out: wknd fnl f* **7/2**[2]
064- **7** *3 ½* **Red Rani**[14] 7987 6-8-0 **55** oh10...(p) JackDuern(7) 7 12
(Reg Hollinshead) *s.i.s: sn outpcd* **66/1**

1m 16.23s (1.23) **Going Correction** +0.25s/f (Slow) **7** Ran SP% **112.6**
Speed ratings (Par 100): **101,100,98,93,91 85,80**
Tote Swingers:1&2:£4.60, 2&3:£5.20, 1&3:£2.50 CSF £18.29 TOTE £2.10: £1.30, £6.00; EX 21.60.
Owner Essex Racing Club (Dreamacha) **Bred** Barry Root **Trained** Newmarket, Suffolk

FOCUS
A competitive looking fillies' handicap. The winner stood out on form and should do better.

114 SPONSOR A RACE BY CALLING 01902 390000 H'CAP 1m 4f 50y(P)
4:35 (4:35) (Class 6) (0-52,52) 4-Y-0+ **£1,535** (£453; £226) **Stalls** Low

Form RPR
503- **1** **Carter**[13] 7996 5-9-0 **49**.. GrahamGibbons 3 65
(Ian Williams) *a.p: led wl over 1f out: rdn clr fnl f: eased towards fin* **7/2**[2]
510- **2** *6* **Prickles**[60] 7407 6-8-13 **48**.. ChrisCatlin 1 54
(Karen George) *chsd ldrs: led over 4f out: rdn and hdd wl over 1f out: no ex fnl f* **10/1**
444- **3** *½* **Marino Prince (FR)**[46] 4912 6-8-12 **47**................................ IanMongan 5 52
(Jim Best) *hld up: hdwy over 5f out: chsd ldr over 4f out: rdn and ev ch wl over 1f out: styd on same pce* **6/4**[1]
335- **4** *hd* **Faith Jicaro (IRE)**[11] 8021 4-8-12 **51**............................... LukeMorris 11 56
(Nicky Vaughan) *hld up: nt clr run over 3f out: hdwy 2f out: styd on: nt rch ldrs* **16/1**
262- **5** *2 ¾* **Dovedon Angel**[33] 7759 5-8-13 **51**...................................... KierenFox(3) 8 51
(Gay Kelleway) *hld up: hdwy 4f out: rdn over 2f out: no ex fnl f* **6/1**[3]
005- **6** *6* **Tinseltown**[27] 3758 5-9-1 **50**.. MickyFenton 10 41
(Brian Rothwell) *hld up: hdwy over 2f out: sn rdn and wknd* **18/1**
005/ **7** *5* **Hardanger (IRE)**[453] 6771 6-8-9 **47**........................(e1) JamesSullivan(3) 7 30
(Tim Fitzgerald) *hld up: hdwy over 4f out: sn rdn: wknd wl over 2f out* **25/1**
00-0 **8** *9* **Fleur De'Lion (IRE)**[3] 79 5-8-11 **46**................................. LiamKeniry 12 14
(Sylvester Kirk) *prom: rdn over 3f out: wknd over 2f out:* **50/1**
300- **9** *12* **Fine Tolerance**[33] 7759 5-9-3 **52**................................ RichardKingscote 6 1
(Sam Davison) *chsd ldr over 7f: rdn and wknd over 3f out: eased over 1f out: t.o* **20/1**
0/ **10** *10* **Crafty George (IRE)**[228] 2484 6-8-4 **46** oh1................ RossCoakley(7) 9 —
(Patrick Allen, Ire) *led over 7f: sn rdn and wknd: t.o* **11/1**
000/ **11** *19* **Big Talk**[50] 7029 4-8-8 **47**..(v) CathyGannon 2 —
(David Bridgwater) *hld up in tch: rdn and lost pl over 5f out: sn bhd: t.o* **25/1**

2m 43.55s (2.45) **Going Correction** +0.25s/f (Slow)
WFA 4 from 5yo+ 4lb **11** Ran SP% **114.5**
Speed ratings (Par 101): **101,97,96,96,94 90,87,81,73,66 54**
Tote Swingers:1&2:£8.10, 2&3:£7.20, 1&3:£3.70 CSF £37.14 CT £74.32 TOTE £4.40: £1.40, £2.80, £2.00; EX 37.20 Trifecta £172.30 Pool £537.86 - 2.31 winning units..
Owner Stratford Bards Racing **Bred** Dr D G St John And Mrs Sherry Collier **Trained** Portway, Worcs
■ Stewards' Enquiry : Kieren Fox caution: used whip with excessive frequency.

FOCUS
A weak race. The favourite didn't translate his jumps form but the rest makes a fair bit of sense at face value.

115 PLAY RAINBOW RICHES AT BLUESQ.COM H'CAP 1m 1f 103y(P)
5:05 (5:05) (Class 6) (0-58,58) 4-Y-0+ **£1,535** (£453; £226) **Stalls** Low

Form RPR
310- **1** **Black Coffee**[12] 8008 6-9-4 **56**...(b) ShaneKelly 9 67
(Mark Brisbourne) *s.i.s: hld up: hdwy 6f out: rdn to ld 1f out: edgd lft r.o* **4/1**[2]
22-0 **2** *3 ¼* **Lucky Diva**[3] 83 4-8-12 **51**.. JamesDoyle 11 55
(Sylvester Kirk) *chsd ldrs: rdn over 1f out: styd on: wnt 2nd last strides* **6/1**
036- **3** *hd* **Verluga (IRE)**[14] 7986 4-9-2 **55**..................................... DuranFentiman 7 59
(Tim Easterby) *led 1f: chsd ldr tl led wl over 3f out: rdn and hdd 1f out: styd on same pce: lost 2nd last strides* **15/2**
651- **4** *1 ¼* **Iguacu**[13] 7996 7-9-1 **53**...(p) JimCrowley 8 54
(George Baker) *s.i.s: hld up: hdwy over 3f out: rdn and ev ch over 1f out: no ex ins fnl f* **9/4**[1]
20-6 **5** *2 ¼* **Kielty's Folly**[8] 14 7-8-13 **51**...................................... GrahamGibbons 10 47
(Brian Baugh) *hld up: racd keenly: hdwy over 2f out: rdn over 1f out: no ex fnl f* **15/2**
50-5 **6** *2 ½* **Dane Cottage**[4] 69 4-8-0 **46**... RPWalsh(7) 6 37+
(David Evans) *hld up: rdn over 2f out: r.o ins fnl f: nvr nrr* **5/1**[3]
403- **7** *1 ½* **Bookiebasher Babe (IRE)**[137] 5455 6-8-7 **45**............. FrannyNorton 4 33
(Michael Quinn) *chsd ldrs: rdn over 2f out: sn wknd* **16/1**
020- **8** *¾* **Dauntsey Park (IRE)**[219] 2753 4-9-5 **58**.......................... CathyGannon 3 44
(Tor Sturgis) *prom: chsd ldr over 3f out: rdn over 1f out: wknd fnl f* **16/1**
000- **9** *1 ¼* **Bobering**[37] 7705 11-8-7 **45**.. KellyHarrison 5 29
(Brian Baugh) *prom: lost pl 5f out: n.d after* **50/1**
506/ **10** *1* **Meydan Style (USA)**[446] 6950 5-8-7 **45**........................... LukeMorris 12 27
(Bruce Hellier) *hld up: plld hrd: hdwy over 3f out: rdn and wknd wl over 1f out* **50/1**
500/ **11** *13* **Rough Sketch (USA)**[461] 6566 6-9-2 **54**............................(t) MartinLane 2 —
(Ian Williams) *plld hrd: led after 1f: hdd wl over 3f out: wknd over 2f out* **16/1**

2m 5.33s (3.63) **Going Correction** +0.25s/f (Slow)
WFA 4 from 5yo+ 1lb **11** Ran SP% **126.8**
Speed ratings (Par 101): **93,90,89,88,86 84,83,82,81,80 69**
Tote Swingers:1&2:£6.80, 2&3:£10.40, 1&3:£3.80 CSF £30.93 CT £181.11 TOTE £5.60: £2.10, £1.20, £3.30; EX 30.00 Trifecta £168.20 Pool £577.67 - 2.54 winning units..
Owner Derek & Mrs Marie Dean **Bred** Mrs M Campbell-Andenaes **Trained** Great Ness, Shropshire

FOCUS
A moderate handicap but a muddliong and messy race and perhaps not form to trust. The winner is rated to last year's best.
Dauntsey Park(IRE) Official explanation: jockey said gelding ran keen and had no more to give
T/Plt: £182.50 to a £1 stake. Pool:£62,263.44. 249.03 winning tickets T/Qpdt: £11.90 to a £1 stake. Pool:£4,984.27. 308.56 winning tickets CR

[102]SOUTHWELL (L-H)
Tuesday, January 11

OFFICIAL GOING: Standard
Wind: Moderate behind Weather: Overcast

116 TODAY'S JOCKEY SPECIALS AT BLUESQ.COM (S) STKS 5f (F)
12:50 (12:50) (Class 6) 4-Y-0+ **£1,535** (£453; £226) **Stalls** High

Form RPR
025- **1** **Spic 'n Span**[34] 7764 6-9-0 **61**..(b) LukeMorris 3 71
(Ronald Harris) *mde all: rdn over 1f out: kpt on wl ins fnl f* **11/8**[1]
2-22 **2** *1 ¼* **Your Gifted (IRE)**[5] 62 4-8-6 **60**............................(e) JamesSullivan(3) 4 62
(Patrick Morris) *trckd ldng pair: hdwy 1/2-way: swtchd lft and rdn to chal over 1f out: ev ch tl drvn and nt qckn wl ins fnl f* **6/4**[2]
356- **3** *4 ½* **First Swallow**[49] 7537 6-8-7 **57**..(t) PNolan(7) 2 50
(David Brown) *cl up: rdn along 1/2-way: sn one pce* **10/1**
560- **4** *2 ¼* **Ingleby Star (IRE)**[28] 7868 6-9-0 **65**...........................(p) JimmyQuinn 1 42
(Noel Wilson) *stmbld s: in tch on outer: rdn along over 2f out: sn one pce* **11/2**[3]

58.73 secs (-0.97) **Going Correction** -0.15s/f (Stan) **4** Ran SP% **106.6**
Speed ratings (Par 101): **101,99,91,88**
CSF £3.65 TOTE £3.00; EX 3.70.There was no bid for winner.
Owner P Nurcombe **Bred** C A Cyzer **Trained** Earlswood, Monmouths

FOCUS
A typically moderate seller. The field kept more towards the stands' side and the winner is rated back to his best.

117 BOOK TICKETS AT SOUTHWELL-RACECOURSE.CO.UK H'CAP 1m 4f (F)
1:20 (1:20) (Class 6) (0-60,61) 4-Y-0+ **£1,535** (£453; £226) **Stalls** Low

Form RPR
04-1 **1** **Stanley Rigby**[8] 16 5-9-1 **51** 6ex.................................... BarryMcHugh 4 64+
(Richard Fahey) *trckd ldrs: hdwy on outer over 3f out: chal over 2f out: rdn to ld wl over 1f out: sn hung lft and kpt on strly ins fnl f* **9/4**[2]
645- **2** *2 ¾* **My Mate Mal**[15] 7985 7-9-3 **60**...(p) LauraPike(7) 6 66
(William Stone) *led: pushed along 4f out: rdn 3f out: sn jnd and drvn: hdd wl over 1f out: kpt on u.p ins fnl f* **12/1**
/42- **3** *5* **Money Money Money**[46] 7579 5-9-5 **55**....................... JamesMillman 8 53
(Rod Millman) *trckd ldng pair: hdwy to chse ldr over 4f out: rdn along 3f out: sn drvn and one pce* **8/1**[3]
33-1 **4** *3 ¾* **Odin's Raven (IRE)**[9] 11 6-9-6 **61** 6ex............................ DaleSwift(5) 3 53
(Brian Ellison) *trckd ldrs on inner: rdn along 4f out: drvn 3f out and sn btn* **5/6**[1]
006/ **5** *½* **Duar Mapel (USA)**[86] 5-9-10 **60**.................................(b) SamHitchcott 7 51
(David Bourton) *hld up towards rr: chsd ldrs 3f out: sn rdn and outpcd fnl 2f* **25/1**
500- **6** *30* **Cragganmore Creek**[40] 7870 8-8-10 **46** oh1................(v) KellyHarrison 2
(Dave Morris) *chsd ldr: pushed along 1/2-way: sn wknd: bhd and eased fnl 2f* **66/1**

2m 41.65s (0.65) **Going Correction** +0.075s/f (Slow)
WFA 4 from 5yo+ 4lb **6** Ran SP% **109.5**
Speed ratings (Par 101): **100,98,94,92,92 72**
toteswingers:1&2: £4.20, 2&3: £3.50, 1&3: £2.00 CSF £25.75 CT £165.41 TOTE £3.40: £2.20, £4.10; EX 30.10 Trifecta £55.90 Pool: £208.72 - 2.76 winning units..
Owner Dean Hardman and Stella Kelsall **Bred** F C T Wilson **Trained** Musley Bank, N Yorks

FOCUS
A low-grade handicap, but there were three last-time-out winners in the line up and it was run at a solid pace. With the favourite disappointing it may not have taken much winning.
Odin's Raven(IRE) Official explanation: jockey said gelding never travelled
Cragganmore Creek Official explanation: trainer said gelding made a noise

118 PLAY GOLF BEFORE RACING H'CAP 2m (F)
1:50 (1:51) (Class 6) (0-60,60) 4-Y-0+ **£1,535** (£453; £226) **Stalls** Low

Form RPR
360- **1** **Delorain (IRE)**[42] 7634 8-8-5 **46** oh1...............................(vt) LauraPike(7) 5 56
(William Stone) *midfield: hdwy to trck ldrs 1/2-way: cl up 4f out: rdn to chal over 2f out: led wl over 1f out: edgd rt wl ins fnl f: jst hld on* **10/1**
05-4 **2** *nk* **Mashdood (USA)**[9] 8 5-9-12 **60**...................................... LukeMorris 7 70
(Peter Hiatt) *led: rdn along 3f out: drvn 2f out: sn hdd: rallied u.p ins fnl f: jst hld* **13/2**[3]
41-2 **3** *1 ¾* **Six Of Clubs**[7] 39 5-8-11 **48**...(b) KierenFox(3) 8 56
(Bill Turner) *hld up in tch: hdwy to trck ldrs over 4f out: effrt 3f out: rdn to chse ldng pair wl over 1f out: sn drvn and kpt on same pce* **15/8**[1]
05-5 **4** *nk* **Silent Lucidity (IRE)**[9] 8 7-9-4 **52**.............................(p) TomEaves 10 59
(Peter Niven) *a.p: effrt over 3f out: rdn over 2f out: drvn and one pce appr fnl f* **16/1**
63-2 **5** *17* **Carnac (IRE)**[8] 16 5-9-0 **48**...(e1) ShaneKelly 1 35
(Alan McCabe) *hld up in rr: hdwy over 6f out: rdn over 3f out: n.d* **3/1**[2]
154- **6** *12* **Escape Artist**[65] 6648 4-8-10 **51**................................(e1) RobertWinston 3 23
(Tim Easterby) *t.k.h: trckd ldrs on inner: hdwy 6f out: rdn along 4f out: drvn 3f out and sn btn* **15/2**
4/6- **7** *12* **Ramvaswani (IRE)**[29] 15 8-9-0 **48**..............................(p) HayleyTurner 6 —
(Neil King) *a towards rr* **50/1**
00-6 **8** *nk* **Sweet Seville (FR)**[9] 11 7-8-9 **48** oh1 ow2............. MarkCoumbe(5) 4 —
(Terry Clement) *a in rr* **50/1**
4 **9** *18* **Sweetest Of Peas (IRE)**[7] 40 4-9-1 **56**........................ PhillipMakin 11 —
(Kevin Ryan) *chsd ldr: rdn along over 4f out: sn wknd* **33/1**

444- **10** *26* **Capable Guest (IRE)**[32] [7805] 9-9-9 **57**................................ ChrisCatlin 2 —
(George Moore) *trckd ldrs: pushed along over 6f out: sn lost pl and bhd fnl 3f* **14/1**

3m 45.85s (0.35) **Going Correction** +0.075s/f (Slow)
WFA 4 from 5yo+ 7lb **10** Ran SP% **113.4**
Speed ratings (Par 101): **102,101,100,100,92 86,80,80,71,58**
toteswingers:1&2: £10.60, 2&3: £3.80, 1&3: £6.50 CSF £70.60 CT £174.22 TOTE £13.80: £4.40, £1.50, £1.30; EX 102.60 Trifecta £245.90 Pool: £378.94 - 1.14 winning units..
Owner Miss Caroline Scott **Bred** Glending Bloodstock **Trained** West Wickham, Cambs

FOCUS
A very weak staying handicap, run at what appeared to be a fair enough pace and the first four came clear. The form is rated through the winner to his best.
Delorain(IRE) Official explanation: trainer said, regarding apparent improvement in form, that the race was run to suit the gelding.
Sweet Seville(FR) Official explanation: jockey said mare ran flat

119 BLUESQ.COM ON YOUR IPHONE H'CAP 6f (F)
2:20 (2:21) (Class 5) (0-70,68) 3-Y-O **£1,813** (£539; £269; £134) **Stalls** Low

Form RPR
22-1 **1** **Finn's Rainbow**[7] [41] 3-9-5 **66** 6ex.................................... PhillipMakin 2 70+
(Kevin Ryan) *led 2f: cl up tl rdn to ld again 1 1/2f out: drvn ins fnl f: kpt on wl towards fin* **8/11**[1]

55-1 **2** *1* **Local Diktator**[9] [10] 3-8-13 **60** 6ex..................................(t) LukeMorris 3 61
(Ronald Harris) *towards rr: hdwy on inner over 2f out: rdn wl over 1f out: styd on ins fnl f: nrst fin* **7/1**[3]

044- **3** *nk* **Cheylesmore (IRE)**[32] [7803] 3-9-3 **64**.............................(e[1]) LiamJones 6 64
(Stuart Williams) *dwlt: towards rr: hdwy on outer 1/2-way: rdn to chse ldrs wl over 1f out: sn drvn and kpt on ins fnl f* **11/1**

04-2 **4** *½* **Close To The Edge (IRE)**[7] [36] 3-9-4 **65**............................ ShaneKelly 1 63
(Alan McCabe) *cl up on inner: led after 2f: rdn along over 2f out: hdd and drvn 1 1/2f out: edgd lft and one pce ent fnl f* **8/1**

20-3 **5** *1 ½* **Je Suis Unrockstar**[10] [4] 3-9-4 **68**...............................(p) BillyCray[(3)] 5 62
(David Nicholls) *chsd ldrs: rdn 2f out: drvn over 1f out: kpt on same pce* **4/1**[2]

500- **6** *8* **Kheya (IRE)**[69] [7301] 3-8-13 **60**.. CathyGannon 4 28
(George Moore) *chsd ldng pair: rdn along 1/2-way: wknd 2f out* **25/1**

1m 17.07s (0.57) **Going Correction** +0.075s/f (Slow) **6** Ran SP% **113.7**
Speed ratings (Par 97): **99,97,97,96,94 83**
toteswingers:1&2: £1.80, 2&3: £5.30, 1&3: £3.10 CSF £6.78 TOTE £1.90: £1.40, £2.40; EX 6.10.
Owner F Gillespie **Bred** Stuart McPhee Bloodstock Ltd **Trained** Hambleton, N Yorks

FOCUS
A moderate 3-y-o handicap, run at a solid pace. Straightforward fornm at face value.

120 SOUTHWELL-RACECOURSE.CO.UK H'CAP 7f (F)
2:50 (2:50) (Class 6) (0-52,56) 4-Y-O+ **£1,535** (£453; £226) **Stalls** Low

Form RPR
21 **1** **Powerful Presence (IRE)**[5] [61] 5-9-6 **56** 6ex.............. JoeFanning 11 72+
(David O'Meara) *trckd ldrs: smooth hdwy on outer 3f out: led on bit 2f out: sn clr: easily* **2/5**[1]

06-3 **2** *4 ½* **Noble Attitude**[8] [19] 5-8-10 **46** oh1.............................. FrannyNorton 8 40
(Richard Guest) *in tch: pushed along 3f out: rdn 2f out: styd on u.p ins fnl f: no ch w wnr* **10/1**

60-0 **3** *1 ¼* **Northumberland**[8] [16] 5-8-10 **46** oh1.......................... KellyHarrison 10 37
(Michael Chapman) *a.p: rdn along wl over 2f out: drvn wl over 1f out and sn one pce* **33/1**

000/ **4** *6* **Cause For Applause (IRE)**[375] [7] 5-8-12 **48** ow1...... PhillipMakin 7 23
(Ray Craggs) *sn led: rdn along and hdd 1/2-way: drvn 2f out: sn one pce* **33/1**

033- **5** *½* **Hambleton**[25] [7911] 4-9-2 **52**...(p) TomEaves 6 25
(Bryan Smart) *chsd ldrs: effrt over 2f out: sn rdn and one pce* **7/2**[2]

53-0 **6** *5* **Rose Bed (IRE)**[5] [57] 4-8-10 **46** oh1..........................(p) BarryMcHugh 9 —
(Michael Quinlan) *a towards rr* **33/1**

00-4 **7** *¾* **Raghdaan**[9] [12] 4-8-10 **46** oh1.. CathyGannon 3 —
(Peter Hiatt) *prom: led 1/2-way: rdn along and hdd 2f out: sn wknd* **6/1**[3]

/60- **8** *4* **Countrycraft**[49] [7538] 4-8-5 **46** oh1.................................. RyanPowell[(5)] 5 —
(Sally Hall) *hld up: a in rr* **33/1**

1m 29.96s (-0.34) **Going Correction** +0.075s/f (Slow) **8** Ran SP% **128.8**
Speed ratings (Par 101): **104,98,97,90,90 84,83,78**
toteswingers:1&2: £2.40, 2&3: £26.00, 1&3: £7.40 CSF £7.34 CT £69.65 TOTE £1.20: £1.02, £2.80, £14.50; EX 7.40 Trifecta £71.50 Pool: £411.19 - 4.25 winning units..
Owner Mrs S O'Meara **Bred** Corduff Stud **Trained** Nawton, N Yorks

FOCUS
All bar two of these were running from just out of the handicap and this was a very weak race, but the winner impressed in a faster time than the 0-70.

121 VISIT NOTTINGHAMSHIRE MAIDEN STKS 1m (F)
3:20 (3:21) (Class 5) 3-Y-O+ **£1,910** (£564; £282) **Stalls** Low

Form RPR
1 **Son Vida (IRE)** 3-8-8 0.. JoeFanning 6 79+
(Mark Johnston) *trckd ldr: cl up 1/2-way: led 3f out: rdn: rn green and hung lft over 1f out: sn clr: eased towards fin: readily* **2/1**[2]

2 *4 ½* **Kishanda** 3-8-3 0.. HayleyTurner 1 61+
(Hughie Morrison) *dwlt and towards rr: hdwy on inner 3f out: rdn along 2f out: styd on u.p ins fnl f: no ch w wnr* **9/1**

54- **3** *3 ½* **Aussie Dollar (IRE)**[13] [8000] 3-8-8 0.......................... KirstyMilczarek 5 58
(Andrew Balding) *led: pushed along 1/2-way: hdd 3f out: drvn and one pce fnl 2f* **10/11**[1]

35-5 **4** *¾* **Chez Vrony**[5] [61] 5-10-0 57.. ChrisCatlin 4 60
(Dave Morris) *chsd ldrs: hdwy on outer and cl up 3f out: rdn over 2f out and ch tl drvn wl over 1f out and sn wknd* **7/1**[3]

5 *2 ¾* **Lyford Lad**[62] 4-10-0 0.. TomEaves 2 54?
(George Moore) *dwlt: sn chsng ldrs: cl up on outer 1/2-way: rdn along 3f out and sn wknd* **66/1**

0- **6** *6* **Dance To Destiny**[13] [8000] 3-8-3 0.................................. CathyGannon 3 31
(Phil McEntee) *chsd ldrs 2f: rdn along 1/2-way: outpcd and bhd fnl 2f* **16/1**

1m 44.57s (0.87) **Going Correction** +0.075s/f (Slow)
WFA 3 from 4yo+ 20lb **6** Ran SP% **115.6**
Speed ratings (Par 103): **98,93,90,89,86 80**
toteswingers:1&2: £3.40, 2&3: £2.70, 1&3: £1.20 CSF £20.39 TOTE £3.10: £2.30, £3.80; EX 13.60.
Owner Jim McGrath, Roger & Dianne Trevitt **Bred** John Fielding **Trained** Middleham Moor, N Yorks

FOCUS
An ordinary maiden and the favourite was below form, but a taking winner in Son Vida.

122 PLAY ROULETTE AT BLUESQ.COM H'CAP 7f (F)
3:50 (3:52) (Class 5) (0-70,74) 4-Y-O+ **£1,878** (£558; £279; £139) **Stalls** Low

Form RPR
043- **1** **Master Leon**[30] [7844] 4-9-4 **67**..(p) TomEaves 6 76+
(Bryan Smart) *trckd ldrs: pushed along 1/2-way: rdn wl over 2f out: hdwy over 1f out: styd on to ld jst ins fnl f: drvn out* **5/1**[3]

511- **2** *nk* **Ingleby King (USA)**[36] [7731] 5-8-13 **62**.................... GrahamGibbons 7 70+
(David O'Meara) *chsd ldrs: hdwy and cl up on outer 3f out: rdn to ld wl over 1f out: sn edgd lft: drvn and hdd jst ins fnl f: rallied and kpt on towards fin* **6/5**[1]

10-1 **3** *2 ¾* **Ace Of Spies (IRE)**[8] [17] 6-9-11 **74** 6ex.................... KirstyMilczarek 3 74
(Conor Dore) *sn led: rdn along 3f out: drvn 2f out: sn hdd and edgd rt over 1f out: one pce appr fnl f* **11/1**

0-43 **4** *1 ¾* **Elusive Warrior (USA)**[8] [17] 8-9-6 **69**..........................(p) ShaneKelly 4 65
(Alan McCabe) *cl up: rdn along over 3f out: drvn over 2f out and grad wknd* **9/2**[2]

050- **5** *4* **Dancing Freddy (IRE)**[15] [7984] 4-8-12 **64**................ RobertLButler[(3)] 2 49
(Michael Chapman) *chsd ldrs on inner: rdn along 3f out: outpcd fnl 2f* **50/1**

450- **6** *2 ¼* **Realt Na Mara (IRE)**[98] [6664] 8-9-7 **70**.............................. TravisBlock 5 49
(Hughie Morrison) *prom: cl up 3f out: sn rdn and wknd wl over 1f out* **7/1**

0/0- **7** *11* **Fools Gold**[28] [7870] 6-8-11 **60**.. FrannyNorton 1 —
(Richard Guest) *a in rr: outpcd and bhd fnl 2f* **11/1**

1m 30.71s (0.41) **Going Correction** +0.075s/f (Slow) **7** Ran SP% **111.4**
Speed ratings (Par 103): **100,99,96,94,89 87,74**
toteswingers:1&2: £2.40 , 1&3 not won, 2&3 not won. CSF £10.83 TOTE £5.40: £2.40, £1.50; EX 16.50.
Owner Alan Zheng **Bred** Ms R A Myatt **Trained** Hambleton, N Yorks

FOCUS
There was a good pace early on in this moderate handicap and the first pair had it to themselves from the furlong marker. The winner is rated back to something like his summer form.
T/Plt: £47.00 to a £1 stake. Pool of £46,961.10 - 728.13 winning tickets. T/Qpdt: £8.90 to a £1 stake. Pool of £4,924.09 - 404.95 winning tickets. JR

[43]KEMPTON (A.W) (R-H)
Wednesday, January 12

OFFICIAL GOING: Standard
Wind: Moderate, behind Weather: Very Overcast, drizzly

123 GREAT SALE OFFERS DAILY AT WILLIAMHILL.COM H'CAP 5f (P)
4:15 (4:15) (Class 7) (0-50,50) 4-Y-O+ **£1,535** (£453; £226) **Stalls** Low

Form RPR
500- **1** **Duke Of Rainford**[22] [7952] 4-9-2 **49**................................ JamieSpencer 8 56
(Michael Herrington) *s.i.s: hld up in last pair: brought wd in st and gd prog over 1f out: sustained effrt to ld last 100yds* **7/2**[1]

20-6 **2** *½* **Bluebok**[3] [102] 10-8-8 **48**..(bt) MatthewCosham[(7)] 6 53
(Milton Bradley) *hld up bhd ldrs: forced to check over 3f out and over 2f out: effrt over 1f out: styd on wl fnl f to take 2nd nr fin* **10/1**

333- **3** *nk* **Force To Spend**[21] [7973] 4-8-11 **49**................................ RyanClark[(5)] 12 53
(Nick Littmoden) *hld up in midfield: prog on outer over 1f out: c to chal last 100yds and w wnr: nt qckn after* **9/1**

550- **4** *1* **Black Baccara**[28] [7877] 4-9-1 **48**......................................(be) AdamKirby 11 48
(Phil McEntee) *pressed ldrs: drvn into narrow ld ent fnl f: hdd and fdd last 100yds* **25/1**

052- **5** *¾* **Jemimaville (IRE)**[28] [7877] 4-9-2 **49**..............................(v) LukeMorris 7 47
(Giles Bravery) *pushed along in midfield after 2f: hanging and nt qckn over 1f out and lost pl: styd on again fnl f* **13/2**

040- **6** *nk* **Spoof Master (IRE)**[21] [7972] 7-9-1 **48**.........................(t) RobertWinston 4 45
(Jeff Pearce) *drvn to hold pl on inner and pressed ldr: upsides ent fnl f: wknd last 100yds* **9/2**[3]

000- **7** *nse* **Tyrannosaurus Rex (IRE)**[12] [8034] 7-9-2 **49**..................(v) TomEaves 5 47+
(Derek Shaw) *s.i.s: pushed along in 9th: trying to make prog whn n.m.r fnl f: nrst fin* **8/1**

002- **8** *¾* **True Red (IRE)**[40] [7676] 4-8-13 **46**..............................(b) AndreaAtzeni 9 40
(Nikki Evans) *chsd ldrs: rdn after 2f: nt qckn over 1f out: wknd ins fnl f* **40/1**

306- **9** *½* **Mr Funshine**[22] [7953] 6-9-2 **49**.. MartinLane 1 41
(Derek Shaw) *s.i.s: hld up last: appeared to be hanging over 1f out: reminders and styd on ins fnl f* **20/1**

600- **10** *½* **Sir Loin**[14] [8005] 10-8-12 **45**.......................................(b) KirstyMilczarek 10 35
(John Gallagher) *wl away fr wd draw: mde most tl hdd & wknd ent fnl f* **16/1**

230- **11** *¾* **Francis Albert**[22] [7952] 5-8-10 **50**............................(b) JosephYoung[(7)] 2 37
(Michael Mullineaux) *cl up bhd ldrs on inner: nt qckn over 1f out: wknd and lost several pls ins fnl f* **4/1**[2]

60.61 secs (0.11) **Going Correction** 0.0s/f (Stan) **11** Ran SP% **120.9**
Speed ratings (Par 97): **99,98,97,96,94 94,94,93,92,91 90**
toteswingers:1&2:£7.30, 1&3:£9.80, 2&3:£14.40 CSF £39.62 CT £304.78 TOTE £3.60: £1.40, £3.00, £3.30; EX 39.70.
Owner P Ringer **Bred** Worksop Manor Stud **Trained** Cold Kirby, N Yorks

FOCUS
A low-grade opener. The principals came from off the pace but the leaders didn't look like they went off too quickly. The form is sound.
Duke Of Rainford Official explanation: jockey said gelding suffered interference in running
Bluebok Official explanation: jockey said gelding suffered interference in running
Tyrannosaurus Rex(IRE) Official explanation: jockey said gelding was denied a clear run
Sir Loin Official explanation: jockey said gelding hung right

124 WILLIAMHILL.COM - ENHANCED SPS ON KEMPTON WINNERS H'CAP 1m 2f (P)
4:45 (4:47) (Class 5) (0-75,76) 4-Y-O+ **£2,047** (£604; £302) **Stalls** Low

Form
3-13 **1** **Kidlat**[7] [54] 6-9-5 **73**.. AdamKirby 9 83
(Alan Bailey) *s.i.s: prog to ld after 1f: mde rest: pressed and rdn over 2f out: pressed again and hrd drvn 1f out: sn drew clr* **5/4**[1]

242- **2** *3* **Professor John (IRE)**[22] [7959] 4-8-9 **65**.............................. JamesDoyle 3 69
(Ian Wood) *chsd ldng pair: urged along 3f out: wnt 2nd jst over 1f out and cl enough: sn outpcd* **5/1**[3]

/25- **3** *½* **Celtic Commitment**[273] [1302] 5-8-13 **67**.......................... HayleyTurner 2 70
(Simon Dow) *led 1f: chsd wnr: rdn to chal over 2f out: stl cl up 1f out: nt qckn* **16/1**

40-5 **4** ¾ **Veroon (IRE)**[8] 38 5-9-6 **74**....................(p) FrannyNorton 6 76
(James Given) *hld up in 4th: clsd on ldrs fr 2f out: tried to chal on inner jst over 1f out: nt qckn and sn hld* **16/1**

046- **5** *nk* **Turjuman (USA)**[28] 7878 6-8-11 **65**.................... JamieMackay 10 66
(Willie Musson) *stdd s: hld up in detached last: coaxed along and no prog over 2f out: styd on whn rdn ins fnl f: nvr nr ldrs* **16/1**

23-5 **6** *2* **Fonterutoli (IRE)**[7] 54 4-9-3 **73**.................... MartinLane 4 70
(Roger Ingram) *hld up in 6th: effrt 2f out: nt qckn over 1f out: wknd ins fnl f* **7/2**[2]

162- **7** ¾ **Strike Force**[14] 8008 7-9-4 **72**....................(t) CathyGannon 5 67
(Olivia Maylam) *stdd s: hld up in 5th: pushed along and no prog 3f out: wknd u.p fnl f* **15/2**

2m 6.49s (-1.51) **Going Correction** 0.0s/f (Stan)
WFA 4 from 5yo+ 2lb 7 Ran SP% **112.7**
Speed ratings (Par 103): **106,103,103,102,102 100,100**
toteswingers:1&2:£1.90, 1&3:£6.10, 2&3:£6.50 CSF £7.62 CT £63.66 TOTE £3.40: £2.50, £2.50; EX 8.20.
Owner John Stocker **Bred** Darley **Trained** Newmarket, Suffolk

FOCUS
A handicap lacking strength in depth. The winner was able to dictate an uneven gallop and the form is rated around the third.
Strike Force Official explanation: vet said gelding lost right-fore shoe

125 TOP FOOTBALL OFFERS TODAY AT WILLIAMHILL.COM H'CAP 5f (P)
5:15 (5:17) (Class 4) (0-85,85) 4-Y-0+ **£3,885** (£1,156; £577; £288) **Stalls** Low

Form RPR

315- **1** **Stratton Banker (IRE)**[34] 7782 4-8-10 **74**.................... JimCrowley 4 87+
(Stuart Williams) *trckd ldng quartet: prog 2f out: rdn to ld 1f out: styd on wl: decisively* **10/3**[2]

21-1 **2** *2* **Feelin Foxy**[8] 29 7-9-6 **84** 6ex.................... FrannyNorton 1 89
(James Given) *led fr ins draw: drvn and hdd 1f out: one pce* **3/1**[1]

00-3 **3** *1 ½* **Absa Lutte (IRE)**[8] 29 8-8-0 **71** oh1....................(t) JosephYoung(7) 2 71
(Michael Mullineaux) *trckd ldrs on inner: disp 2nd and cl enough over 1f out: nt qckn* **9/2**[3]

610- **4** *2 ½* **Ray Of Joy**[13] 8016 5-9-7 **85**.................... FergusSweeney 11 76+
(J R Jenkins) *dwlt: off the pce disputing 6th: shkn up and no ch whn nt clr run over 1f out and swtchd rt: styd on same pce fnl f* **25/1**

4/2- **5** *shd* **Soopacal (IRE)**[16] 7984 6-8-11 **75**.................... JamieSpencer 8 66
(Michael Herrington) *dwlt: off the pce disputing 6th: sme prog over 1f out: nvr threatened: one pce fnl f* **13/2**

00-0 **6** *6* **Nickel Silver**[11] 2 6-9-6 **84**....................(v) TomEaves 6 53
(Bryan Smart) *chsd ldr to wl over 1f out: wknd rapidly* **15/2**

106- **7** *hd* **Pose (IRE)**[13] 8017 4-8-11 **75**.................... MartinLane 3 43
(Roger Ingram) *sn rdn in last and wl bhd: nvr a factor* **50/1**

120- **8** *1 ½* **Earlsmedic**[39] 7697 6-8-13 **82**....................(e) RyanClark(5) 7 45
(Stuart Williams) *pressed ldrs: wd bnd 2f out and wknd rapidly* **9/1**

033- **9** *1 ½* **Grudge**[14] 7998 6-8-9 **73**....................(be) HayleyTurner 9 31
(Conor Dore) *chsng ldrs whn rn v wd bnd over 3f out: rn wd again bnd 2f out: wl bhd after* **10/1**

10-0 **10** *9* **Mo Mhuirnin (IRE)**[11] 2 5-9-0 **85**.................... LauraBarry(7) 5 10
(Richard Fahey) *missed s bdly and lost several l: t.k.h: rn wd bnds over 3f out and 2f out: t.o* **33/1**

59.43 secs (-1.07) **Going Correction** 0.0s/f (Stan) 10 Ran SP% **119.2**
Speed ratings (Par 105): **108,104,102,98,98 88,88,85,83,69**
toteswingers:1&2:£3.70, 1&3:£2.70, 2&3:£5.00 CSF £13.93 CT £45.86 TOTE £6.30: £1.20, £1.20, £1.80; EX 15.90.
Owner James & Sarah **Bred** Pat Grogan **Trained** Newmarket, Suffolk

FOCUS
Quite a decent handicap run at a good clip and one in which the form horses came to the fore. High draws dominated but the form is rated on the positive side and the winner is progressive.
Soopacal(IRE) Official explanation: jockey said gelding hung left
Grudge Official explanation: vet said gelding lost right-fore shoe

126 MOBILE BETTING - VISIT WILLIAMHILL.COM MEDIAN AUCTION MAIDEN STKS 6f (P)
5:45 (5:45) (Class 6) 3-5-Y-O **£1,[illegible]** ([illegible]) **Stalls** Low

Form RPR

044- **1** **Greenhead High**[13] 8020 3-8-12 62.................... J-PGuillambert 6 66
(Jane Chapple-Hyam) *chsd ldng pair: drvn and no imp 2f out: grad clsd over 1f out: styd on to ld last strides* **11/2**

0- **2** *nk* **Sailing North (USA)**[33] 7811 3-8-12 0.................... LukeMorris 5 65
(Ronald Harris) *pressed ldr: rdn to ld 2f out: drvn fnl f: hdd last strides* **8/1**

3 *2* **Sofias Number One (USA)** 3-8-12 0.................... JamieSpencer 9 59+
(Michael Wigham) *dwlt: hld up in 8th: pushed along and prog over 2f out: reminders over 1f out: nursed into 3rd nr fin* **10/1**

005- **4** ¾ **Rambo Will**[13] 8011 3-8-12 63.................... FergusSweeney 3 57
(J R Jenkins) *t.k.h: led to 2f out: grad wknd fnl f* **5/2**[1]

234- **5** ½ **Buddy Miracle**[14] 8002 3-8-7 68.................... HayleyTurner 7 50
(Andrew Balding) *stdd s: hld up in 5th: shkn up and fnd nil 2f out: one pce after* **7/2**[2]

6 *1 ¼* **Striking Eyes** 3-8-7 0.................... RichardKingscote 8 46+
(Roger Charlton) *dwlt: rn green in 6th: no prog 2f out: kpt on ins fnl f* **9/2**[3]

000- **7** *1* **Lady Ellice**[117] 6161 3-8-7 52.................... CathyGannon 4 43
(Phil McEntee) *chsd ldng trio: effrt on inner 2f out: clsd 1f out: wknd qckly last 150yds* **66/1**

63- **8** *2* **Litotes**[12] 8030 3-8-2 0.................... JemmaMarshall(5) 1 36
(Michael Attwater) *a in last trio: no prog 2f out and wl btn after* **16/1**

9 *6* **Speed Awareness** 3-8-12 0.................... LiamKeniry 2 22
(Mark Usher) *sn rdn in detached last: a bhd* **33/1**

1m 13.25s (0.15) **Going Correction** 0.0s/f (Stan) 9 Ran SP% **114.9**
Speed ratings (Par 101): **99,98,95,94,94 92,91,88,80**
toteswingers:1&2:£6.30, 1&3:£4.00, 2&3:£7.90 CSF £48.47 TOTE £3.90: £1.10, £5.90, £4.00; EX 47.80.
Owner Charles Castle **Bred** Wyck Hall Stud Ltd **Trained** Dalham, Suffolk

FOCUS
A weak maiden and not form to be getting carried away with. The form is rated around the winner. The pace looked fair.
Sofias Number One(USA) ◆ Official explanation: jockey said gelding was denied a clear run

127 DOWNLOAD FREE THE RACING POST IPHONE APP! CLAIMING STKS 1m 4f (P)
6:15 (6:15) (Class 6) 4-Y-0+ **£1,535** (£453; £226) **Stalls** Centre

Form RPR

/50- **1** **Muzo (USA)**[34] 7778 5-9-7 65.................... FrannyNorton 4 72
(Chris Dwyer) *led at stdy pce: kicked on 3f out: drvn and narrowly hdd over 1f out: kpt on wl to ld again ins fnl f* **7/2**[3]

14-2 **2** *nk* **Camps Bay (USA)**[9] 24 7-9-11 76.................... HayleyTurner 3 76
(Conor Dore) *trckd ldr: cajoled along to chal 2f out: narrow ld over 1f out: hanging rt after: hdd and outbattled ins fnl f* **10/11**[1]

055- **3** *5* **Home**[15] 7995 6-9-1 52.................... FergusSweeney 2 58
(Brendan Powell) *trckd ldng pair: cl enough on inner wl over 1f out: sn outpcd: fdd fnl f* **25/1**

102- **4** *2* **Talenti (IRE)**[12] 8032 8-9-1 69....................(t) AdamKirby 1 55
(David Flood) *hld up in last pair: outpcd over 2f out: nvr on terms after* **11/4**[2]

046/ **5** *10* **Crazy Colours**[716] 295 5-9-1 60.................... SamHitchcott 5 39
(Zoe Davison) *hld up in last pair: rdn over 2f out: sn wknd* **20/1**

2m 36.72s (2.22) **Going Correction** 0.0s/f (Stan) 5 Ran SP% **109.9**
Speed ratings (Par 101): **92,91,88,87,80**
CSF £7.14 TOTE £5.80: £1.70, £1.40; EX 11.60.Talenti was claimed by Charlie Longsdon for £5,000.
Owner Mrs Shelley Dwyer **Bred** Stonestreet Thoroughbred Holdings LLC **Trained** Burrough Green, Cambs

FOCUS
An uncompetitive claimer run at a steady pace, and muddling form.

128 RACING AT SKYSPORTS.COM FILLIES' H'CAP 7f (P)
6:45 (6:45) (Class 5) (0-70,70) 4-Y-0+ **£2,047** (£604; £302) **Stalls** Low

Form RPR

01- **1** **But Beautiful (IRE)**[35] 7757 4-8-12 **59**.................... JimCrowley 1 66+
(Robert Mills) *hld up in 5th: shkn up over 2f out: swtchd out wd over 1f out and looked in trble: r.o wl fnl f to ld last strides* **5/4**[1]

20-4 **2** *nk* **Bold Ring**[4] 98 5-8-11 **58**.................... JimmyQuinn 10 64
(Edward Creighton) *trckd ldng trio: prog to go 2nd over 1f out: rdn to ld jst ins fnl f and sn over a l clr: collared last strides* **10/1**

420- **3** *1* **Piquante**[27] 7889 5-9-7 **68**....................(v[1]) HayleyTurner 7 71
(Nigel Tinkler) *hld up in 6th: rdn on outer over 2f out: no prog tl styd on wl fr over 1f out: tk 3rd wl ins fnl f: unable to chal* **11/2**[3]

000- **4** *1 ¾* **Poppy Golightly**[12] 8034 4-8-8 **55**.................... RichardKingscote 4 54
(Ron Hodges) *trckd ldng pair: pushed along over 2f out: nt qckn over 1f out: one pce after* **33/1**

00-6 **5** *nk* **Kai Mook**[7] 55 4-9-4 **65**....................(t) FergusSweeney 2 63
(Amy Weaver) *led: rdn 2f out: hdd & wknd jst ins fnl f* **40/1**

6 *1* **Fedora (IRE)**[93] 6821 5-8-13 **65**....................(t) KylieManser(5) 6 60
(Olivia Maylam) *t.k.h: hld up in last trio: pushed along 2f out: styd on nr fin: nvr nrr* **33/1**

04-1 **7** *nse* **Amary (IRE)**[9] 19 4-9-9 **70** 6ex....................(p) JamieSpencer 3 65
(John Harris) *chsd ldr to over 1f out: wknd* **9/2**[2]

005- **8** *1 ½* **Spinning Bailiwick**[12] 8033 5-9-4 **65**.................... GeorgeBaker 9 56
(Gary Moore) *stdd s: dropped in fr wd draw and hld up last: pushed along 2f out: no real prog* **8/1**

100- **9** *1 ¼* **Sunrise Lyric (IRE)**[15] 7991 4-9-1 **62**....................(b[1]) ChrisCatlin 5 50
(Paul Cole) *stdd s: t.k.h: hld up in last trio: effrt on inner 2f out: no prog over 1f out: fdd* **33/1**

1m 25.94s (-0.06) **Going Correction** 0.0s/f (Stan) 9 Ran SP% **109.5**
Speed ratings (Par 100): **100,99,98,96,96 95,94,93,91**
toteswingers:1&2:£3.40, 1&3:£2.90, 2&3:£5.50 CSF £13.18 CT £45.75 TOTE £3.40: £1.50, £1.10, £3.40; EX 12.00.
Owner B Ecclestone, J Humphreys, T G Mills **Bred** Gerrardstown House Stud **Trained** Headley, Surrey

FOCUS
A modest fillies' handicap run at a decent gallop that went the way of the least exposed runner in the field. There is more to come from the winner.

129 SKYSPORTS.COM RACING H'CAP 7f (P)
7:15 (7:15) (Class 7) (0-50,50) 4-Y-0+ **£1,535** (£453; £226) **Stalls** Low

Form RPR

50-4 **1** **Transfixed (IRE)**[6] 70 4-8-10 **50**.................... RPWalsh(7) 5 55
(David Evans) *led: drvn and narrowly hdd over 1f out: kpt on wl fnl f to ld again last stride* **6/1**[2]

000- **2** *shd* **Kenswick**[27] 7885 4-8-10 **48**.................... TobyAtkinson(5) 3 53
(Pat Eddery) *trckd ldrs: prog on inner to go 2nd over 2f out: drvn into narrow ld over 1f out: hdd last stride* **14/1**

433- **3** *nse* **A Pocketful Of Rye (IRE)**[13] 8023 4-8-7 **47**.................... LeonnaMayor(7) 1 52+
(Jane Chapple-Hyam) *trckd ldrs: prog 2f out: wnt 3rd fnl f: pushed along and clsd nr fin* **10/1**

630- **4** *1* **Custard Cream Kid (IRE)**[16] 7986 5-9-2 **49**.................... TomEaves 7 51
(Richard Fahey) *trckd ldrs: effrt over 2f out: tried to cl over 1f out: kpt on same pce fnl f* **13/2**[3]

42-5 **5** ½ **Norcroft**[10] 14 9-8-12 **48**....................(p) KierenFox(3) 10 49
(Christine Dunnett) *hld up towards rr: looking for room over 2f out: prog sn after: nt clr run briefly over 1f out: styd on ins fnl f: nrst fin* **15/2**

550- **6** *1 ¼* **Flying Cherry (IRE)**[28] 7872 4-9-3 **50**.................... IanMongan 2 48
(Jo Crowley) *chsd wnr to over 2f out: nt qckn u.str.p: grad fdd* **11/1**

200- **7** *hd* **Queenie's Star (IRE)**[32] 7829 4-9-3 **50**.................... RobbieFitzpatrick 4 47
(Michael Attwater) *hld up towards rr: prog on inner over 2f out: tried to cl on ldrs over 1f out: no ex after* **8/1**

050- **8** ¾ **Quahadi (IRE)**[35] 7757 5-8-12 **45**....................(t) LiamKeniry 12 40
(Chris Gordon) *sltly awkward s: hld up in last trio: sme prog over 2f out: shkn up and one pce over 1f out* **66/1**

000- **9** *4 ½* **Crystallize**[49] 7555 5-9-0 **47**.................... FergusSweeney 8 30
(Andrew Haynes) *pressed ldng pair to wl over 2f out: sn lost pl and btn* **12/1**

566- **10** *2* **Novillero**[27] 7885 4-9-1 **48**.................... SamHitchcott 14 26
(Jimmy Fox) *racd wd in midfield: rdn fr 1/2-way: lost pl and struggling over 2f out: sn no ch* **9/1**

302- **11** *2* **Jonny Ebeneezer**[27] 7885 12-9-3 **50**....................(be) JamesDoyle 9 22
(David Flood) *chsd ldrs on outer to 1/2-way: sn dropped to rr and struggling* **16/1**

30-0 **12** *1* **Takitwo**[7] 45 8-9-1 **48**....................(v) ChrisCatlin 11 17
(Peter Cundell) *a wl in rr: pushed along bef 1/2-way: sn struggling* **33/1**

56-3 **13** *2 ¾* **Guildenstern (IRE)**[6] 70 9-9-3 **50**.................... RobertWinston 13 12
(Jane Chapple-Hyam) *sn last: struggling bef 1/2-way: no prog* **4/1**[1]

1m 26.78s (0.78) **Going Correction** 0.0s/f (Stan) 13 Ran SP% **122.6**
Speed ratings (Par 97): **95,94,94,93,93 91,91,90,85,83 80,79,76**
toteswingers:1&2:£35.40, 1&3:£33.40, 2&3:£38.70 CSF £89.83 CT £600.36 TOTE £9.00: £2.90, £7.30, £3.70; EX 108.20.
Owner Mrs I M Folkes **Bred** Rathasker Stud **Trained** Pandy, Monmouths
■ The first winner in Britain for R P Walsh, to go with three in Ireland.
■ Stewards' Enquiry : R P Walsh two-day ban: used whip with excessive frequency without giving filly time to respond (Jan 26-27)

FOCUS
Very little recent winning form on show in a low-grade finale contested mostly by exposed performers and perhaps no surprise there was little between the first three at the line. The form is rated on the negative side. The pace was just fair.
T/Plt: £44.80 to a £1 stake. Pool:£67,191.85 - 1,094.35 winning tickets T/Qpdt: £12.80 to a £1 stake. Pool:£7,769.82 - 448.50 winning tickets JN

[94]LINGFIELD (L-H)
Wednesday, January 12

OFFICIAL GOING: Standard
Wind: fresh, behind Weather: overcast

130 PLACE ONLY BETTING AT BLUESQ.COM (S) STKS 6f (P)
12:40 (12:47) (Class 6) 3-Y-O £1,535 (£453; £226) Stalls Low

Form RPR
2-23 **1** **Fifth In Line (IRE)**[6] 66 3-8-7 69 FergusSweeney 8 56
(Jamie Osborne) *mde all: rdn wl over 1f out: kpt on wl and a holding rivals fnl f: rdn out* **10/11**[1]
305- **2** *1 1/4* **Ajaafa**[49] 7552 3-8-12 57 (p) RobbieFitzpatrick 9 57
(Michael Attwater) *dwlt: sn rdn along and outpcd in rr: hdwy jst over 2f out: swtchd rt wl over 1f out: kpt on wl fnl f: wnt 2nd towards fin: nt rch wnr* **16/1**
03-2 **3** *1/2* **Honkers Bonkers**[10] 10 3-8-12 65 (p) JamesDoyle 2 55
(Alan McCabe) *chsd ldrs: wnt 2nd 4f out: rdn to press wnr jst over 2f out: drvn and unable qck over 1f out: one pce and a hld fnl f: lost 2nd towards fin* **15/8**[2]
000- **4** *3/4* **Kitty Fisher**[53] 7520 3-8-7 28 HayleyTurner 5 48
(Ron Hodges) *racd in midfield: rdn over 3f out: outpcd by ldng pair over 2f out: wnt 3rd over 1f out: kpt on fnl f but nvr gng pce to rch ldrs* **100/1**
500- **5** *3* **Sapphire Girl**[16] 7983 3-8-9 55 ow2 TomEaves 3 40
(Richard Fahey) *in tch in midfield: rdn and outpcd by ldng pair over 2f out: no imp u.p over 1f out: wknd fnl 100yds* **12/1**
060- **6** *nk* **Bluberry**[12] 8031 3-8-7 53 LukeMorris 7 37
(Gary Moore) *sn rdn along and outpcd towards rr: hung lft over 1f out: styd on ins fnl f: nvr trbld ldrs* **9/1**[3]
7 *3* **Broughtons Fawn** 3-8-7 0 JamieMackay 1 28
(Willie Musson) *v.s.a: outpcd in rr: n.d* **25/1**
040- **8** *9* **Speed Gene (IRE)**[72] 7271 3-8-0 48 (v[1]) KirstenSmith(7) 6 —
(Martin Bosley) *s.i.s: a towards rr: lost tch 2f out* **50/1**
00- **9** *3* **Lady Titticaca**[72] 7269 3-8-7 0 RichardKingscote 4 —
(Ron Hodges) *chsd ldr tl 4f out: chsd ldng pair after tl wknd qckly wl over 1f out* **100/1**

1m 12.64s (0.74) **Going Correction** +0.075s/f (Slow) 9 Ran SP% **118.5**
Speed ratings (Par 95): **98,96,95,94,90 90,86,74,70**
toteswingers:1&2:£3.50, 1&3:£1.20, 2&3:£3.70 CSF £19.11 TOTE £2.00: £1.02, £2.10, £1.70; EX 11.00 Trifecta £30.00 Pool: £548.39 - 13.52 winning units..The winner was bought in for 5,200gns.
Owner Pennick, Durkan, Hearn **Bred** Me Surrender Syndicate **Trained** Upper Lambourn, Berks

FOCUS
An uncompetitive contest run in a slow time. The winner and third set a fair standard for the grade but the form may not be too solid.

131 LINGFIELD PARK MARRIOTT HOTEL & COUNTRY CLUB H'CAP 2m (P)
1:15 (1:20) (Class 5) (0-75,75) 4-Y-O+ £2,047 (£604; £302) Stalls Low

Form RPR
001- **1** **Coda Agency**[21] 7967 8-10-0 68 JimCrowley 4 74
(David Arbuthnot) *chsd ldr tl led ent fnl 3f: rdn jst over 2f out: hld on wl fnl f* **11/4**[3]
512- **2** *1/2* **Pittodrie Star (IRE)**[28] 7876 4-10-0 75 LiamKeniry 6 80
(Andrew Balding) *stdd after s: hld up in tch in last: clsd to trck rivals over 2f out: rdn and effrt between horses jst over 1f out: hung lft and chsd wnr jst ins fnl f: kpt on but a hld* **9/4**[2]
5/3- **3** *1/2* **Kahfre**[21] 7967 4-9-7 68 (be) GeorgeBaker 5 72
(Gary Moore) *chsd ldng pair: shkn up 5f out: clsd and pressed ldrs on outer 4f out: sn rdn: nt qckn u.p jst over 2f out: no imp and hung lft over 1f out: plugged on reluctantly ins fnl f* **11/8**[1]
600- **4** *2 3/4* **Frameit (IRE)**[21] 7967 4-8-6 53 (v) FrannyNorton 1 54
(James Given) *led tl hdd ent fnl 3f: styd pressing ldrs u.p tl wknd ins fnl f* **12/1**

3m 29.18s (3.48) **Going Correction** +0.075s/f (Slow)
WFA 4 from 6yo+ 7lb 4 Ran SP% **107.2**
Speed ratings (Par 103): **94,93,93,92**
CSF £8.98 TOTE £3.60; EX 7.70.
Owner Banfield, Thompson **Bred** Baydon House Stud **Trained** Compton, Berks
■ Stewards' Enquiry : Liam Keniry one-day ban: careless riding (Jan 26)

FOCUS
Two non-runners made this appear a tactical affair and it came as no surprise to see them race in single file during the early stages. The pace was slow and it is hard to rate the form positively.

132 MARSH GREEN MEDIAN AUCTION MAIDEN STKS 5f (P)
1:50 (1:56) (Class 6) 3-5-Y-O £1,535 (£453; £226) Stalls High

Form RPR
04-2 **1** **Mandy's Hero**[8] 28 3-8-10 66 JamieSpencer 7 67
(Ian Williams) *mde all: pushed clr and edgd rt wl over 1f out: kpt on fnl f: pushed out* **8/15**[1]
00-2 **2** *2* **Pineapple Pete (IRE)**[4] 100 3-8-10 55 (t) ChrisCatlin 6 59
(Paul Cole) *a chsng wnr: rdn ent fnl 2f: styd on same pce fr over 1f out* **15/2**[3]
356- **3** *4* **Kassaab**[14] 7999 3-8-10 63 LukeMorris 5 45
(Jeremy Gask) *chsd ldng pair: rdn and outpcd jst over 2f out: 3rd and wl hld ent fnl f* **8/1**
56- **4** *1 3/4* **Spring Leap**[21] 7960 4-9-11 0 HayleyTurner 2 45
(Robert Cowell) *dwlt: sn outpcd in last trio: no ch w ldrs fnl 2f: kpt on u.p to go modest 4th ins fnl f* **33/1**
060- **5** *1/2* **Ariel Bender**[21] 7973 4-9-11 42 (b) RobbieFitzpatrick 1 43
(Peter Grayson) *sn rdn along and outpcd in last trio: no imp u.p fr over 1f out: n.d* **100/1**
5/2- **6** *1/2* **Mosa Mine**[21] 7960 4-9-6 58 MichaelStainton 3 36
(Jane Chapple-Hyam) *chsd ldrs: rdn wl over 2f out: sn outpcd: wl btn over 1f out* **9/2**[2]
0- **7** *6* **Pharoh Jake**[14] 7999 3-8-7 0 KierenFox(3) 4 14
(John Bridger) *v.s.a: sn rdn along in rr: hdwy into midfield on outer 1/2-way: rn wd and lost pl bnd 2f out: wl bhd after* **100/1**

58.46 secs (-0.34) **Going Correction** +0.075s/f (Slow)
WFA 3 from 4yo 15lb 7 Ran SP% **111.2**
Speed ratings (Par 101): **105,101,95,92,91 91,81**
toteswingers:1&2:£2.10, 1&3:£2.00, 2&3:£2.70 CSF £4.95 TOTE £1.60: £1.10, £3.10; EX 5.40.
Owner Dr Marwan Koukash **Bred** Miss R J Dobson **Trained** Portway, Worcs

FOCUS
This maiden took very little winning and the market pointed strongly towards a victory for Mandy's Hero, who had looked the one to beat on form and didn't need to match his recent best.
Mosa Mine Official explanation: jockey said filly never travelled
Pharoh Jake Official explanation: jockey said gelding was slowly away and hung right

133 FOREST ROW H'CAP 5f (P)
2:25 (2:30) (Class 5) (0-75,73) 4-Y-O+ £2,047 (£604; £302) Stalls High

Form RPR
604- **1** **Garstang**[14] 8005 8-9-4 70 (b) LukeMorris 1 77
(John Balding) *dwlt: sn rcvrd and hld up in midfield: rdn and effrt over 1f out: drvn and hdwy ent fnl f: chal and hung rt ins fnl f: kpt on wl to ld fnl 50yds* **9/2**[3]
012- **2** *1/2* **Picansort**[14] 8004 4-9-2 68 (v) JimmyQuinn 7 73
(Brett Johnson) *chsd ldrs on outer: chsd ldr wl over 1f out: rdn and ev ch ent fnl f: led ins fnl f tl hdd and no ex fnl 50yds* **7/2**[2]
11-2 **3** *nk* **Estonia**[5] 80 4-8-7 59 CathyGannon 5 63+
(Michael Squance) *taken down early: stdd after s: hld up in tch: c wd wl over 1f out: hdwy u.p ent fnl f: r.o wl: nt quite rch ldrs* **5/4**[1]
266- **4** *hd* **Efistorm**[14] 8005 10-9-4 70 HayleyTurner 2 73
(Conor Dore) *stdd after s: hld up in last: effrt on inner over 1f out: edgd rt u.p ent fnl f: ev ch ins fnl f: no ex and btn towards fin* **8/1**
661- **5** *1 1/2* **Brandywell Boy (IRE)**[35] 7764 8-9-4 70 JamesDoyle 6 68
(Dominic Ffrench Davis) *in tch in midfield: rdn and unable qck ent fnl 2f: kpt on ins fnl f: nt pce to chal ldrs* **9/1**
565- **6** *1 1/2* **Step It Up (IRE)**[121] 6018 7-8-5 64 (p) NathanAlison(7) 8 56
(Jim Boyle) *t.k.h: chsd ldr tl led 1/2-way: rdn and hrd pressed ent fnl f: hdd ins fnl f: wknd fnl 100yds* **25/1**
100- **7** *2 1/4* **La Capriosa**[29] 7866 5-9-7 73 IanMongan 3 57
(David Nicholls) *in tch in midfield: lost pl and n.m.r ent fnl 2f: wl hld ent fnl f* **11/1**
500- **8** *3 3/4* **Six Diamonds**[47] 7571 4-8-13 68 RobertLButler(3) 4 39
(Paddy Butler) *sn led: hdd 1/2-way: wkng whn sltly hmpd ent fnl f: wl btn after* **40/1**

58.45 secs (-0.35) **Going Correction** +0.075s/f (Slow) 8 Ran SP% **120.6**
Speed ratings (Par 103): **105,104,103,103,101 98,95,89**
toteswingers:1&2:£2.70, 1&3:£2.50, 2&3:£1.20 CSF £21.93 CT £31.76 TOTE £5.00: £1.30, £1.60, £1.10; EX 17.70 Trifecta £39.60 Pool: £671.25 - 12.52 winning units..
Owner The Foulrice Twenty **Bred** Mrs S E Barclay **Trained** Scrooby, Notts

FOCUS
The early pace looked sound, and it produced a tight finish. The form is rated around the winner.
Picansort Official explanation: jockey said gelding suffered interference at start
Estonia Official explanation: jockey said filly hung right

134 EXCLUSIVE LIVE SHOWS AT BLUESQ.COM H'CAP 6f (P)
3:00 (3:05) (Class 5) (0-75,75) 4-Y-O+ £2,047 (£604; £302) Stalls Low

Form RPR
006- **1** **Waabel**[12] 8033 4-9-4 72 GeorgeBaker 6 78
(Jim Best) *pushed along after s: led after 1f: mde rest: rdn wl over 1f out: kpt on wl u.p fnl f* **7/1**
031- **2** *1/2* **Hinton Admiral**[36] 7737 7-9-6 74 MichaelStainton 2 79
(Jane Chapple-Hyam) *dwlt and pushed along early: t.k.h after 1f and hld up in tch: rdn 2f out: kpt on u.p ins fnl f to snatch 2nd on line: nt quite rch wnr* **5/1**[2]
161- **3** *nse* **Clear Praise (USA)**[14] 8004 4-9-7 75 HayleyTurner 4 79+
(Simon Dow) *taken down early: in tch in midfield: rdn jst over 2f out: no hdwy and drvn jst over 1f out: hrd drvn and hdwy ins fnl f: snatched 3rd on line: nt quite rch wnr* **5/4**[1]
013- **4** *nse* **Incomparable**[14] 8005 6-9-3 71 (bt) IanMongan 1 75
(David Nicholls) *led for 1f: chsd wnr after: rdn and effrt 2f out: ev ch fnl f: unable qck fnl 100yds: lost 2 pls last stride* **6/1**[3]
004- **5** *1/2* **Gwilym (GER)**[53] 7526 8-8-13 67 CathyGannon 7 70
(Derek Haydn Jones) *in tch in rr: rdn along over 3f out: hdwy towards inner ent fnl 2f: kpt on u.p ins fnl f: nt rch ldrs* **33/1**
644- **6** *1/2* **Starwatch**[13] 8014 4-8-12 66 NeilChalmers 5 67
(John Bridger) *in tch: rdn 3f out: lost pl and dropped to rr ent fnl 2f: rallied u.p ins fnl f: kpt on but nt pce to rch ldrs* **20/1**
400- **7** *1/2* **Ivory Silk**[14] 8004 6-9-0 73 (v) TobyAtkinson(5) 3 72
(Jeremy Gask) *stdd s: bhd: no hdwy u.p over 2f out: kpt on ins fnl f: nvr trbld ldrs* **12/1**
5-42 **8** *nk* **Elhamri**[5] 84 7-9-4 72 RobertWinston 8 70
(Conor Dore) *in tch towards rr: rdn and effrt jst over 2f out: kpt on ins fnl f: nvr able to chal* **15/2**

1m 11.34s (-0.56) **Going Correction** +0.075s/f (Slow) 8 Ran SP% **115.1**
Speed ratings (Par 103): **106,105,105,105,104 103,103,102**
toteswingers:1&2:£6.20, 1&3:£3.40, 2&3:£2.50 CSF £42.00 CT £72.69 TOTE £10.00: £2.50, £1.10, £1.40; EX 55.30 Trifecta £147.10 Pool: £765.39 - 3.85 winning units..
Owner M&R Refurbishments Ltd **Bred** Shadwell Estate Company Limited **Trained** Lewes, E Sussex

FOCUS
Considering the horse beaten into last was less than 2 1/2 lengths behind the winner, this probably isn't reliable form. The winner is rated back to his early-season maiden form.
Incomparable ◆ Official explanation: jockey said gelding suffered interference in running
Starwatch Official explanation: jockey said gelding suffered interference in running

135 LINGFIELDPARK.CO.UK H'CAP 1m (P)
3:35 (3:35) (Class 6) (0-60,60) 4-Y-O+ £1,535 (£453; £226) Stalls High

Form RPR
06-2 **1** **Shared Moment (IRE)**[5] 78 5-9-1 54 (v) ChrisCatlin 11 64
(John Gallagher) *s.i.s: hdwy into midfield after 2f out: rdn and effrt to chse ldrs ent fnl f: drvn to ld fnl 100yds: hld on cl home* **9/2**[2]
005- **2** *hd* **Shaded Edge**[15] 7992 7-9-3 56 LiamKeniry 10 65
(David Arbuthnot) *stdd after s: hld up in tch towards rr: rdn and effrt on outer over 1f out: r.o u.p to press wnr wl ins fnl f: hld hd high and nt qckn cl home* **17/2**
34-4 **3** *2* **Goodbye Cash (IRE)**[5] 78 7-9-0 56 AndrewHeffernan(3) 1 61
(Ralph Smith) *sn pushed up to ld: clr over 4f out: rdn ent fnl 2f: hrd pressed ent fnl f: hdd fnl 100yds: sn outpcd by ldng pair: kpt on for 3rd* **16/1**

00-5 **4** *1* **Very Well Red**[11] 7 8-8-10 **49** CathyGannon 7 51
(Peter Hiatt) *led: sn hdd and chsd ldr after: rdn and effrt over 2f out: kpt pressing wnr tl one pce and btn fnl 100yds* **7/1**[3]
040- **5** *nk* **Sadeek**[320] 715 7-9-7 **60** GeorgeBaker 5 62
(Martin Bosley) *in tch: effrt on inner and rdn to chse ldrs jst over 1f out: wknd fnl 100yds* **20/1**
430- **6** *3/4* **Rainsborough**[38] 7717 4-9-3 **56** (e[1]) FergusSweeney 3 56
(Peter Hedger) *in tch: rdn and effrt wl over 1f out: plugged on same pce ins fnl f* **20/1**
63-3 **7** *1/2* **Haveahaarth (IRE)**[2] 112 4-9-2 **60** (p) TobyAtkinson[(5)] 6 59
(Michael Quinlan) *t.k.h: hld up in tch: rdn and unable qck wl over 1f out: styd on same pce and no real imp fnl f* **14/1**
250- **8** *1 1/4* **Fly By Nelly**[15] 7995 5-9-0 **53** JimCrowley 8 49
(Mark Hoad) *racd in last trio: hdwy on inner ent fnl 2f: no hdwy ent fnl f: wknd ins fnl f* **7/1**[3]
02-0 **9** *1/2* **Vezere (USA)**[8] 30 4-9-7 **60** HayleyTurner 9 55
(Simon Dow) *hld up in tch towards rr: rdn and effrt bnd ent fnl 2f: nvr gng pce to trble ldrs* **16/1**
023- **10** *nk* **All Moving Parts (USA)**[32] 7829 4-9-4 **57** (b) JamesDoyle 12 51
(Alan McCabe) *in tch: rdn and nt qckn over 1f out: btn ent fnl f: wknd after* **2/1**[1]
000- **11** *1/2* **Safwaan**[15] 7992 4-9-1 **54** StevieDonohoe 4 47
(Willie Musson) *stdd s: a in rr: n.d* **8/1**
050- **12** *2 3/4* **Cavalry Guard (USA)**[13] 8023 7-8-4 **46** oh1 (b) AmyBaker[(3)] 2 33
(Tim McCarthy) *a in rr: n.d* **66/1**

1m 38.26s (0.06) **Going Correction** +0.075s/f (Slow) 12 Ran SP% **127.6**
Speed ratings (Par 101): **102,101,99,98,98 97,97,96,95,95 94,91**
toteswingers:1&2:£8.80, 1&3:£5.60, 2&3:£19.00 CSF £45.34 CT £595.57 TOTE £5.50: £1.90, £6.80, £5.00; EX 41.20 Trifecta £215.20 Part won. Pool: £290.92 - 0.72 winning units..
Owner Mark Benton **Bred** Mrs E R Cantillon **Trained** Chastleton, Oxon

FOCUS
A modest handicap but the form is straightforward.
Safwaan Official explanation: jockey said gelding moved poorly

136 PLAY FREE BINGO AT BLUESQ.COM MAIDEN STKS 1m 2f (P)
4:05 (4:05) (Class 5) 4-Y-0+ **£1,910** (£564; £282) **Stalls** Low

Form RPR
/35- **1** **Super Collider**[209] 3116 4-9-3 80 JackMitchell 2 68+
(Michael Jarvis) *mde all: shkn and wnt clr over 1f out: pushed out and in command fnl f* **1/4**[1]
23-4 **2** *5* **Bull Five**[11] 1 4-9-3 68 GeorgeBaker 3 58
(Nick Littmoden) *t.k.h early: chsd ldng pair: wnt 2nd over 2f out: rdn and outpcd by wnr over 1f out: wl hld fnl f* **7/2**[2]
3 *1/2* **Olimamu (IRE)** 4-8-12 0 (t) MickyFenton 4 52
(Jeff Pearce) *t.k.h early: hld up in tch: rdn ent fnl 2f: no ch w wnr but pressing for 2nd whn rn green ins fnl f: kpt on* **14/1**[3]
4/ **4** *6* **Perle D'Amour (IRE)**[591] 2514 4-8-12 0 LiamKeniry 6 40
(Martin Bosley) *t.k.h: chsd ldr 9f out tl over 2f out: wknd 2f out: wl btn fnl f* **33/1**
6/0- **5** *1 3/4* **Cullybackey (IRE)**[32] 7835 6-9-0 42 RobbieFitzpatrick 1 36
(John Harris) *t.k.h early: rdn and struggling jst over 2f out: wl btn over 1f out* **66/1**

2m 12.85s (6.25) **Going Correction** +0.075s/f (Slow)
WFA 4 from 6yo 2lb 5 Ran SP% **113.3**
Speed ratings (Par 103): **78,74,73,68,67**
totesuper7: Win: Not won. Place: CSF £1.62 TOTE £1.10: £1.02, £2.10; EX 1.60.
Owner B E Nielsen **Bred** Newsells Park Stud **Trained** Newmarket, Suffolk

FOCUS
Barring an act of God, this looked a simple task for Super Collider, who set a stiff task for his rivals to match. The form is rated loosely around the runner-up but is far from solid.
T/Plt: £18.50 to a £1 stake. Pool:£60,480.54 - 2,381.99 winning tickets T/Qpdt: £4.10 to a £1 stake. Pool:£4,758.18 - 839.90 winning tickets SP

123 KEMPTON (A.W) (R-H)
Thursday, January 13

OFFICIAL GOING: Standard
Wind: Virtually nil Weather: cold

137 GREAT SALE OFFERS DAILY AT WILLIAMHILL.COM CLAIMING STKS 6f (P)
4:20 (4:20) (Class 6) 4-Y-0+ **£1,535** (£453; £226) **Stalls** Low

Form RPR
45-3 **1** **Vhujon (IRE)**[8] 45 6-8-8 76 MatthewCosham[(7)] 1 75
(David Evans) *hld up in 4th: hdwy into 3rd over 3f out: disp 2nd over 2f: drvn and qcknd on inner to ld 1f out: styd on wl* **1/1**[1]
456- **2** *1 1/2* **Matsunosuke**[17] 7984 9-9-9 97 LukeMorris 5 78
(Ronald Harris) *t.k.h: trckd ldr: disp 2nd and drvn over 2f out: styd on fnl f to chse wnr fnl 120yds: no imp* **13/8**[2]
060- **3** *1 1/2* **Athwaab**[91] 6858 4-8-8 65 ChrisCatlin 4 58?
(Michael Quinlan) *led: rdn 2f out: hdd 1f out: styd on same pce and lost 2nd fnl 120yds* **4/1**[3]
/00- **4** *11* **Doctor's Cave**[136] 5586 9-8-7 51 (e[1]) SamHitchcott 3 22
(Ken Cunningham-Brown) *racd in 3rd tl over 3f out: sn btn* **50/1**

1m 12.81s (-0.29) **Going Correction** -0.05s/f (Stan) 4 Ran SP% **110.1**
Speed ratings (Par 101): **99,97,95,80**
CSF £2.99 TOTE £2.10; EX 3.00.Matsunosoke was claimed by Dr R D P Newland for £12,000. Vhujon was claimed by E Grayson for £8,000.
Owner Nick Shutts **Bred** Robert Berns **Trained** Pandy, Monmouths

FOCUS
Straightforward enough claiming form.

138 WILLIAMHILL.COM - BEST ODDS ON KEMPTON FAVOURITES H'CAP 6f (P)
4:50 (4:50) (Class 7) (0-50,50) 4-Y-0+ **£1,535** (£453; £226) **Stalls** Low

Form RPR
606- **1** **Replicator**[22] 7972 6-9-3 **50** (e) JamieMackay 6 59
(Patrick Gilligan) *mde all: rdn 2f out: edgd lft u.p ins fnl f: hld on all out* **4/1**[1]
50-4 **2** *nk* **Black Baccara**[1] 123 4-9-1 **48** (be) AdamKirby 1 56
(Phil McEntee) *chsd ldrs: wnt 2nd u.p 1f out: edgd lft and styd on u.p ins fnl f: a jst hld* **8/1**[3]
040- **3** *1* **Final Rhapsody**[14] 8024 5-9-3 **50** (v[1]) StevieDonohoe 7 55
(Willie Musson) *hld up in rr: rdn and hdwy over 1f out: styd on wl and edgd rt ins fnl f: tk 3rd fnl 120yds: one pce nr fin* **4/1**[1]

550- **4** *1* **Metropolitan Chief**[13] 8035 7-9-1 **48** LiamKeniry 5 50
(Paul Burgoyne) *stdd s and hmpd sn after: drvn and hdwy fr 2f out: styd on ins fnl f: one pce fnl 120yds* **20/1**
0/0- **5** *3/4* **My Best Man**[34] 7810 5-8-12 **48** KierenFox[(3)] 3 47
(Tony Carroll) *chsd ldrs: wnt 2nd and rdn over 2f out: one pce ins fnl f* **25/1**
000- **6** *1 1/4* **Vertumnus**[22] 7972 4-8-10 **48** (be) RyanClark[(5)] 10 43
(Nick Littmoden) *chsd ldr: rdn: hd high and lost 2nd over 2f out: hung lft and btn ins fnl f* **10/1**
00-0 **7** *2* **Tyrannosaurus Rex (IRE)**[1] 123 7-9-2 **49** (v) JoeFanning 9 38
(Derek Shaw) *hmpd after s: in rr: rdn over 2f out: hung rt sn after and sme hdwy over 1f out: sn no imp* **8/1**[3]
405- **8** *1 3/4* **Song Of Praise**[14] 8024 5-9-1 **48** FrannyNorton 4 31
(Michael Blanshard) *in tch: shkn up and no prog fnl 2f* **9/2**[2]
606- **9** *1 1/2* **Woodsley House (IRE)**[29] 7882 9-9-2 **49** (p) NickyMackay 2 27
(Mark Rimmer) *in rr: styd alone far side and sme hdwy fr 2f out but nvr rchd ldrs* **12/1**
646- **10** *nk* **Ever Cheerful**[71] 7299 10-8-10 **50** (p) AaronChave[(7)] 11 27
(Andrew Haynes) *s.i.s: hmpd after s: racd on outside and bhd most of way* **33/1**
52-5 **11** *3/4* **Jemimaville (IRE)**[1] 123 4-9-2 **49** (v) LukeMorris 12 24
(Giles Bravery) *chsd ldrs over 4f* **9/1**

1m 12.73s (-0.37) **Going Correction** -0.05s/f (Stan) 11 Ran SP% **118.7**
Speed ratings (Par 97): **100,99,98,96,95 94,91,89,87,86 85**
toteswingers:1&2 £10.80, 2&3 £8.80, 1&3 £6.80 CSF £35.74 CT £140.77 TOTE £5.90: £2.10, £4.10, £1.10; EX 50.40.
Owner Linton Doolan **Bred** R And Mrs Heathcote **Trained** Newmarket, Suffolk
■ Stewards' Enquiry : Luke Morris two-day ban: careless riding (Jan 27-28)

FOCUS
A bottom-drawer handicap which was more like a classified event with the field being covered by just 2lb.

139 TOP GREYHOUND OFFERS TODAY AT WILLIAMHILL.COM H'CAP 7f (P)
5:20 (5:20) (Class 5) (0-70,70) 4-Y-0+ **£2,047** (£604; £302) **Stalls** Low

Form RPR
003- **1** **Fivefold (USA)**[16] 7992 4-9-2 **65** (p) J-PGuillambert 1 74
(John Akehurst) *trckd ldr: drvn and slt ld ins fnl 2f: hdd over 1f out: rallied u.str.p ins fnl f: responded gamely to ld again last strides* **9/2**[3]
5/4- **2** *hd* **Kenton Street**[40] 7709 6-8-13 **62** SeamieHeffernan 7 70
(Michael J Browne, Ire) *trckd ldrs: chal ins fnl 2f: drvn to ld over 1f out: styd on: hdd and no ex last strides* **9/1**
420- **3** *2* **Collect Art (IRE)**[50] 7561 4-9-0 **63** StevieDonohoe 8 66+
(Andrew Haynes) *t.k.h: towards rr: in tch: hdwy 2f out: sn drvn: kpt on ins fnl f to take 3rd cl home but no imp on ldng duo* **13/2**
03-5 **4** *1/2* **Pytheas (USA)**[8] 55 4-9-7 **70** (p) JoeFanning 4 71
(Michael Attwater) *led tl hdd ins fnl 2f: outpcd by ldng duo ins fnl f and lost 3rd cl home* **13/2**
600- **5** *4 1/2* **Peadar Miguel**[14] 8014 4-9-3 **66** AdamKirby 3 55
(Michael Quinlan) *in tch: rdn over 2f out: sn btn* **11/4**[1]
3-20 **6** *shd* **Musical Script (USA)**[5] 96 8-8-8 **57** (b) ChrisCatlin 5 46
(Mouse Hamilton-Fairley) *in rr: drvn and hdwy 1/2-way: nvr quite rchd ldrs: wknd fr 2f out* **4/1**[2]
420- **7** *1/2* **Pha Mai Blue**[136] 5593 6-8-12 **61** NickyMackay 2 48
(Jim Boyle) *in rr: a outpcd* **7/1**

1m 25.65s (-0.35) **Going Correction** -0.05s/f (Stan) 7 Ran SP% **114.0**
Speed ratings (Par 103): **100,99,97,96,91 91,91**
toteswingers:1&2 £4.40, 2&3 £7.30, 1&3 £6.20 CSF £42.73 CT £260.77 TOTE £5.90: £2.80, £9.40; EX 25.10.
Owner A D Spence **Bred** Calming Syndicate **Trained** Epsom, Surrey
■ Stewards' Enquiry : Seamie Heffernan five-day ban: used whip with excessive frequency without giving gelding time to respond (Jan 27-31)

FOCUS
A moderate handicap with an open look about it. There was a routine pace on and a cracking finish between the first pair.
Pha Mai Blue Official explanation: jockey said gelding hung left on bend

140 MOBILE BETTING - VISIT WILLIAMHILL.COM H'CAP 7f (P)
5:50 (5:50) (Class 5) (0-75,75) 3-Y-O **£2,047** (£604; £302) **Stalls** Low

Form RPR
533- **1** **Odin (IRE)**[57] 7478 3-9-6 **74** RobertWinston 6 79
(David Elsworth) *in tch: rdn: hung rt and lost position over 2f out: rallied: hrd drvn and hdwy over 1f out: hung rt ins fnl f and led fnl 120yds: kpt on wl* **5/2**[1]
051- **2** *1* **Amazon Twilight**[40] 7691 3-9-3 **71** AdamKirby 7 73
(Brett Johnson) *hld up in rr: stdy hdwy over 2f out: led over 1f out: rdn: hdd and one pce fnl 120yds* **11/2**[3]
00-1 **3** *1/2* **City Legend**[3] 109 3-8-12 **66** 6ex (bt) JamesDoyle 1 67
(Alan McCabe) *sn chsng ldr: led 2f out: hdd over 1f out: outpcd by ldng duo fnl 120yds* **9/2**[2]
542- **4** *1 1/4* **Captain Dimitrios**[14] 8012 3-9-0 **75** MatthewCosham[(7)] 5 73
(David Evans) *chsd ldrs: drvn to chal over 1f out: wknd ins fnl f* **13/2**
656- **5** *1 1/4* **Reachtothestars (USA)**[17] 7982 3-8-11 **65** JackMitchell 4 59
(Michael Quinlan) *stdd s: in rr: drvn and styd on fr over 1f out: nvr gng pce to get into contention* **20/1**
013- **6** *7* **Pippa's Gift**[14] 8020 3-9-4 **72** HayleyTurner 2 47
(William Muir) *sn led: rdn and hdd 2f out: wknd qckly appr fnl f* **6/1**
031- **7** *6* **May's Boy**[50] 7552 3-9-3 **71** (p) FergusSweeney 3 30
(Mark Usher) *s.i.s: hdwy and in tch over 2f out: sn rdn: wknd wl over 1f out* **9/2**[2]

1m 25.85s (-0.15) **Going Correction** -0.05s/f (Stan) 7 Ran SP% **112.7**
Speed ratings (Par 97): **98,96,96,94,93 85,78**
toteswingers:1&2 £4.00, 2&3 £3.20, 1&3 £4.60 CSF £16.06 TOTE £3.00: £1.10, £3.70; EX 13.80.
Owner J C Smith **Bred** Littleton Stud **Trained** Newmarket, Suffolk

FOCUS
Not a bad 3-y-o handicap for the class.
Amazon Twilight ◆ Official explanation: jockey said filly hung badly right

141 DOWNLOAD FREE RACING POST IPHONE APP! H'CAP 1m (P)
6:20 (6:20) (Class 4) (0-85,85) 4-Y-0+ **£3,885** (£1,156; £577; £288) **Stalls** Low

Form RPR
615- **1** **Zebrano**[37] 7735 5-9-4 **82** (b) JamesDoyle 3 91
(Andrew Haynes) *trckd ldr: drvn along 2f out: styd on wl to ld fnl 100yds: sn in command: won gng away* **3/1**[2]

650- **2** ¾ **Good Again**[112] 6312 5-9-7 **85** ShaneKelly 8 92
(Gerard Butler) *stdd towards rr: in tch: gd hdwy ins fnl 2f: drvn to take narrow ld jst ins fnl f: hdd and outpcd fnl 100yds* **6/1**

000- **3** 1 ¾ **Big Bay (USA)**[37] 7735 5-9-3 **81** SeamieHeffernan 5 84
(Jane Chapple-Hyam) *s.i.s: sn trcking ldrs: drvn to chal ins fnl 2f and stl upsides ins fnl f: outpcd fnl 100yds* **20/1**

663- **4** *hd* **Tuxedo**[14] 8017 6-8-8 **72** (b) LukeMorris 7 75
(Peter Hiatt) *trckd ldr: t.k.h off modest pce: drvn to chal over 2f out and stl upsides u.p 1f out: wknd fnl 100yds* **8/1**

043- **5** ¾ **Qalahari (IRE)**[54] 7521 5-9-0 **78** AdamKirby 1 79
(Michael Quinlan) *hld up in rr but in tch: drvn and hdwy fr 2f out to chse ldrs 1f out: nvr quite on level terms: wknd fnl 120yds* **9/2**[3]

000- **6** ¾ **Pegasus Again (USA)**[14] 8022 6-9-5 **83** JimCrowley 4 82
(Robert Mills) *set modest pce: drvn and qcknd ins fnl 3f: strly chal fr over 2f out: kpt slt advantage tl hdd & wknd jst ins fnl f* **9/1**

464- **7** ½ **Dubai Miracle (USA)**[103] 6556 4-9-6 **84** MartinLane 2 82
(David Simcock) *s.i.s: in rr: drvn and hdwy over 2f out: sn chsng ldrs: nvr on terms: wknd ins fnl f* **11/4**[1]

100- **8** *8* **Global Village (IRE)**[14] 8017 6-8-11 **80** RyanClark(5) 6 60
(Michael Blake) *in rr: drvn and effrt on outside 3f out: nvr rchd ldrs: sn wknd* **16/1**

1m 39.68s (-0.12) **Going Correction** -0.05s/f (Stan) 8 Ran SP% **115.9**
Speed ratings (Par 105): **98,97,95,95,94 93,93,85**
toteswingers:1&2 £5.50, 2&3 £9.80, 1&3 £17.60 CSF £21.72 CT £306.37 TOTE £3.80: £1.40, £3.60, £3.00; EX 23.80.
Owner Caloona Racing **Bred** P R Attwater **Trained** Limpley Stoke, Bath

FOCUS
A fair handicap, run at an average pace.

142 DOWNLOAD WILLIAM HILL SHAKE-A-BET APP H'CAP 1m (P)
6:50 (6:52) (Class 6) (0-60,60) 3-Y-O £1,535 (£453; £226) **Stalls Low**

Form RPR

050- **1** **Appyjack**[28] 7888 3-8-7 **46** oh1 (t) LukeMorris 6 56
(Tony Carroll) *in tch: pushed along: hung rt and lost pl ins fnl 3f: rdn and str run appr fnl f: led fnl 150yds: gng away whn hung rt again sn after* **20/1**

22-3 **2** 2 ¾ **Mrs Neat (IRE)**[10] 25 3-9-2 **55** (b) JamesDoyle 8 59
(Sylvester Kirk) *s.i.s: in rr: hdwy on ins over 2f out: str run to ld appr fnl f: hdd and outpcd fnl 150yds* **7/2**[2]

644- **3** *4* **Moorland Boy**[13] 8031 3-9-5 **58** FergusSweeney 9 52
(Jamie Osborne) *chsd ldrs: rdn and one pce fr 2f out: styd on again to take 3rd ins fnl f but no ch w ldng duo* **13/2**[3]

62-0 **4** *1* **Three Scoops**[3] 109 3-9-0 **53** (t) HayleyTurner 14 45
(Dominic Ffrench Davis) *chsd ldrs: led over 4f out: rdn over 2f out: hdd appr fnl f: sn btn* **10/1**

06-3 **5** 1 ½ **Titan Diamond (IRE)**[8] 53 3-8-2 **46** oh1 RyanPowell(5) 10 35
(Mark Usher) *chsd ldrs: rdn ins fnl 3f: one pce fnl 2f* **20/1**

504- **6** 1 ¼ **Lovat Lane**[40] 7691 3-8-11 **50** CathyGannon 4 36
(Eve Johnson Houghton) *in rr: rdn and hdwy on outside 3f out: styd on same pce fnl 2f* **16/1**

405- **7** 2 ¾ **High Kickin**[34] 7801 3-9-1 **54** (v) ShaneKelly 3 34
(Alan McCabe) *towards rr: rdn: hung rt and no prog over 2f out* **8/1**

05-4 **8** 4 ½ **Bathwick Freeze**[8] 53 3-8-5 **51** RPWalsh(7) 1 20
(David Evans) *a towards rr* **16/1**

00-4 **9** *9* **Miss Moneypenni**[11] 10 3-9-6 **59** JimCrowley 11 7
(Nick Littmoden) *led tl hdd over 4f out: wknd over 2f out* **40/1**

403- **10** *17* **King Cobra (IRE)**[56] 7496 3-9-2 **55** (v) ChrisCatlin 2 —
(J W Hills) *in rr but in tch: hdwy on ins over 4f out: nt clr run on ins fnl 3f: sn wknd* **8/1**

0-1 **P** **Double Duchess**[12] 5 3-9-7 **60** LiamJones 7 —
(Paul D'Arcy) *s.i.s: sddle slipped sn after: rdn lost irons and p.u 3f out* **13/8**[1]

1m 40.45s (0.65) **Going Correction** -0.05s/f (Stan) 11 Ran SP% **128.7**
Speed ratings (Par 95): **94,91,87,86,84 83,80,76,67,50** —
toteswingers:1&2 £25.30, 2&3 £4.30, 1&3 £37.20 CSF £95.42 CT £538.13 TOTE £6.50: £1.70, £1.50, £3.20; EX 184.20.
Owner Mayden Stud **Bred** Mayden Stud, J A And D S Dewhurst **Trained** Cropthorne, Worcs

FOCUS
A weak 3-y-o handicap, run at a fair pace.
Appyjack Official explanation: trainer said, regarding apparent improvement in form, that the colt seemed to be a slow maturing type who is now coming to hand.
Double Duchess Official explanation: jockey said he hit his leg on stalls causing him to lose an iron.

143 GREAT SALE OFFERS DAILY AT WILLIAMHILL.COM H'CAP 6f (P)
7:20 (7:22) (Class 6) (0-65,65) 4-Y-O+ £1,535 (£453; £226) **Stalls Low**

Form RPR

6/0- **1** **Under Review (IRE)**[39] 7746 5-9-0 **58** (t) SeamieHeffernan 6 67
(Michael J Browne, Ire) *mde all: pushed along ins fnl f: styd on strly fnl 100yds* **10/1**

53-6 **2** *1* **Dvinsky (USA)**[5] 98 10-9-5 **63** (b) RobertWinston 3 69
(Jane Chapple-Hyam) *chsd ldrs: wnt 2nd ins fnl 3f: drvn and styd on to hold that position thrght fnl f: a readily hld by wnr* **7/1**[3]

013- **3** *nk* **Super Frank (IRE)**[14] 8019 8-9-7 **65** (b) IanMongan 10 70
(John Akehurst) *chsd ldrs: drvn to dispute 2nd fr over 1f out: no imp on wnr ins fnl f: dropped to 3rd cl home* **8/1**

000- **4** 2 ¼ **Mogok Ruby**[61] 7441 7-9-2 **60** AdamKirby 5 58
(Brett Johnson) *in tch: rdn and styd on fnl 2f: no imp on ldrs ins fnl f* **12/1**

03-3 **5** *nk* **Norville (IRE)**[5] 97 4-8-12 **63** (b) RPWalsh(7) 7 60
(David Evans) *chsd wnr tl ins fnl 3f: outpcd appr fnl f* **3/1**[1]

010- **6** 1 ¼ **Pragmatist**[44] 7640 7-9-0 **58** JamesMillman 2 51
(Rod Millman) *towards rr: hdwy over 2f out: no imp on ldrs ins fnl f* **12/1**

50-0 **7** *1* **Lord Of The Reins (IRE)**[9] 29 7-9-7 **65** JimCrowley 8 55
(James Given) *in rr: sme prog fr over 1f out: nvr in contention* **10/1**

00-0 **8** 1 ¼ **White Shift (IRE)**[5] 97 5-9-4 **62** MichaelStainton 1 48
(Jane Chapple-Hyam) *in rr: sme prog fr over 1f out* **11/1**

4/1- **9** *4* **Prize Point**[36] 7763 5-9-4 **65** MatthewDavies(3) 9 38
(Jim Boyle) *bhd fr 1/2-way* **6/1**[2]

106- **10** 1 ½ **Nollaig Shona (IRE)**[43] 7655 4-9-4 **62** CathyGannon 11 30
(George Prodromou) *chsd ldrs tl wknd over 2f out* **16/1**

61-0 **11** 1 ¼ **Mary's Pet**[5] 98 4-9-4 **62** J-PGuillambert 4 26
(John Akehurst) *a in rr* **16/1**

1m 12.02s (-1.08) **Going Correction** -0.05s/f (Stan) 11 Ran SP% **116.6**
Speed ratings (Par 101): **105,103,103,100,99 98,96,95,89,87 86**
toteswingers:1&2 £15.70, 2&3 £10.70, 1&3 £11.80 CSF £77.63 CT £605.22 TOTE £13.60: £3.90, £3.10, £2.50; EX 76.70.
Owner Michael J Browne **Bred** James Drynan & Tom Wallace **Trained** Cashel, Co. Tipperary

FOCUS
A tiht handicap, run at a sound pace.
T/Plt: £158.50 to a £1 stake. Pool of £55,047.01 - 253.40 winning tickets. T/Qpdt: £46.70 to a £1 stake. Pool of £7,607.31 - 120.50 winning tickets. ST

116 SOUTHWELL (L-H)
Thursday, January 13

OFFICIAL GOING: Standard
Wind: Moderate behind Weather: Clody, brighter periods

144 BET ON WINNING DISTANCES AT BLUESQ.COM APPRENTICE CLASSIFIED CLAIMING STKS 5f (F)
1:00 (1:00) (Class 6) 4-Y-O+ £1,535 (£453; £226) **Stalls High**

Form RPR

00- **1** **Ridley Didley (IRE)**[56] 7494 6-8-6 62 PaulPickard 6 68
(Noel Wilson) *sn led: rdn wl over 1f out: kpt on wl ins fnl f* **22/1**

316- **2** 2 ½ **Sharp Shoes**[15] 7998 4-8-11 68 (p) AmyRyan 1 64
(Ann Duffield) *prom: chsd wnr 2f out: rdn wl over 1f out: kpt on same pce ins fnl f* **3/1**[2]

21-1 **3** ½ **Residency (IRE)**[10] 15 5-8-4 57 (p) AdamCarter(5) 9 60
(Bryan Smart) *broke wl: trckd ldrs: effrt 2f out: sn rdn: drvn and no imp ent fnl f* **5/2**[1]

006- **4** 1 ¾ **Kylladdie**[15] 8004 4-8-10 70 (p) MartinLane 8 55
(Steve Gollings) *dwlt: sn chsng ldrs: rdn along 2f out: drvn and wknd appr fnl f* **11/2**

21-4 **5** 3 ½ **Kate Skate**[3] 113 4-8-9 65 KierenFox 4 41
(Gay Kelleway) *trckd ldrs: hdwy 1/2-way: rdn wl over 1f out: sn wknd* **7/2**[3]

000- **6** 2 ¼ **Areeg (IRE)**[100] 6643 4-7-13 42 VictorSantos(7) 2 30
(Alan Berry) *chsd ldrs on outer: rdn along 1/2-way: grad wknd* **100/1**

41-6 **7** *5* **Prince James**[11] 13 4-8-4 70 DavidSimmonson(7) 5 17
(Michael Easterby) *dwlt: sn rdn along in rr: outpcd after 1 1/2f and sn bhd* **13/2**

58.87 secs (-0.83) **Going Correction** -0.075s/f (Stan) 7 Ran SP% **109.8**
Speed ratings (Par 101): **103,99,98,95,89 86,78**
toteswingers:1&2 £6.50, 2&3 £1.30, 1&3 £7.40 CSF £80.33 TOTE £16.70: £9.60, £3.50; EX 66.40 Trifecta £115.40 Pool: £237.10 - 1.52 winning units..
Owner Feenan & Tobin **Bred** Peter Molony **Trained** Sandhutton, N Yorks

FOCUS
A moderate apprentice classified claimer. Early pace again proved crucial over this C&D.
Prince James Official explanation: jockey said colt did not face the kickback

145 ROBIN HOOD GB ENDURANCE RIDE SOUTHWELL MAIDEN STKS 1m 3f (F)
1:30 (1:30) (Class 5) 4-Y-O+ £1,910 (£564; £282) **Stalls Low**

Form RPR

2 **1** **Sail Home**[12] 1 4-8-12 65 JimmyQuinn 3 59+
(Julia Feilden) *trckd ldr: cl up 4f out: led 3f out: rdn and qcknd wl over 1f out: kpt on strly* **11/4**[2]

2 **2** 1 ¾ **First Rock (IRE)**[16] 5-9-6 0 GeorgeBaker 4 57
(Alan Swinbank) *trckd ldng pair: hdwy and cl up 4f out: chal 3f out: sn rdn and ev ch tl drvn: edgd lft and one pce fr over 1f out* **40/85**[1]

35-0 **3** 2 ¾ **Mojeerr**[10] 16 5-9-3 43 (e) AndrewHeffernan(3) 5 52
(Alan McCabe) *in tch: hdwy to chse ldng pair wl over 2f out: sn rdn and no imp fr over 1f out* **66/1**

44- **4** *11* **Shouda (IRE)**[33] 7834 5-9-6 0 JoeFanning 2 32
(Barney Curley) *led: rdn along 4f out: hdd 3f out and sn wknd* **14/1**[3]

64-6 **5** *37* **Jingoism (USA)**[7] 61 5-9-6 49 TomEaves 1 —
(Brian Ellison) *in tch: reminders after 3f: rdn along 1/2-way: sn outpcd and bhd* **28/1**

2m 27.59s (-0.41) **Going Correction** +0.025s/f (Slow)
WFA 4 from 5yo 3lb 5 Ran SP% **106.3**
Speed ratings (Par 103): **102,100,98,90,63**
CSF £4.08 TOTE £3.10: £1.30, £1.02; EX 6.10.
Owner Miss J Feilden **Bred** Juddmonte Farms Ltd **Trained** Exning, Suffolk

FOCUS
Despite the proximity of the 43-rated Mojeerr, the front pair in this uncompetitive maiden should still be kept on the right side.

146 GOLF AND RACING AT SOUTHWELL H'CAP 5f (F)
2:00 (2:00) (Class 6) (0-60,60) 3-Y-O £1,535 (£453; £226) **Stalls High**

Form RPR

00-0 **1** **Mini Bon Bon**[9] 41 3-8-11 **50** (v) LiamJones 7 56
(Alan Bailey) *mde all: rdn clr over 1f out: drvn ins fnl f: jst hld on* **20/1**

35-0 **2** *hd* **Bigalo's Vera B**[7] 60 3-8-7 **46** oh1 DuranFentiman 2 51
(Lawrence Mullaney) *trckd ldrs: hdwy 2f out: sn rdn: drvn ent fnl f: styd on wl towards fin: jst hld* **7/1**

065- **3** 2 ¾ **Quadra Hop (IRE)**[73] 7268 3-9-6 **59** CathyGannon 1 54
(Bryn Palling) *prom: chsd wnr over 2f out: rdn wl over 1f out: one pce ent fnl f* **4/1**[2]

610- **4** ½ **Winning Draw (IRE)**[17] 7982 3-9-4 **60** (p) PaulPickard(3) 3 53
(Paul Midgley) *prom: rdn along and outpcd 1/2-way: kpt on u.p ins fnl f* **13/2**

064- **5** *shd* **Bobbyow**[71] 7301 3-9-7 **60** GeorgeBaker 5 53
(Bryn Palling) *in rr and reminders after 1f: rdn along 1/2-way: sme late hdwy* **7/4**[1]

020- **6** *nk* **Gunalt Joy**[62] 7423 3-8-13 **55** JamesSullivan(3) 4 47
(Michael Easterby) *chsd ldrs on outer: rdn along 2f out: sn drvn and grad wknd* **10/1**

604- **7** 3 ¾ **Shutupandrive**[35] 7777 3-8-7 **46** oh1 (v) JimmyQuinn 6 24
(Mark Usher) *prom: rdn along 1/2-way: sn wknd* **11/2**[3]

000- **8** 2 ½ **Zohan (IRE)**[48] 7577 3-8-7 **46** oh1 (b) KirstyMilczarek 8 15
(Peter Grayson) *sn outpcd and a in rr: bhd fr 1/2-way* **100/1**

60.19 secs (0.49) **Going Correction** -0.075s/f (Stan) 8 Ran SP% **112.4**
Speed ratings (Par 95): **93,92,88,87,87 86,80,76**
toteswingers:1&2 £2.10, 2&3 £14.30, 1&3 not won. CSF £146.31 CT £686.91 TOTE £26.80: £5.00, £2.90, £1.10; EX 123.80 TRIFECTA Not won..
Owner A Bailey **Bred** P Balding & W Clifford **Trained** Newmarket, Suffolk

FOCUS
A modest 3-y-o handicap in which the winning time was 1.32 seconds slower than the opening claimer for older horses.

Bobbyow Official explanation: jockey said colt was slowly away

147 BOOK TICKETS ON LINE AT SOUTHWELL-RACECOURSE.CO.UK (S) STKS 7f (F)
2:30 (2:30) (Class 6) 3-Y-O **£1,535** (£453; £226) **Stalls** Low

Form RPR
61-2 **1** **So Is She (IRE)**[7] 59 3-8-13 70 (be[1]) CathyGannon 3 63+
(Alan Bailey) *mde all: clr 2f out: unchal* **1/10**[1]
00-5 **2** *9* **Evelyns Diamond**[12] 5 3-8-4 38 PaulPickard(3) 1 34
(Paul Midgley) *chsd wnr: rdn along 3f out: sn rdn and one pce: hld on for 2nd towards fin* **10/1**[2]
0- **3** *nk* **Ivy And Gold**[121] 6045 3-8-12 0 PatrickMathers 2 38
(Alan Berry) *chsd ldng pair: pushed along to dispute 2nd pl 3f out: sn rdn and one pce* **20/1**[3]
1m 32.73s (2.43) **Going Correction** +0.025s/f (Slow) **3** Ran SP% **104.8**
Speed ratings (Par 95): **87,76,76**
CSF £1.52 TOTE £1.10; EX 1.70.There was no bid for the winner.
Owner Allan McNamee **Bred** Bayview Properties Ltd **Trained** Newmarket, Suffolk
FOCUS
An extremely uncompetitive seller.

148 10% FORECAST BONUS AT BLUESQ.COM H'CAP 1m (F)
3:00 (3:00) (Class 5) (0-70,74) 4-Y-O+ **£1,878** (£558; £279; £139) **Stalls** Low

Form RPR
32-2 **1** **The Lock Master (IRE)**[11] 9 4-9-5 **66** NeilChalmers 7 79
(Michael Appleby) *trckd ldrs: hdwy on outer 1/2-way: rdn to ld wl over 1f out: clr ent fnl f: kpt on* **4/1**[3]
12-4 **2** *2 3/4* **Exopuntia**[10] 19 5-8-9 **56** GregFairley 6 63
(Julia Feilden) *trckd ldrs: hdwy 3f out and sn cl up: ev ch 2f out: sn rdn and kpt on same pce appr fnl f* **11/2**
31-2 **3** *3 1/4* **Bentley**[7] 61 7-9-5 **66** (b) GrahamGibbons 1 65
(Brian Baugh) *in tch on inner: rdn along 1/2-way: drvn wl over 1f out: kpt on ins fnl f* **11/4**[1]
0-13 **4** *1* **Ace Of Spies (IRE)**[2] 122 6-9-13 **74** 6ex KirstyMilczarek 5 71
(Conor Dore) *cl up: led 3f out: sn rdn: drvn and hdd wl over 1f out: grad wknd* **10/1**
232- **5** *4 1/2* **Ubenkor (IRE)**[28] 7895 6-9-2 **66** BillyCray(3) 2 53
(Michael Herrington) *led: rdn along and hdd 3f out: drvn over 2f out and sn wknd* **5/1**
12-2 **6** *1* **Lakeman (IRE)**[11] 12 5-9-4 **65** (be) TomEaves 4 49
(Brian Ellison) *cl up: rdn along 3f out: sn wknd* **7/2**[2]
00- **7** *10* **French Art**[94] 6794 6-9-1 **62** PhillipMakin 3 23
(Nigel Tinkler) *chsd ldrs: rdn along 3f out: wknd over 2f out* **12/1**
1m 43.11s (-0.59) **Going Correction** +0.025s/f (Slow) **7** Ran SP% **117.7**
Speed ratings (Par 103): **103,100,97,96,91 90,80**
toteswingers:1&2 £3.30, 2&3 £1.30, 1&3 £4.70 CSF £27.17 TOTE £24.60: £4.50, £3.40; EX 28.90.
Owner K G Kitchen **Bred** Patrick F Kelly **Trained** Danethorpe, Notts
FOCUS
An ordinary handicap on paper, but six of the seven runners came into the race in decent form and the other was a market springer. Add to that a truly run race resulting from a disputed early lead and the form looks very solid.

149 DINE IN THE PANTRY H'CAP 7f (F)
3:30 (3:30) (Class 5) (0-75,87) 4-Y-O+ **£1,813** (£539; £269; £134) **Stalls** Low

Form RPR
1-11 **1** **Dubai Hills**[4] 105 5-10-0 **87** 12ex AdamCarter(5) 5 102+
(Bryan Smart) *cl up: led after 2f: qcknd clr on bit 2f out: eased towards fin: easily* **30/100**[1]
216- **2** *2* **Conry (IRE)**[51] 7539 5-9-6 **74** StephenCraine 1 79
(Patrick Morris) *trckd ldng pair: hdwy to chse wnr 2f out and sn rdn: drvn over 1f out: sn no imp* **16/1**[3]
102- **3** *14* **Striker Torres (IRE)**[27] 7915 5-9-4 **72** (v) TomEaves 3 41
(Geoffrey Oldroyd) *slt ld 2f: cl up: rdn along 3f out: drvn over 2f out and sn btn* **7/2**[2]
600- **4** *1/2* **Wigram's Turn (USA)**[17] 7088 6-9-11 **68** JamesSullivan(3) 2 36
(Michael Easterby) *in tch: rdn along 1/2-way: sn outpcd* **66/1**
1m 29.09s (-1.21) **Going Correction** +0.025s/f (Slow) **4** Ran SP% **106.5**
Speed ratings (Par 103): **107,104,88,88**
CSF £5.95 TOTE £1.40; EX 4.20.
Owner Mrs F Denniff **Bred** A S Denniff **Trained** Hambleton, N Yorks
FOCUS
An ordinary handicap, but yet another impressive performance from the winner.

150 PLAY MEGAJACKPOTS CLEOPATRA AT BLUESQ.COM H'CAP 6f (F)
4:00 (4:01) (Class 6) (0-60,62) 4-Y-O+ **£1,535** (£453; £226) **Stalls** Low

Form RPR
24-1 **1** **Sir Louis**[11] 13 4-9-2 **62** 6ex GeorgeChaloner(7) 4 74
(Richard Fahey) *t.k.h: chsd ldrs: hdwy over 3f out: led wl over 1f out: sn rdn and kpt on wl* **5/2**[2]
42-2 **2** *2 3/4* **Gold Story**[11] 14 4-8-12 **51** (be) JimmyQuinn 3 54
(Brian Ellison) *hld up: hdwy on inner to chse ldrs over 2f out and sn rdn: drvn over 1f out: kpt on ins fnl f* **2/1**[1]
0-03 **3** *shd* **Errigal Lad**[9] 35 6-9-4 **57** (p) GrahamGibbons 7 60
(John Balding) *led 2f: cl up: rdn and ev ch 2f out: drvn over 1f out and kpt on same pce* **20/1**
00-4 **4** *nk* **Charles Parnell (IRE)**[11] 13 8-9-0 **60** NoraLooby(7) 5 62
(Simon Griffiths) *dwlt: hdwy 1/2-way: chsd ldrs 2f out: sn rdn and no imp appr fnl f* **14/1**
000- **5** *7* **Ponting (IRE)**[30] 7870 5-8-12 **54** PaulPickard(3) 8 34
(Paul Midgley) *cl up: led after 2f: rdn along over 2f out: sn hdd & wknd* **15/2**
0-05 **6** *1* **Flow Chart (IRE)**[4] 107 4-8-7 **46** oh1 (b) KirstyMilczarek 2 22
(Peter Grayson) *chsd ldrs: rdn along 1/2-way: sn wknd* **50/1**
/0-4 **7** *3/4* **Archilini**[7] 57 6-8-7 **46** oh1 GregFairley 9 20
(Matt Sheppard) *in tch on outer: pushed along 1/2-way: sn rdn and wknd* **13/2**
401- **8** *1 1/2* **Final Salute**[58] 7473 5-9-1 **59** (v) AdamCarter(5) 1 28
(Bryan Smart) *chsd ldrs on inner: rdn along 1/2-way: sn wknd* **11/2**[3]
1m 16.57s (0.07) **Going Correction** +0.025s/f (Slow) **8** Ran SP% **115.8**
Speed ratings (Par 101): **100,96,96,95,86 85,84,82**
toteswingers:1&2 £1.02, 2&3 £5.70, 1&3 £3.50 CSF £8.04 CT £77.27 TOTE £3.00: £1.10, £1.10, £11.00; EX 9.90 Trifecta £93.90 Pool: £544.82 - 4.29 winning units..
Owner P Ashton **Bred** Brigadier C K Price **Trained** Musley Bank, N Yorks
FOCUS
They went a good pace in this moderate sprint handicap and the front four pulled well clear. A clear personal best from the winner and the form could be rated a little higher.

Flow Chart(IRE) Official explanation: jockey said gelding hung right
T/Plt: £69.10 to a £1 stake. Pool of £44,121.79 - 465.82 winning tickets. T/Qpdt: £30.60 to a £1 stake. Pool of £3,284.64 - 79.30 winning tickets. JR

[71]MEYDAN (L-H)
Thursday, January 13

OFFICIAL GOING: Tapeta: standard; turf: good
Rail out 4m on Turf course.

151a UAE 1000 GUINEAS TRIAL SPONSORED BY LONGINES (CONDITIONS RACE) (TAPETA) 7f
3:15 (3:15) 3-Y-O
£19,230 (£6,410; £3,205; £1,602; £961; £641)

RPR
1 **Reem (AUS)**[117] 4-9-4 104 PatCosgrave 6 92
(M F De Kock, South Africa) *sn led: kicked clr 2f out: r.o wl* **14/1**
2 *1/2* **Mahbooba (AUS)**[194] 4-9-11 105 ChristopheSoumillon 10 98+
(M F De Kock, South Africa) *mid-div: chsd ldrs 2 1/2f out: r.o wl* **11/4**[1]
3 *3/4* **Abtasaamah (USA)**[89] 6927 3-8-8 85 FrankieDettori 3 87
(Saeed Bin Suroor) *trckd ldrs: ev ch 2f out: one pce fnl 110yds* **7/1**[3]
4 *1 3/4* **Chocolicious (SAF)**[229] 4-9-4 106 RyanMoore 5 84
(H J Brown, South Africa) *settled in rr: r.o fnl 2f but nvr able to chal* **11/4**[1]
5 *3 1/4* **Empire Rose (ARG)**[215] 4-9-4 99 (b) KShea 7 76
(M F De Kock, South Africa) *trckd ldrs: rdn 2 1/2f out: wknd fnl f* **10/1**
6 *1/2* **Quick Val (ARG)**[104] 4-8-11 97 HarryBentley(7) 9 74
(H J Brown, South Africa) *settled in rr: nvr able to chal* **14/1**
7 *1* **Crying Lightening (IRE)**[145] 5322 3-8-8 104 KierenFallon 8 69
(Peter Chapple-Hyam) *trckd ldrs: one pce fnl 1 1/2f* **11/2**[2]
8 *2 3/4* **Najoum (USA)**[124] 5961 3-8-8 86 TedDurcan 1 62
(Saeed Bin Suroor) *broke awkwardly: nvr able to chal* **9/1**
9 *1 1/4* **Energia Cintilante (BRZ)**[61] 4-9-4 88 (t) BReis 4 61
(E Martins, Brazil) *nvr bttr than mid-div* **40/1**
10 *1 1/2* **Artic Rose (IRE)**[14] 8025 3-8-8 87 ErhanYavuz 2 55
(R Bouresly, Kuwait) *in rr of mid-div: rdn 3 1/2f out: sn btn* **50/1**
1m 24.43s (-0.77) **Going Correction** +0.20s/f (Slow)
WFA 3 from 4yo 18lb **10** Ran SP% **118.0**
Speed ratings: **112,111,110,108,104 104,103,100,98,96**
CSF £53.20..
Owner Sheikh Mohammed Bin Khalifa Al Maktoum **Bred** Sheikh Mohammed Bin Khalifa Al Maktoum **Trained** South Africa
FOCUS
Last year this went to Mike De Kock's Raihana, who subsequently underperformed in the UAE 1000 Guineas, but won the Oaks and finished runner-up in the Derby. It again went to the De Kock stable courtesy of the apparent third-string, who set no more than an ordinary gallop. Still, this looks like good form for the division.
NOTEBOOK
Reem(AUS), ex-Australian, defied a 117-day absence on her UAE debut and is clearly smart. There may be more to come as she goes up in trip, but could struggle to confirm form in future with Mahbooba. (op 12-1)
Mahbooba(AUS) ◆, a Grade 1 winner in South Africa, is held in extremely high regard, but had to concede weight all round, was racing over a trip shorter than ideal, and her trainer was concerned the surface might not suit. Still, she easily fared best of those held up, appearing to handle the Tapeta okay. She won't be burdened with a penalty in the Guineas on February 3, when the extra furlong will suit, and there's better to come.
Abtasaamah(USA), a half-sister to Breeders' Cup Juvenile winner (on synthetics) Midshipman, was suited by the surface, but she was too keen early and consequently failed to see her race out. It's unlikely she'll have as much stamina as Mahbooba, and consequently it's difficult to see how she can finish ahead of that rival in the Guineas and Oaks.
Chocolicious(SAF) defeated Mahbooba when 55-1 winner of a 6f Grade 1 in South Africa last May, and was ready for this assignment according to her trainer, so negative hold-up tactics were a surprise, especially as she broke well. In fairness, she was never going that strongly before making only limited progress in the straight, and maybe the surface didn't suit. (tchd 5-2)
Empire Rose(ARG) had every chance but finished her race weakly. (op 9-1)
Crying Lightening(IRE) had been off the track since beaten at odds on in French Group 3 last August and only recently arrived in Dubai, so might have needed this, but even so, it was a run without encouragement.
Najoum(USA) lost ground at the start, and although recovering into mid-division, never featured.

152a DOLCE VITA (H'CAP) (TURF) 7f
3:55 (3:55) (100-110,110) 3-Y-O+
£46,153 (£15,384; £7,692; £3,846; £2,307; £1,538)

RPR
1 **Dandy Boy (ITY)**[120] 6089 5-9-0 106 CO'Donoghue 11 112+
(David Marnane, Ire) *mid-div: chsd ldrs 2 1/2f out: led 1f out: comf* **10/1**
2 *1 3/4* **Hujaylea (IRE)**[89] 6942 8-8-10 102 (p) ShaneFoley 16 103
(M Halford, Ire) *settled in last: r.o wl fnl 2 1/2f: nrest at fin* **10/1**
3 *3/4* **Clearly Silver (SAF)**[159] 5-8-9 101 ChristopheSoumillon 13 100
(M F De Kock, South Africa) *mid-div: chsd ldrs 2 1/2f out: one pce fnl f* **9/1**
4 *1/2* **Escape Route (USA)**[18] 7-8-11 104 (t) RichardMullen 7 101
(S Seemar, UAE) *mid-div: chsd ldrs 2 1/2f out: nt qckn* **12/1**
5 *2 1/4* **Ashram (IRE)**[82] 7083 5-9-2 108 (v) FrankieDettori 4 100+
(Saeed Bin Suroor) *s.i.s: mid-div: r.o wl fnl 2f: nvr nrr* **4/1**[1]
6 *1 1/2* **Munaddam (USA)**[314] 818 9-9-3 109 RichardHills 3 97
(E Charpy, UAE) *chsd ldrs: one pce fnl 1 1/2f* **25/1**
7 *shd* **Sir Gerry (USA)**[89] 6923 6-9-4 110 TadhgO'Shea 14 97
(Doug Watson, UAE) *settled in rr: r.o fnl 2f: nvr nrr* **20/1**
8 *2 1/2* **Happy Dubai (IRE)**[13] 4-8-10 102 DaraghO'Donohoe 6 82
(A Al Raihe, UAE) *mid-div: chsd ldrs 2 1/2f out: wknd fnl f* **20/1**
9 *1 1/4* **McCartney (GER)**[18] 6-8-7 106 (t) HarryBentley(7) 12 83
(S Seemar, UAE) *mid-div: chsd ldrs 3f out: led briefly after 2f out to 1f out: wknd* **13/2**[2]
10 *2 1/4* **Il Grande Maurizio (IRE)**[49] 7624 7-8-9 101 (t) RoystonFfrench 5 72
(A Al Raihe, UAE) *nvr able to chal* **14/1**
11 *1 1/4* **Laa Rayb (USA)**[35] 7792 7-9-1 107 (t) KierenFallon 10 75
(D Selvaratnam, UAE) *nvr nr to chal* **12/1**
12 *nse* **Too Nice Name (FR)**[137] 5574 4-9-0 106 GregoryBenoist 15 74
(X Nakkachdji, France) *wl away: led 2f: led again 2 1/2f out to 2f out: wknd fnl 1 1/2f* **33/1**
13 *2 1/4* **Carnaby Street (IRE)**[94] 6806 4-8-10 102 AhmedAjtebi 8 63
(Mahmood Al Zarooni) *nvr bttr than mid-div* **16/1**

14 2 ½ **Warsaw (IRE)**300 6-8-13 105 (bt) KShea 9 60
(M F De Kock, South Africa) *led after 2f: hdd 2 1/2f out: wknd* **10/1**
15 1 ¾ **Hunting Tower (SAF)**13 9-9-2 108 (t) PatCosgrave 1 58
(M F De Kock, South Africa) *nvr able to chal* **20/1**
16 ¼ **Atlantic Brave**27 5-8-13 105 (vt) WayneSmith 2 54
(M Al Muhairi, UAE) *mid-div: rdn and btn 4f out* **7/1**3
1m 23.12s (83.12) **16** Ran SP% **132.1**
CSF £106.95; Tricast £966.79..
Owner Malih Lahej Al Basti **Bred** Az Ag Rz Emiliana Srl **Trained** Bansha, Co Tipperary

FOCUS
A one-two for Irish-trained runners in this decent, big-field handicap. The leaders went too fast, setting this up for those ridden with patience.

NOTEBOOK
Dandy Boy(ITY)'s trainer was quoted beforehand as saying the colt would "definitely come on for the run", but he was still able to produce a smart performance. The strong pace really suited him seeing as he was given a patient ride by Colm O'Donoghue, and he did this relatively easily. He was travelling much the best on entering the straight and found enough when weaving between horses. This was a career best off a mark of 106 and he'll now step up back up to Listed company on February 10 for the Firebreak Stakes over 1m on Tapeta, the idea being to test him on the surface ahead of a possible tile at the Godolphin Mile.
Hujaylea(IRE), progressive in his native Ireland, was dropped in from the widest draw, sitting last of all at one stage, and that worked in his favour considering the pace. He stayed on well down the outside in the straight, but was always being held by the classy winner.
Clearly Silver(SAF) usually races over shorter in South Africa but, like the first two, he was well placed considering how the race unfolded and stayed on out wide.
Escape Route(USA), 6lb higher than when winning on the Tapeta over this trip at last year's Carnival, raced closer to the pace than the front three yet was still nudged along from some way out to try and keep up, and a more patient ride might have been better.
Ashram(IRE) plugged on from off the speed without offering a great deal.
Munaddam(USA) showed enough to suggest he can still be competitive if coming on for this first run in 314 days.

153a EVIDENZA (H'CAP) (TAPETA) 1m 3f
4:30 (4:30) (95-105,105) 3-Y-O+
£42,307 (£14,102; £7,051; £3,525; £2,115; £1,410)

RPR
1 **Rock N Roll Ransom**96 6738 4-8-8 98 RyanMoore 13 100+
(Mahmood Al Zarooni) *mid-div: wd: chsd ldrs 2f out: led fnl 55yds* **4/1**1
2 ¼ **Halicarnassus (IRE)**88 6977 7-8-9 96 TadhgO'Shea 10 98
(Mick Channon) *mid-div: rdn to ld 1 1/2f out: r.o wl: hdd fnl 55yds* **7/1**3
3 ½ **Prizefighting (USA)**105 6506 4-9-1 105 FrankieDettori 6 106
(Mahmood Al Zarooni) *in rr of mid-div: r.o wl fnl 1 1/2f: nrest at fin* **8/1**
4 2 ¼ **Wonder Lawn (SAF)**14 8028 8-9-2 102 (t) KShea 8 100
(M F De Kock, South Africa) *settled in rr: r.o wl fnl 1 1/2f: nt qckn fnl 110yds* **9/2**2
5 1 **Mojave Moon**145 5291 5-8-10 97 (v) XZiani 3 92
(M bin Shafya, UAE) *sn led: rdn 3f out: hdd & wknd 1 1/2f out* **16/1**
6 ¼ **Colony (IRE)**14 8029 6-8-9 96 (b) PatCosgrave 7 91
(M bin Shafya, UAE) *slowly away: mid-div: chsd ldrs 3f out: nt qckn fnl f* **16/1**
7 1 ½ **Burdlaz (IRE)**250 1911 6-9-3 104 AhmedAjtebi 2 96
(Mahmood Al Zarooni) *trckd ldrs tl 2f out: one pce fnl f* **14/1**
8 ¼ **Meeriss (IRE)**13 6-9-2 102 (t) Christophe-PatriceLemaire 9 95
(D Selvaratnam, UAE) *trckd ldrs tl 2f out: wknd* **8/1**
9 1 ½ **Lion Sands**298 7-9-0 100 (t) CSanchez 5 90
(A bin Huzaim, UAE) *mid-div: n.m.r 6f out: n.d* **25/1**
10 ½ **Rochdale**49 7622 8-9-1 101 (t) RoystonFfrench 12 90
(A Al Raihe, UAE) *mid-div: r.o one pce fnl f* **8/1**
11 5 ¾ **Dr Faustus (IRE)**14 8029 6-8-8 95 (vt) PatDobbs 11 73
(Doug Watson, UAE) *slowly away: settled in rr: nvr able to chal* **20/1**
12 ½ **Birbone (FR)**11 6-8-10 97 RichardMullen 4 74
(S Seemar, UAE) *settled in rr: nvr nr to chal* **20/1**
13 7 ¼ **Man Of Iron (USA)**47 7594 5-9-2 102 KierenFallon 14 67
(Luca Cumani) *settled in rr: n.d* **12/1**
14 3 ¼ **Mister Fasliyev (IRE)**14 8029 9-8-8 95 (bt) WJSupple 1 53
(E Charpy, UAE) *mid-div: ev ch 2f out: wknd fnl f* **33/1**
2m 17.98s (-0.42) **Going Correction** +0.20s/f (Slow)
WFA 4 from 5yo+ 3lb **14** Ran SP% **126.4**
Speed ratings: **109,108,108,106,106 105,104,104,103,103 99,98,93,91**
CSF £31.77; Tricast £224.96..
Owner Godolphin **Bred** Meon Valley Stud **Trained** Newmarket, Suffolk

FOCUS
The pace was steady, resulting in a bunch finish and limited form.

NOTEBOOK
Rock N Roll Ransom was caught wide throughout, which was obviously far from ideal, but it was presumably a calculated decision by Ryan Moore, who didn't want to drop back in search of cover with the gallop a modest one. The tactics paid off narrowly, with the 4-y-o just denying Carnival regular Halicarnassus. The winner, bought out of the Luca Cumani yard for 240,000gns since last seen in October, can be rated better than the result and should have more to offer off a stronger gallop.
Halicarnassus(IRE), a winner on turf at the 2009 and 2010 Carnivals (off 108 and 110 respectively), was clearly on a good mark if back to form and he just failed, being nabbed near the line after looking set to hold on for much of the closing stages. (op 8-1)
Prizefighting(USA), ex-John Gosden, was a little unlucky as he made his move from slightly further back than the winner and had to be switched wide for a clear run around a furlong out.
Wonder Lawn(SAF) was hampered when already well in rear on the first bend and had far too much ground to make up. He can win a similar race. (op 5-1)
Mojave Moon was allowed to build up a clear lead without going particularly fast and is flattered.
Man Of Iron(USA) was bumped when in last place on the first bend, but in truth he was never travelling and has completely lost his way. (op 14-1)

154a PRIMA LUNA (H'CAP) (TURF) 1m 4f 38y
5:05 (5:05) (100-110,110) 3-Y-O+
£46,153 (£15,384; £7,692; £3,846; £2,307; £1,538)

RPR
1 **Wajir (FR)**104 6533 5-8-10 102 TedDurcan 12 111+
(Saeed Bin Suroor) *settled in rr: smooth prog 3 1/2f out: led 1f out: comf* **10/1**
2 4 ¾ **Equiparada (ARG)**166 5-8-9 101 ChristopheSoumillon 2 102
(M F De Kock, South Africa) *mid-div: chsd ldrs 3f out: r.o wl but no ch w wnr* **11/4**1
3 ¾ **Pompeyano (IRE)**109 6388 6-9-0 106 FrankieDettori 13 106
(Saeed Bin Suroor) *trckd ldrs: ev ch 2f out: one pce fnl f* **13/2**3
4 hd **Telluride**137 5575 5-9-1 107 (t) GregoryBenoist 8 107
(J E Hammond, France) *settled in last: r.o wl fnl 2 1/f: nrest at fin* **10/1**
5 1 ¼ **Mikhail Glinka (IRE)**14 8028 4-9-1 110 (t) RyanMoore 9 109
(H J Brown, South Africa) *mid-div: chsd ldrs 3f out: one pce fnl 1 1/2f* **8/1**
6 ¼ **Topclas (FR)**298 5-9-1 107 PatCosgrave 10 104
(M bin Shafya, UAE) *settled in rr: nvr bttr than mid-div* **25/1**
7 2 ¼ **Lawspeaker**103 6590 4-9-0 109 AhmedAjtebi 11 104
(Mahmood Al Zarooni) *settled in rr: nvr nr to chal* **10/1**
8 1 ¼ **Trois Rois (FR)**35 7793 6-8-13 105 (b) WayneSmith 3 97
(I Mohammed, UAE) *mid-div: trckd ldrs 2 1/2f out: led briefly 1 1/2f out: one pce fnl 110yds* **12/1**
9 6 ¾ **Happy Valley (ARG)**166 5-9-3 109 KShea 7 90
(M F De Kock, South Africa) *trckd ldrs tl 3 1/2f out: sn wknd* **6/1**2
10 ¾ **Monte Alto (IRE)**35 7793 7-9-0 106 (t) RichardHills 5 86
(A Al Raihe, UAE) *in rr of mid-div: n.d* **14/1**
11 1 ¼ **Claremont (IRE)**208 3191 5-9-4 110 (v) KierenFallon 4 88
(Mahmood Al Zarooni) *trckd ldrs: led 2 1/2f out to 1f out: rn wd: sn btn* **8/1**
12 21 **Re Barolo (IRE)**298 8-8-9 101 (t) JRosales 1 45
(A bin Huzaim, UAE) *nvr bttr than mid-div* **33/1**
13 1 ¼ **Moiqen (IRE)**13 6-8-8 100 TadhgO'Shea 6 42
(Doug Watson, UAE) *sn led: hdd & wknd 2 1/2f out* **50/1**
2m 30.27s (150.27)
WFA 4 from 5yo+ 4lb **13** Ran SP% **126.9**
CSF £39.43; Tricast £206.11..
Owner Godolphin **Bred** Dayton Investments Ltd **Trained** Newmarket, Suffolk

FOCUS
The early leader Moiqen went through the first 6f in sprinting fractions. The winner is getting closer to his 2009 level.

NOTEBOOK
Wajir(FR), helped by the strong pace, produced an impressive performance, quickening up in taking fashion in the straight. A dual Group-race winner for a different stable in France in 2009, he went 0-6 in Britain last year, but returned with a smart performance. He won't always get the race run to suit, but can rate higher again if he does.
Equiparada(ARG) ◆ was unable to match the winner's change of speed, but had raced closer to the gallop than that one and stayed on well after looking likely to be swamped. Mentioned as a Sheema Classic possible by Mike De Kock, Equiparada had been off for 166 days and there should be more to come, but perhaps the 2m DRC Gold Cup on March 10 will be a better target. After all, her biggest South African success came in a 1m7f Grade 2. (op 3-1)
Pompeyano(IRE), seemingly the choice of Frankie Dettori over the winner, got the decent test he needs and ran his race. (tchd 7-1)
Telluride was well placed out the back considering the pace. (op 8-1)
Mikhail Glinka(IRE) received a bump early on but still responded to pressure in the straight. He needs further, though, and the DRC Gold Cup is presumably his aim. (op 7-1)
Claremont(IRE) was much too free and hung badly right off the final bend. (tchd 15-2)

155a CONQUEST (CONDITIONS RACE) (TAPETA) 6f
5:40 (5:40) 3-Y-O+
£42,307 (£14,102; £7,051; £3,525; £2,115; £1,410)

RPR
1 **Our Giant (AUS)**292 1021 8-8-8 115 (b) ChristopheSoumillon 9 104
(M F De Kock, South Africa) *in rr of mid-div: smooth prog 2 1/2f out: r.o wl: led 110yds out* **9/2**2
2 ¾ **Inxile (IRE)**101 6640 6-8-10 105 MichaelO'Connell(4) 12 107
(David Nicholls) *sn led: rdn clr 2 1/2f out: r.o wl: hdd fnl 110yds* **16/1**
3 shd **Alo Pura**28 7904 7-8-9 104 (e) WJSupple 3 102
(D Selvaratnam, UAE) *in rr of mid-div: chsd ldrs 2f out: no room 1 1/2f out: r.o wl* **7/1**
4 1 **Bankable (IRE)**292 1025 7-9-0 116 (t) RyanMoore 6 104+
(H J Brown, South Africa) *s.i.s: settled in last: r.o wl fnl 2f: nrest at fin* **8/1**
5 1 **Invincible Ash (IRE)**83 7073 6-8-9 104 (p) FrankieDettori 5 96
(M Halford, Ire) *mid-div: r.o: one pce fnl 1 1/2f* **6/1**3
6 shd **Verde-Mar (BRZ)**123 4-8-8 105 BReis 7 94
(E Martins, Brazil) *trckd ldrs tl 1 1/2f out: wknd* **40/1**
7 hd **Atlantic Sport (USA)**123 6-8-8 105 KShea 2 94
(M F De Kock, South Africa) *nvr able to chal* **14/1**
8 shd **Dohasa (IRE)**28 7904 6-9-0 108 AhmedAjtebi 10 99
(I Mohammed, UAE) *a mid-div* **8/1**
9 1 ½ **Mutheeb (USA)**292 1024 6-9-0 112 RichardHills 4 95
(M Al Muhairi, UAE) *chsd ldrs tl 1 1/2f out: wknd* **7/2**1
10 ½ **Rock Jock (IRE)**102 6617 4-8-8 105 TedDurcan 11 87
(Tracey Collins, Ire) *mid-div: chsd ldrs 2 1/2f out: wknd fnl f* **25/1**
11 1 ½ **Force Freeze (USA)**28 7904 6-9-0 112 (t) KierenFallon 8 88
(Doug Watson, UAE) *s.i.s: nvr bttr than mid-div* **6/1**3
12 10 **Montpellier (IRE)**13 8-9-0 105 (t) RoystonFfrench 1 56
(A Al Raihe, UAE) *nvr able to chal* **33/1**
1m 10.76s (-0.24) **Going Correction** +0.25s/f (Slow) **12** Ran SP% **125.5**
Speed ratings: **111,110,109,108,107 107,106,106,104,104 102,88**
CSF £77.67..
Owner Sh Mohd Bin Khalifa Al Maktoum, A Chandler **Bred** Dr Fleming **Trained** South Africa

FOCUS
A quality conditions sprint, more like a Listed race. The pace, set by Inxile, was just fair.

NOTEBOOK
Our Giant(AUS) was seen only once last year, when well beaten in the Al Quoz Sprint on World Cup night after a far from ideal preparation, but he's a dual Grade 1 winner in South Africa and showed his class on his return to action. The surface suited this son of Giant's Causeway, and although he enjoyed a better run through than the third and fourth-placed finishers, he was probably the winner on merit, having the superior speed to take the gaps when they came. It must be remembered that he was getting 6lb from, among others, the runner-up and fourth, so it would be unwise to get carried away and he'll need to improve to win races like the Al Shindagha Sprint (February 3) and/or the Mahab Al Shimaal (Super Thursday, March 3), but he's understandably expected to come on for the run. His next start should tell us whether he's a Golden Shaheen contender. (op 4-1)
Inxile(IRE) ◆, a four-time Listed winner, did really well to stick on for second considering stall 12 has yet to produce a single winner over this C&D (now 0-15) and he'd been hassled by Verde-Mar.
Alo Pura, the current course record holder, was short of room on occasions in the straight, but the winner had picked up that bit earlier, hence that one enjoyed a better trip. She's improving.
Bankable(IRE) ◆, runner-up in the Duty Free when last seen, looked to be ridden with the future in mind on his return. Out the back after a sluggish start, he went for an ambitious run towards the inside rail in the straight, but was soon blocked and consequently didn't get a hard ride. He was going on nicely when finally in the clear late on, crossing the line with plenty left, and this was an encouraging return. The surface suited, opening up the option of the Dubai World Cup. (tchd 9-1)
Invincible Ash(IRE) came into this off the back of a 5f Listed success on Polytrack and maybe the minimum trip suits best.

Mutheeb(USA) was progressive on this surface last year but ran as though in need of the outing. (op 4-1)

156a AL MAKTOUM CHALLENGE R1 SPONSORED BY LONGINES (GROUP 3) (TAPETA) — 1m

6:15 (6:17) 3-Y-0+

£76,923 (£25,641; £12,820; £6,410; £3,846; £2,564)

RPR

1 — **Mendip (USA)**[292] [1023] 4-9-0 113 ..... FrankieDettori 1 — 117+
(Saeed Bin Suroor) *s.i.s: trckd ldng duo: led 1 1/2f out: r.o wl: easily* **1/1**[1]

2 — *2 1/4* — **Imbongi (SAF)**[13] 7-9-0 113 ..... ChristopheSoumillon 10 — 112+
(M F De Kock, South Africa) *settled in rr: r.o wl fnl 2 1/2f: no ch w wnr* **9/1**[3]

3 — *1/4* — **Win For Sure (GER)**[109] [6408] 6-9-0 110 ..... GregoryBenoist 8 — 110
(X Nakkachdji, France) *in rr of mid-div: r.o wl fnl 2f: nrst fin* **25/1**

4 — *shd* — **Colonial (IRE)**[74] [7266] 4-9-0 109 ..... TedDurcan 4 — 110
(Saeed Bin Suroor) *mid-div: r.o wl fnl 2 1/2f: nrst fin* **25/1**

5 — *1 1/4* — **Mr Brock (SAF)**[111] [6344] 8-9-0 115 ..... KShea 3 — 107
(M F De Kock, South Africa) *trckd ldrs: nt qckn fnl f* **12/1**

6 — *1 3/4* — **Green Coast (IRE)**[35] [7792] 8-9-0 113 ..... TadhgO'Shea 11 — 103
(Doug Watson, UAE) *settled in rr: r.o fnl 2f: n.d* **14/1**

7 — *1/4* — **Frozen Power (IRE)**[130] [5803] 4-9-0 109 ..... RoystonFfrench 7 — 103
(Mahmood Al Zarooni) *a mid-div* **25/1**

8 — *1* — **Sea Lord (IRE)**[131] [5775] 4-9-0 115 ..... RichardMullen 12 — 100
(Mahmood Al Zarooni) *sn led: hdd 1 1/2f out: wknd fnl 110yds* **8/1**[2]

9 — *1 1/4* — **My Indy (ARG)**[350] [338] 7-9-0 113 ..... (t) PatCosgrave 6 — 98
(M bin Shafya, UAE) *trckd ldrs: ev ch 2f out: one pce fnl f* **33/1**

10 — *1 1/4* — **King Of Rome (IRE)**[315] [799] 6-9-0 109 ..... PatDobbs 5 — 95
(M F De Kock, South Africa) *racd in rr: n.d* **20/1**

11 — *shd* — **Mabait**[89] [6923] 5-9-0 113 ..... KierenFallon 14 — 94
(Luca Cumani) *in rr of mid-div: nvr able to chal* **9/1**[3]

12 — *1 1/4* — **Mac Love**[90] [6885] 10-9-0 109 ..... MickyFenton 9 — 92
(Stef Higgins) *settled last: nvr nr to chal* **40/1**

13 — *6 1/4* — **Fencing Master**[170] [4456] 4-9-0 110 ..... (t) RyanMoore 2 — 77
(H J Brown, South Africa) *s.i.s: racd in rr: n.d* **14/1**

14 — *18* — **Storm Ultralight (ARG)**[236] [2318] 5-9-0 110 ..... AhmedAjtebi 13 — 36
(Mahmood Al Zarooni) *nvr able to chal: eased fnl 1 1/2f* **12/1**

1m 36.45s (-0.65) **Going Correction** +0.20s/f (Slow) — **14** Ran SP% **131.5**
Speed ratings: **111,108,108,108,107 105,105,104,102,101 101,100,94,76**
CSF: £10.72.
Owner Sheikh Hamdan Bin Mohammed Al Maktoum **Bred** Jayeff B Stables **Trained** Newmarket, Suffolk

FOCUS
This was traditionally the weakest of the three rounds, but not last year when the race went to subsequent World Cup hero Gloria De Campeao, and this season's winner also enters calculations for the latest running of the world's richest race.

NOTEBOOK
Mendip(USA) won his first three starts, including the middle leg of the UAE Triple Crown, the Al Bastakiya, before coming up short in the Derby, after which he apparently suffered a setback. However, he returned with a taking, career-best performance, winning comfortably after being well placed throughout. He has the potential to progress into a Godolphin Mile or World Cup contender, although there is just a slight question mark about his temperament, especially when he faces better competition. The suspicion last year was that he's a bit soft mentally, and that hasn't gone away. He still required a blanket for stalls entry, as well as a blindfold this time, and edged left soon after getting to the front before then flashing his tail on the two occasions he felt the whip. His talent's certainly not in doubt, though, and we'll learn a lot more about him next time, which might be on February 3 for the second round of this series over 1m1f. (op 13-8)
Imbongi(SAF) fared best of the trainer's three runners, but was said to still be in need of the run and was ridden very much with an eye to the future. Set a lot to do, he switched from an outside position to the inside in the straight and ran on well, despite only being nudged out in the last half-furlong. (op 8-1)
Win For Sure(GER), a dual Listed winner in Europe, ran a cracking race but still wasn't good enough.
Colonial(IRE), a [illegible] followed his winning stable companion into the straight, but lacked that one's acceleration.
Mr Brock(SAF) enjoyed a terrific Carnival in 2010, but he'll probably struggle to repeat that level of form this time. (op 10-1)
Sea Lord(IRE) set just an ordinary tempo but his finishing effort was tame. He has won on synthetics, albeit at a much lower level, but had a tough year when most progressive in Britain for Mark Johnston last term and, not the biggest, he looks set to struggle this time around. (op 15-2)
Mabait, a winner on synthetics but in lesser company, seemed to run flat and offered nothing. (op 8-1)
Mac Love refused to settle under a hold-up ride. (op 33-1)

157a MASTER COLLECTION (H'CAP) (TURF) — 1m 1f

6:55 (6:55) (100-118,117) 3-Y-0+

£67,307 (£22,435; £11,217; £5,608; £3,365; £2,243)

RPR

1 — **Steele Tango (USA)**[90] [6885] 6-9-0 110 ..... RyanMoore 12 — 112
(Roger Teal) *in rr of mid-div: smooth prog 2f out: led nr line* **4/1**[1]

2 — *shd* — **Enak (ARG)**[292] [1023] 5-8-11 108 ..... (t) FrankieDettori 5 — 109
(Saeed Bin Suroor) *trckd ldrs: led 1f out: hdd cl to home* **4/1**[1]

3 — *2* — **Across The Rhine (USA)**[89] [6942] 5-8-8 105 ..... WJSupple 4 — 102
(Tracey Collins, Ire) *mid-div: chsd ldrs 2 1/2f out: led briefly 1 1/2f: nt qcknd fnl 110yds* **10/1**[3]

4 — *1/4* — **Hot Six (BRZ)**[112] 6-8-8 105 ..... BReis 9 — 101+
(E Martins, Brazil) *settled in rr: r.o wl fnl 2f: nrst fin* **16/1**

5 — *1/2* — **War Monger (USA)**[39] 7-8-5 100 ..... TadhgO'Shea 8 — 97
(Doug Watson, UAE) *settled in rr: chsd ldrs 2f out: nt qcknd fnl 1f* **18/1**

6 — *1/4* — **Clasp**[14] [8028] 9-8-5 100 ..... (vt) RichardMullen 11 — 96
(Doug Watson, UAE) *nvr bttr than mid-div* **16/1**

7 — *hd* — **Le Drakkar (AUS)**[18] 6-8-8 105 ..... (t) Christophe-PatriceLemaire 1 — 99
(A bin Huzaim, UAE) *nvr bttr than mid-div* **10/1**[3]

8 — *3/4* — **Bronze Cannon (USA)**[14] [8028] 6-9-2 112 ..... TedDurcan 7 — 105
(H J Brown, South Africa) *a mid-div* **12/1**

9 — *shd* — **Fighting Brave (USA)**[90] [6912] 4-8-5 102 ..... (t) KierenFallon 14 — 95
(David Wachman, Ire) *nvr bttr than mid-div* **14/1**

10 — *shd* — **Mr. Crazy Boy (ARG)**[14] [8028] 5-8-5 100 ..... (t) RPCleary 3 — 94
(M F De Kock, South Africa) *a mid-div* **20/1**

11 — *1 1/4* — **Snaafy (USA)**[292] [1025] 7-9-6 117 ..... (b) RichardHills 6 — 106
(M Al Muhairi, UAE) *trckd ldrs tl 2 1/2f out: wknd* **13/2**[2]

12 — *1/4* — **Black Eagle (IRE)**[39] 5-8-6 102 ..... JRosales 2 — 92
(A bin Huzaim, UAE) *in rr of mid-div: n.d* **10/1**[3]

13 — *5 1/4* — **Tam Lin**[292] [1025] 8-9-0 110 ..... (t) PatCosgrave 13 — 89
(M bin Shafya, UAE) *sn led: rdn and hdd 2f out* **16/1**

14 — *15* — **Comradeship (IRE)**[28] [7902] 4-8-5 100 ..... ErhanYavuz 10 — 49
(R Bouresly, Kuwait) *trckd ldrs tl wknd 2 1/2f out* **20/1**

1m 50.15s (110.15)
WFA 4 from 5yo+ 1lb — **14** Ran SP% **127.4**
CSF £19.01 .Placepot: £107.60 to a £1 stake. Pool: £4,489.08. 30.45 winning tickets. Quadpot: £52.20 to a £1 stake. Pool: £572.40. 8.10 winning tickets..
Owner The Thirty Acre Racing Partnership **Bred** Tom Zwiesler **Trained** Ashtead, Surrey

FOCUS
No unexposed progressive types in this contest.

NOTEBOOK
Steele Tango(USA) recorded his third success at the trip, and his fourth in total. He was set plenty to do, being just about last on entering the straight, but crucially he enjoyed a sustained run towards the outside and just got up to defy a 7lb higher mark than when runner-up in last year's Cambridgeshire. Having won this off a rating of 110, he deserves his place in something like the Group 2 Al Rashidiya over C&D January 26, but that will demand more.
Enak(ARG), fourth in the UAE Derby when last seen, coped just fine with the return to turf and stayed on nicely after being well placed. He's entitled to come on for this.
Across The Rhine(USA) showed enough to suggest he can continue to pick up prize money at the Carnival.
Hot Six(BRZ), debuting for a new trainer after nearly four months off, was upsides the winner, well out the back on entering the straight, and unlike that rival, went on to find trouble, which cost him a bit of ground. He can do better.

[130] LINGFIELD (L-H)

Friday, January 14

OFFICIAL GOING: Standard
Wind: Fresh, behind Weather: Light rain before racing, then overcast

158 PLACE ONLY BETTING AT BLUESQ.COM MAIDEN STKS — 7f (P)

12:30 (12:31) (Class 5) 3-Y-0+ — **£1,910** (£564; £282) **Stalls** Low

Form — RPR

1 — **Cassini Flight (USA)** 3-8-9 0 ..... ShaneKelly 3 — 77+
(Jeremy Noseda) *hld up in midfield: rdn over 2f out: styd on to ld last strides* **9/2**[3]

44-2 — 2 — *shd* — **Al Jaadi**[9] [52] 4-9-8 65 ..... JimCrowley 6 — 70
(William Jarvis) *chsd ldrs: led ent st: drvn 2 l clr ent fnl f: jst ct* **5/2**[2]

0/ — 3 — *5* — **Timpanist (USA)**[170] 4-9-8 73 ..... GeorgeBaker 1 — 57
(Simon Dow) *chsd ldrs: wnt 3rd over 2f out: no ex appr fnl f* **25/1**

\- — 4 — *1* — **Loyal N Trusted** 3-8-9 0 ..... AndreaAtzeni 12 — 55
(Michael Wigham) *t.k.h: chsd ldrs: rdn over 2f out: sn outpcd* **50/1**

5 — *1/2* — **Trend Line (IRE)** 3-8-4 0 ..... ChrisCatlin 2 — 48+
(Peter Chapple-Hyam) *in tch: rdn 3f out; styd on same pce* **7/4**[1]

600- — 6 — *3 1/2* — **All Right Now**[282] [1158] 4-9-13 45 ..... MartinLane 8 — 48
(Derek Haydn Jones) *s.s: bhd: shkn up and sme hdwy on inner ent st: no imp* **66/1**

7 — *hd* — **Main Attraction**[205] 4-9-8 0 ..... IanMongan 10 — 42
(Tobias B P Coles) *led tl ent st: wknd over 1f out* **66/1**

8 — *hd* — **Zelenia** 3-8-4 0 ..... LukeMorris 7 — 38
(Peter Winkworth) *mid-div: rdn and outpcd over 3f out: styng on at fin* **50/1**

9 — *1 1/4* — **Tegan (IRE)** 3-8-4 0 ..... FrankieMcDonald 5 — 35
(Richard Hannon) *s.v.s: bhd: rdn 3f out: nvr nr ldrs* **20/1**

00- — 10 — *7* — **Dune Island**[16] [8001] 3-8-6 0 ow2 ..... NeilChalmers 9 — 18
(John Bridger) *in tch tl wknd over 2f out* **100/1**

0- — 11 — *1 1/4* — **Warbond**[174] [4363] 3-8-9 0 ..... LiamKeniry 13 — 17
(Michael Madgwick) *s.s: sn pressing ldr: wknd over 2f out* **100/1**

12 — *4 1/2* — **Have Another** 3-8-10 0 ow1 ..... JamieSpencer 4 — —
(Richard Hannon) *s.s: bhd: hrd rdn on outer over 2f out: no ch after* **6/1**

13 — *13* — **Two Sugars** 3-8-9 0 ..... J-PGuillambert 11 — —
(John Akehurst) *s.s: sn wl bhd and drvn along: nvr any ch* **33/1**

1m 26.71s (1.91) **Going Correction** +0.275s/f (Slow)
WFA [illegible] — **13** Ran SP% **117.8**
Speed ratings (Par 103): **100,99,94,93,92 88,88,88,86,78 77,72,57**
Tote Swingers: 1&2 £2.70, 1&3 £10.80, 2&3 £5.30 CSF £14.93 TOTE £3.60: £1.40, £1.10, £5.00; EX 14.60 Trifecta £161.50 Part won. Pool: £218.31 - 0.73 winning units..
Owner Sanford R Robertson **Bred** Sanford R Robertson **Trained** Newmarket, Suffolk

FOCUS
A moderate maiden and it was no surprise to see it go to one of the newcomers. The time was 0.6secs slower than the following seller.
Tegan(IRE) Official explanation: jockey said filly ran green

159 MARSH GREEN (S) STKS — 7f (P)

1:00 (1:00) (Class 6) 4-Y-0+ — **£1,535** (£453; £226) **Stalls** Low

Form — RPR

50-2 — 1 — **Army Of Stars (IRE)**[11] [17] 5-8-10 73 ..... (p) JimCrowley 3 — 68
(James Given) *trckd ldr: effrt over 2f out: led ins fnl f: rdn out* **4/6**[1]

54-6 — 2 — *1/2* — **Decency (IRE)**[9] [56] 4-8-5 57 ..... LukeMorris 5 — 62
(Harry Dunlop) *handy 3rd and gng wl: shkn up and nt qckn 1f out: hrd rdn and r.o fnl 150yds: a hld* **9/2**[3]

14- — 3 — *1/2* — **The Big Haerth (IRE)**[46] [7627] 5-9-1 70 ..... (t) AndreaAtzeni 1 — 71
(Michael Wigham) *led: rdn ent st: hdd ins fnl f: one pce* **7/2**[2]

00-6 — 4 — *4* — **Desert Dreamer (IRE)**[7] [78] 10-8-3 72 ..... RPWalsh(7) 4 — 55
(David Evans) *dwlt: a last: rdn 3f out: no prog fnl 2f* **11/1**

1m 26.11s (1.31) **Going Correction** +0.275s/f (Slow) — **4** Ran SP% **108.7**
Speed ratings (Par 101): **103,102,101,97**
CSF £4.04 TOTE £1.50; EX 3.50.No bid for the winner.
Owner Peter Swann **Bred** D Johnson **Trained** Willoughton, Lincs

FOCUS
A competitive seller, despite the small field. The time was 0.6secs quicker than the opening maiden.

160 GOLF AT LINGFIELD PARK FILLIES' H'CAP — 1m (P)

1:30 (1:30) (Class 5) (0-75,75) 4-Y-0+ — **£2,047** (£604; £302) **Stalls** High

Form — RPR

36-1 — 1 — **Cat Hunter**[9] [55] 4-9-0 **68** ..... LukeMorris 2 — 74
(Ronald Harris) *trckd ldr: slt ld and qcknd pce 3f out: hld on gamely fnl f* **2/1**[1]

00-3 — 2 — *nk* — **Sasheen**[10] [34] 4-8-7 **61** oh1 ..... (p) NickyMackay 4 — 66
(Jim Boyle) *led: set weak pce: narrowly hdd and rdn 3f out: pressed wnr after: str chal fnl f: kpt on wl* **9/1**

41-3 — 3 — *1* — **Avonrose**[10] [38] 4-8-13 **72** ..... RyanClark(5) 5 — 75+
(Derek Shaw) *hld up in 5th: rdn and outpcd 3f out: rallied and r.o fnl f* **9/4**[2]

410- **4** ½ **Song To The Moon (IRE)**[55] 7521 4-9-4 **75**........(p) MatthewDavies(3) 3 77+
(George Baker) *lost 6 l s: sn in tch in rr: rdn and outpcd 3f out: styd on fnl f* **4/1**[3]

024- **5** *hd* **Miss Bootylishes**[29] 7895 6-9-3 **74**.................................. AmyBaker(3) 1 75
(Andrew Haynes) *dwlt: t.k.h: sn prom: outpcd 3f out: rallied into 3rd over 1f out: no ex* **16/1**

6 2 **Batya (IRE)**[74] 4-8-11 **65**.. IanMongan 6 62
(Tobias B P Coles) *t.k.h: hld up in 4th: jnd ldrs 3f out: rdn over 2f out: wknd over 1f out* **8/1**

1m 43.09s (4.89) **Going Correction** +0.275s/f (Slow) **6** Ran SP% **111.1**
Speed ratings (Par 100): **86,85,84,84,84 82**
Tote Swingers: 1&2 £3.50, 1&3 £1.40, 2&3 £4.30 CSF £19.50 TOTE £2.20: £1.10, £6.40; EX 20.80.
Owner Mrs Kim Sharon Cohen **Bred** Sunny Days Ltd **Trained** Earlswood, Monmouths

FOCUS
A tight fillies' handicap.

161 LINGFIELDPARK.CO.UK MAIDEN STKS — 1m 4f (P)
2:00 (2:00) (Class 5) 4-Y-O+ — **£1,910** (£564; £282) **Stalls** Low

Form — RPR

652- **1** **Mister Frosty (IRE)**[39] 7728 5-9-7 56............................ GeorgeBaker 5 62
(George Prodromou) *hld up: hdwy 5f out: led over 1f out: idled in front fnl f: drvn out* **4/1**[3]

222- **2** ½ **Rosewood Lad**[15] 8013 4-9-3 53.. LukeMorris 6 61
(J S Moore) *towards rr: stmbld and rdn after 50yds: drvn along and styd on fnl 4f: wnt 2nd ins fnl f: clsd on wnr: hld nr fin* **11/4**[1]

43-2 **3** 3 **New Den**[7] 85 4-9-3 58..(v) NickyMackay 2 56
(Jim Boyle) *led tl over 1f out: no ex* **9/1**

/60- **4** 2 **Zafranagar (IRE)**[52] 6957 6-9-0 65......................... GeorgeDowning(7) 8 53
(Tony Carroll) *towards rr: sme hdwy into 5th 4f out: styd on same pce: nvr able to chal* **16/1**

00-0 **5** 16 **Pedasus (USA)**[10] 30 5-9-7 57.................................(v¹) AndreaAtzeni 3 27
(Ronald Harris) *drvn along after s: sn chsng ldr: rdn and wknd 3f out* **33/1**

6 4½ **Western Hope (IRE)** 4-8-12 0.. JimCrowley 7 15
(Simon Dow) *stdd s and missed break: hld up in rr: rdn 4f out: no ch after* **9/2**

4 **7** 4 **Gabrielle Da Vinci**[7] 85 5-8-9 0...................................... RPWalsh(7) 1 —
(David Evans) *prom tl wknd 4f out* **33/1**

00- **8** 3¾ **Maccool (IRE)**[49] 7579 5-9-7 0.. JoeFanning 4 —
(Barney Curley) *t.k.h: chsd ldrs tl wknd over 4f out* **33/1**

0- **9** 2½ **Mr Muddle**[12] 2401 4-9-3 0... JamieGoldstein 9 —
(Sheena West) *chsd ldrs on outer: drvn along and wknd 5f out: sn bhd* **3/1**[2]

2m 33.7s (0.70) **Going Correction** +0.275s/f (Slow)
WFA 4 from 5yo+ 4lb **9** Ran SP% **114.6**
Speed ratings (Par 103): **108,107,105,104,93 90,88,85,83**
Tote Swingers: 1&2 £3.00, 1&3 £4.70, 2&3 £2.70 CSF £15.04 TOTE £3.40: £2.00, £1.10, £3.00; EX 18.10 Trifecta £43.20 Pool: £679.27 - 11.62 winning units..
Owner Matt Bartram **Bred** Thomas McDonogh **Trained** East Harling, Norfolk

FOCUS
A modest older-horse maiden made up of largely exposed sorts. The time, however, was 0.81secs quicker than the following handicap.
Rosewood Lad Official explanation: jockey said gelding suffered interference shortly after start

162 EXCLUSIVE LIVE SHOWS AT BLUESQ.COM H'CAP — 1m 4f (P)
2:30 (2:30) (Class 5) (0-70,70) 4-Y-O+ — **£2,047** (£604; £302) **Stalls** Low

Form — RPR

653- **1** **Beaubrav**[15] 8013 5-9-9 **67**..(t) AdamKirby 1 79
(Michael Madgwick) *prom: rdn 2f out: led over 1f out: pushed clr: comf* **6/1**[2]

221- **2** 4½ **Archie Rice (USA)**[30] 7884 5-9-10 **68**............................. GeorgeBaker 7 73
(Tom Keddy) *sn led: stdd pce after 4f: qcknd tempo over 2f out: hdd over 1f out: nt pce of wnr: jst hld on for 2nd* **2/1**[1]

226- **3** *nk* **Sheila's Bond**[17] 7996 4-8-8 **56**.. LukeMorris 6 60
(J S Moore) *broke best: sn stdd bk to rr: rdn and hdwy into 3rd over 1f out: styd on same pce* **12/1**

60-2 **4** *hd* **Jenny Potts**[7] 79 7-9-2 **65**... TobyAtkinson(5) 4 71+
(Chris Down) *hld up in rr: rdn over 2f out: styd on fnl f: nrst fin* **8/1**[3]

610- **5** 2¼ **Cotton King**[79] 7181 4-9-0 **62**..(vt) IanMongan 5 62
(Tobias B P Coles) *dwlt: sn prom: wnt 2nd 6f out: edgd lft and wknd over 1f out* **10/1**

110- **6** ¾ **Indian Violet (IRE)**[23] 7966 5-9-3 **61**............................ JamieGoldstein 8 60
(Sheena West) *dwlt: t.k.h: trckd ldrs: gng wl tl rdn and wknd wl over 1f out* **8/1**[3]

324- **7** 1 **The Wonga Coup (IRE)**[23] 7963 4-8-5 **56**...................... KierenFox(3) 3 54
(Pat Phelan) *stdd s: t.k.h towards rr: hdwy on inner to chse ldrs over 1f out: sn wknd* **6/1**[2]

654- **8** 3¾ **Relative Strength (IRE)**[37] 7765 6-9-9 **67**...................... AndreaAtzeni 2 59
(Michael Wigham) *chsd ldrs: rdn 3f out: wknd ent st: 7th and btn whn squeezed over 1f out* **11/1**

200- **9** 6 **War Of The Roses (IRE)**[37] 7765 8-9-10 **68**...................(p) TomEaves 9 50
(Roy Brotherton) *hld up in rr on outer: effrt 3f out: sn wknd* **20/1**

2m 34.51s (1.51) **Going Correction** +0.275s/f (Slow)
WFA 4 from 5yo+ 4lb **9** Ran SP% **114.0**
Speed ratings (Par 103): **105,102,101,101,100 99,99,96,92**
Tote Swingers: 1&2 £2.60, 1&3 £10.90, 2&3 £3.60 CSF £18.13 CT £138.99 TOTE £8.00: £2.10, £1.50, £2.50; EX 20.70 Trifecta £178.10 Pool: £657.24 - 2.73 winning units..
Owner The B B Partnership **Bred** Star Pointe Ltd,Brosnan And Williamson **Trained** Denmead, Hants

FOCUS
A modest handicap.

163 LINGFIELD PARK MARRIOTT HOTEL & COUNTRY CLUB H'CAP (DIV I) — 1m 2f (P)
3:00 (3:00) (Class 6) (0-55,55) 4-Y-O+ — **£1,364** (£403; £201) **Stalls** Low

Form — RPR

01-2 **1** **No Complaining (IRE)**[11] 26 4-9-1 **55**.......................... JoeFanning 4 58
(Barney Curley) *trckd ldrs: slt ld and edgd lft over 1f out: disp ld fnl 150yds: jst prevailed: all out* **4/7**[1]

500/ **2** *shd* **Hault**[763] 7645 5-8-12 **50**.. LiamKeniry 2 53
(Gary Moore) *mid-div: hdwy on inner ent st: edgd rt and drvn to dispute ld fnl 150yds: r.o wl: jst pipped* **40/1**

000- **3** 1½ **Tous Les Deux**[14] 8035 8-9-2 **54**................................ FergusSweeney 1 54+
(Dr Jeremy Naylor) *stdd s: hld up in rr: rdn and r.o fnl 2f: nrst fin* **20/1**

/00- **4** ½ **Dalrymple (IRE)**[7] 7727 5-8-7 **45**............................(t) FrankieMcDonald 6 44
(Michael Madgwick) *led tl over 1f out: cl 3rd but hld whn n.m.r sn after: one pce* **66/1**

546- **5** 1½ **Empress Leizu (IRE)**[42] 7685 4-8-12 **55**.......................... KierenFox(3) 3 51
(Tony Carroll) *t.k.h: prom: rdn and swtchd lft over 1f out: no ex* **11/2**[2]

000- **6** 2½ **Inquisitress**[39] 7728 7-8-7 **45**... NeilChalmers 10 36
(John Bridger) *stdd s: mid-div: rdn and no hdwy fnl 2f* **25/1**

000- **7** ½ **Pascalina**[223] 2753 4-8-13 **53**... J-PGuillambert 9 43
(John Akehurst) *stdd s: towards rr: last and pushed along 3f out: n.d after* **16/1**

353- **8** 1 **Starry Mount**[29] 7897 4-9-0 **54**.. JamieSpencer 7 42
(Andrew Haynes) *sn chsng ldr: drvn level 3f out: n.m.r and wknd wl over 1f out* **9/1**

60-0 **9** *nk* **Sweet Possession (USA)**[12] 14 5-9-1 **53**...................... JimCrowley 5 40
(Pat Eddery) *rrd bdly s and nrly fell on landing: wl bhd tl sme hdwy into midfield on outer 3f out: wd and wknd bnd into st* **6/1**[3]

2m 11.47s (4.87) **Going Correction** +0.275s/f (Slow)
WFA 4 from 5yo+ 2lb **9** Ran SP% **121.7**
Speed ratings (Par 101): **91,90,89,89,88 86,85,84,84**
Tote Swingers: 1&2 £9.40, 1&3 £5.60, 2&3 £19.50 CSF £45.28 CT £294.98 TOTE £2.20: £1.10, £18.60, £10.00; EX 39.10 Trifecta £393.00 Pool: £818.04 - 1.54 winning units..
Owner P A Byrne **Bred** Epona Bloodstock Ltd **Trained** Newmarket, Suffolk
■ Stewards' Enquiry : Liam Keniry caution: careless riding
Joe Fanning caution: careless riding

FOCUS
There wasn't much pace on early, but that probably suited the winner.
Sweet Possession(USA) Official explanation: jockey said mare reared when gates were opening, hit her head and was slowly away

164 LINGFIELD PARK MARRIOTT HOTEL & COUNTRY CLUB H'CAP (DIV II) — 1m 2f (P)
3:30 (3:31) (Class 6) (0-55,55) 4-Y-O+ — **£1,364** (£403; £201) **Stalls** Low

Form — RPR

64-2 **1** **Ice Road Trucker (IRE)**[10] 30 4-8-0 **47**...............(v¹) NathanAlison(7) 2 54
(Jim Boyle) *chsd ldrs: hrd rdn 3f out: drvn to dispute ld fnl 150yds: jst prevailed: all out* **3/1**[2]

041- **2** *shd* **Dilys Maud**[29] 7887 4-9-1 **55**..(b) MartinLane 6 61
(Roger Ingram) *dwlt: mid-div: drvn into 3rd over 2f out: disp ld fnl 150yds: r.o wl: jst pipped* **10/1**

030- **3** 1¼ **Sunset Boulevard (IRE)**[17] 7996 8-9-2 **54**..............(b) JamieSpencer 5 58
(Jim Best) *stdd s: patiently rdn in rr: shkn up and hdwy ent st: drvn to chse ldrs fnl f: nt qckn* **2/1**[1]

050- **4** 1¼ **Litenup (IRE)**[37] 7760 5-8-12 **53**.....................................(p) KierenFox(3) 7 55
(Gay Kelleway) *led: hrd rdn and hdd 150yds out: no ex* **5/1**[3]

014- **5** 4½ **Ocean Of Peace (FR)**[17] 7995 8-8-13 **51**................... FergusSweeney 9 44
(Martin Bosley) *towards rr: rdn 3f out: nvr rchd ldrs* **15/2**

632- **6** *nk* **Lunar River (FR)**[17] 7996 8-8-9 **52**.......................(t) JamesRogers(5) 10 44
(David Pinder) *hld up in rr: sme hdwy on outer 3f out: wd and btn ent st* **6/1**

010- **7** ¾ **Denton Ryal**[12] 7874 4-9-0 **54**.. JamieGoldstein 4 44
(Sheena West) *chsd ldrs: outpcd over 2f out: sn btn* **10/1**

000- **8** 5 **Bibiana Bay**[256] 1782 4-8-6 **48** ow1................................. SamHitchcott 3 26
(Gary Moore) *chsd ldrs: drvn along 3f out: sn wknd* **33/1**

000- **9** 15 **Play Up Pompey**[17] 7995 9-8-7 **45**.................................... LukeMorris 8 —
(John Bridger) *in tch: wd bnd after 1f: rdn and wknd over 3f out* **66/1**

2m 7.97s (1.37) **Going Correction** +0.275s/f (Slow)
WFA 4 from 5yo+ 2lb **9** Ran SP% **123.7**
Speed ratings (Par 101): **105,104,103,102,99 99,98,94,82**
Tote Swingers: 1&2 £7.80, 1&3 £3.10, 2&3 £6.10 CSF £35.86 CT £76.27 TOTE £3.00: £1.10, £5.10, £1.70; EX 36.20 Trifecta £382.10 Pool: £748.74 - 1.45 winning units..
Owner Mrs Pippa Boyle **Bred** Albert Conneally **Trained** Epsom, Surrey

FOCUS
They didn't go much quicker in this than the first division.

165 PLAY MEGAJACKPOTS CLEOPATRA AT BLUESQ.COM H'CAP — 5f (P)
4:00 (4:00) (Class 6) (0-65,64) 4-Y-O+ — **£1,535** (£453; £226) **Stalls** High

Form — RPR

23-6 **1** **Decider (USA)**[11] 22 8-9-5 **62**..(p) JoeFanning 6 69
(Ronald Harris) *broke wl: led 1f: chsd ldr after: drvn to ld ins fnl f: a holding runner-up* **20/1**

160- **2** ½ **Pelmanism**[120] 6103 4-9-1 **58**...(b) PhillipMakin 3 63
(Kevin Ryan) *in tch in 5th: drvn to take 2nd fnl 100yds: clsd on wnr: a hld* **11/2**

00-0 **3** 2 **Silver Linnet (IRE)**[7] 80 4-9-2 **59**...................................(b) AdamKirby 2 57
(Michael Quinlan) *led after 1f tl ins fnl f: one pce* **4/1**[3]

131- **4** 2 **Sleepy Blue Ocean**[32] 7860 5-9-7 **64**..........................(p) LukeMorris 1 55
(John Balding) *dwlt: sn chsng ldrs: one pce fnl 2f* **10/3**[1]

001- **5** 1¼ **Anjomarba (IRE)**[23] 7972 4-9-3 **63**.................................... BillyCray(3) 8 49
(Brett Johnson) *outpcd towards rr: sme hdwy over 1f out: nvr rchd ldrs* **9/1**

005- **6** ½ **Electioneer (USA)**[16] 8005 4-9-1 **61**......................... JamesSullivan(3) 4 46
(Michael Easterby) *sn drvn along in rr: styd on fnl f: nvr nrr* **12/1**

606- **7** ¾ **Raimond Ridge (IRE)**[14] 8036 5-8-6 **54**...................(v¹) RyanClark(5) 9 36
(Derek Shaw) *s.i.s: outpcd and bhd: sme hdwy on inner ent st: wknd 1f out* **20/1**

004- **8** 1½ **Straboe (USA)**[14] 8036 5-9-5 **62**.....................................(v) JimCrowley 5 38
(Stuart Williams) *mid-div: outpcd 2f out: sn btn* **7/2**[2]

045- **9** 3½ **Fayre Bella**[30] 7877 4-8-10 **53**... MartinLane 10 17
(John Gallagher) *dwlt: a outpcd and bhd* **25/1**

53-0 **10** 3¾ **Thoughtsofstardom**[5] 102 8-8-11 **54**....................(be) JamieSpencer 7 —
(Phil McEntee) *prom: wknd over 2f out: 6th and btn whn rn wd into st* **33/1**

58.43 secs (-0.37) **Going Correction** +0.275s/f (Slow) **10** Ran SP% **114.7**
Speed ratings (Par 101): **113,112,109,105,103 103,101,99,93,87**
Tote Swingers: 1&2 £14.20, 1&3 £12.90, 2&3 £8.10. Totesuper7: Win: Not won. Place: 18.50. CSF £119.17 CT £538.17 TOTE £17.80: £4.20, £2.50, £1.70; EX 108.10 TRIFECTA Not won..
Owner Robert Bailey **Bred** Green Willow Farms **Trained** Earlswood, Monmouths

FOCUS
A typically competitive 5f handicap for the course.
Electioneer(USA) Official explanation: trainer said a post-race endoscopic examaination had found both blood and mucus
T/Plt: £11.70 to a £1 stake. Pool: £53,697.19. 3,341.81 winning tickets. T/Qpdt: £3.90 to a £1 stake. Pool: £4.389.67. 814.85 winning tickets. LM

[109]WOLVERHAMPTON (A.W) (L-H)

Friday, January 14

OFFICIAL GOING: Standard to slow

Wind: Fresh behind Weather: Cloudy

166 TODAY'S JOCKEY SPECIALS AT BLUESQ.COM H'CAP (DIV I) 5f 216y(P)

4:10 (4:10) (Class 6) (0-55,61) 4-Y-O+ **£1,295** (£385; £192; £96) **Stalls** Low

Form RPR

556- **1** **Welcome Approach**[70] 7334 8-9-1 **54**............................ JimmyQuinn 6 67
(John Weymes) *hld up: hdwy 2f out: rdn to ld and hung rt ins fnl f: r.o* **7/1**

05-2 **2** *3/4* **Libertino (IRE)**[8] 65 4-9-1 **54**.............................. RobertWinston 10 64
(Tony Carroll) *a.p: led over 1f out: sn rdn and edgd lft: hdd ins fnl f: styd on* **6/1[3]**

13-1 **3** *1 1/4* **Kheley (IRE)**[5] 102 5-8-13 **52**.............................. ShaneKelly 7 58
(Mark Brisbourne) *chsd ldrs: rdn and ev ch ins fnl f: styd on same pce* **9/4[1]**

60-4 **4** *3 3/4* **Rightcar Dominic**[10] 28 6-8-7 **46** oh1......................... KellyHarrison 1 40
(Peter Grayson) *s.s: hdwy over 1f out: hung lft ins fnl f: nt rch ldrs* **25/1**

3-12 **5** *3/4* **Double Carpet (IRE)**[5] 107 8-9-8 **61** 6ex.................... KirstyMilczarek 3 53
(Garry Woodward) *hld up: hdwy over 2f out: rdn over 1f out: no ex ins fnl f* **3/1[2]**

560- **6** *1/2* **Royal Blade (IRE)**[31] 7868 4-9-0 **53**.......................... StevieDonohoe 5 43
(Alan Berry) *led: hdd over 4f out: led again over 2f out: rdn and hdd over 1f out: wknd ins fnl f* **14/1**

1-42 **7** *3 3/4* **Lets Move It**[8] 57 4-8-13 **52**..............................(v) PatrickMathers 4 30
(Derek Shaw) *s.i.s: sn pushed along in rr: nvr on terms* **14/1**

004- **8** *1 3/4* **Boxer Shorts**[16] 8006 5-8-0 **46** oh1.........................(t) JosephYoung(7) 8 19
(Michael Mullineaux) *dwlt: outpcd* **40/1**

004- **9** *6* **Suhayl Star (IRE)**[15] 8024 7-8-7 **46** oh1........................... ChrisCatlin 2 —
(Paul Burgoyne) *chsd ldrs: rdn over 2f out: wknd over 1f out* **6/1[3]**

060- **10** *nk* **What Katie Did (IRE)**[147] 5267 6-8-9 **55**.........(p) MatthewCosham(7) 11 —
(Milton Bradley) *w ldr tl led over 4f out: rdn and hdd over 2f out: wknd over 1f out* **25/1**

1m 16.1s (1.10) **Going Correction** +0.175s/f (Slow) **10** Ran SP% **120.3**

Speed ratings (Par 101): **99,98,96,91,90 89,84,82,74,73**

Tote Swingers: 1&2 £8.90, 1&3 £3.40, 2&3 £5.40 CSF £49.25 CT £126.73 TOTE £5.20: £1.80, £3.00, £2.10; EX 50.70.

Owner T A Scothern & Tag Racing **Bred** P Wyatt And Ranby Hall **Trained** Middleham Moor, N Yorks

FOCUS

A low-grade 46-61 handicap and the pace was fast and furious.

Double Carpet(IRE) Official explanation: jockey said gelding ran flat

167 TODAY'S JOCKEY SPECIALS AT BLUESQ.COM H'CAP (DIV II) 5f 216y(P)

4:40 (4:40) (Class 6) (0-55,59) 4-Y-O+ **£1,295** (£385; £192; £96) **Stalls** Low

Form RPR

036- **1** **Almaty Express**[32] 7859 9-8-10 **54**.......................(b) AdamCarter(5) 11 62
(John Weymes) *chsd ldrs: led over 2f out: rdn and hung lft ins fnl f: r.o* **14/1**

314- **2** *1* **Lily Wood**[37] 7761 5-9-0 **53**...(p) LiamJones 3 58
(James Unett) *a.p: chsd wnr wl over 1f out: sn rdn: r.o* **9/2[3]**

00-0 **3** *1 1/4* **Gilderoy**[8] 70 4-8-8 **47**...(be) HayleyTurner 6 48
(Dominic Ffrench Davis) *hld up: hdwy over 2f out: rdn over 1f out: r.o* **16/1**

2-31 **4** *1/2* **Itsthursdayalready**[5] 107 4-9-6 **59** 6ex.......................... ShaneKelly 1 58+
(Mark Brisbourne) *hld up: hmpd over 3f out: hdwy u.p over 1f out: edgd lft ins fnl f: r.o: nt rch ldrs* **5/2[2]**

06-0 **5** *1 1/4* **Brazilian Brush (IRE)**[5] 107 6-8-7 **46** oh1.........(bt) RichardKingscote 9 41
(Milton Bradley) *sn led: rdn and hdd over 2f out: no ex fnl f* **25/1**

05-3 **6** *3/4* **Radiator Rooney (IRE)**[7] 80 8-8-10 **52**......................... AmyRyan(3) 7 45
(Patrick Morris) *hld up: hdwy over 3f out: rdn over 1f out: no ex fnl f* **9/4[1]**

000- **7** *3/4* **Rightcar**[34] 7824 4-8-7 **46** oh1.................................... KirstyMilczarek 4 37
(Peter Grayson) *s.i.s: hld up: hdwy over 1f out: nt trble ldrs* **10/1**

023- **8** *7* **Sweet Mirasol (IRE)**[139] 5535 4-8-12 **51**.......................(t) JimmyQuinn 2 19
(Mandy Rowland) *mid-div: n.m.r and lost pl over 5f out: n.d* **8/1**

000- **9** *3 1/4* **Grand Palace (IRE)**[30] 7883 8-8-7 **46** oh1................(v) PatrickMathers 5 4
(Derek Shaw) *chsd ldrs tl rdn and wknd over 2f out* **40/1**

000- **10** *nk* **Only A Game (IRE)**[48] 7604 6-8-12 **54**...................(vt) GaryBartley(3) 10 11
(Ian McInnes) *hld up in tch: rdn and wknd over 2f out* **16/1**

20-0 **11** *3* **Spirit Of Dixie**[10] 37 4-8-9 **55**.................................(v[1]) LeonnaMayor(7) 8 2
(David Nicholls) *chsd ldrs: rdn over 2f out: sn wknd* **16/1**

1m 16.21s (1.21) **Going Correction** +0.175s/f (Slow) **11** Ran SP% **121.7**

Speed ratings (Par 101): **98,96,95,94,92 91,90,81,77,76 72**

Tote Swingers: 1&2 £9.50, 1&3 £23.20, 2&3 £11.60 CSF £77.65 CT £1062.03 TOTE £18.60: £4.00, £1.50, £1.90; EX 75.40.

Owner Highmoor Racing 2 & Tag Racing **Bred** P G Airey **Trained** Middleham Moor, N Yorks

FOCUS

More of the same and a double for trainer John Weymes.

Itsthursdayalready Official explanation: jockey said gelding suffered interference in running

Rightcar Official explanation: jockey said gelding hung right-handed on bend

168 BLUESQ.COM ON YOUR IPHONE H'CAP 5f 216y(P)

5:10 (5:10) (Class 4) (0-80,80) 4-Y-O+ **£3,561** (£1,059; £529; £264) **Stalls** Low

Form RPR

000- **1** **Lucky Dan (IRE)**[98] 6723 5-9-1 **74**.............................. FrannyNorton 4 85
(Paul Green) *chsd ldrs: rdn over 1f out: led and edgd lft wl ins fnl f: r.o* **25/1**

60-2 **2** *1 3/4* **Onceaponatime (IRE)**[8] 58 6-8-12 **71**.................... KirstyMilczarek 10 76
(Michael Squance) *hld up: hdwy u.p over 1f out: r.o to go 2nd nr fin: nt rch wnr* **12/1**

350- **3** *nk* **Dark Lane**[27] 7934 5-9-3 **76**.. BarryMcHugh 5 80
(Richard Fahey) *a.p: rdn 1/2-way: hung lft ins fnl f: styd on* **15/2**

1-2 **4** *nse* **Methaaly (IRE)**[7] 87 8-8-11 **77**.........................(be) JosephYoung(7) 7 81
(Michael Mullineaux) *w ldrs: led wl over 1f out: sn rdn and edgd lft: hdd wl ins fnl f: lost 2 pls nr fin* **9/2[2]**

514- **5** *hd* **Cardinal**[34] 7826 6-9-5 **78**.. HayleyTurner 9 81
(Robert Cowell) *hld up: r.o ins fnl f: nrst fin* **12/1**

305- **6** *7* **Saharia (IRE)**[28] 7915 4-9-7 **80**.............................. GrahamGibbons 2 61
(Ollie Pears) *hld up: rdn over 1f out: nvr on terms* **11/1**

662- **7** *nk* **Jigajig**[16] 8005 4-8-9 **71**... AmyRyan(3) 1 51
(Kevin Ryan) *led 5f out: hdd 2f out: hung lft and wknd ins fnl f* **13/2**

603- **8** *7* **Excellent Show**[41] 7702 5-9-0 **78**.............................. AdamCarter(5) 3 42
(Bryan Smart) *mid-div: sn pushed along: hdwy over 1f out: hmpd ins fnl f: eased* **6/1[3]**

111- **9** *nk* **Ajara (IRE)**[16] 8005 5-8-12 **71**................................ RichardKingscote 6 38
(Tom Dascombe) *led 1f: remained w ldrs tl led 2f out: sn hdd: wknd ins fnl f* **4/1[1]**

606- **10** *1 1/2* **Rapid Water**[23] 7971 5-8-12 **71**.....................................(b) JimmyQuinn 8 23
(Jane Chapple-Hyam) *s.s: outpcd* **7/1**

1m 14.94s (-0.06) **Going Correction** +0.175s/f (Slow) **10** Ran SP% **117.6**

Speed ratings (Par 105): **107,104,104,104,103 94,94,84,84,82**

Tote Swingers: 1&2 £35.80, 1&3 £64.10, 2&3 £22.80 CSF £297.15 CT £2539.16 TOTE £46.70: £7.70, £3.70, £4.30; EX 301.40.

Owner Paul Green (Oaklea) **Bred** Mountarmstrong Stud **Trained** Lydiate, Merseyside

FOCUS

A highly competitive 71-80 handicap and the three leaders seemed to go too fast for their own good.

Rapid Water Official explanation: jockey said gelding missed break

169 ENJOY THE PARTY PACK GROUP OFFER H'CAP 7f 32y(P)

5:40 (5:41) (Class 6) (0-60,66) 4-Y-O+ **£1,619** (£481; £240; £120) **Stalls** High

Form RPR

44-4 **1** **Pilgrim Dancer (IRE)**[6] 96 4-9-2 **55**.....................(v) StephenCraine 10 66
(Patrick Morris) *chsd ldr tl led over 2f out: rdn over 1f out: r.o* **8/1[3]**

4- **2** *nk* **Mount Hollow**[41] 7706 6-9-4 **57**...............................(p) GrahamGibbons 1 67
(Reg Hollinshead) *a.p: chsd wnr over 1f out: sn rdn: r.o* **2/1[1]**

4-44 **3** *2 3/4* **Downhill Skier (IRE)**[4] 111 7-9-2 **55**............................ EddieAhern 4 58
(Mark Brisbourne) *chsd ldrs: rdn over 1f out: styd on same pce ins fnl f* **11/2[2]**

5-01 **4** *2* **Justcallmehandsome**[7] 90 9-9-13 **66** 6ex............(be) HayleyTurner 6 63
(Dominic Ffrench Davis) *led over 4f: sn rdn: no ex fnl f* **2/1[1]**

540- **5** *shd* **Mr Chocolate Drop (IRE)**[72] 7298 7-9-4 **57**................(t) JimmyQuinn 7 54
(Mandy Rowland) *hld up: hdwy u.p over 1f out: nt trble ldrs* **14/1**

444- **6** *2 1/4* **Farmers Dream (IRE)**[32] 7862 4-8-13 **52**...................... FrannyNorton 9 43
(John Spearing) *s.i.s: hld up: styd on appr fnl f: nvr trbld ldrs* **20/1**

506- **7** *1/2* **Grace And Virtue (IRE)**[32] 7860 4-8-13 **52**...................... ShaneKelly 3 42
(S Donohoe, Ire) *broke wl: hmpd and lost pl sn after s: n.d after* **33/1**

006- **8** *3/4* **Elegant Dancer (IRE)**[72] 7300 4-8-4 **46** oh1....... AndrewHeffernan(3) 12 34
(Paul Green) *hld up: rdn over 1f out: nvr on terms* **22/1**

405- **9** *nk* **Namir (IRE)**[17] 7991 9-9-7 **60**....................................(vt) DuranFentiman 5 47
(James Evans) *hld up: rdn over 2f out: a in rr* **20/1**

000- **10** *3 3/4* **Quadrifolio**[62] 7449 5-8-7 **46** oh1.................................(v) ChrisCatlin 11 23
(Paul Green) *prom: rdn 1/2-way: wknd over 1f out* **33/1**

13-5 **11** *hd* **Boy The Bell**[12] 13 4-8-11 **57**.............................. JosephYoung(7) 2 33
(Michael Mullineaux) *hld up in tch: rdn and wknd over 2f out* **16/1**

1m 30.52s (0.92) **Going Correction** +0.175s/f (Slow) **11** Ran SP% **125.5**

Speed ratings (Par 101): **101,100,97,95,95 92,91,91,90,86 86**

Tote Swingers: 1&2 £6.70, 1&3 £6.30, 2&3 £4.10 CSF £24.43 CT £103.53 TOTE £8.30: £2.50, £1.50, £1.20; EX 39.50.

Owner G Halford **Bred** Sir E J Loder **Trained** Tarporley, Cheshire

FOCUS

A modest handicap and just the first four seriously involved from the halfway mark.

170 STAY AT THE WOLVERHAMPTON HOLIDAY INN CLAIMING STKS 1m 141y(P)

6:10 (6:10) (Class 5) 4-Y-O+ **£2,104** (£626; £312; £156) **Stalls** Low

Form RPR

214- **1** **Star Links (USA)**[32] 7856 5-9-0 73..............................(b) ShaneKelly 3 82
(S Donohoe, Ire) *hld up in tch: chsd ldr over 1f out: shkn up to ld ins fnl f: r.o wl* **11/4[2]**

030- **2** *2 1/2* **She's A Character**[15] 8022 4-9-2 77........................(v[1]) BarryMcHugh 7 79
(Richard Fahey) *s.i.s: rcvrd to chse ldr over 7f out: led over 2f out: rdn over 1f out: hdd and unable qck ins fnl f* **5/2[1]**

050- **3** *2 3/4* **Stand Guard**[30] 7881 7-9-8 78.. JimmyQuinn 1 78
(Jane Chapple-Hyam) *chsd ldrs: rdn over 2f out: styd on same pce appr fnl f* **8/1**

10-1 **4** *1 1/2* **Midnight Strider (IRE)**[4] 112 5-8-10 63.............(t) RichardKingscote 2 62
(Tom Dascombe) *trckd ldrs: pushed along over 3f out: outpcd fr over 2f out* **5/2[1]**

00-1 **5** *hd* **Cobo Bay**[10] 31 6-9-2 78..(b) HayleyTurner 6 68
(Conor Dore) *led: rdn and hdd over 2f out: wknd fnl f* **5/1**

6 *19* **Bold Trumpeter** 5-9-0 0.. RussKennemore 4 —
(Milton Bradley) *dwlt: hld up: rdn over 3f out: wknd over 2f out* **80/1**

1m 50.97s (0.47) **Going Correction** +0.175s/f (Slow)

WFA 4 from 5yo+ 1lb **6** Ran SP% **112.8**

Speed ratings (Par 103): **104,101,99,98,97 80**

Tote Swingers: 1&2 £1.50, 1&3 £3.00, 2&3 £3.40 CSF £10.17 TOTE £4.10: £1.30, £1.60; EX 13.70.Midnight Strider claimed by Mr D. J. Ffrench Davis for £6,000.

Owner G Dolan/M McVitie/G Venamore/Mrs M Dolan **Bred** Shell Bloodstock **Trained** Cootehill Road, Co Cavan

FOCUS

A decent race by claiming standards with just 3lb between the three highest-rated runners on official ratings.

Midnight Strider(IRE) Official explanation: jockey said gelding ran flat

171 HOTEL & CONFERENCING MEDIAN AUCTION MAIDEN STKS 1m 141y(P)

6:40 (6:44) (Class 6) 3-4-Y-O **£1,619** (£481; £240; £120) **Stalls** Low

Form RPR

500- **1** **Tijori (IRE)**[83] 7094 3-8-6 66.. JimmyQuinn 2 73+
(Richard Hannon) *pushed along early: hdwy over 6f out: rdn over 3f out: str run to ld post* **15/2**

2 *hd* **Ekasin** 3-8-6 0.. AndreaAtzeni 5 73+
(Marco Botti) *sn pushed along and prom: hmpd over 1f out: rdn: edgd lft and led wl ins fnl f: hdd post* **12/1**

50- **3** *2* **Flying Phoenix**[16] 8000 3-8-1 0...................................... JamieMackay 8 63
(William Haggas) *led over 7f out: rdn over 1f out: hdd wl ins fnl f: styd on same pce* **20/1**

434- **4** *1 3/4* **Ya Hafed**[163] 4716 3-8-6 66.. ChrisCatlin 7 64
(Ed Dunlop) *led 1f: chsd ldr tl rdn and hung lft over 1f out: no ex ins fnl f* **7/4[1]**

5 *3/4* **Main Beach**[39] 4-9-13 0.. EddieAhern 1 66
(Tobias B P Coles) *dwlt: hld up: hdwy over 1f out: r.o: nt trble ldrs* **8/1**

0- **6** *2 1/4* **Katherine Parr**[30] 7879 3-8-1 0................................. FrannyNorton 9 52+
(Peter Chapple-Hyam) *hld up: hdwy over 2f out: wknd over 1f out* **20/1**

524- **7** *1 1/4* **Farmer's Wife**[46] 7630 3-7-12 59.......................... AndrewHeffernan(3) 10 49
(Bernard Llewellyn) *chsd ldrs: rdn over 1f out: hung lft and wknd fnl f* **7/2[2]**

0-3 **8** *1 1/4* **Mountain Myst**[7] 77 3-8-6 0.. HayleyTurner 6 51
(William Muir) *chsd ldrs: rdn over 3f out: wknd over 2f out* **8/1**

366- **9** *6* **Spread Boy (IRE)**[34] 7833 4-9-13 55.......................... PatrickMathers 4 41
(Alan Berry) *racd keenly: prom: lost pl 7f out: rdn over 2f out: sn lost tch* **40/1**

10 6 **Mushroom** 3-8-1 0 NickyMackay 3 19
(Roger Charlton) *s.s: outpcd: lost tch over 2f out* **4/1**3

1m 52.28s (1.78) **Going Correction** +0.175s/f (Slow)
WFA 3 from 4yo 22lb **10** Ran SP% **132.2**
Speed ratings (Par 101): **99,98,97,95,94 92,91,90,85,79**
Tote Swingers: 1&2 £13.80, 1&3 £20.00, 2&3 £41.90 CSF £102.74 TOTE £8.60: £1.80, £6.60, £8.80; EX 102.50.
Owner Malih Lahej Al Basti **Bred** Polish Belle Partnership **Trained** East Everleigh, Wilts

FOCUS
A fair maiden by mid-winter standards though the pace was not strong.
Mushroom Official explanation: jockey said the filly would not face the kick-back.

172 GREAT OFFERS AT WOLVERHAMPTON-RACECOURSE.CO.UK H'CAP 1m 5f 194y(P)
7:10 (7:11) (Class 6) (0-65,64) 4-Y-0+ **£1,619** (£481; £240; £120) **Stalls** Low

Form RPR
66-1 **1** **French Hollow**[7] 89 6-9-13 **64** 6ex BarryMcHugh 5 77+
(Tim Fitzgerald) *hld up: hdwy over 2f out: led over 1f out: sn clr: eased nr fin* **5/6**1
32-6 **2** 3 ½ **Baltimore Patriot (IRE)**[12] 8 8-9-6 **57** GrahamGibbons 4 63
(Barry Brennan) *a.p: led over 2f out: rdn and hdd over 1f out: styd on same pce fnl f* **20/1**
/45- **3** *nk* **Dot's Delight**[34] 7840 7-8-10 **47** LiamJones 9 53
(Mark Rimell) *hld up: hdwy over 4f out: rdn and ev ch over 1f out: styd on same pce fnl f* **16/1**
401- **4** 2 ¼ **Taste The Wine (IRE)**[31] 7626 5-9-9 **63** AndrewHeffernan(3) 2 65
(Bernard Llewellyn) *hld up: hdwy over 1f out: sn rdn: no imp fnl f* **14/1**
0/2- **5** 8 **Mystified (IRE)**[77] 7213 8-9-4 **55** (tp) TomEaves 7 46
(Roger Fisher) *led: rdn and hdd over 2f out: wknd over 1f out* **7/1**
025/ **6** 5 **Am I Blue**[55] 6543 5-8-11 **48** ChrisCatlin 6 32
(Mrs D Thomas) *prom: chsd ldr 12f out tl rdn 3f out: sn wknd* **13/2**3
500- **7** 16 **Sea Tobougie**[33] 7848 4-8-2 **45** HayleyTurner 3 7
(Mark Usher) *prom: rdn over 3f out: sn wknd: t.o* **50/1**
013- **8** 1 **Bute Street**[111] 6373 6-9-9 **60** GeorgeBaker 10 30
(Ron Hodges) *chsd ldr 2f: remained handy: effrt and nt clr run over 2f out: sn wknd and eased: t.o* **5/1**2

3m 5.88s (-0.12) **Going Correction** +0.175s/f (Slow)
WFA 4 from 5yo+ 6lb **8** Ran SP% **116.3**
Speed ratings (Par 101): **107,105,104,103,98 96,86,86**
Tote Swingers: 1&2 £5.40, 1&3 £6.10, 2&3 £4.90 CSF £22.19 CT £170.28 TOTE £2.50: £1.30, £7.80, £1.90; EX 20.70.
Owner T J Fitzgerald **Bred** T J Fitzgerald **Trained** Norton, N Yorks

FOCUS
A modest stayers' handicap with an emphatic, fast-improving winner.
Bute Street Official explanation: jockey said the gelding had no more to give

173 PLAY FREE BINGO AT BLUESQ.COM H'CAP 1m 4f 50y(P)
7:40 (7:41) (Class 7) (0-50,54) 4-Y-0+ **£1,535** (£453; £226) **Stalls** Low

Form RPR
00-1 **1** **Barodine**[7] 81 8-9-6 **54** 6ex GeorgeBaker 4 66+
(Ron Hodges) *hld up: hdwy over 3f out: chsd ldr over 2f out: led over 1f out: sn clr: eased nr fin* **5/1**3
/00- **2** 4 **Rosenblatt (GER)**[100] 6668 9-9-2 **50** StevieDonohoe 3 54
(John Spearing) *hld up: hdwy over 3f out: rdn to chse wnr ins fnl f: styd on* **12/1**
050/ **3** ½ **Beauchamp Viking**[14] 2912 7-8-12 **46** (t) HayleyTurner 6 49
(Simon Burrough) *hld up: hdwy 2f out: swtchd lft ins fnl f: nt rch ldrs* **20/1**
54-0 **4** *nse* **Barbirolli**[10] 30 9-8-4 **45** LauraPike(7) 7 48
(William Stone) *hld up: hdwy and hung lft over 1f out: r.o: nt rch ldrs* **12/1**
340- **5** 1 ¼ **Derby Desire (IRE)**[16] 8010 7-9-2 **50** (t) ShaneKelly 12 51
(Des Donovan) *chsd ldrs: rdn over 2f out: no ex fnl f* **4/1**2
424- **6** ½ **Escardo (GER)**[56] 7508 8-8-10 **47** RobertLButler(3) 9 47
(David Bridgwater) *chsd ldrs: led over 4f out: rdn and hdd over 1f out: no ex ins fnl f* **11/1**
000/ **7** ¾ **Daggerman**[50] 674 6-8-11 **45** (b1) GrahamGibbons 1 44
(Barry Leavy) *chsd ldrs: rdn over 2f out: no ex fnl f* **16/1**
30-0 **8** 1 **Flyjack (USA)**[7] 86 4-8-6 **47** (p) PatrickDonaghy(3) 5 44
(Lisa Williamson) *s.s: hld up: rdn over 1f out: nvr nrr* **33/1**
052- **9** 8 **Olivino (GER)**[45] 7634 10-8-9 **46** (p) AndrewHeffernan(3) 2 31
(Bernard Llewellyn) *chsd ldrs: rdn over 5f out: wknd 2f out* **7/2**1
065- **10** 1 ¼ **Share Option**[77] 7213 9-8-11 **45** JimmyQuinn 10 28
(Tony Carroll) *hld up: plld hrd: hdwy over 4f out: wknd over 2f out* **11/2**
063- **11** 11 **Barra Raider**[118] 6183 4-8-12 **50** TomEaves 11 15
(Roger Fisher) *chsd ldrs: rdn over 3f out: wknd over 2f out* **12/1**
260- **12** 24 **Jiggalong**[231] 2489 5-8-13 **47** ChrisCatlin 8 —
(Mrs D Thomas) *racd keenly: led 10f out: hdd over 4f out: wknd over 2f out: t.o* **18/1**

2m 43.8s (2.70) **Going Correction** +0.175s/f (Slow)
WFA 4 from 5yo+ 4lb **12** Ran SP% **124.5**
Speed ratings (Par 97): **98,95,95,94,94 93,93,92,87,86 79,63**
Tote Swingers: 1&2 £23.10, 1&3 £32.00, 2&3 £38.20 CSF £67.45 CT £1135.08 TOTE £5.30: £1.70, £5.20, £12.10; EX 104.20.
Owner The Gardens Entertainments Ltd **Bred** Mrs A M Jenkins And E D Kessly **Trained** Charlton Mackrell, Somerset

FOCUS
A rock-bottom 47-54 handicap but a fluent, wide-margin winner.
Share Option Official explanation: jockey said the gelding ran too free
T/Plt: £1,299.30 to a £1 stake. Pool: £84,192.82. 47.30 winning tickets. T/Qpdt: £62.90 to a £1 stake. Pool: £11,148.22. 131 winning tickets. CR

158 LINGFIELD (L-H)
Saturday, January 15

OFFICIAL GOING: Standard
Wind: Very strong, behind Weather: Overcast

174 BET ON TODAY'S FOOTBALL AT BLUESQ.COM H'CAP 1m 2f (P)
12:45 (12:46) (Class 5) (0-70,71) 4-Y-0+ **£2,047** (£604; £302) **Stalls** Low

Form RPR
013- **1** **Lingfield Bound (IRE)**[31] 7881 4-9-5 **70** LukeMorris 5 79
(John Best) *trckd ldrs in 5th: rdn and prog on outer wl over 1f out: led last 150yds: drvn out* **13/2**
012/ **2** ½ **Transformer (IRE)**[279] 6705 5-8-13 **62** JimCrowley 1 70
(William Jarvis) *led: drvn over 1f out: hdd and nt qckn 150yds out: styd on again nr fin* **8/1**
24-1 **3** ½ **Scary Movie (IRE)**[10] 50 6-9-8 **71** CathyGannon 14 78
(Ronald Harris) *hld up in 8th: rdn over 2f out: prog over 1f out: styd on to take 3rd nr fin: nvr able to chal* **10/1**
15-1 **4** *nk* **Lord Theo**[8] 83 7-9-1 **69** RyanClark(5) 4 75
(Nick Littmoden) *hld up in 7th: prog on inner over 2f out: disp 2nd briefly over 1f out: one pce* **10/1**
/31- **5** 1 **Talayeb**[18] 7994 6-9-5 **68** HayleyTurner 2 72
(Marcus Tregoning) *trckd ldng trio: effrt on inner over 2f out: drvn to dispute 2nd briefly over 1f out: nt qckn* **6/1**3
12-1 **6** ½ **Edgeworth (IRE)**[7] 94 5-9-0 **63** (p) ChrisCatlin 8 66+
(Brendan Powell) *hld up in 9th: pushed along 3f out: nt clr run on inner over 2f out: styd on on fnl f* **11/4**1
552- **7** ½ **Green Wadi**[31] 7884 6-9-5 **68** GeorgeBaker 6 70
(Gary Moore) *trckd ldrs in 6th: prog on outer to chse ldr over 2f out to over 1f out: fdd* **9/2**2
000- **8** 3 ¼ **Basra (IRE)**[79] 7190 8-9-7 **70** IanMongan 13 66
(Jo Crowley) *stdd s: hld up last: sme prog 3f out: drvn over 1f out: nvr threatened* **20/1**
664- **9** *hd* **Beau Fighter**[25] 7957 6-8-11 **60** FergusSweeney 9 56
(Gary Moore) *stdd s: hld up in 11th: nvr on terms* **12/1**
063- **10** 1 ½ **Folio (IRE)**[37] 7778 11-9-1 **64** StevieDonohoe 12 57
(Willie Musson) *hld up in last pair: struggling in last trio 3f out: n.d after* **20/1**
600- **11** 4 **Marmooq**[24] 7966 8-8-13 **62** RobbieFitzpatrick 3 47
(Michael Attwater) *mostly chsd ldr to over 2f out: wknd rapidly* **66/1**
050- **12** 2 ½ **Master Of Dance (IRE)**[19] 7985 4-9-5 **70** MickyFenton 11 50
(James Given) *hld up in 10th: struggling in last trio 3f out: no ch after* **66/1**
54-0 **13** 2 ½ **Hierarch (IRE)**[7] 96 4-9-2 **67** (be) StephenCraine 10 42
(David Flood) *t.k.h: pressed ldng pair to wl over 2f out: wknd rapidly* **16/1**

2m 8.04s (1.44) **Going Correction** +0.15s/f (Slow)
WFA 4 from 5yo+ 2lb **13** Ran SP% **127.8**
Speed ratings (Par 103): **100,99,99,98,98 97,97,94,94,93 90,88,86**
Tote Swingers: 1&2 £14.80, 1&3 £8.50, 2&3 £16.60 CSF £60.06 CT £534.33 TOTE £9.60: £3.00, £3.30, £2.50; EX 92.20 TRIFECTA Not won..
Owner Lingfield Park Owners Club **Bred** Mrs Mary Gallagher **Trained** Hucking, Kent
■ Stewards' Enquiry : Stephen Craine three-day ban: careless riding (Jan 29-31)

FOCUS
Several recent winners in a competitive handicap. The ordinary gallop suited the prominent racers and the winner came down the centre in the straight.
Green Wadi Official explanation: jockey said gelding hung left in straight

175 LINGFIELDPARK.CO.UK CLAIMING STKS 1m 2f (P)
1:15 (1:15) (Class 6) 4-Y-0+ **£1,535** (£453; £226) **Stalls** Low

Form RPR
441- **1** **Faithful Ruler (USA)**[18] 7989 7-9-1 78 (p) LukeMorris 4 76
(Ronald Harris) *trckd ldng pair: wnt 2nd over 3f out: rdn to ld over 1f out: styd on* **15/8**1
26-4 **2** ¾ **Dream Of Fortune (IRE)**[7] 94 7-8-4 66 (bt) MatthewCosham(7) 2 70
(David Evans) *t.k.h: hld up in last pair: gd prog on inner over 2f out: chsd wnr fnl f: nt qckn* **9/2**3
105- **3** ¾ **Lang Shining (IRE)**[31] 7251 7-9-11 80 FergusSweeney 5 83
(Jamie Osborne) *hld up bhd ldng quartet: cl up over 2f out: nt qckn over 1f out: styd on* **10/1**
666- **4** ¾ **Sgt Schultz (IRE)**[155] 5034 8-9-5 86 LiamKeniry 9 75
(J S Moore) *hld up bhd ldng quartet: pushed along over 3f out: outpcd 2f out: kpt on fnl f* **14/1**
116- **5** ¾ **Classically (IRE)**[81] 6449 5-9-7 76 GeorgeBaker 1 76
(Hughie Morrison) *led to over 1f out: grad wknd* **4/1**2
50-5 **6** 4 **Thunderball**[6] 105 5-9-2 77 RyanClark(5) 8 68
(David Nicholls) *t.k.h: trckd ldr 1f: styd cl up: wknd wl over 1f out* **9/2**3
000- **7** 7 **Mister Green (FR)**[24] 7971 5-9-11 70 (be) JimCrowley 3 58
(David Flood) *dwlt: t.k.h: hld up in last pair: brief effrt over 2f out: sn wknd* **11/2**
004- **8** 40 **Ting Ting (USA)**[16] 8018 4-7-12 56 (vt1) NickyMackay 7 —
(Jim Boyle) *prog to chse ldr after 1f to over 3f out: wknd rapidly: t.o* **25/1**

2m 6.75s (0.15) **Going Correction** +0.15s/f (Slow)
WFA 4 from 5yo+ 2lb **8** Ran SP% **126.1**
Speed ratings (Par 101): **105,104,103,103,102 99,93,61**
Tote Swingers: 1&2 £3.40, 1&3 £4.20, 2&3 £6.10 CSF £12.10 TOTE £3.10: £1.60, £2.10, £2.30; EX 13.10 Trifecta £57.40 Pool: £403.73 - 5.20 winning units..
Owner Ridge House Stables Ltd **Bred** WinStar Farm LLC **Trained** Earlswood, Monmouths

FOCUS
A fair claimer but a muddling gallop means the bare form is not entirely reliable. The winner came down the centre.
Classically(IRE) Official explanation: jockey said gelding hung right throughout

176 EDENBRIDGE MEDIAN AUCTION MAIDEN STKS 1m (P)
1:50 (1:51) (Class 6) 3-Y-O **£1,535** (£453; £226) **Stalls** High

Form RPR
1 **Western Prize** 3-9-3 0 JimCrowley 3 76+
(Ralph Beckett) *trckd ldng pair: wnt 2nd 2f out: pushed along and clsd to ld 1f out: shkn up and styd on wl* **8/11**1
0- **2** 1 ¼ **Obsession (IRE)**[94] 6849 3-9-3 0 (v) GeorgeBaker 4 72
(Jeremy Noseda) *hld up in 5th: effrt and hanging wl over 1f out: prog to chse wnr ins fnl f: styd on but no imp* **9/2**3
535- **3** 1 ¾ **Tagansky**[123] 6053 3-9-3 71 HayleyTurner 1 68
(Simon Dow) *trckd ldr: led wl over 2f out and sn kicked 2 l clr: hdd and nt qckn 1f out: fdd* **7/2**2
0- **4** 4 ½ **Anna Fontenail**[59] 7478 3-8-12 0 JamesMillman 2 53
(Rod Millman) *t.k.h: hld up bhd ldng pair: racd awkwardly and dropped to last over 2f out: nvr on terms after* **10/1**
0- **5** 1 ¼ **Revolutionary**[24] 7962 3-9-3 0 FergusSweeney 8 55
(Jamie Osborne) *hld up last: pushed along 2f out: modest prog over 1f out: sn no hdwy* **16/1**
0- **6** 9 **Runaway Tiger (IRE)**[52] 7559 3-9-3 0 LiamJones 5 34
(Paul D'Arcy) *led at decent pce into the wind: hdd & wknd wl over 2f out* **33/1**

1m 40.59s (2.39) **Going Correction** +0.15s/f (Slow) **6** Ran SP% **116.2**
Speed ratings (Par 95): **94,92,91,86,85 76**
Tote Swingers: 1&2 £1.50, 1&3 £1.30, 2&3 £1.70 CSF £4.80 TOTE £1.80: £1.40, £1.90; EX 5.10 Trifecta £7.00 Pool: £758.06 - 79.73 winning units..
Owner J C Smith **Bred** Littleton Stud **Trained** Kimpton, Hants

FOCUS
An uncompetitive maiden in which a modest gallop picked up only turning for home. The winner came down the centre and the first three pulled clear.

177 MARSH GREEN H'CAP 1m (P)
2:20 (2:21) (Class 4) (0-85,89) 3-Y-O £3,238 (£963; £481; £240) Stalls High

Form RPR
52-1 **1** **Palm Pilot (IRE)**[12] [27] 3-8-9 **73**........ EddieAhern 2 77+
(Ed Dunlop) *trckd ldng pair: clsd 2f out: pushed into ld over 1f out: hd quite high and cajoled along to hold on* **10/3**[2]
33-3 **2** *nse* **Amwell Pinot**[7] [101] 3-9-11 **89**........(p) CathyGannon 5 93
(Alan Bailey) *trckd ldr to wl over 1f out: rewnewed effrt u.p to chal fnl f: upsides whn edgd lft nr fin: nt qckn* **9/2**[3]
011- **3** *2* **Angelic Upstart (IRE)**[38] [7758] 3-9-0 **78**........ LiamKeniry 3 77
(Andrew Balding) *t.k.h: hld up in 4th: nt qckn over 2f out: kpt on to take 3rd nr fin* **11/10**[1]
341- **4** *½* **Night Witch (IRE)**[29] [7907] 3-8-7 **71** oh1........ JimmyQuinn 4 69
(Edward Creighton) *hld up in 4th: drvn and nt qckn 2f out: one pce after* **16/1**
436- **5** *shd* **Geordie Iris (IRE)**[30] [7891] 3-8-10 **74**........ JimCrowley 1 72
(Richard Hannon) *led to over 1f out: steadily wknd* **11/2**

1m 40.65s (2.45) **Going Correction** +0.15s/f (Slow) **5** Ran SP% **110.1**
Speed ratings (Par 99): **93,92,90,90,90**
CSF £17.85 TOTE £3.10: £1.30, £3.70; EX 13.60.
Owner Cliveden Stud **Bred** Cliveden Stud Ltd **Trained** Newmarket, Suffolk

FOCUS
Three last-time-out winners in a fair handicap. The gallop was again only modest and the winner came down the centre.

178 BLUE SQUARE SPRINT SERIES (ROUND 2) H'CAP (QUALIFIER) 6f (P)
2:55 (2:55) (Class 5) (0-70,70) 4-Y-O+ £2,729 (£806; £403) Stalls Low

Form RPR
12-2 **1** **Picansort**[3] [133] 4-9-5 **68**........(v) JimmyQuinn 1 76
(Brett Johnson) *t.k.h: cl up on inner: wnt 2nd wl over 1f out: narrow ld ins fnl f: jst hld on* **11/4**[1]
/1-0 **2** *nse* **Prize Point**[2] [143] 5-9-2 **65**........ EddieAhern 6 73
(Jim Boyle) *mde most: drvn and narrowly hdd ins fnl f: styd on wl: jst failed* **16/1**
220- **3** *½* **Pipers Piping (IRE)**[16] [8014] 5-9-7 **70**........(p) MichaelStainton 12 76
(Jane Chapple-Hyam) *hld up and sn last: prog fr 2f out: urged along over 1f out: styd on wl to take 3rd last strides* **10/1**
235- **4** *½* **Tislaam (IRE)**[40] [7730] 4-9-5 **68**........(v) RobertWinston 2 72
(Alan McCabe) *t.k.h: n.m.r after 1f: hld up towards rr: prog on inner over 2f out: chsd ldng pair ins fnl f: one pce* **11/2**[2]
10-2 **5** *¾* **Chjimes (IRE)**[7] [98] 7-9-4 **67**........(b) HayleyTurner 8 72+
(Conor Dore) *hld up bhd ldrs: cl up over 1f out: nowhere to go jst ins fnl f: one pce last 75yds* **6/1**[3]
005- **6** *shd* **Al Gillani (IRE)**[17] [8004] 6-9-7 **70**........(tp) GeorgeBaker 3 72
(Jim Boyle) *cl up: pressed ldrs 2f out: nt qckn over 1f out: stl wl there ins fnl f: fdd out of it nr fin* **15/2**
61-5 **7** *1* **Brandywell Boy (IRE)**[3] [133] 8-9-4 **70**........ BillyCray(3) 10 68
(Dominic Ffrench Davis) *chsd ldrs: u.p over 2f out: outpcd after: kpt on again fr over 1f out* **20/1**
20-0 **8** *2* **Desert Strike**[13] [13] 5-9-1 **67**........(p) AndrewHeffernan(3) 9 59
(Alan McCabe) *slowest away: t.k.h early and n.m.r after 1f: nvr on terms* **25/1**
04-5 **9** *¾* **Gwilym (GER)**[3] [134] 8-9-4 **67**........ CathyGannon 4 57
(Derek Haydn Jones) *a towards rr: rdn and no real prog over 2f out* **8/1**
20-6 **10** *nk* **Riflessione**[11] [29] 5-9-6 **69**........(b) JoeFanning 7 61
(Ronald Harris) *pressed ldr to wl over 1f out: wknd and eased* **8/1**
206- **11** *1 ¼* **Whiskey Junction**[41] [7719] 7-9-7 **70**........ ShaneKelly 5 55
(Michael Quinn) *t.k.h early and n.m.r after 1f: a in rr: nvr a factor* **12/1**
00-2 **12** *1 ¼* **Fear Nothing**[11] [20] 4-9-7 **70**........(v) AdamKirby 11 49
(Ian McInnes) *racd wd: pressed ldng pair to over 2f out: sn wknd* **14/1**

1m 11.59s (-0.31) **Going Correction** +0.15s/f (Slow) **12** Ran SP% **128.3**
Speed ratings (Par 103): **108,107,107,106,105 105,104,101,100,100 98,96**
Tote Swingers: 1&2 £18.40, 1&3 £7.10, 2&3 £63.40 CSF £57.21 CT £418.67 TOTE £3.30: £1.40, £6.10, £4.90; EX 89.40 TRIFECTA Not won..
Owner Peter Crate **Bred** Miss Brooke Sanders **Trained** Ashtead, Surrey

FOCUS
A modest handicap in which the gallop was reasonable. The winner, who raced against the inside rail for much of the way, edged towards the centre in the closing stages.
Tislaam(IRE) Official explanation: jockey said colt was denied a clear run
Gwilym(GER) Official explanation: jockey said gelding suffered interference shortly after start
Riflessione Official explanation: jockey said gelding hung right
Whiskey Junction Official explanation: jockey said gelding suffered interference shortly after start

179 ASHURST WOOD MAIDEN STKS 6f (P)
3:30 (3:30) (Class 5) 3-Y-O £1,910 (£564; £282) Stalls Low

Form RPR
332- **1** **Palais Glide**[42] [7686] 3-8-12 70........ EddieAhern 2 66
(Richard Hannon) *mde all: shkn up over 1f out: kpt on wl enough* **1/1**[1]
036- **2** *½* **Christmas Aria (IRE)**[136] [5651] 3-9-3 72........ HayleyTurner 1 69
(Simon Dow) *cl up on inner: chsd wnr wl over 1f out: tried to chal fnl f: a hld* **14/1**
3 *½* **Social Forum (IRE)**[76] [7257] 3-9-3 0........ MartinLane 8 67
(Rodger Sweeney, Ire) *hld up at rr of main gp: rdn and prog on wd outside 2f out: hanging over 1f out: styd on to take 3rd nr fin* **8/1**
034- **4** *1* **Welsh Inlet (IRE)**[17] [7997] 3-8-9 60........ KierenFox(3) 6 59
(John Bridger) *chsd ldrs: rdn 2f out: one pce fr over 1f out* **16/1**
5 *nk* **Beautiful Day** 3-9-3 0........ StevieDonohoe 4 63
(Kevin Ryan) *s.s: in tch at rr of main gp: effrt 2f out: shkn up and one pce over 1f out* **12/1**
20- **6** *2 ½* **Luckbealadytonight (IRE)**[88] [7002] 3-8-12 0........ JoeFanning 5 50
(Mark Johnston) *chsd wnr to wl over 1f out: steadily wknd* **12/1**
356- **7** *2 ¼* **Imogen Louise (IRE)**[58] [7493] 3-8-12 65........(b[1]) CathyGannon 3 43
(Derek Haydn Jones) *t.k.h early: chsd ldrs: lost pl over 2f out: n.d over 1f out* **8/1**
8 *21* **Masie Grey** 3-8-12 0........ JamieSpencer 7 —
(David Elsworth) *swvd bdly rt s: nvr on terms w ldrs: wknd 2f out: t.o* **11/2**[3]
0- **9** *35* **Ajla (IRE)**[168] [4595] 3-8-12 0........ JimCrowley 9 —
(Richard Hannon) *dwlt and then bdly hmpd s: nt rcvr and allowed to coast home fr 4f out* **9/2**[2]

1m 12.57s (0.67) **Going Correction** +0.15s/f (Slow) **9** Ran SP% **133.7**
Speed ratings (Par 97): **101,100,99,98,97 94,91,63,16**
Tote Swingers: 1&2 £7.50, 1&3 £4.70, 2&3 £18.70 CSF £22.71 TOTE £2.10: £1.20, £4.70, £2.60; EX 31.30 Trifecta £93.80 Pool: £720.06 - 5.68 winning units..
Owner Guy Reed **Bred** Theakston Stud **Trained** East Everleigh, Wilts

FOCUS
An uncompetitive maiden, especially with the second and third favourites losing all chance at the start. The gallop was an ordinary one and the winner came down the centre.
Imogen Louise(IRE) Official explanation: jockey said filly hung right
Masie Grey Official explanation: jockey said filly ran green
Ajla(IRE) Official explanation: jockey said filly suffered interference soon after start

180 PLAY FREE BINGO AT BLUESQ.COM H'CAP 1m 2f (P)
4:00 (4:02) (Class 3) (0-95,94) 4-Y-O+ £5,828 (£1,734; £866; £432) Stalls Low

Form RPR
35- **1** **Nice Style (IRE)**[36] [7815] 6-9-7 **94**........ AdamKirby 2 101
(Jeremy Gask) *dwlt: hld up towards rr: prog over 2f out: one of many clsng to chal 1f out: rdn and r.o to ld last 50yds* **9/2**[3]
000- **2** *½* **King Olav (UAE)**[48] [7612] 6-9-3 **90**........ LukeMorris 11 96
(Tony Carroll) *pressed ldr: led briefly over 3f out: styd chalng: led over 1f out: hdd and no ex last 50yds* **25/1**
112- **3** *nk* **Franco Is My Name**[17] [8003] 5-8-12 **85**........ FergusSweeney 10 90
(Peter Hedger) *hld up in midfield: effrt and wdst of all bnd 2f out: ended up against nr side rail fnl f: r.o: nt get there* **6/4**[1]
000- **4** *shd* **The Cayterers**[75] [7012] 9-8-5 **85**........ RPWalsh(7) 5 90
(Tony Carroll) *stdd s: hld up last: sweeping move arnd field fr 5f out to ld jst over 3f out: hdd over 1f out: kpt on* **33/1**
244- **5** *nk* **Audemar (IRE)**[24] [7970] 5-9-3 **90**........ AndreaAtzeni 9 95
(Edward Vaughan) *t.k.h: pressed ldrs: tried to chal and cl enough over 1f out: nt qckn ins fnl f* **14/1**
613- **6** *hd* **Mafeking (UAE)**[24] [7970] 7-9-4 **91**........ ChrisCatlin 13 95
(Mark Hoad) *pressed ldrs: drvn over 2f out: stl cl enough ent fnl f: one pce* **12/1**
000- **7** *nse* **Scamperdale**[17] [8009] 9-8-12 **88**........ KierenFox(3) 3 92
(Brian Baugh) *hld up in last pair: outpcd 3f out: prog on inner fr 2f out: styd on: nvr able to chal* **33/1**
00-0 **8** *1 ½* **Thunderstruck**[14] [6] 6-8-4 **82**........(p) RyanClark(5) 6 83
(David Nicholls) *t.k.h: hld up in midfield: outpcd and rdn 3f out: nvr on terms after: styd on nr fin* **20/1**
14-5 **9** *nk* **Hidden Glory**[14] [6] 4-8-9 **84**........ MickyFenton 4 85
(James Given) *pressed ldrs: rdn over 2f out: stl cl up jst over 1f out: fdd fnl f* **11/1**
024- **10** *nk* **Distinctive Image (USA)**[17] [8009] 6-9-6 **93**........ ShaneKelly 1 94
(Gerard Butler) *trckd ldrs on inner in 6th: effrt 2f out: nt qckn over 1f out: wl hld whn nt clr run ins fnl f* **4/1**[2]
30-5 **11** *4* **Record Breaker (IRE)**[11] [32] 7-8-9 **82**........(v) JoeFanning 7 74
(Mark Johnston) *dwlt: a in rr: struggling fr 3f out* **10/1**
/00- **12** *2 ½* **European Dream (IRE)**[63] [6106] 8-8-12 **85**........(p) JackMitchell 12 72
(Richard Fahey) *dwlt: hld up in rr: brief effrt on outer over 3f out: sn btn* **25/1**
41-0 **13** *18* **Rugell (ARG)**[14] [6] 6-9-3 **90**........ RobbieFitzpatrick 8 41
(Derek Shaw) *led at mod pce to over 3f out: wknd rapidly: t.o* **66/1**

2m 8.91s (2.31) **Going Correction** +0.15s/f (Slow)
WFA 4 from 5yo+ 2lb **13** Ran SP% **129.8**
Speed ratings (Par 107): **96,95,95,95,95 94,94,93,93,93 89,87,73**
Tote Swingers: 1&2 £23.10, 1&3 £3.50, 2&3 £12.60 CSF £126.19 CT £255.03 TOTE £7.10: £1.50, £7.50, £1.20; EX 149.90 Trifecta £469.50 Part won. Pool: £634.51 - 0.73 winning units..
Owner Tony Bloom **Bred** Exors Of The Late Dominic Murphy **Trained** Sutton Veny, Wilts

FOCUS
A good-quality handicap, but few progressive types on show. The gallop, in keeping with the rest of the card, was on the steady side and the winner again came down the centre.

NOTEBOOK
Nice Style(IRE) ◆, who was reportedly turned out too quickly following a run after a long break on his previous start, fared a good deal better back in trip and confirmed himself a very useful performer on Polytrack. He won with a bit in hand and, although this wasn't the strongest race of its type, he's the sort to win again. (op 4-1 tchd 5-1)
King Olav(UAE) had the run of the race and showed a good attitude in the closing stages but things went his way here and he's likely to remain vulnerable to the more progressive sorts in this kind of event.
Franco Is My Name is a bit better than the bare form after drifting to the stands' side in the straight but he wasn't far off his best back over arguably his best trip and he should continue to give a good account. (op 11-4)
The Cayterers, who has slipped in the weights, wasn't disgraced after being sent on some way out but his recent record suggests he wouldn't be certain to build on this next time. (tchd 25-1)
Audemar(IRE) is a reliable yardstick who had the run of the race and was far from disgraced upped to this trip for the first time. He should continue to go well but has little margin for error from this mark. (op 10-1)
Mafeking(UAE) was well placed given the moderate gallop and ran creditably back up in distance but is likely to remain vulnerable to anything progressive or well-handicapped. (op 8-1)
Scamperdale fared better than on his previous start on slowish ground at Wolverhampton but left the impression a stronger overall gallop would have suited him much better.
Distinctive Image(USA), ridden with more patience than when narrowly denied on his last visit to the track, wasn't at his best and, although a better gallop would have suited, he's plenty high enough in the weights at present. (op 5-1 tchd 11-2)
T/Plt: £61.80 to a £1 stake. Pool: £60,004.67 - 708.02 winning tickets. T/Qpdt: £15.00 to a £1 stake. Pool: £4,996.06 - 244.90 winning tickets. JN

[144] SOUTHWELL (L-H)
Sunday, January 16

OFFICIAL GOING: Standard
Wind: Strong 1/2 against Weather: Fine but very windy, rain race 3 onwards

181 PLACE ONLY BETTING AT BLUESQ.COM H'CAP 1m (F)
12:50 (12:51) (Class 6) (0-60,61) 4-Y-O+ £1,489 (£443; £221; £110) Stalls Low

Form RPR
1 **Intyre Trail (IRE)**[65] [7433] 6-9-7 **60**........ LiamKeniry 8 70
(Peter Fahey, Ire) *w ldrs: led over 2f out: edgd lft and styd on fnl f: eased nr fin* **14/1**
211 **2** *2* **Powerful Presence (IRE)**[5] [120] 5-9-8 **61** 6ex........ JoeFanning 6 65
(David O'Meara) *trckd ldr: effrt over 2f out: chsd wnr over 1f out: kpt on same pce* **8/13**[1]

060- **3** ½ **Tomintoul Star**[113] 6375 5-8-13 **55**.......................... JamesSullivan(3) 10 58
(Ruth Carr) *reluctant to load: in rr: hdwy on wd outside over 4f out: kpt on same pce fnl f* **50/1**

400- **4** 3 **Braddock (IRE)**[39] 7763 8-8-7 **46** oh1.............................(t) MartinLane 5 42
(Ken Cunningham-Brown) *trckd ldrs on outer: one pce fnl 2f* **100/1**

30-1 **5** ½ **Zarius**[15] 7 4-8-11 **57**.. NannaHansen(7) 9 52
(Chris Wall) *mde most: hdd over 2f out: wknd fnl f* **3/1**[2]

33-4 **6** 3 ¼ **Bring Sweets (IRE)**[15] 7 4-8-4 **48**.......................... DeanHeslop(5) 7 35
(Brian Ellison) *chsd ldrs: wknd appr fnl f* **20/1**

305- **7** nk **Bestowed**[30] 7920 6-9-4 **60**..............................(v) AndrewHeffernan(3) 3 47
(Tim Vaughan) *hld up in rr: effrt over 2f out: crowded over 1f out: nvr a factor* **28/1**

2-42 **8** 3 ½ **Exopuntia**[3] 148 5-9-3 **56**... GregFairley 1 35
(Julia Feilden) *chsd ldrs: sn drvn along: hung rt and wknd over 1f out* **17/2**[3]

66-1 **9** 3 ½ **Penrod Ballantyne (IRE)**[14] 14 4-9-2 **55**..................... LukeMorris 2 26
(Mike Hammond) *dwlt: sn drvn along in rr: nvr a factor* **14/1**

060- **10** 9 **Orpen Wide (IRE)**[20] 7986 9-8-10 **52**.......................(t) RobertLButler(3) 4 —
(Michael Chapman) *in rr: bhd and reminders 5f out* **80/1**

1m 42.98s (-0.72) **Going Correction** -0.05s/f (Stan) **10** Ran SP% **123.2**
Speed ratings (Par 101): **101,99,98,95,95 91,91,87,84,75**
toteswingers: 1&2 £4.00, 1&3 £45.50, 2&3 £12.00. CSF £24.17 CT £517.38 TOTE £16.30: £2.80, £1.10, £11.00; EX 39.50 TRIFECTA Not won..
Owner Sunday Afternoon Syndicate **Bred** Joe O'Flaherty **Trained** Monasterevin, Co Kildare

FOCUS
A low-grade handicap.

182 ENJOY THE PARTY PACK OFFER MAIDEN STKS 5f (F)
1:20 (1:21) (Class 5) 3-Y-O+ **£2,729** (£806; £403) **Stalls** High

Form RPR

024- **1** **Oh So Kool**[90] 6986 3-8-7 75.. RyanClark(5) 1 73
(Stuart Williams) *mde all: hung rt over 1f out: drvn out* **7/4**[1]

4-24 **2** 2 ¾ **Close To The Edge (IRE)**[5] 119 3-8-7 65..................(v[1]) ShaneKelly 6 58
(Alan McCabe) *chsd ldrs: rdn and hung lft over 1f out: kpt on same pce* **15/8**[2]

3 1 ¾ **Poppy's Rocket (IRE)** 3-8-4 0 ow2............................. DeanHeslop(5) 2 54
(Brian Ellison) *dwlt: sn chsng ldrs: effrt over 1f out: kpt on one pce* **10/1**

5- **4** ¾ **Braehead (IRE)**[18] 8002 3-8-12 62................................ CathyGannon 7 54
(David Evans) *w ldrs stands' side: rdn and wknd appr fnl f* **8/1**

0- **5** 3 ½ **Twisted Wings (IRE)**[224] 2785 3-8-7 0........................ DuranFentiman 4 37
(Tim Easterby) *w ldrs: drvn over 2f out: wknd wl over 1f out* **25/1**

40- **6** 2 ¼ **Prince Titus (IRE)**[123] 6075 3-8-9 0........................ JamesSullivan(3) 5 33
(Linda Stubbs) *chsd ldrs: lost pl over 1f out* **6/1**[3]

- **7** 7 **Bygones For Coins (IRE)** 3-8-7 0............................ PatrickMathers 3 —
(Alan Berry) *s.s: hung lft thrght: lost pl over 2f out: sn bhd* **100/1**

60.20 secs (0.50) **Going Correction** +0.10s/f (Slow) **7** Ran SP% **110.5**
Speed ratings (Par 103): **100,95,92,91,86 82,71**
toteswingers: 1&2 £1.30, 1&3 £3.10, 2&3 £3.80. CSF £4.90 TOTE £2.90: £2.10, £1.10; EX 5.50.
Owner Thompson & Bales **Bred** Old Mill Stud **Trained** Newmarket, Suffolk

FOCUS
A weak maiden.

183 PANTRY RESTAURANT (S) STKS 5f (F)
1:55 (1:56) (Class 6) 3-Y-O **£1,569** (£463; £231) **Stalls** High

Form RPR

40-5 **1** **Princess Dayna**[10] 66 3-8-12 64.......................... RichardKingscote 6 59
(Tom Dascombe) *dwlt: in rr: hdwy over 2f out: styd on to ld last 150yds* **7/1**

00-2 **2** 1 ¼ **Go Maggie Go (IRE)**[10] 64 3-8-9 51.......................... AmyRyan(3) 10 55
(Kevin Ryan) *chsd ldrs: led 1f out: sn hdd and no ex* **7/1**

3-23 **3** nk **Honkers Bonkers**[4] 130 3-9-3 63..................................(p) ShaneKelly 1 58
(Alan McCabe) *dwlt: sn prom: hdwy to chal over 1f out: edgd rt: kpt on same pce* **9/4**[1]

06-5 **4** 1 **Inde Country**[10] 65 3-8-12 40.. LukeMorris 2 51
(Nicky Vaughan) *chsd ldrs: keeping on same pce whn n.m.r 1f out* **100/1**

452- **5** ¾ **Silk Bounty**[20] 7983 3-9-3 62.. MickyFenton 8 52
(James Given) *w ldrs: led over 1f out: sn hdd and fdd* **7/2**[2]

6- **6** 1 ¼ **Blue Ivy**[254] 1879 3-8-12 0.. KellyHarrison 9 43
(Chris Fairhurst) *s.i.s: hung lft and hdwy over 2f out: sn chsng ldrs: fdd fnl f* **66/1**

60-5 **7** nk **Miss Toldyaso (IRE)**[10] 64 3-8-13 54.................... JamesRogers(5) 5 48
(Michael Quinlan) *led tl over 1f out: short of room and sn wknd* **20/1**

00-0 **8** 2 ½ **Look'N'Listen (IRE)**[10] 64 3-8-12 46.................... GrahamGibbons 13 33
(Alan Brown) *in rr stands' side: sme hdwy over 2f out: nvr a factor* **50/1**

00- **9** hd **Bigalo's Princessa**[66] 7400 3-8-12 0........................... DuranFentiman 11 32
(Lawrence Mullaney) *in rr stands' side: sme hdwy over 2f out: sn wknd* **100/1**

131- **10** 2 **Hereselle (IRE)**[20] 7983 3-8-11 65.............................. DavidKenny(7) 4 31
(Michael Chapman) *w ldrs: lost pl over 1f out* **11/2**[3]

450- **11** 2 **Key To The Motion (IRE)**[20] 7983 3-8-9 45.................. PaulPickard(3) 3 17
(Paul Midgley) *dwlt: sn outpcd and drvn along: nvr on terms* **100/1**

6-23 **12** ¾ **Just For Leo (IRE)**[8] 100 3-9-3 62..............................(v) CathyGannon 12 20
(David Evans) *dwlt: sn outpcd and in rr stands' side: bhd fnl 2f* **8/1**

60.24 secs (0.54) **Going Correction** +0.10s/f (Slow) **12** Ran SP% **115.7**
Speed ratings (Par 95): **99,97,96,94,93 91,91,87,86,83 80,79**
toteswingers: 1&2 £6.20, 1&3 £4.40, 2&3 £6.10. CSF £52.09 TOTE £7.10: £2.00, £4.40, £2.00; EX 60.60 Trifecta £200.50 Pool: £371.22 - 1.37 winning units..The winner was bought in for 8,000gns.
Owner Mrs J A Chapman **Bred** Mrs J A Chapman **Trained** Malpas, Cheshire

FOCUS
A competitive seller.
Honkers Bonkers Official explanation: jockey said gelding hung right throughout
Miss Toldyaso(IRE) Official explanation: jockey said filly hung left throughout
Just For Leo(IRE) Official explanation: jockey said gelding was slowly away

184 RACING EXCELLENCE ALL WEATHER "HANDS AND HEELS" APPRENTICE SERIES H'CAP 1m 4f (F)
2:30 (2:30) (Class 6) (0-60,56) 4-Y-O+ **£1,489** (£443; £221; £110) **Stalls** Low

Form RPR

30-2 **1** **Magic Haze**[10] 63 5-9-10 **56**.................................... RichardRowe 7 67+
(Sally Hall) *w ldrs: wnt 2nd over 4f out: led over 1f out: kpt on* **4/1**[2]

45-3 **2** ¾ **Tivers Song (USA)**[13] 16 7-9-1 **47**.............................(b) LucyKBarry 1 56
(John Harris) *led: hdd over 1f out: kpt on ins fnl f: a hld* **8/1**

54- **3** 8 **The Dukes Arch (USA)**[76] 7270 4-8-12 **55**............(b) RossCoakley(7) 10 51
(Peter Fahey, Ire) *sn chsng ldrs: wnt 3rd over 3f out: one pce fnl 2f* **11/4**[1]

3-25 **4** 2 **Carnac (IRE)**[5] 118 5-9-1 **50**...(p) NoraLooby(3) 5 43+
(Alan McCabe) *trckd ldrs: n.m.r on inner over 4f out: styd on to take one pce 4th over 1f out* **9/2**[3]

05-6 **5** 4 ½ **Tinseltown**[6] 114 5-8-13 **50**.................................(p) DavidSimmonson(5) 3 36
(Brian Rothwell) *chsd ldrs: drvn and hung lft over 4f out: lost pl 3f out* **40/1**

606- **6** hd **Beseech (USA)**[17] 8015 4-8-11 **47**.......................... NannaHansen 11 32
(Julia Feilden) *swvd rt s: hdwy on outer 8f out: sn chsng ldrs: wknd fnl 2f* **25/1**

5-03 **7** 2 ¾ **Mojeerr**[3] 145 5-8-13 **45**..(e) MatthewCosham 4 26
(Alan McCabe) *chsd ldrs: drvn 5f out: lost pl over 3f out* **14/1**

200- **8** 3 **Light The City (IRE)**[58] 7504 4-9-1 **51**............................. AlexEdwards 6 27
(Ruth Carr) *hld up in rr: effrt over 4f out: lost pl over 3f out* **25/1**

24-3 **9** 1 ¼ **Yossi (IRE)**[10] 63 7-9-1 **50**.....................................(be) SeanPalmer(3) 2 24
(Richard Guest) *s.i.s: sn bhd: nvr on terms* **17/2**

655- **10** 1 **Asterisk**[25] 7968 4-8-12 **55**.. HannahNunn(7) 9 27
(John Berry) *rrd s: in rr: hdwy on outer over 5f out: outpcd and lost pl over 3f out* **17/2**

00-6 **11** nk **Lord's Seat**[12] 37 4-8-2 **45**... VictorSantos(7) 8 17
(Alan Berry) *mid-div: drvn 6f out: lost pl over 4f out: sn bhd* **100/1**

2m 41.97s (0.97) **Going Correction** -0.05s/f (Stan)
WFA 4 from 5yo+ 4lb **11** Ran SP% **114.8**
Speed ratings (Par 101): **94,93,88,86,83 83,81,79,79,78 78**
toteswingers: 1&2 £6.80, 1&3 £2.90, 2&3 £5.70. CSF £33.83 CT £101.56 TOTE £7.60: £2.30, £4.40, £2.00; EX 45.30 Trifecta £122.00 Pool: £562.26 - 3.41 winning units..
Owner Mrs Joan Hodgson **Bred** Miss S E Hall **Trained** Middleham Moor, N Yorks

FOCUS
They went a good gallop in this apprentice handicap.
Tinseltown Official explanation: jockey said gelding hung left

185 DINE IN THE QUEEN MOTHER RESTAURANT H'CAP 5f (F)
3:05 (3:06) (Class 6) (0-55,55) 4-Y-O+ **£1,619** (£481; £240; £120) **Stalls** High

Form RPR

400- **1** **Shawkantango**[228] 2648 4-8-9 **48**.............................(v) PatrickMathers 12 58
(Derek Shaw) *s.i.s: hdwy stands' side over 1f out: styd on wl to ld nr fin* **33/1**

3-13 **2** hd **Kheley (IRE)**[2] 166 5-8-8 **52**....................................... JamesRogers(5) 6 61
(Mark Brisbourne) *chsd ldrs: styd on and upsides wl ins fnl f: no ex nr fin* **6/4**[1]

506- **3** nk **Dispol Grand (IRE)**[40] 7738 5-9-2 **55**........................... RobertWinston 5 63
(Paul Midgley) *w ldrs: hrd rdn and styd on to ld ins fnl f: edgd lft and hdd towards fin* **4/1**[2]

6-2 **4** ¾ **Cheveyo (IRE)**[7] 102 5-8-0 **46** oh1..........................(e) RossCoakley(7) 4 51
(Patrick Morris) *sn w ldrs: led over 2f out: edgd rt and hdd ins fnl f: crowded and no ex* **7/1**[3]

505- **5** 4 **Fathey (IRE)**[30] 7911 5-8-8 **47**..(v[1]) JoeFanning 3 38
(Charles Smith) *chsd ldrs on outer: wknd over 1f out* **8/1**

00-0 **6** 4 ½ **Head To Head (IRE)**[10] 57 7-8-8 **47**...................(tp) GrahamGibbons 7 22
(Alan Brown) *led tl over 2f out: wknd appr fnl f* **20/1**

00-6 **7** ½ **Egyptian Lord**[13] 15 8-8-8 **47** oh1 ow1..............(b) RobbieFitzpatrick 2 20
(Peter Grayson) *chsd ldrs on outer: wknd over 1f out* **66/1**

00-6 **8** hd **Areeg (IRE)**[3] 144 4-8-0 **46** oh1................................. VictorSantos(7) 1 18
(Alan Berry) *dwlt: sn chsng ldrs on outer: wknd over 1f out* **66/1**

R-33 **9** ½ **Pinball (IRE)**[7] 102 5-8-13 **52**..................................(b) TomEaves 10 22
(Lisa Williamson) *dwlt: sn chsng ldrs: wknd over 1f out* **14/1**

306- **10** 6 **Best One**[17] 8019 7-9-2 **55**..(b) LukeMorris 11 —
(Ronald Harris) *in rr: bhd fnl 2f* **9/1**

600- **11** 1 ¼ **Champagne All Day**[33] 7869 5-8-7 **46** oh1................ MichaelStainton 9 —
(Simon Griffiths) *outpcd and lost pl over 3f out: sn bhd* **100/1**

0/- **12** hd **Saorocain (IRE)**[464] 6653 5-8-7 **46** oh1........................... CathyGannon 8 —
(Patrick Morris) *dwlt: in rr: bhd whn hung lft over 1f out* **20/1**

59.96 secs (0.26) **Going Correction** +0.10s/f (Slow) **12** Ran SP% **116.7**
Speed ratings (Par 101): **101,100,100,99,92 85,84,83,73 71,71**
toteswingers: 1&2 £12.60, 1&3 £20.20, 2&3 £2.90. CSF £79.15 CT £266.64 TOTE £34.10: £7.20, £1.20, £2.40; EX 134.20 TRIFECTA Not won..
Owner Mrs Lyndsey Shaw **Bred** Derek Shaw **Trained** Sproxton, Leics
■ Stewards' Enquiry : Robert Winston caution: used whip with excessive frequency.

FOCUS
A thrilling finish.

186 ENHANCED SP'S AT BLUESQ.COM H'CAP 7f (F)
3:35 (3:35) (Class 4) (0-85,85) 4-Y-O+ **£3,432** (£1,021; £510; £254) **Stalls** Low

Form RPR

14-3 **1** **Everymanforhimself (IRE)**[7] 105 7-9-3 **81**..................(b) TomEaves 3 91
(Kevin Ryan) *trckd ldr: shkn up to ld over 1f out: rdn out* **11/4**[2]

53-1 **2** 1 **Follow The Flag (IRE)**[13] 18 7-9-4 **82**........................(v) ShaneKelly 7 89
(Alan McCabe) *chsd ldrs: styd on to take 2nd last 100yds* **8/1**

53-4 **3** 1 **Trans Sonic**[15] 6 8-9-7 **85**.. JoeFanning 9 90
(David O'Meara) *led: swtchd lft after s: hdd over 1f out: kpt on same pce* **4/1**[3]

4-36 **4** 1 **Elusive Fame (USA)**[7] 105 5-8-11 **75**.........................(b) GregFairley 1 77
(Mark Johnston) *chsd ldrs: upsides 2f out: one pce* **6/1**

426- **5** 2 **Tevez**[17] 8022 6-8-12 **76**...(p) CathyGannon 6 73
(Des Donovan) *dwlt: swtchd wd over 4f out: sn outpcd: sme hdwy 3f out: nvr trbld ldrs* **10/1**

16-2 **6** ¾ **Conry (IRE)**[3] 149 5-8-5 **74**... RyanClark(5) 8 68
(Patrick Morris) *dwlt: t.k.h: sn trcking ldrs on outer: wknd over 1f out* **5/2**[1]

600- **7** ½ **Gala Casino Star (IRE)**[17] 8017 6-9-3 **81**...................... BarryMcHugh 4 74
(Richard Fahey) *hld up towards rr: effrt 3f out: nvr a factor* **25/1**

1m 29.05s (-1.25) **Going Correction** -0.05s/f (Stan) **7** Ran SP% **113.6**
Speed ratings (Par 105): **105,103,102,101,99 98,97**
toteswingers: 1&2 £5.20, 1&3 £2.80, 2&3 £4.50. CSF £24.23 CT £86.15 TOTE £4.10: £2.60, £3.00; EX 19.50 Trifecta £33.30 Pool: £562.96 - 12.50 winning units..
Owner J Duddy B McDonald & A Heeney **Bred** Denis McDonnell **Trained** Hambleton, N Yorks

FOCUS
A decent handicap.
Conry(IRE) Official explanation: jockey said gelding ran too free

187 PLAY RAINBOW RICHES AT BLUESQ.COM H'CAP 7f (F)
4:05 (4:05) (Class 6) (0-60,64) 3-Y-O **£1,489** (£443; £221; £110) **Stalls** Low

Form RPR

006- **1** **West Leake Melody**[48] 7631 3-8-8 **47**.......................... RobertWinston 4 54
(B W Hills) *led: hdd 3f out: regained ld 2f out tl narrowly hdd over 1f out: styd on to ld nr fin: all out* **5/1**[3]

44-2 **2** *hd* **Rhal (IRE)**[12] [41] 3-9-1 **54**.. TomEaves 3 60
(Bryan Smart) *s.i.s: sn trcking ldrs: t.k.h: drvn 3f out: styd on to take narrow ld 100yds out: hdd towards fin* **6/4**[1]

1-03 **3** *½* **Granny Anne (IRE)**[6] [109] 3-9-3 **56**.............................. CathyGannon 6 61
(Alan Bailey) *in rr: drvn over 3f out: hdwy on inner: edgd lft and tk narrow ld over 1f out: hdd and no ex last 100yds* **7/2**[2]

443- **4** *6* **Bachelor Knight (IRE)**[29] [7931] 3-9-4 **60**.................. JamesSullivan(3) 1 49
(Ollie Pears) *t.k.h: trckd ldrs: effrt over 2f out: sltly hmpd and wknd over 1f out* **12/1**

5-12 **5** *3* **Local Diktator**[5] [119] 3-9-11 **64**..(t) LukeMorris 8 45
(Ronald Harris) *t.k.h: w ldr: led 3f out tl over 2f out: sn wknd* **7/2**[2]

00-5 **6** *1¼* **Seadream**[11] [53] 3-8-0 **46** oh1.............................. RachealKneller(7) 2 23
(Mark Usher) *s.s: t.k.h in rr: sme hdwy 4f out: lost pl 3f out* **40/1**

000- **7** *16* **Likeable Lad**[47] [7641] 3-8-8 **47** oh1 ow1......................... BarryMcHugh 7 —
(Ruth Carr) *trckd ldrs on outer: t.k.h: lost pl over 3f out: sn wl bhd* **50/1**

1m 30.94s (0.64) **Going Correction** -0.05s/f (Stan) **7** Ran SP% **113.2**
Speed ratings (Par 95): **94,93,93,86,82 81,63**
toteswingers: 1&2 £3.50, 1&3 £3.80, 2&3 £2.30. CSF £12.69 CT £28.75 TOTE £6.10: £2.50, £1.30; EX 18.20 Trifecta £52.50 Pool: £579.55 - 8.16 winning units..
Owner Henry Barton **Bred** Mrs A Plummer **Trained** Lambourn, Berks
■ Stewards' Enquiry : Cathy Gannon one-day ban: careless riding (Jan 30)

FOCUS
A moderate handicap, but fair form for the grade with the first three clear.
West Leake Melody Official explanation: trainer's rep said, regarding apparent improvement in form, that the colt had jumped smartly away from the stalls, instead of being the usual slow away.
T/Plt: £21.20 to a £1 stake. Pool: £77,369.15 - 2,658.83 winning tickets. T/Qpdt: £11.20 to a £1 stake. Pool: £6,101.28 - 402.04 winning tickets. WG

166 WOLVERHAMPTON (A.W) (L-H)
Monday, January 17

OFFICIAL GOING: Standard to slow changing to standard after race 2 (2:50)
Wind: Light against Weather: Fine

188 BET ON WINNING DISTANCES AT BLUESQ.COM CLAIMING STKS 7f 32y(P)
2:20 (2:21) (Class 6) 4-Y-0+ **£1,535** (£453; £226) **Stalls** High

Form RPR
52-0 **1** **Avon River**[9] [99] 4-9-5 86..(b) DaneO'Neill 1 89
(Richard Hannon) *chsd ldr tl led over 1f out: edgd lft ins fnl f: rdn out* **1/3**[1]

156- **2** *1¼* **Samarinda (USA)**[54] [7557] 8-8-13 78..............................(p) MickyFenton 2 80
(Pam Sly) *led: shkn up and hdd over 1f out: styd on* **4/1**[2]

04-6 **3** *2¾* **Ilie Nastase (FR)**[10] [82] 7-9-0 72................................. HayleyTurner 4 73
(Conor Dore) *chsd ldrs: rdn over 2f out: styd on same pce appr fnl f* **8/1**[3]

0-64 **4** *11* **Desert Dreamer (IRE)**[3] [159] 10-8-7 68..........................(b) CathyGannon 3 37
(David Evans) *dwlt: hdwy over 5f out: rdn over 3f out: wknd 2f out* **25/1**

1m 29.65s (0.05) **Going Correction** +0.15s/f (Slow) **4** Ran SP% **110.0**
Speed ratings (Par 101): **105,103,100,87**
CSF £2.10 TOTE £1.10; EX 2.30.
Owner Jim Horgan **Bred** Poulton Stud **Trained** East Everleigh, Wilts

FOCUS
A steadily run claimer but straightforward form, the winner facing a simple task.

189 RINGSIDE CONFERENCE SUITE - 700 THEATRE STYLE H'CAP 5f 216y(P)
2:50 (2:51) (Class 6) (0-55,55) 3-Y-0 **£1,535** (£453; £226) **Stalls** Low

Form RPR
003- **1** **Joe Le Taxi (IRE)**[76] [7279] 3-9-0 **53**.................................... GregFairley 3 72+
(Mark Johnston) *led 5f out: hdd over 3f out: led again over 2f out: rdn clr fnl f* **3/1**[2]

045- **2** *5* **Torteval (IRE)**[17] [8031] 3-8-0 **46** oh1..............................(v) RPWalsh(7) 11 49
(David Evans) *chsd ldrs: led over 3f out to over 2f out: rdn and edgd lft whn rdr dropped whip over 1f out: styd on same pce fnl f* **9/1**

13-2 **3** *shd* **Shutterbug**[11] [64] 3-8-11 **55**..............................(t) RyanClark(5) 6 58
(Stuart Williams) *[illegible] 1f: chsd ldrs: rdn over 1f out: edgd lft: styd on same pce fnl f* **11/4**[1]

063- **4** *1* **Magical Star**[44] [7691] 3-8-11 **50**.. DaneO'Neill 7 50
(Richard Hannon) *hld up in tch: rdn over 1f out: sn hung lft: no ex fnl f* **15/2**

00-4 **5** *4½* **Scommettitrice (IRE)**[7] [109] 3-9-2 **55**........................... AndreaAtzeni 5 40
(Ronald Harris) *chsd ldrs: rdn over 2f out: wknd fnl f* **5/1**[3]

04-5 **6** *½* **Steel Rain**[10] [88] 3-9-2 **55**.. CathyGannon 2 39
(Nikki Evans) *hld up: hdwy u.p over 1f out: nvr on terms* **20/1**

040- **7** *3¼* **Beach Patrol (IRE)**[42] [7722] 3-8-10 **52**...................... AlanCreighton(3) 4 25
(Edward Creighton) *prom: rdn over 2f out: wknd over 1f out* **20/1**

00-5 **8** *2½* **Sapphire Girl**[5] [130] 3-8-9 **55**........................... GeorgeChaloner(7) 8 20
(Richard Fahey) *s.i.s: a in rr: rdn over 2f out: sn wknd* **16/1**

00-0 **9** *1¾* **Renesmee (IRE)**[11] [64] 3-8-8 **47** oh1 ow1........... RobbieFitzpatrick 10 —
(Peter Grayson) *s.i.s: outpcd* **100/1**

630- **10** *1½* **Crazy In Love**[35] [7857] 3-8-9 **51**.......................................(b) KierenFox(3) 9 —
(Bill Turner) *chsd ldrs: lost pl 1/2-way: wknd sn after* **13/2**

000- **11** *2¼* **Bridget The Fidget**[42] [7722] 3-8-11 **50**................................ JimmyQuinn 1 —
(Edward Creighton) *s.i.s: outpcd* **50/1**

1m 14.85s (-0.15) **Going Correction** +0.15s/f (Slow) **11** Ran SP% **121.8**
Speed ratings (Par 95): **107,100,100,98,92 92,87,84,82,80 77**
toteswingers:1&2:£8.10, 1&3:£3.70, 2&3:£6.20 CSF £30.34 CT £86.77 TOTE £4.60: £2.00, £4.40, £1.10; EX 45.50 Trifecta £430.20 Not won. Pool: £581.48 - 0.63 winning units..
Owner Mark Johnston Racing Ltd **Bred** J Joyce **Trained** Middleham Moor, N Yorks
■ Stewards' Enquiry : Jimmy Quinn caution: used whip when out of contention.

FOCUS
A weak handicap and a very well-treated winner who will have more to offer. The time was fast for the grade although the track was rider faster than the official going, which was changed following this race.

190 BLUESQ.COM ON YOUR IPHONE H'CAP 1m 4f 50y(P)
3:20 (3:20) (Class 5) (0-75,72) 4-Y-0+ **£1,878** (£558; £279; £139) **Stalls** Low

Form RPR
211- **1** **Rhythm Stick**[31] [7921] 4-9-6 **68**.. FrannyNorton 6 75+
(John Berry) *trckd ldrs: racd keenly: rdn to go 2nd 2f out: edgd lft and r.o to ld wl ins fnl f* **15/8**[1]

114- **2** *½* **The Winged Assasin (USA)**[19] [8008] 5-9-10 **68**....(t) RussKennemore 1 74
(Shaun Lycett) *chsd ldr tl led 3f out: shkn up over 1f out: hdd wl ins fnl f* **7/1**

203- **3** *¾* **Kames Park (IRE)**[61] [7480] 9-9-10 **68**......................... JamieSpencer 5 72
(Richard Guest) *hld up: hdwy over 1f out: shkn up ins fnl f: nt qckn towards fin* **5/1**

10-5 **4** *nk* **Cotton King**[3] [162] 4-9-0 **62**..(vt) EddieAhern 2 66
(Tobias B P Coles) *chsd ldrs: rdn over 1f out: styd on same pce ins fnl f* **11/4**[2]

21-2 **5** *1* **Stadium Of Light (IRE)**[16] [3] 4-9-10 **72**................(p) BarryMcHugh 4 74
(Brian Ellison) *hld up: rdn and hdwy over 2f out: styd on same pce ins fnl f* **4/1**[3]

405- **6** *13* **Florio Vincitore (IRE)**[18] [8015] 4-9-0 **62**......................... JimmyQuinn 3 44
(Edward Creighton) *led 9f: sn rdn: wknd over 1f out* **16/1**

2m 43.1s (2.00) **Going Correction** +0.15s/f (Slow)
WFA 4 from 5yo+ 4lb **6** Ran SP% **116.5**
Speed ratings (Par 103): **99,98,98,97,97 88**
toteswingers:1&2:£3.10, 1&3:£2.40, 2&3:£3.90 CSF £16.37 TOTE £2.50: £1.10, £3.30; EX 16.60.
Owner Red Furlongs Partnership **Bred** Mrs M L Parry & P M Steele-Mortimer **Trained** Newmarket, Suffolk

FOCUS
There was a modest pace set (time 7.10 seconds above standard) in this ordinary handicap and they finished in a bunch. The bare form is ordinary and the winner probably didn't have to improve, but remains progressive.
Cotton King Official explanation: jockey said gelding was denied a clear run

191 STAY AT THE WOLVERHAMPTON HOLIDAY INN MAIDEN STKS 1m 1f 103y(P)
3:50 (3:50) (Class 5) 3-Y-0 **£1,813** (£539; £269; £134) **Stalls** Low

Form RPR
3- **1** **Art History (IRE)**[19] [8001] 3-9-3 0.. JoeFanning 3 71+
(Mark Johnston) *led: rn green: hung rt 4f out: hdd 3 out: sn rdn: rallied to ld ins fnl f: r.o* **2/1**[2]

306- **2** *¾* **Maher (USA)**[157] [5049] 3-9-3 75....................................... JamieSpencer 5 70
(David Simcock) *trckd ldr after 1f: hmpd 4f out: pushed along over 2f out: hrd rdn ins fnl f: r.o* **11/10**[1]

63- **3** *1* **Rojo Boy**[118] [6268] 3-9-3 75...(b) RobertWinston 6 68
(David Elsworth) *hld up: hdwy over 4 out: led 3f out: qcknd over 2f out: rdn and hdd ins fnl f: styd on same pce* **5/1**[3]

4 *¾* **Full Bloom** 3-8-12 0.. ShaneKelly 2 61
(Gerard Butler) *chsd ldrs: outpcd over 2f out: rallied over 1f out: r.o* **14/1**

5 *3½* **Ocean's Dream Day (IRE)** 3-9-3 0.................................. EddieAhern 1 59?
(John Ryan) *dwlt: hld up: outpcd wl over 2f out: styd on ins fnl f: nvr on terms* **33/1**

6 *4* **Cadgers Brig** 3-9-3 0... BarryMcHugh 4 50
(Richard Fahey) *hld up: rdn over 3f out: wknd over 2f out* **25/1**

2m 7.88s (6.18) **Going Correction** +0.15s/f (Slow) **6** Ran SP% **111.1**
Speed ratings (Par 97): **78,77,76,75,72 69**
toteswingers:1&2:£1.50, 1&3:£1.60, 2&3:£1.40 CSF £4.44 TOTE £2.90: £1.40, £1.50; EX 5.20.
Owner Sheikh Hamdan Bin Mohammed Al Maktoum **Bred** Kenilworth House Stud **Trained** Middleham Moor, N Yorks

FOCUS
A modest maiden. They went a steady pace, resulting in a time nearly ten seconds above standard and 0.88 seconds slower than the later modestly run 46-60 handicap for 3-y-os. The form is rated loosely around the third and the winner is a potential big improver on the bare figures.

192 WOLVERHAMPTON HOSPITALITY - A PLEASURE CLAIMING STKS 1m 141y(P)
4:20 (4:20) (Class 6) 3-Y-0 **£1,535** (£453; £226) **Stalls** Low

Form RPR
13-5 **1** **Better Self**[14] [27] 3-7-11 65... RPWalsh(7) 3 70
(David Evans) *s.i.s: hld up: hdwy over 2f out: led over 1f out: r.o* **9/2**[3]

114- **2** *1½* **Sheila's Star (IRE)**[37] [7839] 3-8-0 62................................ LukeMorris 4 63
(J S Moore) *led 1f: chsd ldrs: rdn and ev ch over 1f out: styd on same pce ins fnl f* **2/1**[2]

1-4 **3** *2¼* **Coral Moon (IRE)**[9] [101] 3-8-8 75............................. BarryMcHugh 2 65
(Richard Fahey) *trckd ldrs: plld hrd: lost pl over 5f out: styd on ins fnl f* **7/4**[1]

2-23 **4** *1¼* **Ad Vitam (IRE)**[11] [60] 3-8-3 56..................................(tp) DavidProbert 1 58
(Sylvester Kirk) *chsd ldr: led over 7f out: hdd over 5f out: rdn over 2f out: no ex fnl f* **7/1**

311 **5** *shd* **Sir Lunchalott**[18] [8012] 3-8-3 67..................................(b) CathyGannon [illegible] 57
(J S Moore) *chsd ldrs: led over 5f out: rdn and hdd over 1f out: no ex fnl f* **8/1**

1m 52.06s (1.56) **Going Correction** +0.15s/f (Slow) **5** Ran SP% **111.5**
Speed ratings (Par 95): **99,97,95,94,94**
CSF £14.10 TOTE £7.70: £5.00, £2.30; EX 14.70.
Owner Mrs Sally Edwards **Bred** Miss K Rausing **Trained** Pandy, Monmouths

FOCUS
An open claimer run in a time 0.86 seconds slower than the later 61-75 handicap. The favourite disappointed but the form makes sense at face value.

193 ENJOY THE PARTY PACK GROUP OFFER H'CAP 1m 141y(P)
4:50 (4:51) (Class 5) (0-75,74) 3-Y-0 **£1,813** (£539; £269; £134) **Stalls** Low

Form RPR
44-2 **1** **Urban Kode (IRE)**[14] [25] 3-8-0 **60** oh2............... MatthewCosham(7) 3 62
(David Evans) *racd keenly: trckd ldr: led over 6f out: rdn over 2f out: hung rt ins fnl f: styd on* **11/10**[1]

26-1 **2** *½* **Paco Belle (IRE)**[12] [51] 3-8-11 **64**..................................... DaneO'Neill 5 65
(Richard Hannon) *a.p: chsd wnr over 2f out: rdn over 1f out: r.o* **6/1**

53-2 **3** *2¾* **Riot Police (USA)**[14] [23] 3-9-7 **74**...........................(p) JamieSpencer 1 69
(David Simcock) *broke wl: stdd and dropped out in last sn after s: hdwy over 1f out: sn rdn: hung lft ins fnl f: nt run on* **5/2**[2]

610- **4** *2¼* **Diplomasi**[94] [6901] 3-8-12 **65**.. ChrisCatlin 2 55
(Clive Brittain) *sn led: hdd over 6f out: chsd wnr tl rdn over 2f out: no ex fnl f* **9/2**[3]

1m 51.2s (0.70) **Going Correction** +0.15s/f (Slow) **4** Ran SP% **108.7**
Speed ratings (Par 97): **102,101,99,97**
CSF £7.72 TOTE £1.80; EX 8.30.
Owner Mrs B Grainger **Bred** Nils Koop **Trained** Pandy, Monmouths

FOCUS
A moderate little handicap, run at an uneven pace. The winner probably didn't need to improve on his latest effort here.

194 PLAY ROULETTE AT BLUESQ.COM H'CAP 1m 1f 103y(P)
5:20 (5:20) (Class 6) (0-60,60) 3-Y-0 **£1,535** (£453; £226) **Stalls** Low

Form RPR
04-5 **1** **Roi Du Boeuf (IRE)**[14] [25] 3-8-12 **58**......................... AliceHaynes(7) 4 61
(David Simcock) *a.p: rdn to ld ins fnl f: styd on* **12/1**

000- **2** *½* **Jane's Legacy**[37] [7839] 3-8-11 **50**............................... GrahamGibbons 5 52
(Reg Hollinshead) *hld up: hdwy over 6f out: led over 1f out: rdn and hdd ins fnl f: styd on* **16/1**

06-2 **3** *nk* **Not So Bright (USA)**[7] 109 3-9-2 **55**..............................(t) GeorgeBaker 3 56+
(Des Donovan) *hld up: rdn and r.o ins fnl f: nrst fin* **11/8**[1]
441- **4** *¾* **Skeleton (IRE)**[37] 7839 3-9-0 **60**..............................(b) MatthewCosham(7) 1 60
(David Evans) *chsd ldrs: rdn over 2f out: sn outpcd: hung lft over 1f out: r.o* **5/1**[3]
2-32 **5** *1* **Mrs Neat (IRE)**[4] 142 3-9-2 **55**..............................(b) ChrisCatlin 6 53
(Sylvester Kirk) *trckd ldr: plld hrd: led over 4f out: rdn and hdd over 1f out: no ex ins fnl f* **9/4**[2]
60-3 **6** *10* **Rainbows Reach**[14] 23 3-9-0 **53**..............................(bt) ShaneKelly 2 30
(Gay Kelleway) *led: hdd over 4f out: rdn over 2f out: wknd over 1f out* **14/1**

2m 7.00s (5.30) **Going Correction** +0.15s/f (Slow) **6** Ran SP% **109.8**
Speed ratings (Par 95): **82,81,81,80,79 70**
toteswingers:1&2:£8.50, 2&3:£4.30, 1&3:£4.60. totesuper7: WIN: Not won. PLACE: Not won CSF £151.79 TOTE £12.40: £4.80, £6.60; EX 103.40.
Owner Tick Tock Partnership **Bred** Churchtown House Stud & Partners **Trained** Newmarket, Suffolk
■ A first winner for Alice Haynes.

FOCUS
The pace was steady, resulting in a bunch finish, and the form is moderate and muddling. The winner had slipped to a fair mark.
Not So Bright(USA) Official explanation: jockey said gelding was denied a clear run
T/Plt: £39.90 to a £1 stake. Pool:£59,198.24 - 1,082.50 winning tickets T/Qpdt: £24.90 to a £1 stake. Pool:£4,214.91 - 124.90 winning tickets CR

CAGNES-SUR-MER

Monday, January 17

OFFICIAL GOING: Fibresand: standard

195a PRIX DU DOCTEUR GAZAGNAIRE (CONDITIONS) (4YO+) (FIBRESAND) 1m 2f (D)

12:55 (12:00) 4-Y-0+ **£10,775** (£4,310; £3,232; £2,155; £1,077)

RPR
1 **Balajo (FR)**[47] 5-9-4 0.............................. FranckBlondel 3 86
(M Pimbonnet, France) **9/1**
2 *1½* **Konig Bernard (FR)**[97] 6914 5-9-0 0.............................. DominiqueBoeuf 7 79
(W Baltromei, Germany) **11/1**
3 *½* **Villa Molitor (FR)**[337] 558 5-8-10 0.............................. Francois-XavierBertras 8 75
(F Rohaut, France) **5/2**[1]
4 *nk* **Churriana (FR)**[10] 6-9-1 0.............................. FabienLefebvre 6 79
(Mlle A Voraz, France) **20/1**
5 *1½* **Querry Boy (FR)**[128] 5980 4-8-11 0.............................. FabriceVeron 9 74
(H-A Pantall, France) **13/1**
6 *¾* **Street Lair (USA)**[100] 6761 4-9-2 0.............................. IoritzMendizabal 12 78
(J-C Rouget, France) **4/1**[2]
7 *2* **Huangdi (FR)**[14] 5-9-2 0.............................. SebastienMaillot 4 72
(M Boutin, France) **11/2**[3]
8 *shd* **Interian (GER)** 5-9-4 0.............................. ThomasHuet 10 74
(C Ferland, France) **45/1**
9 *1½* **Bencoolen (IRE)**[16] 6 6-9-4 0.............................. NicolasPerret 5 71
(David Nicholls) *towards rr: rdn early in st: no ex* **73/1**
10 *3* **Maroni (IRE)**[708] 463 6-9-0 0.............................. FredericSpanu 2 62
(F Rohaut, France) **13/1**
0 **Kimberley Downs (USA)**[44] 7694 5-9-4 0.............................. SylvainRuis 11 —
(David Nicholls) *racd in midfield: rdn bef st: no ex* **15/1**
0 **Fylarchos (FR)**[112] 4-8-11 0.............................. ThierryThulliez 1 —
(C Laffon-Parias, France) **15/1**

1m 59.24s (119.24)
WFA 4 from 5yo+ 2lb **12** Ran SP% **117.4**
WIN (incl. 1 euro stake): 10.50. PLACES: 3.00, 3.60, 2.00. DF: 57.70. SF: 82.30.
Owner Gilbert Baltus **Bred** Mme G Forien & G Forien **Trained** France

196a PRIX DE GARAVAN (CLAIMER) (4YO+) (FIBRESAND) 6f 110y

1:25 (12:00) 4-Y-0+ **£6,465** (£2,586; £1,939; £1,293; £646)

RPR
1 **Lisselan Muse (USA)**[39] 7-8-8 0.............................. WilliamsSaraiva(3) 9 64
(Mme J Bidgood, France) **44/5**
2 *snk* **Wise Boy (GER)**[90] 4-8-11 0.............................. FlavienPrat 8 64
(Y Fertillet, France) **25/1**
3 *½* **Something (IRE)**[30] 7935 9-9-7 0.............................. IoritzMendizabal 4 73
(David Nicholls) *racd cl up in 3rd: rdn early in st: chal for ld 1f out: r.o wl: hdd for 2nd cl home* **73/10**[3]
4 *nk* **Asulaman (GER)**[21] 4-9-7 0..............................(b) StefanieHofer 16 72
(Mario Hofer, Germany) **10/1**
5 *½* **Abbondanza (IRE)**[13] 35 8-9-4 0.............................. Francois-XavierBertras 15 67
(David Nicholls) *towards rr fr s: rdn and r.o wl in st: fin strly fnl 100yds* **18/1**
6 *¾* **Dikta Melody (FR)**[21] 4-8-6 0..............................(b) StevanBourgois(3) 3 56
(P Demercastel, France) **95/1**
7 *hd* **Grymeos (FR)**[14] 4-9-2 0.............................. SylvainRuis 6 62
(J Heloury, France) **28/1**
8 *3* **Vianello (IRE)**[14] 4-9-11 0..............................(b) ASuborics 5 63
(Mario Hofer, Germany) **14/5**[1]
9 *snk* **Ladouce (FR)**[9] 5-8-7 0.............................. EddyHardouin(8) 13 52
(Robert Collet, France) **30/1**
10 *3* **Green Pride**[40] 8-9-5 0.............................. ThierryThulliez 10 48
(G Martin, Austria) **23/1**
0 **Giant Generation (GER)**[816] 7-8-11 0.............................. FabienLefebvre 2 —
(G Martin, Austria) **24/1**
0 **Time For Gold (FR)**[25] 6-9-2 0..............................(b) GaetanClouet(5) 7 —
(P Monfort, France) **9/1**
0 **Snow Bay**[14] 18 5-10-7 0.............................. NicolasPerret 14 —
(David Nicholls) *towards rr: rdn early in st: no ex: eased fnl f* **25/1**
0 **Good Star (FR)**[100] 5-8-8 0.............................. RonanThomas 11 —
(B Dutruel, France) **57/1**
0 **The Black Lady (GER)**[92] 4-9-1 0.............................. DominiqueBoeuf 12 —
(W Baltromei, Germany) **17/1**
F **Maggi Fong**[81] 5-9-4 0..............................(b) FabriceVeron 1 —
(H-A Pantall, France) *fell at s* **6/1**[2]

1m 17.55s (77.55) **16** Ran SP% **118.1**
WIN (incl. 1 euro stake): 9.80. PLACES: 3.60, 6.90, 3.90. DF: 142.60. SF: 231.60.
Owner Mme J Bidgood **Bred** Triple A Ranch **Trained** France

[188] WOLVERHAMPTON (A.W) (L-H)

Tuesday, January 18

OFFICIAL GOING: Standard
Wind: Fresh half-behind Weather: Fine and sunny

197 TODAY'S JOCKEY SPECIALS AT BLUESQ.COM CLAIMING STKS 5f 20y(P)

2:20 (2:20) (Class 6) 4-Y-0+ **£1,569** (£463; £231) **Stalls** Low

Form RPR
33-1 **1** **Sloop Johnb**[11] 84 5-8-13 74..............................(p) BarryMcHugh 4 75
(Richard Fahey) *chsd ldrs: rdn 1/2-way: r.o to ld wl ins fnl f* **9/4**[2]
33-0 **2** *¾* **Grudge**[6] 125 6-9-5 73..............................(be) HayleyTurner 1 78
(Conor Dore) *led early: chsd ldr: rdn 1/2-way: ev ch ins fnl f: styd on* **7/1**[3]
355- **3** *½* **Lewyn**[20] 7998 4-9-2 79..............................(t) RobertWinston 3 73
(Jeremy Gask) *hld up: rdn over 1f out: r.o ins fnl f: nt rch ldrs* **5/4**[1]
005- **4** *nk* **Rievaulx World**[115] 6374 5-8-10 73..............................(t) JulieBurke(5) 7 71
(Kevin Ryan) *sn led: shkn up over 1f out: edgd rt: hdd and no ex wl ins fnl f* **15/2**
25-1 **5** *2¾* **Spic 'n Span**[7] 116 6-8-7 61..............................(b) LukeMorris 2 53
(Ronald Harris) *dwlt: hdwy 1/2-way: rdn over 1f out: no ex ins fnl f* **9/1**
60-3 **6** *2* **Athwaab**[5] 137 4-8-4 65.............................. ChrisCatlin 6 43
(Michael Quinlan) *chsd ldrs: rdn 1/2-way: wknd over 1f out* **14/1**

61.55 secs (-0.75) **Going Correction** +0.025s/f (Slow) **6** Ran SP% **116.1**
Speed ratings (Par 101): **107,105,105,104,100 96**
.Sloop Johnb claimed by C. R. Dore for £9,000.\n\x\x
Owner Jonathan Gill **Bred** Manor Farm Stud (rutland) **Trained** Musley Bank, N Yorks
■ Stewards' Enquiry : Barry McHugh one-day ban: used whip with excessive frequency (Feb 1)

FOCUS
A decent claimer that went to the 74-rated Sloop Johnb. Only the first two were at their best.
Spic 'n Span Official explanation: jockey said gelding was slowly away

198 WOLVERHAMPTON-RACECOURSE.CO.UK H'CAP 5f 20y(P)

2:50 (2:50) (Class 5) (0-75,73) 3-Y-0 **£2,137** (£635; £317; £158) **Stalls** Low

Form RPR
414- **1** **Mr Optimistic**[45] 7696 3-9-2 **68**.............................. BarryMcHugh 4 77+
(Richard Fahey) *trckd ldrs: nt clr run over 1f out: rdn to ld and hung rt ins fnl f: r.o wl* **11/4**[2]
0-35 **2** *3* **Je Suis Unrockstar**[7] 119 3-8-13 **68**..............................(p) BillyCray(3) 3 66
(David Nicholls) *hld up: pushed along 3f out: hdwy u.p over 1f out: r.o* **10/1**
01-4 **3** *½* **Johnny Hancocks (IRE)**[10] 100 3-9-0 **69**.............................. JamesSullivan(3) 2 65
(Linda Stubbs) *led: hung rt 1/2-way: rdn over 1f out: hdd and unable qck ins fnl f* **5/1**[3]
101- **4** *1¾* **Lady Prodee**[20] 7997 3-8-11 **70**.............................. JakePayne(7) 1 60
(Bill Turner) *dwlt: sn trcking ldrs: rdn over 1f out: no ex ins fnl f* **13/8**[1]
5-4 **5** *½* **Braehead (IRE)**[2] 182 3-8-3 **62**.............................. MatthewCosham(7) 5 50
(David Evans) *chsd ldrs: rdn and ev ch over 1f out: no ex ins fnl f* **12/1**
-230 **6** *1½* **Just For Leo (IRE)**[2] 183 3-8-3 **62**..............................(v) RPWalsh(7) 8 45
(David Evans) *chsd ldrs: rdn 1/2-way: wknd fnl f* **16/1**
00-6 **7** *7* **Lady Brookie**[10] 100 3-8-11 **63**.............................. RobbieFitzpatrick 6 20
(Peter Grayson) *s.i.s: a in rr: wknd 2f out* **33/1**
165- **8** *¾* **Magic Stella**[42] 7734 3-9-7 **73**.............................. DaneO'Neill 7 28
(Alan Jarvis) *sn pushed along in rr: wknd 1/2-way* **11/1**

62.09 secs (-0.21) **Going Correction** +0.025s/f (Slow) **8** Ran SP% **115.4**
Speed ratings (Par 97): **102,97,96,93,92 90,79,78**
Tote Swingers: 1&2 £3.50, 1&3 £3.50, 2&3 £6.90 CSF £30.45 CT £131.26 TOTE £4.60: £1.50, £1.90, £1.50; EX 28.00 Trifecta £113.90 Pool: £563.44 - 3.66 winning units..
Owner Frank Lenny Financial **Bred** C J Murfitt **Trained** Musley Bank, N Yorks

FOCUS
A pretty ordinary sprint handicap, although a nice effort from the winner. The form is rated around the third.
Johnny Hancocks(IRE) Official explanation: jockey said gelding hung right-handed

199 ENHANCED SP'S AT BLUESQ.COM H'CAP 5f 216y(P)

3:20 (3:21) (Class 5) (0-75,75) 4-Y-0+ **£2,201** (£655; £327; £163) **Stalls** Low

Form RPR
/15- **1** **Jack Rackham**[313] 859 7-9-4 **72**..............................(v) TomEaves 1 82
(Bryan Smart) *trckd ldrs: rdn to ld ins fnl f: r.o u.p* **8/1**
13-4 **2** *¾* **Incomparable**[6] 134 6-9-3 **71**..............................(bt) IanMongan 12 79
(David Nicholls) *led: hdd over 4f out: led again over 1f out: rdn and hdd ins fnl f: styd on* **7/1**
515- **3** *1* **Co Dependent (USA)**[18] 8036 5-8-10 **64**.............................. FergusSweeney 11 69+
(Jamie Osborne) *s.i.s: hld up: hdwy 2f out: rdn: edgd rt and r.o ins fnl f: nt rch ldrs* **33/1**
44-0 **4** *nk* **Perlachy**[12] 58 7-8-11 **65**..............................(v) KellyHarrison 7 69
(Derek Shaw) *hld up: r.o ins fnl f: nt trble ldrs* **25/1**
-420 **5** *½* **Elhamri**[6] 134 7-9-4 **72**.............................. HayleyTurner 9 74
(Conor Dore) *chsd ldr: rdn and ev ch wl over 1f out: no ex ins fnl f* **10/1**
66-3 **6** *nk* **Takajan (IRE)**[16] 13 4-8-11 **65**.............................. EddieAhern 10 66
(Mark Brisbourne) *trckd ldrs: rdn over 2f out: styd on same pce fnl f* **18/1**
0-22 **7** *½* **Onceaponatime (IRE)**[4] 168 6-9-3 **71**.............................. LukeMorris 8 73+
(Michael Squance) *chsd ldrs: lost pl after 1f: rdn and nt clr run over 1f out: r.o: nt trble ldrs* **2/1**[1]
063- **8** *¾* **Ballodair (IRE)**[20] 8004 4-9-0 **68**..............................(b[1]) JackMitchell 2 65+
(Richard Fahey) *s.i.s: in rr whn hmpd wl over 3f out: nt clr run ins fnl f: nvr nrr* **4/1**[2]
00-4 **9** *1¼* **Tourist**[14] 35 6-9-7 **75**.............................. JimmyQuinn 6 68
(Derek Shaw) *hld up: rdn over 1f out: nvr on terms* **8/1**
422- **10** *½* **Spin Again (IRE)**[45] 7701 6-9-0 **68**.............................. LiamJones 5 60
(Mark Wellings) *chsd ldrs: rdn and hung lft over 1f out: sn wknd* **14/1**
020- **11** *1* **Devil You Know (IRE)**[46] 7683 5-9-1 **69**..............................(t) GrahamGibbons 4 57
(Michael Easterby) *s.i.s: hdwy to ld over 4f out: rdn and hdd wl over 1f out: wknd fnl f* **5/1**[3]

1m 14.51s (-0.49) **Going Correction** +0.025s/f (Slow) **11** Ran SP% **132.5**
Speed ratings (Par 103): **104,103,101,101,100 100,99,98,96,96 94**
Tote Swingers: 1&2 £35.10, 1&3 £11.90, 2&3 £36.80 CSF £71.41 CT £1857.45 TOTE £11.70: £2.30, £3.30, £11.80; EX 82.40 Trifecta £246.20 Part won. Pool: £332.79 - 0.83 winning units..
Owner Mrs F Denniff **Bred** A S Denniff **Trained** Hambleton, N Yorks

FOCUS
A competitive-looking handicap. It was sound run and the winner is getting closer to his old form.

Tourist Official explanation: trainer's rep said gelding bled from the nose

200 WOLVERHAMPTON HOSPITALITY - A PLEASURE FILLIES' H'CAP 7f 32y(P)
3:50 (3:50) (Class 5) (0-75,74) 4-Y-0+ **£2,137** (£635; £317; £158) **Stalls** High

Form RPR
20-3 **1** **Piquante**[6] 128 5-9-1 **68** HayleyTurner 4 72
(Nigel Tinkler) *led: hdd over 6f out: led again over 5f out: hdd over 3f out: led over 1f out: drvn out* **15/8**[1]
300- **2** ½ **Diapason (IRE)**[159] 4988 5-9-6 **73** (t) RichardKingscote 1 76
(Tom Dascombe) *trckd ldrs: plld hrd: led over 3f out: rdn and hdd over 1f out: styd on* **5/2**[2]
330- **3** 1½ **Catching Zeds**[21] 7992 4-8-8 **61** ow1 TomEaves 5 60
(Ian Williams) *led over 6f out to over 5f out: chsd ldrs: rdn 1/2-way: hung lft over 1f out: sn swtchd rt: r.o* **7/1**[3]
0- **4** *nk* **Lady Excel (IRE)**[160] 4939 5-8-10 **63** MickyFenton 6 61
(Brian Rothwell) *hld up: rdn over 2f out: swtchd rt over 1f out: r.o: nt rch ldrs* **12/1**
150- **5** ½ **Emerald Girl (IRE)**[38] 7841 4-8-12 **72** GeorgeChaloner(7) 3 68
(Richard Fahey) *prom: racd keenly: rdn 1/2-way: styd on same pce fnl f* **5/2**[2]

1m 31.48s (1.88) **Going Correction** +0.025s/f (Slow) **5** Ran SP% **112.1**
Speed ratings (Par 100): **90,89,87,87,86**
CSF £7.03 TOTE £2.60: £1.90, £1.40; EX 7.40.
Owner W F Burton **Bred** Aston House Stud **Trained** Langton, N Yorks

FOCUS
They went just a steady pace in this fillies' handicap. Modest form.
Diapason(IRE) Official explanation: jockey said mare ran too free

201 RACING ALL YEAR AROUND FILLIES' H'CAP 1m 1f 103y(P)
4:20 (4:21) (Class 5) (0-70,65) 4-Y-0+ **£2,137** (£635; £317; £158) **Stalls** Low

Form RPR
62-2 **1** **Catbells (IRE)**[11] 83 4-9-0 **65** (p) NatashaEaton(7) 7 75
(Alan Bailey) *hood removed late and s.s: hdwy to ld over 4f out: clr over 2f out: sn rdn: styd on* **6/4**[1]
16-0 **2** *6* **Princess Lexi (IRE)**[15] 26 4-8-8 **52** TomEaves 1 49
(Ian Williams) *prom: chsd wnr over 3f out: rdn over 2f out: styd on same pce* **5/1**[3]
235- **3** 1½ **Olney Lass**[37] 7845 4-8-9 **53** MartinLane 6 47
(Mike Murphy) *hld up: rdn over 3f out: r.o ins fnl f: nvr trbld ldrs* **13/2**
35- **4** 2¼ **Indefinite Hope (ITY)**[32] 7909 4-9-2 **60** (t) AndreaAtzeni 5 50
(Michael Wigham) *chsd ldrs: rdn over 3f out: wknd wl over 1f out* **7/1**
00-0 **5** *40* **Dubai Legend**[9] 107 5-8-12 **55** DuranFentiman 3 —
(Noel Wilson) *led: hdd over 4f out: sn rdn: wknd over 2f out: t.o* **33/1**
/2-4 **6** *11* **Belles Beau**[11] 88 4-9-2 **60** GrahamGibbons 4 —
(Reg Hollinshead) *sn pushed along and prom: lost pl 7f out: drvn along 6f out: lost tch fnl 3f: t.o* **11/4**[2]

2m 1.54s (-0.16) **Going Correction** +0.025s/f (Slow)
WFA 4 from 5yo+ 1lb **6** Ran SP% **112.1**
Speed ratings (Par 100): **101,95,94,92,56 47**
Tote Swingers: 1&2 £2.70, 1&3 £2.90, 2&3 £3.90 CSF £9.46 TOTE £2.00: £1.80, £2.80; EX 9.50.
Owner C M & Mrs S A Martin **Bred** Mrs Mary Rose Hayes **Trained** Newmarket, Suffolk

FOCUS
A weak handicap, and it's doubtful if the winner had to improve on her recent form.
Belles Beau Official explanation: jockey said filly had no more to give

202 ENJOY THE PARTY PACK GROUP OFFER MAIDEN STKS 1m 141y(P)
4:50 (4:59) (Class 5) 3-Y-0+ **£2,007** (£597; £298; £149) **Stalls** Low

Form RPR
53- **1** **American Smooth**[21] 7994 4-9-13 0 (v) GeorgeBaker 4 58
(Jeremy Noseda) *chsd ldrs: wnt 2nd 2f out: rdn to ld and hung lft wl ins fnl f* **6/1**[2]
06-0 **2** ½ **Kassiodor (GER)**[13] 52 4-9-13 0 MickyFenton 3 57
(Darnay Curley) *plld hrd: led: clr 7f out: shkn up over 1f out: edgd lft and hdd wl ins fnl f* **50/1**[3]
63-2 **3** 1¾ **Duke Of Florence (IRE)**[10] 95 3-8-6 74 (b) ChrisCatlin 5 53
(Richard Hannon) *chsd clr ldr tl rdn 2f out: no ex ins fnl f* **10/11**[1]
0- **4** *15* **Chik's Dream**[111] 6470 4-9-13 0 DaneO'Neill 1 26
(Derek Haydn Jones) *got loose prior to the s: sn bhd* **100/1**

1m 51.88s (1.38) **Going Correction** +0.025s/f (Slow)
WFA 3 from 4yo 22lb **4** Ran SP% **69.6**
Speed ratings (Par 103): **94,93,92,78**
CSF £33.40 TOTE £3.50; EX 13.10.
Owner Budget Stable **Bred** Bottisham Heath Stud **Trained** Newmarket, Suffolk
■ Tornado Force (Evens) was withdrawn. Deduct 45p in the £ under Rule 4.

FOCUS
An eventful contest, the heavily gambled Tornado Force being withdrawn at the start on account of his rider being injured after the horse reared, and 100-1 shot Chik's Dream getting loose. It was slowly run and the form is rated negatively.

203 PLAY RAINBOW RICHES AT BLUESQ.COM H'CAP 1m 1f 103y(P)
5:20 (5:24) (Class 6) (0-60,62) 4-Y-0+ **£1,569** (£463; £231) **Stalls** Low

Form RPR
10-1 **1** **Black Coffee**[8] 115 6-9-9 **62** 6ex (b) ShaneKelly 1 73+
(Mark Brisbourne) *s.i.s: hld up: hdwy over 2f out: chsd ldr 1f out: r.o to ld wl ins fnl f: readily* **7/2**[1]
500- **2** 1½ **Kyle Of Bute**[119] 6269 5-9-4 **57** J-PGuillambert 4 65
(Brian Baugh) *chsd ldr: led over 2f out: sn pushed clr: rdn and hdd wl ins fnl f* **10/1**
503- **3** 2¼ **Una Pelota (IRE)**[32] 7920 5-9-7 **60** (t) RichardKingscote 3 63
(Tom Dascombe) *hld up: hdwy over 4f out: chsd ldr over 2f out: rdn over 1f out: no ex ins fnl f* **5/1**[2]
343- **4** 3¼ **Irish Jugger (USA)**[19] 8015 4-9-5 **59** JamesMillman 12 55
(Rod Millman) *hld up: hdwy over 2f out: rdn and hung lft over 1f out: styd on same pce* **6/1**[3]
40-6 **5** 1¾ **Sennybridge**[11] 83 4-9-4 **58** DaneO'Neill 6 53
(J W Hills) *mid-div: rdn over 2f out: styd on: nt trble ldrs* **20/1**
060- **6** ½ **Watchmaker**[39] 7814 8-9-4 **57** SamHitchcott 2 49
(Tor Sturgis) *mid-div: rdn over 3f out: styd on same pce fnl 2f* **16/1**
12-0 **7** *hd* **Love In The Park**[14] 30 6-9-3 **56** JackMitchell 7 49+
(Roy Brotherton) *s.i.s: hld up: nt clr run over 1f out: n.d* **5/1**[2]
23-0 **8** 2¾ **All Moving Parts (USA)**[6] 135 4-9-3 **57** (b) JamesDoyle 13 42
(Alan McCabe) *hld up: rdn over 1f out: nvr nrr* **10/1**
/0-0 **9** ¾ **Novestar (IRE)**[12] 63 6-9-2 **55** (t) NeilChalmers 9 39
(Michael Appleby) *chsd ldrs: rdn over 3f out: wknd 2f out* **40/1**
244- **10** *shd* **Celtic Ransom**[190] 3957 4-9-6 **60** EddieAhern 8 44
(J W Hills) *chsd ldrs: rdn over 2f out: wknd sn after* **5/1**[2]
300- **11** 3½ **King Of Connacht**[55] 7562 8-9-4 **57** (v) LiamJones 10 33
(Mark Wellings) *hld up: sme hdwy over 1f out: wknd fnl f* **33/1**
20-5 **12** *shd* **Pinsplitter (USA)**[10] 94 4-8-12 **55** (p) AndrewHeffernan(3) 5 31
(Alan McCabe) *set gd pce tl hdd & wknd over 2f out* **20/1**
00-6 **13** *5* **Lytham (IRE)**[15] 21 10-9-4 **57** JimmyQuinn 11 23
(Tony Carroll) *a bhd* **33/1**

2m 0.85s (-0.85) **Going Correction** +0.025s/f (Slow)
WFA 4 from 5yo+ 1lb **13** Ran SP% **128.4**
Speed ratings (Par 101): **104,102,100,97,96 95,95,93,92,92 89,89,84**
Tote Swingers: 1&2 £8.00, 1&3 £5.80, 2&3 £25.10. Totesuper7: WIN: Not won. PLACE: £1,558.90 - 1 winning unit. CSF £40.80 CT £185.58 TOTE £6.30: £2.20, £3.30, £2.90; EX 60.80 Trifecta £320.40 Pool: £571.55 - 1.32 winning units..
Owner Derek & Mrs Marie Dean **Bred** Mrs M Campbell-Andenaes **Trained** Great Ness, Shropshire

FOCUS
The time was fair for the grade and the form looks sound. A clear personal best from the winner.
T/Plt: £277.20 to a £1 stake. Pool:£64,941.05 - 170.98 winning tickets T/Qpdt: £87.60 to a £1 stake. Pool:£4,924.77 - 41.60 winning tickets CR

[137] KEMPTON (A.W) (R-H)
Wednesday, January 19

OFFICIAL GOING: Standard
Wind: Almost Nil Weather: Fine but cloudy

204 BISTRO IN THE PANORAMIC BAR & RESTAURANT H'CAP 1m (P)
4:30 (4:30) (Class 7) (0-50,50) 4-Y-0+ **£1,535** (£453; £226) **Stalls** Low

Form RPR
0-65 **1** **Kielty's Folly**[9] 115 7-9-3 **50** GrahamGibbons 9 59
(Brian Baugh) *t.k.h: cl up: gng easily over 2f out: effrt and pushed firmly into ld jst over 1f out: rdn to assert last 100yds* **9/2**[2]
500- **2** *1* **Holyfield Warrior (IRE)**[168] 4689 7-9-0 **50** AndrewHeffernan(3) 5 57
(Ralph Smith) *led 100yds: styd in ldng trio: led again 2f out to jst over 1f out: tried to rally but no ex last 100yds* **8/1**
24-6 **3** ¾ **Escardo (GER)**[5] 173 8-9-0 **47** LukeMorris 13 52
(David Bridgwater) *hld up in last trio: prog and swtchd lft 2f out: hrd rdn and r.o wl fnl f to take 3rd last strides* **13/2**
53-6 **4** ½ **Cane Cat (IRE)**[13] 70 4-9-2 **49** (t) GeorgeBaker 3 53
(Tony Carroll) *hld up in midfield: swtchd ins and prog over 2f out: tried to chal wl over 1f out: one pce fnl f* **6/1**[3]
0-40 **5** 2¼ **Raghdaan**[8] 120 4-8-13 **46** WilliamCarson 2 45
(Peter Hiatt) *s.i.s: hld up in rr: prog over 2f out: chsd ldrs over 1f out: sn outpcd* **20/1**
00-0 **6** 1¾ **Queenie's Star (IRE)**[7] 129 4-9-3 **50** RobbieFitzpatrick 12 45
(Michael Attwater) *racd wd in midfield: rdn and struggling over 2f out: plugged on* **20/1**
030- **7** *nk* **Boundless Applause**[20] 8023 5-8-12 **45** JamesDoyle 4 39
(Ian Wood) *hld up in midfield: effrt to chse ldrs over 2f out: sn rdn: lft bhd over 1f out* **25/1**
33-3 **8** ½ **A Pocketful Of Rye (IRE)**[7] 129 4-9-0 **47** MichaelStainton 14 40
(Jane Chapple-Hyam) *hld up wl in rr on outer: rdn and no prog over 2f out: struggling after* **8/1**
00-0 **9** 2¼ **Gems**[12] 86 4-8-12 **45** ChrisCatlin 1 33
(Peter Hiatt) *mostly in midfield on inner: n.m.r over 3f out: struggling and no prog 2f out* **33/1**
2-55 **10** ¾ **Norcroft**[7] 129 9-8-10 **48** (p) DyonClark(5) 11 34
(Christine Dunnett) *pressed ldr after 1f: led wl over 2f out to 2f out: wknd rapidly over 1f out* **16/1**
30-4 **11** ½ **Custard Cream Kid (IRE)**[7] 129 5-9-2 **49** JackMitchell 6 34
(Richard Fahey) *hld up in rr: drvn and fnd nil over 2f out: wl btn after* **4/1**[1]
66-0 **12** 3½ **Maitre 'D**[12] 85 4-8-12 **45** JimmyQuinn 8 22
(Christopher Kellett) *awkward s and slowest away: a in last trio: struggling over 2f out* **100/1**
43-5 **13** 2¼ **Suttonia (IRE)**[13] 70 5-8-12 **45** TravisBlock 10 17
(Noel Chance) *led after 100yds to wl over 2f out: wknd qckly* **25/1**
06-0 **14** 3½ **Woodsley House (IRE)**[6] 138 9-8-9 **49** HannahNunn(7) 7 12
(Mark Rimmer) *prom on outer: 3rd 3f out: sn wknd rapidly* **33/1**

1m 40.6s (0.80) **Going Correction** +0.025s/f (Slow) **14** Ran SP% **118.0**
Speed ratings (Par 97): **97,96,95,94,92 90,90,89,87,86 86,82,80,77**
toteswingers:1&2 £14.90, 2&3 £17.80, 1&3 £6.30 CSF £35.83 CT £242.39 TOTE £3.90: £1.10, £5.50, £3.30; EX 60.10.
Owner Saddle Up Racing **Bred** Stanneylands Livery **Trained** Audley, Staffs

FOCUS
A bottom-drawer handicap, run at just an average pace on and racing handily proved an advantage. Straightforward form.

205 RACING UK CLAIMING STKS 1m (P)
5:00 (5:00) (Class 6) 4-Y-0+ **£1,535** (£453; £226) **Stalls** Low

Form RPR
612- **1** **Majuro (IRE)**[38] 7844 7-9-5 87 AndreaAtzeni 3 81
(Michael Wigham) *mde all: rdn 2 l clr wl over 1f out: all out nr fin* **7/4**[1]
40-4 **2** ¾ **Syrian**[12] 82 4-9-3 75 JamieSpencer 6 77
(Ian Williams) *hld up in 4th: hanging fr over 2f out: prog to chse wnr over 1f out: cajoled along to cl reluctantly fnl f: nvr looked likely to go through w it* **7/4**[1]
345- **3** 3¾ **Sovereignty (JPN)**[34] 7890 9-8-8 57 ow1 SamHitchcott 1 59
(Dean Ivory) *t.k.h: hld up last: rdn to go 3rd over 1f out: no threat to ldng pair* **14/1**[3]
15-4 **4** *4* **Slikback Jack (IRE)**[10] 105 4-9-2 79 BillyCray(3) 7 61
(David Nicholls) *chsd wnr: nt qckn over 2f out: lost 2nd over 1f out: wknd* **3/1**[2]
00-0 **5** *17* **Durham Town (IRE)**[15] 34 4-8-5 53 (p) JimmyQuinn 2 —
(Dean Ivory) *t.k.h: trckd ldng pair to over 1f out: wknd rapidly* **33/1**

1m 39.22s (-0.58) **Going Correction** +0.025s/f (Slow) **5** Ran SP% **107.3**
Speed ratings (Par 101): **103,102,98,94,77**
CSF £4.75 TOTE £2.60: £1.20, £2.60; EX 5.70.
Owner S Pecoraro **Bred** Tally-Ho Stud **Trained** Newmarket, Suffolk

FOCUS
A claimer weakened by the non-runners. The well-treated winner dictated and didn't need to be at his best.

206 RACING AT SKYSPORTS.COM H'CAP 1m (P)
5:30 (5:30) (Class 5) (0-75,75) 4-Y-0+ **£2,047** (£604; £302) **Stalls** Low

Form RPR

214- **1** **Gallantry**[20] 8022 9-9-6 **74**.................................... JimmyQuinn 3 84
(Jane Chapple-Hyam) *trckd ldrs in 5th: rdn over 2f out: prog over 1f out: sustained effrt to ld last 150yds: styd on wl* **5/1**[1]

533- **2** *1 ½* **Marching Home**[75] 7338 4-9-2 **70**....................................(t) AdamKirby 7 77
(Walter Swinburn) *pressed ldr: wanting to hang u.p fr 2f out and nt qckn: kpt on to hold on for 2nd* **15/2**[3]

51-6 **3** *nse* **Lisahane Bog**[11] 96 4-9-2 **70**....................................(be) DaneO'Neill 8 76
(Peter Hedger) *slowest away: in tch towards rr: prog u.p fr over 2f out: styd on ins fnl f to press for 2nd* **10/1**

63-4 **4** *shd* **Tuxedo**[6] 141 6-9-4 **72**....................................(b) LukeMorris 1 78
(Peter Hiatt) *trckd ldng pair: hrd rdn and fnd nil 2f out: styd on u.p ins fnl f* **7/1**[2]

36-4 **5** *1 ½* **Visions Of Johanna (USA)**[14] 50 6-9-2 **70**..........(p) JamieSpencer 6 73
(Ian Williams) *led: tried to kick on over 2f out: hdd and fdd u.p last 150yds* **7/1**[2]

4-63 **6** *½* **Ilie Nastase (FR)**[2] 188 7-9-4 **72**.................................... HayleyTurner 4 74
(Conor Dore) *trckd ldng trio: rdn and fnd nil over 2f out: sn lost pl: one pce ins fnl f* **12/1**

10-0 **7** *¾* **Dinner Date**[14] 48 9-8-13 **72**.................................... RyanClark(5) 2 72
(Tom Keddy) *hld up and sn in last pair: prog against rail fr over 2f out: tried to cl on ldrs over 1f out: sn wknd* **33/1**

22-1 **8** *nk* **Hip Hip Hooray**[14] 48 5-9-3 **71**.................................... IanMongan 5 70
(Luke Dace) *racd wd in midfield: lost pl and struggling over 2f out: pushed along and plugged on: nvr a factor* **8/1**

000- **9** *½* **Highly Regal (IRE)**[41] 7781 6-9-7 **75**..............................(b) EddieAhern 9 73
(Roger Teal) *hld up in midfield: drvn and no rspnse 2f out: plugged on ins fnl f* **14/1**

434- **10** *3 ½* **Love Match**[130] 5968 4-8-12 **71**.................................... TobyAtkinson(5) 12 61
(Marco Botti) *heavily restrained s: t.k.h and hld up in last trio: shkn up and limited prog 2f out: sn no hdwy* **8/1**

030- **11** *3 ¾* **Maze (IRE)**[63] 7488 6-9-3 **71**.................................... GeorgeBaker 11 52
(Tony Carroll) *stdd s: t.k.h: hld up in last trio: shkn up and no prog over 2f out* **16/1**

001- **12** *3 ½* **Jodawes (USA)**[34] 7889 4-8-12 **66**.................................... SteveDrowne 13 39
(John Best) *chsd ldrs: 6th 3f out: sn wknd* **7/1**[2]

000- **13** *1 ¼* **Koraleva Tectona (IRE)**[90] 7047 6-8-8 **67**............. AshleyMorgan(5) 10 37
(Mark H Tompkins) *racd wd in midfield: wknd over 2f out* **66/1**

1m 39.21s (-0.59) **Going Correction** +0.025s/f (Slow) **13 Ran SP% 121.9**
Speed ratings (Par 103): **103,101,101,101,99 99,98,98,97,94 90,87,85**
toteswingers:1&2 £7.90, 2&3 £19.00, 1&3 90,£21.50 CSF £42.37 CT £370.79 TOTE £4.70: £1.60, £2.00, £3.70; EX 52.90.
Owner The Circle Bloodstock I Limited **Bred** Cheveley Park Stud Ltd **Trained** Dalham, Suffolk

FOCUS
A modest handicap, but there was a sound pace on and the form is fair for the class. the winner continued his revival.

207 WATCH RACING UK ON SKY 432 H'CAP 1m 4f (P)
6:00 (6:03) (Class 7) (0-50,55) 4-Y-0+ **£1,535** (£453; £226) **Stalls** Centre

Form RPR

03-1 **1** *dht* **Carter**[9] 114 5-9-8 **55** 6ex.................................... GrahamGibbons 4 62
(Ian Williams) *reluctant to enter stalls: hld up in last quartet: rdn and struggling over 2f out: prog on wd outside over 1f out: drvn to dispute ld last 50yds: dead-heated but promoted to outrt wnr* **10/11**[1]

05-4 **2** **Our Kes (IRE)**[12] 86 9-9-0 **47**.................................... JimmyQuinn 6 54
(Jane Chapple-Hyam) *hld up in midfield: dropped to in rr but gng bttr than most 3f out: looking for room over 2f out: angled out wl over 1f out: r.o ins fnl f to dispute ld last 50yds: dead-heated for 1st but disqualified and plcd 2nd* **16/1**

/46- **3** *shd* **Crazy Bold (GER)**[55] 816 8-8-12 **45**.................................... LukeMorris 3 52
(Tony Carroll) *dwlt: t.k.h: hld up in last quartet: prog 2f out: drvn to ld ins fnl f: hung lft and hdd last 50yds: styd on* **14/1**[3]

541- **4** *1 ¾* **Suhailah**[45] 7716 5-9-3 **50**.................................... RobbieFitzpatrick 11 54
(Michael Attwater) *racd wd: trckd ldrs: rdn to chal 2f out: led over 1f out to ins fnl f: outpcd* **14/1**[3]

040- **5** *½* **Acropolis (IRE)**[61] 7508 10-9-0 **47**.................................... RobertWinston 5 50
(Tony Carroll) *t.k.h: hld up in last quartet: gng strly 3f out: prog over 1f out: weaved through and looked dangerous ent fnl f: one pce last 100yds* **25/1**

046- **6** *½* **Wrecking Crew (IRE)**[34] 7896 7-8-12 **45**..................(b) JamesMillman 9 47
(Rod Millman) *t.k.h: hld up but sn trckd ldrs: fnd nil whn asked over 2f out: kpt on ins fnl f: no real danger* **16/1**

04-4 **7** *½* **Rosy Dawn**[15] 33 6-9-2 **49**.................................... MartinLane 12 51
(Luke Dace) *led 2f: styd in ldng trio: drvn to chal over 2f out: on terms over 1f out: swamped by deep clsrs ins fnl f* **20/1**

000- **8** *shd* **Colonel Henry**[45] 7716 4-8-8 **45**..............................(v[1]) HayleyTurner 10 46
(Simon Dow) *prom: frequent reminders and anything but keen to stay there: rdr persevered and stl chalng over 1f out: wknd ins fnl f* **33/1**

560- **9** *3 ¾* **Primera Rossa**[20] 7727 5-8-7 **45**.................................... RyanPowell(5) 1 40
(J S Moore) *hld up towards rr: prog on inner over 2f out: cl enough over 1f out: wknd* **66/1**

64-5 **10** *3 ½* **Etoile Filante (IRE)**[15] 33 4-8-9 **46**.................................... SteveDrowne 14 36
(Jeremy Gask) *led after 2f: hdd u.p over 1f out: wknd* **33/1**

006- **11** *2 ¾* **Jakeys Girl**[50] 7634 4-8-13 **50**.................................... IanMongan 2 35
(Pat Phelan) *racd wd in midfield: lost pl and btn wl over 2f out* **12/1**[2]

44-4 **12** *¾* **Little Meadow (IRE)**[15] 30 4-8-11 **48**.................................... GregFairley 13 32
(Julia Feilden) *chsd ldr tl lost pl qckly wl over 2f out* **12/1**[2]

006- **13** *1 ¼* **Pictures (IRE)**[78] 7286 4-8-6 **48**.................................... RyanClark(5) 7 30
(John Bridger) *w ldrs: stl wl there over 1f out: wknd qckly* **50/1**

2m 35.39s (0.89) **Going Correction** +0.025s/f (Slow)
WFA 4 from 5yo+ 4lb **13 Ran SP% 110.8**
Speed ratings (Par 97): **98,98,97,96,96 96,95,95,93,90 89,88,87**
toteswingers:1&2 £2.50, 2&3 £12.10, 1&3 £6.90 CSF £12.38 CT £87.37 TOTE £6.70: £1.20, £2.90, £3.10; EX 8.50.
Owner Stratford Bards Racing **Bred** Dr D G St John And Mrs Sherry Collier **Trained** Portway, Worcs
■ Galiotto was withdrawn (6/1, unruly in stalls). Deduct 10p in the 3 under R4.
■ Stewards' Enquiry : Jimmy Quinn two-day ban: careless riding (Feb 2-3)
Graham Gibbons one-day ban: excessive use of whip (Feb 2)

FOCUS
A weak handicap. There was a very tight three-way finish and it is doubtful if Carter, who got the race outright after dead-heating, had to match his latest Wolverhampton form.

208 SKYSPORTS.COM RACING H'CAP 6f (P)
6:30 (6:32) (Class 5) (0-75,75) 3-Y-0 **£2,047** (£604; £302) **Stalls** Low

Form RPR

33-4 **1** **Sacrosanctus**[18] 4 3-9-4 **72**.................................... IanMongan 4 74
(David Nicholls) *mde all: drvn 2f out: over a l clr ins fnl f: hld on* **9/4**[1]

314- **2** *nk* **Diamond Charlie (IRE)**[129] 5992 3-9-7 **75**...................... HayleyTurner 7 76+
(Simon Dow) *stdd s and dropped in fr wd draw: plld hrd and hld up in last pair: pushed along and limited prog 2f out: drvn and styd on to take 2nd last 100yds: clsng on wnr fin* **5/1**[3]

42-4 **3** *1* **Captain Dimitrios**[6] 140 3-9-0 **75**....................(v[1]) MatthewCosham(7) 5 73
(David Evans) *chsd wnr: drvn to try to chal 2f out: nt qckn and sn hld: lost 2nd last 100yds* **11/2**

345- **4** *1 ¼* **Restless Bay (IRE)**[23] 7982 3-9-3 **71**...........................(b) GeorgeBaker 1 65
(Reg Hollinshead) *dwlt: hld up in last pair: pushed along and prog to take 3rd briefly over 1f out: sn nt qckn* **4/1**[2]

056- **5** *3 ½* **Acclamatory**[63] 7478 3-8-6 **65**.................................... RyanClark(5) 2 48
(Stuart Williams) *chsd ldng pair: no imp u.p over 1f out: fdd* **5/1**[3]

620- **6** *hd* **Arowana (IRE)**[21] 7997 3-8-7 **61**.................................... SamHitchcott 3 43
(Zoe Davison) *chsd ldrs on inner: drvn to dispute 3rd 2f out to over 1f out: fdd* **25/1**

43- **7** *7* **Eternal Youth (IRE)**[34] 7886 3-9-4 **72**.................................... LukeMorris 6 32
(Ronald Harris) *racd wd bhd ldrs: awkward bnd 3f out: sn gave up* **8/1**

1m 12.86s (-0.24) **Going Correction** +0.025s/f (Slow) **7 Ran SP% 114.4**
Speed ratings (Par 97): **102,101,100,98,93 93,84**
toteswingers:1&2 £2.10, 2&3 £3.90, 1&3 £4.60 CSF £13.88 TOTE £5.00: £2.70, £3.30; EX 13.50.
Owner Paul J Dixon **Bred** Worksop Manor Stud **Trained** Sessay, N Yorks

FOCUS
A modest handicap, run at a fair enough pace and it saw another winner from the front. The form is rated around the winner.
Captain Dimitrios Official explanation: jockey said gelding hung right

209 RACING POST CHASE DAY FEBRUARY 26TH H'CAP 2m (P)
7:00 (7:00) (Class 4) (0-85,85) 4-Y-0+ **£3,885** (£1,156; £577; £288) **Stalls** Low

Form RPR

022- **1** **Phoenix Flight (IRE)**[21] 8007 6-10-0 **85**...................... FergusSweeney 7 92
(James Evans) *stdd s: hld up in last quartet: gd prog on inner over 2f out: led over 1f out: drvn and styd on wl* **9/1**

313- **2** *1 ½* **High On A Hill (IRE)**[21] 8007 4-8-11 **75**.................................... JamesDoyle 2 80
(Sylvester Kirk) *trckd ldr: drvn to chal 2f out: upsides over 1f out: chsd wnr after: kpt on* **11/2**[3]

00-1 **3** *nk* **Porgy**[15] 32 6-9-11 **82**.................................... JamieSpencer 8 87+
(David Simcock) *stdd s: t.k.h: hld up in last pair: looking for room wl over 2f out: hanging and nt keen sn after: urged along and gd prog on outer over 1f out: styd on in ungainly fashion to take 3rd nr fin* **5/1**[2]

225- **4** *hd* **Iron Condor**[21] 8003 4-8-13 **77**.................................... LukeMorris 3 81
(James Eustace) *t.k.h: cl up bhd ldrs: drvn over 2f out: styd on same pce fr over 1f out* **12/1**

041- **5** *1 ¼* **Ethics Girl (IRE)**[21] 8007 5-9-7 **78**..................................(t) RobertHavlin 4 82+
(John Berry) *hld up in midfield: prog 3f out gng strly: shkn up 2f out: limited rspnse and looked hld whn squeezed out 1f out: kpt on* **11/1**

4/4- **6** *hd* **Benhego**[43] 7736 6-9-11 **82**.................................... GeorgeBaker 10 86+
(Gary Moore) *stdd s: t.k.h: hld up in last pair: sme prog over 2f out: trying to cl on ldrs whn no room 1f out: plugged on after* **13/2**

601- **7** *½* **Dalhaan (USA)**[20] 8013 6-9-4 **75**.................................... MartinLane 5 77
(Luke Dace) *trckd ldrs: prog to go 3rd over 2f out gng wl: sn rdn and fnd nil: fdd* **7/1**

65-5 **8** *1 ¾* **Calculating (IRE)**[13] 68 7-8-10 **67**.................................... DaneO'Neill 12 67
(Mark Usher) *hld up in last quartet: pushed along over 2f out: kpt on steadily but nvr nr ldrs* **25/1**

046- **9** *1 ¼* **On Terms (USA)**[115] 6388 5-9-4 **75**.................................... HayleyTurner 6 73
(Simon Dow) *led: kicked on 4f out: hdd & wknd over 1f out* **25/1**

12-2 **10** *7* **Pittodrie Star (IRE)**[7] 131 4-8-11 **75**.................................... DavidProbert 9 65
(Andrew Balding) *t.k.h: racd wd wout cover: wd bnd 3f out and wknd qckly* **4/1**[1]

664- **11** *36* **Dani's Girl (IRE)**[61] 5235 8-9-5 **76**.................................... JackMitchell 1 23
(Pat Phelan) *trckd ldr tl wknd 3f out: eased: t.o* **25/1**

016- **12** *24* **Morar**[41] 7781 5-9-4 **75**.................................... IanMongan 11 —
(Laura Mongan) *trckd ldrs and racd wd: rdn 4f out: sn btn: t.o* **9/1**

3m 31.92s (1.82) **Going Correction** +0.025s/f (Slow)
WFA 4 from 5yo+ 7lb **12 Ran SP% 125.4**
Speed ratings (Par 105): **96,95,95,95,94 94,94,93,92,89 71,59**
toteswingers:1&2 £15.70, 2&3 £9.50, 1&3 £7.20 CSF £60.08 CT £279.65 TOTE £9.10: £3.70, £2.40, £2.10; EX 151.30.
Owner D Ross **Bred** Airlie Stud And Sir Thomas Pilkington **Trained** Broadwas, Worcs

FOCUS
An open staying handicap. There was no pace on early, but still the winner emerged from off the pace. It is hard to be positive about the bare form.

210 KEMPTON.CO.UK H'CAP (DIV I) 7f (P)
7:30 (7:31) (Class 6) (0-55,59) 4-Y-0+ **£1,364** (£403; £201) **Stalls** Low

Form RPR

02-0 **1** **Jonny Ebeneezer**[7] 129 12-8-11 **50**...........................(be) JamesDoyle 3 58
(David Flood) *trckd ldrs in 6th: prog towards inner jst over 2f out: clsd to ld ins fnl f: kpt on* **16/1**

00-3 **2** *½* **Chinese Democracy (USA)**[14] 56 4-8-9 **55**..(v) MatthewCosham(7) 6 61
(David Evans) *t.k.h: hld up in rr: plld out and effrt over 2f out: prog over 1f out: styd on to take 2nd last stride* **5/1**[3]

301- **3** *hd* **Aqua Vitae (IRE)**[34] 7885 4-9-2 **55**.................................... GeorgeBaker 4 60
(Tor Sturgis) *hld up in rr: prog on inner over 2f out: cl enough over 1f out: checked for room briefly jst ins fnl f: chsd wnr after: lost 2nd last stride* **7/1**

500- **4** *1 ¼* **Grey Boy (GER)**[42] 7761 10-8-6 **52**.................................... GeorgeDowning(7) 8 54
(Tony Carroll) *t.k.h: trckd ldr: led jst over 2f out: shovelled along over 1f out: hdd and nt qckn ins fnl f* **12/1**

46-0 **5** *½* **Ever Cheerful**[6] 138 10-8-11 **50**..............................(p) SteveDrowne 5 50
(Andrew Haynes) *racd freely: led to jst over 2f out: lost pl jst over 1f out: nt qckn* **33/1**

-314 **6** *nk* **Itsthursdayalready**[5] 167 4-9-6 **59** 6ex.................................... ShaneKelly 10 58
(Mark Brisbourne) *hld up in last pair: sme prog 2f out: hanging and nt qckn over 1f out: kpt on same pce after: n.d* **3/1**[1]

04-0 **7** *shd* **Suhayl Star (IRE)**^{5} [166] 7-8-7 **46** oh1 .... LukeMorris 1 45
(Paul Burgoyne) *t.k.h: trckd ldng pair: disp 2nd over 1f out: sn nt qckn: wknd ins fnl f* **14/1**
00-0 **8** *shd* **Valentino Swing (IRE)**^{11} [97] 8-8-13 **52** .... NeilChalmers 2 51
(Michael Appleby) *s.s: hld up in last pair: pushed along and appeared to be hanging over 1f out: stuck bhd wall of rivals ins fnl f: keeping on at fin* **14/1**
03-2 **9** *6* **Lord Deevert**^{14} [56] 6-8-8 **54** ....(p) JakePayne$^{(7)}$ 7 37
(Bill Turner) *t.k.h: trckd ldng trio and racd wd: wknd over 2f out* **4/1**^{2}
000/ **10** *7* **Zim Ho**^{462} [6777] 5-8-10 **49** .... DaneO'Neill 9 13
(John Akehurst) *plld hrd bhd ldrs: wknd rapidly over 2f out* **8/1**
1m 26.34s (0.34) **Going Correction** +0.025s/f (Slow) **10** Ran SP% **115.1**
Speed ratings (Par 101): **99,98,98,96,96 95,95,95,88,80**
toteswingers:1&2 £8.80, 2&3 £5.20, 1&3 £19.40 CSF £92.99 CT £621.10 TOTE £20.20: £5.30, £3.30, £1.40; EX 40.70.
Owner DM Partnership **Bred** John Purcell **Trained** Exning, Suffolk

FOCUS
This ordinary handicap was another race where plenty refused to settle. The form does make sense, though, with the winner posting his best figure for two years.
Aqua Vitae(IRE) Official explanation: jockey said filly lost her action
Valentino Swing(IRE) Official explanation: jockey said gelding missed the break and was denied a clear run

211 KEMPTON.CO.UK H'CAP (DIV II) 7f (P)
8:00 (8:01) (Class 6) (0-55,55) 4-Y-0+ **£1,364** (£403; £201) **Stalls** Low

Form RPR
55-0 **1** **West Leake (IRE)**^{11} [97] 5-8-12 **51** .... LiamKeniry 9 60
(Paul Burgoyne) *t.k.h: hld up in 5th: stdy prog gng easily over 2f out: trckd ldr over 1f out: plld out and drvn to ld last 100yds* **6/1**^{3}
00-0 **2** *1 ¼* **Crystallize**^{7} [129] 5-8-8 **47** .... FergusSweeney 1 52
(Andrew Haynes) *trckd ldng pair: chsd ldr over 2f out to over 1f out: kpt on again to take 2nd nr fin* **11/1**
56-0 **3** *½* **Itwasonlyakiss (IRE)**^{13} [57] 4-8-11 **50** .... ChrisCatlin 3 54
(J W Hills) *racd freely: led: drvn 2f out: wknd and hdd last 100yds: lost 2nd fnl strides* **12/1**
4-43 **4** *1 ¼* **Goodbye Cash (IRE)**^{7} [135] 7-8-13 **55** .... AndrewHeffernan$^{(3)}$ 8 56
(Ralph Smith) *t.k.h: chsd ldr to over 2f out: wl btn in 4th over 1f out: plugged on* **7/2**^{2}
40-6 **5** *2 ¼* **Mororless**^{14} [45] 4-8-11 **50** ....(p) SamHitchcott 4 45
(Zoe Davison) *s.i.s: hld up last: u.p sn after 1/2-way: plugged on into 5th over 1f out: n.d* **25/1**
002- **6** *1 ¼* **Grand Honour (IRE)**^{35} [7883] 5-8-13 **52** .... StephenCraine 7 43
(Jim Boyle) *a abt same pl: rdn and nt qckn over 2f out: one pce and no imp after* **2/1**^{1}
530- **7** *2 ½* **Strategic Mover (USA)**^{20} [8024] 6-8-11 **53** ....(vt) RobertLButler$^{(3)}$ 2 37
(Paddy Butler) *a abt same pl: rdn and no prog over 2f out: wl btn over 1f out* **12/1**
042- **8** *2 ½* **Yakama (IRE)**^{20} [8023] 6-9-2 **55** ....(v) DavidProbert 10 33
(Christine Dunnett) *s.i.s: t.k.h and sn trckd ldrs: rdn over 2f out: wknd qckly over 1f out* **7/1**
000- **9** *2 ½* **Jessica Wigmo**^{257} [1884] 8-8-7 **46** oh1 .... LukeMorris 6 17
(Tony Carroll) *dwlt: a in last pair: struggling over 2f out: sn bhd* **16/1**
1m 26.4s (0.40) **Going Correction** +0.025s/f (Slow) **9** Ran SP% **115.8**
Speed ratings (Par 101): **98,96,96,94,92 90,87,84,82**
toteswingers:1&2 £10.60, 2&3 £25.20, 1&3 £11.80 CSF £69.52 CT £772.65 TOTE £8.50: £1.90, £2.30, £4.80; EX 67.60.
Owner L Tomlin **Bred** Rathbarry Stud **Trained** Shepton Montague, Somerset

FOCUS
The second division of the 7f handicap and it was run at a fair pace. The form is rated through the runner-up.
T/Plt: £54.60 to a £1 stake. Pool of £62,531.34 - 834.88 winning tickets. T/Qpdt: £12.30 to a £1 stake. Pool of £7,948.89 - 475.80 winning tickets. JN

174 LINGFIELD (L-H)
Wednesday, January 19

OFFICIAL GOING: Standard
Wind: fairly modest, across Weather: bright and sunny

212 PLACE ONLY BETTING AT BLUESQ.COM MEDIAN AUCTION MAIDEN STKS 7f (P)
12:50 (12:53) (Class 6) 3-Y-0 **£1,535** (£453; £226) **Stalls** Low

Form RPR
3- **1** **Materialism**^{117} [6333] 3-9-3 0 .... GregFairley 1 71+
(Mark Johnston) *chsd ldrs: rdn to chal over 1f out: edgd rt u.p: led ins fnl f: styd on wl* **9/4**^{2}
60-3 **2** *1* **Ana Emarati (USA)**^{14} [52] 3-9-3 67 .... EddieAhern 3 68
(Ed Dunlop) *t.k.h: chsd ldr: rdn and ev ch 2f out: edgd lft u.p: led 1f out: sn hdd and one pce fnl 100yds* **9/2**^{3}
00- **3** *2 ½* **Imperial Fong**^{63} [7479] 3-8-12 0 .... HayleyTurner 5 56
(David Elsworth) *restless in stalls: sn led: rdn and edgd rt 2f out: drvn and hdd 1f out: styng on same pce and hld whn n.m.r ins fnl f: wknd fnl 100yds* **9/1**
05- **4** *nk* **Bedibyes**^{41} [7779] 3-8-9 0 .... RobertLButler$^{(3)}$ 2 55
(Richard Mitchell) *hld up in tch in midfield: rdn to chse ldrs and n.m.r wl over 1f out: flashed tail u.p ent fnl f: styd on same pce fnl 150yds* **33/1**
5 *1 ¼* **Baharat (IRE)** 3-9-3 0 .... GeorgeBaker 8 57+
(Jeremy Noseda) *s.i.s: pushed along early: in tch in rr: hdwy on outer ent fnl 3f: shkn up over 2f out: rdn and hung lft wl over 1f out: no prog and wl hld ins fnl f* **8/13**^{1}
6 *4* **Little Jazz** 3-8-12 0 .... LiamJones 4 41
(Paul D'Arcy) *s.i.s: in tch in rr: pushed along ent fnl 3f: wknd u.p 2f out* **33/1**
7 *8* **Twilight Express (IRE)** 3-8-12 0 .... MickyFenton 6 20
(Emma Lavelle) *s.i.s: sn rcvrd and in tch in midfield: rdn and wknd ent fnl 2f* **33/1**
0 **8** *2* **Five Cool Kats (IRE)**^{14} [43] 3-9-3 0 .... WilliamCarson 7 19
(Paul Burgoyne) *stdd after s: t.k.h: hld up in tch in rr: struggling over 2f out: sn bhd* **33/1**
1m 26.58s (1.78) **Going Correction** +0.125s/f (Slow) **8** Ran SP% **132.6**
Speed ratings (Par 95): **94,92,90,89,88 83,74,72**
toteswingers:1&2 £1.30, 2&3 £2.70, 1&3 £3.60 CSF £14.90 TOTE £2.50: £1.20, £1.40, £1.80; EX 13.70 Trifecta £45.80 Pool: £467.99 - 7.56 winning units..
Owner Sheikh Hamdan Bin Mohammed Al Maktoum **Bred** Darley **Trained** Middleham Moor, N Yorks

FOCUS
An ordinary maiden run in a time 3.58secs outside the standard, about two seconds slower than the 0-70 classified event which followed. The favourite disappointed and the winner is rated up 9lb from his debut.
Baharat(IRE) Official explanation: jockey said colt was slowly away
Five Cool Kats(IRE) Official explanation: jockey said gelding jumped right out of the stalls

213 DORMANSLAND CLASSIFIED CLAIMING STKS 7f (P)
1:20 (1:20) (Class 6) 4-Y-0+ **£1,535** (£453; £226) **Stalls** Low

Form RPR
12-2 **1** **I Confess**^{11} [96] 6-7-11 68 ....(b) RPWalsh$^{(7)}$ 9 75
(David Evans) *mde all: pushed along over 2f out: rdn over 1f out: kpt on ins fnl f* **2/1**^{1}
03-1 **2** *shd* **Fivefold (USA)**^{6} [139] 4-8-4 65 ....(p) ChrisCatlin 2 75
(John Akehurst) *chsd wnr: ev ch and rdn ent fnl 2f: hrd drvn ent fnl f: nt qckn and a jst hld* **6/1**^{3}
3-11 **3** *1* **Rubenstar (IRE)**^{9} [111] 8-8-1 63 .... LukeMorris 8 69
(Patrick Morris) *t.k.h: hld up in tch in midfield: rdn and effrt ent fnl 2f: kpt on u.p ins fnl f: nvr quite gng pce to rch ldrs* **5/2**^{2}
002- **4** *¾* **Frequency**^{73} [6997] 4-8-0 68 ow2 .... JimmyQuinn 5 66
(Amy Weaver) *hld up in tch in midfield: effrt on inner 2f out: drvn to chse ldrs jst over 1f out: hanging rt ins fnl f: no hdwy and btn fnl 75yds* **9/1**
016- **5** *½* **Fleetwoodsands (IRE)**^{110} [6541] 4-8-8 70 ....(t) FrannyNorton 6 73
(Ollie Pears) *taken down early: stdd s: sn t.k.h and hdwy to chse ldrs: rdn and unable qck ent fnl 2f: kpt on again ins fnl f* **9/1**
03-5 **6** *shd* **Harlech Castle**^{13} [58] 6-8-0 69 ....(b) NickyMackay 4 64
(Jim Boyle) *dwlt: racd in last pair: shkn up briefly over 4f out: hrd drvn and no prog wl over 1f out tl styd on ins fnl f: gng on fin: nvr gng pce to rch ldrs* **13/2**
60-0 **7** *2* **Dingaan (IRE)**^{11} [96] 8-8-10 65 .... RobbieFitzpatrick 3 69
(Peter Grayson) *dwlt and bustled along early: racd in last pair: rdn jst over 2f out: drvn and styd on same pce fr over 1f out* **33/1**
1m 24.65s (-0.15) **Going Correction** +0.125s/f (Slow) **7** Ran SP% **112.5**
Speed ratings (Par 101): **105,104,103,102,102 102,99**
toteswingers:1&2 £2.80, 2&3 £3.60, 1&3 £1.70 CSF £14.02 TOTE £2.10: £1.30, £4.30; EX 16.40 Trifecta £69.20 Pool: £293.98 - 293.98 winning units..
Owner J E Abbey **Bred** Gestut Sohrenhof **Trained** Pandy, Monmouths

FOCUS
A modest but tight-knit event that looked to be run at a fairly steady pace, and they finished in a heap. However, the time was around two seconds quicker than the preceding 3-y-o maiden. The form is straightforward at face value but may not prove that solid.
Fleetwoodsands(IRE) Official explanation: jockey said gelding ran too free

214 CROWHURST MAIDEN FILLIES' STKS 1m (P)
1:55 (1:57) (Class 5) 3-Y-0+ **£1,910** (£564; £282) **Stalls** High

Form RPR
1 **Dorcas Lane** 3-8-7 0 .... LukeMorris 3 75+
(Lucy Wadham) *dwlt: sn bustled along and rcvrd to chse ldrs: rdn and effrt on inner to chse ldr 2f out: led jst ins fnl f: styd on strly* **50/1**
22- **2** *4* **Lady Rosamunde**^{22} [7990] 3-8-7 0 ....(v^{1}) HayleyTurner 5 66
(Marcus Tregoning) *chsd ldr: rdn ent fnl 2f: hung lft and outpcd over 1f out: no ch w wnr but plugged on again ins fnl f to go 2nd again fnl 75yds* **10/3**^{2}
32- **3** *½* **Bow River Arch (USA)**^{55} [7567] 3-8-7 0 .... ChrisCatlin 4 65
(Jeremy Noseda) *short of room sn after s: chsd ldrs 5f out: rdn and nt qckn ent fnl 2f: outpcd over 1f out: edging lft and one pce ins fnl f: wnt 3rd towards fin* **8/13**^{1}
4-2 **4** *¾* **Spirit Of Grace**^{9} [110] 3-8-4 0 .... AndrewHeffernan$^{(3)}$ 1 63
(Alan McCabe) *led: rdn ent fnl 2f: hdd jst ins fnl f: no ch w wnr after: lost 2 pls fnl 75yds* **7/1**^{3}
4- **5** *2* **Moresweets 'n Lace**^{215} [3157] 4-9-13 0 .... GeorgeBaker 10 63
(Gary Moore) *stdd and dropped in bhd after s: hdwy into modest 5th over 2f out: kpt on but no real imp fr over 1f out* **14/1**
6 *nk* **Apache Glory (USA)** 3-8-7 0 .... DavidProbert 11 58+
(Richard Hannon) *rn green early: bhd: hdwy jst over 2f out: kpt on steadily ins fnl f: nvr trbld ldrs* **16/1**
7 *2 ¾* **Frosty Reception** 3-8-7 0 .... RichardKingscote 7 51
(Brendan Powell) *hld up towards rr: rdn and struggling over 3f out: wl btn fnl 2f* **66/1**
8 *4* **Lauralu** 3-8-7 0 .... FrannyNorton 9 42
(Michael Blanshard) *dwlt: pushed along early: towards rr but in tch: struggling over 3f out wl btn over 2f out* **66/1**
0 **9** *5* **Bellaboolou**^{11} [95] 3-8-7 0 ....(t) NickyMackay 6 31
(David Pinder) *chsd ldrs: rdn and struggling 4f out: wl bhd over 2f out* **66/1**
\- **10** *nse* **Fulani's (IRE)** 3-8-7 0 .... LiamJones 12 31
(Robert Cowell) *t.k.h early: hld up in rr: struggling 4f out: wl bhd fnl 3f* **66/1**
0-6 **11** *1 ¼* **Katherine Parr**^{5} [171] 3-8-7 0 .... GregFairley 2 28
(Peter Chapple-Hyam) *in tch in midfield: rdn 4f out: lost pl over 3f out: wl btn 2f out* **33/1**
12 *25* **Rich And Reckless** 4-9-13 0 .... IanMongan 8 —
(Tobias B P Coles) *fly-jmpd leaving stalls: bucking and broncing early: immediately t.o* **66/1**
1m 38.89s (0.69) **Going Correction** +0.125s/f (Slow)
WFA 3 from 4yo 20lb **12** Ran SP% **122.4**
Speed ratings (Par 100): **101,97,96,95,93 93,90,86,81,81 80,55**
toteswingers:1&2 £15.00, 2&3 £1.50, 1&3 £12.90 CSF £217.57 TOTE £78.30: £10.10, £1.10, £1.10; EX 305.50 Trifecta £714.70 Part won. Pool £965.82 - 0.72 winning units..
Owner Richard S Keeley **Bred** Elms Stud Co Ltd **Trained** Newmarket, Suffolk

FOCUS
There were some decidedly green fillies on show in what was no more than a modest maiden. It only concerned the first four home from before the home straight. The second and third have not gone on from their debuts but there was no fluke about the winner.
Rich And Reckless Official explanation: jockey said filly reared and missed the break

215 BLUESQ.COM ON YOUR IPHONE H'CAP 5f (P)
2:30 (2:31) (Class 5) (0-75,75) 4-Y-0+ **£2,047** (£604; £302) **Stalls** High

Form RPR
00-6 **1** **Northern Dare (IRE)**^{12} [87] 7-9-0 **68** .... JamieSpencer 1 82
(Richard Fahey) *rdn and sn reminders after s: led after 1f: mde rest: clr 3f out: rdn jst over 2f out: styd on wl and in n.d after: eased towards fin* **8/1**
66-4 **2** *3* **Efistorm**^{7} [133] 10-9-2 **70** .... HayleyTurner 2 73
(Conor Dore) *chsd clr ldng pair: rdn and effrt 2f out: chsd clr wnr ent fnl f: no imp* **7/2**^{3}

233- **3** *1* **Even Bolder**[45] 7719 8-9-7 **75** LiamJones 3 75
(Eric Wheeler) *t.k.h early: hld up in midfield: dropped to last pair over 3f out: rdn and effrt over 1f out: kpt on to go 3rd nr fin: no ch w wnr* **9/4**[1]

42-0 **4** *nk* **Wanchai Whisper**[11] 97 4-8-5 **62** (p) AndrewHeffernan(3) 5 61
(Peter Hedger) *stdd s: hld up in rr: rdn and effrt over 1f out: no ch w wnr but pressing for 2nd ins fnl f: no ex fnl 75yds* **11/2**

550- **5** *5* **Freddie's Girl (USA)**[21] 8005 4-9-4 **72** AdamKirby 4 56
(Stef Higgins) *led for 1f: chsd wnr after: rdn and no imp jst over 2f out: lost 2nd ent fnl f: wknd* **5/2**[2]

00-5 **6** *2* **Clifton Bridge**[12] 84 4-9-0 **68** (b) RobbieFitzpatrick 6 41
(Peter Grayson) *s.i.s: rdn along early: hdwy into midfield: stl wl off the pce 1/2-way: drvn and wknd over 1f out* **33/1**

58.75 secs (-0.05) **Going Correction** +0.125s/f (Slow) **6** Ran SP% **111.0**
Speed ratings (Par 103): **105,100,98,98,90 86**
toteswingers:1&2 £3.30, 2&3 £1.80, 1&3 £3.50 CSF £34.81 TOTE £9.60: £3.30, £2.10; EX 25.40.
Owner Dr Marwan Koukash **Bred** Frank Moynihan **Trained** Musley Bank, N Yorks

FOCUS
A modest sprint handicap which was stolen by the winning rider, and not form to treat too seriously. The winner was very well in on his old form.

216 MARRIOTT PLAY & STAY CLAIMING STKS 2m (P)
3:05 (3:06) (Class 6) 4-Y-O+ **£1,535** (£453; £226) **Stalls** Low

Form RPR
022- **1** **Dansilver**[64] 6855 7-9-3 58 LukeMorris 3 56
(Tony Carroll) *chsd ldng pair: rdn to chal over 1f out: led ins fnl f: styd on wl* **7/2**[2]

4-22 **2** *1 1/4* **Camps Bay (USA)**[7] 127 7-9-7 76 HayleyTurner 1 58
(Conor Dore) *pressed ldr: pushed along to ld 2f out: drvn and edgd lft ent fnl f: hdd ins fnl f: sn btn* **4/7**[1]

45/- **3** *5* **Henry Holmes**[578] 3158 8-9-2 42 RichardThomas 5 47?
(Lydia Richards) *t.k.h: hld up in last pair: clsd and wl in tch over 4f out: rdn and outpcd ent fnl 2f: plugged on to go 3rd ins fnl f* **33/1**

300- **4** *1 1/4* **Rock 'N' Roller (FR)**[20] 8013 7-9-10 68 GeorgeBaker 2 54
(Gary Moore) *led at stdy gallop: hdd and rdn 2f out: btn ent fnl f: wknd* **5/1**[3]

5 *1* **Peintre Du Roi (USA)**[99] 7-9-7 0 AdamKirby 4 49
(Natalie Lloyd-Beavis) *hld up in last: rdn and outpcd over 2f out: n.d after: plugged on again ins fnl f* **40/1**

3m 30.97s (5.27) **Going Correction** +0.125s/f (Slow) **5** Ran SP% **107.9**
Speed ratings (Par 101): **91,90,87,87,86**
CSF £5.70 TOTE £5.20: £1.50, £1.70; EX 7.40.Dansilver was claimed by J. J. Best for £6000.
Owner John W Egan **Bred** Mrs J L Egan **Trained** Cropthorne, Worcs

FOCUS
An uncompetitive and slowly run claimer, and not form to be too positive about. In all likelihood the winner did not need to match his recent handicap form, with the favourite below his best.

217 HOLTYE H'CAP 1m 2f (P)
3:40 (3:40) (Class 5) (0-75,69) 3-Y-O **£2,047** (£604; £302) **Stalls** Low

Form RPR
50-1 **1** **Memorabilia**[16] 25 3-9-3 **65** GregFairley 5 74
(Mark Johnston) *chsd ldr tl swtchd lft 8f out: sn led: hdd over 2f out: rdn and sltly hmpd bnd 2f out: rallied to press ldr 1f out: carried ins lft fnl f: kpt on gamely to ld on post* **5/6**[1]

214- **2** *nse* **Ivan Vasilevich (IRE)**[33] 7916 3-9-6 **68** JamieSpencer 2 77
(Jane Chapple-Hyam) *led tl moved off rail and hdd over 7f out: chsd ldr tl rdn to ld over 2f out: edgd lft and pushed clr ent fnl 2f: c centre st: hrd drvn fr jst over 1f out: hdd on post* **9/2**[2]

4-21 **3** *6* **Urban Kode (IRE)**[2] 193 3-8-9 **64** 6ex RPWalsh(7) 3 61
(David Evans) *chsd ldng pair: rdn over 2f out: outpcd ent fnl 2f: no ch w ldng pair ins fnl f* **6/1**[3]

046- **4** *nse* **Twin Soul (IRE)**[21] 8001 3-9-0 **62** DavidProbert 1 59
(Andrew Balding) *in tch: dropped to last and rdn over 3f out: no ch w ldng pair over 1f out: plugged on ins fnl f to press for 3rd nr fin* **9/1**

42-1 **5** *2* **Dare It And Smile (USA)**[12] 88 3-9-7 **69** MartinLane 4 62
(David Simcock) *awkward leaving stalls: hld up in last: hdwy on outer to chse ldrs over 2f out: rdn and racd awkwardly bnd ent fnl 2f: sn wknd* **6/1**[3]

2m 7.64s (1.04) **Going Correction** +0.125s/f (Slow) **5** Ran SP% **111.3**
Speed ratings (Par 97): **100,99,95,95,93**
CSF £5.03 TOTE £1.90: £1.60, £2.10; EX 6.20.
Owner Sheikh Hamdan Bin Mohammed Al Maktoum **Bred** Whitley Stud **Trained** Middleham Moor, N Yorks

FOCUS
An ordinary 3-y-o handicap, and something of a tactical affair before the pace lifted on the approach to the home turn. The first two drew well clear as they contested a good finish, and both are improved.

218 PLAY RAINBOW RICHES AT BLUESQ.COM APPRENTICE H'CAP 6f (P)
4:10 (4:10) (Class 6) (0-60,60) 4-Y-O+ **£1,535** (£453; £226) **Stalls** Low

Form RPR
5-36 **1** **Radiator Rooney (IRE)**[5] 167 8-8-12 **51** RyanPowell 7 58+
(Patrick Morris) *stdd s: hld up in last pair: hdwy on bit and swtchd lft ent fnl f: rdn and r.o wl to ld wl ins fnl f: gng away fin* **13/2**

00-6 **2** *1 1/4* **Trade Centre**[9] 111 6-9-4 **57** MatthewCosham 3 60
(Milton Bradley) *led: rdn 2f out: kpt on wl tl hdd and no ex wl ins fnl f* **11/2**[3]

42-5 **3** *3/4* **Speak The Truth (IRE)**[12] 80 5-9-7 **60** (p) NathanAlison 5 61
(Jim Boyle) *awkward leaving stalls: t.k.h: hld up in tch: rdn and effrt to chse ldr over 1f out tl ins fnl f: one pce fnl 100yds* **11/2**[3]

216- **4** *3* **Mr Skipiton (IRE)**[19] 8035 6-9-5 **58** JamesRogers 1 49
(Brian McMath) *chsd ldrs: rdn and effrt wl over 1f out: wknd ins fnl f* **11/4**[2]

0/0- **5** *2* **Quick Single (USA)**[20] 8024 5-8-4 **46** oh1 (be) RichardRowe(3) 9 31
(Phil McEntee) *chsd ldrs on outer: rdn ent fnl 2f: outpcd and btn over 1f out* **50/1**

4-00 **6** *1/2* **Memphis Man**[9] 111 8-8-9 **53** RPWalsh(5) 2 36
(David Evans) *taken down early: t.k.h: hld up in rr: c v wd and rdn bnd 2f out: nvr able to chal* **10/1**

21-3 **7** *nk* **Loyal Royal (IRE)**[11] 98 8-9-7 **60** (bt) AdamCarter 4 42
(Milton Bradley) *t.k.h: sn chsng ldr: pressed ldr 4f out tl wknd over 1f out: fdd ins fnl f* **5/2**[1]

1m 13.12s (1.22) **Going Correction** +0.125s/f (Slow) **7** Ran SP% **110.4**
Speed ratings (Par 101): **96,94,93,89,86 86,85**
toteswingers:1&2 £4.50, 2&3 £5.50, 1&3 £4.70 CSF £38.52 CT £197.25 TOTE £6.60: £2.60, £3.40; EX 39.70 Trifecta £176.80 Pool: £645.25 - 2.70 winning units..
Owner Adam Pearson **Bred** Barry Lyons **Trained** Tarporley, Cheshire

FOCUS
A moderate handicap for apprentices. The pace did not seem especially strong and things got a bit messy. The winner took a step closer to his old form.
Loyal Royal(IRE) Official explanation: jockey said gelding ran too free
T/Plt: £32.60 to a £1 stake. Pool of £50,614.26 - 1,130.42 winning tickets. T/Qpdt: £8.60 to a £1 stake. Pool of £4,404.48 - 375.23 winning tickets. SP

195 CAGNES-SUR-MER
Wednesday, January 19
OFFICIAL GOING: Fibresand: standard

219a PRIX DE NICE (H'CAP) (4YO+) (FIBRESAND) 1m 4f
12:40 (12:00) 4-Y-O+
£20,258 (£8,189; £6,034; £3,879; £2,370; £1,508)

RPR
1 **Quatre Tours (FR)**[305] 5-9-0 **0** FranckBlondel 5 81
(F Rossi, France) **117/10**
2 *1* **Silver Valny (FR)**[23] 5-9-11 **0** ThomasMessina 6 90
(Mlle M-L Mortier, France) **7/1**[3]
3 *snk* **Marlow (GER)**[23] 5-8-10 **0** (p) StefanieHofer 15 75
(Mario Hofer, Germany) **9/1**
4 *nse* **Dream Youn (FR)**[27] 6-8-13 **0** (p) SylvainRuis 1 78
(J Van Handenhove, France) **10/1**
5 *nk* **Maidstone Mealy (FR)**[12] 5-8-11 **0** AlexisBadel 13 76
(R Le Gal, France) **34/1**
6 *1/2* **Storming Spirit**[87] 7-8-11 **0** (p) JohanVictoire 2 75
(B Goudot, France) **24/1**
7 *1/2* **Mafra (IRE)**[27] 5-9-3 **0** FlavienPrat 11 80
(P Monfort, France) **11/1**
8 *1/2* **Kel Away (FR)**[23] 4-8-6 **0** DavidBreux 8 72
(Mlle M Henry, France) **62/1**
9 *nk* **Angel Of Rain (FR)**[80] 6-8-10 **0** ThomasHuet 9 72
(Robert Collet, France) **17/2**
10 *nk* **Joly Nelsa (FR)**[52] 6-8-5 **0** Pierre-CharlesBoudot 16 66
(M Cesandri, France) **34/1**
0 **Refik (FR)**[168] 8-9-6 **0** DominiqueBoeuf 12 —
(M Cesandri, France) **21/1**
0 **Spidello (FR)**[23] 6-8-9 **0** FabriceVeron 7 —
(Mme E Siavy-Julien, France) **45/1**
0 **Et Contretout (FR)**[23] 8-8-8 **0** (p) ThierryJarnet 14 —
(Mme C Dufreche, France) **22/1**
0 **Pool Of Knowledge (FR)**[23] 7988 5-8-11 **0** Francois-XavierBertras 3 —
(David Nicholls) *slowly away: racd midfield on settling: smooth prog towards end of bk st: 3rd ent st: rdn: sn no ex: fdd* **16/1**
0 **Enreve (FR)**[169] 5-8-13 **0** ThierryThulliez 10 —
(J-M Capitte, France) **53/10**[1]
0 **Silver Mountain (FR)**[297] 5-8-10 **0** IoritzMendizabal 4 —
(J-C Rouget, France) **6/1**[2]

2m 33.43s (153.43)
WFA 4 from 5yo+ 4lb **16** Ran SP% **116.7**
WIN (incl. 1 euro stake): 12.70. PLACES: 4.10, 2.90, 3.00. DF: 48.00. SF: 100.10.
Owner Jean-Claude Seroul **Bred** Jean-Claude Seroul **Trained** France

220a PRIX DE LA CORNICHE FLEURIE (DIV 1) (CLAIMER) (4YO+) (FIBRESAND) 1m 2f (D)
1:10 (12:00) 4-Y-O+ **£6,896** (£2,758; £2,068; £1,379; £689)

RPR
1 **Indian City (FR)**[23] 7-9-4 0 (b) Pierre-CharlesBoudot 9 64
(J-M Capitte, France) **78/10**
2 *1/2* **King Lou (FR)**[22] 4-8-11 0 FlavienPrat 2 58
(P Demercastel, France) **46/1**
3 *1/2* **Spirit Of The King (FR)**[27] 5-9-0 0 (b) RonanThomas 4 58
(S-A Ghoumrassi, France) **53/1**
4 *nk* **Itathir (FR)**[234] 4-8-8 0 ElliotCanal(8) 5 61
(J-C Rouget, France) **9/2**[1]
5 *hd* **Counterbid (IRE)**[16] 5-9-0 0 SylvainRuis 13 57
(J Heloury, France) **39/1**
6 *nk* **Last Storm**[29] 7-8-11 0 (p) XavierBergeron(8) 3 61
(J-M Capitte, France) **58/10**[2]
7 *1* **Escargot (GER)**[16] 42 5-8-8 0 (b) YoannRousset(6) 15 54
(Y Fertillet, France) **7/1**[3]
8 *nk* **Bank Guard (IRE)**[12] 6-9-4 0 FranckBlondel 6 58
(Rod Collet, France) **7/1**[3]
9 *1* **Sina (GER)**[16] 42 6-8-10 0 (b) FabriceVeron 7 48
(H-A Pantall, France) **15/1**
10 *2* **Monserrat (FR)**[16] 42 5-9-4 0 (p) FredericSpanu 10 52
(P Demercastel, France) **9/1**
0 **Notia (IRE)**[776] 6-8-8 0 ow1 (p) PaulineProd'homme(3) 11 —
(D Prod'Homme, France) **65/1**
0 **Iron Out (USA)**[23] 7985 5-9-0 0 IoritzMendizabal 12 —
(Reg Hollinshead) *prom fr s: wnt 4th bef st: rdn and wnt 3rd early in st: r.o one pce fnl f* **18/1**
0 **Glamstar (FR)**[209] 1197 5-9-0 0 JohanVictoire 8 —
(M Pimbonnet, France) **18/1**
0 **Email Exit (IRE)**[33] 4-8-11 0 FabienLefebvre 1 —
(Mme G Rarick, France) **49/1**
0 **Falcharge**[234] 5-9-4 0 AFiori 14 —
(S Sordi, Italy) **8/1**

2m 3.49s (123.49)
WFA 4 from 5yo+ 2lb **15** Ran SP% **117.1**
WIN (incl. 1 euro stake): 8.80. PLACES: 3.70, 13.50, 14.70. DF: 186.10. SF: 275.30.
Owner Patrick Boudengen **Bred** Patrick Boudengen **Trained** France

221a PRIX DE LA CORNICHE FLEURIE (DIV 2) (CLAIMER) (4YO+) (FIBRESAND) 1m 2f (D)
1:40 (12:00) 4-Y-O+ **£6,896** (£2,758; £2,068; £1,379; £689)

RPR
1 **Renaione (IRE)**[136] 5-9-4 0 (p) ThierryThulliez 10 69
(E Botti, Italy) **5/1**[3]

2 *shd* **Jack Junior (USA)**[12] 7-9-0 0..(p) SylvainRuis 1 65
(C Boutin, France) **3/1**[1]
3 *1* **Zieto (FR)**[362] 272 7-9-4 0.................................. Pierre-CharlesBoudot 13 67
(J-M Capitte, France) **11/1**
4 *1* **Officer In Command (USA)**[43] 7732 5-9-4 0........(b) IoritzMendizabal 2 65
(J S Moore) *prom fr s: racd in 5th along rail: swtchd away fr rail early in st: short of room: hrd rdn whn daylight fnd: r.o wl fnl 100yds to go 4th* **4/1**[2]
5 *snk* **Tudora (AUT)**[993] 6-8-10 0.. ASuborics 6 57
(S Bigus, Austria) **20/1**
6 *snk* **Learco (FR)**[16] 42 10-9-0 0....................................... MathiasSautjeau 4 60
(Y Fertillet, France) **35/1**
7 *hd* **Benaojan (FR)**[27] 5-9-1 0... FredericSpanu 12 61
(X Nakkachdji, France) **13/2**
8 *3/4* **Vera's Moscou (IRE)**[12] 5-9-4 0..................... Francois-XavierBertras 14 63
(Mlle V Dissaux, France) **16/1**
9 *snk* **Corseurasien (FR)**[847] 6222 6-9-4 0.................... StephaneRichardot 3 62
(W J Cargeeg, France) **11/1**
10 *nse* **Duel Au Pistolet (FR)**[79] 4-8-6 0................. AlexandreChampenois(5) 9 57
(Y Fouin, France) **70/1**
0 **Johnmanderville**[196] 3782 5-9-0 0........................... DelphineSantiago 11 —
(Mme F Lauffer, France) **59/1**
0 **Enlil (FR)**[680] 5-9-0 0... ThomasMessina 5 —
(J Parize, France) **20/1**
0 **Simple Mind (GER)**[462] 6-8-8 0...............................(b) YoannRousset(6) 8 —
(Y Fertillet, France) **20/1**
0 **The Wonder Land (FR)**[19] 7-8-10 0......................... RomainPerruchot 7 —
(J-P Perruchot, France) **112/1**

2m 3.29s (123.29)
WFA 4 from 5yo+ 2lb **14** Ran SP% **118.6**
WIN (incl. 1 euro stake): 6.00. PLACES: 2.30, 1.70, 2.90. DF: 12.80. SF: 32.30.
Owner Scuderia Quadrante Rosso **Bred** Giuseppe Rossi **Trained** Italy

212 LINGFIELD (L-H)

Thursday, January 20

OFFICIAL GOING: Standard
Wind: medium, against Weather: light cloud

222 BET ON WINNING DISTANCES AT BLUESQ.COM MAIDEN STKS 1m 4f (P)

12:50 (12:50) (Class 5) 4-Y-0+ **£2,047** (£604; £302) **Stalls** Low

Form RPR
60-4 **1** **Zafranagar (IRE)**[6] 161 6-9-0 65........................... GeorgeDowning(7) 5 70
(Tony Carroll) *stdd s: trckd ldng pair and a gng wl: pushed ahd ent fnl 2f: rdn clr over 1f out: r.o wl: easily* **9/2**
3-23 **2** *6* **New Den**[6] 161 4-9-3 58...(v) NickyMackay 2 60
(Jim Boyle) *led: rdn and hdd ent fnl 2f: sn outpcd by wnr: wl btn fnl f* **3/1**[2]
022- **3** *1* **Wild Geese (IRE)**[36] 5815 4-9-3 64................................... JoeFanning 3 59
(Jonathan Portman) *dwlt: in tch: chsd ldrs and rdn ent fnl 4f: wnt 3rd over 2f out: plugged on same pce and no ch w wnr fr over 1f out* **2/1**[1]
4 *4 1/2* **Vivarini**[59] 7-9-7 0.. FergusSweeney 8 52
(John O'Shea) *s.i.s: pushed along in rr early: clsd and in tch 9f out: rdn and effrt 3f out: chsd ldng trio wl over 1f out: no prog after* **7/2**[3]
5 *6* **Cityar (FR)**[70] 7-9-7 0.. RobertHavlin 6 42
(John O'Shea) *hld up in tch: hdwy into midfield 5f out: struggling u.p wl over 2f out: wknd 2f out* **12/1**
00/ **6** *13* **Little Roxy (IRE)**[18] 455 6-9-2 0..................................... SamHitchcott 1 16
(Anna Newton-Smith) *in tch in midfield: rdn over 8f out: wknd u.p wl over 2f out: sn wl bhd* **50/1**
0 00 **7** *3 1/4* **Rodasus (USA)**[6] 161 5-9-7 53...................................(b) WilliamCarson 7 25
(Ronald Harris) *sn bustled along to chse ldr: rdn and ev ch over 3f out tl over 2f out: sn wknd* **20/1**
5 **8** *23* **Polly's Instinct**[16] 31 6-9-2 0.. ChrisCatlin 4 —
(Peter Hiatt) *stdd s: t.k.h: hld up in tch in last pair: rdn and lost tch over 3f out: t.o fnl 2f* **100/1**

2m 32.28s (-0.72) **Going Correction** +0.125s/f (Slow)
WFA 4 from 5yo+ 4lb **8** Ran SP% **114.1**
Speed ratings (Par 103): **107,103,102,99,95 86,84,69**
toteswingers:1&2:£3.00, 1&3:£3.20, 2&3:£2.10 CSF £18.16 TOTE £6.30: £1.40, £1.30, £1.50; EX 15.20 Trifecta £98.40 Pool: £327.23 - 2.46 winning units..
Owner Paul Downing **Bred** His Highness The Aga Khan's Studs S C **Trained** Cropthorne, Worcs
■ George Downing's first winner.

FOCUS
A very modest older-horse maiden and the field finished spread out all over Surrey. The time was reasonable and suggests the runner-up ran to his best, so the winner rates his best Flat form since he was a 3yo.
Wild Geese(IRE) Official explanation: vet said gelding had lost a left fore shoe

223 HOLTYE H'CAP 1m 5f (P)

1:20 (1:20) (Class 6) (0-65,65) 4-Y-0+ **£1,535** (£453; £226) **Stalls** Low

Form RPR
325- **1** **Dubburg (USA)**[22] 8010 6-9-3 58.................................. StevieDonohoe 8 66
(Willie Musson) *stdd after s: hld up in rr: hdwy 3f out: rdn to chal jst ins fnl f: kpt on wl to ld last strides* **4/1**[1]
226- **2** *hd* **Eagle Nebula**[43] 7765 7-9-7 62.. AdamKirby 12 69
(Brett Johnson) *in tch in midfield: pushed along and hdwy 3f out: rdn and qcknd to ld jst over 2f out: hrd pressed and drvn ins fnl f: hdd wl ins fnl f: kpt on* **9/2**[2]
20-4 **3** *nse* **Squad**[13] 79 5-9-7 62...(v) EddieAhern 1 69
(Simon Dow) *v.s.a: hld up in last pair: gd hdwy towards inner jst over 2f out: chsd wnr over 1f out: ev ch 1f out: edgd rt u.p but led wl ins fnl f: hdd and lost 2 pls last strides* **13/2**[3]
032- **4** *4* **Private Equity (IRE)**[52] 7626 5-8-12 53............................. JoeFanning 9 54
(William Jarvis) *stdd after s: hld up in tch towards rr: effrt and n.m.r jst over 2f out: hdwy between horses 2f out: kpt on but nvr gng pce to chal ldrs* **4/1**[1]
006- **5** *1/2* **Indian Ghyll (IRE)**[203] 3576 5-9-10 65................................ LiamKeniry 11 65
(Roger Teal) *chsd ldr: rdn jst over 2f out: unable qck u.p over 1f out: wknd ent fnl f* **50/1**
300- **6** *1/2* **Cossack Prince**[29] 7967 6-9-3 58.. IanMongan 5 57
(Laura Mongan) *dwlt: sn rcvrd to chse ldrs: gng wl but nt clr run over 2f out tl swtchd lft and rdn over 1f out: btn 1f out: wknd ins fnl f* **25/1**

550- **7** *hd* **Diamond Twister (USA)**[57] 7561 5-9-8 63.......................... GeorgeBaker 4 62
(John Best) *hld up in tch in midfield: lost pl and dropped to rr wl over 2f out: n.m.r on inner bnd ent fnl 2f: styd on same pce fr over 1f out* **16/1**
004- **8** *2 3/4* **Before The War (USA)**[21] 8015 4-8-11 57............................ SteveDrowne 3 53
(Jeremy Gask) *dwlt: sn rcvrd and in tch in midfield: lost pl and dropped to rr over 3f out: rallied on inner ent fnl 2f: no prog and btn 1f out: eased wl ins fnl f* **16/1**
1P0- **9** *1/2* **Vertueux (FR)**[68] 7181 6-8-12 60.............................. GeorgeDowning(7) 10 54
(Tony Carroll) *chsd ldrs: dropped into midfield 5f out: pushed along and wknd wl over 2f out* **33/1**
01-4 **10** *1 1/4* **Juwireya**[13] 89 4-9-3 63..(v) WilliamCarson 2 56
(Peter Hiatt) *led: rdn over 2f out: sn hdd: wknd u.p jst over 2f out: wl btn and eased wl ins fnl f* **16/1**
005- **11** *3 1/4* **Little Richard (IRE)**[56] 7569 12-8-11 52..............................(p) LiamJones 7 39
(Mark Wellings) *in tch in midfield tl dropped to last pair over 5f out: c wd and rdn bnd ent fnl 2f: no prog* **50/1**
00-0 **12** *1 1/2* **Carr Hall (IRE)**[16] 30 8-9-0 55.................................... ShaneKelly 6 40
(Tony Carroll) *stdd s and v.s.a: t.k.h: hld up in last pair tl stdy hdwy on outer 9f out: chsd ldrs 5f out: rdn over 2f out: wkng whn hmpd bnd ent fnl 2f: sn bhd* **13/2**[3]

2m 47.45s (1.45) **Going Correction** +0.125s/f (Slow)
WFA 4 from 5yo+ 5lb **12** Ran SP% **113.2**
Speed ratings (Par 101): **100,99,99,97,97 96,96,94,94,93 91,90**
toteswingers:1&2:£4.60, 1&3:£5.50, 2&3:£6.80 CSF £19.95 CT £111.63 TOTE £5.30: £2.30, £2.00, £2.90; EX 22.80 Trifecta £94.70 Pool: £309.90 - 2.42 winning units..
Owner K A Cosby **Bred** Winchester Farm **Trained** Newmarket, Suffolk

FOCUS
A modest if quite competitive handicap, run at just a fair pace. The first three, who came clear, all came from the rear. The winner had been beaten off this mark on his last six starts and is rated to his winter best.
Carr Hall(IRE) Official explanation: jockey said gelding ran too free and hung right

224 FELBRIDGE H'CAP 5f (P)

1:50 (1:50) (Class 6) (0-60,60) 4-Y-0+ **£1,535** (£453; £226) **Stalls** High

Form RPR
-222 **1** **Your Gifted (IRE)**[9] 116 4-9-0 60........................ MatthewCosham(7) 2 69
(Patrick Morris) *t.k.h: hld up in tch: hdwy to trck ldrs gng wl ent fnl 2f: rdn to chal jst over 1f out: led ins fnl f: r.o wl* **7/2**[2]
65-4 **2** *3/4* **Jimmy Ryan (IRE)**[13] 80 10-9-4 57..........................(t) J-PGuillambert 3 63
(Tim McCarthy) *taken down early and led to post: t.k.h: chsd ldrs: rdn and effrt on outer jst over 1f out: chsd wnr ins fnl f: no imp fnl 75yds* **5/1**
00-0 **3** *1* **Misaro (GER)**[12] 98 10-9-7 60...................................(b) DavidProbert 4 62+
(Ronald Harris) *dwlt and pushed along: rdn and hdwy on inner 2f out: kpt on ins fnl f: nvr able to rch ldrs* **11/4**[1]
/42- **4** *1/2* **Chantilly Jewel (USA)**[38] 7859 6-8-12 51........................(v) EddieAhern 8 52
(Robert Cowell) *in tch in last trio: hdwy and rdn ent fnl 2f: chsd ldrs 1f out: styd on same pce fnl 100yds* **11/2**
04-6 **5** *1/2* **Ten Down**[13] 80 6-8-10 49.. ChrisCatlin 5 48
(Michael Quinn) *led: rdn over 1f out: drvn ent fnl f: hdd ins fnl f: wknd fnl 100yds* **12/1**
0-03 **6** *nk* **Silver Linnet (IRE)**[6] 165 4-9-4 57................................ AdamKirby 10 55
(Michael Quinlan) *s.i.s: bhd: rdn along 1/2-way: styd on ins fnl f: nvr trbld ldrs* **9/2**[3]
240- **7** *1/2* **Papageno**[29] 7960 4-9-2 55....................................(v[1]) StephenCraine 1 51
(J R Jenkins) *chsd ldr: rdn and nt qckn over 1f out: wknd ins fnl f* **25/1**
060- **8** *1 3/4* **Charles Bear**[30] 7953 4-8-7 46 oh1................................ WilliamCarson 6 36
(Bruce Hellier) *in tch: rdn and effrt ent fnl 2f: wknd u.p over 1f out* **66/1**
60-5 **9** *8* **Ariel Bender**[8] 132 4-8-7 46 oh1.............................(b) RobbieFitzpatrick 7 —
(Peter Grayson) *s.i.s: a outpcd in last* **66/1**

59.26 secs (0.46) **Going Correction** +0.125s/f (Slow) **9** Ran SP% **113.6**
Speed ratings (Par 101): **101,99,98,97,96 96,95,92,79**
toteswingers:1&2:£3.60, 1&3:£2.50, 2&3:£3.80 CSF £20.75 CT £53.03 TOTE £4.30: £2.10, £2.20, £1.60; EX 26.60 Trifecta £123.70 Pool: £636.95 - 3.81 winning units..
Owner L Walsh **Bred** Rathasker Stud **Trained** Tarporley, Cheshire

FOCUS
A routine sprint handicap and there was no hanging about. Ordinary form for the grade, rated around the runner-up.
Silver Linnet(IRE) Official explanation: jockey said that the filly jumped right

225 FELCOURT H'CAP 1m (P)

2:20 (2:20) (Class 6) (0-55,55) 4-Y-0+ **£1,535** (£453; £226) **Stalls** High

Form RPR
0-54 **1** **Very Well Red**[8] 135 8-8-10 49.................................... WilliamCarson 3 57
(Peter Hiatt) *chsd ldr: rdn and ev ch ent fnl 2f: led ent fnl f: kpt on wl: rdn out* **9/2**[3]
3/3- **2** *1 1/2* **Abigails Angel**[29] 7969 4-9-1 54.. AdamKirby 6 58
(Brett Johnson) *in tch: reminder over 6f out: hdwy into midfield 5f out: rdn to chse ldng pair over 1f out: hrd drvn and chsd wnr jst ins fnl f: no imp* **4/1**[2]
324- **3** *2 1/4* **Lady Rossetti**[21] 8021 4-8-13 52.................................(p) DaneO'Neill 5 51
(Marcus Tregoning) *in tch in midfield: rdn and effrt over 1f out: kpt on ins fnl f to go 3rd nr fin: no threat to ldng pair* **5/1**
200- **4** *nk* **Brave Decision**[198] 3758 4-8-13 52..............................(p) EddieAhern 1 50
(Robert Cowell) *dwlt: sn rcvrd and led: rdn ent fnl 2f: hdd ent fnl f: wknd fnl 150yds* **14/1**
50-0 **5** *3/4* **Cavalry Guard (USA)**[8] 135 7-8-4 46 oh1....................(b) BillyCray(3) 2 43
(Tim McCarthy) *chsd ldrs: shuffled bk towards rr and n.m.r bnd ent fnl 2f: rallied u.p over 1f out: no imp fnl f* **50/1**
/0-0 **6** *hd* **Softly Killing Me**[16] 30 6-8-7 46 oh1........................(v) DavidProbert 7 42
(Brian Forsey) *rdn and dropped to last sn after s: in tch: rdn over 2f out: no hdwy tl styd on ins fnl f: nvr trbld ldrs* **33/1**
2-02 **7** *3/4* **Lucky Diva**[10] 115 4-8-12 51.. JamesDoyle 8 45
(Sylvester Kirk) *hld up in rr: gd hdwy on outer over 3f out: chsd ldrs and rdn jst over 2f out: wknd over 1f out* **11/4**[1]
50-0 **8** *3 1/2* **Fly By Nelly**[8] 135 5-9-0 53.......................................(p) ChrisCatlin 4 39
(Mark Hoad) *sn bustled along: hdwy to chse ldrs over 6f out: lost pl and rdn over 2f out: wl btn over 1f out* **8/1**
450- **9** *1/2* **Merals Choice**[35] 7889 4-9-2 55...................................... NickyMackay 9 40
(Jim Boyle) *t.k.h: chsd ldrs tl rdn and wknd jst over 2f out: wl btn over 1f out* **10/1**

1m 38.99s (0.79) **Going Correction** +0.125s/f (Slow) **9** Ran SP% **113.3**
Speed ratings (Par 101): **101,99,97,96,96 96,95,91,91**
toteswingers:1&2:£38.00, 1&3:£31.40, 2&3:£31.90 CSF £22.38 CT £91.81 TOTE £4.50: £2.20, £2.00, £1.30; EX 21.40 Trifecta £71.50 Pool: £623.09 - 6.44 winning units..
Owner Phil Kelly **Bred** Butts Enterprises Limited **Trained** Hook Norton, Oxon

FOCUS
A moderate handicap with the top-weight rated just 55. There are grounds for rating the form a little higher.

226 10% FORECAST BONUS AT BLUESQ.COM H'CAP 1m (P)
2:50 (2:50) (Class 4) (0-80,80) 4-Y-0+ **£3,885** (£1,156; £577; £288) **Stalls** High

Form RPR

4-22 **1** **Buaiteoir (FR)**[15] [48] 5-9-2 **78**..(e[1]) LiamJones 2 86+
(Paul D'Arcy) *stdd s: hld up in tch in last: pushed along and qcknd on outer ent fnl f: r.o strly to ld towards fin* **4/1**[2]

00-4 **2** *¾* **Ocean Legend (IRE)**[12] [99] 6-9-3 **79**.............................. ShaneKelly 1 86
(Tony Carroll) *t.k.h: hld up in tch: rdn and hdwy over 1f out: led fnl 75yds: hdd and no ex towards fin* **15/2**

022- **3** *nk* **Miami Gator (IRE)**[21] [8022] 4-9-3 **79**..............................(v) EddieAhern 7 85
(Mrs K Burke) *led: rdn and qcknd 2f out: kpt on wl tl hdd and lost 2 pls fnl 75yds* **7/2**[1]

52- **4** *½* **Wilfred Pickles (IRE)**[51] [7637] 5-9-2 **78**.................... DaneO'Neill 12 84+
(Jo Crowley) *stdd s: hld up in tch in rr: hdwy towards inner over 1f out: nt clr run and swtchd lft 1f out: sn drvn: kpt on* **6/1**[3]

000- **5** *nk* **One Way Or Another (AUS)**[47] [7689] 8-9-4 **80**........... JamesMillman 3 84
(Jeremy Gask) *stdd s: hld up in tch in rr: rdn and hdwy on inner over 1f out: kpt on fnl f* **20/1**

11-0 **6** *¾* **Kiss A Prince**[16] [32] 5-9-4 **80**..............................(b) AdamKirby 4 82
(Dean Ivory) *pushed along early: in tch: chsd ldrs ent fnl 2f: drvn ent fnl f: kpt on same pce ins fnl f* **10/1**

340- **7** *¾* **Bawaardi (IRE)**[33] [7935] 5-8-10 **79**........................ GeorgeChaloner(7) 11 80
(Richard Fahey) *t.k.h: hld up in tch: rdn and unable qck 2f out: drvn 1f out: kpt on again ins fnl f: nt pce to rch ldrs* **16/1**

063- **8** *hd* **King's Colour**[20] [8033] 6-9-4 **80**..............................(v) LiamKeniry 6 80
(Brett Johnson) *t.k.h: chsd ldrs: chal ent fnl 2f: rdn wl over 1f out: stl ev ch tl wknd ins fnl f* **14/1**

211- **9** *nk* **Blue Moon**[21] [8022] 4-8-11 **78**.. JulieBurke(5) 9 78
(Kevin Ryan) *hld up in tch towards rr on outer: effrt bnd 2f out: edging lft and one pce fr over 1f out* **7/1**

40-1 **10** *¾* **Erinjay (IRE)**[16] [31] 5-9-2 **78**.................................... JamieMackay 10 76
(Michael Wigham) *t.k.h: hld up in tch: shuffled bk and lost pl jst over 2f out: kpt on same pce: no imp over 1f out* **12/1**

11 *1 ¾* **Inef (IRE)**[78] 4-9-3 **79**.. IanMongan 8 73
(Laura Mongan) *chsd ldr tl jst over 2f out: wknd ent fnl f* **33/1**

1m 38.34s (0.14) **Going Correction** +0.125s/f (Slow) **11** Ran SP% **117.8**
Speed ratings (Par 105): **104,103,102,102,102 101,100,100,100,99 97**
toteswingers:1&2:£10.50, 1&3:£3.20, 2&3:£6.20 CSF £34.31 CT £117.92 TOTE £5.20: £2.00, £2.70, £1.20; EX 44.80 Trifecta £354.20 Pool: £584.08 - 1.22 winning units..
Owner Laurence Mann **Bred** Ruthyn Bloodstock Limited **Trained** Newmarket, Suffolk

FOCUS
A tight and competitive handicap with just 2lb covering the 11 runners. They didn't go a great pace, though, and it developed into a sprint with a bunch finish. The form is rated at face value for now.

227 MARSH GREEN H'CAP 1m (P)
3:20 (3:20) (Class 6) (0-65,65) 3-Y-O **£1,535** (£453; £226) **Stalls** High

Form RPR

33-1 **1** **Aquilifer (IRE)**[15] [53] 3-9-2 **60**.. ShaneKelly 1 65+
(William Jarvis) *travelled wl: hld up wl in tch: shkn up to ld over 1f out: drvn and r.o fnl f* **5/2**[2]

050- **2** *1 ½* **Sir Randolf (IRE)**[20] [8031] 3-9-7 **65**..............................(t) JamesDoyle 6 67
(Sylvester Kirk) *hld up in tch in last pair: effrt on outer over 1f out: chsd wnr 1f out: edgd lft and no imp fnl f* **5/1**

6-12 **3** *2* **Paco Belle (IRE)**[3] [193] 3-9-6 **64**.. DaneO'Neill 3 61
(Richard Hannon) *in tch: hdwy on outer to join ldrs over 2f out: rdn and nt pce of wnr over 1f out: styd on same pce fnl f* **7/4**[1]

04-6 **4** *½* **Lovat Lane**[7] [142] 3-8-7 **51** oh1..(p) ChrisCatlin 4 47
(Eve Johnson Houghton) *t.k.h: hld up wl in tch in last pair: nt clr run and swtchd lft over 1f out: sn rdn: no prog u.p fnl f* **20/1**

0-55 **5** *1 ¾* **Lynchpin**[10] [109] 3-9-2 **60**..(p) WilliamCarson 7 52
(Ronald Harris) *sn chsng ldr: rdn 3f out: ev ch u.p 2f out: wknd over 1f out* **14/1**

0-1P **6** *2 ¼* **Double Duchess**[7] [142] 3-9-2 **60**.. LiamJones 5 47
(Paul D'Arcy) *led: rdn ent fnl 2f: hdd and short of room over 1f out: sn wknd* **7/2**[3]

1m 40.79s (2.59) **Going Correction** +0.125s/f (Slow) **6** Ran SP% **115.3**
Speed ratings (Par 95): **92,90,88,88,86 84**
toteswingers:1&2:£2.10, 1&3:£1.50, 2&3:£2.70 CSF £15.79 TOTE £3.90: £1.80, £1.50; EX 13.20.
Owner John Kelsey-Fry **Bred** Miss L Magnier **Trained** Newmarket, Suffolk

FOCUS
A moderate handicap and much the slowest of the three C&D times. The form makes sense.

228 PLAY ROULETTE AT BLUESQ.COM H'CAP 7f (P)
3:50 (3:50) (Class 5) (0-70,70) 3-Y-O **£2,047** (£604; £302) **Stalls** Low

Form RPR

44-3 **1** **Cheylesmore (IRE)**[9] [119] 3-9-1 **64**..............................(t[1]) WilliamCarson 1 72
(Stuart Williams) *chsd ldr: rdn and hung lft over 1f out: drvn ahd ins fnl f: sn clr* **7/1**

13-4 **2** *2 ¾* **Irie Ute**[17] [27] 3-8-13 **62**.. LiamKeniry 2 63
(Sylvester Kirk) *chsd clr ldng pair: rdn and effrt 2f out: kpt on same pce u.p fnl f: wnt 2nd towards fin* **12/1**

526- **3** *nk* **Foxtrot Golf (IRE)**[21] [8012] 3-9-5 **68**..............................(p) IanMongan 5 68
(Peter Winkworth) *led: sn clr: rdn over 1f out: drvn ins fnl f: hdd fnl 100yds: sn btn: lost 2nd towards fin* **16/1**

34-2 **4** *1* **Reginald Claude**[15] [44] 3-9-7 **70**.. DaneO'Neill 3 67
(Mark Usher) *racd off the pce in midfield: rdn and hdwy on inner over 1f out: no imp ins fnl f* **10/3**[2]

001- **5** *½* **Roman Strait**[20] [8031] 3-8-12 **61**.. FrannyNorton 7 57+
(Michael Blanshard) *t.k.h: hld up off the pce in last trio: rdn wl over 1f out: no hdwy tl styd on wl ins fnl f: nt rch ldrs* **9/2**[3]

401- **6** *2 ¾* **Magic Of The Sea (IRE)**[63] [7496] 3-9-5 **68**.............................. ChrisCatlin 6 57
(Marco Botti) *t.k.h: hld up off the pce in last trio: rdn and no prog jst over 2f out: n.d* **5/2**[1]

436- **7** *4* **Fantasy Fry**[133] [5874] 3-9-5 **68**.. TravisBlock 4 46
(Hughie Morrison) *hld up off the pce in last trio: short-lived effrt on outer jst over 2f out: sn lost tch* **13/2**

1m 25.7s (0.90) **Going Correction** +0.125s/f (Slow) **7** Ran SP% **109.2**
Speed ratings (Par 97): **99,95,95,94,93 90,86**
toteswingers:1&2:£6.40, 1&3:£15.30, 2&3:£7.20. totesuper7: Abandoned CSF £75.21 CT £1178.22 TOTE £7.70: £4.70, £7.20; EX 36.90 Trifecta £144.10 Pool: £409.19 - 2.10 winning units..
Owner Keith & Meta Pryce **Bred** John Cullinan **Trained** Newmarket, Suffolk

FOCUS
An ordinary handicap and, with the early pace modest, a few of these were inclined to take a pull. It was therefore an advantage to race handily.
T/Plt: £20.70 to a £1 stake. Pool:£59,316.42 - 2,084.44 winning tickets T/Qpdt: 8.90 to a £1 stake. Pool:£5,113.38 - 424.60 winning tickets SP

[197]WOLVERHAMPTON (A.W) (L-H)
Thursday, January 20

OFFICIAL GOING: Standard
Wind: Light across Weather: Misty

229 BET ON WINNING DISTANCES AT BLUESQ.COM H'CAP 7f 32y(P)
4:20 (4:21) (Class 7) (0-50,49) 4-Y-0+ **£1,535** (£453; £226) **Stalls** High

Form RPR

1 **Orpens Peach (IRE)**[41] [7818] 4-9-3 **49**.............................. SeamieHeffernan 11 64
(Seamus Fahey, Ire) *hld up in tch: rdn to ld and hung lft ins fnl f: r.o wl* **12/1**

030- **2** *3 ¾* **Hi Spec (IRE)**[124] [6188] 8-8-11 **48**..............................(t) RyanClark(5) 8 53
(Mandy Rowland) *hld up: hdwy over 2f out: rdn over 1f out: r.o: nt trble wnr* **20/1**

06/0 **3** *hd* **Meydan Style (USA)**[10] [115] 5-8-13 **45**.............................. GregFairley 4 49
(Bruce Hellier) *led: hdd over 6f out: chsd ldr: rdn over 2f out: hmpd ins fnl f: styd on same pce* **33/1**

6-30 **4** *½* **Guildenstern (IRE)**[8] [129] 9-9-3 **49**.............................. JimmyQuinn 1 52
(Jane Chapple-Hyam) *hld up: hdwy over 2f out: rdn over 1f out: styd on same pce ins fnl f* **7/2**[2]

44-0 **5** *nk* **Carnival Dream**[14] [70] 6-8-11 **48**.............................. AdamCarter(5) 2 50
(Hugh McWilliams) *chsd ldr: led over 5f out: rdn and edgd rt over 1f out: hdd and no ex ins fnl f* **13/2**

506- **6** *3 ¾* **Aggbag**[133] [5877] 7-8-13 **45**.. RobertWinston 6 37
(Tony Carroll) *hdwy over 5f out: rdn over 2f out: wknd over 1f out* **5/1**[3]

66-0 **7** *1* **Novillero**[8] [129] 4-9-2 **48**..(b[1]) BarryMcHugh 3 37
(Jimmy Fox) *chsd ldrs: rdn over 2f out: wknd fnl f* **8/1**

00-2 **8** *2 ½* **Kenswick**[8] [129] 4-8-11 **48**.. TobyAtkinson(5) 7 30
(Pat Eddery) *hld up: rdn over 1f out: nvr on terms* **5/2**[1]

056- **9** *11* **Edge End**[22] [8006] 7-8-6 **45**..(p) JosephYoung(7) 10 —
(Lisa Williamson) *hld up: a in rr* **66/1**

00-0 **10** *8* **Hedgerow (IRE)**[14] [69] 4-8-10 **45**..............................(t) AndrewHeffernan(3) 5 —
(David Bourton) *chsd ldrs: rdn 1/2-way: wknd over 2f out: t.o* **25/1**

500- **11** *6* **Pinewood Polly**[273] [1490] 4-8-13 **45**.............................. FrankieMcDonald 9 —
(Shaun Harris) *hld up: a in rr: rdn 1/2-way: sn wknd: t.o* **100/1**

1m 31.0s (1.40) **Going Correction** +0.15s/f (Slow) **11** Ran SP% **113.6**
Speed ratings (Par 97): **98,93,93,92,92 88,87,84,71,62 55**
toteswingers:1&2:£17.90, 1&3:£31.40, 2&3:£41.30 CSF £222.84 CT £7588.56 TOTE £13.70: £3.50, £6.00, £13.80; EX 128.00.
Owner Mrs V Maxwell **Bred** R Grehan & H Maxwell **Trained** Monasterevin, Co. Kildare

FOCUS
This bottom-drawer handicap was run at a decent pace. A clear personal best from the winner, but the third raises doubts.

230 WOLVERHAMPTON-RACECOURSE.CO.UK (S) STKS 5f 216y(P)
4:50 (4:50) (Class 6) 4-Y-O+ **£1,535** (£453; £226) **Stalls** Low

Form RPR

301- **1** **Orpenindeed (IRE)**[111] [6537] 8-9-0 82.............................. AndrewHeffernan(3) 6 71
(Jim Best) *mde virtually all: rdn over 1f out: styd on u.p* **2/7**[1]

35-1 **2** *2 ½* **Apache Ridge (IRE)**[17] [22] 5-9-0 60..............................(p) AmyRyan(3) 1 63
(Kevin Ryan) *hld up: hdwy to chsd wnr over 1f out: sn rdn: styd on same pce ins fnl f* **7/2**[2]

60-4 **3** *2 ½* **Ingleby Star (IRE)**[9] [116] 6-8-12 65..............................(p) RobertWinston 2 50
(Noel Wilson) *broke wl: chsd wnr: rdn over 2f out: styd on same pce appr fnl f* **14/1**[3]

000- **4** *1* **Stormburst (IRE)**[234] [2589] 7-8-7 42.............................. NeilChalmers 5 42
(Adrian Chamberlain) *chsd ldrs: rdn over 2f out: styd on same pce appr fnl f* **66/1**

1m 15.74s (0.74) **Going Correction** +0.15s/f (Slow) **4** Ran SP% **108.1**
Speed ratings (Par 101): **101,97,94,93**
CSF £1.60 TOTE £1.40; EX 1.50.The winner was sold to Frank Sheridan for 6,000gns.
Owner Diamond Racing Ltd **Bred** A Pereira **Trained** Lewes, E Sussex

FOCUS
Orpendeed did not need to be at his best to beat these, and the runner-up is rated close to his recent form.

231 10% FORECAST BONUS AT BLUESQ.COM FILLIES' H'CAP 5f 216y(P)
5:20 (5:21) (Class 5) (0-70,69) 4-Y-O+ **£2,201** (£655; £327; £163) **Stalls** Low

Form RPR

410- **1** **Dualagi**[20] [8034] 7-8-11 **59**.. MartinLane 2 66
(Martin Bosley) *broke wl and led: hdd 4f out: chsd ldrs: rdn to ld over 1f out: r.o* **16/1**

20-5 **2** *½* **Always Dazzling**[17] [19] 4-8-11 **62**.............................. JamesSullivan(3) 1 67
(Ollie Pears) *chsd ldrs: lost pl over 3f out: hdwy over 1f out: rdn and ev ch ins fnl f: r.o* **16/1**

01-5 **3** *¾* **Athaakeel (IRE)**[12] [97] 5-9-3 **65**..............................(b) AndreaAtzeni 5 68
(Ronald Harris) *s.i.s: hld up: hdwy over 1f out: rdn and edgd lft ins fnl f: styd on* **8/1**

0-42 **4** *2* **Bold Ring**[8] [128] 5-8-9 **57**.. JimmyQuinn 7 54
(Edward Creighton) *hld up: hdwy 1/2-way: rdn over 1f out: styd on* **7/2**[3]

00-3 **5** *¾* **Weet A Surprise**[13] [84] 6-9-7 **69**..............................(v) GrahamGibbons 3 63
(James Unett) *hld up: hdwy over 3f out: rdn over 2f out: no ex fnl f* **11/4**[2]

34-4 **6** *½* **Hypnosis**[14] [62] 8-9-2 **64**.. RobertWinston 4 57
(Noel Wilson) *trckd ldr: plld hrd: rdn and ev ch over 1f out: no ex fnl f* **14/1**

60-2 **7** *1 ¾* **Goddess Of Light (IRE)**[10] [113] 4-9-7 **69**..............(b[1]) JamieSpencer 6 56
(Daniel Mark Loughnane, Ire) *chsd ldrs: led 4f out: rdn and hdd over 1f out: wknd ins fnl f* **2/1**[1]

1m 16.12s (1.12) **Going Correction** +0.15s/f (Slow) **7** Ran SP% **111.8**
Speed ratings (Par 100): **98,97,96,93,92 92,89**
toteswingers:1&2:£27.90, 1&3:£13.40, 2&3:£11.90 CSF £214.65 TOTE £23.30: £10.60, £5.90; EX 254.00.
Owner Inca Financial Services **Bred** B Burrough **Trained** Chalfont St Giles, Bucks

FOCUS
A modest fillies' handicap. There was an average pace on which resulted in the runners spread across the track at the furlong marker, but the first three came clear late on. The winner showed his best form since 2008.

Goddess Of Light(IRE) Official explanation: jockey said filly ran too freely

232 DINE IN HORIZONS CLAIMING STKS 1m 5f 194y(P)
5:50 (5:51) (Class 6) 4-Y-O+ **£1,619** (£481; £240; £120) **Stalls** Low

Form RPR
23-3 **1** **Carlton Scroop (FR)**[13] [89] 8-9-4 68 .... AndreaAtzeni 3 73
(Tony Carroll) *a.p: rdn to chse ldr over 2f out: led ins fnl f: hung lft: drvn out* **4/1**[2]
00-1 **2** *2* **Munsef**[17] [24] 9-9-11 94 .... JamieSpencer 1 77
(Ian Williams) *led: shkn up and hung rt over 1f out: hung lft and hdd ins fnl f: styd on same pce* **4/6**[1]
03-3 **3** *2 1/2* **Kames Park (IRE)**[3] [190] 9-9-4 68 .... JimmyQuinn 2 66
(Richard Guest) *hld up: hdwy u.p over 2f out: styd on same pce fnl f* **4/1**[2]
06/5 **4** *1 3/4* **Duar Mapel (USA)**[9] [117] 5-8-9 60 ....(b) AdamCarter(5) 5 60
(David Bourton) *plld hrd: trckd ldr tl rdn over 2f out: no ex fnl f* **16/1**[3]
5 *30* **Puddington Bear**[60] 7-8-9 0 .... MatthewMcGhee(7) 4 20
(Bill Moore) *hld up: plld hrd: rdn and wknd 3f out: t.o* **100/1**

3m 8.18s (2.18) **Going Correction** +0.15s/f (Slow) **5** Ran SP% **106.9**
Speed ratings (Par 101): **99,97,96,95,78**
CSF £6.73 TOTE £3.70: £1.60, £1.10; EX 9.80.Carlton Scroop was claimed by Jim Best for £8,000. Duar Mapel was claimed by Brian Baugh for £4,000.
Owner S Hussain & P O'Neill **Bred** Jonathan Jay **Trained** Cropthorne, Worcs

FOCUS
A muddling claimer and the winner is perhaps the best guide to the form.

233 CALL 01902 390000 TO SPONSOR A RACE MEDIAN AUCTION MAIDEN STKS 5f 216y(P)
6:20 (6:26) (Class 5) 3-5-Y-O **£2,007** (£597; £298; £149) **Stalls** Low

Form RPR
52-3 **1** **Kingscroft (IRE)**[17] [27] 3-8-10 68 .... GregFairley 2 78+
(Mark Johnston) *led 1f: chsd ldr tl led again 2f out: rdn clr fnl f: eased nr fin* **1/3**[1]
2 *9* **Lennoxwood (IRE)** 3-8-10 0 .... RobertWinston 7 45
(Mark Usher) *dwlt: hld up: hdwy over 2f out: rdn over 1f out: styd on to go 2nd nr fin: no ch w wnr* **14/1**[3]
530- **3** *3/4* **Sally's Swansong**[41] [7810] 5-9-7 47 ....(b) GrahamGibbons 1 42
(Eric Alston) *led 5f out: rdn and hdd 2f out: no ex fnl f: lost 2nd nr fin* **18/1**
60-2 **4** *5* **Kristollini**[13] [88] 3-8-5 63 .... JimmyQuinn 8 22
(William Muir) *chsd ldrs: hung rt fnl 4f: wknd wl over 2f out* **11/2**[2]
0-0 **5** *6* **Depden (IRE)**[13] [88] 3-8-10 0 .... DavidProbert 4 —
(Richard Price) *prom: rdn 1/2-way: wknd over 2f out* **66/1**
000/ **6** *3 1/2* **Crystal Bridge**[397] [7816] 4-9-0 30 ....(b1) MatthewMcGhee(7) 3 —
(Bill Moore) *chsd ldrs tl rdn and wknd over 2f out* **100/1**

1m 15.44s (0.44) **Going Correction** +0.15s/f (Slow)
WFA 3 from 4yo+ 16lb **6** Ran SP% **104.8**
Speed ratings (Par 103): **103,91,90,83,75 70**
toteswingers:1&2:£1.70, 1&3:£2.20, 2&3:£6.20 CSF £5.10 TOTE £1.20: £1.02, £5.60; EX 3.80.
Owner Dr Marwan Koukash **Bred** J Beckett **Trained** Middleham Moor, N Yorks
■ Osgoodisgood (13/2) and Evey P (25/1) were withdrawn after bolting to post. Deduct 10p in the £ under R4.

FOCUS
There was a delay to this weak maiden as the two late withdrawals had bolted beforehand. It proved simple for Kingscroft but the time was quicker than the two earlier races and the form could be rated a few pounds higher.
Kristollini Official explanation: jockey said filly hung right

234 GREAT OFFERS AT WOLVERHAMPTON-RACECOURSE.CO.UK H'CAP 1m 4f 50y(P)
6:50 (6:52) (Class 6) (0-65,64) 3-Y-O **£1,619** (£481; £240; £120) **Stalls** Low

Form RPR
02-2 **1** **Investment World (IRE)**[15] [53] 3-8-8 51 .... GregFairley 9 63+
(Mark Johnston) *a.p: chsd ldr over 4f out: led over 2f out: clr fnl f: easily* **7/4**[1]
04-1 **2** *2 1/4* **Blue Cossack (IRE)**[15] [47] 3-8-10 53 .... DavidProbert 4 55+
(Mark Usher) *chsd ldrs: nt clr run over 2f out: rdn to go 2nd ins fnl f: no ch w wnr* **8/1**
50-3 **3** *3/4* **Bathwick Scanno (IRE)**[15] [47] 3-8-4 54 .... MatthewCosham(7) 3 55
(David Evans) *led 1f: chsd clr ldr tl over 4f out: rdn over 2f out: styd on same pce fr over 1f out* **14/1**
6-65 **4** *shd* **Polly Holder (IRE)**[15] [51] 3-9-1 58 ....(v1) RobertWinston 5 59
(Alan Bailey) *prom: rdn over 3f out: edgd lft and styd on same pce appr fnl f* **20/1**
032- **5** *10* **Oratouch (IRE)**[40] [7839] 3-9-6 63 .... AdamKirby 2 48
(Marco Botti) *hld up: rdn over 2f out: nvr on terms* **9/2**[3]
00-4 **6** *1 1/4* **Windsor Knights**[14] [60] 3-9-3 60 ....(bt) JamesDoyle 6 43
(Alastair Lidderdale) *hmpd s: hld up: rdn over 3f out: wknd over 2f out* **33/1**
05-0 **7** *3/4* **High Kickin**[7] [142] 3-8-11 54 ....(p) ShaneKelly 8 36
(Alan McCabe) *led after 1f: clr 9f out to 4f out: rdn and hdd over 2f out: wknd over 1f out* **33/1**
000- **8** *2 3/4* **Danube Dancer (IRE)**[21] [8012] 3-8-7 50 .... JimmyQuinn 11 27
(J S Moore) *s.i.s: a in rr: wknd 3f out* **66/1**
00-0 **9** *9* **Algris**[15] [47] 3-8-7 50 .... LiamJones 1 13
(Sir Mark Prescott Bt) *mid-div: drvn along 7f out: hdwy over 5f out: wknd 2f out* **25/1**
25-2 **10** *6* **Indian Wish (USA)**[15] [47] 3-9-6 63 .... JamieSpencer 10 16
(Michael Quinlan) *s.i.s: hld up: hdwy on outside over 3f out: rdn and wknd 2f out: t.o* **12/1**
065- **11** *14* **More Than Enough (IRE)**[22] [8001] 3-9-7 64 .... JackMitchell 7 —
(Richard Fahey) *hld up: hdwy over 5f out: wknd 3f out: t.o* **5/2**[2]

2m 43.75s (2.65) **Going Correction** +0.15s/f (Slow) **11** Ran SP% **124.6**
Speed ratings (Par 95): **97,95,95,94,88 87,86,85,79,75 65**
toteswingers:1&2:£2.20, 1&3:£9.10, 2&3:£9.50 CSF £17.16 CT £162.60 TOTE £2.90: £1.50, £1.80, £3.00; EX 16.40.
Owner Markus Graff **Bred** Markus Graff **Trained** Middleham Moor, N Yorks

FOCUS
This 3-y-o handicap was run at a solid pace and the first four dominated off the home turn. Modest form but the form seems sound.
Indian Wish(USA) Official explanation: jockey said filly would not face the kickback

235 PLAY ROULETTE AT BLUESQ.COM H'CAP 1m 1f 103y(P)
7:20 (7:20) (Class 4) (0-85,83) 4-Y-O+ **£3,238** (£963; £481; £240) **Stalls** Low

Form RPR
11-2 **1** **Mighty Clarets (IRE)**[12] [94] 4-8-9 72 .... BarryMcHugh 6 80
(Richard Fahey) *chsd ldrs: pushed along over 3f out: rdn to ld ins fnl f: styd on* **8/1**
632- **2** *nk* **Dahaam**[48] [7680] 4-9-4 81 .... JamieSpencer 10 88
(David Simcock) *mid-div: swtchd rt and hdwy over 2f out: hrd rdn and edgd lft ins fnl f: r.o* **3/1**[1]
111- **3** *hd* **Mongoose Alert (IRE)**[20] [8032] 9-9-5 81 .... StevieDonohoe 9 88
(Jim Best) *hld up: hdwy over 1f out: rdn and ev ch ins fnl f: r.o* **5/1**[3]
450- **4** *nk* **Just Bond (IRE)**[140] [5685] 9-8-13 80 .... AdamCarter(5) 2 86
(Geoffrey Oldroyd) *a.p: rdn and ev ch ins fnl f: styd on* **25/1**
505- **5** *3/4* **Snow Dancer (IRE)**[69] [7428] 7-8-10 75 .... JamesSullivan(3) 11 79+
(Hugh McWilliams) *hld up: hdwy over 1f out: nt clr run ins fnl f: r.o* **40/1**
266- **6** *3/4* **Chosen Forever**[142] [5641] 6-9-7 83 .... TomEaves 5 86
(Geoffrey Oldroyd) *sn led: rdn and hung rt over 1f out: hdd and unable qck ins fnl f* **20/1**
0-00 **7** *3/4* **Thunderstruck**[5] [180] 6-9-6 82 ....(p) IanMongan 7 83
(David Nicholls) *chsd ldr: rdn over 2f out: ev ch 1f out: no ex ins fnl f* **15/2**
130- **8** *6* **Granny McPhee**[172] [4619] 5-8-12 81 .... NatashaEaton(7) 8 70
(Alan Bailey) *hld up: rdn over 2f out: nvr on terms* **25/1**
/40- **9** *3 3/4* **Farleigh House (USA)**[22] [8003] 7-9-5 81 .... GeorgeBaker 1 62
(Neil King) *slipped s: sn pushed along and prom: rdn over 1f out: sn wknd* **4/1**[2]
315- **10** *1 1/2* **Pelham Crescent (IRE)**[56] [7568] 8-9-2 78 .... DavidProbert 4 56
(Bryn Palling) *hld up: rdn over 2f out: a in rr* **12/1**
3-12 **11** *11* **Follow The Flag (IRE)**[4] [186] 7-9-6 82 ....(v) ShaneKelly 12 37
(Alan McCabe) *sn pushed along and a in rr* **6/1**

2m 1.81s (0.11) **Going Correction** +0.15s/f (Slow)
WFA 4 from 5yo+ 1lb **11** Ran SP% **121.4**
Speed ratings (Par 105): **105,104,104,104,103 102,102,96,93,92 82**
toteswingers:1&2:£3.20, 1&3:£4.70, 2&3:£3.60 CSF £31.94 CT £137.80 TOTE £6.90: £3.00, £1.10, £3.20; EX 30.80.
Owner The Matthewman Partnership **Bred** Ellesmere Bloodstock Ltd **Trained** Musley Bank, N Yorks

FOCUS
Despite this modest handicap being run at a fair pace the first seven all held a chance of sorts 1f out. The form looks sound enough with the winner rated up a length.
Follow The Flag(IRE) Official explanation: jockey said gelding never travelled
T/Plt: £1,216.00 to a £1 stake. Pool:£65,385.54 - 39.25 winning tickets T/Qpdt: £113.10 to a £1 stake. Pool:£10,504.70 - 68.70 winning tickets CR

151 MEYDAN (L-H)
Thursday, January 20
OFFICIAL GOING: Tapeta: standard; turf: good

236a MARSALA TROPHY (H'CAP) (TAPETA) 7f
2:35 (2:35) (95-105,105) 3-Y-O+
£42,307 (£14,102; £7,051; £3,525; £2,115; £1,410)

Form RPR
460- **1** **Solid Choice (AUS)**[299] [1023] 5-9-1 101 .... ChristopheSoumillon 6 101+
(M F De Kock, South Africa) *s.i.s: settled in rr: led cl home* **8/1**[2]
20/- **2** *1/4* **Yirga**[11] 5-9-0 100 .... PatCosgrave 7 99
(A Al Raihe, UAE) *mid-div: chsd ldrs 2 1/2f out: r.o wl: jst failed* **33/1**
010/ **3** *nse* **Tybalt (USA)**[81] 7-9-3 104 .... AhmedAjtebi 13 102
(Mahmood Al Zarooni) *trckd ldrs: led 2f out: hdd cl home* **14/1**
004- **4** *2 1/4* **Indomito (GER)**[74] [7372] 5-9-4 105 .... WayneSmith 5 97
(P Vovcenko, Germany) *trckd ldrs: ev ch 1 1/2f out: one pce fnl f* **20/1**
32-0 **5** *1/2* **Warsaw (IRE)**[7] [152] 6-9-4 105 ....(b) KShea 8 95
(M F De Kock, South Africa) *mid-div: chsd ldrs 2 1/2f out: one pce fnl fnl f* **14/1**
/20- **6** *shd* **Sahara Kingdom (IRE)**[78] [7304] 4-9-3 104 .... FrankieDettori 3 94
(Saeed Bin Suroor) *a in mid-div* **1/1**[1]
7 *1 1/4* **Nocturnal Affair (SAF)**[208] 5-9-3 104 .... RyanMoore 9 91
(H J Brown, South Africa) *sn led: hdd 2f out: wknd fnl fnl f* **14/1**
340- **8** *[illegible]* **City Style (USA)**[63] [7083] 5-8-8 101 .... AntiocoMurgia(7) 2 [illegible]
(Mahmood Al Zarooni) *slowly away: settled in rr: nvr nr to chal* **25/1**
0/0- **9** *1 1/4* **Aamaaq**[42] [7792] 8-9-1 101 ....(bt) RichardHills 4 85
(A Al Raihe, UAE) *in rr of mid-div: nvr able to chal* **11/1**
240- **10** *1* **Prince Shaun (IRE)**[25] 6-9-2 102 ....(t) TadhgO'Shea 1 83
(Doug Watson, UAE) *nvr bttr than mid-div* **20/1**
435- **11** *1* **Golden Desert (IRE)**[61] [7524] 7-9-0 100 .... JimCrowley 11 78
(Robert Mills) *nvr able to chal* **9/1**[3]
15/0 **12** *3/4* **Il Grande Maurizio (IRE)**[7] [152] 7-9-1 101 ....(t) WJSupple 10 77
(A Al Raihe, UAE) *chsd ldrs tl 2 1/2f out: wknd* **33/1**
1/5- **13** *4* **Swinging Sixties (IRE)**[35] [7905] 6-9-1 101 ....(e) KierenFallon 12 67
(D Selvaratnam, UAE) *trckd ldrs tl 2 1/2f out: sn wknd* **10/1**
100- **14** *2* **Navajo Chief**[36] [7875] 4-9-1 101 .... TedDurcan 14 61
(Alan Jarvis) *trckd ldrs tl 3f out* **33/1**

1m 25.49s (0.29) **Going Correction** +0.275s/f (Slow) **14** Ran SP% **130.7**
Speed ratings: **109,108,108,106,105 105,103,103,102,101 99,99,94,92**
CSF £269.52; Tricast £3,640.51..
Owner Sheikh Mohammed Bin Khalifa Al Maktoum **Bred** Sh Mohd Bin Khalifa Al Maktoum **Trained** South Africa

FOCUS
The pace was modest pace (time 0.31 slower than 2,000 Guineas trial), meaning the field were covered by only around six or seven lengths turning in and most of these struggled to make up significant amounts of ground, but not the winner, who can be rated better than the bare form.

NOTEBOOK
Solid Choice(AUS) ◆, having been ridden patiently after missing the break, was last of all on entering the straight, and even once he'd been taken out wide for a clear run, his rider took a while to get serious. However, he picked up in fine style, passing all of his rivals to lead in the final strides. He should defy a rise. (op 15-2)
Yirga was better positioned than the first and third-placed finishers and is consequently flattered to finish so close.
Tybalt(USA), who showed smart form for John Gosden at the start of his career and was then about Grade 3 standard on a range of surfaces in the US, ran with real credit on his UAE debut. He was stuck wide for much of the way from stall 13, although that at least meant he was able to sit close to the ordinary gallop and he had his chance. There might be a similar in him. (op 12-1)
Indomito(GER) enjoyed a clear run against the inside rail in the straight, but he couldn't quicken. (tchd 22-1)
Warsaw(IRE) had a wide draw, noticeably so into the straight, and can probably do a bit better. (op 12-1)
Sahara Kingdom(IRE) failed to justify strong market support, but he'll be worth another chance. He was poorly positioned following a sluggish start and was always struggling to get involved. (op 11-10)
City Style(USA) had little hope after starting slowest of all.

Golden Desert(IRE) is another who would have preferred a stronger pace.

237a AL HADEERAH TROPHY (H'CAP) (TURF) 5f
3:10 (3:10) (95-115,115) 3-Y-O+

£57,692 (£19,230; £9,615; £4,807; £2,884; £1,923)

Form RPR
/3-0 **1** **Happy Dubai (IRE)**[7] 152 4-8-6 100 AhmedAjtebi 8 109
(A Al Raihe, UAE) *trckd ldrs: led 1f out: r.o wl* **20/1**
106- **2** ½ **Monsieur Joe (IRE)**[112] 6508 4-8-6 100 Christophe-PatriceLemaire 5 107
(Walter Swinburn) *mid-div: chsd ldrs 2 1/2f out: led 1 1/2f out: hdd 1f out: r.o same pce* **10/1**[3]
3 ¾ **Everyday Heroes (USA)**[194] 5-8-6 100 (t) TedDurcan 2 104
(Saeed Bin Suroor) *mid-div: r.o wl fnl 1 1/2f: nt qckn fnl f* **8/1**[2]
220- **4** ¾ **Lui Rei (ITY)**[116] 6390 5-8-5 98 HayleyTurner 7 100
(Robert Cowell) *mid-div: r.o wl fnl 1 1/2f: nrest at fin* **16/1**
300- **5** *shd* **Mister Manannan (IRE)**[175] 4505 4-8-9 104 AdrianNicholls 16 104
(David Nicholls) *s.i.s: led after 1 1/2f: rdn and hdd 1 1/2f out: wknd* **8/1**[2]
000- **6** ¼ **Jimmy Styles**[103] 6735 7-8-6 100 (p) TadhgO'Shea 13 100
(Clive Cox) *mid-div: r.o fnl 2 1/2f: nrest at fin* **16/1**
/00- **7** ¼ **Terrific Challenge (USA)**[20] 9-8-11 106 (vt) RichardMullen 15 104
(S Seemar, UAE) *mid-div: r.o wl fnl 2f* **8/1**[2]
510- **8** ¼ **Rebecca Rolfe**[123] 6238 5-8-8 102 KierenFallon 3 100
(M Gasparini, Italy) *a in mid-div* **14/1**
360/ **9** 2 ¼ **Effort**[34] 5-8-5 95 JRosales 4 89
(A bin Huzaim, UAE) *nvr able to chal* **10/1**[3]
460/ **10** 2 ¼ **Mofarij**[48] 7-8-5 95 (t) RPCleary 1 81
(D Selvaratnam, UAE) *nvr able to chal* **20/1**
040- **11** ½ **War Artist (AUS)**[109] 6608 8-9-6 115 OlivierPeslier 9 94
(Rod Collet, France) *nvr nr to chal* **8/1**[2]
12 ¼ **Noble Heir (SAF)**[166] 6-8-9 104 RyanMoore 10 82
(H J Brown, South Africa) *nvr nr to chal* **7/1**[1]
104- **13** 1 ¼ **Masta Plasta (IRE)**[107] 6663 8-8-6 100 ow1 DaraghO'Donohoe 6 75
(David Nicholls) *nvr nr to chal* **11/1**
/50- **14** *shd* **League Champion (USA)**[35] 7901 8-8-5 95 ErhanYavuz 11 73
(R Bouresly, Kuwait) *led for 1 1/2f: sn struggling* **33/1**
050- **15** ½ **Rain Delayed (IRE)**[144] 5569 5-8-13 107 WJSupple 12 80
(Michael Dods) *s.i.s: nvr able to chal* **14/1**
120- **16** *shd* **Star Crowned (USA)**[299] 1021 8-9-0 108 (t) WayneSmith 14 80
(R Bouresly, Kuwait) *trckd ldrs for 3f: wknd* **16/1**

57.64 secs (57.64) **16** Ran SP% **126.9**
CSF £211.71; Tricast £1,766.51..
Owner Ahmed Al Falasi **Bred** Waterford Hall Stud **Trained** UAE
■ The first race run over this trip on the Meydan turf.

FOCUS
The action unfolded towards the far-side rail and a low draw looked advantageous, indeed the first four were drawn in single figures.

NOTEBOOK
Happy Dubai(IRE) paid for chasing an overly strong pace in a 7f Carnival handicap the previous week, but this drop to the minimum trip suited. The obvious race for him now is a handicap for horses rated 100 and above over C&D on February 10.
Monsieur Joe(IRE) showed good speed but was in a battle from some way out and was softened up by the time the winner challenged. This is his trip and presumably he'll re-oppose the winner on February 10.
Everyday Heroes(USA), a useful sprinter on dirt in the US, handled the turf okay and ran well from his favourable draw. He could try the Tapeta at some stage.
Lui Rei(ITY) was briefly denied a clear run when appearing to be going strongly around 2f out and ran well in the circumstances. Runner-up in a 6f Tapeta handicap here last year, he's got options.
Mister Manannan(IRE) ◆ is one to take from the race, being the second David Nicholls-trained runner this Carnival to run a big race from an unfavourable draw. Not only did stall 16 mean he raced more towards the middle of the track than the principals, but he also started awkwardly, and he did well to show so much speed before understandably tiring.
Jimmy Styles fared second best of those from a double-figure stall.
Terrific Challenge(USA) also ran okay from a high stall. (op 7-1)
War Artist(AUS), making his debut for another new yard, was never really going.
Noble Heir(SAF), a South African Grade 1 winner who was said to have the Al Quoz Sprint as her main objective, was a bit disappointing.

238a UAE 2000 GUINEAS TRIAL SPONSORED BY BAB AL SHAMS (CONDITIONS RACE) (TAPETA) 7f
3:50 (3:50) 3-Y-O

£19,230 (£6,410; £3,205; £1,602; £961; £641)

Form RPR
1 **Zanzamar (SAF)**[173] 4-9-4 104 (b) RichardHills 8 105+
(M F De Kock, South Africa) *in rr of mid-div: smooth prog 2f out: led 1f out: comf* **9/4**[1]
221- **2** 1 **Splash Point (USA)**[87] 7112 3-8-8 83 AhmedAjtebi 13 98
(Mahmood Al Zarooni) *chsd ldrs: led 1 1/2f out: hdd 1f out: r.o* **14/1**
31- **3** 1 ¼ **Bridgefield (USA)**[90] 7058 3-8-8 83 MickaelBarzalona 7 95
(Mahmood Al Zarooni) *mid-div: chsd ldrs 2 1/2f out: r.o same pce fnl f* **11/1**
100- **4** ¾ **Janood (IRE)**[110] 6560 3-8-8 100 FrankieDettori 14 93+
(Saeed Bin Suroor) *in rr of mid-div: r.o fnl 2f: nrest at fin* **5/2**[2]
123- **5** ¾ **Krypton Factor**[110] 6568 3-8-8 100 (b) KierenFallon 9 91
(F Nass, Bahrain) *trckd ldrs: ev ch 1 1/2f out: one pce fnl f* **9/1**[3]
220- **6** 1 ¼ **Introvert (IRE)**[98] 6870 3-8-8 87 RyanMoore 5 87
(Mahmood Al Zarooni) *a in mid-div* **25/1**
061- **7** ¾ **Lord Of The Stars (USA)**[87] 7127 3-8-8 94 TadhgO'Shea 1 85
(David Simcock) *trckd ldrs tl 2f out: one pce fnl f* **16/1**
316- **8** 3 **Signs In The Sand**[89] 7080 3-8-8 98 TedDurcan 6 77
(Saeed Bin Suroor) *settled in rr: nvr nr to chal* **11/1**
312- **9** ¾ **Sonoran Sands (IRE)**[153] 5257 3-8-8 97 HayleyTurner 12 75
(J S Moore) *settled in rr: n.d* **20/1**
623- **10** 9 **Grand Duchy**[21] 8025 3-8-8 88 WayneSmith 10 51
(M Al Muhairi, UAE) *settled in rr: n.d* **33/1**
510- **11** ¼ **Sheer Courage (IRE)**[21] 8025 3-8-2 100 (bt) HarryBentley[(6)] 3 50
(H J Brown, South Africa) *slowly away: n.d* **20/1**
20-0 **12** 1 ½ **Artic Rose (IRE)**[7] 151 3-8-5 86 ow1 ErhanYavuz 2 42
(R Bouresly, Kuwait) *sn led: hdd 1 1/2f out: wknd* **66/1**
13 ¾ **Energia Colonial (BRZ)**[35] 7902 4-9-4 95 BReis 11 47
(E Martins, Brazil) *nvr bttr than mid-div* **33/1**
14 ¾ **Abstrato (BRZ)**[146] 4-9-4 90 KShea 4 45
(M F De Kock, South Africa) *nvr bttr than mid-div* **10/1**

1m 25.18s (-0.02) **Going Correction** +0.275s/f (Slow) **14** Ran SP% **128.4**
WFA 3 from 4yo 18lb
Speed ratings: **111,109,108,107,106 105,104,101,100,89 89,87,87,86**
CSF £34.98..
Owner Hamdan Al Maktoum **Bred** Danika Stud **Trained** South Africa

FOCUS
This has been won by the subsequent UAE 2,000 Guineas winner five times in the last six seasons, and has also produced the last four Derby winners. That sort of record is hard to argue with, but in truth, this form doesn't look that strong by recent standards. The time was 0.31 seconds quicker than the earlier older-horse handicap won by the 101-rated Solid Choice, but that was steadily run.

NOTEBOOK
Zanzamar(SAF), placed in Grade 1 company in South Africa, had blinkers fitted and doesn't look entirely straightforward, being inclined to edge left under pressure and carry his head a touch awkwardly, but he was still too good for this lot. His effort is particularly creditable considering his trainer believes he'll want 1m2f-1m4f in time, and while this may not have been as good a race as in years gone by, he'll still have an obvious chance of Classic success if nothing better emerges. The 2,000 Guineas is on February 10.
Splash Point(USA) needed three goes to win his maiden, getting off the mark over this trip on Kempton's Polytrack in October, but he's smartly bred and showed improved form. Although not well drawn, he was always well placed and had no excuse.
Bridgefield(USA) raced against the inside rail in the straight, which might not have been ideal, but whatever, this Doncaster maiden winner should come on for the run. (op 10-1)
Janood(IRE) didn't progress as expected last year, perhaps being unsuited by soft ground on his last two starts, and there wasn't a great deal of promise this time, although he did have the worst draw. He was sluggish throughout and is going to need to improve for the run as well as a step up in trip if he's going to win the Guineas. (op 11-4)
Krypton Factor, a very useful sprinting juvenile for Sir Mark Prescott, joined these connections for 100,000gns. He ran well for a long way under a positive ride, but ultimately looked a non-stayer.

239a FALCON LOUNGE TROPHY (H'CAP) (TURF) 1m
4:25 (4:25) (100-110,110) 3-Y-O+

£46,153 (£15,384; £7,692; £3,846; £2,307; £1,538)

Form RPR
066- **1** **Derbaas (USA)**[21] 8028 5-8-13 105 (t) RichardHills 11 110
(A Al Raihe, UAE) *trckd ldrs: led 2f out: r.o wl* **14/1**
2 1 ¼ **Here To Win (BRZ)**[173] 5-8-11 104 ChristopheSoumillon 5 105+
(M F De Kock, South Africa) *mid-div: smooth prog 2f out: r.o: nrst at fin* **9/4**[2]
/51- **3** 1 ¼ **Kingsfort (USA)**[82] 7234 4-9-4 110 FrankieDettori 1 109
(Saeed Bin Suroor) *trckd ldrs: ev ch 1 1/2f out: nt qckn* **2/1**[1]
265- **4** 1 ¾ **Invisible Man**[64] 7482 5-9-2 108 (b) TedDurcan 14 103
(Saeed Bin Suroor) *in rr of mid-div: r.o wl fnl 2f: nrest at fin* **12/1**
000- **5** ½ **Classic Blade (IRE)**[25] 5-8-8 100 PatDobbs 2 94
(Doug Watson, UAE) *in rr of mid-div: r.o fnl 2f* **40/1**
50-0 **6** 1 ¼ **Mac Love**[7] 156 10-9-3 109 RichardMullen 3 100
(Stef Higgins) *a in mid-div* **20/1**
00-5 **7** 1 ¼ **War Monger (USA)**[7] 157 7-8-8 100 TadhgO'Shea 8 88
(Doug Watson, UAE) *nvr nr to chal* **16/1**
0- **8** ¾ **Quartier Latin (ARG)**[14] 75 5-8-11 104 (t) WJSupple 6 89
(Doug Watson, UAE) *sn led: hdd 2f out: r.o same pce* **50/1**
120/ **9** 1 ¼ **Third Set (IRE)**[686] 774 8-9-1 107 (t) RyanMoore 13 91
(I Mohammed, UAE) *settled in rr: n.d* **22/1**
/03- **10** 1 **Jaasoos (IRE)**[25] 7-8-10 102 KierenFallon 9 83
(D Selvaratnam, UAE) *nvr bttr than mid-div* **20/1**
0/3- **11** *shd* **Separate Ways (IRE)**[81] 7259 6-8-10 102 (b) CO'Donoghue 12 83
(David Marnane, Ire) *nvr able to chal* **7/1**[3]
12 2 ½ **Florentino (JPN)**[234] 5-9-2 108 AhmedAjtebi 10 83
(Mahmood Al Zarooni) *trckd ldr tl 2 1/2f out: wknd* **20/1**
00-0 **13** 2 ¾ **Black Eagle (IRE)**[7] 157 5-8-10 102 JRosales 4 71
(A bin Huzaim, UAE) *nvr able to chal* **20/1**
1/-0 **14** 12 **Comradeship (IRE)**[7] 157 4-8-8 100 WayneSmith 7 41
(R Bouresly, Kuwait) *v.s.a: racd in last: n.d* **50/1**

1m 36.55s (96.55) **14** Ran SP% **126.6**
CSF £43.27; Tricast £96.82..
Owner Hamdan Al Maktoum **Bred** Shadwell Farm LLC **Trained** UAE

FOCUS
A quality handicap, but the pace was just modest. The time was almost identical to the later Group 2 Cape Verdi Stakes, but they didn't go that quick in that race either.

NOTEBOOK
Derbaas(USA) was well placed considering how the race unfolded and got first run on his chief rivals. That effectively sealed the race, for despite edging left on to the rail under pressure, as well as tending to flash his tail when hit with the whip, he was never in danger. He failed to make any impression at this event last year, but had won two non-Carnival handicaps over this trip on the Tapeta here towards the end of 2010 and is clearly progressing well.
Here To Win(BRZ) ◆, a Grade 1 winner in South Africa, was very much being looked after with an eye to the future. She travelled well, but had been set plenty to do and the jockey then took a while to get serious in the straight before being easy on the filly close to the finish. Clearly the runner-up, mentioned pre-Carnival by her trainer as a possible for Cape Verdi and Balanchine (River Jetez represented trainer in former event), should benefit a good deal from this and ought to show improved form next time. (op 5-2)
Kingsfort(USA), having only his third start since winning the 2009 National Stakes on his final outing for Kevin Prendergast, was racing on ground without soft in the description for the first time and was one-paced under pressure. This was still a smart performance off 110, though, and there really ought to be more to come as he continues to regain full race-sharpness.
Invisible Man, not helped by stall 14, was left with too much to do after being dropped in well off the steady pace.
Classic Blade(IRE) ran okay but wasn't quite up to the level.
Mac Love, keen under restraint early on, was struggling to make a telling impression but keeping on when denied a clear run against the inside rail halfway up the straight, probably costing him a couple of lengths.

240a AL SARAB TROPHY (H'CAP) (TAPETA) 1m 1f 110y
5:10 (5:10) (95-109,109) 3-Y-O+

£57,692 (£19,230; £9,615; £4,807; £2,884; £1,923)

Form RPR
/40- **1** **Spring Of Fame (USA)**[82] 7237 5-9-3 107 FrankieDettori 12 106
(Saeed Bin Suroor) *trckd ldrs: led 1 1/2f out: r.o wl: comf* **8/1**[3]
230- **2** 1 ¼ **Haatheq (USA)**[6] 4-9-0 105 RichardHills 11 100
(A Al Raihe, UAE) *mid-div: r.o wl fnl 1 1/2f: nrest at fin* **10/1**
3 ¼ **Star Empire (SAF)**[166] 5-9-2 106 ChristopheSoumillon 13 99+
(M F De Kock, South Africa) *in rr of mid-div: r.o fnl 2f but nvr able to chal* **7/4**[1]
60/0 **4** *hd* **Rochdale**[7] 153 8-8-11 101 (t) TedDurcan 6 94
(A Al Raihe, UAE) *trckd ldrs: ev ch 2f out: r.o wl* **25/1**
20-0 **5** 1 ¼ **King Of Rome (IRE)**[7] 156 6-9-5 109 KShea 1 100
(M F De Kock, South Africa) *mid-div: r.o fnl 1 1/2f but nvr able to chal* **12/1**
0/6- **6** *hd* **Jalil (USA)**[336] 609 7-9-2 106 AhmedAjtebi 14 96
(Mahmood Al Zarooni) *mid-div: one pce fnl 2f* **16/1**

4/1- **7** 1/2 **Zibimix (IRE)**[98] 6881 7-9-4 108 .... GregoryBenoist 8 97
(X Nakkachdji, France) *mid-div: chsd ldrs 2f out: nt qckn* **14/1**
030- **8** 1/2 **Hattan (IRE)**[56] 7624 9-9-1 105 .... WayneSmith 10 93
(M Al Muhairi, UAE) *sn led: rdn 3f out: hdd 1 1/2f out: r.o same pce* **20/1**
431- **9** 1 1/4 **Kal Barg**[42] 7793 6-9-1 105 .... KierenFallon 9 90
(D Selvaratnam, UAE) *slowly away: settled in rr: nvr able to chal* **7/1**[2]
500- **10** 1/2 **Calvados Blues (FR)**[126] 6123 5-9-4 108 .... RyanMoore 4 92
(Mahmood Al Zarooni) *settled in rr: n.d* **14/1**
11 1 1/2 **Gallahad (BRZ)**[208] 5-8-10 100 .... Christophe-PatriceLemaire 7 81
(A De Royer-Dupre, France) *in rr of mid-div: n.d* **10/1**
/34- **12** 1 1/2 **Famous Warrior (IRE)**[217] 3137 4-8-11 102 .... TadhgO'Shea 2 81
(Doug Watson, UAE) *mid-div on rail: nvr able to chal* **25/1**
300- **13** 3 1/2 **Oroveso (BRZ)**[42] 7793 5-8-13 102 .... BReis 3 74
(E Martins, Brazil) *trckd ldrs: rdn 3f out: sn btn* **25/1**
556- **14** hd **Highland Glen**[79] 7287 5-8-10 100 .... (t) RichardMullen 5 71
(S Seemar, UAE) *settled in rr: nvr nr to chal* **25/1**

1m 59.05s (0.35) **Going Correction** +0.275s/f (Slow)
WFA 4 from 5yo+ 1lb **14** Ran SP% **125.2**
Speed ratings: **109,108,107,107,106 106,106,105,104,104 103,101,99,98**
CSF £82.51; Tricast £201.87..
Owner Godolphin **Bred** Brushwood Stable **Trained** Newmarket, Suffolk

FOCUS
Another modestly run race in which it paid to be handy.

NOTEBOOK
Spring Of Fame(USA) was best placed of the principals, although he was forced wide on the first bend from stall 12. Clearly this isn't form to get carried away with, but the winner was enhancing his impressive record on synthetic tracks. On his only three previous starts off the turf, he had won twice on Polytrack before looking an unlucky loser in a decent conditions event at Kempton. He may have more to offer on this surface.
Haatheq(USA), runner-up in a Listed event on the Jebel Ali dirt the previous week, was trying Tapeta for the first time and kept on well after the winner got first run.
Star Empire(SAF) ◆, a progressive type with smart form to his name in South Africa, had a low head carriage through the first furlong, wanting to go faster than he was allowed, and had to be restrained in behind horses. Consequently he got going too late to pose a serious threat, but he should come on for this and can improve if settling better and/or getting a stronger pace to chase in future. (op 2-1)
Rochdale ran creditably without being good enough.
King Of Rome(IRE), who had no easy under top weight, probably would have preferred a better gallop.
Jalil(USA), who managed only one run last year, showed he retains some ability.

241a CAPE VERDI SPONSORED BY BAB AL SHAMS (GROUP 2) (F&M) (TURF) 1m

5:45 (5:45) 3-Y-O+

£76,923 (£25,641; £12,820; £6,410; £3,846; £2,564)

Form RPR
121- **1** **Aspectoflove (IRE)**[84] 7188 5-9-0 106 .... FrankieDettori 2 103
(Saeed Bin Suroor) *trckd ldng pair: led 1 1/2f out: r.o wl* **3/1**[2]
02- **2** 1/4 **Thai Haku (IRE)**[98] 6881 4-9-0 102 .... Christophe-PatriceLemaire 10 102
(M Delzangles, France) *trckd ldr: led 2 1/2f out: hdd 1 1/2f out: r.o wl* **20/1**
3 1/2 **River Jetez (SAF)**[173] 8-9-0 107 .... ChristopheSoumillon 1 101+
(M F De Kock, South Africa) *trckd ldng pair: no room 2 1/2f out: r.o wl fnl 1 1/2f: nrest at fin* **11/8**[1]
200- **4** 2 3/4 **Ayun Tara (FR)**[77] 4-9-0 104 .... GregoryBenoist 6 95
(X Nakkachdji, France) *mid-div: r.o wl fnl 1 1/2f* **12/1**
353- **5** 1 1/2 **Forest Crown**[84] 7188 4-9-0 100 .... JimCrowley 5 91
(Ralph Beckett) *settled in rr: r.o fnl 1 1/2f* **14/1**
323- **6** 1 1/4 **Kinky Afro (IRE)**[138] 5782 4-9-0 99 .... KierenFallon 4 88
(J S Moore) *nvr bttr than mid-div* **18/1**
/14- **7** 1/2 **Deem (IRE)**[299] 1026 6-9-0 115 .... OlivierPeslier 9 87
(J Barton, Saudi Arabia) *in rr of mid-div: nvr able to chal* **4/1**[3]
8 4 **Summer Games**[62] 6-9-0 95 .... (t) TadhgO'Shea 7 78
(R Bouresly, Kuwait) *s.i.s: n.d* **66/1**
002- **9** 1/4 **Allali Chiara (IRE)**[41] 7916 [illegible] .... CO'Donoghue 3 77
(Andrew Oliver, Ire) *sn led: rdn and hdd 2 1/2f out* **20/1**
10 11 **Emper Holly (ARG)**[389] 5-9-0 98 .... (t) PatCosgrave 8 52
(M bin Shafya, UAE) *s.i.s: a in rr* **33/1**
105/ **11** 7 1/2 **My Sweet Baby (USA)**[236] 5-9-0 100 .... WayneSmith 11 35
(F Nass, Bahrain) *nvr bttr than mid-div* **33/1**

1m 36.52s (96.52) **11** Ran SP% **123.6**
CSF £69.41..
Owner Godolphin **Bred** Patrick Cassidy **Trained** Newmarket, Suffolk

FOCUS
The Cape Verdi was run as a Group 2 for the first time this year, upgraded from Group 3 status, but it was an ordinary contest for the level. Again, they didn't seem to go that quick and the time was very similar to the earlier handicap won by the 105-rated Derbaas, another race run at a modest tempo.

NOTEBOOK
Aspectoflove(IRE) was a close second in both this race and the Balanchine here last year, but she just came out on top this time, thanks in no small part to a brilliant ride from Frankie Dettori. The jockey had his mount well placed throughout, sitting close enough to the modest tempo whilst keeping the favourite locked away against the inside rail some way from the finish, and Dettori's tactical awareness was as good as you'll see. Once in the straight, the rider was reluctant to go too soon, remembering the mare had been caught late on in the second of her two runs here last here, but also ensuring the favourite would struggle for a clear run against the rail. The winner seems unlikely to confirm form with River Jetez in the Balanchine on February 18.
Thai Haku(IRE), an improving French-trained filly, ran a fine race and seems likely to give a good account in the Balanchine, with stamina not an issue.
River Jetez(SAF) ◆, caught in a pocket all the way up the straight, probably would have lost too much momentum by switching around the winner before that one had come under pressure, but the way she finished when finally in the clear suggests she was unlucky. She looks the one to beat in the Balanchine. (op 13-8)
Ayun Tara(FR) wasn't quite up to the class. (op 10-1)
Forest Crown was held by the winner on their last two meetings.
Deem(IRE) won this at Nad Al Sheba in 2009 and landed the Balanchine over 1m1f here last year, but she's a strong stayer these days (fourth in Sheema Classic when last seen) and found a steadily run race at this distance no use to her. (op 7-2)

242a AL FORSAN TROPHY (H'CAP) (TURF) 1m 2f

6:20 (6:20) (100-110,109) 3-Y-O+

£46,153 (£15,384; £7,692; £3,846; £2,307; £1,538)

Form RPR
0/1- **1** **Simon De Montfort (IRE)**[270] 1567 4-9-2 108 .... KierenFallon 13 112+
(Mahmood Al Zarooni) *settled in rr: smooth prog to chse ldrs 2f out: r.o wl: led fnl 110yds* **7/2**[1]
506- **2** 1/2 **Once More Dubai (USA)**[78] 7297 6-8-11 102 .... (bt) TedDurcan 3 104+
(Saeed Bin Suroor) *mid-div: chsd ldrs 2 1/2f out: led 1f out: hdd fnl 110yds* **14/1**
111/ **3** 3 1/4 **Zeitoper**[459] 6889 4-8-8 100 .... WJSupple 8 97
(Mahmood Al Zarooni) *s.i.s: settled in rr: r.o wl fnl 2f: nrest at fin* **9/1**[3]
310- **4** hd **High Twelve (IRE)**[110] 6562 4-8-3 101 ow1 .... AntiocoMurgia(6) 5 96
(Mahmood Al Zarooni) *trckd ldrs: nt qckn fnl f* **14/1**
414- **5** nse **Peligroso (FR)**[71] 7384 5-9-0 105 .... FrankieDettori 6 100+
(Saeed Bin Suroor) *trckd ldr: led 2f out: hdd 1f out* **13/2**[2]
324- **6** 3/4 **Jedi**[89] 7096 5-8-11 102 .... Christophe-PatriceLemaire 9 96
(A bin Huzaim, UAE) *a in mid-div* **10/1**
65-0 **7** 1/2 **Hunting Tower (SAF)**[7] 152 9-9-1 106 .... (t) KShea 14 99
(M F De Kock, South Africa) *settled in rr: r.o fnl 2f but n.d* **16/1**
200- **8** 4 **Dubawi Phantom**[177] 4456 4-8-10 102 .... TadhgO'Shea 11 88
(Ed Dunlop) *settled in rr: n.d* **14/1**
/00- **9** 1/2 **Bon Grain (FR)**[322] 800 6-8-13 104 .... PatCosgrave 7 88
(M bin Shafya, UAE) *sn led: kicked clr 3f out: hdd 2f out* **40/1**
100- **10** 3/4 **Azmeel**[179] 4420 4-9-3 109 .... RyanMoore 4 92
(John Gosden) *nvr bttr than mid-div* **13/2**[2]
303- **11** 1/4 **Heliodor (USA)**[120] 6281 5-8-11 102 .... AhmedAjtebi 10 84
(Mahmood Al Zarooni) *nvr bttr than mid-div* **10/1**
/00- **12** 1 1/4 **Big Creek (IRE)**[123] 4-8-10 102 .... JimCrowley 2 82
(J S Moore) *nvr bttr than mid-div* **25/1**
23-0 **13** 13 **Monte Alto (IRE)**[7] 154 7-9-0 105 .... (t) RichardHills 1 58
(A Al Raihe, UAE) *trckd ldrs tl 2f out: wknd* **14/1**
541- **14** 19 **Shimmering Moment (USA)**[75] 7358 4-9-0 106 ...... (b) CO'Donoghue 12 22
(James J Hartnett, Ire) *nvr bttr than mid-div* **10/1**

2m 1.89s (121.89)
WFA 4 from 5yo+ 2lb **14** Ran SP% **125.0**
CSF £57.74; Tricast £425.94. Placepot: £41.30 to a £1 stake. Pool: £10,933.25. - 193.15 winning tickets. Quadpot: £3.09 to a £1 stake. Pool: £621.70. - 115.10 winning tickets..
Owner Godolphin **Bred** Darley **Trained** Newmarket, Suffolk

FOCUS
This handicap was contested by some interesting types, notably a few runners who had shown Group-race form but hadn't been seen for quite a while.

NOTEBOOK
Simon De Montfort(IRE), whose only defeat in five starts for Andre Fabre came in the Group 1 Criterium de Saint-Cloud in 2009, but who been off the track since winning a Group 3 last April. The gallop was fair, so being held up well off the pace didn't inconvenience the winner, and he picked up in taking fashion when weaving between horses towards the inside in the straight, leading in the final few yards. He was well backed, so clearly plenty was expected, for all that Godolphin's jockey bookings in this race were difficult to read, and in winning off 108 this was a career best. His connections now must decide whether they think he's one for the Duty Free (1m1f) or the Sheema Classic (1m4f). There are mixed messages in his pedigree and his next run, which may be in the Dubai City of Gold over 1m4f on Super Thursday (March 3), will tell us more. (op 4-1)
Once More Dubai(USA) was on good terms with himself, travelling well and finding for pressure, only to be worm down by an exciting prospect.
Zeitoper was unbeaten in three runs as a juvenile and Ahmed Ajtebi thought he could be a Derby horse after winning a French Group 3 on his final outing of that campaign, but he hadn't been seen since. Seemingly far from the owner's first string on his return, he shaped encouragingly and clearly retains a deal of ability.
High Twelve(IRE), sold out of John Gosden's yard for 130,00gns after finishing 12th in the Cambridgeshire, showed enough to suggest he might win a Carnival handicap. According to RPRs his best performance to date came on Polytrack, so he'll be worth a shot on Tapeta.
Peligroso(FR) wasn't good enough.
Jedi ◆, bought out of Sir Michael Stoute's yard for 215,000gns in October, kept on nicely for a horse who wants further. The Listed Nad Al Sheba Trophy over 1m6f on February 17 could be his race.
Azmeel, returning from a 179-day absence, was sweating down his neck and was a bit keen early.

???LINGFIELD (L H)

Friday, January 21

OFFICIAL GOING: Standard
Wind: Light, against Weather: Fine

243 TODAY'S JOCKEY SPECIALS AT BLUESQ.COM CLAIMING STKS 6f (P)

12:55 (12:55) (Class 6) 4-Y-O+ **£1,569** (£463; £231) **Stalls** Low

Form RPR
32U- **1** **Cape Melody**[95] 6987 5-8-10 74 .... MatthewDavies(3) 2 71
(George Baker) *dwlt and rousted along early in last: prog on outer 2f out: coming to chal whn rdr dropped whip 1f out: urged into ld last 150yds* **6/4**[1]
4205 **2** 3/4 **Elhamri**[3] 199 7-8-13 72 .... HayleyTurner 5 69
(Conor Dore) *led: stdd pce after 1f: kicked on 2f out: edgd lft over 1f out: hdd and nt qckn last 150yds* **2/1**[2]
3-56 **3** 1 **Harlech Castle**[2] 213 6-8-10 69 .... (b) NickyMackay 4 63
(Jim Boyle) *chsd ldr to 1/2-way: styd cl up: nt qckn on inner 1f out: kpt on* **7/2**[3]
5-31 **4** 1 1/4 **Vhujon (IRE)**[8] 137 6-9-3 74 .... RobbieFitzpatrick 6 66
(Peter Grayson) *t.k.h: hld up in 4th: rdn to dispute 2nd 2f out: sn nt qckn: fdd ins fnl f* **8/1**
/0-5 **5** 1/2 **Quick Single (USA)**[2] 218 5-8-7 42 .... (v) LukeMorris 3 54?
(Phil McEntee) *chsd ldng pair: rdn to chse ldr 3f out to 2f out: sn last and looked like dropping away: kpt on again nr fin* **66/1**

1m 12.07s (0.17) **Going Correction** +0.075s/f (Slow) **5** Ran SP% **108.2**
Speed ratings (Par 101): **101,100,98,97,96**
CSF £4.59 TOTE £2.40: £1.10, £1.80; EX 6.10.
Owner M Khan X2 **Bred** Mrs A Savage **Trained** Whitsbury, Hants

FOCUS
Quite a competitive claimer on the figures. The form looks dubious with the proximity of the fifth casting doubts.

244 FELBRIDGE H'CAP 2m (P)

1:25 (1:26) (Class 6) (0-65,65) 4-Y-O+ **£1,569** (£463; £231) **Stalls** Low

Form RPR
5-42 **1** **Mashdood (USA)**[10] 118 5-9-9 **60** .... LukeMorris 8 69
(Peter Hiatt) *trckd clr ldr: clsd fr 1/2-way: led over 4f out: drvn over 2f out: styd on wl* **5/2**[1]
405- **2** 2 3/4 **Gandalf**[30] 7967 9-9-13 **64** .... JimCrowley 1 70
(Amy Weaver) *hld up in 4th and wl off the pce: clsd 5f out: prog 4f out: drvn to chse wnr over 2f out: nt qckn over 1f out: hld after* **15/2**

002- **3** 1 ¼ **Rare Coincidence**[69] 6648 10-9-2 **53**...............(p) MartinLane 5 58
(Roger Fisher) *chsd clr ldng pair: wnt 2nd over 4f out to over 2f out: kpt on u.p* **20/1**

220/ **4** 1 ¼ **Dynamic Rhythm (USA)**[555] 4591 8-9-11 **62**............ RobertWinston 4 65
(Peter Brookshaw) *hld up in 5th and wl off the pce: clsd 5f out: urged along over 4f out: sn struggling: tk modest 4th 2f out: plugged on* **10/1**

133- **5** 4 **Tower**[72] 7388 4-8-13 **57**.................. J-PGuillambert 7 55
(George Prodromou) *reluctant to enter stalls: awkward s: hld up in last and wl off the pce: clsd 5f out: shkn up and no rspnse over 3f out: no prog after* **11/4[2]**

112- **6** 11 **Alternative Choice (USA)**[23] 8010 5-10-0 **65**............ GeorgeBaker 6 50
(Nick Littmoden) *stdd s: hld up in 6th and wl off the pce: clsd and in tch 5f out: rdn and lft bhd over 3f out: no ch after* **4/1[3]**

050- **7** 15 **Judgethemoment (USA)**[22] 8013 6-10-0 **65**...........(b[1]) EddieAhern 3 32
(Jane Chapple-Hyam) *led and sn spreadeagled field: c bk fr 1/2-way: hdd & wknd rapidly over 4f out* **12/1**

3m 24.55s (-1.15) **Going Correction** +0.075s/f (Slow)
WFA 4 from 5yo+ 7lb **7** Ran SP% **108.5**
Speed ratings (Par 101): **105,103,103,102,100 94,87**
toteswingers:1&2 £3.30, 2&3 £11.10, 1&3 £9.90 CSF £19.21 CT £263.10 TOTE £3.90: £1.90, £3.30; EX 21.80 Trifecta £82.90 Pool of £600.61 - 5.36 winning units..
Owner Alan Swinburne **Bred** Abbott Properties, Sa **Trained** Hook Norton, Oxon

FOCUS
They went a good pace and the winner was well placed to pick up the pieces. The form seems sound.
Alternative Choice(USA) Official explanation: jockey said gelding ran flat

245 MARSH GREEN (S) STKS 1m 4f (P)
1:55 (1:55) (Class 6) 4-6-Y-0 **£1,569** (£463; £231) **Stalls** Low

Form RPR

26-3 **1** **Sheila's Bond**[7] 162 4-8-8 56.................. LukeMorris 5 62
(J S Moore) *trckd ldng pair: pushed along over 4f out: prog to chse ldr over 3f out: hrd rdn to ld narrowly over 1f out: jst hld on* **2/1[2]**

256- **2** shd **Peace Corps**[23] 8003 5-9-3 73..................(vt) StephenCraine 1 67
(Jim Boyle) *pressed ldr: led over 3f out: drvn and narrowly hdd over 1f out: w wnr after: jst failed* **1/1[1]**

106- **3** 5 **City Stable (IRE)**[25] 7985 6-9-3 67.................. JamieMackay 2 59
(Michael Wigham) *trckd ldng pair: rdn 3f out: sn outpcd: modest 3rd and no imp fnl 2f* **9/2[3]**

4 9 **Lightening Force** 4-8-13 0.................. RobertWinston 4 45
(Peter Brookshaw) *s.i.s: in tch in last: pushed along 4f out: briefly wnt 3rd over 2f out: sn wknd* **16/1**

00-4 **5** 1 ¾ **Dalrymple (IRE)**[7] 163 5-9-3 40..................(t) FrankieMcDonald 3 42
(Michael Madgwick) *led at sensible pce to over 3f out: sn wknd and bhd* **50/1**

2m 34.45s (1.45) **Going Correction** +0.075s/f (Slow)
WFA 4 from 5yo+ 4lb **5** Ran SP% **109.4**
Speed ratings: **98,97,94,88,87**
CSF £4.31 TOTE £2.80: £1.10, £2.00; EX 3.80.The winner was bought by J Flint for 5,000gns.
Owner Ray Styles **Bred** Mrs Anita R Dodd **Trained** Upper Lambourn, Berks

FOCUS
An ordinary seller and muddling form, rated cautiously around the winner.

246 ENHANCED SP'S AT BLUESQ.COM MAIDEN STKS 5f (P)
2:30 (2:30) (Class 5) 3-Y-0 **£2,047** (£604; £302) **Stalls** High

Form RPR

20-2 **1** **Morermaloke**[16] 43 3-9-3 73.................. ShaneKelly 3 66+
(Brian Meehan) *hld up in 5th: smooth prog 2f out: pushed along briefly to cl 1f out: led last 100yds: comf* **1/4[1]**

30-3 **2** 1 ¼ **Fairy Tales**[16] 44 3-8-12 52.................. NeilChalmers 2 56
(John Bridger) *led: kpt on wl whn rdn 2f out: hdd last 100yds: no ch w wnr* **16/1[3]**

0-22 **3** 2 ½ **Pineapple Pete (IRE)**[9] 132 3-9-3 58..................(t) ChrisCatlin 6 52
(Paul Cole) *chsd ldr: rdn over 2f out: nt qckn and hld over 1f out: lost 2nd ins fnl f* **9/2[2]**

05- **4** 1 **Dangerous Illusion (IRE)**[84] 7207 3-8-12 0.................. AndreaAtzeni 1 43
(Michael Quinn) *awkward s: chsd ldng pair: rdn over 2f out: steadily outpcd* **25/1**

U-5 **5** 2 ½ **Pickled Pumpkin**[17] 28 3-9-3 0.................. GeorgeBaker 4 39
(Olivia Maylam) *racd wd: chsd ldng trio to jst over 2f out: sn dropped out* **33/1**

6 2 ¼ **Stoneacre Joe Joe** 3-9-3 0.................. DaneO'Neill 5 31
(Peter Grayson) *dwlt: mostly in 6th and struggling by 1/2-way: wknd ins fnl f* **66/1**

00- **7** 9 **Tough Customer**[81] 7269 3-9-3 0.................. VinceSlattery 7 —
(Gary Brown) *outpcd* **80/1**

59.64 secs (0.84) **Going Correction** +0.075s/f (Slow) **7** Ran SP% **113.6**
Speed ratings (Par 97): **96,94,90,88,84 80,66**
toteswingers:1&2 £1.50, 2&3 £1.20, 1&3 £1.10 CSF £5.81 TOTE £1.20: £1.10, £3.20; EX 5.20.
Owner Decadent Racing **Bred** D R C Elsworth **Trained** Manton, Wilts

FOCUS
A weak maiden and the winner scored with a bit in hand. The form is rated around the runner-up.

247 HARE LANE H'CAP 1m 2f (P)
3:05 (3:05) (Class 6) (0-65,64) 4-Y-0+ **£1,569** (£463; £231) **Stalls** Low

Form RPR

2-16 **1** **Edgeworth (IRE)**[6] 174 5-9-6 **63**..................(p) ChrisCatlin 6 70+
(Brendan Powell) *t.k.h: hld up last: prog on outer over 2f out: trckd ldrs over 1f out: gap appeared jst ins fnl f: rdn and r.o wl to ld last strides* **3/1[2]**

10-6 **2** hd **Indian Violet (IRE)**[7] 162 5-9-4 **61**.................. JamieGoldstein 2 67
(Sheena West) *hld up in midfield: prog on outer to join ldrs 2f out: led over 1f out: r.o ins fnl f: hdd last strides* **13/2[3]**

415- **3** ¾ **Esteem Lord**[30] 7966 5-9-2 **59**.................. JimCrowley 8 63
(Dean Ivory) *hld up in last trio: prog on wd outside over 2f out: rdn to chal jst over 1f out: nt qckn: kpt on nr fin* **7/1**

01-1 **4** 2 **Lord Lansing (IRE)**[14] 86 4-9-4 **63**.................. EddieAhern 4 63+
(Mrs K Burke) *t.k.h: hld up in midfield tl prog to trck ldr 1/2-way: rdn to chal 2f out: nt qckn over 1f out: outpcd after* **11/4[1]**

4- **5** ¾ **Kammamuri (IRE)**[53] 7626 6-9-7 **64**.................. AndreaAtzeni 3 63
(Michael Wigham) *mde most for 3f: styd chsng ldrs: rdn whn pce lifted over 2f out: nt qckn over 1f out: kpt on same pce* **12/1**

060- **6** ¾ **Sir William Orpen**[121] 6290 4-9-0 **59**.................. IanMongan 5 56
(Pat Phelan) *hld up in rr: dropped to last over 2f out: prog on inner wl over 1f out: effrt flattened out ins fnl f* **66/1**

34-3 **7** 2 ¾ **Aflaam (IRE)**[16] 50 6-9-5 **62**..................(t) DavidProbert 7 54
(Ronald Harris) *prom: rdn and nt qckn over 2f out: fdd over 1f out* **7/1**

155- **8** ¾ **Naheell**[35] 7921 5-9-7 **64**..................(p) GeorgeBaker 1 54
(George Prodromou) *prom: lost pl 1/2-way: rdn whn pce lifted over 2f out: steadily fdd* **12/1**

0-05 **9** ½ **Vinces**[14] 83 7-8-13 **56**.................. JamieSpencer 9 45
(Tim McCarthy) *prog to ld after 3f out: kicked on over 2f out: hdd over 1f out: sn btn and eased* **9/1**

2m 8.46s (1.86) **Going Correction** +0.075s/f (Slow)
WFA 4 from 5yo+ 2lb **9** Ran SP% **116.9**
Speed ratings (Par 101): **95,94,94,92,92 91,89,88,88**
toteswingers:1&2 £7.70, 2&3 £9.40, 1&3 £5.90 CSF £23.29 CT £126.73 TOTE £4.40: £1.60, £2.30, £1.60; EX 31.70 Trifecta £142.20 Pool: £980.16 - 5.10 winning units..
Owner K Rhatigan **Bred** Yvonne & Gerard Kennedy **Trained** Upper Lambourn, Berks

FOCUS
They didn't seem to go that fast early but things picked up running down the hill and two of the first three came from the back of the field. The form amongst the principals looks sound.
Lord Lansing(IRE) Official explanation: jockey said gelding hung right
Naheell Official explanation: jockey said horse hung left

248 LINGFIELDPARK.CO.UK H'CAP 1m (P)
3:40 (3:41) (Class 6) (0-65,65) 4-Y-0+ **£1,569** (£463; £231) **Stalls** High

Form RPR

530- **1** **Resuscitator (USA)**[21] 8034 4-9-4 **62**..................(v) EddieAhern 3 72
(Heather Main) *mde virtually all: had most of rivals at full stretch 2f out: rdn over 1f out: battled on wl* **14/1**

642- **2** 1 ½ **Dichoh**[24] 7991 8-9-6 **64**..................(v) ChrisCatlin 9 70
(Michael Madgwick) *chsd ldng pair: drvn and nt qckn over 2f out: lost pl over 1f out: styd on again to take 2nd last 50yds* **15/2**

530- **3** nk **Serious Drinking (USA)**[54] 7611 5-9-4 **62**............ JamieSpencer 10 67
(Walter Swinburn) *dropped in fr wd draw and hld up in last pair: stl there over 1f out: hrd rdn and r.o ins fnl f: tk 3rd last strides* **13/2[3]**

000- **4** ½ **Lopinot (IRE)**[100] 6853 8-9-4 **62**..................(v) JimCrowley 8 66
(Martin Bosley) *hld up in 9th: gng bttr than most whn prog over 2f out: rdn to chse wnr ins fnl f: no imp and fdd out of it nr fin* **20/1**

0-32 **5** hd **Sasheen**[7] 160 4-9-0 **58**..................(p) StephenCraine 11 62
(Jim Boyle) *pressed wnr: rdn and nt qckn 2f out: lost 2nd and one pce ins fnl f* **13/2[3]**

6 **6** 1 ¼ **Fedora (IRE)**[9] 128 5-9-2 **65**..................(t) KylieManser[(5)] 2 66
(Olivia Maylam) *stdd s: hld up in last pair: stl there 2f out: reminders over 1f out: pushed along and styd on steadily ins fnl f: nvr nrr* **25/1**

460- **7** hd **Miss Bounty**[125] 6210 6-8-12 **56**.................. IanMongan 6 57
(Jim Boyle) *cl up: rdn over 2f out: nt qckn wl over 1f out: fdd ins fnl f* **17/2**

20-3 **8** nk **Collect Art (IRE)**[8] 139 4-9-5 **63**.................. StevieDonohoe 4 63
(Andrew Haynes) *settled towards rr: effrt over 2f out: sme prog on inner over 1f out: no hdwy ins fnl f* **9/2[1]**

55-1 **9** 1 ¼ **Wavertree Warrior (IRE)**[18] 26 9-9-4 **62**............ RobertHavlin 12 59
(Nick Littmoden) *racd wd in midfield: rdn 3f out: struggling 2f out: n.d after* **11/1**

001- **10** 3 **Mountrath**[44] 7768 4-9-5 **63**..................(v) DaneO'Neill 7 53
(Brett Johnson) *wl in tch in midfield: rdn over 2f out: lost pl and wknd over 1f out* **6/1[2]**

005- **11** 15 **Prohibition (IRE)**[58] 7561 5-9-5 **63**..................(bt) GeorgeBaker 1 26
(Gary Moore) *prom tl wknd rapidly over 2f out: eased and t.o* **8/1**

1m 37.71s (-0.49) **Going Correction** +0.075s/f (Slow) **11** Ran SP% **116.1**
Speed ratings (Par 101): **105,103,103,102,102 101,101,100,99,96 81**
toteswingers:1&2 £16.80, 2&3 £6.80, 1&3 £20.40 CSF £113.74 CT £768.78 TOTE £17.50: £6.30, £1.30, £2.80; EX 144.20 Trifecta £828.20 Part won. Pool of £1119.29 - 0.52 winning units..
Owner Wetumpka Racing & Donald Kerr **Bred** David Bowman & Dr Carl Chan **Trained** Kingston Lisle, Oxon

FOCUS
The pace held up in this ordinary handicap. The winner is rated back to his early pace.

249 PLAY FREE BINGO AT BLUESQ.COM H'CAP 7f (P)
4:15 (4:15) (Class 5) (0-75,75) 4-Y-0+ **£2,047** (£604; £302) **Stalls** Low

Form RPR

241- **1** **Advertisement (USA)**[158] 5153 4-9-7 **75**..................(t) GeorgeBaker 4 86+
(Jeremy Noseda) *trckd ldng trio: effrt 2f out: clsd to ld last 150yds: drvn out* **11/4[1]**

23-5 **2** 1 ¼ **Lockantanks**[13] 96 4-9-1 **69**.................. ChrisCatlin 6 76
(Michael Appleby) *trckd ldrs in 5th on inner: sltly checked jst over 2f out: prog over 1f out: styd on to take 2nd last 75yds: no ch to chal* **14/1**

00-3 **3** 1 **Cuthbert (IRE)**[16] 55 4-9-2 **70**..................(p) JimCrowley 9 74
(William Jarvis) *pressed ldr: led wl over 1f out: hdd and nt qckn last 150yds* **8/1**

666- **4** ¾ **Chief Exec**[22] 8014 9-9-0 **68**.................. SteveDrowne 7 70
(Jeremy Gask) *dwlt: settled towards rr: rdn over 2f out: nt qckn u.p over 1f out: styd on ins fnl f: nrst fin* **14/1**

040- **5** shd **Cut And Thrust (IRE)**[74] 7377 5-8-13 **67**.................. LiamJones 11 69
(Mark Wellings) *towards rr: prog on outer 3f out: drvn over 2f out: nt qckn over 1f out and no imp: kpt on last 100yds* **20/1**

01-0 **6** nse **Buxton**[13] 96 7-8-13 **67**..................(t) RobertHavlin 13 69+
(Roger Ingram) *hld up last fr wd draw: effrt wl over 1f out: drvn and tried to squeeze through ins fnl f: nvr any ch* **15/2[3]**

205- **7** ½ **Tukitinyasok (IRE)**[87] 7143 4-9-0 **68**..................(p) MartinLane 2 69
(Roger Fisher) *led to wl over 1f out: steadily wknd* **10/1**

05-2 **8** ½ **Lastkingofscotland (IRE)**[16] 55 5-9-6 **74**...............(b) EddieAhern 12 73+
(Conor Dore) *hld up in last trio fr wd draw: stl there over 1f out: reminder ent fnl f: shuffled along and kpt on: nvr nr ldrs* **8/1**

41-4 **9** 1 ¼ **Highland Harvest**[16] 55 7-9-0 **68**.................. IanMongan 5 67
(Jamie Poulton) *t.k.h: pressed ldrs: nt qckn over 1f out: wl hld whn squeezed out nr fin* **11/1**

61-4 **10** nk **Nubar Boy**[13] 97 4-8-9 **63**..................(v) StevieDonohoe 10 58
(David Evans) *hld up in last trio fr wd draw: stl jst abt last over 1f out: shuffled along and no prog* **13/2[2]**

220- **11** 4 **Primo De Vida (IRE)**[182] 4325 4-9-6 **74**.................. StephenCraine 8 64
(Jim Boyle) *prom to over 2f out: wkng qckly whn squeezed out 1f out* **18/1**

1m 24.72s (-0.08) **Going Correction** +0.075s/f (Slow) **11** Ran SP% **114.8**
Speed ratings (Par 103): **103,101,100,99,99 99,98,98,96,96 91**
toteswingers:1&2 £9.50, 2&3 £12.30, 1&3 £4.90 CSF £43.19 CT £279.85 TOTE £3.70: £1.80, £4.40, £2.30; EX 43.50 Trifecta £384.30 Pool of £1012.91 - 1.95 winning units..
Owner M Barber **Bred** Dr & Mrs Walter Zent & Tony Holmes **Trained** Newmarket, Suffolk
■ Stewards' Enquiry : Robert Havlin one-day ban: careless riding (Feb 4)

FOCUS
Most of these looked pretty exposed. The winner looks underestimated and the form is rated around the runner-up.

Lastkingofscotland(IRE) Official explanation: jockey said, regarding running and riding, that his orders were to drop the gelding in from a wide draw, get cover, and challenge up the middle of the straight.
T/Plt: £43.50 to a £1 stake. Pool: of £99,168.64 - 1,661.82 winning tickets. T/Qpdt: £15.30 to a £1 stake. Pool of £8,169.63 - 394.05 winning tickets. JN

229 WOLVERHAMPTON (A.W) (L-H)

Friday, January 21

OFFICIAL GOING: Standard
Wind: Light across Weather: Fine

250 TODAY'S JOCKEY SPECIALS AT BLUESQ.COM H'CAP 5f 216y(P)

4:35 (4:37) (Class 7) (0-50,55) 4-Y-0+ **£1,535** (£453; £226) **Stalls** Low

Form RPR

50-4 **1** **Metropolitan Chief**[8] 138 7-9-2 **48**.................................... LiamKeniry 8 58
(Paul Burgoyne) *mid-div: hdwy over 2f out: led 1f out: edgd lft: rdn out* **10/1**

0-42 **2** *nk* **Black Baccara**[8] 138 4-9-2 **48**..................................(be) AdamKirby 7 57
(Phil McEntee) *hld up: hdwy over 1f out: rdn and edgd lft ins fnl f: r.o* **9/2**[2]

1 **3** *nk* **Orpens Peach (IRE)**[1] 229 4-9-9 **55** 6ex.................. SeamieHeffernan 4 63
(Seamus Fahey, Ire) *hld up: plld hrd: hdwy and swtchd rt 2f out: rdn over 1f out: r.o* **4/1**[1]

/0-5 **4** *¾* **My Best Man**[8] 138 5-8-13 **48**.............................. KierenFox(3) 12 54
(Tony Carroll) *mid-div: sn pushed along: outpcd over 3f out: r.o u.p ins fnl f* **8/1**

33-3 **5** *2* **Force To Spend**[9] 123 4-8-12 **49**............................ RyanClark(5) 5 48
(Nick Littmoden) *trckd ldrs: rdn over 1f out: no ex ins fnl f* **4/1**[1]

53/4 **6** *½* **Valdemar**[12] 102 5-8-13 **45**..(v) GrahamGibbons 6 43
(Alan Brown) *trckd ldr: led wl over 1f out: sn rdn: edgd lft and hdd 1f out: no ex ins fnl f* **7/1**[3]

2-50 **7** *1 ¾* **Jemimaville (IRE)**[8] 138 4-9-3 **49**..................................(v) TravisBlock 3 41
(Giles Bravery) *prom: rdn over 2f out: no ex ins fnl f* **14/1**

00-0 **8** *nse* **Grand Palace (IRE)**[7] 167 8-8-13 **45**..................(v) PatrickMathers 11 40+
(Derek Shaw) *chsd ldrs: rdn over 2f out: cl up whn hmpd 1f out: eased* **40/1**

0-44 **9** *2 ¼* **Rightcar Dominic**[7] 166 6-8-13 **45**........................ RobbieFitzpatrick 9 30
(Peter Grayson) *dwlt: outpcd* **33/1**

06-0 **10** *hd* **Mr Funshine**[9] 123 6-9-3 **49**... JimmyQuinn 10 33
(Derek Shaw) *sn pushed along in rr: sme hdwy and swtchd lft over 1f out: n.d* **20/1**

02-0 **11** *3 ¼* **True Red (IRE)**[9] 123 4-8-11 **46**.........................(b) AndrewHeffernan(3) 1 20
(Nikki Evans) *sn drvn to ld: hdd wl over 1f out: wknd ins fnl f* **33/1**

030- **12** *34* **Miss Polly Plum**[47] 7721 4-9-1 **47**...................................... KellyHarrison 2 —
(Chris Dwyer) *dwlt: outpcd: t.o* **12/1**

1m 15.95s (0.95) **Going Correction** +0.10s/f (Slow) **12** Ran SP% **118.3**
Speed ratings (Par 97): **97,96,96,95,92 91,89,89,86,86 81,36**
toteswingers:1&2 £7.90, 2&3 £4.90, 1&3 £11.10 CSF £52.54 CT £214.73 TOTE £13.30: £2.90, £1.90, £2.00; EX 58.30.
Owner L Tomlin **Bred** J A Prescott And C M Oakshott **Trained** Shepton Montague, Somerset
■ Stewards' Enquiry : Graham Gibbons three-day ban: careless riding (Feb 4,5,7)
Adam Kirby caution: careless riding.

FOCUS
A low-grade handicap run at a sound pace, and the winner came down the centre in the straight. Straightforward form.

251 STAY AT THE WOLVERHAMPTON HOLIDAY INN H'CAP 5f 20y(P)

5:05 (5:08) (Class 6) (0-55,55) 3-Y-0 **£1,619** (£481; £240; £120) **Stalls** Low

Form RPR

00-4 **1** **Kitty Fisher**[9] 130 3-8-7 **46** oh1...................................... HayleyTurner 10 55
(Ron Hodges) *edgd lft sn after s: chsd ldrs: led 4f out: pushed along 1/2-way: rdn and hung rt ins fnl f: styd on* **14/1**

0-04 **2** *1 ¼* **Indie Country**[5] 100 3-8-7 **46** oh1...................................... JimmyQuinn 4 50
(Nicky Vaughan) *plld hrd and prom: trckd wnr 1/2-way: rdn over 1f out: styd on* **8/1**[3]

24-1 **3** *1 ½* **Juarla (IRE)**[15] 64 3-9-2 **55**.. LukeMorris 2 54
(Ronald Harris) *hld up: racd keenly: hdwy 1/2-way: rdn over 1f out: styd on* **5/6**[1]

24-4 **4** *2 ¼* **Misty Morn**[15] 66 3-9-2 **55**.. FrannyNorton 9 46
(Alan Brown) *s.i.s: hld up: hdwy over 1f out: sn rdn: no imp ins fnl f* **8/1**[3]

55-0 **5** *1* **Ladydolly**[15] 64 3-8-4 **46** oh1... BillyCray(3) 7 33
(Roy Brotherton) *chsd ldrs: rdn 1/2-way: styd on same pce fr over 1f out: hung lft ins fnl f* **33/1**

00-4 **6** *1* **Place And Chips**[15] 64 3-9-0 **53**........................(t) RichardKingscote 8 36
(Tom Dascombe) *hld up: rdn over 1f out: nvr trbld ldrs* **7/2**[2]

20-6 **7** *½* **Gunalt Joy**[8] 146 3-8-13 **55**.. JamesSullivan(3) 6 37
(Michael Easterby) *hld up: pushed along 1/2-way: n.d* **14/1**

00-0 **8** *½* **Zohan (IRE)**[8] 146 3-8-8 **47** oh1 ow1.....................(b) RobbieFitzpatrick 3 27
(Peter Grayson) *chsd ldrs: rdn 1/2-way: wknd over 1f out* **80/1**

005- **9** *4 ½* **Bold Deceiver**[36] 7893 3-8-4 **46** oh1.........................(t) AndrewHeffernan(3) 1 10
(Phil McEntee) *led 1f: chsd ldrs: rdn 1/2-way: sn wknd* **50/1**

63.10 secs (0.80) **Going Correction** +0.10s/f (Slow) **9** Ran SP% **118.5**
Speed ratings (Par 95): **97,95,92,89,87 85,85,84,77**
toteswingers:1&2 £4.80, 2&3 £2.90, 1&3 £3.50 CSF £121.48 CT £199.03 TOTE £20.30: £3.60, £2.90, £1.10; EX 76.80.
Owner Miss R Dobson **Bred** Hedsor Stud **Trained** Charlton Mackrell, Somerset

FOCUS
A moderate handicap in which the pace was reasonable. The principals came down the centre in the straight.

252 ENJOY THE PARTY PACK GROUP OFFER H'CAP 1m 4f 50y(P)

5:35 (5:36) (Class 6) (0-60,61) 4-Y-0+ **£1,619** (£481; £240; £120) **Stalls** Low

Form RPR

3-11 **1** **Carter**[2] 207 5-9-6 **61** 12ex... RyanClark(5) 10 77
(Ian Williams) *a.p: led over 1f out: sn rdn and hung rt: r.o wl: eased nr fin* **3/1**[1]

216- **2** *8* **Port Hill**[23] 8010 4-8-12 **52**.. ShaneKelly 2 55
(Mark Brisbourne) *prom: lost pl 8f out: hdwy on outer over 2f out: led over 1f out: sn rdn and hdd: outpcd ins fnl f* **12/1**

54-6 **3** *1 ½* **Escape Artist**[10] 118 4-8-11 **51**................................ RobertWinston 9 52
(Tim Easterby) *hld up: hdwy 8f out: rdn over 2f out: styd on same pce appr fnl f* **12/1**

363- **4** *2* **Amical Risks (FR)**[23] 8010 7-9-8 **58**.............................. BarryMcHugh 6 55
(Ollie Pears) *hld up: rdn over 3f out: hdwy 2f out: nvr trbld ldrs* **8/1**

10-2 **5** *2* **Prickles**[11] 114 6-8-12 **48**.. JoeFanning 11 42
(Karen George) *chsd ldrs: led over 3f out: rdn and hdd over 1f out: wknd ins fnl f* **6/1**[3]

05/0 **6** *2 ¾* **Hardanger (IRE)**[11] 114 6-8-8 **47**..........................(e) JamesSullivan(3) 8 37
(Tim Fitzgerald) *hld up: hdwy over 3f out: rdn and wknd 2f out* **50/1**

302/ **7** *12* **Blockley (USA)**[412] 7649 7-9-9 **59**..................................(t) TomEaves 7 30
(Ian Williams) *hld up: drvn along over 5f out: nvr on terms* **22/1**

0-11 **8** *hd* **Barodine**[7] 173 8-9-11 **61** 6ex................................ RichardKingscote 4 44
(Ron Hodges) *broke wl: sn stdd and lost pl: hdwy over 6f out: rdn over 2f out: wknd and eased wl over 1f out* **4/1**[2]

45-2 **9** *shd* **My Mate Mal**[10] 117 7-9-3 **60**....................................(p) LauraPike(7) 3 30
(William Stone) *prom: jnd ldr over 8f out: led over 5f out: rdn and hdd over 3f out: wknd wl over 1f out* **12/1**

000- **10** *5* **Follow The Dream**[84] 7213 8-9-5 **55**................................ LiamKeniry 5 17
(Karen George) *hld up: a in rr: wknd over 3f out: t.o* **33/1**

20-4 **11** *23* **Abulharith**[18] 24 5-9-4 **54**..(p) LukeMorris 1 —
(Ronald Harris) *s.i.s: sn rcvrd to ld: hdd over 5f out: rdn and wknd over 2f out* **11/1**

12 *4 ½* **Golan Heights (IRE)**[48] 7714 5-9-0 **50**.................(b) SeamieHeffernan 12 —
(J Larkin, Ire) *hld up: hdwy over 8f out: rdn and wknd wl over 3f out: t.o* **16/1**

2m 42.17s (1.07) **Going Correction** +0.10s/f (Slow)
WFA 4 from 5yo+ 4lb **12** Ran SP% **116.9**
Speed ratings (Par 101): **100,94,93,92,91 89,81,81,80,77 62,59**
toteswingers:1&2 £8.90, 2&3 £25.80, 1&3 £8.60 CSF £39.11 CT £382.34 TOTE £5.90: £2.10, £3.50, £2.10; EX 45.00.
Owner Stratford Bards Racing **Bred** Dr D G St John And Mrs Sherry Collier **Trained** Portway, Worcs

FOCUS
An ordinary handicap run at a fair gallop. The winner raced centre-to-far-side down the straight.
Barodine Official explanation: trainer had no explanation for the poor form shown

253 WOLVERHAMPTON - THE BLACK COUNTRY'S ONLY RACECOURSE MAIDEN STKS 7f 32y(P)

6:05 (6:07) (Class 5) 3-Y-0+ **£2,266** (£674; £337; £168) **Stalls** High

Form RPR

230- **1** **Fettuccine (IRE)**[62] 7517 3-8-4 72...................................... HayleyTurner 1 66+
(Jeremy Noseda) *trckd ldrs: nt clr run wl over 1f out: rdn and hung rt ins fnl f: styd on to ld nr fin* **4/1**[3]

2 *nse* **Bint Susu (IRE)** 4-9-8 0... TomEaves 8 70
(Bryan Smart) *chsd ldrs: led 2f out: rdn and edgd lft ins fnl f: hdd nr fin* **4/1**[3]

6- **3** *1 ¼* **Kentish (USA)**[142] 5668 4-9-13 0.. ShaneKelly 3 73
(Michael Quinlan) *a.p: chsd ldr over 1f out: sn rdn and ev ch: styng on same pce whn hmpd nr fin* **7/2**[2]

60- **4** *10* **Apple Dumpling**[24] 7990 3-8-4 0.. NickyMackay 5 35
(Stuart Williams) *chsd ldrs tl rdn and wknd over 1f out* **25/1**

0 **5** *1 ½* **Avon Light**[11] 110 3-8-9 0.. RichardKingscote 4 36
(Milton Bradley) *chsd ldrs: rdn 1/2-way: wknd wl over 1f out* **66/1**

6 *nk* **Hesindamood** 4-9-13 0.. CathyGannon 7 40
(Joanne Priest) *s.s: bhd: styd on ins fnl f: nvr nrr* **33/1**

00- **7** *1 ¼* **Stardust Dancer**[99] 6876 4-9-13 0.................................. FrannyNorton 11 37
(Paul Green) *s.s: outpcd: nvr nrr* **40/1**

8 *½* **Higher Spen Jess** 3-8-1 0.. JamesSullivan(3) 2 25
(Julie Camacho) *s.i.s: hld up: hdwy over 1f out: wknd ins fnl f* **33/1**

6- **9** *6* **Cooke's Bar (IRE)**[42] 7816 4-9-8 0................................ SeamieHeffernan 6 14
(Noel Lawlor, Ire) *hld up: nvr on terms* **50/1**

026- **10** *6* **Elusive Love (IRE)**[31] 7954 3-8-9 64.................................... JoeFanning 9 —
(Mark Johnston) *sn led: rdn and hdd 2f out: edgd rt and wknd over 1f out* **13/8**[1]

6 **11** *8* **Bold Trumpeter**[7] 170 3-9-13 0.................................... RussKennemore 10
(Milton Bradley) *mid-div: drvn along over 4f out: wknd over 2f out: t.o* **100/1**

1m 31.17s (1.57) **Going Correction** +0.10s/f (Slow)
WFA 3 from 4yo+ 18lb **11** Ran SP% **116.9**
Speed ratings (Par 103): **95,94,93,82,80 80,78,78,71,64 55**
toteswingers:1&2 £2.40, 2&3 £3.30, 1&3 £3.80 CSF £19.29 TOTE £5.20: £1.40, £1.30, £1.50; EX 15.90.
Owner Raffles Racing **Bred** Razza Della Sila Srl **Trained** Newmarket, Suffolk
■ Stewards' Enquiry : Hayley Turner one-day ban: careless riding (Feb 4)

FOCUS
An ordinary maiden run at a fair gallop. The market leader disappointed but the first three home pulled clear and the winner raced just off the inside rail in the straight.
Elusive Love(IRE) Official explanation: jockey said colt stopped quickly

254 ENHANCED SP'S AT BLUESQ.COM H'CAP 7f 32y(P)

6:35 (6:37) (Class 4) (0-85,89) 3-Y-0 **£3,561** (£1,059; £529; £264) **Stalls** High

Form RPR

31- **1** **Acclamazing (IRE)**[48] 7700 3-8-12 **76**................................(t) AdamKirby 3 83+
(Marco Botti) *trckd ldrs: shkn up to ld ins fnl f: edgd lft: r.o* **11/4**[1]

3-32 **2** *1 ¼* **Amwell Pinot**[6] 177 3-9-11 **89**...................................(b[1]) CathyGannon 5 93
(Alan Bailey) *a.p: chsd ldr over 5f out: rdn to ld over 1f out: hdd ins fnl f: styd on* **3/1**[2]

21-4 **3** *1 ½* **Swimsuit**[16] 49 3-8-2 **71**.. RyanClark(5) 2 71
(Michael Jarvis) *chsd ldr to over 5f out: remained handy: rdn and ev ch over 1f out: edgd rt: styd on same pce ins fnl f* **15/2**

24-2 **4** *2 ¼* **Il Battista**[12] 106 3-9-6 **84**....................................(p) RobertWinston 6 78
(Alan McCabe) *led: rdn and hdd over 1f out: no ex ins fnl f* **9/2**

5-1 **5** *1 ¾* **Silver Turn**[17] 36 3-8-13 **77**.. TomEaves 1 66
(Bryan Smart) *hld up in tch: lost pl 4f out: styd on u.p fr over 1f out* **10/3**[3]

45-1 **6** *10* **Madam Mayem**[15] 65 3-8-4 **71** oh4........................ RossAtkinson(3) 4 39
(Tom Dascombe) *hld up: hdwy 1/2-way: sn rdn and hung rt: wknd 2f out* **20/1**

1m 30.04s (0.44) **Going Correction** +0.10s/f (Slow) **6** Ran SP% **109.5**
Speed ratings (Par 99): **101,99,97,95,93 81**
toteswingers:1&2 £2.30, 2&3:£4.00, 1&3:£3.50 CSF £10.67 TOTE £4.50: £1.90, £1.50; EX 12.70.
Owner Giuliano Manfredini **Bred** Michael And John Fahy **Trained** Newmarket, Suffolk

FOCUS
Several previous winners in this decent handicap. The gallop was fair and the winner came down the centre in the straight.

255 GREAT OFFERS AT WOLVERHAMPTON-RACECOURSE.CO.UK H'CAP 7f 32y(P)
7:05 (7:07) (Class 6) (0-60,58) 4-Y-O+ £1,619 (£481; £240; £120) Stalls High

Form RPR
64-1 1 **Piccolo Express**[15] 70 5-9-3 **54** J-PGuillambert 3 63
(Brian Baugh) *trckd ldrs: led over 1f out: sn rdn and hung rt: r.o* **9/2**[3]
0-32 2 1 1/4 **Chinese Democracy (USA)**[2] 210 4-8-11 **55**.(v) MatthewCosham(7) 4 61+
(David Evans) *s.i.s: sn pushed along in rr: hdwy u.p over 1f out: r.o* **3/1**[1]
000- 3 nk **Bold Bomber**[84] 7213 5-8-8 **45** FrannyNorton 8 50
(Paul Green) *hld up: plld hrd: hdwy over 2f out: rdn over 1f out: r.o* **33/1**
-443 4 1 1/4 **Downhill Skier (IRE)**[7] 169 7-9-3 **54** ShaneKelly 2 56
(Mark Brisbourne) *hld up: pushed along 1/2-way: hdwy over 1f out: sn rdn: hung rt ins fnl f: styd on* **7/2**[2]
51-2 5 4 **Olympic Dream**[17] 37 5-9-2 **56**(p) BillyCray(3) 6 47
(Michael Herrington) *trckd ldr: racd keenly: rdn and ev ch over 1f out: wknd ins fnl f* **8/1**
600- 6 nse **Scruffy Skip (IRE)**[38] 7870 6-9-3 **57**(p) KierenFox(3) 7 48
(Christine Dunnett) *prom: rdn 1/2-way: outpcd over 2f out: n.d after* **25/1**
0-62 7 1 1/2 **Trade Centre**[2] 218 6-9-6 **57** RussKennemore 10 47
(Milton Bradley) *prom: rdn over 2f out: wknd ins fnl f* **8/1**
000- 8 1/2 **Muqalad (IRE)**[77] 7336 4-9-7 **58** TomEaves 1 43
(Bryan Smart) *led: rdn and hdd over 1f out: wknd ins fnl f* **11/2**
9 1 3/4 **French Express (IRE)**[44] 7774 4-9-3 **54** CathyGannon 5 35
(John C McConnell, Ire) *hld up: plld hrd: rdn over 2f out: wkng whn hung lft over 1f out* **9/1**

1m 30.62s (1.02) **Going Correction** +0.10s/f (Slow) 9 Ran SP% **119.8**
Speed ratings (Par 101): **98,96,96,94,90 90,88,87,85**
toteswingers:1&2 £3.10, 2&3 £35.60, 1&3 £20.10 CSF £19.20 CT £407.71 TOTE £5.80: £2.40, £1.10, £7.70; EX 21.40.
Owner G B Hignett **Bred** G B Hignett **Trained** Audley, Staffs

FOCUS
An average handicap with a moderate gallop which saw several fail to settle early on. The winner edged from the inside rail into the centre down the straight.
French Express(IRE) Official explanation: jockey said filly ran too freely

256 PLAY FREE BINGO AT BLUESQ.COM H'CAP 5f 20y(P)
7:35 (7:36) (Class 7) (0-50,55) 4-Y-O+ £1,535 (£453; £226) Stalls Low

Form RPR
00-0 1 **Rightcar**[7] 167 4-8-12 **45** RobbieFitzpatrick 8 53
(Peter Grayson) *s.i.s: hdwy and swtchd lft over 1f out: rdn to ld wl ins fnl f: r.o* **20/1**
-24 2 1/2 **Cheveyo (IRE)**[5] 185 5-8-12 **45** SeamieHeffernan 12 51
(Patrick Morris) *s.i.s: hld up: hdwy 1/2-way: led ins fnl f: sn rdn and hdd: styd on* **13/2**[2]
0/0- 3 1 **Seeking Rio**[368] 215 4-8-12 **45** HayleyTurner 3 47
(Ron Hodges) *a.p: chsd ldr 1/2-way: rdn over 1f out: hung rt ins fnl f: r.o* **20/1**
0-62 4 shd **Bluebok**[9] 123 10-8-8 **48**(bt) MatthewCosham(7) 2 50
(Milton Bradley) *hld up in tch: rdn over 1f out: ev ch ins fnl f: styd on same pce towards fin* **3/1**[1]
30-0 5 nse **Francis Albert**[9] 123 5-8-10 **50**(b) JosephYoung(7) 9 52
(Michael Mullineaux) *led: clr over 3f out: hung rt fr over 1f out: hdd ins fnl f: nt run on* **10/1**
00-6 6 1 3/4 **Vertumnus**[8] 138 4-8-10 **48**(be) RyanClark(5) 13 44+
(Nick Littmoden) *s.i.s: outpcd: r.o ins fnl f: nrst fin* **11/1**
0-06 7 1 1/4 **Head To Head (IRE)**[5] 185 7-9-0 **47**(bt) JimmyQuinn 10 38
(Alan Brown) *sn pushed along and prom: rdn and hung lft over 1f out: styd on* **20/1**
0-00 8 1 1/4 **Tyrannosaurus Rex (IRE)**[8] 138 7-9-2 **49**(v) TomEaves 11 36
(Derek Shaw) *hld up: rdn over 1f out: no ex ins fnl f* **15/2**[3]
000- 9 hd **Gleaming Spirit (IRE)**[21] 8036 7-8-12 **45**(v) PatrickMathers 5 31
(Peter Grayson) *chsd ldr tl rdn 1/2-way: wknd ins fnl f* **80/1**
45-4 10 1/2 **Southwark Newshawk**[17] 36 4-8-9 **45** KierenFox(3) 7 29
(Christine Dunnett) *hld up: hmpd over 3f out: n.d* **20/1**
00-1 11 1 3/4 **Duke Of Rainford**[9] 123 4-9-8 **55** 6ex ShaneKelly 1 33
(Michael Herrington) *hld up: hmpd wl over 3f out: nvr on terms* **3/1**[1]
60-0 12 hd **Charles Bear**[1] 224 4-8-12 **45** LukeMorris 6 22
(Bruce Hellier) *prom: rdn 1/2-way: wknd ins fnl f* **50/1**
000/ 13 12 **Polish Steps (IRE)**[451] 7089 4-9-0 **47**(be[1]) FrannyNorton 4 —
(Michael Mullineaux) *hld up: plld hrd: wknd 1/2-way* **40/1**

63.31 secs (1.01) **Going Correction** +0.10s/f (Slow) 13 Ran SP% **117.2**
Speed ratings (Par 97): **95,94,92,92,92 89,87,85,85,84 81,81,62**
toteswingers:1&2 £24.40, 2&3 £32.60, 1&3 £74.30 CSF £133.57 CT £2723.09 TOTE £26.60: £5.00, £1.40, £7.70; EX 176.20.
Owner S Kamis & PGRC Ltd **Bred** J M Beever **Trained** Formby, Lancs

FOCUS
Another moderate handicap and one run at a strong gallop. The winner raced towards the centre in the straight.
T/Jkpt: Part won. £41,390.20 to a £1 stake. Pool of £58,296.06 - 0.50 winning tickets. T/Plt: £46.50 to a £1 stake. Pool of £114,203.40 - 1,791.31 winning tickets. T/Qpdt: £23.40 to a £1 stake. Pool of £10,890.01 - 343.00 winning tickets. CR

219 CAGNES-SUR-MER
Friday, January 21
OFFICIAL GOING: Fibresand: standard

257a PRIX DE CLAIREFONTAINE (CONDITIONS) (4YO+) (FIBRESAND) 1m (F)
2:10 (12:00) 4-Y-O+ £10,775 (£4,310; £3,232; £2,155; £1,077)

RPR
1 **Bellinissimo (IRE)**[101] 5-9-4 0 IoritzMendizabal 8 95
(J-C Rouget, France) **7/5**[1]
2 3 **Tuaoi (USA)**[18] 6-9-5 0(p) EricWianny 2 90
(J-P Delaporte, France) **33/10**[2]
3 shd **Ridge City (IRE)**[133] 5935 4-9-4 0 FranckBlondel 6 89
(P Khozian, France) **13/2**[3]
4 1 1/2 **Nareion (GER)**[145] 5573 5-8-11 0 DominiqueBoeuf 4 79
(W Baltromei, Germany) **17/2**
5 2 **Heart Attack (FR)**[131] 5-9-4 0 ASuborics 1 82
(G Martin, Austria) **20/1**
6 3 **Bencoolen (IRE)**[4] 195 6-9-4 0 JohanVictoire 7 76
(David Nicholls) *broke wl: racd 3rd on outer: rdn early in st: no ex: styd on one pce fnl f* **44/1**
7 4 **Fancy Diamond (GER)**[82] 5-8-8 0 Pierre-CharlesBoudot 9 58
(J-M Capitte, France) **34/1**
8 3 **Colwyn (FR)**[124] 6-9-6 0 StefanoLandi 10 64
(Annelies Mathis, Austria) **28/1**
9 5 **Low Budget (FR)**[535] 8-8-13 0 ow2 FranckForesi 3 47
(F Foresi, France) **20/1**
10 10 **Anco Marzio**[593] 2755 5-9-4 0 FabriceVeron 5 32
(H-A Pantall, France) **44/5**

1m 34.58s (94.58) 10 Ran SP% **117.0**
WIN (incl. 1 euro stake): 2.40. PLACES: 1.10, 1.40, 1.50. DF: 3.90. SF: 5.70.
Owner J C Rouget & Mme B Hermelin **Bred** John Carroll **Trained** Pau, France

258a PRIX CHERET (MAIDEN) (3YO) (FIBRESAND) 1m (F)
2:45 (12:00) 3-Y-O £8,620 (£3,448; £2,586; £1,724; £862)

RPR
1 **Filozef (IRE)**[92] 3-9-2 0 ThomasHuet 8 81
(C Ferland, France) **11/10**[1]
2 1 1/2 **Tartampion (IRE)**[73] 3-8-8 0 StevanBourgois(8) 2 78
(Robert Collet, France) **25/1**
3 1 1/2 **Cerences (FR)** 3-9-2 0 IoritzMendizabal 15 75
(J-C Rouget, France) **6/1**[2]
4 1 1/2 **Hugely Exciting**[85] 7186 3-9-2 0 DavyBonilla 3 72
(J S Moore) *prom fr s: racd midfield: rdn early in st: wnt 5th: styd on wl fnl 100yds: wnt 4th on line* **23/1**
5 shd **Bawinanga (USA)**[225] 3-8-13 0 MaximeFoulon 4 69
(J-C Rouget, France) **29/1**
6 nk **Goldtiming (FR)**[81] 3-8-13 0 SylvainRuis 13 68
(D Prod'Homme, France) **13/1**
7 3/4 **Twenty Ten (FR)**[85] 3-9-2 0 StephaneRichardot 10 70
(P Khozian, France) **31/1**
8 nk **High Speed (SWI)** 3-9-2 0 FabriceVeron 1 69
(H-A Pantall, France) **12/1**
9 nse **Quartz (FR)** 3-8-13 0 Francois-XavierBertras 11 66
(F Rohaut, France) **15/1**
10 1 1/2 **Sweet Whip (IRE)**[96] 3-8-13 0 DominiqueBoeuf 5 63
(K Borgel, France) **23/1**
0 **Veri One (FR)**[114] 3-8-13 0 GeraldPardon 6 —
(T Larriviere, France) **34/1**
0 **Vent D'Avril**[78] 3-8-13 0 FranckBlondel 9 —
(D Prod'Homme, France) **78/10**[3]
0 **Great Surprise**[48] 7700 3-9-2 0 JohanVictoire 14 —
(Reg Hollinshead) *in rr fr s: rdn early in st: no ex* **40/1**

1m 37.79s (97.79) 13 Ran SP% **118.3**
WIN (incl. 1 euro stake): 2.10. PLACES: 1.30, 3.50, 2.00. DF: 28.70. SF: 36.80.
Owner Sarl Ecurie Tagada **Bred** E J Loder **Trained** France

259a PRIX DES BOUCHES DU LOUP (CLAIMER) (4YO+) (FIBRESAND) 1m 4f
3:15 (12:00) 4-Y-O+ £6,896 (£2,758; £2,068; £1,379; £689)

RPR
1 **Benjamin (FR)**[29] 6-9-11 0(b) JohanVictoire 8 89
(L A Urbano-Grajales, France) **6/4**[1]
2 hd **Serious Impact (USA)**[13] 6-9-2 0 SylvainRuis 7 80
(F Vermeulen, France) **11/2**[2]
3 1 **Mondovino (FR)**[201] 8-9-2 0 FranckForesi 4 78
(F Foresi, France) **73/10**
4 1 **Rum Chocolate (GER)**[166] 5-8-13 0 ThomasHuet 5 73
(C Ferland, France) **20/1**
5 4 **Higher Ground (FR)**[164] 4-8-11 0 RonanThomas 10 69
(S-A Ghoumrassi, France) **15/1**
6 1/2 **Plutarque (FR)**[24] 4-9-2 0 FabriceVeron 12 73
(H-A Pantall, France) **20/1**
7 6 **Quo Vadis River (FR)**[65] 7-9-6 0 BriceRaballand 6 64
(P Cottier, France) **110/1**
8 4 **Kimberley Downs (USA)**[4] 195 5-9-2 0 IoritzMendizabal 9 53
(David Nicholls) *broke wl to r 2nd: rdn 1/2-way: picked up wl: 2nd ent st: led briefly but sn u.p: no ex: fdd: eased ins fnl f* **15/1**
9 6 **Speranza (FR)**[329] 5-8-11 0 MathieuTavaresDaSilva(6) 3 45
(J-P Roman, France) **24/1**
10 3 **Royal Pepper**[18] 6-8-13 0 BenjaminBoutin(7) 2 43
(C Boutin, France) **6/1**[3]
0 **Monsieur Kiss Kiss**[524] 5019 5-9-2 0 StefanoLandi 11 —
(Annelies Mathis, Austria) **56/1**
0 **Sovietica Zurda (FR)**[462] 5-9-3 0 NicolasPerret 1 —
(K Borgel, France) **19/1**
0 **Don Carlino (POL)** 6-9-2 0 ASuborics 13 —
(S Bigus, Austria) **43/1**

2m 28.0s (148.00)
WFA 4 from 5yo+ 4lb 13 Ran SP% **117.7**
WIN (incl. 1 euro stake): 2.50. PLACES: 1.30, 1.70, 1.70. DF: 6.80. SF: 10.40.
Owner Luis A Urbano Grajales **Bred** Haras De Manneville **Trained** Pau, France

243 LINGFIELD (L-H)
Saturday, January 22
OFFICIAL GOING: Standard
Wind: medium, against Weather: overcast, dry

260 BET ON TODAY'S FOOTBALL AT BLUESQ.COM H'CAP 1m 2f (P)
12:50 (12:50) (Class 6) (0-65,65) 3-Y-O £1,535 (£453; £226) Stalls Low

Form RPR
063- 1 **Medaille D'Or**[24] 8000 3-9-4 **62** JackMitchell 5 74+
(Michael Jarvis) *chsd ldng pair: clsd on ldr 5f out: gng wl over 2f out: pushed into ld ent fnl f: sn in command but rn green ins fnl f: pushed out: comf* **5/4**[1]

-234 **2** *2½* **Ad Vitam (IRE)**[5] 192 3-8-12 **56**....................(tp) JamesDoyle 6 60
(Sylvester Kirk) *racd off the pce in midfield: clsd and in tch over 4f out: lost pl over 2f out: swtchd rt and rdn over 1f out: styd on wl u.p ins fnl f to go 2nd nr fin: no threat to wnr* **10/1**

000- **3** *hd* **Diverting**[24] 8001 3-9-1 **59**.................... SteveDrowne 1 63
(William Jarvis) *hld up in midfield: clsd and wl in tch over 4f out: hdwy u.p over 1f out: chsd clr wnr ins fnl f: no imp: lost 2nd nr fin* **7/1**[3]

44-3 **4** *2* **Moorland Boy**[9] 142 3-9-0 **58**.................... FergusSweeney 7 58
(Jamie Osborne) *t.k.h early: chsd ldr: clsd and pressing ldr over 4f out: led over 2f out: rdn ent fnl 2f: hdd and drvn ent fnl f: sn no ch w wnr: lost 2 pls fnl 100yds* **14/1**

044- **5** *hd* **George Woolf**[158] 5177 3-9-7 **65**.................... RobertWinston 4 65
(Alan McCabe) *short of room and snatched up sn after s: racd off the pce in last pair: clsd and in tch over 4f out: rdn on outer over 2f out: hanging lft over 1f out: r.o wl ins fnl f: nvr trbld ldrs* **16/1**

060- **6** *½* **Bodie**[55] 7610 3-9-2 **60**.................... MickyFenton 9 59
(Pam Sly) *t.k.h: chsd ldrs: clsd and wl in tch over 4f out: rdn and unable qck jst over 2f out: styd on same pce fr over 1f out* **50/1**

-654 **7** *nk* **Polly Holder (IRE)**[2] 234 3-9-0 **58**....................(v) LiamJones 8 56
(Alan Bailey) *s.i.s: bhd and pushed along early: clsd and in tch over 4f out: rdn and no hdwy jst over 2f out: nvr trbld ldrs* **16/1**

24-3 **8** *nk* **Sky Diamond (IRE)**[17] 49 3-9-4 **62**....................(b) FrannyNorton 3 59
(James Given) *led: clr 9f out tl over 4f out: hdd over 2f out: wknd over 1f out* **5/1**[2]

41-4 **9** *1¾* **Skeleton (IRE)**[5] 194 3-8-9 **60**....................(b) RPWalsh[(7)] 2 54
(David Evans) *hld up off the pce in last trio: clsd and in tch over 4f out: effrt u.p and hanging lft over 1f out: sn swtchd rt but no prog fnl f* **10/1**

2m 5.73s (-0.87) **Going Correction** +0.075s/f (Slow) **9** Ran SP% **112.2**
Speed ratings (Par 95): **106,104,103,102,102 101,101,101,99**
Tote Swingers: 1&2 £4.30, 1&3 £3.90, 2&3 £11.60 CSF £14.23 CT £62.50 TOTE £2.00: £1.60, £2.40, £2.40; EX 16.30 Trifecta £252.80 Part won. Pool of £341.66 - 0.50 winning units..
Owner Miss K Rausing **Bred** Miss K Rausing **Trained** Newmarket, Suffolk
■ Medaille D'Or was the last runner of Michale Jarvis's career.

FOCUS
This low-grade 3-y-o handicap was run at something of an uneven pace and the overall form may be worth treating with a degree of caution.
George Woolf Official explanation: jockey said gelding suffered interference shortly after start
Polly Holder(IRE) Official explanation: jockey said filly jumped path across track
Sky Diamond(IRE) Official explanation: jockey ssid gelding ran too free

261 ASHURST WOOD (S) STKS 1m 2f (P)
1:25 (1:25) (Class 6) 4-6-Y-O **£1,535** (£453; £226) **Stalls** Low

Form RPR

4-62 **1** **Unbreak My Heart (IRE)**[12] 112 6-8-11 76.............. RobertLButler[(3)] 4 60+
(Paddy Butler) *chsd ldrs: clsd and jnd ldr over 2f out: led over 1f out: shkn up to assert 1f out: pushed out: comf* **5/4**[1]

2 *¾* **Battle Axe (FR)**[362] 6-8-9 0.................... FergusSweeney 3 51?
(Laura Mongan) *t.k.h: hld up in last: hdwy to trck rivals over 2f out: n.m.r wl over 1f out: rdn to chse wnr ins fnl f: kpt on fnl 75yds* **9/1**

000- **3** *1¾* **Saigon Kitty (IRE)**[41] 7845 4-8-4 53.................... KierenFox[(3)] 1 48
(John Best) *hld up in 3rd: rdn and effrt to press ldrs 3f out: ev ch 2f out: styd on same pce ins fnl f* **9/2**[3]

06-3 **4** *1* **City Stable (IRE)**[1] 245 6-9-0 67.................... JamieMackay 2 51
(Michael Wigham) *led: jnd jst over 3f out: rdn over 2f out: hdd over 1f out: one pce and btn fnl 150yds* **15/8**[2]

2m 9.98s (3.38) **Going Correction** +0.075s/f (Slow)
WFA 4 from 6yo 2lb **4** Ran SP% **107.4**
Speed ratings: **89,88,87,86**
CSF £11.09 TOTE £1.80; EX 10.60.There was no bid for the winner.
Owner Rakebackmypoker.com **Bred** Redpender Stud Ltd **Trained** East Chiltington, E Sussex

FOCUS
An uncompetitive seller.

262 FOURTH "SHAREN BLAQUIERE - CELEBRATE A LIFE" MAIDEN STKS 1m (P)
2:00 (2:01) (Class 5) 3-Y-O £1,910 ([illegible]) Stalls [illegible]

Form RPR

\- **1** **Ruby Brook** 3-9-3 0.................... JimCrowley 2 72+
(Ralph Beckett) *chsd ldng pair: pushed along to chse ldr 2f out: outpcd and rdn over 1f out: swtchd rt and rallied ins fnl f: kpt on wl to ld nr fin* **7/2**[3]

2- **2** *nk* **Crafty Roberto**[24] 8000 3-9-3 0.................... ShaneKelly 9 71+
(Brian Meehan) *led: rdn clr over 1f out: edgd lft u.p: stl clr whn wnt rt fnl 75yds: hdd nr fin* **5/4**[1]

5- **3** *3¾* **Snowy Peak**[38] 7879 3-8-12 0....................(t) EddieAhern 3 57
(Jeremy Noseda) *chsd ldr tl 2f out: sn u.p by ldng pair: kpt on for 3rd but wl hld ent fnl f* **15/8**[2]

0-6 **4** *1¼* **Dance To Destiny**[11] 121 3-9-0 0 ow2.................... AdamKirby 5 57
(Phil McEntee) *t.k.h: hld up in midfield: rdn along 3f out: chsd ldng trio and switching rt 2f out: sn outpcd by ldng pair: styd on same pce after* **66/1**

0 **5** *nk* **Lakota Ghost (USA)**[12] 110 3-9-3 0.................... GeorgeBaker 12 59
(Seamus Durack) *stdd after s: t.k.h: hld up in last pair: rdn and effrt over 1f out: kpt on fnl f: nvr trbld ldrs* **25/1**

0-5 **6** *shd* **Revolutionary**[7] 176 3-9-3 0.................... FergusSweeney 10 59
(Jamie Osborne) *in tch in midfield: rdn and unable qck ent fnl 2f: no threat to ldrs and kpt on same pce fr over 1f out* **25/1**

7 *1¼* **Caravan Rolls On** 3-9-3 0.................... JackMitchell 7 56+
(Peter Chapple-Hyam) *s.i.s: bhd: rdn jst over 2f out: no real hdwy and nt clr run ent fnl f: styd on ins fnl f: nvr trbld ldrs* **25/1**

0 **8** *nk* **Pizzetti (IRE)**[17] 52 3-9-3 0.................... StevieDonohoe 6 55+
(Sir Mark Prescott Bt) *in tch towards rr: pushed along and struggling 3f out: rdn and effrt on inner over 1f out: kpt on but nvr gng pce to rch ldrs* **33/1**

0 **9** *1¼* **Have Another**[8] 158 3-9-3 0.................... DaneO'Neill 8 52
(Richard Hannon) *s.i.s: bhd: rdn along over 2f out: nvr trbld ldrs* **25/1**

0-0 **10** *½* **Talkin Italian**[14] 95 3-8-12 0.................... SteveDrowne 11 46
(Hughie Morrison) *in tch: rdn and struggling over 2f out: lost pl and wd bnd ent fnl 2f: n.d after* **66/1**

00- **11** *¾* **Emerald Royal**[66] 7478 3-9-0 0.................... AlanCreighton[(3)] 4 49
(Edward Creighton) *dwlt: in tch: rdn and unable qck over 2f out: wknd wl over 1f out* **66/1**

1m 40.77s (2.57) **Going Correction** +0.075s/f (Slow) **11** Ran SP% **124.3**
Speed ratings (Par 97): **90,89,85,84,84 84,83,82,81,81 80**
toteswingers:1&2 £2.40, 2&3 £1.40, 1&3 £2.20 CSF £8.24 TOTE £6.30: £1.50, £1.10, £1.30; EX 12.60 Trifecta £25.10 Pool of £717.42 - 21.07 winning units..
Owner A E Frost & A R Adams **Bred** Pollards Stables **Trained** Kimpton, Hants

FOCUS
This maiden was won a year ago by Monterosso, who went on to take the King Edward VII Stakes at Royal Ascot. There was nothing of that quality this year, in a race in which they went 25-1 bar three. The initial pace was fairly steady.

263 ED STANFORD'S 40TH BIRTHDAY (S) STKS 6f (P)
2:35 (2:35) (Class 6) 3-Y-O **£1,535** (£453; £226) **Stalls** Low

Form RPR

56-0 **1** **Imogen Louise (IRE)**[7] 179 3-8-7 62.................... CathyGannon 6 65
(Derek Haydn Jones) *led for 2f: styd trcking ldrs: rdn to chal on inner over 1f out: drvn to ld ins fnl f: r.o strly and drew clr fnl 100yds* **9/1**

141- **2** *3½* **Insolenceofoffice (IRE)**[24] 8002 3-9-3 83.................(p) AdrianNicholls 7 64
(David Nicholls) *t.k.h: chsd wnr tl led 4f out: c towards centre and rdn wl over 1f out: hdd ins fnl f: btn fnl 100yds: wknd* **4/7**[1]

040- **3** *1¾* **Tony Hollis**[43] 7811 3-8-12 56.................... JamesMillman 4 53
(Rod Millman) *t.k.h: chsd ldrs: lost pl jst over 2f out: swtchd rt and rallied 1f out: styd on fnl f to go 3rd towards fin* **33/1**

42-1 **4** *¾* **Slatey Hen (IRE)**[16] 66 3-8-5 67.................... NathanAlison[(7)] 9 51
(Paddy Butler) *t.k.h: chsd ldrs on outer: wnt 2nd over 3f out tl wl over 1f out: wknd u.p 1f out* **7/1**[2]

05-0 **5** *½* **Golden Shine**[14] 100 3-8-12 63....................(v[1]) LukeMorris 8 49
(Alan Bailey) *dwlt: in tch on outer: rdn and hung rt bnd ent fnl 2f: sn outpcd and no threat to ldrs fr over 1f out* **25/1**

60-6 **6** *¾* **Bluberry**[10] 130 3-8-8 53 ow1....................(b[1]) FergusSweeney 1 43
(Gary Moore) *hld up in last trio: rdn and effrt whn n.m.r wl over 1f out: n.d* **33/1**

6 **7** *shd* **Striking Eyes**[10] 126 3-8-7 0.................... RichardKingscote 5 41
(Roger Charlton) *chsd ldrs: rdn and unable qck wl over 1f out: btn jst over 1f out: wknd ins fnl f* **8/1**[3]

50- **8** *2* **Doesn't Care (IRE)**[24] 7999 3-8-12 0.................... TomEaves 3 40
(Richard Fahey) *s.i.s: sn pushed along in rr: sme hdwy between horses 1f out: nvr trbld ldrs* **25/1**

05-2 **9** *1½* **Ajaafa**[10] 130 3-8-12 61....................(p) RobbieFitzpatrick 2 35
(Michael Attwater) *a towards rr: rdn over 2f out: n.d* **14/1**

1m 12.83s (0.93) **Going Correction** +0.075s/f (Slow) **9** Ran SP% **117.5**
Speed ratings (Par 95): **96,91,89,88,87 86,86,83,81**
.The winner was sold to S Arnold for 6,000gns. Insolenceofoffice was claimed by\n\x\x A. Crook for £6000.
Owner Joseph E Keeling **Bred** J Keeling **Trained** Efail Isaf, Rhondda C Taff

FOCUS
Not a bad race for the grade on paper, but the favourite was below par and the form may not prove too solid.

264 BLUE SQUARE SPRINT SERIES (ROUND 3) (H'CAP) (QUALIFIER) 6f (P)
3:05 (3:06) (Class 5) (0-75,74) 4-Y-O+ **£2,729** (£806; £403) **Stalls** Low

Form RPR

021- **1** **Arctic Lynx (IRE)**[70] 7441 4-9-7 **74**.................... GeorgeBaker 3 86+
(John Best) *hld up in tch gng wl: trckd ldng pair over 2f out: swtchd rt and led ins fnl f: idled in front: rdn out* **11/4**[1]

32-1 **2** *¾* **Waterloo Dock**[14] 98 6-8-13 **66**....................(v) ChrisCatlin 1 73
(Michael Quinn) *sn pushed up to chse ldr: rdn and ev ch ent fnl f: styd on same pce fnl 150yds: wnt 2nd towards fin* **20/1**

06-1 **3** *½* **Waabel**[10] 134 4-9-7 **74**.................... JoeFanning 8 79
(Jim Best) *led: rdn wl over 1f out: hdd and styd on same pce ins fnl f: lost 2nd towards fin* **8/1**

0-25 **4** *¾* **Chjimes (IRE)**[7] 178 7-9-0 **67**....................(b) HayleyTurner 6 70
(Conor Dore) *hld up in rr: clsd and in tch 1/2-way: nt clr run bnd ent fnl 2f: rdn and hdwy over 1f out: kpt on wl fnl 100yds: nt rch ldrs* **15/2**

/6-0 **5** *nk* **Jungle Bay**[14] 99 4-9-3 **73**.................... AndrewHeffernan[(3)] 2 75
(Jane Chapple-Hyam) *hld up in tch in midfield: hdwy on inner wl over 1f out: drvn ent fnl f: kpt on same pce u.p fnl f* **33/1**

35-4 **6** *hd* **Tislaam (IRE)**[7] 178 4-9-1 **68**....................(v) RobertWinston 7 69
(Alan McCabe) *in tch: chsd ldrs and rdn 2f out: unable qck over 1f out: kpt on again ins fnl f* **13/2**[3]

[illegible] **7** [illegible] [illegible] **(IRE)**[45] 7754 [illegible].................... KierenFox[(3)] 4 71
(Christine Dunnett) *hld up in midfield: nt clr run bnd ent [illegible]* *towards inner over 1f out: drvn and kpt on same pce fnl f* **12/1**

20-3 **8** *2¾* **Pipers Piping (IRE)**[7] 178 5-9-3 **70**....................(p) MichaelStainton 10 61+
(Jane Chapple-Hyam) *racd in last quartet: clsd and in tch 1/2-way: nt clr run bnd 2f out: swtchd rt and rdn wl over 1f out: one pce and no prog after* **7/1**

405- **9** *2* **Kummel Excess (IRE)**[63] 7526 4-8-12 **72**.................... DavidKenny[(7)] 11 56
(George Baker) *s.i.s: bhd: hdwy on outer over 3f out: wknd u.p wl over 1f out* **33/1**

1-02 **10** *2½* **Prize Point**[7] 178 5-8-13 **66**.................... EddieAhern 5 42
(Jim Boyle) *chsd ldrs: rdn and struggling ent fnl 2f: wknd qckly over 1f out* **6/1**[2]

06-0 **11** *1¼* **Rapid Water**[8] 168 5-9-2 **69**....................(b) JimmyQuinn 12 41
(Jane Chapple-Hyam) *rrd s and v.s.a: clsd and in tch 1/2-way: effrt wl over 1f out: wknd over 1f out* **14/1**

330- **12** *2½* **Comadoir (IRE)**[48] 7719 5-9-4 **71**.................... IanMongan 9 35
(Jo Crowley) *chsd ldrs: wknd 2f out: dropping out whn sltly hmpd wl over 1f out: snl bhd* **16/1**

1m 11.33s (-0.57) **Going Correction** +0.075s/f (Slow) **12** Ran SP% **120.5**
Speed ratings (Par 103): **106,105,104,103,102 102,102,98,95,92 90,87**
Tote Swingers: 1&2 £13.00, 1&3 £7.40, 2&3 £5.20 CSF £67.49 CT £407.04 TOTE £3.90: £1.60, £4.20, £3.50; EX 38.00 Trifecta £311.30 Pool of £517.51 - 1.23 winning units..
Owner Heading For The Rocks Partnership **Bred** Derek Veitch And Saleh Ali Hammadi **Trained** Hucking, Kent

FOCUS
A modest but quite competitive sprint handicap, and the form looks solid. The first three home were all at the front end turning in and the first seven finished clear.
Pipers Piping(IRE) Official explanation: jockey said gelding was denied a clear run
Prize Point Official explanation: trainer said gelding was unsuited by being unable to dominate
Rapid Water Official explanation: jockey said gelding reared and was slowly away

265 VIEW OUR 2011 FIXTURES AT LINGFIELDPARK.CO.UK H'CAP 6f (P)
3:40 (3:40) (Class 3) (0-95,92) 4-Y-O+ **£5,828** (£1,734; £866; £432) **Stalls** Low

Form RPR

112- **1** **Anne Of Kiev (IRE)**[23] 8016 6-9-6 **91**....................(t) SteveDrowne 8 99
(Jeremy Gask) *dropped in bhd after s: hld up in tch: swtchd rt and effrt ent fnl f: r.o wl to ld last stride* **9/2**[3]

33-3 **2** *shd* **Five Star Junior (USA)**[17] 46 5-9-4 **92**.................... JamesSullivan[(3)] 5 99
(Linda Stubbs) *t.k.h early: hld up wl in tch: trckd ldrs gng wl: swtchd lft and hdwy ent fnl f: rdn to ld ins fnl f: hdd last stride* **10/3**[1]

220- **3** *shd* **Sioux Rising (IRE)**[35] 7935 5-8-11 **82**..........................(b[1]) JackMitchell 7 89
(Richard Fahey) *chsd ldrs: rdn wl over 1f out: ev ch ins fnl f: no ex cl home* **7/2**[2]

120- **4** *½* **Vintage (IRE)**[31] 7971 7-8-7 **78**.............................. ChrisCatlin 2 83
(John Akehurst) *led: rdn 2f out: hdd ins fnl f: no ex towards fin* **6/1**

34-6 **5** *¾* **Green Manalishi**[21] 2 10-9-0 **85**..............................(t) TomEaves 6 88
(Kevin Ryan) *t.k.h: chsd ldr: rdn wl over 1f out: ev ch 1f out: one pce fnl 100yds* **16/1**

41-5 **6** *nk* **Perfect Act**[17] 46 6-9-3 **88**.............................. DavidProbert 4 90
(Andrew Balding) *hld up in tch in rr: rdn and effrt ent fnl f: keeping on but hld whn n.m.r wl ins fnl f* **6/1**

31-4 **7** *nk* **Breathless Kiss (USA)**[15] 87 4-8-10 **81**..................(b) JamieSpencer 1 82
(Kevin Ryan) *in tch towards rr: hdwy into midfield 1/2-way: effrt on inner over 1f out: no hdwy ins fnl f* **15/2**

600- **8** *nse* **The Scorching Wind (IRE)**[31] 7970 5-9-0 **90**..............(t) RyanClark(5) 3 91
(Stuart Williams) *v.s.a: in tch in last: c wd and rdn bnd 2f out: styd on ins fnl f: nvr trbld ldrs* **20/1**

1m 11.3s (-0.60) **Going Correction** +0.075s/f (Slow) **8** Ran SP% **114.5**
Speed ratings (Par 107): **107,106,106,106,105 104,104,104**
Tote Swingers: 1&2 £2.40, 1&3 £4.40, 2&3 £3.60 CSF £19.93 CT £57.69 TOTE £3.20: £1.80, £1.40, £2.10; EX 12.80 Trifecta £200.40 Pool of £473.99 - 1.75 winning units..
Owner P Bamford **Bred** Deerfield Farm **Trained** Sutton Veny, Wilts

FOCUS
A fair sprint handicap run in a very similar time to the preceding 61-75 event. The whole field were covered by about two lengths at the line.

NOTEBOOK
Anne Of Kiev(IRE), who was loaded with the help of a blanket, made it three out of three over C&D. She certainly left it late, flying home down the outer to lead on the post after entering the final furlong with only one behind her. She will be seen to even better effect off a faster pace and connections will try to win some black type with her. (op 7-2 tchd 5-1)
Five Star Junior(USA), well supported, travelled nicely and took a slender lead inside the last, only to be nailed in the last stride. He is consistent and obviously capable of winning off this mark. (op 4-1)
Sioux Rising(IRE) was more suited by today's conditions than the 7f on Fibresand she was faced with last time. Tried in blinkers, she ran a solid race but could not quite quicken in the straight. (op 9-2)
Vintage(IRE) ran well on this return from a month's break and gave way only to the finishers inside the final furlong. (op 8-1)
Green Manalishi, dropped 5lb, ran creditably and did not appear to miss the regular cheekpieces. (op 20-1)
Perfect Act beat today's winner at Kempton two runs back but was 7lb higher here. She was not beaten far in sixth. Official explanation: jockey said mare was denied a clear run (op 9-2)
Breathless Kiss(USA) has done all her winning at 5f and off lower marks. (op 8-1)
The Scorching Wind(IRE), sprinting for the first time since the summer of 2009, did well to finish as close as he did after blowing the start. Official explanation: jockey said gelding was slowly away (op 16-1)

266 PLAY MEGAJACKPOTS CLEOPATRA AT BLUESQ.COM H'CAP 1m 4f (P)
4:15 (4:15) (Class 5) (0-70,70) 4-Y-0+ **£2,047** (£604; £302) **Stalls** Low

Form RPR

12/2 **1** **Transformer (IRE)**[7] 174 5-9-5 **64**.............................. JimCrowley 3 70+
(William Jarvis) *chsd ldng pair: effrt to ld and edgd rt wl over 1f out: kpt on fnl f: rdn out* **6/4**[1]

200- **2** *1* **Parhelion**[165] 3519 4-9-7 **70**.............................. JoeFanning 6 74
(Derek Haydn Jones) *chsd ldr: rdn to press ldr over 2f out: edgd lft u.p wl over 1f out: kpt on same pce fnl f* **16/1**

52-1 **3** *½* **Mister Frosty (IRE)**[8] 161 5-9-1 **60**.............................. GeorgeBaker 4 63
(George Prodromou) *chsd ldng trio: effrt and rdn jst over 2f out: chsd ldng pair over 1f out: kpt on but nvr gng pce to chal ldr* **3/1**[2]

120- **4** *3½* **Bariolo (FR)**[24] 8003 7-9-10 **69**.............................. TravisBlock 8 66
(Noel Chance) *stdd s: hld up in rr: rdn and effrt jst over 2f out: n.m.r and swtchd lft jst over 1f out: wnt 4th ins fnl f: nvr threatened ldrs* **12/1**

516- **5** *shd* **Mush Mir (IRE)**[40] 7856 4-9-4 **67**..............................(b) StephenCraine 9 64
(Jim Boyle) *led: hdd and hmpd wl over 1f out: sn btn: wknd over 1f out* **8/1**

64-0 **6** *2* **Beau Fighter**[7] 174 6-8-13 **58**.............................. FergusSweeney 7 52
(Gary Moore) *hld up in last trio: effrt into midfield and rdn ent fnl 2f: no hdwy over 1f out* **13/2**[3]

6/6- **7** *½* **Force Group (IRE)**[214] 3294 7-9-8 **67**.............................. J-PGuillambert 2 60
(Nick Littmoden) *stdd s: hld up in last pair: nt clr run over 2f out tl 2f out: no prog after: n.d* **8/1**

064- **8** *6* **Penang Cinta**[44] 7788 8-8-10 **62**.............................. RPWalsh(7) 1 46
(David Evans) *in tch in midfield: rdn and unable qck ent fnl 3f: wknd jst over 2f out: wl btn fnl 2f* **14/1**

2m 32.81s (-0.19) **Going Correction** +0.075s/f (Slow)
WFA 4 from 5yo+ 4lb **8** Ran SP% **120.8**
Speed ratings (Par 103): **103,102,102,99,99 98,97,93**
Tote Swingers: 1&2 £6.70, 1&3 £2.00, 2&3 £8.20 CSF £30.75 CT £70.51 TOTE £2.70: £1.60, £4.70, £2.10; EX 35.10 Trifecta £100.00 Pool of £732.88 - 5.42 winning units..
Owner M C Banks **Bred** Bryan Ryan **Trained** Newmarket, Suffolk

FOCUS
A moderate handicap run at an ordinary pace, and nothing was able to come from the rear and play a meaningful part.
T/Plt: £6.80 to a £1 stake. Pool of £72,354.55 - 7,729.01 winning tickets. T/Qpdt: £3.70 to a £1 stake. Pool of £5,652.25 - 1,123.76 winning tickets. SP

[257]CAGNES-SUR-MER
Saturday, January 22

OFFICIAL GOING: Turf: heavy

267a PRIX ALBERT TATON (CONDITIONS) (4YO) (TURF) 1m 4f
12:15 (12:00) 4-Y-0 **£10,775** (£4,310; £3,232; £2,155; £1,077)

RPR

1 **War Singer (USA)**[133] 5980 4-9-0 0.............................. IoritzMendizabal 8 83
(J-C Rouget, France) **23/10**[2]

2 *½* **High Figurine (IRE)**[241] 4-8-8 0 ow2..............................(p) JohanVictoire 1 76
(Jean De Roualle, France) **27/1**

3 *1* **Tominator**[64] 7507 4-8-9 0.............................. Francois-XavierBertras 5 75
(Reg Hollinshead) *racd 4th: pulling freely: moved into 2nd 1/2-way down bk st: rdn to ld 2f out: wandered off st line: hdd 1 1/2f out: styd on wl fnl 100yds to keep 3rd* **8/1**[3]

4 *shd* **Singapore Fairy (FR)**[19] 4-7-11 0 ow1.............................. EddyHardouin(8) 4 71
(Robert Collet, France) **16/1**

5 *2½* **Kardo (GER)**[118] 4-8-9 0.............................. DominiqueBoeuf 6 71
(W Baltromei, Germany) **13/1**

6 *nk* **Kenmour (FR)**[121] 6315 4-9-0 0..............................(p) FranckBlondel 3 76
(F Rossi, France) **1/1**[1]

7 *2½* **Passing Chop (FR)**[60] 4-8-2 0..............................(p) BenjaminBoutin(7) 2 67
(C Boutin, France) **32/1**

8 *½* **Ok Coral (FR)**[134] 5935 4-8-9 0.............................. NicolasPerret 7 66
(K Borgel, France) **37/1**

9 *6* **Mambo Star (FR)**[19] 4-8-9 0.............................. SylvainRuis 11 56
(F Vermeulen, France) **28/1**

10 *7* **Viguria (FR)**[247] 4-8-7 0.............................. Pierre-CharlesBoudot 10 43
(M Boutin, France) **92/1**

2m 48.74s (168.74) **10** Ran SP% **118.2**
WIN (incl. 1 euro stake): 3.30. PLACES: 1.90, 6.20, 2.60. DF: 45.20. SF: 61.80.
Owner Ecurie I M Fares **Bred** Hertrich-McCarthy Livestock **Trained** Pau, France

[204]KEMPTON (A.W) (R-H)
Sunday, January 23

OFFICIAL GOING: Standard
Wind: Moderate, against Weather: Overcast

268 RACING UK H'CAP 7f (P)
2:10 (2:10) (Class 6) (0-65,64) 4-Y-0+ **£1,535** (£453; £226) **Stalls** Low

Form RPR

02-5 **1** **Abriachan**[18] 48 4-9-5 **62**.............................. AdamKirby 7 72
(Michael Quinlan) *hld up 2nd last and off the pce: gd hdwy fr 2f out: led 100yds out: drvn out* **7/1**

6/1- **2** *½* **Broughtons Day**[40] 7869 4-9-5 **62**.............................. StevieDonohoe 2 71
(Willie Musson) *mid-div: rdn and hdwy 2f out: led briefly ins fnl f: r.o* **7/2**[1]

24-2 **3** *2¼* **Dancing Welcome**[15] 97 5-9-6 **63**..............................(b) LiamKeniry 1 66
(Milton Bradley) *chsd clr ldrs: hrd rdn and styd on same pce fnl 2f* **5/1**[3]

4-62 **4** *nk* **Decency (IRE)**[9] 159 4-9-2 **59**.............................. LukeMorris 8 61
(Harry Dunlop) *hld up towards rr: rdn and hdwy 2f out: one pce appr fnl f* **10/1**

3-35 **5** *¾* **Norville (IRE)**[10] 143 4-8-13 **63**..............................(b) RPWalsh(7) 5 63
(David Evans) *led at str pce: edgd lft fr 2f out: hdd and edgd rt ins fnl f: wknd* **9/2**[2]

00-6 **6** *2* **Tudor Prince (IRE)**[18] 48 7-9-5 **62**.............................. JimmyQuinn 6 56
(Tony Carroll) *mid-div: rdn 3f out: a wl hld after* **5/1**[3]

05-4 **7** *3¾* **Revelator (IRE)**[19] 38 4-9-7 **64**..............................(tp) JamesDoyle 3 48
(Alan McCabe) *chsd clr ldrs: effrt over 2f out: sn wknd* **8/1**

0-00 **8** *¾* **White Shift (IRE)**[10] 143 5-9-0 **60**.............................. KierenFox(3) 9 42
(Jane Chapple-Hyam) *sn outpcd and rdn along: a bhd* **20/1**

1-00 **9** *7* **Mary's Pet**[10] 143 4-9-5 **62**.............................. J-PGuillambert 4 33
(John Akehurst) *dwlt: sn rdn up to press ldr at str pce: wknd over 2f out: eased whn no ch ins fnl f* **25/1**

1m 25.52s (-0.48) **Going Correction** 0.0s/f (Stan) **9** Ran SP% **115.0**
Speed ratings (Par 101): **102,101,98,98,97 95,91,90,82**
Tote Swingers: 1&2 £6.70, 1&3 £6.70, 2&3 £3.20 CSF £31.61 CT £135.16 TOTE £15.30: £4.40, £3.60, £1.02; EX 49.60 Trifecta £387.00 Pool: £591.06 - 1.13 winning units..
Owner Thomas Mann **Bred** Plantation Stud **Trained** Newmarket, Suffolk

FOCUS
The pace was much too strong in this handicap, setting the race up for those waited with.
Dancing Welcome Official explanation: jockey said mare hung left in straight

269 TURFTV H'CAP 6f (P)
2:40 (2:40) (Class 5) (0-70,69) 4-Y-0+ **£2,047** (£604; £302) **Stalls** Low

Form RPR

004- **1** **Best Trip (IRE)**[25] 8004 4-9-4 **66**.............................. FrannyNorton 8 75
(Richard Guest) *mde all: rdn 3 l ahd 2f out: readily* **5/1**[3]

60-5 **2** *2* **Sherjawy (IRE)**[19] 29 7-9-1 **63**.............................. SamHitchcott 5 66
(Zoe Davison) *chsd wnr: rdn over 2f out: kpt on same pce: a hld* **8/1**

3-62 **3** *1* **Dvinsky (USA)**[10] 143 10-9-3 **65**..............................(b) JimmyQuinn 2 65
(Jane Chapple-Hyam) *in tch in 4th: rdn to chal for 2nd over 1f out: one pce* **9/2**[2]

0-20 **4** *1¾* **Fear Nothing**[8] 178 4-9-7 **69**..............................(p) JoeFanning 1 63
(Ian McInnes) *mid-div: rdn and no hdwy fnl 2f* **11/1**

24-4 **5** *½* **Unlimited**[18] 48 9-8-13 **61**.............................. LukeMorris 6 54
(Tony Carroll) *s.i.s: restrained towards rr: drvn along and mod effrt over 1f out: nvr trbld ldrs* **7/1**

00-4 **6** *¾* **Mogok Ruby**[10] 143 7-8-10 **58**..............................(p) LiamKeniry 4 48
(Brett Johnson) *chsd ldrs: rdn 2f out: sn outpcd* **6/1**

4-04 **7** *¾* **Perlachy**[5] 199 7-9-3 **65**..............................(v) KellyHarrison 7 53
(Derek Shaw) *mid-div on outer: rdn over 2f out: sn btn* **11/1**

64-5 **8** *½* **Desert Icon (IRE)**[15] 98 5-8-8 **63**.............................. AliceHaynes(7) 3 49
(David Simcock) *dwlt: a last: pushed along over 2f out: sn struggling* **7/2**[1]

1m 12.18s (-0.92) **Going Correction** 0.0s/f (Stan) **8** Ran SP% **111.6**
Speed ratings (Par 103): **106,103,102,99,99 98,97,96**
Tote Swingers: 1&2 £12.50, 1&3 £5.30, 2&3 £6.60 CSF £41.91 CT £189.18 TOTE £6.30: £2.70, £2.30, £1.10; EX 61.50 Trifecta £178.90 Pool: £531.88 - 2.20 winning units..
Owner P J Duffen & P Brown **Bred** Limetree Stud **Trained** Stainforth, S Yorks

FOCUS
Form to treat with caution as the winner was allowed a soft lead.
Desert Icon(IRE) Official explanation: jockey said gelding ran too free

270 BOOK KEMPTON TICKETS ON 0844 579 3008 CLASSIFIED CLAIMING STKS 1m (P)
3:15 (3:17) (Class 6) 3-Y-0 **£1,535** (£453; £226) **Stalls** Low

Form RPR

3-51 **1** **Better Self**[6] 192 3-8-4 65.............................. RPWalsh(7) 4 71
(David Evans) *s.i.s and dropped out in last: effrt 2f out: led 1f out: rdn out* **6/4**[1]

533- **2** *1* **Beating Harmony**[43] 7839 3-8-1 58..............................(p) JimmyQuinn 3 58
(Tom Dascombe) *chsd ldr: rdn to ld over 1f out: sn hdd and kpt on same pce* **7/4**[2]

030- **3** *3* **Hackett (IRE)**[23] 8031 3-8-9 62.............................. KellyHarrison 5 59
(Michael Quinn) *racd in 3rd: pushed along over 4f out: effrt on inner 2f out: wknd over 1f out* **13/2**[3]

46-0 **4** *½* **Pyrenean**[13] 109 3-8-1 53..............................(b[1]) FrannyNorton 2 50
(James Given) *led at modest pce: carried hd high and hung rt fr 2f out: hdd & wknd over 1f out* **12/1**

1m 42.71s (2.91) **Going Correction** 0.0s/f (Stan) **4** Ran SP% **97.4**
Speed ratings (Par 95): **85,84,81,80**
CSF £3.49 TOTE £1.40; EX 2.80.Beating Harmony was claimed by Mr Dennis Deacon for £3,000.

Owner Mrs Sally Edwards **Bred** Miss K Rausing **Trained** Pandy, Monmouths

■ So Is She was withdrawn (8/1, deduct 10p in the £).

FOCUS

The field was reduced to four when the quirky So Is She refused to enter the stalls. This claimer was restricted to horses rated 70 or lower and the pace was modest, resulting in a time nearly five second outside standard.

271 PANORAMIC CONDITIONS STKS 1m (P)

3:45 (3:45) (Class 4) 4-Y-0+ **£3,885** (£1,156; £577; £288) **Stalls** Low

Form RPR

64-1 **1** **Bravo Echo**[15] 99 5-9-2 96 .... LukeMorris 9 107+ (Michael Attwater) *travelled wl in 5th: effrt on inner 2f out: led over 1f out: rdn clr: eased nr fin* **8/1**

42-3 **2** *1* **Lowther**[22] 6 6-9-2 96 .... (be) J-PGuillambert 4 102 (Alan Bailey) *s.s: towards rr: rdn and gd hdwy fnl 2f: fin wl: jst snatched 2nd* **7/2**[2]

035- **3** *hd* **Suits Me**[25] 8009 8-9-2 99 .... MickyFenton 3 102 (Tom Tate) *chsd ldr after 1f: rdn to chal over 2f out: nt pce of wnr over 1f out: lost 2nd fnl strides* **15/2**[3]

300- **4** *3 ¾* **Beauchamp Viceroy**[39] 7875 7-9-7 102 .... (b) EddieAhern 7 98 (Gerard Butler) *sn led: rdn and hdd over 1f out: wknd fnl f* **11/4**[1]

430- **5** *1 ¼* **Benandonner (USA)**[119] 6391 8-9-7 95 .... MartinLane 2 95 (Mike Murphy) *chsd ldrs tl outpcd 2f out* **14/1**

540- **6** *½* **Georgebernardshaw (IRE)**[120] 6363 6-9-2 95 .... JamieSpencer 5 89 (David Simcock) *stdd s and dropped out in rr: rdn over 2f out: n.d* **12/1**

006- **7** *½* **Greyfriarschorista**[136] 5879 4-9-2 98 .... JoeFanning 1 88 (Mark Johnston) *broke wl: trckd ldrs tl rdn and wknd 2f out* **7/2**[2]

2/0- **8** *23* **Raine's Cross**[275] 1497 4-9-2 93 .... JimCrowley 8 35 (Peter Winkworth) *fair 6th tl rdn and wknd 3f out: no ch fnl 2f* **25/1**

\- **9** *3 ¼* **Promised Wings (GER)**[301] 4-9-2 0 .... LiamKeniry 6 27 (Chris Gordon) *a in rr: rdn and lost tch over 3f out: sn wl bhd* **66/1**

1m 36.96s (-2.84) **Going Correction** 0.0s/f (Stan) **9** Ran SP% **113.7**

Speed ratings (Par 105): **114,113,112,109,107 107,106,83,80**

Tote Swingers: 1&2 £4.10, 1&3 £6.90, 2&3 £4.40 CSF £35.57 TOTE £8.40: £2.80, £1.90, £2.10; EX 34.40 Trifecta £70.40 Pool: £520.86 - 5.47 winning units..

Owner Canisbay Bloodstock **Bred** Juddmonte Farms Ltd **Trained** Epsom, Surrey

FOCUS

Hard to establish the exact worth of this form, but it was a decent race run at a fair gallop, and on a track riding on the quick side, the time was only 0.38 seconds outside the course record.

272 DAY TIME, NIGHT TIME, GREAT TIME H'CAP 1m 3f (P)

4:15 (4:15) (Class 5) (0-75,75) 4-Y-0+ **£2,047** (£604; £302) **Stalls** Low

Form RPR

60-3 **1** **Eseej (USA)**[14] 104 6-8-8 **62** .... WilliamCarson 7 70 (Peter Hiatt) *anticipated s and broke wl: mde all: wnt 6 l clr 4f out: hrd rdn over 1f out: tired on far rail fnl f: jst hld on* **9/2**[2]

00-3 **2** *nk* **Layla's Dancer**[15] 94 4-8-2 **66** .... LauraPike(7) 1 73 (David Simcock) *hld up in 4th: effrt over 2f out: wnt 2nd over 1f out: mde up 5 l on wnr: jst failed* **5/1**[3]

46-5 **3** *hd* **Turjuman (USA)**[11] 124 6-8-9 **63** .... StevieDonohoe 3 70 (Willie Musson) *hld up in 5th: effrt over 2f out: styd on wl fnl f: clsng at fin* **13/8**[1]

030- **4** *1 ¼* **Aphrodisia**[104] 6797 7-9-1 **74** .... RyanClark(5) 8 79 (Ian Williams) *s.s: hld up in last 15 l off the pce: shkn up over 2f out: hdwy over 1f out: styd on: nrst fin* **5/1**[3]

05-6 **5** *1 ½* **Humungous (IRE)**[18] 54 8-8-13 **67** .... (p) MickyFenton 2 70 (Charles Egerton) *trckd ldrs in 3rd: wnt 2nd 4f out: hrd rdn and one pce appr fnl f: 5th and btn whn n.m.r fnl 50yds* **16/1**

00-0 **6** *13* **Free Tussy (ARG)**[18] 54 7-9-2 **70** .... (bt) GeorgeBaker 5 49 (Gary Moore) *towards rr: drvn along and n.d fnl 3f* **16/1**

531- **7** *6* **Prince Charlemagne (IRE)**[265] 1816 8-8-13 **67** .... FergusSweeney 4 35 (Dr Jeremy Naylor) *towards rr: rdn 3f out: sn bhd* **25/1**

/40- **8** *¾* **Faldal**[72] 7436 5-9-7 **75** .... AdamKirby 6 42 [illegible] **12/1**

2m 19.49s (-2.41) **Going Correction** 0.0s/f (Stan)

WFA 4 from 5yo+ 3lb **8** Ran SP% **112.9**

Speed ratings (Par 103): **108,107,107,106,105 96,91,91**

Tote Swingers: 1&2 £4.50, 1&3 £2.00, 2&3 £3.20 CSF £26.46 CT £50.24 TOTE £5.00: £2.10, £2.50, £1.40; EX 25.00 Trifecta £38.10 Pool: £679.11 - 13.16 winning units..

Owner P W Hiatt **Bred** Shadwell Farm LLC **Trained** Hook Norton, Oxon

■ Stewards' Enquiry : Laura Pike two-day ban: careless riding (Feb 7-8)

FOCUS

There was controversy in this modest handicap with confirmed front-runner Eseej appearing to burst his stall open fractionally before the others and soon establishing a clear lead. Seeing as the winning margin was only a neck, it's possible to argue he gained an advantage that was the difference between victory and defeat, although it's likely he would have been allowed to dominate anyway.

Faldal Official explanation: jockey said mare had no more to give

273 KEMPTON FOR OUTDOOR PURSUITS FILLIES' H'CAP 1m (P)

4:45 (4:45) (Class 5) (0-75,75) 4-Y-0+ **£2,047** (£604; £302) **Stalls** Low

Form RPR

05-0 **1** **Spinning Bailiwick**[11] 128 5-8-10 **64** .... FergusSweeney 3 70 (Gary Moore) *stdd s: hld up in 4th: outpcd 2f out: rallied 1f out: r.o to ld on line* **8/1**

1-33 **2** *nse* **Avonrose**[9] 160 4-9-4 **72** .... JoeFanning 4 78 (Derek Shaw) *led at modest pce: qcknd 2f out: hrd rdn fnl f: ct on line* **2/1**[1]

6-21 **3** *2* **Shared Moment (IRE)**[11] 135 5-8-7 **61** oh3 .... (v) ChrisCatlin 2 62 (John Gallagher) *dwlt: hld up in tch in 5th: rdn and hdwy 2f out: pressed ldrs over 1f out: no ex fnl f* **4/1**[3]

10-4 **4** *1 ½* **Song To The Moon (IRE)**[9] 160 4-9-4 **75** .... (v) MatthewDavies(3) 5 73 (George Baker) *dwlt: sn trcking ldr: rdn 2f out: sn outpcd* **3/1**[2]

120- **5** *nk* **Marksbury**[39] 7874 4-8-7 **61** .... LukeMorris 1 58 (James Eustace) *broke wl: settled in 3rd: rdn to press ldr ins fnl 2f: wknd fnl f* **4/1**[3]

1m 42.82s (3.02) **Going Correction** 0.0s/f (Stan) **5** Ran SP% **109.4**

Speed ratings (Par 100): **84,83,81,80,80**

totesuper7: Win: Not won. Place: £329.10 - 4 winning units. CSF £24.03 TOTE £8.90: £2.60, £1.30; EX 29.30.

Owner Dr Ian R Shenkin **Bred** Mrs M Shenkin **Trained** Lower Beeding, W Sussex

FOCUS

They went a steady pace (time slowest of the three 1m races) and this isn't form to trust.

T/Plt: £20.70 to a £1 stake. Pool of £59,157.57 - 2,078.05 winning tickets. T/Qpdt: £7.20 to a £1 stake. Pool of £4,510.74 - 458.20 winning tickets. LM

[268] KEMPTON (A.W) (R-H)

Monday, January 24

OFFICIAL GOING: Standard

Wind: Moderate, against Weather: Overcast

274 KEMPTON.CO.UK MAIDEN FILLIES' STKS 7f (P)

1:05 (1:06) (Class 5) 3-Y-0+ **£2,115** (£624; £312) **Stalls** Low

Form RPR

0- **1** **She Ain't A Saint**[86] 7232 3-8-10 0 .... SeamieHeffernan 4 76+ (Jane Chapple-Hyam) *mde all: shkn up over 2f out: sn drew clr: pushed out fnl f* **3/1**[2]

2 *2 ¼* **Albaraka** 3-8-10 0 .... StevieDonohoe 5 69+ (Sir Mark Prescott Bt) *settled in 5th: shkn up and prog 2f out: wnt 2nd 1f out: styd on wl enough but no ch w wnr* **11/8**[1]

5-4 **3** *6* **Look Twice**[19] 43 3-8-10 0 .... LiamJones 3 53 (Alex Hales) *mostly chsd wnr: rdn and edgd lft 2f out: outpcd and lost 2nd 1f out: wknd* **10/1**

0 **4** *4 ½* **Zelenia**[10] 158 3-8-10 0 .... LukeMorris 7 40 (Peter Winkworth) *pressed ldrs on outer: bdly outpcd over 2f out: no ch after* **25/1**

63-0 **5** *½* **Litotes**[12] 126 3-8-10 54 .... RobbieFitzpatrick 1 39 (Michael Attwater) *chsd ldrs in 4th: rdn over 2f out: sn wknd* **25/1**

0 **6** *2* **Tegan (IRE)**[10] 158 3-8-11 0 ow1 .... SteveDrowne 6 35 (Richard Hannon) *a abt same pl: shkn up and no prog over 2f out* **8/1**

7 *2 ½* **Adieu** 3-8-11 0 ow1 .... DaneO'Neill 2 28 (Richard Hannon) *s.s: rn green in last: shkn up and no prog over 2f out* **5/1**[3]

1m 26.39s (0.39) **Going Correction** +0.025s/f (Slow) **7** Ran SP% **111.7**

Speed ratings (Par 100): **98,95,88,83,82 80,77**

toteswingers:1&2:£1.70, 1&3:£3.90, 2&3:£2.80 CSF £7.13 TOTE £3.70: £1.30, £2.00; EX 8.40.

Owner Mrs Jane Chapple-Hyam **Bred** Gestut Park Wiedingen **Trained** Dalham, Suffolk

FOCUS

A modest 3-y-o maiden. The first pair can rate higher with the third the best guide.

275 BOOK KEMPTON TICKETS ON 0844 579 3008 CLAIMING STKS 7f (P)

1:35 (1:35) (Class 6) 3-Y-O **£1,535** (£453; £226) **Stalls** Low

Form RPR

31-0 **1** **May's Boy**[11] 140 3-9-5 71 .... (p) DaneO'Neill 2 75+ (Mark Usher) *mde all: rdn clr fr 2f out: in n.d fnl f: eased nr fin* **7/4**[1]

042- **2** *4* **Neytiri**[42] 7857 3-8-2 56 ow1 .... (b[1]) KierenFox(3) 6 50 (Ralph Beckett) *settled in 5th: rdn over 2f out: prog to chse wnr wl over 1f out: no imp* **7/2**[3]

204- **3** *1 ¼* **Littleportnbrandy (IRE)**[24] 8030 3-8-4 70 .... (v[1]) LukeMorris 5 46 (David Evans) *prom: drvn over 2f out: sn outpcd: plugged on u.p to snatch 3rd last strides* **10/1**

50-6 **4** *shd* **Dances With Words (IRE)**[19] 53 3-9-1 57 .... IanMongan 4 56 (Rodney Farrant) *chsd wnr 2f out: styd in tch: hanging whn rdn fr over 2f out: disp 2nd fnl f but continued to hang: no ex and lost 3rd last strides* **20/1**

-231 **5** *5* **Fifth In Line (IRE)**[12] 130 3-8-8 68 .... FergusSweeney 7 36 (Jamie Osborne) *awkward s: t.k.h: chsd wnr after 2f to wl over 1f out: wknd qckly* **15/8**[2]

0 **6** *9* **Broughtons Fawn**[12] 130 3-8-8 0 .... JamieMackay 1 12 (Willie Musson) *v.s.a and swvd bdly lft: ct up at rr of field by 1/2-way: wknd over 2f out* **28/1**

1m 25.93s (-0.07) **Going Correction** +0.025s/f (Slow) **6** Ran SP% **110.7**

Speed ratings (Par 95): **101,96,95,94,89 78**

toteswingers:1&2:£1.90, 1&3:£2.40, 2&3:£2.80 CSF £8.04 TOTE £3.90: £2.70, £1.50; EX 11.70.Littleportnbrandy was claimed by S. Arnold for £5,000.

Owner High Five Racing **Bred** John Richardson **Trained** Upper Lambourn, Berks

FOCUS

A moderate claimer that can be rated around the runner-up and fourth.

Dances With Words(IRE) Official explanation: jockey said gelding hung right

Fifth In Line(IRE) Official explanation: jockey said filly ran flat

276 GOFFS BREEZE-UP AT KEMPTON MARCH 29TH H'CAP 6f (P)

2:10 (2:10) (Class 6) (0-55,56) 4-Y-0+ **£1,535** (£453; £226) **Stalls** Low

Form RPR

465- **1** **Young Simon**[25] 8023 4-9-2 **53** .... (v) IanMongan 4 63 (George Margarson) *trckd ldng pair: effrt on inner to ld over 1f out: in command fnl f: drvn out* **11/2**[3]

-006 **2** *1* **Memphis Man**[5] 218 8-9-0 **51** .... SeamieHeffernan 7 57 (David Evans) *settled in 7th: rdn over 2f out: limited prog over 1f out: styd on wl fnl f to take 2nd nr fin* **20/1**

40-3 **3** *nk* **Final Rhapsody**[11] 138 5-9-0 **51** .... (v) StevieDonohoe 8 56+ (Willie Musson) *hld up in 9th: swtchd lft wl over 1f out and pushed along: stl in last trio ent fnl f: drvn and r.o wl to take 3rd last strides* **4/1**[2]

2-01 **4** *nk* **Jonny Ebeneezer**[5] 210 12-9-5 **56** 6ex .... (be) JamesDoyle 1 60 (David Flood) *trckd ldrs in 5th: effrt 2f out: styd on to take 2nd briefly wl ins fnl f: kpt on* **8/1**

06-1 **5** *¾* **Replicator**[11] 138 6-9-3 **54** .... (e) JamieMackay 5 56 (Patrick Gilligan) *led: drvn over 2f out: hdd over 1f out: fdd and lost pls nr fin* **10/3**[1]

04-1 **6** *1 ¼* **Figaro Flyer (IRE)**[18] 57 8-8-11 **55** .... LewisWalsh(7) 2 53 (Jane Chapple-Hyam) *settled in 8th on inner: reminders wl over 1f out: pushed along and kpt on same pce after* **6/1**

0-45 **7** *1 ½* **Avonvalley**[14] 113 4-9-4 **55** .... RobbieFitzpatrick 12 48 (Peter Grayson) *slowest away and dropped in fr wd draw: pushed along in last bef 1/2-way: struggling after: sme late prog u.p* **25/1**

6-03 **8** *½* **Itwasonlyakiss (IRE)**[5] 211 4-8-13 **50** .... ChrisCatlin 9 42 (J W Hills) *pressed ldr to over 2f out: sn btn* **7/1**

10-0 **9** *1* **Mind The Monarch**[16] 98 4-8-10 **52** .... (v) RyanPowell(5) 10 40 (Roger Teal) *chsd ldng trio to 2f out: sn wknd* **16/1**

06-0 **10** *3* **Best One**[8] 185 7-9-4 **55** .... (b) LukeMorris 11 34 (Ronald Harris) *nvr bttr than midfield: rdn over 2f out: wknd wl over 1f out* **20/1**

1m 12.97s (-0.13) **Going Correction** +0.025s/f (Slow) **10** Ran SP% **115.6**

Speed ratings (Par 101): **101,99,99,98,97 96,94,93,92,88**

toteswingers:1&2:£24.60, 1&3:£6.60, 2&3:£15.10 CSF £110.10 CT £487.67 TOTE £10.60: £3.30, £6.40, £1.10; EX 116.10.

Owner M F Kentish **Bred** M F Kentish **Trained** Newmarket, Suffolk

FOCUS
A weak handicap, run at a sound pace and rated through the runner-up to his recent best.

277 MEYERTIMBER.CO.UK H'CAP 2m (P)
2:45 (2:45) (Class 6) (0-55,55) 4-Y-O+ **£1,535** (£453; £226) **Stalls** Low

Form RPR
60-1 **1** **Delorain (IRE)**[13] [118] 8-8-8 **49**....(vt) LauraPike(7) 7 58+
(William Stone) *settled in rr: trapped bhd rivals in 10th over 3f out: prog over 2f out: drvn over 1f out: styd on wl to ld nr fin* **9/2**[1]

00-4 **2** *nk* **Frameit (IRE)**[12] [131] 4-8-11 **52**....(v) FrannyNorton 11 59
(James Given) *trckd ldrs in 7th: pushed along and prog to go 2nd over 2f out: drvn to ld over 1f out: kpt on but hdd nr fin* **10/1**

003- **3** *3* **Zelos Diktator**[22] [7759] 5-9-7 **55**....(p) GeorgeBaker 6 58
(Gary Moore) *trckd ldng trio: smooth prog to ld 3f out: rdn and hdd over 1f out: fnd nil* **11/2**[2]

/30- **4** *1* **Carbon Print (USA)**[9] [7633] 6-9-4 **52**....(t) DaneO'Neill 9 54
(James Evans) *hld up in rr: prog on outer over 3f out gng strly: rdn over 2f out: kpt on same pce after* **33/1**

42-3 **5** *1 3/4* **Money Money Money**[13] [117] 5-9-6 **54**.... JamesMillman 10 54
(Rod Millman) *chsd ldrs disputing 5th: rdn and cl enough over 2f out: one pce over 1f out* **12/1**

35-4 **6** *1* **Faith Jicaro (IRE)**[14] [114] 4-8-10 **51**.... JamesDoyle 8 50
(Nicky Vaughan) *hld up in rr: stdy prog on outer 4f out: chsd ldrs over 2f out: sn rdn and nt qckn: fdd fnl f* **15/2**

00-0 **7** *3/4* **Fine Tolerance**[14] [114] 5-8-12 **46** oh1....(b1) ChrisCatlin 14 44
(Sam Davison) *hld up in last trio: pushed along 6f out: detached over 3f out: stl pushed along and styd on quite wl fnl 2f: nrst fin* **50/1**

230- **8** *3* **Le Corvee (IRE)**[93] [5873] 9-9-1 **52**.... KierenFox(3) 13 46
(Tony Carroll) *settled towards rr: pushed along and effrt over 3f out: in tch chsng ldrs 2f out: wknd* **10/1**

020- **9** *6* **Astrodiva**[26] [8010] 5-8-11 **50**.... AshleyMorgan(5) 1 37
(Mark H Tompkins) *trckd ldng pair: drvn wl over 2f out: wknd qckly wl over 1f out* **10/1**

50/3 **10** *2 1/2* **Beauchamp Viking**[10] [173] 7-8-12 **46**....(t) EddieAhern 4 30
(Simon Burrough) *trckd ldrs disputing 5th: rdn on inner over 2f out: sn wknd* **12/1**

000- **11** *21* **Whitley Bay (USA)**[84] [7270] 4-8-5 **46** oh1.... LiamJones 12 —
(John Best) *rdn in last after 4f: t.o 5f out* **20/1**

031- **12** *1 3/4* **Torran Sound**[165] [4990] 4-9-0 **55**....(b) LukeMorris 2 —
(James Eustace) *drvn to ld: hdd over 4f out: sn wknd rapidly and eased: t.o* **6/1**[3]

00/ **13** *1 1/4* **Curragh Dancer (FR)**[22] [6593] 8-8-9 **46** oh1.... RobertLButler(3) 3 —
(Paddy Butler) *bmpd s: towards rr and nvr gng wl: drvn 6f out: sn bhd: t.o* **33/1**

30-6 **14** *2* **Dawson Creek (IRE)**[17] [79] 7-9-2 **50**.... IanMongan 5 —
(Luke Dace) *trckd ldr: led over 4f out to 3f out: wknd rapidly and sn heavily eased: t.o* **16/1**

3m 29.62s (-0.48) **Going Correction** +0.025s/f (Slow)
WFA 4 from 5yo+ 7lb **14** Ran SP% **120.8**
Speed ratings (Par 101): **102,101,100,99,98 98,98,96,93,92 81,80,80,79**
toteswingers:1&2:£8.20, 1&3:£6.50, 2&3:£9.90 CSF £47.85 CT £258.34 TOTE £6.90: £1.80, £3.40, £2.00; EX 52.60.
Owner Miss Caroline Scott **Bred** Glending Bloodstock **Trained** West Wickham, Cambs

FOCUS
An ordinary staying handicap where the first pair came clear late on. The winner recorded a small personal best.
Beauchamp Viking Official explanation: jockey said gelding was denied a clear run
Torran Sound Official explanation: jockey said gelding stopped quickly

278 PANORAMIC FILLIES' H'CAP 1m 3f (P)
3:20 (3:20) (Class 5) (0-70,71) 4-Y-O+ **£2,115** (£624; £312) **Stalls** Low

Form RPR
653- **1** **Adoyen Spice**[26] [8008] 4-8-13 **60**.... SeamieHeffernan 5 70+
(Mike Murphy) *t.k.h early: hld up in 8th: shkn up over 2f out: prog to ld over 1f out: styd on wl* **7/2**[1]

30-0 **2** *3/4* **Ocean Countess (IRE)**[21] [26] 5-8-4 **51**.... KierenFox(3) 7 58
(Tony Carroll) *s.s: hld up last: gd prog on outer wl over 1f out: wnt 2nd jst ins fnl f and looked dangerous: edgd rt and nt qckn* **9/1**

41-4 **3** *1/2* **Suhailah**[5] [207] 5-8-7 **51** ow1.... RobbieFitzpatrick 2 57
(Michael Attwater) *trckd ldrs on inner: effrt and edgd towards rail 2f out: drvn and styd on fnl f: tk 3rd nr fin* **14/1**

015- **4** *3/4* **Where's Susie**[47] [7765] 6-9-10 **68**.... GeorgeBaker 8 73
(Michael Madgwick) *trckd ldng pair: wnt 2nd 4f out: rdn to ld for a few strides over 1f out: one pce fnl f* **7/1**[2]

2-21 **5** *1 1/2* **Catbells (IRE)**[6] [201] 4-9-3 **71** 6ex....(p) NatashaEaton(7) 1 76+
(Alan Bailey) *hld up in midfield: sing pulling vigorously fr 6f out and dropped to rr: prog on inner whn nowhere to go wl over 1f out: styd on ins fnl f* **7/2**[1]

60-0 **6** *nse* **It's Dubai Dolly**[17] [79] 5-9-1 **59**.... JamesDoyle 9 61
(Alastair Lidderdale) *led after 1f: tried to kick on over 2f out: hdd and fdd over 1f out* **20/1**

200- **7** *1* **Norse Dame**[173] [4698] 4-9-8 **69**.... RobertWinston 11 69
(David Elsworth) *stdd s: hld up in last pair: lots of urging fr over 2f out: sme late prog: nvr nr ldrs* **14/1**

41-2 **8** *nk* **Dilys Maud**[10] [164] 4-8-11 **58**....(b) RobertHavlin 10 58
(Roger Ingram) *hld up in midfield: prog on outer over 2f out: rdn and fnd nil over 1f out: hanging bdly ins fnl f* **10/1**

05-3 **9** *3 1/4* **My Sister**[17] [90] 4-8-5 **52**.... DavidProbert 6 46
(Mark Usher) *led 1f: chsd ldr to 4f out: wknd 2f out* **12/1**

3/2- **10** *1 1/4* **Josephine Malines**[27] [7015] 7-8-7 **51**....(tp) LukeMorris 3 43
(John Flint) *t.k.h: hld up in midfield: rdn and wknd over 2f out* **16/1**

335- **11** *2* **Affinity**[62] [7541] 4-9-6 **67**.... FrannyNorton 4 55
(James Given) *chsd ldrs on outer: pushed along over 4f out: lost pl u.p over 2f out: sn btn* **8/1**[3]

2m 23.64s (1.74) **Going Correction** +0.025s/f (Slow)
WFA 4 from 5yo+ 3lb **11** Ran SP% **118.8**
Speed ratings (Par 100): **94,93,93,92,91 91,90,90,88,87 85**
toteswingers:1&2:£12.80, 1&3:£11.10, 2&3:£18.00 CSF £36.31 CT £399.30 TOTE £3.20: £1.10, £3.30, £3.20; EX 49.10.
Owner Ronald Bright **Bred** Thorsten Feddern And Mike Murphy **Trained** Westoning, Beds
■ Stewards' Enquiry : Robbie Fitzpatrick one-day ban: careless riding (Feb 7)

FOCUS
A modest fillies' handicap run at an ordinary pace. The form makes sense taken at face value.
Dilys Maud Official explanation: jockey said filly hung right

279 BOOK RACING POST CHASE DAY H'CAP (LONDON MILE QUALIFIER) 1m (P)
3:50 (3:51) (Class 4) (0-85,85) 4-Y-O+ **£3,756** (£1,117; £558; £278) **Stalls** Low

Form RPR
212- **1** **Chilli Green**[25] [8017] 4-8-13 **77**.... DaneO'Neill 2 88+
(John Akehurst) *t.k.h: trckd ldng pair: effrt towards inner to ld over 1f out: in command fnl f: rdn out* **13/8**[1]

310- **2** *1 3/4* **Young Dottie**[55] [7637] 5-8-10 **79**.... JemmaMarshall(5) 1 85
(Pat Phelan) *chsd ldrs in 5th: rdn over 2f out: styd on over 1f out to take 2nd last stride* **16/1**

244- **3** *shd* **Khanivorous**[33] [7965] 4-8-10 **77**....(v1) MatthewDavies(3) 4 83
(Jim Boyle) *racd keenly in ld: drvn and hdd over 1f out: kpt on but lost 2nd last stride* **14/1**

00-2 **4** *nk* **Jake The Snake (IRE)**[19] [45] 10-9-7 **85**.... GeorgeBaker 12 90+
(Tony Carroll) *dwlt: hld up in last: effrt on outer 2f out: styd on fr over 1f out: nt pce to threaten wnr* **9/1**[3]

223- **5** *nse* **Negotiation (IRE)**[25] [8018] 5-8-7 **71**.... FrannyNorton 7 76
(Michael Quinn) *chsd ldng trio: rdn over 2f out: kpt on but lost out in battle for pls nr fin* **10/1**

00-0 **6** *3* **Global Village (IRE)**[11] [141] 6-8-6 **75**.... RyanClark(5) 6 77
(Michael Blake) *hld up in 7th: prog on outer 2f out and tried to cl on ldrs over 1f out: wknd ins fnl f* **20/1**

400- **7** *1/2* **Jordaura**[13] [7121] 5-8-13 **80**.... KierenFox(3) 3 77
(Tony Carroll) *dwlt: hld up in last pair: shuffled along fr over 2f out: nvr nr ldrs* **11/1**

04-0 **8** *3/4* **Rasselas (IRE)**[23] [6] 4-9-2 **80**.... RobertHavlin 9 75
(David Nicholls) *racd wd in midfield: rdn over 2f out: no prog and btn over 1f out* **12/1**

00-3 **9** *6* **Alhaban (IRE)**[16] [99] 5-9-7 **85**....(t) LukeMorris 13 67
(Ronald Harris) *hld up in last trio: rdn on wd outside wl over 2f out: no prog and sn btn* **15/2**[2]

00-3 **10** *3 3/4* **Big Bay (USA)**[11] [141] 5-9-2 **80**.... SeamieHeffernan 10 53
(Jane Chapple-Hyam) *chsd ldr to over 2f out: racd awkwardly after: wknd rapidly fnl f: eased* **15/2**[2]

1m 39.1s (-0.70) **Going Correction** +0.025s/f (Slow) **10** Ran SP% **114.1**
Speed ratings (Par 105): **104,102,102,101,101 98,98,97,91,87**
toteswingers:1&2:£6.50, 1&3:£6.50, 2&3:£16.90 CSF £30.01 CT £250.62 TOTE £2.60: £1.50, £5.70, £3.20; EX 35.10.
Owner Peter M Crane **Bred** P M Crane **Trained** Epsom, Surrey

FOCUS
A modest handicap, run at an ordinary pace. The form is rated around the placed horses.
Alhaban(IRE) Official explanation: jockey said gelding hung left

280 KEMPTON FOR OUTDOOR EVENTS H'CAP 1m (P)
4:25 (4:25) (Class 6) (0-55,55) 4-Y-O+ **£1,535** (£453; £226) **Stalls** Low

Form RPR
00-4 **1** **Poppy Golightly**[12] [128] 4-9-2 **53**.... ChrisCatlin 6 60
(Ron Hodges) *led 1f: trckd ldng pair tl chsd ldr over 2f out: drvn and looked hld over 1f out: styd on fnl f to ld last 50yds* **7/1**[3]

05-0 **2** *nk* **Zeffirelli**[14] [111] 6-9-4 **55**.... SeamieHeffernan 8 61
(Michael Quinn) *chsd ldrs in 5th: rdn over 2f out: grad clsd fr over 1f out: styd on to take 2nd last strides: jst hld* **20/1**

600- **3** *1/2* **Fine Ruler (IRE)**[25] [8024] 7-9-2 **53**.... DaneO'Neill 1 59+
(Martin Bosley) *hld up in midfield on inner: hmpd over 2f out: rallied over 1f out: styd on to take 3rd last strides* **8/1**

34-0 **4** *1/2* **Katmai River (IRE)**[21] [26] 4-8-13 **55**....(v) LeeNewnes(5) 10 59+
(Mark Usher) *pressed ldr's gd pce after 1f: led over 3f out: kicked on over 2f out: looked like holding on tl wilted and hdd last 50yds* **15/2**

50-0 **5** *6* **Quahadi (IRE)**[12] [129] 5-8-9 **46** oh1....(t) EddieAhern 2 36
(Chris Gordon) *hld up in last trio: nt clr run briefly over 2f out: prog to chse ldrs over 1f out: wknd ins fnl f* **10/1**

00-6 **6** *1 1/4* **State General (IRE)**[20] [34] 5-9-2 **53**.... LukeMorris 11 40
(Tony Carroll) *settled in midfield on outer: rdn over 2f out: one pce over 1f out: wknd fnl f* **12/1**

000- **7** *3/4* **Craicajack (IRE)**[69] [7474] 4-8-8 **48**....(b1) AlanCreighton(3) 4 34
(Edward Creighton) *settled in midfield: drvn over 2f out: no real imp on ldrs u.p over 1f out: wknd* **40/1**

00-3 **8** *nse* **Tous Les Deux**[10] [163] 8-9-4 **55**.... FergusSweeney 3 40
(Dr Jeremy Naylor) *trckd ldrs on inner in 6th: rdn and prog to go 3rd briefly wl over 1f out: sn wknd* **3/1**[1]

000- **9** *1 1/2* **First Service (IRE)**[47] [7768] 5-9-1 **52**....(p) RobbieFitzpatrick 12 34
(Michael Attwater) *hld up in last pair: effrt on wd outside over 2f out: only modest late prog* **16/1**

00-0 **10** *2* **Louie's Lad**[20] [28] 5-8-6 **46** oh1.... KierenFox(3) 5 23
(John Bridger) *sn rdn in last and nvr gng wl: plugged on fr over 1f out* **66/1**

600- **11** *3 1/4* **Music Lover**[94] [7064] 4-8-12 **49**.... J-PGuillambert 9 19
(John Panvert) *settled towards rr: rdn 3f out: no prog and sn btn* **16/1**

00/2 **12** *13* **Haulit**[10] [163] 5-9-1 **52**.... GeorgeBaker 13 —
(Gary Moore) *racd wd: chsd ldng trio to 3f out: wknd qckly and sn bhd* **4/1**[2]

00-6 **13** *1/2* **Inquisitress**[10] [163] 7-8-4 **46** oh1....(p) RyanClark(5) 7 —
(John Bridger) *led after 1f at str pce: hdd over 3f out: wknd qckly over 2f out* **20/1**

1m 39.51s (-0.29) **Going Correction** +0.025s/f (Slow) **13** Ran SP% **122.4**
Speed ratings (Par 101): **102,101,101,100,94 93,92,92,91,89 85,72,72**
toteswingers:1&2:£19.30, 1&3:£9.00, 2&3:£36.60 CSF £146.53 CT £1193.68 TOTE £5.50: £2.70, £9.50, £5.10; EX 124.10.
Owner Denis Hardy, Christian Wroe **Bred** Jeremy Gompertz **Trained** Charlton Mackrell, Somerset

FOCUS
A moderate handicap, run at a solid pace. Sound form for the class.
Haulit Official explanation: jockey said gelding ran flat
T/Plt: £88.80 to a £1 stake. Pool:£57,118.50 - 469.12 winning tickets T/Qpdt: £38.90 to a £1 stake. Pool:£4,379.35 - 83.26 winning tickets JN

[250]WOLVERHAMPTON (A.W) (L-H)

Monday, January 24

OFFICIAL GOING: Standard

Wind: Light across Weather: Overcast

281 PLACE ONLY BETTING AT BLUESQ.COM H'CAP 7f 32y(P)

2:20 (2:20) (Class 6) (0-55,54) 3-Y-O **£1,535** (£453; £226) **Stalls** High

Form RPR

000- **1** **Princess Gail**[176] 4614 3-8-9 **47**.................................. GrahamGibbons 2 59
(Mark Brisbourne) *chsd ldrs: rdn to ld and edgd lft over 1f out: drvn clr* **14/1**

6-35 **2** *4 ½* **Titan Diamond (IRE)**[11] 142 3-8-8 **46**.......................... HayleyTurner 8 45
(Mark Usher) *hld up: hdwy over 1f out: rdn to chse wnr ins fnl f: no imp* **7/1**[3]

45-2 **3** *2 ¼* **Torteval (IRE)**[7] 189 3-8-7 **45**..(v) MartinLane 1 38
(David Evans) *led: rdn and hdd over 2f out: edgd lft over 1f out: no ex fnl f* **2/1**[2]

02-6 **4** *½* **William Wainwright (IRE)**[20] 41 3-9-0 **52**................. NickyMackay 5 44
(Ann Duffield) *chsd ldrs: rdn 1/2-way: outpcd over 2f out: styd on ins fnl f* **14/1**

4-22 **5** *nk* **Rhal (IRE)**[8] 187 3-9-2 **54**... TomEaves 3 45
(Bryan Smart) *trckd ldr: racd keenly: led on bit over 2f out: rdn and hdd over 1f out: hung rt and no ex fnl f* **5/6**[1]

0-00 **6** *3* **Look'N'Listen (IRE)**[8] 183 3-8-8 **46**................................ JimmyQuinn 7 29
(Alan Brown) *hld up: rdn over 2f out: nvr on terms* **40/1**

65-5 **7** *3 ¼* **Amore Et Labore**[19] 47 3-9-0 **52**..(b1) LiamKeniry 4 26
(Sylvester Kirk) *hld up in tch: rdn over 2f out: sn wknd* **20/1**

1m 31.28s (1.68) **Going Correction** +0.125s/f (Slow) **7** Ran SP% **120.9**

Speed ratings (Par 95): **95,89,87,86,86 82,79**

toteswingers:1&2:£8.00, 1&3:£5.80, 2&3:£1.50 CSF £112.00 CT £285.95 TOTE £29.90: £8.90, £2.90; EX 74.20 Trifecta £391.70 Part won. Pool of £529.45 - 0.40 winning units..

Owner R Rickett **Bred** Ash Tree Farm Ltd **Trained** Great Ness, Shropshire

FOCUS

A desperately weak three-year-old handicap with the form best rated around the placed horses.

Princess Gail Official explanation: trainer said, regarding apparent improvement in form, that the filly was backward, had suffered from sore shins and, since her last run, had a wind operation.

282 WOLVERHAMPTON RACECOURSE - ALL CONFERENCING NEEDS MET (S) STKS 1m 141y(P)

2:55 (2:55) (Class 6) 4-Y-O+ **£1,535** (£453; £226) **Stalls** Low

Form RPR

0-42 **1** **Syrian**[5] 205 4-9-4 75.. JamieSpencer 2 82
(Ian Williams) *stdd s: hld up: hdwy to ld over 2f out: rdn clr and hung rt over 1f out: styd on* **5/4**[1]

14-5 **2** *5* **Grand Vizier (IRE)**[19] 45 7-9-0 80........................ RichardKingscote 3 66
(Conor Dore) *s.i.s: hld up: r.o ins fnl f: wnt 2nd post: no ch w wnr* **6/1**[3]

6-45 **3** *hd* **Cobo Bay**[10] 170 6-9-5 72..(b) HayleyTurner 6 70
(Conor Dore) *chsd ldrs: rdn over 2f out: styd on same pce appr fnl f: lost 2nd post* **8/1**

56-3 **4** *1 ½* **Final Verse**[20] 31 8-9-0 72..(be) LiamKeniry 1 62
(Matthew Salaman) *hld up in tch: hmpd over 2f out: rdn over 1f out: no imp* **5/2**[2]

50-0 **5** *3 ¾* **Master Of Dance (IRE)**[9] 174 4-8-13 66...................(b1) MickyFenton 5 53
(James Given) *chsd ldrs: led 7f out: rdn and hdd over 2f out: wknd over 1f out* **16/1**

150- **6** *9* **Kildare Sun (IRE)**[26] 8008 9-9-5 63........................(p) GrahamGibbons 4 37
(John Mackie) *led: hdd 7f out: chsd ldr tl rdn over 2f out: wknd wl over 1f out* **9/1**

1m 50.10s (0.01) **Going Correction** +0.125s/f (Slow)

WFA 4 from 6yo+ 1lb **6** Ran SP% **114.3**

Speed ratings (Par 101): **106,101,101,100,96 88**

toteswingers:1&2:£1.40, 1&3:£2.40, 2&3:£3.10 CSF £9.72 TOTE £2.90: £1.60, £2.80; EX 6.90.There was no bid for the winner.

Owner Dr Marwan Koukash **Bred** Barry Walters **Trained** Portway, Worcs

FOCUS

A competitive seller won in decisive fashion with the winner rated in line with previous form for this yard.

283 ENJOY THE PARTY PACK GROUP OFFER H'CAP 1m 141y(P)

3:30 (3:31) (Class 6) (0-55,55) 4-Y-O+ **£1,535** (£453; £226) **Stalls** Low

Form RPR

11-1 **1** **John Potts**[18] 69 6-9-2 **55**.. KellyHarrison 1 64+
(Brian Baugh) *hld up: hdwy wl over 1f out: nt clr run and swtchd lft sn after: r.o to ld wl ins fnl f* **5/1**[2]

33-2 **2** *1 ¼* **Tres Froide (FR)**[17] 86 6-9-0 **53**..................................(p) JoeFanning 3 59
(Nigel Tinkler) *chsd ldrs: rdn over 2f out: nt clr run over 1f out: hmpd ins fnl f: r.o to go 2nd nr fin* **5/1**[2]

062- **3** *¾* **Director General (USA)**[42] 7863 4-9-1 **55**....................(b) PhillipMakin 8 59
(Julie Camacho) *trckd ldrs: plld hrd: rdn over 1f out: ev ch and edgd rt ins fnl f: unable qck towards fin* **9/2**[1]

05-2 **4** *hd* **Fortunate Bid (IRE)**[18] 69 5-8-11 **53**.................. JamesSullivan(3) 12 57
(Linda Stubbs) *plld hrd and prom: wnt 2nd over 5f out: led over 1f out: rdn and hdd wl ins fnl f* **8/1**

41-3 **5** *¾* **Pie Poudre**[21] 26 4-8-11 **51**...(p) TomEaves 10 53
(Roy Brotherton) *hld up: hdwy on outer over 3f out: rdn and ev ch over 1f out: styd on same pce ins fnl f* **15/2**

200- **6** *1 ½* **Libre**[88] 7199 11-8-7 **46**...(p) JimmyQuinn 13 45+
(Violet M Jordan) *hld up: r.o ins fnl f: nvr nrr* **25/1**

0-00 **7** *¾* **Gems**[5] 204 4-8-6 **46** oh1... WilliamCarson 7 43
(Peter Hiatt) *hld up: hdwy over 2f out: sn rdn: styd on* **33/1**

00-5 **8** *3* **Angle Of Attack (IRE)**[18] 57 6-8-7 **46** oh1........... GrahamGibbons 11 36
(Alan Brown) *led: rdn and hdd over 1f out: wknd ins fnl f* **33/1**

6/4- **9** *¾* **No Trimmings (IRE)**[27] 7996 5-8-8 **54**..........................(bt) CTKeane(7) 5 42
(Gerard Keane, Ire) *s.i.s: hld up: plld hrd: hdwy over 6f out: rdn over 1f out: hung lft and wknd fnl f* **5/1**[2]

/56- **10** *¾* **Capacity (IRE)**[27] 7995 4-8-10 **53**.....................(v) AndrewHeffernan(3) 6 40
(T G McCourt, Ire) *plld hrd and prom: hmpd 7f out: rdn over 2f out: wknd over 1f out* **7/1**[3]

604- **11** *2* **Masteeat (USA)**[25] 8023 4-8-6 **46** oh1.............................. HayleyTurner 4 28
(Olivia Maylam) *hld up: rdn over 3f out: wknd over 2f out* **16/1**

1m 52.09s (1.59) **Going Correction** +0.125s/f (Slow)

WFA 4 from 5yo+ 1lb **11** Ran SP% **119.2**

Speed ratings (Par 101): **97,95,95,95,94 93,92,89,89,88 86**

toteswingers:1&2:£3.80, 1&3:£5.90, 2&3:£5.50 CSF £30.11 CT £123.01 TOTE £5.70: £3.00, £1.20, £1.70; EX 16.90 Trifecta £89.20 Pool of £655.08 - 5.43 winning units..

Owner Miss S M Potts **Bred** Miss S M Potts **Trained** Audley, Staffs

FOCUS

An open handicap featuring plenty of in-form horses and rated around the placed horses and the fifth.

284 NAME A RACE TO ENHANCE YOUR BRAND MAIDEN STKS 1m 1f 103y(P)

4:05 (4:05) (Class 5) 4-Y-O+ **£1,813** (£539; £269; £134) **Stalls** Low

Form RPR

042- **1** **Captivator**[136] 5925 4-8-12 71...1 HayleyTurner 3 70+
(James Fanshawe) *hld up: hdwy over 1f out: r.o to ld wl ins fnl f: sn clr: eased towards fin* **2/1**[2]

32- **2** *hd* **Shamardal Phantom (IRE)**[165] 4997 4-8-12 0................ MartinLane 5 66
(David Simcock) *led after 1f: hdd 7f out: chsd ldr tl led again over 2f out: rdn and hdd wl ins fnl f: styd on* **1/1**[1]

3 *2 ¼* **Minsky Mine (IRE)**[162] 5131 4-9-3 77.............................. NeilChalmers 1 66
(Michael Appleby) *led 1f: chsd ldrs: rdn over 1f out: styd on same pce fnl f* **4/1**[3]

0- **4** *6* **Arco Felice (USA)**[135] 5971 4-9-0 0..........................(t) SimonPearce(3) 6 54
(Keith Goldsworthy) *chsd ldrs: rdn over 2f out: wknd fnl f* **25/1**

5 *5* **Jersey Joe (IRE)**[27] 4-8-12 0.. DeanHeslop(5) 2 43
(Brian Ellison) *hld up: rdn over 2f out: sn wknd* **25/1**

005- **6** *1 ½* **Warrior Nation (FR)**[26] 8006 5-8-11 30.................. HarryPoulton(7) 7 40?
(Adrian Chamberlain) *led over 7f out: hdd over 2f out: wknd over 1f out* **150/1**

2m 4.96s (3.26) **Going Correction** +0.125s/f (Slow)

WFA 4 from 5yo 1lb **6** Ran SP% **111.7**

Speed ratings (Par 103): **90,89,87,82,78 76**

toteswingers:1&2:£1.10, 1&3:£1.50, 2&3:£1.40 CSF £4.31 TOTE £2.20: £1.30, £1.90; EX 4.20.

Owner Lord Vestey **Bred** Stowell Park Stud **Trained** Newmarket, Suffolk

FOCUS

A maiden dominated by the two well-bred fillies in the field and rated through the second.

285 BLUESQ.COM ON YOUR IPHONE H'CAP 7f 32y(P)

4:35 (4:35) (Class 4) (0-85,83) 4-Y-O+ **£2,914** (£867; £433; £216) **Stalls** Low

Form RPR

560- **1** **Smalljohn**[161] 5157 5-8-10 **72**..(v) TomEaves 1 78
(Bryan Smart) *led 1f: chsd ldr: rdn over 1f out: led ins fnl f: r.o* **8/1**

02-3 **2** *¾* **Striker Torres (IRE)**[11] 149 5-8-10 **72**..................(v) GrahamGibbons 5 76
(Geoffrey Oldroyd) *led 6f out: rdn and edgd rt over 1f out: hdd ins fnl f: styd on* **7/1**

223- **3** *hd* **Tiradito (USA)**[33] 7965 4-9-3 **79**..................................(p) AndreaAtzeni 6 82+
(Marco Botti) *hld up: hdwy over 1f out: rdn ins fnl f: r.o towards fin* **13/2**[3]

36-2 **4** *hd* **Fishforcompliments**[15] 105 7-8-7 **76**.................. GeorgeChaloner(7) 4 79
(Richard Fahey) *s.i.s: sn prom: rdn over 1f out: styd on* **9/2**[2]

065- **5** *nk* **Vanilla Rum**[142] 5768 4-8-11 **73**.. JimmyQuinn 2 75
(John Mackie) *s.i.s: sn prom: rdn over 1f out: unable qck wl ins fnl f* **16/1**

03-0 **6** *2 ½* **Mastership (IRE)**[16] 99 7-8-12 **77**..........................(v) IanBrennan(3) 7 72
(John Quinn) *hld up: rdn over 2f out: nvr trbld ldrs* **8/1**

021- **7** *¾* **Sarah's Art (IRE)**[24] 8033 8-9-0 **76**.......................................(t) AdamKirby 8 69
(Stef Higgins) *hld up: rdn over 2f out: a in rr* **8/1**

03-5 **8** *1 ¼* **Mr Macattack**[16] 99 6-9-7 **83**................................(t) RichardKingscote 3 73
(Tom Dascombe) *trckd ldrs: rdn and hung rt fr over 1f out: wknd fnl f* **9/4**[1]

1m 29.45s (-0.15) **Going Correction** +0.125s/f (Slow) **8** Ran SP% **114.0**

Speed ratings (Par 105): **105,104,103,103,103 100,99,98**

toteswingers:1&2:£9.20, 1&3:£6.10, 2&3:£5.50 CSF £61.77 CT £388.90 TOTE £11.70: £3.30, £1.20, £1.30; EX 40.00 Trifecta £506.00 Pool of £759.50 - 1.05 winning units

Owner B Smart **Bred** W H R John And Partners **Trained** Hambleton, N Yorks

■ Stewards' Enquiry : Graham Gibbons caution: careless riding.

FOCUS

This looked a wide-open handicap on paper and so it proved. The form looks straightforward rated around the first four.

Sarah's Art(IRE) Official explanation: jockey said gelding had no more to give

Mr Macattack Official explanation: jockey said gelding hung right throughout; vet said gelding finished distressed

286 DINE IN THE HORIZONS RESTAURANT H'CAP 1m 5f 194y(P)

5:05 (5:05) (Class 5) (0-75,72) 4-Y-O+ **£1,813** (£539; £269; £134) **Stalls** Low

Form RPR

12-5 **1** **Dart**[23] 3 7-9-7 **67**.. GrahamGibbons 3 74
(John Mackie) *chsd ldrs: rdn to ld over 1f out: styd on* **7/1**[2]

152- **2** *1 ½* **Accompanist**[45] 7821 8-9-3 **66**...........................(tp) AndrewHeffernan(3) 2 71
(T G McCourt, Ire) *prom: lost pl over 6f out: rdn over 2f out: hdwy over 1f out: styd on to go 2nd post: nt rch wnr* **12/1**

6- **3** *hd* **Lynott (IRE)**[25] 7821 8-9-1 **68**..(tp) CTKeane(7) 5 73
(Gerard Keane, Ire) *s.i.s: hld up: hdwy over 6f out: rdn over 1f out: styd on* **20/1**

13-0 **4** *1* **Bute Street**[10] 172 6-8-13 **59**...................................... RichardKingscote 7 63
(Ron Hodges) *chsd ldr tl led 3f out: rdn and hdd over 1f out: no ex wl ins fnl f* **11/1**[3]

524- **5** *3 ¼* **Ravi River (IRE)**[49] 7729 7-9-1 **61**.................................. BarryMcHugh 1 60
(Brian Ellison) *hld up: rdn over 2f out: nvr on terms* **14/1**

6-11 **6** *¾* **French Hollow**[10] 172 6-9-7 **72**.. DaleSwift(5) 4 70
(Tim Fitzgerald) *hld up: nt clr run over 2f out: hdwy wl over 1f out: sn rdn: styd on same pce* **4/9**[1]

040/ **7** *12* **Bolton Hall (IRE)**[95] 5873 9-8-4 **53** oh8..................(bt) SimonPearce(3) 6 34
(Keith Goldsworthy) *sn led: hung lft fr over 4f out: rdn and hdd 3f out: wknd wl over 1f out* **40/1**

3m 7.09s (1.09) **Going Correction** +0.125s/f (Slow) **7** Ran SP% **111.6**

Speed ratings (Par 103): **101,100,100,99,97 97,90**

toteswingers:1&2:£5.80, 1&3:£8.50, 2&3:£16.80 CSF £78.44 TOTE £4.70: £1.60, £2.90; EX 66.00.

Owner Caroline Lawson and Sarah Underwood **Bred** St Clare Hall Stud **Trained** Church Broughton , Derbys

FOCUS

A modest staying handicap rated around the solid winner and the third.

Bolton Hall(IRE) Official explanation: jockey said gelding hung left

287 PLAY FREE BINGO AT BLUESQ.COM H'CAP 1m 1f 103y(P)
5:35 (5:35) (Class 5) (0-75,75) 4-Y-0+ **£1,813** (£539; £269; £134) **Stalls** Low

Form RPR

2-21 **1** **The Lock Master (IRE)**[11] 148 4-9-4 **73**...................... NeilChalmers 6 81
(Michael Appleby) *hld up: rdn over 3f out: hdwy over 1f out: r.o to ld post* **15/2**

123- **2** *nse* **Loyalty**[38] 7909 4-9-0 **69**..(v) PatrickMathers 10 77
(Derek Shaw) *hld up: hrd rdn over 1f out: fin wl: hit over hd by rivals whip nr fin* **8/1**

0-54 **3** *shd* **Veroon (IRE)**[12] 124 5-9-4 **72**.......................................(p) MickyFenton 9 80
(James Given) *hld up in tch: rdn to ld ins fnl f: hdd post* **10/1**

40-6 **4** *¾* **Brouhaha**[20] 32 7-9-7 **75**......................... RichardKingscote 8 81
(Tom Dascombe) *chsd ldr tl led over 2f out: rdn over 1f out: hdd ins fnl f: styd on* **9/2**[2]

310- **5** *nse* **Lay Claim (USA)**[28] 7985 4-9-4 **73**...............................(bp[1]) ShaneKelly 2 79
(Alan McCabe) *hld up: hdwy over 5f out: rdn and ev ch ins fnl f: styd on* **20/1**

111- **6** *nk* **Querido (GER)**[38] 7919 7-9-0 **68**......................................(t) LiamKeniry 4 74
(Gary Brown) *mid-div: hdwy over 5f out: rdn and ev ch ins fnl f: unable qck towards fin* **5/2**[1]

23-1 **7** *2 ½* **Destiny Of A Diva**[21] 23 4-9-2 **71**.......................... GrahamGibbons 5 71
(Reg Hollinshead) *chsd ldrs: rdn over 2f out: no ex fnl f* **10/1**

052- **8** *nk* **Beetuna (IRE)**[58] 7600 6-9-7 **75**............................... SamHitchcott 7 75
(David Bourton) *hld up: hdwy over 2f out: rdn over 1f out: styd on same pce* **11/2**[3]

55-6 **9** *6* **General Tufto**[20] 38 6-9-3 **71**......................................(b) MartinLane 11 58
(Charles Smith) *s.i.s: hld up: nvr on terms* **33/1**

254- **10** *nk* **Just Timmy Marcus**[44] 7837 5-8-10 **64**.......................... KellyHarrison 1 51
(Brian Baugh) *chsd ldrs: rdn over 1f out: wknd ins fnl f* **10/1**

030- **11** *¾* **Postman**[91] 7128 5-8-11 **65**..(p) TomEaves 3 50
(Bryan Smart) *led: rdn and hdd over 2f out: wknd fnl f* **14/1**

2m 1.65s (-0.05) **Going Correction** +0.125s/f (Slow) **11** Ran SP% **126.7**
WFA 4 from 5yo+ 1lb
Speed ratings (Par 103): **105,104,104,104,104 103,101,101,96,95 95**
toteswingers:1&2:£15.30, 1&3:£26.00, 2&3:£14.70. totesuper7: Win: Not won; Place: Not won. CSF £71.65 CT £623.62 TOTE £9.40: £2.80, £3.20, £4.10; EX 84.70 Trifecta £526.70 Part won. Pool of £711.82 - 0.53 winning units..
Owner K G Kitchen **Bred** Patrick F Kelly **Trained** Danethorpe, Notts

FOCUS
Another tight-knit, competitive handicap illustrated by the fact that less than two lengths separated the first six home. The form looks sound enough at face value rated around the placed horses.
T/Plt: £809.00 to a £1 stake. Pool:£69,242.19 - 62.48 winning tickets T/Qpdt: £24.20 to a £1 stake. Pool:£9,726.98 - 296.32 winning tickets CR

[267]CAGNES-SUR-MER
Monday, January 24

OFFICIAL GOING: Fibresand: standard

288a PRIX DE FORVILLE (CLAIMER) (3YO FILLIES) (FIBRESAND) 1m (F)
2:10 (12:00) 3-Y-0 **£6,465** (£2,586; £1,939; £1,293; £646)

RPR

1 **Cant Catch Cathy (IRE)**[13] 3-8-9 0................................. SylvainRuis 18 74
(P Costes, France) **17/2**

2 *2 ½* **Ulivate (IRE)**[91] 3-8-9 0.. FranckBlondel 10 69
(M Pimbonnet, France) **12/1**

3 *nk* **Danzigs Grandchild (USA)**[19] 51 3-9-0 0............ IoritzMendizabal 4 74
(J S Moore) *broke slowly and suffered interference at s: racd towards rr: hrd rdn early in st towards outside: swtchd towards rail: picked up wl: r.o wl fnl f to go 3rd fnl 100 yds: narrowly missed 2nd spot* **48/10**[1]

4 *1 ½* **Va Bene (FR)**[280] 3-8-9 0.................................... Pierre-CharlesBoudot 2 66
(J-M Capitte, France) **11/1**

5 *¾* **Nova Zarga (IRE)**[129] 3-8-9 0...............................(p) StephaneRichardot 1 64
(S Labate, France) **7/1**[3]

6 *snk* **Avenue Express (IRE)**[27] 3-9-0 0................................ FabriceVeron 11 69
(F-X De Chevigny, France) **9/1**

7 *nse* **Delictuelle (FR)**[105] 3-8-9 0... ThomasMessina 16 64
(R Le Gal, France) **23/1**

8 *2* **Ballagane (FR)** 3-8-9 0.. FabienLefebvre 7 60
(F Foresi, France) **68/1**

9 *nse* **Agonita (FR)**[21] 3-9-0 0.. RonanThomas 5 65
(Mlle S Losch, France) **22/1**

10 *½* **La Route De Lisa (FR)** 3-8-9 0...................(p) Francois-XavierBertras 8 59
(F Rohaut, France) **68/10**[2]

0 **Pinielde (FR)**[17] 3-9-0 0... ThomasHuet 12 —
(C Boutin, France) **9/1**

0 **Nessia (IRE)**[208] 3-8-5 0 ow1...................................(b) YoannRousset[(5)] 3 —
(Y Fertillet, France) **92/1**

0 **Anawin (FR)**[35] 3-8-9 0..(p) ThierryThulliez 15 —
(F Chappet, France) **27/1**

0 **Kyrnollia (FR)**[17] 3-8-9 0...(b) JohanVictoire 17 —
(J Van Handenhove, France) **13/1**

0 **Chip Leader (FR)**[35] 3-8-4 0................................... MatthieuAutier[(5)] 14 —
(R Martens, France) **50/1**

0 **Bretzele**[67] 3-9-0 0... GuillaumeMillet 9 —
(J-P Roman, France) **63/1**

0 **Bella Shara (FR)**[17] 3-8-9 0.. TonyPiccone 13 —
(D Windrif, France) **69/1**

0 **Lady D'Argentelle (FR)** 3-9-0 0.. ASuborics 6 —
(J Parize, France) **53/1**

1m 37.14s (97.14) **18** Ran SP% **117.7**
WIN (incl. 1 euro stake): 9.50. PLACES: 3.20, 4.20, 2.30. DF: 72.50. SF: 134.00.
Owner Henri Philippart **Bred** Lisselan Farms Ltd **Trained** France

[181]SOUTHWELL (L-H)
Tuesday, January 25

OFFICIAL GOING: Standard
Wind: Moderatre behind Weather: Cloudy and dry

289 TODAY'S JOCKEY SPECIALS AT BLUESQ.COM H'CAP 6f (F)
12:50 (12:51) (Class 6) (0-60,60) 4-Y-0+ **£1,535** (£453; £226) **Stalls** Low

Form RPR

64-3 **1** **Toby Tyler**[21] 37 5-9-7 **60**...(v) MickyFenton 10 70
(Paul Midgley) *towards rr: hdwy 1/2-way: rdn to chse ldrs over 1f out: styd on u.p ins fnl f: led last 100yds* **11/1**

2-22 **2** *1* **Gold Story**[12] 150 4-8-8 **52**.......................................(b) DeanHeslop[(5)] 13 59
(Brian Ellison) *in tch and rdn along on outer after 2f: hdwy and wd st: chal over 2f out and sn rdn: drvn and edgd lft ent fnl f: carried hd high and led briefly tl hdd and no ex last 100yds* **3/1**[1]

50-5 **3** *nk* **Dancing Freddy (IRE)**[14] 122 4-9-4 **60**.................(p) RobertLButler[(3)] 8 66
(Michael Chapman) *cl up: wd st: rdn 2f out: led over 1f out: hmpd and carried lft ent fnl f: sn drvn and hdd: no ex last 100yds* **33/1**

0-63 **4** *2 ¼* **Bertbrand**[16] 107 6-8-7 **46** oh1...(v) GregFairley 3 45
(Ian McInnes) *led: rdn along 2f out: drvn over 1f out: hdd & wknd ins fnl f* **20/1**

250- **5** *¾* **Convince (USA)**[127] 6261 10-9-0 **56**................... AndrewHeffernan[(3)] 12 52
(Kevin M Prendergast) *hld up towards rr: hdwy wl over 2f out: rdn and kpt on fr over 1f out: nrst fin* **12/1**

-033 **6** *½* **Errigal Lad**[12] 150 6-9-2 **55**..(p) LukeMorris 11 50
(John Balding) *prom: rdn along wl over 2f out: drvn wl over 1f out and grad wknd* **5/1**[2]

0-44 **7** *2 ¼* **Charles Parnell (IRE)**[12] 150 8-8-12 **58**........................ NoraLooby[(7)] 5 46
(Simon Griffiths) *s.i.s: a towards rr* **8/1**

-420 **8** *2 ½* **Lets Move It**[11] 166 4-9-2 **55**..(v) PatrickMathers 2 35
(Derek Shaw) *towards rr: sme hdwy on inner over 2f out: sn rdn and n.d* **11/1**

-056 **9** *1* **Flow Chart (IRE)**[12] 150 4-8-7 **46** oh1..................(b) RobbieFitzpatrick 6 22
(Peter Grayson) *prom: rdn along wl over 2f out: sn wknd* **50/1**

33-5 **10** *¾* **Hambleton**[14] 120 4-8-11 **50**..(p) TomEaves 9 24
(Bryan Smart) *dwlt: a towards rr* **11/2**[3]

05-5 **11** *¾* **Fathey (IRE)**[9] 185 5-8-8 **47**..(v) JoeFanning 4 19
(Charles Smith) *prom: rdn along over 2f out: sn drvn and wknd* **16/1**

0/4- **12** *9* **Westport**[263] 1885 8-8-11 **50**.. RobertWinston 1 —
(Robin Bastiman) *chsd ldrs: rdn along 1/2-way: sn wknd* **14/1**

1m 17.41s (0.91) **Going Correction** +0.25s/f (Slow) **12** Ran SP% **114.7**
Speed ratings (Par 101): **103,101,101,98,97 96,93,90,88,87 86,74**
toteswingers:1&2 £6.60, 2&3 £24.50, 1&3 £28.50 CSF £41.74 CT £1083.02 TOTE £19.00: £4.20, £1.70, £9.20; EX 39.80 Trifecta £182.30 Part won. Pool of £246.43 - 0.50 winning units..
Owner Anthony D Copley **Bred** Whitsbury Manor Stud **Trained** Westow, N Yorks

FOCUS
A competitive low-grade sprint handicap. Bertbrand took them along at a decent clip and as usual it paid to race close to the pace.

290 MEMBERSHIP OF SOUTHWELL GOLF CLUB (S) STKS 7f (F)
1:20 (1:21) (Class 6) 4-Y-0+ **£1,535** (£453; £226) **Stalls** Low

Form RPR

0-20 **1** **Alpha Tauri (USA)**[16] 105 5-9-5 75.....................................(t) JamesDoyle 4 80
(Frank Sheridan) *mde all: qcknd wl clr over 2f out: rdn ent fnl f: kpt on* **3/1**[2]

1/0- **2** *1 ¾* **Topcroft**[290] 1238 5-9-0 72...(v) PatrickMathers 2 70
(Derek Shaw) *s.i.s and bhd: hdwy over 2f out: sn rdn and edgd lft: styd on u.p: nt rch wnr* **5/1**[3]

0-21 **3** *½* **Army Of Stars (IRE)**[11] 159 5-9-5 71.........................(p) FrannyNorton 7 74
(James Given) *sn chsng wnr: rdn along over 2f out: drvn wl over 1f out: styd on same pce ins fnl f* **13/8**[1]

-434 **4** *4* **Elusive Warrior (USA)**[14] 122 8-8-12 67...................(p) NoraLooby[(7)] 6 63
(Alan McCabe) *chsd ldrs: rdn along over 3f out: sn one pce* **3/1**[2]

04-6 **5** *9* **Vogarth**[23] 12 7-8-11 42...(v) RobertLButler[(3)] 1 34
(Michael Chapman) *chsd ldrs: rdn along 1/2-way: sn wknd* **100/1**

300- **6** *15* **Moon Lightning (IRE)**[74] 6571 5-9-0 69.......................... PJMcDonald 5 —
(Tina Jackson) *chsd ldrs: rdn along 1/2-way: sn wknd* **20/1**

1m 32.05s (1.75) **Going Correction** +0.25s/f (Slow) **6** Ran SP% **110.5**
Speed ratings (Par 101): **100,98,97,92,82 65**
toteswingers:1&2 £2.50, 2&3 £1.80, 1&3 £1.70 CSF £17.42 TOTE £4.70: £2.30, £2.30; EX 18.30.The winner was bought in 6,500gns.
Owner Frank Sheridan **Bred** Flaxman Holdings Ltd **Trained** Wolverhampton, W Midlands
■ Stewards' Enquiry : Patrick Mathers three-day ban: used whip with excessive frequency (Feb 8-10)

FOCUS
A run-of-the-mill seller won in determined fashion.

291 PLAY GOLF BEFORE RACING H'CAP (DIV I) 1m (F)
1:50 (1:50) (Class 6) (0-65,65) 4-Y-0+ **£1,364** (£403; £201) **Stalls** Low

Form RPR

301- **1** **Steed**[44] 7845 4-9-3 **61**...(p) PhillipMakin 4 74
(Kevin Ryan) *cl up: chal over 2f out: rdn wl over 1f out: drvn ent fnl f: styd on to ld last 50yds* **15/8**[1]

1-23 **2** *½* **Bentley**[12] 148 7-9-7 **65**.. GrahamGibbons 10 77
(Brian Baugh) *sn led: rdn along over 2f out: drvn and rdr lost whip over 1f out: hdd and no ex last 50yds* **4/1**[2]

06-2 **3** *4 ½* **Gordy Bee (USA)**[19] 60 5-9-2 **60**.................................(e) FrannyNorton 6 62
(Richard Guest) *cl up: rdn along and outpcd over 2f out: sn drvn and kpt on appr fnl f* **6/1**

04-2 **4** *6* **Positivity**[22] 19 5-8-11 **55**..(p) TomEaves 2 43
(Bryan Smart) *t.k.h: trckd ldrs on inner: effrt 3f out: rdn over 2f out: sn drvn and btn wl over 1f out* **9/2**[3]

46-0 **5** *1 ½* **Buzz Bird**[21] 38 4-9-5 **63**... LeeNewman 7 47
(David Barron) *midfield: rdn along 3f out: drvn 2f out and n.d* **22/1**

6 *1 ¼* **Countess Salome (IRE)**[48] 7773 4-9-2 **60**................. RobertWinston 1 42
(Muredach Kelly, Ire) *chsd ldrs: rdn along wl over 2f out: sn drvn and btn* **20/1**

000- **7** *nk* **Spirit Of Love (IRE)**[28] 7991 4-8-12 **56**.................... WilliamCarson 9 37
(Michael Wigham) *dwlt: sn rdn along and a in rr* **16/1**

606/ **8** *5* **House Of Rules**[463] 6896 4-8-11 **55**.............................. BarryMcHugh 8 24
(Julie Camacho) *racd wd: a towards rr* **14/1**

The Form Book, Raceform Ltd, Compton, RG20 6NL

600- **9** *8* **Flores Sea (USA)**[42] 7870 7-8-13 **57**..............................(b) PJMcDonald 3 —
(Ruth Carr) *s.i.s: a bhd* **33/1**

1m 45.49s (1.79) **Going Correction** +0.25s/f (Slow) **9** Ran SP% **111.9**
Speed ratings (Par 101): **101,100,96,90,88 87,86,81,73**
toteswingers:1&2 £2.50, 2&3 £3.40, 1&3 £3.20 CSF £8.56 CT £35.52 TOTE £3.10: £2.30, £1.10, £1.60; EX 10.70 Trifecta £57.90 Pool: £379.53 - 4.85 winning units..
Owner Mrs J Ryan **Bred** Rosyground Stud **Trained** Hambleton, N Yorks

FOCUS
The first division of the 1m handicap was a competitive affair featuring some in-form performers.

292 PLAY GOLF BEFORE RACING H'CAP (DIV II) 1m (F)
2:20 (2:21) (Class 6) (0-65,65) 4-Y-0+ **£1,364** (£403; £201) **Stalls** Low

Form RPR
045- **1** **San Antonio**[70] 7474 11-9-2 **60**..............................(b) MickyFenton 9 77
(Pam Sly) *led: hdd 4f out: cl up tl led again wl over 2f out: sn rdn clr: kpt on wl* **9/1**
32-5 **2** *9* **Ubenkor (IRE)**[12] 148 6-9-7 **65**.............................. TomEaves 10 61+
(Michael Herrington) *s.i.s and bhd: hdwy on inner 2f out and sn rdn: drvn over 1f out: kpt on ins fnl f: tk 2nd nr line* **4/1**[2]
60-3 **3** *nse* **Tomintoul Star**[9] 181 5-8-8 **55**.............................. JamesSullivan(3) 7 51
(Ruth Carr) *chsd ldrs: rdn along and outpcd over 3f out: hdwy 2f out: chsd wnr over 1f out: sn drvn and no imp: lost 2nd nr line* **3/1**[1]
42-3 **4** *5* **This Ones For Eddy**[23] 9 6-9-1 **59**..............................(b) LukeMorris 4 44
(John Balding) *chsd ldrs on inner: rdn along 3f out: drvn 2f out and sn wknd* **4/1**[2]
3-00 **5** *3 ¾* **All Moving Parts (USA)**[7] 203 4-8-9 **56**..........(b) AndrewHeffernan(3) 1 32
(Alan McCabe) *in tch: rdn along 3f out: sn drvn and no imp* **8/1**[3]
020- **6** *1 ½* **Crocodile Bay (IRE)**[44] 7844 8-8-13 **57**..........(b) FrannyNorton 5 30
(Richard Guest) *cl up on inner: slt ld 1/2-way: rdn and hdd wl over 2f out: drvn and wknd wl over 1f out* **9/1**
005- **7** *4 ½* **Nurai**[167] 4970 4-8-9 **53**..............................(e[1]) LiamJones 8 15
(Paul D'Arcy) *midfield: sme hdwy 3f out: sn rdn and n.d* **20/1**
6 **8** *1 ½* **Batya (IRE)**[11] 160 4-9-5 **63**..............................(b[1]) IanMongan 3 22
(Tobias B P Coles) *midfield: rdn along 1/2-way: sn outpcd and bhd* **20/1**
000- **9** *2* **Ninth House (USA)**[67] 7501 9-8-12 **56**..............................(t) PJMcDonald 2 10
(Ruth Carr) *a in rr* **50/1**
350- **10** *22* **Sarwin (USA)**[111] 6668 8-9-2 **60**.............................. RobertWinston 6 —
(Muredach Kelly, Ire) *chsd ldrs: rdn along 1/2-way: sn wknd* **14/1**

1m 44.36s (0.66) **Going Correction** +0.25s/f (Slow) **10** Ran SP% **114.3**
Speed ratings (Par 101): **106,97,96,91,88 86,82,80,78,56**
toteswingers:1&2 £4.70, 2&3 £3.00, 1&3 £5.60 CSF £42.96 CT £128.47 TOTE £10.60: £2.20, £2.10, £1.20; EX 42.40 Trifecta £399.60 Pool: £567.01 - 1.05 winning units..
Owner Mrs P M Sly **Bred** G Reed **Trained** Thorney, Cambs

FOCUS
They went slightly less of a sedate gallop in this second division of the 1m handicap, resulting in a time nearly a second faster than the first division.

293 10% FORECAST BONUS AT BLUESQ.COM H'CAP 5f (F)
2:50 (2:50) (Class 3) (0-95,94) 4-Y-0+ **£4,533** (£1,348; £674; £336) **Stalls** High

Form RPR
600- **1** **Arganil (USA)**[28] 7993 6-9-7 **94**..............................(b) PhillipMakin 4 105
(Kevin Ryan) *dwlt and sn pushed along in rr: rdn along 1/2-way: hdwy 2f out: swtchd lft over 1f out: styd on to chal ins fnl f: led last 75yds* **3/1**[2]
03-2 **2** *½* **Waveband**[24] 2 4-9-3 **90**.............................. GrahamGibbons 5 99
(David Barron) *led on stands' rail: rdn along 2f out: drvn and hung lft ent fnl f: hdd and no ex last 75yds* **6/4**[1]
21-3 **3** *1 ¼* **Sir Geoffrey (IRE)**[24] 2 5-8-13 **86**..............................(b) IanMongan 1 91
(David Nicholls) *racd wd: chsd ldrs: hdwy over 2f out: rdn wl over 1f out: ev ch ent fnl f: sn drvn and one pce* **4/1**[3]
1-12 **4** *1* **Feelin Foxy**[13] 125 7-8-12 **85**.............................. FrannyNorton 2 86
(James Given) *cl up: effrt 2f out: sn rdn and ch tl drvn and one pce appr fnl f* **7/1**
06-4 **5** *3 ¼* **Luscivious**[24] 2 7-8-11 **87**..............................(b) BillyCray(5) 6 78
(David Nicholls) *chsd ldrs: rdn along 1/2-way: sn wknd* **11/1**
310- **6** *4* **Divertimenti (IRE)**[80] 7352 7-8-7 **80**..............................(b) JimmyQuinn [illegible] [illegible]
(Roy Bowring) *chsd ldrs: rdn along 1/2-way: sn outpcd* **14/1**

58.49 secs (-1.21) **Going Correction** 0.0s/f (Stan) **6** Ran SP% **112.5**
Speed ratings (Par 107): **109,108,106,104,99 93**
toteswingers:1&2 £2.00, 2&3 £1.60, 1&3 £2.60 CSF £7.97 TOTE £3.00: £1.20, £2.20; EX 10.60.
Owner M & Mrs C McGeever **Bred** Colt Neck Stables, Llc **Trained** Hambleton, N Yorks

FOCUS
Southwell put on a terrific programme for good quality sprint handicappers throughout the winter and this was another such event.

NOTEBOOK
Arganil(USA), who was racing off the same mark as when winning a C&D handicap a couple of winters back, came in for plenty of support on this return to 5f. Slowly away, he was driven into contention between runners with 1f to go and asserted in the last 100yds. He is likely to be pushed back up into Listed company on the back of this, but the key to him is clearly 5f on an artificial surface and he shouldn't be discounted under those conditions. (op 10-3 tchd 7-2)
Waveband was sent off favourite on the back of chasing home a horse who had followed up in a higher grade next time out. She did nothing wrong, being fast away and running right the way to the line, but just bumped into a well-treated rival. Compensation shouldn't be far away. (op 13-8 tchd 5-4)
Sir Geoffrey(IRE) travelled sweetly away from the field down the centre of the track. He just couldn't match the front two's finishing burst and is probably handicapped up to the hilt after a recent purple patch. (op 7-2 tchd 9-2)
Feelin Foxy, right at the top of her game of late, was unable to lead and ran well in the circumstances. She is yet to win here despite running creditably in all three starts. (op 13-2 tchd 8-1)

294 GOLF AND RACING AT SOUTHWELL H'CAP 5f (F)
3:20 (3:21) (Class 5) (0-75,75) 4-Y-0+ **£1,813** (£539; £269; £134) **Stalls** High

Form RPR
31-4 **1** **Sleepy Blue Ocean**[11] 165 5-8-10 **64**..............................(p) LukeMorris 3 75
(John Balding) *chsd ldrs towards far side: hdwy 2f out: rdn over 1f out: led ins fnl f: drvn out* **8/1**
310- **2** *hd* **Forever's Girl**[66] 7525 5-9-7 **75**.............................. TomEaves 11 85
(Geoffrey Oldroyd) *sn pushed along and towards rr: swtchd rt and hdwy 2f out: rdn over 1f out: styd on strly on stands' rails ins fnl f: jst hld* **18/1**
200- **3** *hd* **Bookiesindex Boy**[124] 6310 7-9-1 **71**..............................(b) FrannyNorton 4 80
(J R Jenkins) *trckd ldrs gng wl: hdwy on bit wl over 1f out: shkn up to chal and ev ch ins fnl f tl rdn and nt qckn last 75yds* **16/1**
16-2 **4** *1* **Sharp Shoes**[12] 144 4-8-13 **67**..............................(p) SamHitchcott 13 73
(Ann Duffield) *chsd ldrs: hdwy 2f out: sn rdn and kpt on same pce ent fnl f* **20/1**
004- **5** *nk* **Where's Reiley (USA)**[29] 7984 5-9-0 **68**.................... GrahamGibbons 5 73+
(David Barron) *sn outpcd and rdn along in rr: swtchd lft towards far rail 1/2-way: hdwy wl over 1f out: kpt on u.p fnl f: nrst fin* **15/2**[3]
00-0 **6** *½* **La Capriosa**[13] 133 5-9-1 **72**..............................(p) BillyCray(3) 12 75
(David Nicholls) *led: rdn along 2f out: drvn over 1f out: hdd & wknd ins fnl f* **16/1**
641- **7** *¾* **Colorus (IRE)**[29] 7984 8-9-2 **70**..............................(v) WilliamCarson 10 70
(Bill Ratcliffe) *midfield: hdwy to chse ldrs over 2f out: sn rdn and no imp appr fnl f* **14/1**
3-42 **8** *½* **Incomparable**[7] 199 6-9-3 **71**..............................(bt) IanMongan 7 69
(David Nicholls) *prom: rdn along 2f out: sn drvn and wknd appr fnl f* **10/3**[1]
153- **9** *½* **Verinco**[115] 6572 5-9-0 **73**..............................(v) AdamCarter(5) 9 70
(Bryan Smart) *prom: rdn along 2f out: sn drvn and wknd over 1f out* **10/1**
0-00 **10** *1 ¾* **Desert Strike**[10] 178 5-8-11 **65**..............................(p) RobertWinston 6 55
(Alan McCabe) *dwlt: a towards rr* **16/1**
3-02 **11** *¾* **Grudge**[7] 197 6-9-4 **72**..............................(be) HayleyTurner 8 60
(Conor Dore) *a in rr: outpcd and bhd fr 1/2-way* **7/1**[2]
00-1 **12** *¾* **Ridley Didley (IRE)**[12] 144 6-8-11 **68**.............................. PaulPickard(3) 1 53
(Noel Wilson) *prom: rdn along 2f out: sn wknd* **7/1**[2]
250- **13** *¾* **Galpin Junior (USA)**[42] 7866 5-9-2 **70**.............................. PJMcDonald 2 52
(Ruth Carr) *chsd ldrs: rdn along 1/2-way: sn wknd* **14/1**
015- **14** *nk* **First Blade**[42] 7868 5-8-11 **65**..............................(b) JimmyQuinn 14 46
(Roy Bowring) *s.i.s: a bhd* **33/1**

59.48 secs (-0.22) **Going Correction** 0.0s/f (Stan) **14** Ran SP% **124.0**
Speed ratings (Par 103): **101,100,100,98,98 97,96,95,94,91 90,89,88,87**
toteswingers:1&2 £23.20, 2&3 £52.70, 1&3 £33.20 CSF £148.39 CT £2334.47 TOTE £8.40: £2.70, £6.70, £6.10; EX 186.30 TRIFECTA Not won..
Owner Tykes And Terriers Racing Club **Bred** Exors Of The Late N Ahamad & P C Scott **Trained** Scrooby, Notts

FOCUS
A tricky contest featuring plenty of course specialists.

295 GOLF AND RACING AT SOUTHWELL MAIDEN STKS 6f (F)
3:50 (3:53) (Class 5) 3-Y-0+ **£1,910** (£564; £282) **Stalls** Low

Form RPR
36-2 **1** **Christmas Aria (IRE)**[10] 179 3-8-11 72.................... HayleyTurner 2 71
(Simon Dow) *mde most: rdn 2f out: drvn over 1f out: kpt on wl ins fnl f* **11/10**[1]
545- **2** *4 ½* **Eilean Mor**[87] 7224 3-8-11 64.............................. TomEaves 6 57
(Bryan Smart) *cl up: chal over 2f out: sn rdn and ev ch tl drvn and one pce ent fnl f* **9/4**[2]
43- **3** *4* **King Bertolini (IRE)**[42] 7869 4-9-13 0.................... PatrickMathers 1 48
(Alan Berry) *in rr: hdwy 2f out: sn rdn and edgd lft: kpt on one pce* **25/1**
4 *5* **Mcbirney (USA)** 4-9-13 0..............................(b[1]) LiamJones 7 32
(Paul D'Arcy) *chsd ldrs: rapid hdwy on outer and c lose up after 2f: rdn along over 2f out: sn wknd* **8/1**[3]
5 *23* **Marvellous City (IRE)** 3-8-11 0.............................. JimmyQuinn 5 —
(Mandy Rowland) *sn outpcd and bhd: eased fnl 2f* **9/1**
6 *23* **See Vermont** 3-8-11 0.............................. RobertWinston 4 —
(Robin Bastiman) *s.i.s: plld hrd and rapid hdwy to join ldrs after 1f: cl up tl lost pl qckly wl over 2f out: sn bhd and eased fnl 2f* **10/1**

1m 18.7s (2.20) **Going Correction** +0.25s/f (Slow)
WFA 3 from 4yo 16lb **6** Ran SP% **112.4**
Speed ratings (Par 103): **95,89,83,77,46 15**
toteswingers:1&2 £1.20, 2&3 £2.50, 1&3 £1.80 CSF £3.76 TOTE £2.20: £1.70, £1.10; EX 3.80.
Owner John Robinson and Derek Stubbs **Bred** Wiji Bloodstock & Ceka Ltd **Trained** Epsom, Surrey

FOCUS
A desperately weak maiden, even for the time of year.\n

296 PLAY FREE BINGO AT BLUESQ.COM H'CAP 1m (F)
4:20 (4:21) (Class 6) (0-60,60) 3-Y-0 **£1,535** (£453; £226) **Stalls** Low

Form RPR
-1P6 **1** **Double Duchess**[5] 227 3-9-7 **60**.............................. LiamJones 5 75+
(Paul D'Arcy) *mde all: rdn over 2f out: sn clr: easily* **5/1**[3]
06-1 **2** *9* **West Leake Melody**[9] 187 3-9-0 **53** 6ex.................... RobertWinston 4 48
(D W Hills) *trckd ldng pair: hdwy to chse wnr wl over 2f out and sn rdn: drvn wl over 1f out and kpt on same pce* **5/4**[1]
220- **3** *2* **Rath Maeve**[45] 7831 3-9-4 **60**.............................. AndrewHeffernan(3) 2 50
(Alan McCabe) *cl up: rdn along 3f out: drvn over 2f out and sn one pce* **17/2**
2342 **4** *11* **Ad Vitam (IRE)**[3] 260 3-9-3 **56**..............................(tp) LiamKeniry 6 21
(Sylvester Kirk) *sn rdn along and a towards rr* **85/40**[2]
00-0 **5** *3 ¾* **Oh What's Occuring**[15] 109 3-8-7 **46** oh1.................... KellyHarrison 1 —
(Terry Clement) *a in rr: rdn along and outpcd fr 1/2-way* **20/1**
00-0 **6** *8* **Likeable Lad**[9] 187 3-8-4 **46** oh1....................(be[1]) JamesSullivan(3) 3 —
(Ruth Carr) *a in rr: outpcd and bhd fr 1/2-way* **100/1**

1m 47.25s (3.55) **Going Correction** +0.25s/f (Slow) **6** Ran SP% **109.4**
Speed ratings (Par 95): **92,83,81,70,66 58**
toteswingers:1&2 £1.30, 2&3 £2.60, 1&3 £2.00 CSF £11.13 TOTE £6.00: £2.60, £1.10.
Owner Mrs Jan Harris **Bred** Mrs J Harris **Trained** Newmarket, Suffolk

FOCUS
A modest three-year-old handicap.
T/Jkpt: Not won. T/Plt: £258.30 to a £1 stake. Pool of £59,657.24 - 168.55 winning tickets. T/Qpdt: £46.20 to a £1 stake. Pool of £5,268.20 - 84.30 winning tickets. JR

[274]KEMPTON (A.W) (R-H)
Wednesday, January 26

OFFICIAL GOING: Standard
Wind: strong half behind Weather: overcast with light showers

297 BETDAQ JANUARY SALES CLAIMING STKS 1m 2f (P)
4:35 (4:35) (Class 6) 3-Y-0 **£1,535** (£453; £226) **Stalls** Low

Form RPR
36-5 **1** **Geordie Iris (IRE)**[11] 177 3-8-13 72.............................. DaneO'Neill 6 74
(Richard Hannon) *t.k.h: hld up: hdwy fr 3f out: swtchd out wl over 1f out: led ent fnl f: r.o wl: readily* **15/8**[1]
14-2 **2** *3 ¼* **Sheila's Star (IRE)**[9] 192 3-8-7 62.............................. LukeMorris 7 61
(J S Moore) *trckd ldrs: chal over 2f out: led wl over 1f out: hdd ent fnl f: no ex* **5/2**[2]
4-51 **3** *3 ¾* **Roi Du Boeuf (IRE)**[9] 194 3-8-4 58.............................. AliceHaynes(7) 1 58
(David Simcock) *trckd ldrs in 4th: outpcd over 2f out: styd on fr over 1f out: wnt 3rd ins fnl f* **5/1**
000- **4** *nk* **Reach Out**[139] 5892 3-8-10 47.............................. FergusSweeney 4 56?
(Brendan Powell) *trckd ldrs: rdn over 2f out: styd on same pce* **25/1**

5-20 **5** 3 1/4 **Indian Wish (USA)**[6] 234 3-8-4 63....(p) AndreaAtzeni 3 43
(Michael Quinlan) *led tl rdn wl over 1f out: fdd fnl f* **10/3**[3]

00-0 **6** 32 **I Dreamed A Dream**[21] 47 3-8-4 30....(p) LiamJones 5 —
(Dean Ivory) *s.i.s: a last but in tch: rdn over 3f out: wknd over 2f out: t.o* **66/1**

2m 9.19s (1.19) **Going Correction** +0.025s/f (Slow) **6** Ran SP% **108.4**
Speed ratings (Par 95): **96,93,90,90,87 61**
toteswingers:1&2:£1.40, 2&3:£1.60, 1&3:£2.20 CSF £6.31 TOTE £4.90: £2.10, £2.20; EX 6.90.
Owner D R Mean **Bred** Anthony Kirwin **Trained** East Everleigh, Wilts

FOCUS
A modest claimer but the form makes sense at face value rated around the first three.
Indian Wish(USA) Official explanation: jockey said filly had no more to give

298 BETDAQ MULTIPLES H'CAP 5f (P)
5:05 (5:05) (Class 5) (0-70,74) 4-Y-0+ **£2,047** (£604; £302) **Stalls** Low

Form RPR

0-52 **1** **Sherjawy (IRE)**[3] 269 7-9-0 **63**.... SamHitchcott 5 73
(Zoe Davison) *squeezed up sn after s: in tch: rdn 2f out: str run ent fnl f: led fnl 120yds: r.o wl* **7/1**[3]

/34- **2** 1 1/4 **Ability N Delivery**[52] 7746 6-9-4 **67**....(p) SeamieHeffernan 12 73+
(Michael J Browne, Ire) *wnt lft s: towards rr: rdn and hdwy fr wl over 1f out: styd on to go 2nd towards fin: nvr gng to reel in wnr* **8/1**

0-60 **3** nk **Riflessione**[11] 178 5-9-4 **67**....(b) StephenCraine 2 71
(Ronald Harris) *chsd ldrs: rdn 2f out: swtchd rt ent fnl f to chse wnr sn after: lost 2nd nr fin* **15/2**

06-0 **4** 1 1/4 **Whiskey Junction**[11] 178 7-9-4 **67**.... ShaneKelly 7 68
(Michael Quinn) *towards rr of mid-div: rdn and hdwy fr 2f out: cl up whn short of room ins fnl f: no further imp* **16/1**

434- **5** nk **Island Legend (IRE)**[85] 7285 5-9-6 **69**....(p) LukeMorris 1 68
(Milton Bradley) *led: rdn wl over 1f out: drifted lft sn after: hdd fnl 120yds: no ex* **13/2**[2]

6-42 **6** hd **Efistorm**[7] 215 10-9-7 **70**.... HayleyTurner 6 68
(Conor Dore) *mid-div: rdn and hdwy over 1f out: nt clr run briefly ent fnl f: kpt on same pce* **14/1**

0-61 **7** 3/4 **Northern Dare (IRE)**[7] 215 7-9-11 **74** 6ex.... JamieSpencer 3 69
(Richard Fahey) *sn drvn but unable to ld: chsd ldrs: hung lft on bnd fr 3f out and lost pl: nvr bk on terms* **9/4**[1]

-204 **8** hd **Fear Nothing**[3] 269 4-9-6 **69**....(b) JoeFanning 11 64
(Ian McInnes) *chsd ldrs on outer: rdn whn lost pl ent st: nvr bk on terms* **12/1**

424- **9** 2 **Fromsong (IRE)**[26] 8037 13-8-13 **62**....(p) LiamJones 4 50
(Dean Ivory) *chsd ldrs: rdn over 2f out: wknd fnl f* **16/1**

04-0 **10** 2 **Straboe (USA)**[12] 165 5-8-10 **59**....(v) WilliamCarson 9 39
(Stuart Williams) *dwlt: a struggling in rr* **8/1**

2/0- **11** 1 **Orchid Wing**[64] 7539 4-9-2 **65**....(b[1]) IanMongan 8 42
(Tobias B P Coles) *sn struggling towards rr* **50/1**

59.60 secs (-0.90) **Going Correction** +0.025s/f (Slow) **11** Ran SP% **118.7**
Speed ratings (Par 103): **108,106,105,103,103 102,101,101,98,94 93**
toteswingers: 1&2:£9.80, 2&3:£10.80, 1&3:£10.20 CSF £62.61 CT £444.54 TOTE £9.10: £2.50, £2.10, £2.90; EX 71.00.
Owner Charlie's Starrs **Bred** Darley **Trained** Hammerwood, E Sussex
■ Stewards' Enquiry : Stephen Craine caution: careless riding.

FOCUS
With several who like to force it in the line-up this handicap always threatened to be run at a strong pace and be set up for something ridden with a bit more patience. The form is rated around the placed horses.
Whiskey Junction Official explanation: jockey said gelding suffered interference

299 BETDAQ MOBILE FOR IPHONE H'CAP 1m 2f (P)
5:35 (5:35) (Class 6) (0-60,60) 4-Y-0+ **£1,535** (£453; £226) **Stalls** Low

Form RPR

1-21 **1** **No Complaining (IRE)**[12] 163 4-9-4 **59**.... JoeFanning 3 66
(Barney Curley) *in tch: gd run on inner ent st: rdn to ld jst ins fnl f: hrd pressed fnl 100yds: hld on gamely on nod* **7/2**[3]

30-3 **2** nse **Sunset Boulevard (IRE)**[12] 164 8-9-2 **55**....(b) EddieAhern 9 62
(Jim Best) *t.k.h: hld up: hdwy whn swtchd lft over 1f out: rdn for str chal ent fnl f: upsides wnr fnl 100yds: jst failed on nod* **6/1**

4-21 **3** 1 3/4 **Ice Road Trucker (IRE)**[12] 164 4-8-4 **52**....(v) NathanAlison[(7)] 4 58+
(Jim Boyle) *plld hrd: trckd ldr: rdn over 2f out: styng on and abt to chal whn snatched up ent fnl f: kpt on but no ch after* **3/1**[2]

00-5 **4** 1/2 **Etruscan (IRE)**[22] 30 6-9-3 **56**....(p) DaneO'Neill 1 59
(Chris Gordon) *led: rdn over 2f out: hdd jst ins fnl f: no ex* **14/1**

00-0 **5** 1 1/4 **Marmooq**[11] 174 8-9-5 **58**.... RobbieFitzpatrick 2 58
(Michael Attwater) *unsettled stalls: trckd ldrs: rdn wl over 1f out: ch ent fnl f: no ex* **33/1**

20-0 **6** hd **Dauntsey Park (IRE)**[16] 115 4-9-1 **56**.... FergusSweeney 6 56
(Tor Sturgis) *stdd s: bhd: hdwy over 1f out: styd on wout ever threatening* **9/1**

00-0 **7** 1 3/4 **Bibiana Bay**[12] 164 4-8-5 **46** oh1.... LukeMorris 5 42
(Gary Moore) *slowLy into stride: towards rr: short-lived effrt over 1f out* **50/1**

00-2 **8** nk **Kyle Of Bute**[8] 203 5-9-4 **57**.... J-PGuillambert 10 53
(Brian Baugh) *trckd ldrs after 1f: rdn 2f out: grad fdd* **11/4**[1]

00-0 **9** 3/4 **King Of Connacht**[8] 203 8-9-4 **57**....(v) LiamJones 7 51
(Mark Wellings) *t.k.h towards rr: rdn whn c wd ent st: no imp* **33/1**

2m 9.28s (1.28) **Going Correction** +0.025s/f (Slow)
WFA 4 from 5yo+ 2lb **9** Ran SP% **112.7**
Speed ratings (Par 101): **95,94,93,93,92 92,90,90,89**
toteswingers:1&2:£2.50, 2&3:£2.90, 1&3:£2.50 CSF £23.70 CT £68.37 TOTE £5.10: £1.40, £1.50, £3.00; EX 22.20.
Owner P A Byrne **Bred** Epona Bloodstock Ltd **Trained** Newmarket, Suffolk

FOCUS
A moderate handicap but it featured one or two in-form, improving horses. The placed horses are rated to their recent Lingfield form.
Ice Road Trucker(IRE) Official explanation: jockey said gelding hung right

300 BETDAQ MOBILE FOR ANDROID MAIDEN STKS 1m 3f (P)
6:05 (6:05) (Class 5) 3-Y-0+ **£2,047** (£604; £302) **Stalls** Low

Form RPR

0- **1** **Area Fifty One**[42] 7873 3-8-4 0.... NickyMackay 5 78
(John Gosden) *mde all: drvn clr wl over 1f out: unchal: rdn out* **9/4**[2]

2 8 **Stagecoach Danman (IRE)** 3-8-4 0.... JoeFanning 7 63
(Mark Johnston) *chsd wnr: u.p fr 5f out: no ch w wnr fr wl over 1f out: styd on same pce* **6/4**[1]

006- **3** 3/4 **Warrant**[93] 7126 3-8-4 58.... JimmyQuinn 2 62
(Jane Chapple-Hyam) *hld up last but wl in tch: hdwy on inner 3f out: sn rdn to chal for 2nd but no ch w wnr fr wl over 1f out: styd on same pce* **12/1**

5 **4** nse **Hope It Is (USA)**[18] 95 3-8-4 0.... MartinLane 9 62
(David Simcock) *hld up but wl in tch: c wdst ent st: rdn and hdwy over 2f out: styd on same pce* **9/2**[3]

6-0 **5** 11 **Larimar (IRE)**[18] 95 3-8-4 0.... LukeMorris 3 42
(Amanda Perrett) *s.i.s: sn trcking ldrs: rdn over 3f out: wknd over 2f out* **25/1**

6 **6** 1 1/2 **Western Hope (IRE)**[12] 161 4-9-6 0.... HayleyTurner 1 37
(Simon Dow) *trckd ldrs: rdn over 2f out: wknd wl over 1f out* **8/1**

060/ **7** 7 **Two Tone**[549] 4354 5-10-0 40.... KirstyMilczarek 8 30
(Garry Woodward) *s.i.s: sn trcking ldrs: rdn over 3f out: c wd ent st: sn wknd* **66/1**

2m 22.6s (0.70) **Going Correction** +0.025s/f (Slow)
WFA 3 from 4yo 24lb 4 from 5yo 3lb **7** Ran SP% **113.1**
Speed ratings (Par 103): **98,92,91,91,83 82,77**
toteswingers:1&2:£1.80, 2&3:£3.30, 1&3:£4.50 CSF £5.86 TOTE £5.40: £3.70, £2.70; EX 8.50.
Owner Martin Hughes & Michael Kerr-Dineen **Bred** Carmel Stud **Trained** Newmarket, Suffolk

FOCUS
This didn't look like it would take much winning beforehand, and a steady early pace also puts a question mark on the value of the form, which is loosely rated around the third and fourth.

301 TURFTV H'CAP 1m 4f (P)
6:35 (6:36) (Class 6) (0-65,70) 4-Y-0+ **£1,535** (£453; £226) **Stalls** Centre

Form RPR

1/ **1** **My Valley (IRE)**[179] 4610 9-9-6 **60**.... IanMongan 6 68+
(Pat Phelan) *hld up towards rr: c wd ent st: hdwy and hung rt fr 2f out: str run fnl f: led fnl stride: only pushed out* **25/1**

414- **2** hd **Beat Route**[108] 6781 4-9-1 **64**.... JemmaMarshall[(5)] 3 71
(Michael Attwater) *trckd ldrs: rdn to ld over 2f out: sn 2 l clr: kpt on but no ex whn ct fnl stride* **9/2**[2]

42-5 **3** 3/4 **Ramora (USA)**[23] 16 5-8-11 **56**.... KylieManser[(5)] 5 62
(Olivia Maylam) *mid-div: rdn and hdwy fr wl over 1f out: styd on ins fnl f* **12/1**

41-0 **4** 1 1/4 **Burnbrake**[19] 79 6-9-0 **54**....(b) JamesMillman 8 58
(Les Hall) *s.i.s: bhd: gd hdwy on outer fr over 4f out to chse ldrs: sn rdn: styd on same pce* **12/1**

55-3 **5** hd **Home**[14] 127 6-8-12 **52**.... ChrisCatlin 4 55
(Brendan Powell) *trckd ldrs: rdn to chse wnr over 2f out untl ins fnl f: no ex* **7/1**

6 3 **First Smash (GER)**[15] 2837 6-9-7 **61**....(t) SteveDrowne 13 60
(Milton Harris) *hld up towards rr: hdwy over 2f out: sn rdn and edgd lft: swtchd rt to chse ldrs 1f out: styd on* **8/1**

342- **7** 6 **Wasara**[27] 8015 4-9-3 **61**.... FergusSweeney 1 50
(Amy Weaver) *mid-div: hdwy whn nt clr run over 2f out: sn rdn and btn* **3/1**[1]

546- **8** 3 3/4 **Chaqueta**[47] 7814 4-9-0 **58**.... HayleyTurner 7 41
(Chris Wall) *trckd ldr tl rdn 3f out: wknd over 1f out* **11/2**[3]

260- **9** 1 **Magnitude**[106] 6832 6-9-4 **58**.... J-PGuillambert 10 39
(Brian Baugh) *mid-div: rdn 3f out: wknd over 1f out* **12/1**

040- **10** hd **Lady Christie**[152] 5467 4-8-6 **50** oh5.... NeilChalmers 2 31
(Michael Blanshard) *mid-div: rdn wl over 2f out: sn wknd* **66/1**

55-0 **11** 2 3/4 **Cabuchon (GER)**[24] 11 4-8-11 **55**.... JoeFanning 12 32
(Barney Curley) *led tl wl over 2f out: sn wknd* **10/1**

2m 34.63s (0.13) **Going Correction** +0.025s/f (Slow)
WFA 4 from 5yo+ 4lb **11** Ran SP% **119.7**
Speed ratings (Par 101): **100,99,99,98,98 96,92,89,89,89 87**
toteswingers:1&2:£22.30, 2&3:£13.80, 1&3:£29.00 CSF £136.76 CT £1458.47 TOTE £10.40: £2.90, £1.30, £7.70; EX 263.70.
Owner H J F Lang **Bred** John Brophy **Trained** Epsom, Surrey

FOCUS
The pace was decent thanks to handicap debutant and market drifter Cabuchon, who ensured a good gallop. The form is rated around the runner-up to the best of his previous form, backed up by the third and fourth.

302 RACING AT SKYSPORTS.COM H'CAP 6f (P)
7:05 (7:05) (Class 4) (0-85,89) 3-Y-0 **£3,561** (£1,059; £529; £264) **Stalls** Low

Form RPR

3-11 **1** **Fred Willetts (IRE)**[17] 106 3-9-6 **89**....(v) RyanClark[(5)] 4 97
(David Evans) *in tch: pushed along over 3f out: swtchd lft wl over 2f out: sn rdn: r.o strly fnl f: led fnl 30yds* **4/1**[3]

U4-3 **2** nk **Barnet Fair**[23] 20 3-8-4 **71** oh1.... KierenFox[(3)] 5 78
(Richard Guest) *hld up last: swtchd lft over 2f out: qcknd up wl to ld sn after: sn rdn: kpt on but no ex whn hdd fnl 30yds* **14/1**

41-1 **3** 3 **Stirling Bridge**[21] 44 3-8-13 **77**....(b) SteveDrowne 6 74
(William Jarvis) *trckd ldr: rdn over 2f out: kpt on same pce fnl f* **13/8**[1]

45-4 **4** 2 1/2 **Restless Bay (IRE)**[7] 208 3-8-7 **71**....(b) SamHitchcott 3 60
(Reg Hollinshead) *trckd ldrs: nt clr run over 2f out: sn rdn: kpt on same pce* **11/1**

016- **5** 1 3/4 **Toms River Tess (IRE)**[173] 4801 3-9-0 **78**.... KirstyMilczarek 2 62
(Zoe Davison) *in tch: effrt over 2f out: fdd fnl f* **25/1**

20-1 **6** nk **Liberty Green (IRE)**[18] 100 3-8-13 **77**.... JamesDoyle 7 60
(Alan McCabe) *sn pushed into early ld: rdn and hdd 2f out: fdd fnl f* **16/1**

01- **7** 1 1/2 **Mi Regalo**[28] 7999 3-9-1 **79**.... DavidProbert 1 57
(Andrew Balding) *trckd ldr: rdn over 2f out: wknd fnl f* **11/4**[2]

1m 11.67s (-1.43) **Going Correction** +0.025s/f (Slow) **7** Ran SP% **109.5**
Speed ratings (Par 99): **110,109,105,102,99 99,97**
toteswingers:1&2:£8.60, 2&3:£2.90, 1&3:£1.30 CSF £50.19 TOTE £3.70: £1.60, £5.10; EX 29.50.
Owner 24 - 7 / Gap Personnel **Bred** Liam Queally **Trained** Pandy, Monmouths

FOCUS
There was a strong pace on here and the two that appeared to be struggling most to go the gallop early were the ones who eventually benefited and came through to fight out the finish. The winner is rated to his previous Southwell form.
Mi Regalo Official explanation: jockey said gelding ran too free

303 SKYSPORTS.COM FILLIES' H'CAP 7f (P)
7:35 (7:35) (Class 5) (0-70,64) 4-Y-0+ **£2,047** (£604; £302) **Stalls** Low

Form RPR

430- **1** **Perfect Ch'I (IRE)**[27] 8014 4-9-4 **61**.... JamesDoyle 6 70
(Ian Wood) *a.p: led over 2f out: clr ent fnl f: r.o wl: rdn out* **13/2**[3]

01-1 **2** 3 **But Beautiful (IRE)**[14] 128 4-9-7 **64**.... EddieAhern 2 69+
(Robert Mills) *cl up: briefly outpcd whn short of room over 2f out: kpt on fr over 1f out: wnt 2nd wl ins fnl f: no ch w wnr* **8/11**[1]

000- **3** *1 ¼* **Pippbrook Ministar**[26] [8034] 4-8-10 **60**........................ NathanAlison(7) 3 58
(Jim Boyle) *wnt lft s: chsd ldrs: rdn over 2f out: wnt 2nd briefly ins fnl f: no ex towards fin* **33/1**

-424 **4** *½* **Bold Ring**[6] [231] 5-9-3 **60**........................ JimmyQuinn 1 56
(Edward Creighton) *trckd ldrs: rdn over 2f out: chsd wnr over 1f out: kpt on same pce fnl f* **5/1[2]**

10-6 **5** *9* **Pragmatist**[13] [143] 7-9-1 **58**........................ JamesMillman 5 30
(Rod Millman) *rrd leaving stalls: last but in tch: rdn and no imp fr over 2f out: fdd fnl f* **16/1**

30-4 **6** *½* **Profligate (IRE)**[21] [45] 4-9-7 **64**........................(b[1]) SteveDrowne 4 35
(William Jarvis) *bmpd s: sn led: rdn and hdd over 2f out: wknd over 1f out* **13/2[3]**

1m 25.72s (-0.28) **Going Correction** +0.025s/f (Slow) **6** Ran SP% **110.1**
Speed ratings (Par 100): **102,98,97,96,86 85**
toteswingers:1&2:£2.30, 2&3:£5.50, 1&3:£3.60 CSF £11.31 TOTE £6.20: £3.90, £1.10; EX 15.40.
Owner Paddy Barrett **Bred** Glencarrig Stud **Trained** Upper Lambourn, Berks

FOCUS
An interesting fillies' handicap, but the top-weight was rated 6lb below the ceiling for the race. This is rated the winner's best effort since last summer with the runner-up arguably unlucky.
Pragmatist Official explanation: jockey said mare had no more to give
T/Plt: £309.80 to a £1 stake. Pool £58,943.29 - 138.86 winning units T/Qpdt: £55.10 to a £1 stake. Pool £7,539.18 - 101.20 winning units TM

[260]LINGFIELD (L-H)
Wednesday, January 26

OFFICIAL GOING: Standard
Wind: very light, across Weather: overcast

304 BLUE SQUARE WISH CRAWLEY TOWN GOOD LUCK APPRENTICE H'CAP 7f (P)
1:25 (1:25) (Class 6) (0-60,60) 4-Y-0+ **£1,535** (£453; £226) **Stalls** Low

Form RPR

000- **1** **Ede's Dot Com (IRE)**[59] [7614] 7-9-4 **57**........................ LucyKBarry 4 64
(Pat Phelan) *in tch: rdn and effrt on outer 3f out: rdn to press ldrs wl over 1f out: styd on wl under hands and heels ins fnl f to ld fnl 50yds* **7/1**

420- **2** *nk* **Bollywood Style**[63] [7555] 6-9-0 **58**........................ IanBurns(5) 1 64
(John Best) *racd keenly: w ldrs on inner: led ent fnl 2f: rdn over 1f out: edgd rt ins fnl f: hdd and no ex fnl 50yds* **6/1[3]**

630- **3** *½* **Ivory Lace**[74] [7439] 10-9-7 **60**........................ RichardRowe 3 65
(Steve Woodman) *stdd after s: hld up wl bhd in last pair: clsd jst over 2f out: rdn and hdwy on outer ent fnl f: styd on wl to go 3rd wl ins fnl f: nt rch ldrs* **20/1**

4-41 **4** *1 ¼* **Pilgrim Dancer (IRE)**[12] [169] 4-9-4 **60**................(v) GeorgeChaloner(3) 6 61
(Patrick Morris) *t.k.h: w ldrs: ev ch ent fnl 2f: rdn and unable qck over 1f out: no ex and btn ins fnl f* **2/1[1]**

-624 **5** *hd* **Decency (IRE)**[3] [268] 4-8-13 **59**........................ DavidCoyle(7) 7 60
(Harry Dunlop) *taken down early: chsd ldrs: rdn jst over 1f out: styd on same pce ins fnl f* **8/1**

354- **6** *¾* **Laser Ruby**[35] [7972] 4-9-1 **59**........................(v[1]) ThomasBrown(5) 2 58
(Andrew Balding) *stdd after s: t.k.h: hld up in tch: effrt on inner to chse ldrs over 1f out: kpt on same pce and no imp ins fnl f* **6/1[3]**

0-00 **7** *4 ½* **Valentino Swing (IRE)**[7] [210] 8-8-13 **52**........................ NatashaEaton 8 39
(Michael Appleby) *led on outer: hdd ent fnl 2f: wknd u.p jst over 1f out: fdd ins fnl f* **14/1**

-322 **8** *nk* **Chinese Democracy (USA)**[5] [255] 4-8-9 **55**...........(v) KevinLundie(7) 5 41
(David Evans) *stdd and awkward leaving stalls: hld up wl bhd in last pair: rdn and effrt wl over 1f out: no real hdwy: wl hld fnl f* **5/1[2]**

1m 27.2s (2.40) **Going Correction** +0.15s/f (Slow) **8** Ran SP% **113.6**
Speed ratings (Par 101): **92,91,91,89,89 88,83,83**
toteswingers:1&2 £10.60, 2&3 £11.00, 1&3 £21.30 CSF £47.58 CT £797.24 TOTE £14.00. £4.10, £1.90, £3.10; EX 57.20 TRIFECTA Not won..
Owner Ede's (uk) Ltd **Bred** Maurice Burns **Trained** Epsom, Surrey

FOCUS
A moderate apprentice handicap in which there were five horses within a length or so of each other passing the furlong pole. The form is rated on the negative side.

305 DORMANSLAND MAIDEN STKS 6f (P)
1:55 (1:56) (Class 5) 3-Y-O **£1,910** (£564; £282) **Stalls** Low

Form RPR

1 **National Hope (IRE)** 3-8-9 0........................ MatthewDavies(3) 4 70
(George Baker) *s.i.s and nudged along in rr early: chsd ldng trio over 3f out: rdn and effrt on inner wl over 1f out: led u.p 1f out: sn clr: kpt on wl: eased towards fin* **13/2[3]**

3 **2** *2* **Sofias Number One (USA)**[14] [126] 3-9-3 0................ JamieSpencer 5 68
(Michael Wigham) *chsd ldng pair: effrt to press ldrs on outer bnd ent fnl 2f: pushed rt wl over 1f out and sn outpcd: rallied to chse wnr fnl 100yds: kpt on: no threat to wnr* **7/4[2]**

-3 **3** *5* **Liberal Lady**[21] [43] 3-8-12 0........................ SamHitchcott 1 47
(Jimmy Fox) *w ldr: rdn to ld over 1f out: hdd wl over 1f out: sn wknd* **25/1**

5 **4** *hd* **Beautiful Day**[11] [179] 3-9-3 0........................ PhillipMakin 2 51
(Kevin Ryan) *led: rdn and hdd wl over 1f out: wknd qckly 1f out* **11/10[1]**

40- **5** *18* **Suspender Belt**[42] [7879] 3-8-12 0........................ LukeMorris 7 —
(John Best) *bolted bef s: chsd ldrs tl dropped to last over 3f out: lost tch over 2f out: t.o ins fnl f* **14/1**

1m 12.95s (1.05) **Going Correction** +0.15s/f (Slow) **5** Ran SP% **107.8**
Speed ratings (Par 97): **99,96,89,89,65**
CSF £17.59 TOTE £5.50: £1.30, £2.30; EX 13.40.
Owner The No Hope Partnership **Bred** Oghill House Stud & Jimmy Hyland **Trained** Whitsbury, Hants

FOCUS
A weak and uncompetitive maiden, with the favourite disappointing, but they went a good pace thanks to a disputed lead.

306 HOLLOW LANE H'CAP 6f (P)
2:25 (2:25) (Class 6) (0-65,65) 4-Y-0+ **£1,535** (£453; £226) **Stalls** Low

Form RPR

60-2 **1** **Pelmanism**[12] [165] 4-9-1 **59**........................(b) PhillipMakin 8 69
(Kevin Ryan) *towards rr early: hdwy on outer gng wl 3f out: pushed along to chse ldr 2f out: rdn over 1f out: rdn to ld ins fnl f: kpt on wl* **5/2[1]**

-361 **2** *¾* **Radiator Rooney (IRE)**[7] [218] 8-8-2 **51**........................ RyanPowell(5) 2 58
(Patrick Morris) *stdd s: hld up in rr: hdwy to chse ldrs and nt clr run over 1f out: sn swtchd rt: kpt on ins fnl f to go 2nd fnl 50yds: nt rch wnr* **7/2[2]**

3-61 **3** *1* **Decider (USA)**[12] [165] 8-9-7 **65**........................(p) LukeMorris 1 69
(Ronald Harris) *wnt rt s: led and sn clr: rdn over 1f out: hdd ins fnl f: wknd towards fin* **8/1**

44-6 **4** *½* **Starwatch**[14] [134] 4-9-7 **65**........................ NeilChalmers 6 67
(John Bridger) *sn bustled along to chse ldr tl 2f out: styd on same pce fr over 1f out* **7/1**

1-40 **5** *shd* **Nubar Boy**[5] [249] 4-9-5 **63**........................(v) SeamieHeffernan 4 65
(David Evans) *in rr: clsd ent fnl 2f: effrt u.p on inner over 1f out: kpt on same pce and no imp ins fnl f* **4/1[3]**

-620 **6** *1* **Trade Centre**[5] [255] 6-8-11 **55**........................ MartinLane 7 54
(Milton Bradley) *racd off the pce in midfield: rdn along 3f out: styd on same pce and no threat to ldrs fnl 2f* **8/1**

050- **7** *4 ½* **Charles Darwin (IRE)**[57] [7639] 8-8-13 **57**........................ SteveDrowne 5 41
(Michael Blanshard) *racd off the pce in midfield: clsd over 2f out: nt clr run ent bnd 2f out: wknd over 1f out* **12/1**

1m 12.06s (0.16) **Going Correction** +0.15s/f (Slow) **7** Ran SP% **113.2**
Speed ratings (Par 101): **104,103,101,101,100 99,93**
toteswingers:1&2 £2.60, 2&3 £3.70, 1&3 £3.20 CSF £11.13 CT £58.42 TOTE £3.20: £2.50, £4.00; EX 14.00 Trifecta £26.20 Pool: £330.69 - 9.31 winning units..
Owner Guy Reed **Bred** Guy Reed **Trained** Hambleton, N Yorks

FOCUS
A modest sprint handicap, but they certainly went a decent pace thanks to Decider, who is probably the best guide to the form.

307 ENHANCED SP'S AT BLUESQ.COM H'CAP 7f (P)
2:55 (2:55) (Class 5) (0-75,74) 4-Y-0+ **£2,047** (£604; £302) **Stalls** Low

Form RPR

5-20 **1** **Lastkingofscotland (IRE)**[5] [249] 5-9-7 **74**................(b) HayleyTurner 4 82
(Conor Dore) *s.i.s: niggled along in last pair early: hdwy jst over 2f out: n.m.r and squeezed between horses 1f out: rdn to ld fnl 75yds: r.o wl* **6/1**

55-1 **2** *¾* **The Happy Hammer (IRE)**[18] [96] 5-8-11 **64**............ WilliamCarson 8 70
(Eugene Stanford) *chsd ldrs: rdn to press ldrs 2f out: edgd lft u.p over 1f out: led jst ins fnl f: hdd and one pce fnl 75yds* **9/4[1]**

00-0 **3** *nse* **Mister Green (FR)**[11] [175] 5-8-9 **62**................(bt) JamesDoyle 3 68
(David Flood) *dwlt and reminder sn after s: in tch towards rr: swtchd rt and effrt ent fnl f: kpt on wl u.p fnl 100yds* **10/1**

13 **4** *nk* **Rubenstar (IRE)**[7] [213] 8-8-13 **71**........................ RyanClark(5) 1 76
(Patrick Morris) *stdd s: hld up in rr: hdwy on outer 2f out: pressed ldrs u.p ins fnl f: kpt on* **8/1**

6-11 **5** *1* **Cat Hunter**[12] [160] 4-9-3 **70**........................ LukeMorris 7 72
(Ronald Harris) *chsd ldrs: rdn over 2f out: chsd ldr ent fnl 2f: ev ch and hrd drvn over 1f out: no ex fnl 100yds* **11/2[3]**

22-3 **6** *1* **Could It Be Magic**[19] [82] 4-8-12 **72**..................(b) GeorgeChaloner(7) 5 72
(Bill Turner) *in tch in midfield: effrt on inner over 1f out: styd on same pce and no imp ins fnl f* **4/1[2]**

3-54 **7** *¾* **Pytheas (USA)**[13] [139] 4-9-2 **69**........................(p) RobbieFitzpatrick 6 67
(Michael Attwater) *led: rdn over 2f out: kpt on u.p tl hdd jst ins fnl f: wknd fnl 100yds* **14/1**

40-3 **8** *18* **Jack O'Lantern**[23] [22] 4-8-11 **64**........................(t) JamieSpencer 2 29
(Ian Williams) *chsd ldr tl ent fnl 2f: sn lost pl: wl bhd and eased ins fnl f* **14/1**

1m 24.92s (0.12) **Going Correction** +0.15s/f (Slow) **8** Ran SP% **114.0**
Speed ratings (Par 103): **105,104,104,103,102 101,100,80**
toteswingers:1&2 £3.80, 2&3 £7.50, 1&3 £13.10 CSF £19.79 CT £133.45 TOTE £8.40: £2.70, £1.10, £3.80; EX 25.60 Trifecta £372.00 Pool: £618.49 - 1.23 winning units..
Owner Mrs Jennifer Marsh **Bred** Baronrath Stud **Trained** Cowbit, Lincs

FOCUS
A typically competitive Lingfield handicap with barely a length separating seven of the eight runners half a furlong from home. The winner has been rated to last year's best turf form.
Mister Green(FR) Official explanation: jockey said gelding missed the break
Rubenstar(IRE) Official explanation: jockey said gelding jumped awkwardly and missed the break

308 TANDRIDGE CLAIMING STKS 1m 4f (P)
3:25 (3:25) (Class 6) 4-Y-0+ **£1,535** (£453; £226) **Stalls** Low

Form RPR

56-2 **1** **Peace Corps**[5] [249] 5-8-11 73........................(vt) StephenCraine 1 77
(Jim Boyle) *led tl over 10f out: chsd ldr after tl led again over 3f out: rdn 2f out: kpt on and a holding rival ins fnl f* **9/4[2]**

66-4 **2** *3* **Sgt Schultz (IRE)**[11] [175] 8-9-9 82........................ LukeMorris 2 84
(J S Moore) *chsd ldrs: chsd wnr 3f out: rdn ent fnl 2f: unable qck and styd on same pce ins fnl f* **4/5[1]**

-636 **3** *6* **Ilie Nastase (FR)**[7] [206] 7-9-5 72........................ HayleyTurner 4 71
(Conor Dore) *chsd ldr tl led over 10f out: hdd and rdn over 3f out: 3rd and wl hld over 1f out* **11/2[3]**

/65- **4** *13* **Sagunt (GER)**[173] [842] 8-9-1 66........................ JamesDoyle 5 49
(Joanna Davis) *in tch: rdn over 4f out: toiling u.p over 3f out: lost tch over 2f out* **12/1**

430/ **5** *11* **Tifernati**[8] [1458] 7-8-9 79........................(be) FergusSweeney 3 35
(Gary Moore) *stdd s: hld up in tch in rr: clsd 5f out: rdn and toiling over 3f out: wl bhd over 2f out: eased ins fnl f* **10/1**

2m 34.24s (1.24) **Going Correction** +0.15s/f (Slow) **5** Ran SP% **118.5**
Speed ratings (Par 101): **101,99,95,86,79**
CSF £4.88 TOTE £5.20: £3.40, £1.10; EX 4.90.Peace Corps was claimed by M Gates for £6000.
Owner Elite Racing Club **Bred** Cheveley Park Stud Ltd **Trained** Epsom, Surrey

FOCUS
A moderate claimer run at a modest pace. The winner has been rated 3lb off his AW best.

309 LINGFIELD PARK MEDIAN AUCTION MAIDEN STKS 1m 4f (P)
3:55 (3:55) (Class 6) 4-6-Y-O **£1,535** (£453; £226) **Stalls** Low

Form RPR

/3-3 **1** **Kahfre**[14] [131] 4-9-3 68........................(v[1]) GeorgeBaker 1 59+
(Gary Moore) *trckd ldng pair: nt clr run over 2f out tl wl over 1f out: sn rdn to chal on inner: led ins fnl f: fnd ex u.p whn pressed ins fnl f: in command towards fin* **8/11[1]**

3-42 **2** *1 ½* **Bull Five**[14] [136] 4-9-3 67........................ J-PGuillambert 3 57
(Nick Littmoden) *stdd s: t.k.h: hld up in last pair: swtchd rt and effrt on outer 2f out: hanging left over 1f out: pressed wnr ins fnl f: nt gng pce of wnr fnl 75yds* **7/4[2]**

00-6 **3** *2 ½* **Sirdave**[20] [63] 5-9-7 53........................ WilliamCarson 2 53
(Peter Hiatt) *sn led and set stdy gallop: rdn and c centre st: drvn ent fnl f: hdd and no ex ins fnl f: btn fnl 100yds* **12/1[3]**

000- **4** *5* **Harrys**[27] [8021] 4-9-3 52........................ JimmyQuinn 5 45
(Jane Chapple-Hyam) *stdd s: hld up in last pair: outpcd and rdn over 2f out: plugged on to go 4th ins fnl f: no threat to ldrs* **25/1**

000- **5** *¾* **Set Em Up Mo**[49] [7760] 5-9-2 42........................(p) RobbieFitzpatrick 6 39
(Michael Attwater) *chsd ldr after 1f tl 2f out: sn wknd* **50/1**

40 **6** 3 ½ **Gabrielle Da Vinci**[12] 161 5-9-2 0 MartinLane 4 33
(David Evans) *chsd ldrs: effrt on outer to press ldrs over 2f out: wknd qckly over 1f out* **22/1**

2m 40.64s (7.64) **Going Correction** +0.15s/f (Slow)
WFA 4 from 5yo 4lb **6** Ran SP% **112.1**
Speed ratings: **80,79,77,74,73 71**
toteswingers:1&2 £1.10, 2&3 £2.70, 1&3 £2.20 CSF £2.15 TOTE £1.80: £1.20, £1.20; EX 2.50.
Owner SelectRacingClub.co.uk & Dr C A Barnett **Bred** Ballygallon Stud Limited **Trained** Lower Beeding, W Sussex

FOCUS
A weak maiden run at a slow early pace and the winning time was a massive 6.4 seconds slower than the claimer. The third and fifth limit the level.

310 PLAY RAINBOW RICHES AT BLUESQ.COM H'CAP 1m (P)
4:25 (4:25) (Class 5) (0-75,72) 4-Y-0+ **£2,047** (£604; £302) **Stalls** High

Form RPR

3-52 **1** **Lockantanks**[5] 249 4-9-4 **69** NeilChalmers 8 80+
(Michael Appleby) *hld up in tch: gng wl: nt clr run ent fnl 2f: shkn up and qcknd to chal 1f out: led ins fnl f: r.o strly and sn in command: readily* **9/2**[2]

3-44 **2** 2 ¼ **Tuxedo**[7] 206 6-9-6 **71** (b) RobertWinston 4 76+
(Peter Hiatt) *hld up in tch in last pair: nt clr run jst over 2f out tl over 1f out: hdwy u.p 1f out: chsd clr wnr wl ins fnl f: no threat to wnr* **7/1**

1-63 **3** 1 **Lisahane Bog**[7] 206 4-9-5 **70** (b) JimmyQuinn 7 73
(Peter Hedger) *v.s.a and sn bustled along: reminders 4f out: hdwy u.p on inner over 1f out: nt gng pce of wnr ins fnl f* **11/2**[3]

4-13 **4** ½ **Scary Movie (IRE)**[11] 174 6-9-7 **72** DavidProbert 2 74
(Ronald Harris) *hld up wl in tch: rdn and effrt to chal jst over 1f out: led jst ins fnl f: sn hdd and nt gng pce of wnr: lost 2 pls fnl 50yds* **6/1**

21-3 **5** 1 ½ **One Oi**[21] 48 6-8-11 **62** ChrisCatlin 3 60
(David Arbuthnot) *chsd ldrs on outer: effrt ent fnl 2f: ev ch u.p jst over 2f out: outpcd and btn ins fnl f* **4/1**[1]

400- **6** 1 **Prince Of Thebes (IRE)**[51] 7724 10-9-1 **69** KierenFox(3) 6 65
(Michael Attwater) *chsd ldr: rdn and ev ch 2f out tl wknd qckly jst ins fnl f* **16/1**

04-6 **7** 1 ¾ **Masked Dance (IRE)**[20] 58 4-9-7 **72** PhillipMakin 5 64
(Kevin Ryan) *led: rdn and hrd pressed 2f out: hdd jst ins fnl f: sn wknd* **12/1**

05-2 **8** 2 ¼ **Charlie Smirke (USA)**[19] 82 5-9-6 **71** (bt) GeorgeBaker 1 58
(Gary Moore) *in tch in midfield: effrt on inner over 1f out: wknd qckly jst ins fnl f* **4/1**[1]

1m 38.52s (0.32) **Going Correction** +0.15s/f (Slow) **8** Ran SP% **113.9**
Speed ratings (Par 103): **104,101,100,100,98 97,96,93**
toteswingers:1&2 £9.10, 2&3 £10.60, 1&3 £6.30 CSF £35.40 CT £176.51 TOTE £7.90: £2.40, £2.00, £2.50; EX 42.50 Trifecta £423.70 Pool: £687.13 - 1.20 winning units..
Owner Dallas Racing **Bred** Jeremy Green And Sons **Trained** Danethorpe, Notts

FOCUS
An ordinary handicap and the pace looked nothing special, but the last three horses at halfway were the first three home. The runner-up is the guide to the form.
T/Plt: £54.90 to a £1 stake. Pool of £51,026.47 - 678.28 winning tickets. T/Qpdt: £2.50 to a £1 stake. Pool £5,180.98 - 1,489.44 winning tickets. SP

[297]KEMPTON (A.W) (R-H)
Thursday, January 27

OFFICIAL GOING: Standard
Wind: Strong, across towards stands Weather: Overcast, cold

311 WATCH RACING UK ON SKY 432 H'CAP 6f (P)
4:50 (4:51) (Class 7) (0-50,56) 4-Y-0+ **£1,535** (£453; £226) **Stalls** Low

Form RPR

-014 **1** **Jonny Ebeneezer**[3] 276 12-9-9 **56** 6ex (be) JamesDoyle 4 62
(David Flood) *trckd ldng trio: prog to chal over 1f out: chsd ldr after: hung lft but styd on last 100yds to ld fnl strides* **3/1**[1]

00-0 **2** hd **Jessica Wigmo**[8] 211 8-8-9 **45** KierenFox(3) 6 50
(Tony Carroll) *stdd s: hld up in last pair: prog on outer over 2f out: led over 1f out: looked sure to win ins fnl f: edgd lft and hdd last strides* **13/2**

6-00 **3** 1 ¼ **Mr Funshine**[6] 250 6-8-13 **46** MartinLane 1 47
(Derek Shaw) *rrng s: hld up in last pair: prog on outer over 1f out: styd on to chse ldng pair last 150yds: kpt on same pce* **12/1**

046- **4** nse **Novastasia (IRE)**[47] 7835 5-8-12 **45** (b) SamHitchcott 9 46
(Dean Ivory) *awkward s: sn chsd ldng pair: lost pl and rdn jst over 2f out: tried to rally over 1f out but sn nt qckn: kpt on again and nrly snatched 3rd: awkward ride* **6/1**[3]

0-50 **5** 1 ¼ **Ariel Bender**[7] 224 4-8-12 **45** (b) RobbieFitzpatrick 3 42
(Peter Grayson) *led: drvn over 2f out: hdd and btn over 1f out* **33/1**

0-03 **6** 1 ½ **Gilderoy**[13] 167 4-8-12 **45** (be) RobertWinston 7 37
(Dominic Ffrench Davis) *chsd ldrs in 5th: rdn over 2f out: no prog over 1f out: fdd* **7/2**[2]

5-40 **7** nk **Southwark Newshawk**[6] 256 4-8-12 **45** WilliamCarson 8 36
(Christine Dunnett) *t.k.h early: chsd ldr to 2f out: sn btn* **33/1**

0-05 **8** 4 ½ **Quahadi (IRE)**[3] 280 5-8-12 **45** (t) DaneO'Neill 5 22+
(Chris Gordon) *stdd s: hld up in last pair: appeared nt to have clr run over 2f out and over 1f out: wknd* **3/1**[1]

1m 13.86s (0.76) **Going Correction** 0.0s/f (Stan) **8** Ran SP% **113.4**
Speed ratings (Par 97): **94,93,92,92,90 88,87,81**
toteswingers:1&2 £4.80, 2&3 £13.30, 1&3 £6.70 CSF £22.63 CT £201.05 TOTE £6.00: £2.50, £2.10, £4.30; EX 23.30.
Owner DM Partnership **Bred** John Purcell **Trained** Exning, Suffolk

FOCUS
A low-grade handicap with all bar the fourth offically wrong at the weights. The race is rated around her.

312 BISTRO PRICES FROM £42 H'CAP 7f (P)
5:20 (5:20) (Class 7) (0-50,50) 4-Y-0+ **£1,535** (£453; £226) **Stalls** Low

Form RPR

30-2 **1** **Hi Spec (IRE)**[7] 229 8-9-1 **48** (t) AdamKirby 3 57
(Mandy Rowland) *hld up in 10th: prog 2f out: pushed into ld jst ins fnl f: shkn up and in command after: eased last strides* **7/1**

0-20 **2** nk **Kenswick**[7] 229 4-8-11 **49** (v) TobyAtkinson(5) 2 56
(Pat Eddery) *hld up last: prog fr 2f out: clsng whn checked briefly 1f out: styd on to take 2nd last 100yds: clsd: readily hld* **10/1**

0-02 **3** 1 **Crystallize**[8] 211 5-8-12 **45** FergusSweeney 1 49
(Andrew Haynes) *hld up in last quartet: threaded through rivals fr 2f out to chal over 1f out: styd on same pce last 150yds* **6/1**[3]

-550 **4** shd **Norcroft**[8] 204 9-9-1 **48** (p) WilliamCarson 4 52
(Christine Dunnett) *hld up in last quartet: prog 2f out: led jst over 1f out tl jst ins fnl f: nt qckn* **10/1**

30-0 **5** 1 ¼ **Boundless Applause**[8] 204 5-8-12 **45** JamesDoyle 6 45
(Ian Wood) *hld up in midfield: nt qckn 2f out: cl enough 1f out: outpcd after* **11/1**

3-30 **6** shd **A Pocketful Of Rye (IRE)**[8] 204 4-8-8 **48** LauraSimpson(7) 10 48
(Jane Chapple-Hyam) *racd wd in midfield: nt qckn 2f out: pushed along and kpt on same pce after* **12/1**

0-54 **7** ½ **My Best Man**[6] 250 5-8-10 **46** KierenFox(3) 7 45
(Tony Carroll) *t.k.h: led: pressed over 2f out: hdd jst over 1f out: sn btn* **7/2**[1]

504- **8** 1 ½ **Royal Acclamation (IRE)**[185] 4434 6-8-9 **49** (p) DavidKenny(7) 12 44
(Michael Scudamore) *t.k.h: racd wd: pressed ldrs: chal over 2f out: stl upsides jst over 1f out: wknd rapidly* **11/1**

00-2 **9** shd **Holyfield Warrior (IRE)**[8] 204 7-9-0 **50** AndrewHeffernan(3) 5 44
(Ralph Smith) *trckd ldrs on inner: snatched up 1/2-way: effrt 2f out: no prog 1f out: wknd* **9/2**[2]

0-65 **10** 4 ½ **Mororless**[8] 211 4-9-3 **50** (p) SamHitchcott 11 32
(Zoe Davison) *t.k.h: trckd ldr after 2f tl over 2f out: sn wknd u.p* **33/1**

06-0 **11** 1 ½ **Daily Double**[21] 70 5-8-12 **45** (v) MartinLane 8 23
(Martin Bosley) *t.k.h: chsd ldr 2f: rdn over 2f out: no prog over 1f out: wknd* **25/1**

1m 26.78s (0.78) **Going Correction** 0.0s/f (Stan) **11** Ran SP% **116.5**
Speed ratings (Par 97): **95,94,93,93,91 91,91,89,89,84 82**
toteswingers:1&2 £8.00, 2&3 £9.30, 1&3 £5.60 CSF £74.36 CT £347.96 TOTE £8.70: £3.20, £4.30, £1.20; EX 34.20.
Owner Miss M E Rowland **Bred** Mrs Marita Rogers **Trained** Lower Blidworth, Notts

FOCUS
Quite a competitive if moderate handicap, and straightforward form.
Crystallize Official explanation: jockey said gelding lost a near-fore shoe
Boundless Applause Official explanation: jockey said mare was denied a clear run

313 BETDAQ THE BETTING EXCHANGE MEDIAN AUCTION MAIDEN STKS 7f (P)
5:50 (5:51) (Class 6) 3-5-Y-0 **£1,535** (£453; £226) **Stalls** Low

Form RPR

236- **1** **Yes Chef**[142] 5838 4-9-12 72 JamesMillman 1 74
(Rod Millman) *taken down early: sn trckd ldr: clsd 2f out: cajoled along after: eventually persuaded to ld ins fnl f: dwindling advantage nr fin* **6/4**[1]

00- **2** nk **Cold Secret**[228] 3000 3-8-10 0 ow2 RobertWinston 9 70
(David Elsworth) *chsd ldrs in 5th: rdn 1/2-way: prog to take 3rd over 1f out: styd on to chse wnr last 75yds: clsng at fin* **16/1**

20-0 **3** 1 ¾ **Primo De Vida (IRE)**[6] 249 4-9-5 74 (p) NathanAlison(7) 3 68
(Jim Boyle) *led: shkn up over 2f out: pressed over 1f out: hdd ins fnl f: wknd and lost 2nd last 75yds* **8/1**

00- **4** 2 ¾ **Stoppers (IRE)**[271] 1685 4-9-12 0 EddieAhern 2 61
(Robert Mills) *settled in 7th and off the pce: pushed along and stdy prog over 2f out: tk 4th ins fnl f: possible improver* **9/1**

4-5 **5** 3 **Moresweets 'n Lace**[8] 214 4-9-7 0 GeorgeBaker 5 48
(Gary Moore) *restless stalls: mostly in same pl: shkn up and no prog over 2f out: n.d* **5/1**[2]

26-3 **6** nk **Foxtrot Golf (IRE)**[7] 228 3-8-8 68 (p) FergusSweeney 8 47
(Peter Winkworth) *racd wd: chsd ldng pair: hung lft bnd 3f out: wknd tamely fnl 2f* **8/1**

7 13 **Byrons Beau (IRE)** 3-8-5 0 KierenFox(3) 4 12
(Brett Johnson) *rn green and sn struggling in last pair: a bhd: t.o* **12/1**

0 **8** nk **Main Attraction**[13] 158 4-9-7 0 IanMongan 7 11
(Tobias B P Coles) *dwlt: chsd ldng trio: rdn 1/2-way: wknd over 2f out: t.o* **50/1**

9 6 **Sole Bay** 3-8-4 0 ow1 HayleyTurner 6 —
(David Elsworth) *s.s: rn green: a last and wl bhd: t.o* **7/1**[3]

1m 26.13s (0.13) **Going Correction** 0.0s/f (Stan)
WFA 3 from 4yo 18lb **9** Ran SP% **116.9**
Speed ratings (Par 101): **99,98,96,93,90 89,74,74,67**
toteswingers:1&2 £10.70, 2&3 £9.80, 1&3 £3.20 CSF £29.82 TOTE £2.60: £1.10, £5.50, £3.00; EX 47.70.
Owner Coombeshead Racing **Bred** Percys (north Harrow) Ltd **Trained** Kentisbeare, Devon
■ Stewards' Enquiry : Robert Winston four-day ban: weighed in 2lb heavy (Jan 10-14)

FOCUS
A modest maiden, though it was quicker than the previous handicap. The form is rated around the third.
Foxtrot Golf(IRE) Official explanation: jockey said gelding hung left

314 WATCH RACING LIVE @ RACINGUK.COM H'CAP 2m (P)
6:20 (6:21) (Class 5) (0-75,68) 4-Y-0+ **£2,047** (£604; £302) **Stalls** Low

Form RPR

50-1 **1** **Muzo (USA)**[15] 127 5-9-12 **66** FrannyNorton 5 82+
(Chris Dwyer) *trckd clr ldr after 6f: clsd 4f out: led over 2f out but sn pressed: rdn clr over 1f out* **9/2**

46-1 **2** 6 **Inside Knowledge (USA)**[23] 33 5-9-3 **57** KirstyMilczarek 3 68+
(Garry Woodward) *hld up in last: prog to go 3rd 7f out: clsd 4f out: chsd wnr over 2f out and tried to chal: lft bhd over 1f out* **5/2**[1]

3 20 **Galant Star (FR)**[25] 5-10-0 **68** GeorgeBaker 4 53
(Gary Moore) *in tch: nt gng wl bef 1/2-way: struggling in last pair 7f out: plodded into remote 3rd ins fnl f* **10/1**

5-50 **4** 3 ¼ **Calculating (IRE)**[8] 209 7-9-13 **67** DaneO'Neill 6 48
(Mark Usher) *led at gd pce and sn clr: hdd & wknd rapidly over 2f out: lost remote 3rd ins fnl f* **3/1**[2]

23-2 **5** 31 **Master At Arms**[20] 89 8-10-0 **68** EddieAhern 1 12
(Daniel Mark Loughnane, Ire) *chsd ldr 6f: sn pushed along and lost pl: wl bhd in last 5f out: t.o* **7/2**[3]

06- **6** 11 **Lindsay's Dream**[96] 3267 5-9-2 **56** SamHitchcott 2 —
(Zoe Davison) *in tch: drvn and wknd rapidly over 5f out: t.o* **10/1**

3m 28.42s (-1.68) **Going Correction** 0.0s/f (Stan) **6** Ran SP% **112.2**
Speed ratings (Par 103): **104,101,91,89,73 68**
toteswingers:1&2 £1.90, 2&3 £4.60, 1&3 £5.40 CSF £16.11 TOTE £6.10: £2.50, £3.10; EX 15.40.
Owner Mrs Shelley Dwyer **Bred** Stonestreet Thoroughbred Holdings LLC **Trained** Burrough Green, Cambs

FOCUS
They went a fair enough gallop for this 2m handicap and two ended up drawing clear. Both are rated better than the bare form.

Master At Arms Official explanation: jockey said, regarding running and riding, that his orders were, if there was no pace, to make the running.

315 BOOK FOR RACING POST CHASE DAY H'CAP 1m 4f (P)
6:50 (6:51) (Class 5) (0-75,75) 4-Y-0+ **£2,047** (£604; £302) **Stalls** Centre

Form RPR
140- **1** **Taaresh (IRE)**[229] 2961 6-9-10 **75** .... JoeFanning 2 88+
(Kevin Morgan) *trckd ldrs on inner: led 2f out: sn rdn wl clr: 6 l ahd ins fnl f: eased last 50yds* **8/1**
60- **2** *4 ½* **Roilos (IRE)**[51] 7732 5-9-1 **66** .... (t) AndreaAtzeni 7 69
(Michael Wigham) *v awkwardly away: sn in tch in last: effrt 3f out: chsd ldng pair 2f out: kpt on to take 2nd nr fin* **16/1**
21-2 **3** *½* **Archie Rice (USA)**[13] 162 5-8-12 **68** .... RyanClark(5) 1 70
(Tom Keddy) *led 4f: led again 6f out: kicked on 3f out: hdd 2f out and no ch w wnr: lost 2nd nr fin* **7/2**[3]
044- **4** *7* **Encircled**[54] 7687 7-9-10 **75** .... EddieAhern 5 66
(J R Jenkins) *hld up in 5th: taken to outer 1/2-way: sweeping move on wd outside bnd over 3f out: chsd ldng pair briefly over 2f out: sn btn* **9/2**
2-3 **5** *hd* **Al Amaan**[23] 32 6-9-8 **73** .... GeorgeBaker 6 64
(Gary Moore) *prog to ld after 4f tl after 6f: pressed ldr after: rdn and nt qckn wl over 2f out: sn wknd* **5/2**[1]
14-2 **6** *21* **The Winged Assasin (USA)**[10] 190 5-9-3 **68** .... (t) RussKennemore 4 25
(Shaun Lycett) *pressed ldr 4f: nvr looked happy after: rdn 4f out: dropped to last wl over 2f out: t.o* **3/1**[2]

2m 33.29s (-1.21) **Going Correction** 0.0s/f (Stan) **6** Ran SP% **111.0**
WFA 4 from 5yo+ 4lb
Speed ratings (Par 103): **104,101,100,96,95 81**
toteswingers:1&2 £19.30, 2&3 £12.20, 1&3 £5.60 CSF £105.67 TOTE £7.60: £2.40, £8.90; EX 90.70.
Owner Roemex Ltd **Bred** Shadwell Estate Company Limited **Trained** Newmarket, Suffolk

FOCUS
The early pace was a steady one, but it gradually increased. The impressive winner took his form to a new high, though there are doubts over what else ran their races.
The Winged Assasin(USA) Official explanation: jockey said gelding ran flat

316 KEMPTON.CO.UK H'CAP 6f (P)
7:20 (7:20) (Class 4) (0-85,85) 4-Y-0+ **£3,885** (£1,156; £577; £288) **Stalls** Low

Form RPR
61-3 **1** **Clear Praise (USA)**[15] 134 4-8-11 **75** .... HayleyTurner 12 90+
(Simon Dow) *dropped in fr wd draw and hld up last: taken wd and gd prog jst over 2f out: swept into the ld ent fnl f: sn wl in command* **11/2**[2]
20-4 **2** *1 ½* **Vintage (IRE)**[5] 265 7-9-0 **78** .... IanMongan 6 85
(John Akehurst) *led at gd pce: hrd pressed over 1f out: hdd ent fnl f: kpt on: no ch w wnr* **9/2**[1]
152- **3** *shd* **Ebraam (USA)**[29] 7998 8-9-6 **84** .... AndreaAtzeni 10 91+
(Ronald Harris) *hld up in 7th on outer: lost pl 2f out: prog over 1f out: styd on wl ins fnl f: nrly snatched 2nd* **16/1**
50-3 **4** *1 ½* **Dark Lane**[13] 168 5-8-12 **76** .... (v[1]) BarryMcHugh 5 78
(Richard Fahey) *t.k.h: chsd ldr: tried to chal fr 2f out: nrly upsides over 1f out: nt qckn and sn btn* **8/1**
10-4 **5** *¾* **Ray Of Joy**[15] 125 5-9-7 **85** .... DavidProbert 1 84
(J R Jenkins) *chsd ldng quartet: shkn up 2f out: tried to cl over 1f out: nt qckn: fdd* **13/2**
1-24 **6** *hd* **Methaaly (IRE)**[13] 168 8-8-6 **77** .... (be) JosephYoung(7) 3 76
(Michael Mullineaux) *chsd ldrs: urged along over 2f out: sn lost pl: kpt on one pce ins fnl f* **6/1**[3]
24-3 **7** *shd* **Lujeanie**[20] 87 5-9-4 **82** .... (p) AdamKirby 9 81
(Dean Ivory) *hld up in 8th: prog on inner 2f out: nvr able to chal and effrt petered out ins fnl f* **8/1**
03-1 **8** *1* **Diriculous**[20] 87 7-9-7 **85** .... JoeFanning 7 80
(Robert Mills) *t.k.h: trapped wd chsng ldng trio: nt qckn 2f out: steadily lost pl* **9/2**[1]
240- **9** *2 ¼* **Lucky Mellor**[234] 2822 4-8-13 **77** .... SamHitchcott 8 65
(Dean Ivory) *hld up in 8th: [illegible] on inner 2f out: no prog* **40/1**
300- **10** *½* **Bahamian Lad**[100] [illegible] [illegible] **76** .... (p) [illegible] 1 [illegible]
(Reg Hollinshead) *t.k.h: chsd ldng pair to over 1f out: wknd qckly* **25/1**

1m 11.37s (-1.73) **Going Correction** 0.0s/f (Stan) **10** Ran SP% **113.8**
Speed ratings (Par 105): **111,109,108,106,105 105,105,104,101,100**
toteswingers:1&2 £7.90, 2&3 £16.00, 1&3 £16.40 CSF £29.66 CT £380.29 TOTE £9.70: £2.30, £1.50, £3.60; EX 41.40.
Owner Chua, Moore, Goalen & Warner **Bred** Juddmonte Farms Inc **Trained** Epsom, Surrey

FOCUS
A wide-open sprint handicap run at a decent gallop and in a good time. There is more to come from the winner.
Lujeanie Official explanation: jockey said gelding had no more to give

317 BETDAQ ON 0870 178 1221 H'CAP 1m (P)
7:50 (7:51) (Class 6) (0-60,60) 4-Y-0+ **£1,535** (£453; £226) **Stalls** Low

Form RPR
40-5 **1** **Mr Chocolate Drop (IRE)**[13] 169 7-9-2 **55** .... (t) AdamKirby 4 66
(Mandy Rowland) *hld up in 7th: stdy prog over 2f out: rdn to ld 1f out: sn clr* **5/1**[1]
00-0 **2** *3* **French Art**[14] 148 6-9-7 **60** .... (p) EddieAhern 3 64
(Nigel Tinkler) *trckd ldrs in 6th: effrt over 2f out: rdn to chal jst over 1f out: chsd wnr ins fnl f: one pce* **6/1**[3]
00-3 **3** *nk* **El Libertador (USA)**[17] 111 5-9-0 **58** .... (p) TobyAtkinson(5) 5 61
(Jeremy Gask) *hld up in 8th: stdy prog over 2f out: c to chal jst over 1f out: rdn and fnd nil* **5/1**[1]
00-0 **4** *2 ¼* **Spinning Ridge (IRE)**[17] 111 6-9-6 **59** .... (v) DavidProbert 7 57
(Ronald Harris) *s.i.s: t.k.h and scythed through field: led over 4f out and sn clr: hung bdly lft jst over 1f out: hdd & wknd 1f out* **10/1**
360/ **5** *1 ¼* **Lennie Briscoe (IRE)**[485] 6358 5-9-3 **56** .... (t) GeorgeBaker 11 51
(Martin Bosley) *stdd s: hld up in last pair: pushed along over 2f out: nt knocked abt: styd on to take 5th nr fin* **10/1**
42-0 **6** *½* **Yakama (IRE)**[8] 211 6-8-13 **55** .... (v) KierenFox(3) 12 49
(Christine Dunnett) *hld up in last trio and racd wd: rdn and struggling over 2f out: sme modest hdwy over 1f out* **14/1**
00-6 **7** *1 ½* **Scruffy Skip (IRE)**[6] 255 6-9-4 **57** .... (p) WilliamCarson 10 48
(Christine Dunnett) *led 100yds: reminders in 3rd sn after 1/2-way: stl cl up but racd awkwardly over 1f out: fdd* **33/1**
006- **8** *1 ¼* **Sunset Place**[106] 6856 4-9-4 **57** .... (v[1]) SteveDrowne 8 45
(Jonathan Geake) *pushed up to ld after 100yds: hdd over 4f out: wknd over 1f out* **12/1**
64-0 **9** *½* **Munich (IRE)**[23] 30 7-9-5 **58** .... (p) DaneO'Neill 6 45
(Roger Curtis) *s.i.s: hld up in last pair: rdn over 2f out: nvr a factor* **8/1**
2-00 **10** *4* **Vezere (USA)**[15] 135 4-9-5 **58** .... (p) IanMongan 1 36
(Simon Dow) *chsd ldng trio: rdn wl over 2f out: wknd over 1f out* **10/1**
20-0 **11** *2* **Pha Mai Blue**[14] 139 6-9-7 **60** .... (v) NickyMackay 9 33
(Jim Boyle) *t.k.h: racd wd: chsd ldng quartet: hung lft bnd 3f out: sn wknd* **11/2**[2]

1m 39.64s (-0.16) **Going Correction** 0.0s/f (Stan) **11** Ran SP% **118.7**
Speed ratings (Par 101): **100,97,96,94,93 92,91,89,89,85 83**
toteswingers:1&2 £4.40, 2&3 £4.30, 1&3 £1.90 CSF £34.98 CT £141.80 TOTE £5.90: £1.50, £4.00, £2.50; EX 30.90.
Owner Miss M E Rowland **Bred** P J Munnelly **Trained** Lower Blidworth, Notts

FOCUS
The pace was again a fair one. A modest handicap and it's doubtful it took much winning.
Mr Chocolate Drop(IRE) Official explanation: two-day ban: used whip in incorrect place (Feb 10-11)
Pha Mai Blue Official explanation: jockey said gelding hung left
T/Plt: £1,454.20 to a £1 stake. Pool of £72,313.97 - 36.30 winning tickets. T/Qpdt: £628.50 to a £1 stake. Pool of £9,088.59 - 10.70 winning ticket. JN

289 SOUTHWELL (L-H)
Thursday, January 27

OFFICIAL GOING: Standard
Wind: Light across Weather: Overcast

318 PLACE ONLY BETTING AT BLUESQ.COM FILLIES' H'CAP 5f (F)
1:00 (1:00) (Class 5) (0-70,69) 4-Y-0+ **£2,115** (£624; £312) **Stalls** High

Form RPR
000- **1** **Six Wives**[103] 6932 4-8-13 **64** .... AndrewHeffernan(3) 6 76
(David Nicholls) *mde all: rdn and qcknd clr over 1f out: r.o strly* **6/1**
06-0 **2** *3* **Nollaig Shona (IRE)**[14] 143 4-8-13 **61** .... (v[1]) KirstyMilczarek 5 62
(George Prodromou) *trckd wnr: effrt 2f out: sn rdn and ch tl drvn and kpt on same pce appr fnl f* **13/2**
-132 **3** *¾* **Kheley (IRE)**[11] 185 5-8-7 **55** .... ShaneKelly 1 54
(Mark Brisbourne) *chsd ldrs: rdn along 2f out: drvn over 1f out: kpt on same pce* **9/4**[1]
52-1 **4** *5* **Caramelita**[21] 62 4-9-7 **69** .... StephenCraine 4 50
(J R Jenkins) *dwlt: hdwy over 2f out: sn rdn to chse ldrs: drvn and no imp fr wl over 1f out* **7/2**[3]
0/0- **5** *nk* **Little Pandora**[114] 6644 7-8-7 **55** oh10 .... (b) DuranFentiman 8 34
(Lee James) *s.i.s and sn rdn along in rr: sme hdwy u.p fnl 2f: nvr a factor* **100/1**
004- **6** *1 ¾* **Dancing Wave**[37] 7952 5-8-0 **55** oh10 .... JackDuern(7) 2 28
(Michael Chapman) *a towards rr: outpcd and bhd fr 1/2-way* **33/1**
16-3 **7** *1 ¾* **Fashion Icon (USA)**[21] 62 5-9-2 **64** .... (b) JoeFanning 3 31
(David O'Meara) *s.i.s: hdwy on outer and in tch 1/2-way: sn rdn and btn wl over 1f out* **10/3**[2]
00-0 **8** *1 ½* **Six Diamonds**[15] 133 4-9-0 **65** .... (t) RobertLButler(3) 7 26
(Paddy Butler) *racd stands' rail: chsd ldrs: rdn along bef 1/2-way: sn wknd* **33/1**

59.32 secs (-0.38) **Going Correction** 0.0s/f (Stan) **8** Ran SP% **110.6**
Speed ratings (Par 100): **103,98,97,89,88 85,82,80**
toteswingers:1&2 £7.70, 2&3 £2.90, 1&3 £4.10 CSF £40.75 CT £108.22 TOTE £5.90: £2.20, £1.10, £1.50; EX 40.60 Trifecta £314.90 Pool £493.69 - 1.16 winning units..
Owner Sexy Six Partnership **Bred** Cheveley Park Stud Ltd **Trained** Sessay, N Yorks

FOCUS
A low-grade fillies' sprint handicap, where it paid to race up with the pace. The winner is rated back to her C&D nursery form.

319 MEMBERSHIP OF SOUTHWELL GOLF CLUB MEDIAN AUCTION MAIDEN STKS 1m (F)
1:30 (1:30) (Class 6) 3-5-Y-O **£1,535** (£453; £226) **Stalls** Low

Form RPR
34-4 **1** **Ya Hafed**[13] 171 3-8-6 66 .... ChrisCatlin 6 59
(Ed Dunlop) *mde all: rdn wl over 1f out: clr ent fnl f* **4/6**[1]
0- **2** *3 ¾* **Baileys Agincourt**[85] 7302 3-8-6 0 .... JoeFanning 1 50
(Mark Johnston) *dwlt: sn trcking ldrs: pushed along and outpcd wl over 2f out: swtchd rt and rdn wl over 1f out: kpt on to take 2nd ins fnl f* **5/2**[2]
060/ **3** *1* **Ay Tay Tate (IRE)**[461] 7004 5-9-9 50 .... AndrewHeffernan(3) 5 53
(David C Griffiths) *cl up on outer: rdn along to chse wnr over 3f out: drvn over 2f out: sn edgd rt and kpt on same pce: lost 2nd ins fnl f* **16/1**
0-03 **4** *4* **Northumberland**[16] 120 5-9-9 42 .... RobertLButler(3) 3 44
(Michael Chapman) *prom: rdn along over 3f out: drvn over 2f out and sn wknd* **11/1**[3]
5 *12* **Jack's Rocket**[71] 4-9-12 0 .... (e[1]) FrannyNorton 2 11
(Richard Guest) *dwlt: a towards rr* **20/1**
0 **6** *2* **Tobayornottobay**[20] 85 5-9-7 0 .... PatrickMathers 7 —
(Bruce Hellier) *in tch: hdwy 1/2-way: rdn along over 3f out and sn wknd* **50/1**

1m 46.33s (2.63) **Going Correction** +0.225s/f (Slow) **6** Ran SP% **109.5**
WFA 3 from 4yo+ 20lb
Speed ratings (Par 101): **95,91,90,86,74 72**
toteswingers:1&2 £1.10, 2&3 £3.30, 1&3 £2.20 CSF £2.33 TOTE £1.90: £1.30, £2.00; EX 2.40.
Owner Ahmad Al Shaikh **Bred** Lady Bland & Miss Anthea Gibson-Fleming **Trained** Newmarket, Suffolk

FOCUS
A weak maiden run at a steady gallop. The winner basically ran to recent form.

320 TRY BET ANGEL AT TRY.BETANGEL.COM CLAIMING STKS 1m 3f (F)
2:05 (2:05) (Class 6) 4-Y-0+ **£1,457** (£433; £216; £108) **Stalls** Low

Form RPR
3-43 **1** **Trans Sonic**[11] 186 8-9-4 85 .... JoeFanning 1 72
(David O'Meara) *led: rdn along over 2f out: drvn and hdd over 1f out: rallied gamely u.p ins fnl f to ld nr fin* **13/8**[1]
4-30 **2** *hd* **Yossi (IRE)**[11] 184 7-8-9 50 .... (be) FrannyNorton 4 63
(Richard Guest) *trckd wnr: hdwy to chal over 2f out: rdn to ld over 1f out: drvn and edgd rt ins fnl f: hdd and no ex nr fin* **20/1**
1-25 **3** *3 ½* **Stadium Of Light (IRE)**[10] 190 4-8-5 72 .... (p) DeanHeslop(5) 3 60
(Brian Ellison) *hld up in tch: hdwy on inner to chse ldrs 2f out: sn rdn and one pce appr fnl f* **13/8**[1]
1/6- **4** *2 ½* **The Oil Magnate**[280] 1484 6-9-6 80 .... PatrickDonaghy(3) 2 66
(Michael Dods) *trckd ldng pair: hdwy 3f out: rdn to chal over 2f out and ev ch tl drvn and wknd over 1f out* **6/1**[2]
-621 **5** *12* **Unbreak My Heart (IRE)**[5] 261 6-8-9 76 .... RobertLButler(3) 6 33
(Paddy Butler) *in tch: hdwy 5f out: rdn along over 3f out and sn wknd* **12/1**[3]

23-4 **6** *3* **Minortransgression (USA)**[15] [63] 4-8-1 65........(vt[1]) RyanPowell(5) 5 25
(David Evans) *hld up in rr: sme hdwy 1/2-way: rdn along 4f out: sn wknd* **16/1**

2m 29.83s (1.83) **Going Correction** +0.225s/f (Slow)
WFA 4 from 6yo+ 3lb **6** Ran SP% **108.8**
Speed ratings (Par 101): **102,101,99,97,88 86**
toteswingers:1&2 £6.00, 2&3 £6.20, 1&3 £1.40 CSF £33.08 TOTE £3.10: £2.20, £8.80; EX 32.90.
Owner Mrs Lynne Lumley **Bred** I A Balding **Trained** Nawton, N Yorks

FOCUS
A trappy claimer run at a fair clip. The runner-up is rated back to his november form with the others clearly not at their best.

321 PLAY GOLF BEFORE RACING AT SOUTHWELL (S) STKS 6f (F)
2:40 (2:41) (Class 6) 4-Y-0+ **£1,535** (£453; £226) **Stalls** Low

Form RPR

2052 **1** **Elhamri**[6] [243] 7-9-4 70........ HayleyTurner 5 83
(Conor Dore) *trckd ldr: smooth hdwy to ld 2f out: rdn clr appr fnl f: readily* **5/2**[2]

030- **2** *7* **Clear Ice (IRE)**[54] [7701] 4-8-12 60........(v) FrannyNorton 2 55
(Richard Guest) *led: rdn along and hdd 2f out: kpt on same pce* **4/1**[3]

-563 **3** *2* **Harlech Castle**[6] [243] 6-8-12 69........(b) StephenCraine 1 48
(Jim Boyle) *rdn along sn after s and sn outpcd in rr: hdwy over 2f out: kpt on u.p: nvr nr ldrs* **7/4**[1]

05-0 **4** *1 3/4* **Silver Wind**[21] [58] 6-8-12 62........(b) ShaneKelly 7 43
(Alan McCabe) *chsd ldrs: rdn along wl over 2f out: drvn: edgd lft and outpcd fr wl over 1f out* **13/2**

00-0 **5** *11* **Champagne All Day**[11] [185] 5-8-5 38........ NoraLooby(7) 6 —
(Simon Griffiths) *chsd ldrs: rdn along bef 1/2-way: sn outpcd* **100/1**

400- **6** *5* **Excusez Moi (USA)**[63] [7564] 9-8-12 80........(be) PJMcDonald 3 —
(Ruth Carr) *dwlt and sn swtchd to outer: hdwy to chse ldrs 1/2-way: rdn over 2f out: sn wknd* **8/1**

1m 16.27s (-0.23) **Going Correction** +0.225s/f (Slow) **6** Ran SP% **110.4**
Speed ratings (Par 101): **110,100,98,95,81 74**
toteswingers:1&2 £2.10, 2&3 £1.90, 1&3 £1.10 CSF £12.36 TOTE £3.70: £3.30, £1.40; EX 10.90.The winner was bought in for 6,750gns.
Owner Chris Marsh **Bred** Highfield Stud Ltd **Trained** Cowbit, Lincs

FOCUS
An ordinary seller and an improved effort from the winner at face value.
Silver Wind Official explanation: jockey said gelding hung left

322 SOUTHWELL-RACECOURSE.CO.UK H'CAP 6f (F)
3:15 (3:15) (Class 6) (0-60,60) 3-Y-0 **£1,535** (£453; £226) **Stalls** Low

Form RPR

03-1 **1** **Joe Le Taxi (IRE)**[10] [189] 3-9-6 59 6ex........ GregFairley 7 80+
(Mark Johnston) *cl up: led wl over 2f out: rdn clr over 1f out: readily* **1/2**[1]

65-5 **2** *3* **Ridgeway Hawk**[23] [41] 3-8-9 48........(v) RobertHavlin 4 55
(Mark Usher) *dwlt and sn rdn along: hdwy on outer to trck ldng pair after 2f: effrt over 2f out and sn rdn: drvn wl over 1f out: kpt on u.p to take 2nd ins fnl f: no ch w wnr* **7/1**[3]

0-22 **3** *3 3/4* **Go Maggie Go (IRE)**[11] [183] 3-8-12 51........ PhillipMakin 5 46
(Kevin Ryan) *slt ld: rdn along and hdd wl over 2f out: drvn wl over 1f out: sn one pce* **5/1**[2]

566- **4** *3* **These Dreams**[41] [7913] 3-8-7 46 oh1........ ChrisCatlin 2 31
(Richard Guest) *t.k.h: hld up in rr: hdwy on inner over 2f out: sn rdn and no imp* **25/1**

64-5 **5** *3 1/4* **Bobbyow**[14] [146] 3-9-7 60........ DavidProbert 1 35
(Bryn Palling) *chsd ldrs: rdn along 3f out: sn wknd* **10/1**

04-0 **6** *1 3/4* **Ever Roses**[23] [41] 3-8-13 52........ MickyFenton 3 21
(Paul Midgley) *plld hrd: chsd ldrs to 1/2-way: sn wknd* **33/1**

0-06 **7** *10* **Likeable Lad**[2] [296] 3-8-4 46 oh1........(be[1]) JamesSullivan(3) 6 —
(Ruth Carr) *in tch: rdn along bef 1/2-way and sn outpcd* **80/1**

1m 17.25s (0.75) **Going Correction** +0.225s/f (Slow) **7** Ran SP% **112.9**
Speed ratings (Par 95): **104,100,95,91,86 84,71**
toteswingers:1&2 £2.00, 2&3 £2.30, 1&3 £1.10 CSF £4.50 TOTE £1.30: £1.20, £1.30; EX 5.40.
Owner Mark Johnston Racing Ltd **Bred** J Joyce **Trained** Middleham Moor, N Yorks

FOCUS
An uncompetitive handicap, easily landed by the odds-on favourite, who was value for a bit more.

323 BLUESQ.COM ON YOUR IPHONE H'CAP 1m 3f (F)
3:45 (3:45) (Class 5) (0-70,65) 4-Y-0+ **£2,266** (£674; £337; £168) **Stalls** Low

Form RPR

4-11 **1** **Stanley Rigby**[16] [117] 5-9-2 60........ BarryMcHugh 4 69
(Richard Fahey) *hld up in rr: hdwy on outer over 3f out: chal over 2f out: rdn to ld over 1f out: sn drvn and edgd lft: kpt on gamely towards fin* **85/40**[2]

23-2 **2** *nk* **Mediterranean Sea (IRE)**[18] [104] 5-9-7 65........ StephenCraine 2 73
(J R Jenkins) *trckd ldrs: hdwy 3f out: n.m.r over 2f out: rdn to chal whn n.m.r jst over 1f out: drvn and kpt on ins fnl f: ev ch tl no ex nr fin* **7/2**[3]

106- **3** *2 1/4* **Deejan (IRE)**[93] [7147] 6-8-12 56........ DavidProbert 6 60
(Bryn Palling) *led: rdn along and jnd over 2f out: drvn and hdd over 1f out: ev ch tl wknd ins fnl f* **7/1**

0-21 **4** *1 1/2* **Magic Haze**[11] [184] 5-8-5 56........ RichardRowe(7) 5 59
(Sally Hall) *trckd ldng pair: effrt over 3f out: rdn along wl over 2f out: drvn wl over 1f out and sn wknd* **7/4**[1]

610- **5** *10* **Love In The West (IRE)**[117] [6571] 5-9-0 61........(p) GaryBartley(3) 3 44
(John Harris) *chsd ldr: rdn along over 4f out: wknd 3f out* **14/1**

2m 30.61s (2.61) **Going Correction** +0.225s/f (Slow) **5** Ran SP% **109.8**
Speed ratings (Par 103): **99,98,97,96,88**
CSF £9.75 TOTE £6.20: £3.80, £1.70; EX 7.40.
Owner Dean Hardman and Stella Kelsall **Bred** F C T Wilson **Trained** Musley Bank, N Yorks

FOCUS
A competitive handicap ran at a sound gallop. The winner is rated up 5lb but the favourite disappointed.

324 PLAY ROULETTE AT BLUESQ.COM APPRENTICE H'CAP 1m 6f (F)
4:15 (4:15) (Class 6) (0-55,55) 4-Y-0+ **£1,535** (£453; £226) **Stalls** Low

Form RPR

-254 **1** **Carnac (IRE)**[11] [184] 5-8-12 50........(p) NoraLooby(3) 1 58
(Alan McCabe) *trckd ldrs on inner: hdwy 4f out: led over 2f out and sn rdn: kpt on u.p ins fnl f* **6/1**[3]

00-5 **2** *2* **Laura Land**[20] [86] 5-8-6 46 oh1........ IanBurns(5) 4 51
(Mark Brisbourne) *prom: led after 6f: rdn along 4f out: hdd over 2f out: sn drvn and kpt on same pce* **7/1**

-030 **3** *2* **Mojeerr**[11] [184] 5-8-10 50........(v) ThomasBrown(5) 7 52
(Alan McCabe) *in tch on inner: hdwy over 3f out: swtchd rt and rdn to chse ldrs 2f out: drvn and one pce appr fnl f* **25/1**

5-54 **4** *2 3/4* **Silent Lucidity (IRE)**[16] [118] 7-9-0 52........(p) GeorgeChaloner(3) 11 51
(Peter Niven) *midfield: hdwy to trck ldrs 1/2-way: effrt over 3f out: sn rdn along and no imp fnl 2f* **3/1**[1]

005- **5** *1 3/4* **Antoella (IRE)**[67] [7330] 4-7-12 46 oh1........ KevinLundie(7) 2 42
(Philip Kirby) *s.i.s and bhd: hdwy over 4f out: rdn along over 3f out: kpt on fnl 2f: nt rch ldrs* **25/1**

335- **6** *1* **Davana**[37] [7957] 5-8-11 46 oh1........(p) NatashaEaton 6 41+
(Bill Ratcliffe) *hld up in rr: sme hdwy 3f out: nvr a factor* **13/2**

5-32 **7** *2 1/2* **Tivers Song (USA)**[11] [184] 7-8-12 47........(b) LucyKBarry 9 38
(John Harris) *prom: cl up over 4f out: rdn along over 3f out: grad wknd* **7/2**[2]

0-00 **8** *1* **Novestar (IRE)**[9] [203] 6-9-6 55........(t) RichardRowe 8 45
(Michael Appleby) *a towards rr* **16/1**

006- **9** *17* **Solo Choice**[9] [7834] 5-8-6 46 oh1........(e[1]) DavidSimmonson(5) 10 12
(Ian McInnes) *hld up towards rr: hdwy and in tch 5f out: rdn along 4f out and sn wknd* **66/1**

34-5 **10** *2 3/4* **Kingaroo (IRE)**[21] [63] 5-9-3 55........ JakePayne(3) 3 17
(Garry Woodward) *led 6f: prom tl rdn along over 4f out and sn wknd* **8/1**

06/0 **11** *48* **Carlton Mac**[25] [8] 6-8-6 46 oh1........ LukeStrong(5) 5 —
(Simon Griffiths) *prom: lost pce after 4f: bhd fnl 5f: t.o fnl 3f* **66/1**

3m 13.7s (5.40) **Going Correction** +0.225s/f (Slow)
WFA 4 from 5yo+ 6lb **11** Ran SP% **115.0**
Speed ratings (Par 101): **93,91,90,89,88 87,86,85,75,74 46**
toteswingers:1&2 £10.90, 2&3 £39.40, 1&3 £22.10 CSF £45.05 CT £968.55 TOTE £8.20: £2.80, £3.60, £5.70; EX 53.90 TRIFECTA Not won..
Owner Charles Wentworth **Bred** Kilfrush Stud **Trained** Averham Park, Notts

FOCUS
A weak handicap, run at a good gallop with the field finishing well strung out. the winner reversed latest form with the seventh, with the second and third to their recent marks.
Antoella(IRE) Official explanation: jockey said he was late removing blindfold because it had been caught on the cheek piece of the bridle
T/Plt: £20.90 to a £1 stake. Pool of £48,139.71 - 1,675.20 winning tickets. T/Qpdt: £11.60 to a £1 stake. Pool of £3,686.68 - 234.61 winning tickets. JR

288 CAGNES-SUR-MER
Thursday, January 27

OFFICIAL GOING: Fibresand: standard

325a PRIX DU COL DE BRAUS (CLAIMER) (FIBRESAND) 6f 110y
11:50 (12:00) 4-Y-0+ **£6,465** (£2,586; £1,939; £1,293; £646)

RPR

1 **Something (IRE)**[10] [196] 9-9-7 0........ IoritzMendizabal 14 84
(David Nicholls) *broke wl fr wd draw: sn prom on outer: wnt 4th bef st: chal for ld 2f out: cruised to ld 1 1/2f out: sn wnt clr: easily* **42/10**[2]

2 *3* **Wise Boy (GER)**[10] [196] 4-8-11 0........ DominiqueBoeuf 9 65
(Y Fertillet, France) **5/1**[3]

3 *1/2* **Libretto (GER)**[20] [93] 5-9-2 0........ ASuborics 4 69
(H-W Hiller, Germany) **5/2**[1]

4 *3/4* **Richhill Lady**[108] 7-8-11 0........ ThierryThulliez 11 61
(F Chappet, France) **25/1**

5 *shd* **Vianello (IRE)**[10] [196] 4-9-4 0........(b) StefanieHofer 5 68
(Mario Hofer, Germany) **12/1**

6 *1* **Derison (USA)**[27] 9-9-8 0........(b) StephanePasquier 13 69
(P Monfort, France) **12/1**

7 *1* **Chicaya (FR)**[27] 7-8-6 0........ AlexandreChampenois(5) 12 55
(F Vermeulen, France) **39/1**

8 *1/2* **Green Pride**[10] [196] 8-9-5 0........ FranckBlondel 7 62
(G Martin, Austria) **54/1**

9 *snk* **Grymeos (FR)**[10] [196] 4-9-2 0........ AurelienLemaitre 1 58
(J Heloury, France) **41/1**

10 *1* **Staraco (FR)**[27] 7-9-4 0 ow1........ ErwanBureller(5) 15 63
(C Boutin, France) **8/1**

0 **Giant Generation (GER)**[10] [196] 7-8-11 0........ FabienLefebvre 6 —
(G Martin, Austria) **72/1**

0 **La Rogerais (FR)**[153] 6-8-13 0........ SylvainRuis 10 —
(T Doumen, France) **13/1**

0 **Texan Dream (IRE)**[19] 6-8-11 0........ Francois-XavierBertras 2 —
(Mlle V Dissaux, France) **30/1**

0 **Valugny (FR)**[16] 4-9-1 0........ RonanThomas 8 —
(P Van De Poele, France) **32/1**

0 **Mitsui (IRE)** 4-8-11 0........ ThomasMessina 3 —
(H Blume, Germany) **38/1**

1m 16.96s (76.96) **15** Ran SP% **118.8**
WIN (incl. 1 euro stake): 5.20. PLACES: 1.70, 1.70, 1.30. DF: 10.50. SF: 25.80.
Owner Middleham Park Racing LIII **Bred** Newlands House Stud **Trained** Sessay, N Yorks

NOTEBOOK
Something(IRE) trounced his rivals for an easy win.

236 MEYDAN (L-H)
Thursday, January 27

OFFICIAL GOING: Tapeta: standard; turf: good

326a FRIDAY TROPHY (H'CAP) (TAPETA) 1m
2:35 (2:35) (95-105,105) 3-Y-0+
£42,307 (£14,102; £7,051; £3,525; £2,115; £1,410)

RPR

1 **City Style (USA)**[7] [236] 5-8-11 101........ MickaelBarzalona 10 103
(Mahmood Al Zarooni) *in rr of mid-div: rdn 2 1/2f out: r.o wl: led 110yds out* **33/1**

2 *3/4* **Golden Sword**[138] [5938] 5-9-1 105........ ChristopheSoumillon 14 105+
(M F De Kock, South Africa) *settled in rr: r.o wl fnl 2f: nrest at fin* **14/1**

3 *shd* **Final Drive (IRE)**[29] [8009] 5-8-11 101........ JamieSpencer 5 101+
(John Ryan) *settled in rr: rdn 2 1/2f out: r.o wl fnl 1 1/2f* **7/1**

4 *shd* **Rakaan (IRE)**[182] [4509] 4-8-11 101........ TedDurcan 1 101
(Jamie Osborne) *mid-div: r.o wl fnl 1 1/2f: nrest at fin* **11/1**

5 *shd* **Atlantic Sport (USA)**[14] 155 6-9-1 105 .... KShea 2 105
(M F De Kock, South Africa) *mid-div: rdn 2f out: ev ch 110yds out: one pce fnl 55yds* **14/1**
6 *1/2* **Rochdale**[7] 240 8-8-11 101 ....(t) PatCosgrave 12 99
(A Al Raihe, UAE) *trckd ldng pair: led 1f out: hdd and one pce 110yds out* **14/1**
7 *1 3/4* **Sweet Lightning**[117] 6562 6-8-13 102 .... JimCrowley 13 97
(Michael Dods) *settled in rr: n.m.r 1 1/2f out: nvr able to chal* **16/1**
8 *1/2* **Across The Rhine (USA)**[14] 157 5-9-1 105 .... WJSupple 4 98
(Tracey Collins, Ire) *mid-div: chsd ldrs 1 1/2f out: nt qckn fnl 110yds* **12/1**
9 *3/4* **Reynaldothewizard (USA)**[49] 7794 5-9-0 104 ....(t) RichardMullen 3 96
(S Seemar, UAE) *trckd ldng pair tl 2f out: wknd* **4/1[1]**
10 *1* **Yirga**[7] 236 5-8-13 102 .... TadhgO'Shea 8 92
(A Al Raihe, UAE) *mid-div: chsd ldrs 2 1/2f out: one pce fnl f* **9/1**
11 *1 1/2* **Hattan (IRE)**[7] 240 9-9-0 104 .... WayneSmith 9 90
(M Al Muhairi, UAE) *trckd ldrs: led 2f out: hdd and one pce 1f out* **20/1**
12 *1 1/4* **Riggins (IRE)**[61] 7593 7-9-0 104 .... RyanMoore 6 87
(Ed Walker) *in rr of mid-div: no room 1 1/2f out: nt rcvr* **6/1[3]**
13 *6 1/2* **Atlantis Star**[110] 6761 4-9-0 104 ....(p) FrankieDettori 7 72
(Saeed Bin Suroor) *sn led: hdd & wknd 2f out* **9/2[2]**
14 *5 3/4* **Carnaby Street (IRE)**[14] 152 4-8-13 102 .... AhmedAjtebi 11 58
(Mahmood Al Zarooni) *v.s.a: n.d* **33/1**

1m 38.65s (1.55) **Going Correction** +0.275s/f (Slow) **14** Ran SP% **127.5**
Speed ratings: **103,102,102,102,101 101,99,99,98,97 95,94,88,82**
CSF £458.09; Tricast £3,608.47..
Owner Godolphin **Bred** Stonerside Stable **Trained** Newmarket, Suffolk

FOCUS
A competitive handicap run at a fair pace.

NOTEBOOK
City Style(USA) ruined his chance with a slow start in a modestly run race over 7f here last week, and he proved a different proposition over this longer trip off a stronger gallop. He hadn't progressed as expected since winning twice on turf at the 2009 Carnival, indeed this was his first success then, and on occasions he hasn't look straightforward. However, he again showed himself capable of smart form when things drop right, not only benefiting from the fair pace but also being helped by enjoying one continuous run (takes a while to get into his stride). Formerly rated 109, it wouldn't surprise to see him defy a higher mark on this surface or back on turf, where the long straight will suit.
Golden Sword ◆ has been mainly disappointing since leaving Aidan O'Brien (although was third in last year's City of Gold here), including in Britain for Jane Chapple-Hyam when last seen, but he had been "working much better than last year" according to Mike De Kock. Despite being entitled to need the run, and racing over a trip short of his optimum on his first Tapeta start, he finished strongly for second under a less than inspired ride. After being dropped in from the widest stall, his rider took an age to get serious in the straight and challenged between horses, where room was at a premium, rather than going out wide. He could be hard to beat back over 1m2f-plus next time.
Final Drive(IRE), 9lb higher than for his latest impressive Wolverhampton win, showed himself up to this level with a typically strong finishing burst from off the pace.
Rakaan(IRE) had to wait for a gap in the straight before finishing well. This was his first start for 182 days and he can win a similar race.
Atlantic Sport(USA) moved into contention going well early in the straight, but he had raced closer to the pace than those who finished in front of him and also made his bid towards the inside rail, which might not have been ideal.
Rochdale, like Atlantic Sport, deserves credit having raced closer to the pace than the principals.
Sweet Lightning, who needs things to go his way, was continually denied a clear run in the straight. (op 14-1)
Reynaldothewizard(USA), the winner of his last two starts in non-Carnival company, was up in trip and didn't stay.
Riggins(IRE) found little for pressure after moving okay.
Atlantis Star, tried in cheekpieces, pulled too hard early on.

327a GNB SPRINT (H'CAP) (TURF) 6f
3:10 (3:10) (100-110,110) 3-Y-O+
£46,153 (£15,384; £7,692; £3,846; £2,307; £1,538)

RPR
1 **Happy Dubai (IRE)**[7] 237 4-8-13 105 .... FrankieDettori 15 111+
(A Al Raihe, UAE) *mid-div: rdn to ld 1f out: r.o wl: comf* [illegible]
2 *1 3/4* **Dohasa (IRE)**[14] 155 6-9-2 108 .... RyanMoore 12 108
(I Mohammed, UAE) *trckd ldrs: outpcd 2f out: r.o wl fnl f: nrest at fin* **14/1**
3 *1/4* **Rock Jock (IRE)**[14] 155 4-8-13 105 .... TedDurcan 3 104
(Tracey Collins, Ire) *trckd ldrs: led 2f out to 1f out: r.o wl but no ch w wnr: lost 2nd nr fin* **20/1**
4 *2 1/4* **Rileyskeepingfaith**[110] 6752 5-8-8 100 .... AhmedAjtebi 11 92
(Mahmood Al Zarooni) *mid-div: r.o fnl 1 1/2f* **14/1**
5 *1 1/4* **Evens And Odds (IRE)**[117] 6570 7-8-7 102 .... MichaelO'Connell(3) 10 90
(David Nicholls) *sn led: hdd 2f out: r.o same pce* **14/1**
6 *1/4* **Montmorency (IRE)**[18] 5-8-10 102 ....(t) RichardMullen 5 89
(S Seemar, UAE) *s.i.s: trckd ldrs: one pce fnl f* **8/1**
7 *1 3/4* **Mariol (FR)**[59] 8-9-3 109 .... Christophe-PatriceLemaire 1 91
(Rod Collet, France) *a mid-div* **12/1**
8 *1 1/2* **Barney McGrew (IRE)**[131] 6177 8-8-10 102 .... WJSupple 2 79
(Michael Dods) *settled in rr: nvr able to chal* **25/1**
9 *1 3/4* **Clearly Silver (SAF)**[14] 152 5-8-10 102 ow1..(b) ChristopheSoumillon 8 73
(M F De Kock, South Africa) *nvr bttr than mid-div* **5/2[1]**
10 *2 1/4* **Sir Gerry (USA)**[14] 152 6-9-2 108 .... TadhgO'Shea 13 72
(Doug Watson, UAE) *nvr able to chal* **16/1**
11 *3 1/2* **Too Nice Name (FR)**[14] 152 4-9-0 106 ....(t) GregoryBenoist 9 59
(X Nakkachdji, France) *chsd ldrs for 3f: wknd* **20/1**
12 *3/4* **Golden Desert (IRE)**[7] 236 7-8-8 100 .... PatCosgrave 6 50
(Robert Mills) *nvr nr to chal* **14/1**
13 *1/4* **Finjaan**[132] 6147 5-9-4 110 .... RichardHills 7 60
(Doug Watson, UAE) *settled in rr: nvr nr to chal* **14/1**
14 *3/4* **Alsadeek (IRE)**[27] 6-9-2 108 .... PatDobbs 4 55
(Doug Watson, UAE) *trckd ldrs: rdn and wknd 2 1/2f out* **13/2[3]**

69.81 secs (69.81) **14** Ran SP% **127.6**
CSF £90.38; Tricast £1,622.99..
Owner Ahmed Al Falasi **Bred** Waterford Hall Stud **Trained** UAE

FOCUS
Those drawn low were favoured in the first race run on the straight course at this year's Carnival (over 5f the previous week), but there was no sign of a bias this time. They raced middle to far side.

NOTEBOOK
Happy Dubai(IRE) ◆ defied a 5lb rise for his win here over 5f the previous week in the manner of a rapidly improving colt, picking up well after travelling best of all. It's not out of the question that he could develop into an Al Quoz Sprint contender, but before then he has plenty of options in handicaps and conditions company.
Dohasa(IRE) ran well but was no match at all for the progressive winner. (op 16-1)
Rock Jock(IRE) showed good speed towards the far rail and had his chance.
Rileyskeepingfaith, sold out of Mick Channon's yard for 110,000gns since he was last seen, is by no means a typical Godolphin purchase, but he ran well. He has the option of switching to Tapeta.
Evens And Odds(IRE) hasn't gone on as expected since winning the Stewards' Cup, but he showed plenty of speed on his return from a four-month break.
Clearly Silver(SAF), dropped in trip with blinkers back on, seemed to travel okay but found nothing for pressure and was heavily eased around half a furlong out. This was disappointing considering he shaped well on his Dubai debut.

328a AQUARIUS TROPHY (H'CAP) (TAPETA) 1m 3f
4:00 (4:00) (95-109,109) 3-Y-O+
£57,692 (£19,230; £9,615; £4,807; £2,884; £1,923)

RPR
1 **Lost In The Moment (IRE)**[96] 7100 4-8-6 97 .....(p) MickaelBarzalona 13 101
(Saeed Bin Suroor) *mid-div: chsd ldr 3f out: led 1 1/2f out: r.o wl* **11/2[2]**
2 *1/2* **Prizefighting (USA)**[14] 153 4-9-1 106 .... AhmedAjtebi 8 109
(Mahmood Al Zarooni) *mid-div: chsd ldrs 2 1/2f out: ev ch fnl 1 1/2f: nt qckn cl home* **9/2[1]**
3 *4 1/2* **Burdlaz (IRE)**[14] 153 6-9-1 104 .... FrankieDettori 10 98
(Mahmood Al Zarooni) *settled in rr: r.o fnl 2f but n.d* **8/1**
4 *nse* **Halicarnassus (IRE)**[14] 153 7-8-9 98 .... TadhgO'Shea 9 92
(Mick Channon) *mid-div: chsd ldr 3f out: led 2f out: hdd 1 1/2f out: wknd* **11/2[2]**
5 *2 1/4* **King Of Rome (IRE)**[7] 240 6-9-5 108 .... KShea 6 98
(M F De Kock, South Africa) *mid-div: r.o fnl 2f but n.d* **7/1[3]**
6 *1 1/2* **Arqaam**[21] 74 7-8-8 97 .... RichardHills 4 84
(Doug Watson, UAE) *slowly away: racd in rr of mid-div: n.d* **33/1**
7 *1* **Bay Willow (IRE)**[123] 6387 4-8-10 101 .... TedDurcan 2 87
(Saeed Bin Suroor) *trckd ldrs for 2 1/2f then a mid-div* **8/1**
8 *4 1/4* **Bravely Fought (IRE)**[48] 7823 6-8-10 99 .... GFCarroll 11 77
(Sabrina J Harty, Ire) *in rr of mid-div: n.d* **12/1**
9 *2 3/4* **Dr Faustus (IRE)**[14] 153 6-8-6 95 ....(vt) WJSupple 5 68
(Doug Watson, UAE) *slowly away: racd in rr: n.d* **33/1**
10 *1/2* **Dubawi Phantom**[7] 242 4-8-11 102 .... RyanMoore 14 75
(Ed Dunlop) *settled in rr: nvr able to chal* **14/1**
11 *2 1/2* **Lindner (GER)**[13] 6-7-13 95 .... HarryBentley(7) 12 62
(I Mohammed, UAE) *nvr bttr than mid-div* **33/1**
12 *4 3/4* **Happy Valley (ARG)**[14] 154 5-9-6 109 .... ChristopheSoumillon 1 68
(M F De Kock, South Africa) *trckd ldrs for 2 1/2f then mid-div: wknd fnl 2f* **7/1[3]**
13 *24* **Imvula (AUS)**[49] 7793 7-8-10 99 .... XZiani 3 15
(M bin Shafya, UAE) *trckd ldr for 2 1/2f: rdn 4f out: sn btn* **25/1**
14 *15* **Bon Grain (FR)**[7] 242 6-9-1 104 .... PatCosgrave 7 —
(M bin Shafya, UAE) *sn led: clr 7f out: rdn 3 1/2f out: hdd 2f out: wknd qckly* **33/1**

2m 18.33s (-0.07) **Going Correction** +0.275s/f (Slow)
WFA 4 from 5yo+ 3lb **14** Ran SP% **126.1**
Speed ratings: **111,110,107,107,105 104,103,100,98,98 96,93,75,64**
CSF £30.42; Tricast £199.43..
Owner Sheikh Majid Bin Mohammed al Maktoum **Bred** Rockhart Trading Ltd **Trained** Newmarket, Suffolk
■ A 100th Carnival winner for trainer Saeed Bin Suroor.

FOCUS
The pace was strong with Bon Grain soon opening up a huge advantage, only to tire dramatically on the turn into the straight. This didn't look that strong a handicap, but a couple of progressive types pulled nicely clear.

NOTEBOOK
Lost In The Moment(IRE), sold out of Jeremy Noseda's yard for 130,000gns soon after winning a Newbury handicap over 1m2f off 91 last October, showed himself to still be improving. The surface was a question mark considering he had been below form in two starts on Polytrack, but clearly he handled the Tapeta well. His effort is particularly creditable considering he was keen without cover early on and had a wide trip for much of the way. There was also much encouragement to be taken from the way he knuckled down for pressure to see off the runner-up's [illegible] going as he has not always looked entirely straightforward. (op 5-1)
Prizefighting(USA), 1lb higher than when slightly unlucky in a similar race over C&D two [illegible] earlier (just behind Halicarnassus), had his chance this time and, although always held by the winner, kept on strongly to finish a long way ahead of the others.
Burdlaz(IRE) was held by Prizefighting on their recent course meeting, but did reverse placings with Halicarnassus.
Halicarnassus(IRE) was a bit disappointing off 2lb higher than when second over C&D on his previous start.
King Of Rome(IRE) was short of room on the bend into the straight but he was not unlucky.

329a WHEELS TROPHY (H'CAP) (TURF) 1m 6f 11y
4:35 (4:35) (95-115,113) 3-Y-O+
£57,692 (£19,230; £9,615; £4,807; £2,884; £1,923)

RPR
1 **Whispering Gallery**[96] 7096 5-9-4 111 .... TedDurcan 9 115
(Saeed Bin Suroor) *trckd ldng gp: led 1 1/2f out: r.o wl* **6/1[2]**
2 *3/4* **Opinion Poll (IRE)**[95] 7110 5-9-6 113 .... AhmedAjtebi 3 116+
(Mahmood Al Zarooni) *mid-div: r.o wl fnl 1 1/2f: nrest at fin* **6/1[2]**
3 *2 1/2* **Age Of Reason (UAE)**[85] 7297 6-9-1 108 .... FrankieDettori 4 108
(Saeed Bin Suroor) *trckd ldng gp: ev ch 2f out: one pce fnl f* **11/4[1]**
4 *2 1/4* **Drunken Sailor (IRE)**[82] 7368 6-9-5 112 ....(b) RyanMoore 12 108
(Luca Cumani) *mid-div: r.o wl fnl 2f* **7/1[3]**
5 *1/4* **Claremont (IRE)**[14] 154 5-9-3 110 ....(b) MickaelBarzalona 8 106
(Mahmood Al Zarooni) *in rr of mid-div: n.d* **20/1**
6 *2 1/2* **Superstition (FR)**[117] 6591 5-9-0 107 .... Christophe-PatriceLemaire 13 100
(Rod Collet, France) *settled in rr: n.d but r.o fnl 1 1/2f* **14/1**
7 *1/4* **Montaff**[82] 7350 5-8-6 99 .... TadhgO'Shea 1 91
(Mick Channon) *in rr of mid-div: r.o same pce fnl 1 1/2f* **25/1**
8 *1* **Topclas (FR)**[14] 154 5-9-0 107 .... PatCosgrave 14 98
(M bin Shafya, UAE) *trckd ldr: led 2 1/2f out to 1 1/2f out: sn btn* **25/1**
9 *7* **Bank Of Burden (USA)**[81] 4-8-5 100 ....(tp) Per-AndersGraberg 2 85
(Niels Petersen, Norway) *mid-div: nvr able to chal* **16/1**
10 *4 1/4* **Mojave Moon**[14] 153 5-8-5 97 ....(v) XZiani 15 73
(M bin Shafya, UAE) *settled in last: nvr able to chal* **16/1**
11 *10* **Jedi**[7] 242 5-8-9 102 .... JRosales 10 63
(A bin Huzaim, UAE) *nvr bttr than mid-div* **6/1[2]**
12 *1 1/4* **Mr. Crazy Boy (ARG)**[14] 157 5-8-6 100 ....(t) KShea 5 58
(M F De Kock, South Africa) *trckd ldr: rdn 2 1/2f out: wknd fnl 1 1/2f* **25/1**
13 *8 1/4* **New Guinea**[21] 74 8-8-5 95 ....(b) WJSupple 11 46
(E Charpy, UAE) *sn led: hdd & wknd 2 1/2f out* **50/1**

P **Man Of Iron (USA)**[14] 153 5-8-6 99.........................(b) RichardMullen 6 —
(Luca Cumani) *mid-div: p.u 3f out* **25/1**

2m 57.78s (177.78)
WFA 4 from 5yo+ 6lb **14** Ran SP% **122.6**
CSF £38.74; Tricast £124.44..
Owner Godolphin **Bred** Darley **Trained** Newmarket, Suffolk

FOCUS
An early pointer towards the DRC Gold Cup, which will be run as a Group 3 for the first time on March 10. The pace was steady early before gradually increasing.

NOTEBOOK
Whispering Gallery usually races from the front, as when winning over 1m2f on Tapeta off 4lb lower here last year, but clearly he wasn't inconvenienced by being unable to dominate this time. This was a really smart performance off a mark of 111 and, now he's proven himself tactically versatile, it wouldn't surprise to see him improve on last year's fourth in the Gold Cup.
Opinion Poll(IRE), having his first start since leaving Michael Jarvis, might have won under a shrewder ride, but clearly this was still a fine performance off a handicap mark of 113. When going in pursuit of the winner in the straight, he was switched right more than once, but it turned out there was sufficient room to make his move between horses on the final occasion that he edged out, and the way he finished when finally in the clear suggests he would have taken this had he covered less ground. Clearly this was a fine trial for the Gold Cup.
Age Of Reason(UAE), who won a similar race to this last year off 2lb lower before finishing runner-up in the Gold Cup, followed the winner into the straight but wasn't quite good enough.
Drunken Sailor(IRE), last seen running with credit when things didn't go his way in Australia, made a respectable return to Dubai, where he was a winner twice on Tapeta in 2010.
Claremont(IRE) stepped up on his effort here two weeks earlier but didn't quite see his race out.
Man Of Iron(USA) may have picked up an injury rounding the final bend, being pulled up and dismounted. (op 20-1)

330a INSIDEOUT TROPHY (CONDITIONS RACE) (TAPETA) 1m 2f
5:10 (5:10) 3-Y-O+

£42,307 (£14,102; £7,051; £3,525; £2,115; £1,410)

RPR
1 **Bronze Cannon (USA)**[14] 157 6-8-8 112........................(t) RyanMoore 4 101+
(H J Brown, South Africa) *mid-div: smooth prog 2 1/2f out: r.o to ld fnl 110yds* **7/1**
2 ¾ **Mr Brock (SAF)**[14] 156 8-9-0 115.. KShea 13 105
(M F De Kock, South Africa) *trckd ldr: led 1 1/2f out: hdd fnl 110yds* **10/3**[1]
3 *hd* **Enak (ARG)**[14] 157 5-8-8 110...(t) TedDurcan 2 99
(Saeed Bin Suroor) *trckd ldng duo: ev ch 1 1/2f out: one pce fnl 110yds* **9/2**[3]
4 1 ¼ **Trois Rois (FR)**[14] 154 6-9-0 105...........(b) Christophe-PatriceLemaire 3 102
(I Mohammed, UAE) *mid-div: r.o wl fnl 1 1/2f* **20/1**
5 ¼ **Jalil (USA)**[7] 240 7-8-8 106.. AhmedAjtebi 6 96
(Mahmood Al Zarooni) *a mid-div* **16/1**
6 ½ **Monte Alto (IRE)**[7] 242 7-9-0 104......................................(t) TadhgO'Shea 5 101
(A Al Raihe, UAE) *s.i.s: settled in rr: r.o wl fnl 2f* **25/1**
7 ½ **Psychic Ability (USA)**[105] 6877 4-8-13 99........... DaraghO'Donohoe 10 101+
(Saeed Bin Suroor) *settled in rr: r.o fnl 2f but n.d* **14/1**
8 *1* **Pallodio (IRE)**[50] 7776 6-9-0 111.. RichardHills 8 98
(J E Hammond, France) *in rr of mid-div: nvr able to chal* **8/1**
9 *2* **Honour System (IRE)**[91] 4-8-13 99.......................... MickaelBarzalona 9 95
(Saeed Bin Suroor) *in rr of mid-div: n.d* **20/1**
10 ¾ **Wealthy (IRE)**[105] 6881 4-8-13 110................................ FrankieDettori 12 93
(Saeed Bin Suroor) *sn led: clr 4f out: hdd 1 1/2f out: wknd fnl 110yds* **4/1**[2]
11 *hd* **Espiritu (FR)**[342] 627 5-8-8 102.. WayneSmith 7 86
(G Al Marri, UAE) *slowly away: settled in rr: n.d* **22/1**
12 ¼ **Fighting Brave (USA)**[14] 157 4-8-7 102......................(t) ShaneFoley 11 86
(David Wachman, Ire) *trckd ldrs tl 3f out: wknd* **16/1**
13 8 ½ **Noisy Silence (IRE)**[13] 7-8-8 100.. PatDobbs 1 68
(A Manuel, UAE) *nvr bttr than mid-div* **40/1**

2m 4.37s (-0.53) **Going Correction** +0.275s/f (Slow)
WFA 4 from 5yo+ 2lb **13** Ran SP% **123.5**
Speed ratings: **113,112,112,111,111 110,110,109,107,107 107,106,100**
CSF £29.25..
Owner Ramzan Kadyrov **Bred** Hascombe And Valiant Studs **Trained** South Africa

FOCUS
A quality conditions event, more like a Listed contest at the very least, and the pace was good courtesy of Wealthy, who faded soon enough.

NOTEBOOK
Bronze Cannon(USA) gained his first success since the 2009 Hardwicke (when with John Gosden), although this was only his sixth run since then. He needed his first two runs back from a break, both of which were over an inadequate trip, and he was clearly spot on for this third start after the layoff. The fitting of a tongue-tie may also have played its part. He might gain some confidence from this, plus should improve back over further, but he was favourite by these weights (received 6lb from the runner-up) and may struggle to follow up in better company next time.
Mr Brock(SAF), fifth behind Mendip in the first round of the Al Maktoum Challenge on his return, ran a terrific race considering not only was he conceding 6lb to the smart winner, but he was the only runner who really worked to peg back the early leader. (op 7-2)
Enak(ARG), fourth in last year's UAE Derby and a close second to Steele Tango on turf on his reappearance, ran close to form, although he hinted at being a bit lazy, needing to be niggled along early to sit handy. He might find slight improvement for headgear.
Trois Rois(FR) proved suited by the return to Tapeta and kept on reasonably well from off the pace.
Jalil(USA) also plugged on without threatening.

331a AL RASHIDIYA SPONSORED BY GULF NEWS (GROUP 2) (TURF) 1m 1f
5:45 (5:45) 3-Y-O+

£76,923 (£25,641; £12,820; £6,410; £3,846; £2,564)

RPR
1 **Presvis**[225] 3068 7-9-0 116.. RyanMoore 13 122
(Luca Cumani) *settled last: smooth prog 1 1/2f out: led 110yds out: easily* **7/2**[2]
2 4 ¾ **Steele Tango (USA)**[14] 157 6-9-0 113................................ TedDurcan 8 112
(Roger Teal) *settled in rr: r.o wl fnl 2f but no ch w wnr* **6/1**[3]
3 1 ¾ **Caymans (AUS)**[85] 7304 6-9-0 108................................ FrankieDettori 7 108
(Saeed Bin Suroor) *mid-div: smooth prog to ld 2f out: hdd fnl 1f* **6/1**[3]
4 1 ¼ **Irish Flame (SAF)**[180] 5-9-3 119.. KShea 6 109
(M F De Kock, South Africa) *mid-div: r.o fnl 1 1/2f: nt able to chal* **13/8**[1]
5 1 ¼ **Bushman**[124] 6350 7-9-0 110.. JamieSpencer 2 103
(David Simcock) *slowly away: mid-div on rail: r.o fnl 1 1/2f* **16/1**
6 ¾ **Sea Lord (IRE)**[14] 156 4-9-1 115...................................... AhmedAjtebi 1 104
(Mahmood Al Zarooni) *mid-div: chsd ldrs 2f out: nt qcknd fnl 1f* **8/1**
7 2 ¼ **Le Drakkar (AUS)**[14] 157 6-9-0 105........(t) Christophe-PatriceLemaire 5 97
(A bin Huzaim, UAE) *in rr of mid-div: n.d* **25/1**
8 9 ¼ **Frozen Power (IRE)**[14] 156 4-8-13 109................ MickaelBarzalona 11 77
(Mahmood Al Zarooni) *in rr of mid-div: nvr able to chal* **25/1**
9 1 ¼ **Birbone (FR)**[14] 153 6-9-0 97.....................................(v) RichardMullen 4 75
(S Seemar, UAE) *led main gp: rdn and btn 4f out* **50/1**
10 2 ¼ **Grand Hombre (USA)**[13] 11-9-0 95....................................(t) RMBurke 9 70
(R Bouresly, Kuwait) *sn rdn in rr* **100/1**
11 2 ½ **Tequilla Heights (BRZ)**[42] 7905 5-9-0 95..................................(t) BReis 3 65
(E Martins, Brazil) *trckd ldrs tl 2 1/2f out: wknd* **50/1**
12 9 ½ **Third Set (IRE)**[7] 239 8-9-0 107......................................(t) RichardHills 12 45
(I Mohammed, UAE) *in rr of mid-div: n.d* **33/1**
13 *15* **Tam Lin**[14] 157 8-9-0 110..(bt) PatCosgrave 10 13
(M bin Shafya, UAE) *sn led: hdd 2f out: wknd* **28/1**

1m 49.56s (109.56)
WFA 4 from 5yo+ 1lb **13** Ran SP% **124.9**
CSF: £24.68.
Owner Leonidas Marinopoulos **Bred** Mrs M Campbell-Andenaes **Trained** Newmarket, Suffolk
■ The Al Rashidiya had Group 2 status for the first time, upgraded from Group 3 level.

FOCUS
Not a particularly competitive race, but the pace was fair, with Tequilla Heights and Tam Lin taking each other on, and the performance of the reliable Steele Tango, successful in a C&D handicap off 110 two weeks earlier, suggests Presvis returned to his best form.

NOTEBOOK
Presvis hadn't been seen since disappointing at Royal Ascot last year, but this confirmed hold-up performer was ideally suited by the decent gallop and was winning at the Carnival for the third consecutive year. Dropped in from the widest stall, he raced in a detached last under a confident Ryan Moore, who gets on so well with him (partnership now 6-10), and after tanking along under restraint, made fairly effortless headway early in the straight, moving upsides the then leader Caymans over a furlong out without having been seriously asked. He then soon came under just hands-and-heels pressure and drew well clear. All being well, next stop will be the Group 2 Jebel Hatta back over C&D on Super Thursday (March 3), a race he won last year, before his main target, the Duty Free.
Steele Tango(USA) had to wait for an opening early in the straight, allowing the winner first run, but he was only ever going to be second best.
Caymans(AUS), a Group 2 winner in Australia, raced much closer to the pace than the front two and deserves credit.
Irish Flame(SAF), South Africa's Horse of the Year in 2010, was sent off a short-priced favourite owing to doubts about Presvis and a general lack of strength in depth, but Mike De Kock said beforehand he was "not expecting him to win." The trainer proved correct, with this 5-y-o, who had to concede upwards of 3lb all round, simply not having the required speed. He's an out-and-out galloper who wants 1m4f and the City of Gold followed by the Sheema Classic are said to be his main objectives. (op 7-4)
Bushman was produced with every chance but was not at his best.
Sea Lord(IRE) did little change the view that he's going to struggle this year.

332a XPRESS TROPHY (H'CAP) (TURF) 1m
6:25 (6:25) (95-115,113) 3-Y-O+

£57,692 (£19,230; £9,615; £4,807; £2,884; £1,923)

RPR
1 **Win For Sure (GER)**[14] 156 6-9-3 110...................... GregoryBenoist 15 111
(X Nakkachdji, France) *settled in rr: rdn 2 1/2f out: r.o wl fnl 1 1/2f: led nr line* **10/1**
2 ¼ **Navajo Chief**[7] 236 4-8-0 100...................................... HarryBentley(7) 5 100
(Alan Jarvis) *trckd ldr: led 1 1/2f out: r.o wl: hdd cl to home* **50/1**
3 ½ **Raihana (AUS)**[131] 5-9-3 110......................... ChristopheSoumillon 12 109
(M F De Kock, South Africa) *in rr of mid-div: chsd ldrs 2f out: nt qcknd fnl 110yds* **6/1**[2]
4 *nse* **Start Right**[117] 6562 4-8-5 98..................... Christophe-PatriceLemaire 16 97
(Luca Cumani) *in rr of mid-div: r.o wl fnl 2f: nrst fin* **11/4**[1]
5 ¾ **Barbecue Eddie (USA)**[28] 8028 7-8-7 100..................(b) TadhgO'Shea 2 97
(Doug Watson, UAE) *trckd ldng duo: r.o same pce fnl 1 1/2f* **20/1**
6 ¾ **Hujaylea (IRE)**[14] 152 8-8-9 102.......................................(p) ShaneFoley 7 97
(M Halford, Ire) *nvr cl to chal* **7/1**[3]
7 ½ **Oasis Dancer**[160] 5275 4-8-11 105...................................... JimCrowley 10 98
(Ralph Beckett) *a mid-div* **9/1**
8 ¾ **Big Creek (IRE)**[7] 242 4-8-9 102...................................... PatCosgrave 8 94
(J S Moore) *nvr nr to chal* **40/1**
9 *hd* **Lochinver (USA)**[117] 6593 4-9-2 109.................................... TedDurcan 6 101
(Saeed Bin Suroor) *v.s.a: settled in rr: n.d* **7/1**[3]
10 ½ **Munaddam (USA)**[14] 152 9-8-13 106...................................... WJSupple 1 97
(E Charpy, UAE) *nvr bttr than mid-div* **40/1**
11 ¾ **Royal Revival**[88] 7266 4-9-1 108................................ FrankieDettori 3 97
(Saeed Bin Suroor) *nvr bttr than mid-div* **8/1**
12 ½ **Clasp**[14] 157 9-8-8 101 ow1..(vt) PatDobbs 13 88
(Doug Watson, UAE) *nvr bttr than mid-div* **28/1**
13 *1* **Yasoodd**[18] 8-8-7 100..(e) KShea 9 86
(D Selvaratnam, UAE) *nvr bttr than mid-div* **25/1**
14 ¼ **Anam Chara (IRE)**[7] 241 5-8-6 99...................................... WayneSmith 4 84
(Andrew Oliver, Ire) *sn led: hdd 2f out: wknd fnl 1f* **33/1**
15 2 ½ **Tiger Reigns**[117] 6562 5-8-9 102................................ RichardMullen 14 81
(Michael Dods) *settled in rr: n.d* **20/1**
16 ¾ **Fareer**[201] 3888 5-9-0 107.. RichardHills 11 85
(Ed Dunlop) *a mid-div* **12/1**

1m 37.52s (97.52) **16** Ran SP% **130.4**
CSF: £465.16 Tricast: 3286.06. Placepot: £374.30 to a £1 stake. Pool: £9101.99. - 17.75 winning tickets. Quadpot: £11.30 to a £1 stake. Pool: £791.32 - 51.80 winning tickets..
Owner Prime Equestrian S.A.R.L. **Bred** Grosser Fhrhof **Trained** France

FOCUS
The pace was fair, appearing to suit all running styles just about equally, and this was a really competitive contest, one of the best handicaps to be run at the Carnival so far this year. Interestingly, three of the first four finishers were drawn in double figures.

NOTEBOOK
Win For Sure(GER) gave another boost to the form of the first round of the Al Maktoum challenge, having finished third in that race on his Dubai debut, and this performance is all the more creditable considering he made his move out widest of all in the straight. Drawn in stall 15, he sat well off the pace for much of the way and to cover plenty of ground turning into the straight, but he most of an uninterrupted trip. He ran as though he'll benefit from further, so the Jebel Hatta on Super Thursday may be a suitable target, although improvement will be required.
Navajo Chief raced much closer to the pace than the winner, third and fourth-placed finishers, but unlike those runners he had the benefit of a single-figure draw. This was a marked return to form after some poor efforts.
Raihana(AUS), back after an unsuccessful stint in Australia, had to weave her way through in the straight, ending up towards the inside, but she had her chance. Being a big filly, this should bring her on fitness-wise, and she was on edge beforehand, so it may also take the freshness out of her.

Start Right was the second reserve but lined up after Luca Cumani's other two declared runners were pulled out, and he was solid in the market, the impression being that he's thought to still be on a good mark. The widest draw was the worry, but as it turned out that was no excuse - he simply didn't run quite as well as might have been expected. He did, though, show enough to suggest he can win a similar race.
Barbecue Eddie(USA) was always handy from a favourable draw and had his chance, but his trainer has yet to have a winner at the 2011 Carnival.
Hujaylea(IRE) was helped by being held up off an overly strong pace when second here last time and found this tougher.
Oasis Dancer should come on for this first run in 160 days.
Lochinver(USA) ruined his chance with a slow start.
Royal Revival didn't pick up for pressure. (op 15/2)

[304]LINGFIELD (L-H)
Friday, January 28

OFFICIAL GOING: Standard
Wind: Moderate, against Weather: Fine but cloudy, cold

333 BET ON WINNING DISTANCES AT BLUESQ.COM CLAIMING STKS 5f (P)
1:10 (1:10) (Class 6) 3-Y-O **£1,535** (£453; £226) **Stalls** High

Form RPR
121- **1** **Chevise (IRE)**[99] [7040] 3-8-6 74........................ NickyMackay 4 76
(George Baker) *trckd ldr: pushed along 2f out: clsd to ld jst over 1f out: sn clr* **2/7**[1]
34-4 **2** *3 ¾* **Welsh Inlet (IRE)**[13] [179] 3-8-5 62........................ NeilChalmers 3 61
(John Bridger) *led and allowed unchal ld: kicked on over 2f out: hdd jst over 1f out: no ch w wnr* **5/1**[2]
5-45 **3** *2 ½* **Braehead (IRE)**[10] [198] 3-7-12 62........................ RPWalsh(7) 2 52
(David Evans) *settled in 4th: rdn to chse clr ldng pair wl over 1f out: one pce and no imp* **12/1**[3]
0-6 **4** *4* **Fantale**[23] [43] 3-8-5 0........................ MartinLane 5 38
(David Evans) *taken down early: v awkard s and slowly away: in tch in last: rdn 1/2-way: tk modest 4th ins fnl f* **66/1**
000- **5** *2 ¾* **Upark Flyer**[91] [7211] 3-7-9 56........................(e[1]) RyanPowell(5) 1 23
(Patrick Morris) *t.k.h: chsd ldng pair to wl over 1f out: hd high and wknd* **16/1**

59.84 secs (1.04) **Going Correction** +0.125s/f (Slow) 5 Ran SP% **109.5**
Speed ratings (Par 95): **96,90,86,79,75**
CSF £2.10 TOTE £1.20: £1.10, £1.20; EX 1.90.Chevise was subject of a friendly claim.
Owner M Khan X2 **Bred** Paul And Mrs Jenny Green **Trained** Whitsbury, Hants

FOCUS
A moderate and uncompetitive claimer but the form makes sense at face value.

334 LINGFIELDPARK.CO.UK CLASSIFIED CLAIMING STKS 7f (P)
1:40 (1:41) (Class 6) 4-Y-O+ **£1,535** (£453; £226) **Stalls** Low

Form RPR
31-2 **1** **Hinton Admiral**[16] [134] 7-8-8 74 ow2........................ MichaelStainton 6 85
(Jane Chapple-Hyam) *s.i.s: trckd ldrs: wnt 2nd over 2f out: hd at awkward angle but drvn to ld 1f out: styd on wl* **5/4**[1]
3-12 **2** *2 ½* **Fivefold (USA)**[9] [213] 4-8-4 69........................(p) ChrisCatlin 7 74
(John Akehurst) *pressed ldr: led over 3f out: drvn over 2f out: hdd and no ex 1f out* **6/1**[3]
00-1 **3** *1 ½* **Silver Guest**[21] [78] 6-7-13 75........................ AndrewHeffernan(3) 1 68
(Ralph Smith) *hld up bhd ldrs: looking for room over 2f out: prog to chse ldng pair wl over 1f out: nt qckn and no imp* **4/1**[2]
50-5 **4** *1 ¾* **Emerald Girl (IRE)**[10] [200] 4-8-4 72........................ JimmyQuinn 2 65
(Richard Fahey) *sn pushed along to stay in tch: outpcd over 2f out: plugged on fnl f* **12/1**
23-5 **5** *1 ½* **Kipchak (IRE)**[21] [78] 6-8-2 63........................(p) HayleyTurner 3 59
(Conor Dore) *trckd ldrs: pushed along and steadily fdd fnl 2f* **8/1**
2-21 **6** *2 ½* **I Confess**[9] [213] 6-7-11 68........................(b) RPWalsh(7) 5 54
(David Evans) *led to over 3f out: sn u.p: steadily wknd fnl 2f* **6/1**[3]
0-55 **7** *4* **Quick Single (USA)**[7] [243] 5-7-12 42........................(be) DavidProbert 4 38
(Phil McEntee) *sn rdn: a last and struggling* **66/1**

1m 24.24s (-0.56) **Going Correction** +0.125s/f (Slow) 7 Ran SP% **113.3**
Speed ratings (Par 101): **108,105,103,101,99 96,92**
toteswingers:1&2:£2.90, 1&3:£1.80, 2&3:£3.90 CSF £9.17 TOTE £2.90: £1.40, £3.10; EX 10.80.
Owner Rory Murphy **Bred** Gainsborough Stud Management Ltd **Trained** Dalham, Suffolk

FOCUS
A slightly more competitive claimer than the opener, but still a modest affair. The form is rated through the runner-up to his recent best, backed up by the third.

335 BLACKBERRY LANE H'CAP 7f (P)
2:15 (2:15) (Class 6) (0-65,66) 3-Y-O **£1,569** (£463; £231) **Stalls** Low

Form RPR
3-11 **1** **Aquilifer (IRE)**[8] [227] 3-9-9 66 6ex........................ ShaneKelly 9 78+
(William Jarvis) *trckd ldrs in 5th: effrt on outer 2f out: clsd to ld 1f out: drvn clr* **7/4**[1]
01-5 **2** *1 ¾* **Roman Strait**[8] [228] 3-9-4 61........................ LiamKeniry 4 67
(Michael Blanshard) *trckd ldng trio: wnt 2nd over 2f out: drvn to ld briefly jst over 1f out: styd on but outpcd by wnr* **9/2**[2]
40-3 **3** *2 ½* **Tony Hollis**[6] [263] 3-8-13 56........................ JamesMillman 2 56
(Rod Millman) *hld up last: detached and pushed along after 2f: stl last over 1f out: styd on wl fnl f: snatched 3rd on post* **16/1**
060- **4** *nk* **Govenor General (IRE)**[118] [6560] 3-9-3 60........................ GeorgeBaker 3 59
(Jeremy Noseda) *hld up in 8th: gng bttr than most 2f out but plenty to do: shkn up over 1f out: styd on to dispute 3rd nr fin* **6/1**
05- **5** *hd* **Knox Overstreet**[86] [7295] 3-9-5 62........................ SamHitchcott 6 60
(Mick Channon) *drvn to ld and set gd pce: hdd & wknd jst over 1f out: lost 3rd last strides* **5/1**[3]
0-64 **6** *1 ½* **Dances With Words (IRE)**[4] [275] 3-9-0 57........................(p) IanMongan 7 51
(Rodney Farrant) *chsd ldng pair to over 2f out: styd on inner and grad wknd u.p* **14/1**
56-3 **7** *hd* **Kassaab**[16] [132] 3-8-7 57........................ ShirleyTeasdale(7) 8 51
(Jeremy Gask) *pressed ldr at decent pce to 2f out: styd on inner and wknd* **25/1**
003- **8** *6* **Loves Theme (IRE)**[28] [8031] 3-9-3 60........................ J-PGuillambert 1 42
(Alan Bailey) *nvr bttr than 7th: pushed along over 4f out: struggling 3f out: wknd 2f out* **16/1**
54-3 **9** *1* **Monadreen Dancer**[18] [110] 3-9-7 64........................ EddieAhern 10 44
(Daniel Mark Loughnane, Ire) *stdd s: hld up in 6th: effrt on outer 3f out: no prog 2f out: wknd and eased* **10/1**

1m 25.58s (0.78) **Going Correction** +0.125s/f (Slow) 9 Ran SP% **116.9**
Speed ratings (Par 95): **100,98,95,94,94 92,92,85,84**
toteswingers:1&2:£2.60, 1&3:£9.30, 2&3:£10.50 CSF £9.63 CT £95.00 TOTE £2.30: £1.10, £2.60, £5.30; EX 8.10 Trifecta £299.60 Part won. Pool £404.92 - 0.93 winning units..
Owner John Kelsey-Fry **Bred** Miss L Magnier **Trained** Newmarket, Suffolk

FOCUS
A moderate handicap, but they went a fair pace early. The third, fourth and fifth ran close to their marks, so the form looks pretty reliable.
Dances With Words(IRE) Official explanation: jockey said gelding hung right throughout

336 10% FORECAST BONUS AT BLUESQ.COM H'CAP 6f (P)
2:50 (2:50) (Class 5) (0-75,72) 4-Y-O+ **£2,115** (£624; £312) **Stalls** Low

Form RPR
-020 **1** **Prize Point**[6] [264] 5-8-12 66........................ MatthewDavies(3) 4 73
(Jim Boyle) *mde virtually all: stdd pce after 2f: kicked on again over 2f out: hrd pressed fnl f: jst hld on* **3/1**[2]
4-50 **2** *nse* **Desert Icon (IRE)**[5] [269] 5-8-5 63........................ LauraPike(7) 1 70
(David Simcock) *taken down early: hld up in last: gd prog jst over 1f out: r.o to take 2nd nr fin: jst failed* **6/1**[3]
06-0 **3** *½* **Fantasy Fighter (IRE)**[19] [105] 6-9-6 71........................ JimmyQuinn 8 76
(John Quinn) *plld hrd: trckd ldng pair: chsd wnr on inner over 1f out: str chal fnl f: jst hld and lost 2nd nr fin* **8/1**
4-50 **4** *1 ¼* **Gwilym (GER)**[13] [178] 8-9-1 66........................ DaneO'Neill 2 67
(Derek Haydn Jones) *hld up in 7th: prog over 1f out to chse ldrs ins fnl f: nt qckn and no imp last 100yds* **7/1**
0-33 **5** *nk* **Absa Lutte (IRE)**[16] [125] 8-9-0 72........................(t) JosephYoung(7) 7 72+
(Michael Mullineaux) *taken down early: hld up in 5th: sed pulling hrd bef 1/2-way and trapped out wd: lost pl 2f out: no ch 1f out: urged along and kpt on* **15/2**
-254 **6** *½* **Chjimes (IRE)**[6] [264] 7-9-2 67........................(b) HayleyTurner 3 66
(Conor Dore) *trckd ldng pair: chsd wnr 2f out: hanging and nt qckn over 1f out: sn lost pl and btn* **5/2**[1]
22-0 **7** *3 ¼* **Spin Again (IRE)**[10] [199] 6-9-3 68........................ LiamJones 5 56
(Mark Wellings) *w wnr to over 2f out: steadily wknd* **12/1**
0-20 **8** *2 ¾* **Goddess Of Light (IRE)**[8] [231] 4-9-5 70........................ EddieAhern 6 49
(Daniel Mark Loughnane, Ire) *hld up in 6th: rdn and no prog 2f out: wknd fnl f* **9/1**

1m 12.6s (0.70) **Going Correction** +0.125s/f (Slow) 8 Ran SP% **120.9**
Speed ratings (Par 103): **100,99,99,97,97 96,92,88**
toteswingers:1&2:£4.30, 1&3:£6.40, 2&3:£9.70 CSF £22.86 CT £135.82 TOTE £4.00: £1.10, £1.90, £2.50; EX 23.80 Trifecta £164.50 Pool £513.53 - 2.31 winning units.
Owner M Khan X2 **Bred** Mrs B Skinner **Trained** Epsom, Surrey

FOCUS
Quite a competitive little handicap, though the pace was modest for a sprint and a few raced too keenly early. The form is rated through the winner to his recent best.
Fantasy Fighter(IRE) Official explanation: jockey said gelding ran too free
Spin Again(IRE) Official explanation: jockey said gelding hung right

337 FRED & RON GIBSON MEMORIAL H'CAP 5f (P)
3:25 (3:26) (Class 6) (0-62,65) 4-Y-O+ **£1,535** (£453; £226) **Stalls** High

Form RPR
-422 **1** **Black Baccara**[7] [250] 4-8-2 51........................(be) RyanClark(5) 2 61
(Phil McEntee) *trckd ldrs and a gng wl: prog to ld over 1f out: rdn and styd on wl* **11/4**[1]
2-04 **2** *2 ¼* **Wanchai Whisper**[9] [215] 4-9-1 62........................(v[1]) AndrewHeffernan(3) 1 64
(Peter Hedger) *dwlt: hld up in last pair: nudged along and gd prog jst over 1f out: wnt 2nd last 100yds: effrt flattened out and no imp* **9/2**[3]
0-00 **3** *nk* **Steel City Boy (IRE)**[20] [98] 8-8-8 52........................(p) JimmyQuinn 8 53
(Derek Shaw) *s.i.s: hld up in 7th: prog over 1f out: hrd rdn to chse wnr fnl f: no imp and lost 2nd last 100yds* **20/1**
010- **4** *4 ½* **Triskaidekaphobia**[84] [7334] 8-8-12 56........................(t) FrankieMcDonald 7 41
(Paul Fitzsimons) *pressed ldr: led 1/2-way: drvn and hdd over 1f out: wknd* **20/1**
/2-6 **5** *1* **Mosa Mine**[16] [132] 4-9-0 58........................ MichaelStainton 5 39
(Jane Chapple-Hyam) *chsd ldrs on inner: rdn 2f out: steadily wknd* **12/1**
65-6 **6** *½* **Step It Up (IRE)**[16] [133] 7-9-4 62........................ GeorgeBaker 9 41
(Jim Boyle) *chsd ldrs on outer: lost grnd whn wd bnd 2f out: sn wknd* **3/1**[2]
60-0 **7** *1 ¼* **What Katie Did (IRE)**[14] [166] 6-8-5 52........................(b) KierenFox(3) 3 27
(Milton Bradley) *led to 1/2-way: sn u.p: wknd qckly fnl f* **12/1**
-450 **8** *3 ¾* **Avonvalley**[4] [276] 4-8-11 55........................(b[1]) RobbieFitzpatrick 4 16
(Peter Grayson) *dwlt: hld up in last pair: rdn and no prog 2f out* **12/1**
4-65 **9** *2 ¼* **Ten Down**[8] [224] 6-8-7 51 oh2........................(b) AndreaAtzeni 6 4
(Michael Quinn) *pressed ldng pair on outer to 2f out: wknd rapidly* **6/1**

59.45 secs (0.65) **Going Correction** +0.125s/f (Slow) 9 Ran SP% **116.7**
Speed ratings (Par 101): **99,95,94,87,86 85,83,77,73**
toteswingers:1&2:£2.90, 1&3:£11.70, 2&3:£17.20 CSF £15.65 CT £198.62 TOTE £3.30: £1.50, £1.80, £6.80; EX 13.50 Trifecta £180.40 Pool £663.24 - 2.72 winning units.
Owner Eventmaker Racehorses **Bred** Peter Balding **Trained** Newmarket, Suffolk

FOCUS
A moderate sprint handicap run at a solid pace best rated though the runner-up to recent handicap form.

338 ASHURST WOOD H'CAP 5f (P)
4:00 (4:01) (Class 6) (0-60,59) 3-Y-O **£1,535** (£453; £226) **Stalls** High

Form RPR
22-4 **1** **Rylee Mooch**[24] [41] 3-9-4 59........................(e) KierenFox(3) 7 64
(Richard Guest) *pressed ldr: upsides wl over 1f out: pressed new ldr fnl f: forced ahd last 75yds* **9/2**[3]
0-01 **2** *hd* **Mini Bon Bon**[15] [146] 3-9-2 54........................(v) LiamJones 3 58
(Alan Bailey) *trckd ldrs: effrt 2f out: drvn to chal fnl f: pressed wnr nr fin: jst hld* **10/1**
65-3 **3** *¾* **Quadra Hop (IRE)**[15] [146] 3-9-5 57........................ RobertWinston 1 58
(Bryn Palling) *trckd ldrs gng wl: effrt 2f out: led 1f out: drvn and hdd last 75yds: fdd* **13/2**
325- **4** *1 ¾* **Lisselton Cross**[30] [7997] 3-9-5 57........................ GeorgeBaker 9 52+
(Martin Bosley) *chsd ldrs on outer: lost grnd bnd 2f out: hanging and nt qckn over 1f out: kpt on fnl f* **5/2**[1]
04-6 **5** *1 ½* **Mi Sun Donk**[22] [64] 3-9-3 55........................ LiamKeniry 2 45
(Brett Johnson) *s.i.s: hld up in rr: gng wl enough 2f out: sme prog over 1f out: rdn and one pce after* **8/1**

00-0 **6** 3 1/4 **Hey Mambo**[22] 64 3-8-2 **45**.........................(t) RyanClark(5) 6 23
(Roger Ingram) *s.i.s: wl in rr: effrt and hanging over 1f out: rdn and plugged on fnl f* **33/1**
0-32 **7** 3/4 **Fairy Tales**[7] 246 3-9-0 **52**......................... NeilChalmers 4 27
(John Bridger) *led: styd on inner and hdd 1f out: wknd qckly* **7/2**[2]
000- **8** 1 **Veuveveuvevoom**[77] 7418 3-8-7 **45**.................. FrankieMcDonald 5 17
(Gerry Enright) *nvr on terms: struggling in rr fnl 2f* **33/1**
04-0 **9** nk **Shutupandrive**[15] 146 3-8-7 **45**.........................(v) HayleyTurner 10 16
(Mark Usher) *pressed ldng pair on outer to 2f out: sn wknd* **20/1**
0-00 **10** 3/4 **Zohan (IRE)**[7] 251 3-8-7 **45**.........................(b) RobbieFitzpatrick 8 13
(Peter Grayson) *s.i.s: sn detached in last and nt gng wl: nvr a factor* **66/1**

60.35 secs (1.55) **Going Correction** +0.125s/f (Slow) **10** Ran SP% **114.6**
Speed ratings (Par 95): **92,91,90,87,85 80,78,77,76,75**
toteswingers:1&2:£7.00, 1&3:£3.00, 2&3:£8.10 CSF £45.49 CT £295.68 TOTE £6.40: £2.60, £2.80, £3.10; EX 37.50 Trifecta £100.80 Pool £865.79 - 6.35 winning units.
Owner Katie Hughes,Julie McCarlie,Sheila White **Bred** Mrs Sheila White **Trained** Stainforth, S Yorks

FOCUS
A weak 3-y-o sprint handicap in which only one of the ten runners had tasted success before. The form is rated around the placed horses to their upgraded Southwell form.
Zohan(IRE) Official explanation: jockey said gelding hung right throughout

339 PLAY RAINBOW RICHES AT BLUESQ.COM MAIDEN STKS 1m 2f (P)
4:30 (4:32) (Class 5) 3-Y-O **£2,115** (£624; £312) **Stalls** Low

Form RPR
3- **1** **Songjiang**[38] 7954 3-9-3 0.........................(b[1]) RobertHavlin 2 72
(John Gosden) *mde all: dictated stdy pce to 3f out: in command over 1f out: shkn up and styd on fnl f* **14/1**
2 1 3/4 **Blaise Chorus (IRE)** 3-8-12 0......................... RobertWinston 7 64+
(B W Hills) *slowest away: sn in tch in 6th: prog to chse ldng pair 3f out: rdn 2f out: kpt on to take 2nd 1f out: no imp on wnr* **2/1**[2]
0- **3** 3/4 **Ilissos (USA)**[44] 7873 3-9-3 0......................... GeorgeBaker 5 67
(Jeremy Noseda) *trckd ldng pair: rdn and nt qckn over 2f out whn pce lifted: disp 2nd 1f out: one pce* **15/8**[1]
6 **4** nk **Manifestation**[20] 95 3-9-3 0.........................(b[1]) NickyMackay 8 67
(John Gosden) *trckd ldrs in 4th: outpcd whn pce lifted over 2f out: pushed along and styd on steadily fnl f* **5/1**[3]
000- **5** 2 3/4 **Gower Rules (IRE)**[123] 6412 3-9-3 52......................... NeilChalmers 1 61?
(John Bridger) *chsd ldrs in 5th: outpcd over 2f out: no imp after* **100/1**
-4 **6** hd **Loyal N Trusted**[14] 158 3-9-3 0......................... AndreaAtzeni 9 61
(Michael Wigham) *trckd wnr: rdn to chal over 2f out: wknd qckly 1f out* **9/1**
5 **7** 4 1/2 **Ocean's Dream Day (IRE)**[11] 191 3-9-3 0......................... EddieAhern 3 52
(John Ryan) *a in rr: wl outpcd over 2f out: no ch after* **20/1**
-0 **8** 1 1/2 **Westhaven (IRE)**[18] 110 3-9-3 0......................... DaneO'Neill 4 49
(David Elsworth) *s.i.s: a in last trio: racd awkwardly fr 1/2-way: wl adrift and hanging over 1f out* **20/1**
9 25 **Zoriana** 3-8-9 0......................... KierenFox(3) 6 —
(Christine Dunnett) *s.i.s: a in last trio and rn green: wknd rapidly over 2f out: t.o* **66/1**

2m 9.95s (3.35) **Going Correction** +0.125s/f (Slow) **9** Ran SP% **113.5**
Speed ratings (Par 97): **91,89,89,88,86 86,82,81,61**
toteswingers:1&2:£6.80, 1&3:£5.10, 2&3:£2.10. totesuper7: Win: Not won. Place: Not won. CSF £40.61 TOTE £5.30: £1.40, £1.60, £1.30; EX 58.00 Trifecta £116.80 Pool £960.31 - 6.08 winning units.
Owner H R H Princess Haya Of Jordan **Bred** Richard Green And New England Stud **Trained** Newmarket, Suffolk

FOCUS
Some big stables were represented in this maiden, but they only went a steady pace and the winner had things all his own way. The form looks muddling.
T/Plt: £46.10 to a £1 stake. Pool:£45,099.28 - 712.61 winning tickets T/Qpdt: £28.70 to a £1 stake. Pool:£3,958.24 - 101.80 winning tickets JN

281 WOLVERHAMPTON (A.W) (L-H)
Friday, January 28

OFFICIAL GOING: Standard to slow
Wind: Fresh against Weather: Fine

340 BET ON WINNING DISTANCES AT BLUESQ.COM H'CAP 1m 141y(P)
4:40 (4:41) (Class 7) (0-50,55) 4-Y-O+ **£1,535** (£453; £226) **Stalls** Low

Form RPR
-541 **1** **Very Well Red**[8] 225 8-9-7 **54** 6ex......................... WilliamCarson 7 62
(Peter Hiatt) *chsd ldr: rdn over 2f out: styd on u.p to ld ins fnl f* **11/2**[3]
40-4 **2** hd **On The Cusp (IRE)**[22] 61 4-8-4 **45**.........................(p) NathanAlison(7) 1 53
(Michael Chapman) *led: rdn over 1f out: hdd ins fnl f: styd on* **12/1**
6/03 **3** 2 1/4 **Meydan Style (USA)**[8] 229 5-8-12 **45**......................... JoeFanning 4 48
(Bruce Hellier) *plld hrd and prom: rdn over 1f out: no ex wl ins fnl f* **20/1**
-651 **4** hd **Kielty's Folly**[9] 204 7-9-8 **55** 6ex......................... GrahamGibbons 9 57+
(Brian Baugh) *hmpd s: hld up: hdwy over 2f out: rdn over 1f out: styd on* **3/1**[1]
00/- **5** 1 **Ocarito (GER)**[707] 256 10-9-3 **50**......................... StevieDonohoe 3 50
(John Spearing) *hld up: racd keenly: hdwy over 2f out: styd on* **7/1**
06-6 **6** nk **Aggbag**[8] 229 7-8-12 **45**......................... RichardKingscote 5 44+
(Tony Carroll) *hld up: rdn over 2f out: hdwy over 1f out: r.o: nt rch ldrs* **16/1**
3-00 **7** 2 1/4 **Al Rayanah**[21] 86 8-9-2 **49**......................... KirstyMilczarek 2 43
(George Prodromou) *hld up: hdwy 2f out: sn rdn: no ex fnl f* **10/1**
0/2- **8** 7 **Silca Meydan**[386] 75 5-9-3 **50**......................... JamesDoyle 8 27
(Richard Price) *wnt rt s: sn prom: rdn and wknd over 2f out* **14/1**
0-21 **9** 1 **Hi Spec (IRE)**[1] 312 8-9-7 **54** 6ex.........................(t) AdamKirby 6 28
(Mandy Rowland) *sn pushed along and a in rr* **7/1**
/50- **10** 10 **Aurora Lights**[64] 7563 4-8-11 **45**......................... TomEaves 10 —
(Richard Fahey) *chsd ldrs: rdn over 3f out: wknd over 2f out* **5/1**[2]
0/0- **11** 6 **Hill Of Clare (IRE)**[178] 4681 9-8-9 **45**......................... AmyBaker(3) 11 —
(George Jones) *dwlt: a bhd* **100/1**

1m 51.78s (1.28) **Going Correction** +0.125s/f (Slow)
WFA 4 from 5yo+ 1lb **11** Ran SP% **117.1**
Speed ratings (Par 97): **99,98,96,96,95 95,93,87,86,77 72**
toteswingers:1&2:£9.60, 1&3:£12.30, 2&3:£16.90 CSF £69.48 CT £1252.83 TOTE £7.60: £2.90, £5.10, £6.80; EX 68.30.
Owner Phil Kelly **Bred** Butts Enterprises Limited **Trained** Hook Norton, Oxon

FOCUS
The track passed a morning inspection and the going was described as standard to slow. This opening race was a low-grade handicap but there were three last time out winners in the line-up. The pace was not very strong and the first two filled those positions throughout. The form is rated around the first three.
On The Cusp(IRE) Official explanation: jockey said gelding hung right-handed
Hi Spec(IRE) Official explanation: jockey said mare never travelled

341 HOTEL & CONFERENCING AT WOLVERHAMPTON CLASSIFIED CLAIMING STKS 1m 141y(P)
5:10 (5:10) (Class 5) 4-Y-O+ **£2,007** (£597; £298; £149) **Stalls** Low

Form RPR
10-3 **1** **April Fool**[26] 12 7-8-6 65.........................(b[1]) DavidProbert 6 77
(Ronald Harris) *mde all: rdn over 1f out: styd on wl* **9/1**
6-42 **2** 4 1/2 **Dream Of Fortune (IRE)**[13] 175 7-8-8 67.........................(bt) MartinLane 2 69
(David Evans) *hld up: hdwy over 3f out: rdn over 1f out: chsd wnr ins fnl f: no imp: edgd lft towards fin* **4/1**[2]
54-0 **3** 3/4 **What's Up Doc (IRE)**[23] 50 10-8-3 61......................... RichardKingscote 8 62
(Lawney Hill) *chsd wnr to over 2f out: sn rdn: no ex ins fnl f* **22/1**
11-6 **4** 1 3/4 **Querido (GER)**[4] 287 7-8-5 68.........................(vt[1]) ChrisCatlin 9 60
(Gary Brown) *dwlt: pushed along and hdwy 7f out: chsd wnr over 2f out: sn rdn: wknd ins fnl f* **5/6**[1]
10-0 **5** 1/2 **Aviso (GER)**[26] 12 7-8-10 70......................... ShaneKelly 7 64
(Barney Curley) *hld up: hdwy over 5f out: rdn over 3f out: hung lft and wknd over 1f out* **8/1**[3]
50-6 **6** 6 **Kildare Sun (IRE)**[4] 282 9-8-8 63.........................(v) GrahamGibbons 3 48
(John Mackie) *prom: rdn and lost pl over 6f out: n.d after* **16/1**
006- **7** 4 1/2 **Art Scholar (IRE)**[37] 7964 4-8-9 70......................... FergusSweeney 4 40
(Gary Moore) *hld up: rdn over 3f out: wknd over 2f out* **20/1**
0-60 **8** 12 **Lord's Seat**[12] 184 4-8-2 38......................... PatrickMathers 1 —
(Alan Berry) *prom: rdn over 6f out: wknd 4f out* **150/1**
02/0 **9** 9 **Tiger Dream**[21] 82 6-8-8 70.........................(p) FrannyNorton 5 —
(Chris Down) *s.i.s: outpcd: t.o* **12/1**

1m 50.03s (-0.47) **Going Correction** +0.125s/f (Slow)
WFA 4 from 6yo+ 1lb **9** Ran SP% **119.0**
Speed ratings (Par 103): **107,103,102,100,100 95,91,80,72**
toteswingers:1&2:£3.70, 1&3:£26.60, 2&3:£14.60 CSF £45.52 TOTE £11.60: £3.30, £1.50, £7.10; EX 33.10.
Owner G B Balding **Bred** Miss B Swire **Trained** Earlswood, Monmouths

FOCUS
A tight claimer, six of the runners had BHA ratings between 65 and 70. The kickback was flying up and it was probably a big advantage to race prominently but the winner still deserves some credit for a strong front-running effort. He is rated back to his best.
Art Scholar(IRE) Official explanation: jockey said gelding would not face the kick back

342 10% FORECAST BONUS AT BLUESQ.COM H'CAP 2m 119y(P)
5:40 (5:40) (Class 4) (0-85,80) 4-Y-O+ **£3,464** (£1,030; £515; £257) **Stalls** Low

Form RPR
500- **1** **Exemplary**[98] 7053 4-9-4 **80**......................... JoeFanning 4 96
(Mark Johnston) *s.i.s: sn chsng ldr: led 14f out: rdn clr over 1f out: hung rt: comf* **13/8**[1]
41-5 **2** 5 **Ethics Girl (IRE)**[9] 209 5-9-9 **78**.........................(t) FrannyNorton 5 88
(John Berry) *trckd ldrs: racd keenly: hung rt over 4f out: nt clr run over 2f out: chsd wnr over 1f out: sn rdn and no imp* **9/2**[3]
10-3 **3** 5 **Admirable Duque (IRE)**[22] 68 5-9-10 **79**.........................(p) MartinLane 6 83
(Dominic Ffrench Davis) *dwlt: hld up: hdwy over 2f out: rdn over 1f out: wknd ins fnl f* **11/1**
15-1 **4** 2 1/4 **Treacle Tart**[22] 68 6-9-2 **71**......................... AdamKirby 1 72
(Peter Charalambous) *trckd ldrs: wnt 2nd over 3f out: rdn and wknd over 1f out* **2/1**[2]
446- **5** 8 **Taikoo**[95] 7130 6-9-8 **77**......................... TravisBlock 3 69
(Hughie Morrison) *led: hdd 14f out: chsd wnr tl rdn over 3f out: wknd over 2f out* **16/1**
110/ **6** 15 **Kavaloti (IRE)**[576] 3510 7-9-7 **76**.........................(b) AmirQuinn 2 50
(Gary Moore) *hld up: rdn 4f out: sn wknd: t.o* **25/1**

3m 43.14s (1.34) **Going Correction** +0.125s/f (Slow)
WFA 4 from 5yo+ 7lb **6** Ran SP% **107.7**
Speed ratings (Par 105): **101,98,96,95,91 84**
toteswingers:1&2:£34.50, 1&3:£20.60, 2&3:£13.30 CSF £8.50 TOTE £3.50: £3.50, £3.50; EX 10.70.
Owner Sheikh Hamdan Bin Mohammed Al Maktoum **Bred** Darley **Trained** Middleham Moor, N Yorks

FOCUS
A fair staying handicap run at a steady pace. The favourite dictated from some way out and forged clear for a comfortable success. It is probably worth taking the form at face value.
Treacle Tart Official explanation: trainer said mare was unsuited by the compacted polytrack surface

343 ENJOY THE PARTY PACK GROUP OFFER CLAIMING STKS 5f 20y(P)
6:10 (6:10) (Class 6) 4-Y-O+ **£1,637** (£483; £241) **Stalls** Low

Form RPR
3-11 **1** **Sloop Johnb**[10] 197 5-9-1 72.........................(p) KirstyMilczarek 2 70+
(Conor Dore) *chsd ldr 4f out: led 1/2-way: rdn and hung lft ins fnl f: hld on* **5/4**[1]
0-03 **2** 1/2 **Misaro (GER)**[8] 224 10-8-11 60......................... (b) DavidProbert 1 64
(Ronald Harris) *pushed along to ld 1f: hmpd sn after: chsd ldrs: rdn 1/2-way: chsd wnr ins fnl f: r.o* **9/2**[3]
05-4 **3** 5 **Rievaulx World**[10] 197 5-9-1 73.........................(t) PhillipMakin 3 50
(Kevin Ryan) *led 4f out: hdd 1/2-way: rdn over 1f out: wknd ins fnl f* **5/2**[2]
44-6 **4** 1/2 **Gorgeous Goblin (IRE)**[22] 65 4-8-3 39..........(v[1]) JamesSullivan(3) 4 39
(David C Griffiths) *chsd ldrs: rdn 1/2-way: styd on same pce fr over 1f out* **50/1**
60-6 **5** 1 **Royal Blade (IRE)**[14] 166 4-8-10 51......................... PatrickMathers 6 40+
(Alan Berry) *sn outpcd: styd on u.p fr over 1f out: nvr nrr* **33/1**
6-21 **6** 2 1/2 **Punching**[22] 58 7-8-8 76......................... NoraLooby(7) 5 36
(Conor Dore) *prom: rdn 1/2-way: sn wknd* **13/2**
/04- **7** 8 **The Lord**[254] 2229 11-8-5 51......................... JakePayne(7) 7 —
(Bill Turner) *chsd ldrs: rdn 1/2-way: wknd 2f out* **40/1**

62.60 secs (0.30) **Going Correction** +0.125s/f (Slow) **7** Ran SP% **111.9**
Speed ratings (Par 101): **102,101,93,92,90 86,74**
toteswingers:1&2:£1.60, 1&3:£1.40, 2&3:£2.60 CSF £6.98 TOTE £3.20: £1.10, £3.20; EX 8.60.
Owner K F McNulty **Bred** Manor Farm Stud (rutland) **Trained** Cowbit, Lincs
■ Stewards' Enquiry : Jake Payne caution: careless riding.

FOCUS
A fair claimer. The pace was reasonable and the first two pulled clear. The winner is rated to his recent best but the fourth is a doubt over the form.

344 WOLVERHAMPTON-RACECOURSE.CO.UK MAIDEN FILLIES' STKS 1m 141y(P)
6:40 (6:42) (Class 5) 3-Y-O+ **£2,007** (£597; £298; £149) **Stalls** Low

Form RPR

1 **Libritish** 3-8-3 0 ow3 .... TobyAtkinson[5] 6 73+
(Marco Botti) *s.s: hld up: hdwy 2f out: led over 1f out: r.o wl* **9/1**

200- 2 2 1/2 **Beauchamp Xiara**[86] 7307 5-9-13 71 .... JamesDoyle 4 70+
(Hans Adielsson) *prom: rdn and swtchd lft over 1f out: styd on same pce ins fnl f* **2/1**[1]

6- 3 1/2 **Thymesthree (IRE)**[30] 8000 3-8-5 0 .... ChrisCatlin 2 61
(Chris Wall) *led: rdn and hdd over 1f out: edgd lft: styd on same pce ins fnl f* **11/4**[2]

30-0 4 1 1/2 **Jambo Bibi (IRE)**[22] 66 3-8-5 64 .... (b[1]) JoeFanning 8 58?
(Bruce Hellier) *hld up in tch: plld hrd: ev ch over 1f out: sn rdn: hung lft and no ex ins fnl f* **10/1**

4 5 3/4 **Full Bloom**[11] 191 3-8-5 0 .... DavidProbert 1 56
(Gerard Butler) *chsd ldr: rdn over 1f out: no ex ins fnl f* **3/1**[3]

6 6 8 **Refusetosurrender (IRE)**[21] 88 3-8-2 0 .... JamesSullivan[3] 7 38
(Richard Fahey) *plld hrd and prom: rdn and wknd over 1f out* **11/1**

600- 7 19 **Zareena**[42] 7913 3-8-5 40 .... MartinLane 5 —
(David Evans) *sn pushed along in rr: rdn and wknd over 3f out: t.o* **50/1**

1m 53.99s (3.49) **Going Correction** +0.125s/f (Slow)
WFA 3 from 4yo 22lb 4 from 5yo 1lb 7 Ran SP% **114.4**
Speed ratings (Par 100): **89,86,86,85,84 77,60**
toteswingers:1&2:£5.30, 1&3:£5.30, 2&3:£1.90 CSF £27.48 TOTE £13.10: £3.60, £3.20; EX 41.30.
Owner Giuliano Manfredini **Bred** John James **Trained** Newmarket, Suffolk

FOCUS
A weak fillies' maiden but a newcomer overcame a slow start to win with something in hand. It was slowly run and has been rated around the winner.

345 WOLVERHAMPTON HOLIDAY INN H'CAP 5f 216y(P)
7:10 (7:11) (Class 6) (0-65,64) 4-Y-O+ **£1,637** (£483; £241) **Stalls** Low

Form RPR

15-3 1 **Co Dependent (USA)**[10] 199 5-9-7 **64** .... FergusSweeney 4 76
(Jamie Osborne) *s.i.s: hld up: hdwy over 1f out: sn rdn: styd on to ld wl ins fnl f* **7/1**

0-53 2 2 **Dancing Freddy (IRE)**[3] 289 4-9-0 **60** .... (p) RobertLButler[3] 9 66
(Michael Chapman) *led: rdn over 1f out: hdd wl ins fnl f* **8/1**

502- 3 nk **Interchoice Star**[59] 7639 6-9-2 **59** .... (p) DuranFentiman 5 64
(Ray Peacock) *sn pushed along and prom: rdn to chse ldr over 1f out: styd on* **9/1**

3612 4 nk **Radiator Rooney (IRE)**[2] 306 8-8-3 **51** .... RyanPowell[5] 1 55
(Patrick Morris) *hld up: swtchd rt and hdwy over 1f out: sn rdn and hung rt: styd on* **7/2**[1]

5-22 5 3 3/4 **Libertino (IRE)**[14] 166 4-9-0 **57** .... J-PGuillambert 2 49
(Tony Carroll) *chsd ldrs: rdn over 2f out: no ex fnl f* **5/1**[3]

44-6 6 shd **Cheery Cat (USA)**[20] 97 7-9-3 **60** .... (v) MartinLane 7 52
(John Balding) *chsd ldrs: lost pl wl over 3f out: hung lft and styd on ins fnl f* **9/2**[2]

02-2 7 2 **Bel Cantor**[26] 13 8-9-4 **61** .... (p) WilliamCarson 8 46
(Bill Ratcliffe) *mid-div: sn pushed along: lost pl 4f out: n.d after* **6/1**

45-3 8 shd **Colamandis**[22] 65 4-8-8 **54** .... JamesSullivan[3] 3 39
(Hugh McWilliams) *mid-div: rdn over 2f out: wknd over 1f out* **33/1**

000- 9 14 **Eviction (IRE)**[45] 7868 4-9-2 **59** .... (b) AdamKirby 6 —
(Mandy Rowland) *sn drvn along to chse ldrs: rdn over 2f out: wknd over 1f out* **18/1**

1m 15.18s (0.18) **Going Correction** +0.125s/f (Slow) 9 Ran SP% **113.2**
Speed ratings (Par 101): **103,100,99,99,94 94,91,91,72**
toteswingers:1&2:£12.40, 1&3:£6.60, 2&3:£11.80 CSF £60.22 CT £508.20 TOTE £8.10: £2.80, £2.50, £6.00; EX 55.30.
Owner Dr Geraldine O'Sullivan **Bred** Daniel M Ryan **Trained** Upper Lambourn, Berks

FOCUS
A competitive sprint handicap run at a fast pace. The winner continues to improve.

346 PLAY RAINBOW RICHES AT BLUESQ.COM H'CAP 1m 1f 103y(P)
7:40 (7:41) (Class 6) (0-55,55) 4-Y-O+ **£1,637** (£483; £241) **Stalls** Low

Form RPR

455- 1 **Stargazing (IRE)**[62] 7604 5-8-13 **52** .... AdamKirby 11 62+
(Marco Botti) *hld up: hdwy over 3f out: rdn over 1f out: r.o to ld towards fin* **9/2**[2]

36-3 2 3/4 **Verluga (IRE)**[18] 115 4-9-1 **55** .... DuranFentiman 4 61
(Tim Easterby) *a.p: rdn over 1f out: r.o to ld wl ins fnl f: hdd towards fin* **7/2**[1]

000- 3 1/2 **Aine's Delight (IRE)**[24] 6518 5-9-2 **55** .... KirstyMilczarek 7 60
(Andy Turnell) *hld up: hdwy over 3f out: rdn over 1f out: r.o* **25/1**

026- 4 1/2 **Herecomethegirls**[46] 7863 5-8-10 **54** .... (b) KylieManser[5] 8 58
(Olivia Maylam) *s.i.s: hld up: hdwy over 1f out: rdn ins fnl f: r.o* **8/1**

4-63 5 hd **Escardo (GER)**[9] 204 8-8-7 **46** .... WilliamCarson 3 51
(David Bridgwater) *mid-div: hdwy over 3f out: nt clr run over 2f out: rdn over 1f out: styd on same pce ins fnl f* **11/2**

3-20 6 nk **Lord Deevert**[9] 210 6-8-8 **54** .... JakePayne[7] 12 57
(Bill Turner) *chsd ldr tl led over 2f out: rdn over 1f out: hdd wl ins fnl f* **25/1**

32-6 7 2 **Lunar River (FR)**[14] 164 8-8-8 **52** .... (t) JamesRogers[5] 1 52
(David Pinder) *chsd ldrs: rdn over 1f out: no ex wl ins fnl f* **11/1**

00/0 8 3 1/4 **Rough Sketch (USA)**[18] 115 6-8-13 **52** .... (t) TomEaves 6 44
(Ian Williams) *hld up: rdn over 3f out: nvr nrr* **33/1**

000- 9 1 1/4 **Naledi**[222] 2880 7-8-4 **46** .... AndrewHeffernan[3] 2 35
(Richard Price) *led: rdn and hdd over 2f out: wknd ins fnl f* **25/1**

-020 10 3 1/4 **Lucky Diva**[8] 225 4-8-11 **51** .... (p) JamesDoyle 10 33
(Sylvester Kirk) *hld up: rdn over 2f out: edgd lft over 1f out: nvr on terms* **5/1**[3]

0/0- 11 hd **Spares And Repairs**[62] 7599 8-8-0 **46** oh1 .... JackDuern[7] 9 28
(Reg Hollinshead) *hld up: a in rr* **25/1**

-405 12 12 **Raghdaan**[9] 204 4-8-6 **46** .... ChrisCatlin 5 —
(Peter Hiatt) *chsd ldrs tl rdn and wknd over 3f out* **12/1**

2m 2.87s (1.17) **Going Correction** +0.125s/f (Slow)
WFA 4 from 5yo+ 1lb 12 Ran SP% **117.9**
Speed ratings (Par 101): **99,98,97,97,97 97,95,92,91,88 88,77**
toteswingers:1&2:£3.10, 1&3:£53.90, 2&3:£24.70 CSF £18.99 CT £357.31 TOTE £7.50: £3.60, £1.70, £10.80; EX 23.70.
Owner Can Artam **Bred** Paul Green **Trained** Newmarket, Suffolk
■ Stewards' Enquiry : Jake Payne one-day ban: failed to ride to draw (Feb 11)
Kylie Manser one-day ban: used whip without giving mare time to respond (Feb 11)

FOCUS
A modest handicap run at a decent pace. The winner was value for a bit more than the winning margin suggests and the form looks straightforward.
T/Plt: £255.00 to a £1 stake. Pool:£77,605.85 - 222.14 winning tickets T/Qpdt: £26.40 to a £1 stake. Pool:£10,741.88 - 300.40 winning tickets CR

333 LINGFIELD (L-H)
Saturday, January 29

OFFICIAL GOING: Standard
Wind: medium, against Weather: overcast, chilly

347 BLUE SQUARE WISH CRAWLEY TOWN GOOD LUCK MAIDEN STKS 1m (P)
12:50 (12:50) (Class 5) 3-Y-O+ **£1,910** (£564; £282) **Stalls** High

Form RPR

2-4 1 **Wilfred Pickles (IRE)**[9] 226 5-9-13 78 .... DaneO'Neill 3 59+
(Jo Crowley) *stdd s: hld up in last pair: swtchd lft and shkn up over 1f out: pushed ahd ins fnl f: sn clr: v easily* **1/10**[1]

054- 2 3 3/4 **Ippi N Tombi (IRE)**[44] 7893 3-8-2 0 .... LukeMorris 7 41
(Phil McEntee) *chsd ldr: rdn and ev ch 2f out: led over 1f out: drvn and hdd ins fnl f: sn btn but hld on for 2nd* **100/1**

33-3 3 nk **Mr Maximas**[22] 86 4-9-13 47 .... RichardKingscote 5 50
(Bryn Palling) *sn led: rdn over 2f out: hdd over 1f out: nt pce of wnr ins fnl f: kpt on* **12/1**[2]

60- 4 1 **King Of The Titans (IRE)**[89] 7043 8-9-13 0 .... JamieMackay 2 48
(Patrick Gilligan) *chsd ldrs: pushed along and edging lft bnd 2f out: styd on same pce fnl f* **25/1**[3]

0- 5 2 1/2 **Star Danser**[45] 7873 3-8-9 0 ow2 .... SteveDrowne 1 39
(Tom Keddy) *dwlt: sn in tch: rdn and unable qck 2f out: wknd over 1f out* **25/1**[3]

0 6 27 **Bird Dog**[22] 85 5-9-13 0 .... AdamKirby 6 —
(Phil McEntee) *in tch in last pair: rdn along 5f out: hung rt and lost tch jst over 2f out: eased ins fnl f: t.o* **80/1**

1m 40.08s (1.88) **Going Correction** +0.15s/f (Slow)
WFA 3 from 4yo+ 20lb 6 Ran SP% **108.5**
Speed ratings (Par 103): **96,92,91,90,88 61**
toteswingers:1&2:£2.70, 1&3:£1.20, 2&3:£3.50 CSF £26.46 TOTE £1.10: £1.02, £16.90; EX 13.00.
Owner Kilstone Limited **Bred** Eurostrait Ltd **Trained** Whitcombe, Dorset

FOCUS
Despite being sent off at odds of 1-10, this threatened to be less than straightforward for Wilfred Pickles considering he had tended to idle badly when in front on previous outings and was 0-17, but his rivals were not remotely good enough to test him.

348 RICHARD ALDRIDGE 50TH BIRTHDAY H'CAP 1m (P)
1:25 (1:25) (Class 4) (0-85,83) 4-Y-O+ **£2,100** (£2,100; £481; £240) **Stalls** High

Form RPR

400- 1 **Titan Triumph**[93] 7187 7-9-4 **80** .... (t) JimCrowley 1 86
(William Knight) *stdd s: hld up in rr: clsd over 2f out: nt clr run briefly wl over 1f out: rdn and effrt on inner over 1f out: ev ch u.p ins fnl f: jnd ldr on post* **16/1**

11-0 1 dht **Blue Moon**[9] 226 4-9-2 **78** .... PhillipMakin 4 85+
(Kevin Ryan) *chsd ldng trio: clsd to trck ldrs and nt clr run jst over 2f out tl over 1f out: rdn and hdwy between horses ent fnl f: r.o gamely u.p to ld wl ins fnl f: jnd on post* **9/2**[2]

10-1 3 3/4 **Kilburn**[22] 82 7-9-4 **80** .... SteveDrowne 2 84
(Alastair Lidderdale) *chsd ldr: rdn ent fnl 2f: drvn and ev ch over 1f out: led 1f out: hdd and no ex wl ins fnl f* **5/1**[3]

-221 4 nse **Buaiteoir (FR)**[9] 226 5-9-7 **83** .... (e) LiamJones 7 87
(Paul D'Arcy) *stdd s: hld up in midfield: clsd over 2f out: shkn up and effrt jst over 1f out: rdn hands and heels and chal ins fnl f: no ex and no hdwy fnl 75yds* **5/1**[1]

000- 5 1 **Hereford Boy**[278] 1023 7-9-0 **76** .... RobertHavlin 5 70
(Dean Ivory) *hld up in rr: clsd and in tch but stl last 2f out: rdn over 1f out: kpt on ins fnl f: nvr quite gng pce to chal ldrs* **50/1**

1-06 6 shd **Kiss A Prince**[9] 226 5-9-4 **80** .... (p) AdamKirby 3 83+
(Dean Ivory) *hld up in midfield: effrt and rdn whn swtchd lft over 1f out: nvr enough room ins fnl f: nvr able to chal* **13/2**

00-6 7 shd **Pegasus Again (USA)**[16] 141 6-9-4 **80** .... (p) JoeFanning 8 81
(Robert Mills) *led: rdn ent fnl 2f: hdd 1f out: keeping on same pce and hld whn short of room ins fnl f* **10/1**

260- 8 nk **Marvo**[71] 6534 7-8-11 **78** .... AshleyMorgan[5] 6 78
(Mark H Tompkins) *chsd ldng pair: rdn ent fnl 2f: ev ch ent fnl f: no ex and btn fnl 100yds* **28/1**

1m 37.87s (-0.33) **Going Correction** +0.15s/f (Slow) 8 Ran SP% **113.0**
Speed ratings (Par 105): **107,107,106,106,105 105,105,104**WIN: BM £3.40 TT £10.30 PL: BM £1.80, TT £4.40, K £2.20 EX: BM/TT £58.50 TT/BB £38.00 CSF: BM/TT £34.57 TT/BM £42.10 T/C: BM/TT/K £185.00, TT/BM/K £208.96 TRIFECTA: BM/TT/K £244.30, TT/BM/K £237.20. toteswingers:TT&BM:£7.60, TT&K:£9.40, BM&K:£4.00 CT £0.27 TOTE £Owner: £Canisbay Bloodstock, £Bred, £Hesmonds Stud Ltd, £TrainedPatching, W Sussex.
Owner Guy Reed **Bred** Theakston Stud **Trained** Hambleton, N Yorks
■ Stewards' Enquiry : Adam Kirby Fine, £140, used whip that had been modified.

FOCUS
Despite the pace appearing fair, the field finished in a bunch - first two couldn't be separated - and this was a really competitive handicap.
Kiss A Prince ◆ Official explanation: jockey said gelding was denied a clear run

349 DAVE FULLER 50 YEAR'S A WINNER H'CAP 6f (P)
1:55 (1:55) (Class 5) (0-70,69) 3-Y-O **£2,047** (£604; £302) **Stalls** Low

Form RPR

2-31 1 **Kingscroft (IRE)**[9] 233 3-9-6 **68** .... GregFairley 3 76+
(Mark Johnston) *mde all: rdn clr over 1f out: in command and pushed out ins fnl f* **2/7**[1]

254- 2 2 **Captain Loui (IRE)**[80] 7395 3-8-11 **64** .... (p) RyanClark[5] 1 63
(Dai Burchell) *sn outpcd in last and rdn along: reminders 4f out: effrt on outer 2f out: kpt on ins fnl f to snatch 2nd last stride: no threat to wnr* **12/1**[3]

44-1 3 shd **Greenhead High**[17] 126 3-9-4 **66** .... J-PGuillambert 6 65
(Jane Chapple-Hyam) *in tch: nt clr run briefly wl over 1f out: rdn and hdwy over 1f out: chsd wnr ins fnl f: no imp: lost 2nd last stride* **15/2**[2]

2306 4 2 1/4 **Just For Leo (IRE)**[11] 198 3-8-5 **60** .... (v) RPWalsh[7] 5 51
(David Evans) *pressed wnr: ev ch and rdn ent fnl 2f: nt qckn w wnr over 1f out: btn 1f out: lost 2 pls ins fnl f* **20/1**

6-01 **5** 2 **Imogen Louise (IRE)**[7] 263 3-9-4 69 RobertLButler(3) 2 54
(Paddy Butler) *chsd ldrs: sltly hmpd over 5f out: effrt on inner wl over 1f out: unable qck u.p ent fnl f: wknd fnl 150yds* **12/1**[3]

1m 12.99s (1.09) **Going Correction** +0.15s/f (Slow) **5** Ran SP% **109.7**
Speed ratings (Par 97): **98,95,95,92,89**
CSF £4.73 TOTE £1.30: £1.10, £3.40; EX 4.70.
Owner Dr Marwan Koukash **Bred** J Beckett **Trained** Middleham Moor, N Yorks
■ Stewards' Enquiry : Greg Fairley caution: careless riding.

FOCUS
Modest form, but an improving winner.

350 ANDREW'S THREESCORE & TEN YEARS MAIDEN STKS 1m 4f (P)
2:25 (2:25) (Class 5) 4-Y-0+ **£1,910** (£564; £282) **Stalls** Low

Form RPR
2-35 **1** **Money Money Money**[5] 277 5-9-2 54 (b[1]) JamesMillman 6 60
(Rod Millman) *chsd ldr tl led 3f out: rdn clr over 1f out: in command and pushed out fnl f* **5/1**

22-3 **2** 3 ¼ **Wild Geese (IRE)**[9] 222 4-9-3 57 (b[1]) JoeFanning 3 60
(Jonathan Portman) *dwlt and reminders early: chsd ldrs after 2f: rdn to chse ldr over 2f out: styd on same pce u.p fr over 1f out* **11/4**[2]

60-6 **3** 2 ¼ **Sir William Orpen**[8] 247 4-9-3 56 IanMongan 4 56
(Pat Phelan) *hld up in last: hdwy on outer over 3f out: chsd ldng pair jst over 2f out: wanting to hang lft u.p and no prog over 1f out* **8/1**

230- **4** 2 ¾ **Christmas Coming**[246] 2510 4-9-3 68 DaneO'Neill 2 52
(Tony Carroll) *t.k.h: hld up wl in tch: rdn and unable qck ent fnl 2f: styd on same pce and wl hld ent fnl f: eased towards fin* **9/4**[1]

-232 **5** 6 **New Den**[9] 222 4-9-3 55 (v) NickyMackay 5 42
(Jim Boyle) *led: hdd and rdn 3f out: sn struggling: wknd 2f out* **4/1**[3]

4/4 **6** 22 **Perle D'Amour (IRE)**[17] 136 4-8-12 0 LiamKeniry 1 —
(Martin Bosley) *chsd ldrs tl rdn and dropped to rr ent fnl 3f: sn pushed along and struggling: lost tch 2f out* **33/1**

2m 34.64s (1.64) **Going Correction** +0.15s/f (Slow)
WFA 4 from 5yo 4lb **6** Ran SP% **108.2**
Speed ratings (Par 103): **100,97,96,94,90 75**
toteswingers:1&2:£2.10, 1&3:£5.90, 2&3:£5.30 CSF £17.63 TOTE £3.00: £2.50, £1.80; EX 11.90.
Owner Mrs Jenny Willment **Bred** Mrs Jenny Willment **Trained** Kentisbeare, Devon

FOCUS
A moderate maiden - first three finishers rated in the 50s - and not form to dwell on. The pace was just ordinary.

351 BLUE SQUARE SPRINT SERIES (ROUND 4) (H'CAP) (QUALIFIER) 6f (P)
2:55 (2:55) (Class 6) (0-65,65) 4-Y-0+ **£2,729** (£806; £403) **Stalls** Low

Form RPR
4-23 **1** **Dancing Welcome**[6] 268 5-9-5 63 (b) RichardKingscote 12 73
(Milton Bradley) *stdd and dropped in after s: hld up in tch in last trio: c wd and hdwy over 1f out: str run to ld fnl 100yds: sn clr: readily* **8/1**

32-1 **2** 2 **Rio Royale (IRE)**[21] 97 5-9-5 63 (p) JimCrowley 9 67
(Amanda Perrett) *in tch in midfield on outer: rdn and effrt jst over 1f out: drvn and chsd wnr ins fnl f: r.o but no imp* **7/2**[1]

2-53 **3** ¾ **Speak The Truth (IRE)**[10] 218 5-8-12 59 (p) MatthewDavies(3) 10 64+
(Jim Boyle) *stdd s: hld up in last trio: swtchd wd and nt clr run over 1f out: swtchd rt and effrt 1f out: r.o u.p ins fnl f: nvr able to chal* **10/1**

-623 **4** ½ **Dvinsky (USA)**[6] 269 10-9-7 65 (b) JimmyQuinn 8 65
(Jane Chapple-Hyam) *w ldrs on outer: ev ch and rdn wl over 1f out tl outpcd by wnr fnl 100yds: kpt on* **16/1**

-355 **5** hd **Norville (IRE)**[6] 268 4-9-5 63 (b) JamesDoyle 7 62
(David Evans) *stmbld leaving stalls: sn rcvrd and w ldrs: rdn ent fnl f: nt pce of wnr and styd on same pce fnl 100yds* **9/2**[2]

1-53 **6** ½ **Athaakeel (IRE)**[9] 231 5-9-7 65 (b) LukeMorris 6 66+
(Ronald Harris) *wnt lft s: in tch in midfield: effrt and nt clr run over 1f out: r.o fnl 100yds: unable to chal* **15/2**

10-1 **7** ¾ **Dualagi**[9] 231 7-9-4 62 GeorgeBaker 3 57
(Martin Bosley) *in tch in midfield on inner: effrt and rdn over 1f out: pressed ldrs 1f out: no ex and btn fnl 100yds* **11/1**

000- **8** 1 **Sweet Avon**[70] 7518 4-9-0 58 ShaneKelly 1 50
(Matthew Salaman) *led narrowly on inner: rdn ent fnl 2f: kpt on wl tl hdd fnl 100yds: wknd towards fin* **25/1**

054- **9** nk **Royal Box**[45] 7883 4-8-3 52 (b) RyanClark(5) 2 43
(Dai Burchell) *w ldrs: pushed along over 2f out: ev ch tl unable qck and short of room whn swtchd lft and rt 1f out: drvn and one pce fnl f* **33/1**

064- **10** ½ **Do More Business (IRE)**[213] 3567 4-9-4 62 IanMongan 5 52
(Pat Phelan) *short of room sn after s: hld up in last trio: effrt on inner over 1f out: chsd ldrs 1f out: wknd ins fnl f* **11/2**[3]

1-30 **11** ½ **Loyal Royal (IRE)**[10] 218 8-9-2 60 (bt) LiamKeniry 4 52+
(Milton Bradley) *t.k.h: hld up wl in tch: rdn and effrt whn jostled jst over 1f out: nt clr run fnl f: eased fnl 100yds* **16/1**

00-5 **R** **Timeteam (IRE)**[24] 50 5-9-7 65 JamieSpencer 11 —
(Alan Bailey) *taken down early: ref to r: tk no part* **14/1**

1m 12.25s (0.35) **Going Correction** +0.15s/f (Slow) **12** Ran SP% **121.3**
Speed ratings (Par 101): **103,100,99,98,98 97,96,95,95,94 93,—**
toteswingers:1&2:£6.80, 1&3:£12.50, 2&3:£6.90 CSF £36.93 CT £244.72 TOTE £10.90: £2.30, £1.50, £3.70; EX 43.20 Trifecta £138.30 Pool £633.62 - 1.03 winning units..
Owner J M Bradley **Bred** The Hon Mrs E J Wills **Trained** Sedbury, Gloucs

FOCUS
A modest if competitive sprint handicap in which Timeteam refused to exit his stall. The pace was solid enough with four horses disputing the advantage for much of the way.
Loyal Royal(IRE) Official explanation: jockey said gelding was denied a clear run

352 LEWIS COSSTICK 18TH H'CAP 1m 2f (P)
3:30 (3:30) (Class 5) (0-70,70) 4-Y-0+ **£2,047** (£604; £302) **Stalls** Low

Form RPR
5-14 **1** **Lord Theo**[14] 174 7-9-2 70 RyanClark(5) 3 83
(Nick Littmoden) *hld up in rr: gd hdwy on outer to press ldrs bnd 2f out: rdn to ld 1f out: styd on strly: comf* **9/2**[3]

-422 **2** 3 ¼ **Dream Of Fortune (IRE)**[1] 341 7-8-11 67 (bt) RPWalsh(7) 2 73
(David Evans) *in tch in midfield: clsd over 2f out: rdn and edgd lft u.p over 1f out: chsd wnr jst ins fnl f: styd on same pce* **5/1**

42-2 **3** 2 ½ **Professor John (IRE)**[17] 124 4-9-0 65 JamesDoyle 1 66
(Ian Wood) *chsd ldrs: rdn and effrt jst over 2f out: outpcd and wl hld ins fnl f: plugged on to go 3rd nr fin* **4/1**[2]

400- **4** nk **Strong Vigilance (IRE)**[171] 4971 4-9-1 66 JamieSpencer 6 67
(Michael Bell) *chsd ldrs: hdwy to chse ldr wl over 2f out: ev ch 2f out: rdn and unable qck whn sltly hmpd over 1f out: hung lft and rt u.p: wl hld fnl f* **11/2**

6-45 **5** ¾ **Visions Of Johanna (USA)**[10] 206 6-9-6 69 (p) JimCrowley 8 68
(Ian Williams) *chsd ldr tl led over 3f out: rdn and hrd pressed 2f out: hdd 1f out sn outpcd: wl btn fnl 100yds: lost 2 pls nr fin* **7/2**[1]

63-0 **6** ¾ **Folio (IRE)**[14] 174 11-8-13 62 StevieDonohoe 5 59
(Willie Musson) *hld up in rr: clsd and in tch over 2f out: pushed along and no hdwy over 1f out: rdn and wknd fnl f* **10/1**

500- **7** ½ **Saviour Sand (IRE)**[159] 5367 7-8-10 64 (t) KylieManser(5) 7 62
(Olivia Maylam) *s.i.s: towards rr: clsd and in tch over 2f out: rdn and effrt over 1f out: styng on same pce and wl hld whn nt clr run and snatched up ins fnl f* **33/1**

033- **8** 12 **Eton Fable (IRE)**[42] 7932 6-9-2 65 (v) TravisBlock 4 37
(Bill Ratcliffe) *sn bustled up to ld: hdd and rdn over 3f out: sn struggling: wl bhd over 1f out* **10/1**

2m 5.23s (-1.37) **Going Correction** +0.15s/f (Slow)
WFA 4 from 6yo+ 2lb **8** Ran SP% **113.6**
Speed ratings (Par 103): **111,108,106,106,105 104,104,94**
toteswingers:1&2:£4.20, 1&3:£4.50, 2&3:£3.20 CSF £26.80 CT £96.04 TOTE £7.20: £2.30, £1.50, £2.10; EX 21.20 Trifecta £54.50 Pool £706.09 - 9.57 winning units..
Owner Mrs Karen Graham **Bred** Mike Perkins **Trained** Newmarket, Suffolk

FOCUS
The time was good, being 2.58 seconds quicker than the following Class 3 handicap, although that race was run at a muddling pace.
Visions Of Johanna(USA) Official explanation: jockey said gelding hung right
Saviour Sand(IRE) Official explanation: jockey said gelding was denied a clear run

353 PLAY FREE BINGO AT BLUESQ.COM H'CAP 1m 2f (P)
4:05 (4:05) (Class 3) (0-95,94) 4-Y-0+ **£5,828** (£1,734; £866; £432) **Stalls** Low

Form RPR
4-50 **1** **Hidden Glory**[14] 180 4-8-8 83 MickyFenton 3 91
(James Given) *hld up in tch in rr: stl last and effrt on inner over 1f out: rdn and qcknd to ld fnl 100yds: edgd rt but r.o wl* **16/1**

00-0 **2** 1 ¼ **Scamperdale**[14] 180 9-8-12 88 KierenFox(3) 5 94
(Brian Baugh) *wl in tch in midfield: shuffled bk and dropped to last pair over 2f out: rdn and effrt on outer over 1f out: chsd wnr wl ins fnl f: kpt on* **7/1**

335- **3** ¾ **Realisation (USA)**[56] 7698 4-8-8 83 GregFairley 7 87
(Mark Johnston) *led: rdn ent fnl 2f: hdd jst ins fnl f: no ex fnl 100yds* **4/1**[2]

44-5 **4** nse **Audemar (IRE)**[14] 180 5-9-2 89 AndreaAtzeni 4 93
(Edward Vaughan) *chsd ldrs: nt clr run ent fnl 2f: rdn and effrt to press ldrs jst over 1f out: ev ch briefly ins fnl f: styd on same pce fnl 100yds* **15/2**

423- **5** nse **Denton (NZ)**[50] 7815 8-8-13 86 (t) SteveDrowne 2 90
(Jeremy Gask) *taken down early: chsd ldr: ev ch ent fnl 2f: rdn wl over 1f out: led jst ins fnl f tl hdd fnl 100yds* **11/4**[1]

00-4 **6** 1 **The Cayterers**[14] 180 9-8-5 85 RPWalsh(7) 6 87
(Tony Carroll) *s.i.s: hld up in tch in rr: hdwy on outer 3f out: chsd ldrs and rdn over 1f out: unable qck and short of room jst over 1f out: styd on same pce fnl f* **6/1**[3]

50-2 **7** 1 **Good Again**[16] 141 5-9-0 87 ShaneKelly 1 91+
(Gerard Butler) *hld up in tch: trckd ldrs gng wl ent fnl 2f: nt clr run over 1f out and thrght fnl f: nvr able to chal* **7/1**

00-1 **8** ½ **Reve De Nuit (USA)**[28] 6 5-9-7 94 JamesDoyle 8 93
(Alan McCabe) *in tch: hdwy on outer to chse ldrs wl over 2f out: sn rdn: lost pl u.p ent fnl 2f: one pce and wl hld fnl f* **8/1**

2m 7.81s (1.21) **Going Correction** +0.15s/f (Slow)
WFA 4 from 5yo+ 2lb **8** Ran SP% **114.7**
Speed ratings (Par 107): **101,100,99,99,99 98,97,97**
toteswingers:1&2:£13.80, 1&3:£11.60, 2&3:£4.70 CSF £122.20 CT £540.63 TOTE £26.70: £5.70, £3.00, £1.40; EX 123.50 Trifecta £643.20 Pool £869.31 - 1.00 winning units..
Owner Peter Swann **Bred** P Balding **Trained** Willoughton, Lincs
■ Stewards' Enquiry : Andrea Atzeni £140 fine: used whip that had been modified.

FOCUS
A typically messy Lingfield race run in a time 2.58 seconds slower than the earlier Class 5 handicap.

NOTEBOOK
Hidden Glory reversed recent form with a few of these, benefiting from being waited with a bit longer this time according to the winning rider. This was quite a tidy performance and it wouldn't surprise to see him defy a rise if things fall kindly again next time. (tchd 20-1)
Scamperdale, from a stable in good form, couldn't confirm recent placings with Hidden Glory but still ran well. (op 6-1)
Realisation(USA), returning from nearly two months off, slowed the pace on the downhill run before the straight. This was a solid return and he can do better when the emphasis is more on stamina (latest win gained at 1m4f). (op 9-2 tchd 3-1)
Audemar(IRE) had the one-two from this race behind him over C&D last time, but he could find only the one pace for pressure on this occasion. (tchd 8-1)
Denton(NZ) should have been suited by the drop in trip, but he had been off for 50 days and wasn't good enough. (op 10-3 tchd 9-2)
The Cayterers had today's winner, runner-up and fourth behind him here last time, so better could have been expected. (op 15-2)
Good Again had little room to make her move in the straight and was unlucky not to finish quite a bit closer. Official explanation: jockey said mare was denied a clear run (tchd 6-1)
Reve De Nuit(USA) landed a gamble over 1m at Southwell on his previous start, but he was well beaten under these vastly different conditions from 4lb higher. (tchd 9-1)
T/Plt: £22.40 to a £1 stake. Pool:£59,717.00 - 1,939.83 winning tickets T/Qpdt: £8.90 to a £1 stake. Pool:£4,772.56 - 394.96 winning tickets SP

311 KEMPTON (A.W) (R-H)
Sunday, January 30

OFFICIAL GOING: Standard
Wind: Moderate, across Weather: Fine

354 BETDAQ.COM H'CAP (DIV I) 1m 2f (P)
1:45 (1:46) (Class 6) (0-52,58) 4-Y-0+ **£1,364** (£403; £201) **Stalls** Low

Form RPR
14-5 **1** **Ocean Of Peace (FR)**[16] 164 8-9-0 50 LukeMorris 1 60
(Martin Bosley) *trckd ldrs: prog over 2f out: rdn to ld over 1f out: hld on nr fin* **6/1**[3]

235- **2** nk **Broughtons Paradis (IRE)**[170] 5051 5-9-1 51 JamieMackay 5 61
(Willie Musson) *hld up in last trio: prog over 2f out: rdn to chse wnr ins fnl f: clsng at fin* **3/1**[1]

6-02 **3** 7 **Princess Lexi (IRE)**[12] 201 4-8-12 50 JamieSpencer 4 46
(Ian Williams) *trckd ldng pair: effrt on outer to ld 3f out: drvn and hdd over 1f out: hanging bdly rt and wknd* **10/3**[2]

06-0 **4** *1* **Pictures (IRE)**[11] 207 4-8-8 **46** oh1 .... NeilChalmers 9 40
(John Bridger) *t.k.h: hld up last: prog over 2f out: outpcd whn wnt 4th 1f out: no threat* **12/1**

03-0 **5** *3 ¼* **Bookiebasher Babe (IRE)**[20] 115 6-8-10 **46** oh1 .... FrannyNorton 6 33
(Michael Quinn) *sn trckd ldr: awkward bnd 6f out: sn upsides: rdn 3f out: wknd over 2f out* **9/1**

653- **6** *1* **Supatov (USA)**[79] 7429 4-9-0 **52** .... SteveDrowne 8 37
(Hughie Morrison) *led: jnd over 5f out: hdd 3f out: wknd tamely* **10/3**[2]

/00- **7** *3* **Dancing Belle**[29] 7690 6-8-10 **46** oh1 .... DavidProbert 11 25
(J R Jenkins) *t.k.h: chsd ldrs: rdn wl over 3f out: sn wknd and bhd* **40/1**

065- **8** *1* **Green Army**[122] 6517 4-8-10 **48** oh1 ow2 .... SamHitchcott 10 25
(Mick Channon) *in tch: drvn 4f out: last whn looked unwilling to go arnd bnd 2f out: looking at inevitable defeat after* **14/1**

2m 7.43s (-0.57) **Going Correction** -0.05s/f (Stan)
WFA 4 from 5yo+ 2lb **8** Ran SP% **112.2**
Speed ratings (Par 101): **100,99,94,93,90 89,87,86**
toteswingers:1&2:£3.30, 1&3:£3.70, 2&3:£2.40 CSF £23.42 CT £68.81 TOTE £9.80: £1.10, £1.70, £2.70; EX 24.20 Trifecta £97.10 Pool £220.48 - 1.68 winning units..
Owner Mrs Jean M O'Connor **Bred** Raoul Rousset **Trained** Chalfont St Giles, Bucks
■ Stewards' Enquiry : Jamie Spencer caution: used whip without giving filly time to respond.

FOCUS
An extremely moderate contest, and the pace seemed just ordinary. The time was 1.76 seconds quicker than the slowly run second division.
Princess Lexi(IRE) Official explanation: jockey said filly hung right; vet said filly was found to be stiff behind
Green Army Official explanation: jockey said gelding lost its action

355 BETDAQ.COM H'CAP (DIV II) 1m 2f (P)
2:15 (2:17) (Class 6) (0-52,52) 4-Y-0+ **£1,364** (£403; £201) **Stalls** Low

Form RPR

06-0 **1** **Fastinthestraight (IRE)**[23] 86 4-8-9 **47** oh1 ow1 .... (p) DaneO'Neill 5 62+
(Jim Boyle) *plld hrd early: hld up in last trio: on and off the bridle fr 1/2-way: rdn in 8th over 2f out and gng nowhere: picked up over 1f out: rapid prog to ld last 150yds: shot clr* **10/3**[2]

456- **2** *4 ½* **Mayfair's Future**[53] 7760 6-9-0 **50** .... (p) DavidProbert 6 56
(J R Jenkins) *trckd ldng pair tl prog to ld 1/2-way: drvn over 1f out: hdd and brushed aside last 150yds* **7/1**

2/0- **3** *2* **Screaming Brave**[39] 7967 5-9-2 **52** .... (t) JamieGoldstein 9 54
(Sheena West) *hld up in last trio: stl there whn wd bnd 2f out: drvn and styd on wl fnl f to take 3rd last stride* **9/2**[3]

0-60 **4** *hd* **Inquisitress**[6] 280 7-8-10 **46** oh1 .... NeilChalmers 7 48
(John Bridger) *trckd ldrs: prog 2f out: wnt 2nd jst over 1f out and looked threatening: effrt petered out* **33/1**

/2-0 **5** *1* **Josephine Malines**[6] 278 7-8-12 **51** .... (tp) KierenFox[(3)] 1 51
(John Flint) *trckd ldr 3f: styd prom on inner: rdn over 2f out: nt qckn over 1f out: fdd* **8/1**

0-00 **6** *¾* **Sweet Possession (USA)**[16] 163 5-8-7 **48** .... TobyAtkinson[(5)] 3 46
(Pat Eddery) *reluctant to enter stalls: awkward s: t.k.h and sn prom on outer: rdn to chse ldr over 2f out to jst over 1f out: wknd* **8/1**

00-0 **7** *2* **Pascalina**[16] 163 4-8-12 **50** .... J-PGuillambert 2 44
(John Akehurst) *hld up in midfield: rdn and fnd nil wl over 1f out* **14/1**

-635 **8** *¾* **Escardo (GER)**[2] 346 8-8-10 **46** .... WilliamCarson 8 39
(David Bridgwater) *settled in midfield: effrt on outer over 2f out: no prog over 1f out: wknd* **3/1**[1]

/00- **9** *2* **Ring Of Fire**[108] 6871 4-8-10 **48** ow2 .... LiamKeniry 10 37
(John Spearing) *stdd s: hld up last: rdn 2f out: no prog* **50/1**

46/5 **10** *½* **Crazy Colours**[18] 127 5-9-1 **51** .... SamHitchcott 4 39
(Zoe Davison) *led to 1/2-way: wknd over 2f out* **20/1**

2m 8.19s (0.19) **Going Correction** -0.05s/f (Stan)
WFA 4 from 5yo+ 2lb **10** Ran SP% **117.3**
Speed ratings (Par 101): **97,93,91,91,90 90,88,88,86,86**
toteswingers:1&2:£6.30, 1&3:£4.90, 2&3:£6.70 CSF £26.64 CT £106.67 TOTE £3.20: £1.40, £1.10, £2.30; EX 26.70 Trifecta £48.00 Pool £420.67 - 6.48 winning units..
Owner Epsom Equine Spa Partnership **Bred** Patrick J Ryan **Trained** Epsom, Surrey

FOCUS
They went a steady pace and this is moderate form, but the winner and third can rate higher.
Fastinthestraight(IRE) ◆ Official explanation: trainer said, regarding apparent improvement in form, that the gelding is fragile, which has ability but, has had lameness problems in the past and got behind and failed to pick up on its previous run.
Escardo(GER) Official explanation: jockey said gelding ran flat

356 BOOK FOR RACING POST CHASE H'CAP 5f (P)
2:45 (2:45) (Class 5) (0-75,77) 3-Y-O **£2,047** (£604; £302) **Stalls** Low

Form RPR

4-21 **1** **Mandy's Hero**[18] 132 3-9-1 **69** .... (p) JamieSpencer 4 74
(Ian Williams) *mde all: drvn over 1f out: kpt on wl u.p fnl f* **10/3**[3]

14-1 **2** *1* **Mr Optimistic**[12] 198 3-9-2 **77** .... GeorgeChaloner[(7)] 3 79+
(Richard Fahey) *t.k.h: trckd ldng pair: urged along over 1f out: tk 2nd last 100yds: nvr able to chal* **11/4**[2]

1-43 **3** *¾* **Johnny Hancocks (IRE)**[12] 198 3-8-12 **69** .... JamesSullivan[(3)] 2 68
(Linda Stubbs) *chsd wnr: rdn over 1f out: nt qckn and a hld: lost 2nd last 100yds* **13/2**

4-42 **4** *1 ¼* **Welsh Inlet (IRE)**[2] 333 3-8-8 **62** .... NeilChalmers 1 57
(John Bridger) *dwlt: in tch in last pair: tried to cl over 1f out: nt qckn* **6/1**

0-21 **5** *2 ¾* **Morermaloke**[9] 246 3-9-5 **73** .... ShaneKelly 5 58
(Brian Meehan) *dwlt: t.k.h: racd wd in last: lost grnd bnd 2f out: nvr on terms* **9/4**[1]

59.76 secs (-0.74) **Going Correction** -0.05s/f (Stan) **5** Ran SP% **108.1**
Speed ratings (Par 97): **103,101,100,98,93**
CSF £12.27 TOTE £4.20: £1.60, £3.40; EX 8.60.
Owner Dr Marwan Koukash **Bred** Miss R J Dobson **Trained** Portway, Worcs

FOCUS
As is so often the case over 5f here, it proved hard to make up significant amounts of ground, and this is just ordinary form.
Morermaloke Official explanation: jockey said gelding was unsuited by the sharp bend on the inner circuit

357 TRY BETDAQ FOR AN EXCHANGE CLASSIFIED CLAIMING STKS 6f (P)
3:15 (3:15) (Class 6) 4-Y-0+ **£1,535** (£453; £226) **Stalls** Low

Form RPR

360- **1** **Italian Tom (IRE)**[39] 7961 4-9-3 73 .... LukeMorris 8 78
(Ronald Harris) *settled in 5th: rdn on outer 2f out: prog over 1f out: led jst ins fnl f: hld on* **6/1**[2]

0-00 **2** *½* **Lord Of The Reins (IRE)**[17] 143 7-8-9 63 .... FrannyNorton 6 68+
(James Given) *stdd s: hld up last: angled off rail and looking for room 2f out: pushed along over 1f out: prog fnl f: rdn last 100yds: r.o to take 2nd and cl on wnr fin* **13/2**[3]

13-3 **3** *nk* **Super Frank (IRE)**[17] 143 8-8-3 66 .... (b) ChrisCatlin 3 61
(John Akehurst) *rousted along early to chse ldrs: drvn over 2f out: prog on inner to ld over 1f out: hdd and one pce jst ins fnl f* **1/1**[1]

-000 **4** *2 ½* **Desert Strike**[5] 294 5-8-6 65 .... (p) NoraLooby[(7)] 7 63
(Alan McCabe) *t.k.h: pressed ldng pair on outer: wnt 2nd 1/2-way but hanging: stl cl enough 1f out: fdd* **13/2**[3]

-314 **5** *2* **Vhujon (IRE)**[9] 243 6-9-3 74 .... RobbieFitzpatrick 2 61
(Peter Grayson) *led: rdn over 2f out: hdd & wknd over 1f out* **13/2**[3]

0-00 **6** *1* **Mind The Monarch**[6] 276 4-8-3 52 .... DavidProbert 5 44
(Roger Teal) *mostly chsd ldr to 1/2-way: steadily wknd fnl 2f* **16/1**

1m 12.25s (-0.85) **Going Correction** -0.05s/f (Stan) **6** Ran SP% **110.2**
Speed ratings (Par 101): **103,102,101,98,95 94**
toteswingers:1&2:£3.70, 1&3:£1.40, 2&3:£2.50 CSF £40.94 TOTE £7.00: £4.20, £4.20; EX 49.80 Trifecta £34.80 Pool £317.33 - 6.74 winning units..
Owner S & A Mares **Bred** Tom Radley **Trained** Earlswood, Monmouths

FOCUS
A modest claimer.

358 WATCH RACING UK ON SKY 432 H'CAP 7f (P)
3:45 (3:45) (Class 5) (0-75,77) 3-Y-O **£2,047** (£604; £302) **Stalls** Low

Form RPR

23-1 **1** **Kuala Limper (IRE)**[25] 43 3-9-7 **75** .... DaneO'Neill 3 82+
(David Elsworth) *hld up in 4th: prog and carried lft 2f out: rdn to ld wl over 1f out: asserted fnl f* **1/1**[1]

4-24 **2** *1 ½* **Reginald Claude**[10] 228 3-8-11 **70** .... LeeNewnes[(5)] 1 73
(Mark Usher) *trckd ldng pair: brought to chal 2f out: pressed wnr but hung lft over 1f out: nt qckn* **8/1**

104- **3** *5* **Spartic**[56] 7718 3-9-5 **73** .... JamesDoyle 2 63
(Alan McCabe) *led: edging lft bnd 3f out: hung bdly lft 2f out: sn hdd and btn* **13/2**

01-6 **4** *½* **Magic Of The Sea (IRE)**[10] 228 3-8-12 **66** .... AdamKirby 6 54
(Marco Botti) *hld up in last: drvn and in tch 2f out: hung lft and wknd over 1f out* **9/2**[2]

20-5 **5** *2 ½* **Karate (IRE)**[21] 106 3-9-0 **68** .... JoeFanning 5 49
(Mark Johnston) *chsd ldr: rdn over 2f out: sn btn* **5/1**[3]

1m 25.73s (-0.27) **Going Correction** -0.05s/f (Stan) **5** Ran SP% **109.3**
Speed ratings (Par 97): **99,97,91,91,88**
CSF £9.34 TOTE £2.20: £1.10, £5.30; EX 8.50.
Owner John Dwyer **Bred** Oghill House Stud & Jimmy Hyland **Trained** Newmarket, Suffolk
■ Stewards' Enquiry : Lee Newnes one-day ban: used whip in incorrect place (Feb 14)

FOCUS
Only the front two ran to form, but they finished well clear. The pace was fair, and all of these tended to edge towards the stands' rail in the straight, probably following the wayward Spartic.
Spartic Official explanation: jockey said gelding hung left

359 BISTRO PRICES FROM £42 H'CAP 1m 4f (P)
4:15 (4:15) (Class 4) (0-85,85) 4-Y-0+ **£3,885** (£1,156; £577; £288) **Stalls** Centre

Form RPR

015- **1** **Lovers Causeway (USA)**[32] 8007 4-9-3 **82** .... (b) JoeFanning 2 92
(Mark Johnston) *trckd ldr: pushed into ld over 2f out: drvn and in command over 1f out: styd on* **2/1**[1]

032- **2** *3* **Spring Jim**[52] 7781 10-9-7 **82** .... GeorgeBaker 1 87
(James Fanshawe) *trckd ldng pair: shkn up and nt qckn jst over 2f out: kpt on fnl f to take 2nd nr fin* **11/4**[2]

-131 **3** *nk* **Kidlat**[18] 124 6-9-4 **79** .... AdamKirby 4 84
(Alan Bailey) *led: kicked on over 3f out: hdd over 2f out: one pce after: lost 2nd nr fin* **4/1**[3]

1- **4** *½* **Kindlelight Sun (JPN)**[365] 355 5-9-1 **76** .... J-PGuillambert 3 80
(Nick Littmoden) *dwlt: hld up last: shkn up 4f out: effrt on inner to dispute 2nd 2f out: one pce after* **4/1**[3]

60-4 **5** *4 ½* **Hatton Flight**[26] 32 7-9-10 **85** .... (v) DavidProbert 5 82
(Andrew Balding) *settled in 4th: drvn over 3f out: sn dropped to last and struggling* **8/1**

2m 31.91s (-2.59) **Going Correction** -0.05s/f (Stan)
WFA 4 from 5yo+ 4lb **5** Ran SP% **111.1**
Speed ratings (Par 105): **106,104,103,103,100**
CSF £7.85 TOTE £3.10: £1.20, £2.10; EX 9.20.
Owner Crone Stud Farms Ltd **Bred** Skara Glen Stables **Trained** Middleham Moor, N Yorks

FOCUS
A fair handicap run at just an ordinary gallop.

360 KEMPTON.CO.UK MEDIAN AUCTION MAIDEN FILLIES' STKS 1m (P)
4:45 (4:46) (Class 6) 3-5-Y-O **£1,535** (£453; £226) **Stalls** Low

Form RPR

02- **1** **Dazzled**[46] 7872 4-10-0 0 .... HayleyTurner 2 69
(James Fanshawe) *w.w in last trio: prog on inner over 2f out: drvn over 1f out: led jst ins fnl f: styd on* **2/1**[1]

3- **2** *½* **Roman Flame**[58] 7682 3-8-8 75 .... FrannyNorton 4 63
(Michael Quinn) *t.k.h: hld up in last trio: rdn 2f out: prog on outer over 1f out and edgd rt: pressed wnr last 100yds: nt qckn* **2/1**[1]

0 **3** *2 ¼* **Rich And Reckless**[11] 214 4-10-0 0 .... IanMongan 6 63
(Tobias B P Coles) *t.k.h: sn pressed ldr: led over 2f out and shkn up: hdd jst ins fnl f: wknd last 75yds* **66/1**

54- **4** *7* **Asfurah's Image**[48] 7857 3-8-8 60 .... ChrisCatlin 5 42
(Marco Botti) *t.k.h: trckd ldrs: drvn over 2f out: disp 3rd over 1f out: wknd* **13/2**[2]

5 *1 ¾* **Ability Girl** 3-8-8 0 .... NickyMackay 1 38
(Chris Wall) *trckd ldrs: shkn up over 2f out: disp 3rd briefly over 1f out: wknd* **16/1**

6 *1 ½* **Nubian Gem (IRE)** 3-8-5 0 .... KierenFox[(3)] 3 34
(John Best) *difficult to load: v.s.i.s: rn green in detached last: nvr a factor: passed two wkng rivals fnl f* **15/2**

0 **7** *1 ¼* **Mushroom**[16] 171 3-8-8 0 .... (b[1]) SteveDrowne 7 31
(Roger Charlton) *sn led: rdn and hdd over 2f out: wknd over 1f out: eased* **7/1**[3]

8 *5* **Shaunas Spirit (IRE)** 3-8-8 0 .... DavidProbert 8 20
(Dean Ivory) *s.i.s: wnt prom on outer after 3f: wknd qckly wl over 2f out* **33/1**

1m 40.59s (0.79) **Going Correction** -0.05s/f (Stan)
WFA 3 from 4yo 20lb **8** Ran SP% **114.6**
Speed ratings (Par 98): **94,93,91,84,82 81,79,74**
toteswingers:1&2:£2.00, 1&3:£13.10, 2&3:£12.20 CSF £5.74 TOTE £2.70: £1.10, £1.30, £5.70; EX 7.80 Trifecta £159.30 Pool £800.86 - 3.72 winning units..

Owner The Nightcaps **Bred** The Nightcaps **Trained** Newmarket, Suffolk

FOCUS

A modest fillies' maiden and they didn't go that quick. The time was poor, being 1.58 seconds slower than the following Class 6 handicap.

Nubian Gem(IRE) Official explanation: jockey said filly ran green

Mushroom Official explanation: jockey said filly had no more to give

361 WATCH RACES LIVE AT RACINGUK.COM APPRENTICE H'CAP — 1m (P)

5:15 (5:16) (Class 6) (0-65,66) 4-Y-0+ — **£1,535** (£453; £226) **Stalls** Low

Form	Pos	Btn	Horse	Jockey	RPR
/1-2	1		**Broughtons Day**[7] 268 4-9-4 **62** — JulieBurke 9 (Willie Musson) *sn stdd into 6th: shkn up and prog on outer wl over 1f out: rdn and r.o to ld last 75yds* 5/2[1]		69+
45-1	2	1/2	**San Antonio**[5] 292 11-9-1 **66** 6ex — (b) ChristyMews(7) 6 (Pam Sly) *led at gd pce but pressed: drew clr over 2f out: bmpd along and kpt on fnl f: hdd last 75yds* 4/1[2]		72
05-0	3	3/4	**Prohibition (IRE)**[9] 248 5-8-9 **60** — ChelseyBanks(7) 4 (Gary Moore) *s.i.s: t.k.h and sn chsd ldrs in 5th: pushed along fr 2f out: kpt on steadily: nvr threatened to chal* 33/1		64
26-0	4	nk	**Having A Ball**[25] 48 7-9-5 **63** — (v[1]) AmyScott 10 (Peter Cundell) *stdd s: hld up in last pair and detached: prog on outer over 1f out: styd on fnl f: no ch to rch ldrs* 9/1		66
4-46	5	shd	**Join Up**[23] 90 5-9-0 **58** — JamesRogers 2 (Mark Brisbourne) *chsd ldng pair: rdn to chse ldr over 1f out to jst ins fnl f: one pce* 11/2[3]		61
45-3	6	4	**Sovereignty (JPN)**[11] 205 9-8-6 **57** — DavidWarren(7) 3 (Dean Ivory) *t.k.h: pressed ldr to over 2f out: wknd and lost 2nd over 1f out* 12/1		51
000-	7	1	**Illuminative (USA)**[166] 5172 5-8-12 **56** — (p) RyanPowell 7 (Zoe Davison) *s.s: detached in last pair: rdn 3f out: no prog* 40/1		48
24-0	8	1/2	**The Wonga Coup (IRE)**[16] 162 4-8-11 **55** — NathanAlison 8 (Pat Phelan) *t.k.h: sn trckd ldng pair: rdn over 2f out: wknd qckly over 1f out* 9/1		45

1m 39.01s (-0.79) **Going Correction** -0.05s/f (Stan) — 8 Ran SP% **97.0**

Speed ratings (Par 101): **101,100,99,99,99 95,94,93**

toteswingers:1&2:£2.50, 1&3:£19.40, 2&3:£18.20. totesuper7: Win: Not won. Place: £3,647.00 CSF £8.64 CT £125.86 TOTE £2.70: £1.30, £1.50, £7.10; EX 10.00 Trifecta £104.60.

Owner Broughton Thermal Insulation **Bred** Broughton Bloodstock **Trained** Newmarket, Suffolk

FOCUS

This moderate handicap was well run and the winning time was 1.58 seconds quicker than the earlier fillies' maiden.

Illuminative(USA) Official explanation: jockey said gelding was slowly away

T/Plt: £73.90 to a £1 stake. Pool:£58,407.32 - 576.48 winning tickets T/Qpdt: £42.40 to a £1 stake. Pool:£3,784.13 - 66.00 winning tickets JN

340 WOLVERHAMPTON (A.W) (L-H)

Monday, January 31

OFFICIAL GOING: Standard to slow

Wind: Light behind Weather: Fne

362 PLACE ONLY BETTING AT BLUESQ.COM AMATEUR RIDERS' H'CAP (DIV I) — 5f 216y(P)

1:35 (1:36) (Class 6) (0-55,59) 4-Y-0+ — **£1,318** (£405; £202) **Stalls** Low

Form	Pos	Btn	Horse	RPR
4434	1		**Downhill Skier (IRE)**[10] 255 7-10-5 **53** — MissBeckyBrisbourne(7) 4 (Mark Brisbourne) *hld up: hdwy over 2f out: rdn to ld ins fnl f: r.o wl* 6/1	62
65-1	2	2 1/4	**Young Simon**[7] 276 4-10-11 **59** 6ex — (v) MissKMargarson(7) 6 (George Margarson) *a.p: chsd ldr 2f out: rdn and ev ch ins fnl f: styd on same pce* 3/1[1]	61
000-	3	1/2	**Ivestar (IRE)**[53] 7787 6-10-5 **51** — (vt) MissCharlotteHolmes(5) 13 (Ben Haslam) *s.i.s: in rr: r.o ins fnl f: nt rch ldrs* 28/1	51
03-4	4	nk	**Fiancee (IRE)**[22] 107 5-10-0 **46** — (b) MrCMartin(5) 5 (Roy Brotherton) *s.i.s: in rr: rdn over 1f out: r.o ins fnl f: nrst fin* 16/1	45
0-05	5	hd	**Francis Albert**[10] 256 5-10-5 **49** — (be) MissMMullineaux(3) 7 (Michael Mullineaux) *hld up: rdn 1/2-way: r.o ins fnl f: nrst fin* 16/1	48
0-00	6	2	**Grand Palace (IRE)**[10] 250 8-10-5 **46** oh1 — (v) MissADeniel 9 (Derek Shaw) *chsd ldrs: rdn over 1f out: no ex ins fnl f* 16/1	38
020-	7	3/4	**Cocktail Party (IRE)**[53] 7783 5-10-2 **48** — MrFMitchell(5) 3 (James Unett) *hld up in tch: plld hrd: rdn over 1f out: styd on same pce ins fnl f* 8/1	38
-036	8	1 1/4	**Silver Linnet (IRE)**[11] 224 4-10-11 **55** — (b) MrJMQuinlan(3) 8 (Michael Quinlan) *led: rdn over 1f out: hdd & wknd ins fnl f* 9/2[2]	41
040-	9	nk	**Serious Matters (IRE)**[194] 4256 4-10-12 **53** — (t[1]) MissGAndrews 11 (Walter Swinburn) *trckd ldr: plld hrd: rdn over 1f out: hung lft and wknd ins fnl f* 10/1	38
000-	10	2 3/4	**Vintage Quest**[47] 7878 9-10-5 **46** oh1 — (p) MissSBrotherton 1 (Dai Burchell) *s.i.s: sn pushed along in rr: nvr on terms* 14/1	22
000-	11	shd	**St Ignatius**[69] 7537 4-10-11 **55** — MissLMasterton(3) 12 (Michael Appleby) *prom tl rdn and wknd over 2f out* 33/1	31
03-0	12	1 3/4	**Mushy Peas (IRE)**[23] 98 4-10-3 **51** — (v) MrTBellamy(7) 10 (David Evans) *mid-div: rdn over 2f out: sn wknd* 5/1[3]	21
0-65	13	1 3/4	**Royal Blade (IRE)**[3] 343 4-10-5 **51** — MissWGibson(5) 2 (Alan Berry) *prom: rdn over 2f out: wknd over 1f out* 20/1	16

1m 17.24s (2.24) **Going Correction** +0.30s/f (Slow) — 13 Ran SP% **129.8**

Speed ratings (Par 101): **97,94,93,92,92 90,89,87,86,83 83,80,78**

toteswingers:1&2:£3.40, 1&3:£20.80, 2&3:£36.70 CSF £25.98 CT £520.44 TOTE £5.50: £1.70, £2.10, £8.80; EX 29.20 TRIFECTA Not won..

Owner Miss P D Insull **Bred** Swettenham Stud **Trained** Great Ness, Shropshire

FOCUS

The first division of a typically weak handicap for amateur riders. It was a wide-open race, though, and they went a solid gallop in a quicker time than division II. The winner is rated in line with last summer's form.

363 PLACE ONLY BETTING AT BLUESQ.COM AMATEUR RIDERS' H'CAP (DIV II) — 5f 216y(P)

2:05 (2:06) (Class 6) (0-55,55) 4-Y-0+ — **£1,318** (£405; £202) **Stalls** Low

Form	Pos	Btn	Horse	RPR
00-5	1		**Lethal**[27] 37 8-10-9 **53** — MrMPrice(3) 10 (Richard Price) *a.p: rdn to ld wl ins fnl f: r.o* 20/1	59
0-41	2	shd	**Metropolitan Chief**[10] 250 7-10-5 **51** — MrCMartin(5) 11 (Paul Burgoyne) *s.i.s: hld up: hdwy over 1f out: r.o* 8/1	57
424-	3	1	**Monsieur Harvey**[89] 7300 5-10-2 **48** — JustinNewman(5) 6 (Bryan Smart) *sn led: rdn clr over 1f out: hdd wl ins fnl f* 7/1[3]	51
14-2	4	1 1/4	**Lily Wood**[17] 167 5-10-8 **54** — (p) MrFMitchell(5) 5 (James Unett) *hld up in tch: rdn over 1f out: styd on* 3/1[1]	53
0062	5	1 1/4	**Memphis Man**[7] 276 8-10-8 **49** — MissGAndrews 8 (David Evans) *hld up in tch: plld hrd: rdn over 1f out: styd on* 5/1[2]	44
1323	6	3/4	**Kheley (IRE)**[4] 318 5-10-7 **55** — MissBeckyBrisbourne(7) 4 (Mark Brisbourne) *a.p: rdn over 1f out: styd on same pce ins fnl f* 5/1[2]	47
54-0	7	3 1/2	**Royal Box**[2] 351 4-10-11 **52** — (b) MissSBrotherton 13 (Dai Burchell) *chsd ldrs: rdn over 2f out: wknd over 1f out* 9/1	33
3-50	8	1/2	**Boy The Bell**[17] 169 4-10-11 **55** — MissMMullineaux(3) 12 (Michael Mullineaux) *hld up: rdn over 1f out: nvr nrr* 16/1	35
00-3	9	3 3/4	**Bold Bomber**[10] 255 5-9-12 **46** oh1 — (p) MissACraven(7) 9 (Paul Green) *mid-div: hdwy over 2f out: wkng whn hung lft fr over 1f out* 20/1	14
00-4	10	1 3/4	**Stormburst (IRE)**[11] 230 7-10-0 **46** oh1 — MissCLWills(5) 1 (Adrian Chamberlain) *chsd ldrs: n.m.r and lost pl 4f out: n.d after* 33/1	8
400-	11	4	**Commander Wish**[73] 7506 8-10-3 **51** — MrWFeatherstone(7) 2 (Lucinda Featherstone) *s.i.s: a in rr* 10/1	—
30-0	12	2	**Strategic Mover (USA)**[12] 211 6-10-4 **50** — (vt) MissMBryant(5) 7 (Paddy Butler) *s.i.s: a in rr* 25/1	—
650-	13	2 3/4	**Captain Imperial (IRE)**[203] 3948 5-10-0 **46** oh1 — (t) MrSBushby(5) 3 (Robin Bastiman) *chsd ldrs tl wknd over 2f out* 33/1	—

1m 17.77s (2.77) **Going Correction** +0.30s/f (Slow) — 13 Ran SP% **126.2**

Speed ratings (Par 101): **93,92,91,89,88 87,82,81,76,74 69,66,62**

toteswingers:1&2:£47.30, 1&3:£32.20, 2&3:£16.10 CSF £171.57 CT £1258.78 TOTE £25.50: £7.80, £4.60, £3.30; EX 378.40 TRIFECTA Not won..

Owner Ben Edwards **Bred** A S Reid **Trained** Ullingswick, H'fords

FOCUS

This second division of the amateur riders' handicap was another wide open and weak event. It was slower than the first division and the form is of a similar standard. Once again there was a strong pace on. The winner took advantage of a career-low mark.

Captain Imperial(IRE) Official explanation: jockey said that on removing blindfold gelding charged gate causing it to open

364 GREAT OFFERS AT WOLVERHAMPTON-RACECOURSE.CO.UK CLAIMING STKS — 5f 216y(P)

2:40 (2:42) (Class 6) 3-Y-O — **£1,535** (£453; £226) **Stalls** Low

Form	Pos	Btn	Horse	RPR
21-6	1		**Its You Again**[22] 106 3-8-13 78 — AdamKirby 4 (Michael Quinlan) *led: hdd over 4f out: led again 2f out: rdn and edgd lft over 1f out: r.o* 5/2[1]	82
2-43	2	4	**Captain Dimitrios**[12] 208 3-8-13 75 — (v) CathyGannon 5 (David Evans) *chsd ldr tl led over 4f out: hdd 2f out: rdn and hung lft fr over 1f out: styng on same pce whn rdr dropped nrside rein ins fnl f* 3/1[2]	69
311-	3	3/4	**Sugar Beet**[132] 6271 3-8-12 76 — LukeMorris 1 (Ronald Harris) *hld up in tch: rdn over 2f out: chsd wnr over 1f out tl no ex ins fnl f* 7/2[3]	66
54-2	4	3	**Captain Loui (IRE)**[2] 349 3-8-6 64 — (p) RyanClark(5) 2 (Dai Burchell) *prom: rdn over 1f out: wknd fnl f* 7/1	55
65-0	5	4 1/2	**Magic Stella**[13] 198 3-8-9 71 — (v[1]) MatthewDavies(3) 7 (Alan Jarvis) *hld up in tch: rdn 1/2-way: wknd over 2f out* 20/1	42
2-14	6	4 1/2	**Slatey Hen (IRE)**[9] 263 3-8-0 66 — DavidProbert 6 (Paddy Butler) *chsd ldrs tl rdn and wknd over 1f out* 9/1	15

1m 16.16s (1.16) **Going Correction** +0.30s/f (Slow) — 6 Ran SP% **103.1**

Speed ratings (Par 95): **104,98,97,93,87 81**

toteswingers:1&2:£1.30, 1&3:£2.50, 2&3:£1.60 CSF £8.53 TOTE £3.10: £1.70, £2.60; EX 8.90.

Owner Brian Dick **Bred** Springcombe Park Stud **Trained** Newmarket, Suffolk

FOCUS

A middle-of-the-road claimer. The race is rated around the winner, who showed improved form at fave value.

Magic Stella Official explanation: jockey said filly hung right

365 BLUESQ.COM ON YOUR IPHONE H'CAP — 1m 1f 103y(P)

3:15 (3:15) (Class 5) (0-75,70) 3-Y-O — **£1,748** (£520; £260; £129) **Stalls** Low

Form	Pos	Btn	Horse	RPR
0-11	1		**Memorabilia**[12] 217 3-9-6 **69** — JoeFanning 2 (Mark Johnston) *mde all: rdn over 1f out: styd on wl: readily* 6/5[1]	79+
23-4	2	1 3/4	**Imaginary World (IRE)**[28] 25 3-9-5 **68** — (p) JamesDoyle 5 (Alan McCabe) *hld up: hdwy over 2f out: rdn to chse wnr and hung lft ins fnl f: styd on* 10/1	73
-213	3	1 1/4	**Urban Kode (IRE)**[12] 217 3-9-0 **63** — CathyGannon 1 (David Evans) *chsd ldrs: rdn over 2f out: styd on same pce fnl f* 10/1	65
040-	4	nk	**Tidal Star**[80] 7427 3-9-7 **70** — AdamKirby 4 (Michael Quinlan) *chsd wnr: rdn and ev ch over 1f out: no ex ins fnl f* 2/1[2]	72
50-2	5	36	**Sir Randolf (IRE)**[11] 227 3-9-4 **67** — (t) DaneO'Neill 3 (Sylvester Kirk) *prom: rdn over 3f out: wknd over 2f out* 11/2[3]	—

2m 4.04s (2.34) **Going Correction** +0.30s/f (Slow) — 5 Ran SP% **112.4**

Speed ratings (Par 97): **101,99,98,98,66**

CSF £13.75 TOTE £1.40: £1.10, £6.30; EX 9.20.

Owner Sheikh Hamdan Bin Mohammed Al Maktoum **Bred** Whitley Stud **Trained** Middleham Moor, N Yorks

FOCUS

A decent 3-y-o handicap won in good style by a highly progressive sort completing a hat-trick. He rates a small personal best.

Sir Randolf(IRE) Official explanation: jockey had no explanation for the poor form shown

366 HOTEL & CONFERENCING AT WOLVERHAMPTON (S) STKS — 1m 141y(P)

3:50 (3:50) (Class 6) 3-Y-O — **£1,535** (£453; £226) **Stalls** Low

Form	Pos	Btn	Horse	RPR
124-	1		**A Little Bit Dusty**[60] 7664 3-9-1 64 — (b[1]) KierenFox(3) 1 (Bill Turner) *mde all: clr over 2f out: drvn out* 9/2[3]	71
32-5	2	1 1/2	**Oratouch (IRE)**[11] 234 3-8-7 63 — ChrisCatlin 3 (Marco Botti) *sn outpcd: hmpd wl over 3f out: hdwy over 2f out: rdn to chse wnr over 1f out: styd on* 11/10[1]	57+
33-2	3	7	**Beating Harmony**[8] 270 3-8-12 60 — RobertWinston 2 (Tony Carroll) *chsd ldrs: hmpd and lost pl wl over 3f out: nt rcvr* 7/2[2]	45+
00-	4	1 1/2	**Thunderway (IRE)**[194] 4241 3-8-4 0 — PatrickDonaghy(3) 4 (Michael Dods) *hld up in tch: rdn over 2f out: sn btn* 20/1	37
44-5	5	10	**Sir Lunchalott**[14] 192 3-9-4 65 — (b) CathyGannon 6 (J S Moore) *s.i.s: sn prom: chsd wnr 1/2-way tl rdn and wknd wl over 1f out* 10/1	25
04-3	6	4	**Littleportnbrandy (IRE)**[7] 275 3-8-7 70 — (p) RobbieFitzpatrick 5 (Paddy Butler) *chsd wnr tl rdn 1/2-way: hit rails wl over 3f out: wknd over 2f out* 9/1	—

1m 53.81s (3.31) **Going Correction** +0.30s/f (Slow) — 6 Ran SP% **111.9**

Speed ratings (Par 95): **97,95,89,88,79 75**

toteswingers:1&2:£2.00, 1&3:£1.70, 2&3:£1.50 CSF £9.86 TOTE £3.70: £2.70, £1.10; EX 12.60.There was no bid for the winner.

Owner T.O.C.S. Ltd **Bred** T O C S Limited **Trained** Sigwells, Somerset
■ Stewards' Enquiry : Kieren Fox caution: used whip without giving gelding time to respond

FOCUS
A weak seller. The winner is seemingly back to his early form but it's not hard to have doubts.
Oratouch(IRE) Official explanation: jockey said filly suffered interference in running
Sir Lunchalott Official explanation: jockey said gelding ran too free
Littleportnbrandy(IRE) Official explanation: jockey said filly ducked into rails

367 ENJOY THE PARTY PACK GROUP OFFER H'CAP 7f 32y(P)
4:20 (4:20) (Class 5) (0-70,70) 4-Y-0+ **£1,748** (£520; £260; £129) **Stalls** High

Form RPR
200- **1** **Woolfall Sovereign (IRE)**[262] [2093] 5-9-4 **67**................ BarryMcHugh 1 76+
(George Margarson) *a.p: rdn over 1f out: edgd rt and r.o to ld wl ins fnl f* **12/1**
1-06 **2** *1/2* **Buxton**[10] [249] 7-9-4 **67**................(t) RobertHavlin 5 75
(Roger Ingram) *hld up: hdwy 2f out: led over 1f out: sn rdn and hung lft: hdd wl ins fnl f* **8/1**
5-01 **3** *1* **West Leake (IRE)**[12] [211] 5-8-7 **56** oh1................ WilliamCarson 9 61
(Paul Burgoyne) *hld up: hdwy over 1f out: r.o: nt rch ldrs* **14/1**
32-3 **4** *1/2* **Yankee Storm**[23] [96] 6-9-7 **70**................(v) JimmyQuinn 7 74
(Tom Keddy) *hld up: hdwy over 2f out: rdn over 1f out: styng on same pce whn hmpd ins fnl f* **9/2**[2]
510- **5** *2 3/4* **Eastern Hills**[41] [7956] 6-9-3 **66**................(p) ShaneKelly 6 63
(Alan McCabe) *chsd ldr to over 5f out: remained handy: wnt 2nd again over 2f out: led wl over 1f out: sn rdn and hdd: hld whn hmpd ins fnl f* **11/1**
304- **6** *3* **Forward Feline (IRE)**[135] [6210] 5-9-1 **64**................ DavidProbert 3 52
(Bryn Palling) *s.i.s: hld up: rdn and nt clr run over 2f out: n.d* **12/1**
1-21 **7** *nse* **Broughtons Day**[1] [361] 4-8-13 **62**................ ChrisCatlin 2 50
(Willie Musson) *chsd ldrs: rdn over 1f out: no ex ins fnl f* **15/8**[1]
0/0- **8** *shd* **Lastroarofdtiger (USA)**[357] [466] 5-9-4 **67**................ LukeMorris 10 55
(Mrs K Burke) *hld up: hdwy over 1f out: sn rdn: no ex ins fnl f* **20/1**
001- **9** *1* **Nacho Libre**[64] [7614] 6-8-10 **62**................(b) JamesSullivan(3) 8 47
(Michael Easterby) *led: rdn and hdd wl over 1f out: wknd ins fnl f* **12/1**
00-4 **10** *3 1/2* **Wigram's Turn (USA)**[18] [149] 6-9-3 **66**................ GrahamGibbons 4 42
(Michael Easterby) *prom: chsd ldr over 5f out tl rdn over 2f out: wknd fnl f* **6/1**[3]

1m 30.41s (0.81) **Going Correction** +0.30s/f (Slow) **10** Ran SP% **121.2**
Speed ratings (Par 103): **107,106,105,104,101 98,98,97,96,92**
toteswingers:1&2:£24.20, 1&3:£26.60, 2&3:£22.00 CSF £108.40 CT £1406.57 TOTE £18.80: £5.20, £3.00, £3.90; EX 134.80 Trifecta £624.00 Part won. Pool £843.35 - 0.20 winning units..
Owner Graham Lodge Partnership **Bred** Saud Bin Saad **Trained** Newmarket, Suffolk
■ Stewards' Enquiry : Robert Havlin caution: careless riding.
Barry McHugh one-day ban: careless riding (Feb 14)

FOCUS
The Mick Easterby pair of Nacho Libre and Wigram's Turn went off at a breakneck gallop in this competitive handicap, setting it up for those held up. A small personal best from the winner.

368 SPONSOR A RACE BY CALLING 01902 390000 MAIDEN STKS 7f 32y(P)
4:50 (4:51) (Class 5) 3-Y-0 **£1,748** (£520; £260; £129) **Stalls** High

Form RPR
\- **1** **Falmouth Bay (USA)** 3-9-3 0................ JoeFanning 5 81+
(Mark Johnston) *w ldr: racd keenly: led 5f out: shkn up over 1f out: r.o: comf* **4/6**[1]
2-2 **2** *1 3/4* **Crafty Roberto**[9] [262] 3-9-3 0................ ShaneKelly 6 76
(Brian Meehan) *prom: chsd wnr 1/2-way: rdn and hung lft over 1f out: styd on same pce ins fnl f* **15/8**[2]
03- **3** *7* **Miss Firefox**[45] [7913] 3-8-12 0................ LukeMorris 7 52
(Nicky Vaughan) *hld up: hdwy u.p over 2f out: hung lft and wknd ins fnl f* **20/1**
4 *1 1/4* **Rafaaf (IRE)** 3-9-3 0................ NickyMackay 1 54
(Violet M Jordan) *chsd ldrs: rdn over 2f out: wknd fnl f* **10/1**[3]
0- **5** *5* **Unwrapit (USA)**[249] [2461] 3-8-12 0................ TomEaves 3 43
(Bryan Smart) *led 2f: chsd wnr to 1/2-way: rdn whn hmpd 2f out: sn wknd* **25/1**
[illegible]
(Willie Musson) *hld up: shkn up over 2f out: sn wknd* **66/1**

1m 32.34s (2.74) **Going Correction** +0.30s/f (Slow) **6** Ran SP% **114.0**
Speed ratings (Par 97): **96,94,86,84,78 75**
toteswingers:1&2:£1.10, 1&3:£3.50, 2&3:£2.20 CSF £2.15 TOTE £1.90: £1.10, £1.30; EX 3.00 Trifecta £11.20 Pool £1,050.95 - 69.40 winning units..
Owner Sheikh Hamdan Bin Mohammed Al Maktoum **Bred** Gaines-Gentry Thoroughbreds Et Al **Trained** Middleham Moor, N Yorks

FOCUS
A maiden which lacked strength in depth and the front pair came clear. The pace was muddling but the form seems sound enough.

369 PLAY ROULETTE AT BLUESQ.COM FILLIES' H'CAP 1m 4f 50y(P)
5:20 (5:20) (Class 5) (0-75,74) 4-Y-0+ **£1,716** (£510; £255; £127) **Stalls** Low

Form RPR
61-4 **1** **Straversjoy**[25] [67] 4-8-10 **64**................ GrahamGibbons 2 72
(Reg Hollinshead) *chsd ldr tl led over 3f out: rdn clr over 1f out: eased ins fnl f* **5/2**[2]
30-4 **2** *6* **Aphrodisia**[8] [272] 7-9-5 **74**................ RyanClark(5) 4 72
(Ian Williams) *hld up: hdwy 4f out: chsd wnr 3f out: sn rdn: styd on same pce fr over 1f out* **6/4**[1]
300- **3** *3/4* **Bavarica**[129] [6322] 9-9-3 **72**................ TobyAtkinson(5) 5 69
(Julia Feilden) *hld up: hdwy over 2f out: rdn over 1f out: styd on same pce* **4/1**[3]
540- **4** *5* **Sceilin (IRE)**[148] [5786] 7-8-11 **61**................(t) JimmyQuinn 3 52
(John Mackie) *chsd ldrs: rdn over 3f out: wknd over 1f out* **8/1**
603- **5** *5* **Peaceful Means (IRE)**[134] [5635] 8-8-10 **60**................ MickyFenton 1 41
(John Mackie) *led and clr to 1/2-way: rdn and hdd over 3f out: wknd over 2f out* **8/1**

2m 45.31s (4.21) **Going Correction** +0.30s/f (Slow)
WFA 4 from 7yo+ 4lb **5** Ran SP% **110.8**
Speed ratings (Par 100): **97,93,92,89,85**
totesuper7: Abandoned CSF £6.74 TOTE £2.80: £1.20, £1.10; EX 4.50.
Owner E Bennion **Bred** Eric Bennion **Trained** Upper Longdon, Staffs
■ Stewards' Enquiry : Toby Atkinson two-day ban: used whip with excessive frequency (Feb 14-15)

FOCUS
A small-field fillies' handicap which looked steadily run. Not form to be too postive about but the winner rates a 5lb personal best.
T/Plt: £195.80 to a £1 stake. Pool:£83,845.09 - 312.50 winning tickets T/Qpdt: £26.50 to a £1 stake. Pool:£9,541.86 - 265.95 winning tickets CR

325 CAGNES-SUR-MER
Monday, January 31
OFFICIAL GOING: Fibresand: standard

370a PRIX DE GRIMAUD (MAIDEN) (3YO COLTS & GELDINGS) (FIBRESAND) 1m 2f (D)
12:00 (12:00) 3-Y-0 **£8,620** (£3,448; £2,586; £1,724; £862)

RPR
1 **Ujadil Bere (FR)** 3-9-2 0................ DominiqueBoeuf 8 76
(M Pimbonnet, France) **22/5**[2]
2 *1/2* **Par Cinq (FR)**[53] 3-9-2 0................ StephanePasquier 13 76
(P Demercastel, France) **2/1**[1]
3 *nse* **Cenon (IRE)** 3-9-2 0................ IoritzMendizabal 6 75
(J-C Rouget, France) **48/10**[3]
4 *nse* **Dellarte (FR)**[121] [6589] 3-9-2 0................(p) JohanVictoire 14 75
(L A Urbano-Grajales, France) **28/1**
5 *3/4* **Mayday (FR)**[203] 3-9-2 0................ FranckBlondel 2 74
(F Rossi, France) **45/1**
6 *nk* **Parigino (FR)**[14] 3-9-2 0................(p) ThierryThulliez 15 73
(F Chappet, France) **17/1**
7 *nse* **Shirocco Junior** 3-9-2 0................(p) FredericSpanu 1 73
(F Rohaut, France) **70/1**
8 *nse* **Run The Show (FR)**[35] 3-9-2 0................ FabriceVeron 9 73
(H-A Pantall, France) **47/1**
8 *dht* **Haader (USA)** 3-9-2 0................ Francois-XavierBertras 3 73
(F Rohaut, France) **17/2**
10 *1/2* **Baileys Vert (FR)**[53] 3-9-2 0................ ThomasHuet 16 72?
(W Walton, France) **93/1**
0 **Hugely Exciting**[10] [258] 3-9-2 0................ DavyBonilla 11 —
(J S Moore) *broke wl: racd 4th on outer: rdn 2 1/2f out: wnt 3rd u.p 1 1/2f out: ev ch but no ex fnl f: fdd* **11/1**
0 **High Speed (SWI)**[10] [258] 3-8-10 0........... MathieuTavaresDaSilva(6) 4 —
(H-A Pantall, France) **46/1**
0 **Tarkand (FR)** 3-9-2 0................(p) SylvainRuis 5 —
(W Walton, France) **87/1**
0 **Haim (FR)** 3-9-2 0................ NicolasPerret 7 —
(K Borgel, France) **14/1**
0 **Dom'Son (FR)** 3-9-2 0................ FlavienPrat 10 —
(Y Fertillet, France) **36/1**
0 **Scarlet Warrior (AUT)** 3-9-2 0................ FabienLefebvre 12 —
(G Martin, Austria) **62/1**

2m 5.29s (125.29) **16** Ran SP% **117.9**
WIN (incl. 1 euro stake): 5.40. PLACES: 1.50, 1.30, 1.80. DF: 5.70. SF: 14.60.
Owner Gerard Lancry **Bred** Snc Regnier & San Gabriel Inv.Inc **Trained** France

371a PRIX DE TOULOUSE (CONDITIONS) (4YO+) (FIBRESAND) 1m 2f (D)
1:35 (12:00) 4-Y-0+ **£10,775** (£4,310; £3,232; £2,155; £1,077)

RPR
1 **Livandar (FR)**[54] [7776] 5-9-10 0................ RonanThomas 12 109
(P Van De Poele, France) **81/10**
2 *1 1/2* **Tominator**[9] [267] 4-8-9 0................ JohanVictoire 11 93
(Reg Hollinshead) *broke wl to r midfield on outer: gd prog bef st: qcknd wl u.p in st: wnt 2nd 1f out: r.o wl* **22/1**
3 *1 1/2* **Chalsa (FR)**[275] 5-9-4 0................ FranckBlondel 6 97
(P Khozian, France) **19/1**
4 *3/4* **Maroni (IRE)**[14] [195] 6-8-11 0................ FredericSpanu 9 89
(F Rohaut, France) **47/1**
5 *nk* **Tangaspeed (FR)**[72] [7533] 6-8-8 0................ DavyBonilla 15 85
(R Laplanche, France) **23/1**
6 *1/2* **Bling (FR)**[163] 4-9-2 0................ StephanePasquier 3 95
[illegible]
7 *snk* **Villa Molitor (FR)**[14] [195] 5-8-8 0................ Francois-XavierBertras 5 84
(F Rohaut, France) **14/5**[1]
8 *1/2* **Querry Boy (FR)**[14] [195] 4-8-9 0................ FabriceVeron 13 86
(H-A Pantall, France) **17/1**
9 *1* **Konig Bernard (FR)**[14] [195] 5-8-11 0................ DominiqueBoeuf 10 85
(W Baltromei, Germany) **9/2**[2]
10 *1* **Magic Moon (FR)**[54] [7776] 5-8-7 0................ BaptisteChevet(8) 1 87
(T Lemer, France) **21/1**
0 **Eire**[20] 7-9-2 0................ IoritzMendizabal 2 —
(M Nigge, France) **9/1**
0 **Sopran Prince (IRE)**[190] 5-9-4 0................ PierantonioConvertino 16 —
(M Mercalli, Italy) **26/1**
0 **Arlequin**[100] [7084] 4-8-9 0................ SylvainRuis 8 —
(James Bethell) *racd towards rr on outer fr s: rdn early in st: r.o one pce fnl f* **39/1**
0 **Kel Away (FR)**[12] [219] 4-8-6 0................ DavidBreux 4 —
(Mlle M Henry, France) **60/1**
0 **Revolverheld (GER)** 5-9-2 0................(b) ASuborics 7 —
(G Martin, Austria) **58/1**

2m 0.92s (120.92)
WFA 4 from 5yo+ 2lb **15** Ran SP% **116.6**
WIN (incl. 1 euro stake): 9.10. PLACES: 3.80, 6.30, 6.10. DF: 87.40. SF: 157.20.
Owner Christos Theodorakis **Bred** Haras De S A Aga Khan Scea **Trained** France

372a PRIX DE GAND (CLAIMER) (5YO+) (FIBRESAND) 1m 2f (D)
2:40 (12:00) 5-Y-0+ **£6,465** (£2,586; £1,939; £1,293; £646)

RPR
1 **Almaguer**[23] 9-8-9 0................ MathieuTavaresDaSilva(6) 10 66
(F-X Belvisi, France) **14/1**
2 *snk* **Szerelem (FR)**[23] 6-9-1 0................ StephanePasquier 16 66
(F-X De Chevigny, France) **73/10**[2]
3 *2* **West Wing (FR)**[28] 6-9-4 0................ ThomasHuet 6 65
(F-X Belvisi, France) **46/1**
4 *1/2* **Zieto (FR)**[12] [221] 7-9-3 0................ XavierBergeron(8) 14 71
(J-M Capitte, France) **8/1**[3]
5 *1* **Jack Junior (USA)**[12] [221] 7-9-1 0................(p) SylvainRuis 9 59
(C Boutin, France) **5/2**[1]
6 *3/4* **Tudora (AUT)**[12] [221] 6-8-9 0 ow1................ ASuborics 2 52
(S Bigus, Austria) **13/1**

7 hd **Royal Pepper**[10] [259] 6-9-2 0 .... AlexisBadel 13 59
(C Boutin, France) **18/1**
8 ½ **Raganeyev (FR)**[80] 10-9-11 0 .... (b) MorganDelalande 5 67
(X Nakkachdji, France) **17/2**
9 2 **Bencoolen (IRE)**[10] [257] 6-10-3 0 .... JohanVictoire 12 69
(David Nicholls) *in rr on outer fr s: mde prog bef st: u.p early in st: no ex fnl f* **14/1**
10 1½ **Sina (GER)**[12] [220] 6-8-11 0 .... (p) FabriceVeron 3 47
(H-A Pantall, France) **16/1**
0 **Brunoy**[494] 9-9-4 0 .... (p) TonyPiccone 11 —
(J Rossi, France) **15/1**
0 **Sheitan**[277] 6-9-1 0 .... (b) IoritzMendizabal 7 —
(F Brogi, Italy) **20/1**
0 **Notia (IRE)**[12] [220] 6-8-8 0 ow1 .... (b) PaulineProd'homme(4) 8 —
(D Prod'Homme, France) **45/1**
0 **Glamstar (FR)**[12] [220] 5-8-11 0 .... (p) AnthonyTeissieux 1 —
(M Pimbonnet, France) **30/1**
0 **La Tropezienne (FR)** 5-8-8 0 .... (p) SamuelFargeat 4 —
(T Civel, France) **71/1**
P **Aktion Power (GER)**[1667] 8-8-11 0 .... FranckBlondel 15 —
(S Labate, France) **20/1**

2m 2.82s (122.82) **16** Ran SP% **118.6**
WIN (incl 1 euro stake) : 11.80 (Almaguer coupled with West Wing). PLACES: 4.60, 3.70, 15.70. DF : 49.50. SF : 121.10..
Owner Francois-Xavier Belvisi **Bred** Chevington Stud **Trained** France

318 SOUTHWELL (L-H)
Tuesday, February 1

OFFICIAL GOING: Standard
Wind: Light across Weather: Fine and dry

373 BET AND WATCH AT BLUESQ.COM AMATEUR RIDERS' H'CAP 1m 6f (F)
1:30 (1:30) (Class 6) (0-65,65) 4-Y-0+ **£1,483** (£456; £228) **Stalls** Low

Form RPR
415- 1 **William's Way**[64] [7632] 9-10-9 **65** .... (t) MrCMartin(5) 6 77
(Ian Wood) *hld up and bhd: swtchd outside and stdy hdwy 5f out: chal over 2f out: rdn to ld 1 1/2f out: styd on strly and sn clr* **5/2**[1]
2541 2 5 **Carnac (IRE)**[5] [324] 5-9-8 **50** .... (p) MrOGarner(5) 1 54
(Alan McCabe) *cl up on inner: led over 5f out: rdn along 3f out: drvn and hdd 1 1/2f out: sn one pce* **3/1**[2]
00-0 3 2¼ **Light The City (IRE)**[16] [184] 4-8-13 **48** .... WilliamTwiston-Davies(7) 8 49
(Ruth Carr) *in tch: hdwy and cl up 1/2-way: chsd ldr 4f out: rdn along 3f out: drvn 2f out and kpt on same pce* **33/1**
1-40 4 1¼ **Juwireya**[12] [223] 4-10-1 **62** .... (v) MissHannahWatson(5) 3 61
(Peter Hiatt) *trckd ldrs: effrt 4f out: rdn along 3f out: kpt on same pce fnl 2f* **12/1**
-544 5 1¼ **Silent Lucidity (IRE)**[5] [324] 7-10-3 **54** .... (p) MissSBrotherton 9 51
(Peter Niven) *t.k.h: hdwy and cl up after 3f: effrt 4f out: rdn along over 3f out: grad wknd fnl 2f* **6/1**[3]
50-3 6 6 **Astroleo**[28] [39] 5-9-2 **46** oh1 .... MissNMcCaffrey(7) 2 35
(Mark H Tompkins) *led 3f: cl up: pushed along 1/2-way: rdn over 4f out: sn wknd* **25/1**
050- 7 ¾ **Swords**[63] [7634] 9-9-4 **48** oh1 ow2 .... MissSPeacock(7) 5 36
(Ray Peacock) *t.k.h: hdwy on outer to join ldrs after 2f: cl up tl led appr 1/2-way: rdn along over 5f out: sn hdd & wknd wl over 3f out* **50/1**
132- 8 11 **Valantino Oyster (IRE)**[54] [7789] 4-9-10 **57** .... MissCharlotteHolmes(5) 7 30
(Ben Haslam) *in tch: rdn along 6f out: outpcd and bhd fnl 3f* **7/1**
130- 9 20 **Mexican Jay (USA)**[83] [7398] 5-10-2 **58** .... JustinNewman(5) 4 —
(Bryan Smart) *cl up: led after 3f: hdd bef 1/2-way: sn rdn along and lost pl 5f out: bhd fnl 3f* **6/1**[3]

3m 16.41s (8.11) **Going Correction** +0.40s/f (Slow)
WFA 4 from 5yo+ 5lb **9** Ran SP% **111.1**
Speed ratings (Par 101): **92,89,87,87,86 83,82,76,64**
toteswingers:1&2 £2.40, 2&3 £12.70, 1&3 £15.00 CSF £9.35 CT £178.51 TOTE £3.10: £1.30, £1.50, £7.30; EX 10.70 Trifecta £342.20 Pool: £763.09 - 1.65 winning units..
Owner Neardown Stables **Bred** Lewis Caterers **Trained** Upper Lambourn, Berks

FOCUS
Times suggested the surface was on the slow side. A modest handicap run at a reasonable pace, the lead disputed by four runners at one stage. The winner is rated back to last year's form here.

374 PLAY GOLF BEFORE RACING AT SOUTHWELL (S) STKS 1m 4f (F)
2:00 (2:02) (Class 6) 4-Y-0+ **£1,535** (£453; £226) **Stalls** Low

Form RPR
124/ 1 **La Estrella (USA)**[699] [761] 8-9-0 0 .... DaneO'Neill 1 70
(Don Cantillon) *trckd ldrs: hdwy over 3f out: rdn to chse ldr 2f out: drvn to chal over 1f out: led ins fnl f: kpt on wl* **6/4**[1]
-222 2 1¼ **Camps Bay (USA)**[13] [216] 7-9-5 73 .... HayleyTurner 3 73
(Conor Dore) *trckd ldr: hdwy to ld jst over 3f out: rdn over 2f out: drvn and edgd lft over 1f out: hdd ins fnl f: no ex* **7/4**[2]
32-1 3 2½ **Castle Myth (USA)**[23] [103] 5-9-0 63 .... (be) DaleSwift(5) 6 69
(Brian Ellison) *hld up in rr: hdwy 4f out: trckd ldrs 3f out: rdn to chse ldng pair 2f out: sn drvn and no imp appr fnl f* **7/1**
250- 4 9 **Profit's Reality (IRE)**[166] [5235] 9-9-0 77 .... LukeMorris 5 50
(Michael Attwater) *chsd ldng pair: rdn along over 3f out: sn drvn and wknd over 2f out* **11/2**[3]
546- 5 ½ **Greenbelt**[42] [7957] 10-9-0 49 .... PJMcDonald 2 49
(George Moore) *pushed along s and sn led: reminders after 3f: rdn along 4f out: hdd jst over 3f out and sn wknd* **40/1**
4 6 46 **Lightening Force**[11] [245] 4-8-11 0 .... (tp) RobbieFitzpatrick 4 —
(Peter Brookshaw) *a in rr: rdn along over 4f out: sn outpcd and bhd fnl 3f* **66/1**

2m 46.59s (5.59) **Going Correction** +0.40s/f (Slow)
WFA 4 from 5yo+ 3lb **6** Ran SP% **108.2**
Speed ratings (Par 101): **97,96,94,88,88 57**
toteswingers:1&2 £1.10, 2&3 £1.90, 1&3 £1.60 CSF £4.01 TOTE £2.00: £1.10, £1.60; EX 3.30.There was no bid for the winner. Castle Myth was claimed by J. J. Best for £5500.
Owner Don Cantillon **Bred** Five Horses Ltd And Theatrical Syndicate **Trained** Newmarket, Suffolk

FOCUS
A fair seller with the first two and the fourth above average for the grade. The third looks the most likely guide, though.

375 LADIES AT SOUTHWELL GOLF CLUB H'CAP 6f (F)
2:30 (2:30) (Class 6) (0-60,60) 4-Y-0+ **£1,535** (£453; £226) **Stalls** Low

Form RPR
-532 1 **Dancing Freddy (IRE)**[4] [345] 4-9-4 **60** .... (p) RobertLButler(3) 2 68
(Michael Chapman) *chsd ldr on inner: effrt over 2f out: rdn to ld wl over 1f out: drvn ins fnl f and kpt on wl* **7/1**[3]
-222 2 ¾ **Gold Story**[7] [289] 4-8-8 **52** .... DeanHeslop(5) 8 58
(Brian Ellison) *chsd ldrs: hdwy over 2f out: rdn to chse wnr over 1f out: ch tl drvn: carried hd high and edgd lft ins fnl f: no ex towards fin* **3/1**[1]
00-0 3 nse **Muqalad (IRE)**[11] [255] 4-9-0 **53** .... TomEaves 3 58
(Bryan Smart) *chsd ldrs: hdwy 2f out: rdn and ch over 1f out: drvn and kpt on same pce ins fnl f* **6/1**[2]
04-6 4 nk **Dancing Wave**[5] [318] 5-8-0 **46** oh1 .... JackDuern(7) 9 50
(Michael Chapman) *in tch towards outer: wd st: rdn 2f out: styd on wl appr fnl f: nrst fin* **33/1**
0336 5 1¼ **Errigal Lad**[7] [289] 6-9-2 **55** .... (p) LukeMorris 6 55
(John Balding) *chsd ldrs: rdn 2f out: drvn and one pce appr fnl f* **8/1**
3146 6 1¾ **Itsthursdayalready**[13] [210] 4-9-3 **56** .... ShaneKelly 4 51
(Mark Brisbourne) *stdd s and sn swtchd rt: keen and in tch: wd st and hdwy 2f out: sn rdn: edgd lft and no imp fr over 1f out* **3/1**[1]
000- 7 5 **Running Mate (IRE)**[113] [6812] 4-9-6 **59** .... DaneO'Neill 11 38
(Jo Crowley) *chsd ldrs on outer: wd st and sn rdn: drvn and wknd over 1f out* **16/1**
/00- 8 2 **White Ledger (IRE)**[99] [7125] 12-8-7 **46** oh1 .... (v) DuranFentiman 1 18
(Ray Peacock) *a towards rr* **100/1**
00-5 9 nk **Ponting (IRE)**[19] [150] 5-8-10 **49** .... MickyFenton 5 21
(Paul Midgley) *sn led: rdn along over 2f out: drvn and hdd wl over 1f out: sn wknd* **8/1**
00-0 10 1½ **Quadrifolio**[18] [169] 5-8-7 **46** oh1 .... ChrisCatlin 10 13
(Paul Green) *a in rr* **33/1**
05-6 11 8 **Fair Bunny**[23] [107] 4-8-9 **51** .... (b) JamesSullivan(3) 7 —
(Alan Brown) *chsd ldrs: rdn along 1/2-way: sn wknd* **25/1**

1m 19.39s (2.89) **Going Correction** +0.40s/f (Slow) **11** Ran SP% **115.6**
Speed ratings (Par 101): **96,95,94,94,92 90,83,81,80,78 68**
toteswingers:1&2 £2.80, 2&3 £4.40, 1&3 £8.00 CSF £27.04 CT £137.12 TOTE £5.60: £2.70, £1.10, £2.30; EX 18.70 Trifecta £296.30 Pool: £704.89 - 1.76 winning units..
Owner Rakebackmypoker.com **Bred** Vincent Duignan **Trained** Market Rasen, Lincs
■ Stewards' Enquiry : Robert L Butler one-day ban: used whip with excessive frequency (Feb 15)
Dean Heslop five-day ban: used whip with excessive frequency (Feb 15-19)

FOCUS
A moderate handicap run in a time much slower than other two 6f races on the card, a claimer and a Class 5 handicap. The first two were closely matched on recent C&D form.

376 SOUTHWELL-RACECOURSE.CO.UK CLAIMING STKS 6f (F)
3:00 (3:00) (Class 6) 4-Y-0+ **£1,535** (£453; £226) **Stalls** Low

Form RPR
-216 1 **Punching**[4] [343] 7-9-1 76 .... HayleyTurner 6 84
(Conor Dore) *chsd ldr: smooth hdwy to ld wl over 1f out: rdn clr jst over 1f out: drvn ins fnl f: hld on wl* **5/1**
24-1 2 ½ **Bonnie Prince Blue**[28] [35] 8-8-12 80 .... (be) DeanHeslop(5) 2 84
(Brian Ellison) *towards rr: rdn along 1/2-way: hdwy over 1f out: drvn and hung lft ins fnl f: styd on wl towards fin* **5/2**[2]
140- 3 hd **Ingleby Arch (USA)**[51] [7846] 8-9-1 87 .... PhillipMakin 7 82
(David Barron) *chsd ldrs: rdn along bef 1/2-way: drvn wl over 1f out: styd on u.p ins fnl f: nrst fin* **15/8**[1]
15-5 4 4 **Cape Vale (IRE)**[31] [2] 6-9-11 85 .... AdrianNicholls 5 79
(David Nicholls) *led: rdn along over 2f out: hdd wl over 1f out and sn wknd* **3/1**[3]
00-5 5 9 **Hard Rock City (USA)**[30] [12] 11-8-12 77 .... (t) NeilFarley(5) 3 42
(Declan Carroll) *in rr: rdn along 1/2-way: nvr a factor* **25/1**
60-0 6 ½ **Sophie's Beau (USA)**[30] [14] 4-8-11 42 .... RobertLButler(3) 1 38
(Michael Chapman) *trckd ldrs on inner: hdwy and cl up over 2f out: rdn wl over 1f out: sn wknd* **100/1**
00-6 7 14 **Excusez Moi (USA)**[5] [321] 9-8-9 80 .... (be) PJMcDonald 4 —
(Ruth Carr) *dwlt and wnt rt s: a in rr* **25/1**

1m 17.73s (1.23) **Going Correction** +0.40s/f (Slow) **7** Ran SP% **113.7**
Speed ratings (Par 101): **107,106,106,100,88 88,69**
toteswingers:1&2 £2.40, 2&3 £1.60, 1&3 £2.90 CSF £17.65 TOTE £5.60: £3.10, £1.10; EX 18.60.
Owner Liam Breslin **Bred** Cheveley Park Stud Ltd **Trained** Cowbit, Lincs
■ Stewards' Enquiry : Dean Heslop four-day ban: used whip with excessive frequency (Feb 20-23)

FOCUS
A good claimer, but it was slower than the following handicap. The winner produced a big turn around with the runner-up on last month's claimer form.

377 10% FORECAST BONUS AT BLUESQ.COM H'CAP 6f (F)
3:30 (3:30) (Class 5) (0-75,75) 4-Y-0+ **£1,878** (£558; £279; £139) **Stalls** Low

Form RPR
6-36 1 **Takajan (IRE)**[14] [199] 4-8-6 **65** .... JamesRogers(5) 3 75
(Mark Brisbourne) *trckd ldrs: smooth hdwy to ld over 2f out: rdn over 1f out: edgd lft ins fnl f: kpt on* **5/1**[3]
-364 2 nk **Elusive Fame (USA)**[16] [186] 5-8-11 **72** .... (b) JasonHart(7) 2 81
(Mark Johnston) *trckd ldrs: hdwy wl over 2f out: rdn to chse wnr over 1f out: ev ch ins fnl f: nt qckn towards fin* **6/1**
-220 3 2 **Onceaponatime (IRE)**[14] [199] 6-9-2 **70** .... KirstyMilczarek 4 73
(Michael Squance) *trckd ldrs: hdwy over 2f out: rdn wl over 1f out and ch tl drvn and one pce ent fnl f* **7/2**[2]
320- 4 3½ **Beckermet (IRE)**[140] [6048] 9-8-8 **65** .... JamesSullivan(3) 1 56
(Ruth Carr) *led: rdn along wl over 2f out: sn hdd & wknd over 1f out* **40/1**
546- 5 ¾ **Thrust Control (IRE)**[155] [5606] 4-9-2 **75** .... DeanHeslop(5) 5 64
(Brian Ellison) *in rr: hdwy on outer wl over 2f out: sn rdn and no imp* **10/1**
00-3 6 8 **Besty**[26] [58] 4-9-5 **73** .... TomEaves 7 36
(Bryan Smart) *cl up: rdn along wl over 2f out: sn wknd* **10/1**
4-11 7 23 **Sir Louis**[19] [150] 4-8-6 **67** .... GeorgeChaloner(7) 6 —
(Richard Fahey) *akward s and sn t.k.h: hdwy on outer to chse ldrs after 2f: rdn along 1/2-way: wknd qckly over 2f out: sn eased and bhd* **7/4**[1]

1m 17.58s (1.08) **Going Correction** +0.40s/f (Slow) **7** Ran SP% **110.2**
Speed ratings (Par 103): **108,107,104,100,99 88,57**
CSF £31.84 TOTE £6.70: £3.30, £2.30; EX 37.10.
Owner Stephen Jones **Bred** His Highness The Aga Khan's Studs S C **Trained** Great Ness, Shropshire

FOCUS
A reasonable handicap for the class and the time was the quickest of three 6f races on the card. The winner rates pretty much back to his best.
Sir Louis Official explanation: trainer's rep said gelding bled from the nose

378 MEMBERSHIP OF SOUTHWELL GOLF CLUB MAIDEN STKS 1m (F)
4:00 (4:00) (Class 5) 3-Y-O **£1,910** (£564; £282) **Stalls** Low

Form RPR
300- **1** **New Latin (IRE)**[47] 7891 3-9-3 70 .... JoeFanning 4 74+
(Mark Johnston) *cl up: led after 2f: jnd and rdn along wl over 2f out: drvn and hdd briefly 1f out: sn led again and kpt on wl towards fin* **1/1**[1]

2 **2** *½* **Kishanda**[21] 121 3-8-12 0 .... HayleyTurner 3 67
(Hughie Morrison) *trckd ldng pair: hdwy and cl up 3f out: chal over 2f ou: sn rdn and led briefly 1f out: sn hdd and no ex last 75yds* **11/8**[2]

00 **3** *13* **Pizzetti (IRE)**[10] 262 3-9-3 0 .... ChrisCatlin 2 42
(Sir Mark Prescott Bt) *in rr: hdwy over 3f out: pushed along to take mod 3rd over 1f out: no ch w ldng pair* **8/1**[3]

6 **4** *2½* **Cadgers Brig**[15] 191 3-9-3 0 .... FrederikTylicki 1 36
(Richard Fahey) *led 2f: prom tl rdn along over 3f out: outpcd fr wl over 2f out* **14/1**

1m 45.9s (2.20) **Going Correction** +0.40s/f (Slow) **4** Ran SP% **109.9**
Speed ratings (Par 97): **105,104,91,89**
CSF £2.72 TOTE £1.80; EX 2.70.
Owner Sheikh Hamdan Bin Mohammed Al Maktoum **Bred** Stone Ridge Farm **Trained** Middleham Moor, N Yorks

FOCUS
A weak maiden that only concerned two runners, but the time was good, being 1.83 seconds quicker than the 64-rated Aloneinthestreet, a stablemate of New Latin, recorded in the following handicap. The winner is rated back to his 2yo form with the second up 8lb from his recent debut.

379 PLAY FREE BINGO AT BLUESQ.COM H'CAP 1m (F)
4:30 (4:33) (Class 5) (0-75,70) 3-Y-O **£1,813** (£539; £269; £134) **Stalls** Low

Form RPR
400- **1** **Aloneinthestreet (USA)**[104] 7020 3-9-1 **64** .... JoeFanning 1 73
(Mark Johnston) *trckd ldrs on inner: hdwy to chse ldr over 2f out: rdn to ld over 1f out: kpt on wl ins fnl f* **2/1**[2]

1P61 **2** *4* **Double Duchess**[7] 296 3-9-3 **66** 6ex .... LiamJones 3 66
(Paul D'Arcy) *reminders s and sn set brisk pce: jnd and rdn along over 2f out: drvn and hdd over 1f out: one pce ins fnl f* **7/2**[3]

53-3 **3** *6* **Bernisdale**[26] 59 3-8-8 **57** .... TomEaves 4 43
(George Moore) *chsd ldr: rdn along 3f out and sn outpcd: rallied u.p ent fnl f to take 3rd nr fin* **16/1**

061- **4** *½* **Endaxi Mana Mou**[70] 7540 3-9-4 **67** .... KellyHarrison 2 52
(Noel Quinlan) *dwlt and hld up in rr: hdwy whn n.m.r on inner 3f out: rdn along over 2f out: sn drvn and one pce: lost 3rd nr fin* **15/8**[1]

41-4 **5** *1¼* **Night Witch (IRE)**[17] 177 3-9-4 **70** .... AlanCreighton(3) 5 52
(Edward Creighton) *dwlt: hdwy to chse ldng pair 1/2-way: rdn along wl over 2f out: sn drvn and wknd* **15/2**

1m 47.73s (4.03) **Going Correction** +0.40s/f (Slow) **5** Ran SP% **108.0**
Speed ratings (Par 97): **95,91,85,84,83**
CSF £8.88 TOTE £3.20: £1.80, £1.60; EX 11.00.
Owner Sheikh Hamdan Bin Mohammed Al Maktoum **Bred** Mr & Mrs Dick Probert & Robert Cowley **Trained** Middleham Moor, N Yorks
■ Stewards' Enquiry : Liam Jones one-day ban: arrived at stalls after start time (Feb 15)

FOCUS
The time was quite slow, being 1.83 seconds off the time recorded in the earlier 3-y-o maiden. The form is rated around the runner-up and the winner is another big improver on his handicap debut for Johnston.
T/Plt: £77.00 to a £1 stake. Pool of £60,580.06 - 573.72 winning tickets. T/Qpdt: £38.50 to a £1 stake. Pool of £4,024.78 - 77.30 winning tickets. JR

354 KEMPTON (A.W) (R-H)
Wednesday, February 2
OFFICIAL GOING: Standard
Wind: Fresh, half behind Weather: Overcast

380 BETDAQ.COM EVERY WEDNESDAY AT KEMPTON PARK MEDIAN AUCTION MAIDEN STKS 5f (P)
4:50 (4:51) (Class 5) 3-5-Y-O **£2,047** (£604; £302) **Stalls** Low

Form RPR
-33 **1** **Liberal Lady**[7] 305 3-8-9 0 .... EddieAhern 4 60
(Jimmy Fox) *prom: chsd ldr over 2f out: rdn to cl 1f out: led last 150yds: pushed out* **9/2**[2]

05-4 **2** *1* **Rambo Will**[21] 126 3-9-0 63 .... DavidProbert 11 61
(J R Jenkins) *fast away fr wdst draw and led after 1f: drvn and hdd last 150yds: kpt on* **5/1**[3]

U-55 **3** *2¾* **Pickled Pumpkin**[12] 246 3-9-0 0 .... IanMongan 8 51
(Olivia Maylam) *chsd ldrs: wnt 3rd 2f out: rdn and no imp on ldng pair after: kpt on* **33/1**

4 *1½* **Lois Lane** 3-8-9 0 .... RichardKingscote 7 41+
(Ron Hodges) *dwlt and bmpd s: detached in last: promising hdwy on inner over 1f out: tk 4th nr fin* **25/1**

5 *nk* **Evey P (IRE)**[184] 4666 4-9-9 0 .... LiamKeniry 10 46
(Gary Brown) *stdd s fr wd draw: sn chsd ldrs: outpcd wl over 1f out: no ch after* **33/1**

05-4 **6** *1* **Dangerous Illusion (IRE)**[12] 246 3-8-9 47 .... ChrisCatlin 1 36
(Michael Quinn) *chsd ldrs: outpcd fr 2f out: nt on terms after* **14/1**

6- **7** *½* **Cuddly**[155] 5640 3-8-9 0 .... HayleyTurner 5 34
(Robert Cowell) *nvr bttr than midfield: pushed along in 8th 2f out: no real prog* **13/8**[1]

8 *1¾* **Celtic Whisper** 3-8-9 0 .... SteveDrowne 2 28+
(Jeremy Gask) *dwlt: off the pce in last trio: swtchd lft and rn into trble 1f out: keeping on nr fin* **5/1**[3]

20-6 **9** *hd* **Arowana (IRE)**[14] 208 3-8-9 60 .... SamHitchcott 9 27
(Zoe Davison) *prom whn hung lft bnd after 1f: pushed along in midfield 1/2-way: wknd over 1f out* **14/1**

6 **10** *1* **Stoneacre Joe Joe**[12] 246 3-9-0 0 .... RobbieFitzpatrick 6 29
(Peter Grayson) *wnt lft s: a in last trio and struggling* **66/1**

0- **11** *35* **Lagan Lullaby**[255] 2358 3-8-9 0 .... MickyFenton 3 —
(Neil Mulholland) *led 1f: hung lft bnd sn after: chsd ldr to over 2f out: wknd rapidly wl over 1f out: virtually p.u* **25/1**

61.31 secs (0.81) **Going Correction** +0.05s/f (Slow)
WFA 3 from 4yo 14lb **11** Ran SP% **118.0**
Speed ratings (Par 103): **95,93,89,86,86 84,83,80,80,79 23**
toteswingers: 1&2 £2.80, 1&3 £19.70, 2&3 £22.40 CSF £25.90 TOTE £3.30: £1.10, £1.20, £10.20; EX 29.20.
Owner The Fairy Story Partnership **Bred** Deepwood Farm Stud **Trained** Collingbourne Ducis, Wilts

FOCUS
A weak maiden where only the first two mattered in the straight. The winner improved on her initial efforts but not have needed to by much. The form is rated around the second.
Lagan Lullaby Official explanation: jockey said filly hung left, lost her action and had a breathing problem.

381 RACING AT SKYSPORTS.COM H'CAP 1m 2f (P)
5:20 (5:22) (Class 5) (0-75,75) 4-Y-O+ **£2,047** (£604; £302) **Stalls** Low

Form RPR
10-5 **1** **Lay Claim (USA)**[9] 287 4-9-4 **73** .... (b) TomQueally 10 79
(Alan McCabe) *t.k.h: hld up in 10th: plenty to do 2f out: stl only 10th jst over 1f out: gd prog on outer fnl f: led post* **16/1**

330- **2** *nse* **Round Won (USA)**[67] 7597 4-9-3 **72** .... (v[1]) ShaneKelly 3 78
(William Knight) *led: drvn and hrd pressed fnl f: kpt on wl: hdd post* **8/1**[3]

-543 **3** *shd* **Veroon (IRE)**[9] 287 5-9-4 **72** .... (p) MickyFenton 5 78
(James Given) *trckd ldrs in 6th: effrt 2f out: clsd thrght fnl f: jst pipped* **9/1**

23-5 **4** *shd* **Negotiation (IRE)**[9] 279 5-9-3 **71** .... ChrisCatlin 8 77
(Michael Quinn) *trckd ldr: rdn over 2f out: chal fnl f: nrly upsides nr fin: lost 2 pls after* **22/1**

16-5 **5** *1* **Classically (IRE)**[18] 175 5-9-7 **75** .... SteveDrowne 6 79
(Hughie Morrison) *racd wd thrght in midfield: rdn 2f out: tried to cl on ldrs fnl f: nvr quite able to chal* **7/1**[2]

13-1 **6** *nk* **Pertuis (IRE)**[28] 54 5-9-7 **75** .... LukeMorris 9 80+
(Harry Dunlop) *s.i.s: settled in 10th: pushed along over 2f out: sed to run on over 1f out and looking for room: no real ch of winning whn no room ins fnl f: styd on nr fin* **11/4**[1]

0/1- **7** *½* **John Veale (USA)**[53] 7838 5-9-4 **72** .... (t) EddieAhern 14 77+
(Thomas McLaughlin, Ire) *hld up in 8th: prog wl over 1f out: wnt 3rd and clsng jst ins fnl f: probably jst hld whn nowhere to go last 50yds and lost pl* **16/1**

2-23 **8** *1¼* **Professor John (IRE)**[4] 352 4-8-10 **65** .... (p) DavidProbert 4 64
(Ian Wood) *a abt same pl: rdn and no prog over 2f out: one pce after* **8/1**[3]

0-00 **9** *1½* **Dinner Date**[14] 206 9-9-3 **71** .... LiamKeniry 2 67
(Tom Keddy) *prom on inner: chsd ldng pair over 2f out to jst over 1f out: wknd and eased* **33/1**

6-53 **10** *nk* **Turjuman (USA)**[10] 272 6-8-9 **63** .... JamieMackay 11 59
(Willie Musson) *hld up in last pair: stl there over 1f out: hd at awkward angle but kpt on steadily fnl f: nvr involved* **9/1**

25-3 **11** *2¼* **Celtic Commitment**[21] 124 5-8-12 **66** .... HayleyTurner 7 57
(Simon Dow) *chsd ldng pair: rdn over 2f out: sn wknd* **10/1**

116- **12** *11* **Buona Sarah (IRE)**[57] 7732 4-8-5 **67** .... NathanAlison(7) 13 36
(Sheena West) *heavily restrained s and nrly t.o after 100yds: plld hrd and sn in tch in last pair: no prog 2f out: wknd* **16/1**

2m 7.17s (-0.83) **Going Correction** +0.05s/f (Slow)
WFA 4 from 5yo+ 1lb **12** Ran SP% **115.4**
Speed ratings (Par 103): **105,104,104,104,104 103,103,102,101,100 99,90**
toteswingers: 1&2 £16.90, 1&3 £34.70, 2&3 £13.90 CSF £134.99 CT £1231.49 TOTE £20.80: £4.60, £3.20, £3.00; EX 199.30.
Owner Abdul Rahman Al Jasmi **Bred** George Strawbridge Et Al **Trained** Averham Park, Notts
■ Stewards' Enquiry : Eddie Ahern two-day ban: (Feb 16-17_

FOCUS
A modest but competitive handicap, run at a fairly steady pace until it picked up on the approach to the straight. There was a real blanket finish and a couple of hard-luck stories, so the form is ordinary and may not prove entirely solid. That said, it was a race that should produce winners.
Classically(IRE) Official explanation: jockey said that the gelding ran too freely
Pertuis(IRE) Official explanation: jockey said the gelding was denied a clear run
Buona Sarah(IRE) Official explanation: jockey said that the filly missed the break and then ran too freely

382 SKYSPORTS.COM RACING H'CAP 1m (P)
5:50 (5:50) (Class 7) (0-50,50) 4-Y-O+ **£1,535** (£453; £226) **Stalls** Low

Form RPR
6-66 **1** **Aggbag**[5] 340 7-8-12 **45** .... RobertWinston 4 54
(Tony Carroll) *trckd ldrs: clsd 2f out: led over 1f out: sn pressed: drvn and kpt on wl* **11/4**[1]

-304 **2** *2* **Guildenstern (IRE)**[13] 229 9-9-2 **49** .... ShaneKelly 3 53
(Jane Chapple-Hyam) *settled in rr: prog over 2f out: swtchd to inner to take 2nd 1f out and chal: nt qckn last 150yds* **6/1**[3]

0-4 **3** *1¼* **Crianza**[27] 69 5-9-0 **47** .... (p) EddieAhern 5 48
(Nigel Tinkler) *trckd ldr to 1/2-way: wnt 2nd again over 2f out and sn upsides: nt qckn over 1f out: btn fnl f* **4/1**[2]

60-6 **4** *½* **Rigid**[26] 86 4-9-1 **48** .... (be[1]) LukeMorris 2 48
(Tony Carroll) *led: drvn and jnd jst over 2f out: hdd over 1f out: nt qckn* **13/2**

0-06 **5** *1¼* **Queenie's Star (IRE)**[14] 204 4-9-1 **48** .... RobbieFitzpatrick 9 45
(Michael Attwater) *hld up in rr: rdn 3f out: plugged on u.p fnl 2f: nrst fin* **15/2**

0-06 **6** *shd* **Softly Killing Me**[13] 225 6-8-12 **45** .... (v) DavidProbert 7 42
(Brian Forsey) *t.k.h: hld up in rr: drvn and nt qckn wl over 2f out: plugged on after: nrst fin* **12/1**

04-0 **7** *3½* **Masteeat (USA)**[9] 283 4-8-12 **45** .... ChrisCatlin 8 34
(Olivia Maylam) *mounted on crse: t.k.h: trckd ldrs on outer: u.p over 2f out: sn wknd* **18/1**

44-6 **8** *2* **Farmers Dream (IRE)**[19] 169 4-9-3 **50** .... LiamKeniry 11 34
(John Spearing) *dwlt: t.k.h and prog on outer to chse ldr 4f out to over 2f out: wknd* **14/1**

/0-5 **9** *4* **Cullybackey (IRE)**[21] 136 6-8-7 **45** .... JulieBurke(5) 1 20
(John Harris) *prom on inner 2f: steadily lost pl: struggling in last pair 3f out* **20/1**

05-6 **10** *8* **Warrior Nation (FR)**[9] 284 5-8-12 **45** .... (b) NeilChalmers 6 —
(Adrian Chamberlain) *v.s.a: in tch in last pair after 2f: wknd over 2f out: t.o* **80/1**

1m 40.62s (0.82) **Going Correction** +0.05s/f (Slow) **10** Ran SP% **111.7**
Speed ratings (Par 97): **97,95,93,93,92 91,88,86,82,74**
toteswingers: 1&2 £5.10, 1&3 £2.60, 2&3 £4.80 CSF £18.32 CT £62.70 TOTE £2.40: £1.20, £1.90, £1.80; EX 25.50.
Owner Dennis & Andy Deacon **Bred** D R Tucker **Trained** Cropthorne, Worcs

FOCUS
A low-grade handicap run at a steady pace, and few got into it. There were only three previous winners in the race, and they filled the places. The winner ran his best race so far for Carroll.

383 BETDAQ.COM EXCHANGE PRICE MULTIPLES H'CAP — 6f (P)
6:20 (6:21) (Class 6) (0-55,55) 3-Y-O — £1,535 (£453; £226) Stalls Low

Form — RPR

2-33 **1** **Shutterbug**[16] 189 3-9-2 **55**....(vt[1]) WilliamCarson 11 — 59
(Stuart Williams) *trckd ldrs: rdn 2f out: prog to ld jst over 1f out: narrowly hdd ins fnl f: styd on to ld again post* **5/1**[2]

000- **2** *nse* **Tymismoni (IRE)**[49] 7879 3-8-13 **55**....(v[1]) KierenFox(3) 3 — 59
(Brett Johnson) *settled in midfield: pushed along in 6th 1/2-way: prog 2f out: rdn to cl on ldrs 1f out whn whip broke: pushed into narrow ld wl ins fnl f: hdd post* **3/1**[1]

3 *1 1/2* **Ereka (IRE)**[108] 6968 3-8-6 **50**.... RyanPowell(5) 4 — 49
(Murty McGrath) *trckd ldrs: cl up on outer 2f out: kpt on same pce to take 3rd ins fnl f* **16/1**

000- **4** *nk* **Gekko (IRE)**[62] 7666 3-8-13 **52**.... StephenCraine 1 — 50
(Patrick Morris) *trckd ldrs: smooth prog to chal 2f out: rdn and fnd nil over 1f out: one pce after* **8/1**

05-3 **5** *1 1/4* **Una Vita Plus (IRE)**[29] 28 3-8-11 **50**.... JamieMackay 10 — 44
(Patrick Gilligan) *racd freely: disp ld tl def advtange 1/2-way: hdd jst over 1f out: wknd* **10/1**

000- **6** *1 1/4* **High Avon**[105] 7017 3-9-0 **53**....(p) JimCrowley 2 — 43
(Dean Ivory) *t.k.h: hld up in last trio: shkn up 2f out: kpt on after: nrst fin* **5/1**[2]

500- **7** *1/2* **Melbury**[76] 7497 3-9-2 **55**.... ShaneKelly 6 — 43
(Jane Chapple-Hyam) *hld up in 8th: rdn wl over 2f out: kpt on fr over 1f out: n.d* **12/1**

0-60 **8** *3 1/2* **Welsh Dresser (IRE)**[23] 109 3-8-11 **50**.... RobbieFitzpatrick 8 — 27
(Peter Grayson) *sn struggling in rr: nvr a factor* **33/1**

00-0 **9** *2 1/2* **Lady Titticaca**[21] 130 3-8-7 **46** oh1.... HayleyTurner 5 — 15
(Ron Hodges) *t.k.h: hld up in last trio: nvr on terms: no ch fnl 2f* **66/1**

0-66 **10** *1* **Bluberry**[11] 263 3-8-12 **51**....(v[1]) FergusSweeney 12 — 17
(Gary Moore) *racd freely: disp ld to 1/2-way: wknd qckly 2f out* **20/1**

20-0 **11** *21* **Boushra**[23] 109 3-9-1 **54**....(p) LiamKeniry 7 — —
(Sylvester Kirk) *t.k.h: hld up in rr: wknd sn after 1/2-way: eased: t.o* **14/1**

600- **12** *35* **Lord Cornwall (IRE)**[111] 6868 3-8-10 **49** ow1.... JackMitchell 9 — —
(Ed Walker) *chsd ldrs: rdr looking down bef 1/2-way: eased over 2f out: t.o: sddle slipped* **7/1**[3]

1m 13.68s (0.58) **Going Correction** +0.05s/f (Slow) — **12** Ran SP% **120.5**
Speed ratings (Par 95): **98,97,95,95,93 92,91,86,83,82 54,7**
toteswingers: 1&2 £4.40, 1&3 £24.20, 2&3 £29.70 CSF £20.33 CT £232.02 TOTE £3.20: £1.10, £2.40, £8.80; EX 26.80.
Owner Paul W Stevens **Bred** Edmeades, Budgett & Kirtlington Stud **Trained** Newmarket, Suffolk
■ Stewards' Enquiry : William Carson two-day ban: excessive use of whip (Feb 16-17)

FOCUS
A very modest handicap contested largely by fillies and entirely by maidens, and the pace was brisk. The winner probably only had to run up to her best and the runner-up produced a clear personal best.
Lord Cornwall(IRE) Official explanation: jockey said that his saddle slipped

384 LAY BACK AND WIN AT BETDAQ.COM H'CAP — 1m 4f (P)
6:50 (6:50) (Class 5) (0-75,75) 4-Y-O+ — £2,047 (£604; £302) Stalls Centre

Form — RPR

44-4 **1** **Encircled**[6] 315 7-9-7 **75**.... DavidProbert 1 — 82
(J R Jenkins) *trckd ldr in steadily run r: pushed up to ld 2f out: rdn and edgd lft over 1f out: styd on* **8/1**

2222 **2** *1* **Camps Bay (USA)**[1] 374 7-9-5 **73**.... HayleyTurner 4 — 78
(Conor Dore) *hld up in 5th: clsd 3f out: cajoled along and prog on outer to chse wnr jst over 1f out: styd on but nvr really chal* **9/2**[3]

2/21 **3** *1 1/2* **Transformer (IRE)**[11] 266 5-8-13 **67**.... JimCrowley 6 — 70
(William Jarvis) *trckd ldng pair: rdn and nt qckn whn pce lifted: wnt 3rd again 1f out: one pce* **1/1**[1]

42-0 **4** *3 1/4* **Wasara**[7] 301 4-8-4 **61**.... ChrisCatlin 3 — 59
(Amy Weaver) *trckd ldng trio: rdn 3f out: effrt on inner over 2f out: wknd over 1f out* **15/2**

500- **5** *nse* **Time Square (FR)**[49] 6990 4-8-13 **70**....(t) LukeMorris 5 — 68
(Tony Carroll) *stdd s: hld up last: rdn and nt qckn 3f out: no ch whn nt clr run ins fnl f* **33/1**

003- **6** *shd* **Hindu Kush (IRE)**[166] 5272 6-9-2 **70**.... EddieAhern 2 — 68
(Robert Mills) *led at stdy pce: kicked on 3f out: hd high over 2f out: sn hdd: wknd over 1f out* **11/4**[2]

2m 38.44s (3.94) **Going Correction** +0.05s/f (Slow)
WFA 4 from 5yo+ 3lb — **6** Ran SP% **120.7**
Speed ratings (Par 103): **88,87,86,84,84 84**
toteswingers: 1&2 £6.60, 1&3 £2.40, 2&3 £1.10 CSF £46.13 TOTE £10.70: £7.40, £1.90; EX 41.90.
Owner Mrs Wendy Jenkins **Bred** M H Ings **Trained** Royston, Herts

FOCUS
This ordinary handicap was run at a slow pace and became a dash in the straight. The time was over seven seconds outside the standard, and the form is dubious, although it has been rated through the third at face value.

385 BETDAQ MOBILE APPS H'CAP — 7f (P)
7:20 (7:20) (Class 4) (0-85,84) 4-Y-O+ — £3,399 (£1,011; £505; £252) Stalls Low

Form — RPR

41-1 **1** **Advertisement (USA)**[12] 249 4-9-3 **80**....(t) GeorgeBaker 8 — 91+
(Jeremy Noseda) *sn trckd ldr: clsd to ld jst over 1f out: sn drvn to assert: wl in command nr fin* **1/1**[1]

40-0 **2** *1 1/2* **Bawaardi (IRE)**[13] 226 5-9-0 **77**.... JackMitchell 1 — 84+
(Richard Fahey) *hld up in tch: swtchd to inner and prog 2f out: n.m.r briefly over 1f out: styd on to take 2nd last 150yds: no ch to chal* **12/1**

0-42 **3** *1 1/4* **Ocean Legend (IRE)**[13] 226 6-9-3 **80**.... AdamKirby 3 — 84
(Tony Carroll) *trckd ldr: rdn to chal and upsides jst over 1f out: hanging and nt qckn* **3/1**[2]

56-2 **4** *3/4* **Samarinda (USA)**[16] 188 8-9-1 **78**....(p) MickyFenton 6 — 80
(Pam Sly) *led at fair pce: hdd jst over 1f out: sn btn* **20/1**

054- **5** *1 1/2* **Street Power (USA)**[34] 8017 6-9-7 **84**....(p) SteveDrowne 2 — 82
(Jeremy Gask) *t.k.h: hld up bhd ldrs: gng strly over 2f out: shkn up over 1f out: nt qckn* **6/1**[3]

14-1 **6** *2 3/4* **Gallantry**[14] 206 9-8-12 **78**.... AndrewHeffernan(3) 4 — 68
(Jane Chapple-Hyam) *hld up and sn detached in last pair: urged along over 2f out: kpt on fnl f: no ch* **11/1**

063- **7** *1 3/4* **Ongoodform (IRE)**[173] 5031 4-9-3 **80**.... LiamJones 7 — 65
(Paul D'Arcy) *racd wd in tch: rdn over 2f out: wknd qckly over 1f out* **25/1**

00-0 **8** *1/2* **Gala Casino Star (IRE)**[17] 186 6-8-7 **77**.... LauraBarry(7) 5 — 61
(Richard Fahey) *hld up in last pair and sn detached: rdn and fnd nil over 2f out: wl btn after* **50/1**

1m 25.11s (-0.89) **Going Correction** +0.05s/f (Slow) — **8** Ran SP% **115.9**
Speed ratings (Par 105): **107,105,103,103,101 98,96,95**
toteswingers: 1&2 £4.10, 1&3 £2.00, 2&3 £5.30 CSF £15.02 CT £29.78 TOTE £1.70: £1.10, £3.00, £1.10; EX 19.50.
Owner M Barber **Bred** Dr & Mrs Walter Zent & Tony Holmes **Trained** Newmarket, Suffolk

FOCUS
A fair handicap, the best race of the evening, and the pace was reasonable. The winner should do better again and will still be on a good mark after this.
Gallantry Official explanation: jockey said that the gelding lost its action

386 NAME A RACE FOR A BIRTHDAY H'CAP — 7f (P)
7:50 (7:51) (Class 7) (0-50,50) 4-Y-O+ — £1,535 (£453; £226) Stalls Low

Form — RPR

-023 **1** **Crystallize**[6] 312 5-9-1 **48**.... FergusSweeney 1 — 55
(Andrew Haynes) *trckd ldr: led 2f out gng wl: hrd pressed 1f out: edgd rt but hld on* **4/1**[2]

006- **2** *nk* **Royal Envoy (IRE)**[34] 8024 8-8-12 **45**.... MichaelStainton 6 — 51
(Jane Chapple-Hyam) *t.k.h: trckd ldrs: asked for effrt and hanging 2f out: clsd to chal 1f out: hung rt and n.g.t w effrt* **8/1**

-000 **3** *nk* **Valentino Swing (IRE)**[7] 304 8-9-3 **50**....(p) NeilChalmers 10 — 56+
(Michael Appleby) *hld up in last pair: gd prog and threaded through fr over 1f out: tried to chal on inner fnl f: looked hld whn short of room nr fin* **8/1**

46-4 **4** *1/2* **Novastasia (IRE)**[6] 311 5-8-12 **45**....(b) SamHitchcott 5 — 49
(Dean Ivory) *reluctant to enter stalls: trckd ldrs: hrd rdn wl over 2f out: sn lost pl: only 9th over 1f out: styd on wl again last 100yds* **12/1**

-550 **5** *3/4* **Quick Single (USA)**[5] 334 5-8-12 **45**....(v) LukeMorris 8 — 47
(Phil McEntee) *pressed ldrs on outer: hrd rdn and nt qckn over 2f out: one pce after* **20/1**

3-64 **6** *nk* **Cane Cat (IRE)**[14] 204 4-9-1 **48**....(t) GeorgeBaker 3 — 49+
(Tony Carroll) *hld up in rr: prog towards inner over 2f out: looking hld whn sltly hmpd 1f out: one pce* **11/4**[1]

00/0 **7** *3/4* **Zim Ho**[14] 210 5-9-1 **48**.... DaneO'Neill 4 — 47
(John Akehurst) *led to 2f out: steadily wknd fnl f* **14/1**

3-50 **8** *1 3/4* **Suttonia (IRE)**[14] 204 5-8-13 **46** ow1.... AdamKirby 2 — 43
(Noel Chance) *wl in tch: drvn 2f out: trying to cl but looked hld whn hmpd 1f out: no ch after* **14/1**

5504 **9** *1* **Norcroft**[6] 312 9-8-13 **46**....(p) WilliamCarson 11 — 38
(Christine Dunnett) *dropped in fr wd draw and hld up in last pair: effrt on inner 2f out: no real prog whn briefly checked 1f out* **15/2**[3]

-650 **10** *1/2* **Merorless**[6] 312 4-9-2 **49**....(b) IanMongan 9 — 39
(Zoe Davison) *in tch on outer: u.p over 2f out: fnd nil and sn wknd* **25/1**

-050 **11** *5* **Quahadi (IRE)**[6] 311 5-8-12 **45**....(t) LiamKeniry 7 — 22
(Chris Gordon) *hld up towards rr: shkn up and no rspnse over 2f out: sn wl btn* **14/1**

-505 **12** *5* **Ariel Bender**[6] 311 4-8-12 **45**....(b) RobbieFitzpatrick 12 — 8
(Peter Grayson) *in tch on outer: rdn 3f out: sn btn* **50/1**

1m 26.53s (0.53) **Going Correction** +0.05s/f (Slow) — **12** Ran SP% **118.9**
Speed ratings (Par 97): **98,97,97,96,95 95,94,92,91,90 85,79**
toteswingers: 1&2 £6.50, 1&3 £5.80, 2&3 £15.20 CSF £35.47 CT £251.48 TOTE £5.60: £1.10, £3.60, £2.00; EX 41.50.
Owner Mrs A De Weck & P De Weck **Bred** Aiden Murphy **Trained** Limpley Stoke, Bath
■ Stewards' Enquiry : Neil Chalmers four day ban: careless riding (16-19 Feb)
Michael Stainton two-day ban: careless riding (16-17 Feb)

FOCUS
A very weak handicap run at an average pace, and it produced a bunch finish. Poor form, but sound enough.
Royal Envoy(IRE) Official explanation: jockey said that the gelding hung right
Valentino Swing(IRE) Official explanation: jockey said that the gelding was denied a clear run
T/Plt: £92.90 to a £1 stake. Pool: £67,553.15. 530.82 winning tickets. T/Qpdt: £10.40 to a £1 tsake. Pool: £8,977.59. 634.52 winning tickets. JN

347 LINGFIELD (L-H)
Wednesday, February 2

OFFICIAL GOING: Standard
Wind: strong, half behind Weather: overcast, breezy

387 TODAY'S JOCKEY SPECIALS AT BLUESQ.COM APPRENTICE H'CAP — 1m (P)
1:10 (1:10) (Class 6) (0-60,60) 4-Y-O+ — £1,535 (£453; £226) Stalls High

Form — RPR

-213 **1** **Shared Moment (IRE)**[10] 273 5-9-0 **58**....(v) JulieBurke(5) 5 — 64
(John Gallagher) *hld up in tch towards rr: rdn and effrt ent fnl 2f: hdwy u.p over 1f out: r.o wl ins fnl f to ld last strides* **7/2**[1]

410- **2** *hd* **Sonny G (IRE)**[66] 7613 4-9-5 **58**.... KierenFox 7 — 63
(John Best) *led and set stdy gallop: pushed along and wnt clr ent fnl 2f: racd awkwardly over 1f out: drvn 1f out: rdr looked arnd ins fnl f: pushed along fnl 100yds: hdd last strides* **20/1**

433- **3** *1/2* **Ermyntrude**[59] 7717 4-8-9 **53**.... LucyKBarry(5) 8 — 57
(Pat Phelan) *chsd ldr for 1f and again 3f out: rdn and outpcd by ldr ent fnl 2f: kpt on wl again ins fnl f* **9/2**[2]

30-3 **4** *nk* **Ivory Lace**[7] 304 10-9-2 **60**.... RichardRowe(5) 4 — 63
(Steve Woodman) *stdd s: hld up in last pair: rdn and hdwy over 1f out: swtchd lft ins fnl f: r.o wl: nt rch ldrs* **12/1**

00/- **5** *nk* **Bricks And Porter (IRE)**[54] 7818 11-8-13 **52**....(bt) RussKennemore 1 — 54
(Adrian McGuinness, Ire) *chsd ldr after 1f tl 3f out: sn rdn and unable qck: styd on again ins fnl f* **8/1**

40-5 **6** *2 3/4* **Sadeek**[21] 135 7-9-6 **59**.... MartinLane 6 — 55
(Martin Bosley) *hld up in tch in midfield: rdn and unable qck over 2f out: styd on same pce and no imp fr over 1f out* **6/1**[3]

543- **7** *2 1/2* **George Baker (IRE)**[109] 6937 4-9-6 **59**.... MatthewDavies 3 — 49
(George Baker) *in tch in midfield on inner: short of room and swtchd rt 3f out: sn rdn and unable qck: no threat to ldrs after* **9/2**[2]

506- **8** *shd* **Batchworth Blaise**[36] 7991 8-9-4 **57**.... BillyCray 2 — 47
(Eric Wheeler) *stdd after s: hld up in rr: rdn and effrt on outer ent fnl f: no real hdwy: n.d* **9/1**

004- **9** *3* **Stef And Stelio**[47] 7912 4-9-1 **57** .... TobyAtkinson(3) 9 40
(Gerard Butler) *in tch in midfield: rdn and unable qck over 2f out: wknd wl over 1f out* **14/1**

1m 37.96s (-0.24) **Going Correction** +0.025s/f (Slow) 9 Ran SP% **113.1**
Speed ratings (Par 101): **102,101,101,101,100 97,95,95,92**
toteswingers: 1&2 £9.70, 1&3 £4.10, 2&3 £14.40 CSF £73.03 CT £317.65 TOTE £3.90: £1.70, £6.50, £1.60; EX 59.20 TRIFECTA Not won..
Owner Mark Benton **Bred** Mrs E R Cantillon **Trained** Chastleton, Oxon

FOCUS
A competitive apprentice handicap run at a good early pace, with the front five coming home in a bunch. Modest form, rated around the second.

388 HAXTED (S) STKS 6f (P)
1:40 (1:40) (Class 6) 4-Y-O+ **£1,535** (£453; £226) **Stalls** Low

Form RPR

02-4 **1** **Frequency**[14] 213 4-9-2 68 .... (b[1]) EddieAhern 2 70+
(Amy Weaver) *stdd s: hld up in tch: trcking ldrs gng wl whn swtchd rt jst over 1f out: nudged along to chal ins fnl f: rdn to ld fnl 75yds: sn in command: easily* **1/1**[1]

5-12 **2** *2 ¼* **Apache Ridge (IRE)**[13] 230 5-9-2 60 .... (p) JulieBurke(5) 5 67
(Kevin Ryan) *chsd ldrs on outer: ev ch ent fnl 2f: rdn to ld over 1f out: hdd wl ins fnl f: sn btn* **11/4**[2]

01-5 **3** *3 ¼* **Anjomarba (IRE)**[19] 165 4-9-2 63 .... LiamKeniry 3 52
(Brett Johnson) *chsd ldr tl led 2f out: sn rdn: hdd over 1f out: wknd ins fnl f* **3/1**[3]

/0-0 **4** *¾* **Orchid Wing**[7] 298 4-9-2 65 .... (b) IanMongan 1 50
(Tobias B P Coles) *led: rdn and hdd 2f out: wknd u.p jst ins fnl f* **20/1**

00-0 **5** *1 ¾* **Music Lover**[9] 280 4-9-2 49 .... LukeMorris 4 44
(John Panvert) *in tch: rdn and struggling over 2f out: kpt on same pce u.p fnl 2f* **20/1**

1m 11.18s (-0.72) **Going Correction** +0.025s/f (Slow) 5 Ran SP% **111.2**
Speed ratings (Par 101): **105,102,97,96,94**
CSF £4.11 TOTE £2.00: £1.10, £1.50; EX 4.70.The winner was bought in 4,400gns.
Owner Miss A Weaver **Bred** Manor Farm Stud (rutland) **Trained** Newmarket, Suffolk

FOCUS
A modest seller but it was well run. The form is rated around the runner-up.

389 CROWHURST MAIDEN STKS 6f (P)
2:10 (2:10) (Class 5) 3-Y-O+ **£1,910** (£564; £282) **Stalls** Low

Form RPR

0-03 **1** **Primo De Vida (IRE)**[6] 313 4-9-5 73 .... (p) NathanAlison(7) 1 78
(Jim Boyle) *mde all: lft clr wl over 3f out: rdn wl over 1f out: kpt on wl* **2/1**[2]

0-2 **2** *3 ½* **Sailing North (USA)**[21] 126 3-8-11 0 .... LukeMorris 2 63
(Ronald Harris) *chsd ldng pair tl lft chsng clr ldr and rdn over 3f out: hrd drvn and no imp ent fnl f* **7/4**[1]

/ **3** *4* **Stand Beside Me (IRE)** 4-9-12 0 .... (t) LiamKeniry 7 54+
(Sylvester Kirk) *racd in midfield: sltly hmpd over 3f out: outpcd and rdn along over 2f out: no hdwy and wl hld after* **5/1**

00-0 **4** *½* **Lady Ellice**[21] 126 3-8-6 52 .... CathyGannon 5 43
(Phil McEntee) *bhd: rdn and outpcd over 2f out: drvn and pressing for modest 3rd fnl f: n.d* **33/1**

550- **5** *5* **Warm Memories**[115] 6771 4-9-12 65 .... GeorgeBaker 3 36
(Simon Dow) *dwlt: hld up in tch: outpcd and pushed along over 2f out: pressing for 3rd but wl hld over 1f out: wknd fnl f* **9/2**[3]

00 **6** *27* **Main Attraction**[6] 313 4-9-7 0 .... (b[1]) IanMongan 6 —
(Tobias B P Coles) *pressed wnr tl hung rt bnd and lost pl 4f out: wl bhd whn hung rt again bnd 2f out: t.o and eased fnl f* **33/1**

1m 11.57s (-0.33) **Going Correction** +0.025s/f (Slow)
WFA 3 from 4yo+ 15lb 6 Ran SP% **110.4**
Speed ratings (Par 103): **103,98,93,92,85 49**
toteswingers: 1&2 £1.50, 1&3 £2.50, 2&3 £1.50 CSF £5.68 TOTE £3.30: £1.30, £2.20; EX 5.90.
Owner Prime Of Life **Bred** Burgage Stud And Partners **Trained** Epsom, Surrey

FOCUS
An average maiden for the grade run a bit slower than the previous seller. The winner is rated back to his best.
Warm Memories Official explanation: jockey said the gelding hung right under pressure
Main Attraction Official explanation: jockey said that the filly hung right throughout

390 BREATHE SPA AT MARRIOTT LINGFIELD H'CAP (DIV I) 1m 2f (P)
2:40 (2:41) (Class 6) (0-60,60) 4-Y-O+ **£1,364** (£403; £201) **Stalls** Low

Form RPR

00-1 **1** **Ede's Dot Com (IRE)**[7] 304 7-9-5 57 .... IanMongan 7 68
(Pat Phelan) *hld up off the pce in last trio: clsd over 3f out: gd hdwy on inner 2f out: rdn to chal ent fnl f: led ins fnl f: r.o wl: dismntd after fin* **6/1**[3]

05-5 **2** *1 ¼* **Atacama Sunrise**[26] 90 5-9-1 58 .... TobyAtkinson(5) 8 65
(George Prodromou) *stdd s: hld up off the pce in last pair: hdwy 5f out: chsd ldrs over 3f out: led jst over 2f out: drvn over 1f out: hdd ins fnl f: rallied u.p towards fin: a hld* **12/1**

15-3 **3** *1* **Esteem Lord**[12] 247 5-9-7 59 .... JimCrowley 3 64
(Dean Ivory) *chsd ldrs: clsd over 3f out: unable qck u.p 2f out: kpt on again fnl 100yds: nt pce to chal ldrs* **9/4**[1]

625- **4** *5* **Pab Special (IRE)**[36] 7989 8-9-0 52 ow1 .... (v) AdamKirby 4 47
(Brett Johnson) *led tl over 8f out: chsd ldr after tl led again over 2f out: sn hdd and rdn: wknd fnl f* **15/2**

0-00 **5** *2* **Carr Hall (IRE)**[13] 223 8-8-10 55 .... GeorgeDowning(7) 9 46
(Tony Carroll) *stdd s: hld up wl bhd in rr: hdwy on outer over 4f out: nudged along and no prog over 2f out: rdn and wl btn over 1f out* **10/1**

05-2 **6** *½* **Shaded Edge**[21] 135 7-7-7 59 .... LiamKeniry 5 49
(David Arbuthnot) *chsd ldng trio: clsd 4f out: lost pl and short of room over 2f out: no ch w ldrs after: edging out rt over 1f out: wl btn but plugged on fnl f* **6/1**[3]

360- **7** *6* **Bizarrely (IRE)**[36] 7995 4-9-7 60 .... ChrisCatlin 1 38
(Sir Mark Prescott Bt) *awkward leaving stalls and s.i.s: sn swtchd rt and dashed through field to ld over 8f out: rdn and hdd over 2f out: sn wknd* **4/1**[2]

00-3 **8** *shd* **Saigon Kitty (IRE)**[11] 261 4-8-12 54 .... KierenFox(3) 10 32
(John Best) *t.k.h early: hld up in midfield: clsd and wl in tch 4f out: rdn and wknd qckly ent fnl 2f* **16/1**

00-0 **9** *7* **Craicajack (IRE)**[9] 280 4-8-4 48 .... (b) JulieBurke(5) 2 12
(Edward Creighton) *racd off the pce in midfield: lost pl and dropped to rr over 2f out: sn wl bhd* **33/1**

2m 7.01s (0.41) **Going Correction** +0.025s/f (Slow)
WFA 4 from 5yo+ 1lb 9 Ran SP% **116.7**
Speed ratings (Par 101): **99,98,97,93,91 91,86,86,80**
toteswingers: 1&2 £13.80, 1&3 £4.40, 2&3 £7.00 CSF £75.45 CT £210.53 TOTE £6.10: £1.60, £3.80, £1.10; EX 42.70 Trifecta £165.50 Pool: £418.40 - 1.87 winning units..
Owner Ede's (uk) Ltd **Bred** Maurice Burns **Trained** Epsom, Surrey

FOCUS
The first division of the 1m2f handicap, run at a slow gallop and in a time a bit slower than division II. The runner-up is rated back to his November form.

391 BREATHE SPA AT MARRIOTT LINGFIELD H'CAP (DIV II) 1m 2f (P)
3:10 (3:10) (Class 6) (0-60,60) 4-Y-O+ **£1,364** (£403; £201) **Stalls** Low

Form RPR

42-6 **1** **Lean Machine**[25] 94 4-9-7 60 .... (p) LukeMorris 6 65
(Ronald Harris) *chsd ldrs: rdn 2f out: drvn to chse ldr 1f out: led fnl 75yds: all out* **15/2**[3]

003- **2** *nk* **White Deer (USA)**[78] 7472 7-9-3 55 .... (p) FrannyNorton 3 60
(Geoffrey Harker) *in tch in midfield: effrt on inner over 1f out: ev ch and drvn ins fnl f: unable qck nr fin* **15/2**[3]

023- **3** *shd* **Red Willow**[77] 7489 5-9-3 55 .... SamHitchcott 10 60
(John E Long) *chsd ldr tl led wl over 2f out: rdn wl over 1f out: hdd fnl 75yds: kpt on one pce after* **12/1**

310- **4** *¾* **Noah Jameel**[120] 6660 9-9-0 52 .... FergusSweeney 8 56+
(Tony Newcombe) *hld up in last trio: nt clr run over 1f out: gd hdwy ins fnl f: wnt 4th and running on whn nt clr run and swtchd rt towards fin: nvr able to chal* **11/1**

0- **5** *½* **Majestueux (USA)**[34] 8021 4-9-7 60 .... CathyGannon 9 62
(Mark Hoad) *in tch in midfield: rdn and effrt ent fnl 2f: keeping on but hld whn pushed rt towards fin* **25/1**

44-0 **6** *½* **Celtic Ransom**[15] 203 4-9-6 59 .... EddieAhern 7 60
(J W Hills) *chsd ldrs: rdn to chse ldr 2f out tl 1f out: styd on same pce fnl f* **7/1**[2]

00-0 **7** *1 ¼* **Sea Tobougie**[19] 172 4-8-6 45 .... HayleyTurner 5 44
(Mark Usher) *pushed along early: bhd: rdn ent fnl f: r.o u.p fnl 100yds: nvr able to chal* **33/1**

0-02 **8** *1 ½* **Ocean Countess (IRE)**[9] 278 5-8-13 51 .... AdamKirby 4 47
(Tony Carroll) *racd in last pair: stl plenty to do and rdn 3f out: styd on same pce fr over 1f out: nvr trbld ldrs* **1/1**[1]

35-4 **9** *nk* **Indefinite Hope (ITY)**[15] 201 4-9-4 57 .... (t) AndreaAtzeni 2 52
(Michael Wigham) *in tch in midfield: rdn and no prog over 2f out: styd on same pce and no imp fr wl over 1f out* **12/1**

000- **10** *6* **Usquaebach**[25] 7968 4-8-11 55 .... JemmaMarshall(5) 1 38
(Pat Phelan) *led tl wl over 2f out: wknd qckly wl over 1f out* **14/1**

2m 6.91s (0.31) **Going Correction** +0.025s/f (Slow)
WFA 4 from 5yo+ 1lb 10 Ran SP% **123.2**
Speed ratings (Par 101): **99,98,98,98,97 97,96,95,94,90**
toteswingers: 1&2 £7.20, 1&3 £5.60, 2&3 £10.30 CSF £66.34 CT £685.14 TOTE £5.60: £1.50, £2.20, £2.30; EX 48.40 TRIFECTA Not won..
Owner William Jones Lisa Harrington **Bred** Biddestone Stud **Trained** Earlswood, Monmouths

FOCUS
Seemingly a weaker race than the first division, but run in a slightly quicker time. The front six finished in a heap and it's hard to rate the form positively.
Noah Jameel Official explanation: jockey said that the gelding was denied a clear run

392 ENHANCED SP'S AT BLUESQ.COM H'CAP 1m 5f (P)
3:40 (3:40) (Class 5) (0-75,75) 4-Y-O+ **£2,047** (£604; £302) **Stalls** Low

Form RPR

53-1 **1** **Beaubrav**[19] 162 5-9-10 75 .... (t) AdamKirby 2 87+
(Michael Madgwick) *hld up in tch towards rr: hdwy 3f out: chsd ldr wl over 1f out: chal u.p ent fnl f: led ins fnl f: r.o wl* **4/1**[2]

00-2 **2** *2 ½* **Parhelion**[11] 266 4-9-2 71 .... JoeFanning 6 79
(Derek Haydn Jones) *mostly chsd ldr tl led over 2f out: hrd pressed and drvn ent fnl f: hdd and nt pce of wnr ins fnl f* **11/2**[3]

0-24 **3** *2 ¾* **Jenny Potts**[19] 162 7-9-1 66 .... SteveDrowne 1 70
(Chris Down) *chsd ldrs: n.m.r on inner jst over 2f out: outpcd by ldng pair over 1f out: 3rd and kpt on fnl f: no threat to ldng pair* **15/2**

54-3 **4** *¾* **Soundbyte**[26] 79 6-8-10 61 .... FergusSweeney 4 64
(John Gallagher) *in tch towards rr: hdwy 5f out: trcking ldrs over 2f out: rdn and outpcd wl over 1f out: 4th and kpt on same pce fnl f* **10/1**

20-4 **5** *2 ¼* **Bariolo (FR)**[11] 266 7-9-2 67 .... GeorgeBaker 8 66
(Noel Chance) *hld up in last pair: clsd over 4f out: rdn and btn wl over 1f out* **9/1**

533- **6** *nse* **Grande Caiman (IRE)**[84] 7397 7-9-10 75 .... FrannyNorton 7 74
(Geoffrey Harker) *hld up in rr: outpcd wl over 1f out: pushed along over 1f out: wl btn but kpt on ins fnl f* **10/1**

100- **7** *7* **Maslak (IRE)**[35] 8003 7-9-9 74 .... ChrisCatlin 5 63
(Peter Hiatt) *led tl over 2f out: sn struggling: wknd wl over 1f out: wl bhd fnl f* **20/1**

53-3 **8** *15* **Bold Adventure**[22] 67 7-8-11 62 .... TonyCulhane 9 28
(Willie Musson) *hld up in rr: struggling over 4f out: lost tch 3f out: wl bhd fnl 2f: t.o* **12/1**

0-41 **9** *7* **Zafranagar (IRE)**[13] 222 6-8-6 64 .... GeorgeDowning(7) 3 20+
(Tony Carroll) *t.k.h early: chsd ldrs: sddle slipped after 1f: jnd ldrs 6f out tl wknd over 2f out: sn eased: t.o* **3/1**[1]

2m 45.68s (-0.32) **Going Correction** +0.025s/f (Slow)
WFA 4 from 5yo+ 4lb 9 Ran SP% **113.9**
Speed ratings (Par 103): **101,99,97,97,95 95,91,82,78**
toteswingers: 1&2 £4.10, 1&3 £5.60, 2&3 £7.90 CSF £25.89 CT £156.91 TOTE £3.60: £1.50, £1.70, £3.00; EX 21.50 Trifecta £132.10 Pool: £632.34 - 3.54 winning units..
Owner The B B Partnership **Bred** Star Pointe Ltd,Brosnan And Williamson **Trained** Denmead, Hants

FOCUS
A trappy handicap with a number quite tightly matched. The winner is improved and the second is rated back to his 3yo best.
Zafranagar(IRE) Official explanation: jockey said the geldings saddle slipped

393 LINGFIELDPARK.CO.UK H'CAP 2m (P)
4:10 (4:10) (Class 5) (0-70,69) 4-Y-O+ **£2,047** (£604; £302) **Stalls** Low

Form RPR

0-42 **1** **Frameit (IRE)**[9] 277 4-8-3 52 .... (v) FrannyNorton 2 62
(James Given) *hld up in midfield: hdwy to trck ldrs gng wl 3f out: edgd lft bnd ent fnl 2f: chal 1f out: rdn to ld ins fnl f: sn clr: r.o wl* **13/2**

-421 **2** *3 ½* **Mashdood (USA)**[12] 244 5-9-7 64 .... LukeMorris 5 69
(Peter Hiatt) *racd keenly: led: rdn over 2f out: hrd pressed ent fnl f: hdd ins fnl f: sn btn: hld on for 2nd cl home* **2/1**[1]

25-1 **3** *nk* **Dubburg (USA)**[13] 223 6-9-5 62 .... TonyCulhane 3 68
(Willie Musson) *stdd s: hld up in rr: hdwy into midfield 3f out: chsd ldng trio and hmpd bnd ent fnl 2f: rallied u.p and swtchd rt ins fnl f: no ch w wnr but pressing for 2nd cl home* **9/2**[3]

33-5 **4** *1 ½* **Tower**[12] 244 4-8-7 56 .... (p) KirstyMilczarek 6 59
(George Prodromou) *stdd s: hld up in last trio: hdwy 3f out: outpcd and rdn 2f out: kpt on again ins fnl f: no threat to wnr* **13/2**

P0-0 **5** *1¼* **Vertueux (FR)**[13] 223 6-9-0 **57** .... AdamKirby 1 58
(Tony Carroll) *chsd ldrs: reminders 7f out: wnt 2nd over 4f out: ev ch u.p jst over 1f out: sn no ex: wknd ins fnl f* **16/1**

054/ **6** *5* **Drawback (IRE)**[582] 7777 8-9-7 **64** .... StephenCraine 4 59
(Barry Brennan) *stdd s: hld up in rr: effrt and nt clr run 2f out: rdn and no hdwy over 1f out: n.d* **50/1**

01-1 **7** *3½* **Coda Agency**[21] 131 8-9-12 **69** .... JimCrowley 8 60
(David Arbuthnot) *chsd ldr tl over 4f out: sn rdn and struggling: bhd and wl btn 2f out* **10/3**[2]

6-34 **8** *1* **City Stable (IRE)**[11] 261 6-9-8 **65** .... CathyGannon 7 55
(Michael Wigham) *in tch in midfield: wknd u.p over 2f out: wl bhd over 1f out* **25/1**

3m 24.58s (-1.12) **Going Correction** +0.025s/f (Slow)
WFA 4 from 5yo+ 6lb **8** Ran SP% **112.9**
Speed ratings (Par 103): **103,101,101,100,99 97,95,94**
toteswingers: 1&2 £4.10, 1&3 £3.60, 2&3 £3.50 CSF £19.43 CT £64.04 TOTE £7.60: £2.10, £1.70, £1.50; EX 21.50 Trifecta £128.10 Pool: £744.48 - 4.30 winning units..
Owner Peter Swann **Bred** Liam Butler **Trained** Willoughton, Lincs

FOCUS
An ordinary handicap run at a steady pace. the form is rated around the runner-up.

394 PLAY RAINBOW RICHES AT BLUESQ.COM H'CAP 7f (P)
4:40 (4:41) (Class 5) (0-75,73) 4-Y-O+ **£2,047** (£604; £302) **Stalls** Low

Form RPR

134 **1** **Rubenstar (IRE)**[7] 307 8-9-5 **71** .... StephenCraine 5 78
(Patrick Morris) *fly-jmpd s: hld up in rr: stl last but gng wl over 1f out: pushed along and qcknd to ld fnl 75yds: sn in command: readily* **9/2**[3]

6-05 **2** *1¼* **Jungle Bay**[11] 264 4-9-3 **72** .... AndrewHeffernan(3) 6 76
(Jane Chapple-Hyam) *hld up towards rr: hmpd 4f out: hdwy to chse ldrs over 2f out: drvn to ld 1f out: hdd and nt pce of wnr fnl 75yds* **6/1**

-213 **3** *nk* **Army Of Stars (IRE)**[8] 290 5-9-5 **71** ....(p) FrannyNorton 3 74
(James Given) *chsd ldrs: lost pl and dropped to rr over 2f out: rallied ins fnl f: wnt 3rd last strides: gng on fin* **5/1**

40-5 **4** *hd* **Cut And Thrust (IRE)**[12] 249 5-9-0 **66** ....(p) AdamKirby 4 71+
(Mark Wellings) *hld up towards rr: n.m.r sn after s: hdwy 2f out: drvn and ev ch 1f out: nt pce of wnr and short of room wl ins fnl f* **4/1**[2]

006- **5** *2* **Salient**[56] 7766 7-9-5 **71** .... JoeFanning 7 68
(Michael Attwater) *chsd ldrs tl lft 2nd and pushed v wd 4f out: rdn to chal 2f out: led over 1f out: sn hdd: no ex fnl f* **9/1**

500- **6** *1¼* **Highland Bridge**[222] 3413 4-9-1 **67** .... DaneO'Neill 8 61
(David Elsworth) *in tch: swtchd rt and rdn over 1f out: no imp ins fnl f* **12/1**

24-5 **7** *2* **Miss Bootylishes**[19] 160 6-9-0 **73** .... LucyKBarry(7) 1 61
(Andrew Haynes) *led: lft clr 4f out: rdn and hdd over 1f out: wknd fnl f* **14/1**

30-1 **U** **Perfect Ch'l (IRE)**[7] 303 4-9-0 **66** 6ex .... JamesDoyle 2 —
(Ian Wood) *w ldr tl uns rdr 4f out* **7/2**[1]

1m 24.89s (0.09) **Going Correction** +0.025s/f (Slow) **8** Ran SP% **115.7**
Speed ratings (Par 103): **100,98,98,98,95 94,92,—**
toteswingers: 1&2 £4.80, 1&3 £4.10, 2&3 £6.60 CSF £31.90 CT £140.01 TOTE £5.00: £2.10, £2.20, £1.60; EX 30.30 Trifecta £131.20 Pool: £989.90 - 5.58 winning units..
Owner L Walsh **Bred** Schwindibode Ag **Trained** Tarporley, Cheshire

FOCUS
An action packed handicap as Perfect Ch'i was eliminated early from the race when James Doyle was unseated after running about three furlongs, which in turned hampered a number of runners. The field finished in a bunch suggesting that the form is nothing special. The winner posted his best form for over three years.
T/Plt: £56.30 to a £1 stake. Pool: £53,679.13. 695.23 winning tickets. T/Qpdt: £20.10 to a £1 stake. Pool: £4,158.76. 152.50 winning tickets. SP

[370] CAGNES-SUR-MER
Wednesday, February 2

OFFICIAL GOING: Fibresand: standard

395a PRIX DE GRASSE (CLAIMER) (4YO+) (FIBRESAND) 1m 2f (D)
3:25 (12:00) 4-Y-O+ **£6,896** (£2,758; £2,068; £1,379; £689)

RPR

1 **Interian (GER)**[16] 195 5-8-11 0 .... ThomasHuet 8 77
(C Ferland, France) **11/1**

2 *2½* **Torronto (FR)**[42] 8-8-11 0 .... FlavienPrat 5 73
(P Monfort, France) **30/1**

3 *½* **Rum Chocolate (GER)**[12] 259 5-8-8 0 .... DavyBonilla 1 69
(C Ferland, France) **10/1**

4 *1* **Tarpon**[26] 7-9-2 0 ....(p) IoritzMendizabal 15 75
(J C Napoli, France) **3/1**[1]

5 *snk* **Peinture Texane (FR)**[26] 93 5-8-8 0 .... FabriceVeron 2 67
(M Boutin, France) **49/1**

6 *snk* **Officer In Command (USA)**[14] 221 5-8-11 0(b) Francois-XavierBertras 11 70
(J S Moore) *broke wl to r 3rd on outer: settled in 4th: rdn early in st: styd on wl u.p tl fading fnl 100yds* **9/1**

7 *1* **Deacon Blue (FR)**[33] 6-9-2 0 .... AlexisBadel 10 73
(C Boutin, France) **29/1**

8 *nk* **Auzi (FR)**[214] 8-8-11 0 .... TonyPiccone 3 67
(J Rossi, France) **19/1**

9 *1* **Last Storm**[14] 220 7-8-13 0 ....(b) Pierre-CharlesBoudot 12 68
(J-M Capitte, France) **12/1**

10 *snk* **I Love Loup (FR)**[225] 7-9-2 0 .... Jean-MichelSanchez 4 70
(P Khozian, France) **21/1**

0 **Rava (IRE)**[42] 6-8-8 0 .... MorganDelalande 16 —
(X Nakkachdji, France) **48/1**

0 **Darabani (FR)**[37] 6-8-10 0 .... GaetanClouet(6) 9 —
(P Monfort, France) **30/1**

0 **Mr Dob (USA)**[178] 6-9-2 0 .... MlleCarolineBrunaud 14 —
(Mlle C Brunaud, France) **84/1**

0 **Castries (IRE)**[30] 4-8-13 0 ....(p) ThierryThulliez 7 —
(A De Royer-Dupre, France) **9/1**

0 **King Lou (FR)**[14] 220 4-9-2 0 .... StephanePasquier 6 —
(P Demercastel, France) **73/10**[2]

0 **Alicudi (USA)**[22] 4-8-7 0 .... EddyHardouin(6) 13 —
(C Ferland, France) **15/2**[3]

2m 0.41s (120.41)
WFA 4 from 5yo+ 1lb **16** Ran SP% **118.5**
WIN (incl. 1 euro stake): 6.10 (Interian coupled with Rum Chocolate). PLACES: 2.50, 8.00, 7.00. DF: 138.20. SF: 198.00.
Owner Mme Kerstin Kappes **Bred** Gestut Schlenderhan **Trained** France

[373] SOUTHWELL (L-H)
Thursday, February 3

OFFICIAL GOING: Standard
Wind: Moderate across Weather: Fine and dry

396 PLACE ONLY BETTING AT BLUESQ.COM (S) STKS 6f (F)
1:30 (1:30) (Class 6) 3-Y-O **£1,535** (£453; £226) **Stalls** Low

Form RPR

2315 **1** **Fifth In Line (IRE)**[10] 275 3-8-12 68 .... FergusSweeney 5 59
(Jamie Osborne) *cl up: effrt over 2f out: rdn wl over 1f out: drvn ins fnl f: edgd lft and kpt on u.p to ld nr fin* **5/2**[1]

31-0 **2** *nk* **Hereselllie (IRE)**[18] 183 3-8-9 63 .... AndrewHeffernan(3) 2 58
(Michael Chapman) *led: rdn 2f out: edgd lft over 1f out: drvn ins fnl f: hdd and no ex nr fin* **10/1**

10-4 **3** *½* **Winning Draw (IRE)**[21] 146 3-8-12 57 ....(p) TonyCulhane 7 56
(Paul Midgley) *chsd ldrs: hdwy over 2f out: swtchd rt and rdn wl over 1f out: drvn ins fnl f and ev ch: n.m.r and one pce towards fin* **6/1**

43-4 **4** *2* **Bachelor Knight (IRE)**[18] 187 3-9-0 59 .... JamesSullivan(3) 8 55
(Ollie Pears) *in tch: hdwy on outer and cl up after 2f: rdn along over 2f out: sn drvn and kpt on same pce* **4/1**[3]

6-6 **5** *¾* **Blue Ivy**[18] 183 3-8-6 0 .... KellyHarrison 6 41
(Chris Fairhurst) *t.k.h: in tch: effrt over 2f out: sn swtchd to outer and rdn: kpt on u.p fnl f* **11/1**

3 **6** *2¼* **Poppy's Rocket (IRE)**[18] 182 3-8-7 0 ow1 .... TomEaves 1 35
(Brian Ellison) *in tch: effrt wl over 2f out: swtchd rt and rdn wl over 1f out: sn no imp* **10/3**[2]

5-20 **7** *5* **Ajaafa**[12] 263 3-8-11 61 ....(p) RobbieFitzpatrick 3 23
(Michael Attwater) *a in rr* **12/1**

8 *10* **Cumberwell Cracker** 3-7-13 0 .... JakePayne(7) 4 —
(Bill Turner) *a in rr* **40/1**

1m 20.13s (3.63) **Going Correction** +0.325s/f (Slow) **8** Ran SP% **113.5**
Speed ratings (Par 95): **88,87,86,84,83 80,73,60**
toteswingers:1&2:£5.90, 1&3:£3.50, 2&3:£9.20 CSF £28.08 TOTE £3.20: £1.30, £3.10, £2.00; EX 34.60 Trifecta £118.60 Pool: £518.06 - 3.23 winning units..There was no bid for winner.
Owner Pennick, Durkan, Hearn **Bred** Me Surrender Syndicate **Trained** Upper Lambourn, Berks

FOCUS
After the recent dry spell the Fibresand surface had dried out and was reckoned to be riding on the slow side, confirmed by the time in the opener. A run-of-the-mill 3-y-o seller and the first three raced towards the inside rail in the home straight. It may pay not to be too positive about this form, which has been rated around the fourth.

397 SOUTHWELL GOLF CLUB LADY MEMBERS FILLIES' H'CAP 7f (F)
2:00 (2:00) (Class 5) (0-70,64) 4-Y-O+ **£1,813** (£539; £269; £134) **Stalls** Low

Form RPR

02-1 **1** **Feet Of Fury**[30] 37 5-9-6 **63** .... GrahamGibbons 3 81+
(Ian Williams) *cl up: led after 1f: rdn and qcknd clr 2f out: readily* **13/8**[1]

010- **2** *4½* **Clever Omneya (USA)**[49] 7885 5-9-0 **57** .... FrannyNorton 6 57
(J R Jenkins) *led 1f: prom: effrt to chse wnr over 2f out: rdn wl over 1f out: drvn and no imp fnl f* **5/2**[2]

00-0 **3** *2* **Koraleva Tectona (IRE)**[15] 206 6-9-5 **62** .... TomQueally 1 57
(Mark H Tompkins) *trckd ldng pair on inner: effrt to chse wnr 3f out: rdn along over 2f out: drvn wl over 1f out and sn one pce* **20/1**

4-24 **4** *¾* **Positivity**[9] 291 5-8-12 **55** ....(p) TomEaves 5 48
(Bryan Smart) *towards rr and rdn along after 3f: sme hdwy u.p over 2f out: sn drvn and no imp* **11/2**[3]

0-33 **5** *¾* **Tomintoul Star**[9] 292 5-8-9 **55** .... JamesSullivan(3) 2 46
(Ruth Carr) *chsd ldrs: rdn along 3f out: drvn over 2f out and sn wknd* **13/2**

10-6 **6** *27* **Mrs Mogg**[24] 113 4-9-7 **64** .... RichardKingscote 4 —
(Tom Dascombe) *in rr: sn rdn along: bhd fr 1/2-way: eased fnl 2f* **11/1**

1m 31.64s (1.34) **Going Correction** +0.325s/f (Slow) **6** Ran SP% **108.5**
Speed ratings (Par 100): **105,99,97,96,95 65**
toteswingers:1&2:£1.80, 1&3:£5.80, 2&3:£7.90 CSF £5.40 TOTE £2.80: £1.40, £1.80; EX 5.80.
Owner Stratford Bards Racing No 2 **Bred** The National Stud **Trained** Portway, Worcs

FOCUS
A modest 55-64 fillies' handicap but a most emphatic winner who was value for an extra couple of lengths. The second was 7lb off his C&D win.
Mrs Mogg Official explanation: jockey said filly never travelled

398 TICKETS AT SOUTHWELL-RACECOURSE.CO.UK MEDIAN AUCTION MAIDEN STKS 7f (F)
2:30 (2:30) (Class 6) 3-5-Y-O **£1,535** (£453; £226) **Stalls** Low

Form RPR

0-32 **1** **Ana Emarati (USA)**[15] 212 3-8-9 67 .... EddieAhern 2 71
(Ed Dunlop) *mde all: rdn and edgd lft wl over 1f out: clr appr fnl f: readily* **11/10**[1]

45-2 **2** *4* **Eilean Mor**[9] 295 3-8-9 64 .... TomEaves 3 61
(Bryan Smart) *trckd wnr: effrt to chal over 2f out: sn rdn and one pce fr over 1f out* **5/1**[3]

003- **3** *3½* **Laugh Or Cry**[84] 7400 3-8-9 68 .... CathyGannon 7 52
(Peter Makin) *trckd ldrs: hdwy on inner 3f out: rdn over 2f out and sn btn* **13/8**[2]

005- **4** *2½* **Mini's Destination**[156] 5630 3-8-4 51 .... NickyMackay 4 40
(John Holt) *chsd ldrs: rdn along 3f out: sn outpcd* **28/1**

-034 **5** *3½* **Northumberland**[7] 319 5-9-12 42 .... KellyHarrison 6 41
(Michael Chapman) *chsd ldrs: rdn along 3f out: sn outpcd* **16/1**

1m 32.43s (2.13) **Going Correction** +0.325s/f (Slow)
WFA 3 from 4yo+ 17lb **5** Ran SP% **111.7**
Speed ratings (Par 101): **100,95,91,88,84**
CSF £7.28 TOTE £2.10: £1.40, £1.60; EX 4.60.
Owner Abdulla Ahmad Al Shaikh **Bred** Paulyn Limited **Trained** Newmarket, Suffolk

FOCUS
A weak maiden won in easy fashion by Ana Emarati, but the time was slow and he probably didn't need to improve.

399 PLAY GOLF BEFORE RACING AT SOUTHWELL H'CAP 1m 3f (F)
3:00 (3:00) (Class 5) (0-70,69) 4-Y-0+ £1,813 (£539; £269; £134) Stalls Low

Form RPR
0-31 **1** **Eseej (USA)**[11] 272 6-9-6 **68** 6ex................................. WilliamCarson 1 77
(Peter Hiatt) *mde all: rdn along wl over 2f out: drvn over 1f out: styd on strly fnl f* **11/4**[2]
420- **2** *4* **Trachonitis (IRE)**[38] 7985 7-9-7 **69**..................................... ShaneKelly 6 73
(J R Jenkins) *hld up in rr: smooth hdwy on outer over 4f out: effrt 3f out: chal wl over 1f out: ev ch tl rdn and one pce ent fnl f* **3/1**[3]
21 **3** *5* **Sail Home**[21] 145 4-9-1 **65**.. CathyGannon 2 58
(Julia Feilden) *trckd ldrs: hdwy to trck wnr 1/2-way: effrt 3f out: rdn and ch 2f out: sn drvn and wknd over 1f out* **1/1**[1]
366- **4** *5* **Amazing Blue Sky**[72] 7541 5-9-5 **67**............................ PJMcDonald 4 51
(Ruth Carr) *trckd wnr: rdn along 4f out: sn lost pl* **14/1**
000- **5** *shd* **Thundering Home**[105] 7042 4-8-12 **67**.................. JemmaMarshall(5) 5 51
(Michael Attwater) *chsd ldrs on inner: rdn along 4f out: outpcd fnl 3f* **33/1**
060- **6** *60* **Just Zak**[90] 7338 6-8-7 **55** oh1.. GregFairley 3 —
(Owen Brennan) *chsd ldrs: rdn along 1/2-way: sn wknd and wl bhd fnl 3f* **28/1**

2m 30.07s (2.07) **Going Correction** +0.325s/f (Slow)
WFA 4 from 5yo+ 2lb 6 Ran SP% **114.7**
Speed ratings (Par 103): **105,102,98,94,94 51**
toteswingers:1&2:£1.60, 1&3:£1.10, 2&3:£1.40 CSF £11.80 TOTE £3.60: £1.80, £1.50; EX 12.80.
Owner P W Hiatt **Bred** Shadwell Farm LLC **Trained** Hook Norton, Oxon

FOCUS
Modest handicap form. The winner is rated back to last year's form here.

400 EXCLUSIVE LIVE SHOWS AT BLUESQ.COM H'CAP 1m (F)
3:30 (3:30) (Class 5) (0-70,69) 4-Y-0+ £1,878 (£558; £279; £139) Stalls Low

Form RPR
-232 **1** **Bentley**[9] 291 7-9-3 **65**.. GrahamGibbons 7 77
(Brian Baugh) *in tch: rdn along over 3f out: hdwy on inner over 2f out: rdn to ld over 1f out: drvn out* **9/2**[3]
5-12 **2** *1 3/4* **San Antonio**[4] 361 11-9-4 **66** 6ex.................................(b) MickyFenton 4 74
(Pam Sly) *led to 1/2-way: cl up tl rdn and led again 2f out: sn drvn and hdd over 1f out: kpt on same pce* **9/4**[2]
152- **3** *2* **Mr Emirati (USA)**[53] 7845 4-9-4 **66**.................................... TomEaves 8 69
(Bryan Smart) *hld up in tch on outer: hdwy to trck ldrs 1/2-way: effrt 3f out: cl up 2f out: sn rdn and ch tl drvn: edgd lft and one pce appr fnl f* **2/1**[1]
2-52 **4** *3* **Ubenkor (IRE)**[9] 292 6-9-3 **65**... TonyCulhane 3 61
(Michael Herrington) *sn trcking ldrs: hdwy after 2f: slt ld 1/2-way: rdn along 3f out: hdd and drvn 2f out: grad wknd* **10/1**
143- **5** *nk* **King's Counsel (IRE)**[200] 4168 5-8-11 **59**........................ JoeFanning 1 55
(David O'Meara) *sn cl up on inner: pushed along 1/2-way: rdn along 3f out: sn drvn and wknd over 2f out* **10/1**
0-03 **6** *21* **Mister Green (FR)**[8] 307 5-9-0 **62**..............................(bt) JamesDoyle 5 9
(David Flood) *dwlt: a in rr: bhd fr over 2f out* **11/1**
00-6 **7** *2 1/2* **Moon Lightning (IRE)**[9] 290 5-9-7 **69**.......................(p) PJMcDonald 6 11
(Tina Jackson) *chsd ldrs: rdn along 1/2-way: sn wknd* **100/1**
0/0- **8** *2* **Flying Applause**[72] 7539 6-8-12 **60**..............................(b) DaneO'Neill 2 —
(Roy Bowring) *a in rr: bhd fr over 2f out* **40/1**

1m 46.19s (2.49) **Going Correction** +0.325s/f (Slow) 8 Ran SP% **112.2**
Speed ratings (Par 103): **100,98,96,93,92 71,69,67**
toteswingers:1&2:£2.20, 1&3:£3.00, 2&3:£2.20 CSF £14.46 CT £25.59 TOTE £4.20: £1.40, £1.80, £1.10; EX 15.80 Trifecta £31.30 Pool: £709.53 - 16.77 winning units..
Owner The Flying Spur Racing Partnership **Bred** Paul Blows And Jenny Hall **Trained** Audley, Staffs

FOCUS
Quite a competitive 59-69 handicap and there were still four in contention coming to the final furlong. The first pair were well in and the winner is rated to the same level as last time.

401 SOUTHWELL-RACECOURSE.CO.UK H'CAP 5f (F)
4:00 (4:00) (Class 6) (0-60,60) 4-Y-0+ £1,535 (£453; £226) Stalls High

Form RPR
00-1 **1** **Shawkantango**[18] 185 4-8-13 **52**..............................(v) PatrickMathers 6 65
(Derek Shaw) *dwlt: wnt rt s and reminders in rr swtchd lft after 1f: rdn along bef 1/2-way: hdwy 2f out: swtchd rt and drvn over 1f out: qcknd wl to ld jst ins fnl f: kpt on strly* **6/1**[3]
-242 **2** *1 3/4* **Cheveyo (IRE)**[13] 256 5-8-3 **47**....................................(e) JulieBurke(5) 8 54
(Patrick Morris) *slt bump s: hld up towards rr: smooth hdwy 1/2-way: rdn to ld briefly ent fnl f: sn hdd and kpt on same pce* **4/1**[1]
46-0 **3** *1 1/4* **Cape Royal**[27] 80 11-9-7 **60**..............................(bt) RichardKingscote 9 63
(Milton Bradley) *led: rdn wl over 1f out: hdd ent fnl f: kpt on same pce* **12/1**
330- **4** *nk* **We'll Deal Again**[72] 7543 4-9-4 **57**................................ GrahamGibbons 5 58
(Michael Easterby) *prom: rdn 2f out: drvn over 1f out: kpt on same pce* **7/1**
04-3 **5** *1 1/4* **Guto**[31] 15 8-8-11 **57**... MatthewCosham(7) 7 54
(Bill Ratcliffe) *prom: rdn along 2f out: drvn over 1f out and kpt on same pce* **10/1**
30-3 **6** *1/2* **Sally's Swansong**[14] 233 5-8-8 **47**..................................(b) TomEaves 4 42
(Eric Alston) *chsd ldrs: rdn along wl over 1f out: sn drvn and one pce* **20/1**
00-5 **7** *hd* **Lucky Art (USA)**[25] 102 5-8-10 **49**................................ PJMcDonald 12 43
(Ruth Carr) *in tch: smooth hdwy 1/2-way: effrt and ev ch over 1f out tl rdn and wknd ent fnl f* **22/1**
06-3 **8** *hd* **Dispol Grand (IRE)**[18] 185 5-9-4 **57**.............................. TonyCulhane 14 51
(Paul Midgley) *chsd ldrs: rdn along: edgd lft and lost pl 1/2-way: kpt on ins fnl f* **9/2**[2]
260- **9** *shd* **Cavitie**[62] 7683 5-9-7 **60**.. JamesDoyle 2 53
(Andrew Reid) *chsd ldrs on wd outside: rdn along 2f out: sn no imp* **9/2**[2]
530- **10** *1* **Attrition**[99] 7170 4-8-12 **51**.. KellyHarrison 10 41
(Andrew Reid) *s.i.s: a in rr* **22/1**
04-0 **11** *3 1/2* **The Lord**[6] 343 11-8-5 **51**.. JakePayne(7) 1 28
(Bill Turner) *blind removed late and stmbld s: a bhd* **40/1**
300- **12** *1* **Prigsnov Dancer (IRE)**[87] 7380 6-8-7 **46** oh1..............(b[1]) GregFairley 13 20
(Owen Brennan) *chsd ldr 2f: sn rdn along and lost pl: bhd fnl 2f* **28/1**
506- **13** *hd* **Lithaam (IRE)**[120] 6665 7-8-9 **48**....................................(p) BarryMcHugh 3 21
(Milton Bradley) *a towards rr* **20/1**

60.24 secs (0.54) **Going Correction** +0.15s/f (Slow) 13 Ran SP% **124.0**
Speed ratings (Par 101): **101,98,96,95,93 92,92,92,92,90 84,83,83**
toteswinger:1&2:£3.70, 1&3:£20.10, 2&3:£13.90 CSF £28.28 CT £290.97 TOTE £3.90: £1.10, £2.20, £2.70; EX 32.30 Trifecta £303.50 Part won. Pool: £410.15 - 0.50 winning units..
Owner Mrs Lyndsey Shaw **Bred** Derek Shaw **Trained** Sproxton, Leics
■ Stewards' Enquiry : Patrick Mathers one-day ban: used whip in incorrect place (Feb 17)

FOCUS
A wide open 46-60 sprint handicap and a last-to-first winner. The form is rated around the runner-up.
Guto Official explanation: vet said gelding pulled up lame right-fore

402 BET AT BLUESQ.COM H'CAP 6f (F)
4:30 (4:31) (Class 6) (0-65,66) 4-Y-0+ £1,535 (£453; £226) Stalls Low

Form RPR
01-0 **1** **Final Salute**[21] 150 5-8-12 **59**......................................(v) GaryBartley(3) 5 68
(Bryan Smart) *chsd ldrs: hdwy on outer wl over 2f out: rdn to ld wl over 1f out: drvn out* **8/1**
02-3 **2** *1 1/4* **Interchoice Star**[6] 345 6-9-1 **59**..............................(p) DuranFentiman 4 64+
(Ray Peacock) *chsd ldrs: effrt on outer 2f out: rdn to chse wnr ent fnl f: sn drvn and no imp towards fin* **9/2**[3]
2-20 **3** *3 1/2* **Bel Cantor**[6] 345 8-8-10 **61**..............................(p) MatthewCosham(7) 6 55
(Bill Ratcliffe) *cl up: rdn and ev ch over 2f out: drvn wl over 1f out and one pce appr fnl f* **3/1**[2]
15-0 **4** *1 1/4* **First Blade**[9] 294 5-9-7 **65**..(b) DaneO'Neill 3 55
(Roy Bowring) *cl up on inner: rdn and ev ch 2f out: sn drvn and one pce* **15/2**
41-0 **5** *2 1/2* **Cape Of Storms**[32] 13 8-9-6 **64**......................................(b) TomEaves 9 46
(Roy Brotherton) *led on outer: rdn along over 2f out: drvn and hdd wl over 1f out: sn wknd* **8/1**
045- **6** *2* **Louphole**[179] 4875 9-8-9 **60**.. DannyBrock(7) 2 35
(J R Jenkins) *towards rr: hdwy on inner and in tch wl over 2f out: sn rdn and nvr a factor* **16/1**
4-31 **7** *nse* **Toby Tyler**[9] 289 5-9-8 **66** 6ex......................................(v) MickyFenton 7 41+
(Paul Midgley) *rrd s and s.i.s: a bhd* **11/4**[1]
330/ **8** *7* **Bazguy**[781] 7675 6-9-2 **60**...(b) GregFairley 8 13
(Owen Brennan) *sn outpcd in rr and bhd fr 1/2-way* **22/1**

1m 18.19s (1.69) **Going Correction** +0.325s/f (Slow) 8 Ran SP% **114.1**
Speed ratings (Par 101): **101,99,94,93,89 87,86,77**
toteswingers:1&2:£5.20, 1&3:£20.10, 2&3:£3.50. totesuper7: Win: Not won. Place: £77.90. CSF £43.52 CT £132.77 TOTE £13.00: £3.60, £1.60, £1.70; EX 68.70 TRIFECTA Not won..
Owner Crossfields Racing & B Smart **Bred** Bricklow Ltd **Trained** Hambleton, N Yorks

FOCUS
A modest 59-66 handicap and not form to be too positive about.
Final Salute Official explanation: trainer said, regarding apparent improvement in form, that the gelding benefited from being drawn wide and running out of the kickback.
Toby Tyler Official explanation: jockey said gelding missed the break
T/Plt: £13.00 to a £1 stake. Pool:£60,206.91 - 3,372.86 winning tickets T/Qpdt: £5.50 to a £1 stake. Pool:£4,314.13 - 574.60 winning tickets JR

[362]WOLVERHAMPTON (A.W) (L-H)
Thursday, February 3

OFFICIAL GOING: Standard
Wind: Strong, behind Weather: Overcast

403 PLACE ONLY BETTING AT BLUESQ.COM APPRENTICE H'CAP 5f 216y(P)
5:00 (5:01) (Class 5) (0-75,75) 4-Y-0+ £2,039 (£607; £303; £151) Stalls Low

Form RPR
03-0 **1** **Excellent Show**[20] 168 5-9-7 **75**....................................(p) AdamCarter 3 82
(Bryan Smart) *s.i.s: towards rr: hdwy over 2f out: r.o to ld ins fnl f: eased fnl strides* **9/2**[3]
666 **2** *1/2* **Valmina**[107] 6997 4-8-4 **63**.. GeorgeDowning(5) 7 67
(Tony Carroll) *s.i.s: hld up bhd: hdwy 1f out: r.o ins fnl f: fin strly* **10/1**
-335 **3** *nk* **Absa Lutte (IRE)**[6] 336 8-8-13 **72**.................................. JosephYoung(5) 2 75
(Michael Mullineaux) *racd keenly: a.p: led wl over 1f out: hung lft and hdd ins fnl f: nt qckn towards fin* **15/2**
-361 **4** *1/2* **Takajan (IRE)**[2] 377 4-9-3 **71** 6ex.................................. JamesRogers 8 72
(Mark Brisbourne) *hld up: rn wd on bnd over 3f out: effrt and hdwy 2f out: chsd ldrs and hung lft ins fnl f: styd on but nt quite pce of ldrs* **5/1**
63-0 **5** *8* **Ballodair (IRE)**[16] 199 4-8-9 **68**.............................. GeorgeChaloner(5) 5 44
(Richard Fahey) *towards rr: pushed along 3f out: hdwy to chse ldrs wl over 1f out: no real imp: wknd ins fnl f* **7/2**[2]
10-2 **6** *3/4* **Forever's Girl**[9] 294 5-9-7 **75**... RyanPowell 1 48
(Geoffrey Oldroyd) *led: rdn 2f out: hdd wl over 1f out: wekanened fnl 100yds* **5/2**[1]
1-60 **6** *dht* **Prince James**[21] 144 4-8-11 **70**........................... DavidSimmonson(5) 6 43
(Michael Easterby) *chsd ldrs: rdn and outpcd over 2f out: n.d whn hung lft fr over 1f out* **11/1**
0-35 **8** *3 3/4* **Weet A Surprise**[14] 231 6-8-10 **67**.............................(p) AlexEdwards(3) 4 28
(James Unett) *prom: rdn over 2f out: sn wknd* **14/1**

1m 16.21s (1.21) **Going Correction** +0.225s/f (Slow) 8 Ran SP% **120.1**
Speed ratings (Par 103): **100,99,98,98,87 86,86,81**
toteswingers:1&2:£12.60, 1&3:£6.70, 2&3:£8.80 CSF £58.79 CT £406.46 TOTE £8.90: £2.40, £5.60, £3.60; EX 66.30.
Owner A Turton, P Langford & S Brown **Bred** Bearstone Stud And T Herbert Jackson **Trained** Hambleton, N Yorks

FOCUS
A tight sprint handicap, confined to apprentice riders. There was a solid pace on but the time was only a bit quicker than the claimer. The winner's best run since this time last year.
Forever's Girl Official explanation: trainer said race had probably come too soon for mare

404 RINGSIDE SUITE CLASSIFIED CLAIMING STKS 5f 216y(P)
5:30 (5:30) (Class 5) 3-Y-0+ £2,007 (£597; £298; £149) Stalls Low

Form RPR
2-41 **1** **Frequency**[1] 388 4-9-3 68..............................(v[1]) EddieAhern 3 74+
(Amy Weaver) *hld up in last pl: smooth hdwy on bit 1f out: shkn up to ld ins fnl f: easily* **4/5**[1]
260- **2** *1 1/2* **Hand Painted**[71] 7557 5-9-8 70.................................... FergusSweeney 4 73
(Peter Makin) *chsd ldr after 1f: upsides wl over 1f out: sn rdn: nt qckn ins fnl f: no ch w wnr fnl 100yds* **7/2**[2]
0-52 **3** *1/2* **Always Dazzling**[14] 231 4-9-1 63.................................... JamesSullivan(3) 1 67
(Ollie Pears) *racd in 2nd pl for 1f: trckd ldrs after: rdn to ld over 1f out: hdd ins fnl f: no ex fnl 100yds* **11/2**[3]

50-0 **4** *3* **Galpin Junior (USA)**[9] 294 5-9-4 70 .... PhillipMakin 2 57
(Ruth Carr) *led: pushed along 2f out: hdd over 1f out: sn btn and one pce* **6/1**

1m 16.32s (1.32) **Going Correction** +0.225s/f (Slow) **4** Ran SP% **107.4**
Speed ratings (Par 103): **100,98,97,93**
CSF £3.80 TOTE £1.60; EX 4.00.Frequency was claimed by Mr A. Bailey for £3,000.
Owner Miss A Weaver **Bred** Manor Farm Stud (rutland) **Trained** Newmarket, Suffolk

FOCUS
They finished in reverse order to when they jumped off, though, so the pace cannot have been sluggish. The winner seems to have improved for the headgear.

405 EXCLUSIVE LIVE SHOWS AT BLUESQ.COM H'CAP 1m 141y(P)
6:00 (6:00) (Class 4) (0-85,82) 4-Y-0+ **£3,626** (£1,079; £539; £269) **Stalls** Low

Form RPR

14-1 **1** **Star Links (USA)**[20] 170 5-9-0 **75** ....(b) ShaneKelly 5 85
(S Donohoe, Ire) *trckd ldrs: upsides 2f out: led over 1f out: r.o ins fnl f: jst hld on cl home* **11/2**[2]

113- **2** *nse* **Elijah Pepper (USA)**[62] 7680 6-8-12 **73** .... WilliamCarson 9 83
(David Barron) *hld up: rdn over 3f out: hdwy 2f out: r.o and clsd ins fnl f: jst failed* **5/1**[1]

-332 **3** *1 ¾* **Avonrose**[11] 273 4-8-11 **72** .... JoeFanning 7 78
(Derek Shaw) *midfield: rdn and hdwy 2f out: chsd ldrs over 1f out: swtchd lft ins fnl f and wnt 2nd briefly: nt qckn fnl 75yds* **7/1**

22-3 **4** *4* **Miami Gator (IRE)**[14] 226 4-9-4 **79** ....(v) LukeMorris 2 76
(Mrs K Burke) *led: hdd 6f out: remained w ldr: rdn and ev ch over 1f out: no ex fnl 110yds* **5/1**[1]

132- **5** *2 ¼* **Danderek**[272] 1867 5-9-5 **80** .... FrederikTylicki 8 72
(Richard Fahey) *prom: led 6f out: rdn and hdd over 1f out: wknd ins fnl f* **11/2**[2]

044- **6** *¾* **Standpoint**[119] 6701 5-9-3 **78** .... RussKennemore 3 68
(Reg Hollinshead) *midfield: rdn 2f out: no hdwy* **20/1**

64-0 **7** *nk* **Dubai Miracle (USA)**[21] 141 4-9-7 **82** .... MartinLane 1 71
(David Simcock) *trckd ldrs: pushed along over 3f out: lost pl and outpcd 2f out: n.d after* **7/1**

52-0 **8** *3 ¾* **Beetuna (IRE)**[10] 287 6-9-0 **75** .... SamHitchcott 6 56
(David Bourton) *hld up: rdn 2f out: nvr on terms* **9/1**

66-6 **9** *3 ¼* **Chosen Forever**[14] 235 6-9-7 **82** .... GeorgeBaker 4 55
(Geoffrey Oldroyd) *hld up in rr: rdn 2f out: nvr on terms: lame* **6/1**[3]

1m 50.15s (-0.35) **Going Correction** +0.225s/f (Slow) **9** Ran SP% **118.2**
Speed ratings (Par 105): **110,109,108,104,102 102,101,98,95**
toteswingers:1&2:£5.00, 1&3:£9.90, 2&3:£6.20 CSF £33.97 CT £198.72 TOTE £6.60: £2.30, £2.60, £4.60; EX 37.00.
Owner G Dolan/M McVitie/G Venamore/Mrs M Dolan **Bred** Shell Bloodstock **Trained** Cootehill Road, Co Cavan

FOCUS
This was a fair handicap with plenty of previous course form on offer and it looked wide open. There was a fair pace on and it produced a cracking finish between two old rivals. The winner showed his latest form didn't flatter him.
Chosen Forever Official explanation: vet said gelding finished lame

406 DINE IN HORIZONS H'CAP 1m 141y(P)
6:30 (6:31) (Class 6) (0-60,66) 3-Y-0 **£1,569** (£463; £231) **Stalls** Low

Form RPR

53-5 **1** **Lexi's Boy (IRE)**[33] 4 3-9-6 **59** .... PhillipMakin 11 70
(Kevin Ryan) *dwlt: sn prom: led 5f out: rdn over 2f out: edgd rt whn pressed ins fnl f: a doing enough: kpt on gamely* **13/2**[3]

60-6 **2** *¾* **Bodie**[12] 260 3-9-5 **58** ....(b[1]) JoeFanning 3 67
(Pam Sly) *racd keenly: chsd ldrs: wnt 2nd 3f out: chalng fr 2f out: intimidated by drifting wnr ins fnl f: eased whn hld towards fin* **8/1**

6-23 **3** *8* **Not So Bright (USA)**[17] 194 3-9-6 **59** ....(t) AndreaAtzeni 1 50
(Des Donovan) *broke wl: prom: rdn and outpcd by front pair wl over 1f out: n.d after: jst hld on for 3rd* **7/2**[1]

005- **4** *nse* **Delagoa Bay (IRE)**[36] 8000 3-8-12 **51** .... LiamKeniry 9 42+
(Sylvester Kirk) *hld up: hdwy 3f out: rdn over 2f out: styd on ins fnl f: jst failed to get up for 3rd: nt pce to chal front pair* **12/1**

60-4 **5** *2* **Apple Dumpling**[13] 253 3-8-11 **50** .... WilliamCarson 10 36+
(Stuart Williams) *hld up: nt clr run wl over 2f out: pushed along over 1f out: styd on ins fnl f: nt trble ldrs* **15/2**

5-40 **6** *1 ½* **Bathwick Freeze**[21] 142 3-8-8 **47** .... CathyGannon 7 30
(David Evans) *racd keenly in midfield: hdwy to go prom 5f out: rdn and outpcd over 2f out: wl btn ins fnl f* **33/1**

0-56 **7** *nse* **Seadream**[18] 187 3-8-0 **46** oh1 .... RachealKneller(7) 12 29+
(Mark Usher) *dwlt: racd keenly: hld up: pushed along over 1f out: nvr able to trble ldrs* **66/1**

00-3 **8** *1 ¾* **Imperial Fong**[15] 212 3-9-4 **57** .... HayleyTurner 6 36
(David Elsworth) *led: hdd 5f out: rdn and wknd 2f out* **7/2**[1]

005- **9** *2 ½* **Volcanic Lady (IRE)**[158] 5558 3-8-7 **46** oh1 .... MartinLane 5 19
(David Simcock) *hld up: pushed along 2f out: nvr on term w ldrs* **6/1**[2]

50-1 **10** *3 ¼* **Appyjack**[21] 142 3-9-1 **54** ....(t) LukeMorris 4 19
(Tony Carroll) *midfield: rdn 3f out: wknd 2f out* **6/1**[2]

1m 53.27s (2.77) **Going Correction** +0.225s/f (Slow) **10** Ran SP% **121.4**
Speed ratings (Par 95): **96,95,88,88,86 85,85,83,81,78**
toteswingers:1&2:£18.60, 1&3:£8.70, 2&3:£6.20 CSF £60.07 CT £220.38 TOTE £10.80: £3.90, £2.80, £1.30; EX 57.90.
Owner Mrs Margaret Forsyth **Bred** R S Cockerill (farms) Ltd & Peter Dodd **Trained** Hambleton, N Yorks

FOCUS
A weak 3-y-o handicap, but there were some potential improvers lurking. There was an average pace on and it paid to race handily, with the first pair dominating from 2f out. There is a bit of doubt over how much the first two actually improved.
Bathwick Freeze Official explanation: jockey said filly hung right and had no more to give
Imperial Fong Official explanation: trainer's rep said filly ran too free early

407 ENJOY THE PARTY PACK GROUP OFFER H'CAP 2m 119y(P)
7:00 (7:02) (Class 6) (0-60,60) 4-Y-0+ **£1,569** (£463; £231) **Stalls** Low

Form RPR

22-2 **1** **Rosewood Lad**[20] 161 4-9-3 **59** .... CathyGannon 9 71
(J S Moore) *chsd ldrs: reminders after 6f: wnt 2nd over 4f out: led over 3f out: kicked 2f out: sn clr: styd on wl: unchal after* **7/2**[3]

3-04 **2** *7* **Bute Street**[10] 286 6-9-9 **59** .... GeorgeBaker 7 63
(Ron Hodges) *midfield: hdwy 5f out: chsd wnr over 2f out: no imp: no ch fr wl over 1f out* **2/1**[1]

0-11 **3** *3 ½* **Delorain (IRE)**[10] 277 8-9-0 **57** 6ex ....(vt) LauraPike(7) 2 56
(William Stone) *midfield: lost pl briefly over 5f out: sn swtchd rt: hdwy 4f out: chsd wnr 3f out tl over 2f out: sn btn: plugged on at one pce after* **9/4**[2]

/0-0 **4** *13* **Hill Of Clare (IRE)**[6] 340 9-8-7 **46** oh1 .... AmyBaker(3) 4 30
(George Jones) *hld up: pushed along 4f out: sn outpcd: no imp after* **50/1**

25/6 **5** *10* **Am I Blue**[20] 172 5-8-10 **46** .... DavidProbert 5 18
(Mrs D Thomas) *led: hdd over 5f out: rdn and wknd over 3f out* **13/2**

5 **6** *7* **Peintre Du Roi (USA)**[15] 216 7-8-13 **49** .... LukeMorris 3 12
(Natalie Lloyd-Beavis) *chsd ldrs: pushed along 6f out: rdn and wknd 5f out* **22/1**

40-0 **7** *½* **Lady Christie**[8] 301 4-8-4 **46** oh1 .... NeilChalmers 8 9
(Michael Blanshard) *chsd ldr: led over 5f out: rdn and hdd over 3f out: wknd over 2f out* **50/1**

256- **8** *113* **Smarties Party**[237] 1671 8-9-10 **60** .... PaddyAspell 6 —
(Clive Mulhall) *hld up: struggling 5f out: t.o* **10/1**

000- **9** *dist* **Hopefull Blue (IRE)**[59] 7731 5-8-10 **46** oh1 ....(b[1]) FergusSweeney 1 —
(James Evans) *hld up bhd: struggling 6f out: woefully t.o fnl 5f* **50/1**

3m 45.54s (3.74) **Going Correction** +0.225s/f (Slow)
WFA 4 from 5yo+ 6lb **9** Ran SP% **119.0**
Speed ratings (Par 101): **100,96,95,88,84 80,80,—,—**
toteswingers:1&2:£2.70, 1&3:£2.00, 2&3:£1.50 CSF £11.08 CT £18.31 TOTE £4.40: £1.20, £1.10, £2.00; EX 13.90.
Owner Miss D L Wisbey & R J Viney **Bred** Miss D L Wisbey **Trained** Upper Lambourn, Berks

FOCUS
This moderate staying handicap was run at an uneven tempo until the leaders quickened up 6f out. The principals came well clear and the form looks fair, despite the considerable step up from the winner.
Lady Christie Official explanation: jockey said filly hung left
Hopefull Blue(IRE) Official explanation: jockey said mare lost its action

408 GREAT OFFERS ONLINE AT WOLVERHAMPTON-RACECOURSE.CO.UK H'CAP 1m 1f 103y(P)
7:30 (7:32) (Class 7) (0-50,50) 4-Y-0+ **£1,535** (£453; £226) **Stalls** Low

Form RPR

0-0 **1** **Duneen Dream (USA)**[27] 86 6-9-1 **48** .... AndreaAtzeni 11 60
(Nikki Evans) *mde all: kicked clr over 1f out: styd on wl and unchal after* **10/1**[3]

000- **2** *5* **Idol Deputy (FR)**[94] 2337 5-8-8 **48** .... RachealKneller(7) 12 49
(Gavin Blake) *midfield: hdwy 5f out: wnt 2nd over 2f out: rdn and no imp on wnr fr over 1f out* **33/1**

202- **3** *1* **Mary Helen**[77] 7495 4-9-3 **50** .... ShaneKelly 10 49
(Mark Brisbourne) *hld up: hdwy over 3f out: rdn 2f out: styd on ins fnl f: nt pce to get to ldrs* **7/2**[2]

60-0 **4** *nk* **Yorksters Prince (IRE)**[33] 7 4-8-10 **48** .... TobyAtkinson(5) 13 46
(George Prodromou) *chsd ldrs: rdn and nt qckn over 2f out: styd on ins fnl f: nt pce of ldrs* **10/1**[3]

50-3 **5** *2* **Corrib (IRE)**[28] 69 8-9-1 **48** ....(p) DavidProbert 8 42
(Bryn Palling) *midfield: rdn 2f out: kpt on fnl f: no imp* **7/2**[2]

5- **6** *¾* **Sligo All Star**[55] 7814 6-8-12 **45** .... FrannyNorton 5 37
(Thomas McLaughlin, Ire) *prom: rdn over 2f out: sn outpcd* **11/4**[1]

/0-0 **7** *hd* **Spares And Repairs**[6] 346 8-8-5 **45** .... JackDuern(7) 7 37
(Reg Hollinshead) *midfield: pushed along and wknd over 3f out* **33/1**

00/4 **7** *dht* **Cause For Applause (IRE)**[23] 120 5-9-0 **47** .... PhillipMakin 6 39
(Ray Craggs) *hld up: rdn over 2f out: no imp* **20/1**

06-0 **9** *nse* **Grace And Virtue (IRE)**[20] 169 4-9-3 **50** .... CathyGannon 9 42
(S Donohoe, Ire) *prom: rdn and ev ch over 2f out: wknd over 1f out* **14/1**

00-6 **10** *1 ½* **Libre**[10] 283 11-8-13 **46** ....(p) JoeFanning 1 40
(Violet M Jordan) *hld up: trying to keep on whn nt clr run ins fnl f: nvr a danger* **11/1**

60-0 **11** *4 ½* **Jiggalong**[20] 173 5-8-12 **45** .... NeilChalmers 3 24
(Mrs D Thomas) *midfield: lost pl over 4f out: nt clr run over 2f out: bhd after* **25/1**

060/ **12** *3 ¾* **Power Broker**[55] 7819 8-8-12 **45** ....(b) GrahamGibbons 2 16
(Sean Thornton, Ire) *trckd ldrs tl rdn and wknd over 3f out* **11/1**

02-0 **13** *31* **Fitzwarren**[28] 69 10-8-12 **45** ....(tp) SteveDrowne 4 —
(Alan Brown) *prom tl wknd over 2f out: t.o* **33/1**

2m 3.97s (2.27) **Going Correction** +0.225s/f (Slow) **13** Ran SP% **130.1**
Speed ratings (Par 97): **98,93,92,92,90 89,89,89,89,88 84,81,53**
toteswingers:1&2:£70.70, 1&3:£6.60, 2&3:£65.00 CSF £325.59 CT £1399.79 TOTE £13.30: £5.20, £23.10, £1.10; EX 883.20.
Owner John Berry (Gwent) **Bred** Wayne G Lyster III Et Al **Trained** Pandy, Monmouths

FOCUS
A bottom-drawer handicap and not many got involved. the winner is rated back to his old best.
Sligo All Star Official explanation: jockey said mare ran too freely

409 BET AT BLUESQ.COM H'CAP 1m 4f 50y(P)
8:00 (8:00) (Class 6) (0-55,54) 4-Y-0+ **£1,569** (£463; £231) **Stalls** Low

Form RPR

065- **1** **Setter's Princess**[49] 7315 5-9-1 **52** .... GeorgeBaker 6 63
(Ron Hodges) *hld up: hdwy over 3f out: led 1f out: r.o wl and in command ins fnl f* **9/1**

16-2 **2** *2 ¾* **Port Hill**[13] 252 4-8-13 **53** .... ShaneKelly 1 59+
(Mark Brisbourne) *hel.d up: pushed along 6f out: hdwy 2f out: styd on to chse wnr ins fnl f: no imp* **4/1**[1]

4-04 **3** *4* **Barbirolli**[20] 173 9-8-2 **45** ow1 .... LauraPike(7) 2 46
(William Stone) *hld up: hdwy over 1f out: sn rdn: styd on ins fnl f: nt pce to rch front 2* **20/1**

51-4 **4** *¾* **Iguacu**[24] 115 7-9-2 **53** ....(p) DaneO'Neill 9 52
(George Baker) *s.s: hld up: sn in midfield: hdwy 3f out: rdn to chal over 1f out: no ex ins fnl f* **6/1**[3]

040- **5** *3 ¼* **Jackson (BRZ)**[74] 7490 9-8-7 **47** ....(b) AndrewHeffernan(3) 7 41
(Richard Guest) *prom: led over 2f out: rdn and hdd 1f out: wknd ins fnl f* **14/1**

04-0 **6** *8* **Before The War (USA)**[14] 223 4-9-0 **54** ....(b[1]) SteveDrowne 8 35
(Jeremy Gask) *prom: led 5f out: rdn and hdd over 2f out: wknd over 1f out* **14/1**

4-63 **7** *8* **Escape Artist**[13] 252 4-8-10 **50** ....(e) RobertWinston 11 18
(Tim Easterby) *racd keenly: in tch: effrt and ev ch 3f out: weakenee over 1f out* **9/2**[2]

460- **8** *1 ¾* **Bromhead (USA)**[23] 1134 5-8-9 **46** .... AndreaAtzeni 3 11
(Kevin Morgan) *midfield: rdn over 3f out: struggling over 2f out: wl btn after* **8/1**

24-3 **9** *1* **Lady Rossetti**[14] 225 4-8-11 **51** ....(p) HayleyTurner 4 15
(Marcus Tregoning) *trckd ldrs: pushed along 4f out: wknd over 1f out* **6/1**[3]

00-3 **10** *5* **Oak Leaves**[27] 85 4-8-10 **50** .... DavidProbert 5 —
(Nikki Evans) *bhd: niggled along at times: nvr on terms* **22/1**

00-5 **11** *7* **Desert Fairy**[27] 85 5-8-8 **45** ....(t) LiamJones 10 —
(James Unett) *midfield: rdn 6f out: wknd over 2f out* **33/1**

0-52 **12** *22* **Laura Land**[7] 324 5-8-8 **45**... LukeMorris 12 —
(Mark Brisbourne) *led: hdd 5f out: sn rdn: wknd over 3f out: t.o fnl 2f* **7/1**

2m 43.79s (2.69) **Going Correction** +0.225s/f (Slow)
WFA 4 from 5yo+ 3lb **12** Ran SP% **125.7**
Speed ratings (Par 101): **100,98,95,95,92 87,82,81,80,77 72,57**
toteswingers:1&2:£11.30, 1&3:£26.00, 2&3:£7.00 CSF £46.66 CT £733.47 TOTE £14.50: £3.80, £2.20, £3.50; EX 60.70.
Owner Mrs L Sharpe & Mrs S G Clapp **Bred** Mrs P Stocker **Trained** Charlton Mackrell, Somerset

FOCUS
This weak handicap was run at a sound pace. The winner is rated back to her early Flat form with the runner-up to the best view of his recent form.
Port Hill Official explanation: jockey said gelding suffered interference on first bend
T/Plt: £215.00 to a £1 stake. Pool:£81,044.80 - 275.06 winning tickets T/Qpdt: £11.50 to a £1 stake. Pool:£13,458.62 - 865.65 winning tickets DO

395 CAGNES-SUR-MER

Thursday, February 3

OFFICIAL GOING: Fibresand: standard

410a PRIX DE L'ILE SAINT HONORAT (MAIDEN) (3YO COLTS & GELDINGS) (FIBRESAND) 1m (F)

12:30 (12:00) 3-Y-O **£8,620** (£3,448; £2,586; £1,724; £862)

RPR
1 **War Pact (USA)** 3-9-2 0... IoritzMendizabal 2 89
(J-C Rouget, France) **2/5**[1]
2 *5* **Prince Verde (FR)**[37] 3-9-2 0.............................. StephanePasquier 4 80
(P Demercastel, France) **5/1**[2]
3 *2* **Kourdo (FR)**[122] 3-8-13 0..(b) ThomasMessina 9 73
(J Parize, France) **9/1**[3]
4 *nk* **Tibo Tibo (FR)**[237] 2949 3-8-13 0......................... Pierre-CharlesBoudot 6 73
(J-M Capitte, France) **16/1**
5 *1* **Great Surprise**[13] 258 3-8-13 0.................................... JohanVictoire 1 71
(Reg Hollinshead) *trckd ldr tl rdn and nt qckn fr 2f out* **25/1**
6 *1 ½* **Will Of Dream (FR)**[132] 3-8-13 0.................................. FabriceVeron 3 68
(F-X De Chevigny, France) **29/1**
7 *4* **Tobey (IRE)** 3-8-13 0.. DominiqueBoeuf 5 61
(W Baltromei, Germany) **13/1**
8 *3* **Ivory Bird**[146] 3-8-13 0.. GuillaumeMillet 8 56
(P Khozian, France) **31/1**

1m 35.86s (95.86) **8** Ran SP% **121.4**
PARI-MUTUEL (all including 1 euro stakes): WIN 1.40; PLACE 1.10, 1.10, 1.10; DF 2.90; SF 3.00.
Owner Joseph Allen **Bred** J Allen **Trained** Pau, France

326 MEYDAN (L-H)

Thursday, February 3

OFFICIAL GOING: Tapeta: standard; turf: good
The rail was out 12 metres on the turf course.

411a MEYDAN CLASSIC TRIAL SPONSORED BY ETISALAT (CONDITIONS RACE) (TURF) 7f

3:00 (3:00) 3-Y-O **£19,230** (£6,410; £3,205; £1,602; £961; £641)

RPR
1 **Lord Of The Stars (USA)**[14] 238 3-8-8 94.................. TadhgO'Shea 3 102
(David Simcock) *sn led: kicked clr 2 1/2f out: comf* **14/1**
2 *2 ¼* **Krypton Factor**[14] 238 3-8-8 100..................................(b) KierenFallon 1 96
(F Nass, Bahrain) *trckd ldr: rdn 2 1/2f out: r.o wl* **7/1**[3]
3 *1 ¼* **Introvert (IRE)**[14] 238 3-8-8 90.................................... AhmedAjtebi 9 91+
(Mahmood Al Zarooni) *in rr of mid-div: r.o wl fnl 2f: nrst fin* **20/1**
4 *shd* **Ahlaain (USA)**[126] 6507 3-8-8 99.................................... RyanMoore 2 91+
(David Simcock) *mid-div: r.o wl fnl 2f* **6/1**[2]
5 *¾* **Borug (USA)**[120] 6670 3-8-8 89..(p) TedDurcan 7 89
(Saeed Bin Suroor) *trckd ldng pair tl one pce fnl 1 1/2f* **10/1**
6 *1 ¾* **Mayfair Lad**[11] 3-8-8 68..(t) WJSupple 12 84
(A Al Raihe, UAE) *s.i.s: r.o fnl 2 1/2f* **66/1**
7 *½* **Roayh (USA)**[141] 6083 3-8-8 101.................................. FrankieDettori 8 83
(Saeed Bin Suroor) *a mid-div: n.d* **7/4**[1]
8 *2 ¾* **Busker (USA)**[153] 5718 3-8-8 79....................................(t) PatCosgrave 11 75
(M bin Shafya, UAE) *Soon rdn in rr: nvr nr to chal* **33/1**
9 *2* **Major Victory (SAF)**[35] 8022 4-9-4 80.......................... RichardMullen 6 73
(Gay Kelleway) *nvr able to chal* **33/1**
10 *2 ½* **Abstrato (BRZ)**[14] 238 4-9-4 90... KShea 4 66
(M F De Kock, South Africa) *trckd ldrs tl 3f out: sn struggling* **14/1**
11 *¼* **D'Artagnan (SAF)**[31] 21 4-8-11 70.......................... HarryBentley(7) 5 66
(Gay Kelleway) *nvr able to chal* **66/1**
12 *¾* **Energia Carioca (BRZ)**[35] 8025 4-9-4 95...............................(t) BReis 14 64
(E Martins, Brazil) *mid-div: wknd fnl 2f* **8/1**
13 *½* **Calling Elvis (BRZ)**[222] 4-9-4 97.............. Christophe-PatriceLemaire 10 62
(A De Royer-Dupre, France) *nvr bttr than mid-div* **7/1**[3]
14 *2 ¾* **Mutual Force (USA)**[35] 8025 3-8-8 76......................(t) RoystonFfrench 13 52
(A Al Raihe, UAE) *nvr able to chal* **50/1**

1m 24.45s (84.45)
WFA 3 from 4yo 17lb **14** Ran SP% **124.8**
CSF: £107.65..
Owner Ahmad Al Shaikh **Bred** JMJ Racing Stables LLC **Trained** Newmarket, Suffolk

FOCUS
A rare front-running winner, and racing tight against the fence may have been advantageous. The race for which this serves as a trial will be run for only the third time on February 24, a 1m event that has been upgraded to Listed status. However, few were ever seriously competitive here and this form needs treating with caution.

NOTEBOOK
Lord Of The Stars(USA) improved a good deal on the form he showed in the UAE 2,000 Guineas Trial on his Dubai debut and will obviously be worthy of his place in the Meydan Classic, but it's unlikely he'll be gifted such an advantage next time.
Krypton Factor, a non-staying fifth in the Guineas Trial on Tapeta, was ridden conservatively from his low draw and didn't have his stamina severely tested. He kept on but never looked likely to trouble the winner.
Introvert(IRE) is one to take from the race. He raced well off the pace following a slow start and was the only runner to make up a significant amount of ground. In the Guineas Trial he had split today's one-two, and this was anther decent effort.
Ahlaain(USA) shaped as though in need of the run on his return from over four months off. He travelled nicely enough, some way off the lead, but had no hope of getting seriously involved and lost third near the line when clearly getting tired.
Borug(USA), a 1m Polytrack nursery winner off 82 last October, recovered from a sluggish start to sit handier than most, but he lacked the required pace in the straight.
Roayh(USA) was disappointing, even allowing for the lack of pace in the race.

412a UAE 1000 GUINEAS SPONSORED BY ETISALAT (LISTED RACE) (FILLIES) (TAPETA) 1m

3:40 (3:40) 3-Y-O **£96,153** (£32,051; £16,025; £8,012; £4,807; £3,205)

RPR
1 **Mahbooba (AUS)**[21] 151 4-9-4 110.................. ChristopheSoumillon 3 108+
(M F De Kock, South Africa) *mid-div: t.k.h: hrd rdn 1 1/2f out: led 110yds out: comf* **8/11**[1]
2 *3 ¾* **Reem (AUS)**[21] 151 4-9-4 104.. PatCosgrave 5 98
(M F De Kock, South Africa) *trckd ldr: led 2 1/2f out: hdd 110yds out: r.o wl but no ch w wnr* **9/2**[2]
3 *1 ½* **Chocolicious (SAF)**[21] 151 4-9-4 106............................. RyanMoore 4 95
(H J Brown, South Africa) *in rr of mid-div: rdn 3 1/2f out: r.o fnl 1 1/2f* **5/1**[3]
4 *½* **Empire Rose (ARG)**[21] 151 4-9-4 99.................................... KShea 6 93
(M F De Kock, South Africa) *mid-div on rail: r.o fnl 2f* **20/1**
5 *1 ¼* **Abtasaamah (USA)**[21] 151 3-8-8 100......................... FrankieDettori 2 87
(Saeed Bin Suroor) *sn led: hdd 2 1/2f out: kpt on same pce* **10/1**
6 *3 ¼* **Quick Val (ARG)**[21] 151 4-9-4 97...................................... TedDurcan 8 83
(H J Brown, South Africa) *settled in rr: n.d* **20/1**
7 *2 ½* **Amica (SAF)**[27] 92 4-9-4 87.. RoystonFfrench 1 77
(Gay Kelleway) *s.i.s: nvr bttr than mid-div* **50/1**
8 *2 ½* **Crying Lightening (IRE)**[21] 151 3-8-8 104..................... KierenFallon 7 68
(Peter Chapple-Hyam) *settled in rr: nvr able to chal* **14/1**

1m 36.5s (-0.60) **Going Correction** +0.25s/f (Slow)
WFA 3 from 4yo 19lb **8** Ran SP% **120.0**
Speed ratings: **113,109,107,107,106 102,100,97**
CSF: £4.56..
Owner Sheikh Mohammed Bin Khalifa Al Maktoum **Bred** Sheikh Mohammed Bin Khalifa Al Maktoum **Trained** South Africa

FOCUS
The first classic of the Dubai season, and a first UAE 1,000 Guineas success for Mike De Kock, who also had the runner-up and fourth-placed finisher. This year's fillies have so far looked a rank ordinary bunch, but Mahbooba, only the third southern hemisphere winner of the race in 11 runnings, is an obvious exception. The pace was steady.

NOTEBOOK
Mahbooba(AUS) ◆, quite a highly strung type, was unsuited by the lack of pace, being much keener than ideal, but she still proved good enough to reverse placings with her stable companion Reem on 7lb better terms, improving on the form she showed runner-up in the prep race. She took a while to pick up in the straight after coming off the bridle before the runner-up, and briefly looked in a bit of trouble, but her stamina kicked in from around a furlong out. This performance is all the more noteworthy considering her early exertions, and that the pace of the race was hardly conducive to a big performance, and clearly she's really smart. She'll be extremely tough to beat in the Oaks on February 24, when the extra 300m will really suit. (op 4-5 tchd 8-11)
Reem(AUS) looked like she might take a bit of passing when in front early in the straight, but she simply wasn't good enough.
Chocolicious(SAF), fourth in the trial, was well and truly off the bridle turning into the straight but gradually responded. The extra 300m of the Oaks will suit her, but she's unlikely to reverse from with Mahbooba.
Empire Rose(ARG) ran okay without the blinkers this time. (op 16-1)
Abtasaamah(USA), bidding to provide Saeed Bin Suroor with his eighth winner of the race, regressed from the trial, weakening after racing freely in front.
Crying Lightening(IRE) once again offered nothing.

413a ETISALAT ELIFE (H'CAP) (TURF) 1m 4f 93y

4:15 (4:15) (100-113,113) 3-Y-0+ **£67,307** (£22,435; £11,217; £5,608; £3,365; £2,243)

RPR
1 **Star Empire (SAF)**[14] 240 5-8-13 106............... ChristopheSoumillon 2 110+
(M F De Kock, South Africa) *trckd ldr: rdn 2 1/2f out: r.o wl: led cl home* **7/4**[1]
2 *¼* **Calvados Blues (FR)**[14] 240 5-9-1 108..................... RoystonFfrench 1 112
(Mahmood Al Zarooni) *sn led: rdn 3f out: r.o wl: hdd cl home* **20/1**
3 *¾* **Peligroso (FR)**[14] 242 5-8-10 104....................................... TedDurcan 4 106
(Saeed Bin Suroor) *mid-div: r.o wl fnl 2f* **12/1**
4 *1* **Telluride**[21] 154 5-9-0 107.. KierenFallon 8 108
(J E Hammond, France) *settled in rr: rdn 3f out: r.o fnl 2f: nrest at fin* **7/1**
5 *¾* **Mikhail Glinka (IRE)**[21] 154 4-9-1 110...........................(t) RyanMoore 6 111
(H J Brown, South Africa) *in rr of mid-div: r.o fnl 2f: nrest at fin* **10/1**
6 *1 ¼* **Lawspeaker**[21] 154 4-9-0 109................................(b) MickaelBarzalona 7 108
(Mahmood Al Zarooni) *nvr bttr than mid-div* **14/1**
7 *1 ¼* **La De Two (IRE)**[103] 7096 5-9-1 108..........................(t) FrankieDettori 5 104
(Saeed Bin Suroor) *slowly away: settled last: smooth prog 6f out: one pce fnl f* **7/2**[2]
8 *shd* **Buzzword**[151] 5804 4-9-4 113.. AhmedAjtebi 3 110
(Mahmood Al Zarooni) *trckd ldr: rdn 3f out: wknd fnl 1 1/2f* **11/2**[3]
9 *32* **Quality Guitar (BRZ)**[144] 6017 5-8-7 100.................................(t) BReis 9 —
(E Martins, Brazil) *in rr of mid-div: rdn 4 1/2f out: sn btn* **33/1**

2m 36.76s (156.76)
WFA 4 from 5yo 3lb **9** Ran SP% **117.6**
CSF: £42.80; Tricast: £336.92..
Owner Sheikh Mohammed Bin Khalifa Al Maktoum **Bred** Sydney A Muller, F M Ratner & L M Salzman **Trained** South Africa

FOCUS
The impression in the first turf race on the card was that making the running against the inside rail (out 12 metres) was potentially advantageous, and that was confirmed here.

NOTEBOOK
Star Empire(SAF), who raced close to the pace throughout, found just enough after showing a good attitude to take a tight gap between rivals in the straight. Like when a closing third over 1m2f on the Tapeta two weeks earlier, his head carriage was low, suggesting he wanted to go quicker than allowed, and he can do better off a stronger gallop. He was winning off 106, so is probably best kept to handicaps for the time being.
Calvados Blues(FR), who hasn't won since May 2009 and was trying a trip this far for the first time, proved extremely difficult to pass after dictating a steady tempo against the favoured rail, despite having carried his head high throughout and not always looking keen.
Peligroso(FR) improved on the form he showed over 1m2f here last time.

Telluride ◆ is better than he showed. He only had one rival behind him at the top of the straight, and the lack of pace in the race was totally unsuitable, but he finished as well as could have been expected. There's better to come if he can get a stronger pace to chase.
Mikhail Glinka(IRE) didn't run badly considering a stronger pace would have suited better. Last season's Queen's Vase winner should be spot on for the 1m6f Nad Al Sheba Trophy on February 17 and the DRC Gold Cup over 2m on March 10. (op 11-1)
La De Two(IRE), returning from a 103-day break, lost ground with a slow start, and then after being moved up to sit close to the sedate pace before the straight, he found nothing for pressure. (op 4-1)
Buzzword was hugely disappointing on his return from a five-month break, dropping away after racing close up. (op 6-1)

414a AL SHINDAGHA SPRINT SPONSORED BY ETISALAT (GROUP 3) (TAPETA) 6f

4:55 (4:55) 3-Y-O+

£76,923 (£25,641; £12,820; £6,410; £3,846; £2,564)

RPR

1 **Dynamic Blitz (AUS)**[81] 7-9-0 107 .... ODoleuze 10 115+
(P F Yiu, Hong Kong) *chsd ldrs: led 1 1/2f out: r.o wl* **14/1**

2 2 1/4 **Alazeyab (USA)**[328] 5-9-0 106 .... (t) TadhgO'Shea 3 107
(A Al Raihe, UAE) *trckd ldr: nt qckn fnl f but r.o at one pce* **20/1**

3 3/4 **Mutheeb (USA)**[21] [155] 6-9-0 112 .... RichardHills 1 105+
(M Al Muhairi, UAE) *mid-div: r.o fnl 1 1/2f: nrest at fin* **8/1**[3]

4 1/4 **Our Giant (AUS)**[21] [155] 8-9-0 115 .... (b) ChristopheSoumillon 4 104
(M F De Kock, South Africa) *settled in rr: chsd ldrs 2 1/2f out: r.o at one pce fnl f* **7/4**[1]

5 hd **Inxile (IRE)**[21] [155] 6-9-0 108 .... AdrianNicholls 12 103
(David Nicholls) *s.i.s but sn led: hdd 1 1/2f out: r.o same pce* **6/1**[2]

6 3/4 **Dohasa (IRE)**[7] [327] 6-9-0 108 .... RyanMoore 6 101
(I Mohammed, UAE) *a mid-div* **8/1**[3]

7 3 3/4 **Banna Boirche (IRE)**[57] [7772] 5-9-0 108 .... ShaneFoley 2 89
(M Halford, Ire) *settled last: nvr able to chal* **14/1**

8 shd **Prohibit**[123] [6608] 6-9-0 108 .... (p) JamieSpencer 9 88
(Robert Cowell) *nvr bttr than mid-div* **9/1**

9 1 1/4 **Frosty Secret (USA)**[328] 7-9-0 108 .... KShea 5 84
(M F De Kock, South Africa) *nvr bttr than mid-div* **14/1**

10 1/2 **Terrific Challenge (USA)**[14] [237] 9-9-0 106 .... (vt) RichardMullen 7 83
(S Seemar, UAE) *nvr nr to chal* **16/1**

11 2 1/4 **Sangaree (USA)**[186] 6-9-0 107 .... (bt) FrankieDettori 11 76
(Saeed Bin Suroor) *nvr able to chal* **8/1**[3]

12 1/4 **Force Freeze (USA)**[21] [155] 6-9-0 109 .... (t) KierenFallon 8 75
(Doug Watson, UAE) *trckd ldr: no room after 1 1/2f: r.o same pce fnl f* **14/1**

1m 10.47s (-0.53) **Going Correction** +0.25s/f (Slow) **12** Ran SP% **131.3**
Speed ratings: **113,110,109,108,108 107,102,102,100,99 96,96**
CSF: £291.20..
Owner Lam Yin Kee **Bred** D P Esplin & G R Hodgkinson **Trained** Hong Kong

FOCUS
This was won two seasons ago - on the Nad Al Sheba dirt - by subsequent Golden Shaheen winner Big City Man. The latest running didn't look that strong by Group 3 standards, with the runner-up rated just 106, but the winner was quite impressive and the time was just 0.04 seconds outside the track record.

NOTEBOOK
Dynamic Blitz(AUS), from the same stable as the brilliant Sacred Kingdom, was a prolific winner on artificial surfaces in Hong Kong but had never raced left-handed. Having shown good early speed to get a prominent position from his high stall, he sustained his challenge right the way to the line, proving much too good for this lot. He was sufficiently dominant to enter calculations for the Golden Shaheen, although we'll learn more if he takes in the Mahab Al Shimaal, another Group 3 over C&D, on Super Thursday.
Alazeyab(USA), a handicap winner off 102 over C&D as last year's Carnival (runner-up that day was Warsaw, winner of the following race on this card), was the owner's second string, but he represented a yard in really good form and ran a fine race after a 328-day absence.
Mutheeb(USA) ◆ showed enough to suggest he'll be a major player in the Mahab Al Shimaal, a race in which he was runner-up last year from an unfavourable draw. He reversed recent course placings with Our Giant on 6lb better terms, although he wasn't helped by stall one, not always having a great deal of room to play with. Next time out will be his third start after a layoff, which is often a good angle (particularly with sprinters) when the horse in question improved on its comeback run second-time out. (op 7-1)
Our Giant(AUS) was favoured by the weights when winning a conditions race here in January, and this was tougher. He fared best of those held up, but simply didn't pick up sufficiently to get seriously involved. His trainer said beforehand he's keen to step him up to 1m, so maybe the Group 3 Burj Nahaar on Super Thursday will be his target. (op 2-1)
Inxile(IRE) ◆ ran a terrific race to finish second to Our Giant from stall 12 on his previous start, but he faced a tough task from the same draw this time. His chance was further compromised by a sluggish start, and although recovering to lead, he had little chance of sustaining his effort. A drop to handicap company and a more favourable draw might do the trick.
Banna Boirche(IRE) found this trip too short.
Prohibit hadn't been seen for four months and, according to his trainer, the 5f turf conditions event on March 3 is a more important target, with connections eyeing an invite into the Al Quoz Sprint. (op 8-1)
Terrific Challenge(USA) was keeping on at the one pace when short of room, and otherwise would have finished closer. (op 18-1)
Sangaree(USA), on his first start since leaving Bob Baffert, offered little, even allowing for a wide trip.

415a ETISALAT MY PLAN (H'CAP) (TURF) 7f

5:35 (5:35) (100-113,113) 3-Y-O+

£67,307 (£22,435; £11,217; £5,608; £3,365; £2,243)

RPR

1 **Warsaw (IRE)**[14] [236] 6-8-10 104 .... (b) KShea 11 105
(M F De Kock, South Africa) *settled in rr: rdn 2 1/2f out: r.o wl: led fnl 55yds* **14/1**

2 1/4 **Quick Wit**[98] [7187] 4-8-7 100 .... TedDurcan 1 101
(Saeed Bin Suroor) *wl away: trckd ldr: led 110yds out: hdd fnl 55yds* **6/4**[1]

3 1/2 **Hujaylea (IRE)**[7] [332] 8-8-9 102 .... (p) ShaneFoley 6 102
(M Halford, Ire) *settled in rr: r.o wl fnl 1 1/2f: nrst fin* **14/1**

4 3/4 **Iguazu Falls (USA)**[28] [73] 6-8-7 100 .... (t) XZiani 10 98
(M bin Shafya, UAE) *sn led: rdn 2 1/2f out: hdd 110yds out* **33/1**

5 1 1/4 **Munaddam (USA)**[7] [332] 9-8-10 104 .... RichardHills 5 97
(E Charpy, UAE) *mid-div: r.o wl fnl 2f: nvr nrr* **25/1**

6 1/2 **Mabait**[21] [156] 5-9-6 113 .... KierenFallon 8 106
(Luca Cumani) *nvr bttr than mid-div* **9/1**[3]

7 1/2 **Ferneley (IRE)**[190] 7-9-3 110 .... (t) RyanMoore 2 102
(B Cecil, U.S.A) *nvr able to chal* **12/1**

8 1/4 **Colonial (IRE)**[21] [156] 4-9-2 109 .... FrankieDettori 3 100
(Saeed Bin Suroor) *trckd ldng pair: rdn 2 1/2f out: one pce fnl f* **4/1**[2]

9 1 1/2 **Yaa Wayl (IRE)**[124] [6570] 4-9-5 112 .... (p) MickaelBarzalona 7 99
(Saeed Bin Suroor) *nvr bttr than mid-div* **16/1**

10 2 1/2 **Prince Shaun (IRE)**[14] [236] 6-8-8 101 .... (t) TadhgO'Shea 12 81
(Doug Watson, UAE) *in rr of mid-div: n.d* **33/1**

11 3/4 **Solid Choice (AUS)**[14] [236] 5-8-11 105 .... ChristopheSoumillon 4 82
(M F De Kock, South Africa) *slowly away: in rr of mid-div: nvr able to chal* **4/1**[2]

1m 24.1s (84.10) **11** Ran SP% **126.6**
CSF: £37.59..
Owner Mohd Khaleel Ahmed **Bred** Redpender Stud Ltd **Trained** South Africa

FOCUS
This looked a decent handicap beforehand, but it went to one of the exposed runners. The outsider Iguazu Falls set a pace that suited all running styles just about equally.

NOTEBOOK
Warsaw(IRE) finished fifth behind stablemate Solid Choice (failed to beat a rival here) on the Tapeta two weeks earlier, but he didn't mind the return to turf and produced a peak effort on his third start after a layoff. He can be opposed with confidence off a higher mark next time.
Quick Wit, up 6lb for his latest British success, was always handily placed, but he took an age to get past Iguazu Falls, and after finally getting to the front inside the final furlong, he was passed almost immediately by the winner. There was no real excuse, but he looks the type to remain progressive. (op 7-4)
Hujaylea(IRE) was suited by the quick gallop and stayed on well. He didn't get the best of runs through, but his jockey never really had to stop riding.
Iguazu Falls(USA) had the benefit of the favoured rail and briefly looked like causing an upset - he was matched at 2-1 in running.
Munaddam(USA) kept on when switched out wide but wasn't good enough.
Mabait was one-paced after racing keenly, but this was still a smart effort off a mark of 113.
Colonial(IRE) was expected to be suited by the return to turf after his fourth-placed finish in the first round of the Al Maktoum Challenge, but he disappointed. (op 5-1)
Solid Choice(AUS) had come from last to first off a slow pace in a Tapeta handicap here two weeks earlier. Similar tactics were tried, but he failed to pick up and was a beaten horse when badly squeezed out between rivals late on, which exaggerated the margin of defeat.

416a AL MAKTOUM CHALLENGE R2 SPONSORED BY ETISALAT (GROUP 3) (TAPETA) 1m 1f 110y

6:10 (6:10) 3-Y-O+

£76,923 (£25,641; £12,820; £6,410; £3,846; £2,564)

RPR

1 **Bold Silvano (SAF)**[187] 5-9-0 120 .... ChristopheSoumillon 1 119+
(M F De Kock, South Africa) *s.i.s: sn led: hdd 4 1/2f out: led again 2 1/2f out: r.o wl: easily* **7/4**[1]

2 1 1/2 **Spring Of Fame (USA)**[14] [240] 5-9-0 110 .... FrankieDettori 2 111
(Saeed Bin Suroor) *trckd ldr: led 4 1/2f out: hdd 2 1/2f out: r.o wl but no ch w wnr* **13/2**

3 1 1/2 **Interaction (ARG)**[155] [5674] 5-9-0 112 .... Christophe-PatriceLemaire 6 108
(P Bary, France) *settled in rr: r.o wl fnl 2f* **20/1**

4 nse **Al Shemali**[263] [2154] 7-9-0 119 .... (t) RoystonFfrench 3 108
(A Al Raihe, UAE) *trckd ldng pair: ev ch 3f out: r.o same pce* **9/2**[3]

5 1 1/4 **Gitano Hernando**[110] [6925] 5-9-0 118 .... WCMarwing 7 105
(Marco Botti) *settled in last: chsd ldrs 3 out: nt qckn fnl 1 1/2f* **11/4**[2]

6 1 1/2 **My Indy (ARG)**[21] [156] 7-9-0 113 .... (t) PatCosgrave 4 102
(M bin Shafya, UAE) *trckd ldng pair tl 2f out: wknd* **33/1**

7 2 3/4 **Crowded House**[123] [6605] 5-9-0 115 .... (bt) RyanMoore 5 97
(B Cecil, U.S.A) *a in mid-div* **7/1**

8 6 1/2 **Trois Rois (FR)**[7] [330] 6-9-0 110 .... (b) TedDurcan 8 83
(I Mohammed, UAE) *trckd ldng pair: wknd fnl 1 1/2f* **33/1**

9 1 1/4 **Silverside (USA)**[116] 5-9-0 113 .... JulienGrosjean 9 81
(M Delcher-Sanchez, Spain) *settled in rr: nvr able to chal* **25/1**

1m 57.71s (-0.99) **Going Correction** +0.25s/f (Slow) **9** Ran SP% **121.5**
Speed ratings: **113,111,110,110,109 108,106,100,99**
CSF: £14.18.
Owner Sh Mohd Bin Khalifa Al Maktoum & Mrs Thompson **Bred** Ascot Stud Pty Ltd **Trained** South Africa

FOCUS
In 2003 Moon Ballad won this before taking the Dubai World Cup, and last year Allybar was successful en-route to an agonisingly close third in the world's richest race. A few likely World Cup types lined up for this latest running, and it looked a strong edition, but the pace, dictated by the first two finishers, was steady and a few of those in behind were undoubtedly inconvenienced. Regardless, the visual impression created by the winner was stunning, and the runner-up gives the form some substance.

NOTEBOOK
Bold Silvano(SAF) ◆ only had to be nudged along by Christophe Soumillon to go clear early in the straight, and was then gradually eased off from fully a furlong out, with his rider showboating for the final 50 yards or so. He was value for at least treble the winning margin, and although edging right late on, both horse and rider had lost concentration by that point. He was last seen winning the most prestigious race in South Africa, the Grade 1 Durban July in which he defeated the likes of Irish Flame and River Jetez, both of whom have run well in Group company at this year's Carnival, and his official rating of 120 was the highest any of these could boast. However, few could have expected him to win in such style, especially as he was only around "85% ready" according to Mike De Kock. He clearly relished the Tapeta surface, though, and while the World Cup will be a greater test, it could take a special performance to deny him. (op 15-8)
Spring Of Fame(USA), who was 3-4 on synthetics prior to this (looked unlucky for sole defeat), enjoyed an almost identical trip to the way he won a C&D handicap off 107 two weeks earlier. Yet he was no match at all for Bold Silvano.
Interaction(ARG) ◆, the champion 3-y-o male, grass horse and stayer of 2010 in Argentina, fared best of those held up. His effort is all the more noteworthy considering he had little room against the inside rail halfway up the straight. He should do better off over further and off a stronger pace, and maybe his connections will be tempted to switch him back to turf for the Sheema Classic, perhaps via the City of Gold.
Al Shemali, last year's Duty Free winner, lost his place when outpaced on the final bend, before running on quite well. He should come on for this and can do better off a stronger pace, although it remains to be seen whether he'll still be geared towards the World Cup. (op 4-1)
Gitano Hernando was held up in last place off the slow gallop and then made his challenge widest of all on the final bend. He will be worth another chance. (op 3-1)
Crowded House was runner-up in this last year but, now with US connections, he offered little.

417a ETISALAT WASEL (H'CAP) (TURF) 1m 2f

6:45 (6:45) (100-110,110) 3-Y-O+

£67,307 (£22,435; £11,217; £5,608; £3,365; £2,243)

RPR

1 **Lolamar (ITY)**[117] [6763] 4-8-8 100 .... MickaelBarzalona 12 100
(Marco Botti) *mid-div: led 1 1/2f out: r.o wl: jst hld on* **20/1**

2 *shd* **Shimmering Moment (USA)**[14] [242] 4-8-13 105.......... OlivierPeslier 8 105+
(James J Hartnett, Ire) *mid-div: r.o wl fnl 2f: jst failed* **25/1**
3 *1/4* **Senate**[89] [7350] 4-8-9 101.......... TedDurcan 13 101
(Saeed Bin Suroor) *mid-div: r.o wl fnl 1 1/2f* **16/1**
4 *3/4* **Hunting Tower (SAF)**[14] [242] 9-9-0 105..........(t) KShea 3 103
(M F De Kock, South Africa) *trckd ldr: ev ch 1 1/2f out: one pce fnl 110yds* **16/1**
5 *1 1/2* **Kidnapped (AUS)**[74] 5-9-4 109..........(v) FrankieDettori 6 104
(Saeed Bin Suroor) *in rr of mid-div: r.o wl fnl 2f* **7/1**[2]
6 *hd* **Haatheq (USA)**[14] [240] 4-8-13 105.......... RichardHills 14 100
(A Al Raihe, UAE) *trckd ldr: nt qckng fnl 1 1/2f but r.o wl* **8/1**[3]
7 *hd* **Absolute Heretic (AUS)**[277] 5-8-9 100.......... JamieSpencer 4 94
(M F De Kock, South Africa) *s.i.s: settled in rr: rdn 2 1/2f out: r.o wl: nrst fin* **16/1**
8 *shd* **Here To Win (BRZ)**[14] [239] 5-9-1 106.......... ChristopheSoumillon 9 100
(M F De Kock, South Africa) *mid-div: chsd ldrs 2 1/2f out: one pce fnl f* **11/10**[1]
9 *1* **Eddie Jock (IRE)**[20] 7-8-9 100..........(t) RichardMullen 7 92
(S Seemar, UAE) *nvr bttr than mid-div* **33/1**
10 *hd* **Florentino (JPN)**[14] [239] 5-9-3 108.......... AhmedAjtebi 10 100
(Mahmood Al Zarooni) *nvr bttr than mid-div* **20/1**
11 *1/2* **Azmeel**[14] [242] 4-9-3 109.......... RyanMoore 2 100
(John Gosden) *in rr of mid-div: nvr able to chal* **12/1**
12 *3/4* **Hot Six (BRZ)**[21] [157] 6-9-0 105.......... BReis 1 94
(E Martins, Brazil) *in rr of mid-div: n.d* **8/1**[3]
13 *3 1/4* **Gallahad (BRZ)**[14] [240] 5-8-9 100.......... Christophe-PatriceLemaire 5 83
(A De Royer-Dupre, France) *sn led: hdd & wknd 1 1/2f out* **20/1**
14 *dist* **Fencing Master**[21] [156] 4-9-4 110..........(bt) KierenFallon 11 —
(H J Brown, South Africa) *mid-div: nvr able to chal* **16/1**

2m 3.54s (123.54)
WFA 4 from 5yo+ 1lb **14** Ran SP% **134.6**
CSF: £469.66; Tricast: £7,979.49. Placepot: £375.00 to a £1 stake. Pool: £7,141.33. - 13.90 winning tickets. Quadpot: £14.80 to a £1 stake. Pool: £528.00 - 26.40 winning tickets..
Owner Scuderia Siba-Antezzate SRL **Bred** Az Ag Antezzate Srl **Trained** Newmarket, Suffolk

FOCUS
The pace was just ordinary and those held up well off the speed had little chance. There was a bunch finish and this is not strong handicap form.

NOTEBOOK
Lolamar(ITY), a triple winner when trained in Italy, narrowly made a successful debut for Marco Botti after a break of 117 days. Already Group 3 placed in Europe, it wouldn't surprise to see her aimed at the Group 2 Balanchine on February 18, but that will demand more.
Shimmering Moment(USA) was beaten a long way over C&D two weeks earlier, but clearly this was a huge improvement, and she just failed to get up.
Senate shaped nicely on his debut for Godolphin and should do better. (op 14/1)
Hunting Tower(SAF) ran with credit but wasn't quite good enough.
Kidnapped(AUS) fared best of those held up, and this looked a promising Dubai debut, but he was reported to have bled from the nose.
Absolute Heretic(AUS) ◆ was another to keep on well from an unpromising position and might be one to be with next time. (op 14/1)
Here To Win(BRZ) disappointed, even allowing for the steady pace perhaps not suiting. She had shaped nicely over 1m here two weeks earlier and better was expected. (op 11/8)
Fencing Master was reported to have bled from the nose.

387 LINGFIELD (L-H)
Friday, February 4

OFFICIAL GOING: Standard
Wind: Very strong, mostly behind Weather: Overcast

418 BET ON WINNING DISTANCES AT BLUESQ.COM AMATEUR RIDERS' H'CAP — 1m 4f (P)
1:20 (1:20) (Class 5) (0-70,71) 4-Y-0+ **£2,043** (£628; £314) **Stalls** Low

Form RPR
0-43 **1** **Squad**[16] [223] 5-10-6 65..........(v) MrJCoffill-Brown[illegible] 1 73
(Simon Dow) *hld up in rr: prog fr 4f out: chsd ldrs 2f out: rdn to ld 1f out: styd on* **6/1**
-161 **2** *1/2* **Edgeworth (IRE)**[14] [247] 5-10-6 65..........(p) BrendanPowell(7) 3 72
(Brendan Powell) *t.k.h: hld up in rr: prog over 4f out: wnt 3rd over 2f out: brought to chal jst over 1f out: kpt on same pce* **5/1**[2]
43-0 **3** *nk* **Sir Boss (IRE)**[33] [8] 6-10-8 63.......... MissMMullineaux(3) 13 70
(Michael Mullineaux) *racd wd: hld up in tch: prog 3f out: hrd rdn to cl on ldrs 1f out: styd on: nvr quite able to chal* **11/2**[3]
54-0 **4** *1* **Relative Strength (IRE)**[21] [162] 6-11-0 66..........(v) MrMarioBaratti 11 71
(Michael Wigham) *hld up in rr: looking for room 3f out: prog over 2f out: clsd on ldrs on inner 1f out: nt qckn last 150yds* **14/1**
01-4 **5** *1 1/2* **Taste The Wine (IRE)**[21] [172] 5-10-6 63.......... MrRJWilliams(5) 5 66
(Bernard Llewellyn) *trckd ldrs: prog to go 2nd over 4f out: led over 3f out and kicked on: hdd & wknd 1f out* **10/1**
5-20 **6** *5* **My Mate Mal**[14] [252] 7-10-3 62.......... MissCScott(7) 8 57
(William Stone) *led at stdy pce to over 3f out: wknd over 1f out* **33/1**
3/0- **7** *3/4* **Tecktal (FR)**[28] [5536] 8-9-7 52 oh5.......... MissLWilliams(7) 14 46
(Pat Phelan) *stdd s: hld up in rr and racd wd: effrt 3f out: no prog and btn 2f out* **33/1**
300- **8** *1/2* **Buddy Holly**[25] [7694] 6-10-6 65..........(p) MissLMcGuire(7) 9 58
(Violet M Jordan) *rrd s: t.k.h: shuffled bk fr midfield pl and last 5f out: stl there 3f out: styd on fnl 2f* **10/1**
43-4 **9** *2 3/4* **Irish Jugger (USA)**[17] [203] 4-9-12 58.......... MrPMillman(5) 2 47
(Rod Millman) *chsd ldr to 1/2-way: steadily wknd fr 3f out* **8/1**
15-1 **10** *2 3/4* **William's Way**[3] [373] 9-11-0 71 6ex..........(t) MrCMartin(5) 6 55
(Ian Wood) *hld up in rr: rdn and struggling over 4f out: wl btn fnl 3f* **4/1**[1]
-110 **11** *1/2* **Barodine**[14] [252] 8-10-6 63.......... MrPPrince(5) 4 46
(Ron Hodges) *in tch: dropped to rr and struggling 3f out: n.d after* **25/1**
066- **12** *1/2* **Farleigh**[76] [7529] 5-10-5 64.......... MrMMitchell(7) 7 47
(Alex Hales) *hld up in rr: pushed along and struggling over 3f out: sn btn* **66/1**
000- **13** *3* **Corlough Mountain**[60] [7728] 7-9-9 52 oh7..........(be1) MissMBryant(5) 12 30
(Paddy Butler) *t.k.h: prom: chsd ldr 1/2-way to over 4f out: wknd rapidly 2f out* **100/1**
000- **14** *2 1/4* **Set To Go**[79] [7490] 4-9-7 55.......... MrCVitler(7) 10 29
(Tor Sturgis) *prom: lost pl 5f out: sn wl in rr and btn* **66/1**

2m 36.28s (3.28) **Going Correction** +0.15s/f (Slow)
WFA 4 from 5yo+ 3lb **14** Ran SP% **116.0**
Speed ratings (Par 103): **95,94,94,93,92 89,88,88,86,84 84,84,82,80**
Tote Swingers: 1&2 £6.00, 1&3 £6.30, 2&3 £7.00 CSF £33.10 CT £175.40 TOTE £7.90: £2.30, £2.40, £2.50; EX 39.20 Trifecta £171.90 Pool: £376.46 - 1.62 winning units..
Owner Devine, Snell & Chua **Bred** Juddmonte Farms Ltd **Trained** Epsom, Surrey
■ Joe Coffill-Brown's first winner under rules.

FOCUS
They didn't go that quick early but the first three came from off the pace.

419 ASHDOWN FOREST (S) H'CAP — 2m (P)
1:50 (1:50) (Class 6) (0-60,60) 4-Y-0+ **£1,535** (£453; £226) **Stalls** Low

Form RPR
1/4- **1** **Wyeth**[70] [7570] 7-9-10 60..........(p) GeorgeBaker 2 63+
(Gary Moore) *hld up in last trio: prog on outer 3f out: shkn up and clsd to ld jst over 1f out: sn in command* **1/3**[1]
0-50 **2** *1 3/4* **Pinsplitter (USA)**[17] [203] 4-8-9 51..........(p) JamesDoyle 3 52
(Alan McCabe) *t.k.h: hld up in tch: effrt wl over 1f out: styd on to take 2nd ins fnl f: no imp on wnr* **12/1**
5/-3 **3** *hd* **Henry Holmes**[16] [216] 8-8-10 46.......... RichardThomas 8 47
(Lydia Richards) *plld hrd: hld up in tch: cl up whn n.m.r 2f out: effrt to dispute 2nd ins fnl f: kpt on* **14/1**
52-0 **4** *1 1/2* **Olivino (GER)**[21] [173] 10-8-10 46..........(p) DavidProbert 1 45
(Bernard Llewellyn) *trckd ldrs: prog on inner 2f out: led briefly over 1f out: sn outpcd* **10/1**[3]
60-0 **5** *1* **Primera Rossa**[16] [207] 5-8-10 46 oh1.......... LiamKeniry 5 44
(J S Moore) *pressed ldrs: led over 3f out: drvn over 2f out: hdd over 1f out: outpcd* **25/1**
40-5 **6** *shd* **Acropolis (IRE)**[16] [207] 10-8-10 46.......... RobertWinston 7 44+
(Tony Carroll) *hld up last: gng strly but stl only 7th 2f out: asked for effrt and hanging bdly over 1f out: no real prog* **8/1**[2]
440- **7** *5* **Baggsy (IRE)**[25] [7933] 4-8-4 46.......... NickyMackay 6 38
(Julia Feilden) *led at stdy pce for 6f: styd prom tl wknd 2f out* **20/1**
00/0 **8** *13* **Sovereign Spirit (IRE)**[12] [8] 9-8-11 47..........(tp) ChrisCatlin 4 23
(Chris Gordon) *t.k.h: hld up tl allowed to ld after 6f: hdd over 3f out: wknd qckly* **33/1**

3m 33.41s (7.71) **Going Correction** +0.15s/f (Slow)
WFA 4 from 5yo+ 6lb **8** Ran SP% **121.1**
Speed ratings (Par 101): **86,85,85,84,83 83,81,74**
Tote Swingers: 1&2 £2.40, 1&3 £2.80, 2&3 £8.40 CSF £6.33 CT £31.40 TOTE £1.30: £1.02, £2.60, £3.00; EX 7.20 Trifecta £65.50 Pool: £675.36 - 7.62 winning units..There was no bid for the winner.
Owner D R Hunnisett **Bred** Lael Stables **Trained** Lower Beeding, W Sussex

FOCUS
A poor seller run at a steady early pace.
Pinsplitter(USA) Official explanation: jockey said gelding hung both ways
Henry Holmes Official explanation: jockey said gelding hung left
Acropolis(IRE) Official explanation: jockey said gelding hung badly left

420 BLUESQ.COM ON YOUR IPHONE MAIDEN STKS — 1m 2f (P)
2:20 (2:24) (Class 5) 3-Y-0+ **£2,115** (£624; £312) **Stalls** Low

Form RPR
P- **1** **Moonlight Rhapsody (IRE)**[132] [6353] 3-8-0 0.......... FrannyNorton 7 64+
(B W Hills) *mostly trckd ldr: led over 1f out: pushed out: comf* **7/2**[3]
0 **2** *3 1/2* **Fleeting Storm**[27] [95] 3-8-0 0.......... NickyMackay 2 57+
(Hughie Morrison) *hld up disputing 4th: rdn wl over 2f out and outpcd: edgd rt fr over 1f out but styd on wl to take 2nd last strides* **5/2**[2]
40- **3** *nk* **Cecile De Volanges**[37] [8000] 3-8-0 0.......... DavidProbert 3 56
(Tor Sturgis) *difficult to load: disp 2nd pl to 3f out: sn rdn: styd on to chse wnr ins fnl f but no ch: lost 2nd last strides* **6/1**
0-2 **4** *1/2* **Baileys Agincourt**[8] [319] 3-8-5 0.......... JoeFanning 1 60
(Mark Johnston) *led at reasonable pce: drvn over 2f out: hdd and outpcd over 1f out: lost 2 pls ins fnl f* **13/8**[1]
5 *2* **Fifth Estate** 3-8-5 0.......... FrankieMcDonald 6 56
(Jamie Osborne) *dwlt: in tch disputing 4th: rdn and outpcd over 2f out: no imp after* **16/1**
6 *hd* **Roe Valley (IRE)**[16] 4-9-12 0.......... RobertWinston 4 60?
(Linda Jewell) *dwlt: hld up in 6th and in tch: effrt over 2f out: racd [illegible]* **50/1**
7 *54* **Forest** 4-9-12 0.......... RichardThomas 5
(Lydia Richards) *dwlt: sn wl bhd: t.o bef 1/2-way and lost further grnd after* **33/1**

2m 9.78s (3.18) **Going Correction** +0.15s/f (Slow)
WFA 3 from 4yo 22lb **7** Ran SP% **114.0**
Speed ratings (Par 103): **93,90,89,89,87 87,44**
Tote Swingers: 1&2 £2.40, 1&3 £3.10, 2&3 £3.30 CSF £12.61 TOTE £4.90: £2.40, £2.00; EX 13.90 Trifecta £55.90 Pool: £651.69 - 8.62 winning units..
Owner C Wright, P C Barnett & D Nagle **Bred** Barronstown Stud **Trained** Lambourn, Berks

FOCUS
Not too many could be given a chance in this maiden.
Forest Official explanation: jockey said gelding ran green

421 MARRIOTT HOTEL AT LINGFIELD PARK H'CAP — 6f (P)
2:50 (2:52) (Class 6) (0-52,57) 4-Y-0+ **£1,535** (£453; £226) **Stalls** Low

Form RPR
42-4 **1** **Chantilly Jewel (USA)**[15] [224] 6-9-1 50..........(b) JimCrowley 12 59
(Robert Cowell) *trckd ldr: asked to chal over 1f out: hung fire briefly but drvn ahd jst ins fnl f: styd on* **14/1**
4221 **2** *1 1/2* **Black Baccara**[7] [337] 4-9-3 57 6ex..........(be) JulieBurke(5) 4 61
(Phil McEntee) *racd quite keenly: led: drvn over 1f out: hdd and one pce jst ins fnl f* **11/4**[1]
040- **3** *1* **Bubbly Bellini (IRE)**[51] [7882] 4-9-0 52..........(p) MatthewDavies(3) 1 53
(Adrian McGuinness, Ire) *trckd ldrs in 5th: prog on inner to go 3rd over 1f out: hanging lft and styd against rail: nt qckn* **9/1**
02-6 **4** *1 1/4* **Grand Honour (IRE)**[16] [211] 5-9-2 51.......... GeorgeBaker 2 48
(Jim Boyle) *trckd ldng pair: rdn and nt qckn wl over 1f out: one pce after* **9/2**[2]
0625 **5** *1/2* **Memphis Man**[4] [363] 8-8-7 49.......... MatthewCosham(7) 3 44
(David Evans) *taken down early: chsd ldng trio to jst over 2f out: outpcd: styd on again fnl f* **15/2**[3]
06-0 **6** *2 1/2* **Raimond Ridge (IRE)**[21] [165] 5-9-3 52..........(v) PatrickMathers 9 39+
(Derek Shaw) *slowest away: t.k.h early and hld up last: wl off the pce 1/2-way: drvn and styd on fr over 1f out: no ch* **11/1**
-01 **7** *2 3/4* **Rightcar**[14] [256] 4-9-0 49.......... RobbieFitzpatrick 7 28
(Peter Grayson) *nvr bttr than midfield: rdn bef 1/2-way and nt on terms no prog* **25/1**
3-35 **8** *nk* **Force To Spend**[14] [250] 4-9-0 49.......... KellyHarrison 6 27
(Nick Littmoden) *t.k.h: hld up in rr: off the pce bef 1/2-way: no real prog* **8/1**

-540 **9** 2 3/4 **My Best Man**[8] 312 5-8-12 **47**.................... RobertWinston 11 16
(Tony Carroll) *t.k.h: hld up in rr: off the pce by 1/2-way: no prog on outer 2f out* **10/1**

00-0 **10** 1 **Only A Game (IRE)**[21] 167 6-9-0 **52**....................(t[1]) GaryBartley(3) 5 18
(Ian McInnes) *stdd s: hld up in rr: off the pce by 1/2-way: no prog* **33/1**

0-66 **11** 4 1/2 **Vertumnus**[14] 256 4-8-11 **46** oh1....................(be) JoeFanning 8 —
(Nick Littmoden) *plld hrd: hld up in rr: off the pce by 1/2-way: no prog 2f out: wknd* **14/1**

/0-3 **12** 2 1/2 **Seeking Rio**[14] 256 4-8-11 **46** oh1.................... ChrisCatlin 10 —
(Ron Hodges) *racd wd: hld up in rr: off the pce by 1/2-way: no prog 2f out: wknd* **33/1**

1m 11.47s (-0.43) **Going Correction** +0.15s/f (Slow) **12** Ran SP% **118.2**
Speed ratings (Par 101): **108,106,104,103,102 99,95,94,91,89 83,80**
Tote Swingers: 1&2 £8.00, 1&3 £21.50, 2&3 £7.40 CSF £51.37 CT £380.39 TOTE £15.40: £4.40, £1.10, £3.50; EX 58.60 Trifecta £114.80 Pool: £588.35 - 3.79 winning units..
Owner Bottisham Heath Stud **Bred** Two Sisters Stable **Trained** Six Mile Bottom, Cambs

FOCUS
A competitive sprint handicap on paper but the early pace wasn't that great and the first two were in those positions throughout.
Vertumnus Official explanation: jockey said gelding ran too keen

422 SIS LIVE H'CAP 6f (P)
3:25 (3:25) (Class 6) (0-65,64) 3-Y-O **£1,535** (£453; £226) **Stalls** Low

Form RPR

03-0 **1** **Loves Theme (IRE)**[7] 335 3-9-3 **60**....................(b[1]) J-PGuillambert 5 70
(Alan Bailey) *mde virtually all: drew clr over 2f out: styd on wl* **6/1**[3]

10-5 **2** 4 1/2 **Albany Rose (IRE)**[27] 100 3-9-6 **63**.................... SteveDrowne 4 59
(Rae Guest) *chsd ldng pair: rdn over 2f out: hanging sltly but tk 2nd over 1f out: styd on but no ch w wnr* **11/1**

20-6 **3** 4 **Luckbealadytonight (IRE)**[20] 179 3-8-13 **56**.................... JoeFanning 2 39
(Mark Johnston) *w wnr to wl over 2f out: sn fighting losing battle: nt qckn and lost 2nd over 1f out: wknd and jst hld on for 3rd* **5/6**[1]

56-5 **4** 3/4 **Reachtothestars (USA)**[22] 140 3-9-6 **63**....................(t) AdamKirby 7 43
(Noel Quinlan) *hld up in last trio on outer: rdn over 2f out: fnd little and no prog* **11/2**[2]

500- **5** 2 **Two Feet Of Snow (IRE)**[112] 6891 3-9-5 **62**.................... DaneO'Neill 6 36
(Ian McInnes) *dwlt: hld up in last trio: pushed along 1/2-way: no prog after* **20/1**

-242 **6** nk **Close To The Edge (IRE)**[19] 182 3-9-7 **64**............(p) RobertWinston 3 37
(Alan McCabe) *hld up in last trio on inner: pushed along 1/2-way: no rspnse and wl btn fnl 2f* **11/2**[2]

1m 11.38s (-0.52) **Going Correction** +0.15s/f (Slow) **6** Ran SP% **112.7**
Speed ratings (Par 95): **109,103,97,96,94 93**
Tote Swingers: 1&2 £4.20, 1&3 £2.60, 2&3 £2.40 CSF £63.45 TOTE £9.30: £2.80, £3.80; EX 52.30.
Owner Raymond Gomersall **Bred** Deer Forest Stud **Trained** Newmarket, Suffolk

FOCUS
An ordinary handicap.

423 DORMANS PARK CLAIMING STKS 7f (P)
4:00 (4:00) (Class 6) 3-Y-O **£1,535** (£453; £226) **Stalls** Low

Form RPR

1-01 **1** **May's Boy**[11] 275 3-9-1 71....................(p) DaneO'Neill 1 78+
(Mark Usher) *covered up bhd ldng pair: effrt to chal over 1f out: w ldr fnl f: styd on wl to ld nr fin* **15/8**[1]

-511 **2** hd **Better Self**[12] 270 3-8-1 69.................... RPWalsh(7) 2 70
(David Evans) *stdd s: hld up last: quick move towards inner and narrowly ld over 1f out: hrd pressed after: styd on but hdd nr fin* **3/1**[3]

-432 **3** 3 1/2 **Captain Dimitrios**[4] 364 3-8-6 75....................(v) MatthewCosham(7) 4 66
(David Evans) *w ldr: hanging rt 2f out: nt qckn over 1f out and sn outpcd by ldng pair* **9/4**[2]

002- **4** 1 1/4 **Silly Billy (IRE)**[95] 7271 3-8-13 72.................... LiamKeniry 5 62
(Sylvester Kirk) *hld up in 4th: effrt and wd bnd 2f out: rdn and fnd nil over 1f out: wl btn fnl f* **8/1**

-015 **5** 13 **Imogen Louise (IRE)**[6] 349 3-8-6 69.................... RobbieFitzpatrick 3 33
(Paddy Butler) *led to over 1f out: wknd and eased: t.o* **18/1**

1m 25.19s (0.39) **Going Correction** +0.15s/f (Slow) **5** Ran SP% **106.9**
Speed ratings (Par 95): **103,102,98,97,82**
CSF £7.30 TOTE £2.90: £2.10, £1.10; EX 8.00.
Owner High Five Racing **Bred** John Richardson **Trained** Upper Lambourn, Berks

FOCUS
Not a bad claimer.
Captain Dimitrios Official explanation: jockey said gelding hung right throughout

424 PLAY RAINBOW RICHES AT BLUESQ.COM H'CAP 1m 2f (P)
4:35 (4:35) (Class 6) (0-65,65) 3-Y-O **£1,569** (£463; £231) **Stalls** Low

Form RPR

44-5 **1** **George Woolf**[13] 260 3-9-7 **65**.................... RobertWinston 3 68
(Alan McCabe) *hld up last: pushed along and prog on outer fr 3f out: rdn to ld jst ins fnl f: hld on* **2/1**[1]

-325 **2** hd **Mrs Neat (IRE)**[18] 194 3-9-0 **58**....................(p) JamesDoyle 1 61+
(Sylvester Kirk) *patiently rdn: cajoled along to improve fr over 1f out: brought to chal ins fnl f: nudged and hit over hd by rival's whip: nt qckn nr fin* **15/2**

2133 **3** 2 1/4 **Urban Kode (IRE)**[4] 365 3-8-12 **63**.................... MatthewCosham(7) 7 62
(David Evans) *cl up: wnt 2nd 4f out: led 3f out: drvn and hdd jst ins fnl f: nt qckn* **7/1**

0-56 **4** 1/2 **Revolutionary**[13] 262 3-9-2 **60**.................... FergusSweeney 6 58
(Jamie Osborne) *hld up in tch: jnd ldrs 3f out: drvn 2f out: nt qckn over 1f out: one pce after* **5/1**[3]

24-0 **5** 1 **Farmer's Wife**[21] 171 3-9-1 **59**.................... LiamKeniry 2 55
(Bernard Llewellyn) *cl up: trckd ldrs over 2f out: rdn and nt qckn over 1f out: fdd* **25/1**

045- **6** 6 **Lough Corrib (USA)**[137] 6240 3-8-10 **54**.................... JoeFanning 4 38
(Kevin Ryan) *taken down early: led to 3f out: wknd 2f out* **3/1**[2]

6540 **7** 5 **Polly Holder (IRE)**[13] 260 3-9-0 **58**....................(p) J-PGuillambert 5 32
(Alan Bailey) *chsd ldr to 4f out: wknd 3f out: sn bhd* **11/1**

2m 9.43s (2.83) **Going Correction** +0.15s/f (Slow) **7** Ran SP% **111.4**
Speed ratings (Par 95): **94,93,92,91,90 86,82**
Tote Swingers: 1&2 £3.50, 1&3 £3.40, 2&3 £2.70 CSF £16.70 TOTE £2.20: £1.60, £2.10; EX 19.90.
Owner Triple A Partnership **Bred** Wyck Hall Stud Ltd **Trained** Averham Park, Notts

FOCUS
The first two came close in the latter stages of this handicap, and there was an inquiry, but the first past the post kept the race.
T/Plt: £288.90 to a £1 stake. Pool:£60,616.03 - 153,15 winning tickets T/Qpdt: £177.70 to a £1 stake. Pool:£4,515.54 - 18.80 winning tickets JN

403 WOLVERHAMPTON (A.W) (L-H)
Friday, February 4

OFFICIAL GOING: Standard
Wind: Fresh, behind Weather: Overcast, rain race 6

425 BET ON WINNING DISTANCES AT BLUESQ.COM APPRENTICE H'CAP 1m 1f 103y(P)
5:00 (5:02) (Class 6) (0-65,63) 4-Y-O+ **£1,535** (£453; £226) **Stalls** Low

Form RPR

123- **1** **Cyril The Squirrel**[38] 7995 7-9-2 **63**.................... LewisWalsh(5) 5 71
(Karen George) *hld up towards rr early: hdwy on outer 6f out: rdn over 3f out: led 1f out: pushed out* **2/1**[1]

4-5 **2** 1 **Kammamuri (IRE)**[14] 247 6-9-3 **62**....................(b[1]) JakePayne(3) 7 68
(Michael Wigham) *disp ld tl 1f out: nt qckn* **12/1**

0/-5 **3** 1/2 **Bricks And Porter (IRE)**[2] 387 11-8-3 **52**............(bt) RossCoakley(7) 1 57
(Adrian McGuinness, Ire) *disp ld tl 1f out: one pce* **4/1**[2]

1-14 **4** nk **Lord Lansing (IRE)**[14] 247 4-9-2 **63**.................... DavidSimmonson(5) 6 67
(Mrs K Burke) *stdd s: hld up in rr: hdwy on outer 3f out: drvn to chal over 1f out: 4th and hld whn rdr dropped whip 100yds out* **4/1**[2]

30-3 **5** 1 1/2 **Catching Zeds**[17] 200 4-9-1 **60**.................... GeorgeChaloner(3) 3 61
(Ian Williams) *chsd ldrs tl hrd rdn and no ex over 1f out* **5/1**[3]

0-00 **6** 3 3/4 **King Of Connacht**[9] 299 8-8-8 **55**....................(v) IanBurns(5) 8 48
(Mark Wellings) *bolted loose bef s: detached last tl modest effrt 3f out: sn rdn along and nvr able to chal* **33/1**

-005 **7** 1/2 **All Moving Parts (USA)**[10] 292 4-8-8 **55**....................(b) HobieGill(5) 2 47
(Alan McCabe) *rdn leaving stalls then t.k.h: sn chsng ldrs: wknd 3f out* **12/1**

5-6 **8** 31 **Sligo All Star**[1] 408 6-8-7 **49** oh4.................... LucyKBarry 4 —
(Thomas McLaughlin, Ire) *chsd ldrs: wknd qckly over 4f out: sn bhd* **14/1**

2m 3.16s (1.46) **Going Correction** +0.175s/f (Slow) **8** Ran SP% **115.0**
Speed ratings (Par 101): **100,99,98,98,97 93,93,65**
Tote Swingers: 1&2 £4.30, 1&3 £2.70, 2&3 £5.80 CSF £28.49 CT £89.05 TOTE £3.20: £1.90, £2.30, £2.60; EX 22.50.
Owner R E Baskerville **Bred** R E Baskerville **Trained** Higher Eastington, Devon

FOCUS
An ordinary handicap in which the gallop was only fair and the winner raced centre-to-far side in the straight.

426 RINGSIDE CONFERENCE SUITE - 700 THEATRE STYLE H'CAP 7f 32y(P)
5:30 (5:30) (Class 6) (0-60,59) 3-Y-O **£1,535** (£453; £226) **Stalls** High

Form RPR

-033 **1** **Granny Anne (IRE)**[19] 187 3-9-5 **57**.................... CathyGannon 6 63
(Alan Bailey) *hld up in rr: rdn and hdwy whn nt clr run 2f out: bmpd and slt ld 1f out: jnd ins fnl f: jst prevailed* **9/2**[2]

-352 **2** nk **Titan Diamond (IRE)**[11] 281 3-8-1 **46**.................... RachealKneller(7) 5 51
(Mark Usher) *trckd ldrs: no room and shuffled bk over 1f out: rallied and squeezed through to dispute ld ins fnl f: jst pipped* **12/1**

2-64 **3** 3 3/4 **William Wainwright (IRE)**[11] 281 3-9-0 **52**................(p) TomQueally 9 47
(Ann Duffield) *sn prom: edgd rt and slt ld over 1f out: sn hdd and no ex* **16/1**

4-64 **4** nk **Lovat Lane**[15] 227 3-8-11 **49**....................(p) EddieAhern 3 43
(Eve Johnson Houghton) *in tch: effrt on outer over 2f out: drvn to chal over 1f out: one pce* **8/1**[3]

00-1 **5** nk **Princess Gail**[11] 281 3-9-1 **53** 6ex.................... ShaneKelly 1 46
(Mark Brisbourne) *hld up in rr: rdn and sme hdwy over 1f out: sn btn* **8/11**[1]

630- **6** 3/4 **Cinq Heavens (IRE)**[177] 4967 3-9-7 **59**.................... RichardKingscote 8 50
(Tom Dascombe) *led after 1f tl wknd over 1f out* **14/1**

-000 **7** 6 **Zohan (IRE)**[7] 338 3-8-7 **45**....................(b) KirstyMilczarek 4 20
(Peter Grayson) *led 1f: pressed ldr tl wknd 2f out* **100/1**

-555 **8** 32 **Lynchpin**[15] 227 3-9-4 **56**....................(p) LukeMorris 2 —
(Ronald Harris) *chsd ldrs: drvn along over 5f out: sn struggling: bhd and virtually p.u fnl 4f* **12/1**

1m 32.37s (2.77) **Going Correction** +0.175s/f (Slow) **8** Ran SP% **116.1**
Speed ratings (Par 95): **91,90,86,86,85 84,77,41**
Tote Swingers: 1&2 £3.40, 1&3 £12.30, 2&3 £15.20 CSF £56.73 CT £794.05 TOTE £3.00: £1.10, £2.80, £5.40; EX 47.90.
Owner H Herne **Bred** Mrs J A Dene **Trained** Newmarket, Suffolk
■ Stewards' Enquiry : Racheal Kneller three-day ban: careless riding (Feb 18-20)

FOCUS
A moderate handicap but one in which the market leader disappointed. The gallop was an ordinary one and the first two, who finished clear, came down the centre.
Princess Gail Official explanation: jockey said filly ran flat
Lynchpin Official explanation: jockey said colt hung left

427 SPONSOR A RACE BY CALLING 01902 390000 CLAIMING STKS 1m 1f 103y(P)
6:00 (6:01) (Class 5) 4-Y-O+ **£1,813** (£539; £269; £134) **Stalls** Low

Form RPR

12-1 **1** **Majuro (IRE)**[16] 205 7-9-3 85.................... AndreaAtzeni 10 88+
(Michael Wigham) *led after 1f and sn had field stretched out: shkn up and wnt 4 l clr 2f out: a in control: comf* **7/4**[1]

4222 **2** 6 **Dream Of Fortune (IRE)**[6] 352 7-9-1 67....................(bt) TomQueally 5 73+
(David Evans) *hld up and bhd: promising hdwy on outer 2f out: drvn to take 5 l 2nd over 1f out: no ch w wnr* **7/1**

41-1 **3** 2 3/4 **Faithful Ruler (USA)**[20] 175 7-9-3 78....................(p) LukeMorris 11 69
(Ronald Harris) *chsd wnr after 2f tl over 1f out: no ex* **7/2**[2]

/1-0 **4** 3 1/2 **John Veale (USA)**[2] 381 5-9-3 72....................(t) EddieAhern 6 62
(Thomas McLaughlin, Ire) *towards rr: sme hdwy 3f out: sn hrd rdn and nt pce to chal* **4/1**[3]

03-3 **5** 2 1/4 **Una Pelota (IRE)**[17] 203 5-8-11 59....................(t) RichardKingscote 4 51
(Tom Dascombe) *fair 4th tl rdn and outpcd fnl 3f* **16/1**

60-6 **6** 3/4 **Watchmaker**[17] 203 8-8-12 54....................(p) SamHitchcott 3 51
(Tor Sturgis) *led 1f: chsd ldng pair tl rdn and wknd over 2f out* **33/1**

000- **7** 1 3/4 **Sand Tiger (IRE)**[209] 3901 5-9-5 80.................... BarryMcHugh 7 54
(Richard Fahey) *mid-div: drvn along and nt trble ldrs fnl 3f* **14/1**

336- **8** 8 **Plush**[194] 4403 8-8-13 78....................(t) RussKennemore 9 31
(Shaun Lycett) *s.s: bhd: modest hdwy 4f out: wknd 3f out* **9/1**

510- **9** 27 **Novay Essjay (IRE)**[228] 3276 4-9-2 68.................... VinceSlattery 2 —
(Alan Juckes) *mid-div: rdn and struggling 4f out: sn wl bhd* **66/1**

The Form Book, Raceform Ltd, Compton, RG20 6NL

00- **10** *2 ¾* **Upset**[142] 6093 4-8-10 0....................(t) CathyGannon 8 —
(Richard Ford) *sn wl bhd: pushed along 5f out: hrd rdn and no ch 3f out* **100/1**

2m 0.78s (-0.92) **Going Correction** +0.175s/f (Slow) **10** Ran SP% **119.1**
Speed ratings (Par 103): **111,105,103,100,98 97,95,88,64,62**
Tote Swingers: 1&2 £3.50, 1&3 £2.60, 2&3 £3.30 CSF £15.30 TOTE £4.00: £1.90, £2.50, £1.70; EX 18.20.Majuro was subject to a friendly claim.
Owner S Pecoraro **Bred** Tally-Ho Stud **Trained** Newmarket, Suffolk

FOCUS
A fair claimer and one run at a reasonable gallop. The winner raced towards the inside rail throughout.
Upset Official explanation: trainer said gelding had a breathing problem

428 STAY AT THE WOLVERHAMPTON HOLIDAY INN H'CAP 1m 141y(P)
6:30 (6:30) (Class 5) (0-70,71) 4-Y-0+ **£1,878** (£558; £279; £139) **Stalls** Low

Form RPR
30-1 **1** **Resuscitator (USA)**[14] 248 4-9-7 **66**....................(v) EddieAhern 10 80
(Heather Main) *broke wl: prom: hrd rdn 2f out: led ins fnl f: drvn out* **11/2**
4-2 **2** *1 ¾* **Mount Hollow**[21] 169 6-9-2 **61**....................(p) LukeMorris 2 71
(Reg Hollinshead) *trckd ldrs gng wl: led 2f out: hrd rdn and hdd ins fnl f: kpt on* **7/2**[2]
54-0 **3** *4 ½* **Just Timmy Marcus**[11] 287 5-9-5 **64**....................(b) JackMitchell 3 64
(Brian Baugh) *dwlt: towards rr: n.m.r 4f out: promising hdwy over 2f out: hrd rdn over 1f out: one pce* **15/2**
-014 **4** *1 ¼* **Justcallmehandsome**[21] 169 9-9-7 **66**....................(be) GeorgeBaker 9 63
(Dominic Ffrench Davis) *towards rr: rdn and sme hdwy 2f out: nvr able to chal* **4/1**[3]
30-3 **5** *3 ½* **Serious Drinking (USA)**[14] 248 5-9-4 **63**....................(e[1]) StephenCraine 5 52+
(Walter Swinburn) *rrd bdly s and missed break: bhd: rdn over 3f out: sme hdwy 2f out: nvr trbld ldrs* **5/2**[1]
02-0 **6** *3 ½* **Petomic (IRE)**[31] 38 6-9-0 **62**.................... AndrewHeffernan(3) 11 43
(Richard Guest) *sn led: rdn and wknd 2f out* **20/1**
4-5 **7** *9* **Little Luxury (IRE)**[25] 111 4-8-10 **62**....................(v) RossCoakley(7) 8 22
(Denis W Cullen, Ire) *chsd ldrs: hung rt and rdn fr 4f out: wknd over 2f out* **20/1**
6-02 **8** *8* **Kassiodor (GER)**[17] 202 4-9-6 **65**.................... TomQueally 4 —
(Barney Curley) *sn chsng ldr: wknd over 3f out* **14/1**
2-54 **9** *17* **Hector Spectre (IRE)**[28] 90 5-8-10 **55**....................(p) AndreaAtzeni 1 —
(Nikki Evans) *mid-div: rdn 4f out: sn bhd* **12/1**

1m 50.9s (0.40) **Going Correction** +0.175s/f (Slow) **9** Ran SP% **121.8**
Speed ratings (Par 103): **105,103,99,98,95 92,84,77,61**
Tote Swingers: 1&2 £5.20, 1&3 £7.50, 2&3 £7.90 CSF £26.62 CT £147.26 TOTE £7.20: £1.80, £1.10, £3.00; EX 26.90.
Owner Wetumpka Racing & Donald Kerr **Bred** David Bowman & Dr Carl Chan **Trained** Kingston Lisle, Oxon

FOCUS
A modest handicap run at an ordinary gallop. The winner came down the centre in the straight.

429 BLUESQ.COM ON YOUR IPHONE CONDITIONS STKS 5f 216y(P)
7:00 (7:02) (Class 4) 4-Y-0+ **£3,238** (£963; £481; £240) **Stalls** Low

Form RPR
30-2 **1** **Brave Prospector**[30] 46 6-9-7 102....................(t) TomQueally 5 107
(Jane Chapple-Hyam) *in rr: rdn and hdwy ent st: led jst ins fnl f: rdn out* **6/4**[1]
15-4 **2** *2 ¼* **Piscean (USA)**[30] 46 6-9-2 97.................... GeorgeBaker 1 95
(Tom Keddy) *cl up in 4th: trckd ldrs gng wl over 2f out: rdn over 1f out: nt qckn* **5/2**[2]
-124 **3** *2* **Feelin Foxy**[10] 293 7-8-11 85.................... FrannyNorton 3 83
(James Given) *led tl jst ins fnl f: no ex* **7/1**
604- **4** *4* **Atlantic Story (USA)**[51] 7875 9-9-7 102....................(bt) PhillipMakin 2 81
(Michael Easterby) *s.i.s: hld up in 5th: hdwy to press ldr over 2f out: wknd over 1f out* **7/2**[3]
600- **5** *3 ½* **Star Rover (IRE)**[107] 7014 4-9-7 90.................... CathyGannon 6 69
(David Evans) *pressed ldr tl over 2f out: sn wknd* **22/1**
[illegible] **6** *[illegible]* **Luscivious**[10] 293 7-8-13 87....................(p) BillyCray(3) 4 23
(David Nicholls) *pressed ldrs: rdn over 3f out: sn lost pl and struggling in rr* **25/1**

1m 14.78s (-0.22) **Going Correction** +0.175s/f (Slow) **6** Ran SP% **111.5**
Speed ratings (Par 105): **108,105,102,97,92 75**
Tote Swingers: 1&2 £1.50, 1&3 £3.70, 2&3 £6.10 CSF £5.39 TOTE £3.00: £1.60, £1.30; EX 6.00.

Owner Dr Marwan Koukash **Bred** Times Of Wigan Ltd **Trained** Dalham, Suffolk

FOCUS
A decent conditions event run at a reasonable gallop. The winner came down the centre in the straight.
Feelin Foxy Official explanation: jockey said mare hung right throughout

430 ENJOY THE PARTY PACK GROUP OFFER H'CAP 5f 20y(P)
7:30 (7:31) (Class 5) (0-75,75) 4-Y-0+ **£1,942** (£578; £288; £144) **Stalls** Low

Form RPR
34-5 **1** **Island Legend (IRE)**[9] 298 5-9-1 **69**....................(p) RichardKingscote 5 77
(Milton Bradley) *sn led: mde virtually all: wnt clr w runner-up 2f out: hrd rdn over 1f out: hld on whn jnd ins fnl f: all out* **17/2**
-420 **2** *nk* **Incomparable**[10] 294 6-9-5 **73**....................(bt) FrederikTylicki 7 80
(David Nicholls) *chsd wnr: wnt clr w wnr 2f out: hrd rdn over 1f out: hung rt and drew level ins fnl f: nt qckn fnl strides* **7/1**
-603 **3** *½* **Riflessione**[9] 298 5-8-13 **67**....................(b) StephenCraine 3 72
(Ronald Harris) *chsd ldng pair: hrd rdn over 1f out: kpt on wl fnl f* **5/1**[3]
5-46 **4** *hd* **Tislaam (IRE)**[13] 264 4-8-10 **67**....................(p) AndrewHeffernan(3) 6 71
(Alan McCabe) *in tch: rdn over 2f out: r.o fnl f* **9/2**[2]
-426 **5** *½* **Efistorm**[9] 298 10-9-2 **70**.................... CathyGannon 4 73
(Conor Dore) *in rr: drvn along and sme hdwy over 1f out: nrst fin* **14/1**
-020 **6** *1* **Grudge**[10] 294 6-9-5 **73**....................(be) KirstyMilczarek 1 72
(Conor Dore) *restless in stalls: in tch: rdn 3f out: no hdwy fnl 2f* **6/1**
04-1 **7** *½* **Garstang**[23] 133 8-9-5 **73**....................(b) LukeMorris 9 70+
(John Balding) *t.k.h towards rr on outer: rdn over 2f out: hung lft and nt rch ldrs* **9/2**[2]
320- **8** *¾* **Fair Passion**[85] 7405 4-9-7 **75**.................... TomQueally 2 70
(Derek Shaw) *t.k.h towards rr: sme hdwy and rdn 2f out: no ex over 1f out* **4/1**[1]
0-06 **9** *¾* **La Capriosa**[10] 294 5-9-1 **72**.................... BillyCray(3) 8 64
(David Nicholls) *in rr of midfield: rdn and n.d fnl 3f* **20/1**

63.18 secs (0.88) **Going Correction** +0.175s/f (Slow) **9** Ran SP% **121.8**
Speed ratings (Par 103): **99,98,97,97,96 95,94,93,91**
Tote Swingers: 1&2 £14.00, 1&3 £11.60, 2&3 £8.50 CSF £70.17 CT £338.88 TOTE £14.20: £3.80, £2.20, £1.30; EX 67.30.
Owner J M Bradley **Bred** Jerome Casey **Trained** Sedbury, Gloucs

FOCUS
An ordinary handicap and, although the gallop was reasonable, the two leaders didn't come back to the field. Both raced down the centre in the straight.

431 PLAY RAINBOW RICHES AT BLUESQ.COM MEDIAN AUCTION MAIDEN STKS 1m 141y(P)
8:00 (8:00) (Class 5) 3-5-Y-0 **£1,813** (£539; £269; £134) **Stalls** Low

Form RPR
2 **1** **Ekasin**[21] 171 3-8-7 .... AndreaAtzeni 3 78+
(Marco Botti) *mde all: hrd rdn over 1f out: hld on wl fnl f* **13/8**[2]
5 **2** *1 ¾* **Baharat (IRE)**[16] 212 3-8-7 .... ShaneKelly 4 73+
(Jeremy Noseda) *dwlt: sn trcking ldng pair: hrd rdn and outpcd 2f out: styd on to take 2nd fnl 100yds* **4/7**[1]
3 *¾* **One Pursuit (IRE)** 3-8-4 .... BillyCray(3) 5 71
(David Nicholls) *dwlt: hld up in 4th: effrt on outer over 2f out: drvn to chal whn hung lft 1f out: no ex* **22/1**
4 *6* **Freedom Flyer (IRE)** 3-8-2 .... TobyAtkinson(5) 2 57+
(Marco Botti) *stdd s: hld up in last: rdn and struggling fnl 3f* **25/1**
5 *3 ¾* **Reai (IRE)**[60] 4-10-0 .... FrederikTylicki 6 49
(Richard Fahey) *chsd wnr tl wknd 2f out* **20/1**[3]

1m 53.29s (2.79) **Going Correction** +0.175s/f (Slow)
WFA 3 from 4yo 21lb **5** Ran SP% **114.7**
Speed ratings (Par 103): **94,92,91,86,83**
CSF £2.99 TOTE £2.50: £1.10, £1.10; EX 3.10.
Owner A Rosati-Colarieti **Bred** Azienda Agricola Rosati Colarieti **Trained** Newmarket, Suffolk

FOCUS
An uncompetitive maiden run at just a moderate gallop to the straight. The winner came down the centre in the straight.
T/Plt: £41.30 to a £1 stake. Pool:£93,238.02 - 1,644.06 winning tickets T/Qpdt: £10.70 to a £1 stake. Pool:£11,666.55 - 803.30 winning tickets LM

[418]LINGFIELD (L-H)
Saturday, February 5

OFFICIAL GOING: Standard
Wind: very strong, half behind Weather: overcast, very windy

432 BET ON TODAY'S FOOTBALL AT BLUESQ.COM APPRENTICE H'CAP 7f (P)
1:20 (1:20) (Class 6) (0-60,58) 4-Y-0+ **£1,535** (£453; £226) **Stalls** Low

Form RPR
05-6 **1** **Florio Vincitore (IRE)**[19] 190 4-9-2 **58**........(b[1]) JenniferFerguson(5) 11 66
(Edward Creighton) *sn led and clr: c centre st: rdn over 1f out: tiring ins fnl f but battled on gamely fnl 100yds: all out* **9/1**
230- **2** *nk* **Cwmni**[77] 7519 5-9-2 **58**.................... ThomasBrown(5) 5 65+
(Bryn Palling) *taken down early: hld up in rr: nt clr run over 2f out: c wd st and hdwy jst over 1f out: str run ins fnl f: pressing wnr cl home: nt quite get up* **8/1**
40-3 **3** *¾* **Bubbly Bellini (IRE)**[1] 421 4-9-1 **52**....................(p) AshleyMorgan 1 57
(Adrian McGuinness, Ire) *hld up towards rr: effrt and nt clr run jst over 2f out: gd hdwy and edging lft over 1f out: chsd wnr ins fnl f: kpt on: lost 2nd towards fin* **9/2**[1]
3-00 **4** *nk* **Mushy Peas (IRE)**[5] 362 4-8-11 **51**....................(v) MatthewCosham(3) 2 55
(David Evans) *taken down early: prom in main gp: hdwy jst over 2f out: kpt on wl fnl 100yds: unable to chal* **12/1**
500- **5** *3* **Giulietta Da Vinci**[84] 7438 4-8-9 **51**.................... RichardRowe(5) 6 47
(Steve Woodman) *hld up in rr: hdwy on outer 3f out: chsd clr wnr 2f out: no real imp: lost 3 pls fnl f* **14/1**
306- **6** *2* **Crazy Parachute**[73] 7547 4-9-0 **58**.................... ChelseyBanks(7) 8 49
(Gary Moore) *stdd s: racd v wd thrght: wl bhd: hdwy ent fnl f: kpt on: n.d* **22/1**
6206 **7** *1* **Trade Centre**[10] [illegible] [illegible].................... RyanPowell(3) 4 42
(Milton Bradley) *prom in main gp: rdn and unable qck ent fnl 2f: one pce and n.d fr over 1f out* **5/1**[2]
50-0 **8** *nse* **Merals Choice**[16] 225 4-8-12 **52**....................(p) JulieBurke(3) 9 40
(Jim Boyle) *led briefly: chsd clr wnr after tl 2f out: sn struggling u.p: wknd over 1f out* **8/1**
0-00 **9** *¾* **Pha Mai Blue**[9] 317 6-9-4 **58**....................(b[1]) NathanAlison(3) 3 44
(Jim Boyle) *prom in main gp: rdn and effrt jst over 2f out: wknd over 1f out* **13/2**[3]
10-2 **10** *3 ¾* **Sonny G (IRE)**[3] 387 4-9-7 **58**.................... TobyAtkinson 10 34
(John Best) *prom in main gp: rdn and carried hd high u.p ent fnl 2f: wknd wl over 1f out* **9/2**[1]
/56- **11** *8* **Zelos Dream (IRE)**[378] 276 4-9-1 **57**.................... JakePayne(5) 7 11
(Bill Turner) *racd off the pce in midfield: pushed along and dropped to rr wl over 2f out: wl bhd fnl 2f* **25/1**

1m 24.81s (0.01) **Going Correction** +0.10s/f (Slow) **11** Ran SP% **121.1**
Speed ratings (Par 101): **103,102,101,101,98 95,94,94,93,89 80**
Tote Swingers: 1&2 £24.30, 1&3 £18.70, 2&3 £10.60 CSF £81.57 CT £379.67 TOTE £24.50: £5.20, £3.50, £2.10; EX 242.70 TRIFECTA Not won..
Owner Murray & Prosser **Bred** Newsells Park Stud **Trained** Wormshill, Kent

FOCUS
Modest form.
Sonny G(IRE) Official explanation: jockey said colt ran flat

433 CYPRIUM BAR AT MARRIOTT LINGFIELD (S) STKS 1m (P)
1:50 (1:50) (Class 6) 4-Y-0+ **£1,535** (£453; £226) **Stalls** High

Form RPR
4-30 **1** **Aflaam (IRE)**[15] 247 6-8-13 62....................(tp) LukeMorris 8 68
(Ronald Harris) *prom tl led wl over 2f out: rdn and clr wl over 1f out: drvn ent fnl f: styd on wl* **15/8**[1]
0-05 **2** *2 ¾* **Master Of Dance (IRE)**[12] 282 4-8-13 62....................(b) MickyFenton 1 62
(James Given) *led for 1f: styd chsng ldrs: rdn and nt pce of wnr ent fnl 2f: chsd clr wnr jst ins fnl f: plugged on same pce after* **12/1**
0-30 **3** *1 ½* **Collect Art (IRE)**[15] 248 4-8-10 63....................(v) AmyBaker(3) 7 58+
(Andrew Haynes) *t.k.h: hld up in last trio: effrt and nt clr run briefly ent fnl 2f: hdwy and rdn over 1f out: kpt on ins fnl f: nvr threatened ldrs* **7/1**[2]
06-0 **4** *½* **Art Scholar (IRE)**[8] 341 4-8-13 62....................(p) FergusSweeney 2 57
(Gary Moore) *in tch in midfield: hdwy and rdn to chse wnr over 2f out: no imp u.p over 1f out: btn and lost 2nd jst ins fnl f: wknd fnl 100yds* **16/1**
4-52 **5** *6* **Grand Vizier (IRE)**[12] 282 7-8-13 73.................... HayleyTurner 5 43
(Conor Dore) *v.s.a and reluctant early: clsd and in tch 5f out: outpcd wl over 2f out: n.d* **15/8**[1]

240- **6** ¾ **Fever Tree**[127] 6522 4-8-8 57 MartinLane 6 37
(Peter Makin) *t.k.h: rdn and unable qck over 2f out: wknd wl over 1f out* **8/1**[3]

600- **7** 1¾ **Farmers Glory**[8] 4545 4-8-13 54 (b[1]) JimmyQuinn 3 38
(Neil King) *dwlt and rdn along leaving stalls: in tch in last trio: rdn and dropped to last 3f out: sn wl btn* **50/1**

2 **8** 2½ **Battle Axe (FR)**[14] 261 6-8-8 0 GregFairley 4 27
(Laura Mongan) *t.k.h: led after 1f tl wl over 2f out: sn struggling: wl bhd over 1f out* **16/1**

1m 39.42s (1.22) **Going Correction** +0.10s/f (Slow) **8** Ran SP% **114.6**
Speed ratings (Par 101): **97,94,92,92,86 85,83,81**
Tote Swingers: 1&2 £5.70, 1&3 £2.90, 2&3 £7.80 CSF £27.92 TOTE £3.30: £1.10, £3.60, £2.00; EX 25.80 Trifecta £111.40 Pool of £905.01 - 6.01 winning units..No bid for the winner.
Owner Ridge House Stables Ltd **Bred** Shadwell Estate Company Limited **Trained** Earlswood, Monmouths

FOCUS
There wasn't much pace on here.
Grand Vizier(IRE) Official explanation: jockey said gelding was slowly away

434 GILLIAN GRAHAM 60TH BIRTHDAY CELEBRATION MEDIAN AUCTION MAIDEN STKS 1m (P)
2:20 (2:21) (Class 5) 3-5-Y-O **£1,910** (£564; £282) **Stalls** High

Form RPR

1 **Casual Mover (IRE)** 3-8-6 0 KierenFox(3) 3 73+
(John Best) *hld up in tch: effrt and rdn to ld wl over 1f out: clr ent fnl f: r.o strly* **10/1**

35-3 **2** 2¼ **Tagansky**[21] 176 3-8-9 70 HayleyTurner 4 68
(Simon Dow) *hld up in tch in last pair: hdwy 2f out: sn chsng wnr: drvn ent fnl f: kpt on same pce after* **2/1**[2]

6 **3** 2 **Apache Glory (USA)**[17] 214 3-8-4 0 DavidProbert 7 58
(Richard Hannon) *chsd ldrs: wnt 2nd and rdn jst over 2f out: wd bnd and out pce 2f out: one pce and wl hld fr over 1f out* **5/6**[1]

6 **4** ½ **Little Jazz**[17] 212 3-8-4 0 LiamJones 1 57
(Paul D'Arcy) *trckd ldrs on inner: nt clr run and shuffled bk over 2f out: swtchd rt ent fnl 2f: rallied over 1f out: kpt on same pce fnl f* **20/1**

0 **5** 6 **Adieu**[12] 274 3-8-4 0 FrankieMcDonald 6 43
(Richard Hannon) *chsd ldr tl led over 2f out: rdn and hdd wl over 1f out: wknd over 1f out* **25/1**

4- **6** 9 **Yours**[64] 7681 3-8-4 0 ChrisCatlin 2 21
(Kevin Ryan) *led tl over 2f out: wknd u.p jus over 2f out: wl btn over 1f out* **7/1**[3]

7 3¼ **Silent Fury (IRE)** 3-8-4 0 MartinLane 5 13
(Rae Guest) *v.s.a: pushed along early: clsd and in tch after 1f: rdn again 5f out: struggling wl over 3f out: sn wl bhd* **16/1**

1m 40.38s (2.18) **Going Correction** +0.10s/f (Slow) **7** Ran SP% **124.0**
Speed ratings (Par 103): **93,90,88,88,82 73,70**
Tote Swingers: 1&2 £5.60, 1&3 £2.40, 2&3 £19.20 CSF £33.55 TOTE £9.50: £4.00, £1.10; EX 25.20 Trifecta £28.00 Pool of £386.74 - 10.20 winning units..
Owner Steve Gabriel **Bred** M S And C S Griffiths **Trained** Hucking, Kent

FOCUS
Ordinary maiden form.

435 BLUE SQUARE SPRINT SERIES ROUND 5 H'CAP (QUALIFIER) 6f (P)
2:55 (2:57) (Class 6) (0-65,69) 4-Y-O+ **£2,729** (£806; £403) **Stalls** Low

Form RPR

3555 **1** **Norville (IRE)**[7] 351 4-9-4 62 (b) CathyGannon 11 70
(David Evans) *broke wl: racd keenly and pressed ldr: drvn ahd 1f out: hld on wl ins fnl f: all out* **16/1**

6234 **2** nk **Dvinsky (USA)**[7] 351 10-9-6 64 (b) JimmyQuinn 5 71
(Jane Chapple-Hyam) *chsd ldrs: rdn wl over 2f out: kpt on wl and ev ch ins fnl f: no ex nr fin* **20/1**

0-21 **3** ½ **Pelmanism**[10] 306 4-9-6 64 (b) PhillipMakin 9 69
(Kevin Ryan) *pushed along early: in tch towards rr: effrt and rdn wl over 1f out: chsd ldrs 1f out: kpt on wl fnl 100yds: nt quite rch ldng pair* **2/1**[1]

-533 **4** hd **Speak The Truth (IRE)**[7] 351 5-8-12 59 (p) MatthewDavies(3) 6 64
(Jim Boyle) *hld up towards rr: hdwy on inner over 1f out: drvn and pressed ldrs ins fnl f: kpt on same pce fnl 100yds* **8/1**

-502 **5** nse **Desert Icon (IRE)**[8] 336 5-8-13 64 LauraPike(7) 4 69
(David Simcock) *hld up in last pair: hdwy towards inner over 1f out: swtchd lft ins fnl f: kpt on wl u.p towards fin: nt quite rch ldrs* **5/1**[2]

-405 **6** hd **Nubar Boy**[10] 306 4-9-4 62 (v) MartinLane 12 66
(David Evans) *swtchd sharply lft and dropped in bhd after s: hld up in rr: rdn over 1f out: stl last 1f out: str run fnl 100yds: gng on strly fin: nt rch ldrs* **10/1**

-032 **7** shd **Misaro (GER)**[8] 343 10-9-2 60 (b) DavidProbert 2 64
(Ronald Harris) *led: rdn wl over 1f out: hdd 1f out: kpt battling on wl tl no ex fnl 75yds* **12/1**

-231 **8** nk **Dancing Welcome**[7] 351 5-9-11 69 (b) RichardKingscote 7 72
(Milton Bradley) *in tch in midfield: rdn ent fnl 2f: kpt on ins fnl f: nvr quite gng pce to chal ldrs* **13/2**[3]

20-2 **9** 1¼ **Bollywood Style**[10] 304 6-8-13 60 KierenFox(3) 10 59
(John Best) *sn pushed along towards rr: rdn over 1f out: no real hdwy tl styd on fnl 100yds: nvr trbld ldrs* **10/1**

-300 **10** ¾ **Loyal Royal (IRE)**[7] 351 8-9-1 59 (bt) LiamKeniry 1 55
(Milton Bradley) *t.k.h: hld up in tch in midfield: effrt and nt clr run whn swtchd lft over 1f out: nvr able to chal: btn whn eased wl ins fnl f* **33/1**

225- **11** 6 **Green Velvet**[156] 5695 6-9-4 62 GeorgeBaker 8 39
(Peter Makin) *taken down early: in tch on outer: wknd over 1f out: fdd ins fnl f* **10/1**

1m 11.0s (-0.90) **Going Correction** +0.10s/f (Slow) **11** Ran SP% **123.0**
Speed ratings (Par 101): **110,109,108,108,108 108,108,107,106,105 97**
Tote Swingers: 1&2 £15.80, 1&3 £13.50, 2&3 £6.30 CSF £309.88 CT £943.29 TOTE £25.70: £7.20, £3.70, £1.50; EX 169.90 TRIFECTA Not won..
Owner Raymond N R Auld **Bred** R N Auld **Trained** Pandy, Monmouths
■ Stewards' Enquiry : David Probert one-day ban: used whip with excessive frequency (Feb 19)
Matthew Davies one-day ban: used whip with excessive frequency (Feb 19)

FOCUS
This looked pretty competitive on paper, so it was no great surprise that they all finished in a heap.

436 HOLLOW LANE H'CAP 1m 4f (P)
3:25 (3:30) (Class 3) (0-95,91) 4-Y-O+ **£5,828** (£1,734; £866; £432) **Stalls** Low

Form RPR

0-02 **1** **Scamperdale**[7] 353 9-9-1 88 KierenFox(3) 9 99
(Brian Baugh) *hld up in tch: hdwy on outer over 2f out: chsd ldr wl over 1f out: led 1f out: edgd lft but styd on wl fnl 100yds* **6/1**[2]

15-1 **2** 1¼ **Lovers Causeway (USA)**[6] 359 4-9-1 88 6ex (b) JoeFanning 7 97
(Mark Johnston) *t.k.h: chsd ldrs tl led over 2f out: rdn wl over 1f out: hdd 1f out: kpt on same pce fnl 150yds* **11/8**[1]

066- **3** 3½ **Mister New York (USA)**[35] 7507 6-9-6 90 (b) GeorgeBaker 5 93
(Noel Chance) *hld up towards rr: hdwy into midfield over 4f out: chsd ldng pair and rdn over 1f out: styd on same pce and wl hld fnl f* **20/1**

15-0 **4** ¾ **Pelham Crescent (IRE)**[16] 235 8-8-7 77 DavidProbert 2 79
(Bryn Palling) *in tch: lost pl over 3f out: rdn and rallied ent fnl 2f: kpt on same pce and no ch w ldrrs fr over 1f out* **20/1**

00-2 **5** 3 **King Olav (UAE)**[21] 180 6-9-7 91 LukeMorris 1 88
(Tony Carroll) *chsd ldrs: lost pl and dropped to rr of main gp over 3f out: swtchd rt and plugged on fr over 1f out: no ch w ldrs* **13/2**[3]

1-21 **6** 1¾ **Mighty Clarets (IRE)**[16] 235 4-8-4 77 oh2 JimmyQuinn 3 72
(Richard Fahey) *chsd ldrs: looking for room over 2f out: rdn and struggling ent fnl 2f: sn wknd* **11/1**

24-0 **7** 1¾ **Distinctive Image (USA)**[21] 180 6-9-7 91 (p) TomQueally 10 83
(Gerard Butler) *chsd ldr tl led 6f out: hdd and rdn over 2f out: wknd qckly over 1f out* **15/2**

0-50 **8** 14 **Record Breaker (IRE)**[21] 180 7-8-10 80 (b) GregFairley 4 49
(Mark Johnston) *bustled along early: a in rr and nvr gng wl: rdn and losing tch 4f out: wl bhd fnl 2f* **11/1**

40-1 **9** 2 **Taaresh (IRE)**[9] 315 6-9-1 85 JimCrowley 8 61
(Kevin Morgan) *t.k.h: hld up in tch: hdwy to chse ldrs over 4f out: btn ent fnl 2f: c wd and eased over 1f out* **8/1**

1-00 **10** 24 **Rugell (ARG)**[21] 180 6-9-1 85 RobbieFitzpatrick 6 13
(Derek Shaw) *led tl 6f out: lost pl over 4f out: dropped to last over 3f out: sn lost tch: t.o fnl 2f* **50/1**

2m 30.69s (-2.31) **Going Correction** +0.10s/f (Slow)
WFA 4 from 6yo+ 3lb **10** Ran SP% **120.8**
Speed ratings (Par 107): **111,110,107,107,105 104,103,93,92,76**
Tote Swingers: 1&2 £4.60, 1&3 £20.90, 2&3 £16.90 CSF £14.85 CT £163.99 TOTE £13.80: £3.30, £1.02, £4.60; EX 25.90 Trifecta £448.50 Part won. Pool of £606.15 - 0.30 winning units..
Owner Saddle Up Racing **Bred** Mrs J A Prescott **Trained** Audley, Staffs

FOCUS
This was a decent handicap.

NOTEBOOK
Scamperdale won in taking style, sweeping round the outside turning into the straight and running down the favourite inside the last. He'd run well off this mark last time over 1m2f and the extra 2f proved no problem. Indeed, this was probably a career-best effort. (op 10-1)
Lovers Causeway(USA) couldn't quite defy a 6lb penalty for his win at Kempton six days earlier, but considering he raced keenly and wide most of the way it wasn't a bad effort at all. He can probably win again off this sort of mark. (op 13-8 tchd 7-4)
Mister New York(USA) ◆, well beaten over hurdles this winter and out of form in his last few runs on the Flat as well, gave notice that he might be returning to his best with this effort. He could well be able to find a similar race if building on this. (op 22-1)
Pelham Crescent(IRE) remains 2lb above the highest mark he has ever won off. (tchd 22-1)
King Olav(UAE) got outpaced from the turn out of the back straight but stayed on well in the straight. A stronger all-round gallop would have helped him. (op 7-1 tchd 15-2)
Mighty Clarets(IRE), racing from 2lb out of the handicap, didn't get home and is better over shorter. (tchd 10-1)

437 TANDRIDGE MAIDEN STKS 7f (P)
4:00 (4:01) (Class 5) 3-Y-O+ **£1,910** (£564; £282) **Stalls** Low

Form RPR

4-5 **1** **Diplomatic (IRE)**[33] 23 6-9-13 0 AdamKirby 1 68
(Michael Squance) *chsd ldrs: rdn and sltly outpcd jst over 2f out: rallied and swtchd rt over 1f out: kpt on wl u.p to ld fnl 100yds* **33/1**

0/3 **2** hd **Timpanist (USA)**[22] 158 4-9-8 69 GeorgeBaker 2 62
(Simon Dow) *w ldr: rdn and qcknd w ldr over 2f out: ev ch after tl no ex cl home* **13/2**

32 **3** hd **Sofias Number One (USA)**[10] 305 3-8-10 0 JamieSpencer 7 61
(Michael Wigham) *sn led: rdn and qcknd over 2f out: edgd rt and drvn over 1f out: hrd drvn fnl f: hdd and lost 2 pls fnl 50yds* **5/4**[1]

55- **4** 2¼ **Storm Tide**[198] 4299 3-8-5 0 MartinLane 8 50+
(Rae Guest) *in tch in rr: outpcd over 2f out: rn green and hanging lft over 1f out: kpt on ins fnl f: styng on steadily fin* **10/1**

603- **5** 1 **Jo Boy**[66] 7651 4-9-13 64 HayleyTurner 6 58
(David Simcock) *chsd ldrs: rdn and nt qckn w ldrs over 2f out: hung rt and wl hld over 1f out: wl btn whn sltly hmpd and eased towards fin* **4/1**[2]

6 2 **Songburst** 3-8-10 0 DaneO'Neill 4 47+
(Richard Hannon) *s.i.s: pushed at times and in tch in rr: outpcd over 2f out: sme hdwy and edging lft over 1f out: no imp fnl f* **9/2**[3]

7 1¼ **Electric Blue Sky** 3-8-10 0 WilliamCarson 3 44+
(Stuart Williams) *hld up in rr: pushed along and effrt on inner over 1f out: no prog fnl f: n.d* **16/1**

05 **8** 1 **Avon Light**[15] 253 3-8-10 0 RichardKingscote 9 41
(Milton Bradley) *in tch on outer: rdn and struggling over 2f out: plugged on same pce and no threat to ldrs fr over 1f out* **80/1**

9 3¾ **Clonusker (IRE)** 3-8-10 0 RobertWinston 5 31
(Linda Jewell) *dwlt: sn in tch in midfield: rdn and struggling over 2f out: wknd wl over 1f out* **50/1**

1m 27.04s (2.24) **Going Correction** +0.10s/f (Slow)
WFA 3 from 4yo+ 17lb **9** Ran SP% **117.1**
Speed ratings (Par 103): **91,90,90,87,86 84,83,81,77**
Tote Swingers: 1&2 £20.10, 1&3 £13.20, 2&3 £1.60 CSF £235.39 TOTE £42.30: £8.10, £1.10, £1.30; EX 100.10 Trifecta £388.60 Part won. Pool of £525.22 - 0.92 winning units..
Owner Miss K Squance **Bred** Darley **Trained** Newmarket, Suffolk

FOCUS
This didn't look as if it would take much winning and that was confirmed when a 6-y-o, sent off at 33-1, won.
Diplomatic(IRE) Official explanation: trainer said, regarding apparent improvement in form, that the gelding was unsuited by the deeper surface at Wolverhampton and had benefited from the drop in trip.
Avon Light Official explanation: jockey said gelding hung left

438 PLAY ROULETTE AT BLUESQ.COM H'CAP 1m (P)
4:30 (4:30) (Class 3) (0-95,93) 4-Y-O+ **£5,828** (£1,734; £866; £432) **Stalls** High

Form RPR

51-2 **1** **Hazzard County (USA)**[28] 99 7-8-13 92 LauraPike(7) 8 101
(David Simcock) *hld up towards rr: hdwy on outer over 2f out: chal 1f out: rdn to ld fnl 75yds: edgd lft towards fin: kpt on* **6/1**[2]

4-54 **2** shd **Audemar (IRE)**[7] 353 5-9-2 88 (p) AndreaAtzeni 9 97
(Edward Vaughan) *chsd ldrs: rdn and effrt over 1f out: ev ch ins fnl f: jst hld* **6/1**[2]

0-13 **3** *hd* **Kilburn**[7] 348 7-8-8 **80**.. GregFairley 11 89
(Alastair Lidderdale) *chsd ldrs tl wnt 2nd wl over 3f out: rdn to ld over 1f out: hrd pressed jst ins fnl f: hdd fnl 75yds: kpt on* **12/1**
13-6 **4** *3 1/4* **Mafeking (UAE)**[21] 180 7-9-5 **91**.. ChrisCatlin 1 92
(Mark Hoad) *dwlt: sn rcvrd to ld: rdn ent fnl 2f: hdd over 1f out: wknd u.p ins fnl f* **6/1**[2]
15-1 **5** *3/4* **Zebrano**[23] 141 5-9-0 **86**..(b) JamesDoyle 12 85
(Andrew Haynes) *in tch in midfield: rdn and nt qckn over 1f out: styd on same pce and wl hld fnl f* **6/1**[2]
106- **6** *3/4* **Night Lily (IRE)**[108] 7012 5-9-2 **88**.. TonyCulhane 4 86
(Paul D'Arcy) *chsd ldrs on inner: rdn and effrt over 1f out: fnd little u.p and btn jst ins fnl f: wknd fnl 150yds* **10/1**
34-6 **7** *1* **Elna Bright**[28] 99 6-9-7 **93**.. LiamKeniry 6 88
(Brett Johnson) *hld up in rr: hdwy and rdn over 1f out: kpt on fnl f: nvr trbld ldrs* **8/1**[3]
000- **8** *1* **Ezdeyaad (USA)**[155] 5736 7-9-4 **90**.. JackMitchell 10 83
(Ed Walker) *hld up bhd: rdn over 1f out: n.d* **33/1**
220- **9** *1 3/4* **L'Hirondelle (IRE)**[93] 7318 7-8-12 **84**.. RobbieFitzpatrick 5 73
(Michael Attwater) *in tch in midfield: rdn along over 2f out: no hdwy and wl hld over 1f out* **20/1**
4-31 **10** *2 1/2* **Everymanforhimself (IRE)**[20] 186 7-8-12 **84**..(b) PhillipMakin 7 67
(Kevin Ryan) *a in rr: n.d* **5/1**[1]
0-30 **11** *23* **Alhaban (IRE)**[12] 279 5-8-13 **85**..(tp) LukeMorris 2 —
(Ronald Harris) *chsd ldr tl wl over 3f out: wknd qckly jst over 2f out: wl bhd and eased ins fnl f: t.o* **14/1**

1m 36.6s (-1.60) **Going Correction** +0.10s/f (Slow) **11** Ran SP% **116.1**
Speed ratings (Par 107): **112,111,111,108,107 106,105,104,103,100 77**
Tote Swingers: 1&2 £9.70, 1&3 £18.90, 2&3 £23.10 CSF £41.33 CT £420.40 TOTE £7.30: £3.50, £2.60, £4.30; EX 44.70 Trifecta £356.90 Part won. Pool of £482.37 - 0.62 winning units..
Owner Khalifa Dasmal **Bred** Cho, Llc **Trained** Newmarket, Suffolk
■ Stewards' Enquiry : Laura Pike caution: careless riding.

FOCUS
A good quality handicap and a fine ride from Laura Pike.

NOTEBOOK
Hazzard County(USA) is the type that needs to be delivered late and doesn't find much for pressure. Travelling nicely entering the final furlong, when he was asked to go on, he only edged ahead narrowly, and it all got a bit desperate close home as the runner-up rallied, but the line came just in time. Pike, who gave him a good ride, is now 3-7 on him, and the gelding should remain competitive as he can't go up too much for this narrow victory. (op 5-1 tchd 7-1)
Audemar(IRE) remains 3lb above his last winning mark, but he ran well back over 1m, perhaps benefiting from the fitting of cheekpieces for the first time. (op 7-1 tchd 11-2)
Kilburn has a good record over this C&D and this was another sound effort in defeat. He shouldn't go up in the weights, though. (op 10-1)
Mafeking(UAE) ran a game race from the front but he's vulnerable off a mark in the 90s. (op 13-2 tchd 11-2)
Zebrano was a bit slow to pick up and appears happier round Kempton. (op 11-2)
Everymanforhimself(IRE) has run well round here in the past but his recent improvement has come on Fibresand. (op 13-2 tchd 9-2)
T/Plt: £171.00 to a £1 stake. Pool of £66,645.44 284.40 winning tickets. T/Qpdt: £12.30 to a £1 stake. Pool of £5,284.38 - 316.97 winning tickets. SP

410 CAGNES-SUR-MER
Saturday, February 5
OFFICIAL GOING: Turf: very soft

439a PRIX DE CAGNES CENTRE (H'CAP) (5YO+) (TURF) 1m 4f
1:50 (12:00) 5-Y-O+ **£9,482** (£3,793; £2,844; £1,896; £948)

RPR
1 **Korovos (FR)**[59] 6-8-10 **0**.. JohanVictoire 16 75
(L A Urbano-Grajales, France) **16/1**
2 *2* **Miss Tonic (FR)**[79] 7-8-3 **0**..(b) AlexisBadel 8 65
(C Boutin, France) **16/1**
3 *nk* **Parle Toujours (FR)**[500] 5-9-2 **0**.. FabriceVeron 13 78
(H-A Pantall, France) **44/5**
4 *nk* **Suntil Bere (FR)**[322] 5-8-7 **0**..(p) FlavienPrat 18 68
(P Monfort, France) **30/1**
5 *1* **Dream Youn (FR)**[17] 219 6-9-2 **0**..(p) SylvainRuis 7 75
(J Van Handenhove, France) **5/1**[2]
6 *2* **Joly Nelsa (FR)**[17] 219 6-8-7 **0** ow1.. SebastienMaillot 2 63
(M Cesandri, France) **24/1**
7 *3/4* **Zimbabwe (GER)**[144] 6-8-7 **0**.. DavyBonilla 6 62
(P Marion, Germany) **17/1**
8 *1 1/2* **Lord Sam (GER)**[111] 5-8-5 **0**..(b) DominiqueBoeuf 10 58
(K Borgel, France) **9/2**[1]
9 *snk* **Pool Of Knowledge (FR)**[17] 219 5-9-0 **0**.. IoritzMendizabal 15 66
(David Nicholls) *broke wl to r bhd ldrs: rdn bef st: styd on bef fading ins fnl f* **35/1**
10 *1 1/2* **Mondovino (FR)**[15] 259 8-9-1 **0**.. TonyPiccone 12 65
(M Boutin, France) **44/5**
0 **Pralin (FR)**[124] 8-8-11 **0**.. Pierre-CharlesBoudot 1 —
(Mme L Audon, France) **18/1**
0 **Betcherev (IRE)**[36] 7-7-13 **0**..(p) EddyHardouin[(4)] 3 —
(S Cerulis, France) **44/1**
0 **Poincon De France (IRE)**[121] 7-8-11 **0**..(b) FranckBlondel 5 —
(P Monfort, France) **68/10**[3]
0 **Spamix (IRE)**[280] 5-8-13 **0**.. Francois-XavierBertras 9 —
(F Brogi, Italy) **35/1**
0 **Speranza (FR)**[15] 259 5-8-6 **0**..(b) MathieuTavaresDaSilva[(3)] 17 —
(J-P Roman, France) **62/1**
0 **Enreve (FR)**[17] 219 5-9-1 **0**.. ThierryThulliez 14 —
(J-M Capitte, France) **10/1**
0 **Stern Dancer (FR)**[89] 5-7-12 **0**.. SarahCallac[(6)] 11 —
(F Foresi, France) **94/1**

2m 41.56s (161.56) **17** Ran SP% **117.4**
WIN (incl. 1 euro stake): 16.70. PLACES: 5.40, 5.80, 2.60. DF: 146.40. SF: 385.30.
Owner Mlle Helene Mennessier **Bred** Stilvi Compania Financiera S A **Trained** Pau, France

ST MORITZ (R-H)
Sunday, February 6
OFFICIAL GOING: Frozen

440a GRAND PRIX HANDELS & GEWERBEVEREIN ST MORITZ (CONDITIONS) (4YO+) (SNOW) 5f 110y
11:45 (11:45) 4-Y-0+
£5,793 (£2,896; £2,068; £1,379; £689; £413)

RPR
1 **Rushing Dasher (GER)**[714] 652 9-8-10 0 ow5. FrauNatalieFriberg[(6)] 8 —
(Natalie Friberg, Switzerland) **68/10**
2 *1/2* **Freeforaday (USA)**[171] 5247 4-8-11 0.. LukeMorris 2 —
(John Best) *midfield: r.o fnl 1 1/2f: tk 2nd cl home* **42/10**[3]
3 *nk* **Sacho (GER)**[135] 13-9-4 0.. APietsch 1 —
(C Von Der Recke, Germany) **7/2**[2]
4 *hd* **Sweet Venture (FR)**[469] 9-9-6 0.. RobertHavlin 6 —
(M Weiss, Switzerland) **7/10**[1]
5 *6* **Lodano (FR)** 6-9-0 0.. SteveDrowne 3 —
(M Weiss, Switzerland) **137/10**
6 *3/4* **Halsion Chancer**[68] 7637 7-9-6 0.. DPorcu 7 —
(John Best) *bhd fnl 1 1/2f* **89/10**
7 *1/2* **Shetan** 5-9-2 0 ow2..(b) JanRaja 4 —
(M Weiss, Switzerland) **13/1**
8 *7* **Romantic Man (GER)**[685] 8-8-11 0.. MKolb 5 —
(Traugott Stauffer, Switzerland) **108/10**

61.10 secs (61.10) **8** Ran SP% **145.6**
PARI-MUTUEL (all including 1 chf stakes): WIN 7.80; PLACE 1.70, 1.80, 1.60; SF 32.90.
Owner Stall Allegra Racing Club **Bred** H K Gutschow **Trained** Switzerland

441a GRAND PRIX GUARDAVAL IMMOBILIEN (CONDITIONS) (4YO+) (SNOW) 1m 1f
1:15 (1:26) 4-Y-0+ **£5,793** (£2,896; £2,068; £1,379; £689)

RPR
1 **Mascarpone (GER)**[287] 7-9-5 0.. RobertHavlin 8 97
(M Weiss, Switzerland) **41/5**
2 *4* **Pont Des Arts (FR)**[60] 7776 7-9-3 0.. FredericSpanu 7 87
(A Schaerer, Germany) **5/1**[3]
3 *3/4* **Wassiljew (IRE)**[350] 653 7-9-1 0.. MiguelLopez 6 84
(A Schaerer, Germany) **153/10**
4 *3/4* **Winterwind (IRE)**[26] 6-9-3 0.. GeorgBocskai 11 84
(Carmen Bocskai, Switzerland) **21/10**[1]
5 *9* **Bucked Off (SAF)**[350] 653 7-9-1 0.. APietsch 9 65
(C Von Der Recke, Germany) **26/5**
6 *1 1/4* **Fortunato (GER)** 6-9-1 .... KKerekes 10 63
(W Figge, Germany) **144/10**
7 *4* **Glad Panther**[161] 5-9-5 0.. SteveDrowne 2 59
(M Weiss, Switzerland) **29/10**[2]
8 *1 1/4* **Agent Archie (USA)**[95] 7293 4-9-0 0.. LukeMorris 5 52
(John Best) *no imp fr 2f out* **91/10**
9 *nk* **Solapur (GER)**[133] 6-9-3 0.. TonyCastanheira 3 54
(Karin Suter-Weber, Switzerland) **151/10**
10 *2 1/2* **Lapao (GER)**[105] 5-9-3 0..(b) DPorcu 1 49
(W Himmel, Germany) **29/1**
11 *dist* **Russian King (GER)**[26] 5-9-5 0.. PierantonioConvertino 4 —
(R Rohne, Germany) **43/5**

1m 57.7s (117.70) **11** Ran SP% **144.1**
PARI-MUTUEL (all including 1 chf stakes): WIN 9.20; PLACE 2.30, 2.30, 4.00; SF 67.20.
Owner Stall Corviglia **Bred** Gestut Paschberg **Trained** Switzerland

442a GRAND PRIX AMERICAN AIRLINES (CONDITIONS) (4YO+) (SNOW) 1m
1:45 (2:00) 4-Y-0+
£4,344 (£2,172; £1,551; £1,034; £517; £310)

RPR
1 **Northern Glory**[105] 8-9-4 0.. KKerekes 7 72
(W Figge, Germany) **11/5**[2]
2 *1* **Schutzenjunker (GER)**[81] 7492 6-9-6 0.. DPorcu 1 72
(P Schaerer, Switzerland) **8/5**[1]
3 *3/4* **Saphir Bere (FR)**[26] 5-9-6 0.. FredericSpanu 6 71
(Carmen Bocskai, Switzerland) **18/5**[3]
4 *1 1/2* **Sentimento (ISR)**[875] 8-9-13 0.. MTellini 9 75
(Werner Glanz, Germany) **133/10**
5 *3/4* **Song Of Victory (GER)**[350] 653 7-9-4 0.. RobertHavlin 4 64
(M Weiss, Switzerland) **43/10**
6 *1 1/2* **Shakalaka (IRE)**[12] 5-9-4 0.. MissCBurri[(4)] 8 65
(Th Von Ballmoos, Switzerland) **102/10**
7 *7* **Chat De La Burg (USA)**[56] 7844 4-9-8 0.. LukeMorris 5 51
(John Best) *unable to chal ldrs fnl 2f* **102/10**
8 *1 3/4* **Lucidor (GER)**[286] 6692 8-8-11 0.. MiguelLopez 3 37
(M Rulec, Germany) **245/10**
9 *5* **Cayman (IRE)**[41] 4-9-6 0.. APietsch 2 36
(C Von Der Recke, Germany) **157/10**

1m 44.9s (104.90) **9** Ran SP% **145.1**
PARI-MUTUEL (all including 1 chf stakes): WIN 3.20; PLACE 1.70, 1.30, 1.40; SF 3.80.
Owner Stall Salzburg **Bred** Elsdon Farms **Trained** Germany

[425]**WOLVERHAMPTON (A.W)** (L-H)
Monday, February 7

OFFICIAL GOING: Standard
Wind: Strong, behind Weather: Overcast

443 TODAY'S JOCKEY SPECIALS AT BLUESQ.COM H'CAP 5f 20y(P)
2:25 (2:25) (Class 6) (0-65,65) 4-Y-O+ **£1,706** (£503; £252) **Stalls** Low

Form RPR
0004 **1** **Desert Strike**[8] 357 5-9-5 **63**....................................(p) RobertWinston 2 80
(Alan McCabe) *midfield: hdwy over 1f out: led and edgd rt ins fnl f: hld on wl cl home* **9/2**[2]
4-00 **2** *½* **Straboe (USA)**[12] 298 5-8-11 **55**..............................(v) WilliamCarson 12 70
(Stuart Williams) *midfield: rdn and hdwy over 1f out: r.o to take 2nd ins fnl f: sn pressed wnr: looked hld cl home* **9/1**
/00- **3** *1 ¼* **Jolly Ranch**[231] 3255 5-8-11 **55**.................................. FergusSweeney 3 65
(Tony Newcombe) *trckd ldrs: effrt over 1f out: edgd rt ins fnl f: nt qckn* **18/1**
500- **4** *1 ¾* **Steelcut**[112] 6987 7-9-7 **65**.. JamesDoyle 9 69
(Andrew Reid) *in tch: effrt 2f out: nt qckn over 1f out: kpt on towards fin: nt gng pce to chal ldrs* **14/1**
32-0 **5** *1* **The Tatling (IRE)**[31] 80 14-9-5 **63**.......................... RussKennemore 8 63
(Milton Bradley) *swtchd lft s: in rr: hdwy over 1f out: chsd ldrs ins fnl f: one pce fnl 75yds* **16/1**
6-03 **5** *dht* **Cape Royal**[4] 401 11-9-2 **60**...................................(bt) RichardKingscote 7 60
(Milton Bradley) *racd keenly: w ldr: led over 2f out: rdn and hdd ins fnl f: sn wknd* **8/1**
2221 **7** *nk* **Your Gifted (IRE)**[18] 224 4-8-13 **64**.................. MatthewCosham(7) 10 63
(Patrick Morris) *in rr: rdn over 1f out: styd on ins fnl f: nt gng pce to chal* **6/1**[3]
-613 **8** *¾* **Decider (USA)**[12] 306 8-9-7 **65**..................................(p) LukeMorris 6 62
(Ronald Harris) *trckd ldrs: rdn 2f out: wknd ins fnl 110yds* **7/2**[1]
-006 **9** *4* **Grand Palace (IRE)**[7] 362 8-8-7 **51** oh6.....................(v) CathyGannon 5 33
(Derek Shaw) *a towards rr: nvr gng pce to get competitive* **33/1**
6-06 **10** *3 ¼* **Raimond Ridge (IRE)**[3] 421 5-8-8 **52**......................(v) PatrickMathers 1 23
(Derek Shaw) *towards rr: rdn over 2f out: nvr on terms* **6/1**[3]
00-0 **11** *4* **Sir Loin**[26] 123 10-8-2 **51** oh6..(v) JulieBurke(5) 4 —
(John Gallagher) *led: hdd over 2f out: wknd over 1f out* **40/1**

61.77 secs (-0.53) **Going Correction** +0.175s/f (Slow) **11** Ran SP% **113.3**
Speed ratings (Par 101): **111,110,108,105,103 103,103,102,95,90 84**
toteswingers:1&2: £11.50, 2&3: £30.00, 1&3: £16.60 CSF £42.97 CT £669.95 TOTE £5.80: £2.00, £3.80, £8.10; EX 49.30 TRIFECTA Not won..
Owner Southwell Racing Club **Bred** Mrs Mary Rowlands **Trained** Averham Park, Notts

FOCUS
A competitive handicap for the grade. It was well run, though the fierce tailwind in the straight meant that coming from a long way back was difficult. The winner was back to his form of late last year.

444 RACING EXCELLENCE ALL WEATHER "HANDS AND HEELS" APPRENTICE SERIES H'CAP 1m 5f 194y(P)
3:00 (3:01) (Class 6) (0-60,60) 4-Y-O+ **£1,535** (£453; £226) **Stalls** Low

Form RPR
12-0 **1** **Brabazon (IRE)**[34] 33 8-9-5 **60**..............................(bt) RossCoakley(5) 5 66
(Emmet Michael Butterly, Ire) *midfield: hdwy 3f out: led over 1f out: pushed out and styd on ins fnl f* **4/1**[2]
5412 **2** *¾* **Carnac (IRE)**[6] 373 5-9-4 **54**...(p) NoraLooby 6 58
(Alan McCabe) *trckd ldrs: effrt 3f out: styd on to take 2nd fnl 100yds: a looked hld* **11/4**[1]
32-4 **3** *1 ¼* **Private Equity (IRE)**[18] 223 5-8-12 **53**.................. Mary-AnnParkin(5) 7 55
(William Jarvis) *hld up: hdwy and effrt on wd outer 3f out to chse ldrs: nt qckn over 1f out: kpt on towards fin* **4/1**[2]
0/ **4** *1* **Blackriver Boy**[1278] 4342 8-8-10 **46** oh1................................ RPWalsh 4 47
(Niall Moran, Ire) *led: hdd over 1f out: stl chalng 1f no ex fnl 75yds* **7/1**
30-4 **5** *1 ½* **Carbon Print (USA)**[14] 277 6-9-1 **51**..........................(t) RichardRowe 1 50+
(James Evans) *prom tl outpcd over 2f out: kpt on ins fnl f: no imp on ldrs* **9/2**[3]
5-46 **6** *2 ½* **Faith Jicaro (IRE)**[14] 277 4-8-10 **51**............................ NatashaEaton 2 46
(Nicky Vaughan) *hld up bhd: hdwy and effrt on wd outer 3f out to chse ldrs: wknd over 1f out* **8/1**
050- **7** *1 ¼* **Wee Ziggy**[114] 6933 8-8-7 **46** oh1.................................. JosephYoung(3) 8 40
(Michael Mullineaux) *hld up: pushed along and struggling over 2f out* **33/1**
6/00 **8** *10* **Carlton Mac**[11] 324 6-8-10 **46** oh1.......................................(p) LucyKBarry 3 26
(Simon Griffiths) *chsd ldr to 3f out: wknd over 2f out* **100/1**

3m 13.2s (7.20) **Going Correction** +0.175s/f (Slow)
WFA 4 from 5yo+ 5lb **8** Ran SP% **112.4**
Speed ratings (Par 101): **86,85,84,84,83 82,81,75**
toteswingers:1&2: £3.10, 2&3: £2.70, 1&3: £4.30 CSF £14.87 CT £45.06 TOTE £4.60: £1.90, £1.60, £1.20; EX 16.70 Trifecta £36.50 Pool of £486.46 - 9.85 winning units..
Owner James Ferry **Bred** Dermot Cantillon And Forenaghts Stud **Trained** Letterkenny, Co Donegal
■ Ross Coakley's first winner under rules.

FOCUS
An uncompetitive handicap run at a sedate gallop, and the form looks muddling. The winner is rated up 2lb on recent form.

445 ENJOY THE PARTY PACK GROUP OFFER (S) STKS 7f 32y(P)
3:30 (3:31) (Class 6) 3-Y-O+ **£1,535** (£453; £226) **Stalls** High

Form RPR
4-45 **1** **Unlimited**[15] 269 9-9-10 61.. LukeMorris 6 72
(Tony Carroll) *racd keenly: trckd ldrs: effrt over 2f out: led wl over 1f out: styd on wl to draw clr ins fnl f* **10/3**[2]
01-1 **2** *6* **Orpenindeed (IRE)**[18] 230 8-10-0 80.............................. JamesDoyle 1 60
(Frank Sheridan) *led: rdn and hdd wl over 1f out: edgd rt whn wl hld by wnr ins fnl f* **4/9**[1]
5-04 **3** *1 ¾* **Silver Wind**[11] 321 6-9-10 58.......................................(v) RobertWinston 5 51
(Alan McCabe) *pushed along to chse ldr after 1f: lost 2nd over 2f out: btn over 1f out: carried rt whn wl hld ins fnl f* **7/1**[3]
00-0 **4** *5* **St Ignatius**[7] 362 4-9-10 55... NeilChalmers 3 38
(Michael Appleby) *racd keenly: cl up tl rdn and outpcd over 3f out: n.d after* **50/1**
0-05 **5** *4* **Champagne All Day**[11] 321 5-9-10 37.................(v[1]) MichaelStainton 7 27
(Simon Griffiths) *hld up: toiling 4f out: nvr on terms w ldrs* **100/1**
/00- **6** *24* **Mon Mon (IRE)**[72] 7599 4-9-5 35...................................(t) BarryMcHugh 8 —
(Brian Storey) *bhd: toiling 4f out: t.o* **100/1**
0/0- **7** *8* **Bellomi (IRE)**[293] 1457 6-9-10 65.. ChrisCatlin 2 —
(Ken Wingrove) *in rr: toiling 4f out: t.o fnl 2f* **33/1**

1m 30.24s (0.64) **Going Correction** +0.175s/f (Slow) **7** Ran SP% **111.7**
Speed ratings (Par 101): **103,96,94,88,83 56,47**
toteswingers:1&2: £1.90, 2&3: £1.70, 1&3: £1.10 CSF £4.99 TOTE £4.10: £1.60, £1.10; EX 6.50 Trifecta £29.10 Pool of £722.59 - 18.34 winning units..There was no bid for the winner.
Owner M B Clarke **Bred** J Wise **Trained** Cropthorne, Worcs
■ Stewards' Enquiry : James Doyle two-day ban: careless riding (Feb 21-22)

FOCUS
An uncompetitive seller, but it was well run and produced something of a turn up. There were doubts over the current form of all bar the front pair.

446 BLUESQ.COM ON YOUR IPHONE H'CAP 7f 32y(P)
4:05 (4:05) (Class 5) (0-75,75) 4-Y-O+ **£2,072** (£616; £308; £153) **Stalls** High

Form RPR
01-1 **1** **Steed**[13] 291 4-8-12 **66**...(p) PhillipMakin 5 75+
(Kevin Ryan) *pushed along early: in rr: hdwy 2f out: r.o to ld u.str driving fnl 100yds: in command cl home* **5/2**[2]
-125 **2** *¾* **Double Carpet (IRE)**[24] 166 8-8-7 **61**........................... KirstyMilczarek 4 68
(Garry Woodward) *chsd ldrs: led over 1f out: hdd fnl 100yds: no ex cl home* **16/1**
00-2 **3** *4* **Diapason (IRE)**[20] 200 5-9-6 **74**.................................(t) RichardKingscote 8 70
(Tom Dascombe) *hld up: hdwy 3f out: chalng fr 2f out: outpcd by front pair and no ch fnl 150yds* **10/1**
2133 **4** *1 ¾* **Army Of Stars (IRE)**[5] 394 5-9-3 **71**..........................(p) FrannyNorton 7 62
(James Given) *chsd ldrs: nt qckn wl over 1f out: one pce and no imp ins fnl f* **7/2**[3]
4-50 **5** *¾* **Little Luxury (IRE)**[3] 428 4-8-1 **62**.............................(p) RossCoakley(7) 2 51
(Denis W Cullen, Ire) *hld up: hrd at work 3f out: nvr able to get on terms* **22/1**
2-32 **6** *12* **Striker Torres (IRE)**[14] 285 5-9-4 **72**...............................(v) AdamKirby 6 29
(Geoffrey Oldroyd) *sn pressed ldr: led 5f out: rdn and hdd over 1f out: sn wknd* **9/4**[1]
040- **7** *3 ½* **Tasmeem (IRE)**[119] 6799 4-9-7 **75**..............................(b) JamieSpencer 1 23
(David Nicholls) *led: sn pressed: hdd 5f out: sn swtchd rt: rdn and chalng 2f out: wknd over 1f out* **8/1**

1m 30.35s (0.75) **Going Correction** +0.175s/f (Slow) **7** Ran SP% **112.0**
Speed ratings (Par 103): **102,101,96,94,93 80,76**
toteswingers:1&2: £6.80, 2&3: £7.70, 1&3: £3.30 CSF £37.89 CT £337.11 TOTE £4.60: £1.80, £7.20; EX 39.00 Trifecta £546.00 Part won. Pool of £737.84 - 0.30 winning units..
Owner Mrs J Ryan **Bred** Rosyground Stud **Trained** Hambleton, N Yorks
■ Stewards' Enquiry : Phillip Makin caution: careless riding.

FOCUS
Several in-form types in an interesting handicap. It was run at a suicidal pace given the early headwind, with the two front runners dropping right out, and their efforts should be overlooked. Probably not form to take too literally.
Army Of Stars(IRE) Official explanation: jockey said horse was denied a clear run
Striker Torres(IRE) Official explanation: trainer said, regarding running, that the gelding was made too much use of in the early stages.

447 SPONSOR A RACE BY CALLING 01902 390000 CLAIMING STKS 1m 141y(P)
4:35 (4:35) (Class 6) 4-Y-O+ **£1,535** (£453; £226) **Stalls** Low

Form RPR
-421 **1** **Syrian**[14] 282 4-8-10 80.. JamieSpencer 2 85
(Ian Williams) *s.s: plld hrd: sn trckd ldrs: effrt to chal 2f out: r.o to ld fnl 100yds: in command cl home* **1/1**[1]
1-13 **2** *1 ½* **Faithful Ruler (USA)**[3] 427 7-8-11 78..........................(p) LukeMorris 4 83
(Ronald Harris) *led at slow pce: hdd over 6f out: chsd ldr after: rdn to regain ld jst over 1f out: hdd fnl 100yds: nt qckn cl home* **9/2**[3]
220- **3** *½* **Red Somerset (USA)**[137] 6312 8-9-2 90.......................... JulieBurke(5) 5 91
(Mike Murphy) *w ldr: led over 6f out: rdn and hdd jst over 1f out: ev ch tl kpt on same pce fnl 100yds* **11/4**[2]
50-3 **4** *4 ½* **Stand Guard**[24] 170 7-8-6 76..................................... LauraSimpson(7) 1 73
(Jane Chapple-Hyam) *hld up in rr: rdn and outpcd wl over 1f out: no imp* **25/1**
3-06 **5** *1 ½* **Mastership (IRE)**[14] 285 7-8-8 75...............................(p) IanBrennan(3) 3 68
(John Quinn) *hld up: pushed along 2f out: outpcd over 1f out: wl btn after* **8/1**

1m 51.75s (1.25) **Going Correction** +0.175s/f (Slow) **5** Ran SP% **109.8**
Speed ratings (Par 101): **101,99,99,95,93**
CSF £5.89 TOTE £2.00: £1.60, £1.50; EX 5.20.Syrian was subject to a friendly claim.
Owner Dr Marwan Koukash **Bred** Barry Walters **Trained** Portway, Worcs
■ Stewards' Enquiry : Jamie Spencer caution: used whip without giving gelding time to respond.

FOCUS
A good claimer with all the runners rated 75 or more, but it was a cat-and-mouse affair and a prominent position turned out to be a big advantage. Muddling form, rated around the front pair.

448 THE BLACK COUNTRY'S ONLY RACECOURSE MAIDEN STKS 1m 4f 50y(P)
5:05 (5:11) (Class 5) 4-Y-O+ **£1,813** (£539; £269; £134) **Stalls** Low

Form RPR
32-2 **1** **Shamardal Phantom (IRE)**[14] 284 4-8-12 69................ MartinLane 8 69+
(David Simcock) *racd keenly: hld up in rr: hdwy 4f out: led over 2f out: clr over 1f out: edgd rt whn wl in command ins fnl f: easily* **1/1**[1]
2 *5* **Hide The Evidence (IRE)**[131] 6483 10-9-1 0...................... LMcNiff(5) 5 63
(Niall Moran, Ire) *led: rdn and hdd over 2f out: plugged on at one pce and no ch w wnr fr over 1f out* **14/1**
3 *5* **Cloudy Bay (USA)** 4-9-3 0.. LukeMorris 7 55
(Mrs K Burke) *chsd ldr for 4f: chsd ldrs after: rdn over 3f out: sn outpcd: tk mod 3rd over 1f out: no imp* **10/1**[3]
0-4 **4** *3 ¼* **Arco Felice (USA)**[14] 284 4-9-3 0.................................... CathyGannon 3 50
(Keith Goldsworthy) *rn wout declared tongue tie: chsd ldrs tl rdn and wknd over 3f out* **4/1**[2]
30-4 **5** *3* **Christmas Coming**[9] 350 4-9-3 64.............................. FergusSweeney 6 45
(Tony Carroll) *racd keenly in midfield: tk clsr order to chse ldrs after 4f: rdn to chal 3f out: wknd wl over 1f out* **4/1**[2]
6 *5* **Pride Of Mine**[658] 8-9-1 0.. StephenCraine 2 32
(J R Jenkins) *hld up: reminder 7f out: struggling over 3f out: sn wl btn* **20/1**
7 *33* **Charlie's Boy**[48] 5-9-6 0..(t) IanMongan 1 —
(Tobias B P Coles) *midfield: lost pl after 4f: sn in rr: struggling over 3f out: t.o* **40/1**

The Form Book, Raceform Ltd, Compton, RG20 6NL

604- **8** *8* **Better Be Blue (IRE)**[206] 4113 4-8-5 41.................. GeorgeDowning(7) 4 —
(Tony Carroll) *in tch: impr to r w ldr after 4f: lost pl 5f out: wknd 4f out: t.o* **50/1**

2m 43.74s (2.64) **Going Correction** +0.175s/f (Slow)
WFA 4 from 5yo+ 3lb **8** Ran SP% **114.9**
Speed ratings (Par 103): **98,94,91,89,87 83,61,56**
toteswingers:1&2: £5.40, 2&3: £7.60, 1&3: £3.40 CSF £17.37 TOTE £2.60: £1.50, 2.30, £2.80; EX 21.70 Trifecta £162.50 Pool of £1183.83 - 5.39 winning units..
Owner Sultan Ali **Bred** Pier House Stud **Trained** Newmarket, Suffolk
FOCUS
A weak maiden which was slowly run. It is doubtful if the winner had to improve.
Arco Felice(USA) Official explanation: jockey said colt had a breathing problem
Christmas Coming Official explanation: jockey said colt hung right-handed

449 PLAY MEGAJACKPOTS CLEOPATRA AT BLUESQ.COM H'CAP 1m 4f 50y(P)
5:35 (5:35) (Class 6) (0-65,61) 4-Y-0+ **£1,535** (£453; £226) **Stalls** Low

Form RPR
0-54 **1** **Cotton King**[21] 190 4-9-5 **61**..(vt) IanMongan 3 73
(Tobias B P Coles) *hld up: wnt 3rd 7f out: led 3f out: kicked on 2f out: clr over 1f out: r.o wl and unchal after* **6/4**[1]
35-2 **2** *6* **Broughtons Paradis (IRE)**[8] 354 5-8-12 **51**................ TonyCulhane 5 53
(Willie Musson) *hld up in rr: hdwy over 3f out: 2nd wl over 2f out: sn bmpd whn ev ch: sn u.p and outpcd by wnr: no ch ins fnl f* **7/4**[2]
300- **3** *4½* **Horsley Warrior**[79] 7531 5-9-7 **60**....................................... PhillipMakin 1 55
(Ed McMahon) *chsd ldr to 4f out: rdn 3f out: sn outpcd: no imp after* **9/1**
302- **4** *12* **Jeremiah (IRE)**[215] 3783 5-9-5 **58**................................... LukeMorris 2 37
(Laura Young) *chsd ldrs: pushed along and outpcd over 3f out: hung rt wl over 2f out: sn bhd* **6/1**[3]
32-4 **5** *12* **Jasmin Rai**[37] 3 4-8-10 **52**.. ShaneKelly 4 25
(Des Donovan) *led: clr after 2f tl 4f out: hdd 3f out: wknd over 2f out: eased whn wl btn over 1f out* **11/1**

2m 41.84s (0.74) **Going Correction** +0.175s/f (Slow)
WFA 4 from 5yo 3lb **5** Ran SP% **109.0**
Speed ratings (Par 101): **104,100,97,89,81**
CSF £4.31 TOTE £1.70: £1.20, £1.90; EX 4.50.
Owner Mrs Sarah Hamilton **Bred** Meon Valley Stud **Trained** Newmarket, Suffolk
FOCUS
A two-horse race according to the betting and that's how it turned out at the end of a race in which the runaway leader was ignored. The winner is rated up 5lb.
T/Plt: £53.60 to a £1 stake. Pool: of £86,629.84 - 1,178.58 winning tickets. T/Qpdt: £6.60 to a £1 stake. Pool of £8,200.19 - 915.72 winning tickets. DO

[396]SOUTHWELL (L-H)
Tuesday, February 8

OFFICIAL GOING: Standard
Wind: Light across Weather: Fine and dry

450 BET AND WATCH AT BLUESQ.COM AMATEUR RIDERS' H'CAP (DIV I) 1m 3f (F)
1:15 (1:15) (Class 6) (0-52,52) 4-Y-0+ **£1,318** (£405; £202) **Stalls** Low

Form RPR
5-35 **1** **Home**[13] 301 6-10-7 **52**... BrendanPowell(7) 11 65
(Brendan Powell) *hld up in tch: smooth hdwy to trck ldrs 1/2-way: trckd ldr 4f out: led wl over 2f out: sn clr: readily* **15/8**[1]
-520 **2** *7* **Laura Land**[5] 409 5-10-4 **47**......................... MissBeckyBrisbourne(5) 10 47
(Mark Brisbourne) *hld up in tch: hdwy over 3f out: rdn to chse ldrs 2f out: drvn over 1f out: styd on ins fnl f: tk 2nd nr line: no ch w wnr* **11/2**[3]
-320 **3** *hd* **Tivers Song (USA)**[12] 324 7-10-5 **48**..........................(b) MrTGarner(5) 7 48
(John Harris) *cl up: led over 5f out: rdn along and hdd wl over 2f out: sn drvn and one pce: lost 2nd nr line* **9/2**[2]
445- **4** *shd* **Piverina (IRE)**[273] 2012 6-10-3 **46** oh1....................(p) JustinNewman(5) 1 46
(Julie Camacho) *trckd ldrs on inner: hdwy over 3f out: rdn to chse ldng pair over 2f out: sn drvn and no imp* **8/1**
00/- **5** *½* **Revolving World (IRE)**[480] 6818 8-10-1 **46** oh1....... MrAaronJames(7) 5 45
(Lee James) *v s.i.s and bhd: hdwy 1/2-way: rdn along 3f out: styd on on outer fnl 2f: nrst fin* **100/1**
50-0 **6** *3* **Swords**[7] 373 9-10-1 **46** oh1..................................... MissSPeacock(7) 4 40
(Ray Peacock) *hld up in rr: hdwy over 3f out: kpt on fnl 2f: nrst fin* **16/1**
35-3 **7** *2¾* **Olney Lass**[21] 201 4-10-3 **50**................................... MrJordanTaylor(7) 8 39
(Mike Murphy) *racd wd: led 1f: chsd ldrs: rdn along over 3f out: grad wknd fnl 2f* **9/1**
00-0 **8** *3½* **Corlough Mountain**[4] 418 7-10-3 **46** oh1...........(be) MissMBryant(5) 12 28
(Paddy Butler) *racd wd: chsd ldrs: rdn along 4f out: wknd 3f out* **66/1**
06-0 **9** *3½* **Solo Choice**[12] 324 5-10-5 **46** oh1.................................. MrJHamer(3) 3 22
(Ian McInnes) *blindfold removed late: dwlt: rapid hdwy on inner to ld after 1f: pushed along 1/2-way: hdd 5f out: wknd over 3f out* **66/1**
0303 **10** *14* **Mojeerr**[12] 324 5-10-6 **49**...(v) MrOGarner(5) 6 —
(Alan McCabe) *cl up: rdn along 4f out: wknd over 3f out* **8/1**
055- **11** *25* **Isabella Romee (IRE)**[53] 7917 5-10-1 **46**............ MissEClutterbuck(7) 9 —
(Terry Clement) *a in rr: rdn along 5f out: sn bhd* **33/1**

2m 31.78s (3.78) **Going Correction** +0.25s/f (Slow)
WFA 4 from 5yo+ 2lb **11** Ran SP% **113.4**
Speed ratings (Par 101): **96,90,90,90,90 88,86,83,81,70 52**
toteswingers:1&2 £4.90, 2&3 £5.50, 1&3 £3.30 CSF £11.43 CT £39.72 TOTE £2.40: £1.20, £1.70, £1.40; EX 17.90 Trifecta £35.30 Pool: £342.56 - 7.18 winning units..
Owner Mrs Lynn Chapman **Bred** A T Macdonald **Trained** Upper Lambourn, Berks
■ A first winner on just his second ride under Rules for amateur Brendan Powell, the trainer's son.
FOCUS
Times suggested the track was riding slow. Avery moderate contest run at a good pace and quicker than division II. The winner stepped up on his recent Polytrack form.
Solo Choice Official explanation: jockey said on trying to remove the blindfold it was caught on a buckle causing the late romoval.

451 BET AND WATCH AT BLUESQ.COM AMATEUR RIDERS' H'CAP (DIV II) 1m 3f (F)
1:45 (1:45) (Class 6) (0-52,52) 4-Y-0+ **£1,318** (£405; £202) **Stalls** Low

Form RPR
04-4 **1** **Jackie Kiely**[30] 104 10-10-9 **52**...................................(tp) MrCMartin(5) 5 61
(Roy Brotherton) *hld up in rr: stdy hdwy over 4f out: rdn along in tch 3f out: swtchd wd and gd hdwy over 2f out: led wl over 1f out: edgd lft ins fnl f: kpt on* **10/3**[1]
350- **2** *1* **Bright Sparky (GER)**[105] 7145 8-10-10 **48**...........(vt) MissSBrotherton 8 55
(Michael Easterby) *trckd ldrs: hdwy over 3f out: effrt 2f out and sn ev ch: swtchd rt and rdn over 1f out: kpt on* **9/2**[2]
46-6 **3** *1* **Wrecking Crew (IRE)**[20] 207 7-10-1 **46** oh1........... MrsDBamonte(7) 1 51
(Rod Millman) *midfield: hdwy on inner over 3f out: chsd ldrs and n.m.r wl over 1f out: kpt on u.p ins fnl f: nrst fin* **10/1**
000- **4** *3* **Sacco D'Oro**[9] 5203 5-10-5 **46** oh1......................... MissMMullineaux(3) 2 46
(Michael Mullineaux) *trckd ldrs on inner: hdwy 3f out: rdn and ev ch 2f out: sn edgd lft and wknd appr fnl f* **14/1**
-043 **5** *½* **Barbirolli**[5] 409 9-10-1 **46** oh1... MissCScott(7) 9 45
(William Stone) *hld up in rr: stdy hdwy on outer 1/2-way: chsd ldrs 3f out: rdn 2f out: drvn over 1f out and sn one pce* **9/1**
00-6 **6** *2¼* **Credential**[30] 104 9-10-3 **46**.......................................(be[1]) MrTGarner(5) 12 41
(John Harris) *led: rdn along 3f out: drvn and hung rt 2f out: sn hdd & wknd* **40/1**
-006 **7** *2* **Sweet Possession (USA)**[9] 355 5-10-10 **48**................(p) MrSWalker 6 39
(Pat Eddery) *midfield: hdwy on outer 1/2-way: chsd ldrs 3f out: rdn and ch over 2f out: sn btn* **7/1**
5/06 **8** *3½* **Hardanger (IRE)**[18] 252 6-10-5 **46** oh1.................(e) MrJMQuinlan(3) 11 31
(Tim Fitzgerald) *chsd ldrs: hdwy over 3f out: rdn wl over 2f out and sn wknd* **14/1**
445- **9** *½* **Chichen Daawe**[43] 7986 5-10-6 **49**....................................... MrDCottle(5) 3 33
(Brian Ellison) *t.k.h: chsd ldrs: rdn along over 4f out: sn wknd* **13/2**[3]
00/0 **10** *2¼* **Daggerman**[25] 173 6-10-8 **46** oh1..........(b) MissIsabelTompsett 10 26
(Barry Leavy) *prom: rdn along 4f out: sn wknd* **20/1**
/2-0 **11** *5* **Silca Meydan**[11] 340 5-10-7 **48**.. MrMPrice(3) 4 19
(Richard Price) *cl up: rdn along over 3f out: wknd wl over 2f out* **9/1**
/60- **12** *2¼* **Be Kind**[200] 4328 5-10-1 **46** oh1.. MrLMichael(7) 7 13
(Karen George) *dwlt: a in rr: bhd fnl 3f* **33/1**

2m 33.99s (5.99) **Going Correction** +0.25s/f (Slow) **12** Ran SP% **119.7**
Speed ratings (Par 101): **88,87,86,84,84 82,80,78,78,76 72,71**
toteswingers:1&2 £2.10, 2&3 £7.50, 1&3 £6.90 CSF £17.45 CT £138.58 TOTE £5.20: £2.10, £1.10, £3.80; EX 11.80 Trifecta £175.90 Pool: £271.03 - 1.14 winning units..
Owner Mrs Carol Newman **Bred** Mrs M Chaworth Musters **Trained** Elmley Castle, Worcs
FOCUS
Remarkably the one-two from the 2010 running filled the same positions 12 months on. The time was 2.21 seconds slower han the strongly run first division but this looked the slightly stronger race.

452 GOLF AND RACING AT SOUTHWELL H'CAP 5f (F)
2:15 (2:16) (Class 6) (0-65,63) 3-Y-O **£1,535** (£453; £226) **Stalls** High

Form RPR
4-13 **1** **Juarla (IRE)**[18] 251 3-8-13 **55**.. LukeMorris 5 67
(Ronald Harris) *chsd ldrs: hdwy over 2f out: rdn over 1f out: led ins fnl f: kpt on* **4/1**[2]
-223 **2** *½* **Go Maggie Go (IRE)**[12] 322 3-8-12 **54**........................... PhillipMakin 6 64
(Kevin Ryan) *cl up: rdn 2f out: drvn to ld ent fnl f: sn hdd and no ex last 75yds* **7/2**[1]
5-05 **3** *2¼* **Ladydolly**[18] 251 3-8-0 **45**..................................... AndrewHeffernan(3) 8 47
(Roy Brotherton) *led: rdn along 2f out: drvn over 1f out: hdd ent fnl f and kpt on same pce* **50/1**
-542 **4** *1* **Inde Country**[18] 251 3-8-8 **50**.. JimmyQuinn 1 48
(Nicky Vaughan) *chsd ldrs on outer: hdwy 2f out: sn edgd rt and ev ch tl drvn and wknd ent fnl f* **6/1**
000- **5** *1½* **Tancred Spirit**[148] 6035 3-8-7 **49**...................................... PJMcDonald 4 42
(Paul Midgley) *chsd ldng pair: cl up 1/2-way: rdn wl over 1f out and grad wknd* **40/1**
0-51 **6** *shd* **Princess Dayna**[23] 183 3-9-7 **63**............................ RichardKingscote 3 55
(Tom Dascombe) *in tch: rdn along over 2f out: sn no imp* **7/2**[1]
5-33 **7** *9* **Quadra Hop (IRE)**[11] 338 3-9-2 **58**............................... CathyGannon 2 18
(Bryn Palling) *chsd ldrs: pushed along over 2f out: sn rdn: edgd lft and btn* **13/2**
410- **8** *8* **Empress Royal**[126] 6645 3-9-7 **63**...................................... TomEaves 7 —
(Michael Dods) *dwlt: a in rr: outpcd and bhd fnl 2f* **5/1**[3]

61.02 secs (1.32) **Going Correction** +0.225s/f (Slow) **8** Ran SP% **113.1**
Speed ratings (Par 95): **98,97,93,92,89 89,75,62**
toteswingers:1&2 £3.10, 2&3 £14.40, 1&3 £15.80 CSF £17.99 CT £590.87 TOTE £7.20: £1.50, £1.80, £3.10; EX 19.40 Trifecta £293.20 Pool: £499.38 - 1.26 winning units..
Owner Robert & Nina Bailey **Bred** D And Mrs D Veitch **Trained** Earlswood, Monmouths
FOCUS
A modest handicap but the time seemed fair, being almost identical to the following older-horse seller. The winner confirmed Wolverhampton form with the runner-up, but both improved.

453 SOUTHWELL GOLF CLUB MEMBERS (S) STKS 5f (F)
2:45 (2:45) (Class 6) 4-Y-O+ **£1,535** (£453; £226) **Stalls** High

Form RPR
430- **1** **Tsar Bomba (USA)**[105] 7153 4-8-12 57........................... LeeNewman 4 68
(David Barron) *prom: cl up 1/2-way: effrt to chal wl over 1f out: rdn and led appr fnl f: drvn out* **10/1**
41-0 **2** *¾* **Colorus (IRE)**[14] 294 8-9-3 68.................................(v) WilliamCarson 3 70
(Bill Ratcliffe) *chsd ldrs: hdwy 2f out: swtchd rt and rdn over 1f out: drvn to chse wnr ins fnl f: no imp towards fin* **3/1**[1]
0-10 **3** *2* **Ridley Didley (IRE)**[14] 294 6-8-9 67............................... PaulPickard(3) 2 58
(Noel Wilson) *prom on outer: effrt 2f out: sn rdn and ev ch tl drvn and one pce ins fnl f* **6/1**
-002 **4** *3¼* **Lord Of The Reins (IRE)**[9] 357 7-8-12 63..................... FrannyNorton 1 46
(James Given) *towards rr: hdwy 2f out: rdn over 1f out: kpt on same pce* **7/2**[2]
5-43 **5** *¾* **Rievaulx World**[11] 343 5-8-12 67...................................(t) PhillipMakin 5 43
(Kevin Ryan) *led: rdn wl over 1f out: drvn and hdd appr fnl f: sn wknd* **11/2**
300- **6** *1¾* **Spirit Of Coniston**[148] 6031 8-8-12 51.............................. MickyFenton 8 37
(Paul Midgley) *towards rr: hdwy 1/2-way: rdn wl over 1f out: sn edgd lft and wknd* **50/1**
000- **7** *4½* **Turf Time**[132] 6464 4-8-9 48... BillyCray(3) 9 21
(David Nicholls) *towards rr: rdn along and edgd lft 1/2-way: nvr a factor* **22/1**
5-15 **8** *½* **Spic 'n Span**[21] 197 6-9-3 64...(b) LukeMorris 6 24
(Ronald Harris) *chsd ldrs: hdwy over 2f out: rdn wl over 1f out: sn drvn and wknd* **4/1**[3]
660- **9** *¾* **Bombay Mist**[49] 7952 4-8-4 42...........................(be[1]) AndrewHeffernan(3) 7 11
(Richard Guest) *hmpd s: a in rr* **66/1**

61.00 secs (1.30) **Going Correction** +0.225s/f (Slow) **9** Ran SP% **113.8**
Speed ratings (Par 101): **98,96,93,88,87 84,77,76,75**
toteswingers:1&2 £5.90, 2&3 £5.30, 1&3 £6.70 CSF £39.14 TOTE £10.40: £2.50, £1.40, £2.20; EX 56.30 Trifecta £363.60 Part won. Pool: £491.42 - 0.42 winning units..The winner was bought in for 4,750 gns.
Owner Miss N J Barron **Bred** Jim Ryan **Trained** Maunby, N Yorks

FOCUS
A modest seller. The runner-up looks the most reliable guide to the form.

454 GOLF BEFORE RACING AT SOUTHWELL MAIDEN STKS 6f (F)
3:15 (3:18) (Class 5) 3-Y-0+ **£1,910** (£564; £282) **Stalls** Low

Form RPR
250- **1** **Ezra Church (IRE)**[114] 6966 4-9-13 65 LeeNewman 2 80
(David Barron) *trckd ldng pair: hdwy over 2f out: rdn to ld 1 1/2f out: drvn ins fnl f: kpt on* **5/1**[3]
2 2 **Striking The Wind (USA)** 3-8-12 0 JoeFanning 9 72+
(Mark Johnston) *chsd ldrs: hdwy on outer over 2f out: rdn and edgd lft wl over 1f out: chsd wnr whn edgd lft ins fnl f: sn no imp* **2/1**[1]
5-22 **3** 7 **Eilean Mor**[5] 398 3-8-12 64 TomEaves 10 47
(Bryan Smart) *led: rdn along wl over 2f out: drvn and hdd 1 1/2f out: sn wknd* **11/4**[2]
4 2 1/4 **Embassy Pearl (IRE)** 3-8-7 0 ChrisCatlin 4 35+
(Sir Mark Prescott Bt) *dwlt and towards rr: swtchd wd 1/2-way: hdwy over 2f out: kpt on ins fnl f* **7/1**
00- **5** 1/2 **Vantaa (IRE)**[94] 7345 3-8-5 0 LauraBarry(7) 6 38+
(Richard Fahey) *midfield: effrt and sme hdwy on inner 1/2-way: rdn over 2f out and n.d* **6/1**
4-06 **6** 1 1/4 **Ever Roses**[12] 322 3-8-7 50 (v[1]) BarryMcHugh 7 29
(Paul Midgley) *chsd ldrs: rdn along and n.m.r over 3f out: sn drvn and outpcd* **66/1**
7 2 1/2 **Mecca's Team** 3-8-7 0 PJMcDonald 8 21
(Michael Dods) *cl up: rdn along 3f out: wknd over 2f out* **25/1**
0 **8** 7 **Speed Awareness**[27] 126 3-8-5 0 RachealKneller(7) 1 —
(Mark Usher) *sn outpcd and a bhd* **100/1**
4 **9** shd **Mcbirney (USA)**[14] 295 4-9-13 0 (e[1]) LiamJones 5 —
(Paul D'Arcy) *a in rr* **20/1**

1m 17.44s (0.94) **Going Correction** +0.25s/f (Slow)
WFA 3 from 4yo 15lb **9** Ran SP% **114.5**
Speed ratings (Par 103): **103,100,91,88,87 85,82,73,72**
toteswingers:1&2 £4.40, 2&3 £1.90, 1&3:£1.80 CSF £14.90 TOTE £4.40: £1.70, £3.20, £1.02; EX 24.10 Trifecta £87.10 Pool: £176.56 - 1.50 winning units..
Owner Clive Washbourn **Bred** Mrs E Byrne **Trained** Maunby, N Yorks

FOCUS
A modest maiden with little depth, but it was a shade quicker than the following handicap. The winner is rated back to his 3yo best.

455 10% FORECAST BONUS AT BLUESQ.COM H'CAP 6f (F)
3:45 (3:45) (Class 4) (0-80,79) 4-Y-0+ **£2,914** (£867; £433; £216) **Stalls** Low

Form RPR
0521 **1** **Elhamri**[12] 321 7-9-0 72 HayleyTurner 3 81+
(Conor Dore) *prom: effrt 2f out and ev ch whn n.m.r and hmpd over 1f out: swtchd lft ent fnl f and qcknd wl to ld last 75yds* **2/1**[1]
-134 **2** 1 **Ace Of Spies (IRE)**[26] 148 6-9-0 72 KirstyMilczarek 8 76
(Conor Dore) *cl up: rdn and slt ld wl over 1f out: drvn ent fnl f: hdd and no ex last 75yds* **9/2**[3]
004- **3** 3/4 **Marvellous Value (IRE)**[102] 7212 6-9-7 79 FrederikTylicki 1 81
(Michael Dods) *trckd ldrs on inner: hdwy over 2f out: rdn to chal over 1f out and sn edgd rt: drvn and ev ch ins fnl f: no ex last 50yds* **4/1**[2]
4-60 **4** 1/2 **Masked Dance (IRE)**[13] 310 4-8-9 70 (p) AmyRyan(3) 4 70
(Kevin Ryan) *towards rr: swtchd outside and hdwy 2f out: rdn to chse ldrs over 1f out: kpt on ins fnl f* **10/1**
00-1 **5** 3 3/4 **Lucky Dan (IRE)**[25] 168 5-9-7 79 FrannyNorton 5 67
(Paul Green) *in rr: rdn along 1/2-way: n.d* **13/2**
05-0 **6** 2 1/4 **Kummel Excess (IRE)**[17] 264 4-8-12 70 TonyCulhane 7 51
(George Baker) *in tch: rdn along wl over 2f out: sn wknd* **10/1**
10-6 **7** 1/2 **Divertimenti (IRE)**[14] 293 7-9-3 75 (b) JimmyQuinn 6 54
(Roy Bowring) *led 2f: prom tl rdn wl over 2f out and sn wknd* **16/1**
20-0 **8** 8 **Earlsmedic**[27] 125 6-9-7 79 (e) WilliamCarson 2 33
(Stuart Williams) *chsd ldrs on inner: led after 2f: rdn along and hdd over 2f out: sn wknd* **20/1**

1m 17.47s (0.97) **Going Correction** +0.25s/f (Slow) **8** Ran SP% **113.7**
Speed ratings (Par 105): **103,101,100,100,95 92,91,80**
toteswingers:1&2 £2.80, 2&3 £5.70, 1&3 £3.30 CSF £10.91 CT £32.08 TOTE £1.90: £1.20, £1.10, £1.80; EX 8.10 Trifecta £66.30 Pool: £145.32 - 1.62 winning units..
Owner Chris Marsh **Bred** Highfield Stud Ltd **Trained** Cowbit, Lincs

FOCUS
A one-two for trainer Conor Dore. This was a fair handicap but the time was only similar to the previous maiden. The winner rates a bit better than the bare form.

456 BOOK YOUR TICKETS ON-LINE AT SOUTHWELL-RACECOURSE.CO.UK MAIDEN H'CAP 1m (F)
4:15 (4:20) (Class 6) (0-55,54) 3-Y-0 **£1,535** (£453; £226) **Stalls** Low

Form RPR
600- **1** **Jack's Revenge (IRE)**[145] 6118 3-8-12 50 (p) TonyCulhane 3 65
(George Baker) *trckd ldrs on inner: led 1/2-way: rdn 2f out: drvn and edgd lft over 1f out: kpt on strly ins fnl f* **5/4**[1]
005- **2** 3 1/4 **Three Opera Divas**[60] 7803 3-9-2 54 JoeFanning 8 62
(Mark Johnston) *prom: effrt to chse wnr 3f out: rdn to chal 2f out and ev ch tl drvn and one pce ent fnl f* **5/1**[3]
233- **3** 3/4 **Ace Master**[56] 7864 3-8-13 51 JimmyQuinn 12 57
(Roy Bowring) *midfield: hdwy on inner to chse ldrs over 3f out: rdn over 2f out: sn drvn and kpt on same pce* **3/1**[2]
050- **4** 5 **Dance For Livvy (IRE)**[71] 7630 3-8-13 54 PatrickDonaghy(3) 11 49
(Ben Haslam) *towards rr and sn rdn along: hdwy on outer 3f out: rdn 2f out: sn no imp* **9/1**
60- **5** 4 1/2 **Littlepromisedland (IRE)**[80] 7520 3-8-7 45 FrannyNorton 10 29
(Richard Guest) *prom: rdn along over 3f out: grad wknd* **33/1**
05-4 **6** 1/2 **Mini's Destination**[5] 398 3-8-13 51 NickyMackay 13 34
(John Holt) *prom on outer: rdn along 3f out: sn wknd* **20/1**
0-52 **7** 10 **Evelyns Diamond**[26] 147 3-8-7 45 BarryMcHugh 4 —
(Paul Midgley) *dwlt: a towards rr* **40/1**
0-60 **8** nk **Katherine Parr**[20] 214 3-9-0 52 ChrisCatlin 5 —
(Peter Chapple-Hyam) *a towards rr* **12/1**
000- **9** 3 3/4 **Come On Eileen (IRE)**[89] 7400 3-8-4 45 (e) AndrewHeffernan(3) 1 —
(Richard Guest) *a towards rr* **100/1**
000- **10** 1/2 **Jam Maker**[72] 7610 3-8-7 45 DavidProbert 2 —
(J R Jenkins) *a towards rr* **66/1**
5-50 **11** 1 1/2 **Amore Et Labore**[15] 281 3-8-11 49 JamesDoyle 6 —
(Sylvester Kirk) *led to 1/2-way: cl up and rdn along over 3f out: sn wknd* **33/1**
30-5 **12** 87 **Willow's Wish**[33] 60 3-8-12 50 PJMcDonald 9 —
(George Moore) *dwlt: a in rr: wl bhd fnl 3f* **33/1**

1m 45.7s (2.00) **Going Correction** +0.25s/f (Slow) **12** Ran SP% **122.3**
Speed ratings (Par 95): **100,96,96,91,86 86,76,75,71,71 69,—**
toteswingers:1&2 £3.30, 2&3 £3.20, 1&3 £2.10 CSF £7.67 CT £17.40 TOTE £2.30: £1.70, £1.50, £1.80; EX 15.60 Trifecta £31.90 Pool: £500.35 - 11.59 winning units..
Owner Collings, Powner, Sword & Partners **Bred** Con Marnane **Trained** Whitsbury, Hants

FOCUS
Just a 46-55 maiden handicap, but some potential improvers lined up and one of those landed a major gamble. The winner showed big improvement.
Jack's Revenge(IRE) Official explanation: trainer's rep said, regarding apparent improvement in form, that the colt had had a wind operation at the end of last season and has strengthened up.

457 PLAY RAINBOW RICHES AT BLUESQ.COM H'CAP 1m 4f (F)
4:45 (4:45) (Class 5) (0-70,70) 4-Y-0+ **£1,910** (£564; £282) **Stalls** Low

Form RPR
16-5 **1** **Mush Mir (IRE)**[17] 266 4-8-13 65 (b) JoeFanning 4 80
(Jim Boyle) *cl up: led 4f out: rdn and jnd over 2f out: drvn and hdd wl over 1f out: rallied to ld again ins fnl f: kpt on strly towards fin* **9/2**[3]
-453 **2** 2 1/2 **Cobo Bay**[15] 282 6-9-7 70 (b) HayleyTurner 6 81
(Conor Dore) *trckd ldng pair: hdwy 3f out: chsd wnr over 2f out: rdn and slt ld wl over 1f out: sn drvn: carried hd high and hdd ins fnl f: one pce* **8/1**
-504 **3** 4 1/2 **Calculating (IRE)**[12] 314 7-8-9 63 LeeNewnes(5) 5 67
(Mark Usher) *hld up in tch: hdwy to trck ldrs 1/2-way: rdn along and sltly outpcd over 3f out: kpt on u.p fnl 2f* **7/2**[2]
06-3 **4** 7 **Deejan (IRE)**[12] 323 6-8-7 56 oh1 DavidProbert 3 49
(Bryn Palling) *led: rdn along and hdd 4f out: cl up and drvn 3f out: sn wknd* **11/2**
3-22 **5** 5 **Mediterranean Sea (IRE)**[12] 323 5-9-2 65 StephenCraine 2 50
(J R Jenkins) *hld up in rr: hdwy 4f out: rdn along 3f out: sn wknd* **6/5**[1]
31-0 **6** 13 **Prince Charlemagne (IRE)**[16] 272 8-8-6 62 MatthewCosham(7) 1 26
(Dr Jeremy Naylor) *in tch: rdn along over 4f out: sn wknd* **25/1**

2m 41.86s (0.86) **Going Correction** +0.25s/f (Slow)
WFA 4 from 5yo+ 3lb **6** Ran SP% **116.2**
Speed ratings (Par 103): **107,105,102,97,94 85**
toteswingers:1&2 £3.10, 2&3 £2.30, 1&3 £2.70 CSF £39.42 TOTE £4.40: £1.80, £1.70; EX 37.70.
Owner M Khan X2 **Bred** Shadwell Estate Company Limited **Trained** Epsom, Surrey

FOCUS
The front two raced near the inside rail in the straight, but that appeared to be no disadvantage towards the end of the meeting. It looked a modest race and the favourite disappointed, but the winner was unexposed and the second was down to a good mark.
T/Plt: £9.60 to a £1 stake. Pool of £64,693.19 - 4,912.48 winning tickets. T/Qpdt: £5.40 to a £1 stake. Pool £4,883.98 - 665.28 w.tckts JR

458-463a (Foreign Racing) - See Raceform Int.

[380] KEMPTON (A.W) (R-H)
Wednesday, February 9

OFFICIAL GOING: Standard
Wind: Light, behind Weather: Cloudy

464 KEMPTON.CO.UK H'CAP 5f (P)
5:10 (5:10) (Class 7) (0-50,50) 4-Y-0+ **£1,535** (£453; £226) **Stalls** Low

Form RPR
-624 **1** **Bluebok**[19] 256 10-8-9 49 (bt) MatthewCosham(7) 3 55
(Milton Bradley) *pressed ldr: rdn to ld over 1f out: fnd enough u.p fnl f* **3/1**[1]
-003 **2** 1/2 **Steel City Boy (IRE)**[12] 337 8-9-3 50 (p) JimmyQuinn 7 54
(Derek Shaw) *chsd ldrs in 5th: hrd rdn over 1f out: styd on fnl f to take 2nd last 75yds: nt quite able to chal* **13/2**
-000 **3** 1/2 **Tyrannosaurus Rex (IRE)**[19] 256 7-9-0 47 (v) TomEaves 1 49
(Derek Shaw) *trckd ldng pair on inner: nt clr run briefly over 1f out: styd on fnl f to take 3rd nr fin* **6/1**[3]
3-00 **4** 3/4 **Thoughtsofstardom**[26] 165 8-9-3 50 LukeMorris 6 50
(Phil McEntee) *led: drvn and hdd over 1f out: tried to rally ins fnl f: fdd last 75yds* **13/2**
06-0 **5** nse **Lithaam (IRE)**[6] 401 7-9-1 48 (p) RichardKingscote 10 48
(Milton Bradley) *in tch in last trio: shkn up over 1f out: kpt on u.p fnl f: nvr really threatened* **12/1**
-660 **6** 1 **Vertumnus**[5] 421 4-8-12 45 (b) KellyHarrison 4 41
(Nick Littmoden) *t.k.h: hld up in last pair: rdn and fnd nil over 1f out: plugged on* **13/2**
0-30 **7** nk **Seeking Rio**[5] 421 4-8-12 45 HayleyTurner 2 46+
(Ron Hodges) *s.i.s: sn in tch on inner: rdn 1/2-way: prog tl sed to run on 1f out: ch of pl whn trapped bhd rivals last 120yds: eased* **9/2**[2]
006- **8** 2 3/4 **Five Gold Rings (IRE)**[163] 5580 5-8-10 48 RyanPowell(5) 8 33
(Seamus Durack) *racd wd: chsd ldrs: u.p 1/2-way: wknd wl over 1f out* **16/1**
000- **9** 2 1/2 **Mythical Blue (IRE)**[40] 8036 5-9-3 50 RobbieFitzpatrick 12 26
(Peter Grayson) *rring as stalls opened and blindfold late off: slowest away: a in last pair: nvr a factor* **28/1**

60.10 secs (-0.40) **Going Correction** -0.10s/f (Stan) **9** Ran SP% **114.5**
Speed ratings (Par 97): **99,98,97,96,96 94,94,89,85**
toteswingers:1&2:£2.50, 1&3:£5.60, 2&3:£5.20 CSF £22.53 CT £109.82 TOTE £4.30: £1.90, £1.20, £1.90; EX 18.00.
Owner E A Hayward **Bred** E Duggan And D Churchman **Trained** Sedbury, Gloucs

FOCUS
A bottom-drawer sprint handicap. There was a tight finish and a few emerge as being a little better than the bare form. The winner stepped up slightly on his recent level.
Seeking Rio Official explanation: jockey said filly was denied a clear run
Mythical Blue(IRE) Official explanation: jockey said gelding reared as gates opened

465 RACING AT SKYSPORTS.COM H'CAP 5f (P)
5:40 (5:41) (Class 5) (0-75,75) 3-Y-0 **£2,047** (£604; £302) **Stalls** Low

Form RPR
4-32 **1** **Barnet Fair**[14] 302 3-9-4 75 AndrewHeffernan(3) 3 85+
(Richard Guest) *slowest away: patiently rdn in detached last as ldrs set furious pce: prog and plld out over 1f out: drvn to ld last 100yds: styd on wl* **2/1**[1]
32-1 **2** 3/4 **Palais Glide**[25] 179 3-9-2 70 EddieAhern 2 77
(Richard Hannon) *chsd ldrs: prog on inner to ld over 1f out: hdd last 100yds: styd on* **11/2**

01-4 **3** *3* **Lady Prodee**[22] [198] 3-8-13 **70** .... KierenFox(3) 4 67+
(Bill Turner) *racd wd: pushed along to try to match strides w ldrs: struggling over 1f out: kpt on to take 3rd nr fin* **9/2**[3]

-211 **4** *½* **Mandy's Hero**[10] [356] 3-9-7 **75** 6ex ....(p) JamieSpencer 6 70+
(Ian Williams) *sn led and set v fast pce: hrd rdn over 1f out: sn hdd and btn* **9/4**[2]

-352 **5** *¾* **Je Suis Unrockstar**[22] [198] 3-9-0 **68** ....(p) IanMongan 1 60
(David Nicholls) *t.k.h: chsd ldr to wl over 1f out: edgd lft and sn btn* **8/1**

-433 **6** *1¼* **Johnny Hancocks (IRE)**[10] [356] 3-8-11 **68** .... JamesSullivan(3) 5 58
(Linda Stubbs) *chsd ldng pair at str pce: lost pl whn short of room over 1f out: no ch after* **14/1**

59.16 secs (-1.34) **Going Correction** -0.10s/f (Stan) **6** Ran SP% **115.4**
Speed ratings (Par 97): **106,104,100,99,98 96**
toteswingers:1&2:£3.00, 1&3:£3.10, 2&3:£3.90 CSF £13.96 TOTE £2.30: £1.10, £4.40; EX 15.60.
Owner Donald Wheatley **Bred** Mrs J M Russell **Trained** Stainforth, S Yorks

FOCUS
Not a bad 3-y-o sprint handicap for the grade. There was a searching pace on and the time was fast. The winner produced a clear personal best.
Mandy's Hero Official explanation: jockey said gelding moved poorly

466 BETDAQ.COM EVERY WEDNESDAY AT KEMPTON PARK H'CAP 1m 2f (P)
6:10 (6:10) (Class 7) (0-50,56) 4-Y-0+ **£1,535** (£453; £226) **Stalls** Low

Form RPR

6-01 **1** **Fastinthestraight (IRE)**[10] [355] 4-9-3 **51** 6ex ....(p) DaneO'Neill 12 61+
(Jim Boyle) *settled in rr: pushed along and prog over 2f out: drvn on outer over 1f out: stdy on to ld last 150yds: readily* **5/6**[1]

500- **2** *1½* **Kathleen Kennet**[100] [2678] 11-9-0 **47** .... LiamKeniry 3 54
(Jonathan Geake) *hld up in midfield on inner: prog gng strly 2f out: rdn to ld over 1f out: edgd lft and hdd last 150yds: nt qckn* **66/1**

065- **3** *nk* **Hecton Lad (USA)**[93] [7381] 4-8-10 **47** .... KierenFox(3) 4 53
(John Best) *t.k.h: trckd ldr: edgd lft u.p bnd 2f out and lost pl: rallied jst over 1f out to chal: kpt on same pce* **14/1**

4-51 **4** *3¼* **Ocean Of Peace (FR)**[10] [354] 8-9-9 **56** 6ex .... LukeMorris 2 56
(Martin Bosley) *prom: wnt 2nd 2f out: hrd rdn to chal over 1f out: wknd ins fnl f* **7/1**[2]

-661 **5** *1* **Aggbag**[7] [382] 7-9-4 **51** 6ex .... RobertWinston 7 49
(Tony Carroll) *trckd ldrs: rdn 3f out and struggling to hold pl: one pce u.p fnl 2f* **14/1**

600- **6** *shd* **Maydream**[60] [7840] 4-8-12 **46** .... SamHitchcott 9 46
(Jimmy Fox) *in tch on inner: snatched up wl over 3f out and lost pl: rdn after: kpt on fr over 1f out: no ch* **40/1**

4-40 **7** *nse* **Rosy Dawn**[21] [207] 6-9-1 **48** .... IanMongan 1 46
(Luke Dace) *led: hrd rdn and hdd over 1f out: wknd* **12/1**

522/ **8** *3¼* **Inchando (FR)**[379] [4935] 7-8-9 **49** .... GeorgeDowning(7) 6 40
(Tony Carroll) *stdd s: hld up in detached last pair: rdn over 2f out: limited prog over 1f out: no ch* **40/1**

40-5 **9** *2½* **Jackson (BRZ)**[6] [409] 9-8-11 **47** ....(b) AndrewHeffernan(3) 10 33
(Richard Guest) *settled in rr: u.p 3f out: sn lost tch and looked like tailing off: rdr persisted fnl 2f* **8/1**[3]

006- **10** *nse* **Mighty Aphrodite**[71] [7645] 4-8-11 **50** .... KylieManser(5) 5 36
(Olivia Maylam) *stdd s: hld up in detached last pair: rdn and no real prog over 2f out* **66/1**

0/0- **11** *7* **Moment Of Clarity**[146] [6125] 9-9-0 **47** ....(p) JoeFanning 11 19
(Shaun Harris) *racd wd thrght: pressed ldrs tl wknd qckly 2f out* **66/1**

56-2 **12** *12* **Mayfair's Future**[10] [355] 6-9-3 **50** ....(p) DavidProbert 8 —
(J R Jenkins) *prom tl wknd rapidly 3f out: t.o over 1f out* **9/1**

2m 6.19s (-1.81) **Going Correction** -0.10s/f (Stan)
WFA 4 from 6yo+ 1lb **12** Ran SP% **118.5**
Speed ratings (Par 97): **103,101,101,98,98 98,98,95,93,93 87,78**
toteswingers:1&2:£13.70, 1&3:£5.40, 2&3:£74.50 CSF £102.04 CT £500.36 TOTE £1.70: £1.60, £11.10, £3.60; EX 181.70.
Owner Epsom Equine Spa Partnership **Bred** Patrick J Ryan **Trained** Epsom, Surrey

FOCUS
Another bottom-level handicap, but it did feature three last-time-out winners and was a decent race for the grade. It was run at an average pace and the front three came clear. The well-in winner only needed to match his recent C&D victory.
Hecton Lad(USA) Official explanation: jockey said gelding hung left on bend
Maydream Official explanation: jockey said filly was hampered

467 BETDAQ.COM EXCHANGE PRICE MULTIPLES CLAIMING STKS 7f (P)
6:40 (6:40) (Class 6) 3-Y-0+ **£1,535** (£453; £226) **Stalls** Low

Form RPR

1-21 **1** **Hinton Admiral**[12] [334] 7-9-13 78 .... MichaelStainton 1 71
(Jane Chapple-Hyam) *t.k.h: mde all and set stdy pce early: nt asked to kick on tl over 1f out: edgd lft but readily kpt on* **6/4**[2]

0-24 **2** *1* **Jake The Snake (IRE)**[16] [279] 10-10-0 85 .... GeorgeBaker 2 69
(Tony Carroll) *hld up in 4th: clsd 2f out: rdn to chse wnr 1f out: styd on same pce and no imp* **5/6**[1]

-043 **3** *¾* **Silver Wind**[2] [445] 6-9-6 58 ....(v) RobertWinston 4 59
(Alan McCabe) *chsd wnr: rdn and lost 2nd over 2f out: one pce after* **25/1**

-201 **4** *shd* **Lastkingofscotland (IRE)**[14] [307] 5-9-13 77 ....(b) HayleyTurner 3 66
(Conor Dore) *trckd ldng pair: chsd wnr over 2f out: nt qckn and hld over 1f out: sn lost 2nd and one pce* **9/2**[3]

-202 **5** *2¾* **Kenswick**[13] [312] 4-9-0 50 ....(v) TobyAtkinson(5) 7 50
(Pat Eddery) *hld up last: cl enough 2f out: shkn up and nt qckn: wknd* **25/1**

1m 27.31s (1.31) **Going Correction** -0.10s/f (Stan) **5** Ran SP% **120.4**
Speed ratings (Par 101): **88,86,86,85,82**
CSF £3.50 TOTE £2.80: £1.20, £1.60; EX 4.40.
Owner Rory Murphy **Bred** Gainsborough Stud Management Ltd **Trained** Dalham, Suffolk

FOCUS
A falsely run claimer. The front pair did not need to match their recent form.

468 LAY BACK AND WIN AT BETDAQ.COM H'CAP 1m (P)
7:10 (7:10) (Class 4) (0-85,85) 3-Y-0 **£3,885** (£1,156; £577; £288) **Stalls** Low

Form RPR

3-11 **1** **Kuala Limper (IRE)**[10] [358] 3-9-3 **81** 6ex .... DaneO'Neill 1 90+
(David Elsworth) *t.k.h early: sn trckd ldng pair: led over 2f out gng strly: rdn over 1f out: hrd pressed ins fnl f: battled on wl* **7/4**[1]

1 **2** *hd* **Dorcas Lane**[21] [214] 3-9-2 **80** .... LukeMorris 7 87
(Lucy Wadham) *hld up: chsd ldng trio 1/2-way: plld out over 2f out and hanging sltly: rdn to chse wnr over 1f out: clsd to chal last 100yds: styd on but jst hld* **4/1**[3]

44-2 **3** *5* **Whodathought (IRE)**[35] [49] 3-8-2 **71** ....(b) RyanPowell(5) 4 67
(Richard Hannon) *s.i.s: sn pushed up to chse ldr: rdn to chal over 2f out: chsd wnr to over 1f out: fdd* **11/1**

210- **4** *hd* **Malice Or Mischief (IRE)**[54] [7916] 3-9-0 **78** .... NeilChalmers 3 73
(Tony Carroll) *stdd s: hld up last: rdn and in tch over 2f out: no imp over 1f out: outpcd* **20/1**

4-24 **5** *11* **Il Battista**[19] [254] 3-9-7 **85** ....(p) RobertWinston 5 55
(Alan McCabe) *led: rdn 3f out: hdd & wknd over 2f out* **12/1**

00-1 **6** *10* **Aloneinthestreet (USA)**[8] [379] 3-8-6 **70** 6ex .... JoeFanning 6 17
(Mark Johnston) *racd wd and sn nt gng wl: hanging and dropped to last 1/2-way: t.o fnl 2f* **2/1**[2]

1m 39.01s (-0.79) **Going Correction** -0.10s/f (Stan) **6** Ran SP% **110.5**
Speed ratings (Par 99): **99,98,93,93,82 72**
toteswingers:1&2:£1.10, 1&3:£4.30, 2&3:£3.00 CSF £8.84 TOTE £3.10: £1.80, £1.50; EX 7.20.
Owner John Dwyer **Bred** Oghill House Stud & Jimmy Hyland **Trained** Newmarket, Suffolk

FOCUS
This was another fair little 3-y-o handicap for its grade. There was a routine pace on and two progressive horses came nicely clear. The winner is rated a bit better than the bare form but the last two are better at Southwell, which limits the rating.
Aloneinthestreet(USA) Official explanation: trainer had no explanation for the poor form shown

469 BETDAQ MOBILE APPS H'CAP 1m 4f (P)
7:40 (7:47) (Class 6) (0-65,64) 3-Y-0 **£1,535** (£453; £226) **Stalls** Centre

Form RPR

46-4 **1** **Twin Soul (IRE)**[21] [217] 3-9-1 **58** .... DavidProbert 3 64
(Andrew Balding) *trckd ldrs: shkn up and swtchd lft over 2f out: prog after: edgd rt but drvn to ld 1f out: styd on* **6/1**[3]

4-12 **2** *1* **Blue Cossack (IRE)**[20] [234] 3-8-11 **54** .... LiamKeniry 1 59
(Mark Usher) *trckd ldng pair: rdn to ld 2f out: hdd 1f out: kpt on but hld ins fnl f* **5/2**[2]

06-3 **3** *1¾* **Warrant**[14] [300] 3-9-5 **62** .... JimmyQuinn 6 64
(Jane Chapple-Hyam) *stdd s: t.k.h: hld up in last pair: shkn up and prog over 2f out: drvn and nt qckn over 1f out: kpt on to take 3rd last 100yds* **8/1**

54-5 **4** *¾* **Entrance**[33] [77] 3-9-5 **62** .... LukeMorris 2 63
(Julia Feilden) *hld up in tch: prog to chal 2f out: nt qckn over 1f out: grad fdd* **20/1**

00-5 **5** *2* **Gower Rules (IRE)**[12] [339] 3-8-12 **55** .... NeilChalmers 5 53
(John Bridger) *stdd s: hld up last: effrt on inner and in tch 2f out: wl hld whn n.m.r and swtchd lft 1f out* **33/1**

0-33 **6** *nk* **Bathwick Scanno (IRE)**[20] [234] 3-8-11 **54** .... CathyGannon 8 51
(David Evans) *mde most: kicked on over 3f out: hdd 2f out: steadily wknd* **8/1**

603- **7** *10* **Handicraft (IRE)**[98] [7296] 3-8-2 **45** .... JoeFanning 7 26+
(Mark Johnston) *pressed ldr 3f: styd chsng tl hung violently lft over 2f out: ended on on far side rail: eased and wl bhd* **6/4**[1]

65-0 **8** *½* **More Than Enough (IRE)**[20] [234] 3-9-7 **64** .... FrederikTylicki 4 44
(Richard Fahey) *racd wd thrght: chsd ldrs tl wknd 3f out: sn bhd* **12/1**

2m 37.31s (2.81) **Going Correction** -0.10s/f (Stan) **8** Ran SP% **120.5**
Speed ratings (Par 95): **86,85,84,83,82 82,75,75**
toteswingers:1&2:£3.60, 1&3:£11.30, 2&3:£5.70 CSF £22.68 CT £125.16 TOTE £2.40: £1.02, £2.10, £3.80; EX 21.60.Reach Out was withdrawn. Price at time of withdrawal 16-1. Rule 4 does not apply.
Owner N Botica **Bred** Mrs Clodagh McStay **Trained** Kingsclere, Hants

FOCUS
A moderate 3-y-o handicap, run at an uneven pace. The form may not be the most reliable.
Handicraft(IRE) Official explanation: jockey said filly hung left

470 DAY TIME, NIGHT TIME, GREAT TIME H'CAP 6f (P)
8:10 (8:11) (Class 5) (0-70,70) 4-Y-0+ **£2,047** (£604; £302) **Stalls** Low

Form RPR

-464 **1** **Tislaam (IRE)**[5] [430] 4-9-3 **67** ....(p) RobertWinston 4 77+
(Alan McCabe) *hld up in rr: gng easily but nowhere to go 2f out to jst over 1f out: drvn and prog fnl f to ld last 50yds* **11/4**[1]

000- **2** *½* **Tenacestream (CAN)**[55] [7892] 4-9-1 **68** .... KierenFox(3) 3 73
(John Best) *chsd ldrs on inner: clsd over 1f out: rdn to chal and upsides ins fnl f: kpt on* **6/1**[3]

-521 **3** *nk* **Sherjawy (IRE)**[14] [298] 7-9-4 **68** .... SamHitchcott 7 72
(Zoe Davison) *pressed ldr: rdn to ld narrowly 2f out: jnd fnl f: hdd and one pce last 50yds* **8/1**

06-4 **4** *shd* **Kylladdie**[27] [144] 4-9-3 **67** .... JamieSpencer 5 71
(Steve Gollings) *chsd ldrs: rdn over 2f out: clsd u.p over 1f out: upsides 75yds out: nt qckn* **9/1**

05-6 **5** *2½* **Al Gillani (IRE)**[25] [178] 6-9-5 **69** ....(p) GeorgeBaker 8 65
(Jim Boyle) *pressed ldrs: nt qckn wl over 1f out: wl hld fnl f* **4/1**[2]

2040 **6** *1¾* **Fear Nothing**[14] [298] 4-9-3 **67** ....(b) JoeFanning 9 57
(Ian McInnes) *fast away fr wd draw: led to 2f out: wknd fnl f* **25/1**

3353 **7** *¾* **Absa Lutte (IRE)**[6] [403] 8-9-6 **70** .... StephenCraine 11 58
(Michael Mullineaux) *t.k.h: hld up fr wd draw: effrt over 2f out: no prog and btn over 1f out* **4/1**[2]

30-0 **8** *2½* **Comadoir (IRE)**[18] [264] 5-9-4 **68** ....(v[1]) DaneO'Neill 12 48
(Jo Crowley) *in tch in rr: rdn and no room 2f out: btn after and fdd* **20/1**

5-06 **9** *½* **Duplicity**[35] [46] 4-9-6 **70** .... MickyFenton 10 48
(James Given) *t.k.h: hld up fr wd draw: rdn sn after 1/2-way: struggling over 2f out* **33/1**

1m 12.04s (-1.06) **Going Correction** -0.10s/f (Stan) **9** Ran SP% **113.6**
Speed ratings (Par 103): **103,102,101,101,98 96,95,91,91**
toteswingers:1&2:£3.90, 1&3:£4.10, 2&3:£8.00 CSF £18.69 CT £115.59 TOTE £3.00: £1.20, £2.60, £1.80; EX 18.20.
Owner Mrs Z Wentworth **Bred** Airlie Stud **Trained** Averham Park, Notts

■ Stewards' Enquiry : Kieren Fox one-day ban: used whip with excessive frequency (Feb 23)

FOCUS
A very tight sprint handicap with 3lb covering the field. The first four were very closely covered nearing the finish. An ordinary race but the winner is rated better than the bare form.

T/Plt: £27.40 to a £1 stake. Pool:£61,000.03 - 1,622.32 winning tickets T/Qpdt: £8.40 to a £1 stake. Pool:£6,963.34 - 612.60 winning tickets JN

[432]LINGFIELD (L-H)

Wednesday, February 9

OFFICIAL GOING: Standard

Wind: modest, behind Weather: overcast, dry

471 BET ON WINNING DISTANCES AT BLUESQ.COM MAIDEN STKS 1m 2f (P)

1:25 (1:27) (Class 5) 3-Y-0 **£1,910** (£564; £282) **Stalls** Low

Form RPR

00- **1** **Scottish Star**[217] 3794 3-9-3 0 .... LukeMorris 3 77+
(James Eustace) *t.k.h: chsd ldr tl led 6f out: rdn and edgd lft wl over 1f out: kpt on wl u.p: veered bdly rt fnl 100yds: kpt on* **7/4**[1]

3-23 **2** *1* **Riot Police (USA)**[23] 193 3-9-3 73............(p) JamieSpencer 4 75
(David Simcock) *hld up in midfield: trckd ldrs gng wl 3f out: chsd wnr whn nt clr run and swtchd rt over 1f out: rdn to chal jst ins fnl f: ev ch but finding little whn carried bdly rt fnl 100yds: nt rcvr* **11/2**[3]

3 *2 1/4* **Monster Munchie (JPN)** 3-8-12 0............ JimCrowley 5 66+
(William Knight) *hld up in last pair: pushed along whn nt clr run and swtchd rt over 2f out: stl 5th 2f out: gd hdwy to go 3rd ins fnl f: gng on fin* **6/1**

2 **4** *3* **Stagecoach Danman (IRE)**[14] 300 3-9-3 0............ JoeFanning 7 65
(Mark Johnston) *chsd ldrs: wnt 2nd over 4f out: ev ch over 3f out tl over 2f out: wknd u.p over 1f out* **6/1**

5- **5** *hd* **Tornado Force (IRE)**[43] 7990 3-9-3 0............ LiamKeniry 6 64
(J S Moore) *t.k.h: chsd ldrs: rdn to go 2nd over 2f out tl 2f out: wknd over 1f out* **11/4**[2]

6 *3/4* **Jackies Solitaire** 3-8-12 0............ SteveDrowne 2 58+
(Roger Charlton) *s.i.s: bhd: pushed along over 4f out: kpt on same pce and no threat to ldrs fr over 2f out* **50/1**

50 **7** *5* **Ocean's Dream Day (IRE)**[12] 339 3-9-3 0............ KirstyMilczarek 8 53
(John Ryan) *in tch in midfield: rdn and struggling whn edgd lft over 2f out: sn wknd* **80/1**

00 **8** *86* **Have Another**[18] 262 3-9-3 0............ DaneO'Neill 1 —
(Richard Hannon) *led tl 6f out: sn lost pl: t.o and virtually p.u fnl 2f* **80/1**

2m 7.59s (0.99) **Going Correction** +0.10s/f (Slow) 8 Ran SP% **111.4**
Speed ratings (Par 97): **100,99,97,95,94 94,90,21**
toteswingers:1&2:£2.70, 1&3:£3.70, 2&3:£4.00 CSF £11.28 TOTE £2.50: £1.10, £1.40, £2.40; EX 15.40 Trifecta £61.20 Pool: £566.64 - 6.85 winning units..
Owner J C Smith **Bred** Mrs J McCreery **Trained** Newmarket, Suffolk

FOCUS
An interesting maiden on paper run in a relatively good time. The winner had to survive a stewards' enquiry. The runner-up is the most likely guide to the form.
Ocean's Dream Day(IRE) Official explanation: jockey said gelding hung left final bend

472 ASHURST WOOD CLASSIFIED CLAIMING STKS 1m 2f (P)

1:55 (1:55) (Class 6) 4-Y-0+ **£1,535** (£453; £226) **Stalls** Low

Form RPR

-455 **1** **Visions Of Johanna (USA)**[11] 352 6-8-3 67............ JimmyQuinn 3 70
(Ian Williams) *chsd ldrs: chsd ldr wl over 1f out: rdn to ld jst ins fnl f: r.o wl* **3/1**[2]

/6-0 **2** *2* **Force Group (IRE)**[18] 266 7-8-6 65............(b) LukeMorris 5 69
(Nick Littmoden) *s.i.s: sn in tch in midfield: switching rt and effrt on outer bnd 2f out: hung lft u.p over 1f out: chsd ldng pair 1f out: kpt on to go 2nd nr fin: no threat to wnr* **14/1**

00-0 **3** *nk* **Saviour Sand (IRE)**[11] 352 7-7-13 62............(t) JulieBurke(5) 10 66
(Olivia Maylam) *dwlt: t.k.h: in tch tl hdwy to ld 5f out: rdn ent fnl 2f: drvn and hdd jst ins fnl f: styd on same pce after: lost 2nd nr fin* **12/1**

0-06 **4** *1* **Free Tussy (ARG)**[17] 272 7-8-0 65............(bt) RyanPowell(5) 2 65
(Gary Moore) *pushed along early: in tch: lost pl and dropped to last trio over 4f out: rdn and hdwy on inner over 1f out: kpt on fnl f: nt pce to threaten wnr* **25/1**

2222 **5** *1 1/2* **Dream Of Fortune (IRE)**[5] 427 7-8-5 67............(bt) CathyGannon 6 62
(David Evans) *t.k.h: chsd ldr tl led over 6f out tl 5f out: keeping on same pce u.p whn bmpd over 1f out: one pce after* **13/8**[1]

-540 **6** *6* **Pytheas (USA)**[14] 307 4-8-4 68............ JoeFanning 4 50
(Michael Attwater) *t.k.h: in tch in midfield: rdn over 2f out: keeping on same pce whn bmpd over 1f out: sn wknd* **8/1**

43-0 **7** *10* **George Baker (IRE)**[7] 387 4-8-2 59............ NickyMackay 8 36
(George Baker) *w ldr tl chsd ldr 5f out tl wl over 1f out: sn wknd: wl btn and eased ins fnl f* **16/1**

2/00 **8** *1 3/4* **Tiger Dream**[12] 341 6-8-5 65............ ChrisCatlin 1 27
(Chris Down) *led at stdy gallop tl over 6f out: lost pl and last pair whn rdn along over 4f out: lost tch over 2f out* **66/1**

0-13 **9** *1 1/4* **Silver Guest**[12] 334 6-8-1 69............ AndrewHeffernan(3) 9 23
(Ralph Smith) *stdd s: hld up in last: rdn and no hdwy 2f out: n.d: suffered fatal heart attack after r* **6/1**[3]

2m 7.28s (0.68) **Going Correction** +0.10s/f (Slow)
WFA 4 from 6yo+ 1lb 9 Ran SP% **114.1**
Speed ratings (Par 101): **101,99,99,98,97 92,84,82,81**
toteswingers:1&2:£9.70, 1&3:£9.40, 2&3:£23.70 CSF £43.56 TOTE £5.60: £1.50, £2.80, £3.50; EX 48.60 Trifecta £226.70 Not won..
Owner Dr Marwan Koukash **Bred** David S Milch **Trained** Portway, Worcs

FOCUS
An ordinary claimer. Although the early gallop was generous, the tempo steadied after 4f and the form is a bit muddling. It has been rated around the third.

473 EXCLUSIVE LIVE SHOWS AT BLUESQ.COM H'CAP 1m (P)

2:30 (2:31) (Class 5) (0-75,75) 4-Y-0+ **£2,047** (£604; £302) **Stalls** High

Form RPR

5-12 **1** **The Happy Hammer (IRE)**[14] 307 5-8-11 65............ WilliamCarson 4 73
(Eugene Stanford) *fly-jmpd s and s.i.s: in tch: hdwy into midfield 4f out: rdn to chse clr ldr wl over 1f out: no imp tl styd on relentlessly fnl 100yds to ld last stride* **3/1**[1]

00-0 **2** *shd* **Highly Regal (IRE)**[21] 206 6-9-1 72............(b) KierenFox(3) 8 80
(Roger Teal) *chsd ldrs: rdn to ld over 2f out: clr 2f out: drvn ent fnl f: tiring fnl 100yds: hdd last stride* **20/1**

66-4 **3** *1/2* **Chief Exec**[19] 249 9-8-13 67............ LiamKeniry 3 73+
(Jeremy Gask) *hld up in tch in last trio: nt clr run and trying to switch to outer over 2f out: in the clr and hdwy ent fnl f: r.o wl: nt quite rch ldrs* **11/2**[3]

02-5 **4** *nk* **Copperwood**[33] 82 6-9-1 69............ DaneO'Neill 9 75
(Michael Blanshard) *stdd after s: plld hrd: hld up in tch in last trio: hdwy over 2f out: wnt 3rd but stl plenty to do over 1f out: kpt on ins fnl f: nt quite rch ldrs* **9/2**[2]

-442 **5** *nk* **Tuxedo**[14] 310 6-9-4 72............(b) LukeMorris 1 77
(Peter Hiatt) *stdd after s: hld up in last trio: effrt over 2f out: nt clr run wl over 1f out tl ent fnl f: r.o wl fnl 100yds: nt quite rch ldrs* **9/2**[2]

66 **6** *5* **Fedora (IRE)**[19] 248 5-8-8 62............(t) HayleyTurner 2 56
(Olivia Maylam) *in tch on inner: rdn and unable qck over 2f out: wknd over 1f out* **10/1**

06-5 **7** *1* **Salient**[7] 394 7-9-3 71............ JoeFanning 10 62
(Michael Attwater) *in tch in midfield on outer: rdn and no hdwy ent fnl 2f: sn lost pl and wl btn ent fnl f* **12/1**

125- **8** *1 1/4* **Green Earth (IRE)**[88] 7438 4-9-7 75............ IanMongan 6 63
(Pat Phelan) *pressed ldr tl led 6f out tl over 2f out: sn rdn and nt pce of ldr: lost 2nd wl over 1f out: wknd jst over 1f out* **12/1**

441- **9** *2 3/4* **Cativo Cavallino**[119] 6851 8-8-7 64............ NataliaGemelova(3) 5 46
(John E Long) *led for 2f: chsd ldrs after: rdn along over 3f out: wknd ent fnl 2f: wl bhd fnl f* **12/1**

160- **10** *1 1/2* **Heading To First**[140] 6289 4-8-13 70............(p) RobertLButler(3) 7 49
(Paddy Butler) *chsd ldrs for 3f: steadily lost pl: bhd fnl 2f* **100/1**

1m 38.41s (0.21) **Going Correction** +0.10s/f (Slow) 10 Ran SP% **114.7**
Speed ratings (Par 103): **102,101,101,101,100 95,94,93,90,89**
toteswingers:1&2:£11.20, 1&3:£5.80, 2&3:£22.00 CSF £66.60 CT £322.27 TOTE £4.70: £1.30, £7.00, £2.30; EX 63.00 Trifecta £434.90 Not won..
Owner Newmarket Connections Ltd **Bred** Rathbarry Stud **Trained** Newmarket, Suffolk

FOCUS
A competitive handicap for the grade with the first five home pulling clear. The pace looked sound enough and the winner recorded a length personal best.
Chief Exec Official explanation: jockey said gelding was denied a clear run

474 BLACKBERRY LANE CLAIMING STKS 1m 5f (P)

3:00 (3:00) (Class 6) 4-Y-0+ **£1,535** (£453; £226) **Stalls** Low

Form RPR

0-32 **1** **Layla's Dancer**[17] 272 4-8-10 68............ JamieSpencer 1 73
(David Simcock) *chsd clr ldr: clsd over 3f out: rdn and qcknd to ld over 2f out: drvn clr wl over 1f out: in command ins fnl f: eased towards fin* **10/3**[2]

11-3 **2** *3 1/2* **Mongoose Alert (IRE)**[20] 235 9-9-4 82............ SamHitchcott 3 72
(Jim Best) *stdd after s: hld up in last: clsd over 3f out: rdn to chse clr wnr wl over 1f out: edging lft fr over 1f out: one pce and no imp on wnr ins fnl f* **4/7**[1]

041- **3** *1 1/4* **Quinsman**[112] 7011 5-9-8 73............ LiamKeniry 2 74
(J S Moore) *racd in 3rd: clsd over 3f out: rdn and effrt to chse wnr 2f out tl wl over 1f out: one pce and btn 1f out* **9/2**[3]

33-0 **4** *1 3/4* **Eton Fable (IRE)**[11] 352 6-9-0 64 ow1............(p) TravisBlock 4 63
(Bill Ratcliffe) *led: pushed along over 5f out: rdn and c bk to field over 3f out: drven and hdd over 2f out: wknd wl over 1f out: wl hld whn swtchd rt ins fnl f* **25/1**

2m 47.5s (1.50) **Going Correction** +0.10s/f (Slow)
WFA 4 from 5yo+ 4lb 4 Ran SP% **108.8**
Speed ratings (Par 101): **99,96,96,95**
CSF £5.81 TOTE £4.50; EX 6.80.Layla's Dancer was claimed by Mr A. W. Carroll for £8,000.
Owner Dr Marwan Koukash **Bred** Kevin Buckley **Trained** Newmarket, Suffolk

FOCUS
The favourite disappointed and it's doubtful if this took much winning.

475 HOLLOW LANE H'CAP 1m 2f (P)

3:35 (3:35) (Class 5) (0-75,75) 4-Y-0+ **£2,047** (£604; £302) **Stalls** Low

Form RPR

16-0 **1** **Buona Sarah (IRE)**[7] 381 4-8-12 67............ JamesDoyle 4 75
(Sheena West) *in tch towards rr: hdwy ent fnl 2f: sltly hmpd and swtchd rt jst over 1f out: r.o wl fnl f to ld nr fin* **28/1**

3-16 **2** *nk* **Pertuis (IRE)**[7] 381 5-9-7 75............ ChrisCatlin 2 81
(Harry Dunlop) *in tch: rdn and effrt whn edgd rt jst over 1f out: ev ch ins fnl f: kpt on* **11/4**[2]

-215 **3** *nse* **Catbells (IRE)**[16] 278 4-9-3 72............(p) LiamJones 8 78
(Alan Bailey) *chsd ldrs tl pushed along to ld wl over 2f out: rdn ent fnl 2f: drvn over 1f out: kpt on wl tl hdd and lost 2 pls nr fin* **8/1**[3]

-633 **4** *1/2* **Lisahane Bog**[14] 310 4-9-1 70............(p[1]) DaneO'Neill 11 75
(Peter Hedger) *restless in stalls: in tch towards rr: effrt u.p over 1f out: styd on wl ins fnl f* **12/1**

13-1 **5** *shd* **Lingfield Bound (IRE)**[25] 174 4-9-6 75............ LukeMorris 1 80
(John Best) *in tch: effrt and swtchd lft over 1f out: ev ch ins fnl f: no ex towards fin* **5/2**[1]

5433 **6** *shd* **Veroon (IRE)**[7] 381 5-9-5 73............(p) MickyFenton 10 78
(James Given) *hld up in tch in rr: gd hdwy on inner over 1f out: ev ch ins fnl f: no ex fnl 50yds* **8/1**[3]

3-56 **7** *2 3/4* **Fonterutoli (IRE)**[28] 124 4-9-3 72............ RobertHavlin 6 71
(Roger Ingram) *led tl 8f out: chsd ldrs after: rdn and outpcd 2f out: kpt on same pce and no imp fnl f* **10/1**

000- **8** *hd* **Epsom Salts**[111] 7044 6-9-4 72............ IanMongan 9 71
(Pat Phelan) *racd wd tl over 5f out: chsd ldrs tl led 7f out tl wl over 2f out: stl pressing ldr u.p tl wknd ins fnl f: btn and eased towards fin* **12/1**

330- **9** *shd* **Mutajaaser (USA)**[310] 1133 6-8-8 62............ JoeFanning 7 61
(Kevin Morgan) *chsd ldr tl led 8f out tl 7f out: styd chsng ldrs: rdn over 1f out: wknd ins fnl f* **25/1**

01-4 **10** *1 1/4* **Suntrap**[35] 54 4-9-6 75............(v) ShaneKelly 5 73
(William Knight) *in tch: effrt whn hmpd over 1f out: nt rcvr and wl hld after: nt pushed fnl f* **8/1**[3]

6215 **11** *5* **Unbreak My Heart (IRE)**[13] 320 6-9-0 71............ RobertLButler(3) 3 57
(Paddy Butler) *t.k.h: hld up in rr: rdn and btn wl over 1f out* **33/1**

2m 6.07s (-0.53) **Going Correction** +0.10s/f (Slow)
WFA 4 from 5yo+ 1lb 11 Ran SP% **123.3**
Speed ratings (Par 103): **106,105,105,105,105 105,102,102,102,101 97**
toteswingers:1&2:£21.90, 1&3:£25.20, 2&3:£5.50 CSF £107.52 CT £716.86 TOTE £37.10: £10.40, £1.10, £5.20; EX 135.80 Trifecta £494.00 Not won..
Owner Tapestry Partnership **Bred** Peter J Doyle Bloodstock Ltd **Trained** Falmer, E Sussex

FOCUS
A competitive handicap which resulted in a bunched finish. It was the quickest of the three C&D races but the form looks ordinary.

476 HARE LANE H'CAP 6f (P)

4:10 (4:10) (Class 5) (0-75,75) 3-Y-0 **£2,047** (£604; £302) **Stalls** Low

Form RPR

21-1 **1** **Chevise (IRE)**[12] 333 3-9-4 75............ MatthewDavies(3) 5 75
(George Baker) *chsd ldrs: rdn to chal ent fnl f: led ins fnl f: r.o wl: rdn out* **4/1**[2]

4323 **2** *1* **Captain Dimitrios**[5] 423 3-9-7 75............(v) CathyGannon 1 71
(David Evans) *chsd ldrs: rdn and n.m.r ent 2f out: swtchd rt over 1f out: drvn ent fnl f: kpt on to go 2nd last stride* **8/1**

4-13 **3** *shd* **Greenhead High**[11] 349 3-8-13 **67** .... J-PGuillambert 4 63
(Jane Chapple-Hyam) *w ldr: rdn to ld 2f out: drvn ent fnl f: hdd and one pce ins fnl f: lost 2nd last stride* **10/1**

16-5 **4** *shd* **Toms River Tess (IRE)**[14] 302 3-9-7 **75** .... KirstyMilczarek 2 70
(Zoe Davison) *hld up wl in tch in last pair: rdn and effrt ent fnl 2f: drvn and kpt on ins fnl f* **16/1**

3-11 **5** *1 1/4* **Joe Le Taxi (IRE)**[13] 322 3-9-2 **70** .... GregFairley 3 61
(Mark Johnston) *led tl hdd and rdn 2f out: hld hd awkwardly and unable qck over 1f out: wknd ins fnl f* **1/1**[1]

112- **6** *6* **Monsieur Jamie**[54] 7908 3-9-6 **74** .... JimCrowley 6 46
(J R Jenkins) *wnt rt s: wl in tch in last pair: rdn and short lived effrt 2f out: sn wknd and wl btn 1f out* **5/1**[3]

1m 13.01s (1.11) **Going Correction** +0.10s/f (Slow) **6** Ran SP% **112.8**
Speed ratings (Par 97): **96,94,94,94,92 84**
toteswingers:1&2:£19.70, 1&3:£30.20, 2&3:£26.90 CSF £34.14 TOTE £3.40: £1.20, £3.70; EX 26.80.
Owner M Khan X2 **Bred** Paul And Mrs Jenny Green **Trained** Whitsbury, Hants

FOCUS
A fair sprint handicap but it might not have taken too much winning.

477 PLAY ROULETTE AT BLUESQ.COM H'CAP 7f (P)
4:40 (4:40) (Class 6) (0-65,65) 4-Y-0+ **£1,535** (£453; £226) **Stalls** Low

Form RPR

2-00 **1** **Spin Again (IRE)**[12] 336 6-9-0 **65** .... LucyKBarry(7) 9 72
(Mark Wellings) *restless in stalls: led after 1f: mde rest: styd on wl fnl f: rdn out* **8/1**

50-0 **2** *3/4* **Charles Darwin (IRE)**[14] 306 8-8-11 **55** ....(p) LiamKeniry 1 60
(Michael Blanshard) *t.k.h: chsd ldrs: rdn and effrt over 1f out: kpt on ins fnl f: wnt 2nd nr fin* **12/1**

00-0 **3** *nk* **First Service (IRE)**[16] 280 5-8-7 **51** oh2............(e¹) WilliamCarson 6 55
(Michael Attwater) *chsd ldrs: wnt 2nd ent fnl 2f: rdn and pressed wnr jst over 1f out: styd on same pce ins fnl f: lost 2nd nr fin* **12/1**

0-65 **4** *1* **Kai Mook**[28] 128 4-9-3 **61** ....(t) KirstyMilczarek 10 62
(Amy Weaver) *in tch in midfield: n.m.r bnd ent fnl 2f: rdn ent fnl f: kpt on wl fnl 100yds* **15/2**

00-4 **5** *hd* **Lopinot (IRE)**[19] 248 8-9-3 **61** ....(v) GeorgeBaker 8 62
(Martin Bosley) *hld up in tch in rr: rdn and effrt wl over 1f out: kpt on u.p ins fnl f: nt pce to threaten wnr* **5/2**[1]

3220 **6** *hd* **Chinese Democracy (USA)**[14] 304 4-8-12 **56** ....(v) CathyGannon 3 56
(David Evans) *t.k.h: hld up in midfield: effrt u.p on inner over 1f out: styd on same pce ins fnl f* **8/1**

0-34 **7** *3/4* **Ivory Lace**[7] 387 10-8-10 **61** .... RichardRowe(7) 5 59
(Steve Woodman) *stdd after s: hld up in tch in rr: pushed along and effrt on outer bnd 2f out: kpt on fnl f: nvr able to chal* **13/2**[3]

005- **8** *1* **Zagarock**[118] 6862 4-8-9 **53** .... NeilChalmers 4 49
(Bryn Palling) *taken down early: led for 1f: chsd ldrs after tl ent fnl 2f: wknd over 1f out* **16/1**

22-4 **9** *nk* **Penbryn (USA)**[37] 23 4-9-4 **62** ....(be) JimCrowley 7 57
(Nick Littmoden) *stdd after s: hld up in tch in rr: c to outer and effrt over 1f out: no prog: nvr trbld ldrs* **4/1**[2]

0-00 **10** *7* **Six Diamonds**[13] 318 4-8-13 **60** ....(t) RobertLButler(3) 2 36
(Paddy Butler) *hld up in tch towards rr: rdn and no hdwy 2f out: wl bhd fnl f* **40/1**

1m 26.77s (1.97) **Going Correction** +0.10s/f (Slow) **10** Ran SP% **119.6**
Speed ratings (Par 101): **92,91,90,89,89 89,88,87,86,78**
toteswingers:1&2:£20.00, 1&3:£5.30, 2&3:£20.00 CSF £101.93 CT £1180.53 TOTE £16.50: £3.80, £2.60, £5.90; EX 98.30 Trifecta £375.80 Not won..
Owner David Dacosta **Bred** Barry Lyons **Trained** Six Ashes, Shropshire

FOCUS
A weak handicap which was slowly run with the winner allowed an easy lead. Not a race to place too much faith in.
First Service(IRE) Official explanation: jockey said gelding lost both rear shoes
Chinese Democracy(USA) Official explanation: jockey said filly ran too freely
T/Plt: £942.10 to a £1 stake. Pool:£65,627.88 - 50.85 winning tickets T/Qpdt: £90.10 to a £1 stake. Pool:£5,031.79 - 41.30 winning tickets SP

439 CAGNES-SUR-MER
Wednesday, February 9
OFFICIAL GOING: Turf: soft; fibresand: standard

478a PRIX WILLIAM ALEXANDRE RUINAT (CONDITONS) (4YO+) (TURF) 1m 4f 110y
11:30 (12:00) 4-Y-0+ **£10,775** (£4,310; £3,232; £2,155; £1,077)

RPR

1 **Timos (GER)**[16] 6-8-13 0 .... SylvainRuis 1 96
(T Doumen, France) **7/10**[1]

2 *1 1/2* **Salontanzerin (GER)**[71] 7648 6-8-7 0 .... FabriceVeron 6 87
(H-A Pantall, France) **68/10**[3]

3 *2* **Fellini (GER)**[29] 4-8-7 0 ....(p) ThierryJarnet 2 88
(P Monfort, France) **4/1**[2]

4 *3* **A Coeur Ouvert (FR)**[59] 7855 5-8-10 0 .... IoritzMendizabal 3 82
(H-A Pantall, France) **12/1**

5 *2* **Redesignation (IRE)**[88] 7455 6-8-13 0 .... RichardJuteau 7 82
(J-C Sarais, France) **54/1**

6 *2 1/2* **Kardo (GER)**[18] 267 4-8-7 0 .... DominiqueBoeuf 5 76
(W Baltromei, Germany) **24/1**

7 *8* **Tominator**[9] 371 4-8-7 0 .... JohanVictoire 4 63
(Reg Hollinshead) *racd in 4th on outer: rdn early in st: sn no ex: fdd: eased fnl f* **73/10**

2m 46.01s (166.01)
WFA 4 from 5yo+ 3lb **7** Ran SP% **117.2**
WIN (incl. 1 euro stake): 1.70. PLACES: 1.30, 1.90. SF: 4.40.
Owner Marquesa De Moratalla **Bred** Gestut Etzean **Trained** France

479a PRIX DES MIMOSAS (CLAIMER) (4YO+) (TURF) 1m 4f 110y
12:00 (12:00) 4-Y-0+ **£6,896** (£2,758; £2,068; £1,379; £689)

RPR

1 **Refik (FR)**[15] 8-9-5 0 .... DominiqueBoeuf 5 70
(M Cesandri, France) **53/10**[3]

2 *2 1/2* **Mondovino (FR)**[4] 439 8-8-11 0 .... MatthieuAutier(8) 10 66
(M Boutin, France) **9/1**

3 *2 1/2* **Benjamin (FR)**[19] 259 6-9-5 0 ....(b) JohanVictoire 2 63
(L A Urbano-Grajales, France) **6/4**[1]

4 *1* **Divin Tremp**[40] 7-9-5 0 .... StephanePasquier 9 61
(C Scandella, France) **9/1**

5 *1* **Iron Out (USA)**[21] 220 5-9-1 0 ....(p) IoritzMendizabal 4 56
(Reg Hollinshead) *broke wl to r cl to pce fr s: maintained position and r.o wl in st bef fading ins fnl f* **42/1**

6 *1/2* **My Boy Davis (IRE)**[29] 4-9-2 0 ....(p) StephaneRichardot 7 60
(J-P Perruchot, France) **69/1**

7 *10* **Renaione (IRE)**[21] 221 5-9-5 0 ....(p) ThierryThulliez 12 44
(E Botti, Italy) **4/1**[2]

8 *5* **Behma (FR)**[50] 4-8-8 0 ....(b) FabriceVeron 11 29
(Mme J Hendriks, Holland) **62/1**

9 *9* **Kazuri (FR)**[37] 4-8-9 0 ow1 .... ThomasHuet 3 17
(Mme J Hendriks, Holland) **69/1**

10 *3* **Lost Soldier Three (IRE)**[37] 10-8-9 0.....(p) MathieuTavaresDaSilva(5) 6 13
(F-X Belvisi, France) **22/1**

0 **Pacha Des Galas (FR)**[128] 8-8-9 0 .... EddyHardouin(6) 1 —
(F Cheyer, France) **21/1**

0 **Spirit Of The King (FR)**[21] 220 5-9-1 0 ....(b) RonanThomas 8 —
(S-A Ghoumrassi, France) **19/1**

2m 48.04s (168.04)
WFA 4 from 5yo+ 3lb **12** Ran SP% **116.5**
WIN (incl. 1 euro stake): 6.30. PLACES: 1.60, 2.00, 1.20. DF: 21.20. SF: 36.50.
Owner Emile Krief **Bred** Emile Krief **Trained** France

480a PRIX DES MAGNOLIAS (CLAIMER) (3YO) (FIBRESAND) 1m 2f (D)
12:30 (12:00) 3-Y-0 **£6,896** (£2,758; £2,068; £1,379; £689)

RPR

1 **Sheila's Star (IRE)**[14] 297 3-8-8 0 .... Francois-XavierBertras 4 66
(J S Moore) *racd midfield fr s: appeared btn early in st: but picked up wl 1 1/2f out: fnd a split between horses and fin strly to take ld 100yds out: comf* **31/10**[2]

2 *3/4* **Shahighyield (FR)** 3-8-13 0 ....(p) StephaneRichardot 10 69
(P Khozian, France) **15/1**

3 *hd* **Great Surprise**[6] 410 3-8-11 0 .... FabienLefebvre 12 67
(Reg Hollinshead) *broke wl to r 2nd: dropped bk to 3rd early in st: picked up and r.o wl fnl 1 1/2 f to go 2nd: only losing that pl in fnl strides* **18/1**

4 *nse* **Mahya Glaz**[33] 3-8-3 0 ....(p) YoannRousset(5) 6 64
(Y Fertillet, France) **13/2**[3]

5 *nk* **Yosha (IRE)**[54] 3-9-3 0 .... StephanePasquier 2 72
(P Demercastel, France) **23/10**[1]

6 *1* **Mister Segway (IRE)**[48] 3-8-13 0 .... EddyHardouin(7) 9 74
(Robert Collet, France) **13/2**[3]

7 *1 1/2* **Bradbury (IRE)**[114] 6978 3-9-2 0 ....(b) IoritzMendizabal 1 67
(James Bethell) *broke wl to r 3rd along rail: wnt 2nd early in st: hrd rdn: chal for ld: wandered off st line and bmpd eventual wnr: no ex fnl f: fdd* **16/1**

8 *snk* **Asiland (FR)** 3-8-7 0 .... PaulineProd'homme(6) 5 64
(D Prod'Homme, France) **60/1**

9 *1 1/2* **High Speed (SWI)**[9] 370 3-8-11 0 .... FabriceVeron 13 59
(H-A Pantall, France) **23/1**

10 *14* **Sagaway (FR)** 3-9-2 0 ....(b) RonanThomas 11 39
(S-A Ghoumrassi, France) **9/1**

0 **Scarlet Warrior (AUT)**[9] 370 3-8-6 0.....(b) MathieuTavaresDaSilva(5) 3 —
(G Martin, Austria) **42/1**

2m 5.33s (125.33) **11** Ran SP% **116.9**
WIN (incl. 1 euro stake): 4.10. PLACES: 1.80, 3.60, 5.10. DF: 27.70. SF: 59.90.
Owner Ray Styles & J S Moore **Bred** Albert Conneally **Trained** Upper Lambourn, Berks

481a PRIX DES BOUGAINVILLIERS (CLAIMER) (4YO+) (TURF) 7f 110y
2:05 (12:00) 4-Y-0+ **£6,896** (£2,758; £2,068; £1,379; £689)

RPR

1 **Richhill Lady**[13] 325 7-8-8 0 .... ThierryThulliez 14 61
(F Chappet, France) **26/5**[2]

2 *1* **Mikos (FR)**[63] 11-8-4 0 .... EddyHardouin(7) 9 62
(Robert Collet, France) **19/1**

3 *1/2* **Tigron (USA)**[51] 10-9-2 0 ....(b) FredericSpanu 3 65
(Mme C Barande-Barbe, France) **9/1**[3]

4 *3/4* **Pim Pam (IRE)**[49] 4-8-11 0 .... ElliotCanal(6) 2 64
(C Ferland, France) **9/5**[1]

5 *2 1/2* **Snow Bay**[23] 196 5-8-11 0 .... IoritzMendizabal 4 52
(David Nicholls) *broke wl to r in 2nd: pulling freely: swtchd away fr rail early in st: hrd rdn 2f out: no ex: styd on fnl f* **9/1**[3]

6 *3/4* **De Zephyr (FR)**[37] 9-8-8 0 ....(p) StevanBourgois(8) 7 55
(Robert Collet, France) **21/1**

7 *2* **Raganeyev (FR)**[9] 372 10-8-11 0 ....(b) MorganDelalande 6 45
(X Nakkachdji, France) **9/1**[3]

8 *3/4* **Good Bye My Friend (FR)**[89] 5-9-2 0 .... AlexisBadel 1 48
(C Boutin, France) **36/1**

9 *3/4* **Diableside (FR)**[89] 5-8-11 0 .... EricWianny 5 42
(J-P Delaporte, France) **42/1**

10 *2* **Fortune King (AUS)**[71] 6-8-11 0 ....(b) DominiqueBoeuf 15 37
(W Baltromei, Germany) **37/1**

0 **Abbondanza (IRE)**[23] 196 8-8-11 0 .... Francois-XavierBertras 12 —
(C Boutin, France) **50/1**

0 **Captain Bufalo (IRE)**[209] 8-8-11 0 .... Pierre-CharlesBoudot 10 —
(J-M Capitte, France) **46/1**

0 **Maita (GER)**[29] 4-8-13 0 .... SylvainRuis 8 —
(F Vermeulen, France) **32/1**

0 **Vianello (IRE)**[13] 325 4-8-11 0 ....(b) StefanieHofer 11 —
(Mario Hofer, Germany) **19/1**

0 **Revolverheld (GER)**[9] 371 5-9-2 0 ....(b) ASuborics 13 —
(G Martin, Austria) **10/1**

1m 35.4s (95.40) **15** Ran SP% **120.3**
WIN (incl. 1 euro stake): 6.20. PLACES: 2.30, 4.40, 2.80. DF: 42.60. SF: 58.00.
Owner Mme Berthe Klodawski **Bred** Haras De St Pair Du Mont **Trained** France

[464]KEMPTON (A.W) (R-H)

Thursday, February 10

OFFICIAL GOING: Standard

Wind: Light, half behind Weather: Rain before racing, then cloudy

482 KEMPTON.CO.UK H'CAP 6f (P)

5:10 (5:11) (Class 7) (0-50,50) 4-Y-0+ **£1,535** (£453; £226) **Stalls** Low

Form RPR

04-0 **1** **Royal Acclamation (IRE)**[14] [312] 6-8-8 **48**..............(p) DavidKenny(7) 1 58
(Michael Scudamore) *hld up in 5th or 6th: effrt 2f out: led 1f out: rdn out* **7/2**[2]

-500 **2** *2* **Jemimaville (IRE)**[20] [250] 4-8-13 **46**..........................(v) WilliamCarson 3 50
(Giles Bravery) *hld up in rr: plld outside 2f out: hrd rdn and hdwy over 1f out: styd on wl to take 2nd nr fin* **15/2**

010 **3** *1* **Rightcar**[6] [421] 4-9-2 **49**..(b) RobbieFitzpatrick 7 49
(Peter Grayson) *chsd ldng pair: wnt 2nd over 2f out: ev ch over 1f out: nt qckn* **16/1**

000- **4** *½* **Chandrayaan**[165] [5559] 4-8-9 **45**........................(v) NataliaGemelova(3) 10 44
(John E Long) *rdn along most of way: sn in tch on outer: drvn and lost pl over 2f out: styd on ins fnl f* **12/1**

0-00 **5** *2¾* **What Katie Did (IRE)**[13] [337] 6-9-1 **48**................(b) RichardKingscote 5 38
(Milton Bradley) *led: hrd rdn and hdd 1f out: wknd ins fnl f* **9/2**[3]

0-02 **6** *1½* **Jessica Wigmo**[14] [311] 8-8-13 **46**.................................. JamieSpencer 4 31
(Tony Carroll) *hld up towards rr: shkn up and modest effrt 2f out: briefly wnt 4th over 1f out: fnd little* **3/1**[1]

-400 **7** *1¼* **Southwark Newshawk**[14] [311] 4-8-9 **45**......................... KierenFox(3) 2 26
(Christine Dunnett) *chsd ldrs: hrd rdn over 2f out: sn wknd* **33/1**

3/46 **8** *7* **Valdemar**[20] [250] 5-8-7 **45**..(b) DeanHeslop(5) 9 —
(Alan Brown) *wnt lft s: chsd ldr tl hrd rdn and wknd qckly over 2f out* **9/2**[3]

1m 12.39s (-0.71) **Going Correction** -0.025s/f (Stan) 8 Ran SP% **111.9**
Speed ratings (Par 97): **103,100,99,98,94 92,91,81**
toteswingers:1&2 £9.40, 2&3 £15.90, 1&3 £7.90 CSF £28.33 CT £364.98 TOTE £7.00: £2.40, £1.40, £3.90; EX 32.90.
Owner M Scudamore **Bred** The Susie Syndicate **Trained** Bromsash, Herefordshire

FOCUS
A basement grade sprint handicap weakened by a splurge of non-runners. Straightforward form.

483 WATCH RACING UK ON VIRGIN MEDIA 536 CLASSIFIED CLAIMING STKS 1m (P)

5:40 (5:41) (Class 5) 4-Y-0+ **£2,047** (£604; £302) **Stalls** Low

Form RPR

31 **1** **April Fool**[13] [341] 7-8-12 70..(b) DavidProbert 6 77
(Ronald Harris) *mde all: pushed 3 l clr 3f out: hld on wl whn chal fr over 1f out* **7/2**[3]

6-04 **2** *¾* **Having A Ball**[11] [361] 7-8-6 63..(v) ChrisCatlin 1 69
(Jonathan Portman) *sn outpcd in rr: rdn over 3f out: styd on wl fr over 1f out: wnt 2nd nr fin* **10/1**

2-10 **3** *nk* **Hip Hip Hooray**[22] [206] 5-8-12 71..................................... IanMongan 4 75
(Luke Dace) *s.s: towards rr: drvn to chse ldng pair over 2f out: styd on ins fnl f* **8/1**

33-2 **4** *hd* **Marching Home**[22] [206] 4-9-0 70.................................(t) JamieSpencer 2 76
(Walter Swinburn) *chsd wnr 2f then settled in 3rd: regained 2nd over 2f out: rdn to press wnr over 1f out: one pce* **9/4**[2]

/0-2 **5** *8* **Topcroft**[16] [290] 5-8-0 72...(v) LukeMorris 3 44
(Derek Shaw) *reluctant to load: in tch: rdn and outpcd 4f out: drvn along and btn 2f out* **2/1**[1]

-122 **6** *11* **Fivefold (USA)**[13] [334] 4-8-12 69..............................(p) J-PGuillambert 5 43
(John Akehurst) *chsd wnr after 2f: rdn 4f out: wknd over 2f out: bhd and eased over 1f out* **12/1**

1m 38.28s (-1.52) **Going Correction** -0.025s/f (Stan) 6 Ran SP% **114.2**
Speed ratings (Par 103): **106,105,104,104,96 85**
CSF £36.29 TOTE £3.10: £2.00, £11.10; EX 37.30.
Owner G B Balding **Bred** Miss B Swire **Trained** Earlswood, Monmouths

FOCUS
A run-of-the-mill 0-75 classified claimer with a couple of the runners looking very tricky rides. The form makes sense at face value among the front for, but may not prove that reliable.
Fivefold(USA) Official explanation: jockey said the colt stopped quickly

484 BET MULTIPLES - BETDAQ CLAIMING STKS 1m 4f (P)

6:10 (6:10) (Class 6) 4-Y-0+ **£1,535** (£453; £226) **Stalls** Centre

Form RPR

6-55 **1** **Classically (IRE)**[8] [381] 5-9-1 75.................................... SteveDrowne 4 82
(Hughie Morrison) *mde all: set weak pce: wnt 5 l ahd 4f out: effrtlessly drew wl clr: unchal* **4/6**[1]

5-14 **2** *20* **Treacle Tart**[13] [342] 6-9-2 70... GeorgeBaker 2 51
(Peter Charalambous) *hld up in 3rd: rdn to take 8 l 2nd 3f out: no ch w wnr* **15/8**[2]

01-5 **3** *4* **Active Asset (IRE)**[34] [79] 9-8-13 54................................ MartinDwyer 5 42
(David C Griffiths) *t.k.h 10 l off the pce in last: rdn 4f out: no rspnse* **10/1**[3]

0/ **4** *½* **Triple Point (IRE)**[75] 9-8-6 .... StefaanFrancois(7) 1 41
(J-M Plasschaert, Belgium) *chsd wnr: easily outpcd and lost 2nd 3f out: wl btn whn hung bdly lft fnl 2f* **25/1**

2m 34.84s (0.34) **Going Correction** -0.025s/f (Stan)
WFA 4 from 5yo+ 3lb 4 Ran SP% **107.7**
Speed ratings (Par 101): **97,83,81,80**
.Classically was claimed by P. R. Hedger for £8,000.\n\x\x
Owner Ben Arbib **Bred** Bridgewater Equine Ltd **Trained** East Ilsley, Berks

FOCUS
Classically proved in a different league dropped in grade, but he was given a very easy lead. Nothing else ran their race.
Active Asset(IRE) Official explanation: trainer said the gelding pulled up sore
Triple Point(IRE) Official explanation: jockey said the gelding hung left

485 BOOK FOR RACING POST CHASE DAY H'CAP 7f (P)

6:40 (6:41) (Class 6) (0-55,55) 4-Y-0+ **£1,535** (£453; £226) **Stalls** Low

Form RPR

-013 **1** **West Leake (IRE)**[10] [367] 5-9-4 **55**.................................... LiamKeniry 9 64
(Paul Burgoyne) *t.k.h in midfield: effrt over 2f out: led ent fnl f: hld on wl* **11/2**[1]

/3-2 **2** *nk* **Abigails Angel**[21] [225] 4-9-1 **55**...................................... KierenFox(3) 7 63
(Brett Johnson) *towards rr: rdn 3f out: hdwy over 1f out: styd on wl to press wnr fnl 50yds: jst hld* **6/1**[2]

2-64 **3** *1½* **Grand Honour (IRE)**[6] [421] 5-8-7 **51**......................(p) NathanAlison(7) 4 55
(Jim Boyle) *trckd ldrs: rdn to ld over 1f out: hdd ent fnl f: one pce* **6/1**[2]

000- **4** *nk* **Poesmulligan (IRE)**[76] [7570] 5-8-9 **46** oh1................. SteveDrowne 11 49
(Linda Jewell) *bhd: pushed along 4f out: gd hdwy over 1f out: styd on same pce ins fnl f* **66/1**

000- **5** *¾* **Bold Diva**[134] [6455] 6-9-3 **54**..(v) LukeMorris 3 55
(Tony Carroll) *chsd ldrs on inner: rdn to chal 2f out: one pce ins fnl f* **12/1**

420- **6** *½* **Commandingpresence (USA)**[116] [6956] 5-9-3 **54**...... NeilChalmers 10 54
(John Bridger) *towards rr: rdn and styd on fnl 2f: nt rch ldrs* **40/1**

-434 **7** *nse* **Goodbye Cash (IRE)**[22] [211] 7-9-1 **55**............... AndrewHeffernan(3) 2 55
(Ralph Smith) *rdn to ld: hdd & wknd over 1f out* **10/1**

6-44 **8** *3½* **Novastasia (IRE)**[8] [386] 5-8-9 **46** oh1......................(v[1]) SamHitchcott 1 36
(Dean Ivory) *prom tl wknd 2f out* **16/1**

2-06 **9** *1¼* **Yakama (IRE)**[14] [317] 6-9-2 **53**...............................(v) WilliamCarson 6 40
(Christine Dunnett) *in rr of midfield: rdn and sme hdwy 2f out: sn btn* **25/1**

5-02 **10** *1½* **Zeffirelli**[17] [280] 6-9-4 **55**... MartinDwyer 8 38
(Michael Quinn) *prom tl wknd over 2f out* **13/2**[3]

-306 **11** *1½* **A Pocketful Of Rye (IRE)**[14] [312] 4-8-2 **46**.......... LauraSimpson(7) 13 25
(Jane Chapple-Hyam) *bhd: hrd rdn over 2f out: no rspnse* **25/1**

30-6 **12** *nk* **Rainsborough**[29] [135] 4-9-3 **54**..................................(e) DaneO'Neill 14 32
(Peter Hedger) *prom on outer tl wknd 3f out* **10/1**

-412 **13** *½* **Metropolitan Chief**[10] [363] 7-9-0 **51**...................... TomMcLaughlin 12 28
(Paul Burgoyne) *mid-div: wknd 3f out: sn bhd* **12/1**

-225 **14** *1¾* **Libertino (IRE)**[13] [345] 4-9-4 **55**.................................. GeorgeBaker 5 27
(Tony Carroll) *chsd ldrs tl wknd over 2f out* **8/1**

1m 25.54s (-0.46) **Going Correction** -0.025s/f (Stan) 14 Ran SP% **119.5**
Speed ratings (Par 101): **101,100,98,98,97 97,97,93,91,89 88,87,87,85**
toteswingers:1&2 £6.70, 2&3 £8.10, 1&3 £7.50 CSF £36.04 CT £208.41 TOTE £5.60: £2.20, £2.80, £2.90; EX 36.20.
Owner L Tomlin **Bred** Rathbarry Stud **Trained** Shepton Montague, Somerset
■ Stewards' Enquiry : Liam Keniry two-day ban: used whip with excessive frequency (Feb 24-25)

FOCUS
A wide-open handicap run at a breakneck gallop. The form looks sound with the winner getting back to his best.

486 WATCH RACES LIVE AT RACINGUK.COM H'CAP 2m (P)

7:10 (7:10) (Class 4) (0-85,87) 4-Y-0+ **£3,885** (£1,156; £577; £288) **Stalls** Low

Form RPR

00-1 **1** **Exemplary**[13] [342] 4-9-11 **87**....................................... SilvestreDeSousa 2 93
(Mark Johnston) *mde all: set stdy pce: qcknd over 2f out: hld on wl ins fnl f* **3/1**[2]

/4-6 **2** *¾* **Benhego**[22] [209] 6-9-12 **82**... GeorgeBaker 6 87
(Gary Moore) *trckd ldng pair: rdn over 2f out: pressed wnr ins fnl f: a hld* **9/4**[1]

0-11 **3** *nk* **Muzo (USA)**[14] [314] 5-9-5 **75**.. SteveDrowne 4 80
(Chris Dwyer) *trckd wnr: drvn along 2f out: nt qckn ins fnl f* **11/2**

044- **4** *3* **Satwa Gold (USA)**[63] [7781] 5-9-5 **75**.............................. TomQueally 1 76
(Stef Higgins) *hld up in 5th: effrt over 2f out: no imp* **5/1**[3]

-421 **5** *1½* **Frameit (IRE)**[8] [393] 4-8-1 **61** 6ex.............................(v) KellyHarrison 3 62
(James Given) *t.k.h in 4th: outpcd over 2f out: sn btn* **10/1**

01-0 **6** *1* **Dalhaan (USA)**[22] [209] 6-9-5 **75**....................................(t) IanMongan 7 73
(Luke Dace) *hld up in rr: rdn over 2f out: nt trble ldrs* **16/1**

1/1 **7** *2* **My Valley (IRE)**[15] [301] 9-8-8 **64**.................................... ShaneKelly 5 60
(Pat Phelan) *towards rr: rdn over 2f out: n.d* **8/1**

3m 31.43s (1.33) **Going Correction** -0.025s/f (Stan)
WFA 4 from 5yo+ 6lb 7 Ran SP% **113.9**
Speed ratings (Par 105): **95,94,94,92,92 91,90**
toteswingers:1&2 £2.10, 2&3 £5.50, 1&3 £3.20 CSF £10.12 TOTE £3.30: £1.70, £1.90; EX 13.90.
Owner Dr Marwan Koukash **Bred** Darley **Trained** Middleham Moor, N Yorks

FOCUS
The feature handicap turned into a bit of a sprint with the winner allowed to set his own fractions in front. He is progressing, and the form is rated through the next two.

487 BISTRO PRICES FROM £42 FILLIES' H'CAP 6f (P)

7:40 (7:41) (Class 5) (0-70,70) 4-Y-0+ **£2,047** (£604; £302) **Stalls** Low

Form RPR

5-01 **1** **Spinning Bailiwick**[18] [273] 5-9-3 **66**............................(b) GeorgeBaker 6 73
(Gary Moore) *hld up in 4th: effrt and bmpd 2f out: rdn to ld fnl 100yds* **7/2**[2]

2212 **2** *¾* **Black Baccara**[6] [421] 4-8-7 **56**.....................................(be) LukeMorris 7 61
(Phil McEntee) *plld hrd in 5th: nt clr run over 2f out: fnd gap and rdn to ld 1f out: hdd and nt qckn fnl 100yds* **11/4**[1]

2-14 **3** *1½* **Caramelita**[14] [318] 4-9-6 **69**... DavidProbert 4 69
(J R Jenkins) *chsd ldr: rdn over 2f out tl 1f out: one pce* **10/1**

-000 **4** *½* **White Shift (IRE)**[18] [268] 5-8-5 **57**.............................. KierenFox(3) 5 56
(Jane Chapple-Hyam) *hld up in 6th: rdn 3f out: styd on same pce fnl 2f: nt gng pce to chal* **8/1**

0-10 **5** *2¼* **Dualagi**[12] [351] 7-8-13 **62**.. LiamKeniry 1 53
(Martin Bosley) *led tl 2f out: sn btn* **7/1**

00-3 **6** *2¼* **Pippbrook Ministar**[15] [303] 4-8-1 **57**....................... NathanAlison(7) 2 41
(Jim Boyle) *chsd ldrs tl outpcd fnl 2f* **5/1**[3]

-536 **7** *1½* **Athaakeel (IRE)**[12] [351] 5-9-1 **64**..............................(b) WilliamCarson 8 43
(Ronald Harris) *a last: rdn over 3f out: sn bhd* **7/1**

1m 12.12s (-0.98) **Going Correction** -0.025s/f (Stan) 7 Ran SP% **110.8**
Speed ratings (Par 100): **105,104,102,101,98 95,93**
toteswingers:1&2 £1.10, 2&3 £7.50, 1&3 £5.10 CSF £12.66 CT £80.14 TOTE £7.70: £2.60, £2.10; EX 14.10.
Owner Dr Ian R Shenkin **Bred** Mrs M Shenkin **Trained** Lower Beeding, W Sussex
■ Stewards' Enquiry : Luke Morris two-day ban: careless riding (Feb 24-25)

FOCUS
A modest fillies' handicap feauring plenty of in-form horses. The winner was on a good mark based on her old form.

488 BETDAQ THE BETTING EXCHANGE H'CAP (DIV I) 1m (P)

8:10 (8:10) (Class 6) (0-65,65) 4-Y-0+ **£1,364** (£403; £201) **Stalls** Low

Form RPR

33-3 **1** **Ermyntrude**[8] [387] 4-8-4 **53**...................................... JemmaMarshall(5) 5 63
(Pat Phelan) *hld up in 5th: swtchd lft and rdn 2f out: r.o to ld fnl 100yds* **8/1**

11-2 **2** *1¼* **Zafeen's Pearl**[34] [90] 4-9-2 **60**.................................. SamHitchcott 11 67
(Dean Ivory) *disp ld: led over 2f out: hrd rdn and hdd fnl 100yds: nt qckn* **9/1**

42-2 **3** *1* **Dichoh**[20] [248] 8-9-7 **65**..(v) GeorgeBaker 6 70
(Michael Madgwick) *chsd ldrs: rdn 2f out: one pce ins fnl f* **11/2**

4-04 **4** *1 ½* **Katmai River (IRE)**[17] 280 4-8-11 **55**..............................(v) DaneO'Neill 1 57
(Mark Usher) *cl up: rdn to press ldr over 1f out: no ex ins fnl f* **4/1**[2]

1-11 **5** *2 ¾* **John Potts**[17] 283 6-9-2 **60**.. KellyHarrison 7 55
(Brian Baugh) *dwlt: bhd: rdn 2f out: nvr rchd ldrs* **13/2**

00-5 **6** *11* **Peadar Miguel**[28] 139 4-9-7 **65**.. TomQueally 2 35
(Noel Quinlan) *disp ld tl over 2f out: sn wknd* **10/3**[1]

/10- **7** *hd* **Stellarina (IRE)**[150] 6024 5-9-2 **60**..................................(v[1]) JimCrowley 9 29
(William Knight) *s.i.s: bhd: pushed along over 2f out: n.d after* **14/1**

32-3 **8** *80* **Eastern Gift**[34] 93 6-9-1 **62**.. KierenFox(3) 3 —
(Gay Kelleway) *mid-div: pushed along whn n.m.r over 2f out: sn wknd and eased* **5/1**[3]

50- **U** **Holden Eagle**[120] 6846 6-9-5 **63**.. SteveDrowne 8 —
(Tony Newcombe) *hld up in rr gp: no room on inner: hit rail and uns rdr over 2f out* **25/1**

1m 38.47s (-1.33) **Going Correction** -0.025s/f (Stan) **9** Ran SP% **120.1**
Speed ratings (Par 101): **105,103,102,101,98 87,87,7,—**
toteswingers:1&2 £14.20, 2&3 £3.00, 1&3 £12.80 CSF £80.35 CT £439.10 TOTE £13.30: £3.30, £3.40, £2.60; EX 67.50.
Owner Epsom Racegoers No. 2 **Bred** Ermyn Lodge Stud Limited **Trained** Epsom, Surrey

FOCUS
A moderate and eventful handicap, run at a sound pace. It was the pick of the three C&D times and the winner is rated up 3lb.
John Potts Official explanation: jockey said gelding was outpaced

489 BETDAQ THE BETTING EXCHANGE H'CAP (DIV II) 1m (P)
8:40 (8:40) (Class 6) (0-65,65) 4-Y-0+ **£1,364** (£403; £201) **Stalls** Low

Form RPR
-036 **1** **Mister Green (FR)**[7] 400 5-9-5 **63**..............................(bt) JamesDoyle 4 70+
(David Flood) *hld up in 5th: smooth hdwy and led on bit over 1f out: pushed out: shade comf* **9/2**[2]

-052 **2** *½* **Master Of Dance (IRE)**[5] 433 4-9-4 **62**........................(b) MickyFenton 3 68
(James Given) *plld hrd towards rr: rdn over 2f out: styd on wl fr over 1f out: wnt 2nd fnl 100yds: a hld* **15/2**[3]

5-03 **3** *1 ¼* **Prohibition (IRE)**[11] 361 5-9-2 **60**.................................. GeorgeBaker 5 63
(Gary Moore) *chsd ldrs: rdn to press ldrs over 1f out: one pce ins fnl f* **9/2**[2]

606- **4** *1 ¼* **Aldo**[145] 6212 4-9-7 **65**.. J-PGuillambert 8 65
(Alastair Lidderdale) *led: rdn and hdd over 1f out: no ex ins fnl f* **14/1**

0-33 **5** *½* **El Libertador (USA)**[14] 317 5-8-9 **58**..................(p) TobyAtkinson(5) 10 57
(Jeremy Gask) *bhd: rdn over 2f out: sme late hdwy* **9/1**

5-36 **6** *nse* **Sovereignty (JPN)**[11] 361 9-8-13 **57**.............................. SamHitchcott 1 56
(Dean Ivory) *stdd towards rr: hdwy on inner and rdn to chse ldrs over 1f out: no ex* **14/1**

0-02 **7** *1* **French Art**[14] 317 6-9-2 **60**...(p) EddieAhern 2 57
(Nigel Tinkler) *trckd ldr: rdn to chal 2f out: wknd 1f out* **4/1**[1]

630- **P** **Frank Street**[115] 6992 5-8-10 **54**...(t) LiamKeniry 6 —
(Eve Johnson Houghton) *prom: cl 3rd whn wnt lame and p.u wl over 2f out* **8/1**

120- **P** **Signora Frasi (IRE)**[112] 7037 6-9-2 **60**........................ FergusSweeney 7 —
(Tony Newcombe) *hld up in rr: rn into bk of puller-up and bdly hmpd wl over 2f out: p.u* **9/1**

1m 40.25s (0.45) **Going Correction** -0.025s/f (Stan) **9** Ran SP% **112.6**
Speed ratings (Par 101): **96,95,94,93,92 92,91,—,—**
toteswingers:1&2 £5.70, 2&3 £4.60, 1&3 £10.10 CSF £36.87 CT £158.16 TOTE £2.40: £1.10, £5.10, £2.00; EX 43.70.
Owner DM Partnership **Bred** Gainsborough Stud Management Ltd **Trained** Exning, Suffolk
■ Stewards' Enquiry : James Doyle trainer said, regarding that apparent improvement of form, that the gelding was unsuited by the Fibresand surface at Southwell

FOCUS
The second division of the 1m handicap was equally competitve as the first and resulted in a visually impressive winner who will be well treated if building on this. However the pace was steady and this is muddling form.
Signora Frasi(IRE) Official explanation: jockey said the mare suffered interference in running
T/Plt: £175.90 to a £1 stake. Pool of £69,629.31 - 288.85 winning tickets. T/Qpdt: £3.90 to a £1 stake. Pool of £10,363.03 - 1,925.89 winning tickets. LM

450 SOUTHWELL (L-H)
Thursday, February 10

OFFICIAL GOING: Standard
Wind: Light across Weather: Overcast and light rain

490 BET AND WATCH AT BLUESQ.COM H'CAP 1m (F)
1:50 (1:53) (Class 6) (0-52,52) 4-Y-0+ **£1,535** (£453; £226) **Stalls** Low

Form RPR
0-42 **1** **On The Cusp (IRE)**[13] 340 4-8-7 **48**..............................(p) JulieBurke(5) 4 57
(Michael Chapman) *cl up: led after 3f: pushed clr 2f out: rdn and edgd lft over 1f out: kpt on* **11/4**[2]

060- **2** *1 ¼* **Lilli Palmer (IRE)**[119] 6862 4-8-10 **46** oh1........................ MartinLane 10 52
(Mike Murphy) *hld up towards rr: stdy hdwy on outer over 3f out: rdn to chse ldrs wl over 1f out: styd on wl ins fnl f: nt rch wnr* **9/1**

6-32 **3** *½* **Noble Attitude**[30] 120 5-8-7 **46** oh1.................. AndrewHeffernan(3) 11 51
(Richard Guest) *trckd ldrs: hdwy 3f out: chsd wnr over 2f out: rdn wl over 1f out: drvn and one pce ins fnl f* **7/4**[1]

560- **4** *9* **Ledgerwood**[233] 3290 6-8-10 **46** oh1..............................(p) NeilChalmers 8 30
(Adrian Chamberlain) *led 3f: prom tl rdn along 3f out and grad wknd* **50/1**

200- **5** *½* **Castlebury (IRE)**[141] 6298 6-9-1 **51**..............................(b) PJMcDonald 9 34
(Ruth Carr) *chsd ldrs: rdn along 3f out: drvn and kpt on same pce fnl 2f* **18/1**

/4-0 **6** *½* **Westport**[16] 289 8-8-11 **47**.. SilvestreDeSousa 3 29
(Robin Bastiman) *chsd ldrs on inner: rdn along 3f out: drvn and kpt on same pce fnl 2f* **25/1**

50-0 **7** *4 ½* **Captain Imperial (IRE)**[10] 363 5-8-10 **46** oh1..............(t) LeeNewman 7 18
(Robin Bastiman) *midfield: effrt and sme hdwy over 3f out: rdn along wl over 2f out and n.d* **20/1**

00-0 **8** *1 ¾* **Safwaan**[29] 135 4-9-2 **52**.. StevieDonohoe 6 20
(Willie Musson) *upset and taken out of stalls bef s: checked and sn re-stalled: dwlt: sn rdn along and a in rr* **4/1**[3]

006- **9** *hd* **Blue Charm**[150] 6024 7-9-1 **51**.. TomEaves 2 18
(Ian McInnes) *towards rr: effrt over 3f out: sn rdn and nvr a factor* **16/1**

00-0 **10** *29* **Pinewood Polly**[21] 229 4-8-10 **46** oh1..............................(b[1]) LukeMorris 1 —
(Shaun Harris) *dwlt: hdwy on inner and in tch after 2f: effrt to chse ldrs over 3f out: sn rdn and wknd* **100/1**

1m 45.56s (1.86) **Going Correction** +0.125s/f (Slow) **10** Ran SP% **115.7**
Speed ratings (Par 101): **95,93,93,84,83 83,78,77,76,47**
CSF £26.37 CT £55.48 TOTE £4.00: £1.40, £3.50, £1.10; EX 34.60 Trifecta £114.20 Pool: £322.73 - 2.09 winning units..
Owner Rakebackmypoker.com **Bred** J Stan Cosgrove **Trained** Market Rasen, Lincs
■ Stewards' Enquiry : Julie Burke caution: used whip with excessive frequency

FOCUS
A poor contest, with recent winning form conspicuous by its absence, and something of a controversial affair. Half the field were out of the weights and the first three came clear.
Safwaan Official explanation: jockey said the gelding moved poorly

491 PLAY GOLF BEFORE RACING AT SOUTHWELL H'CAP 5f (F)
2:20 (2:20) (Class 5) (0-75,72) 4-Y-0+ **£1,813** (£539; £269; £134) **Stalls** High

Form RPR
00-3 **1** **Bookiesindex Boy**[16] 294 7-9-7 **72**..............................(b) StephenCraine 7 80
(J R Jenkins) *trckd ldrs gng wl: hdwy on bit over 1f out: led ins fnl f: pushed out* **9/1**

04-5 **2** *1* **Where's Reiley (USA)**[16] 294 5-9-3 **68**.................... GrahamGibbons 6 72
(David Barron) *trckd ldrs: rdn along and outpcd wl over 1f out: drvn and styd on wl ins fnl f: nt rch wnr* **7/2**[2]

00-1 **3** *¾* **Six Wives**[14] 318 4-9-0 **72**.. LeonnaMayor(7) 1 74
(David Nicholls) *prom on wd outside: rdn and ev ch over 1f out tl drvn and one pce ins fnl f* **7/1**

-060 **4** *1 ¼* **La Capriosa**[6] 430 5-9-3 **71**...(p) BillyCray(3) 5 68
(David Nicholls) *led: rdn along 2f out: drvn over 1f out: hdd & wknd ins fnl f* **12/1**

6-24 **5** *½* **Sharp Shoes**[16] 294 4-9-2 **67**................................(p) SilvestreDeSousa 8 62
(Ann Duffield) *prom: rdn along 2f out: drvn and one pce appr fnl f* **8/1**

1-41 **6** *nk* **Sleepy Blue Ocean**[16] 294 5-9-2 **67**..............................(p) LukeMorris 9 61
(John Balding) *racd towards stands' rail: in tch: rdn along 2f out: sn no imp* **5/1**[3]

-111 **7** *¾* **Sloop Johnb**[13] 343 5-9-7 **72**..(p) HayleyTurner 2 64
(Conor Dore) *sn prom: rdn along 2f out: grad wknd* **3/1**[1]

260- **8** *1 ¾* **Mata Hari Blue**[133] 6515 5-8-7 **58** oh2.............................. NickyMackay 4 43
(John Holt) *dwlt: a towards rr* **25/1**

1-13 **9** *2 ½* **Residency (IRE)**[28] 144 5-8-6 **62**..............................(p) AdamCarter(5) 3 38
(Bryan Smart) *a towards rr* **11/1**

59.41 secs (-0.29) **Going Correction** +0.025s/f (Slow) **9** Ran SP% **117.4**
Speed ratings (Par 103): **103,101,100,98,97 96,95,92,88**
toteswingers:1&2 £5.50, 2&3 £5.70, 1&3 £9.40 CSF £41.29 CT £239.89 TOTE £23.30: £6.20, £1.10, £1.60; EX 48.40 Trifecta £186.60 Part won. Pool: £252.20 - 0.50 winning units..
Owner Robin Stevens **Bred** D R Tucker **Trained** Royston, Herts

FOCUS
A routine Southwell sprint handicap. The winner is rated back to his best but the second was still a stone off his form of this time last year.

492 HOSPITALITY AT SOUTHWELL RACECOURSE H'CAP 2m (F)
2:50 (2:50) (Class 6) (0-65,71) 4-Y-0+ **£1,535** (£453; £226) **Stalls** Low

Form RPR
6-51 **1** **Mush Mir (IRE)**[2] 457 4-10-1 **71** 6ex..............................(b) StephenCraine 6 83+
(Jim Boyle) *set stdy pce and sn clr: pushed along and qcknd 3f out: unchal* **9/4**[2]

2-21 **2** *3* **Rosewood Lad**[7] 407 4-9-9 **65** 6ex.................................. CathyGannon 1 71
(J S Moore) *hld up towards rr: hdwy over 3f out and sn rdn along: drvn to chse wnr 2f out: sn no imp* **2/1**[1]

000- **3** *3* **Mandalay Prince**[8] 942 7-8-9 **45**.. JamieMackay 2 47
(Willie Musson) *dwlt and in rr: hdwy 1/2-way: rdn to chse ldrs over 3f out: drvn over 2f out and sn one pce* **33/1**

02-1 **4** *5* **Short Supply (USA)**[22] 39 5-9-7 **57**.............................. GrahamGibbons 4 53
(Tim Walford) *prom: hdwy to chse wnr over 4f out: rdn along over 3f out: drvn over 2f out and sn btn* **4/1**[3]

0-03 **5** *nk* **Light The City (IRE)**[9] 373 4-8-3 **48**........................ JamesSullivan(3) 3 44
(Ruth Carr) *trckd ldrs: hdwy on inner 4f out: sn rdn along: drvn over 3f out and sn wknd* **15/2**

20/4 **6** *30* **Dynamic Rhythm (USA)**[20] 244 8-9-12 **62**.................. VinceSlattery 5 22
(Liam Corcoran) *a towards rr: rdn along 1/2-way: wl bhd fnl 4f* **9/1**

60/0 **7** *66* **Two Tono**[15] 300 5-8-9 **45**..(h[1]) KirstyMilczarek 7 —
(Garry Woodward) [illegible] bhd **40/1**

3m 45.76s (0.26) **Going Correction** +0.125s/f (Slow)
WFA 4 from 5yo+ 6lb **7** Ran SP% **111.2**
Speed ratings (Par 101): **104,102,101,98,98 83,50**
toteswingers:1&2 £1.70, 2&3 £12.40, 1&3 £12.50 CSF £6.74 TOTE £3.10: £1.10, £1.70; EX 6.80.
Owner M Khan X2 **Bred** Shadwell Estate Company Limited **Trained** Epsom, Surrey

FOCUS
This was a war of attrition in the conditions and very few ever got into it.the winner built on his latest win but there are doubts over what else ran their race.

493 SOUTHWELL-RACECOURSE.CO.UK CLAIMING STKS 6f (F)
3:20 (3:20) (Class 6) 4-Y-0+ **£1,535** (£453; £226) **Stalls** Low

Form RPR
40-3 **1** **Ingleby Arch (USA)**[9] 376 8-9-1 87.................................. PhillipMakin 5 84
(David Barron) *wnt lft s: prom: rdn along and sltly outpcd 1/2-way: hdwy 2f out: drvn to chse ldr over 1f out: styd on wl u.p to ld ins fnl f* **13/8**[1]

2161 **2** *2* **Punching**[9] 376 7-9-5 75.. HayleyTurner 6 82
(Conor Dore) *sn chsng ldr: cl up 1/2-way: led over 2f out: rdn wl over 1f out: drvn and hdd ins fnl f: one pce* **3/1**[3]

46-5 **3** *1 ¼* **Thrust Control (IRE)**[9] 377 4-8-10 75.................... JacobButterfield(7) 4 76
(Brian Ellison) *sltly hmpd s and towards rr: hdwy on outer 1/2-way: rdn 2f out: kpt on same pce* **14/1**

4-12 **4** *1* **Bonnie Prince Blue**[9] 376 8-9-0 80..............................(v) DaleSwift(5) 3 75
(Brian Ellison) *in rr: effrt and hdwy 1/2-way: sn rdn: drvn 2f out and kpt on same pce* **5/2**[2]

50-6 **5** *16* **Realt Na Mara (IRE)**[30] 122 8-9-0 68 ow1........................ TravisBlock 2 19
(Hughie Morrison) *sn rdn along and a in rr* **10/1**

0-50 **6** *2 ¾* **Ponting (IRE)**[9] 375 5-8-9 49..(b[1]) MickyFenton 1 —
(Paul Midgley) *led: rdn along 1/2-way: hdd over 2f out and sn wknd* **50/1**

1m 16.32s (-0.18) **Going Correction** +0.125s/f (Slow) **6** Ran SP% **109.4**
Speed ratings (Par 101): **106,103,101,100,79 75**
.Bonnie Prince Blue was claimed by J. G. Given for £10,000. \n\x\x
Owner Dave Scott **Bred** Alexander-Groves Thoroughbreds **Trained** Maunby, N Yorks
■ Stewards' Enquiry : Jacob Butterfield caution: use of whip

FOCUS
Five of the six runners ran at the meeting here nine days earlier, three of them in the claimer over this trip, but the 1-2-3 from that race finished 2-4-1 here. This was quite sound run and the form is rated around the front pair.

Realt Na Mara(IRE) Official explanation: jockey said that the gelding was never travelling

494 PLAY GOLF AT SOUTHWELL GOLF CLUB (S) STKS 7f (F)
3:50 (3:50) (Class 6) 3-Y-O **£1,535** (£453; £226) **Stalls** Low

Form RPR

-233 **1** **Honkers Bonkers**[25] [183] 3-8-11 61............................(v[1]) JamesDoyle 7 63
(Alan McCabe) *racd wd: mde all: rdn clr wl over 1f out: kpt on* **2/1**[1]

36-0 **2** *3* **Fantasy Fry**[21] [228] 3-9-3 66.. HayleyTurner 3 61
(Hughie Morrison) *dwlt: t.k.h: sn trcking ldrs: effrt over 2f out and sn rdn: drvn over 1f out: kpt on u.p to take 2nd last 100yds: nt trble wnr* **3/1**[2]

42-2 **3** *1/2* **Neytiri**[17] [275] 3-8-6 56.. CathyGannon 1 49
(Linda Stubbs) *trckd ldng pair: hdwy 3f out: rdn to chse wnr 2f out: sn drvn and one pce: lost 2nd last 100yds* **4/1**[3]

-520 **4** *8* **Evelyns Diamond**[2] [456] 3-8-6 38.................................. BarryMcHugh 2 27
(Paul Midgley) *in rr: rdn along on inner 3f out: nvr a factor* **50/1**

534- **5** *9* **Yorketa**[92] [7396] 3-8-7 55 ow1....................................... TomEaves 6 —
(Michael Dods) *cl up: rdn along 3f out: drvn over 2f out and sn wknd* **3/1**[2]

4-36 **6** *1/2* **Littleportnbrandy (IRE)**[10] [366] 3-8-1 62..................(b[1]) JulieBurke(5) 5 —
(Paddy Butler) *chsd ldrs 2f: lost pl bef 1/2-way and sn bhd* **20/1**

1m 31.28s (0.98) **Going Correction** +0.125s/f (Slow) **6** Ran SP% **110.1**
Speed ratings (Par 95): **99,95,95,85,75 75**
toteswingers:1&2 £1.50, 2&3 £3.40, 1&3 £1.90 CSF £7.93 TOTE £3.50: £2.40, £1.60; EX 9.20.There was no bid for the winner.

Owner Rupert Plersch **Bred** J Atkinson **Trained** Averham Park, Notts

FOCUS
A weak seller, and again few got into it. The winner improved slightly on his recent efforts.

Yorketa Official explanation: trainer was unable to offer any explanation for the poor performance shown

495 ENHANCED SP'S AT BLUESQ.COM H'CAP 7f (F)
4:20 (4:20) (Class 4) (0-80,78) 4-Y-0+ **£2,914** (£867; £433; £216) **Stalls** Low

Form RPR

1-11 **1** **Steed**[3] [446] 4-9-1 72 6ex...(p) PhillipMakin 2 89+
(Kevin Ryan) *dwlt and sn pushed along in rr: hdwy 3f out: rdn to chse ldrs 2f out: styd on to ld over 1f out: clr ins fnl f* **5/2**[1]

210- **2** *4* **Just Five (IRE)**[91] [7403] 5-9-4 78.......................... PatrickDonaghy(3) 3 81
(Michael Dods) *dwlt and sn rdn along in rr: wd st and hdwy on outer over 2f out: rdn to chse ldrs wl over 1f out: drvn and kpt on wl ins fnl f: tk 2nd nr line* **18/1**

44-3 **3** *nk* **Khanivorous**[17] [279] 4-9-6 77......................................(v) StephenCraine 6 79
(Jim Boyle) *prom: hdwy and cl up 3f out: rdn 2f out and ev ch tl drvn and one pce ins fnl f: lost 2nd nr line* **6/1**

4344 **4** *1 3/4* **Elusive Warrior (USA)**[16] [290] 8-8-2 66....................(p) NoraLooby(7) 5 63
(Alan McCabe) *trckd ldrs: rdn along over 2f out: drvn over 1f out and kpt on same pce* **20/1**

52-3 **5** *hd* **Mr Emirati (USA)**[7] [400] 4-8-11 68.................................. TomEaves 7 65
(Bryan Smart) *prom: effrt 3f out and sn cl up: rdn 2f out: drvn over 1f out: sn wknd* **3/1**[3]

1 **6** *hd* **Intyre Trail (IRE)**[25] [181] 6-8-9 66................................ CathyGannon 1 62
(Peter Fahey, Ire) *cl up on inner: effrt over 2f out: rdn wl over 1f out and ev ch tl drvn and wknd ins fnl f* **11/4**[2]

01-5 **7** *3/4* **El Dececy (USA)**[38] [18] 7-9-7 78..........................(p) GrahamGibbons 4 72
(John Balding) *led: rdn along over 2f out: drvn and hdd over 1f out: sn wknd* **11/1**

1m 30.41s (0.11) **Going Correction** +0.125s/f (Slow) **7** Ran SP% **112.9**
Speed ratings (Par 105): **104,99,99,97,96 96,95**
toteswingers:1&2 £10.00, 2&3 £18.10, 1&3 £3.60 CSF £44.15 TOTE £2.90: £1.40, £14.50; EX 59.80.

Owner Mrs J Ryan **Bred** Rosyground Stud **Trained** Hambleton, N Yorks

■ Stewards' Enquiry : Cathy Gannon two-day ban: careless riding (24-25 Feb) caution: used whip with excessive frequency

FOCUS
Not a bad handicap and a disputed lead resulted in a generous pace. Despite that, a little over a length covered the seven runners passing the 2f marker. The winner progressed again and the form is rated around the runner-up.

496 PLAY RAINBOW RICHES AT BLUESQ.COM H'CAP 1m 3f (F)
4:50 (4:51) (Class 5) (0-70,69) 4-Y-0+ **£1,813** (£539; £269; £134) **Stalls** Low

Form RPR

-111 **1** **Stanley Rigby**[14] [323] 5-8-13 61.................................. BarryMcHugh 4 70+
(Richard Fahey) *trckd ldng pair: hdwy on outer over 3f out: led over 2f out: rdn and edgd lft wl over 1f out: drvn ins fnl f: kpt on gamely towards fin* **6/5**[1]

55-0 **2** *2* **Naheell**[20] [247] 5-9-0 62.. KirstyMilczarek 1 67
(George Prodromou) *trckd ldrs: hdwy over 3f out: rdn to chal 2f out: drvn and ev ch over 1f out tl no ex wl ins fnl f* **11/1**

60-0 **3** *2 1/4* **Magnitude**[15] [301] 6-8-7 55...(p) TomEaves 3 56
(Brian Baugh) *led: rdn along over 3f out: hdd over 2f out: sn drvn and kpt on same pce* **15/2**[3]

213- **4** *hd* **Dandarrell**[56] [7898] 4-8-3 56.. JamesSullivan(3) 5 57
(Julie Camacho) *cl up: disp ld after 3f: rdn along over 3f out: drvn over 2f out: sn one pce* **2/1**[2]

5-60 **5** *3 3/4* **General Tufto**[17] [287] 6-9-7 69...(b) MartinLane 2 63
(Charles Smith) *hld up: effrt over 3f out and sn pushed along rdn over 2f out: n.d* **10/1**

2m 30.75s (2.75) **Going Correction** +0.125s/f (Slow)
WFA 4 from 5yo+ 2lb **5** Ran SP% **108.0**
Speed ratings (Par 103): **95,93,91,91,89**
CSF £13.74 TOTE £2.10: £1.70, £4.20; EX 8.90.

Owner Dean Hardman and Stella Kelsall **Bred** F C T Wilson **Trained** Musley Bank, N Yorks

FOCUS
Not much pace on for this ordinary handicap. The winner probably didn't have to improve on his latest effort.

T/Plt: 24.10 to a £1 stake. Pool of £59,312.10 - 1,789.98 winning tickets. T/Qpdt: £5.70 to a £1 stake. Pool of £3,515.47 - 448.77 winning tickets. JR

[458] MEYDAN (L-H)
Thursday, February 10

OFFICIAL GOING: Tapeta: standard; turf: good

497a DUBAI IMTIAZ TROPHY (H'CAP) (TAPETA) 7f
2:25 (2:25) (95-105,105) 3-Y-0+
£42,307 (£14,102; £7,051; £3,525; £2,115; £1,410)

RPR

1 **Rakaan (IRE)**[14] [326] 4-8-11 101.. TedDurcan 6 101
(Jamie Osborne) *mid-div: smooth prog 2f out: led 1f out: r.o wl* **11/2**[2]

2 *1 1/2* **Montmorency (IRE)**[14] [327] 5-8-13 102......................(t) FrankieDettori 1 99
(S Seemar, UAE) *sn led: hdd 1f out: r.o wl* **12/1**

3 *1/2* **Ayun Tara (FR)**[21] [241] 4-9-0 104.................................. GregoryBenoist 2 99+
(X Nakkachdji, France) *trckd ldng pair: ev ch 5f out: nt qckn cl home* **10/1**

4 *1/2* **Atlantic Sport (USA)**[14] [326] 6-9-1 105.. KShea 4 98
(M F De Kock, South Africa) *mid-div: r.o wl fnl 1 1/2f* **5/1**[1]

5 *1/4* **Famous Warrior (IRE)**[21] [240] 4-8-13 102.................. TadhgO'Shea 10 96
(Doug Watson, UAE) *trckd ldr: r.o same pce fnl 2f* **20/1**

6 *1/4* **Clearly Silver (SAF)**[14] [327] 5-8-11 101............ ChristopheSoumillon 7 93+
(M F De Kock, South Africa) *mid-div: chsd ldrs 1 1/2f out: no room 1f out: nt rcvr* **7/1**[3]

7 *1* **Yirga**[14] [326] 5-8-13 102.. RoystonFfrench 8 92
(A Al Raihe, UAE) *in rr of mid-div: r.o fnl 1 1/2f* **11/1**

8 *1* **Indomito (GER)**[21] [236] 5-9-1 105.................................... WayneSmith 5 92
(P Vovcenko, Germany) *trckd ldrs: one pce fnl 1 1/2f* **10/1**

9 *hd* **Nocturnal Affair (SAF)**[21] [236] 5-9-0 104........................ RyanMoore 3 90
(H J Brown, South Africa) *trckd ldng pair tl 2f out: wknd* **14/1**

10 *1/4* **Iver Bridge Lad**[85] [7482] 4-9-1 105....................................(b) JMurtagh 14 90
(John Ryan) *slowly away: settled in rr: nvr nr to chal* **14/1**

11 *hd* **Sir Gerry (USA)**[14] [327] 6-8-8 105.......................... HarryBentley(7) 12 90
(Doug Watson, UAE) *nvr nr to chal* **16/1**

12 *4 1/2* **Lipocco**[110] 7-9-1 105.. KierenFallon 9 78
(Rod Collet, France) *nvr bttr than mid-div* **16/1**

13 *1 1/2* **The Living Room (FR)**[120] [6857] 4-9-0 104..................(t) OlivierPeslier 13 73
(Stephane Chevalier, UAE) *slowly away: settled in rr: nvr able to chal* **12/1**

14 *1/2* **Evens And Odds (IRE)**[14] [327] 7-8-13 102................ AdrianNicholls 11 70
(David Nicholls) *nvr bttr than mid-div* **12/1**

1m 25.14s (-0.06) **Going Correction** +0.225s/f (Slow) **14** Ran SP% **124.0**
Speed ratings: **109,107,106,106,105 105,104,103,103,102 102,97,95,95**
CSF: £72.52; Tricast: £660.65..

Owner David L Dixon **Bred** L Mulryan & M Fahy **Trained** Upper Lambourn, Berks

FOCUS
No unexposed types, so just ordinary handicap form for the level. The pace was no more than fair.

NOTEBOOK
Rakaan(IRE) confirmed the promise he showed when a close fourth over 1m here on his return from a break last month, proving every bit as effective if not more so over this shorter trip. He caused a bit of interference in behind when edging left late on, but was much the best. There might be another one of these in him.
Montmorency(IRE), back up in trip and returned to Tapeta, was able to dominate and, although no match for the winner, stuck on well in the straight. His jockey had to briefly stopped riding when crossed by Rakaan near the line, but he was held by that stage.
Ayun Tara(FR), fourth in the Cape Verdi on her previous start, was keeping on but held when badly hampered against the inside rail in the closing stages. She was not unlucky.
Atlantic Sport(USA) was only just behind Rakaan over 1m here last time, but he lacked that rival's pace on this drop in trip. (op 11-2)
Famous Warrior(IRE) ◆ stepped up a good deal on the form he showed in a slowly run race over further on his Dubai debut. He'll be third off the layoff next time and may be worth having on side.
Clearly Silver(SAF) disappointed when fitted with blinkers and dropped to 6f on turf last time, but this was better and he was unlucky not to finish closer. He was badly squeezed when pointed towards an ambitious gap between rivals inside the final furlong and would have been in the mix for a place with a clear run.

498a DUBAI CASTHOUSE TROPHY (H'CAP) (TAPETA) 1m 3f
3:05 (3:05) (100-110,107) 3-Y-0+
£46,153 (£15,384; £7,692; £3,846; £2,307; £1,538)

RPR

1 **Hunting Tower (SAF)**[7] [417] 9-9-0 105............(t) ChristopheSoumillon 5 104
(M F De Kock, South Africa) *mid-div: chsd ldrs 2 1/2f out: r.o wl: led fnl 110yds* **9/1**[3]

2 *1 1/4* **Sabotage (UAE)**[215] [3922] 5-8-11 102.................................. TedDurcan 8 99
(Saeed Bin Suroor) *trckd ldng duo: ev ch 1 1/2f out: one pce fnl f* **14/1**

3 *shd* **Monte Alto (IRE)**[14] [330] 7-8-13 104..............................(t) RichardHills 9 101
(A Al Raihe, UAE) *mid-div: trckd ldrs 2 1/2f out: led 1 1/2f out: hdd fnl 110yds* **10/1**

4 *1 1/4* **Jedi**[14] [329] 5-8-11 102................................ Christophe-PatriceLemaire 7 96
(A bin Huzaim, UAE) *trckd ldr: rdn 2 1/2f out: led briefly 2f out: r.o one pce* **25/1**

5 *1* **Once More Dubai (USA)**[21] [242] 6-9-0 105............(bt) FrankieDettori 2 98
(Saeed Bin Suroor) *slowly away: settled last: r.o fnl 2 1/2f but nvr able to chal* **9/4**[2]

6 *shd* **Burdlaz (IRE)**[14] [328] 6-8-13 104.................................... AhmedAjtebi 3 96
(Mahmood Al Zarooni) *settled in rr: nvr able to chal* **9/1**[3]

7 *3* **Heliodor (USA)**[21] [242] 5-8-5 102..............................(t) AntiocoMurgia(6) 1 89
(Mahmood Al Zarooni) *sn led: hdd briefly 2f out: hdd & wknd 1 1/2f out* **20/1**

8 *11* **Lost In The Moment (IRE)**[14] [328] 4-8-8 101.....(p) MickaelBarzalona 4 68
(Saeed Bin Suroor) *in rr of mid-div: rdn 6f out: hrd rdn 2 1/2f out: sn btn* **6/4**[1]

2m 20.21s (1.81) **Going Correction** +0.225s/f (Slow)
WFA 4 from 5yo+ 2lb **8** Ran SP% **115.1**
Speed ratings: **102,101,101,100,99 99,97,89**
CSF: £123.25; Tricast: £1,281.21..

Owner Sheikh Mohammed Bin Khalifa Al Maktoum **Bred** Mrs B D Oppenheimer **Trained** South Africa

FOCUS
The only runner with a progressive profile ran well below form, and this slowly run handicap was a weak affair by Carnival standards.

NOTEBOOK
Hunting Tower(SAF), the 2007 Durban July winner, is used as something of a lead horse these days according to Christophe Soumillon, but he showed he's still quite smart, gaining his first success since landing a 61/2f handicap on the Nad Al Sheba turf in 2009. He can be readily opposed in better company next time. (op 8-1)

Sabotage(UAE) was never far away and had his chance against the inside rail in the straight. This was a pleasing comeback from last year's DRC Gold Cup winner and this ought to out him right for a repeat bid. (op 16-1)
Monte Alto(IRE) took over early in the straight but didn't look keen, carrying his head at a slight angle. He wants holding on to longer, but the race wasn't run to suit.
Jedi ran really poorly in a race that should have suited last time, but this was better. A slowly run 1m3f was an insufficient test and he ran as well as could have been expected. (op 20-1)
Once More Dubai(USA) was held up well off the pace, with Frankie Dettori attempting to settle him, but he still proved too keen. He made a brief bid in the straight, but had too much to do considering how events unfolded and his effort soon flattened out. (op 5-2)
Lost In The Moment(IRE) was only 4lb higher than when winning over C&D on his debut for this yard and looked the only progressive runner in the line-up, but he ran terribly. He was being pushed along down the back straight in a bid to keep up with a slow pace and offered absolutely nothing. (op 13-8)

499a DUBAL POTLINES TROPHY (H'CAP) (TAPETA) 1m 1f 110y
3:40 (3:40) (95-105,105) 3-Y-O+

£42,307 (£14,102; £7,051; £3,525; £2,115; £1,410)

RPR
1 **Golden Sword**[14] [326] 5-9-2 105........................ ChristopheSoumillon 5 111+
(M F De Kock, South Africa) *slowly away: settled in rr: smooth prog 2f out: led 110yds out: comf* **2/1**[1]
2 *2 ¼* **Sweet Lightning**[14] [326] 6-9-0 102.............................. JMurtagh 13 104
(Michael Dods) *mid-div: chsd ldrs 3f out: r.o wl but no ch w wnr* **10/1**
3 *1 ½* **Glen Nevis (USA)**[5] [462] 7-8-11 100........................(v) AhmedAjtebi 10 98+
(A Al Raihe, UAE) *in rr of mid-div: r.o wl fnl 2f* **33/1**
4 *½* **Final Drive (IRE)**[14] [326] 5-8-13 101.............................. RyanMoore 11 99
(John Ryan) *settled in rr: r.o fnl 2f* **7/2**[2]
5 *¼* **Royal Destination (IRE)**[118] [6885] 6-9-2 105................(v) WayneSmith 6 102
(F Nass, Bahrain) *a mid-div* **25/1**
6 *hd* **Kal Barg**[21] [240] 6-9-2 105.............................. KierenFallon 14 101
(D Selvaratnam, UAE) *s.i.s: nvr able to chal* **14/1**
7 *½* **Persiste Et Signe (FR)**[55] 4-8-11 101.............................. OlivierPeslier 1 96
(Stephane Chevalier, UAE) *sn led: kicked clr 2 1/2f out: hdd 110yds out: wknd qckly* **14/1**
8 *2 ½* **Rochdale**[14] [326] 8-8-13 101........................(t) RoystonFfrench 3 92
(A Al Raihe, UAE) *a mid-div* **16/1**
9 *6 ½* **Snowmaster (USA)**[320] 5-9-0 102........................(bt) FrankieDettori 12 80
(Saeed Bin Suroor) *trckd ldrs tl one pce 2 1/2f out* **8/1**[3]
10 *1 ½* **Wonder Lawn (SAF)**[6] 8-8-13 101........................(t) KShea 8 76
(M F De Kock, South Africa) *in rr of mid-div: nvr able to chal* **12/1**
11 *2 ¾* **Oroveso (BRZ)**[21] [240] 5-8-11 100.............................. TadhgO'Shea 9 68
(E Martins, Brazil) *in rr of mid-div: n.d* **33/1**
12 *12* **Alrasm (IRE)**[138] [6355] 4-8-13 102.............................. RichardHills 4 47
(E Charpy, UAE) *trckd ldr tl 3f out: sn btn* **20/1**
13 *13* **Dear Bela (ARG)**[453] 5-8-11 100........................(v) TedDurcan 7 17
(Saeed Bin Suroor) *trckd ldrs tl 3 1/2f out: wknd and virtually p.u ins fnl f* **16/1**
14 *7* **Iron Age**[104] 4-8-9 99........................(bt) PatCosgrave 2 —
(M bin Shafya, UAE) *trckd ldng duo tl 3f out: wknd* **25/1**

1m 57.85s (-0.85) **Going Correction** +0.225s/f (Slow) **14** Ran SP% **126.9**
Speed ratings: **112,110,109,108,108 108,107,105,100,99 97,87,77,71**
CSF: £22.92; Tricast: £538.35..
Owner Sh Mohd bin Khalifa Al Maktoum,Wilgerbosdrift **Bred** T E Pocock & Morton Bloodstock **Trained** South Africa

FOCUS
They went a good pace and that suited the resurgent Golden Sword, who produced a last-to-first effort to take advantage of a mark 15lb below his peak RPR.

NOTEBOOK
Golden Sword ◆ hadn't won since taking the 2009 Chester Vase, but he had been working better this year according to Mike De Kock and connections have done well to get his confidence back. He was improving on the form he showed over an inadequate 1m on his Tapeta debut, this time moving into contention going easily out wide early in the straight before drawing away, and clearly hold-up tactics on this synthetic surface now suit a horse who was so often ridden forcefully on turf. [illegible]
Sweet Lightning couldn't reverse recent 1m form with Golden Sword, but this was still a good effort behind the well-handicapped winner.
Glen Nevis(USA) was in the right place considering how the race unfolded and this is as good as he is. (op 25-1)
Final Drive(IRE) was only a short-head behind Golden Sword over 1m here last time, and just ahead of Sweet Lightning, but he wasn't as well suited by the step up in trip as that pair. (op 4-1)
Royal Destination(IRE), bought out of Jeremy Noseda's yard for 40,000gns since last seen in October, was tried in a visor and ran well considering he was forced to switch to the inside in the straight.

500a DUBAL TROPHY (H'CAP) (TURF) 5f
4:15 (4:15) (100-111,111) 3-Y-O+

£67,307 (£22,435; £11,217; £5,608; £3,365; £2,243)

RPR
1 **Prohibit**[7] [414] 6-9-2 108........................(p) ChristopheSoumillon 11 115+
(Robert Cowell) *settled in rr: rdn 2 1/2f out: r.o wl: led fnl 55yds* **7/1**
2 *shd* **Invincible Ash (IRE)**[28] [155] 6-8-11 104........................(p) GFCarroll 9 110
(M Halford, Ire) *chsd ldrs: led 2 1/2f out: r.o wl: hdd fnl 55yds* **7/1**
3 *3 ¼* **Barney McGrew (IRE)**[14] [327] 8-8-8 100........................ RyanMoore 3 95+
(Michael Dods) *mid-div: r.o wl fnl 2f: nrst fin* **20/1**
4 *shd* **Monsieur Joe (IRE)**[21] [237] 4-8-10 102........................ TedDurcan 5 97
(Walter Swinburn) *chsd ldrs: ev ch 1f out: one pce fnl 110yds* **4/1**[2]
5 *1* **Happy Dubai (IRE)**[14] [327] 4-9-5 111........................ RoystonFfrench 6 102
(A Al Raihe, UAE) *trckd ldr: ev ch 1 1/2f out: wknd fnl 110yds* **3/1**[1]
6 *2 ¼* **Mister Manannan (IRE)**[21] [237] 4-8-11 104............... AdrianNicholls 8 86
(David Nicholls) *chsd ldrs: wknd fnl f* **9/2**[3]
7 *½* **Spin Cycle (IRE)**[145] [6194] 5-8-11 103 ow1................(t) OlivierPeslier 10 84
(S Seemar, UAE) *trckd ldrs: one pce fnl f* **14/1**
8 *1 ¼* **Noble Heir (SAF)**[21] [237] 6-8-5 104................(b) HarryBentley(6) 4 80
(H J Brown, South Africa) *sn led: hdd 2 1/2f out: sn wknd* **16/1**
9 *¾* **Compasivo Cat (ARG)**[789] 7-8-11 104........................(t) WJSupple 2 77
(E Charpy, UAE) *sn struggling in rr* **25/1**
10 *2 ¾* **Rebecca Rolfe**[21] [237] 5-8-10 102........................ MickaelBarzalona 7 66
(M Gasparini, Italy) *nvr bttr than mid-div* **14/1**
11 *2 ¼* **Rain Delayed (IRE)**[21] [237] 5-8-13 105........................ JMurtagh 1 61
(Michael Dods) *nvr bttr than mid-div* **25/1**

57.92 secs (57.92) **11** Ran SP% **119.9**
CSF: £54.94; Tricast: £936.95..
Owner K Dasmal, A Rix, F Barr, T Morley, J Penney **Bred** Juddmonte Farms Ltd **Trained** Six Mile Bottom, Cambs

FOCUS
A competitive sprint handicap.

NOTEBOOK
Prohibit did little once in front and the suspicion is he probably wouldn't have seen his race out had he got there much sooner, with his head carriage not overly inspiring. He was never competitive on his reappearance over 6f on the Tapeta a week earlier, but his trainer stated before that race that the Al Quoz Sprint over this C&D was his main aim and victory here will have greatly enhanced his prospects of making the line up.
Invincible Ash(IRE) was suited by the drop in trip and didn't mind the return to turf. She ran right up to her best.
Barney McGrew(IRE) snatched third on the line but was never going to win.
Monsieur Joe(IRE) didn't improve on the form he showed over C&D on his Dubai debut, but he still reversed placings with the below-par Happy Dubai. (op 9-2)
Happy Dubai(IRE), chasing a hat-trick of wins on this straight course, was found out by the combination of a further 6lb rise and his recent busy spell taking its toll. He still fared best of those on the pace, though, finishing just ahead of Mister Manannan.
Mister Manannan(IRE) didn't improve as one might have hoped on his reappearance effort.
Rain Delayed(IRE) was reported by his jockey to have hung outwards throughout.

501a FIREBREAK STKS SPONSORED BY DUBAL (LISTED RACE) (TAPETA) 1m
4:50 (4:50) 3-Y-O+

£67,307 (£22,435; £11,217; £5,608; £3,365; £2,243)

RPR
1 **Skysurfers**[131] [6570] 5-9-0 112........................ FrankieDettori 8 115+
(Saeed Bin Suroor) *mid-div: smooth prog 2 1/2f out: led 1f out: r.o wl* **15/2**
2 *1 ½* **Musir (AUS)**[320] [1023] 5-9-0 117........................ ChristopheSoumillon 13 114+
(M F De Kock, South Africa) *settled in rr: trckd wnr 2 1/2f out: nt qckn fnl f* **6/4**[1]
3 *5 ¼* **Imbongi (SAF)**[28] [156] 7-9-0 113........................ KShea 3 99
(M F De Kock, South Africa) *mid-div: r.o fnl 2f but no ch w first two* **6/1**[3]
4 *1 ¼* **Bankable (IRE)**[28] [155] 7-9-0 116........................(t) RyanMoore 2 97
(H J Brown, South Africa) *mid-div: no room 4f out: r.o fnl 2f but n.d* **5/2**[2]
5 *¾* **Mujaazef**[6] 4-9-0 94........................(t) RichardHills 12 95
(A Al Raihe, UAE) *chsd ldrs: ev ch 2 1/2f out: wknd fnl f* **100/1**
6 *½* **Green Coast (IRE)**[28] [156] 8-9-0 112........................ TadhgO'Shea 9 94
(Doug Watson, UAE) *nvr bttr than mid-div* **20/1**
7 *2 ¼* **Cat Junior (USA)**[117] [6923] 6-9-0 113........................(t) OlivierPeslier 7 89
(Niels Petersen, Norway) *a mid-div* **16/1**
8 *3 ¾* **Lochinver (USA)**[14] [332] 4-9-0 109........................ MickaelBarzalona 6 80
(Saeed Bin Suroor) *nvr able to chal* **33/1**
9 *2 ½* **Gayego (USA)**[96] [7365] 6-9-0 113........................(t) TedDurcan 14 74
(Saeed Bin Suroor) *nvr bttr than mid-div* **12/1**
10 *¾* **Comradeship (IRE)**[5] [462] 4-9-0 100........................ RMBurke 11 72
(R Bouresly, Kuwait) *slowly away: racd in rr: n.d* **66/1**
11 *¾* **Frosty Secret (USA)**[7] [414] 7-9-0 106................ BernardFayd'Herbe 5 71
(M F De Kock, South Africa) *disp ld: rdn to ld 2f out: hdd 1f out: wknd* **66/1**
12 *½* **Dandy Boy (ITY)**[28] [152] 5-9-0 110........................ CO'Donoghue 10 70
(David Marnane, Ire) *nvr bttr than mid-div: stmbld 1 1/2f out: nt rcvr* **12/1**
13 *6 ¾* **Il Grande Maurizio (IRE)**[6] 7-9-0 100........................(v) RoystonFfrench 1 54
(A Al Raihe, UAE) *disp ld tl 2 1/2f out: wknd fnl 1 1/2f* **66/1**
14 *46* **Accountforthegold (USA)**[77] [7625] 9-9-0 93........................ RPCleary 4 —
(R Bouresly, Kuwait) *trckd ldrs for 4 1/2f: sn btn* **100/1**

1m 35.77s (-1.33) **Going Correction** +0.225s/f (Slow) **14** Ran SP% **130.0**
Speed ratings: **115,113,108,107,106 105,103,99,97,96 95,95,88,42**
CSF: £20.23..
Owner Godolphin **Bred** Darley **Trained** Newmarket, Suffolk

FOCUS
A high-quality affair, significantly better than the average Listed contest and more like a Group race. The pace was good, and the track record was lowered, with the time also 1.96 seconds faster than the 2,000 Guineas. The fifth limits the rating.

NOTEBOOK
Skysurfers ◆ had produced a high-class performance in the equivalent race on his return from a four-month break last year, before failing to progress as expected, and he confirmed he's best fresh with another really smart effort, this time after an absence of 131 days. Around a furlong out he looked sure to be passed by Musir, but he found extra and his main rival was eased off near the line, which exaggerated the winning margin. He went on to finish third in the Godolphin Mile last year, despite also taking in Super Thursday, and he could improve on that placing if going straight to World Cup night this time. (op 7-1)
Musir(AUS) ◆ hadn't been seen since winning last year's UAE Derby (also won the Guineas) after failing to pass an x-ray inspection when due to run in Australia. Christophe Soumillon later admitted he thought the colt would be "unbeatable" in this race, which shows the regard in which he's held, but this was still a high-class performance. His stable companion Bold Silvano is favourite for the World Cup in a few lists, but now make no mistake, this horse is now every bit as big a player for what is fast developing into an incredibly hot race. Currently a 12-1 chance, perhaps he'll clash with his aforementioned stablemate before the big day, with the third round of the Al Maktoum Challenge on Super Thursday the logical target if another prep is needed. (op 2-1)
Imbongi(SAF)'s performance suggests Mendip still has a bit to find if he's going to make a genuine World Cup contender. Today's third-placed finisher was just over 2l behind that runner last time.
Bankable(IRE), so eyecatching over 6f on his Tapeta debut, endured a rough trip and couldn't show his best form. He was poorly placed in the straight having been badly hampered on the bend and continually found trouble whilst not being given a hard time in the closing stages.
Mujaazef, who had a recent pipe-opener at Jebel Ali, fared best of those handy and seemed to run the race of his life.
Green Coast(IRE) continues below the form he showed when runner-up in last year's Godolphin Mile.
Cat Junior(USA), sold out of Brian Meehan's yard for 220,000gns since he was last seen, was sweating and ran some way below form. (op 14-1)
Gayego(USA), who had been off since finishing third in the Breeders' Cup Dirt Mile, returned having bled from both nostrils (tchd 14-1)
Dandy Boy(ITY) had a terrible trip in the straight, being kept towards the inside as Musir swept by and consequently running into the back of Il Grande Maurizio, who was weakening quickly. He clipped heels badly and nearly came down in what was a nasty incident.

502a UAE 2000 GUINEAS SPONSORED BY DUBAL (GROUP 3) (TAPETA) 1m
5:30 (5:30) 3-Y-O

£96,153 (£32,051; £16,025; £8,012; £4,807; £3,205)

RPR
1 **Splash Point (USA)**[21] [238] 3-8-8 98.................... MickaelBarzalona 11 104
(Mahmood Al Zarooni) *racd in rr: smooth prog 2f out: led 1f out: r.o wl* **10/1**[3]

2 *1* **Zanzamar (SAF)**[21] [238] 4-9-4 104.....(b) RichardHills 7 100
(M F De Kock, South Africa) *mid-div: trckd ldrs 2 1/2f out: no room 2f out: r.o wl fnl 1f: nrst fin* **4/6**[1]

3 *3/4* **Krypton Factor**[7] [411] 3-8-8 98.....(b) KierenFallon 12 100
(F Nass, Bahrain) *mid-div: chsd ldrs 2f out: ev ch 1d out: one pce fnl 110yds* **16/1**

4 *shd* **Bridgefield (USA)**[21] [238] 3-8-8 96..... AhmedAjtebi 10 100
(Mahmood Al Zarooni) *mid-div: chsd ldrs 2 1/2f out: nt qckn ins fnl f* **11/1**

5 *3/4* **Buffum (USA)**[75] 3-8-8 98..... FrankieDettori 8 98
(Saeed Bin Suroor) *in rr of mid-div: rdn 2 1/2f out: chsd ldrs 1 1/2f out: one pce fnl 110yds* **10/1**[3]

6 *3 3/4* **Sonoran Sands (IRE)**[21] [238] 3-8-8 97..... CO'Donoghue 9 89
(J S Moore) *mid-div: led 2f out: hdd 1f out* **50/1**

7 *1/4* **Paulinho (ARG)**[42] [8025] 4-9-4 109.....(t) RyanMoore 4 87
(H J Brown, South Africa) *a mid-div* **6/1**[2]

8 *1 1/4* **Mayfair Lad**[7] [411] 3-8-8 85.....(t) RoystonFfrench 1 86
(A Al Raihe, UAE) *s.i.s: nvr involved* **66/1**

9 *4 1/4* **Air Of Grace (IRE)**[5] [458] 3-8-8 85..... AntiocoMurgia 6 76
(I Mohammed, UAE) *racd in rr: n.d* **20/1**

10 *2 3/4* **Abjer (FR)**[102] [7265] 3-8-8 104.....(bt) TedDurcan 3 70
(Clive Brittain) *trckd ldr: ev ch 1 1/2f out: nt qckn ins fnl f* **10/1**[3]

11 *1/2* **Hoot (IRE)**[153] [5901] 3-8-8 85.....(t) Christophe-PatriceLemaire 5 69
(A bin Huzaim, UAE) *racd in rr: n.d* **33/1**

12 *20* **Abstrato (BRZ)**[7] [411] 4-9-4 85..... KShea 2 21
(M F De Kock, South Africa) *sn led: hdd & wknd 2 1/2f out* **40/1**

1m 37.73s (0.63) **Going Correction** +0.225s/f (Slow)
WFA 3 from 4yo 19lb 12 Ran SP% **129.4**
Speed ratings: **105,104,103,103,102 98,98,97,92,90 89,69**
CSF 18.09.
Owner Sheikh Hamdan Bin Mohammed Al Maktoum **Bred** WinStar Farm LLC **Trained** Newmarket, Suffolk

FOCUS
The classic crop look an ordinary bunch, both fillies and colts, but Splash Point deserves credit considering the stats suggested those bred in the northern hemisphere were at a disadvantage. Indeed, in the previous ten renewals runners from that section of the world were just 4-77, compared to 6-40 for the southern hemisphere. The pace was just ordinary and the time was 1.96 seconds slower than earlier older-horse Listed race.

NOTEBOOK
Splash Point(USA) could have been at a disadvantage in being held up, but he was always travelling easily and made good headway out wide around the bend into the straight. Despite being on the outside, though, his route to victory still wasn't straightforward as he lost momentum when appearing to take a hefty crack on the head from Frankie Dettori's whip, and he did well to recover, although his chance was aided by Zanzamar also meeting trouble. He was reversing form from the trial with the favourite, having finished second to that rival over 7f, and the step up in trip really suited. By the likeable Street Cry, he has a fine attitude and shapes as though he could stretch out an extra 300m for the Derby, although before then there is middle leg of the Triple Crown to consider, the Al Bastakiya on Super Thursday. (op 10-11)
Zanzamar(SAF) tracked the pace but had nowhere to go when first trying to make his move in the straight and couldn't build up sufficient momentum, having to switch towards the inside rail around a furlong out. He did well to stay on for second and was probably unlucky. Presumably he'll also be considered for the Al Bastakiya before the Derby.
Krypton Factor is probably not really up to this level, but he was always handy and stayed on under a strong drive. (op 14-1)
Bridgefield(USA) was held by Splash Point and Zanzamar on trial form and didn't stay as well as that pair.
Buffum(USA), the winner of a Belmont maiden on his debut before blowing out in an Aqueduct Grade 2, had apparently been pleasing connections but he ran as though in need of this, despite having only been off for 75 days. (op 9-1)
Abjer(FR) offered nothing.

503a DUBAI EXCELLENCE TROPHY (H'CAP) (TURF) 1m 1f
6:15 (6:15) (95-119,119) 3-Y-0+
£57,692 (£19,230; £9,615; £4,807; £2,884; £1,923)

RPR

1 **Raihana (AUS)**[14] [332] 5-8-11 110..... ChristopheSoumillon 6 113+
(M F De Kock, South Africa) *in rr of mid-div: smooth prog 2 1/2f out: led 2f out: comf* **3/1**[2]

2 *3/4* **Fanunalter**[75] [7593] 5-8-7 106..... RyanMoore 2 106
(Marco Botti) *settled in rr: rdn 2 1/2f out: chsd ldrs 1 1/2f out: nt qckn ins fnl f* **12/1**

3 *1/2* **Le Drakkar (AUS)**[14] [331] 6-8-5 102.....(t) Christophe-PatriceLemaire 1 103+
(A bin Huzaim, UAE) *settled in rr: rdn 3f out: r.o wl fnl 2f: nrst fin* **25/1**

4 *1 3/4* **Haatheq (USA)**[7] [417] 4-8-6 105..... RichardHills 11 101
(A Al Raihe, UAE) *in rr of mid-div: r.o wl fnl 2f: nrst fin* **14/1**

5 *1 1/4* **Kingsfort (USA)**[21] [239] 4-8-11 110..... FrankieDettori 9 103
(Saeed Bin Suroor) *mid-div: chsd ldr 2 1/2f out: led 1 1/2f out: hdd 1f out* **5/2**[1]

6 *1/4* **Sahara Kingdom (IRE)**[21] [236] 4-8-5 104..... MickaelBarzalona 13 97
(Saeed Bin Suroor) *trckd ldrs: rdn to ld 2f out: hdd 1 1/2f out: one pce fnl 1f* **12/1**

7 *1* **Irish Flame (SAF)**[14] [331] 5-9-6 119..... KShea 5 109
(M F De Kock, South Africa) *a mid-div* **5/1**[3]

8 *hd* **Iguazu Falls (USA)**[7] [415] 6-8-5 100.....(t) XZiani 10 94
(M bin Shafya, UAE) *sn led: clr 3 1/2f out: hdd 2f out: wknd fnl 1f* **20/1**

9 *1 1/4* **Separate Ways (IRE)**[21] [239] 6-8-5 102.....(bt) ShaneFoley 8 91
(David Marnane, Ire) *in rr of mid-div: nvr able to chal* **25/1**

10 *1/4* **Mac Love**[21] [239] 10-8-8 107..... PatCosgrave 3 94
(Stef Higgins) *nvr bttr than mid-div* **16/1**

11 *1 1/4* **Frozen Power (IRE)**[14] [331] 4-8-7 106..... AhmedAjtebi 7 90
(Mahmood Al Zarooni) *nvr bttr than mid-div* **20/1**

12 *1* **Royal Revival**[14] [332] 4-8-9 108..... TedDurcan 12 90
(Saeed Bin Suroor) *settled in rr: nvr able to chal* **18/1**

13 *8* **Jet Express (SAF)**[6] 9-8-7 104 ow2.....(t) RoystonFfrench 14 71
(A Al Raihe, UAE) *nvr bttr than mid-div* **33/1**

14 *2 1/4* **Bravely Fought (IRE)**[14] [328] 6-8-5 99..... TadhgO'Shea 4 65
(Sabrina J Harty, Ire) *trckd ldrs tl 3f out: sn wknd* **40/1**

1m 49.18s (109.18) 14 Ran SP% **126.0**
CSF: 37.02. Placepot: £766.20 to a £1 stake. Pool: £8817.10 - 8.40 winning tickets. Quadpot: £25.90 to a £1 stake. Pool: £718.62 - 20.50 winning tickets..
Owner Sheikh Mohammed Bin Khalifa Al Maktoum **Bred** Sheikh Mohammad Bin Khalifa Al Maktoum **Trained** South Africa

FOCUS
A good handicap run at a fair gallop, and this was a really smart performance from last year's UAE Oaks winner Raihana, who recorded the quickest time to date over this trip, bettering the recent effort from Presvis by 0.38 seconds.

NOTEBOOK
Raihana(AUS) ◆ has a fine cruising speed, as well as a good change of pace and plenty of stamina, and it doesn't take much imagination to see her being a big player back over C&D in the Duty Free on World Cup night, a race earmarked as a potential target by Mike De Kock pre-Carnival. Before then she could go for the Group 2 Jebel Hatta on Super Thursday, and it's worth noting that her trainer won both of those races with a filly in 2003, Ipi Tombe.
Fanunalter travelled just about as well as the winner into straight, but was caught that bit further back and had to weave his way through, ending up towards the inside rail. He's the sort of horse who probably appreciates seeing little daylight, though, so he can't really be called unlucky.
Le Drakkar(AUS) had to wait for a gap when held up behind the winner in the straight and looked to cross the line with something left, but he wasn't unlucky.
Haatheq(USA) ran a solid race back on turf. (op 3-1)
Kingsfort(USA) didn't progress from a promising enough reappearance and the impression is he doesn't appreciate lively ground.
Sahara Kingdom(IRE) ◆ was slightly disappointing on his reappearance, but showed enough this time to suggest he can win a handicap back on Tapeta, probably over shorter. (op 11-1)
Irish Flame(SAF) ◆ was outpaced halfway up the straight and then became short of room when keeping on again, at which point he was not given a hard time. He was still short of peak fitness according to connections, and 1m1f on quickish ground is not what he wants, so all things considered this was encouraging. Ideally a bit of give underfoot would suit best, but failing that a step up to 1m4f will help and he should be a different proposition next time, which will presumably be in the City of Gold en-route to the Sheema Classic.

[490]SOUTHWELL (L-H)
Friday, February 11

OFFICIAL GOING: Standard
Wind: Light across Weather: Cloudy but dry

504 TODAY'S JOCKEY SPECIALS AT BLUESQ.COM H'CAP 1m (F)
1:15 (1:15) (Class 6) (0-60,58) 4-Y-0+ **£1,535** (£453; £226) **Stalls** Low

Form RPR

03-3 **1** **Almahaza (IRE)**[36] [61] 7-9-7 **58**..... NeilChalmers 5 72
(Adrian Chamberlain) *trckd ldrs: hdwy on inner 3f out: chsd ldr 2f out: rdn and styd on to ld jst ins fnl f: sn clr* **3/1**[1]

-244 **2** *3 3/4* **Positivity**[8] [397] 5-8-12 **54**.....(p) AdamCarter[(5)] 4 59
(Bryan Smart) *sn led: qckcnd clr over 2f out: rdn wl over 1f out: drvn and hdd jst ins fnl f: kpt on same pce* **13/2**

232- **3** *5* **It's A Mans World**[57] [7899] 5-8-13 **53**..... AndrewHeffernan[(3)] 8 47
(Kevin M Prendergast) *t.k.h: prom: effrt 3f out: rdn over 2f out and sn one pce* **7/2**[2]

002- **4** *3/4* **Nevada Desert (IRE)**[80] [7543] 11-9-3 **54**..... MichaelStainton 6 46
(Richard Whitaker) *chsd ldrs: effrt 3f out: rdn over 2f out and sn one pce* **14/1**

1-25 **5** *4* **Olympic Dream**[21] [255] 5-9-5 **56**..... TonyCulhane 3 39
(Michael Herrington) *trckd ldrs: hdwy 1/2-way: rdn wl over 2f out: grad wknd* **8/1**

4-40 **6** *1 1/2* **Little Meadow (IRE)**[23] [207] 4-8-8 **45**..... CathyGannon 10 25
(Julia Feilden) *chsd ldrs on wd outside: rdn along 3f out: sn wknd* **14/1**

6-10 **7** *1/2* **Penrod Ballantyne (IRE)**[26] [181] 4-9-4 **55**..... LukeMorris 7 33
(Mike Hammond) *midfield: effrt 3f out: sn rdn and no imp* **16/1**

660- **8** *3/4* **Lago Indiano (IRE)**[69] [7709] 4-9-0 **51**.....(b[1]) LiamKeniry 11 28
(Peter Fahey, Ire) *sn rdn along and bhd: sme hdwy 2f out: nvr a factor* **5/1**[3]

060- **9** *2 1/2* **Zambuka (FR)**[34] [6629] 4-9-7 **58**.....(t) GrahamGibbons 9 29
(Pat Murphy) *prom: chsd ldr 1/2-way: rdn 3f out: sn wknd* **18/1**

00-0 **10** *1* **Spirit Of Love (IRE)**[17] [291] 4-9-2 **53**..... WilliamCarson 1 22
(Michael Wigham) *s.i.s: a in rr* **40/1**

00-0 **11** *9* **Flores Sea (USA)**[17] [291] 7-9-1 **52**.....(b) PhillipMakin 2 —
(Ruth Carr) *dwlt: a bhd* **66/1**

1m 43.42s (-0.28) **Going Correction** +0.10s/f (Slow) 11 Ran SP% **116.7**
Speed ratings (Par 101): **105,101,96,95,91 90,89,88,86,85 76**
toteswingers:1&2:£5.60, 1&3:£2.30, 2&3:£4.50 CSF £22.63 CT £71.24 TOTE £3.90: £1.30, £2.10, £1.50; EX 20.70 Trifecta £60.80 Pool: £438.98 - 5.34 winning units..
Owner G B Heffaran **Bred** Castletown And Associates **Trained** Ashton Keynes, Wilts

FOCUS
A moderate handicap, but the time was good, being 0.20 seconds quicker than the later Class 5 event. The front pair came clear and the winner is seemingly back to his best.

505 TICKETS AT SOUTHWELL-RACECOURSE.CO.UK H'CAP 6f (F)
1:45 (1:45) (Class 6) (0-65,63) 3-Y-0 **£1,535** (£453; £226) **Stalls** Low

Form RPR

5-52 **1** **Ridgeway Hawk**[15] [322] 3-8-9 **51**.....(v) RobertHavlin 4 55
(Mark Usher) *dwlt and sn swtchd to outer: hdwy 1/2-way: rdn to chse ldr wl over 1f out: drvn and styd on wl fnl f to ld last 50yds* **9/2**[2]

2-41 **2** *nk* **Rylee Mooch**[14] [338] 3-9-4 **63**.....(e) AndrewHeffernan[(3)] 6 66
(Richard Guest) *t.k.h: led: qckcnd clr 2f out: rdn over 1f out: drvn and hung lft ins fnl f: hdd and no ex last 50yds* **11/2**[3]

641- **3** *5* **Verrazano**[61] [7843] 3-9-7 **63**..... PhillipMakin 3 50
(Kevin Ryan) *sltly hmpd s: towards rr and sn pushed along: rdn over 2f out: drvn to chse ldng pair over 1f out: no imp* **1/1**[1]

636- **4** *3/4* **Goal (IRE)**[46] [7983] 3-9-2 **58**..... MartinDwyer 2 43
(David C Griffiths) *in rr: rdn along 1/2-way: hdwy on inner wl over 1f out: n.d* **25/1**

0-43 **5** *3 1/4* **Winning Draw (IRE)**[8] [396] 3-9-1 **57**.....(p) TonyCulhane 1 31
(Paul Midgley) *trckd ldrs: effrt wl over 2f out: sn rdn and wknd* **8/1**

1-02 **6** *6* **Hereselle (IRE)**[8] [396] 3-9-4 **63**..... RobertLButler[(3)] 7 18
(Michael Chapman) *chsd ldr: rdn wl over 2f out: sn drvn and wknd* **16/1**

05-3 **7** *shd* **Diamond Sunrise (IRE)**[35] [88] 3-8-12 **54**..... DuranFentiman 8 —
(Noel Wilson) *chsd ldrs: rdn along 1/2-way: sn wknd* **14/1**

1m 17.82s (1.32) **Going Correction** +0.10s/f (Slow) 7 Ran SP% **111.1**
Speed ratings (Par 95): **95,94,87,86,82 74,74**
toteswingers:1&2:£2.60, 1&3:£1.60, 2&3:£1.70 CSF £27.32 CT £40.70 TOTE £8.20: £3.20, £2.30; EX 20.70 Trifecta £47.20 Pool: £635.19 - 9.94 winning units..
Owner The Goodracing Partnership **Bred** Ridgeway Bloodstock **Trained** Upper Lambourn, Berks

FOCUS
A moderate handicap and pretty weak form. The first pair have been rated up a length.

506 GOLF BEFORE RACING AT SOUTHWELL CLAIMING STKS 5f (F)
2:15 (2:15) (Class 6) 4-Y-0+ **£1,457** (£433; £216; £108) **Stalls** High

Form RPR

/2-5 **1** **Soopacal (IRE)**[30] [125] 6-9-1 **73**..... TonyCulhane 3 69
(Michael Herrington) *chsd ldr: cl up 1/2-way: rdn along 2f out: led over 1f out: sn drvn and hung rt ins fnl f: carried lft and kpt on gamely nr fin* **5/2**[2]

2222 **2** *hd* **Gold Story**[10] [375] 4-8-9 52..(be) BarryMcHugh 4 62
(Brian Ellison) *trckd ldrs: hdwy over 1f out: swtchd rt and rn to chal ent fnl f: ev ch whn hmpd 100yds out: drvn and disp ld whn edgd lft last 50yds: nt go past* **7/1**

0-04 **3** *1 1/4* **Galpin Junior (USA)**[8] [404] 5-8-9 67................................ TomEaves 5 58
(Ruth Carr) *chsd ldng pair: rdn along 2f out: drvn over 1f out: kpt on ins fnl f* **20/1**

1-02 **4** *1 1/2* **Colorus (IRE)**[3] [453] 8-8-13 68....................................(v) WilliamCarson 7 56
(Bill Ratcliffe) *led: jnd over 2f out: rdn wl over 1f out: hdd appr fnl f: sn n.m.r and swtchd lft: one pce* **6/4**[1]

1110 **5** *3 3/4* **Sloop Johnb**[1] [491] 5-9-2 72.......................................(p) HayleyTurner 2 46
(Conor Dore) *sn outpcd and a in rr* **10/3**[3]

60.37 secs (0.67) **Going Correction** +0.175s/f (Slow) **5** Ran SP% **108.9**
Speed ratings (Par 101): **101,100,98,96,90**
CSF £18.27 TOTE £3.20: £2.10, £3.00; EX 15.00.Gold Story was claimed by George Baker for £3,000.
Owner Mrs S Lloyd **Bred** Paul Trainor **Trained** Cold Kirby, N Yorks

FOCUS
An ordinary claimer. The first two came together and the result stood after an enquiry. The runner-up is the key to the form.

507 TICKETS ON LINE AT SOUTHWELL-RACECOURSE.CO.UK (S) H'CAP 1m 4f (F)
2:50 (2:50) (Class 6) (0-60,58) 4-Y-0+ **£1,535** (£453; £226) **Stalls** Low

Form RPR

3-46 **1** **Bring Sweets (IRE)**[26] [181] 4-8-6 **46**.............................. BarryMcHugh 6 56+
(Brian Ellison) *hld up: smooth hdwy on outer 4f out: cl up on bit 2f out: shkn up to ld over 1f out: rdn and edgd lft ins fnl f: styd on* **10/3**[1]

3030 **2** *1 1/2* **Mojeerr**[3] [450] 5-8-5 **49**...(v) RyanTate(7) 10 54
(Alan McCabe) *in tch on inner: hdwy 3f out: rdn wl over 1f out: chsd wnr ins fnl f: kpt on* **22/1**

-302 **3** *2 1/4* **Yossi (IRE)**[8] [320] 7-9-0 **54**................................(be) AndrewHeffernan(3) 4 55
(Richard Guest) *chsd ldrs: hdwy 3f out: rdn over 2f out and ev ch tl drvn and one pce ent fnl f* **9/2**[3]

06-6 **4** *1 1/4* **Beseech (USA)**[26] [184] 4-8-5 **45**.................................... CathyGannon 7 44
(Julia Feilden) *chsd ldrs: hdwy and cl up after 4f: led over 3f out: rdn wl over 2f out: drvn and hdd over 1f out: kpt on same pce* **10/1**

35-6 **5** *3/4* **Davana**[15] [324] 5-8-3 **47** ow2................................(p) MatthewCosham(7) 5 45
(Bill Ratcliffe) *towards rr: hdwy over 2f out: sn rdn and kpt on: nvr rchd ldrs* **11/2**

54-3 **6** *2 1/4* **The Dukes Arch (USA)**[26] [184] 4-9-1 **55**........................(b) LiamKeniry 2 50
(Peter Fahey, Ire) *t.k.h: trckd ldrs: hdwy on outer and cl up 4f out: rdn and ev ch over 2f out: sn drvn and grad wknd* **7/2**[2]

400- **7** *10* **Lady Pacha**[28] [2853] 4-8-5 **45**... MartinLane 1 24
(Tim Pitt) *in rr: rdn along after 3f: nvr a factor* **16/1**

10-5 **8** *3* **Love In The West (IRE)**[15] [323] 5-9-4 **58**...............(p) GaryBartley(3) 3 32
(John Harris) *led 1f: trckd ldrs: rdn along 4f out: drvn 3f out and sn wknd* **25/1**

022- **9** *3/4* **Lady Norlela**[90] [7149] 5-9-3 **54**.. MickyFenton 8 27
(Brian Rothwell) *hld up: a in rr* **10/1**

0-00 **10** *hd* **Spares And Repairs**[8] [408] 8-8-1 **45**.............................. JackDuern(7) 9 17
(Reg Hollinshead) *towards rr: hdwy 1/2-way: rdn along 4f out: sn btn* **40/1**

/00- **11** *1 1/4* **Byron Bay**[9] [7401] 9-8-13 **50**...............................(vt) SilvestreDeSousa 11 20
(Robert Johnson) *led after 1f: rdn along 4f out: hdd over 3f out: sn wknd* **50/1**

2m 42.75s (1.75) **Going Correction** +0.10s/f (Slow)
WFA 4 from 5yo+ 3lb **11** Ran SP% **115.5**
Speed ratings (Par 101): **98,97,95,94,94 92,86,84,83,83 82**
toteswingers:1&2:£14.00, 1&3:£3.90, 2&3:£5.80 CSF £80.17 CT £334.14 TOTE £4.40: £2.20, £5.80, £1.60; EX 89.40 Trifecta £295.10 Pool: £753.90 - 1.89 winning units..There was no bid for the winner.
Owner Koo's Racing Club **Bred** Kilnamoragh Stud **Trained** Norton, N Yorks

FOCUS
[illegible] bit better.
Byron Bay Official explanation: jockey said gelding had no more to give

508 BLUESQ.COM ON YOUR IPHONE FILLIES' H'CAP 1m (F)
3:25 (3:25) (Class 5) (0-75,73) 4-Y-0+ **£1,878** (£558; £279; £139) **Stalls** Low

Form RPR

206- **1** **Hill Tribe**[86] [7476] 4-8-7 **62**................................... AndrewHeffernan(3) 4 72
(Richard Guest) *mde all: jnd and rdn over 2f out: drvn over 1f out: kpt on gamely ins fnl f* **8/1**[3]

3323 **2** *3/4* **Avonrose**[8] [405] 4-9-7 **73**... TomEaves 3 81
(Derek Shaw) *trckd ldng pair: hdwy over 3f out: chal over 2f out: ev ch tl drvn ins fnl f and no ex last 100yds* **8/15**[1]

4-50 **3** *4 1/2* **Miss Bootylishes**[9] [394] 6-9-4 **73**................................ AmyBaker(3) 1 71
(Andrew Haynes) *cl up on inner: rdn over 2f out and ev ch tl drvn and wknd over 1f out* **8/1**[3]

4-10 **4** *6* **Amary (IRE)**[30] [128] 4-9-1 **67**...............................(p) BarryMcHugh 2 51
(John Harris) *chsd ldrs: rdn along 3f out: sn outpcd* **9/2**[2]

004/ **5** *11* **Velvet Band**[246] [2915] 4-8-10 **62**................................ MichaelStainton 6 21
(Richard Whitaker) *chsd ldrs: rdn along over 3f out: sn outpcd* **25/1**

1m 43.62s (-0.08) **Going Correction** +0.10s/f (Slow) **5** Ran SP% **109.5**
Speed ratings (Par 100): **104,103,98,92,81**
CSF £12.93 TOTE £9.90: £3.40, £1.10; EX 15.80.
Owner EERC & Alison Ibbotson **Bred** The Kingwood Partnership **Trained** Stainforth, S Yorks

FOCUS
This looked a weak contest beforehand, but the second-placed filly, who was the pre-race form pick, seemed to run close to her best. The winner's best run since her early efforts.

509 SOUTHWELL-RACECOURSE.CO.UK MAIDEN STKS 7f (F)
4:00 (4:01) (Class 5) 3-Y-0+ **£1,910** (£564; £282) **Stalls** Low

Form RPR

3- **1** **Flynn's Boy**[109] [7119] 3-8-10 0.. MartinLane 3 71
(Rae Guest) *chsd ldrs: rdn along over 2f out: styd on to ld over 1f out: drvn out* **7/2**[2]

0-5 **2** *1 3/4* **Unwrapit (USA)**[11] [368] 3-8-5 0....................................... ChrisCatlin 4 61
(Bryan Smart) *led: rdn and hung rt 2f out: drvn: hung rt and hdd over 1f out: kpt on same pce fnl f* **16/1**

03- **3** *1 3/4* **Cool Luke**[98] [7335] 3-8-10 0.. PJMcDonald 2 62
(Alan Swinbank) *trckd ldr on inner: effrt wl over 2f out: sn: rdn: drvn wl over 1f out and sn one pce* **4/1**[3]

0- **4** *2 3/4* **Old English (IRE)**[93] [7386] 3-8-10 0.......................... SilvestreDeSousa 6 60
(Mark Johnston) *chsd ldng pair: pushed along 3f out: rdn to chal on outer whn bmpd 2f out: drvn whn carried rt and hmpd over 1f out: sn swtchd lft and one pce* **8/11**[1]

43-3 **5** *14* **King Bertolini (IRE)**[17] [295] 4-9-13 56........................ PatrickMathers 1 31
(Alan Berry) *s.i.s and rel to r: a bhd* **28/1**

5 **6** *3/4* **Jack's Rocket**[15] [319] 4-9-6 0.......................................(e) SeanPalmer(7) 5 19
(Richard Guest) *chsd ldrs: rdn along over 3f out: sn wknd* **66/1**

1m 30.72s (0.42) **Going Correction** +0.10s/f (Slow)
WFA 3 from 4yo 17lb **6** Ran SP% **110.9**
Speed ratings (Par 103): **101,99,97,93,77 77**
toteswingers:1&2:£3.60, 1&3:£1.90, 2&3:£3.20 CSF £49.11 TOTE £3.40: £1.60, £7.60; EX 26.50.
Owner C J Murfitt **Bred** C J Murfitt **Trained** Newmarket, Suffolk

FOCUS
Just a modest maiden in which the winner basically matched his debut form.
Unwrapit(USA) Official explanation: jockey said filly hung right

510 PLAY FREE BINGO AT BLUESQ.COM H'CAP 7f (F)
4:35 (4:35) (Class 5) (0-70,68) 3-Y-O **£1,910** (£564; £282) **Stalls** Low

Form RPR

-223 **1** **Eilean Mor**[3] [454] 3-9-0 **64**....................................... GaryBartley(3) 4 65
(Bryan Smart) *mde all: rdn clr 2f out: drvn over 1f out: kpt on* **6/1**[3]

20-3 **2** *1* **Rath Maeve**[17] [296] 3-8-7 **57**................................. AndrewHeffernan(3) 2 56
(Alan McCabe) *trckd wnr: rdn along wl over 1f out: drvn and kpt on same pce fnl f* **14/1**

630- **3** *3/4* **Colebrooke**[111] [7085] 3-9-7 **68**.................................. SilvestreDeSousa 3 65
(Mark Johnston) *trckd ldng pair: niggled along after 3f: rdn over 3f out: drvn 2f out and hung bdly lft over 1f out: hrd drvn and kpt on towards fin* **8/13**[1]

0331 **4** *2 3/4* **Granny Anne (IRE)**[7] [426] 3-8-9 **63** 6ex......................... NatashaEaton(7) 1 54
(Alan Bailey) *trckd ldng pair: rdn along 3f out: swtchd lft to far rail 2f out: sn drvn and btn* **3/1**[2]

1m 31.54s (1.24) **Going Correction** +0.10s/f (Slow) **4** Ran SP% **107.9**
Speed ratings (Par 97): **96,94,94,90**
totesuper7: Win: Not won. Place: 10.90. CSF £50.96 TOTE £10.90; EX 31.40.
Owner Mrs Lucille Bone **Bred** Triple H Stud Ltd **Trained** Hambleton, N Yorks

FOCUS
The only runner who looked open to any improvement was Colebrooke, but he disappointed. Weak form, with the winner rated to his nursery level.
T/Plt: £65.50 to a £1 stake. Pool:£57,458.54 - 640.14 winning tickets T/Qpdt: £15.40 to a £1 stake. Pool:£4,662.33 - 223.60 winning tickets JR

[443]WOLVERHAMPTON (A.W) (L-H)
Friday, February 11

OFFICIAL GOING: Standard
Wind: light half behind Weather: showers

511 TODAY'S JOCKEY SPECIALS AT BLUESQ.COM H'CAP 5f 20y(P)
5:10 (5:12) (Class 6) (0-60,60) 4-Y-0+ **£1,603** (£473; £236) **Stalls** Low

Form RPR

-002 **1** **Straboe (USA)**[4] [443] 5-9-2 **55**.................................(v) WilliamCarson 4 66
(Stuart Williams) *chsd ldrs: chal over 1f out: led last 150yds: edgd rt: hld on wl* **5/4**[1]

30-4 **2** *3/4* **We'll Deal Again**[8] [401] 4-9-1 **57**.........................(v[1]) JamesSullivan(3) 12 65
(Michael Easterby) *dwlt: hld up: hdwy over 2f out: chal over 1f out: edgd lft jst ins fnl f: no ex* **20/1**

02-3 **3** *1 3/4* **Sparking**[32] [113] 4-9-4 **57**.. GrahamGibbons 6 59
(David Barron) *led: edgd lft over 3f out: hdd last 150yds: hld whn n.m.r towards fin* **11/2**[3]

0-43 **4** *3 1/2* **Ingleby Star (IRE)**[22] [230] 6-9-2 **55**.............................(p) JimmyQuinn 9 44
(Noel Wilson) *w ldrs: hung lft 1f out: sn wknd* **16/1**

3230 **5** [illegible] **Kheley (IRE)**[illegible] [illegible] [illegible] 10
(Mark Brisbourne) *chsd ldrs: lost pl over 3f out: swtchd rt and kpt on fnl f* **11/1**

0320 **6** *nk* **Misaro (GER)**[6] [435] 10-9-7 **60**.................................(b) DavidProbert 3 46
(Ronald Harris) *in rr: drvn and n.m.r over 3f out: sme hdwy and hung lft ins fnl f: nvr a threat* **4/1**[2]

36-1 **7** *1 3/4* **Almaty Express**[28] [167] 9-9-0 **58**...............................(b) AdamCarter(5) 10 38
(John Weymes) *in rr: sme hdwy on wd outside over 1f out: nvr a factor* **12/1**

06-0 **8** *hd* **Monte Major (IRE)**[34] [97] 10-8-6 **52**....................(v) GeorgeChaloner(7) 1 31+
(Derek Shaw) *prom on inner: n.m.r and lost pl over 3f out: sme hdwy on ins over 1f out: nvr a threat* **16/1**

/43- **9** *1/2* **Marshal Plat Club**[51] [7960] 4-8-13 **52**............................ J-PGuillambert 13 29
(Alan Bailey) *in rr on outside and drvn over 3f out: nvr a factor* **8/1**

4-00 **10** *2 1/2* **The Lord**[8] [401] 11-8-6 **48**.......................................(p) KierenFox(3) 2 20+
(Bill Turner) *chsd ldrs: hmpd and dropped bk over 3f out: sme hdwy 2f out: sn wknd: hmpd and eased ins fnl f* **50/1**

62.12 secs (-0.18) **Going Correction** +0.225s/f (Slow) **10** Ran SP% **125.5**
Speed ratings (Par 101): **110,108,106,100,99 99,96,96,95,91**
toteswingers:1&2:£9.30, 1&3:£3.30, 2&3:£10.20 CSF £36.16 CT £123.08 TOTE £2.40: £1.10, £7.70, £1.70; EX 44.90.
Owner Brigid & Damian Hennessy-Bourke **Bred** Darley **Trained** Newmarket, Suffolk
■ Stewards' Enquiry : Graham Gibbons two-day ban: careless riding (Feb 25-26)
William Carson two-day ban: careless riding (Feb 25-26)

FOCUS
There was a charge to the first bend here and the pace looked sound enough. The winner built on a better effort latest.
Ingleby Star(IRE) Official explanation: jockey said gelding hung left

512 GREAT OFFERS AT WOLVERHAMPTON-RACECOURSE.CO.UK H'CAP 5f 216y(P)
5:40 (5:43) (Class 6) (0-60,59) 4-Y-0+ **£1,603** (£473; £236) **Stalls** Low

Form RPR

56-1 **1** **Welcome Approach**[28] [166] 8-9-7 **59**.................................. JimmyQuinn 3 67
(John Weymes) *hld up: effrt over 2f out: hdwy on inner over 1f out: r.o to ld last 75yds: jst hld on* **4/1**[2]

230- **2** *shd* **Lake Chini (IRE)**[69] [7699] 9-9-6 **58**..........................(b) GrahamGibbons 5 66
(Michael Easterby) *mid-div: hdwy over 1f out: str run ins fnl f: jst hld* **6/1**

1466 **3** *1/2* **Itsthursdayalready**[10] [375] 4-9-4 **56**................................ ShaneKelly 4 62
(Mark Brisbourne) *mid-div: effrt over 2f out: chsd wnr over 1f out: no ex clsng stages* **8/1**

0-04 **4** ½ **Spinning Ridge (IRE)**[15] 317 6-9-5 **57**.......................(b) DavidProbert 7 61
(Ronald Harris) *w ldr: led over 2f out: edgd lft 1f out: hdd and no ex last 75yds* **9/2**[3]

4-05 **5** *shd* **Carnival Dream**[22] 229 6-8-6 **47**............................ JamesSullivan(3) 11 51
(Hugh McWilliams) *mid-div: hdwy on outer over 1f out: styd on same pce last 100yds* **20/1**

6255 **6** *nse* **Memphis Man**[7] 421 8-8-7 **52**........................... MatthewCosham(7) 10 56
(David Evans) *hld up in rr: hdwy on wd outside over 1f out: styd on wl last 100yds* **20/1**

05-0 **7** ½ **Namir (IRE)**[28] 169 9-9-6 **58**..(vt) DaneO'Neill 9 60
(James Evans) *chsd ldrs: effrt on outer wl over 1f out: kpt on same pce last 75yds* **22/1**

4341 **8** ¾ **Downhill Skier (IRE)**[11] 362 7-9-7 **59** 6ex...................... EddieAhern 8 59
(Mark Brisbourne) *trckd ldrs: effrt and chsd ldr over 1f out: ev ch tl fdd last 75yds* **7/1**

5-12 **9** *4* **Young Simon**[11] 362 4-9-5 **57**.......................................(v) IanMongan 1 44
(George Margarson) *mid-div: lost pl over 1f out* **11/4**[1]

50-0 **10** *6* **Frill A Minute**[36] 57 7-8-7 **45**..................................(v) WilliamCarson 2 13
(Lynn Siddall) *s.i.s: a in rr: nvr on terms* **100/1**

05-0 **11** 1¾ **The Magic Of Rio**[33] 102 5-8-7 **45**...........................(v[1]) CathyGannon 6 —
(David Evans) *led: hdd over 2f out: lost pl over 1f out* **33/1**

1m 16.25s (1.25) **Going Correction** +0.225s/f (Slow) 11 Ran SP% **120.5**
Speed ratings (Par 101): **100,99,99,98,98 98,97,96,91,83 81**
toteswingers:1&2:£7.70, 1&3:£8.70, 2&3:£8.90 CSF £26.99 CT £187.88 TOTE £5.80: £1.40, £1.50, £2.90; EX 22.30.
Owner T A Scothern & Tag Racing **Bred** P Wyatt And Ranby Hall **Trained** Middleham Moor, N Yorks
■ Stewards' Enquiry : David Probert one-day ban: used whip with excessive frequency (Feb 25)

FOCUS
A competitive handicap in which the pace was decent and the first two came from behind. Straightforward form, with the winner pretty much back to his best.
Young Simon Official explanation: jockey said gelding ran flat
The Magic Of Rio Official explanation: jockey said mare had no more to give

513 PARTY PACK GROUP OFFER MEDIAN AUCTION MAIDEN STKS 5f 216y(P)
6:10 (6:14) (Class 6) 3-5-Y-O **£1,603** (£473; £236) **Stalls** Low

Form RPR
4- **1** **Green Apple**[104] 7240 3-8-7 0.................................. FergusSweeney 5 74
(Peter Makin) *trckd ldrs: rdn to ld over 1f out: edgd lft: sn drew clr: eased towards fin* **4/7**[1]

224- **2** *5* **Mazovian (USA)**[46] 7982 3-8-9 69............................ RobertLButler(3) 2 63
(Michael Chapman) *led: hdd over 1f out: no ch w wnr* **4/1**[2]

06- **3** *8* **Pink Sari**[75] 7608 3-8-7 0..(p) CathyGannon 1 32
(Peter Makin) *s.s: last and sn drvn along: hung lft and wnt modest 3rd over 1f out* **20/1**

0- **4** *7* **Everybody Out**[76] 7598 3-8-12 0............................. GrahamGibbons 4 15
(Reg Hollinshead) *chsd ldrs: drvn over 2f out: sn lost pl and bhd* **25/1**

6-0 **5** 2¼ **Cuddly**[9] 380 3-8-7 0.. ShaneKelly 3 —
(Robert Cowell) *s.i.s: sn trcking ldrs: drvn over 3f out: lost pl over 2f out: sn bhd: eased clsng stages* **9/2**[3]

1m 16.57s (1.57) **Going Correction** +0.225s/f (Slow)
WFA 3 from 4yo 15lb 5 Ran SP% **110.4**
Speed ratings (Par 101): **98,91,80,71,68**
CSF £3.19 TOTE £1.50: £1.10, £2.50; EX 3.10.
Owner Ten Of Hearts **Bred** Mrs P J Makin **Trained** Ogbourne Maisey, Wilts
■ Mi Nina Castagna was withdrawn (14/1, unruly & ref to ent stalls). Deduct 5p in the £ under R4.

FOCUS
A weak maiden run in a relatively slow time. There is a bit of doubt over quite what the winner achieved.

514 WOLVERHAMPTON-RACECOURSE.CO.UK H'CAP 1m 5f 194y(P)
6:40 (6:41) (Class 5) (0-75,73) 4-Y-O+ **£2,456** (£725; £362) **Stalls** Low

Form RPR
554- **1** **Mr Plod**[206] 4226 6-8-9 **56**..(p) JamesDoyle 3 62
(Andrew Reid) *trckd ldrs: drvn over 3f out: chal on inner over 1f out: styd on to ld post* **16/1**

2-51 **2** *nse* **Dart**[18] 286 7-9-8 **69**.. GrahamGibbons 1 75
(John Mackie) *s.i.s: hdwy to ld after 1f: edgd lft fnl f: hdd post* **4/1**[3]

2222 **3** 1¼ **Camps Bay (USA)**[9] 384 7-9-12 **73**............................ HayleyTurner 6 77
(Conor Dore) *hld up in rr: hdwy over 2f out: kpt on same pce fnl f* **3/1**[1]

6-31 **4** ¾ **Sheila's Bond**[21] 245 4-8-4 **59**..................................... KierenFox(3) 2 62
(John Flint) *led 1f: chsd ldr: pushed along 3f out: one pce appr fnl f* **9/2**

106- **5** 2¾ **Leyte Gulf (USA)**[43] 8013 8-9-0 **61**.............................. DaneO'Neill 5 62
(Chris Bealby) *hld up in last: hdwy over 2f out: n.m.r on inner and swtchd rt over 1f out: nvr nr to chal* **4/1**[3]

6-12 **6** *2* **Inside Knowledge (USA)**[15] 314 5-9-0 **61**.............. KirstyMilczarek 4 58
(Garry Woodward) *hld up: effrt over 2f out: sn wknd* **7/2**[2]

3m 9.28s (3.28) **Going Correction** +0.225s/f (Slow)
WFA 4 from 5yo+ 5lb 6 Ran SP% **111.3**
Speed ratings (Par 103): **99,98,98,97,96 95**
toteswingers:1&2:£17.70, 1&3:£7.20, 2&3:£2.40 CSF £75.76 TOTE £21.50: £8.40, £2.00; EX 52.30.
Owner A S Reid **Bred** A S Reid **Trained** Mill Hill, London NW7

FOCUS
This looked a pretty tight handicap and it produced a close finish. It was slowly run and the form is muddling.
Inside Knowledge(USA) Official explanation: jockey said gelding hung left

515 BLUESQ.COM ON YOUR IPHONE H'CAP 1m 4f 50y(P)
7:10 (7:10) (Class 4) (0-85,82) 4-Y-O+ **£3,723** (£1,108; £553; £276) **Stalls** Low

Form RPR
630- **1** **Bedouin Bay**[58] 7881 4-8-8 **77**.................................... RosieJessop(5) 6 85
(Alan McCabe) *trckd ldr: t.k.h: chal 3f out: led appr fnl f: styd on wl towards fin* **16/1**

35-3 **2** 1¼ **Realisation (USA)**[13] 353 4-9-4 **82**........................... HayleyTurner 3 88
(Mark Johnston) *led: qcknd 5f out: hdd appr fnl f: styd on same pce* **1/1**[1]

30-0 **3** *7* **Granny McPhee**[22] 235 5-8-13 **79**................................. JulieBurke(5) 2 74
(Alan Bailey) *s.s: hdwy to trck ldrs after 3f: effrt over 3f out: tk modest 3rd over 1f out: edgd lft and one pce* **11/1**

1-41 **4** *hd* **Straversjoy**[11] 369 4-8-6 **70** 6ex............................... GrahamGibbons 4 64
(Reg Hollinshead) *sn trcking ldrs: effrt 3f out: one pce* **6/1**[3]

1-4 **5** *7* **Kindlelight Sun (JPN)**[12] 359 5-9-1 **76**........................... LukeMorris 1 64
(Nick Littmoden) *trckd ldrs: drvn over 4f out: wknd over 2f out: eased fnl f* **5/2**[2]

2m 41.17s (0.07) **Going Correction** +0.225s/f (Slow)
WFA 4 from 5yo+ 3lb 5 Ran SP% **107.1**
Speed ratings (Par 105): **108,107,102,102,97**
CSF £31.47 TOTE £26.80: £7.20, £1.50; EX 35.10.
Owner Mrs Z Wentworth **Bred** Skymarc Farm **Trained** Averham Park, Notts

FOCUS
They didn't go a great gallop here and two came clear, quickening off the front. The winner is rated in line with his French form.

516 BLACK COUNTRY MEDIAN AUCTION MAIDEN STKS 1m 1f 103y(P)
7:40 (7:40) (Class 6) 3-5-Y-O **£1,603** (£473; £236) **Stalls** Low

Form RPR
50-3 **1** **Flying Phoenix**[28] 171 3-8-2 61..................................... CathyGannon 4 66
(William Haggas) *mde all: drvn clr over 1f out: styd on strly* **15/8**[1]

2 *6* **Wily Fox**[172] 4-10-0 82.. LukeMorris 6 63
(James Eustace) *sn trcking ldrs: t.k.h: wnt 2nd 6f out: drvn 3f out: kpt on same pce* **11/4**[3]

00-2 **3** ½ **Jane's Legacy**[25] 194 3-8-2 53...................................... DavidProbert 5 52
(Reg Hollinshead) *hld up in rr: drvn and hdwy 3f out: sn 3rd: one pce* **10/1**

0 **4** *hd* **Caravan Rolls On**[20] 262 3-8-7 0................................ ChrisCatlin 2 57
(Peter Chapple-Hyam) *dwlt: hld up in rr: hdwy to chse ldrs over 5f out: drvn over 3f out: one pce* **2/1**[2]

5/0- **5** *7* **Gracelightening**[252] 2725 4-9-9 64......................... RichardKingscote 1 42
(Bruce Hellier) *trckd ldrs: t.k.h: drvn and outpcd over 3f out: sn lost pl: eased towards fin* **16/1**

0- **6** *6* **Bertie Blu Boy**[100] 7303 3-8-7 0............................... SilvestreDeSousa 3 29
(Paul Green) *trckd ldrs: drvn and lost pl over 4f out: bhd and eased fnl f* **33/1**

2m 4.06s (2.36) **Going Correction** +0.225s/f (Slow)
WFA 3 from 4yo 21lb 6 Ran SP% **112.7**
Speed ratings (Par 101): **98,92,92,92,85 80**
toteswingers:1&2:£1.70, 1&3:£4.40, 2&3:£3.50 CSF £7.50 TOTE £2.80: £1.10, £3.00; EX 8.40.
Owner Winterbeck Manor Stud **Bred** Winterbeck Manor Stud **Trained** Newmarket, Suffolk

FOCUS
They didn't go much of a pace in this weak maiden and it probably didn't take much winning. The winner clearly improved, with the third the best guide.

517 PLAY FREE BINGO AT BLUESQ.COM H'CAP 7f 32y(P)
8:10 (8:11) (Class 7) (0-50,50) 4-Y-O+ **£1,535** (£453; £226) **Stalls** High

Form RPR
0-30 **1** **Bold Bomber**[11] 363 5-8-12 **45**............................ SilvestreDeSousa 10 53
(Paul Green) *mid-div: effrt 3f out: swtchd rt over 1f out: styd on to ld last 75yds* **13/2**

5-30 **2** *1* **Colamandis**[14] 345 4-9-0 **50**................................... JamesSullivan(3) 4 55
(Hugh McWilliams) *sn led: hdd and no ex wl ins fnl f* **25/1**

3042 **3** 1¼ **Guildenstern (IRE)**[9] 382 9-9-2 **49**............................... JimmyQuinn 12 51
(Jane Chapple-Hyam) *in rr: hdwy over 2f out: kpt on same pce fnl f* **9/2**[2]

0-64 **4** ¾ **Rigid**[9] 382 4-9-1 **48**...(be) LukeMorris 6 48
(Tony Carroll) *trckd ldrs: t.k.h: chal over 1f out: kpt on same pce* **4/1**[1]

-634 **5** ½ **Bertbrand**[17] 289 6-8-12 **45**.......................................(v) JamesDoyle 11 44
(Ian McInnes) *mid-div: drvn to chse ldrs over 3f out: kpt on fnl f* **14/1**

-036 **6** 2¾ **Gilderoy**[15] 311 4-8-12 **45**.. HayleyTurner 7 36
(Dominic Ffrench Davis) *chsd ldrs: drvn over 2f out: wknd appr fnl f* **9/1**

00-4 **7** *nk* **Brave Decision**[22] 225 4-9-3 **50**...................................(v[1]) EddieAhern 9 40
(Robert Cowell) *chsd ldrs: wknd fnl f* **4/1**[1]

004- **8** 1¼ **Kheskianto (IRE)**[92] 6077 5-8-9 **45**.......................(bt[1]) RobertLButler(3) 5 32
(Michael Chapman) *s.i.s: sn drvn along: kpt on fnl 2f: nvr nr ldrs* **20/1**

3-44 **9** *nse* **Fiancee (IRE)**[11] 362 5-8-13 **46**.....................................(b) TomEaves 8 33
(Roy Brotherton) *dwlt: sn drvn along: hdwy over 2f out: wknd appr fnl f* **5/1**[3]

000- **10** *19* **Scintillating (IRE)**[336] 870 4-8-12 **45**......................... KirstyMilczarek 1 —
(Ray Peacock) *led early: chsd ldrs: lost pl over 3f out: t.o 2f out* **33/1**

0/0- **11** *26* **Rich Harvest (USA)**[95] 7380 6-8-12 **45**............................ DaneO'Neill 3 —
(Ray Peacock) *dwlt: t.k.h towards rr: bhd fnl 3f: t.o 2f out* **50/1**

1m 31.14s (1.54) **Going Correction** +0.225s/f (Slow) 11 Ran SP% **118.4**
Speed ratings (Par 97): **100,98,97,96,96 92,92,91,91,69 39**
toteswingers:1&2:£19.70, 1&3:£8.70, 2&3:£28.80 CSF £161.95 CT £827.42 TOTE £8.70: £2.60, £3.10, £2.40; EX 291.70.
Owner Paul Green (Oaklea) **Bred** Kingsmead Breeders **Trained** Lydiate, Merseyside
■ Stewards' Enquiry : Jimmy Quinn caution: careless riding.

FOCUS
A bottom-grade handicap. The winner is rated up a length but may not have had to improve.
T/Plt: £43.30 to a £1 stake. Pool:£85,662.34 - 1,441.72 winning tickets T/Qpdt: £9.70 to a £1 stake. Pool:£9,843.55 - 747.89 winning tickets WG

471 LINGFIELD (L-H)
Saturday, February 12

OFFICIAL GOING: Standard
Wind: medium, across Weather: overcast, dry

518 BET ON TODAY'S FOOTBALL AT BLUESQ.COM MAIDEN STKS 5f (P)
1:00 (1:01) (Class 5) 3-Y-O+ **£1,910** (£564; £282) **Stalls** High

Form RPR
4 **1** **Lois Lane**[10] 380 3-8-8 0.................................. RichardKingscote 7 54
(Ron Hodges) *taken down early: hld up in tch: rdn and hdwy on outer jst over 1f out: chsd ldr fnl 100yds: r.o wl to ld on post* **10/1**

05- **2** *nse* **Spontaneity (IRE)**[103] 7269 3-8-8 0.................................. TomEaves 4 54
(Bryan Smart) *led: rdn and forged ahd jst over 1f out: drvn and edgd rt ins fnl f: kpt on wl tl hdd post* **10/3**[2]

3 *1* **Upper Lambourn (IRE)** 3-8-13 0.............................. FergusSweeney 1 55+
(Jamie Osborne) *in tch on inner tl short of room and dropped to rr of main gp 4f out: sn nudged along and rn green: rdn over 1f out: hdwy jst ins fnl f: wnt 3rd fnl 75yds: gng on wl fin: nt rch ldng pair* **5/1**[1]

2-65 **4** *1* **Mosa Mine**[15] 337 4-9-8 55...................................... MichaelStainton 9 52
(Jane Chapple-Hyam) *pressed ldrs: ev ch and rdn wl over 1f out: nt qckn u.p 1f out: no ex fnl 100yds* **16/1**

5 **5** ½ **Evey P (IRE)**[10] 380 4-9-8 0.. LiamKeniry 6 51
(Gary Brown) *taken down early: chsd ldrs: effrt and rdn to chse ldng pair over 1f out: no ex and styd on same pce fnl f* **33/1**

The Form Book, Raceform Ltd, Compton, RG20 6NL

303- **6** ½ **Kokojo (IRE)**[121] 6867 3-8-9 65 ow1 .... DaneO'Neill 10 44
(Brendan Powell) *chsd ldrs: effrt and hanging lft over 1f out tl jst ins fnl f: styd on same pce after: nvr able to chal* **5/1**[3]

7 3¼ **Chenim (IRE)** 3-8-10 0 .... KierenFox(3) 8 36+
(John Best) *s.i.s: sn rdn along and bdly outpcd in last pair: kpt on ins fnl f: n.d* **10/3**[2]

60 **8** 3½ **Stoneacre Joe Joe**[10] 380 3-8-13 0 .... RobbieFitzpatrick 5 24
(Peter Grayson) *sn bustled along: chsd ldrs: rdn 2f out: btn over 1f out: fdd fnl f* **100/1**

9 2¼ **Bella Berti** 3-8-8 0 .... MartinLane 2 10
(Roger Ingram) *s.i.s: a wl outpcd in last* **66/1**

59.42 secs (0.62) **Going Correction** +0.025s/f (Slow)
WFA 3 from 4yo 14lb **9** Ran SP% **111.8**
Speed ratings (Par 103): **96,95,94,92,91 91,85,80,76**
toteswingers:1&2:£6.20, 1&3:£4.40, 2&3:£3.40 CSF £41.46 TOTE £10.30: £2.50, £1.70, £1.40; EX 51.80 Trifecta £235.50 Pool: £467.90 - 1.47 winning units..
Owner Unity Farm Holiday Centre Ltd **Bred** Unity Farm Holiday Centre & R J Hodges **Trained** Charlton Mackrell, Somerset

FOCUS
A weak maiden and much of the interest in the market surrounded two of the three debutants, but no newcomer had taken this in the previous ten years and that trend continued.
Kokojo(IRE) Official explanation: jockey said filly hung left
Chenim(IRE) Official explanation: jockey said gelding ran very green

519 LINGFIELD PARK GOLF CLUB (S) STKS 1m (P)
1:30 (1:32) (Class 6) 3-Y-O **£1,535** (£453; £226) **Stalls** High

Form RPR

24-1 **1** **A Little Bit Dusty**[12] 366 3-9-2 66 .... (b) KierenFox(3) 3 71
(Bill Turner) *t.k.h early: hld up in tch in midfield: swtchd to outer and gd hdwy to chse ldrs over 2f out: rdn to ld ent fnl f: sn clr: comf* **11/10**[1]

30-3 **2** 3¾ **Hackett (IRE)**[20] 270 3-9-0 62 .... MartinDwyer 1 57
(Michael Quinn) *chsd ldrs: ev ch and rdn ent fnl 2f: led wl over 1f out: hdd ent fnl f: no ch w wnr after* **15/2**[3]

3 ¾ **Bountiful Guest** 3-8-7 0 .... CharlesBishop(7) 5 56
(Mick Channon) *s.i.s: sn in tch in midfield: pushed along and outpcd ent fnl 2f: rallied jst ins fnl f: keeping on steadily fin: no ch w wnr* **40/1**

43-0 **4** 1¾ **Eternal Youth (IRE)**[24] 208 3-9-5 70 .... (b) LukeMorris 8 57
(Ronald Harris) *t.k.h: chsd ldr tl led over 2f out: rdn and hdd wl over 1f out: hld hd high u.p over 1f out: wknd ent fnl f* **9/2**[2]

45-6 **5** 1 **Lough Corrib (USA)**[8] 424 3-9-0 54 .... (p) PhillipMakin 2 49
(Kevin Ryan) *taken down early: led tl over 2f out: rdn and struggling ent fnl 2f: no ch and plugged on same pce fnl f* **15/2**[3]

050- **6** 2¼ **Blaze On By**[66] 7755 3-8-9 50 .... NeilChalmers 4 39
(John Bridger) *in tch in midfield: rdn and struggling jst over 2f out: wknd 2f out* **66/1**

40-0 **7** 3 **Beach Patrol (IRE)**[26] 189 3-8-11 52 .... AlanCreighton(3) 7 37
(Edward Creighton) *hld up in last trio: struggling and rdn over 2f out: wknd u.p 2f out* **50/1**

00-6 **8** nk **High Avon**[10] 383 3-9-0 53 .... (b[1]) JimCrowley 10 37
(Dean Ivory) *stdd s: t.k.h: hld up in tch in rr: rdn and struggling whn n.m.r ent fnl 2f: sn wknd* **12/1**

5 **9** 1¾ **Ability Girl**[13] 360 3-8-3 0 ow1 .... NannaHansen(7) 6 29
(Chris Wall) *hld up in last trio: outpcd and losing tch over 2f out: no ch fnl 2f* **16/1**

05 **10** 68 **Adieu**[7] 434 3-8-9 0 .... DaneO'Neill 9 —
(Richard Hannon) *in tch in midfield tl dropped to last wl over 3f out: nt striding out after and sn lost tch: virtually p.u fr over 2f out: t.o* **20/1**

1m 38.81s (0.61) **Going Correction** +0.025s/f (Slow) **10** Ran SP% **113.6**
Speed ratings (Par 95): **97,93,92,90,89 87,84,84,82,14**
toteswingers:1&2:£2.30, 1&3:£14.40, 2&3:£32.50 CSF £9.19 TOTE £2.20: £1.30, £1.70, £10.20; EX 8.70 Trifecta £329.90 Pool: £601.93 - 1.35 winning units..There was no bid for trhe winner.
Owner T.O.C.S. Ltd **Bred** T O C S Limited **Trained** Sigwells, Somerset

FOCUS
A modest seller
Adieu Official explanation: jockey said filly was unruly in stalls

520 LINGFIELD MARRIOTT HOTEL & COUNTRY CLUB MAIDEN STKS 1m (P)
2:05 (2:07) (Class 5) 3-Y-O **£1,910** (£564; £282) **Stalls** High

Form RPR

0-2 **1** **Obsession (IRE)**[28] 176 3-9-3 0 .... (v) GeorgeBaker 6 71
(Jeremy Noseda) *t.k.h early: hld up wl in tch: rdn and qcknd to ld over 1f out: edgd rt and pressed ins fnl f: fnd ex and in command fnl 75yds* **6/4**[1]

3-3 **2** 1 **Rojo Boy**[26] 191 3-9-3 73 .... (b) JamieSpencer 2 68
(David Elsworth) *hld up wl in tch in rr: hdwy to trck ldrs jst over 2f out: rdn to chse wnr jst over 1f out: sn hrd drvn: pressed wnr briefly ins fnl f: nt qckn and btn fnl 75yds* **3/1**[2]

3 2¼ **Strewth (IRE)** 3-9-0 0 .... KierenFox(3) 4 63
(John Best) *hld up in rr of main gp: pushed along and bhd a wall of horses over 2f out: rdn over 1f out: hdwy between horses and r.o wl ins fnl f: wnt 3rd nr fin* **20/1**

4 nk **Gottany O'S** 3-9-3 0 .... SamHitchcott 9 62
(Mick Channon) *in tch in midfield: rdn and effrt 2f out: no hdwy tl styd on wl ins fnl f: wnt 4th nr finsh* **66/1**

5 hd **Crystal Sky (IRE)** 3-8-12 0 .... RobertHavlin 10 57
(Andrew Haynes) *chsd ldrs: pressed ldrs and rdn 2f out: outpcd over 1f out: kpt on same pce fnl f: lost 2 pls nr fin* **100/1**

600- **6** 1¼ **Brandy Alexander**[175] 5294 3-9-3 62 .... DaneO'Neill 11 59
(Richard Hannon) *in tch in midfield: rdn and no hdwy wl over 1f out: hdwy ins fnl f: styd on fnl 100yds: nvr trbld ldrs* **10/1**

0-4 **7** ½ **Anna Fontenail**[28] 176 3-8-12 0 .... JamesMillman 8 53
(Rod Millman) *plld hrd: hld up in tch: switching out rt fr over 1f out: styd on fnl 150yds: nvr able to chal* **16/1**

8 nk **Acorous (FR)**[77] 3-9-3 0 .... StefaanFrancois 5 57
(J-M Plasschaert, Belgium) *w ldr tl led 4f out: rdn and hdd over 1f out: sn outpcd by ldng pair: wknd ins fnl f* **100/1**

05 **9** 1¾ **Lakota Ghost (USA)**[21] 262 3-9-3 0 .... JimCrowley 7 53
(Seamus Durack) *stdd s: hld up in rr: reminder wl over 1f out: pushed along after: kpt on same pce ins fnl f: nvr trbld ldrs* **10/1**

4-6 **10** 1¼ **Yours**[7] 434 3-8-12 0 .... PhillipMakin 12 45
(Kevin Ryan) *hld up in tch towards rr: rdn and effrt on outer bnd 2f out: no prog and wl hld after* **50/1**

0- **11** ½ **Neighbourhood (USA)**[122] 6843 3-9-3 0 .... SilvestreDeSousa 3 49
(Mark Johnston) *led tl 4f out: sn pushed along but styd pressing ldrs tl wknd ent fnl f* **13/2**[3]

12 22 **Sunley Surprise** 3-9-3 0 .... HayleyTurner 1 —
(David Elsworth) *v.s.a: sn rdn along and rn v green in rr: drvn and lost tch over 2f out* **25/1**

1m 40.39s (2.19) **Going Correction** +0.025s/f (Slow) **12** Ran SP% **116.4**
Speed ratings (Par 97): **90,89,86,86,86 85,84,84,82,81 80,58**
toteswingers:1&2:£1.80, 1&3:£6.90, 2&3:£12.10 CSF £5.29 TOTE £2.10: £1.10, £1.10, £6.60; EX 5.30 Trifecta £28.40 Pool: £557.66 - 14.48 winning units..
Owner Miss Yvonne Jacques **Bred** Frank Dunne **Trained** Newmarket, Suffolk

FOCUS
This race had gone to a newcomer in five of the previous seven years, but experience gained the day this time. Despite the winning time being 1.58 seconds slower than the seller, a few of those in behind caught the eye and winners should come out of it.

521 BLUE SQUARE SPRINT SERIES ROUND 6 H'CAP (QUALIFIER) (DIV I) 6f (P)
2:35 (2:36) (Class 5) (0-75,77) 4-Y-0+ **£2,388** (£705; £352) **Stalls** Low

Form RPR

5551 **1** **Norville (IRE)**[7] 435 4-8-10 **64** .... (b) CathyGannon 4 74
(David Evans) *chsd ldr: rdn and nt pce of ldr ent fnl 2f: rallied u.p 1f out: kpt on wl u.p to ld towards fin* **15/2**

-031 **2** ½ **Primo De Vida (IRE)**[10] 389 4-8-9 **70** .... (p) NathanAlison(7) 6 78
(Jim Boyle) *sn led: pushed along and wnt clr ent fnl 2f: tiring ins fnl f: kpt on gamely tl hdd and no ex towards fin* **6/1**[3]

-052 **3** 1¼ **Jungle Bay**[10] 394 4-9-1 **72** .... AndrewHeffernan(3) 5 76+
(Jane Chapple-Hyam) *hld up towards rr: rdn and stl plenty to do wl over 1f out: hdwy u.p over 1f out: styd on wl fnl f to go 3rd nr fin* **3/1**[1]

5334 **4** hd **Speak The Truth (IRE)**[7] 435 5-8-5 **62** oh2 ow1(p) MatthewDavies(3) 2 65
(Jim Boyle) *broke wl: sn stdd to chse ldrs: nt pce of wnr ent fnl 2f: rallied u.p 1f out: swtchd lft and hrd drvn ins fnl f: kpt on same pce towards fin* **16/1**

5-65 **5** ½ **Al Gillani (IRE)**[3] 470 6-9-1 **69** .... (p) GeorgeBaker 1 71
(Jim Boyle) *stdd s: hld up in rr: pushed along and stl plenty to do ent fnl 2f: swtchd rt over 1f out: hdwy 1f out: r.o wl fnl f: keeping on but no threat to wnr whn short of room nr fin* **11/1**

3-01 **6** ½ **Excellent Show**[9] 403 5-9-4 **77** .... (p) AdamCarter(5) 7 77
(Bryan Smart) *wnt rt s: led briefly early: chsd ldrs after: pushed along over 3f out: rdn and nt pce of wnr ent fnl 2f: rallied 1f out: wknd fnl 75yds* **8/1**

2-21 **7** 3½ **Picansort**[28] 178 4-9-2 **70** .... (v) JimmyQuinn 3 59
(Brett Johnson) *t.k.h: hld up in tch in midfield: rdn and outpcd ent fnl 2f: no ch fr over 1f out* **4/1**[2]

6-03 **8** 1¼ **Fantasy Fighter (IRE)**[15] 336 6-9-3 **71** .... TomEaves 10 56
(John Quinn) *stdd s: hld up in rr: rdn and outpcd jst over 2f out: no ch after* **12/1**

4202 **9** 1 **Incomparable**[8] 430 6-9-6 **74** .... (bt) IanMongan 11 56
(David Nicholls) *chsd ldrs: rdn and nt qckn ent fnl 2f: wknd over 1f out* **25/1**

2-12 **10** 8 **Waterloo Dock**[21] 264 6-9-0 **68** .... (v) ChrisCatlin 9 24
(Michael Quinn) *sn rdn along and struggling: dropped to rr 3f out: wl bhd fnl 2f* **12/1**

0-00 **11** 8 **Dingaan (IRE)**[24] 213 8-8-11 **65** .... RobbieFitzpatrick 8 —
(Peter Grayson) *sltly hmpd s: a bhd: lost tch u.p wl over 2f out: wl bhd after* **50/1**

1m 10.82s (-1.08) **Going Correction** +0.025s/f (Slow) **11** Ran SP% **117.6**
Speed ratings (Par 103): **108,107,105,105,104 104,99,97,96,85 75**
toteswingers:1&2:£8.90, 1&3:£8.50, 2&3:£6.60 CSF £52.05 CT £166.63 TOTE £8.80: £3.00, £2.40, £1.20; EX 67.50 Trifecta £424.40 Part won. Pool: £573.58 - 0.62 winning units..
Owner Raymond N R Auld **Bred** R N Auld **Trained** Pandy, Monmouths

FOCUS
Several of the runners in both divisions of this contest had been taking each other on in previous rounds of this sprint series.
Picansort Official explanation: jockey said gelding was too keen early

522 BLUE SQUARE SPRINT SERIES ROUND 6 H'CAP (QUALIFIER) (DIV II) 6f (P)
3:05 (3:06) (Class 5) (0-75,75) 4-Y-0+ **£2,388** (£705; £352) **Stalls** Low

Form RPR

6-13 **1** **Waabel**[21] 264 4-9-7 **75** .... PaulDoe 2 84
(Jim Best) *mde all: pushed and qcknd 2f out: clr over 1f out: edgd lft u.p ins fnl f: tiring towards fin but a holding on* **11/4**[1]

4-10 **2** ½ **Garstang**[8] 430 8-9-5 **73** .... (b) LukeMorris 4 80
(John Balding) *chsd wnr thrght: rdn and clr 2nd wl over 1f out: hanging lft over 1f out: swtchd rt and kpt on to press wnr wl ins fnl f: nvr quite getting up* **14/1**

13-0 **3** 2¾ **Danzoe (IRE)**[21] 264 4-9-0 **71** .... KierenFox(3) 5 69
(Christine Dunnett) *racd in midfield: rdn and nt pce of ldng pair ent fnl 2f: n.m.r over 1f out: hdwy to chse clr ldng pair fnl 150yds: nvr able to chal ldng pair* **11/2**[2]

2310 **4** ½ **Dancing Welcome**[7] 435 5-9-1 **69** .... (b) RichardKingscote 9 66
(Milton Bradley) *racd in midfield: rdn and outpce by ldng pair ent fnl 2f: no threat to ldrs after: kpt on u.p ins fnl f* **8/1**

2546 **5** ½ **Chjimes (IRE)**[15] 336 7-8-12 **66** .... (b) HayleyTurner 7 63
(Conor Dore) *stdd and dropped in bhd after s: effrt but stl plenty to do wl over 1f out: nt clr run ent fnl f: styd on ins fnl f: nvr able to chal* **6/1**[3]

4056 **6** shd **Nubar Boy**[7] 435 4-8-8 **62** .... MartinLane 10 57
(David Evans) *stdd s: bhd: effrt and rdn on outer over 1f out: styd on ins fnl f: nvr trbld ldrs* **8/1**

0-30 **7** hd **Pipers Piping (IRE)**[21] 264 5-9-2 **70** .... (b[1]) MichaelStainton 11 64
(Jane Chapple-Hyam) *stdd s: hld up in last pair: effrt on outer bnd 2f out: styd on ins fnl f: nvr trbld ldrs* **8/1**

4-00 **8** ½ **Hierarch (IRE)**[28] 174 4-8-9 **63** .... (p) JamesDoyle 3 55
(David Flood) *chsd ldrs: rdn and outpcd by ldng pair ent fnl 2f: wnt modest 3rd over 1f out tl fnl 150yds: wknd after* **16/1**

5-66 **9** 1¾ **Step It Up (IRE)**[15] 337 7-8-0 **61** oh3 .... DanielCremin(7) 1 48
(Jim Boyle) *racd in midfield: effrt on inner wl over 1f out: pressing for 3rd but no ch w ldng pair ent fnl f: wknd fnl 150yds* **50/1**

400- **10** nse **Mark Anthony (IRE)**[112] 7082 4-9-3 **71** .... PhillipMakin 6 58
(Kevin Ryan) *rrd s: sn rcvrd to chse ldrs: rdn and outpcd by ldng pair ent fnl 2f: wknd over 1f out* **8/1**

1m 10.93s (-0.97) **Going Correction** +0.025s/f (Slow) **10** Ran SP% **115.3**
Speed ratings (Par 103): **107,106,102,102,101 101,100,100,97,97**
toteswingers:1&2:£4.30, 1&3:£5.00, 2&3:£7.80 CSF £44.08 CT £199.66 TOTE £3.30: £1.10, £3.30, £1.80; EX 34.20 Trifecta £156.60 Pool: £586.30 - 2.77 winning units..
Owner M&R Refurbishments Ltd **Bred** Shadwell Estate Company Limited **Trained** Lewes, E Sussex
■ A winner for Paul Doe on his first ride since June.

FOCUS
This modest handicap was run in a time marginally slower than the first division. It looked an open race on paper, but as it turned out the first two occupied the same positions all the way and nothing else was able to get into it. It may pay to treat the form a little conservatively.

523 MARSH GREEN H'CAP 5f (P)
3:40 (3:41) (Class 4) (0-85,85) 4-Y-0+ **£3,238** (£963; £481; £240) **Stalls** High

Form RPR

1-40 **1** **Breathless Kiss (USA)**[21] 265 4-9-2 **80**......................(b) PhillipMakin 1 99
(Kevin Ryan) *awkward s and dwlt: in tch: smooth hdwy on inner to trck ldr jst over 2f out: rdn to ld over 1f out: clr fnl f: easily* **7/1**

1-33 **2** *4 ½* **Sir Geoffrey (IRE)**[18] 293 5-9-7 **85**..............................(b) IanMongan 6 88
(David Nicholls) *broke v fast and led: rdn and hdd over 1f out: no ch w wnr fnl f but kpt on to hold 2nd* **4/1**[3]

52-3 **3** *¾* **Ebraam (USA)**[16] 316 8-9-6 **84**.. LukeMorris 4 84
(Ronald Harris) *chsd ldr: rdn and outpcd over 1f out: drvn and kpt on same pce fnl f* **9/4**[2]

51-1 **4** *1 ¾* **You'relikemefrank**[36] 80 5-8-7 **71**......................(p) GrahamGibbons 7 65
(John Balding) *in tch: effrt and pushed along 2f out: rdn and outpcd over 1f out: 4th and wl hld fnl f* **15/8**[1]

0206 **5** *3 ¼* **Grudge**[8] 430 6-8-7 **71**..(be) HayleyTurner 5 53
(Conor Dore) *taken down early: chsd ldr tl jst over 2f out: sn wknd: wl btn over 1f out* **20/1**

1243 **6** *4 ½* **Feelin Foxy**[8] 429 7-9-7 **85**... MickyFenton 8 51
(James Given) *taken down early: s.i.s: a in rr: rdn and lost tch wl over 1f out: wl bhd and edgd lft ins fnl f* **16/1**

57.70 secs (-1.10) **Going Correction** +0.025s/f (Slow) **6** Ran SP% **108.7**
Speed ratings (Par 105): **109,101,100,97,92 85**
toteswingers:1&2:£3.90, 1&3:£3.20, 2&3:£2.00 CSF £32.25 CT £73.71 TOTE £8.60: £4.10, £3.10; EX 39.30 Trifecta £102.90 Pool: £652.61 - 4.69 winning units..
Owner Mrs Angie Bailey **Bred** Don Mattox & Pam Mattox **Trained** Hambleton, N Yorks

FOCUS
They went a scorching pace in this sprint and few got into it.

524 HAMMERWOOD H'CAP 1m 4f (P)
4:15 (4:16) (Class 6) (0-52,52) 4-Y-0+ **£1,535** (£453; £226) **Stalls** Low

Form RPR

030- **1** **Captain Cool (IRE)**[44] 8015 4-8-9 **47**............................(b) DaneO'Neill 1 54
(Richard Hannon) *chsd ldrs: rdn to ld wl over 1f out: in command ins fnl f: rdn out* **10/1**

303- **2** *1 ¾* **Minder**[204] 4328 5-9-2 **51**... RichardKingscote 3 55
(Jonathan Portman) *in tch in midfield: hdwy 2f out: rdn over 1f out: chsd wnr ins fnl f: styd on same pce and no imp fnl 100yds* **14/1**

5-41 **3** *nk* **Our Kes (IRE)**[24] 207 9-9-1 **50**.. JimmyQuinn 9 53
(Jane Chapple-Hyam) *stdd s: hld up in rr: hdwy into midfield over 2f out: effrt u.p over 1f out: kpt on same pce ins fnl f* **6/1**[2]

506- **4** *1* **Galiotto (IRE)**[134] 6538 5-9-1 **50**.................................... GeorgeBaker 7 52
(Gary Moore) *hld up in midfield: pushed along and effrt over 2f out: rdn and hdwy over 1f out: kpt on ins fnl f: nvr gng pce to threaten ldrs* **7/4**[1]

-000 **5** *½* **Gems**[19] 283 4-8-7 **45**... WilliamCarson 4 46
(Peter Hiatt) *led: rdn over 2f out: hdd wl over 1f out: lost 2nd ins fnl f: no ex and lost 2 pls after* **25/1**

0-00 **6** *nk* **Pascalina**[13] 355 4-8-9 **47**... LukeMorris 5 48
(John Akehurst) *dwlt: sn rcvrd to chse ldr: rdn and ev ch 2f out: unable qck over 1f out: one pce after* **25/1**

00-0 **7** *nk* **Play Up Pompey**[29] 164 9-8-10 **45**................................ CathyGannon 2 45
(John Bridger) *in tch in midfield: effrt on inner over 1f out: rdn and kpt on same pce fnl f* **66/1**

0-00 **8** *¾* **Fine Tolerance**[19] 277 5-8-10 **45**..............................(b) ChrisCatlin 6 44
(Sam Davison) *in tch in midfield: rdn and hdwy on inner over 1f out: kpt on same pce and no imp fnl f* **25/1**

1-43 **9** *2 ½* **Suhailah**[19] 278 5-9-2 **51**.................................... RobbieFitzpatrick 14 46
(Michael Attwater) *in tch midfield: hdwy to chse ldrs over 1f out: lost pl on outer bnd 2f out: plugged on same pce and n.d after* **8/1**

0-04 **10** *nk* **Yorksters Prince (IRE)**[9] 408 4-8-3 **46**..............(p) TobyAtkinson(5) 11 40
(George Prodromou) *t.k.h early: hld up towards rr: rdn along 4f out: drvn and no hdwy fnl 2f* **20/1**

00-4 **11** *3 ½* **Harrys**[17] 309 4-9-0 **52**.. J-PGuillambert 13 41
(Jane Chapple-Hyam) *stdd s: hld up in last trio: rdn over 2f out: no hdwy: n.d* **33/1**

53-0 **12** *hd* **Starry Mount**[29] 163 4-9-0 **52**...................................... SteveDrowne 12 40
(Andrew Haynes) *hld up in last trio: rdn on inner over 2f out: nvr trbld ldrs* **25/1**

55-0 **13** *shd* **Asterisk**[27] 184 4-9-0 **52**... RobertHavlin 16 40
(John Berry) *stdd s: hld up in rr: rdn and no hdwy jst over 2f out: n.d* **7/1**[3]

6-04 **14** *1 ¼* **Pictures (IRE)**[13] 354 4-8-4 **45**.................................... KierenFox(3) 8 31
(John Bridger) *chsd ldrs: rdn over 2f out: wknd over 1f out: wl btn and eased ins fnl f* **25/1**

2m 35.4s (2.40) **Going Correction** +0.025s/f (Slow)
WFA 4 from 5yo+ 3lb **14** Ran SP% **118.4**
Speed ratings (Par 101): **93,91,91,90,90 90,90,89,88,87 85,85,85,84**
toteswingers:1&2:£10.00, 1&3:£9.00, 2&3:£15.80 CSF £122.48 CT £920.72 TOTE £9.00: £1.70, £4.80, £2.20; EX 117.30 Trifecta £289.00 Pool: £730.56 - 1.87 winning units..
Owner Mrs John Lee **Bred** Jan Revs **Trained** East Everleigh, Wilts

FOCUS
A low-grade handicap run at just a steady pace.

525 PLAY RAINBOW RICHES AT BLUESQ.COM H'CAP 1m 2f (P)
4:50 (4:51) (Class 3) (0-95,94) 4-Y-0+ **£5,828** (£1,734; £866; £432) **Stalls** Low

Form RPR

30-3 **1** **Layline (IRE)**[36] 91 4-9-1 **89**....................................... JamieSpencer 7 97
(Gay Kelleway) *chsd ldng trio: rdn and chal jst over 1f out: led jst ins fnl f: hld on wl u.p* **16/1**

-021 **2** *nk* **Scamperdale**[7] 436 9-9-3 **93**.. KierenFox(3) 4 100
(Brian Baugh) *racd off the pce in midfield: clsd and in tch 4f out: pushed along and hdwy over 2f out: rdn over 1f out: ev ch ins fnl f: no ex nr fin* **8/1**

023- **3** *½* **Baylini**[63] 7828 7-9-1 **88**.. JamesDoyle 13 94
(Jamie Osborne) *taken down early: dwlt: hld up off the pce towards rr: clsd 4f out: swtchd rt ent fnl f: r.o wl fnl f: wnt 3rd last stride* **11/1**

206- **4** *shd* **Emerging Artist (FR)**[154] 5949 5-9-7 **94**.............. SilvestreDeSousa 2 100
(Mark Johnston) *chsd ldng pair: rdn and ev ch over 1f out: no ex fnl 100yds* **4/1**[2]

12-3 **5** *hd* **Franco Is My Name**[28] 180 5-8-13 **86**............................ DaneO'Neill 8 91
(Peter Hedger) *racd off the pce in midfield: pushed along and hdwy over 2f out: pressed ldrs and lugging lft ent fnl f: no ex and btn fnl 75yds* **7/2**[1]

043- **6** *nk* **Resentful Angel**[76] 7612 6-8-9 **87**............................ TobyAtkinson(5) 3 92+
(Pat Eddery) *hld up wl off the pce in last pair: rdn and effrt whn swtchd lft over 1f out: r.o strly ins fnl f: nt rch ldrs* **20/1**

0-20 **7** *nk* **Good Again**[14] 353 5-9-0 **87**....................................... TomQueally 11 91
(Gerard Butler) *racd off the pce in midfield: effrt and rdn jst over 2f out: no imp whn bmpd and pushed rt ent fnl f: r.o fnl 150yds: nt rch ldrs* **9/2**[3]

2-01 **8** *nse* **Avon River**[26] 188 4-8-12 **86**.....................................(b) JimmyQuinn 6 90
(Richard Hannon) *chsd ldrs: rdn over 2f out: stl chsng ldrs and hrd drvn ent fnl f: kpt on same pce* **40/1**

1313 **9** *1 ¾* **Kidlat**[13] 359 6-8-7 **80** oh1.. CathyGannon 1 81
(Alan Bailey) *sn pushed along to ld after 1f: rdn and hdd over 2f out: styd pressing ldrs tl wknd jst ins fnl f* **20/1**

262- **10** *nk* **The Which Doctor**[59] 7881 6-9-0 **87**......................(p) GeorgeBaker 14 87
(Jeremy Noseda) *stdd after s: hld up wl off the pce in rr: rdn and effrt over 1f out: kpt on ins fnl f: nvr able to chal* **10/1**

23-5 **11** *1* **Denton (NZ)**[14] 353 8-8-13 **86**...................................(t) SteveDrowne 10 86
(Jeremy Gask) *led for 1f: chsd ldr after tl led over 2f out: rdn 2f out: hdd jst ins fnl f: btn fnl 100yds: eased towards fin* **16/1**

-501 **12** *5* **Hidden Glory**[14] 353 4-9-0 **88**..................................... MickyFenton 9 76
(James Given) *hld up wl off the pce in last quartet: rdn and effrt on outer over 1f out: no hdwy* **14/1**

/0-0 **13** *31* **Raine's Cross**[20] 271 4-8-11 **85**..................................... JimCrowley 12 11
(Peter Winkworth) *hld up wl off the pce in last quartet: dropped to last ent fnl 3f: lost tch 2f out: eased ins fnl f: t.o* **66/1**

2m 4.43s (-2.17) **Going Correction** +0.025s/f (Slow)
WFA 4 from 5yo+ 1lb **13** Ran SP% **120.8**
Speed ratings (Par 107): **109,108,108,108,108 107,107,107,106,105 105,101,76**
toteswingers:1&2:£23.50, 1&3:£26.70, 2&3:£12.40 CSF £135.05 CT £1490.28 TOTE £22.20: £5.80, £2.30, £3.60; EX 198.50 TRIFECTA Not won..
Owner Miss Gay Kelleway **Bred** Mrs M E Slade **Trained** Exning, Suffolk
■ Stewards' Enquiry : James Doyle one-day ban: careless riding (Feb 26)

FOCUS
A decent and competitive handicap and the pace was a good one, but even so there was less than 2l covering the first eight at the line.

NOTEBOOK
Layline(IRE) had been without a win since his racecourse debut and hasn't always looked an easy ride, but Jamie Spencer found the key to him on his third outing for his new yard. He was always travelling well in a handy position and although pressed on both sides after taking over in front, kept on finding just enough to last home. His trainer believes he will become a Dubai Carnival horse in due course. (tchd 25-1)
Scamperdale was put up 5lb for his success over 1m4f here seven days earlier, which meant that he was no better off with Hidden Glory for his previous defeat by that rival over C&D, but he put up another cracking effort, especially as he made his effort against the inside rail in the straight. It does seem that the longer trip may soon him better now, however. (op 15-2 tchd 13-2)
Baylini got the strong pace she needs and finished with a real flourish down the outside. She is very consistent, but she doesn't win very often these days. (tchd 12-1)
Emerging Artist(FR), making his all-weather debut after five months off, was always handy and never stopped trying. He looks perfectly capable of winning on this surface. (tchd 10-3)
Franco Is My Name came off the bridle approaching the home turn, but although he stayed on in the straight he tended to carry his head to one side and never looked to be doing quite enough. (tchd 3-1)
Resentful Angel ◆ was given a lot to do and still had plenty of ground to make up passing the 2f pole, but she then clicked into gear and was finishing fastest of all. She has won twice over C&D, but may need a stiffer test these days. (tchd 25-1)
Good Again, without a win since October 2009, didn't enjoy much luck when behind three of these over C&D last month and would have finished closer here had she not been bumped by Baylini a furlong out and then carried right by that rival all the way to the line. (op 5-1 tchd 6-1)
Avon River, back in a handicap after winning a 7f Wolverhampton claimer, was trying this trip for the first time and was keen enough early, despite the solid tempo. Under the circumstances he lasted longer than might have been expected. (op 25-1)
T/Plt: £56.30 to a £1 stake. Pool:£55,341.23 - 716.35 winning tickets T/Qpdt: £28.30 to a £1 stake. Pool:£4,345.54 - 113.60 winning tickets SP

511 WOLVERHAMPTON (A.W) (L-H)
Saturday, February 12

OFFICIAL GOING: Standard
Wind: Moderate, half-behind Weather: Dry

526 BET ON TODAY'S FOOTBALL AT BLUESQ.COM AMATEUR RIDERS' H'CAP 1m 141y(P)
6:50 (6:50) (Class 6) (0-60,60) 4-Y-0+ **£1,483** (£456; £228) **Stalls** Low

Form RPR

-465 **1** **Join Up**[13] 361 5-10-7 **58**............................... MissBeckyBrisbourne(5) 5 65
(Mark Brisbourne) *dwlt: midfield: hdwy to trck ldrs 3f out: r.o to ld fnl 100yds: rdn out and on top towards fin* **13/2**[3]

4-03 **2** *½* **What's Up Doc (IRE)**[15] 341 10-11-0 **60**................... MissGAndrews 8 66
(Lawney Hill) *a.p: effrt on inner to ld over 1f out: hdd fnl 100yds: kpt on but hld cl home* **15/2**

1-35 **3** *shd* **Pie Poudre**[19] 283 4-10-2 **51**.................................(p) MrCMartin(3) 2 57
(Roy Brotherton) *hld up: rdn and hdwy over 1f out: r.o to chal fnl 100yds: nt qckn and hld cl home* **6/1**[2]

3-22 **4** *1 ¾* **Tres Froide (FR)**[19] 283 6-10-8 **54**......................(p) MissEJJones 11 56
(Nigel Tinkler) *midfield: rdn and hdwy over 1f out: sn edgd lft: styd on ins fnl f: nt pce to rch ldrs* **5/1**[1]

004- **5** *½* **Provost**[76] 7611 7-10-13 **59**......................................(b) MrOGreenall 12 60
(Michael Easterby) *hld up: hdwy over 3f out: rdn to chse ldrs over 1f out: styd on same pce ins fnl f* **5/1**[1]

0-35 **6** *2 ¼* **Catching Zeds**[8] 425 4-10-7 **58**..................................... MrJHodson(5) 3 53
(Ian Williams) *chsd ldr after 1f: ev ch over 2f out: rdn and lost 2nd over 1f out: no ex fnl 100yds* **7/1**

550- **7** *1* **Prince Golan (IRE)**[158] 5828 7-10-9 **58**........................ MrMPrice(3) 7 51
(Richard Price) *missed break: towards rr: hdwy over 3f out: effrt on outer over 2f out: one pce over 1f out* **25/1**

006- **8** *hd* **Angelena Ballerina (IRE)**[81] 7543 4-10-1 **54**..........(v) MrLMichael(7) 1 47
(Karen George) *led: rdn and hdd over 1f out: wknd ins fnl f* **33/1**

5-24 **9** *¾* **Fortunate Bid (IRE)**[19] 283 5-10-1 **52**................... MissSLWatson(5) 4 45
(Linda Stubbs) *trckd ldrs: hmpd wl over 3f out: sn lost pl: nt clr run 1f out: sn swtchd lft: no imp after* **10/1**

200/ **10** *shd* **Street Crime**[600] 3223 6-10-4 **55**.............................. MrRJWilliams(5) 10 46
(Ron Hodges) *racd keenly: trckd ldrs: rdn over 2f out: wknd over 1f out* **25/1**

03-5 **11** *10* **Peaceful Means (IRE)**[12] 369 8-10-7 **58**............ JonathanEngland(5) 6 26
(Evan Williams) *midfield: lost pl 4f out: struggling and bhd after* **16/1**

16-0 **12** *8* **Sirjosh**[41] [9] 5-10-7 **60**.. MrTHowell(7) 9 —
(Des Donovan) *s.i.s: hld up: sltly hmpd s: a bhd: struggling fnl 3f* **20/1**
1m 52.44s (1.94) **Going Correction** +0.225s/f (Slow) **12** Ran SP% **115.6**
Speed ratings (Par 101): **100,99,99,97,97 95,94,94,93,93 84,77**
toteswingers: 1&2 £10.50, 1&3 £10.60, 2&3 £8.90. CSF £50.35 CT £312.80 TOTE £7.50: £2.50, £3.10, £2.30; EX 48.30.
Owner P R Kirk **Bred** A Reid **Trained** Great Ness, Shropshire
■ Stewards' Enquiry : Miss G Andrews three-day ban: careless riding (April 9,16,May 9)
Miss E J Jones one-day ban: careless riding (Apr 9)
FOCUS
A low-grade amateur riders' handicap and as is often the case in this type of race the pace was sound. There were plenty in with a chance in the home straight.

527 ENJOY THE PARTY PACK GROUP OFFER (S) STKS 1m 1f 103y(P)
7:20 (7:21) (Class 6) 3-Y-O **£1,535** (£453; £226) **Stalls** Low

Form RPR
3424 **1** **Ad Vitam (IRE)**[18] [296] 3-8-12 58..................................(tp) LiamKeniry 1 60
(Sylvester Kirk) *hld up in rr: effrt to cl 2f out: led over 1f out: edgd lft ins fnl f: r.o and in command towards fin* **9/2**[3]
3-23 **2** *¾* **Beating Harmony**[12] [366] 3-8-12 60.............................. HayleyTurner 2 58
(Tony Carroll) *led early: handy: sltly outpcd 2f out: rallied and ev ch fr over 1f out: nt qckn towards fin* **9/4**[2]
5400 **3** *1 ¼* **Polly Holder (IRE)**[8] [424] 3-8-0 56..........................(p) NatashaEaton(7) 4 51
(Alan Bailey) *chsd ldr after 1f: lost 2nd wl over 1f out: ¾ l down and u.p whn n.m.r and hmpd jst ins fnl f: styd on same pce and no imp after* **6/1**
1333 **4** *nk* **Urban Kode (IRE)**[8] [424] 3-8-11 62..............................(v[1]) RPWalsh(7) 3 61
(David Evans) *s.s: racd keenly: sn led: sddle slipped 7f out: rdn 2f out: hdd over 1f out: kpt on same pce ins fnl f* **5/4**[1]
2m 6.76s (5.06) **Going Correction** +0.225s/f (Slow) **4** Ran SP% **107.7**
Speed ratings (Par 95): **86,85,84,83**
CSF £14.36 TOTE £5.70; EX 12.00.The winner was sold to Bernard Llewellyn for 3,000 guineas.
Owner Sylvester Kirk **Bred** Michelle Morgan **Trained** Upper Lambourn, Berks
■ Stewards' Enquiry : Liam Keniry two-day ban: careless riding (Feb 26 & 28)
FOCUS
A moderate seller.

528 WOLVERHAMPTON-RACECOURSE.CO.UK H'CAP 1m 141y(P)
7:50 (7:50) (Class 5) (0-75,75) 4-Y-O+ **£2,137** (£635; £317; £158) **Stalls** Low

Form RPR
0-11 **1** **Resuscitator (USA)**[8] [428] 4-9-4 **72**................................(v) EddieAhern 2 82
(Heather Main) *mde all: kicked on 2f out: rdn over 1f out: pushed out and plld out more towards fin* **2/1**[1]
0-64 **2** *1 ¾* **Brouhaha**[19] [287] 7-9-7 **75**.. RichardKingscote 4 81
(Tom Dascombe) *in tch: effrt 2f out: chsd wnr 1f out: ch ins fnl f: nt qckn towards fin* **85/40**[2]
006- **3** *1 ¾* **Border Owl (IRE)**[88] [7474] 6-8-9 **63**.................................... ChrisCatlin 6 65
(Peter Salmon) *hld up: pushed along over 3f out: hdwy on outer over 2f out: chsd ldrs over 1f out: styd on same pce ins fnl f* **16/1**
65-5 **4** *½* **Vanilla Rum**[19] [285] 4-9-4 **72**.. JimmyQuinn 3 73
(John Mackie) *chsd wnr: u.p and nt qckn 2f out: lost 2nd 1f out: no ex fnl 150yds* **7/1**
030- **5** *3 ¾* **Boy Blue**[200] [4450] 6-8-7 **66**.. TobyAtkinson(5) 1 58
(Peter Salmon) *s.i.s: a bhd: nvr on terms* **12/1**
2321 **6** *1* **Bentley**[9] [400] 7-9-4 **72**.. GrahamGibbons 5 62
(Brian Baugh) *chsd ldrs: pushed along 3f out: rdn and wknd over 1f out* **4/1**[3]
1m 50.26s (-0.24) **Going Correction** +0.225s/f (Slow) **6** Ran SP% **111.4**
Speed ratings (Par 103): **110,108,106,106,103 102**
toteswingers: 1&2 £1.10, 1&3 £6.30, 2&3 £8.20. CSF £6.47 TOTE £3.40: £2.00, £1.30; EX 8.70.
Owner Wetumpka Racing & Donald Kerr **Bred** David Bowman & Dr Carl Chan **Trained** Kingston Lisle, Oxon
FOCUS
An ordinary handicap, though the time was good.

529 WOLVERHAMPTON HOLIDAY INN MAIDEN FILLIES' STKS 1m 141y(P)
8:20 (8:20) (Class 5) 3-Y-O+ **£2,007** (£597; £298; £149) **Stalls** Low

Form RPR
2 **1** **Albaraka**[19] [274] 3-8-5 0.. ChrisCatlin 7 81+
(Sir Mark Prescott Bt) *wnt rt s: chsd ldr 7f out: led over 3f out: kicked clr 2f out: r.o wl: unchal after* **8/13**[1]
2 *6* **Covert Decree** 3-8-5 0.. LukeMorris 1 67+
(Clive Cox) *hld up: rn green: pushed along 5f out: outpcd over 2f out: hdwy to take 2nd over 1f out: hung lft ins fnl f: no ch w wnr: eased fnl 75yds* **22/1**
4-24 **3** *3 ½* **Spirit Of Grace**[24] [214] 3-8-2 69........................... AndrewHeffernan(3) 4 59
(Alan McCabe) *hld up: hdwy 2f out: rdn to chse clr wnr briefly over 1f out: one pce* **13/2**[3]
00-2 **4** *3 ¼* **Beauchamp Xiara**[15] [344] 5-9-12 68............................ JamesDoyle 3 57
(Hans Adielsson) *hld up: hdwy 5f out: pushed along to chse ldrs 3f out: outpcd 2f out: wknd over 1f out* **5/1**[2]
43- **5** *hd* **Surprise (IRE)**[214] [3981] 3-8-5 0.................................... NickyMackay 2 51
(Mark Rimmer) *chsd ldrs: pushed along 3f out: chsd clr wnr 2f out: lost 2nd over 1f out: wl btn ins fnl f* **33/1**
6-3 **6** *2 ¾* **Thymesthree (IRE)**[15] [344] 3-8-2 0........................... SimonPearce(3) 6 45
(Chris Wall) *chsd ldrs: pushed along and wl outpcd over 3f out: n.d after* **10/1**
035- **7** *1 ¼* **Anaya**[30] [7161] 4-9-9 52.. RossAtkinson(3) 5 47
(David Bourton) *led: rdn and hdd over 3f out: outpcd 2f out: wknd over 1f out* **66/1**
1m 50.78s (0.28) **Going Correction** +0.225s/f (Slow) **7** Ran SP% **109.8**
WFA 3 from 4yo+ 21lb
Speed ratings (Par 100): **107,101,98,95,95 93,91**
toteswingers: 1&2 £5.00, 1&3 £1.40, 2&3 £11.70. CSF £17.34 TOTE £1.60: £1.10, £6.20; EX 7.60.
Owner Miss K Rausing **Bred** Miss K Rausing **Trained** Newmarket, Suffolk
FOCUS
A weak maiden, but a wide-margin, unexposed winner.

530 BLUESQ.COM ON YOUR IPHONE FILLIES' H'CAP 7f 32y(P)
8:50 (8:50) (Class 5) (0-75,73) 4-Y-O+ **£2,137** (£635; £317; £158) **Stalls** High

Form RPR
233- **1** **Catherines Call (IRE)**[133] [6577] 4-9-7 **73**............................ AndreaAtzeni 1 81
(Des Donovan) *chsd ldr: effrt to ld 1f out: rdn whn pressed ins fnl f: a doing engough cl home* **3/1**[3]
00-0 **2** *¾* **Ivory Silk**[31] [134] 6-8-13 **70**.. TobyAtkinson(5) 2 76
(Jeremy Gask) *hld up in rr: pushed along over 2f out: clsd over 1f out: wnt 2nd ins fnl f: sn ev ch: nt qckn and hld cl home* **7/1**
0-31 **3** *3 ¼* **Piquante**[25] [200] 5-9-4 **70**..(v) HayleyTurner 3 67
(Nigel Tinkler) *led: rdn and hdd 1f out: edgd rt whn no ex fnl 150yds* **9/4**[2]
34-0 **4** *2 ¼* **Love Match**[24] [206] 4-9-3 **69**.. AdamKirby 4 60
(Marco Botti) *chsd ldrs: rdn and ev ch over 1f out: fdd fnl 75yds: lame* **13/8**[1]
1m 32.24s (2.64) **Going Correction** +0.225s/f (Slow) **4** Ran SP% **106.4**
Speed ratings (Par 100): **93,92,88,85**
CSF £18.93 TOTE £3.90; EX 14.30.
Owner Philip Mclaughlin **Bred** K Maginn **Trained** Newmarket, Suffolk
FOCUS
Just a 4lb weight range in this modest fillies' handicap and all four almost in line a furlong out.
Love Match Official explanation: vet said filly returned lame

531 PLAY RAINBOW RICHES AT BLUESQ.COM H'CAP 1m 4f 50y(P)
9:20 (9:20) (Class 5) (0-75,74) 4-Y-O+ **£2,137** (£635; £317; £158) **Stalls** Low

Form RPR
/50- **1** **Gloucester**[125] [3576] 8-9-5 **72**.. HayleyTurner 3 79
(Michael Scudamore) *hld up in rr: hdwy 3f out: rdn over 1f out: r.o to chal ins fnl f: led post* **6/1**
-111 **2** *hd* **Carter**[22] [252] 5-9-7 **74**.. GrahamGibbons 4 80
(Ian Williams) *chsd ldrs: hdwy 4f out: wnt 2nd wl over 3f out: led over 1f out: sn rdn: pressed ins fnl f: hdd post* **6/5**[1]
620- **3** *1 ¼* **Hallstatt (IRE)**[108] [6538] 5-8-9 **62**.................................(t) JimmyQuinn 6 67
(John Mackie) *hld up: rdn and hdwy over 1f out: styng on whn nt clr run and swtchd lft 150yds out: hld by front pair fnl 50yds* **11/2**[3]
100- **4** *1 ¼* **Goodlukin Lucy**[98] [7349] 4-8-10 **71**................................ TobyAtkinson(5) 2 73
(Pat Eddery) *racd keenly: chsd ldrs: chalng fr over 1f out: styd on same pce fnl 75yds* **8/1**
400- **5** *3* **Jeer (IRE)**[99] [7337] 7-9-5 **72**...(bt) PhillipMakin 1 69
(Michael Easterby) *led: rdn over 2f out: hdd over 1f out: u.p whn carried lft ins fnl f: one pce and no imp after* **5/1**[2]
00-0 **6** *20* **Maslak (IRE)**[10] [392] 7-9-2 **69**.. ChrisCatlin 5 34
(Peter Hiatt) *chsd ldr tl wl over 3f out: sn wknd* **11/1**
2m 41.29s (0.19) **Going Correction** +0.225s/f (Slow)
WFA 4 from 5yo+ 3lb **6** Ran SP% **111.2**
Speed ratings (Par 103): **108,107,107,106,104 90**
toteswingers: 1&2 £2.10, 1&3 £5.10, 2&3 £2.60. CSF £13.49 TOTE £6.40: £2.50, £1.20; EX 12.70.
Owner S M Smith & Keith Hunter **Bred** Juddmonte Farms Ltd **Trained** Bromsash, Herefordshire
FOCUS
A modest but competitive handicap run at a sound pace.
T/Plt: £128.00 to a £1 stake. Pool:£84,189.43 - 479.89 winning tickets. T/Qpdt: £9.60 to a £1 stake. Pool:£7,418.15 - 568.40 winning tickets. DO

478 CAGNES-SUR-MER
Sunday, February 13
OFFICIAL GOING: Fibresand: standard

532a PRIX DE LA CALIFORNIE (LISTED RACE) (3YO) (FIBRESAND) 1m (F)
1:15 (12:00) 3-Y-O **£23,706** (£9,482; £7,112; £4,741; £2,370)

RPR
1 **Mixed Intention (IRE)**[22] 3-8-8 0.. SylvainRuis 4 99
(F Vermeulen, France) **193/10**
2 *2* **Silver Ocean (USA)**[63] [7850] 3-9-2 0.............................. ThierryThulliez 10 103
(Riccardo Santini, Italy) **29/1**
3 *½* **Etive (USA)**[75] 3-8-8 0.. FabriceVeron 7 94
(H-A Pantall, France) **12/1**
4 *nk* **Carnevalo (IRE)**[191] 3-8-11 0.. FranckBlondel 1 96
(F Rossi, France) **1/1**[2]
5 *1* **Redemptor**[104] 3-8-11 0.. IoritzMendizabal 5 [illegible]
(J-C Rouget, France) **1/1**[1]
6 *1* **Filozef (IRE)**[23] [258] 3-8-11 0.. ThomasHuet 9 93
(C Ferland, France) **9/1**
7 *3* **Hugely Exciting**[13] [370] 3-8-11 0.. DavyBonilla 2 87?
(J S Moore) *broke slowly: in rr on rail: rdn bef st: no ex: styd on clsng stages* **66/1**
8 *shd* **Uldiko (FR)**[22] 3-8-11 0..(p) DominiqueBoeuf 8 87
(Mme C Barande-Barbe, France) **21/1**
9 *2 ½* **Domino Rock (FR)**[22] 3-8-11 0.............................. Francois-XavierBertras 3 83
(C Boutin, France) **15/2**[3]
10 *2* **Salorina (USA)**[66] 3-8-8 0.. StephanePasquier 6 76
(D Smaga, France) **22/1**
1m 35.8s (95.80) **10** Ran SP% **118.1**
WIN (incl. 1 euro stake): 20.30. PLACES: 5.20, 8.00, 4.00. DF: 131.40. SF: 268.30.
Owner Jan Romel **Bred** Oghill House Stud **Trained** France

533a PRIX DE LA MEDITERRANEE (CLAIMER) (5YO+) (FIBRESAND) 1m 4f
2:55 (12:00) 5-Y-O+ **£6,465** (£2,586; £1,939; £1,293; £646)

RPR
1 **Almaguer**[13] [372] 9-9-6 0.................................... MathieuTavaresDaSilva 4 69
(F-X Belvisi, France) **11/2**[3]
2 *2* **Lasse (GER)**[189] 8-9-2 0.. ThomasHuet 9 62
(C Ferland, France) **23/10**[1]
3 *1* **Silver's Wish (FR)** 8-9-2 0..(b) RemiCampos 2 61
(T Larriviere, France) **17/1**
4 *½* **Dance The Star (USA)**[41] 6-9-5 0.............................. WilliamsSaraiva 5 63
(Mme J Bidgood, France) **9/2**[2]
5 *3* **Ozzia (GER)**[44] 7-8-13 0..(b) DominiqueBoeuf 13 52
(Y Fertillet, France) **20/1**
6 *snk* **Iron Out (USA)**[4] [479] 5-9-5 0..(p) IoritzMendizabal 3 58
(Reg Hollinshead) *broke wl to be amongst ldrs fr s: rdn and stl prom tl 1 1/2f out whn began to fade* **10/1**
7 *snk* **Monique Bisou (FR)**[41] 5-9-2 0..............................(p) Jean-MichelSanchez 12 55
(Y Fertillet, France) **11/1**
8 *1* **Birdinthehand (FR)**[499] 5-9-5 0..............................(p) StanislavKruglykhin 6 56
(D Rabhi, France) **40/1**
9 *¾* **Pool Of Knowledge (FR)**[8] [439] 5-9-5 0.. ThamiZergane 7 55
(David Nicholls) *prom fr s: sn 3rd: wnt 2nd early in st: rdn: no ex: fdd in st* **38/1**

10 *snk* **Hight Blue Sails (FR)**[654] 7-9-5 0.................................... DavyBonilla 11 55
(J-P Roman, France) **10/1**
0 **West Wing (FR)**[13] 372 6-9-8 0.................................... AMuzzi 8 —
(F-X Belvisi, France) **11/1**
0 **Kimberley Downs (USA)**[23] 259 5-9-5 0................ MichaelSultana 10 —
(David Nicholls) *racd in 5th on outside: moved to 2nd down bk st: rdn bef st: no ex: fdd qckly in st* **41/1**
0 **Ankhor Vat**[37] 6-9-6 0...(b) KhaledMahfoudh 1 —
(J Van Handenhove, France) **63/1**
2m 32.81s (152.81) **13** Ran SP% **118.0**
WIN (incl. 1 euro stake): 4.30 (Almaguer and West Wing couple). PLACES: 2.20, 1.60, 3.70. DF: 8.50. SF: 18.90.
Owner Francois-Xavier Belvisi **Bred** Chevington Stud **Trained** France

440 ST MORITZ (R-H)
Sunday, February 13

OFFICIAL GOING: Frozen

534a GRAND PRIX CHRISTOFFEL BAU TROPHY (CONDITIONS) (4YO+) (SNOW) 1m
1:45 (12:00) 4-Y-0+

£5,793 (£2,896; £2,068; £1,379; £689; £413)

RPR
1 **Rolling Home (GER)**[337] 890 7-9-11 0................................ EPedroza 1 87
(P Schaerer, Switzerland) **3/5**[1]
2 *1* **Halsion Chancer**[7] 440 7-9-6 0.. KierenFox 4 80
(John Best) *chsd ldrs in 4th pl on rail: swtchd outside and wnt 2nd 2 1/2f out: r.o wl fnl f: no imp on wnr fnl 75yds* **191/10**
3 *3* **Rayo (CZE)** 6-9-2 0.. JanRaja 6 70
(M Weiss, Switzerland) **98/10**
4 *2* **Bucked Off (SAF)**[7] 441 7-9-6 0.. APietsch 3 70
(C Von Der Recke, Germany) **42/10**[3]
5 *1 3/4* **Chat De La Burg (USA)**[7] 442 4-9-6 0......................... DavidProbert 5 67
(John Best) *a.p (and led briefly early on): wknd fr 2f out* **98/10**
6 *5* **Barongo (IRE)**[36] 6-9-0 0.. SebastienMaillot 7 51
(U Suter, France) **69/10**
7 *5* **Secret Major (FR)** 7-9-0 0... SteveDrowne 8 41
(M Weiss, Switzerland) **41/10**[2]
8 *dist* **Montecatini (IRE)**[66] 7-9-11 0....................................... RobertHavlin 2 —
(M Weiss, Switzerland) **105/10**
1m 42.93s (102.93) **8** Ran SP% **146.2**
PARI-MUTUEL (all including 1 chf stakes): WIN 1.60; PLACE 1.30, 2.80, 2.00; SF 62.30.
Owner Scuderia Del Clan **Bred** Hannes K Gutschow **Trained** Switzerland

JEBEL ALI (L-H)
Friday, February 11

OFFICIAL GOING: Dirt: fast

535a SHADWELL (H'CAP) (DIRT) 1m 1f 165y
11:30 (11:30) (80-105,101) 3-Y-O£11,599 (£3,866; £2,126; £1,159; £579)

RPR
1 **Meeriss (IRE)**[29] 153 6-9-11 **101**..................................(t) KierenFallon 6 102
(D Selvaratnam, UAE) *trckd ldr: led 1 1/2f out: r.o wl: comf* **10/1**
2 *3 1/2* **Noisy Silence (IRE)**[15] 330 7-9-2 **93**................................. PatDobbs 5 87
(A Manuel, UAE) *mid-div: rdn to chse ldrs 3f out: ev ch 1 1/2f out: nt qckn fnl 100yds* **20/1**
3 *shd* **Stalking Shadow (USA)**[6] 461 6-8-6 **89**..................(t) HarryBentley(7) 8 83
(S Seemar, UAE) *mid-div: r.o fnl 2f* **8/1**[3]
4 *shd* **Submariner (USA)**[7] 5-9-7 **98**.. CSandoval 10 91
(A bin Huzaim, UAE) *trckd ldr: ev ch 2 1/2f out: r.o wl fnl f* **7/2**[1]
5 *1 3/4* **Dynamic Saint (USA)**[36] 74 8-8-6 **83**..........................(e) ShaneFoley 2 73
(Doug Watson, UAE) *settled in rr: r.o same pce fnl 2f* **16/1**
6 *3/4* **Habalwatan (IRE)**[5] 7-7-12 **85**...............................(tp) SAlMazrooei(10) 7 74
(A Al Raihe, UAE) *a mid-div* **25/1**
7 *1 1/4* **Dr Faustus (IRE)**[5] 6-8-5 **82**...(t) TadhgO'Shea 4 68
(Doug Watson, UAE) *slowly away: settled in rr: n.d* **7/1**[2]
8 *1 1/2* **Major Victory (SAF)**[8] 411 4-8-4 **81** ow1............................ WJSupple 9 75
(Gay Kelleway) *sn led: hdd & wknd 2 1/2f out* **14/1**
9 *1/2* **King Charles**[7] 7-8-5 **82**... JRosales 11 65
(A bin Huzaim, UAE) *nvr bttr than mid-div* **12/1**
10 *1* **Tiz Now Tiz Then (USA)**[7] 6-9-1 **91**............................(bt) TedDurcan 3 73
(S Seemar, UAE) *mid-div: rdn 2 1/2f out: wknd fnl 1 1/2f* **16/1**
11 *5 1/2* **Palm Court**[7] 6-9-2 **93**...(tp) RoystonFfrench 13 63
(A Al Raihe, UAE) *nvr able to chal* **8/1**[3]
12 *7* **Pearly King (USA)**[5] 8-9-1 **91**.. WayneSmith 1 50
(M Al Muhairi, UAE) *in rr of mid-div: nvr nr to chal* **7/2**[1]
13 *31* **With Interest**[36] 75 8-9-4 **95**....................................(bt) AhmedAjtebi 12 —
(A Al Raihe, UAE) *nvr able to chal* **14/1**
1m 59.88s (119.88)
WFA 4 from 5yo+ 1lb **13** Ran SP% **129.7**

Owner Sheikh Ahmed Al Maktoum **Bred** Hugo Lascelles **Trained** United Arab Emirates

536a AL SHAFAR GROUP (H'CAP) (DIRT) 7f
12:30 (12:30) 3-Y-0+ **£6,854** (£2,284; £1,256; £685; £342)

RPR
1 **Game Stalker (USA)**[7] 5-8-9 **72**.................................(t) RoystonFfrench 8 70
(A Al Raihe, UAE) *trckd ldrs: rdn 2f out: r.o wl: led last 55yds* **3/1**[2]
2 *1/4* **Glorious Gift (IRE)**[7] 6-9-4 **80**......................................(t) WayneSmith 5 78
(A Al Shamsi, UAE) *trckd ldrs: led 2 1/2f out: r.o wl: hdd 55yds out* **4/1**[3]
3 *12* **Count Paris (USA)**[56] 5-8-3 **65**.. JRosales 6 31
(A bin Huzaim, UAE) *mid-div: r.o fnl 2f but no ch w first two* **14/1**
4 *2 1/4* **Heart Beat (SAF)**[62] 8-7-9 **67**...............................(t) SAlMazrooei(10) 4 27
(A Al Raihe, UAE) *mid-div: r.o fnl 2f but n.d* **2/1**[1]
5 *1 1/4* **Saudi Summer (KSA)**[42] 4-8-11 **74**.................................(t) TedDurcan 7 29
(S Seemar, UAE) *stmbld after 2f: nvr able to chal* **14/1**

6 *1/2* **Street Talk**[6] 459 7-8-9 **72**.. CSanchez 10 26
(A bin Huzaim, UAE) *a mid-div* **16/1**
7 *9 1/4* **Confederation (USA)**[6] 459 9-7-12 **67**....................(t) HarryBentley(7) 2 —
(S Seemar, UAE) *nvr bttr than mid-div* **20/1**
8 *4* **Mutabayen (USA)**[57] 7903 6-8-5 **67** ow2............................ AhmedAjtebi 1 —
(M Ramadan, UAE) *prom nr side: rdn and wknd 3f out* **33/1**
9 *1 1/2* **Musleh (USA)**[36] 76 5-9-4 **80**..................................(bt) RichardHills 11 —
(E Charpy, UAE) *broke awkwardly: led nr side tl 2 1/2f out: sn wknd* **16/1**
10 *hd* **Chaperno (USA)**[7] 4-9-3 **79**....................................(t) PatCosgrave 3 —
(M bin Shafya, UAE) *nvr bttr than mid-div* **16/1**
11 *1/2* **D'Artagnan (SAF)**[8] 411 4-8-3 **70**.................................... TadhgO'Shea 9 —
(Gay Kelleway) *nvr bttr than mid-div* **12/1**
1m 25.27s (85.27) **11** Ran SP% **124.7**

Owner Sheikh Mansoor bin Mohammed al Maktoum **Bred** Darley **Trained** UAE

526 WOLVERHAMPTON (A.W) (L-H)
Monday, February 14

OFFICIAL GOING: Standard
Wind: Slight, across Weather: Dry, sunny spells

537 TODAY'S JOCKEY SPECIALS AT BLUESQ.COM H'CAP 5f 20y(P)
2:10 (2:10) (Class 6) (0-52,55) 4-Y-0+ **£1,535** (£453; £226) **Stalls** Low

Form RPR
05-0 1 **Polemica (IRE)**[39] 70 5-8-12 **48**...................................(bt) JamesDoyle 6 57
(Frank Sheridan) *dwlt: sn midfield: effrt and rdn over 1f out: led wl ins fnl f: drvn and hld on wl* **11/1**
-004 2 *nk* **Thoughtsofstardom**[5] 464 8-9-0 **50**..............................(be) LukeMorris 2 58
(Phil McEntee) *trckd ldrs: rdn to ld over 1f out: hdd wl ins fnl f: kpt on fin* **12/1**
0032 3 *1 1/4* **Steel City Boy (IRE)**[5] 464 8-9-0 **50**...............................(p) JimmyQuinn 5 53
(Derek Shaw) *t.k.h: hld up in tch: rdn and edgd lft over 1f out: kpt on ins fnl f* **11/2**[3]
24-3 4 *3/4* **Monsieur Harvey**[14] 363 5-8-7 **48**................................ AdamCarter(5) 4 48
(Bryan Smart) *t.k.h: prom on outside: effrt and rdn 2f out: kpt on same pce ins fnl f* **9/4**[1]
0-50 5 *1/2* **Lucky Art (USA)**[11] 401 5-8-8 **47**.............................. JamesSullivan(3) 10 46
(Ruth Carr) *pressed ldr: drvn over 2f out: kpt on same pce ins fnl f* **14/1**
000- 6 *1* **Azygous**[111] 7148 8-8-5 **48** ow1.................................. DavidSimmonson(7) 8 43
(G P Kelly) *sn pushed along in rr: hdwy and edgd lft over 1f out: kpt on ins fnl f: no imp* **25/1**
6241 7 *1* **Bluebok**[5] 464 10-8-12 **55** 6ex.............................(bt) MatthewCosham(7) 9 46
(Milton Bradley) *in tch on outside: rdn over 2f out: no ex over 1f out* **25/1**
422 8 *1/2* **Cheveyo (IRE)**[11] 401 5-8-12 **48**.................................(be) JamieSpencer 12 38
(Patrick Morris) *hld up on outside: brought wdst and rdn ent st: nvr able to chal* **9/2**[2]
40-0 9 *1* **Papageno**[25] 224 4-9-2 **52**...(v) EddieAhern 1 38
(J R Jenkins) *led tl hdd over 1f out: nvr able to chal* **16/1**
56-4 10 *4 1/2* **Spring Leap**[33] 132 4-9-2 **52**..(p) JimCrowley 3 22
(Robert Cowell) *dwlt: t.k.h and sn in tch on ins: rdn and wknd 2f out* **9/1**
4500 11 *2 3/4* **Avonvalley**[17] 337 4-9-0 **50**.. RobbieFitzpatrick 13 —
(Peter Grayson) *s.i.s: sn pushed along in rr: nvr on terms* **33/1**
62.84 secs (0.54) **Going Correction** +0.075s/f (Slow) **11** Ran SP% **113.5**
Speed ratings (Par 101): **98,97,95,94,93 91,90,89,87,80 76**
toteswingers:1&2 £17.10, 2&3 £6.00, 1&3 £14.00 CSF £127.66 CT £804.30 TOTE £11.40: £3.80, £3.80, £1.60; EX 150.50 TRIFECTA Not won..
Owner Scuderia A4/5 **Bred** Mervyn Stewkesbury **Trained** Wolverhampton, W Midlands
■ Frank Sheridan's first winner since moving his string to Wolverhampton racecourse.

FOCUS
A low-grade, weak sprint handicap, but a few came here in form. The race is rated around the third.

538 WOLVERHAMPTON-RACECOURSE.CO.UK (S) STKS 5f 216y(P)
2:40 (2:40) (Class 6) 3-Y-O+ **£1,535** (£453; £226) **Stalls** Low

Form RPR
5-44 1 **Restless Bay (IRE)**[19] 302 3-8-7 68................................(v[1]) ChrisCatlin 1 66
(Reg Hollinshead) *t.k.h: hld up in tch: hdwy 1/2-way: rdn to ld ins fnl f: edgd lft and kpt on* **7/2**[2]
-122 2 *1 3/4* **Apache Ridge (IRE)**[12] 388 5-9-13 62.......................(p) PhillipMakin 7 69
(Kevin Ryan) *hld up: hdwy over 1f out: rdn and edgd lft: kpt on wl ins fnl f to take 2nd cl home: no ch w wnr* **13/2**[3]
30-2 3 *shd* **Clear Ice (IRE)**[18] 321 4-9-5 58...........................(v) AndrewHeffernan(3) 10 64
(Richard Guest) *led: rdn 2f out: hdd ins fnl f: kpt on same pce towards fin* **16/1**
6130 4 *1 1/4* **Decider (USA)**[7] 443 8-9-13 65..(p) LukeMorris 5 65
(Ronald Harris) *t.k.h: sn trcking ldr: rdn and ev ch over 1f out: kpt on same pce ins fnl f* **10/1**
-411 5 *1 1/4* **Frequency**[11] 404 4-9-13 70..(v) EddieAhern 9 61+
(Michael Wigham) *hld up on outside: n.m.r briefly 1/2-way: sn rdn: effrt wdst 2f out: edgd lft: kpt on ins fnl f: nvr able to chal* **1/1**[1]
0-20 6 *1 3/4* **Kersivay**[40] 56 5-9-1 57...................................(v) MatthewCosham(7) 3 50
(David Evans) *hld up: rdn whn n.m.r briefly 2f out: no imp appr fnl f* **10/1**
00-5 7 *15* **Two Feet Of Snow (IRE)**[10] 422 3-8-2 58....................... CathyGannon 2 —
(Ian McInnes) *trckd ldrs tl drvn and wknd over 2f out* **33/1**
00/6 8 *2 1/2* **Crystal Bridge**[25] 233 4-8-10 30............................... MatthewMcGhee(7) 4 —
(Bill Moore) *chsd ldrs: rdn over 3f out: sn lost pl: no ch after* **100/1**
1m 15.34s (0.34) **Going Correction** +0.075s/f (Slow)
WFA 3 from 4yo+ 15lb **8** Ran SP% **113.6**
Speed ratings (Par 101): **100,97,97,95,94 91,71,68**
toteswingers:1&2:£3.60, 2&3:£6.30, 1&3:£5.50 CSF £26.01 TOTE £4.90: £2.00, £1.10, £4.60; EX 32.90 Trifecta £101.20 Pool: £622.45 - 4.55 winning units..There was no bid for the winner.
Owner John L Marriott **Bred** Grangemore Stud **Trained** Upper Longdon, Staffs

FOCUS
A modest seller. The winner did not need match his best with the favourite disappointing.
Two Feet Of Snow(IRE) Official explanation: jockey said filly had no more to give

539 ENJOY THE HORIZONS RESTAURANT EXPERIENCE MAIDEN STKS 1m 4f 50y(P)
3:10 (3:12) (Class 5) 4-Y-0+ **£1,813** (£539; £269; £134) **Stalls** Low

Form RPR
2- 1 **Sweet Origin**[238] 3275 4-9-3 0.. JimmyQuinn 1 81+
(Marco Botti) *taken early to post: led at stdy gallop 3f: chsd ldr: shkn up to ld wl over 1f out: sn qcknd wl clr: edgd lft and eased last 100yds* **5/4**[1]

00/ **2** *7* **Accumulate**[260] 2258 8-9-6 0 .... JoeFanning 2 62
(Bill Moore) *trckd ldrs: drvn and outpcd over 3f out: rallied 2f out: edgd lft and chsd clr wnr ins fnl f: no imp* **28/1**

006- **3** *1* **I'Lldoit**[123] 6865 4-8-10 53 .... DavidKenny(7) 4 60
(Michael Scudamore) *hld up: rdn and outpcd 3f out: hdwy over 1f out: nvr able to chal* **33/1**

00-0 **4** *3 1/4* **Norse Dame**[21] 278 4-8-12 67 .... JamieSpencer 6 50
(David Elsworth) *chsd wnr: led after 3f: rdn over 2f out: hdd wl over 1f out: hung lft and sn wknd* **5/2**[2]

3 **5** *1 1/4* **Minsky Mine (IRE)**[21] 284 4-9-3 73 .... NeilChalmers 5 53
(Michael Appleby) *trckd ldrs: drvn and outpcd over 2f out: sn wknd* **11/4**[3]

6 *6* **El'Wringo** 7-9-6 0 .... JamesMillman 3 43
(Rod Millman) *dwlt: hld up last but in tch: struggling over 3f out: sn btn: eased whn no ch over 1f out* **33/1**

2m 42.35s (1.25) **Going Correction** +0.075s/f (Slow)
WFA 4 from 7yo+ 3lb **6** Ran SP% **109.0**
Speed ratings (Par 103): **98,93,92,90,89 85**
toteswingers:1&2 £2.40, 2&3 £6.50, 1&3 £5.90 CSF £33.60 TOTE £1.80: £1.50, £9.40; EX 19.50.
Owner Newsells Park Stud **Bred** Newsells Park Stud Limited **Trained** Newmarket, Suffolk

FOCUS
A visually impressive performance in this modestly run maiden from Sweet Origin, who quickened to lead entering the straight and pulled clear without coming under serious pressure. His two main rivals according to the betting both ran woefully, though, and there is a bit of doubt over what he achieved.

540 THE BLACK COUNTRY'S ONLY RACECOURSE H'CAP 1m 1f 103y(P)
3:40 (3:40) (Class 5) (0-75,74) 3-Y-O **£1,813** (£539; £269; £134) **Stalls** Low

Form RPR

6-51 **1** **Geordie Iris (IRE)**[19] 297 3-9-7 74 .... JamieSpencer 2 85+
(Richard Hannon) *trckd ldrs: effrt and plld out over 1f out: edgd lft u.p and led ins fnl f: kpt on wl* **11/4**[2]

243- **2** *1 3/4* **School For Scandal (IRE)**[61] 7873 3-9-6 73 .... JoeFanning 1 81+
(Mark Johnston) *pressed ldr: rdn over 3f out: led over 1f out to ins fnl f: kpt on same pce and eased whn hld towards fin* **6/4**[1]

3334 **3** *6* **Urban Kode (IRE)**[2] 527 3-8-3 63 ow1 .... (v[1]) MatthewCosham(7) 3 58
(David Evans) *led: rdn over 3f out: hdd over 1f out: no ex ins fnl f* **6/1**

3-42 **4** *6* **Imaginary World (IRE)**[14] 365 3-9-2 69 .... (p) JamesDoyle 4 51
(Alan McCabe) *hld up in tch: rdn along 4f out: short lived effrt over 2f out: sn no imp* **7/2**[3]

4-54 **5** *6* **Entrance**[5] 469 3-8-9 62 .... LukeMorris 5 32
(Julia Feilden) *in tch: rdn and outpcd over 3f out: btn ent st* **16/1**

2m 1.26s (-0.44) **Going Correction** +0.075s/f (Slow) **5** Ran SP% **109.1**
Speed ratings (Par 97): **104,102,97,91,86**
CSF £7.16 TOTE £2.60: £1.20, £1.10; EX 5.50.
Owner D R Mean **Bred** Anthony Kirwin **Trained** East Everleigh, Wilts

FOCUS
A modest handicap in which Urban Kode appeared to go off slightly too fast. The time was relatively fast and the form is taken at something like face value.

541 DOWNLOAD THE BLUE SQUARE IPHONE APP H'CAP 1m 1f 103y(P)
4:10 (4:10) (Class 4) (0-80,80) 4-Y-O+ **£2,914** (£867; £433; £216) **Stalls** Low

Form RPR

05-5 **1** **Snow Dancer (IRE)**[25] 235 7-8-13 75 .... JamesSullivan(3) 6 85
(Hugh McWilliams) *hld up: rdn over 3f out: hdwy over 1f out: kpt on wl ins fnl f: led last stride* **16/1**

-000 **2** *shd* **Thunderstruck**[25] 235 6-9-7 80 .... (p) IanMongan 10 90
(David Nicholls) *cl up: led 1/2-way: rdn over 2f out: kpt on ins fnl f: hdd last stride* **8/1**

23-2 **3** *3/4* **Loyalty**[21] 287 4-8-12 71 .... (v) PatrickMathers 4 79
(Derek Shaw) *prom: chsd wnr and drvn along over 2f out: rallied: kpt on: hld towards fin* **9/2**[2]

13-2 **4** *1 3/4* **Elijah Pepper (USA)**[11] 405 6-9-3 76 .... GrahamGibbons 7 80
(David Barron) *trckd ldrs: effrt and disp 2nd 2f out to over 1f out: no ex ins fnl f* **15/8**[1]

0-11 **5** *1 1/2* **Black Coffee**[21] 203 6-8-9 68 .... (b) ShaneKelly 9 69
(Mark Brisbourne) *dwlt: hld up in midfield on outside: effrt over 2f out: edgd lft and no ex over 1f out* **5/1**[3]

-211 **6** *1 1/2* **The Lock Master (IRE)**[21] 287 4-9-3 76 .... NeilChalmers 5 74
(Michael Appleby) *hld up in tch: niggled along 1/2-way: lost pl over 3f out: sme late hdwy: nvr rchd ldrs* **12/1**

0-51 **7** *1* **Lay Claim (USA)**[12] 381 4-9-2 75 .... (b) TomQueally 3 71
(Alan McCabe) *hld up: n.m.r over 3f out: rdn over 2f out: nvr able to chal* **12/1**

2225 **8** *7* **Dream Of Fortune (IRE)**[5] 472 7-8-2 68 .... (bt) RPWalsh(7) 2 49
(David Evans) *t.k.h: in tch on ins: struggling over 3f out: sn btn* **11/1**

210- **9** *1/2* **West End Lad**[62] 7867 8-9-7 80 .... (b) RussKennemore 1 60
(Roy Bowring) *led at stdy pce to 1/2-way: cl up tl rdn and wknd over 2f out* **25/1**

2m 0.67s (-1.03) **Going Correction** +0.075s/f (Slow) **9** Ran SP% **114.2**
Speed ratings (Par 105): **107,106,106,104,103 102,101,94,94**
toteswingers:1&2 £12.10, 2&3 £8.10, 1&3 £8.60 CSF £135.52 CT £677.55 TOTE £14.60: £3.10, £2.50, £1.70; EX 94.50 Trifecta £341.80 Part won. Pool: £461.90 - 0.10 winning units..
Owner Mrs L Wohlers **Bred** Liam Queally **Trained** Pilling, Lancs

FOCUS
A fair, competitive contest. The pace was modest early, but the time was still 0.59 seconds quicker than the earlier Class 5 handicap for 3-y-os. The winner is rated to something like his best.

542 STAY AT THE WOLVERHAMPTON HOLIDAY INN CONDITIONS STKS 1m 141y(P)
4:40 (4:40) (Class 4) 4-Y-O+ **£3,238** (£963; £481; £240) **Stalls** Low

Form RPR

2-32 **1** **Lowther**[22] 271 6-9-2 97 .... (be) J-PGuillambert 6 104
(Alan Bailey) *trckd ldrs: hdwy to chal over 1f out: edgd lft and led ins fnl f: rdn out* **9/4**[1]

111- **2** *1 3/4* **Norman Orpen (IRE)**[54] 7965 4-9-2 89 .... JamieSpencer 5 100
(Jane Chapple-Hyam) *stdd last but in tch: effrt over 2f out: kpt on ins fnl f: tk 2nd last stride* **9/2**[3]

35-3 **3** *shd* **Suits Me**[22] 271 8-9-2 97 .... MickyFenton 3 100
(Tom Tate) *led: rdn over 2f out: hdd ins fnl f: kpt on same pce: lost 2nd last stride* **5/2**[2]

150- **4** *8* **Mr Hichens**[217] 3969 6-9-2 85 .... ChrisCatlin 1 82
(Karen George) *pressed ldr: ev ch over 3f out to 2f out: sn wknd* **25/1**

312- **5** *3/4* **Fighter Boy (IRE)**[306] 1313 4-9-5 107 .... PhillipMakin 4 83
(David Barron) *t.k.h: trckd ldrs: n.m.r briefly 2f out: sn rdn and wknd* **9/4**[1]

5 **6** *27* **Puddington Bear**[25] 232 7-8-9 0 .... MatthewMcGhee(7) 2 —
(Bill Moore) *t.k.h: hld up in tch: pushed along 1/2-way: sn struggling: t.o* **100/1**

1m 48.78s (-1.72) **Going Correction** +0.075s/f (Slow) **6** Ran SP% **113.1**
Speed ratings (Par 105): **110,108,108,101,100 76**
CSF £13.04 TOTE £4.70: £2.40, £2.20; EX 10.80.
Owner Exors of the Late L J Barratt **Bred** L J Barratt **Trained** Newmarket, Suffolk

FOCUS
A decent conditions race run at what seemed a fair enough gallop. The time was 3.07 seconds quicker than the following Class 5 handicap for 3-y-os. Muddling form as usual for this type of race.

543 SPONSOR A RACE BY CALLING 01902 390000 H'CAP 1m 141y(P)
5:10 (5:10) (Class 5) (0-70,67) 3-Y-O **£1,813** (£539; £269; £134) **Stalls** Low

Form RPR

3-51 **1** **Lexi's Boy (IRE)**[11] 406 3-9-5 65 .... PhillipMakin 4 74+
(Kevin Ryan) *set stdy pce 2f: chsd ldr: led again over 1f out: rdn and hld on wl ins fnl f* **2/1**[2]

5-1 **2** *1/2* **Elvira Delight (IRE)**[38] 77 3-9-7 67 .... HayleyTurner 1 75+
(Jeremy Noseda) *trckd ldrs: n.m.r briefly on ins 2f out: effrt and edgd rt over 1f out: styd on to press wnr ins fnl f: r.o: a hld* **1/1**[1]

0-62 **3** *1 3/4* **Bodie**[11] 406 3-9-2 62 .... (b) MickyFenton 5 66
(Pam Sly) *t.k.h: led after 2f tl rdn and hdd over 1f out: rallied: kpt on same pce ins fnl f* **8/1**

002- **4** *1 1/4* **Crossword**[73] 7677 3-9-1 61 .... AdamKirby 3 62
(Marco Botti) *hld up in tch: hdwy over 2f out: edgd lft and no imp over 1f out* **15/2**[3]

4-05 **5** *7* **Farmer's Wife**[10] 424 3-8-4 57 .... RPWalsh(7) 7 42
(Bernard Llewellyn) *hld up: rdn along and c wd over 2f out: hung bdly lft ent st: sn btn* **25/1**

400- **6** *1 1/4* **Distinguish (IRE)**[112] 7112 3-9-4 64 .... JoeFanning 2 46
(Mark Johnston) *prom tl rdn and wknd fr 2f out* **10/1**

500- **7** *5* **Heart Felt**[103] 7296 3-9-2 62 .... TomEaves 6 33
(Roy Brotherton) *hld up towards rr: struggling over 3f out: sn btn* **66/1**

1m 51.85s (1.35) **Going Correction** +0.075s/f (Slow) **7** Ran SP% **120.6**
Speed ratings (Par 97): **97,96,95,93,87 86,82**
toteswingers:1&2 £2.10, 2&3 £3.20, 1&3:£2.20 CSF £4.72 TOTE £2.70: £1.10, £1.30; EX 7.70.
Owner Mrs Margaret Forsyth **Bred** R S Cockerill (farms) Ltd & Peter Dodd **Trained** Hambleton, N Yorks

FOCUS
This looked a potentially good handicap for the class, with the front four, who can probably all do better at some stage, finishing clear. The form is rated slightly positively around the winner.

544 PLAY FREE BINGO AT BLUESQ.COM H'CAP 7f 32y(P)
5:40 (5:48) (Class 6) (0-60,60) 4-Y-O+ **£1,535** (£453; £226) **Stalls** High

Form RPR

3410 **1** **Downhill Skier (IRE)**[3] 512 7-9-6 59 .... EddieAhern 11 66
(Mark Brisbourne) *hld up in midfield on outside: hdwy to ld wl over 1f out: hld on wl u.p ins fnl f* **6/1**

4-11 **2** *nk* **Piccolo Express**[24] 255 5-9-4 57 .... J-PGuillambert 8 63+
(Brian Baugh) *s.i.s: bhd and checked after 1f: pushed along 1/2-way: gd hdwy 1f out: edgd lft and chsd wnr ins fnl f: r.o* **3/1**[1]

540- **3** *1/2* **Madame Boot (FR)**[87] 7502 4-9-3 56 .... TomQueally 6 61
(Peter Makin) *in tch: rdn whn n.m.r briefly over 2f out: kpt on wl ins fnl f: nrst fin* **12/1**

4663 **4** *1 1/4* **Itsthursdayalready**[3] 512 4-9-3 56 .... ShaneKelly 2 57
(Mark Brisbourne) *only stall that failed to open in false s: trckd ldrs gng wl: effrt and chal ent st: kpt on same pce ins fnl f* **4/1**[2]

00-2 **5** *1 1/4* **Kathleen Kennet**[5] 466 11-8-9 48 ow1 .... LiamKeniry 12 46
(Jonathan Geake) *t.k.h: hld up: rdn along over 2f out: hdwy ins fnl f: nvr able to chal* **12/1**

/0-0 **6** *1/2* **Flying Applause**[11] 400 6-8-13 52 .... (bt) RussKennemore 5 49
(Roy Bowring) *t.k.h: in tch on ins: outpcd over 2f out: rallied over 1f out: no imp* **50/1**

00-0 **7** *2 1/2* **Ninth House (USA)**[20] 292 9-9-0 53 .... (t) PJMcDonald 7 43
(Ruth Carr) *in tch on outside: drvn and outpcd over 2f out: no imp over 1f out* **40/1**

-440 **8** *1* **Charles Parnell (IRE)**[20] 289 8-9-4 57 .... MichaelStainton 9 44
(Simon Griffiths) *dwlt: bhd: rdn and c wd over 2f out: nvr on terms* **16/1**

-414 **9** *5* **Pilgrim Dancer (IRE)**[19] 304 4-9-7 60 .... (v) StephenCraine 3 34
(Patrick Morris) *trckd ldrs: rdn whn checked and wknd 2f out* **9/2**[3]

2206 **10** *1 3/4* **Chinese Democracy (USA)**[5] 477 4-8-10 56 .(v) MatthewCosham(7) 1 25
(David Evans) *led tl hdd wl over 1f out: sn btn: eased whn no ch ins fnl f* **11/1**

1m 30.69s (1.09) **Going Correction** +0.075s/f (Slow) **10** Ran SP% **111.5**
Speed ratings (Par 101): **96,95,95,93,92 91,88,87,81,79**
toteswingers:1&2 £4.90, 2&3 £11.80, 1&3 £10.50 CSF £23.12 CT £202.45 TOTE £6.70: £2.00, £1.40, £4.10; EX 24.40 Trifecta £95.60 Pool: £774.02 - 5.99 winning units..
Owner Miss P D Insull **Bred** Swettenham Stud **Trained** Great Ness, Shropshire

FOCUS
There was a false start to this moderate handicap, caused by Itsthursdayalready, whose gate did not opening properly. Those who did start the first time around covered varying amounts of ground, and a few of them got quite warm, so this form needs treating with caution. It makes sense overall with the winner seemingly back to his best.
Piccolo Express ◆ Official explanation: jockey said gelding hit its nose on gate
T/Plt: £273.00 to a £1 stake. Pool:£65,110.90 - 174.08 winning tickets. T/Qpdt: £36.00 to a £1 stake. Pool of £5,588.70 - 114.65 winning tickets. RY

[504]SOUTHWELL (L-H)
Tuesday, February 15

OFFICIAL GOING: Standard
Wind: Fresh against Weather: Overcast

545 ENHANCED SP'S AT BLUESQ.COM H'CAP 6f (F)
1:50 (1:51) (Class 6) (0-55,55) 4-Y-O+ **£1,535** (£453; £226) **Stalls** Low

Form RPR

30-0 **1** **Attrition**[12] 401 4-8-10 49 .... JamesDoyle 7 62+
(Andrew Reid) *sn led: rdn and qcknd clr wl over 1f out: kpt on ins fnl f* **7/1**[3]

606- **2** *nk* **Premier League**[62] 7877 4-8-11 50 .... (p) RobertWinston 9 59
(Julia Feilden) *trckd ldrs: hdwy over 2f out: rdn to chse wnr over 1f out: drvn and kpt on ins fnl f* **25/1**

0-03 **3** 5 **Muqalad (IRE)**14 375 4-9-0 **53** .... TomEaves 13 46
(Bryan Smart) *chsd ldrs on outer: effrt wl over 2f out: rdn wl over 1f out: kpt on same pce u.p fnl f: tk 3rd nr line* **4/1**1

50-5 **4** shd **Convince (USA)**21 289 10-9-2 **55** .... DavidProbert 14 48
(Kevin M Prendergast) *hld up towards rr: hdwy wl over 2f out: swtchd lft and rdn wl over 1f out: kpt on ins fnl f: nrst fin* **15/2**

6345 **5** hd **Bertbrand**4 517 6-8-7 **46** oh1 .... (v) GregFairley 10 38
(Ian McInnes) *chsd wnr: rdn 2f out: drvn over 1f out: grad wknd: lost 3rd nr line* **11/1**

006- **6** 4 **Dickie Le Davoir**73 7701 7-8-13 **55** .... (v) AndrewHeffernan(3) 8 34
(Richard Guest) *in rr and sn pushed along: hdwy on wd outside over 2f out: sn rdn and kpt on ins fnl f: nvr nr ldrs* **12/1**

4-16 **7** ¾ **Figaro Flyer (IRE)**22 276 8-9-1 **54** .... MichaelStainton 2 31
(Jane Chapple-Hyam) *pushed lft and hmpd s: in rr: rdn along and sme hdwy fnl 2f: nvr a factor* **6/1**2

0-40 **8** 1¼ **Archilini**33 150 6-8-7 **46** oh1 .... (be1) BarryMcHugh 12 19
(Brian Ellison) *a towards rr* **8/1**

603- **9** 1 **Hold On Tiger (IRE)**67 7808 4-8-5 **51** .... (v1) ShirleyTeasdale(7) 11 21
(Keith Dalgleish) *prom: rdn along wl over 2f out: drvn wl over 1f out and sn wknd* **14/1**

0-50 **10** ½ **Angle Of Attack (IRE)**22 283 6-8-7 **46** oh1 .... (vt) SilvestreDeSousa 1 14
(Alan Brown) *sn rdn along in rr: bhd fr 1/2-way* **12/1**

-506 **11** 3½ **Ponting (IRE)**5 493 5-8-9 **48** ow1 .... (b) MickyFenton 5 —
(Paul Midgley) *chsd ldrs on inner: rdn along over 2f out: sn wknd* **25/1**

12 4½ **Indian St Jovite (IRE)**72 7746 4-8-7 **46** oh1 .... CathyGannon 6 —
(Seamus Fahey, Ire) *s.i.s: a bhd* **50/1**

00-0 **13** 6 **Sweet Avon**17 351 4-9-2 **55** .... ShaneKelly 3 —
(Matthew Salaman) *pushed lft s: in tch on inner: rdn along 1/2-way: sn wknd* **10/1**

1m 16.09s (-0.41) **Going Correction** +0.025s/f (Slow) **13** Ran SP% **118.8**
Speed ratings (Par 101): **103,102,95,95,95 90,89,87,86,85 80,74,66**
toteswingers:1&2 £38.70, 2&3 £17.30, 1&3 £5.80 CSF £173.44 CT £824.61 TOTE £7.30: £2.90, £9.30, £1.20; EX 166.70 TRIFECTA Not won..
Owner A S Reid **Bred** Chevington Stud **Trained** Mill Hill, London NW7

FOCUS
A moderate contest and tricky to rate. The first two finished clear but had not shown much previously. They both showed clear personal bests.
Attrition Official explanation: trainer's rep said, regarding apparent improvement in form, that the gelding appeared to benefit from racing prominently from the outset.

546 SOUTHWELL GOLF CLUB LADY MEMBERS MAIDEN STKS 1m (F)
2:20 (2:21) (Class 5) 3-Y-O+ **£1,910** (£564; £282) **Stalls** Low

Form RPR

3 **1** **One Pursuit (IRE)**11 431 3-8-5 0 .... BillyCray(3) 3 60
(David Nicholls) *cl up: led 3f out: rdn wl over 1f out: styd on strly ins fnl f* **6/1**3

60/3 **2** 3 **Ay Tay Tate (IRE)**19 319 5-9-10 50 .... AndrewHeffernan(3) 6 59
(David C Griffiths) *prom: effrt 3f out: rdn 2f out and ev ch tl drvn and one pce appr fnl f* **28/1**

03-5 **3** ½ **Jo Boy**10 437 4-9-13 64 .... MartinLane 8 58
(David Simcock) *trckd ldrs: hdwy over 2f out: rdn edgd lft wl over 1f out: drvn to chse ldng pair ent fnl f: kpt on same pce* **12/1**

2- **4** 2½ **Hermes**134 6635 3-8-8 0 .... JimCrowley 7 46
(Ralph Beckett) *trckd ldrs on outer: effrt 3f out: rdn over 2f out: sn drvn and btn wl over 1f out* **5/6**1

5 3½ **J R Hartley** 3-8-8 0 .... TomEaves 1 38
(Bryan Smart) *led: rdn along and hdd 3f out: drvn over 2f out and grad wknd* **20/1**

6 17 **Carrside Lady** 5-9-8 0 .... SilvestreDeSousa 4 —
(Owen Brennan) *green reminders and outpcd sn after s: hdwy on inner to chse ldrs 1/2-way: rdn 3f out and sn wknd* **100/1**

7 2½ **Barnum (USA)** 3-8-8 0 .... JoeFanning 9 —
(Mark Johnston) *in tch: green and rdn along after 3f: sn outpcd and bhd fr over 3f out* **2/1**2

56 **8** 6 **Jack's Rocket**4 509 4-9-6 0 .... (e) SeanPalmer(7) 5 —
(Richard Guest) *a in rr: outpcd and bhd fr 1/2-way* **100/1**

1m 44.0s (0.30) **Going Correction** +0.025s/f (Slow)
WFA 3 from 4yo+ 19lb **8** Ran SP% **120.1**
Speed ratings (Par 103): **99,96,95,93,89 72,70,64**
toteswingers:1&2 £12.50, 2&3 £16.90, 1&3 £3.20 CSF £139.66 TOTE £6.70: £1.80, £5.60, £2.70; EX 112.90 Trifecta £416.30 Part won. Pool of £562.66 - 0.62 winning units..
Owner Eamon Maher **Bred** Clougher Partnership **Trained** Sessay, N Yorks

FOCUS
A modest maiden run in time 2.58 seconds slower than the 78-rated Sweet Child O'Mine managed later on the card. There is a bit of doubt over what this amounts to with the favourite clearly below his debut form.

547 DINE IN THE PANTRY (S) STKS 7f (F)
2:50 (2:52) (Class 6) 4-Y-O+ **£1,535** (£453; £226) **Stalls** Low

Form RPR

1-50 **1** **El Dececy (USA)**5 495 7-9-4 78 .... (p) GrahamGibbons 7 81
(John Balding) *mde all: rdn clr wl over 1f out: easily* **5/4**1

3444 **2** 6 **Elusive Warrior (USA)**5 495 8-9-4 66 .... (p) RobertWinston 3 65
(Alan McCabe) *chsd ldrs: rdn along on outer 1/2-way: kpt on u.p fnl over 1f out: no ch w wnr* **5/1**3

1334 **3** 1 **Army Of Stars (IRE)**8 446 5-9-4 71 .... (p) JimCrowley 1 63
(James Given) *chsd wnr: rdn along over 2f out: sn one pce* **15/8**2

20-6 **4** hd **Crocodile Bay (IRE)**21 292 8-8-9 55 .... (b) AndrewHeffernan(3) 5 56
(Richard Guest) *in touc h: hdwy over 2f out: rdn to chse wnr wl over 1f out: drvn and wknd ent fnl f* **12/1**

-055 **5** 15 **Champagne All Day**8 445 5-8-12 37 .... MichaelStainton 2 16
(Simon Griffiths) *a in rr: outpcd and bhd fr 1/2-way* **66/1**

0-60 **6** 2¼ **Moon Lightning (IRE)**12 400 5-8-12 60 .... (p) PJMcDonald 6 —
(Tina Jackson) *chsd ldrs: hdwy to chse wnr 1/2-way: rdn wl over 2f out and sn wknd* **66/1**

450- **7** ¾ **Tealing**273 2203 4-8-12 60 .... ChrisCatlin 4 —
(Richard Guest) *a in rr: outpcd and bhd fr 1/2-way* **33/1**

1m 30.8s (0.50) **Going Correction** +0.025s/f (Slow) **7** Ran SP% **109.5**
Speed ratings (Par 101): **98,91,90,89,72 70,69**
toteswingers:1&2 £2.00, 2&3 £1.50, 1&3 £1.40 CSF £7.30 TOTE £1.50: £1.10, £3.50; EX 8.40.There was no bid for the winner.
Owner Brian Morton & Willie McKay **Bred** Shadwell Farm LLC **Trained** Scrooby, Notts

FOCUS
An uncompetitive seller, most of these lacking enthusiasm, and the time was 0.58 seconds slower than the later 3-y-o handicap won by the 51-rated Ace Master. The winner was the clear form pick and probably didn't have to improve.

548 DOWNLOAD THE BLUE SQUARE IPHONE APP H'CAP 1m (F)
3:20 (3:20) (Class 4) (0-85,85) 4-Y-O+ **£2,914** (£867; £433; £216) **Stalls** Low

Form RPR

105- **1** **Sweet Child O'Mine**77 7638 4-8-11 **78** .... AndrewHeffernan(3) 1 94
(Richard Guest) *trckd ldr: smooth hdwy to ld 2f out: sn rdn clr: edgd lft ent fnl f: kpt on strly* **4/1**3

2116 **2** 5 **The Lock Master (IRE)**1 541 4-8-12 **76** .... NeilChalmers 4 80
(Michael Appleby) *in tch: hdwy over 3f out: rdn 2f out: edgd lft over 1f out: kpt on same pce ins fnl f* **5/1**

-431 **3** ¾ **Trans Sonic**19 320 8-9-6 **84** .... (b) SilvestreDeSousa 6 86
(David O'Meara) *sn led and set str pce: hdd and rdn 2f out: swtchd rt and drvn jst ins fnl f: kpt on same pce* **5/2**1

-120 **4** 10 **Follow The Flag (IRE)**26 235 7-9-5 **83** .... (v) ShaneKelly 2 62
(Alan McCabe) *sn rdn along in rr: outpcd and bhd after 2f tl sme late hdwy* **11/2**

0-02 **5** 2½ **Bawaardi (IRE)**13 385 5-9-1 **79** .... FrederikTylicki 7 53
(Richard Fahey) *chsd ldng pair: rdn along 3f out: sn drvn and btn* **7/2**2

206- **6** 2¾ **Exit Smiling**143 6367 6-8-12 **76** .... MickyFenton 5 43
(Paul Midgley) *in tch: pushed along over 4f out: sn rdn and outpcd: bhd fnl 3f* **14/1**

120/ **7** 9 **Hawaass (USA)**664 1460 6-9-7 **85** .... PJMcDonald 3 32
(Ruth Carr) *chsd ldrs: rdn along 3f out: sn wknd* **25/1**

1m 41.42s (-2.28) **Going Correction** +0.025s/f (Slow) **7** Ran SP% **113.4**
Speed ratings (Par 105): **112,107,106,96,93 91,82**
toteswingers:1&2 £4.20, 2&3 £2.30, 1&3 £3.50 CSF £23.64 TOTE £5.40: £2.20, £3.50; EX 25.20.
Owner EERC **Bred** A Reid **Trained** Stainforth, S Yorks

FOCUS
A fair handicap run at a strong pace and the time was quite good, being 2.58 seconds faster than the earlier 3-y-o-plus maiden won by One Pursuit. There is no reason to doubt the improved winner, though.

549 BOOK YOUR TICKETS ON LINE AT SOUTHWELL-RACECOURSE.CO.UK H'CAP 2m (F)
3:50 (3:50) (Class 5) (0-75,77) 4-Y-O+ **£1,813** (£539; £269; £134) **Stalls** Low

Form RPR

-511 **1** **Mush Mir (IRE)**5 492 4-9-10 **77** 12ex .... (b) StephenCraine 5 91+
(Jim Boyle) *mde all: qcknd clr on bridle wl over 2f out: unchal* **6/4**1

5043 **2** 3½ **Calculating (IRE)**7 457 7-9-2 **63** .... DavidProbert 6 67
(Mark Usher) *trckd ldrs: rdn along and sltly outpcd 4f out: drvn 2f out: kpt on to take 2nd ins fnl f: no ch w wnr* **7/2**2

-253 **3** 5 **Stadium Of Light (IRE)**19 320 4-9-2 **69** .... (t) BarryMcHugh 1 67
(Brian Ellison) *chsd wnr: rdn along 4f out: drvn wl over 2f out: sn one pce: lost 2nd ins fnl f* **13/2**

5-10 **4** 12 **William's Way**11 418 9-9-12 **73** .... (t) JamesDoyle 4 57
(Ian Wood) *hld up in rr: hdwy to chse ldrs over 4f out: rdn 3f out: sn outpcd* **16/1**

-113 **5** 21 **Delorain (IRE)**12 407 8-8-9 **56** .... (vt) CathyGannon 2 14
(William Stone) *dwlt and reminders s: trckd ldrs: rdn along over 5f out: sn outpcd and bhd fnl 3f* **10/1**

343- **6** 2½ **King In Waiting (IRE)**258 2659 8-8-12 **59** .... SilvestreDeSousa 3 14
(David O'Meara) *trckd ldng pair: rdn along after 7f: lost pl over 6f out: bhd fnl 3f* **4/1**3

3m 45.04s (-0.46) **Going Correction** +0.025s/f (Slow)
WFA 4 from 7yo+ 6lb **6** Ran SP% **110.5**
Speed ratings (Par 103): **102,100,97,91,81 80**
toteswingers:1&2 £2.30, 2&3 £3.10, 1&3 £2.40 CSF £6.68 TOTE £2.70: £1.60, £3.00; EX 8.50.
Owner M Khan X2 **Bred** Shadwell Estate Company Limited **Trained** Epsom, Surrey
■ Stewards' Enquiry : David Probert caution: used whip with excessive frequency.

FOCUS
A good handicap for the grade won in impressive fashion by Mush Mir, although he had a fairly easy time of it in front. He was value at least twice the winning margin.
Delorain(IRE) Official explanation: jockey said gelding hung right-handed throughout

550 ARENA LEISURE PLC H'CAP 7f (F)
4:20 (4:21) (Class 6) (0-60,59) 3-Y-O **£1,535** (£453; £226) **Stalls** Low

Form RPR

33-3 **1** **Ace Master**7 456 3-8-13 **51** .... JimmyQuinn 6 66
(Roy Bowring) *cl up: hdwy to ld 2f out: rdn clr over 1f out: kpt on strly ins fnl f* **3/1**1

60-4 **2** 4½ **Govenor General (IRE)**18 335 3-9-7 **59** .... GeorgeBaker 5 62
(Jeremy Noseda) *trckd ldrs: hdwy over 2f out: rdn to chse wnr over 1f out: sn edgd lft and no imp* **4/1**3

06-3 **3** 3 **Jay Jays Joy**42 41 3-8-11 **49** .... (b) GrahamGibbons 1 44
(David Barron) *trckd ldrs on inner: hdwy to chse ldr 1/2-way: rdn along over 2f out: drvn over 1f out and kpt on same pce* **10/3**2

-521 **4** shd **Ridgeway Hawk**4 505 3-9-5 **57** 6ex .... (v) RobertHavlin 3 52
(Mark Usher) *hld up in rr: effrt 1/2-way and sn pushed along: rdn on outer over 2f out: sn drvn and no imp* **10/3**2

0-32 **5** 1 **Rath Maeve**4 510 3-9-5 **57** .... RobertWinston 4 49
(Alan McCabe) *led: rdn along 3f out: hdd 2f out and sn drvn: wknd over 1f out* **11/2**

00-0 **6** 10 **Come On Eileen (IRE)**7 456 3-8-4 **45** .... AndrewHeffernan(3) 7 10
(Richard Guest) *chsd ldrs on outer: rdn along 3f out: sn wknd* **66/1**

30-6 **7** 3 **Cinq Heavens (IRE)**11 426 3-9-3 **55** .... RichardKingscote 2 12
(Tom Dascombe) *in tch: rdn along on inner 3f out: sn wknd* **25/1**

1m 30.22s (-0.08) **Going Correction** +0.025s/f (Slow) **7** Ran SP% **111.9**
Speed ratings (Par 95): **101,95,92,92,91 79,76**
toteswingers:1&2 £3.50, 2&3 £3.30, 1&3 £2.30 CSF £14.64 CT £40.09 TOTE £3.20: £1.80, £3.20; EX 17.10 Trifecta £64.30 Pool £655.28 - 7.53 winning units..
Owner S R Bowring **Bred** S R Bowring **Trained** Edwinstowe, Notts

FOCUS
A moderate 3-y-o handicap with the seven runners boasting a combined record of 1-41, although the time was 0.58 quicker than the earlier older-horse seller. A fairly positive view has been taken of the form.

551 PLAY MEGAJACKPOTS CLEOPATRA AT BLUESQ.COM H'CAP — 1m 4f (F)
4:50 (4:50) (Class 6) (0-65,62) 4-Y-0+ — £1,535 (£453; £226) Stalls Low

Form — RPR

4-50 **1** **Kingaroo (IRE)**[19] [324] 5-8-9 **53** .... BillyCray(3) 6 — 62
(Garry Woodward) *led 2f: cl up and niggled along over 7f out: led again 5f out: rdn over 2f out: drvn and kpt on wl ins fnl f* **13/2**[3]

334/ **2** *2* **Sea Cliff (IRE)**[21] [1609] 7-8-5 **53** .... ThomasBrown(7) 4 — 59
(Andrew Crook) *trckd ldrs: cl up on outer 1/2-way: effrt 3f out: chal over 2f out: sn rdn and ev ch whn edgd rt over 1f out: no ex wl ins fnl f* **7/1**

-206 **3** *5* **My Mate Mal**[11] [418] 7-9-5 **60** .... (p) CathyGannon 2 — 58
(William Stone) *sn pushed along in rr: rdn over 4f out: hdwy 3f out: kpt on u.p fnl 2f: n.d* **9/2**[2]

-351 **4** *6* **Home**[7] [450] 6-9-3 **58** 6ex .... ChrisCatlin 3 — 46
(Brendan Powell) *trckd ldrs: cl up 1/2-way: niggled along 4f out: rdn 3f out: sn drvn and wknd 2f out* **4/5**[1]

66-4 **5** *2 ¾* **Amazing Blue Sky**[12] [399] 5-9-4 **62** .... JamesSullivan(3) 1 — 46
(Ruth Carr) *cl up on inner: led after 2f: rdn along and hdd 5f out: wknd over 3f out* **12/1**

2m 43.4s (2.40) **Going Correction** +0.025s/f (Slow) — **5** Ran SP% **107.3**
Speed ratings (Par 101): **93,91,88,84,82**
CSF £43.34 TOTE £6.10: £2.70, £2.30; EX 34.90.
Owner J Pownall **Bred** Kevin Walsh **Trained** Maltby, S Yorks

FOCUS
A moderate handicap and the early pace was steady, resulting in a slow time. The winner is rated back to something like his autumn form.
Home Official explanation: jockey said gelding bled from the nose
T/Plt: £942.00 to a £1 stake. Pool of £63,556.62 - 49.25 winning tickets. T/Qpdt: £16.90 to a £1 stake. Pool of £6,748.01 - 294.04 winning tickets. JR

482 KEMPTON (A.W) (R-H)
Wednesday, February 16

OFFICIAL GOING: Standard
Wind: Brisk, behind Weather: Fine

552 KEMPTON.CO.UK APPRENTICE H'CAP — 1m 2f (P)
5:10 (5:11) (Class 7) (0-50,50) 4-Y-0+ — £1,535 (£453; £226) Stalls Low

Form — RPR

2-60 **1** **Lunar River (FR)**[19] [346] 8-9-0 **50** .... (t) JamesRogers(3) 1 — 60+
(David Pinder) *patiently rdn on inner: wl in rr and plenty to do over 2f out: gd prog wl over 1f out: drvn to ld ins fnl f: sn clr* **5/1**[1]

0-20 **2** *3 ¼* **Holyfield Warrior (IRE)**[20] [312] 7-8-12 **50** .... LucyKBarry(5) 9 — 53
(Ralph Smith) *t.k.h: w ldr: led 4f out: urged along over 1f out: hdd and outpcd ins fnl f* **13/2**[3]

00-2 **3** *2 ¼* **Idol Deputy (FR)**[13] [408] 5-8-9 **47** .... RachealKneller(5) 2 — 46
(Mark Usher) *cl up: nt qckn and outpcd 2f out: urged along and styd on fnl f to take 3rd last strides* **8/1**

-604 **4** *¾* **Inquisitress**[17] [355] 7-8-9 **45** .... (v[1]) MatthewCosham(3) 8 — 42
(John Bridger) *hld up in midfield: prog fr 3f out: rdn to chse ldng pair briefly over 1f out: nt qckn* **12/1**

60-4 **5** *¾* **King Of The Titans (IRE)**[18] [347] 8-8-8 **46** .... (v) AliceHaynes(5) 11 — 42
(Patrick Gilligan) *dwlt: t.k.h: racd wd in midfield: prog to join ldr 4f out: upsides 2f out: hanging and fnd nil over 1f out* **10/1**

0-00 **6** *nk* **Jiggalong**[13] [408] 5-8-7 **45** .... LewisWalsh(5) 3 — 40
(Mrs D Thomas) *s.i.s: sn chsd ldrs: pushed along to chse ldng pair over 2f out to over 1f out: fdd* **33/1**

6/50 **7** *¾* **Crazy Colours**[17] [355] 5-8-9 **45** .... (p) RyanPowell(3) 4 — 38
(Zoe Davison) *rel to r and slowest away: sn in tch: rdn and sme prog fr over 2f out: nvr on terms* **20/1**

-040 **8** *½* **Yorksters Prince (IRE)**[4] [524] 4-8-12 **46** .... TobyAtkinson 6 — 38
(George Prodromou) *settled in midfield: no room and snatched up 3f out: sn rdn: tried to make prog over 1f out: one pce after* **12/1**

6350 **9** *4 ½* **Escardo (GER)**[17] [355] 8-8-12 **45** .... AshleyMorgan 12 — 28
(David Bridgwater) *nvr bttr than midfield: outpcd over 2f out: nvr on terms after* **11/2**[2]

6-00 **10** *1* **Novillero**[11] [229] 4-8-7 **46** .... GemmaElford(5) 10 — 27
(Jimmy Fox) *t.k.h: racd wd in rr: v wd bnd 2f out: nvr a factor* **40/1**

-646 **11** *nk* **Cane Cat (IRE)**[14] [386] 4-8-9 **48** .... (t) GeorgeDowning(5) 14 — 29
(Tony Carroll) *v awkward s: a wl in rr: pushed along and no prog over 2f out* **12/1**

4050 **12** *nk* **Raghdaan**[19] [346] 4-8-8 **45** .... JulieBurke(3) 13 — 25
(Peter Hiatt) *v awkward s: plld hrd: hld up in last trio: no prog over 2f out: nvr a factor* **10/1**

0-00 **13** *nse* **Merals Choice**[11] [432] 4-8-11 **48** .... (p) NathanAlison(3) 5 — 28
(Jim Boyle) *plld hrd: mde most to 4f out: wknd rapidly 3f out* **7/1**

0-45 **14** *1 ½* **Dalrymple (IRE)**[26] [245] 5-8-7 **45** .... (vt) RichardRowe(5) 7 — 22
(Michael Madgwick) *t.k.h: w ldng pair to 4f out: wknd qckly over 3f out* **33/1**

2m 8.41s (0.41) **Going Correction** -0.15s/f (Stan)
WFA 4 from 5yo+ 1lb — **14** Ran SP% **123.3**
Speed ratings (Par 97): **92,89,87,87,86 86,85,85,81,80 80,80,80,79**
toteswingers: 1&2 £7.50, 1&3 £11.00, 2&3 £9.90 CSF £36.36 CT £264.79 TOTE £3.70: £2.20, £3.40, £2.40; EX 41.10.
Owner The Little Farm Partnership **Bred** M Daguzan-Garros & Rolling Hills Farm **Trained** Kingston Lisle, Oxon
■ Stewards' Enquiry : Toby Atkinson caution: used whip when out of contention.
Julie Burke two-day ban: used whip when out of contention (Mar 2 & remedial training tbn)

FOCUS
Although the early gallop appeared steady, things quickened up down the back straight, and it was a fair test.

553 BETDAQ.COM EVERY WEDNESDAY AT KEMPTON PARK H'CAP — 1m 2f (P)
5:40 (5:41) (Class 6) (0-60,60) 4-Y-0+ — £1,535 (£453; £226) Stalls Low

Form — RPR

10-4 **1** **Noah Jameel**[14] [391] 9-8-6 **52** .... DavidKenny(7) 8 — 63+
(Tony Newcombe) *hld up in 12th: nt clr run over 2f out: taken wdr and gd prog to go 2nd jst over 1f out: clsd rapidly to ld last 75yds: sn clr* **11/2**[1]

0-20 **2** *2* **Kyle Of Bute**[21] [299] 5-9-5 **58** .... J-PGuillambert 7 — 65
(Brian Baugh) *led at decent pce: drew away fr over 3f out: 6 l up and drvn over 1f out: collared last 75yds* **7/1**[2]

0-32 **3** *2 ¼* **Sunset Boulevard (IRE)**[21] [299] 8-9-4 **57** .... (b) EddieAhern 3 — 63+
(Jim Best) *hld up in 8th: nt clr run over 2f out: nowhere to go bhd wall of rivals over 1f out: pushed along and r.o wl fnl f to take 3rd last strides* **15/2**[3]

5-52 **4** *hd* **Atacama Sunrise**[14] [390] 5-9-2 **60** .... TobyAtkinson(5) 4 — 62
(George Prodromou) *hld up in 9th: prog on outer fr 3f out: pressed for 2nd bhd clr ldr over 1f out: one pce after* **16/1**

0-60 **5** *½* **Lytham (IRE)**[29] [203] 10-9-2 **55** .... NeilCallan 5 — 56+
(Tony Carroll) *trckd ldrs: shkn up 3f out: nt qckn over 1f out: styd on wl fnl f to press for a pl nr fin* **14/1**

5411 **6** *nse* **Very Well Red**[19] [340] 8-9-5 **58** .... LukeMorris 10 — 59
(Peter Hiatt) *pressed ldng pair: rdn over 3f out: wnt 2nd bhd clr ldr for a few strides over 1f out: one pce after* **15/2**[3]

00-3 **7** *hd* **Aine's Delight (IRE)**[19] [346] 5-9-2 **55** .... KirstyMilczarek 12 — 56
(Andy Turnell) *hld up in 11th: quick prog on wd outside fr 3f out: chalng for a pl over 1f out: fdd* **15/2**[3]

1-04 **8** *3 ¼* **Burnbrake**[21] [301] 6-9-1 **54** .... (b) JamesMillman 9 — 48
(Les Hall) *hld up in last pair: shuffled along and sme prog on outer over 1f out: nvr nr ldrs* **8/1**

1-20 **9** *2 ¼* **Dilys Maud**[23] [278] 4-9-4 **58** .... RobertHavlin 13 — 48
(Roger Ingram) *dwlt: hld up in last pair: shkn up over 2f out: v modest late prog* **16/1**

0-06 **10** *1 ¼* **It's Dubai Dolly**[23] [278] 5-9-4 **57** .... (p) TomQueally 14 — 44
(Alastair Lidderdale) *chsd ldr: rdn over 3f out: sn outpcd: clung on to 2nd tl over 1f out: wknd qckly* **10/1**

5-54 **11** *1 ¾* **Chez Vrony**[36] [121] 5-9-2 **55** .... AdrianMcCarthy 1 — 39
(Dave Morris) *w ldrs: rdn over 3f out: swtchd rt over 1f out: nowhere to go after and wknd fnl f* **33/1**

60/5 **12** *1 ½* **Lennie Briscoe (IRE)**[20] [317] 5-9-3 **56** .... (t) MartinLane 6 — 37+
(Martin Bosley) *s.s: settled in 10th: pushed along and making sme prog on inner whn bdly hmpd over 1f out: nt rcvr* **12/1**

0-54 **13** *½* **Etruscan (IRE)**[21] [299] 6-9-1 **54** .... (p) LiamKeniry 2 — 34
(Chris Gordon) *prom: drvn in 3rd over 3f out: n.m.r on inner 2f out: wknd qckly jst over 1f out* **20/1**

0-05 **14** *22* **Marmooq**[21] [299] 8-9-3 **56** .... RobbieFitzpatrick 11 — —
(Michael Attwater) *chsd ldrs on outer to over 3f out: wknd qckly and eased: t.o* **33/1**

2m 6.15s (-1.85) **Going Correction** -0.15s/f (Stan)
WFA 4 from 5yo+ 1lb — **14** Ran SP% **120.1**
Speed ratings (Par 101): **101,99,97,97,97 97,96,94,92,91 90,88,88,70**
toteswingers: 1&2 £10.50, 1&3 £8.60, 2&3 £8.70 CSF £41.26 CT £292.30 TOTE £6.50: £2.50, £2.80, £1.70; EX 50.20.
Owner A G Newcombe **Bred** Michael Ng **Trained** Yarnscombe, Devon
■ Stewards' Enquiry : Adrian McCarthy four-day ban: careless riding (Mar 2-4,7)

FOCUS
A competitive heat, run in a time 2.26sec quicker than the apprentice handicap earlier on the card.
Sunset Boulevard(IRE) Official explanation: jockey said gelding was denied a clear run
Dilys Maud Official explanation: jockey said filly hung right-handed
Chez Vrony Official explanation: jockey said gelding was denied a clear run

554 BETDAQ.COM EXCHANGE PRICE MULTIPLES H'CAP — 5f (P)
6:10 (6:10) (Class 5) (0-75,74) 4-Y-0+ — £2,047 (£604; £302) Stalls Low

Form — RPR

4-51 **1** **Island Legend (IRE)**[12] [430] 5-9-4 **71** .... (p) RichardKingscote 1 — 82
(Milton Bradley) *mde all: hung lft whn drvn over 1f out: styd on wl fnl f* **3/1**[2]

2122 **2** *1* **Black Baccara**[6] [487] 4-8-2 **60** oh2 .... (be) JulieBurke(5) 7 — 67
(Phil McEntee) *chsd ldng pair: wnt 2nd wl over 1f out: tried to cl on wnr fnl f: a hld* **11/2**

60-1 **3** *¾* **Italian Tom (IRE)**[17] [357] 4-9-6 **73** .... LukeMorris 4 — 77
(Ronald Harris) *sn rdn in 4th bhd str pce: kpt on u.p fr over 1f out to win battle for 3rd* **7/1**

5213 **4** *nse* **Sherjawy (IRE)**[7] [470] 7-9-1 **68** .... SamHitchcott 2 — 72+
(Zoe Davison) *sn pushed along in 5th: tried to cl on ldrs over 1f out: disp 3rd fnl f: nvr able to chal* **5/2**[1]

210 **5** *¾* **Your Gifted (IRE)**[5] [443] 4-8-11 **64** .... StephenCraine 8 — 65
(Patrick Morris) *stdd s: hld up in last pair gng bttr than most: asked to cl on ldrs over 1f out w limited rspnse: rdn and fnd nil last 100yds* **20/1**

6-04 **6** *4 ½* **Whiskey Junction**[21] [298] 7-9-0 **67** .... MartinDwyer 5 — 52
(Michael Quinn) *sn rdn: a in last pair: no ch over 1f out* **5/1**[3]

20-0 **7** *1 ¼* **Fair Passion**[12] [430] 4-9-7 **74** .... JimmyQuinn 9 — 55
(Derek Shaw) *nt wl away but sn rcvrd fr wd draw to chse wnr: wknd wl over 1f out* **14/1**

58.99 secs (-1.51) **Going Correction** -0.15s/f (Stan) — **7** Ran SP% **109.6**
Speed ratings (Par 103): **106,104,103,103,101 94,92**
toteswingers: 1&2 £2.10, 1&3 £2.60, 2&3 £4.40 CSF £17.97 CT £94.83 TOTE £3.30: £1.10, £3.00; EX 16.70.
Owner J M Bradley **Bred** Jerome Casey **Trained** Sedbury, Gloucs

FOCUS
Fast and furious stuff.

555 LAY BACK AND WIN AT BETDAQ.COM H'CAP — 1m (P)
6:40 (6:40) (Class 6) (0-55,55) 4-Y-0+ — £1,535 (£453; £226) Stalls Low

Form — RPR

050- **1** **Allanit (GER)**[112] [7167] 7-9-3 **54** .... TomQueally 12 — 65
(Barney Curley) *taken down early: racd freely: led over 6f out: mde rest: kicked on over 2f out and nvr less than 2 l clr after: hrd rdn over 1f out: styd on* **9/4**[1]

6514 **2** *2 ¼* **Kielty's Folly**[19] [340] 7-9-2 **53** .... GrahamGibbons 5 — 59
(Brian Baugh) *t.k.h: hld up towards rr: squeezed through and prog 2f out: chsd wnr over 1f out: kpt on but nvr able to chal* **6/1**[3]

00-3 **3** *½* **Fine Ruler (IRE)**[23] [280] 7-9-2 **53** .... GeorgeBaker 9 — 58
(Martin Bosley) *stdd s: hld up in last trio: nt clr run briefly 2f out and swtchd lft: prog after: styd on to take 3rd fnl f: nvr able to chal* **8/1**

46-5 **4** *1* **Empress Leizu (IRE)**[33] [163] 4-9-3 **54** .... (v[1]) NeilCallan 7 — 57
(Tony Carroll) *plld hrd: hld up bhd ldrs: rdn whn nt clr run briefly 2f out: kpt on same pce fr over 1f out* **9/1**

3-22 **5** *shd* **Abigails Angel**[6] [485] 4-9-1 **55** .... KierenFox(3) 11 — 57
(Brett Johnson) *hld up in last trio: wd into st: rdn and no prog over 2f out: hdwy over 1f out: styd on same pce fnl f* **7/2**[2]

2025 **6** *½* **Kenswick**[7] [467] 4-8-8 **50** .... (v) TobyAtkinson(5) 8 — 51
(Pat Eddery) *hld up last: shkn up over 2f out: prog over 1f out: kpt on: nvr a threat* **25/1**

0-41 **7** *2* **Poppy Golightly**[23] [280] 4-9-3 **54** .... ChrisCatlin 3 — 51
(Ron Hodges) *t.k.h: hld up bhd ldrs: shkn up over 2f out: nt qckn over 1f out: wknd fnl f* **6/1**[3]

626- **8** 1 1/2 **Gazamali (IRE)**[218] 3975 4-8-8 **52** .... DavidKenny(7) 4 45
(Michael Scudamore) *t.k.h: disp ld to over 6f out: prom tl wknd wl over 1f out* **25/1**

0-30 **9** 1 1/2 **Tous Les Deux**[23] 280 8-9-2 **53** .... DaneO'Neill 2 43
(Dr Jeremy Naylor) *hld up in rr: nt clr run briefly over 2f out: shkn up and no real prog over 1f out* **20/1**

60-0 **10** 1 1/2 **Miss Bounty**[26] 248 6-9-2 **53** .... IanMongan 13 39
(Jim Boyle) *chsd ldrs: rdn over 2f out: wknd over 1f out* **12/1**

050- **11** 1/2 **Christophers Quest**[148] 6275 6-9-0 **51** .... LiamKeniry 6 36
(Natalie Lloyd-Beavis) *nvr bttr than midfield: rdn and no prog over 2f out: sn wknd* **80/1**

000- **12** 2 1/2 **Queen Ranavola (USA)**[212] 4205 4-9-2 **53** .... LukeMorris 14 32
(John Best) *t.k.h: disp ld to over 6f out: chsd wnr to over 2f out: wknd* **50/1**

1m 38.84s (-0.96) **Going Correction** -0.15s/f (Stan) **12 Ran SP% 126.0**
Speed ratings (Par 101): **98,95,95,94,94 93,91,90,88,87 86,84**
toteswingers: 1&2 £5.30, 1&3 £8.80, 2&3 £4.50 CSF £16.44 CT £100.40 TOTE £3.40: £1.30, £2.70, £3.70; EX 31.70.
Owner Curley Leisure **Bred** Gestut Schlenderhan **Trained** Newmarket, Suffolk

FOCUS
The market told the story here.
Allanit(GER) Official explanation: trainer said, regarding apparent improvement in form, that the gelding was suited by being dropped back to a mile, had settled better and was helped by being drawn on the outside as it only has one eye.

556 BETDAQ MOBILE APPS CLASSIFIED CLAIMING STKS 7f (P)
7:10 (7:10) (Class 5) 4-Y-0+ **£2,047** (£604; £302) **Stalls Low**

Form RPR

11 **1** **April Fool**[6] 483 7-8-12 70 .... (b) DavidProbert 7 78
(Ronald Harris) *mde virtually all: abt 2 l clr 2f out: drvn fnl f: jst hld on* **15/8**[1]

30-0 **2** *shd* **Maze (IRE)**[28] 206 6-9-0 68 .... NeilCallan 3 79
(Tony Carroll) *t.k.h: hld up in midfield: prog over 2f out: rdn to chse wnr jst ins fnl f: clsd u.p: jst failed* **12/1**

-216 **3** 1 1/4 **I Confess**[19] 334 6-8-3 70 .... (b) MatthewCosham(7) 4 72
(David Evans) *prom: rdn 1/2-way in 3rd: chsd wnr wl over 2f out: hanging and no imp 1f out: sn lost 2nd: kpt on* **9/1**

16-5 **4** 3 1/2 **Fleetwoodsands (IRE)**[28] 213 4-8-11 69 .... (t) BarryMcHugh 2 64
(Ollie Pears) *t.k.h: hld up in rr: sme prog over 2f out: tk modest 4th over 1f out: no imp* **13/2**[3]

00-4 **5** 3 **Stoppers (IRE)**[20] 313 4-8-10 69 .... EddieAhern 6 54
(Robert Mills) *dwlt: hld up in last: shkn up and sme prog 2f out: one pce in 5th fnl f* **4/1**[2]

3-33 **6** 1 **Super Frank (IRE)**[17] 357 8-8-4 66 .... (b) ChrisCatlin 5 46
(John Akehurst) *hld up and racd wd: effrt over 2f out: no real prog over 1f out* **10/1**

0-05 **7** 3 1/4 **Aviso (GER)**[19] 341 7-9-4 68 .... (b[1]) TomQueally 1 51
(Barney Curley) *settled in rr on inner: shkn up and no prog over 2f out: no ch sn after* **7/1**

3-55 **8** 3/4 **Kipchak (IRE)**[19] 334 6-8-11 62 .... (p) HayleyTurner 8 42
(Conor Dore) *struggling to hold pl on outer after 3f: dropped to rr and wl btn over 2f out* **20/1**

00-0 **9** 2 3/4 **Running Mate (IRE)**[15] 375 4-9-4 55 .... IanMongan 9 42
(Jo Crowley) *chsd wnr to wl over 2f out: wknd qckly* **66/1**

1m 24.36s (-1.64) **Going Correction** -0.15s/f (Stan) **9 Ran SP% 113.7**
Speed ratings (Par 103): **103,102,101,97,94 92,89,88,85**
toteswingers: 1&2 £4.90, 1&3 £4.40, 2&3 £19.90 CSF £26.10 TOTE £1.80: £1.10, £2.10, £3.70; EX 29.90.The winner was claimed by P. D. Evans for £7,000.
Owner G B Balding **Bred** Miss B Swire **Trained** Earlswood, Monmouths

FOCUS
Five of these were within 3lb of each other on adjusted ratings, suggesting it should be a tight contest, and there was indeed a close finish.

557 RACING AT SKYSPORTS.COM H'CAP 7f (P)
7:40 (7:40) (Class 4) (0-85,85) 4-Y-0+ **£2,520** (£2,520; £577; £288) **Stalls Low**

Form RPR

-423 **1** **Ocean Legend (IRE)**[14] 385 6-9-2 **80** .... NeilCallan 6 89
(Tony Carroll) *trckd ldrs in 5th: prog to go 2nd 2f out: rdn to ld jst over 1f out: hrd pressed fnl f: jnd on the nod* **3/1**[2]

366- **1** *dht* **Bowmaker**[157] 6002 4-9-5 **83** .... GregFairley 4 92
(Mark Johnston) *led: drvn and hdd jst over 1f out: battled bk wl fnl f: looked jst hld tl forced dead-heat on the nod* **11/2**[3]

2-36 **3** 1 1/2 **Could It Be Magic**[21] 307 4-8-4 **71** oh1 .... (b) KierenFox(3) 7 76
(Bill Turner) *hld up in last trio: urged along and prog on outer 2f out: chsd ldng pair fnl f: styd on but nvr able to chal* **10/1**

2014 **4** 1 3/4 **Lastkingofscotland (IRE)**[7] 467 5-8-13 **77** .... (b) HayleyTurner 5 77+
(Conor Dore) *dwlt: hld up in last: pushed along fr over 2f out: styd on to take 4th wl ins fnl f: nvr nr ldrs* **16/1**

00-1 **5** 1 1/4 **Woolfall Sovereign (IRE)**[16] 367 5-8-7 **71** oh1 .... BarryMcHugh 9 68
(George Margarson) *t.k.h: disp 2nd pl to 2f out: wknd fnl f* **6/1**

330- **6** 1 **Alfresco**[165] 5750 7-8-12 **76** .... (p) LukeMorris 2 70
(John Best) *plld hrd bhd ldrs: cl up 2f out: wknd over 1f out* **25/1**

/10- **7** 1/2 **Arry's Orse**[137] 6570 4-9-7 **85** .... TomEaves 3 78
(Bryan Smart) *plld hrd: disp 2nd pl to over 2f out: wknd over 1f out* **5/2**[1]

00-0 **8** 1 **Jordaura**[23] 279 5-8-13 **77** .... AdamKirby 1 67
(Tony Carroll) *sltly awkward s and reminder: hld up in last trio: shkn up 2f out: no prog* **7/1**

1m 24.22s (-1.78) **Going Correction** -0.15s/f (Stan) **8 Ran SP% 114.6**
Speed ratings (Par 105): **104,104,102,100,98 97,97,96**WIN: B £4.40, OL £2.60; PL: B £1.40, OL £1.70, CIBM £1.60; EX: B-OL £13.00; OL-B £15.20; CSF: B-OL £11.22, OL-B £9.98; TRICAST: B-OL-CIBM £80.11, OL-B-CIBM £72.35; toteswingers: 1&1 £5.20, 1&3 (B) £9.80, 1&3 (OL) £6.30.
Owner Sheikh Hamdan Bin Mohammed Al Maktoum **Bred** Brook Stud Bloodstock Ltd **Trained** Middleham Moor, N Yorks

FOCUS
Not a bad little handicap.
Alfresco Official explanation: jockey said gelding ran too free

558 GOFFS BREEZE UP AT KEMPTON MARCH 29TH H'CAP 6f (P)
8:10 (8:12) (Class 6) (0-55,55) 3-Y-0 **£1,535** (£453; £226) **Stalls Low**

Form RPR

6-30 **1** **Kassaab**[19] 335 3-9-4 **55** .... (b[1]) SteveDrowne 11 59
(Jeremy Gask) *sn led and crossed fr wd draw: mde virtually all: edgd lft 2f out: hld on u.p* **9/2**[2]

-644 **2** 3/4 **Lovat Lane**[12] 426 3-8-11 **48** .... (b[1]) EddieAhern 5 50
(Eve Johnson Houghton) *chsd ldng pair: drvn to go 2nd wl over 1f out: tried to press wnr fnl f: nt qckn* **12/1**

505- **3** *nk* **Spirit Of Oakdale (IRE)**[154] 6082 3-9-4 **55** .... AdamKirby 4 56
(Walter Swinburn) *rdn in 8th over 3f out: prog u.p over 1f out: styd on fnl f: nvr quite able to chal* **11/4**[1]

0-04 **4** *nse* **Lady Ellice**[14] 389 3-8-11 **48** .... LukeMorris 1 49
(Phil McEntee) *chsd ldrs in 7th: drvn over 2f out: prog over 1f out: styd on u.p fnl f* **14/1**

0-45 **5** 1 1/2 **Scommettitrice (IRE)**[30] 189 3-9-2 **53** .... AndreaAtzeni 2 49
(Ronald Harris) *chsd ldrs in 5th: rdn over 2f out: nt qckn over 1f out: one pce after* **12/1**

4-65 **6** 3/4 **Mi Sun Donk**[19] 338 3-9-2 **53** .... GeorgeBaker 6 47
(Brett Johnson) *chsd ldrs in 4th: drvn and nt qckn over 2f out: grad fdd over 1f out* **14/1**

3 **7** 1 **Ereka (IRE)**[14] 383 3-8-8 **50** .... RyanPowell(5) 7 40
(Murty McGrath) *disp ld w wnr to over 2f out: shovelled along and grad lost pl over 1f out* **7/1**

050 **8** 3/4 **Avon Light**[11] 437 3-9-2 **53** .... RichardKingscote 12 41
(Milton Bradley) *restless stalls: dwlt: wl off the pce in last pair: effrt over 2f out: modest late prog* **40/1**

0-60 **9** *hd* **High Avon**[4] 519 3-9-2 **53** .... (b) SamHitchcott 3 40
(Dean Ivory) *hld up in 9th: effrt on wd outside over 2f out: limited prog over 1f out: fdd fnl f* **8/1**

00-4 **10** *nk* **Gekko (IRE)**[14] 383 3-9-0 **51** .... StephenCraine 8 37
(Patrick Morris) *reluctant to enter stalls: chsd ldrs in 6th: nt qckn over 2f out: sing to lose pl whn nt clr run over 1f out* **11/2**[3]

30-0 **11** 3/4 **Crazy In Love**[30] 189 3-8-13 **50** .... (b) HayleyTurner 10 34
(Olivia Maylam) *s.i.s: a in last trio: rdn and no prog 2f out* **33/1**

0-64 **12** 6 **Fantale**[19] 333 3-8-13 **50** .... MartinLane 9 15
(David Evans) *reluctant to enter stalls: s.s: a in last pair and wl off the pce* **33/1**

1m 13.07s (-0.03) **Going Correction** -0.15s/f (Stan) **12 Ran SP% 120.9**
Speed ratings (Par 95): **94,93,92,92,90 89,88,87,86,86 85,77**
toteswingers: 1&2 £11.00, 1&3 £5.80, 2&3 £11.20 CSF £58.01 CT £181.37 TOTE £5.50: £2.70, £4.10, £2.10; EX 106.20.
Owner Andrew Gauley & Kevin Thomson **Bred** Fernham Farm Ltd **Trained** Sutton Veny, Wilts

FOCUS
First-time blinkers and a drop back in trip did the trick here for the first two home.
T/Plt: £105.00 to a £1 stake. Pool: £70,677.61. 490.95 winning tickets. T/Qpdt: £33.30 to a £1 stake Pool: £7,963.53. 176.69 winning tickets. JN

518 LINGFIELD (L-H)
Wednesday, February 16

OFFICIAL GOING: Standard
Wind: medium, behind Weather: dry, partly cloudy

559 BET ON WINNING DISTANCES AT BLUESQ.COM MAIDEN STKS 7f (P)
2:00 (2:00) (Class 5) 3-Y-O **£1,910** (£564; £282) **Stalls Low**

Form RPR

3 **1** **Social Forum (IRE)**[32] 179 3-9-3 0 .... MartinLane 6 76
(Rodger Sweeney, Ire) *chsd ldr tl led over 2f out: rdn and clr over 1f out: pressed wl ins fnl f: hld on wl towards fin* **7/2**[3]

05- **2** 1/2 **Bosambo**[163] 5814 3-9-3 0 .... PJMcDonald 9 74
(Alan Swinbank) *chsd ldrs: n.m.r briefly jst over 2f out: rdn and hdwy to chse wnr wl over 1f out: kpt on wl u.p and chalng wnr wl ins fnl f: hld towards fin* **12/1**

3 2 3/4 **York Glory (USA)** 3-9-3 0 .... ChrisCatlin 1 67+
(Kevin Ryan) *s.i.s: bhd: gd hdwy on outer 3f out: chal whn rn wd bnd 2f out and sltly outpcd: rallied ent fnl f: wknd fnl 100yds* **9/4**[1]

323 **4** 3/4 **Sofias Number One (USA)**[11] 437 3-9-3 72 .... JamieSpencer 8 65
(Michael Wigham) *hld up towards rr: rdn and effrt ent fnl 2f: nt qckn and no hdwy over 1f out: no threat to ldrs: kpt on u.p ins fnl f* **4/1**

0 **5** 4 1/2 **Frosty Reception**[28] 214 3-8-12 0 .... RichardKingscote 2 48
(Brendan Powell) *chsd ldrs: rdn along 4f out: styd chsng ldrs tl wknd u.p over 1f out: fdd ins fnl f* **50/1**

00- **6** 2 **Salesiano**[91] 7485 3-9-3 0 .... NeilCallan 10 47
(Peter Makin) *stdd after s: in rr: edgd lft after 1f: rdn and no hdwy over 2f out: no ch fnl 2f: plugged on ins fnl f* **16/1**

00-2 **7** 1 3/4 **Cold Secret**[20] 313 3-9-3 73 .... RobertWinston 3 43
(David Elsworth) *racd in last trio: pushed lft after 1f: dropped to last and rdn over 2f out: sn wl btn* **5/2**[2]

00- **8** 13 **Brendan's Gift**[209] 4299 3-8-12 0 .... FrankieMcDonald 5 —
(Brendan Powell) *racd in midfield: u.p and struggling over 2f out: wl bhd fnl 2f* **150/1**

0 **9** 4 1/2 **Masie Grey**[32] 179 3-8-12 0 .... DaneO'Neill 4 —
(David Elsworth) *racd freely: led tl over 2f out: sn wknd: wl bhd over 1f out* **33/1**

1m 25.91s (1.11) **Going Correction** +0.15s/f (Slow) **9 Ran SP% 120.7**
Speed ratings (Par 97): **99,98,95,94,89 87,85,70,65**
toteswingers:1&2 £7.40, 2&3 £6.80, 1&3 £3.30 CSF £46.05 TOTE £6.50: £2.10, £4.10, £1.50; EX 60.60 Trifecta £331.90 Part won. Pool: £448.63 - 0.20 - winning units..
Owner Mrs J B Sweeney **Bred** Finaco Srl **Trained** Castlelyons, Co Cork

FOCUS
An interesting maiden ran at a good early pace.

560 CROWHURST H'CAP 2m (P)
2:30 (2:32) (Class 6) (0-60,60) 4-Y-0+ **£1,535** (£453; £226) **Stalls Low**

Form RPR

2-01 **1** **Brabazon (IRE)**[9] 444 8-9-10 **60** .... (bt) JamieSpencer 7 68+
(Emmet Michael Butterly, Ire) *hld up in rr: hdwy 5f out: rdn and qcknd to ld over 2f out: clr and drvn wl over 1f out: edgd rt u.p ins fnl f: a holding on* **11/4**[1]

-502 **2** 1/2 **Pinsplitter (USA)**[12] 419 4-8-9 **51** .... (p) JamesDoyle 11 56
(Alan McCabe) *hld up in last pair: hdwy 3f out: nt clr run over 2f out tl switching to outer wl over 1f out: hdwy u.p over 1f out: styd on wl ins fnl f: wnt 2nd towards fin: nvr quite getting to wnr* **8/1**

4215 **3** *hd* **Frameit (IRE)**[6] 486 4-9-2 **58** .... (v) MickyFenton 12 63
(James Given) *hld up in midfield: hdwy whn n.m.r and barging match w rival over 2f out: hdwy to chse ldr jst over 1f out: kpt on wl u.p: nt clr run and swtchd sltly rt ins fnl f: lost 2nd towards fin* **9/2**[2]

2-32 **4** 1 1/4 **Wild Geese (IRE)**[18] 350 4-9-2 **58** .... (b) RichardKingscote 4 61
(Jonathan Portman) *chsd ldrs: nt clr run on inner over 2f out tl swtchd ins and effrt over 1f out: chsd ldrs and rdn ent fnl f: kpt on same pce* **15/2**[3]

253/ **5** 2 ¾ **Tobago Bay**[32] 4703 6-9-2 **52**..(b) AdamKirby 10 52
(Gary Moore) *chsd ldr: wnt upsides ldr 8f out: rdn and chsd clr wnr jst over 2f out tl jst over 1f out: no ex ins fnl f* **11/1**

/0-0 **6** ¾ **Tecktal (FR)**[12] 418 8-8-11 **47**.. IanMongan 8 46
(Pat Phelan) *hld up towards rr: clsd and in tch whn nt clr run over 2f out tl over 1f out: styd on fnl f: nvr able to chal* **20/1**

1-23 **7** ¾ **Six Of Clubs**[36] 118 5-8-7 **50**..(b) JakePayne(7) 1 48
(Bill Turner) *hld up in midfield: nt clr run on inner over 2f out tl effrt u.p over 1f out: styd on same pce ins fnl f: nvr able to chal* **12/1**

030/ **8** 2 ¼ **Take A Mile (IRE)**[103] 3084 9-9-3 **53**.. LiamKeniry 6 48
(Seamus Mullins) *hld up towards rr: rdn and effrt towards outer over 2f out: styd on same pce u.p fr over 1f out: nvr trbld ldrs* **16/1**

/2-5 **9** *nk* **Mystified (IRE)**[33] 172 8-9-4 **54**..(tp) NeilCallan 3 49
(Roger Fisher) *led tl rdn and hdd over 2f out: wknd over 1f out* **14/1**

31-0 **9** *dht* **Torran Sound**[23] 277 4-8-12 **54**.. LukeMorris 9 49
(James Eustace) *chsd ldrs: rdn and unable qck over 2f out: wknd over 1f out* **16/1**

3-30 **11** 6 **Bold Adventure**[14] 392 7-9-9 **59**.. StevieDonohoe 5 47
(Willie Musson) *stdd s: hld up in last: nvr on terms* **16/1**

040/ **12** *nk* **Meneur (FR)**[15] 6243 9-9-10 **60**.. GeorgeBaker 2 48
(Gary Moore) *hld up in midfield: hdwy and chsd ldrs over 4f out: rdn over 2f out: short of room and lost pl ent fnl 2f: sn wknd: eased ins fnl f* **20/1**

560- **13** *hd* **Whipperway (IRE)**[10] 1158 4-8-10 **52**.. JamieGoldstein 13 39
(Sheena West) *in tch in midfield on outer: rdn and struggling over 2f out: wl hld fnl 2f* **40/1**

00-0 **14** 9 **Follow The Dream**[26] 252 8-9-0 **50**.. ChrisCatlin 14 27
(Karen George) *in tch in midfield: rdn 4f out: dropped to rr over 3f out: sn lost tch* **50/1**

3m 25.45s (-0.25) **Going Correction** +0.15s/f (Slow)
WFA 4 from 5yo+ 6lb 14 Ran SP% **122.0**
Speed ratings (Par 101): **106,105,105,105,103 103,102,101,101,101 98,98,98,93**
toteswingers:1&2 £6.50, 2&3 £6.90, 1&3 £5.00 CSF £23.80 CT £100.09 TOTE £3.10: £1.80, £2.20, £2.30; EX 28.50 Trifecta £141.70 Pool: £318.07 - 1.66 - winning units..
Owner James Ferry **Bred** Dermot Cantillon And Forenaghts Stud **Trained** Letterkenny, Co Donegal
■ Stewards' Enquiry : Micky Fenton one-day ban: careless riding (Mar 2)

FOCUS
An open-looking race, with the front four pulling clear.
Meneur(FR) Official explanation: trainer said gelding finished distressed

561 LINGFIELD MARRIOTT HOTEL AND COUNTRY CLUB (S) STKS 1m 2f (P)
3:00 (3:02) (Class 6) 4-6-Y-O **£1,535** (£453; £226) **Stalls** Low

Form RPR

0-10 **1** **Erinjay (IRE)**[27] 226 5-9-5 77.. AndreaAtzeni 3 72
(Michael Wigham) *hld up in last: hdwy over 2f out: chsd ldng pair and rdn over 1f out: r.o wl to ld fnl 50yds: sn in command* **2/1**[2]

5-30 **2** 1 **Celtic Commitment**[14] 381 5-8-13 65.. NeilCallan 1 64
(Simon Dow) *led: hrd pressed 2f out: rdn wl over 1f out: forged ahd again ins fnl f: hdd and no ex fnl 50yds* **7/2**[3]

134 **3** ½ **Scary Movie (IRE)**[21] 310 6-9-5 73.. CathyGannon 5 69
(Ronald Harris) *chsd ldr: jnd ldr and nudged along over 2f out: ev ch and drvn wl over 1f out: nt qckn ins fnl f and btn fnl 50yds* **10/11**[1]

00-5 **4** 4 ½ **Giulietta Da Vinci**[11] 432 4-8-7 48.. HayleyTurner 2 49
(Steve Woodman) *t.k.h: chsd ldng pair tl wl over 1f out: wknd jst over 1f out* **25/1**

0050 **5** *shd* **All Moving Parts (USA)**[12] 425 4-8-5 51..(b) RyanTate(7) 4 54
(Alan McCabe) *t.k.h: hld up wl in tch in last pair: rdn and unable qck over 2f out: one pce and no threat to ldrs fnl 2f* **33/1**

2m 8.11s (1.51) **Going Correction** +0.15s/f (Slow)
WFA 4 from 5yo+ 1lb 5 Ran SP% **114.7**
Speed ratings: **99,98,97,94,94**
CSF £9.78 TOTE £3.10: £3.40, £1.40; EX 7.30.There was no bid for the winner.
Owner Seyhan Osman, Michael Wigham **Bred** Bill Benson **Trained** Newmarket, Suffolk

FOCUS
An average seller run at a crawl. There were no claims.
Giulietta Da Vinci Official explanation: trainer said filly was struck into behind

562 DOWNLOAD THE BLUE SQUARE IPHONE APP H'CAP 1m (P)
3:30 (3:30) (Class 5) (0-70,70) 4-Y-O+ **£2,047** (£604; £302) **Stalls** High

Form RPR

0-56 **1** **Peadar Miguel**[6] 488 4-9-2 **65**.. AdamKirby 8 73
(Noel Quinlan) *stdd s: hld up in rr: effrt and swtchd rt over 1f out: squeezed between horses and chal ins fnl f: led fnl 100yds: r.o wl and sn in command* **12/1**

2131 **2** 1 **Shared Moment (IRE)**[14] 387 5-8-11 **60**..(v) ChrisCatlin 1 66
(John Gallagher) *chsd ldrs: swtchd rt and effrt wl over 1f out: ev ch ins fnl f: rdn and nt gng pce of wnr fnl 100yds* **3/1**[1]

6363 **3** *nk* **Ilie Nastase (FR)**[21] 308 7-9-5 **68**.. HayleyTurner 5 73
(Conor Dore) *hld up in rr: effrt and nt clr run over 1f out: sn swtchd lft and hdwy on inner: pressed ldrs ins fnl f: one pce towards fin* **17/2**

05-0 **4** ½ **Tukitinyasok (IRE)**[26] 249 4-9-2 **65**..(p) NeilCallan 6 69
(Roger Fisher) *led: rdn ent fnl 2f: kpt on wl tl hdd fnl 100yds: one pce after* **15/2**

6-34 **5** *nk* **Final Verse**[23] 282 8-9-7 **70**..(be) GeorgeBaker 9 73
(Matthew Salaman) *stdd after s: hld up towards rr: effrt and n.m.r ent fnl 2f: rdn and hdwy over 1f out: kpt on ins fnl f: nt rch ldrs* **5/1**[2]

0-33 **6** 1 ¼ **Cuthbert (IRE)**[26] 249 4-9-4 **70**..(p) KierenFox(3) 4 71
(William Jarvis) *sn bustled up to press ldr: ev ch and rdn over 1f out: unable qck ent fnl f: btn fnl 100yds: n.m.r and eased towards fin* **5/1**[2]

0144 **7** 1 ¼ **Justcallmehandsome**[12] 428 9-8-9 **65**..(be) LucyKBarry(7) 2 63
(Dominic Ffrench Davis) *stdd s: hld up in rr: c wd and effrt bnd ent fnl 2f: kpt on ins fnl f: nvr able to chal* **33/1**

-301 **8** *hd* **Aflaam (IRE)**[11] 433 6-9-5 **68**..(tp) LukeMorris 3 65
(Ronald Harris) *chsd ldrs: rdn over 2f out: unable qck u.p and struggling over 1f out: one pce and wl hld ins fnl f* **7/1**[3]

00-0 **9** 6 **Basra (IRE)**[32] 174 8-9-4 **67**..(v[1]) DaneO'Neill 10 50
(Jo Crowley) *hld up in midfield: hdwy to press ldrs over 2f out: wknd qckly wl over 1f out* **7/1**[3]

10-5 **10** 11 **Eastern Hills**[16] 367 6-9-2 **65**..(p) RobertWinston 7 41
(Alan McCabe) *chsd ldrs: rdn and wknd wl over 1f out: sn bhd: eased ins fnl f* **12/1**

1m 38.49s (0.29) **Going Correction** +0.15s/f (Slow) 10 Ran SP% **124.0**
Speed ratings (Par 103): **104,103,102,102,101 100,99,99,93,82**
toteswingers:1&2 £11.70, 2&3 £7.60, 1&3 £24.70 CSF £51.15 CT £347.37 TOTE £22.00: £4.90, £1.60, £4.80; EX 117.80 TRIFECTA Not won..
Owner Peter J Moran **Bred** A C M Spalding **Trained** Newmarket, Suffolk
■ Noel Quinlan's first winner since taking over the licence from brother Mick.

FOCUS
A competitive-looking handicap, with the first five finishing in a bunch.
Basra(IRE) Official explanation: vet said gelding had a breathing problem
Eastern Hills Official explanation: trainer's rep said gelding was unsuited by the polytrack

563 BLINDLEY HEATH MAIDEN STKS 1m 5f (P)
4:00 (4:00) (Class 5) 4-Y-O+ **£1,910** (£564; £282) **Stalls** Low

Form RPR

024- **1** **Momkinzain (USA)**[125] 6861 4-9-3 76.. SamHitchcott 4 73
(Mick Channon) *chsd ldr: pushed rt bnd 9f out: sn led and mde rest: rdn and drew clr over 1f out: styd on wl: easily* **2/1**[2]

366- **2** 6 **Ned Ludd (IRE)**[68] 6693 8-9-7 57..(b) RichardKingscote 2 64
(Jonathan Portman) *chsd ldrs: wnt 2nd over 8f out: rdn ent fnl 2f: drvn and nt gng pce of wnr over 1f out: no ch w wnr but plugged on to go 2nd fnl 100yds* **13/2**[3]

3 2 **King Kieren (IRE)**[303] 6-9-7 0.. IanMongan 1 61
(Linda Jewell) *dwlt: hld up in tch: hdwy on outer and rdn to press ldrs over 2f out: outpcd by wnr and btn over 1f out: lost 2nd fnl 100yds* **50/1**

2 **4** 4 ½ **First Rock (IRE)**[34] 145 5-9-7 0.. PJMcDonald 3 54
(Alan Swinbank) *led tl hung rt and hdd bnd 9f out: in tch after: shkn up over 2f out: rdn and fnd nil 2f out: wl btn after* **8/11**[1]

00-5 **5** 21 **Set Em Up Mo**[21] 309 5-9-2 42.. RobbieFitzpatrick 5 18
(Michael Attwater) *nvr gng wl and sn nudged along: in tch tl wknd u.p over 2f out: wl bhd and eased ins fnl f* **100/1**

2m 48.84s (2.84) **Going Correction** +0.15s/f (Slow)
WFA 4 from 5yo+ 4lb 5 Ran SP% **107.5**
Speed ratings (Par 103): **97,93,92,89,76**
CSF £13.74 TOTE £3.40: £2.00, £1.70; EX 10.00.
Owner Jaber Abdullah **Bred** Berkshire Stud **Trained** West Ilsley, Berks

FOCUS
A weak maiden run at a moderate gallop.
First Rock(IRE) Official explanation: vet said gelding returned lame behind

564 GOLF AND RACING AT LINGFIELD PARK H'CAP 1m 2f (P)
4:30 (4:30) (Class 6) (0-65,65) 3-Y-O **£1,535** (£453; £226) **Stalls** Low

Form RPR

3252 **1** **Mrs Neat (IRE)**[12] 424 3-9-2 **60**..(p) JamesDoyle 8 68
(Sylvester Kirk) *hld up in last trio: hdwy to trck ldr wl over 1f out: pushed along and effrt to ld fnl 100yds: sn in command: pushed out* **3/1**[2]

606- **2** 1 ½ **Round Turn (IRE)**[83] 7567 3-9-5 **63**.. GrahamGibbons 4 68
(Ed McMahon) *chsd ldng pair: hdwy to join ldr on inner wl over 2f out: rdn to ld ent fnl 2f: hung rt u.p: hdd and nt gng pce of wnr fnl 100yds* **13/8**[1]

-233 **3** 1 **Not So Bright (USA)**[13] 406 3-9-0 **58**..(vt[1]) AndreaAtzeni 2 61
(Des Donovan) *hld up in last trio: shkn up and effrt ent fnl 2f: a wanting to hang lft whn rdn over 1f out: chsd ldrs ins fnl f: kpt on* **6/1**[3]

006- **4** 3 ¾ **Echos Of Motivator**[145] 6334 3-9-7 **65**.. CathyGannon 3 63
(Ronald Harris) *hld up in last: rdn whn hmpd bnd ent fnl 2f: sn swtchd rt: rallied and sme hdwy over 1f out: wnt 4th ins fnl f: hung rt nr fin: nvr trbld ldrs* **12/1**

0-30 **5** 2 ¼ **Mountain Myst**[33] 171 3-9-4 **62**.. MartinDwyer 5 53
(William Muir) *in tch: pushed along briefly 5f out: rdn and unable qck ent fnl 2f: wknd over 1f out* **13/2**

-560 **6** 7 **Seadream**[13] 406 3-8-2 **46** oh1.. DavidProbert 6 23
(Mark Usher) *t.k.h early: led tl hdd ent fnl 2f: wknd qckly wl over 1f out* **25/1**

606- **7** 15 **Varlak**[123] 6936 3-9-1 **62**.. BillyCray(3) 7 —
(Des Donovan) *sn rdn along to press ldr: lost pl and short of room over 2f out: wl bhd fnl 2f* **9/1**

2m 7.84s (1.24) **Going Correction** +0.15s/f (Slow) 7 Ran SP% **112.3**
Speed ratings (Par 95): **101,100,99,96,95 89,77**
toteswingers:1&2 £2.40, 2&3 £3.20, 1&3 £1.60 CSF £7.96 CT £25.02 TOTE £4.30: £1.90, £2.30; EX 9.80 Trifecta £31.10 Pool of £532.98 - 12.68 winning units..
Owner N Pickett **Bred** Dan Major **Trained** Upper Lambourn, Berks

FOCUS
An average handicap.
Varlak Official explanation: jockey said colt hung left

565 PLAY RAINBOW RICHES AT BLUESQ.COM H'CAP 1m 2f (P)
5:00 (5:00) (Class 5) (0-70,70) 4-Y-O+ **£2,047** (£604; £302) **Stalls** Low

Form RPR

0361 **1** **Mister Green (FR)**[6] 489 5-9-7 **69** 6ex..(bt) JamesDoyle 5 75+
(David Flood) *t.k.h: hld up in last trio: hdwy and stl travelling wl over 1f out: swtchd lft jst ins fnl f: rdn: qcknd and r.o wl to ld nr fin* **9/4**[1]

-064 **2** ½ **Free Tussy (ARG)**[7] 472 7-9-3 **65**..(bt) GeorgeBaker 7 70
(Gary Moore) *t.k.h: chsd ldr tl led wl over 1f out: rdn and hung lft over 1f out: kpt on ins fnl f tl hdd nr fin* **16/1**

0-62 **3** *nse* **Indian Violet (IRE)**[26] 247 5-9-0 **62**.. JamieGoldstein 1 67
(Sheena West) *chsd ldrs: swtchd rt and effrt over 1f out: chsd ldr 1f out: ev ch ins fnl f: r.o wl: unable qck nr fin* **7/1**

1612 **4** 1 ½ **Edgeworth (IRE)**[12] 418 5-9-4 **66**..(p) ChrisCatlin 3 68
(Brendan Powell) *t.k.h: in tch: rdn and effrt wl over 1f out: kpt on same pce ins fnl f* **11/4**[2]

6334 **5** 3 ¼ **Lisahane Bog**[7] 475 4-9-7 **70**..(p) DaneO'Neill 2 66
(Peter Hedger) *s.i.s: t.k.h: hld up in tch: rdn and outpcd whn gallop qcknd over 2f out: styd on same pce fnl 2f* **7/2**[3]

01-0 **6** 1 **Jodawes (USA)**[28] 206 4-9-2 **65**.. SteveDrowne 4 59
(John Best) *t.k.h: led and set stdy gallop tl rdn and qcknd wl over 2f out: hdd wl over 1f out: wknd jst ins fnl f* **16/1**

0-11 **7** ½ **Ede's Dot Com (IRE)**[14] 390 7-9-1 **63**.. IanMongan 6 56
(Pat Phelan) *s.i.s: t.k.h: hld up in tch in rr: hdwy on outer 3f out: rdn and unable qck wl over 1f out: one pce and btn after* **8/1**

2m 15.79s (9.19) **Going Correction** +0.15s/f (Slow)
WFA 4 from 5yo+ 1lb 7 Ran SP% **115.0**
Speed ratings (Par 103): **69,68,68,67,64 63,63**
toteswingers:1&2 £7.00, 2&3 £8.50, 1&3 £4.60 CSF £38.50 TOTE £2.40: £3.90, £11.70; EX 40.20.
Owner DM Partnership **Bred** Gainsborough Stud Management Ltd **Trained** Exning, Suffolk

FOCUS
An ordinary handicap and the time was very slow.
T/Plt: £103.40 to a £1 stake. Pool of £55,607.05 - 392.31 winning tickets. T/Qpdt: £23.60 to a £1 stake. Pool of £4,070.47 - 127.60 winning tickets. SP

532 CAGNES-SUR-MER
Wednesday, February 16

OFFICIAL GOING: Fibresand: standard

566a PRIX DES BOURRACHES (CLAIMER) (4YO+) (FIBRESAND) 1m 2f (D)
2:55 (12:00) 4-Y-O+ £6,896 (£2,758; £2,068; £1,379; £689)

RPR
1 **Revolverheld (GER)**7 [481] 5-9-2 0 (b) ASuborics 2 78
(G Martin, Austria) 45/1
2 ½ **Bencoolen (IRE)**16 [372] 6-8-11 0 IoritzMendizabal 7 72
(J Van Handenhove, France) 31/1
3 ¾ **Status (IRE)** 6-8-11 0 MarcoMonteriso 10 71
(M Guarnieri, Italy) 12/1
4 2½ **Szerelem (FR)**16 [372] 6-8-11 0 StephanePasquier 1 66
(F-X De Chevigny, France) 7/2 1
5 ½ **Nolhac (FR)**228 7-8-10 0 (p) YoannRousset(6) 6 70
(Y Fertillet, France) 61/1
6 1 **Galixi (FR)**120 6-8-8 0 DavyBonilla 11 60
(R Laplanche, France) 13/1
7 nk **Class Attraction (IRE)**44 [42] 7-8-3 0 EddyHardouin(5) 14 60
(J E Hammond, France) 19/5 2
8 ½ **Officer In Command (USA)**14 [395] 5-8-11 0(b) Francois-XavierBertras 5 62
(J S Moore) *sn prom: racd in 5th on outside: smooth prog to go 2nd bef st: chal for ld 1 1/2f out: sn u.p: fnd no ex: fdd ins fnl f* 15/1
9 10 **Always In The Sky (FR)**554 5-8-11 0 RemiCampos 3 44
(T Larriviere, France) 35/1
10 10 **Spirit Of The King (FR)**7 [479] 5-8-11 0 (b) DominiqueBoeuf 8 26
(S-A Ghoumrassi, France) 33/1
0 **Satwa Prince (FR)**56 8-9-6 0 (p) JohanVictoire 4 —
(Jean De Roualle, France) 53/10 3
0 **Torronto (FR)**14 [395] 8-8-11 0 FlavienPrat 12 —
(P Monfort, France) 53/10 3
0 **Darabani (FR)**14 [395] 6-8-11 0 FranckBlondel 15 —
(P Monfort, France) 20/1
0 **Tudora (AUT)**16 [372] 6-8-8 0 FabienLefebvre 13 —
(S Bigus, Austria) 40/1

2m 8.34s (128.34) 14 Ran SP% 115.7
WIN (incl.. 1 euro stake); 46.20. PLACES: 13.00, 8.80, 5.20. DF: 284.70. SF: 1,116.70.
Owner Stall Challenger **Bred** Gestut Rietberg **Trained** Austria

545 SOUTHWELL (L-H)
Thursday, February 17

OFFICIAL GOING: Standard
Wind: Nil Weather: Heavy cloud

567 ENHANCED SP'S AT BLUESQ.COM H'CAP 1m (F)
1:50 (1:50) (Class 6) (0-60,57) 3-Y-O £1,535 (£453; £226) Stalls Low

Form RPR
060- 1 **Reachforthebucks**153 [6159] 3-9-3 **50** AndreaAtzeni 3 71+
(Michael Wigham) *hld up: smooth hdwy on outer 2f out and sn trcking ldng pair: shkn up and qcknd to ld ins fnl f: easily* 11/8 1
00-1 2 2½ **Jack's Revenge (IRE)**9 [456] 3-9-6 **56** 6ex (p) MatthewDavies(3) 2 66
(George Baker) *sn led: rdn along 3f out: hdd narrowly 2f out: drvn and rallied ent fnl f: ev ch tl outpcd by wnr last 100yds* 3/1 3
05-2 3 nk **Three Opera Divas**9 [456] 3-9-7 **54** JoeFanning 4 63
(Mark Johnston) *cl up: chal 3f out: rdn to take narrow advantage 2f out: drvn wl over 1f out: hdd and one pce ins fnl f* 17/2
3-31 4 4½ **Ace Master**2 [550] 3-9-10 **57** 6ex JimmyQuinn 1 56
(Roy Bowring) *t.k.h: chsd ldng pair on inner: rdn along wl over 2f out: grad wknd* 9/4 2

1m 42.95s (-0.75) **Going Correction** -0.075s/f (Stan) 4 Ran SP% 108.4
Speed ratings (Par 95): **100,97,97,92**
CSF £5.73 TOTE £1.40 ; EX 4.30.
Owner Reach For The Bucks Racing Partnership **Bred** Miss D Gibbins **Trained** Newmarket, Suffolk

FOCUS
Only four runners but the unexposed, gambled-on winner easily trumped three at the top of their game and this is probably decent form for the grade. It makes sense with the third and fourth running pretty much to the pound from their recent C&D meeting. The pace wasn't strong.

568 BUY TICKETS @ SOUTHWELL-RACECOURSE.CO.UK (S) STKS 1m (F)
2:20 (2:20) (Class 6) 4-Y-O+ £1,535 (£453; £226) Stalls Low

Form RPR
-605 1 **General Tufto**7 [496] 6-9-3 69 (b) MartinLane 3 71
(Charles Smith) *sn rdn along and outpcd in rr: hdwy on outer 3f out: styd on strly to ld 1 1/2f out: clr ent fnl f* 11/4 2
4442 2 3¾ **Elusive Warrior (USA)**2 [547] 8-8-10 66 (p) NoraLooby(7) 4 62
(Alan McCabe) *chsd ldng pair: hdwy over 2f out: rdn wl over 1f out: sn drvn: kpt on to take 2nd ins fnl f* 2/1 1
-060 3 6 **Duplicity**8 [470] 4-8-11 70 J-PGuillambert 2 43
(James Given) *led: hdd 1/2-way: cl up tl led again wl over 2f out: sn rdn and hdd 1 1/2f out: sn drvn and one pce* 11/2
0-64 4 3½ **Crocodile Bay (IRE)**2 [547] 8-8-8 55 (b) AndrewHeffernan(3) 1 35
(Richard Guest) *plld hrd: chsd ldrs on inner: hdwy over 2f out: sn rdn and ch tl drvn and wknd over 1f out* 7/1
030- 5 5 **Bajan Pride**171 [5596] 7-8-11 61 MickyFenton 5 23
(Paul Midgley) *cl up: led 1/2-way: rdn along and hdd wl over 2f out: sn wknd* 7/2 3

1m 42.84s (-0.86) **Going Correction** -0.075s/f (Stan) 5 Ran SP% 110.1
Speed ratings (Par 101): **101,97,91,87,82**
toteswinger: 1&2 £3.60. CSF £8.67 TOTE £4.80 : £4.60, £1.10; EX 8.20.There was no bid for the winner.
Owner Phil Martin & Trev Sleath **Bred** Hascombe And Valiant Studs **Trained** Temple Bruer, Lincs

FOCUS
An ordinary seller run at a decent clip considering the size of the field. It is rated around the runner-up but is not form to be confident about.

569 DINE IN THE PANTRY MEDIAN AUCTION MAIDEN STKS 1m 4f (F)
2:50 (2:50) (Class 6) 4-6-Y-O £1,535 (£453; £226) Stalls Low

Form RPR
5-65 1 **Davana**6 [507] 5-9-1 44 (p) LukeMorris 3 54
(Bill Ratcliffe) *trckd ldrs: hdwy 4f out: led 3f out: rdn clr and hung bdly rt over 2f out: eased ins fnl f* 9/4 2
20-0 2 11 **Astrodiva**24 [277] 5-9-1 49 NeilCallan 4 31
(Mark H Tompkins) *led: rdn along and hdd 3f out: sn drvn and plugged on one pce fr wl over 1f out* 15/8 1
0-63 3 15 **Sirdave**22 [309] 5-9-6 53 ChrisCatlin 1 12
(Peter Hiatt) *trckd ldr: effrt 4f out: rdn along over 3f out: sn outpcd* 5/2 3
0-40 4 36 **Harrys**5 [524] 4-9-3 52 J-PGuillambert 5 —
(Jane Chapple-Hyam) *dwlt and reminders s: sn trcking ldrs: rdn along over 5f out: sn wknd and bhd* 7/1

2m 44.54s (3.54) **Going Correction** -0.075s/f (Stan)
WFA 4 from 5yo 3lb 4 Ran SP% **106.6**
Speed ratings: **85,77,67,43**
CSF £6.63 TOTE £4.10 ; EX 8.20.
Owner T B Tarn **Bred** P T Tellwright **Trained** Newmarket, Suffolk

FOCUS
A very weak maiden indeed, in which the winner was probably the only runner to handle the surface. It is highly unlikely that she improved.

570 DINE IN THE QUEEN MOTHER RESTAURANT CLAIMING STKS 1m 4f (F)
3:25 (3:26) (Class 6) 4-Y-O+ £1,535 (£453; £226) Stalls Low

Form RPR
24/1 1 **La Estrella (USA)**16 [374] 8-9-10 80 DaneO'Neill 2 79
(Don Cantillon) *hld up in tch: hdwy over 4f out: effrt to chse ldng pair 2f out: rdn and edgd lft over 1f out: drvn and kpt on to ld nr fin* 8/11 1
3-04 2 ½ **Eton Fable (IRE)**8 [474] 6-8-10 64 (p) LukeMorris 5 64
(Bill Ratcliffe) *trckd ldr: cl up 1/2-way: rdn to ld over 2f out: drvn over 1f out: edgd rt ins fnl f: hdd and no ex towards fin* 10/1 3
2223 3 ¾ **Camps Bay (USA)**6 [514] 7-9-4 73 HayleyTurner 3 71
(Conor Dore) *hld up in rr: hdwy over 3f out: chsd ldrs 2f out: rdn: n.m.r and swtchd lft ent fnl f: drvn and styd on towards fin* 7/4 2
035- 4 1 **Royal Holiday (IRE)**15 [7899] 4-8-7 58 TomEaves 6 61
(Brian Ellison) *led: rdn along 3f out: hdd over 2f out and sn drvn: ev ch over 1f out: edgd rt ent fnl f: kpt on same pce* 22/1
0-5 5 16 **Bullring (FR)**22 [11] 5-8-10 0 BarryMcHugh 4 36
(Peter Niven) *reminders after s and sn chsng ldng pair: rdn along 5f out: sn wknd* 50/1

2m 41.29s (0.29) **Going Correction** -0.075s/f (Stan)
WFA 4 from 5yo+ 3lb 5 Ran SP% **109.7**
Speed ratings (Par 101): **96,95,95,94,83**
toteswinger: 1&2 £4.80. CSF £8.96 TOTE £2.20 : £1.30, £1.50; EX 8.20.
Owner Don Cantillon **Bred** Five Horses Ltd And Theatrical Syndicate **Trained** Newmarket, Suffolk

FOCUS
Not much between the runners on adjusted official ratings and a tight finish at the end of a steadily-run affair. The winner did not need to match his old form.

571 DOWNLOAD THE BLUE SQUARE IPHONE APP H'CAP 5f (F)
4:00 (4:00) (Class 5) (0-70,68) 4-Y-O+ £2,354 (£695; £347) Stalls High

Form RPR
0-11 1 **Shawkantango**14 [401] 4-8-11 **58** (v) RobbieFitzpatrick 4 70
(Derek Shaw) *dwlt and sltly hmpd s: in rr and swtchd lft to outer after 1f: rdn along 1/2-way: hdwy wl over 1f out: drvn and styd on strly to ld last 100yds* 2/1 1
-416 2 1 **Sleepy Blue Ocean**7 [491] 5-9-6 **67** (p) LukeMorris 6 75
(John Balding) *prom: effrt to chal wl over 1f out: rdn to ld ent fnl f: hdd and nt qckn last 100yds* 7/2 3
-024 3 ¾ **Colorus (IRE)**6 [506] 8-9-0 **68** (v) MatthewCosham(7) 1 73
(Bill Ratcliffe) *led: rdn wl over 1f out: drvn and hdd ent fnl f: one pce* 6/1
60-0 4 2¼ **Mata Hari Blue**7 [491] 5-8-9 **56** KirstyMilczarek 2 53
(John Holt) *chsd ldrs: hdwy 1/2-way: rdn wl over 1f out: sn drvn and one pce fnl f* 33/1
30-1 5 1¾ **Tsar Bomba (USA)**9 [453] 4-9-2 **63** 6ex LeeNewman 3 54
(David Barron) *towards rr: effrt 1/2-way: rdn wl over 1f out: sn no imp* 3/1 2
60-0 6 hd **Cavitie**14 [401] 5-8-11 **58** KellyHarrison 5 48
(Andrew Reid) *chsd ldrs: n.m.r and lost pl after 1f: a towards rr after* 9/1
4-35 7 hd **Guto**14 [401] 8-8-10 **57** MartinLane 7 46
(Bill Ratcliffe) *prom: rdn along over 2f out: drvn and wknd wl over 1f out* 25/1

59.17 secs (-0.53) **Going Correction** -0.025s/f (Stan) 7 Ran SP% **111.6**
Speed ratings (Par 103): **103,101,100,96,93 93,93**
toteswingers: 1&2 £1.90, 1&3 £3.00, 2&3 £2.60. CSF £8.77 TOTE £5.20 : £3.60, £1.50; EX 9.50.
Owner Mrs Lyndsey Shaw **Bred** Derek Shaw **Trained** Sproxton, Leics

FOCUS
Quite a competitive sprint despite the numbers, with nearly half the field coming here in top form. The first two should continue to do well in similar events. The form is rated around the second and third.

572 JOE GOLDING 18TH BIRTHDAY H'CAP 7f (F)
4:35 (4:36) (Class 5) (0-75,80) 4-Y-O+ £1,910 (£564; £282) Stalls Low

Form RPR
-111 1 **Steed**7 [495] 4-9-13 **80** 12ex (p) PhillipMakin 8 94+
(Kevin Ryan) *in tch: hdwy on outer wl over 2f out: rdn along wl over 1f out: led appr fnl f: kpt on wl* 6/5 1
0-56 2 2 **Thunderball**33 [175] 5-8-12 **72** (b) LeonnaMayor(7) 6 80
(David Nicholls) *cl up: led wl over 2f out: rdn wl over 1f out: hdd appr fnl f and kpt on same pce* 15/2
60-1 3 3½ **Smalljohn**24 [285] 5-9-7 **74** (v) TomEaves 1 73
(Bryan Smart) *chsd ldrs on inner: rdn along over 2f out: swtchd rt and drvn over 1f out: sn one pce* 6/1 3
6-05 4 1½ **Buzz Bird**23 [291] 4-8-7 **60** LeeNewman 3 55
(David Barron) *in rr: rdn along and hdwy on inner over 2f out: sn drvn and no imp* 14/1
1342 5 1¼ **Ace Of Spies (IRE)**9 [455] 6-9-5 **72** KirstyMilczarek 2 64
(Conor Dore) *led: rdn along 3f out: hdd over 2f out and grad wknd* 8/1
5211 6 1¼ **Elhamri**9 [455] 7-9-11 **78** 6ex HayleyTurner 5 66
(Conor Dore) *chsd ldng pair: rdn along wl over 2f out: drvn wl over 1f out and sn wknd* 5/1 2

0-00 **7** *nse* **Gala Casino Star (IRE)**[15] 385 6-9-6 **73** .... BarryMcHugh 7 61
(Richard Fahey) *a in rr* **33/1**
1m 28.39s (-1.91) **Going Correction** -0.075s/f (Stan) **7** Ran SP% **108.9**
Speed ratings (Par 103): **107,104,100,99,97 96,96**
toteswingers: 1&2 £2.40, 1&3 £2.80, 2&3 £5.10. CSF £9.67 CT £33.25 TOTE £1.70: £1.10, £4.90; EX 10.70 Trifecta £70.20 Pool: £632.56 - 6.66 winning units..
Owner Mrs J Ryan **Bred** Rosyground Stud **Trained** Hambleton, N Yorks
FOCUS
Three last-time-out winners in opposition but only one the market wanted to know about, and another improved performance from the still-improving winner to defy a double penalty. He may have more to offer. The pace looked decent.

573 PLAY ROULETTE AT BLUESQ.COM APPRENTICE H'CAP 1m (F)
5:05 (5:06) (Class 6) (0-58,64) 4-Y-0+ **£1,535** (£453; £226) **Stalls** Low

Form RPR
3-31 **1** **Almahaza (IRE)**[6] 504 7-9-6 **64** 6ex......................... ThomasBrown(5) 6 81
(Adrian Chamberlain) *hld up in tch: hdwy over 3f out: rdn to ld 2f out: sn hung lft and clr: v easily* **8/11**[1]
4116 **2** *7* **Very Well Red**[1] 553 8-8-12 **58**................................ CharlesBishop(7) 5 59
(Peter Hiatt) *cl up: led over 3f out: rdn and hdd 2f out: kpt on: no ch w wnr* **4/1**[2]
3500 **3** *4 ½* **Escardo (GER)**[1] 552 8-8-2 **46** oh1................................... IanBurns(5) 4 37
(David Bridgwater) *in rr: hdwy 3f out: sn rdn and kpt on same pce: tk modest 3rd nr fin* **13/2**[3]
-400 **4** *hd* **Archilini**[2] 545 6-8-3 **49** oh1 ow3.......................(be) JacobButterfield(7) 2 39
(Brian Ellison) *chsd ldrs on inner: rdn along 3f out: sn outpcd: lost modest 3rd nr fin* **7/1**
500- **5** *16* **Tiger Hawk (USA)**[184] 5171 4-9-4 **57**...........................(b) AlexEdwards 1 —
(Kevin M Prendergast) *led: pushed along 1/2-way: hdd over 3f out and sn wknd* **14/1**
000- **6** *11* **Marron Flore**[281] 2021 8-8-2 **46** oh1..........................(t) GemmaElford(5) 3 —
(Alastair Lidderdale) *chsd ldrs: rdn along over 3f out: sn lost pl and bhd* **66/1**
1m 42.77s (-0.93) **Going Correction** -0.075s/f (Stan) **6** Ran SP% **111.9**
Speed ratings (Par 101): **101,94,89,89,73 62**
toteswingers: 1&2 £1.50, 1&3 £2.30, 2&3 £1.90. toteSuper7: WIN: Not won. PLACE: £20.80. CSF £3.93 TOTE £1.90: £1.10, £1.60; EX 3.30.
Owner G B Heffaran **Bred** Castletown And Associates **Trained** Ashton Keynes, Wilts
FOCUS
Little strength in depth in a modest finale run at a fair pace. Though this was a weak race the winner could be underrated.
T/Plt: £98.80 to a £1 stake. Pool: £54,087.81 - 399.29 winning tickets. T/Qpdt: £16.40 to a £1 stake. Pool: £3,277.26 - 147.80 winning tickets. JR

537 WOLVERHAMPTON (A.W) (L-H)
Thursday, February 17

OFFICIAL GOING: Standard
Wind: Light, across Weather: Dry, cloudy

574 ENHANCED SP'S AT BLUESQ.COM APPRENTICE H'CAP 1m 1f 103y(P)
5:30 (5:30) (Class 6) (0-58,58) 4-Y-0+ **£1,535** (£453; £226) **Stalls** Low

Form RPR
2-06 **1** **Petomic (IRE)**[13] 428 6-9-5 **58**....................................... TobyAtkinson 5 62+
(Richard Guest) *plld hrd early: hld up towards rr: rdn to chse ldrs ent fnl 2f: n.m.r briefly over 1f out: r.o wl ins fnl f to ld nr fin* **5/1**[2]
50-0 **2** *shd* **Aurora Lights**[20] 340 4-8-7 **46** oh1.................................... LeeTopliss 3 50
(Richard Fahey) *s.i.s: hld up in rr: pushed along and hdwy on outer 5f out: c wd and drvn over 1f out: r.o wl fnl f to go 2nd nr fin* **16/1**
-006 **3** *nk* **King Of Connacht**[13] 425 8-8-9 **53**...........................(v) LucyKBarry(5) 2 56+
(Mark Wellings) *t.k.h: hld up in midfield: lost pl and dropped to rr over 4f out: hdwy to chse ldrs and nt clr run ent fnl f: swtchd rt ins fnl f: r.o wl to go 3rd nr fin* **5/1**[2]
-206 **4** *½* **Lord Deevert**[8] 346 6-8-9 **53**...................................... JakePayne(5) 7 55
(Bill Turner) *in tch: hdwy to chse ldrs 5f out: ev ch 2f out: rdn to ld over 1f out: kpt on wl u.p tl hdd and lost 3 pls fnl 50yds* **4/1**[1]
00-0 **5** *1 ¼* **Naledi**[20] 346 7-8-4 **46** oh1................................ JamesRogers(3) 6 45
(Richard Price) *t.k.h: chsd ldr tl 2f out: stl chsng ldrs and rdn over 1f out: kpt on same pce ins fnl f* **17/2**
000- **6** *5* **Clearing House**[142] 6439 6-8-4 **46** oh1......................... RosieJessop(3) 8 35
(John Ryan) *in tch: rdn and ev ch ent fnl 2f: wknd fnl f* **25/1**
353- **7** *hd* **Filun**[157] 6022 6-8-8 **52**...(t) RichardRowe(5) 9 40
(Anthony Middleton) *stdd s: hld up in rr: hdwy 5f out: pressed ldrs on outer and rdn ent fnl 2f: wknd fnl f* **6/1**[3]
05-0 **8** *4 ½* **Bestowed**[21] 181 6-9-5 **58**..(b[1]) AmyBaker 4 37
(Tim Vaughan) *racd keenly: led: rdn and hdd over 1f out: sn wknd* **4/1**[1]
06/0 **9** *8* **House Of Rules**[23] 291 4-8-11 **50**................................... DaleSwift 1 12
(Julie Camacho) *in tch in midfield: rdn and struggling u.p 4f out: sn bhd* **20/1**
2m 4.24s (2.54) **Going Correction** +0.125s/f (Slow) **9** Ran SP% **112.6**
Speed ratings (Par 101): **93,92,92,92,91 86,86,82,75**
toteswingers: 1&2 £13.00, 1&3 £5.40, 2&3 £20.20. CSF £77.79 CT £416.42 TOTE £11.10: £2.80, £7.30, £2.30; EX 56.00.
Owner Johnson Racing **Bred** Neil McGrath **Trained** Stainforth, S Yorks
■ Stewards' Enquiry : Toby Atkinson one-day ban: careless riding (Mar 3)
Lee Topliss one-day ban: used whip with excessive frequency (Mar 3)
FOCUS
Most of the runners were struggling for form in this weak apprentice handicap. There was a lively market and a tight five-way finish in a steadily run race. The winner was a few pounds off last year's turf form.
Bestowed Official explanation: jockey said gelding ran flat

575 SPONSOR A RACE BY CALLING 01902 390000 H'CAP 7f 32y(P)
6:00 (6:01) (Class 7) (0-50,54) 4-Y-0+ **£1,535** (£453; £226) **Stalls** Low

Form RPR
5-01 **1** **Polemica (IRE)**[3] 537 5-9-7 **54** 6ex.............................(bt) JamesDoyle 8 62+
(Frank Sheridan) *hld up in rr of main gp: gd hdwy to trck ldr gng wl over 1f out: pushed along to ld ins fnl f: rdn fnl 100yds: r.o wl* **5/1**[3]
0-04 **2** *¾* **St Ignatius**[10] 445 4-8-10 **50**...............................(p) HobieGill(7) 10 56
(Michael Appleby) *chsd ldr tl led jst over 2f out: rdn over 1f out: hdd ins fnl f: kpt on wl but a hld* **40/1**
5505 **3** *2 ¾* **Quick Single (USA)**[15] 386 5-9-0 **47** ow2.......................(v) AdamKirby 9 46
(Phil McEntee) *racd in last trio: hdwy u.p over 1f out: styd on wl to go 3rd towards fin: nvr trbld ldrs* **14/1**
-301 **4** *½* **Bold Bomber**[6] 517 5-9-4 **51** 6ex........................... SilvestreDeSousa 11 49
(Paul Green) *chsd ldrs: rdn and effrt wl over 1f out: 3rd and nt pce of ldng pair ent fnl f: plugged on same pce after: lost 3rd towards fin* **11/2**
6615 **5** *4 ½* **Aggbag**[8] 466 7-9-3 **50**... RobertWinston 3 44
(Tony Carroll) *racd in tch in midfield: pushed along 6f out: rdn and effrt to chse ldrs over 1f out: wknd 1f out: wl btn and eased ins fnl f* **5/2**[1]
4-30 **6** *2 ½* **Lady Rossetti**[14] 409 4-9-2 **49**.....................................(v[1]) GeorgeBaker 2 28
(Marcus Tregoning) *chsd ldrs: hdwy to press ldrs ent fnl 2f: rdn and sn btn over 1f out: fdd and hung bdly rt fnl f* **9/2**[2]
060- **7** *¾* **Helpmeronda**[329] 979 5-9-2 **49**.................................... GrahamGibbons 5 26
(Ian Williams) *s.i.s: sn outpcd and rdn along in last trio: sme hdwy fnl f: n.d* **20/1**
0/0- **8** *3 ¼* **Eilean Eeve**[113] 7170 5-8-12 **45**...................................... NeilCallan 6 13
(George Foster) *chsd ldrs: c wd and drvn wl over 1f out: sn wknd* **66/1**
/033 **9** *3 ¼* **Meydan Style (USA)**[20] 340 5-8-12 **45**............................ JoeFanning 4 —
(Bruce Hellier) *chsd ldrs: rdn ent fnl 2f: c wd wl over 1f out: sn wknd* **9/2**[2]
06-0 **10** *1 ½* **Five Gold Rings (IRE)**[8] 464 5-8-8 **48**...................... RichardRowe(7) 7 —
(Seamus Durack) *led tl jst over 1f out: wknd qckly over 1f out: fdd fnl f* **66/1**
404- **11** *10* **Happy The Man (IRE)**[187] 5097 4-8-12 **45**..................... CathyGannon 1 —
(John Norton) *sn outpcd and rdn along in rr: lost tch 4f out* **66/1**
00-0 **12** *1* **Ring Of Fire**[18] 355 4-8-12 **45**.....................................(b[1]) SamHitchcott 12 —
(John Spearing) *dwlt: in tch on outer: dropped to rr u.p over 2f out: wl bhd over 1f out* **50/1**
1m 30.26s (0.66) **Going Correction** +0.125s/f (Slow) **12** Ran SP% **117.3**
Speed ratings (Par 97): **101,100,97,96,91 88,87,83,80,78 67,65**
toteswingers: 1&2 £34.70, 1&3 £11.80, 2&3 £26.00. CSF £197.96 CT £2594.99 TOTE £6.60: £1.80, £12.20, £3.40; EX 91.00.
Owner Scuderia A4/5 **Bred** Mervyn Stewkesbury **Trained** Wolverhampton, W Midlands
FOCUS
A weak handicap but it was run at a decent pace and the first two pulled clear. The winner is rated back to her best early form.
Meydan Style(USA) Official explanation: trainer's rep said gelding finished lame
Happy The Man(IRE) Official explanation: jockey said gelding hung badly left-handed throughout

576 ENJOY THE PARTY PACK GROUP OFFER CLAIMING STKS 7f 32y(P)
6:30 (6:31) (Class 6) 3-Y-O **£1,569** (£463; £231) **Stalls** Low

Form RPR
2331 **1** **Honkers Bonkers**[7] 494 3-8-5 **61**...................................(v) LukeMorris 4 67
(Alan McCabe) *sn led: set stdy gallop tl rdn and qcknd over 2f out: hanging lft u.p over 1f out: r.o wl: in command fnl 150yds* **7/2**[3]
112- **2** *3 ½* **My Lord**[71] 7762 3-9-6 **82**.. KierenFox(3) 2 76
(Bill Turner) *t.k.h: trckd ldr tl over 4f out: rdn whn gallop qcknd over 2f out: chsd wnr ent fnl f: no imp and a hld* **13/8**[2]
5112 **3** *¾* **Better Self**[13] 423 3-8-8 **74**.. CathyGannon 1 59
(David Evans) *chsd ldr on outer: wnt 2nd over 4f out: rdn whn gallop qcknd over 2f out: unable qck and lost 2nd ent fnl f: 3rd and wl hld after* **1/1**[1]
200- **4** *7* **Lindo Erro**[134] 6673 3-8-2 **54**...................................... JimmyQuinn 3 37
(John Mackie) *a last: rdn wl over 2f out: outpcd ent fnl 2f: sn wl btn: eased wl ins fnl f* **33/1**
1m 31.79s (2.19) **Going Correction** +0.125s/f (Slow) **4** Ran SP% **113.3**
Speed ratings (Par 95): **92,88,87,79**
CSF £9.98 TOTE £5.10; EX 9.10.Honkers Bonkers was the subject of a friendly claim.
Owner Rupert Plersch **Bred** J Atkinson **Trained** Averham Park, Notts
FOCUS
A tight claimer. The pace was steady and it became very tactical. The winner enjoyed an easy lead but has been rated in line with a best view of his previous form.

577 NAME A RACE TO ENHANCE YOUR BRAND H'CAP 5f 216y(P)
7:00 (7:01) (Class 5) (0-75,75) 4-Y-0+ **£2,266** (£674; £337; £168) **Stalls** Low

Form RPR
40-0 **1** **Tasmeem (IRE)**[10] 446 4-9-7 **75**...................................(b) TomQueally 11 83
(David Nicholls) *t.k.h: chsd ldng pair: rdn to ld jst over 1f out: edgd lft but in command and r.o wl fnl f* **16/1**
0-34 **2** *1* **Dark Lane**[41] [illegible] 5-9-2 [illegible]...(p) LeeTopliss(5) 8 [illegible]
(Richard Fahey) *in tch in midfield: pushed along 1/2-way: hdwy and rdn over 1f out: chsd wnr ins fnl f: kpt on but nvr gng pce to chal wnr* **7/2**[1]
0-23 **3** *hd* **Diapason (IRE)**[10] 446 5-9-6 **74**......................(t) RichardKingscote 12 78+
(Tom Dascombe) *towards rr on outer: c wd and rdn wl over 1f out: hdwy u.p ins fnl f: r.o wl fnl 100yds: nt rch ldrs* **11/1**
65-2 **4** *1* **Valmina**[14] 403 4-8-9 **63**.. LukeMorris 4 64
(Tony Carroll) *chsd ldrs: rdn and unable qck 2f out: styd on same pce u.p fnl f* **7/2**[1]
-030 **5** *1* **Fantasy Fighter (IRE)**[5] 521 6-9-0 **71**........................... KierenFox(3) 9 69+
(John Quinn) *stdd after s: plld hrd early: hld up in rr: hdwy over 1f out: rdn and r.o ins fnl f: nvr able to chal* **15/2**[3]
00-0 **6** *nk* **Bahamian Lad**[21] 316 6-9-5 **73**....................................(p) AdamKirby 5 70
(Reg Hollinshead) *chsd ldr tl wl over 1f out: unable qck u.p ent fnl f: wknd fnl 150yds* **11/1**
0-40 **7** *½* **Tourist**[30] 199 6-9-4 **72**.. JimmyQuinn 6 67
(Derek Shaw) *hld up towards rr on inner: rdn and effrt over 1f out: no imp u.p ins fnl f: kpt on same pce after* **12/1**
030- **8** *hd* **Sir Nod**[147] 6303 9-9-3 **71**... BarryMcHugh 2 66
(Julie Camacho) *rdr removed hood late and slowly away: bhd: rdn ent fnl 2f: swtchd lft and drvn 1f out: kpt on but nvr trbld ldrs* **7/1**[2]
000- **9** *1 ¼* **Defector (IRE)**[illegible] [illegible] [illegible] [illegible]... [illegible] 1 [illegible]
(David Bourton) *led: rdn jst over 2f out: hdd jst over 1f out: wknd ins fnl f* **20/1**
420- **10** *1 ¼* **Avontuur (FR)**[147] 6310 9-8-4 **61**........................ JamesSullivan(3) 7 48
(Ruth Carr) *taken down early: restless in stalls: in tch towards rr: rdn and struggling over 3f out: bhd and no prog fnl 2f* **40/1**
-504 **11** *1* **Gwilym (GER)**[20] 336 8-8-11 **65**................................ DaneO'Neill 3 48
(Derek Haydn Jones) *t.k.h: chsd ldrs: wknd u.p wl over 1f out: bhd and eased wl ins fnl f* **9/1**
1m 15.1s (0.10) **Going Correction** +0.125s/f (Slow) **11** Ran SP% **116.2**
Speed ratings (Par 103): **104,102,102,101,99 99,98,98,96,95 93**
toteswingers: 1&2 £14.00, 1&3 £6.30, 2&3 £7.70. CSF £70.55 CT £516.07 TOTE £37.00: £8.00, £1.60, £5.40; EX 79.60.
Owner Dr Marwan Koukash **Bred** Max Ervine **Trained** Sessay, N Yorks
FOCUS
A fair sprint handicap run in a moderate time. The winner is rated back to his 3yo form with the next two close to their marks.
Tasmeem(IRE) Official explanation: trainer's rep said, regardingapparent improvement in form, that the gelding had benefited from a drop in trip.

Sir Nod Official explanation: jockey said blinds were stuck when he tried to remove them and gelding missed the break

578 DOWNLOAD THE BLUE SQUARE IPHONE APP H'CAP 5f 216y(P)

7:30 (7:30) (Class 4) (0-85,82) 3-Y-O **£3,464** (£1,030; £515; £257) **Stalls** Low

Form RPR

3-41 **1** **Sacrosanctus**^{29} [208] 3-9-1 **76**.. IanMongan 8 86
(David Nicholls) *broke wl to ld and crossed to rail: stdd gallop over 4f out: rdn and qcknd ent fnl 2f: clr and in command 1f out: comf* **10/1**

-441 **2** *4 ½* **Restless Bay (IRE)**^{3} [538] 3-8-13 **74** 6ex........................(v) ChrisCatlin 4 70
(Reg Hollinshead) *t.k.h: chsd ldrs tl wnt 2nd over 4f out: rdn ent fnl 2f: outpcd and swtchd lft 1f out: one pce and no ch w wnr after* **7/1**^{3}

-311 **3** *1 ½* **Kingscroft (IRE)**^{19} [349] 3-9-1 **76**...................................... GregFairley 7 67
(Mark Johnston) *racd wd: towards rr tl hdwy to chse ldrs 4f out: rdn and outpcd ent fnl 2f: no threat to wnr but rallied ins fnl f to snatch 3rd on post* **11/4**^{2}

41-2 **4** *nse* **Insolenceofoffice (IRE)**^{26} [263] 3-9-7 **82**..................(p) GeorgeBaker 6 73
(Andrew Crook) *chsd ldrs: rdn and nt pce of wnr ent fnl 2f: 3rd and wl hld 1f out: lost 3rd on post* **15/2**

0-16 **5** *¾* **Liberty Green (IRE)**^{22} [302] 3-9-1 **76**.............................. JamesDoyle 2 65
(Alan McCabe) *chsd ldr tl over 4f out: rdn and lost pl 1/2-way: styd on same pce and no ch w wnr fr wl over 1f out* **16/1**

3232 **6** *nk* **Captain Dimitrios**^{8} [476] 3-9-0 **75**..............................(v) CathyGannon 3 63
(David Evans) *t.k.h: hld up in midfield: swtchd rt jst over 4f out: rdn 1/2-way: sn outpcd and no ch w wnr whn swtchd lft jst ins fnl f: kpt on* **20/1**

14-2 **7** *1* **Diamond Charlie (IRE)**^{29} [208] 3-9-3 **78**...................... HayleyTurner 5 62
(Simon Dow) *t.k.h: hld up in last pair: bmpd and pushed rt jst over 4f out: rdn and no prog jst over 2f out: n.d: eased towards fin* **9/4**^{1}

-242 **8** *3 ½* **Reginald Claude**^{18} [358] 3-8-10 **71**................................ DaneO'Neill 1 44
(Mark Usher) *dwlt: a in rr: rdn and effrt on inner wl over 1f out: no imp and wl hld 1f out: wknd ins fnl f: eased towards fin* **7/1**^{3}

1m 14.43s (-0.57) **Going Correction** +0.125s/f (Slow) **8** Ran SP% **113.9**
Speed ratings (Par 99): **108,102,100,99,98 98,97,92**
toteswingers: 1&2 £4.10, 1&3 £3.00, 2&3 £2.90. CSF £76.61 CT £248.53 TOTE £17.10: £4.50, £2.40, £1.10; EX 39.60.

Owner Paul J Dixon **Bred** Worksop Manor Stud **Trained** Sessay, N Yorks

FOCUS
A decent handicap, involving three last-time-out winners and four others who finished runner-up on their latest start. The pace was steady and nothing landed a blow behind the trailblazing winner, who was seemingly much improved. The runner-up was close to his best with the rest 10lb+ off.

579 RINGSIDE SUITE MEDIAN AUCTION MAIDEN STKS 1m 141y(P)

8:00 (8:00) (Class 6) 3-5-Y-O **£1,535** (£453; £226) **Stalls** Low

Form RPR

5-32 **1** **Tagansky**^{12} [434] 3-8-8 70 ow1.. NeilCallan 5 68+
(Simon Dow) *hld up in tch: sltly hmpd wl over 3f out: sn rcvrd and travelling wl: rdn and qcknd through gap to ld jst over 1f out: r.o wl: comf* **5/4**^{1}

2 *2 ¼* **Black Pond (USA)** 3-8-7 0.. JoeFanning 2 62+
(Mark Johnston) *chsd ldr tl over 6f out: rdn to press ldr again 3f out: led wl over 1f out: hdd jst over 1f out: nt pce of wnr ins fnl f* **5/2**^{2}

03 **3** *1* **Rich And Reckless**^{18} [360] 4-9-9 0.................................. IanMongan 3 60
(Tobias B P Coles) *hld up in last pair: rdn and effrt on outer to chse ldrs wl over 1f out: nt pce of wnr and styd on same pce fnl f* **11/2**^{3}

0-6 **4** *¾* **Bertie Blu Boy**^{6} [516] 3-8-7 0.............................. SilvestreDeSousa 4 58
(Paul Green) *led: rdn 4f out: hdd wl over 1f out: styd pressing ldrs tl wknd ins fnl f* **80/1**

4 **5** *6* **Freedom Flyer (IRE)**^{13} [431] 3-8-2 0........................ TobyAtkinson(5) 1 44
(Marco Botti) *hld up in last pair: rdn and struggling over 3f out: lost tch jst over 2f out* **11/1**

0- **6** *¾* **Osgoodisgood**^{136} [6635] 3-8-7 0.................................(t) NickyMackay 6 42
(Stuart Williams) *dwlt: sn rcvrd: chsd ldr 6f out tl 3f out: wknd wl over 1f out: sn bhd* **7/1**

1m 51.44s (0.94) **Going Correction** +0.125s/f (Slow)
WFA 3 from 4yo 21lb **6** Ran SP% **110.5**
Speed ratings (Par 101): **100,98,97,96,91 90**
toteswingers: 1&2 £1.50, 1&3 £2.60, 2&3 £5.70. CSF £4.39 TOTE £2.30: £1.50, £1.10; EX 5.40.

Owner Nick Hawkins **Bred** Sir Eric Parker & Mrs Mary Ann Parker **Trained** Epsom, Surrey

FOCUS
An ordinary maiden, in which a fairly exposed sort cashed in on a good opportunity. The form is rated around the winner with the proximity of the fourth dubious.

580 PLAY ROULETTE AT BLUESQ.COM FILLIES' H'CAP 1m 141y(P)

8:30 (8:30) (Class 5) (0-75,63) 4-Y-O+ **£2,007** (£597; £298; £149) **Stalls** Low

Form RPR

55-1 **1** **Stargazing (IRE)**^{20} [346] 5-8-13 **55**.................................... AdamKirby 5 67
(Marco Botti) *hld up in last pair: hdwy 4f out: chsd ldr over 2f out: rdn to ld wl over 1f out: hld on wl ins fnl f* **10/11**^{1}

-211 **2** *½* **No Complaining (IRE)**^{22} [299] 4-9-6 **62**.......................... TomQueally 3 72
(Barney Curley) *racd off the pce in last: hdwy 4f out: wnt 3rd 3f out: rdn to chse wnr over 1f out: sustained chal u.p fnl f: no imp and hld fnl 50yds* **13/8**^{2}

-335 **3** *4 ½* **Tomintoul Star**^{14} [397] 5-8-9 **54**............................(b1) JamesSullivan(3) 4 54
(Ruth Carr) *sn bustled along to ld: racd keenly whn in front: jnd over 4f out: wnt clr 3f out: rdn ent fnl 2f: hdd over 1f out: wknd fnl f* **12/1**

0-4 **4** *14* **Lady Excel (IRE)**^{30} [200] 5-9-6 **62**................................ MickyFenton 2 30
(Brian Rothwell) *chsd ldr: hdwy to join ldr over 4f out tl 3f out: sn struggling: wknd over 2f out: wl bhd ent fnl f* **11/1**^{3}

026/ **5** *2 ¾* **Lilyannabanana**^{523} [5852] 4-9-7 **63**................................ CathyGannon 1 24
(David Evans) *chsd ldrs tl dropped to last 4f out: sn rdn and struggling: wl bhd fnl 2f* **40/1**

1m 51.39s (0.89) **Going Correction** +0.125s/f (Slow) **5** Ran SP% **108.9**
Speed ratings (Par 100): **101,100,96,84,81**
CSF £2.54 TOTE £2.30: £2.70, £1.02; EX 2.40.

Owner Can Artam **Bred** Paul Green **Trained** Newmarket, Suffolk

FOCUS
The two market leaders pulled clear of the rest in this this strongly run fillies' handicap, and look progressive. The form could be out a few pounds either way.

T/Plt: £454.60 to a £1 stake. Pool: £79,368.46 - 127.44 winning tickets. T/Qpdt: £30.50 to a £1 stake. Pool: £8,858.57 - 214.90 winning tickets. SP

497 MEYDAN (L-H)

Thursday, February 17

OFFICIAL GOING: Tapeta: standard; turf: good

The rail was out four meters on the turf course. Times suggested the Tapeta was riding slow.

581a ATTIJARI POINTS REWARD PROGRAM (H'CAP) (TURF) 1m 2f

2:25 (2:25) (100-110,110) 3-Y-O+

£46,153 (£15,384; £7,692; £3,846; £2,307; £1,538)

RPR

1 **Psychic Ability (USA)**^{21} [330] 4-8-10 104......................(v) TedDurcan 3 105
(Saeed Bin Suroor) *sn led: r.o wl fnl 1 1/2f: hld on gamely* **10/3**^{2}

2 *½* **Enak (ARG)**^{21} [330] 5-9-3 109...(t) FrankieDettori 4 110
(Saeed Bin Suroor) *trckd ldr: ev ch 1f out: nt qckn fnl 1/2f* **11/4**^{1}

3 *1 ¼* **Trois Rois (FR)**^{14} [416] 6-9-4 110...........(b) Christophe-PatriceLemaire 5 109
(I Mohammed, UAE) *mid-div on rail: r.o wl fnl 2f* **14/1**

4 *nse* **Lancelot (FR)**^{21} 4-9-3 110.. OlivierPeslier 6 108
(A De Mieulle, Qatar) *settled in rr: chsd ldrs 2f out: one pce fnl f* **7/1**

5 *1 ¼* **Bon Grain (FR)**^{21} [328] 6-8-9 101 ow1............................ PatCosgrave 2 97
(M bin Shafya, UAE) *trckd ldrs: one pce fnl 2f* **33/1**

6 *½* **Emmrooz**^{34} 6-9-2 108...(v) WilliamBuick 1 103+
(D Selvaratnam, UAE) *s.i.s: settled in rr: rdn 4f out: sn btn* **7/2**^{3}

7 *6* **Shimmering Moment (USA)**^{14} [417] 4-9-0 107............. RyanMoore 8 90
(James J Hartnett, Ire) *nvr bttr than mid-div* **5/1**

8 *26* **Florentino (JPN)**^{14} [417] 5-9-2 108................................ AhmedAjtebi 7 39
(Mahmood Al Zarooni) *settled in rr: dropped away 3 1/2f out* **25/1**

2m 4.48s (124.48)
WFA 4 from 5yo+ 1lb **8** Ran SP% **114.6**
CSF: £12.99; Tricast: £110.12..

Owner Godolphin **Bred** Flaxman Holdings Ltd **Trained** Newmarket, Suffolk

FOCUS
They went a steady pace and the first two finishers raced one-two just about throughout. This is ordinary handicap Carnival form.

NOTEBOOK
Psychic Ability(USA) was behind the race-fit pair Enak and Trois Rois over this trip on Tapeta on his reappearance, but he was entitled to come on for that, had a visor reapplied and was back on the grass. He enjoyed the run of the race, dictating a modest tempo, before finding plenty when strongly challenged his stable companion. It's true to say plenty went his way, but he's clearly progressing well and is now 5-9 lifetime, and 5-7 on turf. (op 7-2)
Enak(ARG), seemingly the choice of Frankie Dettori, looked the winner when ranging upsides the long-time leader inside the final 2f, but failed to find extra. On his previous start he failed to convince he was giving everything under pressure and he again shaped as though some headgear might sharpen him. Either that or he needs a drop in trip. (op 5-2)
Trois Rois(FR) found this an insufficient test of stamina.
Lancelot(FR) finished a close third behind Beethoven in the Qatar Derby on his previous start and he gave that form some substance, not beaten far off a handicap mark of 110. Being held up so far off the steady pace didn't help his cause. (op 6-1)
Bon Grain(FR) didn't try to lead this time and offered little.
Emmrooz, whose last three wins have been gained on the Jebel Ali dirt, started slowly and never really travelled.
Shimmering Moment(USA) was nowhere near the form she showed when a close second over C&D on her previous start. (op 6-1)

582a ATTIJARI AL ISLAMI VISA INFINITE CARD (H'CAP) (TAPETA) 6f

3:05 (3:05) (95-122,122) 3-Y-O+

£57,692 (£19,230; £9,615; £4,807; £2,884; £1,923)

RPR

1 **Green Beret (IRE)**^{6} 5-8-5 99... AhmedAjtebi 10 106
(A Al Raihe, UAE) *mid-div: r.o wl fnl 2f: led 55yds out* **16/1**

2 *¾* **Silaah**^{43} [46] 7-8-5 101...(p) AdrianNicholls 9 103
(David Nicholls) *trckd ldr: wd: led 1 1/2f out: hdd fnl 55yds* **9/1**^{3}

3 *shd* **Alazeyab (USA)**^{14} [414] 5-8-6 108..................................(t) RichardHills 3 104
(A Al Raihe, UAE) *trckd ldng trio: ev ch 1 1/2f out: one pce fnl 110yds* **6/1**^{2}

4 *2 ¼* **Rock Jock (IRE)**^{21} [327] 4-8-5 105...................................... WJSupple 4 96
(Tracey Collins, Ire) *sn led: hdd 1 1/2f out: r.o same pce* **16/1**

5 *¼* **Invincible Ash (IRE)**^{7} [500] 6-8-5 107...........................(p) ShaneFoley 8 95
(M Halford, Ire) *nvr able to chal* **6/1**^{2}

6 *½* **Lipocco**^{7} [497] 7-7-12 105.. HarryBentley(7) 12 93
(Rod Collet, France) *mid-div: r.o fnl 2f: nrst fin* **25/1**

7 *1 ¼* **Doncaster Rover (USA)**^{103} [7351] 5-8-6 108.................(b) TedDurcan 6 90+
(David Brown) *s.i.s: sn rdn in rr* **12/1**

8 *1 ½* **Lui Rei (ITY)**^{28} [237] 5-8-5 98... KierenFallon 2 85
(Robert Cowell) *nvr bttr than mid-div* **20/1**

9 *1 ¼* **Star Crowned (USA)**^{28} [237] 8-8-6 108...........................(t) RMBurke 11 82
(R Bouresly, Kuwait) *nvr bttr than mid-div* **20/1**

10 *¼* **Verde-Mar (BRZ)**^{35} [155] 4-8-3 108 ow3.......................... TadhgO'Shea 7 78+
(E Martins, Brazil) *nvr nr to chal* **20/1**

11 *nse* **J J The Jet Plane (SAF)**^{67} [7852] 7-9-6 122......................... PStrydom 5 95
(M Houdalakis, South Africa) *trckd ldr tl 2 1/2f out: sn wknd* **11/8**^{1}

12 *13* **Masta Plasta (IRE)**^{28} [237] 8-8-6 100 ow1............. DaraghO'Donohoe 1 39
(David Nicholls) *nvr able to chal* **25/1**

1m 11.92s (0.92) **Going Correction** +0.40s/f (Slow) **12** Ran SP% **122.1**
Speed ratings: **109,108,107,104,104 103,102,100,98,98 98,80**
CSF: £143.66; Tricast: £974.75..

Owner H R H Princess Haya Of Jordan **Bred** Denis & Teresa Bergin **Trained** UAE

FOCUS
The presence of J J The Jet Plane, who was racing off an official mark of 122, meant that all bar five of these were out of the handicap, and the form looks suspect. The favourite ran a shocker and the first two finishers were some way out of the weights. A strong pace saw the field strung out by halfway, but the final time was 1.49 seconds off the track record, with the Tapeta riding on the slow side throughout the meeting.

NOTEBOOK
Green Beret(IRE) had been in good form in non-Carnival events both on the Meydan Tapeta and more recently the Jebel Ali dirt, and this was a career best from 8lb out of the handicap. There was much to like about the way he travelled, some way off the pace, before picking up out wide, but he'll face a stiffer task next time. (tchd 14-1)
Silaah, 6lb out the handicap, seemed to run as well as he ever has. He's been improving on both Fibresand and Polytrack in Britain recently and showed himself fully effective on Tapeta on this second spell in Dubai. His head carriage was high as usual, but he seemed to try.

Alazeyab(USA) was turned out only two weeks after finishing second in a C&D Group 3 on his return from a lengthy absence. He was sweating between his back legs, but ran another good race. (op 5-1)
Rock Jock(IRE) ran a good race from the front.
Invincible Ash(IRE) also performed creditably, but this trip stretches her.
Doncaster Rover(USA) needed a reminder after a slow start and was never travelling at any stage, only running on past beaten rivals. (op 14-1)
J J The Jet Plane(SAF), who had been off since winning the Hong Kong Sprint in December, was having his first start on the surface, but his trainer was recently quoted as saying "he's flying on the Tapeta." However, he ran poorly, finding next to nothing when asked for his effort having initially shown his customary early pace to race bang on the speed. So limited was the response when he came under pressure that it's hard to believe the Tapeta was solely to blame and he ran like a horse who may have a problem. (op 6-4)

583a ATTIJARI AL ISLAMI (LEG 1 MEYDAN MASTERS) (H'CAP) (TAPETA) 1m

3:40 (3:40) (95-105,105) 3-Y-O+

£42,307 (£14,102; £7,051; £3,525; £2,115; £1,410)

			RPR
1		**Haatheq (USA)**[7] 503 4-9-4 104 ... CHBorel 8 (A Al Raihe, UAE) *settled in rr: smooth prog 2 1/2f out: led 2f out: r.o wl* **8/1**	106
2	*1*	**Kavango (IRE)**[12] 462 4-9-2 101 ... RichardHughes 12 (M bin Shafya, UAE) *mid-div: rdn 2f out: chsd ldrs 2 1/2f out: r.o wl* **14/1**	102
3	*shd*	**Mufarrh (IRE)**[12] 462 4-9-1 100 ... FrankieDettori 4 (A Al Raihe, UAE) *chsd ldrs: ev ch 1f out: one pce fnl 110yds* **10/1**	100
4	*5 1/2*	**Atlantic Sport (USA)**[7] 497 6-9-5 105 ...(b) TJPereira 3 (M F De Kock, South Africa) *trckd ldrs tl 1 1/2f out: wknd fnl 110yds* **7/1**[3]	92
5	*3/4*	**Jaasoos (IRE)**[28] 239 7-9-1 100 ... MaximeGuyon 5 (D Selvaratnam, UAE) *a mid-div* **20/1**	86
6	*hd*	**Golden Arrow (IRE)**[13] 8-9-1 100 ...(bt) JMurtagh 10 (E Charpy, UAE) *in rr of mid-div: r.o fnl 2f* **33/1**	86
7	*1/2*	**Final Drive (IRE)**[7] 499 5-9-2 101 ... RichardHills 6 (John Ryan) *trckd ldrs tl wknd 2f out* **9/2**[2]	85
8	*2 1/4*	**Quick Wit**[14] 415 4-9-2 101 ... WilliamBuick 11 (Saeed Bin Suroor) *trckd ldrs tl 2f out: wknd fnl f* **2/1**[1]	80
9	*1 1/2*	**Comradeship (IRE)**[7] 501 4-9-1 100 ...(b) HiroyukiUchida 2 (R Bouresly, Kuwait) *v.s.a: settled last: nvr nr to chal* **25/1**	76
10	*1 3/4*	**Too Nice Name (FR)**[21] 327 4-9-4 104 ...(t) OlivierPeslier 7 (X Nakkachdji, France) *in rr of mid-div: nvr able to chal* **33/1**	75
11	*2 3/4*	**Kettle River (USA)**[292] 4-9-1 100 ... GeraldMosse 1 (Saeed Bin Suroor) *sn led: hdd 2f out: sn btn* **14/1**	66
12	*14*	**National Pride (USA)**[141] 6-9-3 102 ...(bt) RyanMoore 9 (Mahmood Al Zarooni) *nvr bttr than mid-div* **10/1**	35

1m 38.23s (1.13) **Going Correction** +0.40s/f (Slow) 12 Ran SP% **121.1**
Speed ratings: **110,109,108,103,102 102,101,99,98,96 93,79**
CSF: £111.13; Tricast: £1,137.09..
Owner Hamdan Al Maktoum **Bred** Shadwell Farm LLC **Trained** UAE

FOCUS
They seemed to go a fair enough gallop, but the time was again slow (2.46 seconds off the track record), suggesting the surface was not riding particularly fast. This was an ordinary Carnival handicap.

NOTEBOOK
Haatheq(USA) proved suited by the drop in trip and return to Tapeta and stayed on best under an untypical Borel ride, being brought widest of all by a jockey who so often hugs the inside rail. He could struggle to follow up off a higher mark.
Kavango(IRE) reversed recent C&D (but non-Carnival) form with Mufarrh, though wasn't good enough to trouble the winner.
Mufarrh(IRE), a stable companion of the winner, was clear of the rest.
Atlantic Sport(USA) didn't improve as expected for the step back up in trip and re-fitting of blinkers.
Jaasoos(IRE) would have been slightly closer had he not been short of room halfway up the straight. This was a bit better.
Final Drive(IRE) was ridden closer to the pace than has been the case lately and underperformed. The change in tactics probably didn't suit, but the horse has been kept busy lately - 10th run since debuting for this stable in August - and has probably had enough for now.
Quick Wit received a bump when his rider was trying to keep Mufarrh hemmed away on the entrance to the straight, and he immediately came off the bridle and began to struggle. He had been progressing, but can only be watched next time.

584a NAD AL SHEBA TROPHY SPONSORED BY AL DANA WEALTH MANAGEMENT (LISTED RACE) (TURF) 1m 6f 11y

4:15 (4:15) 3-Y-O+

£67,307 (£22,435; £11,217; £5,608; £3,365; £2,243)

			RPR
1		**Claremont (IRE)**[21] 329 5-9-0 110 ...(b) MickaelBarzalona 1 (Mahmood Al Zarooni) *mid-div: led 2f out: r.o wl* **10/1**	112
2	*1/4*	**Opinion Poll (IRE)**[21] 329 5-9-4 113 ... AhmedAjtebi 4 (Mahmood Al Zarooni) *settled in rr: rdn 3 1/2f out: r.o wl fnl 2f: nrst fin* **15/8**[1]	116+
3	*1 3/4*	**Star Empire (SAF)**[14] 413 5-9-0 109 ... ChristopheSoumillon 8 (M F De Kock, South Africa) *trckd ldr for 4f: ev ch 2f out: wknd fnl 55yds* **3/1**[2]	110
4	*4 1/4*	**Drunken Sailor (IRE)**[21] 329 6-9-0 112 ...(b) KierenFallon 5 (Luca Cumani) *settled in rr: r.o wl fnl 2f but nvr able to chal* **9/2**[3]	104
5	*1/2*	**Pompeyano (IRE)**[35] 154 6-9-0 106 ... FrankieDettori 9 (Saeed Bin Suroor) *settled last: nvr able to chal but r.o fnl 1 1/2f* **6/1**	103
6	*2 1/2*	**Montaff**[21] 329 5-9-0 99 ... JMurtagh 6 (Mick Channon) *s.i.s: in rr of mid-div: r.o fnl 2f* **25/1**	99
7	*1/2*	**Mojave Moon**[11] 5-9-0 98 ...(v) PatCosgrave 7 (M bin Shafya, UAE) *sn led: clr 5f out: hdd 2f out: wknd* **25/1**	99
8	*1/2*	**Royal Bengali (USA)**[11] 4-8-9 95 ... AntiocoMurgia 2 (A bin Huzaim, UAE) *in rr of mid-div: rdn 4f out: n.d* **33/1**	98
9	*1/2*	**Bergo (GER)**[124] 6926 8-9-0 109 ... RyanMoore 3 (Gary Moore) *mid-div: rdn 4f out: sn outpcd* **12/1**	97

2m 59.48s (179.48)
WFA 4 from 5yo+ 5lb 9 Ran SP% **119.7**
CSF: £29.68..
Owner Godolphin **Bred** Darley **Trained** Newmarket, Suffolk

FOCUS
A new name for this staying event, and Listed status for the first time, upgraded from a handicap. The race serves as something of a trial for the Group 3 DRC Gold Cup, which will be run on March 10. However, the pace set by Mojave Moon, who opened up a clear lead down the back straight, was just steady and the runner-up and fourth were not seen at their best.

NOTEBOOK
Claremont(IRE) had been virtually unsteerable around the bend into the straight on his reappearance around here, but he showed more when Mickael Barzalona took over last time and the talented young French jockey got an even better response this time, helping his quirky mount to reverse recent C&D placings with Opinion Poll and Drunken Sailor. However, Claremont can be considered fortunate to hold on from the poorly ridden runner-up.
Opinion Poll(IRE) was arguably unlucky over C&D on his debut for this yard, but there can be little doubt about this defeat - he should have won. Held up last off the steady pace, he covered more ground than most when taken wide around the final bend and was still hopelessly placed at the top of the straight, having around 3l to find on Claremont. He wandered a bit under maximum pressure, probably finding the ground quicker than ideal, but still only just failed to get up. If lining up in the Gold Cup his chance will be obvious, even though he'll still have his Group 2 penalty, although he might not want too many more goes on a quick surface. (op 2-1)
Star Empire(SAF), the winner of a steadily run 1m4f handicap off 106 last time, led the main pack behind the clear leader and plugged on. He didn't conclusively prove his stamina, but is a one-paced sort who was probably found out by the rise in class.
Drunken Sailor(IRE) is the type who needs plenty of cover, but even so he had little hope from so far back and continually found trouble in the straight, not being given a hard time as a result.
Pompeyano(IRE) needs more of a stamina test, but he probably wouldn't have been good enough anyway. (op 11-2)

585a CBD WORLD MASTERCARD (LEG 2 MEYDAN MASTERS) (H'CAP) (TAPETA) 1m 3f

4:55 (4:55) (95-110,110) 3-Y-O+

£57,692 (£19,230; £9,615; £4,807; £2,884; £1,923)

			RPR
1		**Emirates Champion**[222] 3921 5-9-3 102 ...(t) RyanMoore 10 (Saeed Bin Suroor) *settled in rr: smooth prog 2 1/2f out: led 1 1/2f out: r.o wl* **9/2**[2]	106
2	*2*	**Halicarnassus (IRE)**[21] 328 7-8-13 98 ... GeraldMosse 8 (Mick Channon) *mid-div: rdn 2f out: r.o wl fnl f* **6/1**[3]	98
3	*1/4*	**Prizefighting (USA)**[21] 328 4-9-6 108 ... HiroyukiUchida 11 (Mahmood Al Zarooni) *mid-div: chsd ldrs 2f out: nt qckn fnl f* **3/1**[1]	106
4	*1/4*	**Royaaty (IRE)**[13] 5-8-9 95 ... CHBorel 7 (M bin Shafya, UAE) *slowly away: settled in rr: rdn 2 1/2f out: r.o wl fnl 1 1/2f: nrst fin* **8/1**	93
5	*2 1/2*	**Logic Way (USA)**[35] 7-9-7 107 ...(bt) FrankieDettori 12 (Ibrahaim Al Malki, Qatar) *sn led: hdd 1 1/2f out: wknd fnl f* **9/1**	101
6	*1/4*	**Monte Alto (IRE)**[7] 498 7-9-4 104 ...(t) MaximeGuyon 1 (A Al Raihe, UAE) *a mid-div on rail: nvr nrr* **7/1**	97
7	*shd*	**Lion Sands**[13] 7-8-9 95 ...(t) RichardHills 5 (A bin Huzaim, UAE) *trckd ldng pair: nt qckn fnl 2f* **25/1**	88
8	*1 1/4*	**Clasp**[21] 332 9-8-11 97 ...(t) JMurtagh 6 (Doug Watson, UAE) *mid-div: chsd ldrs 2 1/2f out: wknd fnl f* **16/1**	88
9	*1/2*	**Pallodio (IRE)**[21] 330 6-9-11 110 ...(vt) WilliamBuick 9 (J E Hammond, France) *in rr of mid-div: rn wd: n.d* **12/1**	101
10	*2 1/2*	**Mr. Crazy Boy (ARG)**[21] 329 5-9-1 100 ...(t) OlivierPeslier 4 (M F De Kock, South Africa) *trckd ldrs tl 3f out: sn btn* **20/1**	86
11	*1 1/4*	**Bravely Fought (IRE)**[7] 503 6-9-0 99 ... RichardHughes 2 (Sabrina J Harty, Ire) *settled in rr: nvr able to chal* **33/1**	83
12	*4 1/2*	**Bank Of Burden (USA)**[21] 329 4-8-13 100 ...(tp) TJPereira 3 (Niels Petersen, Norway) *trckd ldr tl 2 1/2f out: wknd* **33/1**	76

2m 19.72s (1.32) **Going Correction** +0.40s/f (Slow)
WFA 4 from 5yo+ 2lb 12 Ran SP% **119.1**
Speed ratings: **111,109,109,109,107 107,107,106,105,104 103,99**
CSF: £30.38; Tricast: £93.58..
Owner Godolphin **Bred** Gainsborough Stud Management Ltd **Trained** Newmarket, Suffolk

FOCUS
Another sluggish time (3.94 seconds off track record) on a track that was clearly riding on the slow side. The early pace, set by Logic Way, seemed fair until that runner slowed the gallop a little down the back straight. This was an ordinary handicap by Carnival standards, but a nice enough winner.

NOTEBOOK
Emirates Champion had only been seen once since winning over C&D off 5lb lower this time last year (down the field in the John Smith's Cup in July), having had some "tiny problems" according to Saeed Bin Suroor, but this was a smart effort. He was said by his trainer to be only 80% ready and there could be more to come from this lightly raced 5-y-o.
Halicarnassus(IRE) wasn't at his best when behind Prizefighting here last time, having earlier finished ahead of that rival. This was better.
Prizefighting(USA) went a bit wide into the straight but still had his chance.
Royaaty(IRE) raced in a detached last for much of the way and was probably set a bit too much to do.
Logic Way(USA) had his chance from the front. (op 8-1)

586a AL FAHIDI FORT SPONSORED BY COMMERCIAL BANK OF DUBAI (GROUP 2) (TURF) 1m

5:35 (5:35) 3-Y-O+

£96,153 (£32,051; £16,025; £8,012; £4,807; £3,205)

			RPR
1		**Derbaas (USA)**[28] 239 5-9-0 110 ...(t) RichardHills 2 (A Al Raihe, UAE) *trckd ldr: led 2f out: r.o wl: jst hld on* **8/1**[3]	117
2	*1/2*	**Raihana (AUS)**[7] 503 5-8-9 115 ... ChristopheSoumillon 4 (M F De Kock, South Africa) *mid-div: smooth prog 2 1/2f out: r.o wl fnl 1 1/2f: nrst fin* **11/8**[1]	111+
3	*1 1/4*	**Le Drakkar (AUS)**[7] 503 6-9-0 104 ...(t) OlivierPeslier 5 (A bin Huzaim, UAE) *in rr of mid-div: r.o wl fnl 2f: nrst fin* **20/1**	113
4	*1/4*	**Hearts Of Fire**[145] 6350 4-9-0 117 ...(t) RyanMoore 10 (Ibrahaim Al Malki, Qatar) *slowly away: settled rr: r.o wl fnl 2f: nrst fin* **13/2**[2]	113
5	*3 1/4*	**Thai Haku (IRE)**[28] 241 4-8-9 105 ... Christophe-PatriceLemaire 7 (M Delzangles, France) *mid-div: chsd ldrs 2 1/2f out: one pce fnl 2f* **16/1**	100
6	*1/2*	**Silverside (USA)**[14] 416 5-9-0 113 ... JulienGrosjean 9 (M Delcher-Sanchez, Spain) *sn led: hdd 2f out: wknd fnl 1/2f* **25/1**	104
7	*3/4*	**Finjaan**[21] 327 5-9-0 105 ... PatDobbs 6 (Doug Watson, UAE) *settled in rr: n.d* **33/1**	102
8	*shd*	**Our Giant (AUS)**[14] 414 8-9-0 112 ...(b) KShea 1 (M F De Kock, South Africa) *s.i.s: nvr bttr than mid-div* **9/1**	102
9	*1*	**Invisible Man**[28] 239 5-9-0 108 ...(b) FrankieDettori 8 (Saeed Bin Suroor) *settled in rr: nvr able to chal* **16/1**	100
10	*1 1/2*	**Mabait**[14] 415 5-9-0 113 ... KierenFallon 12 (Luca Cumani) *settled in rr: nvr able to chal* **12/1**	96
11	*2 1/2*	**Snaafy (USA)**[13] 7-9-0 115 ...(v) TadhgO'Shea 11 (M Al Muhairi, UAE) *mid-div: rdn 2 1/2f out: sn btn* **8/1**[3]	90

12 4 1/4 **Bushman**[21] [331] 7-9-0 110 .... WilliamBuick 3 81
(David Simcock) *mid-div on rail: nvr able to chal* **16/1**

1m 37.82s (97.82) 12 Ran SP% **124.5**
CSF: £30.38..
Owner Hamdan Al Maktoum **Bred** Shadwell Farm LLC **Trained** UAE

FOCUS
Traditionally a good pointer towards the Duty Free, with Gladiatorus taking both races two seasons ago, while the winners in 2007, 2008 and last year all subsequently placed in the Group 1 event on World Cup night. Pace was the key - there wasn't much of it (time 1.30 seconds outside course best, albeit the rail was out) and the handily placed Derbass stole a march on his rivals in the straight.

NOTEBOOK
Derbaas(USA) was a good 3l clear of Raihana, and even further ahead of the next two finishers, when left in front by the weakening early leader Silverside around 2f out, and found enough to hold on. This was his fourth straight success following victories in two non-Carnival events on Tapeta and a C&D handicap off 105. However, while he's clearly improving rapidly, this win owed much to the way the race unfolded. (op 15-2)
Raihana(AUS) ◆ was turned out only seven days after defying a handicap mark of 110 around here, and the drop in trip wasn't ideal either. A couple of respected judges described her as looking "lean", and she was on her toes beforehand, but she still ran another terrific race, indeed she probably would have won had she had a stronger pace to chase. She travelled well again but had no chance with the winner by the time she was edged into the clear. Provided her busy spell doesn't take its toll, she will surely go well in the Duty Free. (op 13-8)
Le Drakkar(AUS) ran just as he did the previous week, followed Raihana through having travelled well, but he was again left with too much to do to seriously threaten that rival. He could pick up a nice prize if everything goes his way.
Hearts Of Fire, waited with towards the inside after being dropped in from his wide draw, was another unsuited by the lack of pace. Sold out of Pat Eddery's yard for 550,000gns since he was last seen, he was doing his best work at the finish.
Thai Haku(IRE) was a bit keen and didn't see her race out. (op 14-1)
Our Giant(AUS), up in trip, wasn't given anything like a hard ride once his chance had passed after he met some trouble.
Snaafy(USA), passed over by Richard Hills, had a wide trip and was nowhere near the form he showed when winning a Jebel Ali Listed race on his perhaps favoured dirt surface last time. (op 15-2)

587a CBD FINANCIAL SERVICES (H'CAP) (TURF) 7f
6:10 (6:10) (95-112,112) 3-Y-O+
£57,692 (£14,423; £14,423; £4,807; £2,884; £1,923)

RPR
1 **Across The Rhine (USA)**[21] [326] 5-8-11 104 .... WJSupple 4 102
(Tracey Collins, Ire) *sn led: kicked clr 2f out: r.o gamely* **14/1**
2 1/4 **Swop (IRE)**[125] [6888] 8-8-6 98 .... KierenFallon 3 96+
(Luca Cumani) *mid-div: r.o wl fnl 1 1/2f: nrst fin* **10/1**
2 dht **Mahubo (SAF)**[13] 5-8-7 98 ow1 .... JamieSpencer 5 97+
(M F De Kock, South Africa) *mid-div: rdn 2 1/2f out: r.o wl fnl 1 1/2f: jst failed* **6/1**[2]
4 1/2 **Hujaylea (IRE)**[14] [415] 8-8-4 102 ....(p) CPHoban[(6)] 10 99+
(M Halford, Ire) *settled in rr: r.o fnl 2f but n.d* **5/1**[1]
5 3/4 **Navajo Chief**[21] [332] 4-8-9 101 .... TedDurcan 1 96
(Alan Jarvis) *trckd ldr: r.o same pce fnl 1 1/2f* **13/2**[3]
6 3/4 **Warsaw (IRE)**[14] [415] 6-9-1 107 ....(b) KShea 13 100
(M F De Kock, South Africa) *in rr od main gp: r.o wl fnl 1 1/2f: nrst fin* **5/1**[1]
7 1 1/4 **Classic Blade (IRE)**[12] [462] 5-8-8 100 .... TadhgO'Shea 2 89
(Doug Watson, UAE) *a mid-div* **25/1**
8 1 **Valid Sum (USA)**[124] 5-8-6 98 ....(t) AhmedAjtebi 6 85
(Mahmood Al Zarooni) *nvr bttr than mid-div* **14/1**
9 3/4 **Munaddam (USA)**[14] [415] 9-8-10 102 .... RichardHills 9 87
(E Charpy, UAE) *nvr bttr than mid-div* **10/1**
10 2 1/2 **Golden Desert (IRE)**[21] [327] 7-8-6 98 .... DaraghO'Donohoe 11 76
(Robert Mills) *slowly away: racd in rr: n.d* **28/1**
11 shd **Dubawi Phantom**[21] [328] 4-8-8 100 ....(b) MickaelBarzalona 7 77
(I Mohammed, UAE) *nvr bttr than mid-div* **33/1**
12 1/4 **Montmorency (IRE)**[7] [497] 5-8-10 102 ....(t) RichardMullen 14 79
(S Seemar, UAE) *mid-div: wd: n.d* **10/1**
13 1 1/4 **Yaa Wayl (IRE)**[14] [415] 4-9-6 112 ....(v) FrankieDettori 8 85
(Saeed Bin Suroor) *trckd ldrs tl 2f out: sn btn* **10/1**
14 2 1/4 **Vitznau (IRE)**[173] [5518] 7-8-7 99 .... ShaneFoley 12 66
(Robert Cowell) *slowly away: settled in rr: n.d* **16/1**

1m 25.05s (85.05) CSF: Across The Rhine & Mahubo £76.16, ATR & Swop £49.57. TRICAST: ATR S & M £[illegible].91, 14 Ran SP% 126.8
ATR & S £454.69. Placepot: £79.20 to a £1 stake. Pool: £9,528.54 - 87.80 winning tickets.
Quadpot: £11.10 to a £1 stake. Pool: £630.60 - 41.90 winning tickets. 27.

FOCUS
No obviously progressive types here and Across The Rhine was allowed a soft lead, making just about all in a time 1.93 seconds off the track's best for the distance, although it needs mentioning that the rail was out four meters.

NOTEBOOK
Across The Rhine(USA) wasn't far behind two subsequent winners on the Tapeta last time and this was his third start after a layoff, often a good time to catch such types.
Swop(IRE) showed he remains capable as an 8-y-o, not beaten far after over four months off.
Mahubo(SAF) flopped on the Jebel Ali dirt last time, but clearly the return to turf suited and he ran a fine race. He carried 1lb overweight.
Hujaylea(IRE) was last of all at the top of the straight and did well to get so close considering the lack of pace in the race. (op 6-1)
Navajo Chief was well enough placed but couldn't build on the form of his recent second over 1m, a professional taking over from a 7lb claimer perhaps making his job tougher.
Warsaw(IRE) had everything go his way when winning over C&D the previous week (Hujaylea behind) and couldn't defy a 3lb rise.

559 LINGFIELD (L-H)
Friday, February 18

OFFICIAL GOING: Standard
STANDARD
Wind: Almost nil. Weather: Hazy

588 TODAY'S JOCKEY SPECIALS AT BLUESQ.COM APPRENTICE (S) STKS 1m 4f (P)
1:45 (1:45) (Class 6) 4-Y-O+ **£1,535** (£453; £226) **Stalls** Low

Form RPR
6/1- 1 **The Blue Dog (IRE)**[374] [475] 4-8-6 58 .... DavidKenny[(5)] 6 57+
(George Baker) *w ldrs: led 3f out: shkn up to draw clr over 2f out: in n.d after* **4/9**[1]
1100 2 5 **Barodine**[14] [418] 8-9-10 61 .... MartinLane 2 57
(Ron Hodges) *hld up bhd ldrs: rdn 3f out: wnt 2nd 2f out: hrd drvn and no ch w wnr* **16/1**[3]
0-56 3 3/4 **Acropolis (IRE)**[14] [419] 10-8-12 46 .... GeorgeDowning[(7)] 4 51
(Tony Carroll) *hld up bhd ldrs: waiting for effrt tl 2f out: pushed along to take 3rd 1f out: no ch* **40/1**
41-2 4 6 **Orchard Supreme**[44] [50] 8-9-5 71 .... LucyKBarry[(5)] 1 48
(Ralph Smith) *t.k.h: led after 3f to 3f out: wknd 2f out* **3/1**[2]
20 5 3/4 **Battle Axe (FR)**[13] [433] 6-8-7 0 .... CharlotteJenner[(7)] 3 35
(Laura Mongan) *heavily restrained s: plld hrd in last: effrt 3f out: sn outpcd: hung lft fnl f* **50/1**
00-0 6 nk **Whitley Bay (USA)**[25] [277] 4-9-2 40 .... KierenFox 5 40
(John Best) *led 3f: w ldr to over 4f out: sn u.p: wknd 2f out* **33/1**

2m 34.03s (1.03) **Going Correction** +0.15s/f (Slow)
WFA 4 from 6yo+ 3lb 6 Ran SP% **107.5**
Speed ratings (Par 101): **102,98,98,94,93 93**
Tote Swingers:1&2:£3.50, 2&3:£20.60, 1&3:£8.20 CSF £8.04 TOTE £1.40: £1.10, £3.30; EX 9.30.The winner was bought in for 5,200gns.
Owner Mrs V P Baker & Partners **Bred** Mervyn Stewkesbury **Trained** Whitsbury, Hants

FOCUS
An uncompetitive seller run at a steady gallop. The winner raced centre-to-far-side in the straight and did not need to improve to take this.

589 LINGFIELD MARRIOTT HOTEL & COUNTRY CLUB H'CAP 7f (P)
2:20 (2:20) (Class 6) (0-60,60) 4-Y-O+ **£1,535** (£453; £226) **Stalls** Low

Form RPR
200- 1 **Ymir**[64] [7885] 5-8-10 49 ....(vt) ShaneKelly 10 57
(Michael Attwater) *mde all: clr w runner-up fr over 2f out: drvn over 1f out: styd on wl nr fin* **14/1**
0-66 2 1 1/2 **Tudor Prince (IRE)**[26] [268] 7-9-6 59 .... NeilCallan 6 63
(Tony Carroll) *t.k.h early: chsd wnr thrght: clr of rest over 2f out: tried to chal on inner and sltly hmpd wl over 1f out: nt qckn fnl f: jst hld on for 2nd* **9/2**[1]
230- 3 nk **Patavium Prince (IRE)**[143] [6444] 8-9-5 58 .... DaneO'Neill 1 61
(Jo Crowley) *dwlt: hld up in midfield gng wl: sme prog over 2f out: wnt 3rd bhd clr ldng pair 1f out: styd on: too much to do* **13/2**[3]
2-34 4 1/2 **This Ones For Eddy**[24] [292] 6-9-6 59 .... LukeMorris 2 61
(John Balding) *chsd ldng trio: rdn 1/2-way: wnt 3rd over 2f out to 1f out: kpt on* **11/2**[2]
0/20 5 1/2 **Haulit**[25] [280] 5-8-13 52 .... AdamKirby 12 53
(Gary Moore) *t.k.h: hld up in rr: rdn 3f out: effrt on wd outside over 1f out: styd on: nrst fin* **10/1**
-060 6 hd **Yakama (IRE)**[8] [485] 6-9-0 53 ....(b) WilliamCarson 7 53
(Christine Dunnett) *hld up in last trio: rdn 3f out: styd on fr over 1f out: no ch* **25/1**
30-2 7 1/2 **Cwmni**[13] [432] 5-9-0 60 .... ThomasBrown[(7)] 3 59
(Bryn Palling) *taken down early and thought abt it bef gng: hld up in rr: effrt on inner over 2f out: sme prog over 1f out: no hdwy fnl f* **8/1**
000- 8 1/2 **Simple Rhythm**[82] [7614] 5-9-2 55 .... KirstyMilczarek 8 52
(John Ryan) *hld up in midfield: gng wl 3f out but plenty to do: sme prog over 1f out: nvr nr ldrs and eased nr fin* **25/1**
06-0 9 1 3/4 **Batchworth Blaise**[16] [387] 8-8-13 55 .... KierenFox[(3)] 5 48
(Eric Wheeler) *stdd s: hld up in last: reminders over 4f out: nvr got into it* **17/2**
-340 10 nk **Ivory Lace**[9] [477] 10-9-4 60 .... AndrewHeffernan[(3)] 9 52
(Steve Woodman) *hld up in last trio: rdn 3f out: brought wd in st: no prog* **10/1**
0-02 11 1 1/4 **Charles Darwin (IRE)**[9] [477] 8-9-2 55 ....(p) LiamKeniry 4 44
(Michael Blanshard) *chsd ldrs on outer: rdn over 2f out: no imp: wknd over 1f out* **8/1**
6-05 12 nk **Ever Cheerful**[30] [210] 10-8-9 48 ow1 ....(p) RobertHavlin 11 36
(Andrew Haynes) *chsd ldng pair: rdn 4f out: lost pl over 2f out: wknd* **16/1**

1m 24.7s (-0.10) **Going Correction** +0.15s/f (Slow) 12 Ran SP% **118.1**
Speed ratings (Par 101): **106,104,103,103,102 102,102,101,99,99 97,97**
Tote Swingers:1&2:£43.40, 2&3:£3.90, 1&3:£24.50 CSF £75.64 CT £461.09 TOTE £20.40: £5.80, £2.10, £2.50; EX 165.30 TRIFECTA Not won..
Owner Canisbay Bloodstock **Bred** Canisbay Bloodstock Ltd **Trained** Epsom, Surrey
■ Stewards' Enquiry : William Carson one-day ban: careless riding (Mar 4)

FOCUS
A moderate handicap run at a fair gallop, but one in which it paid to race right up with the pace. The winner raced centre-to-far side in the straight. It is probably not form to treat with too much faith.

590 COWDEN (S) STKS 7f (P)
2:55 (2:55) (Class 6) 3-Y-O+ **£1,535** (£453; £226) **Stalls** Low

Form RPR
2163 1 **I Confess**[2] [556] 6-10-0 70 ....(b) NeilCallan 3 67
(David Evans) *trckd ldr: rdn to ld over 1f out: styd on to assert fnl f* **15/8**[1]
4340 2 1 1/2 **Goodbye Cash (IRE)**[8] [485] 7-9-6 55 .... AndrewHeffernan[(3)] 8 58
(Ralph Smith) *pushed up to ld: hrd rdn 2f out: hdd over 1f out: one pce* **13/2**[3]
001- 3 1 **Lend A Grand (IRE)**[86] [7557] 7-10-0 65 .... DaneO'Neill 6 60
(Jo Crowley) *stdd s: hld up last: shkn up 2f out: wnt 3rd 1f out but hanging: nt qckn* **3/1**[2]
040- 4 1 **Briannsta (IRE)**[188] [5075] 9-9-8 43 ....(b) RichardThomas 1 52?
(John E Long) *stdd s: hld up in 4th: hrd rdn 2f out: disp 3rd 1f out: nt qckn* **33/1**
0-54 5 nk **Emerald Girl (IRE)**[21] [334] 4-9-3 68 .... JimmyQuinn 5 50
(Richard Fahey) *trckd ldng pair: rdn and effrt on inner 2f out: hld whn short of room 1f out: fdd* **15/8**[1]

1m 25.53s (0.73) **Going Correction** +0.15s/f (Slow) 5 Ran SP% **110.8**
Speed ratings (Par 101): **101,99,98,97,96**
CSF £14.33 TOTE £2.00: £1.10, £4.10; EX 11.80 Trifecta £21.90 Pool £402.08 - 13.58 winning units..There was no bid for the winner. Emerald Girl was claimed by Mr S. Arnold for £6,000.
Owner J E Abbey **Bred** Gestut Sohrenhof **Trained** Pandy, Monmouths

FOCUS
A depleted field and no more than a modest seller. The gallop was a moderate one and the winner edged towards the far rail in the closing stages. The winner did not need to match his recent form.
Lend A Grand(IRE) Official explanation: jockey said gelding hung left

Emerald Girl(IRE) Official explanation: jockey said filly never travelled

591 DOWNLOAD BLUE SQUARE IPHONE APP MEDIAN AUCTION MAIDEN STKS — 1m 2f (P)
3:30 (3:37) (Class 6) 3-Y-O — **£2,115** (£624; £312) **Stalls** Low

Form	Pos	Btn	Horse	Jockey	RPR
04	**1**		**Caravan Rolls On**[7] 516 3-9-3 0	JackMitchell 1	71+
			(Peter Chapple-Hyam) *patiently rdn in rr: effrt on wd outside over 3f out: plenty to do but wnt 3rd over 1f out: r.o to ld last 100yds* **13/2**[2]		
	2	¾	**Brilliant Barca** 3-8-10 0	CharlesBishop(7) 6	70
			(Mick Channon) *prom: pushed up on outer to take narrow ld over 2f out: kpt on fr over 1f out: hdd and outpcd last 100yds* **12/1**		
0-3	**3**	2¾	**Ilissos (USA)**[21] 339 3-9-3 0	GeorgeBaker 7	64
			(Jeremy Noseda) *prom: pushed up to chal over 2f out: rdn and nt qckn over 1f out: fdd nr fin* **30/100**[1]		
50-6	**4**	10	**Blaze On By**[6] 519 3-8-9 50	KierenFox(3) 4	39
			(John Bridger) *pressed ldr: led 6f out: hdd & wknd over 2f out* **20/1**		
0	**5**	1	**Twilight Express (IRE)**[30] 212 3-8-12 0	LiamKeniry 2	37
			(Emma Lavelle) *led to 6f out: wknd wl over 2f out* **33/1**		
-00	**6**	7	**Westhaven (IRE)**[21] 339 3-9-3 0	DaneO'Neill 8	28
			(David Elsworth) *s.s: in tch in rr: drvn and reluctant 4f out: sn btn and bhd* **10/1**[3]		
65-	**7**	6	**Elegant Star (IRE)**[70] 7802 3-8-12 0	AdrianMcCarthy 3	11
			(Dave Morris) *prom: lost pl and rdn 5f out: sn wknd and bhd* **66/1**		
	8	shd	**Rapacious** 3-9-3 0	NickyMackay 5	16
			(Mark Rimmer) *s.s: in tch in last: rdn 4f out: wknd 3f out* **33/1**		

2m 7.39s (0.79) **Going Correction** +0.15s/f (Slow) **8** Ran SP% **119.2**
Speed ratings (Par 95): **102,101,99,91,90 84,80,79**
Tote Swingers:1&2:£13.40, 2&3:£2.30, 1&3:£2.60 CSF £73.65 TOTE £5.70: £1.30, £2.90, £1.02; EX 48.60 Trifecta £62.60 Pool £758.32 - 8.96 winning units..
Owner Paul Hancock **Bred** Miss K Rausing **Trained** Newmarket, Suffolk

FOCUS
A weak-looking maiden in which the gallop was no more than fair. The winner came down the centre in the closing stages and the first three pulled clear. The form is rated loosely around the third.

592 BREATHE SPA AT MARRIOTT LINGFIELD H'CAP — 1m 5f (P)
4:05 (4:05) (Class 6) (0-65,64) 4-Y-O+ — **£1,569** (£463; £231) **Stalls** Low

Form	Pos	Btn	Horse	Jockey	RPR
-430	**1**		**Suhailah**[6] 524 5-8-11 51	ShaneKelly 7	58
			(Michael Attwater) *trckd ldng trio: prog to ld over 2f out: drvn over 1f out: jst hld on* **10/1**		
65-1	**2**	hd	**Setter's Princess**[15] 409 5-9-6 60	GeorgeBaker 2	67+
			(Ron Hodges) *hld up in 5th: prog over 2f out: rdn to chse wnr 1f out: clsd grad: jst hld* **2/1**[1]		
-351	**3**	1¼	**Money Money Money**[20] 350 5-9-4 58	(b) JamesMillman 8	63
			(Rod Millman) *trckd ldr: led briefly 3f out: chsd wnr over 2f out to 1f out: nt qckn* **5/1**[3]		
06-4	**4**	1¼	**Galiotto (IRE)**[6] 524 5-8-10 50	(p) LiamKeniry 4	53
			(Gary Moore) *blindfold off late and dwlt: hld up in last pair: bmpd along 4f out: prog to take 4th ins fnl f: nvr on terms* **11/4**[2]		
50-0	**5**	2¼	**Diamond Twister (USA)**[29] 223 5-9-4 61	KierenFox(3) 9	61
			(John Best) *led at mod pce: rdn and hdd 3f out: steadily fdd* **15/2**		
4-06	**6**	1	**Before The War (USA)**[15] 409 4-8-5 52	(b) SimonPearce(3) 6	50
			(Jeremy Gask) *dwlt: hld up in 6th: effrt to chse ldrs over 2f out: steadily fdd over 1f out* **12/1**		
0-63	**7**	¾	**Sir William Orpen**[20] 350 4-8-6 55	JemmaMarshall(5) 5	52
			(Pat Phelan) *plld hrd: hld up in last pair: effrt and in tch 2f out: sn wknd* **12/1**		
135-	**8**	1½	**Miss Wendy**[13] 7397 4-8-13 57	NeilCallan 1	52
			(Mark H Tompkins) *trckd ldng pair: rdn over 2f out: grad wknd over 1f out* **33/1**		

2m 49.82s (3.82) **Going Correction** +0.15s/f (Slow)
WFA 4 from 5yo 4lb **8** Ran SP% **115.8**
Speed ratings (Par 101): **94,93,93,92,90 90,89,88**
Tote Swingers:1&2:£4.60, 2&3:£3.10, 1&3:£7.00 CSF £30.88 CT £113.01 TOTE £12.30: £4.00, £1.10, £1.10; EX 37.70 Trifecta £175.40 Pool £528.81 - 2.23 winning units..
Owner Canisbay Bloodstock **Bred** Canisbay Bloodstock Ltd **Trained** Epsom, Surrey

FOCUS
A moderate handicap, but one run at just a steady gallop to the straight and this bare form may not be entirely reliable. The winner, who came down the centre in the straight, has been rated as running a marginal personal best.
Galiotto(IRE) Official explanation: jockey said blind got caught in gelding's cheek pieces and was slowly away

593 DORMANSLAND MAIDEN STKS — 6f (P)
4:40 (4:42) (Class 5) 3-Y-O+ — **£1,910** (£564; £282) **Stalls** Low

Form	Pos	Btn	Horse	Jockey	RPR
	1		**Chimpunk (USA)**[886] 5980 5-9-12 0	AndreaAtzeni 5	74
			(Michael Wigham) *hld up in 4th: chsd ldng pair over 2f out: clsd and squeezed between them fnl f: urged along and styd on to ld last stride* **5/2**[2]		
222-	**2**	nse	**Midnight Rider (IRE)**[167] 5761 3-8-11 77	NeilCallan 4	70
			(Chris Wall) *awkward s but led: 2 l clr over 2f out: rdn over 1f out: hdd last stride* **8/13**[1]		
	3	nk	**Hoover** 3-8-11 0	StephenCraine 6	69
			(Jim Boyle) *chsd ldr: shkn up over 2f out: signs of greenness but clsd fnl f: lost 2nd and no ex nr fin* **50/1**		
/3	**4**	4½	**Stand Beside Me (IRE)**[16] 389 4-9-12 0	(t) LiamKeniry 2	58
			(Sylvester Kirk) *plld hrd: hld up in 5th: wnt modest 4th over 1f out: reminder ins fnl f: nvr nr ldrs* **10/1**[3]		
66	**5**	3¾	**Refusetosurrender (IRE)**[21] 344 3-8-6 0	JimmyQuinn 3	36
			(Richard Fahey) *plld hrd: disp 2nd to over 3f out: sn dropped away* **33/1**		
	6	7	**Abacist (IRE)** 3-8-11 0	RichardThomas 1	19
			(Ralph Beckett) *a last: lost tch bef 1/2-way* **25/1**		

1m 12.61s (0.71) **Going Correction** +0.15s/f (Slow)
WFA 3 from 4yo+ 15lb **6** Ran SP% **108.3**
Speed ratings (Par 103): **101,100,100,94,89 80**
Tote Swingers:1&2:£1.50, 2&3:£7.40, 1&3:£9.40 CSF £4.06 TOTE £4.50: £1.90, £1.10; EX 4.10.
Owner John Cullinan & Michael Wigham **Bred** Don Mattox & Pam Mattox **Trained** Newmarket, Suffolk

FOCUS
Not too much strength in just a fair maiden in which a modest gallop saw several fail to settle. The first three finished clear and the winner edged towards the centre in the closing stages. The form is rated around the front two.
Stand Beside Me(IRE) Official explanation: jockey said colt ran too freely
Refusetosurrender(IRE) Official explanation: jockey said filly hung left
Abacist(IRE) Official explanation: jockey said gelding ran green

594 PLAY RAINBOW RICHES AT BLUESQ.COM H'CAP — 1m (P)
5:10 (5:10) (Class 5) (0-75,75) 3-Y-O — **£2,115** (£624; £312) **Stalls** High

Form	Pos	Btn	Horse	Jockey	RPR
00-1	**1**		**Tijori (IRE)**[35] 171 3-9-3 71	JimmyQuinn 1	74
			(Richard Hannon) *mde virtually all: set stdy pce to 3f out: urged along and jnd jst over 1f out: asserted again last 100yds* **9/4**[2]		
6-36	**2**	½	**Foxtrot Golf (IRE)**[22] 313 3-8-12 66	(p) DaneO'Neill 2	68
			(Peter Winkworth) *trckd wnr: brought to chal and upsides jst over 1f out: outbattled last 150yds* **7/1**[3]		
-111	**3**	2¼	**Aquilifer (IRE)**[21] 335 3-9-7 75	ShaneKelly 3	72
			(William Jarvis) *trckd ldng pair in slowly run r: rdn and nt qckn over 1f out: one pce after* **10/11**[1]		
260-	**4**	1¼	**Highlife Dancer**[118] 7085 3-8-13 74	CharlesBishop(7) 4	68
			(Mick Channon) *hld up in last but in cl tch: rdn over 2f out: nt qckn and no imp over 1f out* **7/1**[3]		

1m 40.62s (2.42) **Going Correction** +0.15s/f (Slow) **4** Ran SP% **108.2**
Speed ratings (Par 97): **93,92,90,89**
CSF £15.05 TOTE £3.00; EX 9.10.
Owner Malih Lahej Al Basti **Bred** Polish Belle Partnership **Trained** East Everleigh, Wilts

FOCUS
A couple of previous winners in a fair handicap but a slow pace means the bare form isn't entirely reliable. It has been rated around the runner-up. The winner came down the centre in the straight.
T/Plt: £14.50 to a £1 stake. Pool: £42,882.31. 2,157.60 winning tickets. T/Qpdt: £2.30 to a £1 stake. Pool: £3,614.00. 1,120.02 winning tickets. JN

574 WOLVERHAMPTON (A.W) (L-H)
Friday, February 18

OFFICIAL GOING: Standard

595 TODAY'S JOCKEY SPECIALS AT BLUESQ.COM H'CAP — 5f 20y(P)
5:25 (5:25) (Class 6) (0-60,54) 3-Y-O — **£1,535** (£453; £226) **Stalls** Low

Form	Pos	Btn	Horse	Jockey	RPR
2232	**1**		**Go Maggie Go (IRE)**[10] 452 3-9-7 54	PhillipMakin 7	59
			(Kevin Ryan) *w ldr: led over 2f out: rdn over 1f out: drvn ins fnl f: hld on: all out* **1/1**[1]		
000-	**2**	nk	**Porthgwidden Beach (USA)**[142] 6459 3-9-0 47	(t) LiamJones 1	51
			(Stuart Williams) *hld up in tch: swtchd to outer and hdwy over 2f out: rdn to chse wnr jst ins fnl f: kpt on wl* **11/4**[2]		
-553	**3**	1½	**Pickled Pumpkin**[16] 380 3-9-7 54	IanMongan 8	53
			(Olivia Maylam) *s.i.s: sn chsd ldrs towards outer: rdn over 2f out: edgd lft and kpt on ins fnl f* **10/1**		
030-	**4**	2½	**Georgian Silver**[84] 7576 3-9-3 50	LeeNewman 9	40
			(George Foster) *prom on outer: rdn over 2f out: edgd lft over 1f out: no ex ins fnl f* **33/1**		
0-60	**5**	nk	**Gunalt Joy**[28] 251 3-9-5 52	GrahamGibbons 4	41
			(Michael Easterby) *chsd ldrs: rdn and outpcd over 2f out: kpt on same pce ins fnl f* **10/1**		
500-	**6**	1½	**Running Water**[156] 6072 3-8-11 47	JamesSullivan(3) 6	31
			(Hugh McWilliams) *in tch: rdn over 2f out: styd on same pce: edgd rt ins fnl f* **20/1**		
050-	**7**	9	**Taverners Jubilee**[119] 7065 3-8-9 45	LouisBeuzelin(3) 3	—
			(Patrick Morris) *in tch on inner: rdn over 2f out: wknd over 1f out* **25/1**		
5-35	**8**	1½	**Una Vita Pius (IRE)**[16] 383 3-9-2 49	JamieMackay 5	—
			(Patrick Gilligan) *led narrowly: hdd over 2f out: wknd over 1f out: eased ins fnl f* **6/1**		
0000	**9**	1¼	**Zohan (IRE)**[14] 426 3-8-12 45	(b) RobbieFitzpatrick 10	—
			(Peter Grayson) *bmpd and swtchd lft s: a towards rr* **100/1**		
000-	**10**	14	**Regal Rocket (IRE)**[153] 6209 3-8-7 47	(tp) EdwardPierce(7) 2	—
			(John Weymes) *s.i.s: hld up: bhd after 2f: t.o* **40/1**		

63.16 secs (0.86) **Going Correction** +0.125s/f (Slow) **10** Ran SP% **124.1**
Speed ratings (Par 95): **98,97,95,91,90 88,73,71,69,47**
Tote Swingers:1&2:£2.80, 2&3:£5.70, 1&3:£2.50 CSF £3.92 CT £19.19 TOTE £3.30: £1.60, £1.10, £3.30; EX 6.60.
Owner Roger Peel **Bred** Oak Lodge Stud **Trained** Hambleton, N Yorks

FOCUS
On a chilly evening the surface was reckoned to be riding a fraction on the slow side. A low-grade opener but the winner was overdue a first success. It's doubtful if she had to improve on her latest effort.
Gunalt Joy Official explanation: jockey said filly had a breathing problem
Una Vita Pius(IRE) Official explanation: jockey said filly appeared to lose its action but returned sound

596 WOLVERHAMPTON HOSPITALITY - A PLEASURE H'CAP — 1m 5f 194y(P)
6:00 (6:01) (Class 6) (0-65,67) 4-Y-O+ — **£1,535** (£453; £226) **Stalls** Low

Form	Pos	Btn	Horse	Jockey	RPR
-541	**1**		**Cotton King**[11] 449 4-9-9 67 6ex	(vt) IanMongan 2	84+
			(Tobias B P Coles) *midfield on outer: hdwy to trck ldr 6f out: led on bridle over 3f out: rdn clr over 2f out: easily* **10/11**[1]		
06-5	**2**	10	**Leyte Gulf (USA)**[7] 514 8-9-8 61	AdamKirby 6	64
			(Chris Bealby) *slowly away: hld up: hdwy over 4f out: rdn and kpt on fr over 2f out: wnt 2nd ins fnl f: n.d to wnr* **4/1**[2]		
-404	**3**	¾	**Juwireya**[17] 373 4-9-3 61	(v) ChrisCatlin 8	63
			(Peter Hiatt) *prom on outer: led 4f out: sn hdd: rdn and kpt on same pce: lost 2nd ins fnl f* **16/1**		
505-	**4**	1½	**Chocolate Caramel (USA)**[35] 7465 9-9-3 56	FrederikTylicki 7	56
			(Richard Fahey) *hld up in midfield: hdwy 5f out: rdn to chse ldr 3f out: kpt on tl no ex ins fnl f* **14/1**		
63-4	**5**	2½	**Amical Risks (FR)**[28] 252 7-9-4 57	BarryMcHugh 1	53
			(Ollie Pears) *hld up: rdn and hdwy on outer over 2f out: wknd ins fnl f* **8/1**[3]		
/04-	**6**	3	**Ergo (FR)**[18] 1867 7-9-11 64	(v) PJMcDonald 4	56
			(James Moffatt) *hld up in midfield: rdn over 2f out: sn no imp* **25/1**		
000-	**7**	17	**Aureate**[115] 2182 7-9-12 65	DavidProbert 3	33
			(Brian Forsey) *trckd ldrs: rdn over 3f out: sn wknd* **20/1**		
60/	**8**	20	**Ebony Shades (IRE)**[41] 4166 10-9-1 54	(bt[1]) GrahamGibbons 9	—
			(Muredach Kelly, Ire) *led: hdd over 3f out: sn wknd* **12/1**		

/000 9 26 **Carlton Mac**[11] 444 6-8-7 46 oh1 ....(p) SilvestreDeSousa 5 —
(Simon Griffiths) *prom: chsd along 7f out: lost pl over 5f out: wknd fnl 4f: t.o* **80/1**

3m 4.62s (-1.38) **Going Correction** +0.125s/f (Slow)
WFA 4 from 6yo+ 5lb **9** Ran SP% **113.6**
Speed ratings (Par 101): **108,102,101,101,99 97,88,76,61**
Tote Swingers:1&2:£2.10, 2&3:£4.70, 1&3:£3.30 CSF £4.29 CT £31.71 TOTE £2.30: £1.10, £1.10, £3.50; EX 4.70.
Owner Mrs Sarah Hamilton **Bred** Meon Valley Stud **Trained** Newmarket, Suffolk

FOCUS
A modest stayers' handicap run at a sound pace and a wide-margin winner who probably has more to offer. The form is rated around the second and third.
Carlton Mac Official explanation: jockey said gelding had no more to give

597 DOWNLOAD BLUE SQUARE IPHONE APP H'CAP 1m 5f 194y(P)
6:30 (6:30) (Class 4) (0-85,83) 4-Y-0+ **£3,205** (£953; £476; £238) **Stalls** Low

Form RPR
1112 1 **Carter**[6] 531 5-9-3 74 .... GrahamGibbons 6 86+
(Ian Williams) *slowly away: hld up: hdwy to chse ldrs 3f out: rdn over 2f out: led 1f out: kpt on wl* **3/1**[1]
0-22 2 1 1/4 **Parhelion**[16] 392 4-8-11 73 .... JoeFanning 4 82
(Derek Haydn Jones) *chsd ldrs: hdwy to ld over 3f out: rdn whn hdd 2f out: rallied and regained 2nd wl ins fnl f* **4/1**[3]
1-52 3 1/2 **Ethics Girl (IRE)**[21] 342 5-9-8 79 ....(t) RobertHavlin 5 87
(John Berry) *hld up: hdwy 4f out: led on bridle 2f out: sn rdn: hdd 1f out: no ex and lost 2nd wl ins fnl f* **3/1**[1]
101- 4 25 **Dubara Reef (IRE)**[108] 7284 4-8-9 71 ....(p) SilvestreDeSousa 3 44+
(Paul Green) *chsd clr ldr: clsd over 4f out: n.m.r on inner 3f out: wknd over 2f out* **7/2**[2]
000- 5 23 **Far From Old (IRE)**[266] 2509 8-9-12 83 ....(v[1]) HayleyTurner 1 24+
(Michael Bell) *sn led: clr 7f out tl 4f out: hdd over 3f out: wknd qckly: t.o* **7/1**
6 dist **Anak (IRE)**[48] 4184 5-9-6 77 .... PaulDoe 8 —
(Jim Best) *prom: reminders early: lost pl over 9f out: tk little interest and t.o fnl 8f* **16/1**

3m 5.60s (-0.40) **Going Correction** +0.125s/f (Slow)
WFA 4 from 5yo+ 5lb **6** Ran SP% **110.6**
Speed ratings (Par 105): **106,105,105,90,77** —
Tote Swingers:1&2:£2.10, 2&3:£2.90, 1&3:£1.20 CSF £14.73 CT £35.37 TOTE £4.40: £1.50, £2.10; EX 17.00.
Owner Stratford Bards Racing **Bred** Dr D G St John And Mrs Sherry Collier **Trained** Portway, Worcs

FOCUS
A good-class and competitive looking stayers' handicap run at an uneven pace, and in the end a very ready winner who continues to progress. The form is probably sound enough..
Anak(IRE) Official explanation: jockey said gelding was reluctant to race

598 WOLVERHAMPTON HOLIDAY INN H'CAP 1m 4f 50y(P)
7:05 (7:05) (Class 7) (0-50,50) 4-Y-0+ **£1,535** (£453; £226) **Stalls** Low

Form RPR
50-2 1 **Bright Sparky (GER)**[10] 451 8-8-8 48 ....(vt) DavidSimmonson[(7)] 6 55
(Michael Easterby) *sn prom on outer: led 3f out: rdn 2f out: kpt on wl* **7/1**
05-0 2 1 1/4 **Little Richard (IRE)**[29] 223 12-9-0 47 ....(p) AdamKirby 9 52
(Mark Wellings) *in tch: rdn and outpcd over 2f out: rallied over 1f out: kpt on wl to take 2nd fnl 100yds* **33/1**
-413 3 3/4 **Our Kes (IRE)**[6] 524 9-9-3 50 .... StevieDonohoe 5 54
(Jane Chapple-Hyam) *hld up: hdwy on outer over 2f out: rdn to chse ldrs over 1f out: kpt on ins fnl f* **11/2**[2]
0/30 4 1/2 **Beauchamp Viking**[17] 277 7-8-12 45 ....(t) HayleyTurner 3 48
(Simon Burrough) *racd keenly in midfield: rdn and hdwy over 3f out: kpt on ins fnl f* **25/1**
02-3 5 1/2 **Mary Helen**[15] 408 4-8-13 49 .... LiamJones 10 51
(Mark Brisbourne) *s.i.s: hld up: hdwy on outer to chse ldrs over 3f out: rdn over 2f out: chal for 2nd over 1f out: no ex ins fnl f* **8/1**
45-3 6 1/2 **Dot's Delight**[12] 172 7-9-1 48 .... SilvestreDeSousa 4 49
(Mark Rimell) *trckd ldrs on inner: rdn and outpcd 3f out: kpt on again fr over 1f out* **5/1**[1]
655- 7 3 **Lisbon Lion (IRE)**[23] 3965 6-9-2 49 .... PJMcDonald 2 46
(James Moffatt) *hld up: sme late hdwy: n.d* **10/1**
0-30 8 1/2 **Oak Leaves**[15] 409 4-8-12 48 .... DavidProbert 7 44
(Nikki Evans) *led: hdd 3f out: chsd wnr tl over 1f out: wknd ins fnl f* **50/1**
30-0 9 1 1/4 **Le Corvee (IRE)**[25] 277 9-9-3 50 .... LukeMorris 8 44
(Tony Carroll) *prom: wknd over 2f out* **16/1**
560- 10 shd **Paint The Town Red**[112] 7213 6-8-13 46 .... JoeFanning 1 40
(Richard Guest) *hld up in midfield: rdn and lost pl 3f out: wknd fnl 2f* **13/2**
654- 11 3 **Ballade De La Mer**[100] 7398 5-8-13 46 ....(p) LeeNewman 12 35
(George Foster) *trckd ldrs towards outer: n.m.r 4f out: sn rdn: wknd over 2f out* **12/1**
-023 12 dist **Princess Lexi (IRE)**[19] 354 4-8-13 49 .... JamieSpencer 11 —
(Ian Williams) *s.i.s: hld up: lost tch fnl 7f: t.o* **6/1**[3]

2m 43.87s (2.77) **Going Correction** +0.125s/f (Slow)
WFA 4 from 5yo+ 3lb **12** Ran SP% **114.7**
Speed ratings (Par 97): **95,94,93,93,93 92,90,90,89,89 87**,—
Tote Swingers:1&2:£63.70, 2&3:£36.60, 1&3:£4.80 CSF £216.25 CT £1355.48 TOTE £5.50: £1.60, £5.00, £2.30; EX 212.40.
Owner Rupert Armitage & Graham Sparkes **Bred** Graf Und Grafin Von Stauffenberg **Trained** Sheriff Hutton, N Yorks
■ Stewards' Enquiry : David Simmonson two-day ban: used whip with excessive frequency in incorrect place (Mar 4, 7)

FOCUS
A rock-bottom handicap, a seller in all but name and a very limited weight range. Straightforward if limited form.
Princess Lexi(IRE) Official explanation: jockey said filly hung right-handed

599 NAME A RACE TO ENHANCE YOUR BRAND CLAIMING STKS 1m 1f 103y(P)
7:35 (7:35) (Class 5) 4-Y-0+ **£2,007** (£597; £298; £149) **Stalls** Low

Form RPR
4211 1 **Syrian**[11] 447 4-9-0 80 .... JamieSpencer 4 89+
(Ian Williams) *stdd s: plld hrd: hld up: clsd 5f out: upsides and hrd hld 2f out: nudged ahd over 1f out: sn clr: v easily* **4/7**[1]
-132 2 6 **Faithful Ruler (USA)**[11] 447 7-8-12 75 ....(p) LukeMorris 5 69
(Ronald Harris) *trckd ldr in 2nd: led 4f out: drvn whn hdd over 1f out: no ch w wnr* **7/2**[2]
2250 3 6 **Dream Of Fortune (IRE)**[4] 541 7-8-11 68 ....(bt) SilvestreDeSousa 3 55
(David Evans) *chsd ldng pair: outpcd over 4f out: rallied to go 3rd over 2f out: one pce fnl 2f* **7/1**[3]
100- 4 2 3/4 **Ahlawy (IRE)**[102] 7382 8-8-13 81 ....(bt) LeeVickers 1 52
(Frank Sheridan) *slowly away: sn wl bhd: nvr threatened* **9/1**
6 5 9 **Countess Salome (IRE)**[24] 291 4-8-5 56 .... CathyGannon 2 25
(Muredach Kelly, Ire) *led: clr 8f out tl over 5f out: hdd 4f out: wknd over 2f out* **40/1**

2m 2.45s (0.75) **Going Correction** +0.125s/f (Slow) **5** Ran SP% **110.8**
Speed ratings (Par 103): **101,95,90,87,79**
CSF £2.92 TOTE £2.30: £1.50, £1.10; EX 3.20.Syrian was claimed by P. D. Evans for £11,000.
Owner Dr Marwan Koukash **Bred** Barry Walters **Trained** Portway, Worcs

FOCUS
The winner is enjoying himself at this level and is getting closer to his early-season form.
Ahlawy(IRE) Official explanation: jockey said gelding missed the break

600 HOTEL & CONFERENCING AT WOLVERHAMPTON MAIDEN FILLIES' STKS 7f 32y(P)
8:05 (8:06) (Class 5) 3-Y-0+ **£2,007** (£597; £298; £149) **Stalls** High

Form RPR
222- 1 **Strictly Pink (IRE)**[111] 7240 3-8-7 75 .... CathyGannon 5 73
(Alan Bailey) *trckd ldr: racd keenly: led wl over 1f out: edgd lft: rdn clr ins fnl f* **11/8**[1]
02-6 2 4 1/2 **Sottovoce**[44] 52 3-8-7 70 .... HayleyTurner 2 61
(Simon Dow) *trckd ldr: rdn over 2f out: kpt on same pce: wnt 2nd fnl 50yds: no ch w wnr* **7/2**[2]
0-52 3 nk **Unwrapit (USA)**[7] 509 3-8-7 0 .... TomEaves 4 60
(Bryan Smart) *sn led: rdn whn hdd over 1f out: sn no ch w wnr: edgd lft ins fnl f: lost 2nd fnl 50yds* **7/2**[2]
5-46 4 4 1/2 **Mini's Destination**[10] 456 3-8-7 50 .... KirstyMilczarek 9 48
(John Holt) *midfield: hdwy to chse ldrs on outer 3f out: sn rdn: kpt on to go modest 4th ins fnl f* **25/1**
5 nk **Misere** 3-8-7 0 .... SilvestreDeSousa 8 47+
(Kevin Ryan) *slowly away and rn green in rr: hdwy into midfield over 3f out: kpt on same pce: bttr for experience* **13/2**[3]
04-0 6 nk **Lady Mango (IRE)**[39] 110 3-8-7 63 .... LukeMorris 3 46
(Ronald Harris) *chsd ldrs: rdn over 3f out: one pce* **25/1**
0-00 7 4 **Frill A Minute**[7] 512 7-9-5 30 ....(v) DaleSwift[(5)] 7 35
(Lynn Siddall) *in tch on outer: rdn over 3f out: wknd over 1f out* **100/1**
0 8 4 1/2 **Higher Spen Jess**[28] 253 3-8-7 0 .... BarryMcHugh 10 23
(Julie Camacho) *hld up on outer: rdn over 3f out: n.d* **50/1**
000- 9 14 **Lady Of The Knight (IRE)**[172] 5594 3-8-4 0 .... JamesSullivan[(3)] 6 —
(Hugh McWilliams) *dwlt: hld up: a in rr* **50/1**
00 10 35 **Bellaboolou**[30] 214 3-8-7 0 ....(t) ChrisCatlin 1 —
(David Pinder) *s.i.s: sn detached in rr: t.o* **66/1**

1m 30.21s (0.61) **Going Correction** +0.125s/f (Slow)
WFA 3 from 7yo 17lb **10** Ran SP% **114.0**
Speed ratings (Par 100): **101,95,95,90,90 89,85,79,63,23**
Tote Swingers:1&2:£1.70, 2&3:£1.80, 1&3:£2.20 CSF £5.80 TOTE £1.90: £1.02, £1.90, £1.70; EX 7.60.
Owner A J H **Bred** Tally-Ho Stud **Trained** Newmarket, Suffolk

FOCUS
Plenty of deadwood in this modest maiden fillies' race and the first three in the betting had the finish to themselves once in line for home. The easy winner set a far standard and didn't need to match her best.

601 PLAY RAINBOW RICHES AT BLUESQ.COM H'CAP 7f 32y(P)
8:35 (8:36) (Class 5) (0-75,73) 3-Y-0 **£2,007** (£597; £298; £149) **Stalls** High

Form RPR
02-4 1 **Silly Billy (IRE)**[14] 423 3-8-13 72 .... LukeRowe[(7)] 6 76
(Sylvester Kirk) *racd keenly: prom on outer after 2f: led over 2f out: pushed out ins fnl f: kpt on* **14/1**
1 2 3/4 **Dasho**[39] 110 3-9-7 73 .... HayleyTurner 2 75+
(Olivia Maylam) *s.i.s: racd keenly: hld up in rr: swtchd rt to wd outside over 1f out: gd hdwy to chse wnr: drvn and kpt on wl ins fnl f* **13/8**[1]
-133 3 1 1/4 **Greenhead High**[9] 476 3-9-1 67 .... JamieSpencer 1 66+
(Jane Chapple-Hyam) *racd keenly: in tch on inner: short of room 2f out: swtchd rt over 1f out: kpt on to go 3rd ins fnl f* **4/1**[3]
4-24 4 1 3/4 **Captain Loui (IRE)**[18] 364 3-8-13 65 ....(p) LukeMorris 5 59
(Dai Burchell) *prom: rdn and outpcd 2f out: kpt on at one pce ins fnl f* **9/1**
215- 5 3/4 **Saucy Buck (IRE)**[98] 7417 3-9-3 69 ....(v[1]) SamHitchcott 7 61
(Mick Channon) *chsd ldrs on outer: drvn over 1f out: one pce ins fnl f* **11/2**
0-04 6 1 3/4 **Jambo Bibi (IRE)**[21] 344 3-8-8 60 .... JoeFanning 4 47
(Bruce Hellier) *in tch: hdwy over 2f out: edgd lft over 1f out: rdn and wknd ins fnl f* **20/1**
3-01 7 9 **Loves Theme (IRE)**[14] 422 3-9-5 71 ....(b) J-PGuillambert 3 34
(Alan Bailey) *sn led: rdn whn hdd over 2f out: wknd over 1f out* **10/3**[2]

1m 31.05s (1.45) **Going Correction** +0.125s/f (Slow) **7** Ran SP% **118.0**
Speed ratings (Par 97): **96,95,93,91,90 88,78**
Tote Swingers:1&2:£4.80, 2&3:£2.40, 1&3:£9.50 CSF £39.08 TOTE £26.00: £9.90, £3.70; EX 72.60.
Owner Lady Davis **Bred** Sir E J Loder **Trained** Upper Lambourn, Berks
■ Luke Rowe's first winner.

FOCUS
A tight 60-73 3-y-o handicap. It looked a bit of a muddling race and might not be form to take too literally.
T/Plt: £7.00 to a £1 stake. Pool: £82,246.49. 8,549.38 winning tickets. T/Qpdt: £4.70 to a £1 stake. Pool: £7,335.93. 1,151.02 winning tickets. AS

581 MEYDAN (L-H)
Friday, February 18

OFFICIAL GOING: Tapeta: standard; turf: good
The rail was out 15 meters on the turf course.

602a CORPORATE BANKING (H'CAP) (TURF) 6f
3:15 (3:15) (100-115,115) 3-Y-0+
£67,307 (£22,435; £11,217; £5,608; £3,365; £2,243)

RPR
1 **War Artist (AUS)**[29] 237 8-9-6 115 .... OlivierPeslier 6 116+
(Rod Collet, France) *mid-div: smooth prog 3f out: led 1 1/2f out: r.o wl* **10/1**
2 1/4 **Rileyskeepingfaith**[22] 327 5-8-6 100 ....(t) AhmedAjtebi 9 99
(Mahmood Al Zarooni) *racd in rr: racd stands' rail: ev ch 1 1/2f out: r.o wl* **7/1**

3 1/4 **Orife (IRE)**[72] 4-8-6 100........................ GregoryBenoist 1 98
(Stephane Chevalier, UAE) *slowly away: rdn 2 1/2f out: r.o wl fnl 1 1/2f: nrst fin* **16/1**

4 1 **Barney McGrew (IRE)**[8] 500 8-8-6 100.................. RoystonFfrench 3 95
(Michael Dods) *mid-div: r.o wl fnl 2f* **8/1**

5 shd **Mutheeb (USA)**[15] 414 6-9-2 110..........................(v) RichardHills 10 105
(M Al Muhairi, UAE) *trckd ldr: ev ch 1 1/2f out: one pce fnl f* **6/1**[3]

6 2 1/4 **Jimmy Styles**[29] 237 7-8-6 100..........................(p) KierenFallon 7 88
(Clive Cox) *mid-div: chsd ldrs tl 2 1/2f out: nt qckn fnl f* **4/1**[2]

7 1/2 **Inxile (IRE)**[15] 414 6-9-0 108..........................(p) AdrianNicholls 8 94
(David Nicholls) *disp ld: led 2 1/2f out tl 1 1/2f out: wknd* **6/1**[3]

8 1/2 **Musaalem (USA)**[64] 7904 7-8-9 104.................... TadhgO'Shea 4 87
(Doug Watson, UAE) *settled in rr: r.o wl fnl 2f* **16/1**

9 1 1/4 **Everyday Heroes (USA)**[29] 237 5-8-6 100.................. TedDurcan 5 80
(Saeed Bin Suroor) *disp ld tl 2 1/2f out: wknd* **3/1**[1]

10 15 **Compasivo Cat (ARG)**[8] 500 7-8-9 104....................(bt) WJSupple 2 35
(E Charpy, UAE) *disp ld tl 2 1/2f out: wknd qckly* **33/1**

1m 11.67s (71.67) **10** Ran SP% **121.0**
CSF: £81.18; Tricast: £1,130.65..

Owner Rupert Plersch **Bred** S Kirkham **Trained** France

FOCUS
This was a decent sprint handicap, although the time was the slowest of the four races to be run over this C&D so far.

NOTEBOOK
War Artist(AUS) needed the run when finding 5f an inadequate test here on his reappearance, but he was said to look in much better condition this time and returned to form. He was the class act of the field and moved best throughout before finding enough for pressure. Last year he was fourth in the Al Quoz Sprint on World Cup night, but he won't be helped by the distance of that race having changed from 6f to 5f, and he may have to switch back to Tapeta (won on the surface in 2010) next time. The Mahab Al Shimaal on Super Thursday and the Golden Shaheen at the end of March are the obvious races, although he'll have to prove he's still up to such a high level. (op 11-1)

Rileyskeepingfaith wasn't travelling at all well early, but he ended up against the stands' rail in the latter stages and, if that was the intention, it was a shrewd move from Ahmed Ajtebi. Once away from the others and with the fence to guide, the gelding ran on strongly to be closest at the finish, although he still didn't look keen under pressure.

Orife(IRE), who has some useful French form to his name, ran a fine race after a break of 72 days, showing himself well up to this company.

Barney McGrew(IRE), a bit keen early, kept on without threatening. He's not easy to win with these days.

Mutheeb(USA) was unable to get much cover and consequently over-raced.

Jimmy Styles had shaped nicely over 5f on his Dubai debut (War Artist behind), and was expected to appreciate the return to this trip, but he was never travelling.

Inxile(IRE), who had run two good races from the widest stall over this trip on Tapeta, had cheekpieces fitted this time but was unsuited by the switch to turf. He showed his customary early speed, but this track, without a bend to help him get a breather, proved too testing.

Everyday Heroes(USA) had plenty go his way when third over 5f here on his first start in Dubai, and he couldn't repeat that form.

603a ASSET MANAGEMENT (MEYDAN MASTERS INVITATIONAL) (H'CAP) (TURF) 1m 4f 114y

3:50 (3:50) (100-110,109) 3-Y-O+

£46,153 (£15,384; £7,692; £3,846; £2,307; £1,538)

RPR

1 **Calvados Blues (FR)**[15] 413 5-9-5 109........................ JMurtagh 7 112+
(Mahmood Al Zarooni) *mid-div: last 3 1/2f out: smooth prog 2f out: r.o wl: led fnl 55yds* **6/1**[3]

2 1/2 **Mikhail Glinka (IRE)**[15] 413 4-9-2 108....................(t) MaximeGuyon 3 112
(H J Brown, South Africa) *sn led: qcknd 4f out: rdn 2 1/2f out: r.o wl: hdd fnl 55yds* **8/1**

3 1 1/4 **Age Of Reason (UAE)**[22] 329 6-9-4 108.................. RichardHughes 1 108
[illegible]

4 3/4 **Topclas (FR)**[22] 329 5-9-1 105........................ WilliamBuick 5 104
(M bin Shafya, UAE) *settled last: r.o fnl 2f* **16/1**

5 2 3/4 **Telluride**[15] 413 5-9-2 106..........................(t) CHBorel 8 101
(J E Hammond, France) *settled in rr: trckd ldrs 6f out: one pce fnl 2f* **9/2**[2]

6 1/2 **Absolute Heretic (AUS)**[15] 417 5-8-10 100.................. TJPereira 2 94
(M F De Kock, South Africa) *mid-div: no room 2f out: nt rcvr* **9/2**[2]

7 1 1/4 **Bay Willow (IRE)**[22] 328 4-8-9 101........................ GeraldMosse 4 95
(Saeed Bin Suroor) *trckd ldr: ev ch 1 1/2f out: one pce fnl f* **6/1**[3]

P **Lawspeaker**[15] 413 4-9-1 107........................ HiroyukiUchida 6 —
(Mahmood Al Zarooni) *trckd ldng pair tl 2 1/2f out: p.u 1 1/2f out* **14/1**

2m 37.83s (157.83)
WFA 4 from 5yo+ 4lb **8** Ran SP% **113.6**
CSF: £51.78; Tricast: £170.96..

Owner Godolphin **Bred** Thierry De La Herronniere Et Al **Trained** Newmarket, Suffolk

FOCUS
The early gallop, set by Mikhail Glinka, seemed fair, but that one slowed the pace leaving the back straight and very much had the run of the race.

NOTEBOOK
Calvados Blues(FR) had looked flattered by his recent second over C&D considering he was allowed a soft lead against the then favoured inside rail, and he had also displayed an awkward head carriage, but more patient tactics clearly suited at least as well this time. According to Johnny Murtagh, the plan had actually been to race prominently again, but the horse was a bit slow into his stride. This was a really smart performance under top weight seeing as he had been shuffled back to last around the final bend and had to pick up off the muddling pace. The Group 2 Dubai City of Gold over C&D on Super Thursday is the obvious target.

Mikhail Glinka(IRE) had the run of the race but still deserves credit for sticking on so well considering this trip his short of optimum. He reversed last-time out placings with Telluride, and also got a lot closer to Calvados Blues.

Age Of Reason(UAE) tracked the runner-up into the straight but couldn't pick up sufficiently. He needs more of a stamina test and will presumably be aimed at the DRC Gold Cup, a race in which he was runner-up last year.

Topclas(FR), out the back early after missing the break, kept on without threatening.

Telluride, with a tongue-tie re-fitted, was closely matched with today's one-two, but he was unsuited by the lack of pace, even though he made headway before the tempo increased. That said, he's probably not one to make excuses for.

Absolute Heretic(AUS) stayed on from off a slow pace over 1m2f on his Dubai debut, but he was sweating down his neck this time and failed to progress.

Lawspeaker unfortunately seemed to pick up an injury, dropping out early in the straight before being pulled up and dismounted. (op 12-1)

604a PRIVATE BANKING (H'CAP) (TAPETA) 1m

4:30 (4:30) (100-110,110) 3-Y-O+

£46,153 (£15,384; £7,692; £3,846; £2,307; £1,538)

RPR

1 **Famous Warrior (IRE)**[8] 497 4-8-8 101........................ TadhgO'Shea 8 101
(Doug Watson, UAE) *sn led: rdn clr 2f out: r.o wl* **14/1**

2 1 **Sangaree (USA)**[15] 414 6-9-0 107....................(b) MickaelBarzalona 10 105+
(Saeed Bin Suroor) *in rr of mid-div: r.o wl fnl 2f but no ch w wnr* **20/1**

3 1 1/4 **Here To Win (BRZ)**[15] 417 5-8-13 106............ ChristopheSoumillon 11 101+
(M F De Kock, South Africa) *s.i.s: settled in rr: r.o wl fnl 2f: nrst fin* **3/1**[2]

4 1 **Fareer**[22] 332 5-9-0 107........................ RichardHills 5 100
(Ed Dunlop) *mid-div: r.o fnl 2f* **20/1**

5 3/4 **Caymans (AUS)**[22] 331 6-9-1 108........................ FrankieDettori 6 99
(Saeed Bin Suroor) *trckd ldr: ev ch 2f out: one pce fnl f* **5/2**[1]

6 1 **Atlantic Brave**[14] 5-8-11 105..........................(vt) WayneSmith 3 93
(M Al Muhairi, UAE) *broke awkwardly: rdn after 2f: r.o same pce fnl 55yds* **6/1**[3]

7 1/2 **Oasis Dancer**[22] 332 4-8-11 105........................ JimCrowley 7 91
(Ralph Beckett) *trckd ldng trio: ev ch 1 1/2f out: nt qckn fnl 110yds* **14/1**

8 1/4 **Final Drive (IRE)**[1] 583 5-8-8 101........................ RyanMoore 4 88
(John Ryan) *in rr of mid-div: nvr able to chal* **12/1**

9 2 3/4 **My Indy (ARG)**[15] 416 7-9-3 110........................ PatCosgrave 1 90
(M bin Shafya, UAE) *trckd ldr tl 2 1/2f out: wknd* **20/1**

10 2 3/4 **Ayun Tara (FR)**[8] 497 4-8-10 104........................ GregoryBenoist 2 77
(X Nakkachdji, France) *mid-div: wknd fnl 1 1/2f* **10/1**

1m 36.96s (-0.14) **Going Correction** 0.0s/f (Stan) **10** Ran SP% **112.3**
Speed ratings: **100,99,97,96,96 95,94,94,91,88**
CSF: £224.28; Tricast: £790.42..

Owner Mohsin Al Tajir **Bred** Hadi Al Tajir **Trained** United Arab Emirates

FOCUS
After refusing to enter the stalls, Escape Route had to be withdrawn. This was a first winner of the 2011 Carnival for trainer Doug Watson, with Famous Warrior, his 29th runner, making the most of being allowed a soft lead.

NOTEBOOK
Famous Warrior(IRE), formerly trained in Ireland by Kevin Prendergast, ran an encouraging second race for these connections over 7f and built on that on this step back up to 1m, peaking on his third run after a layoff. He's unlikely to get as kind a trip next time, and even if he does, things will be tougher off a higher mark.

Sangaree(USA) showed little from a poor draw in a 6f Group 3 on his debut for this yard, but he was entitled to come on for that and benefited from both the step up in trip and drop in grade.

Here To Win(BRZ), switched to Tapeta and dropped back in trip, having failed to build on a promising Dubai debut last time, lost her race at the start. She was soon out the back after losing a few lengths with an awkward beginning, and she did well to get so close. This was a good run in the circumstances, although she may not be one to follow at short prices.

Fareer ran poorly on turf on his reappearance, but this was better.

Caymans(AUS) didn't start that well and had to use up energy to sit handy. Never a serious threat in the straight, he failed to improve for the switch from turf.

Oasis Dancer may do better next time when he'll be third off the layoff.

Final Drive(IRE), disappointing the previous day, has probably had enough for now.

605a PRIORITY BANKING (LEG 3 MEYDAN MASTERS) (H'CAP) (TURF) 1m 1f

5:05 (5:05) (95-105,104) 3-Y-O+

£42,307 (£14,102; £7,051; £3,525; £2,115; £1,410)

RPR

1 **War Monger (USA)**[29] 239 7-9-1 100........................ OlivierPeslier 11 101
(Doug Watson, UAE) *sn led: rdn clr 2f out: r.o wl: comf* **8/1**[3]

2 2 **Yirga**[8] 497 5-9-3 102..........................(t) RichardHills 7 99+
(A Al Raihe, UAE) *mid-div: r.o wl fnl 2f: nrst fin* **7/1**[2]

3 1 **Marching Time**[13] 462 5-8-9 95........................ FrankieDettori 4 89
(Doug Watson, UAE) *in rr of mid-div: r.o wl fnl 1 1/2f* **13/2**[1]

[illegible]
(Michael Dods) *mid-div: ev ch 2f out: one pce fnl f* **8/1**[3]

5 1/4 **Big Audio (IRE)**[181] 5292 4-8-11 97....................(t) MaximeGuyon 8 90
(Saeed Bin Suroor) *trckd ldng duo: nt qckn fnl 1 1/2f* **7/1**[2]

6 1 1/4 **Eddie Jock (IRE)**[15] 417 7-9-1 100....................(t) TJPereira 10 91
(S Seemar, UAE) *a mid-div* **16/1**

7 2 **Mac Love**[8] 503 10-9-4 104........................ HiroyukiUchida 1 90
(Stef Higgins) *mid-div on rail: r.o same pce fnl 1 1/2f* **12/1**

8 1/2 **Inestimable**[50] 8028 6-9-3 102....................(v) RichardHughes 5 88
(M Al Muhairi, UAE) *slowly away: settled last: nvr nr to chal* **7/1**[2]

9 1/4 **Kal Barg**[8] 499 6-9-4 104........................ WilliamBuick 12 89
(D Selvaratnam, UAE) *mid-div: rn wd: n.d* **8/1**[3]

10 3 1/4 **Big Creek (IRE)**[22] 332 4-9-1 100........................ RyanMoore 2 79
(J S Moore) *trckd ldr tl 2 1/2f out: sn wknd* **20/1**

11 4 1/4 **Brief Encounter (IRE)**[22] 5-9-1 100........................ GeraldMosse 6 70
(Ibrahaim Al Malki, Qatar) *mid-div: wknd fnl 2f* **8/1**[3]

12 1 **Atlantis Star**[22] 326 4-9-4 104..........................(p) CHBorel 3 71
(Saeed Bin Suroor) *settled in rr: nvr able to chal* **9/1**

1m 50.1s (110.10) **12** Ran SP% **123.6**
CSF: £65.91; Tricast: £396.91..

Owner Hamdan Al Maktoum **Bred** Peter Vegso Racing Stable **Trained** United Arab Emirates

FOCUS
This was one of the weakest handicaps run at the Carnival so far this year, and War Monger made the most of being allowed to set soft fractions after easing his way to the front (time 1.31 seconds slower than later Group 2 Balanchine Stakes).

NOTEBOOK
War Monger(USA) was gaining his first success since coming over from the US, but he won't appeal as one to back to follow up.

Yirga returned to form with the tongue-tie re-fitted, finishing well from some way off the pace, but he was no threat to the winner.

Marching Time, represented the same owner and trainer as the winner, and he carried the first colours. He was soon well behind but finished better than the most and this was encouraging. (tchd 6-1)

Tiger Reigns improved on the form he showed on his reappearance and shaped as though he could do better again next time.

Big Audio(IRE) was one-paced under pressure and gave the impression this first run in 181 days was needed.

Mac Love had finished in front of War Monger last time, but the lack of pace didn't suit him. He looked a big threat when arriving on the scene apparently full of running early in the straight, but he had been keen and found little.

Atlantis Star was keen early and the saddle soon slipped, so this performance is best ignored.

606a BUSINESS BANKING (H'CAP) (TAPETA) 7f

5:45 (5:45) (100-110,109) 3-Y-0+

£46,153 (£15,384; £7,692; £3,846; £2,307; £1,538)

RPR

1 **Barbecue Eddie (USA)**[22] 332 7-8-8 100..................(b) RichardHills 10 106+
(Doug Watson, UAE) *trckd ldng gp: led 1 1/2f out: r.o wl: comf* **16/1**

2 2 ¾ **Reynaldothewizard (USA)**[22] 326 5-8-11 104.......(t) RichardMullen 12 101
(S Seemar, UAE) *mid-div: wd: r.o wl fnl 2f* **14/1**

3 shd **As De Trebol (USA)**[71] 7800 5-8-8 100.......................... OlivierPeslier 4 97
(M Delcher-Sanchez, Spain) *sn led: hdd 1 1/2f out: r.o same pce* **16/1**

4 hd **Banna Boirche (IRE)**[15] 414 5-9-0 106............................ JMurtagh 11 103
(M Halford, Ire) *in rr of mid-div: r.o wl fnl 2f* **8/1**

5 hd **Dohasa (IRE)**[15] 414 6-9-2 108............................ MickaelBarzalona 14 104
(I Mohammed, UAE) *settled in rr: nvr nr to chal but r.o fnl 2f* **10/1**

6 2 ¼ **Frosty Secret (USA)**[8] 501 7-9-0 106............ BernardFayd'Herbe 9 96
(M F De Kock, South Africa) *trckd ldr tl 2 1/2f out: one pce fnl f* **16/1**

7 ¼ **Solid Choice (AUS)**[15] 415 5-8-13 105........... ChristopheSoumillon 13 94
(M F De Kock, South Africa) *settled in rr: nvr able to chal* **5/1**[3]

8 ½ **Iver Bridge Lad**[8] 497 4-8-13 105..........................(b) RichardHughes 1 93
(John Ryan) *settled in rr: nvr able to chal* **20/1**

9 1 ¼ **Mariol (FR)**[22] 327 8-9-3 109...................................... GregoryBenoist 3 94
(Rod Collet, France) *nvr bttr than mid-div* **25/1**

10 2 ¼ **Bank Merger (USA)**[132] 4-9-1 107...................................(t) TedDurcan 7 86
(Saeed Bin Suroor) *trckd ldng pair tl 2 1/2f out: wknd* **7/1**

11 5 ¼ **Ashram (IRE)**[36] 152 5-9-2 108...................................(v) FrankieDettori 2 73
(Saeed Bin Suroor) *nvr bttr than mid-div* **9/2**[2]

12 ¼ **Rakaan (IRE)**[8] 497 4-8-13 105... RyanMoore 6 69
(Jamie Osborne) *nvr bttr than mid-div* **7/2**[1]

1m 23.11s (-2.09) **Going Correction** 0.0s/f (Stan) **12 Ran SP% 122.7**
Speed ratings: **111,107,107,107,107 104,104,103,102,99 93,93**
CSF: £229.75; Tricast: £3,634.84..
Owner Hamdan Al Maktoum **Bred** Margaret Addis **Trained** United Arab Emirates

FOCUS
A remarkable third winner on the day for Doug Watson, who had gone 0-28 at this year's Carnival prior to his first success earlier on the card. This was another ordinary handicap, but the pace was strong and the time was the second fastest over C&D to date, just 0.16 seconds off Sirocco Breeze's track record.

NOTEBOOK
Barbecue Eddie(USA) wasn't beaten far in a better race over 1m on turf last time and he proved suited by the return to this C&D, the scene of his only previous success in Dubai. That was at last year's Carnival off 5lb lower, when he was allowed a ridiculously soft lead, but clearly he's not reliant on front-running tactics.
Reynaldothewizard(USA) didn't stay 1m in a hot race around here last time and this was better. His effort is particularly creditable considering he had a wide trip.
As De Trebol(USA) probably would have been second had he not been slightly checked by the winner as that one went past in the closing stages, and this was a big performance considering he set such a good gallop.
Banna Boirche(IRE) improved a little for the step back to a more suitable trip, but not enough.
Solid Choice(AUS) looked the type to progress when going from last to first off a slow pace over this C&D on his reappearance, but he then disappointed on turf (apparently got a bit jarred up) and didn't fare much better on Tapeta, despite the race being run to suit.
Bank Merger(USA) has some quality dirt form to his name in the US, notably second behind the high-class Discreetly Mine in the Grade 1 King's Bishop, but he seemingly failed to act on this synthetic track after a 132-day break.
Rakaan(IRE), 4lb higher than when winning a similar race the previous week, was eased off in the straight after failing to pick up, giving the impression something may have been amiss.

607a BALANCHINE SPONSORED BY EMIRATES NBD (GROUP 2) (FILLIES) (TURF) 1m 1f

6:20 (6:20) 3-Y-0+

£76,923 (£25,641; £12,820; £6,410; £3,846; £2,564)

RPR

1 **River Jetez (SAF)**[29] 241 8-9-2 107.................. ChristopheSoumillon 1 108+
(M F De Kock, South Africa) *in rr of mid-div: smooth prog 2 1/2f out: led 110yds out: r.o wl* **4/5**[1]

2 2 ½ **Reem (AUS)**[15] 412 4-8-9 104.. KShea 11 96
(M F De Kock, South Africa) *mid-div: smooth prog to ld 2f out: r.o wl: hdd fnl 110yds* **12/1**

3 1 **Long Lashes (USA)**[129] 6830 4-9-2 102.........................(tp) TedDurcan 4 101
(Saeed Bin Suroor) *settled in rr: r.o wl fnl 2f: nrst fin* **16/1**

4 1 **Forest Crown**[29] 241 4-9-2 100... JimCrowley 6 99
(Ralph Beckett) *in rr of mid-div: nvr nr to chal* **28/1**

5 hd **Strawberrydaiquiri**[139] 6561 5-9-2 113........................ RyanMoore 7 98
(F Nass, Bahrain) *in rr of mid-div: r.o same pce fnl 2f* **7/2**[2]

6 2 ¼ **Lolamar (ITY)**[15] 417 4-9-2 104............................... MickaelBarzalona 5 93
(Marco Botti) *mid-div on rail: nvr able to chal* **20/1**

7 nse **Aspectoflove (IRE)**[29] 241 5-9-5 106........................... FrankieDettori 2 96
(Saeed Bin Suroor) *settled in rr: nvr able to chal but r.o fnl 2f* **6/1**[3]

8 5 **Kinky Afro (IRE)**[29] 241 4-9-2 99.................................... KierenFallon 8 83
(J S Moore) *nvr bttr than mid-div* **50/1**

9 6 ¾ **Anam Chara (IRE)**[22] 332 5-9-2 97.................................... JMurtagh 3 69
(Andrew Oliver, Ire) *trckd ldr tl 2 1/2f out: sn btn* **66/1**

10 5 ½ **Gallic Star (IRE)**[125] 6950 4-9-2 105........................ RichardHughes 9 57
(Mick Channon) *racd in 3rd: rdn 3f out: sn btn* **25/1**

11 14 **Tinaar (USA)**[125] 6928 5-9-2 95..........................(v) WayneSmith 10 28
(F Nass, Bahrain) *sn led: rdn and hdd 2f out: wknd* **66/1**

1m 48.79s (108.79) **11 Ran SP% 122.6**
CSF: £12.38..
Owner Mr & Mrs C A Amm & Marsh Shirtliff **Bred** Out Of Africa Stud **Trained** South Africa

FOCUS
Only the eighth running of this race, but it already has Group 2 status, upgraded from Group 3 level since last year. This was Mike De Kock's fourth winner of the event, and he also had the runner-up. The pace, set by Strawberrydaiquiri's stablemate, Tinaar, was strong and the time was 1.31 seconds faster than the 100-rated War Monger managed earlier on the card.

NOTEBOOK
River Jetez(SAF), who had looked an unlucky loser when third behind Aspectoflove in the Cape Verdi on her debut in Dubai, made the most of a better trip this time, justifying strong market support, but it was hard work. She was held up some of way off the pace, and her stablemate Reem, who had taken a few lengths out of the field when sent on early in the straight, didn't look like coming back at one stage. However, the favourite gradually responded to strong pressure as the runner-up began to tire, and she was nicely on top at the line. One of Mike De Kock's three previous winners of this, Sun Classique, followed up in the Sheema Classic, and presumably that race will be the target for River Jetez. (op 10-11)
Reem(AUS) ran a fine race for one so young (bred in Southern Hemisphere and yet to have fourth birthday), faring best of those to race close to the strong gallop. (op 10-1)
Long Lashes(USA), passed over by Frankie Dettori, had a tongue-tie re-fitted and ran a fine race after 129 days off. She's yet to really fulfil the potential she showed at two, but is back on the right track.
Forest Crown wasn't quite up to the task but ran well.
Strawberrydaiquiri was switched to the inside when short of room early in the straight, but almost ran into the back her stable companion Tinaar, who was inevitably weakening having made the pace. This daughter of Dansili had raced in front of the held up River Jetez, but found herself in a pocket early in the straight, and even after being switched back out wide she continued to find trouble. This was her first start since leaving Sir Michael Stoute, and she's joined a trainer yet to have a Carnival winner, but while it's hard to know where she would have finished with an uninterrupted trip, clearly she retains ability.
Lolamar(ITY) found this tougher than the recent handicap she won.
Aspectoflove(IRE) always seemed likely to struggle under the penalty picked up for her Cape Verdi win and further compromised her chance with an unusually slow start. (op 5-1)

608a PERSONAL BANKING (CONDITIONS RACE) (TAPETA) 1m 2f

6:55 (6:55) 3-Y-0+

£42,307 (£14,102; £7,051; £3,525; £2,115; £1,410)

RPR

1 **Golden Sword**[8] 499 5-9-0 112........................ ChristopheSoumillon 13 111
(M F De Kock, South Africa) *in rr of mid-div: smooth prog 2 1/2f out: r.o wl: led 1f out: comf* **7/4**[1]

2 2 ¾ **Deem (IRE)**[29] 241 6-8-9 115... OlivierPeslier 9 101
(J Barton, Saudi Arabia) *settled in rr: r.o wl fnl 2f: nrst fin* **5/1**[3]

3 ¾ **Eavesdropper**[258] 2738 4-8-13 95...............................(bt) AhmedAjtebi 6 104
(Mahmood Al Zarooni) *settled in rr: r.o wl fr 2f out but no ch w wnr* **66/1**

4 2 ¾ **Mr Brock (SAF)**[22] 330 8-9-0 115.. KShea 10 99
(M F De Kock, South Africa) *trckd ldrs: one pce fnl f* **11/2**

5 1 ¼ **Jalil (USA)**[22] 330 7-8-8 104...................................(t) MickaelBarzalona 1 90
(Mahmood Al Zarooni) *chsd ldrs: ev ch fnl 2f: one pce fnl f* **16/1**

6 ¾ **Al Shemali**[15] 416 7-9-0 119...................................(t) RoystonFfrench 4 95
(A Al Raihe, UAE) *trckd ldr: led 1 1/2f out: hdd 1f out: wknd fnl 110yds* **4/1**[2]

7 6 ¼ **Bronze Cannon (USA)**[22] 330 6-9-0 112...................(t) RyanMoore 11 82
(H J Brown, South Africa) *led for 1 1/2f: trckd ldng duo: led 3f out: hdd 1 1/2f out: one pce fnl f* **9/1**

8 7 **Balierus (GER)**[49] 4-8-13 95..(b) XZiani 7 68
(M bin Shafya, UAE) *trckd ldr tl 3 1/2f out* **66/1**

9 11 **Wealthy (IRE)**[22] 330 4-8-13 110................................ FrankieDettori 12 46
(Saeed Bin Suroor) *led after 1 1/2f: hdd 3f out: wknd* **10/1**

9 dht **Lindner (GER)**[22] 328 6-8-4 93 ow2........................ AntiocoMurgia(6) 8 40
(I Mohammed, UAE) *nvr nr to chal* **100/1**

11 5 ¾ **Gallahad (BRZ)**[15] 417 5-9-0 98................................(b) GeraldMosse 5 35
(A De Royer-Dupre, France) *trckd ldrs tl 2 1/2f out: wknd* **33/1**

12 5 ¼ **Arqaam**[22] 328 7-8-8 95... RichardHills 2 18
(Doug Watson, UAE) *v.s.a: racd in last: n.d* **16/1**

13 12 **New Guinea**[22] 329 8-8-8 91..(v) KierenFallon 3 —
(H Albloushi, UAE) *n.d* **100/1**

2m 2.40s (-2.50) **Going Correction** 0.0s/f (Stan)
WFA 4 from 5yo+ 1lb **13 Ran SP% 127.2**
Speed ratings: **110,107,107,105,104 103,98,92,84,84 79,75,65**
CSF: £11.28.Placepot: £1,308.80 to a £1 stake. Pool: £7,440.63. 4.15 winning tickets. Quadpot: Part won. £388.30 to a £1 stake. Pool: £524.84. 0.80 winning tickets. Pool of £104.96 carried forward to Meydan Feb 24th..
Owner Sh Mohd bin Khalifa Al Maktoum,Wilgerbosdrift **Bred** T E Pocock & Morton Bloodstock **Trained** South Africa

FOCUS
An impressive performance from Golden Sword, who appreciated the strong pace (set by Wealthy) and took 0.22 seconds off the previous track record - achieved last year by Red Desire in the third round of the Al Maktoum Challenge, a Group 2.

NOTEBOOK
Golden Sword was turned out only eight days after his taking success in handicap company off a mark of 105, and he looks on the way back to the sort of level he showed when runner-up in the 2009 Irish Derby for Aidan O'Brien. He clearly relishes the Tapeta surface, and also appreciates a patient ride these days, in contrast to the forcing tactics that used to be applied. A horse high on confidence, he is now yet another World Cup contender for Mike De Kock, who also has Bold Silvano and Musir, but he probably doesn't have the pace of those two, particularly the latter, and he does seem reliant on a good gallop. (op 2-1)
Deem(IRE), who ran in this rather than defending her crown in the Balanchine earlier on the card, handled the Tapeta well and ran better than in the Cape Verdi on her reappearance. (op 9-2)
Eavesdropper, having his first start since last June, ran a career best with blinkers added for the first time.
Mr Brock(SAF) wasn't good enough but helps give the form a solid look. (op 5-1)
Al Shemali did little for the form of Bold Silvano's win in the second round of the Al Maktoum Challenge, having finished fourth in that contest on his reappearance, but in fairness he was committed much too soon. Last year's Duty Free winner probably would have finished closer under more patient tactics, but looks better on turf.

588 LINGFIELD (L-H)

Saturday, February 19

OFFICIAL GOING: Standard

Wind: Almost nil Weather: Overcast, drizzly

609 BLUE SQUARE WISH CRAWLEY TOWN GOOD LUCK CLAIMING STKS 1m (P)

1:45 (1:46) (Class 6) 3-Y-0 **£1,535** (£453; £226) **Stalls** High

Form RPR

10-4 1 **Malice Or Mischief (IRE)**[10] 468 3-9-0 77......................... NeilCallan 2 80
(Tony Carroll) *awkward to load into stalls: chsd ldng pair: pushed along 3f out: wnt 2nd over 2f out: rdn to ld over 1f out: sn clr* **4/1**[2]

1123 2 3 ¼ **Better Self**[2] 576 3-8-5 74.. CathyGannon 1 64
(David Evans) *hld up last: rdn 3f out: effrt on outer 2f out: kpt on one pce to take 2nd last 100yds* **4/1**[2]

4-11 3 1 ¼ **A Little Bit Dusty**[7] 519 3-8-5 71..............................(b) JakePayne(7) 4 68
(Bill Turner) *led after 2f: rdn and hdd over 1f out: wknd* **9/2**[3]

60- 4 13 **Dream Catcher (FR)**[133] 6737 3-9-8 85........................ JamieSpencer 3 48
(David Nicholls) *led 2f racing v wd: chsd ldr to over 2f out: wknd rapidly: t.o* **1/1**[1]

1m 37.7s (-0.50) **Going Correction** +0.05s/f (Slow) **4 Ran SP% 108.2**
Speed ratings (Par 95): **104,100,99,86**
CSF £18.05 TOTE £4.80; EX 15.30.
Owner Bill Adams **Bred** Kilnamoragh Stud **Trained** Cropthorne, Worcs

The Form Book, Raceform Ltd, Compton, RG20 6NL

FOCUS
Only four runners, but this was a fair claimer. The pace was strong and the time was good. However the favourite disappointed, and the form is not rated as positively as it might have been.

610 LINGFIELD MARRIOTT HOTEL & COUNTRY CLUB MAIDEN STKS — 1m (P)
2:20 (2:20) (Class 5) 3-Y-O — **£1,910** (£564; £282) **Stalls** High

Form — RPR

52 **1** **Baharat (IRE)**[15] [431] 3-9-3 0 ....(v[1]) ShaneKelly 3 — 73
(Jeremy Noseda) *pressed ldr: shkn up to chal over 2f out: cajoled along to ld 1f out: str reminders to maintain advantage after* **8/11**[1]

2 *1* **Fog Cutter (IRE)** 3-9-0 0 ow2 ....(t) JPO'Brien(5) 2 — 73
(James McAuley, Ire) *t.k.h: hld up in 3rd: pushed along and cl enough over 1f out: rdn and styd on same pce to take 2nd last strides* **16/1**

0-4 **3** *shd* **Old English (IRE)**[8] [509] 3-9-3 0 .... JoeFanning 5 — 70
(Mark Johnston) *led at stdy pce: jnd over 2f out: hdd and nt qckn 1f out: lost 2nd last strides* **5/1**[3]

36- **4** *7* **Unex Goya (IRE)**[92] [7503] 3-9-3 0 ....(tp) GeorgeBaker 4 — 54
(George Baker) *trckd ldng trio: rdn wl over 2f out: wknd over 1f out* **4/1**[2]

5 *2 1/2* **Enriching (USA)** 3-9-3 0 .... DaneO'Neill 1 — 49
(David Elsworth) *s.s: rn green in last: in tch to 3f out: sn wknd* **10/1**

1m 40.36s (2.16) **Going Correction** +0.05s/f (Slow) **5** Ran SP% **109.5**
Speed ratings (Par 97): **91,90,89,82,80**
CSF £13.12 TOTE £1.50: £1.10, £6.00; EX 12.10.
Owner Saeed Suhail **Bred** Norelands Bloodstock & Hugo Lascelles **Trained** Newmarket, Suffolk

FOCUS
Some of these may be capable of better in due course, but the bare form looks muddling and it is hard to know what it amounts to. The pace was steady and the final time was slow - 2.66 seconds off the earlier 3-y-o claimer.

611 MARSH GREEN MEDIAN AUCTION MAIDEN STKS — 5f (P)
2:55 (2:56) (Class 6) 3-Y-O — **£1,535** (£453; £226) **Stalls** High

Form — RPR

445- **1** **Grandmas Dream**[131] [6796] 3-8-13 77 ow1 .... PaulDoe 4 — 65
(Jim Best) *led 100yds: chsd ldr: drvn to ld over 1f out: kpt on* **11/8**[1]

00- **2** *3/4* **Midnight Trader (IRE)**[128] [6878] 3-9-3 0 .... LiamJones 3 — 66
(Paul D'Arcy) *hld up in 5th: brought wdst of all bnd 2f out: prog and reminder 1f out: pushed into 2nd last 100yds: nvr chal: do bttr* **8/1**[3]

-424 **3** *1 1/4* **Welsh Inlet (IRE)**[20] [356] 3-8-12 62 .... CathyGannon 1 — 57
(John Bridger) *trckd ldng pair: lost pl on inner 2f out and nt clr run sn after: kpt on to take 3rd wl ins fnl f* **14/1**

54 **4** *1/2* **Beautiful Day**[24] [305] 3-9-3 0 .... PhillipMakin 2 — 60
(Kevin Ryan) *hld up in 4th: prog over 2f out: chsd wnr jst over 1f out: sn rdn and nt qckn: wknd last 100yds* **9/4**[2]

5 *hd* **Bambika** 3-8-12 0 .... IanMongan 5 — 54
(Jo Crowley) *s.s: in tch in last: gng wl enough whn looking for room over 1f out: one pce fnl f* **12/1**

-223 **6** *5* **Pineapple Pete (IRE)**[29] [246] 3-9-3 62 ....(t) JamesDoyle 6 — 41
(Alan McCabe) *pushed up to ld after 100yds: hdd & wknd qckly over 1f out* **9/1**

59.25 secs (0.45) **Going Correction** +0.05s/f (Slow) **6** Ran SP% **108.3**
Speed ratings (Par 95): **98,96,94,94,93 85**
Tote Swingers: 1&2:£3.80, 1&3:£4.40, 2&3:£8.70 CSF £11.99 TOTE £1.90: £1.10, £5.50; EX 10.90.
Owner M&R Refurbishments Ltd **Bred** Mrs Mary Taylor **Trained** Lewes, E Sussex

FOCUS
The 62-rated Welsh Inlet seemed to run her race and looks the best guide to the form of this modest maiden.

612 BLUE SQUARE SPRINT SERIES ROUND 7 H'CAP (QUALIFIER) — 6f (P)
3:25 (3:25) (Class 5) (0-70,72) 4-Y-O+ — **£2,729** (£806; £403) **Stalls** Low

Form — RPR

544/ **1** **Qadar (IRE)**[105] [7357] 9-9-6 69 ....(p) ShaneKelly 5 — 79
(Alan McCabe) *hld up in 7th: decisive burst over 1f out to ld jst ins fnl f: in command after: rdn out* **25/1**

2-34 **2** *3/4* **Yankee Storm**[19] [367] 6-9-6 69 ....(b[1]) JimmyQuinn 3 — 77
(Tom Keddy) *sn chsd ldrs: effrt on inner 2f out: rdn to chal 1f out: sn outpcd by wnr: kpt on* **8/1**

0566 **3** *1/2* **Nubar Boy**[7] [522] 4-8-12 61 ....(v) JamieSpencer 7 — 67
(David Evans) *dwlt: hld up last: gd prog on inner wl over 1f out: tried to cl on ldrs fnl f: styd on same pce* **9/1**

5511 **4** *nk* **Norville (IRE)**[7] [521] 4-9-5 68 ....(b) CathyGannon 1 — 73
(David Evans) *pressed ldr: drvn to ld narrowly 2f out: hdd and one pce jst ins fnl f* **9/2**[2]

-655 **5** *3/4* **Al Gillani (IRE)**[7] [521] 6-9-4 67 ....(p) GeorgeBaker 11 — 70+
(Jim Boyle) *stdd s: hld up in last trio: effrt whn nt clr run wl over 1f out: prog fnl f: styd on: nt rch ldrs* **9/1**

-213 **6** *shd* **Pelmanism**[14] [435] 4-9-1 64 ....(b) PhillipMakin 4 — 67
(Kevin Ryan) *settled in 8th on inner: n.m.r over 2f out: prog over 1f out: one pce fnl f* **10/3**[1]

4641 **7** *hd* **Tislaam (IRE)**[10] [470] 4-9-7 70 ....(p) RobertWinston 8 — 72+
(Alan McCabe) *hld up in last trio: gng strly over 2f out: nt clr run over 1f out: shkn up and styd on fnl f: no ch* **6/1**[3]

0041 **8** *1 1/4* **Desert Strike**[12] [443] 5-9-5 68 ....(p) LukeMorris 6 — 68+
(Alan McCabe) *towards rr: rdn over 2f out: n.m.r wl over 1f out: kpt on same pce fnl f tl no room nr fin* **25/1**

2/ **9** *1 1/4* **Enigma Code (UAE)**[207] [4465] 6-9-2 70 ....(t) JPO'Brien(5) 10 — 64
(James McAuley, Ire) *cl up bhd ldrs: rdn whn nudged by rival over 1f out: sn btn* **40/1**

0201 **10** *1* **Prize Point**[22] [336] 5-9-5 68 .... EddieAhern 2 — 59
(Jim Boyle) *led to 2f out: wknd qckly fnl f* **14/1**

2342 **11** *1 3/4* **Dvinsky (USA)**[14] [435] 10-9-2 65 ....(b) PaulDoe 12 — 50
(Jane Chapple-Hyam) *prom on outer: rdn over 2f out: wknd wl over 1f out* **25/1**

0312 **12** *1 3/4* **Primo De Vida (IRE)**[7] [521] 4-9-2 72 ....(p) NathanAlison(7) 9 — 52
(Jim Boyle) *chsd ldng pair to over 2f out: wknd qckly* **7/1**

1m 11.51s (-0.39) **Going Correction** +0.05s/f (Slow) **12** Ran SP% **119.8**
Speed ratings (Par 103): **104,103,102,101,100 100,100,98,97,95 93,91**
Tote Swingers: 1&2:£37.70, 1&3:£42.70, 2&3:£14.40 CSF £208.76 CT £1963.64 TOTE £37.10: £10.70, £1.90, £3.30; EX 329.50 TRIFECTA Not won..
Owner Mrs Linda Francis **Bred** Martin Francis **Trained** Averham Park, Notts
■ Stewards' Enquiry : Eddie Ahern two-day ban: careless riding (Mar 7-8)

FOCUS
A competitive sprint handicap and the time was 0.56 seconds faster than the following Class 3 event won by Five Star Junior, although they went steady early in that contest.

Norville(IRE) Official explanation: jockey said colt suffered interference in running

613 HAMMERWOOD H'CAP — 6f (P)
4:00 (4:02) (Class 3) (0-95,93) 4-Y-O+ — **£5,828** (£1,734; £866; £432) **Stalls** Low

Form — RPR

3-32 **1** **Five Star Junior (USA)**[28] [265] 5-9-4 93 .... JamesSullivan(3) 9 — 102
(Linda Stubbs) *trckd ldrs in 6th: effrt over 1f out: str run on outer fnl f to ld last 75yds* **5/1**[3]

00-5 **2** *3/4* **Star Rover (IRE)**[15] [429] 4-9-2 88 .... CathyGannon 11 — 94
(David Evans) *pressed ldr: upsides fr 1/2-way: drvn into narrow ld jst ins fnl f: hdd and outpcd last 75yds* **40/1**

1-11 **3** *nse* **Advertisement (USA)**[17] [385] 4-9-1 87 ....(t) GeorgeBaker 8 — 93
(Jeremy Noseda) *cl up in 4th: effrt over 1f out: drvn to chal fnl f: upsides 100yds out: outpcd* **9/4**[1]

003- **4** *nk* **Flipando (IRE)**[98] [7443] 10-9-4 90 .... GrahamGibbons 6 — 95
(David Barron) *rrd s: sn chsd ldrs in 5th: effrt towards inner over 1f out: edgd rt but kpt on fnl f* **10/1**

050- **5** *nk* **Captain Ramius (IRE)**[105] [7348] 5-9-3 89 .... PhillipMakin 4 — 93
(Kevin Ryan) *towards rr in 9th: urged along and no prog over 2f out: drvn and taken to outer 1f out: r.o and clsng at fin* **7/1**

4-65 **6** *nk* **Green Manalishi**[28] [265] 10-8-12 84 ....(p) NeilCallan 5 — 87
(Kevin Ryan) *t.k.h: trckd ldng pair: c between them to chal over 1f out: upsides ent fnl f: fdd last 100yds* **16/1**

111- **7** *1/2* **Humidor (IRE)**[133] [6739] 4-9-2 88 .... JoeFanning 7 — 91
(George Baker) *mde most: jnd 1/2-way: stl disputing ld ent fnl f: fading whn hmpd and snatched up nr fin* **9/2**[2]

1-56 **8** *1* **Perfect Act**[28] [265] 6-9-1 87 .... LiamKeniry 2 — 85
(Andrew Balding) *a abt same pl: shkn up on inner over 1f out: no real imp* **20/1**

000- **9** *3/4* **Fantasy Explorer**[293] [1727] 8-9-2 88 .... JimmyQuinn 10 — 84
(John Quinn) *hld up in 8th: shuffled along over 1f out: nvr remotely involved* **50/1**

00-0 **10** *2* **The Scorching Wind (IRE)**[28] [265] 5-9-3 89 ....(b[1]) WilliamCarson 3 — 79
(Stuart Williams) *s.s: a in last trio: rdn and no prog over 2f out* **11/1**

306- **11** *1 3/4* **New Leyf (IRE)**[140] [6558] 5-9-0 86 .... LukeMorris 12 — 70
(Jeremy Gask) *stdd s: hld up in last trio: shkn up and no prog 2f out* **16/1**

230- **12** *2* **Rocket Rob (IRE)**[182] [5308] 5-9-4 90 .... StevieDonohoe 1 — 68
(Willie Musson) *dwlt: a in last trio: rdn and no prog 2f out* **25/1**

1m 12.05s (0.15) **Going Correction** +0.05s/f (Slow) **12** Ran SP% **120.3**
Speed ratings (Par 107): **101,100,99,99,99 98,98,96,95,93 90,88**
Tote Swingers: 1&2:£30.70, 1&3:£3.70, 2&3:£18.70 CSF £202.28 CT £578.20 TOTE £6.00: £2.00, £11.80, £1.60; EX 146.40 Trifecta £359.40 Pool £694.66 - 1.43 winning units..
Owner Moyns Park Stud **Bred** Robert W Sanford **Trained** Norton, N Yorks
■ Stewards' Enquiry : Graham Gibbons two-day ban: careless riding (Mar 7-8)

FOCUS
A good, competitive handicap, but they didn't go that quick early and the time was 0.56 seconds slower than earlier Class 5 event. This may not be form to take too literally.

NOTEBOOK
Five Star Junior(USA) was more dominant than the winning margin indicates, looking likely to take this from a fair way out having travelled strongest of all. His effort is all the more creditable considering a quicker pace would have suited better and he may come back here shortly for a Listed race. (op 9-2 tchd 4-1)
Star Rover(IRE) was always handily placed and stuck on surprisingly well, improving significantly on the form he showed on his reappearance. (tchd 50-1)
Advertisement(USA), the winner of his last two starts over 7f, was unsuited by the drop in trip and couldn't defy a further 7lb rise. He was just about ideally placed throughout, although he was a bit keen, and he couldn't pick up sufficiently. (op 2-1 tchd 15-8)
Flipando(IRE), returning from a 98-day break, did well to get so close considering he would have preferred a quicker early pace. (op 12-1 tchd 9-1)
Captain Ramius(IRE) had to be switched wide late on but finished well. He had been off since November and his four wins to date have been gained over 7f. (op 12-1)
Green Manalishi probably needs easing slightly in class. (op 20-1)
Humidor(IRE), who won his last three starts of 2010 (first three runs for this yard), resumed off a 5lb higher mark and didn't quite see his race out after being a bit free in front. He was held when squeezed for room late on, but can do better. (op 10-1)
Rocket Rob(IRE), making his debut for this yard after a 182-day break, was not given a hard ride and never featured. (op 20-1)

614 MICHELLE RICH 30TH BIRTHDAY H'CAP — 1m 4f (P)
4:35 (4:35) (Class 4) (0-85,85) 4-Y-O+ — **£3,238** (£963; £481; £240) **Stalls** Low

Form — RPR

100- **1** **Cosmic Sun**[126] [6926] 5-9-0 85 .... GeorgeChaloner(7) 4 — 94
(Richard Fahey) *t.k.h: hld up in midfield: clsd on ldrs fr 2f out: shkn up and qcknd to ld last 100yds: r.o wl* **22/1**

3-11 **2** *1/2* **Beaubrav**[17] [392] 5-9-4 82 ....(t) AdamKirby 3 — 90
(Michael Madgwick) *dwlt: hld up in last trio: gd prog wl over 1f out: c to chal ins fnl f: r.o but jst outpcd* **7/2**[2]

00- **3** *1 1/4* **Broad Meaning**[168] [5774] 5-9-1 84 ....(t) JPO'Brien(5) 8 — 90
(James McAuley, Ire) *trckd ldrs: effrt on inner wl over 1f out: clsd on ldrs ent fnl f: outpcd last 100yds* **40/1**

5-32 **4** *1/2* **Realisation (USA)**[8] [515] 4-9-2 83 .... JoeFanning 7 — 88
(Mark Johnston) *cl up in 3rd: rdn 2f out: led over 1f out tl last 100yds: outpcd* **4/1**[3]

30-1 **5** *1 1/4* **Bedouin Bay**[8] [515] 4-8-9 81 .... RosieJessop(5) 12 — 84
(Alan McCabe) *t.k.h: mostly trckd ldr: led 2f out to over 1f out: fdd ins fnl f* **9/1**

/00- **6** *3/4* **Gunslinger (FR)**[42] [4023] 6-8-9 73 .... HayleyTurner 1 — 75
(Michael Scudamore) *t.k.h: hld up in rr: cajoled along over 2f out: nt qckn over 1f out: kpt on fnl f* **40/1**

-066 **7** *1/2* **Kiss A Prince**[21] [348] 5-9-2 80 ....(p) GeorgeBaker 6 — 81
(Dean Ivory) *t.k.h: hld up in last trio: shkn up 2f out: styd on fnl f: nvr on terms* **13/2**

3611 **8** *1 3/4* **Mister Green (FR)**[3] [565] 5-8-9 73 6ex ....(bt) JamesDoyle 11 — 72
(David Flood) *t.k.h: hld up in last trio: shkn up on outer 2f out: no great prog* **3/1**[1]

5-04 **9** *hd* **Pelham Crescent (IRE)**[14] [436] 8-8-12 76 .... RobertWinston 10 — 74
(Bryn Palling) *awkward s: plld hrd: hld up in midfield: prog 3f out: rdn to chal 2f out: hanging and nt qckn over 1f out: wknd* **11/1**

/45- **10** *3 3/4* **Evident Pride (USA)**[386] [341] 8-9-2 80 .... IanMongan 5 — 72
(Brett Johnson) *t.k.h: hld up towards rr: effrt on wd outside 2f out: sn no prog: wknd fnl f* **25/1**

060- **11** *5* **Chalice Welcome**[52] [8003] 8-9-0 78 .... EddieAhern 2 — 62
(Neil King) *trckd ldrs: effrt on inner whn bdly hmpd wl over 1f out: nt rcvr* **33/1**

/35- **12** ¾ **Soul Heaven**[91] [2261] 4-8-5 **72**................................(tp) CathyGannon 9 55
(James McAuley, Ire) *led at mod pce to 2f out: hanging and wknd qckly*
33/1

2m 32.14s (-0.86) **Going Correction** +0.05s/f (Slow)
WFA 4 from 5yo+ 3lb **12** Ran SP% **117.8**
Speed ratings (Par 105): **104,103,102,102,101 101,100,99,99,97 93,93**
Tote Swingers: 1&2:£19.30, 1&3:£71.10, 2&3:£42.80 CSF £92.57 CT £3101.32 TOTE £23.20: £5.40, £2.20, £9.60; EX 171.60 TRIFECTA Not won..
Owner The Cosmic Cases **Bred** M Wassall **Trained** Musley Bank, N Yorks

FOCUS
This was probably only ordinary form for the grade. The surprise winner is rated in line with last year's turf best.

615 PLAY FREE BINGO AT BLUESQ.COM H'CAP 1m (P)
5:10 (5:10) (Class 3) (0-95,95) 4-Y-0+ **£5,828** (£1,734; £866; £432) **Stalls** High

Form				RPR
06-6	**1**		**Night Lily (IRE)**[14] [438] 5-8-13 **87**.................... LiamJones 10 (Paul D'Arcy) *trckd ldrs in 7th: crept clsr on outer 2f out: rdn and r.o fnl f to ld last 75yds* **15/2**[3]	93
00-1	**2**	½	**Titan Triumph**[21] [348] 7-8-8 **82**....................(t) LukeMorris 8 (William Knight) *stdd s: hld up in last pair: stl there over 1f out: rapid prog on outer fnl f: snatched 2nd last stride* **5/1**[2]	87+
3-64	**3**	hd	**Mafeking (UAE)**[14] [438] 7-9-2 **90**.................... CathyGannon 12 (Mark Hoad) *t.k.h: prom on outer: prog over 2f out: hrd rdn to chal jst over 1f out: styd on: jst outpcd* **12/1**	95
00-0	**4**	nse	**Ezdeyaad (USA)**[14] [438] 7-9-0 **88**.................... JackMitchell 5 (Ed Walker) *trckd ldng pair: drvn to ld narrowly jst over 1f out: hdd last 75yds: lost 2 pls last strides* **25/1**	92
23-3	**5**	nse	**Baylini**[7] [525] 7-9-0 **88**.................... JamesDoyle 9 (Jamie Osborne) *hld up in 8th: drvn over 1f out: r.o ins fnl f: gaining at fin* **9/2**[1]	92
30-5	**6**	hd	**Benandonner (USA)**[27] [271] 8-9-7 **95**.................... NeilCallan 2 (Mike Murphy) *fast away: led: drvn and hdd jst over 1f out: kpt on pressing tl swamped for pls nr fin* **9/1**	99
62-0	**7**	nk	**The Which Doctor**[7] [525] 6-8-13 **87**....................(p) ShaneKelly 6 (Jeremy Noseda) *stdd s: hld up in last quartet: drvn over 1f out: styd on fnl f but nt quite as qckly as other clsrs* **8/1**	90
1204	**8**	¾	**Follow The Flag (IRE)**[4] [548] 7-8-2 **83**....................(p) NoraLooby(7) 11 (Alan McCabe) *t.k.h: trckd ldrs in 5th: bmpd along and nt qckn 2f out: one pce after* **25/1**	84
4-60	**9**	nk	**Elna Bright**[14] [438] 6-9-4 **92**.................... JimmyQuinn 4 (Brett Johnson) *trckd ldrs in 5th on inner: looking for room 2f out and lost pl sltly: nt qckn over 1f out* **14/1**	93
-542	**10**	½	**Audemar (IRE)**[14] [438] 5-9-2 **90**....................(b[1]) AndreaAtzeni 7 (Edward Vaughan) *chsd ldrs to over 1f out: wknd fnl f* **9/2**[1]	90
40-6	**11**	1	**Georgebernardshaw (IRE)**[27] [271] 6-9-5 **93**............ JamieSpencer 3 (David Simcock) *stdd s: hld up in last quartet: looking for room over 2f out: no real prog over 1f out: eased last 100yds* **12/1**	90
20-3	**12**	1 ¾	**Red Somerset (USA)**[12] [447] 8-9-0 **88**.................... MartinLane 1 (Mike Murphy) *s.s: a in last pair: rdn and struggling over 2f out* **12/1**	81

1m 37.32s (-0.88) **Going Correction** +0.05s/f (Slow) **12** Ran SP% **123.3**
Speed ratings (Par 107): **106,105,105,105,105 105,104,103,103,103 102,100**
Tote Swingers: 1&2:£19.00, 1&3:£22.80, 2&3:£12.70 CSF £46.75 CT £454.65 TOTE £11.00: £2.50, £3.00, £4.40; EX 76.10 Trifecta £632.30 Part won..
Owner K Snell **Bred** Keith Wills **Trained** Newmarket, Suffolk

FOCUS
The pace was steady and there was a bunch finish. Muddling form to treat with caution.

NOTEBOOK
Night Lily(IRE) built on the form she showed on her reappearance, reversing C&D placings with Audemar and Mafeking. She should remain competitive. (op 8-1)
Titan Triumph, 2lb higher than when dead-heating over C&D on his reappearance, was set an awful lot to do before being taken extremely wide in the straight. He did well to get so close. (op 6-1 tchd 13-2)
Mafeking(UAE), not helped by stall 12, raced without cover for much of the way but still ran to form. (tchd 14-1)
Ezdeyaad(USA) ◆ improved on the form he showed on his debut for this yard. He briefly looked the winner in the straight, but had been keen and faded late on. Entitled to come on again for this, he could go in next time. (op 33-1)
Baylini needs a good test at this trip, so the steady pace was totally against her, and she ran well in the circumstances. (tchd 4-1)
Audemar(IRE), 2lb higher than when third in this last year, had blinkers replacing cheekpieces, but he proved disappointing. (op 11-2)
T/Plt: £446.90 to a £1 stake. Pool £53,618.09 - 87.57 winning units. T/Qpdt: £102.50 to a £1 stake. Pool £5,073.76 - 36.60 winning units. JN

566 CAGNES-SUR-MER
Saturday, February 19

OFFICIAL GOING: Turf: heavy; fibresand: standard

616a PRIX DU FORT CARRE (MAIDEN) (3YO COLTS & GELDINGS) (TURF) 7f 110y
12:00 (12:00) 3-Y-O **£8,620** (£3,448; £2,586; £1,724; £862)

			RPR
1		**Parigino (FR)**[19] [370] 3-9-2 0....................(p) ThierryThulliez 4 (F Chappet, France) **9/2**[2]	75
2	1 ½	**Mon Julien (USA)** 3-9-2 0.................... IoritzMendizabal 5 (J-C Rouget, France) **2/5**[1]	71
3	2	**Bolt (FR)**[47] 3-8-8 0.................... MatthieuAutier(8) 6 (M Boutin, France) **12/1**	66
4	1	**Baileys Vert (FR)**[19] [370] 3-8-13 0.................... ThomasHuet 1 (W Walton, France) **24/1**	61
5	3	**Pillows Dreams (FR)** 3-9-2 0.................... MorganDelalande 2 (A Spanu, France) **16/1**	56
6	dist	**Hugely Exciting**[6] [532] 3-9-2 0.................... Francois-XavierBertras 3 (J S Moore) *broke wl to go 3rd: dropped bk to 5th bef st: sn u.p: fdd qckly: t.o* **9/1**[3]	—

1m 38.84s (98.84) **6** Ran SP% **117.2**
WIN (incl. 1 euro stake): 5.50. PLACES: 1.30, 1.10. SF: 8.60.
Owner Mme Berthe Klodawski **Bred** Mme Cyril Morange **Trained** France

617a PRIX DE FONTMERLE (CLAIMER) (5YO+) (GENTLEMEN RIDERS) (FIBRESAND) 1m (F)
1:00 (12:00) 5-Y-0+ **£6,465** (£2,586; £1,939; £1,293; £646)

			RPR
1		**Snow Bay**[10] [481] 5-10-11 0.................... MrAlexisLemer 2 (David Nicholls) *broke wl to r 3rd: wnt 2nd early in st: chal for ld 1 1/2 out: led 1f out: sn wnt clr: easily* **124/10**	69
2	3	**Richhill Lady**[10] [481] 7-10-12 0.................... MrJean-PhilippeBoisgontier 1 (F Chappet, France) **5/2**[1]	65
3	1 ½	**El Vettorio (GER)**[81] 8-10-8 0....................(p) MrBrunoVaubernier 7 (C Boutin, France) **63/1**	58
4	1 ½	**Cherma (USA)**[42] 5-10-11 0.................... MrEdouardMonfort 4 (J-P Delaporte, France) **15/1**	59
5	½	**Farlino (FR)**[43] 7-11-8 0....................(b) MrChristopheGuimard 12 (J-P Delaporte, France) **11/2**[3]	69
6	1	**Kecek (IRE)** 8-10-8 0.................... MrYannickMergirie 11 (M Guarnieri, Italy) **68/10**	53
7	¾	**Iron Out (USA)**[6] [533] 5-10-11 0....................(p) MrPatrickDeno 6 (Reg Hollinshead) *prom fr s: u.p early in st: no ex: styd on fnl f* **76/1**	55
8	½	**All Ways To Rome (FR)**[47] 7-10-8 0..........(b) MrJeremieLaurent-Joye 8 (H-A Pantall, France) **7/1**	51
9	nse	**Lord Sandicliffe (IRE)**[43] 6-11-0 0....................(b) MrDickGoossens 14 (Mme J Hendriks, Holland) **120/1**	57
10	2	**Raganeyev (FR)**[10] [481] 10-10-11 0....................(b) MrSvenSchleppi 5 (X Nakkachdji, France) **13/1**	50
0		**Sprint Car (FR)**[99] 7-11-1 0....................(b) MrThibaultMarlin 10 (J-P Delaporte, France) **50/1**	—
0		**Officer In Command (USA)**[3] [566] 5-11-0 0(b) MrChristopheRoberts 13 (J S Moore) *broke wl to r in 6th on wd outside: rdn and no ex early in st: fdd* **34/1**	—
0		**Algon (GER)**[72] 6-10-11 0....................(p) MrFlorentGuy 3 (H Blume, Germany) **9/2**[2]	—
0		**Barateka (FR)** 5-10-8 0.................... MrPabloGredillaZubiria 9 (M Boutin, France) **81/1**	—

1m 36.84s (96.84) **14** Ran SP% **118.0**
WIN (incl. 1 euro stake): 13.40. PLACES: 3.20, 1.60, 9.70. DF: 18.30. SF: 45.50.
Owner Pinnacle Bahamian Bounty Partnership **Bred** West Dereham Abbey Stud **Trained** Sessay, N Yorks

618a (Foreign Racing) - see Raceform Interactive

552 KEMPTON (A.W) (R-H)
Sunday, February 20

OFFICIAL GOING: Standard
Wind: Virtually nil Weather: Overcast

619 BETDAQ H'CAP 7f (P)
1:50 (1:51) (Class 6) (0-55,55) 4-Y-0+ **£1,535** (£453; £226) **Stalls** Low

Form				RPR
-240	**1**		**Fortunate Bid (IRE)**[8] [526] 5-8-12 **52**....................(p) JamesSullivan(3) 7 (Linda Stubbs) *trckd ldrs: drvn and styd on wl appr fnl f: led fnl 75yds: hld on wl* **13/2**	61
4-01	**2**	nk	**Royal Acclamation (IRE)**[10] [482] 6-8-10 **54**..........(p) DavidKenny(7) 10 (Michael Scudamore) *chsd ldrs: led ins fnl 2f: kpt on u.p fnl f: hdd fnl 75yds: no ex cl home* **7/1**	62
0-60	**3**	hd	**Rainsborough**[10] [485] 4-9-2 **53**....................(e) DaneO'Neill 2 (Peter Hedger) *hld up towards rr: hdwy fr 2f out: styd on to chal ins fnl f: no ex clsng stages* **6/1**[3]	60
00-5	**4**	2 ½	**Bold Diva**[10] [485] 6-9-2 **53**....................(v) LukeMorris 1 (Tony Carroll) *in tch: hdwy and n.m.r wl over 1f out: styd on same pce fnl f* **7/2**[1]	54
0/00	**5**	2	**Zim Ho**[18] [386] 5-8-9 **46** oh1.................... ChrisCatlin 9 (John Akehurst) *rrd stalls: sn rcvrd to ld: rdn 3f out: hdd insde fnl 2f: wknd fnl f* **33/1**	41
0003	**6**	hd	**Valentino Swing (IRE)**[18] [386] 8-9-1 **52**....................(p) NeilChalmers 3 (Michael Appleby) *towards rr: hdwy over 2f out: sn rdn: nvr quite rchd ldrs: wknd ins fnl f* **11/2**[2]	47
20-6	**7**	1 ¼	**Commandingpresence (USA)**[10] [485] 5-9-3 **54**.............. NeilCallan 4 (John Bridger) *chsd ldrs: rdn over 2f out: wknd over 1f out* **9/1**	45
0-05	**8**	1 ¾	**Boundless Applause**[24] [312] 5-8-9 **46** oh1.................... JamesDoyle 11 (Ian Wood) *chsd ldr tl over 2f out: wknd u.p over 1f out* **25/1**	33
-210	**9**	1	**Hi Spec (IRE)**[23] [340] 8-9-1 **52** ow1....................(t) AdamKirby 5 (Mandy Rowland) *a outpcd* **8/1**	36
5002	**10**	½	**Jemimaville (IRE)**[10] [482] 4-8-9 **46**....................(v) WilliamCarson 8 (Giles Bravery) *a outpcd* **12/1**	29

1m 25.17s (-0.83) **Going Correction** +0.05s/f (Slow) **10** Ran SP% **113.3**
Speed ratings (Par 101): **106,105,105,102,100 100,98,96,95,94**
toteswingers: 1&2 £8.20, 1&3 £12.40, 2&3 £12.30 CSF £49.91 CT £292.66 TOTE £7.00: £2.20, £1.80, £2.70; EX 64.90 Trifecta £239.90 Part won. Pool: £324.18 - 0.84 winning units..
Owner Jason Button **Bred** E O'Leary **Trained** Norton, N Yorks

FOCUS
A moderate but competitive handicap. The time was fair for for the grade and the winner is rated up a length on his recent form.
Valentino Swing(IRE) Official explanation: jockey said gelding was slowly away
Jemimaville(IRE) Official explanation: trainer said filly finished distressed

620 BET WGC GOLF - BETDAQ CLAIMING STKS 6f (P)
2:20 (2:20) (Class 6) 3-Y-O **£1,535** (£453; £226) **Stalls** Low

Form				RPR
1-11	**1**		**Chevise (IRE)**[11] [476] 3-9-1 **79**.................... MatthewDavies(3) 3 (George Baker) *bmpd after s: trckd ldrs: shkn up and qcknd to ld over 1f out: drvn and styd on strly fnl f: readily* **4/9**[1]	78+
-320	**2**	1 ¾	**Fairy Tales**[23] [338] 3-8-8 **56**.................... LukeMorris 5 (John Bridger) *towards rr but in tch: hdwy over 2f out: drvn to chal wl over 1f out: chsd wnr ins fnl f but a readily hld* **33/1**	62
2326	**3**	2 ¼	**Captain Dimitrios**[3] [578] 3-9-1 **75**....................(v) NeilCallan 4 (David Evans) *led after 1f: jnd over 3f out: sn rdn: hdd over 2f out: hung rt u.p over 1f out: fnd no ex and no ch w ldng duo ins fnl f* **5/2**[2]	62
-146	**4**	3 ½	**Slatey Hen (IRE)**[20] [364] 3-7-12 **63**.................... JulieBurke(5) 1 (Paddy Butler) *led 1f: styd pressing ldr: chal 3f out: slt ld over 2f out: hdd over 1f out: wknd qckly fnl f* **16/1**[3]	39

The Form Book, Raceform Ltd, Compton, RG20 6NL

4-00 **5** *3½* **Shutupandrive**[23] 338 3-8-2 **42**........ HayleyTurner 2 26
(Mark Usher) *bmpd after s: chsd ldrs tl rdn and wknd wl over 2f out* **66/1**

1m 12.47s (-0.63) **Going Correction** +0.05s/f (Slow) **5** Ran SP% **108.1**
Speed ratings (Par 95): **106,103,100,96,91**
CSF £16.75 TOTE £1.40: £1.30, £5.80; EX 9.30.The winner was claimed by S Woodman for £12,000.
Owner M Khan X2 **Bred** Paul And Mrs Jenny Green **Trained** Whitsbury, Hants

FOCUS
An ordinary claimer.
Fairy Tales Official explanation: vet said filly lost a right-fore shoe

621 BET IN RUNNING - BETDAQ H'CAP 1m 4f (P)
2:50 (2:50) (Class 5) (0-70,70) 4-Y-0+ **£2,047** (£604; £302) **Stalls** Centre

Form RPR

3-03 **1** **Sir Boss (IRE)**[16] 418 6-9-1 **64**........ TomEaves 6 72+
(Michael Mullineaux) *trckd ldr: led ins fnl 3f: drvn and styd on strly thrght fnl f* **10/1**

00-5 **2** *1½* **Time Square (FR)**[18] 384 4-9-3 **69**........(t) LukeMorris 8 75
(Tony Carroll) *hld up in rr: drvn and hdwy fr 2f out: styd on u.p fnl f to take 2nd cl home but no imp on wnr* **11/1**

15-4 **3** *½* **Where's Susie**[27] 278 6-9-5 **68**........ GeorgeBaker 3 73
(Michael Madgwick) *trckd ldrs: chsd wnr fr over 2f out: styd on fnl f but a wl hld: lost 2nd cl home* **8/1**

-230 **4** *¾* **Professor John (IRE)**[18] 381 4-8-11 **63**........(b[1]) JamesDoyle 5 67
(Ian Wood) *chsd ldrs: hrd drvn and one pce fnl 2f* **7/1**[3]

14-2 **5** *½* **Beat Route**[25] 301 4-8-10 **67**........ JemmaMarshall[(5)] 10 70
(Michael Attwater) *t.k.h in mid-div: hdwy 4f out: chsd ldrs and hrd drvn fr 2f out: one pce fnl f* **6/1**[2]

6 *2* **Aather (IRE)**[22] 5516 6-9-3 **66**........ LiamKeniry 4 66
(Alan Fleming) *in tch: drvn and hdwy over 2f out: nvr gng pce to rch ldrs: wknd ins fnl f* **7/4**[1]

3-06 **7** *shd* **Folio (IRE)**[22] 352 11-8-10 **59**........ StevieDonohoe 1 59
(Willie Musson) *in rr: hdwy over 2f out: drvn and styd on to chse ldrs ins fnl 2f: nvr on terms: wknd fnl f* **16/1**

5-65 **8** *shd* **Humungous (IRE)**[28] 272 8-9-3 **66**........(b) MickyFenton 2 65
(Charles Egerton) *s.i.s: towards rr: hdwy to chse ldrs 2f out: no imp over 1f out: wknd ins fnl f* **12/1**

20-2 **9** *3¾* **Trachonitis (IRE)**[17] 399 7-9-7 **70**........ ShaneKelly 9 63
(J R Jenkins) *towards rr most of way* **14/1**

60-0 **10** *7* **Heading To First**[11] 473 4-8-10 **65**........(p) RobertLButler[(3)] 7 47
(Paddy Butler) *led tl hdd ins fnl 3f: sn btn* **66/1**

2m 34.05s (-0.45) **Going Correction** +0.05s/f (Slow)
WFA 4 from 6yo+ 3lb **10** Ran SP% **113.4**
Speed ratings (Par 103): **103,102,101,101,100 99,99,99,96,92**
toteswingers: 1&2 £19.10, 1&3 £7.60, 2&3 £16.10 CSF £111.21 CT £921.28 TOTE £15.20: £2.90, £5.20, £2.10; EX 164.50 Trifecta £333.50 Part won. Pool: £450.78 - 0.61 winning units..
Owner I S Ross **Bred** Mrs E R Cantillon **Trained** Alpraham, Cheshire

FOCUS
A modest handicap and they didn't go that quick (time over three seconds outside standard), suiting those who raced prominently.

622 MIX BUSINESS WITH PLEASURE AT KEMPTON H'CAP 2m (P)
3:20 (3:23) (Class 5) (0-70,68) 4-Y-0+ **£2,047** (£604; £302) **Stalls** Low

Form RPR

05-2 **1** **Gandalf**[30] 244 9-9-9 **65**........ HayleyTurner 4 73
(Amy Weaver) *in tch: drvn and qcknd to ld appr fnl 2f: drvn out fnl f: comf* **10/3**[2]

1-06 **2** *2* **Prince Charlemagne (IRE)**[12] 457 8-8-9 **58**...... MatthewCosham[(7)] 1 64
(Dr Jeremy Naylor) *hld up in rr hdwy and rdn over 2f out: styd on to chse wnr appr fnl f but no imp* **33/1**

06-5 **3** *3¼* **Indian Ghyll (IRE)**[31] 223 5-9-7 **63**........ LiamKeniry 5 65
(Roger Teal) *t.k.h: sn led and 8 l clr: jnd 3f out: kpt advantage tl hdd appr fnl 2f: dropped to 4th fnl f but kpt on again to retake 3rd on line* **11/2**

26-2 **4** *nse* **Eagle Nebula**[31] 223 7-9-10 **66**........ AdamKirby 2 68
[illegible] *hdd and lost 3rd on line* **7/2**[3]

2-43 **5** *7* **Private Equity (IRE)**[13] 444 5-8-11 **53**........ JoeFanning 6 47
(William Jarvis) *chsd ldrs: wnt 2nd 4f out: chal ins fnl 3f: sn rdn: wknd qckly over 2f out* **3/1**[1]

3 **6** *3¾* **Galant Star (FR)**[24] 314 5-9-9 **65**........ GeorgeBaker 3 54
(Gary Moore) *chsd ldr to 4f out: sn rdn: wknd over 2f out* **20/1**

630- **7** *10* **King Supreme (IRE)**[88] 7553 6-9-12 **68**........(b) DaneO'Neill 7 45
(Richard Hannon) *in rr: rdn and wd into st: a struggling* **10/1**

-042 **8** *6* **Bute Street**[17] 407 6-9-5 **61**........ RichardKingscote 8 31
(Ron Hodges) *chsd ldrs: rdn over 3f out: sn btn* **8/1**

3m 30.27s (0.17) **Going Correction** +0.05s/f (Slow) **8** Ran SP% **113.6**
Speed ratings (Par 103): **101,100,98,98,94 92,87,84**
toteswingers: 1&2 £12.10, 1&3 £3.60, 2&3 £13.60 CSF £94.83 CT £587.07 TOTE £5.00: £1.60, £7.90, £1.90; EX 65.20 TRIFECTA Not won..
Owner Eddie Partridge **Bred** Cheveley Park Stud Ltd **Trained** Newmarket, Suffolk

FOCUS
A modest staying handicap. The time was over six seconds outside the standard.

623 BOOK NOW FOR RACING POST CHASE H'CAP (LONDON MILE QUALIFIER) 1m (P)
3:55 (3:56) (Class 4) (0-85,83) 4-Y-0+ **£3,561** (£1,059; £529; £264) **Stalls** Low

Form RPR

0-30 **1** **Big Bay (USA)**[27] 279 5-9-4 **80**........ NeilCallan 7 87
(Jane Chapple-Hyam) *in tch: rdn along 3f out: styd on to take slt ld jst ins fnl f: narrowly hdd fnl 120yds: rallied to ld again last stride* **14/1**

-521 **2** *nse* **Lockantanks**[25] 310 4-9-0 **76**........ NeilChalmers 10 83
(Michael Appleby) *hld up in rr: hdwy on outside fr 3f out: drvn to chal 1f out and slt ld fnl 120yds: ct last stride* **6/1**[3]

12-1 **3** *nk* **Chilli Green**[27] 279 4-9-6 **82**........ DaneO'Neill 1 88
(John Akehurst) *chsd ldrs: rdn to take slt ld over 1f out: hdd u.p jst ins fnl f: styd chalng tl no ex nr fin* **7/4**[1]

0-60 **4** *shd* **Pegasus Again (USA)**[22] 348 6-9-2 **78**........ JoeFanning 5 84
(Robert Mills) *hld up in rr: hdwy fr 2f out: styd on thrght fnl f and gng on clsng stages: nt quite pce to chal* **12/1**

6-24 **5** *1¾* **Samarinda (USA)**[18] 385 8-9-1 **77**........(p) MickyFenton 6 79
(Pam Sly) *chsd ldrs: chal fr 2f out tl appr fnl f: one pce ins fnl f* **15/2**

0-02 **6** *1¾* **Highly Regal (IRE)**[11] 473 6-8-8 **73**........(b) JamesSullivan[(3)] 4 71
(Roger Teal) *chsd ldr: chal u.p fr 2f out tl wknd jst ins fnl f* **5/1**[2]

4-16 **7** *1¼* **Gallantry**[18] 385 9-9-2 **78**........ JimmyQuinn 3 73
(Jane Chapple-Hyam) *chsd ldrs: rdn ins fnl 3f: wknd appr fnl f* **9/1**

050- **8** *hd* **Den's Gift (IRE)**[88] 7560 7-9-0 **83**........(b) LucyKBarry[(7)] 2 78
(Clive Cox) *led: sn clr: jnd over 2f out: hdd u.p over 1f out: wknd fnl f* **8/1**

00/ **9** *19* **Focail Eile**[474] 7229 6-8-8 **70**........ ChrisCatlin 9 21
(Noel Quinlan) *a in rr* **25/1**

00-5 **10** *2¾* **Hereford Boy**[22] 348 7-9-0 **76**........ JamieSpencer 8 21
(Dean Ivory) *s.i.s: a towards rr* **11/1**

1m 38.16s (-1.64) **Going Correction** +0.05s/f (Slow) **10** Ran SP% **126.7**
Speed ratings (Par 105): **110,109,109,109,107 106,104,104,85,82**
toteswingers: 1&2 £17.70, 1&3 £9.20, 2&3 £2.70 CSF £103.89 CT £232.40 TOTE £18.40: £4.80, £2.70, £1.20; EX 173.10 TRIFECTA Not won..
Owner Jane Chapple-Hyam & Mrs B J Hirst **Bred** Hermitage Farm LLC **Trained** Dalham, Suffolk

FOCUS
The pace was strong (time by far the quickest of four 1m races), but there was little to separate the first four at the line and this was a really competitive handicap.
Big Bay(USA) Official explanation: trainer said, regarding apparent improvement in form, that the gelding had become upset in the stalls on its previous outing.
Hereford Boy Official explanation: vet said gelding finished lame behind

624 PANORAMIC MAIDEN FILLIES' STKS 1m (P)
4:25 (4:27) (Class 5) 3-Y-0+ **£2,047** (£604; £302) **Stalls** Low

Form RPR

63 **1** **Apache Glory (USA)**[15] 434 3-8-9 0........ JimmyQuinn 9 62
(Richard Hannon) *trckd ldr: drvn to ld over 2f out: c clr fnl f: readily* **13/2**

5-3 **2** *3* **Snowy Peak**[29] 262 3-8-9 0........(t) ShaneKelly 1 55
(Jeremy Noseda) *led tl hdd over 2f out: sn outpcd by wnr but kpt on wl for 2nd* **3/1**[1]

3-2 **3** *¾* **Roman Flame**[21] 360 3-8-9 72........(v[1]) MartinDwyer 8 53
(Michael Quinn) *in rr: hdwy over 2f out: chsd ldng duo ins fnl f and kpt on u.p but no imp* **10/3**[2]

0 **4** *¾* **Sole Bay**[24] 313 3-8-9 0........ DaneO'Neill 3 51
(David Elsworth) *t.k.h: chsd ldrs and stdd in tch: hdwy: green and hd to one side wl over 2f out: rdn and kpt on appr fnl f and r.o cl home to take 4th last strides* **25/1**

5 *nk* **Faith And Hope (IRE)** 3-8-9 0........ HayleyTurner 2 51
(James Fanshawe) *chsd ldrs: rdn over 2f out: one pce ins fnl f: lost 4th last strides* **9/2**[3]

-040 **6** *nk* **Pictures (IRE)**[8] 524 4-10-0 41........ GeorgeBaker 10 56?
(John Bridger) *hld up in rr: pushed along and hdwy fr 2f out: sme prog fnl f but nvr any threat* **33/1**

7 *¾* **Rose Bush (IRE)** 3-8-9 0........ AndreaAtzeni 11 48
(Marco Botti) *in rr: hdwy fr 2f out: kpt on fnl f: nt trble ldrs* **8/1**

06 **7** *dht* **Tegan (IRE)**[27] 274 3-8-9 0........ FrankieMcDonald 5 48
(Richard Hannon) *t.k.h: in rr but in tch: sme prog fr 2f out but nvr nr ldrs: one pce fnl f* **33/1**

04 **9** *1¼* **Zelenia**[27] 274 3-8-9 0........ LukeMorris 7 45
(Peter Winkworth) *chsd ldrs: rdn ins fnl 3f: wknd fr 2f out* **50/1**

10 *16* **Red Copper** 3-8-9 0........ JamieSpencer 6 —
(Michael Bell) *slowly away: rdn and struggling ins fnl 3f: eased* **11/2**

1m 41.79s (1.99) **Going Correction** +0.05s/f (Slow)
WFA 3 from 4yo+ 19lb **10** Ran SP% **117.8**
Speed ratings (Par 100): **92,89,88,87,87 86,86,86,84,68**
toteswingers: 1&2 £3.50, 1&3 £2.80, 2&3 £2.60 CSF £25.85 TOTE £8.00: £2.30, £1.30, £1.40; EX 27.80 Trifecta £50.50 Pool: £502.24 - 7.35 winning units..
Owner Malih Lahej Al Basti **Bred** Malih Al Basti **Trained** East Everleigh, Wilts

FOCUS
The final time, which was the slowest of four 1m races on the card, as well as the proximity of the 41-rated sixth, suggests this is pretty ordinary form. It paid to be handy.

625 BETDAQ THE BETTING EXCHANGE H'CAP (DIV I) 1m (P)
4:55 (4:56) (Class 6) (0-65,65) 4-Y-0+ **£1,364** (£403; £201) **Stalls** Low

Form RPR

[illegible] **1** [illegible][109] 7305 4-8-13 57........(bo[1]) ShaneKelly 1 67
(Gary Moore) *trckd ldrs: hrd drvn and styd on fr 2f out: kpt on wl u.p to ld fnl strides* **7/1**[3]

441- **2** *hd* **Al Aqabah (IRE)**[116] 7168 6-9-5 **63**........(b) NeilCallan 8 72
(Brian Gubby) *chsd ldrs: wnt 2nd over 3f out: rdn to ld wl over 2f out: styd on wl fnl f: hdd fnl strides* **9/2**[2]

0-35 **3** *1* **Serious Drinking (USA)**[16] 428 5-9-4 **62**........(t) JamieSpencer 7 69
(Walter Swinburn) *stdd s: hld up in rr: hdwy on ins fr 2f out: tk 3rd u.p ins fnl f but a jst hld by ldng duo* **9/2**[2]

5-33 **4** *2* **Esteem Lord**[18] 390 5-9-1 **59**........ AdamKirby 6 61
(Dean Ivory) *chsd ldrs: rdn over 2f out: chsd ldng duo 1f out: one pce ins fnl f* **4/1**[1]

-410 **5** *1* **Poppy Golightly**[4] 555 4-8-10 **54**........ ChrisCatlin 4 54
(Ron Hodges) *led: rdn and hdd wl over 2f out: wknd fnl f* **8/1**

0-45 **6** *hd* **Lopinot (IRE)**[11] 477 8-9-3 **61**........(v) HayleyTurner 2 61+
(Martin Bosley) *s.i.s: towards rr: hdwy over 2f out: kpt on same pce and no imp fnl f* **16/1**

0522 **7** *nk* **Master Of Dance (IRE)**[10] 489 4-9-6 **64**........(b) MickyFenton 10 63
(James Given) *s.i.s: towards rr: sme hdwy on outside fr 2f out but nvr in contention* **10/1**

030- **8** *hd* **Powerful Pierre**[97] 7467 4-9-5 **63**........ TomEaves 5 61
(Ian McInnes) *chsd ldrs: rdn over 2f out: btn fnl f* **33/1**

-451 **9** *1¾* **Unlimited**[13] 445 9-9-7 **65**........ LukeMorris 9 59
(Tony Carroll) *t.k.h in rr: hdwy ins fnl 3f: effrt 2f out: nvr on terms and btn appr fnl f* **14/1**

4-64 **10** *1* **Starwatch**[25] 306 4-9-6 **64**........ NeilChalmers 3 56
(John Bridger) *s.i.s: t.k.h in rr: rdn over 2f out and a outpcd* **12/1**

1m 40.73s (0.93) **Going Correction** +0.05s/f (Slow) **10** Ran SP% **112.2**
Speed ratings (Par 101): **97,96,95,93,92 92,92,92,90,89**
toteswingers: 1&2 £9.30, 1&3 £8.50, 2&3 £6.20 CSF £37.00 CT £159.92 TOTE £9.40: £2.60, £2.40, £1.60; EX 57.60 Trifecta £163.60 Pool: £544.15 - 2.46 winning units..
Owner Gallagher Equine Ltd **Bred** Shadwell Estate Company Limited **Trained** Lower Beeding, W Sussex

■ Stewards' Enquiry : Neil Callan one-day ban: used whip with excessive frequency without giving mare time to respond (Mar 7)

FOCUS
They went a muddling pace, although the time was the second quickest of the four 1m races, and 0.39 seconds faster than the other division. Few became involved and this is not form to take too literally.

Starwatch Official explanation: jockey said gelding ran too freely

626 BETDAQ THE BETTING EXCHANGE H'CAP (DIV II) 1m (P)

5:25 (5:27) (Class 6) (0-65,65) 4-Y-0+ £1,364 (£403; £201) Stalls Low

Form				RPR
1-12	1		**But Beautiful (IRE)**[25] 303 4-9-6 **64** ... JoeFanning 3	71+
			(Robert Mills) *trckd ldrs: tk slt advantage 2f out: strly chal sn after and thrght fnl f: jst hld on* **1/1**[1]	
2-30	2	*shd*	**Eastern Gift**[10] 488 6-9-4 **62** ... NeilCallan 2	69
			(Gay Kelleway) *chsd ldrs: str chal fr 2f out and upsides u.p thrght fnl f: edgd lft fnl 50yds: no ex last stride* **8/1**	
2-23	3	*1 ¼*	**Dichoh**[10] 488 8-9-7 **65** ... (p) GeorgeBaker 1	70
			(Michael Madgwick) *led: hdd 2 out: styd pressing ldrs: one pce ins fnl f: hld by ldng duo whn hmpd fnl 50yds but kpt on wl to hold 3rd* **5/1**[2]	
2-2	4	*nse*	**Saddlers Bend (IRE)**[41] 111 5-9-3 **64** ... MatthewDavies(3) 7	68
			(George Baker) *chsd ldrs: rdn and one pce 2f out: rallied and styd on again ins fnl f to cl on 3rd last strides but nt rch ldng duo* **7/1**[3]	
030-	5	*¾*	**Valkov**[54] 7995 4-9-0 **58** ... LukeMorris 4	60
			(Tony Carroll) *in tch: rdn over 2f out: one pce fr over 1f out* **16/1**	
0-51	6	*1*	**Mr Chocolate Drop (IRE)**[24] 317 7-9-3 **61** ... (t) AdamKirby 8	61
			(Mandy Rowland) *in rr: rdn and styd on fr 2f out but nvr in contention: wknd ins fnl f* **10/1**	
-042	7	*7*	**Having A Ball**[10] 483 7-9-5 **63** ... (v) ChrisCatlin 5	47
			(Jonathan Portman) *rdn along 3f out: a in rr* **15/2**	

1m 41.12s (1.32) **Going Correction** +0.05s/f (Slow) **7 Ran SP% 117.0**
Speed ratings (Par 101): **95,94,93,93,92 91,84**
toteswingers: 1&2 £3.60, 1&3 £1.20, 2&3 £4.30. totesuper7: Win: Not won. Place: £303.80. CSF £10.47 CT £29.55 TOTE £1.90: £1.30, £4.20; EX 12.50 Trifecta £49.00 Pool: £933.03 - 49.00 wining units..
Owner B Ecclestone, J Humphreys, T G Mills **Bred** Gerrardstown House Stud **Trained** Headley, Surrey
■ Stewards' Enquiry : Neil Callan caution: careless riding and using whip down the shoulder in the forehand.

FOCUS
The time was slow - 0.39 seconds off the first division - and the first four finishers filled the first four places entering the straight. There are doubts over how reliable this form will prove.
T/Plt: £125.60 to a £1 stake. Pool: £60,130.76. 349.46 winning units. T/Qpdt: £24.40 to a £1 stake. Pool: £4,451.88. 134.80 winning units. ST

534 ST MORITZ (R-H)

Sunday, February 20

OFFICIAL GOING: Frozen

627a GRAND PRIX PRESTIGE (CONDITIONS) (4YO+) (SNOW) 5f 110y

11:40 (12:00) 4-Y-0+

£8,689 (£4,344; £3,103; £2,068; £1,034; £620)

			RPR
1		**Libretto (GER)**[24] 325 5-9-4 0 ... FilipMinarik 3	—
		(H-W Hiller, Germany) **48/10**	
2	*hd*	**Lodano (FR)**[14] 440 6-8-11 0 ... SteveDrowne 5	—
		(M Weiss, Switzerland) **103/10**	
3	*1*	**Sacho (GER)**[14] 440 13-9-2 0 ... APietsch 1	—
		(C Von Der Recke, Germany) **6/1**	
4	*¾*	**Rushing Dasher (GER)**[14] 440 9-9-2 0 ... FrauNatalieFriberg 7	—
		(Natalie Friberg, Switzerland) **39/10**[3]	
5	*¾*	**Sweet Venture (FR)**[14] 440 9-9-2 0 ... RobertHavlin 6	—
		(M Weiss, Switzerland) **23/10**[2]	
6	*1 ¼*	**Shetan**[14] 440 5-8-11 0 ... (b) DPorcu 2	—
		(M Weiss, Switzerland) **97/10**	
7	*7*	**Freeforaday (USA)**[14] 440 4-9-2 0 ... JimCrowley 4	—
		(John Best) *dwlt s: rousted along thrght: racd one fr last: dropped away u.str.p ins fnl 2f* **13/10**[1]	

67.15 secs (67.15) **7 Ran SP% 143.9**
PARI-MUTUEL (all including 1 chf stakes): WIN 5.80; PLACE 2.20, 2.80; SF 173.60.
Owner Ulrich Zerrath **Bred** Gestut Ebbesloh **Trained** Germany

628a GUBELIN 72ND GROSSER PREIS VON ST MORITZ (CONDITIONS) (4YO+) (SNOW) 1m 2f

1:10 (12:00) 4-Y-0+

£35,083 (£17,541; £12,529; £8,353; £4,176; £2,506)

			RPR
1		**Winterwind (IRE)**[14] 441 6-9-4 0 ... GeorgBocskai 13	89
		(Carmen Bocskai, Switzerland)	
2	*¾*	**Pont Des Arts (FR)**[14] 441 7-9-4 0 ... FredericSpanu 1	88
		(A Schaerer, Germany)	
3	*nk*	**Tarkheena Prince (USA)**[161] 6011 6-8-11 0 ... PierantonioConvertino 5	80
		(C Von Der Recke, Germany)	
4	*shd*	**Barongo (IRE)**[7] 534 6-8-11 0 ... SebastienMaillot 17	80
		(U Suter, France)	
5	*1 ¼*	**Schutzenjunker (GER)**[14] 442 6-8-11 0 ... DPorcu 18	78
		(P Schaerer, Switzerland)	
6	*nk*	**Saphir Bere (FR)**[14] 442 5-8-11 0 ... FrankieDettori 15	77
		(Carmen Bocskai, Switzerland)	
7	*1 ½*	**Wassiljew (IRE)**[14] 441 7-8-11 0 ... MiguelLopez 10	74
		(A Schaerer, Germany)	
8	*2*	**Designated Decoy (USA)**[162] 5978 6-8-11 0 ... APietsch 11	71
		(C Von Der Recke, Germany)	
9	*4 ½*	**Mascarpone (GER)**[14] 441 7-9-2 0 ... RobertHavlin 14	68
		(M Weiss, Switzerland)	
10	*1*	**Agent Archie (USA)**[14] 441 4-8-10 0 ... DavidProbert 4	61
		(John Best) *w ldrs: led briefly on bk st: rdn and grad fdd fr 2 1/2f out*	
11	*3*	**Ziking (FR)**[99] 7455 6-9-6 0 ... OlivierPeslier 8	64
		(A Schaerer, Germany)	
12	*2 ½*	**Solapur (GER)**[14] 441 6-9-0 0 ... NicolasGuilbert 12	54
		(Karin Suter-Weber, Switzerland)	
13	*1 ¼*	**Northern Glory**[14] 442 8-9-4 0 ... KKerekes 9	56
		(W Figge, Germany)	
14	*dist*	**Halsion Chancer**[7] 534 7-9-0 0 ... KierenFox 7	—
		(John Best) *chsd ldng gp: wknd fr 3f out: eased and t.o*	
15	*8*	**Rolling Home (GER)**[7] 534 7-9-8 0 ... EPedroza 16	—
		(P Schaerer, Switzerland)	
16	*1 ¾*	**Fight For Freedom (IRE)**[120] 4-8-10 0 ... FilipMinarik 6	—
		(P Schiergen, Germany)	
17	*4*	**Glad Panther**[14] 441 5-9-0 0 ... SteveDrowne 2	—
		(M Weiss, Switzerland)	
18	*1 ¼*	**Palio Square (USA)**[135] 6715 4-8-10 0 ... JimCrowley 3	—
		(Ralph Beckett) *mid-div on outside: bhd fnl 3f: eased and t.o*	

2m 9.38s (129.38)
WFA 4 from 5yo+ 1lb **18 Ran**
PARI-MUTUEL (all including 1 chf stakes): WIN 45.80; PLACE 11.90, 4.40, 12.40; SF 132.20.
Owner Markus Graff **Bred** Denis & Teresa Bergin **Trained** Switzerland

629a GRAND PRIX SPORTMIND (CONDITIONS) (4YO+) (SNOW) 1m 1f

1:50 (12:00) 4-Y-0+

£4,634 (£2,317; £1,655; £1,103; £551; £331)

			RPR
1		**African Art (USA)**[484] 7027 5-9-6 0 ... EPedroza 15	—
		(P Schaerer, Switzerland) **42/10**[2]	
2	*6*	**Rayo (CZE)**[7] 534 6-9-8 0 ... JanRaja 10	—
		(M Weiss, Switzerland) **14/5**[1]	
3	*¾*	**Sentimento (ISR)**[14] 442 8-9-6 0 ... MTellini 8	—
		(Werner Glanz, Germany) **23/5**[3]	
4	*4*	**Bucked Off (SAF)**[7] 534 7-9-8 0 ... APietsch 13	—
		(C Von Der Recke, Germany) **204/10**	
5	*nk*	**Puro (CZE)**[1099] 604 9-9-6 0 ... RobertHavlin 1	—
		(M Weiss, Switzerland) **102/10**	
6	*2*	**Save The Day**[863] 6632 5-8-10 0 ... FrankieDettori 14	—
		(A Schaerer, Germany) **127/10**	
7	*¾*	**Paparazzi (SWI)** 7-8-11 0 ow2 ... NicolasGuilbert 9	—
		(Karin Suter-Weber, Switzerland) **193/10**	
8	*1 ½*	**Peace Keeper (FR)**[48] 42 5-9-8 0 ... SebastienMaillot 2	—
		(U Suter, France) **58/10**	
9	*3*	**Chat De La Burg (USA)**[7] 534 4-9-6 0 ... KierenFox 11	—
		(John Best) *trckd ldng pair in share of 3rd and racd keenly: pushed along 1/2-way to hold pl: no imp u.p fnl 2 1/2f: grad fdd* **18/1**	
10	*6*	**Cayman (IRE)**[14] 442 4-9-2 0 ... PierantonioConvertino 3	—
		(C Von Der Recke, Germany) **30/1**	
11	*1 ¼*	**Nachtschwarmer (GER)**[1236] 7-9-0 0 ... FilipMinarik 6	—
		(Frau Marion Rotering, Germany) **175/10**	
12	*hd*	**Anthology**[202] 4652 5-9-0 0 ... OlivierPeslier 4	—
		(C Von Der Recke, Germany) **211/10**	
13	*1*	**Ritorno (SWI)**[735] 7-9-2 0 ... SteveDrowne 5	—
		(M Weiss, Switzerland) **217/10**	
14	*1 ¾*	**My Xaar In Blue (SWI)** 5-9-0 0 ... DPorcu 12	—
		(P Vovcenko, Germany) **166/10**	
15	*dist*	**Fortunato (GER)**[14] 441 6-9-8 0 ... KKerekes 7	—
		(W Figge, Germany) **77/10**	

1m 59.08s (119.08) **15 Ran SP% 143.9**
PARI-MUTUEL (all including 1 chf stakes): WIN 5.20; PLACE 1.80, 2.10, 2.10; SF 28.30.
Owner Peter Aregger **Bred** Sean Gorman **Trained** Switzerland

595 WOLVERHAMPTON (A.W) (L-H)

Monday, February 21

OFFICIAL GOING: Standard
Wind: Slight against Weather: Overcast

630 TODAY'S JOCKEY SPECIALS AT BLUESQ.COM AMATEUR RIDERS' H'CAP (DIV I) 1m 4f 50y(P)

2:30 (2:30) (Class 6) (0-52,58) 4-Y-0+ £1,318 (£405; £202) Stalls Low

Form				RPR
5202	1		**Laura Land**[13] 450 5-10-3 **46** ... MissBeckyBrisbourne(5) 5	55
			(Mark Brisbourne) *hld up: hdwy over 3f out: led over 1f out: edgd lft: rdn out* **9/1**[3]	
-035	2	*2*	**Light The City (IRE)**[11] 492 4-10-1 **47** ... WilliamTwiston-Davies(5) 8	53
			(Ruth Carr) *chsd ldrs: led over 4f out: rdn and hdd over 1f out: styd on same pce* **10/1**	
0-41	3	*1 ¼*	**Noah Jameel**[5] 553 9-11-1 **58** 6ex ... MrFMitchell(5) 1	62
			(Tony Newcombe) *hld up: hdwy over 2f out: rdn over 1f out: edgd lft ins fnl f: styd on* **11/8**[1]	
0435	4	*1 ½*	**Barbirolli**[13] 451 9-10-1 **46** oh1 ... MissCScott(7) 9	48
			(William Stone) *hld up: rdn over 2f out: styd on fnl f: nt rch ldrs* **16/1**	
400-	5	*1 ½*	**Trumpstoo (USA)**[79] 7704 5-11-0 **52** ... MissADeniel 10	52
			(Richard Fahey) *chsd ldrs: rdn over 2f out: hung lft over 1f out: styd on* **12/1**	
0/00	6	*2 ½*	**Rough Sketch (USA)**[24] 346 6-10-6 **49** ... MrJHodson(5) 3	45
			(Ian Williams) *hld up: hdwy over 2f out: sn rdn: styd on same pce* **9/1**[3]	
0-40	7	*3*	**Abulharith**[11] 252 5-10-13 **51** ... (p) MrOGreenall 7	43
			(Ronald Harris) *chsd ldr: chal over 4f out: rdn over 1f out: wknd fnl f* **14/1**	
60-0	8	*1 ¼*	**Paint The Town Red**[3] 598 6-10-3 **46** ... JustinNewman(5) 2	36
			(Richard Guest) *hood removed late: sn prom: rdn over 2f out: wknd over 1f out* **13/2**[2]	
0005	9	*1 ½*	**Gems**[9] 524 4-10-0 **46** oh1 ... MrTGarner(5) 4	33
			(Peter Hiatt) *prom: pushed along over 5f out: wknd over 2f out* **16/1**	
60-4	10	*24*	**Ledgerwood**[11] 490 6-10-3 **46** oh1 ... (p) BrendanPowell(5) 11	—
			(Adrian Chamberlain) *led: hdd over 4f out: wknd over 3f out: t.o* **66/1**	
240-	U		**Back To Paris (IRE)**[155] 5364 9-10-3 **48** ... (t) MrJMThomas(7) 6	—
			(Philip Kirby) *eventually rrd and uns rdr in stalls* **33/1**	

2m 44.9s (3.80) **Going Correction** +0.225s/f (Slow)
WFA 4 from 5yo+ 3lb **11 Ran SP% 115.1**
Speed ratings (Par 101): **96,94,93,92,91 90,88,87,86,70** —
Tote Swingers: 1&2 £8.40, 1&3 £3.70, 2&3 £4.30 CSF £93.61 CT £198.87 TOTE £7.10: £1.60, £2.20, £1.50; EX 65.50 Trifecta £176.20 Part won. Pool: £238.18 - 0.71 winning units..
Owner Law Abiding Citizens **Bred** Theobalds Stud **Trained** Great Ness, Shropshire

The Form Book, Raceform Ltd, Compton, RG20 6NL

FOCUS
A moderate contest but a solid enough level to the form.

631 TODAY'S JOCKEY SPECIALS AT BLUESQ.COM AMATEUR RIDERS' H'CAP (DIV II) 1m 4f 50y(P)
3:00 (3:01) (Class 6) (0-52,54) 4-Y-0+ **£1,318** (£405; £202) **Stalls** Low

Form RPR
30-1 **1** **Captain Cool (IRE)**[9] 524 4-10-11 **52**....(b) MissEJJones 7 62
(Richard Hannon) *a.p: shkn up over 3f out: chsd ldr over 2f out: led over 1f out: rdn out* **3/1**[1]
0-21 **2** 3 ¼ **Bright Sparky (GER)**[3] 598 8-11-2 **54** 6ex....(vt) MrOGreenall 2 59
(Michael Easterby) *led: rdn and hdd over 1f out: styd on same pce ins fnl f* **3/1**[1]
6-63 **3** 3 ½ **Wrecking Crew (IRE)**[13] 451 7-10-1 **46** oh1.... MrsDBamonte(7) 12 46
(Rod Millman) *hld up: hdwy 5f out: rdn over 1f out: hung lft ins fnl f: no imp* **8/1**
0-06 **4** ½ **Swords**[13] 450 9-10-5 **46** oh1.... MrMPrice(3) 6 45
(Ray Peacock) *hld up: hdwy over 1f out: n.d* **16/1**
55-0 **5** 3 **Dancing Poppy**[46] 69 4-9-12 **46** oh1....(t) MissCEReid(7) 10 41
(Ben De Haan) *prom: rdn over 2f out: wknd over 1f out* **28/1**
00-5 **6** 1 ¼ **Castlebury (IRE)**[11] 490 6-10-6 **49**....(b) WilliamTwiston-Davies(5) 9 42
(Ruth Carr) *chsd ldrs: rdn over 2f out: wknd over 1f out* **16/1**
-563 **7** ¾ **Acropolis (IRE)**[3] 588 10-10-1 **46**.... MrCCarroll(7) 1 38
(Tony Carroll) *mid-div: hdwy over 6f out: rdn over 2f out: sn outpcd* **7/1**[3]
000- **8** 1 ¾ **Truly Magic**[15] 6826 4-10-5 **46** oh1.... MissLHorner 11 35
(Liam Corcoran) *hld up: effrt over 2f out: sn wknd* **80/1**
2-35 **9** *hd* **Mary Helen**[3] 598 4-10-3 **49**.... MissBeckyBrisbourne(5) 8 38
(Mark Brisbourne) *s.i.s: hdwy 10f out: rdn and wknd over 1f out* **5/1**[2]
66-0 **10** 8 **Farleigh**[17] 418 5-10-7 **52**.... MrMMitchell(7) 4 30
(Alex Hales) *w ldr to over 3f out: wknd wl over 1f out* **14/1**
50-0 **11** 10 **Wee Ziggy**[14] 444 8-10-5 **46** oh1.... MissMMullineaux(3) 3 8
(Michael Mullineaux) *mid-div: rdn over 4f out: sn bhd* **40/1**
54-0 **12** 11 **Public Image**[47] 50 5-10-2 **47**.... MrDanielBurchell(7) 5 —
(Jamie Poulton) *s.i.s: a in rr: wknd 4f out: t.o* **50/1**

2m 45.2s (4.10) **Going Correction** +0.225s/f (Slow) **12** Ran SP% **117.8**
WFA 4 from 5yo+ 3lb
Speed ratings (Par 101): **95,92,90,90,88 87,86,85,85,80 73,66**
Tote Swingers: 1&2 £2.80, 1&3 £5.00, 2&3 £5.60 CSF £10.85 CT £65.27 TOTE £4.20: £1.40, £1.10, £2.60; EX 12.90 Trifecta £47.00 Pool: £235.67 - 3.71 winning units..
Owner Mrs John Lee **Bred** Jan Revs **Trained** East Everleigh, Wilts

FOCUS
They once again went a sedate gallop early on in the second division of this amateur riders' handicap, although they did seem to quicken it up with 6f to go. The finish was fought out by the two last-time-out winners in the field. The form is solid at this level with the winner back in good heart.

632 STAY AT THE WOLVERHAMPTON HOLIDAY INN H'CAP 5f 20y(P)
3:30 (3:30) (Class 5) (0-75,74) 3-Y-O **£1,813** (£539; £269; £134) **Stalls** Low

Form RPR
4412 **1** **Restless Bay (IRE)**[4] 578 3-9-8 **74** 6ex....(v) ChrisCatlin 4 79
(Reg Hollinshead) *trckd ldrs: shkn up to ld over 1f out: r.o: readily* **5/2**[1]
412 **2** 1 ½ **Rylee Mooch**[10] 505 3-9-0 **66**....(e) JamieSpencer 2 66
(Richard Guest) *s.s: sn prom: rdn and swtchd lft ins fnl f: r.o to go 2nd and hung rt towards fin* **5/2**[1]
155- **3** ¾ **Overwhelm**[185] 5261 3-9-2 **73**.... LeeTopliss(5) 3 70
(Richard Fahey) *s.i.s: hld up: hdwy over 1f out: sn rdn: styd on same pce ins fnl f* **3/1**[2]
4336 **4** 1 **Johnny Hancocks (IRE)**[12] 465 3-8-12 **67**.... JamesSullivan(3) 1 61
(Linda Stubbs) *chsd ldr tl led 2f out: rdn and hdd over 1f out: no ex ins fnl f* **15/2**
05-2 **5** 4 **Spontaneity (IRE)**[9] 518 3-8-10 **62**.... TomEaves 5 41
(Bryan Smart) *led 3f: sn rdn: wknd ins fnl f* **5/1**[3]

63.05 secs (0.75) **Going Correction** +0.225s/f (Slow) **5** Ran SP% **110.6**
Speed ratings (Par [illegible]): **100,100,[illegible]**
CSF £9.00 TOTE £4.10: £1.80, £1.30; EX 8.30.
Owner John L Marriott **Bred** Grangemore Stud **Trained** Upper Longdon, Staffs

FOCUS
As seemed likely they went a frenetic pace in this 3-y-o handicap. There wasn't much depth to the race but the form has been rated at face value, with a clear personal best from the winner.

633 HOTEL & CONFERENCING AT WOLVERHAMPTON (S) STKS 1m 141y(P)
4:00 (4:00) (Class 6) 4-Y-0+ **£1,535** (£453; £226) **Stalls** Low

Form RPR
-101 **1** **Erinjay (IRE)**[5] 561 5-9-6 77.... AndreaAtzeni 5 77
(Michael Wigham) *hld up: hdwy 3f out: chsd ldr over 1f out: edgd rt: rdn to ld ins fnl f: r.o* **4/7**[1]
1631 **2** ¾ **I Confess**[3] 590 6-9-6 70....(b) JamieSpencer 1 76
(David Evans) *set stdy pce tl rdn over 2f out: hung rt over 1f out: hdd and unable qck ins fnl f* **7/2**[2]
4510 **3** 3 ¼ **Unlimited**[1] 625 9-9-6 65.... LukeMorris 4 69
(Tony Carroll) *prom: rdn over 1f out: styd on same pce fnl f* **14/1**
-303 **4** ¾ **Collect Art (IRE)**[16] 433 4-9-0 62.... StevieDonohoe 7 61
(Andrew Haynes) *hld up: hdwy u.p over 1f out: nvr trbld ldrs* **10/1**[3]
20/0 **5** 3 **Hawaass (USA)**[6] 548 6-9-0 85.... PJMcDonald 6 55
(Ruth Carr) *chsd ldr: rdn and ev ch over 2f out: wknd fnl f* **14/1**
0603 **6** 8 **Duplicity**[4] 568 4-9-0 65....(p) J-PGuillambert 2 38
(James Given) *trckd ldrs: plld hrd: rdn over 2f out: wknd over 1f out: eased ins fnl f* **25/1**

1m 53.7s (3.20) **Going Correction** +0.225s/f (Slow) **6** Ran SP% **112.1**
Speed ratings (Par 101): **94,93,90,89,87 80**
Tote Swingers: 1&2 £1.30, 1&3 £2.80, 2&3 £2.40 CSF £2.82 TOTE £1.70: £1.10, £3.00; EX 2.50.There was no bid for the winner.
Owner Seyhan Osman, Michael Wigham **Bred** Bill Benson **Trained** Newmarket, Suffolk

FOCUS
A run-of-the-mill seller dominated by the first two in the market. The runner-up got first run on the winner and limits the form.

634 DINE IN THE HORIZONS RESTAURANT MAIDEN STKS 1m 1f 103y(P)
4:30 (4:31) (Class 5) 3-Y-0+ **£1,813** (£539; £269; £134) **Stalls** Low

Form RPR
5 **1** **Crystal Sky (IRE)**[9] 520 3-8-0 0.... JimmyQuinn 2 65
(Andrew Haynes) *hld up: hdwy over 2f out: r.o to ld towards fin* **8/1**
-46 **2** ¾ **Loyal N Trusted**[24] 339 3-8-5 0.... AndreaAtzeni 9 68
(Michael Wigham) *led: rdn and edgd lft ins fnl f: hdd towards fin* **16/1**
06-2 **3** 1 ¼ **Maher (USA)**[35] 191 3-8-5 74.... MartinLane 8 65
(David Simcock) *s.i.s and hmpd s: hdwy over 7f out: chsd ldr 4f out: rdn over 2f out: hung lft over 1f out: styd on same pce: wnt 3rd nr fin* **4/5**[1]
03- **4** ½ **Strophic**[87] 7575 4-9-12 0.... JamieSpencer 10 68
(Giles Bravery) *hld up: hdwy over 3f out: chsd ldr over 1f out: rdn and ev ch ins fnl f: hung rt: no ex and lost 3rd nr fin* **9/2**[3]
64 **5** 6 **Cadgers Brig**[20] 378 3-8-5 0.... BarryMcHugh 6 52+
(Richard Fahey) *chsd ldrs: hmpd and lost pl 7f out: outpcd 3f out: styd on fnl f* **66/1**
0- **6** 1 **Khaki (IRE)**[54] 8001 3-8-0 0.... CathyGannon 7 45
(Tor Sturgis) *chsd ldrs tl rdn and hung lft over 2f out: sn wknd* **40/1**
00-6 **7** 3 ¾ **Brandy Alexander**[9] 520 3-8-0 65.... KieranO'Neill(5) 4 42
(Richard Hannon) *chsd ldrs: rdn over 3f out: wknd 2f out* **16/1**
00-0 **8** 5 **Stardust Dancer**[31] 253 4-9-9 0.... PaulPickard(3) 3 35
(Paul Green) *hld up: drvn along 1/2-way: sn wknd* **100/1**
9 1 ¼ **Harry Lime** 3-8-5 0.... JoeFanning 5 29
(Mark Johnston) *hld up: rdn 1/2-way: wknd 3f out* **4/1**[2]

2m 2.80s (1.10) **Going Correction** +0.225s/f (Slow)
WFA 3 from 4yo 21lb **9** Ran SP% **121.5**
Speed ratings (Par 103): **104,103,102,101,96 95,92,87,86**
Tote Swingers: 1&2 £8.80, 1&3 £2.90, 2&3 £5.40 CSF £127.76 TOTE £9.20: £1.70, £3.80, £1.10; EX 105.00 Trifecta £330.50 Pool: £670.08 - 1.50 winning units..
Owner B Fletcher & Partners **Bred** Philip Hore Jnr **Trained** Limpley Stoke, Bath

FOCUS
This looked quite a good maiden for the time of year, but the third disappointed and the second favourite ran poorly. The fourth and fifth set the level. They went no gallop early on but really started to quicken it up with 4f to run.

635 DOWNLOAD BLUE SQUARE IPHONE APP H'CAP 1m 1f 103y(P)
5:00 (5:00) (Class 6) (0-65,64) 4-Y-0+ **£1,535** (£453; £226) **Stalls** Low

Form RPR
00-4 **1** **Strong Vigilance (IRE)**[23] 352 4-9-7 **64**.... JamieSpencer 1 81+
(Michael Bell) *mde all: hung rt wl over 1f out: shkn up and hung lft ins fnl f: r.o wl* **6/4**[1]
-115 **2** 3 **John Potts**[11] 488 6-9-3 **60**.... KellyHarrison 5 71
(Brian Baugh) *hld up: hdwy over 2f out: chsd wnr over 1f out: sn rdn and ev ch: styd on same pce ins fnl f* **9/2**[3]
2-61 **3** 3 ¼ **Lean Machine**[19] 391 4-9-4 **61**....(p) LukeMorris 2 66
(Ronald Harris) *chsd ldrs: wnt 2nd 3f out tl rdn over 1f out: no ex fnl f* **3/1**[2]
0-35 **4** 5 **Corrib (IRE)**[18] 408 8-8-7 **50** oh3....(p) NeilChalmers 4 44
(Bryn Palling) *hld up in tch: rdn over 2f out: wknd over 1f out* **16/1**
0063 **5** ½ **King Of Connacht**[4] 574 8-8-10 **53**....(v) CathyGannon 6 45
(Mark Wellings) *hld up: hdwy over 2f out: wknd over 1f out* **9/2**[3]
4/0- **6** 13 **Gulf Of Aqaba (USA)**[18] 139 5-8-10 **53**.... JoeFanning 3 28
(Ian Williams) *sn chsng wnr tl rdn over 3f out: wkng whn hung lft over 1f out* **14/1**

2m 1.81s (0.11) **Going Correction** +0.225s/f (Slow) **6** Ran SP% **113.9**
Speed ratings (Par 101): **108,105,102,98,97 86**
Tote Swingers: 1&2 £2.60, 1&3 £1.50, 2&3 £2.20 CSF £8.93 TOTE £3.60: £1.40, £1.30; EX 5.90.
Owner Lawrie Inman **Bred** Peter Grimes & John Dwan **Trained** Newmarket, Suffolk

FOCUS
A decent handicap for the grade, won in good style.The runner-up helps with the form.

636 THE BLACK COUNTRY'S ONLY RACECOURSE MAIDEN STKS 7f 32y(P)
5:30 (5:31) (Class 5) 3-Y-0+ **£1,813** (£539; £269; £134) **Stalls** High

Form RPR
4- **1** **Tax Break**[130] 6876 4-9-12 0.... LeeNewman 2 84+
(David Barron) *sn led: hdd over 5f out: chsd ldr tl led again over 2f out: drifted rt: r.o* **7/4**[1]
2 ¾ **Crown Counsel (IRE)** 3-8-9 0.... JoeFanning 1 77+
(Mark Johnston) *a.p: chsd wnr 2f out: sn rdn and ev ch: styd on same pce wl ins fnl f* **9/4**[2]
40 **3** 5 **Mcbirney (USA)**[13] 454 4-9-12 0....(e) LiamJones 5 68
(Paul D'Arcy) *s.i.s: hld up: hdwy over 1f out: styd on same pce fnl f* **66/1**
6-3 **4** nse **Kontich (USA)**[31] 253 4-9-12 0.... ShaneKelly 3 68
(Noel Quinlan) *chsd wnr tl led over 5f out: rdn and hdd over 2f out: no ex fnl f* **10/3**[3]
536- **5** *shd* **Zalano**[151] 6308 3-8-10 61 ow1.... DaneO'Neill 4 64
(Derek Haydn Jones) *trckd ldrs: plld hrd: rdn over 1f out: no ex fnl f* **7/1**
6 1 ¼ **Symphonic Dancer (USA)** 4-9-7 0.... J-PGuillambert 7 60
(Brian Baugh) *hld up: rdn over 1f out: styng on whe n.m.r ins fnl f: nvr trbld ldrs* **33/1**
2 **7** 7 **Lennoxwood (IRE)**[32] 233 3-8-9 0.... HayleyTurner 6 41
(Mark Usher) *s.i.s: hld up: rdn and wknd over 1f out* **11/1**

1m 30.47s (0.87) **Going Correction** +0.225s/f (Slow)
WFA 3 from 4yo 17lb **7** Ran SP% **115.5**
Speed ratings (Par 103): **104,103,97,97,97 95,87**
Tote Swingers: 1&2 £16.70, 2&3 £22.20 CSF £6.09 TOTE £2.30: £1.70, £1.50; EX 10.60.
Owner Connect 4 **Bred** Grangecon Stud **Trained** Maunby, N Yorks

FOCUS
A fair maiden run at an even gallop.

637 PLAY ROULETTE AT BLUESQ.COM H'CAP 7f 32y(P)
6:00 (6:01) (Class 5) (0-70,68) 4-Y-0+ **£1,813** (£539; £269; £134) **Stalls** High

Form RPR
0131 **1** **West Leake (IRE)**[11] 485 5-8-11 **58**.... LiamKeniry 4 70
(Paul Burgoyne) *hld up: hdwy over 1f out: edgd lft ins fnl f: r.o to ld nr fin* **5/1**[3]
-001 **2** 1 **Spin Again (IRE)**[12] 477 6-9-0 **68**.... LucyKBarry(7) 6 77
(Mark Wellings) *sn led: hdd 4f out: led again 3f out: rdn ins fnl f: hdd nr fin* **20/1**
04-6 **3** 1 **Forward Feline (IRE)**[21] 367 5-9-2 **63**.... DavidProbert 5 69
(Bryn Palling) *hld up: rdn over 4f out: hdwy over 1f out: r.o: nt rch ldrs* **18/1**
6-23 **4** nk **Gordy Bee (USA)**[27] 291 5-8-12 **59**....(be) JamieSpencer 2 64
(Richard Guest) *chsd ldrs: rdn over 2f out: styd on same pce ins fnl f* **12/1**
-112 **5** 1 **Piccolo Express**[7] 544 5-8-10 **57**.... J-PGuillambert 9 60
(Brian Baugh) *mid-div: hdwy over 2f out: rdn and hung lft over 1f out: styd on same pce ins fnl f* **7/2**[2]
4-03 **6** 1 ¼ **Just Timmy Marcus**[17] 428 5-9-1 **62**....(b) GrahamGibbons 8 61
(Brian Baugh) *hld up: hdwy over 1f out: one pce ins fnl f* **8/1**
4-22 **7** 1 **Mount Hollow**[17] 428 6-9-4 **65**....(p) LukeMorris 3 63
(Reg Hollinshead) *prom: rdn and n.m.r over 1f out: no ex fnl f* **3/1**[1]
334- **8** 2 ¼ **Dimaire**[195] 4922 4-8-11 **58**.... DaneO'Neill 7 50
(Derek Haydn Jones) *chsd ldrs: rdn over 1f out: wknd ins fnl f* **33/1**

0-54 **9** ½ **Cut And Thrust (IRE)**[19] 394 5-9-5 **66** AdamKirby 1 55
(Mark Wellings) *hld up: hdwy over 2f out: rdn over 1f out: sn hung lft and wknd* **9/1**

2-35 **10** 5 **Mr Emirati (USA)**[11] 495 4-9-5 **66** (p) TomEaves 10 42
(Bryan Smart) *sn chsng ldr: led 4f out to 3f out: sn rdn: wknd over 1f out* **8/1**

1m 30.33s (0.73) **Going Correction** +0.225s/f (Slow) **10** Ran SP% **116.8**
Speed ratings (Par 103): **104,102,101,101,100 98,97,95,94,88**
Tote Swingers: 1&2 £23.20, 1&3 £24.50, 2&3 £26.60; toteSuper7: Win: not won. Place: £28.30. CSF £98.71 CT £1663.13 TOTE £10.40: £4.50, £8.20, £3.60; EX 120.60 TRIFECTA Not won..
Owner L Tomlin **Bred** Rathbarry Stud **Trained** Shepton Montague, Somerset

FOCUS
A competitive handicap to close the card, featuring plenty of in-form horses.
T/Plt: £7.20 to a £1 stake. Pool of £63,745.17 - winning tickets. T/Qpdt: £4.50 to a £1 stake. Pool of £3,739.60 - 610.22 winning tickets. CR

616 CAGNES-SUR-MER
Monday, February 21

OFFICIAL GOING: Fibresand: standard

638a PRIX DE MIRAMAR (CLAIMER) (3YO COLTS & GELDINGS) (3YO) (FIBRESAND) 1m (F)
12:30 (12:00) 3-Y-O **£6,465** (£2,586; £1,939; £1,293; £646)

RPR

1 **Rovos (FR)** 3-8-9 0 Francois-XavierBertras 9 76
(F Rohaut, France) **23/5**[2]

2 nk **Araneide (USA)**[115] 3-8-9 0 StephanePasquier 12 75
(C Scandella, France) **78/10**

3 2½ **Friboy (FR)**[45] 3-8-9 0 NicolasPerret 5 70
(K Borgel, France) **13/1**

4 snk **Germanico (IRE)**[125] 7009 3-8-9 0 (b) Pierre-CharlesBoudot 10 69
(J-M Capitte, France) **41/1**

5 nse **Admirateur (FR)**[133] 3-8-9 0 AnthonyTeissieux 13 69
(M Pimbonnet, France) **27/1**

6 1 **Bradbury (IRE)**[12] 480 3-8-9 0 (b) IoritzMendizabal 3 67
(James Bethell) *broke wl to r in 2nd: travelling easily: tk ld 3f out: led into st: chal 1 1/2f out: rdn but no ex: styd on fnl f* **9/1**

7 hd **Zeetaan (FR)** 3-9-0 0 FranckBlondel 11 71
(P Khozian, France) **53/10**

8 3 **River Prospector (IRE)** 3-9-0 0 GuillaumeMillet 7 64
(P Khozian, France) **43/1**

9 1 **Skipping Stones (IRE)**[45] 3-8-2 0 (p) EddyHardouin(7) 1 57
(Robert Collet, France) **7/2**[1]

10 1 **La Joie De Vivre (USA)**[104] 3-9-0 0 ThierryThulliez 8 60
(R Gibson, France) **5/1**[3]

0 **Aphrodisiac (FR)**[63] 3-8-9 0 JohanVictoire 2 —
(J-L Pelletan, France) **52/1**

0 **Scarlet Warrior (AUT)**[12] 480 3-8-10 0 ow1 (b) FabienLefebvre 6 —
(G Martin, Austria) **32/1**

0 **Eupolis (FR)** 3-8-10 0 ow1 StephaneRichardot 4 —
(D Rabhi, France) **74/1**

1m 37.61s (97.61) **13** Ran SP% **115.6**
WIN (incl. 1 euro stake): 5.60. PLACES: 2.30, 2.70, 3.40. DF: 23.80. SF: 36.10.
Owner Scea Haras De Saint Pair **Bred** 6 C Racing Ltd **Trained** Sauvagnon, France

567 SOUTHWELL (L-H)
Tuesday, February 22

OFFICIAL GOING: Standard
Wind: Virtually nil Weather: Misty and low cloud

639 ENHANCED SP'S AT BLUESQ.COM CLAIMING STKS 1m 6f (F)
1:50 (1:51) (Class 6) 4-Y-O+ **£1,535** (£453; £226) **Stalls** Low

Form RPR

4/11 **1** **La Estrella (USA)**[5] 570 8-9-7 80 DaneO'Neill 3 80
(Don Cantillon) *hld up in rr: hdwy on outer 3f out: chsd ldng pair 2f out: rdn to ld over 1f out: edgd lft and kpt on fnl f* **4/9**[1]

2533 **2** 1 **Stadium Of Light (IRE)**[7] 549 4-8-9 69 BarryMcHugh 5 72
(Brian Ellison) *trckd ldng pair: effrt 4f out: chsd ldr 3f out: rdn to chal 2f out and sn led: drvn and hdd appr fnl f: kpt on same pce* **11/4**[2]

/6-4 **3** 3½ **The Oil Magnate**[26] 320 6-9-7 77 PatrickDonaghy(3) 2 77
(Michael Dods) *plld hrd: chsd ldr: led after 6f: pushed clr over 2f out: jnd and shkn up wl over 1f out: sn hdd and one pce* **10/1**[3]

150/ **4** 5 **Indian Pipe Dream (IRE)**[125] 6281 9-9-2 74 LukeMorris 1 63
(Aytach Sadik) *led 6f: cl up: rdn along over 4f out: wknd over 3f out* **50/1**

0302 **5** 25 **Mojeerr**[11] 507 5-8-6 49 (v) RyanTate(7) 4 27+
(Alan McCabe) *trckd ldrs on inner: sddle slipped after 5f: wknd over 3f out* **33/1**

3m 16.03s (7.73) **Going Correction** -0.075s/f (Stan)
WFA 4 from 5yo+ 5lb **5** Ran SP% **109.9**
Speed ratings (Par 101): **74,73,71,68,54**
CSF £1.92 TOTE £1.30: £1.30, £1.20; EX 1.80.Stadium of Light claimed by J. G. Given for £6,000.
Owner Don Cantillon **Bred** Five Horses Ltd And Theatrical Syndicate **Trained** Newmarket, Suffolk

FOCUS
An uncompetitive claimer and, with no pace on for the first half-mile, a couple took a keen grip early. The winner is a class act for the grade and the fourth looks the key guide to the form.

640 DOWNLOAD THE BLUE SQUARE ANDROID APP H'CAP 1m (F)
2:20 (2:20) (Class 5) (0-70,70) 4-Y-O+ **£1,978** (£584; £292) **Stalls** Low

Form RPR

40-3 **1** **Madame Boot (FR)**[8] 544 4-8-7 **56** LukeMorris 5 64
(Peter Makin) *chsd ldrs: pushed along 1/2-way: rdn 3f out: drvn wl over 1f out: styd on u.p to ld ins fnl f: edgd rt and kpt on wl towards fin* **6/1**

30-0 **2** 1 **Postman**[29] 287 5-8-13 **62** (p) TomEaves 2 68
(Bryan Smart) *dwlt and reminders sn after s: hdwy on inner to trck ldrs after 3f: rdn to chal 2f out: led wl over 1f out and sn drvn: hdd and no ex ins fnl f* **9/1**

214- **3** 3½ **Nolecce**[20] 6930 4-8-10 **62** AndrewHefferman(3) 6 60
(Richard Guest) *in tch: pushed along over 3f out: swtchd lft and rdn 2f out: drvn to chse ldng pair ins fnl f: no imp* **11/4**[2]

0-50 **4** 3¼ **Eastern Hills**[6] 562 6-8-9 **65** (p) HobieGill(7) 4 55
(Alan McCabe) *trckd ldrs: smooth hdwy 3f out: sn chal and led on outer 2f out: rdn: and hdd wl over 1f out: sn edgd lft and wknd* **11/2**[3]

-122 **5** 2½ **San Antonio**[19] 400 11-9-7 **70** (b) HayleyTurner 1 54
(Pam Sly) *led: rdn along 3f out: drvn and hdd 2f out: grad wknd* **6/4**[1]

/0-0 **6** 15 **Fools Gold**[42] 122 6-8-4 **56** oh1 JamesSullivan(3) 3 6
(Richard Guest) *cl up: rdn along over 3f out and sn wknd* **20/1**

1m 42.15s (-1.55) **Going Correction** -0.075s/f (Stan) **6** Ran SP% **111.1**
Speed ratings (Par 103): **104,103,99,96,93 78**
Tote Swingers: 1&2 £5.30, 1&3 £1.40, 2&3 £4.20 CSF £53.18 TOTE £5.20: £3.00, £3.50; EX 83.50.
Owner Mrs B J Carrington **Bred** Haras De Beauvoir & Ecurie Skymarc Farm **Trained** Ogbourne Maisey, Wilts

FOCUS
A pretty weak handicap, though with San Antonio in the field a decent early pace was assured. The form is rated around the principals.

641 GOLF AND RACING AT SOUTHWELL (S) STKS 6f (F)
2:50 (2:50) (Class 6) 3-Y-O+ **£1,535** (£453; £226) **Stalls** Low

Form RPR

1-05 **1** **Cape Of Storms**[19] 402 8-9-13 62 (b) TomEaves 5 68
(Roy Brotherton) *mde all: rdn 2f out: drvn over 1f out: kpt on gamely ins fnl f* **10/1**

-130 **2** 1 **Residency (IRE)**[12] 491 5-9-8 60 (p) AdamCarter(5) 2 65
(Bryan Smart) *chsd wnr on inner: effrt to chal wl over 2f out and sn rdn: ev ch tl drvn jst ins fnl f and no ex last 100yds* **11/2**[3]

3365 **3** 2 **Errigal Lad**[21] 375 6-9-8 54 (p) LukeMorris 6 54
(John Balding) *chsd ldng pair: rdn along and sltly outpcd 2f out: drvn and styd on fnl f* **16/1**

5-06 **4** 10 **Kummel Excess (IRE)**[14] 455 4-9-0 67 (p) MatthewDavies(3) 1 16
(George Baker) *towards rr: hdwy on inner 1/2-way: rdn to chse ldng pair wl over 1f out: sn drvn and btn* **7/2**[2]

404- **5** 3¼ **Tawzeea (IRE)**[117] 7195 6-9-8 60 (p) FrederikTylicki 4 11
(Michael Dods) *dwlt: sn in tch: rdn along over 3f out: sn wknd* **8/1**

240- **6** 2¼ **Cape Kimberley**[115] 7241 4-9-8 64 GeorgeBaker 3 —
(Tony Newcombe) *chsd ldrs: rdn along 1/2-way: wknd 2f out* **6/5**[1]

1m 16.08s (-0.42) **Going Correction** -0.075s/f (Stan) **6** Ran SP% **109.1**
Speed ratings (Par 101): **99,97,95,81,77 74**
Tote Swingers: 1&2 £3.40, 1&3 £10.00, 2&3 £7.40 CSF £58.15 TOTE £11.50: £3.80, £2.90; EX 34.30.There was no bid for the winner.
Owner Arthur Clayton **Bred** R J Turner **Trained** Elmley Castle, Worcs

FOCUS
A modest seller and the race only concerned the front two from a long way out, but with the two market leaders running poorly the form may not amount to much. The winner basically ran to his best.

642 GOLF AND RACING AT SOUTHWELL H'CAP 1m (F)
3:25 (3:25) (Class 6) (0-55,56) 3-Y-O **£1,535** (£453; £226) **Stalls** Low

Form RPR

60-1 **1** **Reachforthebucks**[5] 567 3-9-4 **56** 6ex AndreaAtzeni 5 72+
(Michael Wigham) *trckd ldrs: smooth hdwy over 2f out and sn cl up: shkn up to ld jst ins fnl f: readily* **1/8**[1]

36-4 **2** 1¾ **Goal (IRE)**[11] 505 3-8-13 **54** JamesSullivan(3) 8 59
(David C Griffiths) *sn pushed along in rr: hdwy on inner over 3f out: rdn to ld 2f out: sn drvn: hdd jst ins fnl f: kpt on: no ch w wnr* **14/1**[3]

60-5 **3** 6 **Littlepromisedland (IRE)**[14] 456 3-8-4 **45** AndrewHefferman(3) 7 36
(Richard Guest) *midfield: hdwy 3f out: rdn to chse ldng pair over 1f out: sn no imp* **50/1**

0-00 **4** ¾ **Talkin Italian**[31] 262 3-8-12 **50** GrahamGibbons 2 39
(Hughie Morrison) *cl up: rdn along 3f out: drvn and led briefly over 2f out: sn hdd and one pce* **16/1**

-643 **5** 2 **William Wainwright (IRE)**[18] 426 3-8-11 **49** (b[1]) PhillipMakin 4 34
(Ann Duffield) *reminders s and sn trcking ldrs: hdwy to chse ldr 3f out: rdn over 2f out and sn one pce* **10/1**[2]

06-3 **6** 3¼ **Pink Sari**[11] 513 3-8-12 **50** (p) FergusSweeney 6 27
(Peter Makin) *dwlt: sn trcking ldrs: effrt and hdwy 3f out: rdn over 2f out: sn btn* **20/1**

7 10 **Mariner's Dream (IRE)**[120] 7136 3-8-8 **46** ChrisCatlin 1 —
(C W J Farrell, Ire) *led: rdn along 3f out: hdd over 2f out and wknd qckly* **50/1**

1m 43.08s (-0.62) **Going Correction** -0.075s/f (Stan) **7** Ran SP% **119.2**
Speed ratings (Par 95): **100,98,92,91,89 86,76**
Tote Swingers: 1&2 £2.20, 1&3 £5.40, 2&3 £17.30 CSF £4.02 CT £38.52 TOTE £1.20: £1.10, £2.90; EX 3.70 Trifecta £64.60 Pool: £514.01 - 5.88 winning units..
Owner Reach For The Bucks Racing Partnership **Bred** Miss D Gibbins **Trained** Newmarket, Suffolk

FOCUS
A moderate and uncompetitive handicap, with only the very short-priced winner having been successful before. The form is solid and the winner could have more to offer.

643 SOUTHWELL-RACECOURSE.CO.UK MAIDEN STKS 1m 3f (F)
4:00 (4:00) (Class 5) 3-Y-O+ **£1,910** (£564; £282) **Stalls** Low

Form RPR

0-6 **1** **Runaway Tiger (IRE)**[38] 176 3-8-5 0 (b[1]) LiamJones 6 61
(Paul D'Arcy) *hld up in rr: rapid hdwy on outer over 3f out: led wl over 2f out: sn rdn: drvn and edgd rt ins fnl f: kpt on gamely* **7/2**[2]

0-24 **2** ½ **Baileys Agincourt**[18] 420 3-8-5 63 JoeFanning 4 60
(Mark Johnston) *trckd ldng pair: niggled along 4f out: rdn and sltly outpcd 3f out: chsd wnr fr 2f out and sn drvn: kpt on and ev ch ins fnl f tl no ex last 50yds* **4/11**[1]

00-4 **3** 9 **Thunderway (IRE)**[22] 366 3-7-11 40 JamesSullivan(3) 1 40
(Michael Dods) *prom: rdn along and outpcd over 3f out: kpt on u.p fnl 2f* **12/1**[3]

6 **4** 1 **Pride Of Mine**[15] 448 8-9-9 0 StephenCraine 2 41
(J R Jenkins) *led 3f: prom: rdn along 4f out: drvn over 3f out and sn outpcd* **33/1**

5 4 **Polarity**[105] 5-9-9 0 GrahamGibbons 3 34
(James Bethell) *s.i.s: hdwy to ld after 3f: rdn along 3f out: hdd over 2f out: sn wknd* **12/1**[3]

2m 27.43s (-0.57) **Going Correction** -0.075s/f (Stan)
WFA 3 from 5yo+ 23lb **5** Ran SP% **113.9**
Speed ratings (Par 103): **99,98,92,91,88**
CSF £5.42 TOTE £3.70: £1.40, £1.10; EX 7.90.
Owner Stapleford Racing Ltd **Bred** Darley **Trained** Newmarket, Suffolk

The Form Book, Raceform Ltd, Compton, RG20 6NL

FOCUS
The absence of First Rock rendered this maiden even less competitive than it would otherwise have been. Weak form, rated around the runner-up.

644 PLAY GOLF AT SOUTHWELL GOLF CLUB H'CAP 1m 3f (F)
4:35 (4:36) (Class 5) (0-70,66) 4-Y-0+ **£1,813** (£539; £269; £134) **Stalls** Low

Form RPR
1111 **1** **Stanley Rigby**[12] 496 5-9-7 **66**.. BarryMcHugh 1 77+
(Richard Fahey) *hld up in rr: hdwy over 3f out and sn niggled along: gd hdwy to chse ldrs 2f out: rdn to chal over 1f out: led ins fnl f and kpt on strly* **2/1**[1]
-550 **2** *1 ½* **Kipchak (IRE)**[6] 556 6-9-3 **62**..................................(p) HayleyTurner 7 69
(Conor Dore) *led: hdd and eased sltly 1/2-way: hdwy on inner to ld again 4f out: rdn wl over 2f out: drvn over 1f out: hdd ins fnl f: no ex last 100yds* **25/1**
0/32 **3** *2* **Ay Tay Tate (IRE)**[7] 546 5-8-4 **52** oh2................. AndrewHeffernan(3) 2 55
(David C Griffiths) *trckd ldng pair: effrt 3f out: rdn to chse ldr over 2f out: ev ch tl drvn and one pce appr fnl f* **7/2**[2]
30-0 **4** *1* **Mexican Jay (USA)**[21] 373 5-8-11 **56**...........................(v[1]) TomEaves 5 58
(Bryan Smart) *chsd ldr: hdwy to ld 1/2-way: hdd over 4f out and sn pushed along: rdn 3f out: drvn and one pce fnl 2f* **16/1**
6-22 **5** *nk* **Port Hill**[19] 409 4-8-10 **57**.. ShaneKelly 3 58
(Mark Brisbourne) *chsd ldrs: rdn along and outpcd 3f out: kpt on u.p fnl 2f* **9/2**[3]
-530 **6** *7* **Turjuman (USA)**[20] 381 6-9-5 **64**................................ StevieDonohoe 6 54
(Willie Musson) *hld up: effrt 4f out: rdn along over 3f out: nvr a factor* **5/1**
5-02 **7** *1 ¼* **Naheell**[12] 496 5-9-3 **62**.. KirstyMilczarek 4 50
(George Prodromou) *dwlt: hld up towards rr: hdwy and in tch over 4f out: rdn along over 3f out and sn btn* **6/1**

2m 26.61s (-1.39) **Going Correction** -0.075s/f (Stan)
WFA 4 from 5yo+ 2lb **7** Ran SP% **114.4**
Speed ratings (Par 103): **102,100,99,98,98 93,92**
CSF £52.41 TOTE £2.80: £1.40, £8.30; EX 33.40.
Owner Dean Hardman and Stella Kelsall **Bred** F C T Wilson **Trained** Musley Bank, N Yorks

FOCUS
Apart from a brief lull around 7f from home, the pace was strong in this handicap and the winning time was 0.82 seconds faster than the maiden. It was a weak race and the winner can't go up too much for this.

645 PLAY FREE BINGO AT BLUESQ.COM H'CAP 1m 4f (F)
5:10 (5:10) (Class 6) (0-60,60) 4-Y-0+ **£1,535** (£453; £226) **Stalls** Low

Form RPR
3-40 **1** **Irish Jugger (USA)**[18] 418 4-8-13 **55**.......................... JamesMillman 4 68+
(Rod Millman) *in tch on inner: hdwy 3f out: rdn to chse ldrs wl over 1f out: drvn and styd on ins fnl f to ld nr fin* **12/1**
-461 **2** *hd* **Bring Sweets (IRE)**[11] 507 4-8-8 **50**.......................... BarryMcHugh 11 59+
(Brian Ellison) *hld up in rr: gd hdwy on outer 3f out: cl up 2f out: rdn to chal over 1f out: led narrowly ent fnl f: hdd and no ex nr fin* **9/2**[2]
4-06 **3** *hd* **Beau Fighter**[31] 266 6-8-12 **56**...................................(p) DaleSwift(5) 6 65
(Gary Moore) *t.k.h: cl up: rdn to ld over 2f out: drvn over 1f out: hdd ent fnl f: no ex towards fin* **9/2**[2]
4122 **4** *2* **Carnac (IRE)**[15] 444 5-9-2 **55**..(p) ShaneKelly 7 61
(Alan McCabe) *trckd ldrs: effrt 4f out: rdn along and sltly outpcd over 2f out: kpt on u.p fnl f* **6/1**[3]
6/54 **5** *3* **Duar Mapel (USA)**[33] 232 5-9-2 **55**.......................... GrahamGibbons 5 56
(Brian Baugh) *led: rdn along over 3f out: drvn and hdd over 2f out: grad wknd appr fnl f* **12/1**
0-03 **6** *½* **Magnitude**[12] 496 6-9-0 **53**..(p) TomEaves 9 53
(Brian Baugh) *prom: rdn along 3f out: drvn 2f out and grad wknd* **22/1**
4-41 **7** *2 ½* **Jackie Kiely**[14] 451 10-9-2 **55**..(tp) PhillipMakin 8 51
(Roy Brotherton) *hld up in rr: hdwy over 3f out: rdn along wl over 2f out: nvr nr ldrs* **8/1**
2-13 **8** *2 ¾* **Mister Frosty (IRE)**[31] 266 5-9-7 **60**................................ LukeMorris 2 52
(George Prodromou) *t.k.h: trckd ldrs: n.m.r bnd after 2f: effrt over 4f out: rdn 3f out: wknd fnl 2f* **8/1**
2-45 **9** *8* **Jasmin Rai**[15] 449 4-8-9 **51**.. AndreaAtzeni 1 30
(Des Donovan) *chsd ldrs on inner: rdn along over 4f out: sn wknd* **33/1**
-011 **10** *1 ½* **Fastinthestraight (IRE)**[13] 466 4-9-0 **56**....................(p) DaneO'Neill 12 33
(Jim Boyle) *in tch on outer: effrt over 4f out: rdn along over 3f out: sn drvn and wknd wl over 2f out* **4/1**[1]
200- **11** *11* **Largem**[260] 2811 5-9-0 **53**.. StephenCraine 10 12
(J R Jenkins) *hld up: a in rr* **33/1**

2m 38.8s (-2.20) **Going Correction** -0.075s/f (Stan)
WFA 4 from 5yo+ 3lb **11** Ran SP% **118.5**
Speed ratings (Par 101): **104,103,103,102,100 100,98,96,91,90 82**
CSF £64.63 CT £284.58 TOTE £11.70: £3.80, £1.40, £1.90; EX 82.20 Trifecta £373.50 Part won. Pool: £504.75 - 0.32 winning units..
Owner Rod Millman Racing Club **Bred** Richard S Kaster & Frederick C Wieting **Trained** Kentisbeare, Devon

FOCUS
A moderate handicap, but a competitive one. The winner bounced back to his best, just denying the in-form runner-up.
Irish Jugger(USA) Official explanation: trainer said, regarding the apparent improvement of form, that the gelding struggled with training problems in the past but ran well last time at Chepstow having had a ten month break
T/Plt: £99.60 to a £1 stake. Pool of £44,507.11 - 326.18 winning tickets. T/Qpdt: £16.60 to a £1 stake. Pool of £3,714.40 - 164.82 winning tickets. JR

619 KEMPTON (A.W) (R-H)
Wednesday, February 23

OFFICIAL GOING: Standard
Wind: Almost nil Weather: Overcast

646 BETDAQ.COM EVERY WEDNESDAY AT KEMPTON PARK H'CAP 5f (P)
5:35 (5:35) (Class 5) (0-75,72) 4-Y-0+ **£2,047** (£604; £302) **Stalls** Low

Form RPR
0410 **1** **Desert Strike**[4] 612 5-9-3 **68**..(p) ShaneKelly 9 80
(Alan McCabe) *taken down early: trckd ldng trio: effrt over 1f out: shkn up and r.o to ld last 120yds: sn clr* **15/2**[3]
0-13 **2** *1 ½* **Six Wives**[13] 491 4-9-4 **72**.. BillyCray(3) 6 79
(David Nicholls) *pressed ldr: rdn 2f out: led 1f out: hdd and one pce last 120yds* **15/2**[3]
1-23 **3** *½* **Estonia**[42] 133 4-8-11 **62**.. LukeMorris 4 67
(Michael Squance) *taken down early: trckd ldng pair: rdn whn nt clr run jst over 1f out: styd on same pce ins fnl f* **4/1**[1]
105 **4** *hd* **Your Gifted (IRE)**[7] 554 4-8-6 **64**.......................... MatthewCosham(7) 2 69
(Patrick Morris) *trckd ldrs in 5th gng strly: nt clr run over 1f out tl jst ins fnl f: r.o but ch had gone* **14/1**
6-44 **5** *¾* **Kyladdie**[14] 470 4-9-2 **67**.. JimmyQuinn 7 68
(Steve Gollings) *dwlt: pushed up into 6th: no imp on ldrs u.p over 1f out: kpt on* **6/1**[2]
0024 **6** *¾* **Lord Of The Reins (IRE)**[15] 453 7-8-12 **63**.................. JimCrowley 11 62
(James Given) *dwlt: hld up last: shkn up over 1f out: kpt on ins fnl f: nvr on terms* **25/1**
6033 **7** *nk* **Riflessione**[19] 430 5-9-2 **67**..(b) StephenCraine 5 67
(Ronald Harris) *led to 1f out: wkng whn sltly short of room sn after* **8/1**
3-03 **8** *¾* **Danzoe (IRE)**[11] 522 4-9-5 **70**.................................... WilliamCarson 1 65
(Christine Dunnett) *s.i.s: rdn in 7th after 2f: a struggling to go the pce* **4/1**[1]
3530 **9** *¾* **Absa Lutte (IRE)**[14] 470 8-9-6 **71**..............................(t) GeorgeBaker 10 63
(Michael Mullineaux) *taken down early: stdd s: hld up in last pair: shuffled along on outer over 1f out: nvr involved* **10/1**
3145 **10** *1 ¾* **Vhujon (IRE)**[24] 357 6-9-7 **72**.............................. RobbieFitzpatrick 3 58
(Peter Grayson) *a in last trio: struggling by 1/2-way: no prog* **25/1**

59.23 secs (-1.27) **Going Correction** -0.175s/f (Stan) **10** Ran SP% **112.4**
Speed ratings (Par 103): **103,100,99,99,98 97,96,95,94,91**
toteswingers:1&2:£20.10, 1&3:£7.70, 2&3:£5.40 CSF £60.25 CT £255.16 TOTE £15.60: £3.10, £2.40, £1.40; EX 73.10.
Owner Southwell Racing Club **Bred** Mrs Mary Rowlands **Trained** Averham Park, Notts

FOCUS
Rain during the day resulted in the ground riding slightly on the fast side. A fair, competitive handicap and, as is often the case over this trip here, it paid to race close to the pace. The winner is rated back towards his best and the form makes sense.
Your Gifted(IRE) Official explanation: jockey said the filly was denied a clear run
Lord Of The Reins(IRE) Official explanation: jockey said the gelding missed the break

647 BETDAQ.COM EXCHANGE PRICE MULTIPLES H'CAP 1m 2f (P)
6:05 (6:06) (Class 5) (0-75,75) 4-Y-0+ **£2,047** (£604; £302) **Stalls** Low

Form RPR
30-2 **1** **Round Won (USA)**[21] 381 4-9-4 **73**.................................. ShaneKelly 9 88
(William Knight) *trckd clr ldng pair: wnt 2nd over 3f out: clsd to ld over 2f out and sn kicked away: drvn and maintained advantage fr over 1f out* **3/1**[1]
-642 **2** *4 ½* **Brouhaha**[11] 528 7-9-7 **75**.. RichardKingscote 6 81
(Tom Dascombe) *chsd ldng trio: rdn to go 2nd jst over 2f out: kpt on but no imp on wnr* **4/1**[2]
4-55 **3** *2 ¾* **Moresweets 'n Lace**[27] 313 4-8-9 **64**.......................... FergusSweeney 7 65
(Gary Moore) *settled in midfield: c u.p 4f out: prog to chse clr ldng pair wl over 1f out: one pce after* **16/1**
3-15 **4** *3 ¼* **Lingfield Bound (IRE)**[14] 475 4-9-6 **75**.......................... LukeMorris 10 69
(John Best) *nvr gng wl: drvn in rr after 3f: plugged on fr over 2f out to take modest 4th ins fnl f* **9/2**[3]
244- **5** *3* **Tilsworth Glenboy**[69] 7890 4-8-12 **67**.......................... StephenCraine 5 55
(J R Jenkins) *hld up and sn last: stl there over 3f out but gng bttr than many: rdn on outer over 1f out: limited prog* **25/1**
016- **6** *nse* **Understory (USA)**[235] 3688 4-9-6 **75**.................................. NeilCallan 1 63
(Tim McCarthy) *led 1f: chsd clr ldr to over 3f out: wknd 2f out* **16/1**
3-54 **7** *nse* **Negotiation (IRE)**[21] 381 5-9-4 **72**.................................. MartinDwyer 8 60+
(Michael Quinn) *settled wl in rr: rdn over 3f out: no prog 2f out: eased fnl f* **13/2**
0-34 **8** *4* **Stand Guard**[16] 447 7-9-6 **74**.. JimmyQuinn 12 54
(Jane Chapple-Hyam) *s.i.s: sn chsd ldrs in 5th: rdn 4f out: struggling in rr over 2f out* **13/2**
30-0 **9** *1 ¼* **Mutajaaser (USA)**[14] 475 6-8-2 **61** oh1......................(p) JulieBurke(5) 11 38
(Hugh Morgan) [illegible]
-560 **10** *½* **Fonterutoli (IRE)**[14] 475 4-9-1 **70**.................................. RobertHavlin 3 46
(Roger Ingram) *s.i.s: wl in rr: rdn 4f out: rchd 6th and in tch 3f out: sn wknd* **14/1**

2m 5.19s (-2.81) **Going Correction** -0.175s/f (Stan)
WFA 4 from 5yo+ 1lb **10** Ran SP% **116.9**
Speed ratings (Par 103): **104,100,98,95,93 93,93,89,88,88**
toteswingers:1&2:£2.40, 1&3:£10.00, 2&3:£7.90 CSF £14.81 CT £164.29 TOTE £3.50: £1.10, £2.40, £6.50; EX 15.20.
Owner Bluehills Racing Limited **Bred** Dr & Mrs Thomas Bowman & Rebecca Davis **Trained** Patching, W Sussex

FOCUS
Another fair contest in which Mutajaaser set a good gallop and, like the first race, the time bettered the standard. The winner is thriving and the next two set the level.
Negotiation(IRE) Official explanation: jockey said, regarding the running and riding, that his instructions were to sit in the first three and try and track Round One However, having been slowly away he was forced wide throughout the race and was unable to get into a challenging position.

648 LAY BACK AND WIN AT BETDAQ.COM RACING CLAIMING STKS 7f (P)
6:35 (6:35) (Class 6) 3-Y-0+ **£1,535** (£453; £226) **Stalls** Low

Form RPR
-562 **1** **Thunderball**[6] 572 5-9-5 72..(b) LeonnaMayor(7) 5 80+
(David Nicholls) *mde all: 3 l clr 3f out: rdn 2f out: edgd lft but kpt on wl enough: a holding on* **7/2**[3]
-242 **2** *1 ¾* **Jake The Snake (IRE)**[14] 467 10-10-0 85.............................. NeilCallan 1 77+
(Tony Carroll) *hld up in 4th: pushed along and effrt over 2f out: rdn to chse wnr over 1f out: kpt on but no great imp* **13/8**[1]
-211 **3** *2 ¼* **Hinton Admiral**[14] 467 7-9-13 78.................................. MichaelStainton 3 71+
(Jane Chapple-Hyam) *chsd wnr: rdn 2f out: no imp and lost 2nd over 1f out: wknd nr fin* **2/1**[2]
6-00 **4** *1 ½* **Sirjosh**[11] 526 5-9-8 58.. AndreaAtzeni 4 62
(Des Donovan) *rdn in last after 3f: struggling after: wnt modest 4th over 1f out: plugged on* **33/1**
543- **5** *8* **Euston Square**[151] 6366 5-10-0 73....................................(p) TomEaves 6 47
(David Nicholls) *chsd ldng pair to over 2f out: wknd: wl bhd fnl f* **8/1**

1m 24.08s (-1.92) **Going Correction** -0.175s/f (Stan) **5** Ran SP% **107.7**
Speed ratings (Par 101): **103,101,98,96,87**
CSF £9.20 TOTE £5.10: £2.60, £2.50; EX 9.10.
Owner Paul J Dixon & Brian Morton **Bred** Mrs Yvette Dixon **Trained** Sessay, N Yorks

FOCUS
A decent claimer judged on official ratings, but a race best viewed through the winner and fourth's recent form.

649 BETDAQ MOBILE APPS MEDIAN AUCTION MAIDEN STKS 1m 3f (P)
7:05 (7:06) (Class 6) 3-5-Y-O **£1,535** (£453; £226) **Stalls** Low

Form RPR

64 **1** **Manifestation**[26] 339 3-8-5 0 (b) NickyMackay 10 83+
(John Gosden) *racd freely: mde all and sn clr: 6 l clr after 3f to 3f out: coaxed along after: rdn whn runner-up clsd last 100yds* **11/10**[1]

4 **2** ½ **Gottany O'S**[11] 520 3-8-5 0 SamHitchcott 3 82+
(Mick Channon) *chsd wnr: 6 l down and rdn 4f out: grad clsd fr over 2f out: stl narrowing gap nr fin* **7/2**[2]

02 **3** 11 **Fleeting Storm**[19] 420 3-8-0 0 JimmyQuinn 7 57+
(Hughie Morrison) *chsd ldrs on outer: reminders 5f out: lost pl and struggling bdly u.p in last pair 3f out: rallied 2f out: styd on to take v modest 3rd nr fin* **9/2**[3]

300- **4** ¾ **Lady Morganna (IRE)**[183] 5389 3-8-0 63 KellyHarrison 6 56
(Olivia Maylam) *t.k.h and sn hld up in last pair: rdn and prog over 2f out: chsd clr ldng pair jst over 1f out: no imp: lost 3rd nr fin* **25/1**

-545 **5** 6 **Entrance**[9] 540 3-8-0 60 LukeMorris 1 45
(Julia Feilden) *in tch: rdn to chse clr ldng pair over 3f out: no imp: wknd and lost 3rd jst over 1f out* **9/1**

6 1¼ **Hamilton Hill**[35] 4-9-12 0 AdamKirby 2 51
(Terry Clement) *chsd ldrs: urged along 7f out: rdn 4f out: no imp 3f out: wl btn fnl 2f* **16/1**

00- **7** 2½ **Alhudhud (USA)**[126] 7022 5-10-0 0 (t) AndreaAtzeni 9 46
(Kevin Morgan) *wl in rr and nvr on terms: rdn 4f out: in last pair and no ch whn stmbld bdly wl over 2f out* **100/1**

/ **8** nse **Tango Master**[48] 4-9-12 0 FrankieMcDonald 8 46
(Mouse Hamilton-Fairley) *dwlt: wl in rr: rdn 4f out: rchd 6th over 2f out: nvr on terms and sn wknd* **66/1**

9 15 **Sea Fury (IRE)**[16] 4-9-7 0 JimCrowley 4 14
(Suzy Smith) *chsd ldng pair to over 3f out: wknd rapidly: t.o* **25/1**

6 **10** ¾ **Roe Valley (IRE)**[19] 420 4-9-12 0 SteveDrowne 5 18
(Linda Jewell) *chsd ldrs to 5f out: wknd u.p 4f out: eased: t.o* **50/1**

2m 18.08s (-3.82) **Going Correction** -0.175s/f (Stan)
WFA 3 from 4yo 23lb 4 from 5yo 2lb **10** Ran SP% **116.0**
Speed ratings (Par 101): **106,105,97,97,92 91,90,89,79,78**
toteswingers:1&2:£1.60, 1&3:£1.90, 2&3:£3.20 CSF £4.72 TOTE £2.90: £1.10, £1.20, £1.20; EX 6.10.
Owner H R H Princess Haya Of Jordan **Bred** Mrs S L Brimble **Trained** Newmarket, Suffolk

FOCUS
A modest maiden for 3-y-os plus in which the older runners were relatively inexperienced, and it was dominated by the younger group, with the first two clear.
Roe Valley(IRE) Official explanation: vet said the gelding had lost a right hind shoe

650 SKYSPORTS.COM RACING H'CAP 1m 3f (P)
7:35 (7:35) (Class 5) (0-70,69) 3-Y-O **£2,047** (£604; £302) **Stalls** Low

Form RPR

3-1 **1** **Songjiang**[26] 339 3-9-7 69 RobertHavlin 4 79+
(John Gosden) *led at stdy pce for 4f: trckd ldr: led again 2f out: pushed along to assert over 1f out: comf* **11/8**[1]

-122 **2** 1½ **Blue Cossack (IRE)**[14] 469 3-8-8 56 LiamKeniry 5 62
(Mark Usher) *led after 4f and maintained stdy pce: tried to kick on over 2f out: sn hdd: readily hld after* **5/2**[2]

2333 **3** 1¾ **Not So Bright (USA)**[7] 564 3-8-10 58 (bt[1]) AndreaAtzeni 1 61
(Des Donovan) *hld up last: pushed along on inner and prog to chse ldng pair over 1f out: kpt on same pce after* **7/1**

4-41 **4** 3¼ **Ya Hafed**[27] 319 3-9-4 66 JamieGoldstein 3 64
(Sheena West) *t.k.h: trckd ldng pair: shkn up and nt qckn 2f out: one pce after* **4/1**[3]

0-55 **5** 1½ **Gower Rules (IRE)**[14] 469 3-8-7 55 NeilChalmers 2 51
(John Bridger) *chsd ldng trio: rdn over 2f out: wknd over 1f out* **25/1**

2m 24.73s (2.83) **Going Correction** -0.175s/f (Stan) **5** Ran SP% **107.0**
Speed ratings (Par 97): **82,80,79,77,76**
CSF £4.71 TOTE £2.50: £1.10, £1.20; EX 4.00.
Owner H R H Princess Haya Of Jordan **Bred** Richard Green And New England Stud **Trained** Newmarket, Suffolk

FOCUS
A modest handicap although the majority of the small field came here in reasonable form. The pace was considerably slower than the preceding races on the card. The easy winner was well treated on this handicap bow and can step up again.

651 RACING AT SKYSPORTS.COM H'CAP 6f (P)
8:05 (8:05) (Class 4) (0-85,84) 4-Y-O+ **£3,399** (£1,011; £505; £252) **Stalls** Low

Form RPR

2-33 **1** **Ebraam (USA)**[11] 523 8-9-7 84 LukeMorris 12 95
(Ronald Harris) *hld up in last trio: gd prog fr 2f out: sustained effrt to ld last 100yds: styd on wl* **16/1**

15-1 **2** ¾ **Jack Rackham**[36] 199 7-9-0 77 (v) TomEaves 4 86
(Bryan Smart) *led: kpt on wl whn pressed fr 2f out: hdd and one pce last 100yds* **12/1**

20-3 **3** nk **Sioux Rising (IRE)**[32] 265 5-9-6 83 (p) FrederikTylicki 3 91
(Richard Fahey) *t.k.h: trckd ldng trio: rdn to chal on inner wl over 1f out: nt qckn ins fnl f* **15/2**[3]

1-31 **4** ½ **Clear Praise (USA)**[27] 316 4-9-4 81 HayleyTurner 2 87
(Simon Dow) *t.k.h: trckd ldng pair: wnt 2nd over 2f out: chalng but nt qckn over 1f out: kpt on* **13/8**[1]

RRR- **5** 1¾ **Stefanki (IRE)**[89] 7573 4-9-2 79 ow1 GeorgeBaker 8 80
(Gary Moore) *dwlt: sn in midfield: effrt over 2f out: sn shkn up and nt qckn: one pce after* **10/1**

U16- **6** hd **Liberty Lady (IRE)**[158] 6198 4-9-0 77 AndreaAtzeni 9 78
(Des Donovan) *chsd ldrs in 5th: rdn and cl enough fr 2f out tl jst ins fnl f: fdd* **25/1**

-246 **7** 2 **Methaaly (IRE)**[27] 316 8-8-6 76 (be) JosephYoung[(7)] 1 71
(Michael Mullineaux) *hld up on inner: nt clr run briefly over 2f out: bmpd along furiously and no imp fnl 2f* **12/1**

0-45 **7** dht **Ray Of Joy**[27] 316 5-9-7 84 SteveDrowne 6 79
(J R Jenkins) *hld up towards rr: effrt over 2f out: tried to cl on ldrs over 1f out: wknd ins fnl f* **20/1**

63-0 **9** ½ **Ongoodform (IRE)**[21] 385 4-9-2 79 LiamJones 10 72
(Paul D'Arcy) *racd wd thrght: towards rr: shuffled along fr over 2f out: nvr nr ldrs* **25/1**

-124 **10** shd **Bonnie Prince Blue**[13] 493 8-9-2 79 (b) MickyFenton 7 72
(James Given) *dwlt: hld up in last trio: shkn up 2f out: no real prog* **25/1**

000- **11** shd **Falasteen (IRE)**[128] 6985 4-9-2 79 JamieSpencer 5 71
(David Nicholls) *chsd ldr to over 2f out: btn over 1f out: heavily eased last 50yds and lost several pls* **11/2**[2]

14-5 **12** ¾ **Cardinal**[40] 168 6-9-1 78 JimCrowley 11 68
(Robert Cowell) *hld up in last trio: rdn over 2f out: no prog* **18/1**

1m 11.53s (-1.57) **Going Correction** -0.175s/f (Stan) **12** Ran SP% **117.2**
Speed ratings (Par 105): **103,102,101,100,98 98,95,95,95,94 94,93**
toteswingers:1&2:£12.60, 1&3:£17.80, 2&3:£20.00 CSF £182.07 CT £1573.39 TOTE £14.10: £4.60, £4.00, £3.20; EX 195.80.
Owner Robert & Nina Bailey **Bred** Shadwell Farm LLC **Trained** Earlswood, Monmouths

FOCUS
This good, competitive sprint handicap was run at relatively steady pace. The winner did not need to step up much on his recent level and the form is solid.

652 ALL-WEATHER "HANDS AND HEELS" APPRENTICE H'CAP (PART OF THE RACING EXCELLENCE INITIATIVE) 1m (P)
8:35 (8:36) (Class 7) (0-50,56) 4-Y-O+ **£1,535** (£453; £226) **Stalls** Low

Form RPR

601 **1** **Lunar River (FR)**[7] 552 8-9-9 56 6ex (t) NathanAlison 2 66
(David Pinder) *hld up in last quartet and wl off the pce: gd prog on outer fr 2f out: wnt 2nd ins fnl f: styd on to ld last strides* **9/2**[2]

00-4 **2** nk **Grey Boy (GER)**[35] 210 10-9-0 50 GeorgeDowning[(3)] 6 59
(Tony Carroll) *trckd ldng pair and clr of rest by 1/2-way: led 2f out and sn 3 l clr: tired fnl f: hdd last strides* **5/1**[3]

-202 **3** 1¾ **Holyfield Warrior (IRE)**[7] 552 7-9-3 50 LucyKBarry 3 55
(Ralph Smith) *settled in 7th: pushed along and prog over 2f out: disp 2nd pl over 1f out tl ins fnl f: one pce* **7/2**[1]

0256 **4** 1 **Kenswick**[7] 555 4-9-3 50 (v) AlexEdwards 5 53
(Pat Eddery) *chsd ldrs in 6th: prog over 2f out: disp 2nd pl over 1f out tl ins fnl f: wknd last 75yds* **15/2**

0423 **5** 1¾ **Guildenstern (IRE)**[12] 517 9-8-13 49 (t) LewisWalsh[(3)] 4 48
(Jane Chapple-Hyam) *wl off the pce in 8th: pushed along and sme prog fr over 2f out: kpt on but nt pce to threaten* **11/2**

0-00 **6** ¾ **Sea Tobougie**[21] 391 4-8-9 45 RachealKneller[(3)] 1 42
(Mark Usher) *hld up in last quartet: effrt over 2f out: prog to chse ldrs over 1f out: no hdwy fnl f: fdd* **33/1**

6044 **7** 1 **Inquisitress**[7] 552 7-8-12 45 (v) MatthewCosham 10 40
(John Bridger) *hld up in last quartet: prog 2f out: tried to cl on ldrs over 1f out: effrt petered out fnl f* **12/1**

0-45 **8** 5 **King Of The Titans (IRE)**[7] 552 8-8-10 46 (v) AliceHaynes[(3)] 8 29
(Patrick Gilligan) *pressed ldr at fast pce: led over 4f out: hdd 2f out: wknd rapidly over 1f out* **14/1**

-43 **9** 2¾ **Crianza**[21] 382 5-9-0 47 (p) NoraLooby 9 24
(Nigel Tinkler) *chsd ldrs in 4th: pushed along sn after 1/2-way: wknd rapidly 2f out* **10/1**

06-0 **10** ¾ **Mighty Aphrodite**[14] 466 4-8-7 45 CharlotteJenner[(5)] 7 20
(Olivia Maylam) *led at str pce: hdd over 4f out: stl upsides over 2f out: wknd rapidly over 1f out* **25/1**

04-0 **11** 8 **Boxer Shorts**[40] 166 5-8-9 45 (t) JosephYoung[(3)] 11 —
(Michael Mullineaux) *s.i.s: a wl in rr: wknd 2f out: t.o* **66/1**

12 3½ **Okalydokely (IRE)**[26] 4924 7-9-0 50 ThomasBrown[(3)] 12 —
(Andrew Crook) *chsd ldrs in 5th: wknd 3f out: t.o* **33/1**

1m 39.27s (-0.53) **Going Correction** -0.175s/f (Stan) **12** Ran SP% **118.9**
Speed ratings (Par 97): **95,94,92,91,90 89,88,83,80,79 71,68**
toteswingers:1&2:£7.30, 1&3:£3.50, 2&3:£6.20 CSF £26.54 CT £88.89 TOTE £3.60: £1.10, £2.70, £2.30; EX 33.70.
Owner The Little Farm Partnership **Bred** M Daguzan-Garros & Rolling Hills Farm **Trained** Kingston Lisle, Oxon

FOCUS
A very moderate apprentice handicap in which the early pace was good but the leaders stopped and the winner came from almost last at halfway. Solid form for the grade.
T/Plt: £14.70 to a £1 stake. Pool:£64,942.04 - 3,220.63 winning tickets T/Qpdt: £4.70 to a £1 stake. Pool:£6,512.20 - 1,019.58 winning tickets JN

609 LINGFIELD (L-H)
Wednesday, February 23

OFFICIAL GOING: Standard
Wind: fairly light, behind Weather: rain

653 BET ON WINNING DISTANCES AT BLUESQ.COM MEDIAN AUCTION MAIDEN STKS 6f (P)
1:50 (1:50) (Class 6) 3-5-Y-O **£1,535** (£453; £226) **Stalls** Low

Form RPR

3 **1** **Hoover**[5] 593 3-8-9 0 StephenCraine 3 73+
(Jim Boyle) *chsd ldr tl led 2f out: rdn clr ent fnl f: comf* **2/5**[1]

26-0 **2** 6 **Elusive Love (IRE)**[33] 253 3-8-9 64 JoeFanning 1 52
(Mark Johnston) *t.k.h: led tl hdd and rdn 2f out: btn 1f out: tired fnl f and jst hung on for 2nd nr fin* **6/1**[2]

00- **3** hd **Bianco Boy (USA)**[70] 7872 4-9-10 0 SteveDrowne 2 55+
(John Best) *chsd ldrs: outpcd and chsd ldng pair over 2f out: no ch w wnr but kpt on fnl f: pressing for 2nd nr fin* **12/1**[3]

4 1 **Fleurie Lover (IRE)** 3-8-1 0 AndrewHeffernan[(3)] 6 43+
(Richard Guest) *t.k.h early: hld up in last pair: outpcd and pushed along over 2f out: no ch w wnr but kpt on steadily fnl f* **25/1**

400- **5** 3 **Secret Tycoon (IRE)**[162] 6046 3-8-2 65 RossCoakley[(7)] 4 39
(Patrick Morris) *stdd s: hld up in last pair: outpcd over 2f out: rdn and effrt on inner over 1f out: no imp: n.d* **12/1**[3]

044- **6** 11 **My Mandy (IRE)**[319] 1237 4-9-5 58 LukeMorris 5 —
(Ronald Harris) *chsd ldrs: rdn and struggling over 2f out: bhd fr wl over 1f out* **25/1**

1m 12.3s (0.40) **Going Correction** +0.025s/f (Slow)
WFA 3 from 4yo 15lb **6** Ran SP% **108.8**
Speed ratings (Par 101): **98,90,89,88,84 69**
toteswingers:1&2:£2.20, 1&3:£3.00, 2&3:£2.20 CSF £2.94 TOTE £1.30: £1.10, £1.80; EX 2.80.
Owner The Clean Sweep Partnership **Bred** Paddock Space **Trained** Epsom, Surrey

The Form Book, Raceform Ltd, Compton, RG20 6NL

FOCUS
A seriously uncompetitive maiden and only the front two were ever involved. The time was 0.57 seconds slower than the following Class 6 handicap. Not easy to be confident about the level of the form.

654 BREATHE SPA AT MARRIOTT LINGFIELD H'CAP 6f (P)
2:20 (2:21) (Class 6) (0-65,65) 4-Y-0+ **£1,569** (£463; £231) **Stalls** Low

Form RPR

5465 **1** **Chjimes (IRE)**[11] 522 7-9-7 **65**....(b) HayleyTurner 4 76+
(Conor Dore) *hld up in tch: hdwy to trck ldrs ent fnl 2f: pushed along and qcknd to ld jst ins fnl f: r.o wl and drew clr fnl 100yds* **3/1**[1]

0-20 **2** *2* **Bollywood Style**[18] 435 6-9-1 **59**.... LukeMorris 2 63
(John Best) *in tch: rdn and effrt 2f out: ev ch ent fnl f: sn drvn and one pce ins fnl f* **9/2**[3]

-000 **3** *shd* **Mary's Pet**[31] 268 4-9-0 **61**.... SimonPearce(3) 3 65
(John Akehurst) *chsd ldrs: rdn and effrt on inner ent fnl 2f: ev ch ent fnl f: styd on same pce fnl 100yds* **12/1**

5360 **4** *2* **Athaakeel (IRE)**[13] 487 5-9-5 **63**....(b) CathyGannon 7 61
(Ronald Harris) *led: rdn wl over 1f out: drvn and hdd jst ins fnl f: wknd fnl 100yds* **5/1**

16-0 **5** *7* **South African Gold (USA)**[46] 97 4-9-3 **61**....(p) MickyFenton 6 38
(James Eustace) *unloaded fr stalls as neighbour was unruly: reloaded: a in last pair and nvr travelling: rdn 4f out: lost tch 2f out* **4/1**[2]

0560 **6** *6* **Flow Chart (IRE)**[29] 289 4-8-8 **52** oh6 ow1....(b) RobbieFitzpatrick 1 11
(Peter Grayson) *sson rdn along to press ldr on inner: hdd over 3f out: losing pl whn hmpd bnd jst over 2f out: sn wl bhd* **100/1**

1m 11.73s (-0.17) **Going Correction** +0.025s/f (Slow) **6** Ran SP% **88.5**
Speed ratings (Par 101): **102,99,99,96,87 79**
toteswingers:1&2:£2.40, 1&3:£3.10, 2&3:£3.90 CSF £9.92 TOTE £2.50: £1.10, £1.70; EX 9.40.
Owner Sean J Murphy **Bred** Morgan O'Flaherty **Trained** Cowbit, Lincs

FOCUS
There was a withdrawal at the start after Clear Ice, who was 3-1 joint-favourite, got worked up in his stall. That one's antics meant South African Gold, drawn next door, had to be taken out and reloaded, and he subsequently ran below form. Consequently, this already modest handicap was weakened further, and an overly strong pace, set by Athaakeel and Flow Chart, set the race up for Chjimes. He could be worth another length or more and the form is solid if limited in behind.
South African Gold(USA) Official explanation: jockey said that the colt ran flat

655 COWDEN H'CAP 7f (P)
2:55 (2:57) (Class 6) (0-60,60) 3-Y-O **£1,535** (£453; £226) **Stalls** Low

Form RPR

3522 **1** **Titan Diamond (IRE)**[19] 426 3-8-3 **49**.... RachealKneller(7) 9 56+
(Mark Usher) *in tch: hdwy to chse ldrs gng wl over 1f out: pushed ahd ent fnl f: r.o wl and drew clr ins fnl f: comf* **4/1**[2]

020- **2** *3 ¼* **Majestic Ridge (IRE)**[69] 7894 3-9-5 **58**.... JamieSpencer 5 57
(David Evans) *led: rdn ent fnl 2f: hdd ent fnl f: nt pce of wnr ins fnl f: kpt on for 2nd* **6/1**

00-0 **3** *¾* **Melbury**[21] 383 3-8-13 **52**.... ShaneKelly 10 49
(Jane Chapple-Hyam) *in tch: pushed along and effrt to chse ldrs over 2f out: unable qck u.p over 1f out: rallied ins fnl f: kpt on but no ch w wnr* **14/1**

5550 **4** *nk* **Lynchpin**[19] 426 3-9-2 **55**....(p) CathyGannon 7 52
(Ronald Harris) *chsd ldr: pushed along to press ldr ent fnl 3f: nt qckning u.p whn sltly hmpd 1f out: one pce after* **22/1**

000- **5** *nk* **Bouzy**[132] 6868 3-9-6 **59**.... NeilCallan 3 54
(Simon Dow) *chsd ldrs: rdn and effrt on inner over 1f out: nt qckn u.p ent fnl f: styd on same pce and wl hld after* **5/1**[3]

43-5 **6** *hd* **Surprise (IRE)**[11] 529 3-9-2 **60**.... TobyAtkinson(5) 14 55+
(Mark Rimmer) *swtchd lft after s: hld up towards rr: pushed rt and dropped to last trio over 5f out: stl plenty to do over 1f out: styd on fnl f: nvr trbld ldrs* **14/1**

[illegible] **7** *¾* [illegible] .... [illegible] 8 [illegible]
(Richard Mitchell) *hld up in midfield: sltly hmpd bnd 5f out: swtchd towards inner and effrt over 1f out: flashed tail u.p and no imp fnl f: swtchd lft again ins fnl f* **25/1**

600- **8** *¾* **Alfraamsey**[139] 6694 3-9-4 **57**....(v1) SamHitchcott 6 48
(Mick Channon) *s.i.s: sn rcvrd: moved rt over 5f out: rdn and effrt on outer bnd 2f out: styd on same pce and no real hdwy after* **10/1**

0-40 **9** *nk* **Gekko (IRE)**[7] 558 3-8-5 **51**.... RossCoakley(7) 11 41
(Patrick Morris) *chsd ldrs on outer: rdn and unable qck ent fnl 2f: edgd lft and btn ent fnl f* **16/1**

00-0 **10** *4* **Lord Cornwall (IRE)**[21] 383 3-8-9 **48**.... JackMitchell 2 32
(Ed Walker) *in tch in rr of main gp: switching rt and looking for room over 2f out: rdn and effrt over 1f out: no prog and wl btn ins fnl f* **22/1**

00-2 **11** *½* **Tymismoni (IRE)**[21] 383 3-9-5 **58**....(v) AdamKirby 4 36
(Brett Johnson) *dwlt: sn in midfield: pushed along briefly over 5f out: drvn and no prog 2f out: no threat to ldrs after* **7/2**[1]

-600 **12** *2 ½* **Welsh Dresser (IRE)**[21] 383 3-8-8 **47**.... RobbieFitzpatrick 12 19
(Peter Grayson) *s.i.s: sn outpcd in last pair: rdn over 4f out: nvr on terms* **100/1**

0-00 **13** *14* **Crazy In Love**[7] 558 3-8-11 **50**.... HayleyTurner 13 —
(Olivia Maylam) *wnt rt s: s.i.s: a toiling in rr: lost tch 3f out* **40/1**

00-0 **14** *12* **Emerald Royal**[32] 262 3-8-9 **51**....(t) AlanCreighton(3) 1 —
(Edward Creighton) *dwlt: sn rdn along and rcvrd to r in midfield: rdn and struggling over 2f out: wl bhd and virtually p.u ins fnl f* **33/1**

1m 25.9s (1.10) **Going Correction** +0.025s/f (Slow) **14** Ran SP% **120.4**
Speed ratings (Par 95): **94,90,89,89,88 88,87,86,86,81 81,78,62,48**
toteswingers:1&2:£5.00, 1&3:£12.40, 2&3:£11.20 CSF £26.04 CT £312.72 TOTE £3.90: £1.30, £2.50, £4.00; EX 30.40 TRIFECTA Not won..
Owner I Sheward **Bred** Ballyhane Stud **Trained** Upper Lambourn, Berks
■ A first success as an apprentice for Racheal Kneller, who has had five winners as an amateur.
■ Stewards' Enquiry : Racheal Kneller three-day ban: careless riding (March 9-11)

FOCUS
Plenty of jostling for position from the off and this proved quite a rough race for some. The pace was muddling, suiting those prominent, and this is moderate form (only one previous winner in the line-up), but Titan Diamond is improving at a low level.
Melbury Official explanation: jockey said the filly was struck into shortly after the start
Lynchpin Official explanation: jockey said that the colt hung left
Emerald Royal Official explanation: jockey said that the colt finished lame

656 LINGFIELD PARK OWNERS CLUB (S) STKS 1m 2f (P)
3:30 (3:30) (Class 6) 4-Y-O+ **£1,535** (£453; £226) **Stalls** Low

Form RPR

343 **1** **Scary Movie (IRE)**[7] 561 6-9-6 73....(p) CathyGannon 8 78
(Ronald Harris) *bhd and humoured along at times: clsd and hmpd over 3f out: sn swtchd rt: rdn and chsd clr ldr jst over 1f out: drvn to chal ins fnl f: led towards fin* **4/1**[2]

1-32 **2** *nk* **Mongoose Alert (IRE)**[14] 474 9-9-6 82.... PaulDoe 1 77
(Jim Best) *chsd ldr tl led over 3f out: rdn and clr wl over 1f out: drvn fnl f: jnd ins fnl f: hdd and no ex towards fin* **4/5**[1]

560/ **3** *8* **Superius (IRE)**[13] 6850 6-9-1 88....(v1) MickyFenton 9 57
(Emma Lavelle) *in tch in last trio: clsd over 3f out: rdn and nt qckn over 2f out: wknd 2f out: wl hld whn hung lft over 1f out: wnt modest 3rd last stride* **14/1**

2503 **4** *shd* **Dream Of Fortune (IRE)**[5] 599 7-9-6 68....(bt) JamieSpencer 3 62
(David Evans) *hld up wl in tch: wnt 2nd 3f out: rdn and fnd nil over 1f out: sn btn: tired fnl f and lost 3rd last stride* **9/1**

1-24 **5** *1 ¾* **Orchard Supreme**[5] 588 8-9-6 71....(p) JamieGoldstein 2 59
(Ralph Smith) *hld up in last trio: rdn and fnd nil wl over 2f out: wl btn after* **16/1**

-302 **6** *1 ¾* **Celtic Commitment**[7] 561 5-9-1 65....(v1) NeilCallan 5 50
(Simon Dow) *chsd ldrs: rdn over 3f out: wknd u.p ent fnl 2f: wl btn over 1f out* **9/2**[3]

5/6- **7** *23* **Confide In Me**[310] 256 7-8-13 51 ow1.... RobertLButler(3) 4 8
(Jim Best) *led tl over 3f out: sn rdn: wknd and in rr whn hmpd bnd jst over 2f out: sn lost tch: t.o* **50/1**

2m 4.96s (-1.64) **Going Correction** +0.025s/f (Slow)
WFA 4 from 5yo+ 1lb **7** Ran SP% **118.2**
Speed ratings (Par 101): **107,106,100,100,98 97,79**
toteswingers:1&2:£1.90, 1&3:£7.20, 2&3:£3.90 CSF £7.99 TOTE £6.10: £2.70, £1.10; EX 11.50 Trifecta £106.70 Pool: £708.63 - 4.91 winning units..The winner was bought in for 4,000gns. Mongoose Alert was claimed by K. W. Dalgleish for £6,000.
Owner Ridge House Stables Ltd **Bred** Mrs T Brudenell **Trained** Earlswood, Monmouths

FOCUS
A poor seller in which the first two finished well clear. The form may be rated slightly high. The pace was strong.
Superius(IRE) Official explanation: jockey said that the gelding hung left in the straight

657 DOWNLOAD THE BLUE SQUARE IPHONE APP H'CAP 1m 2f (P)
4:00 (4:00) (Class 5) (0-75,80) 3-Y-O **£2,115** (£624) **Stalls** Low

Form RPR

-511 **1** **Geordie Iris (IRE)**[9] 540 3-9-13 **80** 6ex.... DaneO'Neill 2 83+
(Richard Hannon) *trckd rival tl led 3f out: qcknd and crossed to rail ent fnl 2f: rdn wl over 1f out: pressed wl ins fnl f: r.o and a doing enough* **2/5**[1]

30-3 **2** *nk* **Colebrooke**[12] 510 3-9-1 **68**.... JoeFanning 1 68
(Mark Johnston) *led and set stdy gallop tl hdd 3f out: rdn and swtchd rt 2f out: rallied gamely and pressing wnr wl ins fnl f: kpt on but a hld* **15/8**[2]

2m 13.61s (7.01) **Going Correction** +0.025s/f (Slow) **2** Ran SP% **106.2**
Speed ratings (Par 97): **72,71**
TOTE £1.20.
Owner D R Mean **Bred** Anthony Kirwin **Trained** East Everleigh, Wilts

FOCUS
An intriguing match in which Dane O'Neill proved the more tactically astute of the two jockeys, although in fairness Geordie Iris probably would have won under most circumstances. The time was 8.65 seconds slower than the earlier older-horse seller. It's doubtful if the runner-up stepped up on his previous form.

658 GOLF AND RACING AT LINGFIELD PARK CLAIMING STKS 5f (P)
4:30 (4:30) (Class 6) 4-Y-O+ **£1,535** (£453; £226) **Stalls** High

Form RPR

55-3 **1** **Lewyn**[36] 197 4-8-10 75....(b) HayleyTurner 2 79
(Jeremy Gask) *hld up in tch: shkn up and hdwy to chse ldrs ent fnl 2f: rdn along hands and heels to chse ldr ins fnl f: r.o wl to ld wl ins fnl f* **9/4**[2]

010 **2** *½* **Northern Dare (IRE)**[28] [illegible] 7-9-10 76....(b) JamieSpencer 7 80
(Richard Fahey) *chsd ldrs tl wnt 2nd 3f out: rdn to chal over 1f out: drvn to ld 1f out: kpt on u.p tl hdd and no ex wl ins fnl f* **1/1**[1]

-042 **3** *2* **Wanchai Whisper**[26] 337 4-8-0 60....(v) AndrewHeffernan(3) 1 63
(Peter Hedger) *in tch in last trio: hdwy wl over 1f out: drvn and styd on same pce fnl f* **13/2**[3]

0-36 **4** *2* **Athwaab**[36] 197 4-8-3 57.... AndreaAtzeni 4 56
(Noel Quinlan) *led: rdn wl over 1f out: hdd 1f out: wknd ins fnl f* **20/1**

0243 **5** *1* **Colorus (IRE)**[6] 571 8-8-3 68....(v) TobyAtkinson(5) 3 57
(Bill Ratcliffe) *chsd ldr tl 3f out: wknd u.p jst over 1f out* **8/1**

-660 **6** *¾* **Step It Up (IRE)**[11] 522 7-8-1 58.... DanielCremin(7) 5 55
(Jim Boyle) *in tch: rdn and unable qck wl over 1f out: wknd jst over 1f out* **33/1**

58.40 secs (-0.40) **Going Correction** +0.025s/f (Slow) **6** Ran SP% **112.9**
Speed ratings (Par 101): **104,103,100,96,95 94**
toteswingers:1&2:£1.40, 1&3:£1.90, 2&3:£2.50 CSF £4.92 TOTE £3.30: £1.80, £1.10; EX 5.20.
Owner The Nobles **Bred** Mrs S J Walker **Trained** Sutton Veny, Wilts

FOCUS
A fair claimer run at a strong pace. The winner was the pick of the weights and the second seemed back to his recent front-running form.

659 PLAY MEGAJACKPOTS CLEOPATRA AT BLUESQ.COM H'CAP 6f (P)
5:05 (5:05) (Class 5) (0-75,75) 3-Y-O **£2,115** (£624; £312) **Stalls** Low

Form RPR

-115 **1** **Joe Le Taxi (IRE)**[14] 476 3-8-8 **69**.... DarylByrne(7) 2 69
(Mark Johnston) *chsd ldrs: rdn ent fnl 2f: ev ch ent fnl f: led ins fnl f: r.o wl* **10/3**[2]

500- **2** *¾* **Queen O'The Desert (IRE)**[138] 6722 3-8-13 **70**.... SimonPearce(3) 5 68
(Andrew Balding) *chsd ldr: sltly hmpd wl over 1f out: rdn and ev ch jst ins fnl f: kpt on same pce fnl 75yds* **4/1**[3]

66-4 **3** *¾* **These Dreams**[27] 322 3-7-13 **56** oh11.... AndrewHeffernan(3) 3 52
(Richard Guest) *fly-jmpd s: sn stdd and t.k.h in last pair: rdn and hdwy ent fnl f: pressed ldrs ins fnl f: no ex fnl 75yds* **33/1**

3525 **4** *hd* **Je Suis Unrockstar**[14] 465 3-9-0 **68**....(p) FrederikTylicki 4 63
(David Nicholls) *taken down early: led: stdd gallop 4f out: hung rt bnd 2f out: kpt on wl tl hdd ins fnl f: kpt on same pce after* **4/1**[3]

1333 **5** *½* **Greenhead High**[5] 601 3-8-13 **67**.... J-PGuillambert 6 60
(Jane Chapple-Hyam) *t.k.h: hld up in last pair on outer: rdn ent fnl 2f: styd on same pce and no imp u.p over 1f out* **6/5**[1]

1m 12.54s (0.64) **Going Correction** +0.025s/f (Slow) **5** Ran SP% **111.5**
Speed ratings (Par 97): **96,95,94,93,93**
CSF £16.66 TOTE £3.40: £1.10, £3.50; EX 19.50.

Owner Mark Johnston Racing Ltd **Bred** J Joyce **Trained** Middleham Moor, N Yorks
FOCUS
The early pace was steady (time slowest of three 6f races on the card), and the runner-up, fourth and fifth went noticeably wide into the straight, so the form needs treating with a bit of caution. The winner is rated to the bare form of his recent efforts but could improve.
T/Plt: £6.40 to a £1 stake. Pool:£42,288.28 - 4,790.97 winning tickets T/Qpdt: £5.20 to a £1 stake. Pool:£2,647.40 - 374.50 winning tickets SP

638 CAGNES-SUR-MER
Wednesday, February 23
OFFICIAL GOING: Fibresand: standard

660a PRIX DE CAVAILLON (CLAIMER) (3YO COLTS & GELDINGS) (FIBRESAND) 1m 2f (D)
12:15 (12:00) 3-Y-O £6,465 (£2,586; £1,939; £1,293; £646)

RPR
1 **Twenty Ten (FR)**[33] 258 3-8-8 0 JulienMarquestau(6) 1 74
(P Khozian, France) 93/10
2 1 ½ **Great Surprise**[14] 480 3-9-0 0 FabienLefebvre 4 71
(Reg Hollinshead) *settled in 3rd and then 4th: 3rd and running on over 2 1/2f out: disp ld 1 1/2f out: led ins fnl f: hdd 110yds fr home: jst hld on for 2nd* 8/1
3 shd **Cadologis (FR)** 3-8-9 0 AlexisBadel 10 66
(J-M Capitte, France) 61/1
4 4 **Style D'Or (FR)**[259] 3-8-2 0 (b) EddyHardouin(7) 3 59
(Robert Collet, France) 39/1
5 3 **Bonne Pioche (FR)** 3-8-9 0 (b) ThierryThulliez 5 54
(P Khozian, France) 21/1
6 1 ½ **Un Monde (SPA)** 3-9-0 0 (b) JohanVictoire 9 56
(Mlle A Imaz-Ceca, France) 58/10[3]
7 5 **Talk Of The Nation (USA)**[181] 3-9-4 0 MaximeFoulon 2 51
(J-C Rouget, France) 13/10[1]
8 shd **Propriano (FR)**[47] 3-8-2 0 (p) MatthieuAutier(7) 7 42
(M Boutin, France) 24/1
9 dist **Allegorio (FR)**[178] 3-8-9 0 (p) WilliamsSaraiva 6 —
(Mme J Bidgood, France) 62/1
10 11 **First Mask (FR)** 3-8-9 0 (b[1]) TonyPiccone 8 —
(C Boutin, France) 55/1
11 **Massyaf (IRE)** 3-9-0 0 (b) FranckBlondel 11 —
(Mlle A Imaz-Ceca, France) 4/1[2]

2m 3.47s (123.47) 11 Ran SP% 115.0
PARI-MUTUEL (all including 1 euro stakes): WIN 10.30; PLACE 2.60, 2.90, 10.40; DF 18.30; SF 54.90.
Owner Patrick Dreux **Bred** Haras D'Etreham **Trained** France

661a PRIX DE MONTE CARLO (CONDITIONS) (4YO+) (FIBRESAND) 1m 2f (D)
2:20 (12:00) 4-Y-O+ £10,775 (£4,310; £3,232; £2,155; £1,077)

RPR
1 **Kenmour (FR)**[32] 267 4-9-4 0 (b) DavyBonilla 8 99
(F Rossi, France) 10/1
2 ½ **Chalsa (FR)**[23] 371 5-9-4 0 (p) ThierryThulliez 12 97
(P Khozian, France) 11/2[3]
3 1 **Maroni (IRE)**[23] 371 6-8-11 0 Francois-XavierBertras 11 88
(F Rohaut, France) 9/1
4 snk **Chombo (FR)**[21] 5-8-11 0 (p) JohanVictoire 3 88
(L A Urbano-Grajales, France) 7/2[1]
5 hd **Poussette (FR)** 4-8-13 0 FranckBlondel 7 91
(F Rossi, France) 9/2[2]
6 hd **Tryst**[21] 6-9-4 0 FredericSpanu 6 94
(J E Hammond, France) 9/2[2]
7 nk **Apro Lunare (IRE)**[10] 5-8-11 0 SUrru 1 87
(Laura Grizzetti, Italy) 60/1
8 hd **Gasquet (ITY)**[150] 5-9-2 0 PierantonioConvertino 2 91
(Gianfranco Verricelli, Italy) 38/1
9 ¾ **Tominator**[14] 478 4-9-2 0 ASuborics 10 91
(Reg Hollinshead) *settled in rr: styd on ins fnl 1 1/2f: nvr able to chal* 20/1
10 2 ½ **Arlequin**[23] 371 4-9-2 0 SylvainRuis 5 86
(James Bethell) *hld up: effrt 2f out but no real imp: wknd fnl 150yds* 28/1
0 **Kite Hunter (IRE)**[10] 4-9-4 0 StefanieHofer 4 —
(Mario Hofer, Germany) 22/1
0 **Street Lair (USA)**[37] 195 4-9-2 0 (b[1]) IoritzMendizabal 9 —
(J-C Rouget, France) 11/1

2m 3.50s (123.50)
WFA 4 from 5yo+ 1lb 12 Ran SP% 118.2
PARI-MUTUEL (all including 1 euro stakes): WIN 4.10 (coupled with Poussette); PLACE 7.00, 2.80, 4.20; DF 45.80; SF 120.00.
Owner Jean-Claude Seroul **Bred** Scea Ecurie Bader **Trained** France

646 KEMPTON (A.W) (R-H)
Thursday, February 24
OFFICIAL GOING: Standard
Wind: Light, across Weather: Fine, mild

662 PANORAMIC H'CAP 7f (P)
5:40 (5:42) (Class 7) (0-50,50) 4-Y-O+ £1,535 (£453; £226) Stalls Low

Form RPR
060/ 1 **Stoneacre Gareth (IRE)**[960] 1643 7-8-12 45 AdamKirby 9 70+
(K F Clutterbuck) *trckd ldng pair: wnt 2nd 1/2-way: led over 2f out gng easily: rousted along and sn wl clr* 7/1[3]
0-42 2 6 **Grey Boy (GER)**[1] 652 10-8-10 50 GeorgeDowning(7) 8 57
(Tony Carroll) *hld up wl in rr: taken wd and prog over 2f out: kpt on to take 2nd last 150yds: no ch w wnr* 9/2[1]
00-4 3 ½ **Chandrayaan**[14] 482 4-8-9 45 (v) NataliaGemelova(3) 1 51
(John E Long) *sn last and nt gng wl: gd prog fr 2f out: styd on to take 3rd nr fin and cl on runner-up* 12/1
0-05 4 2 ¼ **Cavalry Guard (USA)**[35] 225 7-8-9 45 (b) BillyCray(3) 4 45
(Tim McCarthy) *led: rdn and hdd over 2f out: steadily fdd: lost 2 pls ins fnl f* 28/1
-440 5 ¾ **Novastasia (IRE)**[14] 485 5-8-12 45 (b) SamHitchcott 3 43
(Dean Ivory) *pushed along towards rr over 4f out: nvr a threat: kpt on fnl f whn no ch* 20/1
-643 6 2 **Grand Honour (IRE)**[14] 485 5-8-10 50 (p) NathanAlison(7) 6 43
(Jim Boyle) *nvr beyond midfield on inner: effrt over 2f out but limited prog and no ch* 11/2[2]
064- 7 2 ½ **Dudley**[111] 7328 4-8-13 46 RichardKingscote 11 33
(Jonathan Portman) *chsd ldrs: given nudge by rival 4f out and nt too enthusiastic after: no prog fnl 2f* 12/1
3060 8 ½ **A Pocketful Of Rye (IRE)**[14] 485 4-8-12 45 MichaelStainton 10 30
(Jane Chapple-Hyam) *hld up in rr and racd wd: shkn up and no real prog fnl 2f* 8/1
00-4 9 1 ¼ **Poesmulligan (IRE)**[14] 485 5-8-12 45 SteveDrowne 14 27
(Linda Jewell) *chsd ldr to 1/2-way: wknd 2f out* 12/1
-042 10 ¾ **St Ignatius**[7] 575 4-8-5 45 (p) HobieGill(7) 12 25
(Michael Appleby) *chsd ldng trio: rdn 3f out: wknd over 2f out* 11/2[2]
000- 11 1 ¼ **Ain't Talkin'**[119] 7191 5-8-13 46 (p) PaulDoe 5 23
(Michael Attwater) *t.k.h: hld up wl in rr: rdn and struggling over 2f out: no ch after* 20/1
/005 12 14 **Zim Ho**[4] 619 5-8-12 45 DaneO'Neill 7 —
(John Akehurst) *t.k.h: chsd ldrs on outer: wknd rapidly over 2f out: t.o* 8/1
56-0 13 15 **Edge End**[35] 229 7-8-12 45 (v) MickyFenton 2 —
(Lisa Williamson) *plld hrd early: hld up bhd ldrs: racd awkwardly and wknd rapidly over 2f out: t.o* 50/1

1m 24.68s (-1.32) **Going Correction** -0.025s/f (Stan) 13 Ran SP% 121.7
Speed ratings (Par 97): **106,99,98,96,95 92,90,89,88,87 85,69,52**
toteswingers:1&2:£4.30, 1&3:£50.60, 2&3:£10.20 CSF £37.48 CT £397.07 TOTE £11.70: £4.00, £2.70, £2.00; EX 46.90.
Owner K F Clutterbuck **Bred** Robert De Vere Hunt **Trained** Exning, Suffolk
FOCUS
A bottom-drawer handicap and a gambled-on winner that did it easily. The winner should be able to score under a penalty.
Edge End Official explanation: jockey said gelding lost its action

663 KEMPTON.CO.UK MEDIAN AUCTION MAIDEN STKS 7f (P)
6:10 (6:10) (Class 6) 3-5-Y-O £1,535 (£453; £226) Stalls Low

Form RPR
1 **Caelis** 3-8-6 0 RichardThomas 7 61+
(Ralph Beckett) *trckd ldng pair: shkn up 2f out: led ent fnl f: styd on: quite readily* 11/1
56- 2 ¾ **Grand Piano (IRE)**[237] 3635 4-9-7 0 ThomasBrown(7) 9 70
(Andrew Balding) *mostly chsd ldr: rdn to chal over 1f out: upsides ent fnl f: chsd wnr after: styd on but readily hld* 7/1[2]
64 3 ¾ **Little Jazz**[19] 434 3-8-6 0 LiamJones 1 57
(Paul D'Arcy) *hld up towards rr: shkn up and prog on outer fr 2f out: styd on fnl f to take 3rd last strides* 8/1[3]
0- 4 hd **Swift Bird (IRE)**[223] 4095 3-8-6 0 AndreaAtzeni 2 57+
(Noel Quinlan) *hld up on inner and sn dropped to 8th: nvr ideally plcd after: effrt 2f out: rdn and styd on same pce fr over 1f out* 4/7[1]
0-0 5 ½ **Warbond**[41] 158 3-8-11 0 FrankieMcDonald 6 60
(Michael Madgwick) *led: set stdy pce to 3f out: urged along sn after: hdd and nt qckn ent fnl f: lost pls after* 50/1
0 6 6 **Celtic Whisper**[22] 380 3-8-6 0 NickyMackay 4 40
(Jeremy Gask) *pressed ldrs on inner: cl enough 2f out: wknd qckly fnl f* 14/1
7 1 **Savinien** 3-8-11 0 NeilCallan 8 42
(David Evans) *s.s: hld up in last pair: effrt over 2f out: nvr on terms w ldrs but plugged on* 14/1
0 8 4 **Clonusker (IRE)**[19] 437 3-8-11 0 EddieAhern 3 32
(Linda Jewell) *t.k.h: hld up towards rr: effrt over 2f out: sn wknd* 50/1
9 1 ¼ **Tinkerbell Will** 4-9-6 0 NataliaGemelova(3) 5 29
(John E Long) *v s.i.s: keen and green in last pair: no prog over 2f out: sn wknd* 50/1
6 10 8 **Hesindamood**[34] 253 4-10-0 0 VinceSlattery 11 14
(Joanne Priest) *racd wd: t.k.h: chsd ldrs 4f: wknd rapidly: t.o* 50/1

1m 26.89s (0.89) **Going Correction** -0.025s/f (Stan)
WFA 3 from 4yo 17lb 10 Ran SP% 116.8
Speed ratings (Par 101): **93,92,91,91,90 83,82,77,76,67**
toteswingers:1&2:£5.60, 1&3:£4.70, 2&3:£5.60 CSF £84.03 TOTE £19.70: £4.50, £1.50, £2.20; EX 81.60.
Owner Belmore Lane Stud Racing Partnership **Bred** S J And Mrs Pembroke **Trained** Kimpton, Hants
■ Stewards' Enquiry : Neil Callan two-day ban: careless riding (Mar 10-11)
FOCUS
An ordinary maiden run at an uneven pace. It is form worth treating with caution for now.

664 KEMPTON FOR OUTDOOR EVENTS H'CAP 6f (P)
6:40 (6:40) (Class 6) (0-55,55) 4-Y-O+ £1,535 (£453; £226) Stalls Low

Form RPR
2-41 1 **Chantilly Jewel (USA)**[20] 421 6-9-4 55 (b) JimCrowley 9 63
(Robert Cowell) *pressed ldr: drvn ahd over 1f out: kpt on wl fnl f and a holding chalrs* 7/1[3]
-012 2 ¾ **Royal Acclamation (IRE)**[4] 619 6-8-10 54 (p) DavidKenny(7) 6 60
(Michael Scudamore) *hld up in rr: taken to outer and shkn up 2f out: prog over 1f out: styd on to take 2nd last strides: couldn't chal* 5/2[1]
00-0 3 nk **Simple Rhythm**[6] 589 5-9-4 55 TomMcLaughlin 2 60
(John Ryan) *pressed ldng pair: rdn to chal and upsides over 1f out: chsd wnr after but hanging lft: hld and lost 2nd last strides* 4/1[2]
2365 4 ½ **Kheley (IRE)**[13] 511 5-9-2 53 ShaneKelly 3 56
(Mark Brisbourne) *chsd ldng trio: rdn to go 3rd over 1f out: styd on but nvr quite able to chal* 9/1
55 5 ½ **Evey P (IRE)**[12] 518 4-8-10 54 LucyKBarry(7) 5 56
(Gary Brown) *hld up and sn detached in last: racd alone on inner and prog fr 2f out: kpt on fnl f: nvr able to chal* 17/2
0-60 6 ½ **Commandingpresence (USA)**[4] 619 5-9-0 54 KierenFox(3) 4 54
(John Bridger) *a in midfield: rdn and nt qckn over 2f out: no imp tl kpt on ins fnl f* 11/1
2556 7 nk **Memphis Man**[13] 512 8-9-0 51 NeilCallan 10 50
(David Evans) *towards rr: urged along over 2f out: no prog but styd on fnl f: nrst fin* 11/1
6-15 8 1 ½ **Replicator**[31] 276 6-8-12 54 (e) TobyAtkinson(5) 8 49
(Patrick Gilligan) *racd wd: chsd ldrs: rdn over 2f out: sn lost pl and btn* 12/1
-654 9 ½ **Mosa Mine**[12] 518 4-9-4 55 MichaelStainton 7 48
(Jane Chapple-Hyam) *racd freely: led to over 1f out: wknd* 33/1

0036 **10** ½ **Valentino Swing (IRE)**[4] 619 8-8-8 **52**.......................... HobieGill(7) 12 44
(Michael Appleby) *dwlt: hld up in last pair: shuffled along on wd outside fr 2f out: nvr involved* **16/1**

1m 12.52s (-0.58) **Going Correction** -0.025s/f (Stan) **10** Ran SP% **114.8**
Speed ratings (Par 101): **102,101,100,99,99 98,98,96,95,94**
toteswingers:1&2:£2.20, 1&3:£4.00, 2&3:£3.70 CSF £24.39 CT £82.17 TOTE £6.20: £1.90, £1.10, £2.80; EX 22.60.
Owner Bottisham Heath Stud **Bred** Two Sisters Stable **Trained** Six Mile Bottom, Cambs
■ Stewards' Enquiry : Tom McLaughlin one-day ban: careless riding (Mar 10)

FOCUS
An ordinary sprint handicap and modest form, with the runner-up probably the best guide.

665 DAY TIME, NIGHT TIME, GREAT TIME CLAIMING STKS 6f (P)
7:10 (7:10) (Class 6) 3-Y-0+ **£1,535** (£453; £226) **Stalls** Low

Form RPR

100- **1** **Roche Des Vents**[222] 4138 3-8-13 78.................................. DaneO'Neill 3 79
(Richard Hannon) *t.k.h: trckd ldr: pushed into ld over 1f out: hrd pressed and drvn fnl f: jst hld on* **5/1**

111 **2** *hd* **April Fool**[8] 556 7-9-9 71...(b) NeilCallan 5 77
(David Evans) *pushed up to ld: rdn and hdd over 1f out: rallied ins fnl f: jst failed* **15/8**[1]

4115 **3** ½ **Frequency**[10] 538 4-9-6 70..(b) AndreaAtzeni 4 73
(Michael Wigham) *sn t.k.h bhd ldng pair: shkn up and nt qckn over 1f out: brought to chal ins fnl f: nt qckn again last 100yds* **7/2**[2]

0144 **4** *nk* **Lastkingofscotland (IRE)**[8] 557 5-9-11 79..................(b) AdamKirby 2 77
(Conor Dore) *settled in last: u.p and no imp fr 2f out: styd on wl last 150yds: gaining at fin* **4/1**[3]

6102 **5** 1½ **Northern Dare (IRE)**[1] 658 7-9-10 76.....................(b) JimCrowley 1 72
(Richard Fahey) *t.k.h: hld up bhd ldng pair: rdn and nt qckn over 1f out: fdd ins fnl f* **11/2**

1m 12.76s (-0.34) **Going Correction** -0.025s/f (Stan)
WFA 3 from 4yo+ 15lb **5** Ran SP% **109.1**
Speed ratings (Par 101): **101,100,100,99,97**
CSF £14.52 TOTE £3.20: £5.30, £1.10; EX 5.10.
Owner Robin Blunt **Bred** G Howard-Spink **Trained** East Everleigh, Wilts

FOCUS
A tricky claimer and a bunched finish. The form is rated around the three immediately behind the winner, who all ran close to their marks.

666 FAMILY FUN AT KEMPTON 02.05.11 H'CAP 7f (P)
7:40 (7:40) (Class 5) (0-75,75) 4-Y-0+ **£2,047** (£604; £302) **Stalls** Low

Form RPR

1252 **1** **Double Carpet (IRE)**[17] 446 8-8-9 **63**.............................. EddieAhern 3 71
(Garry Woodward) *in tch disputing 7th: pushed along 1/2-way: u.p and no prog over 2f out: stl only 7th 1f out: picked up wl and r.o to ld last 50yds* **10/1**

33-1 **2** ¾ **Catherines Call (IRE)**[12] 530 4-9-7 **75**........................ AndreaAtzeni 7 81
(Des Donovan) *trckd ldng pair: clsd to ld over 1f out: drvn and looked like holding on fnl f: hdd and outpcd last 50yds* **15/2**[2]

36-1 **3** ½ **Yes Chef**[28] 313 4-9-4 **72**.. JamesMillman 5 77
(Rod Millman) *t.k.h: hld up in 10th: pushed along 2f out: prog over 1f out looking awkward: eventually r.o wl to snatch 3rd nr fin* **9/2**[1]

000- **4** *hd* **Exceedingly Bold**[140] 6701 4-9-2 **70**................................ DaneO'Neill 1 74
(Jo Crowley) *trckd ldrs in 6th: effrt on inner over 2f out: kpt on fr over 1f out: nvr quite able to chal* **14/1**

6-00 **5** ¾ **Rapid Water**[33] 264 5-8-13 **67**... MartinLane 8 69
(Jane Chapple-Hyam) *cl up bhd ldrs: hrd rdn and nt qckn 2f out: kpt on same pce after* **33/1**

-363 **6** *shd* **Could It Be Magic**[8] 557 4-8-13 **70**.............................(b) KierenFox(3) 12 72
(Bill Turner) *trckd ldr: led jst over 2f out to over 1f out: fdd ins fnl f* **8/1**[3]

000- **7** ¾ **Mountain Cat (IRE)**[157] 6260 7-9-4 **72**........................... JimCrowley 13 74+
(William Knight) *hld up in last trio: effrt over 2f out: no real prog tl styd on ins fnl f: n.d* **16/1**

2-51 **8** 1 **Abriachan**[32] 268 4-9-0 **68**... AdamKirby 9 65
(Noel Quinlan) *hld up in rr: effrt over 2f out: hrd rdn to cl on ldrs over 1f out: one pce after* **10/1**

301- **9** *hd* **Tewin Wood**[64] 7964 4-9-4 **72**... LiamJones 11 69
(Alan Bailey) *racd freely: led: hdd and nt qckn jst over 2f out: wknd fnl f* **16/1**

-103 **10** 4½ **Hip Hip Hooray**[14] 483 5-8-8 **69**.................................. LucyKBarry(7) 6 54
(Luke Dace) *sltly awkward s: t.k.h: hld up in last pair: wd into st: nvr involved* **15/2**[2]

0-06 **11** *nk* **Global Village (IRE)**[31] 279 6-9-5 **73**.......................... SteveDrowne 4 57
(Michael Blake) *hld up in 9th on inner: tried to make prog fr 2f out: no imp 1f out: fdd* **15/2**[2]

4-51 **12** 2¼ **Diplomatic (IRE)**[19] 437 6-9-4 **72**............................... SaleemGolam 10 51
(Michael Squance) *nvr bttr than midfield: u.p 3f out: wknd over 2f out* **28/1**

4425 **13** *nk* **Tuxedo**[15] 473 6-9-4 **72**...(b) ChrisCatlin 14 50
(Peter Hiatt) *awkward s: rushed up on outer and sn prom: lost pl sn after 1/2-way: bhd fnl 2f* **8/1**[3]

1m 25.17s (-0.83) **Going Correction** -0.025s/f (Stan) **13** Ran SP% **118.7**
Speed ratings (Par 103): **103,102,101,101,100 100,99,98,98,93 92,90,89**
toteswingers:1&2:£3.90, 1&3:£10.50, 2&3:£8.90 CSF £82.54 CT £390.82 TOTE £11.90: £3.10, £2.10, £1.80; EX 45.00.
Owner Garry Woodward **Bred** Dr John Waldron **Trained** Maltby, S Yorks

FOCUS
A competitive handicap for the class. The form is limited but looks sound enough.

667 PEPPA PIG AT KEMPTON 02.05.11 CONDITIONS STKS 1m 4f (P)
8:10 (8:10) (Class 4) 4-Y-0+ **£3,885** (£1,156; £577; £288) **Stalls** Centre

Form RPR

0-25 **1** **King Olav (UAE)**[19] 436 6-9-2 91... NeilCallan 2 97
(Tony Carroll) *trckd ldr: led over 2f out and sn kicked 3 l clr: rdn out and in n.d fnl f* **14/1**

442- **2** 2 **Fox Hunt (IRE)**[152] 6355 4-9-2 96.................................... JoeFanning 3 97
(Mark Johnston) *trckd ldng pair to 1/2-way: styd cl up: effrt to chse wnr 2f out: hung lft then rt: nt qckn and readily hld* **8/11**[1]

115- **3** 1¾ **Dirar (IRE)**[167] 5909 6-9-2 0.. EddieAhern 4 91+
(Gordon Elliott, Ire) *settled in 4th tl trckd ldng pair 1/2-way: outpcd 2f out: shuffled along and no meaningful imp after* **2/1**[2]

602- **4** ½ **Into Wain (USA)**[157] 6251 4-8-13 90.................................. DaneO'Neill 6 90
(Steve Gollings) *hld up in last pair: effrt over 2f out: one pce and no imp fr over 1f out* **11/1**[3]

241- **5** 2¼ **Hawaana (IRE)**[203] 4737 6-9-2 86.................................. MickyFenton 5 87
(Gay Kelleway) *plld hrd in last pair: effrt over 2f out: jnd chsers over 1f out: no hdwy after: fdd fnl f* **33/1**

0/3- **6** 13 **Sahrati**[184] 746 7-9-2 72... SteveDrowne 1 66
(Michael Blake) *led at mod pce to over 2f out: immediately dropped out* **66/1**

2m 34.11s (-0.39) **Going Correction** -0.025s/f (Stan)
WFA 4 from 6yo+ 3lb **6** Ran SP% **110.7**
Speed ratings (Par 105): **100,98,97,97,95 87**
toteswingers:1&2:£4.30, 1&3:£8.30, 2&3:£1.02 CSF £24.43 TOTE £13.20: £3.50, £1.10; EX 28.30.
Owner Cover Point Racing **Bred** Darley **Trained** Cropthorne, Worcs

FOCUS
A decent race, but run at a steady pace and the winner got a fine ride. The form should not be trusted implicitly, with the winner th best guide in recording a slight personal best.
Dirar(IRE) ◆ Official explanation: jockey said, regarding running and riding, that his orders were to sit in behind the leaders and remain handy, the pace was slow, which did not suit the gelding, it became tired closing stages having been off the track for a long time.

668 PETER ANDRE AT KEMPTON 06.07.11 H'CAP LONDON MILE (QUALIFIER) 1m (P)
8:40 (8:40) (Class 5) (0-70,62) 3-Y-0 **£2,047** (£604; £302) **Stalls** Low

Form RPR

0-11 **1** **Reachforthebucks**[2] 642 3-9-8 **62** 12ex......................... AndreaAtzeni 1 83+
(Michael Wigham) *trckd ldr tl given nudge by rival 1/2-way: styd cl up: led on bit wl over 1f out: pushed along briefly ent fnl f: cruised home after* **1/3**[1]

001- **2** 3½ **Snow Trooper**[76] 7813 3-9-6 **60**.. SamHitchcott 3 68
(Dean Ivory) *hld up in last pair: rdn wl over 2f out: prog to take 2nd over 1f out: no ch w wnr but drew away fr rest* **8/1**[2]

-232 **3** 10 **Beating Harmony**[12] 527 3-9-4 **58**................................(v[1]) NeilCallan 4 43
(Tony Carroll) *cl up: nudged rival and wnt 2nd 1/2-way: drvn to chal and upsides 2f out: sn wknd* **9/1**[3]

6-54 **4** 2½ **Reachtothestars (USA)**[20] 422 3-9-7 **61**........................ AdamKirby 2 40
(Noel Quinlan) *slowest away but sn pushed up to ld: hdd & wknd wl over 1f out* **16/1**

0-63 **5** *shd* **Luckbealadytonight (IRE)**[20] 422 3-9-2 **56**.................. JoeFanning 5 35
(Mark Johnston) *hld up in last pair: rdn over 2f out: sn btn: wknd over 1f out* **8/1**[2]

1m 39.34s (-0.46) **Going Correction** -0.025s/f (Stan) **5** Ran SP% **113.1**
Speed ratings (Par 97): **101,97,87,85,84**
CSF £4.02 TOTE £1.20: £1.10, £2.60; EX 4.30.
Owner Reach For The Bucks Racing Partnership **Bred** Miss D Gibbins **Trained** Newmarket, Suffolk

FOCUS
The first two came clear here and the winner remains well ahead of the handicapper. The runner-up is probably the best guide to the form.
T/Plt: £70.10 to a £1 stake. Pool:£61,875.63 - 643.52 winning tickets T/Qpdt: £8.10 to a £1 stake. Pool:£8,496.39 - 769.04 winning tickets JN

639 SOUTHWELL (L-H)
Thursday, February 24

OFFICIAL GOING: Standard
Wind: Light across Weather: Fine and dry

669 ENHANCED SP'S AT BLUESQ.COM MEDIAN AUCTION MAIDEN STKS 5f (F)
2:10 (2:10) (Class 6) 3-5-Y-0 **£1,535** (£453; £226) **Stalls** High

Form RPR

024- **1** **Take Your Partner**[65] 7954 3-8-13 60............................(b) PhillipMakin 4 64
(Kevin Ryan) *cl up: effrt 2f out and sn rdn: drvn ent fnl f: kpt on to ld last 75yds* **13/8**[1]

-053 **2** *nk* **Ladydolly**[16] 452 3-8-5 41.. AndrewHeffernan(3) 9 58
(Roy Brotherton) *led: rdn along and jnd wl over 1f out: drvn ent fnl f: hdd and no ex last 75yds* **18/1**

24-2 **3** 2¼ **Mazovian (USA)**[13] 513 3-8-8 69.. JulieBurke(5) 8 55+
(Michael Chapman) *sn pushed along towards rr: rdn 2f out: styd on appr fnl f: nrst fin* **5/2**[2]

4 3¾ **Shakespeares Excel** 4-9-13 0.. PatrickMathers 6 45+
(Derek Shaw) *dwlt: green and sn outpcd towards rr: hdwy over 2f out: styd on appr fnl f: nrst fin* **40/1**

2-00 **5** *nk* **True Red (IRE)**[34] 250 4-9-8 41.....................................(b) DavidProbert 5 39
(Nikki Evans) *chsd ldrs: rdn along 2f out: sn drvn and grad wknd* **66/1**

2236 **6** ½ **Pineapple Pete (IRE)**[5] 611 3-8-13 62......................(vt[1]) JamesDoyle 3 38
(Alan McCabe) *dwlt: hdwy to chse ldrs after 1f: effrt on outer and cl up 1/2-way: rdn along wl over 1f out and sn btn* **6/1**

7 1½ **Princeton Girl** 3-8-8 0.. DuranFentiman 1 28
(Tim Easterby) *racd wd: midfield: rdn along 1/2-way: nvr a factor* **22/1**

0-4 **8** 9 **Everybody Out**[13] 513 3-8-13 0.. GrahamGibbons 7 —
(Reg Hollinshead) *towards rr: outpcd and bhd fr 1/2-way* **40/1**

3- **9** ½ **Deliberation (IRE)**[121] 7142 3-8-13 0.................................. TomEaves 2 —
(Ollie Pears) *dwlt: sn rdn along in rr: outpcd and bhd fr 1/2-way* **5/1**[3]

58.93 secs (-0.77) **Going Correction** -0.125s/f (Stan)
WFA 3 from 4yo 14lb **9** Ran SP% **113.6**
Speed ratings (Par 101): **101,100,96,90,90 89,87,72,72**
Tote Swingers:1&2:£7.40, 1&3:£2.20, 2&3:£4.60 CSF £31.26 TOTE £2.20: £1.10, £3.40, £1.40; EX 30.50 Trifecta £149.70 Pool: £562.58 - 2.78 winning units..
Owner Guy Reed **Bred** G Reed **Trained** Hambleton, N Yorks
■ Stewards' Enquiry : Andrew Heffernan caution: used whip with excessive frequency.

FOCUS
A poor sprint maiden and the form may not amount to much. The fifth is the best guide to the level.

670 PLAY GOLF BEFORE RACING (S) STKS 1m 4f (F)
2:40 (2:40) (Class 6) 4-Y-0+ **£1,535** (£453; £226) **Stalls** Low

Form RPR

-042 **1** **Eton Fable (IRE)**[7] 570 6-9-0 62.....................................(p) WilliamCarson 2 57+
(Bill Ratcliffe) *prom: effrt 3f out: led 2f out and sn rdn: drvn ent fnl f: kpt on wl* **5/6**[1]

05-3 **2** 1 **Sir Haydn**[46] 103 11-8-7 50.. DannyBrock(7) 5 56
(J R Jenkins) *hld up towards rr: stdy hdwy on inner whn n.m.r 3f out: effrt 2f out: rdn to chal over 1f out and ev ch tl edgd rt and no ex last 100yds* **20/1**

35-4 **3** 5 **Royal Holiday (IRE)**[7] 570 4-8-11 58.................................. TomEaves 7 48
(Brian Ellison) *trckd ldrs: hdwy 3f out and sn pushed along: rdn to chse ldng pair whn hung lft wl over 1f out: sn drvn and one pce* **3/1**[2]

0-66 **4** 10 **Credential**[16] 451 9-9-0 43......................................(be) StevieDonohoe 4 33
(John Harris) *led 1f: prom: led again 5f out: rdn over 3f out: drvn and hdd 2f out: sn wknd* **33/1**

-525 **5** *2 ½* **Grand Vizier (IRE)**[19] [433] 7-9-0 70 HayleyTurner 6 29
(Conor Dore) *hld up: hdwy and in tch over 4f out: rdn over 3f out and sn wknd* **4/1**[3]

00-0 **6** *½* **Byron Bay**[13] [507] 9-8-11 48 JamesSullivan(3) 3 29
(Robert Johnson) *hld up in tch: effrt to chse ldrs 4f out: rdn over 3f out and sn wknd* **100/1**

000- **7** *28* **Doric Echo**[148] [6479] 5-8-7 55 (b[1]) AlexEdwards(7) 1 —
(Kevin M Prendergast) *t.k.h: prom: led after 1f: pushed along and hdd 5f out: sn lost pl and bhd* **33/1**

2m 38.93s (-2.07) **Going Correction** -0.15s/f (Stan)
WFA 4 from 5yo+ 3lb 7 Ran SP% **111.2**
Speed ratings (Par 101): **100,99,96,89,87 87,68**
Tote Swingers:1&2:£2.30, 1&3:£1.10, 2&3:£3.70 CSF £20.58 TOTE £1.60: £1.20, £10.60; EX 16.30.The winner was sold to Mr T B Tarn for 5,500gns.
Owner W J H Ratcliffe **Bred** Andrew Christy **Trained** Newmarket, Suffolk

FOCUS
A moderate seller, but a fair early pace. The second is the best guide with the winner below his best.

671 SOUTHWELL-RACECOURSE.CO.UK H'CAP — 1m 6f (F)
3:15 (3:15) (Class 5) (0-75,75) 4-Y-0+ **£1,910** (£564; £282) **Stalls** Low

Form RPR

-311 **1** **Eseej (USA)**[21] [399] 6-9-12 **75** WilliamCarson 1 84
(Peter Hiatt) *mde all: rdn clr over 3f out: kpt on strly* **11/1**

0432 **2** *5* **Calculating (IRE)**[9] [549] 7-8-13 **62** DavidProbert 4 65
(Mark Usher) *trckd ldng pair: effrt 4f out: chsd wnr over 3f out: rdn over 2f out: sn drvn and no imp* **4/1**[2]

23-1 **3** *3 ¼* **Shifting Gold (IRE)**[42] [3] 5-8-9 **61** (b) AmyRyan(3) 6 59
(Kevin Ryan) *dwlt: sn chsng wnr: rdn along 4f out and sn outpcd: wd st and drvn over 2f out: no imp* **4/1**[2]

-512 **4** *22* **Dart**[13] [514] 7-9-8 **71** GrahamGibbons 2 50
(John Mackie) *hld up in tch: pushed along over 5f out: rdn 4f out: sn outpcd and bhd whn eased wl over 1f out* **9/1**[3]

-111 **P** **Luck Of The Draw (IRE)**[48] [79] 4-9-4 **72** StevieDonohoe 5 —
(Sir Mark Prescott Bt) *hld up in rr: in tch whn p.u 5f out: fatally injured* **1/1**[1]

3m 4.38s (-3.92) **Going Correction** -0.15s/f (Stan)
WFA 4 from 5yo+ 5lb 5 Ran SP% **108.3**
Speed ratings (Par 103): **105,102,100,87,—**
CSF £50.13 TOTE £11.10: £3.00, £2.40; EX 25.50.
Owner P W Hiatt **Bred** Shadwell Farm LLC **Trained** Hook Norton, Oxon

FOCUS
A modest staying handicap marred by Luck Of The Draw sadly breaking down at around halfway. The form is pretty straightforward and looks solid enough.

672 COME JUMPING AT SOUTHWELL IN MARCH CLASSIFIED CLAIMING STKS — 6f (F)
3:45 (3:46) (Class 6) 3-Y-0 **£1,535** (£453; £226) **Stalls** Low

Form RPR

6-02 **1** **Fantasy Fry**[14] [494] 3-8-5 65 HayleyTurner 3 73
(Hughie Morrison) *dwlt: sn chsng ldr: effrt and cl up over 2f out: led wl over 1f out: sn rdn clr: readily* **11/4**[2]

-125 **2** *4 ½* **Local Diktator**[39] [187] 3-8-4 63 (t) DavidProbert 2 59
(Ronald Harris) *chsd ldng pair on inner: rdn along wl over 2f out: drvn over 1f out: kpt on to take 2nd ins fnl f: no ch w wnr* **3/1**[3]

3311 **3** *2 ½* **Honkers Bonkers**[7] [576] 3-8-9 63 (v) JamesDoyle 4 56
(Alan McCabe) *led at str pce: rdn along and jnd 2f out: sn hdd: drvn and wknd over 1f out* **5/6**[1]

-026 **4** *15* **Hereselie (IRE)**[13] [505] 3-8-1 60 JulieBurke(5) 5 —
(Michael Chapman) *dwlt and sn pushed along: rdn bef 1/2-way: nvr a factor* **16/1**

0-06 **5** *3 ¼* **Come On Eileen (IRE)**[9] [550] 3-7-13 30 AndrewHeffernan(3) 1 —
(Richard Guest) *a in rr: rdn along bef 1/2-way and sn bhd* **80/1**

1m 14.82s (-1.68) **Going Correction** -0.15s/f (Stan) 5 Ran SP% **113.3**
Speed ratings (Par 95): **105,99,95,75,71**
CSF £11.65 TOTE £4.30: £2.00, £2.10; EX 9.60.
Owner H Morrison **Bred** Meon Valley Stud **Trained** East Ilsley, Berks

FOCUS
A routine claimer in which the majority of these had already met each other here this year. The winner is rated to his previous best with the favourite below form.

673 DOWNLOAD THE BLUE SQUARE ANDROID APP H'CAP — 6f (F)
4:20 (4:21) (Class 5) (0-75,73) 4-Y-0+ **£2,234** (£664; £332; £165) **Stalls** Low

Form RPR

2-32 **1** **Interchoice Star**[21] [402] 6-8-8 **60** (p) WilliamCarson 1 70
(Ray Peacock) *chsd ldrs: hdwy on inner 1/2-way: rdn to ld 2f out: drvn ent fnl f: kpt on wl* **7/1**[3]

4-52 **2** *1 ¾* **Where's Reiley (USA)**[14] [491] 5-9-2 **68** LeeNewman 7 73
(David Barron) *prom: rdn along and outpcd 1/2-way: hdwy on wd outside 2f out: sn rdn: drvn over 1f out: kpt on ins fnl f* **5/2**[1]

3425 **3** *¾* **Ace Of Spies (IRE)**[7] [572] 6-9-7 **73** KirstyMilczarek 3 76
(Conor Dore) *led 2f: prom: rdn 2f out: drvn over 1f out: kpt on same pce* **7/1**[3]

3614 **4** *nk* **Takajan (IRE)**[21] [403] 4-8-12 **69** JamesRogers(5) 6 71
(Mark Brisbourne) *a cl up: effrt 2f out: sn rdn and ev ch tl drvn and one pce appr fnl f* **11/4**[2]

20-4 **5** *2 ½* **Beckermet (IRE)**[23] [377] 9-8-7 **62** JamesSullivan(3) 2 56
(Ruth Carr) *chsd ldrs on inner: rdn along over 2f out: sn drvn and wknd* **28/1**

220- **6** *4 ½* **Desert Falls**[108] [7376] 5-8-8 **60** JimmyQuinn 4 41
(Richard Whitaker) *towards rr: hdwy 1/2-way: rdn along over 2f out: sn no imp* **12/1**

0-36 **7** *1 ¼* **Besty**[23] [377] 4-9-5 **71** (v[1]) TomEaves 5 48
(Bryan Smart) *dwlt: rapid hdwy to ld after 2f: rdn along over 2f out: sn hdd and grad wknd* **16/1**

104- **8** *2 ¼* **Durham Express (IRE)**[117] [7225] 4-9-4 **70** (p) FrederikTylicki 9 40
(Michael Dods) *chsd ldrs on outer: rdn along 1/2-way: sn wknd* **12/1**

00-0 **9** *hd* **Mark Anthony (IRE)**[12] [522] 4-9-4 **70** (b[1]) PhillipMakin 10 40
(Kevin Ryan) *wnt rt s: rdn along and wd st: a towards rr* **8/1**

-606 **10** *1* **Prince James**[21] [403] 4-8-9 **68** DavidSimmonson(7) 8 35
(Michael Easterby) *sn rdn along: a in rr* **50/1**

1m 15.58s (-0.92) **Going Correction** -0.15s/f (Stan) 10 Ran SP% **118.0**
Speed ratings (Par 103): **100,97,96,96,92 86,85,82,82,80**
Tote Swingers:1&2:£3.50, 1&3:£4.90, 2&3:£8.60 CSF £25.15 CT £133.81 TOTE £8.00: £1.80, £2.30, £2.80; EX 30.50 Trifecta £257.50 Part won. Pool: £347.98 - 0.82 winning units..
Owner John P Evitt **Bred** M P Bishop **Trained** Kyre Park, Worcs
■ Stewards' Enquiry : William Carson caution: used whip with excessive frequency.

FOCUS
A moderate sprint handicap, but the early pace was solid. The form looks solid for the grade rated around the winner, third and fourth.

674 CALL 01636 814481 TO SPONSOR A RACE H'CAP — 7f (F)
4:50 (4:52) (Class 6) (0-65,64) 4-Y-0+ **£1,535** (£453; £226) **Stalls** Low

Form RPR

0-15 **1** **Zarius**[39] [181] 4-9-0 **57** JackMitchell 2 67
(Chris Wall) *trckd ldrs on inner: hdwy to chal 2f out: sn rdn: led appr fnl f: drvn out* **5/1**[2]

0-54 **2** *1* **Convince (USA)**[9] [545] 10-8-9 **55** AndrewHeffernan(3) 8 62
(Kevin M Prendergast) *in rr: pushed along 1/2-way: gd hdwy on outer 2f out: sn rdn: styd on strly fnl f: nt rch wnr* **7/1**[3]

-524 **3** *1 ¾* **Ubenkor (IRE)**[21] [400] 6-9-7 **64** PhillipMakin 13 66
(Michael Herrington) *in tch: hdwy on outer 1/2-way: rdn to ld 2f out: drvn: edgd lft and hdd appr fnl f: kpt on same pce* **3/1**[1]

4422 **4** *1 ¾* **Elusive Warrior (USA)**[7] [568] 8-9-7 **64** (p) JamesDoyle 3 62
(Alan McCabe) *led 2f: cl up: rdn along over 2f out: sn drvn and one pce* **7/1**[3]

0-40 **5** *4 ½* **Wigram's Turn (USA)**[24] [367] 6-9-5 **62** GrahamGibbons 1 49
(Michael Easterby) *chsd ldrs: hdwy on inner to ld after 2f: rdn along and hdd 2f out: sn drvn and wknd over 1f out* **20/1**

-203 **6** *1 ¾* **Bel Cantor**[21] [402] 8-9-3 **60** (p) WilliamCarson 7 42
(Bill Ratcliffe) *cl up: rdn along 3f out: drvn and grad wknd fnl 2f* **17/2**

-033 **7** *1 ¾* **Muqalad (IRE)**[9] [545] 4-8-10 **53** TomEaves 4 31
(Bryan Smart) *chsd ldrs: rdn along wl over 2f out: sn drvn and wknd* **8/1**

-644 **8** *1 ½* **Crocodile Bay (IRE)**[7] [568] 8-8-12 **55** (b) JimmyQuinn 10 29
(Richard Guest) *in tch on inner: rdn along wl over 2f out: sn wknd* **28/1**

/60- **9** *5* **Amno Dancer (IRE)**[268] [2620] 4-8-12 **60** LMcNiff(5) 5 22
(David Barron) *a towards rr* **7/1**[3]

01-0 **10** *1 ¾* **Nacho Libre**[24] [367] 6-8-12 **62** (b) DavidSimmonson(7) 14 19
(Michael Easterby) *dwlt: a in rr: outpcd and bhd fr 1/2-way* **25/1**

000- **11** *3 ¼* **Bob Stock (IRE)**[141] [6671] 5-9-0 **57** JamieMackay 6 6
(Willie Musson) *s.i.s: a in rr: bhd fr 1/2-way* **40/1**

600- **12** *1 ¼* **Wotatomboy**[148] [6460] 5-8-4 50 oh2 JamesSullivan(3) 11 —
(Richard Whitaker) *chsd ldrs 3f: sn lost pl and bhd fnl 2f* **40/1**

-044 **13** *nse* **Spinning Ridge (IRE)**[13] [512] 6-8-13 **56** (b) DavidProbert 12 —
(Ronald Harris) *prom: cl up on outer 1/2-way: sn rdn and wknd qckly over 2f out* **16/1**

1m 29.0s (-1.30) **Going Correction** -0.15s/f (Stan) 13 Ran SP% **123.6**
Speed ratings (Par 101): **101,99,97,95,90 88,86,85,79,77 73,72,72**
Tote Swingers:1&2:£8.00, 1&3:£6.10, 2&3:£9.10 CSF £38.96 CT £129.45 TOTE £5.80: £2.20, £2.60, £1.60; EX 65.10 Trifecta £299.10 Part won. Pool: £404.29 - 0.60 winning units..
Owner Mervyn Ayers **Bred** Executive Bloodlines Ltd **Trained** Newmarket, Suffolk

FOCUS
Another moderate handicap, although the early pace was honest. The form looks straightforwrd rated through the runner-up.

675 PLAY RAINBOW RICHES AT BLUESQ.COM H'CAP — 1m (F)
5:20 (5:20) (Class 6) (0-55,55) 4-Y-0+ **£1,535** (£453; £226) **Stalls** Low

Form RPR

2442 **1** **Positivity**[13] [504] 5-8-10 **54** (p) AdamCarter(5) 8 64
(Bryan Smart) *led 2f: chsd ldr tl led again over 2f out: sn rdn clr: drvn ins fnl f and kpt on wl* **7/4**[1]

02-4 **2** *1 ¼* **Nevada Desert (IRE)**[13] [504] 11-9-0 **53** TomEaves 14 59
(Richard Whitaker) *stdd and swtchd lft s: hld up in rr: hdwy on inner wl over 2f out: rdn over 1f out: styd on to chse wnr ins fnl f: nrst fin* **5/1**[2]

-323 **3** *1 ¾* **Noble Attitude**[14] [490] 5-8-4 **46** oh1 AndrewHeffernan(3) 7 48
(Richard Guest) *chsd ldrs: wd st: hdwy 2f out: rdn wl over 1f out: kpt on same pce fnl f* **6/1**[3]

-540 **4** *nk* **Chez Vrony**[8] [553] 5-9-2 **55** AdrianMcCarthy 1 57
(Dave Morris) *a chsng ldrs: rdn along 2f out: drvn over 1f out: kpt on same pce fnl f* **9/1**

0-05 **5** *hd* **Naledi**[7] [574] 7-8-7 **46** oh1 WilliamCarson 3 47
(Richard Price) *in tch on inner: rdn along 3f out: hdwy to chse ldrs 2f out: drvn and kpt on same pce appr fnl f* **20/1**

4004 **6** *4 ½* **Archilini**[7] [573] 6-8-7 **46** oh1 (be) BarryMcHugh 13 37
(Brian Ellison) *t.k.h: hld up in midfield: effrt and sme hdwy 2f out: sn rdn and no imp* **8/1**

0-00 **7** *shd* **Flores Sea (USA)**[13] [504] 7-8-8 **47** (b) PJMcDonald 10 38
(Ruth Carr) *dwlt: rapid hdwy to ld after 2f: rdn along and hdd over 2f out: drvn wl over 1f out: grad wknd* **40/1**

45-0 **8** *1 ½* **Chichen Daawe**[16] [451] 5-8-5 **47** IanBrennan(3) 6 35
(Brian Ellison) *towards rr: hdwy over 2f out: sn rdn and n.d* **10/1**

0/40 **9** *1* **Cause For Applause (IRE)**[21] [408] 5-8-7 **46** oh1 JimmyQuinn 11 32
(Ray Craggs) *midfield: hdwy and in tch on outer 3f out: sn rdn along and wknd over 2f out* **16/1**

4-06 **10** *1 ¾* **Westport**[14] [490] 8-8-7 **46** oh1 LeeNewman 5 28
(Robin Bastiman) *chsd ldrs: rdn along wl over 2f out: sn wknd* **66/1**

600/ **11** *1 ¾* **Prince Samos (IRE)**[575] [4434] 9-8-8 **50** JamesSullivan(3) 4 28
(Clive Mulhall) *a in rr* **50/1**

2-00 **12** *¾* **Silca Meydan**[16] [451] 5-8-2 **46** oh1 JulieBurke(5) 2 22
(Richard Price) *in tch: rdn along 3f out: sn wknd* **14/1**

0/-0 **13** *20* **Sion Hill (IRE)**[53] [14] 10-8-9 **48** (p) KellyHarrison 9 —
(John Harris) *chsd ldrs: rdn along 1/2-way: sn outpcd and bhd* **40/1**

1m 43.16s (-0.54) **Going Correction** -0.15s/f (Stan) 13 Ran SP% **123.2**
Speed ratings (Par 101): **96,94,93,92,92 88,87,86,85,83 81,81,61**
Tote Swingers:1&2:£3.00, 1&3:£2.90, 2&3:£3.00. totesuper7: Win: Not won. Place: £24.10. CSF £9.90 CT £48.20 TOTE £3.00: £1.50, £1.90, £1.40; EX 14.00 Trifecta £28.80 Pool: £260.89 - 6.69 winning units..
Owner Mrs F Denniff **Bred** Mrs Fiona Denniff **Trained** Hambleton, N Yorks

FOCUS
A solid pace for this moderate handicap. The form is weak and the in-form winner is the best guide.
Sion Hill(IRE) Official explanation: jockey said gelding never travelled
T/Plt: £82.60 to a £1 stake. Pool:£51,635.22 - 456.32 winning tickets T/Qpdt: £37.30 to a £1 stake. Pool:£3,371.71 - 66.80 winning tickets JR

[602]MEYDAN (L-H)

Thursday, February 24

OFFICIAL GOING: Tapeta - standard; turf - good

676a JAGUAR XF TROPHY (H'CAP) (TURF) 1m 2f

2:25 (2:25) (100-110,108) 3-Y-O+

£67,307 (£22,435; £11,217; £5,608; £3,365; £2,243)

RPR

1 **Wonder Lawn (SAF)**[14] [499] 8-8-9 100....(t) KShea 4 98
(M F De Kock, South Africa) *mid-div: smooth prog 2 1/2f out: led 2f out: r.o wl* **10/1**

2 *1 3/4* **Yirga**[6] [605] 5-8-13 104....(t) RoystonFfrench 6 99
(A Al Raihe, UAE) *settled in rr: r.o wl fnl 2f: nrst fin* **11/2**

3 *4 3/4* **Espiritu (FR)**[28] [330] 5-8-11 102.... KierenFallon 2 87
(G Al Marri, UAE) *settled in rr: rdn 5f out: r.o one pce fnl 1 1/2f* **10/1**

4 *2 1/2* **Hunting Tower (SAF)**[14] [498] 9-9-3 108....(t) ChristopheSoumillon 1 88
(M F De Kock, South Africa) *mid-div on rail: rdn 3 1/2f out: one pce fnl 2f* **2/1[1]**

5 *3/4* **Lolamar (ITY)**[6] [607] 4-8-11 104.... JMurtagh 3 82
(Marco Botti) *trckd ldr: rdn 4f out: wknd fnl 1 1/2f* **4/1[3]**

6 *23* **War Monger (USA)**[6] [605] 7-9-1 106.... RichardHills 5 80
(Doug Watson, UAE) *sn led: hdd 2f out: wknd fnl f* **10/3[2]**

2m 3.47s (123.47)
WFA 4 from 5yo+ 1lb **6** Ran SP% **110.0**
CSF: £59.01.
Owner Sheikh Mohammed Bin Khalifa Al Maktoum **Bred** Wilgerbosdrift **Trained** South Africa

FOCUS
The rail was out 15 meters on the turf course. Only six runners, they were all fully exposed and most looked too high in the weights. The pace, set by War Monger, was increased much too soon, with most of these in trouble before the long finishing straight, and all things considered, this is weak Carnival form.

NOTEBOOK
Wonder Lawn(SAF) had lost his way on his last couple of starts (beaten over 15l by stablemate Golden Sword last time), but he finally returned to form to build on the promise he showed on Tapeta on the opening night of the Carnival. He'll go up a fair bit in the weights for this and appeals as one to take on next time.
Yirga was well placed considering how the race unfolded but was always held in the straight, carrying his head a bit awkwardly under pressure. He looks one to avoid. (op 9-2, tchd 5-1)
Espiritu(FR) had the race run to suit but never threatened. His only win came in a Beverley maiden.
Hunting Tower(SAF), 3lb higher than when winning a weak race on Tapeta last time, was under strong pressure but gradually responding when almost running into the back of the weakening War Monger. He probably would have been third, or perhaps even second, with a clear run.
Lolamar(ITY) paid for chasing the overly strong gallop, although she was beaten so soon that it seems she was probably below form anyway.
War Monger(USA) defeated Yirga into second when dictating a steady pace over 1m1f the previous week, but he was up 6lb and went too fast this time. (op 7-2)

677a JAGUAR XK TROPHY (H'CAP) (TAPETA) 1m 3f

3:00 (3:00) (100-110,109) 3-Y-O+

£46,153 (£15,384; £7,692; £3,846; £2,307; £1,538)

RPR

1 **Bay Willow (IRE)**[6] [603] 4-8-8 100.... FrankieDettori 2 103+
(Saeed Bin Suroor) *mid-div: smooth prog to ld 2 1/2f out: r.o wl: comf* **11/1**

2 *2 1/2* **Meeriss (IRE)**[13] [535] 6-9-2 106....(t) WilliamBuick 3 103
(D Selvaratnam, UAE) *mid-div: rdn 4f out: r.o wl fnl 2 1/2f: nrst fin* **7/1[3]**

3 *1 1/4* **Prizefighting (USA)**[7] [585] 4-9-2 108.... MickaelBarzalona 8 103
(Mahmood Al Zarooni) *settled in rr: r.o fnl 2f but nvr able to chal* **7/2[2]**

4 *2 1/2* **Jedi**[14] [498] 5-8-11 101.... Christophe-PatriceLemaire 7 91
(A bin Huzaim, UAE) *trckd ldng pair: rdn 3 1/2f out: r.o same pce* **10/1**

5 *1 1/4* **Star Empire (SAF)**[7] [584] 5-9-5 109.... ChristopheSoumillon 5 97
(M F De Kock, South Africa) *slowly away: [illegible]* **6/4[1]**

6 *1 1/2* **Burdlaz (IRE)**[14] [498] 6-8-13 102.... AhmedAjtebi 1 88
(Mahmood Al Zarooni) *settled in rr: r.o one pce fnl 1 1/2f* **12/1**

7 *1 1/4* **Logic Way (USA)**[7] [585] 7-9-2 106....(bt) KierenFallon 6 89
(Ibrahaim Al Malki, Qatar) *trckd ldr: rdn 4 1/2f out: sn btn 2f out* **12/1**

8 *8* **Heliodor (USA)**[14] [498] 5-8-3 100....(vt) AntiocoMurgia(7) 4 69
(Mahmood Al Zarooni) *sn led: clr 7f out: hdd & wknd 2 1/2f out* **20/1**

2m 18.45s (0.05) **Going Correction** +0.30s/f (Slow)
WFA 4 from 5yo+ 2lb **8** Ran SP% **112.3**
Speed ratings: **111,109,108,106,105 104,103,97**
CSF: £81.66; Tricast: £325.37.
Owner Godolphin **Bred** Philip Brady **Trained** Newmarket, Suffolk

FOCUS
Few progressive types here; ordinary Carnival form. The pace was good, with \bHeliodor\p soon racing in a clear lead.

NOTEBOOK
Bay Willow(IRE) was behind both Burdlaz and Prizefighting over C&D on his debut for Saeed Bin Suroor in January, and didn't offer much more on turf last time, but this was more like it. He was a progressive type for Mark Johnston last year and this was an obvious step in the right direction. (op 8-1)
Meeriss(IRE) was found out by a 6lb rise for his recent Jebel Ali win.
Prizefighting(USA) has now placed on all four of his starts this year, but he looked thoroughly awkward under pressure and looks one to avoid for win-only purposes.
Jedi has unsurprisingly failed to progress since leaving Sir Michael Stoute.
Star Empire(SAF), dropped in trip and returned to Tapeta, raced well off the pace after rearing on leaving the stalls, which was far from ideal considering he's so onepaced, and could make no impression in the straight. He was a bit short of room in the closing stages, but was not unlucky. (op 13-8)

678a RANGE ROVER SPORT TROPHY (H'CAP) (TAPETA) 6f

3:40 (3:40) (95-105,105) 3-Y-O+

£42,307 (£14,102; £7,051; £3,525; £2,115; £1,410)

RPR

1 **Charlie's Moment (USA)**[117] 5-8-13 102....(t) MickaelBarzalona 2 109
(Saeed Bin Suroor) *trckd ldr: led 3 1/2f out: r.o wl: comf* **9/1**

2 *1* **Global City (IRE)**[99] [7482] 5-8-11 101....(t) FrankieDettori 6 104
(Saeed Bin Suroor) *trckd ldrs: ev ch 2 1/2f out: r.o same pce fnl 1 1/2f* **4/1[1]**

3 *nk* **Iver Bridge Lad**[6] [606] 4-8-9 102....(b) MichaelO'Connell(4) 10 105
(John Ryan) *mid-div: r.o wl fnl 1 1/2f: nrst fin* **20/1**

4 *1 1/2* **Atlantic Sport (USA)**[7] [583] 6-9-0 104....(b) KShea 3 101
(M F De Kock, South Africa) *mid-div: r.o wl fnl 2f* **7/1[3]**

5 *hd* **Orife (IRE)**[6] [602] 4-8-11 101.... GregoryBenoist 1 98
(Stephane Chevalier, UAE) *trckd ldrs on rail: nt qckn fnl 1 1/2f* **7/1[3]**

6 *1/2* **Silaah**[7] [582] 7-9-1 105....(p) AdrianNicholls 9 100
(David Nicholls) *sn led: hdd 3 1/2f out: one pce fnl 2f: wknd fnl 110yds* **4/1[1]**

7 *3* **Oasis Dancer**[6] [604] 4-8-13 102.... EJMcNamara 12 88
(Ralph Beckett) *a in mid-div* **14/1**

8 *3/4* **Monsieur Joe (IRE)**[14] [500] 4-8-13 102.... TedDurcan 5 86
(Walter Swinburn) *s.i.s: a in rr* **13/2[2]**

9 *nk* **Rain Delayed (IRE)**[14] [500] 5-8-13 102....(p) JMurtagh 4 85
(Michael Dods) *nvr nr to chal* **25/1**

10 *1 1/2* **Lipocco**[7] [582] 7-8-13 102.... WilliamBuick 8 80
(Rod Collet, France) *settled in rr: nvr able to chal* **14/1**

11 *2 3/4* **Star Crowned (USA)**[7] [582] 8-8-13 102....(t) RoystonFfrench 7 71
(R Bouresly, Kuwait) *nvr bttr than mid-div* **18/1**

12 *1 1/4* **Sir Gerry (USA)**[14] [497] 6-8-13 102.... TadhgO'Shea 11 67
(Doug Watson, UAE) *trckd ldr tl 2 1/2f out: sn btn* **16/1**

1m 11.87s (0.87) **Going Correction** +0.375s/f (Slow) **12** Ran SP% **121.4**
Speed ratings: **109,107,107,105,105 104,100,99,98,96 93,91**
CSF: £45.98; Tricast: £723.19.
Owner Godolphin **Bred** McKathan Bros **Trained** Newmarket, Suffolk

FOCUS
It paid to race prominently in this good, competitive sprint handicap.

NOTEBOOK
Charlie's Moment(USA) ◆, a Grade 3 winner on synthetics when trained in the US (has also won on dirt), showed speed to race bang on the pace and managed to get away from his rivals when finding extra at the top of the straight. This effort is particularly creditable considering he apparently didn't look great in his coat for his first run in 117 days, and there may be more to come. (op 8-1)
Global City(IRE), a stable companion of Charlie's Moment, and the choice of Frankie Dettori, was always well placed but lacked the winner's acceleration at the top of the straight. He's entitled to come on for this.
Iver Bridge Lad had been given a chance by the handicapper and showed more on his third run after a break.
Atlantic Sport(USA) was a bit short of room early in the straight, but he basically lacked the required speed when it mattered and was going on at the finish. He'll be suited by a return to further.
Orife(IRE) was below the form he showed when a close third on turf the previous week and perhaps this second run after a break came too soon.
Silaah ran a bit freely and didn't see his race out.

679a JAGUAR XJ TROPHY (H'CAP) (TAPETA) 1m 1f 110y

4:15 (4:15) (95-105,105) 3-Y-O+

£42,307 (£14,102; £7,051; £3,525; £2,115; £1,410)

RPR

1 **Mufarrh (IRE)**[7] [583] 4-8-13 102.... RichardHills 14 113+
(A Al Raihe, UAE) *trckd ldrs: rdn to ld 2f out: r.o wl: comf* **7/1[2]**

2 *4 1/2* **Sahara Kingdom (IRE)**[14] [503] 4-9-0 104.... FrankieDettori 6 105
(Saeed Bin Suroor) *mid-div: chsd ldrs 3f out: r.o wl fnl 1 1/2f but no ch w wnr* **15/2[3]**

3 *hd* **Solid Choice (AUS)**[6] [606] 5-9-1 104.... ChristopheSoumillon 13 105+
(M F De Kock, South Africa) *settled in rr: r.o wl fnl 2f: nrst fin* **8/1**

4 *1/2* **Sweet Lightning**[14] [499] 6-9-1 104.... JMurtagh 8 104
(Michael Dods) *mid-div: chsd ldrs 2f out: one pce fnl 1 1/2f* **7/2[1]**

5 *1 3/4* **Honour System (IRE)**[28] [330] 4-8-10 100.... MickaelBarzalona 11 96
(Saeed Bin Suroor) *settled in rr: r.o wl fnl 2f* **16/1**

6 *shd* **Persiste Et Signe (FR)**[14] [499] 4-8-11 101.... [illegible]
[illegible] *2f out: one pce fnl f* **10/1**

7 *1* **Jalil (USA)**[6] [608] 7-9-0 102....(t) AhmedAjtebi 5 97
(Mahmood Al Zarooni) *trckd ldrs: ev ch 2 1/2f out: r.o same pce* **12/1**

8 *1/4* **Inestimable**[6] [605] 6-8-11 100....(v) WayneSmith 10 93
(M Al Muhairi, UAE) *settled in rr: mod prog fnl 2f* **14/1**

9 *3/4* **Royal Destination (IRE)**[14] [499] 6-9-2 105....(v) KierenFallon 3 97
(F Nass, Bahrain) *a in mid-div* **9/1**

10 *1 1/2* **Glen Nevis (USA)**[14] [499] 7-8-11 100....(v) RoystonFfrench 7 89
(A Al Raihe, UAE) *nvr able to chal* **10/1**

11 *1/2* **Rochdale**[14] [499] 8-8-11 100....(t) WilliamBuick 1 88
(A Al Raihe, UAE) *in rr of mid-div: n.d* **16/1**

12 *1/4* **Separate Ways (IRE)**[14] [503] 6-8-13 101....(b) ShaneFoley 12 89
(David Marnane, Ire) *nvr able to chal* **25/1**

13 *1 1/4* **Bon Grain (FR)**[7] [581] 6-8-11 100.... PatCosgrave 4 84
(M bin Shafya, UAE) *nvr bttr than mid-div* **25/1**

14 *11* **Dear Bela (ARG)**[14] [499] 5-8-11 100.... TedDurcan 2 62
(Saeed Bin Suroor) *sn led: hdd 2 1/2f out: sn btn* **25/1**

1m 58.73s (0.03) **Going Correction** +0.30s/f (Slow) **14** Ran SP% **123.4**
Speed ratings: **111,107,107,106,105 105,104,104,103,102 102,101,100,92**
CSF: £58.93; Tricast: £430.72.
Owner Hamdan Al Maktoum **Bred** Kenilworth House Stud **Trained** UAE

FOCUS
Ordinary form by Carnival standards and they didn't go that quick.

NOTEBOOK
Mufarrh(IRE), the winner of a non-Carnival handicap off 8lb lower on his penultimate start, improved for the step up in trip, the furthest he's tried to date. This isn't strong form, but he's unexposed at around this sort of distance. (op 13-2)
Sahara Kingdom(IRE) was suited by the return to Tapeta, though he hadn't been shaping as though in need of this step up in distance. He ran respectably, but was onepaced under pressure and it's questionable whether this longer trip was in his favour. (op 7-1)
Solid Choice(AUS), upped from 7f, was set far too much to do in a race where few made up significant amounts of ground. The way he stayed on suggests he'll be worth another go at this sort of trip. (op 15-2)
Sweet Lightning, runner-up to the improving Golden Sword in a C&D handicap last time, confirmed form with all of those who were behind him that day and re-opposed, but that doesn't disguise what was a slightly disappointing performance.

Honour System(IRE) was similarly poorly placed to Solid Choice and kept on reasonably well out wide in the straight. He'll be third off the layoff next time and should be capable of a bit better.

680a MEYDAN CLASSIC SPONSORED BY AL TAYER MOTORS (LISTED RACE) (TURF) 1m

4:55 (4:55) 3-Y-O

£57,692 (£19,230; £9,615; £4,807; £2,884; £1,923)

			RPR
1		**Introvert (IRE)**[21] 411 3-8-7 90 ... AhmedAjtebi 8 (Mahmood Al Zarooni) *in rr of mid-div: chsd ldrs 2 1/2f out: r.o wl: led 1f out: comf* **5/1**[2]	97
2	3 1/4	**Ahlaain (USA)**[21] 411 3-8-9 99 ow2 ... WilliamBuick 3 (David Simcock) *slowly away: settled in rr: r.o wl fnl 2f: nrst fin* **11/1**	92
3	1/4	**Lord Of The Stars (USA)**[21] 411 3-8-7 100 ... TadhgO'Shea 11 (David Simcock) *trckd ldr: led 2f out: hdd 1f out: r.o same pce* **5/1**[2]	89
4	shd	**Rosina Grey**[134] 6842 3-8-3 85 ... HarryBentley 7 (S Seemar, UAE) *mid-div: r.o wl fnl 1 1/2f but nvr able to chal* **25/1**	85
5	1/4	**Janood (IRE)**[35] 238 3-8-8 100 ow1 ...(vt) FrankieDettori 5 (Saeed Bin Suroor) *trckd ldng duo: ev ch 1 1/2f out: one pce fnl f* **9/4**[1]	89
6	3/4	**Krypton Factor**[14] 502 3-8-7 100 ...(b) KierenFallon 4 (F Nass, Bahrain) *trckd ldng duo: ev ch 2f out: one pce fnl f* **13/2**[3]	86
7	1/2	**Calling Elvis (BRZ)**[21] 411 4-9-4 97 ... Christophe-PatriceLemaire 2 (A De Royer-Dupre, France) *settled in rr: nvr able to chal but r.o fnl 2f* **20/1**	89
8	3 1/4	**Sonoran Sands (IRE)**[14] 502 3-8-7 95 ...(p) TedDurcan 10 (J S Moore) *nvr bttr than mid-div* **20/1**	78
9	5	**Crying Lightening (IRE)**[21] 412 3-8-3 104 ... MickaelBarzalona 6 (Peter Chapple-Hyam) *sn led: hdd & wknd 2f out* **14/1**	62
10	1 1/2	**Manchester (FR)**[130] 6972 3-8-7 102 ...(t) Per-AndersGraberg 1 (Niels Petersen, Norway) *slowly away: nvr able to chal* **9/1**	63
11	1 1/4	**Energia Colonial (BRZ)**[35] 238 4-9-4 90 ... RichardMullen 9 (E Martins, Brazil) *in rr of mid-div: n.d* **25/1**	64

1m 37.99s (97.99)
WFA 3 from 4yo 19lb **11 Ran SP% 119.7**
CSF: £56.00.
Owner Sheikh Majid Bin Mohammed al Maktoum **Bred** Mrs T Marnane **Trained** Newmarket, Suffolk

FOCUS

The third running of this race and Listed status for the first time, upgraded from conditions class. It wasn't a strong contest and a quick gallop favoured those ridden with patience. The time was 0.38 seconds slower than the 101-rated Navajo Chief recored later on the card.

NOTEBOOK

Introvert(IRE) finished well off a steady pace when third behind Lord Of The Stars and Krypton Factor in the trial over 7f and he confirmed that promise upped in trip, the much quicker gallop very much in his favour. He's an improved colt this year and may be a suitable type for a European classic - last year's winner Frozen Power subsequently landed the German Guineas.

Ahlaain(USA) missed the break, but that probably wasn't a bad thing considering the quick pace. He stayed on out wide in the straight, but it looked hard work and he didn't improve much on the form he showed in the trial.

Lord Of The Stars(USA) had the run of the race when winning the trial, but that certainly wasn't the case this time. He wasn't able to dominate, and was a bit free on the pace, yet he stayed on to fare best of those prominent.

Rosina Grey was last seen winning a 6f Polytrack claimer for Rod Millman, when she didn't look an easy ride, but she had earlier been highly tried, finishing down the field in the Oh So Sharp Stakes (third in that race was subsequent UAE Oaks winner Khawlah). Sold for 17,000gns in October, she ran a fine race, just missing out on some black type.

Janood(IRE), fourth in the UAE 2,000 Guineas trial on his only previous start this year, had a tongue-tie and blinkers added for this switch to turf and step up in trip, but he disappointed. He wasn't help by chasing the quick pace and finished tamely. (op 5-2)

Krypton Factor would have been a bit closer with a clearer run, but he's fully exposed.

681a UAE OAKS SPONSORED BY AL TAYER MOTORS (GROUP 3) (FILLIES) (TAPETA) 1m 1f 110y

5:35 (5:35) 3-Y-O

£96,153 (£32,051; £16,025; £8,012; £4,807; £3,205)

			RPR
1		**Khawlah (IRE)**[146] 6528 3-8-8 95 ... FrankieDettori 5 (Saeed Bin Suroor) *trckd ldr: rdn to ld 2f out: r.o wl: hld on gamely* **9/2**[2]	106+
2	1 1/4	**Mahbooba (AUS)**[21] 412 4-9-4 112 ... ChristopheSoumillon 3 (M F De Kock, South Africa) *mid-div: smooth prog 2 1/2f out: n.m.r 2f out: r.o same pce fnl f* **1/3**[1]	107
3	8 1/4	**Electric Waves (IRE)**[138] 6734 3-8-8 106 ... RichardMullen 4 (Naif Alatawi, Saudi Arabia) *s.i.s: settled in rr: t.k.h: r.o fnl 2f* **16/1**[3]	87
4	3 1/2	**Quick Val (ARG)**[21] 412 4-9-4 95 ... JMurtagh 7 (H J Brown, South Africa) *trckd ldrs: rdn 2 1/2f out: sn btn* **33/1**	83
5	3	**Empire Rose (ARG)**[21] 412 4-9-4 100 ... KShea 6 (M F De Kock, South Africa) *in rr of mid-div: rdn 3 1/2f out: sn btn* **20/1**	77
6	4 1/4	**Amica (SAF)**[21] 412 4-9-4 87 ... RoystonFfrench 1 (Gay Kelleway) *in rr of mid-div: n.d* **80/1**	68
7	1 1/2	**Abtasaamah (USA)**[21] 412 3-8-8 100 ... TedDurcan 2 (Saeed Bin Suroor) *sn led: hdd & wknd 2f out* **20/1**	61

1m 58.51s (-0.19) **Going Correction** +0.30s/f (Slow)
WFA 3 from 4yo 21lb **7 Ran SP% 112.8**
Speed ratings: **112,111,104,101,99 95,94**
CSF: £6.25.
Owner Godolphin **Bred** Darley **Trained** Newmarket, Suffolk

FOCUS

The 11th running of the UAE Oaks, promoted from Listed class to Group 3 level for the first time. They went a good pace thanks to the non-staying Abtasaamah, a stablemate of the winner, and the time was 0.22 seconds quicker than the 102-rated 4-y-o Mufarrh managed earlier on the card. Only two serious contenders, but they're both smart types and finished clear.

NOTEBOOK

Khawlah(IRE) ◆ recorded a seventh victory in the race for Saeed Bin Suroor, causing a minor upset. The winner defeated Mahbooba fair and square, showing that bit more speed than the odds-on favourite. Saeed Bin Suroor's filly won a Newmarket maiden over 1m on her second start last year, before finishing third in the Oh So Sharp Stakes when dropped to 7f for her final juvenile outing, and this was an improved effort on her return. The surface wasn't an issue and she was well suited by the step up in trip, as her breeding suggested (dam 1m2f-1m3f winner). Her performance paid a handsome compliment to the two fillies she finished behind when last seen, namely the winner Havant, who's prominent in the betting for both the English Guineas and Oaks, and runner-up Look At Me, an interesting dark horse for the Newmarket contest. Next stop for the Godolphin filly is apparently the Musidora, and if she does indeed go straight there it could be seen as a fair pointer that Godolphin think she has a real chance of further Oaks success at Epsom. She's 20-1 (from 33-1) with Stan James, but still 33-1 with Coral, and that's probably too big.

Mahbooba(AUS) could have settled better, but that was no real excuse; she was just beaten by a better rival. Time may show she was up against a really decent type, but even so, this performance seems to suggest the Mike De Kock runner is nothing special. That said, she'll still be worth her place in the UAE Derby.

Electric Waves(IRE), despite refusing to settle, won the separate contest for third, although she was nowhere near her official mark of 106. She was last seen winning the Group 3 Cornwallis over 5f for Ed McMahon (sold out of that yard for 200,000gns), and had never previously raced over any further, but she didn't achieve much at all here.

Quick Val(ARG) again offered nothing.

Empire Rose(ARG) didn't build on her Guineas effort.

682a RANGE ROVER TROPHY (H'CAP) (TURF) 1m

6:15 (6:15) (100-113,113) 3-Y-O+

£67,307 (£22,435; £11,217; £5,608; £3,365; £2,243)

			RPR
1		**Navajo Chief**[7] 587 4-8-1 101 ... HarryBentley[(7)] 4 (Alan Jarvis) *sn led: hdd 1 1/2f out: led again 110yds out: r.o wl: jst hld on* **9/1**	102
2	shd	**Kavango (IRE)**[7] 583 4-8-10 104 ... PatCosgrave 5 (M bin Shafya, UAE) *mid-div: chsd ldrs 2f out: r.o wl: jst failed* **8/1**	104
3	3/4	**Fareer**[6] 604 5-8-13 106 ...(v) RichardHills 2 (Ed Dunlop) *in rr of mid-div: chsd ldrs 2 1/2f out: ev ch 1f out: one pce fnl 55yds* **15/2**	105
4	3/4	**Munaddam (USA)**[7] 587 9-8-7 100 ... WJSupple 1 (E Charpy, UAE) *chsd ldrs: led 1 1/2f out: hdd 110yds out: wknd* **25/1**	97
5	1	**Swop (IRE)**[7] 587 8-8-7 100 ... KierenFallon 11 (Luca Cumani) *racd in rr: rdn 2 1/2f out: r.o wl: nrst fin* **4/1**[1]	95
6	1 1/4	**Iguazu Falls (USA)**[14] 503 6-8-7 100 ...(t) XZiani 8 (M bin Shafya, UAE) *trckd ldr: nt qckn fnl f* **20/1**	92
7	3/4	**Hujaylea (IRE)**[7] 587 8-8-3 104 ...(p) CPHoban[(7)] 10 (M Halford, Ire) *settled in rr: nvr able to chal* **7/1**[3]	93
8	1/4	**Warsaw (IRE)**[7] 587 6-9-0 107 ...(b) KShea 7 (M F De Kock, South Africa) *a in mid-div* **6/1**[2]	97
9	1/2	**Sea Lord (IRE)**[28] 331 4-9-6 113 ... AhmedAjtebi 9 (Mahmood Al Zarooni) *nvr bttr than mid-div* **12/1**	102
10	1/2	**Finjaan**[7] 586 5-8-10 104 ... TadhgO'Shea 6 (Doug Watson, UAE) *s.i.s: settled in rr: nvr able to chal* **14/1**	90
11	3/4	**Mahubo (SAF)**[7] 587 5-8-8 101 ... JamieSpencer 12 (M F De Kock, South Africa) *a in rr of mid-div* **7/1**[3]	87
12	1 3/4	**Colonial (IRE)**[21] 415 4-9-2 109 ... FrankieDettori 3 (Saeed Bin Suroor) *mid-div tl 2 1/2f out: wknd qckly* **12/1**	91

1m 37.61s (97.61) **12 Ran SP% 122.8**
CSF: £82.16; Tricast: £580.4. Placepot: £831.50 to a £1 stake. Pool: £7,689.18 - 6.75 winning tickets. Quadpot: £31.00 to a £1 stake. Pool: £1,045.82 - 24.90 winning tickets..
Owner Geoffrey Bishop **Bred** Eurostrait Ltd **Trained** Twyford, Bucks

FOCUS

No progressive types, but this was still a good, competitive handicap. The pace seemed fair and the time was 0.38 seconds quicker than the earlier Meydan Classic, although few of those held up managed to get involved.

NOTEBOOK

Navajo Chief made the running but was passed halfway up the straight, at which point he looked held, but he proved particularly determined and stayed on strongly to get back in front in the final strides. He was a bit disappointing when behind a few of these over 7f here last time, but he was ridden by a professional that day, and the combination of the return of 7lb claimer Harry Bentley and a step up in trip clearly did the trick.

Kavango(IRE), just ahead of Mufarrh (winner earlier on the card) over C&D the previous week, had to settle for his third consecutive second placing, losing out on the nod.

Fareer has worked his way back to form and this was another encouraging enough performance, faring best of those held up. (op 7-1)

Munaddam(USA) was in front just inside the final furlong but he couldn't sustain his effort and failed to even hold on for a place.

Swop(IRE) finished ahead of Navajo Chief over 7f here the previous week, but was disappointing to varying degrees.

Hujaylea(IRE) was another that finished ahead of Navajo Chief over 7f here the previous week, and never got involved.

Mahubo(SAF) failed to get into the race having been held up. (op 13-2)

653 LINGFIELD (L-H)

Friday, February 25

OFFICIAL GOING: Standard

Wind: medium, behind Weather: dry

683 TODAY'S JOCKEY SPECIALS AT BLUESQ.COM H'CAP 6f (P)

2:00 (2:00) (Class 6) (0-60,60) 4-Y-O+ **£1,535** (£453; £226) **Stalls** Low

Form				RPR
060-	1		**Far View (IRE)**[122] 7153 4-8-13 55 ...(tp) MatthewDavies[(3)] 10 (George Baker) *mde all: rdn over 1f out: kpt on u.p ins fnl f* **15/8**[1]	68+
3000	2	3/4	**Loyal Royal (IRE)**[20] 435 8-9-5 58 ...(bt) RichardKingscote 6 (Milton Bradley) *t.k.h: chsd wnr after 1f: rdn over 1f out: kpt on steadily ins fnl f: nvr looked like getting to wnr* **10/1**	68
3206	3	2 1/4	**Misaro (GER)**[14] 511 10-9-5 58 ...(b) TomMcLaughlin 7 (Ronald Harris) *racd wd: hdwy to chse ldrs over 3f out: 3rd and outpcd ent fnl 2f: one pce and a hld after* **11/2**[3]	61
6124	4	hd	**Radiator Rooney (IRE)**[28] 345 8-8-10 54 ... RyanPowell[(5)] 5 (Patrick Morris) *stdd s: t.k.h: dashed up into midfield over 4f out: rdn and unable qck ent fnl 2f: kpt on same pce and no threat to ldrs after* **11/2**[3]	57
550-	5	1/2	**Espy**[57] 8019 6-9-5 58 ... PJMcDonald 2 (Ian McInnes) *t.k.h: hld up in rr: hdwy u.p over 1f out: kpt on u.p ins fnl f: nvr trbld ldrs* **16/1**	59
0004	6	1	**White Shift (IRE)**[15] 487 5-9-0 56 ... KierenFox[(3)] 3 (Jane Chapple-Hyam) *hld up towards rr: wd bnd and rdn 2f out: styd on ins fnl f: nvr trbld ldrs* **9/1**	54
0433	7	nk	**Silver Wind**[16] 467 6-9-2 55 ...(v) ShaneKelly 1 (Alan McCabe) *broke wl: chsd ldr for 1f: hmpd and lost pl over 4f out: bhd and rdn 3f out: plugged on fr over 1f out: no threat to ldrs* **9/2**[2]	52
000-	8	9	**Calabaza**[180] 5557 9-8-7 46 oh1 ...(p) KirstyMilczarek 4 (Michael Attwater) *chsd ldrs tl rdn and wknd qckly 2f out: wl bhd ins fnl f* **66/1**	16
000-	9	7	**Brunelleschi**[203] 4806 8-9-0 60 ... JosephineBruning[(7)] 11 (Patrick Gilligan) *a towards rr: rdn and wknd ent fnl 2f: wl bhd ins fnl f* **25/1**	9

1m 11.6s (-0.30) **Going Correction** +0.075s/f (Slow) **9 Ran SP% 114.0**
Speed ratings (Par 101): **105,104,101,100,100 98,98,86,77**
toteswingers:1&2 £6.40, 2&3 £9.50, 1&3 £5.90 CSF £22.04 CT £87.89 TOTE £3.20: £1.80, £2.80, £2.80; EX 32.20 Trifecta £222.40 Pool: £492.90 - 1.64 winning units..

Owner M Khan X2 **Bred** Mr & Mrs G Middlebrook **Trained** Whitsbury, Hants
■ Stewards' Enquiry : Shane Kelly three-day ban; careless riding (11th, 12th and 15th March)

FOCUS
Few got into this low-grade sprint. The time was respectable, a second outside the standard. The winner is improving and the runner-up sets the level.
Silver Wind Official explanation: jockey said gelding suffered interference in running

684 CROWHURST MEDIAN AUCTION MAIDEN STKS 1m (P)
2:30 (2:30) (Class 6) 3-4-Y-O **£1,535** (£453; £226) **Stalls** High

Form RPR

1 **Loch Fleet (IRE)** 3-8-5 0 .... SimonPearce(3) 7 74+
(Andrew Balding) *hld up in tch: hdwy on outer to press ldr over 2f out: rdn to ld over 1f out: styd on wl and forged ahd ins fnl f* **15/8**[1]

45 **2** *2* **Full Bloom**[28] 344 3-8-3 0 .... NickyMackay 9 64
(Gerard Butler) *in tch: rdn to ld over 2f out: drvn wl over 1f out: hdd over 1f out: styd on same pce ins fnl f* **15/2**

3 *2 ½* **Mutamaleq (IRE)**[173] 5795 4-9-13 75 .... PJMcDonald 2 69
(Ian McInnes) *led tl 6f out: chsd ldrs after tl rdn and outpcd by ldng pair 2f out: edgd lft but kpt on ins fnl f: nvr gng pce to trble ldrs* **5/1**

50- **4** *5* **Crinan Classic**[286] 2122 4-9-13 0 .... AdamKirby 10 58
(Clive Cox) *chsd ldrs tl led 6f out tl rdn and hdd over 2f out: outpcd by ldng pair 2f out: wknd over 1f out* **9/2**[3]

000 **5** *1 ¼* **Bellaboolou**[7] 600 3-8-3 0 ....(t) HayleyTurner 4 44
(David Pinder) *w ldr for 2f: chsd ldrs after tl struggling u.p over 2f out: wl btn over 1f out* **100/1**

-020 **6** *2* **Kassiodor (GER)**[21] 428 4-9-13 62 .... ShaneKelly 8 50
(Barney Curley) *t.k.h: hld up in tch on outer: hdwy to join ldr 5f out tl over 2f out: sn wknd* **14/1**

7 *5* **Hector The Brave (IRE)** 4-9-13 0 .... SamHitchcott 3 39
(John E Long) *in tch in midfield: rdn along over 4f out: struggling and outpcd 3f out: no ch fnl 2f* **40/1**

0- **8** *5* **Ede'Sajolygoodfelo**[144] 6635 3-8-3 0 .... JemmaMarshall(5) 1 21
(Pat Phelan) *in tch towards rr: rdn and dropped into last trio over 5f out: clsd briefly over 3f out: sn lost tch again* **66/1**

04- **9** *nk* **Come On The Irons (USA)**[154] 6333 3-8-8 0 .... JamieGoldstein 5 21
(Ralph Smith) *v awkward leaving stalls and v.s.a: a in last pair: clsd briefly over 3f out: sn lost tch again* **4/1**[2]

10 *2* **La Bambagini** 4-9-3 0 .... KylieManser(5) 6 17
(Olivia Maylam) *v awkward leaving stalls and slowly away: rn green and a struggling in rr* **66/1**

1m 37.99s (-0.21) **Going Correction** +0.075s/f (Slow)
WFA 3 from 4yo 19lb **10** Ran SP% **114.5**
Speed ratings (Par 101): **104,102,99,94,93 91,86,81,80,78**
toteswingers:1&2 £4.10, 2&3 £5.50, 1&3 £3.70 CSF £16.57 TOTE £3.50: £1.30, £2.30, £1.60; EX 14.50 Trifecta £110.60 Pool: £514.60 - 3.44 winning units..
Owner Mick and Janice Mariscotti **Bred** John Malone **Trained** Kingsclere, Hants

FOCUS
Little strength in depth in this ordinary maiden. The form is rated around the placed horses.
Kassiodor(GER) Official explanation: jockey said gelding ran too free
Come On The Irons(USA) Official explanation: jockey said colt jumped awkwardly and ran in snatches and did not face kickback

685 HOLLOW LANE H'CAP 1m (P)
3:05 (3:05) (Class 5) (0-70,70) 4-Y-0+ **£2,047** (£604; £302) **Stalls** High

Form RPR

6-43 **1** **Chief Exec**[16] 473 9-9-4 67 .... GeorgeBaker 2 75
(Jeremy Gask) *hld up towards rr: hdwy to trck ldrs on inner ent fnl 2f: rdn and qcknd between horses to ld 1f out: sn drvn and asserted: r.o wl and in command fnl 75yds* **9/2**[3]

3345 **2** *1* **Lisahane Bog**[9] 565 4-9-7 70 ....(p) DaneO'Neill 5 76
(Peter Hedger) *s.i.s and bustled along early: hdwy into midfield 5f out: rdn and effrt wd on bnd ent fnl 2f: styd on wl ins fnl f: nvr gng pce to chal wnr* **7/1**

-561 **3** *nk* **Peadar Miguel**[8] 502 4-9-6 65 6ex .... AdamKirby 10 74
(Noel Quinlan) *stdd and dropped in bhd after s: t.k.h: hld up in last pair: rdn and hdwy jst over 1f out: r.o ins fnl f: nvr looked like rching wnr* **7/2**[1]

304- **4** *½* **Sunshine Always (IRE)**[171] 5834 5-9-2 70 .... JemmaMarshall(5) 8 78+
(Michael Attwater) *t.k.h: hld up wl in tch: trckd ldrs gng wl whn nt clr run wl over 1f out tl 1f out: rdn and kpt on ins fnl f: nvr able to threaten wnr* **8/1**

00-3 **5** *½* **Tuscan King**[53] 21 4-8-13 62 ....(tp) NeilCallan 3 65
(Bernard Llewellyn) *chsd ldrs: rdn over 2f out: ev ch on inner ent fnl f: nt gng pce of wnr ins fnl f: lost 3 pls wl ins fnl f* **14/1**

3010 **6** *shd* **Aflaam (IRE)**[9] 562 6-9-5 68 ....(tp) TomMcLaughlin 9 70
(Ronald Harris) *pressed ldrs: ev ch 2f out: drvn ent fnl f: wknd u.p fnl 100yds* **12/1**

3633 **7** *¾* **Ilie Nastase (FR)**[9] 562 7-9-5 68 .... HayleyTurner 7 70
(Conor Dore) *t.k.h: hld up in tch: rdn and effrt over 1f out: n.m.r fnl f: nvr able to chal: nt pushed towards fin* **8/1**

2150 **8** *1 ½* **Unbreak My Heart (IRE)**[16] 475 6-9-1 67 ....(p) RobertLButler(3) 4 64
(Paddy Butler) *hld up in tch in rr: rdn and effrt towards inner over 1f out: styd on ins fnl f: nvr trbld ldrs* **66/1**

1440 **9** *½* **Justcallmehandsome**[9] 562 9-9-2 65 ....(be) JamesDoyle 1 61
(Dominic Ffrench Davis) *led: rdn ent fnl 2f: hdd 1f out: sn wknd* **20/1**

-623 **10** *1 ¼* **Indian Violet (IRE)**[9] 565 5-8-13 62 .... JamieGoldstein 6 55
(Sheena West) *w ldr: ev ch and rdn wl over 1f: unable qck u.p over 1f out: wknd ins fnl f* **4/1**[2]

1m 38.38s (0.18) **Going Correction** +0.075s/f (Slow) **10** Ran SP% **115.7**
Speed ratings (Par 103): **102,101,100,100,99 99,98,97,96,95**
toteswingers:1&2 £6.90, 2&3 £6.40, 1&3 £3.30 CSF £35.79 CT £125.78 TOTE £6.50: £2.70, £3.80, £1.30; EX 38.60 Trifecta £334.80 Pool: £651.66 - 1.44 winning units..
Owner Stuart Dobb & Miss Kate Dobb **Bred** C A Cyzer **Trained** Sutton Veny, Wilts

FOCUS
A modest handicap and a bit of a messy race, although the pace was generous enough. The form looks straightforward and solid, rated around the placed horses.
Sunshine Always(IRE) Official explanation: jockey said gelding was denied a clear run
Indian Violet(IRE) Official explanation: trainer said gelding lost a right fore shoe

686 GRUNDFOS WATERMILL CLAIMING STKS 1m 2f (P)
3:40 (3:41) (Class 6) 3-Y-O **£1,535** (£453; £226) **Stalls** Low

Form RPR

0-41 **1** **Malice Or Mischief (IRE)**[6] 609 3-9-3 77 .... NeilCallan 4 78+
(Tony Carroll) *chsd ldng pair tl hdwy to press ldr over 2f out: pushed into ld over 1f out: pushed out and in command ins fnl f* **4/7**[1]

4-51 **2** *2* **George Woolf**[21] 424 3-9-5 68 .... JamesDoyle 3 73
(Alan McCabe) *stdd s: hld up in last: rdn and effrt over 2f out: kpt on u.p ins fnl f to go 2nd wl ins fnl f: no threat to wnr* **6/1**[3]

-123 **3** *½* **Paco Belle (IRE)**[36] 227 3-8-8 65 .... EddieAhern 1 61
(Richard Hannon) *led for 1f: chsd ldr after tl led again over 2f out: rdn 2f out: hdd over 1f out: styd on same pce ins fnl f: lost 2nd wl ins fnl f* **7/2**[2]

4241 **4** *½* **Ad Vitam (IRE)**[13] 527 3-8-6 60 ....(tp) FrannyNorton 2 58
(Bernard Llewellyn) *t.k.h: chsd ldr tl led after 1f: hdd and rdn over 2f out: hmpd bnd ent fnl 2f: styd on same pce fr over 1f out* **16/1**

2m 9.89s (3.29) **Going Correction** +0.075s/f (Slow) **4** Ran SP% **106.0**
Speed ratings (Par 95): **89,87,87,86**
CSF £4.18 TOTE £1.80; EX 4.50.
Owner Bill Adams **Bred** Kilnamoragh Stud **Trained** Cropthorne, Worcs
■ Stewards' Enquiry : Eddie Ahern two-day ban; careless riding (11th-12th March)

FOCUS
An ordinary claimer. The pace was fairly steady and the race only really took shape on the approach to the home turn. The time was nearly six seconds outside the standard and it not form to trust implicitly.

687 DOWNLOAD THE BLUE SQUARE IPHONE APP FILLIES' H'CAP 1m 2f (P)
4:15 (4:17) (Class 5) (0-70,69) 4-Y-0+ **£2,047** (£604; £302) **Stalls** Low

Form RPR

2U6- **1** **Fashionable Gal (IRE)**[87] 7642 4-9-4 66 .... EddieAhern 8 75
(Neil King) *t.k.h: chsd ldrs: rdn to chse ldng pair wl over 1f out: chal ins fnl f: r.o wl to ld nr fin* **10/1**

/1-1 **2** *nk* **The Blue Dog (IRE)**[7] 588 4-8-10 58 .... NickyMackay 3 66
(Mark Rimmer) *chsd ldr tl rdn to ld narrowly 2f out: kpt battling on wl tl hdd and no ex nr fin* **9/2**[3]

23-3 **3** *nk* **Red Willow**[23] 391 5-8-8 55 .... SamHitchcott 9 63
(John E Long) *sn led: rdn and narrowly hdd 2f out: battled on gamely and ev ch after tl no ex wl ins fnl f* **12/1**

666 **4** *4* **Fedora (IRE)**[16] 473 5-8-13 60 ....(t) HayleyTurner 5 60
(Olivia Maylam) *stdd s: hld up in rr: rdn and effrt wl over 1f out: no ch w ldng trio but kpt on to go 4th ins fnl f* **16/1**

53-1 **5** *¾* **Adoyen Spice**[32] 278 4-9-1 63 .... NeilCallan 4 62
(Mike Murphy) *t.k.h: hld up towards rr on outer: rdn and effrt bnd ent fnl 2f: no imp and no threat to ldrs fr over 1f out* **5/2**[1]

-200 **6** *½* **Dilys Maud**[9] 553 4-8-10 58 ....(b) RobertHavlin 7 56
(Roger Ingram) *hld up towards rr: hdwy into midfield 6f out: clsd on outer to chse ldng pair over 2f out: rdn and unable qck ent fnl 2f: 4th and wl btn 1f out* **25/1**

-524 **7** *nk* **Atacama Sunrise**[9] 553 5-8-10 60 .... KierenFox(3) 1 57
(George Prodromou) *hld up in tch in midfield: nt clr run on inner and shuffled bk to rr wl over 2f out: rdn and styd on same pce fr wl over 1f out* **13/2**

6-01 **8** *¾* **Buona Sarah (IRE)**[16] 475 4-9-7 69 .... JamesDoyle 6 65+
(Sheena West) *hld up in tch: rdn and unable qck ent fnl 2f: wknd over 1f out* **3/1**[2]

-545 **9** *2* **Emerald Girl (IRE)**[7] 590 4-9-3 68 .... RobertLButler(3) 2 60
(Paddy Butler) *chsd ldrs tl rdn and struggling over 2f out: wknd u.p over 1f out* **50/1**

2m 8.18s (1.58) **Going Correction** +0.075s/f (Slow)
WFA 4 from 5yo 1lb **9** Ran SP% **113.6**
Speed ratings (Par 100): **96,95,95,92,91 91,91,90,88**
toteswingers:1&2 £7.50, 2&3 £5.30, 1&3 £13.70 CSF £53.64 CT £548.58 TOTE £14.20: £4.00, £1.10, £2.30; EX 62.80 Trifecta £748.90 Part won. Pool of £1012.14 - 0.20 winning units..
Owner John Webb & Neil King **Bred** B D Burnett **Trained** Newmarket, Suffolk

FOCUS
A modest handicap for fillies. The pace was steady and those who were held up towards the back could not get into it. The first three came clear with the winner to her best for her previous trainer and the third to recent form.
Buona Sarah(IRE) Official explanation: jockey said filly lost left hind shoe

688 LINGFIELD PARK OWNERS CLUB MAIDEN STKS 1m 4f (P)
4:45 (4:49) (Class 5) 4-Y-0+ **£1,910** (£564; £282) **Stalls** Low

Form RPR

2 **1** **Wily Fox**[14] 516 4-9-3 75 .... JackMitchell 11 62+
(James Eustace) *t.k.h early: chsd ldrs: rdn and effrt on outer to ld 2f out: edgd lft over 1f out: styd on wl ins fnl f* **9/4**[2]

3 **2** *2 ¼* **King Kieren (IRE)**[9] 563 6-9-6 0 .... EddieAhern 2 58
(Linda Jewell) *in tch in midfield: rdn and effrt in 6th 2f out: swtchd rt over 1f out: plugged on u.p to chse wnr fnl 100yds: no imp* **8/1**[3]

000- **3** *1* **Prince Blue**[82] 7716 4-9-3 40 .... SamHitchcott 8 56
(John E Long) *chsd ldr for 2f: hung rt bnd 9f out: chsd ldr again 7f out: ev ch u.p ent fnl 2f: unable qck over 1f out: plugged on same pce ins fnl f* **50/1**

4 *1 ¼* **River Taff** 4-9-3 0 .... RobertHavlin 4 54+
(Roger Ingram) *stdd s: hld up in tch towards rr: rdn and effrt to chse ldng trio ent fnl 2f: styd on same pce fr over 1f out* **8/1**[3]

5 *1 ¼* **Allez Les Rouges (IRE)**[55] 4-9-3 0 .... MartinDwyer 1 52+
(Andrew Balding) *chsd ldrs tl led 10f out: rdn and hdd 2f out: wknd ent fnl f* **11/8**[1]

6 *8* **Miles Of Sunshine**[12] 6-9-6 0 .... GeorgeBaker 12 40
(Ron Hodges) *hld up in tch in rr: rdn and short-lived effrt over 2f out: sn btn: no ch fr wl over 1f out* **20/1**

6 **7** *nk* **El'Wringo**[11] 539 7-9-6 0 .... JamesMillman 9 39
(Rod Millman) *t.k.h: hld up in tch: rdn and struggling wl over 2f out: no ch fnl 2f* **33/1**

-633 **8** *1 ¼* **Sirdave**[8] 569 5-9-6 53 .... TomMcLaughlin 3 37
(Peter Hiatt) *sn bustled along to ld: hdd 10f out: chsd ldr tl 7f out: styd handy tl wknd u.p wl over 1f out: wl btn ins fnl f* **20/1**

9 *½* **Bearneen Boy (IRE)**[38] 8-9-6 0 .... HayleyTurner 10 36
(Neil King) *s.i.s: a bhd: toiling u.p wl over 2f out: sn wl bhd* **25/1**

2m 33.15s (0.15) **Going Correction** +0.075s/f (Slow)
WFA 4 from 5yo+ 3lb **9** Ran SP% **113.4**
Speed ratings (Par 103): **102,100,99,99,98 92,92,91,91**
toteswingers:1&2 £2.50, 2&3 £60.20, 1&3 £30.80 CSF £17.89 TOTE £3.20: £1.70, £2.10, £6.10; EX 14.10 Trifecta £146.40 Pool: £641.18 - 3.24 winning units..
Owner Blue Peter Racing 10 **Bred** Juddmonte Farms Ltd **Trained** Newmarket, Suffolk

FOCUS
A weak maiden, confined to older horses. Three intended runners were withdrawn at the start and there was a consequent delay. The form is best rated around the first two.

Miles Of Sunshine Official explanation: jockey said gelding ran green

689 PLAY ROULETTE AT BLUESQ.COM FILLIES' H'CAP 7f (P)
5:15 (5:17) (Class 5) (0-70,70) 4-Y-0+ **£2,047** (£604; £302) **Stalls** Low

Form RPR

0-02 **1** **Ivory Silk**[13] 530 6-9-7 **70** AdamKirby 6 83
(Jeremy Gask) *stdd s: hld up in tch in rr: hdwy on outer bnd 2f out: rdn and str run to ld ins fnl f: sn clr: readily* **9/2**[2]

-011 **2** 3 ½ **Spinning Bailiwick**[15] 487 5-9-7 **70** (b) GeorgeBaker 9 74
(Gary Moore) *stdd s: hld up in tch in last pair: hdwy on outer 3f out: effrt over 1f out: rdn and kpt on ins fnl f to go 2nd fnl 75yds: no ch w wnr* **3/1**[1]

-115 **3** ¾ **Cat Hunter**[30] 307 4-9-4 **70** KierenFox(3) 8 72
(Ronald Harris) *t.k.h: in tch on outer: hdwy to join ldrs 3f out: rdn to ld narrowly 2f out: hdd ins fnl f: sn outpcd by wnr: plugged on* **5/1**[3]

-654 **4** ½ **Kai Mook**[16] 477 4-8-12 **61** (t) FergusSweeney 4 62
(Amy Weaver) *chsd ldrs: rdn and ev ch ent fnl 2f: stl ev ch tl nt gng pce of wnr and styd on same pce ins fnl f* **9/1**

0/32 **5** 3 ¼ **Timpanist (USA)**[20] 437 4-9-3 **66** NeilCallan 7 58
(Simon Dow) *wl in tch in midfield: rdn whn barging match w rivals ent fnl 2f: no imp after: wl hld and eased wl ins fnl f* **6/1**

0-66 **6** 1 ½ **Mrs Mogg**[22] 397 4-9-0 **63** (b[1]) RichardKingscote 3 51
(Tom Dascombe) *w ldr tl rdn to ld over 2f out: hdd 2f out: wknd ins fnl f* **20/1**

3402 **7** 2 ¾ **Goodbye Cash (IRE)**[7] 590 7-8-4 **56** oh1 LouisBeuzelin(3) 2 37
(Ralph Smith) *sn bustled up to ld: rdn and hdd over 2f out: wknd over 1f out: bhd ins fnl f* **14/1**

0-1U **8** *nk* **Perfect Ch'l (IRE)**[23] 394 4-9-3 **66** JamesDoyle 1 46
(Ian Wood) *in tch on inner: barging match w rivals and nt clr run ent fnl 2f: rdn and no hdwy over 1f out: wl hld and eased wl ins fnl f* **9/2**[2]

1m 24.31s (-0.49) **Going Correction** +0.075s/f (Slow) **8 Ran SP% 113.7**
Speed ratings (Par 100): **105,101,100,99,95 94,91,90**
toteswingers:1&2 £5.30, 2&3 £2.90, 1&3 £5.60 CSF £18.21 CT £68.79 TOTE £7.00: £3.20, £2.90, £1.10; EX 24.80 Trifecta £93.70 Pool: £634.76 - 5.01 winning units..
Owner Resurrection Partners **Bred** K T Ivory **Trained** Sutton Veny, Wilts

FOCUS
A modest fillies' handicap, but it was run at a decent pace and the form rated around those in the frame behind the winner, should hold up.
T/Plt: £76.80 to a £1 stake. Pool of £54,898.26 - 521.42 winning tickets. T/Qpdt: £11.50 to a £1 stake. Pool of £4,330.42 - 278.64 winning tickets. SP

630 WOLVERHAMPTON (A.W) (L-H)
Friday, February 25

OFFICIAL GOING: Standard
Wind: Light behind becoming fresh behind race 2 onwards Weather: Overcast

690 TODAY'S JOCKEY SPECIALS AT BLUESQ.COM APPRENTICE H'CAP 5f 216y(P)
5:25 (5:26) (Class 7) (0-50,55) 4-Y-0+ **£1,535** (£453; £226) **Stalls** Low

Form RPR

6606 **1** **Vertumnus**[16] 464 4-8-5 **45** (b) JackDuern(7) 5 56
(Nick Littmoden) *hld up: hdwy over 1f out: r.o to ld last strides* **25/1**

0-01 **2** ½ **Attrition**[10] 545 4-9-8 **55** 6ex GeorgeChaloner 2 64
(Andrew Reid) *sn led: clr 2f out: rdn ins fnl f: hdd last strides* **9/4**[1]

06-2 **3** ½ **Premier League**[10] 545 4-9-3 **50** (p) LucyKBarry 6 58
(Julia Feilden) *a.p: chsd ldr over 2f out: rdn over 1f out: r.o* **7/2**[2]

-026 **4** 2 ½ **Jessica Wigmo**[15] 482 8-8-8 **46** GeorgeDowning(5) 10 47
(Tony Carroll) *sn outpcd: nt clr run wl over 1f out: r.o ins fnl f: nvr nrr* **20/1**

-055 **5** 1 ½ **Carnival Dream**[14] 512 6-8-13 **46** ShaneBKelly 4 42
(Hugh McWilliams) *mid-div: rdn over 2f out: r.o ins fnl f: nt rch ldrs* **9/2**[3]

20-0 **6** 2 ¾ **Cocktail Party (IRE)**[25] 362 5-9-0 **47** AlexEdwards 9 34
(James Unett) *s.v.s: hdwy over 2f out: rdn over 1f out: wknd ins fnl f* **12/1**

103 **7** 1 **Rightcar**[15] 482 4-8-8 **48** (b) JasonHart(7) 8 32
(Peter Grayson) *prom: rdn over 2f out: wknd over 1f out* **9/1**

30- **8** *nse* **Leahness (IRE)**[76] 7827 4-8-12 **45** RPWalsh 1 29
(Patrick Morris) *chsd ldrs: rdn over 2f out: wknd over 1f out* **66/1**

00-6 **9** *shd* **Azygous**[11] 537 8-8-9 **47** DavidSimmonson(5) 13 31
(G P Kelly) *broke wl: lost pl after 1f: rdn over 2f out: n.d after* **50/1**

06-0 **10** 1 ¾ **Best Known Secret (IRE)**[50] 57 5-8-9 **45** (b) JakePayne(3) 11 24
(Chris Bealby) *mid-div: rdn over 2f out: n.d* **16/1**

060- **11** *shd* **Thewinnatakesitall**[122] 7153 4-8-7 **45** IanBurns(5) 7 23
(Noel Wilson) *chsd ldrs: lost pl after 1f: rdn over 2f out: n.d after* **40/1**

64- **12** 2 ¼ **Billionaire Boy (IRE)**[113] 7322 4-8-9 **47** RossCoakley(5) 3 19
(Patrick Morris) *sn chsng ldr: rdn over 2f out: wknd over 1f out* **16/1**

1m 16.1s (1.10) **Going Correction** +0.10s/f (Slow) **12 Ran SP% 115.1**
Speed ratings (Par 97): **96,95,94,91,89 85,84,84,84,81 81,78**
toteswingers:1&2 £11.20, 2&3 £2.50, 1&3 £21.40 CSF £76.43 CT £256.85 TOTE £61.90: £18.30, £2.80, £1.10; EX 164.30.
Owner R D Hartshorn **Bred** Shortgrove Manor Stud **Trained** Newmarket, Suffolk

FOCUS
A very weak sprint handicap to open proceedings, confined to apprentice riders. There was a solid pace on and the principals were clear at the finish and the form looks pretty sound for the grade.

691 THE BLACK COUNTRY'S ONLY RACECOURSE H'CAP 5f 20y(P)
5:55 (5:56) (Class 7) (0-50,50) 4-Y-0+ **£1,535** (£453; £226) **Stalls** Low

Form RPR

0323 **1** **Steel City Boy (IRE)**[11] 537 8-9-3 **50** (p) JimmyQuinn 8 59
(Derek Shaw) *a.p: rdn over 1f out: r.o to ld wl ins fnl f* **6/1**[3]

-060 **2** 1 ¼ **Head To Head (IRE)**[35] 256 7-8-12 **45** (bt) TomEaves 9 50
(Alan Brown) *led: rdn and hung lft over 1f out: hdd wl ins fnl f* **40/1**

220 **3** 1 ¼ **Cheveyo (IRE)**[11] 537 5-8-8 **48** RossCoakley(7) 5 48
(Patrick Morris) *dwlt: hld up: hdwy 1/2-way: rdn over 1f out: edgd lft: r.o* **6/1**[3]

6-05 **4** ½ **Lithaam (IRE)**[16] 464 7-8-6 **46** (p) MatthewCosham(7) 2 44
(Milton Bradley) *hld up: hdwy 1/2-way: rdn over 1f out: styd on* **6/1**[3]

0042 **5** *nk* **Thoughtsofstardom**[11] 537 8-8-11 **49** JulieBurke(5) 3 46
(Phil McEntee) *a.p: rdn to chse ldr over 1f out: styd on same pce ins fnl f* **10/3**[1]

-003 **6** ½ **Mr Funshine**[29] 311 6-8-12 **45** MartinLane 1 40
(Derek Shaw) *hld up: rdn over 1f out: r.o: nt rch ldrs* **6/1**[3]

055 **7** ¾ **Francis Albert**[25] 362 5-8-9 **49** (be) JosephYoung(7) 4 44
(Michael Mullineaux) *hld up: hmpd 1/2-way: r.o wl ins fnl f: nrst fin* **11/2**[2]

4-64 **8** 1 ¼ **Gorgeous Goblin (IRE)**[28] 343 4-8-9 **45** (bt[1]) AndrewHeffernan(3) 10 33
(David C Griffiths) *chsd ldrs: rdn over 1f out: wknd ins fnl f* **25/1**

0/0- **9** 6 **Blakeshall Diamond**[162] 6119 6-8-12 **45** (b[1]) JoeFanning 11 12
(Frank Sheridan) *prom: racd keenly: rdn and wknd wl over 1f out* **10/1**

00-0 **10** 3 ¾ **Mythical Blue (IRE)**[16] 464 5-9-3 **50** RobbieFitzpatrick 7 3
(Peter Grayson) *sn rdn along to chse ldrs: wknd 1/2-way* **66/1**

63.05 secs (0.75) **Going Correction** +0.10s/f (Slow) **10 Ran SP% 112.5**
Speed ratings (Par 97): **98,96,94,93,92 91,90,88,79,73**
toteswingers:1&2 £26.00, 2&3 £29.10, 1&3 £6.00 CSF £213.48 CT £1484.01 TOTE £9.90: £1.40, £11.30, £2.50; EX 110.50.
Owner J Medley **Bred** Mrs A B McDonnell **Trained** Sproxton, Leics

FOCUS
Another bottom-drawer sprint handicap in which the third and fourth set a modest standard.

692 WOLVERHAMPTON-RACECOURSE.CO.UK H'CAP 1m 141y(P)
6:25 (6:25) (Class 5) (0-70,68) 4-Y-0+ **£2,266** (£674; £337; £168) **Stalls** Low

Form RPR

113- **1** **Northern Flyer (GER)**[132] 6917 5-8-13 **63** (p) IanBrennan(3) 6 71
(John Quinn) *mde all: set stdy pce tl qcknd over 2f out: rdn over 1f out: r.o* **9/4**[2]

11-0 **2** ¾ **Khajaaly (IRE)**[48] 96 4-9-7 **68** JimmyQuinn 7 74
(Julia Feilden) *trckd ldrs: racd keenly: chsd wnr over 1f out: sn rdn: styd on* **2/1**[1]

-061 **3** *nk* **Petomic (IRE)**[8] 574 6-8-6 **58** TobyAtkinson(5) 4 64
(Richard Guest) *s.s: hld up: shkn up over 3f out: r.o u.p ins fnl f: nrst fin* **5/1**[3]

00-5 **4** *hd* **Thundering Home**[15] 399 4-9-1 **62** JoeFanning 5 67
(Michael Attwater) *a.p: rdn over 1f out: r.o* **10/1**

/00- **5** 3 ¼ **Animator**[106] 7410 6-8-10 **60** RossAtkinson(3) 3 59
(Martin Hill) *chsd wnr tl rdn over 2f out: wknd ins fnl f* **40/1**

50-0 **6** *shd* **Prince Golan (IRE)**[13] 526 7-8-4 **56** JulieBurke(5) 2 54
(Richard Price) *chsd ldrs: rdn over 2f out: wknd ins fnl f* **6/1**

060- **7** ½ **Dragon Slayer (IRE)**[121] 7184 9-8-12 **59** SteveDrowne 1 56
(John Harris) *hld up: rdn over 1f out: wknd ins fnl f* **16/1**

1m 55.67s (5.17) **Going Correction** +0.10s/f (Slow) **7 Ran SP% 112.5**
Speed ratings (Par 103): **81,80,80,79,77 76,76**
toteswingers:1&2 £1.30, 2&3 £3.40, 1&3 £1.50 CSF £6.91 TOTE £4.00: £1.40, £1.60; EX 10.10.

Owner N Chapman **Bred** A Pereira **Trained** Settrington, N Yorks

FOCUS
A tricky handicap. It was run at a crawl and the form is worth treating with some caution.

693 SPONSOR A RACE BY CALLING 01902 390000 MAIDEN STKS 1m 141y(P)
6:55 (6:57) (Class 5) 3-Y-O **£2,007** (£597; £298; £149) **Stalls** Low

Form RPR

1 **Barbican** 3-9-3 0 J-PGuillambert 2 81+
(Alan Bailey) *s.s: rn green in rr early: hld up: hdwy over 2f out: led over 1f out: rdn and hung rt: r.o* **2/1**[2]

43-2 **2** 1 ½ **School For Scandal (IRE)**[11] 540 3-9-3 73 JoeFanning 3 76
(Mark Johnston) *chsd ldr tl led over 2f out: rdn: hung rt and hdd over 1f out: styd on same pce* **4/9**[1]

55-4 **3** ½ **Storm Tide**[20] 437 3-8-12 62 MartinLane 5 70
(Rae Guest) *a.p: chsd ldr 2f out: sn rdn and ev ch: styd on same pce ins fnl f* **16/1**[3]

0-5 **4** 13 **Star Danser**[27] 347 3-9-3 0 SteveDrowne 6 48
(Tom Keddy) *led: rdn and hdd over 2f out: wknd over 1f out* **50/1**

54-2 **5** 2 ¾ **Ippi N Tombi (IRE)**[27] 347 3-8-7 43 JulieBurke(5) 1 37
(Phil McEntee) *chsd ldrs: rdn over 3f out: wknd over 2f out* **50/1**

45- **6** 27 **Big City Boy (IRE)**[56] 8030 3-9-3 0 RobbieFitzpatrick 4 —
(Phil McEntee) *s.i.s: hld up: a in rr: rdn and wknd over 2f out: t.o* **100/1**

1m 51.26s (0.76) **Going Correction** +0.10s/f (Slow) **6 Ran SP% 113.4**
Speed ratings (Par 97): **100,98,98,86,84 60**
toteswingers:1&2 £1.10, 2&3 £2.10, 1&3 £1.10 CSF £3.27 TOTE £3.10: £1.60, £1.10; EX 4.10.
Owner John Stocker **Bred** Hascombe And Valiant Studs **Trained** Newmarket, Suffolk

FOCUS
This moderate maiden saw a gambled-on winner, who can rate higher. The second and third set the level.

694 DOWNLOAD THE BLUE SQUARE IPHONE APP H'CAP 1m 1f 103y(P)
7:25 (7:25) (Class 4) (0-85,82) 4-Y-0+ **£3,238** (£963; £481; £240) **Stalls** Low

Form RPR

3-23 **1** **Loyalty**[11] 541 4-8-10 **71** (v) PatrickMathers 6 85
(Derek Shaw) *hld up: pushed along over 3f out: hdwy over 2f out: led 1f out: r.o wl* **3/1**[2]

3130 **2** 3 ½ **Kidlat**[13] 525 6-9-4 **79** JoeFanning 2 86
(Alan Bailey) *sn pushed along to ld: rdn over 2f out: hdd 1f out: styd on same pce* **5/1**

32-5 **3** ¾ **Danderek**[22] 405 5-9-5 **80** FrederikTylicki 1 86
(Richard Fahey) *chsd ldrs: rdn and swtchd lft over 1f out: styd on same pce ins fnl f* **5/2**[1]

0002 **4** ½ **Thunderstruck**[11] 541 6-9-5 **80** (p) ChrisCatlin 8 85
(David Nicholls) *chsd ldr: rdn over 2f out: ev ch over 1f out: no ex ins fnl f* **7/2**[3]

5-51 **5** *shd* **Snow Dancer (IRE)**[11] 541 7-9-3 **81** 6ex JamesSullivan(3) 5 86
(Hugh McWilliams) *hld up: hdwy over 2f out: rdn over 1f out: no ex ins fnl f* **7/1**

36-0 **6** 3 ¼ **Plush**[21] 427 8-8-11 **75** RossAtkinson(3) 3 74
(Shaun Lycett) *dwlt: hld up: rdn over 1f out: nvr on terms* **33/1**

4/ **7** 14 **Ajdaad (USA)**[136] 4-9-2 **82** RosieJessop(5) 7 54
(Alan McCabe) *hld up: wknd over 2f out* **16/1**

000- **8** 17 **Secret Queen**[125] 7091 4-8-12 **73** SteveDrowne 4 13
(Martin Hill) *chsd ldrs: rdn over 3f out: wknd over 2f out: t.o* **66/1**

1m 59.27s (-2.43) **Going Correction** +0.10s/f (Slow) **8 Ran SP% 115.3**
Speed ratings (Par 105): **114,110,110,109,109 106,94,79**
toteswingers:1&2 £3.10, 2&3 £3.60, 1&3 £1.30 CSF £18.63 CT £42.00 TOTE £4.50: £1.30, £1.10, £1.70; EX 16.20.
Owner Mrs Lyndsey Shaw **Bred** Ecoutila Partnership **Trained** Sproxton, Leics

FOCUS
An open handicap in which there was a fair pace on and it saw a host of chances at the furlong marker. The form looks solid rated around the four immediately behind the winner.

695 HOTEL & CONFERENCING AT WOLVERHAMPTON CLASSIFIED CLAIMING STKS 1m 4f 50y(P)
7:55 (7:55) (Class 6) 4-Y-0+ **£1,706** (£503; £252) **Stalls** Low

Form RPR

4551 **1** **Visions Of Johanna (USA)**[16] 472 6-8-12 **67** JimmyQuinn 2 69+
(Ian Williams) *hld up in tch: shkn up to ld ins fnl f: r.o* **8/13**[1]

The Form Book, Raceform Ltd, Compton, RG20 6NL

6-02 **2** 1 1/4 **Force Group (IRE)**[16] 472 7-8-12 65........................(b) J-PGuillambert 1 67+
(Nick Littmoden) *racd keenly: trckd ldr to 1/2-way: rdn to ld over 1f out: edgd lft: hdd and unable qck ins fnl f* **3/1**[2]
46-1 **3** 5 **Gearbox (IRE)**[19] 85 5-9-5 61.................................. RobbieFitzpatrick 5 67
(Liam Corcoran) *prom: chsd ldr 1/2-way: led 3f out: rdn and hdd over 1f out: eased whn btn ins fnl f* **7/1**[3]
0-50 **4** 13 **Love In The West (IRE)**[14] 507 5-8-9 55....................(p) SteveDrowne 4 37
(John Harris) *led 9f: sn rdn: wknd over 1f out* **12/1**
0-04 **5** 8 **Hill Of Clare (IRE)**[22] 407 9-8-9 40......................... TobyAtkinson(5) 3 30
(George Jones) *s.s: hld up: hdwy over 4f out: sn rdn: wknd over 3f out* **100/1**

2m 44.24s (3.14) **Going Correction** +0.10s/f (Slow) 5 Ran SP% **108.1**
Speed ratings (Par 101): **93,92,88,80,74**
CSF £2.57 TOTE £1.60: £1.10, £1.50; EX 2.50.
Owner Dr Marwan Koukash **Bred** David S Milch **Trained** Portway, Worcs

FOCUS
Straightforward claiming form. The winner did not need to run to recent form with the third and fifth the best guides.

696 PLAY ROULETTE AT BLUESQ.COM H'CAP 5f 20y(P)
8:25 (8:26) (Class 6) (0-65,64) 4-Y-O+ **£1,637** (£483; £241) **Stalls** Low

Form RPR
0021 **1** **Straboe (USA)**[14] 511 5-9-2 59................................(v) J-PGuillambert 11 69
(Stuart Williams) *sn outpcd: hdwy over 1f out: rdn and edgd lft ins fnl f: r.o to ld towards fin* **11/4**[1]
4-46 **2** 1 1/4 **Hypnosis**[36] 231 8-9-5 62.. LeeNewman 1 68
(Noel Wilson) *led: rdn 1/2-way: hdd and unable qck towards fin* **6/1**
1222 **3** 3/4 **Black Baccara**[9] 554 4-8-10 58..............................(be) JulieBurke(5) 2 61
(Phil McEntee) *trckd ldr: racd keenly: rdn over 1f out: styd on* **3/1**[2]
-111 **4** shd **Shawkantango**[8] 571 4-9-2 64 6ex.............................(v) LeeTopliss(5) 7 66+
(Derek Shaw) *s.i.s: outpcd: hdwy 1/2-way: rdn over 1f out: styd on* **4/1**[3]
4120 **5** 2 1/4 **Metropolitan Chief**[15] 485 7-8-10 53.............................. JimmyQuinn 3 47
(Paul Burgoyne) *chsd ldrs: rdn over 1f out: no ex ins fnl f* **10/1**
0-51 **6** 3 3/4 **Lethal**[25] 363 8-8-6 56.. RPWalsh(7) 4 37
(Richard Price) *prom: lost pl over 3f out: n.d after* **12/1**
5321 **7** 1 3/4 **Dancing Freddy (IRE)**[24] 375 4-9-2 62.................(p) RobertLButler(3) 8 37
(Michael Chapman) *chsd ldrs: rdn 1/2-way: wknd over 1f out* **8/1**

62.41 secs (0.11) **Going Correction** +0.10s/f (Slow) 7 Ran SP% **113.8**
Speed ratings (Par 101): **103,101,99,99,96 90,87**
toteswingers:1&2 £5.00, 2&3 £6.20, 1&3 £1.80 CSF £19.39 CT £51.48 TOTE £4.60: £2.50, £2.30; EX 24.40.
Owner Brigid & Damian Hennessy-Bourke **Bred** Darley **Trained** Newmarket, Suffolk

FOCUS
Despite the non-runners this was still a competitive sprint handicap for the class. It was run at a frantic pace and the winner is rated to his best.
T/Plt: £14.00 to a £1 stake. Pool of £75,893.98 - 3,948.49 winning tickets. T/Qpdt: £3.40 to a £1 stake. Pool of £8,928.98 - 1,912.46 winning tickets. CR

683 LINGFIELD (L-H)
Saturday, February 26

OFFICIAL GOING: Standard
Wind: fresh, across Weather: overcast

697 BET ON TODAY'S FOOTBALL AT BLUESQ.COM H'CAP 1m 5f (P)
1:35 (1:35) (Class 5) (0-75,74) 4-Y-O+ **£2,047** (£604; £302) **Stalls** Low

Form RPR
00-6 **1** **Gunslinger (FR)**[7] 614 6-9-7 71...................................... HayleyTurner 4 77
(Michael Scudamore) *stdd s: t.k.h: hld up in last pair: rdn and effrt on inner 3f out: 4th and looked wl hld ent fnl f: styd on wl u.p fnl f to ld nr fin* **7/1**[3]
-321 **2** nk **Layla's Dancer**[17] 474 4-9-4 72....................................... JimmyQuinn 1 77
(Tony Carroll) *led: drew clr ent fnl 2f: rdn over 1f out: tired ins fnl f: hdd nr fin* **9/4**[1]
0-05 **3** shd **Diamond Twister (USA)**[8] 592 5-8-7 60......................... KierenFox(3) 5 65
(John Best) *chsd ldr tl over 2f out: sn rdn and unable qck: rallied fnl f: keeping on whn n.m.r and jostled wl ins fnl f: fin 4th: plcd 3rd* **8/1**
50-4 **4** hd **Profit's Reality (IRE)**[25] 374 9-9-4 68.............................. ShaneKelly 3 73
(Michael Attwater) *hld up: chsd clr ldr over 2f out: drvn and no imp over 1f out: rallied ins fnl f: edgd rt fnl 100yds: styd on: fin 3rd: disqualified and plcd 4th* **25/1**
1-40 **5** 2 1/2 **Suntrap**[17] 475 4-9-6 74.. LukeMorris 6 75
(William Knight) *in tch in midfield: rdn along and dropped to last pair wl over 3f out: 5th and wl hld over 1f out: styd on again ins fnl f* **9/4**[1]
11-2 **6** 1/2 **Jezza**[51] 68 5-9-10 74.. StevieDonohoe 2 75
(Victor Dartnall) *s.i.s: nvr travelling wl in detached last: pushed along 10f out: rdn and no hdwy 5f out: wl btn over 2f out: hdwy over 1f out: styd on fnl f: n.d* **7/2**[2]

2m 46.37s (0.37) **Going Correction** +0.05s/f (Slow)
WFA 4 from 5yo+ 4lb 6 Ran SP% **111.2**
Speed ratings (Par 103): **100,99,99,99,98 97**
Tote Swingers: 1&2 £3.50, 1&3 £5.00, 2&3 £2.60 CSF £22.70 TOTE £13.80: £4.20, £2.00; EX 23.10.
Owner S M Smith & Keith Hunter **Bred** Dayton Investments Ltd **Trained** Bromsash, Herefordshire
■ Stewards' Enquiry : Shane Kelly one-day ban; careless riding (12th March)

FOCUS
An ordinary staying handicap, but something of a controversial race. The pace was sound in view of the size of the field, but even so the first four finished in a heap. The form looks limited.
Suntrap Official explanation: jockey said gelding hung right
Jezza Official explanation: jockey said gelding moved poorly and was never traveling

698 BLUE SQUARE SPRINT SERIES FINAL H'CAP 6f (P)
2:10 (2:10) (Class 5) 4-Y-O+ **£9,714** (£2,890; £1,444; £721) **Stalls** Low

Form RPR
5114 **1** **Norville (IRE)**[7] 612 4-8-13 68...............................(b) CathyGannon 8 78
(David Evans) *broke wl: mde virtually all but hrd pressed thrght: drvn over 1f out: battled on gamely u.p: forged ahd fnl 100yds* **12/1**
2-12 **2** 1 3/4 **Rio Royale (IRE)**[28] 351 5-8-8 63...............................(p) JimCrowley 4 68
(Amanda Perrett) *w wnr: rdn ent fnl 2f: drvn and stl ev ch tl no ex and btn fnl 100yds: tired but hld on for 2nd cl home* **15/2**[3]
44/1 **3** nk **Qadar (IRE)**[7] 612 9-9-5 74..(p) ShaneKelly 7 78
(Alan McCabe) *taken down early: in tch: hmpd and snatched up bnd 5f out: racd on outer after: rdn over 1f out: styd on u.p ins fnl f: pressing for 2nd cl home* **6/1**[2]
4651 **4** nk **Chjimes (IRE)**[3] 654 7-9-2 71 6ex..............................(b) HayleyTurner 6 74
(Conor Dore) *stdd and swtchd lft s: t.k.h: hld up in tch: shkn up and effrt to chse ldrs ent fnl f: rdn and styd on same pce ins fnl f* **14/1**
21-1 **5** 3/4 **Arctic Lynx (IRE)**[35] 264 4-9-10 79................................ GeorgeBaker 2 80
(John Best) *wl in tch on inner: hdwy to press ldrs and rdn over 1f out: fnd little u.p and styd on same pce ins fnl f* **13/8**[1]
3344 **6** 1/2 **Speak The Truth (IRE)**[14] 521 5-8-4 59....................(p) NickyMackay 11 58
(Jim Boyle) *awkward s and s.i.s: sn swtchd lft: bhd in last pair: hdwy on outer ent fnl f: styd on wl fnl 100yds: nt rch ldrs* **18/1**
-131 **7** 2 1/2 **Waabel**[14] 522 4-9-10 79.. PaulDoe 10 71
(Jim Best) *chsd ldrs: rdn and unable qck jst over 2f out: wknd over 1f out* **17/2**
3104 **8** nk **Dancing Welcome**[14] 522 5-8-13 68....................(b) RichardKingscote 9 59
(Milton Bradley) *sn outpcd in rr: sme hdwy on inner over 1f out: styd on ins fnl f: nvr trbld ldrs* **33/1**
-210 **9** 1/2 **Picansort**[14] 521 4-9-1 70..(v) JimmyQuinn 3 59
(Brett Johnson) *chsd ldrs: rdn and struggling ent fnl 2f: wknd u.p over 1f out* **14/1**
5663 **10** 4 **Nubar Boy**[7] 612 4-8-7 62 ow1......................................(v) JamieSpencer 1 43
(David Evans) *in tch towards rr of main gp: short of room bnd ent fnl 2f: drvn and no hdwy over 1f out: eased whn no ch wl ins fnl f* **10/1**
-120 **11** 5 **Waterloo Dock**[14] 521 6-8-13 68..............................(v) MartinDwyer 5 36
(Michael Quinn) *sn bustled along to chse ldrs: rdn and losing pl over 2f out: wl bhd ent fnl f: eased wl ins fnl f* **28/1**

1m 10.54s (-1.36) **Going Correction** +0.05s/f (Slow) course record 11 Ran SP% **116.4**
Speed ratings (Par 103): **111,108,108,107,106 106,102,102,101,96 89**
Tote Swingers: 1&2 £8.40, 1&3 £12.60, 2&3 £8.30 CSF £98.13 CT £600.20 TOTE £9.80: £2.40, £2.10, £2.20; EX 93.80 Trifecta £609.10 Part won. Pool: £823.22 - 0.50 winning units..
Owner Raymond N R Auld **Bred** R N Auld **Trained** Pandy, Monmouths
■ Stewards' Enquiry : Paul Doe two-day ban; careless riding (12th&15th March)

FOCUS
After seven qualifying rounds comprising nine races (two of the qualifying rounds were divided) this final was a very competitive affair with a labyrinth of recent C&D form to unravel. Nine of the 11 runners sported some sort of headgear but the time was good and the form looks solid.

699 BLUE SQUARE SUPPORTING MARIE CURIE CANCER CARE MAIDEN STKS 1m 4f (P)
2:40 (2:40) (Class 5) 3-Y-O **£2,047** (£604; £302) **Stalls** Low

Form RPR
0- **1** **Halifax (IRE)**[136] 6844 3-9-3 0.. JoeFanning 2 81
(Mark Johnston) *chsd ldr: rdn ent fnl 3f: led ins fnl f: styd on wl* **9/2**
222- **2** 1 3/4 **Jacobs Son**[138] 6809 3-9-3 78.. NeilCallan 3 78
(Robert Mills) *led: rdn ent fnl 2f: drvn and hdd ins fnl f: no ex* **7/4**[1]
3 **3** 5 **Monster Munchie (JPN)**[17] 471 3-8-12 0....................... JimCrowley 5 65+
(William Knight) *t.k.h: hld up in rr: hdwy on outer to chse ldng pair over 2f out: no hdwy and outpcd bnd 2f out: 4th and wl btn ent fnl f: wnt 3rd cl home* **5/2**[2]
-232 **4** hd **Riot Police (USA)**[17] 471 3-9-3 73..............................(p) JamieSpencer 1 70
(David Simcock) *hld up in tch: effrt to chse ldng pair ent fnl 2f: rdn and fnd nil over 1f out: wl btn 1f out: wknd ins fnl f: lost 3rd cl home* **3/1**[3]
400- **5** 7 **Laffraaj (IRE)**[122] 7164 3-9-3 46...................................... EddieAhern 4 59
(Pat Eddery) *chsd ldng pair: rdn over 4f out: dropped to last over 2f out: sn wknd* **33/1**

2m 34.99s (1.99) **Going Correction** +0.05s/f (Slow) 5 Ran SP% **111.1**
Speed ratings (Par 97): **95,93,90,90,85**
CSF £12.97 TOTE £4.50: £2.90, £1.10; EX 14.00.
Owner Sheikh Hamdan Bin Mohammed Al Maktoum **Bred** Rabbah Bloodstock Limited **Trained** Middleham Moor, N Yorks

FOCUS
A fair maiden but tricky to pin down formwise.

700 DOWNLOAD BLUE SQUARE IPHONE APP CLEVES STKS (LISTED RACE) 6f (P)
3:10 (3:12) (Class 1) 4-Y-O+
£17,031 (£6,456; £3,231; £1,611; £807; £405) **Stalls** Low

Form RPR
3-22 **1** **Waveband**[36] 293 4-8-9 91.. MartinDwyer 8 101
(David Barron) *mde all: rdn over 1f out: battled on gamely fnl f: hld on wl cl home* **16/1**
12-1 **2** nk **Anne Of Kiev (IRE)**[35] 265 6-8-9 93............................(t) SteveDrowne 1 100
(Jeremy Gask) *dwlt: sn in midfield on inner: rdn and effrt to chse ldrs ent fnl f: ev ch wl ins fnl f: hld cl home* **12/1**
403- **3** shd **Duff (IRE)**[73] 7875 8-9-0 110.. EddieAhern 2 105
(Edward Lynam, Ire) *t.k.h early: in tch on inner: switching rt off of rail over 2f out: swtchd bk lft and rdn jst over 1f out: ev ch wl ins fnl f: r.o* **7/2**[2]
0-21 **4** hd **Brave Prospector**[22] 429 6-9-0 105............................(t) JamieSpencer 12 104
(Jane Chapple-Hyam) *chsd ldrs: ev ch and rdn over 1f out: unable qck u.p ins fnl f* **8/1**
221- **5** 3/4 **Hitchens (IRE)**[98] 7524 6-9-3 105.................................... ShaneKelly 6 105
(David Barron) *in tch in midfield on outer: rdn over 1f out: no imp tl r.o u.p fnl 100yds: nt quite pce to chal ldrs* **5/2**[1]
014- **6** nse **Angel's Pursuit (IRE)**[73] 7875 4-9-0 108......................... DaneO'Neill 4 101
(Richard Hannon) *in tch in midfield: rdn and sltly outpcd over 1f out: rallied ins fnl f: styng on fin but nt quite pce to chal ldrs* **9/2**[3]
-600 **7** 3/4 **Elna Bright**[7] 615 6-9-0 90...(v[1]) JimmyQuinn 11 99
(Brett Johnson) *stdd and swtchd lft after s: bhd: rdn and hdwy ent fnl f: r.o fnl 100yds: nvr able to chal* **25/1**
00-4 **8** nse **Beauchamp Viceroy**[34] 271 7-9-0 100............................(b) NeilCallan 3 99
(Gerard Butler) *chsd ldr: ev ch and rdn over 1f out: styd pressing ldrs tl wknd fnl 75yds* **16/1**
-321 **9** hd **Five Star Junior (USA)**[7] 613 5-9-0 97.......................... JamesSullivan 7 98
(Linda Stubbs) *hld up in tch towards rr on outer: swtchd rt and rdn ent fnl f: r.o ins fnl f: nvr able to chal* **14/1**
-401 **10** 2 **Breathless Kiss (USA)**[14] 523 4-8-9 89..........................(b) AmyRyan 10 87
(Kevin Ryan) *stdd s and sn swtchd lft: bhd: effrt on inner over 1f out: kpt on same pce and no imp fnl f* **33/1**
150- **11** 3/4 **Joe Packet**[149] 6508 4-9-0 97.. JimCrowley 9 89
(Jonathan Portman) *awkward leaving stalls and slowly int stride: t.k.h: hld up in rr: short-lived effrt and no hdwy over 1f out: nvr trbld ldrs* **25/1**
00-1 **12** 2 1/4 **Arganil (USA)**[32] 293 6-9-0 97....................................(b) PhillipMakin 5 82
(Kevin Ryan) *t.k.h: hld up in tch towards rr: rdn and no hdwy wl over 1f out: bhd fnl f* **25/1**

1m 10.74s (-1.16) **Going Correction** +0.05s/f (Slow) 12 Ran SP% **120.7**
Speed ratings (Par 111): **109,108,108,108,107 107,106,106,105,103 102,99**
Tote Swingers: 1&2 £12.20, 1&3 £10.40, 2&3 £7.70 CSF £189.11 TOTE £17.60: £2.70, £2.30, £2.60; EX 125.30 TRIFECTA Not won..

Owner David Redvers **Bred** Stratford Place Stud **Trained** Maunby, N Yorks

FOCUS

The fifth running of this Listed sprint and a fiercely competitive event with only around 3l covering the front nine. This was one for the girls, with females filling the first two places, but the form looks limited for the grade, especially as it was such a bunched finish.

NOTEBOOK

Waveband, representing last year's winning stable, was having her first try here and seemed to be up against it on these terms, but she was given a well-judged ride from the front, and her jockey's decision to bring her out into the centre of the track once into the straight probably made the difference. This adds some value to her.

Anne Of Kiev(IRE) came into this 3-3 over C&D and finished strongly from off the pace. Even though she lost her perfect record, this was still a career-best effort. (op 10-1)

Duff(IRE), best in on official ratings and caught on the line in this race two years ago, travelled well behind the leaders and had every chance, but his finishing effort wasn't quite enough. He looks better over further these days. (op 9-2)

Brave Prospector, beaten just over a length by Hitchens here in November and 3lb better off, turned that form around and had every chance having tracked the winner from the start. (tchd 15-2)

Hitchens(IRE), the winner's stablemate, was never far away on the outside of the field and ran on in the straight without quite managing to land a blow. His 3lb penalty for winning a similar event over C&D in November made this a tough task. (op 9-4 tchd 11-4)

Angel's Pursuit(IRE) didn't get the best of runs when seventh behind Hitchens here in November and enjoyed a 5lb pull, but he didn't click into gear until it was too late and perhaps he does need the extra furlong on this surface. (op 6-1)

Elna Bright, worst in at the weights and visored for the first time, usually races over further and he was doing all his best work late. (tchd 28-1 and 33-1 in a place)

Beauchamp Viceroy has won seven times on Polytrack, but he was racing over a trip this short for the first time in getting on for three years. Having taken a keen grip behind the winner early, he was almost alongside the filly a furlong out but he was racing closer to the inside rail and lost six places inside the last furlong.

Five Star Junior(USA), cosy winner of a C&D handicap seven days earlier, gave the wide outside away to no-one and his finishing burst wasn't quite so potent at his level. (op 16-1)

701 C W SURFACING H'CAP — 5f (P)

3:45 (3:45) (Class 4) (0-85,85) 4-Y-O+ **£3,238** (£963; £481; £240) **Stalls** High

Form RPR

506- **1** **Le Toreador**[118] 7254 6-9-7 **85**........(p) PhillipMakin 6 94
(Kevin Ryan) *dwlt: sn rcvrd to press ldrs: rdn and ev ch over 1f out: led fnl 75yds: styd on wl* **11/2**

-332 **2** ¾ **Sir Geoffrey (IRE)**[14] 523 5-9-7 **85**........(b) FrederikTylicki 1 91
(David Nicholls) *led: rdn wl over 1f out: kpt on wl tl hdd fnl 75yds: no ex towards fin* **2/1**[1]

2436 **3** ¾ **Feelin Foxy**[14] 523 7-9-6 **84**........ FrannyNorton 2 88
(James Given) *taken down early: w ldrs: rdn and unable qck over 1f out: tried to rally u.p jst ins fnl f: no imp fnl 75yds* **10/1**

30-5 **4** ½ **Billy Red**[50] 87 7-9-6 **84**........(b) FergusSweeney 4 86
(J R Jenkins) *chsd ldng trio: rdn and effrt over 1f out: styd on same pce and no imp ins fnl f* **15/2**

350- **5** ½ **Go Nani Go**[208] 4653 5-9-3 **81**........ LukeMorris 5 81
(Ed de Giles) *in tch in last pair: rdn and effrt on outer bnd 2f out: hdwy ent fnl f: no prog and hld fnl 100yds* **5/1**[3]

3-3 **6** 3 ¾ **Even Bolder**[38] 215 8-8-7 **74**........ KierenFox(3) 3 61
(Eric Wheeler) *stdd after s: in tch in rr: hit rail and unbalanced over 2f out: sn rdn: rallied over 1f out: wknd jst ins fnl f* **3/1**[2]

58.32 secs (-0.48) **Going Correction** +0.05s/f (Slow) **6** Ran SP% **111.2**

Speed ratings (Par 105): **105,103,102,101,101 95**

Tote Swingers: 1&2 £3.00, 1&3 £7.00, 2&3 £4.10 CSF £16.64 TOTE £5.50: £2.60, £1.80; EX 16.50.

Owner Guy Reed **Bred** G Reed **Trained** Hambleton, N Yorks

FOCUS

A fairly competitive little sprint in which there was a disputed lead. The form looks straightforward rated around the placed horses and is solid enough.

Even Bolder Official explanation: jockey said that the gelding hit the rail and lost action

702 ENHANCED SP'S AT BLUESQ.COM CONDITIONS STKS — 1m 2f (P)

4:20 (4:20) (Class 3) 4-Y-O+ **£5,828** (£1,734; £866; £432) **Stalls** Low

Form RPR

5-33 **1** **Suits Me**[12] 542 8-8-13 95........ MickyFenton 10 97+
(Tom Tate) *mde all: rdn and qcknd jst over 2f out: fnd ex whn pressed ins fnl f: r.o wl* **10/3**[1]

43-6 **2** ¾ **Resentful Angel**[14] 525 6-8-3 87........ TobyAtkinson(5) 8 91+
(Pat Eddery) *chsd ldrs: wnt 2nd over 3f out: ev ch and drvn over 1f out: no ex and styd on same pce ins fnl f* **9/1**

0-31 **3** hd **Layline (IRE)**[14] 525 4-8-12 91........ JamieSpencer 2 95+
(Gay Kelleway) *hld up in tch: rdn and effrt on inner over 1f out: pressed ldrs ins fnl f: kpt on* **9/2**[2]

06-0 **4** ½ **Greyfriarschorista**[34] 271 4-8-12 93........ JoeFanning 6 94
(Mark Johnston) *chsd wnr tl over 3f out: styd chsng ldrs: swtchd rt ent fnl 2f: pressing ldrs u.p 1f out: no ex and btn fnl 100yds* **6/1**

2-35 **5** nk **Franco Is My Name**[14] 525 5-8-13 86........(p) DaneO'Neill 5 94
(Peter Hedger) *in tch in midfield: rdn and carried hd awkwardly over 1f out: no prog tl styd on wl fnl 100yds: nt pce to chal ldrs* **8/1**

3-35 **6** hd **Baylini**[7] 615 7-8-8 88........ HayleyTurner 1 88
(Jamie Osborne) *hld up in tch towards rr: rdn and effrt 2f out: kpt on fnl f but nvr gng pce to threaten ldrs* **5/1**[3]

510- **7** 1 ¼ **Shamir**[175] 5750 4-8-12 86........ SteveDrowne 3 91
(Jo Crowley) *in tch towards rr: rdn and effrt ent fnl 2f: kpt on but no real imp fnl f* **20/1**

5010 **8** 1 ¼ **Hidden Glory**[14] 525 4-8-12 88........ JimCrowley 7 89
(James Given) *hld up in last pair: rdn and effrt ent fnl f: no imp fnl 150yds: nvr trbld ldrs* **33/1**

66-3 **9** 3 ¾ **Mister New York (USA)**[21] 436 6-9-2 89........(b) GeorgeBaker 4 84
(Noel Chance) *s.i.s and bustled along early: hld up in rr: short-lived effrt on inner over 1f out: n.d* **16/1**

430- **10** 2 **Silver Grey (IRE)**[133] 6950 4-8-7 101........(p) RobertHavlin 9 73
(Roger Ingram) *hld up in tch on outer: hdwy to chse ldrs over 4f out: losing pl bnd 2f out: sn wknd* **7/1**

2m 6.72s (0.12) **Going Correction** +0.05s/f (Slow)

WFA 4 from 5yo+ 1lb **10** Ran SP% **119.4**

Speed ratings (Par 107): **101,100,100,99,99 99,98,97,94,92**

Tote Swingers: 1&2 £7.50, 1&3 £2.80, 2&3 £6.60 CSF £35.23 TOTE £5.10: £1.60, £2.10, £2.10; EX 41.90 Trifecta £159.70 Pool: £1,299.28 - 6.02 winning units..

Owner D E Cook **Bred** R S A Urquhart **Trained** Tadcaster, N Yorks

FOCUS

For the last four years this race was known as the Winter Derby Trial and carried Listed status, but it has now dropped two grades to a Class 3. Admittedly, it resulted in a more competitive race, but the quality has unsurprisingly suffered as the last three winners of the Winter Derby Trial were officially rated 114, 107 and 120, while the highest-rated horse here was 101. The form is rated around the placed horses backed up by the fifth and seventh.

NOTEBOOK

Suits Me came into this with a record of 1-11 over C&D, but most of those races were at Listed level or better. Given his usual attacking ride, he was always finding enough to hold off his rivals, especially once his rider skilfully manoeuvred him away from the inside rail up the home straight. (op 7-2 tchd 4-1 and 3-1)

Resentful Angel ◆ finished behind three of today's rivals when an eye-catching sixth over C&D two weeks ago, but was given a much more prominent ride this time. She never stopped trying and can surely win another race on Polytrack before too long. (op 8-1 tchd 7-1)

Layline(IRE) bounced back to form when gamely landing a decent handicap over C&D a fortnight earlier and ran another good race here, moving up to hold every chance in the home straight. On official ratings he ran right up to form with the front two. (op 7-2)

Greyfriarschorista had been disappointing since being beaten less than a length in last year's Britannia and had yet to prove himself over this far, but he wasn't ridden as though stamina was thought to be an issue and this was a creditable effort. (op 10-1)

Franco Is My Name has plenty of winning form on Polytrack, but he hadn't looked straightforward in his last two starts at this track and again seemed to hang fire when first asked for his effort turning in. He is one to treat with caution. (op 9-1 tchd 15-2)

Baylini has the ability, but she is hard to win with these days (two wins from her last 51 starts) and needs everything to fall just right. Once again her finishing effort was too little too late. (tchd 11-2)

Shamir, not seen since running poorly at Kempton in September, was racing beyond 1m for the first time and didn't fare badly under the circumstances. (tchd 16-1)

Mister New York(USA) Official explanation: jockey said that the gelding missed the break

Silver Grey(IRE) had upwards of 11lb in hand of her rivals at these weights and was last seen finishing ninth in the Grade 1 E P Taylor Stakes at Woodbine in October. She ran well on the Meydan Tapeta early last year, so can act on artificial surfaces, but she dropped out from the home turn here and was disappointing. (op 12-1)

703 PLAY RAINBOW RICHES AT BLUESQ.COM H'CAP — 1m (P)

4:55 (4:55) (Class 4) (0-85,83) 4-Y-O+ **£3,238** (£963; £481; £240) **Stalls** High

Form RPR

2040 **1** **Follow The Flag (IRE)**[7] 615 7-9-6 **82**........(v) NeilCallan 1 92
(Alan McCabe) *in tch: rdn and effrt over 1f out: drvn and chal ins fnl f: r.o strly fnl 75yds to ld nr fin* **20/1**

2-41 **2** hd **Wilfred Pickles (IRE)**[28] 347 5-9-2 **78**........ DaneO'Neill 3 88
(Jo Crowley) *hld up off the pce in midfield: clsd and gng wl jst over 2f out: swtchd ins and hdwy to chse ldrs 1f out: rdn to ld fnl 100yds: hdd and no ex nr fin* **12/1**

1112 **3** 1 ½ **April Fool**[2] 665 7-8-9 **71**........(b) JamieSpencer 12 77
(David Evans) *led: rdn and edgd rt wl over 1f out: kpt on wl u.p tl hdd fnl 100yds: wknd towards fin* **9/1**

5212 **4** 1 **Lockantanks**[6] 623 4-9-0 **76**........ NeilChalmers 10 80
(Michael Appleby) *stdd s: hld up off the pce in rr: clsd over 2f out: stl plenty to do and hdwy jst over 1f out: r.o wl fnl f: nt rch ldrs* **13/2**[3]

1-01 **5** ½ **Blue Moon**[28] 348 4-9-4 **80**........ PhillipMakin 5 83
(Kevin Ryan) *chsd ldng pair: clsd and rdn to chse ldr 2f out: pressing wnr and carried rt wl over 1f out: unable qck u.p ent fnl f: wknd fnl 100yds* **11/2**[2]

2214 **6** nk **Buaiteoir (FR)**[28] 348 5-9-7 **83**........(e) LiamJones 8 85
(Paul D'Arcy) *stdd s: hld up wl off the pce in last: clsd over 2f out: pushed along and switched lft over 1f out: r.o ins fnl f: nvr trbld ldrs* **4/1**[1]

0-12 **7** ½ **Titan Triumph**[7] 615 7-9-6 **82**........(t) JimCrowley 4 83
(William Knight) *stdd s: hld up wl off the pce in rr: clsd over 2f out: rdn and hdwy over 1f out: kpt on fnl f: nvr trbld ldrs* **4/1**[1]

10-2 **8** ½ **Young Dottie**[33] 279 5-8-12 **79**........ JemmaMarshall(5) 11 79
(Pat Phelan) *chsd ldrs: rdn and unable qck ent fnl 2f: edgd rt over 1f out: sn wknd u.p* **20/1**

30-6 **9** ¾ **Alfresco**[10] 557 7-8-12 **74**........(p) LukeMorris 2 72
(John Best) *t.k.h: chsd ldr tl 2f out: drvn and btn jst over 1f out: wknd fnl f* **25/1**

6110 **10** shd **Mister Green (FR)**[7] 614 5-8-9 **71**........(bt) StephenCraine 7 69
(David Flood) *hld up off the pce in midfield: clsd over 2f out: wd and rdn bnd 2f out: sn hung lft and no hdwy: n.d fnl f* **12/1**

-604 **11** hd **Pegasus Again (USA)**[6] 623 6-9-2 **78**........ EddieAhern 6 75
(Robert Mills) *racd off the pce in midfield: lost pl and rdn over 2f out: one pce and no hdwy over 1f out* **8/1**

123- **12** 13 **Skyfire**[208] 4647 4-9-5 **81**........ FrederikTylicki 9 48
(Ed de Giles) *a off the pce in rr: rdn 4f out: last and toiling u.p 3f out: lost tch 2f out* **33/1**

1m 36.41s (-1.79) **Going Correction** +0.05s/f (Slow) **12** Ran SP% **121.5**

Speed ratings (Par 105): **110,109,108,107,106 106,106,105,104,104 104,91**

Tote Swingers: 1&2 £42.80, 1&3 £57.70, 2&3 £8.10 CSF £236.72 CT £2363.27 TOTE £41.90: £9.60, £3.90, £2.70; EX 246.20 Trifecta £708.20 Part won. Pool: £957.06 - 0.10 winning units..

Owner S Gillen **Bred** Martin Francis **Trained** Averham Park, Notts

FOCUS

A decent handicap run at a true pace, but most of the hold-up horses never managed to get involved. The form looks straightforward rated around the winner and third.

T/Plt: £146.30 to a £1 stake. Pool: £79,580.13 - 397.05 winning tickets T/Qpdt: £20.50 to a £1 stake. Pool: £5,878.11 - 211.40 w. tckts SP

704a (Foreign Racing) See Raceform Interactive

660 CAGNES-SUR-MER

Saturday, February 26

OFFICIAL GOING: Turf: good to soft; fibresand: standard

705a GRAND PRIX DU CONSEIL GENERAL DES ALPES MARITIMES (LISTED RACE) (4YO+) (TURF) — 1m 4f 110y

2:08 (12:00) 4-Y-O+ **£32,327** (£12,931; £9,698; £6,465; £3,232)

RPR

1 **Young Tiger (FR)**[76] 7855 10-9-3 0........ Francois-XavierBertras 7 103
(F Rohaut, France) **58/10**[2]

2 1 **Refik (FR)**[17] 479 8-8-13 0........ AntoineSanglard 11 97
(M Cesandri, France) **45/1**

3 hd **Dunaden (FR)**[76] 7855 5-8-13 0........ ThierryThulliez 4 97
(R Gibson, France) **63/10**[3]

4 1 **Griraz (FR)**[33] 6-8-13 0........ Jean-BernardEyquem 14 95
(J-L Dubord, France) **17/1**

5 1 **Diodoros (FR)**33 5-8-13 0 DavyBonilla 15 94
(C Laffon-Parias, France) **78/10**
6 shd **Bridge Of Gold (USA)**192 5220 5-8-13 0 DominiqueBoeuf 10 94
(Mikael Magnusson) *broke smartly to ld to first turn: then settled in 2nd on inner: rdn bef st: u.p to maintain position 2f out: styd on fnl f* **15/1**
6 dht **Fellini (GER)**17 478 4-8-9 0 (p) ThierryJarnet 13 94
(P Monfort, France) **17/1**
8 3/4 **Timos (GER)**17 478 6-8-13 0 SylvainRuis 16 93
(T Doumen, France) **2/1**1
9 1/2 **Silver Valny (FR)**38 219 5-8-13 0 ThomasMessina 6 92
(Mlle M-L Mortier, France) **14/1**
10 5 **A Coeur Ouvert (FR)**17 478 5-8-13 0 IoritzMendizabal 5 84
(H-A Pantall, France) **21/1**
0 **Redesignation (IRE)**17 478 6-8-13 0 RichardJuteau 12 —
(J-C Sarais, France) **102/1**
0 **Lowenherz (GER)**80 7776 7-8-13 0 TonyPiccone 9 —
(H Billot, France) **83/1**
0 **Poincon De France (IRE)**21 439 7-8-13 0 (b) FlavienPrat 8 —
(P Monfort, France) **51/1**
0 **High Figurine (IRE)**10 4-8-6 0 (p) JohanVictoire 3 —
(Jean De Roualle, France) **45/1**
0 **Salontanzerin (GER)**17 478 6-8-9 0 FabriceVeron 1 —
(H-A Pantall, France) **14/1**

2m 45.72s (165.72)
WFA 4 from 5yo+ 3lb **15** Ran SP% **116.8**
WIN (incl. 1 euro stake): 6.80. PLACES: 2.30, 9.60, 2.50. DF: 142.90. SF: 281.50.
Owner Javier Gispert **Bred** Alain De Rose **Trained** Sauvagnon, France

706a PRIX DU GALIBIER (H'CAP) (5YO+) (TURF) 1m 2f 165y
3:10 (12:00) 5-Y-O+ **£7,758** (£3,103; £2,327; £1,551; £775)

RPR
1 **Pumuki (FR)**106 7-9-6 0 SylvainRuis 11 63
(P Chatelain, France) **9/2**1
2 nse **Iron Out (USA)**7 617 5-9-6 0 IoritzMendizabal 14 63
(Reg Hollinshead) *stmbld bdly at s: but sn rdn to ld: maintaining ld tl st whn swtchd to stands rail: r.o wl u.p to ld tl hdd fnl strides* **20/1**
3 3/4 **Frantz De Galais (FR)**57 5-9-2 0 FabriceVeron 5 57
(J-M Lefebvre, France) **17/1**
4 2 **Palea (GER)**46 5-8-13 0 ThierryJarnet 8 50
(S Jesus, France) **19/1**
5 nse **El Vettorio (GER)**7 617 8-9-2 0 (p) DavyBonilla 12 53
(C Boutin, France) **68/10**
6 1/2 **Spirit Of The King (FR)**10 566 5-9-6 0 (b) ThierryThulliez 2 56
(S-A Ghoumrassi, France) **21/1**
7 1 **Armigerent (IRE)**171 7-8-13 0 ASuborics 13 47
(G Collet, France) **26/1**
8 1 1/2 **Blessing Belle (IRE)**46 5-9-0 0 (b) FabienLefebvre 3 45
(Mme G Rarick, France) **20/1**
9 snk **Theorique (FR)**67 8-9-3 0 Pierre-CharlesBoudot 6 48
(M Boutin, France) **58/10**
10 nse **Praha (IRE)**890 6157 5-8-10 0 RichardJuteau 9 41
(J-C Sarais, France) **67/1**
0 **Learco (FR)**38 221 10-9-6 0 (p) MathiasSautjeau 15 —
(Y Fertillet, France) **22/1**
0 **Fair Attitude (IRE)**151 7-9-2 0 NadegeOuakli 1 —
(Robert Collet, France) **5/1**2
0 **Royale Again (FR)**67 6-9-3 0 (b) FranckBlondel 10 —
(P Monfort, France) **11/2**3
0 **Tanaos (FR)**775 5-8-11 0 FranckForesi 7 —
(F Foresi, France) **42/1**
0 **Simple Mind (GER)**38 221 6-9-1 0 (b) YoannRousset(2) 4 —
(Y Fertillet, France) **43/1**

2m 26.79s (146.79) **15** Ran SP% **116.5**
WIN (incl. 1 euro stake): 5.50. PLACES: 2.40, 6.10, 4.80. DF: 50.50. SF: 79.80.
Owner Michel Bouly **Bred** Kmd Holding Sa Fribourg **Trained** France

535 JEBEL ALI (L-H)
Friday, February 25
OFFICIAL GOING: Dirt: fast

707a RACE 2 (H'CAP) (DIRT) 1m 1f
10:45 (10:45) (70-85,85) 3-Y-O+ **£8,435** (£2,811; £1,546; £843; £421)

RPR
1 **Five Cents**14 4-8-8 77 RoystonFfrench 10 78
(A Al Raihe, UAE) *slowly into strd, mid-division, rdn to ld 1 1/2f out, ran on well* **10/1**
2 1 3/4 **Al Marmoom (USA)**14 5-9-0 83 (t) CSanchez 3 81
(A bin Huzaim, UAE) *settled rear, chsd wnr 2f out, not quicken fnl 1f* **6/1**3
3 4 **Hunters' Glen (USA)**42 8-8-5 74 (vt) TadhgO'Shea 5 64
(Doug Watson, UAE) *rear of mid-division, ran on wl fnl 2f, nrst finish* **5/2**1
4 1 1/2 **Dynamic Saint (USA)**14 535 8-8-11 80 (e) PatDobbs 2 67
(Doug Watson, UAE) *mid-division, ran on fnl 2f* **20/1**
5 1/2 **Kala Kanta (IRE)**14 5-8-0 77 (t) HarryBentley(7) 12 62
(S Seemar, UAE) *mid-division, chsd leaders 3f out, one pace fnl 1f* **5/1**2
6 1/2 **Next Move (IRE)**14 4-8-8 77 (t) CSandoval 4 62
(A bin Huzaim, UAE) *always mid-division* **25/1**
7 6 1/2 **Shopton Lane (USA)**98 7-8-6 82 CPHoban(7) 11 55
(Doug Watson, UAE) *soon led, rdn 3f out, wknd fnl 2f* **20/1**
8 1/4 **Major Victory (SAF)**14 535 4-8-5 80 WayneSmith 1 54
(Gay Kelleway) *rear of mid-division, nvr dangerous* **16/1**
9 5 3/4 **Shemoli**21 5-9-0 83 WilliamBuick 9 45
(D Selvaratnam, UAE) *mid-division, not much room 11f out, drpd rear, not recovered* **6/1**3
10 1 1/2 **Stubbs Art (IRE)**21 6-9-2 85 (bt) PatCosgrave 7 44
(A Al Raihe, UAE) *settled rear, chsd leaders 3f out, wknd fnl 1f* **10/1**
11 3 3/4 **Habalwatan (IRE)**14 535 7-8-4 83 (tp) SAlMazrooei(10) 8 35
(A Al Raihe, UAE) *tracked ldr til 2 1/2f out, sn beaten* **12/1**
12 29 **Fareej (USA)**20 463 4-8-9 85 AntiocoMurgia(7) 6 —
(I Mohammed, UAE) *never better than mid-division* **16/1**

1m 51.93s (111.93) **12** Ran SP% **124.8**

Owner Rashid Al Raihe **Bred** Brook Stud Bloodstock Ltd **Trained** UAE

690 WOLVERHAMPTON (A.W) (L-H)
Monday, February 28
OFFICIAL GOING: Standard
Wind: Light against Weather: Light rain

708 10% FORECAST BONUS @ BLUESQ.COM H'CAP 5f 20y(P)
2:30 (2:30) (Class 5) (0-75,75) 4-Y-O+ **£1,813** (£539; £269; £134) **Stalls** Low

Form RPR
-132 1 **Six Wives**5 646 4-9-1 72 BillyCray(3) 7 80
(David Nicholls) *sn pushed along to chse ldrs: rdn 1/2-way: r.o to ld towards fin* **6/1**2
62-0 2 1/2 **Jigajig**45 168 4-9-0 71 (p) AmyRyan(3) 13 77+
(Kevin Ryan) *prom: outpcd wl over 1f out: r.o wl ins fnl f* **12/1**
4101 3 shd **Desert Strike**5 646 5-9-6 74 6ex (p) ShaneKelly 10 80
(Alan McCabe) *s.i.s: hld up: hdwy over 1f out: r.o* **15/2**
2020 4 shd **Incomparable**16 521 6-9-6 74 (bt) FrederikTylicki 8 79
(David Nicholls) *chsd ldrs: rdn over 1f out: led ins fnl f: hdd towards fin* **13/2**3
4265 5 nse **Efistorm**24 430 10-9-1 69 HayleyTurner 5 74
(Conor Dore) *in rr and drvn along over 3f out: r.o wl ins fnl f: nrst fin* **10/1**
40-0 6 nk **Lucky Mellor**32 316 4-9-7 75 AdamKirby 12 79
(Dean Ivory) *chsd ldr: rdn over 1f out: r.o* **16/1**
5040 7 1/2 **Gwilym (GER)**11 577 8-8-9 63 AndreaAtzeni 1 65
(Derek Haydn Jones) *mid-div: rdn 1/2-way: r.o ins fnl f* **25/1**
-511 8 3/4 **Island Legend (IRE)**12 554 5-9-7 75 (p) RichardKingscote 2 75
(Milton Bradley) *led: rdn and hdd ins fnl f: styd on same pce* **9/2**1
5300 9 nk **Absa Lutte (IRE)**5 646 8-8-9 70 (t) JosephYoung(7) 4 68
(Michael Mullineaux) *s.i.s: bhd: r.o wl ins fnl f: nrst fin* **7/1**
0-60 10 2 1/2 **Divertimenti (IRE)**20 455 7-9-2 70 (b) JimmyQuinn 6 59
(Roy Bowring) *hmpd s: a towards rr* **20/1**
0-06 11 1 **Bahamian Lad**11 577 6-9-3 71 (p) LukeMorris 3 57
(Reg Hollinshead) *sn outpcd* **12/1**
0-00 12 nk **Fair Passion**12 554 4-9-4 72 PatrickMathers 9 57
(Derek Shaw) *s.i.s: hdwy over 3f out: rdn: hung lft and wknd over 1f out* **14/1**

61.89 secs (-0.41) **Going Correction** +0.075s/f (Slow) **12** Ran SP% **115.7**
Speed ratings (Par 103): **106,105,105,104,104 104,103,102,101,97 96,95**
Tote Swingers: 1&2 £9.30, 1&3 £6.70, 2&3 £14.40 CSF £74.13 CT £555.86 TOTE £9.00: £3.00, £3.90, £3.40; EX 56.10 Trifecta £272.80 Part won. Pool: £368.75 - 0.10 winning units..
Owner Sexy Six Partnership **Bred** Cheveley Park Stud Ltd **Trained** Sessay, N Yorks

FOCUS
An ultra-competitive sprint handicap featuring plenty of in-form horses. They went a furious gallop throughout and plenty weren't able to lay up with the pace. The form makes sense despite the blanket finish.
Divertimenti(IRE) Official explanation: jockey said gelding was slowly away
Fair Passion Official explanation: jockey said filly failed to handle the bend

709 GREAT OFFERS AT WOLVERHAMPTON-RACECOURSE.CO.UK MAIDEN STKS 5f 216y(P)
3:00 (3:00) (Class 5) 3-Y-O+ **£1,813** (£539; £269; £134) **Stalls** Low

Form RPR
1 **Sound Amigo (IRE)** 3-8-12 0 BarryMcHugh 5 65+
(Ollie Pears) *s.i.s: sn prom: pushed along 1/2-way: shkn up to ld ins fnl f: r.o: readily* **12/1**
0-42 2 1/2 **We'll Deal Again**17 511 4-9-10 58 (v) JamesSullivan(3) 2 65
(Michael Easterby) *chsd ldr tl led over 1f out: rdn: hung lft and hdd ins fnl f: nt qckn* **1/1**1
3 7 **Full Shilling (IRE)** 3-8-7 0 CathyGannon 6 35
(John Spearing) *sn pushed along in rr: rdn 1/2-way: styd on same pce fnl 2f: wnt 3rd nr fin* **16/1**
5- 4 3/4 **Dr Red Eye**259 3020 3-8-9 0 BillyCray(3) 1 38
(David Nicholls) *led: rdn 1/2-way: hdd over 1f out: wknd fnl f: lost 3rd nr fin* **9/4**2
/34 5 2 3/4 **Stand Beside Me (IRE)**10 593 4-9-13 0 (t) JamesDoyle 4 34+
(Sylvester Kirk) *dwlt: hld up: plld hrd: pushed along 1/2-way: nvr on terms* **9/2**3
50- 6 3 1/4 **Macie (IRE)**286 2220 4-9-8 0 PatrickMathers 3 19
(Derek Shaw) *trckd ldrs: rdn 1/2-way: wknd over 1f out* **12/1**

1m 15.13s (0.13) **Going Correction** +0.075s/f (Slow)
WFA 3 from 4yo 15lb **6** Ran SP% **120.2**
Speed ratings (Par 103): **102,101,92,91,87 83**
Tote Swingers: 1&2 £3.60, 1&3 £9.20, 2&3 £4.00 CSF £26.82 TOTE £14.80: £6.70, £1.20; EX 48.70.
Owner Tom McManus **Bred** Sherbourne Lodge **Trained** Norton, N Yorks

FOCUS
A weak sprint maiden limited by the proximity of the runner-up.
Stand Beside Me(IRE) Official explanation: jockey said colt ran too freely

710 HOTEL AND CONFERENCING AT WOLVERHAMPTON RACECOURSE CONDITIONS STKS 7f 32y(P)
3:30 (3:31) (Class 4) 4-Y-O+ **£3,238** (£963; £481; £240) **Stalls** Low

Form RPR
020- 1 **Below Zero (IRE)**118 7289 4-9-2 90 JoeFanning 1 98
(Mark Johnston) *mde all: rdn and hung rt insde fnl f: jst hld on* **9/2**3
0-33 2 nse **Sioux Rising (IRE)**5 651 5-8-11 83 FrederikTylicki 4 93
(Richard Fahey) *a.p: rdn to chse wnr over 1f out: r.o* **8/1**
-111 3 2 **Dubai Hills**46 149 5-8-11 95 AdamCarter(5) 2 93
(Bryan Smart) *sn chsng wnr: rdn 2f out: n.m.r sn after: styd on same pce ins fnl f* **5/4**1
50-5 4 1 **Captain Ramius (IRE)**9 613 5-9-2 89 JamieSpencer 3 92
(Kevin Ryan) *hmpd sn after s: hld up: rdn and hdwy 2f out: swtchd lft 1f out: no ex ins fnl f* **7/4**2

1m 28.53s (-1.07) **Going Correction** +0.075s/f (Slow) **4** Ran SP% **110.1**
Speed ratings (Par 105): **109,108,106,105**
CSF £30.32 TOTE £5.60; EX 22.10.
Owner Sheikh Hamdan Bin Mohammed Al Maktoum **Bred** Darley **Trained** Middleham Moor, N Yorks

FOCUS
A small but select field for this conditions event. The form is rated negatively through the runner-up.

711 DOWNLOAD THE BLUE SQUARE IPHONE APP APPRENTICE H'CAP 1m 1f 103y(P)
4:00 (4:00) (Class 5) (0-70,68) 4-Y-0+ £1,813 (£539; £269; £134) Stalls Low

Form RPR
-115 1 **Black Coffee**[14] 541 6-9-3 **67**....................(b) JamesRogers(3) 2 74
(Mark Brisbourne) *hld up: hdwy and hung rt over 1f out: sn rdn: r.o to ld towards fin* **9/4**[2]
5-11 2 *shd* **Stargazing (IRE)**[11] 580 5-8-12 **59**.................... TobyAtkinson 3 66
(Marco Botti) *trckd ldrs: racd keenly: rdn and ev ch ins fnl f: r.o* **7/4**[1]
4-26 3 *nk* **The Winged Assasin (USA)**[32] 315 5-9-2 **68**..........(t) LucyKBarry(5) 5 74
(Shaun Lycett) *hld up: hdwy over 6f out: pushed along to chse ldr over 2f out: led over 1f out: rdn and hdd ins fnl f: r.o* **13/2**
-032 4 *½* **What's Up Doc (IRE)**[16] 526 10-8-9 **61**.................... LewisWalsh(5) 6 66
(Lawney Hill) *edgd lft s: chsd ldr: hung lft over 2f out: led ins fnl f: sn rdn: hdd towards fin* **4/1**[3]
0-06 5 *7* **Prince Golan (IRE)**[3] 692 7-8-6 **56**.................... DavidKenny(3) 4 46
(Richard Price) *chsd ldrs: pushed along 5f out: rdn 3f out: wknd over 1f out* **16/1**
103- 6 *nk* **High Five Society**[93] 7599 7-9-2 **68**....................(b) LeonnaMayor(5) 1 58
(Roy Bowring) *led: hdd over 1f out: wknd fnl f* **25/1**

2m 2.64s (0.94) **Going Correction** +0.075s/f (Slow) **6 Ran SP% 110.2**
Speed ratings (Par 103): **98,97,97,97,90 90**
Tote Swingers: 1&2 £1.80, 1&3 £2.10, 2&3 £3.20 CSF £6.33 TOTE £2.60: £1.40, £1.90; EX 7.30.
Owner Derek & Mrs Marie Dean **Bred** Mrs M Campbell-Andenaes **Trained** Great Ness, Shropshire

FOCUS
A fair apprentice handicap in which all of the runners had plenty of form over C&D. An easy race to rate and it could be slightly higher.

712 SPONSOR A RACE BY CALLING 01902 390000 H'CAP 1m 141y(P)
4:30 (4:30) (Class 6) (0-60,60) 4-Y-0+ £1,535 (£453; £226) Stalls Low

Form RPR
3-35 1 **Una Pelota (IRE)**[24] 427 5-9-4 **57**....................(b[1]) RichardKingscote 1 69
(Tom Dascombe) *chsd ldr 3f: remained handy: wnt 2nd again over 2f out: sn rdn: led ins fnl f: r.o* **7/1**[3]
-01 2 *1½* **Duneen Dream (USA)**[25] 408 6-9-2 **55**.................... AndreaAtzeni 4 64
(Nikki Evans) *led: rdn over 1f out: hdd and unable qck ins fnl f* **7/2**[1]
-234 3 *2* **Gordy Bee (USA)**[7] 637 5-9-6 **59**....................(e) JamieSpencer 9 63
(Richard Guest) *chsd ldrs: rdn over 3f out: n.m.r over 2f out: r.o* **7/1**[3]
5142 4 *2½* **Kielty's Folly**[12] 555 7-9-1 **54**.................... JackMitchell 7 52
(Brian Baugh) *hld up: hdwy over 2f out: rdn over 1f out: wknd ins fnl f* **7/1**[3]
-020 5 *½* **Ocean Countess (IRE)**[26] 391 5-8-13 **52**.................... CathyGannon 2 49
(Tony Carroll) *s.i.s: hld up: rdn over 1f out: r.o ins fnl f: nrst fin* **12/1**
0/0- 6 *nse* **Echo Dancer**[29] 1508 5-9-6 **59**....................(t) HayleyTurner 3 56
(Trevor Wall) *chsd ldrs: rdn over 2f out: no ex fnl f* **50/1**
04-5 7 *¾* **Provost**[16] 526 7-9-3 **59**....................(b) JamesSullivan(3) 6 54
(Michael Easterby) *hld up: rdn over 2f out: hdwy over 1f out: no imp ins fnl f* **8/1**
4651 8 *nk* **Join Up**[16] 526 5-9-4 **60**.................... RossAtkinson(3) 8 55
(Mark Brisbourne) *prom: rdn and wknd over 1f out* **13/2**[2]
2-40 9 *3½* **Penbryn (USA)**[19] 477 4-9-0 **60**....................(b) DavidKenny(7) 10 46
(Nick Littmoden) *s.i.s: hld up: hdwy over 2f out: rdn: hung lft and wknd over 1f out* **10/1**
62-3 10 *2* **Director General (USA)**[35] 283 4-9-2 **55**....................(b) TomEaves 12 37
(Julie Camacho) *prom: racd keenly: trckd ldr over 5f out tl rdn over 2f out: wknd over 1f out* **8/1**
-100 11 *24* **Penrod Ballantyne (IRE)**[17] 504 4-9-1 **54**....................(v[1]) LukeMorris 5 —
(Mike Hammond) *mid-div: n.m.r over 6f out: rdn over 3f out: wknd sn after: t.o: b.b.v* **25/1**

1m 50.29s (-0.21) **Going Correction** +0.075s/f (Slow) **11 Ran SP% 117.9**
Speed ratings (Par 101): **103,101,99,97,97 97,96,96,93,91 70**
Tote Swingers: 1&2 £6.70, 1&3 £6.30, 2&3 £7.80 CSF £31.75 CT £184.43 TOTE £10.30: £2.90, £1.50, £2.60; EX 40.20 Trifecta £415.80 Pool: £584.39 - 1.04 winning units..
Owner Owen Promotions Limited **Bred** John Fielding **Trained** Malpas, Cheshire

FOCUS
It paid to be handy in this competitive low-grade handicap. The form looks solid.
Penrod Ballantyne(IRE) Official explanation: jockey said gelding ran too freely; trainer said gelding bled from the nose

713 STAY AT THE WOLVERHAMPTON HOLIDAY INN MEDIAN AUCTION MAIDEN STKS 1m 141y(P)
5:00 (5:02) (Class 5) 3-4-Y-0 £1,813 (£539; £269; £134) Stalls Low

Form RPR
1 **Needwood Ridge**[62] 4-10-0 **0**....................(t) JamesDoyle 2 70
(Frank Sheridan) *chsd ldrs: rdn over 2f out: led ins fnl f: r.o* **50/1**[3]
06- 2 *nk* **Sim Sala Bim**[122] 7201 3-8-7 **0**.................... WilliamCarson 4 63
(Stuart Williams) *chsd ldr: rdn over 1f out: ev ch ins fnl f: r.o* **10/11**[1]
2 3 *½* **Black Pond (USA)**[11] 579 3-8-7 **0**.................... JoeFanning 1 62
(Mark Johnston) *led: rdn over 1f out: hdd ins fnl f: styd on* **10/11**[1]
6- 4 *1½* **Arizona High**[120] 7248 3-8-7 **0**.................... DavidProbert 5 59
(Andrew Balding) *plld hrd and prom: rdn over 1f out: styd on same pce ins fnl f* **11/2**[2]
5 *8* **Aimee Tricks** 3-8-2 **0**.................... CathyGannon 3 37+
(Sylvester Kirk) *s.i.s: hld up: rdn over 2f out: wknd over 1f out* **50/1**[3]
6 *2* **Tuscany Red** 3-8-4 **0**.................... AndrewHeffernan(3) 6 38
(Richard Guest) *unruly bhd stalls: hld up: rdn over 2f out: wknd wl over 1f out* **66/1**

1m 52.33s (1.83) **Going Correction** +0.075s/f (Slow)
WFA 3 from 4yo 21lb **6 Ran SP% 125.6**
Speed ratings (Par 103): **94,93,93,91,84 83**
Tote Swingers: 1&2 £10.60, 1&3 £5.50, 2&3 £1.30 CSF £109.46 TOTE £46.50: £10.40, £1.10; EX 115.40.
Owner Tim Maund-Powell **Bred** Mrs Joy Maund-Powell **Trained** Wolverhampton, W Midlands
■ Stewards' Enquiry : William Carson two-day ban: used whip with excessive frequency (Mar 15-16)

FOCUS
A fair maiden notable for a major gamble that went astray in the unlikeliest of circumstances, with the odds-on joint favourites filling the places behind the surprise winner. There are question marks over the form.

714 WOLVERHAMPTON-RACECOURSE.CO.UK MAIDEN STKS 1m 1f 103y(P)
5:30 (5:30) (Class 5) 3-Y-O £1,813 (£539; £269; £134) Stalls Low

Form RPR
5-5 1 **Tornado Force (IRE)**[19] 471 3-9-3 **0**.................... LukeMorris 3 71
(J S Moore) *mde all: rdn over 1f out: hung lft ins fnl f: styd on* **5/1**[3]
2 *1* **Lady Elsie** 3-8-12 **0**.................... LiamJones 2 64+
(William Haggas) *a.p: shkn up to chse wnr ins fnl f: r.o wl* **5/1**[3]
-462 3 *3* **Loyal N Trusted**[7] 634 3-9-3 **0**.................... AndreaAtzeni 6 63
(Michael Wigham) *chsd wnr: rdn over 1f out: no ex ins fnl f* **1/1**[1]
0 4 *1* **Barnum (USA)**[13] 546 3-9-3 **0**.................... JoeFanning 1 61
(Mark Johnston) *hld up: rdn over 1f out: wnt 4th nr fin: nvr trbld ldrs* **4/1**[2]
45 5 *hd* **Freedom Flyer (IRE)**[11] 579 3-9-3 **0**.................... AdamKirby 4 60
(Marco Botti) *prom: rdn over 2f out: wknd fnl f: lost 4th nr fin* **33/1**
6 *3½* **Absolute Princess** 3-8-9 **0**.................... BillyCray(3) 5 48
(David Nicholls) *dwlt: rn green in rr: rdn and hung rt over 2f out: sn wknd* **25/1**

2m 4.38s (2.68) **Going Correction** +0.075s/f (Slow) **6 Ran SP% 110.1**
Speed ratings (Par 97): **91,90,87,86,86 83**
CSF £28.17 TOTE £5.30: £1.90, £2.60; EX 29.50.
Owner Faisal Alsheikh **Bred** Haras Du Mezeray & Ronchalon Racing **Trained** Upper Lambourn, Berks

FOCUS
Quite an interesting 3y-o maiden with the winner a small improver in a race where the level is fluid.

715 PLAY RAINBOW RICHES AT BLUESQ.COM H'CAP 1m 4f 50y(P)
6:00 (6:00) (Class 5) (0-75,73) 4-Y-0+ £1,813 (£539; £269; £134) Stalls Low

Form RPR
2-1 1 **Sweet Origin**[14] 539 4-9-5 **73**.................... JimmyQuinn 3 81+
(Marco Botti) *a.p: rdn over 1f out: led ins fnl f: drvn out* **1/2**[1]
00-5 2 *1½* **Jeer (IRE)**[16] 531 7-9-2 **70**....................(b) JamesSullivan(3) 6 76
(Michael Easterby) *chsd ldr: pushed along over 2f out: led over 1f out: rdn and hdd ins fnl f: styd on same pce* **18/1**
3212 3 *nse* **Layla's Dancer**[2] 697 4-9-4 **72**.................... StevieDonohoe 2 78
(Tony Carroll) *hld up: hdwy over 2f out: rdn and ev ch over 1f out: styd on same pce ins fnl f* **4/1**[2]
20-3 4 *2¾* **Hallstatt (IRE)**[16] 531 5-8-11 **62**....................(t) LukeMorris 5 64
(John Mackie) *hld up: rdn over 3f out: styd on fr over 1f out: nt trble ldrs* **17/2**[3]
-414 5 *4* **Straversjoy**[17] 515 4-9-3 **71**.................... AdamKirby 1 67
(Reg Hollinshead) *chsd ldrs: pushed along to ld over 3f out: rdn and hdd over 1f out: wknd fnl f* **16/1**
2-00 6 *9* **Beetuna (IRE)**[25] 405 6-9-7 **72**.................... CathyGannon 4 54
(David Bourton) *led: hdd over 3f out: sn rdn: wknd wl over 1f out* **16/1**

2m 39.65s (-1.45) **Going Correction** +0.075s/f (Slow)
WFA 4 from 5yo+ 3lb **6 Ran SP% 114.2**
Speed ratings (Par 103): **107,106,105,104,101 95**
CSF £12.42 TOTE £1.50: £1.10, £4.30; EX 14.40.
Owner Newsells Park Stud **Bred** Newsells Park Stud Limited **Trained** Newmarket, Suffolk

FOCUS
The closing 1m4f handicap revolved around one horse. the winner can probably win again while the placed horses help set the level.
T/Plt: £1,118.20 to a £1 stake. Pool:£65,182.76 - 42.55 winning tickets T/Qpdt: £132.20 to a £1 stake. Pool:£4,737.45 - 26.50 winning tickets CR

697 LINGFIELD (L-H)
Tuesday, March 1

OFFICIAL GOING: Standard
Wind: medium, half against Weather: dry but cold

716 AT THE RACES SKY 415 APPRENTICE H'CAP 1m 2f (P)
2:10 (2:10) (Class 6) (0-65,63) 3-Y-O £1,535 (£453; £226) Stalls Low

Form RPR
0-12 1 **Jack's Revenge (IRE)**[12] 567 3-9-5 **58**....................(p) MatthewDavies 4 65+
(George Baker) *hld up wl off the pce towards rr: pushed along and clsd on ldrs on outer 3f out: led over 1f out: hung rt ins fnl f: edgd lft u.p and hld on cl home* **15/8**[1]
06-4 2 *½* **Echos Of Motivator**[13] 564 3-9-10 **63**.................... KierenFox 2 69
(Ronald Harris) *hld up wl off the pce in rr: clsd on ldrs but stl in rr and rdn over 2f out: swtchd lft and hdwy over 1f out: kpt on wl u.p ins fnl f: pressed wnr fnl 50yds: hld cl home* **11/1**
0-40 3 *nk* **Anna Fontenail**[17] 520 3-9-6 **59**.................... JamesMillman 3 64+
(Rod Millman) *stdd s: hld up wl off the pce in rr: clsd on ldrs 3f out: rdn and effrt on outer bnd 2f out: chsd wnr ins fnl f: shied at rivals whip and faltered ins fnl f: edgd lft u.p towards fin* **9/1**
02-4 4 *1¼* **Crossword**[15] 543 3-9-6 **59**....................(p) TobyAtkinson 5 62
(Marco Botti) *hld up wl off the pce in rr: clsd on ldrs 3f out: drvn and chsd ldrs over 1f out: kpt on same pce ins fnl f* **9/2**[2]
-623 5 *2* **Bodie**[15] 543 3-9-4 **62**....................(b) ChristyMews(5) 9 61+
(Pam Sly) *t.k.h: sn clr w ldr: c bk to field over 2f out: stl chsng ldrs and pushed along over 1f out: wknd ins fnl f* **6/1**[3]
501- 6 *½* **Crown Ridge (IRE)**[131] 7035 3-9-5 **58**.................... MartinHarley 6 56
(Mick Channon) *prom in main gp: clsd on ldng pair 3f out: gng wl whn nt clr run and swtchd rt 2f out: nt clr run again over 1f out: sn rdn and fnd little: no prog ins fnl f* **6/1**[3]
4-25 7 *2¾* **Ippi N Tombi (IRE)**[4] 693 3-8-6 **45**.................... AndrewHeffernan 1 38
(Phil McEntee) *racd wl off the pce in midfield: clsd on ldrs 3f out: in tch whn nt clr run and hmpd over 1f out: nt rcvr and no hdwy after* **66/1**
050- 8 *7* **Beach Babe**[155] 6411 3-9-7 **60**.................... MartinLane 8 40
(Jonathan Portman) *prom in main gp: clsd on ldrs 3f out: lost pl jst over 2f out: wl btn over 1f out* **20/1**
0-00 9 *1* **Beach Patrol (IRE)**[17] 519 3-8-6 **50**.................... JenniferFerguson(5) 10 28
(Edward Creighton) *dwlt: sn dashed up to ld and wl clr w rival: hdd wl over 1f out: sn wknd: wl bhd ins fnl f* **40/1**
06-0 10 *21* **Varlak**[13] 564 3-9-6 **59**.................... BillyCray 7 —
(Des Donovan) *prom in main gp tl lost pl and rdn wl over 3f out: lost tch 3f out: t.o* **50/1**

2m 7.35s (0.75) **Going Correction** +0.125s/f (Slow) **10 Ran SP% 110.5**
Speed ratings (Par 96): **102,101,101,100,98 98,96,90,89,72**
toteswingers:1&2 £5.30, 2&3 £10.90, 1&3 £5.00 CSF £22.01 CT £138.51 TOTE £2.50: £1.10, £3.40, £2.90; EX 26.00 Trifecta £547.10 Part won. Pool of £739.38 - 0.91 winning units..

Owner Hendan SD **Bred** Con Marnane **Trained** Whitsbury, Hants
■ Stewards' Enquiry : Martin Harley three-day ban: careless riding (Mar 15-17)

FOCUS
A few of the principals are lazy types, and it showed in the closing stages, but this still looks good form for the grade, and the first three should remain competitive off their new marks.
Anna Fontenail Official explanation: jockey said filly wandered in straight

717 CYPRIUM BAR AT MARRIOTT LINGFIELD (S) STKS — 1m 2f (P)
2:40 (2:40) (Class 6) 3-Y-O — **£1,535** (£453; £226) **Stalls** Low

Form — RPR

-113 **1** **A Little Bit Dusty**[10] 609 3-9-1 71 ....(b) KierenFox(3) 1 — 65
(Bill Turner) *led tl 7f out: chsd ldr after: rdn and ev ch 2f out: led ent fnl f: hld on u.p ins fnl f: bmpd cl home* **11/10**[1]

3 **2** *hd* **Bountiful Guest**[17] 519 3-8-5 0 .... CharlesBishop(7) 4 — 58
(Mick Channon) *stdd s: chsd ldr over 8f out tl led 7f out: rdr in muddle w reins and hdd ent fnl f: kpt on but a jst hld: veered rt and bmpd wnr nr fin* **4/1**[3]

2414 **3** *2 1/4* **Ad Vitam (IRE)**[4] 686 3-9-4 60 ....(tp) LiamKeniry 2 — 60
(Bernard Llewellyn) *chsd ldrs: rdn and nt gng pce of ldng pair over 1f out: edgd rt and rallied ins fnl f: kpt on but nvr gng pce to rch ldrs* **15/2**

03-3 **4** *3 1/2* **Cool Luke**[18] 509 3-8-12 65 .... PJMcDonald 5 — 47
(Alan Swinbank) *in tch: rdn and nt pce of ldng pair over 2f out: no imp and wl hld over 1f out* **5/2**[2]

0 **5** *34* **Zoriana**[32] 339 3-8-7 0 .... WilliamCarson 3 — —
(Christine Dunnett) *a in last: rdn and lost tch qckly 3f out: t.o* **66/1**

2m 11.9s (5.30) **Going Correction** +0.125s/f (Slow) — **5** Ran SP% **109.4**
Speed ratings (Par 96): **83,82,81,78,51**
CSF £5.84 TOTE £2.30: £1.80, £1.20; EX 5.00.There was no bid for the winner. Bountiful Guest was claimed by B. Baugh for £6000.
Owner T.O.C.S. Ltd **Bred** T O C S Limited **Trained** Sigwells, Somerset

FOCUS
The pace was slow and the time was 4.55 seconds slower than earlier 46-65 3-y-o handicap. Weak form, limited by the proximity of the third.

718 LINGFIELDPARK.CO.UK H'CAP — 2m (P)
3:10 (3:10) (Class 5) (0-75,74) 4-Y-O+ — **£2,047** (£604; £302) **Stalls** Low

Form — RPR

3-31 **1** **Kahfre**[11] 309 4-9-1 **68** ....(v) DavidProbert 4 — 76
(Gary Moore) *chsd ldr: shkn up and ev ch ent fnl 2f: led ent fnl f: forged ahd fnl 75yds* **7/1**

222- **2** *1 1/4* **Mohanad (IRE)**[129] 6775 5-9-2 **64** .... JamieGoldstein 5 — 71
(Sheena West) *chsd ldrs: rdn over 2f out: ev ch 1f out tl no ex and btn fnl 75yds* **9/2**[3]

00-0 **3** *1/2* **Epsom Salts**[20] 475 6-9-3 **70** .... JemmaMarshall(5) 2 — 77
(Pat Phelan) *hld up in tch in rr: trcking ldrs gng wl whn nt clr run over 1f out tl eventually swtchd rt ins fnl f: r.o fnl 100yds: nt rch ldrs* **4/1**[2]

44-4 **4** *1 1/2* **Satwa Gold (USA)**[19] 486 5-9-12 **74** .... GeorgeBaker 6 — 78
(Seamus Durack) *hld up wl in tch in last pair: trcking ldrs gng wl and nt clr run ent fnl 2f: swtchd ins and effrt over 1f out: no ex and btn fnl 100yds: wknd towards fin* **7/2**[1]

212 **5** *1/2* **Rosewood Lad**[19] 492 4-9-0 **67** .... CathyGannon 1 — 71
(J S Moore) *led: rdn over 2f out: hdd ent fnl f: wknd fnl 100yds* **4/1**[2]

2153 **6** *3 1/2* **Frameit (IRE)**[13] 560 4-8-7 **60** ....(v) FrannyNorton 3 — 59
(James Given) *t.k.h: trckd ldrs: rdn and unable qck over 1f out: wknd ins fnl f* **11/2**

3m 28.06s (2.36) **Going Correction** +0.125s/f (Slow)
WFA 4 from 5yo+ 5lb — **6** Ran SP% **108.3**
Speed ratings (Par 103): **99,98,98,97,97 95**
toteswingers:1&2 £7.00, 2&3 £4.40, 1&3 £4.80 CSF £34.88 TOTE £8.90: £3.40, £3.50; EX 29.50.
Owner SelectRacingClub.co.uk & Dr C A Barnett **Bred** Ballygallon Stud Limited **Trained** Lower Beeding, W Sussex

FOCUS
A reasonable staying handicap, but the pace was predictably steady, resulting in a time over 8secs above standard. The form seems reasonable, rated around the first three.
Epsom Salts ◆ Official explanation: jockey said gelding was denied a clear run
Frameit(IRE) Official explanation: jockey said gelding ran too free

719 BREATHE SPA AT MARRIOTT LINGFIELD H'CAP — 7f (P)
3:45 (3:45) (Class 6) (0-60,60) 4-Y-O+ — **£1,535** (£453; £226) **Stalls** Low

Form — RPR

0440 **1** **Spinning Ridge (IRE)**[5] 674 6-9-3 **56** ....(b) DavidProbert 3 — 63
(Ronald Harris) *in tch in midfield: rdn and hdwy to chse ldrs over 2f out: led ent fnl f: clr ins fnl f: kpt on wl: rdn out* **13/2**

-054 **2** *1* **Cavalry Guard (USA)**[5] 662 7-8-4 **46** oh1 ....(b) BillyCray(3) 7 — 50
(Tim McCarthy) *towards rr: rdn and hdwy ent fnl 2f: wnt between horses and chsng ldrs 1f out: r.o wl to go 2nd towards fin: nt rch wnr* **20/1**

45-6 **3** *1/2* **Louphole**[26] 402 9-8-12 **58** .... DannyBrock(7) 11 — 61
(J R Jenkins) *stdd and swtchd lft after s: hld up in rr: rdn and hdwy on inner over 1f out: chsd wnr ins fnl f: kpt on lost 2nd towards fin* **33/1**

00-1 **4** *3/4* **Ymir**[11] 589 5-9-0 **53** ....(vt) ShaneKelly 5 — 54
(Michael Attwater) *chsd ldr: rdn and unable qck over 2f out: styd on same pce ins fnl f* **9/2**[2]

-044 **5** *1 1/4* **Katmai River (IRE)**[19] 488 4-8-10 **54** .... LeeNewnes(5) 10 — 52
(Mark Usher) *in tch on outer: rdn and unable qck whn edgd lft over 1f out: styd on u.p fnl 100yds: nvr gng pce to threaten ldrs* **4/1**[1]

-202 **6** *nk* **Bollywood Style**[6] 654 6-9-6 **59** .... LukeMorris 9 — 56
(John Best) *towards rr: rdn along and no hdwy on outer over 2f out: styd on ins fnl f: nvr trbld ldrs* **11/2**[3]

-000 **7** *shd* **Hierarch (IRE)**[17] 522 4-9-7 **60** ....(bt) JamesDoyle 2 — 56
(David Flood) *racd freely: led: rdn wl over 1f out: hdd ent fnl f: wknd fnl 150yds* **9/2**[2]

10-0 **8** *4 1/2* **Stellarina (IRE)**[19] 488 5-9-4 **57** ....(v) JimCrowley 8 — 42
(William Knight) *in tch: rdn and lost pl jst over 2f out: wl btn ent fnl f* **12/1**

4000 **9** *7* **Southwark Newshawk**[19] 482 4-8-7 **46** oh1 .... WilliamCarson 6 — 13
(Christine Dunnett) *a bhd: rdn and toiling over 2f out: sn wl bhd: eased ins fnl f* **66/1**

6-04 **10** *5* **Art Scholar (IRE)**[24] 433 4-9-7 **60** ....(v[1]) GeorgeBaker 1 — 14
(Gary Moore) *chsd ldrs: rdn and nt qckn over 2f out: sn struggling: wl bhd and eased ins fnl f* **15/2**

1m 24.49s (-0.31) **Going Correction** +0.125s/f (Slow) — **10** Ran SP% **113.7**
Speed ratings (Par 101): **106,104,104,103,102 101,101,96,88,82**
toteswingers:1&2 £17.10, 2&3 £34.80, 1&3 £27.50 CSF £123.98 CT £3972.39 TOTE £7.40: £2.10, £4.30, £10.40; EX 104.50 TRIFECTA Not won..
Owner Robert & Nina Bailey **Bred** Eddie O'Leary **Trained** Earlswood, Monmouths

FOCUS
A moderate handicap run at a strong pace. The form looks straightforward.
Art Scholar(IRE) Official explanation: jockey said gelding had no more to give

720 ATR VIRTUALOWNER.COM MAIDEN STKS — 7f (P)
4:20 (4:20) (Class 5) 3-Y-O+ — **£1,910** (£564; £282) **Stalls** Low

Form — RPR

05-2 **1** **Bosambo**[13] 559 3-8-10 77 .... PJMcDonald 3 — 74+
(Alan Swinbank) *w ldr on inner tl led ent fnl 2f: pushed along and rdr looked over wrong shoulder 1f out: nudged along and r.o ins fnl f* **10/11**[1]

520- **2** *1/2* **Uncle Dermot (IRE)**[131] 7035 3-8-10 69 .... DaneO'Neill 2 — 70
(Brendan Powell) *chsd ldrs: swtchd ins and rdn to chse wnr over 1f out: pressed wnr ins fnl f: kpt on: a hld* **6/1**[3]

524/ **3** *10* **Viking Dancer**[518] 6364 4-9-12 75 .... DavidProbert 4 — 50
(Andrew Balding) *led tl hdd ent fnl 2f: wknd u.p over 1f out: wl btn ins fnl f* **7/4**[2]

45-6 **4** *7* **Big City Boy (IRE)**[4] 693 3-8-10 0 ....(v[1]) LukeMorris 1 — 26
(Phil McEntee) *chsd ldrs: rdn wl over 2f out: wknd u.p 2f out: wl bhd over 1f out* **50/1**

1m 25.74s (0.94) **Going Correction** +0.125s/f (Slow)
WFA 3 from 4yo 16lb — **4** Ran SP% **105.0**
Speed ratings (Par 103): **99,98,87,79**
CSF £6.16 TOTE £1.40; EX 4.80.
Owner Guy Reed **Bred** Theakston Stud **Trained** Melsonby, N Yorks

FOCUS
The time of this maiden was 1.25 seconds slower than the earlier Class 6 handicap for the older horses, suggesting they didn't go that quick. The winner had something to spare.

721 AT THE RACES VIRGIN 534 MAIDEN STKS — 6f (P)
4:55 (4:56) (Class 5) 3-Y-O — **£1,910** (£564; £282) **Stalls** Low

Form — RPR

00-2 **1** **Queen O'The Desert (IRE)**[6] 659 3-8-12 70 .... DavidProbert 6 — 67+
(Andrew Balding) *led tl over 4f out: chsd ldr after tl rdn to ld again over 1f out: kpt on wl u.p ins fnl f* **5/2**[2]

3 **2** *nk* **York Glory (USA)**[13] 559 3-9-3 0 .... NeilCallan 3 — 71+
(Kevin Ryan) *in tch: pushed along over 4f out: clsd and nt clr run over 2f out: hung rt and rdn bnd 2f out: hdwy over 1f out: chsd wnr fnl 100yds: clsng towards fin but nvr quite getting to wnr* **1/2**[1]

456- **3** *2 3/4* **Abadejo**[97] 7552 3-9-3 59 .... FergusSweeney 7 — 63
(J R Jenkins) *t.k.h: chsd ldrs tl led over 4f out: hdd and rdn over 1f out: lost 2nd and wknd ins fnl f* **25/1**

3202 **4** *2 1/4* **Fairy Tales**[9] 620 3-8-12 56 .... LukeMorris 4 — 51
(John Bridger) *chsd ldrs: rdn and unable qck ent fnl 2f: styd on same pce and no imp fr over 1f out* **14/1**[3]

5 *2 1/2* **Demoiselle Bond** 3-8-12 0 .... RichardThomas 2 — 44+
(Lydia Richards) *v.s.a: detached in last: rn green bnd 2f out: kpt on ins fnl f: nvr trbld ldrs* **50/1**

00- **6** *4* **Striking Willow**[168] 6053 3-9-3 0 .... JamesMillman 5 — 37
(Rod Millman) *chsd ldrs tl wknd qckly u.p 2f out: sn bhd* **50/1**

1m 13.23s (1.33) **Going Correction** +0.125s/f (Slow) — **6** Ran SP% **109.7**
Speed ratings (Par 98): **96,95,91,88,85 80**
toteswingers:1&2 £1.30, 2&3 £2.50, 1&3 £2.90 CSF £3.89 TOTE £3.20: £1.80, £1.10; EX 5.80.
Owner N Botica **Bred** Rabbah Bloodstock Limited **Trained** Kingsclere, Hants

FOCUS
The front two are fair types, but the remainder have so far shown only modest form at best. The third and fourth are the key to the level.
Demoiselle Bond Official explanation: jockey said filly was slowly away

722 VISIT ATTHERACES.COM/CHELTENHAM H'CAP — 1m (P)
5:25 (5:27) (Class 6) (0-60,59) 4-Y-O+ — **£1,535** (£453; £226) **Stalls** High

Form — RPR

00-6 **1** **Clearing House**[12] 574 6-8-7 **45** .... KirstyMilczarek 4 — 53+
(John Ryan) *unloaded fr stalls and reloaded: hld up in rr: stl plenty to do and looking for run over 1f out: str run and burst between horses to ld wl ins fnl f: sn in command: r.o wl* **20/1**

[illegible]
(Tony Carroll) *in tch: hdwy to chse ldrs over 2f out: carried rt ent st: ev ch u.p 1f out: nt gng pce of wnr wl ins fnl f* **11/2**[2]

5-26 **3** *1/2* **Shaded Edge**[27] 390 7-9-7 **59** .... MartinDwyer 6 — 61
(David Arbuthnot) *chsd ldrs tl wnt 2nd 2f out: sn carried rt: ev ch u.p fr over 1f out: led jst ins fnl f tl hdd and nvr gng pce of wnr wl ins fnl f* **4/1**[1]

00-0 **4** *nk* **Illuminative (USA)**[30] 361 5-9-2 **54** ....(p) SamHitchcott 2 — 55
(Zoe Davison) *dwlt and pushed along early: in tch in midfield: rdn and effrt ent fnl 2f out: swtchd lft ins fnl f: kpt on towards fin* **14/1**

0-00 **5** *1/2* **Miss Bounty**[13] 555 6-8-7 **52** .... NathanAlison(7) 7 — 52
(Jim Boyle) *taken down early: t.k.h: in tch in midfield: rdn and effrt ent fnl 2f: kpt on ins fnl f* **10/1**

1162 **6** *3/4* **Very Well Red**[12] 573 8-9-6 **58** .... WilliamCarson 9 — 56
(Peter Hiatt) *led: c towards centre and rdn wl over 1f out: hdd ins fnl f: wknd towards fin* **4/1**[1]

-006 **7** *nk* **Sea Tobougie**[6] 652 4-8-0 **45** .... RachealKneller(7) 5 — 43
(Mark Usher) *racd in last trio: pushed along and wd bnd 2f out: styd on ins fnl f: nvr gng pce to threaten ldrs* **33/1**

565- **8** *nk* **Officer Lily (USA)**[76] 7872 4-8-12 **53** .... KierenFox(3) 8 — 50
(John Best) *bhd: rdn and effrt wl over 1f out: swtchd lft 1f out: kpt on ins fnl f: nvr able to chal* **11/2**[2]

0606 **9** *4 1/2* **Yakama (IRE)**[11] 589 6-9-0 **52** ....(v) LukeMorris 1 — 39
(Christine Dunnett) *in tch in midfield on inner: rdn over 2f out: unable qck u.p over 1f out: wknd ins fnl f* **10/1**

06-6 **10** *3 1/4* **Crazy Parachute**[24] 432 4-9-3 **55** .... GeorgeBaker 3 — 34
(Gary Moore) *taken down early: plld hrd: chsd ldr tl 2f out: wknd ent fnl f* **9/1**[3]

1m 38.73s (0.53) **Going Correction** +0.125s/f (Slow) — **10** Ran SP% **113.3**
Speed ratings (Par 101): **102,100,100,99,99 98,98,98,93,90**
toteswingers:1&2 £16.00, 2&3 £3.20, 1&3 £16.30 CSF £122.93 CT £549.13 TOTE £26.90: £7.50, £1.70, £2.00; EX 142.70 TRIFECTA Not won..
Owner J Ryan **Bred** Gainsborough Stud Management Ltd **Trained** Newmarket, Suffolk

FOCUS
A moderate contest and they looked like finishing in a bit of a bunch. The third and fourth help set the level.
T/Plt: £358.50 to a £1 stake. Pool of £61,316.19 - 124.85 winning tickets. T/Qpdt: £149.80 to a £1 stake. Pool of £4,049.07 - 20.00 winning tickets. SP

662 KEMPTON (A.W) (R-H)
Wednesday, March 2

OFFICIAL GOING: Standard
Wind: Virtually nil Weather: Light early on

723 FREE ENTRY FOR BETDAQ MEMBERS H'CAP 1m 2f (P)
5:40 (5:40) (Class 4) (0-80,79) 4-Y-O+ **£3,238** (£963; £481; £240) **Stalls** Low

Form RPR
1302 1 **Kidlat**5 694 6-9-7 79 CathyGannon 1 87
(Alan Bailey) *mde all: drvn and stdy on strly fr over 1f out: hld on wl* **13/8**1
0-42 2 3/4 **Aphrodisia**30 369 7-9-2 74 TomEaves 2 81
(Ian Williams) *chsd ldrs: rdn 2f out: styd on to chse wnr ins fnl f: kpt on but a readily hld* **13/2**
-216 3 2 **Mighty Clarets (IRE)**25 436 4-8-12 75 LeeTopliss(5) 9 78
(Richard Fahey) *disp 2nd tl chsd wnr 2f out: no imp: lost 2nd and edgd rt ins fnl f: one pce* **5/1**2
600- 4 nk **Sir Royal (USA)**165 6185 6-9-3 75 FergusSweeney 4 77
(Brendan Powell) *in rr: hdwy on outside fr 2f out: kpt on fnl f but nvr gng pce to rch ldrs* **16/1**
1162 5 nk **The Lock Master (IRE)**15 548 4-9-4 76 NeilChalmers 8 78
(Michael Appleby) *in tch: drvn along 2f out: styd on fnl f but nvr a threat* **6/1**3
-620 6 1 1/4 **Halsion Chancer**10 628 7-9-4 79 KierenFox(3) 7 78
(John Best) *t.k.h: disp 2nd tl rdn 2f out: wknd fnl f: eased whn no ch* **12/1**
-010 7 2 1/4 **Buona Sarah (IRE)**5 687 4-8-4 69 NathanAlison(7) 6 65
(Sheena West) *slowly away: t.k.h: in rr: effrt on ins to chse ldrs over 1f out: no imp: wknd ins fnl f* **12/1**
00-3 8 3/4 **Bavarica**30 369 9-8-8 71 AdamBeschizza(5) 5 67
(Julia Feilden) *in rr effrt on outside 2f out: nvr rchd ldrs and sn wknd* **12/1**
2m 8.93s (0.93) **Going Correction** +0.05s/f (Slow) 8 Ran SP% **111.3**
Speed ratings (Par 105): **98,97,95,95,95 94,92,91**
toteswingers: 1&2 £2.00, 1&3 £2.10, 2&3 £3.80 CSF £11.74 CT £41.08 TOTE £2.30: £1.10, £2.60, £1.90; EX 13.60 Trifecta £72.80 Pool: £8,548.68 - 86.85 winning units..
Owner John Stocker **Bred** Darley **Trained** Newmarket, Suffolk
■ Stewards' Enquiry : Kieren Fox two-day ban: careless riding (March 16 - 17)
Cathy Gannon one-day ban: used whip in the incorrect place (16 Mar)

FOCUS
Very few got into this. The winner got a good ride and is rated to his mark.
Halsion Chancer Official explanation: jockey said that the gelding suffered interference in running
Buona Sarah(IRE) Official explanation: jockey said that the filly missed the break

724 BOOK KEMPTON TICKETS ON 0844 579 3008 CLAIMING STKS 6f (P)
6:10 (6:10) (Class 6) 3-Y-O **£1,535** (£453; £226) **Stalls** Low

Form RPR
1-61 1 **Its You Again**30 364 3-9-4 84 AdamKirby 5 84
(Noel Quinlan) *trckd ldr: led ins fnl 2f: c clr ins fnl f: comf* **7/4**2
12-2 2 2 1/2 **My Lord**13 576 3-8-13 81 KierenFox(3) 3 75
(Bill Turner) *led tl hdd ins fnl 2f: styd on same pce and no ch w wnr fnl f* **13/8**1
3263 3 2 1/4 **Captain Dimitrios**10 620 3-9-0 75 (v) CathyGannon 6 66
(David Evans) *hdwy on outside to chse ldng duo over 3f out: rdn over 2f out and one pce appr fnl f* **15/2**3
3151 4 nk **Fifth In Line (IRE)**27 396 3-8-8 64 SophieDoyle(3) 1 62
(David Flood) *towards rr tl hdwy on ins to dispute 3rd 3f out: nvr gng pce of ldng duo: kpt on one pce to go 4th fnl f* **12/1**
-244 5 1/2 **Captain Loui (IRE)**12 601 3-8-13 64 (b) LukeMorris 7 62
(Dai Burchell) *rdn along over 2f out: a towards rr* **20/1**
-010 6 9 **Loves Theme (IRE)**12 601 3-8-4 71 (v1) NatashaEaton(7) 2 33
(Alan Bailey) *chsd ldrs to 1/2-way: sn wknd* **8/1**
1m 13.2s (0.10) **Going Correction** +0.05s/f (Slow) 6 Ran SP% **109.8**
Speed ratings (Par 96): **101,97,94,94,93 81**
toteswingers: 1&2 £1.10, 1&3 £2.00, 2&3 £2.50 CSF £4.72 TOTE £2.60: £1.70, £1.80; EX 5.90.The winner was subject to a friendly claim.
Owner Brian Dick **Bred** Springcombe Park Stud **Trained** Newmarket, Suffolk

FOCUS
The best two in at the weights had the race between them. The pace was good and the form is straightforward.

725 BETDAQ.COM EXCHANGE PRICE MULTIPLES H'CAP 6f (P)
6:40 (6:40) (Class 5) (0-75,75) 4-Y-O+ **£2,047** (£604; £302) **Stalls** Low

Form RPR
2136 1 **Pelmanism**11 612 4-8-10 64 (b) NeilCallan 1 77+
(Kevin Ryan) *s.i.s: in rr: rdn and hdwy fr 2f out: chsd ldr ins fnl f: led fnl 100yds: won gng away* **9/2**2
04- 2 2 1/4 **Boragh Jamal (IRE)**84 7754 4-8-11 65 (b) MartinDwyer 2 71
(Brian Meehan) *trckd ldrs: rdn and styd on fr 2f out to ld over 1f out: hdd and outpcd fnl 100yds* **10/1**
04-1 3 3 **Best Trip (IRE)**38 269 4-9-5 73 FrannyNorton 4 69
(Richard Guest) *led: rdn over 2f out: hdd over 1f out: wknd ins fnl f* **7/2**1
6555 4 2 1/2 **Al Gillani (IRE)**11 612 6-8-5 66 (p) NathanAlison(7) 10 54
(Jim Boyle) *stdd s: swtchd rt to ins: rdn and hdwy fr over 2f out: sn one pce and no imp on ldng trio* **13/2**3
2134 5 nse **Sherjawy (IRE)**14 554 7-9-0 68 SamHitchcott 5 56
(Zoe Davison) *chsd ldrs: rdn fr 3f out: outpcd fr over 2f out* **14/1**
0-13 6 3 **Italian Tom (IRE)**14 554 4-9-2 73 KierenFox(3) 6 52
(Ronald Harris) *chsd ldr 4f: wknd over 1f out* **8/1**
000- 7 2 **Little Perisher**91 7654 4-8-6 65 (p) AdamBeschizza(5) 3 37
(Karen George) *in rr and sn rdn: sme hdwy u.p over 2f out: nvr rchd ldrs and sn btn* **20/1**
0523 8 1/2 **Jungle Bay**18 521 4-9-4 72 MartinLane 8 43
(Jane Chapple-Hyam) *s.i.s: in rr: rdn and effrt to get in tch 3f out: wknd over 2f out* **9/2**2
-102 9 8 **Garstang**18 522 8-9-7 75 (b) LukeMorris 9 20
(John Balding) *chsd ldrs on outside: rdn: hung rt and wknd ins fnl 3f* **10/1**
06-0 10 24 **Pose (IRE)**49 125 4-9-4 72 (b1) FergusSweeney 7 —
(Roger Ingram) *chsd ldrs: wknd qckly over 2f out: eased fnl f* **33/1**
1m 11.96s (-1.14) **Going Correction** +0.05s/f (Slow) 10 Ran SP% **115.6**
Speed ratings (Par 103): **109,106,102,98,98 94,91,91,80,48**
toteswingers: 1&2 £8.70, 1&3 £1.90, 2&3 £16.10 CSF £48.46 CT £158.62 TOTE £5.20: £2.30, £5.10, £1.50; EX 53.70 Trifecta £411.60 Pool: £3,476.77 - 6.25 winning units..
Owner Guy Reed **Bred** Guy Reed **Trained** Hambleton, N Yorks

FOCUS
The early pace in this sprint was good and that set things up for a closer. The winner is capable of better and the form looks solid as rated.
Al Gillani(IRE) Official explanation: jockey said the gelding reared as the gates opened and was slowly away
Jungle Bay Official explanation: jockey said that the colt lost his action
Pose(IRE) Official explanation: vet said that the filly lost his right fore shoe

726 LAY BACK AND WIN AT BETDAQ.COM MAIDEN STKS 1m (P)
7:10 (7:11) (Class 5) 3-Y-O+ **£2,047** (£604; £302) **Stalls** Low

Form RPR
5- 1 **Carrick A Rede (IRE)**155 6443 3-8-10 0 LukeMorris 1 79+
(Clive Cox) *trckd ldrs: shkn up to go 2nd 3f out: rdn to ld ins fnl f and a in command: edgd lft nr fin* **5/4**1
042- 2 1/2 **Saint Helena (IRE)**126 7164 3-8-5 70 ChrisCatlin 3 73
(Harry Dunlop) *led: rdn over 2f out: hdd ins fnl f: kpt on but a readily hld by wnr* **7/2**3
5 3 6 **Enriching (USA)**11 610 3-8-10 0 DaneO'Neill 4 64
(David Elsworth) *in rr but in tch: pushed along 3f out: hdwy to go 3rd 2f out but nvr any ch w ldng duo* **12/1**
240- 4 7 **Invincibility (IRE)**172 5971 4-10-0 80 NeilCallan 6 54
(Simon Dow) *chsd ldr to 3f out: lost 3rd 2f out: sn wknd* **9/4**2
0 5 16 **Byrons Beau (IRE)**34 313 3-8-10 0 MartinDwyer 2 11
(Brett Johnson) *chsd ldrs to 3f out: sn btn* **33/1**
6 8 **Mr Mackintosh** 3-8-10 0 SamHitchcott 5 —
(Anthony Middleton) *slowly away: a in rr* **33/1**
1m 39.21s (-0.59) **Going Correction** +0.05s/f (Slow)
WFA 3 from 4yo 18lb 6 Ran SP% **111.0**
Speed ratings (Par 103): **104,103,97,90,74 66**
toteswingers: 1&2 £1.80, 1&3 £3.00, 2&3 £3.40 CSF £5.88 TOTE £3.60: £1.60, £1.80; EX 10.00.

Owner Stephen W Barrow **Bred** Anthony Kirwan **Trained** Lambourn, Berks

FOCUS
No more than a fair maiden. The winner stepped up on last season's promising form and the runner-up helps set the level.

727 BETDAQ MOBILE APPS H'CAP 1m (P)
7:40 (7:42) (Class 6) (0-65,64) 4-Y-O+ **£1,535** (£453; £226) **Stalls** Low

Form RPR
41-2 1 **Al Aqabah (IRE)**10 625 6-9-1 63 (b) AdamBeschizza(5) 5 74
(Brian Gubby) *s.i.s: in rr: hdwy on outside over 2f out: hrd rdn and str run thrght fnl f to ld last strides* **3/1**1
5-61 2 hd **Florio Vincitore (IRE)**25 432 4-8-11 61 (b) JenniferFerguson(7) 1 71
(Edward Creighton) *led: sn clr: pushed along over 2f out: kpt narrowing advantage thrght fnl f tl ct last strides* **20/1**
314- 3 1/2 **Regal Rave (USA)**215 4534 4-9-4 61 NeilCallan 3 70
(Mouse Hamilton-Fairley) *towards rr: hdwy fr 3f out: styd on u.p to chse ldr jst ins fnl f but a jst hld: one pce into 3rd fnl 30yds* **16/1**
0-20 4 2 **Sonny G (IRE)**25 432 4-8-13 59 KierenFox(3) 14 63
(John Best) *chsd ldr: rdn and sme prog fr 2f out but nvr a threat: lost 2nd ins fnl f and sn btn* **25/1**
1-35 5 1 **One Oi**35 310 6-9-5 62 LiamKeniry 4 64+
(David Arbuthnot) *s.i.s: in rr: rdn over 2f out: hdwy over 1f out and styd on fnl f but nvr a threat* **5/1**2
5220 6 4 1/2 **Master Of Dance (IRE)**10 625 4-9-7 64 (b) FrannyNorton 9 56
(James Given) *in rr: rdn and hdwy fr 2f out: nvr rchd ldrs* **16/1**
0-56 7 1 1/2 **Sadeek**28 387 7-9-0 57 DaneO'Neill 2 45
(Martin Bosley) *chsd ldrs: rdn ins fnl 3f: outpcd over 2f out* **20/1**
3-31 8 1/2 **Ermyntrude**20 488 4-8-10 58 JemmaMarshall(5) 8 45
(Pat Phelan) *in rr: rdn and hdwy on outside over 2f out: styd on fnl f: nvr nr ldrs* **11/2**3
-353 9 1 3/4 **Serious Drinking (USA)**10 625 5-9-5 62 (t) EddieAhern 7 45
(Walter Swinburn) *in tch: rdn and hdwy to chse ldrs over 2f out tl wknd appr fnl f* **13/2**
050- 10 4 **Gypsy Boy (USA)**237 3831 4-9-7 64 (t) J-PGuillambert 13 38
(Pat Murphy) *in tch: rdn over 2f out and sn btn* **40/1**
005- 11 3/4 **Interakt**181 5677 4-9-7 64 CathyGannon 12 36
(Joseph Tuite) *chsd ldrs tl rdn and wknd 2f out* **25/1**
030- 12 nse **Ajool (USA)**105 7487 4-8-12 55 SamHitchcott 6 27
(Zoe Davison) *bhd most of way* **66/1**
4-06 13 11 **Celtic Ransom**28 391 4-9-0 57 FergusSweeney 10 4
(Gary Moore) *a towards rr* **12/1**
-033 14 10 **Prohibition (IRE)**20 489 5-9-3 60 GeorgeBaker 11 —
(Gary Moore) *chsd ldrs over 5f* **12/1**
1m 39.02s (-0.78) **Going Correction** +0.05s/f (Slow) 14 Ran SP% **118.7**
Speed ratings (Par 101): **105,104,104,102,101 96,95,94,93,89 88,88,77,67**
toteswingers: 1&2 £17.40, 1&3 £4.70, 2&3 £135.90 CSF £72.29 CT £640.70 TOTE £2.80: £1.20, £10.10, £8.10; EX 71.30.
Owner Brian Gubby **Bred** Ocal Bloodstock **Trained** Bagshot, Surrey

FOCUS
A moderate handicap run at a good pace. The likes of the fourth help set the level.
Serious Drinking(USA) Official explanation: jockey said that the the filly stopped quickly
Interakt Official explanation: jockey said that the filly had no more to give
Prohibition(IRE) Official explanation: jockey said that the gelding lost its action

728 SPONSOR AT KEMPTON H'CAP 1m 4f (P)
8:10 (8:12) (Class 6) (0-65,70) 4-Y-O+ **£1,535** (£453; £226) **Stalls** Centre

Form RPR
-031 1 **Sir Boss (IRE)**10 621 6-9-13 70 6ex TomEaves 4 82+
(Michael Mullineaux) *trckd ldrs: led over 2f out: rdn over 1f out: styd on wl: readily* **9/2**2
-605 2 1 1/4 **Lytham (IRE)**14 553 10-8-10 53 NeilCallan 6 62+
(Tony Carroll) *t.k.h: chsd ldrs: rdn over 2f out: chsd wnr over 1f out: kpt on but no imp fnl f* **5/1**3
311/ 3 4 **Camera Shy (IRE)**615 3308 7-8-7 50 AndreaAtzeni 10 53+
(Kevin Morgan) *towards rr but in tch: rdn and hdwy over 1f out: kpt on ins fnl f to go 3rd but no ch w ldng duo* **9/1**
00-0 4 1 1/2 **Largem**8 645 5-8-10 53 NeilChalmers 1 54
(J R Jenkins) *in rr: rdn and hdwy fr 2f out: styd on one pce to take 4th fnl f* **33/1**
0-11 5 1 **Captain Cool (IRE)**9 631 4-8-13 58 6ex (b) DaneO'Neill 5 57
(Richard Hannon) *in tch: rdn and effrt 2f out: nvr gng pce to rch ldrs* **7/2**1
2304 6 1/2 **Professor John (IRE)**10 621 4-9-4 63 JamesDoyle 7 62
(Ian Wood) *led: rdn and tried to qckn ins fnl 3f: hdd over 2f out: sn btn* **9/2**2
0-5 7 nk **Majestueux (USA)**28 391 4-8-13 58 CathyGannon 2 56
(Mark Hoad) *in rr: mod prog fnl f* **7/1**

4301 **8** 1/2 **Suhailah**[12] 592 5-8-11 **54**.................. ShaneKelly 8 51
(Michael Attwater) *in tch: rdn over 2f out: no imp on ldrs and wknd qckly* **12/1**

2-04 **9** 5 **Wasara**[28] 384 4-9-0 **59**.................. FergusSweeney 9 49
(Amy Weaver) *chsd ldr tl over 2f out: wknd qckly fnl f* **14/1**

2m 40.51s (6.01) **Going Correction** +0.05s/f (Slow)
WFA 4 from 5yo+ 2lb **9** Ran SP% **115.1**
Speed ratings (Par 101): **81,80,77,76,75 75,75,74,71**
toteswingers: 1&2 £4.60, 1&3 £2.00, 2&3 £17.00 CSF £27.17 CT £193.56 TOTE £5.40: £1.80, £2.50, £3.30; EX 25.40.
Owner I S Ross **Bred** Mrs E R Cantillon **Trained** Alpraham, Cheshire

FOCUS
They went no pace for most of this race and it turned into a sprint in the straight. Form to treat with caution.

729 KEMPTON FOR OUTDOOR EVENTS FILLIES' H'CAP 7f (P)
8:40 (8:40) (Class 5) (0-70,67) 3-Y-O **£2,047** (£604; £302) **Stalls** Low

Form RPR

5-43 **1** **Storm Tide**[5] 693 3-9-2 **62**.................. MartinLane 5 72+
(Rae Guest) *chsd ldrs: rdn to ld over 1f out: pushed clr ins fnl f: comf* **11/4[2]**

1-64 **2** 2 **Magic Of The Sea (IRE)**[31] 358 3-9-5 **65**..........(b[1]) AdamKirby 4 69
(Marco Botti) *in rr: gd hdwy over 1f out: rdn and styd on to go 2nd fnl 120yds but no imp on wnr* **5/1[3]**

-225 **3** 1 1/2 **Rhal (IRE)**[37] 281 3-8-10 **56**.................. TomEaves 8 56
(Bryan Smart) *led: rdn and qcknd over 2f out: hdd over 1f out: one pce ins fnl f and lost 2nd fnl 120yds* **15/2**

41-3 **4** 1/2 **Verrazano**[19] 505 3-9-3 **63**.................. NeilCallan 1 62
(Kevin Ryan) *chsd ldrs: hrd rdn over 2f out: one pce fr over 1f out* **2/1[1]**

03-6 **5** shd **Kokojo (IRE)**[18] 518 3-8-13 **64**.................. AdamBeschizza(5) 7 62
(Brendan Powell) *trckd ldr: drvn to chal over 1f out: wknd ins fnl f* **14/1**

33-4 **6** 1/2 **Links Drive Lady**[54] 77 3-9-0 **67**.................. HannahNunn(7) 2 64
(Mark Rimmer) *s.i.s: outpcd tl sme prog ins fnl f* **14/1**

-044 **7** 1 1/2 **Lady Ellice**[14] 558 3-8-3 **49**.................. LukeMorris 3 42
(Phil McEntee) *in rr: effrt on ins over 2f out: nvr rchd ldrs and sn btn* **9/1**

030- **8** 9 **Alexs Rainbow (USA)**[139] 6866 3-9-2 **62**.................. ChrisCatlin 6 31
(John Gallagher) *chsd ldrs tl wknd over 2f out* **16/1**

1m 27.21s (1.21) **Going Correction** +0.05s/f (Slow) **8** Ran SP% **117.6**
Speed ratings (Par 95): **95,92,91,90,90 89,88,77**
toteswingers: 1&2 £4.00, 1&3 £2.80, 2&3 £2.30 CSF £17.60 CT £94.31 TOTE £3.50: £1.30, £1.10, £2.90; EX 19.60.
Owner Adrian Smith **Bred** Adrian Smith **Trained** Newmarket, Suffolk
■ Stewards' Enquiry : Adam Beschizza ten-day ban: dropped hands before post (16 - 26 Mar)

FOCUS
A modest fillies' handicap in which nothing really wanted to go on and the early pace was therefore predictably steady. The winner confirmed that she is an improved performer and could be worth a shade more.
T/Plt: £17.30 to a £1 stake. Pool: £64,482.62. 2,711.22 winning tickets. T/Qpdt: £14.70 to a £1 stake. Pool: £6,576.43. 330.40 winning tickets. ST

708 WOLVERHAMPTON (A.W) (L-H)
Wednesday, March 2

OFFICIAL GOING: Standard
Wind: Light against Weather: Cloudy with sunny spells

730 ALL WEATHER "HANDS AND HEELS" APPRENTICE SERIES H'CAP (PART OF THE RACING EXCELLENCE INITIATIVE) 1m 141y(P)
2:30 (2:31) (Class 6) (0-58,57) 4-Y-0+ **£1,535** (£453; £226) **Stalls** Low

Form RPR

-422 **1** **Grey Boy (GER)**[6] 662 10-8-9 **50**.................. GeorgeDowning(3) 6 63+
(Tony Carroll) *hld up in tch: shkn up to ld ins fnl f: r.o wl* **11/4[1]**

000- **2** 3 **Barton Bounty**[75] 7917 4-8-7 **45**..........(b[1]) ShaneBKelly 8 51
(Peter Niven) *dwlt: hld up: hdwy over 1f out: styd on to go 2nd wl ins fnl f: no ch w wnr* **14/1**

/0-0 **3** 3/4 **Moment Of Clarity**[21] 466 9-8-7 **45**..........(p) LucyKBarry 2 49
(Shaun Harris) *led 4f: pushed along to ld again 2f out: hdd over 1f out: styd on same pce ins fnl f* **12/1**

13 **4** hd **Orpens Peach (IRE)**[40] 250 4-9-2 **57**.................. RossCoakley(3) 7 61
(Seamus Fahey, Ire) *a.p: chsd ldr over 2f out: led over 1f out: hdd and no ex ins fnl f* **7/2[2]**

-225 **5** 1 **Abigails Angel**[14] 555 4-9-0 **57**.................. AccursioRomeo(5) 4 59
(Brett Johnson) *plld hrd: trckd ldr over 1f: remained handy: pushed along over 2f out: hung lft over 1f out: styd on* **11/4[1]**

6440 **6** 4 1/2 **Crocodile Bay (IRE)**[6] 674 8-9-3 **55**..........(b) NathanAlison 3 46
(Richard Guest) *plld hrd: trckd ldr 7f out: led over 4f out: pushed along and hdd 2f out: wknd ins fnl f* **9/1**

045/ **7** 1 3/4 **Wednesdays Boy (IRE)**[389] 7174 8-8-10 **48**.................. GeorgeChaloner 1 35
(Peter Niven) *hld up: bhd and pushed along 1/2-way: n.d* **8/1[3]**

04-0 **8** 14 **Briary Mac**[54] 86 4-8-7 **45**..........(p) RichardRowe 9 —
(Peter Pritchard) *hld up: in rr and pushed along 1/2-way: bhd fnl 3f* **40/1**

1m 53.0s (2.50) **Going Correction** +0.175s/f (Slow) **8** Ran SP% **113.5**
Speed ratings (Par 101): **95,92,91,91,90 86,85,72**
toteswingers:1&2 £8.10, 2&3 £13.40, 1&3 £8.90 CSF £41.69 CT £399.57 TOTE £4.20: £1.20, £5.70, £5.60; EX 44.90 Trifecta £392.80 Part won. Pool of £530.87 - 0.30 winning units..
Owner Paul Downing **Bred** J Potempa **Trained** Cropthorne, Worcs

FOCUS
A low-grade 'hands and heels' opener. It had little depth but the form looks sound as rated.

731 LADBROKES.COM H'CAP 1m 4f 50y(P)
3:00 (3:00) (Class 6) (0-65,65) 3-Y-O **£1,535** (£453; £226) **Stalls** Low

Form RPR

1222 **1** **Blue Cossack (IRE)**[7] 650 3-8-12 **56**.................. LiamKeniry 4 64+
(Mark Usher) *hld up: hdwy 5f out: led over 2f out: rdn out* **3/1[1]**

0-33 **2** 2 1/4 **Ilissos (USA)**[12] 591 3-9-6 **64**..........(v[1]) GeorgeBaker 5 68
(Jeremy Noseda) *hld up in tch: chsd wnr over 1f out: sn rdn and hung lft: styd on same pce ins fnl f* **3/1[1]**

4003 **3** 2 3/4 **Polly Holder (IRE)**[18] 527 3-8-10 **54**..........(p) LukeMorris 9 55
(Alan Bailey) *hld up: rdn over 4f out: hdwy over 2f out: no imp ins fnl f* **12/1**

040- **4** 8 **Jelyvator**[153] 6514 3-9-6 **64**.................. JimmyQuinn 8 52
(Alex Hales) *hld up: rdn over 4f out: hung lft and mod late prog fr over 1f out* **25/1**

06-2 **5** 10 **Round Turn (IRE)**[14] 564 3-9-7 **65**.................. GrahamGibbons 2 38
(Ed McMahon) *chsd ldrs: pushed along 4f out: rdn and wknd over 1f out* **4/1[2]**

00-4 **6** 3 3/4 **Reach Out**[35] 297 3-8-10 **54**.................. MartinDwyer 6 21
(Brendan Powell) *chsd ldr: rdn over 3f out: wknd wl over 1f out* **10/1**

000- **7** 6 **The Absent Mare**[106] 7470 3-8-6 **50**..........(t) AndreaAtzeni 1 8
(Frank Sheridan) *led: rdn over 3f out: hdd over 2f out: wknd wl over 1f out: t.o* **16/1**

03-0 **8** 10 **Handicraft (IRE)**[21] 469 3-8-2 **46** oh1..........(b[1]) JoeFanning 3 —
(Mark Johnston) *chsd ldrs: rdn and ev ch over 2f out: sn wknd and eased: t.o* **15/2[3]**

0-23 **9** 21 **Jane's Legacy**[19] 516 3-8-9 **53**.................. ChrisCatlin 7 —
(Reg Hollinshead) *hld up: pushed along 7f out: bhd fnl 4f: t.o* **14/1**

2m 42.98s (1.88) **Going Correction** +0.175s/f (Slow) **9** Ran SP% **114.9**
Speed ratings (Par 96): **100,98,96,91,84 82,78,71,57**
toteswingers:1&2 £1.80, 2&3 £7.80, 1&3 £4.70 CSF £11.73 CT £91.94 TOTE £3.50: £1.80, £1.60, £2.70; EX 13.90 Trifecta £96.80 Pool: £676.83 - 5.17 winning units..
Owner Reg Brookes & Richard Jurd **Bred** Morgan Ferris **Trained** Upper Lambourn, Berks

FOCUS
No hanging about here, and in the end they came home well strung out. The winner was quite impressive and the form looks reliable.
Round Turn(IRE) Official explanation: jockey said that the gelding lost its action
The Absent Mare Official explanation: jockey said that the filly hung right handed
Jane's Legacy Official explanation: vet said filly was in a distressed state

732 ATRCASINOCLUB.COM (S) STKS 5f 20y(P)
3:30 (3:30) (Class 6) 4-Y-0+ **£1,535** (£453; £226) **Stalls** Low

Form RPR

-245 **1** **Sharp Shoes**[20] 491 4-9-5 65..........(p) PaulHanagan 5 72
(Ann Duffield) *chsd ldrs: rdn to ld and hung lft ins fnl f: r.o* **5/2[1]**

1302 **2** 2 1/2 **Residency (IRE)**[8] 641 5-9-0 60..........(p) AdamCarter(5) 2 63
(Bryan Smart) *chsd ldrs: sn pushed along: rdn over 1f out: styd on same pce ins fnl f* **4/1[3]**

1304 **3** 1/2 **Decider (USA)**[16] 538 8-9-5 64..........(p) JoeFanning 3 61
(Ronald Harris) *led: rdn and edgd rt over 1f out: hdd and unable qck ins fnl f* **7/2[2]**

-640 **4** 1/2 **Gorgeous Goblin (IRE)**[5] 691 4-8-6 45..........(vt) JamesSullivan(3) 6 49
(David C Griffiths) *s.i.s: outpcd: hdwy u.p fr over 1f out: nt rch ldrs* **50/1**

-300 **5** 1 **Seeking Rio**[21] 464 4-8-9 44.................. HayleyTurner 4 46
(Ron Hodges) *sn pushed along and prom: rdn 1/2-way: styd on same pce appr fnl f* **14/1**

6036 **6** nk **Duplicity**[9] 633 4-9-0 60..........(b) J-PGuillambert 1 50
(James Given) *sn outpcd: r.o ins fnl f: nvr nrr* **25/1**

0246 **7** 1 1/4 **Lord Of The Reins (IRE)**[7] 646 7-9-0 63.................. FrannyNorton 8 45
(James Given) *sn outpcd* **7/1**

-103 **8** 3/4 **Ridley Didley (IRE)**[22] 453 6-9-0 65.................. LeeNewman 7 43
(Noel Wilson) *w ldr tl rdn over 1f out: wknd ins fnl f* **11/2**

62.99 secs (0.69) **Going Correction** +0.175s/f (Slow) **8** Ran SP% **111.2**
Speed ratings (Par 101): **101,97,96,95,93 93,91,90**
toteswingers:1&2 £2.90, 2&3 £3.80, 1&3 £2.00 CSF £11.88 TOTE £3.30: £1.10, £1.20, £3.80; EX 14.00 Trifecta £33.60 Pool: £679.36 - 14.94 winning units..There was no bid for the winner. Duplicity was claimed by S. Arnold for £6000.
Owner T P McMahon and D McMahon **Bred** Mrs Mary Rowlands **Trained** Constable Burton, N Yorks

FOCUS
The two leaders took each other on and set this selling race up for a closer. Straightforward form.

733 GOT THE FEELING? GET TO LADBROKES H'CAP 1m 5f 194y(P)
4:00 (4:01) (Class 6) (0-65,62) 4-Y-0+ **£1,535** (£453; £226) **Stalls** Low

Form RPR

/0-6 **1** **Gulf Of Aqaba (USA)**[9] 635 5-9-3 **53**..........(b) JoeFanning 5 61
(Ian Williams) *hld up: rdn over 3f out: hdwy over 2f out: led and edgd lft ins fnl f: styd on* **50/1**

6-52 **2** 1 1/2 **Leyte Gulf (USA)**[12] 596 8-9-12 **62**.................. DaneO'Neill 10 68
(Chris Bealby) *s.s: hld up: hdwy over 3f out: led over 1f out: sn rdn: hdd and unable qck ins fnl f* **8/1[3]**

/545 **3** 1 1/4 **Duar Mapel (USA)**[8] 645 5-9-5 **55**.................. JimmyQuinn 8 59
(Brian Baugh) *broke wl: stdd into mid-div after 1f: hdwy 1/2-way: nt clr run 2f out: sn rdn: styd on* **10/1**

00-3 **4** 1/2 **Horsley Warrior**[23] 449 5-9-8 **58**.................. GrahamGibbons 6 62
(Ed McMahon) *chsd ldrs: reminders 1/2-way: rdn over 1f out: styd on same pce ins fnl f* **16/1**

450/ **5** shd **Santera (IRE)**[100] 7721 7-8-6 **45**..........(p) AndrewHeffernan(3) 11 48
(John Flint) *prom: rdn 4f out: sn outpcd: styd on u.p fr over 1f out* **6/4[1]**

5-12 **6** nk **Setter's Princess**[12] 592 5-9-12 **62**.................. GeorgeBaker 3 65
(Ron Hodges) *hld up: hdwy over 1f out: swtchd lft ins fnl f: nt rch ldrs* **7/2[2]**

3513 **7** 1 3/4 **Money Money Money**[12] 592 5-9-8 **58**..........(b) JamesMillman 9 59
(Rod Millman) *hld up: hdwy 5f out: rdn over 2f out: styd on same pce appr fnl f* **12/1**

5-60 **8** shd **Warrior Nation (FR)**[28] 382 5-8-9 **45**.................. DavidProbert 7 46
(Adrian Chamberlain) *hld up: rdn over 3f out: styd on ins fnl f: nvr nrr* **100/1**

9 nse **Tinas Exhibition (IRE)**[46] 3698 4-8-12 **57**.................. MartinHarley(5) 1 58
(Seamus Fahey, Ire) *hld up: rdn over 1f out: styd on ins fnl f: nvr nrr* **18/1**

54-1 **10** 7 **Mr Plod**[19] 514 6-9-9 **59**..........(p) JamesDoyle 12 50
(Andrew Reid) *chsd ldr tl led over 2f out: rdn and hdd over 1f out: wknd ins fnl f* **10/1**

4043 **11** nk **Juwireya**[12] 596 4-9-7 **61**..........(v) ChrisCatlin 4 52
(Peter Hiatt) *led: rdn and hdd over 2f out: wknd over 1f out* **16/1**

0-55 **12** 51 **Bullring (FR)**[13] 570 5-9-5 **55**..........(p) PaulHanagan 2 —
(Peter Niven) *chsd ldrs: rdn over 4f out: wknd over 3f out: t.o* **33/1**

3m 7.18s (1.18) **Going Correction** +0.175s/f (Slow)
WFA 4 from 5yo+ 4lb **12** Ran SP% **122.1**
Speed ratings (Par 101): **103,102,101,101,101 100,99,99,99,95 95,66**
toteswingers:1&2 £40.30, 2&3 £13.60, 1&3 £73.10 CSF £423.74 CT £4339.96 TOTE £62.40: £10.50, £2.20, £2.60; EX 286.80 TRIFECTA Not won..
Owner R S Brookhouse **Bred** Nancy Cole & Bruce Kline **Trained** Portway, Worcs

FOCUS
A modest staying handicap, and the gallop was unrelenting. The winner is rated back to his 3yo form, with the third and fourth offering perspective.
Gulf Of Aqaba(USA) Official explanation: trainer's representative said regarding the apparent improvement of form, that the gelding appeared to benefit from racing over the longer trip of a 1 mile 6 furlongs and the re-application of blinkers

Setter's Princess Official explanation: jockey said that the mare was denied a clear run

734 ATRPOKERCLUB.COM H'CAP 5f 216y(P)
4:30 (4:30) (Class 6) (0-55,61) 4-Y-0+ **£1,535** (£453; £226) **Stalls** Low

Form RPR
0-06 **1** **Flying Applause**[16] 544 6-8-11 **50**...(bt) JimmyQuinn 6 59
(Roy Bowring) *chsd ldrs: rdn over 2f out: r.o to ld wl ins fnl f* **11/1**
0-04 **2** *1 ¼* **Mata Hari Blue**[13] 571 5-9-1 **54**... PaulHanagan 9 59
(John Holt) *hld up: hdwy over 2f out: rdn over 1f out: hung lft ins fnl f: styd on* **7/1**[2]
220- **3** *shd* **Avonlini**[170] 6025 5-8-11 **50**... GrahamGibbons 10 55
(Brian Baugh) *chsd ldrs: rdn to ld ins fnl f: sn hdd and unable qck* **18/1**
5560 **4** *1 ¾* **Memphis Man**[6] 664 8-8-5 **51**... MatthewCosham(7) 7 50
(David Evans) *hld up: hdwy over 1f out: r.o: nt rch ldrs* **11/1**
0-03 **5** *hd* **Simple Rhythm**[6] 664 5-9-1 **54**... KirstyMilczarek 12 53
(John Ryan) *a.p: rdn over 2f out: styd on same pce ins fnl f* **7/1**[2]
550 **6** *hd* **Francis Albert**[5] 691 5-8-3 **49**...(be) JosephYoung(7) 8 47
(Michael Mullineaux) *hld up: plld hrd: hdwy over 2f out: sn outpcd: edgd lft and r.o ins fnl f: nt rch ldrs* **16/1**
60-1 **7** *1 ½* **Far View (IRE)**[5] 683 4-9-1 **61** 6ex...(t) DavidKenny(7) 2 55
(George Baker) *led: hdd over 4f out: led again over 3f out: rdn: hdd and no ex ins fnl f* **6/4**[1]
1205 **8** *½* **Metropolitan Chief**[5] 696 7-9-0 **53**... LiamKeniry 4 45
(Paul Burgoyne) *hld up: hdwy over 2f out: rdn and edgd lft over 1f out: no ex* **8/1**[3]
06-6 **9** *2 ¼* **Dickie Le Davoir**[15] 545 7-8-11 **53**...(b) AndrewHeffernan(3) 3 39
(Richard Guest) *s.s: outpcd* **16/1**
/00- **10** *4* **Lofthouse**[15] 6494 4-8-13 **52**... PJMcDonald 1 26
(Alistair Whillans) *sn outpcd* **80/1**
03-0 **11** *hd* **Hold On Tiger (IRE)**[15] 545 4-8-4 **50**...(p) ShirleyTeasdale(7) 5 23
(Keith Dalgleish) *w ldr tl led over 4f out: hdd over 3f out: rdn over 2f out: sn wknd* **33/1**
-302 **12** *46* **Colamandis**[19] 517 4-8-9 **51**... JamesSullivan(3) 11 —
(Hugh McWilliams) *chsd ldrs: rdn 1/2-way: wknd over 2f out: t.o: b.b.v* **14/1**

1m 15.6s (0.60) **Going Correction** +0.175s/f (Slow) **12** Ran SP% **120.6**
Speed ratings (Par 101): **103,101,101,98,98 98,96,95,92,87 87,25**
toteswingers:1&2 £11.50, 2&3 £14.80, 1&3 £20.00 CSF £87.57 CT £1395.53 TOTE £13.00: £3.90, £3.20, £4.50; EX 108.10 Trifecta £232.40 Part won. Pool of £314.16 - 0.62 winning units..

Owner K Nicholls **Bred** G H Beeby And Viscount Marchwood **Trained** Edwinstowe, Notts

FOCUS
Fast and furious stuff. the form is rated through the third.
Colamandis Official explanation: vet said that the filly bled from the nose

735 LADBROKES MOBILE H'CAP 5f 20y(P)
5:00 (5:00) (Class 6) (0-60,60) 4-Y-0+ **£1,535** (£453; £226) **Stalls** Low

Form RPR
0-36 **1** **Sally's Swansong**[27] 401 5-8-7 **46** oh1...(b) GrahamGibbons 12 55
(Eric Alston) *mid-div: hdwy 2f out: nt clr run and swtchd lft over 1f out: r.o to ld wl ins fnl f* **20/1**
0-06 **2** *½* **Cavitie**[13] 571 5-9-3 **56**...(p) JamesDoyle 9 63
(Andrew Reid) *chsd ldrs: rdn 1/2-way: ev ch ins fnl f: r.o* **8/1**[3]
2-05 **3** *nk* **The Tatling (IRE)**[23] 443 14-9-7 **60**... RichardKingscote 7 67
(Milton Bradley) *hld up: hdwy and nt clr run over 1f out: swtchd rt: fin wl: nt rch ldrs* **12/1**
3231 **4** *½* **Steel City Boy (IRE)**[5] 691 8-9-3 **56** 6ex...(p) JimmyQuinn 13 60
(Derek Shaw) *hld up in tch: rdn over 1f out: r.o* **10/1**
256- **5** *¾* **Rio's Girl**[125] 7194 4-9-2 **58**... AmyRyan(3) 1 59
(Kevin Ryan) *led: rdn and edgd lft over 1f out: hdd and unable qck wl ins fnl f* **5/1**[2]
4-34 **6** *¾* **Monsieur Harvey**[16] 537 5-8-4 **48**... AdamCarter(5) 4 47
(Bryan Smart) *sn pushed along to chse ldrs: nt clr run and swtchd rt over 1f out: sn rdn: eased whn btn wl ins fnl f* **9/2**[1]
2410 **7** *nk* **Bluebok**[16] 537 10-8-5 **51**...(bt) MatthewCosham(7) 6 49
(Milton Bradley) *chsd ldr: rdn over 1f out: no ex ins fnl f* **20/1**
0003 **8** *½* **Tyrannosaurus Rex (IRE)**[91] 404 7-8-8 **47**...(v) PatrickMathers 5 43
(Derek Shaw) *sn pushed along in rr: rdn over 1f out: r.o ins fnl f: nvr nrr* **9/1**
0036 **9** *nk* **Mr Funshine**[5] 691 6-8-7 **46** oh1... JoeFanning 10 41
(Derek Shaw) *hld up: rdn over 1f out: no imp* **16/1**
10-4 **10** *hd* **Triskaidekaphobia**[33] 337 8-9-1 **54**...(t) FrankieMcDonald 11 48
(Paul Fitzsimons) *chsd ldrs: rdn over 1f out: no ex ins fnl f* **33/1**
404- **11** *hd* **Ronnie Howe**[364] 774 7-8-7 **46** oh1...(b) RobbieFitzpatrick 8 39
(Roy Bowring) *prom: rdn 1/2-way: styd on same pce ins fnl f* **40/1**
6-10 **12** *1 ¼* **Almaty Express**[19] 511 9-9-4 **57**...(b) GeorgeBaker 3 46
(John Weymes) *sn pushed along in rr: nvr nrr* **10/1**
2063 **13** *½* **Misaro (GER)**[5] 683 10-9-5 **58**...(b) DavidProbert 2 45
(Ronald Harris) *sn drvn along in mid-div: outpcd 3f out: n.d after* **5/1**[2]

62.86 secs (0.56) **Going Correction** +0.175s/f (Slow) **13** Ran SP% **119.3**
Speed ratings (Par 101): **102,101,100,99,98 97,97,96,95,95 95,93,92**
toteswingers:1&2 £31.50, 2&3 £18.60, 1&3 £38.60 CSF £166.05 CT £2025.20 TOTE £23.60: £8.50, £2.70, £3.10; EX 299.80 TRIFECTA Not won..
Owner Miss F Fenley **Bred** Southern Seafoods **Trained** Longton, Lancs
■ Stewards' Enquiry : Adam Carter one-day ban: careless riding (Mar 16)

FOCUS
Another tight sprint handicap, run at a strong pace. The form is sound enough.
Monsieur Harvey Official explanation: jockey said that the gelding lost its action in the final furlong

736 PLAY ROULETTE AT LADBROKES.COM H'CAP 7f 32y(P)
5:30 (5:30) (Class 4) (0-85,85) 4-Y-0+ **£2,914** (£867; £433; £216) **Stalls** High

Form RPR
3232 **1** **Avonrose**[19] 508 4-8-9 **73**... JoeFanning 3 81
(Derek Shaw) *trckd ldrs: racd keenly: rdn to ld wl ins fnl f: r.o* **9/2**[1]
0-13 **2** *hd* **Smalljohn**[13] 572 5-8-5 **74**...(v) AdamCarter(5) 11 81
(Bryan Smart) *led: rdn over 1f out: hdd wl ins fnl f: r.o* **8/1**[3]
44-6 **3** *shd* **Standpoint**[27] 405 5-8-12 **76**... GrahamGibbons 9 83
(Reg Hollinshead) *a.p: rdn to chse ldr over 1f out: r.o* **9/1**
4-33 **4** *¾* **Khanivorous**[20] 495 4-8-10 **77**...(v) MatthewDavies(3) 7 82
(Jim Boyle) *hld up: drvn along 1/2-way: hdwy u.p over 1f out: hung lft: r.o: nt rch ldrs* **11/2**[2]
-326 **5** *1 ¾* **Striker Torres (IRE)**[23] 446 5-8-8 **72**...(p) JimmyQuinn 2 73
(Geoffrey Oldroyd) *chsd ldrs: rdn over 1f out: styd on same pce ins fnl f* **11/2**[2]
341 **6** *½* **Rubenstar (IRE)**[28] 394 8-8-11 **75**... StephenCraine 8 75
(Patrick Morris) *hld up: rdn and hung lft fnl f: r.o: nrst fin* **11/1**
200- **7** *shd* **Coolminx (IRE)**[130] 7079 4-9-7 **85**... PaulHanagan 4 84
(Richard Fahey) *mid-div: shkn up over 1f out: styd on: nt trble ldrs* **9/2**[1]
3-50 **8** *nk* **Mr Macattack**[37] 285 6-9-4 **82**...(t) RichardKingscote 1 81
(Tom Dascombe) *s.i.s: hld up: rdn over 1f out: nvr on terms* **11/1**
2460 **9** *hd* **Methaaly (IRE)**[7] 651 8-8-5 **76**...(be) JosephYoung(7) 5 74
(Michael Mullineaux) *dwlt: hld up: rdn over 1f out: r.o ins fnl f: nvr on terms* **20/1**
-300 **10** *2* **Alhaban (IRE)**[25] 438 5-9-5 **83**...(tp) DavidProbert 10 76
(Ronald Harris) *awkward leaving stalls: hdwy to chse ldr 6f out: rdn over 2f out: wknd ins fnl f* **16/1**

1m 30.05s (0.45) **Going Correction** +0.175s/f (Slow) **10** Ran SP% **115.6**
Speed ratings (Par 105): **104,103,103,102,100 100,100,99,99,97**
toteswingers:1&2 £5.80, 2&3 £13.80, 1&3 £14.20 CSF £40.20 CT £317.79 TOTE £4.00: £1.10, £5.20, £3.90; EX 25.40 Trifecta £263.70 Part won. Pool of £356.41 - 0.62 winning units..
Owner Moorland Racing **Bred** Mrs Mary Taylor **Trained** Sproxton, Leics

FOCUS
A decent 72-85 handicap for a pitiful first prize. The pace was good and the winner should remain competitive. The third and fourth offer perspective.

737 ENJOY THE PARTY PACK GROUP OFFER MAIDEN FILLIES' STKS 1f 103y(P)
6:00 (6:00) (Class 5) 3-Y-0+ **£1,813** (£539; £269; £134) **Stalls** Low

Form RPR
2 **1** **Covert Decree**[18] 529 3-8-5 0... PaulHanagan 3 71+
(Clive Cox) *mde all: racd keenly: shkn up over 1f out: r.o wl* **30/100**[1]
2 *7* **Silk Lingerie** 3-8-5 0... JimmyQuinn 2 61+
(Mandy Rowland) *s.s: hld up: hdwy to chse wnr over 2f out: sn rdn: no ex ins fnl f* **12/1**[3]
64/ **3** *8* **Danehill Intellect (IRE)**[547] 5547 4-9-11 0... JoeFanning 1 49
(Harry Dunlop) *chsd wnr tl rdn and hung rt over 2f out: sn wknd* **4/1**[2]
0 **4** *nk* **Lauralu**[42] 214 3-8-5 0... WilliamCarson 4 42
(Michael Blanshard) *dwlt: sn chsng ldrs: rdn over 3f out: wknd over 2f out* **33/1**

2m 5.34s (3.64) **Going Correction** +0.175s/f (Slow)
WFA 3 from 4yo 20lb **4** Ran SP% **107.6**
Speed ratings (Par 100): **90,83,76,76**
CSF £4.72 TOTE £1.10; EX 2.10.
Owner Lakes Bathrooms Ltd **Bred** A M Tombs **Trained** Lambourn, Berks

FOCUS
A very weak maiden and in the end, as the betting suggested, only one runner mattered. The race is rated around the slow time and the fourth.
T/Jkpt: Not won. T/Plt: £2,664.70 to a £1 stake. Pool of £72,642.50 - 19.90 winning tickets.
T/Qpdt: £1,028.70 to a £1 stake. Pool of £5,560.90 - 4.00 winning tickets. CR

669 SOUTHWELL (L-H)
Thursday, March 3

OFFICIAL GOING: Standard
Wind: light 1/2 against Weather: overcast and cold

738 ATR CHELTENHAM MEGASITE NOW LIVE H'CAP 1m (F)
2:10 (2:10) (Class 5) (0-75,74) 3-Y-O **£1,813** (£539; £269) **Stalls** Low

Form RPR
31 **1** **One Pursuit (IRE)**[16] 546 3-8-12 **67**... BillyCray(3) 4 69+
(David Nicholls) *dwlt: drvn to sn ld: rdn and wandered fnl 2f: styd on wl ins fnl f* **8/11**[1]
0-16 **2** *1 ½* **Aloneinthestreet (USA)**[22] 468 3-9-7 **73**... JoeFanning 1 71
(Mark Johnston) *chsd ldrs: drvn over 3f out: swtchd rt over 1f out: kpt on same pce fnl f* **9/4**[2]
-523 **3** *shd* **Unwrapit (USA)**[13] 600 3-8-13 **65**...(p) TomEaves 5 63
(Bryan Smart) *led early: w ldr: drvn over 2f out: kpt on same pce fnl f* **4/1**[3]

1m 42.22s (-1.48) **Going Correction** -0.25s/f (Stan) **3** Ran SP% **108.7**
Speed ratings (Par 98): **97,95,95**
CSF £2.67 TOTE £1.50; EX 2.50.
Owner Eamon Maher **Bred** Clougher Partnership **Trained** Sessay, N Yorks

FOCUS
Just a small field for this moderate handicap, weakened by the defection of the likely odds-on favourite. Not easy form to pin down.

739 VISIT ATTHERACES.COM/CHELTENHAM CLAIMING STKS 7f (F)
2:40 (2:40) (Class 6) 3-Y-O **£1,535** (£453; £226) **Stalls** Low

Form RPR
-021 **1** **Fantasy Fry**[7] 672 3-8-12 65... HayleyTurner 2 77
(Hughie Morrison) *w ldr: led over 4f out: drvn clr over 1f out* **11/8**[1]
00-1 **2** *4 ½* **New Latin (IRE)**[30] 378 3-9-2 72... JamesDoyle 3 71
(Frank Sheridan) *narrow ld: hdd over 4f out: hrd drvn over 3f out: wknd fnl 100yds* **5/2**[2]
1-21 **3** *nk* **So Is She (IRE)**[49] 147 3-8-7 68...(be) CathyGannon 5 60
(Alan Bailey) *chsd ldrs: drvn over 4f out: outpcd over 3f out: kpt on fnl 2f* **7/2**[3]
-544 **4** *10* **Reachtothestars (USA)**[7] 668 3-9-0 61...(t) AdamKirby 4 42
(Noel Quinlan) *stdd s: trckd ldrs: lost pl over 4f out: eased ins fnl f* **14/1**
1252 **5** *12* **Local Diktator**[7] 672 3-8-7 63...(tp) LukeMorris 6 —
(Ronald Harris) *trckd ldrs on outer: lost pl over 3f out: eased fnl f* **6/1**

1m 28.61s (-1.69) **Going Correction** -0.25s/f (Stan) **5** Ran SP% **113.9**
Speed ratings (Par 96): **99,93,93,82,68**
CSF £5.34 TOTE £2.10: £1.40, £2.20; EX 5.60.Fantasy Fry was claimed by Alan Solomon for £10,000.
Owner H Morrison **Bred** Meon Valley Stud **Trained** East Ilsley, Berks

FOCUS
A trappy claimer produced an easy winner. The form could be rated 3-5lb more but a little caution has been exercised.

740 ATRVIRTUALOWNER.COM H'CAP 5f (F)
3:10 (3:10) (Class 4) (0-85,81) 3-Y-O **£2,914** (£867; £433; £216) **Stalls** High

Form RPR
12-6 **1** **Monsieur Jamie**[22] 476 3-8-13 **73**... GregFairley 4 78+
(J R Jenkins) *w ldr: led 2f out: drvn clr fnl f* **9/4**[1]
4121 **2** *2 ¾* **Restless Bay (IRE)**[10] 632 3-9-7 **81** 6ex...(v) ChrisCatlin 1 76
(Reg Hollinshead) *swvd rt and hmpd s: hdwy over 3f out: kpt on to take 2nd fnl 100yds* **9/2**
11-3 **3** *1* **Sugar Beet**[31] 364 3-9-2 **76**... LukeMorris 3 68
(Ronald Harris) *wnt lft s: chsd ldrs: hung lft and kpt on same pce appr fnl f* **3/1**[2]
60-4 **4** *¾* **Dream Catcher (FR)**[12] 609 3-9-4 **81**... BillyCray(3) 5 70
(David Nicholls) *led tl 2f out: sn wl outpcd* **11/2**

5254 **5** *nk* **Je Suis Unrockstar**[8] [659] 3-8-1 **68**........................(p) LeonnaMayor(7) 2 57
(David Nicholls) *dwlt: in rr: sme hdwy over 1f out: nvr a factor* **7/2**[3]

59.74 secs (0.04) **Going Correction** +0.05s/f (Slow) **5** Ran SP% **111.6**
Speed ratings (Par 100): **101,96,95,93,93**
CSF £12.65 TOTE £3.20: £1.40, £2.10; EX 12.00.
Owner Mark Goldstein & Stephen Pettman **Bred** Greg Parsons **Trained** Royston, Herts

FOCUS
An open-looking sprint handicap. A personal best from the winner, who has a good record here.
Monsieur Jamie Official explanation: trainer said, regarding apparent improvement in form, that the colt had previously been unruly at the start and upset in the stalls at Lingfield.
Restless Bay(IRE) Official explanation: jockey said gelding was hampered at start

741 HOSPITALITY AT SOUTHWELL RACECOURSE MAIDEN STKS 5f (F)
3:40 (3:46) (Class 5) 3-Y-O **£1,457** (£433; £216; £108) **Stalls** High

Form RPR

4-23 **1** **Mazovian (USA)**[7] [669] 3-9-0 69.................................. RobertLButler(3) 7 64
(Michael Chapman) *chsd ldrs: styd on to ld last 100yds* **3/1**[2]

5-25 **2** *1* **Spontaneity (IRE)**[10] [632] 3-8-12 62.................................. TomEaves 3 54
(Bryan Smart) *led: hdd ins fnl f: no ex* **9/2**[3]

5-02 **3** *1* **Bigalo's Vera B**[49] [146] 3-8-12 50................................ DuranFentiman 1 51
(Lawrence Mullaney) *chsd ldrs on outer: kpt on same pce fnl f* **8/1**

-066 **4** *nk* **Ever Roses**[23] [454] 3-8-12 46.......................................(v) BarryMcHugh 2 50
(Paul Midgley) *mid-div: sn drvn along: swtchd lft to wd outside over 1f out: kpt on* **20/1**

50-0 **5** *5* **Taverners Jubilee**[13] [595] 3-9-0 40............................ LouisBeuzelin(3) 4 37
(Patrick Morris) *chsd ldrs: wknd over 1f out: sddle slipped and eased ins fnl f* **80/1**

0-22 **6** *3/4* **Sailing North (USA)**[29] [389] 3-9-3 66.................................. LukeMorris 8 34
(Ronald Harris) *w ldrs towards stands' side: hung lft and wknd over 1f out* **11/8**[1]

00-5 **7** *3 3/4* **Secret Tycoon (IRE)**[8] [653] 3-9-3 65........................... StephenCraine 6 21
(Patrick Morris) *s.i.s: sme hdwy and hung lft over 2f out: sn wknd* **11/1**

8 *11* **Fawara** 3-8-12 0.. PJMcDonald 9 —
(Ruth Carr) *s.s: sme hdwy stands': side over 2f out: sn wknd: bhd whn eased ins fnl f* **33/1**

60.45 secs (0.75) **Going Correction** +0.05s/f (Slow) **8** Ran SP% **113.7**
Speed ratings (Par 98): **96,94,92,92,84 83,77,59**
toteswingers:1&2:£2.00, 1&3:£3.30, 2&3:£3.30 CSF £16.47 TOTE £4.10: £1.10, £1.10, £1.80; EX 14.50 Trifecta £47.80 Pool: £359.75 - 5.56 winning units..
Owner Mrs M Chapman **Bred** Darley **Trained** Market Rasen, Lincs
■ Silk Bounty was withdrawn on vet's advice (6/1, deduct 10p in the £ under R4.)

FOCUS
A modest maiden run at a fair clip. The favourite didn't run his race and the form is very weak.
Taverners Jubilee Official explanation: jockey said saddle slipped
Sailing North(USA) Official explanation: jockey said gelding stopped quickly

742 SOUTHWELL-RACECOURSE.CO.UK H'CAP 1m 4f (F)
4:10 (4:10) (Class 5) (0-75,72) 4-Y-O+ **£1,813** (£539; £269; £134) **Stalls** Low

Form RPR

532 **1** **Cobo Bay**[23] [457] 6-9-7 **72**..(b) HayleyTurner 4 83+
(Conor Dore) *sn trcking ldr: led over 5f out: drvn clr over 2f out: hung lft 1f out: eased fnl 100yds* **9/4**[1]

561- **2** *9* **Spring Secret**[120] [7306] 5-9-7 **72**... LukeMorris 1 70
(Bryn Palling) *chsd ldrs: drvn 5f out: wnt 3rd over 3f out: wnt 2nd over 1f out: no ch w wnr* **10/3**[3]

00-4 **3** *1 3/4* **Goodlukin Lucy**[19] [531] 4-9-2 **69**.. DaneO'Neill 5 64
(Pat Eddery) *sn chsng ldrs: wnt 2nd over 4f out: one pce fnl 2f* **11/4**[2]

6-45 **4** *6* **Amazing Blue Sky**[16] [551] 5-8-8 **59**................................. PJMcDonald 3 45
(Ruth Carr) *led: reminders 6f out: sn hdd: lost pl over 3f out* **14/1**

-340 **5** *45* **City Stable (IRE)**[29] [393] 6-8-11 **62**................................ PaulHanagan 2 —
(Michael Wigham) *detached in last: pushed along 6f out: sn lost tch: t.o and eased 3f out: virtually p.u* **7/2**

2m 38.21s (-2.79) **Going Correction** -0.25s/f (Stan)
WFA 4 from 5yo+ 2lb **5** Ran SP% **109.4**
Speed ratings (Par 103): **99,93,91,87,57**
CSF £9.84 TOTE £2.10: £1.80, £1.70; EX 13.20.
Owner Patrick Wilmott **Bred** The C H F Partnership **Trained** Cowbit, Lincs

FOCUS
Just a moderate handicap run at a good gallop. The winner was unexposed at the trip and improved on his recent level of form.

743 MEMBERSHIP OF SOUTHWELL GOLF CLUB H'CAP 6f (F)
4:40 (4:41) (Class 6) (0-65,65) 4-Y-O+ **£1,457** (£433; £216; £108) **Stalls** Low

Form RPR

201- **1** **Mottley Crewe**[126] [7195] 4-9-7 **65**.. TomEaves 9 78+
(Michael Dods) *chsd ldrs on outside: wnt 2nd over 3f out: led jst ins fnl f: edgd lft and drew clr* **11/2**[3]

-012 **2** *2 3/4* **Attrition**[6] [690] 4-8-12 **56**..(p) FrederikTylicki 8 61
(Andrew Reid) *w ldr: led over 4f out: wnt clr over 2f out: hdd jst ins fnl f: no ex* **7/4**[1]

030- **3** *1/2* **Jonnie Skull (IRE)**[81] [7847] 5-8-3 **52**..................... DanielleMcCreery(5) 6 55
(Phil McEntee) *mid-div: hdwy on ins over 2f out: styd on to take 3rd last 100yds* **28/1**

-310 **4** *1/2* **Toby Tyler**[28] [402] 5-9-5 **63**...(e[1]) MickyFenton 7 64
(Paul Midgley) *mid-div: hdwy over 2f out: kpt on same pce* **10/1**

1-01 **5** *1* **Final Salute**[28] [402] 5-9-1 **64**.......................................(v) AdamCarter(5) 4 62
(Bryan Smart) *led tl over 4f out: one pce fnl 2f* **5/1**[2]

4101 **6** *1/2* **Downhill Skier (IRE)**[17] [544] 7-9-4 **62**............................... EddieAhern 2 59
(Mark Brisbourne) *s.i.s: bhd: hdwy stands' side 2f out: kpt on fnl f* **7/1**

040- **7** *3 3/4* **Avec Moi**[162] [6285] 4-8-7 **51** oh6......................................(e[1]) LukeMorris 1 36
(Christine Dunnett) *chsd ldrs: outpcd 3f out: wknd over 1f out* **66/1**

5-04 **8** *3/4* **First Blade**[28] [402] 5-9-4 **62**...(b) GrahamGibbons 3 44
(Roy Bowring) *chsd ldrs: wknd fnl 2f* **7/1**

0-65 **9** *1* **Realt Na Mara (IRE)**[21] [493] 8-9-0 **65**............................ JacobMoore(7) 5 44
(Hughie Morrison) *dwlt: a bhd* **14/1**

1m 15.68s (-0.82) **Going Correction** -0.25s/f (Stan) **9** Ran SP% **114.1**
Speed ratings (Par 101): **95,91,90,90,88 88,83,82,80**
toteswingers:1&2:£3.20, 1&3:£17.30, 2&3:£9.80 CSF £15.30 CT £244.93 TOTE £8.20: £3.00, £1.30, £6.20; EX 18.40 TRIFECTA Not won..
Owner Crewe And Nantwich Racing Club **Bred** Longdon Stud Ltd **Trained** Denton, Co Durham

FOCUS
A competitive handicap where few ever got seriously involved. The second and third help with the form.
Downhill Skier(IRE) Official explanation: jockey said gelding did not face the kickback

744 PLAY GOLF BEFORE RACING AT SOUTHWELL APPRENTICE H'CAP 1m (F)
5:10 (5:10) (Class 5) (0-75,74) 4-Y-O+ **£1,813** (£539; £269; £134) **Stalls** Low

Form RPR

6-53 **1** **Thrust Control (IRE)**[21] [493] 4-9-0 **74**.................. JacobButterfield(7) 6 88+
(Brian Ellison) *sn trcking ldr: led over 3f out: wnt clr appr fnl f: readily* **7/1**

0-02 **2** *6* **Postman**[9] [640] 5-8-6 **62**...(p) ShaneBKelly(3) 3 62
(Bryan Smart) *n.m.r s: in rr and sn swtchd wd: hdwy on outside over 4f out: styd on to take 2nd last 100yds* **2/1**[1]

14-3 **3** *1/2* **Nolecce**[9] [640] 4-8-9 **62**... NathanAlison 4 61
(Richard Guest) *trckd ldrs: wnt 2nd over 2f out* **7/1**

6051 **4** *3/4* **General Tufto**[14] [568] 6-9-0 **70**..(b) RPWalsh(3) 1 67
(Charles Smith) *in rr: effrt over 4f out: kpt on one pce fnl 2f* **11/1**

563- **5** *1 1/2* **Jack Dawkins (USA)**[66] [7985] 6-8-6 **64**.......................... LeonnaMayor(5) 5 58
(David Nicholls) *hld up in last: effrt on ins over 2f out: rdn and hung lft over 1f out: nvr nr ldrs* **4/1**[2]

-504 **6** *1/2* **Eastern Hills**[9] [640] 6-8-3 **63**..(p) RyanTate(7) 2 56
(Alan McCabe) *mid-div: effrt over 3f out: sn outpcd: kpt on fnl 2f* **10/1**

3216 **7** *7* **Bentley**[19] [528] 7-9-5 **72**.. LMcNiff 8 49
(Brian Baugh) *led early: chsd ldrs: lost pl 2f out* **6/1**[3]

500- **8** *10* **Vito Volterra (IRE)**[128] [7143] 4-9-1 **73**............................ PeterSword(5) 7 27
(Michael Smith) *sn led: hdd over 3f out: wknd 2f out: sn bhd* **14/1**

1m 41.26s (-2.44) **Going Correction** -0.25s/f (Stan) **8** Ran SP% **116.7**
Speed ratings (Par 103): **102,96,95,94,93 92,85,75**
toteswingers:1&2:£5.50, 1&3:£10.40, 2&3:£3.10. totesuper7: Win: Not won. Place: £156.40. CSF £21.93 CT £104.08 TOTE £10.40: £3.10, £1.50, £1.30; EX 29.30 Trifecta £120.40 Pool: £475.27 - 2.92 winning units..
Owner Koo's Racing Club **Bred** Rathasker Stud **Trained** Norton, N Yorks
■ Jacob Butterfield's first winner, on only his third ride.

FOCUS
A weak apprentice handicap produced an easy winner, who posted a significant personal best. The form could easily rate higher.
T/Plt: £41.80 to a £1 stake. Pool:£58,150.03 - 1,013.20 winning tickets T/Qpdt: £15.60 to a £1 stake. Pool:£3,216.20 - 151.70 winning tickets WG

730 WOLVERHAMPTON (A.W) (L-H)
Thursday, March 3

OFFICIAL GOING: Standard
Wind: Fresh against Weather: Overcast

745 ATRPOKERCLUB.COM H'CAP 5f 216y(P)
5:15 (5:15) (Class 6) (0-65,65) 3-Y-O **£1,569** (£463; £231) **Stalls** Low

Form RPR

5214 **1** **Ridgeway Hawk**[16] [550] 3-8-11 **55**................................(v) RobertHavlin 12 58
(Mark Usher) *hld up in tch: rdn over 1f out: hung lft and led ins fnl f: drvn out* **8/1**

-301 **2** *nk* **Kassaab**[15] [558] 3-9-1 **59**..(b) JimmyQuinn 4 61
(Jeremy Gask) *chsd ldr tl led over 2f out: rdn over 1f out: edgd rt: hdd ins fnl f: r.o* **4/1**[2]

2366 **3** *shd* **Pineapple Pete (IRE)**[7] [669] 3-8-9 **60**.......................(t) NoraLooby(7) 10 62
(Alan McCabe) *hld up: hdwy over 2f out: rdn over 1f out: r.o* **22/1**

6-43 **4** *1 1/4* **These Dreams**[8] [659] 3-7-13 **46** oh1.................. AndrewHeffernan(3) 5 44
(Richard Guest) *s.i.s: hld up: hdwy over 1f out: r.o: nt rch ldrs* **8/1**

402- **5** *1 1/4* **Scoglio**[129] [7124] 3-9-7 **65**...(b) JamesDoyle 9 63+
(Frank Sheridan) *hld up: hdwy over 2f out: disputing cl 2nd: rdn whn struck by rivals whip 1f out: hmpd ins fnl f: no ex* **7/2**[1]

5606 **6** *2 1/2* **Seadream**[15] [564] 3-7-11 **46** oh1...................................... RyanPowell(5) 7 33
(Mark Usher) *s.i.s: hld up: hdwy over 1f out: nvr nrr* **20/1**

20-2 **7** *1 3/4* **Majestic Ridge (IRE)**[8] [655] 3-9-0 **58**................................ NeilCallan 1 40
(David Evans) *led: rdn and hdd 2f out: wknd ins fnl f* **15/2**

6-65 **8** *2 1/4* **Blue Ivy**[28] [396] 3-8-5 **49**.. KellyHarrison 8 24
[illegible]

00-6 **9** *1/2* **Running Water**[13] [595] 3-7-13 **46** oh1...................... JamesSullivan(3) 6 20
(Hugh McWilliams) *mid-div: hdwy over 3f out: rdn over 1f out: wknd fnl f* **50/1**

4-55 **10** *1 3/4* **Bobbyow**[35] [322] 3-8-13 **57**.. DavidProbert 11 25
(Bryn Palling) *mid-div: rdn 1/2-way: wknd over 2f out* **16/1**

020- **11** *hd* **High Class Lady**[119] [7313] 3-9-6 **64**..................................... ShaneKelly 2 32
(Walter Swinburn) *sn pushed along to chse ldrs: rdn and wknd over 2f out* **12/1**

41 **12** *3/4* **Lois Lane**[19] [518] 3-9-5 **63**.................................... RichardKingscote 3 28
(Ron Hodges) *chsd ldrs: ev ch 2f out: sn rdn and wknd* **7/1**[3]

1m 16.19s (1.19) **Going Correction** +0.175s/f (Slow) **12** Ran SP% **117.2**
Speed ratings (Par 96): **99,98,98,96,95 91,89,86,85,83 83,82**
toteswingers:1&2:£5.10, 1&3:£11.80, 2&3:£28.70 CSF £37.69 CT £693.68 TOTE £9.00: £2.30, £2.20, £4.60; EX 73.70.
Owner The Goodracing Partnership **Bred** Ridgeway Bloodstock **Trained** Upper Lambourn, Berks

FOCUS
There was a tight finish and a hard-luck story in this modest handicap. It's hard to be positive about the form but the time was reasonable.

746 STAY AT THE WOLVERHAMPTON HOLIDAY INN (S) STKS 5f 216y(P)
5:40 (5:43) (Class 6) 4-Y-O+ **£1,535** (£453; £226) **Stalls** Low

Form RPR

1222 **1** **Apache Ridge (IRE)**[17] [538] 5-9-3 63...............................(p) AmyRyan(3) 8 69
(Kevin Ryan) *hld up in tch: led 2f out: rdn and hung lft ins fnl f: styd on* **8/1**

1153 **2** *nk* **Frequency**[7] [665] 4-9-6 70..(b) AndreaAtzeni 2 69
(Michael Wigham) *chsd ldrs: nt clr run over 1f out: swtchd lft ins fnl f: sn rdn: r.o* **5/2**[1]

3604 **3** *1* **Athaakeel (IRE)**[8] [654] 5-9-1 63....................................(b) CathyGannon 7 60
(Ronald Harris) *s.i.s: hld up: hdwy over 2f out: rdn and hung lft over 1f out: r.o* **14/1**

-011 **4** *1* **Polemica (IRE)**[14] [575] 5-9-1 59...................................(bt) JamesDoyle 6 57
(Frank Sheridan) *prom: pushed along 1/2-way: rdn and hung lft over 1f out: r.o* **15/2**

304- **5** *hd* **Romantic Queen**[118] [7332] 5-8-6 63.........................(t) MatthewDavies(3) 5 52
(George Baker) *s.i.s: hld up: hdwy and hmpd ins fnl f: r.o: nvr able to chal* **3/1**[2]

600- **6** *3 1/4* **Place The Duchess**[300] [1884] 5-8-9 41.........................(p) RobertHavlin 4 41
(Alastair Lidderdale) *chsd ldr tl led over 2f out: sn hdd: n.m.r and wknd ins fnl f* **100/1**

-206 7 ½ **Kersivay**[17] 538 5-9-0 55 (b) NeilCallan 3 44
(David Evans) *led: racd keenly: rdn and hdd over 2f out: wknd fnl f* **11/1**

2451 8 4 **Sharp Shoes**[1] 732 4-9-1 65 (p) MartinHarley(5) 1 38
(Ann Duffield) *unruly in stalls: dwlt: sn prom: rdn 2f out: wknd fnl f* **4/1**[3]

1m 16.23s (1.23) **Going Correction** +0.175s/f (Slow) 8 Ran SP% **112.4**
Speed ratings (Par 101): **98,97,96,94,94 90,89,84**
toteswingers:1&2:£2.50, 1&3:£9.20, 2&3:£5.00 CSF £27.40 TOTE £8.50: £2.50, £1.10, £5.90; EX 17.40.There was no bid for the winner.
Owner Mrs J Ryan **Bred** Allevamento Ficomontanino Srl **Trained** Hambleton, N Yorks

FOCUS
A tight seller. They were closely grouped off an even pace for a long way. The winner and sixth help with the level.
Sharp Shoes Official explanation: jockey said gelding became upset in stalls and missed the break

747 THE BLACK COUNTRY'S ONLY RACECOURSE FILLIES' H'CAP 1m 141y(P)
6:10 (6:10) (Class 5) (0-70,65) 4-Y-0+ **£2,201** (£655; £327; £163) **Stalls** Low

Form RPR
06-1 1 **Hill Tribe**[20] 508 4-9-3 64 AndrewHeffernan(3) 6 73
(Richard Guest) *mde all: rdn over 1f out: styd on gamely* **9/4**[2]

2-24 2 1 **Saddlers Bend (IRE)**[11] 626 5-8-13 64 DavidKenny(7) 1 71
(George Baker) *a.p: chsd wnr over 1f out: sn rdn: styd on* **7/4**[1]

-054 3 3 **Buzz Bird**[14] 572 4-8-13 57 LeeNewman 2 58
(David Barron) *chsd ldrs: pushed along over 3f out: rdn over 1f out: styd on same pce ins fnl f* **8/1**

522- 4 3 ¼ **Many Welcomes**[218] 4485 6-9-1 59 JimmyQuinn 4 53
(Brian Baugh) *hld up: hdwy u.p over 1f out: wknd ins fnl f* **9/2**[3]

033 5 6 **Rich And Reckless**[14] 579 4-9-7 65 (t) TomMcLaughlin 5 46
(Tobias B P Coles) *racd keenly: trckd ldr tl rdn over 1f out: sn wknd* **8/1**

26/5 6 14 **Lilyannabanana**[14] 580 4-9-2 60 CathyGannon 3 12
(David Evans) *prom: rdn over 3f out: wknd over 2f out* **25/1**

1m 51.93s (1.43) **Going Correction** +0.175s/f (Slow) 6 Ran SP% **111.4**
Speed ratings (Par 100): **100,99,96,93,88 75**
toteswingers:1&2:£1.70, 1&3:£5.00, 2&3:£4.20 CSF £6.49 TOTE £2.40: £1.10, £2.30; EX 7.10.
Owner EERC & Alison Ibbotson **Bred** The Kingwood Partnership **Trained** Stainforth, S Yorks

FOCUS
A fair fillies' handicap. It was tactical and there was an all-the-way winner, who is rated right back to his best. The time was over five seconds slower than standard.
Lilyannabanana Official explanation: jockey said filly hung right-handed throughout

748 ATRCASINOCLUB.COM H'CAP (DIV I) 1m 1f 103y(P)
6:40 (6:40) (Class 6) (0-60,63) 4-Y-0+ **£1,364** (£403; £201) **Stalls** Low

Form RPR
2-42 1 **Nevada Desert (IRE)**[7] 675 11-9-0 53 MichaelStainton 10 62
(Richard Whitaker) *hld up: plld hrd: hdwy over 5f out: nt clr run and swtchd rt over 3f out: rdn over 1f out: r.o to ld nr fin* **8/1**

-202 2 ½ **Kyle Of Bute**[15] 553 5-9-6 59 J-PGuillambert 6 67
(Brian Baugh) *led: hdd over 7f out: chsd ldr tl led again 4f out: rdn clr over 1f out: hdd nr fin* **4/1**[2]

-351 3 1 ¾ **Una Pelota (IRE)**[3] 712 5-9-7 63 6ex (b) RossAtkinson(3) 11 68
(Tom Dascombe) *trckd ldrs: plld hrd: wnt 2nd over 2f out: rdn over 1f out: styd on same pce ins fnl f* **4/1**[2]

0-61 4 2 ¼ **Clearing House**[2] 722 6-8-12 51 6ex KirstyMilczarek 3 51
(John Ryan) *hld up: hdwy u.p over 1f out: nt rch ldrs* **7/2**[1]

0-06 5 4 ½ **Dauntsey Park (IRE)**[36] 299 4-9-2 55 FergusSweeney 9 47
(Tor Sturgis) *s.i.s: hld up: hdwy over 2f out: hrd rdn: hung lft and wknd fnl f* **14/1**

600- 6 2 ¼ **Timber Treasure (USA)**[27] 6040 7-9-1 54 (b) FrannyNorton 2 42
(Paul Green) *hld up: hdwy over 2f out: rdn and wknd over 1f out* **33/1**

134 7 4 **Orpens Peach (IRE)**[1] 730 4-8-13 57 MartinHarley(5) 1 37+
(Seamus Fahey, Ire) *trckd ldrs: plld hrd: rdn and wknd wl over 1f out* **8/1**

60-0 8 6 **Helpmeronda**[14] 575 5-8-7 46 oh1 SaleemGolam 12 15
(Ian Williams) *prom: lost pl over 7f out: wknd 4f out* **22/1**

0-02 9 18 **Aurora Lights**[14] 574 4-8-8 47 PaulHanagan 4 —
(Richard Fahey) *prom: pushed along over 6f out: rdn and wknd 4f out: t.o* **6/1**[3]

00-0 10 27 **Lofthouse**[1] 704 4-8-13 52 PJMcDonald 7 —
(Alistair Whillans) *chsd ldr tl led over 7f out: hdd 4f out: sn rdn: wknd over 2f out: t.o* **50/1**

2m 3.46s (1.76) **Going Correction** +0.175s/f (Slow) 10 Ran SP% **114.6**
Speed ratings (Par 101): **99,98,97,95,91 89,85,80,64,40**
toteswingers:1&2:£5.40, 1&3:£3.50, 2&3:£3.30 CSF £38.68 CT £147.98 TOTE £12.20: £3.10, £1.30, £2.00; EX 41.80.
Owner J Barry Pemberton **Bred** Bryan Ryan **Trained** Scarcroft, W Yorks

FOCUS
A competitive handicap. The pace was fairly steady and the kickback was flying. The runner-up helps set a solid enough level.
Clearing House Official explanation: vet said gelding lost a front shoe
Aurora Lights Official explanation: jockey said filly never travelled

749 ATRCASINOCLUB.COM H'CAP (DIV II) 1m 1f 103y(P)
7:10 (7:10) (Class 6) (0-60,60) 4-Y-0+ **£1,364** (£403; £201) **Stalls** Low

Form RPR
1152 1 **John Potts**[10] 635 6-9-7 60 KellyHarrison 10 73+
(Brian Baugh) *hld up: hdwy on outer over 2f out: chsd ldr over 1f out: rdn to ld and edgd lft ins fnl f: r.o* **2/1**[1]

5/0- 2 ¾ **Five Two**[83] 7819 8-9-4 57 (bt) EddieCreighton 6 68+
(Gavin Patrick Cromwell, Ire) *stdd s: hld up: plld hrd: hdwy over 1f out: sn rdn: r.o to go 2nd wl ins fnl f: nt rch wnr* **20/1**

00-2 3 2 **Barton Bounty**[1] 730 4-8-7 46 oh1 (b) PaulHanagan 8 53
(Peter Niven) *trckd ldrs: led over 2f out: rdn: hung lft and hdd ins fnl f: styd on same pce* **8/1**

2-00 4 2 ¾ **Love In The Park**[44] 203 6-9-2 55 LukeMorris 9 56
(Roy Brotherton) *hld up: rdn over 2f out: hdwy over 1f out: nrst fin* **11/2**[3]

00-5 5 ½ **Always De One**[23] 1 4-8-7 46 oh1 (p) KirstyMilczarek 11 46
(K F Clutterbuck) *w ldr tl led 5f out: rdn and hdd over 2f out: no ex fnl f* **25/1**

660/ 6 ¾ **Final Tune (IRE)**[741] 618 8-9-7 60 AdamKirby 4 58
(Mandy Rowland) *hld up in tch: rdn over 1f out: styd on same pce* **25/1**

03-2 7 1 ¼ **White Deer (USA)**[29] 391 7-9-2 55 (p) FrannyNorton 5 51
(Geoffrey Harker) *hld up: rdn over 1f out: styd on ins fnl f: nvr nrr* **9/2**[2]

6460 8 1 ¼ **Cane Cat (IRE)**[15] 552 4-8-9 48 (t) NeilCallan 7 41
(Tony Carroll) *mid-div: hdwy and nt clr run over 2f out: hmpd ins fnl f: nvr trbld ldrs* **16/1**

0050 9 ½ **Gems**[10] 630 4-8-7 46 oh1 (b[1]) ChrisCatlin 3 38
(Peter Hiatt) *chsd ldrs: rdn over 3f out: wknd over 1f out* **28/1**

0-66 10 5 **Watchmaker**[27] 427 8-9-0 53 (p) SamHitchcott 1 35
(Tor Sturgis) *chsd ldrs: rdn 1/2-way: wknd wl over 1f out* **14/1**

00/0 11 10 **Street Crime**[19] 526 6-8-13 52 RichardKingscote 2 13
(Ron Hodges) *led: t.k.h: jnd bk st: hdd 4f out: grad wknd: heavily eased 1f out* **7/1**

2m 2.74s (1.04) **Going Correction** +0.175s/f (Slow) 11 Ran SP% **119.0**
Speed ratings (Par 101): **102,101,99,97,96 96,94,93,93,88 80**
toteswingers:1&2:£10.10, 1&3:£6.20, 2&3:£51.90 CSF £51.89 CT £277.16 TOTE £4.20: £2.80, £10.50, £4.90; EX 62.60.
Owner Miss S M Potts **Bred** Miss S M Potts **Trained** Audley, Staffs

FOCUS
An ordinary handicap run at a steady tempo. The winner and third help set the level.
Final Tune(IRE) Official explanation: jockey said gelding had no more to give
Cane Cat(IRE) Official explanation: jockey said filly was denied a clear run

750 WOLVERHAMPTON-RACECOURSE.CO.UK H'CAP 1m 141y(P)
7:40 (7:40) (Class 4) (0-85,91) 3-Y-0 **£3,497** (£1,040; £520; £259) **Stalls** Low

Form RPR
-322 1 **Amwell Pinot**[41] 254 3-9-13 91 (b) CathyGannon 4 96
(Alan Bailey) *alawys prom: chsd ldr over 6f out: rdn over 3f out: hung lft and led wl ins fnl f: styd on* **7/1**[3]

-1 2 1 **Falmouth Bay (USA)**[31] 368 3-9-2 80 JoeFanning 1 83+
(Mark Johnston) *chsd ldrs: led over 1f out: rdn: hung lft and hdd wl ins fnl f: styd on same pce* **4/6**[1]

11-3 3 nk **Angelic Upstart (IRE)**[47] 177 3-9-0 78 DavidProbert 3 80
(Andrew Balding) *hld up: pushed along 6f out: hdwy u.p over 2f out: hung lft fr over 1f out: styng on same pce whn nt clr run wl ins fnl f* **5/1**[2]

P612 4 5 **Double Duchess**[30] 379 3-8-8 72 LiamJones 6 65
(Paul D'Arcy) *led: rdn and hdd over 1f out: wknd ins fnl f* **33/1**

2-41 5 4 **Silly Billy (IRE)**[13] 601 3-8-12 76 JamesDoyle 5 59
(Sylvester Kirk) *hld up: rdn and wknd over 2f out* **9/1**

1-43 6 2 **Coral Moon (IRE)**[45] 192 3-8-6 70 PaulHanagan 2 49
(Richard Fahey) *trckd ldrs: racd keen in early: pushed along over 3f out: wknd over 2f out: bhd whn hung lft fr over 1f out* **11/1**

1m 51.56s (1.06) **Going Correction** +0.175s/f (Slow) 6 Ran SP% **110.4**
Speed ratings (Par 100): **102,101,100,96,92 91**
toteswingers:1&2:£1.50, 1&3:£2.50, 2&3:£1.10 CSF £11.84 TOTE £3.20: £1.40, £2.50; EX 13.50.
Owner John Stocker **Bred** Darley **Trained** Newmarket, Suffolk
■ Stewards' Enquiry : Cathy Gannon three-day ban: first incident,two-day ban: careless riding (Mar 17-18); 2nd, one-day ban: careless riding (Mar 19)

FOCUS
A decent handicap. All of the runners had won or finished placed on their previous start. It was run at a bit of stop-start gallop but the first three pulled clear. The form is solid.

751 ENJOY THE PARTY PACK GROUP OFFER MAIDEN FILLIES' STKS 7f 32y(P)
8:10 (8:11) (Class 5) 3-Y-0+ **£2,007** (£597; £298; £149) **Stalls** High

Form RPR
22- 1 **Desert Shine (IRE)**[143] 6803 3-8-8 0 HayleyTurner 2 69+
(Michael Bell) *a.p: chsd ldr over 5f out: led over 1f out: pushed out* **4/9**[1]

6 2 ¾ **Symphonic Dancer (USA)**[10] 636 4-9-10 0 J-PGuillambert 3 73
(Brian Baugh) *prom: pushed along over 4f out: rdn to chse wnr ins fnl f: r.o* **14/1**

3 2 **Step And Fetch (IRE)** 3-8-8 0 PaulHanagan 7 63+
(Ann Duffield) *dwlt: hld up: hdwy over 2f out: r.o to go 3rd wl ins fnl f: nt rch ldrs* **18/1**

-243 4 1 ¼ **Spirit Of Grace**[19] 529 3-8-8 67 (p) JamesDoyle 5 59
(Alan McCabe) *led: rdn and hdd over 1f out: no ex ins fnl f* **5/1**[2]

-464 5 2 ¾ **Mini's Destination**[13] 600 3-8-8 50 NickyMackay 1 52
(John Holt) *chsd ldr to over 5f out: remained handy: rdn over 2f out: sn outpcd* **66/1**

5 6 ¾ **Misere**[13] 600 3-8-8 0 NeilCallan 4 53+
(Kevin Ryan) *hld up: rdn over 2f out: nvr trbld ldrs* **11/1**[3]

7 20 **Shikra** 3-8-8 0 WilliamCarson 6 —
(Eugene Stanford) *s.i.s: sn prom: wknd 1/2-way* **28/1**

1m 31.09s (1.49) **Going Correction** +0.175s/f (Slow)
WFA 3 from 4yo 16lb 7 Ran SP% **111.1**
Speed ratings (Par 100): **98,97,94,93,90 89,66**
toteswingers:1&2:£3.00, 1&3:£3.10, 2&3:£30.70 CSF £7.82 TOTE £2.40: £1.70, £8.90; EX 9.10.
Owner Dr Ali Ridha **Bred** Rabbah Bloodstock Limited **Trained** Newmarket, Suffolk

FOCUS
There did not seem to be much strength in depth in this fillies' maiden and the bare form is probably limited. The winner did not quite need to match her 2yo form.
Step And Fetch(IRE) Official explanation: jockey said, regarding running and riding, that his orders were, on the filly's racecourse debut, to settle early stages, but through greenness it somewhat missed the break and then appeared to resent the kickback, he pulled wide, asked it to make up ground too quickly, which tired it, adding that by riding sympathetically it was able to finish effectively.

752 WOLVERHAMPTON HOSPITALITY - A PLEASURE H'CAP 7f 32y(P)
8:40 (8:42) (Class 7) (0-50,51) 4-Y-0+ **£1,535** (£453; £226) **Stalls** High

Form RPR
60/1 1 **Stoneacre Gareth (IRE)**[7] 662 7-9-5 51 6ex AdamKirby 9 66+
(K F Clutterbuck) *hld up: hdwy over 2f out: led over 1f out: styd on wl: eased nr fin* **4/6**[1]

2 ¾ **Senor Tommie (IRE)**[468] 7471 5-8-10 47 (t) MartinHarley(5) 5 56
(Seamus Fahey, Ire) *chsd ldrs: rdn and ev ch over 1f out: edgd lft fnl f: styd on same pce* **12/1**

4235 3 6 **Guildenstern (IRE)**[8] 652 9-9-3 49 (t) JimmyQuinn 6 43
(Jane Chapple-Hyam) *hld up: hdwy over 1f out: r.o to go 3rd wl ins fnl f: nt trble ldrs* **8/1**[3]

460- 4 ¾ **Avoncreek**[154] 6494 7-9-1 47 KellyHarrison 8 39
(Brian Baugh) *chsd ldrs: rdn over 2f out: hmprd over 1f out: hung lft and wknd fnl f* **12/1**

0-06 5 5 **Cocktail Party (IRE)**[6] 690 5-9-1 47 GrahamGibbons 11 27
(James Unett) *racd keenly: hdwy to ld over 5f out: hung rt over 2f out: hdd wl over 1f out: wknd ins fnl f* **20/1**

3014 6 1 ¾ **Bold Bomber**[14] 575 5-9-2 48 FrannyNorton 1 24
(Paul Green) *hld up: hdwy over 2f out: wknd wl over 1f out* **5/1**[2]

-000 7 1 **Silca Meydan**[7] 675 5-8-13 45 (p) JamesDoyle 3 18
(Richard Price) *hld up: rdn over 2f out: n.d* **14/1**

00-6 8 2 **Marron Flore**[14] 573 8-8-13 45 (p) RobertHavlin 2 14
(Alastair Lidderdale) *prom: rdn 1/2-way: wknd 2f out* **66/1**

000- 9 shd **Rio Sands**[78] 7883 6-9-2 48 MichaelStainton 4 16
(Richard Whitaker) *led: hdd over 5f out: wknd over 1f out* **20/1**

-000 10 *14* **Frill A Minute**[13] [600] 7-8-13 **45**................................(v) WilliamCarson 10 —
(Lynn Siddall) *hld up: hdwy over 4f out: wknd over 3f out: t.o* **66/1**

1m 30.76s (1.16) **Going Correction** +0.175s/f (Slow) **10** Ran SP% **122.3**
Speed ratings (Par 97): **100,99,92,91,85 83,82,80,80,64**
toteswingers:1&2:£2.60, 1&3:£3.30, 2&3:£5.90 CSF £10.81 CT £43.18 TOTE £1.20: £1.02, £4.50, £2.80; EX 16.30.
Owner K F Clutterbuck **Bred** Robert De Vere Hunt **Trained** Exning, Suffolk

FOCUS
A low-grade handicap. The winner is well ahead of the handicapper and the second looks well treated too.
Cocktail Party(IRE) Official explanation: jockey said mare hung right throughout
T/Plt: £23.80 to a £1 stake. Pool:£66,107.47 - 2,025.74 winning tickets T/Qpdt: £5.00 to a £1 stake. Pool:£9,028.63 - 1,310.33 winning tickets CR

676 MEYDAN (L-H)
Thursday, March 3

OFFICIAL GOING: Tapeta: standard; turf: good
Times suggested the Tapeta was riding on the slow side. The rail was out 12m on the turf course.

753a AL BASTAKIYA SPONSORED BY EMIRATES AIRLINE (LISTED RACE) (TAPETA) 1m 1f 110y
3:05 (3:05) 3-Y-0

£96,153 (£32,051; £16,025; £8,012; £4,807; £3,205)

RPR

1 **Reem (AUS)**[13] [607] 4-9-0 104.................... KShea 9 104
(M F De Kock, South Africa) *trckd ldng duo: smooth prog to ld 2f out: r.o wl: comf* **11/10**[1]

2 *5 1/4* **Ahlaain (USA)**[7] [680] 3-8-7 99.................... WilliamBuick 2 93+
(David Simcock) *v.s.a: r.o wl fnl 2f: nrst fin* **6/1**[3]

3 *4 1/4* **Borug (USA)**[28] [411] 3-8-7 89....................(p) TedDurcan 7 85
(Saeed Bin Suroor) *mid-div: r.o same pce fnl 2f* **8/1**

4 *1 1/2* **Sonoran Sands (IRE)**[7] [680] 3-8-7 93....................(p) TadhgO'Shea 6 81
(J S Moore) *trckd ldr: led 7f out: hdd 2f out: r.o same pce* **33/1**

5 *1 1/4* **Bridgefield (USA)**[21] [502] 3-8-7 100.................... AhmedAjtebi 4 79
(Mahmood Al Zarooni) *sn led: hdd 7f out: one pce fnl 4f* **4/1**[2]

6 *1/4* **Paulinho (ARG)**[21] [502] 4-9-4 100....................(t) RyanMoore 1 82
(H J Brown, South Africa) *a in mid-div on rail* **11/1**

7 *3/4* **Energia Carioca (BRZ)**[28] [411] 4-9-4 95.................... RichardMullen 10 81
(E Martins, Brazil) *in rr of mid-div: nvr able to chal* **20/1**

8 *1 1/2* **Air Of Grace (IRE)**[21] [502] 3-8-7 85.................... AntiocoMurgia 5 74
(I Mohammed, UAE) *in rr of mid-div: hrd rdn 4 1/2f out: n.d* **33/1**

9 *6 1/2* **Amica (SAF)**[7] [681] 4-9-0 87.................... RoystonFfrench 8 60
(Gay Kelleway) *in rr of mid-div: n.d* **50/1**

10 *60* **Abjer (FR)**[21] [502] 3-8-9 104....................(t) KierenFallon 3 —
(I Mohammed, UAE) *sn rdn in rr: nvr involved* **12/1**

1m 59.9s (1.20) **Going Correction** +0.40s/f (Slow)
WFA 3 from 4yo 20lb **10** Ran SP% **121.6**
Speed ratings: **111,106,103,102,101 101,100,99,94,46**
CSF: £8.31.
Owner Sheikh Mohammed Bin Khalifa Al Maktoum **Bred** Sheikh Mohammed Bin Khalifa Al Maktoum **Trained** South Africa
■ No filly had ever previously contested this race.

FOCUS
The middle leg of the UAE Triple Crown has been won by some smart types, namely the likes of Asiatic Boy in 2007 and Mendip last year, but this latest running lacked strength in depth. The pace was not strong (the time was 2.90 seconds off the track record) yet they finished spread out.

NOTEBOOK
Reem(AUS), having landed the 1,000 Guineas Trial, Reem had found a couple of stablemates too good, firstly Mahbooba in the Guineas itself, and then River Jetez on turf in the Group 2 Balanchine. However, there was nothing of the calibre of those two here and she outclassed her rivals. This tough filly will definitely go for the UAE Derby according to her trainer. (opnd; 5/4 tchd; 6/5)
Ahlaain(USA) played up in the stalls and lost several lengths when the gates opened (he was also slowly away last time). Consequently, he was well out the back for much of the way, and had no chance with the winner, though he did well to stay on for a clear second. He couldn't be described as unlucky, such was Reem's dominance, but he's still apparently going to run in the UAE Derby if he makes the cut.
Borug(USA) promised to be suited by the step up in trip and return to synthetics, but he wasn't good enough. It was reported that he's unlikely to run again in Dubai this year and is going to head back to the UK at some stage.
Sonoran Sands(IRE) was allowed to set an ordinary pace but still looked a non-stayer.
Bridgefield(USA) was fourth in the UAE 2,000 Guineas last time, but he's bred for speed.

754a EMIRATES AIRLINE TROPHY (CONDITIONS RACE) (TURF) 5f
3:45 (3:45) 3-Y-0+

£67,307 (£22,435; £11,217; £5,608; £3,365; £2,243)

RPR

1 **Happy Dubai (IRE)**[21] [500] 4-9-0 111.................... RoystonFfrench 9 106
(A Al Raihe, UAE) *mid-div: rdn to ld 2f out: r.o wl* **11/2**[2]

2 *1/2* **Monsieur Joe (IRE)**[7] [678] 4-9-0 101....................(v) RyanMoore 4 104
(Walter Swinburn) *mid-div: r.o wl fnl 2f: nrst fin* **12/1**

3 *1 1/4* **Invincible Ash (IRE)**[14] [582] 6-8-9 107....................(p) GFCarroll 8 95
(M Halford, Ire) *mid-div: ev ch 1 1/2f out: one pce fnl 110yds* **11/2**[2]

4 *1* **Prohibit**[21] [500] 6-9-0 112....................(p) ChristopheSoumillon 1 96
(Robert Cowell) *settled in rr: r.o fnl 2 1/2f: nrst fin* **3/1**[1]

5 *1* **Rock Jock (IRE)**[14] [582] 4-8-8 104.................... WJSupple 7 87
(Tracey Collins, Ire) *trckd ldr: nt qckn over 1 1/2f out* **7/1**[3]

6 *1 1/2* **Dohasa (IRE)**[13] [606] 6-9-0 108.................... JMurtagh 3 87
(I Mohammed, UAE) *nvr bttr than mid-div* **11/1**

7 *2 1/4* **Everyday Heroes (USA)**[13] [602] 5-9-0 100.................... FrankieDettori 6 79
(Saeed Bin Suroor) *a in mid-div* **12/1**

8 *1/2* **Mister Manannan (IRE)**[21] [500] 4-9-0 104.................... AdrianNicholls 5 77
(David Nicholls) *a in mid-div* **12/1**

9 *1/2* **Effort**[6] 5-9-0 96.................... Christophe-PatriceLemaire 2 75
(A bin Huzaim, UAE) *nvr able to chal* **22/1**

10 *5* **Mutheeb (USA)**[13] [602] 6-9-0 109....................(v) RichardHills 11 57
(M Al Muhairi, UAE) *led nr side: hdd 2f out: sn btn* **9/1**

11 *4 3/4* **Rock Of Nassau (FR)**[101] [7535] 5-8-8 97.................... MickaelBarzalona 10 34
(F Head, France) *a in rr* **25/1**

58.55 secs (58.55) **11** Ran SP% **117.9**
CSF: £69.96.
Owner Ahmed Al Falasi **Bred** Waterford Hall Stud **Trained** UAE

FOCUS
Only the third race to be run over this C&D and a new contest for Super Thursday, a trial for the Al Quoz Sprint. However, the form is not particularly strong by the standards of a Group 2 prep. All the pace was up the centre of the track and a middle-to-high draw was an advantage. The time was the slowest over this 5f course to date.

NOTEBOOK
Happy Dubai(IRE) had to be re-shod at the start, having pulled off a shoe, but he remained calm. The winner ran a bit flat when behind a few of these here last time, but had previously been in fine form and bounced back to record his third Carnival success of the year. He fully deserves his place in the Al Quoz Sprint, but he's surely going to have to step up on this form considering he was fortunate to confirm earlier placings with Monsieur Joe, who surely would have won granted a better trip, and that runner came into this rated only 101.
Monsieur Joe(IRE) had lost his way since finishing second to Happy Dubai over C&D on these terms in January, but this was just about a career best. He was squeezed out when going for a gap between Invincible Ash and Muthee over a furlong from the finish, and the manner in which he stayed on when finally in the clear suggests he was unlucky.
Invincible Ash(IRE) showed good speed and had her chance. She ran well, but is flattered to reverse February 10 placings with Prohibit.
Prohibit had the worst possible draw, and with no pace on the far side of the track, he was much too keen and soon ended up just about last of all. He did well to get so close and will be worth his place on World Cup night.
Rock Jock(IRE) showed speed but didn't see his race out. (opnd; 9/1 tchd; 8-1)
Everyday Heroes(USA), probably not helped by the brief delay, was sweating and didn't run to form. (op; 11-1)

755a MAHAB AL SHIMAAL SPONSORED BY EMIRATES AIRLINE (GROUP 3) (TAPETA) 6f
4:20 (4:20) 3-Y-0+

£76,923 (£25,641; £12,820; £6,410; £3,846; £2,564)

RPR

1 **Bankable (IRE)**[21] [501] 7-9-0 116....................(t) RyanMoore 6 115+
(H J Brown, South Africa) *s.i.s: smooth prog 2 1/2f out: r.o wl: led fnl 55yds: comf* **11/4**[1]

2 *1* **Conveyance (USA)**[306] [1714] 4-9-0 113....................(t) RichardMullen 8 112
(S Seemar, UAE) *sn led: rdn 2f out: r.o wl: hdd fnl 55yds* **8/1**

3 *1/2* **Force Freeze (USA)**[28] [414] 6-9-0 105....................(t) KierenFallon 5 110
(Doug Watson, UAE) *trckd ldr: ev ch 110yds out: one pce* **25/1**

4 *3/4* **Rileyskeepingfaith**[13] [602] 5-9-0 101....................(t) AhmedAjtebi 11 108
(Mahmood Al Zarooni) *racd in rr: r.o wl fnl 2f: nrst fin* **12/1**

5 *1/2* **Green Beret (IRE)**[14] [582] 5-9-0 107.................... RoystonFfrench 1 106
(A Al Raihe, UAE) *mid-div: short of room 4 1/2f out: r.o fnl 2f* **7/1**[3]

6 *1/4* **Iver Bridge Lad**[7] [678] 4-9-0 102....................(b) MichaelO'Connell 9 106
(John Ryan) *mid-div: chsd ldrs 2 1/2f out: one pce fnl f* **12/1**

7 *1/2* **Indomito (GER)**[21] [497] 5-9-0 104.................... WayneSmith 4 104
(P Vovcenko, Germany) *trckd ldrs whn no room 3f out: nvr rcvrd* **25/1**

8 *1 1/4* **Global City (IRE)**[7] [678] 5-9-0 102....................(t) FrankieDettori 12 100
(Saeed Bin Suroor) *chsd ldrs: one pce fnl f* **6/1**[2]

9 *3/4* **Barbecue Eddie (USA)**[13] [606] 7-9-0 106....................(b) TadhgO'Shea 10 98
(Doug Watson, UAE) *nvr bttr than mid-div* **11/1**

10 *2 1/4* **Silaah**[7] [678] 7-9-0 105....................(p) AdrianNicholls 7 90
(David Nicholls) *chsd ldrs tl one pce fnl 1 1/2f* **12/1**

11 *7* **Bank Merger (USA)**[13] [606] 4-9-0 107....................(t) MickaelBarzalona 2 68
(Saeed Bin Suroor) *nvr able to chal* **16/1**

12 *4 1/4* **Alazeyab (USA)**[14] [582] 5-9-0 108....................(t) RichardHills 3 54
(A Al Raihe, UAE) *trckd ldrs for 3 1/2f: one pce fnl 1 1/2f* **7/1**[3]

1m 11.52s (0.52) **Going Correction** +0.40s/f (Slow) **12** Ran SP% **122.0**
Speed ratings: **112,110,110,109,108 108,107,105,104,101 92,86**
CSF: £25.48.
Owner Ramzan Kadyrov **Bred** Barronstown Stud & Cobra **Trained** South Africa

FOCUS
This has rarely been a key trial for the Golden Shaheen, such has been the US dominance of that race (nine-time winners), but Big City Man was runner-up in this on the Nad Al Sheba dirt in 2009 before winning on World Cup night. The bare form of the latest running is just ordinary by Group 3 standards, but the front two are both classy types who can rate higher.

NOTEBOOK
Bankable(IRE) had luckless trips on his two previous starts this year, when dropped to this distance for the first time on his reappearance and then in the Firebreak Stakes back over 1m, but this race set up nicely for him. He started slowly and was outpaced early, but Ryan Moore shrewdly saved ground around the bend into the straight before switching wide, and this 7-y-o needed only hands-and-heels encouragement to grab the long-time leader near the line. On this evidence he'd struggle to get involved in better company over 6f, and his trainer said beforehand this was being used as a prep for the Duty Free, a race in which he was runner-up last year. This should have helped his confidence and he clearly retains plenty of ability.
Conveyance(USA) won his first four starts for Bob Baffert in the US, the first three on synthetics, including at Grade 3 level, but had been off since setting an unsustainable pace in last year's Kentucky Derby. He's joined a trainer who has yet to have a Carnival winner this year, albeit the horses are in good form domestically, and he was entitled to need the run, but he nearly made all. This was a fine return and he should come on fitness-wise, although he'll have a much tougher job trying to lead the likes of Rocket Man in the Golden Shaheen.
Force Freeze(USA) was always close up and had his chance.
Rileyskeepingfaith did well to finish so close considering he had a wide trip from stall 11, but his proximity supports the view that this is ordinary form for the level. (opnd; 12-1 tchd 14-1)
Green Beret(IRE), a winner from well out of the handicap over C&D last time, pulled much too hard early on and found himself dangerously short of room as a result. He did well to get so close.
Global City(IRE) can be excused this - stall 12 is now 0-17 over this C&D.

756a BURJ NAHAAR SPONSORED BY EMIRATES AIRLINE (GROUP 3) (TAPETA) 1m
4:55 (4:55) 3-Y-0+

£76,923 (£25,641; £12,820; £6,410; £3,846; £2,564)

RPR

1 **Mendip (USA)**[49] [156] 4-9-0 117.................... FrankieDettori 9 102+
(Saeed Bin Suroor) *mid-div: smooth prog 3f out: rdn 2f out: r.o wl: led cl home* **4/5**[1]

2 *1/4* **Zafeen Speed**[26] [461] 4-9-0 100....................(vt) WayneSmith 8 101
(M Al Muhairi, UAE) *mid-div: chsd ldrs 2 1/2f out: ev ch 110yds out: one pce fnl 55yds* **16/1**

3 *1/2* **As De Trebol (USA)**[13] [606] 5-9-0 100.................... OlivierPeslier 4 100
(M Delcher-Sanchez, Spain) *trckd ldng duo: ev ch 1 1/2f out: led 1f out: hdd cl home* **25/1**

4 *1 1/4* **Snaafy (USA)**[14] [586] 7-9-0 112....................(v) RichardHills 12 97
(M Al Muhairi, UAE) *trckd ldr: ev ch 1f out: one pce fnl 110yds* **16/1**

5 *1 1/4* **Banna Boirche (IRE)**[13] [606] 5-9-0 106.................... JMurtagh 2 94
(M Halford, Ire) *mid-div: r.o wl fnl 1 1/2f* **14/1**

6 ¾ **Sangaree (USA)**[13] 604 6-9-0 108 (b) MickaelBarzalona 6 92
(Saeed Bin Suroor) *nvr able to chal* **14/1**
7 ¾ **Our Giant (AUS)**[14] 586 8-9-0 109 (b) ChristopheSoumillon 1 91
(M F De Kock, South Africa) *nvr bttr than mid-div* **11/1**[3]
8 1 ¼ **Famous Warrior (IRE)**[13] 604 4-9-0 105 TadhgO'Shea 5 88
(Doug Watson, UAE) *sn led: hdd 2f out: wknd fnl f* **20/1**
9 ¼ **Crowded House**[28] 416 5-9-0 115 (t) RyanMoore 11 87
(B Cecil, U.S.A) *nvr bttr than mid-div* **7/1**[2]
10 ¾ **Prince Shaun (IRE)**[28] 415 6-9-0 97 (t) PatDobbs 3 85
(Doug Watson, UAE) *nvr bttr than mid-div* **66/1**
11 1 ½ **Falcativ**[26] 462 6-9-0 95 (b) AntiocoMurgia 10 82
(I Mohammed, UAE) *nvr able to chal* **66/1**
12 3 ¼ **Verde-Mar (BRZ)**[14] 582 4-8-8 102 RichardMullen 13 74
(E Martins, Brazil) *n.d* **66/1**
13 1 ¾ **Cat Junior (USA)**[21] 501 6-9-0 113 (vt) WilliamBuick 7 70
(Niels Petersen, Norway) *s.i.s: n.d* **14/1**
14 12 **Kinky Afro (IRE)**[13] 607 4-8-9 99 KierenFallon 14 38
(J S Moore) *n.d* **50/1**

1m 36.77s (-0.33) **Going Correction** +0.40s/f (Slow) **14** Ran SP% **123.2**
Speed ratings: **117,116,116,115,113 113,112,111,110,110 108,105,103,91**
CSF: £15.53.
Owner Sheikh Hamdan Bin Mohammed Al Maktoum **Bred** Jayeff B Stables **Trained** Newmarket, Suffolk

FOCUS
The winners of the 2005 and 2010 Godolphin Mile were beaten in this, namely Grand Emporium (runner-up) and most recently Calming Influence (third). This latest running didn't look a strong race for the grade and those held up struggled to get involved.

NOTEBOOK
Mendip(USA) was expected to prove much the best, but he was forced to work hard. He has only been beaten once in six starts - third in last year's UAE Derby - and returned with a smart performance in the first round of the Al Maktoum Challenge. However, he didn't travel as well as last time according to Frankie Dettori and also failed to quicken when asked, looking in trouble for much of the closing stages and only getting up near the line after producing a sustained challenge. It was interesting to hear Dettori say afterwards he felt something might have been "pinching" Mendip but ,whatever the case, we know he's capable of better and one major plus was the horse's attitude. He's looked immature on occasions, both flashing his tail and edging left here latest, but other than still requiring a blanket for stalls entry, he could not be faulted. He has the option of the Godolphin Mile or the World Cup but will need to raise his game considerably to win the latter event.
Zafeen Speed never made the track when registered with Brian Meehan and only made his debut in November, but he's progressed well in non-Carnival events here lately, winning his last three starts, the latest off a mark of 90. He coped well with this marked step up in class and there could well be more to come, so he'll be worth his place in the Godolphin Mile.
As De Trebol(USA) ran well on his recent Dubai debut, looking unlucky not to take second despite setting a strong pace, and he confirmed that promise. He'll also be worth his place on World Cup night.
Snaafy(USA) was below his official mark of 112.
Banna Boirche(IRE) ran well without threatening.
Our Giant(AUS) has not gone on since winning a 6f conditions race on his return.
Crowded House was never going and looks nowhere near the horse of old.
Cat Junior(USA) was a surprise winner of this last year when with Brian Meehan, but he didn't run to form on his recent debut for this yard and this was even worse.

757a DUBAI CITY OF GOLD SPONSORED BY EMIRATES AIRLINE (GROUP 2) (TURF) 1m 4f 93y
5:30 (5:30) 3-Y-0+
£96,153 (£32,051; £16,025; £8,012; £4,807; £3,205)

RPR
1 **Monterosso**[198] 5185 4-8-11 115 (t) MickaelBarzalona 7 116
(Mahmood Al Zarooni) *trckd ldng duo: led 1 1/2f out: r.o wl* **10/1**
2 1 ¼ **Calvados Blues (FR)**[13] 603 5-9-0 112 FrankieDettori 3 115
(Mahmood Al Zarooni) *trckd ldng pair: ev ch 1 1/2f out: nt qckn fnl f* **4/1**[2]
3 ¾ **Mr Brock (SAF)**[13] 608 8-9-0 108 KShea 4 114
(M F De Kock, South Africa) *trckd ldr: led 2f out: hdd 1 1/2f out: one pce fnl f* **12/1**
4 ½ **Kasbah Bliss (FR)**[161] 6607 9-9-0 110 GeraldMosse 5 113
(F Doumen, France) *in rr of mid-div: r.o wl fnl 2f: nrst fin* **12/1**
5 5 ½ **Topclas (FR)**[13] 603 5-9-0 104 (v) PatCosgrave 9 104
(M bin Shafya, UAE) *settled in rr: nvr nr to chal* **33/1**
6 5 ¼ **Marinous (FR)**[95] 7615 5-9-0 117 (bt) KierenFallon 8 96
(F Head, France) *settled in rr: nvr able to chal* **6/1**[3]
7 3 ¾ **Interaction (ARG)**[28] 416 5-9-0 112 Christophe-PatriceLemaire 2 90
(P Bary, France) *sn led: hdd & wknd 2f out* **4/1**[2]
8 3 **Yirga**[7] 676 5-9-0 105 (t) RoystonFfrench 6 85
(A Al Raihe, UAE) *in rr of mid-div: nvr involved* **25/1**
9 16 **Tam Lin**[35] 331 8-9-0 107 (t) XZiani 1 59
(M bin Shafya, UAE) *slowly away: mid-div: n.d* **50/1**
10 dist **Simon De Montfort (IRE)**[42] 242 4-8-11 113 AhmedAjtebi 10 —
(Mahmood Al Zarooni) *settled in last: rdn 6f out: sn btn* **2/1**[1]

2m 36.09s (156.09)
WFA 4 from 5yo+ 2lb **10** Ran SP% **120.8**
CSF: £51.02.
Owner Godolphin **Bred** Darley **Trained** Newmarket, Suffolk

FOCUS
The pace seemed just ordinary. This has never produced the Sheema Classic winner, and a couple of the likelier types, Interaction and Simon De Montfort, ran well below form in this latest renewal, so it was clearly not as strong a contest as might have been the case.

NOTEBOOK
Monterosso had lost his way when last seen, finishing well beaten in the Great Voltigeur, but he had earlier defeated Arctic Cosmos (later won the St Leger) and Buzzword (won the German Derby next time) in the King Edward VII Stakes at Royal Ascot, and then went off favourite for the Irish Derby, finishing fourth. Despite being the apparent third string on his debut for Godolphin, he gained a straightforward success and clearly retains his ability. He looks a player for the Sheema Classic.
Calvados Blues(FR) has returned to something like his best form this year, winning a handicap off 109 over C&D last time, and this was probably another step forward. He may be the best guide to the form.
Mr Brock(SAF) is not up to seriously challenging the top 1m2f performers on Tapeta anymore, so it made sense to step him up in trip and go back to turf, and he ran well.
Kasbah Bliss(FR) is usually campaigned over staying trips, but was a close third in the 2009 Hong Kong Vase over this distance and ran a fine race after a five-month break.
Marinous(FR) sweated up beforehand and seemed a bit keen in the race itself. He probably found the ground too quick.
Interaction(ARG) was allowed to set just an ordinary pace but was beaten as soon as he was challenged entering the straight.
Simon De Montfort(IRE) created a good impression when staying on from well back to win a handicap on his Dubai debut, and a repeat of those hold-up tactics were tried, but he ran as though he had a problem. He became detached down the back straight and was soon tailed off, not responding to pressure, yet he still completed. He was reported "slow to recover" by the vet, but nothing amiss was found. (opnd; 2-1, tchd 9-4)

758a AL MAKTOUM CHALLENGE R3 SPONSORED BY EMIRATES AIRLINE (GROUP 2) (TAPETA) 1m 2f
6:05 (6:05) 3-Y-0+
£115,384 (£38,461; £19,230; £9,615; £5,769; £3,846)

RPR
1 **Twice Over**[138] 6925 6-9-0 125 TomQueally 13 123+
(Sir Henry Cecil) *mid-div: smooth prog 2 1/2f out: led 2f out: r.o wl* **7/2**[2]
2 2 ¾ **Musir (AUS)**[21] 501 5-9-0 117 ChristopheSoumillon 1 118+
(M F De Kock, South Africa) *mid-div on rail: chsd wnr 2f out: ev ch 1f out: one pce fnl 55yds* **9/4**[1]
3 nse **Gitano Hernando**[28] 416 5-9-0 118 JMurtagh 11 117+
(Marco Botti) *mid-div: chsd ldrs 2 1/2f out: r.o wl fnl 2f* **9/1**
4 1 ¾ **Win For Sure (GER)**[35] 332 6-9-0 113 GregoryBenoist 8 113
(X Nakkachdji, France) *mid-div: r.o wl fnl 2f* **20/1**
5 ¾ **Prince Bishop (IRE)**[137] 6974 4-9-0 118 FrankieDettori 3 112
(Saeed Bin Suroor) *mid-div: chsd ldrs 2 1/2f out: one pce fnl f* **6/1**[3]
6 ¾ **Rajsaman (FR)**[81] 7853 4-9-0 115 KierenFallon 6 110
(F Head, France) *mid-div: r.o fnl 2f* **16/1**
7 nse **Mufarrh (IRE)**[7] 679 4-9-0 112 RichardHills 9 110
(A Al Raihe, UAE) *trckd ldrs: ev ch 2f out: nt qckn fnl f* **16/1**
8 ¾ **Eavesdropper**[13] 608 4-9-0 110 (bt) MickaelBarzalona 2 109
(Mahmood Al Zarooni) *settled in rr: rdn 8 1/2f out: no ex* **33/1**
9 ¾ **Irish Flame (SAF)**[21] 503 5-9-0 119 KShea 14 107
(M F De Kock, South Africa) *trckd ldrs: one pce fnl 2f* **16/1**
10 shd **Richard's Kid (USA)**[151] 6605 6-9-0 119 (bt) RichardMullen 12 107
(S Seemar, UAE) *settled in rr: nvr nr to chal* **12/1**
11 hd **Haatheq (USA)**[14] 583 4-9-0 109 TadhgO'Shea 10 107
(A Al Raihe, UAE) *in rr of mid-div: n.d* **33/1**
12 11 **Hot Six (BRZ)**[28] 417 6-9-0 104 RoystonFfrench 5 85
(E Martins, Brazil) *nvr able to chal* **66/1**
13 3 ¼ **Debussy (IRE)**[117] 7366 5-9-0 120 WilliamBuick 4 78
(Mahmood Al Zarooni) *trckd ldr: led after 2f to 2f out: wknd* **12/1**
14 dist **Etched (USA)**[117] 7367 6-9-0 119 (b) AhmedAjtebi 7 —
(Mahmood Al Zarooni) *sn led: hdd after 2f: rdn 7f out: sn btn* **14/1**

2m 5.44s (0.54) **Going Correction** +0.40s/f (Slow) **14** Ran SP% **129.1**
Speed ratings: **113,110,110,109,108 108,108,107,106,106 106,97,95,—**
CSF: £12.30.
Owner K Abdulla **Bred** Juddmonte Farms Ltd **Trained** Newmarket, Suffolk

FOCUS
The major domestic trial for the World Cup and three winners of this have followed up in the main event, Dubai Millennium (2000), Street Cry (2002) and Electrocutionist (2006). A strong field lined up, although Bold Silvano, who won the second round of this series, was missing owing to a bruised foot.

NOTEBOOK
Twice Over overcame stall 13 and a four-wide trip into the straight. He briefly looked set for a protracted dual with Musir, who was produced going similarly well, but Twice Over readily put that rival away. He managed only tenth in last year's World Cup, but received an early bump on that occasion and was also stuck wide (drawn 11) in what was a messy race. However, he's possibly a better horse now and has proven his ability to act around this tight track.
Musir(AUS) had been due to contest the Burj Nahaar, but was re-routed here to take the place of Bold Silvano. Upped in trip after a fine comeback over 1m, he ran well but was outstayed and probably outclassed by the winner. It will be a surprise if he reverses form at the end of the month.
Gitano Hernando, poorly ridden when behind Bold Silvano in a muddling race last time, had a better trip this time and tracked the winner through. He gives the impression he can step forward again, but unless the World Cup turns into a lottery like it did last year, then he'll probably struggle.
Win For Sure(GER)'s handicap win over 1m on turf last time has worked out really well and he ran a fine race on this significant rise in class.
Prince Bishop(IRE), the winner of his last four starts for Andre Fabre in France, including a Group 3 and a Group 2, had attracted support for the World Cup in recent days, probably owing to being Frankie Dettori's apparent choice here. He ran like a horse in need of the run, but big improvement is required if he's to get involved in the main event.
Rajsaman(FR) was below the form he showed when fourth in the Hong Kong Mile on his previous start and was seemingly unsuited by these vastly different conditions.
Mufarrh(IRE) was up significantly in class after a wide-margin handicap success off 102, but he ran well for a long way, despite having to use up energy to get into a challenging position.
Irish Flame(SAF) was using this as a prep for the Sheema Classic, with connections wanting to avoid another run on firm turf before the big day. He had the worst draw and was not given a hard time once held, so better can be expected next time.
Richard's Kid(USA) won his last two starts in Grade 1 company for Bob Baffert, but was well below form on his debut for a trainer who's still looking for his first Carnival success of 2011.

759a JEBEL HATTA SPONSORED BY EMIRATES AIRLINE (GROUP 2) (TURF) 1m 1f
6:45 (6:45) 3-Y-0+
£96,153 (£32,051; £16,025; £8,012; £4,807; £3,205)

RPR
1 **Wigmore Hall (IRE)**[138] 6925 4-9-0 117 JamieSpencer 7 116+
(Michael Bell) *settled in rr: smooth prog 2 1/2f out: r.o wl: led fnl 55yds* **12/1**
2 ¼ **Poet's Voice**[138] 6925 4-9-0 122 (t) FrankieDettori 12 116+
(Saeed Bin Suroor) *mid-div: chsd ldr 2 1/2f out: r.o wl fnl 1 1/2f: led briefly 110yds out: hdd 55yds out* **3/1**[2]
3 nse **Presvis**[35] 331 7-9-0 120 RyanMoore 1 116+
(Luca Cumani) *slowly away: settled in rr: smooth prog 2f out: r.o wl: nt qckn fnl f* **5/4**[1]
4 1 ¼ **Le Drakkar (AUS)**[14] 586 6-9-0 112 (t) Christophe-PatriceLemaire 5 113
(A bin Huzaim, UAE) *trckd ldng duo: led 2f out: hdd ins fnl f* **20/1**
5 ¼ **Hearts Of Fire**[14] 586 4-9-0 117 (t) KierenFallon 6 112
(Ibrahaim Al Malki, Qatar) *mid-div: r.o wl fnl 1 1/2f* **10/1**[3]
6 ¾ **Steele Tango (USA)**[35] 331 6-9-0 113 JMurtagh 9 111
(Roger Teal) *a in mid-div* **14/1**
7 hd **Lancelot (FR)**[14] 581 4-9-0 109 OlivierPeslier 8 110
(A De Mieulle, Qatar) *a in mid-div* **25/1**
8 1 ¼ **Trois Rois (FR)**[14] 581 6-9-0 110 (b) TadhgO'Shea 11 108
(I Mohammed, UAE) *settled in rr: nvr able to chal* **33/1**
9 ½ **Kavango (IRE)**[7] 682 4-9-0 106 PatCosgrave 10 107
(M bin Shafya, UAE) *trckd ldr: led 2 1/2f out: hdd & wknd 2f out* **33/1**
10 1 ¾ **Al Shemali**[13] 608 7-9-0 119 (t) RoystonFfrench 3 103
(A Al Raihe, UAE) *nvr bttr than mid-div* **10/1**[3]

11 4 1/2 **Ferneley (IRE)**[28] 415 7-9-0 110..........(t) WilliamBuick 2 94
(B Cecil, U.S.A) *in rr of mid-div: n.d* **25/1**
12 9 **Shakespearean (IRE)**[138] 6923 4-9-0 116.......... TedDurcan 4 75
(Saeed Bin Suroor) *sn led: hdd & wknd 2 1/2f out* **16/1**

1m 50.66s (110.66) **12** Ran SP% **126.2**
CSF: £48.29. Placepot: £59.20 to a £1 stake. Pool: £9,975.00 - 123.00 winning tickets. Quadpot: £18.20 to a £1 stake. Pool: £583.50 - 23.70 winning tickets..
Owner M B Hawtin **Bred** K And Mrs Cullen **Trained** Newmarket, Suffolk

FOCUS
A quality Group 2 and form with great relevance to the upcoming Duty Free on World Cup night. Since that aforementioned contest attained Group 1 status, two winners ran in this race en route, Ipi Tombe (winner, 2003) and Jay Peg (third, 2008). They went fast enough to set this up for three high-class hold-up performers, who fought out a terrifically tight finish.

NOTEBOOK
Wigmore Hall(IRE) was last seen finishing fifth in the Champion Stakes behind Twice Over, the dominant winner of the key World Cup trial earlier on the card. He proved he can travel when runner-up in last year's Secretariat Stakes at Arlington in the US and clearly he's thriving in Dubai, this being arguably a career best. Despite having nothing in the hand, he looks a serious contender for the Duty Free, although it's worth noting that Frankie Dettori, aboard Poet's Voice, dropped his whip about a furlong and a half out. (opnd; 11-1)
Poet's Voice may have won had his rider not dropped his whip over a furlong out. Whatever the case the runner-up, last year's Celebration Mile and Queen Elizabeth II Stakes winner, bounced back from a poor effort in the Champion Stales and is himself likely to be a big player on World Cup night. (tchd; 10-3)
Presvis, last year's winner, made his move more towards the inside than the first two finishers, who challenged out wide, but it didn't seem to make a difference. He probably didn't quite match the form of his recent Al Rashidiya success considering he had Steele Tango nearly 5l behind that day, compared to just over 2l this time, but he could still have a say in the Duty Free. (opnd; 11-8)
Le Drakkar(AUS) paid a compliment to both Raihana and Derbass, having finished close-up behind those two (who are both presumably Duty Free bound) recently.
Al Shemali did not improve as one might have hoped for the return to turf and he looks extremely unlikely to retain his crown on World Cup night.

716 LINGFIELD (L-H)
Friday, March 4

OFFICIAL GOING: Standard
Wind: medium, half against Weather: dry, chilly

760 LINGFIELDPARK.CO.UK H'CAP 1m (P)
2:00 (2:01) (Class 6) (0-60,60) 3-Y-O **£1,535** (£453; £226) **Stalls** High

Form RPR
0-42 **1** **Govenor General (IRE)**[17] 550 3-9-6 **59**.......... GeorgeBaker 6 67+
(Jeremy Noseda) *t.k.h: hld up wl in tch: effrt to chse ldr wl over 1f out: rdn to ld ins fnl f: r.o wl: comf* **4/1**[2]
0-32 **2** 1 3/4 **Hackett (IRE)**[20] 519 3-9-7 **60**.......... MartinDwyer 2 64
(Michael Quinn) *led: rdn wl over 1f out: clr w wnr ent fnl f: hdd ins fnl f: no ex* **9/1**
3-56 **3** 1 1/4 **Surprise (IRE)**[9] 655 3-9-7 **60**.......... NickyMackay 5 61
(Mark Rimmer) *t.k.h: hld up in tch towards rr: rdn and hdwy ent fnl 2f: wnt 3rd ins fnl f: kpt on but nvr gng pce to rch ldrs* **12/1**
050 **4** 1/2 **Lakota Ghost (USA)**[20] 520 3-9-7 **60**.......... JimCrowley 3 60
(Seamus Durack) *chsd ldr: rdn and outpcd by ldng pair over 1f out: styd on same pce fnl f* **5/1**[3]
0-30 **5** 3 1/4 **Imperial Fong**[29] 406 3-9-4 **57**.......... J-PGuillambert 10 49
(Ronald Harris) *stdd s: t.k.h: hld up in tch in rr: rdn over 2f out: hdwy but stl plenty to do whn nt clr run and swtchd lft ent fnl f: kpt on fnl f: nvr trbld ldrs* **16/1**
05-3 **6** 1/2 **Spirit Of Oakdale (IRE)**[16] 558 3-9-3 **56**.......... ShaneKelly 9 47
(Walter Swinburn) *t.k.h: chsd ldrs: rdn and unable qck w ldrs ent fnl 2f: no ch w ldrs fr over 1f out* **4/1**[2]
5221 **7** nse **Titan Diamond (IRE)**[9] 655 3-8-9 **55** 6ex.......... RachealKneller(7) 4 46
(Mark Usher) *t.k.h: chsd ldrs: rdn and unable qck ent fnl 2f: outpcd whn nddd lft u.p over 1f out: one pce and wl hld after* **3/1**[1]
0-64 **8** 1 **Blaze On By**[14] 591 3-8-11 **50**.......... CathyGannon [illegible] [illegible]
(John Bridger) *hld up in tch towards rr: rdn and effrt but stl plenty to do whn nt clr run and hmpd ent fnl f: nt rcvr and no ch after* **50/1**
000- **9** 2 1/2 **Fire N'Brimstone**[128] 7163 3-8-13 **52**.......... FrankieMcDonald 1 35
(Mouse Hamilton-Fairley) *taken down early: dwlt: sn rcvrd and in tch: reminder 5f out: rdn over 3f out: wknd 2f out: bhd over 1f out* **100/1**
000- **10** 3 1/4 **Burnem Green**[184] 5667 3-8-11 **50**.......... DaneO'Neill 7 26
(Derek Shaw) *hld up in tch in last pair: nt clr run over 2f out: rdn and no prog 2f out: wl btn and eased wl ins fnl f* **33/1**
216- **11** 2 **Microlight**[95] 7630 3-9-2 **58**..........(e) NataliaGemelova(3) 11 29
(John E Long) *chsd ldrs on outer: rdn and struggling whn wd bnd 2f out: sn wknd and bhd* **14/1**

1m 39.15s (0.95) **Going Correction** +0.125s/f (Slow) **11** Ran SP% **117.8**
Speed ratings (Par 96): **100,98,97,96,93 92,92,91,89,85 83**
Tote Swingers: 1&2 £5.70, 1&3 £10.60, 2&3 £12.10 CSF £39.72 CT £401.57 TOTE £4.20: £1.10, £3.30, £5.20; EX 27.00 Trifecta £250.60 Pool: £701.14 - 2.07 winning units..
Owner G C Stevens **Bred** Ballylinch Stud **Trained** Newmarket, Suffolk
■ Stewards' Enquiry : Racheal Kneller two-day ban; careless riding (18th-19th March)

FOCUS
The pace was not strong, resulting in a time over three seconds above standard. This moderate handicap was won in decisive fashion and the form is rated quite positively.
Microlight Official explanation: jockey said gelding was kicked at start

761 CYPRIUM BAR AT MARRIOTT LINGFIELD (S) STKS 1m (P)
2:35 (2:35) (Class 6) 4-Y-0+ **£1,535** (£453; £226) **Stalls** High

Form RPR
312 **1** **I Confess**[11] 633 6-9-4 70..........(b) NeilCallan 3 64+
(David Evans) *mde all: pushed along and asserted over 1f out: clr and in command fnl f: comf* **4/9**[1]
0/00 **2** 2 3/4 **Street Crime**[1] 749 6-8-12 52.......... JimCrowley 4 52
(Ron Hodges) *chsd wnr thrght: unable qck w wnr u.p over 1f out: kpt on same pce fnl f* **25/1**[3]
0106 **3** 1 1/4 **Aflaam (IRE)**[7] 685 6-9-4 68..........(t) LukeMorris 2 57
(Ronald Harris) *dwlt: bustled along early: in tch: n.m.r on inner and hmpd ent fnl 3f: drvn and nt qckn over 1f out: plugged on same pce fnl f* **2/1**[2]
4-00 **4** 2 1/4 **Public Image**[11] 631 5-8-7 47.......... CathyGannon 1 39
(Jamie Poulton) *s.i.s: in tch in last: rdn and unable qck wl over 1f out: wl hld ent fnl f* **66/1**

1m 40.3s (2.10) **Going Correction** +0.125s/f (Slow) **4** Ran SP% **107.9**
Speed ratings (Par 101): **94,91,90,87**
CSF £11.62 TOTE £1.50; EX 8.30.The winner was bought in for 4,000gns.
Owner J E Abbey **Bred** Gestut Sohrenhof **Trained** Pandy, Monmouths

FOCUS
A weak contest and a muddling race, run in a time 4.30 seconds outside standard. The winner did not need to be at his best to score.

762 LINGFIELDPARK.CO.UK MAIDEN STKS 1m 4f (P)
3:10 (3:10) (Class 5) 3-Y-O+ **£1,910** (£564; £282) **Stalls** Low

Form RPR
22-2 **1** **Jacobs Son**[6] 699 3-8-5 78.......... JimmyQuinn 6 64+
(Robert Mills) *t.k.h early: chsd ldr tl pushed into ld over 2f out: kpt on u.p fnl f: fnd ex whn pressed wl ins fnl f: r.o* **4/9**[1]
06-0 **2** 3/4 **Sunset Place**[36] 317 4-9-12 53.......... RobertHavlin 7 63+
(Jonathan Geake) *stdd s: t.k.h: hld up in tch in rr: rdn and effrt ent fnl 2f: chsd ldrs over 1f out: pressed wnr ins fnl f: no ex and hld fnl 50yds* **25/1**
- **3** nk **Bestwecan (IRE)** 3-8-5 0.......... GregFairley 5 63
(Mark Johnston) *chsd ldrs tl led and qcknd gallop 8f out: rdn and hdd over 2f out: kpt on but one pce u.p after* **6/1**[2]
5- **4** 2 1/4 **No Time For Tears (IRE)**[113] 7413 4-9-7 0.......... DaneO'Neill 2 54+
(Lucinda Featherstone) *stdd s: hld up in tch in last trio: rdn and effrt 2f out: swtchd rt jst over 1f out: kpt on but nvr gng pce to rch ldrs* **50/1**
24 **5** 3 1/2 **First Rock (IRE)**[16] 563 5-10-0 0.......... PJMcDonald 1 54
(Alan Swinbank) *in tch in midfield: pushed along to chse ldrs over 2f out: rdn and little rspnse ent fnl 2f: outpcd and wl btn over 1f out* **7/1**[3]
6 **6** 1/2 **Miles Of Sunshine**[7] 688 6-10-0 0..........(p) GeorgeBaker 4 53
(Ron Hodges) *led at stdy gallop tl hdd 8f out: chsd ldrs after: nt clr run ent fnl 2f: wknd u.p over 1f out* **33/1**
7 29 **Speakers Corner**[9] 5-10-0 0.......... MickyFenton 3 10
(Barney Curley) *in tch in last trio: rdn along 5f out: dropped to last over 3f out: sn lost tch: t.o fnl 2f* **12/1**

2m 34.81s (1.81) **Going Correction** +0.125s/f (Slow)
WFA 3 from 4yo 23lb 4 from 5yo+ 2lb **7** Ran SP% **112.5**
Speed ratings (Par 103): **98,97,97,95,93 93,73**
Tote Swingers: 1&2 £4.80, 1&3 £1.80, 2&3 £8.70 CSF £16.88 TOTE £1.50: £1.30, £10.00; EX 13.60.
Owner Jacobs Construction (Holdings) Limited **Bred** Stowell Park Stud **Trained** Headley, Surrey

FOCUS
A weak maiden and the runner-up helps limit the form. The winner was a good way below his best.

763 PATRICIA HILL MEMORIAL H'CAP 7f (P)
3:45 (3:45) (Class 5) (0-70,76) 4-Y-0+ **£2,047** (£604; £302) **Stalls** Low

Form RPR
-021 **1** **Ivory Silk**[7] 689 6-9-13 **76** 6ex.......... AdamKirby 4 85
(Jeremy Gask) *stdd s: racd in last trio: urged along over 4f out: swtchd rt and effrt wd bnd 2f out: chal 1f out: r.o wl u.p to ld on post* **11/4**[1]
121 **2** nse **The Happy Hammer (IRE)**[23] 473 5-9-4 **67**.......... GeorgeBaker 9 76
(Eugene Stanford) *hld up in tch in midfield: stl gng wl 2f out: shkn up and effrt to chal ent fnl f: rdn to ld jst ins fnl f: r.o wl tl hdd on post* **11/4**[1]
2-54 **3** 3 **Copperwood**[23] 473 6-9-6 **69**.......... DaneO'Neill 8 70
(Michael Blanshard) *t.k.h: chsd ldrs: rdn and ev ch wl over 1f out: led 1f out: sn hdd: outpcd by ldng pair fnl 100yds* **9/2**[2]
-062 **4** nk **Buxton**[32] 367 7-9-5 **68**..........(t) RobertHavlin 6 68
(Roger Ingram) *stdd s: hld up in last: c wd and rdn wl over 1f out: styd on wl ins fnl f: nvr trbld ldrs* **10/1**
1-40 **5** 1 3/4 **Highland Harvest**[42] 249 7-9-5 **68**.......... NeilCallan 7 64
(Jamie Poulton) *chsd ldrs on inner: nt clr run over 2f out tl wl over 1f out: rdn to press ldrs jst over 1f out: wknd ins fnl f* **16/1**
4330 **6** 2 **Silver Wind**[7] 683 6-8-7 **56** oh1..........(v) LukeMorris 1 47
(Alan McCabe) *led: rdn ent fnl 2f: hdd 1f out: wknd ins fnl f* **14/1**
0012 **7** 1 1/4 **Spin Again (IRE)**[11] 637 6-8-12 **68**.......... LucyKBarry(7) 10 55
(Mark Wellings) *w ldr: drvn and ev ch 2f out: unable qck over 1f out: wknd fnl f* **7/1**[3]
2060 **8** 3/4 **Chinese Democracy (USA)**[18] 544 4-8-7 **56** oh1..(b1) CathyGannon 2 41
(David Evans) *dwlt: in tch towards rr: rdn and no prog 2f out: nvr trbld ldrs* **33/1**
3343 **9** nse **Army Of Stars (IRE)**[17] 547 5-9-6 **69**..........(p) JimCrowley 3 54
(James Given) *chsd ldrs: n.m.r over 2f out tl 2f out: sn rdn and unable qck: wknd ent fnl f* **14/1**

1m 24.47s (-0.33) **Going Correction** +0.125s/f (Slow) **9** Ran SP% **113.3**
Speed ratings (Par 103): **106,105,102,102,100 97,96,95,95**
Tote Swingers: 1&2 £2.40, 1&3 £3.70, 2&3 £3.30 CSF £9.90 CT £32.14 TOTE £4.80: £1.10, £3.30, £1.20; EX 13.60 Trifecta £76.30 Pool: £949.03 - 9.20 winning units..
Owner Resurrection Partners **Bred** K T Ivory **Trained** Sutton Veny, Wilts
■ Stewards' Enquiry : Adam Kirby one-day; used whip with excessive force

FOCUS
Not a bad race for the grade, with two in-form, reasonably handicapped runners fighting out a close finish. The first two were clear and the form has a sound look to it.

764 MARSH GREEN H'CAP 7f (P)
4:20 (4:20) (Class 5) (0-75,75) 3-Y-O **£2,047** (£604; £302) **Stalls** Low

Form RPR
3-1 **1** **Flynn's Boy**[21] 509 3-9-5 **73**.......... MartinLane 5 77+
(Rae Guest) *stdd s: hld up in last pair: effrt and nt clr run over 1f out: swtchd rt 1f out: str run ins fnl f to ld fnl 75yds: r.o wl* **6/1**
331- **2** 1/2 **Romantic Wish**[112] 7417 3-9-5 **73**.......... EddieAhern 7 74+
(Robert Mills) *t.k.h early: wl in tch: swtchd rt and effrt over 1f out: rdn and ev ch ins fnl f: r.o but nt quite pce of wnr towards fin* **2/1**[1]
6-21 **3** 1 **Christmas Aria (IRE)**[38] 295 3-9-7 **75**.......... HayleyTurner 3 73
(Simon Dow) *w ldr tl led 2f out: sn rdn: hdd fnl 75yds: outpcd by ldng pair towards fin* **11/2**[3]
1 **4** 3/4 **National Hope (IRE)**[37] 305 3-9-3 **74**.......... MatthewDavies(3) 1 70+
(George Baker) *in tch: rdn and effrt on inner over 1f out: drvn and chsd ldrs 1f out: no ex and no imp fnl 75yds* **3/1**[2]
0-55 **5** 1/2 **Karate (IRE)**[33] 358 3-8-7 **64**.......... SophieDoyle(3) 8 59
(Hans Adielsson) *t.k.h: hld up in last pair: rdn and hdwy ent fnl f: r.o: nt rch ldrs* **20/1**
04-3 **6** nk **Spartic**[33] 358 3-9-4 **72**..........(p) JamesDoyle 2 66
(Alan McCabe) *chsd ldrs: rdn to chse ldr over 1f out: sn drvn: no ex and btn fnl 100yds* **8/1**
3335 **7** nk **Greenhead High**[9] 659 3-8-13 **67**.......... J-PGuillambert 4 61
(Jane Chapple-Hyam) *plld hrd early: chsd ldrs: rdn jst over 1f out: lost pl bnd 2f out: rallied ins fnl f: kpt on* **16/1**
206- **8** 2 **Maggie's Treasure (IRE)**[141] 6868 3-8-7 **61**.......... ChrisCatlin 6 49
(John Gallagher) *led tl 2f out: sn unable qck u.p: wknd jst over 2f out: wknd and in rr whn n.m.r ins fnl f* **33/1**

1m 25.56s (0.76) **Going Correction** +0.125s/f (Slow) **8** Ran SP% **112.7**
Speed ratings (Par 98): **100,99,98,97,96 96,96,93**
Tote Swingers: 1&2 £4.20, 1&3 £4.50, 2&3 £2.80 CSF £17.88 CT £69.23 TOTE £7.70: £2.70, £1.10, £1.70; EX 27.10 Trifecta £51.60 Pool: £706.62 - 10.12 winning units..

Owner C J Murfitt **Bred** C J Murfitt **Trained** Newmarket, Suffolk

FOCUS
The first four finishers had all won last time and had the potential to be better their ratings, so this looks quite strong form. The field did finish quite compressed but the first two in particular can do better.

765 FOREST ROW H'CAP — 1m (P)
4:55 (4:56) (Class 6) (0-65,65) 4-Y-0+ — **£1,535** (£453; £226) **Stalls** High

Form — RPR

-302 **1** **Eastern Gift**[12] 626 6-9-4 **62**.................. NeilCallan 3 — 69+
(Gay Kelleway) *wl in tch: swtchd ins and rdn to chal over 1f out: led jst over 1f out: in command ins fnl f: idling towards fin* **3/1**[1]

-233 **2** *½* **Dichoh**[12] 626 8-9-7 **65**..................(v) GeorgeBaker 5 — 71
(Michael Madgwick) *led: rdn and edgd rt bnd ent st: hdd u.p jst over 1f out: rallied as wnr idled towards fin: a hld* **4/1**[2]

1312 **3** *¾* **Shared Moment (IRE)**[16] 562 5-9-3 **61**..................(v) ChrisCatlin 8 — 65
(John Gallagher) *chsd ldrs: effrt to press ldr and carried rt bnd ent st: rallied ins fnl f: kpt on* **3/1**[1]

-456 **4** *½* **Lopinot (IRE)**[12] 625 8-9-3 **61**..................(v) JimCrowley 1 — 64
(Martin Bosley) *hld up wl in tch in rr: effrt on inner over 1f out: kpt on fnl f: unable to rch ldrs* **8/1**

25-4 **5** *2 ½* **Pab Special (IRE)**[30] 390 8-8-7 **51**..................(v) LiamKeniry 2 — 48
(Brett Johnson) *t.k.h: chsd ldrs: rdn and unable qck ent fnl 2f: styd on same pce fnl f* **16/1**

00-0 **6** *nk* **Commander Wish**[32] 363 8-8-7 **51** oh2..................(p) JimmyQuinn 4 — 48
(Lucinda Featherstone) *stdd s: hld up in last: pushed along and sme hdwy over 1f out: styd on same pce fnl f: n.d* **40/1**

-110 **7** *2* **Ede's Dot Com (IRE)**[16] 565 7-8-13 **62**.................. JemmaMarshall(5) 7 — 54
(Pat Phelan) *t.k.h: hld up wl in tch: rdn and switching rt over 1f out: no imp after* **11/1**

6230 **8** *¾* **Indian Violet (IRE)**[7] 685 5-9-4 **62**.................. JamieGoldstein 11 — 52
(Sheena West) *hld up in last pair: hdwy 4f out: rdn on outer and lost pl bnd 2f out: styd on same pce and no imp after* **7/1**[3]

500- **9** *6* **Tt's Dream**[200] 5159 4-9-0 **58**.................. JamesDoyle 9 — 34
(Alastair Lidderdale) *w ldr: rdn and lost pl qckly ent fnl 2f: bhd ent fnl f* **12/1**

1m 39.77s (1.57) **Going Correction** +0.125s/f (Slow) — **9** Ran SP% **118.0**
Speed ratings (Par 101): **97,96,95,95,92 92,90,89,83**
Tote Swingers: 1&2 £3.10, 1&3 £2.90, 2&3 £2.60 CSF £15.42 CT £39.16 TOTE £4.20: £1.10, £1.30, £2.60; EX 19.90 Trifecta £24.80 Pool: £961.85 - 28.64 winning units..
Owner Mrs D Stanbrook & N Palgrave Brown **Bred** P And Mrs A G Venner **Trained** Exning, Suffolk

FOCUS
Few of these appealed beforehand and they went a steady pace (time nearly four seconds outside standard). The form is modest but straightforward.

766 TANDRIDGE H'CAP — 5f (P)
5:25 (5:29) (Class 5) (0-70,70) 4-Y-0+ — **£2,047** (£604; £302) **Stalls** High

Form — RPR

-233 **1** **Estonia**[9] 646 4-8-13 **62**.................. LukeMorris 3 — 71
(Michael Squance) *hld up in midfield: hdwy to chse ldr 2f out: led over 1f out: r.o wl u.p fnl f* **2/1**[1]

-342 **2** *¾* **Yankee Storm**[13] 612 6-9-7 **70**..................(b) JimmyQuinn 6 — 76
(Tom Keddy) *stdd after s: hld up in last pair: effrt on inner over 1f out: r.o u.p fnl f: wnt 2nd towards fin* **5/2**[2]

2223 **3** *¾* **Black Baccara**[7] 696 4-8-11 **60**..................(be) NeilCallan 5 — 64
(Phil McEntee) *chsd ldrs: clsd over 2f out: ev ch jst over 1f out: drvn ins fnl f: wknd fnl 100yds* **11/4**[3]

2655 **4** *1 ½* **Efistorm**[4] 708 10-9-6 **69**.................. HayleyTurner 2 — 67
(Conor Dore) *chsd clr ldr: clsd over 2f out: lost 2nd 2f out: one pce u.p and btn 1f out* **7/1**

04-5 **5** *½* **Romantic Queen**[1] 746 5-8-11 **63**..................(t) MatthewDavies(3) 4 — 59
(George Baker) *dropped to last sn after s: hld up bhd: rdn and effrt on outer over 1f out: styd on same pce fnl f: nvr able to chal* **7/1**

6606 **6** *1 ¾* **Step It Up (IRE)**[9] 658 7-8-2 **58**..................(v1) DanielCremin(7) 7 — 48
(Jim Boyle) *sn led and clr: c bk to field over 2f out: rdn and hdd over 1f out: wknd fnl f* **25/1**

58.93 secs (0.13) **Going Correction** +0.125s/f (Slow) — **6** Ran SP% **117.4**
Speed ratings (Par 103): **103,101,100,98,97 94**
Tote Swingers: 1&2 £1.80, 1&3 £1.60, 2&3 £1.40 CSF £7.81 CT £13.33 TOTE £3.40: £2.70, £1.30; EX 8.20 Trifecta £11.10 Pool: £388.59 - 25.74 winning units..
Owner Miss K Squance **Bred** Millsec Limited **Trained** Newmarket, Suffolk

FOCUS
The out-of-form Step It Up, visored for the first time, took them along at an unsustainable pace. The winner is rated back to her best.
T/Plt: £11.10 to a £1 stake. Pool:£55,913.51 - 3,675.99 winning tickets T/Qpdt: £2.50 to a £1 stake. Pool:£4,985.26 - 1,450.82 winning tickets SP

745 WOLVERHAMPTON (A.W) (L-H)
Friday, March 4

OFFICIAL GOING: Standard
Wind: Light against Weather: Fine

767 ATRCASINOCLUB.COM £1000 WELCOME BONUS CLASSIFIED CLAIMING STKS — 5f 20y(P)
5:20 (5:20) (Class 5) 4-Y-0+ — **£2,266** (£674; £337) **Stalls** Low

Form — RPR

00-4 **1** **Steelcut**[25] 443 7-8-1 64..................(p) LouisBeuzelin(3) 1 — 75+
(Andrew Reid) *mde all: shkn up over 1f out: r.o wl: eased nr fin* **5/2**[2]

1013 **2** *3 ¼* **Desert Strike**[4] 708 5-8-12 68..................(p) ShaneKelly 4 — 72
(Alan McCabe) *chsd ldrs: rdn over 1f out: wnt 2nd ins fnl f: nt trble wnr* **8/13**[1]

-043 **3** *1 ¼* **Galpin Junior (USA)**[21] 506 5-7-13 60.................. JamesSullivan(3) 2 — 57
(Ruth Carr) *chsd wnr: rdn over 1f out: no ex ins fnl f* **6/1**[3]

62.66 secs (0.36) **Going Correction** +0.375s/f (Slow) — **3** Ran SP% **104.8**
Speed ratings (Par 103): **112,106,104**
CSF £4.44 TOTE £2.30; EX 2.90.Steelcut was claimed by P. D. Evans for £6,000.
Owner A S Reid **Bred** Mrs B Skinner **Trained** Mill Hill, London NW7

FOCUS
A depleted field. The gallop was a moderate one and the winner raced close to the inside rail throughout. He looks likely to be well treated in the short term.

768 ATRCASINOCLUB.COM H'CAP (DIV I) — 2m 119y(P)
5:45 (5:45) (Class 6) (0-60,59) 4-Y-0+ — **£1,364** (£403; £201) **Stalls** Low

Form — RPR

-230 **1** **Six Of Clubs**[16] 560 5-8-9 **50**..................(b) JakePayne(7) 1 — 56
(Bill Turner) *s.i.s: sn prom: 4th whn pulling up 4f out: continued in ld 3f out: drvn clr fnl f* **17/2**

1224 **2** *6* **Carnac (IRE)**[10] 645 5-9-7 **55**..................(p) ShaneKelly 3 — 54+
(Alan McCabe) *chsd ldrs: 3rd whn pulling up 4f out: continued 3f out: chsd ldr 3f out: rdn over 1f out: styd on same pce ins fnl f* **4/1**[2]

-062 **3** *¾* **Prince Charlemagne (IRE)**[12] 622 8-9-3 **58**...... MatthewCosham(7) 2 — 56+
(Dr Jeremy Naylor) *hld up: 7th whn pulling up 4f out: continued 3f out: wnt 3rd ins fnl f: nvr nrr* **8/1**

0-05 **4** *nk* **Vertueux (FR)**[30] 393 6-9-4 **55**.................. LouisBeuzelin(3) 4 — 53+
(Tony Carroll) *mid-div: lost pl 9f out: 8th whn pulling up 4f out: continued 3f out: rdn over 1f out: styd on* **14/1**

0 **5** *½* **Tinas Exhibition (IRE)**[2] 733 4-8-13 **57**.................. MartinHarley(5) 9 — 54+
(Seamus Fahey, Ire) *chsd ldr tl pulling up 4f out: continued 3f out: sn drvnalong: wknd over 1f out* **14/1**

/006 **6** *15* **Rough Sketch (USA)**[11] 630 6-9-1 **49**..................(tp) TomEaves 6 — 28+
(Ian Williams) *mid-div: hdwy over 9f out: 5th whn pulling up 4f out: continued 3f out: sn rdn wknd over 2f out* **11/1**

-064 **7** *15* **Swords**[11] 631 9-8-11 **45**.................. AndreaAtzeni 11 — 6+
(Ray Peacock) *hld up: sme hdwy and 6th whn pulling up 4f out: continued 3f out: sn bhd: t.o* **16/1**

02-3 **8** *94* **Rare Coincidence**[42] 244 10-9-5 **53**..................(p) PaulHanagan 7 — —+
(Roger Fisher) *led tl pulling up 4f out: eventually continued: t.o* **7/2**[1]

00-3 **P** **Mandalay Prince**[22] 492 7-8-11 **45**.................. StevieDonohoe 8 — —+
(Willie Musson) *hld up: 10th whn p.u 4f out* **12/1**

-314 **F** **Sheila's Bond**[21] 514 4-9-3 **59**.................. KierenFox(3) 10 — —
(John Flint) *chsd ldrs: 4th whn broke nr hind over 11f out: fatally injured* **7/1**[3]

00-6 **P** **Maydream**[23] 466 4-8-7 **45**.................. SamHitchcott 5 — —+
(Jimmy Fox) *hld up: 9th whn p.u 4f out* **14/1**

3m 53.09s (11.29) **Going Correction** +0.375s/f (Slow)
WFA 4 from 5yo+ 5lb — **11** Ran SP% **118.3**
Speed ratings (Par 101): **88,85,84,84,84 77,70,26,—,— —**
Tote Swingers: 1&2 £8.70, 1&3 £11.60, 2&3 £4.50 CSF £42.71 CT £288.61 TOTE £12.90: £3.20, £1.10, £2.80; EX 49.10.
Owner Gongolfin **Bred** R V Young **Trained** Sigwells, Somerset

FOCUS
Division one of a moderate handicap but confusion and controversy aplenty. All the riders eased their mounts to a near walk at the end of the back straight to avoid the stricken Sheila's Bond, believing the race had been voided, but were told to continue and a three-furlong sprint ensued. The stop-race procedure was not initated and the horses finished the race, so the stewards had no option but to allow the result to stand. The race is meaningless as a form-guide and the winner is rated only to his pre-race mark.

769 ATRCASINOCLUB.COM H'CAP (DIV II) — 2m 119y(P)
6:15 (6:20) (Class 6) (0-60,60) 4-Y-0+ — **£1,364** (£403; £201) **Stalls** Low

Form — RPR

05-4 **1** **Chocolate Caramel (USA)**[14] 596 9-9-8 **55**.................. PaulHanagan 1 — 62
(Richard Fahey) *hld up: hdwy over 4f out: led over 1f out: drvn out* **4/1**

1536 **2** *1 ¼* **Frameit (IRE)**[3] 718 4-9-8 **60**..................(v) FrannyNorton 5 — 65
(James Given) *hld up: hdwy over 5f out: rdn to chse wnr ins fnl f: styd on* **7/2**[3]

0-45 **3** *4 ½* **Carbon Print (USA)**[11] 444 6-9-5 **52**..................(t) FergusSweeney 7 — 52
(James Evans) *chsd ldrs: rdn over 3f out: styd on same pce fnl f* **11/1**

03-2 **4** *2 ¼* **Minder**[20] 524 5-9-5 **52**.................. RichardKingscote 4 — 49
(Jonathan Portman) *s.i.s: hdwy 14f out: sn chsng ldr: rdn to ld wl over 2f out: hdd over 1f out: no ex fnl f* **3/1**[1]

464- **5** *5* **Trojan Gift (USA)**[172] 6038 4-9-6 **58**.................. BarryMcHugh 8 — 49
(Julie Camacho) *chsd ldr tl led 14f out: rdn and hdd wl over 2f out: wknd over 1f out* **10/3**[2]

-045 **6** *15* **Hill Of Clare (IRE)**[7] 695 9-8-5 **45**..................(p) JackDuern(7) 2 — 18
(George Jones) *s.i.s: hld up: hdwy 11f out: rdn and wknd over 4f out* **66/1**

22/0 **7** *34* **Inchando (FR)**[23] 466 7-8-13 **49**.................. LouisBeuzelin(3) 6 — —
(Tony Carroll) *led: hdd 14f out: chsd ldrs tl rdn and wknd over 3f out: t.o* **7/1**

0000 **8** *6* **Carlton Mac**[14] 596 6-8-12 **45**..................(p) MichaelStainton 3 — —
(Simon Griffiths) *chsd ldrs: lost pl 12f out: last and rdn 7f out: bhd fnl 4f: t.o* **50/1**

3m 47.44s (5.64) **Going Correction** +0.375s/f (Slow)
WFA 4 from 5yo+ 5lb — **8** Ran SP% **114.6**
Speed ratings (Par 101): **101,100,98,97,94 87,71,69**
Tote Swingers: 1&2 £3.70, 1&3 £4.30, 2&3 £5.60 CSF £18.47 CT £140.69 TOTE £5.80: £1.70, £1.20, £5.00; EX 13.90.
Owner Jonathan Gill **Bred** Sierra Thoroughbreds **Trained** Musley Bank, N Yorks

FOCUS
The second division of a moderate handicap and just an ordinary gallop. The winner edged towards the far side in the closing stages. The winner is rated close to his late 2010 form.

770 ATRPOKERCLUB.COM £400 WELCOME BONUS CLAIMING STKS — 1m 141y(P)
6:45 (6:46) (Class 5) 3-Y-O — **£2,558** (£755; £378) **Stalls** Low

Form — RPR

1232 **1** **Better Self**[13] 609 3-8-0 71.................. RPWalsh(7) 2 — 63+
(David Evans) *dwlt: bhd: tk clsr order over 5f out: led 2f out: sn rdn: r.o* **5/2**[2]

-411 **2** *2 ½* **Malice Or Mischief (IRE)**[7] 686 3-9-6 81.................. PaulHanagan 4 — 70
(Tony Carroll) *chsd ldr tl led over 2f out: sn rdn and hdd: styd on same pce ins fnl f* **2/5**[1]

5-65 **3** *1 ¼* **Lough Corrib (USA)**[20] 519 3-9-1 52.................. TomEaves 1 — 62
(Kevin Ryan) *led: rdn and hdd over 2f out: no ex ins fnl f* **25/1**[3]

00-4 **4** *hd* **Lindo Erro**[15] 576 3-8-1 54.................. JamesSullivan(3) 3 — 51
(John Mackie) *chsd ldrs: rdn over 1f out: styd on same pce* **40/1**

1m 53.71s (3.21) **Going Correction** +0.375s/f (Slow) — **4** Ran SP% **106.3**
Speed ratings (Par 98): **100,97,96,96**
CSF £3.82 TOTE £2.70; EX 3.60.
Owner Mrs Sally Edwards **Bred** Miss K Rausing **Trained** Pandy, Monmouths

The Form Book, Raceform Ltd, Compton, RG20 6NL

FOCUS
Another uncompetitive race and one in which a steady gallop - that only picked up turning for home - means this bare form isn't fully reliable. The winner came down the centre and the third will be the key to the leevl of this form.

771 LIVE DEALER GAMES AT ATRCASINOCLUB.COM APPRENTICE H'CAP 1m 4f 50y(P)
7:15 (7:15) (Class 6) (0-55,55) 4-Y-0+ **£1,637** (£483; £241) **Stalls** Low

Form RPR

0 **1** **Golan Heights (IRE)**[42] [252] 5-8-10 **49**..............................(b) LMcNiff 9 56
(Adrian McGuinness, Ire) *mde all: rdn over 1f out: styd on* **20/1**

00-4 **2** *1 1/4* **Sacco D'Oro**[24] [451] 5-8-2 **46** oh1.............................. JosephYoung(5) 5 51+
(Michael Mullineaux) *s.i.s: hld up: hdwy over 2f out: hung lft and r.o wl ins fnl f: nt rch wnr* **9/1**

5-22 **3** *1* **Broughtons Paradis (IRE)**[25] [449] 5-9-1 **54**.......... MatthewCosham 8 58
(Willie Musson) *a.p: racd keenly: rdn and hung lft over 1f out: styd on same pce ins fnl f* **5/2**[1]

2021 **4** *nk* **Laura Land**[11] [630] 5-8-8 **52** 6ex.. IanBurns(5) 1 55
(Mark Brisbourne) *s.i.s: hld up: racd keenly: hdwy 7f out: rdn over 1f out: r.o* **9/2**[2]

5-05 **5** *3/4* **Dancing Poppy**[11] [631] 4-8-2 **46** oh1........................(t) RichardRowe(3) 7 48
(Ben De Haan) *chsd ldrs: rdn and hung lft over 1f out: styd on same pce ins fnl f* **16/1**

5-02 **6** *hd* **Little Richard (IRE)**[14] [598] 12-8-9 **48**......................(p) NathanAlison 11 50+
(Mark Wellings) *hld up: nt clr run over 1f out: r.o ins fnl f: nrst fin* **13/2**

00-0 **7** *2* **Bobering**[53] [115] 11-8-1 **47** oh1 ow1.......................... LauraSimpson(7) 2 46
(Brian Baugh) *chsd ldrs: rdn over 1f out: no ex fnl f* **66/1**

4133 **8** *1* **Our Kes (IRE)**[14] [598] 9-8-7 **51**.................................... LewisWalsh(5) 3 48
(Jane Chapple-Hyam) *trckd ldrs: racd keenly early: rdn over 2f out: styd on same pce appr fnl f* **11/2**[3]

40- **9** *2 1/2* **La Columbina**[139] [6934] 6-9-1 **54**...................................(v) DavidKenny 10 48
(Michael Scudamore) *hld up: hdwy over 7f out: rdn over 3f out: wknd over 1f out* **17/2**

65-0 **10** *4* **Share Option**[49] [173] 9-8-2 **46** oh1........................ GeorgeDowning(5) 12 34
(Tony Carroll) *s.v.s: bhd: clsd on rr of the field 6f out: rdn and wknd wl over 2f out* **18/1**

04-0 **11** *17* **Better Be Blue (IRE)**[25] [448] 4-7-12 **46** oh1............ CharlesBishop(7) 4 8
(Tony Carroll) *prom early: lost pl after 2f: rdn and wknd over 3f out* **66/1**

2m 46.26s (5.16) **Going Correction** +0.375s/f (Slow)
WFA 4 from 5yo+ 2lb **11** Ran SP% **114.9**
Speed ratings (Par 101): **97,96,95,95,94 94,93,92,91,88 77**
Tote Swingers: 1&2 £18.60, 1&3 £15.40, 2&3 £7.20 CSF £183.58 CT £611.16 TOTE £39.30: £9.20, £2.30, £1.10; EX 570.10.
Owner Sean F Gallagher **Bred** The Susie Syndicate **Trained** Lusk, Co Dublin

FOCUS
A moderate handicap but a steady gallop saw several race keenly and this bare form looks suspect. The winner raced against the inside rail throughout and showed something of a return to form.

772 ATRPOKERCLUB.COM FESTIVAL H'CAP 1m 1f 103y(P)
7:45 (7:45) (Class 5) (0-75,75) 4-Y-0+ **£2,266** (£674; £337; £168) **Stalls** Low

Form RPR

1151 **1** **Black Coffee**[4] [711] 6-8-13 **67**..(b) ShaneKelly 3 77
(Mark Brisbourne) *s.i.s: hld up: hdwy over 1f out: r.o to ld post* **11/8**[1]

335- **2** *shd* **Hydrant**[238] [3860] 5-9-3 **71**.. GregFairley 1 81
(Peter Salmon) *led: rdn over 1f out: hdd post* **6/1**[3]

4336 **3** *3/4* **Veroon (IRE)**[23] [475] 5-9-5 **73**.......................................(p) MickyFenton 6 81
(James Given) *hld up: hdwy over 2f out: rdn over 1f out: r.o* **9/2**[2]

30-2 **4** *2 1/2* **She's A Character**[49] [170] 4-9-7 **75**.............................. PaulHanagan 5 79
(Richard Fahey) *a.p: racd keenly: chsd ldr 2f out: rdn over 1f out: no ex ins fnl f* **9/2**[2]

2233 **5** *nk* **Camps Bay (USA)**[15] [570] 7-9-5 **73**......................... KirstyMilczarek 7 76
(Conor Dore) *chsd ldrs: rdn over 1f out: styd on same pce* **11/1**

200- **6** *3 1/4* **Amends (USA)**[120] [illegible] [illegible] **61** oh1 KierenFox(3) 2 57
(John Best) *chsd ldr tl rdn 2f out: wknd fnl f* **12/1**

2m 5.30s (3.60) **Going Correction** +0.375s/f (Slow) **6** Ran SP% **108.8**
Speed ratings (Par 103): **99,98,98,96,95 92**
Tote Swingers: 1&2 £2.70, 1&3 £3.00, 2&3 £1.80 CSF £9.34 TOTE £2.10: £2.30, £2.40; EX 9.90.
Owner Derek & Mrs Marie Dean **Bred** Mrs M Campbell-Andenaes **Trained** Great Ness, Shropshire

FOCUS
A fair handicap but another moderately run race in which the principals came down the centre in the straight. Straightforward form.

773 ATRPOKERCLUB.COM H'CAP 1m 1f 103y(P)
8:15 (8:15) (Class 7) (0-50,50) 4-Y-0+ **£1,535** (£453; £226) **Stalls** Low

Form RPR

3-33 **1** **Mr Maximas**[34] [347] 4-9-0 **47**.................................. RichardKingscote 13 55
(Bryn Palling) *a.p: chsd ldr over 6f out: led over 2f out: rdn and hdd over 1f out: rallied to ld ins fnl f: r.o* **14/1**

0-23 **2** *3/4* **Idol Deputy (FR)**[16] [552] 5-8-7 **47**.............................. RachealKneller(7) 7 54
(Mark Usher) *a.p: chsd wnr over 2f out: led over 1f out: sn rdn: hdd and unable qck ins fnl f* **11/1**

5-30 **3** *2 1/4* **Olney Lass**[24] [450] 4-9-1 **48**.. MartinLane 6 50
(Mike Murphy) *chsd ldrs: rdn over 2f out: styd on* **14/1**

0-40 **4** *2* **Brave Decision**[21] [517] 4-9-1 **48**...................................(p) AndreaAtzeni 5 47
(Robert Cowell) *chsd ldrs: rdn over 2f out: hung lft over 1f out: no ex fnl f* **16/1**

2 **5** *1 1/2* **Senor Tommie (IRE)**[1] [752] 5-8-9 **47**........................(t) MartinHarley(5) 2 43
(Seamus Fahey, Ire) *hld up in tch: rdn and swtchd rt over 1f out: no imp fnl f* **3/1**[1]

-300 **6** *1 3/4* **Oak Leaves**[14] [598] 4-9-0 **47**.. DavidProbert 10 39
(Nikki Evans) *chsd ldrs: rdn over 3f out: wknd over 1f out* **40/1**

-350 **7** *1* **Mary Helen**[11] [631] 4-9-1 **48**... ShaneKelly 8 38
(Mark Brisbourne) *sn pushed along in rr: rdn over 2f out: nvr on terms* **14/1**

65-3 **8** *1/2* **Hecton Lad (USA)**[23] [466] 4-8-11 **47**.............................. KierenFox(3) 4 36
(John Best) *hld up: bhd and rdn 1/2-way: nvr nrr* **4/1**[2]

46-3 **9** *2 1/4* **Crazy Bold (GER)**[22] [207] 8-9-1 **48**............................... PaulHanagan 3 33
(Tony Carroll) *hld up: bhd and rdn over 3f out: n.d* **6/1**[3]

-000 **10** *nk* **Novillero**[16] [552] 4-8-5 **45**.. GemmaElford(7) 1 30
(Jimmy Fox) *sn bhd* **66/1**

0200 **11** *3 1/4* **Lucky Diva**[35] [346] 4-8-10 **50**.. JakePayne(7) 9 28
(Bill Turner) *hld up: pushed along 1/2-way: wknd over 2f out* **25/1**

53-6 **12** *shd* **Supatov (USA)**[33] [354] 4-9-3 **50**.................................. NickyMackay 11 28
(Hughie Morrison) *led: rdn and hdd over 2f out: n.m.r and wknd sn after* **8/1**

0-60 **13** *5* **Libre**[29] [408] 11-8-12 **45**..(p) RobertHavlin 12 14
(Violet M Jordan) *hld up: rdn over 2f out: sn wknd* **33/1**

2m 2.78s (1.08) **Going Correction** +0.375s/f (Slow) **13** Ran SP% **115.3**
Speed ratings (Par 97): **110,109,107,105,104 102,101,101,99,99 96,96,91**
Tote Swingers: 1&2 £39.50, 1&3 £46.10, 2&3 £11.30 CSF £149.73 CT £2190.36 TOTE £20.20: £4.40, £3.70, £5.10; EX 118.60.
Owner Nigel Thomas **Bred** Nigel Thomas **Trained** Tredodridge, Vale Of Glamorgan

FOCUS
A very moderate handicap and an ordinary gallop saw those held up at a disadvantage. The winner raced towards the inside rail in the straight. The form is sound but limited.

774 ATRCASINOCLUB.COM VIP RACING REWARDS MAIDEN STKS 1m 141y(P)
8:45 (8:46) (Class 5) 3-Y-0+ **£2,007** (£597; £298; £149) **Stalls** Low

Form RPR

3-22 **1** **School For Scandal (IRE)**[7] [693] 3-8-7 75................(b[1]) GregFairley 4 70+
(Mark Johnston) *sn led: clr 2f out: canter* **1/5**[1]

0- **2** *8* **Why So Serious**[24] [3901] 5-9-10 0........................... JamesSullivan(3) 1 52
(Peter Salmon) *s.i.s: hld up: hdwy over 1f out: wnt remote 2nd ins fnl f: nvr any ch w wnr* **33/1**

6/ **3** *1/2* **The Gillie**[482] [7289] 4-9-13 0.. PaulHanagan 2 51
(Richard Fahey) *chsd wnr to over 5f out: rdn to chse wnr again over 2f out: sn outpcd: lost 2nd ins fnl f* **4/1**[2]

4 *hd* **General Duke's**[189] [5508] 4-9-13 0..................................... TomEaves 3 46
(Kevin Ryan) *prom: chsd wnr tl rdn and lost pl over 2f out: sn bhd: no ch whn swtchd rt ins fnl f* **20/1**[3]

1m 53.86s (3.36) **Going Correction** +0.375s/f (Slow)
WFA 3 from 4yo+ 20lb **4** Ran SP% **111.0**
Speed ratings (Par 103): **100,92,92,92**
CSF £9.71 TOTE £1.20.
Owner Sheikh Hamdan Bin Mohammed Al Maktoum **Bred** Darley **Trained** Middleham Moor, N Yorks

FOCUS
A most uncompetitive maiden and one in which the gallop was an ordinary one. The easy winner raced centre to far side in the straight. The runner-up is the key to the form and might be flattered.
T/Plt: £218.90 to a £1 stake. Pool:£66,583.69 - 222.02 winning tickets T/Qpdt: £38.60 to a £1 stake. Pool:£10,028.40 - 192.20 winning tickets CR

[108] DEAUVILLE (R-H)
Friday, March 4

OFFICIAL GOING: Fibresand: standard

775a PRIX DE SAINT VALERY (MAIDEN) (3YO FILLIES) (FIBRESAND) 6f 110y
12:15 (12:00) 3-Y-0 **£10,344** (£4,137; £3,103; £2,068; £1,034)

RPR

1 **Mystic Dream** 3-9-0 0.. MichaelHills 4 85
(B W Hills) *wnt 3rd sn after s: proged to 2nd bef st: rdn to ld 1 1/2f out: sn clr: r.o wl: comf* **5/2**[1]

2 *1 1/2* **Boastful (IRE)**[286] [2330] 3-9-0 0.. MaximeGuyon 6 81
(H-A Pantall, France) **7/2**[3]

3 *1* **Nausycaa (IRE)**[66] 3-9-0 0... ThierryJarnet 5 78
(Mlle S-V Tarrou, France) **17/1**

4 *1 1/2* **Good News (FR)**[231] 3-8-10 0.. TheoBachelot(4) 3 74
(C Laffon-Parias, France) **53/10**

5 *2 1/2* **Ensemble (FR)**[124] 3-9-0 0.. MickaelBarzalona 7 66
(F Head, France) **9/1**

6 *2* **Hysterical (USA)** 3-9-0 0.................................... Pierre-CharlesBoudot 1 60
(A Fabre, France) **14/5**[2]

7 *3/4* **Disa (FR)**[190] 3-9-0 0.. AnthonyCrastus 2 58
(D Sepulchre, France) **9/1**

1m 19.6s (79.60) **7** Ran SP% **110.5**
WIN (incl. 1 euro stake): 3.50. PLACES: 1.60, 2.90. SF: 21.70.
Owner K Abdulla **Bred** Millsec Limited **Trained** Lambourn, Berks

776a PRIX DE BACQUEVILLE (MAIDEN) (3YO COLTS & GELDINGS) (FIBRESAND) 6f 110y
12:50 (12:00) 3-Y-0 **£10,344** (£4,137; £3,103; £2,068; £1,034)

RPR

1 **Les Troyens** 3-9-2 0.. MaximeGuyon 1 80
(A Fabre, France) **17/5**[2]

2 *1/2* **Crown Counsel (IRE)**[11] [636] 3-9-2 0................................... JoeFanning 9 79
(Mark Johnston) *sn in 2nd on outer: rdn to ld 1 1/2f out: r.o wl fnl f: hdd cl home* **23/10**[1]

3 *snk* **Taxonomist (USA)**[176] 3-9-2 0................................ MickaelBarzalona 4 79
(A Fabre, France) **6/1**

4 *1/2* **Whistle On By**[97] [7595] 3-9-2 0.. MichaelHills 5 77
(B W Hills) *broke smartly to ld: settled 3rd on rail: rdn early in st: no ex immediately but rallied ins fnl f: r.o wl* **78/10**

5 *snk* **Homajaefef (FR)**[19] 3-9-2 0.. ThierryJarnet 3 77
(Mlle S-V Tarrou, France) **43/10**[3]

6 *1 1/2* **Nektarus (FR)** 3-9-2 0.. TonyPiccone 6 73
(J Rossi, France) **45/1**

7 *1 1/2* **Bizertin (FR)**[56] 3-9-2 0...(p) TheoBachelot 8 68
(D Allard, France) **26/1**

8 *snk* **Les Veys**[60] 3-9-2 0.. ThierryThulliez 2 68
(E Libaud, France) **11/1**

9 *1 1/2* **Konigstreuer (GER)**[257] 3-9-2 0.. DPorcu 7 64
(S Smrczek, Germany) **21/1**

1m 18.5s (78.50) **9** Ran SP% **116.3**
WIN (incl. 1 euro stake): 2.70 (Les Troyens coupled with Taxonomist). PLACES: 1.90, 1.50, 2.40. DF: 7.40. SF: 14.50.
Owner Sheikh Mohammed **Bred** Darley Stud Management Co Ltd **Trained** Chantilly, France

777a PRIX D'AURIGNY (MAIDEN) (UNRACED 3YO COLTS & GELDINGS) (FIBRESAND) 7f 110y
1:50 (12:00) 3-Y-0 **£10,344** (£4,137; £3,103; £2,068; £1,034)

RPR

1 **Glasgow Kid (GER)** 3-9-2 0.. IoritzMendizabal 14 83
(J-C Rouget, France) **11/1**

2 ½ **Moonwalk In Paris (FR)** 3-9-2 0............. Christophe-PatriceLemaire 8 82
(J-C Rouget, France) **53/10[2]**
3 2 **Burgundy (FR)** 3-9-2 0...............................(b[1]) DavyBonilla 7 77
(F Head, France) **9/1**
4 1 **Mandilion (USA)** 3-9-2 0............................. MaximeGuyon 9 75
(A Fabre, France) **33/10[1]**
5 nk **Signorotto (FR)** 3-9-2 0.............................. TonyPiccone 11 74
(J Rossi, France) **53/1**
6 1 ½ **Russell (FR)** 3-9-2 0.................................. ThierryThulliez 2 70
(E Libaud, France) **12/1**
7 nse **Red Lago (IRE)** 3-9-2 0.............................. MichaelHills 13 70
(B W Hills) *broke slowly: rdn to gain position: racd 6th on outside: u.p 1 1/2f out: no ex: styd on fnl f* **15/1**
8 shd **Egotist (IRE)** 3-9-2 0............................... MickaelBarzalona 3 70
(A Fabre, France) **6/1[3]**
9 3 **Passenger (FR)** 3-9-2 0.............................(b[1]) SylvainRuis 4 62
(Mme Pia Brandt, France) **12/1**
10 1 ½ **Marvelloso** 3-9-2 0..................................... RobertWinston 15 59
(E J O'Neill, France) **72/1**
0 **Nolan (FR)** 3-9-2 0....................................... JohanVictoire 12 —
(C Baillet, France) **19/1**
0 **Smaeldadi (FR)** 3-9-2 0............................... SebastienMaillot 1 —
(Robert Collet, France) **22/1**
0 **Cabriac (FR)** 3-9-2 0................................... FranckBlondel 6 —
(G Nicot, France) **53/1**
0 **Lisselan Missile (USA)** 3-9-2 0..................... WilliamsSaraiva 5 —
(Mme J Bidgood, France) **34/1**
0 **White Curtain (USA)** 3-9-2 0........................ AnthonyCrastus 10 —
(D Sepulchre, France) **13/1**

1m 30.7s (90.70) **15** Ran SP% **117.8**
WIN (incl. 1 euro stake): 4.20 (Glasgow Kid and Moonwalk In Paris coupled). PLACES: 4.50, 2.90, 3.10. DF: 28.40. SF: 51.80.
Owner Mme B Hermelin & J C Rouget S A **Bred** Capricorn Stud Sa **Trained** Pau, France

778a PRIX DE MEYDAN (CONDITIONS) (4YO+) (FIBRESAND) 1m 1f 110y
2:20 (12:00) 4-Y-0+ **£14,224** (£5,689; £4,267; £2,844; £1,422)

RPR
1 **Polytechnicien (USA)**[85] 7800 5-9-0 0.............. MickaelBarzalona 9 109
(A Fabre, France) **9/5[1]**
2 3 **Bling (FR)**[19] 4-8-11 0.............................. PhilippeSogorb 6 100
(C Ferland, France) **7/2[2]**
3 nse **Tartan Gigha (IRE)**[153] 6562 6-8-11 0.................. JoeFanning 1 100
(Mark Johnston) *settled in 5th on rail: swtchd away fr rail ent st: rdn but short of room: stdd and swtchd lft: suffered interference 1f out: r.o strly fnl 100yds whn fnd opening: unlucky nt to fin 2nd* **28/1**
4 shd **Capitaine Courage (IRE)**[111] 7455 6-8-11 0............... ThierryThulliez 2 100
(F Doumen, France) **13/1**
5 2 **Mores Wells**[96] 7615 7-9-4 0...........................(b) SebastienMaillot 7 103
(R Gibson, France) **83/10**
6 2 **Cherry Linx (IRE)**[19] 6-8-11 0.......................... NicolasPerret 4 92
(Mme C Barande-Barbe, France) **5/1[3]**
7 hd **Cool Star (FR)**[86] 7776 6-8-11 0....................... MaximeGuyon 8 92
(A Bonin, France) **20/1**
8 3 **Temps Perdus (IRE)**[263] 5-8-11 0...................... DavidMichaux 3 86
(M Cheno, France) **10/1**
9 8 **Schutzenjunker (GER)**[12] 628 6-8-11 0...................... DPorcu 10 71
(P Schaerer, Switzerland) **39/1**
10 10 **Snow Runner (ARG)**[173] 8-8-11 0..........................(p) FranckBlondel 5 52
(Vanja Sandrup, Sweden) **15/1**

1m 57.1s (117.10) **10** Ran SP% **118.5**
WIN (incl. 1 euro stake): 2.80. PLACES: 1.60, 1.60, 5.30. DF: 6.70. SF: 10.30.
Owner Wertheimer & Frere **Bred** Wertheimer & Frere **Trained** Chantilly, France

779 - 785a (Foreign Racing) - See Raceform Interactive

[760]LINGFIELD (L-H)
Monday, March 7

OFFICIAL GOING: Standard
Wind: Moderate, half against Weather: Sunny

786 SUMMER EVENINGS AT LINGFIELD PARK CLAIMING STKS 6f (P)
2:10 (2:10) (Class 6) 4-Y-0+ **£1,535** (£453; £226) **Stalls** Low

Form RPR
1444 1 **Lastkingofscotland (IRE)**[11] 665 5-9-1 77..............(b) HayleyTurner 3 81
(Conor Dore) *trckd ldng pair: brought to chal ins fnl f: urged along and fnd enough to ld narrowly but decisively last 50yds* **5/1[3]**
1025 2 hd **Northern Dare (IRE)**[11] 665 7-8-9 76......................... PaulHanagan 5 75
(Richard Fahey) *led: rdn and pressed 2f out: edgd lft fnl f: hdd and hld last 50yds* **4/1[2]**
1532 3 1 ¼ **Frequency**[4] 746 4-8-3 68...(b) CathyGannon 2 65
(Michael Wigham) *dwlt: hld up in 4th: gng wl enough whn stuck bhd rivals over 1f out: kpt on same pce to take 3rd last strides* **7/4[1]**
-136 4 nk **Italian Tom (IRE)**[5] 725 4-8-13 73................................ LukeMorris 6 74
(Ronald Harris) *pressed ldr: rdn to chal 2f out: hrd drvn and nt qckn over 1f out: fdd* **15/2**
6514 5 nk **Chjimes (IRE)**[9] 698 7-8-13 70.................................(b) KirstyMilczarek 4 73
(Conor Dore) *s.s: plld hrd and hld up in last pair: pushed along on outer over 1f out: kpt on same pce ins fnl f* **4/1[2]**
2060 6 2 **Kersivay**[4] 746 5-7-10 55..(v) KevinLundie[(7)] 1 57
(David Evans) *a in last pair: brief effrt on inner over 1f out: sn btn* **25/1**

1m 12.41s (0.51) **Going Correction** +0.10s/f (Slow) **6** Ran SP% **108.6**
Speed ratings (Par 101): **100,99,98,97,97 94**
toteswingers:1&2 £2.80, 2&3 £1.90, 1&3 £2.00 CSF £23.22 TOTE £3.70: £3.20, £2.40; EX 27.30.Frequency was claimed by K. W. Dalgleish for £5,000.
Owner Mrs Jennifer Marsh **Bred** Baronrath Stud **Trained** Cowbit, Lincs
■ Stewards' Enquiry : Paul Hanagan caution: careless riding.

FOCUS
A small-field claimer. They didn't go that fast early on and a couple of the runners pulling for their heads. The form looks straightforward enough.
Frequency Official explanation: jockey said gelding was denied a clear run
Chjimes(IRE) Official explanation: jockey said gelding jumped awkwardly and ran too free

787 MARRIOTT HOTEL AT LINGFIELD PARK (S) STKS 6f (P)
2:40 (2:40) (Class 6) 3-Y-O **£1,535** (£453; £226) **Stalls** Low

Form RPR
3-04 1 **Eternal Youth (IRE)**[23] 519 3-9-5 66..............................(b) LukeMorris 5 64
(Ronald Harris) *mde all: 2 l clr 2f out: hanging lft fr over 1f out despite jockey's best effrts: hmpd rival and lft clr ins fnl f* **11/4[2]**
2633 2 1 ¼ **Captain Dimitrios**[5] 724 3-8-12 73.....................(v) MatthewCosham[(7)] 2 64
(David Evans) *trckd ldng pair: rdn to chse wnr wl over 1f out: trying to chal on inner whn hmpd ins fnl f: nt rcvr* **10/11[1]**
6442 3 1 ¾ **Lovat Lane**[19] 558 3-8-8 50.................................(b) ChrisCatlin 3 44
(Eve Johnson Houghton) *chsd wnr: nt qckn and lost 2nd wl over 1f out: wl hld after* **11/2[3]**
0-06 4 ¾ **Hey Mambo**[38] 338 3-8-5 34.. KierenFox[(3)] 1 42
(Roger Ingram) *v s.i.s: detached in last to 1/2-way: rdn to go 4th 2f out: no prog after* **66/1**
5-46 5 1 **Dangerous Illusion (IRE)**[33] 380 3-8-8 47.................. FrannyNorton 4 39
(Michael Quinn) *chsd ldrs: nt qckn u.p and sn lft wl bhd: plugged on nr fin* **16/1**
6- 6 10 **Milk Maid (IRE)**[249] 3603 3-8-1 0.................................. JakePayne[(7)] 6 9
(Bill Turner) *dwlt: in tch: rdn over 3f out: wknd 2f out: sn bhd* **11/1**

1m 12.92s (1.02) **Going Correction** +0.10s/f (Slow) **6** Ran SP% **110.1**
Speed ratings (Par 96): **97,95,93,92,90 77**
toteswingers:1&2 £1.40, 2&3 £1.80, 1&3 £1.10 CSF £5.39 TOTE £4.20: £2.40, £1.10; EX 7.30.There was no bid for the winner.
Owner Mrs Ruth M Serrell **Bred** John Malone **Trained** Earlswood, Monmouths

FOCUS
A fair 3-y-o seller. The winner is rated to the balance of his form.
Hey Mambo Official explanation: jockey said filly hung left

788 FURLONGS & FAIRWAYS H'CAP 5f (P)
3:15 (3:15) (Class 6) (0-60,60) 3-Y-O **£1,535** (£453; £226) **Stalls** High

Form RPR
000- 1 **Dorothy's Dancing (IRE)**[187] 5667 3-8-9 **48**............. FergusSweeney 5 61+
(Gary Moore) *t.k.h: hld up and sn in rr: plenty to do whn asked for effrt over 1f out: hanging and green but picked up wl ins fnl f: r.o to ld last strides* **5/1**
2321 2 nk **Go Maggie Go (IRE)**[17] 595 3-9-2 **58**................................ AmyRyan[(3)] 2 69
(Kevin Ryan) *led: rdn and edgd rt fr over 1f out: over a l ahd ins fnl f: collared last strides* **10/3[2]**
-131 3 1 ¾ **Juarla (IRE)**[27] 452 3-9-7 **60**.. LukeMorris 6 65
(Ronald Harris) *s.i.s: sn chsd ldng pair and racd wd: drvn to go 2nd briefly 1f out: nt qckn* **15/8[1]**
-012 4 4 ½ **Mini Bon Bon**[38] 338 3-9-4 **57**...................................(v) LiamJones 3 46
(Alan Bailey) *chsd ldr: rdn 2f out: lost 2nd 1f out: wknd* **6/1**
00-5 5 ¾ **Bouzy**[12] 655 3-9-5 **58**.. TomQueally 1 44
(Simon Dow) *s.i.s: sn chsd ldrs on inner: shkn up 2f out: no prog over 1f out: wknd* **9/2[3]**
00-0 6 4 ½ **Veuveveuvevoom**[38] 338 3-8-7 **46** oh1......................... CathyGannon 4 16
(Gerry Enright) *s.i.s: in tch tl wknd over 1f out* **80/1**

60.20 secs (1.40) **Going Correction** +0.10s/f (Slow) **6** Ran SP% **108.2**
Speed ratings (Par 96): **92,91,88,81,80 73**
toteswingers:1&2 £1.70, 2&3 £1.20, 1&3 £3.90 CSF £20.20 TOTE £5.40: £1.80, £1.90; EX 20.50.
Owner G L Moore **Bred** Patrick Carroll **Trained** Lower Beeding, W Sussex

FOCUS
Quite an interesting 3-y-o handicap that saw Gary Moore land quite a touch. This took little winning but the winner can improve again.
Dorothy's Dancing(IRE) Official explanation: trainer said, regarding apparent improvement in form, that the filly had strengthened up after being off for 187 days, had learnt to settle and ran in a handicap for the first time.

789 BREATHE SPA AT LINGFIELD MARRIOTT H'CAP 1m 4f (P)
3:50 (3:50) (Class 5) (0-75,74) 3-Y-O **£2,047** (£604; £302) **Stalls** Low

Form RPR
6-41 1 **Twin Soul (IRE)**[26] 469 3-8-9 **62**................................ DavidProbert 1 73+
(Andrew Balding) *hld up in 3rd: clsd to dispute ld 3f out: forged clr over 1f out: rdn out* **5/4[1]**
-242 2 7 **Baileys Agincourt**[13] 643 3-8-9 **62**................................ JoeFanning 2 60
(Mark Johnston) *chsd ldr: rdn over 5f out: dropped to last over 3f out: plugged on to take modest 2nd again ins fnl f* **7/1**
-512 3 ½ **George Woolf**[10] 686 3-9-7 **74**.. TomQueally 3 71
(Alan McCabe) *settled in last: rdn over 5f out: prog to dispute ld 3f out and gng more sweetly: btn off over 1f out: wknd and lost 2nd ins fnl f* **5/1[3]**
-332 4 12 **Ilissos (USA)**[5] 731 3-8-11 **64**......................................(v) PaulHanagan 5 42
(Jeremy Noseda) *led and sn set decent pce: hrd rdn and hdd 3f out: wknd tamely: t.o* **15/8[2]**

2m 32.26s (-0.74) **Going Correction** +0.10s/f (Slow) **4** Ran SP% **108.4**
Speed ratings (Par 98): **106,101,101,93**
CSF £9.46 TOTE £3.50; EX 9.30.
Owner N Botica **Bred** Mrs Clodagh McStay **Trained** Kingsclere, Hants

FOCUS
Another small-field 3y-o handicap, but an improving winner. The second favourite failed to give his running.

790 ATR CHELTENHAM MEGASITE NOW LIVE CLAIMING STKS 1m 2f (P)
4:25 (4:25) (Class 6) 4-Y-O+ **£1,535** (£453; £226) **Stalls** Low

Form RPR
6124 1 **Edgeworth (IRE)**[19] 565 5-8-11 66............................(p) ChrisCatlin 6 77
(Brendan Powell) *hld up in last pair: prog on outer over 2f out: urged along and clsd to ld ins fnl f: rdn out* **12/1[3]**
2-11 2 ½ **Majuro (IRE)**[31] 427 7-9-1 85.. JamesDoyle 1 80
(Frank Sheridan) *led after 1f at gd pce: kicked on over 2f out: hdd ins fnl f: styd on* **11/10[1]**
2-00 3 ¾ **The Which Doctor**[16] 615 6-8-12 86..............................(p) TomQueally 4 76
(Jeremy Noseda) *patiently rdn in tch: effrt 2f out: clsd on ldr w wnr over 1f out: nt qckn and n.m.r ins fnl f* **6/4[2]**
1322 4 2 **Faithful Ruler (USA)**[17] 599 7-8-11 76............................(p) LukeMorris 5 71
(Ronald Harris) *prom: chsd ldr 4f out: u.p 2f out: lost 2nd and fdd 1f out* **12/1[3]**
5034 5 4 ½ **Dream Of Fortune (IRE)**[12] 656 7-8-4 66 ow2(bt) MatthewCosham[(7)] 7 62
(David Evans) *dwlt: hld up last: reminders over 2f out: fnd nil and no prog: passed 2 rivals ins fnl f* **33/1**

-334 **6** ¾ **Esteem Lord**[15] 625 5-8-8 59 .... RobertHavlin 3 58
(Dean Ivory) *trckd ldrs: effrt to dispute 2nd over 2f out: losing pl whn tight for room wl over 1f out: wknd* **40/1**

-540 **7** 1 ¾ **Negotiation (IRE)**[12] 647 5-9-1 71 .... FrannyNorton 2 62
(Michael Quinn) *led 1f: chsd ldr to 4f out: sn lost pl and btn* **25/1**

2m 4.07s (-2.53) **Going Correction** +0.10s/f (Slow) **7** Ran SP% **112.2**
Speed ratings (Par 101): **114,113,113,111,107 107,105**
.Majuro was subject to a friendly claim. The Which Doctor was claimed by R. C. Guest for £9,000.\n\x\x
Owner K Rhatigan **Bred** Yvonne & Gerard Kennedy **Trained** Upper Lambourn, Berks

FOCUS
This fair claimer looked to concern only two runners at the weights, but there was a bit of a surprise. The winner's best AW effort but the next two were below form.
Dream Of Fortune(IRE) Official explanation: trainer said gelding had a breathing problem

791 VISIT ATTHERACES.COM/CHELTENHAM MAIDEN FILLIES' STKS 1m (P)
5:00 (5:01) (Class 5) 3-Y-O+ **£1,910** (£564; £282) **Stalls** High

Form RPR

64- **1** **Insieme (IRE)**[139] 7000 3-8-9 0 .... MartinDwyer 8 68+
(Marco Botti) *trcked ldng trio: effrt to chse ldr 2f out clsd to chal ins fnl f sustained effrt to ld nr fin* **6/4**[1]

0-4 **2** hd **Swift Bird (IRE)**[11] 663 3-8-9 0 .... LiamJones 5 68
(Noel Quinlan) *led: kicked on over 2f out: hrd pressed ins fnl f: worn down nr fin* **4/1**[3]

05 **3** 5 **Frosty Reception**[19] 559 3-8-9 0 .... RichardKingscote 6 56
(Brendan Powell) *mostly chsd ldr to 2f out: steadily outpcd u.p* **14/1**

03- **4** 1 **Judgement**[114] 7448 3-8-9 0 .... RobertHavlin 4 54
(John Gosden) *t.k.h: cl up on inner: disp 2nd briefly 2f out: sn brushed aside* **2/1**[2]

0-6 **5** ¾ **Khaki (IRE)**[14] 634 3-8-9 0 .... PaulHanagan 10 53+
(Tor Sturgis) *trckd ldrs on outer: outpcd wl over 2f out and pushed along: kpt on same pce over 1f out* **14/1**

6 1 ½ **Summerandlightning (IRE)**[48] 5-9-8 0 .... LeeNewnes(5) 3 55?
(Mark Usher) *s.i.s: settled in rr: outpcd and pushed along 3f out: no imp on ldrs after* **100/1**

0- **7** 1 ¾ **Fight Or Flight**[114] 7438 4-9-6 0 .... DavidKenny(7) 9 51?
(Brendan Powell) *t.k.h: hld up in rr on outer: drvn over 3f out: sn struggling and lft bhd: no prog after* **100/1**

8 16 **Pippas Prodigy (IRE)** 3-8-9 0 .... EddieCreighton 2 —
(Edward Creighton) *s.i.s: a towards rr: rdn and wknd 3f out: t.o* **40/1**

9 hd **April Belle** 3-8-9 0 .... LukeMorris 1 —
(Tim McCarthy) *v s.i.s: rn v green and constantly urged along to stay in tch: wknd 3f out: t.o* **33/1**

1m 39.55s (1.35) **Going Correction** +0.10s/f (Slow)
WFA 3 from 4yo+ 18lb **9** Ran SP% **114.0**
Speed ratings (Par 100): **97,96,91,90,90 88,86,70,70**
toteswingers:1&2 £2.50, 2&3 £5.60, 1&3 £4.90 CSF £7.75 TOTE £2.50: £1.20, £1.10, £3.40; EX 8.40 Trifecta £85.20 Pool: £7816.91 - 6.79 winning units..
Owner The Great Partnership **Bred** A Panetta **Trained** Newmarket, Suffolk

FOCUS
This maiden revolved around three horses and the market got it right, but only just. The first two came clear.

792 ATR CHELTENHAM MEGASITE NOW LIVE FILLIES' H'CAP 6f (P)
5:30 (5:30) (Class 5) (0-75,79) 4-Y-O+ **£2,047** (£604; £302) **Stalls** Low

Form RPR

0003 **1** **Mary's Pet**[12] 654 4-8-5 61 .... (p) SimonPearce(3) 5 68
(John Akehurst) *mde all: sn at least 2 l clr and untrbld: maintained ld tl hld on to dwindling advantage nr fin* **8/1**

U-1 **2** 1 **Cape Melody**[45] 243 5-9-4 74 .... MatthewDavies(3) 4 78
(George Baker) *chsd ldng pair: pushed along 1/2-way: wnt 2nd 1f out: grad clsd but nvr gng to get there* **2/1**[2]

0112 **3** ¾ **Spinning Bailiwick**[10] 689 5-9-3 70 .... (b) GeorgeBaker 1 72
(Gary Moore) *t.k.h: chsd wnr: nt qckn 2f out: lost 2nd and one pce 1f out* **15/8**[1]

220- **4** 3 ¼ **Mrs Boss**[166] 6284 4-8-11 64 .... JamesMillman 2 56
[illegible] *dnager after* **9/2**[3]

4244 **5** 1 ½ **Bold Ring**[40] 303 5-8-0 60 oh1 .... JenniferFerguson(7) 3 48
(Edward Creighton) *hld up last: pushed along and no prog over 2f out* **8/1**

1m 12.72s (0.82) **Going Correction** +0.10s/f (Slow) **5** Ran SP% **108.5**
Speed ratings (Par 100): **98,96,95,91,89**
CSF £23.63 TOTE £12.50: £3.50, £1.10; EX 32.80.
Owner Mrs I Marshall **Bred** Green Pastures Farm **Trained** Epsom, Surrey

FOCUS
A small-field fillies' sprint. The winner was allowed an easy lead and the form may not prove too solid.
T/Plt: £86.30 to a £1 stake. Pool of £57,992.30 - 490.27 winning tickets. T/Qpdt: £15.40 to a £1 stake. Pool of £4,712.93 - 225.30 winning tickets JN

738 SOUTHWELL (L-H)
Tuesday, March 8

OFFICIAL GOING: Standard
Wind: moderate 1/2 behind Weather: fine and sunny

793 HOSPITALITY AT SOUTHWELL RACECOURSE H'CAP (DIV I) 7f (F)
1:40 (1:42) (Class 6) (0-52,56) 4-Y-O+ **£1,364** (£403; £201) **Stalls** Low

Form RPR

063- **1** **Exceedingly Good (IRE)**[105] 7542 5-8-6 49 .... LeonnaMayor(7) 1 58
(Roy Bowring) *hdwy to ld after 1f: rdr dropped whip over 1f out: edgd rt and kpt on wl: eased nr fin* **16/1**

0330 **2** 1 **Meydan Style (USA)**[19] 575 5-8-10 46 oh1 .... JoeFanning 3 50
(Bruce Hellier) *trckd ldrs: t.k.h: styd on to chse wnr 1f out: no imp* **16/1**

0-54 **3** shd **Bold Diva**[16] 619 6-9-1 51 .... (v) HayleyTurner 13 55
(Tony Carroll) *trckd ldrs: t.k.h: kpt on same pce fnl f* **9/2**[2]

4405 **4** nk **Novastasia (IRE)**[12] 662 5-8-10 46 oh1 .... (b) SamHitchcott 5 49
(Dean Ivory) *dwlt: reminders in rr after 1f: sn drvn and bhd: hdwy over 2f out: swtchd rt appr fnl f: fin wl* **9/1**

32-3 **5** nk **It's A Mans World**[25] 504 5-8-13 52 .... (v) AndrewHeffernan(3) 10 55
(Kevin M Prendergast) *hld up in mid-div: effrt over 2f out: kpt on same pce: nvr nr to chal* **4/1**[1]

-061 **6** nk **Flying Applause**[6] 734 6-9-6 56 6ex .... (bt) JimmyQuinn 4 58
(Roy Bowring) *in rr div: hdwy over 2f out: edgd lft: styd on fnl f* **9/2**[2]

0046 **7** 2 ¼ **Archilini**[12] 675 6-8-10 46 oh1 .... (be) TomEaves 2 42
(Brian Ellison) *dwlt: sn chsng ldrs: wknd fnl 150yds* **15/2**

-060 **8** 7 **Westport**[12] 675 8-8-10 46 oh1 .... (p) LeeNewman 7 25
(Robin Bastiman) *chsd ldrs: wknd over 1f out* **66/1**

/30- **9** 2 ¼ **Compton Micky**[120] 7376 10-8-7 46 oh1 .... (p) PaulPickard(3) 12 19
(Owen Brennan) *t.k.h on outer: trckd ldrs: lost pl over 2f out* **50/1**

3653 **10** 3 ½ **Errigal Lad**[14] 641 6-9-2 52 .... (p) LukeMorris 6 16
(John Balding) *led 1f: chsd ldrs: rdn and hung rt bnd over 3f out: lost pl over 2f out* **11/2**[3]

00-0 **11** 1 ¼ **Wotatomboy**[12] 674 5-8-10 46 .... MichaelStainton 11 7
(Richard Whitaker) *in rr on outside: bhd fnl 3f* **20/1**

/0-0 **12** 13 **Rich Harvest (USA)**[25] 517 6-8-10 46 oh1 .... WilliamCarson 9 —
(Ray Peacock) *w ldrs on outside: drvn and lost pl over 3f out: bhd fnl 2f* **50/1**

1m 30.31s (0.01) **Going Correction** -0.05s/f (Stan) **12** Ran SP% **115.5**
Speed ratings (Par 101): **97,95,95,95,95 94,92,84,81,77 76,61**
toteswingers:1&2:£9.80, 1&3:£9.30, 2&3:£8.90 CSF £234.27 CT £1363.59 TOTE £16.90: £4.50, £5.20, £1.80; EX 174.20 TRIFECTA No won..
Owner S R Bowring **Bred** Martin Francis Ltd **Trained** Edwinstowe, Notts

FOCUS
A very moderate handicap and it paid to be handy. They finished in a heap.
It's A Mans World Official explanation: jockey said, regarding the running and riding, that his instructions were to jump out, get a lead and ride the gelding to get the trip and to finish. He added that he was outpaced and unable to sit handy and the gelding had stayed on at one pace. The trainer confirmed these instructions.
Errigal Lad Official explanation: jockey said the gelding hung right throughout

794 VISIT ATTHERACES.COM/CHELTENHAM H'CAP 5f (F)
2:10 (2:11) (Class 5) (0-75,75) 4-Y-O+ **£1,813** (£539; £269; £134) **Stalls** High

Form RPR

-522 **1** **Where's Reiley (USA)**[12] 673 5-9-0 68 .... (b) LeeNewman 6 88
(David Barron) *w ldr: led over 2f out: shkn up and wnt clr over 1f out: v readily* **4/1**[1]

0204 **2** 4 **Incomparable**[8] 708 6-9-6 74 .... (tp) FrederikTylicki 7 79
(David Nicholls) *chsd ldrs: wnt 2nd over 1f out: no ch w wnr* **8/1**

332- **3** 1 ¾ **Dazeen**[132] 5906 4-8-8 62 .... FrannyNorton 1 60
(Paul Midgley) *in rr far side: hdwy 2f out: styd on wl fnl f* **33/1**

2-51 **4** 1 ¾ **Soopacal (IRE)**[25] 506 6-9-5 73 .... TonyCulhane 8 65
(Michael Herrington) *dwlt: sn trcking ldrs: kpt on same pce over 1f out* **10/1**

4162 **5** nk **Sleepy Blue Ocean**[19] 571 5-9-1 69 .... (p) LukeMorris 13 60
(John Balding) *chsd ldrs stands' side: one pce fnl 2f* **13/2**[3]

3210 **6** 1 ¼ **Dancing Freddy (IRE)**[11] 696 4-8-8 62 .... (p) RobbieFitzpatrick 12 48
(Michael Chapman) *chsd ldrs stands' side: sn drvn along: one pce fnl 2f* **20/1**

6-30 **7** ½ **Fashion Icon (USA)**[40] 318 5-8-5 62 .... (v[1]) NataliaGemelova(3) 2 47
(David O'Meara) *sn in rr towards far side: styd on fnl 2f* **25/1**

-360 **8** hd **Besty**[12] 673 4-9-1 69 .... (v) TomEaves 5 53
(Bryan Smart) *chsd ldrs: hrd rdn and lost pl over 1f out* **20/1**

0-06 **9** 2 **Lucky Mellor**[8] 708 4-9-7 75 .... AdamKirby 11 52
(Dean Ivory) *chsd ldrs: wknd over 1f out* **13/2**[3]

0-31 **10** 2 ¼ **Bookiesindex Boy**[26] 491 7-9-7 75 .... (b) StephenCraine 9 44
(J R Jenkins) *hld up in rr: hdwy 2f out: sn rdn and btn* **5/1**[2]

6-02 **11** hd **Nollaig Shona (IRE)**[40] 318 4-8-7 61 .... (v) KirstyMilczarek 4 29
(George Prodromou) *led tl over 2f out: lost pl over 1f out* **14/1**

0604 **12** 14 **La Capriosa**[26] 491 5-9-2 70 .... AdrianNicholls 10 —
(David Nicholls) *chsd ldrs: heavily eased over 1f out: virtually p.u: lame* **12/1**

58.07 secs (-1.63) **Going Correction** -0.25s/f (Stan) **12** Ran SP% **114.2**
Speed ratings (Par 103): **103,96,93,91,90 88,87,87,84,80 80,57**
toteswingers:1&2:£7.80, 1&3:£14.00, 2&3:£32.20 CSF £32.30 CT £930.66 TOTE £5.70: £2.20, £3.40, £10.80; EX 29.50 Trifecta £176.60 Pool: £425.00 - 1.78 winning units..
Owner Dovebrace Ltd Air-Conditioning-Projects **Bred** Overbrook Farm **Trained** Maunby, N Yorks

FOCUS
This competitive-looking sprint handicap was made to look embarrassingly one-sided, the winner bouncing right back to his best. The form is straightforward.
Lucky Mellor Official explanation: jockey said that the gelding moved poorly
La Capriosa Official explanation: vet said mare was lame post race

795 DINE IN THE PANTRY AT SOUTHWELL CLAIMING STKS 1m 6f (F)
2:40 (2:40) (Class 6) 4-Y-O+ **£1,535** (£453; £226) **Stalls** Low

Form RPR

/111 **1** **La Estrella (USA)**[14] 639 8-9-9 80 .... DaneO'Neill 1 87+
(Don Cantillon) *trckd ldr: chal over 3f out: led on bit over 2f out: wnt easily clr: eased clsng stages* **30/100**[1]

03-6 **2** 1 ¾ **Hindu Kush (IRE)**[34] 384 6-8-13 68 .... JoeFanning 5 72
(Robert Mills) *led: hdd over 2f out: hung lft: kpt on: greatly flattered* **9/2**[2]

6-64 **3** 16 **Beseech (USA)**[25] 507 4-8-2 42 .... JimmyQuinn 2 44
(Julia Feilden) *trckd ldrs: swtchd wd 5f out: sn drvn: outpcd over 3f out: one pce* **10/1**[3]

3025 **4** 4 **Mojeerr**[14] 639 5-8-4 49 .... (v) RyanTate(7) 4 46
(Alan McCabe) *s.v.s: hdwy and in tch after 3f: drvn and outpcd over 4f out: one pce* **20/1**

5 74 **Cosmetic**[28] 6-8-10 0 .... PatrickMathers 3 —
(Colin Teague) *hld up in tch: drvn 8f out: reminders and bhd over 6f out: sn t.o: eventually completed* **66/1**

3m 6.90s (-1.40) **Going Correction** -0.05s/f (Stan)
WFA 4 from 5yo+ 4lb **5** Ran SP% **110.5**
Speed ratings (Par 101): **102,101,91,89,47**
CSF £2.07 TOTE £1.40: £1.10, £1.10; EX 2.30.
Owner Don Cantillon **Bred** Five Horses Ltd And Theatrical Syndicate **Trained** Newmarket, Suffolk

FOCUS
A predictable result for this uncompetitive claimer. The runner-up's recent form sets the level.

796 PLAY GOLF BEFORE RACING AT SOUTHWELL (S) STKS 1m 3f (F)
3:10 (3:10) (Class 6) 4-Y-O+ **£1,535** (£453; £226) **Stalls** Low

Form RPR

5502 **1** **Kipchak (IRE)**[14] 644 6-8-11 65 .... (p) HayleyTurner 12 62
(Conor Dore) *drawn wd: led after 1f: pushed clr 3f out: drvn over 1f out: eased nr fin: unchal* **11/8**[1]

-651 **2** 1 **Davana**[19] 569 5-8-10 51 .... PatrickMathers 2 57
(Colin Teague) *in rr and sn drvn along: hdwy over 3f out: styd on to chse wnr over 1f out: kpt on* **17/2**

0-06 **3** 10 **Byron Bay**[12] 670 9-8-8 42 .... (vt) JamesSullivan(3) 6 42
(Robert Johnson) *led 1f: chsd wnr: rdn over 3f out: one pce* **100/1**

0/05 **4** *3* **Hawaass (USA)**[15] [633] 6-8-11 70........................ PJMcDonald 7 37
(Ruth Carr) *chsd ldrs: wknd over 1f out* **10/1**

3023 **5** *nk* **Yossi (IRE)**[25] [507] 7-8-11 52........................(be) FrannyNorton 3 37+
(Richard Guest) *hmpd s: in rr: effrt over 3f out: kpt on: nvr nr ldrs* **4/1**[2]

0400 **6** *1 ¼* **Yorksters Prince (IRE)**[20] [552] 4-8-10 43........................ LiamKeniry 5 35
(George Prodromou) *dwlt: in rr and reminders 6f out: sme hdwy over 3f out: nvr a factor* **33/1**

35-0 **7** *¾* **Miss Wendy**[18] [592] 4-8-5 54........................ PaulHanagan 1 29
(Mark H Tompkins) *mid-div: drvn over 4f out: hung lft and lost pl over 2f out* **8/1**[3]

-406 **8** *nk* **Little Meadow (IRE)**[25] [504] 4-8-5 44........................ JimmyQuinn 4 28
(Julia Feilden) *in rr: sme hdwy over 3f out: nvr on terms* **14/1**

0500 **9** *15* **Raghdaan**[20] [552] 4-8-10 39........................ ChrisCatlin 9 9
(Peter Hiatt) *sn chsng ldrs: lost pl over 3f out: sn bhd* **33/1**

00-5 **10** *2* **Tiger Hawk (USA)**[19] [573] 4-8-7 55................(b) AndrewHeffernan(3) 11 6
(Kevin M Prendergast) *chsd ldrs: drvn over 4f out: lost pl over 3f out* **20/1**

-664 **11** *6* **Credential**[12] [670] 9-8-6 43........................(be) TobyAtkinson(5) 10 —
(John Harris) *in rr: reminders after 2f: sme hdwy on outside 5f out: hung bdly rt and lost pl over 2f out* **50/1**

0-00 **12** *37* **Pinewood Polly**[26] [490] 4-8-5 20........................ KirstyMilczarek 8 —
(Shaun Harris) *mid-div: drvn over 5f out: sn lost pl and t.o 3f out: sn eased: eventually completed* **100/1**

2m 27.65s (-0.35) **Going Correction** -0.05s/f (Stan)
WFA 4 from 5yo+ 1lb **12** Ran SP% **114.1**
Speed ratings (Par 101): **99,98,91,88,88 87,87,86,76,74 70,43**
toteswingers:1&2:£4.70, 1&3:£28.40, 2&3:£54.00 CSF £12.33 TOTE £1.80: £2.10, £4.10, £23.90; EX 16.60 Trifecta £222.80 Part won. Pool: £301.16 - 0.43 winning units..There was no bid for the winner.
Owner Liam Breslin **Bred** Miss Mary Davidson & Mrs Steffi Von Schilcher **Trained** Cowbit, Lincs

FOCUS
Quite a big field for this seller but it lacked depth and few got into it. The winner is better than this grade at best.
Yossi(IRE) Official explanation: jockey said the gelding was hampered at the start

797 SOUTHWELL-RACECOURSE.CO.UK H'CAP 1m 4f (F)
3:40 (3:42) (Class 6) (0-65,62) 4-Y-0+ **£1,535** (£453; £226) **Stalls** Low

Form RPR

-401 **1** **Irish Jugger (USA)**[14] [645] 4-9-1 **58**........................ JamesMillman 6 67
(Rod Millman) *hld up in rr: effrt over 3f out: styd on outer to ld jst ins fnl f: drvn out* **11/8**[1]

0352 **2** *1 ½* **Light The City (IRE)**[15] [630] 4-8-3 **49**........................ JamesSullivan(3) 7 55
(Ruth Carr) *chsd ldr: led over 4f out: hdd jst ins fnl f: no ex* **15/2**

06-3 **3** *2 ¼* **I'Lldoit**[22] [539] 4-8-8 **58**........................ DavidKenny(7) 2 60
(Michael Scudamore) *chsd ldrs: rdn over 3f out: kpt on same pce fnl 2f* **20/1**

0421 **4** *2* **Eton Fable (IRE)**[12] [670] 6-9-7 **62**........................ PatrickMathers 4 61
(Colin Teague) *led 1f: chsd ldrs: drvn over 5f out: one pce fnl 2f* **8/1**

5-32 **5** *2* **Sir Haydn**[12] [670] 11-8-2 **50**........................ DannyBrock(7) 3 46
(J R Jenkins) *in rr: shkn up and hdwy after 3f: sn chsng ldrs: one pce fnl 2f* **7/1**[3]

00-0 **6** *nse* **War Of The Roses (IRE)**[53] [162] 8-9-7 **62**........................ PaulHanagan 8 58
(Roy Brotherton) *hld up in rr: hdwy 4f out: sn chsng ldrs: wknd over 1f out* **17/2**

0-04 **7** *15* **Mexican Jay (USA)**[14] [644] 5-9-0 **55**........................(v) TomEaves 5 29
(Bryan Smart) *led after 1f: hdd over 4f out: hung rt and wknd over 2f out: sn bhd* **6/1**[2]

435- **8** *3 ½* **Dazakhee**[178] [5942] 4-9-4 **61**........................ TonyCulhane 1 30
(Paul Midgley) *hld up in rr: t.k.h: lost pl 5f out: bhd fnl 3f* **11/1**

2m 40.37s (-0.63) **Going Correction** -0.05s/f (Stan)
WFA 4 from 5yo+ 2lb **8** Ran SP% **115.4**
Speed ratings (Par 101): **100,99,97,96,94 94,84,82**
toteswingers:1&2:£3.50, 1&3:£10.50, 2&3:£17.40 CSF £12.51 CT £143.49 TOTE £3.00: £1.40, £3.50, £6.60; EX 16.20 Trifecta £124.80 Pool: £522.98 - 3.10 winning units.
Owner Rod Millman Racing Club **Bred** Richard S Kaster & Frederick C Wieting **Trained** Kentisbeare, Devon

FOCUS
A modest handicap with little depth and something of a stop-start gallop. The winner confirmed his improvement for the switch to Fibresand.
Mexican Jay(USA) Official explanation: jockey said that the mare hung right

798 SOUTHWELL RACECOURSE FOR CONFERENCES H'CAP 6f (F)
4:10 (4:10) (Class 6) (0-60,59) 4-Y-0+ **£1,535** (£453; £226) **Stalls** Low

Form RPR

000- **1** **Lindoro**[3] [7051] 6-8-12 **53**........................ AndrewHeffernan(3) 1 66
(Kevin M Prendergast) *chsd ldrs: chal 2f out: styd on to ld last 100yds* **16/1**

6-23 **2** *¾* **Premier League**[11] [690] 4-9-2 **54**........................(p) JimmyQuinn 8 65
(Julia Feilden) *trckd ldrs: led over 1f out: edgd rt and hdd ins fnl f: no ex* **7/2**[1]

-255 **3** *4 ½* **Olympic Dream**[25] [504] 5-9-3 **55**........................(p) TonyCulhane 10 53+
(Michael Herrington) *mid-div: hdwy over 2f out: styd on to take 3rd last 100yds* **7/1**

0330 **4** *1 ¾* **Muqalad (IRE)**[12] [674] 4-9-0 **52**........................(v[1]) TomEaves 3 44
(Bryan Smart) *hdwy to ld after 1f: hdd over 1f out: wknd ins fnl f* **6/1**[3]

60-0 **5** *2* **Lago Indiano (IRE)**[25] [504] 4-8-10 **48**........................(b) LiamKeniry 13 34
(Peter Fahey, Ire) *s.i.s: hdwy on outer over 2f out: nvr nr ldrs* **40/1**

421- **6** *½* **Accamelia**[112] [7468] 5-9-6 **58**........................ PaulMulrennan 9 43
(Chris Fairhurst) *chsd ldrs: one pce fnl 2f* **9/2**[2]

0-45 **7** *1* **Beckermet (IRE)**[12] [673] 9-9-7 **59**........................ PJMcDonald 4 41
(Ruth Carr) *led 1f: chsd ldrs: wknd over 1f out* **10/1**

30/0 **8** *2* **Bazguy**[33] [402] 6-9-3 **55**........................(b) AdamKirby 5 31
(Owen Brennan) *chsd ldrs: wknd over 1f out* **22/1**

260- **9** *hd* **Uddy Mac**[144] [6897] 4-9-2 **54**........................ FrannyNorton 7 29
(Neville Bycroft) *in rr: sme hdwy over 2f out: nvr a factor* **16/1**

-005 **10** *5* **True Red (IRE)**[12] [669] 4-8-7 **45**........................(b) DavidProbert 11 —
(Nikki Evans) *chsd ldrs: drvn over 3f out: sn lost pl* **40/1**

00-0 **11** *1 ½* **Doric Echo**[12] [670] 5-8-6 **49**........................(b) DanielleMcCreery(5) 12 —
(Kevin M Prendergast) *s.i.s: in rr: nvr on terms* **66/1**

/0-5 **12** *9* **Little Pandora**[40] [318] 7-8-7 **45**........................(b) DuranFentiman 6 —
(Lee James) *dwlt: in rr dív whn m v wd bnd over 3f out: sn wl bhd* **66/1**

26-0 **13** *3 ½* **Gazamali (IRE)**[20] [555] 4-8-6 **51**........................ DavidKenny(7) 2 —
(Michael Scudamore) *mid-div: effrt over 2f out: sn wknd: eased whn bhd* **10/1**

1m 16.13s (-0.37) **Going Correction** -0.05s/f (Stan) **13** Ran SP% **119.4**
Speed ratings (Par 101): **100,99,93,90,88 87,86,83,83,76 74,62,57**
toteswingers:1&2:£18.80, 1&3:£25.60, 2&3:£6.70 CSF £69.98 CT £456.44 TOTE £29.00: £8.30, £1.50, £2.90; EX 151.70 Trifecta £184.10 Pool: £263.75 - 1.06 winning units.

Owner Alchemy Bloodstock **Bred** Pigeon House Stud **Trained** Malton, N Yorks
■ Stewards' Enquiry : Andrew Heffernan caution: use of whip

FOCUS
A modest sprint handicap and the front pair had the race to themselves from a long way out. Straightforward form.

799 ATR CHELTENHAM MEGASITE NOW LIVE H'CAP 1m (F)
4:40 (4:40) (Class 4) (0-85,85) 4-Y-0+ **£2,914** (£867; £433; £216) **Stalls** Low

Form RPR

4313 **1** **Trans Sonic**[21] [548] 8-8-13 **84**........................ ShaneBKelly(7) 4 91
(David O'Meara) *mde all: drvn 3f out: all out* **4/1**[2]

1625 **2** *nse* **The Lock Master (IRE)**[6] [723] 4-8-12 **76**........................ NeilChalmers 6 83
(Michael Appleby) *chsd ldrs: chal over 1f out: styd on ins fnl f: jst hld* **7/2**[1]

3642 **3** *2* **Elusive Fame (USA)**[35] [377] 5-8-4 **75**........................(b) JasonHart(7) 1 79
(Mark Johnston) *hld up: hdwy to trck ldrs over 3f out: swtchd wd over 2f out: kpt on same pce fnl f* **7/2**[1]

0514 **4** *4 ½* **General Tufto**[5] [744] 6-8-7 **71** oh1........................(b) MartinLane 8 63
(Charles Smith) *in rr on outer: outpcd and lost pl over 4f out: kpt on fnl 2f: nvr a factor* **10/1**

50-4 **5** *5* **Mr Hichens**[22] [542] 6-9-7 **85**........................ ChrisCatlin 3 65
(Karen George) *chsd ldrs: drvn to chse ldr over 3f out: wknd over 1f out* **10/1**

560- **6** *2 ½* **Dubai Dynamo**[150] [6749] 6-9-4 **82**........................ PJMcDonald 5 57
(Ruth Carr) *s.i.s: sn chsng ldrs: wknd over 1f out* **12/1**

60-0 **7** *16* **Marvo**[38] [348] 7-8-12 **76**........................ PaulHanagan 7 14
(Mark H Tompkins) *chsd ldrs on outer: drvn over 3f out: lost pl over 2f out: sn bhd: eased* **5/1**[3]

23-0 **8** *10* **Skyfire**[10] [703] 4-9-2 **80**........................ LukeMorris 2 —
(Ed de Giles) *in rr: drvn over 3f out: sn bhd* **12/1**

1m 42.18s (-1.52) **Going Correction** -0.05s/f (Stan) **8** Ran SP% **114.7**
Speed ratings (Par 105): **105,104,102,98,93 90,74,64**
toteswingers:1&2:£3.40, 1&3:£2.00, 2&3:£3.50 CSF £18.49 CT £53.18 TOTE £4.30: £2.30, £1.10, £1.40; EX 18.40 Trifecta £44.70 Pool: £373.20 - 6.17 winning units.
Owner Mrs Lynne Lumley **Bred** I A Balding **Trained** Nawton, N Yorks

FOCUS
A fair handicap and the pace was honest. Straightforward form.

800 HOSPITALITY AT SOUTHWELL RACECOURSE H'CAP (DIV II) 7f (F)
5:10 (5:10) (Class 6) (0-52,52) 4-Y-0+ **£1,364** (£403; £201) **Stalls** Low

Form RPR

06-0 **1** **Angelena Ballerina (IRE)**[24] [526] 4-9-2 **52**........................(v) KirstyMilczarek 9 63+
(Karen George) *in rr: effrt 4f out: hdwy to ld over 1f out: styd on wl* **7/1**[2]

0420 **2** *3 ¼* **St Ignatius**[12] [662] 4-9-0 **50**........................(p) NeilChalmers 12 53
(Michael Appleby) *chsd ldrs: styd on to go 2nd 1f out: no imp* **9/1**[3]

5040 **3** *1 ¾* **Norcroft**[34] [386] 9-8-3 **46**........................(p) DanielHarris(7) 7 46
(Christine Dunnett) *chsd ldrs: sn drvn along: outpcd 4f out: hdwy over 2f out: n.m.r 1f out: kpt on wl* **10/1**

-000 **4** *1 ¾* **Flores Sea (USA)**[12] [675] 7-8-10 **46** oh1........................(b) PJMcDonald 10 40
(Ruth Carr) *s.s: sn chsng ldrs on outer: outpcd 2f out: styd on fnl f* **12/1**

04-0 **5** *½* **Ronnie Howe**[6] [735] 7-8-10 **46** oh1........................(b) RobbieFitzpatrick 2 39
(Roy Bowring) *led: drvn clr over 3f out: hdd over 1f out: fdd fnl 100yds* **18/1**

30-3 **6** *½* **Jonnie Skull (IRE)**[5] [743] 5-9-2 **52**........................(vt) TomMcLaughlin 4 44
(Phil McEntee) *chsd ldrs: wnt 2nd over 3f out: wknd over 1f out* **6/4**[1]

-606 **7** *1 ½* **Moon Lightning (IRE)**[21] [547] 5-9-2 **52**........................(p) PaulHanagan 6 40
(Tina Jackson) *chsd ldrs: one pce whn edgd rt over 1f out* **22/1**

600- **8** *5* **Chateau Zara**[90] [7761] 4-8-13 **49**........................ JoeFanning 8 24
(Derek Shaw) *chsd ldrs: wknd 2f out* **10/1**

000- **9** *2* **Ochilview Warrior (IRE)**[250] [3595] 4-8-7 **46**........................(b) PaulPickard(3) 3 16
(Robin Bastiman) *a towards rr: bhd fnl 3f* **20/1**

0-00 **10** *1 ¾* **Captain Imperial (IRE)**[26] [490] 5-8-10 **46** oh1........................(tp) LeeNewman 1 12
(Robin Bastiman) *chsd ldrs: wknd 2f out: eased whn bhd* **20/1**

000- **11** *4* **Benamy Boy**[245] [3754] 5-8-10 **46** oh1........................ FrannyNorton 5 —
(Neville Bycroft) *s.i.s: wl bhd fnl 4f* **14/1**

000- **12** *2 ¾* **Spume (IRE)**[268] [2995] 7-8-10 **46** oh1........................ LukeMorris 11 —
(John Balding) *chsd ldrs: lost pl over 4f out: sn bhd* **16/1**

1m 29.00s (-0.02) **Going Correction** -0.05s/f (Stan) **12** Ran SP% **120.1**
Speed ratings (Par 101): **101,97,95,93,92 92,90,84,82,80 75,72**
toteswingers:1&2:£7.80, 1&3:£15.40, 2&3:£14.20. totesuper7: Win: Not won. Place: Not won. CSF £67.36 CT £646.23 TOTE £7.70: £1.70, £2.60, £2.10; EX 65.30 Trifecta £350.50 Pool: £473.70 - 1.00 winning units.
Owner F Michael **Bred** Waterford Hall Stud **Trained** Higher Eastington, Devon

FOCUS
Another moderate handicap, though the winning time was 0.63 seconds faster than the first division. The winner ran to her best form of the last couple of years.
T/Plt: £29.20 to a £1 stake. Pool:£58,069.91 - 1,451.50 winning tickets T/Qpdt: £3.90 to a £1 stake. Pool:£4,301.99 - 807.12 winning tickets WG

723 KEMPTON (A.W) (R-H)
Wednesday, March 9

OFFICIAL GOING: Standard
Wind: Virtually nil Weather: Rain

801 FREE ENTRY FOR BETDAQ MEMBERS MEDIAN AUCTION MAIDEN STKS 1m 2f (P)
5:30 (5:30) (Class 5) 3-Y-0 **£2,047** (£604; £302) **Stalls** Low

Form RPR

2 **1** **Brilliant Barca**[19] [591] 3-9-3 0........................ SamHitchcott 3 65+
(Mick Channon) *trckd ldrs: drvn and qcknd to ld ins fnl f: r.o strly* **9/4**[1]

6-4 **2** *1* **Arizona High**[9] [713] 3-9-3 0........................ JimmyFortune 8 63
(Andrew Balding) *sn led: hdd 5f out: styd chsng ldr: rdn to ld again ins fnl 2f: hdd ins fnl f: styd on same pce* **3/1**[2]

3 *¾* **Peachez** 3-8-13 0 ow1........................(b[1]) AdamKirby 7 58+
(Marco Botti) *s.i.s: in rr: rdn and hdwy fr 2f out: styd on and edgd rt ins fnl f: one pce nr fin* **8/1**

566- **4** *3 ¼* **Dubai Glory**[126] [7296] 3-8-12 60........................ JamesDoyle 5 50
(Sheena West) *chsd ldrs: rdn over 2f out: one pce fnl f* **9/2**[3]

6235 **5** *5* **Bodie**[8] [716] 3-9-3 62........................(b) MickyFenton 1 45
(Pam Sly) *chsd ldr: t.k.h: led 5f out: rdn and hdd 2f out: outpcd ins fnl f* **5/1**

0-36 **6** *7* **Rainbows Reach**[51] [194] 3-8-12 51........................(t) AndreaAtzeni 4 28
(Gay Kelleway) *in rr: but in tch: rdn 3f out and sn wknd* **40/1**

500- **7** *2 ¼* **Beautiful Lando (FR)**[168] [6279] 3-9-3 41........................(b[1]) PaulHanagan 6 27
(Heather Main) *chsd ldrs: rdn 3f out: wknd quickley ins fnl 2f* **25/1**

000- 8 *nk* **On Wings Of Love (IRE)**126 7295 3-8-12 54.................... ChrisCatlin 2 21
(John Gallagher) *chsd ldrs: rdn 3f out: sn wknd* **20/1**

2m 9.36s (1.36) **Going Correction** +0.05s/f (Slow) **8** Ran SP% **112.8**
Speed ratings (Par 98): **96,95,94,91,87 82,80,80**
toteswingers:1&2:£3.30, 1&3:£4.90, 2&3:£8.60 CSF £8.74 TOTE £2.90: £1.30, £1.20, £2.50; EX 5.90 Trifecta £18.80 Pool: £13,435.86 - 528.18 winning units..
Owner The Highlife Racing Club **Bred** Imperial & Mike Channon Bloodstock Ltd **Trained** West Ilsley, Berks

FOCUS
A modest maiden in which it paid to race handy, as is so often the case on Kempton's inner track. They went steady and the time was competitively slow, although these are young horses. The fourth and seventh limit the form but the winner has more to offer.

802 SKYSPORTS.COM RACING H'CAP 1m 2f (P)
6:00 (6:00) (Class 6) (0-65,65) 4-Y-O+ **£1,535** (£453; £226) **Stalls** Low

Form RPR

50-1 **1** **Rezwaan**17 625 4-9-3 **61**...(be) GeorgeBaker 6 82+
(Gary Moore) *trckd ldr: travelling wl whn shkn up to ld over 1f out: sn clr: eased nr fin* **7/2**2

50-1 **2** *3 1/4* **Allanit (GER)**21 555 7-9-2 **60**... TomQueally 8 72+
(Barney Curley) *led: pushed along 2f out: hdd over 1f out: sn no ch w wnr but styd on wl for clr 2nd* **11/4**1

6052 **3** *1 3/4* **Lytham (IRE)**7 728 10-8-9 **53**....................................... J-PGuillambert 7 62+
(Tony Carroll) *in tch: hdwy over 3f out: styd on to take 3rd fnl 2f but nvr gng pce to trble ldng duo* **5/1**3

006- **4** *7* **Waahej**238 4019 5-9-7 **65**.. ChrisCatlin 10 61
(Peter Hiatt) *chsd ldrs in 3rd: rdn and no imp 3f out: wknd into 4th fnl 2f* **14/1**

0-00 **5** *5* **Mutajaaser (USA)**14 647 6-8-13 **57**..............................(p) JoeFanning 4 43
(Kevin Morgan) *chsd ldrs: rdn over 3f out: wknd 2f out* **16/1**

6664 **6** *nk* **Fedora (IRE)**12 687 5-8-10 **59**....................................(t) KylieManser(5) 3 45
(Olivia Maylam) *in rr: rdn along over 4f out: mod prog fnl 2f* **14/1**

5306 **7** *2 1/4* **Turjuman (USA)**15 644 6-9-5 **63**................................ StevieDonohoe 1 44
(Willie Musson) *a towards rr* **8/1**

5450 **8** *10* **Emerald Girl (IRE)**12 687 4-9-1 **62**.......................... RobertLButler(3) 5 24
(Paddy Butler) *a towards rr* **66/1**

0-45 **9** *3/4* **Stoppers (IRE)**21 556 4-9-7 **65**.................................... PaulHanagan 13 26
(Robert Mills) *in tch: rdn 4f out: sn btn* **12/1**

/40- **10** *5* **Integria**203 3581 5-9-7 **65**... TonyCulhane 12 16
(George Baker) *sn in rr* **12/1**

3233 **11** *6* **Noble Attitude**13 675 5-8-7 **51** oh6................................ FrannyNorton 2 —
(Richard Guest) *chsd ldrs: rdn 1/2-way: sn wknd* **16/1**

2m 6.53s (-1.47) **Going Correction** +0.05s/f (Slow) **11** Ran SP% **118.6**
Speed ratings (Par 101): **107,104,103,97,93 93,91,83,82,78 73**
toteswingers:1&2:£3.00, 1&3:£3.20, 2&3:£3.80 CSF £13.67 CT £48.37 TOTE £6.00: £2.10, £1.20, £1.90; EX 18.60 Trifecta £113.80 Pool: £4,723.64 - 30.70 winning units..
Owner Gallagher Equine Ltd **Bred** Shadwell Estate Company Limited **Trained** Lower Beeding, W Sussex

FOCUS
Strong and solid form for the class with a couple of well-handicapped runners dominating and an in-form course specialist taking third. The first three pulled clear. Although the first two finishers filled the front two positions pretty much throughout, the pace was good (field soon unusually strung out) and time was by far the quickest of the three 1m2f races, including 0.98 seconds faster than the 90-rated Georgebernardshaw managed in the conditions event, although that race was modestly run.

803 BETDAQ.COM EXCHANGE PRICE MULTIPLES CONDITIONS STKS 1m 2f (P)
6:30 (6:31) (Class 4) 4-Y-O+ **£3,238** (£963; £481; £240) **Stalls** Low

Form RPR

0-60 **1** **Georgebernardshaw (IRE)**18 615 6-9-2 90............... PaulHanagan 5 93+
(David Simcock) *mde virtually all: rdn over 2f out: edgd lft u.p ins fnl f: wnt rt sn after: drvn out* **8/1**

0-21 **2** *3/4* **Round Won (USA)**14 647 4-9-2 82................................ JimCrowley 1 92+
(William Knight) *chsd wnr to 4f out: rdn and outpcd over 2f out: rallied [illegible] ins fnl f: gng on cl home but a hld* **3/1**2

-313 **3** *1 1/2* **Layline (IRE)**11 702 4-9-2 91.................................. RichardHughes 3 89+
(Gay Kelleway) *rrd stalls: hld up in rr: pushed along and one pce 2f out: drvn and styd on to take 3rd nr fin but nt trble ldng duo* **5/2**1

0-10 **4** *1/2* **Taaresh (IRE)**32 436 6-9-2 85.. JoeFanning 2 88
(Kevin Morgan) *chsd ldrs: rdn to dispute 2nd over 1f out tl ins fnl f: nvr gng pce to rch wnr and wknd nr fin* **16/1**

-356 **5** *1/2* **Baylini**11 702 7-8-11 87.. JamesDoyle 4 82
(Jamie Osborne) *chsd ldrs: wnt 2nd 4f out: rdn and effrt over 2f out: nvr quite rchd wnr: one pce fnl f and wknd fnl 100yds* **11/2**3

0212 **6** *11* **Scamperdale**25 525 9-8-13 94.................................... KierenFox(3) 6 66
(Brian Baugh) *in rr but in tch: rdn 3f out: wknd fr 2f out* **3/1**2

2m 7.51s (-0.49) **Going Correction** +0.05s/f (Slow) **6** Ran SP% **110.9**
Speed ratings (Par 105): **103,102,101,100,100 91**
toteswingers:1&2:£5.10, 1&3:£7.00, 2&3:£1.60 CSF £31.22 TOTE £11.20: £3.60, £2.00; EX 54.10.
Owner Dr Marwan Koukash **Bred** Quay Bloodstock **Trained** Newmarket, Suffolk

FOCUS
They didn't look to go that quick, a view supported by the time being 0.98 seconds slower than the earlier Class 6 handicap, although that was a good race for the grade. This is probably just ordinary conditions race form and the winner didn't need to be anywhere near his best.
Round Won(USA) Official explanation: jockey said gelding was hampered on bend

804 RACING AT SKYSPORTS.COM CLAIMING STKS 7f (P)
7:00 (7:00) (Class 5) 3-Y-O+ **£2,047** (£604; £302) **Stalls** Low

Form RPR

2422 **1** **Jake The Snake (IRE)**14 648 10-9-12 84........................ NeilCallan 1 87
(Tony Carroll) *stdd s: hld up in rr: qcknd and hdwy on outside over 1f out: rdn to ld ins fnl f: readily* **7/4**1

-025 **2** *1 3/4* **Bawaardi (IRE)**22 548 5-10-0 79.................................. PaulHanagan 4 84
(Richard Fahey) *trckd ldrs in 3rd: qcknd to ld ins fnl 2f: hdd u.p ins fnl f: sn one pce* **7/2**3

2113 **3** *3* **Hinton Admiral**14 648 7-9-12 78............................... MichaelStainton 6 75
(Jane Chapple-Hyam) *t.k.h: trckd ldr: rdn and hung rt appr fnl 2f: wknd into 3rd appr fnl f* **7/2**3

-245 **4** *18* **Samarinda (USA)**17 623 8-9-9 77...............................(p) MickyFenton 5 25
(Pam Sly) *led tl hdd ins fnl 2f: sn btn: eased and virtually p.u fnl f* **5/2**2

1m 26.48s (0.48) **Going Correction** +0.05s/f (Slow) **4** Ran SP% **109.4**
Speed ratings (Par 103): **99,97,93,73**
CSF £7.97 TOTE £3.20; EX 10.70.
Owner D Morgan & M B Clarke **Bred** J F Tuthill **Trained** Cropthorne, Worcs

FOCUS
Only four runners, but the form seems straightforward if not a race to put any great faith in. The pace was just ordinary.
Samarinda(USA) Official explanation: jockey said gelding lost its action

805 LAY BACK AND WIN AT BETDAQ.COM CASINO H'CAP 1m 4f (P)
7:30 (7:30) (Class 5) (0-75,75) 4-Y-O+ **£2,047** (£604; £302) **Stalls** Centre

Form RPR

0311 **1** **Sir Boss (IRE)**7 728 6-9-5 **73** 6ex...................................... TomEaves 3 79
(Michael Mullineaux) *chsd ldrs: rdn to ld ins fnl 2f: drvn out ins fnl f: hld on wl* **9/2**3

0-03 **2** *hd* **Epsom Salts**8 718 6-9-2 **70**.. IanMongan 7 75
(Pat Phelan) *s.i.s: in rr: rdn and hung rt over 2f out: styd on u.p ins fnl f: fin wl to take 2nd cl home: nt quite rch wnr* **3/1**1

2335 **3** *nk* **Camps Bay (USA)**5 772 7-9-5 **73**................................ HayleyTurner 5 78
(Conor Dore) *chsd ldrs: rdn and outpcd over 2f out: styd on u.p to chse wnr ins fnl f: kpt on but a jst hld: lost 2nd cl home* **14/1**

603- **4** *1 3/4* **Shades Of Grey**143 6959 4-8-12 **68**................................. AdamKirby 4 70
(Clive Cox) *in rr: drvn along 4f out: hdwy u.p fr 2f out: nvr gng pce to rch ldng trio and one pce ins fnl f* **10/1**

5511 **5** *1* **Visions Of Johanna (USA)**12 695 6-9-0 **68**................ JimmyQuinn 6 69
(Ian Williams) *in rr: hdwy on ins over 2f out: drvn to chse ldrs over 1f out: nvr quite on terms: outpcd ins fnl f* **5/1**

00-4 **6** *1* **Sir Royal (USA)**7 723 6-9-7 **75**................................ FergusSweeney 2 74
(Brendan Powell) *chsd ldr: rdn and ev ch over 2f out: wknd ins fnl f* **10/1**

0-52 **7** *shd* **Time Square (FR)**17 621 4-9-0 **70**................................(t) LukeMorris 1 69
(Tony Carroll) *chsd ldrs: rdn and ev ch 2f out: wknd ins fnl f* **4/1**2

4-25 **8** *2* **Beat Route**17 621 4-8-5 **66**................................ JemmaMarshall(5) 8 62
(Michael Attwater) *led: hdd insde fnl 2f: wknd fnl f* **9/1**

2m 33.91s (-0.59) **Going Correction** +0.05s/f (Slow)
WFA 4 from 6yo+ 2lb **8** Ran SP% **114.7**
Speed ratings (Par 103): **103,102,102,101,100 100,100,98**
toteswingers:1&2:£2.80, 1&3:£11.20, 2&3:£10.60 CSF £18.49 CT £173.05 TOTE £3.30: £1.20, £1.40, £5.00; EX 19.60 Trifecta £224.70 Pool: £6,994.42 - 23.03 winning units..
Owner I S Ross **Bred** Mrs E R Cantillon **Trained** Alpraham, Cheshire

FOCUS
A few in-form runners lined-up and the form looks fair, rated through the tird and fifth. The early pace was just ordinary.

806 BETDAQ MOBILE APPS H'CAP (LONDON MILE QUALIFIER) 1m (P)
8:00 (8:00) (Class 5) (0-70,72) 4-Y-O+ **£2,047** (£604; £302) **Stalls** Low

Form RPR

01-0 **1** **Tewin Wood**13 666 4-9-7 **70**... LiamJones 6 80
(Alan Bailey) *mde all: rdn over 2f out: styd on strly fnl f* **8/1**

1-21 **2** *2 1/4* **Al Aqabah (IRE)**7 727 6-9-9 **72** 6ex..............................(b) NeilCallan 4 77
(Brian Gubby) *in tch: t.k.h: awkward and swtchd to outside bnd 3f out: styd on u.p to chse wnr ins fnl f but no imp* **5/2**1

03-4 **3** *nk* **Strophic**16 634 4-9-2 **65**.. RichardHughes 11 69
(Giles Bravery) *hld up in rr: hdwy and drvn appr fnl 2f: styd on to chse wnr appr fnl f but no imp: one pce into 3rd ins fnl f* **9/2**2

5613 **4** *shd* **Peadar Miguel**12 685 4-9-6 **69**...................................... AdamKirby 7 73
(Noel Quinlan) *in rr: hrd drvn and hdwy over 1f out: styd on u.p ins fnl f to cl on plcd horses nr fnish but no ch w wnr* **5/1**3

6330 **5** *1* **Ilie Nastase (FR)**12 685 7-9-5 **68**................................ HayleyTurner 8 70
(Conor Dore) *in rr: hdwy and swtchd to outside bnd 3f out: styd on u.p fnl 2f and kpt on ins fnl f but nvr gng pce to get into contention* **16/1**

-300 **6** *2* **Pipers Piping (IRE)**25 522 5-9-6 **69**....................(v) MichaelStainton 2 66
(Jane Chapple-Hyam) *chsd ldrs: rdn over 2f out: wknd fnl f* **10/1**

00-4 **7** *3/4* **Exceedingly Bold**13 666 4-9-7 **70**................................ DaneO'Neill 1 65
(Jo Crowley) *chsd ldrs: rdn over 2f out: wknd fnl f* **9/2**2

-050 **8** *3/4* **Aviso (GER)**21 556 7-9-3 **66**...................................... VinceSlattery 5 60
(David Evans) *in rr: sme hdwy on ins fr 3f out: nvr rchd ldrs and wknd wl over 1f out* **33/1**

00-6 **9** *17* **Prince Of Thebes (IRE)**42 310 10-9-4 **67**.................... LukeMorris 10 22
(Michael Attwater) *chsd wnr to 3f out: wknd qckly over 2f out* **20/1**

1500 **10** *10* **Unbreak My Heart (IRE)** [illegible]..........(p) RobertLButler(3) [illegible]
(Paddy Butler) *chsd ldrs tl wknd 3f out* **40/1**

1m 39.54s (-0.26) **Going Correction** +0.05s/f (Slow) **10** Ran SP% **117.8**
Speed ratings (Par 103): **103,100,100,100,99 97,96,95,78,68**
toteswingers:1&2:£9.30, 1&3:£9.40, 2&3:£2.10 CSF £28.13 CT £106.01 TOTE £12.20: £2.70, £2.00, £1.80; EX 36.30 Trifecta £154.10 Pool: £277.11 - 1.33 winning units..
Owner Denco Thermal Limited **Bred** Perle D'Or Partnership **Trained** Newmarket, Suffolk

FOCUS
A modest handicap, but the time was okay, being 0.48 seconds faster than the following Class 7 event. Straightforward form with the winner rated back to his best.

807 GOFFS READY-TO-RUN SALE AT KEMPTON H'CAP 1m (P)
8:30 (8:30) (Class 7) (0-50,50) 4-Y-O+ **£1,535** (£453; £226) **Stalls** Low

Form RPR

-065 **1** **Queenie's Star (IRE)**35 382 4-8-13 **49** ow1..................... AdamKirby 8 56
(Michael Attwater) *in tch: hdwy on outside over 2f out: str run u.p to chal 1f out: slt ld ins fnl f: rdn and styd on wl: on top cl home* **11/1**

2023 **2** *1/2* **Holyfield Warrior (IRE)**14 652 7-8-7 **50**..................... LucyKBarry(7) 5 56
(Ralph Smith) *in rr: hdwy on outside fr over 2f out: drvn to take slt ld 1f out: narrowly hdd ins fnl f: outpcd clsng stages* **5/1**1

60-2 **3** *3/4* **Lilli Palmer (IRE)**27 490 4-8-9 **45**................................ MartinLane 9 49
(Mike Murphy) *chsd ldrs: rdn to chal over 1f out: one pce u.p whn hung lft ins fnl f* **8/1**

06-2 **4** *2 1/4* **Royal Envoy (IRE)**35 386 8-8-11 **47**....................... MichaelStainton 10 46
(Jane Chapple-Hyam) *s.i.s: sn prom: chal 2f out: sn slt ld: hdd 1f out: wknd ins fnl f* **10/1**

6155 **5** *shd* **Aggbag**20 575 7-8-12 **48**.. NeilCallan 12 47
(Tony Carroll) *chsd ldrs: rdn 3f out: outpcd 2f out: styd on again fnl f* **6/1**2

0-00 **6** *1 1/4* **Spirit Of Love (IRE)**26 504 4-8-13 **49**..................(p) AndreaAtzeni 3 45
(Michael Wigham) *in rr tl styd on fr over 1f out: kpt on cl home* **9/1**

0-40 **7** *1* **Poesmulligan (IRE)**13 662 5-8-9 **45**............................ SteveDrowne 7 39
(Linda Jewell) *s.i.s: in rr: hdwy over 1f out: nt rch ldrs* **16/1**

00-0 **8** *1 1/4* **Set To Go**33 418 4-9-0 **50**...(b) ChrisCatlin 14 41
(Tor Sturgis) *chsd ldrs: slt ld over 2f out: sn hdd: wknd fnl f* **25/1**

2564 **9** *1 1/4* **Kenswick**14 652 4-8-6 **49**....................................(v) AlexEdwards(7) 11 37
(Pat Eddery) *chsd ldrs tl wknd fnl f* **12/1**

5003 **10** *2 1/4* **Escardo (GER)**20 573 8-8-9 **45**................................ TonyCulhane 1 28
(David Bridgwater) *in rr: sme hdwy over 1f out: nvr rchd ldrs* **14/1**

0406 **11** *1 1/4* **Pictures (IRE)**17 624 4-8-9 **48**.................................... KierenFox(3) 4 28
(John Bridger) *in rr: brief effrt 2f out: sn wknd* **16/1**

00-4 **12** 1 ¼ **Braddock (IRE)**[52] 181 8-8-2 **45**..............................(t) JakePayne(7) 2 22
(Bill Turner) *chsd ldrs: wknd over 2f out* **12/1**

-421 **13** 2 ½ **On The Cusp (IRE)**[27] 490 4-8-11 **50**..................(p) RobertLButler(3) 6 21
(Michael Chapman) *led tl hdd over 2f out: sn btn* **7/1**[3]

1m 40.02s (0.22) **Going Correction** +0.05s/f (Slow) **13** Ran SP% **119.6**
Speed ratings (Par 97): **100,99,98,96,96 95,94,92,91,89 88,86,84**
toteswingers:1&2:£17.90, 1&3:£17.70, 2&3:£10.50 CSF £65.23 CT £475.96 TOTE £14.50: £4.50, £2.10, £3.80; EX 98.90 Trifecta £175.80 Pool: £237.56 - 1.00 winning units..
Owner The Attwater Partnership **Bred** Noel And Michael Buckley **Trained** Epsom, Surrey

FOCUS
The time was 0.48 seconds slower than the earlier Class 5 handicap. Sound but low-grade form.
T/Plt: £25.80 to a £1 stake. Pool: £61,743.48. 1,743.49 winning tickets. T/Qpdt: £19.90 to a £1 stake. Pool: £7,172.38. 266.10 winning tickets. ST

[786]LINGFIELD (L-H)
Wednesday, March 9

OFFICIAL GOING: Standard
Wind: fresh, across Weather: dry, partly cloudy

808 LINGFIELD PARK OWNERS CLUB H'CAP 1m 5f (P)
2:10 (2:10) (Class 5) (0-70,70) 4-Y-0+ **£2,047** (£604; £302) **Stalls** Low

Form RPR

5-43 **1** **Where's Susie**[17] 621 6-9-7 **68**.................................... GeorgeBaker 3 76+
(Michael Madgwick) *hld up in tch in midfield: n.m.r 3f out: hdwy on inner over 2f out: shkn up and hdwy between horses to ld jst ins fnl f: sn rdn and asserted: pushed out towards fin: comf* **7/2**[1]

5332 **2** 1 **Stadium Of Light (IRE)**[15] 639 4-9-5 **69**.................. PaulMulrennan 7 75
(James Given) *chsd ldr 11f out: pressed ldr 9f out: ev ch and rdn over 2f out: led over 1f out: hdd jst ins fnl f: styd on same pce after* **7/1**

6-53 **3** ½ **Indian Ghyll (IRE)**[17] 622 5-9-2 **63**................................ LiamKeniry 6 68
(Roger Teal) *stdd s: t.k.h: hld up in tch towards rr: hdwy and nt clr run over 2f out tl swtchd rt jst over 1f out: styd on u.p ins fnl f: no threat to wnr* **9/2**[2]

0-43 **4** ¾ **Profit's Reality (IRE)**[11] 697 9-9-7 **68**........................ NeilCallan 2 72
(Michael Attwater) *chsd ldr tl 11f out: styd chsng ldrs: n.m.r over 3f out: pressed ldrs u.p jst over 1f out: styd on same pce ins fnl f* **7/1**

-054 **5** shd **Diamond Twister (USA)**[11] 697 5-8-10 **60**.................... KierenFox(3) 1 64
(John Best) *dwlt and bustled along early: sn hld up in last trio and t.k.h: rdn and effrt jst over 2f out: swtchd lft ent fnl f: styd on u.p fnl f: nt rch ldrs* **11/2**

1002 **6** 2 ½ **Barodine**[19] 588 8-9-0 **61**.. MartinLane 4 61
(Ron Hodges) *chsd ldrs: rdn and unable qck over 2f out: wknd ent fnl f* **25/1**

10- **7** nse **Humor Me Rene (USA)**[92] 7736 4-9-3 **70**............... MatthewDavies(3) 5 70
(George Baker) *stdd s: hld up in tch in last pair: rdn and effrt on outer bnd 2f out: edgd lft u.p 1f out: kpt on ins fnl f: nvr gng pce to rch ldrs* **12/1**

4-34 **8** 3 ¼ **Soundbyte**[35] 392 6-8-13 **60**...................................... FergusSweeney 9 56
(John Gallagher) *sn led: rdn over 2f out: hdd over 1f out: wknd jst ins fnl f* **5/1**[3]

54/6 **9** 2 ¼ **Drawback (IRE)**[35] 393 8-8-12 **59**.............................. StephenCraine 10 51
(Barry Brennan) *t.k.h: hld up in tch: pushed along and nt clr run 2f out: rdn and no rspnse over 1f out: wknd fnl f: eased towards fin* **25/1**

2m 46.73s (0.73) **Going Correction** +0.05s/f (Slow)
WFA 4 from 5yo+ 3lb **9** Ran SP% **112.8**
Speed ratings (Par 103): **99,98,98,97,97 96,95,93,92**
toteswingers:1&2:£3.80, 1&3:£5.50, 2&3:£6.90 CSF £27.54 CT £109.47 TOTE £4.30: £1.10, £2.20, £2.40; EX 14.50 Trifecta £50.80 Pool: £383.60 - 5.58 winning units..
Owner Recycled Products Limited **Bred** Mrs L R Burrage **Trained** Denmead, Hants

FOCUS
The majority of runners were in fair form for this competitive handicap. It was run at a steady pace and quite a few raced keenly in the early stages. They finished quite compressed and the form is limited.

809 MARRIOTT HOTEL AT LINGFIELD PARK APPRENTICE H'CAP 1m (P)
2:40 (2:40) (Class 6) (0-55,58) 4-Y-0+ **£1,535** (£453; £226) **Stalls** High

Form RPR

-005 **1** **Miss Bounty**[8] 722 6-8-12 **52**..............................(p) NathanAlison(3) 11 58
(Jim Boyle) *hld up towards rr: hdwy over 2f out: chsd ldrs 2f out: rdn hands and heels to chal 1f out: led wl ins fnl f: pushed out* **12/1**

0- **2** ¾ **Breezed Well (IRE)**[222] 4563 4-9-4 **55**.......................(t) AshleyMorgan 7 60
(James McAuley, Ire) *chsd ldrs: pushed into ld ent fnl 2f: u.p and hrd pressed 1f out: hdd and one pce wl ins fnl f* **14/1**

4221 **3** nk **Grey Boy (GER)**[7] 730 10-9-2 **58** 6ex.................. GeorgeDowning(5) 3 62
(Tony Carroll) *chsd ldrs: rdn and effrt ent fnl 2f: swtchd lft ent fnl f: styd on same pce ins fnl f* **3/1**[1]

/205 **4** ½ **Haulit**[19] 589 5-9-1 **52**.. KieranO'Neill 1 55
(Gary Moore) *t.k.h: hld up in tch on inner: rdn and effrt 2f out: edging rt ent fnl f: kpt on wl u.p fnl 100yds: nt rch ldrs* **6/1**[2]

0-36 **5** hd **Jonnie Skull (IRE)**[1] 800 5-9-1 **52**...........................(t) TobyAtkinson 5 55
(Phil McEntee) *broke wl: sn stdd and hld up in midfield: rdn and hdwy over 2f out: chsd ldr 2f out: ev ch 1f out: no ex and btn fnl 100yds: nt clr run towards fin* **14/1**

0-04 **6** 5 **Illuminative (USA)**[8] 722 5-9-0 **54**........................(p) RyanPowell(3) 12 45
(Zoe Davison) *stdd s: hld up in last trio: rdn and effrt bnd 2f out: styd on same pce fnl f: nvr trbld ldrs* **11/1**

2006 **7** 1 **Dilys Maud**[12] 687 4-8-13 **55**...............................(b) ShaneBKelly(5) 9 44
(Roger Ingram) *v.s.a: pushed along early: bhd: n.m.r on inner and barging match w rival ent fnl 2f: switching rt and stl nt clr run wl over 1f out tl over 1f out: kpt on u.p fnl f: n.d* **14/1**

0-33 **8** nk **Fine Ruler (IRE)**[21] 555 7-8-13 **53**........................ JamesRogers(3) 8 41
(Martin Bosley) *hld up in midfield: hdwy on outer over 2f out: rdn and unable qck 2f out: wknd ent fnl f* **6/1**[2]

65-0 **9** 3 ¼ **Officer Lily (USA)**[8] 722 4-8-11 **53**............................ IanBurns(5) 6 33
(John Best) *stdd s: hld up in last trio: stl plenty to do whn n.m.r and barging match w rival ent fnl 2f: rdn and no hdwy over 1f out: n.d* **10/1**[3]

-300 **10** 2 ¾ **Tous Les Deux**[21] 555 8-8-12 **52**.....................(p) MatthewCosham(3) 4 26
(Dr Jeremy Naylor) *t.k.h: chsd ldr tl led 5f out: rdn and hdd ent fnl 2f: wknd qckly over 1f out* **20/1**

555 **11** 2 **Evey P (IRE)**[13] 664 4-8-11 **53**.................................. LucyKBarry(5) 2 23
(Gary Brown) *taken down early: t.k.h: in tch in midfield: rdn and nt qckning whn nt clr run and hmpd bnd ent fnl 2f: sn bhd* **6/1**[2]

-020 **12** 22 **Zeffirelli**[27] 485 6-9-4 **55**.. MartinHarley 10 —
(Michael Quinn) *led tl 5f out: chsd ldrs tl lost pl qckly 2f out: bhd and lost tch over 1f out: eased ins fnl f: t.o* **12/1**

1m 38.24s (0.04) **Going Correction** +0.05s/f (Slow) **12** Ran SP% **125.4**
Speed ratings (Par 101): **101,100,99,99,99 94,93,92,89,86 84,62**
toteswingers:1&2:£57.50, 2&3:£16.00, 1&3:£7.50 CSF £178.62 CT £654.28 TOTE £18.80: £5.40, £8.40, £1.10; EX 284.10 TRIFECTA Not won..
Owner Friends Of The Samson Centre Partnership **Bred** J M Beever **Trained** Epsom, Surrey
■ Stewards' Enquiry : Toby Atkinson two-day ban: careless riding (Mar 23-24)

FOCUS
A modest apprentice handicap. The first five were tightly bunched but pulled clear of the rest. Limited form.
Zeffirelli Official explanation: jockey said gelding lost its action

810 BREATHE SPA AT LINGFIELD MARRIOTT H'CAP 7f (P)
3:10 (3:10) (Class 6) (0-60,63) 4-Y-0+ **£1,535** (£453; £226) **Stalls** Low

Form RPR

30-3 **1** **Patavium Prince (IRE)**[19] 589 8-9-5 **58**........................ DaneO'Neill 7 67
(Jo Crowley) *in tch: hdwy to trck ldrs and nt clr run ent fnl 2f: rdn and effrt over 1f out: led 1f out: kpt on wl: rdn out* **9/2**[3]

20-P **2** ¾ **Signora Frasi (IRE)**[27] 489 6-9-0 **60**...................... DavidKenny(7) 12 67
(Tony Newcombe) *hld up in last trio: pushed along and hdwy over 2f out: kpt edging lft fr over 1f out: chsd ldrs jst ins fnl f: kpt on to go 2nd nr fin* **11/1**

0-35 **3** ½ **Tuscan King**[12] 685 4-9-6 **59**.................................(tp) RobertHavlin 3 65
(Bernard Llewellyn) *in tch: lost pl and nudged along 5f out: pushed along and hdwy over 2f out: rdn over 1f out: chsd wnr ins fnl f: no ex fnl 75yds: lost 2nd nr fin* **15/2**

0/11 **4** 2 **Stoneacre Gareth (IRE)**[6] 752 7-9-10 **63** 6ex................ AdamKirby 8 64
(K F Clutterbuck) *sn led and grad crossed to rail: rdn and hdd ent fnl 2f: sn led again: hdd 1f out: wknd ins fnl f* **11/4**[1]

-204 **5** 1 ¼ **Sonny G (IRE)**[7] 727 4-9-3 **59**.................................... KierenFox(3) 1 56
(John Best) *chsd ldrs: effrt u.p on inner over 1f out: unable qck ent fnl f: wknd fnl 150yds* **7/1**

6-60 **6** nk **Crazy Parachute**[8] 722 4-8-9 **55**....................... ChelseyBanks(7) 4 52
(Gary Moore) *taken down early: stdd s and v.s.a: sn swtchd lft: t.k.h: hld up bhd: clsd 4f out: c wd bnd 2f out: rdn ent fnl f: styd on but nvr trbld ldrs* **22/1**

-662 **7** 3 **Tudor Prince (IRE)**[19] 589 7-9-7 **60**............................ NeilCallan 11 49
(Tony Carroll) *racd keenly: chsd ldrs on outer: rdn and ev ch over 2f out: led ent fnl 2f: sn hdd: wknd ent fnl f* **4/1**[2]

000- **8** ¾ **Goose Green (IRE)**[174] 6125 7-8-9 **48**.......................... HayleyTurner 2 35
(Ron Hodges) *in tch in midfield: rdn and struggling over 2f out: wknd wl over 1f out: wl btn fnl f* **33/1**

050- **9** 2 ¼ **Teen Ager (FR)**[69] 8023 7-9-0 **53**................................ LiamKeniry 9 34
(Paul Burgoyne) *t.k.h: chsd ldr: rdn and ev ch over 2f out: wknd over 1f out: fdd fnl f* **18/1**

0002 **10** 90 **Loyal Royal (IRE)**[12] 683 8-9-7 **60**...................(bt) RichardKingscote 10 —
(Milton Bradley) *swtchd lft after s: bhd: lost tch over 2f out: sn eased and virtually p.u fnl f: t.o* **15/2**

1m 24.74s (-0.06) **Going Correction** +0.05s/f (Slow) **10** Ran SP% **121.8**
Speed ratings (Par 101): **102,101,100,98,96 96,93,92,89,—**
toteswingers:1&2:£14.80, 1&3:£4.60, 2&3:£17.40 CSF £55.74 CT £383.18 TOTE £4.50: £1.20, £2.60, £2.50; EX 71.70 TRIFECTA Not won..
Owner Mrs Liz Nelson **Bred** J P Hardiman **Trained** Whitcombe, Dorset

FOCUS
An ordinary handicap run at a fair pace. The winner is rated back to his Polytrack best.
Stoneacre Gareth(IRE) Official explanation: jockey said gelding ran too free
Loyal Royal(IRE) Official explanation: trainer's rep said gelding finished distressed

811 GREAT DEALS ON ANNUAL MEMBERSHIP MAIDEN STKS 7f (P)
3:40 (3:42) (Class 5) 3-Y-O **£1,910** (£564; £282) **Stalls** Low

Form RPR

1 **Cool Macavity (IRE)** 3-8-10 0........................... MatthewLawson(7) 3 75+
(B W Hills) *hld up off the pce in midfield: stl plenty to do and effrt ent fnl 2f: swtchd to outer and hdwy over 1f out: rdn and str run fnl f to ld fnl 75yds: sn in command: quite impressive* **7/2**[2]

2 1 ¾ **Blink Of An Eye** 3-9-3 0.. HayleyTurner 7 68+
(Michael Bell) *sn crossed to rail: chsd ldrs: rdn jst over 2f out: ev ch ent fnl f: outpcd by wnr fnl 75yds* **5/1**

3 ½ **Jackie Love (IRE)** 3-8-12 0..................................... KirstyMilczarek 8 62
(John Ryan) *chsd ldrs: nt clr run and switching lft jst over 2f out: ev ch over 1f out: led 1f out: hdd and outpcd fnl 75yds* **12/1**

0-20 **4** 2 ¼ **Cold Secret**[21] 559 3-9-3 73... DaneO'Neill 9 61
(David Elsworth) *in tch: clsd and chsd ldrs over 2f out: unable qck u.p over 1f out: styd on same pce fnl f* **9/2**[3]

2 **5** 2 **Fog Cutter (IRE)**[18] 610 3-9-3 0...............................(t) CathyGannon 4 55
(James McAuley, Ire) *sn led: rdn ent fnl 2f: hdd 1f out: wknd ins fnl f* **11/4**[1]

6 ½ **Beauchamp Zest** 3-8-12 0...(t) JamesDoyle 5 53+
(Hans Adielsson) *s.i.s: bhd: rdn and effrt on outer bnd ent fnl 2f: unable qck and no hdwy over 1f out: styd on ins fnl f: gng on fin: nvr trbld ldrs* **12/1**

0- **7** nk **Valdaw**[300] 2048 3-9-3 0.. EddieCreighton 11 53
(Joseph Tuite) *stdd and swtchd lft s: sn pushed along towards rr: rdn and no hdwy over 2f out: kpt on fnl f: nvr trbld ldrs* **33/1**

50 **8** 1 ¾ **Ability Girl**[25] 519 3-8-12 0... JackMitchell 2 43
(Chris Wall) *in tch: rdn and unable qck whn nt clr run and hmpd ent fnl 2f: sn wknd* **25/1**

9 ¾ **Shelagh (IRE)** 3-8-12 0... FergusSweeney 1 45+
(Jo Crowley) *hld up in rr: short of room and sltly hmpd ent 2f out: rdn and no hdwy 1f out: pushed along and wl hld ins fnl f* **12/1**

000- **10** 10 **Trust Me Boy**[105] 7550 3-9-3 50................................(v[1]) SamHitchcott 10 19
(John E Long) *sn bhd: rdn in last pair 5f out: lost tch 3f out* **66/1**

11 24 **Lord Sun** 3-9-3 0... RobbieFitzpatrick 6 —
(Peter Grayson) *racd keenly: chsd ldr tl jst over 2f out: sn wknd: t.o fnl f* **66/1**

1m 25.25s (0.45) **Going Correction** +0.05s/f (Slow) **11** Ran SP% **116.6**
Speed ratings (Par 98): **99,97,96,93,91 91,90,88,87,76 48**
toteswingers:1&2:£3.80, 1&3:£11.80, 2&3:£6.00 CSF £20.67 TOTE £4.90: £2.00, £1.20, £6.60; EX 20.40 Trifecta £235.80 Part won. Pool: £318.69 - 0.60 winning units..
Owner Triermore Stud **Bred** C O P Hanbury **Trained** Lambourn, Berks
■ Stewards' Enquiry : Hayley Turner one-day ban: failed to ride to draw (Mar 23)

FOCUS
A modest maiden. The pace was decent and the well-backed winning newcomer was quite impressive. He looks sure to do better.

812 ATR LIVE DAILY FROM CHELTENHAM 8AM H'CAP 5f (P)
4:10 (4:10) (Class 6) (0-60,60) 4-Y-0+ **£1,535** (£453; £226) **Stalls** High

Form RPR
0-40 **1** **Triskaidekaphobia**[7] 735 8-9-1 **54**......................(t) FrankieMcDonald 10 62
(Paul Fitzsimons) *led after 1f: mde rest: rdn over 1f out: r.o wl and a holding runner-up ins fnl f* **33/1**
2233 **2** ¾ **Black Baccara**[5] 766 4-9-2 **60**........................(be) DanielleMcCreery(5) 2 65
(Phil McEntee) *hld up in tch: shuffled bk and lost pl over 3f out: hdwy and nt clr run wl over 1f out: rdn to chse wnr 1f out: r.o but hld by wnr fnl 100yds* **9/2**[2]
-606 **3** 1 ½ **Commandingpresence (USA)**[13] 664 5-8-10 **52**......... KierenFox(3) 7 52
(John Bridger) *bhd: rdn and effrt 2f out: stl plenty to do 1f out: r.o strly ins fnl f to go 3rd nr fin: nvr trbld ldrs* **12/1**
-364 **4** nk **Athwaab**[14] 658 4-9-2 **55**.. AdamKirby 8 54
(Noel Quinlan) *chsd ldrs tl wnt 2nd over 2f out tl unable qck u.p 1f out: wknd fnl 75yds* **8/1**
2314 **5** nk **Steel City Boy (IRE)**[7] 735 8-9-2 **55**............................(p) JimmyQuinn 9 52
(Derek Shaw) *dwlt: bhd: rdn and effrt over 1f out: drvn 1f out: kpt on ins fnl f: nvr gng pce to threaten wnr* **5/1**[3]
5-42 **6** ½ **Jimmy Ryan (IRE)**[48] 224 10-9-5 **58**.........................(t) J-PGuillambert 6 54
(Tim McCarthy) *led to s and taken down v early: in tch towards rr on outer: rdn and effrt over 1f out: kpt on but no real imp fnl f* **6/1**
0-3 **7** 1 **Jolly Ranch**[30] 443 5-9-2 **55**.. FergusSweeney 5 47
(Tony Newcombe) *led for 1f: chsd wnr tl 1/2-way: unable qck u.p wl over 1f out: wknd 1f out* **7/2**[1]
0425 **8** nk **Thoughtsofstardom**[12] 691 8-8-13 **52**............................. LukeMorris 1 43
(Phil McEntee) *in tch: effrt on inner to chse ldrs over 1f out: no prog ent fnl f: wknd ins fnl f* **12/1**
6066 **9** 1 **Step It Up (IRE)**[5] 766 7-8-11 **57**............................(p) DanielCremin(7) 3 44
(Jim Boyle) *t.k.h: in tch: hdwy to chse ldrs over 2f out: rdn and unable qck over 1f out: wknd ins fnl f* **16/1**
-054 **10** 2 **Lithaam (IRE)**[12] 691 7-8-7 **46** oh1.....................(p) RichardKingscote 4 29
(Milton Bradley) *n.m.r sn after s: hdwy towards outer and chsd ldrs 3f out: rdn and unable qck ent fnl 2f: wknd u.p over 1f out* **9/1**

58.45 secs (-0.35) **Going Correction** +0.05s/f (Slow) **10** Ran SP% **116.7**
Speed ratings (Par 101): **104,102,100,99,99 98,97,96,94,91**
toteswingers:1&2:£26.60, 1&3:£32.50, 2&3:£11.70 CSF £176.45 CT £1976.15 TOTE £58.30: £15.10, £3.00, £3.20; EX 233.60 TRIFECTA Not won..
Owner Raymond Tooth And Steve Gilbey **Bred** K Bowen **Trained** Upper Lambourn, Berks
■ The first winner as a trainer for former jockey Paul Fitzsimons. He took over the licence on the death of his partner Julia Tooth.

FOCUS
A modest handicap in which there was a surprise all-the-way winner. Limited form.

813 ATR CHELTENHAM PREVIEW MONDAY 5.30PM CLAIMING STKS 1m 4f (P)
4:40 (4:40) (Class 6) 4-Y-0+ **£1,535** (£453; £226) **Stalls** Low

Form RPR
33-6 **1** **Grande Caiman (IRE)**[35] 392 7-8-9 73.................. SilvestreDeSousa 8 69+
(Geoffrey Harker) *hld up towards rr: sltly hmpd 10f out: stl gng wl ent fnl 2f: nt clr run over 1f out: rdn to chse ldr jst ins fnl f: r.o wl to ld last strides* **6/5**[1]
502- **2** shd **Resplendent Light**[158] 6571 6-8-13 73.........................(t) RobertHavlin 4 73+
(Bernard Llewellyn) *hld up in tch: trckd ldrs gng wl and nt clr run 2f out tl over 1f out: pushed ahd ent fnl f: rdn ins fnl f: r.o tl hdd last strides* **8/1**[3]
45-0 **3** 3 ¼ **Evident Pride (USA)**[18] 614 8-9-7 75.............................. IanMongan 7 76
(Brett Johnson) *chsd ldrs: jinked rt 10f out: rdn and effrt ent fnl 2f: chsd ldng pair ins fnl f: one pce and no imp after* **16/1**
4 2 ½ **Tarwiyna (IRE)** 4-8-4 0.. CathyGannon 5 57
(James McAuley, Ire) *stdd s: hld up in rr: hdwy into midfield 5f out: rdn and chsd ldrs 2f out: wknd ent fnl f* **50/1**
-405 **5** 1 **Suntrap**[11] 697 4-8-9 73...(v) LukeMorris 6 60
(William Knight) *chsd ldrs: hmpd 10f out: rdn and unable qck ent fnl 2f: outpcd and swtchd rt jst over 1f out: no imp fnl f* **3/1**[2]
-022 **6** 1 **Force Group (IRE)**[12] 695 7-8-11 65.......................(b) NeilCallan 3 59
(Nick Littmoden) *s.i.s: t.k.h and chsd ldr over 10f out: wnt wd over 7f out: rdn to ld ent fnl 2f: hdd jst over 1f out: wknd ins fnl f* **8/1**[3]
60/3 **7** 2 **Superius (IRE)**[14] 656 6-8-12 80...................................(b) LiamKeniry 1 56
(Emma Lavelle) *t.k.h: led tl rdn and hdd ent fnl 2f: wknd ent fnl f* **14/1**
0-24 **P** **Beauchamp Xiara**[25] 529 5-8-0 65............................ SophieDoyle(3) 2 —
(Hans Adielsson) *stdd s: t.k.h: hld up in last pair: sddle slipped after 2f: eased and lost tch over 5f out: eventually p.u and dismntd nr fin* **10/1**

2m 32.93s (-0.07) **Going Correction** +0.05s/f (Slow)
WFA 4 from 5yo+ 2lb **8** Ran SP% **116.3**
Speed ratings (Par 101): **102,101,99,98,97 96,95,—**
toteswingers:1&2:£3.00, 1&3:£6.20, 2&3:£6.10 CSF £12.22 TOTE £2.60: £1.30, £1.80, £4.30; EX 14.20 Trifecta £105.30 Pool: £580.91 - 4.08 winning units..
Owner John J Maguire **Bred** Sweet Retreat Syndicate **Trained** Thirkleby, N Yorks

FOCUS
Five of the runners had official rating between 73 and 80 in this fair claimer. It was run at a stop-start gallop and the heavily backed favourite was a last-gasp winner. Straightforward form.
Beauchamp Xiara Official explanation: jockey said saddle slipped

814 ATR LIVE FROM CHELTENHAM 8AM H'CAP 1m 2f (P)
5:10 (5:10) (Class 5) (0-70,70) 4-Y-0+ **£2,047** (£604; £302) **Stalls** Low

Form RPR
013- **1** **Prince Apollo**[156] 6632 6-9-6 **69**...(t) NeilCallan 3 77+
(Gerard Butler) *stdd s: hld up in tch towards rr: nt clr run and hmpd over 2f out: stl plenty to do and hdwy over 1f out: chsd clr ldng pair ins fnl f: str run to ld last strides* **11/4**[1]
U6-1 **2** hd **Fashionable Gal (IRE)**[12] 687 4-9-7 **70**.......................... EddieAhern 7 78
(Neil King) *t.k.h: chsd ldr: rdn clr w rival 2f out: led over 1f out: drvn fnl f: kpt on wl tl hdd last strides* **3/1**[2]
0642 **3** nk **Free Tussy (ARG)**[21] 565 7-9-2 **65**.............................(bt) LiamKeniry 4 72
(Gary Moore) *chsd ldrs: rdn and qcknd on inner to ld over 2f out: clr w rival 2f out: hdd over 1f out: kpt on and ev ch tl no ex nr fin* **11/2**[3]
020- **4** 3 **Silent Oasis**[105] 7548 5-9-4 **67**.................................... FergusSweeney 10 68
(Brendan Powell) *hld up in tch: hdwy on outer over 3f out: wnt 3rd but outpcd by ldng pair 2f out: kpt on same pce fr over 1f out* **7/1**
0-54 **5** nse **Thundering Home**[12] 692 4-8-13 **62**.......................... RobbieFitzpatrick 1 65
(Michael Attwater) *in tch in midfield: rdn and outpcd whn nt clr run 2f out: swtchd rt and rallied jst over 1f out: r.o ins fnl f: no threat to ldrs* **16/1**
0-14 **6** 1 ½ **Midnight Strider (IRE)**[54] 170 5-9-4 **67**........................... DaneO'Neill 6 65
(Joseph Tuite) *hld up in last pair: bhd a wall of horses and nt clr run over 2f out: rdn over 1f out: swtchd rt 1f out: kpt on fnl f: nvr able to chal* **14/1**
00-6 **7** hd **Amends (USA)**[5] 772 4-8-8 **60**.. KierenFox(3) 5 58
(John Best) *t.k.h: hld up in tch: n.m.r over 2f out: sn swtchd rt and rdn: outpcd 2f out: kpt on one pce and no threat to ldrs after* **14/1**
30-5 **8** nse **Valkov**[17] 626 4-8-7 **56**.. LukeMorris 8 53
(Tony Carroll) *in tch: dropped to rr over 5f out: rdn and outpcd jst over 2f out: kpt on but no ch w ldrs fr over 1f out* **12/1**
35-0 **9** 3 ½ **Soul Heaven**[18] 614 4-9-4 **67**.......................................(t) CathyGannon 2 57
(James McAuley, Ire) *led tl over 2f out: sn rdn and struggling ent fnl 2f: wknd over 1f out* **16/1**
000- **10** 2 ½ **Mister Bit (IRE)**[105] 7562 4-8-13 **62**................................... SteveDrowne 9 49
(John Best) *in tch: rdn and unable qck jst over 2f out: lost pl and nt clr run wl over 2f out: sn bhd* **14/1**

2m 9.38s (2.78) **Going Correction** +0.05s/f (Slow) **10** Ran SP% **119.0**
Speed ratings (Par 103): **90,89,89,87,87 85,85,85,82,80**
toteswingers:1&2:£4.00, 1&3:£2.90, 2&3:£2.70 CSF £11.33 CT £42.80 TOTE £4.30: £1.70, £1.10, £2.60; EX 9.90 Trifecta £46.00 Pool: £273.87 - 4.40 winning units..
Owner Asaad Al Banwan **Bred** Juddmonte Farms Ltd **Trained** Newmarket, Suffolk

FOCUS
A fair handicap run at a steady pace. Sound efforts ftom the front trio and the winner is capable of better again.
T/Plt: £568.70 to a £1 stake. Pool:£73,517.75 - 94.36 winning tickets T/Qpdt: £61.00 to a £1 stake. Pool:£4,934.36 - 59.80 winning tickets SP

FONTAINEBLEAU
Wednesday, March 9

OFFICIAL GOING: Turf: good to soft

815a PRIX DU GRAND MAITRE (CONDITIONS) (4YO+) (TURF) 5f 110y
1:05 (12:00) 4-Y-0+ **£12,931** (£5,172; £3,879; £2,586; £1,293)

RPR
1 **Lisselan Diva (IRE)**[151] 5-8-9 0...............................(p) WilliamsSaraiva 7 93
(Mme J Bidgood, France) **14/1**
2 ¾ **Calbuco (FR)**[25] 7-8-13 0.. RaphaelMarchelli 5 95
(B Dutruel, France) **48/10**[3]
3 nk **Salut L'Africain (FR)**[90] 7800 6-8-13 0.........................(p) ThomasHuet 1 94
(Robert Collet, France) **7/1**
4 1 ½ **Personified (GER)**[148] 6830 4-8-9 0.................................. GaryCarter 3 85
(Mme J Bidgood, France) **41/1**
5 shd **Fred Lalloupet**[107] 7535 4-8-13 0.................................. GregoryBenoist 2 89
(D Smaga, France) **2/1**[1]
6 nk **Time Prisoner (USA)**[151] 4-9-5 0.................................. MaximeGuyon 4 94
(A Fabre, France) **14/5**[2]
7 2 **Ajara (IRE)**[54] 168 5-8-9 0.. SylvainRuis 8 77
(Mme L Braem, Belgium) **12/1**
8 4 **Reignier**[186] 5742 4-8-13 0.. RobertWinston 6 68
(Mrs K Burke) *wl away and chsd ldrs: rdn and wknd ins fnl 2f* **7/1**

63.90 secs (63.90) **8** Ran SP% **118.6**
PARI-MUTUEL (all including 1 euro stakes): WIN 11.20 (coupled with Personified); PLACE 3.70, 2.30, 2.70; DF 44.60; SF 154.90.
Owner Haras de Bouquetot Sarl **Bred** Colman O'Flynn **Trained** France

801 KEMPTON (A.W) (R-H)
Thursday, March 10

OFFICIAL GOING: Standard
Wind: Fresh, across Weather: Mainly clear

816 BODUGI.COM LAUNCHES SOCIAL BETTING CLAIMING STKS 1m (P)
5:30 (5:30) (Class 6) 4-Y-0+ **£1,535** (£453; £226) **Stalls** Low

Form RPR
3121 **1** **I Confess**[6] 761 6-8-4 70.......................................(b) MatthewCosham(7) 2 78
(David Evans) *mde all: rdn over 2f out: drvn clr over 1f out: comf* **11/4**[3]
4-00 **2** 2 **Dubai Miracle (USA)**[35] 405 4-9-0 78.............................. MartinLane 4 75
(David Simcock) *chsd ldng pair: rdn 4f out: wnt 2nd over 1f out: no imp* **5/2**[2]
4-12 **3** 1 ¾ **Ours (IRE)**[66] 18 8-9-3 93...(p) BarryMcHugh 5 74
(John Harris) *s.s: sn wl bhd: drvn along 1/2-way: styd on wl ins fnl f: nrst fin* **9/4**[1]
44 **4** 3 **Slikback Jack (IRE)**[50] 205 4-9-3 76........................... AdrianNicholls 6 67
(David Nicholls) *chsd wnr: rdn and hung rt over 2f out: wknd over 1f out* **5/1**
5 1 ¼ **Priority Buy (IRE)** 4-8-13 0.. CathyGannon 1 61
(James McAuley, Ire) *s.s: mod 5th most of way: effrt over 2f out: no ex over 1f out* **14/1**
500- **6** 1 **Ocean Rosie (IRE)**[142] 7006 4-8-5 54.................................. LukeMorris 3 50
(Tony Carroll) *dwlt: mainly 4th: rdn 4f out: wknd over 1f out* **33/1**

1m 40.47s (0.67) **Going Correction** +0.10s/f (Slow) **6** Ran SP% **112.3**
Speed ratings (Par 101): **100,98,96,93,92 91**
toteswingers:1&2 £2.80, 2&3 £1.30, 1&3 £1.70 CSF £10.06 TOTE £5.20: £2.70, £1.10; EX 6.20.
Owner J E Abbey **Bred** Gestut Sohrenhof **Trained** Pandy, Monmouths

FOCUS
This had the look of a tactical affair, but the most straightforward character proved easily the best. The winner didn't need to improve much and this isn't form to place too much faith in.

817 BOOK KEMPTON TICKETS ON 0844 579 3008 CLAIMING STKS 1m (P)
6:00 (6:00) (Class 6) 3-Y-O **£1,535** (£453; £226) **Stalls** Low

Form RPR
4143 **1** **Ad Vitam (IRE)**[9] 717 3-8-9 60...(tp) RobertHavlin 2 64
(Bernard Llewellyn) *plld hrd in 5th: led over 1f out: drvn out* **8/1**
2324 **2** ¾ **Riot Police (USA)**[12] 699 3-9-3 72...................................(p) MartinLane 4 70
(David Simcock) *hld up in 6th: rdn over 2f out: hdwy over 1f out: styd on to take 2nd fnl 75yds* **11/4**[2]
2321 **3** ½ **Better Self**[6] 770 3-8-3 71.. MatthewCosham(7) 3 62
(David Evans) *sn chsng ldr: led 2f out tl over 1f out: kpt on same pce* **11/10**[1]
60-0 **4** 3 **Kyncraighe (IRE)**[64] 52 3-8-0 52.................................(t) KatiaScallan(7) 6 52
(Alastair Lidderdale) *hld up towards rr: hdwy 2f out: no imp ins fnl f* **40/1**

-055 **5** *2 ½* **Farmer's Wife**[24] 543 3-8-4 55........(p) DavidProbert 1 43
(Bernard Llewellyn) *sn prom: wknd over 1f out* **14/1**

2323 **6** *6* **Beating Harmony**[14] 668 3-8-9 58........(p) RichardHughes 7 35
(Tony Carroll) *led and controlled modest pce: increased tempo over 2f out: sn hdd and btn* **13/2**[3]

00-0 **7** *nk* **Heart Felt**[24] 543 3-8-5 57........(p) AndrewHeffernan(3) 8 33
(Roy Brotherton) *chsd ldrs: rdn 3f out: wknd 2f out* **40/1**

0 **8** *4 ½* **Sunley Surprise**[26] 520 3-8-11 0........ DaneO'Neill 9 26
(David Elsworth) *s.s: rdn over 3f out: a bhd* **25/1**

1m 42.43s (2.63) **Going Correction** +0.10s/f (Slow) **8** Ran SP% **114.1**
Speed ratings (Par 96): **90,89,88,85,83 77,76,72**
.Ad Vitam was claimed by J Chapple-Hyam for £4000. Riot Police was claimed by A. W. Carroll for £8000.\n\x\x
Owner B J Llewellyn **Bred** Michelle Morgan **Trained** Fochriw, Caerphilly

FOCUS
The form looks straightforward considering the efforts of the first and third, but the time was almost two seconds slower than the other 1m claimer on the card, which had fewer runners.

818 GOFFS READY-TO-RUN SALE AT KEMPTON MAIDEN STKS 6f (P)
6:30 (6:30) (Class 5) 3-Y-0+ **£2,047** (£604; £302) **Stalls** Low

Form RPR

5-42 **1** **Rambo Will**[36] 380 3-8-12 63........ DavidProbert 6 64
(J R Jenkins) *w ldrs: rdn to ld 1f out: hld on gamely* **10/1**

2- **2** *nk* **Oh My Days (IRE)**[231] 4303 3-8-12 0........ LukeMorris 5 63
(Clive Cox) *hld up towards rr: hdwy over 2f out: rdn to chal over 1f out: kpt on wl: jst hld* **3/1**[2]

0- **3** *¾* **Alpha Delta Whisky**[185] 5808 3-8-12 0........ ChrisCatlin 7 61
(John Gallagher) *slt ld tl rdn and hdd 1f out: kpt on* **50/1**

22-2 **4** *1 ½* **Midnight Rider (IRE)**[20] 593 3-8-12 75........ JackMitchell 3 56
(Chris Wall) *plld hrd in 5th: lost pl and rdn over 2f out: rallied 1f out: styd on same pce* **4/5**[1]

20 **5** *1 ¼* **Lennoxwood (IRE)**[17] 636 3-8-12 0........ LiamKeniry 2 52
(Mark Usher) *hld up in 6th: effrt 2f out: one pce appr fnl f* **20/1**

026/ **6** *2 ¾* **Mymumsaysimthebest**[633] 2980 6-9-12 75........ RobertHavlin 9 47
(Jamie Poulton) *w ldrs tl wknd over 1f out* **8/1**[3]

0 **7** *3 ½* **Savinien**[14] 663 3-8-12 0........ CathyGannon 1 32
(David Evans) *dwlt: bhd: hrd rdn over 2f out: n.d* **66/1**

00 **8** *15* **Masie Grey**[22] 559 3-8-2 0........ DeclanCannon(5) 4 —
(David Elsworth) *chsd ldrs tl hrd rdn and wknd qckly over 2f out* **40/1**

6 **9** *35* **Abacist (IRE)**[20] 593 3-8-12 0........(b1) JimCrowley 10 —
(Ralph Beckett) *rdn leaving stalls: hung lft and v wd thrght: sn t.o* **25/1**

1m 13.68s (0.58) **Going Correction** +0.10s/f (Slow)
WFA 3 from 6yo 14lb **9** Ran SP% **115.3**
Speed ratings (Par 103): **100,99,98,96,94 91,86,66,19**
toteswingers:1&2 £4.50, 2&3 £22.10, 1&3 £66.30 CSF £38.27 TOTE £13.30: £4.40, £2.50, £13.60; EX 44.60.
Owner Mr & Mrs T H Bambridge **Bred** T H Bambridge **Trained** Royston, Herts

FOCUS
With the well-fancied favourite disappointing once again, this didn't look like a stong contest. The winner only needed to reproduce his best form.

819 PANORAMIC, THE PLACE TO DINE H'CAP 1m 4f (P)
7:00 (7:00) (Class 7) (0-50,51) 4-Y-0+ **£1,535** (£453; £226) **Stalls** Centre

Form RPR

-026 **1** **Little Richard (IRE)**[6] 771 12-8-13 49 ow1........(p) AdamKirby 2 56
(Mark Wellings) *trckd ldrs in 5th: led 2f out: drvn out: hld on gamely* **6/1**[3]

-633 **2** *nk* **Wrecking Crew (IRE)**[17] 631 7-8-9 45........ JamesMillman 4 52
(Rod Millman) *t.k.h towards rr: hdwy 2f out: r.o to press wnr fnl 50yds: clsng at fin: jst hld* **9/2**[2]

0-6P **3** *½* **Maydream**[6] 768 4-8-8 47........ LukeMorris 3 52
(Jimmy Fox) *mid-div: rdn 4f out: hdwy 2f out: pressed ldrs ins fnl f: kpt on* **14/1**

00-3 **4** *hd* **Prince Blue**[13] 688 4-8-12 50........ SamHitchcott 1 56
(John E Long) *led 1f: prom: drvn to chse wnr over 1f out: kpt on* **7/1**

53-0 **5** *1 ½* **Filun**[21] 574 6-9-0 50........(t) LiamKeniry 8 53
(Anthony Middleton) *hld up in rr: shkn up 3f out: styd on fnl 2f: nrst fin* **20/1**

6-44 **6** *4 ½* **Galiotto (IRE)**[20] 592 5-9-1 51 ow1........(v1) GeorgeBaker 14 47
(Gary Moore) *dwlt: hdwy to trck ldr after 2f: led on bit over 2f out: sn hdd and rdn: fnd little* **3/1**[1]

0-06 **7** *2* **Tecktal (FR)**[22] 560 8-8-6 47........ JemmaMarshall(5) 11 40
(Pat Phelan) *s.s: bhd: sme hdwy into midfield 1/2-way: wknd 2f out* **8/1**

0-00 **8** *1 ½* **Helpmeronda**[7] 748 5-8-9 45........ GrahamGibbons 7 35
(Ian Williams) *dwlt: towards rr: rdn and hdwy on rail over 2f out: wknd over 1f out* **33/1**

5-63 **9** *6* **Hatch A Plan (IRE)**[62] 81 10-8-11 47........ KirstyMilczarek 10 28
(Mouse Hamilton-Fairley) *towards rr: rdn and hdwy over 3f out: wknd 2f out* **33/1**

0-60 **10** *1* **Dawson Creek (IRE)**[45] 277 7-8-13 49........ IanMongan 13 28
(Luke Dace) *led after 1f tl over 2f out: sn wknd* **25/1**

-404 **11** *½* **Harrys**[21] 569 4-8-7 48........ AndrewHeffernan(3) 6 26
(Jane Chapple-Hyam) *mid-div tl wknd 3f out* **40/1**

0/ **12** *5* **Beech View (IRE)**[508] 6625 6-8-2 45........(t) KirstenSmith(7) 9 15
(Martin Bosley) *mid-div: hdwy and prom after 4f: wknd 4f out: sn bhd* **66/1**

0-66 **13** *10* **State General (IRE)**[45] 280 5-9-0 50........ RichardHughes 12 4
(Tony Carroll) *s.s: rdn 3f out: a bhd* **12/1**

00-0 **14** *10* **Alhudhud (USA)**[15] 649 5-8-9 45........(t) AndreaAtzeni 5 —
(Kevin Morgan) *chsd ldrs tl wknd qckly and eased over 2f out* **25/1**

2m 35.11s (0.61) **Going Correction** +0.10s/f (Slow)
WFA 4 from 5yo+ 2lb **14** Ran SP% **117.7**
Speed ratings (Par 97): **101,100,100,100,99 96,95,94,90,89 89,85,79,72**
toteswingers:1&2 £5.80, 2&3 £13.80, 1&3 £19.10 CSF £29.78 CT £366.92 TOTE £6.00: £2.10, £1.90, £8.60; EX 36.60.
Owner Mark Wellings Racing **Bred** Rathbarry Stud **Trained** Six Ashes, Shropshire

FOCUS
A weak contest at best and the pace in the early stages could hardly be called quick. The tempo only significantly increased 4f out. Limited form.

820 GOFFS READY-TO-RUN SALE MARCH 29TH H'CAP 7f (P)
7:30 (7:30) (Class 5) (0-70,70) 4-Y-0+ **£2,047** (£604; £302) **Stalls** Low

Form RPR

3420 **1** **Dvinsky (USA)**[19] 612 10-9-2 65........(b) PaulDoe 2 72
(Jane Chapple-Hyam) *mde all: hld on gamely u.p fnl 2f* **10/1**

2/0 **2** *½* **Enigma Code (UAE)**[19] 612 6-9-6 69........(t) CathyGannon 7 75
(James McAuley, Ire) *chsd wnr: drvn to chal over 1f out: nt qckn* **8/1**

2521 **3** *nk* **Double Carpet (IRE)**[14] 666 8-9-3 66........ EddieAhern 1 71
(Garry Woodward) *chsd ldng pair: rdn over 2f out: kpt on wl ins fnl f* **7/2**[1]

1311 **4** *½* **West Leake (IRE)**[17] 637 5-9-0 63........ LiamKeniry 6 67
(Paul Burgoyne) *t.k.h in rr of midfield: rdn and no prog 2f out: r.o ins fnl f* **4/1**[2]

000- **5** *¾* **Stevie Gee (IRE)**[129] 7274 7-9-7 70........ RichardKingscote 9 72
(Ian Williams) *t.k.h in midfield: rdn and outpcd over 2f out: styd on ins fnl f* **12/1**

5-31 **6** *hd* **Co Dependent (USA)**[41] 345 5-9-7 70........ FergusSweeney 5 71
(Jamie Osborne) *dwlt: towards rr: rdn and hdwy 2f out: one pce ins fnl f* **13/2**

5-24 **7** *2* **Valmina**[21] 577 4-8-13 62........ LukeMorris 11 58
(Tony Carroll) *bhd: rdn over 2f out: n.d* **12/1**

-510 **8** *nk* **Abriachan**[14] 666 4-9-5 68........ AdamKirby 8 63
(Noel Quinlan) *hld up in 5th: rdn and btn 2f out* **11/2**[3]

-540 **9** *shd* **Cut And Thrust (IRE)**[17] 637 5-8-9 65........ LucyKBarry(7) 4 60
(Mark Wellings) *chsd ldrs tl wknd over 2f out* **11/1**

00- **10** *1* **Major Eradicator (USA)**[274] 2875 4-8-8 57 oh4 ow1... SteveDrowne 10 49
(Alastair Lidderdale) *dwlt: rdn over 2f out: a bhd* **33/1**

1m 26.56s (0.56) **Going Correction** +0.10s/f (Slow) **10** Ran SP% **117.8**
Speed ratings (Par 103): **100,99,99,98,97 97,95,94,94,93**
toteswingers:1&2 £11.70, 2&3 £8.80, 1&3 £5.40 CSF £88.31 CT £348.60 TOTE £10.40: £2.40, £5.60, £1.10; EX 99.70.
Owner David Hardaker **Bred** Eclipse Bloodstock & Tipperary Bloodstock **Trained** Dalham, Suffolk

FOCUS
It paid to race handily in this as the first two early finished in that order, and nothing came quickly enough from the rear to pose them a threat. The form is clearly limited, with the winner as good a guide as any.

821 BODUGI.COM 15K CHELTENHAM GIVEAWAY H'CAP 6f (P)
8:00 (8:00) (Class 7) (0-50,50) 4-Y-0+ **£1,535** (£453; £226) **Stalls** Low

Form RPR

0-00 **1** **Running Mate (IRE)**[22] 556 4-9-0 50........(t) IanMongan 1 57
(Jo Crowley) *prom: drvn to chal 1f out: led fnl 50yds* **15/2**

-440 **2** *nk* **Fiancee (IRE)**[27] 517 5-8-6 45........(p) AndrewHeffernan(3) 4 51
(Roy Brotherton) *led: hrd rdn and kpt on wl fr over 1f out: hdd fnl 50yds* **13/2**[3]

-060 **3** *1 ¼* **Raimond Ridge (IRE)**[31] 443 5-8-5 48........ MatthewCosham(7) 11 50
(Derek Shaw) *s.i.s: bhd: rdn and hdwy 2f out: r.o: nrst fin* **8/1**

630- **4** *1 ½* **Diddums**[327] 1391 5-8-9 50........ AmyScott(5) 5 49
(Alastair Lidderdale) *hld up in rr: pushed along and styd on fnl 2f: nvr nrr* **9/2**[1]

040- **5** *1 ¼* **Stonecrabstomorrow (IRE)**[84] 7885 8-8-12 48........(b) JamesDoyle 8 42
(Frank Sheridan) *prom tl outpcd fnl 2f* **7/1**

0602 **6** *1* **Head To Head (IRE)**[13] 691 7-8-10 46........(bt) TomEaves 9 37
(Alan Brown) *chsd ldr tl hrd rdn and no ex fnl 2f* **15/2**

0264 **7** *shd* **Jessica Wigmo**[13] 690 8-8-9 45........ LukeMorris 7 36
(Tony Carroll) *hld up in rr of midfield: hdwy and hrd rdn 2f out: wknd jst over 1f out* **5/1**[2]

030 **8** *6* **Rightcar**[13] 690 4-8-11 47........(b) RobbieFitzpatrick 3 20
(Peter Grayson) *awkward s and missed break: plld hrd in midfield: hmpd on rail over 4f out: effrt and hrd rdn 2f out: sn wknd* **11/1**

6-40 **9** *5* **Spring Leap**[24] 537 4-8-13 49........(p) JimCrowley 10 7
(Robert Cowell) *chsd ldrs tl 1/2-way* **10/1**

1m 13.89s (0.79) **Going Correction** +0.10s/f (Slow) **9** Ran SP% **112.7**
Speed ratings (Par 97): **98,97,95,93,92 90,90,82,76**
toteswingers:1&2 £6.60, 2&3 £12.00, 1&3 £11.90 CSF £53.90 CT £401.83 TOTE £8.80: £2.30, £3.40, £2.90; EX 41.40.
Owner Kilstone Limited **Bred** Paul Ennis **Trained** Whitcombe, Dorset

FOCUS
This was a competitive race and bookies priced up the field between 9-2 and a miserly 11-1. Weak and limited form, with the winner stepping forward.

822 DAY TIME, NIGHT TIME, GREAT TIME H'CAP 7f (P)
8:30 (8:30) (Class 4) (0-85,85) 4-Y-0+ **£3,885** (£1,156; £577; £288) **Stalls** Low

Form RPR

06-0 **1** **New Leyf (IRE)**[19] 613 5-9-6 84........ SteveDrowne 9 94
(Jeremy Gask) *towards rr: n.m.r after 2f: hdwy 2f out: drvn to dispute ld ins fnl f: jst prevailed* **14/1**

RR-5 **2** *shd* **Stefanki (IRE)**[15] 651 4-9-1 79 ow1........ GeorgeBaker 5 89
(Gary Moore) *chsd ldrs: drvn to dispute ld ins fnl f: jst pipped* **12/1**

4231 **3** *1 ¾* **Ocean Legend (IRE)**[22] 557 6-9-5 83........ RichardHughes 3 88
(Tony Carroll) *chsd ldrs: rdn to dispute 2nd 2f out: nt qckn ins fnl f* **9/4**[1]

360- **4** *1 ¼* **Edgewater (IRE)**[119] 7414 4-8-11 75........ DaneO'Neill 8 77
(John Akehurst) *mid-div: effrt over 2f out: styd on ins fnl f* **16/1**

5621 **5** *nse* **Thunderball**[15] 648 5-8-9 80........(b) LeonnaMayor(7) 6 82
(David Nicholls) *led at gd pce: 4 l clr 1/2-way: hrd rdn over 1f out: hdd & wknd ins fnl f* **10/1**

410- **6** *3 ¼* **Sakhee's Pearl**[146] 6887 5-9-1 79........ IanMongan 11 72
(Jo Crowley) *a abt same pl: rdn and no hdwy fnl 2f* **10/1**

424- **7** *¾* **Space Station**[124] 7352 5-9-5 83........ EddieAhern 14 76
(Simon Dow) *t.k.h towards rr: rdn 3f out: styd on ins fnl f* **7/1**[3]

1240 **8** *1 ¼* **Bonnie Prince Blue**[15] 651 8-8-13 77........(b) PaulMulrennan 1 65
(James Given) *chsd clr ldr tl wknd over 2f out* **33/1**

0-00 **9** *nse* **The Scorching Wind (IRE)**[19] 613 5-9-7 85........(vt1) WilliamCarson 7 75
(Stuart Williams) *mid-div: hmpd and dropped to rr after 2f: rdn 3f out: sme late hdwy* **9/1**

-050 **10** *1 ¼* **Chat De La Burg (USA)**[18] 629 4-8-6 73........ KierenFox(3) 2 58
(John Best) *prom: outpcd and lost pl over 2f out: n.d after* **25/1**

302- **11** *1 ¾* **Poppanan (USA)**[162] 6478 5-8-11 80........ AdamBeschizza(5) 4 62
(Simon Dow) *rdn s: sn in tch: squeezed for room and lost pl after 2f: sme hdwy 2f out: n.d* **16/1**

20-0 **12** *3 ½* **L'Hirondelle (IRE)**[33] 438 7-9-5 83........ JimCrowley 12 54
(Michael Attwater) *bhd: rdn 3f out: n.d* **12/1**

-531 **13** *1 ¼* **Thrust Control (IRE)**[7] 744 4-8-3 74........ JacobButterfield(7) 10 42
(Brian Ellison) *mid-div tl wknd over 2f out* **6/1**[2]

25-0 **14** *3 ¼* **Green Earth (IRE)**[29] 473 4-8-4 73........ JemmaMarshall(5) 13 32
(Pat Phelan) *mid-div: wknd over 3f out: sn bhd* **33/1**

1m 24.68s (-1.32) **Going Correction** +0.10s/f (Slow) **14** Ran SP% **129.3**
Speed ratings (Par 105): **111,110,108,107,107 103,102,101,101,99 97,93,92,88**
toteswingers:1&2 £45.70, 2&3 £6.60, 1&3 £12.20 CSF £181.80 CT £543.04 TOTE £26.20: £6.40, £4.90, £1.80; EX 329.30.
Owner James W Burdett **Bred** John Weld **Trained** Sutton Veny, Wilts

FOCUS
A strongly run race and a fast time which suited those held up. The winner is rated back towards his best and the form has a solid feel.
T/Plt: £243.60 to a £1 stake. Pool of £81,972.89 - 245.61 winning tickets. T/Qpdt: £113.10 to a £1 stake. Pool of £7,694.13 - 50.30 winning tickets. LM

779 MEYDAN (L-H)
Thursday, March 10

OFFICIAL GOING: Tapeta: standard; turf: good

823a DUBAI DUTY FREE TENNIS CHAMPIONSHIPS (CONDITIONS RACE) (TURF) 7f
2:35 (2:35) 3-Y-O

£38,461 (£12,820; £6,410; £3,205; £1,923; £1,282)

RPR
1 **Crying Lightening (IRE)**[14] 680 3-8-3 99 JimmyQuinn 8 102
(Peter Chapple-Hyam) *in rr of mid-div: smooth prog 2f out: r.o wl ins fnl f: led fnl 55yds* **14/1**
2 ¾ **Chocolicious (SAF)**[35] 412 4-9-0 106 RyanMoore 10 105
(H J Brown, South Africa) *mid-div: chsd ldrs 2 1/2f out: led 1f out: hdd cl home* **11/4**[1]
3 2½ **Krypton Factor**[14] 680 3-8-7 100 (b) KierenFallon 4 97
(F Nass, Bahrain) *trckd ldr: led 2f out: hdd 1f out: one pce fnl 110yds* **7/1**
4 ¾ **Abjer (FR)**[7] 753 3-8-5 106 ow2 (b) AntiocoMurgia(6) 3 99
(I Mohammed, UAE) *slowly away: racd in rr: r.o wl fnl 2f: nrst fin* **16/1**
5 ¾ **Lord Of The Stars (USA)**[14] 680 3-8-7 99 TadhgO'Shea 9 93
(David Simcock) *trckd ldrs: ev ch 1 1/2f out: nt qcknd ins fnl f* **5/1**[3]
6 ¼ **Paulinho (ARG)**[7] 753 4-9-4 109 (t) BernardFayd'Herbe 11 98
(H J Brown, South Africa) *settled in rr: r.o fnl 2f but n.d* **14/1**
7 ¾ **Electric Waves (IRE)**[14] 681 3-8-5 106 RichardMullen 5 88
(Naif Alatawi, Saudi Arabia) *mid-div on rail: chsd ldrs 3f out: wknd ins fnl f* **10/3**[2]
8 1¾ **Abtasaamah (USA)**[14] 681 3-8-3 97 AhmedAjtebi 2 82
(Saeed Bin Suroor) *nr bttr than mid-div* **10/1**
9 1¼ **Gold Pearl (USA)**[136] 7116 3-8-7 82 TedDurcan 12 82
(S Seemar, UAE) *in rr of mid-div: n.d* **25/1**
10 8 **Rosina Grey**[14] 680 3-7-11 92 ow1 HarryBentley(7) 7 58
(S Seemar, UAE) *nvr able to chal* **12/1**
11 7 **Calling Elvis (BRZ)**[14] 680 4-9-4 97 ChristopheSoumillon 6 63
(A De Royer-Dupre, France) *a in rr* **12/1**
12 2 **Grand Duchy**[33] 458 3-8-7 79 RoystonFfrench 1 53
(M Al Muhairi, UAE) *sn led: hdd & wknd 2 1/2f out* **66/1**

1m 24.7s (84.70)
WFA 3 from 4yo 16lb **12** Ran SP% **127.9**
CSF: 56.75.
Owner J Barton & C Pizarro **Bred** Paulyn Limited **Trained** Newmarket, Suffolk

FOCUS
The rail was out 15 metres on the turf course. The leaders went off a bit too fast in this ordinary conditions event.

NOTEBOOK
Crying Lightening(IRE) had gone much too fast when finishing well behind a few of these in the Meydan Classic over 1m on her previous start and the combination of the drop in trip and switch to more patient tactics suited. This was her first success since landing a Leicester maiden on her debut, but she ran well in a few pattern races in Britain last year and is smart when at her best.
Chocolicious(SAF) didn't shape as though she wanted a drop in trip when third behind two smart fillies, Mahbooba and Reem, in the UAE 1,000 Guineas on Tapeta, but this more galloping turf track suited her, and so too did the strong pace. As it turned out, she was actually outstayed after being committed sooner than the winner.
Krypton Factor, a tough individual who was having his fifth Carnival start this year, returned to form and deserves credit considering he raced bang on the overly strong pace.
Abjer(FR) lost a few lengths with a slow start, but that wasn't such a bad thing considering the quick gallop and he stayed on well. This was a marked return to form from last year's Autumn Stakes winner, a particularly creditable effort considering that Ascot success came over 1m on soft ground and he's bred for stamina.
Lord Of The Stars(USA) was allowed a soft lead when winning over C&D earlier in the Carnival and hasn't been afforded that advantage in both starts since.
Paulinho(ARG) didn't run badly considering he ended up extremely wide in the straight.
Electric Waves(IRE) pulled much too hard when achieving little in a distant third in the UAE Oaks, and she was again too keen. She's a sprinter and her record suggests she prefers easier ground. (opnd 7-2)

824a DUBAI DUTY FREE GOLF WORLD CUP (H'CAP) (TAPETA) 1m 3f
3:15 (3:15) (100-112,112) 3-Y-O+

£67,307 (£22,435; £11,217; £5,608; £3,365; £2,243)

RPR
1 **Emirates Champion**[21] 585 5-9-2 108 (t) FrankieDettori 5 110+
(Saeed Bin Suroor) *trckd ldrs: led 2f out: r.o wl: comf* **7/4**[1]
2 4¾ **Mr Brock (SAF)**[7] 757 8-9-6 112 KShea 1 105
(M F De Kock, South Africa) *sn led: hdd 2f out: r.o but no ch w wnr* **7/1**[3]
3 ¾ **Bay Willow (IRE)**[14] 677 4-8-11 105 TedDurcan 3 96
(Saeed Bin Suroor) *trckd ldr: one pce fnl 1 1/2f but r.o* **6/1**[2]
4 1 **Prizefighting (USA)**[14] 677 4-9-1 108 (b) AhmedAjtebi 9 102+
(Mahmood Al Zarooni) *settled in rr: r.o fnl 2 1/2f but nvr able to chal* **6/1**[2]
5 1¼ **Monte Alto (IRE)**[11] 7-8-11 104 (t) RichardHills 10 91
(A Al Raihe, UAE) *a mid-div* **14/1**
6 1 **Hunting Tower (SAF)**[14] 676 9-9-2 108 (t) ChristopheSoumillon 8 94+
(M F De Kock, South Africa) *settled in rr: nvr nr to chal* **8/1**
7 ¼ **Sweet Lightning**[14] 679 6-8-11 104 WJSupple 6 88+
(Michael Dods) *nvr bttr than mid-div* **12/1**
8 shd **Kal Barg**[20] 605 6-8-10 102 WilliamBuick 7 87+
(D Selvaratnam, UAE) *settled in rr: rdn 4f out: n.d* **25/1**
9 3½ **Lost In The Moment (IRE)**[28] 498 4-8-8 101 (p) DaraghO'Donohoe 4 80+
(Saeed Bin Suroor) *Mid-div: trckd ldrs 3f out: wknd fnl 2f* **8/1**
10 8¼ **Bronze Cannon (USA)**[20] 608 6-9-2 108 (t) RyanMoore 2 72
(H J Brown, South Africa) *trckd ldrs tl 3f out: sn btn* **10/1**

2m 20.08s (1.68) **Going Correction** +0.35s/f (Slow)
WFA 4 from 5yo+ 1lb **10** Ran SP% **127.0**
Speed ratings: **107,103,103,102,101 100,100,100,97,91**
CSF: 16.20 TRI: 67.58.
Owner Godolphin **Bred** Gainsborough Stud Management Ltd **Trained** Newmarket, Suffolk

FOCUS
This handicap featured some in-form types, and there was an improving winner, but the pace was steady (time 4.30 seconds outside the course record), so it paid to race prominently.

NOTEBOOK
Emirates Champion was always well placed and improved his track record to 3-4, easily defying a 6lb rise for his latest C&D success on his reappearance. Simon Crisford said afterwards the winner is not being considered for World Cup night and also predicted the 5-y-o would struggle back in Europe, as he's so well suited to the Tapeta and would not be easy to place. Consequently, he may be kept in Dubai, but whatever the case, this performance suggested he's up to Group class when conditions are favourable. (opnd 9-4)
Mr Brock(SAF) was allowed a soft lead but he's weighted up to his best.
Bay Willow(IRE), up 5lb for his recent C&D win, was outpaced early in the straight before keeping on again and would have preferred a stronger gallop.
Prizefighting(USA) is difficult to win with, but this wasn't a bad performance seeing as he was keen early and ended up further back than was ideal.
Monte Alto(IRE), a non-Carnival winner last time, was stuck wide without cover for much of the way and is another who was inconvenienced by the lack of pace.
Hunting Tower(SAF) was set far too much to do, but probably wasn't good enough anyway.
Sweet Lightning didn't settle early and is at his best in strongly run races when the leaders come back to him.

825a DUBAI DUTY FREE FINEST SURPRISE (H'CAP) (TURF) 6f
3:50 (3:50) (100-122,122) 3-Y-O+

£67,307 (£22,435; £11,217; £5,608; £3,365; £2,243)

RPR
1 **J J The Jet Plane (SAF)**[21] 582 7-9-6 122 BernardFayd'Herbe 1 125
(M Houdalakis, South Africa) *trckd ldr: led 2f out: r.o wl: comf* **2/1**[1]
2 1¾ **Iver Bridge Lad**[7] 755 4-8-5 105 (b) JimmyQuinn 12 105
(John Ryan) *settled in rr: r.o wl fnl 2f but no ch w wnr* **12/1**
3 1¾ **Green Beret (IRE)**[7] 755 5-8-5 107 RoystonFfrench 10 99
(A Al Raihe, UAE) *trckd ldrs: ev ch 3f out: one pce fnl 1 1/2f* **7/2**[2]
4 ¼ **Doncaster Rover (USA)**[21] 582 5-8-6 108 TedDurcan 2 99
(David Brown) *mid-div: r.o same pce fnl 2f* **12/1**
5 2¼ **Alazeyab (USA)**[7] 755 5-8-5 106 (vt) AhmedAjtebi 3 91
(A Al Raihe, UAE) *sn led: hdd 2 1/2f out: r.o same pce* **6/1**[3]
6 2 **Musaalem (USA)**[20] 602 7-8-5 101 TadhgO'Shea 5 85
(Doug Watson, UAE) *settled in rr: nvr able to chal but r.o fnl 1 1/2f* **25/1**
7 ½ **Indomito (GER)**[7] 755 5-8-5 104 DaraghO'Donohoe 8 83
(P Vovcenko, Germany) *sn rdn in rr: n.d* **18/1**
8 5 **Orife (IRE)**[14] 678 4-8-5 101 (t) GHind 11 67
(Stephane Chevalier, UAE) *nvr bttr than mid-div* **20/1**
9 ¼ **Rock Jock (IRE)**[7] 754 4-8-5 104 WJSupple 7 66
(Tracey Collins, Ire) *nvr bttr than mid-div* **12/1**
10 8¾ **Everyday Heroes (USA)**[7] 754 5-8-5 100 WilliamBuick 6 38
(Saeed Bin Suroor) *trckd ldr tl 3f out: sn wknd* **12/1**
11 ½ **Montmorency (IRE)**[21] 587 5-8-5 102 (vt) RichardMullen 9 37
(S Seemar, UAE) *nvr able to chal* **20/1**
12 ¼ **Mariol (FR)**[20] 606 8-7-12 105 HarryBentley(7) 4 36
(Rod Collet, France) *nvr bttr than mid-div* **20/1**

1m 10.18s (70.18) **12** Ran SP% **124.0**
CSF: 27.79 TRI: 85.85.
Owner H S N Du Preez, C F Strydom et al **Bred** Mrs P J Devine **Trained** South Africa

FOCUS
Most of these were out of the handicap. There seemed no obvious draw bias, but the majority of the runners ended up middle to stands' side.

NOTEBOOK
J J The Jet Plane(SAF) ◆ didn't have to be at his best with most of these out of the weights, but clearly this was still a very smart effort. He had disappointed in a similar handicap on his Tapeta debut when reappearing in Dubai the previous month, but his trainer later admitted the horse was well above his ideal racing weight on that occasion and also said he still wasn't at his peak here, although he was getting there. The gelding travelled strongly throughout, and although edging towards the stands' side in the closing stages, having started from the opposite side of the track, he never looked in any danger. The return to turf evidently suited, although if a lack of fitness was a valid excuse last time then it's probably too early to say whether or not he acts on Tapeta. It's unlikely his connections will want to gamble with the surface on World Cup night, however, and it's almost certain he'll line up for the Al Quoz Sprint back on this turf course, when the drop to 5f shouldn't be too much of a concern. He should be a massive player, with the Dubai sprinting scene having otherwise looked ordinary so far.
Iver Bridge Lad, drawn on the opposite side to the winner, tanked along throughout and picked up when produced with his chance, but he was no match for J J The Jet Plane when that one arrived on the scene. He looks as though he'll be well suited by a drop to 5f, but is surely not an Al Quoz Sprint contender. (opnd 11-1)
Green Beret(IRE), too keen last time, showed speed and seemed to have his chance.
Doncaster Rover(USA), reported to have finished lame on his previous start, fared better this time but was still below his best. He was one of the few in the handicap proper.
Alazeyab(USA) ran better than he did the previous week but never threatened. (opnd 13-2)

826a DRC GOLD CUP SPONSORED BY DUBAI DUTY FREE (GROUP 3) (TURF) 2m
4:30 (4:30) 4-Y-O+

£76,923 (£25,641; £12,820; £6,410; £3,846; £2,564)

RPR
1 **Whispering Gallery**[42] 329 5-9-0 112 FrankieDettori 10 115+
(Saeed Bin Suroor) *trckd ldr: led 2 1/2f out: r.o wl: comf* **10/3**[2]
2 2¼ **Bergo (GER)**[21] 584 8-9-0 109 ChristopheSoumillon 2 112
(Gary Moore) *sn led: hdd 2 1/2f out: r.o wl* **20/1**
3 2¾ **Opinion Poll (IRE)**[21] 584 5-9-3 113 AhmedAjtebi 11 112+
(Mahmood Al Zarooni) *settled in rr: r.o fnl 2f: nrst fin* **5/2**[1]
4 1¼ **Mikhail Glinka (IRE)**[20] 603 4-8-8 110 (t) RyanMoore 5 106
(H J Brown, South Africa) *mid-div: trckd ldrs 7f out: ev ch 2 1/2f out: wknd ins fnl f* **7/1**
5 ½ **Sabotage (UAE)**[28] 498 5-9-0 102 TedDurcan 7 107
(Saeed Bin Suroor) *mid-div on rail: rdn and one pce 3f out* **12/1**
6 ¾ **Drunken Sailor (IRE)**[21] 584 6-9-0 112 (b) KierenFallon 9 106
(Luca Cumani) *in rr of mid-div: nvr able to chal* **8/1**
7 1 **La De Two (IRE)**[35] 413 5-9-0 108 (t) TadhgO'Shea 8 105
(Saeed Bin Suroor) *settled in rr: nvr nr to chal* **16/1**
8 ¼ **Royaaty (IRE)**[11] 5-9-0 100 PatCosgrave 1 104?
(M bin Shafya, UAE) *trckd ldng duo tl 3 1/2f out: wknd fnl 2f* **25/1**
9 1¾ **Age Of Reason (UAE)**[20] 603 6-9-0 108 DaraghO'Donohoe 3 102
(Saeed Bin Suroor) *trckd ldrs tl 2 1/2f out* **12/1**
10 2¼ **Claremont (IRE)**[21] 584 5-9-0 110 (b) WilliamBuick 6 100
(Mahmood Al Zarooni) *nvr bttr than mid-div* **13/2**[3]
11 2¼ **Muller (ARG)**[27] 8-9-0 104 (t) BernardFayd'Herbe 4 98
(S Al Harabi, Saudi Arabia) *a in rr* **25/1**

3m 29.44s (209.44)
WFA 4 from 5yo+ 5lb **11** Ran SP% **122.3**
CSF: 73.97.
Owner Godolphin **Bred** Darley **Trained** Newmarket, Suffolk

FOCUS
Only the third running of the DRC Gold Cup, but the race has already been awarded Group 3 status, upgraded from conditions class since last year. A good field lined up, but this is form to treat with caution as the pace was steady and the first two finishers were in front two for much of the way.

NOTEBOOK
Whispering Gallery didn't see his race out under front-running tactics when only fourth behind a couple of these rivals in this last year, so he was well suited by getting a lead in a race in which there wasn't maximum emphasis on stamina. He had reappeared with smart handicap success off 111 and is evidently as good as ever.
Bergo(GER) failed to beat a rival in the Nad Al Sheba Trophy on his Dubai debut the previous month, but that run was apparently needed and this was clearly a lot better. He was well ridden, though, and may be a bit flattered.
Opinion Poll(IRE) was again poorly ridden by Ahmed Ajtebi. The horse had been given too much to do off a steady pace on his previous start, yet despite this contest being run at a similarly sedate tempo, the jockey once again held his mount up last of all. There's little evidence Mahmood Al Zarooni's runner needs exaggerated waiting tactics and he did well to take third behind two much more sensibly placed runners. He can do even better when returned to his favoured soft surface.
Mikhail Glinka(IRE) ruined his chance by continually wanting to hang left in the straight.
Sabotage(UAE) failed to pick up sufficiently and continues below his best.
Drunken Sailor(IRE), unsuited by the steady pace, was keen for much of the way and couldn't pick up in the relative dash in the straight.
Age Of Reason(UAE) couldn't match the form he showed to be second in this race 12 months ago.
Claremont(IRE) was too keen.

827a DUBAI DUTY FREE DOUBLE MILLIONAIRE (H'CAP) (TAPETA) 1m 1f 110y
5:05 (5:05) (100-116,116) 3-Y-O+

£67,307 (£22,435; £11,217; £5,608; £3,365; £2,243)

RPR
1 **Honour System (IRE)**[14] 679 4-8-5 100 TedDurcan 4 100
(Saeed Bin Suroor) *settled in rr: rdn 3f out: r.o wl fnl 2 1/2f: led fnl 55yds* **14/1**
2 *1* **Haatheq (USA)**[7] 758 4-9-0 109 RichardHills 8 107
(A Al Raihe, UAE) *mid-div: trckd ldr 2 1/2f out: led 1 1/2f out: hdd cl home* **10/1**
3 *½* **Spring Of Fame (USA)**[35] 416 5-9-3 112 FrankieDettori 7 109
(Saeed Bin Suroor) *trckd ldr: ev ch 3f out: r.o same pce fnl 1 1/2f* **2/1**[1]
4 *hd* **Dr Faustus (IRE)**[5] 785 6-8-5 100 (t) TadhgO'Shea 9 97
(Doug Watson, UAE) *s.i.s: settled in rr: r.o wl fnl 2f: nrst fin* **8/1**[3]
5 *¼* **Here To Win (BRZ)**[20] 604 5-8-10 106 ChristopheSoumillon 5 101
(M F De Kock, South Africa) *settled in rr: smooth prog to ld 4 1/2f out: hdd 1 1/2f out: wknd fnl 55yds* **10/3**[2]
6 *1 ¾* **Al Shemali**[7] 759 7-9-6 116 (t) RoystonFfrench 3 107
(A Al Raihe, UAE) *in rr of mid-div: nvr able to chal* **12/1**
7 *½* **Capponi (IRE)**[159] 6562 4-8-8 104 AhmedAjtebi 6 94
(Mahmood Al Zarooni) *mid-div: dropped in rr 3 1/2f out: n.d afterwards* **12/1**
8 *¾* **Trois Rois (FR)**[7] 759 6-9-1 110 (b) RyanMoore 10 100
(I Mohammed, UAE) *trckd ldr: wd: struggling 3f out: sn btn* **12/1**
9 *6 ¼* **Persiste Et Signe (FR)**[14] 679 4-8-5 100 (t) RichardMullen 1 77
(Stephane Chevalier, UAE) *sn led: hdd 4 1/2f out: sn btn* **16/1**
10 *10* **Atlantis Star**[20] 605 4-8-8 104 KierenFallon 2 60
(Mahmood Al Zarooni) *nvr bttr than mid-div* **25/1**
11 *1 ¾* **Lolamar (ITY)**[14] 676 4-8-7 102 WilliamBuick 11 55
(Marco Botti) *trckd ldrs tl 2 1/2f out: one pce fnl 1 1/2f* **14/1**

1m 59.42s (0.72) **Going Correction** +0.35s/f (Slow) **11** Ran SP% **122.8**
Speed ratings: **111,110,109,109,109 108,107,107,102,94 92**
CSF: 152.85 TRI: 407.41.
Owner Sheikh Hamdan Bin Mohammed Al Maktoum **Bred** Darley **Trained** Newmarket, Suffolk

FOCUS
This looked a case of the pace being wound up a bit too soon and those ridden patiently were favoured. Ordinary form.

NOTEBOOK
Honour System(IRE) had struggled to get involved on his two previous starts this year, having been set a bit to do, but he was kept in touch this time and was suited by the way the race unfolded. He was outpaced at the top of the straight, but produced a sustained challenge as the leaders began to wilt and very much gave the impression he'll stay further, a view supported by his rider.
Haatheq(USA) raced slightly closer to the pace than the winner and made his challenge four-wide. His earlier Carnival success came over 1m and he basically didn't see his race out as well as Honour System.
Spring Of Fame(USA) was runner-up, ahead of two of today's rivals, to World Cup candidate Bold Silvano in the second round of the Al Maktoum Challenge, but the beaten runners from that race have now run a total of 12 times between them without success (Silverside made it 0-13 later on this card). He found only the one pace this time and was reportedly said to be hanging to his right in the straight. (opnd 9-4)
Dr Faustus(IRE), the winner of a non-Carnival event here five days earlier, ran on from off the good pace without threatening.
Here To Win(BRZ)'s connections said beforehand the plan was to ride the filly more prominently than had been the case lately, but the tactics were unsuited by the way the race unfolded. She had to expend a fair degree of energy to make her way from the rear to the front midway down the back straight, and by that stage the pace already appeared fair. Although plugging on in the straight, she had little left when strongly challenged.
Al Shemali, another who ran in Bold Silvano's race, continues streets below the form he showed when winning last season's Duty Free.

828a ZABEEL MILE SPONSORED BY DUBAI DUTY FREE (GROUP 2) (TURF) 1m
5:45 (5:45) 3-Y-O+

£96,153 (£32,051; £16,025; £8,012; £4,807; £3,205)

RPR
1 **Rileyskeepingfaith**[7] 755 5-9-0 106 (t) AhmedAjtebi 11 114
(Mahmood Al Zarooni) *in rr of mid-div: led 1f out: r.o wl* **14/1**
2 *2 ¼* **Fareer**[14] 682 5-9-0 106 (v) RichardHills 8 109
(Ed Dunlop) *mid-div: trckd ldrs 2 1/2f out: led 1 1/2f out: hdd 1f out: r.o wl* **10/1**
3 *1 ½* **Fanunalter**[28] 503 5-9-0 107 RyanMoore 10 106+
(Marco Botti) *settled in rr: r.o wl fnl 2f but no ch w wnr* **3/1**[1]
4 *¾* **Kavango (IRE)**[7] 759 4-9-0 106 PatCosgrave 4 104+
(M bin Shafya, UAE) *nvr bttr than mid-div* **14/1**
5 *¼* **Hearts Of Fire**[7] 759 4-9-0 115 (t) ADeVries 12 103
(Ibrahaim Al Malki, Qatar) *slowly away: settled in rr: nvr able to chal but r.o fnl 1 1/2f* **7/2**[2]
6 *½* **Navajo Chief**[14] 682 4-9-0 105 KierenFallon 9 102
(Alan Jarvis) *sn led: hdd 2f out: r.o same pce* **14/1**
7 *¼* **Across The Rhine (USA)**[21] 587 5-9-0 107 WJSupple 3 102
(Tracey Collins, Ire) *trckd ldng pair: ev ch 2f out: wknd fnl 1f* **10/1**
8 *1 ¼* **Invisible Man**[21] 586 5-9-0 107 (b) FrankieDettori 1 99
(Saeed Bin Suroor) *nvr bttr than mid-div* **7/1**[3]
9 *½* **Field Event (SAF)**[62] 7-9-0 105 BernardFayd'Herbe 2 98
(S Al Harabi, Saudi Arabia) *trckd ldr tl 3f out: wknd fnl 1 1/2f* **25/1**
10 *shd* **Silverside (USA)**[21] 586 5-9-0 110 ChristopheSoumillon 7 97
(M Delcher-Sanchez, Spain) *mid-div: trckd ldrs 3f out: wknd fnl 1 1/2f* **10/1**
11 *nse* **Caymans (AUS)**[20] 604 6-9-0 107 TedDurcan 6 97
(Saeed Bin Suroor) *settled in rr: nvr able to chal* **8/1**
12 *2* **Ferneley (IRE)**[7] 759 7-9-0 108 (t) WilliamBuick 5 93
(B Cecil, U.S.A) *a in rr* **20/1**

1m 37.89s (97.89) **12** Ran SP% **126.7**
CSF: 156.89.
Owner Godolphin **Bred** M Barrett **Trained** Newmarket, Suffolk

FOCUS
It will be a surprise if this race retains its current status, although the race did at least get a winner unexposed at the trip, albeit a horse with a rather bizarre profile. The pace seemed just fair.

NOTEBOOK
Rileyskeepingfaith, on his 30th start, was racing beyond 7f for the first time. He's long been exposed as just a smart sprinter, and he looked an unusual Godolphin purchase when picked up out of Mick Channon's yard for 110,000gns last October, but he relished this step up in trip. With the benefit of hindsight, that can hardly be considered a surprise seeing as his dam won over fences. Although he had been running well in defeat over shorter trips lately, evidently this distance suited him well and presumably he'll be persevered with at around 1m. The extra furlong of the Duty Free would be a bit of a question mark and it's highly doubtful he's up to that level anyway, but he'll be worth his place in the Godolphin Mile back on Tapeta.
Fareer reversed recent handicap form with Navajo Chief and Kavango, but was no match for the winner. He's a bit short of this level. (opnd 9-1)
Fanunalter raced off the pace after being dropped in from his double-figure draw but had his chance. He ran well, although maybe not quite to the same level as when runner-up to Raihana in a handicap last time. (opnd 4-1)
Kavango(IRE) stayed on without threatening.
Hearts Of Fire is a bit better than he showed. He lost too much ground when dropped in from his wide draw and then didn't get the best of runs through. That said, he's not one to make too many excuses for. (opnd 100-300)
Navajo Chief defeated Kavango and Fareer when winning a C&D handicap two weeks earlier, but he had the assistance of a 7lb claimer on that occasion and this time struggled to dominate a slightly better quality field.
Invisible Man had little room towards the inside rail in the closing stages and is better than he showed.

829a DUBAI DUTY FREE MILLENNIUM MILLIONAIRE (H'CAP) (TURF) 1m 2f
6:20 (6:20) (100-112,112) 3-Y-O+

£67,307 (£22,435; £11,217; £5,608; £3,365; £2,243)

RPR
1 **Steele Tango (USA)**[7] 759 6-9-6 112 RyanMoore 4 112
(Roger Teal) *mid-div: smooth prog 2f out: led 110yds out: hld on wl* **7/2**[1]
2 *shd* **Enak (ARG)**[21] 581 5-9-4 110 (t) FrankieDettori 3 110
(Saeed Bin Suroor) *mid-div: chsd ldrs 1 1/2f out: r.o wl fnl 1f: jst failed* **7/2**[1]
3 *¾* **Wonder Lawn (SAF)**[14] 676 8-8-13 105 (t) KShea 7 104
(M F De Kock, South Africa) *trckd ldrs: rdn to ld 1 1/2f out: hdd 110yds out: r.o same pce* **5/1**[3]
4 *1 ¼* **Superstition (FR)**[42] 329 5-8-13 105 ChristopheSoumillon 11 101+
(Rod Collet, France) *settled in rr: nvr able to chal* **10/1**
5 *nse* **Psychic Ability (USA)**[21] 581 4-9-1 107 (v) TedDurcan 8 103
(Saeed Bin Suroor) *trckd ldr: rdn 2 1/2f out: one pce fnl 1 1/2f* **9/2**[2]
6 *hd* **Royal Revival**[28] 503 4-9-0 106 DaraghO'Donohoe 5 102+
(Saeed Bin Suroor) *settled in rr: nvr nr to chal but r.o fnl 1 1/2f* **25/1**
7 *¼* **War Monger (USA)**[14] 676 7-9-0 106 TadhgO'Shea 1 101
(Doug Watson, UAE) *trckd ldng duo: wknd fnl 1 1/2f* **14/1**
8 *shd* **Espiritu (FR)**[14] 676 5-8-9 101 ow1 (p) PatCosgrave 2 95+
(G Al Marri, UAE) *settled in rr: r.o wl fnl 1 1/2f: nrst fin* **14/1**
9 *¾* **Yirga**[7] 757 5-8-13 105 (t) RoystonFfrench 10 98
(A Al Raihe, UAE) *a mid-div* **10/1**
10 *¼* **Pallodio (IRE)**[21] 585 6-9-1 107 (vt) RichardHills 9 100
(J E Hammond, France) *in rr of mid-div: nvr able to chal* **16/1**
11 *3* **Logic Way (USA)**[14] 677 7-8-11 104 (bt) ADeVries 6 90
(Ibrahaim Al Malki, Qatar) *sn led: rdn 3f out: sn btn* **20/1**

2m 5.23s (125.23) **11** Ran SP% **125.3**
CSF: 16.46 TRI: 64.48. Placepot: 11.80 to a £1 stake. Pool of £11934.97 - 736.12 winning units. Quadpot: 7.40 to a £1 stake. Pool of 870.88 - 86.30 winning units..
Owner The Thirty Acre Racing Partnership **Bred** Tom Zwiesler **Trained** Ashtead, Surrey

FOCUS
No unexposed performers here, but some decent types fought out the finish and this is solid enough form. That's despite the pace appearing only modest.

NOTEBOOK
Steele Tango(USA) defeated a short-head over 1m1f here on the opening night of the 2011 Carnival and repeated the trick on 1lb better terms over this extra furlong. The winner was a bit warm down his neck and may have preferred a strong pace, although that would have put the emphasis more on stamina, which might not have been ideal. He is a gutsy individual and appreciated the return to handicap company after a couple of decent efforts at Group 2 level. He should get an invite for the Duty Free, but is likely to struggle. In the slightly longer term he reportedly could go to Hong Kong, or return to Britain for the Earl of Sefton.
Enak(ARG) didn't seem to do anything wrong, but he's now been beaten just one length or under on all four of his Carnival starts this year and the view remains that headgear might just make the difference.
Wonder Lawn(SAF) ran well off a 5lb higher mark than when winning over C&D two weeks earlier.
Superstition(FR) found this an insufficient stamina test but ran as well as could have been expected.
Psychic Ability(USA) was on edge beforehand and couldn't repeat the form he showed when winning over C&D last time (allowed soft lead, Enak runner-up), and wasn't allowed to dominate on this occasion.
Royal Revival didn't get the best of runs through and finished as though he may have had something left. This was more encouraging than of late.

[775]DEAUVILLE (R-H)

Thursday, March 10

OFFICIAL GOING: Fibresand: standard

830a PRIX D'AILLY (CONDITIONS) (4YO) (FIBRESAND) 7f 110y

1:50 (12:00) 4-Y-O **£12,068** (£4,827; £3,620; £2,413; £1,206)

Pos	Dist	Horse	RPR
1		**African Story**[107] 4-8-11 0 .... MaximeGuyon 7 (A Fabre, France) **6/4**[1]	94
2	2½	**Robin Du Nord (FR)**[159] 4-9-1 0 .... FranckBlondel 5 (J-P Gauvin, France) **20/1**	92
3	1½	**High Link (FR)**[178] 4-9-4 0 .... Christophe-PatriceLemaire 8 (X Thomas-Demeaulte, France) **9/1**	91
4	4	**Cool Marble (IRE)**[284] 4-9-1 0 .... AnthonyCrastus 1 (Y De Nicolay, France) **9/1**	78
5	1½	**Below Zero (IRE)**[10] [710] 4-9-1 0 .... JoeFanning 2 (Mark Johnston) *broke wl to ld: hdd 1 1/2f out: rdn: no ex: styd on fnl f* **53/10**[3]	74
6	hd	**Menelas**[61] 4-8-11 0 .... TonyPiccone 4 (J Rossi, France) **28/1**	70
7	½	**Lovecraft (USA)**[121] 4-8-11 0 .... (b[1]) Pierre-CharlesBoudot 3 (A Fabre, France) **10/1**	69
8	5	**Silas Marner (FR)**[209] 4-9-1 0 .... IoritzMendizabal 6 (J-C Rouget, France) **3/1**[2]	60

1m 29.1s (89.10) **8** Ran SP% **118.2**

WIN (incl. 1 euro stake): 2.10 (African Story & Lovecraft coupled). PLACES: 1.40, 3.60, 2.60. DF: 24.80. SF: 35.80.

Owner Sheikh Mohammed **Bred** Darley Stud Management Co Ltd **Trained** Chantilly, France

831a PRIX DU MESNIL AUGER (CLAIMER) (4YO) (FIBRESAND) 7f 110y

2:20 (12:00) 4-Y-O **£7,758** (£3,103; £2,327; £1,551; £775)

Pos	Dist	Horse	RPR
1		**Ariete Arrollador**[261] 4-9-4 0 .... IoritzMendizabal 2 (G Arizkorreta Elosegui, Spain) **26/5**[2]	90
2	1½	**John Fitgerald (IRE)** 4-8-11 0 .... StephanePasquier 16 (Y Durepaire, Spain) **44/5**	79
3	½	**Theza Bere (FR)**[66] 4-8-8 0 .... Francois-XavierBertras 14 (P Monfort, France) **63/10**	75
4	2½	**Baron Davis (FR)**[349] 4-9-1 0 .... ThierryJarnet 9 (N Leenders, France) **53/1**	76
5	2	**Miami Gator (IRE)**[35] [405] 4-9-4 0 .... (b) RobertWinston 13 (Mrs K Burke) *broke wl to share ld: rdn to ld 1 1/2f out: hdd 1f out: no ex: styd on* **44/5**	74
6	½	**Grand Lucius (FR)**[66] 4-9-4 0 .... (p) FlavienPrat 5 (D Windrif, France) **9/2**[1]	73
7	3	**Mal And Dave (IRE)**[66] 4-9-2 0 .... MaximeGuyon 6 (Mme Pia Brandt, France) **27/1**	63
8	¾	**Any Given Sunday (GER)**[173] 4-8-8 0 .... DominiqueBoeuf 4 (W Baltromei, Germany) **6/1**[3]	53
9	¾	**Timolin (GER)**[73] 4-8-11 0 .... FranckBlondel 8 (P Monfort, France) **68/10**	54
10	nk	**Valugny (FR)**[42] [325] 4-8-11 0 .... AllanBonnefoy 1 (F Sanchez, France) **78/1**	54
0		**Let It Rock (IRE)**[61] [108] 4-9-2 0 ow1 .... LaurentHuart 10 (Mrs K Burke) *sn prom to r in 4th: rdn early in st: no ex: sn fdd* **58/1**	—
0		**Calvero (FR)**[122] 4-8-11 0 .... RonanThomas 3 (Mme C Barande-Barbe, France) **34/1**	—
0		**Shanaco (FR)**[83] 4-8-11 0 .... (b) SebastienMaillot 12 (Mlle Valerie Boussin, France) **74/1**	—
0		**Oujuu (FR)**[73] 4-9-11 0 .... (p) TonyPiccone 7 (J Rossi, France) **60/1**	—
0		**Wise Boy (GER)**[42] [325] 4-8-9 0 ow1 .... FrankieLeroy(3) 11 (N Milliere, France) **15/1**	—

1m 28.9s (88.90) **15** Ran SP% **116.0**

WIN (incl. 1 euro stake): 6.20. PLACES: 2.80, 3.10, 2.60. DF: 32.00. SF: 66.90.

Owner Juan Benjumea Alarcon **Bred** Loughtown Stud Ltd **Trained** Spain

832a PRIX DE LA FORET DE SAINT GATIEN (H'CAP) (5YO+) (FIBRESAND) 1m 1f 110y

4:00 (12:00) 5-Y-O+ **£6,896** (£2,758; £2,068; £1,379; £689)

Pos	Dist	Horse	RPR
1		**Chamir (FR)**[140] 5-9-4 **0** .... Pierre-CharlesBoudot 7 (J-M Capitte, France) **14/5**[1]	64
2	1½	**Markmanship (FR)**[58] 6-8-0 **0** .... FlavienPrat 11 (Mme V Deiss, France) **36/1**	43
3	hd	**Charming River (FR)**[140] 5-8-8 **0** .... StephanePasquier 13 (Mlle V Dissaux, France) **34/1**	51
4	nse	**El Vettorio (GER)**[12] [706] 8-9-1 **0** .... (p) DavyBonilla 2 (C Boutin, France) **11/1**[3]	57
5	snk	**Iron Out (USA)**[12] [706] 5-9-5 **0** .... (p) Francois-XavierBertras 18 (Reg Hollinshead) *broke wl on wd outside to ld: swtchd to rail after 2f: led into st: rdn 1 1/2f out: r.o wl: hdd 1f out: styd on wl and lost 2nd wl ins fnl f in blanket fin* **15/1**	61
6	snk	**Auenwiese (GER)**[58] 7-9-0 **0** .... (p) MaximeGuyon 6 (S Cerulis, France) **11/1**[3]	56
7	¾	**Decorum (USA)**[61] 5-8-4 **0** .... (p) SoufyaneMoulin(3) 16 (F Vermeulen, France) **43/1**	47
8	snk	**Canalside**[73] 5-9-2 **0** .... (p) IoritzMendizabal 5 (P Monfort, France) **15/1**	56
9	snk	**Montmarin (FR)**[58] 9-8-10 **0** .... (b) FranckBlondel 10 (Mlle V Dissaux, France) **13/1**	50
10	hd	**Learco (FR)**[12] [706] 10-9-2 **0** .... MathiasSautjeau 4 (Y Fertillet, France) **69/1**	55
0		**Peintre Modern (FR)**[58] 8-9-0 **0** .... AntoineHamelin(3) 14 (L Nyffels, France) **22/1**	—
0		**Royal Cyclone (IRE)**[61] 8-8-5 **0** .... SebastienMaillot 1 (M Boutin, France) **47/1**	—
0		**Negramaro (IRE)**[73] 6-8-10 0 .... Christophe-PatriceLemaire 17 (M Boutin, France) **21/1**	—
0		**L'Albatros (FR)**[58] 6-8-2 **0** .... (b) MatthieuAutier 12 (Mme C Barande-Barbe, France) **6/1**[2]	—
0		**Arca (FR)**[58] 6-8-7 **0** .... TonyPiccone 9 (J Rossi, France) **14/1**	—
0		**Escargot (GER)**[50] [220] 5-9-4 **0** .... (b) YoannRousset(2) 3 (Y Fertillet, France) **17/1**	—
0		**Simple Mind (GER)**[12] [706] 6-8-11 **0** .... (b) DominiqueBoeuf 8 (Y Fertillet, France) **48/1**	—
0		**La Terrible (IRE)**[58] 5-9-0 **0** .... SylvainRuis 15 (F Vermeulen, France) **18/1**	—

2m 0.40s (120.40) **18** Ran SP% **116.7**

WIN (incl. 1 euro stake): 3.80. PLACES: 1.70, 9.60, 9.60. DF: 101.50. SF: 97.60.

Owner Bel-Oise SARL **Bred** Societe Civile Ecurie Altima **Trained** France

[767]WOLVERHAMPTON (A.W) (L-H)

Friday, March 11

OFFICIAL GOING: Standard

Wind: Moderate, half-behind Weather: Overcast

833 SPONSOR A RACE BY CALLING 01902 390000 H'CAP 5f 20y(P)

5:50 (5:50) (Class 5) (0-70,70) 4-Y-0+ **£2,169** (£645; £322; £161) **Stalls** Low

Form	Pos	Dist	Horse	RPR
-445	1		**Kylladdie**[16] [646] 4-9-3 **66** .... (b[1]) PaulHanagan 1 (Steve Gollings) *a.p on inner: led over 1f out: rdn and r.o ins fnl f: in command towards fin* **8/1**	77
0211	2	1½	**Straboe (USA)**[14] [696] 5-9-1 **64** .... (v) WilliamCarson 9 (Stuart Williams) *missed break: sn swtchd lft: towards rr: rdn 2f out: hdwy to chal over 1f out: nt qckn ins fnl f: kpt on same pce fnl 50yds* **2/1**[1]	70
3422	3	nse	**Yankee Storm**[7] [766] 6-9-7 **70** .... (b) JimmyQuinn 2 (Tom Keddy) *trckd ldrs: effrt over 1f out: kpt on ins fnl f: nt pce to chal wnr* **4/1**[2]	75
-422	4	shd	**We'll Deal Again**[11] [709] 4-8-6 **58** .... (v) JamesSullivan(3) 6 (Michael Easterby) *rrd s: in tch on outer: effrt 1f out: styng on whn hung lft ins fnl f: hld cl home* **4/1**[2]	63
0330	5	1½	**Riflessione**[16] [646] 5-9-3 **66** .... (b) CathyGannon 3 (Ronald Harris) *led: rdn and hdd over 1f out: keeping on u.p but hld whn n.m.r and eased fnl 50yds* **7/1**[3]	69
3000	6	½	**Absa Lutte (IRE)**[11] [708] 8-9-6 **69** .... (t) GeorgeBaker 4 (Michael Mullineaux) *in tch: nt clr run wl over 1f out: sn pushed along and nt qckn: nt clr run ins fnl f: nt pce to chal* **10/1**	69
6554	7	1	**Efistorm**[7] [766] 10-9-6 **69** .... HayleyTurner 7 (Conor Dore) *in rr: pushed along after 1f: kpt on but nvr able to chal* **16/1**	63
6060	8	½	**Prince James**[15] [673] 4-8-10 **66** .... DavidSimmonson(7) 5 (Michael Easterby) *prom: rdn and losing pl whn n.m.r ins fnl f: sn edgd lft whn btn* **25/1**	58
1450	9	6	**Vhujon (IRE)**[16] [646] 6-9-6 **69** .... RobbieFitzpatrick 8 (Peter Grayson) *a wl bhd and racd wd: nvr on terms* **50/1**	40

62.43 secs (0.13) **Going Correction** +0.25s/f (Slow) **9** Ran SP% **117.7**

Speed ratings (Par 103): **108,105,105,105,102 102,100,99,90**

toteswingers: 1&2 £5.40, 1&3 £5.70, 2&3 £1.90. CSF £24.89 CT £76.45 TOTE £8.60: £1.60, £1.90, £1.20; EX 45.00.

Owner P S Walter **Bred** Horizon Bloodstock Limited **Trained** Scamblesby, Lincs

■ Stewards' Enquiry : James Sullivan three-day ban: careless riding (Mar 25,26,28)

FOCUS

A fair sprint handicap, with the second, third and fourth setting a solid standard. The winner bounced back towards his best AW form.

We'll Deal Again Official explanation: jockey said gelding hung left-handed in home straight

834 ATR CHELTENHAM PREVIEW MONDAY 5.30PM H'CAP 5f 216y(P)

6:20 (6:20) (Class 6) (0-55,55) 3-Y-O **£1,637** (£483; £241) **Stalls** Low

Form	Pos	Dist	Horse	RPR
00-0	1		**Alfraamsey**[16] [655] 3-8-13 **55** .... MartinHarley(5) 4 (Mick Channon) *hld up: pushed along and hdwy 2f out: swtchd rt wl over 1f out: clsng whn edgd lft ins fnl f: r.o to ld fnl 75yds: wl on top at fin* **9/2**[1]	58+
-455	2	¾	**Scommettitrice (IRE)**[23] [558] 3-9-0 **51** .... (b[1]) CathyGannon 3 (Ronald Harris) *led: rdn 2f out: hdd fnl 75yds: hld cl home* **13/2**	52
2-23	3	1	**Neytiri**[29] [494] 3-8-13 **53** .... (p) JamesSullivan(3) 1 (Linda Stubbs) *w ldr: rdn and chalng over 1f out: nt qckn fnl 75yds* **6/1**[3]	51
0440	4	hd	**Lady Ellice**[9] [729] 3-8-12 **49** .... (be[1]) LukeMorris 6 (Phil McEntee) *in tch: rdn 2f out: kpt on ins fnl f: nt quite pce of ldrs* **6/1**[3]	46
2-04	5	¾	**Three Scoops**[57] [142] 3-9-0 **51** .... HayleyTurner 7 (Dominic Ffrench Davis) *w ldrs: rdn and nt qckn over 1f out: one pce whn n.m.r wl ins fnl f: no imp after* **5/1**[2]	46
0-50	6	1½	**Two Feet Of Snow (IRE)**[25] [538] 3-9-4 **55** .... PatrickMathers 8 (Ian McInnes) *towards rr: rdn and hdwy over 1f out: styd on ins fnl f: one pce fnl 100yds* **16/1**	45
6000	7	1¾	**Welsh Dresser (IRE)**[16] [655] 3-8-9 **46** oh1 .... RobbieFitzpatrick 9 (Peter Grayson) *bhd: rdn and hdwy over 1f out: styd on: run flattened out and no imp fnl 100yds* **50/1**	31
63-4	8	5	**Magical Star**[53] [189] 3-8-13 **50** .... NickyMackay 12 (Mark Rimmer) *in tch on outer: rdn and lost pl 2f out: outpcd after* **9/1**	20
00-0	9	7	**Burnem Green**[7] [760] 3-8-13 **50** .... (v[1]) JoeFanning 2 (Derek Shaw) *in tch: rdn and wknd wl over 1f out: eased whn wl btn fnl f* **8/1**	—
640-	10	8	**Libertia**[135] [7177] 3-8-13 **50** .... PaulHanagan 10 (Tony Newcombe) *in tch: n.m.r 2f out: rdn and wknd over 1f out: wl btn after* **14/1**	—
00-0	11	17	**Regal Rocket (IRE)**[21] [595] 3-8-4 **46** oh1 .... (v[1]) DanielleMcCreery(5) 11 (John Weymes) *w ldrs tl rdn and wknd 2f out* **50/1**	—

1m 17.32s (2.32) **Going Correction** +0.25s/f (Slow) **11** Ran SP% **114.3**

Speed ratings (Par 96): **94,93,91,91,90 88,86,79,70,59 36**

toteswingers: 1&2 £9.20, 1&3 £6.60, 2&3 £4.30. CSF £32.55 CT £151.32 TOTE £5.60: £3.20, £1.40, £3.00; EX 39.70.

Owner M Channon **Bred** G Hedley & Mike Channon Bloodstock Limited **Trained** West Ilsley, Berks

■ Martin Harley's first winner since coming to Britain from Ireland.

■ Stewards' Enquiry : Martin Harley two-day ban: careless riding (Mar 25-26)

FOCUS

A very modest handicap, most of the runners were struggling for form and eight of them were maidens. The standard was limited by the second and third.

Regal Rocket(IRE) Official explanation: jockey said filly ran too freely

835 HOTEL & CONFERENCING AT WOLVERHAMPTON H'CAP 1m 4f 50y(P)

6:50 (6:50) (Class 4) (0-85,85) 4-Y-O+ **£3,238** (£963; £481; £240) **Stalls** Low

Form RPR

001- **1** **Jawaab (IRE)**[97] [7694] 7-9-2 **80**.....................(e) AdamKirby 1 90
(Richard Guest) *trckd ldrs: rdn over 2f out: chalng over 1f out: led narrowly wl ins fnl f: r.o u.p and prevailed in driving fin* **15/2**

00-3 **2D** *shd* **Broad Meaning**[20] [614] 5-9-7 **85**.....................(t) CathyGannon 6 95
(James McAuley, Ire) *racd keenly: trckd ldrs: pushed along over 3f out: chalng over 2f out: led narrowly wl over 1f out: hdd wl ins fnl f: r.o u.p: jst hld: subsequently disq: prohibited substance in sample* **9/2[2]**

-040 **2** *3 1/4* **Pelham Crescent (IRE)**[20] [614] 8-8-11 **75**..................... DavidProbert 2 80
(Bryn Palling) *midfield: hdwy over 3f out: kpt on to take 3rd over 1f out: no imp on front pair: fin 3rd, shd & 3 1/4l; subs. plcd 2nd* **5/1[3]**

134- **3** *1 1/2* **Russian George (IRE)**[188] [1889] 5-9-4 **82**..................... PaulHanagan 10 85+
(Steve Gollings) *midfield: rdn and outpcd 3f out: styd on ins fnl f: nt trble ldrs: fin 4th, subs plcd 3rd* **4/1[1]**

41-5 **4** *2 1/2* **Hawaana (IRE)**[15] [667] 6-9-7 **85**..................... MickyFenton 7 84
(Gay Kelleway) *hld up: hdwy to chse ldrs 3f out: one pce ins fnl f: fin 5th, plcd 4th* **10/1**

4/0 **6** *shd* **Ajdaad (USA)**[14] [694] 4-9-0 **80**.....................(p) JamesDoyle 4 79
(Alan McCabe) *hld up: pushed along into midfield 2f out: no imp on ldrs* **16/1**

321 **7** *1 1/2* **Cobo Bay**[8] [742] 6-9-0 **78** 6ex.....................(b) HayleyTurner 5 75
(Conor Dore) *prom: led wl over 4f out: rdn and hdd wl over 1f out: wknd ins fnl f* **9/2[2]**

100- **8** *13* **William Van Gogh**[147] [6904] 4-8-5 **74**..................... JamesSullivan(3) 3 51
(Michael Easterby) *hld up: rdn over 3f out: nvr on terms* **14/1**

-000 **9** *22* **Rugell (ARG)**[34] [436] 6-8-11 **75**..................... RobbieFitzpatrick 8 19
(Derek Shaw) *led: hdd over 5f out: sn pushed along: wknd over 3f out: fin slighly lame* **40/1**

126- **10** *20* **Clear Sailing**[261] [938] 8-9-0 **78**..................... StevieDonohoe 9 —
(Noel Quinlan) *awkward leaving stalls: s.i.s: bhd: hdwy 7f out: prom 6f out: led briefly over 5f out: wknd 3f out* **16/1**

2m 42.24s (1.14) **Going Correction** +0.25s/f (Slow)
WFA 4 from 5yo+ 2lb **10** Ran SP% **114.8**
Speed ratings (Par 105): **106,105,103,102,101 101,100,91,76,63**
toteswingers: 1&2 £5.40, 1&3 £8.10, 2&3 £5.10. CSF £40.54 CT £185.93 TOTE £9.90: £2.90, £2.60, £2.70; EX 55.80.
Owner L & D Racing **Bred** Hascombe And Valiant Studs **Trained** Stainforth, S Yorks

FOCUS
A decent handicap. The first two had a great battle and pulled clear. Solid form.
Rugell(ARG) Official explanation: vet said horse finished lame
Clear Sailing Official explanation: jockey said gelding ran too freely

836 THE BLACK COUNTRY'S ONLY RACECOURSE MEDIAN AUCTION MAIDEN STKS 1m 4f 50y(P)

7:20 (7:20) (Class 6) 3-5-Y-O **£1,535** (£453; £226) **Stalls** Low

Form RPR

42 **1** **Gottany O'S**[16] [649] 3-8-5 0..................... SamHitchcott 2 83+
(Mick Channon) *hld up: hdwy 4f out: wnt 2nd wl over 2f out: rdn to ld over 1f out: sn clr and wl in command: r.o wl: eased towards fin* **4/7[1]**

2/2- **2** *10* **Indochina**[252] [3618] 4-9-12 73..................... MartinLane 3 68
(David Simcock) *led for 1f: chsd ldr tl regained ld 4f out: rdn over 2f out: hdd over 1f out: no ch w wnr fnl f* **11/4[2]**

2- **3** *10* **Stetson**[319] [1572] 5-10-0 0..................... PJMcDonald 1 53
(Alan Swinbank) *chsd ldrs: rdn over 3f out: wl outpcd 2f out: n.d after* **15/2[3]**

5 **4** *1 1/2* **Aimee Tricks**[11] [713] 3-8-0 0..................... CathyGannon 5 43
(Sylvester Kirk) *hld up in rr: pushed along 3f out: nvr able to get on terms w ldrs: n.d* **33/1**

0 **5** *14* **Rapacious**[21] [591] 3-8-5 0..................... NickyMackay 6 27
(Mark Rimmer) *in tch: pushed along 4f out: wknd over 3f out* **66/1**

6 *4 1/2* **Hopes Up**[14] 4-9-7 0..................... RichardKingscote 7 18
(Ian Williams) *led after 1f: hung rt on bnd 6f out: hdd 4f out: rdn and wknd wl over 2f out: eased whn wl bhd wl over 1f out* **33/1**

600- **7** *60* **Roxy Spirit (IRE)**[275] [2860] 4-9-0 30..................... JosephYoung(7) 4 —
(Michael Mullineaux) *chsd ldrs: niggled along after 4f: rdn and wknd over 6f out: t.o over 4f out* **100/1**

2m 41.75s (0.65) **Going Correction** +0.25s/f (Slow)
WFA 3 from 4yo 23lb 4 from 5yo 2lb **7** Ran SP% **110.5**
Speed ratings (Par 101): **107,100,93,92,83 80,40**
toteswingers: 1&2 £1.02, 1&3 £1.60, 2&3 £1.90. CSF £2.11 TOTE £1.70: £1.10, £1.10; EX 2.50.
Owner Dr Marwan Koukash **Bred** Phil Jen Racing **Trained** West Ilsley, Berks

FOCUS
The hot favourite stormed clear in this maiden that lacked strength in depth. The fourth and fifth are the likely key to the form.
Hopes Up Official explanation: jockey said filly hung right-handed

837 WOLVERHAMPTON-RACECOURSE.CO.UK (S) STKS 1m 141y(P)

7:50 (7:50) (Class 6) 4-Y-O+ **£1,535** (£453; £226) **Stalls** Low

Form RPR

1011 **1** **Erinjay (IRE)**[18] [633] 5-9-6 77..................... AndreaAtzeni 3 68
(Michael Wigham) *racd in 3rd pl: rdn and nt qckn over 1f out: styd on ins fnl f: got up towards fin* **2/5[1]**

3346 **2** *1/2* **Esteem Lord**[4] [790] 5-9-0 59..................... AdamKirby 1 61
(Dean Ivory) *chsd ldr: rdn to ld over 1f out: worn down towards fin* **5/1[2]**

-421 **3** *2 1/2* **Nevada Desert (IRE)**[8] [748] 11-9-6 54..................... PaulHanagan 2 62
(Richard Whitaker) *led: rdn and hdd over 1f out: no ex fnl 100yds* **14/1**

5255 **4** *62* **Grand Vizier (IRE)**[15] [670] 7-9-0 68..................... HayleyTurner 4 —
(Conor Dore) *missed break: a bhd: dropped away 3f out: woefully t.o* **17/2[3]**

1m 53.7s (3.20) **Going Correction** +0.25s/f (Slow) **4** Ran SP% **105.3**
Speed ratings (Par 101): **95,94,92,37**
CSF £2.51 TOTE £1.20; EX 2.00.The winner was bought in for 7,500gns.
Owner Seyhan Osman, Michael Wigham **Bred** Bill Benson **Trained** Newmarket, Suffolk

FOCUS
It was hard work for the hot favourite in this seller but he managed to swoop late and improve his strike-rate to 6-11. The form is rated negatively through the second and third.

Grand Vizier(IRE) Official explanation: jockey said gelding hung right-handed

838 ATR LIVE DAILY FROM CHELTENHAM 8AM H'CAP 2m 119y(P)

8:20 (8:20) (Class 5) (0-70,70) 4-Y-O+ **£2,169** (£645; £322; £161) **Stalls** Low

Form RPR

2125 **1** **Rosewood Lad**[10] [718] 4-9-4 **67**..................... CathyGannon 2 75
(J S Moore) *trckd ldrs: effrt and wnt 2nd 3f out: styd on ins fnl f: led towards fin* **11/2[2]**

010- **2** *1/2* **Sunny Spells**[40] [8013] 6-9-4 **62**..................... WilliamCarson 9 69
(Stuart Williams) *sn prom: led after 2f: rdn over 2f out: pressed over 1f out: hdd towards fin* **22/1**

2242 **3** *3/4* **Carnac (IRE)**[7] [768] 5-8-11 **55**.....................(p) JamesDoyle 1 63
(Alan McCabe) *trckd ldrs: nt clr run on bnd wl over 1f out: sn swtchd lft and chalng: edgd rt and styd on same pce towards fin* **5/1[1]**

52-2 **4** *4 1/2* **Accompanist**[46] [286] 8-9-3 **66**.....................(p) MartinHarley(5) 5 67
(T G McCourt, Ire) *in tch: rdn over 3f out: nt qckn over 1f out: swtchd lft ins fnl f: one pce fnl 100yds* **10/1**

0623 **5** *3* **Prince Charlemagne (IRE)**[7] [768] 8-8-10 **61**...... MatthewCosham(7) 7 59
(Dr Jeremy Naylor) *midfield: rdn over 2f out: hdwy to chse ldrs wl over 1f out: no further imp fnl f* **12/1**

5124 **6** *nse* **Dart**[15] [671] 7-9-12 **70**..................... GrahamGibbons 11 67
(John Mackie) *hld up: hdwy over 4f out: effrt whn chsng ldrs over 3f out: wknd over 1f out* **9/1**

050- **7** *hd* **Spiritonthemount (USA)**[126] [6416] 6-8-7 **51** oh6.............(b) ChrisCatlin 3 48
(Peter Hiatt) *midfield: hdwy 1/2-way: rdn briefly 7f out: chsd ldr fr 6f out to 3f out: wknd over 2f out* **28/1**

5-41 **8** *7* **Chocolate Caramel (USA)**[7] [769] 9-9-3 **61** 6ex.......... PaulHanagan 10 50
(Richard Fahey) *hld up: rdn over 3f out: no imp on ldrs: dropped away wl over 1f out* **6/1[3]**

0-61 **9** *4 1/2* **Gulf Of Aqaba (USA)**[9] [733] 5-8-11 **55** 6ex.....................(b) JoeFanning 8 38
(Ian Williams) *hld up: rdn over 3f out: nvr on terms* **6/1[3]**

-300 **10** *5* **Bold Adventure**[23] [560] 7-8-13 **57**..................... StevieDonohoe 4 34
(Willie Musson) *a bhd: hrd at work and lost tch 6f out* **8/1**

01-4 **11** *22* **Dubara Reef (IRE)**[21] [597] 4-9-7 **70**.....................(p) SilvestreDeSousa 6 21
(Paul Green) *led: hdd after 2f: handy tl rdn and wknd 5f out: t.o over 3f out* **9/1**

3m 44.68s (2.88) **Going Correction** +0.25s/f (Slow)
WFA 4 from 5yo+ 5lb **11** Ran SP% **116.3**
Speed ratings (Par 103): **103,102,102,100,98 98,98,95,93,91 80**
toteswingers: 1&2 £27.00, 1&3 £4.30, 2&3 £20.10. CSF £117.20 CT £644.64 TOTE £5.50: £1.10, £7.80, £1.70; EX 148.20.
Owner Miss D L Wisbey & R J Viney **Bred** Miss D L Wisbey **Trained** Upper Lambourn, Berks

FOCUS
A competitive staying handicap, involving two last-time-out winners and five others who finished in the frame on their latest run. The first three pulled clear and the form looks solid, if limited.
Bold Adventure Official explanation: jockey said gelding would not face the kickback
Dubara Reef(IRE) Official explanation: jockey said gelding had no more to give

839 STAY AT THE WOLVERHAMPTON HOLIDAY INN H'CAP 1m 4f 50y(P)

8:50 (8:50) (Class 6) (0-65,64) 4-Y-O+ **£1,637** (£483; £241) **Stalls** Low

Form RPR

1 **Time Travel**[146] [4314] 6-9-3 **60**.....................(t) CathyGannon 5 68+
(James McAuley, Ire) *bmpd s: hld up: hdwy on inner 2f out: led over 1f out: edgd rt wl ins fnl f: r.o wl and wl in command towards fin* **12/1**

1-12 **2** *1 3/4* **The Blue Dog (IRE)**[14] [687] 4-9-2 **61**.....................(b[1]) NickyMackay 6 66
(Mark Rimmer) *midfield: hdwy to chse ldrs 3f out: styd on ins fnl f: tk 2nd post: no imp on wnr* **6/1**

0-34 **3** *nse* **Hallstatt (IRE)**[11] [715] 5-9-5 **62**.....................(t) GrahamGibbons 8 67
(John Mackie) *a.p: chalng 2f out: rdn over 1f out: styd on same pce and wl hld by wnr fnl 50yds* **4/1[1]**

5- **4** *1 1/4* **Horsewithnoname (IRE)**[42] [7711] 4-8-7 **57**.............(p) MartinHarley(5) 1 60
(T G McCourt, Ire) *prom: nt clr run wl over 1f out: nt qckn: styd on same pce ins fnl f* **16/1**

5453 **5** *3/4* **Duar Mapel (USA)**[9] [733] 5-8-11 **54**..................... JimmyQuinn 4 56
(Brian Baugh) *led: rdn and hdd over 1f out: no ex fnl 100yds* **4/1[1]**

12-6 **6** *1 3/4* **Alternative Choice (USA)**[49] [244] 5-9-7 **64** GeorgeBaker 7 60
(Nick Littmoden) *hld up: rdn over 1f out: kpt on ins fnl f: nvr able to chal* **9/2[2]**

033- **7** *1 1/2* **Kingdom Of Munster (IRE)**[13] [6650] 4-9-5 **64**.............. PaulHanagan 2 61
(Richard Fahey) *trckd ldrs: ev ch over 2f out: wknd 1f out* **11/2[3]**

-225 **8** *15* **Port Hill**[17] [644] 4-8-11 **56**..................... LukeMorris 9 31
(Mark Brisbourne) *plld hrd: hld up: rdn and hung rt over 2f out: sn wl outpcd and dropped away* **8/1**

04/5 **9** *10* **Velvet Band**[28] [508] 4-8-12 **57**..................... HayleyTurner 3 17
(Richard Whitaker) *midfield: pushed along 3f out: wknd over 2f out* **40/1**

2m 45.5s (4.40) **Going Correction** +0.25s/f (Slow)
WFA 4 from 5yo+ 2lb **9** Ran SP% **115.0**
Speed ratings (Par 101): **95,93,93,92,92 91,90,80,73**
toteswingers: 1&2 £9.10, 1&3 £11.20, 2&3 £4.90. CSF £81.64 CT £342.97 TOTE £15.90: £5.40, £2.00, £1.60; EX 35.10.
Owner James Gough **Bred** Gainsborough Stud Management Ltd **Trained** Gormanston, Co. Meath

FOCUS
A low-grade handicap. The pace was steady and they were tightly grouped for a long way. Straightforward form.
Port Hill Official explanation: jockey said gelding hung right-handed throughout
T/Plt: £35.90 to a £1 stake. Pool:£90,361.35 - 1,835.10 winning tickets T/Qpdt: £11.50 to a £1 stake. Pool:£8,729.72 - 560.32 winning tickets DO

830 DEAUVILLE (R-H)

Friday, March 11

OFFICIAL GOING: Fibresand: standard

840a PRIX DU PAYS DE BRAY (H'CAP) (4YO) (FIBRESAND) 1m 1f 110y

12:50 (12:00) 4-Y-O

£20,258 (£8,189; £6,034; £3,879; £2,370; £1,508)

RPR

1 **Anaxis (FR)**[63] 4-9-4 **0**..................... JeromeCabre 7 93
(S Wattel, France) **74/10[3]**

2 *1* **Curro Perote (FR)**[160] 4-9-2 **0**..................... JohanVictoire 12 89
(L A Urbano-Grajales, France) **43/10[1]**

3 *snk* **Rhenania (IRE)**[67] 4-8-13 **0**..................... FabriceVeron 15 86
(M Nigge, France) **14/1**

The Form Book, Raceform Ltd, Compton, RG20 6NL

4 *hd* **Silver Green (FR)** 4-9-2 **0**........ Francois-XavierBertras 18 88
(F Rohaut, France) **13/1**

5 *nk* **Issacar (IRE)**^{222} 4-9-0 **0**........(p) Jean-BaptisteHamel 1 86
(A De Watrigant, France) **9/1**

6 *nse* **Zamind (FR)**^{182} [5935] 4-9-2 **0**........ IoritzMendizabal 17 88
(X Thomas-Demeaulte, France) **43/1**

7 *nk* **Mystic Joy (IRE)**^{67} 4-8-10 **0**........ ThierryJarnet 3 81
(N Leenders, France) **18/1**

8 *3/4* **Lucky Harry (FR)**^{113} 4-9-0 **0**........ KarlMartin 5 83
(Alex Fracas, France) **41/1**

9 *snk* **Tominator**^{16} [661] 4-9-6 **0**........(p) RobertWinston 8 89
(Reg Hollinshead) *broke wl to r 2nd: moved to ld bef st: rdn and hdd 1 1/2f out: no ex: styd on one pce fnl f* **51/1**

10 *nse* **Mockingbird (FR)**^{101} 4-8-9 **0**........(b) AnthonyCrastus 14 78
(D Sepulchre, France) **23/1**

0 **California Dreams (SWI)**^{160} 4-8-9 **0**........ SebastienMaillot 4 —
(U Suter, France) **95/1**

0 **Sidney Girl**^{130} 4-8-9 **0**........ StephanePasquier 13 —
(R Gibson, France) **17/1**

0 **Argun River (IRE)**^{136} 4-9-3 **0**........ OlivierPeslier 16 —
(R Gibson, France) **49/1**

0 **Mogadishio (FR)**^{150} 4-9-6 **0**........ MaximeGuyon 2 —
(A Couetil, France) **27/1**

0 **Gonetrio (USA)**^{67} 4-8-9 **0**........ FranckBlondel 9 —
(Rod Collet, France) **12/1**

0 **Kilea (FR)**^{63} 4-9-0 **0**........ DominiqueBoeuf 11 —
(Y Barberot, France) **53/10**^{2}

0 **Le Home (FR)**^{67} 4-8-9 **0**........ TheoBachelot 10 —
(S Wattel, France) **11/1**

0 **Pivoina (IRE)**^{101} 4-9-1 **0**........ ThierryThulliez 6 —
(G Henrot, France) **31/1**

1m 58.0s (118.00) **18** Ran SP% **117.8**
WIN (incl. 1 euro stake): 8.40. PLACES: 3.00, 2.20, 4.50. DF: 24.10. SF: 49.20.
Owner Mathieu Offenstadt **Bred** Scea Haras De La Perelle **Trained** France

841a PRIX DE LA MAYENNE (CONDITIONS) (3YO FILLIES) (FIBRESAND) 7f 110y

1:20 (12:00) 3-Y-O **£14,655** (£5,862; £4,396; £2,931; £1,465)

RPR

1 **Cerveza**^{123} [7383] 3-8-10 0........ GregoryBenoist 6 89
(Mme Pia Brandt, France) **14/1**

2 *1 1/2* **Louvakhova (USA)** 3-9-0 0........ IoritzMendizabal 2 89
(J-C Rouget, France) **9/10**^{1}

3 *3/4* **Heidikly (FR)**^{130} [7276] 3-9-4 0........ ThierryJarnet 3 91
(B De Montzey, France) **4/1**^{2}

4 *2 1/2* **Cheque Book**^{259} [3386] 3-9-0 0........ MichaelHills 7 81
(B W Hills) *broke wl to ld sn after s: led into st: rdn 1 1/2f out: hdd 1f out: no ex: styd on* **9/2**^{3}

5 *1* **Madly In Love (FR)**^{78} [7975] 3-8-10 0........ JohanVictoire 4 75
(J-L Gay, France) **11/1**

6 *1/2* **Passei (FR)**^{59} 3-9-0 0........ ThierryThulliez 1 77
(Mlle V Dissaux, France) **23/1**

7 *6* **Half Truth (IRE)**^{92} 3-9-0 0........ MaximeGuyon 5 62
(H-A Pantall, France) **12/1**

1m 31.5s (91.50) **7** Ran SP% **117.7**
WIN (incl. 1 euro stake): 14.90. PLACES: 3.70, 1.40. SF: 53.40.
Owner J O Trading APS **Bred** B Taylor **Trained** France

842a PRIX DE DOUVILLE (CLAIMER) (4YO) (FIBRESAND) 1m 4f

2:20 (12:00) 4-Y-O **£7,758** (£3,103; £2,327; £1,551; £775)

RPR

1 **Compromis (IRE)** 4-9-4 0........(p) FranckBlondel 3 64
(F Rossi, France) **17/5**^{1}

2 *3/4* **El Bulli (USA)**^{79} 4-8-10 0........(p) ManonScandella$^{(6)}$ 11 61
(F Chappet, France) **15/1**

3 *hd* **Perfect Union (IRE)**^{73} 4-8-9 0........ AnthonyCaramanolis$^{(6)}$ 16 60
(N Clement, France) **43/10**^{2}

4 *2* **Bel Herve (FR)**^{407} 4-9-3 0........ MatthieuAutier$^{(5)}$ 14 63
(J-M Capitte, France) **6/1**^{3}

5 *hd* **Dal'Oro (FR)** 4-8-11 0........(b) AnthonyCrastus 7 52
(Jean De Rouallé, France) **10/1**

6 *nse* **Email Exit (IRE)**^{51} [220] 4-8-11 0........ FabienLefebvre 1 52
(Mme G Rarick, France) **32/1**

7 *nk* **Eagle Cliff**^{147} 4-8-8 0........ TheoBachelot$^{(3)}$ 10 52
(J E Hammond, France) **17/1**

8 *1 1/2* **Nova Med (IRE)**^{59} 4-8-10 0........(b) YoannRousset$^{(6)}$ 8 54
(Y Fertillet, France) **10/1**

9 *1* **Lord Lansing (IRE)**^{35} [425] 4-9-10 0........ LaurentHuart 2 61
(Mrs K Burke) *in rr fr s: swtchd to rail and styd on fnl f* **31/1**

10 *1 1/2* **Nennella (GER)**^{73} 4-8-8 0........(b) DPorcu 13 42
(S Smrczek, Germany) **54/1**

0 **Cloudy Bay (USA)**^{32} [448] 4-9-1 0........ RobertWinston 9 —
(Mrs K Burke) *prom fr s on outer: ev ch ent st: rdn 2f out: no rspnse: grad fdd* **26/1**

0 **Ponderosa (FR)**^{136} 4-8-11 0........ MaximeGuyon 15 —
(J Bertran De Balanda, France) **20/1**

0 **Galant De Giverny (FR)**^{167} 4-8-8 0 ow2........(p) YoannBarille$^{(5)}$ 4 —
(C Diard, France) **119/1**

0 **Lucy In The Sky (FR)**^{84} 4-8-8 0........ GregoryBenoist 6 —
(N Leenders, France) **30/1**

0 **Commando Cat (FR)** 4-8-11 0........ JohanVictoire 5 —
(L A Urbano-Grajales, France) **17/2**

0 **Mick Bora (FR)** 4-8-8 0........ EricMichel 12 —
(Mme E Siavy-Julien, France) **181/1**

2m 34.5s (154.50) **16** Ran SP% **117.4**
WIN (incl. 1 euro stake): 4.40. PLACES: 1.90, 4.20, 1.80. DF: 41.00. SF: 76.60.
Owner Jean-Claude Seroul **Bred** M Henochsberg & Pontchartrain Stud **Trained** France

843a PRIX DE BRANVILLE (CLAIMER) (5YO+) (LADY RIDERS) (FIBRESAND) 1m 4f

3:25 (12:00) 5-Y-O+ **£7,758** (£3,103; £2,327; £1,551; £775)

RPR

1 **Bergonzi (IRE)**^{149} [5788] 7-9-2 0........ SabrinaWandt 2 76
(C Von Der Recke, Germany) **78/10**

2 *1/2* **Law Blade (FR)**^{70} 6-8-11 0........ KarenBeaumard 6 70
(H-A Pantall, France) **63/1**

3 *2* **Runtil Bere (FR)**^{78} 6-8-11 0........ CarlaO'Halloran 11 67
(Mme Pia Brandt, France) **28/1**

4 *1 1/2* **Monique Bisou (FR)**^{26} [533] 5-8-8 0........(b) NadegeOuakli 8 61
(Y Fertillet, France) **13/1**

5 *nse* **West Wing (FR)**^{26} [533] 6-8-11 0........(p) CelineLaunay 5 64
(F-X Belvisi, France) **5/1**^{3}

6 *2* **Icy River (FR)**^{78} 6-8-4 0........(b) MlleAngelaLeCorre$^{(7)}$ 15 61
(P Monfort, France) **54/1**

7 *3/4* **Ramora (USA)**^{44} [301] 5-9-2 0........ KylieManser 13 65
(Olivia Maylam) *racd in 6th: prog bef st: swtchd to mid-trck early in st: rdn 1 1/2f out: no ex: styd on u.p fnl f* **35/1**

8 *1/2* **Premier Violon (IRE)**^{187} 8-9-1 0........ ChrystelleCardenne 9 63
(Mlle C Cardenne, France) **17/1**

9 *snk* **Grandretour**^{410} 7-9-0 0........ ManonScandella$^{(5)}$ 14 67
(J-C Rouget, France) **9/5**^{1}

10 *1/2* **Rouge Emery (FR)**^{74} 5-8-3 0........ MlleZoePfeil$^{(5)}$ 7 55
(J Clais, France) **102/1**

0 **Luberon**^{419} [205] 8-9-2 0........ SilviaCasanova 4 —
(P Schaerer, Switzerland) **25/1**

0 **Alde Gott (FR)**^{10} 8-8-9 0........ PaulineProd'homme$^{(6)}$ 1 —
(D Prod'Homme, France) **19/1**

0 **Wind Of Tea**^{92} 7-9-1 0........(b) CelineCrouzet 3 —
(A Vetault, France) **72/1**

0 **Moon Rock**^{62} 7-8-11 0........(b) MlleAudeDuporte 10 —
(D Menard, France) **145/1**

0 **Lasse (GER)**^{26} [533] 8-8-11 0........ DelphineSantiago 12 —
(C Ferland, France) **9/2**^{2}

0 **Picanina (FR)**^{74} 9-8-8 0........(b) MarieFlahault 16 —
(H Julliot, France) **230/1**

2m 35.3s (155.30) **16** Ran SP% **116.5**
WIN (incl. 1 euro stake): 8.80. PLACES: 3.50, 16.80, 8.90. DF: 338.30. SF: 406.00.
Owner R J Turton **Bred** Deer Forest Stud **Trained** Weilerswist, Germany

833 WOLVERHAMPTON (A.W) (L-H)

Saturday, March 12

OFFICIAL GOING: Standard
Wind: Moderate, half-behind Weather: Overcast with light rain for last two races

844 WILLIAM HILL LADY WULFRUNA STKS (LISTED RACE) 7f 32y(P)

2:10 (2:10) (Class 1) 4-Y-O+

£19,869 (£7,532; £3,769; £1,879; £941; £472) **Stalls** High

Form RPR

200- **1** **Dunelight (IRE)**^{176} [6147] 8-9-3 105........(v) LukeMorris 11 110
(Clive Cox) *racd on outer: chsd ldrs: led over 1f out: edgd lft ins fnl f: drvn out and kpt on wl* **9/1**

502- **2** *1/2* **Docofthebay (IRE)**^{84} [7935] 7-9-3 97........(p) IanMongan 8 109
(David Nicholls) *in tch: effrt to chse ldrs [illegible] 2nd wl ins fnl f: clsng on wnr towards fin* **14/1**

101- **3** *1* **Malcheek (IRE)**^{90} [7846] 9-9-3 100........ DuranFentiman 10 106
(Tim Easterby) *in tch: effrt to chse ldrs 2f out: ch wl over 1f out: styd on ins fnl f: nt quite pce of front pair* **20/1**

03-3 **4** *1 3/4* **Duff (IRE)**^{14} [700] 8-9-3 109........ FMBerry 9 103
(Edward Lynam, Ire) *w ldr: led over 2f out: rdn and hdd over 1f out: no ex fnl 75yds* **4/1**^{1}

124- **5** *1 1/4* **Bohemian Melody**^{166} [6429] 4-9-3 94........ AdamKirby 1 99
(Marco Botti) *trckd ldrs: rdn and outpcd over 1f out: one pce ins fnl f* **7/1**^{3}

011- **6** *nk* **Spirit Of Sharjah (IRE)**^{87} [7875] 6-9-6 105........ JimmyQuinn 6 101+
(Julia Feilden) *hld up: rdn over 2f out: styd on u.p ins fnl f: nt gng pce to rch ldrs* **9/2**^{2}

14-6 **7** *3/4* **Angel's Pursuit (IRE)**^{14} [700] 4-9-3 107........ RichardHughes 7 96
(Richard Hannon) *midfield: rdn and outpcd over 2f out: kpt on ins fnl f: nvr able to chal* **4/1**^{1}

6000 **8** *1* **Elna Bright**^{14} [700] 6-9-3 90........(v) LiamKeniry 4 94
(Brett Johnson) *s.i.s: bmpd sn after s: racd keenly in midfield: rdn and outpcd over 1f out: wl btn ins fnl f* **16/1**

0-20 **9** *nk* **Freeforaday (USA)**^{20} [627] 4-9-3 98........ SteveDrowne 12 93
(John Best) *hld up: pushed along 3f out: kpt on ins fnl f: no imp on ldrs* **40/1**

0-40 **10** *8* **Beauchamp Viceroy**^{14} [700] 7-9-3 98........(bt) NeilCallan 5 74
(Gerard Butler) *led: stdd pce 4f out: hdd over 2f out: rdn wl over 1f out: sn wknd* **12/1**

250- **11** *14* **Desert Creek (IRE)**^{155} [6721] 5-9-3 90........ AdrianNicholls 2 39
(David Nicholls) *hld up: pushed along and bhd over 3f out: nvr on terms* **22/1**

04-4 **12** *96* **Atlantic Story (USA)**^{36} [429] 9-9-3 100........(bt) JamieSpencer 3 —
(Michael Easterby) *hld up: struggling 2f out: bhd over 1f out: virtually p.u ins fnl f: walked across line* **25/1**

1m 28.32s (-1.28) **Going Correction** +0.075s/f (Slow) **12** Ran SP% **116.3**
Speed ratings (Par 111): **110,109,108,106,104 104,103,102,102,93 77,**—
toteswingers: 1&2 £18.60, 1&3 £30.70, 2&3 £26.40. CSF £118.69 TOTE £11.30: £3.70, £4.10, £7.60; EX 107.30 Trifecta £532.10 Part won. Pool: £719.16 - 0.50 winning units..
Owner Mr And Mrs P Hargreaves **Bred** D And B Egan **Trained** Lambourn, Berks

FOCUS
The fifth running of the Lady Wulfruna Stakes as a Listed event and the biggest field to date. The early pace was solid, though it had slowed by halfway. It paid to race handily. Straightforward form, the winner repeating last year's success from placed horses who slightly surprisingly managed to transfer their quite recent Fibresand form back to Polytrack.

NOTEBOOK

Dunelight(IRE) was fit from racing at Meydan when winning this last year, but this was his first outing since September. However, there was no doubting the positive vibes emanating from the stable and they were proved right. The high draw was awkward and he wasn't able to lead early, but as was the case the previous year he showed that he doesn't have to set the pace to be fully effective and he was content with the stalking role on the outside of the leading pack. Sent for home over a furlong out, he was always doing enough to hold on despite hanging away to his left under pressure. (op 11-1)

Docofthebay(IRE) was expected to come on from this with the Lincoln the main target, so this effort must have delighted connections. Always tracking the pace, he came off the bridle turning in but stayed on strongly to press the winner right to the line and will go to Doncaster, for which he remains a top-priced 33-1, with this pleasing prep under his belt.

Malcheek(IRE), returning from a three-month absence, was hammered by Spirit Of Sharjah when they met at Lingfield in November but reversed that form in no uncertain terms. Always held on wide of the field, he ran on well down the centre of the track and this was a decent effort from a horse that is at his most effective when able to dominate. (op 16-1)

Duff(IRE), the highest rated in the field and back over probably his best trip on this surface, looked the one to beat when sent for home off the final bend, but he displayed an awkward head carriage and didn't last in front for long. He seems to have mislaid the winning habit for the time being. (op 9-2)

Bohemian Melody seemed to be travelling better than anything turning in, but didn't find a lot off the bridle. To be fair, he had plenty to find at the weights on this return from six months off. (op 6-1)

Spirit Of Sharjah(IRE) was bidding for a hat-trick and his success in a similar event at Kempton when last seen in December (with a few of today's rivals behind him) meant he had to concede 3lb all round. Held up off the pace, he was keen enough but looked awkward when put under pressure and made very little impression from off the pace. This was his first try here and his style of racing wasn't suited to this contest. (op 5-1 tchd 11-2)

Angel's Pursuit(IRE), not for the first time, didn't enjoy the best of trips and found himself in a poor position on the inside turning in. He needs a change of luck. (op 9-2)

845 WILLIAMHILL.COM H'CAP — 7f 32y(P)

2:45 (2:45) (Class 4) (0-85,94) 3-Y-O — **£3,238** (£963; £481; £240) Stalls High

Form — RPR

3113 **1** — **Kingscroft (IRE)**[23] 578 3-8-11 **75** .... GregFairley 3 — 84
(Mark Johnston) *prom: chsd ldr over 2f out: r.o to ld ins fnl f: kpt on wl and a doing enough towards fin* **6/1**[3]

12 **2** ¾ **Dasho**[22] 601 3-8-11 **75** .... HayleyTurner 11 — 82+
(Olivia Maylam) *sn led: rdn over 1f out: hdd ins fnl f: styd on but a hld after* **9/1**

-415 **3** 2¾ **Silly Billy (IRE)**[9] 750 3-8-12 **76** .... LiamKeniry 10 — 76
(Sylvester Kirk) *midfield: hdwy 2f out: rdn to chse ldrs over 1f out: styd on same pce and no imp fnl 150yds* **16/1**

22-1 **4** 1¾ **Strictly Pink (IRE)**[22] 600 3-8-11 **75** .... CathyGannon 7 — 70+
(Alan Bailey) *hld up: hdwy to chse ldrs over 1f out: sn edgd rt: kpt on same pce fnl 150yds and edgd lft* **10/3**[1]

5-21 **5** ½ **Bosambo**[11] 720 3-8-13 **77** .... PJMcDonald 12 — 71+
(Alan Swinbank) *chsd ldrs: rdn over 1f out: one pce ins fnl f* **9/2**[2]

1- **6** 1½ **Ninita**[99] 7682 3-9-4 **82** .... NickyMackay 2 — 71
(Mark Rimmer) *hld up: pushed along over 3f out: hdwy and edgd lft over 1f out: nt rch ldrs: one pce ins fnl f* **10/1**

1-24 **7** ¾ **Insolenceofoffice (IRE)**[23] 578 3-9-3 **81** .... GeorgeBaker 6 — 68
(Andrew Crook) *hld up: rdn over 1f out: nvr able to trble ldrs* **16/1**

-111 **8** nk **Fred Willetts (IRE)**[45] 302 3-9-13 **94** .... RichardEvans(3) 8 — 81+
(David Evans) *hld up: rdn over 1f out: nvr able to chal* **17/2**

11-4 **9** hd **Dunmore Boy (IRE)**[66] 44 3-8-3 **67** .... PaulHanagan 9 — 53
(Richard Fahey) *towards rr: hdwy into midfield 4f out: rdn over 2f out: no imp on ldrs: wknd fnl f* **11/1**

2-22 **10** 3¾ **My Lord**[10] 724 3-8-13 **80** ....(t) KierenFox(3) 5 — 56
(Bill Turner) *handy: chsd ldr over 5f out tl pushed along over 2f out: rdn and wknd over 1f out* **10/1**

10- **11** 6 **Stamp Duty (IRE)**[140] 7085 3-8-13 **77** .... BarryMcHugh 1 — 37
(Ollie Pears) *broke wl: led early: remained in tch w ldrs: rdn over 2f out: sn wknd* **20/1**

030- **12** 9 **Royal Opera**[140] 7085 3-8-11 **75** .... JamesMillman 4 — 10
(Rod Millman) *a bhd: rdn over 3f out: lost tch over 2f out* **8/1**

1m 29.92s (0.32) **Going Correction** +0.075s/f (Slow) — 12 Ran SP% **130.2**

Speed ratings (Par 100): **101,100,97,95,94 92,91,91,91,87 80,69**

toteswingers: 1&2 £9.40, 1&3 £23.40, 2&3 £13.90. CSF £65.48 CT £869.46 TOTE £5.20: £1.70, £4.10, £5.80; EX 46.30 TRIFECTA Not won..

Owner Dr Marwan Koukash **Bred** J Beckett **Trained** Middleham Moor, N Yorks

FOCUS

A decent handicap contested by some progressive 3-y-os, but another race dominated by those that raced prominently. the form has been rated positively.

Royal Opera Official explanation: jockey said gelding would not face the kickback

846 WILLIAM HILL LINCOLN TRIAL H'CAP — 1m 141y(P)

3:20 (3:23) (Class 2) (0-105,101) 4-Y-O+

£18,693 (£5,598; £2,799; £1,401; £699; £351) Stalls Low

Form — RPR

-321 **1** — **Lowther**[26] 542 6-9-7 **99** ....(be) J-PGuillambert 7 — 108
(Alan Bailey) *in tch: forced wd on bnd wl over 7f out: clsd 4f out: led wl over 1f out: r.o wl to really assert: wandered a little ins fnl f: drvn out: eased whn in full control fnl strides* **5/1**[2]

00-3 **2** ½ **Tartan Gigha (IRE)**[8] 778 6-9-5 **97** .... JoeFanning 10 — 105+
(Mark Johnston) *in tch: forced wd on bnd wl over 7f out: sn lost pl: hdwy over 2f out: styd on to take 2nd 1f out: wanted to lugg lft ins fnl f: clsd on wnr towards fin: nvr gng to get there* **10/1**

006- **3** ¾ **Prime Exhibit**[155] 6721 6-9-3 **95** .... PaulHanagan 2 — 102+
(Richard Fahey) *in tch: hmpd on bnd wl over 7f out: racd in midfield: hdwy to chse ldrs over 1f out: styd on ins fnl f* **4/1**[1]

0-56 **4** 1 **Benandonner (USA)**[21] 615 8-9-3 **95** .... MartinLane 9 — 99
(Mike Murphy) *a.p: rdn over 2f out: nt qckn over 1f out: styd on same pce ins fnl f* **20/1**

11-2 **5** ¾ **Norman Orpen (IRE)**[26] 542 4-9-3 **95** .... JamieSpencer 12 — 97
(Jane Chapple-Hyam) *dwlt: swtchd lft s: hld up: hdwy over 1f out: styd on ins fnl f: nt gng pce to get to ldrs* **6/1**[3]

-601 **6** 2¾ **Georgebernardshaw (IRE)**[3] 803 6-9-4 **96** 6ex.......... RichardHughes 8 — 92
(David Simcock) *led: edgd in on rival on bnd wl over 7f out: hdd over 1f out: wknd fnl f* **16/1**

1113 **7** 3 **Dubai Hills**[12] 710 5-8-12 **95** .... AdamCarter(5) 3 — 84
(Bryan Smart) *dwlt: midfield: pushed along and outpcd over 3f out and dropped to rr: sme hdwy ins fnl f: nvr a threat* **16/1**

1-21 **8** hd **Hazzard County (USA)**[35] 438 7-8-12 **95** .... LauraPike(5) 11 — 83+
(David Simcock) *stmbld s: hld up: wnt lft whn hdwy over 1f out: one pce and no imp on ldrs* **9/1**

3400 **9** ¾ **Final Drive (IRE)**[22] 604 5-9-9 **101** .... StevieDonohoe 13 — 88+
(John Ryan) *dwlt: swtchd lft s: bhd: rdn over 1f out: nvr on terms* **16/1**

050- **10** 2¼ **Prince Of Dance**[141] 7060 5-9-2 **94** .... GrahamGibbons 1 — 76
(Tom Tate) *midfield tl outpcd over 1f out* **18/1**

-331 **11** 10 **Suits Me**[14] 702 8-9-3 **95** .... MickyFenton 4 — 68
(Tom Tate) *prom: n.m.r on inner and hmpd on bnd wl over 7f out: stl up there tl shkn up wl over 1f out: sn wl btn: eased fnl f* **12/1**

311- **12** hd **Licence To Till (USA)**[148] 6910 4-9-2 **94** .... GregFairley 6 — 52
(Mark Johnston) *racd keenly: trckd ldrs: forced wd on bnd wl over 7f out: rdn over 2f out: wknd wl over 1f out* **12/1**

1m 49.35s (-1.15) **Going Correction** +0.075s/f (Slow) — 12 Ran SP% **113.1**

Speed ratings (Par 109): **108,107,106,106,105 102,100,100,99,97 88,88**

toteswingers: 1&2 £11.00, 1&3 £4.40, 2&3 £7.30. CSF £47.25 CT £168.84 TOTE £7.00: £2.00, £3.80, £1.80; EX 42.90 Trifecta £234.80 Pool: £580.82 - 1.83 winning units..

Owner Exors of the Late L J Barratt **Bred** L J Barratt **Trained** Newmarket, Suffolk

■ Nazreef (15/2) was withdrawn after proving unruly in the stalls. R4 applies, deduct 10p in the £.

■ Stewards' Enquiry : Richard Hughes five-day ban: careless riding (Mar 26, 28-31)

FOCUS

A typically competitive renewal of the Lincoln Trial, but another race where the hold-up horses had little chance. There was also early drama with Nazreef being withdrawn after trying to get under his stall, and then plenty of trouble after a furlong when Georgebernardshaw badly hampered Suits Me when crossing to the rail, who in turn hampered Prime Exhibit. The winner is rated better than ever, with the fourtgh and fifth helping with the level.

NOTEBOOK

Lowther was back in a handicap after beating Norman Orpen and Suits Me in a C&D conditions event last time, but although worse off at the weights with both, his trainer remained confident. He was always in a great position up with the leaders and making a dash for home over a furlong out proved to be a race-winning move. He was quoted a top-priced 20-1 for the Lincoln itself immediately afterwards and will head there providing the ground isn't soft. (op 7-1)

Tartan Gigha(IRE), fit from finishing third on the Deauville Fibresand earlier this month, was well held off this mark in this race last year, but this was much better and he was doing all his best work late. His trainer was concerned beforehand that this trip was a little short of his best these days.

Prime Exhibit ◆, last year's Lincoln runner-up, was returning from five months off. Considering that he got knocked back in the early melee here, he did extremely well to finish where he did and the bookmakers seem to think that he will reverse this form with the winner on Town Moor, being a top-priced 16-1 for the Lincoln. (op 11-2)

Benandonner(USA) was always up with the pace and did well to hang in there for so long, though the track was helping his style of running. He remains 8lb above his last winning mark and this effort is unlikely to give the handicapper much reason to drop him.

Norman Orpen(IRE) enjoyed a 4lb pull for a near 2l beating by Lowther over C&D last time, but he was 11lb higher than when completing a Polytrack hat-trick at the end of last year. He finished well down the wide outside, but his style of running was a major disadvantage on the day. (op 13-2 tchd 7-1)

Georgebernardshaw(IRE), carrying a 6lb penalty for his success in a 1m2f Kempton conditions event three days earlier, tried to make his stamina tell but the winner's turn of foot blew him away turning for home.

Dubai Hills wasn't disgraced in a four-runner conditions event here last time but he could never get into the race from off the pace here. He has previously looked invincible on Fibresand and it will be interesting to see how he fares with cut in the ground back on turf.

Hazzard County(USA) goes really well for Laura Pike, but his style of running wasn't suited to these conditions. (op 10-1)

Final Drive(IRE) won six of his last seven starts on Polytrack before heading to Meydan in January, but was off a 9lb higher mark than for his latest success and was never in the contest. (tchd 18-1)

Suits Me Official explanation: jockey said gelding suffered interference in running

847 WILLIAMHILL.COM CLAIMING STKS — 5f 20y(P)

3:55 (3:56) (Class 5) 3-Y-O — **£2,590** (£770; £385; £192) Stalls Low

Form — RPR

3212 **1** — **Go Maggie Go (IRE)**[5] 788 3-8-4 58 .... AmyRyan(3) 8 — 69
(Kevin Ryan) *chsd ldrs: led over 1f out: r.o wl: in command fnl 110yds* **6/1**[3]

0-44 **2** 2¼ **Dream Catcher (FR)**[9] 740 3-9-0 78 .... JamieSpencer 1 — 68
(David Nicholls) *led: rdn and hdd over 1f out: kpt on but hld by wnr fnl 110yds* **4/1**[1]

6332 **3** hd **Captain Dimitrios**[5] 787 3-8-8 71 ....(v) CathyGannon 10 — 61
(David Evans) *hld up in midfield: rdn over 1f out: hdwy whn hung lft ent fnl f: fin strly* **9/1**

3663 **4** 1¼ **Pineapple Pete (IRE)**[9] 745 3-8-0 62 ....(t) NoraLooby(7) 5 — 56
(Alan McCabe) *hld up: rdn and hdwy to chse ldrs over 1f out: nt pce to mount chal: one pce fnl 100yds* **9/1**

1212 **5** 1½ **Restless Bay (IRE)**[9] 740 3-9-3 79 ....(v) ChrisCatlin 9 — 60
(Reg Hollinshead) *hld up: plld wd and hdwy over 1f out: kpt on ins fnl f: nt pce to trble ldrs* **4/1**[1]

010- **6** 1½ **Dolly Parton (IRE)**[224] 4578 3-8-9 71 .... AdrianNicholls 6 — 47
(David Nicholls) *chsd ldrs tl rdn and wknd wl over 1f out* **5/1**[2]

2545 **7** ¾ **Je Suis Unrockstar**[9] 740 3-8-9 66 ....(p) BillyCray(3) 3 — 47
(David Nicholls) *midfield: hdwy on inner wl over 1f out: nt rch ldrs: wknd fnl 110yds* **16/1**

060- **8** ½ **Instructress**[93] 7777 3-8-2 60 .... JimmyQuinn 4 — 35
(Robert Cowell) *hld up in rr: bmpd along briefly jst over 3f out: u.p over 1f out: nvr on terms* **33/1**

1-33 **9** 3¼ **Sugar Beet**[9] 740 3-8-7 74 ....(p) LukeMorris 7 — 29
(Ronald Harris) *midfield: hdwy to chse ldrs 3f out: rdn and hung lft whn wknd over 1f out* **5/1**[2]

0-20 **10** 9 **Majestic Ridge (IRE)**[9] 745 3-8-8 60 ....(v) PaulHanagan 2 — —
(David Evans) *prom tl rdn and wknd over 1f out: eased whn btn ins fnl f* **20/1**

62.37 secs (0.07) **Going Correction** +0.075s/f (Slow) — 10 Ran SP% **121.2**

Speed ratings (Par 98): **102,98,98,96,93 91,90,89,84,69**

toteswingers: 1&2 £4.70, 1&3 £5.90, 2&3 £7.10. CSF £31.56 TOTE £8.10: £2.30, £2.80, £2.40; EX 33.00 Trifecta £136.40 Pool: £781.74 - 4.24 winning units..Dream Catcher was the subject of a friendly claim.

Owner Roger Peel **Bred** Oak Lodge Stud **Trained** Hambleton, N Yorks

FOCUS

A fast and furious sprint claimer in which few got involved. Surprise improvement from the winner, but the form makes sense otherwise.

848 WILLIAM HILL - THE HOME OF BETTING H'CAP — 5f 216y(P)

4:25 (4:26) (Class 2) (0-100,100) 4-Y-O+

£9,969 (£2,985; £1,492; £747; £372; £187) Stalls Low

Form — RPR

03-4 **1** — **Flipando (IRE)**[21] 613 10-8-11 **90** .... GrahamGibbons 12 — 100+
(David Barron) *chsd ldrs: led jst ins fnl f: r.o: a doing enough cl home* **8/1**

205- **2** ½ **Medicean Man**161 6564 5-9-6 99 SteveDrowne 8 108+
(Jeremy Gask) *racd keenly: hld up: hdwy over 2f out: r.o to chal ins fnl 75yds: hld cl home* **6/1**2

0-66 **3** ½ **Jimmy Styles**22 602 7-9-5 98 (p) AdamKirby 4 105
(Clive Cox) *racd keenly: trckd ldrs: effrt to chal over 1f out: nt qckn fnl 50yds* **13/2**3

0-52 **4** nk **Star Rover (IRE)**21 613 4-8-10 89 CathyGannon 7 95
(David Evans) *led: rdn and hrd pressed wl over 1f out: hdd jst ins fnl f: styd on same pce fnl 50yds* **12/1**

5-42 **5** 3 **Piscean (USA)**36 429 6-9-3 96 PaulHanagan 3 93
(Tom Keddy) *racd keenly: hld up: rdn over 1f out: styd on ins fnl f: nt pce to rch ldrs* **4/1**1

614- **6** hd **Secret Asset (IRE)**74 7993 6-9-7 100 GeorgeBaker 5 99
(Jane Chapple-Hyam) *midfield: n.m.r and hmpd 4f out: hdwy wl over 1f out: sn chsd ldrs: no ex fnl 100yds* **7/1**

000- **7** ½ **Rulesn'regulations**112 7522 5-9-4 97 JamieSpencer 13 93
(Matthew Salaman) *prom: n.m.r briefly and lost pl wl over 1f out: sn outpcd: kpt on one pce ins fnl f* **16/1**

020- **8** ½ **Jack My Boy (IRE)**182 5944 4-9-1 94 NeilCallan 6 88
(David Evans) *prom: rdn to chal over 1f out: no ex fnl 100yds* **10/1**

0-54 **9** 1 **Captain Ramius (IRE)**12 710 5-8-10 89 (t) PhillipMakin 2 80
(Kevin Ryan) *hld up towards rr: pushed along over 1f out: nvr able to get on terms w ldrs* **12/1**

302- **10** nk **Wildcat Wizard (USA)**190 5731 5-9-4 97 AdrianNicholls 11 87
(David Nicholls) *racd keenly: hld up: hdwy on outer 3f out: effrt to chse ldrs 2f out: wknd 1f out* **6/1**2

310- **11** 3 **Little Garcon (USA)**112 7524 4-9-3 96 RichardHughes 1 77
(Marco Botti) *racd keenly: hld up: rdn over 1f out: nvr on terms and wl btn fnl f* **10/1**

1m 14.08s (-0.92) **Going Correction** +0.075s/f (Slow) **11** Ran SP% **125.0**
Speed ratings (Par 109): **109,108,107,107,103 103,102,101,100,99 95**
toteswingers: 1&2 £9.20, 1&3 £26.60, 2&3 £12.70. CSF £59.10 CT £347.60 TOTE £11.70: £3.80, £1.50, £4.00; EX 40.50 TRIFECTA Not won..

Owner Mrs J Hazell **Bred** Denis McDonnell **Trained** Maunby, N Yorks

FOCUS
A competitive sprint handicap, but not packed with many established front runners and the pace slowed noticeably before halfway. The favourite had taken the last five runnings of this race, but not this time. The winner was back to his best and there is the promise of more to come on this surface. The form is solid and easy to rate.

NOTEBOOK
Flipando(IRE) was well handicapped on his best form and, with the pace far from breakneck, he had no problem in sitting handy. Set alight over a furlong out, he showed a fine attitude to keep his rivals at bay and he is now three from five here, with his record over C&D 121. (op 7-1)

Medicean Man was returning from 161 days off, but he has won after a similar layoff in the past. Despite the early pace being far from frantic, he had to be niggled along to stay in touch early but he had every chance to get to the winner up the straight and could never quite make it. (op 5-1)

Jimmy Styles, 2lb lower than when winning the 2009 Ayr Gold Cup, was making his all-weather debut on his 28th start. He seemed to get into a spot of bother when the pace slowed before halfway, but he ran on well up the straight and this should have set him up nicely for all the big turf sprint handicaps. (op 12-1)

Star Rover(IRE) signalled a return to form at Lingfield last month and was given a well-judged ride from the front here on a day when the track was favouring front-runners. That enabled him to stay in the thick of the action for as long as he did. Cathy Gannon reported that he had hung right. Official explanation: jockey said gelding hung right-handed (tchd 14-1)

Piscean(USA), still 3lb higher than when winning over C&D in November, didn't find his stride until it was too late and the front-runners weren't coming back. (op 9-1)

Secret Asset(IRE) got into all sorts of trouble against the inside rail on a couple of occasions in the back straight, so it may be best to forgive him this, but he is still 8lb above his last winning mark. (op 6-1)

Rulesn'regulations was having his first start since November and although he has won after a much longer absence in the past, the way he faded late on here suggests that he needed it.

849 WILLIAMHILL.COM - NEW MOBILE PHONE APP H'CAP 1m 5f 194y(P)
4:55 (4:55) (Class 4) (0-85,88) 4-Y-O+ £3,885 (£1,156; £577; £288) **Stalls** Low

Form RPR

0-33 **1** **Admirable Duque (IRE)**43 342 5-9-4 77 (p) NeilCallan 5 87
(Dominic Ffrench Davis) *s.i.s: hld up: hdwy 4f out: effrt on outer 3f out: led 2f out: qcknd away over 1f out: in command whn edgd rt ins fnl f: r.o wl* **16/1**

-113 **2** 2¾ **Muzo (USA)**30 486 5-9-3 76 FrannyNorton 2 82
(Chris Dwyer) *led: rdn and hdd 2f out: one pce and no imp fr over 1f out* **6/1**

0-15 **3** 2½ **Bedouin Bay**21 614 4-9-3 80 JamesDoyle 8 83
(Alan McCabe) *in tch: effrt to chse ldrs 2f out: one pce fr over 1f out and no imp on front pair* **10/1**

0-13 **4** ¾ **Porgy**52 209 6-9-9 82 JamieSpencer 7 84
(David Simcock) *sweating: stdd s: hld up: rdn over 2f out: styd on fr over 1f out: nvr able to rch ldrs* **7/2**2

-500 **5** 2½ **Record Breaker (IRE)**35 436 7-9-3 76 JoeFanning 3 74
(Mark Johnston) *in tch: lost pl 4f out: outpcd 3f out: kpt on steadily fnl f: unable to trble ldrs* **17/2**

2-24 **6** nse **Accompanist**1 838 8-8-7 66 (p) CathyGannon 1 64
(T G McCourt, Ire) *chsd ldrs tl rdn and wknd 2f out* **16/1**

22-1 **7** 2¼ **Phoenix Flight (IRE)**52 209 6-10-0 87 RichardHughes 9 82
(James Evans) *sweating: stdd s: hld up: outpcd 2f out: rdn over 1f out: nvr on terms* **5/1**3

113- **8** 6 **Sherman McCoy**288 2509 5-10-1 88 JamesMillman 4 74
(Rod Millman) *chsd ldr to 4f out: u.p and wknd 3f out* **7/1**

5411 **9** 2¼ **Cotton King**22 596 4-9-1 78 (vt) IanMongan 6 61
(Tobias B P Coles) *racd on outer in midfield: hdwy over 6f out: sn prom: ev ch 3f out: outpcd 2f out: wknd 1f out* **3/1**1

3m 5.28s (-0.72) **Going Correction** +0.075s/f (Slow)
WFA 4 from 5yo+ 4lb **9** Ran SP% **122.1**
Speed ratings (Par 105): **105,103,102,101,100 100,98,95,94**
toteswingers: 1&2 £19.30, 1&3 £22.90, 2&3 £30.10. CSF £114.58 CT £1035.05 TOTE £16.30: £5.30, £2.40, £3.60; EX 94.10 Trifecta £443.90 Part won. Pool: £599.88 - 0.62 winning units..

Owner Exors of the Late Brian W Taylor **Bred** Airlie Stud And R N Clay **Trained** Lambourn, Berks

FOCUS
The pace was far from strong in this staying handicap, so not the test of stamina it might have been. A slight personal best from the winner, with the next three setting the level.

850 WILLIAM HILL - THE HOME OF BETTING MAIDEN STKS 1m 141y(P)
5:25 (5:26) (Class 5) 3-Y-O+ £2,590 (£770; £385; £192) **Stalls** Low

Form RPR

5- **1** **Countermarch**126 7346 3-7-12 0 KieranO'Neill(5) 4 73+
(Richard Hannon) *a.p: led 2f out: asserted over 1f out: in command whn edgd rt ins fnl f: r.o wl* **11/8**1

62 **2** 2¾ **Symphonic Dancer (USA)**9 751 4-9-9 0 J-PGuillambert 10 73
(Brian Baugh) *hld up: hdwy 3f out: styd on to take 2nd ins fnl f: hung lft: no imp on wnr* **4/1**2

035- **3** 3 **X Rated**116 7470 3-8-8 72 LukeMorris 7 65
(Alan McCabe) *trckd ldrs: wnt 2nd 4f out: led wl over 2f out: sn hdd: outpcd by wnr over 1f out: lost 2nd ins fnl f: no ex fnl 75yds* **12/1**

32 **4** 2½ **Bountiful Guest**11 717 3-8-8 0 GrahamGibbons 5 59+
(Brian Baugh) *bhd: pushed along early: nt clr run over 2f out: hdwy over 1f out: kpt on but nt trble ldrs* **11/2**

4 **5** hd **General Duke's**8 774 4-10-0 0 PhillipMakin 3 65+
(Kevin Ryan) *chsd ldr to 4f out: pushed along 3f out: wknd over 1f out* **33/1**

0- **6** 4 **Diocese (USA)**197 5491 3-8-8 0 (t) MartinDwyer 1 50
(Marco Botti) *in tch: outpcd over 2f out: no imp after* **11/2**

64- **7** ½ **Politbureau**203 5288 4-9-11 0 JamesSullivan(3) 9 55
(Michael Easterby) *prom: dropped into midfield after 1f: hdwy on outer to chse ldrs 3f out: wknd 2f out* **8/1**

0/ **8** 6 **Beauchamp Yeoman**498 7146 4-10-0 0 JamesDoyle 11 41
(Hans Adielsson) *midfield: effrt 2f out: no imp on ldrs: wknd over 1f out* **40/1**

3- **9** 1 **Fast Samurai (USA)**210 5085 3-8-8 0 MartinLane 6 32
(David Simcock) *awkward leaving stalls: bhd: pushed along over 2f out: nvr on terms* **5/1**3

060- **10** 18 **Dancing Tara**193 5630 3-8-3 54 CathyGannon 2 —
(David Evans) *led: hdd wl over 2f out: sn wknd* **40/1**

11 nk **Sunblest**18 5-9-9 0 TomEaves 8 —
(Lisa Williamson) *towards rr: toiling and wl bhd over 2f out: nvr on terms* **40/1**

1m 52.1s (1.60) **Going Correction** +0.075s/f (Slow)
WFA 3 from 4yo+ 20lb **11** Ran SP% **138.6**
Speed ratings (Par 103): **95,92,89,87,87 83,83,78,77,61 61**
toteswingers: 1&2 £3.80, 1&3 £8.60, 2&3 £10.60. CSF £8.58 TOTE £3.20: £2.00, £2.20, £3.80; EX 13.10 Trifecta £108.70 Pool: £277.83 - 1.89 winning units..

Owner The Queen **Bred** The Queen **Trained** East Everleigh, Wilts

FOCUS
This maiden lacked strength in depth.

Bountiful Guest Official explanation: jockey said gelding was slow into stride and denied a clear run

Politbureau Official explanation: jockey said gelding hung right-handed on top bend

T/Plt: £2,604.20 to a £1 stake. Pool:£94,895.91 - 26.60 winning tickets. T/Qpdt: £120.90 to a £1 stake. Pool:£7,339.56 - 44.90 winning tickets DO

851a (Foreign Racing) See Raceform Interactive

LE MANS (R-H)
Sunday, March 13

OFFICIAL GOING: Turf: good

852a PRIX CREDIT AGRICOLE (CONDITIONS) (3YO FILLIES) (TURF) 7f
1:30 (12:00) 3-Y-O £4,310 (£1,724; £1,293; £862; £431)

RPR

1 **Navarasa (FR)** 3-9-2 0 FabienLefebvre 11 70
(A Lamotte D'Argy, France) **19/5**2

2 1½ **Finefrenzyrolling (IRE)**197 5531 3-9-2 0 RobertWinston 4 66
(Mrs K Burke) *chsd ldrs: r.o fnl 1 1/2f: nt qckn w wnr* **83/1**

3 ½ **Infidelite** 3-8-11 0 Pierre-CharlesBoudot 3 60
(A Fabre, France) **5/2**1

4 4 **Floriade (IRE)**95 3-9-2 0 GuillaumeFourrier 5 54
(H-A Pantall, France) **39/1**

5 1 **Fast Connection (IRE)**65 3-9-2 0 (b) DavyBonilla 2 51
(F Poulsen, France) **15/1**

6 hd **Nymfia (IRE)** 3-9-2 0 JeromeClaudic 7 51
(C Laffon-Parias, France) **9/2**3

7 nk **Sylphlike (IRE)** 3-8-11 0 SebastienCastellier 6 45
(H-A Pantall, France) **15/1**

8 shd **Daily Dreams (FR)** 3-9-2 0 DavidBreux 9 50
(R Rohne, Germany) **58/1**

9 1 **Selkiss Eria (FR)** 3-9-2 0 AlexandreRoussel 13 47
(C Diard, France) **5/1**

10 1½ **Miyakejima (FR)** 3-8-11 0 FredericSpanu 12 38
(E Libaud, France) **12/1**

11 ¾ **Paperback (IRE)**103 3-8-10 0 FlavienGarnier(6) 1 41
(J-V Toux, France) **102/1**

12 1 **Abandon (FR)**80 7975 3-9-2 0 MorganDelalande 10 38
(C Plisson, France) **70/1**

13 1 **Bio Logique (FR)** 3-9-2 0 RomainLeDrenDoleuze 8 35
(D Allard, France) **25/1**

1m 27.13s (87.13) **13** Ran SP% **116.1**
PARI-MUTUEL (all including 1 euro stakes): WIN 4.80; PLACE 2.10, 14.30, 2.30; DF 65.00; SF 46.10.

Owner Josef Odermatt **Bred** H Kammermann, M Aegerter & D Braun **Trained** France

[793]SOUTHWELL (L-H)
Tuesday, March 15

OFFICIAL GOING: Standard
Wind: virtually nil Weather: fog clearing

853 CHAMPION HURDLE FREE BETS WITH FREEBETTING.CO.UK H'CAP 6f (F)
1:20 (1:20) (Class 5) (0-70,74) 4-Y-0+ **£1,813** (£539; £269; £134) **Stalls** Low

Form RPR
5221 **1** **Where's Reiley (USA)**[7] [794] 5-9-13 **74** 6ex................(b) LeeNewman 1 85
(David Barron) *dwlt: sn rcvrd and led after 1f: mde rest: rdn and hanging rt fr 2f out: kpt on wl fnl f: rdn out* **7/4**[1]
446- **2** *1 ¾* **Klynch**[166] [6494] 5-8-7 **57**................(b) JamesSullivan(3) 4 63
(Ruth Carr) *in tch in midfield: rdn ent fnl 3f: hdwy u.p over 1f out: chsd wnr ent fnl f: kpt on* **33/1**
3104 **3** *2 ½* **Toby Tyler**[12] [743] 5-9-2 **63**................(v) MickyFenton 5 61
(Paul Midgley) *in tch: rdn and unable qck ent fnl 3f: styd on u.p fnl f: snatched 3rd on line: no threat to wnr* **20/1**
-321 **4** *shd* **Interchoice Star**[19] [673] 6-9-4 **65**................(p) AndreaAtzeni 3 63
(Ray Peacock) *chsd ldrs: chsd wnr jst over 2f out: rdn and unable qck wl over 1f out: wknd ins fnl f* **5/1**[3]
-015 **5** *hd* **Final Salute**[12] [743] 5-9-0 **64**................(v) GaryBartley(3) 7 61
(Bryan Smart) *bhd: hung rt and wd bnd 3f out: swtchd lft and styd on u.p ins fnl f: nvr trbld ldrs* **11/1**
-232 **6** *5* **Premier League**[7] [798] 4-8-2 **54**................(p) AdamBeschizza(5) 6 36
(Julia Feilden) *chsd ldrs: rdn and struggling 3f out: wknd 2f out: wl bhd fnl f* **9/4**[2]
6144 **7** *3 ½* **Takajan (IRE)**[19] [673] 4-9-2 **68**................ JamesRogers(5) 2 40
(Mark Brisbourne) *led for 1f: chsd wnr tl jst over 2f out: wknd 2f out: wl bhd and eased wl ins fnl f* **7/1**

1m 15.97s (-0.53) **Going Correction** +0.025s/f (Slow) 7 Ran SP% **112.3**
Speed ratings (Par 103): **104,101,98,98,97 91,86**
toteswingers:1&2:£10.10, 1&3:£4.60, 2&3:£19.40 CSF £53.79 TOTE £2.20: £1.70, £12.70; EX 30.20.
Owner Dovebrace Ltd Air-Conditioning-Projects **Bred** Overbrook Farm **Trained** Maunby, N Yorks

FOCUS
A modest sprint handicap. The winner was well in and should be competitive off his new mark.
Interchoice Star Official explanation: jockey said gelding hung right
Final Salute Official explanation: jockey said gelding hung right throughout
Premier League Official explanation: trainer's rep said gelding ran flat

854 ENJOY THE CHELTENHAM FESTIVAL WITH FREEBETTING.CO.UK CLASSIFIED CLAIMING STKS 1m (F)
1:55 (1:55) (Class 6) 4-Y-0+ **£1,535** (£453; £226) **Stalls** Low

Form RPR
555- **1** **Count Bertoni (IRE)**[222] [4742] 4-8-10 63................ SilvestreDeSousa 10 75
(David O'Meara) *chsd ldrs: rdn to chse ldr over 2f out: led over 1f out: edgd lft jst ins fnl f: rdn out* **8/1**
5021 **2** *¾* **Kipchak (IRE)**[7] [796] 6-8-9 65................(p) HayleyTurner 1 72
(Conor Dore) *taken down early: led: rdn 3f out: hdd over 1f out: kpt on u.p fnl f but a hld* **7/2**[3]
4202 **3** *5* **St Ignatius**[7] [800] 4-8-4 50................(p) NeilChalmers 7 56
(Michael Appleby) *chsd ldr tl ent fnl 3f: wknd u.p over 1f out* **20/1**
040- **4** *1 ½* **Lucayan Dancer**[150] [6915] 11-8-10 58................ AdrianNicholls 6 59
(David Nicholls) *dwlt: sn rdn along and outpcd in rr: drvn 3f out: hdwy over 1f out: r.o fnl f: nvr trbld ldrs* **14/1**
5243 **5** *1* **Ubenkor (IRE)**[19] [674] 6-8-10 63................ TomEaves 9 57
(Michael Herrington) *midfield: pushed along after 2f: no prog 3f out: drvn and plugged on same pce fr over 1f out* **10/3**[2]
4-52 **6** *1* **Kammamuri (IRE)**[39] [425] 6-8-1 62................(bt) AdamBeschizza(5) 3 57+
(Frank Sheridan) *racd off the pce in midfield: pushed along after 2f: no hdwy 3f out: nvr trbld ldrs* **7/4**[1]
-450 **7** *3* **Jasmin Rai**[21] [645] 4-8-4 48................ DavidProbert 2 42
(Des Donovan) *s.i.s: sn rdn along in rr: wknd u.p wl over 2f out: eased fnl f* **33/1**
5046 **8** *½* **Eastern Hills**[12] [744] 6-8-10 60................(p) JamesDoyle 5 47
(Alan McCabe) *trckd ldrs: shkn up to chse ldr ent fnl 3f tl over 2f out: sn wknd* **10/1**
0-50 **9** *7* **Tiger Hawk (USA)**[7] [796] 4-8-2 55 ow1................(b) AndrewHeffernan(3) 4 27
(Kevin M Prendergast) *s.i.s: sn rdn along and a bhd: lost tch over 3f out* **28/1**
10-0 **10** *4* **Novay Essjay (IRE)**[39] [427] 4-8-5 65................ DavidKenny(7) 8 25
(Alan Juckes) *in tch: rdn and struggling over 4f out: c wd 3f out: sn wknd: wl bhd fnl f* **40/1**

1m 42.79s (-0.91) **Going Correction** +0.025s/f (Slow) 10 Ran SP% **122.1**
Speed ratings (Par 101): **105,104,99,97,96 95,92,92,85,81**
toteswingers:1&2:£7.00, 1&3:£15.60, 2&3:£5.80 CSF £36.63 TOTE £6.90: £2.00, £2.50, £4.10; EX 51.60 TRIFECTA Not won..
Owner Mrs S O'Meara **Bred** Le Thenney S A **Trained** Nawton, N Yorks
■ Stewards' Enquiry : Adam Beschizza one-day ban: used whip without giving gelding time to respond (Mar 29)

FOCUS
This claimer was restricted to horses rated 65 or lower. The form is sound but limited with the first pair clear.
Novay Essjay(IRE) Official explanation: jockey said gelding hung badly right

855 CHELTENHAM FESTIVAL FREE BETS WITH FREEBETTING.CO.UK MAIDEN STKS 6f (F)
2:30 (2:30) (Class 5) 3-Y-0 **£1,910** (£564; £282) **Stalls** Low

Form RPR
1 **Twice Red** 3-9-3 0................ LeeNewman 8 77+
(David Barron) *chsd ldrs: rdn to chse ldr wl over 1f out: led over 1f out: r.o wl and drew clr fnl f: rdn out* **7/1**[3]
5-4 **2** *3 ½* **Dr Red Eye**[15] [709] 3-9-0 0................ BillyCray(3) 2 66
(David Nicholls) *led tl over 3f out: ev ch and rdn wl over 2f out: chsd wnr ent fnl f: outpcd by wnr and wl hld fnl f* **6/1**[2]
56 **3** *3 ¾* **Misere**[12] [751] 3-8-12 0................ PhillipMakin 4 53
(Kevin Ryan) *pressed ldr tl led over 3f out: rdn over 2f out: hdd over 1f out: hung rt and wknd fnl f* **8/1**
202- **4** *4 ½* **Sinadinou**[179] [6138] 3-9-3 75................ AdrianNicholls 6 43
(David Nicholls) *w ldr: ev ch and hung rt ent st: sn rdn and struggling: wkng whn swtchd lft ent fnl 2f: wl btn after* **4/6**[1]
265- **5** *4* **Poetically**[190] [5808] 3-9-3 58................ EddieCreighton 3 29
(Joseph Tuite) *sn outpcd in last quartet: struggling u.p 4f out: wl btn fnl 3f* **12/1**
6 *7* **Exocet Missile (IRE)** 3-9-3 0................ SilvestreDeSousa 7 —
(Ann Duffield) *s.i.s: a struggling in last quartet: lost tch over 3f out: eased fnl f* **12/1**
7 *shd* **Hey Up There (IRE)** 3-8-12 0................ PJMcDonald 5 —
(Ruth Carr) *a bhd: lost tch 4f out: wl bhd fnl 3f* **50/1**
3-0 **8** *11* **Deliberation (IRE)**[19] [669] 3-9-3 0................ TomEaves 1 —
(Ollie Pears) *stdd s: t.k.h early: a in rr: lost tch 4f out: t.o fnl 2f* **33/1**

1m 17.89s (1.39) **Going Correction** +0.025s/f (Slow) 8 Ran SP% **118.2**
Speed ratings (Par 98): **91,86,81,75,70 60,60,45**
toteswingers:1&2:£4.60, 1&3:£6.40, 2&3:£3.10 CSF £49.93 TOTE £9.80: £2.00, £1.50, £1.50; EX 46.80 Trifecta £264.80 Part won. Pool: £357.90 - 0.86 winning units..
Owner Y Simova, S Byrne **Bred** Baroness Bloodstock & Redmyre Bloodstock **Trained** Maunby, N Yorks
■ Stewards' Enquiry : Adrian Nicholls caution: used whip without giving gelding time to respond.

FOCUS
The action unfolded against the stands' side in the closing stages. This form looks just modest, but the race should produce a few winners. The winner made a nice debut and the second is the key to the form.
Misere Official explanation: jockey said filly hung right at finish
Exocet Missile(IRE) Official explanation: jockey said colt had no more to give

856 FREE HORSE RACING BETS WITH FREEBETTING.CO.UK (S) STKS 7f (F)
3:05 (3:05) (Class 6) 3-Y-0+ **£1,535** (£453; £226) **Stalls** Low

Form RPR
201 **1** **Alpha Tauri (USA)**[49] [290] 5-10-0 76................(t) JamesDoyle 6 84+
(Frank Sheridan) *mde all: sn crossed to rail: qcknd clr ent fnl 3f: wl clr and in n.d after: rdn ent fnl f: eased wl ins fnl f* **8/11**[1]
0-00 **2** *15* **Wotatomboy**[7] [793] 5-9-0 46................(v[1]) JamesSullivan(3) 2 36
(Richard Whitaker) *chsd wnr thrght: rdn and wl outpcd by wnr 3f out: no ch w wnr after: hld on for 2nd towards fin* **66/1**
5103 **3** *½* **Unlimited**[22] [633] 9-10-0 64................ J-PGuillambert 5 45
(Tony Carroll) *hld up in tch: rdn and wl outpcd over 3f out: wnt modest 3rd over 1f out: no ch w wnr but pressing for 2nd towards fin* **10/1**
6435 **4** *5* **William Wainwright (IRE)**[21] [642] 3-8-6 48......(p) SilvestreDeSousa 7 27
(Ann Duffield) *in tch: swtchd lft and rdn over 4f out: sn struggling: wl btn fnl 3f* **20/1**
116- **5** *1* **Fremen (USA)**[139] [7171] 11-9-8 82................ AdrianNicholls 1 24
(David Nicholls) *dwlt: sn bustled along: sltly hmpd and swtchd rt after 1f: sn chsng ldrs: rdn and wl outpcd by wnr over 3f out: 3rd and wl btn whn racd awkwardly over 1f out: wknd fnl f* **3/1**[2]
452- **6** *7* **Enchanting Smile (FR)**[255] [3662] 4-9-0 70........... MichaelO'Connell(3) 3 —
(David Nicholls) *s.i.s: sn rdn along and a struggling in rr* **7/1**[3]
-000 **7** *nk* **Pinewood Polly**[7] [796] 4-9-3 20................(p) ChrisCatlin 4 —
(Shaun Harris) *chsd ldrs: rdn and struggling 4f out: sn wknd: wl bhd fnl 3f* **100/1**

1m 28.42s (-1.88) **Going Correction** +0.025s/f (Slow)
WFA 3 from 4yo+ 16lb 7 Ran SP% **111.7**
Speed ratings (Par 101): **111,93,93,87,86 78,78**
toteswingers:1&2:£14.60, 1&3:£2.10, 2&3:£21.50 CSF £67.92 TOTE £2.00: £1.80, £17.60; EX 42.40.The winner was bought in for 8,500gns.
Owner Frank Sheridan **Bred** Flaxman Holdings Ltd **Trained** Wolverhampton, W Midlands

FOCUS
This looked to be match on paper, but the second favourite was below par and Alpha Tauri won easily. There was no depth behind him but it's hard to rate the form any lower.

857 CHELTENHAM FESTIVAL FREE BETTING WITH FREEBETTING.CO.UK H'CAP 5f (F)
3:45 (3:46) (Class 6) (0-60,60) 4-Y-0+ **£1,535** (£453; £226) **Stalls** High

Form RPR
05-6 **1** **Electioneer (USA)**[60] [165] 4-9-6 **59**................ GrahamGibbons 14 69+
(Michael Easterby) *midfield: rdn 1/2-way: hdwy u.p jst over 1f out: swtchd lft and str run fnl f to ld fnl 75yds: sn in command* **3/1**[1]
4200 **2** *1* **Lets Move It**[49] [289] 4-9-0 **53**................ RobbieFitzpatrick 7 59
(Derek Shaw) *towards rr: rdn 1/2-way: hdwy over 1f out: pressed ldrs ins fnl f: outpcd by wnr towards fin* **25/1**
0122 **3** *1* **Attrition**[12] [743] 4-9-4 **60**................(p) LouisBeuzelin(3) 3 63
(Andrew Reid) *chsd ldr: rdn to ld jst over 1f out: hung rt ins fnl f: hdd fnl 75yds: wknd towards fin* **7/2**[2]
-053 **4** *½* **The Tatling (IRE)**[13] [735] 14-9-7 **60**................ RichardKingscote 8 61
(Milton Bradley) *dwlt: bhd and swtchd to inner after 1f: hdwy over 1f out: r.o wl ins fnl f: nt rch ldrs* **15/2**[3]
203 **5** *1 ½* **Cheveyo (IRE)**[18] [691] 5-8-4 **48**................(v) KieranO'Neill(5) 4 44
(Patrick Morris) *dwlt: sn rcvrd and chsng ldrs: drvn wl over 1f out: hung rt and wknd ins fnl f* **9/1**
-346 **6** *½* **Monsieur Harvey**[13] [735] 5-8-8 **47**................(v[1]) TomEaves 6 41
(Bryan Smart) *led: rdn ent fnl 2f: hdd jst over 1f out: sn hung rt: wknd ins fnl f* **8/1**
0360 **7** *½* **Silver Linnet (IRE)**[43] [362] 4-9-0 **53**................(b) AdamKirby 2 45
(Noel Quinlan) *sn rdn along: in tch: drvn 1/2-way: wknd u.p jst over 1f out* **9/1**
0433 **8** *2 ¾* **Galpin Junior (USA)**[11] [767] 5-9-5 **58**................ PJMcDonald 13 40
(Ruth Carr) *racd in midfield: rdn and struggling 1/2-way: plugged on same pce and no threat to ldrs fnl 2f* **28/1**
106- **9** *hd* **Tenancy (IRE)**[149] [6965] 7-9-5 **58**................ ChrisCatlin 5 39
(Shaun Harris) *chsd ldrs: rdn 1/2-way and sn struggling: wknd over 1f out* **33/1**
3022 **10** *1 ½* **Residency (IRE)**[13] [732] 5-9-2 **60**................(p) AdamCarter(5) 11 36
(Bryan Smart) *racd in midfield: struggling and rdn whn swtchd lft 2f out: no hdwy after* **8/1**
4-0 **11** *6* **Billionaire Boy (IRE)**[18] [690] 4-8-4 **46** oh1........... JamesSullivan(3) 10 —
(Patrick Morris) *sn rdn along in midfield: struggling 1/2-way: bhd fnl 2f* **50/1**
0540 **12** *hd* **Lithaam (IRE)**[6] [812] 7-8-7 **46** oh1................(p) LukeMorris 12 —
(Milton Bradley) *in tch: rdn and lost pl 3f out: bhd fnl 2f* **40/1**
56-0 **13** *3* **Zelos Dream (IRE)**[38] [432] 4-8-9 **55**................ JakePayne(7) 1 —
(Bill Turner) *a bhd* **66/1**

60.52 secs (0.82) **Going Correction** +0.20s/f (Slow) 13 Ran SP% **117.3**
Speed ratings (Par 101): **101,99,97,97,94 93,93,88,88,85 76,75,71**
toteswingers:1&2:£14.30, 1&3:£4.30, 2&3:£16.80 CSF £87.49 CT £286.41 TOTE £3.80: £1.80, £9.20, £1.10; EX 113.40 Trifecta £340.50 Part won. Pool: £460.15 - 0.71 winning units..
Owner Steve Hull **Bred** Gainsborough Farm Llc **Trained** Sheriff Hutton, N Yorks
■ Stewards' Enquiry : Kieran O'Neill two-day ban: used whip down shoulder in the forehand (Mar 29-30)

FOCUS
A moderate sprint handicap, but not a bad race for the grade. The well treated winner landed a gamble.
Attrition Official explanation: trainer's rep said gelding lost a shoe

858 BIGGEST FREE BETS WITH FREEBETTING.CO.UK H'CAP 1m 4f (F)
4:25 (4:25) (Class 5) (0-75,72) 4-Y-0+ **£1,878** (£558; £279; £139) **Stalls** Low

Form RPR
63-5 **1** **Jack Dawkins (USA)**[12] 744 6-8-11 **62**........................ AdrianNicholls 3 71+
(David Nicholls) *chsd ldrs: pressed ldr over 4f out: rdn to ld wl over 2f out: drvn and kpt on wl fr over 1f out: drvn out* **11/2**[3]
-501 **2** *1 1/4* **Kingaroo (IRE)**[9] 551 5-8-4 **58**........................ BillyCray(3) 1 65
(Garry Woodward) *t.k.h: led for 2f: chsd ldr after tl led again 5f out: rdn and hdd wl over 2f out: hrd drvn and kpt on same pce fr over 1f out* **15/2**
1111 **3** *1* **Stanley Rigby**[21] 644 5-9-7 **72**........................ BarryMcHugh 6 78
(Richard Fahey) *in tch in last pair: hdwy on outer to chse ldrs 7f out: rdn over 3f out: bmpd 2f out: kpt on u.p over 1f out: one pce and no imp ins fnl f* **9/4**[1]
3353 **4** *3/4* **Camps Bay (USA)**[6] 805 7-9-6 **71**........................ HayleyTurner 5 76
(Conor Dore) *stdd s: hld up in last pair: chsd ldng trio over 3f out: drvn and edgd rt 2f out: kpt on same pce u.p fr over 1f out* **9/4**[1]
61-2 **5** *11* **Spring Secret**[12] 742 5-9-7 **72**........................ LukeMorris 2 60
(Bryn Palling) *in tch: pushed along 5f out: dropped to last and u.p 4f out: lost tch over 2f out* **5/1**[2]
4224 **6** *1 1/4* **Elusive Warrior (USA)**[19] 674 8-8-12 **63**........................(p) JamesDoyle 4 49
(Alan McCabe) *chsd ldr tl led after 2f: stdd gallop 7f out: hdd 5f out: rdn and lost pl 4f out: wl bhd over 2f out* **16/1**

2m 39.9s (-1.10) **Going Correction** +0.025s/f (Slow) **6** Ran SP% **111.2**
Speed ratings (Par 103): **104,103,102,102,94 93**
toteswingers:1&2:£9.30, 1&3:£3.10, 2&3:£5.90 CSF £42.77 TOTE £13.00: £5.90, £4.30; EX 42.20.
Owner The Three K's **Bred** Clovelly Farms **Trained** Sessay, N Yorks
■ Stewards' Enquiry : Billy Cray one-day ban: used whip with excessive frequency (Mar 29)
FOCUS
They went steady, yet the time was still 4.06 seconds faster than the following Class 6 event, which run was at an even slower pace. The second and third set a solid enough level.

859 COMPARE FREE BETS WITH FREEBETTING.CO.UK APPRENTICE H'CAP 1m 4f (F)
5:05 (5:07) (Class 6) (0-60,59) 4-Y-0+ **£1,535** (£453; £226) **Stalls** Low

Form RPR
-063 **1** **Beau Fighter**[21] 645 6-9-6 **58**........................(p) DaleSwift 7 70+
(Gary Moore) *t.k.h: hld up in tch: rdn to chal over 2f out: led over 1f out: sn drvn clr: styd on wl* **7/4**[1]
2423 **2** *5* **Carnac (IRE)**[4] 838 5-8-12 **55**........................(p) NoraLooby(5) 5 59
(Alan McCabe) *t.k.h: led and set stdy gallop: pushed along and qcknd ent fnl 3f: hdd over 1f out: sn outpcd by wnr: plugged on same pce fnl f* **3/1**[2]
3522 **3** *3 1/4* **Light The City (IRE)**[7] 797 4-8-4 **49**........................ ShaneBKelly(5) 9 48
(Ruth Carr) *t.k.h: chsd ldr after 3f: rdn ent fnl 3f: wknd over 2f out: wl hld and hung lft fnl f* **9/2**[3]
0214 **4** *1 1/4* **Laura Land**[11] 771 5-8-10 **51**........................ JamesRogers(3) 3 48
(Mark Brisbourne) *t.k.h: chsd ldr for 3f: styd chsng ldrs: rdn ent fnl 3f: sn struggling: no ch fnl 2f* **8/1**
-214 **5** *1/2* **Magic Haze**[47] 323 5-9-2 **59**........................ RichardRowe(5) 1 55
(Sally Hall) *t.k.h: hld up in tch: rdn and outpcd wl over 3f out: plugged on same pce and wl btn fnl 3f* **11/2**
34/2 **6** *2 1/4* **Sea Cliff (IRE)**[9] 551 7-8-12 **55**........................ ThomasBrown(5) 2 48
(Andrew Crook) *hld up in tch: pushed along and struggling 5f out: rdn and no hdwy over 3f out: no ch after* **16/1**
260/ **7** *24* **Trouble Mountain (USA)**[504] 7093 14-8-7 **50**..... DavidSimmonson(5) 8 7
(G P Kelly) *awkward s and slowly away: sn in tch: rdn and lost tch over 3f out: t.o fnl 2f: eased ins fnl f* **80/1**

2m 43.96s (2.96) **Going Correction** +0.025s/f (Slow)
WFA 4 from 5yo+ 2lb **7** Ran SP% **113.2**
Speed ratings (Par 101): **91,87,85,84,84 82,66**
toteswingers:1&2:£2.40, 1&3:£3.40, 2&3:£2.00 CSF £7.00 CT £16.75 TOTE £2.00: £1.10, £1.20; EX 9.80 Trifecta £26.70 Pool: £470.32 - 12.99 winning units..
Owner The Hillians **Bred** Mrs P G Kingston **Trained** Lower Beeding, W Sussex
FOCUS
The pace was slow and most of these were keen. The winner was well treated and is likely to do a bit better than this.
Trouble Mountain(USA) Official explanation: jockey said late removal of blindfold had been caused by being tucked in and was the first time he had to remove one.
T/Plt: £754.00 to a £1 stake. Pool:£51,132.81 - 49.50 winning tickets T/Qpdt: £230.20 to a £1 stake. Pool:£3,484.21 - 11.20 w. tckts SP

860a (Foreign Racing) See Raceform Interactive

[816]KEMPTON (A.W) (R-H)
Wednesday, March 16

OFFICIAL GOING: Standard
Wind: Mild, across Weather: Overcast

861 FREE ENTRY FOR BETDAQ MEMBERS CLASSIFIED CLAIMING STKS 5f (P)
5:50 (5:50) (Class 6) 3-Y-0+ **£1,535** (£453; £226) **Stalls** Low

Form RPR
5-31 **1** **Lewyn**[21] 658 4-9-12 **75**........................(b) FergusSweeney 2 76+
(Jeremy Gask) *chsd ldrs: led over 1f out: r.o: rdn out* **9/5**[2]
0132 **2** *1* **Desert Strike**[12] 767 5-9-11 **74**........................(p) ShaneKelly 1 71
(Alan McCabe) *hld up: swtchd lft and hdwy over 1f out: chsd wnr ent fnl f: rdn and kpt on* **13/8**[1]
4100 **3** *2 1/4* **Bluebok**[14] 735 10-9-4 **50**........................(bt) RichardKingscote 4 56
(Milton Bradley) *chsd ldrs: rdn over 2f out: chsd wnr briefly 1f out: kpt on same pce* **25/1**
0423 **4** *nk* **Wanchai Whisper**[21] 658 4-9-0 **60**........................(p) KierenFox(3) 6 54
(Peter Hedger) *hld up: rdn whn c wd ent st: hdwy sn after: chsd wnr briefly 1f out: no ex fnl 75yds* **9/2**[3]
4-55 **5** *1 3/4* **Romantic Queen**[12] 766 5-9-0 **61**........................(t) MatthewDavies(3) 7 52
(George Baker) *s.i.s: hdwy whn short of room and squeezed out over 1f out: no ch after* **8/1**
5400 **6** *3 3/4* **Litham (IRE)**[1] 857 7-9-4 **45**........................(p) LukeMorris 5 35
(Milton Bradley) *disp ld tl rdn over 1f out: fdd ins fnl f* **33/1**
0-00 **7** *8* **Sir Loin**[37] 443 10-8-12 **43**........................(v) DanielleMcCreery(5) 3 —
(Paul Burgoyne) *racd keenly: disp ld tl rdn over 1f out: sn wknd* **40/1**

59.79 secs (-0.71) **Going Correction** +0.05s/f (Slow) **7** Ran SP% **112.3**
Speed ratings (Par 101): **107,105,101,101,98 92,79**
toteswingers:1&2:£1.10, 1&3:£10.20, 2&3:£16.90 CSF £4.88 TOTE £4.80: £1.50, £1.60; EX 3.20.Wanchai Whisper was claimed by M. E. Rimmer for £3,000.
Owner The Nobles **Bred** Mrs S J Walker **Trained** Sutton Veny, Wilts
FOCUS
A couple of fair sorts in an ordinary claimer. The gallop wasn't overly strong and the winner raced towards the inside rail in the closing stages. He's a good tool in this grade but the third limits the form.

862 BETDAQ.COM EXCHANGE PRICE MULTIPLES H'CAP 1m 2f (P)
6:20 (6:20) (Class 6) (0-60,60) 4-Y-0+ **£1,535** (£453; £226) **Stalls** Low

Form RPR
-005 **1** **Carr Hall (IRE)**[42] 390 8-8-13 **52**........................ LukeMorris 4 59
(Tony Carroll) *trckd ldrs: rdn over 1f out: kpt on to ld fnl 75yds: jst hld on: all out* **14/1**
1-44 **2** *shd* **Iguacu**[41] 409 7-8-13 **52**........................(p) DaneO'Neill 10 59
(George Baker) *s.i.s: sn mid-div: rdn and stdy prog fr 2f out: str run ins fnl f: jst failed* **9/1**
2255 **3** *nse* **Abigails Angel**[14] 730 4-9-3 **56**........................ AdamKirby 8 63
(Brett Johnson) *mid-div: hdwy 2f out: sn rdn: tk narrow advantage ent fnl f: hdd fnl 75yds: kpt on* **9/1**
-223 **4** *1 1/2* **Broughtons Paradis (IRE)**[12] 771 5-9-1 **54**........................ KierenFallon 1 59
(Willie Musson) *trckd ldrs: rdn to chal 2f out: ev ch ent fnl f: kpt on but no ex towards fin* **3/1**[1]
000- **5** *1 1/4* **Boogie Dancer**[124] 770 7-8-10 **49**........................ KirstyMilczarek 2 51
(Stuart Howe) *mid-div: effrt on inner 2f out: styd on same pce* **12/1**
50-U **6** *1/2* **Holden Eagle**[34] 488 6-9-7 **60**........................ SteveDrowne 9 62
(Tony Newcombe) *hld up bhd: rdn and hdwy over 1f out: styng on whn nt clr run ent fnl f: kpt on* **7/1**[3]
4105 **7** *2* **Poppy Golightly**[24] 625 4-9-0 **53**........................ ChrisCatlin 3 50
(Ron Hodges) *led: rdn and hrd pressed fr 2f out: hdd ent fnl f: fdd fnl 120yds* **16/1**
5-00 **8** *hd* **Officer Lily (USA)**[7] 809 4-8-9 **51**........................ KierenFox(3) 6 48
(John Best) *sn prom: hung lft and rdn 5f out: wknd over 1f out* **16/1**
0051 **9** *1 1/4* **Miss Bounty**[7] 809 6-8-4 **50**........................(p) NathanAlison(7) 11 44
(Jim Boyle) *mid-div on outer: rdn over 3f out: wknd over 1f out* **6/1**[2]
-046 **10** *1 1/2* **Illuminative (USA)**[7] 809 5-8-13 **52**........................(p) IanMongan 5 43
(Zoe Davison) *s.i.s: sn cl up: rdn 3f out: wknd wl over 2f out* **25/1**
05-0 **11** *2 1/4* **Zagarock**[35] 477 4-8-10 **49**........................ NeilChalmers 14 36
(Bryn Palling) *sn trcking ldrs: rdn over 3f out: wknd wl over 1f out* **33/1**
26-4 **12** *9* **Herecomethegirls**[47] 346 5-9-1 **54**........................ JimCrowley 7 24
(Olivia Maylam) *a towards rr* **8/1**
006- **13** *1 1/4* **Kingston Folly**[126] 7387 4-9-2 **55**........................ RobertHavlin 12 23
(Andrew Haynes) *s.i.s: rdn 5f out: a towards rr* **20/1**

2m 8.94s (0.94) **Going Correction** +0.05s/f (Slow) **13** Ran SP% **120.6**
Speed ratings (Par 101): **98,97,97,96,95 95,93,93,92,91 89,82,81**
toteswingers: 1&2 £23.10, 1&3 £18.70, 2&3 £12.60 CSF £132.71 CT £1214.21 TOTE £28.80: £6.70, £3.00, £3.70; EX 133.20 TRIFECTA Not won..
Owner The Cropthorne Boys **Bred** R Cody **Trained** Cropthorne, Worcs
FOCUS
A moderate handicap featuring mainly exposed sorts. The pace was an ordinary one and the winner raced centre-to-far-side in the straight. Straightforward form.
Holden Eagle Official explanation: jockey said colt hung right
Kingston Folly Official explanation: jockey said gelding hung left

863 LAY BACK AND WIN AT BETDAQ.COM MEDIAN AUCTION MAIDEN STKS 6f (P)
6:50 (6:52) (Class 6) 3-5-Y-O **£1,535** (£453; £226) **Stalls** Low

Form RPR
0- **1** **Winniepeg**[132] 7309 3-8-7 0........................ JohnFahy(3) 3 59+
(Clive Cox) *led after 1f: pushed clr over 2f out: in command thrght fnl f: readily* **3/1**[2]
56-2 **2** *1 1/2* **Grand Piano (IRE)**[20] 663 4-9-7 65........................ ThomasBrown(5) 7 55
(Andrew Balding) *trckd ldrs: rdn whn briefly outpcd 2f out: r.o to chse wnr ent fnl f: a being hld* **10/11**[1]
50-6 **3** *1 1/2* **Flying Cherry (IRE)**[63] 129 4-9-9 49........................ IanMongan 2 49
(Jo Crowley) *led for 1f: trckd wnr: rdn over 2f out: lost 2nd ent fnl f: kpt on same pce* **7/1**
4 **4** *1* **Fleurie Lover (IRE)**[21] 653 3-8-10 0........................ FrannyNorton 1 46+
(Richard Guest) *in tch: rdn and hung lft fr 2f out: kpt on ins fnl f* **9/2**[3]
5 **5** *1* **Demoiselle Bond**[15] 721 3-8-10 0........................ RichardThomas 8 43
(Lydia Richards) *sn chsng ldrs: rdn over 2f out: fdd ins fnl f* **25/1**
6 *2 3/4* **Add Lib** 3-8-10 0........................ LiamKeniry 5 34
(Matthew Salaman) *dwlt: a in last pair: nvr gng pce to get on terms* **25/1**
0-0 **7** *3/4* **Pharoh Jake**[63] 132 3-8-12 0........................ KierenFox(3) 6 36
(John Bridger) *rdn wl over 2f out: a in last pair: nvr gng pce to get on terms* **66/1**

1m 13.72s (0.62) **Going Correction** +0.05s/f (Slow)
WFA 3 from 4yo 13lb **7** Ran SP% **117.3**
Speed ratings (Par 101): **97,95,93,91,90 86,85**
toteswingers: 1&2 £1.30, 1&3 £1.60, 2&3 £1.60 CSF £6.30 TOTE £4.50: £2.50, £1.40; EX 9.20 Trifecta £40.00 Pool: £7,665.79 - 141.63 winning units..
Owner B D H & R J H Preston **Bred** Darley **Trained** Lambourn, Berks
FOCUS
An uncompetitive maiden in which the gallop was a reasonable one and this form is no more than modest, limited by the second and third. The winner raced centre-to-far side in the straight.

864 BETDAQ MOBILE APPS H'CAP 6f (P)
7:20 (7:20) (Class 4) (0-85,85) 3-Y-O **£3,399** (£1,011; £505; £252) **Stalls** Low

Form RPR
225- **1** **Ceffyl Gwell**[130] 7345 3-8-8 **72**........................ DaneO'Neill 1 76+
(Richard Hannon) *trckd ldrs: rdn wl over 1f out: str run ins fnl f: led post* **4/1**[3]
2-12 **2** *nse* **Palais Glide**[35] 465 3-8-9 **73**........................ EddieAhern 5 77
(Richard Hannon) *led: rdn clr over 1f out: kpt on: ct post* **11/4**[2]
31 **3** *4* **Hoover**[21] 653 3-8-12 **76**........................ StephenCraine 3 67
(Jim Boyle) *trckd ldr: ev ch 2f out: sn rdn: kpt on same pce* **5/1**
6-54 **4** *1 1/4* **Toms River Tess (IRE)**[35] 476 3-8-11 **75**........................ KirstyMilczarek 6 62
(Zoe Davison) *trckd ldrs: swtchd rt for effrt 2f out: one pce sn after* **11/1**
640- **5** *nk* **Satin Love (USA)**[119] 7481 3-9-7 **85**........................ KierenFallon 2 71
(Mark Johnston) *trckd ldr: rdn 2f out: sn one pce* **5/2**[1]

-240 **6** *nk* **Insolenceofoffice (IRE)**[4] 845 3-8-10 **81**................ ThomasBrown(7) 4 66
(Andrew Crook) *cl up in last: rdn over 2f out: nvr gng pce to chal* **15/2**
1m 13.1s **Going Correction** +0.05s/f (Slow) **6** Ran SP% **112.0**
Speed ratings (Par 100): **102,101,96,94,94 94**
toteswingers: 1&2 £4.00, 1&3 £2.60, 2&3 £2.40 CSF £15.29 TOTE £7.90: £3.60, £1.30; EX 26.70.
Owner Derek And Jean Clee **Bred** D D And Mrs Jean P Clee **Trained** East Everleigh, Wilts
■ Stewards' Enquiry : Eddie Ahern three-day ban: used whip with excessive frequency without giving filly time to respond (Mar 30-Apr 1)
Dane O'Neill one-day ban: used whip with excessive frequency down shoulder in the forehand (Mar 30)

FOCUS
A fairly useful handicap in which the gallop was just an ordinary one. The first two came clear down the centre in the straight. A step forward from the winner.

865 RACING AT SKYSPORTS.COM FILLIES' H'CAP 7f (P)
7:50 (7:50) (Class 5) (0-75,75) 4-Y-0+ **£2,047** (£604; £302) **Stalls** Low

Form RPR
-1U0 **1** **Perfect Ch'l (IRE)**[19] 689 4-8-12 **66**................ JamesDoyle 3 74
(Ian Wood) *mde all: rdn over 2f out: hld on wl ins fnl f: rdn out* **7/1**
2321 **2** *nk* **Avonrose**[14] 736 4-9-7 **75**................ DaneO'Neill 2 82
(Derek Shaw) *trckd ldrs: rdn over 2f out: got win a nk of wnr ins fnl f: a being hld off fnl 100yds* **11/4**[2]
12 **3** *1* **Cape Melody**[9] 792 5-9-3 **74**................ MatthewDavies(3) 4 78
(George Baker) *s.i.s: last but in tch: rdn over 2f out: hdwy over 1f out: kpt on ins fnl f* **4/1**[3]
251- **4** *2 ¾* **Sunset Kitty (USA)**[95] 7837 4-9-5 **73**................ AdamKirby 5 70
(Walter Swinburn) *trckd wnr: rdn over 2f out: kpt on same pce* **11/8**[1]
2445 **5** *2* **Bold Ring**[9] 792 5-8-0 **61** oh2................ JenniferFerguson(7) 1 53
(Edward Creighton) *hld up bhd ldrs: effrt 2f out: nt pce to get on terms* **28/1**
-143 **6** *8* **Caramelita**[34] 487 4-9-0 **68**................ StephenCraine 6 39
(J R Jenkins) *t.k.h early: trckd ldrs: rdn over 2f out: wknd over 1f out* **14/1**
1m 25.66s (-0.34) **Going Correction** +0.05s/f (Slow) **6** Ran SP% **111.4**
Speed ratings (Par 100): **103,102,101,98,96 86**
toteswingers: 1&2 £2.80, 1&3 £4.00, 2&3 £1.50 CSF £26.02 TOTE £3.10: £4.70, £2.30; EX 21.20.
Owner Paddy Barrett **Bred** Glencarrig Stud **Trained** Upper Lambourn, Berks
■ Stewards' Enquiry : Dane O'Neill one-day ban: used whip with excessive frequency down the shoulder in the forehand (Mar 31)

FOCUS
A fair fillies' handicap but another race run at just an ordinary gallop. The winner came down the centre in the straight. Not form to get excited about.
Sunset Kitty(USA) Official explanation: jockey said filly hung left 3 1/2f out

866 GOFFS SALE AT KEMPTON MARCH 29TH H'CAP 1m 4f (P)
8:20 (8:21) (Class 5) (0-75,68) 3-Y-O **£2,047** (£604; £302) **Stalls** Centre

Form RPR
-411 **1** **Twin Soul (IRE)**[9] 789 3-9-8 **68** 6ex................ DavidProbert 5 72
(Andrew Balding) *trckd ldrs: rdn wl over 2f out: styd on to ld ent fnl f: hld on: all out* **6/4**[1]
2521 **2** *hd* **Mrs Neat (IRE)**[28] 564 3-9-5 **65**................(p) JamesDoyle 3 69
(Sylvester Kirk) *hld up bhd ldrs: swtchd rt and hdwy over 1f out: sn rdn: styd on wl ins fnl f: iust hld* **15/2**
0-32 **3** *1 ¼* **Colebrooke**[21] 657 3-9-7 **67**................ KierenFallon 1 69
(Mark Johnston) *trckd ldr: rdn over 2f out: styd on fnl f: no ex towards fin* **11/4**[2]
-555 **4** *shd* **Gower Rules (IRE)**[21] 650 3-8-5 **51**................ RichardKingscote 6 53
(John Bridger) *led: rdn wl over 2f out: hdd ent fnl f: styd on but no ex* **16/1**
2221 **5** *1* **Blue Cossack (IRE)**[14] 731 3-9-4 **64**................ LiamKeniry 2 64
(Mark Usher) *trckd ldrs: rdn wl over 2f out: styd on but no ex fnl f* **4/1**[3]
400- **6** *hd* **Dew Reward (IRE)**[159] 6717 3-8-13 **59**................ LukeMorris 4 59
(Eve Johnson Houghton) *little slowly away: trckd ldrs: rdn wl over 2f out: styd on but no ex fnl f* **20/1**
2m 00.03 (2.00) **Going Correction** +0.05s/f (Slow) **6** Ran SP% **109.1**
Speed ratings (Par 98): **94,93,93,92,92 92**
toteswingers: 1&2 £4.10, 1&3 £1.60, 2&3 £1.40 CSF £12.57 TOTE £1.40: £1.50, £4.90; EX 11.10.
Owner N Botica **Bred** Mrs Clodagh McStay **Trained** Kingsclere, Hants
■ Stewards' Enquiry : David Probert one-day ban: used whip with excessive frequency (Mar 30)

FOCUS
A moderate handicap in which a fairly steady pace only picked up around the 2f marker and this bare form may not be entirely reliable. The winner was another to come down the centre and a repeat of her Lingfield figure was enough.

867 GOFFS READY-TO-RUN SALE MARCH 29TH H'CAP 6f (P)
8:50 (8:52) (Class 5) (0-75,75) 4-Y-O+ **£2,047** (£604; £302) **Stalls** Low

Form RPR
1361 **1** **Pelmanism**[14] 725 4-9-2 **70**................(b) PhillipMakin 7 83+
(Kevin Ryan) *s.i.s: steadily rcvrd: hdwy 3f out to trck ldrs: sn rdn: r.o wl ent fnl f: led fnl stride* **9/4**[1]
4-13 **2** *hd* **Best Trip (IRE)**[14] 725 4-9-5 **73**................ FrannyNorton 10 86
(Richard Guest) *led: rdn 2f out: kpt on: hdd fnl stride* **7/1**
3-00 **3** *¾* **Ongoodform (IRE)**[21] 651 4-9-7 **75**................ LiamJones 1 85
(Paul D'Arcy) *mid-div: rdn over 2f out: hdwy over 1f out: styd on fnl f: clsng wl at fin* **7/2**[2]
1345 **4** *1 ½* **Sherjawy (IRE)**[14] 725 7-8-13 **67**................ KirstyMilczarek 9 72
(Zoe Davison) *trckd ldrs: rdn wl over 2f out to chse wnr tl over 1f out: kpt on same pce* **25/1**
1100 **5** *¾* **Mister Green (FR)**[18] 703 5-9-2 **70**................(bt) JamesDoyle 6 73+
(David Flood) *trckd ldrs: rdn over 2f out: no ex ins fnl f* **14/1**
000- **6** *1 ¾* **Rum King (USA)**[137] 7238 4-9-6 **74**................ DaneO'Neill 2 71
(Richard Hannon) *hld up towards rr: rdn and sme hdwy 2f out: no further imp fnl f* **6/1**[3]
0305 **7** *shd* **Fantasy Fighter (IRE)**[27] 577 6-9-2 **70**................ LiamKeniry 3 67
(John Quinn) *s.i.s: towards rr: short lived effrt on outer over 2f out: sn one pce* **16/1**
5554 **8** *2 ½* **Al Gillani (IRE)**[14] 725 6-8-11 **65**................(p) StephenCraine 4 54
(Jim Boyle) *hld up in tch: nt clr run and lost pl over 2f out: nvr any ch after* **8/1**
0-60 **9** *1 ¼* **Alfresco**[18] 703 7-9-4 **72**................(b) KierenFallon 5 57
(John Best) *lft at s whn hood failed to be removed leaving stalls: a in rr* **12/1**
560- **10** *1 ¾* **Caldermud (IRE)**[214] 5073 4-9-5 **73**................ JimCrowley 8 52
(Olivia Maylam) *chsd ldrs: rdn wl over 2f out: wknd wl over 1f out* **25/1**
1m 12.32s (-0.78) **Going Correction** +0.05s/f (Slow) **10** Ran SP% **118.8**
Speed ratings (Par 103): **107,106,105,103,102 100,100,96,95,92**
toteswingers: 1&2 £1.40, 1&3 £6.20, 2&3 £8.90 CSF £19.00 CT £54.44 TOTE £2.50: £1.10, £2.70, £1.80; EX 19.70 Trifecta £69.30 Pool: £429.63 - 4.58 winning units..
Owner Guy Reed **Bred** Guy Reed **Trained** Hambleton, N Yorks

FOCUS
A fair handicap but just an ordinary gallop meant those held up were at a disadvantage. The winner came down the centre in the straight and is progressive.
Alfresco Official explanation: jockey said he was late in removing blindfold as it was caught up on ther bridle.
T/Plt: £68.30 to a £1 stake. Pool: £64,984.26. 694.09 winning tickets. T/Qpdt: £11.60 to a £1 stake. Pool: £5,569.11. 354.17 winning tickets. TM

853 SOUTHWELL (L-H)
Wednesday, March 16

OFFICIAL GOING: Standard
Wind: Light 1/2 against Weather: over cast and misty

868 ENJOY THE CHELTENHAM FESTIVAL WITH FREEBETTING.CO.UK H'CAP 5f (F)
1:55 (1:55) (Class 6) (0-65,61) 3-Y-O **£1,535** (£453; £226) **Stalls** High

Form RPR
-314 **1** **Ace Master**[27] 567 3-9-4 **58**................ JimmyQuinn 6 62
(Roy Bowring) *dwlt: hld up: effrt 2f out: r.o to ld last stride* **4/1**[3]
3012 **2** *shd* **Kassaab**[13] 745 3-9-7 **61**................(b) NickyMackay 7 64
(Jeremy Gask) *mde most: hdd post* **7/2**[2]
1313 **3** *½* **Juarla (IRE)**[9] 788 3-9-6 **60**................ LukeMorris 4 61
(Ronald Harris) *w ldrs: no ex clsng stages* **6/4**[1]
00-5 **4** *¾* **Tancred Spirit**[36] 452 3-8-5 **45**................ FrannyNorton 5 44
(Paul Midgley) *w ldrs: kpt on same pce last 100yds* **12/1**
0-05 **5** *3 ½* **Taverners Jubilee**[13] 741 3-8-2 **45**................ LouisBeuzelin(3) 1 31
(Patrick Morris) *outpcd in rr: hdwy to chse ldrs 2f out: wknd fnl f* **28/1**
000- **6** *¾* **Trading**[162] 6645 3-9-5 **59**................ DuranFentiman 9 42
(Tim Easterby) *chsd ldrs stands' side: wknd over 1f out* **18/1**
-023 **7** *4* **Bigalo's Vera B**[13] 741 3-8-6 **51**................ DeclanCannon(5) 8 20
(Lawrence Mullaney) *dwlt: sn chsng ldrs: lost pl over 1f out* **8/1**
505- **8** *2 ¼* **Freedom Trail**[153] 6867 3-9-6 **60**................(p) PaulMulrennan 3 21
(Tim Fitzgerald) *sn outpcd and swtchd far side: bhd whn hung lft then rt fnl 2f* **16/1**
60.91 secs (1.21) **Going Correction** +0.15s/f (Slow) **8** Ran SP% **115.6**
Speed ratings (Par 96): **96,95,95,93,88 87,80,77**
toteswingers:1&2:£1.90, 1&3:£1.50, 2&3:£1.40 CSF £18.67 CT £29.53 TOTE £4.30: £1.40, £1.50, £1.10; EX 21.30 Trifecta £27.20 Pool: £319.85 - 8.69 winning units..
Owner S R Bowring **Bred** S R Bowring **Trained** Edwinstowe, Notts

FOCUS
A weak sprint handicap, run at a good pace, with little covering the front four at the line. The action all took place down the centre of the track. The third and fourth set the level.

869 CHAMPION CHASE FREE BETS WITH FREEBETTING.CO.UK H'CAP 7f (F)
2:30 (2:30) (Class 5) (0-75,75) 4-Y-O+ **£1,813** (£539; £269; £134) **Stalls** Low

Form RPR
050- **1** **Rio Cobolo (IRE)**[172] 6367 5-9-4 **72**................ AdrianNicholls 3 80
(David Nicholls) *mde all: rdn over 2f out: kpt on wl fnl f* **8/1**
-151 **2** *1 ¾* **Zarius**[20] 674 4-8-7 **61**................ NickyMackay 5 65
(Chris Wall) *sn pushed along: brought wd after 2f: styd on fnl 2f: tk 2nd last 100yds* **6/4**[1]
-350 **3** *½* **Mr Emirati (USA)**[23] 637 4-8-11 **65**................(tp) TomEaves 2 67
(Bryan Smart) *trckd ldrs: effrt over 2f out: styd on same pce fnl f* **9/1**
3265 **4** *hd* **Striker Torres (IRE)**[14] 736 5-9-3 **71**................(p) JimmyQuinn 1 73
(Geoffrey Oldroyd) *trckd ldrs: effrt over 2f out: styd on same pce fnl f* **5/1**[3]
6423 **5** *3 ¾* **Elusive Fame (USA)**[8] 799 5-9-0 **75**................(b) JasonHart(7) 4 68
(Mark Johnston) *sn drvn along in rr: effrt on outside 3f out: sn rdn and wl outpcd* **11/4**[2]
3430 **6** *8* **Army Of Stars (IRE)**[12] 763 5-9-0 **68**................(p) PaulMulrennan 6 41
(James Given) *trckd ldrs: rdn and edgd lft over 2f out: sn lost pl: hung rt fnl f: eased towards fin* **14/1**
1m 29.52s (-0.78) **Going Correction** -0.025s/f (Stan) **6** Ran SP% **111.1**
Speed ratings (Par 103): **103,101,100,100,95 86**
toteswingers:1&2:£1.70, 1&3:£7.50, 2&3:£2.90 CSF £20.17 TOTE £8.30: £2.70, £1.70; EX 31.40.
Owner The Grech Family & The Quinn Family **Bred** Yvonne & Gerard Kennedy **Trained** Sessay, N Yorks
■ Stewards' Enquiry : Jason Hart caution: used whip when out of contention

FOCUS
A reasonable handicap and again the runners all migrated to the centre of the track in the home straight. The winner proved fully effective on the surface and can rate higher.

870 CHELTENHAM FESTIVAL FREE BETS WITH FREEBETTING.CO.UK H'CAP 1m (F)
3:05 (3:06) (Class 5) (0-75,74) 4-Y-O+ **£1,813** (£539; £269; £134) **Stalls** Low

Form RPR
-022 **1** **Postman**[13] 744 5-8-10 **63**................(p) PaulMulrennan 7 72
(Bryan Smart) *chsd ldrs: drvn over 3f out: styd on to ld last 50yds* **9/2**[3]
-311 **2** *½* **Almahaza (IRE)**[27] 573 7-9-7 **74**................ NeilChalmers 5 82
(Adrian Chamberlain) *hld up: effrt on inner over 2f out: led over 1f out: hdd towards fin* **15/8**[1]
6-11 **3** *1 ¼* **Hill Tribe**[13] 747 4-8-10 **68**................ TobyAtkinson(5) 2 73
(Richard Guest) *w ldr: led over 4f out: hdd over 1f out: kpt on same pce last 150yds* **3/1**[2]
4421 **4** *1 ¼* **Positivity**[20] 675 5-8-7 **60** oh2................(p) TomEaves 4 62
(Bryan Smart) *trckd ldrs: hung lft and swtchd rt ins fnl f: wknd towards fin* **13/2**
5144 **5** *hd* **General Tufto**[8] 799 6-9-1 **68**................(b) MartinLane 6 70
(Charles Smith) *dwlt: drvn along on outside: bhd and hung lft over 2f out: styd on strly fnl 150yds* **10/1**
06-6 **6** *3* **Exit Smiling**[29] 548 9-9-7 **74**................ MickyFenton 3 69
(Paul Midgley) *hld up in rr: effrt over 2f out: nvr nr to chal* **12/1**
0-00 **7** *4 ½* **Mark Anthony (IRE)**[20] 673 4-8-9 **67**................ JulieBurke(5) 1 52
(Kevin Ryan) *dwlt: sn chsng ldrs: rdn 3f out: wknd over 1f out* **16/1**
1m 42.73s (-0.97) **Going Correction** -0.025s/f (Stan) **7** Ran SP% **114.0**
Speed ratings (Par 103): **103,102,101,100,99 96,92**
toteswingers:1&2:£2.20, 1&3:£5.40, 2&3:£3.00 CSF £13.30 TOTE £8.30: £6.10, £1.10; EX 18.70.

The Form Book, Raceform Ltd, Compton, RG20 6NL

Owner Crossfields Racing **Bred** Newsells Park Stud **Trained** Hambleton, N Yorks
FOCUS
Just a fair handicap, and straightforward form.

871 BIGGEST FREE BETS WITH FREEBETTING.CO.UK (S) STKS 1m (F)
3:45 (3:45) (Class 6) 3-Y-O **£1,535** (£453; £226) **Stalls** Low

Form RPR
34 **1** **Sofias Number One (USA)**[28] 559 3-8-12 71............ AndreaAtzeni 1 66
(Michael Wigham) *hld up: effrt 3f out: rdn and hung bdly lft appr fnl f: led jst ins fnl f: drvn out* **1/2**[1]
0-33 **2** *1/2* **Tony Hollis**[47] 335 3-8-12 59............ JamesMillman 6 62
(Rod Millman) *t.k.h: trckd ldrs: pushed along over 4f out: wnt modestr 3rd 2f out: styd on to chse wnr last 150yds: no ex* **3/1**[2]
34-5 **3** *8* **Yorketa**[34] 494 3-8-4 55............ PatrickDonaghy(3) 3 38
(Michael Dods) *led: hdd jst ins fnl f: sn wknd: eased nr fin* **11/2**[3]
-065 **4** *41* **Come On Eileen (IRE)**[20] 672 3-8-3 30 ow1............ TobyAtkinson(5) 5 —
(Richard Guest) *led to post: w ldr: drvn over 4f out: lost pl over 2f out: sn bhd: eased ins fnl f: wl t.o* **50/1**

1m 44.33s (0.63) **Going Correction** -0.025s/f (Stan) **4** Ran SP% **109.0**
Speed ratings (Par 96): **95,94,86,45**
CSF £2.33 TOTE £1.10; EX 2.00.There was no bid for winner.
Owner D Hassan **Bred** Rosecrest Farm Llc **Trained** Newmarket, Suffolk
FOCUS
A poor seller with the time 1.6 seconds slower than the preceding handicap. The winner was the clear form choice and is a bit better than a plater.

872 COMPARE FREE BETS WITH FREEBETTING.CO.UK H'CAP 1m 6f (F)
4:25 (4:25) (Class 5) (0-75,75) 4-Y-O+ **£1,813** (£539; £269; £134) **Stalls** Low

Form RPR
222 **1** **Parhelion**[26] 597 4-9-10 75............ JackMitchell 3 82
(Derek Haydn Jones) *sn trcking ldr: drvn over 3f out: led 1f out: edgd lft: drvn out* **3/1**[2]
4322 **2** *1 1/2* **Calculating (IRE)**[20] 671 7-8-12 64............ LeeNewnes(5) 1 69
(Mark Usher) *trckd ldrs: effrt 3f out: upsides appr fnl f: no ex* **7/2**[3]
1-26 **3** *1 3/4* **Jezza**[18] 697 5-9-12 73............ StevieDonohoe 2 76
(Victor Dartnall) *trckd ldrs: hdwy to ld 5f out: hdd 1f out: kpt on same pce* **5/4**[1]
3405 **4** *20* **City Stable (IRE)**[13] 742 6-8-9 56............(b[1]) AndreaAtzeni 4 33
(Michael Wigham) *t.k.h in rr: drvn over 4f out: lost pl over 3f out: sn bhd* **20/1**
0-61 **5** *33* **Gunslinger (FR)**[18] 697 6-9-11 72............ HayleyTurner 5 —
(Michael Scudamore) *t.k.h in front: hdd 5f out: sn rdn: lost pl over 3f out: bhd whn eased 2f out: wl t.o* **7/1**

3m 9.81s (1.51) **Going Correction** -0.025s/f (Stan)
WFA 4 from 5yo+ 4lb **5** Ran SP% **108.9**
Speed ratings (Par 103): **94,93,92,80,61**
CSF £13.26 TOTE £3.70: £1.40, £1.80; EX 13.00.
Owner Ron Williams **Bred** Sheikh Abdulla Bin Isa Al-Khalifa **Trained** Efail Isaf, Rhondda C Taff
FOCUS
Quite a weak staying handicap. The second and third help with the level.

873 FREE HORSE RACING BETS WITH FREEBETTING.CO.UK MAIDEN STKS 7f (F)
5:05 (5:09) (Class 5) 3-Y-O+ **£1,910** (£564; £282) **Stalls** Low

Form RPR
5 **1** **J R Hartley**[29] 546 3-8-12 0............ TomEaves 4 81+
(Bryan Smart) *chsd ldr: led 2f out: drvn out* **12/1**
- **2** *2 1/2* **Honest Deal** 3-8-12 0............ PJMcDonald 6 75+
(Alan Swinbank) *chsd ldrs: wnt 2nd 1f out: kpt on same pce* **7/2**[2]
2 **3** *4* **Striking The Wind (USA)**[36] 454 3-8-12 0............ JoeFanning 12 64
(Mark Johnston) *chsd ldrs: drvn over 4f out: hung lft over 1f out: wnt modest 3rd jst ins fnl f* **1/1**[1]
6-42 **4** *3 1/4* **Goal (IRE)**[22] 642 3-8-9 57............ JamesSullivan(3) 8 56
(David C Griffiths) *mid div: kpt on fnl 2f: nvr nr ldrs* **10/1**
060- **5** *2* **Exchange**[212] 5160 3-8-12 67............ LiamJones 1 51
(William Haggas) *led: hdd 2f out: wknd fnl f* **11/2**[3]
6 **6** *8* **Carrside Lady**[29] 546 5-9-8 0............ GregFairley 11 30
(Owen Brennan) *dwlt: bhd and pushed along: sme hdwy 2f out: nvr a factor* **100/1**
0-4 **7** *5* **Chik's Dream**[57] 202 4-9-13 0............ MartinLane 7 22
(Derek Haydn Jones) *s.i.s: sn bhd: t.o 3f out: sme hdwy fnl 2f: nvr on terms* **33/1**
5 **8** *4* **Marvellous City (IRE)**[50] 295 3-8-12 0............ JimmyQuinn 10 —
(Mandy Rowland) *chsd ldrs: wknd 2f out* **100/1**
250- **9** *1 1/4* **Tombellini (IRE)**[152] 6897 4-9-13 57............ PaulQuinn 5 —
(David Nicholls) *dwlt: sn bhd: t.o 3f out: sme late hdwy* **20/1**
5 **10** *6* **Lyford Lad**[64] 121 4-9-13 0............ PaulMulrennan 2 —
(George Moore) *reluctant to load: s.i.s: sn in mid-div: lost pl over 3f out: sn bhd: fin 11th: plcd 10th* **66/1**
0/- **D** *4 1/2* **Into Mac**[628] 3338 5-9-10 0............ AndrewHeffernan(3) 3 —
(Neville Bycroft) *a towards rr: fin 10th: disqualified - jockey weighed in light* **100/1**
- **U** **Rapid Request (AUS)** 5-9-10 0............ MichaelO'Connell(3) 9 —
(David Nicholls) *gave problems gng to s: green and swvd lft and uns rdr sn after s* **25/1**

1m 29.49s (-0.81) **Going Correction** -0.025s/f (Stan)
WFA 3 from 4yo+ 15lb **12** Ran SP% **120.4**
Speed ratings (Par 103): **103,100,95,91,89 80,74,70,68,56 63,—**
toteswingers:1&2:£4.70, 1&3:£4.40, 2&3:£3.10 CSF £52.90 TOTE £13.80: £2.80, £1.80, £1.20; EX 98.10 Trifecta £291.00 Pool: £589.99 - 1.50 winning units..
Owner The Smart Flyfisher Partnership **Bred** Dunchurch Lodge Stud Co **Trained** Hambleton, N Yorks
■ Stewards' Enquiry : Andrew Heffernan three-day ban: failed to draw correct weight (Mar 30-Apr 1)
FOCUS
Plenty of dead wood in this maiden, but the principals are pretty decent. It was completely dominated by the 3-y-os. The third, seventh and time help with the level.

874 FREE BETTING WITH FREEBETTING.CO.UK H'CAP 6f (F)
5:40 (5:41) (Class 6) (0-60,59) 4-Y-O+ **£1,535** (£453; £226) **Stalls** Low

Form RPR
-042 **1** **Mata Hari Blue**[14] 734 5-9-2 54............ GrahamGibbons 6 67
(John Holt) *trckd ldr: chal over 2f out: led over 1f out: drvn clr: eased clsng stages* **11/4**[1]
6-60 **2** *1 3/4* **Dickie Le Davoir**[14] 734 7-8-9 50............(b) JamesSullivan(3) 1 56
(Richard Guest) *s.s: hdwy on ins over 2f out: styd on to go 2nd jst ins fnl f: no imp* **18/1**
00-1 **3** *nse* **Lindoro**[8] 798 6-9-4 59 6ex............ AndrewHeffernan(3) 10 65
(Kevin M Prendergast) *chsd ldrs: outpcd 3f out: styd on appr fnl f: kpt on wl to take 3rd last 75yds* **10/3**[2]
34-0 **4** *1 1/4* **Dimaire**[23] 637 4-9-6 58............ MartinLane 3 60
(Derek Haydn Jones) *chsd ldrs: rdn and outpcd over 3f out: kpt on fnl f* **10/1**
-035 **5** *1/2* **Simple Rhythm**[14] 734 5-9-0 55............(p) MichaelO'Connell(3) 2 55
(John Ryan) *led: hdd over 1f out: fdd fnl f* **12/1**
40-5 **6** *5* **Stonecrabstomorrow (IRE)**[6] 821 8-8-10 48...(b) RobbieFitzpatrick 12 32
(Frank Sheridan) *in rr-div: sme hdwy 2f out: nvr a factor* **16/1**
0/00 **7** *nk* **Bazguy**[8] 798 6-9-3 55............(b) GregFairley 5 38
(Owen Brennan) *in rr: effrt on outside over 2f out: nvr on terms* **20/1**
0122 **8** *nse* **Royal Acclamation (IRE)**[20] 664 6-8-11 56............ DavidKenny(7) 11 39
(Michael Scudamore) *in rr-div: sme hdwy 2f out: nvr a factor* **9/1**
4-66 **9** *2 3/4* **Cheery Cat (USA)**[47] 345 7-9-0 59............(v) MatthewCosham(7) 13 33
(John Balding) *swtchd lft after s: sn chsng ldrs: rdn 3f out: wknd over 1f out* **14/1**
3-50 **10** *2 1/4* **Hambleton**[50] 289 4-8-10 48............(p) TomEaves 4 15
(Bryan Smart) *s.s: sme hdwy on inner over 2f out: wknd over 1f out* **10/1**
11 *5* **Brockovich (IRE)**[96] 7818 5-8-7 45............ EddieCreighton 7 —
(John Geoghegan, Ire) *s.i.s: in rr: bhd fnl 3f* **8/1**[3]
60-0 **12** *3/4* **Uddy Mac**[8] 798 4-9-2 54............ JimmyQuinn 14 —
(Neville Bycroft) *s.i.s: swtchd lft after s: a bhd* **33/1**
000/ **13** *10* **Count Cougar (USA)**[477] 7503 11-8-8 46............ AdrianNicholls 8 —
(Simon Griffiths) *chsd ldrs: lost pl over 2f out: sn bhd: eased* **66/1**

1m 16.45s (-0.05) **Going Correction** -0.025s/f (Stan) **13** Ran SP% **123.7**
Speed ratings (Par 101): **99,96,96,94,94 87,87,87,83,80 73,72,59**
CSF £56.85 CT £185.70 TOTE £4.10: £1.10, £3.50, £1.80; EX 60.30 Trifecta £189.90 Pool: £351.75 - 1.37 winning units..
Owner M J Golding **Bred** R T And Mrs Watson **Trained** Peckleton, Leics
FOCUS
A moderate 13-runner sprint handicap, but only two counted in the market. The pace was good and very few ever got into this. The form looks solid.
Royal Acclamation(IRE) Official explanation: jockey said gelding did not face the kick-back
T/Plt: £12.90 to a £1 stake. Pool:£50,970.21 - 2,863.71 winning tickets T/Qpdt: £4.80 to a £1 stake. Pool:£3,037.62 - 468.03 winning tickets WG

844 WOLVERHAMPTON (A.W) (L-H)
Thursday, March 17

OFFICIAL GOING: Standard
Wind: mild across Weather: overcast

875 ENJOY THE CHELTENHAM FESTIVAL WITH FREEBETTING.CO.UK H'CAP 5f 20y(P)
5:45 (5:47) (Class 5) (0-75,75) 3-Y-O **£1,813** (£539; £269; £134) **Stalls** Low

Form RPR
2121 **1** **Go Maggie Go (IRE)**[5] 847 3-8-7 64 6ex............ AmyRyan(3) 6 64
(Kevin Ryan) *chsd ldrs: rdn 2f out: c wdst ent st: r.o fnl f: led fnl strides* **15/8**[1]
55-3 **2** *shd* **Overwhelm**[24] 632 3-9-5 73............ PaulHanagan 7 73
(Richard Fahey) *led: rdn 2f out: edgd rt but kpt on whn hrd pressed ins fnl f: hdd fnl strides* **7/2**[2]
45-1 **3** *nk* **Grandmas Dream**[26] 611 3-9-7 75............ PaulDoe 2 74
(Jim Best) *w ldr: rdn over 2f out: kpt on ins fnl f but no ex* **5/1**[3]
-165 **4** *hd* **Liberty Green (IRE)**[28] 578 3-9-7 75............ JamesDoyle 4 73
(Alan McCabe) *awkward leaving stalls: sn pushed along in last pair: rdn wl over 2f out: r.o ent fnl f: nrst fin* **11/2**
5450 **5** *2 1/4* **Je Suis Unrockstar**[5] 847 3-8-9 66............(p) BillyCray(3) 1 56
(David Nicholls) *chsd ldrs: rdn 2f out: kpt on same pce fr over 1f out* **7/1**
3364 **6** *3/4* **Johnny Hancocks (IRE)**[24] 632 3-8-9 66............ JamesSullivan(3) 5 53
(Linda Stubbs) *chsd ldrs: rdn over 2f out: fdd fnl f* **14/1**
-200 **7** *3* **Ajaafa**[42] 396 3-8-3 57............(p) NeilChalmers 3 34
(Michael Appleby) *wnt sltly lft leaving stalls: outpcd 3f out: nvr on terms* **40/1**

61.97 secs (-0.33) **Going Correction** 0.0s/f (Stan) **7** Ran SP% **110.7**
Speed ratings (Par 98): **102,101,101,101,97 96,91**
toteswingers:1&2:£1.90, 1&3:£3.20, 2&3:£3.20 CSF £7.92 TOTE £2.60: £1.40, £2.60; EX 12.00.
Owner Roger Peel **Bred** Oak Lodge Stud **Trained** Hambleton, N Yorks
FOCUS
A modest sprint handicap, but it featured a few in-form horses.

876 BOOKMAKERS FREE BETS WITH FREEBETTING.CO.UK (S) STKS 1m 141y(P)
6:15 (6:15) (Class 6) 4-Y-O+ **£1,535** (£453; £226) **Stalls** Low

Form RPR
-002 **1** **Dubai Miracle (USA)**[7] 816 4-8-12 78............ JamieSpencer 4 69+
(David Simcock) *trckd ldr: led 2f out: r.o: rdn out* **6/4**[1]
-146 **2** *2 1/4* **Midnight Strider (IRE)**[8] 814 5-9-4 67............ DaneO'Neill 1 69
(Joseph Tuite) *sn shkn up to ld: rdn and hdd 2f out: kpt on same pce* **7/1**
3513 **3** *1 1/4* **Una Pelota (IRE)**[14] 748 5-9-4 63............(b) RichardKingscote 2 67
(Tom Dascombe) *trckd ldrs: rdn over 2f out: nvr gng pce to chal* **3/1**[3]
-160 **4** *2 1/2* **Gallantry**[25] 623 9-9-4 77............ JimmyQuinn 3 61
(Jane Chapple-Hyam) *chsd ldng trio: rdn wl over 2f out: nvr any imp* **9/4**[2]

1m 52.16s (1.66) **Going Correction** 0.0s/f (Stan) **4** Ran SP% **108.3**
Speed ratings (Par 101): **92,90,88,86**
CSF £11.00 TOTE £1.60; EX 5.20.The winner was sold for 6,500gns to total plumbing supplies supporters group.
Owner Ahmad Al Shaikh **Bred** BryLynn Farm, Inc **Trained** Newmarket, Suffolk
FOCUS
They raced in single file until rounding the turn into the straight.

877 FREE HORSE RACING BETS WITH FREEBETTING.CO.UK H'CAP 1m 1f 103y(P)
6:45 (6:45) (Class 4) (0-85,85) 4-Y-O+ **£3,238** (£963; £481; £240) **Stalls** Low

Form RPR
3363 **1** **Veroon (IRE)**[13] 772 5-8-8 72............(p) PaulMulrennan 8 83
(James Given) *cl up: pushed along over 3f out: chsd ldr over 1f out: rdn to ld ins fnl f: r.o wl* **10/1**
0024 **2** *3/4* **Thunderstruck**[20] 694 6-9-4 82............(v[1]) IanMongan 7 91
(David Nicholls) *trckd ldrs: led 3f out: rdn wl over 1f out: no ex whn hdd ins fnl f* **5/1**[3]

6422 **3** 5 **Brouhaha**[22] 647 7-8-11 **75** .... RichardKingscote 1 74
(Tom Dascombe) *cl up rdn wl over 2f out: no ch w ldng pair fr over 1f out: kpt on same pce* **9/2**[2]
2124 **4** nk **Lockantanks**[19] 703 4-8-13 **77** .... NeilChalmers 6 75
(Michael Appleby) *hld up: hdwy over 2f out: sn rdn: kpt on same pce fr over 1f out* **8/1**
4-11 **5** 2½ **Star Links (USA)**[42] 405 5-9-1 **79** ....(b) ShaneKelly 4 72
(S Donohoe, Ire) *in last trio but in tch: drvn over 3f out: swtchd rt ent st: no imp* **4/1**[1]
00-4 **6** 1½ **Ahlawy (IRE)**[27] 599 8-9-2 **80** ....(t) JamesDoyle 5 69
(Frank Sheridan) *struggling in rr 1/2-way: passed wkng horses fr over 1f out: nvr a threat* **22/1**
3021 **7** 2¾ **Kidlat**[15] 723 6-9-5 **83** .... AdamKirby 11 67
(Alan Bailey) *sn led: rdn and hdd 3f out: wknd 2f out* **11/2**
133- **8** 1½ **First Post (IRE)**[157] 6813 4-9-2 **80** .... DaneO'Neill 10 61
(Derek Haydn Jones) *t.k.h early: trckd ldrs: ev ch 3f out: sn rdn: wknd over 1f out* **5/1**[3]

1m 59.76s (-1.94) **Going Correction** 0.0s/f (Stan) **8** Ran SP% **111.4**
Speed ratings (Par 105): **108,107,102,102,100 99,96,95**
toteswingers:1&2:£3.50, 1&3:£6.50, 2&3:£4.40 CSF £56.07 CT £252.36 TOTE £13.40: £3.30, £2.40, £1.80; EX 69.10 Trifecta £858.60 Pool: £3,828.98 - 3.30 winning units..
Owner Peter Swann **Bred** C M Farrell **Trained** Willoughton, Lincs

FOCUS
An open handicap.
Kidlat Official explanation: jockey said gelding had no more to give

878 FREE BETTING WITH FREEBETTING MAIDEN STKS 1m 1f 103y(P)
7:15 (7:16) (Class 5) 3-Y-O+ **£1,942** (£578; £288; £144) **Stalls** Low

Form RPR
42-2 **1** **Saint Helena (IRE)**[15] 726 3-8-3 70 ow1 .... ChrisCatlin 11 73
(Harry Dunlop) *trckd ldrs: rdn 2f out: r.o to ld ins fnl f: won gng away* **7/4**[1]
56- **2** 1½ **See The Smile (USA)**[167] 6542 3-8-7 0 .... JamieSpencer 4 74+
(Gay Kelleway) *mid-div: hdwy over 3f out: led 2f out: sn rdn: no ex whn hdd ins fnl f but kpt on for clr 2nd* **5/2**[2]
3 **3** 12 **Mutamaleq (IRE)**[20] 684 4-9-12 72 .... PJMcDonald 1 56
(Ian McInnes) *led: rdn whn hdd 2f out: sn no ch w ldng pair: jst hld on for 3rd* **15/2**
0- **4** nse **Young Jackie**[138] 7231 3-8-3 0 ow1 .... PaulHanagan 6 47
(George Margarson) *towards rr: stdy prog u.p fr 3f out: styd on same pce fnl 2f: wnt 4th fnl f: nvr threatened ldrs* **6/1**
5 4 **I'm A Celebrity** 3-8-7 0 .... AndreaAtzeni 2 44+
(Marco Botti) *s.i.s: sn drvn in rr: nvr a factor* **5/1**[3]
0- **6** 5 **Play The Blues (IRE)**[126] 7406 4-9-7 0 .... FrannyNorton 10 34
(Mark Allen) *trckd ldrs: rdn 3f out: wknd over 1f out* **80/1**
550- **7** ½ **Roose Blox (IRE)**[167] 6540 4-9-12 60 .... TomEaves 5 38
(Roger Fisher) *in tch tl wknd over 2f out* **33/1**
0-0 **8** ¾ **Neighbourhood (USA)**[33] 520 3-8-7 0 .... GregFairley 8 37
(Mark Johnston) *mid-div tl 1/2-way sn drvn in rr* **12/1**
9 3½ **Dawn Auction (IRE)**[19] 4-9-12 0 .... LiamKeniry 3 25
(Anthony Middleton) *trckd ldr: rdn over 3f out: sn wknd* **100/1**
10 21 **Perfect Deal**[17] 4-9-9 0 ....(b[1]) JamesSullivan(3) 7 —
(Michael Easterby) *dwlt v bdly: a towards rr wknd wl over 2f out* **66/1**

2m 1.20s (-0.50) **Going Correction** 0.0s/f (Stan)
WFA 3 from 4yo 19lb **10** Ran SP% **122.0**
Speed ratings (Par 103): **102,100,90,89,86 81,81,80,77,59**
toteswingers:1&2:£2.70, 1&3:£3.40, 2&3:£3.60 CSF £6.56 TOTE £2.80: £1.40, £1.40, £2.50; EX 11.30 Trifecta £43.00 Pool: £3,113.31 - 53.54 winning units..
Owner W R B Racing 47 **Bred** Frank O'Malley **Trained** Lambourn, Berks

FOCUS
The market leaders had this between them up the straight.
I'm A Celebrity Official explanation: jockey said colt was slowly away and ran green

879 COMPARE FREE BETS WITH FREEBETTING.CO.UK CLASSIFIED CLAIMING STKS 1m 4f 50y(P)
7:45 (7:45) (Class 6) 4-Y-O+ **£1,535** (£453; £226) **Stalls** Low

Form RPR
4-U4 **1** **Relative Strength (IRE)**[41] 418 6-8-12 65 ....(bt[1]) JamesDoyle 1 72
(Frank Sheridan) *trckd ldrs: rdn 3f out: chsd ldr 2f out: styd on fnl f: led fnl 75yds* **11/8**[2]
10-0 **2** ¾ **Humor Me Rene (USA)**[8] 808 4-8-9 70 .... NickyMackay 5 70
(George Baker) *trckd ldr: led over 3f out: rdn 2f out: kpt on but no ex whn hdd fnl 75yds* **9/2**[3]
5115 **3** 3¾ **Visions Of Johanna (USA)**[8] 805 6-8-11 68 .... JamieSpencer 2 64
(Ian Williams) *little slowly away: disp 4th: rdn 3f out: squeezed through to chse ldng pair 2f out: kpt on same pce fnl f* **5/4**[1]
0254 **4** 5 **Mojeerr**[9] 795 5-8-6 49 ....(v) AdrianMcCarthy 4 52
(Alan McCabe) *led tl over 3f out: sn rdn: wknd over 1f out* **25/1**
/00- **5** 7 **Noble Edge**[196] 5687 8-8-6 36 ....(p) DuranFentiman 3 41
(Lee James) *disp 4th: rdn over 3f out: sn outpcd: wknd 2f out* **66/1**

2m 40.64s (-0.46) **Going Correction** 0.0s/f (Stan)
WFA 4 from 5yo+ 2lb **5** Ran SP% **110.1**
Speed ratings (Par 101): **101,100,98,94,90**
CSF £7.88 TOTE £2.70: £1.30, £1.30; EX 8.20.
Owner Frank Sheridan **Bred** Holborn Trust Co **Trained** Wolverhampton, W Midlands

FOCUS
There wasn't much to choose between the front three in the market on the ratings, but the money was mostly for the winner and it proved well placed.

880 BIGGEST FREE BETS WITH FREEBETTING.CO.UK H'CAP 5f 216y(P)
8:15 (8:17) (Class 5) (0-70,70) 4-Y-O+ **£1,878** (£558; £279; £139) **Stalls** Low

Form RPR
30-0 **1** **Sir Nod**[28] 577 9-9-7 **70** .... PaulHanagan 10 80
(Julie Camacho) *mde all: pushed clr over 1f out: edgd rt but r.o wl: rdn out* **6/1**[2]
0400 **2** 1¼ **Gwilym (GER)**[17] 708 8-8-13 **62** .... DaneO'Neill 12 68
(Derek Haydn Jones) *chsd wnr thrght: rdn over 2f out: nt pce to chal: kpt on but a being hld* **12/1**
-062 **3** ¾ **Cavitie**[15] 735 5-8-5 **57** ....(p) LouisBeuzelin(3) 6 64
(Andrew Reid) *mid-div tl squeezed up whn lost pl after 1f: sn bmpd: towards rr: hdwy whn short of room and snatched up over 1f out: styd on wl whn clr run ins fnl f: nrst fin* **7/1**[3]
0-41 **4** ¾ **Steelcut**[13] 767 7-8-11 **67** ....(p) MatthewCosham(7) 11 68
(David Evans) *chsd ldrs: rdn whn c wdst ent st: kpt on same pce* **17/2**
0114 **5** shd **Polemica (IRE)**[14] 746 5-8-9 **58** ow1 ....(bt) JamesDoyle 1 59
(Frank Sheridan) *mid-div: effrt over 2f out: hung rt over 1f out: kpt on same pce fnl f* **8/1**
024- **6** 1¼ **Rainy Night**[132] 7331 5-9-6 **69** .... LiamKeniry 9 66
(Reg Hollinshead) *chsd ldrs: rdn 2f out: sn one pce* **9/1**
0006 **7** 1 **Absa Lutte (IRE)**[6] 833 8-9-5 **68** ....(t) GeorgeBaker 8 61
(Michael Mullineaux) *hld up towards rr: hdwy 3f out: rdn wl over 1f out: sn one pce* **7/1**[3]
0606 **8** nse **Kersivay**[10] 786 5-8-0 **56** oh4 ....(v) KevinLundie(7) 7 50
(David Evans) *mid-div: rdn over 2f out: nt clrest of runs over 1f out: sn bmpd: no further imp* **33/1**
2221 **9** ¾ **Apache Ridge (IRE)**[14] 746 5-9-2 **68** ....(p) AmyRyan(3) 4 59
(Kevin Ryan) *sme late hdwy: mainly towards rr* **5/1**[1]
1440 **10** 2¾ **Takajan (IRE)**[2] 853 4-9-0 **68** .... JamesRogers(5) 2 50
(Mark Brisbourne) *mid-div tl wknd 2f out* **14/1**
20-0 **11** 3¼ **Avontuur (FR)**[28] 577 9-8-6 **58** ....(b) JamesSullivan(3) 3 30
(Ruth Carr) *squeezed out sn after s: towards rr whn swtchd to outer after 1f: nvr threatened* **28/1**
013- **12** 8 **Yungaburra (IRE)**[221] 4869 7-9-5 **68** ....(t) MartinDwyer 5 14
(David C Griffiths) *chsd ldrs tl wknd over 2f out* **16/1**

1m 14.53s (-0.47) **Going Correction** 0.0s/f (Stan) **12** Ran SP% **114.2**
Speed ratings (Par 103): **103,101,100,99,99 97,96,96,95,91 87,76**
toteswingers:1&2:£37.80, 1&3:£7.30, 2&3:£31.80 CSF £73.12 CT £520.19 TOTE £4.60: £1.80, £3.40, £3.50; EX 76.30 Trifecta £357.60 Part won. Pool: £483.31 - 0.54 winning units..
Owner Lee Bolingbroke **Bred** B Nordan And Mrs S Camacho **Trained** Norton, N Yorks

FOCUS
A wide-open handicap on paper.

881 CHELTENHAM FESTIVAL FREE BETS WITH FREEBETTING.CO.UK H'CAP 1m 141y(P)
8:45 (8:45) (Class 5) (0-70,68) 4-Y-O+ **£1,813** (£539; £269; £134) **Stalls** Low

Form RPR
1521 **1** **John Potts**[14] 749 6-9-5 **66** .... KellyHarrison 5 74
(Brian Baugh) *mid-div: hdwy 3f out: rdn to ld ent fnl f: kpt on gamely: drvn out* **3/1**[1]
-516 **2** ½ **Mr Chocolate Drop (IRE)**[25] 626 7-9-0 **61** ....(t) AdamKirby 6 68
(Mandy Rowland) *s.i.s: sn in tch: rdn over 2f out: ev ch thrght fnl f: hld nr finsh* **7/1**
1 **3** 1¼ **Needwood Ridge**[17] 713 4-9-5 **66** ....(t) JamesDoyle 7 70
(Frank Sheridan) *hld up in last pair: hdwy on outer fr over 3f out: rdn over 2f out: styd on fnl f* **11/2**
0324 **4** ¾ **What's Up Doc (IRE)**[17] 711 10-9-0 **61** .... DaneO'Neill 3 64
(Lawney Hill) *pressed ldr: led over 3f out: rdn 2f out: hdd ent fnl f: no ex: lost 3rd nr fin* **7/2**[2]
350- **5** ¾ **Dabbers Ridge (IRE)**[141] 7182 9-9-3 **67** .... GaryBartley(3) 8 68
(Ian McInnes) *hld up bhd: hdwy over 2f out: swtchd rt over 1f out to chse ldrs: sn rdn: kpt on same pce* **18/1**
5-04 **6** 22 **Tukitinyasok (IRE)**[29] 562 4-9-4 **65** ....(p) TomEaves 1 20
(Roger Fisher) *chsd ldng pair tl 3f out: wknd 2f out: t.o* **6/1**
000- **7** 20 **Istiqdaam**[173] 6370 6-9-4 **65** ....(b) GrahamGibbons 2 —
(Michael Easterby) *led at str pce tl hdd over 3f out: sn wknd: t.o* **9/2**[3]
0/0 **8** 9 **Focail Eile**[25] 623 6-9-7 **68** .... ChrisCatlin 4 —
(Noel Quinlan) *mid-div tl over 4f out: sn struggling in rr: t.o* **25/1**

1m 50.35s (-0.15) **Going Correction** 0.0s/f (Stan) **8** Ran SP% **116.7**
Speed ratings (Par 103): **100,99,98,97,97 77,59,51**
toteswingers:1&2:£6.20, 1&3:£3.50, 2&3:£3.70 CSF £25.10 CT £110.87 TOTE £8.30: £1.70, £4.80, £3.40; EX 22.90 Trifecta £51.90 Pool: £482.62 - 6.87 winning units..
Owner Miss S M Potts **Bred** Miss S M Potts **Trained** Audley, Staffs
■ Stewards' Enquiry : Adam Kirby caution: used whip with excessive frequency.

FOCUS
A strong pace here, with two horses taking each other on in front.
T/Plt: £50.30 to a £1 stake. Pool:£76,850.90 - 1,114.98 winning tickets T/Qpdt: 11.50 to a £1 stake. Pool:£7,635.77 - 489.74 winning tickets TM

840 DEAUVILLE (R-H)
Thursday, March 17
OFFICIAL GOING: Fibresand: standard

882a PRIX DE CARENTAN (CONDITIONS) (3YO COLTS & GELDINGS) (FIBRESAND) 1m 1f 110y
1:20 (12:00) 3-Y-O **£14,655** (£5,862; £4,396; £2,931; £1,465)

RPR
1 **Durer (FR)**[137] 3-9-0 0 .... ChristopheSoumillon 6 91
(J-C Rouget, France) **7/10**[1]
2 hd **Hurricane Higgins (IRE)**[68] 95 3-9-0 0 .... JoeFanning 1 90
(Mark Johnston) *s.i.s: sn rdn to ld: led into st: rdn and hdd over 1 1/2f out: hrd rdn ent fnl f: rallied wl and only jst failed on line* **5/2**[2]
3 ½ **Clavis (FR)** 3-8-7 0 .... WilliamsSaraiva 5 82
(Mme J Bidgood, France) **34/1**
4 2½ **Victorian Number (FR)**[136] 3-9-0 0 .... RobertWinston 3 84
(E J O'Neill, France) **11/1**
5 ¾ **Air Shot (FR)** 3-9-0 0 .... PhilippeSogorb 2 82
(C Ferland, France) **58/10**[3]
6 snk **De Bon Matin (FR)**[32] 3-9-0 0 .... Jean-BaptisteHamel 4 82
(Mme C Dufreche, France) **23/1**

2m 0.40s (120.40) **6** Ran SP% **117.5**
WIN (incl. 1 euro stake): 1.70. PLACES: 1.20, 1.50. SF: 3.40.
Owner Hamdan Al Maktoum **Bred** Haras Du Quesnay **Trained** Pau, France

NOTEBOOK
Hurricane Higgins(IRE), a winner on Polytrack on his debut in January, battled back once headed and nearly got back in front. He looks a game sort and, closely related to Jukebox Jury, could prove useful once switching to turf.

883a PRIX MONTENICA (LISTED RACE) (3YO COLTS & GELDINGS) (FIBRESAND) 6f 110y
1:55 (12:00) 3-Y-O **£23,706** (£9,482; £7,112; £4,741; £2,370)

RPR
1 **Redemptor**[32] 532 3-9-2 0 .... ChristopheSoumillon 6 106
(J-C Rouget, France) **8/5**[1]
2 1½ **Captain Chop (FR)**[115] 7534 3-9-2 0 .... FlavienPrat 2 102
(D Guillemin, France) **23/10**[2]
3 2 **Bathwick Bear (IRE)**[179] 6230 3-9-2 0 .... IoritzMendizabal 4 96
(David Evans) *led fr s: rdn 1 1/2f out: hdd 1f out: styd on wl: jst hld 3rd on line* **48/10**[3]

4 nse **Bloodson (FR)**[76] 3-9-2 0 .... Roberto-CarlosMontenegro 3 96
(X Thomas-Demeaulte, France) **58/10**
5 snk **King David (FR)**[65] 3-9-2 0 .... Christophe-PatriceLemaire 1 95?
(M Boutin, France) **9/1**
6 hd **Boccalino (GER)**[136] [7277] 3-9-2 0 .... MaximeGuyon 5 95
(H-A Pantall, France) **14/1**
1m 19.6s (79.60) **6** Ran SP% **117.4**
WIN (incl. 1 ewuro stake): 2.60. PLACES: 1.60, 1.60. SF: 6.80.
Owner Hamdan Al Maktoum **Bred** Mme Y Seydoux De Clausonne & E Puerari **Trained** Pau, France

NOTEBOOK
Bathwick Bear(IRE),a Listed winner last season, was making his all-weather debut after six months off and ran pretty well. This should tune him up nicely for a return to turf this spring.

[808] LINGFIELD (L-H)
Friday, March 18

OFFICIAL GOING: Standard
Wind: mild against Weather: light rain

885 ENJOY THE CHELTENHAM FESTIVAL WITH FREEBETTING.CO.UK CLASSIFIED CLAIMING STKS 1m 2f (P)
1:55 (1:55) (Class 6) 4-Y-O+ **£1,535** (£453; £226) **Stalls** Low

Form RPR
1241 **1** **Edgeworth (IRE)**[11] [790] 5-8-6 66 .... (p) ChrisCatlin 6 77
(Brendan Powell) *hld up in last but in tch: hdwy over 2f out: pushed along to chal ent fnl f: led sn after: r.o wl* **5/4**[1]
4600 **2** 2 ¼ **Officer In Command (USA)**[27] [617] 5-8-4 73 .... (b) LukeMorris 3 71
(J S Moore) *little slowly away: sn trcking ldr: rdn to ld 2f out: hdd ins fnl f: kpt on but nt pce of wnr* **9/4**[2]
0-03 **3** nk **Saviour Sand (IRE)**[37] [472] 7-8-0 62 .... (t) SilvestreDeSousa 1 66
(Olivia Maylam) *led: rdn and hdd 2f out: kpt on but no ex ins fnl f* **8/1**
2332 **4** 1 ¾ **Dichoh**[14] [765] 8-8-6 65 .... (v) JimmyQuinn 2 69
(Michael Madgwick) *trckd ldr tl rdn over 2f out: kpt on same pce fr over 1f out* **13/2**[3]
5-20 **5** 1 ¾ **Charlie Smirke (USA)**[51] [310] 5-8-10 70 .... (bt) FergusSweeney 4 69
(Gary Moore) *disp cl 4th: rdn over 2f out: nvr gng pce to chal* **11/1**
060- **6** 15 **Royal Defence (IRE)**[156] [6841] 5-9-0 72 .... FrannyNorton 5 45
(Michael Quinn) *racd in cl 4th/5th: rdn 4f out: sn wknd* **33/1**
2m 5.45s (-1.15) **Going Correction** +0.05s/f (Slow) **6** Ran SP% **110.9**
Speed ratings (Par 101): **106,104,103,102,101 89**
Tote Swingers: 1&2 £1.10, 1&3 £4.10, 2&3 £4.80 CSF £4.12 TOTE £2.20: £1.30, £1.30; EX 5.10.

Owner K Rhatigan **Bred** Yvonne & Gerard Kennedy **Trained** Upper Lambourn, Berks
FOCUS
An evenly run event.

886 GOLD CUP FREE BETS WITH FREEBETTING.CO.UK CLAIMING STKS 7f (P)
2:30 (2:30) (Class 6) 3-Y-O **£1,535** (£453; £226) **Stalls** Low

Form RPR
4153 **1** **Silly Billy (IRE)**[6] [845] 3-8-10 76 .... LukeRowe(7) 5 73
(Sylvester Kirk) *chsd ldrs: clsd on ldrs ent st: led jst ins fnl f: kpt on wl: pushed out* **6/4**[1]
1514 **2** ¾ **Fifth In Line (IRE)**[16] [724] 3-8-10 65 .... SilvestreDeSousa 1 63
(David Flood) *trckd ldrs: led jst over 1f out: rdn and hdd jst ins fnl f: kpt on: hld nr fin* **4/1**[3]
3213 **3** nk **Better Self**[8] [817] 3-8-4 70 .... MartinLane 4 56
(David Evans) *s.i.s: last but in tch: effrt wdst of all ent st: r.o wl ins fnl f* **7/4**[2]
5504 **4** 4 ½ **Lynchpin**[23] [655] 3-8-9 55 .... (b[1]) LukeMorris 2 49
(Ronald Harris) *led for 1f: w ldr: rdn and ev ch over 1f out: fdd ins fnl f* **12/1**
-064 **5** 3 ½ **Hey Mambo**[11] [787] 3-8-4 34 .... FrannyNorton 3 34
(Roger Ingram) *t.k.h: led after 1f: rdn and hdd over 1f out: fdd fnl f* **40/1**
1m 26.36s (1.56) **Going Correction** +0.05s/f (Slow) **5** Ran SP% **106.5**
Speed ratings (Par 96): **93,92,91,86,82**
CSF £7.26 TOTE £2.40: £1.10, £2.60; EX 7.50.
Owner Lady Davis **Bred** Sir E J Loder **Trained** Upper Lambourn, Berks
FOCUS
Just an ordinary claimer with little depth.

887 FREE HORSE RACING BETS WITH FREEBETTING.CO.UK H'CAP 7f (P)
3:05 (3:07) (Class 5) (0-70,68) 3-Y-O **£2,047** (£604; £302) **Stalls** Low

Form RPR
0-43 **1** **Old English (IRE)**[27] [610] 3-9-5 **66** .... KierenFallon 4 69
(Mark Johnston) *sn led: kpt on u.p fnl f: edgd lft nr fin: jst hld on: all out* **13/2**[3]
0-13 **2** shd **City Legend**[64] [140] 3-9-5 **66** .... (bt) JamesDoyle 2 68
(Alan McCabe) *trckd ldrs: rdn over 3f out: kpt on wl ins fnl f: jst failed* **5/1**[2]
060- **3** ½ **Sleeping Brave**[120] [7496] 3-8-1 **55** .... NathanAlison(7) 10 56+
(Jim Boyle) *s.i.s: towards rr: rdn 2f out: styd on strly fnl f: wnt 3rd nr fin* **25/1**
1 **4** hd **Caelis**[22] [663] 3-9-2 **63** .... JimCrowley 6 63+
(Ralph Beckett) *trckd ldrs: rdn over 2f out: styng on whn nt clrest of runs wl ins fnl f* **7/4**[1]
2210 **5** ¼ **Titan Diamond (IRE)**[14] [760] 3-8-6 **58** .... RyanPowell(5) 1 58
(Mark Usher) *mid-div: hdwy u.p over 2f out: styd on fnl f* **12/1**
15-5 **6** ¼ **Saucy Buck (IRE)**[28] [601] 3-9-2 **68** .... (v) MartinHarley(5) 12 67
(Mick Channon) *sn trcking ldrs: rdn to chal briefly 2f out: kpt on same pce fnl f* **11/1**
5-40 **7** ¾ **Bedibyes**[23] [655] 3-8-10 **57** .... HayleyTurner 8 54
(Richard Mitchell) *mid-div: rdn whn nt clr run over 1f out and swtchd rt: swtchd rt again ins fnl f: kpt on but nvr gng to rch ldrs* **40/1**
-555 **8** ¼ **Karate (IRE)**[14] [764] 3-9-1 **62** .... DaneO'Neill 9 58
(Hans Adielsson) *mid-div: hdwy over 2f out: sn rdn: one pce fnl f* **8/1**
0-05 **9** 3 **Warbond**[22] [663] 3-9-1 **62** .... FrankieMcDonald 7 50
(Michael Madgwick) *trckd ldrs: rdn over 2f out: fdd fnl f* **50/1**
055- **10** 1 ¾ **Holcombe Boy**[86] [7962] 3-9-6 **67** .... StevieDonohoe 13 51
(Noel Quinlan) *a towards rr* **16/1**
04-0 **11** ¼ **Come On The Irons (USA)**[21] [684] 3-9-3 **64** .... JamieGoldstein 11 47
(Ralph Smith) *rdn over 3f out: a towards rr* **40/1**
355- **12** 3 ½ **Out Of The Storm**[185] [6052] 3-9-2 **63** .... GeorgeBaker 3 36
(Simon Dow) *hld up towards rr: rdn over 2f out: nvr any imp* **10/1**
-653 **13** 6 **Lough Corrib (USA)**[14] [770] 3-8-8 **60** .... (b[1]) JulieBurke(5) 5 17
(Kevin Ryan) *s.i.s: rcvring but taking t.k.h whn hit rails after 2f: nt rcvr and bhd after* **16/1**
1m 25.7s (0.90) **Going Correction** +0.05s/f (Slow) **13** Ran SP% **125.0**
Speed ratings (Par 98): **96,95,95,95,94 94,93,93,89,87 87,83,76**
Tote Swingers: 1&2 £5.10, 1&3 £67.80, 2&3 £36.40 CSF £39.94 CT £818.52 TOTE £3.90: £2.20, £2.10, £11.10; EX 25.50 Trifecta £359.70.
Owner Sheikh Hamdan Bin Mohammed Al Maktoum **Bred** P G Lyons **Trained** Middleham Moor, N Yorks
■ Stewards' Enquiry : Frankie McDonald caution: careless riding.
FOCUS
Not a strong handicap, but several emerged with credit.
Warbond Official explanation: jockey said gelding hung right throughout
Holcombe Boy Official explanation: jockey said gelding did not handle final bend
Lough Corrib(USA) Official explanation: jockey said gelding ran too free early stages

888 FREE BETTING WITH FREEBETTING.CO.UK MAIDEN STKS 1m (P)
3:45 (3:46) (Class 5) 3-Y-O **£2,047** (£604; £302) **Stalls** High

Form RPR
1 **Protractor (IRE)** 3-9-3 0 .... MichaelHills 2 68+
(B W Hills) *little slowly away: sn trcking ldng pair: pushed along over 3f out: gd run on inner 2f out: led over 1f out: rdn fnl f: drifted rt towards fin: readily* **6/5**[1]
0 **2** hd **Red Copper**[26] [624] 3-8-12 0 .... HayleyTurner 3 60+
(Michael Bell) *trckd ldr: rdn over 2f out: kpt on towards fin but nvr quite gng to get there* **5/1**[3]
3-23 **3** nk **Roman Flame**[26] [624] 3-8-12 70 .... MartinDwyer 4 60
(Michael Quinn) *hld up cl in 4th: rdn to chal for 2nd over 2f out: kpt on ins fnl f* **15/8**[2]
00-0 **4** ¾ **Beautiful Lando (FR)**[9] [801] 3-9-3 41 .... (v[1]) EddieAhern 5 63?
(Heather Main) *led: rdn over 2f out: hdd over 1f out: kpt on but no ex whn lost 2 pls narrowly nring fin* **9/1**
1m 39.81s (1.61) **Going Correction** +0.05s/f (Slow) **4** Ran SP% **106.9**
Speed ratings (Par 98): **93,92,92,91**
CSF £7.09 TOTE £1.90; EX 4.00.
Owner H R Mould **Bred** T G Mills & J Humphreys **Trained** Lambourn, Berks
■ Stewards' Enquiry : Michael Hills caution: careless riding.
FOCUS
A weak maiden in which 70-rated Roman Flame set a modest standard. The fact that they finished in a heap only enhances the feeling that this is modest form, but the winner is totally unexposed and has an eye-catching pedigree.

889 COMPARE FREE BETS WITH FREEBETTING.CO.UK FILLIES' H'CAP 1m (P)
4:25 (4:25) (Class 5) (0-70,70) 4-Y-O+ **£2,047** (£604; £302) **Stalls** High

Form RPR
1626 **1** **Very Well Red**[17] [722] 8-8-8 **57** .... LukeMorris 3 63
(Peter Hiatt) *trckd ldrs: rdn over 2f out: r.o strly fnl f: led towards fin* **12/1**
3123 **2** nk **Shared Moment (IRE)**[14] [765] 5-8-12 **61** .... (v) ChrisCatlin 2 66
(John Gallagher) *chsd ldrs: rdn wl over 1f out: led fnl 120yds: ct towards fin* **5/1**
1-22 **3** nk **Zafeen's Pearl**[36] [488] 4-8-13 **62** .... SamHitchcott 5 67
(Dean Ivory) *led tl 3f out: regained ld 2f out: sn rdn: hdd fnl 120yds: kpt on gamely* **11/4**[2]
-121 **4** 6 **But Beautiful (IRE)**[26] [626] 4-9-5 **68** .... EddieAhern 4 59
(Robert Mills) *trckd ldrs: rdn over 2f out: outpcd wl over 1f out* **11/8**[1]
122- **5** 3 **Inpursuitoffreedom**[106] [7663] 4-9-7 **70** .... KierenFallon 1 54
(Philip McBride) *sn prom: led 3f out tl rdn 2f out: wknd jst over 1f out* **3/1**[3]
1m 38.36s (0.16) **Going Correction** +0.05s/f (Slow) **5** Ran SP% **118.1**
Speed ratings (Par 100): **101,100,100,94,91**
CSF £69.38 TOTE £15.80: £4.90, £2.20; EX 44.10.
Owner Phil Kelly **Bred** Butts Enterprises Limited **Trained** Hook Norton, Oxon
FOCUS
This was run at a reasonable gallop, but that only served to set it up for the closers.
But Beautiful(IRE) Official explanation: trainer said filly did not handle the track

890 SIX NATIONS FREE BETS WITH FREEBETTING.CO.UK H'CAP 1m (P)
5:05 (5:05) (Class 5) (0-70,70) 3-Y-O **£2,047** (£604; £302) **Stalls** High

Form RPR
631 **1** **Apache Glory (USA)**[26] [624] 3-9-2 **65** .... JimmyQuinn 5 74
(Richard Hannon) *trckd ldr: rdn to ld jst over 1f out: jst hld on: all out* **4/1**[3]
65-1 **2** shd **Sammy Alexander**[72] [49] 3-9-4 **67** .... MartinLane 4 76
(David Simcock) *hld up in cl 5th: effrt on outer ent st: chsd wnr ent fnl f: kpt on wl: jst hld off* **3/1**[2]
3350 **3** 5 **Greenhead High**[14] [764] 3-9-3 **66** .... PaulDoe 3 63
(Jane Chapple-Hyam) *led: rdn over 2f out: hdd jst over 1f out: no ex* **10/1**
60-4 **4** ¼ **Highlife Dancer**[28] [594] 3-9-2 **70** .... MartinHarley(5) 2 66
(Mick Channon) *trckd ldrs: rdn wl over 2f out: nt pce to get on terms* **16/1**
-421 **5** ¼ **Govenor General (IRE)**[14] [760] 3-9-2 **65** .... GeorgeBaker 1 61
(Jeremy Noseda) *trckd ldr: rdn 2f out: kpt on same pce* **10/11**[1]
1m 37.49s (-0.71) **Going Correction** +0.05s/f (Slow) **5** Ran SP% **112.4**
Speed ratings (Par 98): **105,104,99,99,99**
CSF £16.43 TOTE £4.40: £1.20, £2.90; EX 14.10.
Owner Malih Lahej Al Basti **Bred** Malih Al Basti **Trained** East Everleigh, Wilts
FOCUS
The market suggested this was all about the favourite, but he proved very disappointing.

891 FOOTBALL FREE BETS WITH FREEBETTING.CO.UK MAIDEN STKS 1m 4f (P)
5:40 (5:41) (Class 5) 3-Y-O **£2,047** (£604; £302) **Stalls** Low

Form RPR
-3 **1** **Bestwecan (IRE)**[14] [762] 3-9-3 0 .... KierenFallon 1 76+
(Mark Johnston) *racd in 4th: rdn to chse ldr over 2f out: led over 1f out: in command fnl f: comf* **4/6**[1]
6-42 **2** 3 ¼ **Echos Of Motivator**[17] [716] 3-9-3 65 .... LukeMorris 2 67
(Ronald Harris) *hld up 5th: rdn to dispute 3rd 2f out: styd on to chse wnr ent fnl f: a hld* **11/4**[2]
66-4 **3** 1 ¼ **Dubai Glory**[9] [801] 3-8-12 60 .... JamesDoyle 3 60
(Sheena West) *trckd ldr: rdn and styd on same pce fnl 2f* **7/1**[3]
3333 **4** 8 **Not So Bright (USA)**[23] [650] 3-9-3 58 .... (bt) GeorgeBaker 5 52
(Des Donovan) *trckd ldr: keen early: led 3f out: rdn and hdd over 1f out: wknd fnl f* **14/1**
05 **5** 9 **Twilight Express (IRE)**[28] [591] 3-8-12 0 .... ChrisCatlin 4 33
(Emma Lavelle) *racd keenly: led tl 3f out: sn btn* **40/1**
2m 33.95s (0.95) **Going Correction** +0.05s/f (Slow) **5** Ran SP% **108.3**
Speed ratings (Par 98): **98,95,95,89,83**
CSF £2.60 TOTE £1.20: £1.10, £1.70; EX 3.10.
Owner Douglas Livingston **Bred** Jim & Anna McCormack **Trained** Middleham Moor, N Yorks

FOCUS
A weak maiden.
T/Plt: £104.90 to a £1 stake. Pool:£43,682.02 - 303.96 winning tickets. T/Qpdt: £39.00 to a £1 stake. Pool:£2,647.12 - 50.20 winning tickets. TM

[875]WOLVERHAMPTON (A.W) (L-H)
Friday, March 18

OFFICIAL GOING: Standard
Wind: almost nil Weather: fine

892 FREEBETS.CO.UK CHELTENHAM FESTIVAL FREE BETS OFFER MAIDEN STKS 5f 20y(P)
5:25 (5:25) (Class 5) 3-Y-O+ **£2,007** (£597; £298; £149) **Stalls** Low

Form RPR
2-33 **1** **Sparking**[35] 511 4-9-5 56 GrahamGibbons 3 58
(David Barron) *mde all: kpt on wl fnl f* **2/1**[2]
6404 **2** 2 1/4 **Gorgeous Goblin (IRE)**[16] 732 4-9-2 47 (vt) JamesSullivan(3) 2 50
(David C Griffiths) *chsd ldrs: drvn over 2f out: chsd wnr jst ins fnl f: kpt on same pce* **40/1**
506 **3** 1/2 **Francis Albert**[16] 734 5-9-10 47 (be) TomEaves 4 53
(Michael Mullineaux) *w ldr: t.k.h: kpt on same pce appr fnl f* **14/1**[3]
00-2 **4** 1 1/2 **Midnight Trader (IRE)**[27] 611 3-8-12 72 TonyCulhane 6 43
(Paul D'Arcy) *trckd ldrs on outside: t.k.h: drvn over 2f out: one pce* **1/2**[1]
5 1 1/4 **Kaminski Kabs** 3-8-2 0 DanielleMcCreery(5) 5 33
(Phil McEntee) *dwlt: drvn along in last: hdwy over 1f out: kpt on: nvr a factor* **100/1**
600 **6** 13 **Stoneacre Joe Joe**[34] 518 3-8-12 40 RobbieFitzpatrick 1 —
(Peter Grayson) *chsd ldrs: drvn and outpcd over 2f out: lost pl over 1f out: eased ins fnl f* **100/1**

62.17 secs (-0.13) **Going Correction** +0.025s/f (Slow)
WFA 3 from 4yo+ 12lb **6** Ran SP% **111.1**
Speed ratings (Par 103): **102,98,97,95,93 72**
Tote Swingers: 1&2 £4.40, 1&3 £1.10, 2&3 £2.60 CSF £44.70 TOTE £1.50: £1.10, £10.20; EX 25.10.
Owner P Bamford **Bred** Dandy's Farm **Trained** Maunby, N Yorks
FOCUS
A most uncompetitive maiden and one weakened further with the below-par showing of the market leader. The gallop was an ordinary one and the winner came down the centre. Straightforward form rated around the first two.

893 FREEBETS.CO.UK CHELTENHAM 2011 FREE BETTING H'CAP 7f 32y(P)
5:50 (5:50) (Class 6) (0-55,55) 4-Y-O+ **£1,637** (£483; £241) **Stalls** High

Form RPR
0445 **1** **Katmai River (IRE)**[17] 719 4-9-0 53 (v) SteveDrowne 3 63
(Mark Usher) *w ldrs: led over 3f out: rdn and hung lft fnl f: all out* **9/2**[2]
3306 **2** nk **Silver Wind**[14] 763 6-8-11 50 (b) ShaneKelly 11 59
(Alan McCabe) *chsd ldrs: wnt 2nd 2f out: styd on fnl f: jst hld* **8/1**
2401 **3** 2 1/4 **Fortunate Bid (IRE)**[26] 619 5-8-13 55 (p) JamesSullivan(3) 7 58
(Linda Stubbs) *in rr: hdwy over 2f out: kpt on same pce appr fnl f* **11/2**
6-00 **4** 3 3/4 **Grace And Virtue (IRE)**[43] 408 4-8-5 47 (p) IanBrennan(3) 9 40
(S Donohoe, Ire) *s.i.s: hdwy over 1f out: kpt on ins fnl f: nvr rchd ldrs* **22/1**
-020 **5** nk **Charles Darwin (IRE)**[28] 589 8-9-2 55 (p) LiamKeniry 8 47
(Michael Blanshard) *in rr: hdwy over 2f out: nvr nr ldrs* **14/1**
200- **6** 1/2 **Belle Park**[153] 6937 4-9-1 54 DarryllHolland 10 45
(Karen George) *hmpd sn after s: in rr: hdwy 2f out: nvr nr ldrs* **18/1**
00-0 **7** 2 **Chateau Zara**[10] 800 4-8-10 49 RobbieFitzpatrick 4 34
(Derek Shaw) *in rr: sme hdwy over 1f out: nvr a factor* **50/1**
- **8** 1/2 **Coolagad Wonder (IRE)**[147] 7077 6-8-11 50 (be) BarryMcHugh 6 34
(Neville Bycroft) *mid-div: drvn 3f out: lost pl over 2f out: no threat after* **4/1**[1]
00-6 **9** 6 **All Right Now**[63] 158 4-8-9 48 PaulHanagan 2 16
(Derek Haydn Jones) *s.i.s: sme hdwy on ins 2f out: hung lft and sn wknd* **12/1**
600- **10** 1 **Dhhamaan (IRE)**[181] 6188 6-9-1 54 (b) PJMcDonald 1 19
(Ruth Carr) *led tl over 3f out: wknd 2f out* **22/1**
63-1 **11** 8 **Exceedingly Good (IRE)**[10] 793 5-8-11 55 6ex DeclanCannon(5) 5 —
(Roy Bowring) *w ldrs: hung rt and wknd over 2f out: sn bhd* **5/1**[3]
2250 **12** 6 **Libertino (IRE)**[36] 485 4-8-8 54 LucyKBarry(7) 12 —
(Tony Carroll) *mid-div: hdwy over 2f out: wknd over 1f out* **14/1**

1m 29.23s (-0.37) **Going Correction** +0.025s/f (Slow) **12** Ran SP% **118.3**
Speed ratings (Par 101): **103,102,100,95,95 94,92,92,85,84 74,68**
Tote Swingers: 1&2 £5.50, 1&3 £4.20, 2&3 £6.80 CSF £39.46 CT £208.16 TOTE £8.10: £2.50, £1.40, £3.80; EX 35.60.
Owner M D I Usher **Bred** Mrs S M Roy **Trained** Upper Lambourn, Berks
FOCUS
Mainly exposed performers in a moderate handicap. Although the gallop was a reasonable one, those held up were at a disadvantage and the winner came down the centre.
All Right Now Official explanation: jockey said gelding hung left-handed
Exceedingly Good(IRE) Official explanation: jockey said mare hung right-handed

894 FREEBETS.CO.UK CHELTENHAM GOLD CUP FREE BETS H'CAP 2m 119y(P)
6:20 (6:20) (Class 4) (0-85,80) 4-Y-O+ **£3,238** (£963; £481; £240) **Stalls** Low

Form RPR
113- **1** **Blackmore**[114] 7553 4-8-9 68 PaulHanagan 2 78+
(Julia Feilden) *sn trcking ldrs: led over 2f out: rdn and edgd rt 1f out: styd on wl clsng stages* **5/2**[1]
-523 **2** 1 1/4 **Ethics Girl (IRE)**[28] 597 5-9-12 80 (t) FrannyNorton 4 89+
(John Berry) *hld up: effrt over 3f out: chsd wnr 2f out: upsides 1f out: kpt on same pce last 75yds* **11/4**[2]
4-44 **3** 9 **Satwa Gold (USA)**[17] 718 5-9-5 73 ShaneKelly 3 71
(Seamus Durack) *hld up: hdwy to trck ldrs 5f out: one pce fnl 2f* **13/2**
3322 **4** 4 1/2 **Stadium Of Light (IRE)**[9] 808 4-8-10 69 PaulMulrennan 5 61
(James Given) *trckd ldr: led 4f out: hdd over 2f out: wknd over 1f out* **7/2**[3]
4/06 **5** 1 **Ajdaad (USA)**[7] 835 4-9-7 80 (p) GrahamGibbons 1 71
(Alan McCabe) *hld up in last: drvn over 3f out: lost pl 2f out* **14/1**
014- **6** 2 3/4 **Gaselee (USA)**[125] 7457 5-9-12 80 SteveDrowne 6 71
(Rae Guest) *led: hdd 4f out: lost pl 2f out: eased nr fin* **8/1**

3m 41.46s (-0.34) **Going Correction** +0.025s/f (Slow)
WFA 4 from 5yo 5lb **6** Ran SP% **108.6**
Speed ratings (Par 105): **101,100,96,94,93 92**
Tote Swingers: 1&2 £1.60, 1&3 £2.50, 2&3 £3.00 CSF £8.96 TOTE £5.10: £2.90, £1.10; EX 7.60.
Owner Good Company Partnership **Bred** Juddmonte Farms Ltd **Trained** Exning, Suffolk

FOCUS
A fair handicap but, although the overall gallop to the straight was steady, the first two, who came down the centre, did well to pull clear in the last furlong.

895 FREEBETS.CO.UK CHELTENHAM 2011 FREE BETS H'CAP (DIV I)1m 141y(P)
6:50 (6:52) (Class 6) (0-55,58) 4-Y-O+ **£1,364** (£403; £201) **Stalls** Low

Form RPR
6-01 **1** **Angelena Ballerina (IRE)**[10] 800 4-9-5 58 6ex (v) KirstyMilczarek 1 67
(Karen George) *mid-div: hdwy over 2f out: led last 100yds: all out* **7/1**
-353 **2** hd **Pie Poudre**[34] 526 4-8-13 52 (p) TomEaves 5 60
(Roy Brotherton) *reluctant to load: s.i.s: hdwy on ins over 2f out: chsng ldrs over 1f out: edgd rt and chal ins fnl f: jst hld* **5/1**[2]
0-23 **3** 3/4 **Barton Bounty**[15] 749 4-8-7 46 oh1 (b) PaulHanagan 6 53
(Peter Niven) *mid-div: effrt and chsd ldrs over 2f out: styd on same pce ins fnl f* **7/2**[1]
6-54 **4** 3/4 **Empress Leizu (IRE)**[30] 555 4-9-0 53 (p) AndreaAtzeni 7 58
(Tony Carroll) *t.k.h: led: hdd last 100yds: no ex* **7/2**[1]
0-03 **5** 2 3/4 **Moment Of Clarity**[16] 730 9-8-4 46 oh1 (p) SimonPearce(3) 4 45
(Shaun Harris) *chsd ldrs: wknd appr fnl f* **25/1**
0616 **6** 1/2 **Flying Applause**[10] 793 6-9-1 54 (bt) RussKennemore 11 52
(Roy Bowring) *chsd ldrs: rdn and outpcd over 2f out: kpt on fnl f* **15/2**
0635 **7** 2 **King Of Connacht**[25] 635 8-8-8 54 (v) LucyKBarry(7) 9 47
(Mark Wellings) *in rr: effrt over 2f out: chsng ldrs over 1f out: kpt on same pce* **20/1**
0-00 **8** 2 3/4 **Ninth House (USA)**[32] 544 9-8-11 50 (bt) PJMcDonald 10 37
(Ruth Carr) *s.i.s: sme hdwy on outer 2f out: nvr on terms* **28/1**
0543 **9** 5 **Buzz Bird**[15] 747 4-9-2 55 GrahamGibbons 2 30
(David Barron) *chsd ldrs: reminders over 4f out: hung lft and lost pl 3f out: sn bhd* **11/2**[3]
2-00 **10** 8 **Fitzwarren**[43] 408 10-8-7 46 oh1 (bt) SilvestreDeSousa 8 —
(Alan Brown) *trckd ldrs: drvn 4f out: lost pl over 1f out: sn bhd and eased: struck into* **50/1**

1m 50.22s (-0.28) **Going Correction** +0.025s/f (Slow) **10** Ran SP% **114.8**
Speed ratings (Par 101): **102,101,101,100,98 97,95,93,88,81**
Tote Swingers: 1&2 £8.50, 1&3 £6.30, 2&3 £2.50 CSF £39.34 CT £143.50 TOTE £9.40: £2.30, £1.30, £2.10; EX 51.20.
Owner F Michael **Bred** Waterford Hall Stud **Trained** Higher Eastington, Devon
FOCUS
Another moderate handicap run at a reasonable gallop. The main action unfolded centre-to far side in the straight.
Buzz Bird Official explanation: jockey said filly hung left-handed
Fitzwarren Official explanation: vet said gelding was struck into

896 FREEBETS.CO.UK CHELTENHAM 2011 FREE BETS H'CAP (DIV II)1m 141y(P)
7:20 (7:20) (Class 6) (0-55,55) 4-Y-O+ **£1,364** (£403; £201) **Stalls** Low

Form RPR
2213 **1** **Grey Boy (GER)**[9] 809 10-8-9 55 GeorgeDowning(7) 9 62
(Tony Carroll) *prom: hdwy 3f out: chsd ldr over 1f out: styd on to ld nr fin* **6/1**
-331 **2** nk **Mr Maximas**[14] 773 4-8-12 51 (t) RichardKingscote 5 57
(Bryn Palling) *trckd ldrs: wnt 2nd over 3f out: led over 1f out: hdd and no ex nr fin* **9/2**[2]
-055 **3** 1 1/2 **Naledi**[22] 675 7-8-4 46 oh1 SophieDoyle(3) 7 49
(Richard Price) *in rr: hdwy 3f out: sn chsng ldrs: styd on same pce fnl f: tk 3rd nr fin* **22/1**
1424 **4** hd **Kielty's Folly**[18] 712 7-9-1 54 GrahamGibbons 6 57
(Brian Baugh) *mid-div: hdwy 3f out: kpt on same pce fnl f* **11/2**[3]
-006 **5** 5 **Spirit Of Love (IRE)**[9] 807 4-8-10 49 (b[1]) AndreaAtzeni 4 41
(Michael Wigham) *s.i.s: rr-div: reminders over 4f out: nvr a factor* **3/1**[1]
4406 **6** nk **Crocodile Bay (IRE)**[16] 730 8-8-8 52 (p) TobyAtkinson(5) 3 44
(Richard Guest) *t.k.h: trckd ldrs: led 4f out: hdd over 1f out: sn wknd* **33/1**
2-30 **7** 1 **Director General (USA)**[18] 712 4-9-1 54 (be) BarryMcHugh 2 44
(Julie Camacho) *led early: chsd ldrs: drvn over 3f out: wknd over 1f out* **6/1**
0030 **8** 1 **Escardo (GER)**[9] 807 8-8-7 46 oh1 (v) WilliamCarson 10 33
(David Bridgwater) *s.i.s: a in rr* **14/1**
-060 **9** 1 1/2 **Celtic Ransom**[16] 727 4-9-2 55 PaulHanagan 1 39
(Gary Moore) *in rr: sme hdwy on outer over 1f out: sn wknd* **7/1**
0-40 **10** 9 **Ledgerwood**[25] 630 6-8-7 46 oh1 (p) NeilChalmers 8 11
(Adrian Chamberlain) *led: hdd 4f out: lost pl over 2f out: sn bhd* **100/1**

1m 50.06s (-0.44) **Going Correction** +0.025s/f (Slow) **10** Ran SP% **114.6**
Speed ratings (Par 101): **102,101,100,100,95 95,94,93,92,84**
Tote Swingers: 1&2 £2.50, 1&3 £9.90, 2&3 £10.30 TOTE £5.40: £1.60, £1.60, £10.20; EX 17.40.
Owner Paul Downing **Bred** J Potempa **Trained** Cropthorne, Worcs
FOCUS
A moderate handicap run at a fair gallop. The first four pulled clear and the winner raced towards the inside rail in the straight.

897 FREEBETS.CO.UK CHELTENHAM BEST FREE BETS H'CAP 1m 1f 103y(P)
7:50 (7:50) (Class 5) (0-70,70) 4-Y-O+ **£2,201** (£655; £327; £163) **Stalls** Low

Form RPR
-356 **1** **Catching Zeds**[34] 526 4-8-7 56 RichardKingscote 12 65
(Ian Williams) *in rr: hdwy over 2f out: styd on on ins to ld last 100yds: hld on towards fin* **18/1**
1511 **2** 3/4 **Black Coffee**[14] 772 6-9-7 70 (b) ShaneKelly 4 78
(Mark Brisbourne) *mid-div: hdwy over 2f out: chsng ldrs whn crowded over 1f out: styd on fnl f* **2/1**[1]
2022 **3** 1 1/4 **Kyle Of Bute**[15] 748 5-8-12 61 J-PGuillambert 8 67
(Brian Baugh) *led after 1f: t.k.h: hdd and no ex ins fnl f* **13/2**[3]
03-6 **4** 1/2 **High Five Society**[18] 711 7-8-9 63 (b) DeclanCannon(5) 1 68
(Roy Bowring) *dwlt: hdwy over 3f out: chsng ldrs and hung lft over 1f out: kpt on same pce* **16/1**
-431 **5** 1 **Chief Exec**[21] 685 9-9-7 70 SteveDrowne 9 73
(Jeremy Gask) *in rr: effrt 2f out: kpt on fnl f: nt rch ldrs* **8/1**
5240 **6** 1 3/4 **Atacama Sunrise**[21] 687 5-8-9 58 LiamKeniry 6 57
(George Prodromou) *sn chsng ldrs: one pce appr fnl f* **33/1**
2343 **7** 3/4 **Gordy Bee (USA)**[18] 712 5-8-4 58 (be) TobyAtkinson(5) 3 56
(Richard Guest) *in rr: bhd and drvn 3f out: kpt on over 1f out: nvr nr ldrs* **12/1**
-006 **8** 1 **Beetuna (IRE)**[18] 715 6-9-6 69 PaulHanagan 10 65
(David Bourton) *sn trcking ldrs: wknd appr fnl f* **11/2**[2]
0226 **9** hd **Force Group (IRE)**[9] 813 7-9-2 65 (b) DarryllHolland 11 61
(Nick Littmoden) *s.s: nvr on terms* **10/1**
13-1 **10** nk **Northern Flyer (GER)**[21] 692 5-9-0 66 (p) IanBrennan(3) 5 61
(John Quinn) *led 1f: t.k.h: wknd appr fnl f* **8/1**

The Form Book, Raceform Ltd, Compton, RG20 6NL

130- **11** *hd* **Colonel Sherman (USA)**[137] 7275 6-8-9 **58**................(t) TonyCulhane 2 53
(Philip Kirby) *mid-div: effrt over 2f out: wknd over 1f out* **33/1**

2m 2.37s (0.67) **Going Correction** +0.025s/f (Slow) **11** Ran SP% **118.1**
Speed ratings (Par 103): **98,97,96,95,94 93,92,91,91,91 91**
Tote Swingers: 1&2 £21.60, 1&3 £17.30, 2&3 £4.00 CSF £54.36 CT £270.98 TOTE £34.40: £10.90, £1.10, £2.60; EX 88.80.
Owner The Ferandlin Peaches **Bred** White Horse Bloodstock Ltd **Trained** Portway, Worcs
■ Stewards' Enquiry : Toby Atkinson one-day ban: used whip without giving gelding time to respond when out of contention (Apr 1)

FOCUS
A modest handicap in which the pace was no more than fair. The winner raced just off the inside rail in the straight.
High Five Society Official explanation: jockey said gelding hung left in home straight
Force Group(IRE) Official explanation: jockey said gelding was slowly away

898 FREEBETS.CO.UK CHELTENHAM EXCLUSIVE FREE BETS H'CAP 1m 1f 103y(P)
8:20 (8:21) (Class 6) (0-60,60) 3-Y-O **£1,671** (£493; £246) **Stalls** Low

Form RPR

2-44 **1** **Crossword**[17] 716 3-9-6 **59**..(b) AndreaAtzeni 3 64
(Marco Botti) *trckd ldrs: styd on to ld over 1f out: hld on towards fin* **9/2**[2]

0504 **2** *½* **Lakota Ghost (USA)**[14] 760 3-9-7 **60**............................... PaulHanagan 8 64+
(Seamus Durack) *in rr: hdwy over 2f out: kpt on wl ins fnl f* **13/2**

643 **3** *½* **Little Jazz**[22] 663 3-9-7 **60**... LiamJones 2 63
(Paul D'Arcy) *in rr: hdwy 5f out: swtchd lft and chsd ldrs over 1f out: kpt on same pce ins fnl f* **9/1**

6-00 **4** *hd* **Varlak**[17] 716 3-9-0 **53**..(v[1]) DarrylHolland 9 56
(Des Donovan) *in rr: hdwy 2f out: styd on same pce appr fnl f* **28/1**

0-64 **5** *nk* **Bertie Blu Boy**[29] 579 3-9-7 **60**............................ SilvestreDeSousa 12 62
(Paul Green) *w ldr: led over 2f out: hdd over 1f out: wknd ins fnl f* **25/1**

5-32 **6** *1* **Snowy Peak**[26] 624 3-9-6 **59**..(t) ShaneKelly 7 59
(Jeremy Noseda) *prom: effrt over 2f out: one pce over 1f out* **7/4**[1]

00-4 **7** *¾* **Lady Morganna (IRE)**[23] 649 3-9-2 **60**..................... KylieManser(5) 4 58
(Olivia Maylam) *in rr: swtchd lft over 1f out: kpt on same pce* **20/1**

-403 **8** *1 ¾* **Anna Fontenail**[17] 716 3-9-7 **60**................................ JamesMillman 1 57
(Rod Millman) *s.i.s: hdwy over 2f out: nt clr run on ins over 1f out: sn wknd* **6/1**[3]

0-45 **9** *½* **Apple Dumpling**[43] 406 3-8-6 **50**................................... RyanClark(5) 10 44
(Stuart Williams) *mid-div: hdwy to chse ldrs over 2f out: wknd fnl f* **14/1**

000- **10** *4 ½* **Generous Genella**[155] 6866 3-9-0 **53**........................ JimmyQuinn 11 40
(Julia Feilden) *prom: lost pl over 1f out: eased towards fin* **12/1**

00-6 **11** *7* **Distinguish (IRE)**[32] 543 3-9-0 **60**............................ DarylByrne(7) 6 29
(Mark Johnston) *mde most: hdd over 2f out: sn lost pl and bhd* **18/1**

2m 2.63s (0.93) **Going Correction** +0.025s/f (Slow) **11** Ran SP% **123.8**
Speed ratings (Par 96): **96,95,95,94,94 93,93,91,91,87 80**
Tote Swingers: 1&2 £5.10, 2&3 £12.10 CSF £35.04 CT £262.10 TOTE £6.30: £2.00, £2.50, £1.70; EX 40.00.
Owner Giuliano Manfredini **Bred** Mrs Clodagh McStay **Trained** Newmarket, Suffolk
■ Stewards' Enquiry : Kylie Manser two-day ban: careless riding (Apr 3-4)
Liam Jones one-day ban: careless riding (Apr 1)

FOCUS
A couple of unexposed performers in a moderate handicap. The gallop was no more than fair and the principals raced centre-to-far side in the straight.
Anna Fontenail Official explanation: jockey said filly suffered interference in running

899 FREEBETS.CO.UK CHELTENHAM FESTIVAL 2011 FREE BETS H'CAP 1m 4f 50y(P)
8:50 (8:50) (Class 7) (0-50,50) 4-Y-O+ **£1,535** (£453; £226) **Stalls** Low

Form RPR

4354 **1** **Barbirolli**[25] 630 9-8-6 **45**.. LauraPike(5) 6 51
(William Stone) *hld up in rr: hdwy on outside over 4f out: styd on fnl 2f: led last 75yds* **12/1**

6332 **2** *nk* **Wrecking Crew (IRE)**[8] 819 7-8-11 **45**..................... JamesMillman 12 51
(Rod Millman) *hld up in rr: hdwy 6f out: styd on over 1f out: kpt on wl to take 2nd nr fin* **3/1**[1]

0-56 **3** *1* **Castlebury (IRE)**[25] 631 6-8-12 **46**............................(b) PJMcDonald 2 51
(Ruth Carr) *trckd ldrs: chal over 3f out: hung lft 1f out: kpt on same pce last 75yds* **25/1**

3500 **4** *½* **Mary Helen**[14] 773 4-8-10 **46**... ShaneKelly 7 50
(Mark Brisbourne) *mid-div: hdwy over 2f out: styd on fnl f: nt rch ldrs* **14/1**

4/ **5** *shd* **Arondo (GER)**[520] 4032 8-8-12 **46**.................................. GrahamGibbons 9 50
(Patrick Martin, Ire) *led: edgd rt over 1f out: hdd and no ex last 75yds* **9/2**[2]

-000 **6** *2* **Fine Tolerance**[34] 524 5-8-11 **45**..................................(b) NeilChalmers 4 46
(Sam Davison) *in rr: drvn 4f out: hdwy on outside over 1f out: nvr rchd ldrs* **25/1**

3-05 **7** *1 ½* **Filun**[8] 819 6-9-2 **50**.. LiamKeniry 3 55+
(Anthony Middleton) *hld up in mid-div: hdwy over 2f out: chsng ldrs whn bdly hmpd ins fnl f: heavily eased towards fin* **8/1**

1330 **8** *1* **Our Kes (IRE)**[14] 771 9-9-2 **50**... PaulDoe 1 47
(Jane Chapple-Hyam) *chsd ldrs: effrt over 2f out: wknd over 1f out* **15/2**

4006 **9** *3* **Yorksters Prince (IRE)**[10] 796 4-8-9 **45**.............(t) SilvestreDeSousa 5 37
(George Prodromou) *in rr: drvn over 3f out: nvr on terms* **16/1**

0232 **10** *2 ½* **Holyfield Warrior (IRE)**[9] 807 7-8-9 **50**..................... LucyKBarry(7) 8 39
(Ralph Smith) *trckd ldrs: t.k.h: wknd 2f out* **5/1**[3]

-660 **11** *shd* **State General (IRE)**[8] 819 5-9-2 **50**........................(tp) J-PGuillambert 10 40
(Tony Carroll) *mid-div: hdwy 7f out: chsng ldrs whn nt clr run over 1f out: sn wknd and eased* **25/1**

0-00 **12** *43* **Bobering**[14] 771 11-8-11 **45**.. KellyHarrison 11 —
(Brian Baugh) *chsd ldrs: lost pl over 3f out: wl bhd and eased over 1f out: t.o* **50/1**

2m 40.68s (-0.42) **Going Correction** +0.025s/f (Slow)
WFA 4 from 5yo+ 2lb **12** Ran SP% **116.5**
Speed ratings (Par 97): **102,101,101,100,100 99,98,97,95,94 94,65**
Tote Swingers: 1&2 £5.20, 1&3 £33.20, 2&3 £37.20 CSF £45.33 CT £904.97 TOTE £19.10: £3.90, £2.10, £13.30; EX 36.40.
Owner Miss Caroline Scott **Bred** Gainsborough Stud Management Ltd **Trained** West Wickham, Cambs
■ Stewards' Enquiry : Graham Gibbons three-day ban: careless riding (Apr 1-3)

FOCUS
A very moderate handicap in which the gallop wasn't strong. The principals came down the centre.
Arondo(GER) Official explanation: jockey said, regarding riding, that approaching the line, he was concerned about gelding's action and felt it prudent to finish sympathetically.
T/Plt: £59.00 to a £1 stake. Pool:£76,582.53 - 946.06 winning tickets. T/Qpdt: £5.10 to a £1 stake. Pool:£11,755.69 - 1,684.41 winning tickets. WG

882 DEAUVILLE (R-H)
Friday, March 18

OFFICIAL GOING: Fibresand: standard

900a PRIX DE COULONCES (CONDITIONS) (4YO) (FIBRESAND) 1m 4f
11:30 (12:00) 4-Y-O **£12,068** (£4,827; £3,620; £2,413; £1,206)

RPR

1 **Fox Hunt (IRE)**[8] 4-9-1 0...(b) JoeFanning 3 101
(Mark Johnston) *broke wl to ld fr s: shared ld down bk st: regained ld bef st: rdn to go clr 2f out: wnt wl clr ent fnl f: easily* **17/10**[1]

2 *5* **Valoro (FR)**[122] 4-8-11 0..(p) MaximeGuyon 6 89
(N Leenders, France) **21/1**

3 *½* **Vivre Libre**[136] 4-8-11 0......................................(b) ChristopheSoumillon 4 89
(E Lellouche, France) **2/1**[2]

4 *1 ½* **Croix Madame (FR)**[125] 4-8-8 0.................................. ThierryThulliez 5 83
(F Doumen, France) **7/2**[3]

5 *2* **Forgotten (FR)**[30] 4-8-6 0...................................... MatthieuAutier(5) 1 83
(B Dutruel, France) **58/10**

6 *20* **Swing Danceur (FR)**[292] 4-9-4 0......................... Jean-BaptisteHamel 2 58
(Mme C Dufreche, France) **14/1**

2m 31.7s (151.70) **6** Ran SP% **118.5**
WIN (incl. 1 euro stake): 2.70. PLACES: 1.90, 5.00. SF: 39.40.
Owner Sheikh Hamdan Bin Mohammed Al Maktoum **Bred** Ballylinch Stud **Trained** Middleham Moor, N Yorks

NOTEBOOK
Fox Hunt(IRE), runner-up here in first-time blinkers the previous week, built on that with an emphatic success and should be able to win again on sand given suitable opportunities.

901a PRIX DE LA CHESNAYE (MAIDEN) (3YO FILLIES) (FIBRESAND) 1m 1f 110y
12:00 (12:00) 3-Y-O **£10,344** (£4,137; £3,103; £2,068; £1,034)

RPR

1 **Galaxie Sud (USA)**[150] 3-9-0 0................................ IoritzMendizabal 10 87
(J-C Rouget, France) **1/1**[1]

2 *3* **Strictly Rhythm**[168] 6528 3-9-0 0...................... Francois-XavierBertras 9 82
(Mme G Rarick, France) **24/1**

3 *1 ½* **Blaise Chorus (IRE)**[49] 339 3-9-0 0........................... RobertWinston 5 79
(B W Hills) *wnt 2nd fr s: rdn to chal for ld 1 1/2f out: hrd rdn ent fnl f: outpcd fnl 100yds: styd on for 3rd* **6/1**[3]

4 *1 ½* **Utopia Jem (FR)**[99] 3-9-0 0.. FabienLefebvre 1 76
(D Sepulchre, France) **16/1**

5 *shd* **Batahola (USA)**[220] 3-9-0 0.............................. Pierre-CharlesBoudot 2 76
(A Fabre, France) **29/1**

6 *1 ½* **Tierceville (IRE)**[81] 3-9-0 0.. OlivierPeslier 8 73
(E Libaud, France) **48/10**[2]

7 *¾* **Threshing Days (IRE)**[165] 3-9-0 0............ Christophe-PatriceLemaire 6 72
(M Delzangles, France) **28/1**

8 *2 ½* **Fille De Famille (FR)**[80] 3-9-0 0....................(b[1]) ChristopheSoumillon 3 67
(R Chotard, France) **8/1**

9 *10* **Royale Celebre (FR)** 3-9-0 0.. MathiasSautjeau 12 49
(Mlle C Rozais, France) **64/1**

10 *2* **Blue Roses (IRE)**[99] 3-9-0 0.. MaximeGuyon 4 46
(H-A Pantall, France) **37/1**

0 **Wedding Dance (FR)** 3-9-0 0.................................. StephanePasquier 11 —
(P Demercastel, France) **36/1**

1m 59.3s (119.30) **11** Ran SP% **116.2**
WIN (incl. 1 euro stake): 2.00. PLACES: 1.30, 3.70, 1.90. DF: 21.40. SF: 27.10.
Owner Nelson Radwan **Bred** Janus Bloodstock Inc. **Trained** Pau, France

NOTEBOOK
Blaise Chorus(IRE) runner-up on her debut on polytrack in January, found this tougher and could not pick up in the closing stages

902a PRIX DE COQUEREL (MAIDEN) (3YO COLTS & GELDINGS) (FIBRESAND) 1m 1f 110y
12:30 (12:00) 3-Y-O **£10,344** (£4,137; £3,103; £2,068; £1,034)

RPR

1 **Baraan (FR)**[177] 3-9-2 0................................ Christophe-PatriceLemaire 1 86
(J-C Rouget, France) **6/4**[1]

2 *3* **Tirion (USA)** 3-9-2 0.. ChristopheSoumillon 14 81
(M Delcher-Sanchez, Spain) **53/10**[3]

3 *2* **The Bells O Peover**[181] 6184 3-9-2 0................................. JoeFanning 2 77
(Mark Johnston) *racd 2nd on rail fr s: rdn and chal for ld 1 1/2f out: briefly led 1f out: sn hrd rdn: no ex: styd on fnl 100yds* **30/1**

4 *hd* **Don Salluste (FR)**[208] 3-8-13 0.................................. TheoBachelot(3) 10 77
(Mme M-C Naim, France) **140/1**

5 *1 ½* **Legendaire (USA)** 3-9-2 0.. MaximeGuyon 12 74
(Mlle H Van Zuylen, France) **13/1**

6 *½* **Egotist (IRE)**[14] 777 3-8-8 0... RufusVergette(8) 8 73
(A Fabre, France) **17/1**

7 *1 ½* **Highdar (FR)**[134] 3-9-2 0.. AnthonyCrastus 3 70
(P Demercastel, France) **44/1**

8 *snk* **Duskill (FR)** 3-9-2 0.. AntoineSamson 5 70
(P Chevillard, France) **119/1**

9 *2 ½* **War Shandar (FR)** 3-9-2 0.. SylvainRuis 7 66
(F Vermeulen, France) **7/2**[2]

10 *2* **Head Held High (USA)** 3-9-2 0.. OlivierPeslier 6 62
(E Libaud, France) **10/1**

0 **United Sport (FR)**[333] 3-8-10 0................................ AntoineHamelin(6) 15 —
(P Chevillard, France) **90/1**

0 **Acorous (FR)**[34] 520 3-9-2 0... StefaanFrancois 4 —
(Sprl Ittech, France) **110/1**

0 **White Curtain (USA)**[14] 777 3-9-2 0...........................(p) StephanePasquier 11 —
(D Sepulchre, France) **26/1**

0 **Candler (IRE)** 3-9-2 0.. Pierre-CharlesBoudot 13 —
(Y De Nicolay, France) **35/1**

0 **Painted Black (ITY)** 3-9-2 0.. IoritzMendizabal 9 —
(G Botti, Italy) **63/1**

1m 57.2s (117.20) **15** Ran SP% **116.9**
WIN (incl. 1 euro stake): 2.50. PLACES: 1.40, 2.00, 4.40. DF: 8.70. SF: 12.50.
Owner H H Aga Khan **Bred** Haras De S A Aga Khan Scea **Trained** Pau, France

NOTEBOOK
The Bells O Peover ran arguably his best race on this step up in trip and all-weather debut after six months off.

903a PRIX DE LESSARD (CLAIMER) (4YO+) (FIBRESAND) 1m 1f 110y
1:05 (12:00) 4-Y-O+ £6,465 (£2,586; £1,939; £1,293; £646)

RPR
1 **Satwa Rose (FR)**593 5-8-13 0 JohanVictoire 16 60
(Jean De Roualle, France) **244/10**
2 nse **Salcedo** 4-9-6 0 ChristopheSoumillon 2 67
(M Delcher-Sanchez, Spain) **48/10**2
3 1 **Josephines Baby (FR)**66 4-8-7 0 MatthieuAutier(6) 10 58
(L A Urbano-Grajales, France) **13/1**
4 1 1/2 **Bold Marc (IRE)**74 [42] 9-9-2 0 RobertWinston 17 58
(Mrs K Burke) *racd bhd ldrs: pulling hrd: proged on wd outside bef st: rdn 1 1/2f out: no ex: styd on u.p fnl f* **34/1**
5 shd **Class Attraction (IRE)**30 [566] 7-8-5 0 TheoBachelot(3) 5 50
(J E Hammond, France) **7/2**1
6 hd **Naidoo (GER)**69 9-8-11 0 DominiqueBoeuf 4 53
(Frau Marion Rotering, Germany) **9/1**
7 snk **Counterbid (IRE)**58 [220] 5-9-2 0 SylvainRuis 8 57
(J Heloury, France) **13/2**3
8 1 **Twin Prince (IRE)**74 [42] 6-9-2 0 (p) MaximeGuyon 12 56
(E Leenders, France) **27/1**
9 hd **The Joe McArdle (GER)**74 [42] 6-9-2 0 (b1) FranckBlondel 11 55
(Alex Fracas, France) **10/1**
10 nk **Torronto (FR)**30 [566] 8-9-1 0 GaetanClouet(5) 15 59
(P Monfort, France) **18/1**
0 **Bencoolen (IRE)**30 [566] 6-9-2 0 IoritzMendizabal 1 —
(D De Waele, France) **10/1**
0 **Nachtschwarmer (GER)**26 [629] 7-9-3 0 (p) FrankieLeroy(3) 14 —
(Frau Marion Rotering, Germany) **22/1**
0 **Sheringarry (FR)**69 5-8-11 0 AnthonyCrastus 9 —
(Mme C Dufreche, France) **75/1**
0 **Yellow Fairy (FR)**738 5-8-13 0 (p) DelphineSantiago 7 —
(B Leclere, France) **98/1**
0 **Lomirana (FR)**74 [42] 5-8-11 0 FredericSpanu 13 —
(A Spanu, France) **65/1**
0 **Pool Of Knowledge (FR)**33 [533] 5-9-2 0 FabienLefebvre 18 —
(D De Waele, France) **38/1**
0 **Lord Howe (GER)**74 4-8-11 0 (b) MorganDelalande 3 —
(J-Y Artu, France) **52/1**
0 **Musk (SAF)**100 5-8-11 0 GuillaumeFourrier 6 —
(S Gouvaze, France) **152/1**

1m 59.3s (119.30) 18 Ran SP% **117.0**
WIN (incl. 1 euro stake): 25.40. PLACES: 7.60, 2.80, 4.60; DF: 83.70; SF: 573.00.
Owner Steven & Gillian Lamprell **Bred** Frank A McNulty **Trained** France

NOTEBOOK
Bold Marc(IRE) is on a long losing run, but ran pretty well in this claimer and it should set him up for a return to turf. He goes well at Catterick so is worth watching out for if turning out there on the first day of the new season.

885 LINGFIELD (L-H)
Saturday, March 19

OFFICIAL GOING: Standard
Wind: light, across Weather: sunny and bright

904 SUMMER EVENINGS AT LINGFIELD PARK CLASSIFIED CLAIMING STKS 6f (P)
1:50 (1:50) (Class 6) 3-Y-O+ £1,535 (£453; £226) Stalls Low

Form RPR
5323 1 **Frequency**12 [786] 4-9-4 68 (b) JoeFanning 5 74+
(Keith Dalgleish) *hld up in tch in last trio: rdn and gd hdwy over 1f out: led ins fnl f: sn in command: readily* **11/4**1
3006 2 2 **Pipers Piping (IRE)**10 [806] 5-9-5 67 (v) KierenFallon 7 67
(Jane Chapple-Hyam) *led for 1f: pressed ldr after tl led again over 2f out: rdn over 1f out: hdd and outpcd by wnr ins fnl f: kpt on to hold 2nd fnl 100yds* **6/1**3
5145 3 nk **Chjimes (IRE)**12 [786] 7-9-5 70 (b) HayleyTurner 6 66
(Conor Dore) *stdd s: swtchd lft and dropped in bhd after s: rdn and effrt on inner over 1f out: kpt on same pce fnl 150yds* **11/4**1
-316 4 1 1/4 **Co Dependent (USA)**9 [820] 5-9-4 70 FergusSweeney 1 62
(Jamie Osborne) *hld up in last pair: effrt and nt clr run over 1f out: hdwy ent fnl f: chsd ldng trio ins fnl f: no imp after* **5/1**2
2203 5 2 **Onceapontime (IRE)**46 [377] 6-9-6 69 LukeMorris 3 57
(Michael Squance) *taken down early: chsd ldrs: rdn and unable qck jst over 2f out: edgd lft and sltly hmpd over 1f out: drvn and styd on same pce fnl f* **15/2**
-336 6 2 **Super Frank (IRE)**31 [556] 8-9-2 65 (b) IanMongan 4 47
(Zoe Davison) *drvn after s: led after 1f: hdd and rdn over 2f out: wknd ent fnl f* **8/1**
0-00 7 4 1/2 **Lord Cornwall (IRE)**24 [655] 3-8-4 44 ow1 (v1) ChrisCatlin 2 35
(Ed Walker) *in tch in midfield: rdn along 3f out: wknd over 1f out* **100/1**

1m 11.65s (-0.25) **Going Correction** 0.0s/f (Stan)
WFA 3 from 4yo+ 13lb 7 Ran SP% **108.2**
Speed ratings (Par 101): **101,98,97,96,93 90,84**
.Frequency claimed by Mr C. R. Dore for £8,000.\n\x\x
Owner Gordon McDowall & Francesca Mitchell **Bred** Manor Farm Stud (rutland) **Trained** Carluke, South Lanarkshire
■ The first training success for former jockey Keith Dalgleish.
■ Stewards' Enquiry : Kieren Fallon one-day ban: failed to ride to draw (Apr 2)

FOCUS
An ordinary claimer.
Pipers Piping(IRE) Official explanation: vet said gelding lost a shoe

905 GREAT DEALS ON ANNUAL MEMBERSHIP MEDIAN AUCTION MAIDEN STKS 7f (P)
2:20 (2:21) (Class 6) 3-5-Y-O £1,535 (£453; £226) Stalls Low

Form RPR
1 **Aanna Heneeih (IRE)** 3-8-11 0 EddieAhern 8 70+
(Ed Dunlop) *dwlt: sn in tch: rdn and effrt ent fnl 2f: chal 1f out: pushed along hands and heels to ld ins fnl f: kpt on wl fnl 100yds* **8/1**3
20-2 2 1/2 **Uncle Dermot (IRE)**18 [720] 3-8-11 70 DaneO'Neill 9 67
(Brendan Powell) *t.k.h early: hld up in last pair: rdn and effrt on outer bnd 2f out: rdn and ev ch ins fnl f: kpt on but hld towards fin* **7/2**2
3- 3 3/4 **Lucky Meadows (IRE)**204 [5489] 3-8-1 0 KieranO'Neill(5) 6 60
(Richard Hannon) *t.k.h early: hld up in tch: chsd ldrs over 2f out: rdn to ld jst over 1f out: hdd and flashed tail u.p ins fnl f: nt qckn and btn fnl 100yds* **4/5**1
60 4 3 1/2 **Abacist (IRE)**9 [818] 3-8-11 0 JimCrowley 4 56
(Ralph Beckett) *in tch: nt clr run and swtchd ins over 2f out: rdn and edgd lft over 1f out: pushed along and outpcd ins fnl f* **33/1**
/325 5 hd **Timpanist (USA)**22 [689] 4-9-7 65 GeorgeBaker 2 55
(Simon Dow) *led for 1f: ev ch u.p over 1f out: outpcd 1f out: wknd ins fnl f* **7/2**2
0 6 3 **Tinkerbell Will**23 [663] 4-9-7 0 SamHitchcott 7 51
(John E Long) *in tch: effrt and n.m.r bnd 2f out: chsd ldrs whn hmpd jst over 1f out: nt rcvr and wl btn fnl f* **66/1**
00 7 3/4 **Five Cool Kats (IRE)**59 [212] 3-8-11 0 WilliamCarson 1 46
(Paul Burgoyne) *led after 1f: rdn jst over 2f out: hdd jst over 1f out: drvn and wknd qckly ins fnl f* **100/1**
0-0 8 2 3/4 **Fight Or Flight**12 [791] 4-9-0 0 DavidKenny(7) 3 42
(Brendan Powell) *s.i.s: hld up in tch towards rr: rdn and struggling over 3f out: kpt on same pce and n.d after: eased ins fnl f* **25/1**
9 10 **Lady Freda** 5-9-7 0 RussKennemore 5 13
(Alan Coogan) *s.i.s: rn green and a in rr* **33/1**

1m 25.89s (1.09) **Going Correction** 0.0s/f (Stan)
WFA 3 from 4yo+ 15lb 9 Ran SP% **123.3**
Speed ratings (Par 101): **93,92,91,87,87 83,83,79,68**
Tote Swingers: 1&2 £3.20, 1&3 £2.70, 2&3 £1.60 CSF £37.29 TOTE £10.50: £2.60, £1.60, £1.10; EX 41.10 Trifecta £67.30 Pool: £762.82 - 8.38 winning units..
Owner Tariq S Al Tayer **Bred** Giuseppe Neri **Trained** Newmarket, Suffolk

FOCUS
An ordinary maiden and only four counted according to the market. Again those who raced down the centre in the straight were favoured. Perhaps not surprisingly, the race was dominated by the 3-y-os.
Abacist(IRE) Official explanation: jockey said gelding hung left throughout

906 TONY'S 60TH CHAMPION H'CAP 1m (P)
2:55 (2:55) (Class 6) (0-60,60) 4-Y-O+ £1,535 (£453; £226) Stalls High

Form RPR
-614 1 **Clearing House**16 [748] 6-8-10 49 KirstyMilczarek 9 59+
(John Ryan) *dwlt: in tch towards rr: rdn and hdwy over 1f out: led ins fnl f: r.o strly* **7/1**3
-353 2 1 1/4 **Tuscan King**10 [810] 4-9-6 59 (tp) RobertHavlin 8 66
(Bernard Llewellyn) *in tch: rdn and unable qck wl over 1f out: rallied and hdwy 1f out: chsd wnr wl ins fnl f: no imp fnl 50yds* **7/1**3
-365 3 1 1/4 **Jonnie Skull (IRE)**10 [809] 5-8-12 51 (vt) KierenFallon 6 55
(Phil McEntee) *led: rdn ent fnl 2f: hrd pressed ent fnl f: hdd ins fnl f: kpt on same pce after* **8/1**
4564 4 nk **Lopinot (IRE)**15 [765] 8-9-7 60 (v) GeorgeBaker 7 64
(Martin Bosley) *hld up in tch: rdn to chal over 1f out: ev ch 1f out: drvn and styd on same pce ins fnl f* **6/1**2
4401 5 nk **Spinning Ridge (IRE)**18 [719] 6-9-5 58 (b) DavidProbert 10 61
(Ronald Harris) *stdd s: hld up in tch in rr: shkn up and effrt ent fnl 2f: hdwy to chse ldrs and drvn ent fnl f: styd on same pce ins fnl f* **10/3**1
-344 6 nk **This Ones For Eddy**29 [589] 6-9-4 57 LukeMorris 4 59
(John Balding) *chsd ldr: rdn 2f out: hrd drvn and unable qck over 1f out: no ex and btn ins fnl f* **8/1**
2023 7 3/4 **St Ignatius**4 [854] 4-8-11 50 (p) NeilChalmers 1 50
(Michael Appleby) *in tch on inner: effrt to chse ldrs and drvn jst over 1f out: nt qckn 1f out: no ex and btn ins fnl f* **16/1**
0-60 8 1 **Amends (USA)**10 [814] 4-9-0 56 KierenFox(3) 12 54
(John Best) *dwlt: in rr: rdn and effrt 2f out: nt clr run and swtchd lft over 1f out: kpt on same pce fnl f: nvr trbld ldrs* **16/1**
-603 9 nk **Rainsborough**27 [619] 4-9-2 55 (e) DaneO'Neill 3 52
(Peter Hedger) *awkward s and s.i.s: hdwy ent fnl 2f: no prog u.p ent fnl f: wl hld whn nt clr run and eased towards fin* **14/1**
-452 10 1 1/4 **Christmas Coming**18 [722] 4-9-6 59 (t) StevieDonohoe 11 54
(Tony Carroll) *dwlt: in tch in midfield on outer: rdn and unable qck ent fnl 2f: drvn and no hdwy over 1f out: plugged on same pce fnl f* **10/1**
0-03 11 1 1/4 **First Service (IRE)**38 [477] 5-8-12 51 (e) WilliamCarson 2 43
(Michael Attwater) *in tch towards rr: effrt u.p on inner 2f out: drvn and no prog over 1f out: wknd ins fnl f* **20/1**
05-0 12 1/2 **Interakt**17 [727] 4-9-2 60 MartinHarley(5) 5 51
(Joseph Tuite) *chsd ldrs: rdn over 1f out: wknd over 1f out* **33/1**

1m 37.31s (-0.89) **Going Correction** 0.0s/f (Stan) 12 Ran SP% **119.8**
Speed ratings (Par 101): **104,102,101,101,100 100,99,98,98,97 96,95**
Tote Swingers: 1&2 £6.30, 1&3 £12.20, 2&3 £10.90 CSF £56.03 CT £407.56 TOTE £9.10: £3.70, £1.90, £2.50; EX 61.60 Trifecta £418.30 Part won. Pool: £565.32 - 0.10 winning units..
Owner J Ryan **Bred** Gainsborough Stud Management Ltd **Trained** Newmarket, Suffolk

FOCUS
A modest handicap, but a typically competitive one for the track and the pace was decent. Despite that, there were plenty still in with every chance a furlong out.
Amends(USA) Official explanation: jockey said gelding never travelled
Christmas Coming Official explanation: jockey said colt hung right throughout

907 MARSH GREEN H'CAP 1m (P)
3:30 (3:30) (Class 4) (0-85,78) 3-Y-O £3,238 (£963; £481; £240) Stalls High

Form RPR
0-1 1 **She Ain't A Saint**54 [274] 3-9-6 77 KierenFallon 4 87+
(Jane Chapple-Hyam) *t.k.h early: chsd ldr: rdn to ld over 1f out: edgd lft but r.o wl fnl f: rdn out* **1/1**1
-221 2 2 1/4 **School For Scandal (IRE)**15 [774] 3-9-4 75 (b) JoeFanning 2 79
(Mark Johnston) *led: rdn jst over 2f out: hdd over 1f out: keeping on same pce and btn whn swtchd rt ins fnl f* **7/2**3
4-36 3 6 **Spartic**15 [764] 3-9-1 72 JamesDoyle 3 62
(Alan McCabe) *stdd after s: hld up in tch: chsd ldng pair 3f out: rdn and outpcd ent fnl 2f: wl btn after* **11/1**
316- 4 3/4 **Ibsaar**174 [6386] 3-9-4 78 GilmarPereira(3) 5 66
(William Haggas) *t.k.h: hld up in tch: pushed along and lost tch over 2f out: racd awkwardly u.p over 1f out: kpt on but no ch fnl f* **3/1**2
10- 5 11 **Miss Boops (IRE)**240 [4305] 3-9-7 78 IanMongan 1 41
(Zoe Davison) *hld up in tch: rdn and lost tch over 2f out: wl bhd fnl 2f* **25/1**

1m 38.32s (0.12) **Going Correction** 0.0s/f (Stan) 5 Ran SP% **109.4**
Speed ratings (Par 100): **99,96,90,90,79**
CSF £4.75 TOTE £2.00: £1.10, £1.50; EX 4.20.
Owner Mrs Jane Chapple-Hyam **Bred** Gestut Park Wiedingen **Trained** Dalham, Suffolk

FOCUS
A fair little handicap though the front pair were the only ones ever in it. The winning time was just over a second slower than the older horses in the preceding handicap.

908 ALL WEATHER "HANDS AND HEELS" APPRENTICE SERIES FINAL H'CAP (RACING EXCELLENCE INITIATIVE) 1m (P)
4:05 (4:05) (Class 4) (0-85,85) 4-Y-O+ **£3,238** (£963; £481; £240) **Stalls** High

Form RPR
220- **1** **Fanditha (IRE)**[155] [6886] 5-9-2 **85**.............................. CharlesBishop(5) 9 93
(Mick Channon) *chsd ldrs: rdn to chal towards inner jst over 1f out: led ins fnl f: r.o wl* **12/1**
2146 **2** *1* **Buaiteoir (FR)**[21] [703] 5-9-5 **83**.............................. MatthewLawson 2 89
(Paul D'Arcy) *stdd s: hld up in last pair: swtchd rt and effrt on outer over 1f out: r.o fnl f to go 2nd nr fin: nt rch wnr* **4/1**[1]
1-01 **3** *nk* **Tewin Wood**[10] [806] 4-8-12 **76**.............................. NatashaEaton 6 81
(Alan Bailey) *led: rdn along wl over 1f out: hdd fnl 100yds: no ex: lost 2nd towards fin* **8/1**
1244 **4** *1 ½* **Lockantanks**[2] [877] 4-8-10 **77**.............................. LeonnaMayor(3) 5 81
(Michael Appleby) *stdd s: hld up in tch in rr: hdwy and gng wl but nt clr run over 1f out: nvr enough room after: kpt on cl home: unable to chal* **5/1**[2]
2313 **5** *nse* **Ocean Legend (IRE)**[9] [822] 6-9-2 **83**.................... GeorgeDowning(3) 3 84
(Tony Carroll) *in tch in midfield: effrt and chsd ldrs 2f out: styd on same pce ins fnl f* **6/1**[3]
-026 **6** *½* **Highly Regal (IRE)**[27] [623] 6-8-9 **73**....................(b) MatthewCosham 8 74
(Roger Teal) *hld up in tch: sltly hmpd and swtchd to outer 3f out: rdn along to chse ldrs ent fnl f: hld hd high and no prog ins fnl f* **9/1**
6206 **7** *3 ¾* **Halsion Chancer**[17] [723] 7-8-11 **78**.............................. ThomasBrown(3) 4 70
(John Best) *chsd ldrs: rdn wl over 1f out: wknd qckly ins fnl f* **9/1**
614- **8** *3 ¼* **Flag Of Glory**[109] [7638] 4-8-9 **73**.............................. NannaHansen 10 57
(Chris Wall) *chsd ldr: rdn 2f out wknd qckly 1f out: fdd ins fnl f* **20/1**
4250 **9** *5* **Tuxedo**[23] [666] 6-8-8 **72**..............................(p) LucyKBarry 1 45
(Peter Hiatt) *in tch: rdn along and lost pl over 2f out: n.d fnl 2f* **16/1**
-301 **10** *4 ½* **Big Bay (USA)**[27] [623] 5-9-1 **82**.............................. LewisWalsh(3) 7 44
(Jane Chapple-Hyam) *s.i.s: nvr gng wl in rr: lost tch over 2f out* **7/1**

1m 36.99s (-1.21) **Going Correction** 0.0s/f (Stan) **10** Ran SP% **112.9**
Speed ratings (Par 105): **106,105,104,103,103 102,98,95,90,86**
Tote Swingers: 1&2 £11.10, 1&3 £18.30, 2&3 £9.90 CSF £57.67 CT £421.18 TOTE £17.70: £5.40, £1.10, £1.60; EX 63.40 TRIFECTA Not won..
Owner Mrs T Burns **Bred** Lynch Bages Ltd & Samac Ltd **Trained** West Ilsley, Berks
■ Charles Bishop's first winner.

FOCUS
A competitive little handicap of its type. The pace was good and the winning time was comfortably the fastest of the three races over 1m on the card.

909 FOREST ROW MAIDEN STKS 1m 2f (P)
4:40 (4:40) (Class 5) 3-Y-O **£2,047** (£604; £302) **Stalls** Low

Form RPR
3- **1** **Failasoof (USA)**[145] [7112] 3-9-3 0.............................. MichaelHills 1 84+
(B W Hills) *led for 1f: chsd ldr after tl led again over 4f out: mde rest: rdn whn pressed ent fnl f: qcknd readily and sn in command: easily* **1/2**[1]
53 **2** *3 ¾* **Enriching (USA)**[17] [726] 3-9-3 0.............................. DaneO'Neill 2 73+
(David Elsworth) *hld up in midfield: hdwy to chse ldrs over 3f out: rdn and wnt 2nd wl over 1f out: pressed wnr ent fnl f: sn outpcd: eased towards fin* **9/1**
04 **3** *1 ¼* **Barnum (USA)**[19] [714] 3-9-3 0.............................. KierenFallon 7 70
(Mark Johnston) *t.k.h early: in tch: hdwy to chse ldrs 7f out: jnd ldr over 3f out: rdn and unable qck wl over 1f out: styd on same pce u.p fnl f* **5/1**[2]
05- **4** *1* **Barnmore**[129] [7386] 3-9-3 0.............................. SteveDrowne 3 68
(Peter Hedger) *s.i.s: hld up in last trio: hdwy into midfield over 3f out: rdn to chse ldng trio jst over 2f out: outpcd over 1f out: plugged on same pce fnl f* **6/1**[3]
6 **5** *¾* **Beauchamp Zest**[10] [811] 3-8-12 0..............................(t) JamesDoyle 4 61
(Hans Adielsson) *hld up in tch: hdwy to chse ldng trio 3f out tl jst over 2f out: sn outpcd u.p: n.d but plugged on fnl f* **16/1**
6 *2 ¼* **Black Feather** 3-8-7 0.............................. DeclanCannon(5) 5 57
(Alan McCabe) *in rr: rdn along over 4f out: kpt on same pce and n.d fnl 2f* **50/1**
-305 **7** *10* **Imperial Fong**[15] [760] 3-8-12 55..............................(p) LukeMorris 6 37
(Ronald Harris) *t.k.h: chsd ldrs tl lost pl u.p 3f out: wl bhd fnl 2f* **20/1**
0-6 **8** *7* **Osgoodisgood**[30] [579] 3-9-3 0..............................(t) JimCrowley 8 28
(Stuart Williams) *led after 1f: hdd over 4f out: lost pl and dropped to last over 2f out: sn lost tch* **20/1**

2m 5.65s (-0.95) **Going Correction** 0.0s/f (Stan) **8** Ran SP% **125.0**
Speed ratings (Par 98): **103,100,99,98,97 95,87,82**
Tote Swingers: 1&2 £2.40, 1&3 £2.10, 2&3 £2.40. CSF £7.18 TOTE £1.90: £2.00, £1.10, £1.50; EX 6.10 Trifecta £16.20 Pool: £768.13 - 35.03 winning units..
Owner Hamdan Al Maktoum **Bred** B Wayne Hughes **Trained** Lambourn, Berks

FOCUS
The 2010 Arlington Million winner Debussy took this maiden two years ago and although this year's winner will have to go some in order to match his achievements, he does look a nice prospect. The 55-rated Imperial Fong was beaten far enough so as not to drag the form down.

910 LUXURY BOOT CAMPS AT LINGFIELD MARRIOTT H'CAP 5f (P)
5:15 (5:15) (Class 5) (0-75,75) 4-Y-O+ **£2,047** (£604; £302) **Stalls** High

Form RPR
3454 **1** **Sherjawy (IRE)**[3] [867] 7-8-13 **67**.............................. KirstyMilczarek 5 73
(Zoe Davison) *pressed ldr: rdn 2f out: led narrowly jst over 1f out: hld on wl fnl f: all out* **13/2**[3]
50-5 **2** *shd* **Freddie's Girl (USA)**[59] [215] 4-9-2 **70**.............................. JimCrowley 4 76
(Seamus Durack) *led: rdn ent fnl 2f: hdd narrowly jst over 1f out: kpt on wl fnl f: a jst hld* **10/1**
135- **3** *nk* **Ajjaadd (USA)**[137] [7285] 5-9-4 **72**.............................. SteveDrowne 7 78
(Ted Powell) *stdd s: hld up in tch in rr: nt clr run and swtchd rt over 1f out: r.o wl ins fnl f: nt quite rch ldrs* **13/2**[3]
-36 **4** *hd* **Even Bolder**[21] [701] 8-9-2 **73**.............................. KierenFox(3) 2 78
(Eric Wheeler) *awkward leaving stalls: hld up in rr: nt clr run and swtchd lft ent fnl f: r.o wl fnl 100yds: nt quite rch ldrs* **8/1**
2331 **5** *shd* **Estonia**[15] [766] 4-8-11 **65**.............................. LukeMorris 3 68
(Michael Squance) *t.k.h: hld up wl in tch: effrt and rdn over 1f out: drvn and hdwy 1f out: kpt on u.p: edgd lft u.p towards fin: nt quite rch ldrs* **2/1**[1]
1020 **6** *nk* **Garstang**[17] [725] 8-9-7 **75**..............................(b) GeorgeBaker 1 77
(John Balding) *t.k.h: chsd ldrs on inner: effrt u.p and ev ch 1f out unable qck fnl 100yds: one pce whn bmpd towards fin* **8/1**
2332 **7** *1 ½* **Black Baccara**[10] [812] 4-8-7 **61** oh1..............................(be) KierenFallon 6 58
(Phil McEntee) *chsd ldrs: effrt bnd 2f out: unable qck over 1f out: btn jst ins fnl f* **4/1**[2]

59.09 secs (0.29) **Going Correction** 0.0s/f (Stan) **7** Ran SP% **111.3**
Speed ratings (Par 103): **97,96,96,96,95 95,93**
Tote Swingers: 1&2 £14.20, 1&3 £6.60, 2&3 £16.00. CSF £62.91 TOTE £9.70: £4.70, £7.40; EX 76.90.
Owner Charlie's Starrs **Bred** Darley **Trained** Hammerwood, E Sussex
■ Stewards' Enquiry : Kirsty Milczarek one-day ban: used whip with excessive frequency (Apr 2)

FOCUS
Races don't come much tighter than this with barely a length covering the front six at the line. The gallop wasn't that strong for a sprint and the front two were on the pace throughout.
T/Plt: £29.10. Pool: £58,258.74 - 1,457.95 winning units. T/Qpdt: £11.60. Pool: £3,760.02 - 237.87 winning units. SP

892 WOLVERHAMPTON (A.W) (L-H)
Saturday, March 19

OFFICIAL GOING: Standard

911 COMPARE FREE BETS WITH FREEBETTING.CO.UK H'CAP 1m 5f 194y(P)
6:20 (6:21) (Class 6) (0-60,59) 4-Y-O+ **£1,535** (£453; £226) **Stalls** Low

Form RPR
302- **1** **Storm Hawk (IRE)**[156] [6871] 4-8-13 **57**....................(p) JamesRogers(5) 5 67
(Pat Eddery) *slowly away: hld up: hdwy on outer 3f out: chsd ldr over 1f out: kpt on to ld nr fin* **5/1**[3]
00/2 **2** *hd* **Accumulate**[33] [539] 8-9-10 **59**.............................. J-PGuillambert 1 69
(Bill Moore) *w ldr: led over 3f out: rdn 2f out: kpt on but hdd nr fin* **11/2**
0261 **3** *2 ¼* **Little Richard (IRE)**[9] [819] 12-9-2 **51**..............................(p) AdamKirby 9 57
(Mark Wellings) *hld up: chsd along 3f out: hdwy 2f out: kpt on ins fnl f* **4/1**[1]
-643 **4** *1 ¾* **Beseech (USA)**[11] [795] 4-8-6 **45**.............................. JimmyQuinn 7 49
(Julia Feilden) *hld up in midfield: rdn and hdwy whn swtchd to outer over 1f out: kpt on ins fnl f* **10/1**
01 **5** *1 ½* **Golan Heights (IRE)**[15] [771] 5-8-13 **53**..............................(b) LMcNiff(5) 6 55
(Adrian McGuinness, Ire) *led narrowly: hdd over 3f out: rdn over 2f out: wknd ins fnl f* **9/2**[2]
5630 **6** *hd* **Acropolis (IRE)**[26] [631] 10-8-4 **46**.............................. ShaneBKelly(7) 8 48
(Tony Carroll) *t.k.h early: midfield: lost pl over 2f out: kpt on ins fnl f: n.d* **16/1**
-036 **7** *2 ½* **Magnitude**[25] [645] 6-9-2 **51**..............................(p) TomEaves 2 49
(Brian Baugh) *trckd ldrs: rdn over 2f out: wknd ins fnl f* **7/1**
0640 **8** *1 ¼* **Swords**[15] [768] 9-8-10 **45**.............................. WilliamCarson 3 41
(Ray Peacock) *trckd ldrs on inner: rdn over 2f out: wknd over 1f out* **20/1**
600- **9** *15* **Weybridge Light**[120] [7504] 6-9-4 **53**..............................(p) LiamKeniry 10 28
(Martin Bosley) *prom on outer tl wknd 3f out* **11/1**
-006 **10** *1* **Jiggalong**[31] [552] 5-8-5 **45**.............................. RyanPowell(5) 4 19
(Mrs D Thomas) *slowly away: hld up: a towards rr* **40/1**

3m 4.30s (-1.70) **Going Correction** +0.025s/f (Slow)
WFA 4 from 5yo+ 4lb **10** Ran SP% **113.2**
Speed ratings (Par 101): **105,104,103,102,101 101,100,99,90,90**
toteswingers: 1&2 £5.50, 1&3 £5.60, 2&3 £4.50. CSF £31.63 CT £119.19 TOTE £10.10: £4.80, £3.50, £1.30; EX 31.60.
Owner Storm Hawk Partnership **Bred** Rodger O'Dwyer **Trained** Nether Winchendon, Bucks

FOCUS
Low-grade fare. It was steadily run for the most part.
Jiggalong Official explanation: trainer said that the filly was left at the start, ran in snatches throughout and on returning to the stables was found to be unwell

912 THE BLACK COUNTRY'S ONLY RACECOURSE H'CAP 5f 216y(P)
6:50 (6:51) (Class 6) (0-52,52) 4-Y-O+ **£1,535** (£453; £226) **Stalls** Low

Form RPR
-602 **1** **Dickie Le Davoir**[3] [874] 7-8-10 **50**..............................(b) JamesSullivan(3) 10 59
(Richard Guest) *hld up: rdn and hdwy on outer over 2f out: chsd ldr over 1f out: edgd rt: r.o wl to ld wl ins fnl f* **15/2**
-543 **2** *¾* **Bold Diva**[11] [793] 6-9-0 **51**..............................(v) JimmyQuinn 1 58
(Tony Carroll) *midfield on inner: rdn over 1f out: r.o wl ins fnl f: wnt 2nd nr line* **11/2**[2]
20-3 **3** *½* **Avonlini**[17] [734] 5-8-13 **50**.............................. GrahamGibbons 8 55
(Brian Baugh) *led: hdd 3f out: led again 2f out: hdd wl ins fnl f* **9/2**[1]
3654 **4** *½* **Kheley (IRE)**[23] [664] 5-8-10 **52**.............................. JamesRogers(5) 5 56
(Mark Brisbourne) *prom: rdn over 2f out: kpt on tl no ex towards fin* **15/2**
4402 **5** *hd* **Fiancee (IRE)**[9] [821] 5-8-11 **48**..............................(p) PaulMulrennan 6 51
(Roy Brotherton) *chsd ldrs: rdn and ev ch over 1f out: no ex towards fin* **16/1**
0603 **6** *1 ½* **Raimond Ridge (IRE)**[9] [821] 5-8-11 **48**.................. RobbieFitzpatrick 9 47
(Derek Shaw) *s.i.s: hld up: rdn over 1f out: kpt on ins fnl f: nrst fin* **12/1**
30-4 **7** *½* **Diddums**[9] [821] 5-8-7 **49**..............................(p) AmyScott(5) 13 46
(Alastair Lidderdale) *dwlt: sn midfield on outer: rdn over 2f out: one pce* **16/1**
2050 **8** *nk* **Metropolitan Chief**[17] [734] 7-9-0 **51**.............................. LiamKeniry 3 47
(Paul Burgoyne) *trckd ldrs on inner: rdn over 1f out: wknd ins fnl f* **16/1**
4-24 **9** *hd* **Lily Wood**[47] [363] 5-9-1 **52**..............................(p) LiamJones 2 48
(James Unett) *sn chsd along towards rr: rdn over 2f out: kpt on ins fnl f: n.d* **13/2**[3]
3304 **10** *nk* **Muqalad (IRE)**[11] [798] 4-8-13 **50**..............................(v) TomEaves 11 45
(Bryan Smart) *w ldr: led 3f out tl 2f out: wknd ins fnl f* **10/1**
6061 **11** *½* **Vertumnus**[22] [690] 4-8-8 **52**..............................(b) JackDuern(7) 12 45
(Nick Littmoden) *dwlt: hld up: hdwy on outer over 2f out: sn rdn: wknd ins fnl f* **20/1**
00- **12** *2 ¾* **My Meteor**[189] [5957] 4-8-13 **50**.............................. BarryMcHugh 4 35
(Tony Newcombe) *midfield: rdn over 2f out: wknd over 1f out* **25/1**
060- **13** *13* **Rileys Crane**[220] [4970] 4-9-1 **52**.............................. WilliamCarson 7 —
(Christine Dunnett) *midfield tl rdn and wknd over 2f out: eased* **50/1**

1m 14.77s (-0.23) **Going Correction** +0.025s/f (Slow) **13** Ran SP% **115.4**
Speed ratings (Par 101): **102,101,100,99,99 97,96,96,96,95 95,91,74**
toteswingers: 1&2 £7.30, 1&3 £7.70, 2&3 £5.60. CSF £45.64 CT £215.34 TOTE £12.60: £3.80, £3.00, £2.00; EX 43.40.
Owner Future Racing (Notts) Limited **Bred** P And Mrs A G Venner **Trained** Stainforth, S Yorks

FOCUS
A run-of-the-mill affair, though it was at least run at a good gallop.

Rileys Crane Official explanation: jockey sasid gelding hung right-handed

913 SIX NATIONS FREE BETS WITH FREEBETTING.CO.UK CLAIMING STKS 5f 216y(P)

7:20 (7:21) (Class 5) 3-Y-O **£1,813** (£539; £269; £134) **Stalls** Low

Form RPR

-220 **1** **My Lord**[7] 845 3-8-9 78 ..... JakePayne(7) 3 72
(Bill Turner) *w ldr: led over 2f out: rdn over 1f out: hld on u.p ins fnl f* **11/10**[1]

0106 **2** ¾ **Loves Theme (IRE)**[17] 724 3-8-9 69 ..... J-PGuillambert 5 63
(Alan Bailey) *led narrowly: rdn whn hdd over 2f out: kpt on but a jst hld ins fnl f* **8/1**

10-6 **3** 2 **Dolly Parton (IRE)**[7] 847 3-8-13 69 ..... AdrianNicholls 2 61
(David Nicholls) *hld up in 4th: rdn over 2f out: kpt on to take 3rd ins fnl f: n.d* **9/2**[3]

0264 **4** ½ **Hereselie (IRE)**[23] 672 3-7-10 58 ..... NoelGarbutt(7) 4 49
(Michael Chapman) *slowly away: sn prom on outer: rdn over 2f out: wknd ins fnl f* **28/1**

16- **5** ½ **Sergeant Suzie**[277] 3059 3-8-4 75 ..... ShaneBKelly(7) 1 55
(Michael Dods) *s.i.s: hld up in 5th: rdn over 1f out: sn edgd rt: kpt on fnl 100yds: nvr on terms* **5/2**[2]

1m 15.42s (0.42) **Going Correction** +0.025s/f (Slow) **5** Ran SP% **108.9**
Speed ratings (Par 98): **98,97,94,93,93**
CSF £10.19 TOTE £2.50: £1.40, £7.40; EX 8.50.
Owner Mrs M S Teversham **Bred** Mrs Monica Teversham **Trained** Sigwells, Somerset

■ Stewards' Enquiry : Jake Payne four-day ban: used whip with excessive frequency without giving gelding time to respond (Apr 2-5)

FOCUS
The market got this one right.

914 GREAT OFFERS AT WOLVERHAMPTON-RACECOURSE.CO.UK (S) STKS 7f 32y(P)

7:50 (7:50) (Class 6) 4-Y-O+ **£1,535** (£453; £226) **Stalls** High

Form RPR

1033 **1** **Unlimited**[4] 856 9-9-4 64 ..... J-PGuillambert 5 79
(Tony Carroll) *hld up in tch: hdwy on inner over 2f out: led over 1f out: rdn clr ins fnl f* **14/1**

6-54 **2** 6 **Fleetwoodsands (IRE)**[31] 556 4-8-12 68 ..... (t) BarryMcHugh 3 57
(Ollie Pears) *trckd ldrs: rdn over 2f out: kpt on to take 2nd ins fnl f: no ch w wnr* **13/2**

1 **3** 3½ **Chimpunk (USA)**[29] 593 5-9-4 76 ..... AndreaAtzeni 4 54
(Michael Wigham) *racd keenly: in tch on outer: hdwy to chal over 2f out tl over 1f out: one pce fnl f* **2/1**[2]

4-3 **4** 2¼ **The Big Haerth (IRE)**[64] 159 5-8-12 69 ..... (t) JamesDoyle 1 41
(Frank Sheridan) *trckd ldrs on inner: rdn to ld over 2f out: edgd rt wl over 1f out: sn hdd: no ex ins fnl f* **7/4**[1]

1-12 **5** 1 **Orpenindeed (IRE)**[40] 445 8-9-4 77 ..... AdamKirby 2 45
(Frank Sheridan) *led narrowly: rdn whn hdd over 2f out: wknd ins fnl f* **9/2**[3]

0-00 **6** 2½ **Novay Essjay (IRE)**[4] 854 4-8-12 65 ..... (v1) GrahamGibbons 7 32
(Alan Juckes) *sn pressed ldr: lost pl over 2f out: wknd over 1f out* **50/1**

200- **7** 12 **Baby Judge (IRE)**[92] 7906 4-8-5 43 ..... NoelGarbutt(7) 6 —
(Michael Chapman) *sn outpcd in rr: bhd fr 1/2-way* **100/1**

1m 28.01s (-1.59) **Going Correction** +0.025s/f (Slow) **7** Ran SP% **110.8**
Speed ratings (Par 101): **110,103,99,96,95 92,78**
toteswingers: 1&2 £3.00, 1&3 £4.00, 2&3 £3.90. CSF £93.31 TOTE £22.00: £13.30, £1.10; EX 45.30.
Owner M B Clarke **Bred** J Wise **Trained** Cropthorne, Worcs

FOCUS
Not the easiest race to assess, but chances are the majority were below their best.

Unlimited Official explanation: trainer's rep said, regarding apparent improvement in form, that the gelding appeared to benefit from a return to the polytrack surface.

915 GRAND NATIONAL FREE BETS WITH FREEBETTING.CO.UK H'CAP 7f 32y(P)

8:20 (8:20) (Class 5) (0-70,70) 4-Y-O+ **£1,813** (£539; £269; £134) **Stalls** High

Form RPR

-543 **1** **Copperwood**[15] 763 6-9-6 69 ..... (p) LiamKeniry 2 76
(Michael Blanshard) *trckd ldr on inner: pushed ahd fnl 100yds: sn drvn: hld on all out* **11/2**[3]

0120 **2** shd **Spin Again (IRE)**[15] 763 6-9-0 70 ..... LucyKBarry(7) 10 77
(Mark Wellings) *sn led: rdn over 2f out: hdd fnl 100yds: kpt on: jst failed* **14/1**

3636 **3** ½ **Could It Be Magic**[23] 666 4-9-6 69 ..... (b) WilliamCarson 6 75
(Bill Turner) *hld up in midfield: rdn over 2f out: swtchd rt over 1f out: r.o strly ins fnl f: nrst fin* **13/2**

1-02 **4** 1½ **Khajaaly (IRE)**[22] 692 4-9-6 69 ..... JimmyQuinn 4 71
(Julia Feilden) *in tch on inner: briefly short of room over 1f out: sn rdn: kpt on ins fnl f* **4/1**[2]

-220 **5** ½ **Mount Hollow**[26] 637 6-9-1 64 ..... (p) GrahamGibbons 8 63
(Reg Hollinshead) *trckd ldr: rdn over 2f out: no ex ins fnl f* **11/2**[3]

1016 **6** ½ **Downhill Skier (IRE)**[16] 743 7-8-13 62 ..... ShaneKelly 7 60
(Mark Brisbourne) *trckd ldr on outer: rdn over 2f out: one pce* **9/1**

0-15 **7** ½ **Woolfall Sovereign (IRE)**[31] 557 5-9-7 70 ..... BarryMcHugh 5 65
(George Margarson) *sn hld up in midfield: rdn over 2f out: kpt on ins fnl f: n.d* **7/2**[1]

-400 **8** 1¼ **Tourist**[30] 577 6-9-7 70 ..... TomEaves 1 64
(Derek Shaw) *dwlt: hld up: rdn over 2f out: n.d* **11/1**

1-00 **9** 1 **Nacho Libre**[23] 674 6-8-9 61 ..... (b) JamesSullivan(3) 9 54
(Michael Easterby) *sn prom: rdn 3f out: wknd over 1f out* **33/1**

4500 **10** ½ **Vhujon (IRE)**[8] 833 6-9-3 66 ..... RobbieFitzpatrick 3 57
(Peter Grayson) *hld up: rdn over 2f out: no imp* **66/1**

1m 29.38s (-0.22) **Going Correction** +0.025s/f (Slow) **10** Ran SP% **115.8**
Speed ratings (Par 103): **102,101,101,99,99 98,97,96,95,94**
toteswingers: 1&2 £12.50, 1&3 £5.70, 2&3 £11.90. CSF £78.66 CT £526.02 TOTE £6.00: £2.40, £5.70, £3.40; EX 68.10.
Owner Mrs Rosemary K Wilkerson **Bred** Hertford Offset Press **Trained** Upper Lambourn, Berks

FOCUS
They didn't go much of a gallop and it paid to race handily, the performance of the third worth marking up slightly.

Nacho Libre Official explanation: trainer said gelding bled

Vhujon(IRE) Official explanation: jockey said gelding hung right-handed

916 HORIZONS RESTAURANT MEDIAN AUCTION MAIDEN STKS 1m 141y(P)

8:50 (8:50) (Class 5) 3-Y-O **£1,813** (£539; £269; £134) **Stalls** Low

Form RPR

324 **1** **Bountiful Guest**[7] 850 3-9-3 67 ..... GrahamGibbons 8 68+
(Brian Baugh) *trckd ldr: chal over 2f out: rdn to ld over 1f out: kpt on wl ins fnl f* **3/1**[3]

4006 **2** ½ **Hugely Exciting**[28] 616 3-9-3 78 ..... LukeMorris 4 67
(J S Moore) *trckd ldr in 2nd: rdn to ld over 2f out: hdd over 1f out: kpt on: hld nr fin* **6/4**[1]

02-5 **3** 2 **Scoglio**[16] 745 3-9-3 65 ..... JamesDoyle 2 62
(Frank Sheridan) *in tch: rdn and swtchd rt over 1f out: styd on ins fnl f* **5/2**[2]

4 ¾ **McCool Bannanas** 3-9-3 0 ..... LiamJones 1 60
(James Unett) *s.i.s: hld up: hdwy on inner over 3f out: rdn to chse ldr over 1f out: one pce ins fnl f* **40/1**

0-04 **5** ¾ **Kyncraighe (IRE)**[9] 817 3-9-3 53 ..... (t) ShaneKelly 5 59?
(Alastair Lidderdale) *midfield: hdwy to chse ldrs over 2f out: rdn over 1f out: no ex ins fnl f* **14/1**

6 13 **Elite Syncopations** 3-8-12 0 ..... RobertHavlin 6 24
(Andrew Haynes) *hld up in tch: wknd fnl 2f* **14/1**

06- **7** 9 **Blazing Apostle (IRE)**[197] 5721 3-8-12 0 ..... WilliamCarson 3 —
(Christine Dunnett) *sn led: rdn whn hdd over 2f out: wknd over 1f out* **66/1**

1m 52.25s (1.75) **Going Correction** +0.025s/f (Slow) **7** Ran SP% **110.8**
Speed ratings (Par 98): **93,92,90,90,89 77,69**
toteswingers: 1&2 £1.30, 1&3 £1.40, 2&3 £1.70. CSF £7.37 TOTE £4.60: £2.20, £2.40; EX 7.50.
Owner Stuart M Mercer **Bred** M Channon B/Stck & G Richardson B/Stck **Trained** Audley, Staffs

FOCUS
Just an ordinary maiden, the proximity of lowly rated Kyncraighe certainly holding the form down. The pace was steady, the race not beginning in earnest until the final 3f.

917 FOOTBALL FREE BETS WITH FREEBETTING.CO.UK H'CAP 1m 4f 50y(P)

9:20 (9:20) (Class 5) (0-70,67) 4-Y-O+ **£1,813** (£539; £269; £134) **Stalls** Low

Form RPR

0-06 **1** **War Of The Roses (IRE)**[11] 797 8-9-1 59 ..... TomEaves 3 64
(Roy Brotherton) *trckd ldng pair: wnt 2nd over 3f out: sn rdn: kpt on ins fnl f: led post* **11/2**[3]

-122 **2** nk **The Blue Dog (IRE)**[8] 839 4-9-2 62 ..... (b) NickyMackay 4 67
(Mark Rimmer) *trckd ldr in 2nd: led over 3f out: rdn 2 l clr 2f out: drvn and edgd lft ins fnl f: hdd post* **11/10**[1]

4535 **3** ½ **Duar Mapel (USA)**[8] 839 5-8-10 54 ..... GrahamGibbons 2 58
(Brian Baugh) *led: hdd over 3f out: sn outpcd: styd on again fr over 1f out* **2/1**[2]

-020 **4** 13 **Naheell**[25] 644 5-8-10 61 ..... MatthewCosham(7) 5 44
(George Prodromou) *slowly away: hld up in 4th: rdn over 3f out: sn wknd* **6/1**

2m 42.64s (1.54) **Going Correction** +0.025s/f (Slow)
WFA 4 from 5yo+ 2lb **4** Ran SP% **110.6**
Speed ratings (Par 103): **95,94,94,85**
CSF £12.40 TOTE £5.40; EX 8.40.
Owner Millend Racing Club **Bred** Mrs Jane Bailey **Trained** Elmley Castle, Worcs

FOCUS
A small field and the pace was predictably on the steady side for a long way.
T/Plt: £89.20 to a £1 stake. Pool:£94,997.69 - 776.70 winning tickets. T/Qpdt: £38.70 to a £1 stake Pool: £6,355.15 - 121.40 w. tckts AS

918-919a (Foreign Racing) See Raceform Interactive

860 SAINT-CLOUD (L-H)

Saturday, March 19

OFFICIAL GOING: Turf: soft

920a PRIX EXBURY (GROUP 3) (4YO+) (TURF) 1m 2f

2:40 (12:00) 4-Y-O+ **£34,482** (£13,793; £10,344; £6,896; £3,448)

RPR

1 **Polytechnicien (USA)**[15] 778 5-8-9 0 ..... OlivierPeslier 9 112
(A Fabre, France) *racd in 4th: qcknd wl 2f out: chal and led 1f out: sn chal by runner-up: r.o wl fnl 100yds to win comf* **11/5**[1]

2 ½ **Cirrus Des Aigles (FR)**[97] 7854 5-9-2 0 ..... FranckBlondel 4 118
(Mme C Barande-Barbe, France) *settled in 3rd after 4f: rdn 2f out: qcknd wl 1f out to go 2nd: chal eventual wnr for ld ins fnl f: no ex fnl 100yds* **5/2**[2]

3 1½ **Silver Pond (FR)**[307] 2160 4-9-2 0 ..... DavyBonilla 3 115
(C Laffon-Parias, France) *settled in rr: last 2f out: rdn and qcknd wl 1 1/2f out: r.o strly fnl f to go 3rd on line* **9/2**[3]

4 nse **Timos (GER)**[21] 705 6-8-11 0 ..... SylvainRuis 6 110
(T Doumen, France) *racd in midfield: hrd rdn 1 1/2f out: r.o wl: wnt 4th cl home* **14/1**

5 ½ **Aizavoski (IRE)**[153] 6974 5-8-11 0 ..... ChristopheSoumillon 7 109
(E Lellouche, France) *racd in 3rd fr s: proged to 2nd down bk st: chal for ld 2f out: tk ld 1 1/2f out: rdn and hdd 1f out: no ex: styd on* **9/1**

6 1½ **Pont Des Arts (FR)**[27] 628 7-8-11 0 ..... FredericSpanu 8 106
(A Schaerer, Germany) *rdn to ld fr s on wd outside: hdd 2f out: styd on fnl f* **23/1**

7 hd **Agent Secret (IRE)**[126] 7455 5-9-0 0 ..... ThierryThulliez 1 109
(F Rohaut, France) *racd in midfield on rail: rdn 2f out: no ex: styd on fnl f* **15/1**

8 snk **Kartica**[128] 7416 4-8-8 0 ..... StephanePasquier 2 102
(P Demercastel, France) *racd towards rr: rdn 2f out: no ex: styd on* **25/1**

9 1½ **Court Canibal**[217] 5107 6-8-11 0 ..... Christophe-PatriceLemaire 5 102
(M Delzangles, France) *a towards rr: hrd rdn and swtchd to rail early in st: no ex: styd on* **14/1**

2m 10.5s (-5.50) **9** Ran SP% **115.6**
WIN (incl. 1 euro stake): 3.20. PLACES: 1.30, 1.30, 1.40. DF: 5.80. SF: 9.30.
Owner Wertheimer & Frere **Bred** Wertheimer & Frere **Trained** Chantilly, France

NOTEBOOK

Polytechnicien(USA) was always in the right place at the right time and moved up to challenge for the lead running into the final furlong and a half. Fabre has been quickly out of the stalls this season and he was winning the Exbury for the eighth occasion. The distance is regarded as perfect for him and he will now be aimed at the Prix d'Harcourt and the Prix Ganay.

Cirrus Des Aigles(FR) challenged the winner in the last furlong but was being held near the line. It was also a fine seasonal debut considering he was conceding 7lb to the winner, and he will renew rivalry in the Harcourt and Ganay.

The Form Book, Raceform Ltd, Compton, RG20 6NL

Silver Pond(FR) ◆, was reappearing after a break of ten months, really caught the eye. Last for much of the race and still with an enormous task halfway up the straight, he mowed down the majority of the field in the final 50 yards. The son of Act One was beaten two lengths but was running against a much fitter winner who was receiving 7lb. He will take on the first two again in the Prix d'Harcourt and Prix Ganay.

CURRAGH (R-H)

Sunday, March 20

OFFICIAL GOING: Soft (soft to heavy in places)

921a TALLY HO STUD EUROPEAN BREEDERS FUND MAIDEN — 5f

2:35 (2:35) 2-Y-O **£10,706** (£2,482; £1,086; £620)

RPR

1 — **Whip Rule (IRE)** 2-9-3 ...... KJManning 1 — 87
(J S Bolger, Ire) *trckd ldr in 2nd: pushed along fr 2f out: carried bdly rt ins fnl f: kpt on u.p: jst failed: fin 2nd, hd: awrdd r* **10/1**

2 — **Tough As Nails (IRE)** 2-9-0 ...... GFCarroll(3) 6 — 87
(Michael Mulvany, Ire) *mde all: drvn along fr 2f out: hung bdly rt ins fnl f: kpt on u.p: hld on: fin 1st: disq: plcd 2nd* **8/1**

3 *2* **Pinkisthecolour (IRE)** 2-8-12 ...... DPMcDonogh 3 — 74
(Kevin Prendergast, Ire) *towards rr: hdwy between horses to go 3rd over 1f out: rdn and no imp ins fnl f: kpt on one pce* **4/1[2]**

4 *2* **Gold Lace (IRE)** 2-8-12 ...... FMBerry 5 — 67
(P J Prendergast, Ire) *chsd ldrs in mainly 4th: rdn and no imp over 1f out: kpt on one pce ins fnl f* **6/1[3]**

5 *12* **Lost City (IRE)** 2-9-3 ...... PaulHanagan 2 — 29
(Richard Fahey) *s.i.s: sn trcking ldrs on outer in 3rd: rdn and no ex fr over 1f out: wknd* **8/11[1]**

64.92 secs (2.42) **Going Correction** +0.625s/f (Yiel) **5 Ran SP% 112.4**
Speed ratings: **104,105,101,98,79**
CSF £76.26 TOTE £7.10: £2.10, £2.90; DF 53.70.
Owner Mrs June Judd **Bred** J S Bolger **Trained** Coolcullen, Co Carlow
■ Stewards' Enquiry : G F Carroll advice: careless riding

FOCUS
The ground, officially soft-heavy, was described as horrible and tacky by the riders.

NOTEBOOK
Whip Rule(IRE) was rightly awarded the race in the Stewards' room after he was hampered by Tough As Nails in the closing stages. He should be more at home over a furlong longer on this evidence as his two brothers won over 6f and 1m going back.
Tough As Nails(IRE) bounced out of the gate to soon lead and passing the furlong pole had his chasing rivals in trouble. He lost valuable ground by not keeping a straight line and it was long odds-on he'd lose the race in the Stewards' room. The son of Dark Angel had a head to spare at the line but, despite his rider holding his whip in the right hand, the colt drifted right under pressure inside the final furlong and in doing so hindered the challenge of Jim Bolger's runner, especially in the final 50 yards. (op 16/1)
Pinkisthecolour(IRE) had to be mounted on the track and was on her toes beforehand. She never looked likely to impose her presence but should learn plenty from this initial experience. (op 10/3 tchd 3/1)
Lost City(IRE) missed the break and passing the halfway stage was niggled along after taking closer order then was the first horse beaten. The market indicated he was sharp enough to do himself justice and is probably better than this bare form suggests, especially when he gets some better ground. Official explanation: jockey said colt ran green and hung right (op 4/6 tchd 4/5)

923a NEWBRIDGE & OCALA TWINNING H'CAP — 6f

3:35 (2:37) 3-Y-O+ **£11,206** (£3,275; £1,551; £517)

RPR

1 — **Blue Dahlia (IRE)**[190] 5973 4-7-8 83 oh5 ...... SAGray(10) 7 — 88+
(T Stack, Ire) *trckd ldrs: 5th 1/2-way: smooth hdwy to ld over 1f out: rdn and kpt on wl ins fnl f* **9/2[2]**

2 *2* **Three Way Stretch (IRE)**[266] 3489 5-8-3 85 ......(t) BACurtis(3) 13 — 84
(J T Gorman, Ire) *towards rr: swtchd rt 2f out: rdn to go 6th on outer over [illegible] fnl f* **25/1**

3 *shd* **Luisant**[140] 7259 8-9-11 109 ...... JPO'Brien(5) 11 — 108+
(J A Nash, Ire) *hld up in rr: 11th 1/2-way: 9th over 1f out: kpt on wl ins fnl f wout rching wnr* **7/2[1]**

4 *1* **The Tooth Fairy (IRE)**[197] 5774 5-8-8 90 ...... GFCarroll(3) 9 — 85
(Michael Mulvany, Ire) *chsd ldrs: 6th 1/2-way: rdn into 4th 1f out: no imp and kpt on same pce fnl f* **14/1**

5 *hd* **Moonreach (IRE)**[312] 2036 4-8-13 92 ...... FMBerry 8 — 87
(James J Hartnett, Ire) *a.p: 2nd 1/2-way: chal fr 2f out: 3rd 1f out: no imp u.p ins fnl f* **16/1**

6 *1 1/4* **Jeannie Galloway (IRE)**[184] 6142 4-8-8 87 ...... WMLordan 2 — 78
(Richard Fahey) *prom on outer: 3rd 1/2-way: rdn to go 2nd briefly over 1f out: no ex u.p ins fnl f* **10/1**

7 *2* **Libano (IRE)**[140] 7259 5-9-7 100 ...... PJSmullen 5 — 84
(D K Weld, Ire) *in rr of mid-div: nvr a factor: sme hdwy into 8th 2f out: no imp and kpt on one pce fr 1f out* **12/1**

8 *2 1/2* **Sioux Rising (IRE)**[20] 710 5-8-5 84 ...... WJSupple 6 — 60
(Richard Fahey) *chsd ldrs: 6th 1/2-way: drvn along 2f out: no ex fr 1f out* **7/1[3]**

9 *3/4* **Mo Mhuirnin (IRE)**[67] 125 5-8-4 83 ...... PaulHanagan 14 — 57
(Richard Fahey) *led: strly pressed 2f out: hdd over 1f out: sn no ex: wknd* **10/1**

10 *nk* **Jembatt (IRE)**[197] 5774 4-9-0 93 ...... JMurtagh 12 — 66
(Edward Lynam, Ire) *in rr of mid-div: short of room over 2f out: sme late hdwy wout threatening* **12/1**

11 *2* **Six Of Hearts**[197] 5774 7-9-2 95 ...... CO'Donoghue 1 — 62
(Cecil Ross, Ire) *chsd ldrs on outer: 9th 1/2-way: 7th and pushed along 2f out: sn no ex* **16/1**

12 *3* **Miss Eze**[134] 7355 5-8-4 83 ...... DJMoran 3 — 40
(Paul Cashman, Ire) *a towards rr* **20/1**

13 *6* **Thats A Fret (IRE)**[134] 7348 5-8-11 90 ...... NGMcCullagh 10 — 28
(Liam McAteer, Ire) *mid-div: 8th 1/2-way: no ex fr 2f out* **16/1**

14 *8* **Alshahbaa (IRE)**[184] 4-8-9 88 ...... RPCleary 4 — —
(Ms Joanna Morgan, Ire) *a towards rr: nvr a factor* **16/1**

15 *1* **Moran Gra (USA)**[381] 796 4-8-13 92 ...... KJManning 16 — —
(Ms Joanna Morgan, Ire) *a towards rr* **16/1**

16 *9* **What About Me (IRE)**[301] 2370 4-8-5 91 ...... RPWhelan(7) 15 — —
(Brian Nolan, Ire) *prom: 3rd 1/2-way: sn rdn and no ex: wknd* **20/1**

1m 17.38s (2.38) **Going Correction** +0.625s/f (Yiel) **16 Ran SP% 135.9**
Speed ratings: **109,106,106,104,104 102,100,96,95,95 92,88,80,70,68 56**
CSF £128.87 CT £466.08 TOTE £5.00: £1.50, £6.90, £1.50, £2.50; DF 203.30.
Owner Richard Barnes **Bred** Grangecon Stud **Trained** Golden, Co Tipperary

FOCUS
This looked an open handicap on paper but the winner travelled well and is on the up. The form's rated around the next two.

NOTEBOOK
Blue Dahlia(IRE) could be called the winner passing the 2f pole and she stuck to her task well under a polished ride from her inexperienced 10lb claimer. She was a model of consistency last season after winning her maiden over this C&D 12 months ago, and on this evidence she can win another.
Three Way Stretch(IRE) hadn't been seen since last June and he stayed on under pressure to take second and in the process showed a return his best form. He'll appreciate another furlong or two on this evidence.
Luisant stayed on well inside the final furlong, conceding weight all round, and will appreciate another furlong. (op 4/1)
The Tooth Fairy(IRE) had every chance if good enough approaching the final furlong but was unable to raise his game. (op 16/1)
Moonreach(IRE)
Jeannie Galloway(IRE) was another to race prominently but the distress signals went up after halfway. (op 10/1 tchd 12/1)
Sioux Rising(IRE), fit from the AW and the shorter-priced of the stable's pair, was on the retreat approaching the final furlong. (op 8/1)
Mo Mhuirnin(IRE) made the running but had nothing more to offer when challenged. (op 8/1)

924a LODGE PARK STUD EUROPEAN BREEDERS FUND PARK EXPRESS STKS (GROUP 3) (F&M) — 1m

4:05 (4:08) 3-Y-O+ **£44,827** (£13,103; £6,206; £2,068)

RPR

1 — **Lolly For Dolly (IRE)**[267] 3467 4-9-13 107 ......(b[1]) WMLordan 5 — 107
(T Stack, Ire) *trckd ldrs: 5th 1/2-way: swtchd rt to chal over 1f out: rdn to ld ins fnl f: edgd rt and kpt on wl u.p* **5/2[1]**

2 *2* **Gemstone (IRE)**[161] 6784 3-8-9 98 ...... CO'Donoghue 2 — 96
(A P O'Brien, Ire) *trckd ldrs: cl 3rd 1/2-way: travelled wl to dispute 2f out: sn led and rdn: hdd u.p ins fnl f: kpt on same pce* **7/1[2]**

3 *nk* **Banimpire (IRE)**[175] 6401 3-8-9 95 ...... KJManning 7 — 95
(J S Bolger, Ire) *trckd ldr: disp ld fr 1/2-way: drvn along and narrowly hdd over 2f out: rallied fr over 1f out: kpt on one pce u.p* **12/1**

4 *3/4* **Termagant (IRE)**[301] 2370 4-9-10 105 ...... DPMcDonogh 3 — 97
(Kevin Prendergast, Ire) *hld up in rr: 6th 2f out and sn rdn: kpt on u.p ins fnl f wout troubling ldrs* **5/2[1]**

5 *shd* **Paraphernalia (IRE)**[140] 7259 4-9-10 99 ...... WJLee 9 — 96
(David Wachman, Ire) *settled towards rr: drvn along in 7th over 1f out: kpt on u.p fnl f* **10/1**

6 *6* **Princess Severus (IRE)**[204] 5519 3-8-9 98 ...... NGMcCullagh 1 — 80
(James J Hartnett, Ire) *chsd ldrs on outer: 4th 1/2-way: pushed along after 1/2-way: no ex fr over 1f out* **7/1[2]**

7 *hd* **Enchanted Evening (IRE)**[203] 5568 5-9-10 95 ...... PJSmullen 6 — 82
(D K Weld, Ire) *led: jnd 1/2-way: hdd u.p over 1f out: sn no ex: wknd* **8/1[3]**

8 *nk* **Mid Mon Lady (IRE)**[149] 7076 6-9-10 100 ......(b) FMBerry 4 — 81
(H Rogers, Ire) *hld up in rr: drvn along 2f out: no ex fr over 1f out* **16/1**

9 *15* **Burn The Floor (IRE)**[254] 3881 3-8-9 ...... DJMoran 8 — 44
(J S Bolger, Ire) *chsd ldrs: 6th 1/2-way: dropped to rr 2f out: wknd* **66/1**

1m 49.42s (3.42) **Going Correction** +0.70s/f (Yiel)
WFA 3 from 4yo+ 17lb **9 Ran SP% 117.4**
Speed ratings: **110,108,107,106,106 100,100,100,85**
CSF £21.46 TOTE £2.90: £1.20, £1.60, £3.50; DF 14.00.
Owner David Keoghan **Bred** J Jamgotchian **Trained** Golden, Co Tipperary

FOCUS
Confirmation that the Stack team is in good heart again for the early part of the campaign, winning the first Pattern race of the season, as they had last year with Pollen. The form is rated through the winner and third.

NOTEBOOK
Lolly For Dolly(IRE), blinkered for the first time on her first outing since contesting the 1m2f Pretty Polly Stakes at the venue last June, stuck to her task well despite edging slightly to the right in the closing stages. She did not seem to stay in the Pretty Polly, though the Group 1 attempt was probably a bit ambitious for a filly who finished down the field in the Irish 1000 Guineas before a fourth placing in the Sandringham Handicap at Royal Ascot. On this evidence she can prove a solid Group 3 performer at around one mile. (op 15/8)
Gemstone(IRE), one of four three-year-olds in this field, was a C&D winner on the final start of her juvenile career, and this was a satisfactory reappearance considering she will probably benefit from stepping up in trip. (op 7/1 tchd 8/1)
Banimpire(IRE), prominently ridden, seemed to be struggling around a quarter of a mile down, and it was to her credit that she battled well through the final furlong. She was found wanting last season when raised in class after a maiden win, but she seems to have matured along the right lines, and is the sort of tough filly with whom her trainer does so well.
Termagant(IRE), having won the Moyglare on the second of two runs at two, did not race again after finishing just behind Lolly For Dolly when ninth in the Irish 1000 Guineas. She was backed down to share favouritism as Lolly For Dolly drifted in the betting, but never looked like imposing her presence under a hold-up ride. It will take another run before one could say with more certainty what the future may hold for her after last season's truncated campaign. (op 3/1)
Paraphernalia(IRE), who was rated a modest 75 when Listed-placed at a big price at Naas last October, ran a race in keeping with her revised mark of 99 here, finishing clear of the remainder. (op 12/1)
Princess Severus(IRE), an import from Britain, attracted some market support on her Irish debut.
Enchanted Evening(IRE), who was lightly raced last season, faded after making the early running. (op 10/1)

925a WWW.THETOTE.COM IRISH LINCOLNSHIRE (PREMIER H'CAP) — 1m

4:35 (4:36) 4-Y-O+

£31,034 (£9,827; £4,655; £1,551; £1,034; £517)

RPR

1 — **Drombeg Dawn (IRE)**[187] 6068 5-8-13 85 ...... BACurtis(3) 16 — 91
(A J McNamara, Ire) *trckd ldrs: 4th 1/2-way: rdn to chal over 1f out: disp early fnl f: kpt on wl u.p: led on line* **25/1**

2 *shd* **Toraidhe (IRE)**[140] 7262 5-9-10 93 ...... KJManning 14 — 98
(J S Bolger, Ire) *a.p: cl up 3rd 1/2-way: disp and drvn along fr over 2f out: kpt on wl u.p fnl f: jst failed* **12/1**

3 *hd* **Kyllachy Star**[134] 7348 5-9-6 94 ...... LeeTopliss(5) 12 — 99
(Richard Fahey) *mid-div: 7th 1/2-way: rdn 2f out: 5th 1f out: kpt on wl u.p ins fnl f* **12/1**

4 *1/2* **Rory Anna (IRE)**[28] 4033 5-8-9 78 ...... CDHayes 13 — 82
(John J Walsh, Ire) *in rr of mid-div: drvn along on stands' side over 2f out: 8th over 1f out: kpt on wl u.p fnl f wout rching ldrs* **11/1**

5 *3/4* **Money Trader (IRE)**[114] 7586 4-8-13 82 ...... WMLordan 4 — 84
(J T Gorman, Ire) *in rr of mid-div: wnt 5th on far side 2f out: chal over 1f out: no imp and kpt on same pce u.p ins fnl f* **33/1**

6 nk **Gimli's Rock (IRE)**29 6971 5-9-7 90....(b) FMBerry 10 91
(Mrs John Harrington, Ire) *prom: disp ld 1/2-way: drvn along and hdd over 2f out: sn lost pl and dropped to 9th 1f out: rallied wl ins fnl f* **15/2**3

7 1 **The Fifth Member (IRE)**103 7735 7-9-6 89.... StephenCraine 3 88
(Jim Boyle) *prom: disp ld 1/2-way: hdd over 1f out: sn no ex* **14/1**

8 1 1/4 **Hawkhill (IRE)**66 7262 5-9-0 86....(p) GFCarroll(3) 11 82
(M Halford, Ire) *in rr of mid-div: 11th 1/2-way: kpt on one pce u.p fr over 1f out wout threatening* **16/1**

9 1 1/4 **Blue Moon**22 703 4-8-11 80.... NeilCallan 1 73
(Kevin Ryan) *trckd ldrs: 5th 1/2-way: drvn along in 6th over 1f out: no imp ins fnl f* **12/1**

10 7 **Photo Opportunity**197 5774 4-9-8 91.... PJSmullen 9 68
(D K Weld, Ire) *trckd ldrs: 6th 1/2-way: rdn and no ex fr over 1f out* **5/2**1

11 4 1/2 **Osirixamix (IRE)**21 5708 8-8-4 73.... DJMoran 6 40
(A J Martin, Ire) *hld up towards rr: no imp fr 2f out* **20/1**

12 2 1/2 **Blue Ridge Lane (IRE)**147 7567 5-8-4 80....(bt) CPHoban(7) 2 41
(John C McConnell, Ire) *a towards rr* **33/1**

13 3 **Our Joe Mac (IRE)**183 6180 4-9-11 94.... PaulHanagan 15 48
(Richard Fahey) *mid-div: 9th 1/2-way: no ex fr 2f out* **3/1**2

14 1 1/2 **Steed**31 572 4-9-5 88....(p) PhillipMakin 8 39
(Kevin Ryan) *a towards rr* **11/1**

1m 50.93s (4.93) **Going Correction** +0.70s/f (Yiel) **14** Ran SP% **132.1**
Speed ratings: **103,102,102,102,101 101,100,98,97,90 86,83,80,79**
CSF £316.02 CT £2282.50 TOTE £27.00: £5.10, £4.40, £4.00; DF 234.50.
Owner Cian McAuliffe **Bred** Windflower Overseas **Trained** Croom, Co Limerick
■ Stewards' Enquiry : C D Hayes three-day ban: improper and excessive use of the whip (Apr 3,5,8)

FOCUS
After Big Robert at 33-1 last year bookmakers got another result this time with a 25-1 chance successful.

NOTEBOOK
Drombeg Dawn(IRE)'s final two starts last season blotted her race record, but she had seldom run a bad race until then and enjoyed a profitable spell as a three-year-old in 2009. She had shown the ability to run well when fresh, and this was an important factor as she dug deep to prevail in a tight finish to the first big handicap of the season, a good result for the handicapper with the first six covered by less than two lengths.
Toraidhe(IRE), who failed to win again after a C&D maiden success on the corresponding day last season, put in a spirited effort and was only just touched off after running prominently throughout. (op 20/1)
Kyllachy Star, the Fahey second string, finished well to take third place. (op 16/1)
Rory Anna(IRE) had the advantage of race-fitness after a spell over hurdles. (op 12/1)
Money Trader(IRE) started last season with a second in the Madrid Handicap on this card and was a long-priced winner over this trip at Leopardstown last June. He climbed a bit high in the ratings thereafter, but was back on a competitive mark here.
Gimli's Rock(IRE), last of three behind Dunguib in the Red Mills Trial Hurdle at Gowran, is an effective dual-purpose performer. He ran a good race over a trip short of his best here and on ground that might have been expected to be a bit slow for him, finding a second wind after looking in difficulties over a furlong out. He won the October Handicap over 1m4f at Naas last season, so it was not surprising that he was tapped for speed before renewing his effort late. (op 8/1 tchd 7/1)
Photo Opportunity was a well-supported favourite, but failed to run to expectations. The lightly raced half-brother to the talented Famous Name won on quickish ground at Killarney last August and the going may not have suited him. (op 9/4 tchd 2/1)
Osirixamix(IRE) Official explanation: vet said gelding was found to have low grade blood and mucus following an endoscopic examination post-race
Our Joe Mac(IRE) had ground conditions to suit but was disappointing. (op 10/3 tchd 7/2)

922 - 927a (Foreign Racing) - See Raceform Interactive

911 WOLVERHAMPTON (A.W) (L-H)
Monday, March 21

OFFICIAL GOING: Standard
Wind: nil Weather: fine

928 SPONSOR A RACE BY CALLING 01902 390000 H'CAP 5f 216y(P)
2:20 (2:21) (Class 6) (0-65,63) 4-Y-0+ **£1,535** (£453; £226) **Stalls** Low

Form RPR

30-0 1 **Powerful Pierre**29 625 4-9-0 **61**....(v) LeeTopliss(5) 6 68
(Ian McInnes) *in tch on inner: hdwy 2f out: rdn over 1f out: kpt on wl to ld fnl 50yds* **6/1**2

50-5 2 hd **Espy**24 683 6-9-1 **57**.... PJMcDonald 7 63
(Ian McInnes) *dwlt: hld up: gd hdwy over 1f out: rdn and ev ch ins fnl f: kpt on* **10/1**3

6043 3 1/2 **Athaakeel (IRE)**18 746 5-9-5 **61**....(b) LukeMorris 10 66
(Ronald Harris) *in tch: gd hdwy over 2f out: rdn to ld over 1f out: edgd lft and hdd fnl 50yds* **10/1**3

0500 4 1 1/2 **Aviso (GER)**12 806 7-9-7 **63**.... CathyGannon 4 63+
(David Evans) *dwlt: in rr: pushed along over 3f out: kpt on strly ins fnl f: nrst fin* **12/1**

-450 5 1 1/2 **Beckermet (IRE)**13 798 9-8-12 **57**.... JamesSullivan(3) 11 52
(Ruth Carr) *w ldr: rdn 2f out: one pce* **20/1**

-051 6 shd **Cape Of Storms**27 641 8-9-7 **63**....(b) TomEaves 2 58
(Roy Brotherton) *led: rdn whn hdd over 1f out: wknd ins fnl f* **12/1**

20-4 7 1/2 **Mrs Boss**14 792 4-9-7 **63**.... JamesMillman 12 56
(Rod Millman) *hld up on outer: rdn over 2f out: nvr threatened* **12/1**

-516 8 nk **Lethal**24 696 8-8-13 **55**.... JamesDoyle 9 47
(Richard Price) *chsd ldrs: rdn over 2f out: wknd ins fnl f* **20/1**

6-11 9 nk **Welcome Approach**38 512 8-9-5 **61**.... DarryllHolland 1 52
(John Weymes) *hld up: pushed along over 3f out: nvr threatened* **9/2**1

0166 10 3/4 **Downhill Skier (IRE)**2 915 7-9-6 **62**.... EddieAhern 5 51
(Mark Brisbourne) *hld up in midfield: rdn over 2f out: no imp* **9/2**1

30-2 11 8 **Lake Chini (IRE)**38 512 9-9-3 **59**....(b) GrahamGibbons 8 22
(Michael Easterby) *trckd ldrs on inner: rdn over 2f out: wknd over 1f out* **9/2**1

1m 14.28s (-0.72) **Going Correction** -0.05s/f (Stan) 11 Ran SP% **119.6**
Speed ratings (Par 101): **102,101,101,99,97 96,96,95,95,94 83**
toteswingers:1&2 £17.50, 2&3 £19.40, 1&3 £20.80 CSF £65.92 CT £589.26 TOTE £6.60: £1.80, £5.50, £2.00; EX 93.60 Trifecta £297.30 Part won. Pool of £401.77 - 0.20 winning units..
Owner Richard Mustill **Bred** Hedsor Stud **Trained** Catwick, E Yorks

FOCUS
An open-looking sprint handicap and the form is solid but limited.
Aviso(GER) Official explanation: jockey said gelding hung left-handed
Mrs Boss Official explanation: jockey said filly hung right-handed
Welcome Approach Official explanation: jockey said gelding ran flat

929 NAME A RACE TO ENHANCE YOUR BRAND (S) STKS 5f 20y(P)
2:50 (2:50) (Class 6) 3-Y-O **£1,535** (£453; £226) **Stalls** Low

Form RPR

340- 1 **Lord Avon**157 6900 3-9-1 79.... KierenFox(3) 1 79+
(Bill Turner) *w ldr: led wl over 1f out: rdn clr ins fnl f: comf* **5/2**2

136- 2 3 1/2 **Second Encore**129 7424 3-8-13 68.... LiamKeniry 4 61
(J S Moore) *led narrowly: hdd wl over 1f out: kpt on but no ch w wnr* **6/1**

3323 3 1 1/4 **Captain Dimitrios**9 847 3-9-4 69....(v) CathyGannon 6 62
(David Evans) *hld up: rdn and outpcd over 2f out: drvn and kpt on ins fnl f: wnt 3rd fnl strides* **13/8**1

-041 4 nk **Eternal Youth (IRE)**14 787 3-9-4 70....(b) LukeMorris 5 61
(Ronald Harris) *trckd ldng pair: rdn over 2f out: one pce: hung lft ins fnl f and lost 3rd fnl strides* **4/1**3

60-0 5 1 1/2 **Instructress**9 847 3-8-13 57.... EddieAhern 2 50
(Robert Cowell) *trckd ldng pair: rdn over 1f out: one pce* **18/1**

0 6 6 **Fawara**18 741 3-8-7 0.... PJMcDonald 3 23
(Ruth Carr) *hld up: rdn over 2f out: sn wknd* **50/1**

61.41 secs (-0.89) **Going Correction** -0.05s/f (Stan) **6** Ran SP% **108.2**
Speed ratings (Par 96): **105,99,97,96,94 84**
toteswingers:1&2 £2.20, 2&3 £2.00, 1&3 £1.80 CSF £16.09 TOTE £3.30: £4.10, £1.70; EX 12.70.The winner was bought in for 5,500gns.
Owner Mrs M S Teversham **Bred** Mrs Monica Teversham **Trained** Sigwells, Somerset

FOCUS
What had looked a competitive seller produced a facile winner. He looks better than this grade with the third the best guide to the form.

930 GREAT OFFERS AT WOLVERHAMPTON-RACECOURSE.CO.UK MAIDEN STKS 1m 4f 50y(P)
3:20 (3:21) (Class 5) 3-Y-O+ **£1,813** (£539; £269; £134) **Stalls** Low

Form RPR

00- 1 **Birdwatcher (IRE)**131 7385 3-8-5 0.... JoeFanning 4 65
(Mark Johnston) *mde all: chsd along over 3f out: kpt on wl: comf* **9/2**2

00-0 2 5 **The Absent Mare**19 731 3-8-0 45....(t) SilvestreDeSousa 6 52?
(Frank Sheridan) *in tch: hdwy to chse wnr over 2f out: sn rdn: one pce* **33/1**

/30- 3 3 1/2 **Highland Park (IRE)**158 6876 4-9-11 0.... AndreaAtzeni 2 53
(Michael Wigham) *trckd ldng pair: swtchd to outer over 4f out: rdn over 3f out: chsd wnr 2f out: sn drvn and no imp* **4/11**1

5 4 7 **Polarity**27 643 5-9-8 0.... GrahamGibbons 5 37
(James Bethell) *w ldr: rdn over 3f out: wknd over 1f out* **22/1**

540- 5 5 **Bussell Along (IRE)**196 5813 5-9-8 46....(t) CathyGannon 1 29
(Pam Ford) *in tch: rdn over 2f out: sn wknd* **28/1**

6 1 **Green Ensign (IRE)** 4-9-11 0.... JamesDoyle 3 32
(Alan McCabe) *hld up: rdn over 4f out: wknd over 2f out* **16/1**3

2m 40.07s (-1.03) **Going Correction** -0.05s/f (Stan)
WFA 3 from 4yo 22lb 4 from 5yo 2lb **6** Ran SP% **108.1**
Speed ratings (Par 103): **101,97,95,90,87 86**
toteswingers:1&2 £10.80, 2&3 £5.40, 1&3 £1.70 CSF £101.78 TOTE £5.10: £2.00, £11.10; EX 81.20.
Owner Sheikh Hamdan Bin Mohammed Al Maktoum **Bred** Jeremy Gompertz **Trained** Middleham Moor, N Yorks

FOCUS
A weak maiden that produced a surprise winner and the form is very modest.

931 RINGSIDE CONFERENCE SUITE, 700 THEATRE STYLE H'CAP 1m 1f 103y(P)
3:50 (3:50) (Class 5) (0-75,72) 3-Y-O **£1,878** (£558; £279; £139) **Stalls** Low

Form RPR

521 1 **Baharat (IRE)**30 610 3-9-4 **69**....(v) ShaneKelly 5 79
(Jeremy Noseda) *dwlt: trckd ldrs: rdn and hung lft fr over 1f out: chal ins fnl f: led fnl strides* **7/2**1

533- 2 hd **Standout**154 6979 3-9-3 **68**.... JimmyFortune 8 77
(Richard Hannon) *midfield: chsd along 3f out: hdwy on outer 2f out: drvn to chse ldr over 1f out: edgd lft: led narrowly ins fnl f: kpt on but hdd fnl strides* **7/2**1

5-51 3 3 **Tornado Force (IRE)**21 714 3-9-3 **68**.... LukeMorris 1 71
(J S Moore) *trckd ldr: led 2f out: sn rdn: hdd ins fnl f: no ex* **7/2**1

3-42 4 3 1/4 **Irie Ute**60 228 3-8-11 **62**.... LiamKeniry 3 58
(Sylvester Kirk) *in tch on inner: hdwy to chse ldr over 1f out: rdn and wknd ins fnl f* **14/1**

51 5 1 1/4 **Crystal Sky (IRE)**28 634 3-9-1 **66**.... RobertHavlin 6 60
(Andrew Haynes) *hld up: hdwy on outer 3f out: rdn over 2f out: no imp over 1f out* **8/1**3

-162 6 2 1/2 **Aloneinthestreet (USA)**18 738 3-9-7 **72**....(b1) JoeFanning 7 60
(Mark Johnston) *led: rdn whn hdd 2f out: wknd over 1f out* **11/1**

01-2 7 3 1/2 **Snow Trooper**25 668 3-8-11 **62**.... SamHitchcott 4 43
(Dean Ivory) *racd keen in midfield: rdn over 2f out: sn wknd* **11/2**2

0-25 8 4 1/2 **Sir Randolf (IRE)**49 365 3-9-2 **67**....(t) JamesDoyle 2 39
(Sylvester Kirk) *s.i.s: hld up: rdn over 3f out: wknd over 2f out* **28/1**

2m 2.28s (0.58) **Going Correction** -0.05s/f (Stan) **8** Ran SP% **111.6**
Speed ratings (Par 98): **95,94,92,89,88 85,82,78**
toteswingers:1&2 £2.70, 2&3 £3.60, 1&3 £3.70 CSF £14.71 CT £43.46 TOTE £3.30: £1.10, £2.30, £1.30; EX 15.40 Trifecta £54.30 Pool of £479.91 - 6.53 winning units..
Owner Saeed Suhail **Bred** Norelands Bloodstock & Hugo Lascelles **Trained** Newmarket, Suffolk

FOCUS
A tight handicap dominated by the co-favourites. There were steps up from the first two but the form looks sound.

932 WOLVERHAMPTON-RACECOURSE.CO.UK H'CAP 1m 141y(P)
4:20 (4:23) (Class 4) (0-80,80) 4-Y-0+ **£2,914** (£867; £433; £216) **Stalls** Low

Form RPR

0-46 1 **Ahlawy (IRE)**4 877 8-9-7 **80**....(bt) JamesDoyle 1 87
(Frank Sheridan) *trckd ldrs on inner: rdn over 1f out: kpt on ins fnl f: led fnl strides* **11/1**

50-4 2 nk **Just Bond (IRE)**60 235 9-9-7 **80**.... SilvestreDeSousa 4 87
(Geoffrey Oldroyd) *midfield: hdwy and short of room over 1f out: swtchd lft: kpt on wl ins fnl f: wnt 2nd fnl strides* **9/2**3

3-24 3 shd **Elijah Pepper (USA)**35 541 6-9-3 **76**.... GrahamGibbons 5 82
(David Barron) *trckd ldr: led 2f out: sn rdn: edgd rt fr over 1f out: hdd fnl strides* **11/8**1

/20- 4 2 1/4 **Gracious Melange**229 4699 4-9-7 **80**.... AdamKirby 8 81
(Marco Botti) *midfield: hdwy on outer over 2f out: rdn to chse ldr over 1f out: one pce* **7/2**2

000- 5 nse **Desert Auction (IRE)**273 3271 4-9-6 **79**.... GeorgeBaker 3 80
(Dean Ivory) *hld up: rdn over 1f out: kpt on ins fnl f* **16/1**

60-6 **6** *nk* **Dubai Dynamo**[13] 799 6-9-7 **80** .... PJMcDonald 6 81
(Ruth Carr) *sn settled into midfield: rdn over 2f out: one pce* **14/1**

050- **7** *5* **Legal Eagle (IRE)**[143] 7212 6-9-5 **78** .... FrannyNorton 7 68
(Paul Green) *racd keenly: hld up: n.d* **22/1**

040- **8** *hd* **Handsome Falcon**[251] 3973 7-9-2 **75** .... BarryMcHugh 2 65
(Ollie Pears) *sn led: rdn whn hdd 2f out: sn wknd* **16/1**

1m 49.74s (-0.76) **Going Correction** -0.05s/f (Stan) **8** Ran SP% **113.6**
Speed ratings (Par 105): **101,100,100,98,98 98,93,93**
toteswingers:1&2 £6.40, 2&3 £2.00, 1&3 £3.30 CSF £58.96 CT £112.92 TOTE £13.80: £2.70, £1.50, £1.10; EX 44.50 Trifecta £262.40 Part won. Pool of £354.61 - 0.70 winning units..
Owner Frank Sheridan **Bred** Castlemartin Stud And Skymarc Farm **Trained** Wolverhampton, W Midlands

FOCUS
A fair handicap with the majority closely matched and the form best rated around the placed horses.

933 WOLVERHAMPTON HOSPITALITY - A PLEASURE H'CAP 7f 32y(P)

4:50 (4:56) (Class 6) (0-60,60) 4-Y-O+ **£1,535** (£453; £226) **Stalls** High

Form RPR

3034 **1** **Collect Art (IRE)**[28] 633 4-9-7 **60** .... StevieDonohoe 10 72
(Andrew Haynes) *mde most: rdn 2f out: drvn over 1f out: kpt on wl ins fnl f* **9/1**

3302 **2** *3/4* **Meydan Style (USA)**[13] 793 5-8-7 **46** .... JoeFanning 7 56
(Bruce Hellier) *chsd wnr: drvn over 1f out: kpt on* **16/1**

-335 **3** *3/4* **El Libertador (USA)**[39] 489 5-9-1 **57** .... (b) KierenFox(3) 5 65
(Jeremy Gask) *dwlt: hld up: rdn over 1f out: kpt on wl ins fnl f: nrst fin* **3/1**[1]

1125 **4** *1/2* **Piccolo Express**[28] 637 5-9-6 **59** .... J-PGuillambert 2 67
(Brian Baugh) *midfield on inner: rdn 2f out: kpt on ins fnl f* **4/1**[2]

1145 **5** *1/2* **Polemica (IRE)**[4] 880 5-9-4 **57** .... (bt) JamesDoyle 6 62
(Frank Sheridan) *in tch on outer: hdwy to chse ldng pair over 1f out: no ex ins fnl f* **7/1**

0205 **6** *1/2* **Charles Darwin (IRE)**[3] 893 8-9-2 **55** .... (p) LiamKeniry 4 59
(Michael Blanshard) *hld up in midfield: swtchd to outer over 1f out: sn rdn: kpt on ins fnl f* **20/1**

020 **7** *1 1/4* **French Art**[39] 489 6-9-7 **60** .... (p) EddieAhern 1 61
(Nigel Tinkler) *trckd ldrs: rdn over 2f out: drvn over 1f out: wknd fnl 100yds* **9/1**

-036 **8** *3/4* **Just Timmy Marcus**[28] 637 5-9-7 **60** .... (b) GrahamGibbons 8 61
(Brian Baugh) *s.i.s: hld up: n.d* **9/2**[3]

0146 **9** *1 1/4* **Bold Bomber**[18] 752 5-8-8 **47** .... (p) SilvestreDeSousa 11 42
(Paul Green) *hld up: drvn over 1f out: n.d* **16/1**

-100 **10** *1 1/2* **Almaty Express**[19] 735 9-9-3 **56** .... (b) DarryllHolland 3 49
(John Weymes) *t.k.h early: trckd ldrs: rdn 3f out: wknd over 1f out* **25/1**

1m 29.13s (-0.47) **Going Correction** -0.05s/f (Stan) **10** Ran SP% **116.1**
Speed ratings (Par 101): **100,99,98,97,97 96,95,94,92,91**
toteswingers:1&2 £9.90, 2&3 £17.10, 1&3 £7.80 CSF £141.40 CT £535.29 TOTE £11.50: £5.60, £8.70, £1.50; EX 101.10 TRIFECTA Not won..
Owner Miss C Berry **Bred** Pier House Stud **Trained** Limpley Stoke, Bath

FOCUS
Just a modest contest but straightforward form rated around the first four.

934 DINE IN HORIZONS H'CAP 5f 20y(P)

5:20 (5:23) (Class 6) (0-65,64) 4-Y-O+ **£1,535** (£453; £226) **Stalls** Low

Form RPR

2112 **1** **Straboe (USA)**[10] 833 5-9-7 **64** .... (v) WilliamCarson 10 74
(Stuart Williams) *chsd ldrs: rdn over 2f out: hdwy over 1f out: led ins fnl f: kpt on wl* **9/4**[1]

0534 **2** *1 3/4* **The Tatling (IRE)**[6] 857 14-9-3 **60** .... RichardKingscote 8 64
(Milton Bradley) *hld up: rdn over 2f out: hdwy over 1f out: kpt on wl ins fnl f: wnt 2nd fnl strides* **7/1**[3]

3043 **3** *1/2* **Decider (USA)**[19] 732 8-9-6 **63** .... (b) LukeMorris 7 65
(Ronald Harris) *led after 1f: rdn over 1f out: hdd ins fnl f: lost 2nd fnl strides* **10/1**

3145 **4** *3/4* **Steel City Boy (IRE)**[12] 812 8-8-12 **55** .... (p) JoeFanning 12 55
(Derek Shaw) *midfield on outer: rdn over 2f out: hdwy over 1f out: kpt on ins fnl f* **16/1**

401 **5** *1 1/4* **Triskaidekaphobia**[12] 812 8-9-0 **57** .... (t) FrankieMcDonald 4 52
(Paul Fitzsimons) *led for 1f: remained prom: rdn 2f out: wknd ins fnl f* **16/1**

-361 **6** *3/4* **Sally's Swansong**[19] 735 5-8-7 **50** oh1 .... (b) GrahamGibbons 5 42
(Eric Alston) *midfield: rdn over 2f out: kpt on* **7/1**[3]

063 **7** *1* **Francis Albert**[3] 892 5-8-0 **50** oh3 .... (be) JosephYoung(7) 1 39
(Michael Mullineaux) *t.k.h early: midfield on inner: rdn 2f out: kpt on* **8/1**

56-5 **8** *1 1/4* **Rio's Girl**[19] 735 4-8-12 **58** .... AmyRyan(3) 9 42+
(Kevin Ryan) *chsd ldrs: rdn over 2 out: wknd ins fnl f* **11/2**[2]

50-6 **9** *2* **Macie (IRE)**[21] 709 4-8-7 **50** .... RobbieFitzpatrick 11 27
(Derek Shaw) *s.i.s: hld up: n.d* **40/1**

220- **10** *3* **Madam Isshe**[171] 6536 4-9-1 **58** .... TomMcLaughlin 3 24
(Malcolm Saunders) *trckd ldrs: short of room and lost pl over 3f out: rdn over 2f out: sn wknd* **20/1**

0600 **11** *2 3/4* **Prince James**[10] 833 4-9-4 **64** .... JamesSullivan(3) 6 20
(Michael Easterby) *a outpcd in rr* **20/1**

-150 **12** *1* **Spic 'n Span**[41] 453 6-9-5 **62** .... (b) ChrisCatlin 2 15
(Ronald Harris) *rrd bdly s: a towards rr* **28/1**

61.52 secs (-0.78) **Going Correction** -0.05s/f (Stan) **12** Ran SP% **118.5**
Speed ratings (Par 101): **104,101,100,99,97 96,94,92,89,84 80,78**
toteswingers:1&2 £4.30, 2&3 £11.20, 1&3 £5.40 CSF £16.72 CT £134.40 TOTE £2.30: £1.10, £3.40, £5.30; EX 25.90 Trifecta £253.60 Pool of £521.10 - 1.52 winning units..
Owner Brigid & Damian Hennessy-Bourke **Bred** Darley **Trained** Newmarket, Suffolk
■ Stewards' Enquiry : William Carson three-day ban: careless riding (Apr 4-6)
Graham Gibbons three-day ban: weighed-in 2lb heavy (Apr 4-6)

FOCUS
A low-grade sprint handicap run at a strong gallop with the runner-up in good form and a fair guide.
Madam Isshe Official explanation: jockey said filly suffered interference early
Prince James Official explanation: jockey said colt suffered interference early
Spic 'n Span Official explanation: jockey said gelding fly-leapt on leaving stalls
T/Plt: £866.30 to a £1 stake. Pool of £58,292.65 - 49.12 winning tickets. T/Qpdt: £34.60 to a £1 stake. Pool of £5,412.75 - 115.60 winning tickets. AS

COMPIEGNE (L-H)

Monday, March 21

OFFICIAL GOING: Turf: heavy

935a PRIX D'AIGUISY (CLAIMER) (5YO+) (LADY RIDERS) (TURF) 1m

3:55 (12:00) 5-Y-O+ **£6,465** (£2,586; £1,939; £1,293; £646)

RPR

1 **Jack Junior (USA)**[49] 372 7-8-11 0 .... (p) MlleNathalieDesoutter 1 69
(C Boutin, France) **41/10**[2]

2 *4* **Moody Tunes**[135] 7352 8-9-2 0 .... KellyHarrison 4 64
(Mrs K Burke) *shared ld tl rdn early in st: led 2f out: wandered off st line: surrendered ld 1f out: dropped to 3rd 100yds out: r.o again u.p to regain 2nd on line* **38/1**

3 *snk* **Solaria (FR)**[9] 5-8-8 0 ow1 .... PaulineProd'homme(6) 3 62
(Mlle V Dissaux, France) *fin 4th: promoted to 3rd* **16/1**

4 *1 1/2* **Nakaling (FR)**[72] 8-8-11 0 .... (p) CarlaO'Halloran 8 59
(E Danel, France) *fin 3rd: disqualified and plcd 4th* **25/1**

5 *1 1/2* **Rendelsham (FR)**[123] 7500 8-8-11 0 .... CelineLaunay 5 52
(J-P Gallorini, France) **8/1**

6 *2 1/2* **Atlantico (SPA)**[517] 6-8-10 0 .... (b) ManonScandella(6) 9 51
(Y Durepaire, Spain) **33/10**[1]

7 *1/2* **Indran (FR)**[111] 6-9-6 0 .... (b) DelphineSantiago 6 54
(B Dutruel, France) **11/1**

8 *1* **Mikos (FR)**[9] 11-8-11 0 .... NadegeOuakli 12 43
(Robert Collet, France) **13/1**

9 *1* **Criticize (USA)**[8] 5-9-2 0 .... SabrinaWandt 2 46
(C Von Der Recke, Germany) **13/2**[3]

10 *3* **De Zephyr (FR)**[11] 9-8-8 0 .... EmilieDorigny(8) 11 39
(Robert Collet, France) **13/1**

0 **Un Amor (FR)**[185] 10-8-11 0 .... MlleAnnelieAckermann 10 —
(D De Waele, France) **62/1**

0 **Farlino (FR)**[11] 7-9-2 0 .... (b) SandrineHouben 13 —
(J-P Delaporte, France) **83/10**

0 **Speed Oway** 5-8-6 0 .... MllePaolaBeacco(5) 7 —
(D Cros, France) **84/1**

1m 42.64s (102.64) **13** Ran SP% **115.7**
WIN (incl. 1 euro stake): 5.10. PLACES: 2.20, 7.70, 4.60. DF: 74.10. SF: 96.80.
Owner M-B Rougier & R Marot **Bred** Marablue Farm **Trained** France

868 SOUTHWELL (L-H)

Tuesday, March 22

OFFICIAL GOING: Standard
Wind: almost nil Weather: fine

936 LADBROKES.COM H'CAP 6f (F)

2:20 (2:20) (Class 5) (0-70,66) 3-Y-O **£1,813** (£539; £269; £134) **Stalls** Low

Form RPR

24-1 **1** **Take Your Partner**[26] 669 3-9-7 **66** .... (b) PhillipMakin 3 83+
(Kevin Ryan) *trckd ldr: led over 2f out: clr over 1f out: eased towards fin* **5/2**[2]

2141 **2** *4 1/2* **Ridgeway Hawk**[19] 745 3-8-13 **58** .... (v) RobertHavlin 1 58
(Mark Usher) *trckd ldrs: swtchd outside 3f out: chsd wnr over 1f out: no imp* **9/4**[1]

-434 **3** *3 1/4* **These Dreams**[19] 745 3-8-8 **53** .... PaulHanagan 6 43
(Richard Guest) *hld up: effrt over 2f out: hung rt over 1f out: kpt on to take n.d 3rd last 100yds* **11/1**

03-4 **4** *1 1/2* **Speedy Joe**[78] 20 3-9-5 **64** .... TomEaves 2 50
(Bryan Smart) *led tl over 2f out: wknd ins fnl f* **8/1**

6-02 **5** *9* **Elusive Love (IRE)**[27] 653 3-9-1 **60** .... JoeFanning 4 19
(Mark Johnston) *stdd s: hld up: effrt over 2f out: sn wknd* **11/2**[3]

6634 **6** *2* **Pineapple Pete (IRE)**[10] 847 3-8-10 **62** .... (t) NoraLooby(7) 7 15
(Alan McCabe) *in rr: effrt over 3f out: hung lft over 1f out: nvr a factor* **9/1**

2644 **7** *14* **Hereselle (IRE)**[3] 913 3-8-8 **58** .... JamesRogers(5) 5 —
(Michael Chapman) *drvn along to chse ldrs: lost pl over 2f out: sn bhd* **18/1**

1m 16.08s (-0.42) **Going Correction** -0.075s/f (Stan) **7** Ran SP% **109.4**
Speed ratings (Par 98): **99,93,88,86,74 72,53**
toteswingers: 1&2 £1.70, 1&3 £4.30, 2&3 £4.20 CSF £7.75 TOTE £3.90: £2.80, £1.90; EX 8.90.
Owner Guy Reed **Bred** G Reed **Trained** Hambleton, N Yorks

FOCUS
An uncompetitive handicap won easily but the race is rated negatively through the runner-up.

937 GOT THE FEELING, GET TO LADBROKES MEDIAN AUCTION MAIDEN STKS 1m (F)

2:55 (2:56) (Class 6) 3-5-Y-O **£1,535** (£453; £226) **Stalls** Low

Form RPR

6 **1** **Absolute Princess**[22] 714 3-8-1 0 .... BillyCray(3) 4 74+
(David Nicholls) *mde all: drvn clr over 1f out: eased towards fin* **33/1**

35-3 **2** *5* **X Rated**[10] 850 3-8-9 71 .... JamesDoyle 7 67
(Alan McCabe) *trckd ldrs: wnt 2nd over 2f out: no ch w wnr* **9/2**

22 **3** *2 1/2* **Kishanda**[49] 378 3-8-4 0 .... HayleyTurner 5 58
(Hughie Morrison) *hld up in rr: drvn over 3f out: kpt on to take n.d 3rd last 100yds* **5/4**[1]

4 *5* **Long Live Love (USA)** 3-8-9 0 .... JoeFanning 2 51
(Mark Johnston) *dwlt: sn trcking ldrs: hung lft over 2f out: wknd over 1f out* **7/2**[2]

00-0 **5** *12* **Ochilview Warrior (IRE)**[14] 800 4-9-12 43 .... (b) LeeNewman 1 29
(Robin Bastiman) *mid-div: lost pl over 3f out: sn bhd* **100/1**

6 *1/2* **Excuse Me** 3-8-9 0 .... PJMcDonald 6 23
(Alan Swinbank) *dwlt: sn chsng ldrs: hung lft and wknd over 2f out* **4/1**[3]

000- **7** *nk* **Mistress Shy**[202] 5658 4-9-7 37 .... PaulHanagan 3 22
(Robin Dickin) *trckd ldrs: lost pl and hmpd 3f out: sn bhd* **66/1**

8 *12* **Nha Trang (IRE)** 4-9-12 0 .... SilvestreDeSousa 8 —
(Deborah Sanderson) *lost pl after 1f: swtchd wd after 2f: bhd 3f out: t.o* **25/1**

1m 43.02s (-0.68) **Going Correction** -0.075s/f (Stan)
WFA 3 from 4yo 17lb **8** Ran SP% **114.1**
Speed ratings (Par 101): **100,95,92,87,75 75,74,62**
toteswingers:1&2: £10.10, 2&3: £2.00, 1&3: £5.20 CSF £171.29 TOTE £47.10: £8.30, £1.40, £1.02; EX 166.20 Trifecta £623.00 Part won. Pool of £842.00 - 0.60 winning units..

Owner Paul J Dixon **Bred** Mrs Yvette Dixon **Trained** Sessay, N Yorks
FOCUS
The winner was a big improver but a few of the likelier types disappointed, while the 71-rated runner-up didn't convince that he was at his best and the form looks ordinary.
Excuse Me Official explanation: trainer's representative said the gelding had a breathing problem

938 LADBROKES MOBILE H'CAP 1m 3f (F)
3:30 (3:30) (Class 5) (0-75,69) 4-Y-0+ **£1,813** (£539; £269; £134) **Stalls** Low

Form RPR
0631 **1** **Beau Fighter**[7] 859 6-8-11 **59**....(p) FergusSweeney 3 70
(Gary Moore) *hld up wl in tch: hdwy to trck ldrs over 4f out: wnt cl 2nd over 2f out: narrow ld over 1f out: kpt on wl towards fin* **10/11**[1]
5012 **2** *1* **Kingaroo (IRE)**[7] 858 5-8-7 **58**.... BillyCray(3) 1 67
(Garry Woodward) *led: jnd over 3f out: narrowly hdd over 1f out: kpt on same pce last 150yds* **4/1**[2]
0-20 **3** *8* **Trachonitis (IRE)**[30] 621 7-9-7 **69**.... PaulHanagan 5 66
(J R Jenkins) *hld up in last: hdwy over 4f out: kpt on down wd outside to take modest 3rd jst ins fnl f* **5/1**[3]
0-06 **4** *1 1/4* **Maslak (IRE)**[38] 531 7-9-4 **66**.... ChrisCatlin 4 61
(Peter Hiatt) *chsd ldrs: drvn 5f out: outpcd over 3f out: kpt on ins fnl f: tk modest 4th nr fin* **12/1**
3305 **5** *3/4* **Ilie Nastase (FR)**[13] 806 7-9-5 **67**.... HayleyTurner 2 60
(Conor Dore) *trckd ldrs: chal over 3f out: wknd over 1f out* **14/1**
0235 **6** *17* **Yossi (IRE)**[14] 796 7-8-4 **55** oh4....(be) JamesSullivan(3) 6 21
(Richard Guest) *dwlt: in rr: drvn over 6f out: lost pl over 3f out: sn wl bhd* **12/1**

2m 26.35s (-1.65) **Going Correction** -0.075s/f (Stan) **6** Ran SP% **111.1**
Speed ratings (Par 103): **103,102,96,95,95 82**
toteswingers: 1&2 £2.30, 2&3 £1.50, 1&3 £2.30 CSF £4.68 TOTE £2.40: £2.10, £2.90; EX 4.10.
Owner The Hillians **Bred** Mrs P G Kingston **Trained** Lower Beeding, W Sussex
FOCUS
An ordinary handicap and they didn't go that quick but the form looks sound enough.

939 PLAY ROULETTE AT LADBROKES.COM (S) STKS 1m 4f (F)
4:05 (4:05) (Class 6) 4-Y-0+ **£1,535** (£453; £226) **Stalls** Low

Form RPR
-325 **1** **Sir Haydn**[14] 797 11-8-6 48....(v) DannyBrock(7) 7 56
(J R Jenkins) *in rr: hdwy over 7f out: sn chsng ldrs: outpcd over 3f out: hdwy on inner to chal over 1f out: edgd rt: styd on to ld last 100yds* **7/1**
0212 **2** *1* **Kipchak (IRE)**[7] 854 6-9-5 65....(p) HayleyTurner 1 61
(Conor Dore) *swvd rt s: led: t.k.h: rdn and edgd rt 2f out: hdd and no ex last 100yds* **11/4**[1]
2063 **3** *1 1/4* **My Mate Mal**[35] 551 7-8-8 58....(p) LauraPike(5) 8 53
(William Stone) *trckd ldrs: wnt cl 2nd over 2f out: kpt on same pce ins fnl f* **3/1**[2]
4214 **4** *nk* **Eton Fable (IRE)**[14] 797 6-9-5 60....(p) WilliamCarson 5 58
(Colin Teague) *trckd ldrs: t.k.h: drvn over 4f out: kpt on one pce fnl 2f* **3/1**[2]
40-4 **5** *18* **Lucayan Dancer**[7] 854 11-8-13 58.... PaulQuinn 2 25
(David Nicholls) *in rr: hdwy on outside to chse ldrs over 5f out: lost pl over 3f out: sn bhd* **5/1**[3]
000- **6** *3 1/4* **Silken Aunt**[200] 5729 4-8-6 49....(b[1]) JoeFanning 6 15
(Kevin McAuliffe) *shkn up after s: sn trcking ldrs: t.k.h: lost pl over 2f out* **33/1**
00-6 **7** *2* **Cragganmore Creek**[70] 117 8-8-13 33.... ChrisCatlin 3 17
(Dave Morris) *prom early: sn mid-div: reminders 7f out: lost pl over 4f out: sn bhd* **50/1**
0000 **8** *46* **Carlton Mac**[18] 769 6-8-13 26....(p) MichaelStainton 4 —
(Simon Griffiths) *in rr: sn drvn along: lost tch 6f out: sn t.o* **100/1**

2m 40.49s (-0.51) **Going Correction** -0.075s/f (Stan)
WFA 4 from 6yo+ 2lb **8** Ran SP% **111.7**
Speed ratings (Par 101): **98,97,96,96,84 82,80,50**
toteswingers:1&2 £2.60, 2&3 £4.40, 1&3 £6.80 CSF £25.32 TOTE £12.50: £3.90, £2.20, £1.10; EX 30.20 Trifecta £140.60 Pool of £636.93 - 3.35 winning units..There was no bid for the winner.
Owner R.M.G.R. Syndicate **Bred** D Leggate, Miss N Kent & Helshaw Grange Stud **Trained** Royston, Herts
FOCUS
A moderate seller run at a steady pace, resulting in a time nearly five seconds outside standard. The third looks the best guide to the form.

940 SOUTHWELL RACECOURSE FOR CONFERENCES H'CAP 5f (F)
4:40 (4:42) (Class 4) (0-85,77) 3-Y-O **£2,914** (£867; £433; £216) **Stalls** High

Form RPR
1-14 **1** **Even Stevens**[72] 106 3-9-2 **75**.... BillyCray(3) 1 92
(David Nicholls) *mde all: clr over 2f out: edgd lft over 1f out: eased nr fin* **9/4**[2]
15- **2** *9* **Oneladyowner**[290] 2757 3-9-4 **74**.... PhillipMakin 5 59
(David Brown) *gave problems in stalls: dwlt: sn chsng ldrs: kpt on to take modest 2nd over 1f out* **7/2**[3]
-231 **3** *1 1/2* **Mazovian (USA)**[19] 741 3-8-5 **66**.... JamesRogers(5) 6 45
(Michael Chapman) *racd stands' side: sn wl outpcd: hdwy over 1f out: styd on to take n.d 3rd post* **12/1**
1654 **4** *nse* **Liberty Green (IRE)**[5] 875 3-9-5 **75**....(p) JamesDoyle 4 54
(Alan McCabe) *chsd wnr: kpt on same pce appr fnl f* **12/1**
2125 **5** *1 1/2* **Restless Bay (IRE)**[10] 847 3-9-7 **77**....(v) ChrisCatlin 3 51
(Reg Hollinshead) *racd towards far side: sn outpcd: sme hdwy 2f out: nvr a factor* **6/1**
2-61 **U** **Monsieur Jamie**[19] 740 3-9-7 **77**.... GregFairley 2 —
(J R Jenkins) *ducked down in stalls: plunged and uns rdr whn stalls opened* **2/1**[1]

58.16 secs (-1.54) **Going Correction** -0.075s/f (Stan) **6** Ran SP% **116.0**
Speed ratings (Par 100): **109,94,92,92,89** —
toteswingers: 1&2 £3.10, 1&3 £5.70, 2&3 £8.20 CSF £11.07 TOTE £3.60: £1.30, £2.20; EX 13.10.
Owner Paul J Dixon **Bred** Mrs Yvette Dixon **Trained** Sessay, N Yorks
FOCUS
This 3-y-o sprint was severely weakened when the favourite Monsieur Jamie unseated his rider in the stalls. However, it would be unwise to underestimate the performance of the winner, who recorded a time 2.10 seconds faster than the following older-horse Class 6 event.

941 QUEEN MOTHER RESTAURANT H'CAP 5f (F)
5:10 (5:10) (Class 6) (0-55,55) 4-Y-O+ **£1,535** (£453; £226) **Stalls** High

Form RPR
-505 **1** **Lucky Art (USA)**[36] 537 5-8-4 **46**.... JamesSullivan(3) 8 52
(Ruth Carr) *mde all centre: hrd rdn over 1f out: jst hld on* **12/1**
3455 **2** *nse* **Bertbrand**[35] 545 6-8-7 **46** oh1....(b) GregFairley 1 52
(Ian McInnes) *racd far side: chsd ldrs: styd on to chal jst ins fnl f: jst hld* **8/1**[3]
6544 **3** *1/2* **Kheley (IRE)**[3] 912 5-8-8 **52**.... JamesRogers(5) 14 56
(Mark Brisbourne) *racd stands' side: sn in rr: gd hdwy over 1f out: edgd lft: styd on wl towards fin* **5/1**[1]
0355 **4** *3/4* **Simple Rhythm**[6] 874 5-8-13 **55**....(p) MichaelO'Connell(3) 7 57
(John Ryan) *chsd ldrs: edgd lft over 1f out: kpt on same pce* **11/2**[2]
4250 **5** *1 3/4* **Thoughtsofstardom**[13] 812 8-8-6 **50**....(be) DanielleMcCreery(5) 4 45
(Phil McEntee) *chsd ldrs: kpt on same pce over 1f out* **16/1**
-065 **6** *hd* **Cocktail Party (IRE)**[19] 752 5-8-7 **46** oh1....(p) GrahamGibbons 12 40
(James Unett) *mid-div: hdwy 2f out: kpt on: nvr rchd ldrs* **20/1**
00-6 **7** *1/2* **Place The Duchess**[19] 746 5-8-8 **47** oh1 ow1....(v[1]) RobertHavlin 5 40
(Alastair Lidderdale) *towards rr: hdwy 2f out: kpt on ins fnl f* **33/1**
0-00 **8** *2* **Papageno**[36] 537 4-8-11 **50**....(v) PaulHanagan 6 35
(J R Jenkins) *s.i.s: sn chsng ldrs: wknd ins fnl f: eased nr fin* **12/1**
2002 **9** *nk* **Lets Move It**[7] 857 4-9-0 **53**.... RobbieFitzpatrick 9 37
(Derek Shaw) *sn outpcd and in rr: nvr a factor* **8/1**[3]
400- **10** *1 1/4* **Pavement Games**[148] 7131 4-8-10 **49**.... JamesDoyle 13 29
(Richard Guest) *racd stands' side: chsd ldrs: wknd over 1f out* **25/1**
0050 **11** *1/2* **True Red (IRE)**[14] 798 4-8-4 **46** oh1....(b) SophieDoyle(3) 2 24
(Nikki Evans) *chsd ldrs: far side: outpcd 2f out: sn lost pl* **33/1**
5-00 **12** *hd* **The Magic Of Rio**[39] 512 5-8-0 **46** oh1....(v) RPWalsh(7) 3 23
(David Evans) *racd far side: chsd ldrs: outpcd 2f out: sn wknd* **16/1**
4-05 **13** *1/2* **Ronnie Howe**[14] 800 7-8-2 **46** oh1....(b) DeclanCannon(5) 11 22
(Roy Bowring) *chsd ldrs: wknd over 1f out* **5/1**[1]
6026 **14** *1/2* **Head To Head (IRE)**[12] 821 7-8-7 **46**....(bt) SilvestreDeSousa 10 20
(Alan Brown) *dwlt: racd stands' side: a bhd* **10/1**

60.26 secs (0.56) **Going Correction** -0.075s/f (Stan) **14** Ran SP% **121.7**
Speed ratings (Par 101): **92,91,91,89,87 86,86,82,82,80 79,79,78,77**
toteswingers: 1&2 £14.60, 1&3 £18.10, 2&3 £3.80 CSF £101.57 CT £566.04 TOTE £10.70: £5.10, £3.20, £2.20; EX 119.70 Trifecta £343.10 Part won. Pool of £463.69 - 0.61 winning units..
Owner David W Chapman **Bred** Gaines-Gentry Thoroughbreds **Trained** Huby, N Yorks
FOCUS
A moderate, but competitive sprint handicap and the winner did not need to step up much on recent form to score.

942 SOUTHWELL-RACECOURSE.CO.UK APPRENTICE H'CAP 1m (F)
5:40 (5:41) (Class 6) (0-60,60) 3-Y-O **£1,535** (£453; £226) **Stalls** Low

Form RPR
-424 **1** **Goal (IRE)**[6] 873 3-9-4 **57**.... KieranO'Neill 4 65
(David C Griffiths) *s.i.s: hdwy over 4f out: chsd ldrs over 3f out: led over 1f out: kpt on u.p* **6/4**[1]
066- **2** *1 3/4* **Trojan Touch (USA)**[160] 6850 3-8-4 **46** oh1....(b[1]) JamesRogers(3) 7 49
(Chris Dwyer) *gave problems bef s: led: hung rt and hdd over 1f out: styd on same pce* **14/1**
-045 **3** *7* **Kyncraighe (IRE)**[3] 916 3-8-11 **53**....(t) AmyScott(3) 5 41
(Alastair Lidderdale) *hld up in rr: wnt modest 3rd over 2f out: one pce* **7/1**
500 **4** *3 1/4* **Ocean's Dream Day (IRE)**[41] 471 3-9-1 **57**.... RyanPowell(3) 6 38
(John Ryan) *hld up: effrt over 3f out: 4th and one pce whn hung lft and rt over 1f out* **5/2**[2]
-450 **5** *10* **Apple Dumpling**[4] 898 3-8-11 **50**.... RyanClark 3 —
(Stuart Williams) *chsd ldrs: drvn over 3f out: wknd over 2f out* **10/1**
-563 **6** *7* **Surprise (IRE)**[18] 760 3-9-7 **60**....(b[1]) TobyAtkinson 1 —
(Mark Rimmer) *t.k.h: sn trcking ldrs: wknd over 2f out* **13/2**[3]
0-53 **7** *3 1/4* **Littlepromisedland (IRE)**[28] 642 3-8-4 **46** oh1.... NathanAlison(3) 2 —
(Richard Guest) *s.s: a bhd* **16/1**

1m 43.35s (-0.35) **Going Correction** -0.075s/f (Stan) **7** Ran SP% **116.0**
Speed ratings (Par 96): **98,96,89,86,76 69,65**
toteswingers: 1&2 £8.00, 1&3 £3.10, 2&3 £18.80. totesuper7: Win: Not won. Place: £180.40 CSF £24.99 TOTE £1.70: £1.10, £11.90; EX 23.10.
Owner D Kilpatrick W McKay **Bred** A M F Persse **Trained** Bawtry, S Yorks
FOCUS
A seriously uncompetitive handicap, although the winner could rate a little higher.
T/Plt: £23.10 to a £1 stake. Pool of £60,154.92 - 1,897.12 winning tickets. T/Qpdt: £13.50 to a £1 stake. Pool of £4,151.13 - 226.60 winning tickets. WG

861 KEMPTON (A.W) (R-H)
Wednesday, March 23

OFFICIAL GOING: Standard
Wind: Moderate, half behind Weather: Sunny, mild

943 FREE ENTRY FOR BETDAQ MEMBERS H'CAP (DIV I) 1m 2f (P)
5:50 (5:50) (Class 6) (0-60,64) 4-Y-O+ **£1,364** (£403; £201) **Stalls** Low

Form RPR
4-33 **1** **Nolecce**[20] 744 4-9-7 **60**.... PaulHanagan 3 71+
(Richard Guest) *taken down early: t.k.h: trckd ldrs in 6th: prog over 2f out: plld out and decisive move to ld jst over 1f out: rdn out* **9/2**[2]
2553 **2** *1 3/4* **Abigails Angel**[7] 862 4-9-3 **56**....(p) AdamKirby 2 63
(Brett Johnson) *mde most: kicked on over 2f out: hdd jst over 1f out: fought on and clr of rest but readily hld last 150yds* **4/1**[1]
004- **3** *3 3/4* **Market Puzzle (IRE)**[210] 5411 4-8-12 **51**.... GrahamGibbons 6 51
(Mark Brisbourne) *settled in last quartet: prog on inner jst over 2f out: styd on fnl f to take 3rd last stride* **9/1**
2131 **4** *nse* **Grey Boy (GER)**[5] 896 10-9-4 **64** 6ex.... GeorgeDowning(7) 1 63
(Tony Carroll) *t.k.h: trckd ldr 3f: styd prom: rdn in 3rd 2f out: nt qckn over 1f out: lost 3rd last stride* **7/1**
-004 **5** *1 1/4* **Love In The Park**[20] 749 6-9-1 **54**.... LukeMorris 7 51
(Roy Brotherton) *rn in snatches in last pair: struggling over 3f out: prog u.p on inner 2f out: kpt on: n.d* **11/1**
0-30 **6** *1 1/4* **Aine's Delight (IRE)**[35] 553 5-9-2 **55**.... SteveDrowne 10 51
(Andy Turnell) *t.k.h: hld up in last quartet: pushed along over 2f out: nt clr run briefly wl over 1f out: sme late prog: nvr involved* **13/2**[3]
060- **7** *1* **Double Fortune**[278] 3155 4-9-7 **60**.... IanMongan 9 53
(Jamie Poulton) *racd wd in midfield: rdn over 2f out: no prog over 1f out: fdd* **20/1**
0-50 **8** *1 1/2* **Majestueux (USA)**[21] 728 4-9-4 **57**.... CathyGannon 11 47
(Mark Hoad) *prog and prom after 3f: chsd ldr over 5f out: drvn over 2f out: lost 2nd over 1f out: wknd qckly and eased* **16/1**
-442 **9** *2* **Iguacu**[7] 862 7-8-13 **52**....(p) DaneO'Neill 12 38
(George Baker) *s.s: rcvrd to trck ldrs in 5th: rdn 3f out: wknd over 1f out* **9/2**[2]

4060 **10** ½ **Pictures (IRE)**[14] 807 4-8-4 **46** oh1..............................(v[1]) KierenFox(3) 5 31
(John Bridger) *s.s: hld up in last pair: brought wd and effrt bnd 2f out: sn no prog* **25/1**

00-0 **11** ½ **Tt's Dream**[19] 765 4-9-0 **53**.. JamesDoyle 8 37
(Alastair Lidderdale) *chsd ldr after 3f tl over 5f out: wknd qckly wl over 2f out* **33/1**

000/ **12** 2 **Fast Elaine (IRE)**[552] 6034 4-8-7 **46** oh1.......................... DavidProbert 4 26
(Martin Bosley) *chsd ldrs on inner: lost pl u.p 3f out: sn wl in rr* **50/1**

2m 8.84s (0.84) **Going Correction** +0.05s/f (Slow) 12 Ran SP% **119.9**
Speed ratings (Par 101): **98,96,93,93,92 91,90,89,87,87 87,85**
toteswingers: 1&2 £4.00, 1&3 £12.00, 2&3 £6.20 CSF £22.19 CT £158.93 TOTE £6.10: £2.20, £1.40, £6.30; EX 29.10 Trifecta £1020.30 Pool: £ 2,334.81 - 1.69 winning units..
Owner Future Racing (Notts) Limited **Bred** Hedsor Stud **Trained** Stainforth, S Yorks

FOCUS
They went no pace early in this ordinary handicap, and few got into it but the form looks solid rated around the third and fourth.
Majestueux(USA) Official explanation: jockey said gelding lost its action home straight
Iguacu Official explanation: jockey said gelding hung badly right
Pictures(IRE) Official explanation: jockey said filly missed the break

944 FREE ENTRY FOR BETDAQ MEMBERS H'CAP (DIV II) 1m 2f (P)
6:20 (6:22) (Class 6) (0-60,60) 4-Y-0+ **£1,364** (£403; £201) **Stalls** Low

Form RPR
00- **1** **Addikt (IRE)**[179] 6372 6-9-0 **60**.. DavidKenny(7) 6 70+
(Michael Scudamore) *settled in midfield: prog fr 3f out: shuffled along and sustained effrt fr over 1f out to ld ins fnl f: won gng away* **7/2**[1]

-012 **2** 1½ **Duneen Dream (USA)**[23] 712 6-9-4 **57**......................... AndreaAtzeni 1 63
(Nikki Evans) *led: wound up the pce fr over 3f out: drvn over 1f out: hdd and outpcd ins fnl f* **9/2**[2]

0051 **3** 1 **Carr Hall (IRE)**[7] 862 8-9-5 **58** 6ex.................................... LukeMorris 4 62
(Tony Carroll) *trckd ldng pair after 3f: rdn over 2f out: clsd to dispute 2nd briefly 1f out: outpcd* **11/2**[3]

00-5 **4** 2¼ **Animator**[26] 692 6-9-3 **56**.. JimCrowley 7 56
(Martin Hill) *chsd ldr: rdn 3f out: nt qckn wl over 1f out: lost 2nd and wknd 1f out* **8/1**

0060 **5** ½ **Dilys Maud**[14] 809 4-9-1 **54**..(b) RobertHavlin 3 53
(Roger Ingram) *s.s: sn in midfield: shkn up over 2f out: nt qckn wl over 1f out: no imp after* **14/1**

000/ **6** nk **Now**[639] 3209 5-8-13 **52**... JamesMillman 9 52
(Rod Millman) *hld up in last trio: t.k.h and rn into trble more than once on ins: reminder 3f out: last sn after: taken wd wl over 1f out: fin to sme gd effect fnl f* **33/1**

5-60 **7** 1 **Sligo All Star**[47] 425 6-8-7 **46** oh1................................ CathyGannon 11 42
(Thomas McLaughlin, Ire) *awkward s: hld up in last: effrt on outer 3f out: no prog and btn over 1f out* **33/1**

-050 **8** ½ **Vinces**[61] 247 7-9-0 **53**... J-PGuillambert 2 48
(Tim McCarthy) *prom: rdn in 4th wl over 2f out: wknd over 1f out* **20/1**

5-30 **9** ½ **Hecton Lad (USA)**[19] 773 4-8-8 **47**............................... SteveDrowne 5 42
(John Best) *t.k.h early: hld up towards rr: lost pl and in last pair wl over 2f out: reminders over 1f out: keeping on nr fin* **7/1**

0613 **10** hd **Petomic (IRE)**[26] 692 6-9-4 **60**................................. JamesSullivan(3) 8 54
(Richard Guest) *hld up in last trio: effrt and sme prog fr 3f out: no hdwy 2f out: wknd* **7/1**

200- **11** 14 **Shoot The Pot (IRE)**[123] 7531 4-8-11 **55**................. DeclanCannon(5) 10 23
(John Mackie) *chsd ldrs tl wknd rapidly 3f out: t.o* **14/1**

2m 7.75s (-0.25) **Going Correction** +0.05s/f (Slow) 11 Ran SP% **115.9**
Speed ratings (Par 101): **103,101,101,99,98 98,97,97,96,96 85**
toteswingers: 1&2 £3.00, 1&3 £7.30, 2&3 £2.00 CSF £18.05 CT £82.97 TOTE £6.00: £2.10, £1.90, £1.80; EX 26.00 Trifecta £147.30 Pool: £3,446.53 - 17.30 winning units..
Owner Good Breed Limited **Bred** Deerpark Stud **Trained** Bromsash, Herefordshire

FOCUS
The second division of this moderate handicap and run faster than the first. The form looks straightforward rated through the second.
Dilys Maud Official explanation: jockey said filly hung right
Hecton Lad(USA) Official explanation: jockey said gelding hung right on bend

945 BETDAQ.COM EXCHANGE PRICE MULTIPLES MEDIAN AUCTION MAIDEN STKS 1m 2f (P)
6:50 (6:51) (Class 5) 3-5-Y-0 **£2,047** (£604; £302) **Stalls** Low

Form RPR
036- **1** **Futurism**[193] 5969 3-8-8 64.. DaneO'Neill 7 71+
(Richard Hannon) *mde all: set stdy pce tl 3f out: booted clr fr 2f out: in n.d after: eased last 75yds* **9/2**[3]

-553 **2** 5 **Moresweets 'n Lace**[28] 647 4-9-9 63............................... GeorgeBaker 1 59
(Gary Moore) *trckd ldng pair: wnt 2nd 3f out: rdn and lft bhd by wnr fnl 2f* **6/1**

60 **3** ½ **Roe Valley (IRE)**[28] 649 4-10-0 0... IanMongan 3 63?
(Linda Jewell) *stdd s: hld up in last pair: prog 3f out: chsd ldng pair over 2f out: one pce and no ch over 1f out* **100/1**

5- **4** 1½ **Tropical Beat**[143] 7248 3-8-8 0... NickyMackay 2 57+
(John Gosden) *tk fierce hold and hld up in 4th: lost pl over 3f out: racd awkwardly over 2f out: sn no ch* **11/8**[1]

3 **5** 3 **Peachez**[14] 801 3-8-3 0..(b) AndreaAtzeni 6 46
(Marco Botti) *s.s: hld up in last pair: outpcd over 2f out: kpt on same pce fnl f* **3/1**[2]

2 **6** 9 **Silk Lingerie**[21] 737 3-8-3 0.. LukeMorris 4 28
(Mandy Rowland) *hld up in 5th: prog to dispute 2nd briefly 3f out: sn rdn: wknd 2f out: bhd after* **14/1**

7 37 **Sevivon**[26] 4-9-6 0.. PatrickHills(3) 5 —
(J W Hills) *t.k.h: chsd wnr to 3f out: wknd v rapidly: wl t.o and virtually p.u* **40/1**

2m 9.88s (1.88) **Going Correction** +0.05s/f (Slow)
WFA 3 from 4yo 20lb 7 Ran SP% **109.7**
Speed ratings (Par 103): **94,90,89,88,86 78,49**
toteswingers: 1&2 £3.00, 1&3 £13.90, 2&3 £16.70 CSF £28.49 TOTE £6.40: £3.30, £4.30; EX 41.30.
Owner Longview Stud & Bloodstock Ltd **Bred** Wyck Hall Stud Ltd **Trained** East Everleigh, Wilts

FOCUS
A modest maiden lacking early pace and best rated through the runner-up.
Tropical Beat Official explanation: jockey said colt ran too free

946 LAY BACK AND WIN AT BETDAQ.COM H'CAP 5f (P)
7:20 (7:20) (Class 5) (0-75,75) 4-Y-0+ **£2,047** (£604; £302) **Stalls** Low

Form RPR
-132 **1** **Best Trip (IRE)**[7] 867 4-9-5 **73**.. FrannyNorton 6 82
(Richard Guest) *fast away: mde all: drvn and more than a l clr 1f out: hld on* **7/2**[1]

4451 **2** ½ **Kylladdie**[12] 833 4-9-3 **71**...(b) PaulHanagan 3 78
(Steve Gollings) *hld up in 5th: plld out and effrt over 1f out: r.o fnl f: tk 2nd last strides: nt quite rch wnr* **7/2**[1]

1322 **3** nk **Desert Strike**[7] 861 5-9-6 **74**...(p) NeilCallan 1 80
(Alan McCabe) *trckd ldng pair: rdn to chse wnr over 1f out: clsd last 150yds but lost 2nd fnl strides* **7/2**[1]

0060 **4** ¾ **Absa Lutte (IRE)**[6] 880 8-8-13 **67**..................................(bt[1]) TomEaves 5 70
(Michael Mullineaux) *sltly awkward s: hld up last: effrt on inner over 1f out: styd on to take 4th wl ins fnl f: unable to land a blow* **10/1**

1364 **5** hd **Italian Tom (IRE)**[16] 786 4-9-3 **71**................................... LukeMorris 2 74
(Ronald Harris) *chsd ldng trio: rdn 2f out: wnt 3rd over 1f out: no imp ins fnl f: lost two pls nr fin* **8/1**[3]

04-2 **6** 5 **Boragh Jamal (IRE)**[21] 725 4-8-11 **65**..........................(b) ShaneKelly 8 50
(Brian Meehan) *s.i.s: a in last pair: rdn and struggling wl over 1f out* **4/1**[2]

-310 **7** 2 **Bookiesindex Boy**[15] 794 7-9-7 **75**..........................(b) StephenCraine 7 53
(J R Jenkins) *trckd wnr: gng wl enough 2f out: wknd rapidly over 1f out* **16/1**

59.53 secs (-0.97) **Going Correction** +0.05s/f (Slow) 7 Ran SP% **112.8**
Speed ratings (Par 103): **109,108,107,106,106 98,95**
toteswingers: 1&2 £1.80, 1&3 £2.40, 2&3 £1.80 CSF £15.46 CT £44.32 TOTE £4.40: £2.30, £2.40; EX 18.50 Trifecta £58.40 Pool: £5,015.84 - 63.49 winning units..
Owner P J Duffen & P Brown **Bred** Limetree Stud **Trained** Stainforth, S Yorks

FOCUS
A competitive little sprint on paper and the form looks reliable if limited.

947 RACING AT SKYSPORTS.COM H'CAP 6f (P)
7:50 (7:52) (Class 6) (0-60,60) 4-Y-0+ **£1,535** (£453; £226) **Stalls** Low

Form RPR
06U- **1** **Boldinor**[201] 5714 8-9-3 **59**.. GeorgeBaker 2 68
(Martin Bosley) *mde all: hrd pressed fr over 1f out: hld on wl fnl f* **14/1**

0421 **2** ½ **Mata Hari Blue**[7] 874 5-9-4 **60** 6ex............................. GrahamGibbons 6 67
(John Holt) *a chsng wnr: drvn and persistent chal fr over 1f out: a jst hld fnl f* **5/2**[1]

2460 **3** ½ **Lord Of The Reins (IRE)**[21] 732 7-9-4 **60**................. PaulMulrennan 1 66
(James Given) *t.k.h on inner: trckd ldng pair: rdn 2f out: tried to chal fr jst over 1f out: nt qckn ins fnl f* **7/1**

-411 **4** ½ **Chantilly Jewel (USA)**[27] 664 6-9-3 **59**.......................(b) JimCrowley 7 63
(Robert Cowell) *t.k.h: hld up towards rr: prog on inner to take 4th wl over 1f out: tried to cl on ldng trio fnl f: nvr getting there in time* **7/2**[2]

525- **5** 1¾ **Durgan**[91] 7960 5-9-4 **60**... SteveDrowne 10 59
(Linda Jewell) *chsd ldng trio tl wl over 1f out: nt qckn and wl hld after* **12/1**

00-0 **6** 1 **Little Perisher**[21] 725 4-9-4 **60**.....................................(p) DarryllHolland 5 56
(Karen George) *awkward to load: t.k.h: hld up in detached last: pushed along fr 2f out: modest late prog* **11/1**

0141 **7** shd **Jonny Ebeneezer**[55] 311 12-9-2 **58**........................(b) StephenCraine 8 53
(David Flood) *taken down early: hld up towards rr: effrt 2f out: one pce and no imp on ldrs* **14/1**

-120 **8** ½ **Young Simon**[40] 512 4-9-3 **59**...(v) DaneO'Neill 9 53
(George Margarson) *hld up towards rr: rdn over 2f out: no imp on ldrs who dominated thrght* **6/1**[3]

000- **9** 3¼ **Wellington Fair**[119] 7556 4-9-3 **59**..................................(b) AdamKirby 3 43
(Tor Sturgis) *taken down early: loaded in stalls wout rdr aboard: chsd ldng quartet to 2f out: wknd u.p over 1f out* **16/1**

1m 13.19s (0.09) **Going Correction** +0.05s/f (Slow) 9 Ran SP% **112.8**
Speed ratings (Par 101): **101,100,99,99,96 95,95,94,90**
toteswingers: 1&2 £14.40, 1&3 £19.20, 2&3 £6.40 CSF £47.98 CT £273.95 TOTE £19.60: £7.00, £1.90, £1.90; EX 77.60 TRIFECTA Not won..
Owner Ron Collins **Bred** Ron Collins **Trained** Chalfont St Giles, Bucks

FOCUS
The pace held up well in this sprint handicap and the form looks straightforward.

948 BETDAQ MOBILE APPS H'CAP 1m 4f (P)
8:20 (8:20) (Class 4) (0-85,83) 4-Y-0+ **£3,399** (£1,011; £505; £252) **Stalls** Centre

Form RPR
2-11 **1** **Sweet Origin**[23] 715 4-9-0 **78**.. AdamKirby 6 88
(Marco Botti) *mde all: stretched on fr 4f out: 4 l clr 2f out: reminders over 1f out: advantage eroded fnl f but only pushed out* **1/1**[1]

3111 **2** 1 **Sir Boss (IRE)**[14] 805 6-9-0 **76**.. TomEaves 2 84
(Michael Mullineaux) *sn hld up in 5th: effrt whn chopped off over 2f out: prog to chse clr wnr over 1f out: clsd the gap fnl f but nvr able to chal* **9/2**[3]

0/0- **3** 2¼ **Blue Spartan (IRE)**[289] 2821 6-8-13 **75**......................... JamesMillman 7 79
(Rod Millman) *hld up in 6th: pushed along over 2f out: stl same pl over 1f out: styd on fnl f to take 3rd last strides* **40/1**

34-4 **4** nk **Russian George (IRE)**[12] 835 5-9-5 **81**........................ PaulHanagan 1 84
(Steve Gollings) *chsd ldng pair: pushed along over 3f out: hrd rdn to dispute 2nd over 2f out to over 1f out: fdd* **4/1**[2]

104- **5** ¾ **Arizona John (IRE)**[131] 7428 6-9-2 **83**..................... DeclanCannon(5) 4 85
(John Mackie) *trckd ldng trio: rdn 3f out: no hdwy 2f out: fdd over 1f out* **14/1**

-153 **6** 1 **Bedouin Bay**[11] 849 4-9-2 **80**.. JamesDoyle 5 81
(Alan McCabe) *sn chsd wnr: pushed along over 3f out: wknd u.p wl over 1f out* **7/1**

26-0 **7** 5 **Clear Sailing**[12] 835 8-9-0 **76**.. StevieDonohoe 3 69
(Noel Quinlan) *awkward s and slowly away: t.k.h: hld up and a last: shkn up and no prog over 2f out* **40/1**

2m 33.95s (-0.55) **Going Correction** +0.05s/f (Slow)
WFA 4 from 5yo+ 2lb 7 Ran SP% **112.2**
Speed ratings (Par 105): **103,102,100,100,100 99,96**
toteswingers: 1&2 £1.10, 1&3 £17.30, 2&3 £18.90 CSF £5.60 TOTE £1.70: £1.10, £1.40; EX 4.20.
Owner Newsells Park Stud **Bred** Newsells Park Stud Limited **Trained** Newmarket, Suffolk

FOCUS
The fourth race in a row on the card to be dominated from the front but the form looks sound with a progressive sort beating the in-form runner-up.

949 SKYSPORTS.COM RACING H'CAP (LONDON MILE QUALIFIER) 1m (P)
8:50 (8:50) (Class 5) (0-75,75) 4-Y-0+ **£2,047** (£604; £302) **Stalls** Low

Form RPR
3021 **1** **Eastern Gift**[19] 765 6-8-11 **65** NeilCallan 7 74
(Gay Kelleway) *hld up in midfield: rdn and prog on outer fr over 2f out: disp ld jst ins fnl f: narrow ld nr fin* **13/2**
04-4 **2** *hd* **Sunshine Always (IRE)**[26] 685 5-8-11 **70** JemmaMarshall(5) 5 78
(Michael Attwater) *led 100yds: styd handy in chsng gp: effrt to cl fr 2f out: disp ld jst ins fnl f: nt qckn nr fin* **5/1**[3]
00-0 **3** *nse* **Mountain Cat (IRE)**[27] 666 7-9-4 **72** JimCrowley 9 80
(William Knight) *prom in chsng gp: wnt 2nd over 3f out: rdn to cl on ldr fr 2f out: disp ld jst ins fnl f: nt qckn nr fin* **7/2**[1]
-612 **4** *1 ¼* **Florio Vincitore (IRE)**[21] 727 4-8-2 **63** (b) JenniferFerguson(7) 12 68
(Edward Creighton) *led after 100yds and sn clr: 8 l ahd 1/2-way: c bk to rivals fr 2f out: hdd jst ins fnl f: kpt on* **14/1**
60-4 **5** *2 ¾* **Edgewater (IRE)**[13] 822 4-9-6 **74** GeorgeBaker 1 73
(John Akehurst) *prom: chsd clr ldr 5f out to over 3f out: styd wl there: tried to cl over 1f out: fdd fnl f* **4/1**[2]
020- **6** *2* **Dr Wintringham (IRE)**[132] 7403 5-9-2 **70** DarryllHolland 3 64
(Karen George) *wl enough plcd on inner bhd ldrs: effrt over 2f out: nt qckn wl over 1f out: fdd* **22/1**
5213 **7** *¾* **Double Carpet (IRE)**[13] 820 8-8-13 **67** FergusSweeney 2 59
(Garry Woodward) *hld up in midfield on inner: effrt over 2f out: no prog and wl btn over 1f out* **10/1**
0-50 **8** *7* **Hereford Boy**[31] 623 7-9-7 **75** RobertHavlin 11 51
(Dean Ivory) *t.k.h: hld up in 10th: outpcd whn brief effrt 2f out: no ch after: wknd rapidly fnl f* **33/1**
0420 **9** *¾* **Having A Ball**[31] 626 7-8-9 **63** ChrisCatlin 6 38
(Jonathan Portman) *hld up in last trio: nvr really a factor: v modest late prog* **25/1**
120- **10** *1 ½* **Advertise**[176] 6444 5-9-6 **74** EddieCreighton 13 45
(Joseph Tuite) *plld hrd: hld up but wd: u.p over 3f out: wl btn over 2f out* **33/1**
1-04 **11** *1 ½* **John Veale (USA)**[47] 427 5-8-12 **71** (t) MartinHarley(5) 8 39
(Thomas McLaughlin, Ire) *chsd clr ldr after 1f to 5f out: u.p and wknd over 2f out* **14/1**
60-0 **12** *3* **Ensnare**[75] 82 6-9-0 **68** StevieDonohoe 4 29
(Noel Quinlan) *dwlt: a in last trio: rdn and no prog wl over 2f out: sn bhd* **20/1**
3452 **13** *9* **Lisahane Bog**[26] 685 4-9-2 **70** (p) DaneO'Neill 10 10
(Peter Hedger) *slowest away: hld up in last trio: rdn 3f out: no rspnse: eased and wl bhd after* **11/1**

1m 39.29s (-0.51) **Going Correction** +0.05s/f (Slow) **13** Ran SP% **121.8**
Speed ratings (Par 103): **104,103,103,102,99 97,97,90,89,87 86,83,74**
toteswingers: 1&2 £9.00, 1&3 £3.10, 2&3 £6.90 CSF £37.02 CT £134.36 TOTE £7.80: £2.20, £1.10, £1.20; EX 55.70 Trifecta £327.50 Pool: £ 560.74 - 1.26 winning units..
Owner Davies, Palgrave-Brown & Stanbrook **Bred** P And Mrs A G Venner **Trained** Exning, Suffolk

FOCUS
A good gallop was guaranteed here with Florio Vincitore in the line-up. The form looks solid but limited.

950 BOOK KEMPTON TICKETS ON 0844 579 3008 H'CAP 7f (P)
9:20 (9:21) (Class 7) (0-50,55) 4-Y-0+ **£1,535** (£453; £226) **Stalls** Low

Form RPR
4600 **1** **Cane Cat (IRE)**[20] 749 4-8-13 **46** (t) LukeMorris 2 53
(Tony Carroll) *t.k.h: hld up in 8th: prog jst over 2f out: drvn and r.o to take narrow ld ins fnl f: jst hld on* **16/1**
6141 **2** *nse* **Clearing House**[4] 906 6-9-5 **55** 6ex MichaelO'Connell(3) 7 62+
(John Ryan) *hld up towards rr: nt clr run and swtchd lft 2f out: prog over 1f out: str chal last 100yds: jst failed* **3/1**[1]
6-24 **3** *1 ¼* **Royal Envoy (IRE)**[14] 807 8-9-0 **47** ShaneKelly 11 51
(Jane Chapple-Hyam) *trckd ldng pair: clsd to chal 2f out: narrow ld over 1f out: hdd and one pce ins fnl f* **13/2**[2]
604- **4** *1 ¼* **Lend A Light**[97] 7885 5-9-2 **49** GeorgeBaker 14 50
(Philip Hobbs) *t.k.h: sn trckd ldr fr wd draw: led 2f out to over 1f out: stl upsides ins fnl f: wknd last 100yds* **10/1**
0-40 **5** *nk* **Diddums**[4] 912 5-9-2 **49** (p) LiamJones 13 49
(Alastair Lidderdale) *hld up in last pair: prog fr 2f out: drvn and styd on fnl f: nrst fin* **25/1**
50-0 **6** *¾* **Teen Ager (FR)**[14] 810 7-9-3 **50** LiamKeniry 6 48
(Paul Burgoyne) *dwlt: hld up wl in rr: sme prog on inner over 2f out: looking for room over 1f out: kpt on: no threat* **18/1**
0542 **7** *shd* **Cavalry Guard (USA)**[22] 719 7-8-10 **46** (b) BillyCray(3) 3 44
(Tim McCarthy) *plld hrd bhd ldrs: cl enough over 1f out: sn nt qckn and btn* **12/1**
1555 **8** *nk* **Aggbag**[14] 807 7-9-0 **47** NeilCallan 1 44
(Tony Carroll) *trckd ldrs: cl up bhd them fr 2f out: nt qckn jst over 1f out: fdd* **7/1**[3]
5640 **9** *shd* **Kenswick**[14] 807 4-9-1 **48** FergusSweeney 12 44
(Pat Eddery) *hld up last: sme prog over 1f out: reminder sn after: kpt on fnl f: nvr nr ldrs* **14/1**
6436 **10** *1 ¾* **Grand Honour (IRE)**[27] 662 5-9-3 **50** StevieDonohoe 8 42
(Jane Chapple-Hyam) *hld up in 7th: lost pl wl over 1f out: pushed along and n.d after* **14/1**
2100 **11** *nk* **Hi Spec (IRE)**[31] 619 8-9-3 **50** (t) AdamKirby 10 41
(Mandy Rowland) *dwlt: hld up wl in rr: pushed along 2f out: no real imp on ldrs* **20/1**
0-06 **12** *½* **Commander Wish**[19] 765 8-9-2 **49** (p) DaneO'Neill 9 39
(Lucinda Featherstone) *hld up in last trio: effrt on wd outside 3f out: no prog 2f out* **40/1**
5-45 **13** *1 ½* **Pab Special (IRE)**[19] 765 8-9-2 **49** (v) IanMongan 5 35
(Brett Johnson) *racd freely: led to 2f out: sn wknd* **16/1**
0-06 **14** *3 ¾* **Fools Gold**[29] 640 6-9-3 **50** PaulHanagan 4 26
(Richard Guest) *t.k.h: trckd ldng trio: wknd qckly 2f out* **12/1**

1m 27.26s (1.26) **Going Correction** +0.05s/f (Slow) **14** Ran SP% **116.7**
Speed ratings (Par 97): **94,93,92,91,90 89,89,89,89,87 86,86,84,80**
toteswingers: 1&2 £15.30, 1&3 £20.50, 2&3 £8.60 CSF £60.21 CT £365.41 TOTE £19.30: £4.60, £2.60, £2.10; EX 57.60 Trifecta £289.40 Pool: £391.14 - 1.00 winning units..
Owner John W Egan **Bred** Mrs G P Booth And J Porteous **Trained** Cropthorne, Worcs

FOCUS
A moderate handicap rated conservatively around the winner and third. The early pace didn't look too hot but the first two came from off the pace.
Teen Ager(FR) Official explanation: jockey said gelding was denied a clear run

T/Plt: £108.80 to a £1 stake. Pool £88,266.68. 591.90 winning tickets. T/Qpdt: £34.00 to a £1 stake. Pool: £8,784.58. 190.92 winnign tickets. JN

943 KEMPTON (A.W) (R-H)
Thursday, March 24

OFFICIAL GOING: Standard
Wind: light, across Weather: dry

951 REWARDS4RACING.COM CLAIMING STKS 1m (P)
5:40 (5:41) (Class 6) 3-Y-O **£1,535** (£453; £226) **Stalls** Low

Form RPR
4112 **1** **Malice Or Mischief (IRE)**[20] 770 3-9-11 **80** NeilCallan 5 79
(Tony Carroll) *t.k.h early: chsd ldrs: pushed along over 3f out: clsd on ldr 2f out: ev ch over 1f out: drvn 1f out: led ins fnl f: r.o wl* **7/4**[1]
1233 **2** *hd* **Paco Belle (IRE)**[27] 686 3-8-8 **63** KieranO'Neill(5) 2 66
(Richard Hannon) *chsd ldr: rdn and clsd ent fnl 2f: rdn to ld over 1f out: hdd ins fnl f: r.o* **4/1**[3]
2133 **3** *8* **Better Self**[6] 886 3-8-7 **68** RPWalsh(7) 1 53
(David Evans) *v.s.a: sn rcvrd: c wd and effrt wl over 2f out: no threat to ldr after: kpt on to go 3rd ins fnl f* **5/1**
1431 **4** *1* **Ad Vitam (IRE)**[14] 817 3-8-13 **64** (tp) LauraSimpson(7) 6 53
(Jane Chapple-Hyam) *stdd after s: t.k.h: hld up in midfield: rdn and effrt over 2f out: styd on fnl f: no threat to ldrs* **20/1**
341 **5** *2 ¾* **Sofias Number One (USA)**[8] 871 3-9-6 **71** AndreaAtzeni 3 46
(Michael Wigham) *hld up in last trio: effrt and rdn over 2f out: no threat to ldrs after: plugged on fnl f* **3/1**[2]
033- **6** *¾* **Captain Sharpe**[154] 7034 3-9-5 **70** (p) RobertHavlin 4 44
(Bernard Llewellyn) *stdd s: hld up in rr: lost grnd 1/2-way: rdn and effrt over 2f out: no ch w ldrs but kpt on ins fnl f* **10/1**
0555 **7** *3 ¼* **Farmer's Wife**[14] 817 3-8-12 **54** (b[1]) DavidProbert 7 29
(Bernard Llewellyn) *led at stdy gallop: allowed to go clr 4f out: rdn over 2f out: drvn and hdd over 1f out: fdd ins fnl f* **50/1**

1m 41.58s (1.78) **Going Correction** +0.075s/f (Slow) **7** Ran SP% **113.8**
Speed ratings (Par 96): **94,93,85,84,82 81,78**
toteswingers:1&2:£1.90, 1&3:£1.80, 2&3:£4.80 CSF £9.03 TOTE £2.90: £1.30, £3.00; EX 9.10.Malice Or Mischief was subject to a friendly claim. Paco Belle was claimed by Mr A. Crook for £5,000.
Owner Bill Adams **Bred** Kilnamoragh Stud **Trained** Cropthorne, Worcs

FOCUS
This opening claimer was run at an ordinary early pace, but front-running Farmer's Wife opened up a clear advantage turning for home and that caught out most of her rivals. The first pair took it up nearing the final furlong and fought out a driving finish. Straightforward claiming form, rated around the front pair.

952 GOFFS READY-TO-RUN SALE NEXT TUESDAY MAIDEN FILLIES' STKS 1m (P)
6:10 (6:11) (Class 5) 3-Y-O+ **£2,047** (£604; £302) **Stalls** Low

Form RPR
1 **Dubaianswer** 3-8-11 **0** AdamKirby 6 79+
(Marco Botti) *hld up in last trio: hdwy to trck ldrs over 2f out: rdn to ld ent fnl f: r.o wl: comf* **2/1**[1]
2 *2 ¼* **Greenflash** 3-8-11 **0** JimmyFortune 1 73+
(Richard Hannon) *chsd ldr for 1f: in tch after: rdn and effrt ent fnl 2f: chsd wnr fnl f: styd on same pce* **13/2**[3]
0-42 **3** *1 ¼* **Swift Bird (IRE)**[17] 791 3-8-11 **72** LiamJones 4 70
(Noel Quinlan) *led: rdn ent fnl 2f: hdd ent fnl f: one pce fnl f* **2/1**[1]
4 *1* **Neat Sweep (IRE)** 3-8-11 **0** JamesDoyle 2 68
(Alan McCabe) *chsd ldrs: rdn and effrt to press ldrs wl over 1f out: styd on same pce fnl f* **40/1**
5- **5** *1 ½* **Tinaheely (IRE)**[148] 7164 3-8-11 **0** CathyGannon 9 64
(Jonathan Portman) *t.k.h: pressed ldr after 1f: rdn jst over 2f out: wknd ent fnl f* **25/1**
40- **6** *3 ¾* **Fortunateencounter (FR)**[150] 7113 3-8-11 **0** RobertHavlin 10 56
(John Gosden) *hld up in last pair: rdn and effrt over 2 out: no real hdwy: plugged on same pce and nd fnl 2f* **5/1**[2]
0- **7** *½* **Kalendar Girl (IRE)**[188] 6158 3-8-11 **0** JamieMackay 8 54
(Willie Musson) *t.k.h: hld up in rr: effrt over 2f out: sn struggling: one pce and wl hld fnl 2f* **50/1**
8 *8* **Mistress Quick** 3-8-11 **0** LukeMorris 3 36
(Ben De Haan) *in tch in midfield: rdn over 2f out: sn struggling: wl bhd fnl 2f* **50/1**
6 **9** *1 ½* **Summerandlightning (IRE)**[17] 791 5-9-9 **0** LeeNewnes(5) 11 33
(Mark Usher) *in tch: rdn and struggling over 3f out: wl bhd fnl 2f* **66/1**

1m 39.93s (0.13) **Going Correction** +0.075s/f (Slow)
WFA 3 from 5yo 17lb **9** Ran SP% **116.4**
Speed ratings (Par 100): **102,99,98,97,96 92,91,83,82**
toteswingers:1&2:£3.90, 1&3:£2.40, 2&3:£3.80 CSF £16.13 TOTE £2.50: £1.10, £2.70; EX 15.70.
Owner Giuliano Manfredini **Bred** Dave Curran & Eric Cantillon **Trained** Newmarket, Suffolk

FOCUS
An ordinary fillies' maiden, run at a fair pace. A nice start from the winner and the form has been given a chance.

953 WATCH RACING UK ON SKY 432 MAIDEN STKS 7f (P)
6:40 (6:41) (Class 5) 3-Y-O **£2,047** (£604; £302) **Stalls** Low

Form RPR
0 **1** **Shelagh (IRE)**[15] 811 3-8-12 **0** IanMongan 5 62+
(Jo Crowley) *hld up in tch in rr: gd hdwy on inner ent fnl 2f: led over 1f out: r.o wl fnl f* **4/1**[3]
2 *1 ¼* **Precocious Kid (IRE)** 3-9-3 **0** GeorgeBaker 1 64
(Chris Wall) *in tch: swtchd lft and effrt ent fnl 2f: edgd rt over 1f out: ev ch ent fnl f: no ex and btn fnl 100yds* **5/4**[1]
04 **3** *2 ¾* **Sole Bay**[32] 624 3-8-12 **0** DaneO'Neill 2 51
(David Elsworth) *chsd ldr tl 4f out: rdn to ld wl over 1f out: sn hdd: styd on same pce fnl f* **9/4**[2]
00- **4** *4 ½* **Cara Carmela**[132] 7418 3-8-12 **0** WilliamCarson 6 39
(Stuart Williams) *led: rdn ent fnl 2f: hdd over 1f out: wknd fnl f* **16/1**
5 *½* **Sing Alana Sing** 3-8-5 **0** JakePayne(7) 4 38
(Bill Turner) *chsd ldrs: wnt 2nd 4f out tl ent fnl 2f: sn wknd* **14/1**
00 **6** *9* **Clonusker (IRE)**[28] 663 3-9-3 **0** SteveDrowne 3 18
(Linda Jewell) *hld up in tch: pushed along 4f out: lost tch over 2f out* **40/1**

1m 28.06s (2.06) **Going Correction** +0.075s/f (Slow) **6** Ran SP% **110.2**
Speed ratings (Par 98): **91,89,86,81,80 70**
toteswingers:1&2:£1.50, 1&3:£1.20, 2&3:£1.80 CSF £9.09 TOTE £3.70: £1.20, £1.10; EX 12.00.
Owner Kilstone Limited **Bred** Levent Zumreoglu **Trained** Whitcombe, Dorset

FOCUS
A weak 3-y-o maiden, run at an average pace. The time was slow and it's hard to be positive about the form.

954 TURFTV.CO.UK H'CAP — 1m 4f (P)
7:10 (7:12) (Class 6) (0-65,65) 4-Y-0+ — **£1,535** (£453; £226) **Stalls** Centre

Form — RPR
0122 **1** **Kingaroo (IRE)**[2] 938 5-8-12 **58** .... BillyCray(3) 7 — 67
(Garry Woodward) *mde all: hrd pressed and rdn ent fnl 2f: hld on gamely fnl f* **9/2**[2]
6-02 **2** *nk* **Sunset Place**[20] 762 4-9-1 **60** .... RobertHavlin 1 — 68
(Jonathan Geake) *in tch in midfield: hdwy over 2f out: rdn and ev ch over 1f out: kpt on wl but a jst hld fnl f* **11/1**
-250 **3** *3/4* **Beat Route**[15] 805 4-9-1 **65** .... JemmaMarshall(5) 8 — 72
(Michael Attwater) *chsd ldrs: wnt 3rd 4f out: swtchd lft over 2f out: rdn and ev ch ent fnl f: unable qck and hld fnl 100yds* **11/2**[3]
11 **4** *2 1/4* **Lunar River (FR)**[29] 652 8-8-13 **61** .... (t) JamesRogers(5) 2 — 64
(David Pinder) *in tch in midfield: effrt on inner over 2f out: ev ch ent fnl f: wknd ins fnl f* **7/1**
11/3 **5** *1/2* **Camera Shy (IRE)**[22] 728 7-8-7 **50** .... AndreaAtzeni 5 — 53
(Kevin Morgan) *hld up in midfield: rdn and effrt to chse ldrs wl over 1f out: kpt on ins fnl f: nvr gng quite pce to rch ldrs* **13/2**
505- **6** *1 1/4* **Perfect Vision**[140] 7316 4-9-5 **64** .... LukeMorris 6 — 65
(Clive Cox) *t.k.h: hld up in tch towards rr: rdn and hung rt over 2f out: styd on fnl f: nt rch ldrs* **11/1**
-650 **7** *3/4* **Humungous (IRE)**[32] 621 8-9-7 **64** .... (bt) MickyFenton 4 — 63
(Charles Egerton) *stdd s: hld up in rr: rdn 3f out: switching rt over 2f out: styd on ins fnl f: nvr trbld ldrs* **14/1**
00-5 **8** *1/2* **Boogie Dancer**[8] 862 7-8-7 **50** oh1 .... CathyGannon 9 — 49
(Stuart Howe) *s.i.s: rdn and effrt over 2f out: no real hdwy: nvr trbld ldrs* **20/1**
9 *nk* **Landesherr (GER)**[172] 4-9-6 **65** .... IanMongan 10 — 63
(Steve Gollings) *dwlt: t.k.h: sn rcvrd to chse wnr: rdn and unable qck ent fnl 2f: lost 2nd wl over 1f out: wknd ent fnl f* **7/2**[1]
-545 **10** *1 1/2* **Thundering Home**[15] 814 4-9-2 **61** .... NeilCallan 11 — 57
(Michael Attwater) *s.i.s: hld up in last trio: rdn and effrt over 2f out: drvn over 1f out: nvr rchd ldrs* **10/1**
64/3 **11** *42* **Danehill Intellect (IRE)**[22] 737 4-9-1 **60** .... ChrisCatlin 3 — —
(Harry Dunlop) *t.k.h: chsd ldrs tl rdn and lost pl over 3f out: t.o fnl 2f* **25/1**
2m 34.9s (0.40) **Going Correction** +0.075s/f (Slow)
WFA 4 from 5yo+ 2lb — **11** Ran SP% **122.7**
Speed ratings (Par 101): **101,100,100,98,98 97,97,96,96,95 67**
toteswingers:1&2:£10.90, 1&3:£6.60, 2&3:£16.30 CSF £55.95 CT £286.08 TOTE £5.00: £1.90, £4.90, £2.70; EX 67.10.
Owner J Pownall **Bred** Kevin Walsh **Trained** Maltby, S Yorks
FOCUS
An open-looking handicap, run at a fair enough pace. Solid but limited form, the winner proving fully effective on this surface.
Humungous(IRE) Official explanation: jockey said gelding resented tongue strap

955 BOOK KEMPTON TICKETS ON 0844 579 3008 H'CAP — 2m (P)
7:40 (7:40) (Class 6) (0-65,65) 4-Y-0+ — **£1,535** (£453; £226) **Stalls** Low

Form — RPR
/34- **1** **Kadouchski (FR)**[7] 7649 7-8-9 **48** .... RobertHavlin 4 — 60+
(John Berry) *hld up in tch in last trio: smooth hdwy on inner ent fnl 2f: rdn to ld ent fnl f: r.o wl* **9/4**[1]
1/10 **2** *1 3/4* **My Valley (IRE)**[42] 486 9-9-10 **63** .... IanMongan 9 — 70
(Pat Phelan) *chsd ldr tl led over 4f out: rdn over 2f out: drvn and hdd ent fnl f: no ex fnl 150yds* **6/1**
/2-5 **3** *2 3/4* **L'Homme De Nuit (GER)**[13] 89 7-9-12 **65** .... (p) PaulDoe 7 — 69
(Jim Best) *hld up in tch in rr: pushed along and hdwy ent fnl 3f: chsd ldng pair fnl f: kpt on but nvr gng pce to rch ldrs* **12/1**
014- **4** *3/4* **Foreign King (USA)**[134] 7388 7-9-1 **54** .... LiamKeniry 2 — 57
(Seamus Mullins) *t.k.h: chsd ldrs tl wnt 2nd over 4f out: [illegible] unable qck jst over 2f out: no ch w ldng pair fnl f* **11/2**[3]
1135 **5** *4 1/2* **Delorain (IRE)**[37] 549 8-8-11 **55** .... (vt) LauraPike(5) 8 — 52
(William Stone) *in tch on outer: chsd ldrs and rdn ent fnl 2f: nt qckn and sn outpcd: wl hld and hung rt fnl f* **7/1**
-126 **6** *11* **Inside Knowledge (USA)**[41] 514 5-9-8 **61** .... MartinLane 5 — 45
(Garry Woodward) *hld up in tch in last trio: hung lft bnd over 4f out: hdwy over 3f out: hung lft again bnd 3f out: sn wknd* **4/1**[2]
5/65 **7** *1/2* **Am I Blue**[49] 407 5-8-0 **46** oh1 .... LewisWalsh(7) 6 — 30
(Mrs D Thomas) *led tl over 4f out: rdn and lost pl over 3f out: wl bhd over 2f out* **25/1**
250- **8** *1 3/4* **Party Palace**[156] 6416 7-8-7 **46** oh1 .... CathyGannon 3 — 27
(Stuart Howe) *in tch in midfield: pushed along over 7f out: rdn and dropped to last over 3f out: wl bhd over 2f out* **12/1**
3m 30.79s (0.69) **Going Correction** +0.075s/f (Slow) — **8** Ran SP% **112.2**
Speed ratings (Par 101): **101,100,98,98,96 90,90,89**
toteswingers:1&2:£6.60, 1&3:£7.40, 2&3:£9.10 CSF £15.41 CT £128.37 TOTE £3.70: £2.10, £1.10, £3.00; EX 14.50.
Owner John Berry **Bred** Henrietta Charlet & Danny Charlesworth **Trained** Newmarket, Suffolk
FOCUS
A weak staying handicap, run at an average pace. The winner was well on top and can do better again.
Delorain(IRE) Official explanation: jockey said gelding hung right
Inside Knowledge(USA) Official explanation: jockey said gelding hung left

956 PANORAMIC H'CAP — 7f (P)
8:10 (8:10) (Class 4) (0-85,84) 4-Y-0+ — **£3,885** (£1,156; £577; £288) **Stalls** Low

Form — RPR
6215 **1** **Thunderball**[14] 822 5-8-10 **80** .... (b) LeonnaMayor(7) 3 — 87
(David Nicholls) *t.k.h: led over 6f out: mde rest: clr over 3f out: rdn over 1f out: kpt on and a jst holding on: eased last strides* **6/1**
4221 **2** *nk* **Jake The Snake (IRE)**[15] 804 10-9-7 **84** .... NeilCallan 8 — 90
(Tony Carroll) *dropped in bhd after s: hld up in last: swtchd lft and effrt 2f out: hdwy over 1f out: drvn ins fnl f: chsd wnr fnl 100yds: r.o wl: nvr quite getting to wnr* **6/1**
54-5 **3** *1/2* **Street Power (USA)**[50] 385 6-9-5 **82** .... (p) SteveDrowne 7 — 87
(Jeremy Gask) *stdd and dropped in bhd after s: hld up in last trio: swtchd lft and hdwy 2f out: r.o wl fnl f: wnt 3rd fnl 100yds: nt rch wnr* **9/2**[2]
-500 **4** *1 1/2* **Mr Macattack**[22] 736 6-9-3 **80** .... (t) RichardKingscote 4 — 81
(Tom Dascombe) *stdd s: t.k.h: hld up in last trio: effrt on inner 2f out: kpt on ins fnl f: snatched 4th on line: nvr gng to rch wnr* **14/1**
3-12 **5** *nse* **Catherines Call (IRE)**[28] 666 4-8-13 **76** .... DarryllHolland 2 — 77
(Des Donovan) *in tch: rdn to chse wnr over 1f out: hrd drvn jst over 1f out: kpt on same pce fnl f: lost 3 pls fnl 100yds* **11/2**[3]
211 **6** *1 1/4* **I Confess**[14] 816 6-8-2 **72** .... (b) MatthewCosham(7) 1 — 69
(David Evans) *led tl over 6f out: chsd wnr after tl 2f out: outpcd u.p over 1f out: one pce fnl f* **8/1**
300- **7** *nse* **Nezami (IRE)**[152] 7092 6-9-0 **77** .... AndreaAtzeni 6 — 74
(John Akehurst) *in tch: rdn and unable qck ent fnl 2f: styd on same pce fr over 1f out* **9/1**
6410 **8** *shd* **Tislaam (IRE)**[33] 612 4-8-7 **70** .... (p) LukeMorris 5 — 67
(Alan McCabe) *t.k.h: chsd ldrs: rdn to chse wnr 2f out tl over 1f out: wknd jst ins fnl f* **7/2**[1]
1m 25.07s (-0.93) **Going Correction** +0.075s/f (Slow) — **8** Ran SP% **112.1**
Speed ratings (Par 105): **108,107,107,105,105 103,103,103**
toteswingers:1&2:£4.80, 1&3:£4.70, 2&3:£2.90 CSF £39.88 CT £176.53 TOTE £6.80: £2.70, £2.00, £1.40; EX 27.00.
Owner Paul J Dixon & Brian Morton **Bred** Mrs Yvette Dixon **Trained** Sessay, N Yorks
FOCUS
A fair handicap, and straightforward but limited form. The winner was allowed a pretty soft lead.

957 WATCH RACES LIVE AT RACINGUK.COM H'CAP — 1m (P)
8:40 (8:40) (Class 6) (0-58,58) 4-Y-0+ — **£1,535** (£453; £226) **Stalls** Low

Form — RPR
015 **1** **Spinning Ridge (IRE)**[5] 906 6-9-5 **58** .... (b) DavidProbert 4 — 65
(Ronald Harris) *dwlt: hld up in tch in last trio: hdwy on inner 2f out: rdn to chal 1f out: led ins fnl f: r.o wl* **11/2**[2]
3-00 **2** *hd* **George Baker (IRE)**[43] 472 4-9-3 **56** .... TonyCulhane 1 — 63
(George Baker) *in tch: effrt to chal 2f out: ev ch u.p ent fnl f: led ins fnl f: sn hdd and unable qck nr fin* **16/1**
6030 **3** *nk* **Rainsborough**[5] 906 4-9-2 **55** .... (e) DaneO'Neill 2 — 61
(Peter Hedger) *hld up in tch in midfield: n.m.r over 2f out tl swtchd ins and gd hdwy ent fnl 2f: ev ch 1f out: no ex towards fin* **14/1**
4244 **4** *nk* **Kielty's Folly**[6] 896 7-9-1 **54** .... CathyGannon 3 — 59
(Brian Baugh) *chsd ldrs: rdn to ld over 1f out: drvn 1f out: hdd ins fnl f: nt qckn fnl 100yds* **9/2**[1]
0205 **5** *5* **Ocean Countess (IRE)**[24] 712 5-8-12 **51** .... NeilCallan 6 — 45
(Tony Carroll) *hld up in tch: nt clr run and swtchd lft over 1f out: chsd clr ldng quartet fnl f: kpt on: nvr able to chal* **11/2**[2]
60/6 **6** *1 1/2* **Final Tune (IRE)**[21] 749 8-9-5 **58** .... AdamKirby 10 — 48
(Mandy Rowland) *stdd s: hld up in tch in rr: rdn and effrt wl over 1f out: kpt on same pce and no ch ldrs fnl f* **14/1**
4013 **7** *nk* **Fortunate Bid (IRE)**[6] 893 5-8-13 **55** .... (p) JamesSullivan(3) 11 — 45
(Linda Stubbs) *taken down early: t.k.h: in tch: bmpd and pushed rt over 2f out: sn rdn and effrt on outer: wknd ent fnl f* **8/1**[3]
0651 **8** *3/4* **Queenie's Star (IRE)**[15] 807 4-8-13 **52** .... LukeMorris 7 — 40
(Michael Attwater) *in tch in midfield: swtchd lft and bmpd rival over 2f out: drvn 2f out: wknd jst over 1f out* **8/1**[3]
0/50 **9** *1 1/4* **Lennie Briscoe (IRE)**[36] 553 5-9-0 **53** .... (t) MartinLane 14 — 38
(Martin Bosley) *dwlt: t.k.h: sn rcvrd and chsd ldr tl wl over 1f out: wknd jst over 1f out* **25/1**
-330 **10** *2* **Fine Ruler (IRE)**[15] 809 7-9-1 **54** ow1 .... GeorgeBaker 9 — 36
(Martin Bosley) *t.k.h: hld up wl in tch in midfield: nt clr run fr over 2f out: nvr able to chal* **9/1**
0510 **11** *hd* **Miss Bounty**[8] 862 6-8-9 **55** .... (p) NathanAlison(7) 12 — 35
(Jim Boyle) *taken down early: chsd ldrs: rdn and unable qck over 2f out: wknd over 1f out* **16/1**
/002 **12** *1/2* **Street Crime**[20] 761 6-8-13 **52** .... JimCrowley 8 — 31
(Ron Hodges) *t.k.h: led: rdn and hdd over 1f out: wknd qckly jst over 1f out* **16/1**
-630 **13** *16* **Sir William Orpen**[15] 592 4-9-0 **53** .... IanMongan 13 — —
(Pat Phelan) *stdd s: t.k.h: hld up in tch in rr: rdn and effrt 3f out: btn and hung lft 2f out: eased ins fnl f* **33/1**
1m 39.82s (0.02) **Going Correction** +0.075s/f (Slow) — **13** Ran SP% **118.9**
Speed ratings (Par 101): **102,101,101,101,96 94,94,93,92,90 90,89,79**
toteswingers:1&2:£26.40, 1&3:£22.30, 2&3:£36.90 CSF £90.15 CT £815.87 TOTE £7.60: £3.10, £6.70, £5.40; EX 117.80.
Owner Robert & Nina Bailey **Bred** Eddie O'Leary **Trained** Earlswood, Monmouths
■ Stewards' Enquiry : Luke Morris one-day ban: careless riding (Apr 7)
FOCUS
The first four came well clear in a driving finish in this weak handicap, which was run at an ordinary early pace and that resulted in most taking a keen hold. The first four home came out of the top four boxes and the form is clearly limited.
Fine Ruler(IRE) Official explanation: jockey said gelding was denied a clear run
T/Plt: £45.30 to a £1 stake. Pool:£69,542.06 - 1,118.33 winning tickets T/Qpdt: £19.40 to a £1 stake. Pool:£7,939.69 - 302.44 winning tickets SP

904 LINGFIELD (L-H)
Friday, March 25

OFFICIAL GOING: Standard
Wind: Almost nil Weather: Sunny, warm

958 FOREST ROW H'CAP — 5f (P)
2:30 (2:33) (Class 6) (0-65,65) 3-Y-0 — **£1,569** (£463; £231) **Stalls** High

Form — RPR
00-1 **1** **Dorothy's Dancing (IRE)**[18] 788 3-8-11 **55** .... FergusSweeney 5 — 58+
(Gary Moore) *t.k.h: cl up: trckd ldr 1/2-way: chal over 1f out: carried rt but rdn to ld ins fnl f: jst hld on* **8/15**[1]
4243 **2** *nse* **Welsh Inlet (IRE)**[34] 611 3-9-5 **63** .... CathyGannon 2 — 66
(John Bridger) *led: drvn over 1f out: edgd rt and hdd ins fnl f: fought on wl: jst failed* **14/1**
25-4 **3** *3 1/4* **Lisselton Cross**[56] 338 3-8-12 **56** .... (p) JimCrowley 1 — 47
(Martin Bosley) *chsd ldr to 1/2-way: rdn and cl enough over 1f out: fdd ins fnl f* **8/1**[3]
550- **4** *nk* **Cristaliyev**[125] 7528 3-9-6 **64** .... StephenCraine 6 — 54
(Jim Boyle) *hld up in last trio: effrt 2f out: rdn and cl enough over 1f out: fdd ins fnl f* **20/1**
6346 **5** *4 1/2* **Pineapple Pete (IRE)**[3] 936 3-9-4 **62** .... (t) NeilCallan 7 — 36
(Alan McCabe) *t.k.h: hld up in last trio and racd wd: shkn up and nt qckn wl over 1f out: wknd ins fnl f* **15/2**[2]
0645 **6** *3* **Hey Mambo**[7] 886 3-8-4 **53** oh6 ow2 .... RyanClark(5) 4 — 16
(Roger Ingram) *dwlt: t.k.h: hld up in last trio: wknd over 2f out* **66/1**
59.77 secs (0.97) **Going Correction** +0.20s/f (Slow) — **6** Ran SP% **101.0**
Speed ratings (Par 96): **100,99,94,94,87 82**
toteswingers:1&2 £1.60, 2&3 £2.10, 1&3 £1.60 CSF £6.66 TOTE £1.60: £1.10, £3.10; EX 5.50.

Owner G L Moore **Bred** Patrick Carroll **Trained** Lower Beeding, W Sussex
■ Sailing North (5/1) was withdrawn after breaking out of the stalls. Deduct 5p in the £ under R4.

FOCUS
A weakish sprint handicap. The winner probably didn't need to improve on his previous C&D win.
Welsh Inlet(IRE) Official explanation: jockey said filly hung right

959 MR & MRS ARNOLD'S WEDDING DAY MAIDEN FILLIES' STKS 7f (P)
3:00 (3:02) (Class 5) 3-Y-0+ **£2,047** (£604; £302) **Stalls** Low

Form RPR
3-3 **1** **Lucky Meadows (IRE)**[6] 905 3-8-9 0 DaneO'Neill 1 69
(Richard Hannon) *mde all: rdn 2f out: swished tail but hld on to dwindling ld nr fin* **4/1**[2]
05- **2** 1/2 **Baqaat (USA)**[204] 5691 3-8-9 0 EddieAhern 5 68
(Ed Dunlop) *hld up in 4th: pushed along and prog fr 3f out: chsd wnr over 1f out: grad clsd gap but nvr quite got there* **10/11**[1]
0- **3** 1 1/4 **Eljowzah (IRE)**[301] 2505 3-8-9 0 PhilipRobinson 2 65
(Clive Brittain) *chsd wnr: shkn up 2f out: lost 2nd over 1f out: kpt on same pce ins fnl f* **6/1**[3]
3 **4** 4 1/2 **Jackie Love (IRE)**[16] 811 3-8-8 0 ow2 MichaelO'Connell(3) 7 54
(John Ryan) *hld up in 5th: effrt over 2f out: sn lft bhd by ldrs* **4/1**[2]
06 **5** 3 3/4 **Celtic Whisper**[29] 663 3-8-9 0 NickyMackay 6 42
(Jeremy Gask) *chsd ldng pair to 1/2-way: wknd 2f out* **50/1**
0 **6** 2 1/2 **Shaunas Spirit (IRE)**[54] 360 3-8-9 0 WilliamCarson 4 36
(Dean Ivory) *plld hrd and sn restrained in last: rdn whn hung rt and wd bnd 2f out: sn bhd* **66/1**

1m 25.78s (0.98) **Going Correction** +0.20s/f (Slow)
WFA 3 from 4yo 15lb **6** Ran SP% **110.1**
Speed ratings (Par 100): **102,101,100,94,90 87**
toteswingers:1&2 £1.80, 2&3 £1.60, 1&3 £2.10 CSF £7.75 TOTE £4.50: £2.00, £1.30; EX 9.10.
Owner Mike Hawkett & Robin Heffer **Bred** Summerhill Parkes Syndicate **Trained** East Everleigh, Wilts
■ Stewards' Enquiry : Michael O'Connell Fine £140, Rule (C) 43.5.3. One-day ban: Rule (D) 46.5.2, attempted to weigh-in without chamois.

FOCUS
No more than a modest maiden, but a pleasing performance from the winner who rates a small personal best.
Shaunas Spirit(IRE) Official explanation: jockey said filly hung right

960 MARRIOTT PLAY & STAY CLAIMING STKS 6f (P)
3:35 (3:35) (Class 6) 4-Y-0+ **£1,535** (£453; £226) **Stalls** Low

Form RPR
1133 **1** **Hinton Admiral**[16] 804 7-8-12 77 NeilCallan 2 84
(Jane Chapple-Hyam) *mde all: set stdy pce: kicked on over 2f out: drvn over 1f out: hld on* **13/8**[2]
-560 **2** 1/2 **Perfect Act**[34] 613 6-8-10 85 DavidProbert 1 80
(Andrew Balding) *cl up in 3rd: chsd wnr 2f out: rdn over 1f out: clsd ins fnl f: no imp nr fin* **5/6**[1]
2400 **3** 4 **Bonnie Prince Blue**[15] 822 8-8-9 75 (b) PaulMulrennan 3 67
(James Given) *chsd wnr: rdn and nt qckn whn pce lifted over 2f out: sn lost 2nd and btn* **13/2**[3]

1m 13.38s (1.48) **Going Correction** +0.20s/f (Slow) **3** Ran SP% **106.0**
Speed ratings (Par 101): **98,97,92**
CSF £3.34 TOTE £2.20; EX 2.80.Hinton Admiral was claimed by K. W. Dalgleish for £9000.
Owner Rory Murphy **Bred** Gainsborough Stud Management Ltd **Trained** Dalham, Suffolk

FOCUS
With just the three runners, this was always going to be tactical. The winner got an easy lead and the form is rated around him.

961 LINGFIELD PARK OWNERS CLUB H'CAP 6f (P)
4:10 (4:12) (Class 4) (0-85,85) 4-Y-0+ **£3,464** (£1,030; £515; £257) **Stalls** Low

Form RPR
406- **1** **Curtains**[119] 7574 4-9-5 83 NeilCallan 3 93
(Simon Dow) *prom in chsng gp: wnt 3rd over 3f out: drvn and clsd to ld jst ins fnl f: hld on wl* **6/1**[3]
1141 **2** nk **Norville (IRE)**[27] 698 4-8-10 74 (b) CathyGannon 8 83
(David Evans) *dwlt: wl in rr: rdn and gd prog fr 2f out: wnt 2nd and clsd on wnr ins fnl f: hld nr fin* **9/2**[1]
1-15 **3** 2 **Arctic Lynx (IRE)**[27] 698 4-9-1 79 (t) GeorgeBaker 10 82
(John Best) *sn off the pce in midfield: rdn and prog fr 2f out: styd on to take 3rd ins fnl f: nt gng pce to threaten* **9/2**[1]
4441 **4** 1 1/2 **Lastkingofscotland (IRE)**[18] 786 5-8-13 77 (b) HayleyTurner 5 75
(Conor Dore) *hld up in last pair: pushed along firmly over 2f out: styd on fr over 1f out: tk 4th last strides* **10/1**
0-54 **5** nk **Billy Red**[27] 701 7-9-5 83 (b) FergusSweeney 2 80
(J R Jenkins) *blasted off in front and sn clr: hdd & wknd jst ins fnl f* **16/1**
4/13 **6** nk **Qadar (IRE)**[27] 698 9-8-10 74 (p) ShaneKelly 11 70
(Alan McCabe) *settled in rr: effrt over 2f out: sme prog on outer over 1f out: nt gng pce to threaten* **11/2**[2]
560- **7** 1 3/4 **Rocker**[162] 6858 7-8-4 73 HarryBentley(5) 9 64+
(Gary Moore) *settled in midfield on inner: shuffled along fnl 2f: nvr nr ldrs* **50/1**
0-42 **8** 1 1/4 **Vintage (IRE)**[57] 316 7-8-11 78 SimonPearce(3) 6 65
(John Akehurst) *a abt same pl on inner: tended to run-in snatches: no prog over 1f out* **8/1**
00-0 **9** nk **Fantasy Explorer**[34] 613 8-9-7 85 MickyFenton 1 71
(John Quinn) *chsd clr ldr: tried to cl over 1f out: sn wknd qckly* **16/1**
1310 **10** nk **Waabel**[27] 698 4-9-1 79 PaulDoe 7 64
(Jim Best) *prom in chsng gp: hanging lft u.p over 1f out: wknd* **10/1**
1612 **11** 2 1/4 **Punching**[43] 493 7-8-8 79 LukeRowe(7) 4 61
(Conor Dore) *prom in chsng gp: lost pl 1/2-way: wkng whn sltly hmpd ins fnl f* **33/1**
320- **12** 1 1/2 **Fawley Green**[168] 6714 4-8-10 74 JimCrowley 12 47
(William Muir) *racd wd: mostly last: wl btn fnl 2f* **20/1**

1m 11.29s (-0.61) **Going Correction** +0.20s/f (Slow) **12** Ran SP% **116.8**
Speed ratings (Par 105): **112,111,108,106,106 106,103,102,101,101 98,96**
toteswingers:1&2 £7.00, 2&3 £3.20, 1&3 £7.20 CSF £31.96 CT £136.14 TOTE £5.40: £3.10, £2.10, £1.50; EX 39.80 Trifecta £136.50 Pool: £771.30 - 4.18 winning units..
Owner The Pull Yourself Together Partnership **Bred** Sir Eric Parker **Trained** Epsom, Surrey

FOCUS
Thanks to Billy Red they went a really good gallop in this competitive handicap. The form is solid.

962 BARRY GURR MEMORIAL H'CAP 1m 5f (P)
4:45 (4:45) (Class 5) (0-75,74) 4-Y-0+ **£2,047** (£604; £302) **Stalls** Low

Form RPR
-615 **1** **Gunslinger (FR)**[9] 872 6-9-5 72 HayleyTurner 5 77
(Michael Scudamore) *hld up last: prog 3f out: effrt on inner 2f out and sn pressing ldr: persistent chal after: drvn ahd last 50yds* **13/2**
-431 **2** shd **Where's Susie**[16] 808 6-9-7 74 RobertHavlin 6 79
(Michael Madgwick) *hld up: prog to trck ldr over 3f out: led 2f out: sn hrd pressed: hdd and no ex last 50yds* **3/1**[2]
-533 **3** hd **Indian Ghyll (IRE)**[16] 808 5-8-11 64 DaneO'Neill 2 68
(Roger Teal) *hld up bhd ldrs: cl 4th over 2f out: drvn to go 3rd over 1f out: clsd on ldng pair last 150yds: nt quite get there* **10/3**[3]
-434 **4** 5 **Profit's Reality (IRE)**[16] 808 9-9-1 68 ShaneKelly 1 65
(Michael Attwater) *led to over 8f out: led again 5f out to 2f out: wknd ins fnl f* **8/1**
21 **5** 5 **Wily Fox**[28] 688 4-9-2 72 JackMitchell 3 62
(James Eustace) *trckd ldr 3f: styd handy tl lost pl over 3f out: wknd over 1f out* **5/2**[1]
126/ **6** 13 **Rollin 'n Tumblin**[1069] 1501 7-8-6 64 JemmaMarshall(5) 4 34
(Michael Attwater) *hld up tl plld way through to ld over 8f out: hdd 5f out: wknd 3f out* **8/1**

2m 48.22s (2.22) **Going Correction** +0.20s/f (Slow)
WFA 4 from 5yo+ 3lb **6** Ran SP% **112.2**
Speed ratings (Par 103): **101,100,100,97,94 86**
toteswingers:1&2 £3.40, 2&3 £1.40, 1&3 £3.30 CSF £26.09 TOTE £6.60: £2.90, £2.00; EX 23.70.
Owner S M Smith & Keith Hunter **Bred** Dayton Investments Ltd **Trained** Bromsash, Herefordshire

FOCUS
A modest handicap and a three-way photo. It was a bit of a muddling race and it's hard to be positive about the form.
Gunslinger(FR) Official explanation: trainer said, regarding apparent improvement in form, that the gelding was better suited by hold-up tactics.

963 LINGFIELD PARK SPORTING MEMBERSHIP H'CAP 1m 2f (P)
5:20 (5:20) (Class 4) (0-85,85) 4-Y-0+ **£3,464** (£1,030; £515; £257) **Stalls** Low

Form RPR
20-1 **1** **Fanditha (IRE)**[6] 908 5-9-0 85 CharlesBishop(7) 4 93
(Mick Channon) *trckd ldr after 3f in slowly run r: led 3f out: hrd pressed fr over 1f out: edgd rt but hld on wl* **9/4**[1]
3565 **2** nk **Baylini**[16] 803 7-9-4 85 SophieDoyle(3) 8 92
(Jamie Osborne) *prom in slowly run r: wnt cl 2nd over 2f out: chal fr over 1f out: nt qckn last 100yds* **9/2**[3]
-551 **3** 1 1/4 **Classically (IRE)**[43] 484 5-8-12 76 DaneO'Neill 5 81
(Peter Hedger) *rring whn stalls opened and slowly away: sn in tch in last trio: prog 2f out: styd on to take 3rd ins fnl f: unable to chal* **7/1**
1-55 **4** 1/2 **Hawaana (IRE)**[14] 835 6-9-5 83 MickyFenton 3 87
(Gay Kelleway) *t.k.h bhd ldrs in slowly run r: effrt over 2f out: nt qckn over 1f out: kpt on same pce* **8/1**
0660 **5** 3/4 **Kiss A Prince**[34] 614 5-9-2 80 (b) JimmyFortune 1 82
(Dean Ivory) *hld up in last trio in slowly run r: poorly plcd whn pce lifted 3f out: styd on ins fnl f: n.d* **4/1**[2]
16-6 **5** dht **Understory (USA)**[30] 647 4-8-10 74 EddieAhern 6 76
(Tim McCarthy) *led after 2f and maintained stdy pce: hdd 3f out: cl up tl fdd ins fnl f* **33/1**
-000 **7** 1 1/2 **The Scorching Wind (IRE)**[15] 822 5-9-2 80 (vt) WilliamCarson 7 79
(Stuart Williams) *s.v.s: sn in tch in slowly run r: poorly plcd whn pce lifted 3f out: one pce after* **14/1**
-010 **8** nk **Avon River**[41] 525 4-9-2 85 (b) KieranO'Neill(5) 2 83
(Richard Hannon) *led at slow pce for 2f: rdn 3f out: lost pl and struggling over 1f out* **7/1**

2m 9.67s (3.07) **Going Correction** +0.20s/f (Slow) **8** Ran SP% **114.7**
Speed ratings (Par 105): **95,94,93,93,92 92,91,91**
toteswingers:1&2 £2.70, 2&3 £7.20, 1&3 £3.60 CSF £12.53 CT £59.95 TOTE £1.90: £1.02, £2.90, £3.70; EX 9.80 Trifecta £31.00 Pool: £325.95 - 7.76 winning units..
Owner Mrs T Burns **Bred** Lynch Bages Ltd & Samac Ltd **Trained** West Ilsley, Berks

FOCUS
They went a steady early pace here before sprinting from the turn in, and it paid to race prominently. Another race where it's hard to be positive about the form.
The Scorching Wind(IRE) Official explanation: jockey said gelding was slowly away
T/Plt: £22.30 to a £1 stake. Pool of £60,435.90 - 1,977.28 winning tickets. T/Qpdt: £14.20 to a £1 skake. Pool of £3,198.37 - 165.60 winning tickets. JN

928 WOLVERHAMPTON (A.W) (L-H)
Friday, March 25

OFFICIAL GOING: Standard
Wind: Almost nil Weather: Sunny

964 STAY AT THE WOLVERHAMPTON HOLIDAY INN H'CAP 5f 216y(P)
5:15 (5:15) (Class 6) (0-60,60) 3-Y-O **£1,637** (£483; £241) **Stalls** Low

Form RPR
2253 **1** **Rhal (IRE)**[23] 729 3-9-2 55 TomEaves 8 63
(Bryan Smart) *checked sn after s: cl up: led centre over 1f out: drvn out ins fnl f* **4/1**[1]
5444 **2** 2 **Reachtothestars (USA)**[22] 739 3-9-5 58 (t) AdamKirby 10 60
(Noel Quinlan) *plld hrd: led and sn crossed to ins rail: rdn and hdd over 1f out: kpt on u.p ins fnl f* **9/2**[2]
4354 **3** hd **William Wainwright (IRE)**[10] 856 3-8-9 48 (v[1]) PhillipMakin 6 49
(Ann Duffield) *hmpd sn after s: t.k.h: in tch on outside: rdn over 2f out: no imp tl styd on ins fnl f: nrst fin* **11/1**
4552 **4** nse **Scommettitrice (IRE)**[14] 834 3-9-0 53 (b) LukeMorris 3 54
(Ronald Harris) *in tch: drvn over 2f out: hdwy over 1f out: kpt on ins fnl f: nvr nrr* **13/2**
3-44 **5** nk **Bachelor Knight (IRE)**[50] 396 3-9-6 59 (p) BarryMcHugh 4 59
(Ollie Pears) *trckd ldrs: effrt and rdn over 2f out: kpt on same pce ins fnl f* **8/1**
4-06 **6** 2 1/2 **Lady Mango (IRE)**[35] 600 3-9-6 59 TomMcLaughlin 7 51
(Ronald Harris) *hld up towards rr on outside: rdn over 2f out: edgd lft over 1f out: sn no imp* **20/1**
0-01 **7** 2 3/4 **Alfraamsey**[14] 834 3-9-7 60 SamHitchcott 2 43
(Mick Channon) *sn pushed into midfield: drvn and outpcd 2f out: no imp after* **6/1**[3]

6066 **8** *1 1/4* **Seadream**[22] [745] 3-8-0 **46** oh1 RachealKneller(7) 5 25
(Mark Usher) *s.i.s: bhd: sme hdwy on ins over 1f out: nvr able to chal* **16/1**

460- **9** *1 1/4* **Gothic Chick**[135] [7395] 3-9-0 **60** NoraLooby(7) 11 35
(Alan McCabe) *bhd: drvn along 1/2-way: nvr on terms* **20/1**

06-0 **10** *nk* **Maggie's Treasure (IRE)**[21] [764] 3-9-3 **56** ChrisCatlin 1 30
(John Gallagher) *t.k.h: trckd ldrs tl rdn and wknd wl over 1f out* **8/1**

0000 **11** *2 1/4* **Welsh Dresser (IRE)**[14] [834] 3-8-7 **46** oh1 RobbieFitzpatrick 9 13
(Peter Grayson) *sn bhd on outside: struggling 1/2-way: nvr on terms* **66/1**

1m 14.87s (-0.13) **Going Correction** -0.075s/f (Stan) **11** Ran SP% **113.3**
Speed ratings (Par 96): **97,94,94,94,93 90,86,84,83,82 79**
toteswingers:1&2 £5.70, 2&3 £7.90, 1&3 £6.50 CSF £20.23 CT £180.01 TOTE £7.50: £2.30, £3.20, £4.80; EX 34.80.
Owner Crossfields Racing **Bred** Epona Bloodstock Ltd **Trained** Hambleton, N Yorks
FOCUS
They didn't seem to go that quick and this is moderate form, although sound enough for the grade.

965 SPONSOR A RACE BY CALLING 01902 390000 H'CAP 1m 5f 194y(P)
5:45 (5:45) (Class 5) (0-75,75) 4-Y-0+ **£2,331** (£693; £346; £173) **Stalls** Low

Form RPR

0/22 **1** **Accumulate**[6] [911] 8-8-10 **59** J-PGuillambert 4 68
(Bill Moore) *trckd ldr: pushed along over 2f out: led centre over 1f out: pushed clr ins fnl f* **5/4**[1]

220- **2** *3 3/4* **Red Kestrel (USA)**[130] [7465] 6-9-6 **69** PhillipMakin 2 73
(Kevin Ryan) *set pce: rdn over 2f out: hdd over 1f out: kpt on same pce ins fnl f* **9/2**[3]

2123 **3** *3/4* **Layla's Dancer**[25] [715] 4-9-6 **73** StevieDonohoe 6 76
(Tony Carroll) *in tch: pushed along over 2f out: hdwy and hung lft over 1f out: sn no imp* **3/1**[2]

5-03 **4** *7* **Evident Pride (USA)**[16] [813] 8-9-12 **75** IanMongan 3 68
(Brett Johnson) *t.k.h: prom: rdn 3f out: wknd wl over 1f out* **11/2**

50-0 **5** *11* **Roose Blox (IRE)**[8] [878] 4-8-7 **60** (p) TomEaves 5 38
(Roger Fisher) *t.k.h: prom on outside: lost pl after 6f: rdn and struggling fr 1/2-way* **66/1**

00-0 **6** *21* **William Van Gogh**[14] [835] 4-9-4 **71** GrahamGibbons 7 19
(Michael Easterby) *dwlt: hld up: hdwy on ins to trck ldrs after 6f: rdn and wknd over 3f* **20/1**

3m 4.07s (-1.93) **Going Correction** -0.075s/f (Stan)
WFA 4 from 6yo+ 4lb **6** Ran SP% **109.3**
Speed ratings (Par 103): **102,99,99,95,89 77**
toteswingers:1&2 £1.90, 2&3 £2.00, 1&3 £1.10 CSF £6.86 TOTE £1.80: £1.20, £2.10; EX 9.70.
Owner C W Moore **Bred** Raymond Cowie **Trained** Ledsham, Cheshire
FOCUS
An uncompetitive contest. They went a steady pace until the tempo increased early on the final circuit and the first two were always handy. The winner probably only had to run to his latest form.

966 ENJOY THE PARTY PACK GROUP OFFER H'CAP (DIV I) 7f 32y(P)
6:15 (6:17) (Class 6) (0-55,55) 3-Y-0 **£1,364** (£403; £201) **Stalls** High

Form RPR

000- **1** **Century Dancer**[84] [8031] 3-8-5 **49** RyanPowell(5) 10 55
(Tor Sturgis) *hld up: plenty to do 2f out: gd hdwy on outside to ld wl ins fnl f: kpt on strly* **22/1**

660- **2** *3/4* **Cheers**[249] [4203] 3-9-1 **54** FrankieMcDonald 9 58
(Paul Fitzsimons) *t.k.h: trckd ldrs: hdwy to ld over 1f out: sn rdn: hdd wl ins fnl f: kpt on same pce* **7/1**[3]

60-3 **3** *2 1/4* **Sleeping Brave**[7] [887] 3-8-9 **55** NathanAlison(7) 7 53
(Jim Boyle) *midfield: drvn and outpcd wl over 2f out: rallied over 1f out: kpt on: no ex wl ins fnl f* **5/4**[1]

3-40 **4** *2 1/4* **Magical Star**[14] [834] 3-8-10 **49** SteveDrowne 4 41
(Mark Rimmer) *hld up towards rr: effrt and hdwy 2f out: kpt on ins fnl f: nvr able to chal* **16/1**

-233 **5** *3/4* **Neytiri**[14] [834] 3-9-0 **53** DarryllHolland 6 43
(Linda Stubbs) *in tch: rdn over 2f out: kpt on same pce ins fnl f* **5/1**[2]

00-0 **6** *1 1/2* **On Wings Of Love (IRE)**[16] [801] 3-8-13 **52** (b1) ChrisCatlin 2 38
(John Gallagher) *led: rdn and hdd over 1f out: wknd ins fnl f* **11/1**

000- **7** *1 1/4* **Complicate** [illegible] 3-8-4 [illegible] oh1 [illegible] 0 [illegible]
(Andrew Reid) *midfield on ins: drvn and outpcd over 2f out: n.d after* **20/1**

5044 **8** *1/2* **Lynchpin**[7] [886] 3-9-2 **55** (b) LukeMorris 8 36
(Ronald Harris) *cl up: drvn over 3f out: wknd over 1f out* **11/1**

606- **9** *1 3/4* **Sister Sioux (IRE)**[202] [5762] 3-8-7 **46** oh1 LeeNewman 1 22
(Robin Bastiman) *trckd ldrs: rdn 3f out: wknd ent st* **33/1**

066- **10** *4 1/2* **Back For Tea (IRE)**[210] [5483] 3-8-11 **50** StevieDonohoe 5 14
(Willie Musson) *dwlt: bhd: struggling 3f out: btn whn veered rt over 1f out* **8/1**

1m 29.78s (0.18) **Going Correction** -0.075s/f (Stan) **10** Ran SP% **119.3**
Speed ratings (Par 96): **95,94,91,89,88 86,85,84,82,77**
toteswingers:1&2 £41.40, 2&3 £3.60, 1&3 £13.30 CSF £168.62 CT £342.25 TOTE £35.40: £8.90, £2.90, £1.10; EX 236.80.
Owner Century Racing **Bred** Redmyre Bloodstock And S Hillen **Trained** Upper Lambourn, Berks
FOCUS
They went a strong pace and the time was 1.40 seconds faster than the second division. Fair form for the grade, with a personal best from the first two.

967 ENJOY THE PARTY PACK GROUP OFFER H'CAP (DIV II) 7f 32y(P)
6:45 (6:45) (Class 6) (0-55,55) 3-Y-0 **£1,364** (£403; £201) **Stalls** High

Form RPR

556- **1** **Onlyfoalsandhorses (IRE)**[226] [4967] 3-8-8 **52** RyanPowell(5) 3 56
(J S Moore) *prom: pushed along 3f out: hdwy against far rail to ld ins fnl f: sn hrd pressed: hld on wl* **9/1**

3236 **2** *nk* **Beating Harmony**[15] [817] 3-9-2 **55** DarryllHolland 9 58
(Tony Carroll) *hld up: pushed along over 3f out: hdwy on wd outside over 1f out: edgd lft and chal ins fnl f: jst hld* **9/2**[1]

-045 **3** *2* **Three Scoops**[14] [834] 3-8-11 **50** (tp) JamesDoyle 10 48
(Dominic Ffrench Davis) *t.k.h: led tl edgd rt u.p and hdd ins fnl f: kpt on same pce* **9/2**[1]

0453 **4** *1 3/4* **Kyncraighe (IRE)**[3] [942] 3-8-7 **53** (tp) KatiaScallan(7) 2 46
(Alastair Lidderdale) *prom: outpcd 3f out: rallied fnl f: nvr rchd ldrs* **11/2**[2]

0-44 **5** *nk* **Lindo Erro**[21] [770] 3-8-10 **54** DeclanCannon(5) 5 46
(John Mackie) *s.i.s: sn midfield on towards outside: effrt over 2f out: no ex ins fnl f* **10/1**

-506 **6** *3/4* **Two Feet Of Snow (IRE)**[14] [834] 3-9-0 **53** PJMcDonald 6 43
(Ian McInnes) *prom: effrt and ev ch over 1f out: wknd ins fnl f* **7/1**[3]

530 **7** *1 1/2* **Littlepromisedland (IRE)**[3] [942] 3-8-7 **46** oh1 KirstyMilczarek 4 32
(Richard Guest) *hld up on ins: drvn over 3f out: no imp fnl 2f* **12/1**

4404 **8** *6* **Lady Ellice**[14] [834] 3-8-10 **49** (be) LukeMorris 1 19
(Phil McEntee) *t.k.h: trckd ldrs: rdn and outpcd 4f out: n.d after* **15/2**

-004 **9** *3* **Talkin Italian**[31] [642] 3-8-9 **48** (b1) SteveDrowne 7 10
(Hughie Morrison) *t.k.h: w ldr to 1/2-way: rdn and wknd 2f out* **8/1**

1m 31.18s (1.58) **Going Correction** -0.075s/f (Stan) **9** Ran SP% **113.9**
Speed ratings (Par 96): **87,86,84,82,82 81,79,72,69**
toteswingers:1&2 £14.30, 2&3 £3.20, 1&3 £19.30 CSF £48.53 CT £208.52 TOTE £16.80: £5.30, £1.40, £1.70; EX 99.10.
Owner Colin Powell & T Wilkinson **Bred** Tally-Ho Stud **Trained** Upper Lambourn, Berks
FOCUS
The time was 1.40 seconds slower than the strongly run first division, suggesting they didn't go that quick. Limited form, rated through the third.

968 DINE IN HORIZONS RESTAURANT (S) STKS 1m 1f 103y(P)
7:15 (7:15) (Class 6) 4-Y-0+ **£1,535** (£453; £226) **Stalls** Low

Form RPR

-340 **1** **Stand Guard**[30] [647] 7-8-12 72 DarryllHolland 7 66
(Jane Chapple-Hyam) *hld up in tch: stdy hdwy to trck ldrs on outside whn hung rt over 2f out: rdn to ld over 1f out: sn clr* **7/2**[2]

6-06 **2** *4* **Plush**[28] [694] 8-8-12 72 RussKennemore 3 58
(Shaun Lycett) *dwlt: hld up: rdn over 3f out: hdwy and edgd lft over 1f out: chsd (clr) wnr wl ins fnl f: r.o* **7/2**[2]

613 **3** *1/2* **Lean Machine**[32] [635] 4-9-4 61 (p) LukeMorris 4 63
(Ronald Harris) *trckd ldrs: effrt and ev ch over 1f out: rdn and kpt on same pce ins fnl f* **10/1**

1462 **4** *3/4* **Midnight Strider (IRE)**[8] [876] 5-9-4 65 ChrisCatlin 8 61
(Joseph Tuite) *prom: rdn 3f out: rallied and ev ch over 1f out: nt qckn ins fnl f* **15/2**[3]

0300 **5** *1 1/2* **Escardo (GER)**[7] [896] 8-8-12 41 (v) RobbieFitzpatrick 5 52
(David Bridgwater) *hld up in tch: rdn over 3f out: edgd lft and no imp over 1f out* **66/1**

6002 **6** *1 1/4* **Officer In Command (USA)**[7] [885] 5-9-4 73 (b) LiamKeniry 6 55
(J S Moore) *t.k.h: cl up: led 2f out to over 1f out: wknd ins fnl f* **15/8**[1]

-600 **7** *8* **Sligo All Star**[2] [944] 6-8-7 43 KirstyMilczarek 2 28
(Thomas McLaughlin, Ire) *hld up in tch on ins: struggling 3f out: sn wknd* **18/1**

-450 **8** *16* **Stoppers (IRE)**[16] [802] 4-8-12 63 IanMongan 1 —
(Robert Mills) *led tl hdd over 2f out: sn struggling: t.o* **16/1**

2m 0.28s (-1.42) **Going Correction** -0.075s/f (Stan) **8** Ran SP% **112.7**
Speed ratings (Par 101): **103,99,99,98,97 95,88,74**
toteswingers:1&2 £4.00, 2&3 £4.50, 1&3 £7.80 CSF £15.69 TOTE £3.80: £1.10, £2.20, £1.80; EX 21.00.There was no bid for the winner.
Owner The Circle Bloodstock I Limited **Bred** Juddmonte Farms Ltd **Trained** Dalham, Suffolk
FOCUS
A muddling seller and a few of these limit the form, notably the fifth.

969 GREAT OFFERS AT WOLVERHAMPTON-RACECOURSE.CO.UK H'CAP 1m 1f 103y(P)
7:45 (7:45) (Class 7) (0-50,55) 4-Y-0+ **£1,535** (£453; £226) **Stalls** Low

Form RPR

-233 **1** **Barton Bounty**[7] [895] 4-8-12 **45** (b) PhillipMakin 6 63
(Peter Niven) *hld up: nt clr run over 2f out: swtchd to outside and hdwy to ld over 1f out: kpt on wl ins fnl f* **8/1**

3322 **2** *3/4* **Wrecking Crew (IRE)**[7] [899] 7-8-13 **46** JamesMillman 5 62
(Rod Millman) *in tch: hdwy and ev ch wl over 1f out: rdn and kpt on ins fnl f: hld towards fin* **4/1**[2]

-303 **3** *8* **Olney Lass**[21] [773] 4-9-0 **47** MartinLane 4 46
(Mike Murphy) *t.k.h: prom: effrt over 1f out: plugged on ins fnl f: no ch w first two* **8/1**

-232 **4** *1 1/2* **Idol Deputy (FR)**[21] [773] 5-8-9 **49** RachealKneller(7) 12 45
(Mark Usher) *trckd ldrs: effrt whn nt clr run briefly ent st: edgd lft and sn outpcd* **13/2**[3]

/04- **5** *1/2* **Darfour**[291] [1983] 7-9-1 **48** (t) LukeMorris 9 43
(Martin Hill) *towards rr: pushed along and outpcd 4f out: hdwy over 1f out: nvr able to chal* **28/1**

1412 **6** *1 3/4* **Clearing House**[2] [950] 6-9-8 **55** 6ex KirstyMilczarek 3 46
(John Ryan) *hld up in midfield on ins: effrt whn nt clr run over 2f out: sn rdn and no imp* [illegible]

-020 **7** *nk* **Aurora Lights**[22] [748] 4-9-0 **47** (p) TonyHamilton 11 38
(Richard Fahey) *hld up on outside: effrt 4f out: sn outpcd: sme late hdwy: nvr on terms* **22/1**

-450 **8** *6* **Pab Special (IRE)**[2] [950] 8-9-2 **49** (v) IanMongan 1 27
(Brett Johnson) *prom: effrt and rdn over 2f out: wknd over 1f out* **14/1**

6600 **9** *2* **State General (IRE)**[7] [899] 5-8-13 **46** (tp) J-PGuillambert 2 20
(Tony Carroll) *led tl hdd over 1f out: sn wknd* **22/1**

-563 **10** *7* **Castlebury (IRE)**[7] [899] 6-8-13 **46** (b) PJMcDonald 13 —
(Ruth Carr) *cl up: rdn over 3f out: wkng whn hmpd over 2f out* **12/1**

000/ **11** *16* **Buckers Beauty (IRE)**[889] [6787] 5-8-9 **49** HobieGill(7) 8 —
(Alan McCabe) *bhd: lost tch 4f out: t.o* **50/1**

2m 0.93s (-0.77) **Going Correction** -0.075s/f (Stan) **11** Ran SP% **114.8**
Speed ratings (Par 97): **100,99,92,90,90 88,88,83,81,75 61**
toteswingers:1&2 £3.90, 2&3 £5.50, 1&3 £3.80 CSF £37.34 CT £266.40 TOTE £8.50: £3.10, £1.90, £2.70; EX 29.70.
Owner Francis Green Racing Ltd **Bred** Mrs M L Parry **Trained** Barton-le-Street, N Yorks
FOCUS
A weak race in which the front two did well to pull so far clear. The time was 0.65 seconds off the earlier seller won by the 72-rated Stand Guard.

970 WOLVERHAMPTON-RACECOURSE.CO.UK H'CAP 5f 20y(P)
8:15 (8:15) (Class 4) (0-85,85) 4-Y-0+ **£3,238** (£963; £481; £240) **Stalls** Low

Form RPR

405- **1** **Baby Strange**[143] [7289] 7-9-5 **83** TomEaves 2 90
(Derek Shaw) *chsd ldng gp: pushed along after 2f: hdwy over 1f out: styd on wl to ld towards fin* **8/1**

-656 **2** *hd* **Green Manalishi**[34] [613] 10-9-5 **83** (p) PhillipMakin 1 89
(Kevin Ryan) *prom: effrt and drvn over 1f out: led briefly wl ins fnl f: jst hld* **7/2**[2]

3322 **3** *1* **Sir Geoffrey (IRE)**[27] [701] 5-9-7 **85** (b) IanMongan 8 88
(David Nicholls) *t.k.h: led: rdn 2f out: hdd and no ex wl ins fnl f* **5/2**[1]

16-6 **4** *hd* **Liberty Lady (IRE)**[30] [651] 4-8-12 **76** DarryllHolland 3 78
(Des Donovan) *hld up: hdwy on ins over 1f out: no further imp wl ins fnl f* **5/1**[3]

00-0 **5** *shd* **Falasteen (IRE)**[30] [651] 4-8-13 **77** StevieDonohoe 5 79
(David Nicholls) *stdd in rr: effrt and hdwy over 1f out: kpt on ins fnl f* **13/2**

50- **6** *2 1/2* **Taurus Twins**[236] [4625] 5-8-4 **71** oh2 (b) BillyCray(3) 4 64
(Richard Price) *trckd ldrs: drvn and c wd ent st: sn outpcd: kpt on ins fnl f: no imp* **14/1**

200- **7** 2 3/4 **Living It Large (FR)**[147] 7212 4-9-4 82 TonyHamilton 6 65
(Roger Fisher) *cl up tl rdn and wknd over 1f out* **8/1**
366- **8** 1 1/4 **Chosen One (IRE)**[209] 5513 6-8-7 71 oh1 PJMcDonald 7 49
(Ruth Carr) *cl up: rdn over 2f out: wknd over 1f out* **22/1**
61.24 secs (-1.06) **Going Correction** -0.075s/f (Stan) **8** Ran SP% **114.0**
Speed ratings (Par 105): **105,104,103,102,102 98,94,92**
toteswingers:1&2 £8.20, 2&3 £2.10, 1&3 £4.90 CSF £35.93 CT £91.02 TOTE £10.40: £2.90, £2.10, £1.30.
Owner Market Avenue Racing Club Ltd **Bred** Michael John Williamson **Trained** Sproxton, Leics
FOCUS
A fair sprint handicap run at a good pace. The form makes sense at face value.

971 THE BLACK COUNTRY'S ONLY RACECOURSE MAIDEN STKS 5f 216y(P)
8:45 (8:48) (Class 5) 3-Y-O+ **£2,007** (£597; £298; £149) **Stalls** Low

Form RPR
/24- **1** **Bandstand**[389] 751 5-9-8 73 AdamCarter(5) 6 84
(Bryan Smart) *t.k.h: sn pressing ldr: led 2f out: edgd rt and drew clr ins fnl f* **10/3**[2]
323- **2** 4 **Lady Platinum Club**[113] 7667 3-8-9 70 (p) TomEaves 4 62
(Geoffrey Oldroyd) *chsd ldrs: drvn and outpcd over 2f out: rallied to chse wnr ins fnl f: no imp* **9/1**
2-2 **3** 4 1/2 **Oh My Days (IRE)**[15] 818 3-9-0 0 LukeMorris 8 53
(Clive Cox) *t.k.h: led tl rdn and hdd 2f out: wknd ins fnl f* **10/11**[1]
3 **4** 3/4 **Full Shilling (IRE)**[25] 709 3-8-9 0 ChrisCatlin 3 45
(John Spearing) *prom: drvn and outpcd 1/2-way: no imp fnl 2f* **33/1**
6/3 **5** 1/2 **The Gillie**[21] 774 4-9-13 0 TonyHamilton 1 53+
(Richard Fahey) *bhd and sn pushed along: nvr able to chal* **8/1**[3]
5 **6** 1/2 **Kaminski Kabs**[7] 892 3-8-4 0 DanielleMcCreery(5) 5 42
(Phil McEntee) *s.i.s: rn green in rr: nvr rchd ldrs* **50/1**
7 3 1/2 **Passing Moment** 3-8-9 0 GrahamGibbons 7 31
(Brian Baugh) *s.i.s: bhd and green: nvr on terms* **12/1**
4 **8** 21 **Shakespeares Excel**[29] 669 4-9-13 0 RobbieFitzpatrick 2 —
(Derek Shaw) *trckd ldrs: drvn 1/2-way: hung lft and wknd 2f out: eased whn no ch* **8/1**[3]
1m 14.52s (-0.48) **Going Correction** -0.075s/f (Stan)
WFA 3 from 4yo+ 13lb **8** Ran SP% **120.3**
Speed ratings (Par 103): **100,94,88,87,87 86,81,53**
toteswingers:1&2 £4.30, 2&3 £2.00, 1&3 £2.10 CSF £35.01 TOTE £4.60: £1.20, £2.50, £1.10; EX 40.20.
Owner Crossfields Racing **Bred** D J And Mrs Brown **Trained** Hambleton, N Yorks
FOCUS
An ordinary sprint maiden but a fair performance from the winner. He appeared to improve but there is a bit of doubt with the favourite disappointing.
T/Plt: £59.30 to a £1 stake. Pool of £65,498.35 805.00 winning tickets. T/Qpdt: £15.90 to a £1 stake. Pool of £10,874.26 - 504.00 winning tickets. RY

DUNDALK (A.W) (L-H)
Friday, March 25
OFFICIAL GOING: Standard

972a IRISH STALLION FARMS EUROPEAN BREEDERS FUND AUCTION MAIDEN 5f (P)
6:30 (6:31) 2-Y-O **£7,732** (£1,793; £784; £448)

RPR
1 **Snowflake Dancer (IRE)** 2-9-0 KJManning 5 72
(J S Bolger, Ire) *prom: sn chsd ldr in 2nd: impr to ld under 2f out: rdn and strly pressed fr over 1f out: kpt on u.p: jst hld on* **9/2**[3]
2 shd **One Kool Dude** 2-9-0 DPMcDonogh 7 72
(Richard Fahey) *prom early: sn chsd ldrs: 5th 1/2-way: rdn into 3rd over 1f out: kpt on wl ins fnl f: jst hld* **3/1**[2]
3 hd **Battleroftheboyne (IRE)** 2-8-8 GFCarroll(3) 9 68
(Michael Mulvany, Ire) *chsd ldrs: 3rd 1/2-way: rdn to chal in 2nd over 1f out: kpt on ins fnl f: lost 2nd last strides* **8/1**
4 nk **Rockview Diamond (IRE)** 2-8-8 ShaneFoley(3) 1 71+
(John C McConnell, Ire) *hld up towards rr: rdn into 5th 1f out: kpt on ins fnl f* **20/1**
5 1 3/4 **Bible Black (IRE)** 2-8-11 KLatham 3 68+
(G M Lyons, Ire) *chsd ldrs: 4th 1/2-way: veered rt under 2f out: sltly hmpd over 1f out: no clr run ins fnl f: hmpd in clsng stages* **11/4**[1]
6 2 1/2 **French Emperor (IRE)** 2-9-0 CO'Donoghue 8 53
(Edward Lynam, Ire) *chsd ldrs early: sn dropped towards rr: rdn into 6th over 1f out: no imp ins fnl f* **6/1**
7 1 3/4 **Exactness** 2-8-6 CDHayes 2 38
(K J Condon, Ire) *a towards rr* **16/1**
8 1 1/2 **Diamond Rainbow (IRE)** 2-9-0 PJSmullen 6 52+
(Rodger Sweeney, Ire) *towards rr early: 6th 1/2-way: hmpd under 2f out: sn no ex* **16/1**
9 shd **Yo Credo (IRE)** 2-8-6 DJMoran 4 31
(Irene J Monaghan, Ire) *prom: sn led: rdn and hdd under 2f out: wknd over 1f out* **22/1**
60.12 secs (60.12) **9** Ran SP% **116.1**
CSF £18.53 TOTE £4.70: £1.40, £1.70, £2.30; DF 15.20.
Owner Mrs June Judd **Bred** Barronstown Stud **Trained** Coolcullen, Co Carlow
■ Stewards' Enquiry : K Latham advice: careless riding
FOCUS
A pretty eventful start to the Dundalk season, not surprising with a bunch of unraced juveniles racing on the turn. They finished in a heap and the form is rated around the averages for the track and time of year.
NOTEBOOK
Snowflake Dancer(IRE) came home in front. He showed no shortage of speed but displayed signs of greenness and when asked to quicken he took a bit of sorting out and tended to drift right under pressure inside the last furlong. For all that, he wasn't stopping and was professional enough with the promise of a fair bit more to come. (op 4/1 tchd 5/1)
One Kool Dude will appreciate stepping up in trip. He was ridden in the early stages to go the pace and didn't look entirely comfortable but the further they went the more momentum he built up and he came home well. (op 11/4)
Battleroftheboyne(IRE) represented the same connections who saw their two-year-old disqualified on opening day at the Curragh. This one probably ran his race but just wasn't good enough. Ridden through to make his challenge a furlong out, he had every chance and probably wasn't done too many favours by the winner drifting to his right, but his effort just flattened out inside the final 100 yards. He looks a typical early season speedy juvenile. (op 6/1)
Rockview Diamond(IRE) was drawn on the inside rail but such was the melee that developed he had to be pulled to the wide outside inside the last furlong and when getting there it took him a few strides to get on an even keel. When he did, he came home best of all. Another furlong would not be a problem and he should go close to winning one of these.
Bible Black(IRE) ran very green and was involved in a fair bit of mayhem. He was caught in behind horses but, in trying to find racing room. (op 3/1 tchd 5/2)
French Emperor(IRE), who opened at 14/1, struggled to go the pace and never made an impression. (op 14/1)
Diamond Rainbow(IRE) was starting to make nice headway, and got involved in some scrimmaging. (op 14/1)

973a WWW.DUNDALKSTADIUM.COM H'CAP 6f (P)
7:00 (7:03) (47-70,69) 3-Y-O **£4,758** (£1,103; £482; £275)

RPR
1 **Big Tex (IRE)**[251] 4161 3-9-3 67 JPO'Brien(5) 7 73
(W McCreery, Ire) *sn led: rdn and chal 1 1/2f out: kpt on u.p ins fnl f: jst hld on* **10/1**
2 shd **Red Army Blues (IRE)**[222] 5126 3-9-6 65 KLatham 1 71+
(G M Lyons, Ire) *dwlt: towards rr: gd hdwy on inner into 5th 2f out: rdn into 3rd 1f out: kpt on wl ins fnl f: jst failed* **14/1**
3 1 1/4 **Beau Bunny (IRE)**[139] 7356 3-9-1 60 CDHayes 2 62
(P D Deegan, Ire) *chsd ldrs: 3rd 1/2-way: 2nd 2f out: rdn to chal 1 1/2f out: kpt on ins fnl f: no ex cl home* **9/1**[3]
4 3 **Extra Steps (IRE)**[154] 7074 3-8-13 65 RPWhelan(7) 14 57+
(Paul Cashman, Ire) *hld up towards rr: hdwy into 7th 2f out: rdn into 5th 1f out: no ex ins fnl f: kpt on same pce* **14/1**
5 2 **Elusive Express (IRE)**[110] 7748 3-9-9 68 PJSmullen 13 54+
(H Rogers, Ire) *hld up towards rr: rdn into 7th 1f out: kpt on same pce ins fnl f* **9/1**[3]
6 nk **More Than A Lot (IRE)**[105] 7817 3-9-2 64 ShaneFoley(3) 4 49
(M Halford, Ire) *chsd ldrs: 6th 1/2-way: impr to 3rd 2f out: rdn in 4th 1f out: no ex and kpt on same pce* **7/1**[2]
7 1 1/4 **Princess Theophane (IRE)**[110] 7750 3-8-5 50 NGMcCullagh 5 31
(Liam McAteer, Ire) *chsd ldrs: 5th 1/2-way: rdn in 6th under 2f out: kpt on same pce fr over 1f out* **33/1**
8 1/2 **Late Debate (USA)**[187] 6229 3-8-13 58 KJManning 12 37
(J S Bolger, Ire) *in rr of mid-div: rdn and no imp over 2f out: kpt on one pce* **12/1**
9 1 **Teriyaki (IRE)**[236] 4628 3-9-6 68 GFCarroll(3) 3 44
(Daniel Mark Loughnane, Ire) *mid-div: rdn in 9th 2f out: no ex* **14/1**
10 nk **Big Bad Lily (IRE)**[173] 6616 3-8-7 55 BACurtis(3) 8 30
(Augustine Leahy, Ire) *mid-div: rdn and no ex over 2f out* **16/1**
11 1/2 **Old English (IRE)**[7] 887 3-9-10 69 FMBerry 9 43
(Mark Johnston) *chsd ldr: 2nd 1/2-way: rdn in 4th 2f out: no ex over 1f out: wknd ins fnl f* **13/8**[1]
12 nk **Solo Whisper (IRE)**[207] 5594 3-9-5 64 (b[1]) DPMcDonogh 11 37
(Adrian McGuinness, Ire) *a towards rr* **28/1**
13 1/2 **Future Impact (IRE)**[181] 6380 3-9-10 69 CO'Donoghue 10 40
(P D Deegan, Ire) *mid-div: rdn and no imp 2f out: wknd* **12/1**
14 9 **Lake Wanaka (IRE)**[194] 6010 3-8-4 49 oh2 RPCleary 6 —
(Ms Joanna Morgan, Ire) *chsd ldrs: 4th 1/2-way: rdn and wknd 2f out* **25/1**
1m 12.11s (72.11) **14** Ran SP% **131.2**
CSF £152.68 CT £1379.22 TOTE £19.90: £3.90, £3.80, £1.90; DF 210.20.
Owner Mrs Amanda McCreery **Bred** McMac Syndicate **Trained** The Curragh, Co.Kildare
FOCUS
It paid to be prominent. The form is rated around the third.
NOTEBOOK
Big Tex(IRE), who opened at 25/1, was smartly away and travelled well in front, pulling out plenty inside the final furlong when Joseph O'Brien got stuck in to him. He would have been caught in another half stride but it was a good effort from the front at a track his trainer thought wouldn't suit. There's no reason why he shouldn't progress and he shouldn't get too much of a penalty. (op 25/1)
Red Army Blues(IRE) ◆ was very unlucky. He missed the break by a stride or two and in addition his rider had to snatch him up as he was interfered with off the first bend, causing him to drop back to nearly last. From there he had a reasonable passage but had to switch a couple of horses wide inside the final furlong. He came home best of all and it would have been justified had he got up. He shouldn't be long making up for this though at this venue. (op 18/1)
Beau Bunny(IRE) ran a fair race and may just be worth trying over the minimum trip again. She showed plenty of speed in a race not many managed to get into and kept it up until just fading well inside the last. She has enough speed on this evidence to be competitive over 5f. (op 8/1)
Extra Steps(IRE) gave notice that she might step up to 7f as she did some reasonable late work to be nearest at the finish.
Elusive Express(IRE) was trapped a bit wide in the straight and got buffeted around a bit, so she didn't do badly in staying on to finish fifth. (op 8/1)
More Than A Lot(IRE) tracked the leaders to the 2f pole but just wasn't good enough. (op 15/2)
Teriyaki(IRE) Official explanation: jockey said colt checked off heels on the first bend
Old English(IRE) was biting off a bit more than he could chew here in the end. He didn't have enough pace to get to the front despite being hard ridden in the attempt to do so. He faded inside the last furlong and a half. Official explanation: jockey said colt struggled over the shorter trip and was outpaced in the straight (op 7/4)

977a FUNDRAISING MADE EASY AT DUNDALK H'CAP 1m (P)
9:00 (9:01) (50-75,75) 4-Y-O+ **£4,758** (£1,103; £482; £275)

RPR
1 **Opening Nite (IRE)**[56] 6961 4-9-9 70 (b) PTownend 11 74
(Denis W Cullen, Ire) *hld up towards rr: hdwy in 9th 2f out: rdn into 4th 1f out: styd on wl ins fnl f to ld last strides* **25/1**
2 hd **King's Bastion (IRE)**[110] 7751 7-9-6 72 JPO'Brien(5) 8 76
(Luke Comer, Ire) *chsd ldrs: 3rd 1/2-way: 2nd 1 1/2f out: rdn to chal ins fnl f and led last 100yds: hdd last strides* **20/1**
3 hd **Scary Movie (IRE)**[30] 656 6-9-11 75 (p) GFCarroll(3) 7 78
(C Moore, Ire) *mid-div: rdn 2f out: styd on in 6th 1f out: kpt on ins fnl f* **11/2**[1]
4 1 **Mac Tiernan (IRE)**[107] 7771 4-9-2 73 CTKeane(10) 9 74
(Michael Fitzsimons, Ire) *led: rdn and chal ins fnl f: hdd fnl 100yds: no ex* **13/2**[3]
5 3/4 **Mount Abora (IRE)**[105] 7818 4-8-8 58 ShaneFoley(3) 5 57
(Charles O'Brien, Ire) *in rr of mid-div: hdwy into 6th 2f out: rdn in 7th 1f out: kpt on same pce ins fnl f* **16/1**
6 nk **Breezed Well (IRE)**[16] 809 4-8-9 56 (t) CO'Donoghue 1 54
(James McAuley, Ire) *chsd ldrs: 5th 1/2-way: rdn in 3rd 1 1/2f out: no ex fnl f* **7/1**
7 1 **Gracchus (USA)**[111] 7712 5-9-6 67 (bt) CDHayes 14 63
(Noel Meade, Ire) *hld up towards rr: sme late hdwy in 8th 1f out: no imp and kpt on same pce* **14/1**
8 1/2 **Noble Jack (IRE)**[50] 2926 5-9-8 72 BACurtis(3) 10 67
(Muredach Kelly, Ire) *towards rr for most: nvr a factor* **20/1**

9 1 1/4 **Elusive Fame (USA)**[9] 869 5-9-12 73 ....(b) SeamieHeffernan 3 65
(Mark Johnston) *chsd ldr in 2nd: rdn 2f out: no ex in 4th 1 1/2f out: wknd fnl f* **6/1**[2]

10 3 1/2 **Curl Cat (USA)**[364] 1000 5-10-0 75 .... DPMcDonogh 12 59
(K J Condon, Ire) *chsd ldrs: 6th 1/2-way: rdn in 7th 2f out: no ex and wknd* **6/1**[2]

11 hd **Gala Casino Star (IRE)**[36] 572 6-9-8 69 .... KLatham 4 53
(Richard Fahey) *chsd ldrs: 7th 1/2-way: rdn in 8th 2f out: no ex and wknd* **6/1**[2]

12 1 **Lily's Star (IRE)**[151] 7138 4-9-0 61 .... PJSmullen 13 42
(H Rogers, Ire) *a towards rr* **12/1**

13 3/4 **Global Recovery (IRE)**[154] 7078 4-8-12 59 ....(p) KJManning 6 39
(J S Bolger, Ire) *chsd ldrs: 3rd 1/2-way: rdn in 5th 2f out: no ex and wknd* **14/1**

1m 38.72s (98.72) **13** Ran SP% **124.4**
CSF £461.75 CT £3150.55 TOTE £21.10: £4.40, £6.60, £2.30; DF 221.40.
Owner LMBP Partnership **Bred** Conor Murphy & Rathmore Stud **Trained** Newlands, Co Kildare

FOCUS
The first four were close to their marks.

NOTEBOOK
Opening Nite(IRE) improved his position entering the straight and despite having to make his challenge between horses inside the last, he sustained his effort to get his head in front close home. He won't get much of a penalty for this and his trainer feels he could still be improving. (op 28/1)
King's Bastion(IRE) was almost good enough here. Racing reasonably close to the pace, he responded well to hit the front inside the final furlong, but was just mugged on the line. He's capable of winning a similar race.
Scary Movie(IRE) has been busy on similar surfaces but didn't look the easiest of rides. Held up, he began to make ground, but had to move to the outside of the field to make his challenge. He took his time to get organised but ran on well inside the last. (op 9/2)
Mac Tiernan(IRE) may have gone off too quickly. Despite travelling well enough when still in front a furlong out, he weakened close home. (op 8/1)
Mount Abora(IRE) tried to make her challenge up the inside in the straight and didn't get enough daylight.
Breezed Well(IRE) was close enough to the leaders in the straight, but could only keep on at one pace.
Gala Casino Star(IRE) Official explanation: jockey said gelding was boxed in uin the straight and was unable to deliver a challenge

974 - 976a, 978 - 979a (Foreign Racing) - See Raceform Interactive

1010 DEAUVILLE (R-H)
Friday, March 25

OFFICIAL GOING: Fibresand: standard

980a PRIX D'ALMENECHES (MAIDEN) (3YO COLTS & GELDINGS) (FIBRESAND) 7f 110y
1:50 (12:00) 3-Y-O **£10,344** (£4,137; £3,103; £2,068; £1,034)

RPR

1 **Moonwalk In Paris (FR)**[21] 777 3-9-2 0 .... IoritzMendizabal 3 83
(J-C Rouget, France) **7/2**[2]

2 nk **Crown Counsel (IRE)**[21] 776 3-9-2 0 .... RobertWinston 2 82
(Mark Johnston) *rdn to ld initially: then settled 2nd: rdn early in st: grabbed ld 1 1/2f out: r.o u.p: hdd 100yds out: r.o wl to hold 2nd* **10/1**

3 hd **Toss The Dice (IRE)**[157] 3-9-2 0 .... Christophe-PatriceLemaire 8 82
(A De Royer-Dupre, France) **15/2**

4 snk **Masteroftherolls (IRE)** 3-9-2 0 .... MaximeGuyon 13 81
(A Fabre, France) **9/1**

5 hd **Forceful Appeal (USA)**[159] 3-9-2 0 .... StephanePasquier 7 81
(Mme C Head-Maarek, France) **5/2**[1]

6 2 **Touch Of Roc**[18] 3-9-2 0 .... DavyBonilla 11 76
(C Lerner, France) **24/1**

7 snk **Signorotto (FR)**[21] 777 3-9-2 0 .... TonyPiccone 4 76
(J Rossi, France) **37/1**

8 snk **Bolero (GER)** 3-9-2 0 .... ASuborics 12 75
(Manfred Hofer, Germany) **75/1**

9 hd **Becquarey (FR)**[115] 3-9-2 0 .... GregoryBenoist 5 75
(A Trybuhl, Germany) **29/1**

10 1 **Taxonomist (USA)**[21] 776 3-9-2 0 .... MickaelBarzalona 1 72
(A Fabre, France) **63/10**[3]

0 **Holy Roman (FR)**[169] 3-9-2 0 .... ThierryThulliez 6 —
(J Van Handenhove, France) **59/1**

0 **Asanga (USA)**[81] 3-8-13 0 .... TheoBachelot(3) 9 —
(J E Hammond, France) **12/1**

0 **Nektarus (FR)**[21] 776 3-9-2 0 .... JohanVictoire 10 —
(J Rossi, France) **49/1**

1m 32.0s (92.00) **13** Ran SP% **118.0**
WIN (incl 1 euro stake): 4.50. PLACES: 1.70, 2.70, 2.20. DF: 20.80. SF: 27.30.
Owner SARL Ecurie J-L Tepper **Bred** Neustrian Associates & Dandy's Farm **Trained** Pau, France

981a PRIX D'ARGENTELLES (MAIDEN) (3YO FILLIES) (FIBRESAND) 7f 110y
2:55 (12:00) 3-Y-O **£10,344** (£4,137; £3,103; £2,068; £1,034)

RPR

1 **Nuit Polaire (IRE)**[21] 3-9-0 0 .... IoritzMendizabal 10 82
(J-C Rouget, France) **29/10**[2]

2 1 1/2 **Uklanie (FR)** 3-9-0 0 .... ThierryThulliez 2 78
(F Chappet, France) **11/1**

3 snk **Joie De Deauville (FR)**[18] 3-9-0 0 .... DavyBonilla 14 78
(M Figge, Germany) **21/1**

4 nk **Zelkova (FR)** 3-9-0 0 .... GregoryBenoist 7 77
(M Delzangles, France) **15/1**

5 hd **Disluiquejelaime**[202] 3-8-10 0 .... TheoBachelot(4) 15 77
(C Ferland, France) **56/1**

6 nk **Grande Amore (IRE)** 3-9-0 0 .... ASuborics 13 76
(Manfred Hofer, Germany) **67/1**

7 snk **Rose The One (FR)** 3-9-0 0 .... ThomasMessina 5 76
(J-M Beguigne, France) **10/1**

8 3/4 **Boastful (IRE)**[21] 775 3-9-0 0 .... MaximeGuyon 1 74
(H-A Pantall, France) **5/2**[1]

9 hd **Rizella (FR)**[211] 3-9-0 0 .... JohanVictoire 4 73
(Mme C Head-Maarek, France) **13/2**[3]

10 3/4 **Rock An Run (IRE)**[132] 3-8-8 0 .... PaulineProd'homme(6) 8 71
(D Prod'Homme, France) **55/1**

0 **Vauville (IRE)**[207] 5622 3-9-0 0 .... Christophe-PatriceLemaire 16 —
(Y De Nicolay, France) **25/1**

0 **Finefrenzyrolling (IRE)**[12] 852 3-9-0 0 .... AndrewElliott 6 —
(Mrs K Burke) *settled 3rd on rail: rdn 1 1/2f out: no ex: qckly fdd* **29/1**

0 **Back On Stage (FR)** 3-9-0 0 .... ThierryJarnet 9 —
(Mlle S-V Tarrou, France) **36/1**

0 **Minerva (FR)**[21] 3-9-0 0 .... FlavienPrat 3 —
(Mme M Bollack-Badel, France) **68/1**

0 **Ventiane (GER)** 3-9-0 0 .... StephanePasquier 12 —
(H-W Hiller, Germany) **21/1**

0 **Quest Of Paradise (FR)** 3-9-0 0 .... MickaelBarzalona 11 —
(Mlle S-V Tarrou, France) **52/1**

1m 30.6s (90.60) **16** Ran SP% **118.5**
WIN (incl 1 euro stake): 3.90. PLACES: 1.80, 4.90, 4.40. DF: 27.20. SF: 62.80.
Owner Ecurie Des Monceaux **Bred** Alex Pereira **Trained** Pau, France

951 KEMPTON (A.W) (R-H)
Saturday, March 26

OFFICIAL GOING: Standard
Wind: Across, fresh becoming strong Weather: Overcast becoming bright

982 BETFRED THE BONUS KING MAIDEN STKS 5f (P)
2:30 (2:30) (Class 4) 2-Y-O **£2,752** (£818; £409; £204) **Stalls** Low

Form RPR

1 **Redair (IRE)** 2-8-12 0 .... CathyGannon 4 80+
(David Evans) *chsd ldr and sn clr of rest: led over 1f out: immediately hung lft and rn green: drvn out and kpt on wl* **11/4**[2]

2 1 3/4 **Bubbly Ballerina** 2-8-7 0 .... DeclanCannon(5) 7 73
(Alan Bailey) *fast away: led and sn clr w wnr: sltly wd bnd 2f out: hdd over 1f out: styd on but readily hld* **7/1**[3]

3 6 **He's So Cool (IRE)** 2-9-0 0 .... KierenFox(3) 1 54+
(Bill Turner) *sn outpcd in 4th: pushed along bef 1/2-way: kpt on to take modest 3rd ins fnl f* **5/4**[1]

4 3 **Ciara Boo (IRE)** 2-8-12 0 .... PaulDoe 5 37
(David Evans) *chsd ldng pair but sn outpcd: no imp over 1f out: lost 3rd ins fnl f* **16/1**

5 4 1/2 **Snowed In (IRE)** 2-9-3 0 .... LiamKeniry 8 24+
(J S Moore) *s.s: wl bhd in last: nvr a factor: passed 2 rivals ins fnl f* **8/1**

6 1/2 **Umph (IRE)** 2-9-3 0 .... TomMcLaughlin 2 22
(David Evans) *sn outpcd in 6th: a bhd* **10/1**

7 2 1/4 **Lilygloves** 2-8-12 0 .... SamHitchcott 6 8
(Mick Channon) *sn wl outpcd in 5th: nvr a factor: wknd fnl f* **10/1**

60.46 secs (-0.04) **Going Correction** -0.05s/f (Stan) **7** Ran SP% **118.8**
Speed ratings (Par 94): **98,95,85,80,73 72,69**
toteswingers:1&2:£5.70, 1&3:£1.10, 2&3:£7.10 CSF £23.40 TOTE £4.00: £2.30, £2.10; EX 26.30.
Owner Mrs S Edwards,Mrs J Potter,J Potter **Bred** Noel O'Callaghan **Trained** Pandy, Monmouths

FOCUS
Britain's first two-year-old event of 2011 was contested by five trainers whose juveniles invariably make a fast start to the season. The front two dominated from some way out, with track position proving crucial. The form is rated around the race averages.

NOTEBOOK
Redair(IRE), the most expensive purchase in the line-up, was a major morning plunge. She landed the gamble cosily, too, but not before showing distinct signs of greenness by wandering violently in the home straight. She came home strongly, though, and, bred to stay longer trips, will surely improve for this first experience. (op 5-2 tchd 10-3 and 4-1 in a places and 7-2 in places)
Bubbly Ballerina, bred to stay a good deal further in time, was fastest away and had established a decent lead before the turn for home. She began to tread water approaching the final furlong, however, and could not respond when the winner swept past. (op 13-2 tchd 15-2 and 8-1 in places)
He's So Cool(IRE), a January foal from a speedy family, was a well-backed favourite. He could not match the early pace of the first two, though, and was only fourth entering the home straight. He stayed on late and may do better next time. (op 6-4 tchd 6-5 and 15-8 in places)
Ciara Boo(IRE), a half-sister to five winners, broke quite well and was soon in third. She tired noticeably in the closing stages, though, and may just have needed this.
Snowed In(IRE), from the first crop of a Middle Park Stakes winner, was outpaced in the early stages and seemed likely to finish tailed off. He made late progress, however, and will probably be more streetwise next time. (op 10-1)
Umph(IRE), whose sire did well as a freshman last term, was never going the pace. (op 12-1)
Lilygloves, a mid-April foal, faded after racing in fifth for the first half of the contest. (op 12-1)

983 BETFRED "IT'S GOALS GALORE" MEDIAN AUCTION MAIDEN STKS 1m 3f (P)
3:00 (3:00) (Class 6) 3-4-Y-O **£1,535** (£453; £226) **Stalls** Low

Form RPR

44- 1 **Tweedledrum**[257] 3953 4-9-9 0 .... DavidProbert 6 68
(Andrew Balding) *settled in 6th: clsd on ldrs 3f out: drvn 2f out: styd on to ld jst over 1f out: drew clr* **5/1**[3]

03- 2 2 3/4 **Rasam Aldaar**[173] 6618 3-8-8 0 .... SamHitchcott 5 65
(Mick Channon) *trckd ldrs: rdn over 3f out: clsd to ld 2f out: hdd and one pce jst over 1f out* **11/8**[1]

3 1 1/2 **Clarion Call** 3-8-8 0 .... CathyGannon 7 62
(Eve Johnson Houghton) *settled in last: lost tch 4f out: shkn up over 2f out and m green: gd prog sn after: wnt 3rd 1f out and threatened briefly: no ex* **14/1**

4 2 3/4 **Gawaarib (USA)** 3-8-8 0 .... NickyMackay 1 57
(John Gosden) *trckd ldr 4f: lost pl qckly 1/2-way: rdn and lost tch in last trio 4f out: styd on again fnl 2f to take 4th last strides* **3/1**[2]

000- 5 nk **Phoenix Fantasy (IRE)**[173] 6635 3-8-8 50 .... HayleyTurner 8 57?
(Jonathan Portman) *trckd ldr after 4f: rdn to ld over 2f out to 2f out: wknd jst over 1f out* **20/1**

3 6 1/2 **Olimamu (IRE)**[73] 136 4-9-6 0 ....(t) SimonPearce(3) 3 54
(Lydia Pearce) *t.k.h: trckd ldrs: cl 4th and gng wl whn nt clr run over 2f out: sn rdn and wknd tamely* **8/1**

7 6 **Blowing A Hoolie (IRE)** 3-8-3 0 .... KellyHarrison 4 40
(Gay Kelleway) *t.k.h: hld up in last pair: lost tch 4f out: bhd after* **12/1**

8 11 **Graceful Spirit**[10] 4-9-6 0 .... KierenFox(3) 2 23
(Des Donovan) *led to over 2f out: wknd qckly* **20/1**

2m 23.07s (1.17) **Going Correction** -0.05s/f (Stan)
WFA 3 from 4yo 21lb **8** Ran SP% **118.8**
Speed ratings (Par 101): **93,91,89,87,87 87,82,74**
toteswingers:1&2:£2.40, 1&3:£14.10, 2&3:£4.20 CSF £12.83 TOTE £3.80: £1.10, £1.70, £4.00; EX 16.60.
Owner Kingsclere Racing CLub **Bred** Kingsclere Stud **Trained** Kingsclere, Hants

FOCUS
This looked a modest maiden, judged on the form of those to have run. It was steadily run and there are doubts over the reliability of the form.

984 BETFRED H'CAP 7f (P)
3:35 (3:35) (Class 6) (0-65,63) 4-Y-O+ **£1,535** (£453; £226) **Stalls** Low

Form RPR
4451 **1** **Katmai River (IRE)**[8] 893 4-9-1 **57**....(v) DavidProbert 6 68
(Mark Usher) *trckd ldrs in 4th: rdn over 2f out: prog to take narrow ld over 1f out: hrd pressed fnl f: hld on wl* **2/1**[1]
-240 **2** *hd* **Valmina**[16] 820 4-8-12 **61**....(t) GeorgeDowning(7) 3 71
(Tony Carroll) *dwlt: hld up in last pair: shkn up over 2f out: prog on outer over 1f out: chal fnl f: r.o but nt qckn* **8/1**
3114 **3** *2¼* **West Leake (IRE)**[16] 820 5-9-7 **63**.... TomMcLaughlin 2 67
(Paul Burgoyne) *trckd ldng pair: effrt on inner and upsides wl over 1f out: nt qckn ent fnl f* **3/1**[2]
5400 **4** *4* **Cut And Thrust (IRE)**[16] 820 5-9-7 **63**....(v[1]) JamesDoyle 4 56
(Mark Wellings) *pressed ldr: led over 2f out to over 1f out: wknd* **7/1**
50-4 **5** *1¼* **Crinan Classic**[29] 684 4-9-0 **59**....(p) JohnFahy(3) 1 49
(Clive Cox) *rousted along to ld: hdd over 2f out: wknd over 1f out* **5/1**[3]
-004 **6** *3* **Sirjosh**[20] 648 5-9-2 **58**.... CathyGannon 5 40
(Des Donovan) *dwlt: t.k.h and hld up in last pair: c u.p after 3f and struggling after* **6/1**

1m 25.91s (-0.09) **Going Correction** -0.05s/f (Stan) **6** Ran SP% **112.9**
Speed ratings (Par 101): **98,97,95,90,89 85**
toteswingers:1&2:£5.50, 1&3:£2.00, 2&3:£5.80 CSF £18.56 TOTE £3.30: £1.40, £12.50; EX 21.70.
Owner M D I Usher **Bred** Mrs S M Roy **Trained** Upper Lambourn, Berks
■ Stewards' Enquiry : David Probert one-day ban: used whip with excessive frequency (Apr 9)

FOCUS
A low-grade handicap, with the top-weight rated just 63, and the early pace was steady. Limited but sound form.
Sirjosh Official explanation: jockey said gelding never travelled

985 BETFRED "WHEN BOTH TEAMS SCORE..." H'CAP 6f (P)
4:10 (4:11) (Class 5) (0-70,72) 4-Y-O+ **£2,047** (£604; £302) **Stalls** Low

Form RPR
4223 **1** **Yankee Storm**[15] 833 6-9-2 **70**....(b) RyanClark(5) 5 78
(Tom Keddy) *chsd ldr to over 3f out: wnt 2nd again over 2f out: drvn to ld v narrowly jst over 1f out: hrd pressed after: jst hld on* **9/2**[2]
4201 **2** *nse* **Dvinsky (USA)**[16] 820 10-9-4 **67**....(b) ShaneKelly 11 75
(Jane Chapple-Hyam) *sn led: drvn and narrowly hdd jst over 1f out: fought on wl and upsides fnl f: jst pipped* **10/1**
3164 **3** *1* **Co Dependent (USA)**[7] 904 5-9-6 **69**.... FergusSweeney 3 74+
(Jamie Osborne) *dwlt: hld up in last trio: prog on outer over 2f out: tk 3rd fnl f and clsd on ldng pair: effrt flattened out nr fin* **13/2**
303- **4** *½* **The Wee Chief (IRE)**[205] 5695 5-9-0 **68**.... SeanLevey(5) 10 71
(Jimmy Fox) *sltly awkward s: t.k.h: hld up in tch: effrt 2f out: nt qckn over 1f out: kpt on same pce* **13/2**
60-2 **5** *1½* **Hand Painted**[51] 404 5-9-5 **68**.... JimmyFortune 1 66
(Peter Makin) *hld up bhd ldrs: effrt to go 3rd over 1f out on inner: nt qckn sn after: fdd fnl f* **3/1**[1]
4541 **6** *nk* **Sherjawy (IRE)**[7] 910 7-9-6 **69**.... KirstyMilczarek 7 66
(Zoe Davison) *prom on outer: chsd ldr over 3f out tl over 2f out: one pce u.p* **17/2**
3231 **7** *½* **Frequency**[7] 904 4-9-9 **72**.... HayleyTurner 6 68+
(Conor Dore) *v awkward s and slowly away: settled in last: jst pushed along fr over 2f out: kpt on: nvr nr ldrs* **5/1**[3]
2035 **8** *¾* **Onceaponatime (IRE)**[7] 904 6-9-5 **68**.... LeeNewman 2 61
(Michael Squance) *prom: rdn over 2f out: steadily wknd over 1f out* **11/1**
5-00 **9** *¾* **Green Earth (IRE)**[16] 822 4-9-2 **70**.... JemmaMarshall(5) 4 61
(Pat Phelan) *settled in last trio: rdn over 2f out: no prog* **16/1**
1114 **10** *¾* **Shawkantango**[29] 696 4-9-1 **64**.... RobbieFitzpatrick 12 53
(Derek Shaw) *nvr bttr than midfield: u.p and no rspnse over 2f out: sn dropped to last pair and btn* **20/1**

1m 12.69s (-0.41) **Going Correction** -0.05s/f (Stan) **10** Ran SP% **125.1**
Speed ratings (Par 103): **100,99,98,97,95 95,94,93,92,91**
toteswingers:1&2:£7.50, 1&3:£5.50, 2&3:£13.70 CSF £52.90 CT £310.01 TOTE £3.60: £1.10, £4.30, £4.00; EX 48.30.
Owner R L Maynard **Bred** Mark Johnston Racing Ltd **Trained** Newmarket, Suffolk

FOCUS
Only a modest contest, with the top-weight rated 72, but it looked fiercely competitive on paper. The winner basically ran to his best, with the second running his best race since last summer.
Dvinsky(USA) Official explanation: jockey said gelding hung right on bend

986 BETFRED.COM POKER CONDITIONS STKS 6f (P)
4:40 (4:41) (Class 3) 3-Y-O+ **£5,180** (£1,541; £770; £384) **Stalls** Low

Form RPR
0362 **1** **Iver Bridge Lad**[16] 825 4-9-1 0....(b) MichaelO'Connell(3) 7 96
(John Ryan) *trckd ldrs in 4th: pushed along and prog to ld over 1f out: drvn and styd on stoutly* **15/8**[2]
-331 **2** *1* **Ebraam (USA)**[31] 651 8-9-4 88.... LukeMorris 5 93
(Ronald Harris) *hld up last: effrt 2f out: hrd rdn to take 2nd jst ins fnl f: styd on but a hld* **8/1**
4-60 **3** *1¾* **Angel's Pursuit (IRE)**[14] 844 4-9-11 105....(b[1]) JimmyFortune 1 94
(Richard Hannon) *trckd ldng pair: effrt to chal wl over 1f out: nt qckn ent fnl f: wl hld after* **11/8**[1]
060- **4** *1* **Mac Gille Eoin**[239] 4536 7-9-4 85.... FergusSweeney 4 84
(John Gallagher) *led: hung bdly lft fr 2f out and ended against nr side rail: hdd over 1f out: n.d fnl f* **16/1**
000- **5** *6* **Absolute Music (USA)**[123] 7545 4-8-13 93.... AdamKirby 3 60
(Marco Botti) *chsd ldr to jst over 2f out: sn wknd* **5/1**[3]

1m 11.61s (-1.49) **Going Correction** -0.05s/f (Stan) **5** Ran SP% **110.5**
Speed ratings (Par 107): **107,105,103,102,94**
CSF £15.98 TOTE £3.10: £1.70, £1.30; EX 13.80.
Owner The Iver Lads **Bred** Jcs Wilson Bloodstock **Trained** Newmarket, Suffolk
■ Stewards' Enquiry : Fergus Sweeney one-day ban: careless riding (Apr 9)

FOCUS
An interesting conditions event. The form pair were not at their best and this is probably not one to be too positive about.

NOTEBOOK
Iver Bridge Lad, second off a mark of 105 in Dubai on his most recent outing, was a game winner. Smartly away but soon reined back slightly, he raced in fourth until the 2f pole and then quickened decisively. He was strongly pressed by the runner-up but always seemed likely to hold on. This was not his best effort and he almost certainly did not run to his rating but his victory was well deserved. He may now head for the Cammidge Trophy at Doncaster next Saturday. (tchd 13-8)

Ebraam(USA), successful off a rating of 84 in a handicap here a month earlier, was held up in the early stages. He began to make progress in the home straight, though, and threw down a decent challenge under strong driving. His handicap mark will suffer for this.

Angel's Pursuit(IRE), fitted with first-time blinkers after twice disappointing this year, was again well below his peak. Never closer than third, he was losing ground on the first two in the closing stages. (op 13-8 tchd 7-4 and 15-8 in a place)

Mac Gille Eoin, without a victory since the summer of 2009, broke more quickly than his rivals and soon established a useful lead. He drifted badly left in the home straight, though, finishing the race under the stands' rail, and that put paid to his chance. (op 14-1)

Absolute Music(USA), decent as a two-year-old and making her first appearance for new connections, ran as if the race was needed after a 123-day layoff. She chased the pace until the 2f marker but then faded quickly. (tchd 9-2)

987 BETFRED "BUNDLES" H'CAP 7f (P)
5:15 (5:15) (Class 6) (0-65,64) 3-Y-O **£1,535** (£453; £226) **Stalls** Low

Form RPR
025- **1** **Avalon Bay**[142] 7313 3-9-3 **60**.... DaneO'Neill 6 65
(Pat Eddery) *mde all: sn 3 l clr: hld together tl shkn up 2f out: rdn out fnl f: unchal* **13/2**
3334 **2** *2¼* **Not So Bright (USA)**[8] 891 3-9-0 **57**....(tp) CathyGannon 3 56
(Des Donovan) *settled in last pair: prog on inner over 2f out: chsd wnr over 1f out: kpt on but no real imp* **6/1**[3]
-010 **3** *2* **Alfraamsey**[1] 964 3-8-10 **60**.... CharlesBishop(7) 1 54
(Mick Channon) *chsd wnr after 2f: drvn and no imp over 2f out: lost 2nd over 1f out: fdd* **6/1**[3]
205 **4** *hd* **Lennoxwood (IRE)**[16] 818 3-8-10 **53**.... DavidProbert 5 46
(Mark Usher) *dwlt: chsd ldng pair after 2f to 2f out: one pce u.p* **9/2**[2]
504- **5** *3½* **Danceyourselfdizzy (IRE)**[159] 6988 3-9-7 **64**.... JimmyFortune 7 53
(Richard Hannon) *wnt lft s: hld up in last: rdn and modest prog over 2f out: no hdwy over 1f out: wl btn after* **11/8**[1]
20-0 **6** *4½* **High Class Lady**[23] 745 3-9-3 **60**.... AdamKirby 8 31
(Walter Swinburn) *bmpd s: chsd wnr 2f out: sn lost pl and u.p: wl btn 3f out* **16/1**
16-0 **7** *1* **Microlight**[22] 760 3-8-12 **58**....(e) NataliaGemelova(3) 4 27
(John E Long) *in tch: drvn and struggling in rr 3f out: sn btn* **20/1**

1m 26.34s (0.34) **Going Correction** -0.05s/f (Stan) **7** Ran SP% **112.8**
Speed ratings (Par 96): **96,93,91,90,86 81,80**
toteswingers:1&2:£5.00, 1&3:£6.40, 2&3:£5.50 CSF £43.11 CT £244.54 TOTE £7.70: £4.40, £1.60; EX 42.50.
Owner Pat Eddery Racing (Reference Point) **Bred** Manor Farm Stud (rutland) **Trained** Nether Winchendon, Bucks

FOCUS
A modest 3-y-o handicap. The winner got an easy lead and the form is rated around him.

988 BETFRED TEXT KEMP TO 89660 H'CAP (LONDON MILE QUALIFIER) 1m (P)
5:50 (5:50) (Class 3) (0-95,94) 3-Y-O **£5,180** (£1,541; £770; £384) **Stalls** Low

Form RPR
313- **1** **Tinkertown (IRE)**[150] 7165 3-9-3 **90**.... ChrisCatlin 1 102
(Paul Cole) *hld up in tch: shkn up and prog to go 3rd 2f out: clsd to ld 1f out: forged clr: readily* **9/2**
-111 **2** *4* **Kuala Limper (IRE)**[45] 468 3-8-12 **85**.... DaneO'Neill 2 88
(David Elsworth) *t.k.h: led after 3f: hrd pressed over 2f out: fending off rival whn wnr stormed past 1f out: no answer* **9/4**[1]
3221 **3** *nk* **Amwell Pinot**[23] 750 3-9-7 **94**....(b) CathyGannon 3 96
(Alan Bailey) *cl up: pressed ldr over 4f out: chal fr 3f out: upsides over 1f out: sn outpcd* **11/4**[2]
0604 **4** *2¾* **Sonoran Sands (IRE)**[23] 753 3-9-4 **91**....(p) HayleyTurner 6 87
(J S Moore) *led at modest pce for 3f: sn settled in 3rd: shkn up and nt qckn over 2f out: n.d after* **9/1**
1 **5** *¾* **Loch Fleet (IRE)**[29] 684 3-8-7 **80**.... DavidProbert 5 74
(Andrew Balding) *cl up: drvn and no qckn over 2f out: wl btn sn after* **3/1**[3]
404- **6** *3¼* **Bussa**[200] 5830 3-8-1 **81**.... MatthewCosham(7) 4 67
(David Evans) *awkward s: a last: struggling fr 3f out* **25/1**

1m 38.48s (-1.32) **Going Correction** -0.05s/f (Stan) **6** Ran SP% **114.5**
Speed ratings (Par 102): **104,100,99,96,96 92**
toteswingers:1&2:£2.10, 2&3:£1.70, 1&3:£3.40. totesuper7: Win: £168.91. Place: £52.36 CSF £15.49 TOTE £5.20: £2.90, £1.10; EX 16.40.
Owner Mrs Fitri Hay **Bred** Corrin Stud **Trained** Whatcombe, Oxon

FOCUS
A decent finale in which, beforehand at least, all the runners appeared to have claims. The favourite was below form but the winner is generally progressive.

NOTEBOOK
Tinkertown(IRE), twice successful as a 2-y-o in 2010, decisively regained the winning thread. Held up in the early stages, he was briefly outpaced coming off the home turn but quickened well when switched left around rivals and then drew clear for a smooth success. His rating will rise markedly for this, but he should score again at some stage. (op 11-2 tchd 7-2)

Kuala Limper(IRE), 4lb higher than when completing a hat-trick over course and distance in February, was quite keen early on and, perhaps as a result, his saddle slipped forward. That clearly did not improve his prospects, but the winner beat him too easily for him to be called unlucky. (op 15-8)

Amwell Pinot was up 5lb since his most recent success at Wolverhampton 23 days earlier and racing from his new mark proved beyond him. He was always prominent and slightly impeded by the runner-up inside the final furlong, but the interference certainly did not cost him the race. (op 10-3 tchd 4-1)

Sonoran Sands(IRE), lowered in the ratings after a sequence of modest efforts in Dubai this year, led in the early stages. He had been overtaken by halfway, however, and could not muster a change of pace in the home straight. (op 11-1 tchd 8-1)

Loch Fleet(IRE), well backed when taking a maiden on his only previous outing, never looked likely to collect again. No closer than fourth at any stage, he does not seem particularly well handicapped on this evidence. (op 10-3 tchd 7-2)

Bussa, making his AW debut and his first appearance of 2011, was awkward leaving the stalls and, from then on, always struggling to stay with his rivals. (op 20-1)

T/Plt: £259.40 to a £1 stake. Pool:£42,132.61 - 118.55 winning tickets T/Qpdt: £45.20 to a £1 stake. Pool:£2,916.48 - 47.70 winning tickets JN

958 LINGFIELD (L-H)

Saturday, March 26

OFFICIAL GOING: Standard

Wind: Almost nil Weather: Overcast

989 SPORTINGBET SUPPORTS HEROS HEVER SPRINT STKS (LISTED RACE) 5f (P)

2:00 (2:00) (Class 1) 4-Y-0+

£17,031 (£6,456; £3,231; £1,611; £807; £405) **Stalls** High

Form RPR

2-12 **1** **Anne Of Kiev (IRE)**[28] 700 6-8-9 95............................(t) SteveDrowne 5 101
(Jeremy Gask) *n.m.r and shuffled to rr sn after s: hdwy on ins 2f out: kpt on wl ins fnl f to ld towards fin* **7/1**

1260 **2** *hd* **Silaah**[23] 755 7-9-0 105...(p) DaneO'Neill 2 105
(David Nicholls) *cl up: led over 1f out: rdn and edgd lft: kpt on ins fnl f: hdd towards fin* **5/1**[2]

0-40 **3** *¾* **Lui Rei (ITY)**[37] 582 5-9-0 0.. JimCrowley 1 102
(Robert Cowell) *s.i.s: sn prom on ins: effrt and ev ch ins fnl f: hld towards fin* **25/1**

3210 **4** *nk* **Five Star Junior (USA)**[28] 700 5-9-0 97...................... DarryllHolland 3 101
(Linda Stubbs) *trckd ldrs: effrt over 1f out: kpt on same pce wl ins fnl f* **12/1**

21-5 **5** *½* **Hitchens (IRE)**[28] 700 6-9-3 104............................ GrahamGibbons 6 102
(David Barron) *lw: in tch: rdn and outpcd 2f out: rallied and kpt on ins fnl f: nrst fin* **9/4**[1]

-221 **6** *nk* **Waveband**[28] 700 4-8-12 96... EddieAhern 8 96
(David Barron) *led to over 1f out: rallied: kpt on same pce wl ins fnl f* **13/2**[3]

620- **7** *1* **Fratellino**[317] 2058 4-9-0 96...................................... RobertWinston 4 95
(Alan McCabe) *trckd ldrs: drvn over 2f out: one pce ins fnl f: eased whn hld towards fin* **20/1**

-524 **8** *1¾* **Star Rover (IRE)**[14] 848 4-9-0 89................................. JimmyFortune 9 88
(David Evans) *sn bhd on outside: hdwy u.p over 1f out: nvr able to chal* **20/1**

14-6 **9** *1¾* **Secret Asset (IRE)**[14] 848 6-9-0 99................................ NeilCallan 10 82
(Jane Chapple-Hyam) *hld up on outside: struggling over 2f out: sn btn* **8/1**

034- **10** *12* **Rowe Park**[126] 7524 8-9-0 100.. IanMongan 7 39
(Linda Jewell) *lw: in tch: struggling over 2f out: sn btn* **10/1**

58.46 secs (-0.34) **Going Correction** +0.125s/f (Slow) **10** Ran SP% **114.5**

Speed ratings (Par 111): **107,106,105,105,104 103,102,99,96,77**

toteswingers:1&2 £5.40, 2&3 £29.70, 1&3 £31.90 CSF £39.85 TOTE £7.60: £2.50, £1.60, £8.00; EX 37.90 Trifecta £323.50 Pool: £1,189.27 - 2.72 winning units..

Owner P Bamford **Bred** Deerfield Farm **Trained** Sutton Veny, Wilts

FOCUS

Useful form in this Listed sprint with a small personal best from the winner. They went a sound pace and there were no obvious hard-luck stories.

NOTEBOOK

Anne Of Kiev(IRE) has thrived this winter and went one better than at a similar level last time, needing all of this shorter trip to prevail (recent wins had all come at 6f). Her improvement started on turf last summer, so she's not necessarily just an AW specialist, and there could easily be more to come from her. (op 5-1)

Silaah was at the top of his game when last seen in this country, and put a couple of below-par efforts in Dubai behind him. A bit more will be required in turf races at this level, but he's yet another example of his trainer's knack with sprinters and he's not necessarily reached his peak yet, for all he's seven. (op 7-1)

Lui Rei(ITY)'s best form before this had come over further but he showed he has the speed for the minimum trip. He's not been long with a trainer who tends to get the best out of this type, and he shouldn't be too hard to place to advantage if his sights aren't set too high. (op 20-1)

Five Star Junior(USA) didn't have things go his way last time and showed he can be competitive at this level, though he will have to take his form up another notch to prevail in this company, particularly on turf. (tchd 14-1)

Hitchens(IRE) didn't have quite the chance the market suggested conceding weight all round, and wasn't discredited, particularly as this trip is probably shorter than ideal (all wins at 6f). He's just as effective on turf. (, tchd 7-2 in a place and 10-3 in a place)

Waveband had justed edged out Anne of Kiev here last time, but had a 3lb penalty to shoulder and, perhaps more importantly, wasn't able to dominate as she had on that occasion, fading inside the last. (op 5-1 tchd 7-1)

Fratellino showed enough to suggest he retains all his ability after a ten-month absence, though he's unlikely to be the easiest to place near to hand, being too high in the weights for handicaps and probably not quite good enough for conditions races. (op 16-1)

Secret Asset(IRE) was always caught a bit wide but wasn't at his best in any case. (op 15-2 tchd 9-1)

990 SPORTINGBET SUPPORTS HEROS SPRING CUP (LISTED RACE) 7f (P)

2:35 (2:38) (Class 1) 3-Y-O

£17,031 (£6,456; £3,231; £1,611; £807; £405) **Stalls** Low

Form RPR

410- **1** **Dubawi Gold**[154] 7081 3-9-1 100................................ JimmyFortune 5 105
(Richard Hannon) *stdd in last pl: effrt and plenty to do ent st: edgd lft and gd hdwy against ins rail ins fnl f to ld towards fin* **7/4**[1]

22- **2** *hd* **Elshabakiya (IRE)**[298] 2616 3-8-10 0........................ PhilipRobinson 4 99
(Clive Brittain) *h.d.w: t.k.h: chsd ldr: rdn and led ins fnl f: hdd towards fin* **5/1**[3]

111- **3** *3* **Vanguard Dream**[170] 6690 3-9-1 95................................ DaneO'Neill 2 96
(Richard Hannon) *t.k.h early: led: rdn 2f out: edgd lft and hdd ins fnl f: sn outpcd* **9/4**[2]

015- **4** *5* **Conducting**[142] 7317 3-9-1 78.. ShaneKelly 1 82
(Brian Meehan) *s.i.s: hld up in tch: effrt over 2f out: wknd wl over 1f out* **25/1**

521- **5** *¾* **Oceanway (USA)**[142] 7312 3-8-10 87................................ GregFairley 6 75
(Mark Johnston) *str: lw: in tch on outside: pushed along fr 1/2-way: wknd fr 2f out* **11/2**

03-3 **6** *4½* **Bathwick Bear (IRE)**[9] 883 3-9-3 101.......................... RichardEvans 3 70
(David Evans) *on toes: lw: chsd ldrs tl drvn and wknd fr 2f out* **12/1**

1m 23.74s (-1.06) **Going Correction** +0.125s/f (Slow) **6** Ran SP% **110.7**

Speed ratings (Par 106): **111,110,107,101,100 95**

toteswingers:1&2 £2.60, 2&3 £2.20, 1&3 £1.10 CSF £10.61 TOTE £2.40: £1.10, £4.00; EX 13.00.

Owner Andrew Tinkler **Bred** A H Bennett **Trained** East Everleigh, Wilts

FOCUS

A much smaller field than usual for this listed 3-y-o prize, but the race was well run and this looks good form. The winner confirmed his Ascot improvement.

NOTEBOOK

Dubawi Gold ◆ could turn out to be one of its best winners of this after justifying hefty market support on his first outing for Richard Hannon. He'd often taken a good hold in his races for Michael Dods last term and new connections were obviously keen to get him settled. That did result in him having quite a lot to do entering the straight, but he showed a good turn of foot to get up near the line. He'll get 1m this year on this evidence and will be well worth his place in a Guineas trial, the Free Handicap mentioned as a likely target. (op 7-2)

Elshabakiya(IRE), runner-up in a couple of sprint maidens early last summer, showed marked improvement on her return, failing only narrowly to emulate Nashmiah's success in this for the same connections in 2009, seeing things out well considering she was keen enough early on. There's every reason to believe she can go on from this but, knowing her trainer, there's a good chance her sights will be set pretty high now (entered in Guineas and Oaks). (op 3-1)

Vanguard Dream, a stablemate of the winner, couldn't maintain his unbeaten record on his return but confirmed himself a useful colt, making the running and possibly just needing this for fitness in the end. He stays 1m and his three wins as a juvenile came on good going or softer. (tchd 5-2)

Conducting won't prove up to this level in all probability, but there was plenty to like in the way he travelled for a long way and at least his eventual margin of defeat should ensure he doesn't do too much damage to a BHA mark of 78. His maiden win came at this trip on soft ground. (op 18-1)

Oceanway(USA) was progressive in maidens last year, culminating with a success over 7f at Kempton in November, and might have been expected to make more of an impact up in class. It's still early days with her, however, and the fact she was pitched in at this level suggests she must be fairly highly regarded. (op 5-1)

Bathwick Bear(IRE) was always likely to be vulnerable under his penalty, but this was still disappointing, particularly as he'd seemed to run creditably on his return at Deauville earlier in the month. Official explanation: was always likely to be vulnerable under his penalty, but this was still disappointing, particularly as he'd seemed to run creditably on his return at Deauville earlier in the month.

991 SPORTINGBET SUPPORTS HEROS WINTER DERBY (GROUP 3) 1m 2f (P)

3:10 (3:11) (Class 1) 4-Y-0+

£28,385 (£10,760; £5,385; £2,685; £1,345; £675) **Stalls** Low

Form RPR

112- **1** **Nideeb**[119] 7594 4-9-0 107.. PhilipRobinson 3 112
(Clive Brittain) *lw: -racd freely: led 1f: cl up: led on ins over 2f out: rdn and qcknd over 1f out: edgd both ways and kpt on strly ins fnl f* **9/4**[1]

501- **2** *1½* **Dansili Dancer**[143] 7297 9-9-0 110................................ AdamKirby 10 109
(Clive Cox) *hld up towards rr: hdwy and prom over 2f out: effrt and chsd wnr appr fnl f: kpt on* **4/1**[2]

651- **3** *3¾* **Pachattack (USA)**[140] 7371 5-8-11 106..........................(b) NeilCallan 9 98
(Gerard Butler) *t.k.h: cl up: ev ch briefly over 2f out: sn rdn and outpcd: kpt on ins fnl f: nt gng pce of first two* **4/1**[2]

3310 **4** *¼* **Suits Me**[14] 846 8-9-0 95.. DarryllHolland 11 101
(Tom Tate) *led after 1f: rdn and hdd over 2f out: kpt on same pce fr over 1f out* **12/1**

036- **5** *2¼* **Cockney Class (USA)**[162] 6885 4-9-0 95.......................... LiamJones 4 96
(Brian Meehan) *bit bkwd: midfield: effrt on outside over 2f out: drvn and outpcd wl over 1f out: styd on towards fin: no imp* **12/1**

-355 **6** *1* **Franco Is My Name**[28] 702 5-9-0 88..............................(p) DaneO'Neill 8 94
(Peter Hedger) *hld up: pushed along over 2f out: edgd rt and kpt on over 1f out: nvr able to chal* **20/1**

3133 **7** *½* **Layline (IRE)**[17] 803 4-9-0 91...................................... RobertWinston 2 93
(Gay Kelleway) *b: b.hind: dwlt: t.k.h and sn prom: rdn and outpcd over 2f out: n.d after* **20/1**

35-1 **8** *2¼* **Nice Style (IRE)**[70] 180 6-9-0 97................................... SteveDrowne 12 89
(Jeremy Gask) *lw: t.k.h: hld up: drvn over 2f out: edgd lft and no imp over 1f out* **7/1**[3]

30-0 **9** *1¾* **Silver Grey (IRE)**[28] 702 4-8-11 95..............................(p) MartinLane 6 82
(Roger Ingram) *towards rr: drvn and outpcd wl over 2f out: sn btn* **33/1**

10-0 **10** *hd* **Shamir**[28] 702 4-9-0 86.. IanMongan 7 85
(Jo Crowley) *in tch on outside: drvn over 2f out: wknd ent st* **33/1**

-000 **11** *hd* **Big Creek (IRE)**[36] 605 4-9-0 0....................................(p) LukeMorris 5 84
(J S Moore) *t.k.h: cl up tl rdn and wknd over 2f out* **33/1**

0100 **12** *1¾* **Hidden Glory**[28] 702 4-9-0 87...................................... PaulMulrennan 1 81
(James Given) *hld up on ins: drvn over 2f out: sn btn* **50/1**

1005 **13** *18* **Mister Green (FR)**[10] 867 5-9-0 71...............................(bt) TonyCulhane 13 45
(David Flood) *stdd s: hld up and bhd: rdn over 2f out: sn lost tch* **100/1**

2m 3.42s (-3.18) **Going Correction** +0.125s/f (Slow) **13** Ran SP% **120.0**

Speed ratings (Par 113): **117,115,112,112,110 110,109,107,106,106 106,104,90**

CSF £10.01 TOTE £3.20: £1.40, £1.80, £1.50; EX 12.10 Trifecta £23.00 Pool: £2,287.12 - 73.58 winning units..

Owner Saeed Manana **Bred** Rabbah Bloodstock Limited **Trained** Newmarket, Suffolk

■ Stewards' Enquiry : Philip Robinson caution: used whip without giving colt time to respond.

FOCUS

By no means a vintage renewal of the Winter Derby in depth, but the three in the line-up rated in excess of 100 did come to the fore. An up-to-scratch effort from the winner. The tempo steadied once Suits Me got across to lead early, and it didn't pay to sit too far back.

NOTEBOOK

Nideeb ended last year in really good heart, winning a listed race over C&D, but almost certainly took his form up another notch in taking this in good style, travelling smoothly and always doing enough after quickening to the front at the top of the straight. His third in a Listed race at Newmarket last autumn showed he's just as good on turf and this should set him up perfectly for a profitable campaign. (op 11-4)

Dansili Dancer has a really good record on this surface and lost little in defeat against a progressive rival, seeing off the rest comfortably. Something like the Magnolia Stakes at Kempton would be an obvious next target for him. He's not quite as good on turf but did win a handicap off 99 a couple of years back and is now lower in the weights on grass, so there'll be plenty of options for him even when opportunities on AW dry up. (op 9-2)

Pachattack(USA), a three-time winner last year, including a couple of Listed events on turf, was by no means discredited on her return, able only to keep on rather than quicken once the tempo increased. She's a tough and reliable mare and is sure to pay her way again, particularly in races against her own sex. (tchd 7-2)

Suits Me doesn't seem quite as good as last year and couldn't match his second in this 12 months ago, being soon across to dictate but readily brushed aside in the straight.

Cockney Class(USA) got his career back on track at the end of last year and showed he has returned in good heart, seeing out the longer trip well, albeit with the emphasis on speed. He's versatile regards ground, having shown won on good to firm and also shown his form on a softish surface. (op 14-1 tchd 11-1)

Franco Is My Name had a bit to find and fared about as well as could be expected, though he doesn't look the easiest of rides these days, once again carrying his head a shade awkwardly. (op 25-1)

Layline(IRE) was another who had a bit to find and also ran as well as could be expected. (op 16-1)

Nice Style(IRE) was well worth her place in this company after winning a handicap off 94 last time but got little chance to show what she could do, caught too far back. She's worth another chance. Official explanation: jockey said gelding did not face the kickback (op 8-1)

Mister Green(FR) Official explanation: trainer said gelding bled from the nose

992 SPORTINGBET SUPPORTS HEROS MAIDEN STKS — 1m 2f (P)
3:40 (3:41) (Class 5) 3-Y-0+ — **£1,942** (£578; £288; £144) **Stalls** Low

Form — RPR

42- **1** **Musawama (IRE)**[197] [5916] 3-8-7 0 ... RobertHavlin 5 — 78+
(John Gosden) *lw: hld up in tch: smooth hdwy on wd outside to ld over 2f out: pushed out ins fnl f: comf* **13/8**[1]

00- **2** *1 ½* **Viking Storm**[154] [7094] 3-8-7 0 ... ChrisCatlin 7 — 71
(Harry Dunlop) *hld up last: effrt and swtchd centre over 1f out: gd hdwy to chse (clr) wnr ins fnl f: r.o* **33/1**

3 *nk* **Tasheyaat** 3-8-2 0 ... WilliamCarson 2 — 65+
(B W Hills) *w'like: hld up in tch: n.m.r over 2f out: effrt and hdwy over 1f out: kpt on ins fnl f: no imp towards fin* **15/8**[2]

0- **4** *2 ¾* **Yahafedh Alaih**[256] [3991] 3-8-9 0 ow2 ... PhilipRobinson 6 — 67
(Clive Brittain) *hld up towards rr: hdwy on outside to chse (clr) wnr over 1f out to ins fnl f: kpt on same pce* **7/1**[3]

0 **5** *3* **Harry Lime**[33] [634] 3-8-7 0 ... GregFairley 1 — 59
(Mark Johnston) *t.k.h early: led to over 2f out: outpcd over 1f out* **12/1**

32 **6** *nse* **King Kieren (IRE)**[29] [688] 6-9-13 0 ... EddieAhern 4 — 63?
(Linda Jewell) *trckd ldrs: effrt over 2f out: wknd appr fnl f* **12/1**

5-4 **7** *3 ½* **No Time For Tears (IRE)**[22] [762] 4-9-8 0 ... DaneO'Neill 3 — 51
(Lucinda Featherstone) *s.i.s: hld up: shkn up over 1f out: nvr nr ldrs* **20/1**

66 **8** *4* **Miles Of Sunshine**[22] [762] 6-9-13 0 ... (p) JimCrowley 9 — 48
(Ron Hodges) *t.k.h: trckd ldrs tl rdn and wknd over 1f out* **40/1**

0-6 **9** *2 ¾* **Diocese (USA)**[14] [850] 3-8-8 0 ow1 ... (t) SteveDrowne 8 — 39
(Marco Botti) *trckd ldrs: rdn over 2f out: wknd over 1f out* **20/1**

2m 7.45s (0.85) **Going Correction** +0.125s/f (Slow)
WFA 3 from 4yo+ 20lb — **9** Ran SP% **115.7**
Speed ratings (Par 103): **101,99,99,97,94 94,92,88,86**
toteswingers: 1&2 £14.50, 1&3 £1.10, 2&3 £53.10 CSF £65.57 TOTE £3.00: £1.20, £14.00, £1.10; EX 44.20 Trifecta £93.50 Pool: £849.81 - 6.72 winning units..
Owner Hamdan Al Maktoum **Bred** Shadwell Estate Company Limited **Trained** Newmarket, Suffolk

FOCUS
Not much strength in depth in this maiden but there was promise amongst the principals. The winner probably didn't need to improve on his 2yo form but can rate higher.

993 SPORTINGBET.COM SUPPORTS HEROS MAIDEN STKS — 1m (P)
4:15 (4:15) (Class 5) 3-Y-0+ — **£1,942** (£578; £288; £144) **Stalls** High

Form — RPR

50- **1** **Great Shot**[154] [7094] 3-8-10 0 ... LiamKeniry 8 — 74+
(Sylvester Kirk) *swtg: plld hrd: stdd in tch: effrt and rn wd bnd ent st: hdwy to ld ins fnl f: styd on strly* **5/2**[2]

43-4 **2** *1* **Whistle On By**[22] [776] 3-8-10 75 ... DarryllHolland 6 — 72
(B W Hills) *swtg: cl up: led over 2f out: rdn and edgd lft over 1f out: hdd ins fnl f: kpt on same pce* **7/4**[1]

23 **3** *nk* **Black Pond (USA)**[26] [713] 3-8-10 0 ... NeilCallan 7 — 71
(Mark Johnston) *lengthy: str: chsd ldrs on outside: hdwy and ev ch 2f out: sn rdn and edgd lft: kpt on same pce ins fnl f* **4/1**[3]

4 *2 ¾* **Prime Mover** 3-8-10 0 ... EddieAhern 3 — 65+
(Ed Dunlop) *w'like: leggy: s.i.s: bhd: hdwy and rn green 2f out: styd on ins fnl f: nvr able to chal* **8/1**

6-34 **5** *1 ¼* **Kentish (USA)**[33] [636] 4-9-8 73 ... KieranO'Neill[(5)] 4 — 66
(Noel Quinlan) *led at stdy pce tl hdd over 2f out: no ex over 1f out* **8/1**

6 **6** *6* **Black Feather**[7] [909] 3-8-0 0 ... DeclanCannon[(5)] 5 — 42
(Alan McCabe) *leggy: trckd ldrs: drvn and struggling over 2f out: sn btn* **20/1**

006- **7** *nk* **Cinderella**[131] [7461] 4-9-3 35 ... RyanPowell[(5)] 2 — 46
(Lucinda Featherstone) *trckd ldrs tl rdn and wknd over 2f out* **66/1**

1m 38.44s (0.24) **Going Correction** +0.125s/f (Slow)
WFA 3 from 4yo 17lb — **7** Ran SP% **113.4**
Speed ratings (Par 103): **103,102,101,98,97 91,91**
toteswingers: 1&2 £1.40, 1&3 £3.40, 2&3 £1.30 CSF £7.16 TOTE £4.30: £3.10, £2.00; EX 11.30 Trifecta £98.60 Pool: £778.81 - 5.84 winning units..
Owner J C Smith **Bred** Littleton Stud **Trained** Upper Lambourn, Berks

FOCUS
Probably a similar ordinary standard to the other maiden on the card, the 75-rated runner-up very much the guide to the form. The winner was up a stone on his 2yo level.

994 SPORTINGBET.COM SUPPORTS HEROS H'CAP — 1m 4f (P)
4:45 (4:45) (Class 3) (0-95,93) 4-Y-0+ — **£5,828** (£1,734; £866; £432) **Stalls** Low

Form — RPR

-112 **1** **Beaubrav**[35] [614] 5-8-13 **85** ... (t) JimCrowley 6 — 95+
(Michael Madgwick) *prom: shkn up and qcknd to ld appr fnl f: comf* **10/3**[2]

2000 **2** *1 ¾* **Tominator**[15] [840] 4-9-2 **90** ... TonyCulhane 8 — 95+
(Reg Hollinshead) *stdd in last pl: effrt and plenty to do ent st: rdn and styd on to go 2nd towards fin: no ch w wnr* **13/2**

062- **3** *nk* **Bowdler's Magic**[150] [7173] 4-8-13 **87** ... NeilCallan 5 — 92
(Mark Johnston) *lw: trckd ldrs: effrt and ev ch over 2f out to appr fnl f: kpt on same pce: lost 2nd towards fin* **11/4**[1]

66- **4** *2* **Langley**[13] 4-8-10 **84** ... RobertHavlin 2 — 85?
(Pat Murphy) *hld up in tch: rdn whn edgd lft over 1f out: kpt on ins fnl f: nvr able to chal* **40/1**

-324 **5** *½* **Realisation (USA)**[35] [614] 4-8-9 **83** ... GregFairley 4 — 84
(Mark Johnston) *dictated ordinary gallop: rdn and hdd appr fnl f: sn outpcd* **11/2**[3]

13-0 **6** *½* **Sherman McCoy**[14] [849] 5-8-13 **85** ... JamesMillman 1 — 85
(Rod Millman) *t.k.h: cl up: drvn and outpcd over 2f out: sn n.d* **10/1**

2126 **7** *1* **Scamperdale**[17] [803] 9-9-4 **93** ... KierenFox[(3)] 7 — 91
(Brian Baugh) *prom on outside: rdn and edgd lft over 1f out: wknd ins fnl f* **8/1**

303- **8** *2 ¾* **Gomrath (IRE)**[115] [7653] 4-8-7 **81** ... SamHitchcott 3 — 75
(Mick Channon) *t.k.h: trckd ldrs: struggling over 2f out: sn btn* **15/2**

2m 34.34s (1.34) **Going Correction** +0.125s/f (Slow)
WFA 4 from 5yo+ 2lb — **8** Ran SP% **112.9**
Speed ratings (Par 107): **100,98,98,97,96 96,95,94**
toteswingers: 1&2 £5.90, 1&3 £2.10, 2&3 £5.10 CSF £24.50 CT £65.67 TOTE £4.00: £1.50, £2.60, £1.40; EX 24.90 Trifecta £44.60 Pool: £554.65 - 9.20 winning units..
Owner The B B Partnership **Bred** Star Pointe Ltd,Brosnan And Williamson **Trained** Denmead, Hants

FOCUS
A useful handicap. The gallop was just a modest one, not really increasing until the final 4f. The winner continued his progress and was value for a bit extra, but there is a slight doubt over the reliability of the form.

NOTEBOOK
Beaubrav just keeps getting better, particularly at this venue, making it five wins in his last seven starts here, the modest gallop playing to the strengths of one with form over shorter, quickening to the front around 1f out. There may not be many options for him on AW in the near future, but he'll be of interest back on turf off his much lower mark in that sphere. (op 4-1)
Tominator, who came here fit from a spell in France, is unexposed at this sort of trip and may be capable of adding to his success at Wolverhampton in November, being better than the result here having still been last at the top of the straight. (op 8-1)
Bowdler's Magic couldn't justify favouritism but this was still an encouraging return to action, the fact he could keep on only at one pace in the end perfectly understandable given he's more about stamina than speed (second over 2m on turf on final start last year). He should build on this. (op 3-1 tchd 10-3)
Langley, a dual winner on the Flat in Germany, had shown little for his current yard over hurdles and clearly appreciated the return to the level, keeping on steadily. (tchd 33-1)
Realisation(USA) was closely matched with Beaubrav on their latest efforts and might have been expected to do better, weakening in the end having dictated the pace. (op 5-1)
Sherman McCoy has been below par on both recent starts since returning from a break. (op 8-1)
Scamperdale is another who has now been below his best the last twice. (tchd 15-2)
Gomrath(IRE) showed no immediate promise after a four-month break. (tchd 7-1 and 8-1)

995 SPORTINGBET SUPPORTS HEROS H'CAP — 1m (P)
5:20 (5:20) (Class 4) (0-85,85) 4-Y-0+ — **£3,238** (£963; £481; £240) **Stalls** High

Form — RPR

-412 **1** **Wilfred Pickles (IRE)**[28] [703] 5-9-2 **80** ... IanMongan 8 — 87
(Jo Crowley) *trckd ldrs on ins: effrt 2f out: led ins fnl f: hld on wl u.p* **3/1**[1]

1462 **2** *hd* **Buaiteoir (FR)**[7] [908] 5-9-5 **83** ... TonyCulhane 5 — 89+
(Paul D'Arcy) *prom on outside: effrt and rdn over 1f out: hdwy to chse wnr wl ins fnl f: jst hld* **7/2**[2]

3631 **3** *½* **Veroon (IRE)**[9] [877] 5-8-13 **77** ... (p) PaulMulrennan 6 — 82
(James Given) *swtg: led 1f: pressed ldr: disp ld 2f out to ins fnl f: kpt on towards fin* **14/1**

212 **4** *nk* **The Happy Hammer (IRE)**[22] [763] 5-8-8 **72** ... WilliamCarson 4 — 76+
(Eugene Stanford) *dwlt: hld up: effrt over 1f out: sn rdn: no imp tl styd on wl towards fin* **11/2**

50-0 **5** *nk* **Den's Gift (IRE)**[34] [623] 7-9-2 **83** ... (b) JohnFahy[(3)] 7 — 87
(Clive Cox) *led after 1f: rdn and jnd 2f out: hdd ins fnl f: kpt on same pce towards fin* **9/2**[3]

-120 **6** *nk* **Titan Triumph**[28] [703] 7-9-4 **82** ... (t) JimCrowley 2 — 85
(William Knight) *hld up: smooth hdwy appr st: effrt on outside over 1f out: one pce ins fnl f* **13/2**

0401 **7** *2* **Follow The Flag (IRE)**[28] [703] 7-9-7 **85** ... (v) NeilCallan 1 — 83
(Alan McCabe) *prom: rdn and outpcd 2f out: no imp ins fnl f* **10/1**

2060 **8** *2 ¼* **Halsion Chancer**[7] [908] 7-8-12 **76** ... SteveDrowne 3 — 69
(John Best) *hld up in tch: drvn and outpcd 2f out: sn btn* **25/1**

1m 37.75s (-0.45) **Going Correction** +0.125s/f (Slow) — **8** Ran SP% **113.7**
Speed ratings (Par 105): **107,106,106,105 105,103,101**
toteswingers:1&2 £2.10, 2&3 £13.10, 1&3 £4.50 CSF £13.46 CT £123.13 TOTE £5.60: £3.30, £1.60, £5.30; EX 12.30 Trifecta £98.90 Pool: £549.387 - 4.11 winning units..
Owner Kilstone Limited **Bred** Eurostrait Ltd **Trained** Whitcombe, Dorset
■ Stewards' Enquiry : Neil Callan caution: used whip without giving gelding time to respond.

FOCUS
A fairly useful contest in which they didn't go much of a gallop once Den's Gift got sole possession of the lead, resulting in a bunched finish. The first two are basically rated to form.
T/Plt: £22.20 to a £1 stake. Pool of £99,422.24 - 3,264.73 winning tickets. T/Qpdt: £2.90 to a £1 stake. Pool of £5,423.55 - 1,355.18 winning tickets. RY

[823] MEYDAN (L-H)
Saturday, March 26

OFFICIAL GOING: Turf: good; tapeta: standard
The Tapeta was riding on the slow side.

996a AL QUOZ SPRINT SPONSORED BY EMIRATES NBD (GROUP 2) (TURF) — 5f
1:15 (1:15) 3-Y-0+
£384,615 (£128,205; £64,102; £32,051; £19,230; £12,820)

RPR

1 **J J The Jet Plane (SAF)**[16] [825] 7-9-0 122 ... BernardFayd'Herbe 11 — 118+
(M Houdalakis, South Africa) *prom centre: effrt and rdn whn n.m.r over 1f out: edgd lft and styd on wl fnl f: led towards fin* **6/4**[1]

2 *hd* **War Artist (AUS)**[36] [602] 8-9-0 116 ... OlivierPeslier 9 — 116
(Rod Collet, France) *hld up: gd hdwy on nr side of gp to ld over 1f out: kpt on fnl f: hdd towards fin* **11/1**[3]

3 *hd* **Better Be The One (AUS)**[48] 5-9-0 110 ... (b) DannyBeasley 4 — 115
(M Freedman, Singapore) *prom centre: effrt and ev ch ins fnl f: kpt on fnl f: hld towards fin* **16/1**

4 *shd* **Invincible Ash (IRE)**[23] [754] 6-8-9 107 ... (p) JMurtagh 8 — 110
(M Halford, Ire) *hld up and bhd centre: effrt and hdwy on nr side of gp over 1f out: kpt on wl u.p fnl f: jst hld* **33/1**

5 *2 ¼* **Prohibit**[23] [754] 6-9-0 112 ... (p) FrankieDettori 5 — 107
(Robert Cowell) *hld up: effrt towards far side of gp over 1f out: swtchd lft and kpt on fnl f: no imp* **16/1**

6 *nk* **Inxile (IRE)**[36] [602] 6-9-0 108 ... (p) AdrianNicholls 13 — 106
(David Nicholls) *mde most centre tl hdd over 1f out: kpt on same pce fnl f* **20/1**

7 *½* **Triple Aspect (IRE)**[168] [6735] 5-9-0 107 ... RyanMoore 15 — 104
(William Haggas) *hld up: hdwy nr side of gp over 1f out: kpt on fnl f: nvr able to chal* **16/1**

8 *nk* **Quick Enough (USA)**[26] 7-9-0 108 ... (t) RBejarano 10 — 103
(Doug O'Neill, U.S.A) *hld up centre: rdn 1/2-way: no imp tl edgd lft and hdwy over 1f out: kpt on fnl f: nvr rchd ldrs* **16/1**

9 *1* **Mar Adentro (FR)**[145] [7278] 5-9-0 110 ... (tp) ChristopheSoumillon 7 — 99
(R Chotard, France) *hld up centre: rdn and effrt over 1f out: sn in tch: no ex ins fnl f* **25/1**

10 *shd* **Happy Dubai (IRE)**[23] [754] 4-9-0 113 ... RoystonFfrench 2 — 99
(A Al Raihe, UAE) *hld up midfield on far side of gp: effrt and drvn 2f out: btn fnl f* **14/1**

11 *½* **Spin Cycle (IRE)**[15] 5-9-0 110 ... (t) RichardMullen 3 — 97
(S Seemar, UAE) *prom on far side of gp: effrt 2f out: wknd fnl f* **20/1**

12 *½* **Monsieur Joe (IRE)**[23] [754] 4-9-0 112 ... (v) JamieSpencer 6 — 95
(Walter Swinburn) *hld up towards nr side of gp: effrt over 1f out: nvr able to chal* **12/1**

13 ¾ **Stradivinsky (USA)**[62] 8-9-0 110 .... (t) JRLeparoux 14 93
(Richard Dutrow Jr, U.S.A) *prom centre: rdn whn nt clr run over 1f out: sn lost pl* **14/1**

14 *nse* **Sole Power**[218] 5276 4-9-0 117 .... WMLordan 12 92
(Edward Lynam, Ire) *cl up centre: drvn over 2f out: wknd over 1f out* **10/1**[2]

15 ½ **Piccadilly Filly (IRE)**[174] 6608 4-8-9 106 .... EddieCreighton 1 86
(Edward Creighton) *disp ld centre: rdn 1/2-way: wknd ent fnl f* **33/1**

16 2½ **Mr Gruff (USA)**[298] 7-9-0 111 .... (t) JRosario 16 82
(Ronald W Ellis, U.S.A) *dwlt: sn cl up in centre: rdn: edgd lft and wknd over 1f out* **14/1**

59.14 secs (59.14) **16** Ran SP% **127.9**
CSF: 17.61.

Owner H S N Du Preez, C F Strydom et al **Bred** Mrs P J Devine **Trained** South Africa

FOCUS
The distance had been decreased by a furlong and the level upped to a Group 2 since last season, but race lacked depth and the proximity of the likes of Invincible Ash (officially rated 107), Inxile (108) and Triple Aspect (107) suggests J J The Jet Plane didn't have to be anywhere near top form to prevail after a troubled trip. The race was run in thick mist until about halfway and viewing was restricted. All the pace was up the middle of the track and there didn't seem to be a major draw bias.

NOTEBOOK
J J The Jet Plane(SAF) was below his peak, but this was still a commendable performance as he was badly squeezed for room over 400m out and had to be brave to take a narrow gap once switched left, staying on well to secure a victory that looked unlikely for much of the journey. He was only 1lb off his career-high RPR when defying an official mark of 122 in a 6f handicap just 16 days earlier, so that could well have taken the edge off him and the drop in trip wasn't ideal. According to connections he could be set for another spell in Britain, with the July Cup (third in 2009) a target, before possibly then going to France. (op 7/4)
War Artist(AUS), who defeated Rileyskeepingfaith in a 6f handicap here off a mark of 115 last time, was possibly a bit unlucky as he raced more towards the near side than the winner and third-placed finisher and had no company for most of the last furlong.
Better Be The One(AUS), formerly a smart sprinter in Australia when known as Common Interest (defeated Starspangledbanner as a 2-y-o), is trained in Singapore these days and had been in winning form recently. He was produced with every chance and was only reeled back in the final few yards.
Invincible Ash(IRE) has yet to win above Listed level and had been held in handicaps here this year, but she ran a fine race, staying on from well back.
Prohibit travelled strongly but had to be switched in order to find a clear run and was never getting there. (op 14/1)
Inxile(IRE) showed his customary early speed before fading. He could now go for the Palace House at Newmarket.
Triple Aspect(IRE), returning from a 168-day break, stayed on from last place.
Mar Adentro(FR) ran a bit better than his finishing position suggests, making a brief effort before tiring on his first start in 145 days.
Happy Dubai(IRE), a triple Carnival winner this year, raced away from the main action towards the far side and seemed a bit flat.
Monsieur Joe(IRE) is better than he showed as he used up energy to move from stall six towards the stands' side in the early stages, before understandably getting tired.
Sole Power ran poorly on his first start since his shock Nunthorpe win.

997a GODOLPHIN MILE SPONSORED BY ETISALAT (GROUP 2) (TAPETA) 1m

1:50 (1:51) 3-Y-0+

£384,615 (£128,205; £64,102; £32,051; £19,230; £12,820)

RPR

1 **Skysurfers**[44] 501 5-9-0 115 .... FrankieDettori 13 118+
(Saeed Bin Suroor) *midfield: smooth hdwy to ld and hrd pressed over 1f out: rdn and hld on wl fnl f* **4/1**[1]

2 ½ **Mufarrh (IRE)**[23] 758 4-9-0 112 .... RichardHills 1 117
(A Al Raihe, UAE) *t.k.h: trckd ldrs: hdwy to dispute ld over 1f out tl wl ins* [illegible] **25/1**

3 3¼ **Red Jazz (USA)**[161] 6923 4-9-0 120 .... MichaelHills 6 110
(B W Hills) *in tch: hdwy on outside over 2f out: rdn and edgd lft ent fnl f: kpt on same pce* **5/1**[2]

4 ½ **Premio Loco (USA)**[176] 6529 7-9-0 119 .... GeorgeBaker 3 108
(Chris Wall) *hld up in tch: effrt over 2f out: hung lft over 1f out: kpt on fnl f: no imp* **8/1**[3]

5 *nse* **Zafeen Speed**[23] 756 4-9-0 111 .... (vt) WayneSmith 8 108
(M Al Muhairi, UAE) *hld up: rdn along 1/2-way: rallied over 2f out: kpt on fnl f: nrst fin* **16/1**

6 1¾ **Le Drakkar (AUS)**[23] 759 6-9-0 113 ...... (t) Christophe-PatriceLemaire 14 104
(A bin Huzaim, UAE) *hld up on outside: outpcd 1/2-way: edgd lft and rallied 2f out: kpt on: nvr able to chal* **16/1**

7 1¼ **Make Music For Me (USA)**[48] 4-9-0 113 .... (t) MESmith 9 101
(Alexis Barba, U.S.A) *bhd: outpcd and plenty to do 1/2-way: hdwy on outside over 1f out: nvr on terms* **20/1**

8 ¼ **Conveyance (USA)**[23] 755 4-9-0 113 .... (t) RichardMullen 2 101
(S Seemar, UAE) *sn led: hdd & wknd fnl 1 1/2f* **10/1**

9 ½ **Hearts Of Fire**[16] 828 4-9-0 112 .... (t) JMurtagh 11 100
(Ibrahaim Al Malki, Qatar) *s.i.s: bhd: rdn and sme hdwy over 2f out: nvr rchd ldrs* **16/1**

10 1¼ **I Want Revenge (USA)**[49] 5-9-0 110 .... (bt) RADominguez 10 97
(Richard Dutrow Jr, U.S.A) *trckd ldr tl 2 1/2f out: wknd fnl f* **8/1**[3]

11 4 **As De Trebol (USA)**[23] 756 5-9-0 110 .... OlivierPeslier 4 87
(M Delcher-Sanchez, Spain) *cl up tl rdn and wknd wl over 1f out: eased whn no ch* **25/1**

12 1½ **Rileyskeepingfaith**[16] 828 5-9-0 115 .... (t) AhmedAjtebi 12 84
(Mahmood Al Zarooni) *hld up midfield: drvn over 2f out: nvr on terms* **8/1**[3]

13 ¾ **Imbongi (SAF)**[44] 501 7-9-0 113 .... ChristopheSoumillon 5 82
(M F De Kock, South Africa) *s.i.s: t.k.h: hld up towards ins: pushed along over 2f out: nvr able to chal* **8/1**[3]

14 3¼ **Crowded House**[23] 756 5-9-0 112 .... (vt) JRosario 7 75
(B Cecil, U.S.A) *hld up: outpcd 1/2-way: nvr on terms* **33/1**

1m 37.65s (0.55) **14** Ran SP% **123.2**
CSF: 116.45.

Owner Godolphin **Bred** Darley **Trained** Newmarket, Suffolk

FOCUS
Godolphin's two trainers had been responsible for half of the ten previous winners of this Group 2, and Saeed Bin Suroor improved on his impressive record. The form is rated through the second and fifth.

NOTEBOOK
Skysurfers, the winner of a Listed race over C&D in February on his sole appearance at this year's Carnival, had finished third in this last season. A horse who needs time between races, he was not ideally drawn but jumped well and tracked the pace early before making good ground to challenge in the straight. It looked at one point as if the runner-up was holding him, but Frankie Dettori, using all his experience, put his whip down inside the last furlong and his mount then ran on to score a shade cosily. He is nowhere near as good on turf so connections are likely to race him in the US in the autumn before a return here. (op 9/2)
Mufarrh(IRE), a dual winner over this track this winter, over C&D and further, was not up to competing with the likes of Twice Over in the Al Maktoum Challenge last time. However, given a good ride by Richard Hills, who had him tucked in on the rail before making his move early in the straight, he battled on well and was only worn down well inside the last furlong.
Red Jazz(USA), the winner of the Challenge Stakes at Newmarket when last seen, was making his debut on a synthetic surface on his first start since October. A market drifter, he was never far away if racing on the outside of his field. He was being ridden when Michael Hills let the winner up his inside off the turn, from which point his mount could only keep on at the one pace. His trainer believes he was not that as happy on the surface as he is on turf, and he might send him to Hong Kong, either next month if he gets over this well enough, or at the end of the year. (11/2)
Premio Loco(USA), who finished behind subsequent Dubai World Cup winner Gloria De Campeao on his only previous appearance at the Carnival in January 2010, had been winning at this level on turf either side of that, and he also came here with a 5-5 record over 1m on Polytrack. Another having his first start since October, he raced upsides the winner for much of the way and came through at about the same time, but failed to pick up as well when asked. His trainer felt the ground was not fast enough for his gelding.
Zafeen Speed, a dual C&D winner in handicaps at the carnival before running Mendip close here in a Group 3 last time, was held up early and ran on in the straight without threatening, doing best of those coming from the back. He is usually ridden more prominently and might have been placed using those tactics.
Le Drakkar(AUS) had finished well beaten in this last year on his last run on synthetics but had been performing creditably on turf at the Carnival this season. He was held up and raced wide from his outside draw, so this was a creditable effort.
Make Music For Me(USA), whose wins in the US last season were at around this trip but on turf, handles synthetics as well but never figured.
Conveyance(USA), a front-runner who was narrowly beaten in a 6f race on his Dubai debut earlier in the month, was stepping up to a trip over which he scored twice in the US early last year. He made the running but did not get much peace and, although battling on, was beaten off well before the last furlong.
Hearts Of Fire had been confined to turf in three starts at the Carnival. Making his debut on synthetics, he was being ridden some way from home.
I Want Revenge(USA), a Grade 1 winner at this trip in the USA on dirt, had also shown in the past he handled synthetics. He helped to make the running but was troubled by the too keen As De Trebol and was struggling soon after turning in.
As De Trebol(USA), placed on all three starts on an artificial surface, including when third to Dubai Duty Free contender Mendip over C&D earlier in the month, failed to settle in the early stages and dropped away tamely.
Rileyskeepingfaith couldn't match the form he showed when winning a turf Group 2 on his first try at this distance last time. After pulling up, it was established that he had injured his left-fore leg and he was transported to the Dubai Equine Hospital for further observatio. It was subsequently reported that he was lame on his left fore.
Imbongi(SAF) had a lot to find with Skysurfers judged on his most recent effort, but did not even run up to that form. (op 17/2)

998a UAE DERBY SPONSORED BY THE SAEED & MOHAMMED AL NABOODAH GROUP (GROUP 2) (TAPETA) 1m 1f 110y

2:25 (2:29) 3-Y-0

£769,230 (£256,410; £128,205; £64,102; £38,461; £25,641)

RPR

1 **Khawlah (IRE)**[30] 681 3-8-4 113 .... MickaelBarzalona 11 111
(Saeed Bin Suroor) *midfield on outside: hdwy over 2f out: styd on wl u.p fnl f: led last stride* **4/1**[1]

2 *nse* **Master Of Hounds (USA)**[140] 7360 3-8-8 113 .... RyanMoore 9 115
(A P O'Brien, Ire) *trckd ldr: rdn to ld over 1f out: kpt on wl u.p: hdd last stride* **11/1**

3 3½ **Mahbooba (AUS)**[illegible] [illegible] [illegible] .... ChristopheSoumillon 5 108
(M F De Kock, South Africa) *prom: rdn and outpcd 2f out: rallied fnl f: kpt on: nt rch first two* **9/2**[2]

4 ¼ **Zanzamar (SAF)**[44] 502 4-9-5 104 .... (b) RichardHills 8 111
(M F De Kock, South Africa) *t.k.h: in tch on outside: effrt and drvn 2f out: sn outpcd: styd on fnl f: no imp* **8/1**

5 1¼ **Xin Xu Lin (BRZ)**[105] 4-9-5 115 .... FrankieDettori 13 110
(Mahmood Al Zarooni) *crossed to ins rail after 2f: led at modest gallop: rdn and hdd over 1f out: kpt on same pce fnl f* **11/2**[3]

6 3¼ **Alexander Pope (IRE)**[108] 7770 3-8-8 100 .... JamieSpencer 2 98
(A P O'Brien, Ire) *hld up on ins: effrt and drvn over 2f out: hdwy over 1f out: styd on fnl f: nvr able to chal* **14/1**

7 ¾ **Ahlaain (USA)**[23] 753 3-8-8 102 .... Christophe-PatriceLemaire 4 97
(David Simcock) *s.s: bhd tl hdwy over 2f out: kpt on fnl f: nvr rchd ldrs* **50/1**

8 4 **Reem (AUS)**[23] 753 4-9-1 107 .... KShea 1 88
(M F De Kock, South Africa) *t.k.h: trckd ldr: rdn 2f out: edgd lft and wknd appr fnl f* **14/1**

9 3¼ **Laser Bullet (JPN)**[35] 3-8-8 102 .... ShinjiFujita 10 82
(Kiyoshi Hagiwara, Japan) *hld up and bhd: rdn over 2f out: nvr on terms* **40/1**

10 *shd* **Splash Point (USA)**[44] 502 3-8-9 104 ow1 .... JMurtagh 3 83
(Mahmood Al Zarooni) *t.k.h in midfield: drvn and outpcd over 2f out: btn over 1f out* **9/1**

11 ½ **Utley (USA)**[140] 7360 3-8-8 110 .... WilliamBuick 12 81
(John Gosden) *hld up on outside: shortlived effrt over 2f out: wknd ent st* **12/1**

12 14 **Introvert (IRE)**[30] 680 3-8-8 104 .... AhmedAjtebi 7 52
(Mahmood Al Zarooni) *hld up towards rr: struggling 4f out: sn btn* **33/1**

13 6¾ **Sweet Ducky (USA)**[55] 3-8-8 110 .... TomQueally 6 38
(H J Brown, South Africa) *midfield: struggling 4f out: sn wknd* **12/1**

14 7¼ **Mantoba**[140] 7360 3-8-8 105 .... (bt) MartinDwyer 14 23
(Brian Meehan) *racd in rr: rdn 3 1/2f out: sn btn* **25/1**

1m 58.83s (0.13)
WFA 3 from 4yo 19lb **14** Ran SP% **122.9**
CSF: 48.19.

Owner Godolphin **Bred** Darley **Trained** Newmarket, Suffolk

■ Khawlah became the first filly to win the race. Aidan O'Brien's runners were his first in Dubai since 2005.

FOCUS

Between them Mike De Kock (five) and Saeed Bin Suroor (six) had won the 11 previous runnings and that trend continued, but only just. The record of runners bred in the northern hemisphere now stands at 7-96, compared to 5-58 for the southern hemisphere. A deep field assembled for this latest running - ten of the 13 runners to have been awarded RPRs had achieved three-figure ratings - and this is strong form. The pace wasn't strong.

NOTEBOOK

Khawlah(IRE), the UAE Oaks winner, sported the Godolphin second colours, although Frankie Dettori had no chance of doing the weight. She was waited with a little way off the pace and raced wide without much cover, although it was probably no bad thing to be away from the inside rail and she made good headway turning into the straight. Once in line for the finish she took a while to get the better of the runner-up, but her increasingly impressive young jockey, Mickael Barzalona, forced her head in front in the final strides. Provided a couple of tough races that have come relatively early in her physical development don't have a negative impact and she acclimatises when back in Britain, she could be an Oaks candidate, and will reportedly go straight for that race. (op 9/2)

Master Of Hounds(USA) didn't run as well as expected in the Breeders' Cup Juvenile Turf when last seen, but he had earlier finished third in the Group 1 Racing Post Trophy and gave that form a boost of sorts, just being denied by a potentially high-class filly. Always well placed by Ryan Moore, he looked likely to hold on for much of the closing stages, being matched at 1.05 in running, but his connections felt he got a bit tired. The step up in trip and switch to this surface suited, but he'll apparently now be considered for the 2,000 Guineas.

Mahbooba(AUS) had her limitations exposed when runner-up to Khawlah in the Oaks and it was the same story this time, but she showed a fine attitude to stick on for third. She should stay further. (op 5/1)

Zanzamar(SAF) fared best of the classic generation colts to have already raced in Dubai this year but was still well held, confirming the impression that the fillies were a better bunch. A bit unlucky when second in the UAE 2,000 Guineas, he had no excuses this time. (op 15/2)

Xin Xu Lin(BRZ), a four-time Group 1 winner in South America, including a Derby and the continent's equivalent of the Arc, looks a stayer and was ridden from the front. He ran well but couldn't pick up sufficiently and may be more of a long-term prospect.

Alexander Pope(IRE), sold to new owners since his last start but still with Aidan O'Brien, was in an unpromising position turning into the straight and lacked the pace to get involved.

Ahlaain(USA) missed the break once again and was doing his best work at the finish.

Reem(AUS) won the middle leg of the UAE Tripe Crown, the Al Bastakiya, but that was a weak edition.

Splash Point(USA), the UAE 2,000 Guineas winner, carried 1lb overweight and proved disappointing.

Mantoba reportedly swallowed his tongue.

999a DUBAI GOLDEN SHAHEEN SPONSORED BY GULF NEWS (GROUP 1) (TAPETA) 6f

3:05 (3:05) 3-Y-O+

£769,230 (£256,410; £128,205; £64,102; £38,461; £25,641)

			RPR
1		**Rocket Man (AUS)**[20] 6-9-0 121 .... FCoetzee 8 (Patrick Shaw, Singapore) *pressed ldr: effrt and rdn 2f out: led ins fnl f: kpt on strly* **1/1**[1]	126
2	2 ¼	**Euroears (USA)**[63] 7-9-0 113 .... (t) MESmith 6 (Bob Baffert, U.S.A) *led: rdn 2f out: hdd ins fnl f: kpt on same pce* **4/1**[2]	119
3	¼	**Sunny King (IRE)**[20] 8-9-0 115 .... GeraldMosse 5 (J Moore, Hong Kong) *hld up bhd ldng gp on outside: effrt and hdwy over 1f out: styd on to go 3rd towards fin: no ch w first two* **10/1**	118+
4	¼	**Green Birdie (NZ)**[49] 8-9-0 116 .... BrettPrebble 9 (C Fownes, Hong Kong) *s.i.s: outpcd and bhd: rdn and hdwy on outside wl over 1f out: edgd lft: kpt on same pce wl ins fnl f* **16/1**	117+
5	3 ¼	**Charlie's Moment (USA)**[30] [678] 5-9-0 108 .... (t) FrankieDettori 2 (Saeed Bin Suroor) *prom: effrt and rdn wl over 1f out: edgd lft and wknd ins fnl f* **20/1**	107
6	¼	**Escape Route (USA)**[15] 7-9-0 111 .... (t) RichardMullen 7 (S Seemar, UAE) *s.i.s: outpcd in last pl: hdwy on ins over 1f out: nvr able to chal* **40/1**	106
7	2 ½	**Dim Sum**[49] 7-9-0 115 .... (v) DarrenBeadman 1 (J Moore, Hong Kong) *chsd ldrs: drvn over 2f out: wknd appr fnl f* **10/1**	98
8	¾	**Dynamic Blitz (AUS)**[51] [414] 7-9-0 113 .... ODoleuze 4 (P F Yiu, Hong Kong) *chsd ldng gp: n.m.r after 1f: rdn and ouptaced over 2f out: no ch after* **7/1**[3]	95
9	5 ¼	**Force Freeze (USA)**[15] 6-9-0 108 .... (t) KierenFallon 3 (Doug Watson, UAE) *trckd ldrs on outside: drvn 1/2-way: edgd lft and wknd over 1f out* **40/1**	79

1m 11.28s (0.28) **9** Ran SP% **116.2**

CSF: 4.94.

Owner Alfredo Leonardo Arnaldo Crabbia **Bred** D R Fleming **Trained** Singapore

FOCUS

This lacked the depth expected for a Group 1 sprint, with only two of the runners having won at the top level in international company and the late withdrawal of last year's winner Kinsale King (swelling on his right-fore leg) didn't help matters. The first two finishers filled the front two positions more or less throughout and the time was 0.85 seconds off the track record.

NOTEBOOK

Rocket Man(AUS) gained a thoroughly deserved success. He had been beaten into second on the four previous occasions he'd contested international sprints at this level, but he arguably should have won here last year and there's little doubt he's one of the best sprinters around. He has a sustained finishing effort rather than an ability to quicken noticeably, so took a while to get past Euroears, but he was well on top at the line and was basically a class apart. It's likely he'll now try and improve on two consecutive second placings in the International Sprint at Kranji before maybe going to Royal Ascot. (op 11/10)

Euroears(USA), a Grade 2 winner on the Santa Anita dirt two months earlier, would probably have preferred a quicker surface but he made the most of a surprisingly soft lead to hold on for second. His connections mentioned the Breeders' Cup Sprint as a possible target.

Sunny King(IRE) ran about as well as could have been expected considering he would have been better suited by a stronger pace.

Green Birdie(NZ) was another who needed a stronger pace. He could go to Royal Ascot.

Charlie's Moment(USA) won a C&D Carnival handicap off just 102 on his previous start and clearly this was a lot tougher.

Escape Route(USA), out of his depth, gave trouble at the start and needed a blanket for stalls entry, but he made some late headway.

Dim Sum was well below the form he showed when winning in Group 1 company in Hong Kong on his previous start.

Dynamic Blitz(AUS) had been off since winning a C&D Group 3 in February and was never going. (op 13/2)

1000a DUBAI DUTY FREE SPONSORED BY DUBAI DUTY FREE (GROUP 1) (TURF) 1m 1f

3:45 (3:49) 3-Y-O+

£1,923,076 (£641,025; £320,512; £160,256; £96,153; £64,102)

			RPR
1		**Presvis**[23] [759] 7-9-0 120 .... RyanMoore 6 (Luca Cumani) *slowly away: settled in rr: smooth prog 2 1/2f out: led 110yds out: r.o wl* **5/1**[1]	123
2	¾	**River Jetez (SAF)**[36] [607] 8-8-9 110 .... BernardFayd'Herbe 3 (M F De Kock, South Africa) *trckd ldrs: rdn and hdwy to ld appr fnl f: hdd ins fnl f: kpt on* **6/1**[3]	116
3	1 ½	**Wigmore Hall (IRE)**[23] [759] 4-9-0 117 .... JamieSpencer 5 (Michael Bell) *hld up: no room fr 3f out tl swtchd to outside and gd hdwy 1f out: edgd lft and styd on strly fnl f: nt rch first two* **11/2**[2]	118
4	¼	**Royal Bench (IRE)**[104] [7853] 4-9-0 116 .... OlivierPeslier 4 (Robert Collet, France) *hld up on ins: effrt whn nt clr run briefly over 1f out: styd on wl fnl f: nrst fin* **14/1**	117
5	1 ¾	**Victor's Cry (USA)**[48] 6-9-0 115 .... (t) VEspinoza 14 (Eoin Harty, U.S.A) *settled in rr: nvr able to chal: r.o fnl 2f* **40/1**	114
6	1	**Mendip (USA)**[23] [756] 4-9-0 117 .... FrankieDettori 7 (Saeed Bin Suroor) *midfield: effrt over 2f out: kpt on same pce fnl f* **8/1**	112
7	½	**Strawberrydaiquiri**[36] [607] 5-8-9 113 .... JMurtagh 8 (F Nass, Bahrain) *t.k.h: trckd ldrs: led over 2f out tl appr fnl f: kpt on same pce* **20/1**	106
8	shd	**Beauty Flash (NZ)**[20] 6-9-0 118 .... (t) GeraldMosse 2 (A S Cruz, Hong Kong) *led at modest gallop: hdd over 2f out: one pce fr over 1f out* **10/1**	110
9	¼	**Beethoven (IRE)**[30] 4-9-0 117 .... (b) SebSanders 11 (Ahmed Kobeissi, Qatar) *hld up on outside: effrt over 2f out: nvr able to chal* **66/1**	110
10	¼	**Rajsaman (FR)**[23] [758] 4-9-0 115 .... KierenFallon 10 (F Head, France) *racd wd: hld up: hdwy into midfield 4f out: rdn and outpcd fnl 2f* **33/1**	109
11	shd	**Raihana (AUS)**[37] [586] 5-8-9 113 .... ChristopheSoumillon 16 (M F De Kock, South Africa) *s.i.s: hld up and sn angled towards ins: effrt whn nt clr run over 1f out: nvr rchd ldrs* **16/1**	104
12	1 ¼	**Tazeez (USA)**[162] [6885] 7-9-0 118 .... TadhgO'Shea 13 (John Gosden) *trckd ldrs: rdn over 2f out: wknd over 1f out* **18/1**	106
13	¾	**Bankable (IRE)**[23] [755] 7-9-0 116 .... (t) KShea 9 (H J Brown, South Africa) *mid-div: chsd ldrs 2f out: wknd fnl f* **10/1**	105
14	1 ¼	**Better Than Ever (AUS)**[13] 5-9-0 119 .... (t) SJumaat 12 (L Laxon, Singapore) *t.k.h in midfield: rdn and wknd 2f out* **12/1**	102
15	2 ¼	**Debussy (IRE)**[23] [758] 5-9-0 120 .... AhmedAjtebi 1 (Mahmood Al Zarooni) *trckd ldrs: rdn over 2f out: wkng whn hmpd over 1f out* **20/1**	97
16	2	**Derbaas (USA)**[37] [586] 5-9-0 115 .... (t) RichardHills 15 (A Al Raihe, UAE) *t.k.h: hld up in tch on outside: rdn: edgd lft and wknd over 1f out* **14/1**	93

1m 50.21s (110.21) **16** Ran SP% **124.2**

CSF: 32.57.

Owner Leonidas Marinopoulos **Bred** Mrs M Campbell-Andenaes **Trained** Newmarket, Suffolk

■ A first winner at the World Cup meeting for Luca Cumani and Ryan Moore.

FOCUS

A competitive renewal of this Group 1 with just 7lb covering the entire field judged on official ratings. The pace did not look strong and was steadied before the home turn, but that did not stop four of the first five coming from well back. Presvis recorded a slight personal best.

NOTEBOOK

Presvis finished a close third to Wigmore Hall here this month and had won four of his eight races at the Carnival, but had been runner-up and seventh in the two previous renewals of this. Held up at the back as usual after a tardy start, he picked up really well this time and got a dream run through the pack to catch the mare inside the final furlong. It's likely he'll take the same route as in the last two years now, going to Sha Tin next month for the QE II Cup, which he won in 2009, and then to Singapore in May. The only problem is that Ryan Moore might not be available for the former as it is Guineas weekend at Newmarket. That is a blow, as he is now 7-11 on the horse whereas all other riders are 1-12 (op 11/2)

River Jetez(SAF), a top mare in South Africa, had been placed over 1m here before winning a Group 2 over 1m1f (both fillies' races). Never far away, she ran a brave race against the colts and geldings and it was only the late surge of the winner that proved too strong.

Wigmore Hall(IRE) narrowly beat Poet's Voice and today's winner in a Group 2 over C&D this month and seemed to be improving. He was held up at the back with his old rival, but his rider pulled towards the outside early in the straight and failed to get a clear run when he needed it. He finished really strongly and looked to be unlucky, but he might get a chance for revenge if taking on the winner again in Hong Kong. Whatever his fate there, he can win good races in Britain this summer and is young enough to come back here for the next few years.

Royal Bench(IRE), a useful miler in France, having won a Group 2 at the Arc meeting before running Beauty Flash close in the Hong Kong Mile, was hampered on the inside early and ended up at the back, next to the winner, turning in. He tried to make his move at the same time but had weakening rivals in front of him, and had to let the winner get first run before switching out behind him. He finished well and is another who is progressing and, as he handles any ground, could be set for a good season.

Victor's Cry(USA), a high-class turf performer in the US, was another to come from well back when the race was over. He was held up from his wide draw and, still last a furlong and a half out, he rattled home down the outside.

Mendip(USA), lightly raced and useful on synthetics, being a dual winner at the Carnival this year, was tackling turf for the first time and was up in grade. The different surface probably found him out at this level.

Strawberrydaiquiri, a useful mare at up to Group 2 level for Sir Michael Stoute but beaten in all three tries in Group 1s, looked held by River Jetez judged on their form here in February. She showed up well and kicked on early in the straight, but was run down by the strong late finishers.

Beauty Flash(NZ), the winner of the Hong Kong Mile in December, had won both starts since in Hong Kong Group 1s. He made the running and stacked up his rivals going into the home turn. However, he was headed early in the straight and, despite staying on, could not produce a change of gear. (op 11/1)

Beethoven(IRE), a Dewhurst winner for Aidan O'Brien but with a lot to find with Beauty Flash and a couple of others on Hong Kong form, had done well since joining new connections and racing in Qatar. He found this a bit too hot, only running on late having been held up.

Rajsaman(FR) another useful French miler, having finished fourth to Beauty Flash in Hong Kong in December, had been well beaten by Twice Over on synthetics here earlier in the month. He was unable to get competitive.

Raihana(AUS), the winner of a handicap over C&D in February before being narrowly beaten by Derbaas in a Group2 over 1m last time, was up in grade and was always towards the rear from her outside draw.

Tazeez(USA), an improved performer late last season, finishing third to Debussy in the Arlington Million before winning twice at Newmarket over this trip, still had something to find here and, after showing up early from his wide draw, weakened in the straight.
Bankable(IRE) had done well for his new trainer, winning a Group 2 here last year before finishing second in this race but had raced only on Tapeta at this year's Carnival and won over 6f last time. He ran quite well, tracking the leaders on the inside, and was not that far away when hampered and eased in the final furlong. He was reportedly jarred up afterwards and might now be retired.
Better Than Ever(AUS), a high-class Singapore performer, having been beaten just once in 15 starts, was a winner on both grass and Polytrack but did not look up to this class.
Debussy(IRE), winner of the Arlington Million for John Gosden but beaten a long way by Twice Over here this month, tracked the leaders but was on the retreat when buffeted about in the straight. He has now been beaten on all three tries here.
Derbaas(USA) failed to shine when coming here last year from Ed Dunlop but had acclimatised since and had been a winner here three times this winter, all at 1m and twice on turf. However, he was up in grade and racing over a longer trip, and that combined with his wide draw found him out. (op 12/1)

1001a DUBAI SHEEMA CLASSIC (GROUP 1) (TURF) — 1m 4f 11y

4:50 (5:00) 3-Y-O+

£1,923,076 (£641,025; £320,512; £160,256; £96,153; £64,102)

RPR

1 — **Rewilding**[196] [5945] 4-8-13 121 .... FrankieDettori 8 — 124+
(Mahmood Al Zarooni) *hld up midfield: stdy hdwy over 2f out: rdn over 1f out: led ins fnl f: sn clr: comf* **2/1**[1]

2 *3¼* **Redwood**[104] [7851] 5-9-0 115 .... MichaelHills 5 — 117
(B W Hills) *t.k.h: hld up midfield on ins: hdwy to trck ldrs over 3f out: effrt and ev ch ins fnl f: edgd lft and kpt on: nt pce of wnr* **8/1**

3 *nk* **Calvados Blues (FR)**[23] [757] 5-9-0 112 .... AhmedAjtebi 4 — 117
(Mahmood Al Zarooni) *t.k.h in midfield: stmbld and lost grnd after 2f: stdy hdwy 4f out: effrt whn nt clr run fr over 2f out tl swtchd lft ent fnl f: sn rdn and hung lft: kpt on wl to take 3rd nr fin* **20/1**

4 *1¾* **Laaheb**[181] [6389] 5-9-0 115 .... RichardHills 1 — 114
(Roger Varian) *set stdy pce 4f: chsd ldr: effrt and ch over 1f out: kpt on same pce fnl f* **12/1**

5 *½* **Chinchon (IRE)**[161] [6951] 6-9-0 115 .... GeraldMosse 3 — 113
(C Laffon-Parias, France) *hld up on ins: stdy hdwy over 3f out: rdn and outpcd over 2f out: rallied whn n.m.r ins fnl f: no imp* **28/1**

6 *1* **Rulership (JPN)**[69] 4-8-13 117 .... ChristopheSoumillon 10 — 113
(Katsuhiko Sumii, Japan) *plld hrd: cl up: led after 4f: rdn and hdd ins fnl f: sn outpcd* **5/1**[3]

7 *2¾* **Irish Flame (SAF)**[23] [758] 5-9-0 116 .... (b) KShea 6 — 107
(M F De Kock, South Africa) *hld up and bhd: stdy hdwy into midfield over 2f out: rdn and no imp fr over 1f out* **14/1**

8 *2½* **Deem (IRE)**[36] [608] 6-8-10 115 ow1 .... OlivierPeslier 2 — 99
(J Barton, Saudi Arabia) *trckd ldrs: effrt and rdn 2f out: keeping on same pce whn bdly hmpd ent fnl f: nt rcvr and eased* **16/1**

9 *2½* **King Dancer (IRE)**[27] 5-9-0 113 .... (b) RyanMoore 14 — 99
(S Woods, Hong Kong) *hld up: stdy hdwy on ins over 3f out: rdn 2f out: sn outpcd* **25/1**

10 *shd* **Marinous (FR)**[23] [757] 5-9-0 117 .... KierenFallon 11 — 99
(F Head, France) *t.k.h: hld up: effrt on wd outside over 3f out: nvr able to chal* **25/1**

11 *8¾* **Bourbon Bay (USA)**[35] 5-9-0 115 .... (vt) RBejarano 9 — 85
(Neil Drysdale, U.S.A) *prom: rdn and outpcd 4f out: sn btn* **25/1**

12 *6* **Champ Pegasus (USA)**[35] 5-9-0 118 .... (t) JRosario 7 — 76
(Richard E Mandella, U.S.A) *hld up: struggling over 4f out: nvr on terms* **16/1**

13 *14* **Al Shemali**[16] [827] 7-9-0 115 .... (t) RoystonFfrench 13 — 53
(A Al Raihe, UAE) *t.k.h: hld up in midfield on outside: rdn over 3f out: sn wknd* **40/1**

14 *31* **Dangerous Midge (USA)**[140] [7366] 5-9-0 122 .... (b) MartinDwyer 12 — 4
(Brian Meehan) *t.k.h: cl up: rdn and struggling 3f out: sn wknd* **9/2**[2]

2m 29.01s (149.01)
WFA 4 from 5yo+ 2lb — **14** Ran SP% **127.6**
CSF: 17.01.
Owner Godolphin **Bred** Watership Down Stud **Trained** Newmarket, Suffolk

FOCUS
This Group 1 has had its share of high-profile winners in recent years, with Nayef, Sulamani and last year Dar Re Mi (a half-sister to Rewilding) all successful. This year's renewal included last year's Dubai Duty Free winner and Breeders' Cup Turf victor in what looked another competitive contest judged on the ratings. The pace was decent but it proved to be a rough race.

NOTEBOOK
Rewilding, a high-class colt in Britain last year, having finished third in the Derby and then winning the Great Voltigeur before finishing well beaten in the St Leger, was having his first run since but appears to go well fresh. Settled off the pace, he came with an sustained run down the centre of the track, and at the line was a decisive winner. Apparently he is a little fragile and needs time between his races, but looks potentially a major player in the big European middle-distance races this season. He could go for the Coronation Cup next if everything goes well but the Prince Of Wales's stakes at Royal Ascot is a more likely target. (op 5/2)
Redwood developed into a high-class international performer last autumn, winning a Grade 1 in Canada before finishing a close third in the Canadian International and then second in the Hong Kong Vase. His rider believes the 5-y-o is better than last year, he is obviously suited by travel and could improve again.
Calvados Blues(FR), the winner of a handicap here in February, was then runner-up to subsequent World Cup third Monterosso. He was hampered in the early parts but then was making good headway when caught up in the general bunching on the inside rail in the closing stages. He finished well once switched outside again, and would probably have been second with a clear passage.
Laaheb, first runner as a trainer for Michael Jarvis's former assistant Roger Varian, is a consistent performer for whom this is an optimum trip. He was improving when last seen in September and seems to have continued that trend, running well on this step up in grade. He should be up to winning good races back in Europe in the summer and could well have an international campaign in the autumn.
Chinchon(IRE), a dual Group 3 winner in France but held at a higher level, ran a decent race despite not getting the best of passages near the rail. He has been lightly raced but can do well back in Europe if his trainer has a clear run with him.
Rulership(JPN), a high-class performer at a slightly lower level in Japan, pulled too hard in the early stages and only settled once in front. However, despite battling on quite well, he paid for his efforts in the straight.
Irish Flame(SAF) ran well on turf at shorter earlier in the Carnival but had finished well behind Twice Over on synthetics last time. The fitting of blinkers and racing over a longer trip failed to bring about the required improvement.
Deem(IRE), fourth in this last year and seventh the year before, usually races at shorter. She ran really well here and was battling for a place when the chief sufferer in the general bunching that occurred near the rail in the closing stages, which forced her rider to snatch up.
King Dancer(IRE) finished sixth when Redwood was second in the Hong Kong Vase but failed to repeat that effort.
Marinous(FR) beat Redwood in the Grade Prix de Deauville on soft ground last season but had finished behind Calvados Blues here on his most recent start. He was too keen under restraint early which cost him.
Bourbon Bay(USA), a high-class US performer who was closely matched with compatriot Champ Pegasus on their home form, showed up for a long way before fading.
Champ Pegasus(USA), who finished second to Dangerous Midge in the Breeders' Cup Turf, ran no sort of race, being out the back and detached for much of the way and only passing a couple of beaten horses in the straight.
Al Shemali won the Dubai Duty Free on this day last year but had not scored since and had struggled a little at this year's carnival. He probably does not stay this far but was not helped by racing wide from his high draw.
Dangerous Midge(USA) improved last season after winning the Old Newton Cup, and then took the Breeders' Cup Turf at Churchill Downs from Champ Pegasus. He ran very disappointingly on this first start since, being under pressure 5f from home and eventually tailing off. Something must have been amiss although nothing was found to be wrong immediately after the race.

1002a DUBAI WORLD CUP SPONSORED BY EMIRATES AIRLINE (GROUP 1) (TAPETA) — 1m 2f

5:35 (5:37) 3-Y-O+

£3,846,153 (£1,282,051; £641,025; £320,512; £192,307; £128,205)

RPR

1 — **Victoire Pisa (JPN)**[27] 4-9-0 121 .... MircoDemuro 6 — 120+
(Katsuhiko Sumii, Japan) *settled last: rapid hdwy on outside to join ldr over 4f out: rdn to ld appr fnl f: hld on gamely* **12/1**

2 *½* **Transcend (JPN)**[34] 5-9-0 116 .... ShinjiFujita 9 — 119
(Takayuki Yasuda, Japan) *led at stdy gallop: jnd over 4f out: rdn and hdd appr fnl f: kpt on but a hld* **40/1**

3 *¼* **Monterosso**[23] [757] 4-9-0 115 .... (t) MickaelBarzalona 2 — 118
(Mahmood Al Zarooni) *trckd ldrs: effrt and rdn 2f out: kpt on u.p fnl f* **40/1**

4 *¼* **Cape Blanco (IRE)**[174] [6612] 4-9-0 126 .... JamieSpencer 4 — 118
(A P O'Brien, Ire) *trckd ldr to 1/2-way: cl up: ev ch over 2f out: drvn and sltly outpcd 2f out: hrd rdn and styd on fnl f* **4/1**[2]

5 *¾* **Gio Ponti (USA)**[140] [7364] 6-9-0 121 .... RADominguez 5 — 116+
(Christophe Clement, U.S.A) *plld hrd: prom: effrt on wd outside 2f out: kpt on fnl f: hld towards fin* **12/1**

6 *1* **Gitano Hernando**[23] [758] 5-9-0 118 .... JMurtagh 8 — 114+
(Marco Botti) *trckd ldrs: effrt and drvn along over 2f out: kpt on same pce fnl f* **14/1**

7 *½* **Musir (AUS)**[23] [758] 5-9-0 117 .... ChristopheSoumillon 7 — 113+
(M F De Kock, South Africa) *plld hrd: hld up: stdy hdwy whn nt clr run briefly over 2f out: sn rdn and edgd lft over 1f out: kpt on fnl f: nvr able to chal* **12/1**

8 *½* **Buena Vista (JPN)**[90] 5-8-9 121 .... RyanMoore 13 — 107+
(Hiroyoshi Matsuda, Japan) *hld up and bhd: stdy hdwy over 2f out: effrt and swtchd centre over 1f out: sn rdn: kpt on fnl f: nvr able to chal* **7/1**[3]

9 *1¼* **Twice Over**[23] [758] 6-9-0 125 .... TomQueally 12 — 110+
(Sir Henry Cecil) *t.k.h in midfield on outside: checked after 2f: effrt on outside over 2f out: no rspnse* **2/1**[1]

10 *¼* **Prince Bishop (IRE)**[23] [758] 4-9-0 117 .... AhmedAjtebi 3 — 109+
(Saeed Bin Suroor) *hld up in tch: blkd after 2f: drvn along 3f out: edgd lft and wknd wl over 1f out* **25/1**

11 *2¼* **Golden Sword**[36] [608] 5-9-0 117 .... KShea 14 — 105+
(M F De Kock, South Africa) *t.k.h: hld up and bhd: effrt on outside 2f out: edgd lft: nvr able to chal* **12/1**

12 *½* **Richard's Kid (USA)**[23] [758] 6-9-0 119 .... (bt) RichardMullen 11 — 104+
(S Seemar, UAE) *s.i.s: hld up: stdy hdwy on ins over 3f out: wknd fnl 2f* **50/1**

13 *12* **Fly Down (USA)**[49] 4-9-0 123 .... (t) JRLeparoux 1 — 80+
(Nicholas Zito, U.S.A) *in tch on ins: bdly hmpd and lost pl after 2f: struggling fr over 4f out* **25/1**

14 *1¼* **Poet's Voice**[23] [759] 4-9-0 122 .... (t) FrankieDettori 10 — 100+
(Saeed Bin Suroor) *t.k.h: hld up midfield: n.m.r and edgd rt after 2f: effrt and rdn 2f out: sn wknd: eased whn no ch* **11/1**

2m 5.94s (1.04) — **14** Ran SP% **126.1**
CSF: 447.77; Placepot: £7.80 to a £1 stake. Pool of £15,820.00 - 1,407.10 winning units;
Quadpot: £5.40 to a £1 stake. Pool of £1,800.74 - 245.96 winning units..
Owner Yoshimi Ichikawa **Bred** Shadai Farm **Trained** Japan
■ A first victory in the race for Japan, and they also had the runner-up.

FOCUS
Just like last year, when the World Cup was run at Meydan for the first time, a steady pace rendered the race something of a $10 million lottery. Between them this lot had recorded 26 top-level victories, including ten individual Grade or Group 1 winners, but while perhaps a thrilling spectacle for many a neutral, the lack of pace denied the majority of the runners the chance to run to their full potential and the race is close to meaningless from a form perspective. The first four home were the first four turning in and only 3l covered the first seven finishers. A number of these, including the winner, are better than the bare form. The time was 3.54 seconds outside Golden Sword's track record - desperately slow, even allowing for the way the surface was riding, and the slowest race over this 1m2f trip at the Carnival this year.

NOTEBOOK
Victoire Pisa(JPN) is a high-class colt and may have won off a truer pace anyway, but one thing's for sure, he received a great ride tactical from Mirco Demuro. The steady gallop meant few runners made up significant amounts of ground in the closing stages, but Demuro was as alert as anyone as to how the race was unfolding. Victoire Pisa was last of all early having apparently hit his head in the stalls, but once he'd negotiated the first bend he was taken around runners down the back straight, quickly moving into second spot without expending as much energy as would normally be the case with such a bold move. Once there, it was clear he was still travelling strongly and was ideally placed for the relative dash in the closing stages. He has improved since finishing seventh in last year's Arc and should continue to be a major force in some of the world's top middle-distance events.
Transcend(JPN), one of the leading dirt performers in his homeland, where he'd won the Japan Cup Dirt and most recently the prestigious February Stakes, he had to prove himself on this surface, as well as show he was up to such international company. However, he was allowed a really soft lead and stuck on well, having initially looked set to be swamped on entering the straight. This was a fine effort, but he's flattered.
Monterosso, who had some high-class form over 1m4f for Mark Johnston last year, had returned to something like his best when winning the trial for the Sheema Classic on Super Thursday when debuting for Mahmood Al Zarooni. However, the decision to run here instead of in the turf event was fully justified. He was well placed and stayed on strongly after getting a gap when required in the straight, although his rider thought he might have been second with a clearer run. Seeing as he stays so well, the steady pace cannot have been ideal and he deserves extra credit. (op 33/1)
Cape Blanco(IRE) had been the subject of a partial sale since he was last seen, but remained with Aidan O'Brien and was the trainer's first runner in the race. Trying a synthetic surface for the first time, last year's Irish Derby and Irish Champion Stakes winner was handily placed but couldn't find sufficient speed. This was a good effort, although one would have expected him to finish better than Monterosso judged on their respective achievements last year.

Gio Ponti(USA), last year's fourth-placed finisher, was again unsuited by a lack of pace. He was keen down the back straight, before going wide on the final bend, and did well to get so close.
Gitano Hernando, recently sold but said to be having one last run for Marco Botti before joining Herman Brown, had no excuse other than obvious one - the slow tempo.
Musir(AUS) travelled strongly but was too far back on entering the straight to make an impression.
Buena Vista(JPN) comprehensively defeated Victoire Pisa when first past the post in last year's Japan Cup, and was only a nose behind that rival in the Arima Kinen on her last start, but she's a confirmed hold-up performer whose main asset is a strong, late finishing burst, so the slow gallop was no use to her at all. She would have been slightly closer with a clear run in the straight and this was the first time she has finished outside the top three in an 18-race career. (op 8/1 tchd 15/2)
Twice Over didn't have things go his way when tenth in this last year, but was made favourite after an impressive success in the key domestic trial. However, it was a similar story to 12 months ago. Again drawn in double figures, he was caught wide through the opening stages and received an early bump, after which he could make no impression. (op 9/4)
Golden Sword was faced with a totally different scenario to when winning impressively on his last two starts - better rivals and no pace to run at.
Fly Down(USA) lost his chance when badly squeezed out on the first turn.
Poet's Voice didn't settle, much like when below form in last year's Champion Stakes on his only previous try at this distance.

1003 - (Foreign Racing) - See Raceform Interactive

LEOPARDSTOWN (L-H)
Sunday, March 27

OFFICIAL GOING: Good to yielding

1004a LEOPARDSTOWN 2,000 GUINEAS TRIAL STKS (GROUP 3) (C&G) 1m
3:00 (3:09) 3-Y-O £26,616 (£7,780; £3,685)

RPR
1 **Dunboyne Express (IRE)**[155] 7081 3-9-0 114 .... DPMcDonogh 2 99+
(Kevin Prendergast, Ire) *settled in 3rd: clsd ent st: qcknd nicely on outer to ld 1f out: pushed out and kpt on wl fnl f* 5/4[1]
2 1 3/4 **Exodus**[134] 7456 3-9-0 98 .... SeamieHeffernan 3 94
(A P O'Brien, Ire) *led early: trckd ldr in 2nd: rdn early st: 2nd 1f out but sn no ch w wnr: kpt on same pce* 9/2[2]
3 nk **Whipless (IRE)**[161] 6969 3-9-0 95 .... KJManning 4 93
(J S Bolger, Ire) *led after 1f: strly pressed fr early st: hdd u.p and dropped to 3rd 1f out: kpt on one pce* 12/1[3]

1m 41.36s (0.16) 3 Ran SP% 70.3
CSF £2.24 TOTE £1.10; DF 1.80.
Owner J Connaughton **Bred** John Connaughton **Trained** Friarstown, Co Kildare

FOCUS
Cocozza (6/4) was withdrawn after sitting down in the stalls. Deduct 40p in the £ under R4. The winner did not need to run to his juvenile best.

NOTEBOOK
Dunboyne Express(IRE), who had easily the best two-year-old form, was more than equal to the task, coming from behind his two rivals to lead just over 1f out. He was well on top in the closing stages and trainer Kevin Prendergast said: "It was a satisfactory performance, although not one to rave about it. We would have learned more if the withdrawn horse had run. Our horse should come on a good bit for the race and will run next in the Irish 2,000 Guineas." An eight-length winner of the Group 3 Anglesey Stakes over 6f, the winner had raced keenly when fifth in the Racing Post Trophy and, according to Prendergast, has been held up in his preparation for that Doncaster event and again after the race. (op 11/10 tchd 11/8)
Exodus, who is entered for the Investec Derby, was a nine-length winner of a 1m maiden in October before finishing fourth behind stablemate Recital in a Group 1 event over 1m2f at Saint-Cloud in November. Soon second, he was unable to quicken when the winner made his move but stayed on in the closing stages and will appreciate going back up in trip. (op 5/1 tchd 11/2)
Whipless(IRE), winner of a 6f maiden at the Curragh in August before being unplaced when highly tried in a Group 1 in France and in a nursery at Naas, was soon in front. Unable to raise his effort when taken on and headed by the winner, he kept on. (op 10/1 tchd 14/1)

1006a LEOPARDSTOWN 1,000 GUINEAS TRIAL STKS (GROUP 3) (FILLIES) 7f
4:00 (4:06) 3-Y-O £26,616 (£7,780; £3,685; £1,228)

RPR
1 **Empowering (IRE)**[107] 7817 3-9-1 84 ow1 .... JPO'Brien 12 104
(A P O'Brien, Ire) *sn led and mde virtually all: pushed along and 2 l advantage 2f out: kpt on wl u.p fnl f* 11/2[3]
2 1 3/4 **Wild Wind (GER)**[177] 6530 3-9-0 103 .... CO'Donoghue 9 98+
(A P O'Brien, Ire) *trckd ldrs: 6th 1/2-way: rdn into 4th under 2f out: kpt on u.p to go 2nd cl home* 5/1[2]
3 shd **History Note (IRE)**[167] 6817 3-9-0 .... JMurtagh 2 98
(John M Oxx, Ire) *settled towards rr: 11th on inner appr st: stdy hdwy to go 5th ins fnl f: kpt on wl between horses fnl 100yds* 3/1[1]
4 shd **Manieree (IRE)**[147] 7256 3-9-0 91 .... NGMcCullagh 6 98
(John M Oxx, Ire) *prom: 2nd 1/2-way: drvn along ent st: 3rd and no imp 1f out: kpt on same pce u.p ins fnl f* 11/1
5 nk **Seeharn (IRE)**[231] 4879 3-9-0 99 .... DPMcDonogh 5 97
(Kevin Prendergast, Ire) *trckd ldrs: 3rd 1/2-way: drvn along to go 2nd over 1f out: no imp ins fnl f and dropped to 5th clsng stages* 8/1
6 1 1/4 **Juliet Capulet (IRE)**[170] 6727 3-9-0 90 .... PJSmullen 13 94
(A P O'Brien, Ire) *towards rr: sme hdwy on outer early st: kpt on ins fnl f wout threatening* 25/1
7 hd **Hurricane Havoc (IRE)**[162] 6927 3-9-0 94 ....(b[1]) KJManning 8 93
(J S Bolger, Ire) *chsd ldrs on outer: 5th 1/2-way: drvn along in 6th ent st: no imp fr over 1f out* 10/1
8 1 3/4 **Katla (IRE)**[146] 7277 3-9-0 103 .... WJLee 4 88
(J F Grogan, Ire) *mid-div best: nvr a factor* 8/1
9 1/2 **Gatamalata (IRE)**[210] 5570 3-9-0 90 .... CDHayes 1 87
(Joseph G Murphy, Ire) *trckd ldrs on inner: 4th 1/2-way: no ex fr under 2f out: wknd* 33/1
10 shd **Redskin Dancer (IRE)**[161] 6968 3-9-0 90 .... BACurtis 14 87
(John M Oxx, Ire) *towards rr: nvr a factor: kpt on one pce in st* 14/1
11 3 **Gossamer Seed (IRE)**[162] 6940 3-9-0 82 .... SeamieHeffernan 11 79
(John Joseph Murphy, Ire) *mid-div: 8th 1/2-way: no ex fr 2f out* 25/1
12 hd **Radharcnafarraige (IRE)**[263] 3792 3-9-0 100 ....(p) DJMoran 3 78
(J S Bolger, Ire) *mid-div on inner: nvr a factor: no threat in st* 12/1
13 1 1/4 **Emerald Ring (IRE)**[161] 6969 3-9-0 92 ....(b) WMLordan 7 75
(David Wachman, Ire) *nvr a factor* 33/1
14 1 1/2 **Knock Stars (IRE)**[156] 7073 3-9-0 97 .... PBBeggy 10 71
(Patrick Martin, Ire) *mid-div: pushed along in 9th appr st: no ex fr 2f out* 20/1

1m 29.09s (0.39) 14 Ran SP% 129.4
CSF £33.60 TOTE £11.40: £3.20, £2.10, £1.10; DF 50.10.
Owner Mrs A M O'Brien **Bred** Whisperview Trading Ltd **Trained** Ballydoyle, Co Tipperary

FOCUS
This was a typically competitive Group 3 fillies' race. Joseph O'Brien put up 1lb overweight and was unable to claim but those negatives were entirely offset by a brilliantly judged ride on Empowering. The sixth looks the best guide to the form.

NOTEBOOK
Empowering(IRE) went into this with a relatively modest rating of 84. Despite being drawn in 12, O'Brien was able to guide the Dundalk maiden winner to the front and he was clearly intent on making use of her stamina. She looked ripe for picking off early in the straight but kept on galloping and ultimately won a shade snugly, thanks in no small measure to her jockey. This may yet turn out to be her cup final and she had the run of the race, but her attitude is endearing and she looks worth stepping up in trip and would be an interesting Irish Guineas runner if ridden positively. "She is very well bred and has been working very well," said Aidan O'Brien. He added that she might even go for to Newmarket for the English Guineas. (op 12/1)
Wild Wind(GER) ran a perfectly solid race. Unlike the winner, she was weak in the betting and was ridden to get a lead after breaking well. She travelled smoothly in midfield but it could be argued that her stablemate got first run on her. She ran on gamely and is a filly worth stepping up in trip. (op 9/2 tchd 4/1)
History Note(IRE) ◆ was perhaps the one to pick out with a view to the future on just her second start. She had to wait behind a glut of horses early in the straight before passing around six of them and was powering on at the finish. Considering that this trip is very much on the sharp side for her - and the relatively sympathetic handling she got from her rider - this was a cracking run. John Oxx will now appreciate he has a filly on his hands with Classic potential. (op 11/4 tchd 7/2)
Manieree(IRE) was ridden positively and gave a good account of herself. She was just denied black-type placing and will also easily get further than this. (op 12/1)
Seeharn(IRE) ultimately had every chance but ran a little better than her finishing position would suggest. Her trainer has been keen to stress that his string are a little behind and she can improve.
Juliet Capulet(IRE) is fairly exposed and ran about as well as could have been expected.
Hurricane Havoc(IRE) did not have the pace to go with the principals and probably needs further. (op 11/1 tchd 12/1)
Katla(IRE) was disappointing and this performance was inconclusive with regard to what trip she might get as a three-year-old. She is well worth another chance. (op 7/1)

1005 & 1007 - 1009a (Foreign Racing) - See Raceform Interactive

900 DEAUVILLE (R-H)
Thursday, March 24

OFFICIAL GOING: Fibresand: standard

1010a PRIX DU DUN (CONDITIONS) (3YO COLTS & GELDINGS) (FIBRESAND) 7f 110y
1:50 (12:00) 3-Y-O £12,500 (£5,000; £3,750; £2,500; £1,250)

RPR
1 **Cool Dude (FR)**[272] 3-8-9 0 .... JohanVictoire 7 86
(Mme C Head-Maarek, France) 9/1
2 nk **Numbers Talk (IRE)**[75] 3-9-2 0 ....(p) Roberto-CarlosMontenegro 1 92
(X Thomas-Demeaulte, France) 48/10[3]
3 nk **Malthouse (GER)**[173] 6560 3-8-9 0 .... RobertWinston 2 85
(Mark Johnston) *shared ld on inner on settling: tk ld 3f out: rdn 2 1/2f out: hdd 1 1/2f out: styd on u.p: rallied ins fnl f: r.o wl fnl 100yds* 11/1
4 2 **Les Troyens**[20] 776 3-9-2 0 .... MaximeGuyon 4 87
(A Fabre, France) 1/1[1]
5 2 1/2 **Ouilly (IRE)** 3-8-9 0 .... IoritzMendizabal 9 74
(J-C Rouget, France) 9/2[2]
6 hd **Pam (IRE)**[114] 7647 3-8-7 0 .... EddyHardouin[(6)] 6 78
(Robert Collet, France) 18/1
7 2 1/2 **Uighur (FR)**[302] 3-8-2 0 .... RufusVergette[(7)] 8 68
(A Fabre, France) 25/1
8 2 **Lockhart (FR)**[9] 3-8-9 0 .... StephanePasquier 3 63
(Mlle V Dissaux, France) 33/1
9 2 **Dom Tom (USA)**[202] 3-8-9 0 .... TonyPiccone 5 58
(Mme C Head-Maarek, France) 39/1

1m 31.7s (91.70) 9 Ran SP% 118.3
WIN (incl. 1 euro stake): 8.10 (Cool Dude coupled with Dom Tom). PLACES: 3.10, 2.00, 3.90. DF: 25.90. SF: 81.60.
Owner Marquesa De Moratalla **Bred** S C E A La Poterie **Trained** Chantilly, France

1011a PRIX D'HUDIMESNIL (CONDITIONS) (4YO+) (LADY RIDERS) (FIBRESAND) 1m 1f 110y
2:55 (12:00) 4-Y-O+ £9,482 (£3,793; £2,844; £1,896; £948)

RPR
1 **Satwa Pearl**[183] 5-8-6 0 .... CelineLaunay 3 78
(Jean De Roualle, France) 19/1
2 1 1/2 **Sand Skier**[145] 7233 4-8-9 0 .... BrigitteRenk 2 79
(Mark Johnston) *racd midfield on settling: rdn and proged bef st: u.p 2f out: r.o wl whn swtchd towards stands' side: styd on wl fnl 100yds to claim 2nd on line* 73/10
3 hd **Presumably (IRE)** 4-8-6 0 .... NadegeOuakli 8 75
(Robert Collet, France) 70/1
4 1 1/2 **Ideology**[81] 5-8-9 0 ....(b[1]) StefanieHofer 14 76
(Mario Hofer, Germany) 7/1
5 hd **Darizi (FR)**[299] 2557 4-8-4 0 .... ManonScandella[(5)] 10 75
(J-C Rouget, France) 7/2[1]
6 shd **Imasci**[476] 4-9-0 0 .... DelphineSantiago 5 80
(Manfred Hofer, Germany) 9/2[2]
7 nse **Distinctive Image (USA)**[47] 436 6-8-9 0 .... SabrinaWandt 6 75
(C Von Der Recke, Germany) 20/1
8 1 **Gris D'Honneur (FR)** 4-8-9 0 .... KellyHarrison 7 73
(D De Watrigant, France) 11/1
9 1 **Tally Ho (FR)**[150] 4-8-2 0 .... MlleAmelieFoulon[(7)] 1 71
(A Fabre, France) 9/1
10 nk **Baan Rim Pa (FR)**[130] 5-8-7 0 .... PaulineProd'homme[(2)] 12 71
(D Prod'Homme, France) 42/1
0 **Ordenstreuer (IRE)**[124] 7532 5-9-4 0 .... MlleNathalieDesoutter 11 —
(H-W Hiller, Germany) 63/10[3]
0 **Maroon Machine (IRE)**[241] 4446 4-8-9 0 .... KirstyMilczarek 9 —
(E J O'Neill, France) 21/1
0 **Acid Test (FR)** 4-8-9 0 .... MarieFlahault 4 —
(C Boutin, France) 81/1

0 **Atromos (FR)** 4-8-9 0 .... KarenBeaumard 13 —
(L Nyffels, France) **76/1**

1m 58.1s (118.10) **14** Ran SP% **117.5**
WIN (incl. 1 euro stake): 20.00. PLACES: 6.20, 3.20, 15.50. DF: 95.30. SF: 224.90.
Owner Steven & Gillian Lamprell **Bred** E Puerari And Dominique Ades-Hazan **Trained** France

1012a PRIX DE LA VERONNE (CLAIMER) (4YO) (FIBRESAND) 1m 4f

3:25 (12:00) 4-Y-0 **£6,465** (£2,586; £1,939; £1,293; £646)

RPR

1 **Helly (FR)**[72] 4-8-9 0 .... FrankieLeroy(4) 5 57
(R Pritchard-Gordon, France) **15/2[3]**

2 *snk* **Email Exit (IRE)**[13] 842 4-8-11 0 .... FabienLefebvre 15 55
(Mme G Rarick, France) **15/1**

3 *hd* **Gemo Lotus (IRE)**[72] 4-8-11 0 .... MaximeGuyon 6 55
(Mme Pia Brandt, France) **4/1[2]**

4 *1 1/2* **Gobi (FR)** 4-8-11 0 ....(b) Pierre-CharlesBoudot 7 52
(J-M Capitte, France) **24/1**

5 *hd* **Lord Lansing (IRE)**[13] 842 4-9-11 0 .... AndrewElliott 1 66
(Mrs K Burke) *settled midfield on rail: proged bef st: rdn and picked up wl 2f out: u.p to stay w ldrs 1f out: no ex: styd on fnl 100yds* **19/1**

6 *snk* **El Bulli (USA)**[13] 842 4-9-2 0 ....(p) ThierryThulliez 16 57
(F Chappet, France) **2/1[1]**

7 *2* **Nova Med (IRE)**[13] 842 4-9-5 0 ....(b) YoannRousset(6) 10 63
(Y Fertillet, France) **11/1**

8 *nk* **Jo Mania (IRE)** 4-8-11 0 .... GaetanMasure 13 48
(J-M Capitte, France) **18/1**

9 *3* **Refuse To Davis (IRE)**[87] 4-9-2 0 .... ArnaudBourgeais 12 49
(N Leenders, France) **26/1**

10 *1 1/2* **Tintalle (FR)**[231] 4-8-8 0 .... IoritzMendizabal 3 39
(Mlle C Brunaud, France) **17/2**

0 **Playa Blanca (FR)**[12] 4-8-3 0 .... EddyHardouin(5) 8 —
(Robert Collet, France) **42/1**

0 **Sandinnar (FR)**[72] 4-8-8 0 ....(b) FranckBlondel 4 —
(J Boisnard, France) **17/1**

0 **Kin Super (FR)**[105] 4-8-9 0 ow1 ....(b[1]) SylvainBellanger 14 —
(F Leralle, France) **112/1**

0 **Cycladelle (FR)** 4-8-13 0 .... DavidFournier 2 —
(C Restout, France) **88/1**

0 **Fiesta Becquerel (FR)** 4-8-13 0 .... EricMichel 9 —
(Mme E Siavy-Julien, France) **111/1**

2m 33.5s (153.50) **15** Ran SP% **119.0**
WIN (incl. 1 euro stake): 8.50. PLACES: 2.40, 4.90, 2.00. DF: 60.20. SF: 115.90.
Owner George-William Haine **Bred** Haras Du Quesnay **Trained** France

1013a PRIX DE LA LEZARDE (CLAIMER) (5YO+) (FIBRESAND) 1m 4f

3:55 (12:00) 5-Y-0+ **£6,465** (£2,586; £1,939; £1,293; £646)

RPR

1 **West Wing (FR)**[13] 843 6-9-2 0 ....(b) ThomasHuet 8 66
(F-X Belvisi, France) **18/1**

2 *1/2* **Sicyus De Juilley (FR)**[895] 10-8-11 0 .... FabriceVeron 1 61
(J-L Guillochon, France) **24/1**

3 *1* **Almaguer**[14] 9-9-11 0 .... IoritzMendizabal 10 73
(F X Belvisi, France) **63/10[2]**

4 *1 1/2* **L'Impressioniste (FR)**[156] 7-9-2 0 .... ThierryThulliez 7 62
(F Chappet, France) **4/1[1]**

5 *3/4* **Ainebe Crocus (FR)**[75] 10-8-10 0 ....(b) TheoBachelot(6) 11 61
(S Wattel, France) **4/1[1]**

6 *nse* **Secundus (GER)**[20] 6-9-2 0 ....(b) Francois-XavierBertras 16 61
(M Nigge, France) **11/1**

7 *2* **Bergonzi (IRE)**[13] 843 7-9-6 0 .... SabrinaWandt 3 62
(C Von Der Recke, Germany) **8/1[3]**

8 *1* **Willow Weep For Me (FR)**[20] 8-9-2 0 ....(b) MichaelMartinez 13 56
(J M Lefebvre, France) **11/1**

9 *3* **Fedora (IRE)**[15] 802 5-8-13 0 .... KylieManser 5 45
(Olivia Maylam) *racd midfield: moved away fr rail down bkst: dropped bk bef st: short of room early in st: rdn 2f out: no ex* **64/1**

10 *1/2* **Chocapix (IRE)**[20] 5-8-13 0 .... FabienLefebvre 12 48
(C Le Lay, France) **13/1**

0 **Ksaros (FR)**[20] 8-9-2 0 ....(b) SylvainBellanger 15 —
(F Leralle, France) **98/1**

0 **Ka Nordik (FR)**[7] 9-8-8 0 ....(p) DavidFournier 4 —
(N Leenders, France) **77/1**

0 **Premier Violon (IRE)**[13] 843 8-9-2 0 ....(p) AlexandreRoussel 6 —
(Mlle C Cardenne, France) **16/1**

0 **Arca (FR)**[14] 832 6-8-11 0 .... TonyPiccone 9 —
(J Rossi, France) **47/1**

0 **Counterbid (IRE)**[6] 903 5-9-2 0 .... SylvainRuis 14 —
(J Heloury, France) **17/1**

0 **Rouge Emery (FR)**[13] 843 5-8-13 0 .... AdrienFouassier 2 —
(J Clais, France) **67/1**

2m 34.3s (154.30) **16** Ran SP% **116.7**
WIN (incl. 1 euro stake): 5.20 (West Wing and Almaguer coupled). PLACES: 4.20, 7.20, 3.50. DF: 154.90. SF: 254.60..
Owner Francois-Xavier Belvisi **Bred** Takashi Watanabe **Trained** France

964 WOLVERHAMPTON (A.W) (L-H)

Monday, March 28

OFFICIAL GOING: Standard
Wind: almost nil Weather: fine and sunny

1014 NEW SEASON AT ATRVIRTUALOWNER.COM CLAIMING STKS 7f 32y(P)

2:20 (2:20) (Class 6) 4-Y-0+ **£1,535** (£453; £226) **Stalls** High

Form RPR

-564 **1** **Benandonner (USA)**[16] 846 8-9-9 94 .... MartinLane 2 95
(Mike Murphy) *trckd ldrs: effrt over 2f out: led over 1f out: drew clr ins fnl f: readily* **4/11[1]**

4000 **2** *4* **Tourist**[9] 915 6-8-13 68 .... JimmyQuinn 4 74
(Derek Shaw) *hld up in last: effrt 3f out: kpt on to chse wnr fnl f: no imp* **28/1**

011 **3** *2* **Alpha Tauri (USA)**[13] 856 5-9-4 78 ....(t) JamesDoyle 1 74
(Frank Sheridan) *led: drvn over 2f out: hdd over 1f out: one pce* **7/1[3]**

0331 **4** *shd* **Unlimited**[9] 914 9-8-13 72 .... J-PGuillambert 3 68
(Tony Carroll) *chsd ldng pair: drvn 3f out: one pce fnl f* **9/2[2]**

1m 28.26s (-1.34) **Going Correction** +0.10s/f (Slow) **4** Ran SP% **107.4**
Speed ratings (Par 101): **111,106,104,104**
CSF £10.72 TOTE £1.10; EX 9.20.
Owner Phil Woods **Bred** Gainsborough Farm Llc **Trained** Westoning, Beds

FOCUS
An above-average claimer run at a reasonable pace. There is a bit of doubt over the form and the winner is rated 5lb off his recent best.

1015 DINE IN THE HORIZONS RESTAURANT MAIDEN STKS 7f 32y(P)

2:50 (2:51) (Class 5) 3-Y-0+ **£1,813** (£539; £269; £134) **Stalls** High

Form RPR

32- **1** **Wiqaaya (IRE)**[181] 6441 3-8-7 0 .... RichardHills 2 69+
(Ed Dunlop) *mde all: qcknd clr over 2f out: v easily* **1/14[1]**

2 *6* **Brent Pelham** 4-9-13 0 .... TomMcLaughlin 1 49
(Tobias B P Coles) *trckd ldrs: drvn over 2f out: wnt 2nd over 1f out: no ch w wnr* **8/1[2]**

0- **3** *3/4* **Chillianwallah**[164] 6899 3-8-12 0 .... RichardKingscote 4 42
(James Unett) *dwlt: in rr: reminders after 2f: rdn over 2f out: kpt on same pce* **20/1[3]**

60 **4** *1* **Hesindamood**[32] 663 4-9-13 0 .... CathyGannon 3 44
(Joanne Priest) *trckd wnr: t.k.h: drvn over 2f out: fdd fnl f* **25/1**

0 **5** *5* **Lady Freda**[9] 905 5-9-8 0 .... RussKennemore 5 26
(Alan Coogan) *t.k.h towards rr: drvn over 3f out: hung rt and lost pl over 2f out* **40/1**

1m 34.58s (4.98) **Going Correction** +0.10s/f (Slow)
WFA 3 from 4yo+ 15lb **5** Ran SP% **115.5**
Speed ratings (Par 103): **75,68,67,66,60**
CSF £1.56 TOTE £1.10: £1.02, £2.00; EX 2.00.
Owner Hamdan Al Maktoum **Bred** Shadwell Estate Company **Trained** Newmarket, Suffolk

FOCUS
A desperately weak and uncompetitive maiden.

1016 ATTHERACES.COM EXCLUSIVE HUGH TAYLOR TIPPING H'CAP 2m 119y(P)

3:20 (3:20) (Class 5) (0-75,73) 4-Y-0+ **£1,813** (£539; £269; £134) **Stalls** Low

Form RPR

544- **1** **Bravo Bravo**[162] 6955 4-8-3 55 .... ChrisCatlin 3 63
(Mick Channon) *hld up: hdwy 6f out: sn chsng ldrs: led over 1f out: drvn out* **11/2**

1251 **2** *1 1/4* **Rosewood Lad**[17] 838 4-9-5 71 .... CathyGannon 6 78+
(J S Moore) *trckd ldrs: reminders over 6f out: chsd ldrs 5f out: n.m.r and lost pl 3f out: hdwy over 1f out: styd on wl to take 2nd nr fin* **6/4[1]**

-104 **3** *1/2* **William's Way**[41] 549 9-9-9 70 ....(t) JamesDoyle 1 76
(Ian Wood) *dwlt: in rr: hdwy to chse ldrs 5f out: chal over 2f out: kpt on same pce fnl f* **20/1**

333- **4** *3* **Dr Finley (IRE)**[103] 6816 4-8-10 65 ....(p) SimonPearce(3) 5 67
(Lydia Pearce) *trckd ldrs: drvn over 2f out: wknd fnl f* **11/1**

5353 **5** *1 1/4* **Duar Mapel (USA)**[9] 917 5-8-8 55 ow1 ....(p) GrahamGibbons 2 56
(Brian Baugh) *led: hdd over 7f out: led over 3f out: hdd over 1f out: sn wknd* **4/1[3]**

41-3 **6** *33* **Quinsman**[47] 474 5-9-7 73 .... RyanPowell(5) 4 34+
(J S Moore) *t.k.h towards rr: sddle slipped after abt 3f: jnd ldr after 6f: led 8f out tl over 3f out: sn lost pl and bhd: eased* **7/2[2]**

3m 43.47s (1.67) **Going Correction** +0.10s/f (Slow)
WFA 4 from 5yo+ 5lb **6** Ran SP% **110.7**
Speed ratings (Par 103): **100,99,99,97,97 81**
toteswingers:1&2:£2.50, 1&3:£4.20, 2&3:£4.40 CSF £13.86 TOTE £4.10: £1.50, £2.20; EX 16.70.
Owner Derek And Jean Clee **Bred** D & Jean Clee & Burlington Bloodstock **Trained** West Ilsley, Berks

FOCUS
A low-grade staying handicap and a bit of a messy race. The level is set around the third.

1017 STAY AT THE WOLVERHAMPTON HOLIDAY INN H'CAP 1m 141y(P)

3:50 (3:50) (Class 5) (0-75,75) 4-Y-0+ **£1,813** (£539; £269; £134) **Stalls** Low

Form RPR

-542 **1** **Fleetwoodsands (IRE)**[9] 914 4-8-13 67 ....(t) BarryMcHugh 6 74
(Ollie Pears) *tk fierce hold: sn trcking ldr: led 2f out: sn narrowly hdd: styd on to ld towards fin: jst hld on* **5/1**

26-5 **2** *nse* **Tevez**[71] 186 6-9-2 75 .... MartinHarley(5) 4 82
(Des Donovan) *dwlt: hld up: hdwy on outside over 1f out: chal wl ins fnl f: jst hld* **13/2**

3224 **3** *3/4* **Faithful Ruler (USA)**[21] 790 7-9-7 75 ....(p) LukeMorris 7 80
(Ronald Harris) *trckd ldrs: drvn over 2f out: narrow ld appr fnl f: rdr dropped reign and drifted lft: hdd and no ex towards fin* **11/4[1]**

00-5 **4** *2 1/2* **Stevie Gee (IRE)**[18] 820 7-9-1 69 .... RichardKingscote 3 68
(Ian Williams) *trckd ldrs: effrt over 2f out: chsd wnr over 1f out: fdd* **9/2[3]**

622 **5** *3 1/4* **Symphonic Dancer (USA)**[16] 850 4-9-4 72 .... J-PGuillambert 5 64
(Brian Baugh) *hld up: effrt over 2f out: nvr trbld ldrs* **7/2[2]**

030- **6** *1 1/4* **Baltimore Jack (IRE)**[178] 6543 7-8-13 67 .... GrahamGibbons 1 56
(G P Kelly) *led: hdd 2f out: wknd over 1f out* **9/1**

640- **7** *5* **Valdan (IRE)**[210] 5333 7-8-11 65 ....(t) PaulHanagan 2 42
(Maurice Barnes) *dwlt: hld up towards rr: drvn over 3f out: sme hdwy on ins 2f out: sn wknd* **16/1**

1m 51.2s (0.70) **Going Correction** +0.10s/f (Slow) **7** Ran SP% **113.0**
Speed ratings (Par 103): **100,99,99,97,94 93,88**
toteswingers:1&2:£4.60, 1&3:£2.10, 2&3:£3.40 CSF £35.74 TOTE £4.80: £1.40, £2.70; EX 47.80.
Owner Ollie Pears **Bred** Gary O'Reilly **Trained** Norton, N Yorks

FOCUS
The early pace was steady and the winner very much stole the race. It's hard to be positive about this muddling form although the runner-up ran as well as ever at face value.

1018 SPONSOR A RACE BY CALLING 01902 390000 H'CAP 1m 4f 50y(P)

4:20 (4:27) (Class 6) (0-60,60) 3-Y-0 **£1,535** (£453; £226) **Stalls** Low

Form RPR

50-4 **1** **Dance For Livvy (IRE)**[48] 456 3-9-0 53 .... PJMcDonald 9 61
(Ben Haslam) *mid-div: hdwy to chse ldrs over 2f out: styd on to ld 1f out: drvn out* **14/1**

0-02 **2** *1 1/4* **The Absent Mare**[7] 930 3-8-7 46 oh1 ....(t) SilvestreDeSousa 8 52+
(Frank Sheridan) *dwlt: in rr: hdwy on outside 3f out: styd on fnl f: tk 2nd towards fin* **7/1[3]**

05-4 **3** *3/4* **Delagoa Bay (IRE)**[53] 406 3-8-12 51 .... JamesDoyle 7 56
(Sylvester Kirk) *awkward to load: mid-div: hdwy and 3rd over 2f out: kpt on same pce fnl f* **4/1[1]**

455 **4** *shd* **Freedom Flyer (IRE)**[28] 714 3-9-6 **59** AdamKirby 12 63
(Marco Botti) *sn trcking ldrs: led over 3f out: hdd 1f out: one pce* **5/1**[2]
600- **5** *5* **Hi Note**[145] 7296 3-8-3 **49** CharlesBishop(7) 5 45
(Mick Channon) *mid-div: effrt on outer 3f out: kpt on: nvr rchd ldrs* **16/1**
000- **6** *5* **Ivanov (IRE)**[200] 5894 3-8-7 **46** oh1 JamieMackay 2 34
(Willie Musson) *dwlt: in rr: effrt 3f out: kpt on fnl f: nvr on terms* **7/1**[3]
40-4 **7** *½* **Jelyvator**[26] 731 3-9-7 **60** JimmyQuinn 6 48
(Alex Hales) *mid-div: effrt 3f out: nvr a factor* **14/1**
0-46 **8** *2* **Reach Out**[26] 731 3-8-13 **52** PaulHanagan 10 36
(Brendan Powell) *led rdrless to s: chsd ldrs: lost pl over 2f out* **16/1**
-004 **9** *1* **Varlak**[10] 898 3-9-0 **53** (v) DarryllHolland 3 36
(Des Donovan) *gave problems s: in rr: hung lft and reminders over 4f out: nvr on terms* **10/1**
0-00 **10** *1* **Neighbourhood (USA)**[11] 878 3-9-5 **58** GregFairley 11 39
(Mark Johnston) *led: hdd over 3f out: lost pl over 2f out* **25/1**
023 **11** *3 ¾* **Fleeting Storm**[33] 649 3-9-6 **59** (p) SteveDrowne 1 34
(Hughie Morrison) *chsd ldrs: sn pushed along: lost pl over 2f out* **4/1**[1]
0-00 **12** *4 ½* **Heart Felt**[18] 817 3-8-13 **52** (p) TomEaves 4 20
(Roy Brotherton) *sn chsng ldrs: lost pl 3f out* **50/1**

2m 42.06s (0.96) **Going Correction** +0.10s/f (Slow) 12 Ran SP% **121.7**
Speed ratings (Par 96): **100,99,98,98,95 91,91,90,89,88 86,83**
toteswingers:1&2:£25.00, 1&3:£14.10, 2&3:£3.80 CSF £111.68 CT £476.84 TOTE £17.50: £3.80, £2.70, £1.40; EX 139.10 Trifecta £397.00 Part won. Pool: £536.62 - 0.44 winning units..
Owner Mark James **Bred** Lynn Lodge Stud **Trained** Middleham Moor, N Yorks

FOCUS
The early pace was a steady one for this 1m4f 3-y-o handicap. A tricky race to pin down, but the first four were clear and the form has been given a chance.

1019 THE BLACK COUNTRY'S ONLY RACECOURSE H'CAP 5f 216y(P)
4:50 (4:50) (Class 4) (0-85,85) 3-Y-O **£2,914** (£867; £433) **Stalls** Low

Form RPR
1151 **1** **Joe Le Taxi (IRE)**[33] 659 3-8-8 **72** GregFairley 3 76
(Mark Johnston) *chsd ldr: sn pushed along: rdn over 2f out: styd on to take narrow ld ins fnl f: hld on wl nr fin* **1/1**[1]
0- **2** *nk* **Tom Sawyer**[221] 5245 3-9-7 **85** PaulHanagan 2 88
(Julie Camacho) *led: shkn up and qcknd over 2f out: narrowly hdd ins fnl f: no ex nr fin* **2/1**[2]
5-56 **3** *4 ½* **Saucy Buck (IRE)**[10] 887 3-8-0 **71** oh4 (v) CharlesBishop(7) 1 60
(Mick Channon) *trckd ldrs: effrt over 2f out: plld wd over 1f out: sn wl outpcd* **7/2**[3]

1m 15.75s (0.75) **Going Correction** +0.10s/f (Slow) 3 Ran SP% **105.6**
Speed ratings (Par 100): **99,98,92**
CSF £3.14 TOTE £1.40; EX 2.10.
Owner Mark Johnston Racing Ltd **Bred** J Joyce **Trained** Middleham Moor, N Yorks

FOCUS
Quite competitive, despite there being just three runners. The winner is rated close to his Southwell win and it's hard to be too confident about the form.
T/Plt: £124.40 to a £1 stake. Pool:£50,124.48 - 294.06 winning tickets T/Qpdt: £40.10 to a £1 stake. Pool:£3,703.32 - 68.20 winning tickets WG

989 LINGFIELD (L-H)
Tuesday, March 29

OFFICIAL GOING: Standard
Wind: Almost nil Weather: Hazy but fine

1020 SUMMER EVENINGS AT LINGFIELD PARK MAIDEN STKS 5f (P)
2:10 (2:11) (Class 5) 3-Y-O **£2,047** (£604; £302) **Stalls** High

Form RPR
0- **1** **Fair Value (IRE)**[169] 6811 3-8-12 **0** NeilCallan 6 77
(Simon Dow) *rn green thrght but sn chsd ldng pair: wnt 2nd over 2f out: urged along to cl and led jst over 1f out: galloped on strly and sn clr: quite impressive* **5/1**
544 **2** *4 ½* **Beautiful Day**[38] 611 3-9-3 **66** (b[1]) PhillipMakin 1 66
(Kevin Ryan) *led: rdn and hdd jst over 1f out: kpt on wl enough but no ch w wnr* **9/2**[3]
5550 **3** *2 ¾* **Karate (IRE)**[11] 887 3-9-3 **61** JamesDoyle 7 56
(Hans Adielsson) *in tch: pushed along after 2f: outpcd over 2f out: kpt on u.p to take 3rd last 100yds* **4/1**[2]
5 **4** *1 ¼* **Bambika**[38] 611 3-8-12 **0** IanMongan 3 47
(Jo Crowley) *chsd ldr to over 2f out: rdn and steadily wknd over 1f out* **2/1**[1]
5 *nk* **Miakora** 3-8-12 **0** MartinDwyer 2 46
(Michael Quinn) *s.i.s: in tch: pushed along wl over 2f out: brief effrt on inner over 1f out: sn no hdwy* **14/1**
55 **6** *3 ½* **Demoiselle Bond**[13] 863 3-8-12 **0** RichardThomas 4 33
(Lydia Richards) *fractious coming on to crse: a in last pair: outpcd over 2f out: sn no ch* **66/1**
7 *5* **Miming** 3-8-12 **0** SteveDrowne 5 15
(Hughie Morrison) *a in last pair: outpcd fr 1/2-way: no ch after* **7/1**

58.58 secs (-0.22) **Going Correction** +0.175s/f (Slow) 7 Ran SP% **108.8**
Speed ratings (Par 98): **108,100,96,94,93 88,80**
Tote Swingers: 1&2 £3.30, 1&3 £4.00, 2&3 £2.90 CSF £24.80 TOTE £3.80: £1.40, £2.00; EX 28.80.
Owner Edward Hyde **Bred** Edward Hyde **Trained** Epsom, Surrey

FOCUS
A modest sprint maiden, but quite a good performance from the winner and the time was fair. The form is rated around the runner-up.

1021 GREAT DEALS ON ANNUAL MEMBERSHIP (S) STKS 1m (P)
2:40 (2:40) (Class 6) 3-Y-O+ **£1,535** (£453; £226) **Stalls** High

Form RPR
4-34 **1** **The Big Haerth (IRE)**[10] 914 5-10-0 **68** (t) JamesDoyle 1 70
(Frank Sheridan) *t.k.h: cl up in 3rd: pushed firmly into 2nd over 1f out: clsd and rdn to ld last 150yds: styd on wl* **3/1**[2]
116 **2** *1 ¼* **I Confess**[5] 956 6-9-11 **72** (b) RichardEvans(3) 5 67
(David Evans) *led: set stdy pce: kicked on over 2f out: hdd and readily outpcd last 150yds* **7/4**[1]
1604 **3** *1 ¾* **Gallantry**[12] 876 9-10-0 **75** DarryllHolland 3 63
(Jane Chapple-Hyam) *settled in 4th: pushed along whn pce lifted over 2f out: kpt on u.p to take 3rd ins fnl f: nvr a threat* **3/1**[2]
5142 **4** *2* **Fifth In Line (IRE)**[11] 886 3-8-6 **66** MartinDwyer 7 48
(David Flood) *t.k.h: sn trckd ldr: pushed along over 2f out: lost 2nd jst over 1f out: wknd* **4/1**[3]
/00- **5** *1* **Mumtaz Begum**[219] 5325 6-9-3 **39** (v) SamHitchcott 2 45?
(John E Long) *a in last pair: steadily outpcd once pce lifted over 2f out* **125/1**
000- **6** *½* **Final Try**[217] 5379 4-9-1 **40** NathanAlison(7) 4 49?
(Paddy Butler) *plld hrd: dropped to rr after 3f and last fr 1/2-way: steadily outpcd fr over 2f out* **100/1**

1m 39.25s (1.05) **Going Correction** +0.175s/f (Slow)
WFA 3 from 4yo+ 17lb 6 Ran SP% **108.1**
Speed ratings (Par 101): **101,99,98,96,95 94**
Tote Swingers: 1&2 £1.50, 1&3 £1.70, 2&3 £2.10 CSF £7.99 TOTE £3.10: £1.40, £1.10; EX 10.90.Winner bought by David Evans for 6,200gns.
Owner Dr D F Moretti **Bred** Hong Kong Breeders Club **Trained** Wolverhampton, W Midlands

FOCUS
Mixed abilities in this seller, and a four-horse race judged on the ratings. The pace was steady until the home turn. Muddling form, rated loosely around the winner.

1022 LINGFIELD PARK OWNERS CLUB H'CAP 1m (P)
3:10 (3:11) (Class 6) (0-65,65) 3-Y-O **£1,535** (£453; £226) **Stalls** High

Form RPR
6-25 **1** **Round Turn (IRE)**[27] 731 3-9-7 **65** DarryllHolland 10 70
(Ed McMahon) *sn t.k.h: trckd ldrs on outer: quick move to ld jst over 3f out: drvn over 1f out: edgd rt fnl f: hld on wl* **8/1**[3]
-424 **2** *¾* **Irie Ute**[8] 931 3-9-4 **62** LiamKeniry 1 65
(Sylvester Kirk) *t.k.h: trckd ldrs: lost pl over 3f out: prog again over 1f out to press ldr ins fnl f: fnd little and hld nr fin* **8/1**[3]
1-6 **3** *hd* **Crown Ridge (IRE)**[28] 716 3-8-9 **58** MartinHarley(5) 4 61
(Mick Channon) *led to over 6f out: lost pl on inner 3f out: effrt again and prog on inner over 1f out: drvn and kpt on fnl f* **7/1**[2]
001- **4** *1 ½* **Slumbering Sioux**[161] 7004 3-9-4 **62** AdamKirby 6 61
(Harry Dunlop) *prom: rdn to chse ldng pair over 2f out: disp 2nd over 1f out: nt qckn* **14/1**
55-0 **5** *nk* **Out Of The Storm**[11] 887 3-9-2 **60** NeilCallan 11 58
(Simon Dow) *hld up in last trio: prog over 4f out to trck ldrs 3f out: rdn and cl enough 2f out: one pce* **17/2**
-332 **6** *shd* **Tony Hollis**[13] 871 3-9-2 **60** JamesMillman 2 58+
(Rod Millman) *hld up and racd wd: nt wl plcd whn pce lfted fr 3f out: nvr on terms after: styd on fnl f* **11/1**
600- **7** *¾* **Lemon Drop Red (USA)**[196] 6053 3-9-6 **64** EddieAhern 7 60+
(Ed Dunlop) *stdd s: t.k.h and hld up towards rr: trbld passage in slowly run event and only 10th over 2f out: no ch after: kpt on fnl f* **3/1**[1]
405- **8** *½* **Looksmart**[141] 7379 3-9-4 **62** JimmyFortune 5 57
(Richard Hannon) *plld way into ld over 6f out but set v stdy pce: hdd jst over 3f out: shkn up and racd awkwardly on inner over 2f out: nt qckn after* **12/1**
000 **9** *1* **Five Cool Kats (IRE)**[10] 905 3-8-9 **53** WilliamCarson 8 46
(Paul Burgoyne) *prom: jnd wnr jst over 3f out: nt qckn over 2f out: wknd fnl f* **66/1**
060 **10** *2 ¼* **Tegan (IRE)**[37] 624 3-8-9 **53** FrankieMcDonald 3 41+
(Richard Hannon) *bmpd after 2f: dropped to last pair 5f out: detached 3f out: no ch after* **20/1**
4-00 **11** *½* **Come On The Irons (USA)**[11] 887 3-9-4 **62** JamieGoldstein 12 49
(Ralph Smith) *hld up in last pair fr wd draw: detached fr 3f out once pce lifted: bhd after* **40/1**
-322 **12** *1 ½* **Hackett (IRE)**[25] 760 3-9-5 **63** MartinDwyer 9 46
(Michael Quinn) *racd wd towards rr: prog to chse ldrs over 2f out: nt qckn over 1f out: sn eased* **7/1**[2]

1m 40.75s (2.55) **Going Correction** +0.175s/f (Slow) 12 Ran SP% **114.1**
Speed ratings (Par 96): **94,93,93,91,91 91,90,89,88,86 86,84**
Tote Swingers: 1&2 £15.90, 1&3 £9.50, 2&3 £8.20 CSF £66.73 CT £477.00 TOTE £10.90: £3.50, £3.00, £2.90; EX 81.60 Trifecta £174.90 Pool: £546.25 - 2.31 winning units..
Owner J C Fretwell **Bred** C O'Reilly & Co **Trained** Lichfield, Staffs
■ Stewards' Enquiry : Darryll Holland three-day ban: careless riding (Apr 12-14); one-day ban: careless riding (Apr 15)

FOCUS
A modest but competitive-looking handicap in which the very steady pace caused all sorts of traffic problems, and there were several hard-luck stories. The level is set around the second and third.

1023 LUXURY BOOT CAMPS AT LINGFIELD MARRIOTT H'CAP 7f (P)
3:40 (3:45) (Class 4) (0-85,83) 3-Y-O **£3,399** (£1,011; £505) **Stalls** Low

Form RPR
1131 **1** **Kingscroft (IRE)**[17] 845 3-9-5 **81** GregFairley 2 85
(Mark Johnston) *dwlt: t.k.h and sn trckd ldr: pushed along over 2f out: drvn to chal over 1f out: edgd ahd ins fnl f* **10/11**[1]
211- **2** *nk* **Bunce (IRE)**[176] 6627 3-9-7 **83** JimmyFortune 3 86
(Richard Hannon) *led at stdy pce: shkn up whn pressed over 1f out: narrowly hdd and hrd rdn ins fnl f: nt qckn* **Evs**[2]
-544 **3** *4* **Toms River Tess (IRE)**[13] 864 3-8-12 **74** KirstyMilczarek 1 66
(Zoe Davison) *taken down early: uns rdr and bolted bef s: clattering through rails: restless in stalls: cl up tl steadily outpcd over 1f out* **14/1**[3]

1m 27.15s (2.35) **Going Correction** +0.175s/f (Slow) 3 Ran SP% **109.1**
Speed ratings (Par 100): **93,92,88**
CSF £2.21 TOTE £1.90; EX 1.80.
Owner Dr Marwan Koukash **Bred** J Beckett **Trained** Middleham Moor, N Yorks

FOCUS
A decent handicap, despite the small field, and it resulted in a good tussle between the market leaders, both of whom are progressive. The pace was slow.

1024 FREE REPLAYS AT ATTHERACES.COM FILLIES' H'CAP 6f (P)
4:10 (4:11) (Class 5) (0-75,74) 4-Y-O+ **£2,047** (£604; £302) **Stalls** Low

Form RPR
443- **1** **Dream Number (IRE)**[139] 7390 4-8-7 **60** MartinDwyer 5 66
(William Muir) *hld up in 4th: effrt 2f out: drvn and r.o to ld last 150yds: jst hld on* **5/1**[3]
00-0 **2** *shd* **Secret Queen**[32] 694 4-9-0 **67** LukeMorris 6 73
(Martin Hill) *stdd s: hld up in last pair: rdn on outer over 1f out: styd on wl fnl f: jst failed* **25/1**
123 **3** *¾* **Cape Melody**[13] 865 5-9-7 **74** JimmyFortune 3 78
(George Baker) *hld up in last pair: effrt on inner over 2f out: drvn and styd on fr over 1f out: nt pce to chal* **15/8**[1]
1321 **4** *¾* **Six Wives**[29] 708 4-9-0 **74** LeonnaMayor(7) 4 75
(David Nicholls) *pressed ldr: pushed along and nt qckn over 1f out: outpcd ins fnl f* **4/1**[2]
0031 **5** *½* **Mary's Pet**[22] 792 4-8-8 **64** (p) SimonPearce(3) 1 64
(John Akehurst) *led: more than a l clr 2f out: hdd & wknd last 150yds* **4/1**[2]

1436 **6** 4 1/2 **Caramelita**[13] 865 4-9-0 **67** .... DavidProbert 2 52
(J R Jenkins) *chsd ldng pair to wl over 1f out: wknd* **13/2**
1m 12.0s (0.10) **Going Correction** +0.175s/f (Slow) **6** Ran SP% **108.6**
Speed ratings (Par 100): **106,105,104,103,103 97**
Tote Swingers: 1&2 £8.30, 1&3 £2.20, 2&3 £6.30 CSF £88.85 TOTE £8.20: £4.60, £19.70; EX 65.00.
Owner Linkslade Lottery **Bred** James Waldron **Trained** Lambourn, Berks
FOCUS
A fair fillies' sprint, with several of these having shown good recent form. It was a race of changing fortunes in the straight. The form is rated through the runner-up.

1025 NEW SEASON AT ATRVIRTUALOWNER.COM H'CAP 1m 5f (P)
4:40 (4:40) (Class 6) (0-60,60) 4-Y-0+ **£1,535** (£453; £226) **Stalls** Low

Form RPR
22-1 **1** **Dansilver**[15] 216 7-9-7 **58** .... PaulDoe 5 65
(Jim Best) *trckd ldng pair: poised to chal over 2f out: rdn on inner over 1f out: led last 150yds: drvn out* **5/2**[2]
-022 **2** 1/2 **Sunset Place**[5] 954 4-9-6 **60** .... RobertHavlin 1 66
(Jonathan Geake) *hld up in last: wnt 4th 6f out: poised to chal over 2f out: drvn on outer over 1f out: upsides ins fnl f: nt qckn nr fin* **11/8**[1]
0-34 **3** nk **Prince Blue**[19] 819 4-8-10 **50** .... SamHitchcott 6 56
(John E Long) *led at mod pce: drvn 2f out: hdd last 150yds: styd on but hld nr fin* **4/1**[3]
3010 **4** 5 **Suhailah**[27] 728 5-8-13 **53** .... KierenFox(3) 7 51
(Michael Attwater) *trckd ldr: moved upsides 4f out: drvn over 2f out: wknd over 1f out* **8/1**
4040 **5** 1 1/2 **Harrys**[19] 819 4-8-5 **45** .... (b[1]) JimmyQuinn 4 41
(Jane Chapple-Hyam) *hld up in 4th: dropped to last 6f out: struggling to stay w ldrs 3f out: fdd 2f out* **12/1**
2m 49.84s (3.84) **Going Correction** +0.175s/f (Slow)
WFA 4 from 5yo+ 3lb **5** Ran SP% **109.5**
Speed ratings (Par 101): **95,94,94,91,90**
CSF £6.29 TOTE £2.40: £1.10, £1.50; EX 6.70.
Owner Leon Best **Bred** Mrs J L Egan **Trained** Lewes, E Sussex
FOCUS
A low-grade handicap but another close finish. Muddling and limited form.

1026 FOLLOW @ATTHERACES ON TWITTER H'CAP 1m (P)
5:10 (5:10) (Class 5) (0-75,75) 4-Y-0+ **£2,047** (£604; £302) **Stalls** High

Form RPR
41-0 **1** **Cativo Cavallino**[48] 473 8-8-7 **64** .... NataliaGemelova(3) 4 68
(John E Long) *mde all: increased tempo fr over 2f out: rdn and had rest in trble over 1f out: hld on nr fin* **4/1**[3]
0-60 **2** 1/2 **Prince Of Thebes (IRE)**[20] 806 10-8-10 **64** .... NeilCallan 2 67
(Michael Attwater) *trckd wnr to 1/2-way: rdn over 2f out: wnt 2nd again wl over 1f out but no imp: clsd fnl f: nt quite get there* **11/4**[2]
4315 **3** 2 **Chief Exec**[11] 897 9-9-2 **70** .... LiamKeniry 6 68
(Jeremy Gask) *blindfold off late and dwlt: hld up last: wnt 4th over 2f out gng wl: nt qckn over 1f out: rdn and kpt on same pce after* **5/4**[1]
-510 **4** 1/2 **Diplomatic (IRE)**[33] 666 6-9-2 **70** .... LukeMorris 3 67
(Michael Squance) *hld up in 4th: rdn and dropped to last over 2f out: tried to rally on inner over 1f out: one pce* **10/1**
5/0- **5** 3 **Come On Safari (IRE)**[313] 2253 4-9-2 **75** .... MartinHarley(5) 5 65
(Joseph Tuite) *cl up: trckd wnr fr 1/2-way to wl over 1f out: wknd* **8/1**
1m 38.41s (0.21) **Going Correction** +0.175s/f (Slow) **5** Ran SP% **111.3**
Speed ratings (Par 103): **105,104,102,102,99**
CSF £15.36 TOTE £9.90: £10.70, £2.00; EX 15.40.
Owner P Saxon **Bred** Miss A M Rees **Trained** Caterham, Surrey
■ Stewards' Enquiry : Natalia Gemelova one-day ban: used whip in incorrect place (Apr 12)
FOCUS
A modest handicap, but one featuring a couple of recent winners. It was another muddling race and it's hard to be confident about the form.
Cativo Cavallino Official explanation: trainer said, regarding apparent improvement in form, that the gelding was suited by being able to dominate.
T/Jkpt: Not won. T/Plt: £505.30 to a £1 stake. Pool:£60,729.17 - 87.72 winning tickets T/Qpdt: £72.50 to a £1 stake. Pool:£4,658.34 - 47.50 winning tickets JN

936 SOUTHWELL (L-H)
Tuesday, March 29

OFFICIAL GOING: Standard
Wind: Virtually nil Weather: Fine and dry

1027 SOUTHWELL-RACECOURSE.CO.UK MAIDEN STKS 1m (F)
2:30 (2:30) (Class 5) 3-Y-0 **£1,910** (£564; £282) **Stalls** Low

Form RPR
03- **1** **Ashva (USA)**[188] 6293 3-9-3 0 .... TomEaves 3 80+
(Michael Dods) *cl up: led 2f out: sn shkn up: rdn over 1f out: kpt on* **8/11**[1]
3- **2** 2 1/4 **Roninski (IRE)**[178] 6566 3-9-3 0 .... PaulMulrennan 4 75
(Bryan Smart) *chsd ldng pair: led after 1 1/2f: pushed along and jnd 3f out: hdd 2f out and sn rdn: drvn and ev ch whn wandered appr fnl f: kpt on same pce* **3/1**[2]
0- **3** nk **Georgey Girl**[130] 7503 3-8-12 0 .... PJMcDonald 5 69
(Alan Swinbank) *in tch: hdwy to chse ldng pair 3f out: rdn 2f out: kpt on wl fnl f: nrst fin* **40/1**
4 15 **Carrowbeg (IRE)** 3-9-3 0 .... SilvestreDeSousa 2 40
(Mark Johnston) *led 2f: cl up on inner: pushed along over 3f out: sn rdn: rn green and outpcd* **9/1**
04- **5** 2 1/4 **Fine Style (IRE)**[216] 5413 3-9-3 0 .... HayleyTurner 7 34
(Michael Bell) *in tch: pushed along after 2f: rdn along 1/2-way: outpcd fnl 3f* **15/2**[3]
6 **6** 27 **Tuscany Red**[29] 713 3-9-0 0 .... RobertLButler(3) 6 —
(Richard Guest) *dwlt: a in rr: rdn along 1/2-way: sn wl bhd* **150/1**
1m 42.89s (-0.81) **Going Correction** -0.075s/f (Stan) **6** Ran SP% **107.8**
Speed ratings (Par 98): **101,98,98,83,81 54**
CSF £2.78 TOTE £1.90: £1.50, £1.50; EX 3.90.
Owner Andrew Tinkler **Bred** Brook Stud Bloodstock Ltd **Trained** Denton, Co Durham

FOCUS
An above-average maiden for the track. The front pair stepped on the fair standard they set, with the first three clear.

1028 WORK, LIFE BALANCE MEDIAN AUCTION MAIDEN STKS 1m 4f (F)
3:00 (3:00) (Class 5) 3-5-Y-0 **£1,910** (£564; £282) **Stalls** Low

Form RPR
2422 **1** **Baileys Agincourt**[22] 789 3-8-5 62 .... SilvestreDeSousa 3 59+
(Mark Johnston) *mde all: pushed along over 3f out: rdn wl over 2f out: drvn over 1f out and kpt on wl: eased towards fin* **4/1**[2]
6433 **2** 1 **Little Jazz**[11] 898 3-8-0 60 .... KellyHarrison 4 50
(Paul D'Arcy) *in tch: hdwy to trck ldrs over 4f out: effrt on inner and cl up 3f out: rdn to chal 2f out and ev ch tl drvn and one pce ins fnl f* **13/2**[3]
00-5 **3** hd **Laffraaj (IRE)**[31] 699 3-8-5 50 .... (v[1]) ChrisCatlin 5 55
(Pat Eddery) *trckd wnr: effrt 4f out and sn cl up: rdn to chal 3f out and ev ch tl drvn and one pce ent fnl f* **25/1**
4 2 1/4 **Karasenir (IRE)**[11] 5-9-13 0 .... JamieSpencer 2 53
(Philip Hobbs) *hld up in tch: trckd ldrs on outer 1/2-way: reminders 4f out: rdn over 3f out: drvn and edgd lft over 2f out: hrd drvn appr fnl f: sn edgd rt and no imp* **4/9**[1]
0-2 **5** 2 **Why So Serious**[25] 774 5-9-8 0 .... TobyAtkinson(5) 6 50
(Peter Salmon) *hld up in rr: hdwy 4f out: rdn to chse ldrs 3f out: drvn and no imp fr wl over 1f out* **50/1**
05 **6** dist **Rapacious**[18] 836 3-8-5 0 .... NickyMackay 1 —
(Mark Rimmer) *chsd ldrs: pushed along bef 1/2-way: lost pl over 4f out and sn wl bhd* **150/1**
2m 43.52s (2.52) **Going Correction** -0.075s/f (Stan)
WFA 3 from 5yo 22lb **6** Ran SP% **109.1**
Speed ratings (Par 103): **88,87,87,85,84** —
CSF £25.84 TOTE £3.50: £2.00, £4.10; EX 12.60.
Owner G R Bailey Ltd (Baileys Horse Feeds) **Bred** P And Mrs A G Venner **Trained** Middleham Moor, N Yorks
■ Stewards' Enquiry : Jamie Spencer two-day ban: used whip with excessive frequency with arm above shoulder height (Apr 12-13)
FOCUS
A weak maiden run in a slow time (over eight seconds above standard) in which the winner, officially rated 62, looks the best guide to the form. He probably didn't have to improve.
Karasenir(IRE) Official explanation: jockey said gelding never travelled

1029 DINE IN THE QUEEN MOTHER RESTAURANT H'CAP 5f (F)
3:30 (3:31) (Class 6) (0-60,60) 4-Y-0+ **£1,535** (£453; £226) **Stalls** High

Form RPR
6021 **1** **Dickie Le Davoir**[10] 912 7-9-1 **54** .... (b) JamieSpencer 6 68
(Richard Guest) *in tch: hdwy to trck ldr 1/2-way: rdn to ld 1f out: sn edgd lft and clr* **8/1**
23 **2** 1 3/4 **Clear Ice (IRE)**[43] 538 4-9-2 **58** .... (v) RobertLButler(3) 8 66
(Richard Guest) *sn led: rdn wl over 1f out: hdd 1f out: sn edgd lft and kpt on same pce* **13/2**[3]
3040 **3** 1 1/4 **Muqalad (IRE)**[10] 912 4-8-10 **49** .... (vt) TomEaves 3 53
(Bryan Smart) *wnt rt s: sn chsng ldrs: hdwy on outer and cl up 1/2-way: rdn wl over 1f out: kpt on same pce fnl f* **7/1**
5443 **4** shd **Kheley (IRE)**[7] 941 5-8-8 **52** .... JamesRogers(5) 2 55
(Mark Brisbourne) *chsd ldrs: rdn 2f out: drvn over 1f out: sn one pce* **7/2**[1]
4224 **5** 1/2 **We'll Deal Again**[18] 833 4-9-4 **60** .... (v) JamesSullivan(3) 4 61
(Michael Easterby) *sltly hmpd s: sn chsng ldrs: rdn along wl over 1f out: sn wknd* **7/2**[1]
4552 **6** 1 1/4 **Bertbrand**[7] 941 6-8-7 **46** oh1 .... (b) PaulHanagan 1 43
(Ian McInnes) *prom: rdn along 2f out: sn drvn and wknd* **4/1**[2]
0020 **7** 3/4 **Lets Move It**[7] 941 4-9-2 **55** .... GrahamGibbons 7 49
(Derek Shaw) *in tch: rdn along 2f out: sn btn* **12/1**
0-60 **8** 6 **Egyptian Lord**[72] 185 8-8-7 **46** oh1 .... (b) RobbieFitzpatrick 5 19
(Peter Grayson) *in tch: rdn along after 2f: sn outpcd and bhd* **80/1**
60.22 secs (0.52) **Going Correction** +0.15s/f (Slow) **8** Ran SP% **110.3**
Speed ratings (Par 101): **101,98,96,96,95 93,92,82**
CSF £54.43 CT £363.29 TOTE £11.80: £2.40, £1.90, £2.10; EX 25.10.
Owner Future Racing (Notts) Limited **Bred** P And Mrs A G Venner **Trained** Stainforth, S Yorks
FOCUS
A few in-form types lined up in this low-grade handicap. The form is rated around the runner-up.

1030 MEMBERSHIP OF SOUTHWELL GOLF CLUB H'CAP 1m 6f (F)
4:00 (4:00) (Class 3) (0-95,90) 4-Y-0+ **£4,533** (£1,348; £674; £336) **Stalls** Low

Form RPR
1111 **1** **La Estrella (USA)**[21] 795 8-9-6 **80** .... DaneO'Neill 7 92
(Don Cantillon) *trckd ldrs: hdwy to chse ldr wl over 2f out: rdn to chal wl over 1f out: kpt on to ld appr fnl f: rdn out* **4/1**[2]
5111 **2** 1 1/4 **Mush Mir (IRE)**[42] 549 4-9-10 **88** .... (b) StephenCraine 4 98
(Jim Boyle) *led 3f: trckd ldr tl led again 3f out: jnd wl over 1f out: shkn up and hdd appr fnl f: sn edgd lft and one pce* **7/2**[1]
2221 **3** 6 **Parhelion**[13] 872 4-9-1 **79** .... JackMitchell 5 81
(Derek Haydn Jones) *hld up in tch: hdwy on outer 4f out: rdn to chse ldng pair over 2f out: drvn wl over 1f out and kpt on same pce* **5/1**
3222 **4** 5 **Calculating (IRE)**[13] 872 7-8-0 **67** oh1 .... RachealKneller(7) 1 62
(Mark Usher) *hld up in tch: effrt over 3f out: rdn along over 2f out: sn no imp* **12/1**
11-0 **5** 10 **Palio Square (USA)**[37] 628 4-9-8 **86** .... JimCrowley 2 67
(Ralph Beckett) *chsd ldng pair on inner: rdn along 4f out: wknd 3f out* **7/2**[1]
0-11 **6** 3 1/4 **Exemplary**[47] 486 4-9-12 **90** .... SilvestreDeSousa 6 66
(Mark Johnston) *t.k.h: trckd ldr tl led after 3f: rdn along and hdd 3f out: wknd over 2f out* **9/2**[3]
5232 **7** 14 **Ethics Girl (IRE)**[11] 894 5-9-10 **84** .... (t) PaulHanagan 3 41
(John Berry) *hld up in tch: effrt 4f out: rdn along over 3f out and sn wknd* **16/1**
3m 5.21s (-3.09) **Going Correction** -0.075s/f (Stan)
WFA 4 from 5yo+ 4lb **7** Ran SP% **112.9**
Speed ratings (Par 107): **105,104,100,98,92 90,82**
CSF £17.86 TOTE £6.30: £3.80, £2.40; EX 16.40.
Owner Don Cantillon **Bred** Five Horses Ltd And Theatrical Syndicate **Trained** Newmarket, Suffolk
FOCUS
Several in-form types lined up and the first two finishers were a combined 10-10 on the Southwell Fibresand coming into the race. Clearly this is good form, and sound enough.
NOTEBOOK
La Estrella(USA), a four-time winner here in selling and claiming company since returning from a lengthy absence, coped well with this tougher contest to take his overall record on the Southwell Fibresand to a remarkable 8-8. He proved more resolute than the runner-up and may now switch to the turf. (op 7-2)

Mush Mir(IRE) was 3-3 at the track coming into this, but he hadn't been seriously challenged for his last two victories and this was a lot tougher off 11lb higher than his latest success. He again travelled well, but was eventually forced off the bridle and didn't find a great deal. (op 4-1)
Parhelion was up 4lb for winning a lesser race over C&D on his previous start and this was solid effort in defeat, confirming form with Calculating. (op 6-1)
Calculating(IRE) was a bit out of his depth. (op 16-1)
Palio Square(USA), progressive on Polytrack for Henry Cecil last year before being sold for 20,000gns, was well beaten on the St Moritz ice on his debut for this yard. Stepped back up in trip and trying Fibresand for the first time, he was solid in the market but was beaten going down the back straight. (op 4-1 tchd 10-3)
Exemplary, bidding for a hat-trick after wins over 2m on Polytrack, was up a further 3lb and still had to prove himself on Fibresand. He dropped away after failing to settle and this was a poor performance. Official explanation: jockey said gelding ran too free (op 4-1 tchd 5-1)
Ethics Girl(IRE) Official explanation: jockey said mare did not handle the Fibresand surface

1031 JUSTBOOKIES.COM H'CAP — 7f (F)
4:30 (4:32) (Class 5) (0-75,73) 3-Y-O — **£1,813** (£539; £269; £134) **Stalls** Low

Form — RPR
-321 **1** **Ana Emarati (USA)**[54] 398 3-9-6 **72** .... JamieSpencer 2 — 85+
(Ed Dunlop) *led: edgd rt and hdd after 1 1/2f: cl up: led over 2f out: rdn and edgd lft over 1f out: drvn clr ins fnl f: eased nr fin* **11/8**[1]
1-34 **2** 2 1/4 **Verrazano**[27] 729 3-8-7 **62** .... AmyRyan(3) 1 — 66
(Kevin Ryan) *cl up on inner: led after 1 1/2f: rdn wl over 2f out and sn hdd: swtchd rt and rallied jst over 1f out: drvn and one pce ins fnl f* **13/2**[3]
2231 **3** 4 **Eilean Mor**[46] 510 3-9-0 **66** .... TomEaves 3 — 59
(Bryan Smart) *chsd ldrs: rdn along wl over 2f out: drvn wl over 1f out: sn one pce* **13/2**[3]
430- **4** 1 1/2 **Coax**[132] 7478 3-9-0 **66** .... SilvestreDeSousa 4 — 55
(Mark Johnston) *in tch: rdn along and rn green 1/2-way: sn outpcd and bhd: swtchd wd home turn: styd on appr fnl f* **11/4**[2]
022- **5** hd **Justbookie Dot Com (IRE)**[114] 7715 3-9-7 **73** .... PaulHanagan 5 — 62
(Louise Best) *chsd ldrs: rdn over 2f out: sn wknd* **8/1**

1m 29.97s (-0.33) **Going Correction** -0.075s/f (Stan) — **5** Ran SP% **106.5**
Speed ratings (Par 98): **98,95,90,89,88**
CSF £9.79 TOTE £1.40: £1.02, £4.60; EX 11.50.
Owner Abdulla Ahmad Al Shaikh **Bred** Paulyn Limited **Trained** Newmarket, Suffolk

FOCUS
A low-grade 3-y-o handicap, but the time was respectable and the winner produced a significant personal best.

1032 GREAT OFFERS AT SOUTHWELL-RACECOURSE.CO.UK H'CAP — 2m (F)
5:00 (5:00) (Class 6) (0-65,64) 4-Y-O+ — **£1,535** (£453; £226) **Stalls** Low

Form — RPR
3-62 **1** **Hindu Kush (IRE)**[21] 795 6-9-7 **64** .... SeanLevey(5) 8 — 74
(Robert Mills) *mde all: rdn 3f out: sn jnd and drvn whn edgd lft wl over 1f out: styd on gamely fnl f* **9/2**[2]
2301 **2** 3 1/2 **Six Of Clubs**[25] 768 5-8-5 **50** .... (b) JakePayne(7) 1 — 56
(Bill Turner) *trckd ldrs: swtchd ins and smooth prog 4f out: trckd wnr on bit 3f out: chal on inner whn n.m.r wl over 1f out: sn shkn up and fnd nil* **11/4**[1]
3000 **3** 2 **Bold Adventure**[18] 838 7-9-2 **54** .... StevieDonohoe 9 — 58
(Willie Musson) *hld up in rr: effrt over 4f out and sn rdn along: wd st: styd on fnl 2f: nrst fin* **9/1**
50-0 **4** 2 3/4 **Spiritonthemount (USA)**[7] 838 6-8-10 **48** .... (b) ChrisCatlin 4 — 48
(Peter Hiatt) *swtchd rt to outer and reminders s: sn chsng ldrs: rdn along over 4f out: wknd 3f out* **12/1**
0-34 **5** 3/4 **Horsley Warrior**[27] 733 5-9-5 **57** .... GrahamGibbons 5 — 56
(Ed McMahon) *trckd ldrs: hdwy and cl up 1/2-way: effrt and ev ch over 3f out: rdn wl over 2f out and sn wknd* **5/1**[3]
500- **6** 24 **Gulf Punch**[124] 2780 4-8-2 **45** .... (p) SilvestreDeSousa 3 — 16
(Milton Harris) *prom: rdn along 5f out: sn wknd* **16/1**
300- **7** 5 **They All Laughed**[175] 6648 8-8-9 **50** .... (p) RobertLButler(3) 6 — 15
(Marjorie Fife) *hld up: effrt 6f out: sn rdn along and lost pl and bhd* **9/1**
605- **8** 35 **Spruzzo**[273] 3535 5-8-9 **47** .... KellyHarrison 7 — —
(Chris Fairhurst) *chsd ldrs: rdn along 1/2-way: sn lost pl and bhd* **33/1**
6512 **9** dist **Davana**[21] 796 5-9-2 **54** .... PaulHanagan 2 — —
(Colin Teague) *racd wd: hld up in rr: rdn along 5f out: sn wl bhd: t.o fnl 3f* **11/2**

3m 43.54s (-1.96) **Going Correction** -0.075s/f (Stan)
WFA 4 from 5yo+ 5lb — **9** Ran SP% **113.4**
Speed ratings (Par 101): **101,99,98,96,96 84,82,64,—**
Tote Swingers: 1&2 £3.00, 1&3 £9.30, 2&3 £3.30 CSF £16.93 CT £104.67 TOTE £6.90: £2.80, £1.10, £3.40; EX 20.40.
Owner R A Mills **Bred** Anne Marie O' Brien & Joseph Crowley & Peter Magni **Trained** Headley, Surrey

FOCUS
Form to treat with caution. The early pace was slow, resulting in a time over nine seconds above standard, yet the field were strung out. The race is rated around the winner.
Gulf Punch Official explanation: jockey said filly had no more to give
Davana Official explanation: jockey said mare never travelled
T/Plt: £34.00 to a £1 stake. Pool:£72,815.07 - 1,559.87 winning tickets T/Qpdt: £72.50 to a £1 stake. Pool:£5,591.85 - 312.36 winning tickets JR

935 COMPIEGNE (L-H)
Tuesday, March 29
OFFICIAL GOING: Turf: soft

1033a PRIX DE SAINT-SAUVEUR (CLAIMER) (4YO) (TURF) — 1m
2:20 (12:00) 4-Y-O — **£7,758** (£3,103; £2,327; £1,551; £775)

RPR
1 **Pim Pam (IRE)**[48] 481 4-8-13 0 .... EddyHardouin(3) 13 — 78
(C Ferland, France) **21/10**[1]
2 2 1/2 **Style De Lois (FR)**[119] 4-8-10 0 .... MatthieuAutier(8) 4 — 74
(M Boutin, France) **10/1**
3 nk **Cloudy Bay (USA)**[18] 842 4-8-11 0 .... (p) DavyBonilla 3 — 66
(Mrs K Burke) *settled 3rd on rail: travelling wl: proged 3f out: rdn to chal for ld 2f out: no ex: styd on wl fnl f* **45/1**
4 2 **Celebrity Choice (IRE)**[102] 4-9-2 0 .... (b[1]) AnthonyCaramanolis(3) 8 — 70
(B Dutruel, France) **48/10**[2]
5 nse **Malariska (FR)**[18] 4-8-4 0 .... MathieuTavaresDaSilva(7) 12 — 62
(A Lyon, France) **11/1**
6 nk **Alamona (GER)**[177] 4-8-8 0 .... DominiqueBoeuf 2 — 58
(C Sprengel, Germany) **53/10**[3]
7 1 1/2 **Miami Gator (IRE)**[19] 831 4-9-4 0 .... (b) AndrewElliott 11 — 64
(Mrs K Burke) *broke wl on wd outside: rdn to ld into st: u.p 2 1/2f out: styd on: no ex ins fnl f* **13/1**
8 1/2 **Formalite (FR)**[96] 4-8-11 0 .... (b) StephanePasquier 5 — 56
(T Larriviere, France) **10/1**
9 1 1/2 **Illusio (FR)**[85] 4-8-11 0 .... GregoryBenoist 10 — 53
(D Smaga, France) **30/1**
10 3/4 **Acid Test (FR)**[5] 1011 4-8-10 0 .... BenjaminBoutin(8) 1 — 58
(C Boutin, France) **61/1**
0 **King Des Aigles (FR)**[11] 4-8-11 0 .... (p) FredericSpanu 9 — —
(Mme C Barande-Barbe, France) **20/1**
0 **Spirituoso (FR)**[294] 4-9-1 0 .... SamuelFargeat 7 — —
(E Lellouche, France) **44/1**
0 **Skiryades (FR)** 4-8-4 0 .... SoufyaneMoulin(7) 14 — —
(C Boutin, France) **114/1**
0 **Becagand** 4-8-13 0 .... PaulineProd'homme(5) 6 — —
(D Prod'Homme, France) **49/1**

1m 38.55s (98.55) — **14** Ran SP% **115.9**
WIN (incl. 1 euro stake): 3.10. PLACES: 1.70, 2.80, 8.30. DF: 13.20. SF: 20.60.
Owner J-C Rouget **Bred** Kenilworth House Stud **Trained** France

CATTERICK (L-H)
Wednesday, March 30
OFFICIAL GOING: Good (good to firm in places; 8.1)
The opening day of the turf season and of the jockeys' championship.
Wind: moderate 1/2 behind Weather: overcast, light rain

1034 WILLIAM HILL - HOME OF BETTING APPRENTICE H'CAP — 5f
2:20 (2:21) (Class 6) (0-65,65) 4-Y-O+ — **£1,706** (£503; £252) **Stalls** Low

Form — RPR
423- **1** **Ballarina**[107] 7860 5-8-5 **54** .... NeilFarley(5) 14 — 70+
(Eric Alston) *racd wd: chsd ldrs: hdwy wl over 1f out: rdn and styd on strly to ld ins fnl f* **15/2**[3]
6060 **2** 2 1/2 **Kersivay**[13] 880 5-8-3 **52** .... (v) MatthewCosham(5) 1 — 59
(David Evans) *chsd ldrs: swtchd rt and rdn wl over 1f out: styd on ins fnl f: tk 2nd nr line* **11/2**[1]
00-6 **3** nk **Spirit Of Coniston**[50] 453 8-8-7 **51** oh1 .... PaulPickard 12 — 57
(Paul Midgley) *qckly away and wnt lft s: sn led and drifted to far rail: rdn wl over 1f out: drvn and hdd ins fnl f: wknd towards fin: lost 2nd nr line* **33/1**
1030 **4** 1/2 **Ridley Didley (IRE)**[28] 732 6-9-4 **62** .... MichaelO'Connell 11 — 66
(Noel Wilson) *hmpd s: sn chsng ldr: effrt 2f out: sn rdn and ev ch tl drvn and wknd ent fnl f* **14/1**
0406 **5** 1 1/2 **Fear Nothing**[49] 470 4-9-4 **65** .... (b) LeeTopliss(3) 15 — 64
(Ian McInnes) *racd wd: in tch: rdn along and outpcd 1/2-way: styd on appr fnl f* **16/1**
6-50 **6** 3/4 **Rio's Girl**[9] 934 4-9-0 **58** .... (p) AmyRyan 7 — 54
(Kevin Ryan) *wnt rt s: chsd ldrs: rdn along wl over 1f out: sn drvn: edgd rt and grad wknd* **7/1**[2]
6000 **7** 1/2 **Prince James**[9] 934 4-8-8 **59** .... DavidSimmonson(7) 2 — 53
(Michael Easterby) *midfield: hdwy on inner 2f out: sn rdn and no imp appr fnl f* **18/1**
4234 **8** 1 1/4 **Wanchai Whisper**[14] 861 4-9-1 **59** .... BillyCray 4 — 49
(Mark Rimmer) *towards rr whn n.m.r after 1f: hdwy 1/2-way: rdn along wl over 1f out: n.d* **8/1**
000- **9** 2 1/4 **Silvanus (IRE)**[189] 6299 6-9-3 **61** .... IanBrennan 8 — 43
(Paul Midgley) *hmpd s: n.m.r after 1f: nvr bttr than midfield* **20/1**
1244 **10** hd **Radiator Rooney (IRE)**[33] 683 8-8-9 **53** .... JamesSullivan 3 — 34
(Patrick Morris) *hmpd s: sn chsd ldrs: rdn along over 2f out: sn wknd* **12/1**
-300 **11** nse **Fashion Icon (USA)**[22] 794 5-8-13 **60** .... (b) SeanLevey(3) 10 — 41
(David O'Meara) *hmpd s: sn in midfield: effrt to chse ldrs over 2f out: sn rdn and wknd* **10/1**
13-0 **12** 2 3/4 **Yungaburra (IRE)**[13] 880 7-8-8 **57** .... (t) NoraLooby(5) 6 — 28
(David C Griffiths) *hmpd s: towards rr whn hmpd after 1f: nvr a factor* **16/1**
205- **13** 1 1/4 **Kyzer Chief**[239] 4672 6-8-9 **58** .... GarryWhillans(5) 5 — 24+
(Ron Barr) *hmpd s: dwlt: a towards rr: sddle slipped* **14/1**
130- **14** 3 1/4 **King Of Swords (IRE)**[214] 5513 7-9-4 **62** .... (p) LouisBeuzelin 13 — 17
(Nigel Tinkler) *chsd ldrs: rdn along bef 1/2-way: sn wknd* **25/1**
1-45 **15** 3 3/4 **Kate Skate**[76] 144 4-9-4 **65** .... AdamBeschizza(3) 9 — —
(Gay Kelleway) *hmpd s: a in rr* **14/1**

59.79 secs (-0.01) **Going Correction** +0.15s/f (Good) — **15** Ran SP% **116.1**
Speed ratings (Par 101): **106,102,101,100,98 97,96,94,90,90 90,85,83,78,72**
toteswingers: 1&2 £6.30, 1&3 £50.30, 2&3 £69.90 CSF £44.96 CT £1313.79 TOTE £6.90: £2.30, £2.40, £13.20; EX 59.70 TRIFECTA Not won..
Owner Mrs P O Morris **Bred** Mrs D Du Feu And Trickledown Stud **Trained** Longton, Lancs
■ Stewards' Enquiry : Paul Pickard five-day ban: careless riding (Apr 13-16,18); one-day ban: failed to ride to draw (Apr 19); one-day ban: used whip with excessive frequency (Apr 20)

FOCUS
Only 1mm of rain overnight, and the ground was given as good, good to firm in places (GoingStick 8.1). An ordinary apprentices' event to kick off the Flat turf season. Two came stands' side, including the winner, while the rest stuck to the far side. Few got involved, but this is sound enough early-season form.
Yungaburra(IRE) Official explanation: jockey said gelding suffred interference shortly after start
Kyzer Chief Official explanation: jockey said saddle slipped

1035 WILLIAMHILL.COM H'CAP — 7f
2:50 (2:51) (Class 5) (0-75,75) 4-Y-O+ — **£2,072** (£616; £308; £153) **Stalls** High

Form — RPR
-604 **1** **Masked Dance (IRE)**[50] 455 4-9-7 **75** .... (p) PhillipMakin 11 — 85
(Kevin Ryan) *trckd ldrs: led over 1f out: drvn out* **12/1**
000- **2** 1 3/4 **Frognal (IRE)**[181] 6501 5-9-3 **74** .... JamesSullivan(3) 2 — 79
(Ruth Carr) *t.k.h in midfield: effrt over 2f out: styd on fnl f: tk 2nd towards fin* **25/1**
-132 **3** 3/4 **Smalljohn**[28] 736 5-9-7 **75** .... (v) TomEaves 9 — 78
(Bryan Smart) *w ldrs: kpt on same pce ins fnl f* **8/1**
1123 **4** 1/2 **April Fool**[32] 703 7-9-5 **73** .... (b) LeeVickers 8 — 75
(David Evans) *chsd ldrs: kpt on same pce appr fnl furlong* **9/1**
0-13 **5** 1 1/2 **Lindoro**[14] 874 6-8-3 **62** .... DanielleMcCreery(5) 6 — 60
(Kevin M Prendergast) *mid-div: rdn and hdwy over 3f out: one pce fnl 2f* **10/1**

000- **6** ½ **Fazza**[160] 7046 4-8-7 **61** .... BarryMcHugh 13 57
(Edwin Tuer) *mid-div: outpcd over 3f out: kpt on fnl 2f* **25/1**
240- **7** 1½ **Legal Legacy**[173] 6709 5-9-7 **75** .... FrederikTylicki 7 67+
(Michael Dods) *s.s: bhd tl styd on fnl 2f* **7/1**[2]
32-3 **8** *nk* **Dazeen**[22] 794 4-8-8 **62** .... FrannyNorton 10 53
(Paul Midgley) *in rr: effrt over 2f out: styd on ins fnl f* **12/1**
3131 **9** 1¼ **Trans Sonic**[22] 799 8-9-2 **75** .... SeanLevey(5) 14 63
(David O'Meara) *chsd ldrs: drvn over 3f out: wknd appr fnl f* **5/1**[1]
202- **10** 2¾ **So Bazaar (IRE)**[270] 3668 4-9-0 **68** .... PJMcDonald 1 49
(Alan Swinbank) *mid-div: kpt on fnl 2f: nvr on terms* **12/1**
245- **11** 1½ **Violent Velocity (IRE)**[110] 7804 8-8-7 **64** .... IanBrennan(3) 12 41
(John Quinn) *s.i.s: hdwy u.p over 3f out: lost pl over 1f out* **15/2**[3]
430- **12** *nse* **Ryedane (IRE)**[130] 7525 9-9-2 **70** .... DavidAllan 5 46
(Tim Easterby) *in rr: rdn and sme hdwy 2f out: sn wknd* **18/1**
220- **13** 7 **Raleigh Quay (IRE)**[63] 6984 4-9-7 **75** .... PaulMulrennan 15 32
(Micky Hammond) *in rr: bhd fnl 2f* **16/1**
105- **14** 3 **Grand Stitch (USA)**[118] 7668 5-8-11 **70** ....(b[1]) NeilFarley(5) 4 19
(Declan Carroll) *led: hdd over 1f out: wknd* **40/1**
64-0 **15** 3¼ **Politbureau**[18] 850 4-8-4 **65** .... DavidSimmonson(7) 3 6
(Michael Easterby) *s.i.s: a in rr* **20/1**

1m 26.48s (-0.52) **Going Correction** +0.15s/f (Good) **15** Ran SP% **120.2**
Speed ratings (Par 103): **108,106,105,104,102 102,100,100,98,95 93,93,85,82,78**
toteswingers: 1&2 £90.60, 1&3 £22.80, 2&3 £42.90 CSF £290.33 CT £2599.79 TOTE £18.80: £5.70, £10.00, £1.90; EX 248.90 TRIFECTA Not won..
Owner Mrs L D Edwards **Bred** Canice Farrell Jnr **Trained** Hambleton, N Yorks

FOCUS
They went a strong gallop here, thanks to Grand Stitch. The form looks straightforward enough.

1036 WILLIAM HILL H'CAP 1m 3f 214y
3:20 (3:20) (Class 4) (0-80,80) 4-Y-O+ **£3,885** (£1,156; £577; £288) **Stalls** Low

Form RPR
20-1 **1** **Kiama Bay (IRE)**[83] 67 5-8-13 **74** .... IanBrennan(3) 4 86+
(John Quinn) *hld up in tch: hdwy over 3f out: rdn to chal wl over 1f out: led appr fnl f: edgd lft and drvn out* **11/4**[1]
150- **2** ¾ **Royal Swain (IRE)**[145] 7337 5-9-5 **77** .... PJMcDonald 9 86
(Alan Swinbank) *hld up in rr: hdwy 3f out: rdn to ld briefly 1 1/2f out: drvn and hdd appr fnl f: kpt on u.p towards fin* **4/1**[2]
636- **3** 3¼ **Chookie Hamilton**[18] 8007 7-9-7 **79** .... TomEaves 8 83
(Keith Dalgleish) *trckd ldrs: hdwy on outer over 3f out: led over 2f out: sn rdn and hdd over 1 1/2f out: sn one pce* **11/1**
6-43 **4** 4 **The Oil Magnate**[36] 639 6-9-5 **77** .... FrederikTylicki 5 75
(Michael Dods) *hld up in tch: hdwy over 3f out: rdn to chse ldrs 2f out: no imp appr fnl f* **5/1**[3]
126- **5** 2¼ **Pertemps Networks**[151] 7226 7-9-3 **75** .... GrahamGibbons 3 69
(Michael Easterby) *led 1 1/2f: trckd ldrs on inner: effrt and ev ch 2f out: sn rdn and wknd over 1f out* **13/2**
614- **6** 1½ **Mason Hindmarsh**[137] 6622 4-8-8 **68** .... PaulMulrennan 10 60
(Karen McLintock) *hld up towards rr: sme hdwy on outer over 2f out: sn rdn and no imp* **11/2**
055- **7** 1¼ **Donna Elvira**[171] 6781 4-8-10 **70** .... TonyHamilton 6 60
(Edwin Tuer) *prom: hdwy to chse ldr 1/2-way: rdn along over 3f out: sn wknd* **11/1**
453- **8** 5 **Oddsmaker (IRE)**[154] 7176 10-8-7 **65** oh7........(t) JamieMackay 2 47
(Maurice Barnes) *dwlt: hdwy to ld after 1 1/2f: rdn along over 3f out: hdd over 2f out: sn drvn and wknd* **22/1**
1/5- **9** 23 **Tayarat (IRE)**[16] 5360 6-8-9 **70** ....(bt) RobertLButler(3) 1 15
(Michael Chapman) *chsd ldrs to 1/2-way: sn lost pl and bhd fnl 3f* **66/1**

2m 39.39s (0.49) **Going Correction** +0.15s/f (Good)
WFA 4 from 5yo+ 2lb **9** Ran SP% **114.6**
Speed ratings (Par 105): **104,103,101,98,97 96,95,92,76**
toteswingers: 1&2 £3.70, 1&3 £9.10, 2&3 £5.00 CSF £13.52 CT £102.27 TOTE £3.40: £1.70, £2.10, £3.30; EX 12.80 Trifecta £77.10 Pool: £377.58 - 3.62 winning units..
Owner Dr Marwan Koukash **Bred** Tipper House Stud **Trained** Settrington, N Yorks

FOCUS
A fairly open handicap. The front pair are less exposed than most and both progressed.

1037 WILLIAMHILL.COM CLAIMING STKS 7f
3:50 (3:50) (Class 6) 3-Y-O+ **£1,706** (£503; £252) **Stalls** High

Form RPR
5310 **1** **Thrust Control (IRE)**[20] 822 4-10-0 84 .... SilvestreDeSousa 7 88
(Brian Ellison) *sn led: rdn wl over 1f out: sn clr: styd on strly* **2/1**[1]
2210 **2** 4½ **Apache Ridge (IRE)**[13] 880 5-9-7 72 ....(p) PhillipMakin 5 69
(Kevin Ryan) *trckd ldrs: hdwy 1/2-way: chsd wnr over 2f out: rdn wl over 1f out and kpt on same pce ins fnl f* **13/2**
106- **3** *hd* **Kingswinford (IRE)**[228] 5082 5-9-11 75 .... RichardEvans(3) 3 78+
(David Evans) *hld up towards rr: hdwy on inner over 2f out: swtchd rt to outer and rdn over 1f out: styd on ins fnl f* **4/1**[2]
16-5 **4** *nk* **Fremen (USA)**[15] 856 11-9-8 82 .... AdrianNicholls 9 69
(David Nicholls) *dwlt: sn cl up on outer: effrt over 2f out and sn rdn along: drvn and one pce fr over 1f out* **9/2**[3]
444 **5** 1 **Slikback Jack (IRE)**[20] 816 4-9-11 75 ....(p) BillyCray(3) 8 72
(David Nicholls) *hld up in rr: effrt over 2f out: sn rdn and kpt on ins fnl f: nrst fin* **15/2**
345- **6** 1½ **Royal Dignitary (USA)**[238] 4713 11-9-4 77........ MichaelO'Connell(5) 1 63
(David Nicholls) *dwlt: hld up: hdwy to trck ldrs 1/2-way: effrt 2f out: sn rdn and no imp fr over 1f out* **8/1**
465- **7** 2 **No Quarter (IRE)**[173] 6710 4-9-8 54 .... MartinLane 2 56
(Tracy Waggott) *cl up on inner: rdn along wl over 2f out: drvn wl over 1f out and sn wknd* **22/1**
00-0 **8** 9 **Baby Judge (IRE)**[11] 914 4-9-3 49 .... RobertLButler(3) 4 30
(Michael Chapman) *prom: rdn along bef 1/2-way: sn wknd* **125/1**
0P0/ **9** 26 **Glencairn Star**[491] 7503 10-9-10 46 ....(p) TomEaves 6 —
(Frederick Watson) *a in rr: bhd fnl 3f* **100/1**

1m 27.39s (0.39) **Going Correction** +0.15s/f (Good) **9** Ran SP% **113.9**
Speed ratings (Par 101): **103,97,97,96 94,92,81,52**
toteswingers: 1&2 £2.90, 1&3 £3.50, 2&3 £4.60 CSF £15.30 TOTE £2.30: £1.10, £2.50, £1.80; EX 14.60 Trifecta £95.10 Pool: £511.91 - 3.98 winning units..Apache Ridge was claimed by K Dalgleish for £5,000.
Owner Koo's Racing Club **Bred** Rathasker Stud **Trained** Norton, N Yorks

FOCUS
Not many could be fancied in this claimer. The winner ran to a similar standard as his Southwell win.

Kingswinford(IRE) Official explanation: jockey said gelding was unsuited by the track

1038 WILLIAM HILL MAIDEN STKS 5f 212y
4:20 (4:21) (Class 5) 3-Y-O+ **£2,072** (£616; £308; £153) **Stalls** Low

Form RPR
003- **1** **Another Wise Kid (IRE)**[195] 6111 3-9-1 68 .... MickyFenton 9 73
(Paul Midgley) *chsd ldrs: chal over 2f out: led over 1f out: drvn out* **6/1**[2]
0 **2** 2½ **Mecca's Team**[50] 454 3-8-10 0 .... TomEaves 7 60
(Michael Dods) *led tl over 1f out: styd on same pce ins fnl f* **16/1**
500- **3** *shd* **Philharmonic Hall**[159] 7050 3-9-1 65 .... TonyHamilton 2 65
(Richard Fahey) *drvn along to sn chse ldrs: styd on same pce ins fnl f* **17/2**
02-4 **4** 6 **Sinadinou**[15] 855 3-9-1 75 .... AdrianNicholls 4 46
(David Nicholls) *chsd ldrs: drvn over 3f out: wknd over 1f out* **11/8**[1]
0/5- **5** 2 **Idealism**[347] 1386 4-10-0 0 .... FrederikTylicki 6 43+
(Micky Hammond) *in rr: sme hdwy over 1f out: nvr on terms* **10/1**
000- **6** *nk* **Twennyshortkid**[196] 6070 3-9-1 50 .... PaulMulrennan 5 38
(Paul Midgley) *hld up in mid-div: effrt over 2f out: hung rt: wknd over 1f out* **100/1**
7 ¾ **Drive Home (USA)**[339] 1550 4-10-0 0 .... LeeNewman 10 40
(Noel Wilson) *chsd ldrs: wknd over 1f out* **16/1**
550- **8** 1¾ **Barkston Ash**[249] 4388 3-9-1 62 ....(b) DavidAllan 8 30
(Eric Alston) *mid-div: effrt on outside over 3f out: wknd over 1f out* **13/2**[3]
55- **9** *shd* **Oldmeldrum (IRE)**[176] 6646 3-8-10 0 .... PJMcDonald 1 25+
(Ben Haslam) *s.s: in rr: hung rt and kpt on fnl 2f* **12/1**
0-60 **10** ½ **Areeg (IRE)**[73] 185 4-9-2 42 .... VictorSantos(7) 11 28
(Alan Berry) *s.i.s: a in rr* **150/1**
11 6 **Hardrock Diamond** 3-9-1 0 .... PhillipMakin 12 —
(Ben Haslam) *a towards rr: bhd fnl 2f* **50/1**
0 **12** 7 **Princeton Girl**[34] 669 3-8-10 0 .... DuranFentiman 3 —
(Tim Easterby) *s.i.s: sme hdwy over 3f out: wknd over 1f out: bhd whn eased nr fin* **28/1**

1m 14.34s (0.74) **Going Correction** +0.15s/f (Good)
WFA 3 from 4yo 13lb **12** Ran SP% **115.9**
Speed ratings (Par 103): **101,97,97,89,86 86,85,83,83,82 74,65**
toteswingers: 1&2 £20.00, 1&3 £6.70, 2&3 £17.20 CSF £93.40 TOTE £7.10: £2.80, £6.20, £1.50; EX 116.50 Trifecta £299.10 Part won. Pool: £404.26 - 0.44 winning units..
Owner Michael Ng **Bred** Paul Kavanagh **Trained** Westow, N Yorks

FOCUS
No more than a fair maiden, and very few got into it. The favourite was again way off his 2yo best, leaving this looking modest form.
Twennyshortkid Official explanation: jockey said gelding hung right-handed in straight
Oldmeldrum(IRE) Official explanation: jockey said filly hung right throughout

1039 WILLIAMHILL.COM - NEW IPHONE APP H'CAP 1m 5f 175y
4:50 (4:50) (Class 5) (0-75,70) 4-Y-O+ **£2,072** (£616; £308; £153) **Stalls** Low

Form RPR
662- **1** **Madamlily (IRE)**[131] 6921 5-9-0 **58** .... TomEaves 6 68+
(John Quinn) *trckd ldrs: smooth hdwy to join ldr 3f out: led on bit over 2f out: pushed clr wl over 1f out: rdn ins fnl f and kpt on* **6/1**[2]
22-0 **2** 2¼ **Lady Norlela**[47] 507 5-8-3 **54** .... ShaneBKelly(7) 5 59
(Brian Rothwell) *hld up in rr: hdwy 4f out: rdn 2f out: styd on strly appr fnl f: nt rch wnr* **20/1**
034- **3** 2¾ **Leaving Alone (USA)**[155] 7149 4-8-4 **55** .... JamesSullivan(3) 11 56
(Edwin Tuer) *hld up towards rr: hdwy over 4f out: rdn 2f out: styd on wl u.p appr fnl f: nrst fin* **16/1**
100- **4** 4 **Eijaaz (IRE)**[134] 7475 10-9-0 **58** ....(p) SilvestreDeSousa 1 54
(Geoffrey Harker) *hld up in rr: hdwy over 4f out: chsd ldrs 2f out: rdn wl over 1f out and kpt on same pce* **6/1**[2]
624- **5** 1 **Puy D'Arnac (FR)**[148] 7284 8-9-12 **70** .... PJMcDonald 4 64
(George Moore) *hld up towards rr: hdwy over 5f out: chsd ldrs 3f out: rdn 2f out and sn one pce* **12/1**
500- **6** 5 **Classic Contours (USA)**[15] 7147 5-8-13 **57** .... MartinLane 9 44
(Tracy Waggott) *chsd ldrs: rdn along over 4f out: drvn along 3f out: wknd fnl 2f* **18/1**
142- **7** 2½ **Danceintothelight**[76] 7116 4-9-0 **65** .... KellyHarrison 8 49
(Micky Hammond) *prom: chsd ldr over 4f out: rdn along 3f out: sn drvn and wknd* **7/2**[1]
105- **8** 2¼ **Drop The Hammer**[36] 7145 5-8-11 **60** ....(b) SeanLevey(5) 7 41
(David O'Meara) *led and sn clr: rdn along over 4f out: hdd wl over 2f out and sn wknd* **8/1**[3]
002- **9** 11 **Flora's Pride**[21] 7147 7-8-9 **53** .... PaulMulrennan 3 18
(Keith Reveley) *a towards rr: outpcd and bhd fnl 4f* **10/1**
065- **10** 5 **Amir Pasha (UAE)**[7] 6306 6-9-3 **61** ....(v) FrederikTylicki 2 19
(Micky Hammond) *prom: rdn along over 4f out: sn wknd* **17/2**
601- **11** 41 **Emirate Isle**[15] 7147 7-8-4 **51** ....(p) IanBrennan(3) 12 —
(Brian Storey) *a towards rr: outpcd and bhd fr over 4f out* **33/1**
031- **12** 2½ **Moonlight Blaze**[13] 7145 4-8-5 **53** .... DuranFentiman 10 —
(Chris Fairhurst) *chsd ldrs: lost pl 1/2-way: sn bhd: b.b.v* **14/1**

3m 6.14s (2.54) **Going Correction** +0.15s/f (Good)
WFA 4 from 5yo+ 4lb **12** Ran SP% **114.7**
Speed ratings (Par 103): **98,96,95,92,92 89,88,86,80,77 54,52**
toteswingers:1&2 £25.40, 2&3 £44.20, 1&3 £25.90 CSF £115.36 CT £1809.78 TOTE £3.90: £1.10, £5.80, £5.30; EX 122.40 TRIFECTA Not won..
Owner Bob McMillan **Bred** Dermot Brennan And Associates Ltd **Trained** Settrington, N Yorks

FOCUS
This looked quite competitive on paper, albeit the top weight was rated 5lb below the ceiling. The pace was fair but this is not the most convincing of form.
Drop The Hammer Official explanation: jockey said mare had no more to give
Emirate Isle Official explanation: jockey said gelding hung right throughout
Moonlight Blaze Official explanation: trainer's rep said gelding broke a blood vessel

1040 WILLIAM HILL 0800 44 40 40 H'CAP 5f
5:20 (5:33) (Class 6) (0-60,60) 3-Y-O **£1,706** (£503; £252) **Stalls** Low

Form RPR
4-44 **1** **Misty Morn**[68] 251 3-9-0 **53** .... PaulMulrennan 7 57
(Alan Brown) *led tl jst ins fnl f: sn regained ld and kpt on wl* **12/1**
0-54 **2** ¾ **Tancred Spirit**[14] 868 3-8-7 **46** oh1........(p) PJMcDonald 5 47
(Paul Midgley) *chsd wnr: hrd rdn and led briefly jst ins fnl f: no ex* **4/1**[2]
00-6 **3** 1¼ **Trading**[14] 868 3-9-3 **56** .... DavidAllan 6 53
(Tim Easterby) *chsd ldrs: edgd rt 1f out: styd on* **9/2**[3]
600- **4** *hd* **Majestic Millie (IRE)**[148] 7279 3-8-4 **46** oh1........ NataliaGemelova(3) 1 42
(David O'Meara) *w ldrs: rdn over 2f out: kpt on same pce ins fnl f* **6/1**
4-60 **5** ¾ **Yours**[46] 520 3-9-1 **54** .... PhillipMakin 2 47+
(Kevin Ryan) *rrd s: bhd tl kpt on ins fnl f* **6/1**

30-4 **6** *nse* **Georgian Silver**[40] 595 3-8-10 **49**.................................... LeeNewman 3 42
(George Foster) *chsd ldrs on ins: fdd last 150yds* **14/1**

-055 **7** *1 ½* **Taverners Jubilee**[14] 868 3-8-4 **46** oh1..................... LouisBeuzelin(3) 8 34
(Patrick Morris) *chsd ldrs: wknd last 150yds* **28/1**

0-60 **8** *¾* **Running Water**[27] 745 3-8-4 **46** oh1..................... JamesSullivan(3) 10 31
(Hugh McWilliams) *chsd ldrs on outside: outpcd over 2f out: no threat after* **16/1**

304- **9** *½* **Ezzles (USA)**[105] 7880 3-9-4 **57**............................ SilvestreDeSousa 9 40
(Paul Cole) *sn outpcd and drvn along in rr: sme hdwy 2f out: nvr on terms* **5/2**[1]

61.57 secs (1.77) **Going Correction** +0.15s/f (Good) **9** Ran SP% **119.0**
Speed ratings (Par 96): **91,89,87,87,86 86,83,82,81**
toteswingers: 1&2 £8.30, 1&3 £10.10, 2&3 £4.20. totesuper7: Win: Not won. Place: £1575.00 CSF £61.43 CT £256.35 TOTE £17.60: £4.10, £1.20, £1.20; EX 79.70 Trifecta £356.50 Part won. Pool: £481.82 - 0.44 winning units..
Owner Rangers Racing **Bred** P A Mason **Trained** Yedingham, N Yorks
■ Irish Boy (11/1) was withdrawn after bursting out of the stalls. Deduct 5p in the £ under R4.
■ Stewards' Enquiry : P J McDonald one-day ban: used whip with excessive frequency (Apr 13)

FOCUS

A moderate sprint handicap won by the only previous winner in the field. Few got involved and this looks weak form.
Yours Official explanation: jockey said filly reared as stalls opened
Ezzles(USA) Official explanation: jockey said colt never travelled
T/Jkpt: Part won. £28,430.50 - 0.50 winning units. T/Plt: £803.40 to a £1 stake. Pool of £79,432.83 - 72.17 winning tickets. T/Qpdt: £30.50 to a £1 stake. Pool of £5,865.05 - 142.20 winning tickets. JR

1020 LINGFIELD (L-H)

Wednesday, March 30

OFFICIAL GOING: Standard

Wind: Strong, behind Weather: Overcast with rain before racing

1041 L & M BODY REPAIRS LEGENDARY H'CAP (DIV I) 6f (P)

2:00 (2:00) (Class 6) (0-60,60) 4-Y-0+ **£1,364** (£403; £201) **Stalls** Low

Form RPR

0020 **1** **Loyal Royal (IRE)**[21] 810 8-9-7 **60**......................(bt) RichardKingscote 6 70
(Milton Bradley) *dwlt: hld up last: plenty to do 2f out: gd prog towards inner after: urged along and styd on wl ins fnl f to ld last strides* **8/1**

0-10 **2** *nk* **Far View (IRE)**[28] 734 4-9-7 **60**......................(tp) JimmyFortune 2 69
(George Baker) *chsd ldr: clr of rest 2f out: drvn to chal 1f out: led last 150yds: hanging lft and bmpd rival after: hdd fnl strides* **9/4**[1]

2505 **3** *½* **Thoughtsofstardom**[8] 941 8-8-11 **50**.......................... KierenFallon 7 57
(Phil McEntee) *led at str pce: drvn over 1f out: edgd rt and hdd last 150yds: bmpd rival after: no ex nr fin* **16/1**

0630 **4** *1 ½* **Misaro (GER)**[28] 735 10-9-4 **57**..............................(b) WilliamCarson 3 60
(Ronald Harris) *chsd ldng pair: outpcd over 2f out: hanging and nt qckn over 1f out: lost 3rd ins fnl f* **17/2**

5432 **5** *¾* **Bold Diva**[11] 912 6-8-13 **52**.......................................(v) JimmyQuinn 9 52
(Tony Carroll) *s.i.s: hld up in 9th: effrt and rdn 2f out: kpt on ins fnl f: n.d* **4/1**[2]

0360 **6** *1 ½* **Mr Funshine**[28] 735 6-8-7 **46** oh1.................................. PaulHanagan 4 41
(Derek Shaw) *towards rr: rdn 2f out: plugged on: n.d* **25/1**

1410 **7** *1 ¼* **Jonny Ebeneezer**[7] 947 12-9-5 **58**......................(be) StephenCraine 5 49
(David Flood) *nvr bttr than midfield: rdn and no prog over 2f out* **20/1**

46-6 **8** *1* **Dancing Again**[85] 28 5-8-2 **46** oh1.......................... HarryBentley(5) 1 34
(Eric Wheeler) *chsd ldrs: rdn over 2f out: no imp in 4th over 1f out: wknd* **100/1**

1200 **9** *7* **Young Simon**[7] 947 4-9-3 **59**...............................(v) SimonPearce(3) 8 25
(George Margarson) *chsd ldrs on outer: rdn wl over 2f out: wknd sn after* **8/1**

2056 **10** *8* **Charles Darwin (IRE)**[9] 933 8-9-1 **54**.......................(p) LiamKeniry 10 —
(Michael Blanshard) *forced to r wd: chsd ldrs to 1/2-way: sn wknd: t.o* **11/2**[3]

1m 11.73s (-0.17) **Going Correction** +0.05s/f (Slow) **10** Ran SP% **114.4**
Speed ratings (Par 101): **103,102,101,99,98 96,95,93,84,73**
toteswingers: 1&2 £3.70, 1&3 £10.60, 2&3 £9.30 CSF £25.36 CT £290.20 TOTE £7.80: £2.80, £1.40, £7.00; EX 31.40.
Owner JMB Racing.co.uk **Bred** J F Tuthill **Trained** Sedbury, Gloucs

FOCUS

The first and slightly stronger division of this class 6 handicap was run at a strong gallop. Straightforward, sound form.

1042 PREMIER SHOWFREIGHT YEARLING BONUS SCHEME MAIDEN STKS 5f (P)

2:30 (2:30) (Class 5) 2-Y-0 **£2,047** (£604; £302) **Stalls** High

Form RPR

1 **Miss Work Of Art** 2-8-12 0.. PaulHanagan 4 85+
(Richard Fahey) *chsd ldng trio: effrt and wd bnd 2f out: rdn and clsd to ld ins fnl f: sn clr* **11/8**[1]

2 *3 ¼* **Launch On Line** 2-8-9 0....................................... KierenFox(3) 6 72
(Bill Turner) *led: rdn over 1f out: hdd ins fnl f: qckly lft bhd by wnr* **12/1**[3]

3 *1 ½* **Choice Of Remark (IRE)** 2-9-3 0.............................. NeilCallan 2 71
(David Evans) *chsd ldr over 3f out: rdn and no imp over 1f out: sn lost 2nd and fdd* **7/4**[2]

4 *3* **The Dancing Lord** 2-8-10 0.................................. JakePayne(7) 1 59
(Bill Turner) *chsd ldr to over 3f out: styd wl in tch tl wknd qckly 1f out* **20/1**

5 *3 ¼* **Sabusa (IRE)** 2-9-3 0.. TomQueally 5 46
(Alan McCabe) *s.s: sn wl outpcd: nvr a factor* **14/1**

6 *¾* **Night Angel (IRE)** 2-8-12 0.................................... JamesMillman 3 38
(Rod Millman) *v s.i.s: outpcd and nvr on terms* **16/1**

7 *9* **Bookiesindexdotnet** 2-8-12 0.................................... JimCrowley 7 —
(J R Jenkins) *s.s: outpcd and a bhd: t.o* **16/1**

59.77 secs (0.97) **Going Correction** +0.05s/f (Slow) **7** Ran SP% **109.4**
Speed ratings (Par 92): **94,88,86,81,76 75,60**
toteswingers: 1&2 £1.90, 1&3 £1.10, 2&3 £4.60 CSF £17.16 TOTE £2.80: £2.10, £4.80; EX 11.50.
Owner Mel Roberts & Ms Nicola Meese 1 **Bred** Newsells Park Stud **Trained** Musley Bank, N Yorks

FOCUS

An interesting maiden with all of the field making their racecourse debut. Only the front four got involved. The winner impressed and as it was a Racing Post Yearling Bonus race it could have been above-average for the track/grade/time of year.

NOTEBOOK

Miss Work Of Art ran out an impressive winner, looking a class above her rivals. Costing £29,000 as a yearling, she looks money well spent for her stable, who have started the season well with their 2-y-os. Quickening nicely in the home straight, she drew clear, shaping as though she will get further. Though the quality of this race will not become apparent for some time, she created a lovely visual impression on debut and looks one to keep on-side this campaign. (op 5-4 tchd 6-4 in places)
Launch On Line is an April foal, but showed some good early pace and looks a likely candidate to win her fair share of races from the front. (op 10-1 tchd 9-1)
Choice Of Remark(IRE), a half-brother to the useful Anna Pavlova, cost 13,000 euro as a yearling and was another to make a solid racecourse debut. Tiring in the closing stages, he should come on plenty for the run and looks to have a decent future. (op 5-2 tchd 13-8)
The Dancing Lord travelled well for a long way, and with his dam's previous two foals both winning as juveniles, he looks a likely sort to win a race this season, but will probably need further than this. (op 14-1)
Night Angel(IRE) Official explanation: jockey said filly ran green

1043 L & M BODY REPAIRS LEGENDARY H'CAP (DIV II) 6f (P)

3:00 (3:00) (Class 6) (0-60,60) 4-Y-0+ **£1,364** (£403; £201) **Stalls** Low

Form RPR

3446 **1** **Speak The Truth (IRE)**[32] 698 5-9-5 **58**......................(p) TomQueally 6 66
(Jim Boyle) *chsd ldrs disputing 5th: effrt on outer and rdn 2f out: gd run ins fnl f to ld last strides* **7/2**[2]

3320 **2** *¾* **Black Baccara**[11] 910 4-9-7 **60**................................(be) KierenFallon 10 66
(Phil McEntee) *trckd ldr: rdn to chal over 1f out: narrow ld ins fnl f: jst asserting whn hdd and outpcd last strides* **9/2**[3]

4114 **3** *1* **Chantilly Jewel (USA)**[7] 947 6-9-6 **59**........................(b) JimCrowley 9 62
(Robert Cowell) *led at mod pce: rdn and narrowly hdd 1f out: kpt on but lost 2nd nr fin* **10/3**[1]

-160 **4** *¾* **Figaro Flyer (IRE)**[43] 545 8-9-0 **53**................................. ShaneKelly 3 53
(Jane Chapple-Hyam) *settled towards rr: shkn up over 2f out: no prog tl styd on ins fnl f: nrst fin* **14/1**

530- **5** *nse* **Miss Firefly**[189] 6284 6-9-4 **57**...................................... GeorgeBaker 1 57
(Ron Hodges) *t.k.h: chsd ldng pair to 1f out: one pce* **12/1**

0300 **6** *1 ¼* **Rightcar**[20] 821 4-8-7 **46**..(b) RobbieFitzpatrick 4 42
(Peter Grayson) *dwlt then bmpd s: hld up in last trio: effrt on inner 2f out: kpt on same pce: n.d* **33/1**

6036 **7** *nse* **Raimond Ridge (IRE)**[11] 912 5-8-8 **47**...................... WilliamCarson 7 43
(Derek Shaw) *settled in last trio: rdn 2f out: kpt on but nvr a threat* **6/1**

2640 **8** *shd* **Jessica Wigmo**[20] 821 8-8-7 **46** oh1............................. HayleyTurner 5 42
(Tony Carroll) *chsd ldrs disputing 5th: nt qckn 2f out: fdd ins fnl f* **20/1**

6063 **9** *1 ¼* **Commandingpresence (USA)**[21] 812 5-8-9 **51**......... KierenFox(3) 11 43
(John Bridger) *forced to r wd in midfield: u.p and struggling over 2f out: hanging and wl btn over 1f out* **14/1**

00-0 **10** *1 ¾* **Calabaza**[33] 683 9-8-2 **46** oh1...............................(p) JemmaMarshall(5) 8 32
(Michael Attwater) *t.k.h: hld up last: shkn up over 1f out: no prog* **100/1**

00-3 **11** *hd* **Bianco Boy (USA)**[35] 653 4-9-5 **58**.............................. SteveDrowne 2 44
(John Best) *chsd ldng trio to 2f out: wknd qckly* **16/1**

1m 12.71s (0.81) **Going Correction** +0.05s/f (Slow) **11** Ran SP% **113.4**
Speed ratings (Par 101): **96,95,93,92,92 90,90,90,89,86 86**
toteswingers: 1&2 £3.90, 1&3 £2.80, 2&3 £3.20 CSF £18.51 CT £55.49 TOTE £3.40: £1.70, £1.10, £1.50; EX 20.90.
Owner Inside Track Racing Club **Bred** Gerard Mulligan **Trained** Epsom, Surrey

FOCUS

No early pace in the second division of the 6f handicap, and the field ended up in a bit of a heap at the finish. Ordinary if sound form.
Commandingpresence(USA) Official explanation: jockey said mare hung left

1044 TAGWORLDWIDE.COM (S) STKS 6f (P)

3:30 (3:31) (Class 6) 3-Y-0+ **£1,706** (£503; £252) **Stalls** Low

Form RPR

4003 **1** **Bonnie Prince Blue**[5] 960 8-10-0 75..............................(b) TomQueally 3 72
(James Given) *chsd ldrs on inner: drvn 2f out: styd on fr over 1f out: led last 75yds: hld on* **6/1**

2310 **2** *nk* **Frequency**[4] 985 4-10-0 72...(b) HayleyTurner 1 71
(Conor Dore) *dwlt: wl in rr: taken to outer and only 7th 2f out: str run u.p ins fnl f: snatched 2nd on post* **2/1**[1]

1200 **3** *nse* **Waterloo Dock**[32] 698 6-10-0 66...............................(b[1]) MartinDwyer 2 71
(Michael Quinn) *led: beat off chalr 2f out: hdd and no ex last 75yds: lost 2nd on post* **7/1**

5540 **4** *1 ¾* **Al Gillani (IRE)**[14] 867 6-9-9 63.................................(b[1]) GeorgeBaker 7 60
(Jim Boyle) *pressed ldr: upsides 2f out: sn rdn and nt qckn: one pce after* **3/1**[2]

40-4 **5** *2 ½* **Briannsta (IRE)**[40] 590 9-9-9 43.................................(b) RichardThomas 5 52
(John E Long) *chsd ldng pair to over 3f out: lost pl: kpt on ins fnl f but n.d* **33/1**

000- **6** *hd* **Boga (IRE)**[147] 7300 4-9-4 49.. JimCrowley 6 46
(Ron Hodges) *in tch: effrt over 2f out: rdn and no imp on ldrs over 1f out* **50/1**

0433 **7** *1 ¼* **Athaakeel (IRE)**[9] 928 5-9-9 61...............................(b) WilliamCarson 4 47
(Ronald Harris) *chsd ldrs: wnt 3rd over 3f out: hrd rdn 2f out: sn fdd* **9/2**[3]

-400 **8** *10* **Poesmulligan (IRE)**[21] 807 5-9-9 44...........................(p) SteveDrowne 8 15
(Linda Jewell) *dwlt: hld up: struggling in last pair over 2f out: sn wl bhd* **33/1**

000- **9** *11* **Terrys Flutter**[140] 7393 3-8-5 45.. ChrisCatlin 9 —
(Mark Allen) *a in last pair: wknd over 2f out: t.o* **66/1**

1m 12.22s (0.32) **Going Correction** +0.05s/f (Slow)
WFA 3 from 4yo+ 13lb **9** Ran SP% **112.6**
Speed ratings (Par 101): **99,98,98,96,92 92,90,77,62**
toteswingers: 1&2 £3.40, 1&3 £8.70, 2&3 £8.00 CSF £17.64 TOTE £7.90: £2.00, £1.10, £2.20; EX 15.80.Frequency was subject to a friendly claim.
Owner Danethorpe Racing Partnership **Bred** George Joseph Hicks **Trained** Willoughton, Lincs
■ Stewards' Enquiry : Hayley Turner one-day ban: used whip with excessive frequency without giving gelding time to respond (Apr 13)

FOCUS

An ordinary seller. The form seems sound but the winner didn't need to match his Southwell best.

1045 H & V SERVICEPLAN H'CAP 7f (P)

4:00 (4:01) (Class 6) (0-60,60) 4-Y-0+ **£1,706** (£503; £252) **Stalls** Low

Form RPR

2353 **1** **Guildenstern (IRE)**[27] 752 9-8-8 **47**............................. HayleyTurner 7 56
(Jane Chapple-Hyam) *chsd ldrs: effrt over 2f out: prog to dispute 2nd 1f out: drvn and clsd after: led last strides* **20/1**

5-63 **2** *nk* **Louphole**[29] 719 9-8-11 **57**.. DannyBrock(7) 2 65
(J R Jenkins) *s.s: sn in midfield: 6th over 2f out on inner: prog to dispute 2nd 1f out: clsd on ldr after: upsides nr fin: jst outpcd* **16/1**

0-14 **3** *nk* **Ymir**[29] 719 5-8-13 **52**........(vt) NeilCallan 14 59
(Michael Attwater) *led 1f: led again 4f out: kicked clr over 2f out: 3 l up 1f out: collared last strides* **6/1**

500- **4** *4 1/2* **Prince Namid**[147] 7298 9-9-6 **59**........ WilliamCarson 9 54
(Jonathen de Giles) *dwlt: hld up in last pair: stl there and wl off the pce over 2f out: drvn on wd outside over 1f out: r.o wl ins fnl f to take 4th nr fin: no ch* **33/1**

3653 **5** *1 1/4* **Jonnie Skull (IRE)**[11] 906 5-8-12 **51**........(t) KierenFallon 4 42
(Phil McEntee) *led after 1f to 4f out: drvn and nt qckn w ldrs over 2f out: wknd and lost 2nd 1f out* **11/2[3]**

600- **6** *nk* **Fitz**[130] 7519 5-9-5 **58**........ JimCrowley 12 49
(Matthew Salaman) *hld up towards rr: plenty to do over 2f out and shkn up: no prog tl styd on ins fnl f: n.d* **16/1**

-040 **7** *hd* **Art Scholar (IRE)**[29] 719 4-9-5 **58**........(p) GeorgeBaker 1 48
(Gary Moore) *chsd ldng pair: rdn and nt qckn 2f out: hanging and wknd over 1f out* **25/1**

3532 **8** *3/4* **Tuscan King**[11] 906 4-9-7 **60**........(tp) RobertHavlin 10 48
(Bernard Llewellyn) *hld up towards rr: plenty to do whn effrt in midfield over 2f out: no prog and wl btn 1f out* **5/1[2]**

044- **9** *1* **Bahkov (IRE)**[308] 2441 5-8-7 **51**........ HarryBentley(5) 3 36
(Eric Wheeler) *chsd ldrs: struggling to hold pl fr 1/2-way: no prog and wl btn over 1f out* **33/1**

0-36 **10** *1/2* **Pippbrook Ministar**[48] 487 4-8-10 **56**........(p) NathanAlison(7) 8 40
(Jim Boyle) *prom: rdn 3f out: sn lost pl and struggling* **14/1**

-263 **11** *hd* **Shaded Edge**[29] 722 7-9-5 **58**........ MartinDwyer 6 42
(David Arbuthnot) *hld up towards rr: pushed along 3f out: dropped to last trio over 2f out: no prog after* **4/1[1]**

-606 **12** *2* **Crazy Parachute**[21] 810 4-8-11 **50**........ TomQueally 13 28
(Gary Moore) *s.v.s: t.k.h and hld up in last pair: limited prog 2f out: wknd ins fnl f* **16/1**

0-06 **13** *2 1/4* **Teen Ager (FR)**[7] 950 7-8-11 **50**........ LiamKeniry 5 22
(Paul Burgoyne) *t.k.h: trckd ldrs: wknd qckly 2f out* **8/1**

520- **14** *16* **Moonlight Serenade**[357] 1162 4-9-0 **53**........ SteveDrowne 11 —
(Simon Earle) *a towards rr: wknd over 2f out: eased: t.o* **50/1**

1m 24.44s (-0.36) **Going Correction** +0.05s/f (Slow) **14** Ran SP% **118.2**
Speed ratings (Par 101): **104,103,103,98,96 96,96,95,94,93 93,91,88,70**
toteswingers: 1&2 £50.00, 1&3 £23.00, 2&3 £12.20 CSF £290.73 CT £2216.28 TOTE £28.00: £5.70, £7.60, £2.30; EX 165.80.
Owner Brian Johnson **Bred** Peter E Daly **Trained** Dalham, Suffolk

FOCUS
A wide-open handicap, in which the front three pulled well clear. The winner is rated back to his latter 2010 form.
Moonlight Serenade Official explanation: jockey said filly lost its action

1046 NICHOLAS HALL H'CAP — 1m 4f (P)
4:30 (4:30) (Class 5) (0-75,75) 4-Y-0+ **£2,729** (£806; £403) **Stalls** Low

Form RPR

002- **1** **Deauville Post (FR)**[167] 6872 4-9-7 **75**........ RyanMoore 2 83+
(Richard Hannon) *mde all: set stdy pce for 7f: pressed 3f out: shkn up 2f out: styd on strly and in command ins fnl f* **5/6[1]**

-064 **2** *1 3/4* **Maslak (IRE)**[8] 938 7-9-0 **66**........ ChrisCatlin 6 71
(Peter Hiatt) *trckd wnr thrght: chal and upsides 3f out: nt qckn 2f out: wl hld ins fnl f* **25/1**

3534 **3** *2* **Camps Bay (USA)**[15] 858 7-9-7 **73**........ HayleyTurner 3 75
(Conor Dore) *hld up in last trio: pushed along over 4f out: struggling in 7th over 2f out: styd on fr over 1f out to take 3rd nr fin* **14/1**

02-2 **4** *1/2* **Resplendent Light**[21] 813 6-9-6 **72**........(t) RobertHavlin 1 73
(Bernard Llewellyn) *cl up in 4th: chsd ldng pair 3f out: rdn and cl enough wl over 1f out: wknd ins fnl f* **11/2[2]**

043- **5** *1/2* **Opera Prince**[123] 7323 6-8-12 **64**........ KierenFallon 7 64
(Lady Herries) *hld up in last trio: rdn and sme prog 3f out: nt qckn 2f out: no imp after* **8/1**

5450 **5** *dht* **Thundering Home**[6] 954 4-8-7 **61**........ RobbieFitzpatrick 8 61
(Michael Attwater) *s.i.s: hld up in last trio: effrt on wd outside 3f out: drvn and no prog 2f out: one pce after* **25/1**

-154 **7** *3 1/2* **Lingfield Bound (IRE)**[33] 647 4-9-7 **79**........ SteveDrowne 6 70
(John Best) *chsd ldrs in 5th: rdn over 2f out: no imp wl over 1f out: wknd ins fnl f* **13/2[3]**

4344 **8** *4* **Profit's Reality (IRE)**[5] 962 9-8-9 **68**........ AaronChave(7) 4 56
(Michael Attwater) *dwlt: t.k.h and sn trckd ldng pair: wknd 3f out* **25/1**

2m 34.44s (1.44) **Going Correction** +0.05s/f (Slow)
WFA 4 from 6yo+ 2lb **8** Ran SP% **112.6**
Speed ratings (Par 103): **97,95,94,94,93 93,91,88**
toteswingers: 1&2 £5.20, 1&3 £3.40, 2&3 £11.40 CSF £28.91 CT £175.49 TOTE £1.90: £1.10, £8.40, £3.40; EX 17.10.
Owner Sir Robert Ogden **Bred** Haras D'Etreham **Trained** East Everleigh, Wilts

FOCUS
A race that went to script for the well-supported favourite. It was slowly run and may not have taken too much winning.

1047 RUDRIDGE MAIDEN STKS — 7f (P)
5:00 (5:00) (Class 5) 3-Y-0 **£2,047** (£604; £302) **Stalls** Low

Form RPR

222- **1** **Choral**[151] 7232 3-8-12 77........ RyanMoore 5 66
(Richard Hannon) *chsd ldr to over 2f out: sn shkn up: cajoled along to cl over 1f out: led last 100yds: rdn out* **1/3[1]**

00- **2** *1 1/2* **Court Applause (IRE)**[181] 6497 3-9-3 0........ MartinDwyer 4 67
(William Muir) *trckd ldng pair: wnt 2nd over 2f out: clsd to ld 1f out: hdd and one pce last 100yds* **9/1[3]**

0-04 **3** *1 1/2* **Beautiful Lando (FR)**[12] 888 3-9-3 50........(v) KierenFallon 1 63
(Heather Main) *led: set stdy pce for 1f then blasted clr: hdd and no ex 1f out* **14/1**

0- **4** *4 1/2* **Spartan Spirit (IRE)**[193] 6190 3-9-3 0........ JimmyFortune 2 51+
(Hughie Morrison) *hld up in 4th: wl off the pce after 2f: virtually t.o over 2f out: kpt on steadily fr over 1f out: nt disgracd* **5/1[2]**

0-0 **5** *25* **Ede'Sajolygoodfelo**[33] 684 3-9-3 0........ JackMitchell 3 —
(Pat Phelan) *hld up last: wl outpcd and pushed along after 2f: t.o fnl 3f* **40/1**

1m 24.89s (0.09) **Going Correction** +0.05s/f (Slow) **5** Ran SP% **110.8**
Speed ratings (Par 98): **101,99,97,92,63**
CSF £4.28 TOTE £1.20: £1.10, £4.50; EX 3.00.
Owner Longview Stud & Bloodstock Ltd **Bred** Longview Stud & Bloodstock Ltd **Trained** East Everleigh, Wilts

FOCUS
An interesting maiden with a couple of improving types taking their chance, but still weakish form. The winner had plenty in hand of these on her previous form.

T/Plt: £81.10 to a £1 stake. Pool of £61,173.46 550.00 winning tickets T/Qpdt: £17.60 to a £1 stake. Pool of £5,050.69 - 211.70 winning tickets. JN

[1014] WOLVERHAMPTON (A.W) (L-H)
Wednesday, March 30

OFFICIAL GOING: Standard
Wind: Light, behind

1048 WOLVERHAMPTON-RACECOURSE.CO.UK H'CAP — 5f 20y(P)
5:30 (5:32) (Class 5) (0-75,75) 4-Y-0+ **£1,942** (£578; £288; £144) **Stalls** Low

Form RPR

3223 **1** **Desert Strike**[7] 946 5-9-6 **74**........(p) RobertWinston 9 86
(Alan McCabe) *chsd ldrs: shkn up over 1f out: rdn to ld wl ins fnl f: r.o* **5/1[3]**

5110 **2** *1 1/2* **Island Legend (IRE)**[30] 708 5-9-7 **75**........(p) RichardKingscote 7 82
(Milton Bradley) *led: rdn and edgd lft over 1f out: hdd wl ins fnl f* **13/2**

2042 **3** *hd* **Incomparable**[22] 794 6-9-6 **74**........(bt) IanMongan 1 80
(David Nicholls) *chsd ldr: rdn over 1f out: r.o* **4/1[2]**

4512 **4** *1* **Kylladdie**[7] 946 4-9-3 **71**........(b) PaulHanagan 3 73
(Steve Gollings) *sn pushed along in rr: hdwy 1/2-way: rdn over 1f out: r.o* **15/8[1]**

-000 **5** *1/2* **Fair Passion**[30] 708 4-9-0 **68**........ AdamKirby 6 68
(Derek Shaw) *hld up: hdwy over 1f out: r.o: nt trble ldrs* **16/1**

-600 **6** *1 1/2* **Divertimenti (IRE)**[30] 708 7-8-13 **67**........(b) JimmyQuinn 5 62
(Roy Bowring) *chsd ldrs: rdn over 1f out: no ex ins fnl f* **25/1**

-514 **7** *5* **Soopacal (IRE)**[22] 794 6-9-3 **71**........ TonyCulhane 4 48
(Michael Herrington) *hld up: sme hdwy u.p over 1f out: wknd fnl f* **12/1**

2065 **8** *3/4* **Grudge**[46] 523 6-9-1 **69**........(be) LukeMorris 2 43
(Conor Dore) *sn pushed along and prom: rdn 1/2-way: wknd 2f out* **16/1**

1105 **9** *2 3/4* **Sloop Johnb**[47] 506 5-9-2 **70**........(p) KirstyMilczarek 8 34
(Conor Dore) *s.s: a in rr: bhd fnl 3f* **16/1**

61.71 secs (-0.59) **Going Correction** +0.05s/f (Slow) **9** Ran SP% **114.0**
Speed ratings (Par 103): **106,103,103,101,100 98,90,89,84**
toteswingers: 1&2 £6.70, 1&3 £3.10, 2&3 £4.90 CSF £36.86 CT £141.93 TOTE £4.60: £1.10, £2.20, £2.10; EX 37.70 Trifecta £101.90 Pool: £7,772.68 - 56.40 winning units..
Owner Southwell Racing Club **Bred** Mrs Mary Rowlands **Trained** Averham Park, Notts

FOCUS
A reasonable race for the grade run at a good pace. The winner, better than ever, reversed recent form with the third and fourth.

1049 NAME A RACE TO ENHANCE YOUR BRAND FILLIES' MAIDEN AUCTION STKS — 5f 20y(P)
6:00 (6:01) (Class 5) 2-Y-0 **£1,942** (£578; £288; £144) **Stalls** Low

Form RPR

1 **Dijarvo** 2-8-5 0........ LiamJones 4 66+
(Tony Carroll) *chsd ldrs: rdn to ld over 1f out: hung lft: r.o* **9/2[3]**

2 *2 1/2* **Queen Of The Hop** 2-8-4 0........ LukeMorris 2 55+
(J S Moore) *chsd ldr: rdn and ev ch over 1f out: styd on same pce ins fnl f* **5/2[1]**

3 *1 3/4* **Nannerl (IRE)** 2-8-5 0........ PaulHanagan 8 49+
(Kevin Ryan) *led: rdn and edgd rt wl over 1f out: sn hdd: nt clr run: hung rt and no ex ins fnl f* **5/1**

4 *4 1/2* **Mousie** 2-8-4 0........ NickyMackay 5 30
(Alan McCabe) *hld up: hdwy 1/2-way: wknd over 1f out* **20/1**

5 *1* **Aquasulis (IRE)** 2-8-6 0........ CathyGannon 1 28+
(David Evans) *dwlt: sn pushed along in rr: nvr on terms* **4/1[2]**

6 *2* **Early Ambition** 2-8-4 0........ JimmyQuinn 3 18
(Andrew Haynes) *s.i.s: sn chsng ldrs: rdn 1/2-way: wknd over 1f out* **9/2[3]**

7 *5* **Jettie** 2-7-12 0........ RPWalsh(7) 7 —
(David Evans) *chsd ldrs: rdn 1/2-way: sn wknd* **20/1**

63.48 secs (1.18) **Going Correction** +0.05s/f (Slow) **7** Ran SP% **111.1**
Speed ratings (Par 89): **92,88,85,78,76 73,65**
toteswingers: 1&2 £3.00, 1&3 £5.60, 2&3 £2.00 CSF £15.23 TOTE £7.40: £3.70, £2.30; EX 28.10 Trifecta £150.30 Pool: £7,522.13 - 37.03 winning units..
Owner The Dijarvo Partnership **Bred** B Minty **Trained** Cropthorne, Worcs

FOCUS
Probably just a modest juvenile fillies' maiden, but a few of these seemed quietly fancied and Dijarvo, who was much the best, created a good impression. The race averages and the time provide an early guide to the form.

NOTEBOOK
Dijarvo ◆ travelled nicely just in behind the leaders, and although carried wide into the straight, she quickly responded to a couple of sharp reminders to pull clear, winning tidily despite edging left late on. She only cost £3,000 but is bred to be speedy, being a half-sister to a few sprint winners, out of a 5f juvenile scorer, and she could add to this.
Queen Of The Hop came under pressure before halfway to hold her position, but although responding, she lacked the natural pace of the winner. This should sharpen her up. (op 3-1)
Nannerl(IRE) displayed loads speed but lost ground when going wide around the bend into the straight and was one-paced thereafter. (op 11-2 tchd 6-1)
Mousie, weak in the market, kept on from off the pace without seriously threatening. She showed enough to suggest she can win a seller or suchlike.
Aquasulis(IRE) was extremely green. She unseated her rider when jinking slightly on the way to the start, and in the race itself she started slowly and looked awkward, carrying her head to the side at times. This experience should bring her on, but she'll still be best watched next time. (op 11-4)
Early Ambition didn't see her race out at all, but she wasn't given a hard time. (op 5-1 tchd 11-2)

1050 STAY AT THE WOLVERHAMPTON HOLIDAY INN (S) STKS — 1m 5f 194y(P)
6:30 (6:30) (Class 6) 4-Y-0+ **£1,535** (£453; £226) **Stalls** Low

Form RPR

6306 **1** **Acropolis (IRE)**[11] 911 10-9-2 44........ LukeMorris 4 55+
(Tony Carroll) *a.p: racd keenly: chsd ldr over 5f out: led over 2f out: sn edgd rt and pushed clr: eased ins fnl f* **11/1**

10/6 **2** *5* **Kavaloti (IRE)**[9] 342 7-9-2 69........(b) FergusSweeney 5 44
(Gary Moore) *chsd ldr after 2f: led over 6f out: rdn and hdd over 2f out: sn btn* **4/1[2]**

110- **3** *15* **Gremlin**[325] 1357 7-8-13 72........(p) KierenFox(3) 1 23
(Ronald Harris) *chsd ldrs: hmpd wl over 5f out: reminders 4f out: rdn and wknd 2f out* **4/6[1]**

0 **4** *74* **Sevivon**[7] 945 4-8-7 0........ LiamJones 3 —
(J W Hills) *led: pushed along 8f out: rdn and hdd over 6f out: sn wknd: t.o* **80/1**

2325 U **New Den**[12] 350 4-8-12 55..........(vt) NickyMackay 2 —
(Jim Boyle) *stmbld and uns rdr leaving stalls* **9/2**[3]
3m 6.56s (0.56) **Going Correction** +0.05s/f (Slow)
WFA 4 from 7yo+ 4lb **5** Ran SP% **107.7**
Speed ratings (Par 101): **100,97,88,46,—**
CSF £49.62 TOTE £7.10: £3.10, £2.80; EX 23.90.There was no bid for the winner.
Owner A W Carroll **Bred** Quay Bloodstock And Samac Ltd **Trained** Cropthorne, Worcs
FOCUS
This was a weak seller and the form looks close to worthless. New Den unseated his rider after stumbling on leaving the stalls, and the three beaten runners who completed all ran woefully.

1051 ENJOY THE PARTY PACK GROUP OFFER H'CAP 1m 1f 103y(P)
7:00 (7:00) (Class 4) (0-85,80) 3-Y-O **£3,238** (£963; £481; £240) **Stalls** Low

Form RPR
2-11 **1** **Palm Pilot (IRE)**[74] 177 3-9-3 **76**.......... PaulHanagan 4 81+
(Ed Dunlop) *chsd ldr 4f: remained handy: r.o u.p to ld nr fin* **3/1**[3]
2212 **2** *hd* **School For Scandal (IRE)**[11] 907 3-9-4 **77**..........(b) JimmyQuinn 3 81
(Mark Johnston) *sn led: hrd rdn and hung rt ins fnl f: hdd nr fin* **9/4**[2]
5211 **3** *½* **Baharat (IRE)**[9] 931 3-9-2 **75** 6ex..........(v) ShaneKelly 1 78
(Jeremy Noseda) *a.p: chsd ldr over 5f out: rdn and hung rt over 1f out: styd on* **6/4**[1]
236- **4** *17* **Focail Maith**[133] 7481 3-9-7 **80**.......... AdamKirby 2 47
(Noel Quinlan) *hld up: rdn over 2f out: sn wknd* **8/1**
2m 2.88s (1.18) **Going Correction** +0.05s/f (Slow) **4** Ran SP% **106.9**
Speed ratings (Par 100): **96,95,95,80**
CSF £9.68 TOTE £2.80; EX 6.60.
Owner Cliveden Stud **Bred** Cliveden Stud Ltd **Trained** Newmarket, Suffolk
FOCUS
Only four runners and it was steadily run, but a good 3-y-o handicap for the grade. The form makes some sense.

1052 HORIZONS RESTAURANT H'CAP 1m 141y(P)
7:30 (7:31) (Class 6) (0-65,64) 4-Y-O+ **£1,603** (£473; £236) **Stalls** Low

Form RPR
4-63 **1** **Forward Feline (IRE)**[37] 637 5-9-1 **63**.......... DeclanCannon(5) 11 71
(Bryn Palling) *hld up: hdwy over 2f out: rdn to ld 1f out: hung rt: r.o* **20/1**
3530 **2** *½* **Serious Drinking (USA)**[28] 727 5-9-5 **62**..........(t) JamieSpencer 4 69
(Walter Swinburn) *hld up: hdwy u.p over 1f out: swtchd lft fnl f: r.o* **11/1**
06-4 **3** *hd* **Aldo**[48] 489 4-9-6 **63**..........(t) JamesDoyle 8 69
(Alastair Lidderdale) *led: rdn and hdd 1f out: hung rt: r.o* **20/1**
0223 **4** *½* **Kyle Of Bute**[12] 897 5-9-4 **61**.......... J-PGuillambert 3 67+
(Brian Baugh) *hld up: nt clr run: swtchd rt and hdwy over 1f out: r.o: nt rch ldrs* **8/1**
-112 **5** *¾* **Stargazing (IRE)**[30] 711 5-9-3 **60**.......... AdamKirby 7 64
(Marco Botti) *prom: nt clr run over 1f out: swtchd lft: styd on u.p* **7/4**[1]
610- **6** *1½* **Twisted**[154] 7167 5-9-7 **64**..........(b) GrahamGibbons 6 64
(Michael Easterby) *prom: chsd ldr over 6f out: rdn over 2f out: no ex fnl f* **4/1**[2]
35-0 **7** *1* **Dazakhee**[22] 797 4-8-12 **55**.......... TonyCulhane 1 53+
(Paul Midgley) *hld up: rdn over 2f out: styd on ins fnl f: nrst fin* **25/1**
3561 **8** *2½* **Catching Zeds**[12] 897 4-9-4 **61**.......... RichardKingscote 2 53
(Ian Williams) *stmbld s: hld up in tch: rdn over 1f out: sn wknd* **15/2**[3]
6510 **9** *hd* **Join Up**[30] 712 5-9-0 **60**.......... RossAtkinson(3) 10 52
(Mark Brisbourne) *chsd ldrs: rdn over 2f out: wknd over 1f out* **20/1**
0360 **10** *1* **Just Timmy Marcus**[9] 933 5-8-12 **60**.......... JemmaMarshall(5) 12 49
(Brian Baugh) *hld up: effrt over 1f out: nvr on terms* **22/1**
-006 **11** *1¾* **Novay Essjay (IRE)**[11] 914 4-9-1 **58**..........(v) PaulHanagan 5 43
(Alan Juckes) *chsd ldr 2f: remained handy: rdn over 2f out: wknd over 1f out* **50/1**
4400 **12** *3¾* **Justcallmehandsome**[33] 685 9-8-12 **62**..........(be) RachealKneller(7) 9 39
(Dominic Ffrench Davis) *mid-div: hdwy 6f out: rdn and wknd over 1f out* **20/1**
1m 50.27s (-0.23) **Going Correction** +0.05s/f (Slow) **12** Ran SP% **116.8**
Speed ratings (Par 101): **103,102,102,101,101 99,99,96,96,95 94,90**
toteswingers: 1&2 £35.90, 1&3 £26.40, 2&3 £25.60 CSF £201.40 CT £4487.35 TOTE £16.40: £4.70, £2.70, £7.80; EX 81.70 Trifecta £2790.50 Pool: £5,279.50 - 1.40 winning units..
Owner Derek And Jean Clee **Bred** D D And Mrs Jean P Clee **Trained** Tredodridge, Vale Of Glamorgan
FOCUS
A modest but competitive handicap. The pace looked muddling (time over three second above standard) and field bunched up rounding the final bend. The form is sound enough.

1053 SPONSOR A RACE BY CALLING 01902 390000 MEDIAN AUCTION MAIDEN STKS 1m 141y(P)
8:00 (8:02) (Class 6) 3-5-Y-O **£1,637** (£483; £241) **Stalls** Low

Form RPR
50-0 **1** **Beach Babe**[29] 716 3-8-4 56.......... NickyMackay 9 51
(Jonathan Portman) *trckd ldr: rdn to ld over 2f out: sn hrd pressed: hld on gamely fnl f* **12/1**
2-53 **2** *nse* **Scoglio**[11] 916 3-8-9 63..........(t) JamesDoyle 8 56
(Frank Sheridan) *prom: smooth hdwy to chal over 2f out: sn rdn: kpt on fnl f: jst hld* **5/2**[2]
0-0 **3** *½* **Valdaw**[21] 811 3-8-9 0.......... EddieCreighton 4 55
(Joseph Tuite) *hld up on ins: drvn and outpcd over 2f out: rallied appr fnl f: r.o* **12/1**
4 **4** *nse* **McCool Bannanas**[11] 916 3-8-9 0.......... LiamJones 10 55
(James Unett) *t.k.h: in tch on outside: hdwy to chse ldrs 2f out: hung lft and kpt on fnl f* **8/1**[3]
0/- **5** *1½* **Missprint**[488] 7556 4-9-4 0.......... JemmaMarshall(5) 7 51
(Brian Baugh) *hld up in midfield: stdy hdwy over 2f out: rdn and edgd lft fnl f: one pce* **66/1**
00- **6** *1½* **Smart George (IRE)**[182] 6473 3-8-9 0.......... LukeMorris 2 48
(Clive Cox) *towards rr and sn niggled along: drvn and outpcd over 3f out: rallied and green over 1f out: no imp fnl f* **5/4**[1]
7 *2¾* **Sienna Blue** 3-8-4 0.......... CathyGannon 3 37
(Malcolm Saunders) *missed break: bhd: drvn over 3f out: edgd lft and sme late hdwy: nvr on terms* **16/1**
8 *½* **John The Glass**[27] 4-10-0 0.......... AdamKirby 5 45?
(Mark Wellings) *s.i.s: bhd: drvn over 3f out: outpcd fnl 2f* **100/1**
6 **9** *4* **Elite Syncopations**[11] 916 3-8-4 0.......... JimmyQuinn 6 26
(Andrew Haynes) *led at slow pce: rdn and hdd over 2f out: wknd over 1f out* **33/1**
00 **10** *6* **Higher Spen Jess**[40] 600 3-8-4 0..........(p) PaulHanagan 1 12
(Julie Camacho) *t.k.h: trckd ldrs tl rdn and wknd 2f out* **33/1**
1m 54.6s (4.10) **Going Correction** +0.05s/f (Slow)
WFA 3 from 4yo 19lb **10** Ran SP% **113.8**
Speed ratings (Par 101): **83,82,82,82,81 79,77,76,73,68**
toteswingers: 1&2 £4.20, 1&3 £6.50, 2&3 £3.80 CSF £40.72 TOTE £17.20: £4.30, £1.20, £3.10; EX 43.00 Trifecta £264.10 Pool: £392.61 - 1.10 winning units..
Owner Mrs R F Knipe **Bred** R F And S D Knipe **Trained** Compton, Berks
FOCUS
They went a steady gallop and the time was desperately slow, being 4.33 seconds off the earlier Class 6 handicap - a race which also lacked pace. This is modest form at best, but the race could produce the odd winner. Beach Babe did not need to match her 2yo best.

1054 WOLVERHAMPTON FILLIES' H'CAP 7f 32y(P)
8:30 (8:30) (Class 5) (0-70,70) 4-Y-O+ **£1,942** (£578; £288; £144) **Stalls** High

Form RPR
1455 **1** **Polemica (IRE)**[9] 933 5-8-8 **57** ow1..........(bt) JamesDoyle 2 65
(Frank Sheridan) *hld up: hdwy 2f out: rdn to ld ins fnl f: edgd lft: kpt on strly* **5/2**[2]
6544 **2** *2¾* **Kai Mook**[33] 689 4-8-8 **60**..........(t) KierenFox(3) 6 61
(Roger Ingram) *pressed ldr: led and rdn over 2f out: hdd ins fnl f: kpt on same pce* **6/1**
602- **3** *½* **Gemma's Delight (IRE)**[159] 7064 4-8-7 **56** oh1..........(p) LiamJones 5 56
(James Unett) *t.k.h: trckd ldrs: effrt 2f out: kpt on same pce fnl f* **4/1**[3]
1123 **4** *6* **Spinning Bailiwick**[23] 792 5-9-7 **70**..........(b) GeorgeBaker 3 53
(Gary Moore) *t.k.h: hld up in tch: rdn over 2f out: edgd lft and wknd 1f out* **15/8**[1]
-104 **5** *½* **Amary (IRE)**[47] 508 4-9-2 **65**..........(p) BarryMcHugh 1 47
(John Harris) *hld up in tch on ins: rdn whn n.m.r briefly and outpcd over 1f out: n.d after* **10/1**
010- **6** *3¾* **Ellies Image**[229] 5024 4-9-0 **63**.......... GrahamGibbons 4 35
(Brian Baugh) *t.k.h: trckd ldrs tl hung lft and wknd over 1f out* **12/1**
0P0- **7** *9* **First Term**[166] 6903 4-8-7 **56** oh1.......... LukeMorris 7 —
(Malcolm Saunders) *led: rdn and hdd over 2f out: edgd lft and wknd over 1f out* **33/1**
1m 29.15s (-0.45) **Going Correction** +0.05s/f (Slow) **7** Ran SP% **117.4**
Speed ratings (Par 100): **104,100,100,93,92 88,78**
toteswingers: 1&2 £3.90, 1&3 £3.80, 2&3 £4.60 CSF £18.66 TOTE £2.00: £1.10, £3.00; EX 18.20.
Owner Scuderia A4/5 **Bred** Mervyn Stewkesbury **Trained** Wolverhampton, W Midlands
FOCUS
A modest fillies' handicap which probably didn't take much winning. A length personal best from the winner.
T/Plt: £951.90 to a £1 stake. Pool £74,956.74. 57.48 winning tickets. T/Qpdt: £121.80 to a £1 stake. Pool: £9,151.62. 55.60 winning tickets. CR

LEICESTER (R-H)
Thursday, March 31

OFFICIAL GOING: Good (8.3)
Wind: Fresh half-behind Weather: Cloudy

1055 LADBROKES.COM KNIGHTON MEDIAN AUCTION MAIDEN STKS 5f 2y
2:20 (2:21) (Class 5) 2-Y-O **£1,942** (£578; £288; £144) **Stalls** High

Form RPR
1 **Jack Who's He (IRE)** 2-9-3 0.......... NeilCallan 6 83+
(David Evans) *mde virtually all: rdn over 1f out: hung rt: r.o wl* **4/1**[2]
2 *4* **Dawn Lightning** 2-8-12 0.......... RobertWinston 4 64
(Alan McCabe) *a.p: rdn to chse wnr fnl f: edgd rt: styd on same pce* **11/2**
3 *2¼* **Dougie Boy** 2-9-0 0.......... KierenFox(3) 1 61
(Bill Turner) *chsd ldrs: pushed along and edgd rt fr 1/2-way: styd on same pce appr fnl f* **4/1**[2]
4 *1¼* **Copper Falls** 2-8-12 0.......... FergusSweeney 2 51
(Brendan Powell) *w wnr tl rdn over 1f out: edgd rt and wknd ins fnl f* **9/1**
5 *hd* **Dream Whisperer** 2-8-12 0.......... JamesDoyle 7 50
(Dominic Ffrench Davis) *hld up in tch: pushed along 1/2-way: rdn and hung rt fr over 1f out: no ex fnl f* **9/2**[3]
6 *28* **Zeeman** 2-8-12 0.......... DeclanCannon(5) 3 —
(Nicky Vaughan) *dwlt: sn pushed along in rr: wknd 1/2-way: t.o* **33/1**
7 *1¼* **Waybuloo (IRE)** 2-8-12 0.......... PaulHanagan 5 —
(Gay Kelleway) *prom: rdn 1/2-way: sn hung rt: wknd over 1f out: t.o* **3/1**[1]
61.19 secs (1.19) **Going Correction** -0.05s/f (Good) **7** Ran SP% **111.5**
Speed ratings (Par 92): **88,81,78,76,75 30,28**
toteswingers:1&2:£3.50, 1&3:£2.60, 2&3:£5.00 CSF £24.60 TOTE £3.00: £2.30, £4.30; EX 20.70.
Owner Barry McCabe **Bred** Knocklong House Stud **Trained** Pandy, Monmouths
FOCUS
Smart types have won this maiden, including subsequent Coventry winners Hellvelyn (2006) and Art Connoisseur (2008), but this year's race didn't look particularly strong and it would be surprising if it contained a Royal Ascot winner. Jack Who's He did it well though, and the time was good.
NOTEBOOK
Jack Who's He(IRE), whose trainer has already had a 2-y-o winner this season, was one of the most well-grown horses in the line-up and showed a professional attitude under a positive ride to win on debut. Considering his size, there should be more to come and he ought to hold his own in fair company. (op 3-1)
Dawn Lightning, said to be a handful in the paddock, missed the kick slightly but soon got back on terms and travelled quite nicely while others struggled. She stayed on well once under pressure and looks the type to win a race early on. (tchd 6-1)
Dougie Boy, already gelded, is related to a winner and kept on respectably after hitting a flat spot at about halfway. His trainer reported beforehand that his horse has a knee action, so will probably need ease in the ground to be at his best. (op 9-2 tchd 5-1)
Copper Falls, a half-sister to Leelu, a winner at 7f-1m, showed early dash but could not sustain her effort in the final stages. She was reported to have been making noises in the paddock, and dragged her lass around while doing so. (tchd 12-1)
Dream Whisperer was strong in the market but looked smaller than her rivals, and tended to hang inside the final furlong. (op 6-1)
Waybuloo(IRE) was keen early but soon came under pressure and wasn't a factor. (op 7-2 tchd 9-4)

1056 LADBROKES.COM (S) STKS 5f 218y
2:50 (2:50) (Class 6) 3-Y-O **£1,619** (£481; £240; £120) **Stalls** High

Form RPR
200- **1** **Cootehill Lass (IRE)**[131] 7527 3-8-9 65.......... SilvestreDeSousa 2 59
(Geoffrey Harker) *s.i.s: hdwy 1/2-way: rdn to ld 1f out: edgd lft: r.o* **9/4**[1]

0414 **2** *2* **Eternal Youth (IRE)**[10] 929 3-9-5 70 .... (b) LukeMorris 5 62
(Ronald Harris) *led: rdn: edgd rt and hdd over 1f out: styd on same pce* **8/1**

2445 **3** *1* **Captain Loui (IRE)**[29] 724 3-9-5 62 .... (p) PaulHanagan 1 59
(Dai Burchell) *chsd ldrs: rdn to ld over 1f out: sn hdd: no ex ins fnl f* **6/1**[3]

3233 **4** *2 1/4* **Captain Dimitrios**[10] 929 3-9-5 69 .... (v) NeilCallan 3 52
(David Evans) *chsd ldrs: rdn over 2f out: no ex fnl f* **5/2**[2]

60-0 **5** *nk* **Dancing Tara**[19] 850 3-8-9 50 .... CathyGannon 6 41
(David Evans) *prom: rdn over 2f out: styd on same pce appr fnl f* **22/1**

5 **6** *11* **Sing Alana Sing**[7] 953 3-8-2 0 .... (t) JakePayne(7) 8 —
(Bill Turner) *sn pushed along and prom: rdn 1/2-way: sn hung rt and wknd* **25/1**

7 *1 1/2* **The Blind Side (IRE)** 3-9-0 0 .... NeilChalmers 4 —
(Michael Appleby) *s.s: outpcd* **50/1**

-465 **8** *2* **Dangerous Illusion (IRE)**[24] 787 3-8-9 45 .... AndreaAtzeni 9 —
(Michael Quinn) *chsd ldrs: rdn over 2f out: hung rt over 1f out: wknd and eased fnl f* **28/1**

-025 **9** *3 1/2* **Elusive Love (IRE)**[9] 936 3-9-0 60 .... KierenFallon 7 —
(Mark Johnston) *s.i.s: sme hdwy u.p 1/2-way: wknd over 2f out* **7/1**

1m 13.15s (0.15) **Going Correction** -0.05s/f (Good) **9** Ran SP% **110.8**
Speed ratings (Par 96): **97,94,93,90,89 74,72,70,65**
toteswingers:1&2:£5.10, 1&3:£3.70, 2&3:£6.10 CSF £18.68 TOTE £2.70: £1.40, £2.10, £2.20; EX 26.80 Trifecta £82.80 Pool: £839.50 - 7.50 winning units..There was no bid for the winner.

Owner An Englishman, Irishman & Scotsman **Bred** Speers Bloodstock Ltd **Trained** Thirkleby, N Yorks

FOCUS
A competitive but ordinary seller. The winner is rated close to her maiden best.

1057 LADBROKES.COM KIBWORTH H'CAP — 1m 3f 183y
3:20 (3:20) (Class 4) (0-85,82) 3-Y-O **£3,238** (£963; £481; £240) **Stalls** Low

Form RPR

301- **1** **Sadler's Risk (IRE)**[170] 6831 3-9-7 **82** .... JoeFanning 4 94+
(Mark Johnston) *mde all: shkn up over 1f out: sn clr: readily* **4/6**[1]

2-21 **2** *4* **Jacobs Son**[27] 762 3-9-2 **77** .... RyanMoore 3 79
(Robert Mills) *a.p: rdn to chse wnr over 1f out: no imp* **7/2**[2]

5212 **3** *4 1/2* **Mrs Neat (IRE)**[15] 866 3-8-1 **67** .... (p) KieranO'Neill(5) 5 62
(Sylvester Kirk) *hld up: hdwy to chse wnr over 2f out: sn rdn and hung rt: wknd over 1f out* **12/1**

21 **4** *9* **Brilliant Barca**[22] 801 3-8-7 **68** .... SamHitchcott 1 53
(Mick Channon) *chsd wnr tl rdn over 2f out: wknd over 1f out* **9/2**[3]

2m 35.31s (1.41) **Going Correction** +0.125s/f (Good) **4** Ran SP% **108.1**
Speed ratings (Par 100): **100,97,94,88**
CSF £3.28 TOTE £1.50; EX 3.80.

Owner R S Brookhouse **Bred** Smythson **Trained** Middleham Moor, N Yorks

FOCUS
A decent performance from the winner, who improved considerably on his maiden win and looks sure to rate higher. The form is rated through the runner-up.

1058 LADBROKES.COM GRANBY H'CAP — 1m 60y
3:50 (3:51) (Class 5) (0-70,70) 4-Y-O+ **£1,942** (£578; £288; £144) **Stalls** Low

Form RPR

20-4 **1** **Silent Oasis**[22] 814 5-9-2 **65** .... FergusSweeney 6 74
(Brendan Powell) *hld up: hdwy over 2f out: rdn to ld 1f out: edgd rt: styd on* **6/1**[3]

260- **2** *3/4* **Formulation (IRE)**[159] 7090 4-9-6 **69** .... JimmyFortune 1 76
(Hughie Morrison) *hld up in tch: rdn and swtchd lft over 1f out: sn ev ch: styd on* **4/1**[1]

3430 **3** *3 1/2* **Gordy Bee (USA)**[13] 897 5-8-3 **57** .... (b) TobyAtkinson(5) 5 56
(Richard Guest) *led: rdn over 2f out: hdd 1f out: no ex* **10/1**

050- **4** *2 3/4* **Tanforan**[166] 6935 9-8-8 **57** .... KellyHarrison 3 50
(Brian Baugh) *hld up: hdwy over 1f out: nt trble ldrs* **40/1**

100 **5** *2 1/2* **Sennockian Storm (USA)**[162] 7012 4-9-7 **70** .... JoeFanning 2 57
(Mark Johnston) *chsd ldr tl rdn and wknd over 1f out* **10/1**

0221 **6** *12* **Postman**[15] 870 5-9-4 **67** .... (p) TomEaves 7 27
(Bryan Smart) *prom: rdn over 2f out: wknd over 1f out* **4/1**[1]

0060 **7** *1 1/4* **Beetuna (IRE)**[13] 897 6-9-2 **65** .... (b) PaulHanagan 10 22
(David Bourton) *hld up: plld hrd: hdwy over 2f out: rdn and wknd over 1f out* **5/1**[2]

14-3 **8** *8* **Regal Rave (USA)**[29] 727 4-8-13 **62** .... NeilCallan 8 —
(Mouse Hamilton-Fairley) *chsd ldrs: rdn over 3f out: wknd 2f out* **4/1**[1]

1m 46.3s (1.20) **Going Correction** +0.125s/f (Good) **8** Ran SP% **114.2**
Speed ratings (Par 103): **99,98,94,92,89 77,76,68**
toteswingers:1&2:£5.60, 1&3:£8.70, 2&3:£7.80 CSF £30.13 CT £237.05 TOTE £8.80: £2.80, £1.80, £5.80; EX 41.40 Trifecta £494.70 Pool: £681.97 - 1.02 winning units..

Owner Dr E Semple & Russ Pendleton **Bred** Paulyn Limited **Trained** Upper Lambourn, Berks

FOCUS
A moderate handicap. The winner is rated back to her best previous form, which came here last season.

Beetuna(IRE) Official explanation: jockey said gelding lost its action

1059 LADBROKES.COM CONDITIONS STKS — 5f 218y
4:20 (4:21) (Class 3) 3-Y-O **£5,504** (£1,637; £818; £408) **Stalls** High

Form RPR

1- **1** **Retainer (IRE)**[351] 1309 3-9-7 0 .... RyanMoore 4 105
(Richard Hannon) *trckd ldr: plld hrd: led 4f out: drvn out: edgd rt nr fin* **4/9**[1]

614- **2** *1* **Glas Burn**[153] 7204 3-8-11 93 .... KierenFallon 3 92
(Jonathan Portman) *led 2f: remained w wnr: rdn fr over 1f out: r.o* **6/1**[3]

32- **3** *6* **Breedj (IRE)**[321] 2095 3-8-11 0 .... PhilipRobinson 1 73
(Clive Brittain) *chsd ldrs: rdn over 2f out: edgd lft over 1f out: wknd fnl f* **7/2**[2]

1255 **4** *2* **Restless Bay (IRE)**[9] 940 3-9-2 77 .... (v) ChrisCatlin 2 71
(Reg Hollinshead) *dwlt: hld up: hdwy 1/2-way: rdn and wknd over 1f out* **40/1**

1m 12.69s (-0.31) **Going Correction** -0.05s/f (Good) **4** Ran SP% **108.2**
Speed ratings (Par 102): **100,98,90,88**
CSF £3.61 TOTE £1.40; EX 2.70.

Owner B Bull **Bred** Des Vere Hunt & Jack Ronan Farming Co **Trained** East Everleigh, Wilts

FOCUS
An interesting 3-y-o event, rated around the runner-up. The winner is potentially smart.

NOTEBOOK
Retainer(IRE) landed a Newmarket novice contest on his debut last April, in which three of the five behind him won at least one race subsequently. Absent since due to breaking a leg while exercising on the gallops, connections had evidently been hoping to get him to the Super Sprint or a valuable sales race at some stage, but decided against it and gave him the time off. Quickly away, albeit a bit keen, he was far from impressive, but he was giving 10lb to the winner and it seems sure that there is plenty of improvement to come. He can be placed to advantage by a trainer adept at finding the right opportunities. (op 8-15)

Glas Burn made improvement with each run as a 2-y-o and proved she hasn't gone backwards through the winter with a good performance. One would imagine connections will hope to get some black type for her. (op 5-1)

Breedj(IRE) is evidently highly regarded (entered in the 1,000 Guineas and Oaks), but was beaten both times over 5f as a juvenile, the latter a Listed contest. Outpaced at around halfway, she kept on but was a bit disappointing. However, up in trip, she is one to keep an eye out for in handicaps before anything at a higher level is considered. (op 4-1)

Restless Bay(IRE) has plenty of experience, but faced a stiff task at these weights on official figures and was readily held. (op 28-1)

1060 LADBROKES.COM BARKBY MAIDEN FILLIES' STKS — 7f 9y
4:50 (4:52) (Class 5) 3-Y-O **£2,266** (£674; £337; £168) **Stalls** High

Form RPR

3- **1** **Sand Owl**[171] 6796 3-9-0 0 .... RyanMoore 2 79
(Peter Chapple-Hyam) *hld up: hdwy 1/2-way: rdn to ld over 1f out: r.o* **15/8**[1]

442- **2** *1* **Mother Jones**[204] 5865 3-9-0 74 .... TomEaves 3 76
(Bryan Smart) *plld hrd: led: rdn and hdd over 1f out: styd on* **11/1**

3- **3** *1* **Hunza Dancer (IRE)**[163] 7001 3-9-0 0 .... WilliamBuick 1 73
(John Gosden) *hld up: hdwy 1/2-way: rdn over 1f out: styd on same pce ins fnl f* **11/4**[2]

03- **4** *3 1/4* **Glyn Ceiriog**[183] 6469 3-9-0 0 .... TonyCulhane 10 65
(George Baker) *s.i.s: hld up: r.o fr over 1f out: nvr nrr* **16/1**

060- **5** *1* **Merrjanah**[195] 6154 3-9-0 62 .... PhilipRobinson 5 62
(Clive Brittain) *chsd ldrs: rdn over 2f out: sn outpcd* **20/1**

6 *1* **Alkhawarah (USA)** 3-9-0 0 .... RichardHills 8 59
(Mark Johnston) *chsd ldr tl rdn over 1f out: wknd ins fnl f* **10/3**[3]

04- **7** *5* **Talkative Guest (IRE)**[227] 5147 3-8-11 0 .... SimonPearce(3) 12 46
(George Margarson) *chsd ldrs: rdn over 2f out: wknd over 1f out* **25/1**

52- **8** *2* **Spring Bouquet (IRE)**[255] 4187 3-9-0 0 .... SamHitchcott 11 40
(Mick Channon) *s.i.s: sn mid-div: rdn and wknd over 2f out* **16/1**

500- **9** *2 1/4* **Rural Pursuits**[181] 6521 3-9-0 54 .... NickyMackay 4 34
(Christine Dunnett) *s.i.s: hdwy 1/2-way: wknd wl over 1f out* **200/1**

06-0 **10** *1 1/2* **Blazing Apostle (IRE)**[12] 916 3-9-0 49 .... DavidProbert 7 30
(Christine Dunnett) *hld up: a in rr: lost tch fr over 2f out* **200/1**

6 **11** *nk* **Add Lib**[15] 863 3-9-0 0 .... LiamKeniry 6 29
(Matthew Salaman) *mid-div: rdn and wknd over 2f out* **100/1**

1m 26.41s (0.21) **Going Correction** -0.05s/f (Good) **11** Ran SP% **115.2**
Speed ratings (Par 95): **96,94,93,90,88 87,82,79,77,75 75**
toteswingers:1&2:£3.60, 1&3:£2.00, 2&3:£4.50 CSF £23.19 TOTE £4.20: £1.60, £1.60, £1.10; EX 16.50 Trifecta £40.50 Pool: £896.61 - 16.37 winning units..

Owner The Triple Crown Partnership **Bred** Executive Bloodlines **Trained** Newmarket, Suffolk

FOCUS
A reasonable event without a great deal of depth, and the form is rated around the first three.

Glyn Ceiriog ◆ Official explanation: jockey said, regarding running and riding, that his orders were to ride the filly as he found it, try to settle and get its head down, adding that it settled well but came off the bridle 4f out and would appreciate a longer trip; trainer confirmed adding that the filly was weak as a 2yo, had strengthened during the winter and was still rather buzzy and would possibly appreciate easier ground.

1061 LADBROKES.COM H'CAP — 7f 9y
5:20 (5:21) (Class 4) (0-85,85) 4-Y-O+ **£2,590** (£770; £385; £192) **Stalls** High

Form RPR

331- **1** **Nimue (USA)**[243] 4601 4-9-2 **80** .... JamieSpencer 1 88
(Paul Cole) *mde all: racd centre tl c towards stands' side 1/2-way: shkn up ins fnl f: r.o* **4/1**[2]

5001 **2** *nk* **Mr Macattack**[7] 956 6-8-11 **75** .... (t) RichardKingscote 9 82
(Tom Dascombe) *s.i.s: racd stands' side: hdwy over 2f out: rdn and swtchd rt over 1f out: ev ch ins fnl f: r.o* **10/1**

4-63 **3** *3/4* **Standpoint**[29] 736 5-8-13 **77** .... GrahamGibbons 7 82
(Reg Hollinshead) *led stands' side to 1/2-way: chsd wnr thereafter tl rdn over 1f out: styd on* **5/1**[3]

24-0 **4** *hd* **Space Station**[21] 822 5-9-5 **83** .... (b) NeilCallan 4 87
(Simon Dow) *racd centre: prom: jnd stands' side 1/2-way: rdn over 1f out: edgd rt: unable qck towards fin* **5/2**[1]

4414 **5** *1 3/4* **Lastkingofscotland (IRE)**[6] 961 5-8-13 **77** .... (b) HayleyTurner 6 77
(Conor Dore) *racd stands' side: chsd ldrs: rdn over 1f out: styd on* **12/1**

301- **6** *1/2* **Dancing Maite**[248] 4431 6-8-10 **74** .... JimmyQuinn 5 72
(Roy Bowring) *racd centre: chsd wnr jnd stands' side 1/2-way: rdn and ev ch over 1f out: no ex ins fnl f* **16/1**

-123 **7** *1 3/4* **Ours (IRE)**[21] 816 8-9-0 **78** .... (p) BarryMcHugh 10 72
(John Harris) *s.s: racd stands' side: outpcd: r.o ins fnl f: nrst fin* **25/1**

030- **8** *3/4* **Barren Brook**[165] 6963 4-9-1 **82** .... JamesSullivan(3) 11 74
(Michael Easterby) *racd stands' side: mid-div: hdwy 1/2-way: rdn over 2f out: sn outpcd* **16/1**

613- **9** *nk* **Merchant Of Medici**[162] 7012 4-9-2 **80** .... MartinDwyer 2 71
(William Muir) *racd centre: prom: jnd stands' side 1/2-way: rdn and wknd over 1f out* **13/2**

214- **10** *3/4* **Aerodynamic (IRE)**[164] 6990 4-9-7 **85** .... PaulMulrennan 3 74
(Clive Mulhall) *racd centre: hld up in tch: jnd stands' side 1/2-way: wknd 2f out* **28/1**

005- **11** *13* **Urban Space**[91] 8018 5-8-3 **74** .... NoraLooby(7) 8 28
(Conor Dore) *racd stands' side: chsd ldrs tl rdn and wknd over 2f out* **66/1**

1m 24.92s (-1.28) **Going Correction** -0.05s/f (Good) **11** Ran SP% **115.9**
Speed ratings (Par 105): **105,104,103,103,101 101,99,98,97,96 82**
toteswingers:1&2:£14.10, 1&3:£4.20, 2&3:£15.90 CSF £42.26 CT £207.93 TOTE £6.40: £2.40, £1.50, £1.30; EX 70.30 Trifecta £479.80 Pool: £972.75 - 1.50 winning units..

Owner Mrs Fitri Hay **Bred** William A Carl **Trained** Whatcombe, Oxon

FOCUS
There was a difference of opinion among the jockeys about where to race, but the groups merged together about 3f out and a tight finished ensued. An ordinary handicap, run at a fair pace, and rated around the runner-up.

T/Plt: £76.20 to a £1 stake. Pool:£80,160.91 - 767.91 winning tickets T/Qpdt: £8.70 to a £1 stake. Pool:£6,146.01 - 520.90 winning tickets CR

[1048]WOLVERHAMPTON (A.W) (L-H)

Thursday, March 31

OFFICIAL GOING: Standard

Wind: Moderate, behind Weather: Fine

1062 FREE REPLAYS AT ATTHERACES.COM CLAIMING STKS 5f 20y(P)

5:45 (5:46) (Class 6) 3-Y-O £1,637 (£483; £241) Stalls Low

Form RPR

40-1 1 **Lord Avon**[10] 929 3-9-1 79 KierenFox(3) 3 85
(Bill Turner) *w ldr: def advantage 1/2-way: rdn 1f out: r.o wl: pushed out whn in command wl ins fnl f* **4/5**[1]

-330 2 2 **Sugar Beet**[19] 847 3-8-9 72 (b[1]) LukeMorris 2 69
(Ronald Harris) *chsd ldrs: rdn 1/2-way: styd on to take 2nd ins fnl f: no imp on wnr* **15/2**

36-2 3 hd **Second Encore**[10] 929 3-7-13 68 RyanPowell(5) 4 63
(J S Moore) *racd keenly: led narrowly to 1/2-way: rdn and nt qckn over 1f out: lost 2nd ins fnl f: kpt on same pce* **3/1**[2]

3-44 4 19 **Speedy Joe**[9] 936 3-8-2 64 (v[1]) AdamCarter(5) 1 —
(Bryan Smart) *bustled along coming out of stalls: a bhd: nvr able to go pce of others: dropped away wl over 1f out* **6/1**[3]

61.44 secs (-0.86) **Going Correction** +0.05s/f (Slow) 4 Ran SP% **106.6**
Speed ratings (Par 96): **108,104,104,74**
CSF £6.76 TOTE £1.10; EX 6.40.
Owner Mrs M S Teversham **Bred** Mrs Monica Teversham **Trained** Sigwells, Somerset

FOCUS
The runners encountered a blustery wind blowing up the course in the straight but the reverse in the back straight. A better than average claimer despite the small field, with nothing rated lower than 64. The winner is rated back towards his early 2yo form.

1063 BUSCADOR H'CAP 1m 4f 50y(P)

6:15 (6:15) (Class 6) (0-60,56) 4-Y-0+ £1,569 (£463; £231) Stalls Low

Form RPR

2234 1 **Broughtons Paradis (IRE)**[15] 862 5-9-4 **53** StevieDonohoe 6 60
(Willie Musson) *hld up: hdwy over 2f out: sn trckd ldrs: rdn 1f out: chalng ins fnl f: sn led: r.o and on top at fin* **14/1**

2356 2 1/2 **Yossi (IRE)**[9] 938 7-9-2 **51** (be) PaulHanagan 7 57
(Richard Guest) *racd keenly in midfield: hdwy to ld after 3f: rdn over 1f out: hdd wl ins fnl f: hld fnl strides* **14/1**

344- 3 nk **Blackstone Vegas**[110] 7840 5-9-2 **51** JoeFanning 3 57
(Derek Shaw) *led for 3f: remained handy: rdn to chal ins fnl f: hld and nt qckn fnl strides* **9/2**[1]

2144 4 2 1/4 **Laura Land**[16] 859 5-9-3 **52** ShaneKelly 9 54
(Mark Brisbourne) *hld up: hdwy to trck ldrs 6f out: rdn over 2f out: nt qckn over 1f out: hung lft ins fnl f: one pce fnl 100yds* **9/2**[1]

5004 5 nk **Mary Helen**[13] 899 4-8-8 **45** LukeMorris 4 47
(Mark Brisbourne) *trckd ldrs for 2f: midfield after: niggled along 4f out: kpt on ins fnl f: nt pce of ldrs* **6/1**[3]

3541 6 3/4 **Barbirolli**[13] 899 9-8-7 **47** LauraPike(5) 10 48
(William Stone) *midfield: hdwy to go prom 7f out: 2nd 6f out tl rdn wl over 1f out: fdd fnl 100yds* **6/1**[3]

5630 7 2 1/4 **Castlebury (IRE)**[6] 969 6-8-11 **46** (b) PJMcDonald 1 43
(Ruth Carr) *in tch: outpcd 2f out: no imp on ldrs after* **8/1**

200- 8 6 **Orpen Bid (IRE)**[7] 5202 6-8-4 **46** ow1 (p) JosephYoung(7) 2 34
(Michael Mullineaux) *hld up: struggling 4f out: nvr on terms* **50/1**

2406 9 1 3/4 **Atacama Sunrise**[13] 897 5-9-4 **56** AmyBaker(3) 5 41
(George Prodromou) *prom: lost pl over 7f out but stl hld up: effrt and hdwy on outer to chse ldrs 2f out: wknd wl over 1f out* **14/1**

000- 10 25 **The Chester Giant**[206] 5815 4-8-3 **45** RyanPowell(5) 8 —
(Patrick Morris) *prom: pushed along over 3f out: sn wknd* **20/1**

2m 44.2s (3.10) **Going Correction** +0.05s/f (Slow)
WFA 4 from 5yo+ 2lb 10 Ran SP% **112.8**
Speed ratings (Par 101): **91,90,90,88,88 88,86,82,81,64**
toteswingers: 1&2 £11.60, 1&3 £2.90, 2&3 £6.40. CSF £69.84 CT £334.16 TOTE £5.60: £3.70, £4.80, £1.10; EX 76.60.
Owner Broughton Thermal Insulation **Bred** Mount Coote Stud **Trained** Newmarket, Suffolk

FOCUS
A moderate but fairly competitive handicap named after a multiple course winner. it was a bit of a muddling race and the form is only ordinary.

1064 STAY AT THE WOLVERHAMPTON HOLIDAY INN H'CAP 5f 216y(P)

6:45 (6:45) (Class 5) (0-75,75) 3-Y-O £1,942 (£578; £288; £144) Stalls Low

Form RPR

4-11 1 **Take Your Partner**[9] 936 3-9-4 **72** 6ex (b) PhillipMakin 4 83+
(Kevin Ryan) *mde all: qcknd over 3 l clr ent st under 2f out: a in command: eased down fnl 50yds* **8/13**[1]

146- 2 2 1/4 **Da Ponte**[226] 5187 3-9-7 **75** ShaneKelly 3 74
(Walter Swinburn) *hld up: chsd ldrs over 4f out: rdn over 2f out and nt qckn: kpt on ins fnl f: wnt 2nd fnl 75yds: no ch w wnr* **2/1**[2]

530- 3 1 1/4 **Consistant**[92] 7999 3-8-13 **67** J-PGuillambert 2 62
(Brian Baugh) *racd in 2nd pl: rdn and nt qckn over 2f out: sn outpcd by wnr: lost 2nd and wl hld fnl 75yds* **17/2**[3]

2525 4 3 **Local Diktator**[28] 739 3-8-8 **62** (t) LukeMorris 1 47
(Ronald Harris) *hld up in rr over 4f out: effrt wl over 1f out but no threat to wnr: wknd fnl 100yds* **20/1**

1m 15.12s (0.12) **Going Correction** +0.05s/f (Slow) 4 Ran SP% **110.5**
Speed ratings (Par 98): **101,98,96,92**
CSF £2.18 TOTE £1.60; EX 2.80.
Owner Guy Reed **Bred** G Reed **Trained** Hambleton, N Yorks

FOCUS
The 3-y-os in this handicap covered a ratings spread similar to those in the opening claimer and the betting suggested it was a match. However, it proved to be a one-horse race. The winner was well in and showed he is just as good here as Southwell, value for 4l.

1065 ENJOY THE PARTY PACK GROUP OFFER MAIDEN STKS 5f 20y(P)

7:15 (7:16) (Class 5) 3-Y-O+ £1,942 (£578; £288; £144) Stalls Low

Form RPR

1 **Royal Bajan (USA)** 3-9-0 0 PaulHanagan 9 60+
(James Given) *in tch: swtchd rt over 1f out: qcknd to ld fnl 75yds: edgd lft whn wl on top cl home* **7/4**[1]

065- 2 1 1/4 **My Love Fajer (IRE)**[124] 7592 3-9-0 69 KirstyMilczarek 10 56
(George Prodromou) *chsd ldrs: rdn over 1f out: led ins fnl f: hdd fnl 75yds: nt pce of wnr and wl hld cl home* **9/2**[3]

3 nk **Hootys Agogo** 3-8-9 0 NeilFarley(5) 2 55
(Declan Carroll) *midfield: pushed along 2f out: edgd rt and hdwy over 1f out: styd on ins fnl f: gng on at fin* **10/1**

0630 4 3/4 **Francis Albert**[10] 934 5-9-5 48 (be) JosephYoung(7) 6 57
(Michael Mullineaux) *racd keenly: led narrowly: rdn over 1f out: hdd ins fnl f: one pce fnl 50yds* **10/1**

50 5 1 1/2 **Marvellous City (IRE)**[15] 873 3-9-0 0 KellyHarrison 4 47
(Mandy Rowland) *w ldr: rdn and stl ev ch over 1f out: no ex fnl 75yds* **40/1**

40 6 2 **Shakespeares Excel**[6] 971 4-9-12 0 JoeFanning 11 44
(Derek Shaw) *hld up in midfield: effrt over 1f out: no imp on ldrs: one pce ins fnl f* **28/1**

7 1/2 **Take Root** 3-9-0 0 LiamKeniry 5 38
(Reg Hollinshead) *chsd ldrs: rdn and edgd rt over 1f out: outpcd by ldrs fnl 110yds* **17/2**

0 8 1 **Lord Sun**[22] 811 3-9-0 0 RobbieFitzpatrick 1 34
(Peter Grayson) *towards rr: pushed along wl over 1f out: kpt on fnl f wout threatening* **50/1**

03/ 9 1 **Invincible Hero (IRE)**[559] 6065 4-9-12 0 (t) DavidNolan 7 35
(Declan Carroll) *in rr: pushed along over 2f out: nvr on terms* **4/1**[2]

56 10 7 **Kaminski Kabs**[6] 971 3-8-4 0 DanielleMcCreery(5) 8 —
(Phil McEntee) *towards rr: pushed along over 3f out: rn wd on bnd wl over 2f out: nvr on terms* **28/1**

/0- 11 1 3/4 **Exceedingthestars**[211] 5668 4-9-7 0 LukeMorris 3 —
(Michael Squance) *pushed along in midfield: wknd 3f out: eased whn wl btn over 1f out* **25/1**

0000 12 2 3/4 **Pinewood Polly**[16] 856 4-9-7 16 (p) ChrisCatlin 12 —
(Shaun Harris) *hld up: rdn over 2f out: nvr on terms* **100/1**

62.48 secs (0.18) **Going Correction** +0.05s/f (Slow)
WFA 3 from 4yo+ 12lb 12 Ran SP% **119.4**
Speed ratings (Par 103): **100,98,97,96,93 90,89,88,86,75 72,68**
toteswingers: 1&2 £1.50, 1&3 £6.10, 2&3 £11.90. CSF £8.94 TOTE £1.60: £1.10, £1.20, £14.20; EX 11.00.
Owner Mrs B E Wilkinson **Bred** West Wind Farm **Trained** Willoughton, Lincs

FOCUS
A very moderate maiden despite the relatively large field; the time was over a second slower than the opening claimer and it produced a bunched finish. Limited form, with the runner-up 10lb off even his latter 2yo form.

My Love Fajer(IRE) Official explanation: vet said gelding had a fibrillating heart
Exceedingthestars Official explanation: jockey said saddle slipped

1066 ATRVIRTUALOWNER.COM YEARLING SALES H'CAP 1m 1f 103y(P)

7:45 (7:45) (Class 5) (0-75,73) 4-Y-O+ £1,942 (£578; £288; £144) Stalls Low

Form RPR

0-41 1 **Strong Vigilance (IRE)**[38] 635 4-9-6 **72** JamieSpencer 3 79
(Michael Bell) *awkward s: hdwy to ld 1 m out: rdn whn pressed 3f out: hdd 2f out: regained ld over 1f out: hld on wl fnl strides* **11/8**[1]

-263 2 nk **The Winged Assasin (USA)**[31] 711 5-9-2 **68** PaulHanagan 2 74
(Shaun Lycett) *prom: lost pl but hld up in last over 7f out: hdwy on outer 3f out: led 2f out: rdn and hdd over 1f out: nt qckn ins fnl f: rallied fnl strides but hld* **3/1**[2]

5112 3 shd **Black Coffee**[13] 897 6-9-7 **73** (b) ShaneKelly 4 79
(Mark Brisbourne) *stdd s: hld up: hdwy 2f out: effrt to chse ldrs over 1f out: nt qckn: r.o and clsd fnl strides* **11/2**[3]

5211 4 2 3/4 **John Potts**[14] 881 6-9-5 **71** KellyHarrison 1 71
(Brian Baugh) *led: hdd 1 m out: remained handy: rdn to chal over 1f out: no ex fnl 50yds* **8/1**

242- 5 1 **Laconicos (IRE)**[237] 4804 9-8-2 **59** (t) LauraPike(5) 6 57
(William Stone) *racd keenly: in tch: wnt prom 5f out: rdn over 2f out: sn outpcd: no imp after* **11/1**

06-4 6 nk **Waahej**[22] 802 5-8-11 **63** ChrisCatlin 5 60
(Peter Hiatt) *trckd ldrs: wnt 2nd over 6f out: upsides but lost 2nd 3f out: stl ev ch 2f out: btn over 1f out* **13/2**

2m 2.32s (0.62) **Going Correction** +0.05s/f (Slow) 6 Ran SP% **115.3**
Speed ratings (Par 103): **99,98,98,96,95 95**
toteswingers: 1&2 £2.90, 1&3 £1.20, 2&3 £3.20. CSF £5.95 TOTE £2.80: £2.10, £1.90; EX 8.00.
Owner Lawrie Inman **Bred** Peter Grimes & John Dwan **Trained** Newmarket, Suffolk

FOCUS
Quite a competitive handicap with several coming into this in good form. The form is limited and the winner probably didn't need to improve on his previous C/D win.

Black Coffee Official explanation: jockey said, regarding running and riding, that his orders were to obtain a position close behind the leaders, which he was able to do, adding that the gelding may have benefited from a stronger pace throughout, picking up well in the home straight, and ran on to be narrowly beaten.

1067 WOLVERHAMPTON-RACECOURSE.CO.UK H'CAP 5f 216y(P)

8:15 (8:15) (Class 4) (0-85,85) 4-Y-O+ £3,238 (£963; £481; £240) Stalls Low

Form RPR

5-12 1 **Jack Rackham**[36] 651 7-9-0 **78** (v) TomEaves 11 88
(Bryan Smart) *chsd ldrs: rdn over 1f out: r.o ins fnl f: led fnl strides* **7/1**[3]

000- 2 hd **Capercaillie (USA)**[196] 6113 4-9-6 **84** LukeMorris 5 93
(Clive Cox) *midfield: hdwy 2f out: swtchd lft wl over 1f out: sn led: rdn ins fnl f: hdd fnl strides* **6/1**[2]

100- 3 1 1/2 **Icelandic**[131] 7522 9-9-7 **85** (t) JamesDoyle 7 89
(Frank Sheridan) *bhd: niggled along over 3f out: rdn and hdwy ins fnl f: wnt 3rd fnl 75yds: styd on but nt pce to rch front pair* **8/1**

0-01 4 3/4 **Tasmeem (IRE)**[42] 577 4-9-0 **78** (b) AdrianNicholls 9 80
(David Nicholls) *racd keenly in midfield: effrt over 2f out: edgd lft ins fnl f: kpt on but nt pce of ldrs* **15/2**

01-1 5 1 **Mottley Crewe**[28] 743 4-8-9 **73** FrederikTylicki 10 72
(Michael Dods) *prom: rdn and ev ch over 1f out: kpt on same pce fnl 100yds* **6/1**[2]

600- 6 2 **Great Charm (IRE)**[117] 7697 6-8-13 **77** GrahamGibbons 6 69
(Eric Alston) *prom: rdn and ev ch 2f out: one pce fnl 150yds* **8/1**

3-10 7 hd **Diriculous**[63] 316 7-9-6 **84** PaulHanagan 3 76+
(Robert Mills) *towards rr: nt clr run 2f out: rdn and nt qckning whn bmpd ins fnl f: eased whn no ch fnl 75yds* **10/3**[1]

4253 8 2 **Ace Of Spies (IRE)**[35] 673 6-8-8 **72** KirstyMilczarek 2 57
(Conor Dore) *a bhd: nvr gng pce to threaten* **33/1**

2116 9 3/4 **Elhamri**[42] 572 7-8-12 **76** HayleyTurner 4 59
(Conor Dore) *prom: rdn over 1f out: sn wknd* **16/1**

135- 10 1/2 **Westwood**[155] 7180 6-9-3 **81** NeilCallan 8 62
(Derek Haydn Jones) *led: rdn and hdd over 1f out: wknd ins fnl f* **14/1**

103- **11** *8* **Comptonspirit**[206] 5809 7-8-9 **73** ow2 J-PGuillambert 1 29
(Brian Baugh) *a bhd* **20/1**

1m 14.33s (-0.67) **Going Correction** +0.05s/f (Slow) **11** Ran SP% **118.4**
Speed ratings (Par 105): **106,105,103,102,101 98,98,95,94,94 83**
toteswingers: 1&2 £7.80, 1&3 £22.10, 2&3 £16.40. CSF £49.04 CT £354.61 TOTE £4.50: £1.20, £1.80, £3.80; EX 60.70.
Owner Mrs F Denniff **Bred** A S Denniff **Trained** Hambleton, N Yorks

FOCUS
The feature race on the card and a decent, competitive sprint for the money, with a stone covering the field on official ratings. It was a race of changing fortunes. The winner is rated as getting close to his old form, with the runner-up better than ever.

1068 THE BLACK COUNTRY'S ONLY RACETRACK H'CAP 1m 141y(P)
8:45 (8:45) (Class 6) (0-52,52) 4-Y-0+ **£1,569** (£347; £347) **Stalls** Low

Form RPR

0-23 **1** **Lilli Palmer (IRE)**[22] 807 4-8-10 **46** oh1 MartinLane 7 62
(Mike Murphy) *hld up: hdwy 2f out: led over 1f out: edgd lft whn drawing clr ins fnl f: readily* **9/2**[2]

630- **2** *6* **Forzarzi (IRE)**[206] 5821 7-8-11 **50** JamesSullivan(3) 9 52
(Hugh McWilliams) *racd keenly in midfield: hdwy 4f out: rdn and chalng over 1f out: nt pce of wnr ins fnl f but kpt on whn duelling for 2nd* **25/1**

2320 **2** *dht* **Holyfield Warrior (IRE)**[13] 899 7-8-13 **52** KierenFox(3) 10 54
(Ralph Smith) *hld up: hdwy on inner 2f out: rdn over 1f out: kpt on whn chalng for 2nd ins fnl f: no ch w wnr* **7/1**[3]

4066 **4** *½* **Crocodile Bay (IRE)**[13] 896 8-8-13 **49** (b) PaulHanagan 8 50
(Richard Guest) *racd keenly: a.p: led 2f out: rdn and hdd over 1f out: one pce ins fnl f* **7/1**[3]

-035 **5** *nk* **Moment Of Clarity**[13] 895 9-8-10 **46** oh1 (p) ChrisCatlin 2 46
(Shaun Harris) *midfield: rdn over 1f out: styd on same pce ins fnl f* **12/1**

0-25 **6** *1¾* **Kathleen Kennet**[45] 544 11-8-12 **48** LiamKeniry 4 44
(Jonathan Geake) *midfield: rdn and outpcd wl over 1f out: no imp* **9/1**

4210 **7** *hd* **On The Cusp (IRE)**[22] 807 4-8-10 **49** (p) RobertLButler(3) 3 45
(Richard Guest) *sn led: rdn and hdd 2f out: wknd over 1f out* **17/2**

-544 **8** *nk* **Empress Leizu (IRE)**[13] 895 4-9-2 **52** NeilCallan 1 47
(Tony Carroll) *led early: remained handy: rdn 2f out: n.m.r and eased briefly wl over 1f out: pushed along appr fnl f: no imp after* **2/1**[1]

0-0 **9** *1¾* **Major Eradicator (USA)**[21] 820 4-8-7 **50** KatiaScallan(7) 6 41
(Alastair Lidderdale) *a bhd* **14/1**

000- **10** *½* **Machinate (USA)**[308] 2477 9-8-9 **48** RossAtkinson(3) 5 38
(Mark Brisbourne) *a bhd* **28/1**

6350 **11** *12* **King Of Connacht**[13] 895 8-9-2 **52** (v) LukeMorris 11 14
(Mark Wellings) *prom on outer: rdn and ev ch 2f out: wknd over 1f out* **16/1**

1m 50.78s (0.28) **Going Correction** +0.05s/f (Slow) **11** Ran SP% **124.6**
Speed ratings (Par 101): **100,94,94,94,93 92,92,91,90,89 79**toteswingers: 1& Hollyfield Warrior £2.40, 1& Forzazi £17.20, HW & F £29.20. WIN: £7.10, PLACES: £2.40, HW £4.40, F £11.80. CSF: LP & HW £19.29, LP & F £58.33. EXACTA: LP & HW £16.80, LP & F £67.00, TRICAST: LP, HW & F £366.98, LP, F & HW £400.69. CT £0.27 TOTE £Owner: £M Murphy, £Bred, £Mrs Vanessa Hutch, £TrainedWestoning, Beds.

FOCUS
This selling-grade handicap was run at a reasonable gallop but several of the runners did not have much room to operate on the home turn. In the end though the winner came from the back. She turned around Kempton running with the third but the form is taken at face value.
Empress Leizu(IRE) Official explanation: jockey said gelding was denied a clear run
T/Plt: £44.70 to a £1 stake. Pool:£83,623.23 - 1,365.57 winning tickets T/Qpdt: £13.30 to a £1 stake. Pool:£9,285.71 - 513.36 winning tickets DO

1069 - 1070a (Foreign Racing) - See Raceform Interactive

MUSSELBURGH (R-H)
Friday, April 1

OFFICIAL GOING: Good to soft (good in places on round course; 5.9)
Wind: Strong, against Weather: Bright and breezy

1071 FASTER GREENER CENTRAL TAXIS EBF MAIDEN STKS 5f
2:20 (2:24) (Class 5) 2-Y-0 **£3,238** (£963; £481; £240) **Stalls** High

Form RPR

1 **Hamza (IRE)** 2-9-3 0 PhillipMakin 6 85+
(Kevin Ryan) *mde virtually all: shkn up to go clr appr fnl f: kpt on strly: readily* **4/1**[3]

2 *3¼* **Stonefield Flyer** 2-9-0 0 MichaelO'Connell(3) 7 72+
(Keith Dalgleish) *green and unruly in preliminaries: dwlt: sn in tch: effrt and hung rt over 1f out: hdwy to chse (clr) wnr ins fnl f: no imp* **14/1**

3 *4* **Devlin** 2-9-3 0 PaulHanagan 8 56+
(Richard Fahey) *sn pushed along in tch: edgd rt and outpcd 2f out: styd on ins fnl f: nt rch first two* **11/4**[1]

4 *1¼* **Idler (IRE)** 2-9-3 0 JoeFanning 1 51+
(Mark Johnston) *wnt rt s: sn cl up on outside: rdn and rn green over 1f out: btn ins fnl f: bttr for r* **7/2**[2]

5 *1½* **Profile Star (IRE)** 2-9-3 0 LeeNewman 5 45
(David Barron) *disp ld to wl over 1f out: sn outpcd: wknd ins fnl f* **16/1**

6 *1½* **Made In The Shade** 2-8-9 0 PaulPickard(3) 3 34
(Paul Midgley) *sn rn green and outpcd: sme late hdwy: nvr on terms* **50/1**

7 *¾* **Art Dzeko** 2-9-3 0 DavidAllan 2 36
(Tim Easterby) *trckd ldrs: rdn along 1/2-way: outpcd whn carried sltly rt over 1f out: sn btn* **9/1**

8 *4* **Pontius Pilate (IRE)** 2-9-3 0 PaulMulrennan 4 20
(Bryan Smart) *missed break: drvn along and a detached* **4/1**[3]

62.78 secs (2.38) **Going Correction** +0.225s/f (Good) **8** Ran SP% **113.4**
Speed ratings (Par 92): **89,83,77,75,73 70,69,63**
toteswingers:1&2 £7.20, 2&3 £3.70, 1&3 £3.70 CSF £55.79 TOTE £5.90: £1.90, £3.20, £1.20; EX 68.40 Trifecta £382.50 Pool: £604.85 - 1.17 winning units..
Owner Mubarak Al Naimi **Bred** Castlemartin Stud And Skymarc Farm **Trained** Hambleton, N Yorks

FOCUS
The winning rider in the first reported that the ground was "just the soft side of good." The time was over four seconds slower than the standard, but they were racing into quite a stiff headwind. Winners should emerge from this race, which was probably a decent early-season maiden.

NOTEBOOK
Hamza(IRE) cost £25,000 and is out of a half-sister to smart sprinter Dandy Man. From the first crop of a sire who did so well for the Ryan yard, he knew his job and made just about all the running, pulling clear to win in nice style. An April foal and one of the youngest in the line-up, he will be given time to strengthen up before he's seen out again. More should be heard of him. (op 7-1)
Stonefield Flyer played up beforehand, probably unsettled by the blustery conditions, and took a lot of persuading to go down to the start. He ran surprisingly well in the circumstances, staying on for second after wandering and running decidedly green. This experience will have done him good. (op 10-1 tchd 16-1)
Devlin isn't the biggest but looked fit. Representing a yard which got off the mark with its powerful team of juveniles earlier in the week, he was a little slow to break from the inside stall and took time to get the hang of things, but came through well late on to secure third. A maiden should soon be found for him. (op 2-1 tchd 3-1)
Idler(IRE), out of a very smart sprinter in Australia, is a well-grown colt who was relaxed in the preliminaries. Rather trapped wide after swerving to his right from the outside stall, he recovered to chase the leaders but could only stick on at the same pace in the final furlong. His trainer's juveniles often improve for a run. (tchd 5-2)
Profile Star(IRE), a relatively cheap buy, is closely related to last season's Listed-placed juvenile sprinter Moonlit Garden. A sturdy sort, he showed bright pace to match strides with the winner before fading. (op 22-1)
Made In The Shade, whose dam won at 5-7f, may need more time. (op 66-1)
Art Dzeko, a well-grown colt, out of a half-sister to Nell Gwyn winner Reunion, should certainly improve for the run. (op 8-1 tchd 6-1)
Pontius Pilate(IRE), who had yet to come in his coat, is a half-brother to Mill Reef Stakes winner Cool Creek and was the most expensive purchase in this field at 50,000gns. After being walked most of the way to post, he fell out of the stalls and trailed throughout. (op 11-2)

1072 BDO LLP CLASSIFIED (S) STKS 1m 4f 100y
2:50 (2:50) (Class 6) 4-Y-0+ **£1,619** (£481; £240; £120) **Stalls** Low

Form RPR

20-2 **1** **Red Kestrel (USA)**[7] 965 6-8-13 69 PhillipMakin 3 71+
(Kevin Ryan) *mde all at stdy gallop: shkn up briefly and qcknd clr 2f out: easily* **5/4**[1]

416- **2** *4½* **Grand Diamond (IRE)**[9] 5852 7-8-13 69 (p) KierenFallon 6 61
(Jim Goldie) *t.k.h: chsd ldrs: effrt and wnt 2nd over 2f out: kpt on: no imp* **7/4**[2]

2144 **3** *3¼* **Eton Fable (IRE)**[10] 939 6-9-4 64 (p) PatrickMathers 1 61
(Colin Teague) *t.k.h: pressed wnr: rdn over 3f out: lost 2nd over 2f out: n.d after* **14/1**

230- **4** *4½* **Royal Straight**[153] 7228 6-8-13 69 PaulHanagan 5 52
(Linda Perratt) *stdd last but in tch: effrt on outside 3f out: sn no imp: btn over 1f out* **4/1**[3]

2m 50.89s (8.89) **Going Correction** +0.225s/f (Good)
WFA 4 from 6yo+ 1lb **4** Ran SP% **107.5**
Speed ratings (Par 101): **79,76,73,70**
toteswinger: 1&2 £1.70. CSF £3.68 TOTE £2.20; EX 4.10.The winner was bought in for 12,500gns.
Owner Hambleton Racing Ltd XII **Bred** Darley **Trained** Hambleton, N Yorks

FOCUS
This was quite a tight seller on official figures. The winner had an easy lead and it's doubtful if he had to improve on his recent AW form. The third looks the best guide.

1073 CORE OIL AND GAS LTD H'CAP 5f
3:20 (3:20) (Class 4) (0-80,79) 4-Y-0+ **£3,885** (£1,156; £577; £288) **Stalls** High

Form RPR

522- **1** **Nadeen (IRE)**[129] 7539 4-9-6 **78** KierenFallon 14 89
(Michael Smith) *hld up: pushed along and hdwy 2f out: rdn to ld ins fnl f: kpt on strly* **11/2**[1]

53-0 **2** *½* **Verinco**[66] 294 5-8-10 **73** (v) AdamCarter(5) 10 82
(Bryan Smart) *led: rdn 2f out: hdd ins fnl f: kpt on u.p* **6/1**[2]

000- **3** *1½* **Oldjoesaid**[175] 6723 7-9-7 **79** PhillipMakin 5 83
(Kevin Ryan) *trckd ldrs: effrt and swtchd lft over 1f out: sn drvn: kpt on u.p fnl f* **13/2**[3]

400- **4** *3¾* **Mon Brav**[165] 6985 4-9-3 **75** (v) DavidNolan 4 65
(Declan Carroll) *in tch: effrt and rdn 2f out: kpt on same pce fnl f* **10/1**

0252 **5** *shd* **Northern Dare (IRE)**[25] 786 7-9-3 **75** (b) PaulHanagan 8 65
(Richard Fahey) *towards rr: drvn 1/2-way: hdwy over 1f out: kpt on fnl f: nvr rchd ldrs* **12/1**

66-0 **6** *1* **Chosen One (IRE)**[7] 970 6-8-9 **70** JamesSullivan(3) 9 56
(Ruth Carr) *trckd ldrs: effrt and drvn over 1f out: wknd ins fnl f* **14/1**

4510 **7** *1* **Sharp Shoes**[29] 746 4-8-9 **67** (p) SilvestreDeSousa 6 50
(Ann Duffield) *towards rr: drvn 1/2-way: no imp fr over 1f out* **18/1**

030- **8** *hd* **Ignatieff (IRE)**[222] 5335 4-9-0 **79** KristinStubbs(7) 12 61
(Linda Stubbs) *w ldrs tl rdn and wknd over 1f out* **18/1**

313 **9** *hd* **Highland Warrior**[156] 7175 12-8-9 **70** PaulPickard(3) 1 51
(Paul Midgley) *dwlt and swtchd centre s: hld up: rdn and sme hdwy over 1f out: nvr rchd ldrs* **10/1**

043- **10** *¾* **Berbice (IRE)**[153] 7225 6-8-7 **65** DavidAllan 7 43
(Linda Perratt) *dwlt: hld up: effrt and rdn 2f out: nt pce to chal* **14/1**

000- **11** *2* **Mandurah (IRE)**[200] 6031 7-8-9 **67** AdrianNicholls 13 38
(David Nicholls) *midfield on ins: effrt and pushed along 1/2-way: wknd over 1f out* **8/1**

000- **12** *1¼* **Argentine (IRE)**[141] 7405 7-8-6 **64** LeeNewman 3 31
(George Foster) *towards rr: effrt on outside 1/2-way: wknd over 1f out* **50/1**

00- **13** *8* **Go Go Green (IRE)**[233] 4942 5-9-7 **79** JamieSpencer 11 17
(Jim Goldie) *dwlt: bhd: rdn and veered sharply rt 1/2-way: sn btn* **9/1**

015- **14** *5* **Lesley's Choice**[156] 7175 5-9-1 **73** (v) PaulMulrennan 2 —
(Linda Perratt) *in tch on outside: drvn and outpcd 1/2-way: wknd wl over 1f out* **16/1**

60.78 secs (0.38) **Going Correction** +0.225s/f (Good) **14** Ran SP% **121.7**
Speed ratings (Par 105): **105,104,101,95,95 94,92,92,91,90 87,85,72,64**
toteswingers: 1&2 £8.50, 1&3 £3.50, 2&3 £12.50. CSF £37.72 CT £230.47 TOTE £4.90: £1.50, £2.30, £2.90; EX 70.00 Trifecta £300.80 Pool: £495.99 - 1.22 winning units..
Owner Miss Rebecca Smith **Bred** Rabbah Bloodstock Limited **Trained** Kirkheaton, Northumberland

FOCUS
An ordinary sprint handicap but a fair race for the grade. The first three came clear and the form should be sound enough. the winner was up a length on his AW form.

1074 BOOGIE IN THE MORNING H'CAP 7f 30y
3:50 (3:50) (Class 5) (0-70,70) 3-Y-0 **£2,331** (£693; £346; £173) **Stalls** Low

Form RPR

022- **1** **Las Verglas Star (IRE)**[149] 7296 3-9-7 **70** PaulHanagan 9 82
(Richard Fahey) *prom: smooth hdwy to ld over 1f out: edgd rt and rdn clr fnl f* **6/1**[3]

2313 **2** *5* **Eilean Mor**[3] 1031 3-8-12 **66** AdamCarter(5) 3 64
(Bryan Smart) *t.k.h: mde most tl edgd lft and hdd over 1f out: kpt on same pce fnl f* **8/1**

254- **3** *¾* **Dotty Darroch**[153] 7224 3-8-7 **56** LeeNewman 5 52
(Robin Bastiman) *pressed ldr: effrt and ev ch over 2f out to 1f out: kpt on same pce ins fnl f* **40/1**

341- **4** *½* **Delaney's Dream**[150] 7279 3-9-5 **68** AdrianNicholls 1 63
(David Nicholls) *t.k.h: trckd ldrs: rdn and outpcd 2f out: edgd lft and kpt on ins fnl f* **5/4**[1]

000- **5** 1 3/4 **Byron Bear (IRE)**[214] 5595 3-8-2 **54** ow3 .... PaulPickard(3) 7 47+
(Paul Midgley) *s.i.s: bhd: pushed along 3f out: hdwy on outside over 1f out: edgd rt and kpt on fnl f: nrst fin* **66/1**

041- **6** 2 1/2 **Chilledtothebone**[186] 6425 3-9-7 **70** ....(v) KierenFallon 4 53
(Linda Stubbs) *sn pushed along in midfield: rdn and outpcd 3f out: no imp fnl 2f* **9/1**

406- **7** 3/4 **Peppercorn Rent (IRE)**[161] 7050 3-8-2 **51** ....(e) DuranFentiman 6 32
(Tim Easterby) *towards rr: drvn and outpcd 1/2-way: nvr rchd ldrs* **33/1**

066- **8** nk **Monel**[219] 5404 3-8-5 **54** .... SilvestreDeSousa 8 34
(Jim Goldie) *t.k.h: hld up ins: nt clr run bnd 4f out: rdn and edgd rt over 2f out: nvr rchd ldrs* **10/1**

306- **9** 2 1/4 **Mr Khan**[305] 2577 3-8-6 **55** .... JoeFanning 11 29
(Linda Perratt) *plld hrd in midfield: pushed along over 2f out: wknd over 1f out* **25/1**

032- **10** 1 3/4 **Good Boy Jackson**[184] 6457 3-9-4 **67** .... PhillipMakin 10 37
(Kevin Ryan) *dwlt: hld up towards rr on outside: struggling over 2f out: sn btn* **11/2**[2]

1m 31.63s (2.63) **Going Correction** +0.225s/f (Good) **10** Ran SP% **115.0**
Speed ratings (Par 98): **93,87,86,85,83 81,80,79,77,75**
toteswingers: 1&2 £5.70, 1&3 £19.20, 2&3 £22.80. CSF £50.46 CT £1779.60 TOTE £5.50: £2.80, £2.70, £8.10; EX 38.90 Trifecta £131.80 Pool: £632.55 - 3.55 winning units..
Owner CBWS Partnership **Bred** Brendan Holland And P Connell **Trained** Musley Bank, N Yorks

FOCUS
Few got into this modest handicap, and the first four home were always prominent. There is a slight doubt aboyt taking the form literally, but it has been rated around the second and third.
Monel Official explanation: jockey said gelding ran too free

1075 PETER DOWELL IS ALMOST 50 H'CAP 1m
4:20 (4:20) (Class 4) (0-85,85) 4-Y-O+ **£3,885** (£1,156; £577; £288) **Stalls** Low

Form RPR

4051 **1** **Snow Bay**[41] 617 5-9-4 **82** .... AdrianNicholls 2 93
(David Nicholls) *t.k.h: mde all: rdn over 2f out: edgd lft and styd on strly ins fnl f* **12/1**

462- **2** 2 1/2 **Guest Book (IRE)**[181] 6556 4-9-7 **85** .... JoeFanning 4 90
(Mark Johnston) *pressed wnr: rdn 2f out: edgd rt 1f out: kpt on towards fin: nt gng pce of wnr* **5/4**[1]

-243 **3** hd **Elijah Pepper (USA)**[11] 932 6-8-12 **76** .... LeeNewman 3 80
(David Barron) *dwlt: sn prom on ins: effrt over 2f out: kpt on same pce ins fnl f* **8/1**

000- **4** 4 1/2 **Northern Fling**[153] 7227 7-9-6 **84** .... KierenFallon 8 78
(Jim Goldie) *hld up on ins: effrt and rdn over 3f out: kpt on ins fnl f: nvr able to chal* **9/1**

2-53 **5** 3/4 **Danderek**[35] 694 5-9-1 **79** .... PaulHanagan 7 71
(Richard Fahey) *cl up on outside: rdn and outpcd over 2f out: edgd rt and no imp ins fnl f* **4/1**[2]

13-1 **6** 2 1/4 **Prince Apollo**[23] 814 6-8-11 **75** ....(t) NeilCallan 5 62
(Gerard Butler) *t.k.h: in tch: rdn and edgd lft 2f out: edgd rt and wknd ent fnl f* **5/1**[3]

43-5 **7** 3 1/2 **Euston Square**[37] 648 5-8-9 **73** .... PaulMulrennan 1 52
(Alistair Whillans) *missed break: bhd: drvn along over 3f out: sn btn* **33/1**

1m 41.88s (0.68) **Going Correction** +0.225s/f (Good) **7** Ran SP% **112.9**
Speed ratings (Par 105): **105,102,102,97,97 94,91**
toteswingers: 1&2 £3.40, 1&3 £6.70, 2&3 £2.60 CSF £26.92 CT £131.94 TOTE £12.20: £5.20, £1.90; EX 39.40 Trifecta £92.50 Pool: £655.25 - 5.24 winning units..
Owner Pinnacle Bahamian Bounty Partnership **Bred** West Dereham Abbey Stud **Trained** Sessay, N Yorks

FOCUS
Ordinary handicap form. The all-the-way winner is only rated in line with the best view of his early form last year.
Euston Square Official explanation: jockey said gelding was slowly away

1076 MATT ON-COURSE BOOKMAKER TAKES FORECAST BETS MAIDEN STKS 1m 1f
4:50 (4:50) (Class 5) 3-Y-O+ **£1,942** (£578; £288; £144) **Stalls** Low

Form RPR

222- **1** **Calypso Magic (IRE)**[181] 6566 3-8-11 76 .... PaulHanagan 1 84+
(Howard Johnson) *mde all: rdn and qcknd clr over 1f out: unchal* **7/2**[2]

2 4 1/2 **Rainy Champion (USA)** 3-8-11 0 .... NeilCallan 2 72
(Gerard Butler) *dwlt: sn trcking ldrs: rdn and outpcd over 2f out: rallied to chse (clr) wnr ins fnl f: no imp* **7/1**

543- **3** 1 1/4 **Dressing Room (USA)**[183] 6514 3-8-11 73 .... KierenFallon 7 69
(Mark Johnston) *prom: rdn after 3f: rallied and edgd lft over 2f out: edgd rt and chsd (clr) wnr over 1f out: no imp and lost 2nd ins fnl f* **5/6**[1]

4 12 **Dancing Gizmo**[44] 6-9-11 0 .... MichaelO'Connell(3) 4 44
(Alistair Whillans) *t.k.h: hld up in tch: effrt and hung lft over 2f out: sn outpcd: edgd rt and btn over 1f out* **66/1**

56-2 **5** 7 **See The Smile (USA)**[15] 878 3-8-11 72 .... JamieSpencer 3 36
(Gay Kelleway) *trckd wnr: rdn and edgd lft over 2f out: wknd over 1f out: eased whn no ch last 100yds* **9/2**[3]

6 2 **Abernethy (IRE)** 3-8-11 0 .... PaulMulrennan 5 25
(Linda Perratt) *s.i.s: hld up: rdn 3f out: sn btn* **50/1**

7 21 **Serenata Mia** 4-9-9 0 .... SilvestreDeSousa 6 —
(Michael Smith) *plld hrd: in tch: green and outpcd after 3f: sn struggling: t.o* **50/1**

1m 56.09s (2.19) **Going Correction** +0.225s/f (Good)
WFA 3 from 4yo+ 17lb **7** Ran SP% **112.9**
Speed ratings (Par 103): **99,95,93,83,77 75,56**
tteswingers: 1&2 £2.50, 2&3 £1.70, 1&3 not won. CSF £26.23 TOTE £3.70: £1.10, £6.00; EX 15.90.
Owner Transcend Bloodstock LLP **Bred** J Quigley **Trained** Billy Row, Co Durham

FOCUS
A modest maiden which saw a wide-margin winner, with the first three coming well clear. The race has been rated around the winner's 2yo form.

1077 LADBROKES & WILLIAM HILL SUPPORTING FREE RACEDAY APPRENTICE H'CAP 1m
5:20 (5:20) (Class 6) (0-60,60) 4-Y-O+ **£1,619** (£481; £240; £120) **Stalls** Low

Form RPR

530- **1** **Hits Only Jude (IRE)**[141] 7403 8-9-0 **56** ....(v) NeilFarley(3) 4 67
(Declan Carroll) *midfield on ins: effrt over 2f out: led ins fnl f: hld on wl* **7/1**

24-5 **2** nk **Ravi River (IRE)**[49] 286 7-9-2 **60** .... JacobButterfield(5) 8 70
(Brian Ellison) *prom: effrt over 2f out: edgd rt and led briefly 1f out: kpt on: jst hld* **12/1**

60-0 **3** 4 1/2 **Amno Dancer (IRE)**[36] 674 4-9-2 **58** .... LMcNiff(3) 12 58
(David Barron) *trckd ldrs: led over 2f out tl ins fnl f: edgd lft and sn no ex* **12/1**

455- **4** 1/2 **Ra Junior (USA)**[147] 7327 5-9-2 **60** .... ShaneBKelly(5) 10 59
(Paul Midgley) *hld up: hdwy over 2f out: kpt on fnl f: nvr able to chal* **6/1**[3]

550- **5** 1 3/4 **Whaston (IRE)**[60] 7958 6-8-7 **46** oh1 ....(vt) LeeTopliss 2 41
(Pauline Robson) *led: rdn and hdd over 2f out: sn outpcd: kpt on same pce ins fnl f* **7/1**

553- **6** 3/4 **Miss Blink**[157] 7153 4-8-4 **48** .... GeorgeChaloner(5) 7 41+
(Robin Bastiman) *s.i.s: sn wl bhd: hdwy on outside over 2f out: kpt on ins fnl f: nvr able to chal* **9/1**

6-32 **7** 3 3/4 **Verluga (IRE)**[40] 346 4-9-3 **56** .... LanceBetts 5 40
(Tim Easterby) *hld up towards rr: rdn over 2f out: sn no imp* **11/2**[2]

000- **8** 3/4 **Classic Descent**[213] 5641 6-9-2 **55** ....(t) SeanLevey 9 38
(Ruth Carr) *hld up towards rr: rdn over 2f out: nvr able to chal* **12/1**

532- **9** 2 1/4 **My One Weakness (IRE)**[116] 7730 4-9-2 **55** .... DaleSwift 6 33
(Brian Ellison) *hld up on outside: struggling over 2f out: sn btn* **3/1**[1]

3-00 **10** 3 1/2 **Hold On Tiger (IRE)**[30] 734 4-8-3 **49** .... ShirleyTeasdale(7) 14 18
(Keith Dalgleish) *w ldr: drvn over 3f out: edgd rt and wknd fr 2f out* **50/1**

503- **11** 3 1/4 **Bahamian Kid**[118] 7701 6-9-4 **60** ....(v) JulieBurke(3) 3 22
(George Foster) *hld up: rdn over 2f out: nvr on terms* **14/1**

000- **12** 1 1/2 **Shunkawakhan (IRE)**[183] 6495 8-8-3 **47** ow1 ...... DavidSimmonson(5) 1 —
(Linda Perratt) *prom tl rdn and wknd over 2f out* **28/1**

1m 43.88s (2.68) **Going Correction** +0.225s/f (Good) **12** Ran SP% **124.8**
Speed ratings (Par 101): **95,94,90,89,87 87,83,82,80,76 73,72**
toteswingers:1&2 £17.70, 2&3 £29.90, 1&3 £18.60 CSF £93.10 CT £1030.67 TOTE £6.90: £2.00, £4.90, £4.90; EX 108.20 Trifecta £365.70 Part won. Pool of £494.25 - 0.83 winning units..
Owner Dreams **Bred** Swordlestown Stud **Trained** Sledmere, E Yorks
■ Stewards' Enquiry : Neil Farley four-day ban: used whip with excessive frequency without giving gelding time to respond (Apr 15,16,18)
Shirley Teasdale two-day ban: careless riding (Apr 15-16)
L McNiff three-day ban: careless riding (Apr 15,16,18)

FOCUS
A low-grade handicap for apprentices, run at a solid pace. The first two were clear but the form is not rated too positively.
T/Plt: £111.30 to a £1 stake. Pool of £68,530.56 - 449.14 winning tickets. T/Qpdt: £28.20 to a £1 stake. Pool of £5,005.20 - 131.10 winning tickets. RY

1062 WOLVERHAMPTON (A.W) (L-H)
Friday, April 1

OFFICIAL GOING: Standard
Wind: Fresh behind Weather: Overcast

1078 GEOFFREY EVANS 84TH BIRTHDAY H'CAP 5f 216y(P)
5:40 (5:40) (Class 6) (0-60,61) 3-Y-O **£1,706** (£503; £252) **Stalls** Low

Form RPR

000- **1** **Paradise Place**[116] 7723 3-8-13 **50** .... TomQueally 9 58
(Robert Cowell) *hld up: hdwy u.p over 2f out: hung lft ins fnl f: styd on to ld nr fin* **25/1**

2531 **2** shd **Rhal (IRE)**[7] 964 3-9-7 **61** 6ex .... GaryBartley(3) 2 69
(Bryan Smart) *chsd ldr: led over 4f out: rdn ins fnl f: edgd rt and hdd nr fin* **4/5**[1]

5524 **3** 3 1/4 **Scommettitrice (IRE)**[7] 964 3-9-2 **53** ....(b) TomMcLaughlin 4 51
(Ronald Harris) *chsd ldrs: rdn and hung lft over 1f out: styd on same pce ins fnl f* **15/2**[3]

3543 **4** 3/4 **William Wainwright (IRE)**[7] 964 3-8-7 **47** ....(v) JohnFahy(3) 5 42
(Ann Duffield) *led: hdd over 4f out: chsd ldr: rdn over 1f out: styd on same pce ins fnl f* **11/2**[2]

500 **5** 2 **Ability Girl**[23] 811 3-9-4 **55** .... JackMitchell 7 44
(Chris Wall) *hld up: rdn over 2f out: hung lft over 1f out: styd on ins fnl f: nvr nrr* **14/1**

006- **6** 1/2 **Rattleyurjewellery**[119] 7681 3-8-3 **45** .... DeclanCannon(5) 6 32
(David Brown) *in tch: rdn over 2f out: styd on same pce appr fnl f* **12/1**

2000 **7** 8 **Ajaafa**[15] 875 3-9-4 **55** ....(p) NeilChalmers 3 17
(Michael Appleby) *chsd ldrs: rdn over 3f out: n.m.r and wknd over 2f out* **50/1**

5066 **8** 6 **Two Feet Of Snow (IRE)**[7] 967 3-9-2 **53** .... PJMcDonald 1 —
(Ian McInnes) *s.s: outpcd* **17/2**

1m 15.38s (0.38) **Going Correction** +0.10s/f (Slow) **8** Ran SP% **113.4**
Speed ratings (Par 96): **101,100,96,95,92 92,81,73**
toteswingers:1&2 £8.60, 2&3 £2.20, 1&3 £13.70 CSF £45.27 CT £184.57 TOTE £31.00: £5.40, £1.10, £1.40; EX 74.30.
Owner Jim Furlong **Bred** The Lavington Stud **Trained** Six Mile Bottom, Cambs

FOCUS
The time was 0.18 seconds quicker than the following Class 4 handicap but that comparison is misleading as they went steady in the later contest. This was just a moderate 3-y-o sprint, but the front two both look ahead of their current marks. The favourite gave the third and fourth a bigger beating than over C&D latest.
Paradise Place ◆ Official explanation: trainer's rep said, regarding apparent improvement in form, that the filly appeared to have matured over the winter and may have been suited by the shorter trip of 6f.

1079 BETFAIR LAMBOURN OPEN DAY ON 22ND APRIL H'CAP 5f 216y(P)
6:10 (6:10) (Class 4) (0-85,83) 3-Y-O **£3,238** (£963; £481; £240) **Stalls** Low

Form RPR

31-1 **1** **Acclamazing (IRE)**[70] 254 3-9-6 **82** ....(t) AdamKirby 3 90+
(Marco Botti) *dwlt: sn trcking ldrs: rdn to ld ins fnl f: r.o wl: comf* **8/15**[1]

113- **2** 1 **Sadafiya**[185] 6445 3-9-7 **83** .... RichardHills 2 87
(Ed Dunlop) *led 1f: chsd ldr tl led over 1f out: rdn: hung lft and hdd ins fnl f: styd on same pce* **2/1**[2]

1-40 **3** 3 1/4 **Dunmore Boy (IRE)**[20] 845 3-8-7 **69** oh4 ....(p) BarryMcHugh 1 63
(Richard Fahey) *w ldr tl led at stdy pce 5f out: qcknd over 2f out: rdn and hdd over 1f out: no ex ins fnl f* **18/1**[3]

315- **4** nse **Tro Nesa (IRE)**[150] 7280 3-9-1 **77** .... TomQueally 5 70
(Ann Duffield) *hld up: hdwy over 1f out: sn rdn: no ex ins fnl f* **20/1**

1m 15.56s (0.56) **Going Correction** +0.10s/f (Slow) **4** Ran SP% **108.6**
Speed ratings (Par 100): **100,98,94,94**
CSF £1.85 TOTE £1.50; EX 1.90.
Owner Giuliano Manfredini **Bred** Michael And John Fahy **Trained** Newmarket, Suffolk

FOCUS
A steady early pace resulted in final a time 0.18 seconds slower than the earlier Class 6 handicap, also for 3-y-os. However, hand times show the field covered the closing 2f around three seconds faster than the earlier contest - something close to a swift 22.75 seconds. The form is rated through the runner-up and the third is a slight doubt.

1080 ENJOY THE PARTY PACK GROUP OFFER H'CAP 1m 5f 194y(P)
6:40 (6:40) (Class 6) (0-65,64) 4-Y-O+ **£1,706** (£503; £252) **Stalls** Low

Form RPR
-061 **1** **War Of The Roses (IRE)**[13] 917 8-9-8 **61**.................... GeorgeBaker 7 69
(Roy Brotherton) *hld up: hdwy over 3f out: chsd ldr 2f out: rdn to ld 1f out: jst hld on* **11/2[3]**
5130 **2** *nk* **Money Money Money**[30] 733 5-9-4 **57**..................(b) JamesMillman 2 64
(Rod Millman) *chsd ldr tl led over 3f out: rdn and hdd over 2f out: rallied ins fnl f: r.o* **7/1**
-054 **3** *1 ½* **Vertueux (FR)**[21] 768 6-9-2 **55**.................................. LukeMorris 1 60
(Tony Carroll) *chsd ldrs: pushed along 4f out: nt clr run and lost pl over 2f out: rallied over 1f out: r.o* **11/2[3]**
2613 **4** *½* **Little Richard (IRE)**[13] 911 12-8-13 **51** ow1.................(p) AdamKirby 5 56
(Mark Wellings) *chsd ldrs: rdn over 2f out: styd on* **11/4[1]**
-522 **5** *3 ¼* **Leyte Gulf (USA)**[30] 733 8-9-10 **64**.................................. DaneO'Neill 3 63
(Chris Bealby) *dwlt: sn prom: lost pl over 3f out: rdn over 2f out: hdwy over 1f out: hung lft and no ex ins fnl f* **3/1[2]**
6400 **6** *1 ¾* **Swords**[13] 911 9-8-1 **45**..(v[1]) KieranO'Neill[(5)] 4 42
(Ray Peacock) *hld up: plld hrd: hdwy over 2f out: rdn over 1f out: no ex* **50/1**
5223 **7** *8* **Light The City (IRE)**[17] 859 4-8-9 **51**............................ PJMcDonald 6 37
(Ruth Carr) *led: rdn and hdd over 3f out: wknd over 1f out* **7/1**
3m 6.66s (0.66) **Going Correction** +0.10s/f (Slow)
WFA 4 from 5yo+ 3lb **7** Ran SP% **109.4**
Speed ratings (Par 101): **102,101,100,100,98 97,93**
toteswingers:1&2 £6.60, 2&3 £6.20, 1&3 £6.00 CSF £38.90 TOTE £6.30: £3.40, £2.10; EX 33.00.
Owner Millend Racing Club **Bred** Mrs Jane Bailey **Trained** Elmley Castle, Worcs
FOCUS
A moderate contest and a final time over six seconds above standard suggests they didn't go that quick. The winner built slightly on his recent win.

1081 FOLLOW @ATTHERACES ON TWITTER CLAIMING STKS 1m 1f 103y(P)
7:10 (7:10) (Class 5) 4-Y-O+ **£1,942** (£578; £288; £144) **Stalls** Low

Form RPR
-112 **1** **Majuro (IRE)**[25] 790 7-9-2 **85**...(t) JamesDoyle 1 86+
(Frank Sheridan) *mde all: clr fnl 2f: easily* **30/100[1]**
-062 **2** *8* **Plush**[7] 968 8-8-6 **72**.. HayleyTurner 4 57
(Shaun Lycett) *s.i.s: hld up: rdn over 2f out: sn outpcd: hung lft over 1f out: wnt 2nd ins fnl f: nvr any ch w wnr* **10/1[3]**
3562 **3** *1 ¾* **Yossi (IRE)**[1] 1063 7-8-11 **51**.......................................(be) FrannyNorton 3 58
(Richard Guest) *chsd wnr: rdn over 2f out: hung lft and wknd over 1f out: lost 2nd ins fnl f* **33/1**
-003 **4** *2* **The Which Doctor**[25] 790 6-8-10 **84**......................(p) RobertLButler[(3)] 2 56
(Richard Guest) *chsd ldrs: wnt 2nd briefly 3f out: sn rdn: wknd wl over 1f out* **9/2[2]**
2m 0.92s (-0.78) **Going Correction** +0.10s/f (Slow) **4** Ran SP% **107.1**
Speed ratings (Par 103): **107,99,98,96**
.Majuro was claimed by J Balding £13,000.\n\x\x
Owner Dr D F Moretti **Bred** Tally-Ho Stud **Trained** Wolverhampton, W Midlands
FOCUS
An uncompetitive claimer, and easy for the winner with his form rivals disappointing.
Yossi(IRE) Official explanation: jockey said gelding hung left-handed

1082 WOLVERHAMPTON-RACECOURSE.CO.UK H'CAP 1m 141y(P)
7:40 (7:40) (Class 6) (0-60,60) 3-Y-O **£1,706** (£503; £252) **Stalls** Low

Form RPR
-645 **1** **Bertie Blu Boy**[14] 000 0 0 0 59.................... GregFairley 10 70
(Paul Green) *led 1f: chsd ldr tl led again over 2f out: rdn over 1f out: styd on wl* **11/1**
66-2 **2** *3 ½* **Trojan Touch (USA)**[10] 942 3-8-7 **46** oh1..................(b) FrannyNorton 2 49
(Chris Dwyer) *led over 7f out: rdn and hdd over 2f out: styd on same pce ins fnl f* **15/2[3]**
050- **3** *nse* **Twinkled**[141] 7408 3-9-7 **60**... HayleyTurner 7 63
(Michael Bell) *chsd ldrs: rdn over 1f out: styd on same pce ins fnl f* **13/8[1]**
4241 **4** *2* **Goal (IRE)**[10] 942 3-8-13 **57**... KieranO'Neill[(5)] 1 55
(David C Griffiths) *chsd ldrs: rdn over 1f out: no ex* **11/4[2]**
0-15 **5** *3 ¼* **Princess Gail**[56] 426 3-9-6 **59**... ShaneKelly 5 50
(Mark Brisbourne) *hld up: nt clr run and swtchd rt over 7f out: hdwy over 3f out: rdn over 2f out: wkng whn hung lft ins fnl f* **16/1**
000- **6** *7* **Kwik Lightening**[195] 6182 3-8-7 **46** oh1......................(v[1]) PJMcDonald 8 21
(Ben Haslam) *prom: rdn over 2f out: sn wknd* **8/1**
2362 **7** *1 ¾* **Beating Harmony**[7] 967 3-9-2 **55**.................................. DarryllHolland 6 26
(Tony Carroll) *sn pushed along in rr: nvr on terms* **17/2**
60-0 **8** *1 ¾* **Gothic Chick**[7] 964 3-9-7 **60**..(p) TomQueally 4 27
(Alan McCabe) *mid-div: rdn over 3f out: wknd over 2f out* **50/1**
000- **9** *shd* **Mariyah**[153] 7242 3-8-7 **46** oh1.. LukeMorris 9 —
(Michael Blanshard) *hld up: hmpd over 7f out: rdn over 4f out: a bhd* **100/1**
-000 **10** *59* **Lord Cornwall (IRE)**[13] 904 3-8-7 **46** oh1...................(b[1]) ChrisCatlin 3 —
(Ed Walker) *s.i.s and hmpd s: sn wl bhd: virtually p.u fnl 3f: t.o* **100/1**
1m 51.69s (1.19) **Going Correction** +0.10s/f (Slow) **10** Ran SP% **116.3**
Speed ratings (Par 96): **98,94,94,93,90 83,82,80,80,28**
toteswingers:1&2 £9.60, 2&3 £3.50, 1&3 £7.30 CSF £90.24 CT £209.15 TOTE £13.70: £3.40, £2.70, £1.10; EX 70.80.
Owner B & B Hygiene Limited **Bred** H Bourchier **Trained** Lydiate, Merseyside
FOCUS
A few of these are pretty limited and not many got involved from off the pace. the winner is rated up 5lb with the second to form. The time was nearly five seconds above standard, suggesting they didn't go that quick, but it was still 2.35 seconds faster than the following slowly run Class 5 event.
Beating Harmony Official explanation: jockey said gelding never travelled

1083 READ BARRY GERAGHTY'S BLOG AT ATTHERACES.COM H'CAP 1m 141y(P)
8:10 (8:10) (Class 5) (0-75,75) 4-Y-O+ **£1,942** (£578; £288; £144) **Stalls** Low

Form RPR
/5P- **1** **African Cheetah**[420] 430 5-9-7 **75**...................................... AdamKirby 6 82
(Reg Hollinshead) *mde all: set stdy pce tl qcknd 3f out: drvn out* **13/2**
13 **2** *½* **Needwood Ridge**[15] 881 4-8-12 **66**..............................(t) JamesDoyle 5 72
(Frank Sheridan) *chsd wnr: rdn over 2f out: r.o* **2/1[1]**
6130 **3** *1 ¾* **Petomic (IRE)**[9] 944 6-8-7 **61** oh1....................................... HayleyTurner 2 63
(Richard Guest) *hld up: racd keenly: hdwy u.p over 1f out: r.o: nt rch ldrs* **13/2**
0211 **4** *1 ¾* **Eastern Gift**[9] 949 6-8-12 **71** 6ex............................ AdamBeschizza[(5)] 4 69
(Gay Kelleway) *chsd ldrs: rdn over 2f out: no ex ins fnl f* **5/2[2]**
3503 **5** *8* **Mr Emirati (USA)**[16] 869 4-8-10 **64**..........................(tp) FrederikTylicki 3 44
(Bryan Smart) *plld hrd and prom: rdn over 2f out: wknd over 1f out* **4/1[3]**
1m 54.04s (3.54) **Going Correction** +0.10s/f (Slow) **5** Ran SP% **108.6**
Speed ratings (Par 103): **88,87,86,84,77**
CSF £19.31 TOTE £9.00: £4.80, £1.80; EX 28.10.
Owner Ray Robinson **Bred** Sheikh Abdulla Bin Isa Al-Khalifa **Trained** Upper Longdon, Staffs
FOCUS
An ordinary handicap. The winner dictated a steady pace and the time was over seven seconds above standard. It was also 2.35 seconds off the earlier Class 6 event but hand times show the final 2f were covered about 2.30 seconds faster than that contest. The third helps set the standard.

1084 STAY AT THE WOLVERHAMPTON HOLIDAY INN MEDIAN AUCTION MAIDEN STKS 7f 32y(P)
8:40 (8:42) (Class 6) 3-4-Y-O **£1,706** (£503; £252) **Stalls** High

Form RPR
0- **1** **Amelia's Surprise**[169] 6878 3-8-8 0................................ HayleyTurner 5 60
(Michael Bell) *chsd ldr: rdn to ld 1f out: r.o* **9/2**
453- **2** *1 ¼* **Crucis Abbey (IRE)**[153] 7240 3-8-13 75........................ WilliamCarson 6 61
(James Unett) *set stdy pce tl qckned over 2f out: sn rdn: hdd 1f out: styd on same pce* **5/2[2]**
66- **3** *nk* **Stravsambition**[179] 6626 3-8-8 0.. LiamKeniry 2 55
(Reg Hollinshead) *s.i.s: hld up: hdwy over 1f out: sn rdn: no ex ins fnl f* **33/1**
6- **4** *1 ½* **Prince Of Passion (CAN)**[263] 3945 3-8-13 0.............. FrederikTylicki 1 56
(Michael Dods) *hld up: hdwy over 4f out: rdn over 2f out: styd on same pce ins fnl f* **11/4[3]**
2500 **5** *1 ¼* **Libertino (IRE)**[14] 893 4-9-6 53.............................. GeorgeDowning[(7)] 3 58
(Tony Carroll) *plld hrd and prom: rdn over 2f out: no ex ins fnl f* **20/1**
3 **6** *9* **Step And Fetch (IRE)**[29] 751 3-8-8 0........................... DarryllHolland 8 24
(Ann Duffield) *sn chsng ldrs: drvn along 4f out: wknd over 2f out: eased ins fnl f* **9/4[1]**
1m 31.96s (2.36) **Going Correction** +0.10s/f (Slow)
WFA 3 from 4yo 14lb **6** Ran SP% **111.9**
Speed ratings (Par 101): **90,88,88,86,85 74**
toteswingers:1&2 £2.70, 2&3 £11.50, 1&3 £26.20 CSF £16.03 TOTE £6.50: £2.20, £3.10; EX 15.50.
Owner R A Pegum **Bred** Cranford Stud **Trained** Newmarket, Suffolk
FOCUS
The visual impression was that they went a steady pace early - a few of these were keen - and that was backed up by the final time, which was the best part of five seconds above standard. Consequently, a few of these may be flattered and the form needs treating with caution. It is limited by the fifth, and the race may not have taken that much winning.
Step And Fetch(IRE) Official explanation: jockey said filly never travelled
T/Plt: 108.60 to a £1 stake. Pool of £71,868.66 - 483.03 winning tickets. T/Qpdt: £65.10 to a £1 stake. Pool of £7,116.05 - 80.80 winning tickets. CR

1085 - 1091a (Foreign Racing) - See Raceform Interactive

DONCASTER (L-H)
Saturday, April 2

OFFICIAL GOING: Good (7.8)
Wind: Fresh, half against Weather: fine, becoming sunny but breezy

1092 WILLIAM HILL SPRING MILE (H'CAP) 1m (S)
2:05 (2:05) (Class 2) 4-Y-O+
£24,924 (£7,464; £3,732; £1,868; £932; £468) **Stalls** High

Form RPR
100 **1** **Eton Forever (IRE)**[210] 3696 4-9-7 **92**............................ NeilCallan 10 110
(Roger Varian) *trckd ldrs stands' side: led over 1f out: r.o strly: 1st of 10 that side* **10/1[3]**
061- **2** *3 ¾* **Dance And Dance (IRE)**[184] 6510 5-9-3 **93**......... AdamBeschizza[(5)] 19 102
(Edward Vaughan) *hld up in mid-div stands' side: effrt over 2f out: styd on to take 2nd ins fnl f: 2nd of 10 that side* **16/1**
060- **3** *1 ¾* **Manassas (IRE)**[175] 6752 6-9-5 **93**........................... LouisBeuzelin[(3)] 22 98
(Brian Meehan) *trckd ldr stands' side: led that side over 2f out: hdd over 1f out: kpt on same pce: 3rd of 10 that side* **16/1**
410- **4** *1 ½* **Justonefortheroad**[147] 7348 5-9-5 **90**........................... PaulHanagan 10 92
(Richard Fahey) *hld up in rr far side: gd hdwy 2f out: styd on wl to ld that gp ins fnl f: 1st of 12 that gp* **14/1**
1-25 **5** *nk* **Norman Orpen (IRE)**[21] 846 4-9-4 **89**............................ RyanMoore 17 90
(Jane Chapple-Hyam) *s.i.s: in rr stands' side: hdwy over 2f out: kpt on wl fnl f: 4th of 10 that side* **10/1[3]**
260- **6** *nk* **Smarty Socks (IRE)**[147] 7348 7-9-6 **91**................. SilvestreDeSousa 15 91
(David O'Meara) *dwlt: sn chsng ldrs stands' side: kpt on same pce fnl 2f: 5th of 10 that side* **25/1**
310- **7** *2 ¾* **Oriental Scot**[196] 6203 4-9-5 **90**...................................... SteveDrowne 12 84+
(William Jarvis) *in rr far side: hdwy over 2f out: styd on fnl f: 2nd of 12 that gp* **16/1**
125- **8** *shd* **Sir George (IRE)**[176] 6709 6-9-2 **87**................................ BarryMcHugh 21 81
(Ollie Pears) *trckd ldrs stands' side: effrt over 2f out: fdd fnl f: 6th of 10 that side* **25/1**
312- **9** *hd* **Pintura**[175] 6749 4-9-0 **90**...(p) LauraPike[(5)] 6 83
(David Simcock) *trckd ldrs far side: one pce fnl 2f: 3rd of 12 that gp* **20/1**
000- **10** *1* **Marajaa (IRE)**[169] 6888 9-9-3 **88**...................................... JamieMackay 7 79
(Willie Musson) *in rr far side: gd hdwy 2f out: chsng ldrs that side 1f out: sn wknd: 4th of 12 that gp* **50/1**
00-3 **11** *nse* **Kyllachy Star**[13] 925 5-9-2 **92**... LeeTopliss[(5)] 4 83
(Richard Fahey) *chsd ldrs far side: effrt over 2f out: swtchd lft and sn wknd: 5th of 12 that gp* **11/1**
325- **12** *2* **Charlie Cool**[175] 6749 8-9-5 **93**.....................................(b) JamesSullivan[(3)] 20 79
(Ruth Carr) *in rr stands' side: nvr nr ldrs: 7th of 10 that side* **40/1**
365- **13** *1 ¼* **Highland Knight (IRE)**[183] 6534 4-9-3 **88**.......................(t) DavidProbert 3 71
(Andrew Balding) *trckd ldrs far side: upsides that gp over 1f out: sn wknd: 6th of 12 that gp* **16/1**
131- **14** *1 ½* **Kalk Bay (IRE)**[179] 6659 4-9-7 **92**..................................... JMurtagh 1 72
(William Haggas) *trckd ldrs far side: effrt over 2f out: sn wknd: 7th of 12 that gp* **13/2[1]**
554- **15** *1 ¼* **Linnens Star (IRE)**[182] 6564 4-9-2 **87**................................ JimCrowley 8 64
(Ralph Beckett) *trckd ldrs far side: wknd 2f out: 8th of 12 that gp* **14/1**

000- **16** ½ **Pleasant Day (IRE)**[238] 4828 4-9-5 **90** TonyHamilton 2 66
(Richard Fahey) *led far side gp: hdd & wknd 2f out: 9th of 12 that gp* **33/1**

050- **17** 1½ **Breakheart (IRE)**[182] 6562 4-9-5 **90** TomEaves 9 62
(Michael Dods) *trckd ldrs far side: wknd over 2f out: 10th of 12 that gp* **12/1**

001- **18** 1 **Medicinal Compound**[167] 6961 4-9-5 **90** PhillipMakin 13 60
(Kevin Ryan) *in rr stands' side: nvr a factor: 8th of 10 that gp* **33/1**

060- **19** hd **Champagne Style (USA)**[133] 7522 4-9-3 **88** AdamKirby 14 58
(Richard Guest) *swtchd rt and racd stands' side: in rr: nvr on terms: 9th of 10 that side* **66/1**

530- **20** hd **Camerooney**[147] 7348 8-9-1 **91** DaleSwift(5) 18 60
(Brian Ellison) *led stands' side tl over 2f out: sn wknd: last of 10 that side* **25/1**

215- **21** nk **Mata Keranjang (USA)**[217] 5516 4-9-5 **90** JamieSpencer 5 58
(Paul Cole) *trckd ldrs far side: effrt over 2f out: sn hmpd: hung lft and lost pl over 1f out: 11th of 12 that gp* **8/1**[2]

4010 **22** ½ **Follow The Flag (IRE)**[7] 995 7-9-3 **88** 5ex (v) TomQueally 11 55
(Alan McCabe) *in rr far side: bhd fnl 2f: last of 12 that gp* **40/1**

1m 38.68s (-0.62) **Going Correction** +0.075s/f (Good) **22 Ran SP% 126.0**
Speed ratings (Par 109): **106,102,100,99,98 98,95,95,95,94 94,92,91,89,88 87,86,85,85,84 84,84**
toteswingers: 1&2 £34.10, 1&3 £56.90, 2&3 £45.80 CSF £143.91 CT £2564.19 TOTE £10.30: £2.80, £3.50, £4.80, £2.90; EX 122.90 Trifecta £1027.60 Pool: £1944.14 - 1.40 winning units..
Owner H R H Sultan Ahmad Shah **Bred** Mrs Brid Cosgrove **Trained** Newmarket, Suffolk
■ Roger Varian's first runner in Britain, after taking over the licence from Michael Jarvis.
■ Stewards' Enquiry : Lee Topliss one-day ban: careless riding (Apr 16)

FOCUS
Following a harsh winter there was a poor covering of grass. The ground had been watered during the week and riders were uncomplimentary, one describing it as "dead, slow and sticky". There was only a 6lb weight range in this valuable handicap, a consolation race for the Lincoln which was first run in 1993. The time was just a second outside the standard and the form should work out, although it did appear that those drawn high were favoured. The form looks more interesting than the Lincoln with positives about the first three. The winner can hold his own in better grade.

NOTEBOOK
Eton Forever(IRE) ◆ was the least exposed member of this line-up. He tracked the pace on the near side and, once easing to the front, quickly came clear for a very comfortable victory. A big, burly sort who had been gelded over the winter, he looks a potentially smart performer. He will be suited by better ground and should get 1m2f. (op 17-2)
Dance And Dance(IRE) ran on well to take second inside the last and clearly goes well fresh, having scored on his seasonal debut last spring. He ended the campaign with a win at Newmarket and resumed here off 3lb higher, but remains on the up.
Manassas(IRE) won this race in 2009 and was just 1lb higher here. Drawn nearest the rail, he took the overall lead over 2f out but was soon put in his place by the winner. He spent much of last season running over shorter and this was a pleasing return at a venue he likes.
Justonefortheroad, one of three runners from the Richard Fahey yard which won this event 12 months ago with Irish Heartbeat, 'won' the far side race. He came home well and has clearly resumed in good heart, but is currently operating off a career-high mark. (op 20-1 tchd 12-1)
Norman Orpen(IRE), who had not raced on turf since his racecourse debut, was able to run off 6lb lower than when fifth to Lowther in the Lincoln Trial at Wolverhampton. He came home nicely after switching to the outer of the stands' group, and a handicap on this surface should come his way.
Smarty Socks(IRE) had been eased 2lb since his last appearance, but was still 6lb higher than his latest winning mark. He travelled quite well but could not quicken up when let down. (op 33-1)
Oriental Scot ◆ finished nicely from the back of the centre group and gave the definite impression that he has more to offer. He goes well when fresh. (op 18-1 tchd 20-1)
Sir George(IRE), a half-brother to the 2008 Spring Mile winner Don't Panic, ran his race with no apparent excuses.
Pintura travelled nicely for a long way and finished third in his group, albeit comfortably held in the end. He progressed well last term, when he showed a preference for genuine soft ground. (op 25-1)
Marajaa(IRE) was also tenth in this event last season before being placed in the Newbury Spring Cup and the Victoria Cup. He showed enough to suggest that he will pay his way at nine.
Kyllachy Star had the advantage of a recent run but could not make it count. (op 12-1)
Kalk Bay(IRE) was a leading ante-post fancy for the Lincoln but failed to make the cut. Lightly raced and progressive in his first season, he had a similar profile to Penitent, who won the Lincoln for the Haggas yard a year ago, and raced out of the same number 1 stall. He proved disappointing, but was not persevered with when his chance had gone and should be afforded another chance. (op 8-1)
Mata Keranjang(USA) has undergone a recent gelding operation. Already under pressure when he was carried to his left 2f out, he was quickly in trouble and beat just one home. He still has plenty to prove. (op 13-2)

1093 WILLIAMHILL.COM CAMMIDGE TROPHY (LISTED RACE) 6f
2:35 (2:36) (Class 1) 3-Y-0+
£17,031 (£6,456; £3,231; £1,611; £807; £405) **Stalls** High

Form RPR

-663 **1** **Jimmy Styles**[21] 848 7-9-2 99 (p) AdamKirby 5 111
(Clive Cox) *hld up: swtchd lft and hdwy over 1f out: led ins fnl f: rdn out* **22/1**

3621 **2** 1¼ **Iver Bridge Lad**[7] 986 4-9-2 105 (b) JimmyQuinn 7 107
(John Ryan) *hld up in tch: rdn and ev ch over 1f out: styd on* **13/2**[2]

-214 **3** 1 **Brave Prospector**[35] 700 6-9-2 104 (t) JamieSpencer 14 104
(Jane Chapple-Hyam) *hld up: hdwy over 1f out: rdn and ev ch ins fnl f: unable qck* **12/1**

1-55 **4** 1¼ **Hitchens (IRE)**[7] 989 6-9-5 102 SilvestreDeSousa 11 103+
(David Barron) *hld up: r.o ins fnl f: nt rch ldrs* **7/1**[3]

030- **5** ¾ **Lovelace**[249] 4457 7-9-2 105 AdrianNicholls 4 97
(David Nicholls) *hld up in tch: rdn to ld over 1f out: hdd and no ex ins fnl f* **14/1**

/60- **6** hd **Royal Rock**[175] 6735 7-9-2 105 GeorgeBaker 12 97+
(Chris Wall) *hld up: hdwy nt clr run and swtchd lft over 1f out: swtchd rt ins fnl f: r.o: nt trble ldrs* **14/1**

400- **7** 1¼ **Prime Defender**[181] 6608 7-9-2 109 RobertWinston 2 93
(B W Hills) *chsd ldrs: rdn and ev ch over 1f out: no ex ins fnl f* **13/2**[2]

3-04 **8** 1½ **Doncaster Rover (USA)**[23] 825 5-9-2 106 TedDurcan 6 91+
(David Brown) *chsd ldrs: rdn whn nt clr run over 1f out: wknd ins fnl f* **17/2**

-000 **9** ½ **Rain Delayed (IRE)**[37] 678 5-9-2 100 JMurtagh 9 86+
(Michael Dods) *hld up: nt clr run over 1f out: nvr trble ldrs* **28/1**

134- **10** 2 **Bated Breath**[217] 5526 4-9-2 107 SteveDrowne 13 80+
(Roger Charlton) *hld up: hmpd wl over 2f out: nvr trbld ldrs* **5/2**[1]

20-0 **11** ¾ **Jack My Boy (IRE)**[21] 848 4-9-2 93 (b) NeilCallan 8 78
(David Evans) *led: rdn and hdd over 1f out: wknd ins fnl f* **33/1**

200- **12** ½ **Rash Judgement**[162] 7060 6-9-2 89 DavidAllan 1 76
(Eric Alston) *w ldr: rdn over 2f out: wknd over 1f out* **80/1**

464- **13** 3¾ **Fitz Flyer (IRE)**[148] 7329 5-9-2 96 TomEaves 3 64
(Bryan Smart) *s.i.s: sn prom: rdn over 4f out: wknd over 1f out* **33/1**

150- **14** 1 **Tajneed (IRE)**[162] 7060 8-9-2 102 PaulHanagan 10 61
(David Nicholls) *chsd ldrs: rdn over 2f out: wknd over 1f out* **14/1**

1m 12.38s (-1.22) **Going Correction** +0.075s/f (Good) **14 Ran SP% 120.9**
Speed ratings (Par 111): **111,109,108,106,105 105,103,101,100,98 97,96,91,90**
toteswingers: 1&2 £27.30, 1&3 £26.30, 2&3 £9.80 CSF £154.43 TOTE £29.50: £6.20, £2.20, £4.00; EX 179.20 Trifecta £1216.90 Part won. Pool of £1644.58 - 0.10 winning units..
Owner Gwyn Powell and Peter Ridgers **Bred** Barry Minty **Trained** Lambourn, Berks

FOCUS
A fair Listed sprint on paper, contested largely by exposed types, but an unsatisfactory race as a number found trouble in the tightly bunched field. Some caution should be exercised over the form. The winner looked better than ever and the race has been rated around him and the third.

NOTEBOOK
Jimmy Styles, third in a Wolverhampton handicap last week after a spell in Dubai, notched his first win since the 2009 Ayr Gold Cup. Only settling when buried in the pack, he ran on between horses towards the far side of the group to forge ahead inside the last. He is likely to go next for the Abernant Stakes at Newmarket's Craven meeting. (op 25-1 tchd 33-1 in a place)
Iver Bridge Lad, like the winner, had enjoyed some winter sunshine in Dubai. The recent Kempton scorer came to have his chance but found one too strong. (op 9-1)
Brave Prospector was drawn in the highest stall but was dropped out and came down the outside, which helped him to avoid the trouble. This consistent sort had been running well in Polytrack sprints and transferred his solid form back to turf. (tchd 11-1)
Hitchens(IRE) has been performing creditably in Listed races at Lingfield, winning one in November. Held up at the back, he did not get the gaps when his rider wanted them but came home very nicely for fourth and remains in good heart. (op 12-1)
Lovelace, whose trainer won this event a year ago with Inxile, came wide and had his chance before fading. Having his first run at a trip as short as this for nearly three years, he had reportedly undergone a knee operation since his last start in July. (op 11-1 tchd 16-1 in a place)
Royal Rock was apparently a sick horse during 2010, when he ran just twice. He showed promising signs of a revival, running on from the back after needing to be switched. (op 9-1)
Prime Defender, who won this in 2009 and was runner-up last year, was unplaced in Group 1 company on his final six starts of last season. He shaped as if this was just needed and it would not be a surprise to see him bid for a repeat win in the Duke Of York Stakes in May. (tchd 6-1)
Doncaster Rover(USA), who reportedly finished lame after both his starts at Meydan, was already under pressure when he encountered trouble. (op 9-1)
Rain Delayed(IRE), also back from the UAE, was another who didn't get the breaks. (tchd 25-1)
Bated Breath had not been seen since being held in this grade at the end of August. He was trapped against the rail from his high draw and was quite badly hampered not long after halfway. He met more trouble when trying to improve, and this run can be written off. Official explanation: jockey said colt was denied a clear run (op 3-1)

1094 WILLIAM HILL LINCOLN (HERITAGE H'CAP) 1m (S)
3:10 (3:13) (Class 2) 4-Y-0+
£62,310 (£18,660; £9,330; £4,670; £2,330; £1,170) **Stalls** High

Form RPR

0240 **1** **Sweet Lightning**[23] 824 6-9-4 **104** JMurtagh 16 114
(Michael Dods) *racd stands' side: hld up in mid-div: hdwy over 2f out: led jst ins fnl f: styd on wl: 1st of 10 that side* **16/1**

030- **2** 2½ **Brae Hill (IRE)**[175] 6752 5-8-9 **95** JamieSpencer 19 99
(Richard Fahey) *trckd ldrs stands' side: led that side 2f out: hdd and no ex jst ins fnl f: 2nd of 10 that side* **22/1**

1130 **3** 6 **Dubai Hills**[21] 846 5-8-9 **95** TomEaves 6 85
(Bryan Smart) *racd far side: mid-div: hdwy over 2f out: led that gp over 1f out: r.o: 1st of 11 that gp* **40/1**

100- **4** ¾ **Axiom**[147] 7348 7-9-1 **101** NeilCallan 15 89
(Ed Walker) *in rr stands' side: hdwy over 2f out: kpt on fnl f: 3rd of 10 that side* **50/1**

222- **5** ¾ **Eton Rifles (IRE)**[147] 7348 6-8-8 **94** PaulMulrennan 9 81
(Howard Johnson) *trckd ldrs far side: led that gp over 2f out tl over 1f out: kpt on same pce: 2nd of 11 that gp* **18/1**

02-2 **6** 1½ **Docofthebay (IRE)**[21] 844 7-8-11 **97** (p) IanMongan 13 80
(David Nicholls) *chsd ldrs stands' side: one pce fnl 2f: 4th of 10 that side* **11/1**

3211 **7** ½ **Lowther**[21] 846 6-9-2 **102** 5ex (be) RobertWinston 17 84+
(Alan Bailey) *hld up in mid-div stands' side: effrt and nt clr run 3f out: swtchd lft over 1f out: styd on: nvr nr ldrs: 5th of 10 that side* **11/1**

530- **8** nk **Light From Mars**[189] 6349 6-8-11 **97** TomQueally 8 78
(David Nicholls) *trckd ldrs far side: effrt over 2f out: kpt on same pce: 3rd of 11 that gp* **14/1**

/50- **9** nse **Fremont (IRE)**[336] 1703 4-8-8 **94** RyanMoore 21 75
(Richard Hannon) *hld up in rr stands' side: effrt over 2f out: kpt on: nvr nr ldrs: 6th of 10 that side* **8/1**[3]

153- **10** shd **Irish Heartbeat (IRE)**[175] 6752 6-8-10 **96** PaulHanagan 7 77+
(Richard Fahey) *t.k.h in rr far side: hdwy 2f out: kpt on fnl f: 4th of 11 that gp* **6/1**[1]

44-0 **11** 2 **Our Joe Mac (IRE)**[13] 925 4-8-8 **94** TonyHamilton 14 71
(Richard Fahey) *trckd ldrs stands' side: effrt over 2f out: one pce: 7th of 10 that side* **16/1**

06-3 **12** ½ **Prime Exhibit**[21] 846 6-8-4 **95** LeeTopliss(5) 1 70
(Richard Fahey) *w ldrs far side: wknd 2f out: 5th of 11 that gp* **9/1**

006- **13** nk **Castles In The Air**[189] 6349 6-9-2 **102** FrederikTylicki 5 77
(Richard Fahey) *mid-div far side: hdwy over 2f out: wknd over 1f out: 6th of 11 that gp* **33/1**

100- **14** 1½ **Kiwi Bay**[147] 7348 6-8-9 **95** PJMcDonald 12 66
(Michael Dods) *hld up in rr far side: nvr a factor: 7th of 11 that gp* **40/1**

521- **15** ½ **Gunner Lindley (IRE)**[175] 6749 4-8-7 **93** MichaelHills 18 63
(B W Hills) *w ldr stands' side: led that gp over 3f out: hdd 2f out: sn wknd: 8th of 10 that side* **13/2**[2]

50-0 **16** ½ **Prince Of Dance**[21] 846 5-8-8 **94** TedDurcan 3 63
(Tom Tate) *racd far side: mid-div: effrt over 2f out: wknd over 1f out: 8th of 11 that gp* **33/1**

550- **17** ¾ **Dream Lodge (IRE)**[94] 8009 7-8-5 **94** BillyCray(3) 20 61
(David Nicholls) *chsd ldrs stands' side: wknd over 2f out: 9th of 10 that side* **25/1**

0-32 **18** ¾ **Tartan Gigha (IRE)**[21] 846 6-8-10 **96** SilvestreDeSousa 2 61
(Mark Johnston) *racd far side: trckd ldrs: wknd over 2f out: 9th of 11 that gp* **12/1**

010- **19** nk **Harrison George (IRE)**[168] 6923 6-9-3 **110** GeorgeChaloner(7) 4 75
(Richard Fahey) *led far side gp: hdd over 2f out: sn wknd: 10th of 11 that gp* **40/1**

060- **20** 2½ **Al Muheer (IRE)**[226] 5247 6-8-8 **94** AdrianNicholls 10 53
(David Nicholls) *racd far side: a in rr: last of 11 that gp* **28/1**

41/- **21** *38* **Doctor Crane (USA)**[678] 2296 5-8-10 **96**..................(e[1]) RobertHavlin 22 —
(John Gosden) *led stands' side tl over 3f out: hung rt and sn dropped rt away: t.o 1f out: virtually p.u: last of 10 that side* **16/1**

1m 38.38s (-0.92) **Going Correction** +0.075s/f (Good) **21** Ran SP% **129.5**
Speed ratings (Par 109): **107,104,98,97,97 95,95,94,94,94 92,92,91,90,89 89,88,87,87,84 46**
toteswingers: 1&2 £79.50, 1&3 £380.40, 2&3 Not won CSF £349.30 CT £13231.23 TOTE £18.80: £4.30, £6.70, £9.40, £11.70; EX 497.60 Trifecta £8723.20 Part won. Pool of £11788.17 - 0.20 winning units..
Owner Andrew Tinkler **Bred** Mrs M Lavell **Trained** Denton, Co Durham

FOCUS
More competitive a Lincoln than had looked likely as a result of the late withdrawal on account of the ground of long-term ante-post favourite and potential blot on the handicap Taqleed and, all in all, the form looks pretty ordinary for the standard of the race. As expected they split into two groups, and just like in the Spring Mile, those on the stands' side came out on top, with the first two pulling clear. The winner improved but the time was no better than the Spring Mile and the form, rated loosely around the runner-up, has its limits.

NOTEBOOK
Sweet Lightning has done most of his racing over middle distances and looked handicapped to the hilt, but he was fit from racing in Dubai and, as he's been a strong traveller throughout his career, there was always the chance that he would appreciate dropping back in trip and getting to race off a strong gallop. Tracking the pace on the stands' side, he came through to challenge Brae Hill 1f out, and he was always going to stay on strongly once in front. He won here off a mark of 102, and whether he'd be so effective over this trip in Listed company is open to question, so carrying a big weight in races like the Hunt Cup looks more likely to bring out the best in him. (op 25-1)
Brae Hill(IRE) didn't look badly treated on his best form. There should be improvement to come from him on the back of this and, having run well at Chester on more than one occasion in the past, he'll no doubt be aimed for a race at the May meeting. (op 33-1)
Dubai Hills, who ran up a sequence on the Fibresand over the winter, was reappearing off a 30lb higher mark than when last seen on turf. This fine effort, winning his race on the far side, confirms him to be a much improved performer and not just a Fibresand specialist. The Spring Cup could be on his agenda, providing there is some give in the ground. (op 66-1)
Axiom, third on the stands' side, is at his best with cut in the ground. A gelding who seems to go well fresh, he looks to have run close to his mark and, although pretty exposed now, is likely to continue to be a fixture in these big-field handicaps. He might go to Sandown next.
Eton Rifles(IRE), another at his best with some give in the ground, has been largely campaigned over 6f-7f in previous years and, although he ran well to finish second on the far side, he'll surely be suited by a return to shorter. (op 20-1)
Docofthebay(IRE) ran a fine race in Listed company on the AW last time and was officially 6lb well in at the weights. He had his chance, but 7f seems to suit him better these days - last four wins over that trip. (op 12-1)
Lowther, 2lb well in under his penalty, could only keep on at the one pace once in the clear. He has never run that well here and might be happier on a sharper track. (op 12-1)
Light From Mars, another who has run well fresh before, finished third on the far side on his debut for David Nicholls. He finished third in the Bunbury Cup last season off this mark but probably needs to drop a little to get his head in front in one of these.
Fremont(IRE), held up on the stands' side, found little off the bridle, but he'd been off the track for 11 months and probably needs 7f and the ground rattling to be seen at his best. (op 9-1)
Irish Heartbeat(IRE), winner of the Spring Mile last year, was well supported and came to have his chance on the far side, but he weakened out of it in the closing stages and perhaps the fact that he raced quite keenly early told in the end. (op 17-2)
Our Joe Mac(IRE), who ran a shocker in Ireland last time, was again below his best.
Prime Exhibit likes to get his toe in and perhaps this ground just didn't suit him. (tchd 8-1)
Gunner Lindley(IRE) showed early speed on the stands' side but failed to see his race out. (op 7-1)
Tartan Gigha(IRE), officially 3lb well in at the weights, never got competitive from off the pace on the far side. He needs fast summer ground to be seen at his best. (op 11-1 tchd 10-1)
Doctor Crane(USA) Official explanation: jockey said gelding hung right

1095 WILLIAMHILL.COM BROCKLESBY CONDITIONS STKS 5f
3:40 (3:44) (Class 4) 2-Y-O **£6,476** (£1,927; £963; £481) **Stalls** High

Form RPR

3 **1** **He's So Cool (IRE)**[7] 982 2-8-8 0.................................. KierenFox(3) 5 83
(Bill Turner) *mde all: rdn over 1f out: r.o: eased nr fin* **8/1**

1 **2** *¾* **Redair (IRE)**[7] 982 2-8-10 0.................................. CathyGannon 2 79
(David Evans) *chsd wnr: pushed along 1/2-way: rdn over 1f out: r.o* **9/4**[1]

3 *1 ¼* **Crowning Star (IRE)** 2-8-11 0.................................. JamieSpencer 9 76+
(J S Moore) *dwlt: bhd and swtchd lft over 3f out: hdwy over 1f out: r.o: nt rch ldrs* **12/1**

4 *hd* **Tyre Giant Dot Com** 2-8-11 0.................................. TomEaves 4 75+
(Geoffrey Oldroyd) *s.i.s: hld up: hdwy over 1f out: r.o* **12/1**

5 *2 ½* **Jimmy The Lollipop (IRE)** 2-8-11 0.................................. PhillipMakin 3 66+
(Kevin Ryan) *prom: rdn 1/2-way: no ex fnl f* **7/1**[3]

6 *nk* **Triggerlo** 2-8-11 0.................................. SamHitchcott 6 65+
(Mick Channon) *s.i.s: sn pushed along in rr: rdn over 1f out: r.o ins fnl f: nvr nrr* **25/1**

7 *½* **Beau Mistral (IRE)** 2-8-6 0.................................. SilvestreDeSousa 7 60+
(Paul Green) *mid-div: nt clr run over 1f out: r.o ins fnl f: nvr trbld ldrs* **40/1**

8 *4* **Joey Hayes** 2-8-11 0.................................. AdamKirby 1 49
(Noel Quinlan) *prom: rdn over 1f out: wknd fnl f* **40/1**

9 *½* **Adranian (IRE)** 2-8-11 0.................................. NeilCallan 11 47
(David Evans) *sn pushed along in rr: wknd over 1f out* **11/1**

10 *1* **Outlaw Torn (IRE)** 2-8-11 0.................................. RobertWinston 10 43
(Alan McCabe) *chsd ldrs tl rdn and wknd over 1f out* **16/1**

11 *nk* **King Fong** 2-8-8 0.................................. MichaelO'Connell(3) 8 42
(John Ryan) *sn pushed along and a in rr* **33/1**

12 *hd* **Our Boy Jack (IRE)** 2-8-11 0.................................. PaulHanagan 13 41
(Richard Fahey) *prom tl rdn and wknd over 1f out* **10/3**[2]

61.70 secs (1.20) **Going Correction** +0.075s/f (Good) **12** Ran SP% **118.7**
Speed ratings (Par 94): **93,91,89,89,85 85,84,77,77,75 74,74**
toteswingers: 1&2 £5.10, 1&3 £13.90, 2&3 £8.20 CSF £25.52 TOTE £9.90: £2.60, £1.30, £3.50; EX 32.90 Trifecta £319.50 Pool of £958.64 - 2.22 winning units..
Owner E A Brook **Bred** Crone Stud Farms Ltd **Trained** Sigwells, Somerset

FOCUS
This is usually the first 2yo event of the season, but not this year, and previous experience told as the first two home came out of a Kempton maiden on Polytrack last week. The runner-up in that Kempton contest, Bubbly Ballerina, was declared here but was an absentee. The last Brocklesby runner to come here with a previous outing behind him was Spoof Master, the winner in 2006, while five of the field the year before had already been seen out including the first three home.

NOTEBOOK
He's So Cool(IRE) was well held in third at Kempton first time, but reportedly had his head turned when the stalls opened and could never get to grips with the first two. The switch to racing on turf suited and he made all, holding off the Kempton winner Redair who was 4lb worse off here. Trainer Bill Turner's fourth Brocklesby winner in a decade, he is set to go for Chester's Lily Agnes Stakes early next month. The Lord won both races for the stable in 2002 and was runner-up at Newmarket in between. (op 11-1 tchd 12-1)
Redair(IRE) had been green when winning at Kempton but knew her job this time. Under a penalty, she chased her rival all the way and went down fighting after being switched to the rail late on. Likely to stay a bit further, she could continue to pay her way. (op 5-2)
Crowning Star(IRE) ◆ was the oldest in the field and this well-grown colt ran well. Keen in rear until he was switched to race on the outside of the field, he came home nicely for third and can win an early maiden. (tchd 16-1)
Tyre Giant Dot Com, who is already gelded, is still a couple of weeks short of his real second birthday. Another who was not best away, he also benefited from racing on the outside of the bunch and made a pleasing start to his career. (tchd 11-1 and 16-1)
Jimmy The Lollipop(IRE) is a 27,000gns yearling by Amadeus Wolf, who sired a winner for the Ryan yard at Musselburgh on Friday, out of a half-sister to Gimcrack winner Carrowkeel. He had a harder race than some on this debut but showed enough to suggest that an ordinary event will be found for him before long. (op 6-1 tchd 15-2)
Triggerlo is by a sprinter out of a dam who won at up to 1m4f. He took time to get the hang of things but came home in decent style and should benefit from the experience. (op 20-1 tchd 16-1)
Beau Mistral(IRE) is a half-sister to two plating-class sprint maidens out of a mare who was unplaced on her only start. She belied her pedigree with a promising display, running on nicely at the end after encountering traffic problems. Official explanation: jockey said filly suffered interference in running (op 33-1)
Our Boy Jack(IRE) faded after showing prominently against the stands' rail. He might need an extra furlong. (op 4-1 tchd 3-1)

1096 BOB BEEVERS MEMORIAL MAIDEN STKS 1m 2f 60y
4:15 (4:16) (Class 5) 3-Y-O **£2,978** (£886; £442; £221) **Stalls** Low

Form RPR

22- **1** **Sud Pacifique (IRE)**[192] 6279 3-9-3 0.................................. RyanMoore 1 90+
(Jeremy Noseda) *trckd ldrs: led 3f out: styd on strly to forge clr appr fnl f: v readily* **10/3**[2]

4- **2** *3 ¾* **Canna (IRE)**[183] 6532 3-9-3 0.................................. MichaelHills 4 82
(B W Hills) *dwlt: sn mid-div: hdwy over 3f out: chsd wnr over 1f out: no imp* **3/1**[1]

62-3 **3** *2 ½* **The Bells O Peover**[15] 902 3-9-3 70.................................. RichardHills 15 77
(Mark Johnston) *chsd ldrs: chal 3f out: styd on same pce over 1f out* **8/1**

-2 **4** *nse* **Honest Deal**[17] 873 3-9-3 0.................................. PJMcDonald 14 77
(Alan Swinbank) *chsd ldrs: kpt on same pce fnl 2f* **16/1**

30- **5** *½* **Ryton Runner (IRE)**[182] 6560 3-9-3 0.................................. RobertHavlin 13 76+
(John Gosden) *mid-div: hdwy 3f out: hung lft over 1f out: styd on wl towards fin: will improve* **14/1**

4- **6** *4* **Communicator**[155] 7202 3-9-3 0.................................. JamieSpencer 9 68+
(Michael Bell) *hld up towards rr: hdwy over 4f out: chsng ldrs 3f out: wknd over 1f out* **7/1**

445- **7** *1* **Nabah**[154] 7235 3-8-12 97.................................. PhilipRobinson 3 61
(Clive Brittain) *trckd ldrs: rdn 3f out: wknd over 1f out* **7/2**[3]

8 *5* **Penang Pacific** 3-9-3 0.................................. RobertWinston 7 56
(Alan McCabe) *in rr: bhd and drvn 3f out* **50/1**

9 *8* **Tartan Jura** 3-9-3 0.................................. SilvestreDeSousa 12 40
(Mark Johnston) *s.i.s: last and drvn along: green and hung rt over 3f out* **25/1**

5-32 **10** *8* **X Rated**[11] 937 3-9-3 70.................................. JamesDoyle 11 24
(Alan McCabe) *led tl 3f out: sn wknd* **25/1**

0- **11** *4* **Silver Tiger**[172] 6828 3-9-3 0.................................. GeorgeBaker 6 16
(Chris Wall) *stdd s: t.k.h in rr: sme hdwy over 3f out: wknd over 2f out* **40/1**

66 **12** *nk* **Black Feather**[7] 993 3-8-13 0 ow1.................................. AdamKirby 10 11
(Alan McCabe) *mid-div: sn drvn along: bhd fnl 3f* **66/1**

00- **13** *4 ½* **May Burnett (IRE)**[150] 7303 3-8-7 0.................................(t) SeanLevey(5) 8 1
(Brian Rothwell) *chsd ldrs: drvn over 5f out: lost pl over 3f out* **100/1**

2m 10.7s (1.30) **Going Correction** +0.075s/f (Good) **13** Ran SP% **121.0**
Speed ratings (Par 98): **97,94,92,91,91 88,87,83,77,70 67,67,63**
toteswingers: 1&2 £3.60, 1&3 £6.80, 2&3 £7.00 CSF £13.28 TOTE £4.10: £1.50, £1.70, £3.00; EX 16.70 Trifecta £96.60 Pool of £1183.40 - 9.06 winning units..
Owner Sir Robert Ogden **Bred** Eduard Mordukhovitch **Trained** Newmarket, Suffolk

FOCUS
One or two interesting horses in this maiden but not form with which to get carried away. It was the slowest of the four C&D races. The winner is rated up 10lb.

1097 WILLIAMHILL.COM H'CAP (DIV I) 1m 2f 60y
4:50 (4:51) (Class 4) (0-85,85) 4-Y-O+ **£4,954** (£1,474; £736; £367) **Stalls** Low

Form RPR

000- **1** **Mirrored**[182] 6562 5-9-7 **85**.................................. DuranFentiman 14 94
(Tim Easterby) *t.k.h in last: gd hdwy and nt clr run over 2f out: burst through to ld 1f out: r.o strly* **18/1**

060- **2** *2 ¼* **Oneofapear (IRE)**[162] 7053 5-9-5 **83**.................................. PJMcDonald 11 88
(Alan Swinbank) *mid-div: hdwy over 3f out: led over 1f out: sn hdd and no ex* **11/1**

120- **3** *nk* **Veiled Applause**[19] 7243 8-9-1 **82**.................................. IanBrennan(3) 5 86
(John Quinn) *mid-div: hdwy on outer over 2f out: edgd lft and styd on same pce fnl f* **14/1**

-554 **4** *1 ½* **Hawaana (IRE)**[8] 963 6-9-5 **83**.................................. JamieSpencer 1 84
(Gay Kelleway) *hld up towards rr: smooth hdwy 4f out: chsng ldrs 2f out: kpt on same pce appr fnl f* **8/1**[3]

5 *¾* **White Diamond**[24] 7141 4-8-9 **73**.................................. TomEaves 10 73
(Malcolm Jefferson) *chsd ldrs: styd on same pce fnl 2f* **20/1**

041- **6** *¾* **Tres Coronas (IRE)**[175] 6753 4-9-6 **84**.................................. LeeNewman 7 82
(David Barron) *stdd s: t.k.h sn in rr: hdwy to chse ldrs over 2f out: kpt on same pce fnl f* **9/1**

3-50 **7** *¾* **Denton (NZ)**[49] 525 8-9-7 **85**.................................(t) SteveDrowne 12 82
(Jeremy Gask) *chsd ldrs: led over 2f out: hdd over 1f out: sn fdd* **11/1**

010- **8** *½* **Mainland (USA)**[182] 6573 5-8-11 **75**.................................. PaulMulrennan 13 71
(Tracy Waggott) *hld up in rr: gd hdwy on inner 3f out: sn chsng ldrs: wknd over 1f out* **33/1**

402- **9** *3 ½* **Ejteyaaz**[175] 6753 4-9-3 **81**.................................. PaulHanagan 4 70
(Richard Fahey) *sn chsng ldrs: wknd fnl 2f* **8/1**[3]

200- **10** *4* **Valiant Knight (FR)**[173] 6813 4-9-0 **78**.................................. RyanMoore 3 59
(Richard Hannon) *chsd ldrs: effrt over 3f out: lost pl over 1f out* **4/1**[1]

000- **11** *1* **Hail Promenader (IRE)**[249] 4459 5-8-9 **80**............ MatthewLawson(7) 9 59
(B W Hills) *in rr: hdwy on outer over 4f out: rdn over 3f out: wknd 2f out* **11/1**

220- **12** *3 ¾* **Lord Raglan (IRE)**[189] 6355 4-9-0 **78**.................................. AndrewElliott 2 49
(Mrs K Burke) *led: hdd over 2f out: sn wknd* **11/1**

-231 **13** *1 1/4* **Loyalty**[36] 694 4-9-1 **79**..(v) PatrickMathers 8 48
(Derek Shaw) *s.i.s: sn in mid-div: drvn over 5f out: chsng ldrs on ins 3f out: hung lft: wknd 2f out* **11/2**[2]

2m 9.77s (0.37) **Going Correction** +0.075s/f (Good) **13** Ran SP% **120.6**
Speed ratings (Par 105): **101,99,98,97,97 96,95,95,92,89 88,85,84**
toteswingers: 1&2 £43.00, 1&3 £45.10, 2&3 £31.20 CSF £205.26 CT £2860.26 TOTE £20.00: £5.40, £5.50, £5.20; EX 361.50 Trifecta £627.60 Part won. Pool of £848.10 - 0.30 winning units..

Owner Middleham Park Racing XXX **Bred** Millsec Limited **Trained** Great Habton, N Yorks

FOCUS
A fair handicap run at an ordinary pace. It was nearly a second slower than division II but the form looks sound enough. The winner showed his best form since he was a 3yo.
Loyalty Official explanation: jockey said gelding never travelled

1098 WILLIAMHILL.COM H'CAP (DIV II) 1m 2f 60y
5:20 (5:21) (Class 4) (0-85,85) 4-Y-0+ **£4,954** (£1,474; £736; £367) **Stalls** Low

Form RPR
220- **1** **Bonfire Knight**[143] 5913 4-9-7 **85**...................................... PaulHanagan 8 97+
(John Quinn) *hld up: hdwy over 3f out: led over 1f out: shkn up and edgd lft ins fnl f: r.o* **10/3**[1]
-515 **2** *1 1/2* **Snow Dancer (IRE)**[36] 694 7-8-9 **76**...................... JamesSullivan(3) 13 84
(Hugh McWilliams) *hld up: hdwy over 1f out: rdn to chse wnr ins fnl f: r.o* **14/1**
163- **3** *2 3/4* **The Galloping Shoe**[12] 4830 6-9-5 **83**.............................. JimCrowley 6 86
(Alistair Whillans) *hld up: hdwy over 1f out: r.o: nt rch ldrs* **18/1**
242- **4** *nk* **Abergavenny**[196] 6185 4-9-7 **85**...................................... TomEaves 9 87
(Brian Ellison) *prom: rdn over 3f out: styd on u.p* **4/1**[2]
410- **5** *1/2* **Jonny Lesters Hair (IRE)**[211] 5736 6-9-4 **82**.................... DavidAllan 7 83+
(Tim Easterby) *hld up: plld hrd: hdwy over 2f out: rdn over 1f out: styd on same pce ins fnl f* **9/1**
35-2 **6** *2 1/4* **Hydrant**[29] 772 5-8-9 **73**.. GregFairley 12 69
(Peter Salmon) *chsd ldr to 1/2-way: remained handy: led over 2f out: rdn and hdd over 1f out: no ex ins fnl f* **14/1**
1536 **7** *1 1/2* **Bedouin Bay**[10] 948 4-9-0 **78**.. JamesDoyle 11 71
(Alan McCabe) *chsd ldrs: rdn over 2f out: hung lft over 1f out: no ex* **18/1**
6252 **8** *nk* **The Lock Master (IRE)**[25] 799 4-9-0 **78**........................ NeilChalmers 14 71
(Michael Appleby) *hld up: rdn over 2f out: nvr trbld ldrs* **20/1**
500- **9** *5* **Lucky Dance (BRZ)**[17] 7233 9-9-0 **78**................................ NickyMackay 4 61
(Mark Rimmer) *hld up: sme hdwy u.p over 1f out: sn wknd* **25/1**
503- **10** *nse* **Monkton Vale (IRE)**[150] 7307 4-8-7 **71**....................(b) FrederikTylicki 2 54
(Richard Fahey) *led: rdn and hdd over 2f out: wknd over 1f out* **6/1**[3]
160- **11** *5* **Lucky Windmill**[185] 6467 4-9-2 **80**.................................. PJMcDonald 1 53
(Alan Swinbank) *chsd ldrs: rdn over 2f out: wknd over 1f out* **11/1**
0242 **12** *66* **Thunderstruck**[16] 877 6-9-2 **80**....................................(v) IanMongan 10 —
(David Nicholls) *prom: chsd ldr 1/2-way tl wknd and eased over 2f out: t.o* **9/1**

2m 8.80s (-0.60) **Going Correction** +0.075s/f (Good) **12** Ran SP% **118.2**
Speed ratings (Par 105): **105,103,101,101,100 99,97,97,93,93 89,36**
toteswingers: 1&2 £12.50, 1&3 £11.40, 2&3 £26.00 CSF £51.44 CT £741.36 TOTE £4.40: £2.10, £3.50, £4.20; EX 69.60 TRIFECTA Not won..
Owner Ross Harmon **Bred** Wyck Hall Stud Ltd **Trained** Settrington, N Yorks

FOCUS
This race was run in a time 0.97sec quicker than the first division. The winner can probably do better and the second confirmed his recent AW form.
Jonny Lesters Hair(IRE) Official explanation: jockey said gelding ran too free
Thunderstruck Official explanation: jockey said gelding hung right throughout

1099 UNIVERSALRECYCLINGCOMPANY.CO.UK APPRENTICE H'CAP 1m 2f 60y
5:55 (5:55) (Class 5) (0-70,70) 4-Y-0+ **£2,115** (£624; £312) **Stalls** Low

Form RPR
460- **1** **Frontline Phantom (IRE)**[162] 7054 4-8-7 **59**.............. HarryBentley(3) 1 75+
(Mrs K Burke) *trckd ldrs: led 3f out: wnt clr ins fnl f: heavily eased towards fin* **11/1**
-410 **2** *2 1/2* **Zafranagar (IRE)**[28] 392 6-8-10 **64**........................ GeorgeDowning(5) 5 72
(Tony Carroll) *mid-div: hdwy over 3f out: chsd wnr over 2f out: no imp* **8/1**[2]
0000 **3** *1/2* **Gala Casino Star (IRE)**[8] 977 6-9-6 **69**............................ LeeTopliss 8 76
(Richard Fahey) *mid-div: hdwy over 3f out: kpt on wl ins fnl f* **8/1**[2]
066- **4** *1/2* **Rosbay (IRE)**[176] 6724 7-9-6 **69**.. LanceBetts 14 75
(Tim Easterby) *rr-div: hdwy over 3f out: styd on fnl 2f: nt rch ldrs* **8/1**[2]
43-5 **5** *3 1/2* **King's Counsel (IRE)**[18] 400 5-8-10 **59**......................(v) SeanLevey 11 58
(David O'Meara) *mid-div: sn drvn along: styd on fnl 3f: nvr nr to chal* **14/1**
340- **6** *3 3/4* **Sharakti (IRE)**[155] 7205 4-9-7 **70**................................... DeclanCannon 20 62
(Alan McCabe) *chsd ldrs: wknd over 1f out* **25/1**
046- **7** *1* **Law To Himself (IRE)**[175] 6753 4-9-2 **68**..................... GarryWhillans(3) 6 58
(Alan Swinbank) *prom: swtchd rt 3f out: one pce* **14/1**
552- **8** *3/4* **Zaplamation (IRE)**[182] 6573 6-9-1 **69**........................ ShaneBKelly(5) 18 57
(John Quinn) *hld up in rr: hdwy over 2f out: kpt on ins fnl f* **7/1**[1]
613- **9** *1* **Swiftly Done (IRE)**[173] 6794 4-9-2 **68**............................ NeilFarley(3) 2 54
(Declan Carroll) *s.i.s: kpt on fnl 2f: nvr nr ldrs* **14/1**
445- **10** *nk* **Easy Terms**[164] 7015 4-8-11 **60**.. AdamCarter 3 45
(Edwin Tuer) *trckd ldrs: chal over 4f out: wknd 2f out* **22/1**
132- **11** *1* **Hong Kong Island (IRE)**[157] 7176 4-9-0 **66**.............. JamesRogers(3) 7 49
(Micky Hammond) *hld up towards rr: effrt 3f out: nvr a factor* **16/1**
000- **12** *5* **Blue Spinnaker (IRE)**[150] 7306 12-8-9 **63**......... DavidSimmonson(5) 15 36
(Michael Easterby) *s.i.s: nvr on terms* **16/1**
213 **13** *2* **Sail Home**[58] 399 4-9-0 **63**.. AdamBeschizza 16 32
(Julia Feilden) *mid-div: effrt over 3f out: sn wknd* **20/1**
60-0 **14** *nk* **Dragon Slayer (IRE)**[36] 692 9-8-12 **61**............................ TobyAtkinson 9 30
(John Harris) *dwlt: hdwy over 3f out: swtchd rt 2f out: nvr a factor* **66/1**
300- **15** *2 1/2* **Scarab (IRE)**[150] 7306 6-9-5 **68**.................................... AshleyMorgan 10 32
(Tim Walford) *mid-div: effrt 3f out: sn wknd* **28/1**
113- **16** *8* **Sharp Sovereign (USA)**[154] 7228 5-9-4 **70**.................. LMcNiff(3) 13 18
(David Barron) *chsd ldrs: lost pl over 2f out* **9/1**[3]
1445 **17** *nk* **General Tufto**[17] 870 6-9-1 **67**.............................(b) MatthewLawson(3) 12 14
(Charles Smith) *in rr: sme hdwy and drvn 4f out: lost pl over 2f out* **40/1**
640- **18** *3/4* **Koo And The Gang (IRE)**[214] 5641 4-8-12 **61**................. DaleSwift 4 7
(Brian Ellison) *led: hdd 3f out: sn wknd* **14/1**
230- **19** *10* **Red Skipper (IRE)**[107] 7899 6-8-4 **56**............................ JulieBurke(3) 17 —
(Noel Wilson) *chsd ldrs: lost pl over 2f out: eased over 1f out* **40/1**
010- **20** *10* **Star Addition**[113] 7814 5-8-5 **57**................................. DavidKenny(3) 19 —
(Eric Alston) *dwlt: in rr: eased over 1f out* **40/1**

2m 8.95s (-0.45) **Going Correction** +0.075s/f (Good) **20** Ran SP% **127.8**
Speed ratings (Par 103): **104,102,101,101,98 95,94,94,93,92 92,88,86,86,84 77,77,77,69,61**
toteswingers: 1&2 £48.20, 1&3 £50.30, 2&3 £36.00 CSF £89.88 CT £767.52 TOTE £17.90: £5.50, £2.90, £2.40, £2.40; EX 212.40 TRIFECTA Not won..
Owner Frontline Bathrooms **Bred** Joe Rogers **Trained** Middleham Moor, North Yorks

FOCUS
The winning time of this apprentice handicap compared favourably with the times of the previous handicaps for higher-rated horses. The improved winner was value for 4l.
T/Jkpt: Not won. T/Plt: £19,426.50 to a £1 stake. Pool: £203,579.28. 7.65 winning tickets. T/Qpdt: £554.90 to a £1 stake. Pool: £13,048.58. 17.40 winning units. WG

982 KEMPTON (A.W) (R-H)
Saturday, April 2

OFFICIAL GOING: Standard
Wind: moderate across Weather: Fine but cloudy

1100 WILLIAMHILL.COM MAGNOLIA STKS (LISTED RACE) 1m 2f (P)
2:20 (2:21) (Class 1) 4-Y-0+
£17,031 (£6,456; £3,231; £1,611; £807; £405) **Stalls** Low

Form RPR
/64- **1** **Shamali**[311] 2444 6-8-13 **99**.. EddieAhern 9 103
(William Haggas) *b.hind: dwlt: rcvrd to trck ldr in modly run event: rdn 2f out: led jst ins fnl f: styd on* **12/1**
3-62 **2** *1 1/2* **Resentful Angel**[35] 702 6-8-8 **87**...................................... DaneO'Neill 4 95
(Pat Eddery) *swtg: led at mod pce: kicked on over 2f out: hdd and one pce jst ins fnl f* **25/1**
002- **3** *1* **Pink Symphony**[192] 6281 4-8-8 **105**................................. ChrisCatlin 2 93
(Paul Cole) *a chsng ldng pair: drvn over 2f out: nt qckn over 1f out: one pce after* **11/2**[2]
125- **4** *1 3/4* **Penitent**[154] 7237 5-9-2 **111**.. FrankieDettori 3 98
(William Haggas) *b.hind: lw: a 4th: rdn whn pce lifted over 2f out: kpt on same pce: nvr able to chal* **11/8**[1]
644- **5** *1* **Cumulus Nimbus**[133] 7523 4-8-13 **99**............................ JimmyFortune 5 93
(Richard Hannon) *stdd s: hld up in 7th: rdn whn pce lifted over 2f out: kpt on ins fnl f: no ch* **8/1**
325- **6** *nk* **Mr Willis**[141] 7430 5-8-13 **89**.. MarcHalford 1 92
(Terry Clement) *chsd ldrs in 5th: rdn wl over 2f out: no imp over 1f out* **50/1**
535- **7** *hd* **Saphira's Fire (IRE)**[133] 7523 6-8-8 **102**.......................... MartinDwyer 8 87
(William Muir) *hld up in 8th: rdn and struggling over 2f out: no ch after: mod late prog* **15/2**[3]
346- **8** *3/4* **Chapter And Verse (IRE)**[94] 8009 5-8-13 **99**................ TonyCulhane 6 90
(Mike Murphy) *swtg: stdd s: hld up last: gng wl enough but stl in last pair 2f out: pushed along over 1f out: nvr remotely involved* **9/1**
653- **9** *1 3/4* **Bikini Babe (IRE)**[147] 7358 4-8-8 **103**................................ JoeFanning 7 82
(Mark Johnston) *lw: hld up in 6th: rdn over 2f out: no prog wl over 1f out: wknd* **8/1**

2m 4.62s (-3.38) **Going Correction** +0.025s/f (Slow) **9** Ran SP% **115.0**
Speed ratings (Par 111): **114,112,112,110,109 109,109,108,107**
toteswingers:1&2 £26.10, 2&3 £31.70, 1&3 £7.40 CSF £261.45 TOTE £11.20: £3.30, £6.00, £1.70; EX 104.20 Trifecta £265.50 Pool of £703.40 - 1.96 winning units..
Owner Abdulla Al Khalifa **Bred** Sheikh Abdulla Bin Isa Al-Khalifa **Trained** Newmarket, Suffolk

FOCUS
A race that has been won by some Group-class performers - notably Kandidate and Dansant - since Polytrack was laid in 2006 but, although the winner is smart, this race lacked something in the way of strength (runner-up only rated 87, market leader bit disappointing) and a gallop that was no more than fair (despite a reasonable final time) saw those up with the pace hold a big advantage. Not form to be confident about. The winner raced just off the inside rail in the straight.

NOTEBOOK
Shamali, absent and gelded since turned over at a short price at Ffos Las last May, was always well positioned in a moderately run race and didn't have to improve to beat an 87-rated rival and to maintain his unbeaten record on Polytrack. While things were in his favour here, he's not fully exposed and may be able to take his form to a higher level on either turf or synthetics.
Resentful Angel, the lowest rated of these, is a reliable type who was allowed an easy time of it in front and seemed to run extremely well in the face of a stiff task. She's almost certainly flattered to a large degree by the way things panned out, though, and life will be a fair bit tougher back in handicaps after reassessment. (op 28-1 tchd 33-1)
Pink Symphony, who looked very fit beforehand, had a good chance at the weights and, although fairly easy to back on this reappearance run and first outing on an artificial surface, had the run of the race and was far from disgraced. A stronger gallop would have suited her much better and she may be capable of picking up a race of this nature against the girls. (op 9-2)
Penitent, a stable-companion of the winner and from the yard that won this last year, looked to have solid claims despite conceding weight all round but, although his stamina wasn't fully tested, he again failed to improve for the step up to this trip after attracting plenty of market support. A more truly run race over 1m should suit better and he's worth another chance. (op 13-8 tchd 7-4)
Cumulus Nimbus, who didn't look great in his coat, showed improved form in last weekend's Winter Derby and wasn't able to show what he was capable of here, but he fared best of those that attempted to come from off the pace and he's a bit better than this bare form. A stronger overall gallop would have suited. (op 9-1)
Mr Willis, having his first run for his new stable, wasn't disgraced in the face of a stiff task in this muddling event but he'll be suited by the return to handicaps and also by the switch back to Lingfield, the scene of his five career victories.
Saphira's Fire(IRE) looked fit beforehand but was another that wasn't seen to best effect in this tactical race on this first run after a break. She is a fairly consistent sort but a losing run that stretches back nearly three years is becoming a bit of a worry. (op 8-1)
Chapter And Verse(IRE), who sweated up beforehand, wasn't suited by the way things unfolded. (op 11-1 tchd 12-1)

1101 WILLIAMHILL.COM E B F MAIDEN STKS 5f (P)
2:55 (2:55) (Class 5) 2-Y-O **£3,561** (£1,059; £529; £264) **Stalls** Low

Form RPR
1 **Jawking** 2-9-3 **0**.. PaulDoe 1 66
(David Evans) *leggy: pushed up to ld and mde rest: urged along over 1f out: jst hld on* **12/1**
6 **2** *shd* **Umph (IRE)**[7] 982 2-9-3 **0**.. TomMcLaughlin 2 66
(David Evans) *leggy: mostly chsd wnr: drvn over 1f out: kpt chalng ins fnl f: jst failed* **20/1**
5 **3** *1* **Sabusa (IRE)**[3] 1042 2-9-3 **0**... SebSanders 5 62
(Alan McCabe) *w'like: racd wd: chsd ldng pair: rdn and struggling 2f out: plugged on ins fnl f* **11/2**[2]
4 *3/4* **Kyllasie** 2-8-12 **0**.. JimmyFortune 4 58
(Richard Hannon) *athletic: hld up in 4th: wnt for run up inner over 1f out and sn chopped off: rdn and nt qckn after* **4/11**[1]
5 *3 3/4* **She's Reel Dusty** 2-8-12 **0**.. LukeMorris 3 39
(Bill Turner) *neat: b: sn last: rdn bef 1/2-way: wl btn over 1f out* **10/1**[3]

62.59 secs (2.09) **Going Correction** +0.025s/f (Slow) **5** Ran SP% **110.2**
Speed ratings (Par 92): **84,83,82,81,75**
CSF £153.89 TOTE £8.30: £4.90, £5.00; EX 73.30.
Owner J A Wilcox **Bred** Mrs D J Hughes **Trained** Pandy, Monmouths
■ Stewards' Enquiry : Paul Doe two-day ban: careless riding (Apr 16,18)

FOCUS
A race that threw up a smart type in Richard Hannon's subsequent triple Listed winner Fat Boy in 2007 but, given the proximity of the two with previous experience and with the short-priced favourite disappointing, this form has a distinctly modest feel to it. The winner raced close to the inside rail throughout. The time was relatively slow.

NOTEBOOK
Jawking, a gelded second foal of a modest dual 6f turf winner, is a half-brother to a claiming Fibresand scorer and, after being nibbled at a double-figure price beforehand, did enough after running green to beat his more experienced stablemate and to provide his trainer with his third debut juvenile winner of the season. Although this form is nothing special, he hadn't quite come in his coat and he's the type to progress again for this yard. (op 14-1)
Umph(IRE), easy in the market beforehand, showed the benefit of having a previous run at this stage and fared considerably better than over course-and-distance a week earlier. This isn't strong form but he showed a reasonable attitude and should be able to pick up a similarly uncompetitive event. (op 14-1 tchd 12-1)
Sabusa(IRE), who has a bit of size about him, attracted support and easily bettered the form shown at Lingfield earlier in the week, but this race lacked much in the way of strength and, although he'll have an experience advantage in the coming weeks, he'll be vulnerable to anything half decent in this grade. (op 8-1)
Kyllasie is slightly on the leg and hadn't quite come in her coat. A sister to useful sprinter Doric Lady, she was the first juvenile runner of the season for an in-form yard that won this race last year and in 2007. She was backed as though defeat was out of the question on this racecourse debut so this has to go down as disappointing, even taking into account her greenness and the fact that she was checked at a crucial stage (unlikely that made much difference to the result). However she has obviously been showing a fair bit at home and she is well worth another chance with this experience behind her. (op 2-5 after 1-2 in places tchd 4-9 in places)
She's Reel Dusty, whose dam was a very useful sort over sprint distances on turf and Polytrack, is a late foal who was fairly easy to back and was well beaten after running green on this racecourse debut. She should improve a fair bit for this experience but she'll have to if she is to win a race in the near future. (op 8-1)

1102 WILLIAMHILL.COM ROSEBERY H'CAP — 1m 3f (P)
3:25 (3:29) (Class 2) (0-105,99) 4-Y-0+
£18,693 (£5,598; £2,799; £1,401; £699; £351) **Stalls** Low

Form — RPR
00-1 **1** — **Cosmic Sun**[42] [614] 5-9-0 **89** .... JackMitchell 15 — 100
(Richard Fahey) *hld up in last pair fr wd draw: gd prog towards inner over 2f out: drvn to chse clr ldr over 1f out: clsd and led last 100yds: won gng away* **14/1**
220- **2** *1 1/4* **Red Cadeaux**[168] [6926] 5-9-10 **99** .... EddieAhern 1 — 108
(Ed Dunlop) *lw: won early battle for ld: drvn at least 3 l clr 2f out: kpt on but hdd and outpcd last 100yds* **9/1**
212- **3** *3 1/4* **Lunar Victory (USA)**[211] [5728] 4-8-12 **87** .... WilliamBuick 16 — 90+
(John Gosden) *h.d.w: lw: hld up in rr fr wd draw: drvn and prog on outer over 2f out: kpt on to take 3rd 1f out: no imp after* **13/2**[2]
156- **4** *3/4* **Ramona Chase**[166] [6990] 6-8-6 **81** .... (t) RobbieFitzpatrick 11 — 83
(Michael Attwater) *hld up in midfield: rdn over 2f out: styd on fr over 1f out to take 4th wl ins fnl f* **66/1**
514- **5** *2* **Captain John Nixon**[113] [7815] 4-8-10 **85** .... AndreaAtzeni 10 — 84
(Pat Eddery) *lw: hld up towards rr: effrt whn nt clr run over 2f out: drvn and kpt on one pce after: n.d* **16/1**
432- **6** *1/2* **Averroes (IRE)**[179] [6654] 4-9-1 **90** .... LukeMorris 3 — 88
(Clive Cox) *trckd ldng pair after 3f: chsd ldr over 3f out: drvn and no imp 2f out: wknd over 1f out* **9/2**[1]
203- **7** *6* **Plymouth Rock (IRE)**[168] [6926] 5-9-8 **97** .... (v) DarryllHolland 8 — 85
(Jeremy Noseda) *dwlt: hld up in last trio: gng wl enough 3f out: drvn and outpcd 2f out: no ch after: plugged on* **14/1**
400- **8** *1 1/2* **Gaily Noble (IRE)**[196] [6205] 5-8-11 **86** .... FergusSweeney 4 — 71
(Andrew Haynes) *cl up: drvn to dispute 3rd briefly 2f out: wknd rapidly jst over 1f out* **28/1**
5-12 **9** *1 1/4* **Lovers Causeway (USA)**[56] [436] 4-9-2 **91** .... (b) FrankieDettori 7 — 74
(Mark Johnston) *lw: chsd ldng pair 3f: styd prom: drvn over 2f out: wknd qckly over 1f out* **7/1**[3]
0-04 **10** *nk* **[illegible]**[35] [70?] 4-9-? **91** .... JoeFanning 5 — 74
(Mark Johnston) *settled in midfield: effrt and sme prog whn [illegible] 2f out: sn wknd* **14/1**
0-06 **11** *nk* **Montaff**[44] [584] 5-9-3 **97** .... MartinHarley(5) 14 — 79
(Mick Channon) *racd wd in midfield: prog to dispute 2nd over 3f out: wknd wl over 2f out* **25/1**
-212 **12** *15* **Round Won (USA)**[24] [803] 4-8-13 **88** .... DaneO'Neill 13 — 45
(William Knight) *nvr bttr than midfield: rdn and wknd wl over 2f out: t.o* **12/1**
-251 **13** *3 3/4* **King Olav (UAE)**[37] [667] 6-9-2 **91** .... SebSanders 9 — 41
(Tony Carroll) *sn towards rr: rdn and wknd wl over 2f out: sn wl bhd: t.o* **15/2**
010- **14** *6* **Missionaire (USA)**[29] [7061] 4-8-8 **83** .... FrannyNorton 2 — 23
(Tony Carroll) *tried to ld but unable to match strides w ldr: 2nd tl wknd rapidly over 3f out: t.o* **40/1**
2111 **15** *29* **Syrian**[43] [599] 4-9-1 **90** .... PatCosgrave 12 — —
(David Evans) *b: s.v.s: sn in tch in last pair: rdn over 3f out: wknd and eased over 2f out: wl t.o* **25/1**

2m 17.17s (-4.73) **Going Correction** +0.025s/f (Slow) **15** Ran SP% **114.4**
Speed ratings (Par 109): **118,117,114,114,112 112,108,106,106,105 105,94,91,87,66**
toteswingers:1&2 £26.30, 2&3 £25.40, 1&3 £20.30 CSF £114.88 CT £785.42 TOTE £19.00: £5.10, £3.30, £3.10; EX 195.00 Trifecta £458.00 Pool of £619.03 - 1.00 winning units..
Owner The Cosmic Cases **Bred** M Wassall **Trained** Musley Bank, N Yorks

FOCUS
A competitive handicap on paper and one won in the recent past by horses that have gone on to show smart form such as Kandidate, Philatelist and, most recently, Dansili Dancer. This year's renewal saw a progressive winner who isn't far off being smart run close to his best. Although the early gallop was decent, it steadied a shade around halfway and very few got involved in a race run in course-record time. The first six finished clear and the winner raced towards the inside rail in the straight.

NOTEBOOK
Cosmic Sun ◆ confirmed himself an improved performer with a career-best effort that saw him make up a good deal of ground in the straight to collar a rival that very much got first run (but wasn't stopping) to maintain his unbeaten record on artificial surfaces. He'll be equally at home back over 1m4f or returned to turf and he appeals strongly as the type to win another decent handicap. (op 12-1)
Red Cadeaux ◆, an improver up to 2m2f last year, was nibbled at in the market and ran as well as he ever has done under an enterprising ride. Down a fair bit in trip on this first run since October, he fared easily the best of those that raced up with the pace. The return to further or the switch back to turf won't inconvenience and he should be able to make amends. He would be interesting if targeted at the Chester Cup. (op 12-1)
Lunar Victory(USA) ◆, who isn't fully exposed, ran as well as he ever has done from his outside draw after making up his ground much wider than either the winner or runner-up on this first run over 1m3f and only this second run in a handicap. He is in good hands and there's almost certainly more to come.
Ramona Chase is fully exposed but he ran creditably in this competitive handicap, leaving the impression that an even stiffer test of stamina would have suited. He'll be interesting in a lesser grade but it's worth remembering that consistency hasn't always been his strongest suit. (op 50-1)
Captain John Nixon, who looked well but became warm, shaped as though retaining much of his ability on this first run since the first half of December. His record last year was one of improvement and he's capable of winning a handicap away from progressive sorts from his current mark granted an even stiffer test of stamina.
Averroes(IRE) only has a maiden win to his name but showed bits of very useful turf form up to 1m4f last year and, after attracting support, ran as though this race was just needed on this all-weather debut and first start since early October. He isn't fully exposed and is worth another chance. (tchd 5-1 in places)
Plymouth Rock(IRE), a bit on edge beforehand, again didn't look entirely straightforward on this reappearance run once pressure was applied. He shaped as though a much stiffer test of stamina would have suited better. (op 12-1)
Lovers Causeway(USA) had been in good form when last seen in February but disappointed on this occasion. However he will be worth another chance back over a bit further in due course. (op 15-2)
Round Won(USA) disappointed but isn't fully exposed and will be worth another chance back over 1m2f.

1103 WILLIAM HILL H'CAP (LONDON MILE QUALIFIER) — 1m (P)
4:00 (4:00) (Class 4) (0-85,87) 4-Y-0+ **£3,885** (£1,156; £577; £288) **Stalls** Low

Form — RPR
5652 **1** — **Baylini**[8] [963] 7-9-6 **87** .... SophieDoyle(3) 1 — 95
(Jamie Osborne) *trckd ldrs: shkn up over 2f out: prog on inner to ld jst over 1f out: rdn out* **13/2**
0100 **2** *1 3/4* **Avon River**[8] [963] 4-9-7 **85** .... DaneO'Neill 2 — 89
(Richard Hannon) *pushed up to ld and allowed untrbld advantage: kicked on over 2f out: hdd and one pce jst over 1f out* **9/2**[3]
055- **3** *1 3/4* **Getcarter**[159] [7114] 5-8-11 **75** .... JimmyFortune 3 — 75
(Richard Hannon) *t.k.h: hld up in 7th: prog on inner over 2f out: wnt 3rd over 1f out: edgd lft and nt qckn u.p: kpt on* **9/2**[3]
0-30 **4** *2* **Red Somerset (USA)**[42] [615] 8-9-7 **85** .... MartinLane 5 — 80
(Mike Murphy) *lw: chsd ldrs: rdn fr 1/2-way: struggling in rr over 2f out: styd on u.p ins fnl f* **7/2**[1]
00-5 **5** *1/2* **Desert Auction (IRE)**[12] [932] 4-8-13 **77** .... MartinDwyer 4 — 71
(Dean Ivory) *trckd ldr: rdn over 2f out: lost 2nd and wknd over 1f out* **10/1**
/00- **6** *nk* **Roodle**[174] [6776] 4-9-4 **85** .... JohnFahy(3) 7 — 79
(Eve Johnson Houghton) *b: hld up in tch: rdn and nt qckn over 2f out: sn outpcd and btn* **18/1**
0050 **7** *1 1/2* **Mister Green (FR)**[7] [991] 5-8-12 **71** oh1 .... (bt) JemmaMarshall(5) 6 — 61
(David Flood) *hld up in last: shkn up and no rspnse over 2f out: no ch after* **12/1**
3135 **8** *2 1/4* **Ocean Legend (IRE)**[14] [908] 6-9-5 **83** .... SebSanders 8 — 68
(Tony Carroll) *cl up: rdn to dispute 2nd 2f out: wknd rapidly over 1f out* **4/1**[2]

1m 38.63s (-1.17) **Going Correction** +0.025s/f (Slow) **8** Ran SP% **114.0**
Speed ratings (Par 105): **106,104,102,100,100 99,98,95**
toteswingers:1&2 £7.90, 2&3 £4.30, 1&3 £6.30 CSF £35.48 CT £132.03 TOTE £6.10: £1.50, £1.60, £1.70; EX 21.10.
Owner J P Doyle **Bred** Templeton Stud **Trained** Upper Lambourn, Berks

FOCUS
A useful handicap but one comprising exposed performers and a steady gallop that only lifted around 2f from home means this bare form has a shaky look to it. Those held up were again at a disadvantage and the winner raced close to the inside rail in the straight. The winner looks the best guide to the form.

1104 WILLIAM HILL SNOWDROP FILLIES' STKS (LISTED RACE) — 1m (P)
4:35 (4:36) (Class 1) 4-Y-0+
£17,031 (£6,456; £3,231; £1,611; £807; £405) **Stalls** Low

Form — RPR
522- **1** — **Agony And Ecstasy**[130] [illegible] 4-8-12 **94** .... (t) RichardKingscote 6 — 99
(Ralph Beckett) *mde all: stretched on over 2f out: more than 2 l clr over 1f out: jst hld on* **14/1**
6-61 **2** *hd* **Night Lily (IRE)**[42] [615] 5-8-12 **89** .... LiamJones 9 — 99
(Paul D'Arcy) *lw: dwlt: hld up in last trio: prog on inner over 2f out: sustained effrt to go 2nd jst ins fnl f: clsd on wnr fin: jst failed* **14/1**
063- **3** *1 1/4* **Maid In Heaven (IRE)**[227] [5222] 4-8-12 **92** .... JoeFanning 2 — 96
(Walter Swinburn) *chsd wnr 3f and again 3f out: drvn and no imp 2f out: lost 2nd jst ins fnl f: kpt on* **10/1**[3]
-600 **4** *3/4* **Kinky Afro (IRE)**[30] [756] 4-8-12 **95** .... LiamKeniry 4 — 94
(J S Moore) *hld up towards rr: rdn and prog over 2f out: kpt on same pce fr over 1f out* **25/1**
066- **5** *2 3/4* **Yer Woman (IRE)**[133] [7522] 4-8-12 **91** .... JimmyFortune 10 — 88
(Richard Hannon) *restrained after s: hld up and sn last: taken to wd outside over 2f out: stl last over 1f out: drvn and r.o: no ch* **33/1**
550- **6** *shd* **Totally Ours**[169] [6886] 4-8-12 **97** .... MartinDwyer 3 — 87
(William Muir) *prom: rdn and outpcd fr over 2f out: n.d after: kpt on nr fin* **14/1**
022- **7** *nk* **Mosqueras Romance**[108] [7875] 5-8-12 **100** .... FrankieDettori 1 — 87
(Marco Botti) *dwlt: rcvrd to trck ldrs in 5th: effrt to chse ldng pair over 2f out: no imp over 1f out: fdd ins fnl f: lost 2 pls last strides* **11/10**[1]
0-11 **8** *3/4* **Fanditha (IRE)**[8] [963] 5-8-12 **88** .... DarryllHolland 8 — 85
(Mick Channon) *racd wd in midfield: rdn and no prog wl over 2f out: sn btn* **12/1**
31- **9** *1/2* **Fun Affair (USA)**[204] [5925] 4-8-12 **80** .... WilliamBuick 5 — 87
(John Gosden) *lengthy: scope: lw: t.k.h: chsd wnr after 3f to 3f out: sn lost pl u.p: wknd* **4/1**[2]
542- **10** *1* **Bahati (IRE)**[161] [7097] 4-8-12 **92** .... StephenCraine 11 — 82
(Jonathan Portman) *v awkward s: hld up in last trio: rdn 3f out: sn struggling* **25/1**

1m 37.87s (-1.93) **Going Correction** +0.025s/f (Slow) **10** Ran SP% **115.0**
Speed ratings (Par 108): **110,109,108,107,105 104,104,103,103,102**
toteswingers:1&2 £10.40, 2&3 £7.80, 1&3 £11.70 CSF £184.93 TOTE £15.80: £5.20, £5.40, £2.60; EX 295.20.
Owner Miss Rachel Tregaskes **Bred** Downfield Cottage Stud **Trained** Kimpton, Hants

FOCUS
Not the strongest of Listed races with only the disappointing market leader going into the race rated in triple figures. An ordinary gallop increased early in the straight and this was another race in which very few figured. The winner raced centre-to-far-side late on. It's doubtful whether this is form to trust.

NOTEBOOK

Agony And Ecstasy is largely a consistent sort who confirmed she retains all her ability under an enterprising ride back over this trip and back on Polytrack on this first run since November. She's a very useful sort on both turf and artificial surfaces and she will remain of interest at a similar level when a similarly easy lead looks likely. The Group 3 Athasi Stakes at the Curragh is reportedly on the agenda. (tchd 16-1)

Night Lily(IRE) ◆ looked to have a bit to find at the weights but ran as well as she ever has done on returned to Listed company and she deserves extra credit from coming from as far off an ordinary gallop as she did. A stronger pace would have suited and she's capable of winning one of these when things pan out to her liking. (op 11-1 tchd 10-1)

Maid In Heaven(IRE), on her toes beforehand, developed into a very useful performer up to this trip on turf last year and, although well placed given the ordinary tempo, shaped as though retaining much of her ability on this first run since August. She showed a willing attitude late and and should be able to pick up the winning thread this season. (tchd 8-1)

Kinky Afro(IRE), fit from a campaign in Dubai, fared better than in Group 3 company on Tapeta last time but, although a stronger gallop would have helped her, she hasn't won for over a year and is going to have to raise her game to win a similar race. (op 20-1)

Yer Woman(IRE) was far from disgraced on her first run over this trip on her first run in Listed company in a race where the prominent-racers again held the edge. The return to 7f in a more truly run race should suit better but she'll have to improve to win a similar event or to defy her current mark in handicaps. (op 20-1)

Totally Ours, a very useful sort on turf who had won two of her three outings at this course, left the impression that the return to 1m2f would be more to her liking. She is worth another chance granted a stiffer test.

Mosqueras Romance, the pick of these weights, was a long way below the form shown in Listed events at this course and at Lingfield on her last two starts in the latter months of last year and was the disappointment. She's obviously better than this but doesn't look one for maximum faith. (tchd Evens and 5-4 in places)

Fun Affair(USA), who showed useful form to beat a couple of subsequent winners in a Wolverhampton maiden in September, had a fair bit to find in this much tougher company and, although she was priced up more on potential, she still proved a bit disappointing in a race where improving sorts where thin on the ground. She will be worth another chance. Official explanation: jockey said filly ran flat (op 5-1 tchd 6-1)

1105 WILLIAMHILL.COM QUEEN'S PRIZE (H'CAP) — 2m (P)

5:05 (5:06) (Class 2) (0-105,92) 4-Y-0+

£7,788 (£2,332; £1,166; £583; £291; £146) **Stalls** Low

Form	Pos	Dist	Horse / Comment	SP	RPR
0-	1		**Battleoftrafalgar**[29] 7736 4-8-13 **83** ....(b) JoeFanning 9 (Michael Attwater) *swtg: led after 2f: mde rest: urged along over 2f out: pressed on all sides over 1f out: hld on wl*	**40/1**	88
/32-	2	¾	**Right Stuff (FR)**[11] 1020 8-9-5 **85** .... EddieAhern 2 (Gary Moore) *trckd ldrs: shkn up over 2f out and sltly outpcd: drvn over 1f out: styd on ins fnl f to take 2nd last stride*	**7/1**[3]	89
244-	3	*shd*	**Aurorian (IRE)**[187] 6423 5-9-3 **83** .... JimmyFortune 10 (Richard Hannon) *bit bkwd: prom: trckd wnr over 6f out: drvn over 2f out: chal over 1f out: hld ins fnl f: lost 2nd last stride*	**11/2**[2]	87
360-	4	*shd*	**Desert Sea (IRE)**[204] 5908 8-9-12 **92** .... MartinDwyer 4 (David Arbuthnot) *dwlt: hld up in 7th: rdn over 2f out: prog over 1f out: kpt on to dispute 2nd ins fnl f: a hld*	**3/1**[1]	96+
1132	5	½	**Muzo (USA)**[21] 849 5-8-11 **77** .... FrannyNorton 8 (Chris Dwyer) *led 2f: trckd wnr to over 6f out: styd cl up: drvn to chal again 2f out: stl cl enough ins fnl f: lost pls last strides*	**7/1**[3]	80
02-4	6	2¼	**Into Wain (USA)**[37] 667 4-9-5 **89** .... DarryllHolland 11 (Steve Gollings) *hld up in 8th: drvn and hanging over 2f out: styd on fr over 1f out: nvr gng pce to rch ldrs*	**8/1**	89
044-	7	1½	**Crocus Rose**[162] 7061 5-8-13 **79** .... LukeMorris 6 (Harry Dunlop) *bit bkwd: hld up in 6th: effrt to chse ldng trio 2f out and cl enough: wknd ins fnl f*	**12/1**	78
66-4	8	2	**Langley**[7] 994 4-8-12 **82** .... DaneO'Neill 5 (Pat Murphy) *lw: hld up in last pair: rdn and no prog over 2f out: one pce after*	**25/1**	78
2-10	9	*nk*	**Phoenix Flight (IRE)**[11] 849 6-9-7 **87** .... FergusSweeney 7 (James Evans) *lw: hld up in last pair: shkn up and no rspnse over 2f out: one pce after*	**11/2**[2]	83
	10	4½	**Emrani (USA)**[22] 5934 4-9-1 **85** ....(p) SebSanders 1 (Donald McCain) *lw: prom: u.p over 5f out: wknd over 2f out*	**14/1**	75

3m 28.15s (-1.95) **Going Correction** +0.025s/f (Slow)
WFA 4 from 5yo+ 4lb — **10** Ran SP% **112.5**
Speed ratings (Par 109): **105,104,104,104,104 103,102,101,101,99**
toteswingers:1&2 £24.50, 2&3 £7.00, 1&3 £27.30 CSF £289.92 CT £1795.52 TOTE £42.80: £9.60, £2.60, £2.60; EX 282.20.
Owner Bagden Wood Building Services Limited **Bred** J M Beever **Trained** Epsom, Surrey

FOCUS

A traditionally competitive handicap but mainly exposed sorts and an ordinary gallop that only picked up passing the intersection saw those held up at a disadvantage. The winner came down the centre in the straight and the form is rated around the third and fifth.

NOTEBOOK

Battleoftrafalgar, useful up to 1m4f for Aidan O'Brien, was fit from a recent hurdle spin and left behind his previous below-par Flat run on this first outing over 2m with his usual blinkers refitted. He handles fast and softish ground and, while he was allowed an easy lead, he did show a good attitude for pressure and it will be interesting to see if this can be built on when returned to turf. (tchd 33-1)

Right Stuff(FR), also fit from a recent hurdle run, is a consistent sort on Polytrack and ran up to his best, despite racing with the choke out, to fill the same position he had done in this race last year. A stronger overall gallop would have suited and he should continue to give a good account on Polytrack or on a sound surface over hurdles. (op 8-1)

Aurorian(IRE) is a consistent sort effective over a variety of distances and he ran creditably after being well placed in a moderately run race on this first start since September. He is high enough in the weights but should continue to give it his best shot. (op 6-1 tchd 7-1)

Desert Sea(IRE) ◆, who won this race in 2009, shaped better than the bare result suggests after faring the best of those held up on this first outing since September. He too would have been suited by a much stronger overall gallop and last year's Northumberland Plate third is capable of winning a reasonable staying handicap this term. (op 11-4)

Muzo(USA)'s record is one of steady improvement and, although ideally placed throughout, ran creditably in this stronger grade returned to this longer trip. There's almost certainly more to come from one who has only had nine races. (op 8-1)

Into Wain(USA) wasn't disgraced in a race that wasn't run to suit the hold-up horses on this first run over this trip. A more truly run race over shorter should see him in a more favourable light.

Emrani(USA) Official explanation: jockey said gelding had no more to give

1106 WILLIAMHILL.COM H'CAP — 7f (P)

5:40 (5:41) (Class 4) (0-85,81) 3-Y-0 — **£3,885** (£1,156; £577; £288) **Stalls** Low

Form	Pos	Dist	Horse / Comment	SP	RPR
P21-	1		**Indian Jack (IRE)**[136] 7478 3-9-5 **79** .... LukeMorris 4 (Alan Bailey) *h.d.w: tall: scope: hld up in 4th: stoked up over 2f out: drvn and clsd over 1f out: led jst ins fnl f: forged clr*	**10/11**[1]	86+
-011	2	2¾	**May's Boy**[57] 423 3-9-6 **80** ....(p) DaneO'Neill 5 (Mark Usher) *trckd ldr: rdn to ld wl over 1f out: hdd jst ins fnl f: outpcd*	**8/1**	80
213	3	¾	**Christmas Aria (IRE)**[29] 764 3-9-1 **75** .... HayleyTurner 1 (Simon Dow) *led: rdn and hdd wl over 1f out: already hld in 3rd whn rdr dropped whip 1f out*	**15/2**[3]	73
500-	4	¾	**Persian Herald**[175] 6745 3-9-7 **81** .... MartinDwyer 3 (William Muir) *stdd s: hld up last: shkn up over 2f out: no imp tl plugged on ins fnl f*	**10/1**	77
25-1	5	*nk*	**Ceffyl Gwell**[17] 864 3-9-2 **76** .... JimmyFortune 2 (Richard Hannon) *trckd ldng pair: effrt 2f out: nt qckn over 1f out: wknd ins fnl f*	**11/4**[2]	71

1m 25.99s (-0.01) **Going Correction** +0.025s/f (Slow) — **5** Ran SP% **111.0**
Speed ratings (Par 100): **101,97,97,96,95**
CSF £8.98 TOTE £1.80: £1.40, £4.10; EX 8.90.
Owner Forza Azzurri **Bred** Waterford Hall Stud **Trained** Newmarket, Suffolk

FOCUS

A fairly useful handicap in which all of the runners had won races. The gallop was an ordinary one and the winner came down the centre. He's progressing nicely, but his task was eased by the poor run of the fifth.

T/Plt: £4,951.60 to a £1 stake. Pool of £63,082.75 - 9.30 winning ticket. T/Qpdt: £125.50 to a £1 stake. Pool of £5,922.18 - 34.90 winning tickets. JN

[1092] DONCASTER (L-H)

Sunday, April 3

OFFICIAL GOING: Good (good to firm in places)

Wind: Cloudy, rain between races 5 and6 Weather: light, half against

1107 AJA GENTLEMAN AMATEUR RIDERS' H'CAP — 1m 4f

1:40 (1:40) (Class 5) (0-70,70) 4-Y-0+ — **£2,307** (£709; £354) **Stalls** Low

Form	Pos	Dist	Horse / Comment	SP	RPR
0-52	1		**Jeer (IRE)**[34] 715 7-10-13 **69** ....(b) MrDHDunsdon 19 (Michael Easterby) *mde all: sn 3 to 4 l up: rdn over 2f out: hld on ins fnl f*	**11/1**	78
122-	2	1	**Sancho Panza**[174] 6816 4-9-11 **57** .... MrRBirkett(3) 12 (Julia Feilden) *in tch: swtchd rt over 3f out: hdwy over 2f out: chsd wnr ins fnl f: kpt on*	**12/1**	64
045-	3	2½	**Hail Tiberius**[151] 7307 4-10-11 **68** .... MrSWalker 2 (Tim Walford) *hld up in midfield: rdn and outpcd over 3f out: hdwy over 2f out: kpt on wl ins fnl f: wnt 3rd cl home*	**8/1**[2]	73
-041	4	*nse*	**Relative Strength (IRE)**[17] 879 6-11-0 **70** ....(bt) MrMarioBaratti 16 (Frank Sheridan) *midfield: hdwy over 3f out: rdn over 2f out: kpt on ins fnl f*	**17/2**[3]	73
146-	5	¾	**James Pollard (IRE)**[37] 7778 6-10-2 **63** ....(t) MrRJWilliams(5) 17 (Bernard Llewellyn) *midfield: hdwy over 3f out: chsd wnr 2f out: no ex ins fnl f*	**28/1**	65
266-	6	2½	**Tenhoo**[127] 7599 5-9-9 **56** oh4 .... MrARawlinson(5) 7 (Eric Alston) *midfield on inner: rdn over 3f out: kpt on one pce*	**20/1**	54
3-45	7	1½	**Amical Risks (FR)**[44] 596 7-9-9 **56** oh1 .... WilliamTwiston-Davies(5) 6 (Ollie Pears) *hld up: rdn and hdwy on outer over 3f out: kpt on ins fnl f*	**17/2**[3]	51
200-	8	2¼	**Arashi**[176] 6754 5-10-4 **65** ....(v) MrJPFeatherstone(5) 1 (Lucinda Featherstone) *hld up: kpt on fnl 2f: n.d*	**14/1**	57
1-45	9	1¼	**Taste The Wine (IRE)**[26] 418 5-9-11 **58** .... BrendanPowell(5) 13 (Bernard Llewellyn) *v.s.a: hld up: kpt on fnl 3f: n.d*	**14/1**	48
0513	10	*nk*	**Carr Hall (IRE)**[11] 944 8-9-12 **61** .... MrCCarroll(7) 10 (Tony Carroll) *hld up in midfield: hdwy over 3f out: wknd over 1f out*	**20/1**	50
5022	11	½	**Pinsplitter (USA)**[46] 560 4-9-8 **56** oh2 ....(p) MrTGarner(5) 5 (Alan McCabe) *hld up: rdn over 3f out: n.d*	**16/1**	44
/323	12	1¼	**Ay Tay Tate (IRE)**[40] 644 5-9-12 **57** .... MrCMartin(3) 18 (David C Griffiths) *trckd ldr: rdn over 2f out: sn wknd*	**33/1**	43
600-	13	2¼	**Jenny Soba**[41] 7634 8-9-10 **59** oh9 ow3 .... MrWFeatherstone(7) 3 (Lucinda Featherstone) *hld up in midfield: rdn over 3f out: no imp*	**66/1**	42
110-	14	¾	**Dean Iarracht (IRE)**[155] 7228 5-10-8 **64** .... MrSDobson 4 (Tracy Waggott) *dwlt: hld up and keen: hdwy 3f out: wknd over 1f out*	**20/1**	46
-431	15	*nk*	**Squad**[58] 418 5-10-8 **69** ....(v) MrJCoffill-Brown(5) 11 (Simon Dow) *hld up in midfield: brief hdwy towards outer over 3f out: wknd 2f out*	**15/2**[1]	50
450-	16	2½	**Simple Jim (FR)**[170] 6895 7-9-9 **58** .... MrSMurray(7) 21 (David O'Meara) *midfield on outer: wknd fnl 3f*	**14/1**	35
414-	17	2¾	**Mustajed**[93] 8032 10-10-1 **62** .... MrPMillman(5) 22 (Rod Millman) *trckd ldrs: wknd fnl 3f*	**18/1**	35
1-53	18	7	**Active Asset (IRE)**[52] 484 9-9-9 **56** oh2 .... JustinNewman(5) 15 (David C Griffiths) *midfield: wknd over 3f out*	**50/1**	18
3535	19	1¾	**Duar Mapel (USA)**[6] 1016 5-9-9 **56** oh2 .... MrOGarner(5) 20 (Brian Baugh) *trckd ldrs: rdn over 3f out: sn wknd*	**33/1**	15
320-	20	5	**Vittachi**[13] 6109 4-9-10 **58** .... GrantCockburn(5) 9 (Alistair Whillans) *midfield: rdn over 3f out: sn wknd*	**40/1**	9
050-	21	5	**Global**[156] 6534 5-10-6 **69** .... MrJohnWilley(7) 14 (Brian Ellison) *midfield on outer: wknd over 4f out*	**25/1**	12

2m 35.08s (0.18) **Going Correction** +0.075s/f (Good)
WFA 4 from 5yo+ 1lb — **21** Ran SP% **124.5**
Speed ratings (Par 103): **102,101,99,99,99 97,96,94,94,93 93,92,91,90,90 88,87,82,81,77 74**
Tote Swingers: 1&2 £45.70, 1&3 £13.10, 2&3 £28.60 CSF £119.32 CT £1135.00 TOTE £12.00: £2.20, £5.30, £2.80, £3.00; EX 152.10 Trifecta £226.70 Part won. Pool: £306.48 - 0.10 winning units..
Owner Mrs Jean Turpin **Bred** Floors Farming And Side Hill Stud **Trained** Sheriff Hutton, N Yorks

FOCUS

Following a dry night the going was given as good, good to firm in places. They didn't go that quick early here. The winner showed his best form since this time last year.

Taste The Wine(IRE) Official explanation: jockey said on trying to remove blindfold that it caught on a buckle and caused a delay

1108 CROWNHOTEL-BAWTRY.COM MAIDEN STKS 7f
2:10 (2:13) (Class 4) 3-Y-O **£3,561** (£1,059; £529; £264) **Stalls** High

Form RPR

23- **1** **King Of Jazz (IRE)**[309] 2547 3-9-3 0... RyanMoore 4 90+
(Richard Hannon) *trckd ldr in centre: led over 2f out: rdn over 1f out: edgd rt jst ins fnl f: kpt on* **13/8**[1]

2 *1 3/4* **Firebeam** 3-9-3 0... KierenFallon 9 85+
(William Haggas) *in tch in centre: hdwy over 3f out: chsd wnr over 1f out: kpt on ins fnl f* **12/1**

230- **3** *3 3/4* **With Hindsight (IRE)**[246] 4578 3-9-3 77... PhilipRobinson 6 75
(Clive Cox) *t.k.h: hld up in centre: rdn over 2f out: kpt on wl ins fnl f: wnt 3rd cl home* **20/1**

00- **4** *hd* **Tiberius Claudius (IRE)**[215] 5626 3-9-3 0... TomQueally 2 74
(George Margarson) *dwlt: hld up in midfield centre: hdwy over 1f out: kpt on ins fnl f* **50/1**

435- **5** *3/4* **Early Applause**[185] 6505 3-9-3 74... MichaelHills 12 72
(B W Hills) *racd cl up stands' side: rdn over 2f out: one pce* **4/1**[2]

30- **6** *3 1/4* **Shamdarley (IRE)**[183] 6560 3-9-3 0... FrederikTylicki 5 64+
(Michael Dods) *in tch in centre: rdn over 1f out: no imp* **16/1**

7 *1/2* **Muffin McLeay (IRE)** 3-9-3 0... LeeNewman 8 62
(David Barron) *dwlt: hld up centre: swtchd rt to r stands' side over 3f out: rdn over 2f out: n.d* **100/1**

633- **8** *1/2* **Cultural Desert**[156] 7201 3-9-3 76... JimCrowley 11 61
(Ralph Beckett) *trckd ldr stands' side: rdn 3f out: wknd over 1f out* **4/1**[2]

2 **9** *4 1/2* **Blink Of An Eye**[25] 811 3-9-3 0... JamieSpencer 3 49
(Michael Bell) *led in centre: rdn whn hdd over 2f out: wknd over 1f out* **10/1**[3]

10 *4* **Ellemental** 3-8-12 0... AndrewElliott 10 33
(Mrs K Burke) *dwlt: hld up in centre: rdn over 2f out: sn hung rt: n.d* **100/1**

255- **11** *shd* **Icy Blue**[148] 7347 3-9-3 69... TomEaves 1 38
(Richard Whitaker) *hld up in midfield in centre: wknd fnl 2f* **40/1**

26- **12** *17* **In Babylon (GER)**[177] 6704 3-9-3 0... PaulHanagan 7 —
(Tom Dascombe) *trckd ldr in centre and keen: wknd qckly over 2f out* **33/1**

1m 26.06s (-0.24) **Going Correction** +0.075s/f (Good) **12** Ran SP% **114.8**
Speed ratings (Par 100): **104,102,97,97,96 92,92,91,86,82 81,62**
Tote Swingers: 1&2 £5.20, 1&3 £5.60, 2&3 £20.80 CSF £21.72 TOTE £2.60: £1.20, £3.50, £4.00; EX 15.30 Trifecta £170.10 Pool: £545.02 - 2.37 winning units..

Owner Justin Dowley & Michael Pescod **Bred** T M Jennings **Trained** East Everleigh, Wilts

FOCUS
They split into two groups here, with the bulk of the runners coming up the centre of the track and just two horses coming up the stands' side. The first four came from the larger group up the centre. Fair maiden form, rated around the third and arguably worth a bit more.

1109 WILLIAM HILL HOME OF BETTING H'CAP (DIV I) 7f
2:45 (2:45) (Class 4) (0-85,85) 4-Y-O+ **£3,238** (£963; £481; £240) **Stalls** High

Form RPR

126- **1** **Lord Aeryn (IRE)**[155] 7238 4-9-1 79... PaulHanagan 9 91
(Richard Fahey) *racd centre tl gps merged 1/2-way: hld up: hdwy over 2f out: swtchd lft over 1f out: rdn to ld wl ins fnl f* **11/2**[2]

030- **2** *1/2* **Internationaldebut (IRE)**[159] 7146 6-9-4 82... KierenFallon 14 93
(Paul Midgley) *racd stands' side: hld up: in tch: led over 1f out: sn rdn: edgd lft and hdd wl ins fnl f* **9/2**[1]

6-01 **3** *2* **New Leyf (IRE)**[24] 822 5-9-0 78... SteveDrowne 4 84
(Jeremy Gask) *racd centre tl gps merged 1/2-way: hld up: hdwy over 2f out: ev ch over 1f out: sn rdn: styd on same pce ins fnl f* **13/2**[3]

320- **4** *1 1/4* **Imperial Djay (IRE)**[181] 6029 6-8-13 77... PJMcDonald 1 79+
(Ruth Carr) *racd centre tl gps merged 1/2-way: dwlt: hld up: hdwy over 1f out: r.o: nrst fin* **28/1**

353- **5** *1 1/2* **Ming Meng (IRE)**[168] 6963 4-8-12 76... HayleyTurner 5 74
(Michael Bell) *racd centre tl gps merged 1/2-way: chsd ldrs: rdn and ev ch over 1f out: no ex ins fnl f* **9/1**

025- **6** *2* **Cyflymder (IRE)**[122] 7665 5-8-5 74... NeilFarley(5) 6 67
(Declan Carroll) *racd centre tl gps merged 1/2-way: hld up: hdwy over 2f out: rdn over 1f out: no ex ins fnl f* **12/1**

4622 **7** *1 1/4* **Buaiteoir (FR)**[8] 995 5-9-6 84... TonyCulhane 12 73
(Paul D'Arcy) *racd stands' side: hld up: hdwy and nt clr run over 2f out: nt knocked arnd whn btn fnl f* **15/2**

000- **8** *6* **My Gacho (IRE)**[189] 6394 9-8-8 75... MichaelO'Connell(3) 2 48
(David Nicholls) *led centre tl gps merged 1/2-way: rdn over 2f out: wknd over 1f out* **12/1**

421- **9** *1/2* **Little Pete (IRE)**[42] 6-8-9 73... PatrickMathers 3 45
(Ian McInnes) *racd centre tl gps merged 1/2-way: chsd ldrs: rdn 3f out: wknd over 1f out* **40/1**

040- **10** *1 3/4* **Academy Blues (USA)**[177] 6721 6-9-0 85... PNolan(7) 16 52
(David Nicholls) *racd stands' side: chsd ldr tl led over 2f out: rdn and hdd over 1f out: wknd fnl f* **18/1**

260- **11** *4* **Night Trade (IRE)**[148] 7352 4-9-0 78... SilvestreDeSousa 8 34+
(Deborah Sanderson) *racd centre tl gps merged 1/2-way: prom: rdn over 2f out: wknd over 1f out* **22/1**

100- **12** *1* **Rough Rock (IRE)**[155] 7238 6-8-4 73... AdamBeschizza(5) 11 27
(Chris Dwyer) *racd stands' side: prom tl wknd 2f out* **20/1**

-501 **13** *5* **El Dececy (USA)**[47] 547 7-8-7 76...(p) KieranO'Neill(5) 13 16
(John Balding) *led stands' side over 4f: sn wknd* **16/1**

640- **14** *4* **Ursula (IRE)**[168] 6963 5-8-13 77... AndrewElliott 7 —
(Mrs K Burke) *racd centre tl gps merged 1/2-way: prom 4f* **22/1**

020- **15** *1* **Antoniola (IRE)**[199] 6105 4-8-11 75... TedDurcan 10 —
(Tim Easterby) *racd centre tl gps merged 1/2-way: a in rr: bhd fnl 3f* **11/1**

1m 26.06s (-0.24) **Going Correction** +0.075s/f (Good) **15** Ran SP% **122.9**
Speed ratings (Par 105): **104,103,101,99,98 95,94,87,86,84 80,79,73,68,67**
Tote Swingers: 1&2 £4.30, 1&3 £8.00, 2&3 £7.30 CSF £28.50 CT £173.84 TOTE £6.20: £2.40, £2.70, £2.90; EX 21.40 Trifecta £150.10 Pool: £466.74 - 2.30 winning units..

Owner Mrs H Steel **Bred** Woodhouse Syndicate **Trained** Musley Bank, N Yorks

■ Stewards' Enquiry : Kieran O'Neill caution: used whip down shoulder in the forehand.

FOCUS
A bit of a messy race, with the whole field eventually clustering towards the stands' side and getting in each other's way, but the right horses came to the fore at the finish and the form makes enough sense among the principals.

1110 WILLIAM HILL HOME OF BETTING H'CAP (DIV II) 7f
3:20 (3:21) (Class 4) (0-85,84) 4-Y-O+ **£3,238** (£963; £481; £240) **Stalls** High

Form RPR

360- **1** **King Of Eden (IRE)**[210] 5789 5-9-0 77... DavidAllan 6 87
(Eric Alston) *hld up: hdwy to trck ldrs 3f out: rdn to ld over 1f out: hld on drvn out* **10/1**[3]

0211 **2** *hd* **Ivory Silk**[30] 763 6-8-10 73... RyanMoore 8 82
(Jeremy Gask) *s.i.s: hld up: swtchd lft and gd hdwy over 2f out: chsd wnr ins fnl f: edgd rt: kpt on but jst hld towards fin kpt on* **9/2**[1]

-065 **3** *1 1/4* **Mastership (IRE)**[55] 447 7-9-0 80...(p) IanBrennan(3) 5 86
(John Quinn) *hld up: hdwy over 2f out: swtchd rt over 1f out: kpt on wl ins fnl f* **14/1**

50-1 **4** *nk* **Rio Cobolo (IRE)**[18] 869 5-8-10 76... MichaelO'Connell(3) 3 81
(David Nicholls) *chsd ldrs: chal over 2f out: led over 1f out: sn hdd: kpt on* **16/1**

130- **5** *hd* **Magic Cat**[148] 7352 5-9-5 82... AndrewElliott 9 87
(Mrs K Burke) *hld up: rdn over 2f out: hdwy over 1f out: swtchd lft 1f out: kpt on wl ins fnl f* **16/1**

000- **6** *1/2* **Extraterrestrial**[160] 7121 7-9-6 83... PaulHanagan 2 86
(Richard Fahey) *hld up: hdwy over 2f out: rdn over 1f out: kpt on ins fnl f* **7/1**[2]

210- **7** *1 1/4* **Another Try (IRE)**[148] 7352 6-8-9 77... HarryBentley(5) 12 77
(Alan Jarvis) *prom: led over 2f out: rdn whn hdd over 1f out: no ex ins fnl f* **12/1**

0-66 **8** *shd* **Dubai Dynamo**[13] 932 6-9-1 78... PJMcDonald 1 78
(Ruth Carr) *hld up: rdn over 1f out: kpt on ins fnl f: n.d* **12/1**

55-1 **9** *shd* **Count Bertoni (IRE)**[19] 854 4-8-11 74... SilvestreDeSousa 4 73
(David O'Meara) *in tch on outer: rdn and hdwy over 2f out: no ex ins fnl f* **16/1**

060- **10** *1 1/4* **Fibs And Flannel**[152] 7283 4-8-10 73... DuranFentiman 10 69
(Tim Easterby) *midfield: pushed along over 3f out: one pce* **25/1**

011- **11** *5* **Not My Choice (IRE)**[190] 6370 6-8-5 71...(t) JamesSullivan(3) 11 54
(David C Griffiths) *cl up: led 4f out: rdn whn hdd over 2f out: wknd over 1f out* **33/1**

000- **12** *nk* **Karaka Jack**[167] 6984 4-8-9 75... BillyCray(3) 14 57
(David Nicholls) *chsd ldrs: rdn over 2f out: wknd 1f out* **7/1**[2]

140- **13** *1 1/4* **Solar Spirit (IRE)**[107] 7915 6-9-2 79... PaulMulrennan 16 57
(Tracy Waggott) *rrd s: plld hrd: trckd ldrs: lost pl over 1f out: wknd ins fnl f* **16/1**

121- **14** *3* **Cara's Request (AUS)**[152] 7283 6-9-7 84... PaulQuinn 15 54
(David Nicholls) *led: hdd 4f out: wknd over 2f out* **11/1**

013 **15** *1 3/4* **Tewin Wood**[15] 908 4-8-10 76... AmyBaker(3) 13 42
(Alan Bailey) *chsd ldrs: wknd over 1f out* **20/1**

10-2 **16** *8* **Just Five (IRE)**[52] 495 5-8-12 78... PatrickDonaghy(3) 7 22
(Michael Dods) *hld up: a towards rr* **28/1**

1m 25.93s (-0.37) **Going Correction** +0.075s/f (Good) **16** Ran SP% **121.2**
Speed ratings (Par 105): **105,104,103,103,102 102,100,100,100,99 93,93,91,88,86 77**
Tote Swingers: 1&2 £5.90, 1&3 £24.40, 2&3 £22.00 CSF £51.49 CT £648.67 TOTE £9.90: £2.00, £1.60, £4.50, £4.90; EX 62.40 TRIFECTA Not won..

Owner The Grumpy Old Geezers **Bred** Gainsborough Stud Management Ltd **Trained** Longton, Lancs

FOCUS
They seemed to go a better early gallop in this division, the winning time was marginally quicker, and the first three came from off the pace. A similar standard of form to division one, the winner continuing his progress.

1111 WILLIAMHILL.COM H'CAP 6f
3:55 (3:55) (Class 2) (0-100,100) 4-Y-O+ **£9,390** (£2,794; £1,396; £697) **Stalls** High

Form RPR

301- **1** **Horseradish**[148] 7010 4-9-0 96... HayleyTurner 4 105+
(Michael Bell) *a.p: led and edgd rt over 1f out: rdn out* **5/1**[1]

/55- **2** *3/4* **Waffle (IRE)**[162] 7079 5-9-6 99... SilvestreDeSousa 17 106+
(David Barron) *hld up: t.k.h: nt clr run over 2f out to over 1f out: r.o wl ins fnl f: nt rch wnr* **14/1**

500- **3** *shd* **Our Jonathan**[162] 7079 4-9-0 93... JamieSpencer 8 99
(Kevin Ryan) *hld up: swtchd lft and hdwy over 1f out: chsd wnr ins fnl f: r.o* **8/1**[3]

103- **4** *3/4* **Lutine Bell**[120] 7689 4-8-13 92...(b) NeilCallan 14 96
(Mike Murphy) *chsd ldrs: rdn over 1f out: r.o* **18/1**

000- **5** *3/4* **Advanced**[148] 7348 8-8-8 90... AmyRyan(3) 10 92
(Kevin Ryan) *chsd ldrs: rdn over 1f out: styd on same pce ins fnl f* **20/1**

600- **6** *1/2* **Quest For Success (IRE)**[148] 7348 6-9-2 95... PaulHanagan 13 95
(Richard Fahey) *chsd ldrs: rdn and ev ch over 1f out: no ex ins fnl f* **11/1**

003- **7** *3/4* **Nasri**[174] 6806 5-8-13 92... WilliamCarson 16 90
(David Nicholls) *chsd ldr tl led over 2f out: rdn and hdd over 1f out: no ex ins fnl f* **20/1**

05-2 **8** *nk* **Medicean Man**[22] 848 5-9-2 95... SteveDrowne 6 92
(Jeremy Gask) *hld up: swtchd lft and hdwy over 1f out: r.o: nt rch ldrs* **6/1**[2]

400- **9** *nk* **Kellys Eye (IRE)**[163] 7060 4-8-10 92... BillyCray(3) 7 88
(George Foster) *s.i.s: hld up: hdwy u.p over 2f out: styd on same pce ins fnl f* **18/1**

110- **10** *hd* **Colonel Mak**[176] 6752 4-9-2 100... LMcNiff(5) 20 95+
(David Barron) *hld up: r.o ins fnl f: nvr nrr* **28/1**

002- **11** *3/4* **Esprit De Midas**[163] 7060 5-8-12 91... PhillipMakin 1 84+
(Kevin Ryan) *hld up: rdn over 2f out: r.o ins fnl f: nvr trbld ldrs* **25/1**

030- **12** *1/2* **Johannes (IRE)**[162] 7079 8-9-3 96... TonyHamilton 21 87
(Richard Fahey) *prom: rdn over 1f out: no ex fnl f* **16/1**

265- **13** *1/2* **Layla's Hero (IRE)**[191] 6321 4-8-13 92... TomQueally 3 81
(David Nicholls) *half-rrd s: hld up: rdn over 2f out: nvr trbld ldrs* **16/1**

406- **14** *nse* **Parisian Pyramid (IRE)**[148] 7348 5-9-2 95... StephenCraine 19 84+
(Kevin Ryan) *hld up: nvr on terms* **14/1**

3-41 **15** *1/2* **Flipando (IRE)**[22] 848 10-9-1 94... LeeNewman 2 82
(David Barron) *s.s: a in rr* **20/1**

50-0 **16** *2 1/4* **Joe Packet**[36] 700 4-9-2 95... JimCrowley 22 75
(Jonathan Portman) *prom: rdn over 1f out: wknd fnl f* **20/1**

310- **17** *hd* **Osteopathic Remedy (IRE)**[148] 7348 7-9-1 97... PatrickDonaghy(3) 15 77
(Michael Dods) *mid-div: rdn over 2f out: wknd over 1f out* **40/1**

20-0 **18** *1* **Fratellino**[8] 989 4-9-2 95... RobertWinston 11 81+
(Alan McCabe) *led over 3f: hmpd and wknd over 1f out* **25/1**

000- **19** *6* **Hotham**[162] 7079 8-8-12 **91**.. BarryMcHugh 5 48
(Noel Wilson) *chsd ldrs: rdn over 2f out: wknd over 1f out* **50/1**
02-0 **20** *4* **Wildcat Wizard (USA)**[22] 848 5-8-11 **93**.......... MichaelO'Connell(3) 18 38
(David Nicholls) *hld up: wknd over 2f out* **14/1**
1m 12.22s (-1.38) **Going Correction** +0.075s/f (Good) **20** Ran SP% **127.3**
Speed ratings (Par 109): **112,111,110,109,108 108,107,106,106,106 105,104,103,103,103 100,99,98,90,85**
Tote Swingers: 1&2 £10.20, 1&3 £6.60, 2&3 £14.60 CSF £63.96 CT £583.94 TOTE £6.90: £1.70, £3.40, £2.10, £5.30; EX 74.80 Trifecta £192.30 Pool: £670.73 - 2.58 winning units..
Owner Mrs G Rowland-Clark **Bred** Mrs F A Veasey **Trained** Newmarket, Suffolk

FOCUS
A good-quality handicap run at a sound pace. The winner is progressive but this is probably not form to get carried away with.

NOTEBOOK
Horseradish, who scored four times last year, including first time out, showed that quick ground is not a problem for him, even if a bit of cut suits him best. He had this won when quickening clear a furlong out and, while the margin was cut down close home, he was value for further. He looks just the type who could make a successful move into Pattern company as the season develops, although the Victoria Cup could be his next port of call (he's equally effective over 7f). (op 6-1)
Waffle(IRE) ◆, a relatively lightly raced five-year-old, didn't have the clearest of runs as he tried to make up ground from off the pace, but he finished better than anything once in the clear and looks to have been a good purchase by current connections. Providing he can be kept sound, it'll be a surprise if his new trainer can't find a race for him off this sort of mark. (op 12-1)
Our Jonathan, dropped in at the tail of the field, made his move around the outside, down the centre of the track, but he could never quite get to the winner. He has dropped to a favourable mark and is equally effective over 5f, granted a decent pace. (op 6-1)
Lutine Bell shaped encouragingly on his reappearance, over a trip thought to be short of his best. He was running off a career-high mark here, but clearly remains on the upgrade.
Advanced, runner-up in this race two years ago, ran at this meeting last year off a 15lb higher mark. Never far off the pace, he showed he's no back number yet. (op 28-1)
Quest For Success(IRE) tends to need his first run of the season so this was a perfectly respectable effort. (op 16-1 tchd 10-1)
Nasri, who was having his first outing for David Nicholls, showed plenty of pace for a long way.
Medicean Man may have found the ground a bit quick as he hung under pressure. (op 8-1)
Kellys Eye(IRE) is probably another at his best on a slightly easier surface.
Colonel Mak faced a stiff task under top weight and didn't run too badly in the circumstances.

1112 WILLIAMHILL.COM DONCASTER SHIELD (CONDITIONS STKS) 1m 4f
4:25 (4:25) (Class 2) 4-Y-0+ **£9,390** (£2,794; £1,396; £697) **Stalls** Low

Form RPR
410- **1** **Cracking Lass (IRE)**[148] 7350 4-8-8 94.......................... PaulHanagan 4 100
(Richard Fahey) *hld up in rr: chsd along over 4f out: hdwy wl over 2f out: chsd ldr over 1f out: led ins fnl f: kpt on* **11/1**
023- **2** *½* **Moyenne Corniche**[114] 7823 6-9-0 97.......................... TomEaves 3 104
(Brian Ellison) *led: rdn over 3f out: hdd ins fnl f: kpt on* **8/1**
206- **3** *6* **Prompter**[148] 7350 4-8-13 103.......................... JamieSpencer 2 94
(Michael Bell) *hld up in tch: hdwy over 3f out: rdn over 2f out: drvn over 1f out: no imp: eased fnl 75yds* **2/1**[2]
221- **4** *6* **Times Up**[148] 7350 5-9-0 102.......................... DaneO'Neill 6 85
(John Dunlop) *trckd ldr in 2nd: rdn over 4f out: wknd 2f out* **5/4**[1]
554- **5** *38* **Nanton (USA)**[127] 7594 9-9-0 103.......................... PhillipMakin 1 —
(Jim Goldie) *trckd ldng pair: rdn 4f out: sn wknd* **11/2**[3]
2m 35.78s (0.88) **Going Correction** +0.075s/f (Good)
WFA 4 from 5yo+ 1lb **5** Ran SP% **112.6**
Speed ratings (Par 109): **100,99,95,91,66**
CSF £83.64 TOTE £7.50: £3.20, £4.20; EX 44.00.
Owner Mel Roberts and Ms Nicola Meese **Bred** Thomas Doherty **Trained** Musley Bank, N Yorks

FOCUS
A tight race on paper, with just 6lb covering the entire field on adjusted ratings. The form trio were disappointing and this is ordinary form for the grade.

NOTEBOOK
Cracking Lass(IRE) was the outsider of the field. She had done her previous winning with plenty of cut in the ground and these conditions had to be a concern, but she coped with them well. She doesn't look short of stamina, and it wouldn't be a surprise to see her step up to 1m6f at some point. Her connections have a fillies' Listed race at Goodwood at the end of the month in mind for her. (op 10-1)
Moyenne Corniche dominated from the outset and looked to have been given a well-judged ride by Tom Eaves, but he was eventually collared by the winner. He's another at his best with some cut in the ground, but he had the run of the race here and no other excuse. (op 11-1 tchd 7-1)
Prompter travelled up well looking a big danger but his response when put under pressure was disappointing. He only has a maiden win to his name and might not be one to trust completely. (op 9-4)
Times Up ran a bit like he did on his reappearance last year. He probably needed the outing, and should be a lot sharper next time (he won second time out last year). (op 11-8, tchd 13-8 and 6-1 in places)
Nanton(USA) finished second in a Group 2 on his reappearance last year but he was nowhere near that level here. He dropped out very tamely, with his rider looking down, so perhaps something was amiss. (op 5-1)

1113 SEP H'CAP 1m 2f 60y
4:55 (4:58) (Class 3) (0-90,85) 3-Y-O **£5,828** (£1,734; £866; £432) **Stalls** Low

Form RPR
1 **1** **Barbican**[37] 693 3-9-1 79.......................... J-PGuillambert 4 90+
(Alan Bailey) *in tch: pushed along 4f out: hdwy over 2f out: rdn to ld ins fnl f: kpt on* **7/4**[1]
12 **2** *1* **Dorcas Lane**[53] 468 3-9-5 83.......................... RyanMoore 7 92+
(Lucy Wadham) *dwlt: hld up: pushed along 4f out: hdwy on outer over 2f out: drvn and kpt on wl ins fnl f: wnt 2nd fnl 50yds* **6/1**[3]
10- **3** *2* **Well Sharp**[162] 7095 3-9-4 82.......................... TomEaves 2 87
(Michael Dods) *led at stdy pce: rdn over 3f out: drvn whn hdd ins fnl f: no ex fnl 100yds* **8/1**
120- **4** *1¼* **Goldenveil (IRE)**[163] 7059 3-9-4 82.......................... PaulHanagan 6 85
(Richard Fahey) *t.k.h: trckd ldr: rdn over 3f out: one pce fr over 1f out* **14/1**
01- **5** *1* **Beatrice Aurore (IRE)**[198] 6155 3-8-13 77.......................... TedDurcan 5 78
(John Dunlop) *racd keenly: trckd ldr in 2nd: rdn over 3f out: one pce over 1f out: no ex ins fnl f* **2/1**[2]
1121 **6** *7* **Malice Or Mischief (IRE)**[10] 951 3-9-2 80.......................... NeilCallan 8 67
(Tony Carroll) *midfield: rdn over 3f out: sn no imp* **20/1**
41- **7** *4½* **Stansonnit**[131] 7536 3-9-7 85.......................... PJMcDonald 10 63
(Alan Swinbank) *hld up: rdn over 3f out: sn wknd* **16/1**
1-6 **8** *44* **Ninita**[22] 845 3-9-4 82.......................... NickyMackay 3 —
(Mark Rimmer) *midfield: rdn over 4f out: sn wknd: eased over 1f out* **28/1**
2m 14.7s (5.30) **Going Correction** +0.075s/f (Good) **8** Ran SP% **115.9**
Speed ratings (Par 102): **81,80,78,77,76 71,67,32**
Tote Swingers: 1&2 £2.70, 2&3 £4.20 CSF £13.19 CT £66.89 TOTE £2.80: £1.50, £1.70, £2.00; EX 14.90 Trifecta £99.40 Pool: £974.70 - 7.25 winning units..
Owner John Stocker **Bred** Hascombe And Valiant Studs **Trained** Newmarket, Suffolk

FOCUS
An interesting 3-y-o handicap, albeit the top-weight weighed in 5lb below the ceiling for the race. They went no pace early. There is probably more to come from the first two.

NOTEBOOK
Barbican ◆ landed a bit of a gamble on his debut and he confirmed the favourable impression he left that day by taking this a shade cosily. Still showing signs of inexperience, his rider didn't have to go for everything, and clearly there's plenty more to come. He should get further as well, and his connections are eyeing up a tilt at the King George V Handicap at Royal Ascot. (op 5-2)
Dorcas Lane was held up at the back of the field, which wasn't the place to be in a tactical affair. She finished well to take second, though, and will be seen to better effect in a more strongly run race. (op 11-2 tchd 7-1)
Well Sharp enjoyed the run of things out in front, dictating a modest gallop, so he was in the best place to quicken when the sprint for home began. He may be flattered by the bare form, but he did run in the Horris Hill last autumn so is evidently well thought of by connections. (tchd 15-2)
Goldenveil(IRE), one of the more exposed runners in the line-up, raced keenly early. She has a pedigree that's a mixture of speed and stamina and perhaps she'll eventually prove to be at her best over a mile.
Beatrice Aurore(IRE) also proved hard to settle off the steady early gallop, and probably not too much should be read into this performance. (op 15-8 tchd 9-4)
Malice Or Mischief(IRE) has been in good form on the all-weather of late, but she's been doing her winning at a much lower level than this. (op 16-1)

1114 STOBART FILLIES' H'CAP 1m (S)
5:25 (5:26) (Class 4) (0-85,85) 4-Y-O+ **£3,561** (£1,059; £529; £264) **Stalls** High

Form RPR
0-24 **1** **She's A Character**[30] 772 4-8-9 73.......................... PaulHanagan 4 86
(Richard Fahey) *trckd ldrs: rdn over 2f out: led jst over 1f out: drvn clr ins fnl f* **13/2**[3]
156- **2** *4* **Frontline Girl (IRE)**[163] 7063 5-8-8 72.......................... AndrewElliott 6 76
(Mrs K Burke) *cl up: led after 2f: rdn whn hdd jst over 1f out: kpt on but no ch w wnr* **11/1**
6261 **3** *2* **Very Well Red**[16] 889 8-8-8 72.......................... WilliamCarson 11 71
(Peter Hiatt) *cl up: rdn over 3f out: drvn and outpcd over 1f out: kpt on again ins fnl f: wnt 3rd towards fin* **12/1**
051- **4** *1* **Law Of The Range**[200] 6090 4-9-4 82.......................... AdamKirby 10 79
(Marco Botti) *led for 2f: remained prom: rdn over 2f out: no ex ins fnl f: lost 3rd towards fin* **5/2**[1]
0-44 **5** *4½* **Song To The Moon (IRE)**[70] 273 4-8-6 73........(b) MatthewDavies(3) 5 60
(George Baker) *hld up: rdn along over 4f out: one pce: nvr threatened* **14/1**
1/0- **6** *4* **Golden Aria (IRE)**[332] 1850 4-9-0 78.......................... RyanMoore 8 55
(Richard Hannon) *prom tl wknd over 2f out* **13/2**[3]
145- **7** *1¼* **Viewing**[233] 5056 4-8-13 77.......................... PaulMulrennan 12 51
(James Given) *hld up in tch: rdn over 3f out: sn no imp: wknd over 1f out* **14/1**
141- **8** *2½* **Snow Magic (IRE)**[164] 7042 4-9-0 78.......................... PatCosgrave 1 52
(James Fanshawe) *hld up: rdn over 2f out: sn no imp: eased ins fnl f* **9/2**[2]
42P- **9** *10* **Cheers For Thea (IRE)**[189] 6395 6-9-7 85......................(bt) DavidAllan 9 31
(Tim Easterby) *hld up: rdn over 2f out: sn wknd* **8/1**
1m 41.36s (2.06) **Going Correction** +0.075s/f (Good) **9** Ran SP% **113.9**
Speed ratings (Par 102): **92,88,86,85,80 76,75,72,62**
Tote Swingers: 1&2 £11.90, 1&3 £9.70, 2&3 £13.20. totesuper7: Win: Not won. Place: £493.50. CSF £73.78 CT £837.94 TOTE £6.40: £2.20, £3.80, £2.60; EX 87.80 Trifecta £448.60 Part won. Pool: £606.27 - 0.60 winning units..
Owner Aykroyd And Sons Ltd **Bred** Genesis Green & Deerpark Stud **Trained** Musley Bank, N Yorks

FOCUS
This looked a fairly competitive handicap on paper but the winner bolted up. The form is rated around the front two and there's a chance this made the winner look better than she is.
T/Jkpt: Not won. T/Plt: £740.90 to a £1 stake. Pool of £129,556 - 127.64 winning tickets. T/Qpdt: £175.00 to a £1 stake. Pool of £9,176 - 38.80 winning tickets. AS

1115 & 1117a - (Foreign Racing) - See Raceform Interactive

921 CURRAGH (R-H)
Sunday, April 3

OFFICIAL GOING: Straight course - heavy; round course - soft (soft to heavy in places)

1116a ANNE BREWSTER MEMORIAL LOUGHBROWN STKS (LISTED RACE) 7f
2:25 (2:26) 3-Y-O **£22,413** (£6,551; £3,103; £1,034)

RPR
1 **Sing Softly (USA)**[14] 922 3-8-12.......................... CO'Donoghue 5 102
(A P O'Brien, Ire) *a.p: disp ld bef 1/2-way: led wl over 1f out: drvn out and kpt on wl fnl f* **7/2**[3]
2 *1* **Defining Year (IRE)**[14] 926 3-9-1 98.......................... GFCarroll 2 102
(M Halford, Ire) *broke wl and settled in 3rd: pushed along to go 2nd 1f out: no imp on wnr and kpt on same pce ins fnl f* **7/4**[1]
3 *1¾* **Deire Na Sli (IRE)**[154] 7258 3-8-12 90.......................... DJMoran 4 94
(J S Bolger, Ire) *chsd ldrs: 6th 1/2-way: hdwy on outer under 2f out: 3rd 1f out: no imp ins fnl f* **20/1**
4 *2½* **Triple Eight (IRE)**[182] 6616 3-9-1 98..........................(b) PJSmullen 1 91
(D K Weld, Ire) *settled towards rr: wnt 4th 1/2-way: no imp fr over 1f out: kpt on one pce* **12/1**
5 *½* **Tell The Wind (IRE)**[168] 6969 3-8-12 95.......................... DPMcDonogh 7 86
(Kevin Prendergast, Ire) *sn led: jnd bef 1/2-way: pressed and hdd wl over 1f out: sn no ex: kpt on one pce* **14/1**
6 *14* **Glor Na Mara (IRE)**[169] 6924 3-9-1 113.......................... KJManning 6 81
(J S Bolger, Ire) *settled towards rr: 5th 1/2-way: pushed along in 4th 2f out: sn no ex: eased whn btn fnl f* **15/8**[2]
1m 33.71s (2.91) **Going Correction** +0.35s/f (Good) **6** Ran SP% **112.5**
Speed ratings: **97,95,93,91,90 74**
CSF £10.13 TOTE £4.10: £1.60, £1.30; DF 13.50.
Owner Michael Tabor **Bred** Summer Wind Farm **Trained** Ballydoyle, Co Tipperary

FOCUS
The runner-up sets the standard.

NOTEBOOK
Sing Softly(USA), winner of a 6f maiden over the same course last month, followed up here in good style. She led and disputed throughout and was on top from just over a furlong out from where she kept on well. Afterwards winning trainer Aidan O'Brien said: "We weren't sure about her getting the trip on heavy ground but she didn't seem to have a problem. She might get a mile on better ground and we'll consider one of the 1000 Guineas for her."

Defining Year(IRE), winner of a handicap over the course and trip last month, produced a good effort here. He goes on the ground and after settling in third he began his challenge over a furlong out and kept on quite well without seriously troubling the winner. (op 5/2)
Deire Na Sli(IRE), who came good on her final start least season when landing a nursery over this trip at Leopardstown, made an encouraging return. She made headway two furlongs out and went third under a furlong out, keeping on without troubling the first two.
Triple Eight(IRE) had shown his best form on much quicker ground last season. Held up, he was under pressure two furlongs out and could make little impression thereafter although keeping on in the closing stages. (op 11/1)
Tell The Wind(IRE), a maiden winner and Listed placed at Dundalk last season, led and disputed here until weakening entering the final furlong. (op 14/1 tchd 16/1)
Glor Na Mara(IRE) was the clear pick on official ratings. Although a maiden, he had been placed a couple of times at Group 1 level last season including when third in the Dewhurst. He had been found wanting in the National Stakes here in September on the only occasion he had encountered soft ground and it is quite likely that the heavy conditions here contributed to what was a very disappointing effort. Held up, he was ridden two furlongs out and was quickly done with before dropping behind and being eased inside the final furlong. Official explanation: jockey said colt did not handle today's ground (op 5/4 tchd 2/1)

1118a BIG BAD BOB GLADNESS STKS (GROUP 3) 7f
3:30 (3:32) 4-Y-0+ £33,620 (£9,827; £4,655; £1,551)

RPR
1 **Lolly For Dolly (IRE)**[14] 924 4-9-1 107..........................(b) WMLordan 1 114
(T Stack, Ire) *settled towards rr: hdwy into 4th over 1f out: sn rdn to chal: kpt on wl u.p to ld clsng stages* **9/2**[3]
2 *shd* **The Cheka (IRE)**[127] 7593 5-9-1 .... JMurtagh 9 113
(Eve Johnson Houghton) *sn led: jnd over 2f out: advantage again 1 1/2f out: sn strly pressed: kpt on wl ins fnl f: hdd clsng stages* **8/1**
3 *4* **Luisant**[14] 923 8-9-1 109.. FMBerry 7 102
(J A Nash, Ire) *settled in rr: rdn in 7th over 1f out: kpt on u.p fnl f wout threatening principals* **9/2**[3]
4 *shd* **Croisultan (IRE)**[148] 7351 5-9-1 106............................... NGMcCullagh 6 102
(Liam McAteer, Ire) *prom: cl 2nd 1/2-way: disp over 2f out: hdd 1 1/2f out: sn no imp u.p: no ex ins fnl f* **33/1**
5 *2* **Regal Parade**[182] 6611 7-9-7 .... AdrianNicholls 2 108+
(David Nicholls) *trckd ldrs: cl 5th 1/2-way: drvn along fr over 2f out: 3rd over 1f out: sn no ex: wknd fnl f* **9/4**[1]
6 *1* **Emulous**[168] 6970 4-9-1 111... PJSmullen 8 99
(D K Weld, Ire) *trckd ldrs: 4th 1/2-way: rdn in 5th under 2f out: no ex ins fnl f* **4/1**[2]
7 *4 ½* **Across The Rhine (USA)**[24] 828 5-9-1 105.................... PShanahan 5 92
(Tracey Collins, Ire) *trckd ldrs: 3rd 1/2-way: rdn and dropped to 6th over 1f out: no ex* **20/1**
8 *1 ¼* **Youm Mutamiez (USA)**[135] 7511 4-9-1 .... WJSupple 3 78
(P D Deegan, Ire) *settled bhd ldrs: 6th 1/2-way: rdn under 2f out: no ex fr over 1f out: eased whn btn ins fnl f* **10/1**
9 *shd* **Paraphernalia (IRE)**[14] 924 4-8-12 99..................................... WJLee 4 75
(David Wachman, Ire) *a towards rr: in tch 2f out: no ex fr over 1f out* **25/1**

1m 30.9s (0.10) **Going Correction** +0.35s/f (Good) 9 Ran SP% **118.9**
Speed ratings: **113,112,108,108,105 104,99,98,98**
CSF £40.18 TOTE £5.50: £1.50, £2.30, £1.70; DF 36.90.
Owner David Keoghan **Bred** J Jamgotchian **Trained** Golden, Co Tipperary

FOCUS
A decent renewal of the Gladness.

NOTEBOOK
Lolly For Dolly(IRE) secured a third Group 3 win, all of them at this track, getting up in the last few strides to foil the runner-up. A tough filly who clearly relishes testing conditions, she was dropping back in distance following her win over 1m in the Park Express Stakes last month. The Athasi Stakes, which she won a year ago, on May 2 is a possible target, although the Dahlia Stakes over 1m1f at Newmarket on the previous day will also be considered. (op 5/1)
The Cheka(IRE) was having his first run of the season. Soon in front, after forging ahead well over 1f out he kept on well and was only touched off. He gets 1m and should be able to build on this encouraging effort.
Luisant, a seven-time winner, twice at Listed level, had run third in a 6f handicap on his reappearance here last month. Held up, he made headway under 2f out and looked as if he might get seriously involved before failing to make much impression inside the final furlong. (op 6/1)
Croisultan(IRE), suited by the ground, has done his winning over shorter trips. Having his first run of the year, he was soon second and was disputing the lead over 2f out, but after being headed well over 1f out he had no more to offer.
Regal Parade looked the form pick here on his performances last season, but despite being given a racecourse gallop at Catterick four days earlier he ran here as if needing it. After tracking the leaders and then moving into contention under 2f out, he was quickly done with entering the final furlong. (op 9/4 tchd 3/1)
Emulous, a Group 3 winner over a slightly longer trip on soft ground last year, tracked the leaders, but she could make little impression after coming under pressure one and a half furlongs out. (op 4/1 tchd 3/1)

1119a GEEGEEZ.CO.UK ALLEGED STKS (LISTED RACE) 1m 2f
4:00 (4:02) 4-Y-0+ £22,413 (£6,551; £3,103; £1,034)

RPR
1 **Unaccompanied (IRE)**[16] 5571 4-8-12 90.......................... PJSmullen 3 98
(D K Weld, Ire) *trckd ldr in 2nd: rdn to ld under 2f out: kpt on wl u.p fnl f* **4/1**[2]
2 *2 ½* **Cilium (IRE)**[245] 4631 5-8-12 87.. WJSupple 4 93
(Jeffrey Ian Mulhern, Ire) *trckd ldrs in 3rd: rdn to go 2nd over 1f out: no imp on wnr fnl f: kpt on same pce* **33/1**
3 *4* **St Nicholas Abbey (IRE)**[337] 1699 4-9-1 119.......... SeamieHeffernan 2 88+
(A P O'Brien, Ire) *settled in 5th: wnt 4th appr st: pushed along and no imp 2f out: 3rd early fnl f: kpt on one pce* **4/11**[1]
4 *1 ¼* **Few Are Chosen (IRE)**[198] 6171 5-8-12 88....................... PShanahan 7 82+
(Tracey Collins, Ire) *towards rr: nvr a factor: kpt on u.p fr over 1f out wout threatening principals* **33/1**
5 *3* **Mount Helicon**[109] 6686 6-9-1 103...(t) FMBerry 1 83
(T Hogan, Ire) *led: pushed along ent st: hdd under 2f out: dropped to 4th early fnl f: no ex* **20/1**
6 *4* **Waydownsouth (IRE)**[154] 7262 4-9-1 96............................... DMGrant 5 75+
(Patrick J Flynn, Ire) *chsd ldrs in 4th: rdn and dropped to rr early st: no ex* **11/1**[3]

2m 24.26s (9.96) **Going Correction** +1.20s/f (Soft) 6 Ran SP% **112.3**
Speed ratings: **101,99,95,94,92 89**
CSF £96.10 TOTE £4.00: £1.90, £14.20; DF 67.40.
Owner Moyglare Stud Farm **Bred** Moyglare Stud Farm Ltd **Trained** The Curragh, Co Kildare

FOCUS
Two non-runners and deep ground for this race which was supposed to be all about the return of a superstar. The pace was steady and the first two were in the best place up front. They have been rated on the upgrade, but St Nicholas Abbey was disappointing.

NOTEBOOK
Unaccompanied(IRE) was quite well fancied on the back of a ultra-smart hurdling campaign and she underlined her progressive nature. She loves this type of ground and is the ultimate horse in that she handles summer conditions too and is thoroughly uncomplicated. The filly tracked the pacesetter and basically was in command once she took the lead. She is now a Listed winner on the Flat and it will be fascinating to see how far she can go in this sphere. She next runs over hurdles at Punchestown and should go close.
Cilium(IRE), 87-rated, probably ran above that. The mare's connections will be delighted with this effort and she is another who is adaptable ground-wise. It is to her trainer's credit that she produced her career best effort as a five-year-old and she now has some black-type placing.
St Nicholas Abbey(IRE), not seen since finishing sixth in last season's 2,000 Guineas, had a rating of 119 and ran about two stone below that. He got a shade revved up before the start and ran a little keenly off the modest early gallop, but with the guts of a half a mile to go, you got the feeling Seamie Heffernan sensed he was in trouble. He did not get after him until as late as possible and the response was decidedly underwhelming. He should have been plenty fit enough to go close in this and it is hard to take any positives from the race. (op 1/3)
Few Are Chosen(IRE) was discarded in the market and ran in the manner of a horse somewhat outclassed. She was not disgraced. (op 40/1)
Mount Helicon faded away after making the speed and wants further than this.
Waydownsouth(IRE) ran well below his mark but can improve plenty from this - that was all he did last season, going up 46lb in the space of six runs. (op 12/1 tchd 10/1)

1120 - 1121a (Foreign Racing) - See Raceform Interactive

815 FONTAINEBLEAU
Friday, April 1

OFFICIAL GOING: Turf: very soft

1122a PRIX COR DE CHASSE (LISTED RACE) (3YO+) (TURF) 5f 110y
1:50 (12:00) 3-Y-0+ £22,413 (£8,965; £6,724; £4,482; £2,241)

RPR
1 **Fred Lalloupet**[23] 815 4-9-6 0.. OlivierPeslier 13 108
(D Smaga, France) **43/5**
2 *3* **Lisselan Diva (IRE)**[23] 815 5-9-3 0.........................(p) WilliamsSaraiva 7 95
(Mme J Bidgood, France) **83/10**[3]
3 *hd* **Move In Time**[174] 6734 3-8-13 0... TomEaves 11 99
(Bryan Smart) *broke wl: a.p stands' side: rdn 2f out: styd on wl fnl f: wnt cl for 2nd* **11/1**
4 *¾* **Bluster (FR)**[130] 7535 5-9-10 0..................................... IoritzMendizabal 4 98
(Robert Collet, France) **12/1**
5 *¾* **Calbuco (FR)**[23] 815 7-9-6 0.. ThierryThulliez 9 92
(B Dutruel, France) **9/1**
6 *snk* **Clairvoyance (IRE)**[130] 7535 4-9-6 0............................... MaximeGuyon 6 92
(H-A Pantall, France) **63/10**[2]
7 *snk* **Tiza (SAF)**[151] 7278 9-9-10 0...(p) FranckBlondel 8 95
(F Rossi, France) **11/1**
8 *nk* **Personified (GER)**[23] 815 4-9-3 0.. GaryCarter 5 87
(Mme J Bidgood, France) **25/1**
9 *snk* **Dam D'Augy (FR)**[84] 92 6-9-6 0..................................(b) ThierryJarnet 10 90
(Mlle S-V Tarrou, France) **18/1**
10 *2 ½* **Le Valentin (FR)**[113] 5-9-6 0.. AnthonyCrastus 3 81
(Y De Nicolay, France) **11/2**[1]
0 **Something (IRE)**[48] 9-9-6 0...................................... StephanePasquier 14 —
(P Monfort, France) **63/10**[2]
0 **Reignier**[23] 815 4-9-6 0..(b[1]) AndrewElliott 2 —
(Mrs K Burke) *rdn to ld far side: swtchd towards stands' side at 1/2-way: hrd rdn: no ex: qckly fdd* **65/1**
0 **Satu Mare (FR)**[295] 3-8-6 0.. StefanieHofer 12 —
(Mario Hofer, Germany) **35/1**
0 **Kagura (USA)**[154] 7222 3-8-9 0...................................... MickaelBarzalona 1 —
(G Henrot, France) **15/1**

64.70 secs (64.70)
WFA 3 from 4yo+ 11lb 14 Ran SP% **118.0**
WIN (incl. 1 euro stake): 9.60. PLACES: 3.20, 2.60, 4.00. DF: 75.90. SF: 99.80.
Owner Maurice Laqasse **Bred** Maurice Lagasse & Pontchartrain Stud **Trained** Lamorlaye, France

1123 - 1124a (Foreign Racing) - See Raceform Interactive

1069 SAINT-CLOUD (L-H)
Sunday, April 3

OFFICIAL GOING: Turf: heavy

1125a PRIX EDMOND BLANC (GROUP 3) (4YO+) (TURF) 1m
2:40 (12:00) 4-Y-0+ £34,482 (£13,793; £10,344; £6,896; £3,448)

RPR
1 **Skins Game**[22] 851 5-8-11 0................................ ChristopheSoumillon 5 110
(J-C Rouget, France) *wl in rr on settling: hrd rdn 2f out: responded wl to cl on ldrs 1 1/2f out: disp ld w eventual 2nd ent fnl f: r.o wl to take ld fnl 50yds: jst hld on* **7/5**[1]
2 *nse* **Rostrum (FR)**[22] 851 4-8-11 0.. MaximeGuyon 2 110
(A Fabre, France) *racd 5th: rdn bef st: picked up wl ent fnl f: disp ld w eventual wnr fnl 100yds: failed narrowly* **4/1**[2]
3 *2* **Silverside (USA)**[24] 828 5-8-11 0.............................. StephanePasquier 3 105
(F Sanchez, France) *racd 3rd on rail on settling: swtchd away fr rail 1 1/2f out to chal for ld 1f out: qcknd wl to ld 1f out: hdd 100yds out: r.o wl* **25/1**
4 *½* **Pink Gin (FR)**[136] 7500 4-8-11 0....................................... OlivierPeslier 7 104
(J-M Beguigne, France) *racd 3rd on settling: rdn to ld 1 1/2f out: hdd 1f out: styd on wl* **53/10**[3]
5 *¾* **Rysckly (FR)**[22] 851 4-8-11 0.. GregoryBenoist 9 102
(Y De Nicolay, France) *racd in 6th: rdn 2f out: no ex: styd on fnl f* **16/1**
6 *½* **Gotlandia (FR)**[172] 6857 4-8-8 0................... Christophe-PatriceLemaire 8 98
(M Delzangles, France) *racd towards rr: rdn 2 1/2f out on outer: styd on wl fnl f* **15/1**
7 *3* **Flash Dance (IRE)**[22] 851 5-8-8 0............................ MickaelBarzalona 6 91
(F Head, France) *sn led: in front ent st: rdn 2f out: hdd 1 1/2f out: no ex: fdd: eased towards fin* **10/1**
8 *3* **Courchevel (IRE)**[131] 7545 4-8-8 0................................ IoritzMendizabal 1 84
(Robert Collet, France) *racd towards rr: rdn 2 1/2f out on outside: no ex: nvr a factor* **9/1**
9 *6* **Ransom Hope**[16] 6-8-11 0.. CristianDemuro 4 74
(L Riccardi, Italy) *settled 4th: rdn early in st: no ex: sn fdd* **21/1**

1m 48.1s (0.60) 9 Ran SP% **117.2**
WIN (incl. 1 euro stake): 2.40. PLACES: 1.20, 1.60, 4.10. DF: 4.10. SF: 6.60.
Owner Marquesa De Moratalla **Bred** Mr & Mrs J G Davis **Trained** Pau, France

SAN SIRO (R-H)
Sunday, April 3

OFFICIAL GOING: Turf: good

1126a PREMIO ANGELO GARDENGHI - TROFEO ITS (MAIDEN) (UNRACED 3YO) (TURF) 1m 1f
2:35 (12:00) 3-Y-O **£7,758** (£3,413; £1,862; £931)

RPR
1 **King's Star (IRE)** 3-9-2 0 MSanna 2 —
(D Gambarota, Italy) **54/10**
2 2 1/4 **Mazzore (IRE)** 3-9-2 0 GSanna 11 —
(M Gasparini, Italy) **161/10**
3 1 1/4 **Arbalo (IRE)** 3-9-2 0 StefanoLandi 4 —
(R Feligioni, Italy) **39/10**[3]
4 10 **Shumy Forever (ITY)** 3-9-2 0 SMulas 3 —
(G Marras, Italy) **30/1**
5 5 **Jenio Horse (IRE)** 3-9-2 0 MarcoMonteriso 9 —
(E Botti, Italy) **91/10**
6 2 1/2 **Silent Land** 3-8-13 0 MircoDemuro 5 —
(Noel Quinlan) *midfield early racing freely: sn chsng ldrs in 3rd: wnt 2nd over 4f out: sn shkn up: rdn 2 1/2f out: wknd ins fnl 2f: eased fnl f* **7/5**[1]
7 8 **Tamarix Boy (IRE)** 3-9-2 0 PierantonioConvertino 7 —
(M Marcialis, Italy) **705/100**
8 10 **Ornella Vanoni** 3-8-13 0 UmbertoRispoli 8 —
(B Grizzetti, Italy) **19/5**[2]
9 1 1/2 **Nanni Pepi (ITY)** 3-9-2 0 GCongiu 10 —
(M Innocenti, Italy) **36/1**
10 3 1/2 **Rusticano (FR)** 3-9-2 0 WVarchetta 1 —
(Gabriele Miliani, Italy) **213/10**

1m 52.3s (-5.60) **10** Ran SP% **137.1**
PARI-MUTUEL (all including 1 euro stakes): WIN 6.40; PLACE 2.23, 4.10, 2.16; DF 31.07.
Owner Doris Schoenherr **Bred** Rabbah Bloodstock Ltd **Trained** Italy

1127a PREMIO GARDONE (LISTED RACE) (3YO COLTS & GELDINGS) (TURF) 1m
3:10 (12:00) 3-Y-O **£24,137** (£10,620; £5,793; £2,896)

RPR
1 **Cazals (IRE)** 3-8-11 0 UmbertoRispoli 2 96
(B Grizzetti, Italy) **20/75**[1]
2 2 1/4 **Ekasin**[58] 431 3-8-11 0 MarcoMonteriso 3 91
(Marco Botti) *broke wl to ld: set gd pce: chal by eventual wnr ent fnl 2 1/2f: hrd rdn whn hdd 2f out: btn and eased fnl 150yds* **22/5**[3]
3 3 1/4 **Gold Sprinter (IRE)**[7] 3-8-11 0 CColombi 5 83
(B Grizzetti, Italy) **41/10**[2]
4 3 1/4 **Crafty Roberto**[62] 368 3-8-11 0 PierantonioConvertino 1 76
(Noel Quinlan) *stdd at s to trck ldrs tl ent st: rdn to chal ldrs briefly 2 1/2f out: sn btn and eased fnl f* **13/2**

1m 37.7s (-4.40) **4** Ran SP% **130.4**
PARI-MUTUEL (all including 1 euro stakes): WIN 1.27; PLACE 1.06, 1.37; DF 3.74.
Owner Allevamento Dei Sette **Bred** Giovanni Faldutto **Trained** Italy

COLOGNE (R-H)
Sunday, April 3

OFFICIAL GOING: Turf: soft

1128a YOOBET.DE GRAND PRIX PREMIERE (GROUP 3) (4YO+) (TURF) 1m 2f 110y
4:10 (4:16) 4-Y-0+ **£27,586** (£9,482; £4,741; £2,586; £1,724; £1,293)

RPR
1 **Illo (GER)**[182] 6606 5-9-0 0 ADeVries 4 108
(J Hirschberger, Germany) *broke fast to ld: set gd pce: qcknd bef end of bk st: wnt wl clr ent st: r.o wl: easily* **43/5**
2 3 **Altair Star (IRE)**[162] 7102 4-8-11 0 AStarke 5 99
(P Schiergen, Germany) *racd in 3rd on settling: proged bef fnl turn: rdn to catch ldr: r.o wl in st* **235/10**
3 10 **Appel Au Maitre (FR)**[203] 6017 7-9-2 0 GaetanMasure 7 85
(Wido Neuroth, Norway) *settled towards rr: proged smoothly down st: styd on wl* **8/1**[3]
4 hd **Russian Tango (GER)**[182] 6606 4-9-2 0 EPedroza 8 84
(A Wohler, Germany) *broke wl to r bhd ldr: pulling freely: looked threatening early in st: r.o: lost 3rd ins fnl f* **17/5**[2]
5 2 **Zazou (GER)**[147] 7373 4-9-4 0 THellier 2 82
(Mario Hofer, Germany) *broke slowly: settled midfield: sn dropped bk to rr: forced wd ent st: rdn but no ex fnl 2f* **1/2**[1]
6 4 1/2 **Zaungast (IRE)**[162] 7102 7-8-11 0 APietsch 3 66
(W Hickst, Germany) *settled towards rr: proged in bk st: no ex in st* **236/10**
7 6 **Titurel (GER)**[19] 860 6-9-0 0 ASuborics 9 58
(Manfred Hofer, Germany) *broke wl to r bhd ldr: shkn up ent st: no ex: sn fdd* **104/10**
8 7 **Touch Of Hawk (FR)**[162] 7102 5-9-2 0 LennartHammer-Hansen 1 46
(Wido Neuroth, Norway) *racd midfield: r.o in st but nvr threatened: qckly wknd* **28/1**

2m 16.68s (136.68) **8** Ran SP% **131.3**
WIN (incl. 10 euro stake): 96. PLACES: 24, 36, 21. SF: 1,106..
Owner Gestut Schlenderhan **Bred** Gestut Schlenderhan **Trained** Germany

FOLKESTONE (R-H)
Monday, April 4

OFFICIAL GOING: Good (good to soft in places; 6.5)
Wind: fresh across Weather: cloudy

1129 CLAYDON HORSE EXERCISERS MEDIAN AUCTION MAIDEN STKS 5f
2:20 (2:23) (Class 6) 2-Y-O **£1,706** (£503; £252) **Stalls** High

Form RPR
4 1 **The Dancing Lord**[5] 1042 2-8-12 0 RyanClark(5) 6 75+
(Bill Turner) *mde all: a gng best: rdn clr over 1f out: eased ins fnl f: v easily* **9/4**[2]
2 2 6 **Queen Of The Hop**[5] 1049 2-8-12 0 LukeMorris 2 46
(J S Moore) *sltly hmpd sn after s: chsd ldng pair: sn rdn along: outpcd by wnr and wl btn over 1f out: wnt 2nd nr fin* **6/4**[1]
3 shd **Thorpe Bay** 2-9-3 0 NickyMackay 5 51
(Mark Rimmer) *wnt rt s: chsd wnr: rdn ent fnl 2f: outpcd and btn over 1f out: edgd rt after and lost 2nd nr fin* **33/1**
4 5 **First Rebellion** 2-9-3 0 KierenFallon 4 33+
(Joseph Tuite) *sltly hmpd s and s.i.s: sn rdn along: effrt on outer 1/2-way: wknd wl over 1f out* **9/2**[3]
5 1 **Sea Poet** 2-9-3 0 NeilCallan 1 32+
(Andrew Haynes) *v.s.a: sn rdn and outpcd in last pair* **6/1**
6 5 **The Coulbeck Kid** 2-9-3 0 DavidProbert 3 11
(Des Donovan) *dwlt: rn green and sn outpcd in last pair: rdn after 1f: lost tch 1/2-way* **14/1**

61.30 secs (1.30) **Going Correction** -0.10s/f (Good) **6** Ran SP% **112.8**
Speed ratings (Par 90): **85,75,75,67,65 57**
CSF £6.10 TOTE £3.60: £1.60, £1.10; EX 6.80.
Owner Mrs M S Teversham **Bred** Mrs Monica Teversham **Trained** Sigwells, Somerset

FOCUS
After a dry night the ground was changed to good, good to soft in places for Folkestone's opening meeting of the season. There was reported to be a strip of ground up the stands' rail riding quicker than the rest of the track and, while the winner could be rated much higher, it's likely the bare form isn't quite as good as it looks.

NOTEBOOK
The Dancing Lord made the most of being drawn against the stands' rail with an alert exit from the stalls. Always in front, he drew further and further away, winning by a wide margin. His trainer thought he would benefit from the switch to turf (made his debut on Polytrack five days previously), and being from a family who come to hand early this was a prime opportunity. A novice event would seem his likely destination and he can probably follow up before the nicer types come out. (tchd 5-2)
Queen Of The Hop was sent off favourite on the back of finishing runner-up in a Wolverhampton maiden auction five days earlier. Drawn out in the centre of the track, she could never get on terms with the winner but did run on for second She is very small and will need to find a weak contest soon. (op 7-4 tchd 15-8 and 11-8)
Thorpe Bay, drawn next to the winner, was close up throughout but couldn't respond when that rival kicked 2f out. There is plenty of speed on the dam's side of his pedigree and he should be up to winning soon. (op 28-1)
First Rebellion looked of interest on his debut with Kieren Fallon booked, but he had it all to do racing down the centre of the track. He has a bit of substance and should be able to put up a better show with this run under his belt. (op 5-1 tchd 4-1)
Sea Poet was always towards the rear after missing the break. He did run on in the last furlong though, and can improve on this. (op 13-2)
The Coulbeck Kid was restless in the stalls and showed little. (op 11-1)

1130 CLAYDON.COM MEDIAN AUCTION MAIDEN STKS 6f
2:50 (2:51) (Class 6) 3-Y-O **£1,706** (£503; £252) **Stalls** High

Form RPR
60- 1 **Chokurei (IRE)**[188] 6441 3-8-12 0 LukeMorris 4 65+
(Clive Cox) *chsd ldrs: swtchd rt and effrt ent fnl 2f: drvn to chal over 1f out: led ins fnl f: r.o wl* **9/4**[2]
0-3 2 1 **Alpha Delta Whisky**[25] 818 3-9-3 0 ChrisCatlin 1 67
(John Gallagher) *w ldr: rdn ent fnl 2f: led wl over 1f out: drvn and hdd ins fnl f: no ex* **11/2**
255- 3 1 1/2 **His Grace (IRE)**[182] 6626 3-9-3 71 NeilCallan 2 62
(Andrew Haynes) *led and crossed to stands' rail: hung rt thrght: rdn over 2f out: hdd wl over 1f out: wknd fnl 100yds* **5/4**[1]
050- 4 7 **Bahri Sheen (IRE)**[168] 6988 3-9-3 70 JimmyQuinn 3 40
(John Best) *trckd ldrs: rdn and effrt 2f out: fnd little and sn btn* **9/2**[3]

1m 12.79s (0.09) **Going Correction** -0.10s/f (Good) **4** Ran SP% **108.8**
Speed ratings (Par 96): **95,93,91,82**
CSF £13.07 TOTE £4.60; EX 18.50.
Owner H E Sheikh Sultan Bin Khalifa Al Nahyan **Bred** Sheikh Sultan Bin Khalifa Al Nayhan **Trained** Lambourn, Berks

FOCUS
A weak median auction maiden for 3-y-os rated around the winner to her 2-y-o best.
His Grace(IRE) Official explanation: jockey said that the gelding hung right

1131 SPIFFING CRABBIE'S ALCOHOLIC GINGER BEER H'CAP 6f
3:20 (3:20) (Class 5) (0-75,73) 3-Y-O **£2,388** (£705; £352) **Stalls** High

Form RPR
426- 1 **Apollo D'Negro (IRE)**[173] 6849 3-8-11 **66** JohnFahy(3) 2 72
(Clive Cox) *w ldr: rdn to ld over 1f out: r.o wl ins fnl f* **7/4**[1]
50-4 2 1 **Cristaliyev**[10] 958 3-8-10 **62** PatCosgrave 6 65
(Jim Boyle) *sn led: rdn and edging rt wl over 1f out: hdd over 1f out: styd on same pce ins fnl f* **4/1**[3]
212- 3 3/4 **Queen Of Cash (IRE)**[145] 7395 3-9-6 **72** RobertWinston 4 73
(Hughie Morrison) *t.k.h early: chsd ldrs: effrt on rail but nt clr run fr wl over 1f out: swtchd rt ent fnl f: drvn and one pce fnl 150yds* **2/1**[2]
300- 4 1 1/2 **Arctic Mirage**[168] 6988 3-9-4 **70** LiamKeniry 3 66
(Michael Blanshard) *t.k.h: chsd ldrs: edgd lft u.p and outpcd over 1f out: styd on again fnl 100yds* **13/2**
036- 5 10 **Snow Ridge**[170] 6919 3-9-2 **68** SebSanders 1 32
(Andrew Haynes) *swtchd lft s: a in last and sn rdn along: lost tch 2f out* **11/1**

1m 12.36s (-0.34) **Going Correction** -0.10s/f (Good) **5** Ran SP% **111.4**
Speed ratings (Par 98): **98,96,95,93,80**
CSF £9.18 TOTE £2.10: £1.30, £2.20; EX 9.20.
Owner Gwyn Powell and Peter Ridgers **Bred** Patrick Cummins **Trained** Lambourn, Berks

FOCUS
A small field 3-y-o handicap. The front two held those positions throughout. The runner-up has been rated back to something like his best, and the third has been rated close to her AW mark.

1132 CLAYDON HORSE EXERCISERS (S) STKS 7f (S)
3:50 (3:52) (Class 6) 3-Y-O **£1,535** (£453; £226) **Stalls** High

Form RPR
656- **1** **Red Zeus (IRE)**[255] 4323 3-8-12 67 LiamKeniry 7 54
(J S Moore) *w ldrs tl 1/2-way: sn lost pl: drvn over 1f out: str run on stands' rails ins fnl f: led last strides* **3/1**[2]
3326 **2** *hd* **Tony Hollis**[6] 1022 3-8-12 60 JamieSpencer 1 53
(Rod Millman) *stdd and swtchd lft s: hld up in tch: hdwy 1/2-way: drvn to chal over 1f out: led fnl 100yds: edgd lft and hdd last strides* **6/4**[1]
000- **3** *1* **Chillie Peppar**[157] 7201 3-8-12 54 KierenFallon 5 51
(George Prodromou) *led: rdn 2f out: drvn ent fnl f: hdd fnl 100yds: no ex and btn whn n.m.r nr fin* **5/1**
34 **4** *1 1/4* **Jackie Love (IRE)**[10] 959 3-8-7 0 KirstyMilczarek 3 42
(John Ryan) *in tch towards rr: rdn and effrt 1/2-way: drvn to chse ldrs over 1f out: wknd ins fnl f* **7/2**[3]
-404 **5** *nse* **Magical Star**[10] 966 3-8-7 48 NickyMackay 4 42
(Mark Rimmer) *trckd ldrs: wnt 2nd 3f out: rdn and fnd nil over 1f out: nt qckning whn n.m.r ins fnl f wkng fnl 100yds* **20/1**
56 **6** *4* **Sing Alana Sing**[4] 1056 3-8-7 0 (t) DavidProbert 8 31
(Bill Turner) *w ldrs tl 1/2-way: sn struggling: wl btn over 1f out* **28/1**
606- **7** *10* **Senor Tibor (USA)**[176] 6779 3-8-12 60 (b[1]) EddieCreighton 2 9
(Edward Creighton) *s.i.s: a in rr: lost tch over 2f out* **16/1**
6456 **8** *7* **Hey Mambo**[10] 958 3-8-7 45 MartinLane 6 —
(Roger Ingram) *awkward leaving stalls and slowly away: t.k.h in rr: lost tch wl over 2f out: t.o* **50/1**

1m 29.09s (1.79) **Going Correction** -0.10s/f (Good) 8 Ran SP% **119.9**
Speed ratings (Par 96): **85,84,83,82,82 77,66,58**
toteswingers:1&2 £2.50, 2&3 £3.10, 1&3 £3.70 CSF £8.22 TOTE £4.80: £1.50, £1.02, £2.90; EX 10.30.There was no bid for the winner.
Owner John E McClenaghan & J S Moore **Bred** Paul Hardy **Trained** Upper Lambourn, Berks
■ Stewards' Enquiry : Kieren Fallon one-day ban: careless riding

FOCUS
A weak 3-y-o seller rated around the runner-up to his AW form and the third to a personal best.
Senor Tibor(USA) Official explanation: jockey said that the gelding was slowly away

1133 CLAYDON HORSE EXERCISERS MAIDEN FILLIES' STKS 7f (S)
4:20 (4:21) (Class 5) 3-Y-O+ **£1,910** (£564; £282) **Stalls** High

Form RPR
0- **1** **Here To Eternity (USA)**[249] 4517 3-8-10 0 JackMitchell 3 62+
(Peter Chapple-Hyam) *hld up: hdwy to press ldrs 3f out: pushed ahd to ld jst over 1f out: rdn whn pressed ins fnl furlng: kpt on wl* **7/4**[2]
0-6 **2** *3/4* **Play The Blues (IRE)**[18] 878 4-9-5 0 RyanPowell[(5)] 4 65
(Mark Allen) *stdd s: t.k.h: chsd ldrs: n.m.r and swtchd rt over 1f out: drvn and hdwy in centre 1f out: pressed ldr fnl 100yds: a hld* **33/1**
3255 **3** *1* **Timpanist (USA)**[16] 905 4-9-10 63 SebSanders 2 62
(Simon Dow) *w ldr tl rdn to ld 2f out: hdd and unable qck jst over 1f out: one pce* **7/1**[3]
023- **4** *5* **Gay Gallivanter**[217] 5583 3-8-10 73 KierenFallon 5 44
(Michael Quinn) *t.k.h and led at stdy gallop: qcknd 3f out: hdd and rdn 2f out: sn hung rt u.p and wknd* **8/11**[1]
06 **5** *1* **Tinkerbell Will**[16] 905 4-9-10 0 SamHitchcott 1 46
(John E Long) *chsd ldrs: rdn and unable qck ent fnl 2f: wknd over 1f out* **33/1**

1m 28.52s (1.22) **Going Correction** -0.10s/f (Good)
WFA 3 from 4yo 14lb 5 Ran SP% **112.6**
Speed ratings (Par 100): **89,88,87,81,80**
CSF £38.56 TOTE £2.90: £1.40, £9.40; EX 28.40.
Owner Miss K Rausing **Bred** Kirsten Rausing **Trained** Newmarket, Suffolk

FOCUS
A modest fillies' maiden and, with the favourite bombing out, the winner had little to beat.

1134 CLAYDON HORSE EXERCISERS H'CAP 1m 1f 149y
4:50 (4:52) (Class 5) (0-70,69) 3-Y-O **£1,910** (£564; £282) **Stalls** Centre

Form RPR
-414 **1** **Ya Hafed**[40] 650 3-9-3 64 JamesDoyle 4 71+
(Sheena West) *mde all: rdn clr and in command 2f out: eased wl ins fnl f* **4/1**[2]
3342 **2** *4* **Not So Bright (USA)**[9] 987 3-8-10 57 (tp) DavidProbert 1 56
(Des Donovan) *in tch: rdn to chse ldng pair over 2f out: sn outpcd by wnr: wnt 2nd over 1f out: no imp* **9/2**[3]
530- **3** *1 3/4* **Sixty Roses (IRE)**[186] 6513 3-9-8 69 ow1 MartinLane 7 64+
(John Dunlop) *s.i.s: hld up in last pair: stl plenty to do and rdn 3f out: nt clr run over 2f out tl 2f out: swtchd lft over 1f out: styd on u.p to go 3rd wl ins fnl f* **2/1**[1]
5636 **4** *3/4* **Surprise (IRE)**[13] 942 3-8-12 59 NickyMackay 2 52
(Mark Rimmer) *chsd ldrs: wnt 2nd 3f out: sn rdn and outpcd by wnr: lost 2nd over 1f out: plugged on* **20/1**
00-0 **5** *3 3/4* **Generous Genella**[17] 898 3-8-7 54 oh4 JimmyQuinn 5 39
(Julia Feilden) *chsd ldrs: rdn and swtchd lft bnd over 2f out: sn wknd* **20/1**
5004 **6** *8* **Ocean's Dream Day (IRE)**[13] 942 3-8-8 55 KirstyMilczarek 3 24
(John Ryan) *dwlt: sn rcvrd and in midfield: unable qck u.p whn pushed lft bnd over 2f out: wl btn whn hung rt over 1f out* **10/1**
0-40 **7** *27* **Lady Morganna (IRE)**[17] 898 3-8-9 56 ow1 KierenFallon 6 —
(Olivia Maylam) *chsd ldr tl 3f out: wkng whn pushed lft bnd over 2f out: sn bhd and eased: t.o* **5/1**
053 **8** *1/2* **Frosty Reception**[28] 791 3-9-1 62 SebSanders 8 —
(Brendan Powell) *dwlt: a in rr: rdn and lost tch over 3f out: virtually p.u fr over 1f out: t.o* **8/1**

2m 8.94s (4.04) **Going Correction** +0.40s/f (Good) 8 Ran SP% **117.9**
Speed ratings (Par 98): **99,95,94,93,90 84,62,62**
toteswingers:1&2 £2.20, 2&3 £3.20, 1&3 £2.80 CSF £23.15 CT £44.99 TOTE £2.90: £1.50, £1.10, £1.70; EX 16.10.
Owner Ashley Head **Bred** Lady Bland & Miss Anthea Gibson-Fleming **Trained** Falmer, E Sussex

FOCUS
A low-grade 3-y-o handicap and, with doubts about most of the runners, the form is not convincing.

1135 STONE STREET APPRENTICE H'CAP 1m 4f
5:20 (5:22) (Class 6) (0-60,56) 4-Y-O+ **£1,535** (£453; £226) **Stalls** High

Form RPR
0500 **1** **Gems**[32] 749 4-8-9 45 LucyKBarry 2 53
(Peter Hiatt) *mde all: clr whn hung lft u.p fr over 1f out: kpt on wl* **9/1**
050- **2** *3 1/4* **Musashi (IRE)**[25] 6668 6-9-0 56 CharlotteJenner[(7)] 1 59
(Laura Mongan) *hld up in midfield: effrt and rdn 3f out: chsd wnr 1f out: kpt on* **9/1**
0500 **3** *4* **Vinces**[12] 944 7-8-13 53 IanBurns[(5)] 5 50
(Tim McCarthy) *hld up in last pair: sme hdwy whn nt clr run on inner over 1f out: sn swtchd lft: styd on: nvr trbld ldrs* **6/1**[3]
40-5 **4** *2 1/4* **Derby Desire (IRE)**[80] 173 7-8-9 49 ThomasBrown[(5)] 7 42
(Des Donovan) *chsd ldrs: wnt 2nd and rdn wl over 2f out: drvn and no imp 2f out: lost 2nd 1f out: wknd* **10/3**[2]
3251 **5** *3 3/4* **Sir Haydn**[13] 939 11-8-8 48 (v) DannyBrock[(5)] 9 35
(J R Jenkins) *hld up in rr: rdn and effrt on outer 3f out: no imp and wl hld whn hung rt over 1f out* **7/1**
454- **6** *2* **Rose Aurora**[165] 7039 4-8-5 46 (v) KatiaScallan[(5)] 4 30
(Marcus Tregoning) *chsd ldrs: wnt 2nd 8f out tl 3f out: sn rdn and struggling: wknd wl over 1f out* **11/4**[1]
0104 **7** *3 1/4* **Suhailah**[6] 1025 5-8-11 53 AaronChave[(7)] 8 32
(Michael Attwater) *racd wd: in tch: chsd clr ldng trio 5f out tl wl over 2f out: wl btn whn hmpd wl over 1f out* **10/1**
050/ **8** *9* **Hereditary**[26] 6643 9-8-10 45 (tp) AlexEdwards 6 —
(Linda Jewell) *in tch in midfield: struggling and dropped in rr whn hmpd 4f out: sn bhd: t.o* **16/1**
006/ **9** *3/4* **Birthday Star (IRE)**[25] 7642 9-8-5 45 (tp) GeorgeDowning[(5)] 3 —
(Linda Jewell) *dwlt: a in rr: lost tch over 3f out: t.o* **40/1**
00/0 **10** *21* **Fast Elaine (IRE)**[12] 943 4-8-2 45 KirstenSmith[(7)] 10 —
(Martin Bosley) *w wnr tl 8f out: steadily lost pl: wl t.o fnl 2f* **20/1**

2m 45.13s (4.23) **Going Correction** +0.40s/f (Good)
WFA 4 from 5yo+ 1lb 10 Ran SP% **118.7**
Speed ratings (Par 101): **101,98,96,94,92 90,88,82,82,68**
toteswingers:1&2 £20.60, 2&3 £13.70, 1&3 £16.00 CSF £88.74 CT £531.83 TOTE £14.40: £4.40, £2.60, £2.10; EX 110.10.
Owner R Robinson **Bred** Bishop Wilton Stud **Trained** Hook Norton, Oxon

FOCUS
A low-grade apprentice handicap. As in the first race on the round course the winner, who is not an obvious improver, made all.
Gems Official explanation: trainer said, regarding the apparent improvement of form, that the filly was better suited by being able to dominate in this race
Hereditary Official explanation: jockey said that the gelding suffered interference in running
T/Plt: £47.50 to a £1 stake. Pool of £51,918.83 - 796.51 winning tickets. T/Qpdt: £19.30 to a £1 stake. Pool of £3,569.54 - 136.50 winning tickets. SP

WINDSOR (R-H)
Monday, April 4

OFFICIAL GOING: Good to firm (good in places; 9.0)
Wind: Moderate, behind Weather: Overcast becoming fine

1136 EUROPEAN BREEDERS' FUND MAIDEN STKS 5f 10y
2:40 (2:44) (Class 5) 2-Y-O **£3,238** (£963; £481; £240) **Stalls** Low

Form RPR
1 **Silverheels (IRE)** 2-9-3 0 SilvestreDeSousa 10 90+
(Paul Cole) *veered lft after s and reminder: sn chsd ldrs disputing 5th: stl running green whn shkn up to cl over 1f out: r.o to ld last 150yds: sn clr* **6/1**[3]
2 *3 1/4* **Lord Ofthe Shadows (IRE)** 2-9-3 0 RyanMoore 1 74+
(Richard Hannon) *trckd ldng trio: clsd 2f out: rn green but shkn up to ld over 1f out: hdd and outpcd last 150yds* **5/4**[1]
3 *1 1/4* **Sea Odyssey (IRE)** 2-9-3 0 MichaelHills 7 69+
(B W Hills) *pressed ldr: led over 3f out: rdn and hdd over 1f out: one pce* **9/4**[2]
4 *3* **Tango Sky (IRE)** 2-9-3 0 JimCrowley 6 57
(Ralph Beckett) *gd spd and w ldrs over 3f: grad fdd* **14/1**
4 **5** *3/4* **Ciara Boo (IRE)**[9] 982 2-8-12 0 CathyGannon 5 49
(David Evans) *led to over 3f out: rdn 1/2-way: outpcd wl over 1f out: n.d after* **8/1**
6 *6* **Bella Ponte** 2-8-12 0 DaneO'Neill 9 25
(John Gallagher) *chsd ldrs but nt on terms: outpcd fr 1/2-way* **40/1**
7 *2 1/2* **Joli Colourful (IRE)** 2-9-3 0 FergusSweeney 11 20
(Tony Newcombe) *dwlt: chsd ldrs in 5th: outpcd by 1/2-way: n.d after* **50/1**
8 *3 1/4* **Seven Year Itch (IRE)** 2-8-12 0 PaulDoe 3 —
(David Evans) *s.s: bdly outpcd and a wl bhd* **40/1**
9 *11* **Middleton Flyer (IRE)** 2-8-12 0 TomMcLaughlin 4 —
(David Evans) *s.s: bdly outpcd and sn t.o* **33/1**
10 *3* **Garrarufa (IRE)** 2-9-3 0 JamesMillman 8 —
(Rod Millman) *dwlt: bdly outpcd and sn t.o* **33/1**

59.37 secs (-0.93) **Going Correction** -0.30s/f (Firm) 10 Ran SP% **120.0**
Speed ratings (Par 92): **95,89,87,83,81 72,68,63,45,40**
toteswingers:1&2 £3.00, 2&3 £2.30, 1&3 £3.00 CSF £13.98 TOTE £6.20: £1.90, £1.10, £1.60; EX 19.90 Trifecta £27.30 Pool of £530.15 - 14.34 wining units..Cool Kittiwake was withdrawn. Price at time of withdrawal 100/1. Rule 4 does not apply.
Owner Goldswain Hunter Jefferson Williams **Bred** Castlemartin Stud And Skymarc Farm **Trained** Whatcombe, Oxon

FOCUS
The last two winners of this maiden went on to win in Group company - Red Clubs in 2009 and Zebedee last year. This latest edition was run at a fast pace, with three horses vying for the early lead, and the final time was only 0.62 seconds outside the juvenile track record, although there was a following wind. The field were soon strung out, with several of these noticeably green, but the 'right' horses came to the fore and this looks strong early season juvenile form.

NOTEBOOK
Silverheels(IRE) ◆, a 30,000gns first foal of an unraced dam, was born in January so was fully entitled to be an early type. He was extremely green early, hanging left soon after leaving the stalls and needing to be corrected twice with the whip, but being left some way off the pace was no bad thing considering the leaders went quick. Once getting the idea, he picked up in taking fashion to readily overhaul two well-fancied runners from powerful stables and draw some way clear. He looks Royal Ascot class, although that's a little way off and Paul Cole suggested he could go to France at some stage. (op 9-2)
Lord Ofthe Shadows(IRE) ◆, representing last year's winning stable, was strong in the market, although Richard Hannon's only other juvenile to have run this year was beaten at odds of 4-11. This colt's sales price increased from 30,000gns as a foal to 70,000gns as a yearling and he showed plenty of ability, picking up well after having to be niggled to stay in touch with the early leaders. He can be expected to win next time before stepping up in class. (tchd 6-5 and 6-4)
Sea Odyssey(IRE) ◆'s sales price increased from 9,000euros as a foal to 65,000gns last year and he represented Barry Hills, who won this in 2009. Strong in the market, he showed good early pace but couldn't dominate outright and looked to do too much too soon. He saw off the other two pacesetters, though, and his natural speed should see him reach quite a useful level. (op 3-1 tchd 10-3)

Tango Sky(IRE), a £22,000 purchase, was another who went off plenty fast enough and didn't see his race out. (tchd 16-1)

Ciara Boo(IRE) was the only runner with previous experience, but she had recorded an RPR of just 36 on her debut and struggled to see her race out, having been the third member of the trio who battled for the early lead. (op 11-1 tchd 7-1)

1137 OVERTONES AT ROYAL WINDSOR RACECOURSE 25TH JUNE CLAIMING STKS — 1m 2f 7y

3:10 (3:12) (Class 6) 3-Y-O £1,706 (£503; £252) Stalls High

Form				RPR
005-	1		**Certral**[128] 7602 3-8-7 56 (p) TonyCulhane 3 (George Baker) *trckd ldng pair: effrt 3f out: rdn to ld jst over 2f out: styd on* **15/8**[1]	53
00-6	2	1 ¼	**Dew Reward (IRE)**[19] 866 3-9-0 61 CathyGannon 5 (Eve Johnson Houghton) *pressed ldr: led over 4f out: sn rdn: hdd u.p jst over 2f out: kpt on* **5/2**[2]	57
500-	3	3	**Quite A Catch (IRE)**[167] 6994 3-9-6 62 JimCrowley 1 (Jonathan Portman) *hld up in cl tch: rdn and nt qckn over 2f out: one pce and no imp after* **7/1**[3]	57
33-6	4	hd	**Captain Sharpe**[11] 951 3-8-11 70 (p) RobertHavlin 6 (Bernard Llewellyn) *hld up in cl tch: pushed along over 3f out: rdn and nt qckn over 2f out: one pce* **5/2**[2]	48
006	5	6	**Clonusker (IRE)**[11] 953 3-9-1 45 (p) JimmyFortune 4 (Linda Jewell) *led at mod pce: hdd and rdn over 4f out: kpt pressing ldrs tl wknd wl over 1f out* **66/1**	40
0000	6	3	**Welsh Dresser (IRE)**[10] 964 3-8-7 36 RobbieFitzpatrick 2 (Peter Grayson) *a in last: outpcd over 3f out: rdn and no imp over 2f out: wknd ins fnl f* **66/1**	26

2m 10.5s (1.80) **Going Correction** -0.35s/f (Firm) 6 Ran SP% **107.4**
Speed ratings (Par 96): **78,77,74,74,69 67**
toteswingers:1&2 £1.80, 2&3 £2.60, 1&3 £1.60 CSF £6.20 TOTE £2.70: £1.50, £1.10; EX 8.40.Certral was claimed by L. S. Keys for £8000.

Owner Mrs C E S Baker **Bred** Whatton Manor Stud **Trained** Whitsbury, Hants

FOCUS
A moderate contest run at a steady pace, resulting in a time over four seconds above standard and 3.97 seconds slower than the later 3-y-o maiden. It has been rated around the runner-up to his recent AW form.

1138 PHARMALINK CONSULTING SPRING H'CAP — 1m 67y

3:40 (3:40) (Class 4) (0-85,85) 4-Y-O+ £3,885 (£1,156; £577; £288) Stalls Low

Form				RPR
400-	1		**Uncle Fred**[187] 6449 6-8-12 76 JimCrowley 8 (Patrick Chamings) *hld up last: waiting for room tl pushed along firmly and gd prog between rivals 2f out: rdn to ld jst ins fnl f: styd on wl* **9/1**	84
6-13	2	nk	**Yes Chef**[39] 666 4-8-8 72 JamesMillman 3 (Rod Millman) *t.k.h: hld up in 4th: shkn up and wanting to hang lft fr over 2f out: kpt on to chal ins fnl f: a jst hld* **4/1**[1]	79
014-	3	1 ½	**Ellemujie**[152] 7292 6-9-5 83 AdamKirby 6 (Dean Ivory) *hld up and sn in 5th: shkn up 3f out: cl enough u.p over 1f out: nt qckn* **11/1**	87
000-	4	½	**Guilded Warrior**[161] 7121 8-9-7 85 FergusSweeney 2 (Stuart Kittow) *led: drvn 2f out: hdd and one pce jst ins fnl f* **9/2**[2]	88
33-0	5	4	**First Post (IRE)**[18] 877 4-9-2 80 DaneO'Neill 5 (Derek Haydn Jones) *lost pl and in last pair bef 1/2-way: rdn on outer over 2f out: no prog over 1f out: wknd* **4/1**[1]	74
321-	6	4	**Kingsdine (IRE)**[255] 4325 4-8-13 77 TomMcLaughlin 1 (Malcolm Saunders) *t.k.h: trckd ldng pair: rdn over 2f out: wknd wl over 1f out: eased* **11/2**[3]	65
-133	7	hd	**Kilburn**[58] 438 7-9-4 82 SteveDrowne 7 (Alastair Lidderdale) *trckd ldr to 2f out: sn wknd: eased ins fnl f* **4/1**[1]	68

1m 40.75s (-3.95) **Going Correction** -0.35s/f (Firm) 7 Ran SP% **111.9**
Speed ratings (Par 105): **105,104,103,102,98 94,94**
toteswingers:1&2 £9.70, 2&3 £8.40, 1&3 £8.40 CSF £42.62 CT £398.24 TOTE £13.30: £4.10, £2.90; EX 63.60 Trifecta £176.90 Pool: £398.56 - 1.66 winning units..

Owner Inhurst Players **Bred** Netherfield House Stud **Trained** Baughurst, Hants

FOCUS
A combination of quick ground and a following wind contributed to a time 1.75 seconds under standard, but clearly the pace was fast. This was a fair handicap and the winner has been rated back to last year's best.

1139 DOWNLOAD TRAINER MAGAZINE ON ITUNES MAIDEN STKS — 1m 2f 7y

4:10 (4:15) (Class 5) 3-Y-O £2,388 (£705; £352) Stalls High

Form				RPR
33-	1		**Discoteca**[187] 6473 3-9-3 0 JimmyFortune 3 (Andrew Balding) *sn led: urged along 3f out: hrd rdn over 1f out: drew clr ins fnl f* **13/8**[1]	84+
00-	2	4	**Lucky Legs (IRE)**[184] 6559 3-8-12 0 MichaelHills 7 (B W Hills) *hld up in tch: stdy prog gng wl on outer over 2f out: wnt 2nd over 1f out: shkn up and lft bhd by wnr ins fnl f* **14/1**	71
	3	1 ¾	**Informed Award** 3-9-3 0 WilliamBuick 2 (John Gosden) *hld up in tch: pushed along over 2f out: swtchd lft and shkn up 1f out: styd on wl to take 3rd nr fin* **9/1**	73+
62-	4	nk	**Elfine (IRE)**[169] 6953 3-8-12 0 DaneO'Neill 1 (Harry Dunlop) *cl up: pushed along over 3f out: drvn and in tch 2f out: fdd* **6/1**	67
044-	5	2	**Silverware (USA)**[173] 6844 3-9-3 73 RyanMoore 5 (Richard Hannon) *mostly chsd wnr: rdn and cl enough 2f out: lost 2nd and fdd over 1f out* **11/2**[3]	68
0-	6	nk	**Atlas Shrugged (IRE)**[163] 7099 3-9-3 0 AdamKirby 4 (Clive Cox) *chsd ldrs: pushed along sn after 1/2-way: grad fdd u.p fnl 2f* **4/1**[2]	67
3	7	1 ½	**Strewth (IRE)**[51] 520 3-9-0 0 KierenFox[(3)] 10 (John Best) *prog arnd outer on bnd 6f out to join ldrs 1/2-way: rdn over 2f out: wknd over 1f out* **16/1**	64
0-	8	7	**Like A Boy**[145] 7385 3-9-3 0 SteveDrowne 6 (Peter Makin) *t.k.h: hld up in rr: lost tch w ldng gp 3f out: pushed along and nvr on terms after* **40/1**	50
	9	½	**May Contain Nuts** 3-9-3 0 FergusSweeney 8 (Brendan Powell) *s.s: hld up in rr: reminder over 4f out: sn lost tch w ldng gp: pushed along and no imp after* **50/1**	49
00-	10	6	**Laafhd**[196] 6249 3-8-12 0 JamesMillman 9 (Tony Newcombe) *a in rr: rdn 4f out: sn struggling* **100/1**	32
0	11	41	**Pippas Prodigy (IRE)**[28] 791 3-8-5 0 JenniferFerguson[(7)] 11 (Edward Creighton) *a in rr: hung lft and wknd over 4f out: wl t.o* **200/1**	—

2m 6.53s (-2.17) **Going Correction** -0.35s/f (Firm) 11 Ran SP% **116.2**
Speed ratings (Par 98): **94,90,89,89,87 87,86,80,80,75 42**
toteswingers:1&2 £8.30, 2&3 £15.10, 1&3 £4.30 CSF £27.74 TOTE £3.00: £1.60, £3.00, £2.80; EX 36.10 Trifecta £140.50 Pool: £776.61 - 4.09 winning units..

Owner David Brownlow **Bred** Usk Valley Stud **Trained** Kingsclere, Hants

FOCUS
A good 3-y-o maiden and probably ordinary form overall, with the fourth and fifth rated close to their marks.

Strewth(IRE) Official explanation: jockey said the colt failed to handle the bend

1140 TOBY LE RONE H'CAP — 5f 10y

4:40 (4:43) (Class 4) (0-85,80) 4-Y-O+ £3,561 (£1,059; £529; £264) Stalls Low

Form				RPR
0-6	1		**Taurus Twins**[10] 970 5-8-13 72 (b) TomQueally 13 (Richard Price) *led after 1f: mde rest: drvn and in command ins fnl f: styd on wl* **16/1**	84
-364	2	2	**Even Bolder**[16] 910 8-8-11 73 KierenFox[(3)] 14 (Eric Wheeler) *chsd ldrs: prog towards outer to chse wnr jst over 1f out: styd on but no imp after* **10/1**	78
35-3	3	1	**Ajjaadd (USA)**[16] 910 5-8-13 72 SteveDrowne 2 (Ted Powell) *hld up wl in rr: nt clr run briefly over 2f out: prog over 1f out: styd on ins fnl f: snatched 3rd on line* **11/2**[1]	73+
50-5	4	nse	**Go Nani Go**[37] 701 5-9-7 80 WilliamBuick 10 (Ed de Giles) *towards rr: prog on outer fr 1/2-way: rdn over 1f out: kpt on: nvr able to chal* **7/1**[2]	81
035-	5	hd	**Equuleus Pictor**[111] 7866 7-9-0 73 CathyGannon 1 (John Spearing) *lost midfield position 1/2-way: wl in rr 2f out: drvn and styd on ins fnl f: clsng at fin* **16/1**	77+
263-	6	nse	**Atlantic Beach**[153] 7281 6-9-2 75 JimCrowley 11 (Milton Bradley) *chsd ldrs: rdn over 1f out: kpt on same pce: nvr able to chal* **20/1**	75
046-	7	¾	**Evelyn May (IRE)**[129] 7573 5-8-9 75 MatthewLawson[(7)] 15 (B W Hills) *s.i.s: prog fr rr on outer 1/2-way: nvr on terms w ldrs: kpt on* **9/1**	72
60-0	8	hd	**Rocker**[10] 961 7-8-8 72 HarryBentley[(5)] 5 (Gary Moore) *mostly in midfield: urged along and no prog 2f out: edgd lft over 1f out: kpt on* **7/1**[2]	69
035	9	nse	**Cape Royal**[56] 443 11-9-4 77 (bt) RichardKingscote 16 (Milton Bradley) *prom: rdn to dispute 2nd over 1f out: no imp ins fnl f: wknd nr fin* **16/1**	73
101-	10	hd	**Victorian Bounty**[145] 7399 6-9-7 80 MickyFenton 12 (Stef Higgins) *led 1f: chsd wnr to jst over 1f out: fdd* **22/1**	76
5540	11	1	**Efistorm**[24] 833 10-9-6 79 HayleyTurner 3 (Conor Dore) *hld up in rr: no prog 2f out: swtchd lft and styd on ins fnl f: nvr nr ldrs* **8/1**[3]	71
-060	12	1 ¼	**Lucky Mellor**[27] 794 4-9-1 74 (b) AdamKirby 6 (Dean Ivory) *hld up in midfield on inner: nudged along and no prog over 1f out: nvr nr ldrs* **20/1**	62
125-	13	2 ½	**Bronze Beau**[196] 6245 4-9-2 78 (t) JamesSullivan[(3)] 9 (Linda Stubbs) *chsd ldrs on inner: n.m.r briefly 2f out: shkn up over 1f out: wknd* **14/1**	57
411-	14	11	**Galatian**[205] 5956 4-9-4 77 JamesMillman 7 (Rod Millman) *s.i.s: nvr on terms w ldrs: wknd and eased over 1f out* **8/1**[3]	56

58.08 secs (-2.22) **Going Correction** -0.30s/f (Firm) course record 14 Ran SP% **119.9**
Speed ratings (Par 105): **105,101,100,100,99 99,98,98,98,97 96,94,90,72**
CSF £162.13 CT £1032.76 TOTE £18.80: £4.70, £3.00, £2.40; EX 202.00 TRIFECTA Not won..

Owner G E Amey **Bred** G E Amey **Trained** Ullingswick, H'fords

FOCUS
A good sprint handicap and the course record was lowered by 0.22 seconds thanks to quick ground and a following wind. The first two finishers emerged from wide stalls, but there was no obvious draw bias. The third and fifth are the best guide to the level.

Atlantic Beach Official explanation: vet said the gelding had lost a left fore shoe

Galatian Official explanation: jockey said the gelding hung left and was never travelling

1141 ROYAL WINDSOR RACING CLUB CLASSIFIED STKS — 6f

5:10 (5:14) (Class 5) 3-Y-O £2,388 (£705; £352) Stalls Low

Form				RPR
15-2	1		**Oneladyowner**[13] 940 3-9-0 73 PhillipMakin 7 (David Brown) *trckd ldrs: rdn to chal 2f out: narrow ld ins fnl f: drvn out* **6/1**	75
350-	2	hd	**Roman Dancer (IRE)**[109] 7891 3-9-0 74 TomQueally 3 (John Gallagher) *pressed ldr: led over 3f out: hrd rdn 2f out: narrowly hdd ins fnl f: kpt on* **16/1**	74
541-	3	nk	**Camache Queen (IRE)**[199] 6161 3-9-0 75 CathyGannon 1 (Denis Coakley) *pressed ldng pair on inner: lost pl sltly 1/2-way: renewed effrt 2f out: chal u.p ins fnl f: nt qckn nr fin* **8/1**	73
004-	4	2 ¼	**Firstknight**[185] 6520 3-9-0 74 AdamKirby 4 (Marco Botti) *in tch in rr: rdn over 2f out: clsd on ldrs over 1f out: hanging and nt qckn ins fnl f* **11/4**[2]	66
41-	5	½	**Soweto Star (IRE)**[172] 6878 3-9-0 74 LukeMorris 6 (John Best) *in tch: stmbld sltly jst over 2f out: drvn to chse ldrs over 1f out: one pce after* **5/2**[1]	64
5-13	6	½	**Grandmas Dream**[18] 875 3-9-0 75 PaulDoe 2 (Jim Best) *led to over 3f out: styd pressing ldr tl fdd 1f out* **10/1**	63
235-	7	6	**Park Ballet (IRE)**[196] 6258 3-8-9 71 HarryBentley[(5)] 9 (Jonathan Portman) *awkward s: in tch in last: rdn over 2f out: no prog over 1f out: wknd* **20/1**	44
4-1	8	2 ½	**Green Apple**[52] 513 3-9-0 75 FergusSweeney 8 (Peter Makin) *wl in tch on outer: rdn over 2f out: wknd over 1f out* **5/1**[3]	36

1m 11.25s (-1.75) **Going Correction** -0.30s/f (Firm) 8 Ran SP% **117.0**
Speed ratings (Par 98): **99,98,98,95,94 94,86,82**
toteswingers:1&2 £11.10, 2&3 £19.20, 1&3 £7.10 CSF £95.04 TOTE £7.30: £2.10, £2.90, £2.80; EX 136.40 TRIFECTA Not won..

Owner Bolland, Watson, Gregory, Lloyd & Oades **Bred** Barry Minty **Trained** Averham Park, Notts

FOCUS
The final time suggests they didn't go that quick (two races on the card dipped well under standard) and it paid to race prominently. Oridnary form rated through the runner-up and third.

T/Plt: £379.20 to a £1 stake. Pool of £72,069.55 - 138.73 winning tickets. T/Qpdt: £229.10 to a £1 stake. Pool of £5,387.39 - 17.40 winning tickets. JN

LONGCHAMP (R-H)

Monday, April 4

OFFICIAL GOING: Turf: heavy

1142a PRIX DE PONTOISE (CLAIMER) (5YO+) (TURF) 1m 2f

3:20 (12:00) 5-Y-O+ **£7,758** (£3,103; £2,327; £1,551; £775)

RPR

1 **I Love Loup (FR)**[7] 7-9-1 0......................... Christophe-PatriceLemaire 2 78
(M Boutin, France) **10/1**

2 *snk* **Touching Kings (FR)**[16] 6-9-1 0................................ GregoryBenoist 7 78
(X Nakkachdji, France) **13/10[1]**

3 *4* **Class Attraction (IRE)**[17] [903] 7-8-11 0.......... ChristopheSoumillon 12 66
(Mme C Barande-Barbe, France) **63/10[3]**

4 *hd* **Auzi (FR)**[61] [395] 8-8-11 0.. TonyPiccone 3 65
(J Rossi, France) **16/1**

5 *snk* **Same As Gold (FR)**[91] [42] 7-8-11 0...................... MickaelBarzalona 8 65
(D De Waele, France) **44/1**

6 *snk* **Question D'Or (FR)**[16] 5-9-2 0................................(p) IoritzMendizabal 4 70
(Robert Collet, France) **12/1**

7 *½* **Bencoolen (IRE)**[17] [903] 6-8-11 0.............................. MaximeGuyon 10 64
(D De Waele, France) **24/1**

8 *½* **Montnamix (FR)**[562] 6-9-4 0.. OlivierPeslier 11 70
(J-Y Artu, France) **21/1**

9 *½* **Farhan (FR)**[125] 5-9-1 0..(b) DavyBonilla 6 66
(C Lerner, France) **24/1**

10 *snk* **Lowenherz (GER)**[7] 7-9-4 0.. ThierryThulliez 1 68
(J-P Perruchot, France) **6/1[2]**

0 **Once Upon A Cat (IRE)**[881] 7-8-8 0.............................. ThomasHuet 5 —
(Mrs K Burke) *s.i.s: a in rr: nvr a factor* **52/1**

0 **Pick Well (FR)**[102] 5-9-1 0.. JohannBensimon 9 —
(Mme L Audon, France) **70/1**

0 **Peinture Texane (FR)**[25] 5-8-0 0............................ MatthieuAutier(8) 13 —
(M Boutin, France) **28/1**

2m 15.2s (11.20) **13** Ran SP% **115.6**
WIN (incl. 1 euro stake): 7.60 (I Love Loup coupled with Peinture Texane). PLACES: 2.20, 1.30, 2.00. DF: 9.30. SF: 32.40.
Owner Mme Mathieu Boutin **Bred** Mme Charlotte Thoreau **Trained** France

1100 KEMPTON (A.W) (R-H)

Tuesday, April 5

OFFICIAL GOING: Standard
Wind: Moderate, across Weather: Overcast

1143 WILLIAM HILL, HOME OF BETTING MAIDEN AUCTION STKS 5f (P)

2:20 (2:20) (Class 5) 2-Y-O **£2,417** (£713; £357) **Stalls** Low

Form RPR

5 **1** **Snowed In (IRE)**[10] [982] 2-8-11 0.. LiamKeniry 4 66
(J S Moore) *prom early: dropped to last and pushed along 1/2-way: sltly hmpd wl over 1f out: clsd to chal fnl f: edgd rt but led narrowly last 100yds: drvn out* **9/2[3]**

2 *shd* **That's Dangerous** 2-8-11 0.. SteveDrowne 1 66+
(Roger Charlton) *dwlt: rcvrd and in tch after 1f: prog 2f out: led briefly ins fnl f: upsides after: jst hld* **11/8[1]**

3 *2½* **Mrs Mop (IRE)** 2-8-8 0.. RichardHughes 2 55
(Richard Hannon) *hmpd s: rcvrd to ld after 2f: hdd and fdd ins fnl f* **2/1[2]**

4 *12* **Multi Blessing** 2-8-9 0... NeilCallan 3 11
(Alan Jarvis) *wnt rt s: led 2f: hanging lft after: wknd over 1f out* **9/2[3]**

62.28 secs (1.78) **Going Correction** +0.075s/f (Slow) **4** Ran SP% **111.8**
Speed ratings (Par 92): **88,87,83,64**
CSF £11.49 TOTE £5.60; EX 11.40.
Owner Norton Common Farm Racing **Bred** T Cahalan & D Cahalan **Trained** Upper Lambourn, Berks
■ Stewards' Enquiry : Liam Keniry one-day ban: careless riding (Apr 19); caution: used whip with excessive frequency on a 2yo, 2nd run.

FOCUS
Only four runners but, although not easy to get a solid handle on the form given the winner (the only one with previous experience) had been well beaten on his debut, it is unlikely to be anything out of the ordinary. The gallop was a reasonable one and the winner edged towards the inside rail late on.

NOTEBOOK
Snowed In(IRE), well beaten after a slow start on his debut in a race that has worked out well, jumped off better this time and put his experience to good use against three newcomers with a much-improved display. He'll be better suited by 6f, but it will be a surprise if he confirms placings with the runner-up should the pair meet again in the near future. (op 4-1 tchd 5-1)
That's Dangerous ◆, the first runner for impressive Coventry scorer and Dewhurst runner-up Three Valleys, and his trainer's first juvenile runner of the season, has physical scope and showed more than enough on this debut - missed the break, ran green and carried off a true line in the closing stages - to suggest he should be capable of picking up a similar event at least with this run behind him. His pedigree suggests 6f should suit even better and he should be able to leave this bare form behind. (op 5-4)
Mrs Mop(IRE), a sparely made daughter of Middle Park winner Amadeus Wolf (whose son Hamza ran out an impressive winner at Musselburgh last week) and the only filly in the race, showed plenty of toe after being baulked at the start on this racecourse debut. She should be all the wiser for this experience and should be able to pick up a small race. (op 7-4 tchd 13-8)
Multi Blessing, whose dam is a half-sister to the yard's former Princess Margaret winner Mixed Blessing, attracted support on this racecourse debut but was eventually well beaten after taking a strong hold and after looking ill-at-ease on the track. He too should improve for this experience.
Official explanation: jockey said colt ran green (op 14-1)

1144 SHAKE-A-BET DOWNLOAD @ WILLIAMHILL.COM H'CAP 1m 2f (P)

2:50 (2:51) (Class 5) (0-75,74) 4-Y-O+ **£2,417** (£713; £357) **Stalls** Low

Form RPR

6-65 **1** **Understory (USA)**[11] [963] 4-9-5 72... NeilCallan 5 79
(Tim McCarthy) *racd freely: mde all: kicked on over 2f out: 2 l clr and drvn 1f out: jst lasted* **15/2[3]**

312- **2** *hd* **Crunched**[276] [3689] 4-9-7 74.................................... HayleyTurner 7 81
(Michael Bell) *trckd wnr 3f: wnt 2nd over 2f out: drvn and no imp tl clsd qckly last 75yds: jst failed* **4/1[2]**

422- **3** *2¾* **Loyaliste (FR)**[130] [7575] 4-9-4 71.................................. RichardHughes 2 73
(Richard Hannon) *n.m.r s: hld up in rr: rdn and prog on inner over 2f out: wnt 3rd over 1f out: kpt on but no real imp* **3/1[1]**

543- **4** *1½* **Potentiale (IRE)**[164] [7089] 7-9-4 74.............................(p) PatrickHills(3) 6 73
(J W Hills) *hld up in rr: prog on outer over 2f out: rdn to dispute 3rd over 1f out: fdd fnl f* **10/1**

401- **5** *4* **Dark Ranger**[18] [5636] 5-8-10 63.......................................(p) RobertHavlin 3 54
(Tim Pitt) *squeezed out s: hld up last: shkn up and lft bhd over 2f out: no ch after: fin w a flourish* **12/1**

44-5 **6** *1* **Tilsworth Glenboy**[41] [647] 4-8-12 65............................ StephenCraine 4 54
(J R Jenkins) *n.m.r s: t.k.h: chsd wnr after 3f to over 2f out: wknd* **14/1**

6423 **7** *1½* **Free Tussy (ARG)**[27] [814] 7-8-12 65.......................(bt) FergusSweeney 8 51
(Gary Moore) *t.k.h: hld up bhd ldrs: rdn and nt qckn over 2f out: wknd over 1f out* **8/1**

315- **8** *11* **Morning Chief (IRE)**[145] [7414] 4-9-5 72............................ LukeMorris 1 45
(Clive Cox) *restless stalls: t.k.h: trckd ldrs: lost pl and shkn up 1/2-way: struggling over 2f out: wknd and eased* **3/1[1]**

2m 6.54s (-1.46) **Going Correction** +0.075s/f (Slow) **8** Ran SP% **116.3**
Speed ratings (Par 103): **108,107,105,104,101 100,99,90**
toteswingers:1&2:£6.40, 1&3:£3.90, 2&3:£2.30 CSF £38.22 CT £111.04 TOTE £7.90: £1.70, £1.40, £1.10; EX 30.10.
Owner The Bordeaux Fine Wines Racing Club **Bred** Darley **Trained** Godstone, Surrey
■ Stewards' Enquiry : Hayley Turner three-day ban: careless riding (Apr 19-21)

FOCUS
No more than a fair handicap. A steady gallop to the home straight meant those held up were at a disadvantage and, although the overall time compared to Racing Post Standard was respectable, the bare form looks unreliable. The winner raced close to the inside rail throughout.

1145 WILLIAMHILL.COM H'CAP 5f (P)

3:20 (3:20) (Class 4) (0-85,79) 3-Y-O **£3,478** (£1,204) **Stalls** Low

Form RPR

-111 **1** **Chevise (IRE)**[44] [620] 3-9-2 79...................................... HarryBentley(5) 4 83
(Steve Woodman) *trckd rival: shkn up over 1f out: clsd to ld last 150yds: styd on* **5/2[2]**

2432 **2** *¾* **Welsh Inlet (IRE)**[11] [958] 3-8-7 65...................................... LukeMorris 3 66
(John Bridger) *led: shkn up over 1f out: hdd and nt qckn last 150yds* **7/2[3]**

5-32 **U** **Overwhelm**[19] [875] 3-8-11 74... LeeTopliss(5) 2 —
(Richard Fahey) *veered rt: sddle slipped and uns rdr s* **5/6[1]**

61.12 secs (0.62) **Going Correction** +0.075s/f (Slow) **3** Ran SP% **105.3**
Speed ratings (Par 100): **98,96,—**
CSF £8.89 TOTE £2.90; EX 5.60.
Owner The Chevise Partnership **Bred** Paul And Mrs Jenny Green **Trained** East Lavant, W Sussex

FOCUS
A very disappointing turnout in a race contested solely by fillies and one that turned into a match when odds-on favourite Overwhelm parted company with her rider as the stalls opened. The gallop was only fair and the winner raced just off the inside rail in the straight.

1146 PLAY FTSE WITH TRADER @ WILLIAMHILL.COM MEDIAN AUCTION MAIDEN FILLIES' STKS 1m (P)

3:50 (3:50) (Class 6) 3-5-Y-O **£1,748** (£516; £258) **Stalls** Low

Form RPR

1 **Metropolitain Miss (IRE)** 3-8-12 0................................ SamHitchcott 8 75
(Mick Channon) *trckd ldr: shkn up to ld jst over 2f out: pushed along firmly and steadily drew clr* **20/1**

0- **2** *3½* **Ssafa**[157] [7232] 3-8-12 0.. SebSanders 7 66
(J W Hills) *hld up in last trio: prog on outer to take 3rd 2f out: pushed along and kpt on steadily fnl f to snatch 2nd last stride* **33/1**

033- **3** *shd* **Destiny Of Dreams**[120] [7723] 3-8-12 68............................ DaneO'Neill 2 66
(Jo Crowley) *led: rdn and hdd jst over 2f out: one pce and no ch w wnr over 1f out: lost 2nd last stride* **9/2[2]**

4 *2½* **Dark Spirit (IRE)** 3-8-12 0.. RobertHavlin 3 60
(Tim Pitt) *hld up in tch: effrt over 2f out: pushed along and tk 4th over 1f out: no imp after* **33/1**

366- **5** *3* **September Draw (USA)**[176] [6809] 3-8-12 66............... RichardHughes 5 50
(Richard Hannon) *hld up in last trio: pushed along over 2f out: sn outpcd* **5/1[3]**

6 *1* **Gennie** 3-8-7 0.. KieranO'Neill(5) 1 50
(Richard Hannon) *s.i.s: rcvrd to trck ldng pair to 2f out: rn green and wknd* **11/1**

7 *6* **Zanoubiatta (USA)** 3-8-12 0.. EddieAhern 4 36
(Ed Dunlop) *s.i.s: rcvrd to trck ldng trio: shkn up over 2f out: sn wknd and eased* **11/10[1]**

8 *shd* **Daliana** 3-8-12 0.. HayleyTurner 6 36
(Michael Bell) *stdd s and hld up in last trio: shkn up and no prog over 2f out: wknd over 1f out* **7/1**

1m 40.44s (0.64) **Going Correction** +0.075s/f (Slow) **8** Ran SP% **113.9**
Speed ratings (Par 98): **99,95,95,92,89 88,82,82**
toteswingers:1&2:£17.50, 1&3:£7.90, 2&3:£12.80 CSF £477.14 TOTE £21.90: £3.30, £6.30, £1.40; EX 104.40.
Owner Saeed Misleh **Bred** Rabbah Bloodstock Limited **Trained** West Ilsley, Berks

FOCUS
An uncompetitive maiden in which a couple of the newcomers disappointed and the third horse looks the best guide to the level of the form. The gallop was an ordinary one and the winner came down the centre.

1147 WILLIAM HILL, HOME OF BETTING FILLIES' H'CAP 7f (P)

4:20 (4:20) (Class 5) (0-75,74) 4-Y-O+ **£2,417** (£713; £357) **Stalls** Low

Form RPR

203- **1** **Leadenhall Lass (IRE)**[229] [5238] 5-9-0 67......................... IanMongan 5 73
(Pat Phelan) *settled disputing 4th: shkn up and effrt on outer 2f out: clsd 1f out: drvn and kpt on to ld post* **14/1**

51-4 **2** *shd* **Sunset Kitty (USA)**[20] [865] 4-9-6 73...........................(v[1]) EddieAhern 2 79
(Walter Swinburn) *restless stalls: trckd ldng pair: rdn to go 2nd 2f out: clsd to ld jst ins fnl f: hdd post* **7/2[3]**

1U01 **3** *hd* **Perfect Ch'I (IRE)**[20] [865] 4-9-2 69.................................... JamesDoyle 6 74
(Ian Wood) *chsd ldr to 2f out: rallied u.p jst over 1f out: chal nr fin: jst hld* **7/1**

-212 **4** *¾* **Al Aqabah (IRE)**[27] [806] 6-9-1 73.........................(b) AdamBeschizza(5) 3 76
(Brian Gubby) *dwlt: hld up disputing 4th: rdn wl over 2f out and struggling: rallied over 1f out: kpt on nr fin* **5/2[1]**

061- **5** *nse* **Leelu**[128] [7613] 5-8-13 66... LiamKeniry 4 69
(David Arbuthnot) *led: drvn over 1f out and more than a l clr: hdd jst ins fnl f: lost pls nr fin* **11/4[2]**

1233 **6** 2 3/4 **Cape Melody**[7] 1024 5-9-7 **74**....(p) JimmyFortune 1 70
(George Baker) *rel to r and reminder: sn in tch: rdn 3f out: no imp over 1f out* **11/2**

1m 25.86s (-0.14) **Going Correction** +0.075s/f (Slow) **6** Ran SP% **112.0**
Speed ratings (Par 100): **103,102,102,101,101 98**
toteswingers:1&2:£4.10, 1&3:£8.10, 2&3:£4.30 CSF £61.26 TOTE £16.40: £8.10, £2.00; EX 55.30.

Owner The Lime Street Syndicate **Bred** R N Auld **Trained** Epsom, Surrey

FOCUS

A fair fillies' handicap run at an ordinary gallop and one in which the first five finished in a heap. The winner came down the centre in the straight.

Cape Melody Official explanation: jockey said mare was slowly away

1148 WILLIAMHILL.COM H'CAP 2m (P)

4:50 (4:51) (Class 5) (0-70,70) 4-Y-0+ **£2,417** (£713; £357) **Stalls** Low

Form RPR

22-2 **1** **Mohanad (IRE)**[20] 718 5-9-2 **65**.... HarryBentley(5) 3 69
(Sheena West) *in tch though shuffled bk towards rr by 1/2-way: shkn up and prog on outer over 2f out: styd on wl fnl f: led last strides* **15/2**

1-10 **2** *hd* **Coda Agency**[33] 393 8-9-11 **69**.... NeilCallan 8 73
(David Arbuthnot) *led: rdn over 2f out: pressed and jnd all sides after: battled on really wl: hdd last strides* **16/1**

6-24 **3** *nse* **Eagle Nebula**[15] 622 7-9-5 **66**.... KierenFox(3) 7 70
(Brett Johnson) *hld up in last pair: gd prog on inner over 2f out: drvn to chal ins fnl f: upsides last strides: jst pipped* **16/1**

5-21 **4** 1/2 **Gandalf**[44] 622 9-9-12 **70**.... HayleyTurner 5 73
(Amy Weaver) *trckd ldr: rdn to chal over 2f out: upsides fnl f tl no ex nr fin* **7/1**[3]

P55- **5** *1* **Corr Point (IRE)**[165] 7067 4-9-8 **70**.... FergusSweeney 1 72+
(Jamie Osborne) *hld up in last trio: plenty to do whn swtchd lft 2f out: rdn and styd on wl fnl f: gaining at fin* **4/1**[2]

34-1 **6** *1* **Kadouchski (FR)**[12] 955 7-8-10 **54**.... RobertHavlin 10 55
(John Berry) *mostly trckd ldng pair: rdn to chal over 2f out: sn upsides: looked jst hld whn short of room last 100yds and lost pl* **13/8**[1]

5333 **7** 1 1/4 **Indian Ghyll (IRE)**[11] 962 5-9-7 **65**.... DaneO'Neill 4 64
(Roger Teal) *t.k.h: wnt prom 10f out: rdn and nt qckn over 2f out: one pce and no imp after* **12/1**

0/62 **8** 3/4 **Kavaloti (IRE)**[6] 1050 7-9-11 **69**....(be) GeorgeBaker 2 71
(Gary Moore) *trckd ldrs: drvn over 2f out: styng on and ch whn gap clsd ins fnl f: snatched up and nt rcvr* **28/1**

02-1 **9** 3 3/4 **Storm Hawk (IRE)**[17] 911 4-8-10 **63**....(p) JamesRogers(5) 6 57
(Pat Eddery) *stdd s: hld up in last pair: tried to make prog on wd outside bnd 4f out: nt qckn over 2f out: hung rt over 1f out* **7/1**[3]

26/6 **10** *23* **Rollin 'n Tumblin**[11] 962 7-8-10 **59**.... JemmaMarshall(5) 9 25
(Michael Attwater) *stdd s: hld up tl plld way through to go prom 1/2-way: wknd over 2f out: t.o* **33/1**

3m 33.4s (3.30) **Going Correction** +0.075s/f (Slow)
WFA 4 from 5yo+ 4lb **10** Ran SP% **120.7**
Speed ratings (Par 103): **94,93,93,93,93 92,92,91,89,78**
toteswingers:1&2:£16.80, 1&3:£15.80, 2&3:£16.90 CSF £123.63 CT £1875.69 TOTE £11.20: £2.70, £4.80, £4.60; EX 122.50.

Owner Heart Of The South Racing **Bred** Ms Ashley O'Leary **Trained** Falmer, E Sussex

■ Stewards' Enquiry : Harry Bentley two-day ban: used whip with excessive frequency (Apr 19-20)

FOCUS

A couple of in-form sorts in a modest handicap. The gallop, like so many over 2m at this track, was an uneven one and the winner came down the centre.

Kavaloti(IRE) ◆ Official explanation: jockey said gelding was denied a clear run

1149 SHAKE-A-BET DOWNLOAD @ WILLIAMHILL.COM H'CAP 6f (P)

5:20 (5:20) (Class 6) (0-65,65) 3-Y-0 **£1,748** (£516; £258) **Stalls** Low

Form RPR

000- **1** **Ellie In The Pink (IRE)**[256] 4317 3-8-7 **56**.... HarryBentley(5) 2 62
(Alan Jarvis) *dwlt: sn in tch: effrt over 2f out: prog over 1f out: shkn up and r.o to ld last 150yds* **20/1**

206- **2** 3/4 **Delira (IRE)**[197] 6259 3-9-4 **62**.... RichardKingscote 9 66
(Jonathan Portman) *sltly awkward s: hld up in 8th: prog wl over 1f out: styd on wl to take 2nd last 75yds: nt rch wnr* **16/1**

2024 **3** 1 1/4 **Fairy Tales**[35] 721 3-9-4 **62**.... LukeMorris 1 62
(John Bridger) *trckd ldng trio: drvn on inner to dispute 2nd over 1f out and tried to chal: one pce fnl f* **25/1**

25-1 **4** *nk* **Avalon Bay**[10] 987 3-9-7 **65**.... DaneO'Neill 5 64
(Pat Eddery) *chsd ldng pair: wnt 2nd over 2f out: drvn and cl enough jst over 1f out: nt qckn and sn outpcd* **7/4**[1]

0-1 **5** *1* **Winniepeg**[20] 863 3-9-1 **62**.... JohnFahy(3) 4 58
(Clive Cox) *led: drvn over 1f out: hdd & wknd last 150yds* **4/1**[2]

40-6 **6** 1/2 **Encore View**[85] 110 3-9-4 **62**....(t) GeorgeBaker 8 56
(Nick Littmoden) *settled towards rr: coaxed along and no real prog 2f out: one pce whn rdn ins fnl f: nvr nr ldrs* **10/1**

4423 **7** 2 3/4 **Lovat Lane**[29] 787 3-8-7 **51** oh1....(b) LiamKeniry 7 36
(Eve Johnson Houghton) *in tch: rdn over 2f out: nt qckn and wl btn over 1f out* **14/1**

3503 **8** *1* **Greenhead High**[18] 890 3-9-6 **64**.... J-PGuillambert 6 46
(Jane Chapple-Hyam) *chsd ldr to over 2f out: steadily wknd u.p* **11/2**[3]

00-6 **9** *19* **Salesiano**[48] 559 3-9-2 **60**....(b[1]) NeilCallan 3 —
(Peter Makin) *s.s: hung bdly lft thrght: a bhd: t.o* **15/2**

1m 12.98s (-0.12) **Going Correction** +0.075s/f (Slow) **9** Ran SP% **113.8**
Speed ratings (Par 96): **103,102,100,99,98 97,94,92,67**
toteswingers:1&2:£36.40, 1&3:£20.00, 2&3:£27.30 CSF £292.94 CT £7833.03 TOTE £29.20: £6.10, £7.00, £10.20; EX 302.90.

Owner Allen B Pope & Jarvis Associates **Bred** J Jamgotchian **Trained** Twyford, Bucks

FOCUS

A mix of exposed and lightly raced sorts in this modest handicap. The gallop was a reasonable one and the winner raced centre to far side in the closing stages.

Ellie In The Pink(IRE) Official explanation: trainer said, regarding apparent improvement in form, that the filly had improved from two to three and had been running in better company.

Salesiano Official explanation: jockey said colt never travelled

T/Plt: £1,679.20 to a £1 stake. Pool:£45,110.57 - 19.61 winning tickets T/Qpdt: £134.20 to a £1 stake. Pool:£3,702.06 - 20.40 winning tickets JN

PONTEFRACT (L-H)

Tuesday, April 5

OFFICIAL GOING: Good to firm (7.9)

Wind: almost nil Weather: overcast

1150 PONTEFRACT LOYALTY CARD H'CAP 1m 4y

2:10 (2:11) (Class 5) (0-70,70) 4-Y-0+ **£2,422** (£715; £357) **Stalls** Low

Form RPR

30-1 **1** **Hits Only Jude (IRE)**[4] 1077 8-8-2 **56**....(v) NeilFarley(5) 6 68
(Declan Carroll) *in tch: effrt over 2f out: led over 1f out: styd on wl to forge clr* **5/1**[1]

00-0 **2** 4 1/2 **Classic Descent**[4] 1077 6-8-4 **56** oh1....(bt) JamesSullivan(3) 4 58
(Ruth Carr) *s.s: t.k.h: hdwy over 5f out: effrt on ins 2f out: chsd wnr fnl f: no imp* **20/1**

050- **3** 3/4 **Tribal Myth (IRE)**[200] 6144 4-8-13 **62**.... PhillipMakin 1 62
(Kevin Ryan) *trckd ldrs: effrt over 1f out: kpt on same pce* **5/1**[1]

020- **4** 2 1/4 **Bajan Flash**[175] 6832 4-9-4 **67**.... AdrianNicholls 2 62
(David Nicholls) *in tch: effrt on ins 2f out: n.m.r: kpt on same pce fnl f* **8/1**[3]

600- **5** 1 1/4 **Sedgwick**[193] 6328 9-9-5 **68**.... ChrisCatlin 11 60+
(Shaun Harris) *in rr: effrt over 2f out: edgd lft and kpt on fnl f: nvr nr ldrs* **28/1**

-331 **6** 2 1/4 **Nolecce**[13] 943 4-9-0 **63**.... AdamKirby 14 50
(Richard Guest) *hld up in rr: effrt on outside 2f out: nvr nr ldrs* **6/1**[2]

600- **7** 1 1/4 **Carlitos Spirit (IRE)**[165] 7063 7-9-2 **65**....(v) PJMcDonald 13 49
(Ian McInnes) *stdd s: t.k.h in rr: sme hdwy 2f out: nvr a factor* **40/1**

306- **8** 1 1/4 **Desert Hunter (IRE)**[201] 6117 8-8-8 **57**.... KellyHarrison 7 38
(Micky Hammond) *w ldr: t.k.h: led over 2f out: hdd over 1f out: wknd* **14/1**

3-10 **9** *2* **Northern Flyer (GER)**[18] 897 5-9-2 **65**....(p) PaulHanagan 12 41
(John Quinn) *mid-div: effrt over 2f out: wknd fnl f* **8/1**[3]

040- **10** *5* **Wiseman's Diamond (USA)**[143] 7453 6-8-11 **60**.... BarryMcHugh 10 25
(Paul Midgley) *chsd ldrs on outer: drvn over 2f out: lost pl over 1f out* **16/1**

540- **11** 4 1/2 **Viking Warrior (IRE)**[172] 6897 4-9-3 **66**.... FrederikTylicki 8 21
(Michael Dods) *sn prom on outer: drvn over 2f out: lost pl over 1f out* **20/1**

260- **12** *8* **Aussie Blue (IRE)**[162] 7128 7-9-5 **68**.... MichaelStainton 3 —
(Richard Whitaker) *led: hdd over 2f out: sn wknd: eased towards fin* **25/1**

1m 43.81s (-2.09) **Going Correction** -0.30s/f (Firm) **12** Ran SP% **101.6**
Speed ratings (Par 103): **98,93,92,90,89 87,85,84,82,77 73,65**
toteswingers:1&2:£19.90, 1&3:£3.90, 2&3:£23.80 CSF £86.87 CT £374.63 TOTE £6.00: £2.10, £7.40, £2.00; EX 97.20 Trifecta £273.80 Part won. Pool: £370.03 - 0.62 winning units..

Owner Dreams **Bred** Swordlestown Stud **Trained** Sledmere, E Yorks

FOCUS

With 1mm of rain overnight the clerk of the course reported that there was plenty of moisture in the ground and that it might ride on the dead side. The jockeys felt it was just on the fast side of good. A modest but competitive handicap to start the season here. A low draw has been an advantage in previous runnings and that was again the case. The winner has been rated back to the sort of form he showed this time last year.

1151 HIGH-RISE MEDIAN AUCTION MAIDEN STKS 1m 2f 6y

2:40 (2:43) (Class 4) 3-Y-O **£4,144** (£1,233; £616; £307) **Stalls** Low

Form RPR

233- **1** **Halfsin (IRE)**[143] 7452 3-9-3 83.... AdamKirby 2 85
(Marco Botti) *mde all: qcknd over 2f out: edgd rt and lft: styd on wl: unchal* **5/2**[1]

2 *2* **Munbaher (IRE)** 3-9-3 0.... RichardHills 1 81
(Mark Johnston) *trckd ldrs: effrt and chsd wnr over 2f out: edgd lft 1f out: styd on same pce* **5/2**[1]

3 *4* **Eternal Heart (IRE)** 3-9-3 0.... GregFairley 3 73
(Mark Johnston) *trckd ldrs: drvn over 4f out: one pce fnl 2f* **8/1**[3]

22-2 **4** *5* **Lady Rosamunde**[76] 214 3-8-12 72.... WilliamBuick 7 58
(Marcus Tregoning) *t.k.h in rr: hdwy over 2f out: styd on wl fnl f* **4/1**[2]

4- **5** *1* **Getabuzz**[172] 6894 3-9-3 0.... DavidAllan 11 61
(Tim Easterby) *s.i.s: t.k.h: swtchd lft after 1f: towards rr: kpt on fnl 2f: nvr on terms* **22/1**

\- **6** *nse* **Charles De Mille** 3-9-3 0.... PJMcDonald 6 61
(George Moore) *trckd ldrs: outpcd over 2f out: wknd over 1f out* **66/1**

0- **7** *6* **Karmarouge (IRE)**[234] 5066 3-8-8 0 ow1....(t) SeanLevey(5) 5 45
(Brian Rothwell) *in rr: drvn over 3f out: nvr nr ldrs* **100/1**

5204 **8** 4 1/2 **Evelyns Diamond**[54] 494 3-8-12 38.... BarryMcHugh 8 35
(Paul Midgley) *chsd ldrs: drvn over 3f out: lost pl over 2f out* **200/1**

5- **9** *20* **Sobea Star (IRE)**[196] 6268 3-8-12 0.... MickyFenton 4 —
(Pam Sly) *in rr: lost pl over 3f out: sn wl bhd: t.o* **33/1**

326- **10** 1 3/4 **Lady Bridget**[139] 7486 3-8-12 70.... MichaelHills 9 —
(B W Hills) *chsd ldrs: effrt over 2f out: sn wl outpcd: eased over 1f out: sn bhd: t.o* **9/1**

11 *14* **Word To The Wise (IRE)** 3-9-3 0.... KierenFallon 10 —
(Michael Smith) *s.i.s: in rr and drvn along: wl bhd over 3f out: sn t.o* **20/1**

2m 14.22s (0.52) **Going Correction** -0.30s/f (Firm) **11** Ran SP% **113.3**
Speed ratings (Par 100): **85,83,80,76,75 75,70,66,50,49 38**
toteswingers:1&2:£2.70, 1&3:£4.20, 2&3:£6.50 CSF £7.69 TOTE £2.40: £1.10, £1.30, £3.90; EX 9.60 Trifecta £29.80 Pool: £642.79 - 15.91 winning units..

Owner Giuliano Manfredini **Bred** Glending Bloodstock **Trained** Newmarket, Suffolk

FOCUS

A fair maiden with a couple of interesting newcomers. The early pace was steady and nothing got into it from the rear. The winner has been rated to his 2-y-o form.

Lady Bridget Official explanation: trainer's rep said filly was unsuited by the good to firm ground

1152 DALBY STAND H'CAP 6f

3:10 (3:10) (Class 3) (0-95,92) 3-Y-O

£6,449 (£1,931; £965; £483; £241; £121) **Stalls** Low

Form RPR

2-14 **1** **Strictly Pink (IRE)**[24] 845 3-8-4 **75**.... CathyGannon 7 83
(Alan Bailey) *s.i.s: in rr: hdwy over 1f out: swtchd lft: styd on wl to ld towards fin* **9/1**

150- **2** *nk* **Lexi's Hero (IRE)**[178] 6734 3-9-1 **86**.... PhillipMakin 2 93
(Kevin Ryan) *w ldr: led after 2f: 3 l clr over 1f out: hdd and no ex fnl 50yds* **4/1**[1]

140- **3** 3/4 **My Single Malt (IRE)**[180] 6690 3-8-6 **77**.... JamieSpencer 1 82
(Tom Tate) *towards rr: effrt over 2f out: plld wd over 1f out: sn chsng ldrs: no ex last 75yds* **4/1**[1]

40-5 **4** *5* **Satin Love (USA)**[20] 864 3-8-11 **82**.... KierenFallon 4 71
(Mark Johnston) *chsd ldrs: sn drvn along: one pce whn n.m.r on ins 1f out* **10/1**

331- **5** *nse* **State Of Mind**[200] 6153 3-8-3 **81** ow1 .... DuilioDaSilva(7) 10 69
(Paul Cole) *trckd ldrs: effrt over 2f out: wknd fnl f* **15/2**[3]
300- **6** *3/4* **Chiswick Bey (IRE)**[185] 6568 3-9-0 **92** .... GeorgeChaloner(7) 9 78
(Richard Fahey) *chsd ldrs: outpcd and lost pl over 2f out: kpt on appr fnl f* **6/1**[2]
501- **7** *nk* **Another Citizen (IRE)**[201] 6102 3-8-7 **78** .... DavidAllan 11 63
(Tim Easterby) *hld up in rr: effrt on outside 2f out: kpt on: nvr nr ldrs: will improve* **16/1**
0-2 **8** *2 1/2* **Tom Sawyer**[8] 1019 3-9-0 **85** .... PaulHanagan 5 62
(Julie Camacho) *led 2f: w ldrs: lost pl over 1f out: eased towards fin* **10/1**
266- **9** *2 3/4* **Blaze Of Thunder (IRE)**[200] 6139 3-8-5 **76** .... PJMcDonald 8 44
(Alan Swinbank) *chsd ldrs: lost pl 2f out* **25/1**
010- **10** *16* **Mutajare (IRE)**[173] 6870 3-9-0 **85** .... RichardHills 12 —
(Mark Johnston) *hld up in midfield on outside: effrt over 2f out: lost pl over 1f out: eased ins fnl f* **11/1**
560- **11** *21* **Jeeran**[166] 7036 3-8-4 **75** oh1 ow2 .... ChrisCatlin 3 —
(Clive Brittain) *in rr: bhd fnl 2f: virtually p.u ins fnl f: t.o* **50/1**

1m 14.88s (-2.02) **Going Correction** -0.30s/f (Firm) **11** Ran SP% **114.3**
Speed ratings (Par 102): **101,100,99,92,92 91,91,88,84,63 35**
toteswingers:1&2:£8.00, 1&3:£6.70, 2&3:£4.80 CSF £43.55 CT £170.81 TOTE £11.50: £3.60, £1.70, £1.10; EX 49.40 Trifecta £411.80 Part won. Pool: £556.52 - 0.60 winning units..
Owner A J H **Bred** Tally-Ho Stud **Trained** Newmarket, Suffolk
■ Stewards' Enquiry : Cathy Gannon two-day ban: careless riding (Apr 19-20)

FOCUS
A decent 3-y-o sprint handicap in which the pace was good and it produced a close finish. The first three finished clear and the race has been rated a bit above average.

NOTEBOOK
Strictly Pink(IRE) came into this off a good spell on Polytrack during the winter. She missed the break slightly and was last early, but she made good headway in the straight and her rider squeezed her through a narrow gap, doing the fourth few favours in the process, but then found plenty for pressure to run down the leader near the line. (op 7-1)
Lexi's Hero(IRE) was a pretty consistent juvenile and showed plenty of pace on this reappearance. He made the running from his low draw and looked like holding on entering the last furlong before being run down near the line. If given time to get over this, he can gain compensation before long. (op 9-2 tchd 7-2)
My Single Malt(IRE) had the inside stall but did not break that well. He was forced to come wide off the bend, but had his chance entering the last furlong before being unable to find extra. He will not mind a step back up in trip. (op 11-2)
Satin Love(USA) did not go on from last season's debut, but he came into this off a recent start on Polytrack. He chased the leaders into the straight but was making no impression on them when hampered by the winner as she went by. (op 8-1)
State Of Mind ran reasonably on this handicap debut, but looks high enough in the weights and might get dropped a little now. (op 8-1)
Chiswick Bey(IRE) did well after winning the Brocklesby last season and was backed on this seasonal return. He looked in trouble at halfway, but stayed on again in the straight. (op 10-1)
Another Citizen(IRE) improved to win on his third start last season and ran on late on this return to action. Much better can be expected from him with this under his belt. (op 14-1)
Tom Sawyer Official explanation: jockey said gelding had no more to give

1153 JAMAICAN FLIGHT H'CAP 2m 1f 216y
3:40 (3:40) (Class 5) (0-75,74) 4-Y-0+ **£4,435** (£1,309; £655) **Stalls** Low

Form RPR
156- **1** **Descaro (USA)**[16] 7061 5-9-12 **69** .... SilvestreDeSousa 17 72
(David O'Meara) *trckd ldrs: effrt 3f out: styd on to ld clsng stages* **13/2**[3]
13-1 **2** *3/4* **Blackmore**[18] 894 4-9-12 **74** .... PaulHanagan 2 76
(Julia Feilden) *in tch: chal 3f out: led jst ins fnl f: hdd and no ex clsng stages* **3/1**[1]
210- **3** *3/4* **Marcus Antonius**[174] 6855 4-8-10 **58** .... PatCosgrave 4 59
(Jim Boyle) *in tch: hdwy 6f out: led over 2f out: hdd over 1f out: kpt on same pce last 150yds* **9/1**
010- **4** *hd* **Terenzium (IRE)**[15] 6224 9-8-12 **55** ....(p) PJMcDonald 9 56
(Micky Hammond) *in rr: hdwy 4f out: chsng ldrs on inner over 1f out: kpt on same pce* **33/1**
-410 **5** *1* **Chocolate Caramel (USA)**[illegible] 838 9-9-3 **60** .... FrederikTylicki [illegible] [illegible]
(Richard Fahey) *mid-div: hdwy to trck ldrs 6f out: narrow ld over 1f out: hdd jst ins fnl f: no ex* **20/1**
345- **6** *hd* **Heart Of Dubai (USA)**[130] 5687 6-8-7 **50** oh5 .... KellyHarrison 10 50
(Micky Hammond) *dwlt: hld up in rr: hdwy 7f out: kpt on one pce fnl 2f: nvr a real threat* **25/1**
003- **7** *nk* **I Got Music**[32] 6649 4-7-13 **50** oh4 .... JamesSullivan(3) 7 49
(Keith Reveley) *in rr: gd hdwy on outside over 3f out: kpt on same pce fnl f* **40/1**
0-50 **8** *1 1/4* **Jackson (BRZ)**[37] 466 9-8-13 **56** ow1 .... AdamKirby 6 54
(Richard Guest) *in rr: hrd drvn 6f out: hdwy 2f out: kpt on one pce: nvr trbld ldrs* **28/1**
6/0- **9** *1/2* **Pegasus Prince (USA)**[23] 7284 7-8-11 **54** .... TomEaves 14 51
(Keith Reveley) *mid-div: drvn over 4f out: one pce fnl 2f* **4/1**[2]
43-6 **10** *6* **King In Waiting (IRE)**[16] 549 8-9-0 **57** ....(t) PaulMulrennan 5 48
(David O'Meara) *chsd clr ldr: upsides 7f out: wknd over 2f out* **10/1**
130- **11** *10* **Ultimate Quest (IRE)**[46] 7695 6-9-4 **68** ....(b) DavidKenny(7) 13 48
(Michael Chapman) *in tch: hdwy to ld 4f out: hdd over 2f out: sn lost pl* **25/1**
00- **12** *3/4* **Treason Trial**[59] 6921 10-8-2 **50** oh5 ....(p) NeilFarley(5) 15 29
(Andrew Crook) *in rr: sme hdwy 5f out: lost pl over 2f out: sn bhd* **50/1**
021- **13** *1 3/4* **Dan Buoy (FR)**[152] 6983 8-9-7 **67** ....(b) BillyCray(3) 11 44
(Richard Guest) *led and sn clr: jnd 7f out: hdd 4f out: wknd over 1f out* **13/2**[3]
640/ **14** *10* **Feeling Peckish (USA)**[13] 4848 7-8-4 **50** oh5...(t) AndrewHeffernan(3) 3 16
(Michael Chapman) *chsd ldrs: lost pl 6f out: sn bhd* **40/1**
10-2 **15** *22* **Sunny Spells**[25] 838 6-9-8 **65** .... JamieSpencer 1 7
(Stuart Williams) *chsd ldrs: reminders 6f out: lost pl 3f out: bhd whn heavily eased ins fnl f: t.o* **16/1**

3m 58.15s (1.95) **Going Correction** -0.30s/f (Firm)
WFA 4 from 5yo+ 5lb **15** Ran SP% **122.3**
Speed ratings (Par 103): **83,82,82,82,81 81,81,81,80,78 73,73,72,68,58**
toteswingers:1&2:£6.20, 1&3:£10.30, 2&3:£9.50 CSF £23.99 CT £183.41 TOTE £6.10: £2.50, £2.60, £3.50; EX 23.80 Trifecta £234.30 Part won. Pool: £316.66 - 0.60 winning units..
Owner R Fell & K Everitt **Bred** Langley House Stud **Trained** Nawton, N Yorks

FOCUS
A big field of varying ability in this first in the series of stayers' races run here during the season, and named in honour of a former course specialist. The sixth and seventh, who both ran from out of the handicap, finished close up, limiting the form.

Sunny Spells Official explanation: jockey said gelding had no more to give

1154 PADDOCK PACKAGE H'CAP 1m 2f 6y
4:10 (4:12) (Class 2) (0-105,101) 4-Y-0+
£7,788 (£2,332; £1,166; £583; £291; £146) **Stalls** Low

Form RPR
221- **1** **Ingleby Spirit**[176] 6813 4-8-6 **86** .... BarryMcHugh 5 96
(Richard Fahey) *mde all: qcknd over 2f out: styd on to forge clr last 100yds: unchal* **9/1**
004- **2** *3 1/2* **Changing The Guard**[154] 7287 5-8-4 **84** .... PaulHanagan 1 87
(Richard Fahey) *chsd ldrs: wnt 2nd over 2f out: kpt on same pce fnl f* **5/2**[1]
0-04 **3** *1* **Tiger Reigns**[46] 605 5-9-7 **101** .... FrederikTylicki 2 102
(Michael Dods) *trckd ldrs: effrt over 2f out: styd on same pce fnl f* **4/1**[2]
0-00 **4** *1 1/2* **Arlequin**[41] 661 4-8-8 **88** ow1 .... PhilipRobinson 9 86+
(James Bethell) *in rr: hdwy on outside over 1f out: hung lft and kpt on: nvr nr to chal* **5/1**[3]
400- **5** *nk* **Crackentorp**[144] 7084 6-8-9 **89** .... RobertWinston 10 86
(Tim Easterby) *hld up in mid-div: drvn over 2f out: kpt on appr fnl f: nvr a factor* **16/1**
300- **6** *1 1/2* **Doctor Zhivago**[271] 3824 4-8-6 **86** .... AdrianNicholls 11 80
(David Nicholls) *trckd ldrs: chal over 2f out: wknd over 1f out* **16/1**
220- **7** *1/2* **Speed Dating**[17] 6562 5-8-7 **87** ow1 ....(b) JamieSpencer 8 80
(John Quinn) *dwlt: in rr: effrt over 3f out: hdwy on outside over 1f out: nvr a factor* **10/1**
10- **8** *hd* **Itlaaq**[206] 5955 5-8-8 **91** .... JamesSullivan(3) 3 84
(Michael Easterby) *dwlt: mid-div: sme hdwy over 1f out: nvr nr ldrs* **20/1**
510- **9** *3 1/4* **Full Speed (GER)**[357] 1274 6-8-8 **88** .... PJMcDonald 7 75
(Alan Swinbank) *mid-div: effrt over 2f out: wknd over 1f out* **40/1**
05-1 **10** *3 1/2* **Sweet Child O'Mine**[49] 548 4-8-7 **87** .... KierenFallon 6 67
(Richard Guest) *trckd ldrs: drvn over 2f out: wknd 1f out: eased towards fin* **8/1**
/66- **11** *1 1/4* **Overrule (USA)**[254] 4405 7-8-6 **86** .... TomEaves 4 63
(Brian Ellison) *in rr: drvn over 3f out: nvr on terms* **22/1**

2m 10.73s (-2.97) **Going Correction** -0.30s/f (Firm) **11** Ran SP% **118.8**
Speed ratings (Par 109): **99,96,95,94,93 92,92,89,86 85**
toteswingers:1&2:£3.30, 1&3:£6.80, 2&3:£2.90 CSF £31.34 CT £108.17 TOTE £12.10: £3.60, £1.40, £1.20; EX 41.20 Trifecta £261.60 Pool: £614.98 - 1.73 winning units..
Owner Percy/Green Racing **Bred** Barton Stud And Peter Botham **Trained** Musley Bank, N Yorks

FOCUS
Decent prizemoney resulted in a good-class handicap and yet another win in the race for Richard Fahey, who was responsible for the first two home. The time was under standard and just under 3.5secs faster than the earlier maiden, but few got involved from off the pace. The winner has been rated as running another personal best, following on from his final start last year, but he did get the run of things.

NOTEBOOK
Ingleby Spirit is well suited by soft ground and, with the going remaining fast, his trainer switched the champion jockey to his other runner. However, the gelding made the running and his rider astutely slowed the pace before kicking on rounding the home turn. He was always holding his stable companion from that point, but will be switched back to an easier surface in future. (op 8-1 tchd 10-1)
Changing The Guard, whose rider was switched to ride instead of being aboard the winner, chased his stablemate from the start but could never reel him in. He was clear of the remainder though, and should be better for the outing. (op 11-4 tchd 3-1)
Tiger Reigns, last seen running in Dubai, was quite keen behind the leaders but could not keep up with them once they quickened off the bend. He will not find winning easy off his current mark, but he is another who might appreciate some cut in the ground. (op 5-1 tchd 7-2)
Arlequin, who did not run that well on a recent spell in the south of France, did best of those that came from off the pace, especially as he did not get the clearest of runs and had to come wide in the straight, with his rider reporting that the gelding hung left. This should set him up for another crack at the handicap at York's May meeting which he won last year. Official explanation: jockey said colt hung left (op 6-1)
Crackentorp has never won on turf but is a useful performer in this grade, although he is best suited by further. He ran creditably on this return to action though, and is another who could be heading to York for the handicap he finished runner-up in last season. (op 22-1)
Doctor Zhivago is lightly raced but showed up well until tiring in the straight on this first run for a new trainer. (op 14-1)
Itlaaq, having his first start for the yard, ran well without being given a hard race on this seasonal debut and will appreciate a return to a soft surface. (op 16-1)

1155 PONTEFRACT-RACES.CO.UK MAIDEN FILLIES' STKS 6f
4:40 (4:44) (Class 5) 3-Y-O **£2,422** (£715; £357) **Stalls** Low

Form RPR
224- **1** **Florestans Match**[195] 6286 3-9-0 84 .... JimCrowley 11 85+
(Ralph Beckett) *swtchd lft after s: chsd ldrs: led over 1f out: forged clr: eased towards fin* **11/8**[1]
2 *4* **Clara Zetkin** 3-9-0 0 .... PhillipMakin 10 69+
(David Brown) *sn chsng ldrs: wnt 2nd 1f out: kpt on same pce* **10/1**
3 *shd* **Flashbang** 3-9-0 0 .... SilvestreDeSousa 9 69+
(Paul Cole) *chsd ldrs: styd on same pce fnl f* **4/1**[2]
4 *2* **Ziraun** 3-9-0 0 .... PhilipRobinson 8 62
(Clive Brittain) *chsd ldrs: effrt over 2f out: one pce appr fnl f* **6/1**[3]
244- **5** *3* **Suddenly Susan (IRE)**[118] 7758 3-8-11 67 .... BillyCray(3) 7 53
(David Nicholls) *led tl over 2f out: wknd over 1f out* **10/1**
44 **6** *2 1/4* **Fleurie Lover (IRE)**[20] 863 3-9-0 0 .... FrannyNorton 6 46
(Richard Guest) *w ldrs: led over 2f out: hdd over 1f out: hung rt and sn wknd* **28/1**
7 *1/2* **Canashito** 3-9-0 0 .... MichaelHills 12 44+
(B W Hills) *dwlt: hld up in rr: effrt over 2f out: nvr a factor* **10/1**
8 *nk* **Daisyclipper** 3-9-0 0 .... PaulHanagan 4 43
(Ann Duffield) *in rr: sme hdwy on ins over 2f out: wknd over 1f out* **20/1**
406- **9** *2* **Cool In The Shade**[211] 5818 3-8-11 47 .... PaulPickard(3) 1 37
(Paul Midgley) *in rr: drvn and outpcd over 2f out: nvr a factor* **80/1**
0 **10** *1* **Passing Moment**[11] 971 3-9-0 0 .... RobertWinston 2 34
(Brian Baugh) *hld up in rr: sme hdwy and swtchd outside 2f out: sn wknd* **100/1**
11 *11* **Catallout (IRE)** 3-8-9 0 .... NeilFarley(5) 14 —
(Declan Carroll) *trckd ldrs on outer: effrt over 2f out: sn wknd and bhd* **50/1**

1m 16.04s (-0.86) **Going Correction** -0.30s/f (Firm) **11** Ran SP% **116.1**
Speed ratings (Par 95): **93,87,87,84,80 77,77,76,74,72 58**
toteswingers:1&2:£5.20, 1&3:£2.60, 2&3:£10.30 CSF £15.70 TOTE £2.00: £1.02, £4.80, £2.60; EX 19.60 Trifecta £59.40 Pool: £800.81 - 9.96 winning units..
Owner Newsells Park Stud **Bred** Newsells Park Stud **Trained** Kimpton, Hants

FOCUS
A wide variation in levels of ability amongst those with previous experience in this fillies' maiden, but several interesting newcomers, including three southern raiders. The time was 1.16secs slower than the earlier handicap over the trip. The winner didn't have to run to her best to win easily.

Fleurie Lover(IRE) Official explanation: jockey said filly hung right in straight

1156 RACING ON TUESDAY 19TH APRIL H'CAP 1m 4f 8y
5:10 (5:10) (Class 5) (0-75,75) 4-Y-0+ **£2,422** (£715; £357) **Stalls** Low

Form RPR

5005 **1** **Record Breaker (IRE)**[24] 849 7-9-5 **73**..............(b) SilvestreDeSousa 7 85
(Mark Johnston) *drvn to ld: mde all: drvn over 2f out: styd on wl: eased towards fin* **3/1**[1]

-343 **2** 3 1/4 **Hallstatt (IRE)**[25] 839 5-8-9 **63**......................(t) PaulHanagan 3 69
(John Mackie) *trckd ldrs: wnt 2nd over 2f out: sn rdn and no imp* **10/3**[2]

6151 **3** 6 **Gunslinger (FR)**[11] 962 6-9-6 **74**...................... KierenFallon 1 70
(Michael Scudamore) *dwlt: hld up in rr: drvn over 3f out: sn chsng ldrs: kpt on same pce fnl 2f* **13/2**

026- **4** 5 **Rowan Tiger**[166] 7045 5-9-7 **75**...................... PatCosgrave 5 63
(Jim Boyle) *hld up in mid-div: effrt over 2f out: fdd over 1f out* **4/1**[3]

400- **5** 2 3/4 **Folk Tune (IRE)**[22] 6750 8-9-4 **72**......................(p) TomEaves 6 56
(John Quinn) *in rr: effrt 4f out: outpcd over 2f out: n.d after* **8/1**

050- **6** 11 **Agapanthus (GER)**[65] 6832 6-9-2 **70**...................... TomQueally 4 36
(Barney Curley) *hld up in rr: hdwy 6f out: sn shkn up: rdn and lost pl over 2f out: sn bhd* **8/1**

-454 **7** shd **Amazing Blue Sky**[33] 742 5-8-7 **64**...................... JamesSullivan(3) 2 30
(Ruth Carr) *chsd wnr: drvn 5f out: lost pl over 2f out: sn bhd* **12/1**

2m 35.51s (-5.29) **Going Correction** -0.30s/f (Firm) 7 Ran SP% **111.3**
Speed ratings (Par 103): **105,102,98,95,93 86,86**
toteswingers:1&2:£2.10, 1&3:£5.30, 2&3:£1.90. totesuper7: Win: Not won. Place: Not won. CSF £12.46 TOTE £4.20: £3.80, £2.80; EX 15.80.
Owner Triplin Racing **Bred** Sir E J Loder **Trained** Middleham Moor, N Yorks

FOCUS
Just a fair handicap that ended up in something of a procession. It has been rated through the runner-up to his recent AW form.
T/Jkpt: £21,382.30 to a £1 stake. Pool:£30,116.05 - 1.00 winning ticket T/Plt: £15.80 to a £1 stake. Pool:£83,729.49 - 3,862.72 winning tickets T/Qpdt: £5.90 to a £1 stake. Pool:£4,962.56 - 612.63 winning tickets WG

1157 - 1163a (Foreign Racing) - See Raceform Interactive

BEVERLEY (R-H)
Wednesday, April 6

OFFICIAL GOING: Good to firm (8.0)
Wind: Moderate against Weather: Fine and dry

1164 WELCOME BACK TO BEVERLEY (S) STKS 1m 100y
2:10 (2:12) (Class 6) 3-Y-0+ **£1,661** (£494; £247; £123) **Stalls** Low

Form RPR

000- **1** **Rowan Lodge (IRE)**[189] 6463 9-9-7 62......................(b) PaulHanagan 1 68
(Ollie Pears) *t.k.h: hld up in midfield: hdwy to trck ldrs 2f out: effrt and bmpd over 1f out: rdn to chal whn n.m.r ent fnl f: kpt on gamely u.p to ld nr fin* **17/2**

3-20 **2** 1/2 **White Deer (USA)**[34] 749 7-9-7 65......................(p) SilvestreDeSousa 6 67
(Geoffrey Harker) *trckd ldng pair: hdwy over 2f out: rdn to chal over 1f out: drvn and edgd lft ins fnl f: led last 100yds: hdd and no ex nr fin* **7/1**[3]

50-5 **3** shd **Dabbers Ridge (IRE)**[20] 881 9-9-4 75...................... GaryBartley(3) 3 67
(Ian McInnes) *hld up in midfield: hdwy on outer 3f out: rdn to chse ldng pair whn edgd rt over 1f out: drvn to ld and edgd rt ent fnl f: hdd and no ex last 100yds* **10/3**[2]

65-2 **4** 2 1/4 **Opus Maximus (IRE)**[92] 31 6-9-7 83...................... GregFairley 9 61
(Mark Johnston) *cl up: led wl over 2f out: rdn and edgd rt over 1f out: sn drvn and hdd: kpt on same pce* **11/10**[1]

30-5 **5** 6 **Bajan Pride**[48] 568 7-9-7 61...................... MickyFenton 11 48
(Paul Midgley) *hld up in rr: hdwy over 2f out: sn rdn and n.d* **33/1**

04-0 **6** 1 1/2 **Kheskianto (IRE)**[54] 517 5-9-2 47......................(bt) RussKennemore 4 39
(Michael Chapman) *trckd ldrs: hdwy to chse ldng pair 3f out: rdn 2f out: sn drvn and ev ch tl wknd appr fnl f* **100/1**

030- **7** 2 1/2 **Bold Indian (IRE)**[28] 7149 7-9-2 52...................... DaleSwift(5) 8 38
(Mike Sowersby) *s.i.s: a towards rr* **80/1**

2206 **8** nk **Master Of Dance (IRE)**[35] 727 4-9-7 69......................(b) FrannyNorton 5 38
(James Given) *chsd ldrs: rdn along over 2f out: sn wknd* **7/1**[3]

-500 **9** 1 **Tiger Hawk (USA)**[22] 854 4-9-4 45......................(p) AndrewHeffernan(3) 2 35
(Kevin M Prendergast) *led: rdn along and jnd 3f out: sn hdd & wknd* **100/1**

0-00 **10** 1 1/4 **Avontuur (FR)**[20] 880 9-9-4 68...................... JamesSullivan(3) 7 33
(Ruth Carr) *a in rr* **25/1**

1m 47.73s (0.13) **Going Correction** -0.05s/f (Good) 10 Ran SP% **116.2**
Speed ratings (Par 101): **97,96,96,94,88 86,84,83,82,81**
toteswingers:1&2:£10.00, 1&3:£4.50, 2&3:£7.00 CSF £63.75 TOTE £11.90: £2.30, £1.90, £1.50; EX 51.90.There was no bid for winner. Opus Maximus was claimed by Ms Jennie Candlish for £6,000.
Owner K C West & Venture Racing **Bred** M P B Bloodstock Ltd **Trained** Norton, N Yorks
■ Stewards' Enquiry : James Sullivan caution: used whip when out of contention.

FOCUS
On a bright and breezy afternoon the watered ground was described as 'on the quick side of good'. Plenty of familiar faces in this selling race and in the end the cream came to the top with the first four in the market virtually in line with 100yds to run.

1165 RACING UK ON SKY 432 MAIDEN AUCTION STKS 5f
2:40 (2:47) (Class 5) 2-Y-0 **£2,298** (£684; £341; £170) **Stalls** Low

Form RPR

1 **Lily's Angel (IRE)** 2-8-6 0...................... BarryMcHugh 6 70+
(Richard Fahey) *trckd ldrs on inner: swtchd lft and hdwy to chal over 1f out: rdn to ld ins fnl f: kpt on wl* **9/2**[2]

2 **2** 1/2 **One Kool Dude**[12] 972 2-8-11 0...................... PaulHanagan 4 73+
(Richard Fahey) *led: rdn and jnd over 1f out: drvn and hdd ins fnl f: kpt on* **4/6**[1]

3 7 **Nellie Pickersgill** 2-8-6 0...................... DavidAllan 2 43
(Tim Easterby) *midfield: hdwy on inner 2f out: rdn over 1f out: kpt on ins fnl f* **16/1**

4 3 1/2 **Red Tyke (IRE)** 2-8-11 0...................... MickyFenton 7 35
(John Quinn) *chsd ldrs: rdn 2f out: edgd rt and wknd over 1f out* **8/1**[3]

5 1 **Always Ends Well (IRE)** 2-8-4 0...................... SilvestreDeSousa 9 25
(Mark Johnston) *cl up on outer: rdn 2f out and ev ch tl edgd rt and wknd appr fnl f* **14/1**

6 2 **Flying Pickets (IRE)** 2-8-9 0...................... LeeNewman 3 22
(David Brown) *in tch: rdn along 2f out: grad wknd* **16/1**

7 2 1/4 **Bertie Dancing (IRE)** 2-8-9 0...................... RobertWinston 1 14
(Nigel Tinkler) *dwlt and bhd: hdwy 2f out: n.m.r over 1f out: n.d* **50/1**

8 nk **Headstight (IRE)** 2-8-4 0...................... PJMcDonald 8 8
(Paul Midgley) *dwlt: sn cl up: rdn along 2f out and sn wknd* **40/1**

9 6 **Just Dixie** 2-8-1 0...................... JamesSullivan(3) 10 —
(John Weymes) *dwlt: a towards rr* **66/1**

10 hd **Mick Slates (IRE)** 2-8-6 0...................... NeilFarley(5) 5 —
(Declan Carroll) *dwlt: rn green and a in rr* **33/1**

65.84 secs (2.34) **Going Correction** +0.175s/f (Good) **10** Ran SP% **116.5**
Speed ratings (Par 92): **88,87,76,70,68 65,62,61,51,51**
toteswingers:1&2:£1.10, 1&3:£10.30, 2&3:£5.50 CSF £7.68 TOTE £4.20: £1.10, £1.10, £3.20; EX 9.60.
Owner Middleham Park Racing XLVIII **Bred** N And Mrs N Nugent **Trained** Musley Bank, N Yorks

FOCUS
Another delayed start after Red Tyke unseated Micky Fenton on the way to the start. Paul Hanagan again found himself on his feet and had to lead One Cool Dude the final 2f to the stalls. Richard Fahey warned beforehand that there was little to choose between his two runners and he was proved spot on, the pair some way clear.

NOTEBOOK
Lily's Angel(IRE), a daughter of first-season sire Dark Angel, who retired to stud after his successful juvenile campaign, certainly knew her job. The pair came clear and she edged it near the line. She can surely win again. (op 13-2)
One Kool Dude, beaten a whisker at Dundalk first time, took them along and went down fighting. He should make it third time lucky. (tchd 8-13 and 8-11)
Nellie Pickersgill, quite a late foal, cost £10,000. She stayed on after getting outpaced and her stable's juveniles generally improve a good deal for their first run.
Red Tyke(IRE) and his rider were clearly none the worse. A £9,500 purchase and son of first-season sire Red Clubs, the experience will not be lost on him. (op 9-1)
Always Ends Well(IRE), a daughter of a middle-distance performer, cost just 2,000gns. From her outside draw she showed bags of toe and should improve for the experience. (op 10-1)
Bertie Dancing(IRE) Official explanation: jockey said gelding was denied a clear run

1166 SPRING INTO RACING AT BEVERLEY H'CAP 5f
3:10 (3:15) (Class 3) (0-95,94) 4-Y-0+ **£5,828** (£1,734; £866; £432) **Stalls** Low

Form RPR

4010 **1** **Breathless Kiss (USA)**[39] 700 4-9-2 **89**......................(b) PhillipMakin 9 98
(Kevin Ryan) *hld up towards rr: hdwy wl over 1f out: styng on whn hmpd ent fnl f: sn swtchd rt and rdn: qcknd wl to ld nr fin* **14/1**

0-05 **2** nk **Falasteen (IRE)**[12] 970 4-8-10 **83**...................... FrederikTylicki 6 91
(David Nicholls) *blind removed late and dwlt: hdwy to trck ldrs 1/2-way: swtchd lft and rdn ent fnl f: led last 40yds: edgd rt and hdd nr line* **20/1**

401- **3** nse **Beat The Bell**[180] 6706 6-8-13 **86**...................... LeeNewman 4 94
(David Barron) *trckd ldrs: hdwy over 1f out: rdn to ld ent fnl f: sn drvn: hdd and nt qckn fnl 40yds* **8/1**[3]

100- **4** 2 **Confessional**[165] 7079 4-9-5 **92**......................(e) RobertWinston 13 93
(Tim Easterby) *swtchd rt s: hdwy to trck ldrs on inner after 1f: swtchd lft over 1f out and effrt to chal ent fnl f: sn rdn and one pce* **20/1**

031- **5** 3/4 **Whozthecat (IRE)**[142] 7466 4-8-11 **89**...................... NeilFarley(5) 8 87
(Declan Carroll) *cl up: effrt 2f out: sn rdn and ev ch tl drvn and one pce ent fnl f* **13/2**[1]

000- **6** 1 3/4 **Tabaret**[172] 6918 8-8-13 **86**...................... MichaelStainton 7 78
(Richard Whitaker) *chsd ldrs: rdn along wl over 1f out: kpt on ins fnl f* **33/1**

0-10 **7** nk **Arganil (USA)**[39] 700 6-8-12 **90**......................(b) JulieBurke(5) 14 81+
(Kevin Ryan) *s.i.s and bhd: pushed along and hdwy 2f out: swtchd rt and rdn ent fnl f: kpt on wl: nrst fin* **20/1**

042- **8** shd **Midnight Martini**[188] 6509 4-9-5 **92**......................(t) DavidAllan 15 82
(Tim Easterby) *nvr bttr than midfield* **20/1**

050- **9** nk **Duchess Dora (IRE)**[165] 7079 4-9-0 **87**...................... PaulHanagan 16 76+
(John Quinn) *midfield: on outer: swtchd rt wl over 1f out: styd on ins fnl f: nrst fin* **7/1**[2]

010- **10** 3/4 **Hamoody (USA)**[250] 4536 7-8-5 **85**...................... PNolan(7) 10 72+
(David Nicholls) *v.s.a and bhd: swtchd wd and hdwy over 1f out: nvr nr ldrs* **22/1**

324- **11** nk **Lenny Bee**[120] 7740 5-8-12 **90**...................... DaleSwift(5) 2 76
(George Foster) *led: rdn along and hdd 2f out: drvn and wknd over 1f out* **10/1**

11-0 **12** 1 **Humidor (IRE)**[46] 613 4-8-12 **88**...................... MatthewDavies(3) 3 70
(George Baker) *in tch: hdwy 2f out: swtchd lft and rdn over 1f out: sn btn* **7/1**[2]

000- **13** hd **Solemn**[167] 7041 6-8-8 **81**......................(b) SilvestreDeSousa 1 62
(Milton Bradley) *cl up on inner: led 2f out: rdn and hdd ent fnl f: sn wknd* **14/1**

30-0 **14** 1 1/4 **Rocket Rob (IRE)**[46] 613 5-9-1 **88**...................... JamieMackay 12 65
(Willie Musson) *dwlt: a in rr* **33/1**

110- **15** 2 **Green Park (IRE)**[172] 6918 8-9-7 **94**......................(b) DavidNolan 17 63
(Declan Carroll) *a towards rr* **50/1**

414- **16** 2 **Noodles Blue Boy**[180] 6706 5-8-13 **86**...................... FrannyNorton 5 48
(Ollie Pears) *chsd ldrs: rdn along 2f out: wkng whn hmpd over 1f out: sn in rr* **17/2**

040- **17** 21 **Fol Hollow (IRE)**[180] 6706 6-9-3 **90**...................... AdrianNicholls 11 —
(David Nicholls) *chsd ldrs: rdn along over 2f out: sn lost pl and eased in rr* **9/1**

63.39 secs (-0.11) **Going Correction** +0.175s/f (Good) 17 Ran SP% **123.6**
Speed ratings (Par 107): **107,106,106,103,102 99,98,98,98,96 96,94,94,92,89 86,52**
toteswingers:1&2:£81.30, 1&3:£50.10, 2&3:£34.30 CSF £273.31 CT £2404.61 TOTE £18.40: £4.30, £3.70, £2.70, £5.80; EX 424.70.
Owner Mrs Angie Bailey **Bred** Don Mattox & Pam Mattox **Trained** Hambleton, N Yorks
■ Stewards' Enquiry : Matthew Davies one-day ban: careless riding (Apr 20)

FOCUS
A wide open and good class sprint handicap and the action that mattered was towards the far side - the low drawn runners under the new directive.

NOTEBOOK
Breathless Kiss(USA), better than ever on the AW this winter, had cut no ice in Listed company on her previous start. She improved from the rear and burst between horses to snatch the prize near the line. There may be even better to come.
Falasteen(IRE), back with his previous handler who took this twice in the last four years, is much better suited by turf than the AW. Now just 1lb higher than for his last success, he too came from off the pace and should have little difficulty going one better. Official explanation: jockey said blindfold became entangled in the bridle, was difficult to remove and gelding missed the break
Beat The Bell, 2lb higher than when signing off with success at Musselburgh, showed ahead but could not quite last home. Equally effective over five and six, he looks sure to add to his record this time. (op 15-2)
Confessional, a winner twice in 2010, did best of those drawn in double figures. He had to search for racing room and should come on for the outing. (op 25-1)
Whozthecat(IRE), just 1lb higher than for his win at Wolverhampton on his final start last year, looks capable of better this time. He ran without his usual visor here. (op 15-2)
Tabaret, who won first time out over this C&D last season, is just 1lb higher than for his last success.

Humidor(IRE) Official explanation: trainer's rep said gelding was struck into

1167 CELEBRATE YOUR BIRTHDAY AT BEVERLEY FILLIES' STKS (H'CAP) 1m 1f 207y

3:40 (3:41) (Class 5) (0-70,68) 4-Y-0+ **£2,298** (£684; £341; £170) **Stalls** Low

Form RPR

445- **1** **Dance For Julie (IRE)**[82] 7642 4-9-4 **68**................. PatrickDonaghy(3) 4 72
(Ben Haslam) *hld up in rr: swtchd ins and gd hdwy 2f out: rdn to chal over 1f out: drvn and edgd lft ins fnl f: styd on to ld last 50yds* **4/1**

1222 **2** *nk* **The Blue Dog (IRE)**[18] 917 4-9-2 **63**...........................(b) PhillipMakin 6 67
(Mark Rimmer) *hld up in rr: smooth hdwy on outer 3f out and sn cl up: led wl over 1f out: rdn ins fnl f: hdd and no ex last 50yds* **3/1[3]**

113 **3** *3 1/4* **Hill Tribe**[21] 870 4-9-4 **68**........................... JamesSullivan(3) 3 65
(Richard Guest) *led: rdn along over 2f out: drvn and hdd wl over 1f out: sn one pce* **11/4[2]**

301- **4** *3 1/2* **Leitzu (IRE)**[9] 7037 4-8-12 **64**............................ MartinHarley(5) 1 54
(Mick Channon) *trckd ldr: hdwy and cl up 3f out: rdn along over 2f out and ev ch tl drvn and wknd over 1f out* **5/2[1]**

300- **5** *19* **Swish Dish (CAN)**[184] 6632 4-9-4 **65**.......................... FrederikTylicki 2 17
(Micky Hammond) *chsd ldng pair: effrt over 3f out: rdn wl over 2f out: sn wknd and eased* **11/1**

2m 6.82s (-0.18) **Going Correction** -0.05s/f (Good) **5** Ran SP% **108.6**
Speed ratings (Par 100): **98,97,95,92,77**
CSF £15.61 TOTE £2.80: £1.70, £1.70; EX 11.30.
Owner Mark James **Bred** Lynn Lodge Stud **Trained** Middleham Moor, N Yorks

FOCUS
No hanging about in this modest fillies' handicap.

1168 RACING UK H'CAP 1m 1f 207y

4:10 (4:10) (Class 4) (0-80,78) 3-Y-O **£4,131** (£1,229; £614; £306) **Stalls** Low

Form RPR

3-1 **1** **Art History (IRE)**[79] 191 3-9-5 **76**........................... SilvestreDeSousa 2 91
(Mark Johnston) *trckd ldrs on inner: swtchd lft and hdwy 3f out: rdn to chal wl over 1f out: kpt on to ld ent fnl f: drvn out* **5/1[3]**

31- **2** *1 1/2* **Hawaafez**[120] 7733 3-9-5 **76**.. RichardHills 3 88
(Marcus Tregoning) *prom: trckd ldr after 3f: effrt over 2f out: sn rdn and wandered: drvn and ev ch ent fnl f: one pce last 100yds* **5/4[1]**

2122 **3** *4 1/2* **School For Scandal (IRE)**[7] 1051 3-9-6 **77**..................(b) GregFairley 6 80
(Mark Johnston) *led: rdn along 2f out: drvn and hdd ent fnl f: grad wknd* **7/1**

21- **4** *1 3/4* **Corsicanrun (IRE)**[197] 6268 3-9-4 **75**............................ PaulHanagan 4 74
(Richard Fahey) *t.k.h: chsd ldr 3f: trckd ldrs on inner: pushed along over 2f out: rdn wl over 1f out and sn no imp* **3/1[2]**

235- **5** *1 1/4* **Celani**[145] 7427 3-9-1 **72**... PJMcDonald 7 69
(Tim Walford) *hld up in rr: sme hdwy over 3f out: rdn along wl over 2f out: n.d* **40/1**

601- **6** *2 1/4* **Oasis Storm**[179] 6743 3-9-7 **78**.................................... FrederikTylicki 5 70
(Michael Dods) *hld up in tch: hdwy on outer to chse ldrs 3f out: rdn along over 2f out: sn wknd* **10/1**

446- **7** *26* **Fimias (IRE)**[167] 7035 3-8-10 **67**.............................. RoystonFfrench 1 —
(Geoffrey Harker) *a in rr: rdn along and outpcd over 3f out: sn bhd* **25/1**

2m 6.34s (-0.66) **Going Correction** -0.05s/f (Good) **7** Ran SP% **114.0**
Speed ratings (Par 100): **100,98,95,93,92 91,70**
toteswingers:1&2:£2.00, 1&3:£1.80, 2&3:£1.50 CSF £11.62 TOTE £7.80: £2.40, £1.70; EX 14.80.
Owner Sheikh Hamdan Bin Mohammed Al Maktoum **Bred** Kenilworth House Stud **Trained** Middleham Moor, N Yorks

FOCUS
A very interesting 3-y-o handicap run at a sound pace, and both the first two look sure to make serious progress.

1169 WHISTLEJACKETS CAFE STKS (H'CAP) 7f 100y

4:40 (4:41) (Class 5) (0-70,68) 3-Y-O **£2,298** (£684; £341; £170) **Stalls** Low

Form RPR

-132 **1** **City Legend**[19] 887 3-9-6 **67**.....................................(bt) RobertWinston 7 74
(Alan McCabe) *trckd ldr: effrt over 2f out: rdn wl over 1f out: drvn ins fnl f: styd on to ld nr fin* **13/2[3]**

-342 **2** *hd* **Verrazano**[8] 1031 3-9-1 **62**.. PhillipMakin 1 68
(Kevin Ryan) *led: rdn along 2f out: drvn ent fnl f: hdd and no ex towards fin* **4/1[1]**

63 **3** *3 1/2* **Crown Ridge (IRE)**[8] 1022 3-8-6 **58**.............................. MartinHarley(5) 14 55+
(Mick Channon) *hld up in midfield: hdwy to chse ldrs over 3f out: rdn and edgd rt wl over 1f out: kpt on u.p fnl f* **10/1**

200- **4** *3/4* **Vetvey (IRE)**[170] 6986 3-8-8 **55**.............................. SilvestreDeSousa 9 50
(Mark Johnston) *chsd ldng pair: rdn along over 2f out: drvn over 1f out and sn one pce* **8/1**

506- **5** *3/4* **Rational Act (IRE)**[151] 7345 3-9-1 **62**................................ DavidAllan 12 56
(Tim Easterby) *trckd ldrs: hdwy 1/2-way: rdn along to chse ldng pair over 2f out: drvn and wknd appr fnl f* **33/1**

055- **6** *3/4* **Eduardo**[169] 7004 3-8-7 **57**... PatrickDonaghy(3) 6 49
(Jedd O'Keeffe) *towards rr: hdwy on outer over 2f out: sn rdn and no imp appr fnl f* **16/1**

655- **7** *1 1/4* **Anddante (IRE)**[222] 5498 3-9-1 **67**................................ LanceBetts(5) 8 56
(Tim Easterby) *chsd ldrs: rdn along over 2f out: sn one pce* **25/1**

204- **8** *1/2* **Ventura Sands (IRE)**[207] 5936 3-9-7 **68**........................... DavidNolan 11 55
(Richard Fahey) *stdd s and hld up in rr: sme hdwy fnl 2f: n.d* **14/1**

613- **9** *1 1/4* **Reason To Believe (IRE)**[181] 6694 3-9-4 **65**.................. PJMcDonald 3 49
(Ben Haslam) *chsd ldrs on inner: rdn along 3f out: sn wknd* **6/1[2]**

5233 **10** *1 1/4* **Unwrapit (USA)**[34] 738 3-9-3 **64**.............................(v[1]) RoystonFfrench 2 45
(Bryan Smart) *a towards rr* **14/1**

335- **11** *1/2* **Inside**[178] 6777 3-8-11 **58**.. PaulHanagan 10 38
(Richard Fahey) *dwlt: sn in tch: rdn along 3f out and sn wknd* **13/2[3]**

32P- **12** *1 1/4* **Chadford**[169] 7004 3-8-7 **57**...................................... JamesSullivan(3) 5 34
(Tim Walford) *a in rr* **33/1**

660- **13** *8* **Rapturous Applause**[183] 6646 3-8-13 **60**.......................... FrederikTylicki 4 17
(Micky Hammond) *a towards rr* **14/1**

1m 34.33s (0.53) **Going Correction** -0.05s/f (Good) **13** Ran SP% **116.8**
Speed ratings (Par 98): **94,93,89,88,88 87,85,85,83,82 81,80,71**
toteswingers:1&2:£3.70, 1&3:£6.90, 2&3:£9.70 CSF £31.17 CT £265.33 TOTE £6.80: £2.00, £1.30, £3.80; EX 26.30.
Owner Contango Syndicate **Bred** Contango Bloodstock Ltd **Trained** Averham Park, Notts

FOCUS
A low-grade 3-y-o handicap run at a sound pace and the first two were one-two throughout.

1170 RACING HERE AGAIN NEXT THURSDAY H'CAP 1m 4f 16y

5:10 (5:10) (Class 5) (0-75,73) 3-Y-O **£2,298** (£684; £341; £170) **Stalls** Low

Form RPR

065- **1** **Pretty Diamond (IRE)**[132] 7567 3-8-9 **61**.......................... GregFairley 5 68
(Mark Johnston) *trckd ldr: hdwy to chal over 2f out: rdn to ld over 1f out: drvn and edgd lft ins fnl f: kpt on wl towards fin* **13/2[3]**

043- **2** *3/4* **Prince Freddie**[189] 6471 3-9-1 **67**.................................... PaulHanagan 4 73
(Philip Kirby) *trckd ldrs: hdwy on outer over 2f out: chal over 1f out and sn rdn: ev ch whn hmpd ins fnl f: no ex last 100yds* **13/2[3]**

P-1 **3** *3/4* **Moonlight Rhapsody (IRE)**[61] 420 3-9-2 **68**............ RobertWinston 1 73
(B W Hills) *trckd ldrs: effrt 2f out: rdn over 1f out: ch ent fnl f: sn drvn and one pce* **4/1[2]**

-31 **4** *1/2* **Bestwecan (IRE)**[19] 891 3-9-6 **72**........................ SilvestreDeSousa 2 76
(Mark Johnston) *led: rdn along over 2f out: drvn and hdd over 1f out: one pce ins fnl f* **8/11[1]**

0-44 **5** *7* **Highlife Dancer**[19] 890 3-9-2 **73**................................ MartinHarley(5) 3 66
(Mick Channon) *hld up in rr: effrt and sme hdwy over 2f out: rdn wl over 1f out: sn btn* **16/1**

2m 39.76s (-0.04) **Going Correction** -0.05s/f (Good) **5** Ran SP% **110.5**
Speed ratings (Par 98): **98,97,97,96,92**
CSF £43.41 TOTE £6.40: £2.50, £2.70; EX 46.70.
Owner Markus Graff **Bred** Maddenstown Equine Enterprise Ltd **Trained** Middleham Moor, N Yorks

FOCUS
A modest 3-y-o stayers' handicap and all but one of the five runners still had every chance inside the final furlong.
Pretty Diamond(IRE) Official explanation: trainer said, regarding apparent improvement in form, he only viewed it as a small improvement and the filly ran up to its handicap mark.
T/Plt: £114.90 to a £1 stake. Pool:£57,459.16 - 364.75 winning tickets T/Qpdt: £22.70 to a £1 stake. Pool:£5,182.60 - 168.86 winning tickets JR

1143 KEMPTON (A.W) (R-H)

Wednesday, April 6

OFFICIAL GOING: Standard
Wind: Light, across Weather: Fine, warm

1171 FREE ENTRY FOR BETDAQ MEMBERS H'CAP 6f (P)

5:40 (5:41) (Class 6) (0-65,65) 4-Y-O+ **£1,748** (£516; £258) **Stalls** Low

Form RPR

4603 **1** **Lord Of The Reins (IRE)**[14] 947 7-9-2 **60**................. PaulMulrennan 3 70
(James Given) *hld up in last pair: gd prog through rivals over 2f out: led over 1f out: styd on wl* **6/1[3]**

5005 **2** *3/4* **Libertino (IRE)**[5] 1084 4-8-9 **53**...................................... NeilCallan 5 61
(Tony Carroll) *chsd ldrs in 6th: n.m.r but sme prog over 2f out: nt qckn over 1f out: styd on to take 2nd nr fin* **5/1[1]**

0350 **3** *1/2* **Onceaponatime (IRE)**[11] 985 6-9-7 **65**.......................(b[1]) LukeMorris 2 71
(Michael Squance) *hld up in last trio: nt clr run wl over 2f out: prog through rivals to chse wnr 1f out: no imp: lost 2nd nr fin* **7/1**

6U-1 **4** *1* **Boldinor**[14] 947 8-9-4 **62**.. DavidProbert 8 65
(Martin Bosley) *t.k.h: trckd ldr after 2f: led over 2f out to over 1f out: one pce* **7/1**

-020 **5** *2 3/4* **Nollaig Shona (IRE)**[29] 794 4-9-2 **60**......................... StevieDonohoe 6 54
(George Prodromou) *settled in rr: rdn and struggling on outer over 2f out: kpt on ins fnl f* **12/1**

0046 **6** *nk* **White Shift (IRE)**[40] 683 5-8-10 **54**............................... WilliamBuick 1 47
(Jane Chapple-Hyam) *hld up and sn in last trio: nt clr run on inner wl over 2f out: prog wl over 1f out: sn fdd* **6/1[3]**

40-6 **7** *nk* **Cape Kimberley**[17] 941 4-9-2 **60**.. MartinLane 10 52
(Tony Newcombe) *racd on outer: chsd ldrs: rdn and outpcd over 2f out: n.d after: plugged on* **11/1**

541- **8** *5* **Spinning Spirit (IRE)**[162] 7144 4-9-7 **65**........................ JimCrowley 7 41
(Milton Bradley) *prom: cl 3rd 2f out: wknd qckly over 1f out* **11/2[2]**

40-0 **9** *2 3/4* **Avec Moi**[34] 743 4-8-0 **51** oh6... DanielHarris(7) 9 19
(Christine Dunnett) *dwlt: racd wd thrght: lost grnd bnd 3f out: sn btn* **40/1**

3/0- **10** *12* **Excellent Vision**[386] 894 4-9-7 **65**................................ PatCosgrave 12 —
(Milton Bradley) *dwlt: rushed arnd field and sn led: hdd & wknd rapidly over 2f out: t.o* **16/1**

06-0 **U** **Cinderella**[11] 993 4-8-8 **52** oh6 ow1........................ FergusSweeney 11 25
(Lucinda Featherstone) *chsd ldr 2f: losing pl whn n.m.r over 2f out: trying to rally over 1f out whn stmbld and uns rdr* **33/1**

1m 13.18s (0.08) **Going Correction** 0.0s/f (Stan) **11** Ran SP% **112.9**
Speed ratings (Par 101): **99,98,97,96,92 91,91,84,81,65** —
toteswingers:1&2 £9.10, 2&3 £11.50, 1&3 £7.90 CSF £34.51 CT £180.47 TOTE £4.50: £1.70, £2.90, £2.70; EX 38.90.
Owner Danethorpe Racing Partnership **Bred** C Farrell **Trained** Willoughton, Lincs

FOCUS
A fairly open sprint handicap.

1172 BETDAQ.COM EXCHANGE PRICE MULTIPLES CLAIMING STKS 1m (P)

6:10 (6:10) (Class 6) 4-Y-0+ **£1,535** (£453; £226) **Stalls** Low

Form RPR

03/ **1** **Ivory Jazz**[624] 4176 4-8-11 0.. JimCrowley 1 80
(Dean Ivory) *trckd ldr: clsd over 2f out: rdn to ld wl over 1f out: asserted ins fnl f: pushed out* **25/1[3]**

5641 **2** *2 1/4* **Benandonner (USA)**[9] 1014 8-9-7 94................................ MartinLane 2 85
(Mike Murphy) *led and untrbld in front: rdn 2f out: sn hdd and nt qckn: one pce after* **4/6[1]**

2212 **3** *1* **Jake The Snake (IRE)**[13] 956 10-9-1 85............................ NeilCallan 3 77
(Tony Carroll) *hld up in 3rd: rdn to cl over 2f out: chal and upsides over 1f out: fdd ins fnl f* **13/8[2]**

350- **4** *35* **Alqaahir (USA)**[210] 5867 9-8-5 68.................................... AmyScott(5) 5 —
(Paddy Butler) *settled in detached last: rdn and no prog over 3f out: t.o* **33/1**

1m 39.25s (-0.55) **Going Correction** 0.0s/f (Stan) **4** Ran SP% **104.9**
Speed ratings (Par 101): **102,99,98,63**
Ivory Jazz was claimed by S. Arnold for £6000.
Owner John Khan & Dean Ivory **Bred** New England Stud & Mount Coote Stud **Trained** Radlett, Herts

FOCUS
Not the duel it was expected to be.

1173 RACING AT SKYSPORTS.COM MEDIAN AUCTION MAIDEN STKS 1m 4f (P)
6:40 (6:40) (Class 6) 3-5-Y-0 **£1,748** (£516; £258) **Stalls** Centre

Form RPR
4 **1** **Gawaarib (USA)**[11] 983 3-8-7 0................................(b[1]) WilliamBuick 8 74
(John Gosden) *rousted along leaving stalls: led after 1f: jnd 4f out: rdn over 2f out: styd on and asserted ins fnl f* **5/1**
03-2 **2** 2 1/2 **Rasam Aldaar**[11] 983 3-8-7 72.. SamHitchcott 5 70
(Mick Channon) *trckd wnr after 4f: chal and upsides 4f out: drvn over 2f out: stl upsides over 1f out: nt qckn* **4/1**[3]
064- **3** 1 3/4 **Major Domo (FR)**[196] 6279 3-8-8 71 ow1.................... RichardHughes 7 68
(Harry Dunlop) *t.k.h: hld up bhd ldrs: rdn to try to chal 2f out: hd high and nt qckn* **9/4**[2]
553- **4** 2 **Roanstar**[201] 6152 4-9-13 70... JimmyFortune 6 66
(Andrew Balding) *t.k.h: led 1f: settled disputing 3rd after 4f: cl up and urged along 2f out: fnd nil* **13/8**[1]
5 6 **Pearl Mountain (IRE)**[90] 4-9-5 0.......................... SimonPearce(3) 4 51
(Lydia Pearce) *hld up: wnt prom over 7f out: shkn up and wd bnd 4f out: lft bhd by ldrs fr 3f out: nt disgracd* **20/1**
0 **6** 14 **La Bambagini**[40] 684 4-9-3 0.. KylieManser(5) 2 29
(Olivia Maylam) *in tch: reminder 1/2-way: wknd over 3f out: sn wl bhd* **66/1**
00-0 **7** 3/4 **Mistress Shy**[15] 937 4-9-8 37... SebSanders 1 28
(Robin Dickin) *in tch tl wknd over 3f out: sn wl bhd* **66/1**
0/00 **8** 36 **Two Tone**[31] 492 5-10-0 35.. TomMcLaughlin 3 —
(Garry Woodward) *in tch in last pair to 4f out: sn wl bhd: t.o: lame* **100/1**

2m 35.98s (1.48) **Going Correction** 0.0s/f (Stan)
WFA 3 from 4yo 21lb 4 from 5yo 1lb **8** Ran SP% **114.3**
Speed ratings (Par 101): **95,93,92,90,86 77,77,53**
toteswingers:1&2 £1.60, 2&3 £4.90, 1&3 £3.10 CSF £24.56 TOTE £6.10: £2.00, £1.02, £1.20; EX 12.00.
Owner Hamdan Al Maktoum **Bred** Castleton Lyons **Trained** Newmarket, Suffolk

FOCUS
An ordinary maiden run at a steady pace.
Two Tone Official explanation: jockey said gelding finished lame

1174 SPONSOR A RACE AT KEMPTON H'CAP 1m 4f (P)
7:10 (7:10) (Class 5) (0-70,69) 4-Y-0+ **£2,417** (£713; £357) **Stalls** Centre

Form RPR
623- **1** **Seaside Sizzler**[138] 7504 4-9-3 66.................................... JimCrowley 5 75
(Ralph Beckett) *settled in 5th: pushed along bef 1/2-way and then reminders: appeared to be struggling bdly after: fnlly r.o over 2f out: clsd to ld jst over 1f out: styd on strly* **5/2**[1]
2503 **2** 1 1/4 **Beat Route**[13] 954 4-9-5 68.. NeilCallan 4 75
(Michael Attwater) *trckd ldrs: gng best 3f out: sn wnt 2nd: clsd and rdn to ld briefly over 1f out: styd on wl enough but outpcd ins fnl f* **7/2**[3]
43-5 **3** 5 **Opera Prince**[7] 1046 6-9-2 64..(p) SebSanders 2 63
(Lady Herries) *led at fair pce: rdn over 2f out: hdd and fdd over 1f out* **8/1**
03-4 **4** 4 **Shades Of Grey**[28] 805 4-9-5 68.......................................(b[1]) AdamKirby 3 61
(Clive Cox) *trckd ldr: rdn and nt qckn 3f out: sn lost 2nd and btn* **10/3**[2]
6-00 **5** 9 **Clear Sailing**[14] 948 8-9-7 69.. StevieDonohoe 1 47
(Noel Quinlan) *rrd s: sn t.k.h in last: cl up over 3f out: rdn and wknd over 2f out* **20/1**
4011 **6** 3/4 **Irish Jugger (USA)**[29] 797 4-9-1 64.................................. JamesMillman 6 41
(Rod Millman) *trckd ldng pair: pushed along over 3f out: wknd tamely over 2f out* **9/2**

2m 32.68s (-1.82) **Going Correction** 0.0s/f (Stan)
WFA 4 from 6yo+ 1lb **6** Ran SP% **107.9**
Speed ratings (Par 103): **106,105,101,99,93 92**
toteswingers:1&2 £2.10, 2&3 £4.40, 1&3 £3.30 CSF £10.50 TOTE £4.70: £2.60, £1.30; EX 10.00.
Owner I J Heseltine **Bred** Redmyre Bloodstock And S Hillen **Trained** Kimpton, Hants

FOCUS
A fairly modest handicap.
Clear Sailing Official explanation: jockey said gelding ran too free

1175 LAY BACK AND WIN AT BETDAQ.COM H'CAP (LONDON MILE QUALIFIER) 1m (P)
7:40 (7:41) (Class 4) (0-85,85) 3-Y-0 **£4,129** (£1,228; £614; £306) **Stalls** Low

Form RPR
21-1 **1** **Indian Jack (IRE)**[4] 1106 3-9-7 85 6ex................................ LukeMorris 6 90+
(Alan Bailey) *hld up in tch: shkn up whn pce lifted over 2f out: drvn and prog over 1f out: styd on wl fnl f to ld last stride* **7/4**[1]
312- **2** shd **Tasfeya**[155] 7280 3-9-0 78.. KierenFallon 7 83
(Mark Johnston) *led at mod pce: kicked on over 2f out: drvn and 2 l ahd over 1f out: styd on: hdd post* **8/1**[3]
01- **3** shd **Club Oceanic**[133] 7559 3-9-2 80.. GeorgeBaker 1 85+
(Jeremy Noseda) *cl up on inner: chsd ldr 2f: rdn and clsd fnl f: nrly upsides nr fin but lost 2nd* **9/4**[2]
1- **4** 1 1/2 **John Biscuit (IRE)**[219] 5587 3-9-7 85................................. JimmyFortune 3 87+
(Andrew Balding) *hld up in tch: effrt on inner 2f out and looked dangerous over 1f out: kpt on same pce fnl f* **12/1**
511- **5** 6 **Muntasib (USA)**[126] 7652 3-9-6 84.................................. TadhgO'Shea 2 72
(Marcus Tregoning) *t.k.h: hld up in tch: pushed along over 2f out: nt qckn over 1f out: wknd* **17/2**
032- **6** hd **Planet Waves (IRE)**[137] 7528 3-9-2 80..........................(b) PhilipRobinson 8 67
(Clive Brittain) *s.i.s: t.k.h and sn prom: rdn to dispute 2nd over 2f out: wknd wl over 1f out* **25/1**
231- **7** shd **Sirius Prospect (USA)**[147] 7386 3-9-2 80........................ JimCrowley 5 67
(Dean Ivory) *taken down early: restless stalls: plld hrd: chsd ldr to 2f out: sn wknd* **12/1**
210- **8** 2 1/2 **Custom House (IRE)**[192] 6386 3-9-5 83.......................... RichardHughes 4 64
(Richard Hannon) *hld up last: pushed along over 2f out: no prog: eased fnl f* **12/1**

1m 39.78s (-0.02) **Going Correction** 0.0s/f (Stan) **8** Ran SP% **115.7**
Speed ratings (Par 100): **100,99,99,98,92 92,92,89**
toteswingers:1&2 £2.80, 2&3 £6.30, 1&3 £2.50 CSF £16.96 CT £32.66 TOTE £2.30: £1.10, £3.30, £2.10; EX 16.10.
Owner Forza Azzurri **Bred** Waterford Hall Stud **Trained** Newmarket, Suffolk

FOCUS
A good-looking 3-y-o handicap. The pace was again unsatisfactory and Kieren Fallon nearly stole it aboard Tasfeya.
Muntasib(USA) Official explanation: jockey said colt hung left

1176 BETDAQ MOBILE APPS H'CAP 7f (P)
8:10 (8:10) (Class 5) (0-70,70) 3-Y-0 **£2,417** (£713; £357) **Stalls** Low

Form RPR
-043 **1** **Beautiful Lando (FR)**[7] 1047 3-8-7 56 oh6.........(v) FrankieMcDonald 10 63
(Heather Main) *awkward s and rousted along in rr early: gd prog on inner over 2f out: led over 1f out but pressed: pushed out and a holding on ins fnl f* **16/1**
625- **2** nk **Homeboy (IRE)**[139] 7493 3-9-2 65.................................... HayleyTurner 9 71
(Marcus Tregoning) *settled in rr: rousted along 3f out: gd prog on outer over 2f out: chal over 1f out: edgd rt and styd on: a hld* **15/2**[3]
1- **3** 4 1/2 **Seeking Magic**[118] 7779 3-9-7 70.. AdamKirby 8 64+
(Clive Cox) *t.k.h despite fierce pce: hld up disputing 4th: nt qckn as others swept past 2f out: styd on to take 3rd jst ins fnl f* **6/5**[1]
0-24 **4** 1/2 **Midnight Trader (IRE)**[19] 892 3-9-7 70.............................. TonyCulhane 2 63
(Paul D'Arcy) *heavily restrained s: hld up in last pair: shuffled along on inner fnl 2f: styd on steadily: nvr nr ldng pair* **12/1**
60-5 **5** 7 **Exchange**[21] 873 3-9-2 65...(b[1]) EddieAhern 1 39
(William Haggas) *blasted off in front but pressed for 2f: clr 3f out: tied up and hdd over 1f out* **8/1**
1424 **6** 5 **Fifth In Line (IRE)**[8] 1021 3-8-12 66............................(b[1]) SeanLevey(5) 4 26
(David Flood) *tried to press ldr at str pce but forced to drop in bhd after 2f: wknd rapidly and lost 2nd 2f out* **33/1**
310- **7** 3 3/4 **Brave Battle**[151] 7347 3-9-5 68.. RichardHughes 5 18
(Richard Hannon) *disp 4th bhd clr ldrs: rdn wl over 2f out: sn wknd* **12/1**
61-4 **8** 2 1/4 **Endaxi Mana Mou**[64] 379 3-9-4 67.................................... JackMitchell 6 11
(Noel Quinlan) *stdd s: hld up in last pair: no prog over 2f out: sn wl bhd* **20/1**
4310 **9** 4 1/2 **Old English (IRE)**[12] 973 3-9-5 68.................................... KierenFallon 3 —
(Mark Johnston) *chsd clr ldng pair to over 2f out: wknd rapidly* **11/2**[2]

1m 25.52s (-0.48) **Going Correction** 0.0s/f (Stan) **9** Ran SP% **112.7**
Speed ratings (Par 98): **102,101,96,95,87 82,77,75,70**
toteswingers:1&2 £11.20, 2&3 £2.70, 1&3 £7.70 CSF £126.63 CT £253.96 TOTE £27.80: £6.50, £3.60, £1.02; EX 260.70.
Owner Les Chevaliers **Bred** Jean-Pierre Deroubaix **Trained** Kingston Lisle, Oxon

FOCUS
A race to treat with caution, this time not because of a dawdle, but due to the hard-pulling Exchange setting a searching gallop and the field being strung out turning in.
Old English(IRE) Official explanation: jockey said colt had no more to give

1177 BOOK KEMPTON PARK TICKETS ON 0844 579 3008 H'CAP 7f (P)
8:40 (8:41) (Class 6) (0-65,65) 4-Y-0+ **£1,748** (£516; £258) **Stalls** Low

Form RPR
1143 **1** **West Leake (IRE)**[11] 984 5-9-5 63..................................... LiamKeniry 2 70
(Paul Burgoyne) *trckd ldrs on inner: effrt 2f out: sustained chal over 1f out: led narrowly last 50yds: jst hld on* **8/1**
6124 **2** nse **Florio Vincitore (IRE)**[14] 949 4-9-5 63....................(b) EddieCreighton 6 70+
(Edward Creighton) *missed break: t.k.h and grad worked way through field to trck ldrs 1/2-way: drvn and edgd lft 2f out: styd on u.p to chal ins fnl f: jst failed* **9/4**[1]
245- **3** nk **Eager To Bow (IRE)**[174] 6864 5-9-5 63............................ JimCrowley 11 69+
(Patrick Chamings) *hld up wl in rr: looking for room over 2f out: prog and drvn over 1f out: r.o fnl f: tk 3rd last strides and clsng on ldng pair* **5/1**[2]
4511 **4** 1/2 **Katmai River (IRE)**[11] 984 4-9-3 61..........................(v) SteveDrowne 4 66
(Mark Usher) *mde most: drvn and hrd pressed fr over 1f out: hdd and no ex last 50yds* **11/2**[3]
0231 **5** 1 3/4 **Crystallize**[63] 386 5-8-7 51... LukeMorris 5 51
(Andrew Haynes) *pressed ldrs: drvn over 2f out: stl chsng over 1f out: fdd ins fnl f* **20/1**
6620 **6** nk **Tudor Prince (IRE)**[28] 810 7-9-1 59................................. NeilCallan 12 58
(Tony Carroll) *in tch in midfield: looking for room and swtchd sharply lft over 2f out: drvn over 1f out: one pce* **9/1**
-060 **7** 3/4 **Teen Ager (FR)**[7] 1045 7-8-7 51 oh1........................ FrankieMcDonald 9 48
(Paul Burgoyne) *in tch in midfield: effrt on outer and bmpd over 2f out: one pce and no imp over 1f out* **20/1**
4100 **8** 2 **Jonny Ebeneezer**[7] 1041 12-9-0 58.............................(be) StephenCraine 3 50
(David Flood) *in tch in midfield: effrt to chse ldrs 2f out: sn drvn: fdd ins fnl f* **50/1**
3531 **9** 1/2 **Guildenstern (IRE)**[7] 1045 9-8-9 53 6ex......................... HayleyTurner 14 43
(Jane Chapple-Hyam) *hld up in 12th: jst pushed along fr over 2f out: nvr involved* **11/1**
200- **10** 3 3/4 **Motty's Gift**[232] 5171 4-8-12 56......................................(v) EddieAhern 1 36
(Walter Swinburn) *a abt same pl: shkn up and no prog over 2f out* **25/1**
0403 **11** 1 1/2 **Norcroft**[29] 800 9-8-0 51 oh5..(p) DanielHarris(7) 10 27
(Christine Dunnett) *pressed ldr: wknd over 2f out* **33/1**
0-00 **12** 2 1/4 **Ensnare**[14] 949 6-9-7 65... StevieDonohoe 7 35
(Noel Quinlan) *restless stalls: detached in last: a bhd* **33/1**
005- **13** 3 **Footstepsofspring (FR)**[169] 7007 4-8-12 56................. TonyCulhane 8 18
(Willie Musson) *racd v wd: w ldr: hung bdly lft bnd 3f out and lost all ch* **16/1**

1m 26.01s (0.01) **Going Correction** 0.0s/f (Stan) **13** Ran SP% **119.4**
Speed ratings (Par 101): **99,98,98,96 95,94,92,91,87 85,83,79**
toteswingers:1&2 £3.50, 2&3 £6.80, 1&3 £7.10 CSF £24.05 CT £106.93 TOTE £4.60: £1.70, £1.50, £3.10; EX 35.20.
Owner L Tomlin **Bred** Rathbarry Stud **Trained** Shepton Montague, Somerset

FOCUS
A tight finish.
Footstepsofspring(FR) Official explanation: jockey said gelding failed to handle right-hand bend
T/Plt: £511.70 to a £1 stake. Pool of £58,692.92 - 83.72 winning tickets. T/Qpdt: £6.60 to a £1 stake. Pool of £8,321.20 - 924.20 winning tickets. JN

1041 LINGFIELD (L-H)
Wednesday, April 6

OFFICIAL GOING: Standard
Wind: fresh, behind Weather: sunny, warm breezy

1178 GODSTONE CLAIMING STKS 7f (P)
2:30 (2:30) (Class 6) 3-Y-0+ **£1,535** (£453; £226) **Stalls** Low

Form RPR
0-02 **1** **Maze (IRE)**[49] 556 6-9-12 72.. NeilCallan 4 81
(Tony Carroll) *t.k.h: chsd ldr tl led 5f out: mde rest: qcknd over 2f out: drvn ent fnl f: styd on wl* **5/2**[2]

The Form Book, Raceform Ltd, Compton, RG20 6NL

2201 **2** *1 1/4* **My Lord**[18] 913 3-8-4 78.................................... JakePayne(7) 3 72
(Bill Turner) *led tl 5f out: chsd ldrs on inner after: swtchd rt and effrt wl over 1f out: chsd wnr over 1f out: styd on same pce fnl f* **9/2**[3]

01-3 **3** *3/4* **Lend A Grand (IRE)**[47] 590 7-9-7 65.................................... IanMongan 2 71
(Jo Crowley) *hld up up in tch in last pair: swtchd rt and effrt over 1f out: kpt on u.p ins fnl f: nvr trbld ldrs* **11/1**

416 **4** *2* **Rubenstar (IRE)**[35] 736 8-9-8 74.................................... RichardHughes 6 66
(Patrick Morris) *stdd s: hld up in tch in last pair: shkn up and effrt wl over 1f out: drvn and no prog 1f out: one pce and wl hld fnl f* **7/4**[1]

10-1 **5** *1/2* **Caprio (IRE)**[91] 45 6-10-0 79.................................... NickyMackay 1 71
(Jim Boyle) *bustled along leaving stalls: chsd ldrs: rdn 3f out: sn chsng ldr: drvn 2f out: sn outpcd and btn 1f out* **6/1**

6-00 **6** *12* **Microlight**[11] 987 3-8-9 55.................................... RichardThomas 5 28
(John E Long) *chsd ldrs: dropped to rr and struggling over 2f out: wl bhd fnl f* **100/1**

1m 25.65s (0.85) **Going Correction** +0.175s/f (Slow)
WFA 3 from 6yo+ 14lb **6** Ran SP% **106.7**
Speed ratings (Par 101): **102,100,99,97,96 83**
toteswingers:1&2:£3.60, 1&3:£4.10, 2&3:£3.40 CSF £12.52 TOTE £3.00: £1.10, £2.40; EX 12.60.
Owner Centaur Global Partnership I **Bred** Millsec Limited **Trained** Cropthorne, Worcs

FOCUS
With four horses rated in the 70s, this was probably a fair race of its type, although there wasn't a great deal of pace on early.

1179 LINGFIELDPARK.CO.UK MAIDEN STKS 7f (P)
3:00 (3:00) (Class 5) 3-Y-O **£2,115** (£624; £312) **Stalls** Low

Form RPR
2 **1** **Greenflash**[13] 952 3-8-12 0.................................... RichardHughes 2 67+
(Richard Hannon) *mde all: rdn and asserted over 1f out: clr and in command fnl f: comf* **4/9**[1]

0-22 **2** *1 3/4* **Uncle Dermot (IRE)**[18] 905 3-9-3 70.................................... FergusSweeney 4 67
(Brendan Powell) *hld up in tch in midfield: rdn and effrt wl over 1f out: drvn and hdwy ent fnl f: chsd wnr fnl 150yds: nvr gng pce to threaten wnr* **9/2**[2]

3 *1 1/2* **Poyle Punch** 3-9-3 0.................................... JimCrowley 6 63+
(Ralph Beckett) *dwlt: in tch in rr: rdn and hdwy jst over 1f out: styd on wl fnl f: gng on fin but no threat to wnr* **7/1**[3]

30 **4** *2* **Ereka (IRE)**[49] 558 3-8-12 48.................................... LiamKeniry 1 53?
(Murty McGrath) *chsd ldrs: rdn to chse wnr wl over 1f out: outpcd and btn 1f out: wknd and lost 2 pls ins fnl f* **50/1**

05- **5** *1 1/4* **Lady Deanie (IRE)**[163] 7123 3-8-12 0.................................... DavidProbert 5 50
(Bryn Palling) *chsd ldr: rdn 3f out: lost 2nd wl over 1f out: wknd fnl f* **16/1**

0- **6** *3 1/4* **Excellence (IRE)**[252] 4474 3-8-12 0.................................... ChrisCatlin 3 41
(Karen George) *stdd s: t.k.h: hld up in last pair: rdn wl over 1f out: sn wknd* **100/1**

005- **7** *11* **Tsarina Louise**[183] 6658 3-8-12 0.................................... PaulMulrennan 8 11
(James Given) *in tch in midfield: rdn and wknd qckly wl over 1f out: wl bhd fnl f* **66/1**

1m 26.24s (1.44) **Going Correction** +0.175s/f (Slow) **7** Ran SP% **110.3**
Speed ratings (Par 98): **98,96,94,92,90 86,74**
toteswingers:1&2:£1.10, 1&3:£2.20, 2&3:£2.80 CSF £2.52 TOTE £1.60: £1.10, £1.50; EX 2.20.
Owner Terry Neill & Sir Eric Parker **Bred** Sir Eric Parker **Trained** East Everleigh, Wilts

FOCUS
A weak maiden using the fourth as a guide.

1180 DORMANSLAND (S) STKS 6f (P)
3:30 (3:30) (Class 6) 3-Y-O+ **£1,535** (£453; £226) **Stalls** Low

Form RPR
3102 **1** **Frequency**[7] 1044 4-9-12 72.................................... (b) KirstyMilczarek 2 74+
(Conor Dore) *hld up in midfield: hdwy wl over 1f out: rdn to chse clr ldr jst over 1f out: led ins fnl f: sn clr: comf* **13/8**[2]

6304 **2** *2 1/2* **Misaro (GER)**[7] 1041 10-9-7 57.................................... (b) DavidProbert 4 61
(Ronald Harris) *led: pushed clr ent fnl 2f: drvn ent fnl f: hdd ins fnl f: sn [illegible]* **7/1**

0031 **3** *5* **Bonnie Prince Blue**[7] 1044 8-9-12 73.................................... (b) PaulMulrennan 1 50
(James Given) *chsd ldr tl over 3f out: rdn to chse clr ldr again 2f out: no imp and lost 2nd jst over 1f out: wl btn fnl f* **9/2**[3]

13 **4** *1 3/4* **Chimpunk (USA)**[18] 914 5-9-12 75.................................... AndreaAtzeni 3 44
(Michael Wigham) *dwlt: hld up in last pair: rdn and effrt whn pushed sltly rt bnd 2f out: sn drvn and no real hdwy: 4th and wl btn fnl f* **6/4**[1]

3005 **5** *4* **Seeking Rio**[35] 732 4-8-9 44.................................... JakePayne(7) 5 22
(Ron Hodges) *chsd ldrs: wnt 2nd over 3f out: rdn over 2f out: edgd rt and lost pl bnd 2f out: sn wknd* **100/1**

0-45 **6** *1/2* **Briannsta (IRE)**[7] 1044 9-9-7 43.................................... (b) RichardThomas 7 25
(John E Long) *a towards rr: bhd and pushed along 4f out: no ch fnl 2f* **66/1**

1m 11.8s (-0.10) **Going Correction** +0.175s/f (Slow) **6** Ran SP% **111.3**
Speed ratings (Par 101): **107,103,97,94,89 88**
toteswingers:1&2:£3.20, 1&3:£1.10, 2&3:£3.70 CSF £12.99 TOTE £2.70: £1.10, £8.10; EX 11.60.The winner was bought in for 9,200gns.
Owner Patrick Wilmott **Bred** Manor Farm Stud (rutland) **Trained** Cowbit, Lincs

FOCUS
After the first two races on the card were basically stolen by decent front-running rides, it was pleasing to see a horse win after being given a well-judged hold-up ride.
Bonnie Prince Blue Official explanation: jockey said gelding hung badly right

1181 ASHURST WOOD H'CAP 2m (P)
4:00 (4:01) (Class 6) (0-60,64) 4-Y-O+ **£1,910** (£564; £282) **Stalls** Low

Form RPR
-6P3 **1** **Maydream**[27] 819 4-8-6 46.................................... FrankieMcDonald 5 52
(Jimmy Fox) *hld up in last trio: pushed along and hdwy over 2f out: chsd ldng pair 2f out: pressing ldrs but n.m.r thrght fnl f tl pushed along and wnt between horses to ld on post* **11/2**[3]

35/ **2** *nse* **Mac Federal (IRE)**[1453] 458 9-9-2 55.................................... SophieDoyle(3) 1 61
(Sheena West) *chsd ldr tl led wl over 2f out: rdn and hdd narrowly 2f out: stl ev ch and kpt on gamely to ld again fnl 75yds: hdd on post* **9/4**[1]

2-11 **3** *nk* **Dansilver**[8] 1025 7-10-0 64 6ex.................................... PaulDoe 7 69
(Jim Best) *stdd s: hld up in rr: hdwy to chse ldrs over 4f out: drvn to ld narrowly 2f out: hrd drvn 1f out: hdd fnl 75yds: no ex* **7/2**[2]

0/5- **4** *9* **Sommersturm (GER)**[96] 1984 7-9-4 54.................................... TomQueally 4 48
(Barney Curley) *sn led: hdd wl over 2f out: wknd qckly wl over 1f out: wl btn fnl f* **8/1**

660 **5** *9* **Miles Of Sunshine**[11] 992 6-9-3 53.................................... JimCrowley 6 36
(Ron Hodges) *chsd ldrs: rdn and wknd qckly over 2f out: wl bhd over 1f out* **9/1**

6235 **6** *15* **Prince Charlemagne (IRE)**[26] 838 8-9-10 60.................................... FergusSweeney 8 25
(Dr Jeremy Naylor) *stdd and dropped in bhd after s: rdn and short-lived effrt over 2f out: wl bhd fnl 2f: eased ins fnl f* **7/1**

6434 **7** *11* **Beseech (USA)**[18] 911 4-8-2 47 oh1 ow1.................................... AdamBeschizza(5) 3 —
(Julia Feilden) *chsd ldrs tl rdn and dropped to last over 3f out: lost tch over 2f out: t.o and eased ins fnl f* **8/1**

3m 27.8s (2.10) **Going Correction** +0.175s/f (Slow)
WFA 4 from 6yo+ 4lb **7** Ran SP% **113.1**
Speed ratings (Par 101): **101,100,100,96,91 84,78**
toteswingers:1&2:£3.80, 1&3:£5.20, 2&3:£1.80 CSF £17.90 CT £48.61 TOTE £5.60: £2.30, £1.60; EX 25.30.
Owner The Dancing Partners **Bred** The Dancing Partners **Trained** Collingbourne Ducis, Wilts

FOCUS
An open-looking contest, with the outsider of seven going off at only 9-1. The early gallop was sedate, which meant this was not a proper test of stamina.

1182 GREAT DEALS ON ANNUAL MEMBERSHIP H'CAP 5f (P)
4:30 (4:30) (Class 6) (0-60,60) 4-Y-O+ **£1,910** (£564; £282) **Stalls** High

Form RPR
352- **1** **Rebecca Romero**[182] 6665 4-8-12 51.................................... (v) RichardHughes 8 60
(Denis Coakley) *in tch in midfield: rdn and effrt 2f out: hdwy and edgd lft u.p 1f out: str run to ld fnl 75yds: sn in command* **9/2**[2]

-426 **2** *3/4* **Jimmy Ryan (IRE)**[28] 812 10-9-4 57.................................... (t) J-PGuillambert 1 63
(Tim McCarthy) *taken down early: in tch in midfield on inner: rdn and hdwy over 1f out: hrd drvn and ev ch fnl 100yds: no ex and comf hld by wnr towards fin* **7/1**[3]

0630 **3** *nk* **Commandingpresence (USA)**[7] 1043 5-8-7 51.................................... SeanLevey(5) 6 56+
(John Bridger) *towards rr: n.m.r and shuffled bk jst over 2f out: hdwy and edgd lft jst ins fnl f: r.o wl u.p towards fin: nt rch ldrs* **20/1**

1500 **4** *1/2* **Spic 'n Span**[16] 934 6-9-7 60.................................... (b) ChrisCatlin 2 63
(Ronald Harris) *taken down early: w ldr tl led after 1f out: rdn over 1f out: drvn ins fnl f: hdd fnl 75yds: wknd and lost 2 pls towards fin* **25/1**

1220 **5** *1/2* **Royal Acclamation (IRE)**[21] 874 6-8-9 55.................................... DavidKenny(7) 5 56+
(Michael Scudamore) *sn outpcd in last: swtchd lft and hdwy on inner 1f out: styd on wl ins fnl f: nt rch ldrs* **9/1**

5053 **6** *1* **Thoughtsofstardom**[7] 1041 8-8-5 49.................................... DanielleMcCreery(5) 4 47
(Phil McEntee) *chsd ldrs: rdn to chse ldr jst over 1f out tl ins fnl f: no ex and btn whn n.m.r towards fin* **12/1**

3554 **7** *2* **Simple Rhythm**[15] 941 5-9-1 54.................................... KirstyMilczarek 9 45
(John Ryan) *in tch in midfield: rdn and effrt but nt clr run over 1f out tl ent fnl f: one pce and no imp after* **12/1**

015 **8** *1 1/2* **Triskaidekaphobia**[16] 934 8-9-4 57.................................... (t) FrankieMcDonald 10 42
(Paul Fitzsimons) *led for 1f: w ldr after tl over 1f out: wknd fnl f* **12/1**

-102 **9** *nk* **Far View (IRE)**[7] 1041 4-9-7 60.................................... (vt[1]) JimmyFortune 3 44+
(George Baker) *hld up in midfield: nt clr run over 2f out tl 2f out: rdn and hung lft over 1f out: no hdwy and wl btn whn eased wl ins fnl f* **11/8**[1]

59.31 secs (0.51) **Going Correction** +0.175s/f (Slow) **9** Ran SP% **114.5**
Speed ratings (Par 101): **102,100,100,99,98 97,93,91,91**
toteswingers:1&2:£2.90, 1&3:£18.60, 2&3:£15.50 CSF £35.59 CT £569.79 TOTE £4.20: £1.40, £2.30, £6.90; EX 31.30.
Owner Keepers Racing Ii **Bred** D W Armstrong **Trained** West Ilsley, Berks

FOCUS
With so many horses in this that like to get on with things, indeed a couple were taken down steadily to the start, there was little chance the early gallop was going to be anything else but quick. The front few went off at a rapid rate, which undoubtedly helped the winner.
Simple Rhythm Official explanation: jockey said mare hung left
Far View(IRE) Official explanation: trainer said gelding was unsuited by the shorter trip

1183 GRAND NATIONAL MICROSITE NOW LIVE H'CAP 1m 2f (P)
5:00 (5:00) (Class 4) (0-85,83) 4-Y-O+ **£3,238** (£963; £481; £240) **Stalls** Low

Form RPR
6-12 **1** **Fashionable Gal (IRE)**[28] 814 4-8-9 71.................................... EddieAhern 2 77
(Neil King) *chsd ldr: clsd and pressed ldr ent fnl 2f: rdn to ld over 1f out: drvn fnl f: a doing enough* **11/10**[1]

0210 **2** *hd* **Kidlat**[20] 877 6-9-0 83.................................... AlexOwen(7) 5 88
(Alan Bailey) *led: pushed along and qcknd [illegible] 1f out: [illegible] along and kpt on gamely ins fnl f* **3/1**[2]

0-30 **3** *1 1/2* **Bavarica**[35] 723 9-8-2 69.................................... AdamBeschizza(5) 3 71
(Julia Feilden) *chsd ldng pair: clsd and in tch 2f out: drvn ent fnl f: kpt on same pce ins fnl f* **13/2**[3]

1232 **4** *11* **Shared Moment (IRE)**[19] 889 5-8-7 69 oh8.................................... (v) ChrisCatlin 4 49
(John Gallagher) *stdd s: a same pl: rdn and no rspnse 3f out: wl btn fnl 2f* **15/2**

3000 **5** *14* **Alhaban (IRE)**[35] 736 5-9-4 80.................................... (t) TomMcLaughlin 1 32
(Ronald Harris) *stdd s: a last: rdn and struggling 4f out: lost tch wl over 2f out: t.o* **8/1**

2m 7.71s (1.11) **Going Correction** +0.175s/f (Slow) **5** Ran SP% **108.8**
Speed ratings (Par 105): **102,101,100,91,80**
CSF £4.46 TOTE £2.10: £1.60, £2.30; EX 5.80.
Owner John Webb & Neil King **Bred** B D Burnett **Trained** Newmarket, Suffolk

FOCUS
They all kept in one long line throughout the early section of the race, and nothing happened until the leader injected some much needed pace over 4f out.

1184 VISIT ATTHERACES.COM/NATIONAL H'CAP 1m (P)
5:30 (5:31) (Class 6) (0-60,60) 4-Y-O+ **£1,910** (£564; £282) **Stalls** High

Form RPR
-011 **1** **Angelena Ballerina (IRE)**[19] 895 4-9-7 60.................................... (v) KirstyMilczarek 2 68
(Karen George) *dwlt: pushed along in tch in rr: drvn and effrt ent fnl 2f: swtchd rt over 1f out: chal ins fnl f: led towards fin: rdn out* **11/2**

4126 **2** *1/2* **Clearing House**[12] 969 6-8-13 57.................................... AdamBeschizza(5) 7 64
(John Ryan) *wl in tch in last trio: hdwy to chse ldng pair over 2f out: rdn to ld 1f out: hdd and no ex towards fin* **9/4**[1]

0020 **3** *4 1/2* **Street Crime**[13] 957 6-8-4 50.................................... JakePayne(7) 6 46
(Ron Hodges) *t.k.h: w ldrs: ev ch and rdn wl over 2f out: led wl over 1f out tl 1f out: wknd ins fnl f* **16/1**

4520 **4** *1 1/2* **Christmas Coming**[18] 906 4-9-6 59.................................... (p) EddieAhern 3 52
(Tony Carroll) *wl in tch in midfield: rdn and effrt to chse ldng trio 2f out: drvn jst over 1f out: wknd ins fnl f* **5/1**[3]

2045 **5** *shd* **Sonny G (IRE)**[28] 810 4-9-1 57.................................... KierenFox(3) 5 50
(John Best) *chsd ldr tl led 4f out: rdn wl over 2f out: hdd over 1f out: wknd 1f out* **6/1**

2054 **6** *1/2* **Haulit**[28] 809 5-8-13 52.................................... (p) LiamKeniry 1 44
(Gary Moore) *t.k.h: chsd ldrs on inner: rdn and fnd nil over 1f out: sn btn* **7/2**[2]

5420 **7** 1 ¼ **Cavalry Guard (USA)**[14] 950 7-8-2 **46**....................(b) HarryBentley(5) 8 35
(Tim McCarthy) *in tch in last trio: rdn and effrt on outer over 2f out: no prog and wl btn over 1f out* **12/1**
00-6 **8** 12 **Final Try**[8] 1021 4-8-0 **46** oh1.. NathanAlison(7) 4 —
(Paddy Butler) *led tl 4f out: sn lost pl: lost tch 2f out: t.o* **50/1**
1m 39.83s (1.63) **Going Correction** +0.175s/f (Slow) **8** Ran SP% **114.9**
Speed ratings (Par 101): **98,97,93,91,91 90,89,77**
toteswingers:1&2:£2.90, 1&3:£11.60, 2&3:£12.70 CSF £18.40 CT £186.80 TOTE £4.20: £1.40, £1.70, £5.00; EX 12.30.
Owner F Michael **Bred** Waterford Hall Stud **Trained** Higher Eastington, Devon
■ Stewards' Enquiry : Nathan Alison one-day ban: careless riding (Apr 20)

FOCUS
A modest handicap run at a steady gallop early. The field were stacked up coming round the final bend, but they soon thinned out and the finish was fought out by the two form horses.
T/Plt: £157.60 to a £1 stake. Pool:£54,628.32 - 252.97 winning tickets T/Qpdt: £88.10 to a £1 stake. Pool:£4,133.09 - 34.68 winning tickets SP

NOTTINGHAM (L-H)
Wednesday, April 6
OFFICIAL GOING: Outer course - firm (good to firm in places; 9.5)
Wind: Fresh against Weather: Fine

1185 E B F / BET ON TOTEPLACEPOT AT TOTESPORT.COM NOVICE STKS 5f 13y
2:20 (2:22) (Class 4) 2-Y-O **£4,533** (£1,348; £674; £336) **Stalls** High

Form RPR
1 **The Penny Horse (IRE)** 2-9-0 0...................................... JamesDoyle 8 76
(J S Moore) *hld up: hdwy 2f out: led ins fnl f: hung lft: r.o* **12/1**
3 **2** hd **Choice Of Remark (IRE)**[7] 1042 2-9-0 0....................... CathyGannon 6 75
(David Evans) *led: rdn: hung lft and hdd over 1f out: r.o* **9/4**[2]
6 **3** 2 **Triggerlo**[4] 1095 2-9-0 0.. SamHitchcott 7 68
(Mick Channon) *chsd ldrs: rdn over 1f out: styng on same pce whn hung lft ins fnl f* **6/4**[1]
4 2 ¼ **Choisirez (IRE)** 2-8-3 0 ow1................................ MatthewCosham(7) 2 55
(David Evans) *prom: outpcd 3f out: styd on ins fnl f* **8/1**[3]
5 ¾ **Latte** 2-9-0 0.. KierenFallon 3 57+
(Linda Stubbs) *chsd ldrs: rdn: hung lft and led over 1f out: hdd & wknd ins fnl f* **17/2**
6 1 ¾ **Sonko (IRE)** 2-8-6 0.. AmyRyan(3) 5 45+
(Tim Pitt) *prom: rdn over 1f out: hung lft and wknd fnl f* **16/1**
7 5 **Lone Star State (IRE)** 2-8-9 0................................ KieranO'Neill(5) 1 32
(Ian Patrick Browne, Ire) *s.i.s and wnt lft s: hdwy 3f out: wknd 2f out* **25/1**
62.79 secs (1.79) **Going Correction** -0.025s/f (Good) **7** Ran SP% **109.8**
Speed ratings (Par 94): **84,83,80,76,75 72,64**
toteswingers:1&2:£5.00, 1&3:£4.10, 2&3:£1.60 CSF £36.27 TOTE £16.70: £7.40, £1.50; EX 50.80 Trifecta £96.70 Pool: £396.20 - 3.03 winning units..
Owner Mrs Emma Ambrose & J S Moore **Bred** Padraig Murphy **Trained** Upper Lambourn, Berks

FOCUS
The going was officially described as firm, good to firm in places. After a false patch of ground was discovered on the inner course on the morning of racing, all races were switched to the outer course.

NOTEBOOK
The Penny Horse(IRE) landed a small gamble for the in-form Stan Moore stable. He got a nice tow into the race, travelling smoothly behind horses, and once finding a gap he took up the running easily. He survived notable greenness in the closing stages when veering across the track and was worth more than the winning margin suggests. The trainer reported he may have some time off to mature, but he is a promising horse for the future. (op 20-1)
Choice Of Remark(IRE), third on his debut on Polytrack last week, may have been flattered to get as close to the winner as he did. He was more professional than his rivals and kept straight under pressure but was ultimately no match. He should be able to score in a novice event before the better types come out. (op 2-1 tchd 11-4)
Triggerlo, who was sixth in the Brocklesby last weekend, broke alertly but struggled to get on terms with the speedier Choice Of Remark next to him, and looks to need further already by the way he just stayed on at the one pace. (op 15-8 tchd 11-8)
Choisirez(IRE), whose jockey put up 1lb overweight so could only claim 6lb, was under pressure from some way out, and although not responding initially, she did make headway inside the last furlong. She will come on for the run. (op 7-1 tchd 13-2)
Latte made good progress down the centre of the track but lacked the pace when it mattered. One would think a small novice sprint could come his way. Official explanation: jockey said, regarding dropping hands before win post, that the gelding hung throughout and appeared to lose its action and felt it prudent to ease. (op 7-1)
Sonko(IRE) raced with enthusiasm but threw away any chance when hanging left from 1f out. (tchd 12-1)
Lone Star State(IRE) gave himself a huge task after edging left after leaving the stalls. This experience should set him straighter for next time. (op 28-1)

1186 FREE RACING POST FORM AT TOTESPORT.COM CONDITIONS STKS 5f 13y
2:50 (2:50) (Class 3) 3-Y-O+ **£5,828** (£1,734; £866; £432) **Stalls** High

Form RPR
6212 **1** **Iver Bridge Lad**[4] 1093 4-9-7 105........................(b) MichaelO'Connell(3) 6 111
(John Ryan) *hld up: hdwy and nt clr run over 1f out: led ins fnl f: r.o wl* **11/4**[1]
4-60 **2** 2 **Secret Asset (IRE)**[11] 989 6-9-1 97.................................. RyanMoore 4 95
(Jane Chapple-Hyam) *chsd ldrs: led over 1f out: sn rdn: hdd and unable qck ins fnl f* **9/2**[3]
100- **3** 1 ¼ **Face The Problem (IRE)**[208] 5907 3-8-7 101.................. MichaelHills 7 88
(B W Hills) *hld up: swtchd lft and hdwy over 1f out: styd on same pce ins fnl f* **11/2**
2104 **4** ¾ **Five Star Junior (USA)**[11] 989 5-9-1 94......................... KierenFallon 9 88
(Linda Stubbs) *hld up: swtchd lft and hdwy over 1f out: sn rdn: styd on same pce ins fnl f* **3/1**[2]
6-64 **5** ¾ **Liberty Lady (IRE)**[12] 970 4-8-10 76............................. JamesDoyle 8 80
(Des Donovan) *chsd ldrs: rdn over 1f out: no ex fnl f* **66/1**
421- **6** 1 ¾ **Captain Dunne (IRE)**[183] 6663 6-9-12 104................. DuranFentiman 2 90
(Tim Easterby) *chsd ldr: rdn and ev ch over 1f out: wknd ins fnl f* **10/1**
000- **7** hd **Judd Street**[270] 3891 9-9-1 99...(v) DaneO'Neill 3 78
(Eve Johnson Houghton) *s.i.s: hld up: hdwy 1/2-way: rdn and wknd over 1f out* **20/1**
5240 **8** ½ **Star Rover (IRE)**[11] 989 4-9-7 89............................ RichardEvans(3) 5 85
(David Evans) *led: rdn 1/2-way: hdd over 1f out: wknd ins fnl f* **22/1**
265- **9** 4 ½ **Corporal Maddox**[312] 2537 4-9-1 104............................ JamieSpencer 1 60
(Jamie Osborne) *hld up: rdn 2f out: a in rr* **12/1**
59.63 secs (-1.37) **Going Correction** -0.025s/f (Good)
WFA 3 from 4yo+ 11lb **9** Ran SP% **112.6**
Speed ratings (Par 107): **109,105,103,102,101 98,98,97,90**
toteswingers:1&2:£3.90, 1&3:£3.70, 2&3:£5.50 CSF £14.60 TOTE £3.70: £1.10, £1.80, £2.40; EX 17.10 Trifecta £55.70 Pool: £325.58 - 4.32 winning units..
Owner The Iver Lads **Bred** Jcs Wilson Bloodstock **Trained** Newmarket, Suffolk

FOCUS
An interesting conditions sprint in which the favourite had won five of the last eight runnings.

NOTEBOOK
Iver Bridge Lad, well backed, enhanced that statistic further with an emphatic victory. He sat behind the pace early before powering through a gap between rivals a furlong out and registered a ready success. Trainer John Ryan said "he's a tough horse who is more straightforward than he used to be". His second behind J J The Jet Plane in Meydan has proved to be no fluke judged by his recent results, and he may go for a conditions race at Newbury. (op 10-3 tchd 7-2)
Secret Asset(IRE) tracked the pace and quickened to lead 1f out but had no answer to the winner's pace once he came alongside. He acts well under these quick conditions and this should set him up nicely for next time. (op 4-1)
Face The Problem(IRE) put in a pleasing display. Although receiving weight from all of his rivals he shaped better than most. He was switched left 2f out but his challenge came a little too late, which may have cost him a chance of second. He won a Listed contest last season, still holds an entry in the Duke Of York and remains interesting. (op 9-2)
Five Star Junior(USA), a consistent hold-up performer, was switched left to come with his challenge after finding trouble behind horses, and was another to hit top gear too late. He's better over further. (op 4-1)
Liberty Lady(IRE) ran better than many may have expected given her starting price. The handicapper may punish her too much for this.
Captain Dunne(IRE) broke well and dictated matters from the offset. He couldn't sustain his pace from 2f out though, and looked in need of the run. (op 8-1 tchd 15-2)
Judd Street was slowly away. He also often needs his first run of the season and never got into serious contention. (tchd 22-1)
Star Rover(IRE), who won here as a juvenile, showed bags of early pace but isn't good enough at this level. (op 20-1)
Corporal Maddox has run better with cut in the ground so would never have been in love with this ground. His new trainer may look for a race over further for him. (op 11-1)

1187 BET ON TONIGHT'S FOOTBALL AT TOTESPORT.COM H'CAP 5f 13y
3:20 (3:20) (Class 5) (0-75,73) 3-Y-O **£2,266** (£674; £337; £168) **Stalls** High

Form RPR
3465 **1** **Pineapple Pete (IRE)**[12] 958 3-8-1 **60**..........................(t) RyanTate(7) 8 62
(Alan McCabe) *hld up: swtchd lft 2f out: hdwy over 1f out: edgd lft: rdn to ld wl ins fnl f: r.o* **14/1**
040- **2** ½ **Indian Shuffle (IRE)**[147] 7392 3-9-3 **69**.......................... KierenFallon 6 69
(Jonathan Portman) *led: rdn over 1f out: hdd wl ins fnl f* **13/2**[2]
230- **3** nk **Perfect Pastime**[190] 6445 3-9-7 **73**.......................... AdamKirby 2 72
(Walter Swinburn) *chsd ldr: rdn over 1f out: ev ch ins fnl f: unable qck towards fin* **10/11**[1]
-215 **4** 1 ¼ **Morermaloke**[66] 356 3-9-2 **73**.. LeeTopliss(5) 7 68
(Ian McInnes) *s.i.s and hmpd s: sn prom: rdn 1/2-way: sn outpcd: styd on ins fnl f* **10/1**[3]
10-0 **5** 1 **Empress Royal**[57] 452 3-8-11 **63**.................................. TonyHamilton 4 54
(Michael Dods) *hld up: hdwy over 1f out: sn rdn and hung lft: no ex ins fnl f* **13/2**[2]
000- **6** 8 **Meandmyshadow**[165] 7087 3-8-13 **65**................................ TedDurcan 9 27
(Alan Brown) *chsd ldrs tl rdn and wknd over 1f out* **13/2**[2]
62.07 secs (1.07) **Going Correction** -0.025s/f (Good) **6** Ran SP% **108.1**
Speed ratings (Par 98): **90,89,88,86,85 72**
toteswingers:1&2:£6.30, 1&3:£2.40, 2&3:£1.30 CSF £89.65 CT £147.81 TOTE £8.20: £4.90, £3.50; EX 38.70 Trifecta £61.50 Pool: £219.56 - 2.64 winning units..
Owner Jaber Ali Alsabah **Bred** Stratford Place Stud **Trained** Averham Park, Notts

FOCUS
After the defection of the likely favourite this had the look of a tricky handicap, but the favourite was extremely well supported.
Morermaloke Official explanation: jockey said gelding hung right

1188 TOTESPORT.COM "FURTHER FLIGHT" STKS (LISTED RACE) 1m 6f 15y
3:50 (3:51) (Class 1) 4-Y-O+
£17,031 (£6,456; £3,231; £1,611; £807; £405) **Stalls** Low

Form RPR
342- **1** **The Betchworth Kid**[25] 7350 6-9-0 97............................ HayleyTurner 1 104
(Alan King) *hld up: rdn over 3f out: hung lft and r.o ins fnl f: led post* **8/1**
412- **2** shd **Free Agent**[192] 6388 5-9-0 107....................................... RyanMoore 8 104
(Richard Hannon) *hld up in tch: lost pl 9f out: hdwy over 3f out: rdn to ld over 1f out: hdd post* **6/4**[1]
005- **3** 1 ¼ **Askar Tau (FR)**[185] 6607 6-9-0 105..........................(v) GeorgeBaker 2 102
(Marcus Tregoning) *hld up: hdwy 9f out: rdn and ev ch whn hung lft over 1f out: no ex towards fin* **5/1**[3]
065- **4** 1 ¼ **Apprimus (IRE)**[130] 7594 5-9-0 98...................................... AdamKirby 7 100
(Marco Botti) *led after 1f: hdd 10f out: chsd ldr: rdn over 2f out: no ex ins fnl f* **7/1**
004- **5** 5 **Akmal**[172] 6929 5-9-0 108.. TadhgO'Shea 5 93
(John Dunlop) *dwlt: sn chsng ldrs: led 10f out: rdn and hdd over 1f out: wknd ins fnl f* **5/2**[2]
026/ **6** 55 **Peppertree Lane (IRE)**[482] 6306 8-9-0 96.................... JamieSpencer 4 —
(Peter Bowen) *led 1f: chsd ldrs: rdn 4f out: wknd wl over 2f out: t.o* **40/1**
3m 1.91s (-5.39) **Going Correction** -0.125s/f (Firm) **6** Ran SP% **111.3**
Speed ratings (Par 111): **110,109,109,108,105 74**
toteswingers:1&2:£1.70, 1&3:£3.60, 2&3:£2.60 CSF £20.23 TOTE £8.40: £2.30, £2.10; EX 17.60 Trifecta £58.60 Pool: £522.87 - 6.60 winning units..
Owner W H Ponsonby **Bred** R P Williams **Trained** Barbury Castle, Wilts

FOCUS
A strong renewal of this Listed race with three Group winners present.

NOTEBOOK
The Betchworth Kid has found it hard to win lately over hurdles but came here fit from that sphere. He was switched off in the rear in the hope of having a fast pace to run at and he got it courtesy of firstly Apprimus, who took them along early, and then by Akmal, who injected more pace down the back straight. He was a fair way behind rivals and was briefly short of room as the second home tried to pen him in, but he picked up well down the wide outside to land a last-gasp victory. Hayley Turner gets on well with him and he will be aimed at the big Flat handicaps in the summer, off seemingly a guaranteed higher mark for winning this. (tchd 9-1)
Free Agent, second in a Listed race at Ascot when last seen, made a sustained run to the outside of runners 2f from home and responded well for Ryan Moore's urgings to grab the lead from Askar Tau inside the last 1f but was mugged on the line. He remains on an upward curve and will be better with a little ease in the ground. (op 5-4 tchd 13-8)

Askar Tau(FR), whose career high came in the Group 2 Doncaster Cup two seasons ago, travelled powerfully on the heels of the leaders coming into the home straight, looking like the one to be on, but he edged left under pressure inside the final furlong and went down in the dying strides. He often needs his first run massively so this good effort was highly encouraging, and he holds a Yorkshire Cup entry. (op 15-2)
Apprimus(IRE) led early and settled well once headed by the front-running Akmal. He got outpaced once the pace quickened noticeably in the home straight, and he responded moderately, looking like he would appreciate a step up in trip. (op 15-2)
Akmal, highly progressive in 2009 and winner of a Group 2 at Sandown in May last year, was slow away and couldn't get the lead initially before taking it up entering the back straight. He tried to respond for pressure entering the home straight but looked in need of the run. He's a big, strapping individual who seems certain to come on for this, and he'll be more effective over further, with the Yorkshire Cup a possibility. (op 11-4)
Peppertree Lane(IRE) could never land a blow and was out of his depth. (tchd 50-1)

1189 GET LIVE FOOTBALL STATS AT TOTESPORT.COM H'CAP — 1m 2f 50y
4:20 (4:21) (Class 5) (0-70,70) 3-Y-O — **£4,209** (£1,252; £625; £312) **Stalls** Low

Form — RPR
214- **1** **Amistress**[170] 6979 3-8-7 **56** ..... CathyGannon 4 — 66
(Eve Johnson Houghton) *chsd ldrs: led 2f out: sn rdn and hdd: rallied to ld post* **10/1**
33-2 **2** *nse* **Standout**[16] 931 3-9-5 **68** ..... RyanMoore 11 — 78
(Richard Hannon) *hld up: hdwy over 2f out: led over 1f out: sn rdn: hdd post* **11/8**[1]
-323 **3** *3* **Colebrooke**[21] 866 3-9-4 **67** ..... FrankieDettori 7 — 71
(Mark Johnston) *chsd ldr tl led over 2f out: sn rdn and hdd: styd on same pce ins fnl f* **7/1**[2]
654- **4** *1* **Anton Dolin (IRE)**[169] 7004 3-8-11 **60** ..... TedDurcan 2 — 62
(John Dunlop) *hld up in tch: rdn over 2f out: edgd lft and no ex fnl f* **8/1**[3]
0-06 **5** *4 1/2* **Bradbury (IRE)**[44] 638 3-9-1 **64** ..... JamieSpencer 9 — 57
(James Bethell) *hld up: rdn over 2f out: hung lft and styd on ins fnl f: nvr nrr* **16/1**
060- **6** *4* **Royal Reason**[160] 7185 3-9-4 **67** ..... DarryllHolland 3 — 52
(Mick Channon) *chsd ldrs: rdn over 3f out: wknd over 2f out* **10/1**
665- **7** *3/4* **Smart Step**[183] 6647 3-8-9 **65** ..... DarylByrne(7) 6 — 49
(Mark Johnston) *led over 7f: wknd over 1f out* **9/1**
063- **8** *1 1/4* **Cuban Piece (IRE)**[200] 6211 3-9-7 **70** ..... RichardKingscote 5 — 51
(Tom Dascombe) *s.i.s: sn prom: rdn over 3f out: wknd over 2f out* **16/1**
400- **9** *3* **Deep Applause**[170] 6978 3-9-4 **67** ..... TomEaves 8 — 42
(Michael Dods) *s.i.s: hld up: hdwy and nt clr run over 3f out: wknd over 2f out* **14/1**
005- **10** *2 3/4* **Bobby Dazzler (IRE)**[121] 7723 3-8-11 **60** ..... JamesDoyle 1 — 30
(Sylvester Kirk) *hld up: rdn and wknd over 2f out* **40/1**
2m 10.74s (-0.96) **Going Correction** -0.125s/f (Firm) **10 Ran SP% 114.8**
Speed ratings (Par 98): **98,97,95,94,91 87,87,86,83,81**
toteswingers:1&2:£4.00, 1&3:£4.10, 2&3:£2.70 CSF £23.69 CT £106.57 TOTE £11.40: £1.90, £1.10, £1.40; EX 33.30 Trifecta £69.90 Pool: £483.26 - 5.11 winning units..
Owner Mrs P Robeson **Bred** Southcourt Stud **Trained** Blewbury, Oxon
FOCUS
The field was decimated by withdrawals following the faster than anticipated conditions. A low-grade handicap with many potential improvers in the line-up.

1190 BET ON LIVE GOLF AT TOTESPORT.COM H'CAP — 1m 75y
4:50 (4:50) (Class 6) (0-65,65) 4-Y-O+ — **£1,942** (£578; £288; £144) **Stalls** Centre

Form — RPR
5162 **1** **Mr Chocolate Drop (IRE)**[20] 881 7-8-10 **54** ..... (t) JimmyQuinn 6 — 60
(Mandy Rowland) *a.p: chsd ldr over 2f out: styd on u.p to ld post* **11/4**[2]
06-3 **2** *nk* **Border Owl (IRE)**[53] 528 6-9-4 **62** ..... FrankieDettori 13 — 67
(Peter Salmon) *chsd ldrs: led over 2f out: rdn fnl f: hdd post* **2/1**[1]
4500 **3** *1/2* **Jasmin Rai**[22] 854 4-8-7 **51** oh3 ..... CathyGannon 3 — 55
(Des Donovan) *hld up: hdwy over 2f out: rdn over 1f out: edgd lft: r.o* **20/1**
33 **4** *1/2* **Mutamaleq (IRE)**[20] 878 4-9-2 **65** ..... LeeTopliss(5) 2 — 59
(Ian McInnes) *sn led: rdn and hdd over 2f out: no ex fnl f: fin 5th: plcd 4th* **11/2**[3]
300- **5** *hd* **Guga (IRE)** [illegible] ..... (p) SaleemGolam 15 — 50
(John Mackie) *plld hrd and prom: rdn over 3f out: styd on same pce ins fnl f: fin 6th: plcd 5th* **6/1**
001- **6** *12* **Bishopbriggs (USA)**[97] 8023 6-9-2 **60** ..... JamesDoyle 9 — 26
(K F Clutterbuck) *chsd ldr tl rdn over 3f out: wknd over 2f out: fin 7th: plcd 6th* **10/1**
00-0 **7** *3 1/4* **Spacecraft (IRE)**[93] 16 4-8-7 **51** oh6 ..... NeilChalmers 1 — 9
(Christopher Kellett) *s.s: a in rr: rdn and wknd 3f out: fin 8th: plcd 7th* **80/1**
1045 **D** *3 3/4* **Amary (IRE)**[7] 1054 4-9-4 **65** ..... (p) PatrickHills(3) 7 — 60
(John Harris) *hld up: rdn over 2f out: r.o ins fnl f: nrst fin: fin 4th disqualified and plcd last: jockey failed to weigh in* **12/1**
1m 45.21s (-0.39) **Going Correction** -0.125s/f (Firm) **8 Ran SP% 112.5**
Speed ratings (Par 101): **96,95,95,90,90 78,75,91**
toteswingers:1&2:£2.70, 1&3:£7.40, 2&3:£9.40 CSF £8.34 CT £84.80 TOTE £4.50: £2.00, £1.80, £3.30; EX 10.00 Trifecta £58.10 Pool: £415.91 - 5.29 winning units..
Owner Miss M E Rowland **Bred** P J Munnelly **Trained** Lower Blidworth, Notts
■ Stewards' Enquiry : Patrick Hills three-day ban: failed to weigh-in (Apr 20,21,23)
FOCUS
Another field which was weakened by several withdrawals. A wide-open handicap run at a generous pace, and it produced a good finish.

1191 BET ON THE MASTERS AT TOTESPORT.COM H'CAP — 1m 75y
5:20 (5:21) (Class 5) (0-75,74) 3-Y-O — **£2,266** (£674; £337; £168) **Stalls** Centre

Form — RPR
530- **1** **Buzz Law (IRE)**[192] 6386 3-8-13 **66** ..... AndrewElliott 10 — 73
(Mrs K Burke) *prom: racd keenly: led over 1f out: rdn out* **7/4**[1]
000- **2** *1/2* **Pivot Bridge**[168] 7020 3-8-10 **63** ..... MichaelHills 7 — 69
(B W Hills) *chsd ldr tl led over 3f out: rdn and hdd over 1f out: styd on* **2/1**[2]
-250 **3** *2 3/4* **Sir Randolf (IRE)**[16] 931 3-8-11 **64** ..... (t) JamesDoyle 6 — 64
(Sylvester Kirk) *chsd ldrs: rdn and ev ch over 2f out: styd on same pce ins fnl f* **14/1**
135- **4** *2 1/4* **Hawk Moth (IRE)**[162] 7151 3-9-0 **67** ..... CathyGannon 5 — 62
(John Spearing) *hld up: racd keenly: hdwy over 2f out: sn rdn: no ex fnl f* **7/1**
1626 **5** *13* **Aloneinthestreet (USA)**[16] 931 3-9-3 **70** ..... (b) FrankieDettori 4 — 35
(Mark Johnston) *led 5f: wknd over 1f out* **4/1**[3]
1m 47.94s (2.34) **Going Correction** -0.125s/f (Firm) **5 Ran SP% 108.9**
Speed ratings (Par 98): **83,82,79,77,64**
totesuper7: Win: Not won. Place: £435.80 CSF £5.41 TOTE £2.70: £1.10, £1.80; EX 6.10 Trifecta £34.70 Pool: £262.21 - 5.59 winning units..
Owner Mrs Elaine M Burke **Bred** C J Wall **Trained** Middleham Moor, North Yorks
FOCUS
Another race with many non-runners. A field of unexposed horses in handicap company.
Hawk Moth(IRE) Official explanation: jockey said gelding ran keen
T/Jkpt: £7,100.00 to a £1 stake. Pool:£10,000.00 - 1.00 winning ticket T/Plt: £82.30 to a £1 stake. Pool:£60,043.10 - 532.30 winning tickets T/Qpdt: £15.50 to a £1 stake. Pool:£3,834.72 - 182.50 winning tickets CR

1171 KEMPTON (A.W) (R-H)
Thursday, April 7

OFFICIAL GOING: Standard
Wind: Fairly light, across Weather: Dry and warm

1192 KEMPTON.CO.UK MEDIAN AUCTION MAIDEN FILLIES' STKS — 5f (P)
5:55 (5:58) (Class 6) 2-Y-O — **£1,748** (£516; £258) **Stalls** Low

Form — RPR
1 **Majestic Rose** 2-8-9 0 ..... MartinHarley(5) 4 — 75+
(Mick Channon) *chsd ldr: wnt upsides 1/2-way: rdn to ld over 1f out: styd on strly and drew clr fnl 100yds: comf* **9/4**[1]
2 *2 1/4* **Van Go Go** 2-9-0 0 ..... RichardKingscote 5 — 65
(Tom Dascombe) *led: set stdy gallop: shkn up and qcknd wl over 1f out: rdn and hdd over 1f out: outpcd by wnr fnl 100yds* **9/4**[1]
3 *2 1/2* **Xyzzy** 2-9-0 0 ..... RoystonFfrench 2 — 56
(Linda Stubbs) *chsd ldrs: rdn and effrt wl over 1f out: outpcd by ldrs over 1f out: styd on same pce and wl hld fnl f* **13/2**[2]
4 *4* **Sister Guru** 2-9-0 0 ..... DaneO'Neill 1 — 42
(Peter Hedger) *v.s.a: rn green in detached last: clsd and in tch over 3f out: disputing 3rd and rdn wl over 1f out: wknd ent fnl f* **9/1**[3]
62.19 secs (1.69) **Going Correction** -0.025s/f (Stan) **4 Ran SP% 84.9**
Speed ratings (Par 87): **85,81,77,71**
CSF £4.36 TOTE £3.30; EX 5.90.
Owner Jaber Abdullah **Bred** Mike Channon Bloodstock Ltd **Trained** West Ilsley, Berks
■ Stewards' Enquiry : Richard Kingscote one-day ban: failed to ride to draw (Apr 21)
FOCUS
Only four runners after Marygold refused to enter the stalls (5/2, deduct 25p in the £ under R4) and no form to go on, but the two who dominated seemed reasonably well fancied. They seemed to go steady early, and this is very guesy form. The winner should progress.
NOTEBOOK
Majestic Rose is bred to be precocious, being a February foal and a half-sister to three juvenile winners, and all of those were successful on Polytrack. Although being both a bit green and keen through the early stages, she lengthened well when asked in the straight and was much the best. She looks a useful type for the time of year and could win a nice prize. (op 11-4 tchd 3-1)
Van Go Go looked well educated but simply found the winner too good. She showed enough to suggest she should win a similar race, although her dam failed to progress after finishing runner-up on her first two starts. (op 15-8 tchd 13-8)
Xyzzy is bred to be an early type but she was weak in the market and was too green under pressure to get seriously involved. She displayed a quick-ground action but was rather climbing a bit in the closing stages and should have learnt plenty. (op 5-1 tchd 7-1)
Sister Guru, the youngest runner in the line-up, has nice enough breeding (sister to useful 7f winner) and ran better than the beaten margin suggests. She missed the break and lacked both early and end-race speed, but she made a brief effort in the straight and has ability. (op 11-1 tchd 14-1)

1193 FAMILY FUN DAYS AT KEMPTON H'CAP — 5f (P)
6:25 (6:25) (Class 6) (0-65,64) 3-Y-O — **£1,748** (£516; £258) **Stalls** Low

Form — RPR
-421 **1** **Rambo Will**[28] 818 3-9-6 **63** ..... DavidProbert 5 — 68
(J R Jenkins) *broke wl and led for 1f: chsd ldrs after: drvn over 1f out: rallied gamely to go between horses ins fnl f: led last strides* **10/3**[3]
3646 **2** *1/2* **Johnny Hancocks (IRE)**[21] 875 3-9-7 **64** ..... RoystonFfrench 2 — 67
(Linda Stubbs) *sn rdn: led after 1f: drvn and hrd pressed ent fnl f: kpt on wl tl hdd last strides* **7/1**
0-11 **3** *nk* **Dorothy's Dancing (IRE)**[13] 958 3-9-2 **59** ..... FergusSweeney 6 — 61
(Gary Moore) *hld up in tch: effrt to chse ldr over 1f out: rdn and pressed ldr ent fnl f: fnd little u.p and hld fnl 100yds* **7/4**[1]
603- **4** *9* **Brave Tiger (IRE)**[169] 7017 3-8-13 **56** ..... (bt1) NeilCallan 7 — 26
(Hugo Palmer) *sn rdn along: chsd ldr after 1f tl 2f out: wknd u.p over 1f out: wl btn whn swtchd lft ins fnl f* **3/1**[2]
660- **5** *7* **Kingfisher Blue (IRE)**[179] 6769 3-8-11 **57** ..... SophieDoyle(3) 3 — —
(Jamie Osborne) *hmpd s and s.i.s: sn outpcd in last pair: lost tch 1/2-way* **9/1**
410 **6** *1 3/4* **Lois Lane**[35] 745 3-9-4 **61** ..... RichardKingscote 4 — —
(Ron Hodges) *wnt rt s: sn outpcd in last pair: rn wd and lost tch over 3f out: no ch after* **14/1**
60.25 secs (-0.25) **Going Correction** -0.025s/f (Stan) **6 Ran SP% 113.6**
Speed ratings (Par 96): **101,100,99,85,82 71**
toteswingers: 1&2 £4.70, 1&3 £2.40, 2&3 3.80. CSF £26.26 TOTE £3.30: £2.80, £1.20; EX 13.70.
Owner Mr & Mrs T H Bambridge **Bred** T H Bambridge **Trained** Royston, Herts
■ Stewards' Enquiry : Royston Ffrench one-day ban: used whip with excessive frequency (Apr 21)
David Probert one-day ban: used whip with excessive frequency (Apr 21)
FOCUS
A modest sprint handicap run at a good pace and in a fair time for the grade. The winner is rated back to his early-season maiden form.

1194 BISTRO IN THE PANORAMIC CLASSIFIED STKS — 1m 2f (P)
6:55 (6:55) (Class 5) 3-Y-O — **£2,417** (£713; £357) **Stalls** Low

Form — RPR
42-1 **1** **Musawama (IRE)**[12] 992 3-9-0 75 ..... RichardHills 3 — 83+
(John Gosden) *led over 8f out: mde rest: hung lft bnd 2f out: sn rdn: styd on wl ins fnl f* **4/9**[1]
01- **2** *1 1/4* **Swindy**[155] 7302 3-9-0 75 ..... KierenFallon 2 — 80+
(Paul Cole) *led tl over 8f out: chsd wnr: clsd and pressed wnr 3f out: sn hung lft and dropped to last wl over 1f out: rallied to chse wnr again 1f out: r.o but a hld* **3/1**[2]
36-1 **3** *7* **Futurism**[15] 945 3-9-0 74 ..... RichardHughes 1 — 71
(Richard Hannon) *hld up in last: pushed along and clsd on inner 3f out: lft w ev ch and rdn wl over 1f out tl ent fnl f: btn and eased fnl 75yds* **6/1**[3]
2m 6.51s (-1.49) **Going Correction** -0.025s/f (Stan) **3 Ran SP% 108.5**
Speed ratings (Par 98): **104,103,97**
CSF £2.12 TOTE £1.40; EX 2.30.
Owner Hamdan Al Maktoum **Bred** Shadwell Estate Company Limited **Trained** Newmarket, Suffolk

FOCUS
Only three runners, but the first two are decent types. the pace was sound and the form is rated on the positive sound.

1195 RACING UK CLASSIFIED CLAIMING STKS — 1m 2f (P)
7:25 (7:26) (Class 6) 4-Y-O+ — £1,535 (£453; £226) Stalls Low

Form — RPR

-345 **1** **Kentish (USA)**[12] 993 4-9-2 68 .... AdamKirby 1 — 73
(Noel Quinlan) *mde all: set stdy gallop tl rdn and qcknd 3f out: pressed and hrd drvn jst ins fnl f: kpt on* **11/8**[1]

445 **2** ¾ **Slikback Jack (IRE)**[8] 1037 4-9-4 75 .... (p) IanMongan 2 — 74
(David Nicholls) *stdd s: t.k.h: trckd rivals tl wnt 2nd over 2f out: swtchd lft and drvn over 1f out: ev ch jst ins fnl f: nt qckn and a hld after* **13/8**[2]

-245 **3** 7 **Orchard Supreme**[43] 656 8-8-10 67 .... JamieGoldstein 4 — 52
(Ralph Smith) *chsd ldr: rdn whn gallop qcknd over 2f out: sn dropped to last: wknd ent fnl f* **11/4**[3]

2m 13.51s (5.51) **Going Correction** -0.025s/f (Stan) — 3 Ran SP% **106.9**
Speed ratings (Par 101): **76,75,69**
CSF £3.81 TOTE £1.70; EX 3.70.
Owner R P Gallagher **Bred** Juddmonte Farms Inc **Trained** Newmarket, Suffolk

FOCUS
A slowly run claimer and not form to dwell on. The winner probably only had to match his maiden form.

1196 "WATCH RACING UK ON SKY 432" H'CAP — 5f (P)
7:55 (7:55) (Class 5) (0-75,75) 4-Y-O+ — £2,417 (£713; £357) Stalls Low

Form — RPR

1102 **1** **Island Legend (IRE)**[8] 1048 5-9-7 75 .... (p) RichardKingscote 3 — 85
(Milton Bradley) *stmbld s but sn led: pushed clr wl over 1f out: kpt on wl and a in command fnl f* **10/3**[1]

0005 **2** 1 ½ **Fair Passion**[8] 1048 4-9-0 68 .... AdamKirby 4 — 73
(Derek Shaw) *sltly hmpd s: hld up in tch towards rr: hdwy and pushed rt bnd 2f out: r.o to chse wnr jst ins fnl f: r.o but nvr gng to rch wnr* **6/1**[3]

3315 **3** nk **Estonia**[19] 910 4-8-11 65 .... NeilCallan 6 — 69
(Michael Squance) *hld up in midfield: swtchd lft and hdwy ent fnl 2f: chsd ldng pair and hung rt ins fnl f: r.o and pressed for 2nd fnl 75yds* **11/2**[2]

2231 **4** 2 ¾ **Yankee Storm**[12] 985 6-9-1 74 .... (b) RyanClark(5) 11 — 68+
(Tom Keddy) *dwlt: hld up in rr: swtchd lft and gd hdwy u.p jst ins fnl f: r.o wl: nvr able to chal* **15/2**

3214 **5** 1 **Six Wives**[9] 1024 4-9-6 74 .... IanMongan 9 — 64
(David Nicholls) *chsd ldrs: rdn to chse clr wnr over 1f out: no imp and wl hld 1f out: lost 3 pls ins fnl f* **10/1**

3100 **6** hd **Bookiesindex Boy**[15] 946 7-9-6 74 .... (t) StephenCraine 2 — 63
(J R Jenkins) *rrd s and s.i.s: hld up in tch in last trio: effrt but nt clr run over 1f out tl swtchd lft ins fnl f: kpt on cl home: nvr able to chal* **25/1**

0423 **7** ¾ **Incomparable**[8] 1048 6-9-3 74 .... (bt) BillyCray(3) 7 — 61
(David Nicholls) *racd in midfield on outer: hdwy to chse ldrs 1/2-way: rdn and nt qckn over 1f out: wknd fnl f* **7/1**

0650 **8** hd **Grudge**[8] 1048 6-9-1 69 .... (be) HayleyTurner 1 — 55
(Conor Dore) *chsd wnr tl over 1f out: wknd u.p ent fnl f* **22/1**

9 1 ½ **Gala Spirit (IRE)**[224] 5458 4-8-13 67 .... AndreaAtzeni 8 — 47
(Michael Wigham) *stdd s: hld up in tch in last trio: rdn and effrt over 1f out: nvr trbld ldrs* **8/1**

60-0 **10** ¾ **Caldermud (IRE)**[22] 867 4-8-11 70 .... SeanLevey(5) 5 — 48
(Olivia Maylam) *stdd s: t.k.h: hld in tch towards rr: effrt and pushed wd bnd 2f out: n.d after* **50/1**

0-52 **11** ¾ **Freddie's Girl (USA)**[19] 910 4-9-3 71 .... JimCrowley 10 — 46
(Seamus Durack) *chsd ldrs: rdn and struggling over 1f out: btn whn short of room ent fnl f: wknd* **16/1**

60.12 secs (-0.38) **Going Correction** -0.025s/f (Stan) — 11 Ran SP% **113.3**
Speed ratings (Par 103): **102,99,99,94,93 92,91,91,88,87 86**
toteswingers: 1&2 £7.40, 1&3 £3.20, 2&3 £6.20. CSF £21.32 CT £105.16 TOTE £2.80: £1.02, £4.10, £2.50; EX 34.80.
Owner J M Bradley **Bred** Jerome Casey **Trained** Sedbury, Gloucs

FOCUS
This looked a good contest for the class, but the story of the race was Island Legend being allowed a soft lead, and Richard Kingscote shrewdly saved plenty for the finish. the runner-up built on her better recent effort.

1197 BRITISH BIG BAND 22.06.11 H'CAP — 6f (P)
8:25 (8:25) (Class 4) (0-85,85) 4-Y-O+ — £3,691 (£1,098; £548; £274) Stalls Low

Form — RPR

1321 **1** **Best Trip (IRE)**[15] 946 4-8-12 76 .... FrannyNorton 8 — 86
(Richard Guest) *taken down early: broke v fast: mde all and crossed to rail: rdn and clr 2f out: drvn ent fnl f: a holding on* **13/2**[3]

052- **2** 1 **Shifting Star (IRE)**[156] 7289 6-9-6 84 .... AdamKirby 4 — 91
(Walter Swinburn) *chsd ldrs: rdn to chse clr wnr over 1f out: sn drvn: kpt on ins fnl f but nvr gng to chal wnr* **13/2**[3]

-314 **3** nse **Clear Praise (USA)**[43] 651 4-9-3 81 .... NeilCallan 7 — 88+
(Simon Dow) *stdd s: hld up in rr: effrt and nt clr run over 2f out: swtchd lft and hdwy ent fnl 2f: r.o wl u.p fnl f: nvr gng to rch wnr* **9/4**[1]

304- **4** 3 ¼ **We Have A Dream**[156] 7289 6-9-7 85 .... MartinDwyer 2 — 81
(William Muir) *chsd ldrs: rdn 3f out: outpcd u.p over 2f out: styd on again u.p ins fnl f but no ch w ldrs* **5/1**[2]

60-4 **5** ½ **Mac Gille Eoin**[12] 986 7-9-7 85 .... JimCrowley 3 — 80
(John Gallagher) *hld up in last trio: effrt on inner ent fnl 2f: kpt on fnl f: nvr trbld ldrs* **8/1**

540/ **6** nk **Quaroma**[698] 1880 6-9-4 82 .... DaneO'Neill 9 — 76
(Peter Hedger) *stdd and dropped in bhd after s: stl last and shkn up wl over 1f out: kpt on ins fnl f: nvr trbld ldrs* **40/1**

304- **7** nk **Baldemar**[179] 6776 6-9-5 83 .... TonyHamilton 6 — 76
(Richard Fahey) *in tch: effrt and hung rt whn rdn over 2f out: no real prog: nvr trbld ldrs* **5/1**[2]

6120 **8** ½ **Punching**[13] 961 7-8-13 77 .... KirstyMilczarek 1 — 68
(Conor Dore) *chsd wnr: rdn and outpcd by wnr 2f out: lost 2nd over 1f out: wknd fnl f* **20/1**

1160 **9** hd **Elhamri**[7] 1067 7-8-12 76 .... HayleyTurner 5 — 66
(Conor Dore) *hld up in midfield: effrt and looking to switch lft over 2f out: no hdwy: wl btn ent fnl f* **25/1**

1m 11.55s (-1.55) **Going Correction** -0.025s/f (Stan) — 9 Ran SP% **112.9**
Speed ratings (Par 105): **109,107,107,103,102 102,101,101,100**
toteswingers: 1&2 £7.60, 1&3 £1.90, 2&3 £5.00. CSF £45.73 CT £123.80 TOTE £11.00: £2.40, £2.40, £1.10; EX 48.20.
Owner P J Duffen & P Brown **Bred** Limetree Stud **Trained** Stainforth, S Yorks

FOCUS
A fair sprint handicap, but Best Trip was allowed an uncontested lead and was was one of five consecutive winners from the front. The form is rated through the second.

1198 PEPPA PIG AT KEMPTON 02.05.11 H'CAP (LONDON MILE QUALIFIER) — 1m (P)
8:55 (8:55) (Class 5) (0-75,75) 4-Y-O+ — £2,417 (£713; £357) Stalls Low

Form — RPR

323- **1** **Willow Dancer (IRE)**[157] 7274 7-9-7 75 .... (p) AdamKirby 4 — 81
(Walter Swinburn) *mde all: rdn and qcknd 2f out: clr and edgd lft u.p over 1f out: styd on wl* **4/1**[2]

4-42 **2** 1 **Sunshine Always (IRE)**[15] 949 5-8-13 72 .... JemmaMarshall(5) 7 — 76
(Michael Attwater) *chsd ldrs: rdn and effrt wl over 1f out: chsd clr wnr ent fnl f: kpt on* **5/2**[1]

-500 **3** ¾ **Hereford Boy**[15] 949 7-9-4 72 .... RobertHavlin 1 — 74
(Dean Ivory) *stdd after s: hld up in rr: effrt and nt clr run 2f out: sn swtchd rt and hdwy on inner over 1f out: wnt 3rd ins fnl f: r.o: nt rch wnr* **20/1**

3055 **4** 1 **Ilie Nastase (FR)**[16] 938 7-8-12 66 .... HayleyTurner 3 — 66
(Conor Dore) *chsd ldng pair: rdn to chse clr wnr jst over 2f out tl ent fnl f: styd on same pce u.p fnl f* **8/1**[3]

500- **5** 1 ¼ **Cool Hand Jake**[182] 6701 5-9-6 74 .... FergusSweeney 2 — 71
(Peter Makin) *stdd s: hld up in tch: rdn and effrt towards inner 2f out: drvn and styd on same pce fnl f* **12/1**

052- **6** 3 ¾ **Striding Edge (IRE)**[164] 7111 5-9-0 68 .... JamesDoyle 5 — 56
(Hans Adielsson) *stdd after s: t.k.h: hld up in tch towards rr: rdn and effrt 2f out: drvn and btn ent fnl f: wknd* **5/2**[1]

-060 **7** 6 **Global Village (IRE)**[42] 666 6-9-0 68 .... SteveDrowne 6 — 43
(Michael Blake) *chsd wnr tl jst over 2f out: sn struggling u.p: wl bhd fnl f* **14/1**

061/ **8** 7 **Spice Run**[507] 7411 8-8-13 67 .... MickyFenton 8 — 26
(Stef Higgins) *s.i.s: sn rcvrd and in tch on outer: wknd qckly over 2f out: sn bhd* **16/1**

1m 39.77s (-0.03) **Going Correction** -0.025s/f (Stan) — 8 Ran SP% **113.3**
Speed ratings (Par 103): **99,98,97,96,95 91,85,78**
toteswingers: 1&2 £2.90, 1&3 £21.10, 2&3 £11.10. CSF £14.14 CT £174.79 TOTE £2.90: £1.02, £2.10, £8.30; EX 15.20.
Owner Mrs G Godfrey & Mrs A Horner **Bred** Exors Of The Late R E Sangster **Trained** Aldbury, Herts

FOCUS
A modest handicap in which Willow Dancer became the fifth winner to make just about all of the running on this seven-race card. Probably not form to be too positive about.
T/Plt: £49.50 to a £1 stake. Pool:£50,118.97 - 739.04 winning tickets. T/Qpdt: £7.10 to a £1 stake. Pool:£5,255.71 - 541.64 winning tickets. SP

RIPON (R-H)
Thursday, April 7

OFFICIAL GOING: Good (8.5)
Wind: Fresh, half behind Weather: Cloudy, fine

1199 E B F EAT SLEEP & DRINK AT NAGS HEAD PICKHILL MAIDEN STKS — 5f
2:10 (2:11) (Class 5) 2-Y-O — £3,561 (£1,059; £529; £264) Stalls High

Form — RPR

1 **Queens Revenge** 2-8-12 0 .... DavidAllan 4 — 82+
(Tim Easterby) *missed break: bhd: hdwy 1/2-way: rdn to ld ins fnl f: kpt on wl* **11/2**[3]

2 hd **Alejandro (IRE)** 2-9-3 0 .... PaulHanagan 3 — 85+
(Richard Fahey) *cl up gng wl: led 1/2-way: rdn and hdd ins fnl f: kpt on fin* **11/2**[3]

3 4 ½ **Almond Branches** 2-8-12 0 .... PJMcDonald 1 — 64+
(George Moore) *cl up on outside: ev ch 1/2-way to over 1f out: outpcd ins fnl f* **9/2**[2]

4 4 **Princess Banu** 2-8-12 0 .... EddieCreighton 6 — 50
(Mick Channon) *trckd ldrs: drvn along after 2f: edgd rt over 1f out: btn ins fnl f* **6/1**

5 2 ½ **Kodiac King (IRE)** 2-9-3 0 .... PhillipMakin 8 — 46+
(Kevin Ryan) *t.k.h: hld up in tch: rdn and hung rt 2f out: sn wknd* **7/2**[1]

6 nk **Topcoat (IRE)** 2-9-3 0 .... SilvestreDeSousa 2 — 45
(Mark Johnston) *in tch: effrt on outside 1/2-way: wknd wl over 1f out* **6/1**

7 4 **Red Shadow** 2-8-12 0 .... PaulMulrennan 5 — 25
(Alan Brown) *led to 1/2-way: rdn and wknd wl over 1f out* **25/1**

8 26 **No Legs (IRE)** 2-8-12 0 .... CathyGannon 7 — —
(David Evans) *dwlt: bhd: lost tch after 2f: t.o* **10/1**

60.15 secs (-0.55) **Going Correction** -0.125s/f (Firm) — 8 Ran SP% **112.7**
Speed ratings (Par 92): **99,98,91,85,81 80,74,32**
toteswingers:1&2:£4.10, 1&3:£7.10, 2&3:£4.20 CSF £34.53 TOTE £9.90: £2.30, £1.40, £1.60; EX 31.20 TRIFECTA Not won..
Owner W H Ponsonby **Bred** Mickley Stud & C J Whiston **Trained** Great Habton, N Yorks

FOCUS
A traditionally strong early-season maiden. The time was decent and the winner quite imperssive, in a race rated at the better edge of the averages.

NOTEBOOK
Queens Revenge, woolly in her coat and the second oldest in the line-up, was slowly away crossing on to the rail behind the field. She loomed up travelling well at the furlong marker, but didn't head the winner until the last 100yds, appearing to idle for a few strides in front. She held on well enough in the end, though, and can be considered much the best in this field. A half-sister to three 2-y-o winners out of a mare who also won at two, she is very likely to stay 6f and can be considered an exciting prospect. She is a first winner for freshman sire Multiplex and it will be interesting to see if she follows the same path as the stable's winner last year, who reappeared in a novice contest at the Dante meeting. (tchd 5-1)
Alejandro(IRE), an April foal from the first crop of Dark Angel, was much more professional than the winner as he was quickly away, bagged the rail, and had most of the field beaten off with 2f to run. He kept on gamely to the line, displaying a likeable attitude, and will be a short-price favourite to go one better next time. (op 13-2)
Almond Branches was disadvantaged by having to race well off the rail. From the first crop of Dutch Art, she was the oldest in the field but didn't show the same professionalism as the runner-up. Her dam only won a seller as a 2-y-o, but she could be up to winning a small maiden. (op 5-1)
Princess Banu cost 33,000gns as a yearling and is out of a 5f winner at two. She ran with credit despite being green, but is a small first foal and would want to be doing her winning soon. (op 11-2)
Kodiac King(IRE) was awkward out of the gates and looked as if this outing would bring him on mentally. (tchd 9-2)
Topcoat(IRE) showed early speed before fading and will need further in time. (op 15-2 tchd 11-2)

Red Shadow is very small and will need to be found a very easy 5f.

1200 SIS LIVE H'CAP (DIV I) — 6f
2:45 (2:45) (Class 4) (0-85,85) 4-Y-0+ **£4,209** (£1,252; £625; £312) **Stalls** High

Form RPR

5-54 **1** **Cape Vale (IRE)**[65] 376 6-9-6 **84** ... AdrianNicholls 2 93
(David Nicholls) *sn crossed over to stands' rail: mde all: rdn and drifted rt over 2f out: kpt on strly fnl f* **8/1**

600- **2** 1 1/4 **Discanti (IRE)**[181] 6723 6-9-6 **84** ... (t) DavidAllan 8 89
(Tim Easterby) *trckd wnr: effrt and rdn 2f out: kpt on ins fnl f* **5/1**[2]

3223 **3** 2 3/4 **Sir Geoffrey (IRE)**[13] 970 5-9-4 **85** ... (p) BillyCray(3) 10 81
(David Nicholls) *trckd ldrs: drvn over 2f out: kpt on same pce fnl f* **8/1**

04-3 **4** 1 1/4 **Marvellous Value (IRE)**[58] 455 6-9-1 **79** ... FrederikTylicki 12 71+
(Michael Dods) *hld up: hmpd over 3f out: effrt and edgd rt over 1f out: styd on fnl f: nrst fin* **10/3**[1]

055- **5** 3/4 **Ventura Cove (IRE)**[226] 5390 4-8-10 **74** ... PaulHanagan 3 64
(Richard Fahey) *prom: rdn and outpcd over 2f out: kpt on fnl f: nrst fin* **8/1**

/00- **6** 1 1/2 **Jobe (USA)**[327] 2134 5-9-4 **82** ... PhillipMakin 4 67
(Kevin Ryan) *taken early to post: dwlt: sn swtchd rt and racd wd in midfield: outpcd over 2f out: r.o fnl f* **14/1**

060- **7** 1/2 **River Falcon**[152] 7352 11-8-10 **74** ... PaulMulrennan 13 57
(Jim Goldie) *hld up: pushed along over 3f out: sme hdwy over 1f out: nvr able to chal* **22/1**

316- **8** nse **Feel The Heat**[292] 3215 4-9-0 **78** ... TomEaves 11 61
(Bryan Smart) *tubed: dwlt: sn pushed along towards rr: edgd rt over 3f out: rdn and no imp fnl 2f* **7/1**[3]

6006 **9** 3 1/2 **Divertimenti (IRE)**[8] 1048 7-9-2 **80** ... (b) JimmyQuinn 7 52
(Roy Bowring) *cl up tl rdn and wknd over 1f out* **25/1**

-125 **10** 5 **Catherines Call (IRE)**[14] 956 4-8-12 **76** ... DarryllHolland 1 32
(Des Donovan) *dwlt: sn in tch on outside: edgd rt and wknd fr 2f out* **7/1**[3]

000- **11** 9 **Niran (IRE)**[133] 7566 4-8-13 **77** ... PJMcDonald 5 4
(Ruth Carr) *s.i.s: sn pushed along in rr: struggling fr 1/2-way* **33/1**

1m 11.45s (-1.55) **Going Correction** -0.125s/f (Firm) **11** Ran SP% **115.9**
Speed ratings (Par 105): **105,103,99,98,97 95,94,94,89,82 70**
toteswingers:1&2:£8.40, 1&3:£7.80, 2&3:£6.70 CSF £45.94 CT £338.87 TOTE £12.50: £3.20, £1.50, £2.80; EX 50.40 Trifecta £142.80 Pool: £368.63 - 1.91 winning units..
Owner Lady O'Reilly **Bred** Derek Veitch **Trained** Sessay, N Yorks

FOCUS
It paid to be handy in this competitive 71-85 handicap. The time was 0.77sec faster than division II and the winner's rated back to his best.

1201 RIPON SILVER BOWL CONDITIONS STKS — 1m 1f 170y
3:20 (3:21) (Class 3) 4-Y-0+ **£6,623** (£1,982; £991; £495; £246) **Stalls** Low

Form RPR

150- **1** **St Moritz (IRE)**[194] 6349 5-9-0 102 ... AdrianNicholls 2 108
(David Nicholls) *set stdy pce: mde all: rdn and hrd pressed fr over 2f out: edgd lft and hld on gamely fnl f* **13/2**[3]

322- **2** 3/4 **Kings Gambit (SAF)**[181] 6720 7-9-5 110 ... JamieSpencer 5 111
(Tom Tate) *trckd wnr: rdn and ev ch fr over 2f out: edgd rt over 1f out: kpt on fnl f: jst hld* **8/11**[1]

653- **3** 4 **Monitor Closely (IRE)**[193] 6389 5-9-0 110 ... GeorgeBaker 1 98
(Michael Bell) *t.k.h: trckd ldrs: effrt and swtchd lft over 2f out: edgd rt and outpcd over 1f out* **9/4**[2]

0-00 **4** 11 **Silver Grey (IRE)**[12] 991 4-8-9 100 ... (p) MartinLane 4 70
(Roger Ingram) *hld up in tch: drvn and outpcd 4f out: n.d after* **28/1**

10-0 **5** 7 **West End Lad**[52] 541 8-9-0 80 ... (b) JimmyQuinn 3 60
(Roy Bowring) *prom tl rdn and wknd fr 3f out* **100/1**

2m 2.16s (-3.24) **Going Correction** -0.075s/f (Good) **5** Ran SP% **106.4**
Speed ratings (Par 107): **109,108,105,96,90**
CSF £11.12 TOTE £5.50: £1.20, £1.10; EX 12.30.
Owner Billy Hughes **Bred** Newsells Park Stud **Trained** Sessay, N Yorks

FOCUS
The feature conditions race turned up somewhat of a surprise. Slightly muddling form, rated around the winner to the best view of his Bunbury Cup form.

NOTEBOOK
St Moritz(IRE), bought for 105,000gns by David Nicholls at the Horses In Training Sale at the end of last turf season, repaid a small fraction of that outlay, making all for a game success. Winner of last season's Bunbury Cup when trained by Mark Johnston, he had stamina to prove stepping up to 1m2f (hadn't raced beyond 1m in Britain) but seemed to actually improve for the extra distance. He had 3lb to find with the penalised runner-up at the weights and has now shown he is up to contesting Listed/Group 3 races with the summit of his stamina not yet known. He wasn't stopping at the line. (tchd 6-1 and 15-2)
Kings Gambit(SAF), placed on his last five starts without winning, was given every chance having tracked the pace throughout. Winner of this race last year, he failed to show the same tenacity as the winner in the finish and probably needs to get his own way in front to be seen at his best. He's well up to winning races of this nature, if not slight better, but is unlikely to be improving as a 7-y-o. (op 4-5 tchd 4-6)
Monitor Closely(IRE) loomed up going equally as well as the front pair with over 1f to run, but didn't see his race out. His injury problems are well documented and if kept sound this time around, he can nick a small Group race with this race certain to have brought him on a good deal. (tchd 5-2)
Silver Grey(IRE) was injured on her travels at Woodbine at the end of her 3-y-o season and has yet to convince in three runs now as a 4-y-o. (op 22-1)

1202 RIPON "COCK O' NORTH" H'CAP — 1m
3:55 (3:55) (Class 3) (0-95,92) 3-Y-0 **£6,623** (£1,982; £991; £495; £246) **Stalls** Low

Form RPR

321- **1** **Polar Kite (IRE)**[272] 3874 3-8-10 **81** ... PaulHanagan 5 92
(Richard Fahey) *trckd ldrs: rdn and edgd rt over 1f out: hdwy to ld ins fnl f: kpt on wl* **9/2**[3]

1- **2** 1 **Eternal Ruler (IRE)**[167] 7049 3-8-4 **75** ... PJMcDonald 8 84+
(Alan Swinbank) *dwlt: hld up: hdwy on ins whn nt clr run over 2f out: swtchd lft and carried hd high fr over 1f out: kpt on wl to take 2nd nr fin* **4/1**[2]

213- **3** 3/4 **Nawaashi**[173] 6920 3-8-5 **76** ... TadhgO'Shea 3 83
(Mark Johnston) *cl up: led over 3f out: rdn and hdd ins fnl f: kpt on same pce* **10/1**

012- **4** 7 **Mariachi Man**[167] 7059 3-9-5 **90** ... DavidAllan 4 81
(Tim Easterby) *t.k.h: trckd ldrs: rdn and carried hd high over 2f out: edgd rt and wknd over 1f out* **3/1**[1]

1110 **5** 3/4 **Fred Willetts (IRE)**[26] 845 3-8-9 **87** ... MatthewCosham(7) 1 76
(David Evans) *hld up: rdn along over 3f out: no imp fr 2f out* **12/1**

00-3 **6** 5 **Malthouse (GER)**[14] 1010 3-9-2 **87** ... FrankieDettori 7 65
(Mark Johnston) *in tch on outside: outpcd over 4f out: rallied over 2f out: wknd wl over 1f out* **4/1**[2]

125- **7** 1/2 **Piceno (IRE)**[111] 7916 3-8-7 **78** ... AdrianNicholls 9 55
(David Nicholls) *led to over 3f out: wknd over 1f out* **10/1**

-245 **8** 6 **Il Battista**[57] 468 3-8-3 **74** ... AndrewMullen 6 37
(Alan McCabe) *hld up: struggling 3f out: nvr on terms* **25/1**

1m 40.21s (-1.19) **Going Correction** -0.075s/f (Good) **8** Ran SP% **112.9**
Speed ratings (Par 102): **102,101,100,93,92 87,87,81**
toteswingers:1&2:£3.40, 1&3:£5.70, 2&3:£5.80 CSF £22.22 CT £168.92 TOTE £4.40: £2.10, £1.80, £3.20; EX 18.70 Trifecta £105.90 Pool: £695.99 - 4.86 winning units..
Owner Mr And Mrs J D Cotton **Bred** Holborn Trust Co **Trained** Musley Bank, N Yorks

FOCUS
An open 0-95 3-y-o handicap. With top-weight Nasharra a non-runner, the race was 5lb below the ceiling, but a fairly positive view has been taken of the form with the winner up 10lb.

NOTEBOOK
Polar Kite(IRE) showed some smart form as a 2-y-o, including when winning a maiden on his third and final outing, and appeared to start his 3-y-o career on a realistic mark. Prominent throughout, he showed a good attitude to battle past the front-running Nawaashi and looks the type of strapping gelding who is up to winning races off a higher mark. He is likely to bid to follow up in the valuable Totesport Silver Bowl at Haydock next month. (op 4-1 tchd 7-2)
Eternal Ruler(IRE), a winner of a 1m maiden at Ayr on his sole start as a 2-y-o, came home like a train to get up for second having been outpaced with 3f to run. He looks to have started handicaps on a fair mark and has a bright future, with the likelihood that he'll stay further as he matures. (op 6-1)
Nawaashi chased home subsequent Princess Margaret winner Soraaya on her racecourse debut before winning her maiden next time out. She ended her 2-y-o season when a beaten favourite in a Catterick nursery and appeared to have started her 3-y-o career on a fair mark. She only gave best inside the last furlong and can find a similar race soon. Like most from the Mark Johnston stable, she promises to be a better 3-y-o. (op 8-1)
Mariachi Man was seven lengths back in fourth, but this was a hot race and he is likely to be up to winning off this sort of mark when finding more juice in the ground. (op 7-2 tchd 4-1)
Malthouse(GER) failed to pick up once pulled to the outside. He didn't go on after winning an Ascot maiden on debut last year and despite running a fair race on the AW at Deauville last month, hasn't started off his 3-y-o career in auspicious fashion. (op 7-2)

1203 BET TOTEPOOL TO SUPPORT YOUR SPORT MAIDEN STKS — 1m
4:30 (4:40) (Class 5) 3-Y-O **£2,590** (£770; £385; £192) **Stalls** Low

Form RPR

222 **1** **Crown Counsel (IRE)**[13] 980 3-9-3 82 ... FrankieDettori 10 82+
(Mark Johnston) *cl up: led over 2f out: edgd rt over 1f out: kpt on strly fnl f* **5/2**[1]

06- **2** 1 1/4 **Muhandis (IRE)**[210] 5892 3-9-3 0 ... TadhgO'Shea 4 79
(Ed Dunlop) *reluctant to enter stalls: dwlt: sn midfield: hdwy to chse wnr over 1f out: edgd rt: kpt on fnl f: nt pce to chal* **16/1**

3 2 1/4 **Agiaal (USA)** 3-9-3 0 ... WilliamBuick 9 74+
(John Gosden) *midfield: pushed along and rn green over 2f out: hdwy over 1f out: shkn up and styd on wl fnl f: bttr for r* **3/1**[2]

232- **4** nk **King Of The Celts (IRE)**[204] 6070 3-9-3 76 ... DavidAllan 5 73
(Tim Easterby) *led to over 2f out: sn rdn: kpt on same pce fnl f* **6/1**

20- **5** 1/2 **Calaf**[167] 7058 3-9-3 0 ... PaulHanagan 6 72
(Jane Chapple-Hyam) *t.k.h: trckd ldrs: rdn over 2f out: kpt on same pce appr fnl f* **12/1**

242- **6** 4 **Yojimbo (IRE)**[176] 6849 3-9-3 79 ... SamHitchcott 12 63
(Mick Channon) *prom: effrt over 2f out: wknd fnl f* **5/1**[3]

4- **7** 1 1/2 **Pintrada**[250] 4568 3-9-3 0 ... DarryllHolland 16 59
(James Bethell) *midfield on outside: pushed along and green fr 3f out: edgd rt and outpcd 2f out* **12/1**

046- **8** 2 3/4 **Benidorm**[162] 7178 3-9-3 63 ... AndrewMullen 2 53
(Alan McCabe) *in tch: effrt over 2f out: wknd over 1f out* **100/1**

464- **9** 6 **Tarantella Lady**[200] 6222 3-8-12 72 ... TomEaves 7 34
(George Moore) *loose bef s: in tch: drvn and outpcd over 3f out: n.d after* **28/1**

10 3 1/2 **Azurinta (IRE)** 3-8-12 0 ... JamieSpencer 8 26
(Michael Bell) *dwlt: hld up towards rr: pushed along 3f out: nvr able to chal* **28/1**

11 1 **Camporosso** 3-9-3 0 ... SilvestreDeSousa 3 29
(Mark Johnston) *dwlt: bhd: shortlived effrt on outside over 3f out: sn btn* **18/1**

0- **12** hd **Short Takes (USA)**[188] 6532 3-9-3 0 ... SaleemGolam 11 28
(John Gosden) *bhd: drvn along 1/2-way: sn no imp* **40/1**

00- **13** 1 3/4 **Mint Imperial (IRE)**[145] 7452 3-9-3 0 ... GeorgeBaker 13 24
(Amy Weaver) *hld up: rdn along 1/2-way: nvr able to chal* **150/1**

14 1 1/4 **Joe Rocco (IRE)** 3-9-3 0 ... PJMcDonald 1 21
(Alan Swinbank) *hld up on ins: rdn over 4f out: sn struggling* **50/1**

060- **15** 1 1/2 **Go**[171] 6988 3-9-3 60 ... FrederikTylicki 15 18
(Micky Hammond) *towards rr: struggling over 3f out: sn btn* **100/1**

00- **16** 8 **Bollin Harry**[162] 7179 3-9-3 0 ... DuranFentiman 14 —
(Tim Easterby) *prom tl rdn and wknd qckly over 2f out* **100/1**

1m 41.42s (0.02) **Going Correction** -0.075s/f (Good) **16** Ran SP% **126.0**
Speed ratings (Par 98): **96,94,92,92,91 87,86,83,77,73 72,72,71,69,68 60**
toteswingers:1&2:£11.40, 1&3:£4.30, 2&3:£15.70 CSF £45.80 TOTE £3.70: £1.50, £6.20, £1.20; EX 58.80 TRIFECTA Pool: £801.45 - 1.79 winning units..
Owner Sheikh Hamdan Bin Mohammed Al Maktoum **Bred** Gerrardstown House Stud **Trained** Middleham Moor, N Yorks

FOCUS
Nothing had set too high a standard in this big-field maiden, therefore it was a wide-open affair. Tarantella Lady got loose and played up behind the stalls once caught, which caused a lengthy delay to the start. Pretty straightforward maiden form. the winner has improved with each run.

1204 ATTHERACES.COM APPRENTICE H'CAP — 5f
5:00 (5:04) (Class 5) (0-70,70) 4-Y-0+ **£2,331** (£693; £346; £173) **Stalls** High

Form RPR

5051 **1** **Lucky Art (USA)**[16] 941 5-8-7 **58** ... ShaneBKelly(3) 4 65
(Ruth Carr) *mde all: hrd pressed fnl f: kpt on wl: jst lasted* **13/2**[3]

3000 **2** shd **Fashion Icon (USA)**[8] 1034 5-8-7 **60** ... (b) LauraBarry(5) 6 67
(David O'Meara) *trckd ldrs: effrt and swtchd lft appr fnl f: kpt on wl: jst hld* **12/1**

320- **3** 3/4 **Choc'A'Moca (IRE)**[155] 7300 4-7-13 **57** ... (v) MichaelKenny(10) 9 61
(Declan Carroll) *midfield: sn pushed along: hdwy fnl f: kpt on wl* **13/2**[3]

-500 **4** hd **Boy The Bell**[66] 363 4-8-5 **56** oh2 ... NatashaEaton(3) 5 59+
(Brian Ellison) *midfield: hdwy and edgd rt over 1f out: kpt on wl fnl f: nrst fin* **11/2**[1]

522- **5** 3/4 **Sandwith**[162] 7169 8-9-2 **64** ... (v) JulieBurke 3 65
(George Foster) *cl up: effrt and ev ch ent fnl f: no ex last 50yds* **7/1**

644- **6** nk **Angelo Poliziano**[126] 7668 5-9-7 **69** ... (p) RosieJessop 11 69
(Ann Duffield) *hld up in tch: effrt over 1f out: kpt on steadily fnl f* **8/1**

006- **7** nk **Baybshambles (IRE)**[220] 5601 7-8-10 **58** ... JamesRogers 12 56+
(Ron Barr) *bhd and outpcd: hdwy and drifted rt fnl f: nrst fin* **7/1**

000- **8** *1 ¼* **Sea Crest**[164] [7132] 5-8-5 **56** oh9 JohnCavanagh(3) 7 50
(Mel Brittain) *s.i.s: bhd: effrt and edgd rt 2f out: no imp fnl f* **25/1**
440- **9** *1 ½* **Nomoreblondes**[260] [4243] 7-9-2 **69** (p) DavidSimmonson(5) 10 58
(Paul Midgley) *prom: outpcd 1/2-way: no imp fr over 1f out* **18/1**
000- **10** *3 ¼* **Pearly Wey**[174] [6903] 8-8-12 **60** GarryWhillans 2 37
(Ian McInnes) *towards rr on outside: drvn along 1/2-way: btn over 1f out* **20/1**
14 **11** *4 ½* **Steelcut**[21] [880] 7-9-5 **70** (p) MatthewCosham(3) 1 31
(David Evans) *trckd ldrs tl rdn and wknd over 1f out* **6/1**[2]
605- **12** *11* **Ya Boy Sir (IRE)**[167] [7052] 4-8-10 **58** LMcNiff 8 —
(Noel Wilson) *slowly away: bhd: nt clr run 1/2-way: sn rdn and btn* **33/1**

59.68 secs (-1.02) **Going Correction** -0.125s/f (Firm) **12** Ran SP% **117.0**
Speed ratings (Par 103): **103,102,101,101,100 99,99,97,94,89 82,64**
toteswingers:1&2:£26.40, 1&3:£10.80, 2&3:£21.10 CSF £78.74 CT £536.73 TOTE £8.80: £2.50, £5.60, £2.60; EX 89.60 TRIFECTA Part won. Pool: £531.13 - 0.10 winning units..
Owner David W Chapman **Bred** Gaines-Gentry Thoroughbreds **Trained** Huby, N Yorks
■ Stewards' Enquiry : Rosie Jessop one-day ban: used whip without giving gelding time to respond (Apr 21)

FOCUS
A wide-open apprentice handicap over 5f which resulted in a very tight finish. Not many got involved. The winner is rated back to last summer's form.

1205 SIS LIVE H'CAP (DIV II) 6f
5:30 (5:30) (Class 4) (0-85,85) 4-Y-0+ **£4,209** (£1,252; £625; £312) **Stalls** High

Form RPR
040- **1** **Lucky Numbers (IRE)**[194] [6364] 5-9-7 **85** JamieSpencer 7 94
(Paul Green) *hld up in tch on outside: hdwy over 1f out: drvn to ld wl ins fnl f: kpt on wl* **7/1**
000- **2** *½* **Medici Time**[171] [6981] 6-9-2 **80** (v) GrahamGibbons 1 87
(Tim Easterby) *cl up: rdn and led over 1f out: hdd wl ins fnl f: r.o* **11/1**
600- **3** *¾* **Invincible Lad (IRE)**[180] [6739] 7-8-12 **79** MichaelO'Connell(3) 8 84
(David Nicholls) *trckd ldrs: hdwy and ev ch over 1f out to ins fnl f: kpt on: hld towards fin* **12/1**
00-0 **4** *¾* **Coolminx (IRE)**[36] [736] 4-9-1 **84** LeeTopliss(5) 10 86+
(Richard Fahey) *in tch: n.m.r and lost pl over 4f out: hdwy wl over 1f out: edgd rt and kpt on fnl f* **5/1**[1]
521- **5** *nse* **Grissom (IRE)**[162] [7169] 5-9-0 **78** DuranFentiman 12 80+
(Tim Easterby) *hld up in midfield: nt clr run over 2f out: rallied fnl f: nrst fin* **13/2**[3]
0-01 **6** *1 ½* **Sir Nod**[21] [880] 9-8-10 **74** PaulHanagan 4 71
(Julie Camacho) *led tl rdn and hdd over 1f out: kpt on same pce* **11/2**[2]
310- **7** *1 ¼* **Illustrious Prince (IRE)**[178] [6798] 4-8-12 **81** NeilFarley(5) 11 74
(Declan Carroll) *dwlt: bhd and sn pushed along: edgd rt and hdwy over 1f out: nvr able to chal* **8/1**
520- **8** *½* **Di Stefano**[154] [7320] 4-8-11 **75** AdrianNicholls 5 67
(David Nicholls) *in tch: rdn along 1/2-way: no imp fr over 1f out* **8/1**
50U- **9** *2 ¾* **Red Cape (FR)**[210] [5884] 8-9-1 **82** JamesSullivan(3) 6 65
(Ruth Carr) *cl up tl rdn and wknd over 1f out* **16/1**
646- **10** *5* **Commanche Raider (IRE)**[259] [4288] 4-8-13 **77** FrederikTylicki 9 44
(Michael Dods) *dwlt: hld up: rdn over 2f out: btn over 1f out* **14/1**
000- **11** *8* **Floor Show**[181] [6723] 5-8-8 **72** LeeNewman 3 13
(Noel Wilson) *dwlt: sn prom: drvn and wknd 2f out: eased whn btn fnl f* **14/1**

1m 12.22s (-0.78) **Going Correction** -0.125s/f (Firm) **11** Ran SP% **115.3**
Speed ratings (Par 105): **100,99,98,97,97 95,93,92,89,82 71**
CSF £79.90 CT £923.08 TOTE £6.20: £3.00, £5.10, £4.00; EX 74.60 Trifecta £165.00 Part won. Pool: £223.00 - 0.50 winning units..
Owner Men Behaving Badly Two **Bred** Rory O'Brien **Trained** Lydiate, Merseyside
■ Stewards' Enquiry : Neil Farley Fine: £140, breach of Rule (D)49, failed to report at scales.

FOCUS
The second division of the 6f handicap looked equally as competitive as the first, but was a little slower. Similar sort of form with not many getting involved again.
Illustrious Prince(IRE) Official explanation: jockey said, regarding running and riding, that his orders were to get cover and to obtain the best possible placing, the gelding stumbled shortly after the start and briefly lost its action and did not handle the undulating track.
T/Plt: £109.40 to a £1 stake. Pool:£50,387.11 - 336.16 winning tickets T/Qpdt: £26.00 to a £1 stake. Pool:£4,606.60 - 130.95 winning tickets RY

MAISONS-LAFFITTE (R-H)
Thursday, April 7

OFFICIAL GOING: Turf: good

1206a PRIX DJEBEL (GROUP 3) (3YO COLTS & GELDINGS) (TURF) 7f (S)
2:20 (12:00) 3-Y-0 **£34,482** (£13,793; £10,344; £6,896; £3,448)

RPR
1 **Surfrider (IRE)**[27] 3-9-2 OlivierPeslier 3 111+
(E Libaud, France) *covered up at bk of field fr s: swtchd towards stands' rail 2f out: qcknd wl 1f out: fin strly to ld fnl 50yds: all out* **61/10**
2 *hd* **Havane Smoker**[158] [7265] 3-9-2 IoritzMendizabal 2 110
(J-C Rouget, France) *racd in 4th on settling: wnt 3rd 2f out: chal for ld 1 1/2f out: qcknd wl to ld 100yds out: hdd fnl 50yds* **7/2**[2]
3 *1 ½* **Redemptor**[21] [883] 3-9-2 ChristopheSoumillon 6 106+
(J-C Rouget, France) *settled at rr fr s: swtchd towards stands' rail 2f out: travelling easily: rdn to ld 1 1/2f out: sn chal and hdd 1f out: rdn and no ex: styd on fnl f* **1/1**[1]
4 *¾* **Al Hazim (CAN)**[33] 3-9-2 AnthonyCrastus 1 104
(J-L Pelletan, France) *sn led: hdd 1 1/2f out: rdn and no ex fnl f: styd on* **8/1**
5 *2* **Captain Chop (FR)**[21] [883] 3-9-2 FlavienPrat 4 99
(D Guillemin, France) *prom fr s: dropped bk to 4th 2f out: rdn and no ex: styd on fnl f* **48/10**[3]
6 *6* **Domino Rock (FR)**[53] [532] 3-9-2 BenjaminBoutin 5 82
(C Boutin, France) *racd in 3rd on outer on settling: rdn 2f out: no ex: fdd* **18/1**

1m 26.9s (-1.40) **6** Ran SP% **119.9**
WIN (incl. 1 euro stake): 7.10. PLACES: 3.50, 2.00. SF: 26.00.
Owner Michel Delauzun **Bred** Ecoutila Partnership **Trained** France

NOTEBOOK
Surfrider(IRE) won this with more in hand than the margin would suggest. His rider believes he will get 1m and he will now be aimed at the French Guineas.

1207a PRIX IMPRUDENCE (GROUP 3) (3YO FILLIES) (TURF) 7f (S)
2:55 (12:00) 3-Y-0 **£34,482** (£13,793; £10,344; £6,896; £3,448)

RPR
1 **Moonlight Cloud**[186] [6610] 3-9-0 DavyBonilla 7 111+
(F Head, France) *led fr s: swtchd towards stands' rail: r.o strly fnl f: nvr threatened: easily* **26/5**[2]
2 *2* **Helleborine**[186] [6609] 3-9-0 StephanePasquier 1 106
(Mme C Head-Maarek, France) *broke wl: settled in 4th on rail following eventual wnr: rdn 2f out: appeared short of room whn trying to chal1 1/2f out: r.o wl whn clr wout threatening wnr* **1/1**[1]
3 *1* **Miss Fifty (IRE)**[186] [6609] 3-9-0 SebastienMaillot 2 103
(U Suter, France) *racd towards rr on rail bhd eventual runner-up: rdn 1 1/2f out: picked up wl: fin strly fnl 100yds* **69/1**
4 *½* **Etive (USA)**[21] [884] 3-9-0 MaximeGuyon 4 102
(H-A Pantall, France) *settled bhd ldrs: picked up wl 1 1/2f out: r.o wl fnl f wout threatening ldrs* **21/1**
5 *¾* **Whip And Win (FR)**[135] [7544] 3-9-0 GregoryBenoist 8 100
(Robert Collet, France) *racd towards rr: rdn to cl on outer 1 1/2f out: r.o fnl f* **16/1**
6 *shd* **Nova Step**[21] [884] 3-9-0 Francois-XavierBertras 3 99
(F Rohaut, France) *broke wl to r cl to eventual wnr: rdn 1 1/2f out: no ex: styd on fnl f* **9/1**
7 *1* **Madly In Love (FR)**[27] [841] 3-9-0 JohanVictoire 6 97?
(J-L Gay, France) *racd towards rr: rdn 1 1/2f out: r.o wl fnl f* **55/1**
8 *1 ½* **Wizz Kid (IRE)**[157] [7277] 3-9-0 ChristopheSoumillon 5 93
(Robert Collet, France) *covered up in midfield fr s: rdn 1 1/2f out: no ex* **13/1**
9 *shd* **Mambia**[186] [6609] 3-9-0 Christophe-PatriceLemaire 11 92
(J-C Rouget, France) *a towards rr: nvr a factor* **78/10**[3]
10 *½* **Izalia (FR)**[157] [7276] 3-9-0 FranckBlondel 9 91
(F Rossi, France) *racd towards rr on outer: rdn 2f out: no ex: fdd* **13/1**
0 **Action Chope (FR)**[198] [6277] 3-9-0 ThierryJarnet 10 —
(D Guillemin, France) *broke wl to r in 3rd on outer: rdn 1 1/2f out: no ex: wknd qckly* **32/1**

1m 26.1s (-2.20) **11** Ran SP% **118.5**
WIN (incl. 1 euro stake): 6.20. PLACES: 1.80, 1.20, 8.50. DF: 4.00. SF: 11.40.
Owner George Strawbridge **Bred** George Strawbridge **Trained** France

NOTEBOOK
Moonlight Cloud was there to be shot at in front, but kept on finding plenty when asked. She will now head for the Newmarket 1,000 Guineas for which she is currently a top-price 8-1.
Helleborine had every chance to pick up the winner, but failed to do so. Her trainer believed that the winner was fitter, but it's still uncertain whether she will join her conqueror at Newmarket.

1208 - (Foreign Racing) - See Raceform Interactive

NEWCASTLE (L-H)
Friday, April 8

OFFICIAL GOING: Round course - good to soft (good in places); straight course - good (good to soft in places from 1m to 6f)
Wind: Breezy, across Weather: Hot, sunny

1209 SWARLANDSELFSTORAGE.CO.UK MEDIAN AUCTION MAIDEN STKS 5f
2:20 (2:21) (Class 6) 2-Y-0 **£1,942** (£578; £288; £144) **Stalls** High

Form RPR
1 **Marford Missile (IRE)** 2-9-3 RichardKingscote 2 72
(Tom Dascombe) *mde virtually all: jnd and rdn over 1f out: edgd lft ins fnl f: hld on wl* **3/1**[2]
2 *½* **Shevington** 2-9-3 PaulHanagan 3 70+
(Richard Fahey) *dwlt: sn trcking ldrs: rdn 2f out: hdwy appr fnl f: styd on wl ins fnl f: tk 2nd cl home* **11/4**[1]
3 *shd* **Forevertheoptimist (IRE)** 2-9-3 KierenFallon 1 70
(Linda Stubbs) *trckd ldrs: hdwy to dispute ld 1f out: kpt on ins fnl f: hld and lost 2nd cl home* **3/1**[2]
4 *6* **Ortea** 2-9-3 NeilCallan 5 48
(David Evans) *pressed wnr: pushed along 2f out: wknd ent fnl f* **11/4**[1]
5 *5* **Egyptian Cross** 2-9-3 PaulMulrennan 4 30
(John Weymes) *dwlt: sn pushed along in rr: rdn and wknd fr 2f out* **14/1**[3]

64.23 secs (3.13) **Going Correction** +0.175s/f (Good) **5** Ran SP% **110.0**
Speed ratings (Par 90): **81,80,80,70,62**
CSF £11.51 TOTE £4.10: £1.90, £1.70; EX 8.60.
Owner The MHS 4x10 Partnership **Bred** Miss Mary Davidson & Mrs Steffi Von Schilcher **Trained** Malpas, Cheshire

FOCUS
An interesting little maiden despite the small field with all five contestants seeing the racecourse for the first time. The jockeys after the first race described the ground as "a bit dead".

NOTEBOOK
Marford Missile(IRE) won his race with a swift exit. He may have been headed by the third horse for a few strides inside the last furlong, but rallied gamely and this half-brother to three winners including the prolific Kipchak ought to get a bit further in time. (op 9-2)
Shevington ◆ missed the break completely and took a while to get into stride. He stayed on well in the latter stages as he went for a gap between the two leaders, but couldn't quite get there. This £20,000 foal can be considered the best horse in the race and should go one better soon. (op 5-2 tchd 9-4 and 3-1)
Forevertheoptimist(IRE), who is already gelded, ran well considering he raced green on the outside of the field and had every chance until the last few strides. Whilst the front pair are both January foals, he was by far the youngest having not been born until April, so is entitled to improve. (op 9-4 tchd 10-3)
Ortea, representing a yard that has already had three 2-y-o winners this season, showed speed against the stands' rail but got tired inside the last furlong. (op 7-2)
Egyptian Cross, out of a winner at up to 1m6f on the Flat, was always in trouble after fluffing the start. (tchd 16-1)

1210 METNOR GROUP MAIDEN STKS 1m 3y(S)
2:55 (2:56) (Class 5) 3-Y-0+ **£2,590** (£770; £385; £192) **Stalls** High

Form RPR
5-4 **1** **Tropical Beat**[16] [945] 3-8-12 NickyMackay 11 86
(John Gosden) *cl up: led over 2f out: rdn and hrd pressed fnl f: edgd rt: kpt on wl towards fin* **5/1**[3]

2 *1* **Miss Aix** 3-8-8 0 ow1 JamieSpencer 1 81
(Michael Bell) *prom: smooth hdwy over 2f out: rdn to chal ins fnl f: kpt on: hld nr fin* **7/2[2]**

0- 3 *13* **Honest Buck**[318] 2425 4-9-13 0 FrederikTylicki 13 58
(Kate Walton) *led tl hdd over 2f out: outpcd by ldng pair ins fnl f* **20/1**

00- 4 *3/4* **Gud Day (IRE)**[125] 7693 3-8-12 0 SilvestreDeSousa 8 52+
(Deborah Sanderson) *missed break: bhd tl edgd lft and styd on steadily ins fnl f: nvr nr to chal* **100/1**

3- 5 *3/4* **Trumpington Street (IRE)**[190] 6504 3-8-12 0 WilliamBuick 9 50
(John Gosden) *chsd ldrs: drvn and ev ch over 2f out: wknd ins fnl f* **7/4[1]**

25- 6 *7* **Apache Warrior**[214] 5815 4-9-13 0 TomEaves 7 38
(George Moore) *in tch: rdn and effrt 3f out: wknd over 1f out* **8/1**

7 *nk* **Silvers Spirit**[30] 5-9-8 0 PaulHanagan 6 33
(Keith Reveley) *missed break: bhd: pushed along 3f out: nvr able to chal* **50/1**

8 *13* **Friday Night Lad (IRE)** 4-9-13 0 PJMcDonald 2 —
(Alan Swinbank) *hld up towards rr: rdn over 3f out: sn btn* **25/1**

00- 9 *3 1/2* **Three White Socks (IRE)**[367] 1143 4-9-8 0 DaleSwift(5) 14 —
(Brian Ellison) *racd alone stands' side: rdn and edgd lft over 4f out: sn btn* **50/1**

10 *17* **Higher Spen Rose** 3-8-7 0 BarryMcHugh 5 —
(Julie Camacho) *hld up in tch: rdn over 3f out: wknd over 2f out* **9/1**

- 11 *28* **Situation Vacant** 4-9-13 0 JoeFanning 10 —
(Mark Johnston) *towards rr: rdn and green after 3f: sn struggling* **11/1**

12 *31* **Poosie Nansie (IRE)** 4-9-8 0 LeeNewman 12 —
(George Foster) *dwlt: sn prom: rdn and wknd fr 1/2-way: eased whn no ch ins fnl f* **100/1**

1m 40.9s (-2.50) **Going Correction** -0.20s/f (Firm)
WFA 3 from 4yo+ 15lb 12 Ran SP% 119.2
Speed ratings (Par 103): **104,103,90,89,88 81,81,68,64,47 19,—**
toteswingers:1&2 £5.40, 2&3 £22.60, 1&3 £26.70 CSF £21.96 TOTE £6.70: £2.30, £2.00, £9.10; EX 33.90 Trifecta £263.00 Pool: £355.49 - 1.0 winning units..
Owner Normandie Stud Ltd **Bred** Normandie Stud Ltd **Trained** Newmarket, Suffolk

FOCUS
A modest older-horse maiden with few getting into it and the first two pulled miles clear. The finish brought back memories of the Eider. There was little strength in depth but the time was relatively good.
Gud Day(IRE) Official explanation: jockey said gelding hung left throughout
Poosie Nansie(IRE) Official explanation: jockey said filly lost its action

1211 FREEBETTING.CO.UK MAIDEN STKS (DIV I) 1m 4f 93y
3:30 (3:31) (Class 5) 3-Y-O+ £2,266 (£674; £337; £168) Stalls Low

Form RPR

3- 1 **Lady Chaparral**[266] 4115 4-9-8 0 TomEaves 7 75
(George Moore) *cl up: led after 2f: mde rest: qcknd clr over 2f out: pushed along and hld on wl ins fnl f* **11/2[2]**

6- 2 *3/4* **Raajih**[176] 6873 3-8-7 0 RichardHills 9 77
(John Gosden) *t.k.h early: prom: chsd wnr after 4f: rdn: edgd lft and outpcd over 2f out: styd on wl ins fnl f* **5/4[1]**

3 *nk* **Gogeo (IRE)**[58] 4-9-13 0 PJMcDonald 11 78+
(Alan Swinbank) *hld up: pushed along 1/2-way: hdwy over 2f out: styd on fnl f: no imp last 75yds* **12/1**

4 *6* **Chapter Five**[31] 4-9-8 0 PaulHanagan 1 64
(Keith Reveley) *slowly away: hld up: pushed along over 3f out: hdwy over 2f out: styd on ins fnl f: no imp* **7/1[3]**

5 *2* **Doynosaur**[50] 4-9-8 0 RobertWinston 6 61
(Mrs K Burke) *in tch: rdn over 3f out: no imp fr 2f out* **14/1**

4 6 *6* **River Dragon (IRE)**[12] 11 6-10-0 0 BarryMcHugh 8 56
(Neville Bycroft) *midfield: edgd lft and outpcd wl over 2f out: sn outpcd* **12/1**

05 7 *4* **Harry Lime**[13] 992 3-8-7 0 JoeFanning 3 48
(Mark Johnston) *trckd ldrs tl rdn and wknd fr 2f out* **15/2**

8 *nk* **Serenader**[35] 4-9-13 0 DanielTudhope 5 49
(David O'Meara) *s.i.s: hld up: rdn over 3f out: sn no imp* **66/1**

0/3- 9 *hd* **Across The Sea (USA)**[347] 1572 4-9-13 0 SilvestreDeSousa 10 49
(Geoffrey Harker) *t.k.h: hld up: struggling over 4f out: sme late hdwy: nvr on terms* **8/1**

00- 10 *5* **Diamond City (IRE)**[181] 6742 3-8-7 0 DuranFentiman 2 39
(Deborah Sanderson) *t.k.h: led 2f: cl up tl rdn and wknd over 2f out* **100/1**

00- 11 *92* **Pengula (IRE)**[173] 6966 4-9-8 0 PhillipMakin 4 —
(Robert Johnson) *plld hrd in midfield: struggling over 4f out: sn btn: eased whn no ch fnl 4f* **100/1**

2m 47.49s (1.89) **Going Correction** +0.225s/f (Good)
WFA 3 from 4yo 21lb 4 from 6yo 1lb 11 Ran SP% 120.7
Speed ratings (Par 103): **102,101,101,97,95 91,89,89,88,85 24**
toteswingers:1&2 £3.70, 2&3 £6.00, 1&3 £12.10 CSF £13.08 TOTE £6.10: £1.40, £1.10, £2.50; EX 15.30 Trifecta £191.70 Pool: £494.92 -1.91 winning units..
Owner Geoff & Sandra Turnbull **Bred** Geoff & Sandra Turnbull **Trained** Middleham Moor, N Yorks

FOCUS
This was a modest maiden and again few got into it with the first two holding those places throughout. Little form to go on but the first two may do better.
Across The Sea(USA) Official explanation: jockey said gelding had a breathing problem

1212 FREEBETTING.CO.UK MAIDEN STKS (DIV II) 1m 4f 93y
4:05 (4:06) (Class 5) 3-Y-O+ £2,266 (£674; £337; £168) Stalls Low

Form RPR

2- 1 **Ittirad (USA)**[163] 7178 3-8-7 0 NeilCallan 4 81+
(Roger Varian) *t.k.h: trckd ldrs: smooth hdwy to ld over 2f out: sn clr: comf* **1/3[1]**

2 *3 3/4* **War Poet** 4-9-13 0 DanielTudhope 7 77
(David O'Meara) *hld up: hdwy 3f out: hung lft and chsd (clr) wnr appr fnl f: kpt on: no imp* **33/1**

44- 3 *2 1/4* **Almarmooq (USA)**[197] 6313 4-9-13 0 RichardHills 11 73
(John Gosden) *cl up: led over 3f out to 2f out: one pce whn lost 2nd appr fnl f* **4/1[2]**

06- 4 *6* **Judicious**[195] 6356 4-9-13 0 SilvestreDeSousa 1 63
(Geoffrey Harker) *dwlt: t.k.h in rr: outpcd over 4f out: styd on fr 2f out: nvr able to chal* **25/1**

5 *3 1/2* **Lure of The Night (IRE)**[53] 4-9-8 0 SeanLevey(5) 5 58
(Brian Rothwell) *hld up in tch on ins: rdn and outpcd over 2f out: sn n.d* **50/1**

5- 6 *1 3/4* **Garth Mountain**[236] 5116 4-9-10 0 RichardEvans(3) 6 55
(David Evans) *t.k.h early: trckd ldrs: drvn over 2f out: sn wknd* **16/1[3]**

7 *1* **Pete**[53] 8-9-7 0 (t) GarryWhillans(7) 10 53
(Barry Murtagh) *hld up in midfield on outside: rdn over 2f out: sn btn* **33/1**

0 8 *3 3/4* **Nha Trang (IRE)**[17] 937 4-9-8 0 LanceBetts(5) 9 47
(Deborah Sanderson) *in tch: drvn and outpcd over 3f out: sn btn* **66/1**

50 9 *16* **Lyford Lad**[23] 873 4-9-13 0 PJMcDonald 3 22
(George Moore) *t.k.h: led to over 3f out: wknd over 2f out* **80/1**

10 *51* **Molannarch**[29] 5-9-9 0 PaulHanagan 8 —
(Keith Reveley) *hld up in midfield: struggling 4f out: sn btn* **25/1**

2m 47.24s (1.64) **Going Correction** +0.225s/f (Good)
WFA 3 from 4yo 21lb 4 from 5yo+ 1lb 10 Ran SP% 119.2
Speed ratings (Par 103): **103,100,99,95,92 91,90,88,77,43**
toteswingers:1&2 £5.00, 2&3 £8.80, 1&3 £1.10 CSF £24.86 TOTE £1.70: £1.02, £6.60, £1.10; EX 17.10 Trifecta £38.60 Pool: £643.21 - 12.32 winning units..
Owner Sheikh Ahmed Al Maktoum **Bred** Darley **Trained** Newmarket, Suffolk

FOCUS
With the market going 16-1 bar two, that tells you everything you need to know about the competitiveness of the second division of this maiden. A couple of the beaten horses did catch the eye, though. The winner did not need to improve on his 2yo debut form. The winning time was 0.25 seconds faster than the first division.
Judicious ◆ Official explanation: jockey said gelding ran too free

1213 LA TAXIS H'CAP 5f
4:40 (4:42) (Class 6) (0-60,60) 4-Y-O+ £1,942 (£578; £288; £144) Stalls High

Form RPR

434 1 **Ingleby Star (IRE)**[56] 511 6-9-7 **60** (p) LeeNewman 4 71
(Noel Wilson) *trckd ldrs: rdn and led over 1f out: kpt on strly ins fnl f* **20/1**

0-63 2 *1 1/4* **Spirit Of Coniston**[9] 1034 8-8-11 **50** KierenFallon 12 56
(Paul Midgley) *midfield: pushed along 1/2-way: gd hdwy ins fnl f: tk 2nd last stride* **10/1**

06-0 3 *shd* **Tenancy (IRE)**[24] 857 7-9-5 **58** (b) JamieSpencer 6 64
(Shaun Harris) *led tl hdd over 1f out: kpt on u.p ins fnl f* **16/1**

23-1 4 *hd* **Ballarina**[9] 1034 5-8-10 **54** NeilFarley(5) 10 59
(Eric Alston) *taken early to post: w ldr: ev ch and rdn over 1f out: kpt on ins fnl f: hld nr fin* **13/8[1]**

033- 5 *shd* **Bouncy Bouncy (IRE)**[164] 7154 4-9-2 **55** (t) HayleyTurner 16 60
(Michael Bell) *hld up: hdwy on outside to press ldrs over 1f out: kpt on same pce wl ins fnl f* **8/1[3]**

1140 6 *nk* **Shawkantango**[13] 985 4-9-6 **59** (v) PatrickMathers 11 62
(Derek Shaw) *bhd and outpcd: gd hdwy on outside over 1f out: kpt on ins fnl f* **16/1**

0030 7 *1 1/4* **Tyrannosaurus Rex (IRE)**[37] 735 7-8-7 **46** (v) JoeFanning 1 45
(Derek Shaw) *in tch: effrt over 2f out: kpt on same pce ins fnl f* **20/1**

030/ 8 *shd* **Big Slick (IRE)**[639] 3730 6-8-13 **52** RobertWinston 8 51
(Mel Brittain) *midfield: drvn and outpcd 1/2-way: hdwy against far rail ins fnl f: nrst fin* **22/1**

4330 9 *nse* **Galpin Junior (USA)**[24] 857 5-9-3 **56** PJMcDonald 9 54
(Ruth Carr) *trckd ldrs tl rdn and no ex ins fnl f* **9/1**

05-0 10 *1* **Kyzer Chief**[9] 1034 6-9-5 **58** SilvestreDeSousa 7 53
(Ron Barr) *prom: rdn over 2f out: one pce over 1f out* **20/1**

0602 11 *1 1/4* **Kersivay**[9] 1034 5-8-13 **52** (v) NeilCallan 2 42
(David Evans) *in tch: drvn 1/2-way: outpcd over 1f out* **6/1[2]**

000- 12 *1/2* **Lady Lube Rye (IRE)**[294] 3161 4-8-10 **49** DuranFentiman 3 38
(Noel Wilson) *bhd and sn pushed along: sme late hdwy: nvr on terms* **50/1**

/0-0 13 *1 1/4* **Eilean Eeve**[50] 575 5-8-4 **46** oh1 (p) JamesSullivan(3) 14 30
(George Foster) *midfield on outside: struggling 2f out: sn btn* **100/1**

0220 14 *5* **Residency (IRE)**[24] 857 5-9-3 **56** (p) TomEaves 5 22
(Bryan Smart) *bhd and sn outpcd: no ch fr 1/2-way* **22/1**

0260 15 *3 3/4* **Head To Head (IRE)**[17] 941 7-8-7 **46** oh1 (bt) PaulHanagan 15 —
(Alan Brown) *s.i.s: sn wl bhd: no ch fr 1/2-way* **40/1**

61.77 secs (0.67) **Going Correction** +0.175s/f (Good) 15 Ran SP% 122.7
Speed ratings (Par 101): **101,99,98,98,98 97,95,95,95,94 92,91,89,81,75**
toteswingers:1&2 £14.00, 2&3 £32.70, 1&3 £34.70 CSF £194.20 CT £3372.13 TOTE £26.10: £4.70, £3.20, £4.10; EX 190.50 Trifecta Not won..
Owner P M Watson and Mrs N Wilson **Bred** Pat Cosgrove **Trained** Sandhutton, N Yorks

FOCUS
A moderate 46-60 sprint handicap, albeit a competitive one. The stalls may have been placed against the stands' rail, but the runners ended up racing closer to the far rail. Apart from the winner, they finished in a heap. Straightforward form.
Head To Head(IRE) Official explanation: jockey said gelding missed the break

1214 SURGO CONSTRUCTION H'CAP 7f
5:15 (5:15) (Class 4) (0-85,82) 3-Y-O £2,784 (£828; £414; £206) Stalls High

Form RPR

252- 1 **Maverik**[190] 6488 3-8-11 **72** FrederikTylicki 8 80
(Michael Dods) *plld hrd: hld up: hdwy on outside over 2f out: led over 1f out: edgd rt and kpt on strly ins fnl f* **13/2[3]**

22-1 2 *1 1/4* **Las Verglas Star (IRE)**[7] 1074 3-9-1 **76** 6ex PaulHanagan 5 81
(Richard Fahey) *prom: hdwy to chal over 1f out: rdn and edgd lft: kpt on same pce ins fnl f* **11/10[1]**

534- 3 *1 3/4* **Dads Amigo**[168] 7059 3-9-7 **82** KierenFallon 2 82
(George Foster) *led tl hdd over 1f out: rdn and kpt on same pce ins fnl f* **9/1**

16-5 4 *5* **Sergeant Suzie**[20] 913 3-8-4 **72** ShaneBKelly(7) 1 59
(Michael Dods) *w ldr: rdn and outpcd 2f out: n.d after* **20/1**

10-0 5 *nk* **Stamp Duty (IRE)**[27] 845 3-9-0 **75** BarryMcHugh 3 61
(Ollie Pears) *stdd in tch: effrt over 2f out: no imp wl over 1f out* **16/1**

04-6 6 *2 3/4* **Bussa**[13] 988 3-9-3 **78** NeilCallan 9 57
(David Evans) *hld up: drvn over 2f out: nvr able to chal* **16/1**

424- 7 *2* **Brave Dream**[186] 6619 3-8-10 **71** PhillipMakin 4 44
(Kevin Ryan) *trckd ldrs tl rdn and wknd over 1f out* **11/2[2]**

2406 8 *2* **Insolenceofoffice (IRE)**[23] 864 3-8-10 **78** (p) ThomasBrown(7) 6 46
(Andrew Crook) *hld up in tch: struggling over 2f out: sn btn* **33/1**

5-15 9 *1/2* **Silver Turn**[77] 254 3-9-0 **75** TomEaves 7 41
(Bryan Smart) *dwlt: hld up: rdn over 2f out: sn wknd* **14/1**

1m 27.89s (0.09) **Going Correction** -0.20s/f (Firm) 9 Ran SP% 112.5
Speed ratings (Par 100): **96,94,92,86,86 83,81,78,78**
toteswingers:1&2 £2.90, 2&3 £3.20, 1&3 £3.40 CSF £13.54 CT £64.22 TOTE £7.30: £1.50, £1.20, £2.30; EX 17.30 Trifecta £44.70 Pool: £792.26 - 13.09 winning units..
Owner Andrew Tinkler **Bred** J G Davis & Star Pointe Ltd **Trained** Denton, Co Durham
■ Freddie Tylicki's first winner since breaking his shoulder last June.

FOCUS
Unlike in the previous contest, the runners came down the centre of the track. The first three pulled right away from the rest and are the ones to concentrate on. The winner is rated up 8lb and the form makes sense.

1215 NORTH SEA LOGISTICS H'CAP 2m 19y
5:50 (5:50) (Class 4) (0-85,86) 4-Y-O+ £2,978 (£886; £442; £221) Stalls Low

Form RPR
/3-3 **1** **Agglestone Rock**[24] 3 6-8-7 **66** oh1 PaulHanagan 2 83
(Philip Kirby) *t.k.h: chsd ldr and clr of rest: led gng wl 3f out: drew clr fnl 2f: easily* **7/2**[2]
040- **2** *15* **Nemo Spirit (IRE)**[71] 6750 6-9-7 **80** (tp) RichardKingscote 9 78
(Tom Dascombe) *led and clr w one other: hdd 3f out: plugged on same pce fnl 2f* **7/1**
-116 **3** *4* **French Hollow**[74] 286 6-8-7 **66** oh1 BarryMcHugh 7 60
(Tim Fitzgerald) *hld up: rdn and outpcd 3f out: rallied and chsd first two ins fnl f: no imp* **7/1**
600- **4** *3* **Yahrab (IRE)**[132] 7591 6-9-7 **85** NeilFarley(5) 5 75
(Declan Carroll) *hld up: rdn and chsd clr ldng pair fr 2f out to ins fnl f: wknd* **15/2**
2/5- **5** *4* **Bin End**[373] 1069 5-9-10 **83** JamieSpencer 4 68
(Michael Bell) *t.k.h: stdd in tch: rdn and chsd clr ldng pair over 3f out to 2f out: sn btn* **4/1**[3]
030/ **6** *1/2* **Burnt Oak (UAE)**[20] 6948 9-8-7 **66** oh6 KellyHarrison 8 51
(Chris Fairhurst) *hld up: rdn over 3f out: edgd lft and sn btn* **11/1**
246- **7** *9* **High Ransom**[21] 6955 4-8-4 **67** (p) PJMcDonald 6 41
(Micky Hammond) *chsd clr ldng pair: rdn over 3f out: wknd over 2f out* **3/1**[1]

3m 34.65s (-4.75) **Going Correction** -0.15s/f (Firm)
WFA 4 from 5yo+ 4lb **7 Ran SP% 112.3**
Speed ratings (Par 105): **105,97,95,94,92 91,87**
toteswingers:1&2 £4.80, 2&3 £7.70, 1&3 £2.80 CSF £26.65 CT £159.52 TOTE £4.20: £2.70, £3.30; EX 13.60 Trifecta £46.90 Pool: £384.00 - 6.05 winning units..
Owner Geoff Kirby Basil Holian Michael Buckley **Bred** Mrs Fiona Denniff **Trained** Castleton, N Yorks

FOCUS
A strange staying handicap in that the front pair appeared to go off at a generous early pace and soon put daylight between themselves and the rest, but if the other riders thought that they would come back then they were mistaken. The winner was potentially well treated on the Flat.

1216 GOSFORTH DECORATING & BUILDING SERVICES APPRENTICE H'CAP 1m 3y(S)
6:25 (6:25) (Class 6) (0-60,60) 4-Y-O+ £1,942 (£578; £288; £144) Stalls High

Form RPR
00 **1** **French Art**[18] 933 6-9-7 **60** (p) TobyAtkinson 13 73
(Nigel Tinkler) *prom: hdwy to ld wl over 1f out: rdn out ins fnl f* **14/1**
4-52 **2** *1 1/2* **Ravi River (IRE)**[7] 1077 7-9-7 **60** DaleSwift 14 69
(Brian Ellison) *cl up: led 3f out to wl over 1f out: kpt on ins fnl f* **2/1**[1]
/24- **3** *2 1/4* **Prince Rhyddarch**[175] 6890 6-9-1 **54** SeanLevey 9 58
(Michael Dods) *hld up: hdwy to chse ldng pair over 1f out: kpt on ins fnl f* **7/1**[3]
450- **4** *6* **Machir Bay**[157] 7282 4-8-0 **46** ShirleyTeasdale(7) 16 36
(Keith Dalgleish) *prom: drvn along 3f out: kpt on same pce fr 2f out* **20/1**
5-65 **5** *1 1/2* **Tinseltown**[52] 184 5-8-3 **47** ow1 DavidSimmonson(5) 1 34
(Brian Rothwell) *bhd tl edgd lft and hdwy 2f out: kpt on fnl f: nt gng pce to chal* **16/1**
3353 **6** *1 1/2* **Tomintoul Star**[50] 580 5-8-4 **48** (b) ShaneBKelly(5) 11 31
(Ruth Carr) *t.k.h: trckd ldrs: effrt over 2f out: wknd over 1f out* **7/1**[3]
050- **7** *1 1/4* **Petrocelli**[14] 6890 4-9-0 **56** LMcNiff(3) 3 36
(Wilf Storey) *hld up: hdwy over 2f out: btn ins fnl f* **25/1**
020- **8** *2 1/4* **Broctune Papa Gio**[164] 7153 4-8-10 **49** LeeTopliss 2 24
(Keith Reveley) *hld up bhd ldng gp: effrt over 2f out: sn outpcd* **14/1**
043- **9** *9* **Carragold**[205] 6076 5-8-7 **49** (b) JohnCavanagh(3) 5 —
(Mel Brittain) *bmpd sn after s: bhd and sn rdn along: nvr on terms* **12/1**
121- **10** *3/4* **Gadobout Dancer**[228] 5361 4-9-3 **56** NeilFarley 4 —
(Declan Carroll) *prom tl rdn and wknd fr 2f out* **6/1**[2]
020- **11** *4 1/2* **Funky Munky**[12] 7402 6-8-7 **46** AdamCarter 10 —
(Alistair Whillans) *sn pushed along in midfield: struggling 3f out: sn btn* **12/1**
000- **12** *2 3/4* **Catcher Of Dreams (IRE)**[160] 7230 5-8-4 **46** oh1 AmyScott(3) 7 —
(George Foster) *cl up: led after 3f to 3f out: sn wknd* **40/1**
3020 **13** *2 3/4* **Colamandis**[37] 734 4-8-11 **50** DeclanCannon 8 —
(Hugh McWilliams) *led 3f: cl up tl rdn and wknd fr 3f out* **50/1**

1m 41.45s (-1.95) **Going Correction** -0.20s/f (Firm) **13 Ran SP% 120.2**
Speed ratings (Par 101): **101,99,97,91,89 88,87,84,75,75 70,67,65**
toteswingers:1&2 £9.00, 2&3 £4.80, 1&3 £22.00. totesuper7: Win: Not won. Place: Not won. CSF £40.95 CT £226.73 TOTE £12.60: £4.20, £1.40, £2.50; EX 39.20 TRIFECTA Not won..
Owner Jim O'Doherty **Bred** Newsells Park Stud Limited **Trained** Langton, N Yorks
■ Stewards' Enquiry : Dale Swift two-day ban: used whip with excessive frequency (Apr 23-24)

FOCUS
A moderate apprentice handicap and the field finished well spread out. They raced centre to far side. The winner is rated back to the sort of form he was in this time last year.
T/Plt: £87.80 to a £1 stake. Pool of £37,363.00 - 310.55 winning tickets. T/Qpdt: £5.50 to a £1 stake. Pool £3,413.00 - 459.10 winning tickets. RY

1078 WOLVERHAMPTON (A.W) (L-H)
Friday, April 8

OFFICIAL GOING: Standard
Wind: fairly light, half against Weather: dry and warm

1217 FREEBETS.CO.UK GRAND NATIONAL FREE BET OFFERS MEDIAN AUCTION MAIDEN STKS 5f 20y(P)
6:15 (6:16) (Class 5) 3-5-Y-O £1,748 (£520; £260; £129) Stalls Low

Form RPR
1 **Odd Ball (IRE)** 4-9-11 0 StephenCraine 5 59
(Patrick Morris) *dwlt: sn rcvrd and in tch: rdn to chse ldng pair 2f out: unable qck and outpcd over 1f out: rallied u.p ins fnl f: r.o strly fnl 100yds to ld nr fin* **12/1**
- **2** *nk* **Ginzan** 3-8-10 0 ow1 TomMcLaughlin 6 49
(Malcolm Saunders) *s.i.s: sn rcvrd and in tch on outer: rdn and outpcd bnd 2f out: rallied 1f out: r.o wl to press ldrs wl ins fnl f: wnt 2nd last stride* **6/1**[3]
0 **3** *shd* **Take Root**[8] 1065 3-9-0 0 ChrisCatlin 8 52
(Reg Hollinshead) *t.k.h: chsd ldr after 1f: ev ch 2f out: rdn wl over 1f out: drvn to ld fnl 100yds: hdd nr fin: lost 2nd last stride* **6/1**[3]
040- **4** *1 3/4* **Chester Deelyte (IRE)**[158] 7268 3-8-6 48 PatrickDonaghy(3) 4 41
(Lisa Williamson) *led: rdn 2f out: drvn over 1f out: edgd lft u.p and hdd fnl 100yds: wknd towards fin* **20/1**
2035 **5** *3/4* **Cheveyo (IRE)**[24] 857 5-9-8 47 (b) RossAtkinson(3) 3 48
(Patrick Morris) *hld up wl in tch: rdn and effrt wl over 1f out: nt qckn u.p over 1f out: one pce and no threat to ldrs fnl f* **11/2**[2]
0-00 **6** *nk* **Renesmee (IRE)**[81] 189 3-8-9 31 RobbieFitzpatrick 7 38
(Peter Grayson) *chsd ldr for 1f: sn rdn: lost pl 2f out: rallied u.p 1f out: chsng ldrs and keeping on whn pushed lft and hmpd ins fnl f: nt rcvr* **125/1**
3 **7** *2 3/4* **Hootys Agogo**[8] 1065 3-9-0 0 DavidNolan 1 39
(Declan Carroll) *stmbld bdly leaving stalls: t.k.h: hld up wl in tch on inner: rdn and effrt 2f out: keeping on same pce and hld whn short of room and hmpd ins fnl f: eased fnl 100yds* **11/10**[1]
8 *7* **Right Credentials** 3-8-9 0 LukeMorris 2 —
(Bruce Hellier) *s.i.s: sn rdn and bdly outpcd in rr: sme hdwy 1/2-way: wknd over 1f out* **9/1**

63.25 secs (0.95) **Going Correction** +0.125s/f (Slow)
WFA 3 from 4yo+ 11lb **8 Ran SP% 114.8**
Speed ratings (Par 103): **97,96,96,93,92 91,87,76**
toteswingers:1&2:£10.10, 1&3:£11.40, 2&3:£7.60 CSF £81.82 TOTE £14.10: £3.80, £2.80, £2.20; EX 121.50.
Owner James Jamieson **Bred** Ms S Pettigrew & J Jamieson **Trained** Tarporley, Cheshire
■ Stewards' Enquiry : Patrick Donaghy two-day ban: careless riding (Apr 23-24)

FOCUS
A poor maiden won by a 4-y-o newcomer and weak form limited by the proximity of fourth and sixth.
Hootys Agogo Official explanation: jockey said gelding stumbled leaving stalls

1218 FREEBETS.CO.UK GRAND NATIONAL FREE BETTING H'CAP 1m 5f 194y(P)
6:45 (6:45) (Class 6) (0-60,57) 4-Y-O+ £1,535 (£453; £226) Stalls Low

Form RPR
1302 **1** **Money Money Money**[7] 1080 5-9-7 **57** (b) JamesMillman 1 66
(Rod Millman) *trckd ldrs and a travelling wl: nt clr run 3f out tl wl over 1f out: sn rdn to ld: clr jst ins fnl f: comf* **2/1**[1]
5-36 **2** *3 1/2* **Dot's Delight**[42] 598 7-8-11 **47** LiamJones 6 51
(Mark Rimell) *stdd s: hld up in rr: rdn and effrt 3f out: drvn to chse ldrs and wd bnd 2f out: kpt on to go 2nd ins fnl f: no ch w wnr* **9/2**[2]
44-4 **3** *1 1/2* **Shouda (IRE)**[85] 145 5-8-13 **49** TomQueally 5 51
(Barney Curley) *chsd ldr: ev ch and hanging rt bnd 2f out: rdn to ld wl over 1f out: sn hdd and outpcd by wnr: hung rt u.p and lost 2nd ins fnl f* **5/1**[3]
2-30 **4** *1* **Rare Coincidence**[29] 768 10-9-3 **53** (p) MartinLane 2 54
(Roger Fisher) *led: rdn over 2f out: hdd wl over 1f out: outpcd by wnr and btn over 1f out: plugged on same pce fnl f* **5/1**[3]
3061 **5** *3/4* **Acropolis (IRE)**[9] 1050 10-9-1 **51** 6ex LukeMorris 3 50
(Tony Carroll) *hld up in last pair: rdn and effrt ent fnl 2f: styd on same pce fr over 1f out* **9/2**[2]
0006 **6** *8* **Fine Tolerance**[21] 899 5-8-9 **45** (b) JimmyQuinn 4 33
(Sam Davison) *dwlt: sn rcvrd and in tch in midfield: rdn 4f out: wknd over 2f out* **10/1**

3m 6.20s (0.20) **Going Correction** +0.125s/f (Slow) **6 Ran SP% 112.1**
Speed ratings (Par 101): **104,102,101,100,100 95**
toteswingers:1&2:£1.70, 1&3:£1.10, 2&3:£6.20 CSF £11.20 TOTE £3.00: £1.40, £2.60; EX 8.50.
Owner Mrs Jenny Willment **Bred** Mrs Jenny Willment **Trained** Kentisbeare, Devon

FOCUS
A limited but sound handicap rated around the placed horses.

1219 FREEBETS.CO.UK GRAND NATIONAL FREE BETS CLASSIFIED STKS 5f 216y(P)
7:15 (7:16) (Class 5) 3-Y-O £1,780 (£529; £264; £132) Stalls Low

Form RPR
300- **1** **Golden Taurus (IRE)**[231] 5261 3-9-0 69 SebSanders 4 76+
(J W Hills) *dwlt: hld up in last: gd hdwy on outer wl over 1f out: rdn along hands and heels to ld ent fnl f: sn clr and r.o strly: easily* **11/8**[1]
2313 **2** *4* **Mazovian (USA)**[17] 940 3-8-7 64 DavidKenny(7) 2 63
(Michael Chapman) *led: rdn ent fnl 2f: drvn and hdd ent fnl f: no ch w wnr fnl f: kpt on* **13/2**[3]
452- **3** *nk* **Roodee Queen**[228] 5358 3-9-0 70 StephenCraine 3 62
(Patrick Morris) *chsd ldng pair: effrt and rdn to chal wl over 1f out: outpcd by wnr and btn 1f out: kpt on* **13/2**[3]
1062 **4** *9* **Loves Theme (IRE)**[20] 913 3-9-0 69 (v) J-PGuillambert 1 43
(Alan Bailey) *pressed ldr on inner: rdn 1/2-way: drvn and unable qck ent fnl 2f: wknd ent fnl f: wl btn and eased fnl 100yds* **13/8**[2]

1m 15.16s (0.16) **Going Correction** +0.125s/f (Slow) **4 Ran SP% 106.9**
Speed ratings (Par 98): **103,97,97,85**
CSF £9.46 TOTE £1.90; EX 7.30.
Owner N Hubbard P Saunders L Cowan **Bred** Lynch Bages And Samac **Trained** Upper Lambourn, Berks

FOCUS
A modest classifiied stakes and a strong pace set things up perfectly for the winner. The form is best rated through the runner-up.
Loves Theme(IRE) Official explanation: trainer said, regarding running, that the filly was unable to dominate.

1220 FREEBETS.CO.UK GRAND NATIONAL FREE BET MAIDEN FILLIES' STKS 7f 32y(P)
7:45 (7:46) (Class 5) 3-Y-O+ £1,748 (£520; £260; £129) Stalls High

Form RPR
4 **1** **Embassy Pearl (IRE)**[59] 454 3-8-10 0 SebSanders 1 78
(Sir Mark Prescott Bt) *mde virtually all: set stdy gallop: rdn and qcknd 2f out: drvn clr over 1f out: r.o strly: readily* **7/4**[2]
0-20 **2** *8* **Finefrenzyrolling (IRE)**[14] 981 3-8-10 0 AndrewElliott 4 55
(Mrs K Burke) *chsd ldrs on outer: rdn to chse wnr ent fnl 2f: outpcd by wnr and btn ent fnl f: kpt on for modest 2nd* **13/8**[1]
3 *1 1/4* **Lady of Burgundy** 5-9-10 0 LiamKeniry 6 57
(Mark Usher) *s.i.s: racd in last trio: rdn and hdwy over 2f out: 4th and no ch w wnr over 1f out: kpt on fnl f to go modest 3rd last strides* **16/1**
033- **4** *hd* **Hoppy's Flyer (FR)**[136] 7536 3-8-10 75 RussKennemore 3 51
(Philip Kirby) *taken down early: chsd wnr tl ent fnl 2f: sn outpcd u.p: wl btn fnl f: lost 3rd last strides* **11/2**[3]

00-6 **5** *5* **Ocean Rosie (IRE)**[29] [816] 4-9-10 52 .... LukeMorris 8 43
(Tony Carroll) *s.i.s: nvr travelling wl in rr: rdn over 4f out: nvr on terms* **14/1**

6 *1 1/4* **Chipofftheoldblock** 3-8-10 0 .... LiamJones 2 35
(Bruce Hellier) *plld hrd: chsd ldrs: rdn and wknd ent fnl 2f: fdd over 1f out* **50/1**

34 **7** *9* **Full Shilling (IRE)**[14] [971] 3-8-10 0 .... ChrisCatlin 5 10
(John Spearing) *restless in stalls: plld hrd: hld up in midfield: rdn and lost pl 3f out: sn bhd: t.o* **14/1**

P0-0 **8** *6* **First Term**[9] [1054] 4-9-10 55 .... TomMcLaughlin 7 —
(Malcolm Saunders) *hld up in last trio: rdn and lost tch 3f out: t.o fnl f* **40/1**

1m 29.72s (0.12) **Going Correction** +0.125s/f (Slow)
WFA 3 from 4yo+ 14lb **8** Ran SP% **113.5**
Speed ratings (Par 100): **104,94,93,93,87 86,75,68**
toteswingers:1&2:£1.30, 1&3:£7.20, 2&3:£7.80 CSF £4.86 TOTE £2.50: £1.60, £1.10, £4.10; EX 5.70.
Owner Mrs June Rooney **Bred** T J Rooney And Corduff Stud **Trained** Newmarket, Suffolk

FOCUS
An ordinary maiden but the level is fluid.

1221 FREEBETS.CO.UK GRAND NATIONAL BEST FREE BETS H'CAP 7f 32y(P)
8:15 (8:16) (Class 5) (0-75,74) 4-Y-0+ **£1,813** (£539; £269; £134) **Stalls** High

Form RPR
3314 **1** **Unlimited**[11] [1014] 9-9-5 72 .... J-PGuillambert 5 80
(Tony Carroll) *t.k.h: chsd ldrs: rdn to chal over 1f out: led ins fnl f: r.o wl* **15/2**

6363 **2** *1/2* **Could It Be Magic**[20] [915] 4-9-0 70 ....(b) KierenFox(3) 4 77
(Bill Turner) *hld up wl in tch in midfield: rdn over 2f out: nt clr run and swtchd rt 1f out: drvn to chse wnr fnl 100yds: r.o* **9/2**[1]

5431 **3** *2 1/4* **Copperwood**[20] [915] 6-9-5 72 ....(p) LiamKeniry 7 73
(Michael Blanshard) *t.k.h: hld up in tch on outer: chsd ldng pair and rdn wl over 1f out: fnd little and outpcd 1f out: drvn ins fnl f: kpt on again fnl 100yds* **7/1**

1202 **4** *hd* **Spin Again (IRE)**[20] [915] 6-8-12 72 .... LucyKBarry(7) 3 72
(Mark Wellings) *broke wl: led and set stdy gallop: rdn and qcknd 3f out: drvn over 1f out: hdd ins fnl f: wknd fnl 75yds* **7/1**

5-54 **5** *hd* **Vanilla Rum**[55] [528] 4-9-3 70 .... GrahamGibbons 2 70
(John Mackie) *dwlt: sn bustled along and rcvrd to chse ldng pair: rdn and unable qck over 2f out: drvn and styd on one pce fr over 1f out* **9/2**[1]

0002 **6** *nk* **Tourist**[11] [1014] 6-9-1 68 .... JimmyQuinn 8 67
(Derek Shaw) *hld up in last trio: swtchd rt and effrt over 1f out: drvn and kpt on ins fnl f: nvr able to chal* **6/1**[2]

050- **7** *shd* **Paradise Spectre**[175] [6896] 4-8-12 65 .... AndrewElliott 6 64
(Mrs K Burke) *hld up in last trio: rdn and effrt on inner over 1f out: kpt on but nvr able to chal* **13/2**[3]

5/0- **8** *1/2* **Sumbe (USA)**[322] [2290] 5-9-5 72 .... AndreaAtzeni 9 69
(Michael Wigham) *restless in stalls: stdd and dropped in bhd after s: hld up in last: c wd over 1f out: rdn ent fnl f: kpt on ins fnl f: n.d* **7/1**

1m 29.35s (-0.25) **Going Correction** +0.125s/f (Slow) **8** Ran SP% **113.2**
Speed ratings (Par 103): **106,105,102,102,102 102,101,101**
toteswingers:1&2:£5.70, 1&3:£2.90, 2&3:£3.70 CSF £40.27 CT £246.31 TOTE £7.90: £2.30, £2.10, £1.90; EX 37.40.
Owner M B Clarke **Bred** J Wise **Trained** Cropthorne, Worcs

FOCUS
A fair and competitive handicap but the early pace wasn't hectic. The first two set the level.

1222 FREEBETS.CO.UK GRAND NATIONAL HOT FREE BETS H'CAP 1m 1f 103y(P)
8:45 (8:45) (Class 5) (0-75,74) 4-Y-0+ **£1,813** (£539; £269; £134) **Stalls** Low

Form RPR
0-03 **1** **Mountain Cat (IRE)**[16] [949] 7-9-7 74 .... JimCrowley 5 84+
(William Knight) *t.k.h: hld up in last trio: hdwy on outer over 1f out: rdn and r.o wl fnl f to ld nr fin* **3/1**[1]

1125 **2** *nk* **Stargazing (IRE)**[9] [1052] 5-8-7 60 .... AndreaAtzeni 2 67
(Marco Botti) *led: rdn and ... fnl f: r.o wl tl hdd and no ex nr fin* **3/1**[1]

6-46 **3** *2 1/2* **Waahej**[8] [1066] 5-8-10 63 .... ChrisCatlin 4 65
(Peter Hiatt) *stdd after s: t.k.h: hld up in last trio: effrt towards inner wl over 1f out: drvn and styd on wl fnl f: wnt 3rd fnl 75yds* **11/1**

62-0 **4** *1/2* **Strike Force**[86] [124] 7-9-0 72 ....(t) AdamBeschizza(5) 6 73
(Clifford Lines) *chsd ldrs: wnt 3rd 4f out: rdn over 2f out: styd on same pce u.p fr over 1f out* **16/1**

132 **5** *hd* **Needwood Ridge**[7] [1083] 4-8-13 66 ....(t) JamesDoyle 1 66
(Frank Sheridan) *awkward leaving stall: sn chsng ldr: rdn wl over 2f out: hrd drvn and unable qck over 1f out: one pce and btn fnl f* **4/1**[2]

2654 **6** *3/4* **Striker Torres (IRE)**[23] [869] 5-9-3 70 .... JimmyQuinn 7 71
(Geoffrey Oldroyd) *stdd and dropped in bhd after s: hld up in last: effrt and hdwy towards inner over 1f out: keeping on but no threat to ldrs whn nt clr run fnl 150yds: nvr able to chal* **9/1**

1123 **7** *nk* **Black Coffee**[8] [1066] 6-9-6 73 ....(b) ShaneKelly 3 71
(Mark Brisbourne) *chsd ldrs: rdn 2f out: sn unable qck and drvn: wknd ent fnl f* **9/2**[3]

2m 3.01s (1.31) **Going Correction** +0.125s/f (Slow) **7** Ran SP% **112.4**
Speed ratings (Par 103): **99,98,96,96,95 95,94**
toteswingers:1&2:£2.60, 1&3:£7.10, 2&3:£5.90 CSF £11.63 TOTE £4.40: £2.80, £2.10; EX 8.10.
Owner S Rudolf **Bred** Mrs Mary Gallagher **Trained** Patching, W Sussex

FOCUS
A fair handicap but the pace was steady and the form is muddling, with the second looking the best guide.
Striker Torres(IRE) Official explanation: jockey said gelding was denied a clear run
Black Coffee Official explanation: jockey said gelding ran too free and was unsuited by the slow pace

1223 FREEBETS.CO.UK GRAND NATIONAL EXCLUSIVE FREE BETS H'CAP 1m 4f 50y(P)
9:15 (9:15) (Class 4) (0-85,84) 4-Y-0+ **£3,238** (£963; £481; £240) **Stalls** Low

Form RPR
1112 **1** **Sir Boss (IRE)**[16] [948] 6-9-4 80 .... TomQueally 2 89
(Michael Mullineaux) *hld up in last pair: smooth hdwy to join ldrs travelling wl 2f out: rdn to ld ent fnl f: pushed out: comf* **11/4**[2]

422- **2** *1 1/2* **Saint Thomas (IRE)**[147] [7428] 4-8-12 75 .... JimmyQuinn 3 81
(John Mackie) *chsd ldr tl 9f out: chsd ldrs after: rdn ent fnl 2f: chsd wnr ins fnl f: kpt on* **5/2**[1]

1233 **3** *3* **Layla's Dancer**[14] [965] 4-8-10 73 .... LukeMorris 4 74
(Tony Carroll) *chsd ldr 9f out: rdn to ld 2f out: sn hung lft: hdd ent fnl f: wknd* **7/2**[3]

-461 **4** *2 1/2* **Ahlawy (IRE)**[18] [932] 8-9-6 82 ....(bt) JamesDoyle 1 79
(Frank Sheridan) *stdd s: hld up in last pair: rdn and struggling over 2f out: wl hld whn swtchd rt over 1f out* **6/1**

114- **5** *1 1/4* **Christmas Carnival**[223] [5529] 4-9-7 84 .... GrahamGibbons 5 79
(Michael Easterby) *led tl rdn and hdd 2f out: wknd over 1f out* **9/2**

2m 42.84s (1.74) **Going Correction** +0.125s/f (Slow)
WFA 4 from 6yo+ 1lb **5** Ran SP% **109.9**
Speed ratings (Par 105): **99,98,96,94,93**
CSF £9.94 TOTE £2.90: £1.60, £1.40; EX 8.60.
Owner I S Ross **Bred** Mrs E R Cantillon **Trained** Alpraham, Cheshire

FOCUS
This always had the potential to be a bit of a messy race, and so it proved with the form muddling, despite the placed horses being the best guides.
T/Plt: £338.60 to a £1 stake. Pool:£46,007.00 - 99.18 winning tickets T/Qpdt: £16.60 to a £1 stake. Pool:£5,962.00 - 265.40 winning tickets SP

1085 DUNDALK (A.W) (L-H)
Friday, April 8

OFFICIAL GOING: Standard

1228a CROWNE PLAZA LEADING JOCKEY & TRAINER CHAMPIONSHIP H'CAP 1m (P)
8:30 (8:30) 4-Y-0+ **£11,206** (£3,275; £1,551; £517)

RPR
1 **Lightening Sticks (IRE)**[125] [7707] 4-8-13 82 ....(t) FMBerry 4 91+
(Richard Brabazon, Ire) *chsd ldrs: 4th 1/2-way: hdwy in 3rd 1 1/2f out: chal 1f out: sn led and rdn clr: kpt on wl: comf* **11/4**[2]

2 *2 1/2* **Dahindar (IRE)**[7] [1088] 6-10-5 102 .... PBBeggy 7 104
(Edward Lynam, Ire) *hld up towards rr: clsr in 7th 1 1/2f out: rdn in 6th 1f out: kpt on to take 2nd ins fnl f: no ch w wnr* **5/2**[1]

3 *1/2* **Captain Ramius (IRE)**[27] [848] 5-9-4 87 .... PJSmullen 8 88
(Kevin Ryan) *hld up towards rr: rdn in 8th 1f out: r.o wl fnl f* **7/1**

4 *3/4* **Barrow Island (IRE)**[14] [976] 4-8-11 80 .... JMurtagh 10 79
(M Halford, Ire) *chsd ldr in 2nd: rdn to ld briefly over 1f out: no ex ins fnl f* **4/1**[3]

5 *1 3/4* **Mountain Coral (IRE)**[12] [1005] 7-9-2 85 .... NGMcCullagh 9 80
(F Oakes, Ire) *settled bhd ldrs: 5th 1/2-way: rdn over 1f out: kpt on same pce fnl f* **7/1**

6 *nk* **Macnas (USA)**[14] [974] 4-8-1 73 .... ShaneFoley(3) 5 67
(James J Hartnett, Ire) *led after 1f: rdn and hdd over 1f out: no ex* **7/1**

7 *1/2* **Cornakill (USA)**[245] [4813] 4-9-6 96 .... SHJames(7) 6 89
(Kevin Prendergast, Ire) *mid-div: 7th 1/2-way: rdn 2f out: no imp 1 1/2f out: kpt on one pce* **25/1**

8 *3/4* **Patrickswell (IRE)**[7] [1086] 7-8-5 77 ....(p) BACurtis(3) 2 68
(Marcus Callaghan, Ire) *led early: hdd after 1f: 3rd 1/2-way: rdn in 4th over 1f out: no ex fnl f* **16/1**

9 *4 1/2* **Maundy Money**[159] [7262] 8-9-12 95 .... CO'Donoghue 1 76
(David Marnane, Ire) *settled bhd ldrs: 6th 1/2-way: rdn in 7th and hmpd 1f out: eased fnl f* **20/1**

1m 38.1s (98.10) **9** Ran SP% **127.2**
CSF £11.36 CT £47.19 TOTE £2.80: £1.40, £1.40, £2.90; DF 20.90.
Owner Mrs Alice Perry **Bred** Darley **Trained** Curragh, Co Kildare

NOTEBOOK
Lightening Sticks(IRE), the subject of a substantial gamble when landing a maiden here in December, once again proved popular with punters and won with a fair bit to spare. In a tightly bunched field, he moved up travelling ominously well passing the 2f pole and once he hit the front the result was never in doubt. (op 11/2)
Dahindar(IRE) was shouldered with 10st 5lb after making a winning seasonal reappearance last week and didn't enjoy the clearest of passages as Padraig Beggy attempted to come with his trademark late run. A wall of traffic greeted Beggy when he turned for home and, although he wasn't severely hampered, he would have finished a lot closer to the winner with a smoother passage. His mount remains capable of winning more races off this mark. (op 2/1 tchd 3/1)
Captain Ramius(IRE) made the journey from Kevin Ryan's British stable and ran on well in the closing stages to grab third, suggesting a further step up in trip could benefit. (op 15/2 tchd 13/2)
Barrow Island(IRE) was never far away, but when the winner kicked for home he had no answers and faded into fourth.
Mountain Coral(IRE) has a string of decent placed efforts to his name, but after being forced to race wide throughout he could never land a blow. (op 13/2)

1229 - 1230a (Foreign Racing) - See Raceform Interactive

1124 SAINT-CLOUD (L-H)
Friday, April 8

OFFICIAL GOING: Turf: good to soft

1231a PRIX RIGHT ROYAL (LISTED RACE) (4YO+) (TURF) 1m 7f 100y
4:00 (12:00) 4-Y-0+ **£22,413** (£8,965; £6,724; £4,482; £2,241)

RPR
1 **Kasbah Bliss (FR)**[36] [757] 9-9-0 0 .... ThierryThulliez 5 106
(F Doumen, France) **17/5**[2]

2 *3/4* **Gentoo (FR)**[166] [7110] 7-9-8 0 ....(p) Christophe-PatriceLemaire 6 113
(A Lyon, France) **14/5**[1]

3 *1* **Le Larron (IRE)**[188] [6590] 4-9-0 0 .... ChristopheSoumillon 8 107
(A De Royer-Dupre, France) **10/1**

4 *3/4* **Los Cristianos (FR)**[187] [6607] 5-9-0 0 .... OlivierPeslier 7 103
(A Couetil, France) **23/1**

5 *1 1/2* **Mashoor (FR)**[24] [860] 4-9-0 0 .... MaximeGuyon 2 105
(A Fabre, France) **4/1**[3]

6 *1 1/2* **Americain (USA)**[117] [7851] 6-9-8 0 .... GeraldMosse 1 108
(A De Royer-Dupre, France) **9/2**

7 *2 1/2* **Blek (FR)**[166] [7110] 6-9-6 0 .... AnthonyCrastus 4 103
(E Lellouche, France) **11/1**

8 *8* **Snape Maltings (IRE)**[143] 4-8-11 0 ....(p) FabriceVeron 9 88
(H-A Pantall, France) **19/1**

9 *10* **Lamool (GER)**[166] 4-9-0 0 ....(p) FilipMinarik 3 80
(Mario Hofer, Germany) **47/1**

3m 22.8s (202.80)
WFA 4 from 5yo+ 3lb **9** Ran SP% **115.9**
WIN (incl. 1 euro stake): 4.40. PLACES: 1.60, 1.50, 2.60. DF: 11.30. SF: 22.10.
Owner Henri De Pracomtal **Bred** Haras D'Ecouves Et H De Pracomtal **Trained** Bouce, France

NOTEBOOK
Kasbah Bliss(FR) quickened up well to win and his trainer believed that everything was in his favour here. He will only come over for the Gold Cup if conditions are suitable.
Gentoo(FR) ran well on this seasonal reappearance as his trainer felt that the ground was against him. He is likely to contest the Gold Cup.
Americain(USA), winner of last year's Melbourne Cup, didn't enjoy a clear run at all in the home straight. He won't be aimed at the Gold Cup and is more likely to be supplemented for the Coronation Cup with the Prix Barbeville his next port of call.

1178 LINGFIELD (L-H)
Saturday, April 9

OFFICIAL GOING: Standard
Race times were not that quick, suggesting the hot weather slowed up the track.
Wind: mild breeze Weather: Sunny

1232 GRAND NATIONAL GUIDE AT FREEBETTING.CO.UK H'CAP — 7f (P)
2:00 (2:00) (Class 5) (0-70,70) 4-Y-O+ — **£2,388** (£705; £352) **Stalls** Low

Form	Pos	Dist	Horse / Trainer / Comment	RPR
350-	1		**Rondeau (GR)**[148] 7421 6-9-7 **70** ... GeorgeBaker 6 (Patrick Chamings) *hld up bhd ldrs: smooth hdwy to ld ent fnl f: r.o wl: readily* **13/2**[3]	79+
-341	2	1 ½	**The Big Haerth (IRE)**[11] 1021 5-9-4 **70** ow1 ... (t) RichardEvans(3) 9 (David Evans) *trckd ldrs: rdn 2f out: kpt on ins fnl f: wnt 2nd towards fin: nt pce of wnr* **9/1**	75
1242	3	nk	**Florio Vincitore (IRE)**[3] 1177 4-9-0 **63** ... (b) EddieCreighton 2 (Edward Creighton) *s.i.s: bhd: rdn and sme prog 2f out: styd on fnl f: wnt 3rd nr fin* **6/4**[1]	67
6-50	4	¾	**Salient**[59] 473 7-9-5 **68** ... NeilCallan 8 (Michael Attwater) *trckd ldr: rdn to ld wl over 1f out: hdd ent fnl f: no ex and lost 2 pls towards fin* **8/1**	70
0-02	5	¾	**Secret Queen**[11] 1024 4-9-6 **69** ... LukeMorris 1 (Martin Hill) *hld up: rdn 2f out: styd on but nt pce to get on terms* **11/1**	69
-122	6	5	**Rio Royale (IRE)**[42] 698 5-9-1 **64** ... (p) JimCrowley 7 (Amanda Perrett) *led: rdn and hdd wl over 1f out: wknd fnl f* **5/1**[2]	51
5104	7	nk	**Diplomatic (IRE)**[11] 1026 6-9-5 **68** ... KirstyMilczarek 4 (Michael Squance) *cl up: rdn whn bmpd on bnd 2f out: wknd 1f out* **20/1**	54
0	8	½	**Do More Business (IRE)**[70] 351 4-8-6 **60** ... JemmaMarshall(5) 10 (Pat Phelan) *hld up: rdn and c wd ent st: no imp* **33/1**	44
0624	9	1 ¾	**Buxton**[36] 763 7-9-5 **68** ... (t) MartinLane 3 (Roger Ingram) *cl up: rdn whn hmpd on bnd 2f out: sn wknd* **10/1**	48+

1m 26.13s (1.33) **Going Correction** +0.275s/f (Slow) — 9 Ran SP% **116.2**
Speed ratings (Par 103): **103,101,100,100,99 93,93,92,90**
toteswingers:1&2:£36.70, 1&3:£4.50, 2&3:£10.30 CSF £63.64 CT £133.32 TOTE £6.90: £2.00, £4.20, £1.10; EX 84.00 Trifecta £199.80 Part won. Pool: £270.02 - 0.44 winning units..
Owner The Foxford House Partnership **Bred** Ippotour Stud **Trained** Baughurst, Hants

FOCUS
A modest handicap and the pace seemed just steady (time more than three seconds above standard), but there was a tidy winner. The second and fourth help set the standard.
Florio Vincitore(IRE) Official explanation: jockey said gelding was slowly away
Diplomatic(IRE) Official explanation: jockey said gelding suffered interference in running

1233 GRAND NATIONAL FREE BETTING WITH FREEBETTING.CO.UK H'CAP — 1m 2f (P)
2:30 (2:32) (Class 6) (0-60,60) 4-Y-O+ — **£1,706** (£503; £252) **Stalls** Low

Form	Pos	Dist	Horse / Trainer / Comment	RPR
5532	1		**Moresweets 'n Lace**[17] 945 4-9-7 **60** ... GeorgeBaker 3 (Gary Moore) *trckd ldrs: dropped to mid-div 5f out: hdwy fr 3f out: rdn over 2f out: running on wl whn swtchd rt 1f out: led ins fnl f: comf* **5/1**[1]	71
0065	2	2 ½	**Spirit Of Love (IRE)**[22] 896 4-8-7 **46** oh1 ... AndreaAtzeni 6 (Michael Wigham) *prom: led 4f out: rdn 2f out: hung rt ent fnl f: sn hdd: kpt on but no ex* **11/2**[2]	52
42-5	3	nk	**Laconicos (IRE)**[9] 1066 9-8-13 **57** ... (t) LauraPike(5) 2 (William Stone) *hld up towards rr: r.o strly whn pushed along fr over 1f out: wnt 3rd ins fnl f: fin wl* **7/1**	62+
4505	4	1 ¼	**Thundering Home**[10] 1046 4-9-6 **59** ... RobbieFitzpatrick 11 (Michael Attwater) *pushed along early towards rr: rdn and hdwy on inner 2f out: styd on fnl f* **8/1**	62
0-55	5	½	**Always De One**[24] 749 4-8-7 **46** oh1 ... (p) KirstyMilczarek 10 (K F Clutterbuck) *trckd ldrs: rdn 2f out: kpt on same pce fnl f* **25/1**	48
3202	6	1 ½	**Holyfield Warrior (IRE)**[9] 1068 7-8-9 **51** ... KierenFox(3) 5 (Ralph Smith) *hld up towards rr: rdn 2f out: styd on fnl f: nvr trbld ldrs* **6/1**[3]	50
0-00	7	shd	**Heading To First**[48] 621 4-8-8 **54** ... (p) NathanAlison(7) 9 (Paddy Butler) *nvr bttr than mid-div* **33/1**	52
4-00	8	1 ¼	**The Wonga Coup (IRE)**[35] 361 4-8-9 **53** ... JemmaMarshall(5) 7 (Pat Phelan) *chsd ldrs: rdn 2f out: ch ent fnl f: fdd fnl 120yds* **11/1**	49
4060	9	½	**Atacama Sunrise**[9] 1063 5-9-0 **53** ... LiamKeniry 1 (George Prodromou) *mid-div: rdn 2f out: wknd fnl f* **8/1**	48
-060	10	6	**Folio (IRE)**[48] 621 11-9-4 **57** ... StevieDonohoe 12 (Willie Musson) *rdn over 2f out: a towards rr* **10/1**	40
0605	11	2 ½	**Dilys Maud**[17] 944 4-9-0 **53** ... (b) RobertHavlin 8 (Roger Ingram) *s.i.s: hdwy on outer to trck ldrs after 3f out: rdn over 2f out: wknd over 1f out* **16/1**	31
04-5	12	7	**Darfour**[15] 969 7-8-9 **48** ... (t) LukeMorris 4 (Martin Hill) *led tl 4f out: sn rdn: wknd 2f out* **14/1**	12
00-5	13	5	**Mumtaz Begum**[11] 1021 6-8-7 **46** oh1 ... (v) SamHitchcott 13 (John E Long) *mid-div: rdn 3f out: wknd 2f out* **66/1**	—

2m 6.83s (0.23) **Going Correction** +0.275s/f (Slow) — 13 Ran SP% **119.3**
Speed ratings (Par 101): **110,108,107,106,106 105,105,104,103,98 96,91,87**
toteswingers:1&2:£6.10, 1&3:£4.60, 2&3:£5.50 CSF £31.24 CT £196.17 TOTE £3.70: £1.30, £1.30, £4.50; EX 27.60 Trifecta £263.40 Part won. Pool: £356.00 - 0.44 winning units..
Owner Darrell Hinds **Bred** Jeremy Hinds **Trained** Lower Beeding, W Sussex
■ Stewards' Enquiry : Andrea Atzeni two-day ban: careless riding (Apr 23-24)
George Baker caution: careless riding.

FOCUS
A moderate handicap run at a fair pace, but it went to the least exposed runner-up in the line-up. The winner posted a personal best.

1234 FREE GRAND NATIONAL BETS WITH FREEBETTING.CO.UK INTERNATIONAL TRIAL STKS (LISTED RACE) — 1m (P)
3:00 (3:03) (Class 1) 3-Y-O
£17,031 (£6,456; £3,231; £1,611; £807; £405) **Stalls** High

Form	Pos	Dist	Horse / Trainer / Comment	RPR
10-1	1		**Dubawi Gold**[14] 990 3-9-0 101 ... RichardHughes 8 (Richard Hannon) *racd keenly: broke wl: trckd ldr: qcknd up wl to ld over 1f out: r.o: pushed out* **10/11**[1]	101+
3-	2	½	**Hamlool (IRE)**[303] 2887 3-9-0 0 ... PhilipRobinson 7 (Clive Brittain) *s.i.s: rcvrd to trck ldrs after 1f: rdn 2f out: r.o ins fnl f: wnt 2nd towards fin: clsng on wnr* **8/1**[3]	99
112-	3	¾	**Burj Alzain (IRE)**[108] 7974 3-9-0 92 ... NeilCallan 4 (Gerard Butler) *in tch: tk clsr order over 2f out: sn rdn: chsd wnr over 1f out: kpt on: lost 2nd nr fin* **9/1**	97
6044	4	2 ¼	**Sonoran Sands (IRE)**[14] 988 3-9-0 89 ... TadhgO'Shea 2 (J S Moore) *s.i.s: sn pushed along: led after 1f: rdn and hdd over 1f out: no ex fnl f* **66/1**	92?
13-1	5	2	**Tinkertown (IRE)**[14] 988 3-9-0 99 ... JamieSpencer 6 (Paul Cole) *trckd ldrs tl outpcd over 2f out* **8/1**[3]	87
333-	6	2 ½	**Sylvestris (IRE)**[197] 6317 3-8-9 78 ... JimCrowley 5 (Ralph Beckett) *towards rr: rdn over 2f out: nt pce to cl on ldrs* **33/1**	77
640-	7	7	**Emma's Gift (IRE)**[245] 4842 3-8-9 94 ... JimmyQuinn 1 (Julia Feilden) *mid-div: rdn over 2f out: wknd over 1f out* **66/1**	61
260-	8	55	**Stentorian (IRE)**[203] 6200 3-9-0 98 ... FrankieDettori 3 (Mark Johnston) *chsd ldrs tl struggling 4f out: sn wl bhd* **20/1**	—
122-	U		**Unex El Greco**[168] 7085 3-9-0 90 ... WilliamBuick 9 (John Gosden) *v.s.a and uns rdr leaving stalls* **7/1**[2]	—
1-	P		**Atraaf (IRE)**[136] 7558 3-9-0 0 ... RichardHills 10 (Marcus Tregoning) *s.i.s: towards rr: pushed along whn lost action and p.u over 1f out* **9/1**	—

1m 37.26s (-0.94) **Going Correction** +0.275s/f (Slow) — 10 Ran SP% **117.8**
Speed ratings (Par 106): **115,114,113,111,109 107,100,45,—,—**
toteswingers:1&2:£5.00, 1&3:£4.20, 2&3:£12.10 CSF £8.70 TOTE £1.80: £1.10, £2.80, £2.90; EX 15.80 Trifecta £135.30 Pool: £705.81 - 3.86 winning units..
Owner Andrew Tinkler **Bred** A H Bennett **Trained** East Everleigh, Wilts

FOCUS
Only three of the previous nine winners of this race have managed to win again in Britain. The form of this latest edition is limited by a few of the beaten runners, but the winner has more ability than the margins suggest. he is rated 10lb off his reappearance form. They seemed to go a quick pace.

NOTEBOOK
Dubawi Gold ◆, who had a tendency to be keen when with Michael Dods last year, was held up when landing the 7f Listed Spring Cup (stable took the race with Paco Boy in 2008) on his debut for Richard Hannon but almost broke too well this time. He soon found himself in second place, and despite getting a lead from Sonoran Sands, wouldn't drop his head. Being able to overcome expending so much energy before the race got serious is a clear sign that he's a colt of considerable ability, but clearly he will have to learn to settle if he's to fulfil his potential. His connections think plenty of him and understandably they'll consider the 2,000 Guineas at Newmarket. Incidentally, he's bred along similar lines to last year's Guineas winner Makfi, being a son of Dubawi out of a Green Desert mare. (op 11-10 tchd 6-5 in a place)
Hamlool(IRE) ◆, off the track since recording an RPR of 80 over 6.5f in a Newbury maiden on his debut last June, made a highly promising return. A horse with plenty of size, a track this tight might not have been ideal and he looked in need of the run when off the bridle before the final bend, but he kept responding to pressure. He's open to significant improvement and, bred to stay further, will be worth his place in a Derby trial. (tchd 15-2)
Burj Alzain(IRE) won his first two starts over 1m at Kempton but seemed to have his limitations exposed when a close second over 1m2f in a Deauville conditions race when last seen in December. He found the front two a bit too good, but this was still a respectable return. (op 8-1)
Sonoran Sands(IRE) reversed recent Kempton form with the disappointing Tinkertown but still found this a bit hot. He has an official mark of only 89 and is probably a fair guide to the form. (op 50-1)
Tinkertown(IRE) impressed when a 4l winner off 90 on his return but was never going that well this time and the race probably came too soon.
Stentorian(IRE) Official explanation: jockey said colt never travelled
Unex El Greco lost several lengths when standing still as the stalls opened and then veered left when finally consenting to step forward, in the process unbalancing William Buick, who was unseated. The horse's attitude could be called into question. (tchd 10-1)
Atraaf(IRE) had looked a decent prospect when providing Marcus Tregoning with a rare debut winner over C&D on his sole juvenile start but was weak in the market for this return. He never travelled and was eventually pulled up, apparently having lost his action. (tchd 10-1)

1235 COMPARE FREE BETS AT FREEBETTING.CO.UK MAIDEN AUCTION STKS — 5f (P)
3:30 (3:36) (Class 6) 2-Y-O — **£1,706** (£503; £252) **Stalls** High

Form	Pos	Dist	Horse / Trainer / Comment	RPR
2	1		**Dawn Lightning**[9] 1055 2-7-13 0 ... KieranO'Neill(5) 1 (Alan McCabe) *trckd ldrs: swtchd rt jst over 1f out: r.o wl but drifted rt: led towards fin: pushed out* **13/8**[1]	64
62	2	1 ¾	**Umph (IRE)**[7] 1101 2-8-13 0 ... TomMcLaughlin 3 (David Evans) *led: rdn and hrd pressed fr jst over 1f out: no ex whn hdd towards fin* **13/2**	67
0	3	1 ½	**Joey Hayes**[7] 1095 2-8-9 0 ... JamieSpencer 4 (Noel Quinlan) *sn chsng ldr: rdn 2f out: ev ch ent fnl f: no ex fnl 100yds* **2/1**[2]	58
	4	3	**Si Sealy (IRE)** 2-8-11 0 ... CathyGannon 2 (David Evans) *s.i.s: in last pair but wl in tch: rdn over 2f out: nt pce to get involved* **7/2**[3]	49
	5	1 ½	**Ermyn Flyer** 2-7-13 0 ... JemmaMarshall(5) 5 (Pat Phelan) *s.i.s: in last pair but wl in tch: rdn over 2f out: nt pce to get involved* **14/1**	36

62.66 secs (3.86) **Going Correction** +0.275s/f (Slow) — 5 Ran SP% **113.7**
Speed ratings (Par 90): **80,77,74,70,67**
CSF £12.78 TOTE £2.30: £1.90, £2.40; EX 5.10.
Owner A J Wittering **Bred** P A Mason **Trained** Averham Park, Notts

FOCUS
The first two had both recorded RPRs in the 60s last time and the third-placed finisher just 50, while the other two were making their debuts, so it is probably just modest form.

NOTEBOOK
Dawn Lightning found trouble in the straight, having to be switched around her two main rivals, but she still picked up well to confirm the promise she showed on her debut at Leicester. She was getting plenty of weight from most of these and the conditions of the race suited her. (op 11-10 tchd 10-11)

Umph(IRE), beaten just a short-head at Kempton last time, edged left on to the sometimes unfavoured inside rail in the straight and found the winner much too strong. (op 9-2 tchd 4-1)
Joey Hayes couldn't justify strong on-course support but still stepped up on the form he showed in the Brocklesby on his debut. (op 9-2)
Si Sealy(IRE), an 8,000euros purchase who has already been gelded, never threatened after a slow start but still fared best of the two newcomers. (op 11-2 tchd 13-2)
Ermyn Flyer is bred to want further and never recovered from a slow start. (tchd 16-1)

1236 EBF GRAND NATIONAL BETTING WITH FREEBETTING.CO.UK MAIDEN STKS 6f (P)

4:00 (4:04) (Class 5) 3-Y-O **£3,412** (£1,007; £504) **Stalls** Low

Form RPR
0- **1** **Munaaseb**[172] [7002] 3-9-3 0 .... RichardHills 6 88+
(Ed Dunlop) *trckd ldr: led over 1f out: qcknd clr: impressive* **7/4**[1]
5- **2** *8* **Trojan Rocket (IRE)**[101] [7999] 3-9-3 0 .... KirstyMilczarek 3 62
(George Prodromou) *hmpd leaving stalls: towards rr: hdwy on inner 2f out: wnt 2nd ent fnl f but nvr any ch w wnr* **10/1**[3]
3 *nk* **Dark Isle** 3-9-3 0 .... SebSanders 5 61
(J W Hills) *trckd ldrs: rdn over 2f out: kpt on to chal for 2nd ins fnl f: no ex towards fin* **6/1**[2]
4 *7* **A'Faal** 3-8-12 0 .... PhilipRobinson 7 34
(Clive Brittain) *rn green: s.i.s: sn pushed along in tch: nvr trbld ldrs* **14/1**
00- **5** *1* **Fully Armed (IRE)**[172] [7001] 3-8-12 0 .... MartinLane 2 26
(Rae Guest) *trckd ldrs: rdn 3f out: sn btn* **80/1**
50-4 **6** *1 1/2* **Bahri Sheen (IRE)**[5] [1130] 3-9-0 70 .... KierenFox(3) 8 27
(John Best) *hld up: rdn over 2f out: nvr any imp* **12/1**
00 **7** *1 1/2* **Savinien**[30] [818] 3-9-3 0 .... CathyGannon 4 22
(David Evans) *wnt lft leaving stalls: in tch: rdn 3f out: wknd over 1f out* **50/1**
0- **D** *1 1/4* **Black Cadillac (IRE)**[190] [6532] 3-9-3 0 .... JimmyFortune 1 35
(Andrew Balding) *led tl rdn over 1f out: sn no ch w wnr: wknd fnl f* **7/4**[1]

1m 13.63s (1.73) **Going Correction** +0.275s/f (Slow) **8** Ran SP% **113.7**
Speed ratings (Par 98): **99,88,87,78,75 73,71,76**
toteswingers:1&2:£3.90, 1&3:£3.60, 2&3:£5.80 CSF £21.78 TOTE £2.70: £1.10, £1.50, £2.80; EX 21.10.
Owner Hamdan Al Maktoum **Bred** Mrs Sheila Oakes **Trained** Newmarket, Suffolk

FOCUS
Not much strength in depth, but a useful winner even though he had little to beat.
A'Faal Official explanation: jockey said filly was very green
Bahri Sheen(IRE) Official explanation: jockey said gelding reared in stalls
Savinien Official explanation: jockey said gelding hung left
Black Cadillac(IRE) Official explanation: jockey said colt stopped quickly

1237 FREE FOOTBALL BETS WITH FREEBETTING.CO.UK H'CAP 7f (P)

5:05 (5:06) (Class 3) (0-95,92) 4-Y-O+ **£5,828** (£1,734) **Stalls** Low

Form RPR
/45- **1** **Son Of The Cat (USA)**[322] [2316] 5-9-1 92 .... (t) AdamBeschizza(5) 1 98
(Brian Gubby) *awkward leaving stalls: racd keenly trcking ldr: upsides over 2f out: rdn over 1f out: tk narrow advantage fnl 100yds: drvn out* **5/2**[2]
-113 **2** *nk* **Advertisement (USA)**[49] [613] 4-9-2 88 .... (t) GeorgeBaker 2 93
(Jeremy Noseda) *led: jnd over 2f out: rdn ent fnl f: narrowly hdd fnl 100yds: kpt on* **2/7**[1]

1m 29.51s (4.71) **Going Correction** +0.275s/f (Slow) **2** Ran SP% **106.3**
Speed ratings (Par 107): **84,83**
TOTE £3.50.
Owner Brian Gubby **Bred** Andover Stable Llc **Trained** Bagshot, Surrey

FOCUS
Only two runners after the race was almost boycotted completely, with the prize money falling short of the tariff set by the Horsemen's Group. Advertisement set a modest tempo, resulting in a time over six seconds outside standard. It's hard to rate the worth of the form.

NOTEBOOK
Son Of The Cat(USA) was said by his trainer to have only been declared because he needed a run before next week's Abernant Stakes at Newmarket, having been off since last May, but the gelding is not entered at Newmarket, reportedly due to an oversight. Despite being keen early, the winner picked up well and clearly retains a deal of ability. There are no immediate plans, but the trainer said this trip stretches the gelding's stamina and he wouldn't want the ground too fast. (op 11-4 tchd 3-1)
Advertisement(USA)'s jockey took a while to get serious, allowing the winner to get upsides entering the straight, and the runner-up was one-paced when under pressure, eventually being run out of it. He was returning from a 49-day break and it's hard to gauge exactly what he achieved, but according to Jeremy Noseda he only took his chance because he's due to go the sales at Doncaster on April 21. (tchd 1-4 tchd 3-10 in places)

1238 FREE BETTING WITH FREEBETTING.CO.UK H'CAP 1m 4f (P)

5:40 (5:40) (Class 2) (0-105,92) 4-Y-O+ **£8,095** (£2,408; £1,203; £601) **Stalls** Low

Form RPR
1121 **1** **Beaubrav**[14] [994] 5-9-7 91 .... (t) JimCrowley 1 99
(Michael Madgwick) *racd in cl 4th: drew upsides over 1f out: shkn up to ld ent fnl f: rdn and sn in command* **4/5**[1]
2510 **2** *1 3/4* **King Olav (UAE)**[7] [1102] 6-9-7 91 .... NeilCallan 3 95
(Tony Carroll) *led for 4f: trckd ldr: rdn whn sltly hmpd over 2f out: kpt on to regain 2nd ins fnl f* **7/2**[3]
0002 **3** *1* **Tominator**[14] [994] 4-9-7 92 .... TonyCulhane 2 94
(Reg Hollinshead) *stdd s: trckd ldrs racing keenly: led wl over 2f out: rdn over 1f out: hdd ent fnl f: no ex* **11/4**[2]
504- **4** *3/4* **Magicalmysterytour (IRE)**[162] [7208] 8-9-2 86 .... StevieDonohoe 4 87
(Willie Musson) *trckd ldr: led after 4f: rdn and hdd wl over 2f out: kpt on same pce* **12/1**

2m 34.15s (1.15) **Going Correction** +0.275s/f (Slow)
WFA 4 from 5yo+ 1lb **4** Ran SP% **112.1**
Speed ratings (Par 109): **107,105,105,104**
CSF £4.17 TOTE £1.60; EX 6.20.
Owner The B B Partnership **Bred** Star Pointe Ltd,Brosnan And Williamson **Trained** Denmead, Hants

FOCUS
Another race in which prize money fell short of the tariff set by the Horsemen's Group and consequently only four runners. Predictably enough they went a steady pace, so the form needs treating with caution.

NOTEBOOK
Beaubrav was held up last of the four runners, but he remained in touch throughout and, having travelled best into the straight, was always doing enough for pressure. He's now 6-8 at Lingfield and was defying a 6lb rise for his latest course win. (op 6-5 tchd 4-6)
King Olav(UAE) was outpaced on the downhill run before the straight and was short of room against the inside rail approaching the final bend, before staying on dourly. He wasn't unlucky, though. (tchd 10-3 and 4-1)
Tominator was keen without cover down the back straight and had little left when coming under pressure. (tchd 7-2)
Magicalmysterytour(IRE) has won when fresh, but he shaped as though in need of this first start after a 162-day break and a steadily run race probably didn't suit. (op 13-2 tchd 14-1)
T/Plt: £63.90 to a £1 stake. Pool:£43,836.89 - 500.25 winning tickets T/Qpdt: £19.80 to a £1 stake. Pool:£2,175.44 - 81.00 winning tickets TM

THIRSK (L-H)

Saturday, April 9

OFFICIAL GOING: Good (7.4)
Wind: Breezy, half against Weather: Hot, sunny

1239 THOMAS LORD STKS (H'CAP) 6f

1:35 (1:36) (Class 5) (0-70,70) 4-Y-O+ **£2,914** (£867; £433; £216) **Stalls** High

Form RPR
0211 **1** **Dickie Le Davoir**[11] [1029] 7-9-1 67 .... (b) JamesSullivan(3) 10 82
(Richard Guest) *dwlt: hld up: hdwy on outside of gp over 2f out: led ins fnl f: kpt on strly* **20/1**
300- **2** *2 1/2* **Mandalay King (IRE)**[200] [6267] 6-9-3 66 .... PaulMulrennan 4 73
(Marjorie Fife) *midfield: drvn over 2f out: hdwy to chse wnr wl ins fnl f: r.o* **18/1**
326- **3** *1 1/4* **Carrie's Magic**[277] [3751] 4-9-1 69 .... (b[1]) LMcNiff(5) 13 72
(David Barron) *mde most tl hung lft and hdd ins fnl f: kpt on same pce* **9/1**[3]
000- **4** *1/2* **Timeless Elegance (IRE)**[189] [6572] 4-9-5 68 .... FrederikTylicki 2 69
(Howard Johnson) *racd alone far side: a.p: rdn 2f out: kpt on same pce fnl f* **14/1**
00-0 **5** *2* **Mandurah (IRE)**[8] [1073] 7-9-2 65 .... AdrianNicholls 8 60
(David Nicholls) *cl up: ev ch and hung lft over 1f out: kpt on same pce ins fnl f* **16/1**
0-01 **6** *shd* **Powerful Pierre**[19] [928] 4-8-10 64 .... (v) LeeTopliss(5) 15 59
(Ian McInnes) *trckd ldrs: drvn 1/2-way: one pce fnl 2f* **9/1**[3]
311- **7** *nk* **Henry Morgan**[234] [5211] 4-9-2 65 .... TomEaves 16 59
(Bryan Smart) *tubed: in tch: drvn over 2f out: no imp over 1f out* **11/2**[2]
340- **8** *2 1/2* **Northern Bolt**[158] [7283] 6-9-7 70 .... (b) PatrickMathers 9 56
(Ian McInnes) *prom: drvn over 2f out: sn one pce* **33/1**
2106 **9** *1/2* **Dancing Freddy (IRE)**[32] [794] 4-9-4 70 .... (p) RobertLButler(3) 6 54
(Richard Guest) *cl up: effrt and ev ch over 2f out: no ex over 1f out* **66/1**
200- **10** *1/2* **Cawdor (IRE)**[132] [7613] 5-9-0 70 .... KristinStubbs(7) 12 53
(Linda Stubbs) *towards rr and sn pushed along: nvr able to chal* **20/1**
030- **11** *nk* **Cheyenne Red (IRE)**[169] [7051] 5-9-1 64 .... PJMcDonald 11 46
(Michael Dods) *trckd ldrs tl rdn and wknd 2f out* **12/1**
4100 **12** *6* **Tislaam (IRE)**[16] [956] 4-9-3 66 .... (p) RobertWinston 14 28
(Alan McCabe) *dwlt: bhd: rdn over 2f out: nvr on terms* **11/2**[2]
3611 **13** *6* **Pelmanism**[24] [867] 4-9-2 65 .... (b) PhillipMakin 3 —
(Kevin Ryan) *towards rr: pushed along over 2f out: sn btn* **4/1**[1]
30-0 **14** *3/4* **Ryedane (IRE)**[10] [1035] 9-9-2 70 .... (b) LanceBetts(5) 1 —
(Tim Easterby) *swtchd rt and hld up on outside of gp sn after s: struggling over 2f out: sn btn* **25/1**
24-6 **15** *2 3/4* **Rainy Night**[23] [880] 5-9-5 68 .... (p) PaulHanagan 7 —
(Reg Hollinshead) *towards rr: struggling over 2f out: sn btn* **12/1**

1m 14.26s (1.56) **Going Correction** +0.35s/f (Good) **15** Ran SP% **121.8**
Speed ratings (Par 103): **103,99,98,97,94 94,94,90,90,89 89,81,73,72,68**
toteswingers: 1&2 £74.70, 1&2 £56.60, 2&3 £45.20. CSF £327.19 CT £3520.90 TOTE £12.90: £2.90, £6.10, £3.70; EX 295.50 TRIFECTA Not won..
Owner Future Racing (Notts) Limited **Bred** P And Mrs A G Venner **Trained** Stainforth, S Yorks

FOCUS
The opening event was a modest handicap, with the top-weight rated 70, but it looked ultra-competitive on paper. All bar one of the runners made for the stands' rail when the stalls opened. This rates as the winner's best run since July 2009.
Tislaam(IRE) Official explanation: jockey said gelding never travelled

1240 BET ON TOTESCOOP6 AT TOTESPORT.COM H'CAP 7f

2:10 (2:11) (Class 3) (0-90,90) 4-Y-O+ **£8,418** (£2,505; £1,251; £625) **Stalls** Low

Form RPR
040- **1** **Joseph Henry**[169] [7060] 9-9-2 86 .... AdrianNicholls 10 97
(David Nicholls) *mde all: rdn over 1f out: styd on wl* **18/1**
040- **2** *1 3/4* **Hacienda (IRE)**[191] [6510] 4-9-6 90 .... JoeFanning 2 96
(Mark Johnston) *a.p: chsd wnr 1/2-way: rdn over 1f out: no imp ins fnl f* **6/1**[2]
525- **3** *1 3/4* **Ancient Cross**[169] [7060] 7-9-2 89 .... (t) JamesSullivan(3) 13 91+
(Michael Easterby) *dwlt: hld up: hdwy over 2f out: swtchd rt over 1f out: styd on* **12/1**
106- **4** *1 1/2* **Dhaular Dhar (IRE)**[141] [6709] 9-9-5 89 .... KierenFallon 14 87
(Jim Goldie) *hld up: hdwy over 1f out: styd on: nt rch ldrs* **14/1**
030- **5** *nk* **Zomerlust**[176] [6888] 9-8-12 87 .... (p) SeanLevey(5) 4 84
(John Quinn) *mid-div: hdwy 1/2-way: outpcd over 2f out: styd on ins fnl f* **16/1**
1110 **6** *nk* **Steed**[20] [925] 4-9-4 88 .... (p) PhillipMakin 8 84
(Kevin Ryan) *s.i.s: hld up: hdwy and nt clr run: swtchd rt over 1f out: r.o: nrst fin* **8/1**
066- **7** *1 3/4* **Collateral Damage (IRE)**[203] [6178] 8-9-4 88 .... (t) DavidAllan 3 79
(Tim Easterby) *mid-div: rdn over 2f out: hdwy over 1f out: nt trble ldrs* **8/1**
456- **8** *2 1/4* **Oratory (IRE)**[177] [6877] 5-9-6 90 .... SilvestreDeSousa 1 75
(Geoffrey Harker) *s.s: nvr nrr* **4/1**[1]
160- **9** *2 1/4* **San Cassiano (IRE)**[222] [5605] 4-9-6 90 .... PJMcDonald 6 69
(Ruth Carr) *chsd wnr to 1/2-way: wknd over 1f out* **20/1**
66-1 **10** *9* **Bowmaker**[52] [557] 4-9-2 86 .... GregFairley 9 41
(Mark Johnston) *sn pushed along and a in rr* **7/1**[3]
0-04 **11** *1* **Ezdeyaad (USA)**[49] [615] 7-9-6 90 .... JackMitchell 11 42
(Ed Walker) *prom: rdn over 2f out: wkng whn hmpd over 1f out* **14/1**
033- **12** *2* **Celtic Sultan (IRE)**[203] [6178] 7-9-6 90 .... (b) MickyFenton 5 37
(Tom Tate) *mid-div: hmpd after 1f: sn prom: hung rt over 4f out: wknd over 2f out* **10/1**
200- **13** *1* **Glenridding**[143] [7488] 7-9-2 86 .... (p) PaulMulrennan 7 30
(James Given) *plld hrd and prom: lost pl 4f out: wknd 1/2-way* **28/1**

1m 29.44s (2.24) **Going Correction** +0.50s/f (Yiel) **13** Ran SP% **118.5**
Speed ratings (Par 107): **107,105,103,101,100 100,98,96,93,83 82,79,78**
toteswingers: 1&2 £41.30, 1&3 £58.70, 2&3 £15.30. CSF £121.52 CT £1411.59 TOTE £22.20: £4.70, £1.90, £3.50; EX 192.50 TRIFECTA Not won..
Owner Billy Hughes **Bred** John Brown & Megan Dennis **Trained** Sessay, N Yorks
■ Stewards' Enquiry : Phillip Makin caution: careless riding.

FOCUS
A decent handicap, with all the runners rated from 86-90, and few could be confidently discounted beforehand. The front pair were 1-2 for much of the race and the form's rated around them.

NOTEBOOK
Joseph Henry, fourth in this race in 2010 and generally a reliable yardstick, led throughout. Quickly away, he was soon in a clear lead and, despite tiring slightly late on, always looked likely to hold his advantage. He cannot be improving at nine, but surely faces a rise from the handicapper after this. Connections believe he is best with some cut and may now target an event at Naas. (op 16-1)
Hacienda(IRE), gelded since last season and dropping back from 1m for this return to action, will probably benefit from a step back up in trip. He could not match the winner's early pace, racing in about sixth, and, although he stayed on well in the final furlong, was unable to get to grips with his conqueror. (op 11-2)
Ancient Cross had proved thoroughly consistent in 2010 and again posted a sound effort. No closer than mid-division in the early stages, he tried hard to close the first two down towards the finish, but could not raise a significant change of gear.
Dhaular Dhar(IRE), 4lb higher than when scoring over 1m1f last season, appears, on this evidence, to need a little help from the handicapper. He was far from disgraced but never seemed likely to make the first three. (op 12-1)
Zomerlust, wearing cheekpieces for just the second time, was always in about the same place. He rarely wins at this time of year and, if his overall record proves a good guide, will probably come into his own in highsummer. (op 20-1)
Steed, who ran up a sequence of wins on the AW over the winter, had disappointed on his latest turf outing. This was a much better effort, though, and he plugged on gamely in the home straight. (op 11-1)

1241 TOTESPORT.COM H'CAP 5f
2:45 (2:47) (Class 3) (0-95,95) 3-Y-O **£8,418** (£2,505; £1,251; £625) **Stalls** High

Form RPR
500- **1** **On The High Tops (IRE)**[175] 6916 3-8-2 **76**.............. AndrewMullen 12 83
(Tom Tate) *taken early to post: cl up: effrt and ev ch over 1f out: bmpd ins fnl f: hung rt and kpt on wl to ld towards fin* **18/1**
123- **2** 3/4 **Flash City (ITY)**[113] 7908 3-8-6 **80**................................(v[1]) TomEaves 15 84
(Bryan Smart) *led: rdn whn edgd lft and blkd ins fnl f: kpt on: hdd nr fin* **16/1**
410- **3** 2 **Boundaries**[183] 6719 3-8-9 **83**...................................(v) PaulMulrennan 16 80
(Tim Easterby) *trckd ldrs: effrt over 1f out: kpt on same pce ins fnl f* **25/1**
200- **4** 1/2 **Jamesway (IRE)**[189] 6568 3-9-2 **90**................................ TonyHamilton 5 85+
(Richard Fahey) *taken early to post: bhd and outpcd: swtchd rt 1/2-way: kpt on wl fnl f: nrst fin* **18/1**
224- **5** 1 **Cocktail Charlie**[222] 5604 3-9-7 **95**............................. RobertWinston 10 86
(Tim Easterby) *towards rr: hdwy 1/2-way: rdn over 1f out: kpt on same pce ins fnl f* **9/1**
-141 **6** 3/4 **Even Stevens**[18] 940 3-8-13 **90**... BillyCray[(3)] 6 79
(David Nicholls) *trckd ldrs: rdn and edgd lft over 1f out: kpt on same pce fnl f* **7/1[2]**
031- **7** 1 3/4 **Indieslad**[206] 6075 3-8-6 **80**....................................... SilvestreDeSousa 2 62+
(Ann Duffield) *dwlt: bhd and outpcd: hdwy over 1f out: nrst fin* **17/2**
001- **8** 1 **El Viento (FR)**[175] 6916 3-8-7 **88**....................................... LauraBarry[(7)] 9 67
(Richard Fahey) *towards rr: drvn after 2f: hdwy over 1f out: n.d* **20/1**
030- **9** nk **Ballista (IRE)**[182] 6751 3-9-7 **95**................................ RichardKingscote 7 73
(Tom Dascombe) *dwlt: bhd and outpcd: sme late hdwy: nvr rchd ldrs* **14/1**
-411 **10** shd **Sacrosanctus**[51] 578 3-8-11 **85**...................................... TomQueally 13 62
(David Nicholls) *bhd: hmpd over 3f out: sn outpcd: styd on fnl f: nvr on terms* **12/1**
1- **11** 1 3/4 **Above The Stars**[360] 1294 3-8-10 **84**............................. PaulHanagan 11 55
(Richard Fahey) *in tch: rdn and hung lft over 2f out: wknd over 1f out* **13/2[1]**
001- **12** 3 3/4 **Berberana (IRE)**[164] 7174 3-8-7 **81**.................................. DavidAllan 8 39
(Tim Easterby) *in tch: drvn along 1/2-way: sn wknd* **8/1[3]**
315- **13** 3 1/2 **Barbieri (IRE)**[162] 7204 3-9-2 **90**....................................... SteveDrowne 3 35
(Jeremy Gask) *midfield on outside: struggling over 2f out: sn btn* **20/1**
310- **14** 3 1/4 **Watts Up Son**[183] 6719 3-8-0 **79**......................................(t) NeilFarley[(5)] 4 12
(Declan Carroll) *bhd and sn drvn along: nvr on terms* **33/1**
000- **15** 8 **Boundless Spirit**[204] 6139 3-8-6 **80**............................. AdrianNicholls 1 —
(David Nicholls) *spd centre tl rdn and wknd fr 2f out* **16/1**
041- **R** **Magnini (IRE)**[165] 7142 3-8-5 **79**................................... PJMcDonald 14 —
(Kevin Ryan) *taken early to post: in tch: hmpd over 3f out: sn veered rt and crashed through stands' rail: fatally injured* **9/1**

60.23 secs (0.63) **Going Correction** +0.35s/f (Good) **16** Ran SP% **120.4**
Speed ratings (Par 102): **108,106,103,102,101 100,97,95,95,94 92,86,80,75,62** —
toteswingers: 1&2 £77.70, 1&3 £14.60, 2&3 £7.10. CSF £264.01 CT £3796.20 TOTE £25.40: £3.80, £4.30, £6.00, £4.10; EX 324.70 TRIFECTA Not won..
Owner The Ivy Syndicate **Bred** Mrs Clodagh McStay **Trained** Tadcaster, N Yorks

FOCUS
Another wide-open handicap, this time featuring several lightly raced runners, and predictably the whole field came towards the stands' side. The first three were all drawn high and the winner is rated back to his 2yo form.

NOTEBOOK
On The High Tops(IRE), whose early-season two-year-old form gave him a decent chance, fared much better than in some of his more recent races. Always in the first three, racing up against the stands' rail, he just got the better of a hard-fought battle, involving a bit of a barging match, with the runner-up. His immediate future seems dependent on how the handicapper reacts.
Flash City(ITY) was fitted with a first-time visor for this seasonal reappearance and it certainly did him no harm. He was in front at an early stage and lost out only in the dying strides. If his rating does not suffer too much for this, he should remain competitive.
Boundaries, 6lb higher than when scoring at Chester in September 2010, tried hard to overcome that rise. He was always in the first half-dozen but, although he did nothing wrong in the final furlong, he never quite looked capable of troubling the first two. (tchd 28-1)
Jamesway(IRE) has been gelded since last season, but the surgery does not, on this evidence, appear to have made enough difference to suggest he is likely to overcome what looks a less-than-generous mark. (op 25-1)
Cocktail Charlie, gelded since his fourth in a Listed event at Ripon last August, was a little outpaced in the early stages. He made up some ground from halfway, but it was not enough for him to take a major role at the business end. (op 17-2)
Even Stevens had been raised 15lb since scoring by nine lengths at Southwell in March and this run suggests that was an overreaction from the handicapper. He was close to the pace from the start and held his place until halfway, but could not quicken when it really mattered. (op 11-2)

1242 MICHAEL FOSTER MEMORIAL EBF CONDITIONS STKS 6f
3:15 (3:20) (Class 2) 4-Y-O+
£9,346 (£2,799; £1,399; £700; £349; £175) **Stalls** High

Form RPR
4-50 **1** **Evens And Odds (IRE)**[58] 497 7-9-0 102....................... KierenFallon 6 105
(David Nicholls) *a.p: pushed along over 2f out: rdn to ld ins fnl f: edgd lft: r.o* **6/1**
110- **2** 1/2 **Redford (IRE)**[182] 6735 6-9-0 111...................................... TomQueally 2 103
(David Nicholls) *hld up: hdwy to ld over 1f out: hung rt: hdd and unable qck ins fnl f* **7/2[2]**
444- **3** 1 3/4 **Hamish McGonagall**[191] 6508 6-9-0 107............................ DavidAllan 7 98
(Tim Easterby) *led: rdn and hdd over 1f out: styd on same pce ins fnl f* **10/3[1]**
06-0 **4** 2 1/4 **Castles In The Air**[7] 1094 6-9-0 102................................. PaulHanagan 3 91
(Richard Fahey) *w ldrs: rdn and ev ch whn hung lft over 1f out: no ex ins fnl f* **10/3[1]**
00-0 **5** 3/4 **Rash Judgement**[7] 1093 6-9-0 89.................................. RobertWinston 5 88?
(Eric Alston) *dwlt: hld up: swtchd lft and rdn over 2f out: no imp fnl f* **16/1**
000- **6** shd **Damika (IRE)**[176] 6888 8-9-0 95................................... MichaelStainton 4 88
(Richard Whitaker) *hld up: rdn over 2f out: nt trble ldrs* **12/1**
320- **7** 2 **Tax Free (IRE)**[154] 7351 9-9-0 102................................... AdrianNicholls 1 81
(David Nicholls) *w ldrs: rdn and ev ch over 1f out: wknd ins fnl f* **5/1[3]**

1m 13.28s (0.58) **Going Correction** +0.35s/f (Good) **7** Ran SP% **112.9**
Speed ratings (Par 109): **110,109,107,104,103 102,100**
toteswingers: 1&2 £10.00, 1&3 £2.00, 2&3 £2.60. CSF £26.47 TOTE £6.70: £3.40, £2.00; EX 25.20.
Owner Dab Hand Racing **Bred** Old Carhue Stud **Trained** Sessay, N Yorks
■ Stewards' Enquiry : Tom Queally one-day ban: careless riding (Apr 23)

FOCUS
Official ratings indicated an ability range of 22lb in this conditions event and, on that basis, just five had realistic claims. The winner is probably the best guide, but the form of these races is rarely reliable.

NOTEBOOK
Evens And Odds(IRE), winner of the 2010 Stewards' Cup from a mark of 98 and now 4lb higher, seemed to run right up to his best. Always in the leading quartet close to the stands' rail, he quickened smartly in the final furlong and held on well under pressure. This was a good effort, especially as he had suffered a bout of colic while in Dubai earlier in the year. (op 5-1 tchd 9-2)
Redford(IRE), successful off 103 over 7f last season and now rated 111, ran as if this race would bring him on. He travelled smoothly most of the way, making his challenge wide of the winner, but appeared to get tired in the closing stages. His next target is the Duke of York Stakes. (op 10-3 tchd 4-1)
Hamish McGonagall, admirably consistent over 5f last season, was another arguably below his peak. He broke well, as usual, and led up against the stands' rail, but could not engage a higher gear when the first two quickened up. The minimum trip probably suits him better. (op 3-1)
Castles In The Air, dropping back in trip after finishing towards the rear in the Lincoln a week previously, looked more at home over this shorter distance. He raced in the leading trio from the outset and, although he was outpaced in the closing stages, plugged on gamely. (op 5-1)
Rash Judgement, whose official mark of 89 made him easily the lowest-rated runner, ran as well as could be expected. Steadied at the start, he simply could not get to grips with the leading contenders. (op 20-1 tchd 25-1)
Damika(IRE), successful in the 2010 Great St Wilfrid off 94, missed the kick from the stalls and was not quite fast enough to recoup the lost ground against rivals as talented as the first four. He will probably be more at home in a handicap. (op 25-1)
Tax Free(IRE), twice successful at Pattern level in 2009 but without a win last season, is becoming disappointing. He tried to match strides with the pace-setter early on, but faded quickly at the business end. At nine, he looks past his best. (op 4-1)

1243 SQUIRE FREDERICK BELL H'CAP 1m 4f
3:50 (3:50) (Class 5) (0-75,75) 4-Y-O+ **£2,914** (£867; £433; £216) **Stalls** Low

Form RPR
562- **1** **Ubi Ace**[34] 6050 5-9-5 **72**.. GrahamGibbons 11 85
(Tim Walford) *prom: smooth hdwy to ld over 2f out: rdn and edgd lft over 1f out: drvn out fnl f* **6/1[2]**
-520 **2** 3/4 **Time Square (FR)**[31] 805 4-9-2 **70**................................(t) TomQueally 3 82
(Tony Carroll) *prom: effrt 3f out: edgd lft and hdwy to press wnr over 1f out: kpt on fnl f* **12/1**
134- **3** 8 **Patavium (IRE)**[16] 5215 8-9-3 **70**.................................. TonyHamilton 13 69
(Edwin Tuer) *t.k.h: cl up: effrt and ev ch over 2f out: outpcd by ldng pair appr fnl f* **16/1**
0642 **4** 1/2 **Maslak (IRE)**[10] 1046 7-9-1 **68**.. ChrisCatlin 9 66
(Peter Hiatt) *trckd ldrs: led 4f out to over 2f out: sn rdn and nt qckn* **11/1**
45 **5** hd **General Duke's**[28] 850 4-8-9 **63** ow1................................ PhillipMakin 8 61
(Kevin Ryan) *hld up: rdn and outpcd over 3f out: styd on fnl 2f: nvr able to chal* **16/1**
40-0 **6** 3/4 **Valdan (IRE)**[12] 1017 7-8-7 **63**..............................(t) AndrewHeffernan[(3)] 1 60
(Maurice Barnes) *dwlt: bhd: drvn over 5f out: hrd rdn and styd on fnl 2f: n.d* **14/1**
32-6 **7** nse **Houston Dynimo (IRE)**[93] 68 6-8-9 **62**..................... PaulMulrennan 6 59
(Nicky Richards) *midfield on ins: hdwy and prom 2f out: sn rdn and nt qckn* **16/1**
325- **8** nk **Elmfield Giant (USA)**[157] 7293 4-9-7 **75**.......................... PaulHanagan 10 71
(Richard Fahey) *hld up in tch: effrt and drvn over 3f out: edgd lft 2f out: kpt on same pce* **8/1**
62-1 **9** 3 1/2 **Madamlily (IRE)**[10] 1039 5-9-0 **67**....................................... TomEaves 7 58
(John Quinn) *in tch: drvn and outpcd 3f out: no imp fnl 2f* **4/1[1]**
005- **10** 1 3/4 **Think Its All Over (USA)**[170] 7042 4-9-5 **73**.............. FrederikTylicki 14 61
(Julie Camacho) *hld up: rn wd first bnd after 2f: effrt on outside over 3f out: nvr able to chal* **14/1**
060/ **11** 6 **Dar Es Salaam**[351] 6995 7-8-12 **70**.................................. DaleSwift[(5)] 2 48
(Brian Ellison) *hld up on ins: struggling over 5f out: n.d after* **16/1**
1443 **12** 10 **Eton Fable (IRE)**[10] 1072 6-8-11 **64**..................................(p) TravisBlock 4 26
(Colin Teague) *led to 4f out: rdn and wknd fr 3f out* **33/1**
/21- **13** nk **Jackday (IRE)**[323] 2295 6-9-5 **72**......................................(p) DavidAllan 5 34
(Tim Easterby) *hld up: pushed along 5f out: nvr on terms* **15/2[3]**
366- **14** 32 **Streets Of War (USA)**[170] 7042 4-9-2 **70**.............. SilvestreDeSousa 12 —
(Geoffrey Harker) *hld up: reminders and outpcd over 5f out: sn btn: eased whn no ch fnl 2f* **10/1**

2m 41.38s (5.18) **Going Correction** +0.50s/f (Yiel)
WFA 4 from 5yo+ 1lb **14** Ran SP% **122.1**
Speed ratings (Par 103): **102,101,96,95,95 95,95,94,92,91 87,80,80,59**
toteswingers: 1&2 £21.20, 1&3 £7.80, 2&3 £10.30. CSF £77.48 CT £1114.18 TOTE £8.80: £3.40, £4.40, £3.90; EX 109.90 TRIFECTA Not won..
Owner N J Maher **Bred** Steel's Thoroughbred Breeding **Trained** Sheriff Hutton, N Yorks

FOCUS
Just a run-of-the-mill handicap, with the top-weight rated 75, but it was run at a decent pace and the first two drew well clear of the rest. Not easy form to pin down.
Houston Dynimo(IRE) Official explanation: jockey said gelding was denied a clear run
Streets Of War(USA) Official explanation: jockey said gelding never travelled

1244 MARIE JOWETT "MILESTONE" BIRTHDAY H'CAP (DIV I) 7f
4:55 (4:57) (Class 5) (0-75,77) 4-Y-O+ **£2,729** (£806; £403) **Stalls** Low

Form RPR
-135 **1** **Lindoro**[10] 1035 6-8-4 **61** oh1................................... AndrewHeffernan[(3)] 8 70
(Kevin M Prendergast) *chsd ldr: led over 2f out: drvn out* **6/1[2]**

0042 **2** *1/2* **Mr Macattack**[9] 1061 6-9-6 **77**....(t) RossAtkinson(3) 7 84
(Tom Dascombe) *hld up: hdwy over 2f out: rdn over 1f out: styd on u.p* **4/1**[1]

430- **3** *3/4* **Mujaadel (USA)**[165] 7143 6-9-7 **75**.... PaulMulrennan 9 80
(David Nicholls) *hld up: hdwy 4f out: rdn over 1f out: edgd rt ins fnl f: styd on* **15/2**[3]

300- **4** *3 1/4* **Elusive Sue (USA)**[165] 7146 4-9-2 **75**.... LeeTopliss(5) 14 72
(Richard Fahey) *hld up: hdwy 2f out: rdn over 1f out: edgd lft fnl f: nt rch ldrs* **20/1**

10R- **5** *5* **Just The Tonic**[227] 5421 4-8-12 **66**.... LeeNewman 1 49
(Marjorie Fife) *hdwy to go prom over 5f out: rdn over 1f out: wknd fnl f* **28/1**

20-0 **6** *1 1/2* **Raleigh Quay (IRE)**[10] 1035 4-9-6 **74**.... FrederikTylicki 2 53
(Micky Hammond) *hld up: r.o ins fnl f: nvr nrr* **22/1**

000- **7** *1 1/2* **Come And Go (UAE)**[217] 5756 5-9-5 **73**.... DanielTudhope 4 48
(Ian McInnes) *prom: rdn over 1f out: wknd fnl f* **20/1**

0366 **8** *1/2* **Duplicity**[38] 732 4-8-7 **61** oh1....(p) WilliamCarson 12 35
(Richard Guest) *led to over 2f out: rdn and wknd over 1f out* **16/1**

020- **9** *7* **Jupiter Fidius**[168] 7082 4-8-10 **64**....(p) PhillipMakin 13 19
(Kate Walton) *hld up: wknd 1/2-way* **14/1**

0155 **10** *1 1/2* **Final Salute**[25] 853 5-8-9 **63**....(v) TomEaves 6 14
(Bryan Smart) *chsd ldrs: rdn over 3f out: wknd 2f out* **20/1**

1- **11** *6* **Hakuna Matata**[174] 6966 4-9-3 **71**.... PaulHanagan 10 —
(Brian Ellison) *sn bhd* **4/1**[1]

1m 30.97s (3.77) **Going Correction** +0.50s/f (Yiel) **11** Ran SP% **100.7**
Speed ratings (Par 103): **98,97,96,92,87 85,83,83,75,73 66**
toteswingers: 1&2 £5.60, 1&3 £7.20, 2&3 £5.40. CSF £19.75 CT £112.47 TOTE £7.00: £1.70, £2.00, £2.00; EX 33.40 Trifecta £48.00 Part won. Pool: £67.96 - 0.71 winning units..
Owner Alchemy Bloodstock **Bred** Pigeon House Stud **Trained** Matlon, N Yorks
■ Stewards' Enquiry : Andrew Heffernan one-day ban: used whip with excessive frequency (Apr 23)
Ross Atkinson one-day ban: used whip with excessive frequency (Apr 23)

FOCUS
No superstars in this handicap, but plenty with chances on form. Pretty ordinary form, but the winner used to be a lot better than this.
Final Salute Official explanation: jockey said gelding failed to handle the bend

1245 MARIE JOWETT "MILESTONE" BIRTHDAY H'CAP (DIV II) 7f
5:25 (5:26) (Class 5) (0-75,76) 4-Y-0+ **£2,729** (£806; £403) **Stalls** Low

Form RPR

230- **1** **George Benjamin**[180] 6800 4-9-6 **74**.... AdrianNicholls 12 86
(David Nicholls) *racd wd: hld up: gd hdwy on outside over 2f out: edgd lft and led over 1f out: styd on strly* **7/1**[3]

230- **2** *2* **High Rolling**[75] 7988 4-8-7 **61**.... RobertWinston 2 67
(Tim Easterby) *prom: ev ch over 2f out: chsng wnr and rdn whn swtchd rt appr fnl f: r.o* **18/1**

6-52 **3** *2* **Tevez**[12] 1017 6-9-3 **76**.... SeanLevey(5) 8 77
(Des Donovan) *dwlt: hld up and bhd: gd hdwy on outside to chse ldrs over 1f out: kpt on same pce fnl f* **7/1**[3]

00-6 **4** *3/4* **Fazza**[10] 1035 4-8-7 **61** oh2.... DavidAllan 1 60
(Edwin Tuer) *midfield: hdwy on ins over 2f out: sn rdn: nt qckn fnl f* **11/1**

50-1 **5** *hd* **Ezra Church (IRE)**[60] 454 4-9-4 **72**.... LeeNewman 4 70
(David Barron) *prom: rdn over 2f out: kpt on same pce fnl f* **9/1**

042- **6** *3 1/2* **Mozayada (USA)**[324] 2262 7-8-7 **61** oh1.... SilvestreDeSousa 3 50
(Mel Brittain) *cl up: led 1/2-way to over 1f out: wknd fnl f* **20/1**

1331 **7** *1* **Hinton Admiral**[15] 960 7-9-7 **75**.... JoeFanning 11 61
(Keith Dalgleish) *t.k.h in midfield: effrt over 2f out: sn hung lft: no imp fr over 1f out* **8/1**

600- **8** *2 3/4* **Rock 'N' Royal**[158] 7283 4-9-5 **73**.... PaulHanagan 7 52
(Richard Fahey) *midfield: drvn along over 2f out: no imp over 1f out* **11/2**[1]

1323 **9** *1 1/4* **Smalljohn**[10] 1035 5-9-7 **75**....(v) TomEaves 9 50
(Bryan Smart) *trckd ldrs: drvn along 3f out: wknd over 1f out* **6/1**[2]

026- **10** *1/2* **Fama Mac**[164] 7183 4-8-10 **64**.... PhillipMakin 6 38
(Neville Bycroft) *towards rr: rdn after 3f: nvr on [illegible]* **22/1**

000- **11** *3 1/2* **Child Of Our Time (IRE)**[177] 6864 4-8-11 **65**.... PatrickMathers 14 30
(Colin Teague) *hld up: pushed along 1/2-way: shortlived effrt over 2f out: sn n.d* **50/1**

144- **12** *6* **Salerosa (IRE)**[112] 7935 6-9-0 **68**.... PaulMulrennan 10 16
(Ann Duffield) *hld up: rdn along over 2f out: nvr able to chal* **16/1**

402- **13** *44* **Captain Macarry (IRE)**[175] 6922 6-9-6 **74**....(v) WilliamCarson 13 —
(Stuart Williams) *led to 1/2-way: wknd qckly over 2f out* **14/1**

14 *74* **Giant Among Men (USA)**[1024] 3188 6-9-2 **70**.... KierenFallon 5 —
(Richard Guest) *towards rr: drvn along 1/2-way: sn lost tch: eased* **10/1**

1m 30.43s (3.23) **Going Correction** +0.50s/f (Yiel) **14** Ran SP% **122.1**
Speed ratings (Par 103): **101,98,96,95,95 91,90,87,85,85 81,74,23,—**
toteswingers: 1&2 £23.60, 1&3 £8.00, 2&3 £33.40. CSF £125.56 CT £954.45 TOTE £7.70: £2.50, £6.00, £3.30; EX 121.60 TRIFECTA Not won..
Owner C M & M A Scaife **Bred** Mascalls Stud **Trained** Sessay, N Yorks

FOCUS
The second division of this 7f handicap did not appear to have quite the depth of the first. The winner is rated to his best.
Salerosa(IRE) Official explanation: jockey said mare hung right throughout
Giant Among Men(USA) Official explanation: jockey said gelding finished distressed

1246 BILSDALE MEDIAN AUCTION MAIDEN STKS 6f
6:00 (6:03) (Class 5) 3-4-Y-0 **£2,914** (£867; £433; £216) **Stalls** High

Form RPR

5- **1** **Youhavecontrol (IRE)**[192] 6458 3-9-0 0.... FrederikTylicki 9 79+
(Michael Dods) *t.k.h early: midfield: effrt whn nt clr run over 2f and over 1f out: swtchd and qcknd to ld last 100yds: hld on wl* **13/2**

442- **2** *hd* **Bertiewhittle**[161] 7224 3-9-0 65.... LeeNewman 3 78
(David Barron) *midfield: hdwy to ld over 1f out: rdn and edgd rt: hdd last 100yds: rallied* **6/1**[3]

23-2 **3** *5* **Lady Platinum Club**[15] 971 3-8-9 67....(p) PaulHanagan 14 57
(Geoffrey Oldroyd) *prom: drvn over 2f out: kpt on fnl f: no ch w first two* **7/2**[1]

4042 **4** *4* **Gorgeous Goblin (IRE)**[22] 892 4-9-4 47....(vt) JamesSullivan(3) 13 47
(David C Griffiths) *cl up: rdn and led briefly over 1f out: carried rt and sn no ex* **25/1**

2-44 **5** *3/4* **Sinadinou**[10] 1038 3-9-0 70....(b[1]) AdrianNicholls 7 50
(David Nicholls) *led: rdn 1/2-way: hdd over 1f out: n.m.r appr fnl f: sn btn* **13/2**

5442 **6** *nk* **Beautiful Day**[11] 1020 3-9-0 66.... PhillipMakin 11 46
(Kevin Ryan) *t.k.h: trckd ldrs: nt clr run over 2f out: sn rdn: wknd fnl f* **15/2**

36- **7** *3/4* **Iceblast**[154] 7346 3-9-0 0.... GrahamGibbons 8 43
(Michael Easterby) *dwlt: bhd and sn pushed along: sme hdwy whn n.m.r ins fnl f: n.d* **4/1**[2]

500- **8** *nse* **Alensgrove (IRE)**[166] 7124 3-8-9 62.... MickyFenton 6 38
(Paul Midgley) *cl up: rdn 1/2-way: ev ch over 1f out: sn btn* **18/1**

9 *2* **The Nifty Duchess** 3-8-9 0.... DavidAllan 10 32
(Tim Easterby) *dwlt: bhd and sn pushed along: nvr on terms* **20/1**

0 **10** *2 1/2* **Hardrock Diamond**[10] 1038 3-9-0 0.... PaulMulrennan 15 29
(Ben Haslam) *hld up on stands' rail: rdn over 2f out: sn btn* **66/1**

11 *9* **Maxamillion Bounty** 3-9-0 0.... TomEaves 1 —
(Michael Dods) *dwlt and wnt lft s: rn green in rr: struggling fr 1/2-way* **28/1**

1m 14.7s (2.00) **Going Correction** +0.35s/f (Good)
WFA 3 from 4yo 12lb **11** Ran SP% **113.8**
Speed ratings (Par 103): **100,99,93,87,86 86,85,85,82,79 67**
toteswingers: 1&2 £8.40, 1&3 £5.30, 2&3 £5.50. CSF £41.74 TOTE £8.70: £2.40, £2.20, £1.50; EX 68.70 TRIFECTA Part won. Pool: £247.46 - 0.90 winning units..
Owner Andrew Tinkler **Bred** Chameleon Syndicate **Trained** Denton, Co Durham
■ Stewards' Enquiry : Lee Newman one-day ban: careless riding (Apr 23)

FOCUS
Seemingly a modest maiden, made a little more interesting by a clutch of previously unraced three-year-olds from decent stables. The first two finished clear and the form has been rated a little conservatively, but could be better than it first appears.
T/Plt: £3,124.70 to a £1 stake. Pool:£52,222.18 - 12.20 winning tickets. T/Qpdt: £121.30 to a £1 stake. Pool:£3,214.78 - 19.60 winning tickets. RY

1217 WOLVERHAMPTON (A.W) (L-H)
Saturday, April 9

OFFICIAL GOING: Standard
Wind: Light across Weather: Fine

1247 FREEBETS.CO.UK GRAND NATIONAL 2011 BETTING OFFERS AMATEUR RIDERS' H'CAP (DIV I) 5f 216y(P)
6:20 (6:20) (Class 6) (0-60,63) 4-Y-0+ **£1,318** (£405; £202) **Stalls** Low

Form RPR

0201 **1** **Loyal Royal (IRE)**[10] 1041 8-10-10 **63**....(bt) MissHDavies(7) 2 71
(Milton Bradley) *s.i.s: hld up: hdwy over 1f out: r.o to ld nr fin* **7/1**

0656 **2** *1* **Cocktail Party (IRE)**[18] 941 5-9-7 **46** oh1....(p) MissCHJones(7) 11 51
(James Unett) *mid-div: hdwy 1/2-way: rdn to ld wl ins fnl f: hdd nr fin* **28/1**

0-52 **3** *1* **Espy**[19] 928 6-10-13 **59**.... MrSDobson 4 61
(Ian McInnes) *s.i.s: hld up: hdwy over 2f out: led 1f out: rdn and hdd wl ins fnl f: styd on same pce* **4/1**[2]

0403 **4** *1/2* **Muqalad (IRE)**[11] 1029 4-9-12 **49**....(vt) JustinNewman(5) 13 49
(Bryan Smart) *chsd ldrs: rdn and ev ch 1f out: styd on same pce* **10/1**

6634 **5** *3/4* **Itsthursdayalready**[54] 544 4-10-5 **56**.... MissBeckyBrisbourne(5) 3 54
(Mark Brisbourne) *hld up: hdwy over 1f out: styd on: nt trble ldrs* **9/2**[3]

6-30 **6** *nk* **Dispol Grand (IRE)**[65] 401 5-10-6 **57**.... MissWGibson(5) 7 54
(Paul Midgley) *prom: rdn and ev ch ins fnl f: no ex* **10/1**

0-33 **7** *1 1/4* **Avonlini**[21] 912 5-10-4 **50**.... MrSWalker 9 43
(Brian Baugh) *chsd ldr: rdn and ev ch over 2f out: styd on same pce fnl f* **7/2**[1]

6304 **8** *hd* **Francis Albert**[9] 1065 5-10-1 **50**....(be) MissMMullineaux(3) 6 42
(Michael Mullineaux) *led: rdn over 2f out: hdd 1f out: no ex* **11/1**

-004 **9** *3* **Mushy Peas (IRE)**[63] 432 4-10-5 **51**....(v) MissSBrotherton 12 34
(David Evans) *s.i.s: hld up: hdwy over 1f out: nvr trbld ldrs* **15/2**

005- **10** *1* **Karate Queen**[206] 6077 6-9-9 **46**.... MissVBarr(5) 10 25
(Ron Barr) *mid-div: hdwy 1/2-way: wknd over 1f out* **25/1**

0-0 **11** *1 3/4* **Leahness (IRE)**[43] 690 4-9-9 **48** oh1 ow2.... MrDRogerson(7) 5 22
(Ken Wingrove) *hld up: rdn over 2f out: a in rr* **50/1**

00-6 **12** *1/2* **Boga (IRE)**[10] 1044 4-9-11 **48**.... MrPPrince(5) 8 20
(Ron Hodges) *chsd ldrs tl wknd 2f out* **20/1**

0-60 **13** *3* **Place The Duchess**[18] 941 5-10-0 **46** oh1....(vt) MissZoeLilly 1 9
(Alastair Lidderdale) *prom tl rdn and wknd over 2f out* **25/1**

1m 15.18s (0.18) **Going Correction** 0.0s/f (Stan) **13** Ran SP% **129.0**
Speed ratings (Par 101): **98,96,95,94,93 93,91,91,87,86 83,83,79**
toteswingers:1&2:£21.20, 1&3:£4.30, 2&3:£45.70 CSF £205.10 CT £939.28 TOTE £11.50: £3.00, £6.30, £2.10; EX 394.20.
Owner JMB Racing.co.uk **Bred** J F Tuthill **Trained** Sedbury, Gloucs
■ Stewards' Enquiry : Miss M Mullineaux caution: used whip down shoulder in the forehand.

FOCUS
A modest handicap for amateur riders run at a good pace and the winner was able to overcome a position well back on the home turn. The winner's best effort since 2007.
Avonlini Official explanation: trainer said mare finished distressed

1248 FREEBETS.CO.UK GRAND NATIONAL 2011 BETTING OFFERS AMATEUR RIDERS' H'CAP (DIV II) 5f 216y(P)
6:50 (6:50) (Class 6) (0-60,60) 4-Y-0+ **£1,318** (£405; £202) **Stalls** Low

Form RPR

0060 **1** **Novay Essjay (IRE)**[10] 1052 4-10-4 **50**....(b[1]) MrSWalker 2 57
(Alan Juckes) *chsd ldrs: rdn over 1f out: r.o to ld post* **11/1**

-240 **2** *nse* **Lily Wood**[21] 912 5-9-12 **51**....(p) MissCHJones(7) 1 58
(James Unett) *chsd ldr tl led over 4f out: hung rt fr over 2f out: hdd ins fnl f: r.o* **9/1**

0623 **3** *shd* **Cavitie**[23] 880 5-10-4 **57**....(p) MrAJones(7) 4 64
(Andrew Reid) *chsd ldrs: rdn to ld ins fnl f: hdd post* **5/2**[1]

60-4 **4** *1/2* **Avoncreek**[37] 752 7-10-0 **46**.... MissSBrotherton 5 51
(Brian Baugh) *hld up: hdwy over 2f out: rdn and swtchd lft ins fnl f: r.o* **7/1**[3]

0500 **5** *1/2* **Metropolitan Chief**[21] 912 7-9-10 **49**.... MrZBaker(7) 6 52
(Paul Burgoyne) *s.i.s: hld up: hdwy over 1f out: r.o* **12/1**

5160 **6** *1/2* **Lethal**[19] 928 8-10-5 **54**.... MrMPrice(3) 3 56
(Richard Price) *led: hdd over 4f out: chsd ldrs: rdn over 1f out: styd on* **12/1**

5342 **7** *nk* **The Tatling (IRE)**[19] 934 14-10-7 **60**.... MissHDavies(7) 8 61
(Milton Bradley) *dwlt: hld up: hdwy over 1f out: no imp towards fin* **13/2**[2]

30-5 **8** *3/4* **Miss Firefly**[10] 1043 6-10-5 **56**.... MrPPrince(5) 12 54
(Ron Hodges) *trckd ldrs: rdn keenly: rdn over 1f out: styd on* **8/1**

300- **9** *5* **Imaginary Diva**[137] 7537 5-9-11 **50**.... MissKMargarson(7) 10 32
(George Margarson) *prom: rdn over 1f out: sn wknd* **25/1**

4025 **10** *1 1/2* **Fiancee (IRE)**[21] 912 5-9-12 **47**....(p) MrCMartin(3) 7 25
(Roy Brotherton) *sn outpcd: eased ins fnl f* **7/1**[3]

500- 11 2 3/4 **Charity Fair**[161] [7229] 4-9-9 46 oh1 .... MissVBarr(5) 9 15
(Ron Barr) *sn outpcd: bhd fr 1/2-way* **25/1**

1m 15.88s (0.88) **Going Correction** 0.0s/f (Stan) **11** Ran SP% **119.4**
Speed ratings (Par 101): **94,93,93,93,92 91,91,90,83,81 78**
toteswingers:1&2:£30.30, 1&3:£5.50, 2&3:£3.20 CSF £107.86 CT £288.07 TOTE £13.70: £4.80, £3.50, £1.60; EX 193.70.

Owner Whispering Winds **Bred** Camogue Stud Ltd **Trained** Abberley, Worcs

■ Stewards' Enquiry : Mr S Walker caution: used whip down shoulder in the forehand.

FOCUS
The second division of the amateur riders handicap in which the first three were always close to the pace, the time was 0.7 seconds slower than the opener and little got into from behind. A bunch finish and the form is rated through the second and third.

Fiancee(IRE) Official explanation: jockey said mare never travelled

1249 FREEBETS.CO.UK GRAND NATIONAL 2011 FREE BET BONUSES H'CAP 5f 216y(P)
7:20 (7:20) (Class 6) (0-65,69) 3-Y-0 **£1,619** (£481; £240; £120) **Stalls** Low

Form RPR
1 1 **Sound Amigo (IRE)**[40] [709] 3-9-5 63 .... BarryMcHugh 1 69+
(Ollie Pears) *trckd ldrs: shkn up over 2f out: rdn to ld ins fnl f: r.o* **7/4**[1]

5312 2 1 1/4 **Rhal (IRE)**[8] [1078] 3-9-6 69 .... AdamCarter(5) 3 71
(Bryan Smart) *w ldr tl led over 1f out: rdn and hdd ins fnl f: styd on same pce* **7/2**[3]

453- 3 shd **Piccoluck**[175] [6919] 3-9-7 65 .... DuranFentiman 4 67
(Deborah Sanderson) *pushed along early in rr: hdwy over 2f out: rdn over 1f out: styd on* **7/1**

0122 4 7 **Kassaab**[24] [868] 3-9-4 62 ....(b) SteveDrowne 2 41
(Jeremy Gask) *led: rdn: edgd lft and hdd over 1f out: wknd ins fnl f* **2/1**[2]

65-5 5 3 1/2 **Poetically**[25] [855] 3-8-11 55 .... EddieCreighton 5 23
(Joseph Tuite) *chsd ldrs: rdn over 2f out: wknd wl over 1f out* **16/1**

1m 14.78s (-0.22) **Going Correction** 0.0s/f (Stan) **5** Ran SP% **110.3**
Speed ratings (Par 96): **101,99,99,89,85**
CSF £8.22 TOTE £1.80: £1.20, £2.50; EX 10.60.

Owner Tom McManus **Bred** Sherbourne Lodge **Trained** Norton, N Yorks

FOCUS
A modest handicap run at a fair pace and not form to be getting carried away with for all the winner is sure to rate higher in time. The second and third set the standard.

1250 FREEBETS.CO.UK GRAND NATIONAL 2011 FREE BET EXCLUSIVES (S) STKS 1m 141y(P)
7:50 (7:51) (Class 6) 3-Y-0+ **£1,535** (£453; £226) **Stalls** Low

Form RPR
221/ 1 **Troopingthecolour**[6] [7550] 5-9-11 80 .... JamieSpencer 1 76
(Steve Gollings) *chsd ldrs: rdn to ld 2f out: hrd drvn and hung lft ins fnl f: styd on* **2/1**[1]

1162 2 2 1/4 **I Confess**[11] [1021] 6-9-9 70 ....(b) MatthewCosham(7) 6 76
(David Evans) *led 1f: chsd ldr tl led again over 2f out: sn hdd: rdn and nt clr run ins fnl f: swtchd rt: styd on same pce* **9/4**[2]

0111 3 7 **Erinjay (IRE)**[29] [837] 5-9-9 77 .... TCCarroll(7) 3 60
(Emmet Michael Butterly, Ire) *hld up: hdwy over 1f out: sn rdn: no ex fnl f* **2/1**[1]

4624 4 5 **Midnight Strider (IRE)**[15] [968] 5-9-11 65 ....(b[1]) MartinHarley(5) 5 48
(Joseph Tuite) *chsd ldrs: rdn over 3f out: wknd over 2f out* **9/2**[3]

46 5 10 **Lightening Force**[67] [374] 4-9-6 0 .... KieranO'Neill(5) 4 20
(Ian Patrick Browne, Ire) *pushed along to ld after 1f: rdn and hdd over 2f out: wknd over 1f out* **14/1**

60 6 42 **Bold Trumpeter**[78] [253] 5-9-11 0 .... RichardKingscote 2 —
(Milton Bradley) *hld up: rdn 1/2-way: wknd wl over 2f out: t.o* **66/1**

1m 49.98s (-0.52) **Going Correction** 0.0s/f (Stan) **6** Ran SP% **123.8**
Speed ratings (Par 101): **102,100,93,89,80 43**
toteswingers:1&2:£3.80, 1&3:£1.10, 2&3:£1.70 CSF £7.88 TOTE £2.30: £1.60, £2.00; EX 9.40.The winner was bought in for 7,250gns

Owner P J Martin **Bred** Meon Valley Stud **Trained** Scamblesby, Lincs

FOCUS
A fair seller run at a respectable pace, though the betting was of as much interest as the action with the forecast favourite Erinjay freely available to back on the exchanges at nearly twice his starting price before finishing a well-held third. The runner-up helps with the level.

Erinjay(IRE) Official explanation: jockey said gelding moved poorly

1251 FREEBETS.CO.UK GRAND NATIONAL 2011 FREE BETS FILLIES' H'CAP 1m 141y(P)
8:20 (8:20) (Class 5) (0-70,70) 3-Y-0 **£3,238** (£963; £481; £240) **Stalls** Low

Form RPR
100- 1 **Dazzling Valentine**[169] [7066] 3-9-4 70 .... AmyBaker(3) 7 77
(Alan Bailey) *hld up: rdn over 3f out: hdwy over 1f out: r.o to ld nr fin* **16/1**

003- 2 3/4 **Cinta**[163] [7185] 3-9-7 70 .... MichaelHills 6 75
(Marco Botti) *trckd ldrs: racd keenly: led 2f out: rdn ins fnl f: hdd nr fin* **3/1**[2]

403- 3 2 **Set To Music (IRE)**[206] [6071] 3-9-7 70 .... JamieSpencer 1 71
(Michael Bell) *chsd ldr: rdn and ev ch over 2f out: edgd lft over 1f out: styd on same pce ins fnl f* **7/4**[1]

-445 4 3 **Lindo Erro**[15] [967] 3-8-2 56 oh4 .... DeclanCannon(5) 5 50
(John Mackie) *prom: rdn over 3f out: styd on* **22/1**

505- 5 1/2 **Fairlie Dinkum**[173] [6979] 3-9-6 69 .... GregFairley 4 62
(Bryan Smart) *led: rdn and hdd 2f out: wknd ins fnl f* **8/1**

034- 6 1 1/2 **Miss Chicane**[192] [6468] 3-9-6 69 .... ShaneKelly 3 58
(Walter Swinburn) *prom: rdn over 1f out: wknd ins fnl f* **4/1**[3]

245- 7 1 **Zamina (IRE)**[150] [7393] 3-9-1 64 .... JamesDoyle 2 51
(Sylvester Kirk) *hld up: rdn 1/2-way: sn wl outpcd: styd on ins fnl f* **8/1**

04-0 8 19 **Talkative Guest (IRE)**[9] [1060] 3-9-1 64 .... TomQueally 8 —
(George Margarson) *hld up: bhd fr 1/2-way* **16/1**

1m 49.35s (-1.15) **Going Correction** 0.0s/f (Stan) **8** Ran SP% **119.7**
Speed ratings (Par 95): **105,104,102,99,99 98,97,80**
toteswingers:1&2:£7.90, 1&3:£7.00, 2&3:£1.50 CSF £66.83 CT £132.55 TOTE £17.70: £4.10, £2.80, £1.02.

Owner The Glenbuccaneers **Bred** Chippenham Lodge Stud Ltd **Trained** Newmarket, Suffolk

FOCUS
Probably an uncompetitive handicap in which all bar one of the unexposed runners disappointed and the rank outsider well out of the weights not beaten far in fourth. The pace looked fair and the form is rated around the third.

1252 FREEBETS.CO.UK GRAND NATIONAL 2011 FREE BETTING MAIDEN FILLIES' STKS 1m 1f 103y(P)
8:50 (8:50) (Class 5) 3-Y-0+ **£2,266** (£674; £337; £168) **Stalls** Low

Form RPR
33 1 **Monster Munchie (JPN)**[42] [699] 3-8-5 0 .... HarryBentley(5) 1 57
(William Knight) *led: hdd 6f out: chsd clr ldr: rdn to ld over 1f out: r.o* **5/6**[1]

2 1 1/4 **Sizzle (FR)** 3-8-10 0 .... RichardKingscote 2 54
(Tom Dascombe) *trckd ldrs: shkn up over 2f out: nt clr run over 1f out: styd on* **Evs**[2]

3 hd **Redhotdoc**[531] 7-9-6 0 .... MatthewMcGhee(7) 4 58
(Bill Moore) *s.s: hdwy to chse ldr over 7f out: pushed along to ld 6f out: sn clr: rdn over 2f out: hdd over 1f out: unable qck towards fin* **40/1**

36 4 7 **Olimamu (IRE)**[14] [983] 4-9-10 0 ....(t) SimonPearce(3) 5 43
(Lydia Pearce) *chsd ldrs: rdn over 3f out: outpcd fr over 2f out* **10/1**[3]

5 23 **Ellielusive (IRE)** 4-9-13 0 .... ShaneKelly 3 —
(Mark Brisbourne) *hld up: rdn over 3f out: wknd over 2f out* **14/1**

2m 2.65s (0.95) **Going Correction** 0.0s/f (Stan)
WFA 3 from 4yo+ 17lb **5** Ran SP% **122.8**
Speed ratings (Par 100): **95,93,93,87,67**
CSF £2.32 TOTE £2.90: £1.50, £1.10; EX 3.50.

Owner A Black **Bred** Shadai Farm **Trained** Patching, W Sussex

FOCUS
An extremely weak maiden but even so not a result to take at face value with the rank outsider and eventual third allowed to steal a long lead. It;s doubtful if the winner had to match his previous level.

1253 FREEBETS.CO.UK GRAND NATIONAL 2011 BEST FREE BETS H'CAP 1m 4f 50y(P)
9:20 (9:20) (Class 6) (0-60,57) 4-Y-0+ **£1,706** (£503; £252) **Stalls** Low

Form RPR
44-3 1 **Blackstone Vegas**[9] [1063] 5-9-2 52 .... RobbieFitzpatrick 10 61
(Derek Shaw) *chsd ldr: rdn over 2f out: led over 1f out: styd on gamely* **7/2**[2]

-050 2 nk **Filun**[22] [899] 6-9-0 50 .... LiamKeniry 6 59
(Anthony Middleton) *hld up: hdwy over 4f out: chsd wnr over 1f out: sn ev ch: r.o* **4/1**[3]

0045 3 2 3/4 **Mary Helen**[9] [1063] 4-8-8 45 .... LiamJones 1 49
(Mark Brisbourne) *hld up: hdwy over 2f out: rdn over 1f out: styd on* **8/1**

0355 4 7 **Moment Of Clarity**[9] [1068] 9-8-6 45 ....(p) SimonPearce(3) 3 38
(Shaun Harris) *led: rdn over 2f out: hdd over 1f out: wknd ins fnl f* **10/1**

0553 5 1 **Naledi**[22] [896] 7-8-6 45 .... SophieDoyle(3) 8 38
(Richard Price) *hld up in tch: lost pl over 4f out: n.d after* **10/1**

005/ 6 hd **Graycliffe (IRE)**[606] [4874] 5-9-3 53 .... StephenCraine 5 44
(Patrick Morris) *prom: rdn over 2f out: wknd fnl f* **22/1**

1444 7 1 1/2 **Laura Land**[9] [1063] 5-9-1 51 .... ShaneKelly 7 40
(Mark Brisbourne) *hld up: hdwy over 5f out: rdn over 3f out: wknd fnl f* **6/1**

3005 8 3/4 **Escardo (GER)**[15] [968] 8-8-4 47 .... JoshBaudains(7) 2 34
(David Bridgwater) *chsd ldrs: rdn over 1f out: wknd fnl f* **22/1**

466- 9 20 **Sure Fire (GER)**[369] [1134] 6-9-5 55 .... TomQueally 9 —
(Barney Curley) *sn prom: pushed along 6f out: rdn over 3f out: wknd over 2f out* **9/4**[1]

2m 39.65s (-1.45) **Going Correction** 0.0s/f (Stan)
WFA 4 from 5yo+ 1lb **9** Ran SP% **125.3**
Speed ratings (Par 101): **104,103,101,97,96 96,95,95,81**
toteswingers:1&2:£4.70, 1&3:£5.20, 2&3:£6.90 CSF £19.78 CT £107.53 TOTE £5.20: £2.10, £2.50, £2.50; EX 14.00.

Owner Shakespeare Racing **Bred** Elms Stud Co Ltd **Trained** Sproxton, Leics

FOCUS
A low-grade finale after the withdrawal of the top weight and one run at a very muddling gallop, so in all likelihood probably unreliable form despite the first three coming clear. The winner confirmed recent C&D form with the third.

Sure Fire(GER) Official explanation: jockey said gelding never travelled

T/Plt: £21.80 to a £1 stake. Pool £61, 046.13 - 2,035.16 winning units. T/Qpdt: £4.70 to a £1 stake. Pool £6,386.20 - 999.34 winning units. CR

1254 - 1258a (Foreign Racing) - See Raceform Interactive

[1003]LEOPARDSTOWN (L-H)
Sunday, April 10

OFFICIAL GOING: Good to firm (good in places)

1259a P.W.MCGRATH MEMORIAL BALLYSAX STKS (GROUP 3) 1m 2f
3:45 (3:47) 3-Y-0 **£26,616** (£7,780; £3,685; £1,228)

RPR
1 **Banimpire (IRE)**[21] [924] 3-8-12 99 .... KJManning 1 105
(J S Bolger, Ire) *chsd ldrs: 3rd 1/2-way: rdn 2f out: styd on to ld 1f out: kpt on wl u.p fnl f* **14/1**

2 1/2 **Regent Street (IRE)**[121] [7822] 3-9-1 81 .... CO'Donoghue 3 107
(A P O'Brien, Ire) *led: disp 1/2-way: rdn over 2f out: hdd 1f out: kpt on: no ex cl home* **25/1**

3 1 **Recital (FR)**[148] [7456] 3-9-6 114 .... RyanMoore 7 111+
(A P O'Brien, Ire) *t.k.h and settled towards rr: checked over 2f out: pushed along into 5th 1 1/2f out: 4th 1f out: hung lft u.p and no ex ins fnl f* **8/13**[1]

4 shd **Rich Tapestry (IRE)**[177] [6909] 3-9-1 88 .... PJSmullen 4 105
(D K Weld, Ire) *hld up towards rr: hdwy into 5th 4f out: rdn into 4th 2f out: 3rd 1f out: no ex ins fnl f: kpt on same pce* **14/1**

5 3 1/2 **Adilapour (IRE)**[21] [926] 3-9-1 93 .... JMurtagh 2 98+
(John M Oxx, Ire) *settled bhd ldrs: 5th 1/2-way: rdn and dropped to rr over 2f out: 6th 1 1/2f out: kpt on one pce* **5/1**[2]

6 5 1/2 **Exodus**[14] [1004] 3-9-1 100 .... SeamieHeffernan 5 89
(A P O'Brien, Ire) *chsd ldr: disp 1/2-way: rdn in 2nd 2f out: no ex over 1f out: wknd* **9/1**[3]

7 8 **Mawaakef (IRE)**[196] [6403] 3-9-1 100 .... DPMcDonogh 6 75
(Kevin Prendergast, Ire) *chsd ldrs: 4th 1/2-way: rdn in 5th 2f out: no ex and wknd over 1f out* **9/1**[3]

2m 4.73s (-3.47) **Going Correction** -0.025s/f (Good) **7** Ran SP% **115.8**
Speed ratings: **113,112,111,111,108 104,98**
CSF £275.90 TOTE £14.40: £3.90, £17.10; DF 345.50.

Owner Mrs J S Bolger **Bred** Kilcarn Stud **Trained** Coolcullen, Co Carlow

FOCUS
The time was the fastest since the race was moved from the Curragh to Leopardstown in 1993 that probably had a lot to do with the good, good to firm in places ground description, which was quicker than what is usually associated with this track in April. The pace set by Regent Street (in what appeared a pacemaking role for Recital) was decent. The form is rated around the fifth and Recital still comes out best at the weights.

NOTEBOOK
Banimpire(IRE), the only filly in the line-up, had finished third over 7f on soft ground last month and was tackling this trip for the first time. Always close up, she was third into the straight and challenged under pressure to hit the front entering the final furlong. She was kept up to her work, keeping on quite well. She is entered for the Qipco 1,000 Guineas (she is also in the Irish equivalent, the Investec Oaks and the Irish Oaks) and trainer Jim Bolger is in no rush to decide on Newmarket, although he did indicate that middle distances might suit the her best. (op 12/1)
Regent Street(IRE) won over just short of 1m3f at Dundalk on his second and final start last season and he came out of this race with plenty of credit. He made the running, keeping on well when headed, and on pedigree he will be suited by 1m4f. (op 33/1)
Recital(FR) won a 1m maiden on good ground at Navan in October before winning the Group 1 Criterium de Saint-Cloud over this trip on heavy ground in November. He raced keenly at the back of the field and had plenty to do rounding the final bend, but was beginning to improve on the turn when he was checked to avoid clipping heels before picking up to deliver his challenge over 1f out. However, he was unable to make much impression inside the final furlong and only just shaded the verdict for third. Aidan O'Brien indicated that a return to Leopardstown for the Derrinstown Derby Trial on May 8 is on the cards, but it will take a much more convincing performance than this if he is to shorten up for Epsom. Official explanation: jockey said colt ran fresh early on and had to check off heels turning for home (op 4/7)
Rich Tapestry(IRE), winner of a 1m maiden at Dundalk in October, made an encouraging return, coming from behind to get into contention in the straight and keeping on for pressure.
Adilapour(IRE), a maiden winner over 1m at Gowran Park on his only start last year, had been only touched off in a 7f handicap at the Curragh last month. He lost his place off the final bend and, although keeping on, never posed a threat thereafter. (op 11/2)

1260 - 1262 & 1264a (Foreign Racing) - See Raceform Interactive

DUSSELDORF (R-H)
Sunday, April 10

OFFICIAL GOING: Turf: soft

1263a GROSSER PREIS DES VOLKSWAGEN ZENTRUM NORDRHEIN (GROUP 3) (4YO+) (TURF) 1m
4:00 (12:00) 4-Y-0+
£27,586 (£9,482; £4,741; £2,586; £1,724; £1,293)

RPR
1 **Alianthus (GER)**161 [7266] 6-9-4 0 ... ADeVries 1 109
(J Hirschberger, Germany) *mde all: rdn over 2f out: styd on wl u.p fnl f* **3/5**1
2 1/2 **Magic Eye (IRE)**161 6-8-10 0 ... AHelfenbein 6 99
(Andreas Lowe, Germany) *racd on heels of ldng gp in 5th: hdwy on outside 2f out: bmpd w rival ins fnl f: styd on wl to take 2nd on line* **41/5**
3 hd **Sanjii Danon (GER)**143 [7500] 5-8-11 0 ... APietsch 2 100
(W Hickst, Germany) *a.p: pressed ldr 1 1/2f out: r.o: no ex fnl 75yds: lost 2nd cl home* **7/1**3
4 2 **Kite Hunter (IRE)**46 [661] 4-9-0 0 ... THellier 4 98
(Mario Hofer, Germany) *chsd ldrs early: trckd ldr after 2f: rdn and nt qckn 1 1/2f out: fdd ins fnl 110yds* **89/10**
5 7 **Murcielago (GER)**169 4-8-11 0 ... ASuborics 7 79
(M Keller, Germany) *settled in rr: passed btn horses fnl f: nvr in contention* **223/10**
6 1 1/2 **Beltanus (GER)**259 7-8-11 0 ... FilipMinarik 5 76
(T Potters, Germany) *prom: 3rd over 3 1/2f out: nt qckn u.p: wknd fnl f* **37/1**
7 nk **Querari (GER)**225 [5542] 5-9-6 0 ... EPedroza 8 84
(A Wohler, Germany) *nvr plcd to chal* **14/5**2
8 [illegible] **[illegible] Beauty (GER)**34 4-8-10 0 ... VSchulepov 3 73
(M Figge, Germany) *nvr threatened* **29/1**
1m 35.8s (-5.36) **8** Ran SP% **132.5**
WIN (incl. 10 euro stake): 16. PLACES: 10, 12, 11. SF: 64..
Owner Baron G Von Ullmann **Bred** Gestut Karlshof **Trained** Germany

1142 LONGCHAMP (R-H)
Sunday, April 10

OFFICIAL GOING: Turf: good

1265a PRIX LA FORCE (GROUP 3) (3YO) (TURF) 1m 2f 110y
2:40 (12:00) 3-Y-0 **£34,482** (£13,793; £10,344; £6,896; £3,448)

RPR
1 **Baraan (FR)**23 [902] 3-9-2 0 ... Christophe-PatriceLemaire 1 111+
(J-C Rouget, France) *led sn after s tl hdd briefly 1 1/2f out: changed legs: qcknd wl to regain ld 1f out: r.o wl: comf* **17/5**3
2 3/4 **Prairie Star (FR)**148 [7456] 3-9-2 0 ... ChristopheSoumillon 5 109+
(E Lellouche, France) *settled in 2nd: rdn to ld briefly 1 1/2f out: hdd 1f out: r.o wl* **6/4**1
3 3/4 **Pour Moi (IRE)**168 3-9-2 0 ... MickaelBarzalona 2 108+
(A Fabre, France) *racd 4th initially: ref to settle: moved into 3rd at 1/2-way: rdn early in st: r.o wl fnl f* **12/1**
4 2 **Staros (IRE)**22 [919] 3-9-2 0 ... AnthonyCrastus 4 104
(E Lellouche, France) *hld up in rr: t.k.h: rdn early in st: styd on fnl f* **4/1**
5 hd **Maxios**185 [6702] 3-9-2 0 ... StephanePasquier 3 104
(J E Pease, France) *settled in 3rd: dropped bk to 4th at 1/2-way: rdn 1 1/2f out: no ex ins fnl f: styd on* **14/5**2
2m 15.3s (5.10) **Going Correction** +0.425s/f (Yiel) **5** Ran SP% **116.7**
Speed ratings: **98,97,96,95,95**
WIN (incl. 1 euro stake): 4.40. PLACES: 2.20, 1.50. SF: 11.80.
Owner H H Aga Khan **Bred** Haras De S A Aga Khan Scea **Trained** Pau, France

NOTEBOOK
Baraan(FR) enjoyed an uncontested lead early and quickened up well when challenged to give his owner his fourth win in this race in the past six years. He is likely to be aimed at the Jockey Club with another race before then a possibility.
Prairie Star(FR) was thought by his trainer to have needed it and will now be aimed at the Prix Hocquart.
Maxios wouldn't have been suited by the moderate pace on this return to action, but was still disappointing.

1266a PRIX D'HARCOURT (GROUP 2) (4YO+) (TURF) 1m 2f
3:10 (12:00) 4-Y-0+ **£63,879** (£24,655; £11,767; £7,844; £3,922)

RPR
1 **Planteur (IRE)**119 [7854] 4-9-1 0 ... ChristopheSoumillon 5 121+
(E Lellouche, France) *settled in 3rd on rail: swtchd to rail 1 1/2f out: qcknd wl to take ld 1f out: sn clr: easily* **7/5**1
2 2 1/2 **Ley Hunter (USA)**171 [7048] 4-8-11 0 ... MickaelBarzalona 1 109
(A Fabre, France) *settled at rr of field: rdn early in st on outside: r.o wl fnl f to take 2nd fnl strides* **7/1**3
3 snk **Agent Secret (IRE)**22 [920] 5-8-11 0 ... OlivierPeslier 4 109
(F Rohaut, France) *settled in 4th: rdn 2f out: r.o wl fnl f: lost 2nd fnl strides* **18/1**
4 hd **Silver Pond (FR)**22 [920] 4-9-1 0 ... DavyBonilla 2 113
(C Laffon-Parias, France) *led sn after s: r.o wl in st: hdd 1f out: styd on wl clsng stages* **23/10**2
5 snk **Timos (GER)**22 [920] 6-8-11 0 ... SylvainRuis 8 108
(T Doumen, France) *settled in 6th: rdn 2f out: qcknd wl: styd on wl fnl 100yds* **22/1**
6 hd **Akarlina (FR)**176 [6950] 5-8-8 0 ... ThierryThulliez 6 105
(N Clement, France) *racd 5th: rdn early in st: swtchd to rail 1f out: r.o wl fnl 100yds* **10/1**
7 2 **Wiener Walzer (GER)**189 [6612] 5-8-11 0 ... MaximeGuyon 3 104
(A Fabre, France) *settled in 2nd: rdn 2f out: r.o u.p: no ex fnl f* **12/1**
8 3 **Celtic Celeb (IRE)**168 [7110] 4-9-1 0 ... GeraldMosse 7 102
(F Doumen, France) *settled towards rr of field: rdn early in st: no ex fnl 1 1/2f* **15/1**
2m 4.30s (0.30) **Going Correction** +0.425s/f (Yiel) **8** Ran SP% **117.1**
Speed ratings: **115,113,112,112,112 112,110,108**
WIN (incl. 1 euro stake): 2.40. PLACES: 1.50, 2.30, 3.60. DF: 8.90. SF: 16.10.
Owner Ecurie Wildenstein **Bred** Dayton Investments Ltd **Trained** Lamorlaye, France

NOTEBOOK
Planteur(IRE) showed an impressive turn of foot to win going away and could hardly have been more impressive. He is likely to go for the Ganay next, with the Eclipse and Prince Of Wales's potential targets later on.

1136 WINDSOR (R-H)
Monday, April 11

OFFICIAL GOING: Good to firm (good in places; watered; 9.0)
Straight at full width, top bend at normal configuration and distances as advertised.
Wind: Brisk across Weather: Cloudy

1267 PITMEN PAINTERS AT THEATRE ROYAL WINDSOR APPRENTICE H'CAP 6f
5:00 (5:00) (Class 5) (0-75,75) 4-Y-0+ **£2,115** (£624; £312) **Stalls** Low

Form RPR
-342 1 **Dark Lane**53 [577] 5-9-7 **75** ... (p) LeeTopliss 3 83
(Richard Fahey) *hld up in rr but in tch: drvn and hdwy over 1f out: str run u.p ins fnl f to ld last strides* **3/1**1
0-54 2 hd **Stevie Gee (IRE)**14 [1017] 7-9-1 **69** ... (b) RyanClark 2 76
(Ian Williams) *chsd ldrs: drvn to take slt ld ins fnl f: hdd last strides* **9/2**2
3062 3 1 1/4 **Silver Wind**24 [893] 6-8-6 **65** ... (b) HobieGill(5) 5 68
(Alan McCabe) *w ldr tl led jst ins fnl 2f: sn hanging bdly lft: hdd ins fnl f: no ex* **8/1**
500- 4 1 1/4 **Kings 'n Dreams**179 [6879] 4-9-2 **70** ... (b) AdamBeschizza 9 69
(Dean Ivory) *in tch: rdn over 2f out: edging lft ins fnl and nvr gng pce to rch ldrs* **9/1**
[illegible] 5 [illegible] **[illegible]**7 [1140] [illegible] **73** ... HarryBentley 8 66
(Eric Wheeler) *in tch: pushed along over 2f out: nvr gng pce to chal and wknd fnl f* **9/2**2
4002 6 1 **Gwilym (GER)**25 [880] 8-8-9 **63** ... RyanPowell 1 53
(Derek Haydn Jones) *t.k.h: slt ld tl hdd ins fnl 2f: wknd 1f out* **5/1**3
5540 7 3 **Simple Rhythm**5 [1182] 5-8-2 **61** oh2 ... (p) NatashaEaton(5) 7 42
(John Ryan) *s.i.s: pushed along and prog 2f out but nvr in contention: wknd over 1f out* **16/1**
20-0 8 1 3/4 **Fawley Green**17 [961] 4-8-13 **70** ... (p) JamesRogers(3) 4 45
(William Muir) *s.i.s: a in rr* **12/1**
1m 11.3s (-1.70) **Going Correction** -0.20s/f (Firm) **8** Ran SP% **112.7**
Speed ratings (Par 103): **103,102,101,99,97 95,91,89**
toteswingers:1&2:£4.90, 1&3:£4.00, 2&3:£7.60 CSF £15.95 CT £95.03 TOTE £3.20: £1.40, £2.40, £2.70; EX 15.95 Trifecta £98.60 Pool: £4,360.31 - 32.72 winning units..
Owner David W Armstrong **Bred** David Jamison Bloodstock **Trained** Musley Bank, N Yorks
■ Stewards' Enquiry : Ryan Clark three-day ban: used whip with excessive frequency (Apr 25-27)

FOCUS
A modest apprentice handicap. The winner didn't have to improve much on recent Polytrack efforts.

1268 E B F SPORTINGBET.COM MAIDEN STKS 5f 10y
5:30 (5:30) (Class 5) 2-Y-0 **£3,238** (£963; £481; £240) **Stalls** Low

Form RPR
2 1 **Lord Ofthe Shadows (IRE)**7 [1136] 2-9-3 0 ... RichardHughes 6 75+
(Richard Hannon) *mde all: shkn up over 1f out: styd on strly fnl f: easily* **4/11**1
2 1 1/4 **Serious Spender (IRE)** 2-9-3 0 ... JimCrowley 8 68+
(Ralph Beckett) *in tch: hdwy to chse wnr over 2f out: drvn and styd on wl thrght fnl f but a comf hld* **11/2**2
5 3 2 **Aquasulis (IRE)**12 [1049] 2-8-12 0 ... NeilCallan 4 55
(David Evans) *chsd wnr tl over 2f out: styd on but nt gng pce of ldng duo fnl f* **33/1**
4 1/2 **Safari Storm (USA)** 2-9-3 0 ... MartinDwyer 1 59+
(Brian Meehan) *towards rr but in tch: pushed along 2f out: kpt on ins fnl f but nvr gng pce to rch ldrs* **9/1**3
0 5 3/4 **Middleton Flyer (IRE)**7 [1136] 2-8-12 0 ... TomMcLaughlin 2 52+
(David Evans) *chsd ldrs tl outpcd after 2f: styd on again fnl f but nvr any threat* **66/1**
6 9 **Witty Buck** 2-9-3 0 ... RobertWinston 9 23
(Alan McCabe) *chsd ldrs: rdn 1/2-way: wknd ins fnl 2f* **33/1**
7 2 1/4 **Courtland King (IRE)** 2-9-3 0 ... PaulDoe 5 15
(David Evans) *slowly away: a outpcd in rr* **20/1**

8 4 **Foolscap (IRE)** 2-9-3 0 .... StephenCraine 7 1
(Jim Boyle) *slowly away: a outpcd in rr* **40/1**

9 nk **Illustrious Lad (IRE)** 2-9-3 0 .... PatCosgrave 3 —
(Jim Boyle) *slowly away: rcvrd to get into mid-div 1/2-way: wknd qckly 2f out* **25/1**

60.13 secs (-0.17) **Going Correction** -0.20s/f (Firm) **9** Ran SP% **117.1**
Speed ratings (Par 92): **93,91,87,87,85 71,67,61,60**
toteswingers:1&2:£1.70, 1&3:£3.20, 2&3:£8.40 CSF £2.39 TOTE £2.00: £1.02, £1.70, £5.70; EX 4.10 Trifecta £33.00 Pool: £9,973.35 - 223.19 winning units..
Owner Richard Hitchcock Alan King **Bred** Max Morris **Trained** East Everleigh, Wilts

FOCUS
Not a particularly strong maiden.

NOTEBOOK
Lord Ofthe Shadows(IRE), second in a similar event over C&D on debut, showed the benefit of that experience by travelling strongly out in front and only needed to be shaken up by Richard Hughes to put the contest to bed. It's not easy to tell whether this colt is above average but he's done nothing wrong and we'll learn plenty more about him next time, possibly in a conditions race. (op 1-3 tchd 2-5)
Serious Spender(IRE) made a hugely encouraging debut and will take a deal of beating next time with this experience under his belt. He travelled every bit as well as the winner for a long way before lacking the experience of that rival in the final furlong. A Super Sprint entry suggests connections think a bit of him and this was a good start. (op 6-1)
Aquasulis(IRE) stepped up on his modest Wolverhampton debut.
Safari Storm(USA), who ran with promise, is bred to appreciate further than this in time. Newcomers from this yard often improve significantly for their first outing so this was a noteworthy effort. (op 10-1)
Middleton Flyer(IRE) Official explanation: jockey said filly lost its action

1269 SPORTINGBET.COM H'CAP 1m 67y
6:00 (6:00) (Class 4) (0-85,83) 4-Y-O+ **£3,885** (£1,156; £577; £288) **Stalls** Low

Form RPR

400- **1** **Kay Gee Be (IRE)**[193] 6510 7-9-6 **82** .... PaulHanagan 1 92
(Richard Fahey) *disp ld 2f then trckd ldr: rdn over 2f out: kpt on to ld jst ins fnl f: drvn out* **5/2**[1]

0-45 **2** 3/4 **Edgewater (IRE)**[19] 949 4-8-11 **73** .... DaneO'Neill 6 81
(John Akehurst) *in tch: hdwy over 2f out: sn rdn: styd on wl fnl f to take 2nd last stride but no imp on wnr* **12/1**

0-11 **3** nse **Rezwaan**[33] 802 4-8-13 **75** .... (be) RyanMoore 2 83
(Gary Moore) *disp ld tl def advantage after 2f: rdn along 3f out: hdd ins fnl f: styd on same pce and lost 2nd last stride* **8/1**

6521 **4** 3/4 **Baylini**[9] 1103 7-8-12 **77** .... SophieDoyle(3) 8 83
(Jamie Osborne) *chsd ldrs: rdn over 2f out: styd on thrght fnl f but nvr gng pce to chal* **4/1**[2]

2444 **5** 5 **Lockantanks**[23] 908 4-8-9 **71** .... NeilChalmers 11 66
(Michael Appleby) *in rr: drvn along 3f out: styd on fr over 1f out but nvr any ch of rching ldrs* **12/1**

350- **6** 1 1/2 **Jewelled**[216] 5833 5-8-10 **72** .... WilliamBuick 5 63
(Lady Herries) *in rr: pushed along over 3f out: kpt on fnl f but nvr gng pce to rch ldrs* **20/1**

20-6 **7** 1 1/4 **Dr Wintringham (IRE)**[19] 949 5-8-11 **73** .... DarryllHolland 14 61
(Karen George) *t.k.h in mid-div: sme hdwy 3f out: nvr in contention and no ch fnl 2f* **20/1**

20-0 **8** 3/4 **Advertise**[19] 949 5-8-10 **72** .... EddieCreighton 13 59
(Joseph Tuite) *bhd: mod prog fnl 2f* **33/1**

1330 **9** nk **Kilburn**[7] 1138 7-9-6 **82** .... SteveDrowne 4 68
(Alastair Lidderdale) *s.i.s: in rr: sme hdwy 1/2-way: wknd over 2f out* **22/1**

200- **10** 1 **Bramshaw (USA)**[178] 6888 4-9-7 **83** .... NeilCallan 3 72
(Amanda Perrett) *chsd ldrs: rdn 3f out: wknd over 1f out: eased whn no ch fnl f* **9/2**[3]

000- **11** 6 **Aspectus (IRE)**[179] 6877 8-9-7 **83** .... FergusSweeney 10 53
(Jamie Osborne) *chsd ldrs: rdn over 3f out: wknd over 2f out* **22/1**

1m 40.8s (-3.90) **Going Correction** -0.35s/f (Firm) **11** Ran SP% **114.4**
Speed ratings (Par 105): **105,104,104,103,98 96,95,94,94,93 87**
toteswingers:1&2:£7.80, 1&3:£3.80, 2&3:£10.00 CSF £29.72 CT £213.50 TOTE £4.10: £1.80, £4.70, £1.60; EX 30.10 Trifecta £154.50 Pool: £3,191.91 -15.28 winning units..
Owner G H Leatham & M A Leatham **Bred** Pursuit Of Truth Syndicate **Trained** Musley Bank, N Yorks

FOCUS
Quite a competitive little handicap. The winner had plenty going for him and is basically rated to last year's turf form.
Bramshaw(USA) Official explanation: jockey said colt moved poorly
Aspectus(IRE) Official explanation: jockey said horse was struck into behind

1270 AFFORDABLE RACEHORSE SYNDICATION WITH JAMASITR RACING MAIDEN FILLIES' STKS 1m 67y
6:35 (6:35) (Class 5) 3-Y-O **£2,388** (£705; £352) **Stalls** Low

Form RPR

0- **1** 1/2 **Lunar Phase (IRE)**[163] 7231 3-9-0 0 .... LukeMorris 5 76+
(Clive Cox) *chsd ldrs: drvn and styd on wl fnl 2f: qcknd ins fnl f to chse wnr fnl 75yds but a hld* **9/1**

6- **2** 1 1/2 **Crystal Etoile**[206] 6150 3-9-0 0 .... RyanMoore 11 73
(Sir Michael Stoute) *chsd ldrs: chal fr over 2f out and stl ev ch over 1f out: no ex: fdd fnl 75yds and lost 2nd* **9/2**[2]

3 2 1/2 **Serial Sinner (IRE)** 3-9-0 0 .... PaulHanagan 2 67+
(Paul Cole) *t.k.h in tch: hdwy to chse ldrs fr 3f out: kpt on fnl f but nvr gng pce to chal* **28/1**

4- **4** nk **Shelovestobouggie**[208] 6092 3-9-0 0 .... TomQueally 12 66
(Sir Henry Cecil) *chsd ldrs: drvn to take slt ld over 2f out: sn hdd: wknd ins fnl f* **7/1**[3]

606- **5** 1 3/4 **Corvette**[158] 7312 3-9-0 65 .... FergusSweeney 13 62
(J R Jenkins) *in rr: pushed along fr 3f out: styd on fnl 2f: nt rch ldrs* **100/1**

4- **6** hd **Apparel (IRE)**[165] 7198 3-9-0 0 .... EddieAhern 3 61
(Ed Dunlop) *s.i.s: in rr: sme hdwy fr 3f out but stl green: kpt on same pce fnl 2f* **14/1**

50- **7** 3 **Viking Rose (IRE)**[168] 7113 3-9-0 0 .... DarryllHolland 6 54
(James Eustace) *chsd ldrs: rdn over 2f out: wknd wl over 1f out* **50/1**

8 3/4 **Ambala** 3-9-0 0 .... TedDurcan 1 52
(Chris Wall) *s.i.s: in rr tl sme prog fnl 2f* **80/1**

00- **9** 1 **Allez Leulah (IRE)**[157] 7325 3-9-0 0 .... SilvestreDeSousa 10 50
(Mark Johnston) *led tl hdd over 2f out: sn wknd* **66/1**

06 **10** 17 **Shaunas Spirit (IRE)**[17] 959 3-9-0 0 .... LiamJones 9 —
(Dean Ivory) *t.k.h: chsd ldrs 5f* **100/1**

0530 **11** 9 **Frosty Reception**[7] 1134 3-9-0 62 .... JimCrowley 14 —
(Brendan Powell) *a in rr* **100/1**

0 **12** nse **April Belle**[35] 791 3-9-0 0 .... J-PGuillambert 7 —
(Tim McCarthy) *a in rr* **100/1**

2- **D** **Izzi Top**[171] 7057 3-9-0 0 .... WilliamBuick 4 78+
(John Gosden) *plld hrd: chsd ldrs and bit c through mouth after 2f: swtchd lft over 3f out: drvn and qcknd to chal 2f out: led sn after: styd on strly fnl f: fin 1st, 1/2l: subs. disq: prohibited substance in sample* **8/11**[1]

1m 43.62s (-1.08) **Going Correction** -0.35s/f (Firm) **13** Ran SP% **117.3**
Speed ratings (Par 95): **90,89,86,86,84 84,81,80,79,62 53,53,91**
toteswingers:1&2:£2.90, 1&3:£2.00, 2&3:£7.40 CSF £7.98 TOTE £1.70: £1.10, £2.10, £2.30; EX 9.10 Trifecta £26.00.
Owner H E Sheikh Sultan Bin Khalifa Al Nahyan **Bred** Arctic Tack Stud **Trained** Lambourn, Berks

FOCUS
The first two home are held in quite high regard and there was a lot to like about the runs of the third and fourth, so this might turn out to be a decent fillies' maiden. The time was relatively slow but the form makes a fair bit of sense. The winner only matched her 2yo effort but is sure to do better.

1271 SPORTINGBET.COM MAIDEN STKS 1m 2f 7y
7:05 (7:05) (Class 5) 3-Y-O+ **£2,388** (£705; £352) **Stalls** Centre

Form RPR

5- **1** **Laughing Jack**[178] 6883 3-8-9 0 .... EddieAhern 5 80+
(Ed Dunlop) *mde virtually all: pushed along over 2f out: styd on wl whn strly chal ins fnl f: edgd lft and drvn out cl home* **7/4**[1]

4/0- **2** shd **Nibani (IRE)**[364] 1268 4-10-0 0 .... RyanMoore 10 84+
(Sir Michael Stoute) *in tch: hdwy 3f out to chse wnr ins fnl 2f: str chal ins fnl f: edgd lft and kpt on cl home but a jst hld* **11/2**

2- **3** 5 **Aldedash (USA)**[126] 7723 3-8-9 0 .... TomQueally 12 70
(Sir Henry Cecil) *chsd ldrs: drvn and styd on to take wl hld 3rd ins fnl f* **5/1**[3]

0- **4** 3/4 **Ugo (USA)**[227] 5491 3-8-9 0 .... LukeMorris 8 69
(Heather Main) *chsd ldrs: rdn over 2f out: styd on same pce fr over 1f out* **66/1**

3 **5** 1/2 **Informed Award**[7] 1139 3-8-9 0 .... WilliamBuick 14 68
(John Gosden) *chsd wnr: rdn over 2f out: styd on same pce* **4/1**[2]

6 3 1/2 **Native Colony** 3-8-9 0 .... NeilCallan 11 61+
(Roger Varian) *s.i.s: in rr pushed along and hdwy 2f out: drvn and kpt on thrght fnl f: gng on cl home but nvr any ch* **33/1**

00- **7** nk **Sum Satisfaction**[176] 6953 3-8-9 0 .... JamesDoyle 2 60
(Dominic Ffrench Davis) *in rr: hdwy on outside fr 3f out: nvr rchd ldrs and styd on same pce fr over 1f out* **80/1**

6- **8** hd **Musical Flight**[205] 6190 3-8-9 0 .... MichaelHills 13 60
(B W Hills) *t.k.h: chsd ldrs tl wknd fr 2f out* **7/1**

0 **9** 1 **May Contain Nuts**[7] 1139 3-8-9 0 .... FergusSweeney 1 58
(Brendan Powell) *s.i.s: in rr: hdwy to get in bhd ldrs over 2f out: sn pushed along: fdd over 1f out* **100/1**

10 2 1/2 **Korabushka** 3-8-4 0 .... HayleyTurner 9 48
(Jeremy Noseda) *s.i.s: nvr beyond mid-div* **25/1**

11 1 1/4 **Host The Band** 7-9-9 0 .... DaneO'Neill 4 49
(Tony Newcombe) *s.i.s: a towards rr* **100/1**

12 1 1/2 **Refusal** 3-8-6 0 .... SophieDoyle(3) 6 47
(Andrew Reid) *a towards rr* **100/1**

13 4 **One London (IRE)** 4-9-7 0 .... DuilioDaSilva(7) 3 43
(Paul Cole) *chsd ldrs tl wknd qckly 3f out* **50/1**

2m 6.63s (-2.07) **Going Correction** -0.35s/f (Firm)
WFA 3 from 4yo+ 19lb **13** Ran SP% **115.4**
Speed ratings (Par 103): **94,93,89,89,88 86,85,85,84,82 81,80,77**
toteswingers:1&2:£2.00, 1&3:£3.90, 2&3:£7.90 CSF £10.78 TOTE £3.50: £1.60, £1.80, £1.90; EX 12.80 Trifecta £40.50.
Owner Sir Thomas Pilkington **Bred** Sir Thomas Pilkington **Trained** Newmarket, Suffolk

FOCUS
A good-looking field and a race that should throw up a few winners, but it was a typically muddling Windsor maiden. The first two came clear and are likely to do better.

1272 MATTHEW TROUNCE 21ST BIRTHDAY CELEBRATION H'CAP 1m 3f 135y
7:35 (7:35) (Class 5) (0-75,75) 3-Y-O **£2,388** (£705; £352) **Stalls** Centre

Form RPR

040- **1** **First Battalion (IRE)**[164] 7202 3-9-6 **74** .... (v1) RyanMoore 3 76
(Sir Michael Stoute) *trckd ldrs: swtchd lft and hdwy over 1f out: hrd drvn fnl f: chal between horses: carried lft and led cl home: all out* **5/2**[1]

43-3 **2** shd **Dressing Room (USA)**[10] 1076 3-9-4 **72** .... (v1) SilvestreDeSousa 5 74
(Mark Johnston) *disp ld 2f: styd chsng ldrs: drvn to ld over 1f out: hrd drvn whn chal ins fnl f: hung lft and hdd cl home* **10/3**[3]

2113 **3** nk **Baharat (IRE)**[12] 1051 3-9-7 **75** .... (v) DarryllHolland 6 77
(Jeremy Noseda) *in tch: pushed along over 4f out: hdwy fr 2f out: drvn to chal wl ins fnl f: styng on and ev ch whn bmpd and carried lft cl home* **4/1**

5554 **4** 1 1/2 **Gower Rules (IRE)**[26] 866 3-8-7 **61** oh10 .... LukeMorris 1 60?
(John Bridger) *disp ld 2f: sn chsd ldr: drvn to chal over 2f out: outpcd fnl f* **40/1**

32-3 **5** nk **Bow River Arch (USA)**[82] 214 3-9-3 **71** .... GeorgeBaker 2 69
(Jeremy Noseda) *led after 2f: rdn whn chal fr over 2f out: hdd over 1f out: styd on same pce ins fnl f* **11/4**[2]

4-23 **6** 9 **Whodathought (IRE)**[61] 468 3-9-3 **71** .... RichardHughes 4 54
(Richard Hannon) *a in last: shkn up and no imp on ldrs over 2f out: sn dropped away* **13/2**

2m 29.7s (0.20) **Going Correction** -0.35s/f (Firm) **6** Ran SP% **114.1**
Speed ratings (Par 98): **85,84,84,83,83 77**
toteswingers:1&2:£2.90, 1&3:£2.00, 2&3:£7.40 CSF £11.49 TOTE £2.80: £1.70, £4.70; EX 8.90.
Owner D Smith, Mrs J Magnier, M Tabor **Bred** Mubkera Syndicate **Trained** Newmarket, Suffolk

■ Stewards' Enquiry : Silvestre De Sousa three-day ban: careless riding (Apr 25-27)

FOCUS
A good little contest, but the two horses visored for the first time on handicap debut finished first and second. It was slowly run and the fourth casts doubt on the form, so it's hard to be too positive about the race.

T/Plt: £8.00 to a £1 stake. Pool:£65,938.25 - 5,963.03 winning tickets T/Qpdt: £4.70 to a £1 stake. Pool:£6,430.15 - 1,005.20 winning tickets ST

[1247]WOLVERHAMPTON (A.W) (L-H)

Monday, April 11

OFFICIAL GOING: Standard

Wind: Fresh behind Weather: Overcast

1273 SPONSOR A RACE BY CALLING 01902 390000 H'CAP 1m 141y(P)

2:10 (2:10) (Class 6) (0-55,55) 4-Y-0+ £1,706 (£503; £252) Stalls Low

Form RPR

3532 **1** **Pie Poudre**[24] 895 4-9-0 **53**....(v[1]) TomEaves 7 60
(Roy Brotherton) *s.i.s: hld up: hdwy over 1f out: rdn to ld wl ins fnl f: r.o* **9/2**[1]

3312 **2** *nse* **Mr Maximas**[24] 896 4-9-0 **53**....(tp) RichardKingscote 11 60
(Bryn Palling) *chsd ldrs: rdn and edgd lft over 1f out: sn swtchd rt: ev ch ins fnl f: r.o* **9/2**[1]

-005 **3** *3/4* **Mutajaaser (USA)**[33] 802 6-9-1 **54**....(e[1]) AndreaAtzeni 1 59
(Kevin Morgan) *chsd ldrs: rdn over 2f out: ev ch ins fnl f: unable qck towards fin* **9/1**[3]

2331 **4** *1/2* **Barton Bounty**[17] 969 4-8-13 **52**....(b) PaulMulrennan 2 56
(Peter Niven) *s.i.s: hld up: rdn over 2f out: hdwy over 1f out: r.o* **9/2**[1]

506- **5** *1/2* **Hathaway (IRE)**[262] 4337 4-9-1 **54**.... GrahamGibbons 3 57
(Mark Brisbourne) *led: rdn over 1f out: hdd and no ex wl ins fnl f* **16/1**

0/66 **6** *3/4* **Final Tune (IRE)**[18] 957 8-9-2 **55**.... JimmyQuinn 12 56
(Mandy Rowland) *chsd ldrs: rdn over 2f out: styd on same pce fnl f* **14/1**

30-2 **7** *1/2* **Forzarzi (IRE)**[11] 1068 7-8-7 **49**.... JamesSullivan(3) 4 49
(Hugh McWilliams) *prom: rdn over 2f out: no ex ins fnl f* **14/1**

2444 **8** *1 1/4* **Kielty's Folly**[18] 957 7-9-1 **54**.... CathyGannon 10 51
(Brian Baugh) *hld up: styng on whn nt clr run ins fnl f: nvr trbld ldrs* **8/1**[2]

-065 **9** *hd* **Dauntsey Park (IRE)**[39] 748 4-9-0 **53**.... FergusSweeney 8 49
(Tor Sturgis) *hld up: rdn over 1f out: nt trble ldrs* **9/1**[3]

0203 **10** *1* **Street Crime**[5] 1184 6-8-4 **50**.... JakePayne(7) 9 44
(Ron Hodges) *chsd ldr: rdn over 2f out: hung lft and wknd ins fnl f* **25/1**

000- **11** *3/4* **Luv U Noo**[154] 7377 4-9-2 **55**.... TonyCulhane 5 47
(Brian Baugh) *stdd s: hld up: a in rr* **25/1**

00-6 **12** *4 1/2* **Belle Park**[24] 893 4-9-1 **54**.... JamieSpencer 6 36
(Karen George) *hld up: rdn and hung lft over 1f out: a in rr* **16/1**

6-00 **13** *hd* **Farleigh**[49] 631 5-8-10 **49**....(t) LiamJones 13 31
(Alex Hales) *s.i.s: hld up: rdn over 3f out: a in rr* **33/1**

1m 50.19s (-0.31) **Going Correction** -0.075s/f (Stan) **13** Ran SP% **121.4**
Speed ratings (Par 101): **98,97,97,96,96 95,95,94,94,93 92,88,88**
toteswingers:1&2:£2.80, 1&3:£11.30, 2&3:£10.40 CSF £22.51 CT £185.98 TOTE £8.00: £1.20, £1.10, £5.50; EX 13.30 Trifecta £51.20 Pool: £203.48 - 2.94 winning units..
Owner Bredon Hill Racing Club **Bred** Peter Holmes **Trained** Elmley Castle, Worcs

FOCUS
Low-grade fare, and a bit muddling, though in-form horses came to the fore and there's no reason why it won't prove solid form for the level. The winner matched his latest form.

Luv U Noo Official explanation: jockey said, regarding running and riding, that his orders were to get a good position in fourth or fifth and try to achieve the best possible placing, the filly was slow into its stride, then met with a wall of horses and had nowhere to go when the pace picked up on the final bend, having been outpaced he pushed to the line.

1274 WOLVERHAMPTON HOSPITALITY - A PLEASURE CLAIMING STKS 5f 20y(P)

2:40 (2:40) (Class 6) 3-Y-0+ £1,706 (£503; £252) Stalls Low

Form RPR

5400 **1** **Efistorm**[7] 1140 10-9-1 67.... KirstyMilczarek 4 73
(Conor Dore) *mde all: rdn and hung rt fr over 1f out: r.o* **5/1**

0433 **2** *1 1/4* **Decider (USA)**[21] 934 8-9-0 63....(p) LukeMorris 1 68
(Ronald Harris) *trckd wnr: racd keenly: rdn over 1f out: edgd rt: no imp ins fnl f* **9/2**[2]

20-0 **3** *1 1/4* **Devil You Know (IRE)**[83] 199 5-9-0 68....(t) GrahamGibbons 5 63
(Michael Easterby) *a.p: rdn over 1f out: r.o* **10/3**[2]

140- **4** *1/2* **Desperate Dan**[172] 7033 10-9-4 75....(b) JamieSpencer 2 65
(Andrew Haynes) *hood removed late and s.i.s: sn pushed along in rr: r.o u.p ins fnl f: nvr trbld ldrs* **6/1**

1003 **5** *3* **Bluebok**[26] 861 10-9-0 50....(bt) RichardKingscote 8 50
(Milton Bradley) *chsd ldrs tl rdn and wknd over 1f out* **28/1**

0/60 **6** *9* **Crystal Bridge**[56] 538 4-8-8 30....(b) MatthewMcGhee(7) 7 19
(Bill Moore) *sn outpcd* **200/1**

-311 **7** *34* **Lewyn**[26] 861 4-9-9 75....(b) FergusSweeney 9 —
(Jeremy Gask) *rrd and lost all ch s: t.o* **5/2**[1]

61.35 secs (-0.95) **Going Correction** -0.075s/f (Stan) **7** Ran SP% **104.7**
Speed ratings (Par 101): **104,102,100,99,94 80,25**
toteswingers:1&2:£3.80, 1&3:£4.00, 2&3:£3.20 CSF £22.78 TOTE £7.20: £2.60, £2.50; EX 26.90 TRIFECTA Part won. Pool: £243.31 - 0.50 winning units..
Owner Sean J Murphy **Bred** E Duggan And D Churchman **Trained** Cowbit, Lincs
■ Kersivay (14/1) was withdrawn after breaking through the stalls. Deduct 5p in the £ under R4.

FOCUS
To-form efforts from the leading pair in a claimer in which few got competitive. The race was weakened by the effective non-participation of the favourite Lewyn.

Lewyn Official explanation: jockey said filly reared at start and missed the break

1275 ENJOY THE PARTY PACK GROUP OFFER H'CAP 5f 216y(P)

3:10 (3:10) (Class 4) (0-80,80) 3-Y-0 £3,238 (£963; £481) Stalls Low

Form RPR

-111 **1** **Take Your Partner**[11] 1064 3-9-7 **80**....(b) PhillipMakin 1 84
(Kevin Ryan) *chsd ldr: rdn 2f out: hung rt and styd on u.p to ld wl ins fnl f* **1/5**[1]

005- **2** *hd* **Thirteen Shivers**[185] 6719 3-8-5 **71**.... DavidSimmonson(7) 2 74
(Michael Easterby) *chsd ldrs: rdn over 2f out: r.o* **11/1**[3]

016- **3** *2* **Nine Before Ten (IRE)**[177] 6916 3-9-2 **75**.... SilvestreDeSousa 4 72
(Deborah Sanderson) *led: rdn and edgd rt over 1f out: hdd and no ex wl ins fnl f* **13/2**[2]

1m 14.32s (-0.68) **Going Correction** -0.075s/f (Stan) **3** Ran SP% **105.0**
Speed ratings (Par 100): **101,100,98**
CSF £2.77 TOTE £1.10; EX 2.70.
Owner Guy Reed **Bred** G Reed **Trained** Hambleton, N Yorks

FOCUS
A small field but there was a tight finish. There may be be a bit more to come from Take Your Partner.

1276 WOLVERHAMPTON-RACECOURSE.CO.UK H'CAP 7f 32y(P)

3:40 (3:40) (Class 6) (0-65,64) 4-Y-0+ £1,706 (£503; £252) Stalls High

Form RPR

3353 **1** **El Libertador (USA)**[21] 933 5-9-0 **57**....(b) JamieSpencer 6 67
(Jeremy Gask) *hld up: pushed along 1/2-way: hdwy and swtchd lft over 1f out: shkn up to ld wl ins fnl f: r.o* **11/4**[1]

0664 **2** *1/2* **Crocodile Bay (IRE)**[11] 1068 8-8-7 **50** oh2....(e[1]) FrannyNorton 7 59
(Richard Guest) *hld up in tch: racd keenly: led over 1f out: sn rdn: hdd wl ins fnl f* **7/1**

5004 **3** *1 3/4* **Aviso (GER)**[21] 928 7-9-6 **63**.... JamesDoyle 2 67
(David Evans) *prom: rdn over 1f out: r.o* **3/1**[2]

6166 **4** *1 3/4* **Flying Applause**[24] 895 6-8-11 **54**....(bt) JimmyQuinn 3 53
(Roy Bowring) *chsd ldr 2f: remained handy: rdn over 1f out: styd on same pce fnl f* **7/1**

151 **5** *2 1/2* **Spinning Ridge (IRE)**[18] 957 6-9-3 **60**....(b) DavidProbert 10 52
(Ronald Harris) *hld up: hdwy over 2f out: rdn over 1f out: no ex ins fnl f* **11/2**[3]

5000 **6** *2* **Vhujon (IRE)**[23] 915 6-9-6 **63**.... RobbieFitzpatrick 1 50
(Peter Grayson) *hld up: rdn over 2f out: r.o ins fnl f: nvr nrr* **66/1**

23-0 **7** *2 1/2* **Sweet Mirasol (IRE)**[87] 167 4-8-5 **51**....(t) SimonPearce(3) 4 31
(Mandy Rowland) *led: rdn and hdd over 1f out: wknd ins fnl f* **33/1**

00-0 **8** *4 1/2* **Istiqdaam**[25] 881 6-9-3 **63**....(b) JamesSullivan(3) 9 31
(Michael Easterby) *prom: chsd ldr 5f out: rdn and ev ch over 2f out: wknd over 1f out* **11/1**

041/ **9** *2 1/2* **Magical Illusion**[979] 4706 5-9-3 **60**.... CathyGannon 5 21
(David Evans) *trckd ldrs: racd keenly: rdn 1/2-way: wknd over 2f out* **18/1**

0-06 **10** *3 1/2* **Little Perisher**[19] 947 4-9-1 **58**....(p) ChrisCatlin 11 10
(Karen George) *s.i.s: a in rr: lost tch fnl 3f* **25/1**

1m 29.17s (-0.43) **Going Correction** -0.075s/f (Stan) **10** Ran SP% **113.9**
Speed ratings (Par 101): **99,98,96,94,91 89,86,81,78,74**
toteswingers:1&2:£5.50, 1&3:£3.50, 2&3:£7.30 CSF £21.55 CT £61.89 TOTE £4.30: £1.90, £2.10, £2.40; EX 22.90 Trifecta £52.90 Pool: £426.90 - 5.97 winning units..
Owner J L Day **Bred** Kingswood Farm **Trained** Sutton Veny, Wilts

FOCUS
Reasons to view this form positively for the level, with the fourth and fifth both reasonable yardsticks, and the principals look ahead of their marks.

1277 HOTEL & CONFERENCING AT WOLVERHAMPTON MEDIAN AUCTION MAIDEN STKS 1m 141y(P)

4:10 (4:10) (Class 5) 3-5-Y-0 £2,266 (£674; £337; £168) Stalls Low

Form RPR

233- **1** **My Mate Jake (IRE)**[157] 7324 3-8-11 71.... PaulMulrennan 10 65+
(James Given) *mde all: rdn and hung rt over 1f out: hung lft ins fnl f: styd on* **10/11**[1]

44 **2** *3/4* **McCool Bannanas**[12] 1053 3-8-11 0.... JamieSpencer 2 63
(James Unett) *trckd wnr: racd keenly: rdn 2f out: hmpd over 1f out: styd on u.p* **5/1**[3]

0 **3** *3/4* **Sienna Blue**[12] 1053 3-8-6 0.... CathyGannon 8 56
(Malcolm Saunders) *hld up: rdn over 3f out: hdwy over 2f out: r.o to go 3rd post: nt rch ldrs* **22/1**

-532 **4** *nse* **Scoglio**[12] 1053 3-8-11 62....(bt) JamesDoyle 1 61
(Frank Sheridan) *chsd ldrs: rdn over 2f out: styd on same pce ins fnl f: lost 3rd post* **7/2**[2]

05/ **5** *8* **Mrs E**[535] 6982 4-9-6 0.... JamesSullivan(3) 3 42
(Michael Easterby) *plld hrd and prom: rdn and wknd over 2f out* **20/1**

0/-5 **6** *1* **Missprint**[12] 1053 4-9-4 0.... JemmaMarshall(5) 5 39
(Brian Baugh) *hld up: sme hdwy u.p over 2f out: sn wknd* **33/1**

7 *nk* **Mundesley** 3-8-11 0....(t) RichardKingscote 4 40
(Tom Dascombe) *hld up: pushed along 1/2-way: lost tch fnl 3f* **11/1**

0 **8** *3 3/4* **John The Glass**[12] 1053 4-10-0 0.... RobbieFitzpatrick 6 35
(Mark Wellings) *hld up: plld hrd: rdn over 3f out: sn wknd* **100/1**

1m 50.02s (0.12) **Going Correction** -0.075s/f (Stan)
WFA 3 from 4yo 17lb **8** Ran SP% **112.6**
Speed ratings (Par 103): **95,94,93,93,86 85,85,82**
toteswingers:1&2:£1.90, 1&3:£6.20, 2&3:£10.70 CSF £5.39 TOTE £1.70: £1.10, £1.60, £5.10; EX 6.00 Trifecta £45.40 Pool: £561.80 - 9.14 winning units..
Owner Alex Owen **Bred** Crandon Park Stud **Trained** Willoughton, Lincs

FOCUS
Modest form in what was a slowly run maiden. The winner didn't need to match his 2yo best.

McCool Bannanas Official explanation: caution: careless riding.

1278 BEST WISHES TO PAUL RUSSELL CLAIMING STKS 1m 1f 103y(P)

4:45 (4:45) (Class 6) 4-Y-0+ £1,706 (£503; £252) Stalls Low

Form RPR

0034 **1** **The Which Doctor**[10] 1081 6-9-0 80....(e[1]) RobertLButler(3) 4 76
(Richard Guest) *hld up: rdn and no rspnse over 2f out: swtchd rt over 1f out: fnlly r.o ins fnl f to ld post* **5/1**[3]

100- **2** *shd* **Uphold**[205] 6203 4-9-11 90....(b[1]) JamieSpencer 1 84
(Jamie Osborne) *chsd ldrs: rdn over 1f out: led wl ins fnl f: hdd post* **10/11**[1]

303 **3** *1/2* **Cloudy Bay (USA)**[13] 1033 4-9-5 72....(p) AndrewElliott 6 77
(Mrs K Burke) *hld up: rdn over 3f out: hdwy over 2f out: rdn and ev ch ins fnl f: unable qck towards fin* **14/1**

133 **4** *2* **Lean Machine**[17] 968 4-8-7 65....(p) CathyGannon 5 61
(Ronald Harris) *chsd ldr: led over 1f out: sn rdn: hdd and no ex wl ins fnl f* **11/2**

2122 **5** *nk* **Kipchak (IRE)**[20] 939 6-8-9 65....(p) KirstyMilczarek 3 62
(Conor Dore) *led: plld hrd: clr 7f out to over 3f out: rdn over 2f out: hdd over 1f out: no ex ins fnl f* **9/2**[2]

2m 0.32s (-1.38) **Going Correction** -0.075s/f (Stan) **5** Ran SP% **109.3**
Speed ratings (Par 101): **103,102,102,100,100**
CSF £9.98 TOTE £3.60: £1.10, £1.70; EX 11.10.
Owner Rakebackmypoker.com **Bred** Limestone And Tara Studs **Trained** Stainforth, S Yorks

FOCUS
Fairly useful form in this claimer, but it was a muddling race and they finished in a heap.

1279 GREAT OFFERS AT WOLVERHAMPTON-RACECOURSE.CO.UK FILLIES' H'CAP 5f 216y(P)

5:20 (5:20) (Class 4) (0-80,78) 4-Y-0+ £3,238 (£963; £481; £240) Stalls Low

Form RPR

0-26 **1** **Forever's Girl**[67] 403 5-9-6 **77**.... PaulMulrennan 5 85
(Geoffrey Oldroyd) *mde all: shkn up over 1f out: styd on* **9/1**

4551 **2** 3/4 **Polemica (IRE)**[12] 1054 5-8-5 **62**....(bt) AndreaAtzeni 2 68+
(Frank Sheridan) *s.i.s: hld up: rdn over 2f out: hdwy over 1f out: r.o to go 2nd wl ins fnl f: nt rch wnr* **9/2**[3]

0604 **3** 3/4 **Absa Lutte (IRE)**[19] 946 8-8-6 **66**....(bt) SimonPearce(3) 3 69
(Michael Mullineaux) *a.p: chsd wnr 2f out: sn rdn: styd on: lost 2nd wl ins fnl f* **6/1**

4330 **4** 1 1/2 **Athaakeel (IRE)**[12] 1044 5-8-5 **62**....(b) CathyGannon 8 60
(Ronald Harris) *s.i.s: hld up: rdn over 2f out: r.o ins fnl f: nrst fin* **18/1**

-645 **5** 1 1/2 **Liberty Lady (IRE)**[5] 1186 4-9-5 **76**.... DavidProbert 4 70
(Des Donovan) *prom: rdn over 2f out: styd on same pce appr fnl f* **7/2**[1]

033- **6** 1 **Starclass**[230] 5396 4-9-7 **78**.... ShaneKelly 1 68
(Walter Swinburn) *s.i.s: hld up: hdwy over 2f out: rdn over 1f out: no further prog* **4/1**[2]

10- **7** 1/2 **Bella Noir**[170] 7097 4-9-7 **78**.... AndrewElliott 7 67
(Mrs K Burke) *chsd ldrs: rdn over 3f out: outpcd fr over 2f out* **8/1**

-016 **8** 2 3/4 **Excellent Show**[58] 521 5-9-5 **76**....(p) TomEaves 6 56
(Bryan Smart) *chsd wnr: shkn up 1/2-way: rdn 2f out: wknd fnl f* **6/1**

1m 13.56s (-1.44) **Going Correction** -0.075s/f (Stan) **8** Ran SP% **115.3**
Speed ratings (Par 102): **106,105,104,102,100 98,98,94**
toteswingers:1&2:£6.40, 1&3:£10.70, 2&3:£6.80. totesuper7: Win: Not won. Place: £42.70 CSF £49.54 CT £265.46 TOTE £10.70: £4.60, £1.20, £2.60; EX 58.90 Trifecta £218.20 Part won. Pool: £294.92 - 0.61 winning units..
Owner R C Bond **Bred** R C Bond **Trained** Brawby, N Yorks

FOCUS
Just run-of-the-mill fare and it's probably not woth getting carried away with this form, but the winner is rated back to her best.
T/Plt: £47.60 to a £1 stake. Pool:£48,641.23 - 745.12 winning tickets T/Qpdt: £3.30 to a £1 stake. Pool:£4,048.85 - 896.84 winning tickets CR

1129 FOLKESTONE (R-H)

Tuesday, April 12

OFFICIAL GOING: Good to firm (8.7)
Wind: Light, behind Weather: Fine

1280 FRIENDS OF BUTTERCUPS (S) STKS 5f
2:30 (2:30) (Class 6) 3-Y-O **£1,706** (£503; £252) **Stalls** High

Form RPR

425- **1** **Novabridge**[194] 6489 3-9-4 63....(b) KierenFallon 2 65
(Andrew Haynes) *led after 1f: mde rest: shkn up and drew clr 1f out* **2/7**[1]

4650 **2** 4 **Dangerous Illusion (IRE)**[12] 1056 3-8-7 45.... MartinDwyer 1 40
(Michael Quinn) *chsd wnr over 3f out: cl enough over 1f out: sn outpcd* **12/1**[3]

4045 **3** 1 1/4 **Magical Star**[8] 1132 3-8-7 48....(b[1]) NickyMackay 4 35
(Mark Rimmer) *hld up: swtchd outside and effrt 2f out: sn outpcd and btn* **5/1**[2]

0-06 **4** 1/2 **Veuveveuvevoom**[36] 788 3-8-4 36....(p) SimonPearce(3) 3 33
(Gerry Enright) *led 1f: rdn 2f out: sn outpcd* **25/1**

58.99 secs (-1.01) **Going Correction** -0.275s/f (Firm) **4** Ran SP% **106.0**
Speed ratings (Par 96): **97,90,88,87**
CSF £4.23 TOTE £1.10; EX 4.20.There was no bid for the winner.
Owner Dajam Ltd **Bred** Bishopswood Bloodstock & Trickledown Stud **Trained** Limpley Stoke, Bath

FOCUS
Underfoot conditions were officially good to firm, with 5-7mm of water having been applied to the course the previous day. The weather was dry and bright, but there was a keen, blustery wind. Racing began with a poor seller. The form is rated around the winner.

1281 BUTTERCUPS CORPORATE MEMBERSHIP H'CAP 5f
3:00 (3:00) (Class 5) (0-75,74) 4-Y-O+ **£2,388** (£705; £352) **Stalls** High

Form RPR

3202 **1** **Black Baccara**[13] 1043 4-8-8 **61**....(be) KierenFallon 4 68
(Phil McEntee) *racd against nr side rail: led after 100yds: mde rest: coaxed along w hd high over 1f out: a holding on* **7/4**[2]

120- **2** 1/2 **Magical Speedfit (IRE)**[185] 6739 6-9-4 **74**.... SimonPearce(3) 2 79
(George Margarson) *hld up: sn outpcd by other pair and pushed along: clsd over 1f out: wnt 2nd last 150yds and tried to chal: a hld* **9/4**[3]

43-1 **3** 2 1/4 **Dream Number (IRE)**[14] 1024 4-9-0 **67**.... MartinDwyer 1 67
(William Muir) *led 100yds: pressed wnr after tl rdn and nt qckn jst over 1f out: lost 2nd last 150yds: eased* **13/8**[1]

58.18 secs (-1.82) **Going Correction** -0.275s/f (Firm) course record **3** Ran SP% **105.2**
Speed ratings (Par 103): **103,102,98**
CSF £5.37 TOTE £2.40; EX 5.50.
Owner Eventmaker Racehorses **Bred** Peter Balding **Trained** Newmarket, Suffolk

FOCUS
Just an ordinary sprint handicap, with the top weight rated 74, but aided by the blustery wind, it was run in course record time. The winner probably only ran to her recent AW form.

1282 DIESEL ADOPTION H'CAP 1m 7f 92y
3:30 (3:30) (Class 5) (0-75,74) 4-Y-O+ **£2,388** (£705; £352) **Stalls** High

Form RPR

/102 **1** **My Valley (IRE)**[19] 955 9-9-1 **65**.... IanMongan 4 72
(Pat Phelan) *hld up last: sweeping move rnd field over 3f out: rdn to ld jst over 2f out: drvn and styd on wl* **8/1**

254- **2** 1 1/4 **Stormy Morning**[104] 8010 5-9-0 **64**.... LiamKeniry 5 69
(J S Moore) *hld up in 4th gng wl: wnt 3rd 2f out and looked sure to threaten: shkn up over 1f out: kpt on same pce to take 2nd nr fin* **6/1**[3]

024- **3** 1/2 **Not Til Monday (IRE)**[22] 8013 5-9-1 **65**.... KierenFallon 6 69
(J R Jenkins) *led after 2f and set decent pce: urged along over 5f out: hdd over 4f out: rousted to ld briefly over 2f out: one pce u.p* **3/1**[2]

10-3 **4** 2 1/4 **Marcus Antonius**[7] 1153 4-8-5 **58**.... NickyMackay 3 59
(Jim Boyle) *hld up in 3rd: trapped bhd rivals over 3f out: rdn over 2f out: hanging and nt qckn after* **1/1**[1]

202- **5** 14 **Swordsman (GER)**[203] 4745 9-9-4 **68**....(vt) ChrisCatlin 2 51
(Chris Gordon) *led 2f: chsd ldr: led over 4f out to over 2f out: n.m.r sn after and wknd rapidly* **9/1**

3m 23.64s (-6.06) **Going Correction** -0.325s/f (Firm)
WFA 4 from 5yo+ 3lb **5** Ran SP% **110.4**
Speed ratings (Par 103): **103,102,102,100,93**
CSF £50.11 TOTE £7.10: £3.40, £3.10; EX 34.90.
Owner H J F Lang **Bred** John Brophy **Trained** Epsom, Surrey

FOCUS
A run-of-the-mill handicap which probably didn't take much winning. The first three all ran close to their recent marks.

1283 BUTTERCUPS SANCTUARY FOR GOATS APPRENTICE H'CAP 6f
4:00 (4:02) (Class 6) (0-60,60) 4-Y-O+ **£1,706** (£503; £252) **Stalls** High

Form RPR

2315 **1** **Crystallize**[6] 1177 5-9-1 **57**.... SeanPalmer(3) 6 61
(Andrew Haynes) *prom: wnt 2nd 2f out: shkn up to ld over 1f out: hld on wl* **4/1**[3]

-405 **2** 1/2 **Diddums**[20] 950 5-9-2 **55**....(p) KatiaScallan 3 57
(Alastair Lidderdale) *hld up in 4th: trckd ldrs over 1f out: effrt to chse wnr last 150yds and sn chalng: nt qckn nr fin* **7/1**

2222 **3** 1 3/4 **Gold Story**[60] 506 4-9-7 **60**.... CharlesBishop 2 56
(George Baker) *dwlt: hld up in last pair: shkn up and nt qckn over 1f out: kpt on fnl f to take 3rd nr fin* **9/4**[1]

0536 **4** 3/4 **Thoughtsofstardom**[6] 1182 8-8-12 **51**.... LeonnaMayor 5 45
(Phil McEntee) *t.k.h: led against nr side rail: edgd rt fr 2f out: hdd over 1f out: fdd fnl f* **3/1**[2]

5550 **5** 2 **Evey P (IRE)**[34] 809 4-8-13 **52**.... JosephYoung 1 40
(Gary Brown) *racd on outer: chsd ldr to 2f out: wknd fnl f* **5/1**

005- **6** 26 **Stargazy**[250] 4738 7-8-11 **50**.... AliceHaynes 4 —
(Alastair Lidderdale) *dwlt: a in last pair: wknd 1/2-way: t.o* **14/1**

1m 11.63s (-1.07) **Going Correction** -0.275s/f (Firm) **6** Ran SP% **111.6**
Speed ratings (Par 101): **96,95,93,92,89 54**
Tote Swingers: 1&2 £3.30, 1&3 £2.40, 2&3 £2.50 CSF £30.19 TOTE £5.30: £2.80, £7.30; EX 21.50.
Owner Mrs A De Weck & P De Weck **Bred** Aiden Murphy **Trained** Limpley Stoke, Bath

FOCUS
A low-grade handicap in which the top weight was rated 60. Weak form with the winner up 6lb on recent AW figures.

1284 BUTTERCUPS GUARDIANSHIP MAIDEN STKS 7f (S)
4:30 (4:31) (Class 5) 3-Y-O+ **£2,388** (£705; £352) **Stalls** High

Form RPR

232- **1** **Yair Hill (IRE)**[182] 6825 3-8-13 80.... TedDurcan 4 78+
(John Dunlop) *mde all: easily drew clr 2f out* **1/5**[1]

2 5 **Deerslayer (USA)** 5-9-13 0.... PaulDoe 2 58
(Jim Best) *dwlt: rn green but sn in tch: shkn up and prog to take 2nd over 1f out: no ch w wnr but kpt on* **12/1**[3]

-205 **3** 4 1/2 **Indian Wish (USA)**[76] 297 3-8-8 60....(t) WilliamCarson 3 31
(Tim McCarthy) *mostly chsd wnr to over 2f out: rdn and sn lft bhd* **8/1**[2]

4 4 **Casternova** 3-8-8 0.... JimmyQuinn 7 21
(Hughie Morrison) *s.s: rn green and detached in last early: nvr a factor: pushed along to take modest 4th nr fin* **16/1**

00-0 **5** 2 1/2 **Trust Me Boy**[34] 811 3-8-13 48....(v) SamHitchcott 1 19
(John E Long) *racd wd: prom: rdn 1/2-way: chsd wnr over 2f out to over 1f out: wknd rapidly* **100/1**

05- **6** 15 **Heavenly Pursuit**[135] 7608 3-8-1 0.... NathanAlison(7) 5 —
(Jim Boyle) *plld hrd bhd ldrs: wknd rapidly 1/2-way: t.o* **20/1**

1m 25.68s (-1.62) **Going Correction** -0.275s/f (Firm)
WFA 3 from 5yo 14lb **6** Ran SP% **113.8**
Speed ratings (Par 103): **98,92,87,82,79 62**
Tote Swingers: 1&2 £1.60, 1&3 £1.60, 2&3 £2.30 CSF £4.15 TOTE £1.40: £1.02, £6.30; EX 3.90.
Owner The Earl Cadogan **Bred** The Earl Cadogan **Trained** Arundel, W Sussex

FOCUS
Precious little depth to this weak maiden. It is doubtful if the easy winner had to improve on his 2yo form.
Deerslayer(USA) Official explanation: jockey said that the gelding hung left

1285 BUTTERCUPS ADOPT A GOAT MAIDEN STKS 1m 4f
5:05 (5:05) (Class 5) 3-Y-O+ **£2,388** (£705; £352) **Stalls** High

Form RPR

00-2 **1** **Viking Storm**[17] 992 3-8-7 70.... ChrisCatlin 3 74
(Harry Dunlop) *trckd ldng pair: wnt 2nd over 5f out: pushed into ld over 2f out: steadily drew rt away* **4/6**[1]

540- **2** 10 **History Girl (IRE)**[138] 7567 3-8-2 65.... JimmyQuinn 6 59
(Sir Henry Cecil) *hld up in last pair: trckd ldng pair 5f out: shkn up to chse wnr 2f out: sn no ch* **7/4**[2]

66-0 **3** 14 **Back For Tea (IRE)**[18] 966 3-8-7 47.... WilliamCarson 4 36
(Phil McEntee) *t.k.h: led 1f: trckd ldr tl led 1/2-way: hdd over 2f out: wknd rapidly* **80/1**

4 9 **Frolic Along (IRE)**[17] 4-9-8 0.... DavidProbert 2 16+
(J R Jenkins) *dwlt: hld up in last pair: pushed along over 5f out: lft bhd fnl 4f: t.o* **8/1**[3]

5 4 1/2 **Shalamiyr (FR)**[91] 6-10-0 0.... EddieCreighton 7 14
(Edward Creighton) *s.s: rcvrd to ld after 1f: hdd 1/2-way: lost pl qckly: t.o* **50/1**

2m 38.05s (-2.85) **Going Correction** -0.325s/f (Firm)
WFA 3 from 4yo 21lb 4 from 6yo+ 1lb **5** Ran SP% **110.7**
Speed ratings (Par 103): **96,89,80,74,71**
CSF £2.09 TOTE £1.40: £1.02, £2.50; EX 2.30.
Owner Be Hopeful Partnership **Bred** Charlie Wyatt **Trained** Lambourn, Berks

FOCUS
A weak maiden in which few had obvious claims. The winner improved 3lb on her reappearance effort.

1286 OPEN DAYS AT BUTTERCUPS H'CAP 1m 1f 149y
5:40 (5:41) (Class 5) (0-75,73) 3-Y-O **£2,388** (£705; £352) **Stalls** Centre

Form RPR

1- **1** **Zain Al Boldan**[250] 4736 3-9-7 **73**.... SamHitchcott 3 80+
(Mick Channon) *t.k.h: hld up: trckd ldr over 5f out: rdn over 2f out: hung lft and rn green over 1f out: rallied wl fnl f: led post* **85/40**[2]

4141 **2** hd **Ya Hafed**[8] 1134 3-9-4 **70** 6ex.... JamesDoyle 2 76
(Sheena West) *led: kicked on 3f out: styd on fnl f: hdd post* **4/6**[1]

515 **3** 4 **Crystal Sky (IRE)**[22] 931 3-8-13 **65**.... RobertHavlin 1 63
(Andrew Haynes) *trckd ldr to over 5f out: rdn over 2f out: edgd lft and fdd fnl f* **11/2**[3]

2m 7.40s (2.50) **Going Correction** -0.325s/f (Firm) **3** Ran SP% **107.4**
Speed ratings (Par 98): **77,76,73**
CSF £4.02 TOTE £2.30; EX 3.50.
Owner Jaber Abdullah **Bred** Tweenhills & R & L Warner Bloodstock **Trained** West Ilsley, Berks

FOCUS
No more than an ordinary handicap, even though the winner lined up with Classic engagements. Slightly muddling form.

T/Plt: £69.20 to a £1 stake. Pool:£38,606.57 - 407.14 winning tickets T/Qpdt: £16.80 to a £1 stake. Pool:£2,919.20 - 128.28 winning tickets JN

[1027] SOUTHWELL (L-H)

Tuesday, April 12

OFFICIAL GOING: Standard

Wind: Strong behind Weather: Fine and dry

1287 32RED H'CAP 5f (F)
2:10 (2:10) (Class 6) (0-60,60) 4-Y-0+ **£1,706** (£503; £252) **Stalls** High

Form RPR

5004 **1** **Spic 'n Span**[6] 1182 6-9-7 **60**....(b) CathyGannon 4 70
(Ronald Harris) *prom: led over 3f out: rdn clr over 1f out: drvn out* **7/1**

0511 **2** *hd* **Lucky Art (USA)**[5] 1204 5-8-7 **49**.... JamesSullivan(3) 2 58
(Ruth Carr) *a.p: rdn and sltly outpcd over 1f out: styd on wl u.p fnl f: jst hld* **3/1**[1]

0424 **3** *1 ½* **Gorgeous Goblin (IRE)**[3] 1246 4-8-3 **47**....(vt) KieranO'Neill(5) 3 51
(David C Griffiths) *chsd ldrs: rdn along wl over 1f out: kpt on u.p fnl f* **14/1**

406 **4** *shd* **Shakespeares Excel**[12] 1065 4-8-8 **47**.... RobbieFitzpatrick 1 51
(Derek Shaw) *in tch on wd outside: hdwy to chse ldng pair wl over 1f out: sn rdn and one pce fnl f* **16/1**

1223 **5** *4* **Attrition**[28] 857 4-9-6 **59**....(p) PaulHanagan 8 48
(Andrew Reid) *sn trcking ldrs: effrt to chse ldng pair 1/2-way: rdn 2f out and sn wknd* **7/2**[2]

2 **6** *¾* **Clear Ice (IRE)**[14] 1029 4-9-3 **59**....(v) RobertLButler(3) 6 45
(Richard Guest) *prom: rdn along 1/2-way: sn btn* **5/1**[3]

0355 **7** *1* **Cheveyo (IRE)**[4] 1217 5-8-6 **48** ow1....(v) RossAtkinson(3) 10 31
(Patrick Morris) *dwlt: a in rr* **14/1**

4434 **8** *nse* **Kheley (IRE)**[14] 1029 5-8-8 **52**.... JamesRogers(5) 7 35
(Mark Brisbourne) *led over 1f: prom tl rdn along 1/2-way: sn drvn and outpcd wl over 1f out* **8/1**

0-00 **9** *1 ½* **Avec Moi**[6] 1171 4-8-0 **46** oh1.... DanielHarris(7) 9 23
(Christine Dunnett) *sn outpcd and bhd fr 1/2-way* **100/1**

5604 **10** *2* **Memphis Man**[41] 734 8-8-10 **49**.... SilvestreDeSousa 5 19
(David Evans) *in rr and early reminders: sn outpcd and bhd* **11/1**

58.33 secs (-1.37) **Going Correction** -0.175s/f (Stan) **10** Ran SP% **116.0**

Speed ratings (Par 101): **103,102,100,100,93 92,90,90,88,85**

Tote Swingers: 1&2 £21.50, 1&3 £33.70, 2&3 £10.70 CSF £28.13 CT £248.32 TOTE £9.70: £3.10, £1.70, £3.40; EX 34.90 Trifecta £247.80 Part won. Pool: £334.99 - 0.44 winning units..

Owner P Nurcombe **Bred** C A Cyzer **Trained** Earlswood, Monmouths

FOCUS

A moderate sprint handicap, though no shortage of recent form with half the field having run within the previous six days. All the action took place centre to far side.

1288 SOUTHWELL-RACECOURSE.CO.UK MEDIAN AUCTION MAIDEN STKS 7f (F)
2:40 (2:41) (Class 6) 3-4-Y-0 **£1,706** (£503; £252) **Stalls** Low

Form RPR

050- **1** **Lightning Cloud (IRE)**[172] 7058 3-8-13 69.... PhillipMakin 3 79+
(Kevin Ryan) *led 1f: cl up: led on bit over 2f out: pushed clr over 1f out: rn green and jinked rt ins fnl f: comf* **8/11**[1]

-320 **2** *5* **X Rated**[10] 1096 3-8-13 68.... RobertWinston 2 67
(Alan McCabe) *rdn along early and led after 1f: pushed along and hdd over 2f out: drvn wl over 1f out: and sn one pce: clr 2nd whn stmbld bdly nr line: fatally injured* **5/2**[2]

2 **3** *3 ¼* **Precocious Kid (IRE)**[19] 953 3-8-13 0.... JackMitchell 5 57
(Chris Wall) *in rr: rdn along and outpcd over 3f out: hdwy 2f out: drvn and kpt on same pce appr fnl f: tk 3rd nr fin* **6/1**[3]

4645 **4** *shd* **Mini's Destination**[40] 751 3-8-3 59.... JamesRogers(5) 6 52
(John Holt) *chsd ldng pair: rdn along wl over 2f out: sn drvn and outpcd fr wl over 1f out: lost 3rd towards fin* **40/1**

05- **5** *4* **Areef (IRE)**[165] 7210 3-8-8 0.... MartinLane 4 42
(Michael Bell) *hld up in rr: hdwy to chse ldrs 1/2-way: rdn along wl over 2f out: sn wknd* **16/1**

1m 30.49s (0.19) **Going Correction** +0.05s/f (Slow) **5** Ran SP% **109.1**

Speed ratings (Par 101): **100,94,90,90,85**

CSF £2.69 TOTE £1.20: £1.02, £2.10; EX 2.90.

Owner Hambleton Racing Ltd XVIII **Bred** John Cullinan **Trained** Hambleton, N Yorks

■ Stewards' Enquiry : James Rogers ten-day ban: failed to ride out for third place (Apr 26 - May 5)

FOCUS

An uncompetitive maiden.

1289 PLAY GOLF BEFORE RACING AT SOUTHWELL CLAIMING STKS 6f (F)
3:10 (3:10) (Class 6) 3-Y-0+ **£1,706** (£503; £252) **Stalls** Low

Form RPR

0313 **1** **Bonnie Prince Blue**[6] 1180 8-9-3 73....(b) TomQueally 4 83
(James Given) *in rr: rdn along and outpcd after 2f: hdwy 3f out: rdn to chse ldr wl over 1f out: sn drvn and hung lft to far rail: styd on to ld fnl 100yds* **9/2**[3]

0-31 **2** *2* **Ingleby Arch (USA)**[61] 493 8-9-7 83.... PhillipMakin 2 81
(David Barron) *cl up: led 1/2-way: rdn and hung rt fr wl over 1f out: drvn ins fnl f: hdd and one pce last 100yds* **8/11**[1]

0516 **3** *12* **Cape Of Storms**[22] 928 8-9-3 62....(b) TomEaves 5 38
(Roy Brotherton) *cl up: rdn along over 2f out: sn one pce* **10/1**

11-4 **4** *3 ¼* **Benato The Great (IRE)**[96] 58 5-9-5 72.... AdrianNicholls 6 30
(David Nicholls) *t.k.h: cl up on outer: effrt to chse ldr wl over 2f out: sn rdn and edgd lft wl over 1f out: sn wknd* **4/1**[2]

0-00 **5** *9* **First Term**[4] 1220 4-9-0 53....(p) CathyGannon 3 —
(Malcolm Saunders) *prom: rdn along 1/2-way: sn wknd* **66/1**

0-06 **6** *2 ½* **Sophie's Beau (USA)**[70] 376 4-8-9 42.... DavidKenny(7) 1 —
(Michael Chapman) *reminders s and sn led on inner: rdn along over 3f out: sn hdd & wknd* **125/1**

1m 16.15s (-0.35) **Going Correction** +0.05s/f (Slow) **6** Ran SP% **107.5**

Speed ratings (Par 101): **104,101,85,81,69 65**

Tote Swingers: 1&2 £1.10, 1&3 £3.80, 2&3 £2.00 CSF £7.48 TOTE £4.40: £2.80, £1.20; EX 6.80.

Owner Danethorpe Racing Partnership **Bred** George Joseph Hicks **Trained** Willoughton, Lincs

FOCUS

An uncompetitive claimer in which the pair best in at the weights dominated the finish, but not in the order most would have expected.

1290 GOLF AND RACING AT SOUTHWELL MAIDEN STKS 5f (F)
3:40 (3:40) (Class 5) 2-Y-0 **£2,388** (£705; £352) **Stalls** High

Form RPR

1 **Mitchum** 2-9-3 0.... PhillipMakin 2 85+
(David Barron) *cl up: slt ld after 2f: shkn up wl over 1f out and sn qcknd clr: easily* **7/2**[2]

3 **2** *8* **Dougie Boy**[12] 1055 2-9-0 0.... KierenFox(3) 7 56
(Bill Turner) *racd nr stands' rail: chsd ldng pair: rdn along wl over 1f out: drvn appr fnl f: edgd lft and kpt on same pce* **15/8**[1]

4 **3** *¾* **Mousie**[13] 1049 2-8-5 0.... RyanTate(7) 1 48
(Alan McCabe) *in tch on outer: hdwy 1/2-way: rdn to chse wnr over 1f out: sn drvn and one pce* **14/1**

4 *2 ¼* **Bojangle (IRE)** 2-8-12 0.... PaulHanagan 5 40
(Dominic Ffrench Davis) *chsd ldrs: rdn along 1/2-way: sn outpcd and hung lft fr over 1f out* **12/1**

5 *nk* **Darnathean** 2-9-3 0....(v[1]) TonyCulhane 3 44
(Paul D'Arcy) *led 3f: cl up: rdn 2f out: sn wknd* **7/1**[3]

6 *4 ½* **Manderston** 2-9-3 0.... SilvestreDeSousa 4 28
(Mark Johnston) *s.i.s: a in rr* **7/1**[3]

7 *1 ½* **Abercandy (IRE)** 2-8-12 0.... TomQueally 6 18
(David Evans) *sn outpcd and a in rr* **7/1**[3]

8 *9* **Cotes Du Rhone (IRE)** 2-9-3 0.... CathyGannon 8 —
(David Evans) *s.i.s: a bhd* **28/1**

60.05 secs (0.35) **Going Correction** -0.175s/f (Stan) **8** Ran SP% **112.3**

Speed ratings (Par 92): **90,77,76,72,71 64,62,47**

Tote Swingers: 1&2 £1.70, 1&3 £4.70, 2&3 £4.30 CSF £10.07 TOTE £4.10: £1.40, £1.02, £2.90; EX 10.20 Trifecta £244.30 Part won. Pool: £330.27 - 0.20 winning units..

Owner A J Duffield **Bred** Conor J C Parsons & Brian M Parsons **Trained** Maunby, N Yorks

FOCUS

An ordinary maiden, but a very taking winner.

NOTEBOOK

Mitchum, a half-brother to a winning sprinter, comes from a stable always to be feared here and his sire had a good record (12-75) and a healthy level-stake profit at the track coming into this. Always up with the pace in the centre, his rider sent him about his business passing the 2f pole and he was soon in a completely different parish. The beaten horses may not have been up to much, but the way he went about this was very impressive and connections weren't even sure beforehand whether he would need it or not. (op 3-1 tchd 11-4)

Dougie Boy, just behind a subsequent winner when third on his Leicester debut, is a half-brother to a winner on this surface. Although not far away towards the nearside, he was being ridden from some way out but battled on to win the separate race for second. He ran into one here and should be up to winning a small maiden. (op 5-2 tchd 11-4)

Mousie, a well-beaten fourth of seven on her Wolverhampton debut, didn't run badly but her previous experience may have been a help.

Bojangle(IRE), a half-sister to four winners including the Listed winner Fashionable, ran on again after getting outpaced and looks the type to improve. (op 11-1 tchd 10-1)

Darnathean matched the winner until halfway, but the fact that he was visored for this racecourse debut wasn't encouraging. (op 5-1)

1291 MEMBERSHIP OF SOUTHWELL GOLF CLUB H'CAP 1m 6f (F)
4:10 (4:14) (Class 5) (0-75,79) 4-Y-0+ **£2,388** (£705; £352) **Stalls** Low

Form RPR

46-5 **1** **Taikoo**[74] 342 6-9-2 **72**.... JacobMoore(7) 6 83
(Hughie Morrison) *prom: led after 3f: hdd after 4f and chsd clr ldr: tk clsr order over 3f out: led over 2f out: rdn and edgd rt over 1f out: kpt on gamely* **7/1**

2224 **2** *2 ¼* **Calculating (IRE)**[14] 1030 7-8-12 **66**.... LeeNewnes(5) 7 73
(Mark Usher) *hld up in tch: swtchd ins and hdwy 4f out: rdn to chse ldrs 2f out: drvn over 1f out: styd on ins fnl f: edgd rt and no imp towards fin* **9/2**[2]

64-5 **3** *nk* **Trojan Gift (USA)**[39] 769 4-8-5 **57**.... BarryMcHugh 1 64
(Julie Camacho) *t.k.h early: hld up in rr: stdy hdwy 4f out: rdn to chse ldrs on outer 2f out: drvn and kpt on same pce fnl f* **12/1**

0051 **4** *5* **Record Breaker (IRE)**[7] 1156 7-10-2 **79** 6ex....(b) SilvestreDeSousa 2 79
(Mark Johnston) *reminders s: swtchd outside after 1 1/2f and gd hdwy to ld after 4f: sn clr: pushed along over 3f out: rdn and hdd over 2f out: sn drvn and wknd over 1f out* **11/4**[1]

0-20 **5** *10* **Sunny Spells**[7] 1153 6-8-11 **65**.... RyanClark(5) 8 51
(Stuart Williams) *prom: rdn along 1/2-way: sn outpcd and bhd fnl 3f* **9/2**[2]

500- **6** *3* **Shy**[190] 6639 6-9-0 **63**.... JamesMillman 4 45
(Rod Millman) *chsd ldrs: rdn along and lost pl 1/2-way: bhd fnl 3f* **20/1**

045- **7** *15* **Persian Peril**[210] 6050 7-9-9 **72**.... TomEaves 3 33
(Alan Swinbank) *a in rr: rdn along over 4f out: sn outpcd and bhd: t.o and eased fnl 2f* **8/1**

3230 **8** *13* **Ay Tay Tate (IRE)**[9] 1107 5-8-8 **57**.... PaulHanagan 5 —
(David C Griffiths) *led 3f: chsd ldrs: rdn along 5f out: sn wknd and bhd: t.o and eased fnl 2f* **6/1**[3]

3m 7.20s (-1.10) **Going Correction** +0.05s/f (Slow)

WFA 4 from 5yo+ 3lb **8** Ran SP% **113.4**

Speed ratings (Par 103): **105,103,103,100,94 93,84,77**

Tote Swingers: 1&2 £8.00, 1&3 £18.40, 2&3 £4.10 CSF £37.74 CT £370.70 TOTE £20.30: £5.20, £1.40, £6.50; EX 34.30 Trifecta £364.70 Part won. Pool: £492.92 - 0.44 winning units..

Owner Mrs M D W Morrison **Bred** Miss B Swire **Trained** East Ilsley, Berks

■ A first winner on only his second ride for Jacob Moore.

FOCUS

Quite a test of stamina with Record Breaker setting a strong pace once in front.

Shy Official explanation: jockey said the mare was never travelling

1292 DINE IN THE QUEEN MOTHER RESTAURANT H'CAP 1m (F)
4:40 (4:40) (Class 5) (0-75,73) 4-Y-0+ **£2,388** (£705; £352) **Stalls** Low

Form RPR

2216 **1** **Postman**[12] 1058 5-9-1 **67**....(p) TomEaves 8 76
(Bryan Smart) *cl up on outer: smooth hdwy to ld 2f out: rdn ent fnl f: edgd lft and drvn out* **5/1**[3]

60-2 **2** *¾* **Formulation (IRE)**[12] 1058 4-9-6 **72**.... JimmyFortune 6 79
(Hughie Morrison) *sn led: rdn along and hdd 2f out: drvn and rallied over 1f out: ev ch ins fnl f tl edgd lft and no ex fnl 50yds* **9/4**[1]

2350 **3** *2 ¾* **Elusive Fame (USA)**[18] 977 5-8-13 **72**....(b) JasonHart(7) 5 73
(Mark Johnston) *t.k.h: hld up in tch: hdwy over 3f out: chsd ldng pair 2f out: rdn and ch over 1f out: drvn and one pce fnl f* **15/2**

166- **4** *1 ½* **I'm Super Too (IRE)**[258] 4483 4-9-0 **73**.... GarryWhillans(7) 3 70
(Alan Swinbank) *trckd ldrs: hdwy 3f out: rdn 2f out: sn drvn: edgd rt over 1f out and sn one pce* **15/2**

4450 **5** *2* **General Tufto**[10] 1099 6-8-13 **65**....................(b) MartinLane 2 58
(Charles Smith) *sn rdn along and outpcd: bhd tl hdwy and wd st: kpt on u.p fnl 2f: nvr nr ldrs* **16/1**

2246 **6** *½* **Elusive Warrior (USA)**[28] 858 8-8-8 **60**....................(p) RobertWinston 4 51
(Alan McCabe) *chsd ldrs: rdn along over 2f out: sn drvn and wknd* **12/1**

133 **7** *5* **Hill Tribe**[6] 1167 4-9-2 **68**.................... PaulHanagan 7 48
(Richard Guest) *cl up: rdn along over 3f out: wknd wl over 2f out* **4/1**[2]

6-66 **8** *48* **Exit Smiling**[27] 870 9-9-5 **71**.................... MickyFenton 1 —
(Paul Midgley) *a in rr: outpcd and bhd 3f out: eased fnl 2f* **10/1**

1m 43.73s (0.03) **Going Correction** +0.05s/f (Slow) **8** Ran SP% **113.6**
Speed ratings (Par 103): **101,100,97,96,94 93,88,40**
Tote Swingers: 1&2 £4.20, 1&3 £10.00, 2&3 £3.30 CSF £16.46 CT £82.38 TOTE £5.30: £1.10, £1.10, £3.40; EX 17.80 Trifecta £105.80 Pool: £477.56 - 3.34 winning units..
Owner Crossfields Racing **Bred** Newsells Park Stud **Trained** Hambleton, N Yorks
FOCUS
Not a bad little handicap and one run at a decent pace.
Exit Smiling Official explanation: vet said gelding finished distressed

1293 MEALS IN THE PANTRY AT SOUTHWELL H'CAP 1m (F)
5:10 (5:10) (Class 6) (0-60,60) 3-Y-O **£1,706** (£503; £252) **Stalls** Low

Form RPR
6-33 **1** **Jay Jays Joy**[56] 550 3-8-10 **49**....................(b) LeeNewman 8 58+
(David Barron) *s.i.s and bhd: gd hdwy on inner to trck ldrs 1/2-way: led over 3f out: rdn 2f out: kpt on gamely u.p fnl f* **11/2**

4332 **2** *5* **Little Jazz**[14] 1028 3-9-7 **60**.................... LiamJones 3 57
(Paul D'Arcy) *trckd ldrs: hdwy 3f out: swtchd rt and rdn to chse wnr over 1f out: sn drvn and ev ch tl one pce ins fnl f* **9/2**[3]

006- **3** *2¼* **Goodmanyourself**[277] 3874 3-8-7 **46**.................... MickyFenton 4 38
(Paul Midgley) *chsd ldr: cl up 1/2-way: rdn to chse wnr 3f out: drvn wl over 1f out: sn one pce* **7/1**

125- **4** *10* **Geronimo Chief (IRE)**[122] 7831 3-9-6 **59**.................... PhillipMakin 2 28
(Ben Haslam) *led: rdn along and hdd over 3f out: sn drvn and wknd over 2f out* **7/2**[1]

043- **5** *7* **Ad Value (IRE)**[202] 6300 3-9-0 **53**.................... RobertWinston 5 —
(Alan Swinbank) *hld up in tch: effrt over 3f out: sn rdn and nvr a factor* **4/1**[2]

0-05 **6** *½* **Dancing Tara**[12] 1056 3-8-11 **50**.................... TomQueally 7 —
(David Evans) *towards rr: rdn along over 3f out: nvr a factor* **20/1**

65-0 **7** *14* **Elegant Star (IRE)**[53] 591 3-8-7 **46** oh1....................(v[1]) AdrianMcCarthy 1 —
(Dave Morris) *chsd ldrs: rdn along wl over 3f out: sn wknd* **50/1**

6-12 **8** *22* **West Leake Melody**[77] 296 3-8-11 **50**.................... PaulHanagan 6 —
(Patrick Morris) *prom on outer: rdn along wl over 3f out: sn wknd and bhd whn eased fnl 2f* **9/2**[3]

1m 45.52s (1.82) **Going Correction** +0.05s/f (Slow) **8** Ran SP% **113.2**
Speed ratings (Par 96): **92,87,84,74,67 67,53,31**
Tote Swingers: 1&2 £7.90, 2&3 £17.10 CSF £29.74 CT £175.21 TOTE £8.10: £2.70, £1.10, £6.90; EX 33.50 Trifecta £240.50 Part won. Pool: £325.07 - 0.61 winning units..
Owner Jada Johnson & GJSS **Bred** Mrs F S Williams **Trained** Maunby, N Yorks
FOCUS
A modest 3-y-o handicap in which the front trio pulled a long way clear of the rest and they finished spread out all over Nottinghamshire.
West Leake Melody Official explanation: jockey said that the gelding was never travelling
T/Plt: £45.60 to a £1 stake. Pool:£48,450.05 - 774.14 winning tickets T/Qpdt: £7.40 to a £1 stake. Pool:£3,687.73 - 368.42 winning tickets JR

1273 WOLVERHAMPTON (A.W) (L-H)
Tuesday, April 12

OFFICIAL GOING: Standard
Wind: Fine Weather: Light behind

1294 32RED CASINO OF THE DECADE H'CAP 5f 20y(P)
2:20 (2:20) (Class 6) (0-60,60) 3-Y-O **£1,706** (£503; £252) **Stalls** Low

Form RPR
006- **1** **Dreams Of Glory**[184] 6769 3-8-7 **46**.................... HayleyTurner 3 55
(Ron Hodges) *mde all: rdn over 1f out: edgd rt: r.o* **16/1**

000- **2** *2* **Palindromic (IRE)**[177] 6954 3-8-10 **49**....................(b) SteveDrowne 1 51
(Jeremy Gask) *a.p: chsd wnr 2f out: sn rdn: styd on same pce ins fnl f* **11/1**[3]

3133 **3** *nse* **Juarla (IRE)**[27] 868 3-9-7 **60**.................... LukeMorris 5 62
(Ronald Harris) *chsd ldrs: rdn over 1f out: styd on same pce ins fnl f* **5/1**[2]

1 **4** *2¾* **Royal Bajan (USA)**[12] 1065 3-9-7 **60**.................... PaulMulrennan 2 52
(James Given) *prom: n.m.r and lost pl 4f out: hdwy u.p over 1f out: no imp ins fnl f* **4/11**[1]

40-4 **5** *7* **Chester Deelyte (IRE)**[4] 1217 3-8-6 **48**.................... PatrickDonaghy[(3)] 4 15
(Lisa Williamson) *chsd ldrs tl rdn and wknd 1/2-way* **25/1**

5424 **6** *nk* **Inde Country**[63] 452 3-8-6 **50**.................... DeclanCannon[(5)] 6 16
(Nicky Vaughan) *chsd ldrs: rdn over 1f out: sn hung lft and wknd* **14/1**

61.64 secs (-0.66) **Going Correction** -0.125s/f (Stan) **6** Ran SP% **114.7**
Speed ratings (Par 96): **100,96,96,92,81 80**
Tote Swingers: 1&2 £6.60, 1&3 £4.50, 2&3 £2.70 CSF £163.84 TOTE £20.80: £6.10, £4.70; EX 133.70.
Owner P E Axon **Bred** P E Axon **Trained** Charlton Mackrell, Somerset
FOCUS
A very ordinary and uncompetitive handicap that took less winning than seemed likely with the short-priced market leader disappointing. The gallop was reasonable and the winner came down the centre.
Dreams Of Glory Official explanation: trainer said, regarding the apparent improvement of form, that the colt had strenthen up over the summer
Royal Bajan(USA) Official explanation: trainer's representative was unable to offer any explanation for the poor performance shown

1295 32RED.COM (S) STKS 7f 32y(P)
2:50 (2:50) (Class 6) 3-Y-O+ **£1,706** (£503; £252) **Stalls** High

Form RPR
1622 **1** **I Confess**[3] 1250 6-9-9 70....................(b) RichardEvans[(3)] 5 74
(David Evans) *led 2f: chsd ldr tl led again over 1f out: sn rdn: hung lft ins fnl f: styd on u.p* **6/4**[1]

2060 **2** *1¼* **Master Of Dance (IRE)**[6] 1164 4-9-7 62....................(b) PaulMulrennan 4 66
(James Given) *chsd ldrs: led 5f out: rdn over 2f out: hdd over 1f out: hung lft ins fnl f: styd on* **6/1**[3]

4164 **3** *2* **Rubenstar (IRE)**[6] 1178 8-9-12 74.................... StephenCraine 1 66
(Patrick Morris) *hood removed late and s.s: bhd: tk clsr over 5f out: hdwy over 2f out: rdn over 1f out: hung lft: styd on same pce fnl f* **3/1**[2]

4306 **4** *2¾* **Army Of Stars (IRE)**[27] 869 5-9-9 67....................(p) TjadeCollier[(3)] 2 58
(James Given) *chsd ldrs: rdn over 2f out: wknd fnl f* **12/1**

4453 **5** *3½* **Captain Loui (IRE)**[12] 1056 3-8-7 65....................(p) LukeMorris 3 44
(Dai Burchell) *chsd ldrs: rdn over 2f out: wknd over 1f out* **3/1**[2]

1m 29.23s (-0.37) **Going Correction** -0.125s/f (Stan)
WFA 3 from 4yo+ 14lb **5** Ran SP% **112.0**
Speed ratings (Par 101): **97,95,93,90,86**
CSF £11.10 TOTE £2.50: £1.70, £3.10; EX 12.20.There was no bid for the winner. Army Of Stars was claimed by Michael Blake for £6,000.
Owner J E Abbey **Bred** Gestut Sohrenhof **Trained** Pandy, Monmouths
FOCUS
Exposed performers in an ordinary seller. The gallop was no more than fair and the winner came down the centre.
Rubenstar(IRE) Official explanation: jockey said the blinds were removed late as they got stuck when he tried to remove them

1296 GREAT OFFERS AT WOLVERHAMPTON-RACECOURSE.CO.UK H'CAP 7f 32y(P)
3:20 (3:21) (Class 4) (0-80,79) 4-Y-O+ **£3,238** (£963; £481; £240) **Stalls** High

Form RPR
23-3 **1** **Tiradito (USA)**[78] 285 4-9-7 **79**....................(p) AdamKirby 1 88
(Marco Botti) *hld up: hdwy over 2f out: rdn to ld ins fnl f: r.o* **9/4**[1]

0130 **2** *1½* **Tewin Wood**[9] 1110 4-8-11 **76**.................... NatashaEaton[(7)] 8 81
(Alan Bailey) *chsd ldr tl led 1/2-way: rdn over 1f out: hdd and unable qck ins fnl f* **5/1**[3]

60-0 **3** *hd* **Night Trade (IRE)**[9] 1109 4-9-6 **78**....................(p) PaulMulrennan 4 82
(Deborah Sanderson) *a.p: chsd ldr 2f out: rdn and ev ch ins fnl f: unable qck* **16/1**

4145 **4** *1* **Lastkingofscotland (IRE)**[12] 1061 5-9-4 **76**....................(b) HayleyTurner 7 78
(Conor Dore) *s.i.s: pushed along in rr early: r.o ins fnl f: nrst fin* **6/1**

145- **5** *¾* **Spa's Dancer (IRE)**[183] 6805 4-9-3 **78**.................... PatrickHills[(3)] 5 78+
(J W Hills) *s.s: bhd: hdwy on ins over 1f out: no ex ins fnl f* **9/2**[2]

300- **6** *3¼* **Feeling Fresh (IRE)**[161] 7283 6-8-12 **70**.................... GregFairley 3 61
(Paul Green) *chsd ldrs: rdn and hung rt over 2f out: wknd over 1f out* **8/1**

050- **7** *3* **Arachnophobia (IRE)**[171] 7091 5-9-5 **77**.................... GeorgeBaker 2 60
(Martin Bosley) *broke wl: sn lost pl: rdn over 2f out: sn wknd* **6/1**

2530 **8** *1* **Ace Of Spies (IRE)**[12] 1067 6-8-13 **71**.................... KirstyMilczarek 6 51
(Conor Dore) *led to 1/2-way: rdn and wknd 2f out* **25/1**

1m 28.09s (-1.51) **Going Correction** -0.125s/f (Stan) **8** Ran SP% **115.0**
Speed ratings (Par 105): **103,101,101,99,99 95,91,90**
Tote Swingers: 1&2 £4.30, 1&3 £11.60, 2&3 £17.20 CSF £13.76 CT £143.52 TOTE £2.20: £1.10, £2.40, £6.10; EX 17.00.
Owner El Catorce **Bred** F J F M Llc **Trained** Newmarket, Suffolk
FOCUS
Mainly exposed sorts in a fair handicap. The gallop was a reasonable one and the winner raced centre-to-far-side in the straight.

1297 32RED H'CAP 2m 119y(P)
3:50 (3:51) (Class 6) (0-65,65) 4-Y-O+ **£1,706** (£503; £252) **Stalls** Low

Form RPR
-011 **1** **Brabazon (IRE)**[37] 560 8-9-9 **64**....................(bt) MartinHarley[(3)] 6 69
(Emmet Michael Butterly, Ire) *s.i.s: hld up: hdwy over 2f out: led ins fnl f: styd on wl* **11/8**[1]

623- **2** *2¾* **Haldibari (IRE)**[230] 4362 7-9-0 **52**.................... RussKennemore 4 54
(Shaun Lycett) *led 1f: chsd ldr: rdn to ld over 2f out: hung lft and hdd ins fnl f: styd on same pce* **10/1**

312- **3** *1¼* **Motirani**[111] 7967 4-9-9 **65**.................... TomMcLaughlin 7 66
(Lydia Pearce) *hld up: hdwy over 2f out: rdn over 1f out: edgd lft and styd on same pce fnl f* **6/4**[2]

055- **4** *½* **Royal Patriot (IRE)**[20] 7450 4-8-0 **45**.................... LouisBeuzelin[(3)] 1 45
(Paul Green) *hld up: hdwy over 3f out: rdn over 1f out: nt clr run ins fnl f: styd on same pce* **20/1**

0-04 **5** *½* **Spiritonthemount (USA)**[14] 1032 6-8-9 **47**....................(b) LukeMorris 2 46
(Peter Hiatt) *s.i.s: pushed along to ld at stdy pce after 1f: hdd 6f out: rdn over 3f out: styd on same pce fr over 1f out* **13/2**[3]

616- **6** *1½* **Court Wing (IRE)**[152] 7407 5-8-12 **53**.................... AndrewHeffernan[(3)] 3 51
(Richard Price) *chsd ldrs: rdn over 1f out: no ex ins fnl f* **8/1**

266- **7** *3* **Blinka Me**[15] 5260 4-9-2 **58**.................... DaneO'Neill 5 52
(Alex Hales) *prom: qcknd to ld 6f out: rdn and hdd over 2f out: wknd ins fnl f* **20/1**

3m 46.11s (4.31) **Going Correction** -0.125s/f (Stan)
WFA 4 from 5yo+ 4lb **7** Ran SP% **125.2**
Speed ratings (Par 101): **84,82,82,81,81 80,79**
Tote Swingers: 1&2 £2.70, 1&3 £1.60, 2&3 £3.60 CSF £18.54 TOTE £1.80: £1.10, £11.00; EX 29.80.
Owner James Ferry **Bred** Dermot Cantillon And Forenaghts Stud **Trained** Letterkenny, Co Donegal
FOCUS
A modest staying handicap in which the gallop was steady to the home turn and the bare form doesn't look reliable. The winner came down the centre.

1298 32RED MEDIAN AUCTION MAIDEN STKS 1m 1f 103y(P)
4:20 (4:22) (Class 6) 3-Y-O **£1,774** (£523; £262) **Stalls** Low

Form RPR
6- **1** **Fadhaa (IRE)**[172] 7058 3-9-3 0.................... RichardHills 7 82+
(B W Hills) *chsd ldrs: led over 2f out: rdn out* **1/1**[1]

325- **2** *¾* **Zakon (IRE)**[180] 6859 3-9-3 70.................... EddieAhern 4 78
(Denis Coakley) *broke wl: stdd and lost pl 7f out: hdwy over 2f out: rdn to chse wnr over 1f out: r.o* **11/2**[3]

02- **3** *3¼* **Praxios**[143] 7530 3-9-3 0.................... KirstyMilczarek 3 71
(Luca Cumani) *hld up: hdwy over 3f out: rdn over 1f out: edgd lft and no ex ins fnl f* **3/1**[2]

0- **4** *3¼* **Greyfriars Drummer**[188] 6676 3-9-3 0.................... GregFairley 8 64+
(Mark Johnston) *s.s: hdwy to chse ldr and rn wd over 7f out: led over 6f out: hdd over 3f out: hung lft and wknd over 1f out* **14/1**

5 *1¼* **Play Music** 3-8-9 0.................... MartinHarley[(3)] 5 57
(Mick Channon) *sn led: hdd over 6f out: chsd ldr tl led again over 3f out: hdd over 2f out: wknd ins fnl f* **10/1**

35 **6** *½* **Peachez**[20] 945 3-8-12 0.................... AdamKirby 2 56
(Marco Botti) *hld up: rdn over 2f out: wknd over 1f out* **16/1**

0- **7** *12* **Joe Strummer (IRE)**[160] 7303 3-9-3 0.................... HayleyTurner 1 35
(Michael Bell) *chsd ldrs tl rdn and wknd over 2f out* **20/1**

2m 0.15s (-1.55) **Going Correction** -0.125s/f (Stan) **7** Ran SP% **116.8**
Speed ratings (Par 96): **101,100,97,94,93 93,82**
Tote Swingers: 1&2 £2.40, 1&3 £1.70, 2&3 £2.20 CSF £7.46 TOTE £2.20: £1.60, £1.70; EX 6.60.
Owner Hamdan Al Maktoum **Bred** Shadwell Estate Company Limited **Trained** Lambourn, Berks

The Form Book, Raceform Ltd, Compton, RG20 6NL

FOCUS
A race won emphatically last year by subsequent St Leger winner Arctic Cosmos but, although this race should throw up winners, it'll be a surprise if any of these go on to make a mark in Group company. The gallop was a modest one and the winner came down the centre in the straight.

1299 32REDPOKER.COM H'CAP — 1m 1f 103y(P)
4:55 (4:56) (Class 6) (0-65,64) 3-Y-O — £1,706 (£503; £252) Stalls Low

Form — RPR
040- **1** **Romeo Montague**[143] [7530] 3-9-6 **63**.......................... TomMcLaughlin 8 — 71+
(Ed Dunlop) *s.s: hld up: hdwy over 2f out: led over 1f out: rdn out* **15/8**[1]
650- **2** ½ **Iron Green (FR)**[183] [6802] 3-9-3 **60**.................................... EddieAhern 1 — 67
(Heather Main) *chsd ldrs: rdn and ev ch over 1f out: r.o* **5/1**[3]
600- **3** 2½ **C P Joe (IRE)**[180] [6875] 3-9-1 **58**...................................... FrannyNorton 2 — 60
(Paul Green) *a.p: rdn over 3f out: edgd lft ins fnl f: styd on* **12/1**
4314 **4** 1½ **Ad Vitam (IRE)**[19] [951] 3-9-0 **64**..............................(t) LauraSimpson(7) 3 — 63+
(David C Griffiths) *hld up: hmpd wl over 3f out: hdwy over 1f out: nt trble ldrs* **18/1**
004- **5** 1½ **Valley Tiger**[158] [7335] 3-9-7 **64**..................................... GeorgeBaker 6 — 60
(William Muir) *hld up: hdwy over 1f out: nvr trbld ldrs* **13/2**
-022 **6** 1 **The Absent Mare**[15] [1018] 3-8-4 **50**..........................(t) LouisBeuzelin(3) 7 — 44
(Frank Sheridan) *led after 1f: rdn and hdd over 1f out: wknd ins fnl f* **6/1**
004- **7** 2½ **Desert Location**[134] [7631] 3-9-4 **61**................................. HayleyTurner 5 — 50
(Michael Bell) *led 1f: chsd ldrs: rdn over 2f out: wknd ins fnl f* **4/1**[2]
660- **8** 2¾ **Tahitian Princess (IRE)**[168] [7142] 3-8-10 **53**................ PaulMulrennan 9 — 36
(Ann Duffield) *chsd ldrs: rdn over 3f out: wknd and eased fnl f* **25/1**
52-0 **9** 26 **Spring Bouquet (IRE)**[12] [1060] 3-9-4 **64**...................... MartinHarley(3) 4 — —
(Mick Channon) *hld up: bhd fnl 5f: t.o* **14/1**

2m 0.30s (-1.40) **Going Correction** -0.125s/f (Stan) — 9 Ran SP% **122.5**
Speed ratings (Par 96): **101,100,98,97,95 94,92,90,67**
Tote Swingers: 1&2 £21.00, 1&3 £5.90, 2&3 £18.60 CSF £12.37 CT £93.14 TOTE £2.50: £1.10, £4.60, £5.20; EX 14.90.
Owner Mrs G A Rupert **Bred** Issa Syndicate **Trained** Newmarket, Suffolk

FOCUS
A few unexposed sorts in a modest handicap. The gallop was an ordinary one and the winner raced centre-to-far-side in the straight.

1300 32REDBET.COM H'CAP — 1m 4f 50y(P)
5:25 (5:25) (Class 6) (0-65,65) 3-Y-O — £1,706 (£503; £252) Stalls Low

Form — RPR
00-1 **1** **Birdwatcher (IRE)**[22] [930] 3-9-5 **63**................................... GregFairley 3 — 71+
(Mark Johnston) *n.m.r s: chsd ldr 10f out: led over 2f out: rdn out* **2/1**[1]
0033 **2** ¾ **Polly Holder (IRE)**[41] [731] 3-8-6 **53**..............................(p) AmyBaker(3) 1 — 60
(Alan Bailey) *chsd ldr 2f: remained handy tl lost pl 6f out: hdwy over 1f out: r.o* **7/1**
54-0 **3** ¾ **Szabo's Destiny**[99] [25] 3-9-7 **65**................................... PaulMulrennan 2 — 71
(James Given) *hld up: hdwy over 3f out: rdn over 1f out: styd on* **25/1**
-422 **4** 3¼ **Echos Of Motivator**[25] [891] 3-9-7 **65**................................ LukeMorris 5 — 66
(Ronald Harris) *hld up: hdwy over 6f out: sn pushed along: rdn over 2f out: no ex fnl f* **3/1**[3]
645- **5** 2½ **Operateur (IRE)**[178] [6936] 3-9-6 **64**.................................... EddieAhern 6 — 61
(Ben Haslam) *chsd ldrs tl wknd over 1f out* **9/4**[2]
-230 **6** ¾ **Jane's Legacy**[41] [731] 3-8-2 **53**.. JackDuern(7) 4 — 48
(Reg Hollinshead) *hmpd at s: hld up: hdwy over 5f out: rdn over 3f out: wknd over 1f out* **33/1**
660- **7** 5 **Dancing Cavalier (IRE)**[158] [7335] 3-8-8 **52**............... GrahamGibbons 7 — 39
(Reg Hollinshead) *sn led at stdy pce: qcknd over 3f out: rdn and hdd over 2f out: wknd over 1f out* **7/1**

2m 42.26s (1.16) **Going Correction** -0.125s/f (Stan) — 7 Ran SP% **120.9**
Speed ratings (Par 96): **91,90,90,87,86 85,82**
CSF £18.20 CT £280.32 TOTE £4.90: £3.80, £5.70; EX 18.80.
Owner Sheikh Hamdan Bin Mohammed Al Maktoum **Bred** Jeremy Gompertz **Trained** Middleham Moor, N Yorks

FOCUS
A modest handicap run at just an ordinary gallop. The progressive winner came down the centre in the straight.
T/Jkpt: £4,453.50 to a £1 stake. Pool:£602,375.16 - 110.38 winning tickets T/Plt: £333.00 to a £1 stake. Pool:£88,000.01 - 188.88 winning tickets T/Qpdt: £8.90 to a £1 stake. Pool:£6,975.15 - 774.14 winning tickets CR

[1034] CATTERICK (L-H)
Wednesday, April 13

OFFICIAL GOING: Good to firm (watered; 9.3)
Wind: Fresh half behind Weather: Overcast and showers

1301 XTREMEADVENTURES.COM (S) STKS — 5f
2:00 (2:00) (Class 6) 2-Y-O — £1,706 (£503; £252) Stalls Low

Form — RPR
0 **1** **Seven Year Itch (IRE)**[9] [1136] 2-8-6 0.......................... RoystonFfrench 1 — 58
(David Evans) *mde all: rdn 2f out: edgd rt and styd on wl fnl f* **14/1**
2 2½ **Becksies** 2-8-6 0.. BarryMcHugh 7 — 49
(Paul Midgley) *cl up: rdn along and sltly outpcd over 1f out: kpt on u.p ins fnl f to take 2nd nr line* **11/1**[3]
3 **3** shd **Nannerl (IRE)**[14] [1049] 2-8-3 0.. AmyRyan(3) 3 — 49
(Kevin Ryan) *dwlt and hmpd s: sn swtchd rt and hdwy to chse ldrs after 1 1/2f: effrt to dispute ld 2f out and ev ch: rdn and hung lft ent fnl f: sn one pce: lost 2nd nr line* **4/9**[1]
0 **4** shd **Lilygloves**[18] [982] 2-8-6 0.. SamHitchcott 4 — 48
(Mick Channon) *cl up: rdn 2f out and ev ch tl drvn and one pce appr fnl f* **6/1**[2]
0 **5** 3¾ **Just Dixie**[7] [1165] 2-8-6 0.. DuranFentiman 2 — 35
(John Weymes) *chsd ldrs: rdn along 1/2-way: sn outpcd and bhd* **33/1**
0 **6** 39 **No Legs (IRE)**[6] [1199] 2-7-13 0.. KevinLundie(7) 6 — —
(David Evans) *awkward s: s.i.s and a bhd* **16/1**

60.95 secs (1.15) **Going Correction** -0.15s/f (Firm) — 6 Ran SP% **107.4**
Speed ratings (Par 90): **84,80,79,79,73 11**
toteswingers:1&2:£22.80, 1&3:£3.90, 2&3:£1.40 CSF £129.93 TOTE £13.30: £4.00, £5.50; EX 126.80.The winner bought by James Bethel for 7,000gns.
Owner Mrs E Evans **Bred** M Phelan & Lawman Syndicate **Trained** Pandy, Monmouths

FOCUS
It was dry overnight and the going was good to firm. A seller for 2-y-os and most of the runners had not shown much. The form is rated around the third and the average.

NOTEBOOK
Seven Year Itch(IRE) was always outpaced after a slow start when 40-1 for a Windsor maiden on debut, but she broke well this time and put in a strong front-running display to win with plenty of authority. The form probably does not amount to much but it was a good step forward, and this Lawman second foal of a 1m Italian winner is bred to get quite a bit further in time. She was sold to James Bethell for 7,000gns at the auction. (tchd 16-1)
Becksies, the first foal of an unraced mare, looked inexperienced before staying on late to snatch second on debut. (op 8-1)
Nannerl(IRE) was the clear form pick on her third in a 5f Wolverhampton maiden auction on debut. She was sent off a hot favourite and things looked to be going well for a long way, but she didn't pick up when ranging alongside the leader and had no response when that rival kicked on again. (op 1-2 tchd 2-5 and 4-7 in a place)
Lilygloves was a bit keen but did quite well to keep battling away with the chasing trio. She still has a bit to learn but has progressed from her low-key debut run. (op 13-2 tchd 7-1)
Just Dixie, a distant 66-1 ninth of ten in a Beverley maiden on debut, struggled for pace. (op 28-1)
No Legs(IRE) trailed home after an awkward start. (op 10-1)

1302 RACINGUK.COM MAIDEN STKS — 7f
2:35 (2:35) (Class 5) 3-Y-O — £2,072 (£616; £308; £153) Stalls Centre

Form — RPR
533- **1** **Shadow Catcher**[196] [6458] 3-9-3 68................................ FrederikTylicki 5 — 70+
(Michael Dods) *led 1f: cl up on inner tl led again 1/2-way: rdn 2f out: drvn ent fnl f and kpt on wl* **6/4**[2]
23- **2** 2 **Abidhabidubai**[310] [2813] 3-8-12 0... TomEaves 8 — 60+
(John Quinn) *trckd ldrs: effrt over 2f out: sn rdn and sltly outpcd: kpt on u.p fnl f: tk 2nd nr fin* **11/8**[1]
55-3 **3** ½ **His Grace (IRE)**[9] [1130] 3-9-3 71.. PhillipMakin 7 — 63
(Andrew Haynes) *plld hrd early: cl up tl led after 1f: hdd 1/2-way: rdn and ev ch 2f out tl drvn and one pce ins fnl f: lost 2nd nr fin* **7/2**[3]
00- **4** 1¼ **Bailadeira**[158] [7345] 3-8-10 0 ow3.. DaleSwift(5) 1 — 58
(Tim Etherington) *chsd ldrs on inner: rdn along over 2f out: sn drvn and kpt on same pce* **25/1**
0-3 **5** 4 **Ivy And Gold**[90] [147] 3-9-3 0... PatrickMathers 2 — 49
(Alan Berry) *in tch: rdn along 1/2-way: outpcd fr over 2f out* **80/1**
0 **6** 17 **The Blind Side (IRE)**[13] [1056] 3-8-10 0................................. HobieGill(7) 6 — —
(Michael Appleby) *a in rr: outpcd and bhd fr 1/2-way* **125/1**

1m 27.08s (0.08) **Going Correction** -0.075s/f (Good) — 6 Ran SP% **110.2**
Speed ratings (Par 98): **96,93,93,91,87 67**
toteswingers:1&2:£1.02, 1&3:£1.30, 2&3:£1.30 CSF £3.75 TOTE £2.90: £1.10, £1.70; EX 3.70.
Owner A Wynn-Williams, D Graham, D Neale **Bred** Mascalls Stud **Trained** Denton, Co Durham
■ Stewards' Enquiry : Dale Swift one-day ban: used whip down shoulder in the forehand (Apr 27)

FOCUS
The three market leaders dominated this strongly run minor maiden. Ordinary form, rated at face value.

1303 SUSAN AND ALMA CHINA TREK H'CAP — 7f
3:10 (3:12) (Class 6) (0-60,59) 3-Y-O — £1,706 (£503; £252) Stalls Centre

Form — RPR
0-63 **1** **Trading**[14] [1040] 3-9-3 **55**.. DuranFentiman 1 — 64
(Tim Easterby) *sn led: rdn and qcknd clr wl over 1f out: styd on strly* **13/2**
633 **2** 2¾ **Crown Ridge (IRE)**[7] [1169] 3-9-7 **59**................................ SamHitchcott 6 — 61+
(Mick Channon) *towards rr: hdwy over 2f out: rdn to chse ldrs over 1f out: drvn and kpt on fnl f: nt rch wnr* **9/4**[1]
00-6 **3** ½ **Twennyshortkid**[14] [1038] 3-8-12 **50**................................... BarryMcHugh 3 — 50
(Paul Midgley) *trckd ldrs: hdwy wl over 2f out: rdn to chse wnr over 1f out: drvn and one pce fnl f* **7/2**[2]
54-3 **4** 2 **Dotty Darroch**[12] [1074] 3-9-3 **55**... LeeNewman 10 — 50
(Robin Bastiman) *trckd ldrs: effrt over 2f out: sn rdn and no imp appr fnl f* **9/2**[3]
6530 **5** nk **Lough Corrib (USA)**[26] [887] 3-9-6 **58**..........................(b) PhillipMakin 7 — 52
(Kevin Ryan) *in rr: hdwy 2f out: sn rdn: styd on wl fnl f: nrst fin* **10/1**
4534 **6** hd **Kyncraighe (IRE)**[19] [967] 3-8-13 **51**.........................(tp) FrederikTylicki 5 — 44
(Alastair Lidderdale) *chsd ldrs: rdn over 2f out: drvn and one pce fr over 1f out* **14/1**
460- **7** 4½ **Commander Veejay**[243] [5020] 3-8-8 **46**...........................(p) MickyFenton 9 — 27
(Brian Rothwell) *cl up: rdn along 3f out: drvn over 2f out and sn wknd* **25/1**
040- **8** 12 **Whipperoo (IRE)**[138] [7572] 3-8-4 **45**........................... JamesSullivan(3) 8 — —
(Patrick Morris) *a in rr* **40/1**
002- **9** 17 **Bigalo's Laura B (IRE)**[203] [6294] 3-8-8 **53**........(e) DavidSimmonson(7) 2 — —
(G P Kelly) *dwlt: a towards rr* **18/1**
260- **P** **Blind Stag (IRE)**[226] [5602] 3-9-4 **56**................................ TonyHamilton 4 — —
(David Thompson) *chsd ldrs on outer: rn wd home turn and sn lost pl: bhd whn p.u over 1f out* **28/1**

1m 26.41s (-0.59) **Going Correction** -0.075s/f (Good) — 10 Ran SP% **115.3**
Speed ratings (Par 96): **100,96,96,94,93 93,88,74,55,—**
toteswingers:1&2:£2.50, 1&3:£4.60, 2&3:£4.10 CSF £20.84 CT £61.54 TOTE £5.90: £2.40, £1.10, £3.60; EX 15.00.
Owner Habton Farms **Bred** Major And Mrs R B Kennard **Trained** Great Habton, N Yorks

FOCUS
There was a lively market for this low-grade handicap. It was run at a decent pace but not many made any impression behind the well-drawn trailblazing winner. He is rated back to his early 2yo form.
Blind Stag(IRE) Official explanation: jockey said colt hung badly right-handed and lost its action

1304 BETFAIR RICHMOND CONDITIONS STKS — 1m 3f 214y
3:45 (3:45) (Class 3) 3-Y-O — £6,231 (£1,866; £933; £467) Stalls Low

Form — RPR
421 **1** **Gottany O'S**[33] [836] 3-8-12 82... SamHitchcott 1 — 82+
(Mick Channon) *trckd ldr: led 1/2-way: rdn along wl over 1f out: styd on wl* **2/9**[1]
601- **2** 1¾ **Mica Mika (IRE)**[195] [6513] 3-8-12 79.................................. TonyHamilton 5 — 77
(Richard Fahey) *t.k.h early: led to 1/2-way: chsd wnr: rdn to chal 2f out: sn drvn and one pce ent fnl f* **7/2**[2]
3 23 **The Snorer** 3-8-4 0.. JamesRogers(5) 2 — 37
(John Holt) *trckd ldng pair: effrt over 3f out: sn rdn along and outpcd fnl 2f* **80/1**[3]
0- **4** 5 **Big Zaf**[226] [5594] 3-8-12 0.. MickyFenton 4 — 32
(Paul Midgley) *a in rr: outpcd and bhd fr over 2f out* **100/1**

2m 41.13s (2.23) **Going Correction** -0.075s/f (Good) — 4 Ran SP% **106.3**
Speed ratings (Par 102): **89,87,72,69**
CSF £1.23 TOTE £1.20; EX 1.20.
Owner Dr Marwan Koukash **Bred** Phil Jen Racing **Trained** West Ilsley, Berks

FOCUS
They went a steady early pace in this conditions event but the hot favourite seized the initiative some way out and surged to a fairly comfortable success over his main form danger. Muddling form, the front pair close to their marks on paper.

NOTEBOOK

Gottany O'S achieved a personal best when storming clear at odds-on in a 1m4f Wolverhampton maiden last month. He had leading form claims and put in another likeable display on his turf debut to provide Mick Channon with a fifth winner in the last six runnings of this race. This big, long-striding type should continue to progress and could head towards a valuable 1m4f handicap. (op 1-3)

Mica Mika(IRE) showed steady improvement last year, winding up with a win off 70 in a 7f Warwick nursery. His pedigree raised some doubts about whether this big step up in trip would suit on his reappearance, and was a reluctant leader in the early stages racing keenly, but he showed a good attitude and some stamina to keep rallying behind the potentially useful winner. He could have scope for progress in handicaps and should be a little less revved up after this comeback run. (op 11-4 tchd 5-2)

The Snorer, a cheaply bought gelding, was well beaten thrown in at the deep end on debut. (op 50-1 tchd 100-1)

Big Zaf struggled at 100-1 in a Newcastle maiden last August and was out of his depth stepped up almost 5f in trip on this reappearance.

1305 GO RACING IN YORKSHIRE H'CAP — 1m 3f 214y

4:20 (4:20) (Class 5) (0-70,67) 4-Y-0+ **£4,209** (£1,252; £625; £312) **Stalls** Low

Form / RPR

3-55 **1** **King's Counsel (IRE)**[11] 1099 5-8-13 **59**.................(v) DanielTudhope 2 67
(David O'Meara) *cl up: led 3 1/2f out and sn clr: rdn wl over 1f out: drvn ins fnl f and kpt on gamely* **11/4**[2]

00-4 **2** *1 1/4* **Eijaaz (IRE)**[14] 1039 10-8-8 **57**.................(p) MichaelO'Connell(3) 5 63
(Geoffrey Harker) *hld up in rr: stdy hdwy over 4f out: chsd wnr over 1f out: rdn and edgd lft ent fnl f: kpt on same pce* **9/1**

32-0 **3** *nk* **Valantino Oyster (IRE)**[71] 373 4-8-5 **55**............. PatrickDonaghy(3) 7 60+
(Ben Haslam) *hld up: effrt 3f out: rdn along 2f out: styd on wl u.p fnl f: nrst fin* **25/1**

1-40 **4** *nse* **Dubara Reef (IRE)**[33] 838 4-9-6 **67**.................(p) PhillipMakin 3 72
(Paul Green) *trckd ldrs: hdwy over 3f out: rdn 2f out: drvn and one pce ent fnl f* **12/1**

34-3 **5** *1 1/4* **Leaving Alone (USA)**[14] 1039 4-8-5 **55**............. JamesSullivan(3) 6 58
(Edwin Tuer) *in tch: hdwy to chse ldrs over 3f out: rdn over 2f out: drvn wl over 1f out and kpt on same pce* **17/2**[3]

00-4 **6** *2* **Blue Nymph**[40] 68 5-9-7 **67**................. TomEaves 12 67
(John Quinn) *in tch: effrt 3f out: rdn along 2f out: sn no imp* **7/4**[1]

250- **7** *1 1/4* **Weetfromthechaff**[158] 2583 6-8-7 **53** oh1.............(t) JamieMackay 8 51
(Maurice Barnes) *t.k.h: chsd ldrs: hdwy 4f out: rdn to chse ldr over 2f out: drvn wl over 1f out and grad wknd* **33/1**

000- **8** *6* **Dimashq**[179] 6915 9-8-7 **53** oh8................. MickyFenton 11 41
(Paul Midgley) *nvr bttr than midfield* **50/1**

2-02 **9** *1* **Lady Norlela**[14] 1039 5-8-4 **57**................. ShaneBKelly(7) 10 44
(Brian Rothwell) *hld up: a in rr* **14/1**

05-0 **10** *3/4* **Drop The Hammer**[14] 1039 5-8-10 **59**............. NataliaGemelova(3) 9 44
(David O'Meara) *hld up: a in rr* **14/1**

526/ **11** *2* **Michevious Spirit (IRE)**[282] 4-8-7 **54**............. BarryMcHugh 4 36
(David Thompson) *in tch: pushed along 5f out: rdn over 3f out and sn wknd* **80/1**

140- **12** *50* **Always Dixie (IRE)**[148] 7475 4-8-10 **57**............. RobertWinston 1 —
(Andrew Crook) *led: rdn along over 4f out: hdd 3 1/2f out: sn wknd and bhd whn eased wl over 1f out* **80/1**

2m 38.02s (-0.88) **Going Correction** -0.075s/f (Good)
WFA 4 from 5yo+ 1lb **12** Ran SP% **115.8**
Speed ratings (Par 103): **99,98,97,97,97 95,94,90,90,89 88,55**
toteswingers:1&2:£3.90, 1&3:£18.60, 2&3:£62.00 CSF £26.08 CT £507.68 TOTE £6.40: £2.60, £1.80, £6.30; EX 28.70.
Owner W R B Racing 44 **Bred** Peter And Jackie Grimes **Trained** Nawton, N Yorks
■ Stewards' Enquiry : Patrick Donaghy three-day ban: weighed in 2lb heavy (Apr 27-29)

FOCUS
This was steadily run. The well-backed winner seized the initiative some way out before scoring in game style in this ordinary handicap, recording a small personal best.
King's Counsel(IRE) Official explanation: trainer said, regarding apparent improvement in form, that the gelding was able to dominate in a less competitive race.

1306 TURFTV H'CAP — 5f

4:55 (4:56) (Class 6) (0-60,66) 3-Y-0 **£1,706** (£503; £252) **Stalls** Low

Form / RPR

330- **1** **Irish Boy (IRE)**[120] 7864 3-8-9 **48**................. DuranFentiman 6 54
(Noel Wilson) *in tch on outer: hdwy wl over 1f out: rdn and kpt on to ld wl ins fnl f* **7/1**

-542 **2** *2 1/4* **Tancred Spirit**[14] 1040 3-8-8 **47**.................(p) BarryMcHugh 2 45
(Paul Midgley) *led: rdn 2f out: drvn and edgd rt 1f out: hdd and no ex wl ins fnl f* **7/2**[1]

00-4 **3** *3/4* **Majestic Millie (IRE)**[14] 1040 3-8-1 **47** oh1 ow1.......... ShaneBKelly(7) 5 45
(David O'Meara) *trckd ldrs: effrt and n.m.r over 1f out: swtchd lft and rdn jst ins fnl f: rdr dropped reins: kpt on same pce towards fin* **4/1**[2]

-252 **4** *1 1/4* **Spontaneity (IRE)**[41] 741 3-9-7 **60**................. TomEaves 4 51
(Bryan Smart) *cl up on outer: ev ch 2f out: sn rdn and wknd ent fnl f* **8/1**

-605 **5** *1* **Yours**[14] 1040 3-9-1 **54**................. PhillipMakin 1 41
(Kevin Ryan) *chsd ldrs: rdn along 2f out: sn drvn and one pce* **4/1**[2]

-441 **6** *1* **Misty Morn**[14] 1040 3-8-13 **57**................. DaleSwift(5) 3 41
(Alan Brown) *cl up: effrt 2f out and ev ch: rdn wl over 1f out: swtchd lft and drvn ent fnl f: sn wknd* **9/2**[3]

4651 **7** *1 1/2* **Pineapple Pete (IRE)**[7] 1187 3-9-13 **66** 6ex.............(t) RobertWinston 7 44
(Alan McCabe) *dwlt and swtchd lft s: a in rr* **10/1**

59.48 secs (-0.32) **Going Correction** -0.15s/f (Firm) **7** Ran SP% **113.1**
Speed ratings (Par 96): **96,92,91,89,87 86,83**
toteswingers:1&2:£5.20, 1&3:£7.00, 2&3:£4.10 CSF £30.87 TOTE £10.60: £5.80, £3.40; EX 48.30.
Owner Annwell Inn Syndicate **Bred** Seamus McMullan **Trained** Sandhutton, N Yorks

FOCUS
A competitive sprint handicap run at a strong pace. Ordinary for for the low grade.
Misty Morn Official explanation: jockey said filly lost its action

1307 WE AGAIN 3RD MAY APPRENTICE H'CAP — 5f 212y

5:30 (5:36) (Class 6) (0-65,64) 4-Y-0+ **£1,706** (£503; £252) **Stalls** Low

Form / RPR

0341 **1** **Collect Art (IRE)**[23] 933 4-9-6 **63**................. AmyScott 10 75
(Andrew Haynes) *mde all: rdn clr wl over 1f out: drvn out* **13/2**[3]

2245 **2** *1 3/4* **We'll Deal Again**[15] 1029 4-8-10 **58**.................(v) DavidSimmonson(5) 6 64
(Michael Easterby) *dwlt and towards rr: hdwy 1/2-way: rdn to chse wnr wl over 1f out: drvn and no imp ins fnl f* **7/1**

-110 **3** *2 3/4* **Welcome Approach**[23] 928 8-8-4 **50**................. ShaneBKelly(3) 1 48
(John Weymes) *towards rr: hdwy 2f out: sn rdn and kpt on wl fnl f: nrst fin* **17/2**

4212 **4** *hd* **Mata Hari Blue**[21] 947 5-9-7 **64**................. JamesRogers 12 61
(John Holt) *sn cl up: rdn along 2f out: edgd lft over 1f out and kpt on same pce* **11/4**[1]

400- **5** *nse* **Bahamian Jazz (IRE)**[180] 6897 4-9-0 **57**................. LMcNiff 5 54
(Robin Bastiman) *chsd ldrs: rdn along over 2f out: drvn and one pce fr over 1f out: eased nr fin* **22/1**

306- **6** *2* **Two Turtle Doves (IRE)**[215] 5905 5-9-1 **63**............. JosephYoung(5) 7 53
(Michael Mullineaux) *chsd ldrs on inner: hdwy and ch 2f out: sn rdn and grad wknd* **14/1**

0230 **7** *1/2* **St Ignatius**[25] 906 4-8-2 **50**.................(p) HobieGill(5) 8 39+
(Michael Appleby) *t.k.h: racd wd: in tch: rdn along 2f out: n.d* **11/1**

46-2 **8** *1/2* **Klynch**[29] 853 5-8-9 **57**.................(b) LauraBarry(5) 3 44+
(Ruth Carr) *s.i.s and bhd: sme hdwy 2f out: sn rdn and n.d* **4/1**[2]

05-0 **9** *1 1/2* **Ya Boy Sir (IRE)**[6] 1204 4-9-1 **58**................. DarylByrne 2 40
(Noel Wilson) *cl up on inner: ev ch 2f out: sn rdn and wknd* **50/1**

350- **10** *5* **Quaestor (IRE)**[168] 7168 4-9-0 **57**................. GarryWhillans 11 23
(Andrew Crook) *a towards rr* **33/1**

565- **11** *1 3/4* **Real Diamond**[162] 7281 5-8-13 **56**................. JulieBurke 9 17
(Ollie Pears) *chsd ldrs: rdn along 1/2-way: wknd 2f out* **8/1**

1m 12.88s (-0.72) **Going Correction** -0.075s/f (Good) **11** Ran SP% **118.4**
Speed ratings (Par 101): **101,98,95,94,94 92,91,90,88,82 79**
toteswingers:1&2:£10.00, 1&3:£9.40, 2&3:£11.40 CSF £50.95 CT £401.12 TOTE £6.90: £2.70, £1.50, £4.10; EX 63.70.Yungaburra was withdrawn. Price at time of withdrawal 25/1. Rule 4 does not apply
Owner Miss C Berry **Bred** Pier House Stud **Trained** Limpley Stoke, Bath
■ Stewards' Enquiry : L McNiff four-day ban: failed to ride out for fourth (Apr 27-29,May 2)

FOCUS
A modest apprentice handicap. The winner was the fourth on the card to make all and is rated back to his 3yo best.
T/Plt: £393.60 to a £1 stake. Pool:£35,808.91 - 66.40 winning tickets T/Qpdt: £10.40 to a £1 stake. Pool:£4,531.18 - 320.00 winning tickets JR

1192 KEMPTON (A.W) (R-H)

Wednesday, April 13

OFFICIAL GOING: Standard
Wind: Moderate, across Weather: Overcast

1308 FREE ENTRY FOR BETDAQ MEMBERS APPRENTICE H'CAP — 1m 2f (P)

6:00 (6:00) (Class 6) (0-60,59) 4-Y-0+ **£1,748** (£516; £258) **Stalls** Low

Form / RPR

300- **1** **Bubbly Braveheart (IRE)**[119] 7878 4-9-7 **59**................. LucyKBarry 3 67
(Pat Phelan) *mde all: hrd rdn and hld on wl fr over 1f out: a in control* **7/2**[1]

-514 **2** *3/4* **Ocean Of Peace (FR)**[63] 466 8-8-9 **54**................. KirstenSmith(7) 6 60
(Martin Bosley) *chsd ldng pair: wnt 2nd over 1f out: kpt on wl: a hld* **10/1**

-413 **3** *2 3/4* **Noah Jameel**[51] 630 9-9-2 **59**................. CharlesBishop(5) 2 60
(Tony Newcombe) *chsd ldrs: rdn 2f out: kpt on fnl f* **4/1**[2]

3033 **4** *1/2* **Olney Lass**[19] 969 4-8-8 **46**................. JakePayne 9 46
(Mike Murphy) *sn chsng wnr: lost 2nd over 1f out: one pce* **15/2**

2515 **5** *1 3/4* **Sir Haydn**[9] 1135 11-9-1 **58**.................(v) DannyBrock(5) 4 54
(J R Jenkins) *s.s: in rr: rdn 3f out: nvr rchd ldrs* **25/1**

5130 **6** *1 1/2* **Carr Hall (IRE)**[10] 1107 8-9-0 **57**................. GeorgeDowning(5) 7 50
(Tony Carroll) *towards rr: rdn 3f out: nvr able to chal* **13/2**

04-3 **7** *4* **Market Puzzle (IRE)**[21] 943 4-8-8 **51**................. ThomasBrown(5) 5 36
(Mark Brisbourne) *hld up in 5th: rdn 3f out: wknd 2f out* **8/1**

0000 **8** *2* **Novillero**[40] 773 4-8-2 **45**................. GemmaElford(5) 1 26
(Jimmy Fox) *rdn 3f out: a in rr gp* **50/1**

5532 **9** *1 1/2* **Abigails Angel**[21] 943 4-9-0 **59**................. JasonHart(7) 8 37
(Brett Johnson) *plld hrd on outer in midfield: wnt wd and wknd bnd into st* **9/2**[3]

2m 7.72s (-0.28) **Going Correction** 0.0s/f (Stan) **9** Ran SP% **111.5**
Speed ratings (Par 101): **101,100,98,97,96 95,92,90,89**
toteswingers: 1&2 £8.50, 1&3 £5.50, 2&3 £2.00 CSF £37.03 CT £140.61 TOTE £3.50: £1.40, £3.10, £2.10; EX 58.00.
Owner The Only Pub In The World **Bred** Albert Conneally **Trained** Epsom, Surrey
■ Stewards' Enquiry : Kirsten Smith three-day ban: careless riding (Apr 27-29)

FOCUS
Races over this C&D are rarely truly run and the tempo to the home turn in this moderate handicap was a steady one. Those held up were at a disadvantage and the winner raced close to the inside rail throughout. Straightforward form.

1309 BETDAQ.COM EXCHANGE PRICE MULTIPLES H'CAP — 5f (P)

6:30 (6:30) (Class 5) (0-70,69) 4-Y-0+ **£2,417** (£713; £357) **Stalls** Low

Form / RPR

6031 **1** **Lord Of The Reins (IRE)**[7] 1171 7-9-4 **66** 6ex............ PaulMulrennan 2 75
(James Given) *chsd ldrs: effrt 2f out: r.o to ld fnl 50yds* **4/1**

0052 **2** *1* **Fair Passion**[6] 1196 4-9-5 **67**................. StephenCraine 1 72
(Derek Shaw) *dwlt: sn led: stl on bit over 1f out: rdn and nt qckn ins fnl f: hdd fnl 50yds* **7/4**[1]

6500 **3** *nk* **Grudge**[6] 1196 6-9-5 **67**.................(be) GeorgeBaker 4 71
(Conor Dore) *prom: drvn to dispute 2nd over 1f out: hld whn edgd lft ins fnl f* **12/1**

3153 **4** *shd* **Estonia**[6] 1196 4-9-3 **65**................. LukeMorris 3 69
(Michael Squance) *hld up in 5th: rdn and hdwy to dispute 2nd over 1f out: styd on same pce* **10/3**[3]

5416 **5** *2 1/2* **Sherjawy (IRE)**[18] 985 7-9-7 **69**................. KirstyMilczarek 5 64
(Zoe Davison) *in tch tl rdn and dropped to rr over 2f out: sme late hdwy* **3/1**[2]

00-0 **6** *6* **Gleaming Spirit (IRE)**[82] 256 7-8-7 **55** oh10.......(v) RobbieFitzpatrick 8 28
(Peter Grayson) *drvn to ld early: pressed ldr after tl drvn along and wknd qckly over 1f out* **100/1**

0-56 **7** *3/4* **Clifton Bridge**[84] 215 4-9-0 **62**................. FergusSweeney 7 32
(Peter Grayson) *sn outpcd and bhd* **40/1**

60.05 secs (-0.45) **Going Correction** 0.0s/f (Stan) **7** Ran SP% **115.6**
Speed ratings (Par 103): **103,101,100,100,96 87,85**
toteswingers: 1&2 £2.30, 1&3 £7.70, 2&3 £4.70 CSF £11.71 CT £75.71 TOTE £4.00: £2.10, £1.10; EX 12.60.
Owner Danethorpe Racing Partnership **Bred** C Farrell **Trained** Willoughton, Lincs

FOCUS
Exposed performers in a modest handicap. The gallop was sound and the winner came down the centre in the straight. He is rated back to his autumn form.
Grudge Official explanation: jockey said gelding hung left

Clifton Bridge Official explanation: vet said gelding was lame left-fore

1310 LAY BACK AND WIN AT BETDAQ.COM H'CAP 1m 4f (P)

7:00 (7:00) (Class 6) (0-55,55) 4-Y-0+ **£1,748** (£516; £258) **Stalls** Centre

Form RPR

1/35 **1** **Camera Shy (IRE)**[20] [954] 7-8-13 **50**........................ AndreaAtzeni 6 61+
(Kevin Morgan) *chsd ldr: led over 3f out: qcknd 7 l clr 2f out: in n.d after: rdn out* **6/1**[3]

0502 **2** *1 ¾* **Filun**[4] [1253] 6-8-13 **50**........................ LiamKeniry 8 56
(Anthony Middleton) *hld up in rr: nt clr run over 2f out: rapid hdwy to go 2nd and clsd on wnr ins fnl f: too much to do* **9/2**[2]

3-24 **3** *2 ½* **Minder**[22] [769] 5-9-1 **52**........................(tp) StephenCraine 13 54
(Jonathan Portman) *prom: wnt 2nd and easily outpcd by wnr 2f out: sn btn: lost 2nd ins fnl f: kpt on* **33/1**

0-04 **4** *½* **Largem**[42] [728] 5-8-12 **49**........................ DavidProbert 7 50
(J R Jenkins) *stdd s: hld up towards rr: rdn over 3f out: styd on fnl 2f: nrst fin* **16/1**

250- **5** *1 ¼* **Motarjm (USA)**[123] [7840] 7-9-1 **52**........................(t) ChrisCatlin 4 51
(Lydia Pearce) *chsd ldrs tl outpcd and btn 2f out* **20/1**

-435 **6** *¾* **Private Equity (IRE)**[52] [622] 5-9-2 **53**........................ JoeFanning 5 51
(William Jarvis) *t.k.h: in tch: rdn and similar position fnl 3f: styd on same pce: no imp* **8/1**

5003 **7** *nk* **Vinces**[9] [1135] 7-9-2 **53**........................ GeorgeBaker 10 51
(Tim McCarthy) *mid-div: rdn and lost pl 3f out: styd on fnl f* **22/1**

6134 **8** *nse* **Little Richard (IRE)**[12] [1080] 12-9-1 **52**........................(p) JamesDoyle 2 49
(Mark Wellings) *mid-div: outpcd 3f out: drvn along and wl btn whn edgd rt over 1f out: nvr able to chal* **9/1**

0523 **9** *1* **Lytham (IRE)**[35] [802] 10-9-4 **55**........................ SebSanders 3 51+
(Tony Carroll) *t.k.h: in tch: hdwy on outer to join ldrs over 4f out: wknd wl over 1f out* **5/2**[1]

3300 **10** *½* **Our Kes (IRE)**[26] [899] 9-8-11 **48**........................ ShaneKelly 12 43
(Michael Squance) *bhd: rdn 3f out: nvr nr ldrs* **20/1**

5-40 **11** *½* **No Time For Tears (IRE)**[18] [992] 4-9-2 **54**........................ TomMcLaughlin 11 48
(Lucinda Featherstone) *chsd ldrs: drvn along 3f out: sn wknd* **9/1**

5416 **12** *½* **Barbirolli**[13] [1063] 9-8-5 **47**........................ LauraPike(5) 14 40
(William Stone) *bhd: mod effrt on rail over 2f out: wknd wl over 1f out* **33/1**

5/0- **13** *7* **Blazing Buck**[152] [6454] 5-9-0 **51**........................ LukeMorris 9 38
(Tony Carroll) *led tl over 3f out: hrd rdn and wknd over 2f out: no ch whn hmpd over 1f out* **25/1**

2m 37.35s (2.85) **Going Correction** 0.0s/f (Stan)
WFA 4 from 5yo+ 1lb **13 Ran SP% 121.6**
Speed ratings (Par 101): **90,88,87,86,86 85,85,85,84,84 83,83,78**
toteswingers: 1&2 £4.00, 1&3 £40.60, 2&3 £42.70 CSF £30.36 CT £833.57 TOTE £7.00: £2.70, £1.20, £12.20; EX 38.90.
Owner Michael Ogburn **Bred** Haras D'Etreham And Madame Lily Ades **Trained** Newmarket, Suffolk
■ Stewards' Enquiry : James Doyle three-day ban: careless riding (Apr 27-29)

FOCUS
A weak handicap and one run at a steady gallop to the home turn. The winner raced towards the inside rail in the straight. He's rated back to his 2009 form.
Little Richard(IRE) Official explanation: jockey said gelding was denied a clear run

1311 BETDAQ MOBILE APPS MEDIAN AUCTION MAIDEN STKS 1m 3f (P)

7:30 (7:30) (Class 6) 3-5-Y-0 **£1,748** (£516; £258) **Stalls** Low

Form RPR

5- **1** **Sandusky**[172] [7094] 3-8-8 0........................ AhmedAjtebi 1 74+
(Mahmood Al Zarooni) *chsd ldrs on ins rail: effrt and drifted bdly lft towards outside rail fr 2f out: drvn to ld 100yds out* **3/1**[2]

0/- **2** *¾* **Tappanappa (IRE)**[536] [7029] 4-10-0 0........................ JimmyFortune 10 76+
(Andrew Balding) *s.s: towards rr: effrt over 3f out: styd on u.p to snatch 2nd on line* **9/4**[1]

2 **3** *nse* **Lady Elsie**[44] [714] 3-8-3 0........................ LiamJones 6 68
(William Haggas) *led and rn green: hrd rdn over 1f out: edgd lft and hdd 100yds out: kpt on gamely: lost 2nd on line* **5/1**

[illegible] **4** [illegible] [illegible] (USA)[18] [illegible] [illegible]........................ [illegible] 7 [illegible]
([illegible]) *[illegible]*
swtchd rt over 1f out: no ex **7/2**[3]

0-53 **5** *1 ¾* **Laffraaj (IRE)**[15] [1028] 3-8-8 62........................(v) ChrisCatlin 8 59
(Pat Eddery) *chsd ldrs: rdn over 3f out: wknd u.str.p over 1f out* **40/1**

6 *1* **The Tiger** 3-8-3 0........................ HarryBentley(5) 2 57
(Ed Dunlop) *s.s: bhd: rdn 3f out: nt pce to chal* **33/1**

7 *1 ½* **Take A Spin** 3-8-3 0 ow2........................ DuilioDaSilva(7) 4 57
(Paul Cole) *sn bhd: pushed along over 2f out: nt trble ldrs* **66/1**

8 *2 ¼* **Mina's Boy** 3-8-8 0........................ EddieAhern 9 50
(Ed Dunlop) *s.s: towards rr: rdn 5f out: struggling fnl 3f* **16/1**

5 **9** *1 ¼* **I'm A Celebrity**[27] [878] 3-8-8 0........................ AndreaAtzeni 3 48
(Marco Botti) *in tch: rdn 5f out: wknd 3f out* **18/1**

0405 **10** *1 ¾* **Harrys**[15] [1025] 4-10-0 39........................ ShaneKelly 5 48
(Michael Squance) *mid-div: rdn 3f out: sn wknd* **150/1**

2m 20.0s (-1.90) **Going Correction** 0.0s/f (Stan)
WFA 3 from 4yo 20lb **10 Ran SP% 113.3**
Speed ratings (Par 101): **106,105,105,101,99 99,97,96,95,94**
toteswingers: 1&2 £2.90, 1&3 £4.20, 2&3 £2.90 CSF £9.69 TOTE £3.90: £1.10, £1.10, £2.40; EX 11.20.
Owner Godolphin **Bred** Genesis Green Stud Ltd **Trained** Newmarket, Suffolk
■ Stewards' Enquiry : Liam Jones one-day ban: careless riding (Apr 27); one-day ban: failed to ride to draw (Apr 28)

FOCUS
An ordinary maiden. The first three, who ended up towards the stands' side, pulled clear of the rest in the closing stages. The first two should improve on the bare form.

1312 RACING AT SKYSPORTS.COM H'CAP 1m 3f (P)

8:00 (8:01) (Class 6) (0-60,60) 3-Y-O **£1,748** (£516; £258) **Stalls** Low

Form RPR

5544 **1** **Gower Rules (IRE)**[2] [1272] 3-8-12 **51**........................ RichardKingscote 6 55
(John Bridger) *mde virtually all: rdn 3 l clr 2f out: drvn to hold on fnl f* **10/1**[3]

000- **2** *1 ¼* **Watered Silk**[247] [4902] 3-8-12 **51**........................ PatDobbs 11 53+
(Marcus Tregoning) *s.s: hld up in rr: shkn up over 2f out: mde up 15 l fr over 1f out: fin fast to take 2nd on line* **14/1**

006- **3** *shd* **Sukhothai (USA)**[176] [7004] 3-9-3 **56**........................ KierenFallon 10 58
(James Fanshawe) *prom: rdn to chse wnr over 2f out: kpt on fnl f: lost 2nd on line* **11/1**

2-21 **4** *shd* **Investment World (IRE)**[83] [234] 3-9-7 **60**........................ JoeFanning 4 61
(Mark Johnston) *hld up in midfield: hdwy to press for 2nd over 2f out: kpt on u.p* **4/5**[1]

0-62 **5** *1 ½* **Dew Reward (IRE)**[9] [1137] 3-9-5 **58**........................ CathyGannon 12 57
(Eve Johnson Houghton) *chsd ldrs: rdn and hung rt over 2f out: styd on same pce* **20/1**

040- **6** *¾* **Subramaniam**[191] [6618] 3-9-7 **60**........................ PaulMulrennan 2 57
(James Given) *broke wl: dropped bk several pls after 3f: reminders 6f out: effrt over 2f out: no imp* **10/1**[3]

000- **7** *3 ¾* **Captain Bellamy (USA)**[178] [6953] 3-9-2 **55**........................ SteveDrowne 9 46
(Hughie Morrison) *in tch on outer: rdn 3f out: sn outpcd* **5/1**[2]

055 **8** *1 ½* **Twilight Express (IRE)**[26] [891] 3-8-8 **47** oh1 ow1........................ LiamKeniry 7 35
(Emma Lavelle) *towards rr: pushed along whn n.m.r over 2f out: nt trble ldrs* **100/1**

0-60 **9** *6* **Diocese (USA)**[18] [992] 3-9-4 **57**........................(t) AndreaAtzeni 8 34
(Marco Botti) *mid-div: rdn over 3f out: sn outpcd in rr* **20/1**

00-0 **10** *½* **Mariyah**[12] [1082] 3-8-7 **46** oh1........................ LukeMorris 3 22
(Michael Blanshard) *a bhd* **100/1**

600- **11** *nk* **Little Book**[224] [5660] 3-9-5 **58**........................ ShaneKelly 5 34
(Edward Vaughan) *in rr: gd hdwy to chse wnr after 4f: wknd over 2f out* **50/1**

00-5 **12** *2 ¾* **Phoenix Fantasy (IRE)**[18] [983] 3-9-7 **60**........................ StephenCraine 1 31
(Jonathan Portman) *towards rr: n.m.r and rdn 6f out: struggling fnl 3f* **33/1**

2m 22.47s (0.57) **Going Correction** 0.0s/f (Stan) **12 Ran SP% 121.8**
Speed ratings (Par 96): **97,96,96,95,94 94,91,90,86,85 85,83**
toteswingers: 1&2 £15.00, 1&3 £19.90, 2&3 £13.20 CSF £132.79 CT £1580.05 TOTE £6.30: £1.10, £5.80, £2.80; EX 225.60.
Owner Mrs Liz Gardner **Bred** Michael O'Mahony **Trained** Liphook, Hants
■ Stewards' Enquiry : Kieren Fallon seven-day ban (reduced from 10 days on appeal): failed to take all reasonable and permissible measures to obtain best possible placing (Apr 27-May 3)

FOCUS
A few unexposed sorts in a moderate handicap in which the modest gallop picked up turning for home. Very few figured and the winner, who had an easy lead, came down the centre in the straight. Muddling form.
Subramaniam Official explanation: jockey said colt ran too freely and hung left
Twilight Express(IRE) Official explanation: jockey said filly ran too freely

1313 RACING UK H'CAP (LONDON MILE QUALIFIER) 1m (P)

8:30 (8:30) (Class 4) (0-85,83) 3-Y-O **£4,129** (£1,228; £614; £306) **Stalls** Low

Form RPR

210- **1** **The Shrew**[193] [6563] 3-9-3 **79**........................ WilliamBuick 3 89+
(John Gosden) *trckd ldr: rdn to ld 2f out: clr fnl f: kpt up to work: readily* **3/1**[2]

301- **2** *3* **Double Dealer**[185] [6777] 3-9-7 **83**........................ AhmedAjtebi 4 85+
(Mahmood Al Zarooni) *stdd s: hld up in 5th: effrt and hung lft 2f out: stened and r.o strly fnl f: snatched 2nd on line* **3/1**[2]

16-4 **3** *nse* **Ibsaar**[25] [907] 3-9-1 **77**........................ TadhgO'Shea 6 79
(William Haggas) *led: rdn and hdd 2f out: sn outpcd by wnr: lost 2nd on line* **7/1**[3]

122 **4** *3 ½* **Dasho**[32] [845] 3-9-3 **79**........................ IanMongan 5 73+
(Olivia Maylam) *stdd s: sn pulling hrd in 4th: hrd rdn 2f out: one pce* **9/4**[1]

1511 **5** *hd* **Joe Le Taxi (IRE)**[16] [1019] 3-8-12 **74**........................ GregFairley 2 67
(Mark Johnston) *trckd ldng pair: rdn over 2f out: one pce* **7/1**[3]

36-4 **6** *hd* **Focail Maith**[14] [1051] 3-9-1 **77**........................ AdamKirby 1 70
(Noel Quinlan) *hld up in rr: rdn and no prog over 2f out: styng on at fin* **20/1**

1m 39.23s (-0.57) **Going Correction** 0.0s/f (Stan) **6 Ran SP% 110.5**
Speed ratings (Par 100): **102,99,98,95,95 95**
toteswingers: 1&2 £3.30, 1&3 £10.40, 2&3 £4.20 CSF £11.98 TOTE £2.00: £1.20, £3.10; EX 11.90.
Owner W J Gredley **Bred** Middle Park Stud Ltd **Trained** Newmarket, Suffolk

FOCUS
A useful handicap but one run at a steady gallop to the intersection and this bare form doesn't look strictly reliable. The winner raced close to the inside rail in the straight and the form is rated around the third.

1314 [illegible] [illegible]

9:00 (9:00) (Class 5) (0-70,70) 4-Y-O+ **£2,417** (£713; £178; £178) **Stalls** Low

Form RPR

3645 **1** **Italian Tom (IRE)**[21] [946] 4-9-7 **70**........................ LukeMorris 1 76
(Ronald Harris) *led: hrd rdn and hdd 1f out: rallied gamely to get bk up nr fin* **11/2**[3]

1643 **2** *nk* **Co Dependent (USA)**[18] [985] 5-9-7 **70**........................ FergusSweeney 5 75
(Jamie Osborne) *dwlt: hld up in 6th: hdwy 2f out: slt ld 1f out: edgd rt fnl 100yds: hdd nr fin* **6/1**

2012 **3** *nse* **Dvinsky (USA)**[18] [985] 10-9-7 **70**........................(v) KierenFallon 4 75
(Michael Squance) *trckd wnr: drvn to chal over 1f out: n.m.r fnl 50yds: kpt on* **7/2**[1]

3503 **3** *dht* **Onceaponatime (IRE)**[7] [1171] 6-9-2 **65**........................(b) AdamKirby 9 70
(Michael Squance) *t.k.h in rr: rdn over 2f out: gd hdwy fnl f to dead-heat for 3rd on line* **12/1**

144- **5** *¾* **Doc Hay (USA)**[165] [7239] 4-9-5 **68**........................(t) ChrisCatlin 7 72+
(Paul Cole) *plld hrd: prom: drvn to press ldrs fnl f: r.o: 4th and hld whn n.m.r nr fin* **11/2**[3]

4461 **6** *¾* **Speak The Truth (IRE)**[14] [1043] 5-8-13 **62**........................(p) PatCosgrave 6 62
(Jim Boyle) *t.k.h: chsd ldrs: rdn over 2f out: one pce* **5/1**[2]

2402 **7** *¾* **Valmina**[18] [984] 4-8-8 **64**........................(t) GeorgeDowning(7) 3 62
(Tony Carroll) *in tch in 5th: lost pl 3f out: sn rdn and btn: styng on at fin* **7/1**

400- **8** *3 ¼* **Knightfire (IRE)**[164] [7255] 4-9-3 **66**........................ ShaneKelly 8 60
(Walter Swinburn) *t.k.h towards rr: hdwy to chse ldrs over 1f out: hmpd on ins rail 150yds out: snatched up: nt rcvr* **17/2**

1m 13.19s (0.09) **Going Correction** 0.0s/f (Stan) **8 Ran SP% 114.7**
Speed ratings (Par 103): **99,98,98,98,97 96,95,91**
PL: D £1.30, O £2.80; TRICAST: IT-CD-D £65.68, IT-CD-O £191.01; toteswingers: 1&2 £6.90, 1&3(D) £2.10, 1&3(O) £5.80, 2&3(D) £3.60, 2&3 (O) £4.20 CSF £38.31 TOTE £4.80: £1.10, £1.30; EX 53.80.
Owner S & A Mares **Bred** Tom Radley **Trained** Earlswood, Monmouths

FOCUS
Mainly exposed sorts in an ordinary handicap in which the early gallop was just fair and several finished in a heap. The winner raced towards the inside rail in the straight. The form is rated through Divinsky.
Knightfire(IRE) Official explanation: jockey said gelding was denied a clear run
T/Plt: £309.40 to a £1 stake. Pool: £58,244.20. 137.39 winning tickets. T/Qpdt: £140.50 to a £1 stake. Pool: £5,260.78. 27.70 winning tickets. LM

NEWMARKET (R-H)

Wednesday, April 13

OFFICIAL GOING: Good to firm (good in places; watered; 8.7)

Far side track used with stalls on far side.

Wind: Fresh half-behind Weather: Overcast

1315 ALEX SCOTT MAIDEN STKS (C&G) 7f

1:50 (1:52) (Class 4) 3-Y-O £4,533 (£1,348; £674; £336) Stalls Low

Form RPR

022- **1** **Commended**[166] 7201 3-9-0 81 .... MichaelHills 1 86
(B W Hills) *mde virtually all: rdn over 1f out: edgd lft ins fnl f: jst hld on* **11/4**[1]

2- **2** *hd* **Afkar (IRE)**[320] 2486 3-9-0 0 .... PhilipRobinson 5 85
(Clive Brittain) *led for a few strides: chsd wnr: rdn over 1f out: edgd lft: r.o* **7/2**[2]

0- **3** *2½* **L'Ami Louis (IRE)**[186] 6748 3-9-0 0 .... DaneO'Neill 10 78
(Henry Candy) *hld up: hdwy over 4f out: rdn over 1f out: styd on same pce fnl f* **7/1**[3]

00- **4** *3¼* **L'Hermitage (IRE)**[182] 6849 3-9-0 0 .... MartinDwyer 4 69
(Brian Meehan) *prom: reminders 1/2-way: wknd over 1f out* **25/1**

226- **5** *1¾* **Battle Of Britain**[271] 4111 3-9-0 68 ....(t) WilliamCarson 9 65
(Giles Bravery) *hld up: rdn over 1f out: r.o ins fnl f: nvr nrr* **25/1**

6 *nse* **Lieutenant Kojak** 3-8-11 0 .... SimonPearce(3) 2 65
(Peter Charalambous) *sn pushed along in rr: r.o ins fnl f: nvr trbld ldrs* **100/1**

05- **7** *½* **Misk Khitaam (USA)**[194] 6532 3-9-0 0 .... RichardHills 7 63
(John Dunlop) *chsd ldrs: rdn over 2f out: wknd over 1f out* **7/2**[2]

8 *1¾* **Dunseverick (IRE)** 3-9-0 0 .... TedDurcan 8 59
(David Lanigan) *s.s: hdwy 1/2-way: wknd wl over 1f out* **14/1**

9 *8* **Who Loves Ya Baby** 3-9-0 0 .... KirstyMilczarek 6 37
(Peter Charalambous) *prom: lost pl after 2f: sn bhd* **100/1**

10 *1½* **Pagan Warrior (IRE)** 3-9-0 0 .... AdamKirby 3 33
(Clive Cox) *rn green and a in rr: bhd fr 1/2-way* **7/1**[3]

1m 25.56s (0.16) **Going Correction** -0.025s/f (Good) **10** Ran SP% **112.5**

Speed ratings (Par 100): **98,97,94,91,89 89,88,86,77,75**

toteswingers:1&2:£2.80, 1&3:£4.70, 2&3:£3.80 CSF £11.56 TOTE £3.90: £1.30, £1.40, £2.30; EX 11.90 Trifecta £67.40 Pool: £588.78 - 6.13 winning units..

Owner E D Kessly **Bred** Mrs A M Jenkins And E D Kessly **Trained** Lambourn, Berks

FOCUS

Watering took place the previous day, with 10mm being applied, but it was dry overnight and the going was given as good to firm, good in places. There was a tailwind. Often quite a good maiden, this year's event looked pretty average on paper. The form is rated around the front pair, and the third was a big improver.

Misk Khitaam(USA) Official explanation: jockey said colt stopped quickly

Pagan Warrior(IRE) Official explanation: jockey said colt ran green

1316 EQUINE PRODUCTS UK CONDITIONS STKS 5f

2:25 (2:26) (Class 3) 2-Y-O £6,476 (£1,927; £963; £481) Stalls Low

Form RPR

1 **1** **Jack Who's He (IRE)**[13] 1055 2-9-2 0 .... CathyGannon 2 85
(David Evans) *chsd ldr tl led 1/2-way: rdn and hdd over 1f out: rallied to ld nr fin* **5/4**[1]

2 *hd* **Tell Dad** 2-8-9 0 .... RichardHughes 5 77+
(Richard Hannon) *dwlt: sn prom: jnd ldrs 1/2-way: led over 1f out: rdn and edgd lft ins fnl f: hdd nr fin* **7/4**[2]

3 *2* **Chillie Billie** 2-8-9 0 .... KierenFallon 1 70
(Phil McEntee) *hld up in tch: shkn up 1/2-way: rdn and swtchd lft over 1f out: styd on same pce ins fnl f* **12/1**

53 **4** *2½* **Sabusa (IRE)**[11] 1101 2-8-12 0 .... WilliamBuick 4 64
(Alan McCabe) *chsd ldrs: rdn over 1f out: styd on same pce* **16/1**

41 **5** *5* **The Dancing Lord**[9] 1129 2-8-5 0 .... JakePayne(7) 3 46
(Bill Turner) *led to 1/2-way: rdn over 1f out: wknd fnl f* **5/1**[3]

59.81 secs (0.71) **Going Correction** -0.025s/f (Good) **5** Ran SP% **111.0**

Speed ratings (Par 96): **93,92,89,85,77**

CSF £3.75 TOTE £2.00: £1.20, £1.40; EX 3.80.

Owner Barry McCabe **Bred** Knocklong House Stud **Trained** Pandy, Monmouths

FOCUS

In the last five years this race has been a fine pointer to Royal Ascot success, with Queen Mary winner Gilded successful in 2006 and Coventry Stakes winner Art Connoisseur victorious in 2008. The winner in 2009, Monsieur Chevalier, was also unlucky not to win that year's Norfolk Stakes, while Spirit Of Sharjah, the 2007 winner, was third in his Norfolk. Seven of the last ten winners had had a previous outing, and experience proved crucial this time. It was fast run and the third is the key to the level of the form.

NOTEBOOK

Jack Who's He(IRE), who was on his toes in the paddock, just saw off the newcomer Tell Dad close home. The winner had taken a Leicester maiden by 4l first time up and, with the runner-up giving the form a boost by going in next time, he was strong in the market. He faced no easy task giving weight all round, and had to be pushed along to hold his prominent position, but he was possibly at an advantage in racing next to the far rail and, finding plenty for pressure, eventually outbattled the smooth travelling newcomer. The Lily Agnes at Chester probably wouldn't suit him ideally, given the need for early speed over that 5f trip and that he's quite a big sort, and so he could go for a conditions race at Ascot next, as his trainer believes he needs 6f already, and the stiff 5f there should suit him better. (op 7-4 tchd 15-8)

Tell Dad ◆, whose trainer had sent out five of the previous seven winners of this race (stable not represented in one of the other two years), had to be of interest, even allowing for it being his debut. He missed the break slightly but travelled like the best horse in the race and came there apparently full of running, but when he was asked to go and win his inexperience came to the fore and he edged left, and then right, before coming up a little short, having been done at 1.07 in running. He will have no trouble going one better and it wouldn't be at all surprising to see him develop into a pattern-class performer in time. His dam is a half-sister to Icesolator, who could only finish ninth for Hannon in this race in 2008, but that colt still went and won his next three starts, including the Listed National Stakes. (op 6-4 tchd 11-8)

Chillie Billie, the youngest of these, got a bit unbalanced and ran green but showed plenty of ability to finish third. He has plenty of speed and will have no trouble getting off the mark. (op 20-1)

Sabusa(IRE) looked to face a stiff task and didn't run too badly on this switch to turf. (tchd 20-1)

The Dancing Lord had a lot more to do than when making all at Folkestone second time out. He showed speed early but was another who got unbalanced. (op 7-2)

1317 £150,000 TATTERSALLS MILLIONS 3-Y-O SPRINT 6f

3:00 (3:01) (Class 2) 3-Y-O £83,653 (£38,011; £15,214; £7,599; £4,571; £3,042) Stalls Low

Form RPR

520- **1** **Sir Reginald**[193] 6560 3-9-3 102 .... PaulHanagan 10 91
(Richard Fahey) *chsd ldrs: rdn and bmpd over 1f out: led and edgd lft ins fnl f: r.o* **4/1**[2]

300- **2** *¾* **Madany (IRE)**[193] 6559 3-8-12 90 .... RichardHills 3 87+
(B W Hills) *a.p: nt clr run: swtchd lft and hmpd over 1f out: rdn and r.o ins fnl f* **7/1**

310- **3** *nk* **Khor Sheed**[194] 6530 3-8-12 104 .... KierenFallon 7 83
(Luca Cumani) *mid-div: pushed along 1/2-way: hdwy over 1f out: r.o* **10/3**[1]

000- **4** *½* **Button Moon (IRE)**[198] 6419 3-8-12 78 ....(p) MartinLane 5 81
(Ian Wood) *a.p: chsd ldr 1/2-way: led over 1f out: rdn and hdd ins fnl f: styd on same pce* **100/1**

410- **5** *1¼* **Cruiser**[193] 6560 3-9-3 83 .... RichardHughes 4 82+
(William Muir) *hld up: hdwy over 1f out: swtchd lft ins fnl f: r.o: nt rch ldrs* **12/1**

431- **6** *shd* **Masaya**[193] 6559 3-8-12 99 .... PhilipRobinson 6 77
(Clive Brittain) *led: rdn and hdd over 1f out: styd on same pce ins fnl f* **9/2**[3]

4 **7** *3¼* **Rafaaf (IRE)**[72] 368 3-9-3 0 .... AndreaAtzeni 9 71
(Robert Eddery) *chsd ldrs: rdn over 2f out: wknd fnl f* **150/1**

212- **8** *4* **Neebras (IRE)**[279] 3823 3-9-3 110 .... MickaelBarzalona 8 58+
(Mahmood Al Zarooni) *s.s: a bhd* **4/1**[2]

030- **9** *nk* **Shafgaan**[193] 6560 3-9-3 90 .... ChrisCatlin 11 58
(Clive Brittain) *s.i.s: in rr and pushed along: sme hdwy on outer over 2f out: sn wknd* **22/1**

1113 **10** *½* **Aquilifer (IRE)**[54] 594 3-9-3 75 ....(t) ShaneKelly 12 56
(William Jarvis) *pushed along in rr early: nvr on terms* **50/1**

010- **11** *10* **Shim Sham (IRE)**[179] 6927 3-8-12 87 .... MartinDwyer 1 19
(Brian Meehan) *chsd ldr to 1/2-way: wknd 2f out* **15/2**

1m 11.33s (-0.87) **Going Correction** -0.025s/f (Good) **11** Ran SP% **121.2**

Speed ratings (Par 104): **104,103,102,101,100 100,95,90,90,89 76**

toteswingers:1&2:£8.00, 1&3:£3.70, 2&3:£5.40 CSF £32.79 TOTE £4.70: £1.90, £3.20, £1.10; EX 34.20 Trifecta £167.10 Pool: £917.25 - 4.06 winning units..

Owner Jim McGrath **Bred** Jeremy Green And Sons **Trained** Musley Bank, N Yorks

■ Stewards' Enquiry : Richard Hills one-day ban: careless riding (Apr 27)

FOCUS

Not as big a field as one might have expected given the prize money on offer in this new sales race, and a mix of abilities on show. The form could be rated higher on time, but the fourth and fifth limit it.

NOTEBOOK

Sir Reginald found live 1000 Guineas candidate I Love Me just too good in another one of these over 7f last autumn, and he may have had to settle for second again had Madany enjoyed a clear run, but Hanagan held his ground and made the most of his rival's troubled passage. This quick ground really suited Sir Reginald, and the gelding operation he had over the winter has apparently done him the world of good. This was his big race, so future targets are up in the air, but if he were to make a quick return to the track the Listed Pavillion Stakes, over this trip at Ascot in a fortnight's time, looks a possible target, as it's restricted to 3-y-os. (op 7-1)

Madany(IRE), fairly consistent at two, had a nice run through on the far side, behind the pace, but once switched for a run she found Hanagan to her left in determined mood to ensure she didn't get a run between his mount and Button Moon. Forced to switch around the winner, she finished well once in the clear, but the line came too soon. She looked unlucky, and appears to have done well from two to three. (op 14-1)

Khor Sheed, whose trainer was concerned beforehand that she might be a bit short of peak fitness, put up a good effort. She promises to stay a bit further this year. (op 11-4)

Button Moon(IRE) ran her best race at two on the July course when narrowly denied by Zebedee in one of these valuable sales races, and she ran another fine race to finish fourth here. Although still a maiden after ten starts, she has won her fair share of prize money.

Cruiser was running on quite nicely at the finish, but the quick ground was a question mark coming into the race, and it's quite possible he'll be better suited by some cut. (op 20-1)

Masaya, who won one of these for fillies last October, showed pace on the far side but was treading water from a furlong out. She's another who might be better with a bit of dig. (op 7-1)

Neebras(IRE) held a clear chance on the book, but he was very keen to post, missed the break and was struggling throughout. Official explanation: trainer's rep said, regarding running, that the colt ran too free to post. (op 9-4 tchd 2-1, 5-1 and 6-1 in places)

Shafgaan was on his toes beforehand. (op 25-1)

Aquilifer(IRE) Official explanation: jockey said gelding hung right throughout

Shim Sham(IRE) showed early speed but dropped out very quickly from over 2f out and presumably something was amiss. Official explanation: jockey said filly stopped quickly (op 8-1 tchd 7-1)

1318 BET AT BLUESQ.COM EUROPEAN FREE H'CAP (LISTED RACE) 7f

3:35 (3:35) (Class 1) 3-Y-O £17,031 (£6,456; £3,231; £1,611; £807; £405) Stalls Low

Form RPR

112- **1** **Pausanias**[186] 6737 3-8-12 **101** .... RichardHughes 6 105+
(Richard Hannon) *trckd ldrs: led and edgd rt over 1f out: rdn out* **10/3**[2]

414- **2** *1* **Rerouted (USA)**[164] 7265 3-9-4 **107** .... MichaelHills 1 108
(B W Hills) *led: rdn and hdd over 1f out: styd on u.p* **6/1**

50-0 **3** *1¼* **Utley (USA)**[18] 998 3-9-7 **110** .... WilliamBuick 2 108
(John Gosden) *a.p: rdn over 1f out: styd on* **12/1**

244- **4** *¾* **The Paddyman (IRE)**[195] 6507 3-9-3 **106** .... RyanMoore 4 102
(William Haggas) *hld up: swtchd lft and hdwy over 1f out: nt rch ldrs* **9/2**[3]

233- **5** *2¼* **Elzaam (AUS)**[172] 7095 3-9-7 **110** ....(v[1]) RichardHills 5 100
(Roger Varian) *prom: chsd ldr over 2f out: sn rdn: n.m.r over 1f out: wknd wl ins fnl f* **15/8**[1]

011- **6** *1½* **Majestic Dubawi**[207] 6176 3-8-11 **100** .... NeilCallan 3 86
(Mick Channon) *chsd ldr over 3f: sn rdn: wknd fnl f* **7/1**

1m 24.06s (-1.34) **Going Correction** -0.025s/f (Good) **6** Ran SP% **110.5**

Speed ratings (Par 106): **106,104,103,102,100 98**

toteswingers:1&2:£2.40, 1&3:£8.10, 2&3:£5.70 CSF £22.12 TOTE £3.90: £2.30, £1.90; EX 19.70.

Owner Sir Alex Ferguson & Sotirios Hassiakos **Bred** Granham Farm And P Hearson Bloodstock **Trained** East Everleigh, Wilts

FOCUS

Not much of a Classic pointer in recent years, with the exception of Indian Haven, who went on to take the Irish Guineas in 2003, and this year's race looks unlikely to have any impact on the English Guineas. The first two progressed and the next pair are rated to form.

NOTEBOOK

Pausanias ◆ certainly has the look of a smart colt in the making, and he could well be heading for the German Guineas on the back of this taking display. He's done well from two to three, has plenty of size about him, and travelled well through this race, despite some reservations about the ground being on the quick side for him. He quickened up well to assert, shouldn't have any trouble with a return to 1m, and looks one to keep on the right side. (op 3-1 tchd 7-2)

Rerouted(USA), fourth behind Roderic O'Connor in the Group 1 Criterium International on his final start at two, didn't do that form any harm with this solid effort in defeat. Up there all the way on the far side, he showed he's trained on, and it wouldn't be a surprise to see him turn up in the Jersey Stakes later in the year. (tchd 11-2)

Utley(USA) had the benefit of a previous outing this season, albeit a well-beaten effort in the UAE Derby. He put up a fair effort back on turf, but he could well prove a difficult horse to place this season. (tchd 14-1)

The Paddyman(IRE) struggled to get to the principals from off the pace. He was beaten over a length by Rerouted in the Somerville Tattersall Stakes here last September and, despite the conditions arguably being more in his favour, couldn't reverse the form. (tchd 5-1 in places)

Elzaam(AUS) was beating a retreat when hampered. He shaped like a blatant non-stayer and a return to sprinting surely beckons for him now. (op 5-2 tchd 11-4 in places)

Majestic Dubawi won a Group 3 at Ayr last autumn (Nell Gwyn winner later on this card back in third), but one got the impression that had she trained on she would be contesting the Nell Gwyn itself rather than this handicap. Weak in the market, she ran poorly and has a lot to prove now. (op 6-1 tchd 8-1)

1319 LANWADES STUD NELL GWYN STKS (GROUP 3) (FILLIES) 7f

4:10 (4:10) (Class 1) 3-Y-O

£28,385 (£10,760; £5,385; £2,685; £1,345; £675) **Stalls** Low

Form				RPR
132-	**1**		**Barefoot Lady (IRE)**[186] 6751 3-8-12 97 .... PaulHanagan 11 (Richard Fahey) *hld up: hdwy over 2f out: rdn ins fnl f: edgd rt and r.o to ld post* **14/1**	104
1	**2**	*nk*	**Sing Softly (USA)**[10] 1116 3-8-12 100 .... RyanMoore 9 (A P O'Brien, Ire) *a.p: led over 1f out: sn rdn and edgd rt: r.o: hdd post* **9/4**[1]	103
143-	**3**	*¾*	**Maqaasid**[194] 6530 3-9-1 105 .... RichardHills 2 (John Gosden) *hld up: swtchd lft and hdwy over 1f out: rdn and ev ch ins fnl f: unable qck nr fin* **4/1**[2]	104+
221-	**4**	*1 ¾*	**Show Rainbow**[170] 7123 3-8-12 82 .... NeilCallan 3 (Mick Channon) *chsd ldr to over 4f out: remained handy: led over 2f out: rdn and hdd over 1f out: no ex towards fin* **25/1**	96
131-	**5**	*1*	**Ladies Are Forever**[193] 6568 3-8-12 103 .... SilvestreDeSousa 7 (Geoffrey Oldroyd) *hld up: hdwy 1/2-way: rdn over 1f out: no ex ins fnl f* **5/1**[3]	94
401-	**6**	*½*	**Sweet Cecily (IRE)**[166] 7204 3-8-12 100 .... RichardHughes 1 (Richard Hannon) *led: rdn and hdd over 2f out: no ex ins fnl f* **16/1**	92
22-2	**7**	*½*	**Elshabakiya (IRE)**[18] 990 3-8-12 95 .... PhilipRobinson 10 (Clive Brittain) *s.i.s: hld up: rdn over 2f out: hung rt and styd on ins fnl f: nrst fin* **6/1**	91
0001	**8**	*1 ½*	**Crying Lightening (IRE)**[34] 823 3-8-12 104 .... JimmyQuinn 5 (Peter Chapple-Hyam) *hld up: hdwy 1/2-way: outpcd over 2f out: n.d after* **14/1**	87
550-	**9**	*1*	**Lily Again**[172] 7098 3-8-12 96 .... FrankieDettori 4 (Paul Cole) *mid-div: hdwy to chse ldr over 4f out: rdn and ev ch over 2f out: wknd fnl f* **16/1**	84
31-	**10**	*¾*	**Qushchi**[165] 7232 3-8-12 80 .... JimCrowley 6 (William Jarvis) *s.i.s: rdn over 2f out: a in rr* **22/1**	82
-141	**11**	*2*	**Strictly Pink (IRE)**[8] 1152 3-8-12 75 .... CathyGannon 8 (Alan Bailey) *chsd ldrs: rdn and ev ch over 2f out: wknd fnl f* **40/1**	77

1m 24.44s (-0.96) **Going Correction** -0.025s/f (Good) **11** Ran SP% **117.5**

Speed ratings (Par 105): **104,103,102,100,99 99,98,96,95,94 92**

toteswingers:1&2:£6.50, 1&3:£6.60, 2&3:£2.70 CSF £44.74 TOTE £15.10: £3.40, £1.30, £2.10; EX 69.70 Trifecta £356.20 Pool: £1,376.45 - 2.85 winning units..

Owner Mrs H Steel **Bred** Arbawny Ventures 2000uc **Trained** Musley Bank, N Yorks

■ Stewards' Enquiry : Ryan Moore caution: used whip down shoulder in the forehand.

FOCUS

The overall impression was that, with the first three finishing in a bit of a heap, this is a trial that will not have much of an impact on the 1,000 Guineas. The winning time was 0.38sec slower than the Free Handicap earlier on the card, equating to 6l, and the form is ordinary for the grade.

NOTEBOOK

Barefoot Lady(IRE) doesn't hold an entry in the Guineas but showed she's improved from two to three with a strong late run to get up close home. Returning to quick ground suited her and, given that she's a daughter of that tough mare Lady Angharad, there must be a chance that she'll take her racing well and connections will get a good campaign out of her. They have the option to supplement her for the Guineas, but she was fit for this and perhaps this was her big day. (tchd 12-1)

Sing Softly(USA) had the benefit of race-fitness having already won twice this year, but the form of those victories didn't amount to a great deal and improvement was needed for her to take this. She also had to prove herself on this quicker ground, but as a daughter of Hennessy that was never likely to be a problem. She looked the likeliest winner running into the Dip but edged right when asked to quicken and didn't quite see her race out as well as the winner. It was a solid effort and she remains on an upward curve, but Ballydoyle would appear to have stronger candidates for the Guineas at his stage. (op 5-2 tchd 11-4 in places)

Maqaasid, shouldering a 3lb penalty, travelled strongly in behind the pace and was brought to have every chance a furlong out, but she was one-paced from there and, despite finishing third, the seventh furlong didn't appear to be in her favour. She might still go down the Classic route, much like Lady Of The Desert last year (France is an option), but just like that filly she looks a sprinter really and, while the programme is not easy for 3-y-o sprinters, it will surely be over shorter that she will eventually be seen at her best this year. (tchd 9-2)

Show Rainbow ◆, a well-made filly, only had a heavy-ground maiden success last autumn to her name and had plenty to find on the ratings, but it looked significant that her connections chose to run her in this race rather than the Group 3 winner Majestic Dubawi, who contested the Free Handicap earlier on the card. She ran a blinder in defeat and, based on her pedigree, has the potential to improve further for a step up to 1m. (tchd 33-1 in a place)

Ladies Are Forever travelled quite well but got unbalanced and failed to pick up out of the Dip and lost a little bit of momentum when crossed by the runner-up soon afterwards. It looks as if she's another who will have to drop back to sprinting now. (op 6-1 tchd 9-2)

Sweet Cecily(IRE) showed early pace but failed to see out the trip and she's another who'll presumably now be dropped back in distance.

Elshabakiya(IRE) was another who got rather unbalanced and hung right in the closing stages. Perhaps this ground was on the quick side for this daughter of Diktat. (op 11-2 tchd 5-1)

Crying Lightening(IRE) had a fitness edge having been campaigned in Dubai, but she was struggling from some way out here. (op 16-1)

1320 BLUE SQUARE FEILDEN STKS (LISTED RACE) 1m 1f

4:45 (4:45) (Class 1) 3-Y-O

£17,031 (£6,456; £3,231; £1,611; £807; £405) **Stalls** Low

Form				RPR
13-	**1**		**Dordogne (IRE)**[180] 6884 3-8-13 95 .... FrankieDettori 4 (Mark Johnston) *mde virtually all: rdn over 1f out: styd on gamely: edgd rt nr fin* **7/2**[1]	103+
41-	**2**	*hd*	**Happy Today (USA)**[226] 5582 3-8-13 83 .... MartinDwyer 5 (Brian Meehan) *a.p: chsd wnr over 3f out: rdn over 1f out: ev ch ins fnl f: unable qck nr fin* **15/2**	102
211-	**3**	*shd*	**Moriarty (IRE)**[208] 6149 3-8-13 94 .... RichardHughes 6 (Richard Hannon) *stdd s: hld up: hdwy over 1f out: r.o* **4/1**[2]	102+
41-	**4**	*3*	**Specific Gravity (FR)**[189] 6676 3-8-13 96 .... TomQueally 2 (Sir Henry Cecil) *chsd ldrs: rdn over 1f out: hung lft and no ex ins fnl f* **9/2**[3]	100+
140-	**5**	*1 ¾*	**Toolain (IRE)**[172] 7081 3-9-2 105 .... NeilCallan 1 (Roger Varian) *prom: rdn over 2f out: styd on same pce fr over 1f out* **13/2**	100
530-	**6**	*nk*	**Musharakaat (IRE)**[193] 6559 3-8-8 97 .... RichardHills 7 (Ed Dunlop) *hld up: hdwy u.p over 2f out: styd on same pce appr fnl f* **10/1**	91
231-	**7**	*7*	**Fulgur**[188] 6689 3-8-13 83 .... KierenFallon 3 (Luca Cumani) *plld hrd: trckd wnr over 7f out: rdn over 2f out: wknd wl over 1f out* **5/1**	80+

1m 52.16s (0.46) **Going Correction** -0.025s/f (Good) 7 Ran SP% **111.3**

Speed ratings (Par 106): **96,95,95,95,93 93,87**

toteswingers:1&2:£4.90, 1&3:£2.80, 2&3:£6.10 CSF £27.96 TOTE £3.60: £2.20, £3.80; EX 29.00.

Owner Sheikh Hamdan Bin Mohammed Al Maktoum **Bred** Mr & Mrs G Middlebrook **Trained** Middleham Moor, N Yorks

FOCUS

This looked an interesting race on paper, featuring several promising types and, while the betting suggested it was an open race, and the result - something of a bunch finish - appeared to suggest it was an ordinary renewal, there's a case to be made that the form might be all right. The first four all improved.

NOTEBOOK

Dordogne(IRE) ◆, whose trainer had sent out three of the previous seven winners of this race, improved that record further. By Singspiel out of that tough and prolific mare Riberac, he set out to make all and, despite being tackled on both sides heading into the Dip and also by Moriarty late on, kept finding extra and stuck his neck out in willing fashion to hold off his rivals. He looks just the sort that should improve further as the season goes on and as he steps up in distance. Dettori suggested that the Sandown Classic Trial might be a suitable next step. (tchd 10-3)

Happy Today(USA), who missed his intended engagement in the Royal Lodge last autumn on account of a foot abscess, is bred to enjoy this sort of ground and ran a promising race in defeat. He's closely related to St James's Palace winner Zafeen and he should be up to contesting Group races in time. (op 17-2)

Moriarty(IRE) was reported to have thrived over the winter but should improve for this run. Expected to appreciate the step up in trip, he came through from off the pace to join issue well inside the last, and there should be more to come from him. (op 5-1)

Specific Gravity(FR) quickened up well to join the winner with 2f to run but he then got unbalanced and hung before dropping out of contention. His form at two came on soft ground and it might be that he needs cut to be seen at his best. He's not one to write off. (op 10-3)

Toolain(IRE), who showed a quirk or two as a juvenile, is another who might have found this ground on the quick side. He's by Diktat and the quickest surface he'd encountered before was described as good. (op 11-2 tchd 5-1)

Musharakaat(IRE) had a solid chance at the weights but proved a little disappointing. (op 14-1 tchd 16 -1 in a place)

Fulgur didn't help his cause by failing to settle through the early stages. He had flashed his tail repeatedly in the paddock, so may have got upset before arriving at the start. (op 11-2)

1321 DOWNLOAD BLUE SQUARE IPHONE APP MAIDEN STKS 1m 2f

5:20 (5:20) (Class 4) 3-Y-O **£4,533** (£1,348; £674; £336) **Stalls** Low

Form				RPR
5-	**1**		**Ocean War**[239] 4490 3-9-3 0 .... MickaelBarzalona 3 (Mahmood Al Zarooni) *a.p: rdn to chse ldr over 2f out: led ins fnl f: edgd lft: styd on* **4/1**[3]	101
5-	**2**	*1*	**Maqaraat (IRE)**[166] 7203 3-9-3 0 .... RichardHills 7 (B W Hills) *hld up: hdwy over 1f out: hung rt and r.o ins fnl f: nt rch wnr* **5/2**[2]	99
5-	**3**	*1 ¾*	**Dream Achieved**[264] 4318 3-9-3 0 .... MichaelHills 4 (B W Hills) *led: rdn over 1f out: hdd and unable qck ins fnl f* **13/2**	95
	4	*2 ¼*	**Alkimos (IRE)** 3-9-3 0 .... KierenFallon 2 (Luca Cumani) *hld up: hdwy over 2f out: rdn over 1f out: styd on same pce* **14/1**	91
	5	*2 ¼*	**Midsummer Sun** 3-9-3 0 .... TomQueally 6 (Sir Henry Cecil) *prom: rdn over 2f out: wknd over 1f out* **6/4**[1]	86
0-	**6**	*6*	**Elrasheed**[243] 5049 3-9-3 0 .... TadhgO'Shea 8 (John Dunlop) *chsd ldr 8f out tl rdn and wknd over 2f out* **14/1**	74
	7	*37*	**Hab Reeh** 3-9-3 0 .... PhilipRobinson 5 (Clive Brittain) *s.s: hld up: a in rr: bhd fnl 4f: t.o* **50/1**	—

2m 4.70s (-1.10) **Going Correction** -0.025s/f (Good) 7 Ran SP% **117.2**

Speed ratings (Par 100): **103,102,100,99,97 92,62**

toteswingers:1&2:£2.50, 1&3:£3.50, 2&3:£2.90 CSF £15.06 TOTE £5.30: £2.70, £1.10; EX 15.90 Trifecta £101.10 Pool: £507.21 - 3.71 winning units..

Owner Godolphin **Bred** Newsells Park Stud Limited **Trained** Newmarket, Suffolk

■ A winner on his first day's riding in England for talented French jockey Mickael Barzalona.

FOCUS

This had the look of a classy maiden on paper, with a hyped-up favourite facing some well-bred rivals representing prominent connections. The form is rated fairly positively.

Hab Reeh Official explanation: jockey said colt lost its action

1322 JOIN BLUESQ.COM FOR £20 OF FREE BETS H'CAP 6f

5:55 (5:55) (Class 2) (0-100,100) 3-Y-O **£10,361** (£3,083; £1,540; £769) **Stalls** Low

Form				RPR
1-11	**1**		**Acclamazing (IRE)**[12] 1079 3-8-10 **89** ow1 .... (t) AdamKirby 3 (Marco Botti) *hld up: hdwy over 2f out: led ins fnl f: r.o wl* **9/4**[1]	95+
225-	**2**	*2 ¾*	**Avonmore Star**[191] 6636 3-9-1 **94** .... RichardHughes 2 (Richard Hannon) *sn led: rdn over 1f out: hdd and unable qck ins fnl f* **8/1**	91
054-	**3**	*1 ¼*	**Cape To Rio (IRE)**[172] 7080 3-9-7 **100** .... RyanMoore 7 (Richard Hannon) *hld up: hdwy over 2f out: sn rdn: outpcd over 1f out: r.o ins fnl f* **6/1**[3]	93
111-	**4**	*shd*	**Indian Ballad (IRE)**[187] 6719 3-8-7 **86** .... GrahamGibbons 8 (Ed McMahon) *chsd ldrs: rdn over 1f out: styd on same pce* **7/2**[2]	79

3-36 **5** ½ **Bathwick Bear (IRE)**[18] 990 3-9-4 **100** RichardEvans(3) 4 91
(David Evans) *led early: chsd ldr: rdn over 1f out: no ex ins fnl f* **20/1**
005- **6** ½ **Remotelinx (IRE)**[214] 5965 3-8-9 **88** DaneO'Neill 6 77
(J W Hills) *hld up: r.o ins fnl f: nvr trbld ldrs* **16/1**
250- **7** *nk* **Chilworth Lad**[216] 5880 3-9-0 **96** MartinHarley(3) 10 85
(Mick Channon) *hld up: sme hdwy over 1f out: n.d* **10/1**
4-20 **8** 2½ **Diamond Charlie (IRE)**[55] 578 3-8-2 **81** oh3 SilvestreDeSousa 9 62
(Simon Dow) *hld up in tch: plld hrd: rdn over 1f out: sn wknd* **12/1**
556- **9** 9 **Waltz Darling (IRE)**[214] 5943 3-9-2 **95** PaulHanagan 1 47
(Richard Fahey) *chsd ldrs tl rdn and wknd 2f out* **7/1**

1m 12.51s (0.31) **Going Correction** -0.025s/f (Good) **9** Ran SP% **118.3**
Speed ratings (Par 104): **96,92,90,90,89 89,88,85,73**
toteswingers:1&2:£6.30, 1&3:£3.50, 2&3:£7.10. totesuper7: Win: Not won. Place:£74.40 CSF £21.77 CT £98.20 TOTE £2.50: £1.10, £1.40, £3.00; EX 20.90 Trifecta £170.40 Pool: £366.17 - 1.59 winning units..
Owner Giuliano Manfredini **Bred** Michael And John Fahy **Trained** Newmarket, Suffolk

FOCUS
A good-quality sprint handicap for 3-y-os, but a modest time compared with the sales race. The winner carried over his Polytrack progress and may do better again.

NOTEBOOK
Acclamazing(IRE) made the most of his fitness from the AW and saw off his rivals inside the last furlong with a taking turn of foot. Clearly he is just as effective on fast turf as he is on Polytrack and the 1lb overweight his rider put up proved inconsequential. He could well win again while in this form. (op 5-2)
Avonmore Star ◆ was below his best on his last two starts at two, but those efforts came on soft ground and he was much happier back on a sound surface. He found the race-fit winner too strong but is fully entitled to come on for this and should go close next time. (op 7-1)
Cape To Rio(IRE) stayed on well close home to grab third. He might not be the easiest to place this year as he's rated 100 and giving weight away in handicaps could well prove just as tough as taking on better horses in Listed company. Connections may have to look for conditions races.
Indian Ballad(IRE) showed enough to suggest that he might be able to continue the improvement he showed last autumn. He's versatile with regard to ground conditions. (op 9-2 tchd 5-1)
Bathwick Bear(IRE), like the winner, had the benefit of race-fitness from the AW. He's another whose mark will not make things easy for him in the coming weeks. (op 16-1)
Remotelinx(IRE) was held up out the back and given plenty to do. He made modest late headway without being given a hard time and should come on plenty for this reappearance effort. (op 14-1)
Chilworth Lad, who was ridden by a 3lb claimer, is another who showed enough to suggest he might be of interest for a similar race in the coming weeks with this run under his belt. (op 12-1)
Diamond Charlie(IRE) Official explanation: jockey said colt ran too free
T/Jkpt: Not won. T/Plt: £25.00 to a £1 stake. Pool:£71,405.72 - 2,081.16 winning tickets T/Qpdt: £16.80 to a £1 stake. Pool:£4,858.88 - 212.84 winning tickets CR

1164 BEVERLEY (R-H)
Thursday, April 14

OFFICIAL GOING: Good to firm (firm in places on the back straight; 8.9)
Rail around inside of bottom bend moved out 2m.
Wind: Light half against Weather: Overcast but dry

1323 BEVERLEY MINSTER CLAIMING STKS 5f
2:00 (2:00) (Class 6) 3-Y-O **£1,075** (£1,075; £246; £123) **Stalls** Low

Form RPR
0-55 **1** **Exchange**[8] 1176 3-8-6 65 (b) LiamJones 5 58
(William Haggas) *hld up in tch: swtchd outside and hdwy 2f out: rdn to chal over 1f out: drvn to ld ins fnl f: edgd rt and put hd in air nr fin: jnd on line* **9/4**[2]
00-6 **1** *dht* **Meandmyshadow**[8] 1187 3-8-1 65 (b[1]) SilvestreDeSousa 1 53
(Alan Brown) *cl up on inner: rdn to ld wl over 1f out: hdd ent fnl f: sn drvn and rallied wl towards fin to join ldr on line* **13/2**
0664 **3** *nk* **Ever Roses**[42] 741 3-8-1 51 (v) DuranFentiman 7 52
(Paul Midgley) *in tch: rdn along and outpcd 1/2-way: edgd rt to inner and hdwy over 1f out: styd on wl u.p ins fnl f: nrst fin* **20/1**
-600 **4** 2¼ **Running Water**[15] 1040 3-8-6 37 BarryMcHugh 3 49
(Hugh McWilliams) *trckd ldrs: hdwy 2f out: rdn to ld briefly ent fnl f: sn drvn and hdd: kpt on same pce* **50/1**
2154 **5** 5 **Morermaloke**[8] 1187 3-8-9 73 DanielTudhope 6 34
(Ian McInnes) *chsd ldng pair: pushed along 2f out: sn rdn and wknd over 1f out* **7/2**[3]
-403 **6** ¾ **Dunmore Boy (IRE)**[13] 1079 3-8-11 65 (p) PaulHanagan 4 33
(Richard Fahey) *led: rdn along 2f out: drvn and hdd wl over 1f out: sn wknd* **6/4**[1]
0 **7** 2 **Hey Up There (IRE)**[30] 855 3-7-12 0 JamesSullivan(3) 2 16
(Ruth Carr) *s.i.s: a in rr* **100/1**

63.99 secs (0.49) **Going Correction** -0.125s/f (Firm) **7** Ran SP% **114.0**
Speed ratings (Par 96): **91,91,90,86,78 77,74**
WIN: Exchange £1.50, Meandmyshadow £3.30 PL: Exchange £2.40, Meandmyshadow £2.20. EX: E/M £11.00 M/E £8.70 CSF: E/M £8.37 M/E 10.70 toteswingers: E&3: £4.80, E&M: £2.90, M&3 £5.50.
Owner G Morrill **Bred** M J Dawson **Trained** Yedingham, N Yorks
Owner Highclere Thoroughbred Racing(Buchan II) **Bred** Southill Stud **Trained** Newmarket, Suffolk

FOCUS
A dead-heat in this weak claimer, and dubious form.

1324 RAPID LAD H'CAP 1m 1f 207y
2:35 (2:36) (Class 5) (0-70,69) 4-Y-O+ **£2,298** (£684; £341; £170) **Stalls** Low

Form RPR
50-3 **1** **Tribal Myth (IRE)**[9] 1150 4-8-9 **62** JulieBurke(5) 15 73
(Kevin Ryan) *trckd ldng pair: cl up 1/2-way: chal over 2f out: rdn to ld over 1f out: kpt on wl ins fnl f* **9/1**
004- **2** 1½ **Brockfield**[251] 4781 5-8-12 **60** SilvestreDeSousa 9 68
(Mel Brittain) *led: rdn along over 2f out: drvn and hdd over 1f out: kpt on wl ins fnl f* **17/2**
52-0 **3** 1¼ **Zaplamation (IRE)**[12] 1099 6-9-7 **69** TomEaves 13 74
(John Quinn) *trckd ldrs: hdwy over 2f out: rdn wl over 1f out: kpt on same pce u.p ins fnl f* **7/1**[3]
6/0- **4** ¾ **Brasingaman Eric**[328] 2290 4-8-2 **55** oh5 NeilFarley(5) 14 59
(George Moore) *midfield: hdwy on outer over 4f out: chsd ldrs 3f out: rdn to chal 2f out and ev ch tl drvn and one pce appr fnl f* **100/1**
2222 **5** 2¼ **The Blue Dog (IRE)**[8] 1167 4-9-1 **63** (b) NickyMackay 5 62
(Mark Rimmer) *hld up in tch: effrt whn n.m.r and swtchd lft wl over 1f out: sn rdn and no imp ins fnl f* **9/2**[1]
40-6 **6** 1½ **Sharakti (IRE)**[12] 1099 4-9-6 **68** SebSanders 11 64
(Alan McCabe) *chsd ldrs: effrt over 2f out: rdn wl over 1f out: drvn and wknd appr fnl f* **13/2**[2]

563- **7** ½ **Eltheeb**[67] 6856 4-9-7 **69** GregFairley 1 64
(George Moore) *dwlt and in rr: hdwy on wd outside over 2f out: sn rdn: kpt on: nt rch ldrs* **10/1**
524- **8** *nk* **Aegean Destiny**[162] 7307 4-8-10 **63** DeclanCannon(5) 7 57
(John Mackie) *in tch: hdwy to chse ldrs 3f out: rdn along 2f out: sn drvn and btn wl over 1f out* **11/1**
55-0 **9** 2 **Donna Elvira**[15] 1036 4-9-5 **67** TonyHamilton 10 57
(Edwin Tuer) *chsd ldrs: rdn along over 2f out: grad wknd* **22/1**
33-0 **10** 2¼ **Kingdom Of Munster (IRE)**[29] 839 4-9-0 **62** (b[1]) PaulHanagan 8 48
(Richard Fahey) *chsd ldrs: rdn along over 2f out: sn wknd* **15/2**
00-0 **11** ½ **Blue Spinnaker (IRE)**[12] 1099 12-8-6 **61** DavidSimmonson(7) 12 46
(Michael Easterby) *a towards rr* **25/1**
30-6 **12** 6 **Baltimore Jack (IRE)**[17] 1017 7-9-7 **69** DavidNolan 3 42
(G P Kelly) *a in rr* **25/1**
4-00 **13** *hd* **Politbureau**[15] 1035 4-8-12 **63** JamesSullivan(3) 6 36
(Michael Easterby) *a in rr* **50/1**
106- **14** 6 **Bollin Freddie**[160] 7330 7-8-5 **60** ShaneBKelly(7) 4 21
(Alan Lockwood) *a in rr: fin lame* **18/1**
425- **15** 28 **Tilos Gem (IRE)**[208] 6187 5-8-11 **59** AdrianNicholls 2 —
(David Nicholls) *rrd and lost several l s: a bhd: eased and t.o fnl 2f* **10/1**

2m 4.86s (-2.14) **Going Correction** -0.125s/f (Firm) **15** Ran SP% **123.1**
Speed ratings (Par 103): **103,101,100,100,98 97,96,96,94,93 92,87,87,83,60**
toteswingers:1&2 £23.70, 2&3 £19.50, 1&3 £20.80 CSF £80.73 CT £580.28 TOTE £13.80: £5.50, £4.70, £3.50; EX 78.90.
Owner Mr & Mrs K Hughes and Dr J Gozzard **Bred** Norelands Stallions **Trained** Hambleton, N Yorks
■ Stewards' Enquiry : Julie Burke one-day ban: used whip with excessive frequency (Apr 28)

FOCUS
Modest fare and a handy position proved vital, nothing ever threatening to get in a serious blow from off the pace. The winner built on a good comeback with a 5lb personal best.
Eltheeb Official explanation: jockey said gelding stumbled at start
Bollin Freddie Official explanation: vet said gelding finished lame
Tilos Gem(IRE) Official explanation: jockey said gelding moved poorly throughout

1325 GET MARRIED AT BEVERLEY RACECOURSE H'CAP 1m 4f 16y
3:10 (3:10) (Class 4) (0-85,85) 4-Y-O+ **£4,144** (£1,233; £616; £307) **Stalls** Low

Form RPR
600- **1** **Granston (IRE)**[173] 7084 10-9-7 **84** GrahamGibbons 3 92
(James Bethell) *trckd ldrs on inner: hdwy 2f out: rdn to chal ent fnl f: sn led and kpt on* **16/1**
0-21 **2** 1½ **Red Kestrel (USA)**[13] 1072 6-8-7 **75** JulieBurke(5) 10 80
(Kevin Ryan) *led: rdn along over 2f out: drvn over 1f out: hdd jst ins fnl f: no ex* **11/1**
440- **3** ¾ **Nave (USA)**[173] 7084 4-9-7 **85** GregFairley 7 89
(Mark Johnston) *trckd ldr: hdwy and cl up 3f out: rdn to chal 2f out: drvn and one pce ent fnl f* **13/2**[3]
04-5 **4** 3¾ **Arizona John (IRE)**[22] 948 6-9-0 **82** DeclanCannon(5) 9 80
(John Mackie) *trckd ldrs: hdwy on outer 3f out: rdn to chal 2f out and ev ch tl drvn and wknd appr fnl f* **9/1**
520- **5** ½ **Mons Calpe (IRE)**[160] 7337 5-8-7 **70** oh1 (b) SilvestreDeSousa 5 67
(Paul Cole) *trckd ldrs: effrt 3f out: rdn 2f out: wknd over 1f out* **16/1**
301- **6** ½ **Alubari**[131] 7703 4-8-7 **71** MartinLane 4 67
(David Simcock) *prom: pushed along over 3f out: rdn over 2f out and sn btn* **7/1**
/05- **7** 1¼ **Dr Livingstone (IRE)**[88] 6565 6-9-6 **83** SebSanders 1 77
(Charles Egerton) *hld up: a towards rr* **28/1**
U42- **8** 1¼ **Bahamian Music (IRE)**[165] 7253 4-9-3 **81** PaulHanagan 8 73
(Richard Fahey) *hld up: effrt and sme hdwy 3f out: sn rdn and btn 2f out* **3/1**[1]
600- **9** 2¼ **Green Lightning (IRE)**[212] 6050 4-9-2 **80** AdrianNicholls 2 69
(Mark Johnston) *a in rr* **11/1**
12-2 **10** 21 **Crunched**[9] 1144 4-8-3 **74** IanBurns(7) 6 29
(Michael Bell) *in tch: rdn along 4f out: wknd 3f out: sn bhd and eased fnl 2f: fin lame* **7/2**[2]

2m 36.71s (-3.09) **Going Correction** -0.125s/f (Firm)
WFA 4 from 5yo+ 1lb **10** Ran SP% **114.9**
Speed ratings (Par 105): **105,104,103,101,100 100,99,98,97,83**
toteswingers:1&2 £25.80, 2&3 £7.00, 1&3 £10.50 CSF £177.14 CT £1265.11 TOTE £20.80: £4.80, £3.70, £3.90; EX 169.20.
Owner Richard T Vickers **Bred** Yeomanstown Stud **Trained** Middleham Moor, N Yorks
■ Stewards' Enquiry : Ian Burns three-day ban: careless riding (Apr 19-21)

FOCUS
A fairly useful contest. As in the previous race it didn't pay to sit too far back, and not that many ever threatened a serious blow.
Crunched Official explanation: vet said gelding finished lame

1326 RACING UK STKS (H'CAP) 7f 100y
3:45 (3:46) (Class 3) (0-95,92) 3-Y-O **£6,676** (£1,986; £992; £495) **Stalls** Low

Form RPR
004- **1** **Belle Royale (IRE)**[192] 6627 3-9-0 **85** FrannyNorton 6 89
(Mark Brisbourne) *hld up: hdwy over 2f out: swtchd rt and rdn over 1f out: styd on wl u.p ins fnl f to ld last 50yds* **16/1**
14- **2** ½ **Common Touch (IRE)**[221] 5784 3-8-9 **80** PaulHanagan 3 83
(Richard Fahey) *trckd ldr: hdwy over 2f out and sn ev ch: rdn to ld over 1f out: sn drvn and edgd rt: hdd and no ex last 50yds* **5/4**[1]
1311 **3** 1¼ **Kingscroft (IRE)**[16] 1023 3-8-12 **83** GregFairley 5 83
(Mark Johnston) *led: rdn along and jnd 2f out: drvn and hdd appr fnl f: kpt on same pce* **7/2**[2]
100- **4** 2¼ **Orientalist**[200] 6386 3-9-2 **87** EddieAhern 4 81
(Eve Johnson Houghton) *trckd ldng pair: hdwy 3f out and sn cl up: rdn to chal and ev ch 2f out: drvn and wknd appr fnl f* **4/1**[3]
100- **5** 8 **Nasharra (IRE)**[194] 6568 3-9-7 **92** TomEaves 2 66
(Kevin Ryan) *hld up: effrt and sme hdwy on inner 3f out: rdn over 2f out and sn btn* **11/2**

1m 33.52s (-0.28) **Going Correction** -0.125s/f (Firm) **5** Ran SP% **107.9**
Speed ratings (Par 102): **96,95,94,91,82**
CSF £35.63 TOTE £16.60: £9.90, £1.02; EX 41.30.
Owner Peter Mort **Bred** Dxb Bloodstock Ltd **Trained** Great Ness, Shropshire

FOCUS
A bit of a surprise result with the outsider of the quintet prevailing, though there was no fluke about her success. The runner-up is probably the best long-term prospect, however.

NOTEBOOK
Belle Royale(IRE) took a busy juvenile campaign well, winning four of her 14 starts, and showed she's trained on well, the longer trip clearly suiting. She won twice at Chester last year and connections reportedly have a race in mind for her at the May meeting but, likeable though she is, it's hard to believe she won't prove vulnerable to something more progressive there. She's just as effective on a softer surface. (op 9-1)

Common Touch(IRE) has now been beaten at short odds on both starts in handicaps, but this was still an encouraging return and he'll improve as he gains in experience, particularly as he learns to settle - he was plenty keen enough in the first half of this race. (op 13-8 tchd Evens and 7-4 in a place)
Kingscroft(IRE) couldn't maintain his winning run on turf, but he clearly acts on it. Another small rise in the weights was just enough to find him out. (op 11-4)
Orientalist wasn't discredited on his reappearance, but he's had a fair bit of racing now and the overriding impression was that he'll always be vulnerable to less-exposed types off a mark in the mid-80s. (op 9-2)
Nasharra(IRE) boasted some pretty useful form as a juvenile but there was little encouragement to be drawn from this, as he was beaten before stamina should have been an issue. He's unlikely to be the easiest to place near to hand. (op 5-1 tchd 7-1)

1327 MOORENDS HOTEL'S OUTING H'CAP — 1m 1f 207y

4:20 (4:21) (Class 5) (0-70,69) 3-Y-O — **£2,298** (£684; £341; £170) **Stalls** Low

Form — RPR

022- **1** **Bouggatti**[188] 6717 3-9-3 **65** .... PaulHanagan 5 71+
(William Jarvis) *trckd ldrs: hdwy to chal over 2f out and sn rdn: drvn ent fnl f: kpt on to ld last 75yds: jst hld on* **11/4**[1]

441- **2** *shd* **Unknown Rebel (IRE)**[178] 6978 3-9-3 **65** .... SilvestreDeSousa 2 71
(Kevin Ryan) *led: rdn along 2f out: drvn over 1f out: hdd last 75yds: rallied wl nr line* **11/4**[1]

040- **3** *nk* **Jeu De Vivre (IRE)**[152] 7447 3-9-0 **62** .... GregFairley 3 68+
(Mark Johnston) *trckd ldng pair: effrt on inner whn n.m.r over 1f out: sn rdn and kpt on wl ins fnl f* **6/1**[2]

400- **4** *nk* **Kodicil (IRE)**[178] 6978 3-8-8 **56** oh8 ow1 .... GrahamGibbons 6 61
(Tim Walford) *awkward s: sn trcking ldr: effrt to chal over 2f out: sn rdn and ev ch tl drvn and nt qckn ins fnl f* **40/1**

500- **5** *2 1/2* **Dark Dune (IRE)**[204] 6300 3-9-1 **63** .... DavidAllan 4 63
(Tim Easterby) *hld up in rr: hdwy 2f out: rdn over 1f out: kpt on same pce ins fnl f* **12/1**[3]

-424 **6** *shd* **Imaginary World (IRE)**[59] 540 3-9-7 **69** .... SebSanders 7 68
(Alan McCabe) *hld up: swtchd outside and hdwy over 2f out: rdn to chal wl over 1f out and ev ch tl drvn and wknd ent fnl f* **16/1**

036- **7** *3 1/4* **Plattsburgh (USA)**[187] 6742 3-9-6 **68** .... AhmedAjtebi 1 61
(Mahmood Al Zarooni) *hld up in tch on inner: swtchd lft and hdwy over 2f out: rdn wl over 1f out and sn btn* **11/4**[1]

2m 6.50s (-0.50) **Going Correction** -0.125s/f (Firm) — **7** Ran SP% **110.3**
Speed ratings (Par 98): **97,96,96,96,94 94,91**
toteswingers:1&2 £2.60, 2&3 £4.00, 1&3 £3.90 CSF £9.44 TOTE £3.50: £1.90, £1.50; EX 11.50.

Owner E A Randall, A M Mitchell & G B Turnbull **Bred** Chippenham Lodge Stud **Trained** Newmarket, Suffolk

FOCUS
A tight betting affair and it worked out that way on the track, too, with under a length separating the first four. The form seems sound despite the fourth's proximity.
Plattsburgh(USA) Official explanation: jockey said gelding ran too free

1328 CONSTANT SECURITY MAIDEN STKS — 1m 100y

4:55 (4:56) (Class 5) 3-Y-O+ — **£2,298** (£684; £341; £170) **Stalls** Low

Form — RPR

0- **1** **Ektibaas**[251] 4803 3-8-12 0 .... SebSanders 5 76+
(B W Hills) *trckd ldrs: hdwy over 2f out: rdn and rn green over 1f out: drvn to chse ldr ins fnl f: styd on to ld on line* **8/15**[1]

23 **2** *nse* **Striking The Wind (USA)**[29] 873 3-8-12 0 .... GregFairley 8 76
(Mark Johnston) *led: rdn along 2f out: drvn 2 l clr ent fnl f: edgd lft and ct on line* **6/1**[2]

4 **3** *1* **Prime Mover**[19] 993 3-8-12 0 .... EddieAhern 4 74+
(Ed Dunlop) *hld up in tch: hdwy on inner 2f out: rdn ent fnl f: kpt on* **15/2**

465- **4** *9* **Flodden (USA)**[186] 6779 3-8-12 73 .... SilvestreDeSousa 6 53
(Paul Cole) *chsd ldng pair: hdwy and cl up over 2f out: rdn and ev ch wl over 1f out: sn edgd rt and wknd* **7/1**[3]

5 *2 1/2* **American Lover (FR)**[51] 4-9-3 0 .... DaleSwift(5) 3 46
(John Wainwright) *s.i.s: a in rr* **100/1**

6 *3 3/4* **Khalashan (FR)**[45] 5-9-13 0 .... TonyHamilton 7 43
(Peter Niven) *s.i.s: a in rr* **100/1**

02 **7** *4 1/2* **Red Copper**[27] 888 3-8-7 0 .... PaulHanagan 1 23
(Michael Bell) *chsd ldr: rdn along wl over 2f out: wknd wl over 1f out* **14/1**

1m 46.92s (-0.68) **Going Correction** -0.125s/f (Firm)
WFA 3 from 4yo+ 15lb — **7** Ran SP% **112.4**
Speed ratings (Par 103): **98,97,96,87,85 81,77**
toteswingers:1&2 £1.20, 2&3 £2.70, 1&3 £2.00 CSF £4.14 TOTE £1.50: £1.10, £1.70; EX 3.80.
Owner Hamdan Al Maktoum **Bred** Shadwell Estate Company Limited **Trained** Lambourn, Berks

FOCUS
Probably ordinary maiden form for the track, rated around the race averages. The first three came clear.

1329 NEXT RACEDAY HERE MONDAY 2ND MAY H'CAP — 7f 100y

5:30 (5:30) (Class 5) (0-70,73) 3-Y-O — **£2,298** (£684; £341; £170) **Stalls** Low

Form — RPR

316- **1** **Lady Gar Gar**[174] 7059 3-9-2 **65** .... SilvestreDeSousa 6 71
(Geoffrey Oldroyd) *trckd ldrs: pushed along and sltly outpcd 3f out: hdwy over 2f out: swtchd outside and rdn over 1f out: led ins fnl f: sn drvn and hung rt: jst hld on* **7/2**[3]

0062 **2** *shd* **Hugely Exciting**[26] 916 3-9-7 **70** ....(p) SamHitchcott 2 76
(J S Moore) *hld up towards rr: hdwy on inner over 2f out: chsd ldrs over 1f out: rdn and ev ch ins fnl f: no ex nr fin* **20/1**

00-3 **3** *1 3/4* **Philharmonic Hall**[15] 1038 3-9-2 **65** ....(p) PaulHanagan 4 67
(Richard Fahey) *stmbld s: sn chsng ldrs: hdwy over 2f out: rdn over 1f out: drvn to ld briefly ent fnl f: sn hdd and hld whn n.m.r towards fin* **13/2**

3422 **4** *3 1/4* **Verrazano**[8] 1169 3-8-9 **61** .... AmyRyan(3) 8 55
(Kevin Ryan) *cl up: rdn over 2f out: drvn and ev ch over 1f out: wknd ent fnl f* **9/4**[1]

1321 **5** *2 3/4* **City Legend**[8] 1169 3-9-10 **73** 6ex ....(bt) SebSanders 3 60
(Alan McCabe) *hld up in rr: sme hdwy on outer over 2f out: rdn wl over 1f out: sn no imp* **3/1**[2]

3132 **6** *nk* **Eilean Mor**[13] 1074 3-9-2 **65** .... TomEaves 1 51
(Bryan Smart) *led: rdn along over 2f out: drvn over 1f out: hdd & wknd ent fnl f* **8/1**

004- **7** *7* **Melancholy Hill (IRE)**[148] 7484 3-8-9 **58** .... EddieAhern 7 26
(Paul Cole) *s.i.s: a bhd* **14/1**

040- **8** *8* **Wolds Agent**[181] 6894 3-8-7 **56** oh1 ....(b[1]) DuranFentiman 5 —
(Tim Easterby) *chsd ldrs: rdn along 1/2-way: sn wknd* **33/1**

1m 33.82s (0.02) **Going Correction** -0.125s/f (Firm) — **8** Ran SP% **116.8**
Speed ratings (Par 98): **94,93,91,88,85 84,76,67**
toteswingers:1&2 £12.80, 2&3 £20.30, 1&3 £5.70 CSF £68.90 CT £442.43 TOTE £6.10: £1.70, £6.70, £3.10; EX 80.40.

Owner R C Bond **Bred** R C Bond **Trained** Brawby, N Yorks
■ Stewards' Enquiry : Silvestre De Sousa caution: careless riding.

FOCUS
The leaders went off too hard here, setting it up for those coming from off the pace. A clear personal best from the winner.
T/Plt: £177.50 to a £1 stake. Pool of £43,616.78 - 179.32 winning tickets. T/Qpdt: £16.90 to a £1 stake. Pool of £3,432.28 - 150.14 winning tickets JR

1308 KEMPTON (A.W) (R-H)

Thursday, April 14

OFFICIAL GOING: Standard
Wind: virtually nil Weather: dry

1330 JD PROMOTIONS FILLIES' H'CAP — 7f (P)

6:15 (6:15) (Class 5) (0-75,73) 4-Y-O+ — **£2,417** (£713; £357) **Stalls** Low

Form — RPR

42 **1** **Saddlers Bend (IRE)**[42] 747 5-8-11 **66** .... MatthewDavies(3) 4 77
(George Baker) *chsd ldng pair: rdn to chal over 1f out: drvn to ld 1f out: r.o wl: in command fnl 100yds* **9/1**

035- **2** *1 1/4* **Russian Rave**[186] 6772 5-9-4 **70** .... StephenCraine 6 78
(Jonathan Portman) *stdd s: hld up in last pair: pushed along and hdwy over 2f out: swtchd lft and gd hdwy 2f out: chsd wnr 1f out: r.o: a hld* **14/1**

1-42 **3** *3/4* **Sunset Kitty (USA)**[9] 1147 4-9-7 **73** ....(v) AdamKirby 7 79
(Walter Swinburn) *stdd s: hld up in last pair: shkn up and hdwy over 2f out: swtchd lft and hdwy u.p ent fnl f: styd on same pce ins fnl f* **11/4**[1]

566- **4** *1 3/4* **Suzy Alexander**[267] 4248 4-8-6 **63** .... LauraPike(5) 5 64
(David Simcock) *hld up in midfield: rdn and effrt on outer over 1f out: styd on same pce and no imp ins fnl f* **8/1**[3]

U013 **5** *3/4* **Perfect Ch'l (IRE)**[9] 1147 4-9-3 **69** .... JamesDoyle 3 68
(Ian Wood) *sn bustled along and led: rdn jst over 2f out: drvn and hdd 1f out: wknd ins fnl f* **4/1**[2]

1234 **6** *7* **Spinning Bailiwick**[15] 1054 5-9-3 **69** ....(b) GeorgeBaker 2 49
(Gary Moore) *hld up in tch in midfield: rdn and nt qckn ent fnl 2f: wknd over 1f out* **8/1**[3]

021- **7** *1 1/2* **Majestic Bright**[138] 7596 4-8-13 **65** .... KirstyMilczarek 1 41
(Luca Cumani) *w ldr tl jst over 2f out: wknd qckly over 1f out: wl bhd ins fnl f* **11/4**[1]

1m 24.82s (-1.18) **Going Correction** -0.125s/f (Stan) — **7** Ran SP% **112.2**
Speed ratings (Par 100): **101,99,98,96,95 87,86**
toteswingers:1&2 £12.20, 2&3 £12.00, 1&3 £4.00 CSF £113.49 TOTE £5.80: £2.20, £4.90; EX 65.50.
Owner Mrs Christine Cone **Bred** J F Tuthill **Trained** Whitsbury, Hants

FOCUS
A fair fillies' handicap run at a reasonable gallop. Straightforward form.

1331 CELEBRITYAPPEARANCE.CO.UK CLASSIFIED STKS — 6f (P)

6:45 (6:45) (Class 6) 3-Y-O+ — **£1,748** (£516; £258) **Stalls** Low

Form — RPR

000- **1** **Invigilator**[206] 6249 3-8-10 53 .... LukeMorris 4 56
(Harry Dunlop) *chsd ldrs: wnt 2nd 3f out: drvn to ld 1f out: styd on wl u.p ins fnl f* **7/2**[2]

0052 **2** *1* **Libertino (IRE)**[8] 1171 4-9-8 53 .... NeilCallan 9 56
(Tony Carroll) *in tch: rdn and effrt to chse ldng trio jst over 2f out: kpt on u.p ins fnl f: wnt 2nd nr fin* **9/4**[1]

445/ **3** *hd* **Bobby's Doll**[502] 7584 4-9-8 51 .... StevieDonohoe 1 55
(Terry Clement) *led: rdn wl over 1f out: drvn and hdd 1f out: styd on same pce ins fnl f: lost 2nd nr fin* **20/1**

5505 **4** *2 1/4* **Evey P (IRE)**[2] 1283 4-9-8 52 .... LiamKeniry 2 48+
(Gary Brown) *stdd s: t.k.h: hld up in rr: nt clr run wl over 2f out: switching lft 2f out: styd on u.p ins fnl f: nt rch ldrs* **7/1**

0-63 **5** *1 3/4* **Flying Cherry (IRE)**[29] 863 4-9-8 52 .... DaneO'Neill 6 42
(Jo Crowley) *hld up towards rr: hdwy and rdn jst over 2f out: plugged on u.p ins fnl f: nvr trbld ldrs* **8/1**

3660 **6** *2 1/4* **Duplicity**[5] 1244 4-9-5 55 ....(p) RobertLButler(3) 5 35
(Richard Guest) *t.k.h: chsd ldrs: rdn to chse ldng pair over 2f out: hrd drvn and unable qck over 1f out: wknd ins fnl f* **6/1**[3]

6-0U **7** *8* **Cinderella**[8] 1171 4-9-8 35 .... TomMcLaughlin 12 —
(Lucinda Featherstone) *dwlt: in midfield on outer: rn wd bnd 4f out: rdn and short-lived effrt over 2f out: wknd 2f out: wl bhd ins fnl f* **33/1**

000- **8** *1/2* **Sleights Boy (IRE)**[178] 6980 3-8-10 55 .... KellyHarrison 11 —
(Ian McInnes) *in tch in midfield: hung lft bnd 4f out: lost pl over 3f out: towards rr and wkng whn hmpd 2f out: wl btn after* **33/1**

065 **9** *1 1/4* **Celtic Whisper**[20] 959 3-8-10 53 ....(t) SteveDrowne 3 —
(Jeremy Gask) *in tch in midfield: rdn along and effrt on inner wl over 2f out: no hdwy and btn 2f out: sn wknd* **10/1**

5005 **10** *1* **Ability Girl**[13] 1078 3-8-10 54 .... JackMitchell 8 —
(Chris Wall) *dwlt: a in rr: rdn and no prog over 2f out: lost tch 2f out* **16/1**

005- **11** *12* **Pappas Fc**[314] 2692 4-9-8 30 ....(b[1]) RichardKingscote 10 —
(Milton Bradley) *chsd ldr tl 3f out: wknd u.p over 2f out: t.o ins fnl f* **100/1**

1m 12.64s (-0.46) **Going Correction** -0.125s/f (Stan)
WFA 3 from 4yo 12lb — **11** Ran SP% **117.5**
Speed ratings (Par 101): **98,96,96,93,91 88,77,76,75,73 57**
toteswingers:1&2 £2.60, 2&3 £8.90, 1&3 £10.20 CSF £11.36 TOTE £6.50: £2.40, £1.30, £2.70; EX 15.20 Trifecta £1329.90.
Owner David & Paul Hearson **Bred** Granham Farm And P Hearson Bloodstock **Trained** Lambourn, Berks

FOCUS
A very weak classified event and an unlikely source of future winners. The unexposed winner showed his first real form.
Bobby's Doll Official explanation: jockey said filly was struck on head by another's whip
Sleights Boy(IRE) Official explanation: jockey said gelding hung left on the bend
Pappas Fc Official explanation: jockey said gelding was unable to handle the bend

1332 ADEVENTS & HOSPITALITY MAIDEN FILLIES' STKS — 1m 4f (P)

7:15 (7:15) (Class 5) 3-4-Y-O — **£2,417** (£713; £357) **Stalls** Centre

Form — RPR

4- **1** **Field Of Miracles (IRE)**[166] 7232 3-8-8 0 .... WilliamBuick 7 84
(John Gosden) *mde virtually all: rdn ent fnl 2f: asserted over 1f out: styd on wl ins fnl f: gng away at fin: rdn out* **5/6**[1]

0- **2** *3* **Galivant (IRE)**[209] 6154 3-8-8 0 .... RobertWinston 1 79
(J W Hills) *chsd ldrs: rdn to chse wnr jst over 2f out tl over 1f out: chsd wnr again and swtchd lft jst ins fnl f: no imp* **9/1**[3]

0- **3** 2½ **Moment Juste**166 7231 3-8-8 0 .... RobertHavlin 8 75
(John Gosden) *in rr of main gp: pushed along 1/2-way: hdwy 3f out: chsd ldng pair wl over 1f out: wnt 2nd over 1f out tl jst ins fnl f: wknd fnl 100yds* **10/1**

0- **4** 7 **Armoise**174 7057 3-8-8 0 .... MartinDwyer 3 64
(Marco Botti) *chsd ldrs: chsd wnr 3f out tl jst over 2f out: wknd over 1f out* **15/8**2

0- **5** 15 **Pyjoma**192 6624 4-10-0 0 .... TonyCulhane 2 42
(Julia Feilden) *stdd s: detached in last tl clsd 1/2-way: struggling over 3f out: wnt modest 5th and no ch fnl 2f* **33/1**

6 2 **Willow The Rose**39 4-10-0 0 .... StephenCraine 4 39
(J R Jenkins) *s.i.s: sn in midfield: rdn and struggling over 3f out: wl bhd over 2f out* **33/1**

7 6 **Himalayan Moon** 4-10-0 0 .... JamesDoyle 5 29
(Ian Wood) *chsd wnr tl 3f out: sn rdn and lost pl qckly: t.o over 1f out* **33/1**

04 **8** 27 **Lauralu**43 737 3-8-8 0 .... LiamKeniry 6 —
(Michael Blanshard) *in tch in midfield tl dropped to last over 4f out: sn lost tch: t.o fr wl over 2f out* **50/1**

2m 32.18s (-2.32) **Going Correction** -0.125s/f (Stan)
WFA 3 from 4yo 21lb **8** Ran SP% **119.2**
Speed ratings (Par 100): **102,100,98,93,83 82,78,60**
toteswingers:1&2 £2.80, 2&3 £9.10, 1&3 £3.70 CSF £10.10 TOTE £2.20: £1.02, £3.10, £3.90; EX 9.50 Trifecta £37.40.
Owner Cheveley Park Stud **Bred** Epona Bloodstock Ltd **Trained** Newmarket, Suffolk

FOCUS
Not much strength in depth to this maiden for all three of them held an entry in the Oaks, including the first and second. The pace was only fair with the field still well bunched turning for home. Probably ordinary maiden form.
Lauralu Official explanation: trainer said filly lost its action

1333 PETER ANDRE AT KEMPTON 06.07.11 H'CAP — 1m (P)
7:45 (7:45) (Class 6) (0-65,65) 4-Y-0+ **£1,748** (£516; £258) **Stalls** Low

Form RPR
-325 **1** **Sasheen**83 248 4-9-3 **61** .... (p) AdamKirby 2 72
(Jeremy Gask) *mde virtually all: rdn and clr wl over 1f out: in command after: r.o wl* **15/2**3

0-45 **2** 3 **Crinan Classic**19 984 4-8-12 **56** .... LukeMorris 11 60+
(Clive Cox) *hld up in midfield: swtchd ins 5f out: rdn and hdwy over 2f out: pressing for placings ent fnl f: chsd wnr ins fnl f: no imp* **25/1**

-355 **3** ½ **One Oi**43 727 6-9-3 **61** .... LiamKeniry 1 64
(David Arbuthnot) *chsd ldrs: rdn to chse wnr wl over 1f out: drvn and no imp ent fnl f: styd on same pce after: lost 2nd fnl 100yds* **6/1**1

0-31 **4** hd **Madame Boot (FR)**51 640 4-9-2 **60** .... SteveDrowne 6 62
(Peter Makin) *sn pushed along and hdwy to chse wnr after 2f: drvn and nt gng pce of wnr 2f out: kpt on same pce u.p fr over 1f out* **7/1**2

1262 **5** ¾ **Clearing House**8 1184 6-8-13 **57** .... KirstyMilczarek 12 58+
(John Ryan) *hld up in midfield: hdwy 4f out: rdn and outpcd over 2f out: rallied u.p over 1f out: kpt on ins fnl f: no threat to ldrs* **6/1**1

-602 **6** 3¼ **Prince Of Thebes (IRE)**16 1026 10-9-7 **65** .... NeilCallan 4 58
(Michael Attwater) *dwlt: sn rdn along and rcvrd to r in midfield after 1f: rdn and unable qck over 2f out: wknd over 1f out* **15/2**3

0303 **7** 1¼ **Rainsborough**21 957 4-8-11 **55** .... (e) DaneO'Neill 10 45
(Peter Hedger) *stdd s: t.k.h: hld up in rr: swtchd lft and hdwy wl over 1f out: styd on ins fnl f: n.d* **8/1**

012- **8** ½ **Room For A View**141 7561 4-9-6 **64** .... (p) TedDurcan 14 53
(Marcus Tregoning) *hld up in rr: rdn and effrt jst over 2f out: styd on ins fnl f: nvr trbld ldrs* **15/2**3

0-50 **9** ½ **Valkov**36 814 4-8-4 **55** .... GeorgeDowning(7) 9 43
(Tony Carroll) *racd in midfield on outer: effrt and rdn ent fnl 2f: no prog* **20/1**

0-65 **10** 1 **Ocean Rosie (IRE)**6 1220 4-8-8 **52** .... JimmyQuinn 13 38
(Tony Carroll) *in tch: rdn and lost pl wl over 2f out: no ch fnl 2f* **50/1**

560- **11** ¾ **Hambledon Hill**371 1188 5-8-10 **54** .... RobertHavlin 3 38
(Paul Burgoyne) *hld up in rr: hdwy over 2f out: sn rdn: wknd wl over 1f out* **33/1**

4200 **12** nk **Having A Ball**22 949 7-9-3 **61** .... ChrisCatlin 8 44
(Jonathan Portman) *a in rr: n.d* **20/1**

4-30 **13** nk **Regal Rave (USA)**14 1058 4-9-4 **62** .... WilliamBuick 7 45
(Mouse Hamilton-Fairley) *chsd wnr for 2f: rdn and wknd qckly 2f out: wl btn 1f out* **8/1**

40-0 **14** 19 **Integria**36 802 5-9-5 **63** .... (p) TonyCulhane 5 —
(George Baker) *in tch in midfield: rdn and struggling over 2f out: wl bhd and eased ins fnl f: t.o* **33/1**

1m 38.82s (-0.98) **Going Correction** -0.125s/f (Stan) **14** Ran SP% **119.8**
Speed ratings (Par 101): **99,96,95,95,94 91,90,89,89,88 87,87,86,67**
toteswingers:1&2 £59.70, 2&3 £40.70, 1&3 £9.10 CSF £191.39 CT £1237.17 TOTE £6.50: £3.50, £10.30, £3.30; EX 253.60.
Owner Sashay Partnership **Bred** Edward J G Young **Trained** Sutton Veny, Wilts

FOCUS
A modest handicap and something of a tactical affair with the pace only fair and little getting into the race from behind. The first two are rated back to their maiden best.

1334 BRITISH BIG BAND 22.06.11 CLAIMING STKS — 6f (P)
8:15 (8:15) (Class 6) 3-Y-0 **£1,748** (£516; £258) **Stalls** Low

Form RPR
4142 **1** **Eternal Youth (IRE)**14 1056 3-8-11 67 .... (b) LukeMorris 2 62
(Ronald Harris) *t.k.h: hld up wl in tch: pushed along to chal between horses ent fnl f: pushed ahd fnl 75yds: kpt on* **9/2**2

04-0 **2** hd **Ezzles (USA)**15 1040 3-9-1 55 .... (t) ChrisCatlin 5 65
(Paul Cole) *led: rdn ent fnl 2f: hrd drvn 1f out: hdd fnl 75yds: r.o u.p: a jst hld* **14/1**

2012 **3** 2¼ **My Lord**8 1178 3-9-0 78 .... KierenFox(3) 3 60
(Bill Turner) *chsd ldr for 2f: wnt 2nd again and n.m.r over 2f out: drvn and ev ch 1f out: wknd fnl 75yds* **5/6**1

4246 **4** 1¼ **Fifth In Line (IRE)**8 1176 3-8-4 65 .... JimmyQuinn 6 43
(David Flood) *taken down early: hld up wl in tch: effrt on outer 2f out: drvn to chse ldrs over 1f out: wknd jst ins fnl f* **9/2**2

10-0 **5** 1¾ **Brave Battle**8 1176 3-9-9 68 .... DaneO'Neill 4 57
(Richard Hannon) *t.k.h: chsd ldr after 2f tl over 2f out: stl ev ch and rdn 2f out: wknd ent fnl f* **10/1**3

60- **6** 16 **Sue's Dream**185 6804 3-8-5 0 .... HarryBentley(5) 1 —
(Alan Jarvis) *awkward leaving stalls and s.i.s: sn rdn along: clsd and in tch 1/2-way: rdn and wknd wl over 2f out: t.o* **33/1**

1m 12.66s (-0.44) **Going Correction** -0.125s/f (Stan) **6** Ran SP% **109.6**
Speed ratings (Par 96): **97,96,93,92,89 68**
toteswingers:1&2 £4.70, 2&3 £4.70, 1&3 £1.50 CSF £54.86 TOTE £11.80: £2.00, £8.50; EX 38.80.
Owner Mrs Ruth M Serrell **Bred** John Malone **Trained** Earlswood, Monmouths

FOCUS
A fair claimer if something of a messy race and muddling form guide with the second causing a bit of trouble when finally across to the rail round the home bend. The winner is the best guide to the form.

1335 BISTRO IN THE PANORAMIC H'CAP — 7f (P)
8:45 (8:45) (Class 4) (0-80,80) 3-Y-0 **£4,129** (£1,228; £614; £306) **Stalls** Low

Form RPR
313- **1** **Rossetti**257 4578 3-9-4 **77** .... 1 PatCosgrave 4 84
(James Fanshawe) *hld up in rr: hdwy and swtchd lft over 1f out: str run u.p ins fnl f: led nr fin* **6/1**3

422- **2** ½ **Avid Kale**157 7379 3-9-0 **73** .... AdamKirby 8 79+
(Marco Botti) *hld up in rr: n.m.r over 2f out: stl last trio over 1f out: swtchd lft and hdwy ent fnl f: str run fnl 150yds: snatched 2nd last stride* **12/1**

011- **3** shd **Tamareen (IRE)**199 6426 3-8-13 **72** .... TadhgO'Shea 2 77
(Ed Dunlop) *in tch in midfield: pushed along and hmpd over 3f out: n.m.r 2f out: edgd rt and gd hdwy to chal over 1f out: drvn to ld jst over 1f out: hdd and lost 2 pls nr fin* **11/2**2

0112 **4** ¾ **May's Boy**12 1106 3-9-7 **80** .... (p) DaneO'Neill 9 83
(Mark Usher) *t.k.h: chsd ldrs: n.m.r on inner tl rdn and effrt ent fnl 2f: chsd ldr 1f out: styd on same pce and lost 2 pls fnl 100yds* **8/1**

211- **5** 1 **Ree's Rascal (IRE)**162 7296 3-8-8 **67** .... NickyMackay 10 68
(Jim Boyle) *in tch: pushed along over 3f out: rdn wl over 2f out: chsd ldrs u.p over 1f out: no ex and one pce ins fnl f* **14/1**

3-11 **6** 3 **Flynn's Boy**41 764 3-9-4 **77** .... MartinLane 5 70+
(Rae Guest) *short of room sn after s and dropped in rr: rdn over 4f out: hdwy on outer over 1f out: kpt on u.p ins fnl f: nvr trbld ldrs* **13/2**

1531 **7** 1¼ **Silly Billy (IRE)**27 886 3-8-10 **76** .... LukeRowe(7) 1 65
(Sylvester Kirk) *chsd ldrs: sltly hmpd and lost pl after 2f: swtchd ins and pushed along ent fnl 2f: kpt on same pce and no imp after* **25/1**

25-2 **8** nk **Homeboy (IRE)**8 1176 3-8-7 **66** oh1 .... HayleyTurner 6 54
(Marcus Tregoning) *chsd ldrs: wnt 2nd after 2f: pushed ahd over 2f out: drvn over 1f out: sn hdd and btn: wknd qckly ins fnl f* **9/2**1

401- **9** ½ **Adorable Choice (IRE)**168 7185 3-9-0 **73** .... RichardKingscote 11 60
(Tom Dascombe) *racd wd in midfield: rdn and effrt over 2f out: no imp and no threat to ldrs fnl 2f* **20/1**

231- **10** hd **Never Never Land**167 7210 3-9-2 **75** .... WilliamBuick 12 61+
(John Gosden) *chsd ldrs: rdn and unable qck jst over 2f out: nt clr run 2f out: swtchd rt and rdn 1f out: no prog: eased towards fin* **6/1**3

10-5 **11** 2¼ **Miss Boops (IRE)**26 907 3-9-1 **74** .... IanMongan 7 54
(Zoe Davison) *short of room s and sn bhd: edgd lft ins fnl f: n.d* **50/1**

522- **12** 1¾ **Khaleeji**174 7065 3-9-5 **78** .... ChrisCatlin 3 54
(J W Hills) *led: crossed to rail after 2f: rdn and hdd over 2f out: wkng whn pushed rt 2f: sn bhd* **12/1**

1m 24.87s (-1.13) **Going Correction** -0.125s/f (Stan) **12** Ran SP% **119.2**
Speed ratings (Par 100): **101,100,100,99,98 94,93,93,92,92 89,87**
toteswingers:1&2 £30.00, 2&3 £18.30, 1&3 £8.10 CSF £74.67 CT £429.72 TOTE £10.20: £4.00, £4.60, £3.30; EX 97.10.
Owner Dragon Gate **Bred** Bricklow Ltd **Trained** Newmarket, Suffolk

FOCUS
A fairly useful handicap with several progressive sorts on show. It was run at a good pace, the front-runners setting things up for those behind, and the form is probably decent for the grade. Personal bests from the first two.

1336 RACING UK H'CAP — 6f (P)
9:15 (9:15) (Class 6) (0-55,55) 4-Y-0+ **£1,748** (£516; £258) **Stalls** Low

Form RPR
064- **1** **Dashwood**113 7960 4-9-2 **55** .... WilliamCarson 9 70+
(Giles Bravery) *stdd s: hld up in rr: c wd and effrt 2f out: str run and hung rt fr jst over 1f out: led jst ins fnl f: sn clr: r.o wl* **7/4**1

-001 **2** 2¾ **Running Mate (IRE)**35 821 4-9-0 **53** .... (t) IanMongan 11 59
(Jo Crowley) *in tch: rdn effrt jst over 2f out: hdwy u.p over 1f out: chsd wnr fnl 50yds: no imp* **11/1**

4325 **3** ½ **Bold Diva**15 1041 6-8-13 **52** .... (v) LukeMorris 5 56
(Tony Carroll) *hld up in tch: swtchd ins and hdwy ent fnl 2f: chsd ldrs over 1f out: chsd ldr over 1f out and wnr ins fnl f: no imp: lost 2nd fnl 50yds* **8/1**

3042 **4** 1 **Misaro (GER)**8 1180 10-9-2 **55** .... (b) DavidProbert 8 56+
(Ronald Harris) *chsd ldrs on outer: unable qck u.p and outpcd 2f out: rallied under ins fnl f: no ch w wnr* **4/1**3

0466 **5** ½ **White Shift (IRE)**8 1171 5-8-12 **54** .... KierenFox(3) 12 54
(Michael Squance) *stdd s: sn outpcd and detached in last: rdn and hdwy over 1f out: styd on ins fnl f: nt rch ldrs* **25/1**

1606 **6** 1 **Lethal**5 1248 8-8-10 **54** .... (t) AdamBeschizza(5) 4 50
(Richard Price) *chsd ldr: rdn and unable qck 2f out: lost 2nd over 1f out: wknd 1f out* **20/1**

3644 **7** hd **Athwaab**36 812 4-9-0 **53** .... AdamKirby 1 49
(Noel Quinlan) *led: rdn and wnt clr 2f out: hdd jst ins fnl f: sn wknd* **15/2**

/02- **8** shd **River Bounty**137 7607 6-8-8 **52** .... HarryBentley(5) 7 47
(Alan Jarvis) *chsd ldrs: rdn and effrt jst over 2f out: wknd u.p ent fnl f* **14/1**

2205 **9** 7 **Royal Acclamation (IRE)**8 1182 6-8-9 **55** .... (p) DavidKenny(7) 3 28
(Michael Scudamore) *chsd ldrs tl wknd u.p wl over 1f out: wl bhd ins fnl f* **10/3**2

1m 11.9s (-1.20) **Going Correction** -0.125s/f (Stan) **9** Ran SP% **125.9**
Speed ratings (Par 101): **103,99,98,97,96 95,95,94,85**
toteswingers:1&2 £7.60, 2&3 £6.50, 1&3 £7.30 CSF £26.09 CT £136.78 TOTE £3.50: £1.90, £4.30, £1.80; EX 41.00 Trifecta £296.30.
Owner Macattack, William Lea Screed & Form IT **Bred** Darley **Trained** Cowlinge, Suffolk

FOCUS
A modest handicap run at a decent pace and a win for the unexposed, gambled-on Dashwood. He should do better. The second ran to his C&D latest.
T/Plt: £1,218.60 to a £1 stake. Pool of £56,926.67 - 34.10 winning tickets. T/Qpdt: £73.00 to a £1 stake. Pool of £6,760.75 - 68.45 winning tickets. SP

1315 NEWMARKET (R-H)

Thursday, April 14

OFFICIAL GOING: Good to firm (good in places; 9.1)

Far side track used with stalls on stands' side.

Wind: Light half-behind Weather: Overcast

1337 EBF JOHN FAIREY RETIREMENT MAIDEN FILLIES' STKS 5f

1:50 (1:50) (Class 4) 2-Y-O **£4,533** (£1,348; £674; £336) **Stalls** High

Form RPR

4 **1** **Princess Banu**[7] 1199 2-9-0 0 .... ChrisCatlin 3 80+
(Mick Channon) *mde all: rdn out* **11/1**

2 *1¾* **Royal Blush** 2-9-0 0 .... FrankieDettori 8 74+
(Paul Cole) *hld up in tch: pushed along 1/2-way: r.o to go 2nd wl ins fnl f: nt rch wnr* **4/1**[2]

3 *¾* **Guru Girl** 2-9-0 0 .... AndrewElliott 7 71
(Mrs K Burke) *chsd wnr 4f out: rdn over 1f out: styd on same pce and lost 2nd wl ins fnl f* **25/1**

4 *1* **Dark Ages (IRE)** 2-9-0 0 .... AdamKirby 9 67
(Noel Quinlan) *chsd ldrs: rdn over 1f out: styd on same pce ins fnl f* **11/2**[3]

5 *2¾* **Marie's Fantasy** 2-9-0 0 .... KierenFallon 1 58
(Gay Kelleway) *prom: pushed along 1/2-way: styd on same pce appr fnl f* **25/1**

6 *½* **My Solitaire (IRE)** 2-9-0 0 .... LukeMorris 6 56
(Clive Cox) *sn pushed along in rr: styd on ins fnl f: nvr nrr* **7/1**

7 *2¼* **Steady The Buffs** 2-9-0 0 .... NeilCallan 4 48
(Hugo Palmer) *chsd ldrs: rdn 1/2-way: hung lft and wknd over 1f out* **66/1**

8 *3½* **Tea Cup** 2-9-0 0 .... RichardHughes 2 44+
(Richard Hannon) *s.s: outpcd* **6/4**[1]

9 *nk* **Liesl (IRE)** 2-9-0 0 .... PhillipMakin 5 34+
(Kevin Ryan) *s.i.s: sn pushed along and a in rr* **11/1**

60.22 secs (1.12) **Going Correction** +0.075s/f (Good) **9** Ran SP% **113.7**

Speed ratings (Par 91): **94,91,90,88,84 83,79,74,73**

toteswingers:1&2 £7.10, 2&3 £12.50, 1&3 £20.60 CSF £52.94 TOTE £10.90: £2.30, £1.70, £4.40; EX 52.80 Trifecta £402.80 Pool of £544.39 - 1.00 winning units..

Owner Mrs T Burns **Bred** T R G Vestey **Trained** West Ilsley, Berks

FOCUS

This maiden has produced some decent sorts in recent years including Flashy Wings (2005) and Silk Blossom (2006), both of whom went on to win the Lowther. A timely reminder, were it needed, of how much of an advantage a previous run can be at this time of year. The time was decent and the winner is rated at the top end of the race averages.

NOTEBOOK

Princess Banu was the only one with experience, having finished fourth of eight at Ripon seven days earlier. That form is nothing special, but she knew her job here, breaking well and soon getting across to the stands' rail. She knew too much for her rivals where it mattered and she had obviously learned a great deal from her debut performance. A small filly, Chester may be next, where the track ought to suit her. (op 12-1 tchd 10-1)

Royal Blush ◆, a half-sister to six winners over a variety of trips, stayed on very nicely up the nearside rail to grab second and Frankie was by no means hard on her. Her performance can be raised a notch as she didn't see much daylight passing the 2f pole and she shouldn't take long in going one better. (op 5-1)

Guru Girl, a £10,000 filly out of a 7f winner, was always in about the same place and kept on well. She can win races and shapes as though an extra furlong will suit eventually.

Dark Ages(IRE) ◆, a 36,000gns half-sister to six winners (mainly over sprint distances), also kept on well having been handy from the off. She is a May foal, so was much the youngest in the field and should therefore have a fair amount of improvement in her. (tchd 6-1 in places)

Marie's Fantasy, a 4,500gns half-sister to a couple of winners at up to 7f, showed some ability.

Tea Cup was all the rage in the market, but she took an age to get into stride and lost her race there and then. She wasn't knocked about once all hope had gone Richard Hughes reported that the filly moved poorly after leaving the stalls. This 65,000euros half-sister to the useful 7f winner Forest Storm seems sure to leave this debut running well behind. Official explanation: jockey said filly moved poorly after leaving stalls (op 11-8 tchd 13-8 and 7-4 in places)

1338 GREVILLE STARKEY WOOD DITTON STKS 1m

2:25 (2:26) (Class 4) 3-Y-O **£5,180** (£1,541; £770; £384) **Stalls** High

Form RPR

1 **Midsummer Fair (USA)** 3-9-3 0 .... MickaelBarzalona 9 89+
(Mahmood Al Zarooni) *led: hdd over 6f out: chsd ldrs tl led again over 2f out: styd on wl* **6/1**[3]

2 *3* **Air Traffic** 3-9-3 0 .... TomQueally 8 82+
(Sir Henry Cecil) *s.i.s: hld up: hdwy over 2f out: r.o to go 2nd ins fnl f: no ch w wnr* **6/1**[3]

3 *1¾* **Laashak (USA)** 3-9-3 0 .... RichardHills 13 78+
(Sir Michael Stoute) *hld up: hdwy over 2f out: swtchd rt over 1f out: r.o: nrst fin* **12/1**

4 *2* **England Rules (IRE)** 3-9-3 0 .... WilliamBuick 11 73
(Jeremy Noseda) *chsd ldrs: rdn over 2f out: styd on same pce ins fnl f* **16/1**

5 *½* **Above Standard (IRE)** 3-9-3 0 .... MichaelHills 3 72
(B W Hills) *prom: rdn and ev ch over 1f out: wknd ins fnl f* **7/2**[1]

6 *nk* **Ashiri (IRE)** 3-9-0 0 .... LouisBeuzelin(3) 7 71+
(Sir Michael Stoute) *mid-div: hdwy over 4f out: rdn over 2f out: styd on same pce fr over 1f out* **10/1**

7 *1¼* **The Guru Of Gloom (IRE)** 3-9-3 0 .... RichardHughes 2 68+
(William Muir) *hld up: swtchd lft over 1f out: r.o ins fnl f: nvr nrr* **33/1**

8 *½* **Enjoy Today (USA)** 3-9-3 0 .... MartinDwyer 5 67
(Brian Meehan) *prom: lost pl over 5f out: hdwy over 3f out: wknd over 1f out* **10/1**

9 *2¾* **Arch Fire (USA)** 3-9-3 0 .... RyanMoore 4 60+
(Sir Michael Stoute) *s.i.s: sn pushed along in rr: nvr nrr* **9/2**[2]

10 *1* **Dffra (IRE)** 3-8-12 0 .... PhilipRobinson 10 53
(Clive Brittain) *plld hrd: led over 6f out: hdd over 2f out: wknd over 1f out* **16/1**

11 *1¼* **Nuzool (IRE)** 3-9-3 0 .... TadhgO'Shea 14 55
(John Dunlop) *s.i.s: a in rr* **66/1**

12 *¾* **Galloping Minister (IRE)** 3-9-3 0 .... RichardKingscote 6 53
(Tom Dascombe) *chsd ldrs tl wknd over 1f out* **66/1**

13 *65* **Donnaconna (CAN)** 3-9-3 0 .... FrankieDettori 12 —
(Mark Johnston) *prom tl rdn over 3f out: sn wknd: t.o* **12/1**

1m 39.76s (1.16) **Going Correction** +0.075s/f (Good) **13** Ran SP% **120.2**

Speed ratings (Par 100): **97,94,92,90,89 89,88,87,84,83 82,81,16**

toteswingers:1&2 £8.20, 2&3 £15.10, 1&3 £16.60 CSF £41.90 TOTE £7.30: £2.60, £3.00, £4.40; EX 50.30 Trifecta £363.30 Part won. Pool of £490.96 - 0.20 winning units..

Owner Godolphin **Bred** Diane Harrington **Trained** Newmarket, Suffolk

■ The name of former top jockey Greville Starkey, who died last year, has been added to the race title.

FOCUS

It's a long time since the Wood Ditton produced a winner of any real significance but this may have been a fair renewal. It threatened to be run at a crawl until Dffra pulled her way to the front after 2f. It's hard not to be taken by the performance of the winner, however, whilst there were some eye-catching performances in behind.

The Guru Of Gloom(IRE) ◆ Official explanation: jockey said gelding was denied a clear run

Arch Fire(USA) Official explanation: jockey said colt missed the break

1339 £250,000 TATTERSALLS MILLIONS 3-Y-O TROPHY 1m 2f

3:00 (3:02) (Class 2) 3-Y-O

£139,449 (£57,046; £25,382; £12,665; £6,332; £2,522) **Stalls** High

Form RPR

466- **1** **Auld Burns**[194] 6560 3-9-3 96 .... JamieSpencer 13 100+
(Richard Hannon) *stdd s: hld up: hdwy over 2f out: rdn and hung lft over 1f out: r.o to ld nr fin* **25/1**

242- **2** *½* **Measuring Time**[166] 7236 3-9-3 105 .... RichardHughes 3 99
(Richard Hannon) *a.p: chsd ldr over 2f out: led over 1f out: sn rdn: hdd nr fin* **9/2**[2]

15- **3** *1* **Questioning (IRE)**[194] 6560 3-9-3 93 .... WilliamBuick 6 97+
(John Gosden) *hld up: hdwy over 2f out: rdn over 1f out: edgd lft: styd on* **11/2**[3]

613- **4** *¾* **Namibian (IRE)**[174] 7059 3-9-3 82 .... RichardHills 9 97+
(Mark Johnston) *chsd ldrs: rdn over 3f out: styng on whn hmpd wl ins fnl f: nt rcvr* **40/1**

235- **5** *2* **Together (IRE)**[160] 7340 3-8-12 0 .... CO'Donoghue 5 86
(A P O'Brien, Ire) *hld up in tch: rdn and n.m.r over 1f out: styng on same pce whn hmpd wl ins fnl f* **15/8**[1]

1- **6** *nk* **Chef**[185] 6802 3-9-3 78 .... JimmyFortune 8 91+
(Andrew Balding) *hld up in tch: racd keenly: outpcd over 2f out: r.o ins fnl f* **25/1**

01-1 **7** *nk* **Sadler's Risk (IRE)**[14] 1057 3-9-3 94 .... JoeFanning 4 91
(Mark Johnston) *led: rdn over 2f out: hdd over 1f out: no ex ins fnl f* **15/2**

165- **8** *½* **Date With Destiny (IRE)**[180] 6927 3-8-12 96 .... RyanMoore 2 84
(Richard Hannon) *hld up: rdn over 1f out: r.o ins fnl f: nrst fin* **14/1**

404- **9** *3¼* **Madawi**[173] 7095 3-9-3 96 ....(b[1]) PhilipRobinson 1 83
(Clive Brittain) *hld up: hdwy on outer over 6f out: rdn and wkng whn hmpd over 1f out* **20/1**

0-45 **10** *1¼* **Janood (IRE)**[49] 680 3-9-3 0 ....(vt) FrankieDettori 14 80
(Saeed Bin Suroor) *hld up: rdn over 2f out: nvr trbld ldrs* **16/1**

-32 **11** *1* **Rojo Boy**[61] 520 3-9-3 72 ....(b) DaneO'Neill 11 78?
(David Elsworth) *hld up: nvr on terms* **150/1**

00-2 **12** *nk* **Lucky Legs (IRE)**[10] 1139 3-8-12 0 .... MichaelHills 10 72
(B W Hills) *hld up: hdwy over 4f out: rdn over 2f out: n.m.r and wknd over 1f out* **66/1**

2-33 **13** *13* **The Bells O Peover**[12] 1096 3-9-3 73 .... RoystonFfrench 7 51
(Mark Johnston) *chsd ldrs tl wknd over 2f out* **100/1**

10- **14** *15* **State Opera**[194] 6560 3-9-3 92 .... KierenFallon 12 21
(Mark Johnston) *chsd ldrs: rdn over 3f out: wkng whn hmpd over 2f out* **12/1**

2m 4.47s (-1.33) **Going Correction** +0.075s/f (Good) **14** Ran SP% **118.4**

Speed ratings (Par 104): **108,107,106,106,104 104,104,103,101,100 99,99,88,76**

toteswingers:1&2 £20.60, 2&3 £5.50, 1&3 £24.90 CSF £128.10 TOTE £34.40: £7.40, £1.90, £2.10; EX 160.00 Trifecta £916.50 Part won. Pool: £1238.51 - 0.03 winning units..

Owner P A Byrne **Bred** Simon Tindall **Trained** East Everleigh, Wilts

FOCUS

The early pace looked ordinary but the time was significantly faster than the later handicap. It resulted in a 1-2 for trainer Richard Hannon. The winner produced a 6lb personal best to reverse last year's form with the second and third.

NOTEBOOK

Auld Burns, gelded since last season, put up a remarkable performance to win this. Occupying last place for much of the way, his rider was forced to take him out wide in order to get a run and, despite hanging running out of the Dip, he stayed on to mug his stablemate close to the line. His stamina wasn't assured, so the modest early pace would have helped him. (op 33-1)

Measuring Time, a Dante entry, had already proved his stamina for this trip over C&D on his final start at two and previously had six of today's rivals behind him when fourth in the Tattersalls Millions 2-Y-O Trophy. He was brought with his effort at just the right time, but couldn't stamp his authority on the contest and was run out of it. (op 5-1)

Questioning(IRE) ◆ had suggested that the step up to this trip would suit in both outings last year. He looked dangerous when produced with his effort entering the last quarter-mile, but his head-carriage suggested that he wasn't handling the Dip very well and he couldn't quicken up the final climb. The best of him is still to be seen. (op 5-1 tchd 6-1)

Namibian(IRE), one of four from the yard, had plenty to find on form but he is bred to have appreciated this longer trip. Unfortunately he endured a nightmare run inside the last furlong when still in with every chance, but his problems may have been partly of his own making as he was hanging. Richard Hills reported that he was denied a clear run and the colt can continue to improve. Official explanation: jockey said colt was denied a clear run (op 33-1)

Together(IRE), by far the highest-rated horse in the field, was tried at the very highest level after winning a Group 3 at Leopardstown last July, though she was a beaten favourite in a valuable fillies' sales race on soft ground here in October. Having been keen early, she had every chance a furlong out but then faded as though not staying. (op 9-4)

Chef ◆, a Derby entry and winner of a 7f maiden on his one start at two, wasn't guaranteed to stay on pedigree and seemed to be ridden with that in mind. Keen enough early, the way he ran on late suggests that the trip wasn't a problem and there should be better to come from him. (op 20-1)

Sadler's Risk(IRE) held an advantage in fitness having easily won a four-runner handicap over nearly 1m4f on his Leicester return. Attempting to make all once again, he did his best but was picked off inside the last furlong and was beaten when hampered close to the line. Joe Fanning reported that he was denied a clear run. Official explanation: jockey said colt was denied a clear run (op 8-1)

Date With Destiny(IRE), a 1,000 Guineas and Oaks entry, wasn't disgraced in the Prestige and Rockfel in her last two starts at two and was trying beyond 7f for the first time. She didn't run badly considering she saw plenty of daylight on the outside and seemed to be hating the track. (op 16-1)

The Bells O Peover Official explanation: jockey said gelding hung both ways inside final furlong

1340 CONNAUGHT ACCESS FLOORING ABERNANT STKS (LISTED RACE) 6f

3:35 (3:37) (Class 1) 3-Y-O+

£17,031 (£6,456; £3,231; £1,611; £807; £405) **Stalls** High

Form RPR

342- **1** **Genki (IRE)**[187] 6735 7-9-5 111 ....(v) SteveDrowne 7 112
(Roger Charlton) *hld up: hdwy over 2f out: rdn to ld ins fnl f: jst hld on* **12/1**

2121 **2** *nk* **Iver Bridge Lad**[8] 1186 4-9-5 105..........(b) JimmyQuinn 4 111
(John Ryan) *chsd ldrs: rdn to ld ins fnl f: edgd lft and sn hdd: r.o* **11/2**[2]

024- **3** *nse* **Dinkum Diamond (IRE)**[187] 6734 3-8-7 106.......... DaneO'Neill 9 108+
(Henry Candy) *hld up: hdwy and nt clr run over 1f out: swtchd rt: r.o wl* **10/1**

-121 **4** *1* **Anne Of Kiev (IRE)**[19] 989 6-9-4 98..........(t) LukeMorris 5 107
(Jeremy Gask) *hld up: r.o ins fnl f: nrst fin* **28/1**

561- **5** *nk* **Inler (IRE)**[173] 7083 4-9-5 106.......... MartinDwyer 12 107
(Brian Meehan) *chsd ldrs: rdn over 2f out: styd on* **8/1**[3]

00-0 **6** *nk* **Prime Defender**[12] 1093 7-9-5 107.......... RobertWinston 13 106
(B W Hills) *chsd ldr: rdn and ev ch over 1f out: styd on same pce ins fnl f* **14/1**

156- **7** *½* **Bounty Box**[200] 6390 5-9-0 102.......... GeorgeBaker 6 99
(Chris Wall) *led: rdn over 1f out: hdd and no ex ins fnl f* **20/1**

6631 **8** *nk* **Jimmy Styles**[12] 1093 7-9-9 107..........(p) AdamKirby 10 107
(Clive Cox) *s.i.s: hld up: r.o ins fnl f: nvr nrr* **12/1**

100- **9** *¾* **Poet's Place (USA)**[187] 6752 6-9-5 102.......... PhillipMakin 3 101
(David Barron) *prom: rdn whn hmpd 1f out: no ex* **8/1**[3]

220- **10** *nk* **Society Rock (IRE)**[279] 3870 4-9-5 115.......... PatCosgrave 8 100
(James Fanshawe) *hld up: hdwy over 1f out: no ex ins fnl f* **11/4**[1]

-040 **11** *2* **Doncaster Rover (USA)**[12] 1093 5-9-5 104.......... FrankieDettori 11 93
(David Brown) *chsd ldrs: sn pushed along: lost pl wl over 2f out* **16/1**

340- **12** *1* **Himalya (IRE)**[180] 6923 5-9-5 110.......... JamieSpencer 1 90
(Jeremy Noseda) *dwlt: a in rr* **12/1**

2143 **13** *3½* **Brave Prospector**[12] 1093 6-9-5 104..........(t) TomQueally 2 79
(Jane Chapple-Hyam) *sn pushed along and a in rr* **25/1**

1m 11.12s (-1.08) **Going Correction** +0.075s/f (Good)
WFA 3 from 4yo+ 12lb **13** Ran SP% **121.0**
Speed ratings (Par 111): **110,109,109,108,107 107,106,106,105,104 102,100,96**
toteswingers:1&2 £7.40, 2&3 £11.10, 1&3 £12.10 CSF £75.87 TOTE £10.20: £3.90, £3.20, £4.20; EX 58.00 TRIFECTA Not won..
Owner Ms Gillian Khosla **Bred** Rathbarry Stud **Trained** Beckhampton, Wilts

FOCUS

A competitive Abernant with five of these having clashed in the Cammidge Trophy at Doncaster earlier this month. That said this looked an ordinary renewal, best rated around the front pair.

NOTEBOOK

Genki(IRE) was one of the highest rated in the field and ended last season with a narrow defeat in an Ascot Group 3. Although he has gone well fresh in the past, his trainer felt he may need it this time but his fears proved unfounded. He ran on well down the outside of the field when asked and hit the front well inside the last furlong. He looks better than ever and may go for the Duke Of York next month. (op 9-1)

Iver Bridge Lad was weighted to reverse Cammidge Trophy form with Jimmy Styles and duly did so, holding every chance until the winner pounced late. This effort is all the more meritorious considering he was off the bridle earlier than most and he holds his form remarkably well. He may be given a short break now. (op 6-1tched 13-2 in places)

Dinkum Diamond(IRE), a smart juvenile sprinter last season including finishing runner-up in the Flying Childers, was bidding to become the first 3-y-o to win this since 1996 (though few have tried in the meantime). His trainer was keen to find out whether he stays 6f and this staying-on performance suggested he does.

Anne Of Kiev(IRE), who has been in cracking form on Polytrack during the winter, ran on well down the wide outside to finish a very respectable fourth, and this was as good a performance as she has ever put up. (op 40-1)

Inler(IRE), having only his sixth outing, was travelling as well as anything coming to the last furlong but didn't find as much off the bridle as had looked likely. His trainer thought he might need it and he should attract interest when he goes to the sales.

Prime Defender has been disappointing since winning the Duke Of York last May, but he had every chance here and this was a better effort than in the Cammidge Trophy. (op 12-1)

Bounty Box, winner of a fillies' Listed race at Pontefract last August, made the running until carrying her head to one side and hanging racing out of the Dip.

Poet's Place(USA) ended last season on a low note, but he was in great form before that including winning the Portland. He ran well for a long way here and should come on for it. (tchd 15-2 and 9-1)

Society Rock(IRE), the highest rated in the field on account of his second in last season's Golden Jubilee, hadn't been seen since finishing seventh in the following month's July Cup, but he did win on his reappearance last season and was reported to have thrived during his absence. He never managed to land a blow but was later reported to be coughing. (op 10-3 tchd 7-2 in places)

1341 BREEZE UP VENDORS CRAVEN STKS (GROUP 3) (C&G) 1m

4:10 (4:11) (Class 1) 3-Y-O

£28,385 (£10,760; £5,385; £2,685; £1,345; £675) **Stalls** High

Form RPR

114- **1** **Native Khan (FR)**[173] 7081 3-8-12 111.......... KierenFallon 1 111+
(Ed Dunlop) *racd keenly: sn trcking ldrs: led over 1f out: styd on: in command whn hung lft towards fin* **8/11**[1]

165- **2** *2* **Libranno**[208] 6192 3-9-1 112.......... RyanMoore 5 109
(Richard Hannon) *led: rdn and hdd over 1f out: styd on same pce ins fnl f* **4/1**[2]

21- **3** *hd* **Yaseer (IRE)**[120] 7873 3-8-12 85.......... RichardHills 6 105+
(Marcus Tregoning) *chsd ldr: rdn and ev ch over 2f out: outpcd over 1f out: styd on u.p towards fin* **9/2**[3]

100- **4** *3¼* **Casual Glimpse**[196] 6507 3-8-12 97.......... RichardHughes 3 98
(Richard Hannon) *prom: rdn over 2f out: wknd ins fnl f* **16/1**

4220 **5** *2¼* **Ahlaain (USA)**[19] 998 3-8-12 100.......... WilliamBuick 4 93
(David Simcock) *s.i.s: in rr: rdn over 2f out: wknd over 1f out* **20/1**

0-4 **6** *10* **Yahafedh Alaih**[19] 992 3-8-12 0.......... PhilipRobinson 2 70?
(Clive Brittain) *hld up: rdn over 2f out: stmbld and wknd wl over 1f out* **66/1**

1m 37.56s (-1.04) **Going Correction** +0.075s/f (Good) **6** Ran SP% **108.2**
Speed ratings (Par 108): **108,106,105,102,100 90**
toteswingers:1&2 £1.20, 2&3 £1.90, 1&3 £1.80 CSF £3.57 TOTE £1.70: £1.20, £1.30; EX 3.80.
Owner V I Araci **Bred** Aliette Forien And Gilles Forien **Trained** Newmarket, Suffolk

FOCUS

The Craven can still be won by a top-notcher such as Twice Over three years ago and Haafhd in 2004, but the absence of one of last season's very top juveniles suggested that this year's renewal was going to have little impact on the classic markets. It remains to be seen how strong the form is, even though the winning time was 2.2 seconds faster than the Wood Ditton. Native Khan has been rated to his Racing Post Trophy mark, with the second to form and the third a big improver.

NOTEBOOK

Native Khan(FR) had decent form at two, narrowly beating Measuring Time (runner-up in the earlier sales race) in the Solario before finishing a running-on fourth behind Casamento in the Racing Post Trophy. He wasn't an intended runner in this, but he had been working so well that connections had a change of heart. However, he got himself into quite a state beforehand, which wasn't ideal, so the fact that he quickened up so well to hit the front a furlong out and win comfortably does him credit. Whether this was 2,000 Guineas-winning form has to be doubtful, though, and he is still available at 16-1 for the first Classic. The French Guineas is the alternative. (op 4-5 after early 10-11 and eavens in places, tchd 5-6)

Libranno, winner of the July Stakes and Richmond Stakes last season, was therefore conceding 3lb to his five rivals for those successes. Trying beyond 6f for the first time, he took quite a hold in front, which wasn't ideal with his stamina in doubt, and he could do little when the winner pounced. A drop back in trip looks in order, but his Group 2 penalty may continue to make him hard to place. (tchd 7-2)

Yaseer(IRE) ◆ was impressive considering he still looked green when beating four subsequent individual winners in a Kempton maiden in December, but this was a major step up in class. He ran creditably, though, staying on again after seeming to get outpaced and he probably has a lot more to offer. (op 5-1)

Casual Glimpse was well held on the three occasions he tackled Pattern company last season and he was never able to trouble the leaders here. He seems to have a class barrier. (op 11-1 tchd 10-1)

Ahlaain(USA), winner of just one of his ten starts and in action at Meydan earlier this year, made a difficult task even harder by missing the break and he could never land a blow. (op 16-1 tchd 14-1)

Yahafedh Alaih was predictably out of his depth. (op 80-1)

1342 WEATHERBYS EARL OF SEFTON STKS (GROUP 3) 1m 1f

4:45 (4:45) (Class 1) 4-Y-O+

£28,385 (£10,760; £5,385; £2,685; £1,345; £675) **Stalls** High

Form RPR

010- **1** **Ransom Note**[194] 6562 4-8-12 106.......... MichaelHills 8 114
(B W Hills) *mde all: shkn up over 1f out: rdn and edgd rt ins fnl f: styd on* **6/1**

1-11 **2** *1½* **Polytechnicien (USA)**[26] 920 5-9-1 0.......... OlivierPeslier 9 115
(A Fabre, France) *chsd ldrs: wnt 2nd over 2f out: sn rdn: styd on* **7/2**[2]

/15- **3** *1* **Elusive Pimpernel (USA)**[348] 1699 4-8-12 115.......... RyanMoore 2 109+
(John Dunlop) *a.p: rdn and edgd rt fr over 1f out: styd on* **2/1**[1]

1261 **4** *½* **Steele Tango (USA)**[35] 829 6-8-12 114.......... TedDurcan 6 108
(Roger Teal) *hld up: hdwy over 2f out: rdn and hung rt over 1f out: styd on* **5/1**

/50- **5** *9* **World Heritage**[202] 6344 5-8-12 108.......... AndreaAtzeni 7 89
(Robert Eddery) *chsd wnr tl rdn over 2f out: hung rt and wknd over 1f out* **100/1**

011- **6** *9* **Forte Dei Marmi**[208] 6193 5-8-12 111.......... KierenFallon 4 70
(Luca Cumani) *hld up: rdn: hung rt and wknd over 1f out* **4/1**[3]

655- **7** *1¾* **Bullet Train**[204] 6281 4-8-12 109.......... TomQueally 3 66
(Sir Henry Cecil) *hld up: rdn and wknd over 2f out* **16/1**

1m 49.42s (-2.28) **Going Correction** +0.075s/f (Good) **7** Ran SP% **113.4**
Speed ratings (Par 113): **113,111,110,110,102 94,92**
toteswingers:1&2 £5.10, 2&3 £2.50, 1&3 £3.20 CSF £26.70 TOTE £6.90: £2.30, £3.60; EX 21.00 Trifecta £123.30 Pool: £985.31 - 5.91 winning units..
Owner H R Mould **Bred** Rabbah Bloodstock Limited **Trained** Lambourn, Berks

FOCUS

The first Group race of the season on turf for older horses, the Earl Of Sefton has been won in recent years by the subsequently top-class Notnowcato (2006) and Manduro (2007). This was a race where it paid to be up there. This was tight renewal and probably not form for maximum faith.

NOTEBOOK

Ransom Note was in the ideal position out in front. A winner three times over 1m last season including the Britannia, he was last seen finishing in midfield over C&D in the Cambridgeshire, but he wasn't ridden as though his stamina for the trip was thought to be in question and he kept responding to his rider's urgings when asked. Connections think he will get another furlong and he may be given an international campaign eventually. (tchd 11-2)

Polytechnicien(USA), from the yard that sent out Manduro to win this four years ago, came into the contest race-fit and bidding for a four-timer. He travelled well behind the winner, but he couldn't get on terms when asked to close up the hill. This was still a fair effort under his penalty. (tchd 4-1)

Elusive Pimpernel(USA) was an impressive winner of the Craven on this card last year, but hadn't been seen since finishing fifth in the 2,000 Guineas the following month. He came through to hold every chance, but hung away to the far rail and was by no means given a hard time. Provided he comes out of this in one piece, he should be able to return to winning ways sooner rather than later. (op 5-2 tched 11-4 in places)

Steele Tango(USA), second and fourth in the last two runnings of this, came into this fit from a successful spell in Dubai and ran his race again, pulling miles clear of the rest without being good enough. (op 9-2)

World Heritage, placed a few times for Pascal Bary in France two years ago, lost his way afterwards but ran well for a long way here.

Forte Dei Marmi, a winner four times over 1m2f last season including in three fiercely competitive handicaps, was dropped right out early but found absolutely nothing off the bridle and hung all over the place. (tchd 7-2 and 9-2 in places)

Bullet Train became disappointing after winning the Lingfield Derby Trial just under a year ago and he was never in the race here, with the shorter trip doing nothing for him. (op 14-1)

1343 ROSSDALES MAIDEN FILLIES' STKS 7f

5:20 (5:20) (Class 4) 3-Y-O

£4,533 (£1,348; £674; £336) **Stalls** High

Form RPR

1 **Deity** 3-9-0 0.......... RyanMoore 1 82+
(Jeremy Noseda) *a.p: led over 1f out: shkn up and r.o wl* **15/2**

3 **2** *2¼* **Flashbang**[9] 1155 3-9-0 0.......... JamieSpencer 5 76
(Paul Cole) *led 1f: chsd ldr tl led again 1/2-way: rdn: hung lft and hdd over 1f out: styd on same pce ins fnl f* **10/3**[3]

3 *¾* **To The Spring** 3-9-0 0.......... KierenFallon 4 74+
(William Haggas) *a.p: shkn up over 1f out: styd on* **11/2**

4- **4** *1* **Heatherbird**[191] 6651 3-9-0 0.......... JimCrowley 8 71
(William Jarvis) *free to post: stdd s: hld up: plld hrd: hdwy 1/2-way: rdn over 1f out: no ex ins fnl f* **3/1**[2]

5 *4¼* **Elraabeya (CAN)** 3-9-0 0.......... RichardHills 2 60
(Sir Michael Stoute) *hld up: hdwy over 2f out: wknd over 1f out* **11/4**[1]

4- **6** *½* **Tanassuq (USA)**[185] 6803 3-9-0 0.......... TadhgO'Shea 3 58
(John Dunlop) *s.s: bhd 1/2-way: nvr nrr* **10/1**

0- **7** *5* **Queens Troop**[178] 6986 3-9-0 0.......... PhilipRobinson 6 45
(Dean Ivory) *plld hrd: led 6f out: hdd 1/2-way: wknd over 2f out* **100/1**

00- **8** *6* **Golden Compass**[183] 6849 3-9-0 0.......... WilliamCarson 9 29
(Giles Bravery) *hld up: rdn 1/2-way: wknd over 2f out* **66/1**

1m 27.4s (2.00) **Going Correction** +0.075s/f (Good) **8** Ran SP% **113.5**
Speed ratings (Par 97): **91,88,87,86,83 83,77,70**
toteswingers:1&2 £3.70, 2&3 £4.40, 1&3 £5.60 CSF £32.20 TOTE £7.40: £3.30, £1.50, £2.50; EX 25.00 Trifecta £204.40 Pool: £549.76 - 1.99 winning units..
Owner Highclere Thoroughbred Racing-Blue Peter **Bred** Plantation Stud **Trained** Newmarket, Suffolk

FOCUS
Not much previous form to go on and the moderate winning time suggests there isn't much depth to this maiden, so the race has not been rated too positively. The last ten winners of this contest had previous racecourse experience which makes the winner's effort look a bit better.

1344 GLYN HOPKIN H'CAP — 1m 2f
5:50 (5:53) (Class 3) (0-95,94) 3-Y-O **£7,771** (£2,312; £1,155; £577) **Stalls** High

Form — RPR

3-11 **1** **Art History (IRE)**[8] 1168 3-8-9 **82** 6ex.......................... FrankieDettori 2 90+
(Mark Johnston) *chsd ldr centre gp over 8f out: led that gp over 3f out: rdn ro ld overall and hung lft over 1f out: styd on* **9/4**[2]

21- **2** *½* **Glencadam Gold (IRE)**[181] 6894 3-8-11 **84**..................... TomQueally 4 91+
(Sir Henry Cecil) *dwlt: hld up: racd centre over 8f out: hdwy over 5f out: rdn and ev ch over 1f out: styd on* **7/1**

150- **3** *1* **Sergeant Ablett (IRE)**[194] 6560 3-9-2 **89**..................... PaulMulrennan 5 94
(James Given) *overall ldr: racd alone stands' side fr over 8f out: rdn and hdd over 1f out: kpt on* **11/1**

641- **4** *1* **Labarinto**[196] 6514 3-9-0 **87**.. RyanMoore 1 90+
(Sir Michael Stoute) *hld up: racd centre over 8f out: hdwy over 1f out: no imp ins fnl f* **7/4**[1]

313- **5** *7* **Poplin**[196] 6505 3-9-1 **88**... KierenFallon 7 77
(Luca Cumani) *racd centre over 8f out: prom: drifted lft over 2f out: wknd over 1f out* **6/1**[3]

1-33 **6** *1½* **Angelic Upstart (IRE)**[42] 750 3-8-7 **80** oh2.................. DavidProbert 9 66
(Andrew Balding) *hld up: racd centre over 8f out: rdn and drifted lft over 2f out: n.d* **25/1**

1 **7** *4* **Casual Mover (IRE)**[68] 434 3-8-4 **80** oh3....................... KierenFox(3) 6 58
(John Best) *hld up: racd centre over 8f out: rdn over 2f out: wknd over 1f out* **33/1**

441- **8** *19* **Golden Hinde**[228] 5546 3-8-13 **86**...................................... RichardHills 8 52
(Mark Johnston) *led centre gp over 8f out: rdn and hdd over 3f out: wknd over 2f out: t.o* **25/1**

2m 5.95s (0.15) **Going Correction** +0.075s/f (Good) **8** Ran SP% **112.9**
Speed ratings (Par 102): **102,101,100,100,94 93,90,74**
toteswingers: 1&2 £3.00, 1&3 £4.50, 2&3 £7.10. Tote Super 7: Win: Not won. Place: Not won.
CSF £17.55 CT £139.90 TOTE £2.90: £1.20, £2.70, £3.70; EX 15.80 Trifecta £215.40 Pool: £695.83 - 2.39 - 5.91 winning units..
Owner Sheikh Hamdan Bin Mohammed Al Maktoum **Bred** Kenilworth House Stud **Trained** Middleham Moor, N Yorks

FOCUS
The majority of these had plenty of scope for improvement and there is no reason to think that we will not be hearing plenty more of a few of these, not just the winner. The first four finsihed clear and the form has been rated on the positive side. There was a difference of opinion amongst the jockeys with the majority switching to race up the centre whilst Sergeant Ablett ran a solo up the stands' rail, but the way they finished suggested there wasn't any great advantage.

NOTEBOOK
Art History(IRE), a lean sort already proven at the trip, was bidding for a hat-trick under a 6lb penalty, but he was still 4lb well in compared to his revised mark. With race-fitness on his side, it made sense for him to be ridden prominently and he saw his race out best up the final climb. Things will be much harder for him from now on, but he looks a typical improver from the yard and it would be dangerous to assume that he cannot continue to thrive. (tchd 2-1 and 5-2)
Glencadam Gold(IRE) ◆ looked a real stayer when winning over 1m at Redcar on his second and final start at two, but was given a more patient ride on this reappearance. He impressed with the way he quickened up from off the pace to just about hit the front passing the 2f pole, but lack of a recent run then appeared to take its toll. He should go one better soon and may well turn out to be the best of these. (op 8-1)
Sergeant Ablett(IRE), ex-Mark Johnston and having his first start for the yard, looked as though he might have stolen it against the nearside rail around 3f from home and he kept on well when the challengers arrived out towards the centre of the track. He should do well for his new stable. (op 16-1 tchd 10-1)
Labarinto, progressive in three outings at two, was up 3f in trip. He came home well enough from off the pace and should be winning again now that he has this run under his belt. (tchd 13-8)
Poplin, a progressive filly last autumn who was bred to relish this longer trip, ran as though the outing was badly needed. (op 13-2 tchd 7-1)
T/Jkpt: Not won. T/Plt: £189.40 to a £1 stake. Pool of £76,777.89 - 295.78. T/Qpdt: £23.00 to a £1 stake. Pool of £6,915.44 - 221.86 winning tickets. CR

1345 - 1352a (Foreign Racing) - See Raceform Interactive

BRIGHTON (L-H)
Friday, April 15

OFFICIAL GOING: Good to firm (watered; 9.0)
Course at inner configuration and distances as advertised.
Wind: virtually nil Weather: dry and bright

1353 CASINO AT BET365 H'CAP — 1m 1f 209y
4:30 (4:30) (Class 5) (0-70,70) 4-Y-O+ **£2,590** (£770; £385; £192) **Stalls** High

Form — RPR

3-16 **1** **Prince Apollo**[14] 1075 6-9-7 **70**...(t) NeilCallan 7 79
(Gerard Butler) *stdd s: t.k.h: hld up in tch: trckd ldrs 4f out: swtchd rt and effrt 2f out: rdn to ld 1f out: in command fnl 100yds: r.o wl: rdn out* **15/8**[1]

215 **2** *2* **Wily Fox**[21] 962 4-9-5 **68**... SebSanders 4 73
(James Eustace) *taken down early: led after 1f: rdn over 2f out: hdd and unable qck u.p over 1f out: chsd wnr and no imp ins fnl f* **11/2**[3]

045- **3** *2¾* **Scorn (USA)**[140] 7575 4-9-3 **66**.. PatDobbs 3 66
(Richard Hannon) *led for 1f: chsd ldr after: upsides and travelling wl over 2f out: rdn to ld over 1f out: hdd 1f out: fnd little u.p and sn btn: wknd fnl 100yds* **11/2**[3]

216- **4** *1* **Lady Lam**[149] 7490 5-9-1 **64**..(t) GeorgeBaker 1 62
(Sylvester Kirk) *stdd s: t.k.h: hld up in last trio: rdn and effrt over 1f out: kpt on ins fnl f: no ch w ldrs* **4/1**[2]

0330 **5** *½* **Prohibition (IRE)**[44] 727 5-8-5 **59**.............................. HarryBentley(5) 2 56
(Gary Moore) *stdd s: t.k.h: sn in midfield: chsd ldrs 5f out: n.m.r on inner over 2f out: rdn and fnd little over 1f out: wknd ent fnl f* **15/2**

0-54 **6** *2¼* **Derby Desire (IRE)**[11] 1135 7-8-4 **56** oh7.................... SophieDoyle(3) 5 48
(Des Donovan) *chsd ldrs: rdn and unable qck over 2f out: plugged on same pce and no ch w ldrs fr over 1f out* **12/1**

430- **7** *½* **Rock With You**[360] 1450 4-8-13 **67**............................ JemmaMarshall(5) 6 58
(Pat Phelan) *t.k.h: hld up in last trio: pushed along and unable qck wl over 2f out: bhd whn edgd lft over 1f out* **12/1**

2m 2.53s (-1.07) **Going Correction** -0.125s/f (Firm) **7** Ran SP% **112.7**
Speed ratings (Par 103): **99,97,95,94,94 92,91**
toteswingers: 1&2 £2.30, 1&3 £2.90, 2&3 £3.80 CSF £12.14 TOTE £2.50: £1.50, £2.90; EX 13.20.
Owner Asaad Al Banwan **Bred** Juddmonte Farms Ltd **Trained** Newmarket, Suffolk

FOCUS
The going was good to firm on a watered track. They went a fairly steady pace in this handicap and the performance of the winner can be marked up because he was very keen under restraint for a long way. The form is rated around him.
Rock With You Official explanation: trainer's rep said filly was unsuited by the track

1354 BET365.COM CLASSIFIED STKS — 7f 214y
5:00 (5:00) (Class 6) 3-Y-O+ **£1,878** (£558; £279; £139) **Stalls** Low

Form — RPR

0332 **1** **Polly Holder (IRE)**[3] 1300 3-8-3 **53**................................(p) AmyBaker(3) 4 59
(Alan Bailey) *led at stdy gallop: hdd and rdn over 2f out: battled on gamely and kpt pressing ldr after tl led towards fin* **3/1**[3]

-231 **2** *nk* **Lilli Palmer (IRE)**[15] 1068 4-9-7 **55**...................................... MartinLane 3 62
(Mike Murphy) *t.k.h: chsd wnr tl led narrowly over 2f out: drvn over 1f out: kpt on u.p tl hdd and no ex towards fin* **13/8**[1]

0-33 **3** *2¼* **Sleeping Brave**[21] 966 3-7-13 **55**..........................(b[1]) NathanAlison(7) 5 53
(Jim Boyle) *stdd s: t.k.h: chsd ldng pair: rdn and hung rt ent fnl 2f: keeping on same pce and hld whn hung lft u.p ins fnl f* **5/1**

040- **4** *5* **Flinty**[199] 6443 3-8-1 **55**.. KieranO'Neill(5) 2 41
(Richard Hannon) *stdd s: hld up in tch in last pair: rdn and outpcd ent fnl 3f: 4th and wl hld fr over 1f out* **5/2**[2]

0-00 **5** *6* **Fight Or Flight**[27] 905 4-9-0 **52**.. DavidKenny(7) 1 32
(Brendan Powell) *stdd s: hld up in last pair: hdwy to press ldrs 3f out: sn rdn and unable qck: wknd ent fnl 2f* **33/1**

1m 37.49s (1.49) **Going Correction** -0.125s/f (Firm)
WFA 3 from 4yo 15lb **5** Ran SP% **111.3**
Speed ratings (Par 101): **87,86,84,79,73**
CSF £8.43 TOTE £3.20: £1.80, £1.50; EX 7.70.
Owner A Bailey **Bred** M Doyle **Trained** Newmarket, Suffolk

FOCUS
The first two had a good battle in this 0-55 classified event. Obviously limited form, with the first pair to their turf latest.

1355 BET365.COM H'CAP — 7f 214y
5:30 (5:30) (Class 5) (0-70,70) 4-Y-O+ **£2,590** (£770; £385; £192) **Stalls** Low

Form — RPR

0230 **1** **Princess Lexi (IRE)**[56] 598 4-8-7 **56** oh2.............................. MartinLane 6 69
(Ian Williams) *dwlt: bustled along and rcvrd to press ldr after 1f: led over 4f out: drvn over 1f out: kpt on wl u.p: forged ahd fnl 100yds* **9/1**

3411 **2** *1¾* **Collect Art (IRE)**[2] 1307 4-9-1 **64** ow1............................ GeorgeBaker 5 73
(Andrew Haynes) *led: hdd over 4f out: styd upsides wnr: rdn wl over 1f out: btn fnl 100yds: wknd towards fin* **4/5**[1]

2114 **3** *1½* **Eastern Gift**[14] 1083 6-9-7 **70**.. NeilCallan 3 76
(Gay Kelleway) *in tch: chsd ldrs and rdn over 2f out: swtchd rt over 1f out: kpt on same pce and no imp fnl f* **5/2**[2]

0500 **4** *15* **Mister Green (FR)**[13] 1103 5-9-6 **69**...........................(t) TonyCulhane 4 40
(David Flood) *stdd s: t.k.h: hld up in tch: hdwy to press ldrs ent fnl 3f: shkn up and fnd nil over 2f out: sn btn: wl bhd 1f out* **13/2**[3]

600- **5** *1½* **Mut'Ab (USA)**[25] 5859 6-9-4 **70**.........................(v[1]) AlanCreighton(3) 1 38
(Edward Creighton) *chsd ldrs: dropped to last and rdn over 3f out: wknd u.p over 2f out: wl bhd over 1f out* **25/1**

1m 34.39s (-1.61) **Going Correction** -0.125s/f (Firm) **5** Ran SP% **111.3**
Speed ratings (Par 103): **103,101,99,84,83**
CSF £17.28 TOTE £10.70: £4.00, £1.30; EX 24.80.
Owner Dr Marwan Koukash **Bred** Epona Bloodstock Ltd And P A Byrne **Trained** Portway, Worcs

FOCUS
A fair handicap with a clear personal best from the winner. The first two had a sustained duel up front.

1356 BET365 H'CAP — 6f 209y
6:00 (6:00) (Class 4) (0-85,84) 4-Y-O+ **£3,280** (£981; £490) **Stalls** Low

Form — RPR

6240 **1** **Buxton**[6] 1232 7-8-7 **70**..(t) MartinLane 5 79
(Roger Ingram) *hld up in last: pushed along and clsd 2f out: rdn and qcknd to ld 1f out: sn in command: r.o wl* **15/8**[2]

[illegible] **2** *2¼* **April Fool**[8] 1035 7-8-0 77 [illegible] (b) CathyGannon 3 [illegible]
(David Evans) *led at decent gallop: jnd and rdn over 2f out: hdd 1f out: nt pce of wnr ins fnl f* **5/6**[1]

136- **3** *8* **Lady Florence**[199] 6439 6-8-11 **74**.. MarcHalford 1 55
(Alan Coogan) *chsd ldr tl hdwy to join ldr over 2f out: rdn over 1f out: wknd ent fnl f* **9/2**[3]

1m 22.16s (-0.94) **Going Correction** -0.125s/f (Firm) **3** Ran SP% **107.5**
Speed ratings (Par 105): **100,97,88**
CSF £3.87 TOTE £3.90; EX 3.90.
Owner Peter J Burton **Bred** Sharon Ingram **Trained** Epsom, Surrey

FOCUS
They went a reasonable pace, despite the small turnout for this handicap. The winner is rated to last year's form.

1357 POKER AT BET365 H'CAP — 6f 209y
6:35 (6:36) (Class 6) (0-60,58) 4-Y-O+ **£1,878** (£558; £279; £139) **Stalls** Low

Form — RPR

2300 **1** **St Ignatius**[2] 1307 4-8-13 **50**...(p) JamesDoyle 10 58
(Michael Appleby) *chsd ldng pair: rdn to chse ldr over 2f out: hld hd high u.p: drvn and ev ch 1f out: led ins fnl f: rdn out* **13/2**[3]

303- **2** *½* **Mandhooma**[198] 6456 5-9-7 **58**.. ChrisCatlin 1 67+
(Peter Hiatt) *hld up in rr: hdwy into midfield ent fnl 2f: nt clr run over 1f out: swtchd rt jst over 1f out: str run ins fnl f: wnt 2nd towards fin: nvr quite getting to wnr* **10/1**

0-00 **3** *¾* **Set To Go**[37] 807 4-8-9 **46**..(b) HayleyTurner 9 50
(Tor Sturgis) *chsd ldr and clr of field: led over 2f out: rdn wl over 1f out: drvn and hdd ins fnl f: styd on same pce fnl 100yds* **14/1**

4052 **4** *1¼* **Diddums**[3] 1283 5-9-4 **55**...(v[1]) LiamJones 6 56
(Alastair Lidderdale) *t.k.h: hld up in midfield: clsd and in tch over 3f out: rdn to chse ldrs over 1f out: one pce and no imp fnl f* **13/2**[3]

5442 **5** *4½* **Kai Mook**[16] 1054 4-8-11 **51**.. KierenFox(3) 8 40
(Roger Ingram) *chsd ldng trio: clsd 4f out: rdn and unable qck jst over 2f out: rdn and wknd jst over 1f out* **4/1**[2]

0400 **6** *2¾* **Art Scholar (IRE)**[16] 1045 4-9-4 **55**...............................(p) GeorgeBaker 4 36
(Gary Moore) *racd off the pce in midfield: clsd 4f out: effrt and rdn on inner jst over 2f out: fnd little u.p and btn over 1f out: wknd fnl f* **9/1**

30-0 **7** *2½* **Miss Polly Plum**[84] 250 4-8-8 **45**...............................(p) WilliamCarson 7 20
(Chris Dwyer) *led at fast gallop: hdd over 2f out: rdn jst over 2f out: wknd wl over 1f out: fdd ins fnl f* **40/1**

0040 **8** *3* **Mushy Peas (IRE)**[6] 1247 4-9-0 **51**...............................(v) CathyGannon 11 18
(David Evans) *a in rr: nvr toubled ldrs* **12/1**

0-46 **9** *6* **Mogok Ruby**^{82} [269] 7-9-1 **52** .... PatDobbs 2 —
(Brett Johnson) *sn detached in last: nvr on terms* **25/1**

3151 **10** *7* **Crystallize**^{3} [1283] 5-9-6 **57** .... NeilCallan 3 —
(Andrew Haynes) *restless in stalls: stmbld s: racd off the pce in midfield: clsd and in tch over 2f out: rdn and unable qck ent fnl 2f: wkng whn pushed rt jst over 1f out: wl btn and eased ins fnl f* **9/4**^{1}

1m 22.51s (-0.59) **Going Correction** -0.125s/f (Firm) **10** Ran SP% **117.2**
Speed ratings (Par 101): **98,97,96,95,90 86,84,80,73,65**
toteswingers:1&2:£8.50, 1&3:£15.20, 2&3:£19.30 CSF £69.98 CT £900.82 TOTE £8.20: £3.70, £4.10, £10.20; EX 122.30.

Owner Dallas Racing **Bred** Simon And Helen Plumbly **Trained** Danethorpe, Notts

FOCUS
They went a fast pace in this modest handicap and there was a hard-luck story in the runner-up. The winner is up slightly on this year's AW form.

Mandhooma Official explanation: jockey said mare was denied a clear run

Mushy Peas(IRE) Official explanation: jockey said gelding hung left

Crystallize Official explanation: jockey said gelding became up and stumbled on leaving stalls

1358 BET365 MAIDEN STKS 5f 213y
7:10 (7:12) (Class 5) 3-Y-O+ **£2,590** (£770; £385; £192) **Stalls** Low

Form RPR

202- **1** **Freckenham (IRE)**^{224} [5720] 3-8-10 72 .... HayleyTurner 7 77
(Michael Bell) *mde all: pushed along to assert ent fnl f: styd on wl: pushed out: comf* **7/4**^{1}

00- **2** *1 ¾* **Mixed Emotions (IRE)**^{305} [3034] 3-8-10 0 .... PatDobbs 4 71
(Richard Hannon) *chsd ldng pair: rdn and effrt ent fnl 2f: chsd wnr ins fnl f: kpt on but no threat to wnr* **14/1**

254- **3** *1 ¼* **Bakoura**^{169} [7185] 3-8-10 72 .... MartinLane 1 67
(John Dunlop) *w wnr tl hmpd 4f out: chsd wnr after: rallied and pressed wnr over 2f out: rdn and edgd rt wl over 1f out: nt qckn ent fnl f: styd on same pce: lost 2nd ins fnl f* **2/1**^{2}

4 *2 ¼* **Bahia Emerald (IRE)** 3-8-10 0 .... SebSanders 5 60+
(Jeremy Noseda) *s.i.s: in rr: wnt rt and hdwy wl over 2f out: chsd ldng trio 2f out: kpt on but no imp after* **7/2**^{3}

60 **5** *13* **Add Lib**^{15} [1060] 3-8-10 0 .... CathyGannon 2 19
(Matthew Salaman) *in tch in midfield: rdn and effrt whn sltly hmpd over 2f out: wkng whn pushed lft and hmpd wl over 1f out: sn lost tch* **50/1**

05 **6** *10* **Lady Freda**^{18} [1015] 5-9-8 0 .... MarcHalford 8 —
(Alan Coogan) *wnt rt s: t.k.h: hld up in tch in rr: rdn: rn green and wkng whn bdly hmpd wl over 1f out: sn lost tch: eased wl ins fnl f: t.o* **100/1**

/0-0 **7** *6* **Exceedingthestars**^{15} [1065] 4-9-8 0 .... WilliamCarson 6 —
(Michael Squance) *taken down early: t.k.h: hld up in tch: hdwy on outer to chse ldrs 3f out: rdn and hung bdly lft 2f out: sn btn and lost tch: virtually p.u ins fnl f: t.o* **66/1**

69.58 secs (-0.62) **Going Correction** -0.125s/f (Firm)
WFA 3 from 4yo+ 12lb **7** Ran SP% **103.0**
Speed ratings (Par 103): **99,96,95,92,74 61,53**
toteswingers:1&2:£3.10, 1&3:£1.02, 2&3:£3.00 CSF £20.11 TOTE £2.90: £2.60, £6.40; EX 16.50.

Owner Sheikh Marwan Al Maktoum **Bred** Darley **Trained** Newmarket, Suffolk

FOCUS
They finished well strung out in this modest but interesting maiden. It;s doubtful if the winner had to improve on her best form. Silent Fright got worked up and was withdrawn at the start (7/1, deduct 10p in the £ under R4.)

1359 FINANCIALS AT BET365 H'CAP 5f 213y
7:40 (7:40) (Class 5) (0-70,69) 3-Y-O **£2,590** (£770; £385; £192) **Stalls** Low

Form RPR

160- **1** **Native Picture (IRE)**^{199} [6445] 3-9-6 **68** .... PatDobbs 4 74
(Richard Hannon) *chsd ldng pair: rdn to ld ent fnl f: kpt on wl: rdn out* **11/4**^{1}

1-23 **2** *1 ¼* **Shostakovich (IRE)**^{96} [106] 3-9-6 **68** .... (tp) JamesDoyle 6 70
(Sylvester Kirk) *chsd ldr: ev ch ent fnl 2f: hld hd high and nt qckn u.p over 1f out: chsd wnr and styd on same pce ins fnl f* **7/2**^{2}

-200 **3** *1* **Majestic Ridge (IRE)**^{34} [847] 3-8-8 **56** .... (v) CathyGannon 7 55
(David Evans) *sn led: jnd and rdn ent fnl 2f: hdd ent fnl f: no ex and btn fnl 100yds* **12/1**

132- **4** *nk* **Stunning In Purple (IRE)**^{243} [5111] 3-9-6 **68** .... NeilCallan 3 66
(Andrew Haynes) *chsd ldng trio: rdn along and effrt wl over 1f out: kpt on same pce ins fnl f* **4/1**^{3}

0624 **5** *4 ½* **Loves Theme (IRE)**^{7} [1219] 3-9-4 **69** .... (p) AmyBaker$^{(3)}$ 8 52
(Alan Bailey) *racd wd: in tch: effrt 3f out: no prog and btn over 1f out: plugged on same pce fnl f* **9/1**

0243 **6** *2 ½* **Fairy Tales**^{10} [1149] 3-8-11 **62** .... KierenFox$^{(3)}$ 2 37
(John Bridger) *stdd s: a towards rr: rdn and effrt over 2f out: no prog and wl hld over 1f out* **12/1**

0103 **7** *shd* **Alfraamsey**^{20} [987] 3-8-8 **59** .... MartinHarley$^{(3)}$ 1 34
(Mick Channon) *hld up in last pair: rdn and effrt over 2f out: drvn and no hdwy wl over 1f out: wknd fnl f* **9/2**

0000 **8** *¾* **Ajaafa**^{14} [1078] 3-9-0 **62** .... (b^{1}) LiamJones 5 35
(Michael Appleby) *hld up in rr: hdwy wl over 2f out: wknd wl over 1f out: bhd fnl f* **33/1**

69.90 secs (-0.30) **Going Correction** -0.125s/f (Firm) **8** Ran SP% **115.4**
Speed ratings (Par 98): **97,95,94,93,87 84,84,83**
toteswingers:1&2:£2.70, 1&3:£5.90, 2&3:£12.30 CSF £12.64 CT £97.19 TOTE £3.30: £1.10, £1.10, £4.40; EX 7.40.

Owner Malih Lahej Al Basti **Bred** P McCutcheon **Trained** East Everleigh, Wilts

FOCUS
The first four pulled clear in this sprint handicap which was won by an unexposed and very well-related type. Reasonable form for the grade.

T/Plt: £455.80 to a £1 stake. Pool:£41,803.56 - 66.95 winning tickets T/Qpdt: £269.70 to a £1 stake. Pool:£4,192.14 - 11.50 winning tickets SP

NEWBURY (L-H)
Friday, April 15

OFFICIAL GOING: Good to firm
Rail realignment on home bend increased distances on round course by about 15m.
Wind: Nil Weather: White cloud

1360 ERIK PENSER BANK EBF MAIDEN STKS 5f 34y
1:35 (1:35) (Class 4) 2-Y-O **£4,857** (£1,445; £722; £360) **Stalls** High

Form RPR

1 **Magic City (IRE)** 2-9-3 0 .... RichardHughes 7 93+
(Richard Hannon) *disp ld tl def advantage 3f out: shkn up and hung lft ins fnl 2f: pushed clr over 1f out: comf* **4/1**^{1}

2 *6* **Signifer (IRE)** 2-9-0 0 .... MartinHarley$^{(3)}$ 6 71
(Mick Channon) *chsd ldrs: wnt 2nd ins fnl 2f: kpt on wl ins fnl f: nvr any ch w wnr* **33/1**

3 *¾* **Commissar** 2-9-3 0 .... SilvestreDeSousa 3 69+
(Paul Cole) *chsd ldrs: pushed along 1/2-way: kpt on ins fnl f but nvr any ch w wnr* **4/1**^{1}

4 *2 ¾* **Letsgoroundagain (IRE)** 2-9-3 0 .... MichaelHills 12 63+
(B W Hills) *in rr: green and stl plenty to do 2f out: shkn up and str run ins fnl f: fin wl: should improve* **14/1**

5 *1* **Chunky Diamond (IRE)** 2-9-3 0 .... JackMitchell 9 55
(Peter Chapple-Hyam) *chsd ldrs: pushed along 1/2-way: kpt on same pce ins fnl f* **5/1**^{2}

6 *½* **Pitt Rivers** 2-9-3 0 .... SamHitchcott 5 53+
(Mick Channon) *s.i.s: sn in tch: rdn and one pce 2f out: kpt on again ins fnl f* **25/1**

7 *¾* **Tioman Legend** 2-9-3 0 .... SteveDrowne 2 51
(Roger Charlton) *in tch: drvn to chse ldrs over 2f out: wknd ins fnl f* **10/1**

8 *1* **Arabian Falcon** 2-9-3 0 .... MartinDwyer 10 47
(Brian Meehan) *chsd ldrs: rdn 1/2-way: wknd over 1f out* **12/1**

9 *1 ¼* **Coach Montana (IRE)** 2-9-3 0 .... KierenFallon 4 43
(Jane Chapple-Hyam) *broke wl: sn green and pushed along in rr: kpt on ins fnl f but nvr gng pce to get into contention* **8/1**

10 *¾* **B Fifty Two (IRE)** 2-9-3 0 .... SebSanders 1 40
(J W Hills) *sn pushed along in rr and green: sme late prog* **40/1**

11 *2 ½* **Stepper Point** 2-9-3 0 .... HayleyTurner 13 31+
(William Muir) *disp ld 2f: wknd 2f out* **40/1**

12 *¾* **Meloneras** 2-8-12 0 .... JamesMillman 15 23
(Rod Millman) *green and pushed along in rr: sme late prog* **66/1**

13 *3 ¼* **Powerful Wind (IRE)** 2-9-3 0 .... DavidProbert 8 17
(Ronald Harris) *gd spd 3f* **100/1**

P **Regal Entrance** 2-9-3 0 .... (v^{1}) FrankieDettori 11 —
(Jeremy Noseda) *in rr: p.u and dismntd 1/2-way* **6/1**^{3}

61.11 secs (-0.29) **Going Correction** +0.075s/f (Good) **14** Ran SP% **119.7**
Speed ratings (Par 94): **105,95,94,89,88 87,86,84,82,81 77,76,71,—**
toteswingers:1&2 £17.40, 2&3 £23.90, 1&3 £3.40 CSF £150.53 TOTE £4.90: £2.00, £9.60, £1.60; EX 161.90 TRIFECTA Not won..

Owner D W Barker **Bred** Miss Annmarie Burke **Trained** East Everleigh, Wilts

FOCUS
Three of the last seven winners of this race went on to win in Group company, namely in 2004 Tournedos (Molecomb), in 2007 Winker Watson (Norfolk and July Stakes) and last year Klammer (Horris Hill). In this latest running they raced middle to stands' side. No form to go on, but a big field lined up, with plenty of powerful yards represented, and several of these took the eye in the paddock. Magic City impressed, and there was definite promise from the third and fourth.

NOTEBOOK
Magic City(IRE) ◆ showed good speed from off and sustained his challenge in taking style, despite edging left for much of the closing stages, albeit he straightened up okay near the line. It's probably worth pointing out, though, that the middle of the track looked the place to be on the straight course, so he was not at a disadvantage. Whatever the case, this £42,000 purchase looks Royal Ascot class.
Signifer(IRE), a 15,000gns purchase representing Mick Channon, who had a nice juvenile winner at Newmarket the previous day, looked a bit on the weak side, but showed enough to suggest he will win a maiden before stepping up in class. (op 28-1)
Commissar ◆, a 32,000gns half-brother to, among others, useful 6f-7f 2-y-o winner Lily Again, has plenty of size and scope for an early type. He was under pressure by halfway and lacked the natural speed of the winner, but kept on. His stable introduced a particularly decent type at Windsor earlier in the month (Silverheels) and this one also has the potential to be above average. (op 6-1 tchd 7-2)
Letsgoroundagain(IRE) ◆ was just about as eyecatching a debutant as you will see. He raced out the back for much of the way, but gradually got the idea when switched wide and stayed on very well without being subjected to anything like a hard time. There should be significant improvement to come and he could be smart. (op 11-1)
Chunky Diamond(IRE), a £42,000 purchase whose dam was a 5f winner on 2yo debut, is only medium sized, but was solid in the market and showed ability. (op 11-2 tchd 13-2)
Pitt Rivers, a stablemate of the runner-up, looked as though the run would bring him on and he didn't help himself with a slow start. There should be a lot better to come.
Tioman Legend looks the type to do better in time. (op 9-1 tchd 11-1)
Arabian Falcon, who was slightly on his toes beforehand, should come on for the outing. (op 16-1 tchd 10-1)
Coach Montana(IRE) was representing last year's winner stable, but he needed the experience. (op 15-2 tchd 7-1)
Stepper Point ◆ looked as though he'd be better for the run, but showed plenty of early speed against the possibly unfavoured near-side rail. (op 50-1)
Regal Entrance, sporting a visor on debut, was pulled up and dismounted at about halfway and looked lame on his near hind. (op 5-1)

1361 DUBAI DUTY FREE FULL OF SURPRISES H'CAP 7f (S)
2:10 (2:10) (Class 3) (0-95,92) 3-Y-O
£7,165 (£2,145; £1,072; £537; £267; £134) **Stalls** High

Form RPR

210- **1** **Sikeeb (IRE)**^{195} [6568] 3-9-1 **86** .... PhilipRobinson 6 97
(Clive Brittain) *chsd ldrs: drvn to ld 1f out: styd on strly fnl 120yds* **8/1**

61- **2** *2 ¾* **Attracted To You (IRE)**^{244} [5078] 3-8-13 **84** .... RichardHughes 4 88
(Richard Hannon) *t.k.h: hld up in rr but in tch: hdwy 2f out: drvn and styd on between horses ins fnl f: styd on wl to take 2nd nr fin but no imp on wnr* **11/2**^{2}

030- **3** *¾* **Rigolleto (IRE)**^{153} [7456] 3-9-7 **92** .... KierenFallon 2 94
(Mick Channon) *pressed ldrs: drvn to take slt ld wl over 1f out: hdd ins fnl f: styd on same pce and lost 2nd cl home* **16/1**

010- **4** *1* **Norse Blues**[174] 7095 3-8-9 **80**........ LiamKeniry 1 79
(Sylvester Kirk) *led main gp in centre and overall ldr over 3f out: rdn 2f out: hdd wl over 1f out: styd disputing 2nd tl last 110yds* **10/1**
421- **5** *3 ¼* **Gentle Lord**[213] 6047 3-8-10 **81**........(t) RichardKingscote 8 72
(Tom Dascombe) *chsd ldrs: rdn over 2f out: wknd ins fnl f* **10/1**
346- **6** *1 ¼* **None Shall Sleep (IRE)**[172] 7116 3-9-5 **90**........ JamieSpencer 10 77
(Paul Cole) *awkward leaving stalls and v.s.a: wnt lft to outer after 2f: hdwy and hrd rdn 2f out: nvr on terms w ldrs and wknd ins fnl f* **22/1**
01- **7** *5* **Celebrity**[273] 4095 3-9-0 **85**........ RyanMoore 7 59
(Richard Hannon) *s.i.s: in rr: pushed along over 2f out: sme prog ins fnl f but nvr any ch* **6/1**[3]
210- **8** *1 ½* **Penny's Pearl (IRE)**[218] 5882 3-9-5 **90**........ JimmyFortune 11 60
(Richard Hannon) *trckd ldr on stands' rail tl drvn to chal main gp 3f out: wknd ins fnl 2f* **33/1**
422- **9** *1 ¼* **El Muqbil (IRE)**[182] 6883 3-9-2 **87**........ RichardHills 9 53
(Brian Meehan) *trckd ldrs: shkn up 3f out: wknd over 2f out* **5/2**[1]
010- **10** *14* **Basilica**[199] 6445 3-8-12 **83**........ JamesMillman 3 11
(Rod Millman) *overall ldr: racd w one other stands' side: hdd 3f out: sn btn* **80/1**
021- **11** *9* **Home Office**[161] 7335 3-8-7 **78**........ SilvestreDeSousa 5 —
(Mark Johnston) *chsd ldrs: rdn over 3f out: sn wknd* **6/1**[3]

1m 24.91s (-0.79) **Going Correction** +0.075s/f (Good) **11** Ran SP% **116.2**
Speed ratings (Par 102): **107,103,103,101,98 96,91,89,87,71 61**
toteswingers:1&2 £9.20, 2&3 £14.30, 1&3 £26.50 CSF £50.21 CT £692.37 TOTE £9.50: £3.00, £2.00, £4.50; EX 55.90 Trifecta £386.50 Pool: £841.01 - 1.61 winning units..
Owner Saeed Manana **Bred** Ms Dolores Jones **Trained** Newmarket, Suffolk

FOCUS
The last four editions of this handicap have produced some really nice types. This might not have been quite as strong as some previous runnings, but it was a good 3-y-o handicap nonetheless and the form is rated on the positive side. The majority of these raced away from the fence towards the middle of the track for much of the way.

NOTEBOOK
Sikeeb(IRE) was probably unsuited by soft ground when well beaten in the Redcar Two-Year-Old Trophy when last seen. He was being niggled along some way out, but gradually responded and was nicely on top at the line - his chance maybe helped a little by challenging furthest away from the stands' rail. There should be improvement to come, especially over 1m, so perhaps he'll be a Britannia horse. (op 11-1)
Attracted To You(IRE), off the track since winning a 6f maiden on easy ground here last August, got going too late to challenge the winner. Although she managed to win over a sprint trip, there is stamina in her pedigree and she looks in need of further. (op 4-1)
Rigolleto(IRE) was last of ten in the Group 1 Criterium De Saint-Cloud on his final juvenile start. He was faced with vastly different conditions for his return, but ran respectably. (op 20-1)
Norse Blues was quite a free-going type last year but he settled okay this time, leading the group up the middle. However, he ultimately shaped as though the run was needed. (op 14-1)
Gentle Lord, absent since winning a 6f maiden on soft ground last September, had a tongue-tie fitted for the first time but had stamina to prove. He made his bid towards the stands' rail, which might not have been ideal, and didn't convince that he got the trip. (tchd 9-1)
None Shall Sleep(IRE) ruined his chance with a really awkward start. He'll have a bit to prove next time. (op 18-1 tchd 25-1)
Celebrity, a stable-companion of the runner-up, had been off the track since winning a 6f maiden here last July and shaped as though badly in need of the outing, never threatening after starting slowly. (tchd 11-2)
El Muqbil(IRE), who looked as though this run would bring him forward, was well fancied to build on the promise he showed in juvenile maidens, but his yard have yet to really get going and he ran a lacklustre race, finding little for pressure. (op 3-1)

1362 COLN VALLEY STUD BRIDGET MAIDEN FILLIES' STKS 7f (S)
2:40 (2:43) (Class 4) 3-Y-O **£4,857** (£1,445; £722; £360) **Stalls** High

Form RPR
1 **Hezmah** 3-9-0 0........ RichardHills 4 83
(John Gosden) *trckd ldr: chal 2f out: led wl over 1f out: pushed clr ins fnl f: readily* **4/1**[1]
2 *2 ¼* **Cheherazad (IRE)** 3-9-0 0........ SilvestreDeSousa 5 77
(Paul Cole) *led: rdn and jnd 2f out: hdd wl over 1f out: nt gng pce of wnr ins fnl f but kpt on wl for 2nd* **11/1**
3 *[illegible]* **[illegible] (USA)** 3-9-0 0........ WilliamBuick [illegible] [illegible]
(John Gosden) *green towards rr: hdwy and n.m.r over 2f out: drvn and styd on wl ins fnl f to take 3rd fnl 75yds: nt rch ldng duo* **6/1**[2]
4 *1 ¼* **Rougette** 3-9-0 0........ MichaelHills 9 68+
(B W Hills) *in rr hdwy and n.m.r 2f out: styng on whn nt clr run 1f out: swtchd lft and kpt on: gng on cl home* **13/2**[3]
5 *shd* **Sure Route** 3-9-0 0........ RichardHughes 6 68
(Richard Hannon) *chsd ldrs: rdn to go 3rd 1f out but no imp on ldng duo: outpcd into 4th fnl 75yds: lost 4th cl home* **9/1**
6 *3 ½* **Vicona (IRE)** 3-9-0 0........ JamieSpencer 3 59
(Paul Cole) *chsd ldrs: drvn to dispute 3rd over 1f out but no imp and hung rt u.p: wknd fnl 120yds* **22/1**
7 *hd* **Federation** 3-9-0 0........ SteveDrowne 11 58
(Roger Charlton) *in tch: pushed along over 2f out: kpt on ins fnl f but nvr in contention* **14/1**
8 *2 ½* **Pinch Of Posh (IRE)** 3-9-0 0........ KierenFallon 14 51
(Paul Cole) *chsd ldrs: rdn over 2f out: wknd ins fnl f* **10/1**
9 *½* **Lightning Spirit** 3-9-0 0........ LiamKeniry 2 50
(Gary Moore) *chsd ldrs: rdn over 2f out: wknd ins fnl f* **33/1**
10 *hd* **Doricemay (IRE)** 3-9-0 0........ AdamKirby 7 49
(Clive Cox) *chsd ldrs: rdn and outpcd over 2f out: kpt on again cl home* **11/1**
11 *1 ½* **Golden Slipper** 3-9-0 0........ TedDurcan 12 45
(Chris Wall) *s.i.s: in rr: kpt on fnl 2f but nvr any ch* **20/1**
12 *½* **Saktoon (USA)** 3-9-0 0........ PhilipRobinson 1 44
(Clive Brittain) *wnt bdly lft s: sn rcvrd and in tch but green: wknd over 1f out* **14/1**
13 *3 ¼* **Duchess Of Magenta (IRE)** 3-9-0 0........ TomQueally 16 35
(Eve Johnson Houghton) *in rr: sme prog ins fnl f* **50/1**
- **14** *nse* **Polly McGinty** 3-9-0 0........ LukeMorris 10 35
(Nicky Vaughan) *rdn 1/2-way: a in rr* **100/1**
15 *4* **Queen Myrine (IRE)** 3-9-0 0........ RyanMoore 15 24
(Richard Hannon) *green: bhd most of way* **12/1**
16 *2 ½* **Mandatori (IRE)** 3-9-0 0........ JimCrowley 13 17
(Nicky Vaughan) *chsd ldrs to 1/2-way* **100/1**

1m 25.78s (0.08) **Going Correction** +0.075s/f (Good) **16** Ran SP% **120.4**
Speed ratings (Par 97): **102,99,97,95,95 91,91,88,87,87 86,85,81,81,77 74**
toteswingers: 1&2 £11.50, 1&3 £24.80, 2&3 £15.40 CSF £44.80 TOTE £4.20: £1.80, £4.30, £3.10; EX 46.20 Trifecta £311.90 Part won. Pool: £421.57 - 0.80 winning units..
Owner Hamdan Al Maktoum **Bred** Andrew Buxton **Trained** Newmarket, Suffolk

FOCUS
This fillies' maiden has gone to a subsequent Group-race winner three times in the last seven seasons - Illustrious Miss in 2004, Silver Touch in 2006 and Promising Lead in 2008. The time of this latest running was a highly respectable 0.87 seconds slower than earlier Class 3 handicap. No form by which to judge these, but plenty of them looked nice types. They raced up the middle of the track and the front pair were always 1-2.
Saktoon(USA) Official explanation: jockey said filly ran green

1363 ROBERT SANGSTER MEMORIAL MAIDEN FILLIES' STKS (DIV I) 1m 2f 6y
3:15 (3:15) (Class 4) 3-Y-O **£4,533** (£1,348; £674; £336) **Stalls** Low

Form RPR
1 **Imperial Pippin (USA)** 3-9-0 0........ WilliamBuick 3 85+
(John Gosden) *trckd ldrs on ins: pushed along over 2f out: drvn and qcknd to press ldr over 1f out: upsides ins fnl f: asserted fnl 50yds: kpt on wl* **7/1**[2]
4- **2** *nk* **Caraboss**[225] 5692 3-9-0 0........ RyanMoore 2 84+
(Sir Michael Stoute) *disp ld tl slt advantage over 5f out: styd strly chal but narrow ld over 1f out: kpt on ins fnl f tl hdd and nt qckn fnl 50yds* **8/11**[1]
3 *2 ¼* **Stella Point (IRE)** 3-9-0 0........ RichardHughes 11 80+
(Mick Channon) *stdd s and bhd: hdwy over 2f out: styd on wl ins fnl f to take 3rd nr fin: gng on cl home* **11/1**
4 *nk* **Creme Anglaise** 3-9-0 0........ HayleyTurner 6 79
(Michael Bell) *chsd ldrs: drvn and kpt on to chse ldng duo ins fnl 2f: no imp and lost 3rd cl home* **50/1**
3- **5** *3* **Hidden Valley**[187] 6779 3-9-0 0........ LiamKeniry 7 73
(Andrew Balding) *chsd ldrs: rdn over 2f out: styd on same pce fr over 1f out* **16/1**
5 **6** *¾* **Trend Line (IRE)**[91] 158 3-9-0 0........ JackMitchell 8 72+
(Peter Chapple-Hyam) *in rr: swtchd to outside over 2f out: drvn and styd on fnl f but nvr gng pce to rch ldrs* **12/1**
7 *2 ¾* **Tarkeeba (IRE)** 3-9-0 0........ RichardHills 10 66+
(Roger Varian) *in rr: pushed along over 2f out: kpt on ins fnl f but nvr any ch* **8/1**[3]
0- **8** *1 ½* **Supreme Seductress (IRE)**[175] 7057 3-9-0 0........ MichaelHills 4 63
(B W Hills) *disp ld tl over 5f out: styd upsides and str chal fr 3f out tl wl over 1f out: wknd qckly ins fnl f* **20/1**
9 *2* **Sharp Relief (IRE)** 3-9-0 0........ JimmyFortune 5 59
(Hughie Morrison) *in rr but in tch: drvn and green over 2f out: sn btn* **28/1**
00- **10** *3 ¾* **High Fallutin (IRE)**[196] 6521 3-8-9 0........ AmyScott(5) 12 52
(Eve Johnson Houghton) *in tch: chsd ldrs 5f out: wknd over 2f out* **100/1**
11 *8* **Formal Dining (USA)** 3-9-0 0........ TedDurcan 1 36
(Edward Vaughan) *slowly away: t.k.h and sn in tch: wknd ins fnl 3f* **40/1**

2m 10.38s (1.58) **Going Correction** -0.125s/f (Firm) **11** Ran SP% **117.0**
Speed ratings (Par 97): **88,87,85,85,83 82,80,79,77,74 68**
toteswingers: 1&2 £2.90, 1&3 £4.50, 2&3 £4.20 CSF £11.91 TOTE £8.10: £1.80, £1.10, £2.50; EX 17.60 Trifecta £72.50 Pool: £714.93 - 7.29 winning units..
Owner K Abdulla **Bred** Juddmonte Farms Inc **Trained** Newmarket, Suffolk

FOCUS
Some really smart fillies have won a division of this maiden in recent times, including subsequent Group 1 winners Islington, Eswarah and Folk Opera, as well as Irish St Leger runner-up Clowance. Hand times show the field covered the first 5f around 3.20 seconds slower than the second division, and the final time was 2.65 seconds slower, so something of a dash to the line ensued, making the performance of the winner all the more impressive. The form is rated around the race averages.

1364 ROBERT SANGSTER MEMORIAL MAIDEN FILLIES' STKS (DIV II) 1m 2f 6y
3:50 (3:50) (Class 4) 3-Y-O **£4,533** (£1,348; £674; £336) **Stalls** Low

Form RPR
2- **1** **Dancing Rain (IRE)**[178] 7000 3-9-0 0........ KierenFallon 1 87+
(William Haggas) *disp ld tl def advantage 6f out: jnd fr 2f out: drvn ins fnl f: asserted and styd on strly ins fnl 120yds: readily* **7/2**[3]
04- **2** *1 ¼* **Highest**[198] 6469 3-9-0 0........ WilliamBuick 10 84
(John Gosden) *trckd ldrs: drvn to chal fr 2f out: styd pressing for ld ins fnl f tl outpcd by wnr fnl 120yds but hld on wl for 2nd* **7/1**
3 **3** *½* **Tasheyaal**[20] 992 3-9-0 0........ RichardHills 6 83
(B W Hills) *trckd ldrs: chsd wnr 3f out and str chal 2f out: ev ch ins fnl f tl outpcd fnl 120yds and one pce into 3rd sn after* **5/2**[1]
2- **4** *4 ½* **Sunday Bess (JPN)**[169] 7186 3-9-0 0........ RichardKingscote 2 74+
(Tom Dascombe) *wl there tl lost position over 3f out: swtchd rt to outside and kpt on again fr over 1f out to take 4th ins fnl f but nvr a threat* **11/4**[2]
5 *4* **Cape Princess** 3-9-0 0........ JamieSpencer 5 66
(Michael Bell) *in rr: drvn and hdwy 3f out: styd on to take 4th 2f out but nvr nr ldng trio and wknd into 5th ins fnl f* **14/1**
6 *2* **Golden City (IRE)** 3-9-0 0........ JackMitchell 4 62
(Chris Wall) *s.i.s: in rr: pushed along over 3f out: nvr gng pce to rch ldrs* **100/1**
00- **7** *2 ½* **Miss Topsy Turvy (IRE)**[174] 7094 3-9-0 0........ TedDurcan 8 57+
(John Dunlop) *in rr: rdn 3f out and stl green: nvr gng pce to get nr ldrs* **66/1**
65 **8** *nk* **Beauchamp Zest**[27] 909 3-9-0 0........(t) JamesDoyle 11 56
(Hans Adielsson) *rdn over 3f out: a towards rr* **66/1**
9 *nk* **All Time** 3-9-0 0........ TomQueally 3 56+
(Sir Henry Cecil) *chsd ldrs: rdn: green and wknd qckly 2f out* **6/1**
53- **10** *½* **Monicalew**[146] 7530 3-9-0 0........ AdamKirby 7 55
(Walter Swinburn) *sn disputing ld tl dropped to 2nd 6f out: wknd qckly 3f out* **33/1**
11 *3 ¼* **Dawn Gale (IRE)** 3-9-0 0........ SteveDrowne 9 48
(Hughie Morrison) *a in rr* **50/1**

2m 7.73s (-1.07) **Going Correction** -0.125s/f (Firm) **11** Ran SP% **119.8**
Speed ratings (Par 97): **99,98,97,94,90 89,87,86,86,86 83**
toteswingers: 1&2 £4.70, 1&3 £3.30, 2&3 £4.80 CSF £28.28 TOTE £5.00: £2.20, £2.40, £1.80; EX 26.70 Trifecta £72.50 Pool: £1162.82 - 11.86 winning units..
Owner M J & L A Taylor **Bred** Swettenham Stud **Trained** Newmarket, Suffolk

FOCUS
Often a strong fillies' maiden. They went an ordinary pace and the time, although 2.65 seconds quicker than the steadily run first leg, was 0.91 seconds slower than the following conditions event. The winner built on her debut effort and the form is rated around the race averages.

1365 DUBAI DUTY FREE GOLF WORLD CUP CONDITIONS STKS 1m 2f 6y
4:25 (4:25) (Class 3) 3-Y-O **£7,788** (£2,332; £1,166; £583; £291) **Stalls** Low

Form RPR
011- **1** **Cai Shen (IRE)**[225] 5690 3-8-13 90........ RichardHughes 1 103
(Richard Hannon) *hld up off pce in 5th: swtchd rt to outside: 3f out: drvn and rapid hdwy to qckn into 3 l ld ins fnl 2f: in n.d ins fnl f: readily: enterprising ride* **8/1**[3]

51- **2** 2 3/4 **Al Kazeem**[174] 7094 3-8-13 95 SteveDrowne 2 97+
(Roger Charlton) *t.k.h: chsd ldrs and disputing 3rd tl outpcd whn pce qcknd sharply over 2f out and swtchd rt to outside: styd on to chse enterprisingly rdn wnr appr fnl f but no imp: jst hld on for 2nd* **5/2**[2]

2- **3** *shd* **Thimaar (USA)**[174] 7094 3-8-13 0 RichardHills 3 97+
(John Gosden) *t.k.h: trckd ldrs and disputing 3rd: drvn to chse enterprisingly rdn wnr whn pce qcknd sharply 2f out: one pce into 3rd appr fnl f: rallied to press for 2nd nr fin but no ch w wnr* **5/6**[1]

041- **4** *11* **Argocat (IRE)**[182] 6883 3-8-13 88 JamieSpencer 4 75
(Paul Cole) *sn trcking ldr: led 4f out: rdn 3f out: hdd ins fnl 2f: sn wknd* **16/1**

3-1 **5** *9* **Failasoof (USA)**[27] 909 3-8-13 83 TadhgO'Shea 5 57
(B W Hills) *sn led: hdd 4f out: wknd ins fnl 3f: eased whn no ch ins fnl f* **9/1**

2m 6.82s (-1.98) **Going Correction** -0.125s/f (Firm) **5** Ran SP% **110.1**
Speed ratings (Par 102): **102,99,99,90,83**
CSF £27.91 TOTE £6.70: £2.90, £1.20; EX 23.30.
Owner Mrs J Wood **Bred** Wardstown Stud Ltd **Trained** East Everleigh, Wilts

FOCUS
Over the years this conditions event has been contested by several smart types - now too many to mention them all but the most high profile of recent times is Light Shift, who took this en-route to her 2007 Oaks success. The beaten runners are often worth following too, and last season Myplacelater, a subsequent Listed winner, defeated Bullet Train, who later won the Lingfield Derby Trial. It was quicker than the previous maidens and the winner is progressive.

NOTEBOOK
Cai Shen(IRE) ◆ had stamina to prove (not sure to stay on breeding) on his seasonal return and was the only one of these not entered in the Dante. Visually he looked to outpace his rivals when committed around 2f out, quickening well to go clear, and that may have been the case. However, hand times show the field covered the first 5f quicker than both divisions of the fillies' maiden (final time also faster), and even though they didn't go quick in either of those races, particularly the first division, it at least shows that this race wasn't run at a crawl so it might be dangerous to assume he's grossly flattered. Admittedly the next two finishers are open to significant improvement, but he's clearly a talented colt and if anything he still looked green when in front, appearing to idle somewhat. There was a suggestion afterwards that the Dee Stakes could be a suitable target, with his speed a potential asset around Chester. (op 13-2 tchd 6-1)
Al Kazeem ◆, who landed a separate division to the maiden won by Carlton House here (1m, good to soft) on his final juvenile outing, is a sizeable type and looked as though the run would do him good. He can improve. (op 3-1 tchd 9-4)
Thimaar(USA) ◆, runner-up to Al Kazeem on his only start at two, just failed to reverse form. He looked as though he'd come on for the run fitness-wise and can do a lot better. (op Evens tchd 5-4 and 11-8 in a place)
Argocat(IRE) didn't offer much after a six-month break, but faced stiff company. (op 14-1 tchd 12-1)
Failasoof(USA) ran as though something was amiss. (op 7-1 tchd 13-2)

1366 DUBAI DUTY FREE DOUBLE MILLIONAIRE H'CAP 5f 34y
4:55 (4:57) (Class 2) (0-110,102) 4-Y-0+
£9,346 (£2,799; £1,399; £700; £349; £175) Stalls High

Form RPR
221- **1** **Noble Storm (USA)**[161] 7329 5-9-7 102 GrahamGibbons 5 114
(Ed McMahon) *disp ld tl def advantage over 3f out: rdn ins fnl f: r.o strly* **6/1**[3]

0000 **2** 1/2 **Rain Delayed (IRE)**[13] 1093 5-9-4 99 RichardHughes 1 109+
(Michael Dods) *t.k.h: in tch: gd hdwy over 1f out: str run to chse wnr ins fnl f: kpt on wl but a hld* **8/1**

544- **3** *3* **Captain Carey**[251] 4814 5-8-12 93 TomMcLaughlin 2 92
(Malcolm Saunders) *chsd ldrs: wnt 2nd and drvn 2f out: no imp over 1f out: wknd into 3rd ins fnl f* **20/1**

-602 **4** *nk* **Secret Asset (IRE)**[9] 1186 6-9-2 97 RyanMoore 8 95+
(Jane Chapple-Hyam) *drvn along and outpcd in rr tl hdwy appr fnl f: kpt on but nvr gng pce to rch ldrs* **5/1**[1]

000- **5** *1* **Run For The Hills**[146] 7524 5-9-0 95 WilliamBuick 4 90
(Roger Charlton) *in tch: drvn and hdwy fr 2f out: chsd ldrs over 1f out: hung rt u.p and fnd no ex ins fnl f* **14/1**

130- **6** 1 3/4 **Sohraab**[199] 6446 7-8-7 88 EddieAhern 3 76
(Hughie Morrison) *chsd ldrs: rdn over 2f out: wknd ins fnl f* **11/1**

00-2 **7** *2* **Capercaillie (USA)**[15] 1067 4-8-7 88 oh3 LukeMorris 10 69
(Clive Cox) *in rr: pushed along 1/2-way: kpt on ins fnl f* **8/1**

1044 **8** *5* **Five Star Junior (USA)**[9] 1186 5-8-13 94 KierenFallon 7 57
(Linda Stubbs) *chsd ldrs to 1/2-way* **17/2**

600- **9** *4* **Moorhouse Lad**[181] 6918 8-9-2 97 TomEaves 9 46
(Bryan Smart) *dispute ld tl over 3f out: wknd ins fnl 2f* **25/1**

020- **10** 2 1/4 **Noverre To Go (IRE)**[146] 7524 5-9-2 97 (t) RichardKingscote 12 38
(Tom Dascombe) *rdn 1/2-way: a outpcd* **20/1**

032- **11** *6* **Courageous (IRE)**[210] 6142 5-8-11 92 JimmyFortune 11 11
(David Nicholls) *chsd ldrs to 1/2-way* **7/1**

000- **12** 4 1/2 **Striking Spirit**[209] 6177 6-9-2 97 AdrianNicholls 13 —
(David Nicholls) *chsd ldrs to 1/2-way* **11/2**[2]

60.63 secs (-0.77) **Going Correction** +0.075s/f (Good) **12** Ran SP% **120.0**
Speed ratings (Par 109): **109,108,103,102,101 98,95,87,80,77 67,60**
toteswingers: 1&2 £10.00, 1&3 £15.60, 2&3 £31.90 CSF £52.48 CT £914.92 TOTE £7.80: £2.00, £2.60, £5.70; EX 46.30 Trifecta £693.90 Part won. Pool of £937.80 - 0.10 winning units..
Owner R L Bedding **Bred** Brereton C Jones **Trained** Lichfield, Staffs

FOCUS
Usually a quality sprint handicap - subsequent Group 1 winner Kyllachy took the 2002 running. There was a feeling that the middle of the track was favoured on the straight course at this meeting and that was borne out here. They raced middle to stands' side, but those who raced away from the fence fared best with five of the first six finishers drawn in the bottom five stalls. The form might not be the most solid.

NOTEBOOK
Noble Storm(USA) ◆ is a strong, proper sprinting type physically, but he looked as though the run would do him good. He was favoured by where he raced, but this was still a smart performance on his return - he blitzed his rivals and had this won from some way out before getting tired. There can be little doubt he's Group class. (op 9-2)
Rain Delayed(IRE) was patiently ridden and stayed on well to finish clear of the rest, but he looks flattered to get to so close to the winner. (op 15-2 tchd 7-1)
Captain Carey has a gradually progressive profile and this was a fine return from a 251-day absence, especially as his stable has yet to really get going yet. He could be one to keep on side this year. (op 25-1)
Secret Asset(IRE) is due to be eased 2lb, which should help. (op 15-2)
Run For The Hills has been gelded and had a wind operation since last seen. His head carriage was a bit awkward on occasions and he hung under pressure, not making a telling impression. Apparently he's now off to race in Singapore. (op 16-1)
Sohraab, well drawn, was 10lb lower than when fifth in this last year and 7lb lower than when runner-up the year before, but he can't be relied upon these days. (op 8-1)
Five Star Junior(USA) Official explanation: jockey said gelding lost its action
Noverre To Go(IRE) raced towards the unfavoured nearside rail and was entitled to need this comeback run. (op 22-1 tchd 25-1)
Courageous(IRE), poorly drawn, was eased once held. He can do better. (op 15-2 tchd 8-1)
Striking Spirit ◆ was heavily eased once held and had raced against the unfavoured near rail. Official explanation: jockey said gelding lost its action (op 15-2)

1367 DREWEATTS 1759 H'CAP 2m
5:25 (5:25) (Class 4) (0-85,82) 4-Y-0+ £3,885 (£1,156; £577; £288) Stalls Low

Form RPR
022- **1** **Warne's Way (IRE)**[41] 7181 8-8-13 67 (b) KierenFallon 12 76
(Brendan Powell) *trckd ldrs in 3rd: led over 3f out: drvn clr fr 2f out: in n.d after* **16/1**

2 *3* **Zakatal**[20] 5-9-12 80 (t) JamieSpencer 1 85
(Philip Hobbs) *mid-div: drvn and outpcd 4f out: swtchd sharply rt to outside over 2f out: hrd rdn and styd on ins fnl f to take 2nd last strides but nvr any ch w wnr* **7/2**[2]

202- **3** *nk* **Albeed**[180] 6955 4-9-0 72 TedDurcan 8 77+
(John Dunlop) *chsd ldrs: wnt 2nd and drvn over 2f out: sn hanging lft and no imp: lost wl hld 2nd last strides* **12/1**

2213 **4** 2 1/2 **Parhelion**[17] 1030 4-9-7 79 TomQueally 2 81
(Derek Haydn Jones) *chsd ldr tl over 3f out then chsd wnr tl over 2f out: styd on same pce* **14/1**

13-2 **5** 1 1/4 **High On A Hill (IRE)**[86] 209 4-9-3 75 TravisBlock 10 75
(Sylvester Kirk) *mid-div: hdwy over 3f out: rdn and one pce fnl 2f* **22/1**

24-1 **6** *4* **Momkinzain (USA)**[58] 563 4-9-4 76 SamHitchcott 14 71
(Mick Channon) *in rr: hrd drvn and hdwy on outside fr 3f out: chsd ldrs and no imp fnl 2f* **12/1**

40-2 **7** *shd* **Nemo Spirit (IRE)**[7] 1215 6-9-12 80 (vt[1]) RichardKingscote 4 75
(Tom Dascombe) *sn led: hdd over 3f out: grad wknd fr 2f out* **20/1**

531- **8** 1 1/2 **Sula Two**[180] 6955 4-9-4 76 JimCrowley 13 69
(Ron Hodges) *in rr: hdwy on outside over 2f out but nvr any threat* **12/1**

243/ **9** 2 3/4 **Non Dom (IRE)**[44] 6552 5-9-7 75 SteveDrowne 3 65
(Hughie Morrison) *chsd ldrs: rdn 3f out: wknd fr 2f out* **11/4**[1]

1-36 **10** 2 1/4 **Quinsman**[18] 1016 5-9-5 73 LiamKeniry 6 60
(J S Moore) *in rr: brief effrt fr 3f out but nvr nr ldrs* **28/1**

-032 **11** *53* **Epsom Salts**[37] 805 6-9-4 72 IanMongan 9 —
(Pat Phelan) *in rr: hdwy to get in tch 3f out but nvr on terms: wknd over 2f out: eased whn no ch ins fnl f: t.o* **8/1**[3]

-443 **12** *5* **Satwa Gold (USA)**[28] 894 5-9-3 71 (t) RichardHughes 5 —
(Seamus Durack) *mid-div and sme prog over 3f out: nvr any threat: eased whn no ch ins fnl f: t.o* **9/1**

100- **13** *9* **Lajidaal (USA)**[18] 5747 4-9-10 82 WilliamBuick 11 —
(Gary Moore) *sn rdn and nvr travelling in rr: eased whn no ch fnl 3f: t.o* **40/1**

3m 32.88s (0.88) **Going Correction** -0.125s/f (Firm)
WFA 4 from 5yo+ 4lb **13** Ran SP% **120.6**
Speed ratings (Par 105): **92,90,90,89,88 86,86,85,84,83 56,54,49**
toteswingers: 1&2 £14.40, 1&3 £22.50, 2&3 £15.30. Tote Super 7: Win: Not won. Place: Not won. CSF £69.04 CT £723.36 TOTE £22.80: £4.90, £1.60, £5.30; EX 125.00 TRIFECTA Not won..
Owner Nigel Stafford **Bred** Mrs Ann Kennedy **Trained** Upper Lambourn, Berks

FOCUS
A race won in 2007 by subsequent Royal Ascot and Cheltenham Festival winner Junior. This looked a competitive contest. The winner recorded a Flat personal best.
Lajidaal(USA) Official explanation: jockey said colt never travelled
T/Jkpt: Not won. T/Plt: £50.00 to a £1 stake. Pool of £71,344.95 - 1040.40 winning units. T/Qpdt: £5.20 to a £1 stake. Pool of £5,278.59 - 743.30 winning units. ST

1294 WOLVERHAMPTON (A.W) (L-H)
Friday, April 15

OFFICIAL GOING: Standard
Wind: Light across Weather: Cloudy with sunny spells

1368 PPDG FILL YOUR VACANCIES FOR FREE H'CAP 7f 32y(P)
2:30 (2:31) (Class 5) (0-75,74) 4-Y-0+ £2,266 (£674; £337; £168) Stalls High

Form RPR
00U- **1** **Khandaq (USA)**[148] 7499 4-9-7 74 PaulMulrennan 6 81
(Keith Dalgleish) *s.i.s: hld up: hdwy over 2f out: led over 1f out: rdn out* **18/1**

4313 **2** 3/4 **Copperwood**[7] 1221 6-9-5 72 (p) DaneO'Neill 9 77
(Michael Blanshard) *hld up: hdwy 2f out: rdn over 1f out: edgd lft ins fnl f: r.o* **5/1**[3]

5114 **3** 1 1/4 **Katmai River (IRE)**[9] 1177 4-8-8 61 (v) PaulHanagan 4 63
(Mark Usher) *chsd ldrs: rdn over 2f out: ev ch over 1f out: no ex wl ins fnl f* **9/4**[1]

066- **4** 1/2 **Tamasou (IRE)**[227] 5634 6-9-0 67 RichardMullen 7 67
(Ed McMahon) *hld up: rdn 1/2-way: hdwy over 1f out: r.o nt rch ldrs* **7/2**[2]

1043 **5** *4* **Toby Tyler**[31] 853 5-8-9 62 (v) MickyFenton 5 51
(Paul Midgley) *hld up: rdn over 2f out: styd on ins fnl f: nvr trbld ldrs* **18/1**

/136 **6** *3* **Qadar (IRE)**[21] 961 9-9-0 74 (p) NoraLooby[(7)] 3 55
(Alan McCabe) *trckd ldrs: racd keenly: wknd ins fnl f* **15/2**

2130 **7** *4* **Double Carpet (IRE)**[23] 949 8-9-0 67 KirstyMilczarek 1 38
(Garry Woodward) *led: rdn and hdd over 1f out: wknd ins fnl f* **6/1**

01-0 **8** 2 1/4 **Bishopbriggs (USA)**[9] 1190 6-8-10 63 FrankieMcDonald 2 28
(K F Clutterbuck) *chsd ldr tl rdn over 2f out: wknd over 1f out* **25/1**

1m 29.05s (-0.55) **Going Correction** 0.0s/f (Stan) **8** Ran SP% **110.1**
Speed ratings (Par 103): **103,102,100,100,95 92,87,85**
toteswingers: 1&2 £32.90, 1&3 £10.70, 2&3 £1.50 CSF £97.34 CT £270.67 TOTE £23.00: £11.90, £1.60, £1.02; EX 78.30.
Owner Gordon McDowall **Bred** Shadwell Farm LLC **Trained** Carluke, South Lanarkshire

FOCUS
A fair level of form in a handicap which was run at a good pace. Straightforward form.

1369 PPDG.CO.UK (S) STKS 7f 32y(P)
3:00 (3:00) (Class 6) 3-Y-O £1,706 (£503; £252) Stalls High

Form RPR
52-3 **1** **Roodee Queen**[7] 1219 3-8-7 70 PaulHanagan 4 52
(Patrick Morris) *mde all: pushed clr over 1f out: edgd rt ins fnl f: rdn out* **5/4**[1]

5305 **2** 3/4 **Lough Corrib (USA)**[2] 1303 3-8-12 58 (b) PhillipMakin 3 55
(Kevin Ryan) *hld up: rdn over 2f out: hdwy over 1f out: chsd wnr ins fnl f: r.o* **4/1**[3]

5-55 **3** *3 1/4* **Poetically**[6] 1249 3-8-12 55 .... EddieCreighton 2 47
(Joseph Tuite) *plld hrd and prom: chsd wnr over 2f out: sn rdn: no ex and lost 2nd ins fnl f* **10/1**

344 **4** *3/4* **Jackie Love (IRE)**[11] 1132 3-8-7 0 .... KirstyMilczarek 1 39
(John Ryan) *s.i.s: hdwy over 4f out: rdn over 2f out: styd on same pce appr fnl f* **9/4**[2]

06-0 **5** *hd* **Senor Tibor (USA)**[11] 1132 3-8-5 60 ....(v[1]) JenniferFerguson[(7)] 5 43
(Edward Creighton) *chsd wnr 6f out tl over 2f out: styd on same pce appr fnl f* **50/1**

06 **6** *26* **Fawara**[25] 929 3-8-4 0 .... JamesSullivan[(3)] 6 —
(Ruth Carr) *chsd wnr 1f: remained handy: rdn 1/2-way: wknd over 2f out: t.o* **40/1**

1m 30.76s (1.16) **Going Correction** 0.0s/f (Stan) **6** Ran SP% **108.7**
Speed ratings (Par 96): **93,92,88,87,87 57**
toteswingers: 1&2 £2.40, 1&3 £2.90, 2&3 £2.20 CSF £6.21 TOTE £1.90: £1.10, £1.70; EX 5.60.The winner was bought in for 4,750gns.

Owner Chester Racing Club Ltd **Bred** Tom & Evelyn Yates **Trained** Tarporley, Cheshire

FOCUS
A weak seller. The winner was a stone+ off her 2yo best.

1370 PPDG 100,000 LIVES CHANGED FOREVER MAIDEN STKS 7f 32y(P)
3:35 (3:35) (Class 5) 3-Y-O+ **£2,266** (£674; £337; £168) **Stalls** High

Form RPR

3-2 **1** **Roninski (IRE)**[17] 1027 3-8-13 0 .... PaulMulrennan 1 74
(Bryan Smart) *mde all: rdn clr fr over 1f out: eased towards fin* **1/6**[1]

22-5 **2** *6* **Wishformore (IRE)**[100] 56 4-9-3 60 ....(p) RyanPowell[(5)] 4 58
(J S Moore) *chsd wnr thrght: rdn over 1f out: sn outpcd* **6/1**[2]

00 **3** *4* **Passing Moment**[10] 1155 3-8-3 0 .... AndrewElliott[(5)] 3 42
(Brian Baugh) *plld hrd and prom: rdn over 2f out: sn outpcd* **50/1**

4 *nk* **Fiftynotout (IRE)** 4-9-13 0 .... BarryMcHugh 2 51
(Roger Fisher) *s.s: hld up: hdwy 2f out: sn rdn and outpcd* **20/1**

2 **5** *13* **Brent Pelham**[18] 1015 4-9-13 0 .... StevieDonohoe 5 16
(Tobias B P Coles) *prom: rdn 1/2-way: wknd over 2f out* **14/1**[3]

1m 31.68s (2.08) **Going Correction** 0.0s/f (Stan)
WFA 3 from 4yo 14lb **5** Ran SP% **113.4**
Speed ratings (Par 103): **88,81,76,76,61**
CSF £1.93 TOTE £1.30: £1.02, £2.00; EX 1.60.

Owner Ron Hull **Bred** Peter Hodgson And Star Pointe Limited **Trained** Hambleton, N Yorks

FOCUS
A dire maiden, and litle to go on with the runer-up no guide. The form is rated loosely around the winner.

1371 PPDG 4TH BEST UK COMPANY H'CAP 5f 20y(P)
4:10 (4:11) (Class 4) (0-85,85) 4-Y-O+ **£3,238** (£963; £481; £240) **Stalls** Low

Form RPR

000- **1** **Magical Macey (USA)**[179] 6985 4-9-0 78 .... LeeNewman 2 86
(David Barron) *chsd ldrs: rdn to ld 1f out: edgd lft: jst hld on* **3/1**[2]

0206 **2** *nse* **Garstang**[27] 910 8-8-10 74 ....(b) PaulHanagan 6 82
(John Balding) *hld up in tch: racd keenly: rdn over 1f out: hung lft ins fnl f: r.o* **8/1**

6043 **3** *2 1/4* **Absa Lutte (IRE)**[4] 1279 8-8-4 71 oh5 ....(bt) SimonPearce[(3)] 5 71
(Michael Mullineaux) *hld up: hdwy over 1f out: sn rdn and ev ch: styd on same pce ins fnl f* **5/1**

6562 **4** *shd* **Green Manalishi**[21] 970 10-9-7 85 ....(p) PhillipMakin 7 84
(Kevin Ryan) *hld up: hdwy over 1f out: sn rdn: no ex ins fnl f* **9/4**[1]

-545 **5** *2* **Billy Red**[21] 961 7-9-3 81 ....(b) FergusSweeney 3 73
(J R Jenkins) *w ldr tl led 2f out: rdn and hdd 1f out: wknd ins fnl f* **9/2**[3]

4363 **6** *1 1/2* **Feelin Foxy**[48] 701 7-9-5 83 .... PaulMulrennan 1 70
(James Given) *led 3f: sn rdn: wknd ins fnl f* **6/1**

005- **7** *1 3/4* **Diamond Johnny G (USA)**[233] 5417 4-8-12 76 ....(t) EddieCreighton 4 56
(Edward Creighton) *s.i.s: hdwy over 2f out: rdn 1/2-way: wknd over 1f out* **33/1**

61.28 secs (-1.02) **Going Correction** 0.0s/f (Stan) **7** Ran SP% **119.0**
Speed ratings (Par 105): **108,107,104,104,100 98,95**
toteswingers:1&2 £5.30, 2&3 £6.70, 1&3 £3.50 CSF £28.29 TOTE £4.20: £2.30, £3.90; EX 35.80.

Owner K J Alderson **Bred** Silver Springs Stud Farm Inc & Mrs J Costelloe **Trained** Maunby, N Yorks

FOCUS
A fairly useful sprint handicap. The winner is rated to his 3yo best and the second back to his 2009 form.

Feelin Foxy Official explanation: jockey said mare hung right-handed

1372 PPDG VALUES CHAMPION 2011 H'CAP 1m 4f 50y(P)
4:45 (4:45) (Class 6) (0-65,65) 4-Y-O+ **£1,706** (£503; £252) **Stalls** Low

Form RPR

403 **1** **Mcbirney (USA)**[53] 636 4-9-2 64 .... AndrewHeffernan[(3)] 6 76
(Paul D'Arcy) *hld up: hdwy over 2f out: led over 1f out: rdn out* **11/4**[2]

2341 **2** *3* **Broughtons Paradis (IRE)**[15] 1063 5-9-0 58 .... StevieDonohoe 7 65
(Willie Musson) *hld up: hdwy over 3f out: chsd ldr over 2f out: led over 1f out: sn rdn and hdd: styd on same pce ins fnl f* **3/1**[3]

063- **3** *2* **Ghufa (IRE)**[165] 7275 7-9-4 65 .... SimonPearce[(3)] 3 69
(Lydia Pearce) *a.p: chsd ldr over 5f out: led over 3f out: rdn and hdd over 1f out: no ex ins fnl f* **9/4**[1]

30-0 **4** *3/4* **Colonel Sherman (USA)**[28] 897 6-9-0 58 .... RussKennemore 1 61
(Philip Kirby) *chsd ldr over 6f: remained handy tl outpcd over 2f out: styd on u.p ins fnl f* **9/1**

1225 **5** *11* **Kipchak (IRE)**[4] 1278 6-9-7 65 ....(p) KirstyMilczarek 4 50
(Conor Dore) *led and clr to 1/2-way: rdn and hdd over 3f out: wknd 2f out* **7/1**

0-06 **6** *4 1/2* **William Van Gogh**[21] 965 4-9-2 64 .... JamesSullivan[(3)] 2 42
(Michael Easterby) *hld up: hdwy over 4f out: sn rdn: wknd over 2f out* **20/1**

2m 39.85s (-1.25) **Going Correction** 0.0s/f (Stan)
WFA 4 from 5yo+ 1lb **6** Ran SP% **109.7**
Speed ratings (Par 101): **104,102,100,100,92 89**
toteswingers:1&2 £2.30, 2&3 £1.90, 1&3 £1.80 CSF £10.84 TOTE £5.50: £3.30, £1.90; EX 16.00.

Owner D'Arcy & Saunders **Bred** Charles H Wacker **Trained** Newmarket, Suffolk

FOCUS
A moderate handicap, run at a fair pace. The winner looks progressive k.and the second ran her best race so far on Polytrack.

1373 PERTEMPS PEOPLE DEVELOPMENT GROUP H'CAP 1m 141y(P)
5:20 (5:20) (Class 6) (0-65,65) 4-Y-O+ **£1,706** (£503; £252) **Stalls** Low

Form RPR

-631 **1** **Forward Feline (IRE)**[16] 1052 5-9-2 65 .... DeclanCannon[(5)] 8 73
(Bryn Palling) *hld up: hdwy over 2f out: nt clr run and swtchd rt over 1f out: rdn to ld ins fnl f: r.o* **11/2**[3]

6-43 **2** *1* **Aldo**[16] 1052 4-9-5 63 ....(t) FergusSweeney 9 69
(Alastair Lidderdale) *a.p: rdn over 1f out: ev ch and hung lft ins fnl f: styd on same pce* **11/2**[3]

526 **3** *2* **Kammamuri (IRE)**[31] 854 6-9-4 62 ....(bt) DaneO'Neill 1 63
(Frank Sheridan) *a.p: rdn to chse ldr over 2f out: led ins fnl f: sn hdd and no ex* **3/1**[1]

4-44 **4** *2* **Bold Marc (IRE)**[28] 903 9-9-4 62 .... AndrewElliott 5 59
(Mrs K Burke) *chsd ldrs tl led over 6f out: rdn over 1f out: hdd and no ex ins fnl f* **15/2**

0-02 **5** *2 1/2* **Classic Descent**[10] 1150 6-8-5 52 ....(t) JamesSullivan[(3)] 2 43
(Ruth Carr) *s.s: hld up: r.o ins fnl f: nvr nrr* **6/1**

0454 **6** *shd* **Amary (IRE)**[9] 1190 4-9-6 64 ....(p) BarryMcHugh 7 55
(John Harris) *chsd ldrs: rdn over 3f out: wknd ins fnl f* **20/1**

0053 **7** *nse* **Mutajaaser (USA)**[4] 1273 6-8-10 54 ....(be[1]) PaulHanagan 10 45
(Kevin Morgan) *s.s: hld up: hdwy over 2f out: rdn over 1f out: wknd ins fnl f* **4/1**[2]

/0-6 **8** *5* **Echo Dancer**[5] 712 5-8-12 56 ....(t) LeeNewman 4 35
(Trevor Wall) *prom: rdn over 3f out: wknd over 1f out* **40/1**

-046 **9** *5* **Tukitinyasok (IRE)**[29] 881 4-9-6 64 ....(b[1]) TonyHamilton 6 32
(Roger Fisher) *led: hdd over 6f out: chsd ldr tl rdn over 2f out: wknd over 1f out* **16/1**

500- **10** *15* **Bernix**[175] 7068 9-8-13 57 ....(p) J-PGuillambert 3 —
(Mark Campion) *hld up in tch: lost pl 4f out: rdn and wknd over 2f out: t.o* **25/1**

1m 49.8s (-0.70) **Going Correction** 0.0s/f (Stan) **10** Ran SP% **118.7**
Speed ratings (Par 101): **103,102,100,98,96 96,96,91,87,73**
toteswingers:1&2 £5.50, 2&3 £3.60, 1&3 £4.90 CSF £35.69 CT £111.12 TOTE £6.70: £2.20, £1.10, £2.70; EX 24.40.

Owner Derek And Jean Clee **Bred** D D And Mrs Jean P Clee **Trained** Tredodridge, Vale Of Glamorgan

FOCUS
There was a sound pace on here and it is straightforward form.

1374 PPDG SUPPORTING YOUNG TALENT APPRENTICE H'CAP 1m 1f 103y(P)
5:50 (5:50) (Class 6) (0-55,55) 4-Y-O+ **£1,706** (£503; £252) **Stalls** Low

Form RPR

3314 **1** **Barton Bounty**[4] 1273 4-8-13 52 ....(b) ShaneBKelly 7 65+
(Peter Niven) *hld up: hdwy over 2f out: rdn to ld and hung lft 1f out: styd on* **9/4**[1]

44-3 **2** *1/2* **Marino Prince (FR)**[24] 114 6-8-3 47 .... DavidSimmonson[(5)] 4 57
(Paul Midgley) *hld up: hdwy over 2f out: rdn to chse wnr ins fnl f: r.o* **8/1**

-354 **3** *4* **Corrib (IRE)**[53] 635 8-8-3 47 ow1 ....(p) ThomasBrown[(5)] 3 49
(Bryn Palling) *s.s: hld up: hdwy u.p over 1f out: r.o: nrst fin* **12/1**

2324 **4** *1 1/4* **Idol Deputy (FR)**[21] 969 5-8-10 49 .... RachealKneller 5 48
(Mark Usher) *chsd ldrs: shkn up over 2f out: nt clr run and swtchd rt ins fnl f: styd on same pce* **11/2**[3]

0050 **5** *hd* **Escardo (GER)**[6] 1253 8-8-1 47 ....(p) JoshBaudains[(7)] 6 46
(David Bridgwater) *prom: chsd ldr over 4f out: chal 3f out: rdn over 2f out: rdr dropped whip over 1f out: styd on same pce* **20/1**

6460 **6** *1/2* **Fedora (IRE)**[22] 1013 5-8-11 55 ....(t) JenniferFerguson[(5)] 8 53
(Olivia Maylam) *led: rdn over 2f out: hdd and no ex 1f out* **20/1**

4-30 **7** *3* **Market Puzzle (IRE)**[2] 1308 4-8-12 51 .... LucyKBarry 11 42
(Mark Brisbourne) *hld up: hdwy over 3f out: rdn over 2f out: wknd over 1f out* **9/1**

50-4 **8** *1 1/2* **Machir Bay**[7] 1216 4-8-0 46 .... JasonHart[(7)] 10 34
(Keith Dalgleish) *chsd ldr 5f: rdn and wknd over 2f out* **9/1**

5-40 **9** *2 3/4* **Indefinite Hope (ITY)**[72] 391 4-8-10 54 ....(t) GeorgeDowning[(5)] 9 26
(Frank Sheridan) *prom: lost pl over 7f out: pushed along and hdwy 6f out: wknd over 2f out* **5/1**[2]

-504 **10** *7* **Love In The West (IRE)**[49] 695 5-8-7 51 ....(b[1]) CharlesBishop[(5)] 1 19
(John Harris) *prom: lost pl over 4f out: sn bhd* **22/1**

050- **11** *7* **Miss Tenacious**[180] 6956 4-8-7 46 oh1 .... JakePayne 2 —
(Ron Hodges) *chsd ldrs: rdn and wkng whn n.m.r over 3f out* **66/1**

2m 1.95s (0.25) **Going Correction** 0.0s/f (Stan) **11** Ran SP% **117.0**
Speed ratings (Par 101): **98,97,94,92,92 92,89,88,85,79 73**
toteswingers: 1&2 £5.30, 1&3 £7.40, 2&3 £16.50 CSF £19.49 CT £179.81 TOTE £3.20: £1.30, £2.70, £3.20; EX 19.90.

Owner Francis Green Racing Ltd **Bred** Mrs M L Parry **Trained** Barton-le-Street, N Yorks

FOCUS
A moderate handicap, run to suit the closers. the winner is progressing and looks a bit better than the bare form.

T/Plt: £57.90 to a £1 stake. Pool of £49,279.95 - 621.11 winning units. T/Qpdt: £24.20 to a £1 stake. Pool of £3,336.92 - 101.90 winning units. CR

1375 - 1380a (Foreign Racing) - See Raceform Interactive

1224 DUNDALK (A.W) (L-H)
Friday, April 15

OFFICIAL GOING: Standard

1381a WWW.DUNDALKSTADIUM.COM H'CAP 1m 4f (P)
9:25 (9:39) (60-100,95) 4-Y-O+ **£11,206** (£3,275; £1,551; £517)

RPR

1 **Mount Athos (IRE)**[188] 6736 4-9-12 94 .... WMLordan 5 102+
(David Wachman, Ire) *mid-div: 8th 1/2-way: hdwy in 5th 1 1/2f out: rdn to ld 1f out: kpt on wl fnl f* **6/1**[3]

2 *2* **Dreamy Gent (IRE)**[211] 4772 9-8-7 77 .... ShaneFoley[(3)] 3 81
(Mrs John Harrington, Ire) *chsd ldrs: 7th 1/2-way: hdwy into 3rd 1 1/2f out: chal over 1f out: 2nd and no ex ins fnl f: kpt on same pce* **16/1**

3 *1/2* **High Importance (USA)**[128] 7772 4-8-12 80 .... SeamieHeffernan 10 83
(A J Martin, Ire) *in rr of mid-div: hdwy under 2f out: 6th 1 1/2f out: rdn into 4th 1f out: kpt on same pce fnl f* **66/1**

4 *nk* **Grey Soldier (IRE)**[28] 5083 6-10-0 95 ....(bt) DPMcDonogh 1 98
(Gordon Elliott, Ire) *chsd ldrs: 4th 1/2-way: hdwy in 2nd 2f out: rdn to dispute over 1f out: no ex ins fnl f: kpt on same pce* **8/1**

5 1 3/4 **Denny Crane**[126] 7823 5-9-3 84 JMurtagh 6 84
(Edward Lynam, Ire) *mid-div: 10th 1/2-way: rdn over 2f out: styd on into 5th 1f out: kpt on same pce fnl f* **9/2**[2]

6 2 1/2 **Blue Ridge Lane (IRE)**[7] 1229 5-8-12 79 (bt) GFCarroll 11 75
(John C McConnell, Ire) *hld up towards rr: sme late hdwy in 9th 1f out: kpt on same pce fnl f* **18/1**

7 nk **Toraidhe (IRE)**[14] 1088 5-10-0 95 (tp) KJManning 8 91
(J S Bolger, Ire) *mid-div: 9th 1/2-way: rdn into 7th 1f out: no ex fnl f and kpt on same pce* **14/1**

8 1 1/2 **Emerging Artist (FR)**[62] 525 5-9-13 94 GregFairley 4 87
(Mark Johnston) *chsd ldr in 2nd: led 4f out: rdn and hdd over 1f out: no ex* **7/4**[1]

9 shd **Zaralabad (IRE)**[180] 6971 7-9-12 93 FMBerry 14 86
(C F Swan, Ire) *hld up towards rr: no imp in 10th 1f out: kpt on one pce* **20/1**

10 nk **Bravely Fought (IRE)**[5] 1262 6-9-5 93 CPHoban(7) 2 86
(Sabrina J Harty, Ire) *chsd ldrs: 6th 1/2-way: hdwy into 3rd 2f out: rdn in 4th 1 1/2f out: no ex fr over 1f out* **7/1**

11 3 **Pires**[19] 1007 7-9-11 95 RMMoran(3) 9 83
(A J Martin, Ire) *towards rr for most: nvr a factor* **33/1**

12 1 3/4 **Broad Meaning**[7] 1229 5-9-4 88 (t) JPO'Brien(3) 13 73
(James McAuley, Ire) *chsd ldrs: 5th 1/2-way: rdn and no ex 2f out: wknd* **33/1**

13 1 1/2 **Beau Michael**[12] 4216 7-8-12 79 (bt) CO'Donoghue 12 62
(Adrian McGuinness, Ire) *chsd ldrs: 3rd 1/2-way: rdn in 4th 2f out: no ex and wknd* **25/1**

14 dist **Dancera (GER)**[298] 2194 7-8-7 74 DMGrant 7 —
(Mervyn Torrens, Ire) *led: rdn and hdd 4f out: no ex and wknd* **28/1**

2m 29.63s (149.63)
WFA 4 from 5yo+ 1lb **14** Ran SP% **129.7**
Daily Double: 138.50 euros to a 5 euro stake. CSF £97.49 CT £5803.58 TOTE £5.30: £1.20, £11.60, £23.10; DF 279.00.
Owner Dr Marwan Koukash **Bred** David Magnier And Cobra Bloodstock **Trained** Goolds Cross, Co Tipperary

FOCUS
The runner-up and third have been rated to their marks.

NOTEBOOK
Mount Athos(IRE), formerly trained by John Hills in Britain, had not been seen since finishing a disappointing 12th when fancied for a valuable Class 2 handicap at Ascot last October. A three-time winner for Hills, he was given a mark of 94 on his first start for Wachman and won with a bit to spare. Settled in mid-division, he was eased to the outside in the home straight to make his challenge. He quickened up well and put the race to bed in a couple of strides. He cruised home under a hands-and-heels ride and the winning margin could have been doubled. There could be a valuable handicap, perhaps on Guineas weekend at the Curragh, within his grasp, but the Chester Cup will also surely come into consideration (now 8-1 favourite for that race). (op 6/1 tchd 7/1)
Dreamy Gent(IRE) ran a cracker on his first start for seven months. A trailblazer in the past, more patient tactics were deployed here and, after tracking the pace, the 9-y-o stayed on well for second. A 2m handicap chase at Fairyhouse over Easter could be next on the agenda. (op 20/1)
High Importance(USA) looked to have lost the plot but this was a surprising upturn in fortunes for the son of Arch, who belied his 66-1 starting price with a fine run, making up ground down the wide outside in the home straight. No doubt his astute handler has a plan in place over hurdles in the coming months. (op 50/1)
Grey Soldier(IRE) was the subject of encouraging vibes from his trainer, who stated that he worked like a Champion Hurdle horse prior to his disappointing showing in the County Hurdle at Cheltenham. Always in the perfect position tracking the pace here, Declan McDonogh seemed to be producing his mount with a winning challenge when hitting the front just after the 2f pole. But he didn't find as much as expected off the bridle. Still, this was a promising display under top weight. (op 10/1 tchd 12/1)
Denny Crane travelled with his usual fluency but was unable to quicken inside the final furlong and wasn't knocked about once his chance had gone. (op 7/2)
Toraidhe(IRE) appeared not to stay after travelling well for a long way. (op 11/1)
Emerging Artist(FR) was heavily backed but, after adopting his customary front-running tactics, he was unable to sustain that pace after turning into the straight and trailed home a disappointing eighth. (op 2/1 tchd 9/4)
Pires fly-jumped out of the stalls, losing a couple of lengths in the process, and never got into contention.
T/Jkpt: @1,875.00. Pool of @5,000.00 - 2 winning units. T/Plt: @207.10. Pool of @16,067.67 - 58.18 winning units. II

[1107]DONCASTER (L-H)
Saturday, April 16

OFFICIAL GOING: Good to firm (good in places on round course)
Wind: Virtually nil Weather: Clody but dry

1382 AJA LADY RIDERS' H'CAP (LADY AMATEUR RIDERS) 7f
4:35 (4:36) (Class 4) (0-80,80) 4-Y-O+ £3,123 (£968; £484; £242) Stalls High

Form RPR

0252 1 **Bawaardi (IRE)**[38] 804 5-10-0 80 MissTSyddall(7) 5 87
(Richard Fahey) *hld up: stdy hdwy over 2f out: rdn over 1f out: led and edgd lft ins fnl f: kpt on* **7/1**[3]

0-05 2 1/2 **Den's Gift (IRE)**[21] 995 7-10-2 80 (b) MissRachelKing(5) 12 86
(Clive Cox) *prom on stands' rail: effrt to ld 2f out: rdn over 1f out: hdd and no ex ins fnl f* **5/1**[2]

020- 3 3/4 **Summer Dancer (IRE)**[223] 5789 7-10-2 80 MissWGibson(5) 6 84
(Paul Midgley) *hld up in centre: hdwy over 2f out: rdn over 1f out: kpt on wl fnl f* **14/1**

1310 4 hd **Trans Sonic**[17] 1035 8-9-8 74 (b) MissRHeptonstall(7) 1 77
(David O'Meara) *overall ldr far side: rdn along and hdd 2f out: edgd lft appr fnl f and one pce* **8/1**

5 1 **Power Force (SAF)**[346] 5-9-13 77 MissKECooper(5) 13 78
(Tom Tate) *towards rr: hdwy over 2f out: sn rdn and kpt on fnl f: nrst fin* **16/1**

0-00 6 4 **Ryedane (IRE)**[7] 1239 9-9-4 70 MissRRichardson(7) 14 60
(Tim Easterby) *prom stands' rail: rdn along 3f out: wknd fnl 2f* **28/1**

4600 7 1 **Methaaly (IRE)**[45] 736 8-9-9 71 (be) MissMMullineaux(3) 8 64
(Michael Mullineaux) *chsd ldrs towards stands' rail: rdn along over 2f out: sn no imp* **11/1**

000- 8 1 3/4 **Kavachi (IRE)**[137] 7637 8-10-2 80 MissHayleyMoore(5) 10 63
(Gary Moore) *s.i.s: a towards rr* **18/1**

0-14 9 2 1/2 **Rio Cobolo (IRE)**[13] 1110 5-9-10 76 MissJWalker(7) 11 52
(David Nicholls) *rrd s and s.i.s: swtchd to stands' rails and hdwy to chse ldrs 3f out: sn rdn and wknd fnl 2f* **9/2**[1]

6-54 10 hd **Fremen (USA)**[17] 1037 11-9-13 79 MissKBannon(7) 2 54
(David Nicholls) *chsd overall ldr far side: rdn along 3f out: sn wknd* **14/1**

-650 11 1 **Realt Na Mara (IRE)**[44] 743 8-9-6 72 MissNDumelow(7) 3 45
(Hughie Morrison) *prom centre: rdn along 3f out: wknd over 2f out* **22/1**

0-03 12 1 1/2 **Night Trade (IRE)**[4] 1296 4-9-11 77 (p) MissDLenge(7) 9 45
(Deborah Sanderson) *prom centre: effrt wl over 2f out and ev ch tl rdn: edgd lft and wknd wl over 1f out* **17/2**

25-6 13 7 **Cyflymder (IRE)**[13] 1109 5-9-6 72 MissCLWhitehead(7) 7 22
(Declan Carroll) *prom centre: rdn along 3f out: sn wknd* **8/1**

1m 26.68s (0.38) **Going Correction** -0.15s/f (Firm) **13** Ran SP% **120.7**
Speed ratings (Par 105): **91,90,89,89,88 83,82,80,77,77 76,74,66**
toteswingers:1&2:£5.30, 1&3:£14.60, 2&3:£18.60 CSF £42.32 CT £504.15 TOTE £8.60: £2.90, £1.90, £4.60; EX 47.10 Trifecta £332.00 Pool £547.39 - 1.22 winning units..
Owner The Matthewman One Partnership **Bred** Millsec Limited **Trained** Musley Bank, N Yorks
■ Stewards' Enquiry : Miss D Lenge two-day ban: careless riding (tbn)

FOCUS
The field spread across the track in this lady amateur riders' handicap and there appeared to be little bias. Straightforward enough form, rated around the front pair.
Methaaly(IRE) Official explanation: jockey said gelding lost its action
Cyflymder(IRE) Official explanation: jockey said gelding never travelled

1383 CROWNHOTEL-BAWTRY.COM MAIDEN STKS 5f
5:10 (5:10) (Class 4) 2-Y-O £3,432 (£1,021; £510; £254) Stalls High

Form RPR

1 **Lilbourne Lad (IRE)** 2-9-3 0 PatDobbs 4 80+
(Richard Hannon) *trckd ldrs: green and sltly outpcd 2f out: swtchd lft and rdn to chal ent fnl f: qcknd wl to ld last 100yds* **4/5**[1]

2 1 **Pea Shooter** 2-9-3 0 PhillipMakin 3 76+
(Kevin Ryan) *trckd ldrs: swtchd rt to rails and hdwy over 1f out: rdn to ld appr fnl f: drvn and edgd lft ins fnl f: hdd and nt qckn last 100yds* **11/2**[3]

22 3 1 1/4 **One Kool Dude**[10] 1165 2-9-3 0 PaulHanagan 2 72+
(Richard Fahey) *chsd ldrs: pushed along 2f out: n.m.r and swtchd lft over 1f out: sn rdn and ev ch ent fnl f: edgd rt and one pce last 100yds* **3/1**[2]

4 nk **Choisan (IRE)** 2-9-3 0 RobertWinston 7 71
(Tim Easterby) *towards rr: hdwy 2f out: swtchd lft and rdn to chal ent fnl f: sn one pce* **20/1**

5 1 3/4 **Liebesziel** 2-9-3 0 TadhgO'Shea 5 64
(Alan McCabe) *s.i.s and bhd: hdwy on outer 2f out: rdn and ev ch ent fnl f: sn one pce* **80/1**

5 6 hd **Profile Star (IRE)**[15] 1071 2-9-3 0 GrahamGibbons 10 63
(David Barron) *led: rdn along 2f out: hdd & wknd over 1f out* **16/1**

622 7 1/2 **Umph (IRE)**[7] 1235 2-9-3 0 TomMcLaughlin 8 62
(David Evans) *cl up: rdn 2f out: drvn and wknd over 1f out* **25/1**

6 8 2 **Flying Pickets (IRE)**[10] 1165 2-9-3 0 LukeMorris 1 54
(David Brown) *chsd ldrs: rdn along over 2f out: wkng whn n.m.r wl over 1f out* **40/1**

9 3/4 **J J Leary (IRE)** 2-9-3 0 AdrianNicholls 6 51
(David Nicholls) *s.i.s: a towards rr* **25/1**

10 5 **Johnny Cavagin** 2-9-3 0 (t) LiamKeniry 9 33
(Richard Guest) *in tch: effrt 1/2-way: sn rdn and wknd* **100/1**

59.85 secs (-0.65) **Going Correction** -0.15s/f (Firm) **10** Ran SP% **118.9**
Speed ratings (Par 94): **99,97,95,94,92 91,91,87,86,78**
toteswingers:1&2:£2.80, 1&3:£1.40, 2&3:£3.70 CSF £5.45 TOTE £1.90: £1.20, £2.10, £1.10; EX 8.80 Trifecta £17.10 Pool £4,565.61 - 196.50 winning units..
Owner Andrew Russell **Bred** Swordlestown Little **Trained** East Everleigh, Wilts

FOCUS
A decent juvenile maiden, rated around the third. Winners should emerge from the race.

NOTEBOOK
Lilbourne Lad(IRE) proved all the rage beforehand, but things didn't look good for supporters as he lost ground when losing his pitch on the inside 2f out. He picked up strongly once getting himself organised, though, and rates value for further. The experience should bring him on nicely and he can follow up in novice company, with a sixth furlong expected to suit in time. (op 11-10 tchd 6-5)
Pea Shooter ◆ showed his inexperience, but still came through with a bold bid and only got reeled in near the finish. There should be on of these in him soon. (op 5-1)
One Kool Dude had finished second on his two previous outings and likely ran up to form, so rates a solid benchmark. He will certainly appreciate another furlong in due course. (op 11-4)
Choisan(IRE), another with a speedy pedigree, showed definite ability first time up and left the impression he would come on a good deal. (tchd 18-1)
Liebesziel is out of a dual winner at this trip and he was doing some encouraging late work after a sluggish start.
Profile Star(IRE) Official explanation: jockey said colt hung left throughout

1384 SPRINGWELLCARCARE.CO.UK H'CAP 1m (S)
5:40 (5:40) (Class 3) (0-95,95) 3-Y-O £6,152 (£1,830; £914; £456) Stalls High

Form RPR

126- 1 **Belgian Bill**[198] 6507 3-9-4 92 (t) TonyCulhane 6 99+
(George Baker) *trckd ldrs: swtchd rt and hdwy 2f out: rdn to ld appr fnl f: kpt on wl* **9/4**[1]

1105 2 1 **Fred Willetts (IRE)**[9] 1202 3-8-4 85 (v) MatthewCosham(7) 1 90
(David Evans) *hld up towards rr: hdwy on outer 3f out: rdn to ld wl over 1f out: edgd rt and hdd appr fnl f: kpt on u.p towards fin* **12/1**

116- 3 1 3/4 **Azrael**[175] 7095 3-9-7 95 RobertWinston 2 96
(Alan McCabe) *chsd ldrs: effrt over 2f out: sn rdn and kpt on same pce fnl f* **8/1**[3]

03-1 4 nk **Ashva (USA)**[18] 1027 3-8-5 79 RoystonFfrench 9 79
(Michael Dods) *dwlt: hdwy to ld after 1 1/2f: rdn along over 2f out: drvn: edgd lft and hdd wl over 1f out: wknd ent fnl f* **9/2**[2]

150- 5 2 1/4 **Rhythm Of Light**[194] 6619 3-8-4 78 RichardKingscote 8 73
(Tom Dascombe) *t.k.h: led after 1 1/2f: prom tl rdn along over 2f out and kpt on same pce* **33/1**

014- 6 1 **Bridle Belle**[198] 6505 3-8-11 85 PaulHanagan 7 78
(Richard Fahey) *trckd ldrs: effrt and cl up 1/2-way: rdn wl over 2f out: sn wknd* **9/4**[1]

251- 7 3 3/4 **El Torbellino (IRE)**[199] 6457 3-8-4 78 DuranFentiman 4 62
(David O'Meara) *prom: rdn along 3f out: sn wknd* **22/1**

01- 8 3 1/4 **Orange Ace**[157] 7385 3-8-4 78 TadhgO'Shea 3 54
(Paul Cole) *hld up in rr: rdn along over 2f out: sn outpcd* **11/1**

2450 9 9 **Il Battista**[9] 1202 3-7-9 76 oh7 RyanTate(7) 5 32
(Alan McCabe) *a in rr: outpcd and bhd fnl 3f* **66/1**

1m 37.51s (-1.79) **Going Correction** -0.15s/f (Firm) **9** Ran SP% **115.6**
Speed ratings (Par 102): **102,101,99,98,96 95,91,88,79**
toteswingers:1&2:£2.80, 1&3:£1.40, 2&3:£3.70 CSF £31.88 CT £187.17 TOTE £3.30: £1.60, £3.70, £1.40; EX 37.20 Trifecta £114.80 Pool £7,093.33 - 45.71 winning units..
Owner PJL, Cooper & Heath **Bred** Wickfield Stud And Hartshill Stud **Trained** Whitsbury, Hants

FOCUS
An interesting 3-y-o handicap. There was a sound pace on and the form should work out. The winner looks progressive.

NOTEBOOK

Belgian Bill was equipped with a first-time tongue tie on this seasonal return and, well backed, ran out a ready winner. He was confidently ridden and probably idled somewhat after hitting the front. The step up in trip was in his favour and there is very likely more to come from him. (op 2-1 tchd 5-2)

Fred Willetts(IRE), well held the last twice, ran a blinder with the visor reapplied and is clearly up to his current rating. He deserves to go one better again. (tchd 14-1)

Azrael developed into a very useful juvenile last year. He proved easy to back first time up under top weight and shaped as though the run was needed. There should be improvement in him, but a mark of 95 makes him tricky to place. (op 17-2)

Ashva(USA)'s Fibresand maiden win got a boost when the runner-up won easily next time and it looked as though he could have got in lightly on this handicap debut. He was still travelling easily 3f out, but ultimately paid for his early exertions and this probably isn't the way to ride him. (op 5-1 tchd 4-1)

1385 FERGUSSON COAL DONCASTER MILE STKS (LISTED RACE) 1m (R)
6:15 (6:15) (Class 1) 4-Y-O+ **£17,778** (£6,723; £3,360; £1,680) **Stalls** Low

Form RPR

50-1 **1** **St Moritz (IRE)**[9] 1201 5-8-12 104 .... AdrianNicholls 1 108
(David Nicholls) *trckd ldrs: effrt and nt clr run 2f out: sn pushed along: rdn and qcknd to ld appr fnl f: drvn and edgd rt towards fin: hld on wl* **7/4**[1]

414- **2** ½ **Off Chance**[267] 4347 5-8-7 100 .... DuranFentiman 3 102
(Tim Easterby) *hld up in rr: effrt and n.m.r wl over 1f out and again ent fnl f: rdn and kpt on ins fnl f: n.m.r and nt qckn towards fin* **14/1**

000- **3** *nk* **Balcarce Nov (ARG)**[189] 6749 6-8-12 93 .... GrahamGibbons 2 106
(Tom Tate) *stdd s and hld up in rr: hdwy on inner over 2f out: nt clr run and swtchd lft over 1f out: rdn ent fnl f: ev ch tl nt qckn towards fin* **20/1**

010- **4** *shd* **Set The Trend**[196] 6562 5-8-12 100 .... LiamKeniry 6 106
(Andrew Balding) *t.k.h: cl up: rdn to ld briefly wl over 1f out: hdd and drvn appr fnl f: no ex towards fin* **5/1**[3]

0432 **5** 1¾ **Fareer**[37] 828 5-8-12 109 ....(v) TadhgO'Shea 5 102
(Ed Dunlop) *t.k.h early: trckd ldrs on outer: effrt and cl up over 2f out: sn rdn and one pce ent fnl f* **15/8**[2]

016- **6** 1¼ **The Rectifier (USA)**[273] 4166 4-8-12 109 .... MickyFenton 4 99
(Jim Boyle) *set stdy pce: qckng 3f out: sn rdn and hdd wl over 1f out: grad wknd* **10/1**

1m 37.42s (-2.28) **Going Correction** -0.10s/f (Good) **6** Ran SP% **108.3**
Speed ratings (Par 111): **107,106,106,106,104 103**
toteswingers:1&2:£3.90, 1&3:£9.80, 2&3:£10.70 CSF £23.25 TOTE £3.10: £1.90, £4.00; EX 20.20.
Owner Billy Hughes **Bred** Newsells Park Stud **Trained** Sessay, N Yorks
■ Stewards' Enquiry : Liam Keniry three-day ban: weighed in 2lb+ heavy (May 2-4)

FOCUS
A tight-looking Listed event. It was run at an unsatisfactory pace and the field were covered by around a length as the sprint developed from 2f out. The second and third help with the level but the overall form needs treating with some caution.

NOTEBOOK

St Moritz(IRE) dug deep when asked for maximum effort and it made it 2-2 since joining current connections. He dictated when scoring on his seasonal debut upped to near 1m2f nine days earlier, but was content to let others get on with it here and is obviously most versatile. It marginally rates a career-best and it's hard to gauge just how much improvement he has in him just yet. (op 15-8 tchd 2-1)

Off Chance faced a stiff task on this first run back, but she was suited by the way the race unfolded and went close despite not getting the best of runs. This was a pleasing display. Official explanation: jockey said mare was denied a clear run (op 10-1)

Balcarce Nov(ARG) has gone close in this class before, but his form tailed off last year and he arrived with plenty to prove. He posted a much more encouraging effort, however, and has clearly benefited for his time off the track.

Set The Trend looked up against it on his debut in such company. However, he held every chance, just paying late on for running freely through the early stages and he should only improve for the outing. (op 7-1)

Fareer disappointed, even allowing for the race not being run to suit and he now has something to prove again. (op 13-8 tchd 6-4)

The Rectifier(USA) held a leading chance on paper, but had changed stables since his final outing last year and proved very easy to back. He dictated at a steady tempo and blatantly needed the [illegible] (op [illegible])

1386 ATTEYS MAIDEN STKS 1m 4f
6:45 (6:46) (Class 4) 3-Y-O+ **£4,079** (£1,214; £606; £303) **Stalls** Low

Form RPR

3 **1** **Gogeo (IRE)**[8] 1211 4-9-12 0 .... RobertWinston 3 82+
(Alan Swinbank) *trckd ldrs: swtchd rt and hdwy over 3f out: sn cl up: shkn up to ld wl over 1f out: rdn and hung lft appr fnl f: sn clr* **7/2**[3]

2 **2** 4½ **Rainy Champion (USA)**[15] 1076 3-8-7 0 .... DarryllHolland 7 72
(Gerard Butler) *trckd ldr: hdwy over 3f out: led wl over 2f out and sn rdn: drvn and hdd wl over 1f out: n.m.r and hmpd on inner appr fnl f: sn one pce* **5/4**[1]

2 **3** 2¼ **War Poet**[8] 1212 4-9-12 0 .... SilvestreDeSousa 1 71
(David O'Meara) *hld up in rr: gd hdwy on inner 3f out: rdn to chal over 2f out and ev ch tl drvn and one pce over 1f out* **9/4**[2]

2300 **4** 7 **Ay Tay Tate (IRE)**[4] 1291 5-9-10 55 ....(tp) AndrewHeffernan[(3)] 2 59
(David C Griffiths) *set stdy pce: rdn and qcknd 4f out: hung rt and hdd wl over 2f out: sn wknd* **14/1**

0 **5** 15 **Serenader**[8] 1211 4-9-7 0 .... SeanLevey[(5)] 6 35
(David O'Meara) *trckd ldng pair: rdn along 4f out: wknd over 3f out* **50/1**

6 ¾ **Amtired**[32] 5-9-8 0 .... DaleSwift[(5)] 4 34
(Brian Ellison) *in tch: rdn along 4f out: wknd over 3f out* **20/1**

2m 31.93s (-2.97) **Going Correction** -0.10s/f (Good)
WFA 3 from 4yo 20lb 4 from 5yo 1lb **6** Ran SP% **110.8**
Speed ratings (Par 105): **105,102,100,95,85 85**
toteswingers:1&2:£1.80, 1&3:£1.20, 2&3:£1.30 CSF £8.09 TOTE £5.00: £2.30, £1.40; EX 12.20.
Owner Mrs J Porter **Bred** Peter Nolan **Trained** Melsonby, N Yorks
■ Stewards' Enquiry : Darryll Holland caution: careless riding.

FOCUS
An ordinary maiden, but it was quite well run and the winner looks potentially useful.

1387 CHARLOTTE GREAVES HAPPY 40TH BIRTHDAY H'CAP 1m 2f 60y
7:20 (7:20) (Class 3) (0-95,91) 4-Y-O+ **£6,152** (£1,830; £914; £456) **Stalls** Low

Form RPR

-004 **1** **Arlequin**[11] 1154 4-9-2 86 .... PhilipRobinson 3 94+
(James Bethell) *dwlt: sn trcking ldrs: hdwy wl over 2f out and sn swtchd rt: rdn and hung lft appr fnl f: led 1f out and sn clr* **7/2**[2]

350- **2** 1¾ **Embsay Crag**[294] 3432 5-8-8 78 .... PaulMulrennan 2 83
(Kate Walton) *trckd ldrs: rdn 2f out and sltly outpcd whn n.m.r over 1f out: styd on u.p to chse wnr ins fnl f: no imp* **12/1**

112- **3** ½ **Northside Prince (IRE)**[212] 6106 5-9-2 86 .... RobertWinston 12 92+
(Alan Swinbank) *hld up towards rr: hdwy over 2f out: nt clr run over 1f out: swtchd rt and drvn ent fnl f: kpt on wl towards fin* **11/1**

50-0 **4** *nk* **Breakheart (IRE)**[14] 1092 4-9-5 89 .... FrederikTylicki 11 92
(Michael Dods) *hld up towards rr: hdwy on outer 3f out: rdn wl over 1f out: chsd ldrs ent fnl f: kpt on same pce* **9/2**[3]

10-0 **5** 1 **Itlaaq**[11] 1154 5-9-6 90 .... GrahamGibbons 8 91
(Michael Easterby) *led: rdn along 3f out: jnd and drvn 2f out: n.m.r and hdd 1f out: wknd ins fnl f* **22/1**

04-2 **6** ½ **Changing The Guard**[11] 1154 5-9-1 85 .... PaulHanagan 7 87+
(Richard Fahey) *hld up in midfield: effrt and hdwy over 2f out: n.m.r and rdn over 1f out: sn no imp* **10/3**[1]

00-6 **7** *hd* **Doctor Zhivago**[11] 1154 4-9-0 84 .... AdrianNicholls 1 84
(David Nicholls) *prom: hdwy and cl up over 2f out: rdn and ev ch whn hmpd appr fnl f: no ch after* **10/1**

20-0 **8** ½ **Speed Dating**[11] 1154 5-8-8 85 ....(p) ShaneBKelly[(7)] 4 84
(John Quinn) *in rr: hdwy on inner 2f out: rdn and kpt on ins fnl f: n.d* **16/1**

103- **9** 1¼ **Destinys Dream (IRE)**[210] 6185 6-9-2 86 .... KellyHarrison 6 82
(Tracy Waggott) *hld up in rr: hdwy wl over 2f out: n.m.r and rdn over 1f out: sn no imp* **16/1**

10- **10** 1¾ **Pass Muster**[313] 2816 4-8-13 83 .... RoystonFfrench 5 76
(Geoffrey Harker) *hld up: effrt and sme hdwy 3f out: rdn along over 2f out and n.d* **25/1**

25-0 **11** 7 **Charlie Cool**[14] 1092 8-9-4 91 ....(b) JamesSullivan[(3)] 9 70
(Ruth Carr) *t.k.h: chsd ldrs: rdn along 3f out: sn wknd* **22/1**

1-11 **12** 23 **Dontpaytheferryman (USA)**[49] 104 6-8-12 82 .... WilliamCarson 10 15
(Brian Ellison) *sn prom: rdn along 4f out: wknd over 3f out* **14/1**

2m 7.96s (-1.44) **Going Correction** -0.10s/f (Good) **12** Ran SP% **119.6**
Speed ratings (Par 107): **101,99,99,98,98 97,97,97,96,94 89,70**
toteswingers:1&2:£13.10, 1&3:£12.30, 2&3:£15.60 CSF £44.47 CT £427.80 TOTE £4.70: £1.80, £6.90, £2.10; EX 63.20 Trifecta £696.50 Pool £3,576.65 - 3.80 winning units..
Owner J Carrick **Bred** Dr A J F Gillespie **Trained** Middleham Moor, N Yorks

FOCUS
A fair and competitive handicap, but it was a bit messy and muddling. The winner did not need to match his 3yo best.

NOTEBOOK

Arlequin stayed on after getting behind at Pontefract on his previous outing, but was ridden more sensibly here and scored readily off a 2lb lower mark. He had his optimum conditions here and may well defy a higher mark while in this sort of mood. (op 3-1)

Embsay Crag ◆ failed to win last year, but on the evidence of this pleasing comeback effort his turn is not far off again. It should put him spot on for a return to Chester next month. (op 18-1)

Northside Prince(IRE) ◆ progressed dramatically last summer and he looks set for even better things this year. He would have gone closer with a better passage and is one to be with next time out. (op 12-1)

Breakheart(IRE) badly needed his seasonal debut for his new connections at Doncaster a fortnight earlier and got well backed this time. He posted an improved effort without seriously threatening and is entitled to come on again. (op 11-2)

Itlaaq showed more than on his first run for current connections 11 days earlier, but was allowed to dictate and probably needs to drop the handicap before coming good again. (op 25-1)

Changing The Guard finished in front of four of these, including the winner, off this mark at Pontefract last time out. However, he was ridden much more patiently and the switch of tactics backfired. (op 3-1 tchd 7-2)

Dontpaytheferryman(USA) Official explanation: jockey said gelding hung left

1388 SIS LIVE FILLIES' H'CAP 1m 2f 60y
7:55 (7:56) (Class 4) (0-85,83) 4-Y-O+ **£3,885** (£1,156; £577; £288) **Stalls** Low

Form RPR

42-1 **1** **Captivator**[82] 284 4-8-13 75 .... HayleyTurner 5 88+
(James Fanshawe) *hld up: smooth hdwy to trck ldrs over 3f out: chal on bit 11/2f out: shkn up to ld ent fnl f and sn clr* **7/2**[2]

5 **2** 2¼ **White Diamond**[14] 1097 4-8-11 73 .... PaulHanagan 7 77
(Malcolm Jefferson) *led: rdn along 3f out: jnd and drvn 11/2f out: hdd ent fnl f and kpt on same pce* **9/2**[3]

45-0 **3** 1¾ **Viewing**[13] 1114 4-8-13 75 .... PaulMulrennan 2 76
(James Given) *hld up in rr: hdwy on inner over 2f out: rdn over 1f out: styd on ins fnl f: swtchd rt and tk 3rd nr fin* **20/1**

2010 **4** *hd* **Very Well Red**[13] 1111 [illegible] .... WilliamCarson [illegible] [illegible]
(Peter Hiatt) *chsd ldrs: rdn along over 2f out: drvn and n.m.r over 1f out: swtchd rt ent fnl f:kpt on same pce* **14/1**

023- **5** *hd* **Countess Comet (IRE)**[167] 7253 4-9-3 79 .... JimCrowley 1 79
(Ralph Beckett) *trckd ldrs on outer: hdwy 3f out: rdn over 2f out: drvn and wknd wl over 1f out* **9/2**[3]

-121 **6** 7 **Fashionable Gal (IRE)**[10] 1183 4-8-12 74 .... J-PGuillambert 9 60
(Neil King) *hld up towards rr: hdwy on outer over 3f out: rdn over 2f out: sn btn* **7/1**

060- **7** 1 **Bollin Dolly**[228] 5638 8-9-3 79 .... RobertWinston 3 63
(Tim Easterby) *chsd ldr: rdn along over 3f out: drvn over 2f out and sn wknd* **12/1**

323- **8** 22 **Sing Sweetly**[108] 8003 4-9-7 83 ....(t) DarryllHolland 4 23
(Gerard Butler) *sn chsng ldrs: rdn along on outer over 3f out: sn btn and bhd fnl 2f* **3/1**[1]

2m 7.69s (-1.71) **Going Correction** -0.10s/f (Good) **8** Ran SP% **115.2**
Speed ratings (Par 102): **102,100,98,98,98 92,92,74**
toteswingers::1&2:£5.90, 1&3:£7.60, 2&3:£20.50 CSF £19.84 CT £272.12 TOTE £4.10: £1.60, £2.00, £4.50; EX 28.70 Trifecta £437.30 Part won. Pool £591.00 - 0.60 winning units..
Owner Lord Vestey **Bred** Stowell Park Stud **Trained** Newmarket, Suffolk

FOCUS
A competitive fillies' handicap and a progressive winner.

Sing Sweetly Official explanation: trainer's rep had no explanation for the poor form shown
T/Plt: £61.80 to a £1 stake. Pool £45,300.87 - 534.63 winning units. T/Qpdt: £21.10 to a £1 stake. Pool £4,817.01 - 168.60 winning units. JR

HAYDOCK (L-H)
Saturday, April 16

OFFICIAL GOING: Good to firm (good in places; 7.6)
All races on outer home straight with races on round course reduced by 6yds.
Wind: Light, half-against Weather: Cloudy

1389 ST HELENS MAIDEN STKS 1m 3f 200y
5:00 (5:02) (Class 5) 3-Y-O **£2,914** (£867; £433) **Stalls** Centre

Form RPR

22- **1** **Nathaniel (IRE)**[219] 5878 3-9-3 0 .... WilliamBuick 2 82+
(John Gosden) *chsd ldr after nrly 2f: led under 2f out: stretched clr fnl f: eased down fnl 100yds* **1/20**[1]

6- **2** *9* **Madrasa (IRE)**[186] 6831 3-9-3 0 .... SebSanders 3 68
(Ed McMahon) *racd keenly: led: hdd under 2f out: sn rdn: no ch w wnr after* **20/1**[2]

0 **3** *2 1/4* **Tartan Jura**[14] 1096 3-9-3 0 .... GregFairley 1 64
(Mark Johnston) *green and broke loose in paddock: chsd ldr: j. road in first f: lost 2nd after nrly 2f: racd in rr after: rdn and outpcd over 2f out: wl btn* **22/1**[3]

2m 31.41s (-2.59) **Going Correction** -0.35s/f (Firm) **3** Ran SP% **104.3**
Speed ratings (Par 98): **94,88,86**
CSF £1.82 TOTE £1.10; EX 1.50.
Owner Lady Rothschild **Bred** Kincorth Investments Inc **Trained** Newmarket, Suffolk

FOCUS
An uncompetitive maiden run at just a fair pace and won as easily by the long odds-on favourite as the betting suggested. He is understandably rated a fair bit off his 2yo best.

1390 TOM JONES LIVE ON 18TH JUNE H'CAP 1m 2f 95y
5:30 (5:31) (Class 4) (0-80,80) 4-Y-0+ **£5,180** (£1,541; £770; £384) **Stalls** High

Form RPR

051- **1** **Prince Of Johanne (IRE)**[180] 6990 5-9-5 **78** ....(p) FrannyNorton 8 89
(Tom Tate) *midfield: hdwy 2f out: rdn over 1f out: r.o to ld ins fnl f: sn edgd lft: in command fnl 75yds* **12/1**

666- **2** *2* **Oriental Cavalier**[152] 7463 5-8-13 **72** ....(v) SebSanders 11 79
(Mark Buckley) *in tch: effrt 2f out: rdn to chal fr over 1f out: ev ch ins fnl f: nt qckn fnl 75yds* **25/1**

420- **3** *2 1/4* **One Scoop Or Two**[166] 7274 5-9-5 **78** .... RussKennemore 14 81
(Reg Hollinshead) *a.p: led 2f out: rdn and edgd lft over 1f out: hdd ins fnl f: no ex fnl 75yds* **50/1**

311- **4** *hd* **Piano**[175] 7090 4-9-7 **80** .... WilliamBuick 7 83+
(John Gosden) *hld up in rr: hdwy on outer wl over 1f out: styd on and edgd lft ins fnl f: nt quite pce to rch ldrs* **6/4**[1]

-535 **5** *1 1/2* **Danderek**[15] 1075 5-9-5 **78** .... TonyHamilton 13 78
(Richard Fahey) *led early: remained prom: rdn 2f out: kpt on same pce fr over 1f out* **9/1**[3]

110- **6** *nk* **Grams And Ounces**[33] 6447 4-9-3 **76** .... CathyGannon 6 75+
(Amy Weaver) *in rr: rdn 3f out: hdwy over 1f out: kpt on ins fnl f: nt pce to get competitive* **20/1**

120- **7** *3/4* **King Zeal (IRE)**[176] 7062 7-9-1 **79** .... JamesRogers(5) 10 77
(Barry Leavy) *sn led: pushed along and hdd 2f out: rdn whn stl chsng ldrs over 1f out: wknd ins fnl f* **12/1**

500- **8** *1 1/4* **That'll Do Nicely (IRE)**[127] 7815 8-9-2 **75** .... DavidNolan 2 70
(Nicky Richards) *hld up: pushed along over 2f out: kpt on modly ins fnl f: nvr a threat* **33/1**

1153 **9** *2 1/4* **Visions Of Johanna (USA)**[30] 879 6-8-9 **68** .... JimmyQuinn 15 59
(Ian Williams) *hld up: rdn and hdwy into midfield over 2f out: no imp on ldrs: wknd over 1f out* **12/1**

20-0 **10** *3/4* **Antoniola (IRE)**[13] 1109 4-9-1 **74** .... DavidAllan 5 64
(Tim Easterby) *midfield: rdn over 2f out: no imp* **33/1**

11 *8* **Strong Knight**[280] 4-9-2 **75** .... DanielTudhope 4 49
(Tim Walford) *chsd ldrs: rdn over 2f out: hung lft and wknd over 1f out* **66/1**

241- **12** *4 1/2* **Music City (IRE)**[220] 5860 4-9-5 **78** .... GregFairley 16 44
(Mark Johnston) *in tch: pushed along and lost pl over 4f out: sn bhd* **4/1**[2]

5P-1 **13** *1/2* **African Cheetah**[15] 1083 5-9-5 **78** .... JamesDoyle 3 43
(Reg Hollinshead) *midfield: rdn over 2f out: wknd over 1f out* **16/1**

310- **14** *18* **Mistoffelees**[223] 5790 5-8-11 **77** .... TalibHussain(7) 1 8
(Luca Cumani) *hld up: bhd and struggling fnl 3f* **12/1**

2m 11.08s (-4.92) **Going Correction** -0.35s/f (Firm) **14** Ran SP% **124.6**
Speed ratings (Par 105): **105,103,101,101,100 100,99,98,96,96 89,86,85,71**
toteswingers:1&2:£47.90, 1&3:£35.30, 2&3:£120.20 CSF £295.44 CT £13569.71 TOTE £12.30: £3.50, £7.00, £4.50; EX 158.60.
Owner David Storey **Bred** T J Rooney And Corduff Stud **Trained** Tadcaster, N Yorks

FOCUS
A fair handicap in which the field were soon strung out despite the pace not obviously being a strong one and the third deserves credit in the circumstances. The winner is rated back to his best with the next two to their marks.
Strong Knight Official explanation: jockey said gelding hung left-handed in home straight
African Cheetah Official explanation: jockey said horse stopped quickly

1391 ARICABEAU RACING H'CAP 5f
6:00 (6:01) (Class 4) (0-85,84) 3-Y-O **£5,180** (£1,541; £770; £384) **Stalls** High

Form RPR

4-12 **1** **Mr Optimistic**[76] 356 3-8-9 **77** .... LeeTopliss(5) 9 83
(Richard Fahey) *midfield: hdwy over 1f out: edgd lft ent fnl f: r.o to ld fnl stride* **8/1**

540- **2** *hd* **Defence Council (IRE)**[182] 6916 3-8-11 **74** .... FrannyNorton 7 79
(Mel Brittain) *w ldr: rdn over 1f out: led ins fnl f: hdd fnl stride* **14/1**

164- **3** *3/4* **Riverdale (IRE)**[204] 6325 3-9-0 **77** .... SebSanders 14 80
(Ann Duffield) *towards rr: hdwy into midfield 1/2-way: r.o ins fnl f: gng on at fin* **7/1**[3]

23-2 **4** *hd* **Flash City (ITY)**[7] 1241 3-9-4 **84** ....(v) GaryBartley(3) 6 86
(Bryan Smart) *sn led: rdn over 1f out: hdd ins fnl f: continued to chal: nt qckn towards fin* **4/1**[1]

-442 **5** *nk* **Dream Catcher (FR)**[35] 847 3-8-12 **75** .... WilliamBuick 1 76
(David Nicholls) *midfield: effrt over 1f out: styd on ins fnl f: nt quite pce of ldrs* **7/1**[3]

2554 **6** *1 1/2* **Restless Bay (IRE)**[16] 1059 3-8-13 **76** ....(v) RussKennemore 4 72
(Reg Hollinshead) *s.i.s: hld up: hdwy over 1f out: chsd ldrs ins fnl f: one pce fnl 110yds* **33/1**

-32U **7** *1/2* **Overwhelm**[11] 1145 3-8-11 **74** .... TonyHamilton 5 68
(Richard Fahey) *hld up: rdn and hdwy to chse ldng bunch over 1f out: hung lft ins fnl f: nt pce to chal* **14/1**

10-0 **8** *1/2* **Watts Up Son**[7] 1241 3-9-0 **77** ....(t) DavidNolan 2 69
(Declan Carroll) *hld up: rdn 2f out: nvr able to chal* **33/1**

00-0 **9** *1* **Boundless Spirit**[7] 1241 3-8-9 **75** ....(t) MichaelO'Connell(3) 3 63
(David Nicholls) *plld hrd: prom: rdn over 1f out: unbalanced ent fnl f: wknd fnl 120yds* **20/1**

313- **10** *nse* **Captain Kolo (IRE)**[182] 6916 3-9-0 **77** .... DavidAllan 12 65
(Tim Easterby) *chsd ldrs: rdn 2f out: wknd over 1f out* **9/2**[2]

110 **11** *3 1/4* **Sacrosanctus**[7] 1241 3-9-0 **80** .... BillyCray(3) 15 56
(David Nicholls) *towards rr: sn pushed along: in midfield 1/2-way: wknd over 1f out* **8/1**

445- **12** *4 1/2* **Style And Panache (IRE)**[133] 7696 3-9-0 **77** .... CathyGannon 10 37
(David Evans) *a outpcd in rr* **16/1**

6544 **13** *2 3/4* **Liberty Green (IRE)**[25] 940 3-8-12 **75** .... JamesDoyle 11 25
(Alan McCabe) *chsd ldrs tl wknd over 1f out: eased whn wl btn ins fnl f* **25/1**

61.52 secs (0.72) **Going Correction** +0.125s/f (Good) **13** Ran SP% **119.1**
Speed ratings (Par 100): **100,99,98,98,97 95,94,93,92,92 86,79,75**
toteswingers:1&2:£50.70, 1&3:£23.80, 2&3:£30.20 CSF £109.00 CT £824.31 TOTE £8.10: £2.60, £5.30, £3.10; EX 154.10.
Owner F L F S Ltd **Bred** C J Murfitt **Trained** Musley Bank, N Yorks

FOCUS
A fair handicap in which the action unfolded down the centre with the third doing best of those that stayed stand side. Another personal best from the winner, who's been progressive on the AW.
Sacrosanctus Official explanation: jockey said gelding never travelled

1392 TURFTV.CO.UK H'CAP 1m 30y
6:30 (6:31) (Class 5) (0-75,74) 3-Y-O **£2,914** (£867; £433; £216) **Stalls** Low

Form RPR

353- **1** **Franciscan**[172] 7151 3-9-0 **67** .... KirstyMilczarek 12 71+
(Luca Cumani) *towards rr: hdwy 2f out: rdn over 1f out: r.o ins fnl f to ld cl home* **15/2**

603- **2** *hd* **Matavia Bay (IRE)**[171] 7163 3-8-4 **62** .... HarryBentley(5) 10 65
(Alan Jarvis) *in tch: chalng 2f out: rdn to ld over 1f out: hdd and hld cl home* **14/1**

355- **3** *1/2* **Number Theory**[186] 6828 3-9-3 **70** .... JimmyQuinn 9 72
(John Holt) *midfield: hdwy to chse ldrs over 2f out: ev ch ins fnl f: hld towards fin* **40/1**

00-1 **4** *hd* **Dazzling Valentine**[7] 1251 3-9-4 **74** .... AmyBaker(3) 8 75+
(Alan Bailey) *bhd: pushed along 2f out: hdwy over 1f out: r.o and clsd towards fin* **13/2**[2]

356- **5** *1 1/2* **Adlington**[229] 5595 3-9-4 **71** .... TonyHamilton 6 69
(Richard Fahey) *chsd ldrs: rdn over 1f out: ev ch ins fnl f: no ex fnl 50yds* **16/1**

5123 **6** *1/2* **George Woolf**[40] 789 3-9-7 **74** .... JamesDoyle 3 71
(Alan McCabe) *in tch: rdn 2f out: nvr able to chal: one pce ins fnl f* **12/1**

140- **7** *3* **Regimental (IRE)**[184] 6875 3-9-3 **70** .... SebSanders 5 60
(Ann Duffield) *hld up: pushed along and nt clr run 2f out: hdwy over 1f out: one pce ins fnl f* **20/1**

6451 **8** *hd* **Bertie Blu Boy**[15] 1082 3-9-0 **67** .... FrannyNorton 4 56
(Paul Green) *led: hdd over 5f out: remained w ldr: regained ld over 2f out: rdn and hdd over 1f out: wknd fnl 100yds* **8/1**

000- **9** *1 1/4* **Control Chief**[186] 6827 3-8-12 **65** .... RichardThomas 11 52
(Ralph Beckett) *bhd: pushed along over 4f out: nt clr run ent fnl 2f: kpt on one pce ins fnl f: nvr threatened ldrs* **9/1**

51- **10** *10* **Cape Of Dance (IRE)**[241] 5210 3-9-7 **74** .... GregFairley 1 38
(Mark Johnston) *w ldr: led over 5f out: hdd over 2f out: sn u.p: wknd over 1f out* **7/1**[3]

000- **11** *11* **Coracle**[207] 6268 3-8-5 **61** .... TjadeCollier(3) 2 —
(David Nicholls) *midfield: rdn and wknd 2f out* **33/1**

61- **12** *1 1/4* **Rasheed**[108] 8000 3-9-7 **74** .... WilliamBuick 7 —
(John Gosden) *chsd ldrs: c wd ent st over 4f out: short-lived effrt over 2f out: sn wknd: eased whn wl btn ins fnl f* **11/4**[1]

1m 42.62s (-2.08) **Going Correction** -0.35s/f (Firm) **12** Ran SP% **115.8**
Speed ratings (Par 98): **96,95,95,95,93 93,90,89,88,78 67,66**
toteswingers:1&2:£13.20, 1&3:£19.10, 2&3:£21.30 CSF £102.70 CT £2450.26 TOTE £10.80: £3.30, £5.70, £9.40; EX 71.50.
Owner Fittocks Stud For Camilla Millbank **Bred** Fittocks Stud **Trained** Newmarket, Suffolk
■ Stewards' Enquiry : Harry Bentley two-day ban: used whip with excessive frequency (May 2-3)

FOCUS
A modest handicap, if one contested largely by unexposed types, run at a decent gallop with the principals coming from off the pace. The winner can be expected do fair bit better.
Rasheed Official explanation: jockey said gelding hung right on bend

1393 WATCH RACING UK ON SKY 432 MAIDEN FILLIES' STKS 1m 30y
7:05 (7:06) (Class 5) 3-Y-0+ **£2,914** (£867; £433; £216) **Stalls** Low

Form RPR

45- **1** **Wrekin Sunset**[164] 7302 3-9-0 0 .... AndrewElliott 7 79
(Mrs K Burke) *a.p: led jst over 2f out: rdn over 1f out: pressed thrght fnl f: a doing enough cl home* **20/1**

2 *3/4* **Inklet** 3-9-0 0 .... SebSanders 6 78
(Marco Botti) *in tch: wnt prom over 4f out: chalng fr 2f out: pressed wnr thrght fnl f tl nt qckn cl home* **10/1**

23- **3** *hd* **Rainbow Springs**[195] 6609 3-9-0 0 .... WilliamBuick 1 77
(John Gosden) *hld up: nt clr run 2f out: swtchd rt wl over 1f out: prog whn edgd rt briefly ins fnl f: styd on wl towards fin: nvr gng to get there* **2/5**[1]

2- **4** *1 1/4* **Baisse**[130] 7733 3-9-0 0 .... JimmyQuinn 4 74
(Sir Henry Cecil) *racd keenly: trckd ldrs: effrt to chal over 2f out: nt qckn over 1f out: styd on same pce ins fnl f* **4/1**[2]

43- **5** *2 3/4* **Beso (IRE)**[154] 7447 3-9-0 0 .... KirstyMilczarek 2 68
(Luca Cumani) *in tch: outpcd and lost pl 3f out: kpt on fnl f: nvr able to chal* **8/1**[3]

6- **6** *nk* **Adaria**[214] 6046 3-9-0 0 .... RobbieFitzpatrick 8 67
(David C Griffiths) *dwlt: swtchd lft s: hld up: rdn wl over 1f out: nvr able to chal* **80/1**

50- **7** *8* **Decadence**[162] 7335 3-9-0 0 .... DavidAllan 5 49
(Eric Alston) *led: hdd jst over 2f out: wknd over 1f out* **25/1**

5 **8** *18* **Ellielusive (IRE)**[7] 1252 4-10-0 0 .... TomMcLaughlin 3 —
(Mark Brisbourne) *hld up: effrt and hdwy 3f out: wknd under 2f out* **100/1**

1m 42.92s (-1.78) **Going Correction** -0.35s/f (Firm)
WFA 3 from 4yo 14lb **8** Ran SP% **122.5**
Speed ratings (Par 100): **94,93,93,91,89 88,80,62**
toteswingers:1&2:£9.10, 1&3:£2.90, 2&3:£2.50 CSF £203.46 TOTE £24.50: £5.40, £3.20, £1.02; EX 280.70.
Owner Ray Bailey **Bred** Ray Bailey **Trained** Middleham Moor, North Yorks

FOCUS
A maiden that looked straightforward for the favourite but ultimately produced something of an upset at the end of a muddling race, the pace only fair. It was the slowest of the three C&D times and the form is rated loosely around the fourth and fifth.

1394 HAYDOCK PARK RAILS AND RING BOOKMAKERS H'CAP 1m 30y
7:35 (7:36) (Class 5) (0-70,70) 4-Y-0+ **£2,914** (£867; £433; £216) **Stalls** Low

Form RPR

250- **1** **Cono Zur (FR)**[229] 5596 4-9-4 **67** .... SebSanders 10 78
(Ruth Carr) *mde all: rdn over 1f out: r.o ins fnl f and a in control* **14/1**

20-4 **2** *1 1/2* **Bajan Flash**[11] 1150 4-8-13 **65** .... MichaelO'Connell(3) 6 73
(David Nicholls) *a.p: chsd wnr fnl 2f: rdn over 1f out: no imp* **9/2**[3]

103- **3** *2 1/4* **Tarooq (USA)**[156] 7414 5-9-7 **70**.................................. TonyHamilton 2 72
(Richard Fahey) *in tch: effrt under 2f out: wnt 3rd 1f out: wanted to lug lft ins fnl f: kpt on but no imp on front 2* **10/3**[1]

01 **4** *hd* **French Art**[8] 1216 6-8-12 **66**.....................................(p) TobyAtkinson(5) 1 68
(Nigel Tinkler) *hld up: rdn 2f out: swtchd lft u.p over 1f out: styd on ins fnl f: nt pce to chal* **6/1**

-320 **5** *3/4* **Verluga (IRE)**[15] 1077 4-8-7 **56** oh1..................................... DavidAllan 7 56
(Tim Easterby) *midfield: effrt 2f out: chsd ldrs over 1f out: one pce fnl f* **14/1**

0-11 **6** *1 3/4* **Hits Only Jude (IRE)**[11] 1150 8-9-1 **64**.........................(v) DavidNolan 12 60
(Declan Carroll) *hld up: rdn 2f out: no imp and one pce ins fnl f* **4/1**[2]

10-0 **7** *3/4* **Star Addition**[14] 1099 5-8-7 **56** oh2.................................... BarryMcHugh 3 50
(Eric Alston) *racd keenly: trckd ldrs: rdn 2f out: wknd fnl 110yds* **18/1**

0026 **8** *3 3/4* **Tourist**[8] 1221 6-8-9 **58**.. JimmyQuinn 8 44
(Derek Shaw) *rrd s: hld up: u.p 2f out: nvr on terms* **12/1**

655- **9** *15* **Madame Excelerate**[164] 7305 4-9-4 **67**........................ TomMcLaughlin 4 18
(Mark Brisbourne) *in rr: hdwy after 2f: in tch w ldrs: rdn 3f out: wknd 2f out* **14/1**

10-6 **10** *6* **Ellies Image**[17] 1054 4-8-13 **62**.. CathyGannon 11 —
(Brian Baugh) *prom: pushed along over 3f out: wknd wl over 1f out* **20/1**

5035 **11** *2 1/2* **Mr Emirati (USA)**[15] 1083 4-9-1 **64**...................................(tp) TomEaves 9 —
(Bryan Smart) *hld up in rr: pushed along 3f out: nvr on terms* **18/1**

1m 41.62s (-3.08) **Going Correction** -0.35s/f (Firm) **11** Ran SP% **118.5**
Speed ratings (Par 103): **101,99,97,97,96 94,93,90,75,69 66**
toteswingers:1&2:£23.60, 1&3:£10.90, 2&3:£2.40 CSF £76.61 CT £270.98 TOTE £19.30: £5.00, £1.90, £1.60; EX 112.30.
Owner Ruth Carr Racing **Bred** Jean-Pierre-Joseph Dubois **Trained** Huby, N Yorks

FOCUS
A modest handicap and one run at just a fair gallop with the first two in the van throughout but the winner did it well and didn't look flattered. He is rated back to last year's winning for in a seller. This was the quickest of the three C&D times.
Tourist Official explanation: jockey said gelding ran too free
T/Plt: £589.10 to a £1 stake. Pool £36,562.32 - 45.30 winning units. T/Qpdt: £62.50 to a £1 stake. Pool £5,528.25 - 65.40 winning units. DO

1055 LEICESTER (R-H)
Saturday, April 16

OFFICIAL GOING: Good to firm (good in places)
Wind: Light behind Weather: Sunny

1395 BET ON TOTEPLACEPOT AT TOTESPORT.COM H'CAP 5f 218y
2:15 (2:16) (Class 4) (0-85,85) 4-Y-0+ **£2,590** (£770; £385; £192) **Stalls** High

Form RPR

2111 **1** **Dickie Le Davoir**[7] 1239 7-8-9 **76**..............................(b) RobertLButler(3) 3 86
(Richard Guest) *s.i.s: in rr: hdwy over 2f out: led over 1f out: edgd lft: rdn out* **14/1**

2112 **2** *1* **Ivory Silk**[13] 1110 6-8-12 **76**.. RoystonFfrench 4 83
(Jeremy Gask) *hld up: hdwy over 1f out: rdn over 1f out: styd on* **9/1**

321- **3** *1 1/2* **Hot Pursuits**[238] 5285 4-9-0 **78**.. JimCrowley 12 80
(Hughie Morrison) *dwlt: hld up: hdwy over 1f out: r.o* **8/1**

0-00 **4** *nk* **Jordaura**[59] 557 5-8-10 **74**... AndreaAtzeni 11 75+
(Tony Carroll) *hld up: hdwy over 1f out: edgd rt ins fnl f: r.o* **14/1**

52-2 **5** *1/2* **Shifting Star (IRE)**[9] 1197 6-9-7 **85**.................................. ShaneKelly 10 85
(Walter Swinburn) *a.p: rdn over 1f out: styd on* **15/2**

01-6 **6** *nk* **Dancing Maite**[16] 1061 6-8-10 **74**.. JimmyQuinn 6 73
(Roy Bowring) *mid-div: hdwy over 2f out: rdn over 1f out: styd on same pce ins fnl f* **7/1**[3]

50-0 **7** *1 3/4* **Legal Eagle (IRE)**[26] 932 6-8-7 **78**..........................(p) DuilioDaSilva(7) 7 71
(Paul Green) *w ldrs: rdn over 2f out: led wl over 1f out: sn hdd: no ex ins fnl f* **28/1**

3312 **8** *2 1/2* **Ebraam (USA)**[21] 986 8-8-9 **73**.. LukeMorris 8 58
(Ronald Harris) *prom: racd keenly: rdn over 1f out: wknd ins fnl f* **13/2**[2]

1000 **9** *3/4* **Elhamri**[9] 1107 7-9-10 **74**.. HayleyTurner 2 57
(Conor Dore) *chsd ldrs: rdn 2f out: wknd fnl f* **40/1**

24-1 **10** *6* **Bandstand**[22] 971 5-8-9 **78**... AdamCarter(5) 9 41
(Bryan Smart) *w ldr tl led over 2f out: sn rdn: hdd wl over 1f out: wknd fnl f* **12/1**

400- **11** *3* **Tyfos**[203] 6358 6-9-3 **81**.. J-PGuillambert 14 35
(Brian Baugh) *led over 3f: wknd over 1f out* **12/1**

2231 **12** *2 1/2* **Desert Strike**[17] 1048 5-8-11 **75**..................................... RobertWinston 15 21
(Alan McCabe) *s.i.s: hdwy over 4f out: rdn and hung rt over 2f out: sn wknd* **16/1**

100- **13** *8* **Kakapuka**[251] 4865 4-8-12 **76**.. StevieDonohoe 13 —
(Anabel K Murphy) *hdwy over 4f out: wknd over 2f out* **40/1**

-052 **14** *9* **Falasteen (IRE)**[10] 1166 4-9-7 **85**..................................... AdrianNicholls 5 —
(David Nicholls) *s.i.s: rdn and wknd over 2f out: eased fnl f* **11/2**[1]

1m 11.41s (-1.59) **Going Correction** -0.325s/f (Firm) **14** Ran SP% **117.0**
Speed ratings (Par 105): **97,95,93,93,92 92,89,86,85,77 73,70,59,47**
toteswingers:1&2 £10.50, 2&3 £6.80, 1&3 £46.60 CSF £15.15 CT £6.26 TOTE £11.70: £3.10, £3.00, £2.90; EX 40.30.
Owner Future Racing (Notts) Limited **Bred** P And Mrs A G Venner **Trained** Stainforth, S Yorks

FOCUS
This was a competitive sprint handicap, although the leaders went too fast, setting this up for the hold-up horses. The race should produce a few winners in the coming weeks. They were spread across the track but there was no sign of a draw bias. The winner is rated back to his very best post-3yo form.
Falasteen(IRE) Official explanation: jockey said gelding lost its action

1396 FREE RACING POST FORM AT TOTESPORT.COM MEDIAN AUCTION MAIDEN STKS 5f 2y
2:45 (2:48) (Class 6) 2-Y-0 **£1,706** (£503; £252) **Stalls** High

Form RPR

1 **Cockney Fire** 2-8-12 0.. CathyGannon 10 73+
(David Evans) *hld up: hdwy 1/2-way: rdn over 1f out: led ins fnl f: r.o: hung rt towards fin* **11/2**[3]

63 **2** *1 1/2* **Triggerlo**[10] 1185 2-9-0 0... MartinHarley(3) 4 72
(Mick Channon) *led: rdn over 1f out: hdd and unable qck ins fnl f* **5/2**[2]

3 *1 3/4* **Summathisnthat** 2-8-12 0.. DavidProbert 3 61
(Des Donovan) *chsd ldrs: rdn over 1f out: styd on* **33/1**

4 *3/4* **Reina Sofia** 2-8-12 0... LukeMorris 1 58
(Tony Carroll) *mid-div: hdwy 2f out: rdn over 1f out: styd on* **20/1**

4 **5** *2 1/2* **First Rebellion**[12] 1129 2-9-3 0....................................... EddieCreighton 9 54
(Joseph Tuite) *chsd ldrs: rdn 1/2-way: hung rt fr over 1f out: wknd ins fnl f* **40/1**

6 *2* **Xinbama (IRE)** 2-9-0 0.. PatrickHills(3) 11 47
(J W Hills) *hld up: rdn over 1f out: nvr on terms* **25/1**

3 **7** *nk* **Thorpe Bay**[12] 1129 2-9-3 0... NickyMackay 2 46
(Mark Rimmer) *chsd ldr: rdn 1/2-way: wknd ins fnl f* **11/1**

8 *1/2* **Monumental Man** 2-9-3 0.. ShaneKelly 6 44
(James Unett) *s.s: outpcd* **66/1**

9 *2* **Apostle (IRE)** 2-9-3 0... HayleyTurner 8 37
(Michael Bell) *sn outpcd and bhd* **9/4**[1]

P **En Ete** 2-8-5 0 .... JakePayne(7) 5 —
(Bill Turner) *sn hung rt and outpcd: t.o whn p.u over 3f out: dismntd* **12/1**

60.79 secs (0.79) **Going Correction** -0.325s/f (Firm) **10** Ran SP% **106.2**
Speed ratings (Par 90): **80,77,74,73,69 66,65,65,61,—**
toteswingers:1&2 £3.90, 2&3 £11.40, 1&3 £23.80 CSF £15.32 TOTE £6.90: £1.50, £1.20, £4.70; EX 20.40.
Owner G Amey & P D Evans **Bred** G E Amey **Trained** Pandy, Monmouths
■ Casa Bex (9/1) was withdrawn (ref to ent stalls). Deduct 10p in the £ under R4.

FOCUS
Overall this was probably just an ordinary juvenile maiden, although there is little previous form to go on. The race is related twards the bottom end of the race averages.

NOTEBOOK
Cockney Fire looked green once in front, but was much the best. She's a half-sister to Kumbeshwar, who progressed to a useful rating over middle-distances on the Flat for this yard before making a high-class juvenile hurdler for Alan King, and this one can be expected to take her racing well and improve. Incidentally, this was a first winner as a sire for Cockney Rebel, who won the 2,000 Guineas in 2007. (op 13-2)
Triggerlo showed speed but wasn't good enough. To this point he has shown his limitations, but he should find a race. (tchd 3-1)
Summathisnthat, who was bought back for just 800gns, couldn't go with the front two but kept on well for third.
Reina Sofia showed enough to suggest she can make her mark for a stable that has already had a juvenile winner this year. (op 25-1)
First Rebellion stepped up a little on his debut effort. (op 50-1)
Xinbama(IRE) hinted at ability and should be better for the run. (op 40-1)
Monumental Man lost ground with a slow start but made some late headway. (op 50-1)
Apostle(IRE) cost £60,000 and was a strong favourite for his debut, but he didn't convince in the paddock that he was ready to make a winning start and he showed nothing. He didn't miss the break, but was soon behind and did not respond to pressure. It seems that he needs more time. (tchd 15-8 and 5-2 in places)
En Ete Official explanation: jockey said filly lost its action

1397 TOTETENTOFOLLOW.CO.UK LEICESTERSHIRE STKS (LISTED RACE) 7f 9y
3:15 (3:16) (Class 1) 4-Y-0+
£17,031 (£6,456; £3,231; £1,611; £807; £405) **Stalls** High

Form RPR

233- **1** **Flambeau**[175] 7083 4-8-11 98.. DaneO'Neill 7 113
(Henry Candy) *chsd ldrs: led over 1f out: sn clr: eased towards fin* **6/1**[3]

300- **2** *4 1/2* **Field Of Dream**[183] 6885 4-9-2 105.................................... J-PGuillambert 4 106
(Luca Cumani) *s.i.s: hdwy 1/2-way: rdn over 2f out: chsd wnr ins fnl f: no imp* **25/1**

312- **3** *1 1/2* **Side Glance**[203] 6349 4-9-2 106... DavidProbert 9 102
(Andrew Balding) *hld up: hdwy over 1f out: r.o: nt rch ldrs* **9/4**[1]

3-34 **4** *1 1/4* **Duff (IRE)**[35] 844 8-9-2 106..(v) ShaneKelly 2 99
(Edward Lynam, Ire) *led: rdn and hdd over 1f out: no ex* **10/1**

356- **5** *1 1/4* **High Standing (USA)**[182] 6923 6-9-2 109.............................. JimCrowley 6 95
(William Haggas) *hood removed late: dwlt: hld up: hdwy over 1f out: no imp ins fnl f* **9/2**[2]

00-1 **6** *3/4* **Dunelight (IRE)**[35] 844 8-9-5 105.....................................(v) LukeMorris 1 96
(Clive Cox) *chsd ldr: rdn over 2f out: wknd ins fnl f* **16/1**

221- **7** *nse* **Fathsta (IRE)**[189] 6752 6-9-2 103.................................... StevieDonohoe 3 93
(David Simcock) *chsd ldrs: rdn over 2f out: wknd over 1f out* **22/1**

30-5 **8** *3* **Lovelace**[14] 1093 7-9-2 105... AdrianNicholls 5 85
(David Nicholls) *hld up: rdn over 2f out: hung rt over 1f out: n.d* **6/1**[3]

11-6 **9** *1/2* **Spirit Of Sharjah (IRE)**[35] 844 6-9-5 98..................... FrankieDettori 10 87
[illegible]

504- **10** *nk* **Flowing Cape (IRE)**[190] 6577 6-9-2 79.............................. GeorgeBaker 8 83
(Reg Hollinshead) *hld up: racd keenly: hdwy 1/2-way: wknd over 1f out* **100/1**

1m 21.92s (-4.28) **Going Correction** -0.325s/f (Firm) **10** Ran SP% **116.0**
Speed ratings (Par 111): **111,105,104,102,101 100,100,96,96,96**
toteswingers:1&2:£14.60, 2&3:£16.50, 1&3:£3.60 CSF £143.51 TOTE £6.70: £2.00, £5.90, £1.30; EX 184.10.
Owner Major M G Wyatt **Bred** Dunchurch Lodge Stud Co **Trained** Kingston Warren, Oxon
■ Stewards' Enquiry : J-P Guillambert three-day ban: used whip in incorrect place (May 2-4)

FOCUS
This looked a decent Listed race, but a few of the likely types disappointed to varying degrees. An impressive return from the winner, but just bit of doubt over what else ran their race.

NOTEBOOK
Flambeau ◆ did well last year, being placed in Listed company after winning a maiden on her reappearance, and being a big filly, she is thought to have strengthened up a fair bit during her break. She got warm beforehand, but settled well in the race and quickened once asked. She has a high cruising speed, so should be effective over 6f, but Dane O'Neill feels she settles well enough to get 1m, although he thinks that will be the limit of her stamina. The manner of this success suggests she'll be comfortable in a higher grade and the plan is the Group 3 Chartwell Fillies' Stakes over this trip on the Lingfield turf on Derby Trial day. (op 5-1)
Field Of Dream lost his way after winning a Newmarket Listed race last May, but the winter break seems to have freshened him up and this was a solid return. (op 33-1 tchd 20-1)
Side Glance had to wait for a gap but was one-paced when in the clear. He progressed well last year and should have more to offer this time, but he shaped as though this first start in 203 days was needed. (op 3-1 tchd 10-3)
Duff(IRE) is probably not quite as good as he used to be but this was a respectable effort. (op 11-1)
High Standing(USA) looked to hold obvious claims on his return, not only because he was the clear pick on official ratings, but he had won first-time out for the last three seasons and was successful on his last start at Listed level. However, he was a major market drifter - he had been a 9-4 shot with two bookies who priced up the previous evening. He was immediately out the back after Jim Crowley was slow to remove the blindfold and made only minor progress, leaving himself with a bit to prove next time. (op 10-3 tchd 5-1)
Dunelight(IRE) had a tough task under the penalty picked up for his recent Wolverhampton success at this level.
Fathsta(IRE) didn't run badly considering he was last seen winning on soft ground over 6f in a handicap off 94 last October. He was keen and this should have taken the freshness out of him. (op 16-1)
Lovelace didn't come on as expected from a promising reappearance in the Cammidge Trophy. (op 15-2)

Spirit Of Sharjah(IRE) was well short of his best, even allowing for a 3lb penalty. (op 15-2 tchd 8-1)

1398 BET ON TODAY'S FOOTBALL AT TOTESPORT.COM H'CAP 1m 1f 218y
3:50 (3:51) (Class 5) (0-70,69) 4-Y-O+ **£2,590** (£770; £385; £192) **Stalls** Low

Form RPR

620- **1** **Boa**[343] 1920 6-8-10 **58** DavidProbert 7 65
(Reg Hollinshead) *a.p: rdn to chse ldr over 1f out: styd on u.p to ld post* **7/1**

00-0 **2** *nse* **Buddy Holly**[29] 418 6-9-0 **62** AndreaAtzeni 3 69
(Robert Eddery) *sn led: shkn up over 1f out: styd on: hdd post* **3/1**[1]

1303 **3** *2* **Petomic (IRE)**[15] 1083 6-9-2 **64** HayleyTurner 1 67
(Richard Guest) *hld up: hdwy over 3f out: rdn over 1f out: styd on same pce ins fnl f* **7/1**

100- **4** *2 1/4* **Kayaan**[13] 7167 4-8-13 **61** MickyFenton 5 60
(Pam Sly) *s.s: hld up: hdwy and hung rt fr over 1f out: no imp ins fnl f* **9/2**[3]

60-6 **5** *8* **Royal Defence (IRE)**[29] 885 5-9-2 **67** MartinHarley(3) 4 50
(Michael Quinn) *prom: racd keenly: pushed along over 4f out: wknd over 2f out* **25/1**

6134 **6** *1/2* **Peadar Miguel**[38] 806 4-9-2 **69** AdamBeschizza(5) 2 51
(Noel Quinlan) *chsd ldrs tl rdn and wknd over 2f out* **13/2**

50-0 **7** *hd* **Tombellini (IRE)**[31] 873 4-8-7 **55** FrankieMcDonald 6 42
(David Nicholls) *chsd ldr: rdn over 2f out: wknd and eased fnl f: lost 2 pls nr fin* **20/1**

246- **8** *15* **Brigadoon**[226] 5679 4-9-4 **66** JimCrowley 8 —
(William Jarvis) *racd wd tl jnd main gp 8f out: chsd ldrs: rdn over 2f out: wknd over 1f out* **10/3**[2]

2m 8.26s (0.36) **Going Correction** +0.125s/f (Good) **8** Ran SP% **113.2**
Speed ratings (Par 103): **103,102,101,99,93 92,92,80**
toteswingers: 1&2 £5.00, 1&3 £12.70, 2&3 £2.60 CSF £27.73 CT £152.22 TOTE £10.20: £2.70, £1.20, £1.50; EX 29.50.
Owner Geoff Lloyd **Bred** R Hollinshead **Trained** Upper Longdon, Staffs
■ Stewards' Enquiry : Andrea Atzeni one-day ban: careless riding (May 2)

FOCUS
Few appealed in this modest handicap. The race is rated around the third to his turf form.

1399 MORE LIVE FOOTBALL BETTING AT TOTESPORT.COM MAIDEN STKS 1m 1f 218y
4:25 (4:27) (Class 5) 3-Y-O+ **£2,914** (£867; £433; £216) **Stalls** Low

Form RPR

1 **Mezyaad (USA)** 3-8-10 0 FrankieDettori 7 77+
(Roger Varian) *a.p: chsd ldr 3f out: led 2f out: shkn up over 1f out: edgd rt ins fnl f: styd on* **8/13**[1]

00- **2** *hd* **High Samana**[171] 7163 3-8-10 0 JimCrowley 2 76
(Ralph Beckett) *led: rdn and hdd 2f out: ev ch whn bmpd wl ins fnl f: styd on* **8/1**

00- **3** *10* **Veloce (IRE)**[175] 7099 3-8-10 0 ShaneKelly 8 56
(John Dunlop) *hld up: hdwy over 3f out: wknd 2f out: wnt 3rd sn after* **22/1**

4 *6* **Star Alliance (IRE)** 3-8-10 0 DaneO'Neill 6 44
(John Dunlop) *s.s: hdwy over 2f out: sn wknd* **7/1**[3]

0 **5** *8* **Graceful Spirit**[21] 983 4-9-8 0 DavidProbert 10 26
(Des Donovan) *hld up: hdwy 3f out: sn hung rt and wknd* **40/1**

66 **6** *1 3/4* **Carrside Lady**[31] 873 5-9-8 0 FrankieMcDonald 9 23
(Owen Brennan) *s.i.s: hld up: a in rr* **50/1**

4 **7** *1/2* **Neat Sweep (IRE)**[23] 952 3-8-5 0 AndreaAtzeni 5 19
(Alan McCabe) *plld hrd: hld up in tch: rdn over 2f out: sn wknd* **9/2**[2]

66 **8** *3/4* **Western Hope (IRE)**[80] 300 4-9-8 0 HayleyTurner 4 20
(Simon Dow) *chsd ldrs: pushed along 6f out: wknd wl over 2f out* **28/1**

6 **9** *40* **Green Ensign (IRE)**[26] 930 4-9-13 0 PatCosgrave 3 —
(Alan McCabe) *chsd ldr: pushed along over 4f out: hung lft and wknd wl over 2f out: eased: t.o* **20/1**

2m 8.07s (0.17) **Going Correction** +0.125s/f (Good)
WFA 3 from 4yo+ 17lb **9** Ran SP% **120.7**
Speed ratings (Par 103): **104,103,95,91,84 83,82,82,50**
CSF £6.32 TOTE £1.50: £1.10, £1.10, £5.30; EX 5.20.
Owner Sheikh Ahmed Al Maktoum **Bred** Darley **Trained** Newmarket, Suffolk

FOCUS
Little strength in depth to this maiden with the majority of these looking pretty limited, and two runners pulled well clear. The time was 0.19 seconds quicker than the earlier Class 5 handicap, although that race seemed to be steadily run. The first pair are rated slightly above the race averages.
Graceful Spirit Official explanation: jockey said filly hung left
Neat Sweep(IRE) Official explanation: jockey said filly ran too free

1400 GET LIVE FOOTBALL STATS AT TOTESPORT.COM H'CAP 7f 9y
4:55 (4:59) (Class 5) (0-70,68) 3-Y-O **£1,942** (£578; £288; £144) **Stalls** High

Form RPR

003- **1** **Konstantin (IRE)**[128] 7779 3-8-13 **60** HayleyTurner 2 70+
(Marcus Tregoning) *chsd ldrs: rdn over 1f out: led ins fnl f: r.o* **9/2**[2]

061- **2** *2* **Classic Voice (IRE)**[175] 7087 3-9-7 **68** GeorgeBaker 1 71
(Hugo Palmer) *chsd ldrs tl led over 2f out: hdd and no ex ins fnl f* **13/2**[3]

240- **3** *2 1/2* **Bajan Bear**[199] 6465 3-9-6 **67** DaneO'Neill 10 63
(Michael Blanshard) *s.i.s: hld up: hdwy over 1f out: rdn and hung rt ins fnl f: styd on same pce* **11/1**

14 **4** *3* **Caelis**[29] 887 3-9-2 **63** JimCrowley 4 51
(Ralph Beckett) *chsd ldrs: rdn over 2f out: hung rt and no ex ins fnl f* **5/2**[1]

2330 **5** *4 1/2* **Unwrapit (USA)**[10] 1169 3-8-11 **63** (p) AdamCarter(5) 6 39
(Bryan Smart) *led over 4f: wknd ins fnl f* **12/1**

3422 **5** *dht* **Not So Bright (USA)**[12] 1134 3-8-10 **57** (tp) AndreaAtzeni 7 33
(Des Donovan) *mid-div: hdwy over 2f out: sn rdn: wknd ins fnl f* **15/2**

5503 **7** *4* **Karate (IRE)**[18] 1020 3-9-2 **66** SophieDoyle(3) 8 31
(Hans Adielsson) *hld up in tch: rdn and wknd 2f out* **16/1**

-233 **8** *nk* **Roman Flame**[29] 888 3-9-5 **66** PatCosgrave 9 30
(Michael Quinn) *sn pushed along in rr: rdn over 2f out: hung rt and wknd sn after* **25/1**

336- **9** *6* **Eyes On**[191] 6695 3-8-10 **62** AdamBeschizza(5) 3 —
(Philip McBride) *hld up: rdn over 2f out: sn wknd* **8/1**

1m 25.74s (-0.46) **Going Correction** -0.325s/f (Firm) **9** Ran SP% **108.7**
Speed ratings (Par 98): **89,86,83,80,75 75,70,70,63**
CSF £30.37 CT £269.62 TOTE £6.00: £1.80, £1.80, £3.80; EX 26.90.
Owner Lady Tennant **Bred** Miss Annmarie Burke **Trained** Lambourn, Berks

FOCUS
A modest handicap with the favourite disappointing. The winner looks slightly better than the bare form. Close To The Edge (16/1) was deemed a non-runner by the stewards under new rules brought in this season.

1401 BET TOTEPOOL AT TOTESPORT.COM H'CAP 1m 3f 183y
5:10 (5:10) (Class 3) (0-95,72) 3-Y-O **£3,885** **Stalls** Low

Form RPR

2-21 **1** **Saint Helena (IRE)**[30] 878 3-8-9 **72** DavidCoyle(7) 1 —
(Harry Dunlop) *walked over*

ms (-153.90) **1** Ran

.
Owner W R B Racing 47 **Bred** Frank O'Malley **Trained** Lambourn, Berks

FOCUS
This event produced a walkover after it was boycotted by trainers because the prize money was below the Horsemen's Group tariff. It provided David Coyle with a first 'winner' on only his third ride.
T/Plt: £116.30 to a £ 1 stake. Pool of £50,110.72 - 314.42 winning units. T/Qpdt: £26.20 to £1 stake. Pool of £3,043.70 - 85.90 winning units. CR

1360 NEWBURY (L-H)
Saturday, April 16

OFFICIAL GOING: Good to firm (7.0)
Rail realignment on home bend increased distance son round course by 8m.
Wind: Virtually nil Weather: White cloud

1402 DUBAI DUTY FREE MILLENNIUM MILLIONAIRE H'CAP 1m 2f 6y
1:35 (1:36) (Class 4) (0-85,85) 4-Y-O+ **£5,180** (£1,541; £770; £384) **Stalls** Low

Form RPR

12- **1** **Modun (IRE)**[177] 7045 4-9-6 **84** RyanMoore 14 103+
(Sir Michael Stoute) *hld up in rr: stdy hdwy on outer over 2f out: pushed along to ld jst ins fnl f: sn clr: easily* **7/2**[1]

516- **2** *4* **Udabaa (IRE)**[327] 2386 4-9-2 **80** RichardHills 3 91
(Marcus Tregoning) *sn trcking ldr: chal fr 3f out tl rdn to take narrow ld appr fnl f: hdd jst ins fnl f: kpt on but no ch w wnr* **9/1**

520- **3** *1 1/2* **Satwa Moon (USA)**[196] 6565 5-9-6 **84** EddieAhern 10 92
(Ed Dunlop) *chsd ldrs: drvn to chal ins fnl 2f tl outpcd ins fnl f* **7/1**

/11- **4** *hd* **Bourne**[176] 7062 5-9-4 **82** KierenFallon 7 90+
(Luca Cumani) *pushed lft after 1f: in rr: hdwy fr 2f out: styd on wl ins fnl f: gng on cl home but nvr gng pce to rch ldng trio* **9/2**[2]

110- **5** *1 1/4* **Cashpoint**[371] 1220 6-9-5 **83** WilliamBuick 13 88
(Anthony Middleton) *racd wd early and sn led: jnd fr 3f out but kpt narrow ld tl hdd appr fnl f: wknd fnl 120yds* **50/1**

441- **6** *1 1/2* **All Action (USA)**[196] 6557 4-9-7 **85** TomQueally 6 87+
(Sir Henry Cecil) *in rr: wnt lft after 1f: n.m.r ins fnl 3f: hdwy fr 2f out: styd on ins fnl f but nvr a threat* **13/2**[3]

/50- **7** *nse* **Red Courtier**[337] 2079 4-9-2 **80** JimmyFortune 11 82
(Paul Cole) *chsd ldrs: rdn 3f out: sn one pce: kpt on again ins fnl f* **12/1**

541- **8** *1* **All The Winds (GER)**[143] 7548 6-9-2 **80** RussKennemore 8 80
(Shaun Lycett) *in rr: rdn and hdwy on wd outside fr over 2f out: kpt on fnl f but nvr rchd ldrs* **33/1**

321- **9** *1* **Significant Move**[192] 6678 4-9-1 **79** IanMongan 9 77
(Stuart Kittow) *in tch: drvn to chse ldrs fr 3f out: no imp fr 2f out: wknd ins fnl f* **12/1**

201- **10** *1* **Warlu Way**[201] 6422 4-8-13 **77** TedDurcan 5 73+
(John Dunlop) *mid-div: pushed along and no prog fr over 2f out* **25/1**

322- **11** *nk* **Rock The Stars (IRE)**[50] 7307 4-8-2 **71** oh2 AmyScott(5) 15 66
(J W Hills) *racd on outside: chsd ldrs 3f out: wknd over 1f out* **22/1**

514- **12** *1* **Tinshu (IRE)**[140] 7591 5-9-7 **85** MichaelHills 2 78
(Derek Haydn Jones) *chsd ldrs: rdn and n.m.r on ins over 2f out: sn btn* **20/1**

136- **13** *2* **Rosco Flyer (IRE)**[130] 7736 5-8-9 **76** JohnFahy(3) 12 65
(Roger Teal) *chsd ldrs: rdn 3f out: wknd wl over 2f out* **50/1**

00-0 **14** *2 1/4* **Hail Promenader (IRE)**[14] 1097 5-8-6 **77** MatthewLawson(7) 4 62
(B W Hills) *pressed ldrs: ev ch 3f out: wknd 2f out* **33/1**

-162 **15** *3 1/4* **Pertuis (IRE)**[66] 475 5-8-12 **76** ChrisCatlin 1 54
(Harry Dunlop) *hmpd on ins after 1f: swtchd to outer and sme hdwy 3f out: nvr rchd ldrs and no ch fnl 2f* **25/1**

2m 7.12s (-1.68) **Going Correction** -0.025s/f (Good) **15** Ran SP% **118.2**
Speed ratings (Par 105): **105,101,100,100,99 98,98,97,96,95 95,94,93,91,88**
Tote Swingers: 1&2 £7.90, 1&3 £8.50, 2&3 £18.60 CSF £30.28 CT £210.33 TOTE £4.60: £2.10, £3.00, £2.70; EX 37.40 Trifecta £162.20 Pool: £603.74 - 2.75 winning units..
Owner Ballymacoll Stud **Bred** Ballymacoll Stud Farm Ltd **Trained** Newmarket, Suffolk
■ Stewards' Enquiry : Eddie Ahern three-day ban: careless riding (May 2-4)
Tom Queally four-day ban: careless riding (May 2-5)

FOCUS
Only one of these had raced within the last month, so there ought to be plenty more to come from the majority of the field. It featured some exposed types, but also a couple that could go on to prove up to Listed company or higher before the season is over, and is hot form for the grade. The race is rated fairly posiitively and should work out. The early gallop didn't look strong, and it only appeared to significantly increase about 4f out.

1403 DUBAI DUTY FREE FINEST SURPRISE STKS (REGISTERED AS THE JOHN PORTER STAKES) (GROUP 3) 1m 4f 5y
2:05 (2:05) (Class 1) 4-Y-O+
£28,385 (£10,760; £5,385; £2,685; £1,345; £675) **Stalls** Low

Form RPR

160- **1** **Indian Days**[125] 7851 6-9-3 113 TomQueally 4 117
(James Given) *hld up in rr but in tch: hdwy fr 3f out: drvn to take slt ld jst ins fnl 2f and sn hanging lft: rdn and styd on wl u.p fnl f: jst hld on* **7/1**[3]

03-6 **2** *hd* **Bridge Of Gold (USA)**[49] 705 5-8-12 106 ChristopheSoumillon 3 112
(Mikael Magnusson) *disp 2nd to 7f out: styd chsng ldrs: rdn 3f out: one pce 2f out: c rt to outside and rallied fnl f: str run clsng stages: fin wl: jst failed* **8/1**

342- **3** *2 1/2* **Poet**[175] 7096 6-8-12 114 AdamKirby 2 108
(Clive Cox) *led: drvn along fr 3f out: narrowly hdd jst ins fnl 2f: styd pressing ldrs and ev ch ins fnl f tl outpcd fnl 150yds* **10/3**[2]

550- **4** *2* **Allied Powers (IRE)**[202] 6410 6-8-12 113 JamieSpencer 8 105
(Michael Bell) *s.i.s: in rr: pushed along 4f out: styd on fr 2f out and r.o ins fnl f but nvr gng pce to rch ldng trio* **8/1**

311- **5** *nk* **Verdant**[262] 4470 4-8-11 103 RyanMoore 5 104
(Sir Michael Stoute) *trckd ldrs: drvn and qcknd over 2f out and sn chalng: stl upsides wl over 1f out: wknd ins fnl f: lost 4th nr fin* **6/4**[1]

The Form Book, Raceform Ltd, Compton, RG20 6NL

-242 **6** *7* **Halicarnassus (IRE)**[58] 585 7-8-12 98................................ NeilCallan 6 93
(Mick Channon) *disp 2nd tl chsd ldr 7f out: rdn 3f out: wknd 2f out* **16/1**

44-5 **7** *3 ¼* **Cumulus Nimbus**[14] 1100 4-8-11 99............................ RichardHughes 1 88
(Richard Hannon) *slowly away: t.k.h and sn in tch: rdn over 3f out: btn sn after* **14/1**

2m 32.11s (-3.39) **Going Correction** -0.025s/f (Good)
WFA 4 from 5yo+ 1lb **7** Ran SP% **110.3**
Speed ratings (Par 113): **110,109,108,106,106 102,99**
Tote Swingers: 1&2 £4.80, 1&3 £3.50, 2&3 £4.00 CSF £55.59 TOTE £8.10: £3.50, £3.10; EX 63.10 Trifecta £525.10 Pool: £709.71 - 1.00 winning units..

Owner D J Fish **Bred** Mrs C Regalado-Gonzalez **Trained** Willoughton, Lincs

FOCUS

This looked an ordinary renewal in terms of quality, and it seems highly unlikely at this stage that we witnessed another Harbinger in action, who took this race last year. The last ten winners of this race had all won at the trip before, which looked to rule a couple of these out, and the quick going also counted against quite a few. The first two basically ran to form.

NOTEBOOK

Indian Days, carrying a penalty, held his form at a high level last season, which finished with a down-the-field effort in Hong Kong during December. James Given felt his horse would benefit from this outing, so it bodes well that Indian Days proved good enough to take this despite hanging under pressure at one stage. Connections plan to aim him towards the Singapore Airlines International Cup at Kranji next, before attacking races like the Coronation Cup. (tchd 13-2 and 15-2)

Bridge Of Gold(USA), who ran at Cagnes-Sur-Mer in February, had something to find in this company even on his best form, so this was a really encouraging effort on the face of it. He is certainly up to winning a race at this level, and it will be interesting to see how he is campaigned.

Poet got to the lead early and ran his race on ground that was most probably too quick for him considering his best form. (op 4-1)

Allied Powers(IRE), 12th of 15 in this last season, collected a couple of Group 3s in France before running well in Group 1 company twice - he was reported to have lost his action on his final start. Michael Bell feels his horse always needs his first start of the year, which looked the case again here. This should set him up for a repeat bid on the Prix d'Hedouville. (tchd 9-1)

Verdant was the most interesting participant for a trainer with a good record in the race. The colt was seemingly well thought of last year, but didn't make it out of handicap company, which wasn't a particular concern here considering connections. Related to plenty of nice types, he reportedly had a small setback late last summer, although nothing serious and his trainer gave him plenty of time to recover. Well supported, it's best to give him the benefit of the doubt for now as to whether he is up to this class or not. (tchd 11-8 and 13-8)

Halicarnassus(IRE) has been around for what seems like forever, and still knows how to run a big race, as he showed out in Dubai during January and February. Tenth in this race last year, he was hard ridden quite early in the home straight and faded late on. (tchd 14-1)

Cumulus Nimbus didn't look to have any obvious chance in this grade, and so it proved. He broke slowly and pulled really hard under restraint. Official explanation: jockey said colt ran too free (op 16-1 tchd 12-1)

1404 DUBAI DUTY FREE STKS (REGISTERED AS THE FRED DARLING STAKES) (GROUP 3) 7f (S)

2:40 (2:40) (Class 1) 3-Y-O

£28,385 (£10,760; £5,385; £2,685; £1,345; £675) **Stalls** Centre

Form RPR

202- **1** **Rimth**[197] 6530 3-9-0 105.. ChristopheSoumillon 10 106
(Paul Cole) *hld up in rr: swtchd rt: drvn and rapid hdwy fnl f to ld fnl 120yds: readily* **13/2**[3]

103- **2** *1 ¼* **Sharnberry**[169] 7204 3-9-0 95.. KierenFallon 11 103
(Ed Dunlop) *t.k.h towards rr but in tch: drvn and hdwy fr 2f out to ld 1f out: hdd fnl 120yds: kpt on but nt pce of wnr* **12/1**

111- **3** *1 ¾* **Eucharist (IRE)**[219] 5882 3-9-0 96................................ RichardHughes 7 98
(Richard Hannon) *t.k.h: hld up in rr: hdwy wl over 1f out: styd on insde fnl f to take 3rd nr fin but no imp on ldng duo* **7/1**

135- **4** *½* **Pontenuovo (FR)**[191] 6702 3-9-0 111....................... StephanePasquier 5 97+
(Roger Charlton) *hld up towards rr: hdwy fr 2f out: styd on ins fnl f to take one pce 3rd fnl 120yds: dropped bk to 4th nr fin* **5/1**[2]

100 **5** *½* **Mortitia**[176] [illegible] [illegible].. [illegible] 12 [illegible]
(Brian Meehan) *in tch: hrd drvn over 1f out: styd on ins fnl f but nvr gng pce to rch ldrs* **50/1**

262- **6** *nk* **Cochabamba (IRE)**[182] 6927 3-9-0 104........................... JackMitchell 8 94
(Roger Teal) *in rr: rdn 2f out: styd on u.p fnl f: gng on cl home but nvr a threat* **10/1**

131- **7** *½* **Cape Dollar (IRE)**[182] 6927 3-9-0 105.............................. RyanMoore 1 93
(Sir Michael Stoute) *chsd ldrs: drvn and effrt over 1f out but nvr quite gng pce to chal: wknd fnl 120yds* **5/2**[1]

32-3 **8** *nk* **Breedj (IRE)**[16] 1059 3-9-0 82.. PhilipRobinson 13 92?
(Clive Brittain) *led: rdn over 2f out: hdd 1f out: wknd ins fnl f* **40/1**

123- **9** *2 ½* **Darajaat (USA)**[189] 6734 3-9-0 99.................................... RichardHills 14 86
(Marcus Tregoning) *t.k.h: trckd ldrs: pushed along 2f out: styd wl there tl wknd ins fnl f* **14/1**

116- **10** *¾* **Tallahasse (IRE)**[210] 6176 3-9-0 90................................. JimmyFortune 9 84
(Alan Swinbank) *in tch: drvn along fr over 2f out and nvr gng pce to get into contention* **33/1**

130- **11** *hd* **Perfect Tribute**[240] 5246 3-9-0 100.................................... AdamKirby 6 83
(Clive Cox) *plld hrd: chsd ldrs: rdn 2f out: sn btn* **20/1**

14-2 **12** *½* **Glas Burn**[16] 1059 3-9-0 93.. EddieAhern 4 82
(Jonathan Portman) *chsd ldrs: drvn 2f out: stl wl there 1f out: eased whn wkng ins fnl f* **40/1**

414- **13** *4* **Aneedah (IRE)**[168] 7235 3-9-0 95...................................... WilliamBuick 3 71
(John Gosden) *t.k.h: chsd ldrs: rdn and effrt 2f out: wknd qckly fnl f* **8/1**

000- **14** *12* **Yarooh (USA)**[264] 4429 3-9-0 75.. ChrisCatlin 2 38
(Clive Brittain) *chsd ldrs: rdn 3f out: wknd qckly ins fnl 2f* **125/1**

1m 25.34s (-0.36) **Going Correction** -0.10s/f (Good) **14** Ran SP% **121.0**
Speed ratings (Par 108): **98,96,94,94,93 93,92,92,89,88 88,87,83,69**
Tote Swingers: 1&2 £13.10, 1&3 £6.70, 2&3 £15.30 CSF £77.83 TOTE £7.60: £2.50, £3.50, £2.00; EX 83.80 Trifecta £849.80 Part won. Pool: £71148.48 - 020 winning units..

Owner Denford Stud **Bred** Belgrave Bloodstock Ltd **Trained** Whatcombe, Oxon

■ Stewards' Enquiry : Eddie Ahern caution: allowed filly to coast home with no assistance, Rule (B) 59.4.

FOCUS

Recent winners of this don't go on to prove successful in the 1,000 Guineas at Newmarket, but some have run with distinction, albeit not many. The field came down the centre of the course, and the early pace did not look that strong. This looked a fairly limited renewal, with the third and fifth the best initial guide.

NOTEBOOK

Rimth showed classy form at two but the trip here looked of some concern considering the pace she displayed as a juvenile. Runner-up in the Group 1 Cheveley Park on her final start of 2010, she was given a wonderful ride by Christophe Soumillon, who got his mount settled nicely in rear before weaving his way to the front at the right time. Not in the Guineas at the moment, she is probably worth her place in the field if supplemented but it would be surprising if there wasn't stronger stayers up against her at Newmarket to beat her. The French Guineas looks like a sensible alternative. (op 5-1)

Sharnberry, who got warm beforehand, finished her juvenile season with a third in the Listed Bosra Sham Stakes after being behind Rimth in the Cheveley Park - she may not have been at her best at the time. Things didn't look promising while she was being knocked about in the pack, but she found a way clear and ran on strongly to probably put up a career-best performance. It remains to be seen whether she'll stay any further, but the jockey felt she is worth supplementing for Newmarket. (op 11-1)

Eucharist(IRE) ◆ won four races at two, including two nurseries, and ran a similar race to Rimth here without being quite as good. On this evidence, she is clearly a Group filly and one would imagine connections will have no trouble finding a suitable contest for her. (op 8-1 tchd 6-1)

Pontenuovo(FR) ◆ was well thought of in France and ran some nice races without hitting the heights connections seemingly had for her. Having her first start for Roger Charlton, and rated 6lb clear on official ratings, connections weren't sure the trip (dam stayed 6.5f) or ground would be suit, so this was a fact-finding mission. It appeared that the jockey was following Cape Dollar, and got forced very wide to make her challenge as the field panned out. This was probably a good effort to finish fourth and she can be given another chance. (op 9-2 tchd 11-2)

Mortitia, whose trainer felt she was unlucky not to win at Doncaster last year, stayed on after hitting a flat spot, and ran well. (op 66-1)

Cochabamba(IRE) showed good form for her small stable as a juvenile, but her trainer warned before this contest that the run was designed to bring her on. Settled in rear, she needed strong pressure when the pace lifted, but kept on in pleasing style to promise better to come. (op 9-1 tchd 11-1)

Cape Dollar(IRE) didn't look to have any potential stamina issues, and won here over C&D on her second start, but this was a lacklustre effort as she failed to make any impression. She looked a little uneasy as the tempo quickened so, in this company, maybe she appreciates more cut in the ground than she got here. (op 4-1)

Darajaat(USA) was tried in the 5f Cornwallis Stakes on her final start of 2010, so the trip here looked a possible issue considering what she did last year - her trainer indicated thought she may revert to sprinting if she didn't get competitive here. After showing up early, she failed to get home and a drop in distance must be on the cards. (op 12-1 tchd 16-1)

Perfect Tribute, on toes beforehand, pulld hard and finished well beaten. Official explanation: jockey said filly ran too free (op 28-1)

Aneedah(IRE) quickly made up into useful juvenile last year with fourths at Newmarket in valuable sales race (7f) and a fillies' Listed event (1m). On her toes at the start, she raced a bit keen and will need to settle better. (op 10-1)

1405 TOTESPORT.COM GREENHAM STKS (GROUP 3) 7f (S)

3:10 (3:12) (Class 1) 3-Y-O

£28,385 (£10,760; £5,385; £2,685; £1,345; £675) **Stalls** Centre

Form RPR

111- **1** **Frankel**[182] 6924 3-9-0 126.. TomQueally 3 124+
(Sir Henry Cecil) *sn trcking ldr: qcknd to chal 3f out: led sn after: shkn up and edgd lft 2f out: drvn and qcknd clr fnl f: easily* **1/4**[1]

411- **2** *4* **Excelebration (IRE)**[267] 4332 3-9-0 89................................ AdamKirby 1 113
(Marco Botti) *t.k.h early: trckd ldrs in 3rd: drvn and qcknd to chal wnr 2f out: styd on terms tl readily outpcd appr fnl f: clr 2nd best* **25/1**

10- **3** *6* **Shropshire (IRE)**[241] 5219 3-9-0 94.................................... MichaelHills 2 97
(B W Hills) *t.k.h: chsd ldrs: styd on to take wl hld 3rd fnl 2f* **18/1**[3]

11-3 **4** *1 ½* **Vanguard Dream**[21] 990 3-9-0 95.................................... RyanMoore 4 93
(Richard Hannon) *t.k.h early: in rr: rdn and outpcd 3f out: drvn and styd on fnl f to take wl hld 4th nr fin* **20/1**

113- **5** *1 ¼* **Picture Editor**[168] 7236 3-9-0 99...................................... IanMongan 5 89
(Sir Henry Cecil) *sn led: jnd by wnr 3f out: sn hdd: wknd fr 2f out* **33/1**

132- **6** *hd* **Strong Suit (USA)**[197] 6531 3-9-0 113........................(t) RichardHughes 6 89
(Richard Hannon) *stdd s: t.k.h in rr: sme hdwy to dispute wl hld 3rd ins fnl 2f: wknd over 1f out and hung rt ins fnl f* **9/2**[2]

1m 24.6s (-1.10) **Going Correction** -0.10s/f (Good) **6** Ran SP% **115.0**
Speed ratings (Par 108): **102,97,90,88,87 87**
Tote Swingers: 1&2 £2.90, 1&3 £2.90, 2&3 £6.30 CSF £12.45 TOTE £1.30: £1.10, £5.30; EX [illegible]

Owner K Abdulla **Bred** Juddmonte Farms Ltd **Trained** Newmarket, Suffolk

FOCUS

A straightforward return from Frankel with his sole realistic form rival disappointing, and the favourite is rated 8lb off his Dewhurst form. The second clearly improved and the form is rated loosely around the race averages. The winning time was quicker than the Fred Darling, which had eight more runners in it.

NOTEBOOK

Frankel, who was a bit noisy in the pre-parade ring, was running in a trial well known for not producing winners at Newmarket in a few weeks, but the last horse to do the double, Wollow, was trained by Henry Cecil, back in 1976, so backers should not get too worried by that statistic yet. Such has been the hype about Frankel this year that he reportedly outpaced a Newmarket-to-Cambridge passenger trainer earlier in the year. His credentials were there for all to see, unbeaten in four starts, which finished with a Group 1 success in the Dewhurst Stakes three weeks after winning the Group 2 Royal Lodge by an impressive ten lengths. Said to not have grown a great deal during the winter, which isn't surprising considering his size at two, the one worry with him was whether this big, strong colt would settle and give himself a chance of running a race. Connections had taken the step of employing a pacemaker in Picture Editor, but Frankel was in the lead inside the 3f marker. Tom Queally looked to be racing a bit more freely than he'd have wanted, but his mount saw off the rival that dared to eyeball him and put up a workmanlike, if not spectacular, performance. Bookmakers shortened his price for the Guineas a fraction (his Derby odds unsurprisingly remained roughly the same), and it's definitely worth remembering that this victory came when Henry Cecil's horses had appeared to be needing the run. Judged on this performance alone, he doesn't look the type to thrive at much further than a mile, if anything he looks capable of holding his own at sprinting trips, much like his dam. Connections will no doubt be pleased to get this run out of the way, and can now concentrate on his first big target. He is likely to have a pacemaker again in the Guineas. (op 1-3 tchd 2-9 and 2-5 in a place and 4-11 in places)

Excelebration(IRE) ◆ poses a real problem with regard to the value of the form. He was the lowest rated of the field on official figures, but had won two of his three starts as a juvenile. A winter on his back may well have done him the world of good and connections have a decent animal on their hands. He is in the German Guineas but the trainer feels the horse's trip will be 7f, so next stop could be at Ascot for the Jersey Stakes. (op 28-1 tchd 33-1 in places)

Shropshire(IRE) still looks a bit green and may leave this effort behind in due course. His pedigree suggests he'll be a sprinter. (op 20-1 tchd 16-1)

Vanguard Dream did have the benefit of a recent start, and made some good late ground after getting outpaced. (op 25-1)

Picture Editor, in as a pacemaker for Frankel, had proved himself to be a talented performer as a juvenile. He seemed guaranteed to make this a decent test considering he was proven over at least 1m (he was one of the second favourites for the Derby before his Zetland Stakes defeat), but even he couldn't hang on for as long as some may have thought. (op 28-1)

Strong Suit(USA) won on his debut at the course (6f) in good style before winning the Coventry at Royal Ascot by the skin of his teeth - Klammer, who has form tied in with the favourite, was beaten six lengths in that contest. He then went in search of a Group 1 victory in Ireland but was beaten by Zoffany (who was behind him at Ascot). A defeat in ground far from ideal in the Middle Park was the last we saw of him in 2010, but he looked by far the most realistic challenger to the favourite here. Representing a stable that sent out Redback, Major Cadeaux, Paco Boy and Dick Turpin to win this in the past ten years, he was most disappointing, as he never made any impression on the runner-up let alone the winner in the final stages. This leaves him with plenty to prove. Official explanation: jockey said colt lost its action (op 4-1 tchd 5-1)

1406 TOTESCOOP6 SPRING CUP (H'CAP) 1m (S)

3:45 (3:48) (Class 2) 4-Y-0+

£18,693 (£5,598; £2,799; £1,401; £699; £351) **Stalls** Centre

Form RPR

30-0 **1** **Light From Mars**[14] [1094] 6-9-7 **97**.......................... MickaelBarzalona 10 106
(David Nicholls) *w ldr: led 3f out: hld on towards fin: all out* **14/1**

12-0 **2** *nk* **Pintura**[14] [1092] 4-8-9 **90**.......................... LauraPike(5) 8 98
(David Simcock) *mid-div: hdwy far side over 2f out: chal ins fnl f: no ex nr fin* **25/1**

2110 **3** *1/2* **Lowther**[14] [1094] 6-9-10 **100**..........................(be) AdamKirby 7 107
(Alan Bailey) *w ldrs: rdn over 2f out: str chal fnl f: no ex clsng stages* **16/1**

300- **4** *3/4* **Proponent (IRE)**[175] [7100] 7-9-5 **95**.......................... TedDurcan 3 100+
(Roger Charlton) *hld up in rr: hdwy over 2f out: kpt on wl fnl f* **16/1**

311- **5** *hd* **Nazreef**[116] [7955] 4-8-11 **87**..........................(t) TravisBlock 12 92
(Hughie Morrison) *w ldrs: kpt on same pce fnl f* **16/1**

30-2 **6** *nk* **Brae Hill (IRE)**[14] [1094] 5-9-8 **98**.......................... JamieSpencer 25 102+
(Richard Fahey) *hld up in mid-div: hdwy stands' side over 2f out: kpt on ins fnl f: nt rch ldrs* **12/1[3]**

200- **7** *1/2* **Leviathan**[183] [6888] 4-8-11 **87**.......................... SteveDrowne 11 90
(Tony Newcombe) *chsd ldrs: edgd lft over 2f out: one pce* **16/1**

60-3 **8** *1 1/4* **Manassas (IRE)**[14] [1092] 6-9-0 **93**.......................... LouisBeuzelin(3) 24 93
(Brian Meehan) *trckd ldrs: drvn over 2f out: one pce* **16/1**

-612 **9** *nk* **Night Lily (IRE)**[14] [1104] 5-8-1 **82**.......................... KieranO'Neill(5) 19 82+
(Paul D'Arcy) *mid-div stands' side: hdwy over 2f out: kpt on: nrst fin* **12/1[3]**

13-0 **10** *1* **Merchant Of Medici**[16] [1061] 4-8-4 **80**.......................... ChrisCatlin 13 77
(William Muir) *mid-div: hdwy over 2f out: kpt on: nt rch ldrs* **50/1**

60-0 **11** *3* **Al Muheer (IRE)**[14] [1094] 6-9-2 **92**..........................(b) MichaelHills 5 82
(David Nicholls) *in rr: sme hdwy over 3f out: nvr nr ldrs* **33/1**

215- **12** *1 1/2* **Signor Verdi**[168] [7233] 4-8-10 **86**.......................... MartinDwyer 15 73+
(Brian Meehan) *mid-div: drvn over 2f out: nvr a threat* **12/1[3]**

621- **13** *nk* **South Cape**[171] [7182] 8-8-13 **89**.......................... RyanMoore 2 75
(Gary Moore) *in rr: sme hdwy over 2f out: nvr a factor* **25/1**

00-0 **14** *1 3/4* **Marajaa (IRE)**[14] [1092] 9-8-10 **86**.......................... JamieMackay 23 68
(Willie Musson) *in rr: sme hdwy 2f out: swtchd rt: nvr on terms* **20/1**

4-11 **15** *1* **Bravo Echo**[83] [271] 5-9-2 **92**.......................... NeilCallan 9 72
(Michael Attwater) *in tch: effrt over 2f out: wknd over 1f out* **14/1**

1303 **16** *3 1/4* **Dubai Hills**[14] [1094] 5-9-5 **95**.......................... TomEaves 20 67
(Bryan Smart) *in tch stands' side: drvn 3f out: sn wknd* **20/1**

410- **17** *hd* **Mujood**[198] [6510] 8-8-8 **87**.......................... JohnFahy(3) 14 59
(Eve Johnson Houghton) *chsd ldrs: rdn over 2f out: sn wknd* **100/1**

3212 **18** *1 3/4* **Avonrose**[31] [865] 4-8-1 **77**.......................... AdrianMcCarthy 4 45
(Derek Shaw) *a towards rr* **66/1**

101- **19** *3 1/2* **Brick Red**[168] [7233] 4-9-3 **93**.......................... JimmyFortune 17 53
(Andrew Balding) *mid-div: effrt over 2f out: sn wknd* **10/1[2]**

6-30 **20** *8* **Prime Exhibit**[14] [1094] 6-9-3 **93**.......................... WilliamCarson 1 34
(Richard Fahey) *led tl 3f out: sn lost pl: bhd whn eased ins fnl f* **22/1**

-040 **21** *hd* **Greyfriarschorista**[14] [1102] 4-9-0 **90**..........................(b[1]) RichardHills 18 31
(Mark Johnston) *chsd ldrs: lost pl over 2f out* **14/1**

011- **22** *1 3/4* **Saint Pierre (USA)**[198] [6503] 4-8-12 **88**.......................... KierenFallon 16 25
(Luca Cumani) *t.k.h: trckd ldrs: drvn 3f out: sn lost pl* **9/1[1]**

211- **23** *2 1/4* **Suited And Booted (IRE)**[283] [3796] 4-9-6 **96**.......................... RichardHughes 21 28
(Richard Hannon) *t.k.h in rr: effrt 3f out: sn lost pl and bhd: eased* **9/1[1]**

-200 **24** *4 1/2* **Freeforaday (USA)**[35] [811] 4-9-4 **97**.......................... KierenFox(3) 6 18
(John Best) *w ldrs: rdn over 4f out: lost pl 3f out: sn bhd: eased* **66/1**

130- **P** **Capital Attraction (USA)**[224] [5741] 4-9-10 **100**.......................... TomQueally 22 —
(Sir Henry Cecil) *in rr: heavily eased 3f out: sn t.o: p.u over 1f out* **33/1**

1m 36.98s (-2.72) **Going Correction** -0.10s/f (Good) **25** Ran SP% **135.0**
Speed ratings (Par 109): **109,108,108,107,107 106,106,105,104,103 100,99,99,97,96 93,92,91,87,79 79,77,75,70,—**
Tote Swingers: 1&2 £159.60, 2&3 £107.80 CSF £347.89 CT £5618.01 TOTE £17.30: £4.20, £10.00, £5.40, £7.00; EX 839.20 TRIFECTA Not won..
Owner Dr Marwan Koukash **Bred** Harts Farm And Stud **Trained** Sessay, N Yorks

FOCUS
A race that has provided plenty of shocks recently, as one would expect for such a wide-open and competitive handicap. Only one joint-favourite had won in the preceding ten renewals, and seven winners in that period were sent off at double-figure odds. It was a good finish for owner Dr Marwan Koukash, who had the 1-2 as well as the sixth. Probably ordinary form of its type, with the winner the best guide.

NOTEBOOK
Light From Mars managed to reverse form with a couple of those he met again in the Lincoln under a prominent ride. He looked there to be shot at over 2f out, but he kept on finding and gained a first success since October 2009. (op 16-1)
Pintura had proved best with ease in the ground, so the way he kept on here suggests he'll handle most ground now. His problem is that the handicapper seems to have him.
Lowther came under pressure and then ran on to look a likely winner before weakening in the final stages. (op 20-1)
Proponent(IRE), said to still look a bit wintry and not come to himself yet, didn't appear well treated on his winning handicap form but stayed on through horses to make a pleasing return. (op 20-1)
Nazreef has only ever won on the AW, but he proved he isn't a one-trick pony with a fair performance on his return from a break. The way he faded in the final stages suggests he'll have more to come. (op 20-1)
Brae Hill(IRE), runner-up in the Lincoln last time, fought on well towards the stands' side but couldn't confirm his Doncaster form with Light From Mars and Lowther. (op 11-1)
Leviathan made late progress and should be straighter for this run. (op 20-1 tchd 25 -1 in a place)
Manassas(IRE) was always thereabout but lacked a change of gear to make an impact.
Saint Pierre(USA) appeared to be caught out by a lack of experience after racing keenly. Official explanation: jockey said colt hung left-handed (tchd 10-1)
Suited And Booted(IRE) was solid in the betting but ran disappointingly after taking a strong hold in rear. Official explanation: vet said colt moved poorly post-race (op 10-1)
Capital Attraction(USA) Official explanation: jockey said gelding lost its action

1407 TOTESPORT 0800 221 221 MAIDEN STKS 1m 3f 5y

4:15 (4:18) (Class 4) 3-Y-O **£5,180** (£1,541; £770; £384) **Stalls** Low

Form RPR

1 **World Domination (USA)** 3-9-3 0.......................... TomQueally 8 100+
(Sir Henry Cecil) *trckd ldrs: qcknd to chal ins fnl 3f: led appr fnl 2f: pushed clr fnl f: r.o strly* **3/1[2]**

2 *3 3/4* **Solar Sky** 3-9-3 0.......................... IanMongan 5 93+
(Sir Henry Cecil) *in rr: green and pushed along 3f out: swtchd rt to outside and gd hdwy fr 2f out: str run thrght fnl f to take 2nd fnl 120yds: gng on on cl home: should improve* **20/1**

04- **3** *3 1/4* **Reflect (IRE)**[229] [5582] 3-9-3 0.......................... RichardHughes 2 87
(Richard Hannon) *chsd ldrs: rdn over 2f out: swtchd rt sn after and styd on to chse wnr wl over 1f out but nvr any ch: one pce and lost 2nd fnl 120yds* **6/1[3]**

02- **4** *shd* **Wayward Glance**[171] [7179] 3-9-3 0.......................... ChristopheSoumillon 11 87
(Michael Bell) *in rr: hdwy 4f out: drvn and one pce ins fnl 3f: rdn and styd on again fnl f to press for 3rd cl home but nvr a threat* **10/1**

5 *2 3/4* **Fiorente (IRE)** 3-9-3 0.......................... RyanMoore 1 82+
(Sir Michael Stoute) *mid-div: hdwy to trck ldrs fr 3f out: shkn up 2f out and kpt on wl tl outpcd fnl f* **8/1**

0- **6** *3/4* **Ardlui (IRE)**[164] [7302] 3-9-3 0.......................... FergusSweeney 12 81+
(Henry Candy) *in rr: pushed along 3f out: hdwy fr 2f out: styd on fnl f but nvr gng pce to rch ldrs* **33/1**

3- **7** *2* **Suhaili**[183] [6883] 3-9-3 0.......................... NeilCallan 3 77
(Roger Varian) *led 3f: styd w ldr tl led over 5f out: hdd over 3f out: wknd fnl f* **7/4[1]**

0- **8** *7* **Sirius Superstar**[175] [7099] 3-9-3 0.......................... JimmyFortune 6 64
(Andrew Balding) *mid-div: drvn along and no imp fr 3f out: no ch after* **16/1**

9 *nk* **Sacred Sound (IRE)** 3-9-3 0.......................... TedDurcan 13 64
(Mick Channon) *in rr: pushed along and sme prog 4f out: rdn and bhd fr 3f out* **80/1**

10 *1 3/4* **Kuda Huraa (IRE)** 3-9-3 0..........................(t) JamieSpencer 14 61
(Paul Cole) *t.k.h: chsd ldr tl led after 3f: hdd over 5f out: drvn to take slt ld again over 3f out: hdd over 2f out: wknd appr fnl f* **33/1**

0-6 **11** *3 3/4* **Atlas Shrugged (IRE)**[12] [1139] 3-9-3 0.......................... AdamKirby 10 54
(Clive Cox) *in tch: hdwy to chse ldrs 4f out: wknd fr 3f out* **40/1**

4- **12** *5* **Navigation Track**[185] [6845] 3-9-3 0.......................... MartinDwyer 9 45
(David Simcock) *pushed along in rr 5f out: sme prog into mid-div 3f out: wknd sn after* **100/1**

0 **13** *4* **Camporosso**[9] [1203] 3-9-3 0.......................... KierenFallon 7 38
(Mark Johnston) *chsd ldrs tl wknd over 2f out* **33/1**

0- **14** *12* **Strength And Stay (IRE)**[213] [6087] 3-9-3 0.......................... EddieAhern 4 16
(Eve Johnson Houghton) *prom early: bhd fr 1/2-way* **100/1**

2m 19.64s (-1.56) **Going Correction** -0.025s/f (Good) **14** Ran SP% **121.0**
Speed ratings (Par 100): **104,101,98,98,96 96,94,89,89,88 85,81,78,70**
Tote Swingers: 1&2 £14.70, 1&3 £5.90, 2&3 £18.10 CSF £68.60 TOTE £3.90: £2.20, £5.20, £2.10; EX 52.80 Trifecta £450.00 Part won. Pool of £608.21 - 0.44 winning units..
Owner K Abdulla **Bred** Juddmonte Farms Inc **Trained** Newmarket, Suffolk

FOCUS
Mixed messages can be gleaned from the horses who have taken this race in the past. Sight Unseen looked to have the potential to do anything after his win in 2009 but disappointed thereafter, Tighnabruaich (2008) and Western Adventure (2007) didn't scale any huge heights after they proved successful, but Hala Bek won this on debut in 2006, and then went on to finish fourth in the Epsom Derby on his next start. The winner already looks smart at least.

1408 DUBAI DUTY FREE TENNIS CHAMPIONSHIPS MAIDEN STKS (DIV I) 1m (S)

4:50 (4:53) (Class 4) 3-Y-O **£4,857** (£1,445; £722; £360) **Stalls** Centre

Form RPR

5- **1** **Laajooj (IRE)**[173] [7112] 3-9-3 0.......................... MickaelBarzalona 7 84+
(Mahmood Al Zarooni) *hld up in mid div: effrt and edgd rt 2f out: led ins fnl f: edgd lft: drvn out* **11/4[2]**

53- **2** *1* **Discovery Bay**[184] [6873] 3-9-3 0.......................... SteveDrowne 2 82
(Roger Charlton) *w ldrs: led over 1f out: hdd and no ex ins fnl f* **14/1**

3 *nse* **Danehill Dante (IRE)** 3-9-3 0.......................... RichardHughes 12 82+
(Richard Hannon) *hld up stands' side: hdwy to chse ldrs over 1f out: kpt on wl: will improve* **12/1**

5- **4** *1* **Tanfeeth**[248] [4962] 3-9-3 0.......................... RichardHills 11 79+
(Ed Dunlop) *stdd s: hld up in rr: n.m.r over 2f out: r.o ins fnl f: will improve* **10/1**

5 *1 3/4* **Eshtibaak (IRE)** 3-9-3 0.......................... RobertHavlin 5 79+
(John Gosden) *s.s: in rr: hdwy 2f out: sn swtchd rt: styd on wl fnl f: promising* **25/1**

32- **6** *2 3/4* **Blue Deer (IRE)**[200] [6436] 3-9-3 0.......................... NeilCallan 9 69
(Mick Channon) *led: hdd over 1f out: sn fdd* **22/1**

0 **7** *nk* **Red Lago (IRE)**[43] [777] 3-9-3 0.......................... MichaelHills 1 68
(B W Hills) *mid-div: effrt on far side over 2f out: kpt on fnl f* **50/1**

2- **8** *3/4* **Kirthill (IRE)**[176] [7058] 3-9-3 0.......................... KierenFallon 8 67
(Luca Cumani) *trckd ldrs: effrt over 2f out: fdd appr fnl f* **2/1[1]**

9 *hd* **Change The Subject (USA)** 3-9-3 0.......................... TomQueally 14 66
(Sir Henry Cecil) *in rr: drvn over 2f out: kpt on: nvr nr ldrs: will improve* **14/1**

10 *nse* **Crimson Knight** 3-9-3 0.......................... MartinDwyer 3 66
(Brian Meehan) *chsd ldrs: drvn 3f out: hung rt and grdaually wknd* **50/1**

11 *2* **Plimsoll Line (USA)** 3-9-3 0.......................... JamieSpencer 4 61
(Michael Bell) *chsd ldrs: wknd over 1f out* **8/1[3]**

00- **12** *2* **Xclaim**[175] [7094] 3-9-3 0.......................... AdamKirby 6 57
(Clive Cox) *t.k.h: trckd ldrs: wknd over 1f out* **28/1**

3- **13** *1* **Ringstead Bay (FR)**[139] [7609] 3-9-3 0.......................... JimmyFortune 13 55
(Ralph Beckett) *in rr: nvr on terms* **28/1**

14 *6* **Montegonian (USA)** 3-9-3 0.......................... RyanMoore 10 41
(Marcus Tregoning) *dwlt: in rr: drvn and n.m.r over 2f out: sn bhd* **40/1**

1m 38.5s (-1.20) **Going Correction** -0.10s/f (Good) **14** Ran SP% **122.7**
Speed ratings (Par 100): **102,101,100,99,98 95,95,94,94,94 92,90,89,83**
Tote Swingers: 1&2 £11.60, 1&3 £7.70, 2&3 £19.80 CSF £38.83 TOTE £4.00: £1.10, £4.10, £3.10; EX 64.30 Trifecta £240.80 Pool: £829.91 - 2.55 winning units..
Owner Godolphin **Bred** Kildaragh Stud **Trained** Newmarket, Suffolk
■ Stewards' Enquiry : Mickael Barzalona caution: careless riding.

FOCUS
The first division of the 7f maiden looked slightly the weaker on paper, but this is usually a race that produces plenty of future winners. Diamond Tycoon's victory in 2007 was a particularly good contest, as he had Lucarno (St Leger winner) and Pipedreamer (that year's Cambridgeshire victor) behind him.

1409 DUBAI DUTY FREE TENNIS CHAMPIONSHIPS MAIDEN STKS (DIV II) 1m (S)

5:25 (5:30) (Class 4) 3-Y-O **£4,857** (£1,445; £722; £360) **Stalls** Centre

Form RPR

1 **Dubawi Sound** 3-9-3 0 .... NeilCallan 8 88+
(Roger Varian) *in rr: gd hdwy over 2f out: drvn and r.o strly to ld ins fnl f: edgd lft: won gng away: readily* **50/1**

25- 2 2 **General Synod**[218] 5916 3-9-3 0 .... RichardHughes 7 83
(Richard Hannon) *chsd ldrs: led ins fnl 2f: sn rdn: hdd ins fnl f: hld whn hung lft u.p fnl 140yds* **7/4[1]**

3- 3 1 **Colombian (IRE)**[210] 6190 3-9-3 0 .... RobertHavlin 2 82+
(John Gosden) *trckd ldrs: drvn along 2f out: ev ch appr fnl f: one pce and hld by wnr whn hmpd fnl 140yds: styd on again last strides* **2/1[2]**

4 4 **Quadrant (IRE)** 3-9-3 0 .... MartinDwyer 12 72
(Brian Meehan) *in tch: drvn and hdwy over 2f out: rdn and styd on fnl f but nvr gng pce to rch ldrs* **18/1**

5 3/4 **Strategic Bid** 3-9-3 0 .... JamieSpencer 9 70+
(Paul Cole) *t.k.h in rr: hdwy fr 2f out: kpt on fnl f but nvr a threat* **13/2[3]**

6 nse **Voodoo Prince** 3-9-3 0 .... EddieAhern 4 70+
(Ed Dunlop) *s.i.s: t.k.h and sn chsng ldrs: pushed along and one pce 2f out: kpt on again ins fnl f* **8/1**

35- 7 nk **Mariners Lodge (USA)**[185] 6843 3-9-3 0 .... AhmedAjtebi 5 69
(Mahmood Al Zarooni) *t.k.h: led tl hdd ins fnl 2f: wknd 1f out* **16/1**

8 3 1/2 **Jumeira Field (USA)** 3-9-3 0 .... RyanMoore 11 61
(Sir Michael Stoute) *in tch: pushed along ins fnl 3f: wknd ins fnl 2f* **28/1**

6- 9 3/4 **Red Inca**[210] 6196 3-9-3 0 .... KierenFallon 1 59
(Brian Meehan) *in tch: pushed along 3f out: wknd 2f out* **14/1**

- 10 1 1/4 **Billy Buttons** 3-9-3 0 .... JimmyFortune 3 57
(Andrew Balding) *chsd ldrs tl wknd over 2f out* **33/1**

30 11 2 **Strewth (IRE)**[12] 1139 3-9-0 0 .... KierenFox(3) 6 52
(John Best) *chsd ldrs 5f* **50/1**

12 2 **Junoob** 3-9-3 0 .... RichardHills 14 47
(John Dunlop) *s.i.s: pushed along and green fr 1/2-way: hung lft sn after: a bhd* **66/1**

13 3/4 **Edgware Road** 3-9-3 0 .... SteveDrowne 13 46
(Roger Charlton) *in tch: chsd ldrs 3f out: wknd over 2f out* **40/1**

1m 38.45s (-1.25) **Going Correction** -0.10s/f (Good) **13** Ran SP% **126.2**
Speed ratings (Par 100): **102,100,99,95,94 94,93,90,89,88 86,84,83**
Tote Swingers: 1&2 £29.70, 1&3 £25.90, 2&3 £2.00 CSF £142.10 TOTE £69.80: £14.60, £1.60, £1.40; EX 238.00 TRIFECTA Not won..
Owner Cromhall Stud **Bred** Derek R Price **Trained** Newmarket, Suffolk

FOCUS
Some nice-looking horses took their chance in this, and the race looks sure to produce winners. There wasn't a great of difference between the winning times of the two divisions, but this was a bit quicker.
Edgware Road Official explanation: jockey said gelding stopped quickly
T/Jkpt: £20,118.60. Pool of £28,336.08 - 1 winning unit. T/Plt: £2,181.70 to a £1 stake. Pool of £119,993.90 - 40.15 winning units. T/Qpdt: £151.30 to a £1 stake. Pool of £8,844.66 - 43.24 winning units. ST

1199 RIPON (R-H)

Saturday, April 16

OFFICIAL GOING: Good to firm (good in places; 8.9)
Rail on bend into home straight moved out 6m adding 11m to race son round course.
Wind: Virtually nil Weather: Cloudy

1410 BET ON TOTESCOOP6 AT TOTESPORT.COM H'CAP 1m

2:00 (2:01) (Class 3) (0-90,90) 4-Y-O+ **£8,256** (£2,472; £1,236; £618; £308; £155) **Stalls** Low

Form RPR

0511 1 **Snow Bay**[15] 1075 5-9-4 **87** .... FrannyNorton 14 98
(David Nicholls) *prom: led over 3f out: rdn 2f out: drvn and hld on wl ins fnl f* **11/1**

3104 2 1 1/4 **Suits Me**[21] 991 8-9-4 **87** .... PhillipMakin 9 95
(David Barron) *w ldr: rdn over 1f out: kpt on but nvr quite rch wnr* **13/2[2]**

5-15 3 1 **Zebrano**[70] 438 5-8-9 **78** ....(b) MartinLane 17 84+
(Andrew Haynes) *hld up: n.m.r over 2f out: swtchd lft over 1f out: sn gd hdwy: drvn and kpt on wl ins fnl f: wnt 3rd nr line* **33/1**

003- 4 hd **Douze Points (IRE)**[202] 6400 5-9-6 **89** ....(p) PatCosgrave 6 94
(Ed de Giles) *in tch on inner: rdn and hdwy over 1f out: drvn and kpt on ins fnl f* **20/1**

363- 5 1 1/4 **Arabian Spirit**[148] 7227 6-9-3 **86** .... PaulHanagan 1 88
(Richard Fahey) *trckd ldrs on inner: pushed along over 3f out: rdn over 2f out: no ex fnl 100yds: fin 6th: plcd 5th* **8/1[3]**

0-00 6 2 1/2 **Prince Of Dance**[14] 1094 5-9-6 **89** .... GrahamGibbons 18 84
(Tom Tate) *chsd ldrs: rdn over 2f out: no ex fr over 1f out: fin 7th: plcd 6th* **14/1**

404- 7 3/4 **Keys Of Cyprus**[172] 7143 9-8-12 **81** .... PaulQuinn 3 76+
(David Nicholls) *midfield: rdn over 1f out: kpt on: n.d: fin 8th: plcd 7th* **16/1**

30-0 8 nse **Cameroonеy**[14] 1092 8-9-2 **90** .... DaleSwift(5) 4 85
(Brian Ellison) *led: hdd over 3f out: sn rdn: wknd over 1f out: fin 9th: plcd 8th* **20/1**

000- 9 hd **Spying**[156] 7411 4-8-10 **79** .... PaulMulrennan 10 73
(Ann Duffield) *midfield: rdn over 2f out: sn no imp: fin 10th: plcd 9th* **16/1**

25-0 10 1 1/4 **Sir George (IRE)**[14] 1092 6-9-4 **87** .... BarryMcHugh 12 79
(Ollie Pears) *hld up in midfield: rdn over 2f out: sn no imp: fin 11th: plcd 10th* **16/1**

60-6 11 1 **Smarty Socks (IRE)**[14] 1092 7-9-7 **90** .... SilvestreDeSousa 15 79+
(David O'Meara) *s.i.s: hld up in midfield: n.m.r over 2f out tl over 1f out: nvr threatened: fin 12th: plcd 11th* **6/1[1]**

150- 12 1 3/4 **Shadowtime**[196] 6567 6-8-12 **81** .... PatrickMathers 11 66
(Colin Teague) *in tch: rdn over 2f out: wknd over 1f out: fin 13th: plcd 12th* **66/1**

112- 13 hd **Amethyst Dawn (IRE)**[168] 7227 5-9-5 **88** .... DavidAllan 2 73
(Tim Easterby) *s.i.s: hld up: pushed along over 2f out: n.d: fin 14th: plcd 13th* **12/1**

654- 14 hd **Tartan Gunna**[217] 5955 5-9-4 **87** ....(v) JoeFanning 7 71
(Mark Johnston) *s.i.s: hld up: rdn over 2f out: sn no imp: plcd 15th: plcd 14th* **12/1**

040- 15 1 **City Of The Kings (IRE)**[168] 7227 6-9-0 **86** .... MichaelO'Connell(3) 13 68
(Geoffrey Harker) *hld up in midfield: rdn 2f out: n.d: fin 16th: plcd 15th* **28/1**

1106 16 1/2 **Steed**[7] 1240 4-8-12 **86** ....(p) JulieBurke(5) 5 67
(Kevin Ryan) *midfield: rdn over 2f out: wknd over 1f out: fin 17th: plcd 16th* **18/1**

60-0 17 1 1/4 **San Cassiano (IRE)**[7] 1240 4-9-3 **89** .... JamesSullivan(3) 8 67
(Ruth Carr) *trckd ldrs tl wknd over 2f out: fin 18th: plcd 17th* **40/1**

30-0 18 1 1/4 **Barren Brook**[16] 1061 4-8-5 **81** .... DavidSimmonson(7) 20 56
(Michael Easterby) *slowly away: hld up: a in rr: fin 19th: plcd 18th* **40/1**

14-0 19 1 1/2 **Aerodynamic (IRE)**[16] 1061 4-9-1 **84** .... TonyHamilton 19 56
(Clive Mulhall) *hld up: a bhd: fin 20th: plcd 19th* **50/1**

62-2 D hd **Guest Book (IRE)**[15] 1075 4-8-9 **85** .... DarylByrne(7) 16 90+
(Mark Johnston) *hld up: rdn and gd hdwy on outer over 2f out: chsd ldrs over 1f out: kpt on one pce ins fnl f: disqualified and plcd last rdr failed to weigh in* **8/1[3]**

1m 39.33s (-2.07) **Going Correction** -0.075s/f (Good) **20** Ran SP% **127.4**
Speed ratings (Par 107): **107,105,104,104,103 100,99,99,99,98 97,95,95,95,94 93,92,91,89,104**
toteswingers:1&2 £20.10, 2&3 £23.70, 1&3 £27.20 CSF £75.47 CT £2388.79 TOTE £12.60: £3.20, £2.10, £7.50, £5.30; EX 93.50 TRIFECTA Not won..
Owner Pinnacle Bahamian Bounty Partnership **Bred** West Dereham Abbey Stud **Trained** Sessay, N Yorks

■ Stewards' Enquiry : Michael O'Connell two-day ban: careless riding (May 2-3)
Daryl Byrne three-day ban: failed to weigh in (May 2-4)

FOCUS
The early pace was no more than fair for this competitive 1m handicap. The winner confirmed he is better than ever, with the fourth helping with the standard.

NOTEBOOK
Snow Bay, who did well to get across from stall 14, could be called the winner soon after passing 3f out. A ready scorer off 5lb lower at Musselburgh previously, this free-wheeling type is clearly in the form of his life and probably deserves a crack at a good handicap now. He could be of interest around Chester for the big May meeting. (op 12-1)
Suits Me, making his debut for David Barron, was in fair form on the AW over the winter, finishing fourth in the Winter Derby at Lingfield last time. Rated 12lb lower on turf compared to the AW, he was soon on the pace and ran right up to his previous turf best. (op 8-1 tchd 11-2)
Zebrano always faced a stiff ask from stall 17, and found himself widest of all when trying to challenge in the straight. He did well, staying on strongly close home to just get up for third and can be rated better than the bare form.
Douze Points(IRE), who has won just once from 25 starts, seemed suited by the step back up in trip and ran well from a mark of 89. (op 18-1)
Arabian Spirit, unsuccessful when tried hurdling in November, simply wasn't good enough from this mark returned to turf.
Prince Of Dance will be of interest once the handicapper relents. (op 18-1)
Smarty Socks(IRE) always faced an uphill task following his sluggish start and can be given another chance. (op 17-2)
Amethyst Dawn(IRE) Official explanation: jockey said mare missed the break
Barren Brook Official explanation: jockey said gelding failed to handle bend
Aerodynamic(IRE) Official explanation: jockey said gelding slipped on bend turning in
Guest Book(IRE) was always poorly positioned and can be rated better than the bare form. His rider failed to weigh in subsequently, though, leading to his disqualification. (op 10-1)

1411 STOWE FAMILY LAW LLP H'CAP 5f

2:30 (2:31) (Class 5) (0-75,75) 4-Y-O+ **£4,209** (£1,252; £625; £312) **Stalls** High

Form RPR

0-05 1 **Mandurah (IRE)**[7] 1239 7-8-7 **64** .... MichaelO'Connell(3) 13 74
(David Nicholls) *mde virtually all stands' side: hotly chal ins fnl f: jst hld on* **15/2[3]**

006- 2 shd **Bosun Breese**[106] 7239 6-9-4 **72** .... LeeNewman 11 82
(David Barron) *racd stands' side: w wnr: styd on ins fnl f: jst denied* **20/1**

015- 3 1 3/4 **Senate Majority**[151] 7473 4-8-7 **61** oh1 .... DavidAllan 2 65+
(Tim Easterby) *racd far side: in rr: hdwy 2f out: led that side jst ins fnl f: r.o: 1st of 6 that gp* **18/1**

140- 4 hd **Lees Anthem**[215] 6031 4-8-9 **63** .... PatrickMathers 7 66
(Colin Teague) *swtchd lft s to r stands' side: rr-div: sn drvn along: hdwy towards centre over 2f out: styd on ins fnl f: no ex fnl 75yds* **50/1**

2145 5 1/2 **Six Wives**[9] 1196 4-8-8 **65** .... BillyCray(3) 16 66
(David Nicholls) *racd stands' side: chsd ldrs: kpt on same pce ins fnl f* **12/1**

2-02 6 shd **Jigajig**[47] 708 4-9-0 **71** ....(p) AmyRyan(3) 3 72
(Kevin Ryan) *racd far side: chsd ldrs: kpt on same pce ins fnl f: 2nd 0f 6 that gp* **17/2**

123- 7 nk **Supreme Spirit (IRE)**[246] 5054 4-9-7 **75** .... FrannyNorton 15 75
(David Nicholls) *s.s: r stands' side: bhd: hdwy 2f out: styd on wl ins fnl f* **11/2[1]**

040- 8 1 **Select Committee**[171] 7175 6-8-13 **74** ....(p) ShaneBKelly(7) 6 70
(John Quinn) *racd far side: chsd ldr: kpt on same pce appr fnl f: 3rd of 6 that gp* **20/1**

5100 9 nk **Sharp Shoes**[15] 1073 4-8-11 **65** ....(p) PhillipMakin 9 60
(Ann Duffield) *racd stands' side: chsd ldrs towards centre: kpt on same pce appr fnl f* **25/1**

05-0 10 1/2 **Grand Stitch (USA)**[17] 1035 5-9-1 **69** ....(v) DavidNolan 5 62
(Declan Carroll) *led 5 others far side: hdd that side jst ins fnl f: wknd: 4th of 6 that gp* **25/1**

2340 11 hd **Wanchai Whisper**[17] 1034 4-8-7 **61** oh3 ....(p) LiamJones 10 54
(Mark Rimmer) *swtchd lft s to r stands' side: mid-div: effrt over 2f out: edgd rt nvr a factor* **40/1**

4341 12 1 **Ingleby Star (IRE)**[8] 1213 6-8-11 **65** ....(p) DuranFentiman 1 54
(Noel Wilson) *racd far side: in rr: hdwy 2f out: nvr nr ldrs: 5th of 6 that gp* **10/1**

4230 13 1/2 **Incomparable**[9] 1196 6-9-0 **73** ....(bt) SeanLevey(5) 18 60
(David Nicholls) *racd stands' side: mid-div: hung rt and lost pl over 1f out* **12/1**

6-06 14 nk **Chosen One (IRE)**[15] 1073 6-8-12 **69** .... JamesSullivan(3) 8 55
(Ruth Carr) *racd stands' side: chsd ldrs towards centre: wknd appr fnl f* **25/1**

0002 15 1 3/4 **Fashion Icon (USA)**[9] 1204 5-8-8 **62** .... SilvestreDeSousa 12 42
(David O'Meara) *chsd ldrs stands' side: lost pl over 1f out* **17/2**

512- **16** *nse* **Oondiri (IRE)**[202] 6392 4-8-9 **63**.. PaulHanagan 4 43
(Tim Easterby) *dwlt: racd far side: effrt 2f out: nvr a factor: last of 6 that gp* **7/1**[2]

00-0 **17** *shd* **Pearly Wey**[9] 1204 8-8-7 **61** oh2.. BarryMcHugh 17 40
(Ian McInnes) *s.s: racd stands' side: a bhd* **33/1**

58.79 secs (-1.91) **Going Correction** -0.30s/f (Firm) **17** Ran SP% **118.8**
Speed ratings (Par 103): **103,102,100,99,98 98,98,96,96,95 95,93,92,92,89 89,89**
toteswingers:1&2 £50.10, 2&3 £83.40, 1&3 £65.10 CSF £152.64 CT £2672.98 TOTE £9.80: £2.30, £4.70, £4.50, £7.40; EX 268.40 TRIFECTA Not won..

Owner Simple Technology UK **Bred** Michael Lyons **Trained** Sessay, N Yorks

FOCUS
The field split into two groups and it was those who raced stands' side that came out on top. The winner is rated in line with last year's form, with the runner-up to form.

1412 ENTER THE FLAT TOTETENTOFOLLOW H'CAP 2m
3:00 (3:05) (Class 2) (0-105,98) 4-Y-0+
£12,773 (£3,825; £1,912; £957; £477; £239) **Stalls** Low

Form RPR

-060 **1** **Montaff**[14] 1102 5-9-11 **97**.. SamHitchcott 8 103
(Mick Channon) *hld up: hdwy over 3f out: rdn over 2f out: squeezed through gap 1f out: led fnl 110yds: kpt on* **8/1**

350- **2** *1 ¼* **Montparnasse (IRE)**[187] 6808 4-8-10 **86**.. PhillipMakin 4 90
(Kevin Ryan) *trckd ldr: rdn over 2f out: led jst ins fnl f: sn hdd: kpt on* **3/1**[1]

-116 **3** *½* **Exemplary**[18] 1030 4-9-0 **90**.. JoeFanning 2 93
(Mark Johnston) *led: rdn over 2f out: hdd jst ins fnl f: one pce* **8/1**

330- **4** *1 ½* **Halla San**[43] 3447 9-9-7 **98**.. LeeTopliss(5) 10 100
(Richard Fahey) *midfield: rdn over 3f out: kpt on wl ins fnl f: nrst fin* **25/1**

5 *1 ½* **English Summer**[151] 4-9-1 **91**.. SilvestreDeSousa 9 91
(Mark Johnston) *prom: rdn over 2f out: wknd ins fnl f* **6/1**[3]

300- **6** *nk* **Deauville Flyer**[182] 6926 5-9-6 **92**.. PaulHanagan 6 91
(Tim Easterby) *in tch: rdn over 2f out: chsd ldrs over 1f out: no ex ins fnl f* **7/2**[2]

-134 **7** *6* **Porgy**[35] 849 6-8-10 **82**.. MartinLane 3 74
(David Simcock) *s.i.s: hld up: hdwy on outer over 3f out: wknd over 2f out:* **14/1**

510- **8** *1* **My Arch**[115] 6926 9-9-3 **89**.. BarryMcHugh 5 80
(Ollie Pears) *hld up: hdwy on outer over 6f out: rdn over 3f out: sn wknd* **7/1**

9 *1 ¼* **Kayef (GER)**[31] 4-8-12 **88**..(p) FrederikTylicki 1 78
(Michael Scudamore) *hld up: pushed along over 4f out: sn struggling* **16/1**

000- **10** *14* **Rangefinder**[161] 7350 7-8-12 **89**.. SeanLevey(5) 7 62
(Andrew Crook) *trckd ldrs: rdn over 3f out: wknd over 2f out* **40/1**

3m 31.76s (-0.04) **Going Correction** -0.075s/f (Good)
WFA 4 from 5yo+ 4lb **10** Ran SP% **115.1**
Speed ratings (Par 109): **97,96,96,95,94 94,91,90,90,83**
toteswingers:1&2 £2.50, 2&3 £5.60, 1&3 £1.40 CSF £31.78 CT £200.71 TOTE £10.30: £3.00, £1.90, £2.80; EX 51.00 Trifecta £388.60 Part won. Pool: £525.27 - 0.10 winning units..

Owner Barry Walters Catering **Bred** Barry Walters **Trained** West Ilsley, Berks
■ Stewards' Enquiry : Paul Hanagan one-day ban: failed to ride out for 5th (May 2)

FOCUS
A useful staying event. This was the winner's easiest task on paper for some time and he is rated to last year's form. The fourth helps with the standard.

NOTEBOOK
Montaff had been struggling off similar marks at Meydan this year, and again when returning to Britain in the Rosebery. This wasn't as competitive, though, and he produced a nice change of gear to settle it. The return to 2m in this company clearly suited him well, but in winning this off 97, he clearly isn't going to be the easiest to place in future. (op 12-1)
Montparnasse(IRE), formerly with Brian Meehan, travelled well just in behind the speed and held every chance, but he couldn't quicken when asked. (tchd 11-4 and 10-3)
Exemplary bounced back to form on this return to turf, battling on well without being able to find any extra. (op 6-1 tchd 9-1)
Halla San, who failed to complete on three starts over jumps this winter, ran better than expected under top weight on this return to the level. (op 20-1)
English Summer, who had some useful form to his name, had never tackled ground this lively before so probably ran well. He's entitled to improve. (op 8-1)
Deauville Flyer, who needed his reappearance run last season, remains 8lb above his last winning mark and it was no surprise to see him come up short. (op 9-2)

1413 PLAY BLACKJACK AT TOTESPORT.COM (S) STKS 1m 1f 170y
3:35 (3:37) (Class 5) 3-4-Y-0 **£2,266** (£674; £337; £168) **Stalls** Low

Form RPR

-445 **1** **Highlife Dancer**[10] 1170 3-8-7 68.. SamHitchcott 2 59
(Mick Channon) *hld up: hdwy over 3f out: rdn to chal 2f out: led ins fnl f: drvn and kpt on* **11/10**[1]

005- **2** *¾* **Pinotage**[173] 7126 3-8-7 46.. MichaelStainton 4 57
(Richard Whitaker) *hld up: hdwy over 3f out: led over 2f out: sn drvn: hdd ins fnl f* **9/1**

3-33 **3** *5* **Bernisdale**[74] 379 3-8-2 60.. PaulHanagan 5 42
(George Moore) *led narrowly: hdd 7f out: led again over 3f out: sn rdn: hdd over 2f out: wknd over 1f out* **3/1**[2]

0-0 **4** *1 ½* **Karmarouge (IRE)**[11] 1151 3-7-13 0..(t) AndrewHeffernan(3) 8 39
(Brian Rothwell) *hld up: hdwy over 3f out: sn rdn: no imp on ldrs fnl 2f* **12/1**

0-43 **5** *5* **Thunderway (IRE)**[53] 643 3-7-13 43.. JamesSullivan(3) 9 28
(Michael Dods) *trckd ldrs: rdn over 3f out: wknd over 1f out* **8/1**[3]

0-05 **6** *17* **Ochilview Warrior (IRE)**[25] 937 4-9-10 41..(p) LeeNewman 10 —
(Robin Bastiman) *w ldr: led narrowly 7f out: hdd over 3f out: wknd qckly* **28/1**

2040 **7** *53* **Evelyns Diamond**[11] 1151 3-8-2 38.. DuranFentiman 6 —
(Paul Midgley) *sn pushed along in rr: t.o* **33/1**

006- **8** *7* **River Blade**[128] 7785 3-8-7 45.. LiamJones 3 —
(Mark Brisbourne) *hld up: a in rr: t.o* **22/1**

2m 5.51s (0.11) **Going Correction** -0.075s/f (Good)
WFA 3 from 4yo 17lb **8** Ran SP% **112.2**
Speed ratings (Par 103): **96,95,91,90,86 72,30,24**
toteswingers:1&2 £2.50, 2&3 £5.60, 1&3 £1.40 CSF £11.47 TOTE £2.20: £1.10, £2.30, £1.40; EX 13.60 Trifecta £38.60 Pool: £488.39 - 9.35 winning units..There was no bid for the winner.

Owner The Highlife Racing Club **Bred** Imperial & Mike Channon Bloodstock Ltd **Trained** West Ilsley, Berks
■ Stewards' Enquiry : Michael Stainton two-day ban: used whip with excessive frequency (May 2-3)

FOCUS
A lowly seller. It has been rated around the third and is arguably worth a bit more.

1414 PLAY ROULETTE AT TOTESPORT.COM MAIDEN AUCTION FILLIES' STKS 5f
4:10 (4:12) (Class 5) 2-Y-0 **£2,978** (£886; £442; £221) **Stalls** High

Form RPR

1 **Ponty Acclaim (IRE)** 2-8-4 0.. DuranFentiman 6 76+
(Tim Easterby) *trckd ldrs: led 1f out: rdn clr ins fnl f: comf* **10/1**

0 **2** *2 ¼* **Beau Mistral (IRE)**[14] 1095 2-8-1 0.. JamesSullivan(3) 8 68
(Paul Green) *led narrowly: rdn whn hdd 1f out: kpt on but no ch w wnr* **4/1**[1]

3 *1 ½* **Sweet Chilli (IRE)** 2-8-6 0.. LeeNewman 9 65
(David Barron) *trckd ldrs: rdn 2f out: kpt on same pce ins fnl f* **7/1**[3]

0 **4** *3 ¼* **Red Shadow**[9] 1199 2-8-1 0.. AndrewHeffernan(3) 10 51
(Alan Brown) *trckd ldrs: rdn 2f out: one pce ins fnl f* **40/1**

2 **5** *hd* **Launch On Line**[17] 1042 2-8-6 0.. JoeFanning 2 52
(Bill Turner) *w ldr: rdn over 1f out: wknd ins fnl f* **9/2**[2]

6 *½* **Mebsuta (IRE)** 2-8-8 0.. PaulMulrennan 12 52+
(Kevin Ryan) *outpcd in rr tl kpt on fr over 1f out: nrst fin* **8/1**

7 *shd* **Arcticality (IRE)** 2-8-8 0.. FrederikTylicki 4 52
(Richard Fahey) *sn pushed along in midfield: kpt on ins fnl f* **10/1**

8 *3 ½* **Dora's Sister (IRE)** 2-8-5 0.. SeanLevey(5) 11 41
(John Quinn) *in tch: rdn over 2f out: wknd over 1f out* **4/1**[1]

9 *½* **Vieira Da Silva (IRE)** 2-8-8 0.. SamHitchcott 5 38
(Mick Channon) *midfield: outpcd over 2f out: wknd over 1f out* **12/1**

10 *½* **Flurry Of Hands (IRE)** 2-8-6 0.. MartinLane 1 34
(Ann Duffield) *wnt rt s: a outpcd in rr* **33/1**

11 *hd* **Pendle Lady (IRE)** 2-8-6 0.. LiamJones 3 33
(Mark Brisbourne) *dwlt: a outpcd towards rr* **50/1**

12 *1 ¼* **First Fast Now (IRE)** 2-8-6 0.. SilvestreDeSousa 7 29
(Nigel Tinkler) *s.i.s: hld up: sme hdwy whn short of room over 1f out: n.d* **20/1**

59.70 secs (-1.00) **Going Correction** -0.30s/f (Firm) **12** Ran SP% **119.8**
Speed ratings (Par 89): **96,92,90,84,84 83,83,77,77,76 76,74**
toteswingers:1&2 £26.50, 2&3 £9.80, 1&3 £28.40 CSF £48.79 TOTE £13.60: £4.40, £1.60, £3.20; EX 74.40 TRIFECTA Not won..

Owner Rapcalone **Bred** T Darcy & Vincent McCarthy **Trained** Great Habton, N Yorks
■ Stewards' Enquiry : Sean Levey caution: careless riding.

FOCUS
Just an ordinary juvenile contest. A nice start from the winner and the form is rated at the mid point of the averages.

NOTEBOOK
Ponty Acclaim(IRE), representing a yard that has already had a first-time-up juvenile winner this season, wasn't expensive but is from a good sprinting family and her trainer gave the impression he thinks a bit of her. It will be interesting to see where she goes next. (tchd 12-1)
Beau Mistral(IRE) looked a likely future winner when finishing a promising seventh in the Brockelsby on debut and had the advantage of the stands' rail, but she just found one too speedy. (op 11-2)
Sweet Chilli(IRE) is bred to want further than this and made a promising debut. (op 15-2)
Red Shadow was going on well close home and has clearly learnt from her debut effort.
Launch On Line was disappointing, considering the abundant promise she had shown on debut. (op 7-2 tchd 3-1)
Mebsuta(IRE), a daughter of Amadeus Wolf, stayed on encouragingly and should improve. (op 12-1)
Dora's Sister(IRE), a daughter of Dark Angel and related to plenty of sprint winners, failed to live up to expectations, but newcomers from this yard often improve markedly for an outing. (op 9-2)

1415 BET BINGO AT TOTESPORT.COM MAIDEN STKS 1m 1f 170y
4:45 (4:47) (Class 5) 3-Y-0 **£2,978** (£886; £442; £221) **Stalls** Low

Form RPR

1 **Beaten Up** 3-9-3 0.. LiamJones 1 88+
(William Haggas) *trckd ldrs: rdn to ld wl over 1f out: kpt on wl* **13/2**[3]

-24 **2** *3 ¾* **Honest Deal**[14] 1096 3-9-3 0.. PaulMulrennan 12 80
(Alan Swinbank) *led after 2f: rdn whn hdd wl over 1f out: no ch w wnr* **9/2**[2]

4 **3** *7* **Carrowbeg (IRE)**[18] 1027 3-9-3 0.. SilvestreDeSousa 3 66+
(Mark Johnston) *led for 2f: remained prom: rdn over 4f out: wknd over 1f out* **10/1**

4 *2 ¾* **Dervisher (IRE)** 3-8-10 0.. CharlesEddery(7) 2 60+
(Sir Henry Cecil) *sn trckd ldrs: rdn and lost pl over 4f out: kpt on again fr over 1f out* **14/1**

30- **5** *1 ¾* **Madison Square (USA)**[164] 7302 3-8-10 0.. AntiocoMurgia(7) 7 56
(Mahmood Al Zarooni) *hld up: rdn over 3f out: no imp tl sme late hdwy: n.d* **10/1**

4-0 **6** *¾* **Pintrada**[9] 1203 3-9-3 0.. JoeFanning 11 55
(James Bethell) *in tch on outer: hdwy to chse ldrs over 3f out: sn rdn: wknd over 1f out* **16/1**

323- **7** *nk* **Galloping Queen (IRE)**[209] 6222 3-8-12 74.. SamHitchcott 6 49
(Mick Channon) *midfield: rdn over 3f out: no imp* **8/1**

4-5 **8** *4* **Getabuzz**[11] 1151 3-9-3 0.. MartinLane 4 46+
(Tim Easterby) *dwlt: hld up: rdn over 4f out: nvr threatened* **18/1**

05- **9** *4 ½* **White Fusion**[229] 5595 3-9-3 0.. FrederikTylicki 10 37
(Howard Johnson) *midfield: rdn over 4f out: wknd over 3f out* **50/1**

4- **10** *¾* **Goodness**[175] 7094 3-9-3 0.. RichardMullen 8 35
(Sir Michael Stoute) *trckd ldrs: rdn and outpcd over 4f out: wknd over 1f out* **15/8**[1]

5-0 **11** *8* **Sobea Star (IRE)**[11] 1151 3-8-9 0.. SimonPearce(3) 9 —
(Pam Sly) *s.i.s: hld up: a bhd* **66/1**

2m 4.07s (-1.33) **Going Correction** -0.075s/f (Good) **11** Ran SP% **116.9**
Speed ratings (Par 98): **102,99,93,91,89 89,88,85,82,81 75**
toteswingers:1&2 £4.30, 1&3 £10.40, 2&3 £12.20 CSF £35.60 TOTE £7.80: £2.90, £1.20, £3.40; EX 45.10 Trifecta £362.70 Pool: £598.10 - 1.22 winning units..

Owner B Haggas **Bred** J B Haggas **Trained** Newmarket, Suffolk

FOCUS
No more than a fair maiden overall, but the first two came clear and are useful prospects.
Goodness Official explanation: jockey said colt never travelled
Sobea Star(IRE) Official explanation: jockey said filly had a breathing problem

1416 PLAY POKER AT TSPOKER.COM CONDITIONS STKS 1m 4f 10y
5:15 (5:16) (Class 3) 4-Y-0+ **£8,256** (£2,472; £1,236; £618; £308) **Stalls** Low

Form RPR

200- **1** **Dandino**[139] 7615 4-8-8 113.. PaulMulrennan 2 116
(James Given) *trckd ldr: led over 3f out: clr over 1f out: rdn out: easily* **4/6**[1]

650- **2** *11* **Icon Dream (IRE)**[173] 7140 4-8-8 99 .... MartinLane 5 98
(David Simcock) *s.i.s: hld up: hdwy over 3f out: sn rdn: wnt 2nd over 2f out: no ch w wnr* **9/1**

53-0 **3** *2 1/2* **Bikini Babe (IRE)**[14] 1100 4-8-3 100 .... SilvestreDeSousa 4 89
(Mark Johnston) *hld up: hdwy over 3f out: sn rdn: one pce* **13/2**[3]

1112 **4** *nk* **Mush Mir (IRE)**[18] 1030 4-8-8 92 ....(b) JoeFanning 1 94
(Jim Boyle) *led: rdn whn hdd over 3f out: one pce* **12/1**

300- **5** *8* **Total Command**[217] 5945 4-8-12 106 .... RichardMullen 3 92
(Sir Michael Stoute) *in tch: rdn over 3f out: wknd over 2f out* **9/2**[2]

2m 31.4s (-5.30) **Going Correction** -0.075s/f (Good) **5** Ran SP% **109.2**
Speed ratings (Par 107): **114,106,105,104,99**
CSF £7.24 TOTE £1.60: £1.02, £6.00; EX 9.80.
Owner Elite Racing Club **Bred** Elite Racing Club **Trained** Willoughton, Lincs

FOCUS

An interesting conditions race. An impressive return from Dandino, but this is not form to go overboard about.

NOTEBOOK

Dandino, a rapid improver last season who hadn't run since finishing 11th in the Japan Cup, ran out an easy winner. Although his main rival Total Command failed to run up to his best, it was hard not to be taken with the way in which he galloped clear and a return to Group company now beckons with the Jockey Club Stakes at Newmarket's Guineas meeting the likely aim. (op 10-11)
Icon Dream(IRE) may not be worth his rating of 99 but is still a decent type who was well and truly put in his place by the winner. (op 11-1 tchd 8-1)
Bikini Babe(IRE), well below par at Kempton earlier in the month, never threatened under a hold-up ride. (tchd 5-1)
Mush Mir(IRE), much improved on Fibresand of late, attempted to make all on this return to turf, but it was always going to be tough against a horse of the winners calibre. (op 10-1)
Total Command failed to progress last season, beating just one home in both the Great Voltigeur and St Leger, but he'd been gelded over the winter and was expected to give the winner a race, despite being poorly in at the weights. He was unable to do so, however, fading rather tamely under pressure, and is once again left with plenty to prove. (op 3-1)
T/Plt: £508.40 to a £1 stake. Pool of £54,713.36 - 78.55 winning units. T/Qpdt: £34.70 to a £1 stake. Pool of 3,638.92 - 77.60 winning units. AS

1417 - 1419a (Foreign Racing) - See Raceform Interactive

NAAS (L-H)
Saturday, April 16

OFFICIAL GOING: Yielding to soft

1420a WOODLANDS STKS (LISTED RACE) 5f
3:40 (3:41) 3-Y-0+ **£22,413** (£6,551; £3,103; £1,034)

RPR

1 **Inxile (IRE)**[21] 996 6-9-9 ....(p) FMBerry 9 116+
(David Nicholls) *prom early: sn led: clr over 1f out: kpt on strly: easily* **5/4**[1]

2 *3* **Knock Stars (IRE)**[20] 1006 3-8-10 97 .... PBBeggy 8 97+
(Patrick Martin, Ire) *mid-div early: 6th 1/2-way: rdn in 5th 2f out: 3rd and no imp 1f out: kpt on to take 2nd ins fnl f: no ch w wnr* **12/1**

3 *3* **Lui Rei (ITY)**[21] 989 5-9-9 .... SeamieHeffernan 5 94
(Robert Cowell) *chsd ldrs: 5th 1/2-way: rdn in 4th 2f out: no imp over 1f out: kpt on same pce ins fnl f* **9/1**

4 *1/2* **Partner (IRE)**[15] 1085 5-9-9 96 ....(b) CO'Donoghue 10 92
(David Marnane, Ire) *mid-div: 9th 1/2-way: rdn into 6th 1f out: kpt on same pce ins fnl f* **9/1**

5 *1 3/4* **Bay Knight (IRE)**[188] 6702 5-9-9 97 .... DPMcDonogh 11 [illegible]
(K J Condon, Ire) *towards rr: rdn into 9th 1f out: kpt on ins fnl f* **25/1**

6 *hd* **Calm Bay (IRE)**[15] 1085 5-9-9 89 ....(bt) ShaneFoley 7 85
(H Rogers, Ire) *prom early: sn chsd ldr in 2nd: rdn and no ex over 1f out: wknd ins fnl f* **20/1**

7 *2* **Snaefell (IRE)**[188] 6783 7-9-12 108 ....(p) JMurtagh 3 81+
(M Halford, Ire) *mid-div: 7th 1/2-way: rdn in 6th 2f out: no imp in 5th 1f out: kpt on one pce* **9/2**[2]

8 *1 3/4* **Look Busy (IRE)**[190] 6706 6-9-6 90 ....(p) CDHayes 4 69+
(P J Prendergast, Ire) *mid-div: 8th 1/2-way: rdn and no imp 2f out: kpt on one pce* **11/1**

9 *2* **Ibelieveinmiracles (IRE)**[2] 1346 4-9-6 63 ....(t) NGMcCullagh 2 62
(Paul A Roche, Ire) *a towards rr* **100/1**

10 *3 1/2* **Above Limits (IRE)**[181] 6976 4-9-6 .... PJSmullen 6 49
(David Simcock) *prom early: sn chsd ldrs: 3rd 1/2-way: rdn 2f out: no ex over 1f out: eased ins fnl f* **15/2**[3]

11 *4 1/2* **What About Me (IRE)**[27] 923 4-9-6 90 ....(b[1]) RPWhelan 1 33
(Brian Nolan, Ire) *chsd ldrs early: 4th 1/2-way: rdn and no ex over 2f out: wknd* **50/1**

60.53 secs (-1.47)
WFA 3 from 4yo+ 10lb **11** Ran SP% **122.0**
CSF £18.81 TOTE £2.10: £1.70, £2.30, £2.30; DF 24.70.
Owner D Nicholls **Bred** Denis And Mrs Teresa Bergin **Trained** Sessay, N Yorks

FOCUS

The winner, fit from Dubai, looked as good as ever and is now 3-3 at this track. The runner-up has been rated as running a personal best, with the fourth to his Dundalk figure.

NOTEBOOK

Inxile(IRE) slammed his rivals to register his fifth career win. Clearly freshened up from his stint in Dubai, where he ran sixth behind J J The Jet Plane in a Group 2 at Meydan on World Cup night, he was on his toes beforehand. He played up in the stalls but once the gate opened he was always in command. At halfway, he was clear of his chasing rivals and, despite idling, still had three lengths to spare over his nearest pursuer. In 2009 he returned to the Kildare track six weeks later to win the Naas Sprint Stakes and it's likely he'll take the same route. (op 5/4 tchd 11/8)
Knock Stars(IRE), who trailed home last of 14 in a Group 3 at Leopardstown last month, was nibbled at in the market at fancy prices. She finished best of the rest back over her favoured trip. (op 14/1 tchd 11/1)
Lui Rei(ITY) was another who had a stint in Dubai before his third on the AW at Lingfield, and he clearly struggled in this soft ground. (op 9/1 tchd 8/1)
Partner(IRE) was another who never got going on this surface. (op 8/1)
Calm Bay(IRE), the winner of this race in 2008 and a close third last year, never got competitive on his first start since October, despite having his ground. Hopefully he'll be sharper for this next time. (op 16/1)

1421 - 1426a (Foreign Racing) - See Raceform Interactive

NAVAN (L-H)
Sunday, April 17

OFFICIAL GOING: Straight course - good to yielding; round course - yielding (yielding to soft in places in back straight)

1427a VINTAGE CROP STKS (LISTED RACE) 1m 5f
4:05 (4:06) 4-Y-0+ **£22,413** (£6,551; £3,103; £1,034)

RPR

1 **Fame And Glory**[196] 6612 5-9-9 124 .... JamieSpencer 1 115+
(A P O'Brien, Ire) *settled in 4th: hdwy early st: 2nd 2f out: rdn to ld early ins fnl f: drvn out* **2/9**[1]

2 *1/2* **Nebula Storm (IRE)**[168] 7263 4-9-1 91 .... JMurtagh 2 107
(John M Oxx, Ire) *chsd ldr in 2nd: clsr 1/2-way: drvn along and dropped to 4th 3f out: 3rd and swtchd rt 1f out: styd on wl u.p ins fnl f: nt rch wnr* **8/1**[2]

3 *1* **Fictional Account (IRE)**[203] 6388 6-9-2 103 .... FMBerry 3 106
(V C Ward, Ire) *led and sn 5 l clr: reduced advantage 1/2-way: pushed along 2f out: strly pressed and hdd early ins fnl f: no imp and lost 2nd clsng stages* **10/1**[3]

4 *3* **Unity (IRE)**[259] 4631 4-8-12 98 ....(p) WMLordan 7 98
(David Wachman, Ire) *settled in 3rd: pushed along fr over 2f out: no imp in 4th whn sltly hmpd 1f out: kpt on one pce* **20/1**

5 *11* **Sense Of Purpose (IRE)**[225] 5776 4-8-12 98 .... PJSmullen 6 82
(D K Weld, Ire) *a in rr: in tch tl pushed along and no ex fr 2f out* **14/1**

2m 55.89s (-4.11)
WFA 4 from 5yo+ 1lb **5** Ran SP% **113.5**
CSF £3.02 TOTE £1.10: £1.02, £2.90; DF 2.70.
Owner Mrs Fitri Hay **Bred** Ptarmigan Bloodstock And Miss K Rausing **Trained** Ballydoyle, Co Tipperary

FOCUS

The lightly raced runner-up has been rated as running a personal best, while the third and fourth help set the level.

NOTEBOOK

Fame And Glory was clearly the pick at the weights, even with his 7lb Group 1 penalty, for his first start of the season and first attempt beyond 1m4f. He duly won without being impressive but there were no clues either in the race, or immediately afterwards, regarding his possible participation in the Ascot Gold Cup. The race was run at an uneven gallop and the winner settled quite well despite the on-off tempo. Held up, he began to close early in the straight but, after going second 2f out, it took him a while to get to and master the front-running Fictional Account inside the final furlong. And no sooner had he done that than the runner-up came at him hard in the closing stages. The winner looked quite ready in terms of fitness but it would be reasonable to expect improvement. Where he goes next is unclear, with trainer Aidan O'Brien stating that no decision about the Gold Cup will be made until after the four-time Group 1 winner's next race. O'Brien said: "We have the Mooresbridge Stakes, the Coronation Cup and the Saval Beg Stakes to choose from and we'll make a decision about Ascot afterwards".
Nebula Storm(IRE) went into this rated 92 having raced only three times. Winner of a 7f maiden as a 2-y-o, he ran only once last season, finishing second in a 1m4f handicap. He came out of this race with plenty of credit. After racing in second place, he lost his place when the tempo increased early in the straight before running on well after being switched right 1f out. He finished the race well and was reeling in the winner near the finish.
Fictional Account(IRE), a Listed winner over 2m at Ascot in September, made the running and only gave best early in the final furlong. She kept on and only lost second spot close home.
Unity(IRE), placed at Listed and Group 3 level last year (both small field events like this), raced in third place and was unable to raise her effort before being slightly hampered about 1f out.
Sense Of Purpose(IRE), runner-up in the Galtres Stakes last year, raced in rear. Pushed along into the straight, she was unable to make any impresion from 3f out.

1428 - 1430a (Foreign Racing) - See Raceform Interactive

CAPANNELLE (R-H)
Sunday, April 17

OFFICIAL GOING: Turf: soft

1431a PREMIO PARIOLI (GROUP 3) (3YO COLTS) (TURF) 1m
3:50 (12:00) 3-Y-0 **£73,275** (£32,241; £17,586; £8,793)

RPR

1 **Al Rep (IRE)**[14] 3-9-2 0 .... SSulas 10 105
(D Camuffo, Italy) *settled midfield: plld hrd ent fnl bnd: settled in st to go 6th 3f out: clr run on inner to produce effrt over 2f out: hrd rdn 1 1/2f out: gained upper hand fnl 100yds* **97/10**

2 *3/4* **Duchamp (FR)** 3-9-2 0 .... ASanna 12 103
(O Pessi, Italy) *hld up midfield on outer: rdn to produce effrt in centre of trck 2 1/2f out: prog to ld briefly 1f out: chal and hrd rdn tl btn fnl 100yds* **73/10**[3]

3 *1/2* **The Confessor (ITY)**[203] 3-9-2 0 .... CristianDemuro 11 102
(L Riccardi, Italy) *broke wl to ld after 1f: rdn 2f out to keep one-l ld: chal and hdd over 1f out: n.m.r: squeezed on rail by eventual wnr fnl 150yds* **105/10**

4 *2 1/2* **Insciaveghen (ITY)**[21] 3-9-2 0 .... MircoDemuro 5 96
(Vittorio Caruso, Italy) *midfield on rail tl ent st: rdn and outpcd 3f out: railled u.str ride: styd on fnl f* **6/4**[1]

5 *3/4* **Free Winner (IRE)**[210] 3-9-2 0 .... UmbertoRispoli 9 95
(B Grizzetti, Italy) *fr wd draw sn swtchd to r on rail after 1f: hld up in rr: moved to centre of trck 2 1/2f out: prog under hrd ride on outer to stay on fnl f* **238/10**

6 *1* **Samysilver (USA)** 3-9-2 0 .... GBietolini 4 92
(Gianluca Bietolini, Italy) *broke wl to ld briefly then trckd ldrs tl st: effrt 2f out: sn btn* **159/10**

7 *3/4* **Doquet (IRE)**[266] 3-9-2 0 .... DarioVargiu 3 91
(B Grizzetti, Italy) *trckd ldrs oin 4th tl st: rdn and outpcd 2 1/2f out: sn btn* **92/10**

8 *3* **Passaggio (ITY)**[21] 3-9-2 0 .... ACorniani 14 84
(A Cascio, Italy) *in rr: effrt on inner 2f out: nvr chal* **49/1**

9 *1* **Come Il Vento (ITY)** 3-9-2 0 .... AntonioFadda 6 81
(A Cottu, Italy) *in rr tl ent st: rdn and struggling in last tl 2 1/2f out: styd on under hrd ride fnl f* **183/10**

10 *1 1/2* **Lowawatha**[21] 3-9-2 0 .... StefanoLandi 7 78
(D Grilli, Italy) *6th ent st: outpcd fnl 3f* **129/10**

11 *nk* **Rue Du Soleil (USA)**[21] 3-9-2 0 ....(b) GMarcelli 1 77
(R Menichetti, Italy) *midfield on inner: effrt over 3f out to stay in tch: sn btn* **48/1**

12 1 1/2 **Regarde Moi** 3-9-2 0 FabioBranca 13 74
(S Botti, Italy) *trckd ldrs: chal to dispute ld 2 1/2f out: hrd rdn and btn 2f out: eased fnl 1 1/2f* **33/10**[2]
13 2 1/2 **Tellovoi (IRE)** 3-9-2 0 MEsposito 8 68
(L Polito, Italy) *5th tl ent st: btn over 2f out* **114/10**
14 4 **Cast Away (IRE)**[14] 3-9-2 0 PierantonioConvertino 2 59
(S Cannavo', Italy) *nr rr on inner: nvr figured* **30/1**
15 10 **Alabama Song (ITY)**[14] 3-9-2 0 CFiocchi 15 36
(R Menichetti, Italy) *in rr: outpcd 3f out* **48/1**
1m 38.1s (-1.70) **15** Ran SP% **142.8**
WIN (incl. 1 euro stake): 10.67. PLACES: 3.53, 2.98, 3.68. DF: 96.42.
Owner Scuderia Colle Papa **Bred** John Cullinan **Trained** Italy

1432a PREMIO CARLO CHIESA (GROUP 3) (3YO+ FILLIES & MARES) (TURF) 6f
4:25 (12:00) 3-Y-O+ **£34,482** (£15,172; £8,275; £4,137)

RPR
1 **Sandslash (IRE)**[44] 3-8-5 0 FabioBranca 10 105
(L Riccardi, Italy) *hld up in rr on outer: produced to chal on outer 2f out: rdn to ld ent fnl f: rdn out to hold on comf fnl 100yds* **48/10**[3]
2 1 1/4 **Charming Woman (IRE)**[154] [7459] 4-9-2 0 MircoDemuro 2 101
(Vittorio Caruso, Italy) *v.s.a: hld up in rr: n.m.r whn midfield 2 1/2f out: fnd spce to produce run on outer 1 1/2f out: styd on fnl f* **23/10**[1]
3 nk **Madda's Force (ITY)**[154] [7459] 5-9-2 0 MPasquale 9 100
(R Belli, Italy) *broke wl to trck ldrs: rdn and 2nd 2f out: styd on under hrd ride fnl f* **43/5**
4 hd **Rebecca Rolfe**[66] [500] 5-9-2 0 MKolmarkaj 8 99
(M Gasparini, Italy) *shared ld after 1f: rdn 2 1/2f out to stay in tch: btn 1 1/2f out* **89/10**
5 1/2 **Cry Of Liberty (IRE)**[182] [6976] 4-9-2 0 CristianDemuro 12 98
(L Riccardi, Italy) *shared ldr after 1f: led after 2f: hdd ent fnl f: styd on under hrd ride* **112/10**
6 2 **Rockatella (IRE)**[190] [6765] 4-9-2 0 DominiqueBoeuf 1 91
(W Hefter, Germany) *in rr on rail for 3f: rdn to stay in tch 2 1/2f out: sn no ex* **12/5**[2]
7 3/4 **Malikayah (IRE)**[175] 3-8-5 0 SSulas 4 89
(D Camuffo, Italy) *trckd ldrs in 4th for 3f: hrd rdn and outpcd fnl 2 1/2f* **215/10**
8 hd **Nebbia Di Latte (ITY)**[54] 4-9-2 0 (b) MarcoMonteriso 6 88
(M Massimi Jr, Italy) *in rr: nvr figured* **234/10**
9 nse **Zobenigo (IRE)**[315] 4-9-2 0 MEsposito 5 88
(L Polito, Italy) *midfield: sltly hmpd by eventual 2nd 2 1/2f out: one pce and eased fnl 100yds* **94/10**
10 4 **Soir De Lune (IRE)** 3-8-5 0 DarioVargiu 7 75
(B Grizzetti, Italy) *racd midfield: outpcd 3f out and lost position* **131/10**
11 3/4 **Kagera**[161] 3-8-5 0 UmbertoRispoli 13 73
(B Grizzetti, Italy) *trckd ldrs on outer for 3f: outpcd and hrd rdn 2 1/2f out: sn btn: eased* **112/10**
12 8 **Spinning Yarn**[162] [7370] 4-9-2 0 GBietolini 11 47
(A Renzoni, Italy) *midfield on outer for 2 1/2f: no ex ent fnl 3f* **118/10**
13 5 **Elusive Force (ITY)**[63] 5-9-2 0 GErcegovic 3 31
(P Riccioni, Italy) *shared ld after 1f: outpcd and sltly hmpd on rail 3f out* **72/1**

69.10 secs (-1.20)
WFA 3 from 4yo+ 11lb **13** Ran SP% **148.3**
WIN (incl. 1 euro stake): 5.41. PLACES: 2.03, 1.59, 2.46. DF: 23.99.
Owner Scuderia Lechereo **Bred** Azienda Agricola Valle Falcone Srl **Trained** Italy

KREFELD (R-H)
Sunday, April 17
OFFICIAL GOING: Turf: good

1433a GROSSER PREIS DER KREFELDER WIRTSCHAFT - DR BUSCH MEMORIAL (GROUP 3) (3YO) (TURF) 1m 110y
4:10 (4:25) 3-Y-O
£27,586 (£9,482; £4,741; £2,586; £1,724; £1,293)

RPR
1 **Lindenthaler (GER)**[210] [9990] 3-9-2 0 ADeVries 7 108
(P Schiergen, Germany) *broke wl: led early then settled in 2nd: gd prog ent st: tk ld 2f out: r.o wl: easily* **41/10**[3]
2 2 1/2 **Rubber Duck (GER)** 3-9-2 0 DPorcu 3 102
(S Smrczek, Germany) *racd 4th: plld hrd: r.o wl in st: chsd wnr home* **28/1**
3 1 1/2 **Nice Danon**[182] [6972] 3-9-2 0 JBojko 2 99
(A Wohler, Germany) *hld up in midfield: rdn early in st: picked up wl: r.o* **9/2**
4 1/2 **Silvaner (GER)**[182] [6972] 3-9-2 0 AStarke 5 98
(P Schiergen, Germany) *a towards rr: nvr travelling smoothly: swung wd into st: hrd rdn: no imp* **13/10**[1]
5 5 **Quinindo (GER)**[155] [7456] 3-9-2 0 EPedroza 4 87
(A Wohler, Germany) *racd freely in 3rd: btn sn after ent st* **17/10**[2]
6 8 **Apilado (GER)** 3-9-2 0 Jan-ErikNeuroth 6 69
(Wido Neuroth, Norway) *broke wl: sn led: qckly chal in st: hdd 2f out: rdn: no ex: fdd* **214/10**
7 4 1/2 **Diego (GER)**[182] [6972] 3-9-2 0 (b) THellier 1 59
(T Mundry, Germany) *a in rr: nvr a factor* **156/10**
1m 45.05s (-1.55) **7** Ran SP% **132.2**
WIN (incl. 10 euro stake): 51. PLACES: 18, 32, 18. SF: 761.
Owner Gestut Ebbesloh **Bred** Gestut Ebbesloh **Trained** Germany

REDCAR (L-H)
Monday, April 18
OFFICIAL GOING: Firm (good to firm in places; watered; 8.4)
Wind: moderate 1/2 behind Weather: changeable

1434 WIN A VIP DAY OUT @ REDCARRACING.CO.UK MAIDEN AUCTION STKS 5f
2:20 (2:21) (Class 5) 2-Y-O **£1,942** (£578; £288; £144) **Stalls** High

Form RPR
2 1 **Van Go Go**[11] [1192] 2-8-4 0 RichardKingscote 7 63+
(Tom Dascombe) *w ldrs: led over 2f out: drvn out* **10/3**[1]
2 1 **Flambard House (IRE)** 2-8-12 0 PaulMulrennan 4 67+
(Howard Johnson) *chsd ldrs: kpt on ins fnl f: no ex* **16/1**
05 3 nk **Middleton Flyer (IRE)**[7] [1268] 2-8-7 0 RoystonFfrench 3 61
(David Evans) *led: edgd lft and hdd over 2f out: kpt on same pce fnl f* **9/2**[3]
4 1/2 **Fayr Fall (IRE)** 2-8-9 0 DuranFentiman 9 61
(Tim Easterby) *chsd ldrs: styd on same pce fnl f* **16/1**
5 5 hd **Latte**[12] [1185] 2-8-9 0 TomEaves 10 60
(Linda Stubbs) *dwlt: sn chsng ldrs: one pce appr fnl f* **7/2**[2]
6 2 3/4 **First Bid** 2-8-9 0 RichardMullen 6 50
(Kevin Ryan) *dwlt: hdwy to chse ldrs over 2f out: wknd appr fnl f* **9/1**
7 1 3/4 **Economic Crisis (IRE)** 2-8-4 0 PatrickMathers 8 39+
(Alan Berry) *s.i.s: hdwy and hung bdly lft over 2f out: wknd over 1f out* **100/1**
8 1 1/2 **Gone By Sunrise** 2-9-2 0 PaulHanagan 5 45
(Richard Fahey) *wnt rt s: sn chsng ldrs: drvn over 2f out: wknd over 1f out* **6/1**
9 7 **Storm Fairy** 2-8-5 0 ow1 AndrewElliott 2 —
(Mrs K Burke) *dwlt: sn w ldrs: wknd 2f out* **22/1**
53 10 nk **Aquasulis (IRE)**[7] [1268] 2-8-7 0 RobertWinston 1 —
(David Evans) *wnt lft s: t.k.h: w ldrs: hung lft over 2f out: sn lost pl* **8/1**
58.71 secs (0.11) **Going Correction** -0.175s/f (Firm) **10** Ran SP% **116.0**
Speed ratings (Par 92): **92,90,89,89,88 84,81,79,68,67**
toteswingers:1&2:£12.20, 1&3:£3.80, 2&3:£16.70 CSF £56.73 TOTE £2.80: £2.00, £5.50, £1.80; EX 54.00 TRIFECTA Not won..
Owner A Black **Bred** A Black **Trained** Malpas, Cheshire

FOCUS
The jockeys reported that the ground was quick, but with a good covering of grass. The stalls were placed next to the stands' rail, but as the race progressed the runners ended up all over the track. The field finished compressed and this is probably weak form, but it makes sense.

NOTEBOOK
Van Go Go was one of those with previous experience having finished second of four in a Kempton Polytrack fillies' maiden on debut. Always up with the pace, she battled on well to score and should continue to do well at a modest level. (tchd 3-1 and 7-2)
Flambard House(IRE) ◆, an 11,500euros gelding out of a half-sister to three winners including the very useful Rich Ground, did best of the newcomers and came home in good style. He has a bit of scope and can go one better before too long. (op 28-1)
Middleton Flyer(IRE) was another with previous experience and kept on to reverse Windsor form with her stablemate Aquasulis, but she may need to be dropped in grade if she is to win a race. (op 5-1)
Fayr Fall(IRE), a 2,000euros gelding from a yard with a record of 2-5 with its juveniles so far this season, ran a promising debut as he is very much bred to stay on the dam's side of his pedigree. (op 25-1)
Latte showed plenty of early speed when fifth of seven on his Nottingham debut and did so again, but he couldn't quicken under pressure when in with every chance. (op 7-1)
Aquasulis(IRE) Official explanation: jockey said filly hung left

1435 ALASTAIR DOWN GRAVESTONE (S) STKS 5f
2:50 (2:50) (Class 6) 2-Y-O **£1,706** (£503; £252) **Stalls** High

Form RPR
1 **Spiders Of Spring (IRE)** 2-8-12 0 PaulHanagan 3 55
(Richard Fahey) *mde all: rdn over 1f out: edgd lft: all out* **10/3**[3]
45 2 nk **Ciara Boo (IRE)**[14] [1136] 2-8-7 0 RobertWinston 5 49
(David Evans) *w wnr: drvn over 2f out: styd on towards fin: jst hld* **11/10**[1]
22 3 3 3/4 **Queen Of The Hop**[14] [1129] 2-8-7 0 (p) RichardKingscote 1 35
(J S Moore) *dwlt: sn chsng ldrs on outside: rdn and hung lft over 2f out: one pce* **5/2**[2]
4 2 1/4 **Mad For Fun (IRE)** 2-8-7 0 MickyFenton 4 27
(Paul Midgley) *wnt rt s: sn chsng ldrs: edgd rt over 1f out: sn wknd* **10/1**
60.00 secs (1.40) **Going Correction** -0.175s/f (Firm) **4** Ran SP% **108.4**
Speed ratings (Par 90): **81,80,74,70**
CSF £7.50 TOTE £4.20; EX 8.30.There was no bid for the winner.
Owner R A Fahey **Bred** Brendan Peoples **Trained** Musley Bank, N Yorks

FOCUS
A weak juvenile seller and the winning time was 1.29 seconds slower than the maiden. The runner-up sets the level.

NOTEBOOK
Spiders Of Spring(IRE) made just about every yard and the key to this victory was when he quickened from the front 1f out and took a length or so out of his nearest rival. A half-brother to two prolific winners at up to 7f, the form is moderate but he is entitled to improve. (op 5-2)
Ciara Boo(IRE) had already shown ability in a couple of maidens at Kempton and Windsor and both races have since produced winners. The money came for her and she had every chance, but she became slightly outpaced when the winner quickened and had insufficient time to get back up. (op 6-4)
Queen Of The Hop was tried in cheekpieces after finishing runner-up in a couple of moderate maidens at Wolverhampton and Folkestone, but she was being ridden along almost from the start and never looked happy. This was a step backwards. (op 9-4)
Mad For Fun(IRE) betrayed her inexperience by missing the break and was never competitive, but as she out of a half-sister to a couple of smart middle-distance performers in Savarain and Forte Dei Marmi so she may improve for a bit for further. (op 11-1 tchd 8-1)

1436 BECOME AN ANNUAL BADGE HOLDER TODAY MEDIAN AUCTION MAIDEN STKS 7f
3:20 (3:21) (Class 5) 3-Y-O **£1,942** (£578; £288; £144) **Stalls** High

Form RPR
2 1 **Clara Zetkin**[13] [1155] 3-8-12 0 PhillipMakin 3 67+
(David Brown) *dwlt: hdwy to trck ldrs over 3f out: wnt 2nd over 2f out: led appr fnl f: edgd lft: drvn out* **11/8**[1]
0- 2 1 **Auto Mac**[216] [6047] 3-9-3 0 PaulMulrennan 5 69
(Neville Bycroft) *chsd ldrs: drvn over 3f out: edgd rt over 1f out: kpt on wl ins fnl f: tk 2nd nr fin* **66/1**

42-2 **3** *hd* **Mother Jones**[18] 1060 3-8-12 76 TomEaves 8 64
(Bryan Smart) *led: t.k.h: hdd appr fnl f: edgd lft: kpt on same pce* **9/4**[2]
364- **4** *1/2* **Moral Issue**[182] 6980 3-9-0 70 PatrickDonaghy(3) 6 67
(Jedd O'Keeffe) *trckd ldrs: outpcd over 1f out: kpt on last 100yds* **12/1**
5 *6* **Full Pelt (USA)** 3-9-3 0 RichardKingscote 7 51
(Tom Dascombe) *s.i.s: sn chsng ldrs: drvn and outpcd 3f out: wknd over 1f out* **8/1**
04- **6** *11* **Wong Again**[192] 6712 3-8-12 0 PaulHanagan 1 16
(J W Hills) *hld up: hdwy to trck ldrs over 3f out: wknd 2f out* **7/1**[3]
7 *22* **This Is Us (IRE)** 3-8-12 0 DavidAllan 4 —
(Eric Alston) *s.v.s: sme hdwy 3f out: sn wknd and bhd: t.o* **22/1**
8 *3/4* **Lucky Cap** 3-9-3 0 MickyFenton 9 —
(Paul Midgley) *dwlt: sn chsng ldrs: hung lft and lost pl over 3f out: sn bhd: t.o* **50/1**

1m 24.39s (-0.11) **Going Correction** -0.175s/f (Firm) **8** Ran SP% **112.0**
Speed ratings (Par 98): **93,91,91,84 71,46,45**
toteswingers:1&2:£11.30, 1&3:£1.70, 2&3:£14.50 CSF £108.01 TOTE £1.80: £1.10, £11.10, £1.30; EX 86.80 TRIFECTA Not won..
Owner Norton Common Farm Racing **Bred** Howard Barton Stud **Trained** Averham Park, Notts

FOCUS
Just an ordinary maiden, although a couple did offer some encouragement. The time was slow and the runner-up lends doubt to the form.
This Is Us(IRE) Official explanation: jockey said filly missed the break

1437 JOHN SMITH'S REDCAR STRAIGHT-MILE CHAMPIONSHIP (H'CAP) (QUALIFIER) 1m
3:50 (3:50) (Class 5) (0-75,75) 3-Y-O **£3,820** (£1,136; £568; £283) **Stalls** High

Form RPR
30-1 **1** **Buzz Law (IRE)**[12] 1191 3-9-1 **69** AndrewElliott 8 82
(Mrs K Burke) *hld up: smooth hdwy 3f out: led over 1f out: rdn and edgd lft: kpt on towards fin* **9/4**[1]
-215 **2** *1 1/4* **Bosambo**[37] 845 3-9-6 **74** RobertWinston 5 84
(Alan Swinbank) *hld up in rr: hdwy 3f out: chsng wnr over 1f out: carried lft ins fnl f: no ex* **6/1**[3]
443- **3** *4 1/2* **Chosen Character (IRE)**[226] 5761 3-9-3 **71** (t) RichardKingscote 3 71
(Tom Dascombe) *trckd ldrs: rdn 3f out: kpt on same pce over 1f out* **9/2**[2]
50-0 **4** *1 1/2* **Barkston Ash**[19] 1038 3-8-4 **58** DuranFentiman 6 54
(Eric Alston) *t.k.h: led tl over 1f out: one pce* **25/1**
026- **5** *7* **Hartforth**[168] 7272 3-9-2 **70** (b) GrahamGibbons 2 50
(James Bethell) *sn chsng ldrs: rdn and lost pl over 3f out: detached last over 1f out: kpt on towards fin* **9/1**
401- **6** *3/4* **Lady Del Sol**[185] 6891 3-9-7 **75** PaulMulrennan 1 54
(Marjorie Fife) *hld up in rr: t.k.h: hdwy over 3f out: upsides over 2f out: sn wknd* **6/1**[3]
55-0 **7** *nse* **Anddante (IRE)**[12] 1169 3-8-11 **65** DavidAllan 9 43
(Tim Easterby) *t.k.h: w ldrs: lost pl over 2f out* **9/1**
003- **8** *2 3/4* **Inca Chief**[185] 6894 3-8-8 **62** PaulHanagan 7 34
(Ann Duffield) *s.i.s: sn chsng ldrs: lost pl over 2f out* **8/1**

1m 36.19s (-1.81) **Going Correction** -0.175s/f (Firm) **8** Ran SP% **112.5**
Speed ratings (Par 98): **102,100,96,94,87 87,86,84**
toteswingers:1&2:£3.80, 1&3:£2.90, 2&3:£2.50 CSF £15.43 CT £54.78 TOTE £2.90: £1.10, £2.30, £2.00; EX 12.40 Trifecta £65.20 Pool: £422.10 - 65.20 winning units..
Owner Mrs Elaine M Burke **Bred** C J Wall **Trained** Middleham Moor, North Yorks

FOCUS
Not a bad little handicap of its type with the first two horses having both already been successful this year. The front pair came clear and the winner is rated up 6lb.
Lady Del Sol Official explanation: jockey said filly ran too free

1438 COME RACING AGAIN ON EASTER MONDAY H'CAP 6f
4:20 (4:20) (Class 4) (0-85,84) 3-Y-O+ **£2,590** (£770; £385; £192) **Stalls** High

Form RPR
200- **1** **Doctor Parkes**[219] 5941 5-10-0 **84** RobertWinston 2 93
(Eric Alston) *hld up: hdwy over 2f out: hung lft: styd on to ld last 100yds* **11/2**[3]
[illegible]
(Tracy Waggott) *w ldrs: led over 3f out: hdd ins fnl f: no ex* **10/1**
00-0 **3** *1 1/4* **Karaka Jack**[15] 1110 4-9-1 **74** MichaelO'Connell(3) 10 78
(David Nicholls) *hld up in rr: hdwy over 1f out: swtchd lft and chsng ldrs jst ins fnl f: kpt on same pce* **5/1**[2]
10-0 **4** *1 3/4* **Arry's Orse**[61] 557 4-9-13 **83** TomEaves 5 81
(Bryan Smart) *t.k.h: w ldrs: fdd last 100yds* **6/1**
002- **5** *1 3/4* **Jarrow (IRE)**[185] 6904 4-9-7 **77** AdrianNicholls 6 70
(David Nicholls) *hld up towards rr: effrt and swtchd lft 2f out: sn chsng ldrs: wknd last 100yds* **11/2**[3]
3421 **6** *2* **Dark Lane**[7] 1267 5-9-5 **75** (p) PaulHanagan 4 61
(Richard Fahey) *chsd ldrs: drvn over 2f out: wknd over 1f out* **11/4**[1]
0U-0 **7** *1/2* **Red Cape (FR)**[11] 1205 8-9-8 **81** JamesSullivan(3) 8 66
(Ruth Carr) *chsd ldrs: wknd 2f out* **20/1**
200- **8** *1 1/4* **Prince Of Vasa (IRE)**[176] 5606 4-9-9 **79** MichaelStainton 7 60
(Michael Smith) *s.i.s: effrt over 2f out: nvr a factor* **50/1**
/10- **9** *1/2* **Ghost (IRE)**[233] 5524 4-9-5 **82** PNolan(7) 1 61
(David Nicholls) *stdd s: hld up in rr: sme hdwy over 2f out: carried hd high: nvr a threat* **18/1**
503- **10** *1/2* **Stonehaugh (IRE)**[232] 5545 8-9-0 **70** oh4 TonyHamilton 3 48
(Howard Johnson) *led tl over 3f out: wknd 2f out* **25/1**
010- **11** *12* **Captain Royale (IRE)**[173] 7180 6-9-6 **76** (p) PatrickMathers 11 15
(Colin Teague) *racd alone stands' side: bhd fnl 2f: eased* **40/1**

69.91 secs (-1.89) **Going Correction** -0.175s/f (Firm) **11** Ran SP% **115.8**
Speed ratings (Par 105): **105,104,102,100,98 95,94,93,92,91 75**
toteswingers:1&2:£15.10, 1&3:£9.10, 2&3:£10.70 CSF £55.65 CT £298.16 TOTE £6.60: £2.30, £3.20, £3.10; EX 89.00 TRIFECTA Not won..
Owner Joseph Heler **Bred** Joseph Heler **Trained** Longton, Lancs

FOCUS
A decent sprint handicap and the form looks sound with the front pair to form. All bar one raced up the centre of the track.
Dark Lane Official explanation: trainer had no explanation for the poor form shown

1439 BOOK TICKETS ON-LINE @ REDCARRACING.CO.UK APPRENTICE CLAIMING STKS 6f
4:50 (4:50) (Class 6) 3-4-Y-O **£1,706** (£503; £252) **Stalls** High

Form RPR
1021 **1** **Frequency**[12] 1180 4-10-0 72 (b) MartinHarley 8 71+
(Conor Dore) *stdd s: hld up: effrt over 2f out: led over 1f out: pushed out towards fin* **6/4**[1]
0-00 **2** *1/2* **Uddy Mac**[33] 874 4-8-13 52 (b) LeeTopliss(2) 3 52
(Neville Bycroft) *chsd ldrs: hrd rdn and kpt on wl to chse wnr ins fnl f* **10/1**
-435 **3** *nk* **Winning Draw (IRE)**[66] 505 3-8-0 58 (p) DeclanCannon(2) 6 46
(Paul Midgley) *mid-div: hdwy over 2f out: kpt on wl ins fnl f* **12/1**
2335 **4** *1/2* **Neytiri**[24] 966 3-8-4 52 (b) JamesSullivan 9 47
(Linda Stubbs) *in rr: hdwy over 2f out: chsng ldrs 1f out: kpt on same pce* **20/1**
5434 **5** *hd* **William Wainwright (IRE)**[17] 1078 3-8-7 48 (v) AmyRyan 11 49
(Ann Duffield) *led: edgd lft and hdd over 1f out: one pce* **20/1**
0-63 **6** *1 1/4* **Dolly Parton (IRE)**[30] 913 3-8-0 68 ow2 LeonnaMayor(4) 1 42
(David Nicholls) *trckd ldrs on outside: ev ch over 1f out: wknd towards fin* **9/4**[2]
-650 **7** *1* **Royal Blade (IRE)**[77] 362 4-9-5 48 TjadeCollier 7 46
(Alan Berry) *chsd ldrs: edgd lft over 1f out: sn wknd* **40/1**
65-0 **8** *1/2* **No Quarter (IRE)**[19] 1037 4-9-2 54 GarryWhillans(4) 2 45
(Tracy Waggott) *chsd ldrs: wkng whn hmpd and swtchd rt over 1f out* **8/1**[3]
00- **9** *1/2* **Du Plessis**[316] 2787 4-9-8 0 DaleSwift(2) 5 48
(Brian Ellison) *s.i.s: in rr: bhd and edgd lft over 1f out: kpt on ins fnl f* **40/1**
000- **10** *2 3/4* **Isle Of Ellis (IRE)**[215] 6076 4-9-2 38 ShaneBKelly(4) 4 35
(Ron Barr) *prom: lost pl over 2f out: sn bhd* **80/1**
000- **11** *nk* **Chardonnay Star (IRE)**[215] 6077 4-9-1 36 (v) PatrickDonaghy 10 29
(Colin Teague) *in rr: lost pl 3f out: sn bhd* **100/1**

1m 11.81s (0.01) **Going Correction** -0.175s/f (Firm)
WFA 3 from 4yo 11lb **11** Ran SP% **115.3**
Speed ratings (Par 101): **92,91,90,90,90 88,87,86,85,82 81**
toteswingers:1&2:£4.30, 1&3:£5.20, 2&3:£9.70 CSF £16.06 TOTE £3.00: £1.30, £2.90, £3.30; EX 23.70 Trifecta £77.60 Pool: £496.32 - 4.73 winning units..Frequency was claimed by Mrs Francesca Mitchell for £10,000.
Owner Patrick Wilmott **Bred** Manor Farm Stud (rutland) **Trained** Cowbit, Lincs
■ Stewards' Enquiry : Lee Topliss one-day ban: used whip with excessive frequency (May 2)

FOCUS
A weak claimer featuring a mixed bag of abilities. The winner had little to beat and the level is set around the fourth and fifth.

1440 FOLLOW REDCAR RACING ON FACEBOOK FILLIES' H'CAP 1m 2f
5:25 (5:25) (Class 5) (0-70,63) 3-Y-O+ **£1,942** (£578; £288; £144) **Stalls** Low

Form RPR
45-0 **1** **Easy Terms**[16] 1099 4-9-7 **59** JamesSullivan(3) 3 72
(Edwin Tuer) *led 1f: trckd ldr: led 3f out: styd on wl fnl f: readily* **9/2**[3]
000- **2** *2 1/2* **Lady Chloe**[221] 5878 3-8-8 **60** PaulHanagan 4 65
(Philip Kirby) *fly-jmpd s: hld up: hdwy over 3f out: hung lft and chsd wnr over 1f out: no imp* **2/1**[1]
500- **3** *3 1/4* **Talk Of Saafend (IRE)**[22] 5408 6-9-7 **56** TonyHamilton 2 58
(Dianne Sayer) *in rr: effrt 3f out: kpt on fnl f: nvr trbld ldrs* **16/1**
032- **4** *1 1/2* **Spavento (IRE)**[212] 6188 5-9-8 **57** DavidAllan 5 56
(Eric Alston) *trckd ldrs: wnt 2nd over 2f out: one pce* **3/1**[2]
40-0 **5** *1/2* **Wiseman's Diamond (USA)**[13] 1150 6-9-9 **58** MickyFenton 1 56
(Paul Midgley) *hld up in rr: effrt 3f out: nvr nr to chal* **15/2**
030- **6** *2 1/4* **Cool Baranca (GER)**[28] 7055 5-9-13 **62** DuranFentiman 7 55
(Dianne Sayer) *hld up towards rr: effrt over 2f out: nvr a factor* **11/2**
00-0 **7** *16* **Child Of Our Time (IRE)**[9] 1245 4-10-0 **63** PatrickMathers 6 24
(Colin Teague) *drvn to ld after 1f: t.k.h: hdd 3f out: sn lost pl and bhd: t.o* **33/1**

2m 6.27s (-0.83) **Going Correction** -0.175s/f (Firm)
WFA 3 from 4yo+ 17lb **7** Ran SP% **112.5**
Speed ratings (Par 100): **96,94,91,90,89 88,75**
toteswingers:1&2:£2.30, 1&3:£6.40, 2&3:£9.60. Tote Super 7: Win: £5,843.20. Place: £64.30. CSF £13.47 TOTE £5.50: £2.50, £1.30; EX 19.60.
Owner E Tuer **Bred** T E Pocock **Trained** Great Smeaton, N Yorks

FOCUS
A modest fillies' handicap in which recent winning form was conspicuous by its absence. The winner is rated back to something like her best. The early pace was strong.
T/Plt: £95.50 to a £1 stake. Pool:£49,610.10 - 379.20 winning tickets T/Qpdt: £11.00 to a £1 stake. Pool:£4,720.15 - 317.50 winning tickets WG

1267 WINDSOR (R-H)
Monday, April 18

OFFICIAL GOING: Good to firm (good in places; 8.4)
Straight at full width, top bend at normal configuration and distances as advertised.
Wind: Moderate, against Weather: Fine

1441 SPORTINGBET.COM MAIDEN AUCTION FILLIES' STKS 5f 10y
5:20 (5:21) (Class 5) 2-Y-O **£2,388** (£705; £352) **Stalls** Low

Form RPR
1 **Best Terms** 2-8-8 0 RichardHughes 2 82+
(Richard Hannon) *trckd ldng pair: pushed into ld over 1f out: hrd pressed and drifted lft fnl f: pushed along firmly and styd on wl* **7/4**[1]
2 *1/2* **Heyward Girl (IRE)** 2-8-4 0 AndreaAtzeni 15 76+
(Robert Eddery) *racd wdst of all: prog fr rr 1/2-way: drvn to chal and upsides fnl f: hld fnl 50yds* **9/2**[2]
3 *3* **Poetic Dancer** 2-8-4 0 LukeMorris 9 65
(Clive Cox) *racd wd: in tch: effrt 2f out: kpt on same pce fr over 1f out* **25/1**
4 *3/4* **Supreme Quest** 2-8-13 0 SteveDrowne 10 72
(Roger Charlton) *chsd ldrs on outer: effrt 2f out: cl enough over 1f out: outpcd fnl f* **8/1**
5 *1 1/2* **Misty Conquest (IRE)** 2-8-4 0 HayleyTurner 8 57+
(Tom Dascombe) *chsd ldrs: outpcd over 1f out: kpt on again ins fnl f* **20/1**
6 *1 1/4* **Marygold** 2-8-1 0 SimonPearce(3) 12 53
(John Akehurst) *wl in rr on outer: styd on fr over 1f out: nrst fin* **33/1**
7 *3/4* **Raspberry Fizz** 2-8-6 0 CathyGannon 13 52
(Eve Johnson Houghton) *dwlt: wl in rr: nvr a threat: late prog on outer* **40/1**
3 **8** *1* **Mrs Mop (IRE)**[13] 1143 2-8-10 0 RyanMoore 3 53
(Richard Hannon) *racd against nr side rail: chsd ldrs: outpcd fr wl over 1f out: fdd* **7/1**[3]
9 *1 1/4* **Red Larkspur (IRE)** 2-8-1 0 KierenFox(3) 6 42
(Roger Teal) *pressed ldr: led over 2f out to over 1f out: rn green and wknd* **8/1**

10 *nse* **Ida Inkley (IRE)** 2-8-4 0 NickyMackay 11 42
(Jonathan Portman) *dwlt: wl in rr: pushed along and no prog 2f out: modest late prog on outer* **80/1**

11 *1 3/4* **Red Hearts (IRE)** 2-8-6 0 JimmyQuinn 14 38
(Julia Feilden) *hld up in midfield: no prog 2f out: sn lost pl and fdd* **66/1**

12 *2 1/4* **Imperial Weapon (IRE)** 2-8-4 0 WilliamCarson 5 30
(John Spearing) *s.s: a in rr: no ch whn n.m.r over 1f out: fdd* **50/1**

13 *1/2* **Miss Noble** 2-8-4 0 SilvestreDeSousa 7 26
(Stuart Williams) *chsd ldrs and cl up: lost pl 2f out: sn wknd* **25/1**

14 *3 1/4* **Rooknrasbryripple** 2-8-6 0 ChrisCatlin 1 16
(Mick Channon) *led to over 2f out: wknd qckly over 1f out* **16/1**

61.66 secs (1.36) **Going Correction** +0.10s/f (Good) **14** Ran SP% **117.7**
Speed ratings (Par 89): **93,92,87,86,83 81,80,79,77,76 74,70,69,64**
toteswingers:1&2:£3.60, 1&3:£12.20, 2&3:£21.40 CSF £7.77 TOTE £2.60: £1.30, £1.90, £4.60; EX 15.10 Trifecta £287.90 Pool: £3,307.95 - 8.50 winning units..
Owner R Barnett **Bred** W And R Barnett Ltd **Trained** East Everleigh, Wilts

FOCUS
An auction maiden restricted to fillies and few of these seemed strongly fancied. Not easy form to assess, but the front two in the betting came to the fore and both can do better.

NOTEBOOK
Best Terms ◆ is a May 19 foal and is a half-sister to two 1m2f winners, so this was a noteworthy effort. Travelling well when switched into the clear early in the straight, she had to be shaken up to take care of her main rival, who was initially away from her, more towards the middle of the track, but Hughes didn't have to go for absolutely everything. The successful rider feels the filly will definitely get 6f and, considering her breeding, there should be more to come as the year progresses. (tchd 13-8 and 15-8 and 2-1 in places)
Heyward Girl(IRE) is a much earlier foal than Best Terms - born January 23 - and is out of a prolific winner. She was well fancied, but a wide draw did her no favours. Having shown good pace from the off, she briefly looked the winner about 2f out (touched 1.24 in running), but she had been caught really wide throughout and had to give best to the favourite. There should be a similar race in her. (op 13-2)
Poetic Dancer, a 5,000gns half-sister to dual 1m Polytrack winner Tactful, was unfancied in the market but showed ability.
Supreme Quest cost £18,000 and had to concede weight to all of her rivals. She showed up well to a point but was one-paced under pressure. (op 9-1 tchd 10-1 in a place)
Misty Conquest(IRE) was weak in the market, despite her stable having made a fast start with their juveniles, but she showed ability. (op 25-1)
Marygold was strong in the market before refusing to enter the stalls on her intended debut at Kempton earlier in the month. She lacked the speed of some of these but kept on. (op 25-1)
Mrs Mop(IRE) was weak in the market and didn't build on her debut effort. She was never travelling and looks best watched for now. (op 11-2)

1442 ROYAL WINDSOR RACING CLUB H'CAP — 1m 3f 135y
5:50 (5:50) (Class 5) (0-70,67) 3-Y-O — **£2,388** (£705; £352) **Stalls** High

Form RPR

6-43 **1** **Dubai Glory**[31] 891 3-8-12 **58** JamesDoyle 5 68
(Sheena West) *prom: trckd ldr 1/2-way: led and kicked on 4f out: hrd pressed and edgd lft fnl f: hld on wl* **10/1**

65-1 **2** *nk* **Pretty Diamond (IRE)**[12] 1170 3-9-4 **64** SilvestreDeSousa 7 73
(Mark Johnston) *hld up in 5th: prog 3f out: rdn to chse wnr jst over 2f out: clsd to chal fnl f: nt qckn last 50yds* **4/5**[1]

66-5 **3** *8* **September Draw (USA)**[13] 1146 3-9-3 **63** RichardHughes 1 59
(Richard Hannon) *trckd ldr to 1/2-way: pushed along over 3f out: outpcd fr 2f out: plugged on to take 3rd ins fnl f* **8/1**[3]

050- **4** *3/4* **Breton Star**[188] 6831 3-9-1 **61** MartinLane 8 56
(David Simcock) *hld up: detached in last and shkn up 4f out: sme prog 3f out: wnt modest 3rd over 1f out: wknd ins fnl f* **20/1**

214 **5** *1 1/4* **Brilliant Barca**[18] 1057 3-9-5 **65** SamHitchcott 3 57
(Mick Channon) *s.i.s: sn chsd ldng trio: rdn to chse wnr briefly over 2f out: sn lft bhd* **9/1**

63-0 **6** *8* **Cuban Piece (IRE)**[12] 1189 3-9-7 **67** (b[1]) JimmyFortune 4 46
(Tom Dascombe) *led: rdn and hdd 4f out: chsd wnr to over 2f out: capitulated rapidly* **16/1**

3324 **7** *22* **Ilissos (USA)**[42] 789 3-9-7 **67** (v) RyanMoore 2 —
(Jeremy Noseda) *hld up in last pair: effrt 3f out: hrd drvn and no rspnse over 2f out: wknd qckly: eased and t.o* **9/2**[2]

2m 27.83s (-1.67) **Going Correction** -0.025s/f (Good) **7** Ran SP% **114.6**
Speed ratings (Par 98): **104,103,98,97,97 91,77**
toteswingers:1&2:£2.50, 1&3:£9.20, 2&3:£2.70 CSF £18.68 CT £71.49 TOTE £12.90: £2.50, £1.20; EX 27.40 Trifecta £220.10 Pool: £4,525.46 - 15.21 winning units..
Owner The Affordable (2) Partnership **Bred** Hascombe And Valiant Studs **Trained** Falmer, E Sussex

FOCUS
An ordinary handicap. The early pace seemed fair, although as usual the gallop slowed noticeably as the field negotiated the sharp turn on the run back towards the straight. The winner is rated back to the best view of her early 2yo form.

1443 PLAY MECCA BINGO ON YOUR IPHONE H'CAP — 1m 3f 135y
6:20 (6:21) (Class 4) (0-80,80) 4-Y-O+ — **£3,561** (£1,059; £529; £264) **Stalls** High

Form RPR

112- **1** **New Code**[93] 7963 4-9-3 **77** RyanMoore 16 83+
(Gary Moore) *hld up in 12th: prog over 3f out: swtchd outside and effrt 2f out: drvn and r.o to ld last 100yds: readily* **7/1**[3]

426/ **2** *1* **Advisor (FR)**[86] 4709 5-9-7 **80** JamieSpencer 10 84
(Michael Bell) *led at mod pce: drvn over 2f out: kpt on wl but hdd and outpcd last 100yds* **14/1**

660- **3** *shd* **Meglio Ancora**[90] 6639 4-8-10 **70** EddieAhern 6 74
(Jonathan Portman) *trckd ldrs: rdn 3f out: prog u.p 2f out: chal and upsides fnl f: kpt on* **22/1**

/0-3 **4** *1 1/2* **Blue Spartan (IRE)**[26] 948 6-8-13 **75** LouisBeuzelin(3) 3 76
(Rod Millman) *trckd ldrs in abt 8th: effrt 3f out: drvn and cl up over 1f out: one pce after* **12/1**

012- **5** *nse* **Saborido (USA)**[171] 7208 5-9-2 **75** PatDobbs 4 76
(Amanda Perrett) *trckd ldng pair on inner: drvn over 2f out: cl up over 1f out: nt qckn* **14/1**

0-46 **6** *3/4* **The Cayterers**[24] 353 9-9-6 **79** LukeMorris 12 79
(Tony Carroll) *slowest away: wl in rr: rousted along over 3f out: prog 2f out: chsd ldrs over 1f out: one pce after* **9/1**

-303 **7** *1 1/4* **Bavarica**[12] 1183 9-8-4 **68** AdamBeschizza(5) 1 66
(Julia Feilden) *t.k.h: hld up in last quartet: sme prog over 2f out: rdn and tried to cl on ldrs over 1f out: one pce fnl f* **14/1**

233- **8** *1 1/4* **Kerchak (USA)**[190] 6781 4-9-1 **75** JimCrowley 15 71
(William Jarvis) *trckd ldr: rdn to chal over 2f out: upsides wl over 1f out: fdd* **5/1**[1]

030- **9** *1* **Crystal Celebre (IRE)**[203] 6427 5-8-6 **70** AmyScott(5) 9 64
(Henry Candy) *hld up last: stl there whn reminders 2f out: prog over 1f out: no ch of rching ldrs* **25/1**

23-3 **10** *3/4* **Eshtyaaq**[106] 11 4-8-8 **68** CathyGannon 8 63
(David Evans) *t.k.h: hld up in 10th: effrt on outer whn sltly hmpd jst over 2f out and lost pl: nvr on terms after* **16/1**

0021 **11** *1 1/4* **Dubai Miracle (USA)**[32] 876 4-9-3 **77** (t) KirstyMilczarek 14 68
(Laura Young) *wl in tch bhd ldrs: effrt over 3f out: cl enough on outer wl over 1f out: wknd* **18/1**

4223 **12** *1/2* **Brouhaha**[32] 877 7-8-13 **75** (p) RossAtkinson(3) 2 65
(Tom Dascombe) *hld up in last quartet: no real prog on inner fnl 2f* **12/1**

5513 **13** *2* **Classically (IRE)**[24] 963 5-9-3 **76** SteveDrowne 13 62
(Peter Hedger) *hld up in 11th: effrt 3f out: no prog and btn 2f out: wknd* **18/1**

010- **14** *hd* **Ancient Greece**[235] 5456 4-8-11 **74** (t) MatthewDavies(3) 5 60
(George Baker) *trckd ldrs in 4th: effrt 3f out: nt qckn 2f out: wknd* **13/2**[2]

300- **15** *2 3/4* **Mecox Bay (IRE)**[183] 6957 4-8-9 **69** DavidProbert 7 50
(Andrew Balding) *trckd ldrs: rdn 3f out: steadily wknd* **8/1**

6/0- **16** *1/2* **Pergamon (IRE)**[262] 2860 5-8-11 **70** RussKennemore 11 51
(Claire Dyson) *prom: rdn 4f out: wknd over 2f out* **100/1**

2m 27.63s (-1.87) **Going Correction** -0.025s/f (Good)
WFA 4 from 5yo+ 1lb **16** Ran SP% **124.6**
Speed ratings (Par 105): **105,104,104,103,103 102,101,101,100,99 99,98,97,97,95 95**
toteswingers:1&2:£12.90, 1&3:£73.00, 2&3:£118.20 CSF £102.01 CT £2079.01 TOTE £5.80: £1.70, £3.00, £5.70, £3.60; EX 85.90 Trifecta £947.20 Part won. Pool: £1,280.04 - 0.88 winning units..
Owner Mrs Elizabeth Kiernan **Bred** Foursome Thoroughbreds **Trained** Lower Beeding, W Sussex

FOCUS
They didn't seem to go that quick, and the time was only 0.20sec faster than the earlier Class 5 handicap for 3-y-os. Fair form, rated around the third and fourth.
Dubai Miracle(USA) Official explanation: jockey said gelding hung right

1444 READING POST H'CAP — 6f
6:50 (6:51) (Class 5) (0-75,75) 4-Y-O+ — **£2,266** (£674; £337; £168) **Stalls** Low

Form RPR

000- **1** **Spanish Bounty**[201] 6478 6-9-7 **75** EddieAhern 14 91
(Jonathan Portman) *mde all: shkn up and drew clr fr 2f out: r.o wl* **7/1**[2]

26/6 **2** *5* **Mymumsaysimthebest**[39] 818 6-9-2 **70** RyanMoore 13 70
(Gary Moore) *hld up in last quintet: prog on wd outside over 2f out: wnt 2nd over 1f out: no imp on clr wnr* **15/2**[3]

0-25 **3** *1/2* **Hand Painted**[23] 985 5-8-13 **67** (p) TravisBlock 4 65
(Peter Makin) *hld up in midfield: effrt 2f out: rdn and styd on to take 3rd wl ins fnl f* **8/1**

35-5 **4** *nk* **Equuleus Pictor**[14] 1140 7-9-4 **72** CathyGannon 3 69
(John Spearing) *prom: drvn to dispute 2nd 2f out but sn no ch w wnr: kpt on* **8/1**

350- **5** *1/2* **Seamus Shindig**[196] 6625 9-9-1 **74** AmyScott(5) 7 70+
(Henry Candy) *hld up in last quintet: effrt over 1f out: styd on fnl f: no ch* **10/1**

211- **6** *1 1/4* **Wooden King (IRE)**[140] 7628 6-8-12 **66** TomMcLaughlin 15 58
(Malcolm Saunders) *mostly chsd wnr: lft bhd fr 2f out: lost 2nd and fdd over 1f out* **16/1**

03-4 **7** *1 1/4* **The Wee Chief (IRE)**[23] 985 5-8-13 **67** PatDobbs 12 55
(Jimmy Fox) *hld up last: looking for room over 2f out: swtchd lft and prog over 1f out: one pce fnl f* **4/1**[1]

63-6 **8** *1 1/2* **Atlantic Beach**[14] 1140 6-9-1 **74** HarryBentley(5) 16 57
(Milton Bradley) *pressed ldrs: shkn up 2f out: sn outpcd: wknd fnl f* **12/1**

106- **9** *1 3/4* **Elusive Hawk (IRE)**[179] 7033 7-9-4 **72** TomQueally 9 49
(Barney Curley) *hld up bhd ldrs: effrt towards outer and in tch w chsng gp wl over 1f out: fdd* **12/1**

03-0 **10** *3* **Comptonspirit**[18] 1067 7-9-6 **74** J-PGuillambert 5 42
(Brian Baugh) *pressed ldrs: rdn and lost pl over 1f out: wknd rapidly last 150yds* **28/1**

0P0- **11** *nk* **Polar Annie**[195] 6656 6-8-11 **65** MartinLane 10 32
(Malcolm Saunders) *chsd ldrs on outer: effrt over 2f out: wknd wl over 1f out* **40/1**

00-6 **12** *1/2* **Rum King (USA)**[33] 867 4-9-4 **72** RichardHughes 8 37
(Richard Hannon) *hld up in last quintet: pushed along and no prog 2f out: no ch after* **17/2**

100- **13** *1 1/4* **Zowington**[167] 7285 9-9-0 **68** (v) WilliamCarson 1 29
(Stuart Williams) *hld up in last quintet: effrt on inner 2f out: nt clr run after and no ch* **28/1**

000- **14** *1/2* **The Strig**[156] 7441 4-8-13 **67** JimCrowley 2 27
(Stuart Williams) *chsd ldrs: rdn over 2f out: hanging and wknd over 1f out* **16/1**

1m 13.03s (0.03) **Going Correction** +0.10s/f (Good) **14** Ran SP% **122.6**
Speed ratings (Par 103): **103,96,95,95,94 92,91,89,86,82 82,81,80,79**
toteswingers:1&2:£13.50, 1&3:£30.80, 2&3:£17.10 CSF £58.88 CT £450.47 TOTE £9.30: £3.70, £3.00, £3.90; EX 69.60 TRIFECTA Not won..
Owner J G B Portman **Bred** Farleigh Court Racing Partnership **Trained** Compton, Berks

FOCUS
This looked a typically competitive sprint beforehand, but nothing could live with Spanish Bounty, who was formerly rated 96 and returned to form to take advantage of being able to contest a Class 5 handicap for the first time. The form could be worth a bit more.

1445 SPORTINGBET.COM MAIDEN STKS — 1m 2f 7y
7:20 (7:21) (Class 5) 3-Y-O — **£2,388** (£705; £352) **Stalls** High

Form RPR

02- **1** **Purification (IRE)**[205] 6365 3-9-3 0 WilliamBuick 1 87+
(John Gosden) *mde all: increased tempo fr 4f out: shkn up and in command over 1f out: styd on wl* **7/4**[1]

4-6 **2** *3* **Communicator**[16] 1096 3-9-3 0 JamieSpencer 8 81
(Michael Bell) *trckd ldng pair: dropped to 5th briefly over 2f out but gng easily: shuffled along and prog to chse wnr jst over 1f out: no imp but kpt on* **4/1**[3]

3-32 **3** *2 3/4* **Dressing Room (USA)**[7] 1272 3-9-3 72 (v) SilvestreDeSousa 3 75
(Mark Johnston) *trckd wnr: rdn over 2f out: sn lost 2nd: bmpd by rivals over 1f out: one pce* **5/1**

223- **4** *1/2* **Tiger Webb**[179] 7036 3-9-3 79 TomQueally 9 74
(Sir Henry Cecil) *hld up in 5th: prog over 3f out to chse wnr over 2f out: wandered u.p and nt qckn: fdd over 1f out* **7/2**[2]

05- **5** *2 1/2* **Canaveral**[208] 6279 3-9-3 0 MartinDwyer 6 69
(Brian Meehan) *t.k.h: hld up in 4th: pushed along over 3f out: no prog 2f out: wknd* **11/1**

6 ¾ **Planetoid (IRE)** 3-9-3 0.. TedDurcan 4 68+
(David Lanigan) *s.s: in tch in last pair: outpcd and pushed along 4f out: sn adrift: kpt on fr over 1f out* **8/1**

0-0 **7** 1 **Short Takes (USA)**[11] 1203 3-9-3 0.............................. SaleemGolam 5 66
(John Gosden) *hld up in last pair: outpcd and pushed along 4f out: sn adrift: lost no further grnd fnl 2f* **40/1**

2m 7.47s (-1.23) **Going Correction** -0.025s/f (Good) **7** Ran SP% **117.1**
Speed ratings (Par 98): **103,100,98,98,96 95,94**
toteswingers:1&2:£4.40, 1&3:£2.70, 2&3:£6.20 CSF £9.49 TOTE £2.50: £1.50, £2.20; EX 9.90 Trifecta £20.50 Pool: £4,526.66 - 163.16 winning units..
Owner Martin Hughes & Michael Kerr-Dineen **Bred** Tullamaine Castle Stud **Trained** Newmarket, Suffolk

FOCUS
A race won by subsequent St Leger winner Sixties Icon in 2006 and multiple Listed scorer Dansant the following year. This season's running looked a fair contest, but it was a bit muddling and it remains to be seen how reliable this form is, though it makes sense initially

1446 DOWNLOAD TRAINER MAGAZINE FROM APP STORE H'CAP 1m 67y
7:50 (7:50) (Class 5) (0-75,75) 3-Y-O **£2,388** (£705; £352) **Stalls** Low

Form RPR

41-5 **1** **Soweto Star (IRE)**[14] 1141 3-9-6 **74**.................................. LukeMorris 2 82
(John Best) *pushed along in midfield: disputing 5th whn lft in ld after melee bnd over 4f out: drvn 2f out: styd on wl fnl f* **12/1**

613- **2** 1½ **My Vindication (USA)**[143] 7572 3-9-5 **73**........................ RyanMoore 11 78
(Richard Hannon) *hld up last: effrt whn lft 3rd after melee bnd over 4f out: rdn to chse wnr wl over 1f out: clsd fnl f: nt qckn after* **8/1**

31-2 **3** 5 **Romantic Wish**[45] 764 3-9-2 **75**.................................... SeanLevey(5) 6 69
(Robert Mills) *dwlt: hld up: 7th whn lft 2nd after melee bnd over 4f out: rdn over 2f out: lost 2nd and fdd wl over 1f out* **17/2**

540- **4** nk **Al Andalyya (USA)**[297] 3386 3-9-3 **71**................................ TedDurcan 9 64
(David Lanigan) *wl in rr: lft in cl tch after melee bnd over 4f out: rdn over 3f out: sn struggling* **16/1**

1- **5** nk **The Holyman (IRE)**[181] 6994 3-9-7 **75**........................ FergusSweeney 4 67
(Jo Crowley) *hld up in rr: lft in 4th pl after melee bnd over 4f out: rdn and struggling over 3f out: sn btn* **9/2**[2]

046- **6** 8 **Sergeant Troy (IRE)**[177] 7099 3-8-13 **67**.................... SteveDrowne 13 41+
(Roger Charlton) *chsd ldrs: disputing 5th whn bdly hmpd bnd over 4f out: nvr able to rcvr* **9/2**[2]

303- **7** 21 **Green Pearl (IRE)**[213] 6163 3-9-4 **72**.............................. JimCrowley 3 —+
(Ralph Beckett) *chsd ldrs: 4th whn bdly hmpd bnd over 4f out: lost all ch* **15/2**[3]

44-5 **8** 54 **Silverware (USA)**[14] 1139 3-9-5 **73**............................. RichardHughes 1 —+
(Richard Hannon) *trckd ldng pair: veered lft bnd over 4f out: lost all ch and allowed to coast home* **3/1**[1]

006- **9** dist **No Larking (IRE)**[193] 6688 3-8-11 **65**.............................. DaneO'Neill 10 —+
(Henry Candy) *led: rn off the crse bnd over 4f out: hacked bk eventually* **12/1**

30-0 **10** 2¾ **Royal Opera**[37] 845 3-9-7 **75**.. JamesMillman 8 —+
(Rod Millman) *t.k.h: trckd ldr tl carried off the crse bnd over 4f out: hacked bk eventually* **25/1**

1m 44.25s (-0.45) **Going Correction** -0.025s/f (Good) **10** Ran SP% **119.9**
Speed ratings (Par 98): **101,99,94,94,94 86,65,11,—,—**
toteswingers:1&2:£16.00, 1&3:£12.40, 2&3:£2.80 CSF £107.23 CT £889.62 TOTE £12.90: £4.00, £3.30, £2.90; EX 68.80 TRIFECTA Not won..
Owner Hucking Horses IV **Bred** Lady Of Talent Syndicate **Trained** Hucking, Kent

FOCUS
Half the field lost their chance on the final part of the bend heading back in the direction of the straight, around 4f out. They all seemed to negotiate the sharpest point of the turn okay, but the trouble started when early leader No Larking veered badly left just before the field straightened up. He ended up on the opposite side of the track (Dane O'Neill did well to prevent his mount from crashing through the rails) and took Royal Opera with him. Independently, Silverware, who had been chasing the pace, did likewise, carrying Green Pearl and Sergeant Troy across the track. There was a small group of people on the infield at exactly the point where the trouble occurred and it seems probable that the two runners responsible for the carnage were shying away having been spooked. So, this was effectively a five-runner race. The front pair had unexposed profiles and did draw clear.
T/Jkpt: Not won. T/Plt: £110.00 to a £1 stake. Pool: £88,762.46 - 330.64 winning tickets. T/Qpdt: £52.50 to a £1 stake Pool: £10,503.09 148.00 w. tckts JN

1447a (Foreign Racing) See RI

BATH (L-H)
Tuesday, April 19

OFFICIAL GOING: Firm (10.0)
Wind: Virtually nil Weather: Sunny periods

1448 LINDLEY CATERING H'CAP 1m 5y
5:00 (5:00) (Class 5) (0-75,75) 4-Y-O+ **£2,422** (£715; £357) **Stalls** Low

Form RPR

052- **1** **Boom And Bust (IRE)**[184] 6958 4-9-2 **70**........................ MartinDwyer 3 84
(Marcus Tregoning) *mde all: shkn up over 1f out: c readily clr ins fnl f: v easily* **11/10**[1]

0-60 **2** 5 **Dr Wintringham (IRE)**[8] 1269 5-9-5 **73**...................... RichardHughes 1 76
(Karen George) *stdd s: hld up in rr: hdwy over 2f out: edgd rt over 1f out and disp 2nd ins fnl f: chsd wnr fnl 120yds but nvr any ch* **7/2**[2]

0-P2 **3** 1¾ **Signora Frasi (IRE)**[41] 810 6-8-7 **61**.......................... FergusSweeney 2 59
(Tony Newcombe) *sn racing in 3rd: rdn over 2f out: styd on to dispute 2nd ins fnl f but nvr any ch w wnr: one pce into 3rd fnl 120yds* **14/1**

5320 **4** nk **Tuscan King**[20] 1045 4-8-2 **56**.......................................(tp) DavidProbert 6 54
(Bernard Llewellyn) *chsd wnr: rdn over 2f out but nvr any ch: wknd into 4th ins fnl f* **7/1**

2243 **5** 5 **Faithful Ruler (USA)**[22] 1017 7-9-7 **75**............................(p) LukeMorris 4 61
(Ronald Harris) *chsd ldrs: rdn 3f out: no ch and wkng whn pushed rt over 1f out* **4/1**[3]

1m 39.05s (-1.75) **Going Correction** -0.125s/f (Firm) **5** Ran SP% **109.0**
Speed ratings (Par 103): **103,98,96,95,90**
CSF £5.07 TOTE £1.70: £1.02, £3.80; EX 7.60.
Owner Jas Singh **Bred** Duncan A McGregor **Trained** Lambourn, Berks

FOCUS
A modest handicap whoch probably took little winning, but the easy winner's form has been given a chance.

1449 LINDLEY CATERING MEDIAN AUCTION MAIDEN STKS 5f 161y
5:30 (5:30) (Class 5) 3-4-Y-O **£2,422** (£715; £357) **Stalls** Centre

Form RPR

40-2 **1** **Indian Shuffle (IRE)**[13] 1187 3-9-3 70................................ EddieAhern 4 63
(Jonathan Portman) *sn pressing for ld: chal 3f out: slt ld 2f out: jnd again appr fnl f: styd on u.p ins fnl f: asserted fnl 50yds* **15/8**[2]

-056 **2** ¾ **Dancing Tara**[7] 1293 3-8-12 50.................................. TomMcLaughlin 1 55
(David Evans) *pressed ldr over 1f: outpcd into 4th 4f out: swtchd rt and hdwy over 2f out: str run to chal appr fnl f and stl upsides u.p fnl 120yds: no ex and outpcd fnl 50yds* **16/1**

226 **3** 1¼ **Sailing North (USA)**[47] 741 3-9-3 65.................................. LukeMorris 6 56
(Ronald Harris) *in tch: hrd rdn fr over 2f out: styd on to take one pce 3rd ins fnl f* **5/1**[3]

060- **4** 1 **Make My Mark (IRE)**[144] 7577 3-8-12 46........................ TadhgO'Shea 2 48
(John Gallagher) *in tch: pushed along and one pce 1/2-way: hdwy appr fnl f: styd on ins fnl f but nt rch ldng trio* **16/1**

5 2 **Waterbury Girl** 3-8-12 0.. DavidProbert 9 41+
(Bryn Palling) *s.i.s: in rr and green: pushed over 3f out: stl green fr 2f out but kpt on ins fnl f* **12/1**

5-33 **6** 4 **His Grace (IRE)**[6] 1302 3-9-3 70.. NeilCallan 7 33
(Andrew Haynes) *sn in slt ld: jnd over 3f out and sn rdn: hdd 2f out: wknd appr fnl f* **7/4**[1]

0-6 **7** 8 **Excellence (IRE)**[13] 1179 3-8-12 0.................................... ChrisCatlin 5 —
(Karen George) *slowly away: a outpcd* **33/1**

05-0 **8** 7 **Pappas Fc**[5] 1331 4-10-0 30.. FergusSweeney 3 —
(Milton Bradley) *a outpcd* **100/1**

0-0 **9** 2½ **Lagan Lullaby**[76] 380 3-8-9 0.................................(t) SimonPearce(3) 8 —
(Neil Mulholland) *chsd ldrs: rdn 3f out: wkng whn hmpd over 2f out* **100/1**

1m 11.03s (-0.17) **Going Correction** -0.375s/f (Firm)
WFA 3 from 4yo 11lb **9** Ran SP% **112.2**
Speed ratings (Par 103): **86,85,83,82,79 74,63,54,50**
toteswingers:1&2:£14.00, 2&3:£21.90, 1&3:£2.10 CSF £30.11 TOTE £3.60: £1.70, £7.00, £2.20; EX 21.60.
Owner Out To Grass Partnership **Bred** Anglia Bloodstock And Tsarina Stud **Trained** Compton, Berks

FOCUS
A poor maiden with little depth, run at a strong pace. The fourth and fifth limit the form.
Lagan Lullaby Official explanation: jockey said filly had a breathing problem

1450 R & R ICES H'CAP 1m 2f 46y
6:00 (6:00) (Class 4) (0-80,76) 4-Y-O+ **£2,866** (£846; £423) **Stalls** Low

Form RPR

/15- **1** **Huff And Puff**[340] 2079 4-9-7 **76**.. NeilCallan 2 82+
(Amanda Perrett) *racd in 2nd to 6f out: styd cl 3rd: drvn to chal 2f out: rdn to ld appr fnl f: styd on wl cl home* **11/10**[1]

43-4 **2** ¾ **Potentiale (IRE)**[14] 1144 7-9-1 **73**.............................(p) PatrickHills(3) 3 78
(J W Hills) *trckd ldrs: swtchd rt ins fnl 2f: styd on to chse wnr ins fnl f: kpt on: a hld* **8/1**

2411 **3** 1¾ **Edgeworth (IRE)**[22] 885 5-9-5 **74**..................................(p) ChrisCatlin 4 75
(Brendan Powell) *plld hrd in rr tl plld way to press ldr 6f out and stl pulling whn led appr fnl 3f: rdn over 2f out and kpt slt advantage tl hdd appr fnl f: no ex fnl 150yds* **7/1**

15-0 **4** 4½ **Morning Chief (IRE)**[14] 1144 4-9-1 **70**.............................. LukeMorris 1 62
(Clive Cox) *led: jnd 6f out: hdd appr fnl 3f: wknd appr fnl f* **6/1**[3]

324- **5** 8 **Sunny Future (IRE)**[241] 5286 5-9-3 **72**........................ TomMcLaughlin 5 48
(Malcolm Saunders) *t.k.h: hld up in rr: sme hdwy to get in tch over 4f out: wknd over 2f out* **3/1**[2]

2m 10.23s (-0.77) **Going Correction** -0.125s/f (Firm) **5** Ran SP% **110.5**
Speed ratings (Par 105): **98,97,96,92,86**
CSF £10.48 TOTE £2.00: £1.30, £3.60; EX 10.70.
Owner A D Spence **Bred** Sir Eric Parker **Trained** Pulborough, W Sussex

FOCUS
A tight little handicap, run at a muddling pace and the progressive winner rates value for a bit further. the form is rated around the third.

1451 BRITISH STALLION STUDS SUPPORTING BRITISH RACING EBF MEDIAN AUCTION MAIDEN STKS 5f 11y
6:30 (6:31) (Class 5) 2-Y-O **£3,343** (£987; £493) **Stalls** Centre

Form RPR

1 **Factory Time (IRE)** 2-9-3 0.. ChrisCatlin 5 78+
(Mick Channon) *sn chsng ldr: rdn to ld over 1f out: styd on strly ins fnl f* **11/8**[1]

4 **2** 2 **Copper Falls**[19] 1055 2-8-12 0...................................... FergusSweeney 2 66
(Brendan Powell) *plld hrd and awkward on ins after 120yds: chsd ldrs: swtchd rt to outside over 2f out: chsd wnr appr fnl f: styd on: a readily hld* **11/4**[2]

3 1¾ **Worth** 2-8-12 0.. MartinDwyer 3 59+
(Brian Meehan) *s.i.s: in rr: green and sn pushed along: hdwy fr 2f out: styd on to take 3rd ins fnl f but no imp on ldng duo* **11/2**[3]

5 **4** 1½ **Sea Poet**[15] 1129 2-9-3 0.. SamHitchcott 4 58
(Andrew Haynes) *in tch: pushed along 3f out: styd on ins fnl f but nvr any ch w ldng trio* **20/1**

5 3¼ **Spring Daisy (IRE)** 2-8-12 0...................................... RichardSmith 1 41
(Tom Dascombe) *sn pushed along: a outpcd* **12/1**

0 **6** 2¾ **Courtland King (IRE)**[8] 1268 2-9-3 0.................................. NeilCallan 6 36
(David Evans) *sn led: hdd & wknd qckly over 1f out* **11/2**[3]

61.55 secs (-0.95) **Going Correction** -0.375s/f (Firm) **6** Ran SP% **112.0**
Speed ratings (Par 92): **92,88,86,83,78 74**
toteswingers:1&2 £1.10, 2&3 £1.60, 1&3 £2.70 CSF £5.31 TOTE £4.00: £2.30, £1.10; EX 7.30.
Owner Jaber Abdullah **Bred** Tally-Ho Stud **Trained** West Ilsley, Berks

FOCUS
An average juvenile maiden. The well backed winner was well on top and the second is improving.

NOTEBOOK
Factory Time(IRE) landed some decent bets, winning readily enough on debut, and ought to come on nicely for the run. This ground was probably as quick as he wants it and it will be interesting to see how this scopey son of first-season sire Baltic King acquits himself in novice company. (op 6-4)
Copper Falls was backed to improve on her Leicester debut and did just that, but was always being held by the winner. She may be able to nick a small maiden at this time of year. (tchd 3-1)
Worth left the impression she would sharpen up a deal for this initial racecourse experience and was doing her best work late on. She ought to go close next time out. (op 6-1)
Sea Poet, the outsider of the field, was taken off his feet early on. He stayed on nicely once the penny dropped, though, and posted an encouraging effort. (op 16-1)

Spring Daisy(IRE) was hopelessly outpaced and looks to need more time. (op 9-1)
Courtland King(IRE) showed up well early, but was done with in between the final 2f and will struggle to win a maiden. (op 13-2)

1452 CELEBRATING 200YRS OF RACING AT LANSDOWN H'CAP 5f 11y
7:00 (7:00) (Class 4) (0-85,84) 3-Y-O £2,719 (£809; £404; £202) Stalls Centre

Form RPR
0-11 1 **Lord Avon**[19] 1062 3-9-4 84 .... KierenFox(3) 3 92
(Bill Turner) *mde all: hrd drvn appr fnl f styd on gamely fnl 120yds* 15/2[3]
22-1 2 ¾ **Quality Art (USA)**[105] 28 3-8-9 72 .... RichardHughes 2 77
(Gary Moore) *trckd wnr: jnd for 2nd over 2f out: n.m.r and swtchd rt appr fnl f: rdn and qcknd ins fnl f but a hld by wnr and no ex cl home* 10/11[1]
222- 3 2 ¾ **Millyluvstobougie**[191] 6769 3-8-13 76 .... LukeMorris 6 71
(Clive Cox) *chsd ldrs in 3rd tl drvn to dispute 2nd over 2f out: one pce whn sltly hmpd appr fnl f* 15/8[2]
0211 4 6 **Fantasy Fry**[47] 739 3-9-0 77 .... RichardSmith 5 51
(Tom Dascombe) *in tch: rdn over 2f out: no imp and wknd sn after* 14/1
313- 5 8 **Wolf Slayer**[110] 8011 3-8-7 73 .... RossAtkinson(3) 1 18
(Tom Dascombe) *sn drvn along in rr and outpsced: wknd 2f out* 22/1

60.60 secs (-1.90) **Going Correction** -0.375s/f (Firm) 5 Ran SP% **109.9**
Speed ratings (Par 100): **100,98,94,84,72**
CSF £15.04 TOTE £6.20: £4.00, £1.10; EX 17.50.
Owner Mrs M S Teversham **Bred** Mrs Monica Teversham **Trained** Sigwells, Somerset

FOCUS
A modest 3-y-o sprint handicap run in an ordinary time. The form is rated around the runner-up.

1453 DIGIBET H'CAP 5f 161y
7:30 (7:30) (Class 6) (0-60,60) 4-Y-O+ £1,753 (£517; £259) Stalls Centre

Form RPR
1103 1 **Welcome Approach**[6] 1307 8-8-11 50 .... LukeMorris 8 61
(John Weymes) *broke wl: stdd in mid-div: hdwy on outer over 2f out: hrd drvn and qcknd to ld fnl 150yds: gng clr cl home* 6/1[3]
5005 2 2 **Metropolitan Chief**[10] 1248 7-8-4 48 .... DanielleMcCreery(5) 2 52
(Paul Burgoyne) *s.i.s: in rr: hdwy on ins fr 2f out: styd on to chse ldrs ins fnl f: tk 2nd cl home but no ch w wnr* 20/1
530- 3 hd **Bateleur**[192] 6741 7-8-13 59 .... CharlesBishop(7) 4 63
(Mick Channon) *chsd ldrs: led over 1f out: sn pushed along: hdd and outpcd by wnr fnl 150yds: lost 2nd cl home* 15/2
3420 4 1 ½ **The Tatling (IRE)**[10] 1248 14-9-2 58 .... SimonPearce(3) 9 62+
(Milton Bradley) *in rr: nt clr run over 2f out: hdwy over 1f out: styd on ins fnl f but nt rch ldng trio* 8/1
2011 5 ½ **Loyal Royal (IRE)**[10] 1247 8-9-7 60 ....(bt) FergusSweeney 3 57+
(Milton Bradley) *in rr: pushed along and nt clr run 2f out: hdwy on outside over 1f out: styd on ins fnl f: nt rch ldrs* 13/2
600- 6 1 **Kyllachy Storm**[201] 6515 7-9-6 59 .... GeorgeBaker 1 53
(Ron Hodges) *sn led but hrd pressed: hdd over 1f out: wknd fnl 75yds* 11/2[2]
0055 7 2 ½ **Seeking Rio**[13] 1180 4-8-4 46 oh1 .... KierenFox(3) 6 32
(Ron Hodges) *pressed ldrs: ev ch 2f out: wknd over 1f out* 28/1
2326 7 dht **Premier League**[35] 853 4-9-3 56 ....(p) RichardHughes 5 42
(Julia Feilden) *trckd ldrs: pushed along and n.m.r over 1f out: no imp jst ins fnl f: sn btn* 4/1[1]
0-60 9 3 ¼ **Boga (IRE)**[10] 1247 4-8-9 48 .... SamHitchcott 11 23
(Ron Hodges) *chsd ldrs: rdn over 2f out: wknd over 1f out: hung lft ins fnl f* 40/1
0424 10 ½ **Misaro (GER)**[5] 1336 10-9-4 57 ....(b) DavidProbert 12 30
(Ronald Harris) *pressed ldrs: rdn over 2f out: wknd wl over 1f out* 11/2[2]
200- 11 1 ½ **Talamahana**[248] 5076 6-9-1 54 ....(v) ChrisCatlin 10 22
(Andrew Haynes) *in tch: outpcd 1/2-way: sme hdwy on outside over 2f out: wknd wl over 1f out* 20/1

1m 10.75s (-0.45) **Going Correction** -0.375s/f (Firm) 11 Ran SP% **116.7**
Speed ratings (Par 101): **88,85,85,83,82 81,77,77,73,72 70**
toteswingers:1&2:£12.50, 2&3:£21.50, 1&3:£21.50 CSF £122.26 CT £931.08 TOTE £7.30: £1.60, £4.40, £3.40; EX 154.60.
Owner T A Scothern & Tag Racing **Bred** P Wyatt And Ranby Hall **Trained** Middleham Moor, N Yorks

FOCUS
This moderate sprint handicap was a typically open event for the class. Straightforward form with the third a decent guide.
The Tatling(IRE) Official explanation: jockey said gelding was denied a clear run

1454 BATH RUGBY COMMUNITY FOUNDATION H'CAP 1m 2f 46y
8:00 (8:00) (Class 6) (0-65,63) 4-Y-O+ £1,753 (£517; £259) Stalls Low

Form RPR
0122 1 **Duneen Dream (USA)**[27] 944 6-8-10 52 .... DavidProbert 7 64
(Nikki Evans) *led after 1f: jnd over 1m out: def advantage again over 5f out: travelling wl appr fnl 2f: rdn clr over 1f out: readily* 5/2[1]
20- 2 2 ¼ **Timocracy**[180] 7038 6-9-7 63 .... SamHitchcott 2 70
(Andrew Haynes) *t.k.h: in tch: swtchd rt to outside over 2f out: drvn and styd on wl fr over 1f out: tk 2nd ins fnl f and styd on but no imp on wnr* 5/1
305- 3 2 **Annelko**[128] 7848 4-8-7 49 oh1 .... FergusSweeney 4 52
(Andrew Haynes) *led 1f: styd prom tl lost position but styd in tch over 4f out: hdwy 3f out: drvn to chse ldrs 2f out but no imp on wnr: styd on to hold one pce in 3rd ins fnl f* 8/1
64-0 4 1 ¼ **Penang Cinta**[87] 266 8-9-3 59 .... NeilCallan 3 60
(David Evans) *in tch: rn wd bnd 5f out: hdwy 3f out: drvn to chse wnr over 2f out but no imp: lost 2nd ins fnl f and sn wknd* 7/2[2]
005- 5 17 **Mister Fantastic**[19] 6848 5-8-2 51 .... LiamLewis-Salter(7) 1 18
(Dai Burchell) *plld hrd and pressed wnr after 1f tl over 5f out: wknd: appr fnl 3f* 11/1
3046 6 7 **Professor John (IRE)**[48] 728 4-9-5 61 ....(v) MartinLane 8 14
(Ian Wood) *t.k.h: chsd ldrs: rn wd bnd 5f out: rdn to chse wnr over 3f out but no imp: lost 2nd and wknd over 2f out: eased whn no ch ins fnl f* 4/1[3]
3500 7 40 **King Of Connacht**[19] 1068 8-8-8 50 ....(p) LukeMorris 6 —
(Mark Wellings) *in rr: rn wd bnd 5f out and no ch after: t.o* 14/1

2m 9.77s (-1.23) **Going Correction** -0.125s/f (Firm) 7 Ran SP% **113.6**
Speed ratings (Par 101): **99,97,95,94,81 75,43**
toteswingers:1&2 £4.10, 2&3 £10.30, 1&3 not won. CSF £15.11 CT £85.09 TOTE £3.90: £2.80, £1.70; EX 9.60.
Owner John Berry (Gwent) **Bred** Wayne G Lyster III Et Al **Trained** Pandy, Monmouths

FOCUS
An ordinary handicap, run at an uneven pace. The winner basically carried over his recent AW improvement.
T/Plt: £59.80 to a £1 stake. Pool -of £41,451.86 - 505.46 winning units. T/Qpdt: £15.20 to a £1 stake. Pool of £4,051.24 - 196.88 winning units. ST

1150 PONTEFRACT (L-H)
Tuesday, April 19

OFFICIAL GOING: Good to firm (8.9)
Wind: almost nil Weather: fine and sunny

1455 IRISH NIGHT ON FRIDAY EVENING 27TH MAY MAIDEN FILLIES' STKS 5f
2:10 (2:12) (Class 5) 2-Y-O £2,422 (£715; £357) Stalls Low

Form RPR
1 **Ebony Clarets** 2-9-0 0 .... PaulHanagan 10 72+
(Richard Fahey) *s.s: hdwy and edgd lft 3f out: swtchd rt and chsng ldrs over 1f out: edgd lft and styd on to ld nr fin* 5/1[2]
5 2 ½ **Always Ends Well (IRE)**[13] 1165 2-9-0 0 .... SilvestreDeSousa 6 70
(Mark Johnston) *led: edgd rt ins fnl f: hdd and no ex nr fin* 8/1[3]
3 1 ¼ **Pyman's Theory (IRE)** 2-9-0 0 .... RichardKingscote 8 66+
(Tom Dascombe) *trckd ldr: keeping on same pce whn n.m.r nr fin* 4/5[1]
4 5 **Springleaf (IRE)** 2-9-0 0 .... TonyHamilton 11 48+
(Richard Fahey) *s.i.s: sn chsng ldrs: outpcd over 2f out: kpt on ins fnl f* 33/1
5 3 **Oneniteinheaven (IRE)** 2-9-0 0 .... PaulMulrennan 7 37
(Ann Duffield) *chsd ldrs: fdd over 1f out* 25/1
6 3 **Stormin Gordon (IRE)** 2-9-0 0 .... NeilChalmers 1 26
(Michael Appleby) *in rr: kpt on ins fnl f: nvr nr ldrs* 40/1
7 ¾ **Tallula (IRE)** 2-9-0 0 .... FrederikTylicki 4 23
(Micky Hammond) *chsd ldrs: drvn over 2f out: wknd over 1f out* 40/1
8 7 **Lyricist** 2-9-0 0 .... GrahamGibbons 5 —
(Kevin Ryan) *hld up: sn trcking ldrs: lost pl over 2f out* 20/1
9 3 ½ **Red Samantha (IRE)** 2-8-11 0 .... TjadeCollier(3) 2 —
(Alan Berry) *hld up in rr: bhd fnl 2f* 100/1
0 10 1 ¾ **Waybuloo (IRE)**[19] 1055 2-9-0 0 ....(b[1]) KierenFallon 9 —+
(Gay Kelleway) *chsd ldrs: drvn over 2f out: wknd over 1f out: bit slipped* 11/1
11 ½ **Punchie** 2-9-0 0 .... DavidAllan 3 —
(Tim Easterby) *dwlt: sn outpcd and in rr: bhd fnl 2f* 10/1

63.16 secs (-0.14) **Going Correction** -0.275s/f (Firm) 11 Ran SP% **118.2**
Speed ratings (Par 89): **90,89,87,79,74 69,68,57,51,48 48**
toteswingers:1&2 £5.00, 2&3 £3.40, 1&3 £2.80 CSF £40.98 TOTE £5.80: £2.00, £1.80, £1.10; EX 28.80 Trifecta £269.50 Part won. Pool: £364.30 - 0.93 winning units..
Owner The Matthewman Partnership **Bred** Michael E Broughton **Trained** Musley Bank, N Yorks

FOCUS
Not much form to go on in this fillies' maiden, but the front three, all of whom seemed fancied to varying degrees, pulled clear and look to have run to a fair level at least. They are rated a bit better than the race averages.

NOTEBOOK
Ebony Clarets ◆, a 14,000gns half-sister to 1m2f winner Broughtons Swinger, did well to make a winning debut and looks above average. Having been slowest away, she had to be niggled along throughout and although gradually responding, she raced further back the next two finishers who were always in the front rank. Once in the straight she always looked like getting up, showing a good attitude out wide. She'll be a lot sharper next time, but shapes as though she'll get 6f. (op 6-1 tchd 15-2)
Always Ends Well(IRE), although ultimately well beaten on her debut at Beverley, had shown ability and she put her experience to good use, having her chance after showing plenty of speed. (op 13-2)
Pyman's Theory(IRE), the highest priced of these bought at auction, having cost £42,000, was the subject of a significant gamble, but in the paddock she looked as though the run would bring her on. She seemed to know what was required, being well placed just off the front-running Always Ends Well, but she was unable to get past that rival in the straight, getting tired late on. (op 5-4 tchd 11-8 in a place)
Springleaf(IRE) ◆, the winner's stable companion, started slowly and was caught wide for much of the way, so a lot better can be expected in due course. (op 28-1)
Oneniteinheaven(IRE) was weak in the market and shaped as though the run was needed. (op 20-1)
Waybuloo(IRE) Official explanation: jockey said bit slipped through filly's mouth

1456 CORNMARKET H'CAP 1m 4f 8y
2:40 (2:41) (Class 5) (0-75,73) 3-Y-O £2,422 (£715; £357) Stalls Low

Form RPR
4-03 1 **Szabo's Destiny**[7] 1300 3-8-13 65 .... PaulMulrennan 3 72
(James Given) *led: qcknd 3f out: hrd drvn and edgd rt ins fnl f: all out* 12/1
43-2 2 ¾ **Prince Freddie**[13] 1170 3-9-2 68 .... PaulHanagan 5 74
(Philip Kirby) *chsd ldrs: effrt over 2f out: almost upsides 1f out: keeping on same pce whn carried rt clsng stages* 5/2[1]
16- 3 1 ¾ **Devoted (IRE)**[214] 6160 3-9-7 73 .... JimCrowley 1 76
(Ralph Beckett) *s.s: hld up in rr: effrt over 2f out: chsng ldrs over 1f out: styd on same pce* 4/1[2]
456- 4 1 ¾ **Mojolika**[197] 6618 3-9-0 66 .... DavidAllan 6 66
(Tim Easterby) *chsd ldr: one pce fnl 2f* 5/1[3]
-314 5 1 ½ **Bestwecan (IRE)**[13] 1170 3-9-6 72 .... KierenFallon 2 70
(Mark Johnston) *in rr: sn nudged along: hrd drvn over 4f out: reminders over 2f out: kpt on: nvr a threat* 5/2[1]
35-5 6 18 **Celani**[13] 1168 3-9-4 70 .... GrahamGibbons 4 39
(Tim Walford) *trckd ldrs: drvn over 2f out: wknd over 1f out: bhd whn eased clsng stages* 8/1

2m 37.63s (-3.17) **Going Correction** -0.275s/f (Firm) 6 Ran SP% **112.6**
Speed ratings (Par 98): **99,98,97,96,95 83**
toteswingers: 1&2 £4.80, 1&3 £7.50, 2&3 £3.00 CSF £42.31 TOTE £15.60: £5.80, £1.10; EX 34.10.
Owner Danethorpe Racing Partnership **Bred** Limestone And Tara Studs **Trained** Willoughton, Lincs

FOCUS
An ordinary 3-y-o handicap and straightforward form. The winner confirmed her recent good run and the second progressed again. The pace was a steady one.

1457 RIU PALACE MELONERAS H'CAP 6f
3:10 (3:10) (Class 2) (0-100,100) 4-Y-O+
£7,788 (£2,332; £1,166; £583; £291; £146) Stalls Low

Form RPR
-410 1 **Flipando (IRE)**[16] 1111 10-9-1 94 .... GrahamGibbons 7 101
(David Barron) *trckd ldrs: led over 1f out: hld on wl* 7/1[3]
30-2 2 ¾ **Internationaldebut (IRE)**[16] 1109 6-8-7 86 .... MickyFenton 3 91
(Paul Midgley) *hld up towards rr: gd hdwy over 1f out: sn chsng ldrs: wnt 2nd ins fnl f: no ex towards fin* 7/2[2]

140- **3** *nk* **Crown Choice**[269] 4358 6-9-0 **93** .... AdamKirby 9 97+
(Walter Swinburn) *hld up in rr: effrt over 1f out: swtchd outside 1f out: styd on strly* **5/2**[1]
10-0 **4** *1/2* **Osteopathic Remedy (IRE)**[16] 1111 7-9-4 **97** .... FrederikTylicki 5 99
(Michael Dods) *hld up towards rr: hdwy over 1f out: styd on wl: n.m.r ins fnl f* **18/1**
00-2 **5** *3/4* **Discanti (IRE)**[12] 1200 6-8-7 **86** oh1 .... (t) DavidAllan 13 86
(Tim Easterby) *chsd ldrs: wknd clsng stages* **7/1**[3]
2-00 **6** *hd* **Wildcat Wizard (USA)**[16] 1111 5-8-12 **91** .... (b[1]) AndrewMullen 11 90
(David Nicholls) *t.k.h in midfield: effrt over 1f out: kpt on same pce* **12/1**
00-0 **7** *3/4* **Judd Street**[13] 1186 9-9-2 **95** .... (v) DaneO'Neill 1 92
(Eve Johnson Houghton) *trckd ldrs: kpt on same pce appr fnl f* **16/1**
00-6 **8** *1 1/4* **Tabaret**[13] 1166 8-8-7 **86** oh1 .... MichaelStainton 8 79
(Richard Whitaker) *in tch: effrt 2f out: one pce* **14/1**
10-0 **9** *3* **Green Park (IRE)**[13] 1166 8-9-0 **93** .... (b) AndrewElliott 10 76
(Declan Carroll) *led: swtchd lft after s: hdd over 1f out: sn wknd* **33/1**
505- **10** *3/4* **Tombi (USA)**[226] 5787 7-8-11 **93** .... MichaelO'Connell(3) 6 74
(Geoffrey Harker) *t.k.h in rr: bhd fnl 2f* **8/1**
051- **11** *1* **Haajes**[193] 6723 7-8-7 **86** .... BarryMcHugh 12 63
(Paul Midgley) *trckd ldrs: wknd 2f out: sn bhd* **22/1**

1m 15.34s (-1.56) **Going Correction** -0.275s/f (Firm) **11** Ran SP% **119.7**
Speed ratings (Par 109): **99,98,97,96,95 95,94,93,89,88 86**
toteswingers: 1&2 £6.70, 1&3 £5.60, 2&3 £3.10 CSF £32.29 CT £81.73 TOTE £9.10: £3.60, £1.60, £1.10; EX 49.80 Trifecta £153.30 Pool: £538.92 - 2.60 winning units..
Owner Mrs J Hazell **Bred** Denis McDonnell **Trained** Maunby, N Yorks

FOCUS
This sprint lost some of its interest when Hoof It was declared a non-runner, and in that one's absence it looked just a fair race for the class. It was competitive enough, but the pace didn't seem that strong for a sprint and those held up may have been at a slight disadvantage. The winner is an admirable veteran but this form might not be the most reliable.

NOTEBOOK
Flipando(IRE) was always well placed by Graham Gibbons considering how the race unfolded and returned to form after a below-par effort at Doncaster last time. This stiff track probably helped him considering he was formerly better known as a miler and has won at up to 1m2f. (op 15-2 tchd 8-1)
Internationaldebut(IRE) just failed to take advantage of a mark 3lb lower than when runner-up in this race last year. This followed on from a good second over 7f at Doncaster (off 4lb lower) and he's started the season well. (op 9-2 tchd 11-2)
Crown Choice ◆ won a maiden on his reappearance last year, proving he can go well fresh, but this was a tough race for his first start in 269 days. He had been shaping as though worth a try over 6f and was well backed, and although unable to justify the support this was a noteworthy effort, faring best of those held up. This could prove to be his trip and there should be more to come. (op 7-2 tchd 9-4)
Osteopathic Remedy(IRE) stepped up significantly on the form he showed on his reappearance and is another who deserves extra credit considering he raced some way off the ordinary gallop. (op 16-1 tchd 25-1)
Discanti(IRE), 1lb out of the handicap, didn't quite see out this stiff 6f. (tchd 6-1)
Wildcat Wizard(USA) showed a bit more in first-time blinkers.
Tombi(USA), returning from a 226-day break, has a good record when fresh but he proved disappointing on his debut for a new yard. (op 5-1)

1458 PONTEFRACT MARATHON H'CAP 2m 5f 122y
3:40 (3:40) (Class 5) (0-75,75) 4-Y-0+ **£4,209** (£1,252; £625; £312) **Stalls** Low

Form RPR
05-0 **1** **Spruzzo**[21] 1032 5-8-7 **56** oh11 .... KellyHarrison 10 63
(Chris Fairhurst) *chsd ldrs: wnt 2nd 10f out: led over 4f out: edgd lft over 1f out: hld on gamely* **100/1**
04-3 **2** *1 1/2* **Night Orbit**[26] 8 7-8-8 **57** .... GregFairley 2 62
(Julia Feilden) *mid-div: hdwy to chse ldrs 7f out: wnt 2nd over 2f out: styd on same pce ins fnl f* **16/1**
56-1 **3** *1 1/2* **Descaro (USA)**[14] 1153 5-9-10 **73** .... SilvestreDeSousa 8 77
(David O'Meara) *hld up in midfield: hdwy 6f out: sn chsng ldrs: hrd drvn over 2f out: kpt on same pce ins fnl f* **13/8**[1]
5/5- **4** *16* **King's Revenge**[18] 7626 8-8-11 **60** .... (b) RussKennemore 9 48
(Shaun Lycett) *s.s: in rr: sme hdwy 6f out: nvr on terms* **33/1**
30-0 **5** *3/4* **Ultimate Quest (IRE)**[14] 1153 6-8-4 **60** .... (b) DavidKenny(7) 12 47
(Michael Chapman) *swtchd lft after s: in rr: hdwy 3f out: nvr nr ldrs* **20/1**
10-4 **6** *hd* **Terenzium (IRE)**[14] 1153 9-8-7 **56** .... (p) PaulMulrennan 5 43
(Micky Hammond) *hld up in rr: sme hdwy 6f out: nvr nr ldrs* **14/1**
03-0 **7** *6* **I Got Music**[14] 1153 4-7-12 **56** oh6 .... JamesSullivan(3) 3 37
(Keith Reveley) *hld up in rr: hrd drvn 6f out: nvr on terms* **12/1**
1-00 **8** *7* **Torran Sound**[28] 560 4-7-10 **56** oh4 .... RyanPowell(5) 11 30
(James Eustace) *chsd ldrs: led 11f out: hdd over 4f out: wknd over 2f out* **18/1**
-500 **9** *17* **Jackson (BRZ)**[14] 1153 9-8-5 **57** oh1 ow1 .... (b) TjadeCollier(3) 6 14
(Richard Guest) *trckd ldrs: drvn 4f out: sn wknd* **28/1**
4105 **10** *70* **Chocolate Caramel (USA)**[14] 1153 9-8-11 **60** .... PaulHanagan 7 —
(Richard Fahey) *in rr: bhd fnl 5f: t.o 3f out: virtually p.u* **9/1**
21-0 **11** *19* **Dan Buoy (FR)**[14] 1153 8-9-4 **67** .... (b) AdamKirby 4 —
(Richard Guest) *led: clr after 3f: jnd after 8f: hdd 11f out: sn lost pl: t.o 3f out: virtually p.u* **17/2**[3]
000- **12** *1 1/2* **Markington**[12] 6423 8-9-12 **75** .... (b) KierenFallon 1 —
(Peter Bowen) *in rr: sn pushed along: t.o 3f out: virtually p.u* **7/2**[2]

4m 48.4s (-2.60) **Going Correction** -0.275s/f (Firm)
WFA 4 from 5yo+ 6lb **12** Ran SP% **118.5**
Speed ratings (Par 103): **93,92,91,86,85 85,83,81,74,49 42,41**
toteswingers: 1&2 £92.00, 1&3 £42.10, 2&3 £5.70 CSF £1244.92 CT £4146.06 TOTE £62.30: £13.50, £3.80, £1.40; EX 1238.20 TRIFECTA Not won..
Owner 980 Racing **Bred** C And Mrs Wilson **Trained** Middleham Moor, N Yorks

FOCUS
A marathon trip, so form that might not count for a lot in normal staying events. The race has been rated at face value initially. They went a good pace from the off, yet it paid to race handily.
Spruzzo Official explanation: trainers representative said regarding apparent improvement in for that gelding was better
Terenzium(IRE) Official explanation: trainer said gelding was unsuited by good to firm ground
Dan Buoy(FR) Official explanation: trainer said gelding was unsuited by good to firm going
Markington Official explanation: trainer said gelding was unsuited by good to firm ground

1459 SUBSCRIBE ONLINE @ RACINGUK.COM MAIDEN STKS 6f
4:10 (4:11) (Class 5) 3-Y-0+ **£2,422** (£715; £357) **Stalls** Low

Form RPR
52- **1** **Chiefdom Prince (IRE)**[174] 7183 4-9-11 0 .... RyanMoore 2 92
(Sir Michael Stoute) *fast away: mde virtually all: drvn clr over 1f out: edgd rt ins fnl f: kpt up to work* **8/15**[1]
03- **2** *3* **Redvers (IRE)**[186] 6899 3-9-0 0 .... JimCrowley 5 79
(Ralph Beckett) *chsd ldrs: wnt 2nd over 1f out: kpt on: no imp* **10/1**[3]
40- **3** *1/2* **Obiter Dicta**[171] 7232 3-8-9 0 .... DaneO'Neill 13 73
(Henry Candy) *s.i.s: in rr: hdwy over 2f out: tk 3rd 1f out: styd on* **12/1**
426- **4** *6* **Tilliemint (IRE)**[283] 3897 3-8-9 70 .... DavidAllan 6 54
(Tim Easterby) *chsd ldrs: wknd ins fnl f* **12/1**
0 **5** *3/4* **Daisyclipper**[14] 1155 3-8-9 0 .... PaulHanagan 10 51
(Ann Duffield) *hld up towards rr: effrt over 2f out: kpt on ins fnl f* **40/1**
6 *4 1/2* **Colourbearer (IRE)** 4-9-11 0 .... RichardKingscote 9 45
(Milton Bradley) *hld up in midfield: hdwy on ins over 2f out: wknd over 1f out* **100/1**
0 **7** *3/4* **Catallout (IRE)**[14] 1155 3-8-9 0 .... AndrewElliott 11 34
(Declan Carroll) *sn bhd: kpt on fnl 2f: nvr a factor* **66/1**
8 *nk* **Alive And Kicking** 3-9-0 0 .... PhilipRobinson 3 38
(James Bethell) *s.i.s: sn chsng ldrs: wknd over 1f out* **20/1**
00 **9** *9* **Hardrock Diamond**[10] 1246 3-9-0 0 .... PaulMulrennan 14 —
(Ben Haslam) *sn bhd: sme hdwy on outer over 1f out: nvr on terms* **100/1**
-0 **10** *7* **Bygones For Coins (IRE)**[93] 182 3-8-9 0 .... TonyHamilton 12 —
(Alan Berry) *chsd ldrs: wknd* **100/1**
0- **11** *8* **Vintage Grape (IRE)**[339] 2130 3-8-9 0 .... DuranFentiman 8 —
(Eric Alston) *chsd ldrs: lost pl over 2f out* **66/1**
6 **12** *19* **Alkhawarah (USA)**[19] 1060 3-8-9 0 .... RichardHills 7 —
(Mark Johnston) *w ldrs: rdn and lost pl over 2f out: eased over 1f out: virtually p.u: t.o* **5/1**[2]

1m 15.33s (-1.57) **Going Correction** -0.275s/f (Firm)
WFA 3 from 4yo 11lb **12** Ran SP% **119.5**
Speed ratings (Par 103): **99,95,94,86,85 79,78,77,65,56 45,20**
toteswingers: 1&2 £3.90, 1&3 £3.40, 2&3 £7.10 CSF £6.88 TOTE £1.60: £1.10, £2.00, £2.80; EX 7.30 Trifecta £33.20 Pool: £634.46 - 14.12 winning units..
Owner Saeed Suhail **Bred** New England Stud, Myriad And N Wright **Trained** Newmarket, Suffolk

FOCUS
A race won last year the smart Bated Breath. This year's running looked a good contest, especially by the usual standards of an older-horse sprint maiden. The time was decent and a fairly posiitve view has been taken of the form, with the first three clear.
Alive And Kicking Official explanation: trainer said gelding was unsuited by good to firm going
Hardrock Diamond Official explanation: trainer said gelding was unsuited by good to firm ground
Alkhawarah(USA) Official explanation: trainer had no explination as to poor running

1460 YORKSHIRE BUSINESS FORUM H'CAP 1m 4y
4:40 (4:41) (Class 5) (0-75,75) 4-Y-0+ **£2,422** (£715; £357) **Stalls** Low

Form RPR
5-10 **1** **Count Bertoni (IRE)**[16] 1110 4-9-4 **72** .... SilvestreDeSousa 14 83
(David O'Meara) *mde all: styd on wl fnl 2f: drew clr last 150yds* **11/1**
13-0 **2** *3 1/2* **Swiftly Done (IRE)**[17] 1099 4-9-0 **68** .... (b[1]) AndrewElliott 2 71
(Declan Carroll) *prom: effrt over 2f out: styd on to take 2nd jst ins fnl f: no imp* **16/1**
433- **3** *3* **Azimuth (USA)**[249] 5026 4-9-5 **73** .... PaulHanagan 8 69
(Ann Duffield) *trckd ldrs: effrt over 2f out: kpt on same pce* **8/1**
110- **4** *1* **Hail Bold Chief (USA)**[192] 6753 4-9-6 **74** .... RobertWinston 1 68
(Alan Swinbank) *trckd ldrs: effrt over 2f out: kpt on same pce over 1f out* **2/1**[1]
/5-5 **5** *1 1/2* **Idealism**[20] 1038 4-8-11 **65** .... FrederikTylicki 10 55
(Micky Hammond) *hld up in rr: effrt and n.m.r over 2f out: kpt on: nvr trbld ldrs* **20/1**
215- **6** *1/2* **Private Joke**[118] 7965 4-9-6 **74** .... WilliamBuick 12 63
(John Gosden) *trckd ldrs: rn wd bnd after 2f: one pce appr fnl f* **6/1**[2]
60-0 **7** *1* **Aussie Blue (IRE)**[14] 1150 7-8-12 **66** .... MichaelStainton 7 53
(Richard Whitaker) *mid-div: effrt on ins whn n.m.r over 2f out: kpt on: nvr nr ldrs* **22/1**
333- **8** *nk* **Effigy**[184] 6958 7-9-2 **75** .... AmyScott(5) 11 61
(Henry Candy) *hld up in rr: effrt over 2f out: kpt on: nvr nr ldrs* **15/2**
0-06 **9** *1/2* **Raleigh Quay (IRE)**[10] 1244 4-9-4 **72** .... KellyHarrison 3 57
(Micky Hammond) *in rr: drvn over 2f out: nvr on terms* **12/1**
1206 **10** *10* **Titan Triumph**[24] 995 7-9-1 **69** .... (t) JimCrowley 6 31
(William Knight) *hld up in rr: hdwy on outside over 3f out: chsng ldrs over 1f out: heavily eased jst ins fnl f* **7/1**[3]
440- **11** *22* **Raqeeb (USA)**[241] 5304 4-9-4 **75** .... JamesSullivan(3) 15 —
(Ruth Carr) *w ldr: wknd qckly over 2f out: sn bhd* **10/1**
1040 **12** *dist* **Diplomatic (IRE)**[10] 1232 6-8-12 **66** .... WilliamCarson 5 —
(Michael Squance) *s.i.s: a in rr: bhd whn heavily eased over 1f out: wl t.o: eventually completed* **50/1**

1m 43.83s (-2.07) **Going Correction** -0.275s/f (Firm) **12** Ran SP% **118.4**
Speed ratings (Par 103): **99,95,92,91,90 89,88,88,87,77 55,—**
toteswingers: 1&2 £18.60, 1&3 £13.90, 2&3 £19.80 CSF £165.67 CT £1510.06 TOTE £15.20: £4.60, £5.60, £3.10; EX 171.10 Trifecta £385.20 Part won. Pool: £520.54 - 0.10 winning units..
Owner Equality Racing **Bred** Le Thenney S A **Trained** Nawton, N Yorks

FOCUS
This looked a competitive handicap beforehand, but it provided a clear-cut winner. It's perhaps best not to get carried away with the form.
Titan Triumph Official explanation: trainer said gelding was unsuited by good to firm ground

1461 NRC DAY ON EASTER WEDNESDAY 27TH APPRENTICE H'CAP 1m 2f 6y
5:10 (5:10) (Class 5) (0-70,70) 4-Y-0+ **£2,422** (£715; £357) **Stalls** Low

Form RPR
32-0 **1** **Hong Kong Island (IRE)**[17] 1099 4-9-0 **66** .... EdmondLinehan(3) 4 83
(Micky Hammond) *hld up in midfield: stdy hdwy on ins over 2f out: chsng ldrs whn swtchd rt over 1f out: led jst ins fnl f: drvn out* **13/2**
66-6 **2** *1* **Tenhoo**[16] 1107 5-8-7 **56** oh4 .... NathanAlison 5 70
(Eric Alston) *stdd s: t.k.h towards rr: hdwy and n.m.r over 2f out: styd on to chse wnr ins fnl f: no ex* **12/1**
0003 **3** *4 1/2* **Gala Casino Star (IRE)**[17] 1099 6-9-3 **69** .... GeorgeChaloner(3) 9 74
(Richard Fahey) *trckd ldrs: hmpd bnd after 2f: led and edgd lft over 1f out: hdd jst ins fnl f: eased towards fin* **4/1**[2]
4102 **4** *3/4* **Zafranagar (IRE)**[17] 1099 6-8-10 **64** .... GeorgeDowning(5) 12 67
(Tony Carroll) *detached in rr: hdwy over 4f out: edgd rt and kpt on over 1f out: nvr nr to chal* **9/2**[3]
0220 **5** *1 1/4* **Pinsplitter (USA)**[16] 1107 4-8-2 **56** oh2 .... RyanTate(5) 1 57
(Alan McCabe) *sn chsng ldrs: edgd rt and one pce over 1f out* **16/1**
4505 **6** *1 1/2* **General Tufto**[7] 1292 6-9-2 **65** .... (b) MatthewLawson 7 63
(Charles Smith) *detached in rr and sn drvn along: hdwy and swtchd outside over 1f out: kpt on: nvr rchd ldrs* **28/1**
0-02 **7** *3 1/2* **Buddy Holly**[3] 1398 6-8-13 **62** .... MatthewCosham 10 53
(Robert Eddery) *chsd ldrs: hmpd bnd after 2f: swtchd outside over 3f out: wknd jst ins fnl f* **7/2**[1]
50-0 **8** *5* **Global**[16] 1107 5-8-11 **65** .... DavidSimmonson(5) 2 46
(Brian Ellison) *chsd ldrs: led after 2f: hdd over 1f out: sn wknd* **14/1**
06-0 **9** *1/2* **Desert Hunter (IRE)**[14] 1150 8-8-7 **56** oh1 .... ShaneBKelly 6 36
(Micky Hammond) *chsd ldrs: wknd jst ins fnl f* **22/1**

13-0 **10** *14* **Sharp Sovereign (USA)**[17] 1099 5-9-7 **70**.................. AntiocoMurgia 11 22
(David Barron) *led 2f: drvn over 3f out: lost pl over 2f out: sn bhd: eased over 1f out* **8/1**

063- **11** *1 1/4* **Cornish Beau (IRE)**[204] 6424 4-9-7 **70**........................ CharlesEddery 13 19
(Mark H Tompkins) *w ldrs: lost pl over 2f out: bhd whn eased 1f out* **12/1**

2m 10.03s (-3.67) **Going Correction** -0.275s/f (Firm) **11** Ran SP% **120.6**
Speed ratings (Par 103): **103,102,98,98,97 95,93,89,88,77 76**
toteswingers:1&2 £16.10, 2&3 £14.90, 1&3 £7.80. Tote Super 7: Win: Not won. Place: Not won. CSF £84.07 CT £357.48 TOTE £9.20: £2.80, £3.30, £1.80; EX 109.90 TRIFECTA Not won..
Owner Miss Terri Anne Nixon **Bred** The Goldsmith Bloodstock Partnership **Trained** Middleham Moor, N Yorks

FOCUS
This looked just an ordinary apprentices' handicap and the leaders may have gone off a bit too fast. The first two came clear.
Cornish Beau(IRE) Official explanation: trainer said gelding was unsuited by good to firm ground
T/Jkpt: Not won. T/Plt: £93.60 to a £1 stake. Pool of £56,962.86 - 444.1 winning units. T/Qpdt: £34.60 to a £1 stake. Pool of £3,968.29 - 84.82 winning units. WG

1287 SOUTHWELL (L-H)
Tuesday, April 19

OFFICIAL GOING: Standard
Wind: Light across Weather: Fine and dry

1462 32RED CLAIMING STKS 7f (F)
2:00 (2:02) (Class 6) 3-Y-O+ **£1,706** (£503; £252) **Stalls** Low

Form RPR

45-6 **1** **Royal Dignitary (USA)**[20] 1037 11-10-0 75.................. AdrianNicholls 4 83
(David Nicholls) *chsd wnr: rdn along 3f out: chal and carried bdly rt over 1f out: led ins fnl f: edgd lft and kpt on wl towards fin* **15/2**[3]

113 **2** *1 1/4* **Alpha Tauri (USA)**[22] 1014 5-10-0 78............................(t) JamesDoyle 5 80
(Frank Sheridan) *rn free and set str pce: pushed clr wl over 2f out: rdn and hung bdly rt over 1f out: sn jnd and drvn: hdd ins fnl f: kpt on same pce* **5/6**[1]

-116 **3** *2 1/2* **Hits Only Jude (IRE)**[3] 1394 8-9-10 79..........................(v) DavidNolan 6 69
(Declan Carroll) *sn rdn along and outpcd in rr: hdwy 1/2-way: rdn to chse ldng pair wl over 2f out: drvn and one pce appr fnl f* **13/8**[2]

00-0 **4** *38* **Niran (IRE)**[12] 1200 4-9-4 70.................................. SebSanders 3 —
(Ruth Carr) *sn pushed along: a in rr: outpcd and bhd fr over 2f out* **25/1**

1m 29.57s (-0.73) **Going Correction** 0.0s/f (Stan) **4** Ran SP% **108.3**
Speed ratings (Par 101): **104,102,99,56**
CSF £14.58 TOTE £6.30; EX 15.00.Alpha Tauri was claimed by R. C. Guest for £10,000.
Owner Middleham Park Racing XXXVI **Bred** Bentley Smith, J Michael O'Farrell Jr , Joan Thor **Trained** Sessay, N Yorks
■ Stewards' Enquiry : Adrian Nicholls one-day ban: careless riding (May 3)
James Doyle two-day ban: careless riding (May 3-4)

FOCUS
Fair form in this small-field claimer, with the veteran winner rated back to last season's level.
Alpha Tauri(USA) Official explanation: jockey said gelding hung right

1463 MEMBERSHIP OF SOUTHWELL GOLF CLUB H'CAP 6f (F)
2:30 (2:31) (Class 5) (0-70,70) 4-Y-O+ **£2,047** (£604; £302) **Stalls** Low

Form RPR

5163 **1** **Cape Of Storms**[7] 1289 8-8-10 **62**.......................(b) AndrewHeffernan[(3)] 3 71
(Roy Brotherton) *mde all: rdn 2f out: drvn ent fnl f: kpt on gamely* **4/1**[1]

1454 **2** *3/4* **Steel City Boy (IRE)**[29] 934 8-8-4 **56** oh2....................... BillyCray[(3)] 10 63
(Garry Woodward) *prom on outer: chsd wnr fr 1/2-way: rdn to chal wl over 1f out: drvn and ev ch ent fnl f: kpt on same pce towards fin* **14/1**

0460 **3** *2 1/2* **Eastern Hills**[35] 854 6-8-8 **57**...............................(p) JamesDoyle 1 56
(Alan McCabe) *prom on inner: rdn 2f out: drvn over 1f out: kpt on same pce* **9/1**

40-0 **4** *1 1/2* **Koo And The Gang (IRE)**[17] 1099 4-8-11 **60**.................. PhillipMakin 6 54
(Brian Ellison) *chsd ldrs: pushed along and sltly outpcd 1/2-way: rdn 2f out: kpt on ins fnl f* **4/1**[1]

3214 **5** *1 1/4* **Interchoice Star**[35] 853 6-8-11 **65**..........................(p) LeeTopliss[(5)] 9 55
(Ray Peacock) *in tch: hdwy on outer to chse ldrs over 2f out: rdn wl over 1f out and sn no imp* **7/1**[3]

500- **6** *3 1/2* **Fulford**[258] 4706 6-8-8 **57**.. FrannyNorton 4 36
(Mel Brittain) *chsd ldrs: rdn over 2f out: sn drvn and grad wknd* **20/1**

2-30 **7** *2 1/4* **Dazeen**[20] 1035 4-8-13 **62**.. TonyCulhane 11 33
(Paul Midgley) *a towards rr* **7/1**[3]

1060 **8** *1/2* **Dancing Freddy (IRE)**[10] 1239 4-8-10 **62**.............(p) RobertLButler[(3)] 7 32
(Richard Guest) *dwlt: sn swtchd to inner: a towards rr* **14/1**

2200 **9** *1 1/2* **Residency (IRE)**[11] 1213 5-8-10 **59**..........................(p) TomEaves 8 24
(Bryan Smart) *a towards rr* **28/1**

4-04 **10** *14* **Dimaire**[34] 874 4-8-8 **57**... AndreaAtzeni 2 —
(Derek Haydn Jones) *chsd ldrs: rdn along 1/2-way: sn wknd* **13/2**[2]

00-0 **11** *3 1/2* **Floor Show**[12] 1205 5-9-7 **70**.................................... LeeNewman 5 —
(Noel Wilson) *rrd s: a in rr: bhd and eased fnl 2f* **14/1**

1m 16.12s (-0.38) **Going Correction** 0.0s/f (Stan) **11** Ran SP% **116.5**
Speed ratings (Par 103): **102,101,97,95,94 89,86,85,83,65 60**
toteswingers:1&2 £9.90, 2&3 £9.40, 1&3 £24.20 CSF £62.80 CT £486.73 TOTE £7.20: £2.50, £3.90, £4.40; EX 61.60.
Owner Arthur Clayton **Bred** R J Turner **Trained** Elmley Castle, Worcs

FOCUS
Just an ordinary handicap, full of exposed horses. It paid to race prominently with nothing ever threatening to get into it from behind. The winner is rated back to his old best with the second up a length on his recent form.
Dazeen Official explanation: jockey said gelding resented kickback

1464 32RED CASINO H'CAP 5f (F)
3:00 (3:00) (Class 6) (0-55,55) 4-Y-O+ **£2,047** (£604; £302) **Stalls** High

Form RPR

-632 **1** **Spirit Of Coniston**[11] 1213 8-8-12 **51**............................ TonyCulhane 9 62
(Paul Midgley) *led: rdn along 2f out: hdd and n.m.r over 1f out: swtchd lft and drvn to ld again ins fnl f: kpt on wl* **11/2**[2]

3550 **2** *1 1/4* **Cheveyo (IRE)**[7] 1287 5-8-1 **47**..........................(v) NoelGarbutt[(7)] 6 51
(Patrick Morris) *dwlt and sn rdn along towards rr: hdwy 1/2-way: rdn to ld over 1f out and sn hung rt: hdd ins fnl f and kpt on same pce* **22/1**

4340 **3** *1 1/4* **Kheley (IRE)**[7] 1287 5-8-8 **52**.................................. JamesRogers[(5)] 11 52
(Mark Brisbourne) *in tch on wd outside: hdwy to chse ldrs 2f out: sn rdn and n.m.r ent fnl f: swtchd lft and kpt on wl towards fin* **17/2**

4243 **4** *hd* **Gorgeous Goblin (IRE)**[7] 1287 4-8-4 **48**.................(vt) KieranO'Neill[(5)] 7 47
(David C Griffiths) *dwlt and bhd: rdn along and hdwy on stands' rail wl over 1f out: styng on whn n.m.r ent fnl f: sn swtchd lft and kpt on towards fin* **11/2**[2]

4064 **5** *nk* **Shakespeares Excel**[7] 1287 4-8-8 **47**........................ RobbieFitzpatrick 10 45
(Derek Shaw) *trckd ldrs: hdwy 2f out and sn ev ch: rdn and n.m.r ent fnl f: sn one pce* **7/1**[3]

006- **6** *1 1/2* **Lujiana**[154] 7468 6-9-2 **55**....................................... FrannyNorton 5 47
(Mel Brittain) *prom: rdn along over 2f out: wknd over 1f out* **11/2**[2]

5526 **7** *2* **Bertbrand**[21] 1029 6-8-9 **48**.................................(b) JamesDoyle 2 33
(Ian McInnes) *chsd ldrs on outer: rdn along wl over 1f out: sn one pce* **16/1**

4034 **8** *2 1/2* **Muqalad (IRE)**[10] 1247 4-8-9 **48**.............................(vt) TomEaves 8 24
(Bryan Smart) *cl up: rdn along over 2f out: sn wknd* **5/1**[1]

02-3 **9** *nse* **Gemma's Delight (IRE)**[20] 1054 4-9-2 **55**.....................(p) LiamJones 3 31
(James Unett) *a towards rr* **7/1**[3]

1/6- **10** *1/2* **Mission Impossible**[274] 4199 6-9-1 **54**........................ PatrickMathers 1 28
(Colin Teague) *a towards rr* **40/1**

-050 **11** *2* **Ronnie Howe**[28] 941 7-8-4 **46** oh1.........................(bt) DeclanCannon[(3)] 4 13
(Roy Bowring) *chsd ldrs: rdn along 1/2-way: sn wknd* **22/1**

60.35 secs (0.65) **Going Correction** +0.15s/f (Slow) **11** Ran SP% **115.4**
Speed ratings (Par 101): **100,98,96,95,95 92,89,85,85,84 81**
toteswingers:1&2 £20.10, 2&3 £14.90, 1&3 £38.30 CSF £120.39 CT £1034.70 TOTE £5.80: £1.90, £6.10, £2.50; EX 158.50.
Owner P O'Gara & N Kelly **Bred** Green Square Racing **Trained** Westow, N Yorks

FOCUS
A run-of-the-mill sprint. The main action unfolded middle to stands' side and the winner is rated a shade better than the bare form.

1465 SOUTHWELL-RACECOURSE.CO.UK MAIDEN STKS 5f (F)
3:30 (3:30) (Class 5) 3-Y-O **£2,047** (£604; £302) **Stalls** High

Form RPR

2- **1** **Jamaican Bolt (IRE)**[164] 7345 3-9-3 0.............................. TomEaves 1 81
(Bryan Smart) *wnt lft s: sn cl up: led after 2f: pushed clr over 1f out: kpt on* **2/11**[1]

4426 **2** *3 3/4* **Beautiful Day**[10] 1246 3-9-3 66...................................... PhillipMakin 7 67
(Kevin Ryan) *led 2f: cl up: rdn along wl over 1f out: drvn and kpt same pce* **17/2**[3]

6643 **3** *1 3/4* **Ever Roses**[5] 1323 3-8-12 51......................................(v) TonyCulhane 4 56
(Paul Midgley) *outpcd and rdn along in rr: hdwy wl over 1f out: kpt on ins fnl f* **20/1**

6-0 **4** *2 1/2* **See The Storm**[105] 28 3-9-3 0.................................... StephenCraine 2 52
(Patrick Morris) *prom: rdn along 1/2-way: drvn and outpcd wl over 1f out* **100/1**

532 **5** *4* **Ladydolly**[54] 669 3-8-9 60.................................(p) AndrewHeffernan[(3)] 3 33
(Roy Brotherton) *prom: rdn along 1/2-way: sn drvn and outpcd* **7/1**[2]

000- **6** *2* **Deveze (IRE)**[169] 7268 3-8-12 48.................................(p) JamesDoyle 5 25
(Dean Ivory) *chsd ldrs: rdn along 1/2-way: sn outpcd* **66/1**

0 **7** *3 1/4* **Miming**[21] 1020 3-8-12 0.. TravisBlock 6 —
(Hughie Morrison) *sn rdn along: a in rr* **50/1**

60.65 secs (0.95) **Going Correction** +0.15s/f (Slow) **7** Ran SP% **116.8**
Speed ratings (Par 98): **98,92,89,85,78 75,70**
toteswingers:1&2 £1.50, 2&3 £1.40, 1&3 £2.60 CSF £2.75 TOTE £1.60: £1.10, £2.00; EX 3.30.
Owner R C Bond & C S Bond **Bred** Swordlestown Stud **Trained** Hambleton, N Yorks

FOCUS
A weak and one-sided maiden and the winner did not need to improve on his 2yo debut form..

1466 32REDPOKER.COM H'CAP 1m 6f (F)
4:00 (4:00) (Class 6) (0-65,63) 4-Y-O+ **£1,706** (£503; £252) **Stalls** Low

Form RPR

0116 **1** **Irish Jugger (USA)**[13] 1174 4-9-8 **63**.............................. JamesMillman 2 76
(Rod Millman) *hld up in tch: hdwy over 3f out: chal 2f out: rdn to ld over 1f out: styd on* **9/2**[3]

245 **2** *1/2* **First Rock (IRE)**[46] 762 5-9-2 **55**................................. TomEaves 8 67
(Alan Swinbank) *trckd ldrs: smooth hdwy to ld 3f out: jnd and rdn 2f out: hdd over 1f out: drvn and one pce ins fnl f* **9/2**[3]

0003 **3** *11* **Bold Adventure**[21] 1032 7-9-1 **54**................................... TonyCulhane 5 51
(Willie Musson) *hld up and bhd: niggled along 5f out: rdn and wd st: kpt on u.p ins fnl f: tk remote 3rd nr fin* **15/8**[1]

2-14 **4** *nk* **Short Supply (USA)**[18] 492 5-9-4 **57**.......................... DanielTudhope 6 54
(Tim Walford) *cl up: rdn along 3f out: drvn over 2f out and sn one pce: lost 3rd nr line* **7/1**

1221 **5** *10* **Kingaroo (IRE)**[26] 954 5-9-7 **63**................................. BillyCray[(3)] 4 46
(Garry Woodward) *cl up: led after 2f: rdn along and hdd 3f out: sn drvn and wknd* **7/2**[2]

0-3P **6** *15* **Mandalay Prince**[46] 768 7-8-6 **45**............................. AdrianMcCarthy 7 —
(Willie Musson) *s.i.s: a in rr: outpcd and bhd fnl 4f* **25/1**

006- **7** *5* **December**[8] 7604 5-8-8 **47**...(t) SaleemGolam 1 —
(Christine Dunnett) *t.k.h: led 2f: cl up tl rdn along and wknd 5f out: sn bhd* **66/1**

500- **8** *49* **Simone Martini (IRE)**[145] 1462 6-8-10 **49**.................(vt) RobertHavlin 3 —
(Milton Harris) *chsd ldrs: rdn along 1/2-way: sn wknd and bhd fnl 4f* **40/1**

3m 8.29s (-0.01) **Going Correction** 0.0s/f (Stan)
WFA 4 from 5yo+ 2lb **8** Ran SP% **113.6**
Speed ratings (Par 101): **100,99,93,93,87 78,76,48**
toteswingers: 1&2 £5.00, 1&3 £2.70, 2&3 £1.20 CSF £24.43 CT £49.67 TOTE £5.00: £1.90, £2.10, £1.10; EX 27.90.
Owner Rod Millman Racing Club **Bred** Richard S Kaster & Frederick C Wieting **Trained** Kentisbeare, Devon

FOCUS
Quite a few patently failed to give their running here, but it's probably still best to take a reasonably positive view of the leading pair's performances. The form could easily be rated 3-5lb higher.
Bold Adventure Official explanation: jockey said gelding was never travelling

1467 SOUTHWELL GOLF CLUB LADY MEMBERS H'CAP 7f (F)
4:30 (4:30) (Class 4) (0-85,85) 4-Y-O+ **£2,914** (£867; £433; £216) **Stalls** Low

Form RPR

3112 **1** **Almahaza (IRE)**[34] 870 7-8-13 **77**.............................. NeilChalmers 2 87
(Adrian Chamberlain) *trckd ldrs: hdwy 3f out: rdn to ld over 1f out: drvn ins fnl f and kpt on wl* **8/1**

320- **2** *3/4* **Masai Moon**[311] 2971 7-9-7 **85**................................... JamesMillman 6 93
(Rod Millman) *cl up: rdn to ld over 2f out: drvn and hdd over 1f out: rallied ins fnl f: no ex towards fin* **14/1**

40-0 **3** *1 1/4* **Academy Blues (USA)**[16] 1109 6-9-7 **85**..................... AdrianNicholls 3 90
(David Nicholls) *s.i.s and bhd: t.k.h and gd hdwy on inner and cl up after 2f: effrt 2f out: sn rdn and ev ch tl drvn and one pce ins fnl f* **7/1**

1121 **4** *1* **Majuro (IRE)**[18] 1081 7-9-7 **85**..(t) TonyCulhane 1 87
(Richard Guest) *led: rdn along and hdd over 2f out: sn drvn and kpt on same pce* **4/1**[2]

02-0 **5** *15* **Esprit De Midas**[16] 1111 5-9-6 **84**.......................... PhillipMakin 7 46
(Kevin Ryan) *chsd ldrs on outer: rdn along 1/2-way: drvn 3f out and sn outpcd* **2/1**[1]

200- **6** *¾* **Gobama**[173] 7188 4-9-7 **85**.. SebSanders 8 44
(J W Hills) *a in rr* **16/1**

00-3 **7** *1½* **Icelandic**[19] 1067 9-9-7 **85**...(t) JamesDoyle 5 40
(Frank Sheridan) *midfield: rdn along over 3f out: sn outpcd* **5/1**[3]

4445 **8** *nk* **Lockantanks**[8] 1269 4-8-8 **77**.. SeanLevey(5) 4 32
(Michael Appleby) *chsd ldrs: rdn along over 3f out: sn wknd* **14/1**

1m 29.1s (-1.20) **Going Correction** 0.0s/f (Stan) **8** Ran SP% **112.8**
Speed ratings (Par 105): **106,105,103,102,85 84,82,82**
toteswingers: 1&2 £11.20, 1&3 £9.10, 2&3 £12.00 CSF £106.61 CT £822.82 TOTE £6.40: £2.20, £4.00, £2.00; EX 119.00.
Owner G B Heffaran **Bred** Castletown And Associates **Trained** Ashton Keynes, Wilts

FOCUS
The best-quality race of the afternoon. The front four came well clear and the winner took his form to a new high.
Academy Blues(USA) Official explanation: jockey said gelding hung right

1468 32REDBINGO.COM H'CAP — 1m (F)
5:05 (5:06) (Class 6) (0-55,55) 4-Y-0+ **£1,706** (£503; £252) **Stalls** Low

Form RPR

5-00 **1** **Dazakhee**[20] 1052 4-9-2 **55**.. TonyCulhane 3 66
(Paul Midgley) *hld up in tch: smooth hdwy on inner 3f out: sn trcking ldr: effrt to ld 2f out: rdn over 1f out: drvn and edgd lft ins fnl f: kpt on* **11/4**[1]

2100 **2** *1¼* **On The Cusp (IRE)**[19] 1068 4-8-6 **50** ow1....................(p) JulieBurke(5) 7 58
(Richard Guest) *sn led: rdn along and hdd 2f out: rallied u.p ins fnl f: no ex last 100yds* **17/2**

5430 **3** *1¾* **Buzz Bird**[32] 895 4-9-1 **54**... LeeNewman 13 58
(David Barron) *chsd ldrs: n.m.r and lost pl 3f out: rdn and styd on wl fr over 1f out* **9/2**[2]

4054 **4** *1¾* **Novastasia (IRE)**[42] 793 5-8-7 **46**....................................(b) LiamJones 9 46
(Dean Ivory) *hld up: gd hdwy on outer 3f out: rdn to chse ldng pair 2f out: sn rdn and one pce* **20/1**

3536 **5** *4* **Tomintoul Star**[11] 1216 5-9-0 **53**....................................(b) PhillipMakin 14 44
(Ruth Carr) *prom: rdn along to chse ldng pair 3f out: drvn 2f out and grad wknd* **5/1**[3]

2330 **6** *5* **Noble Attitude**[41] 802 5-8-4 **46** oh1..................................... BillyCray(3) 6 25
(Richard Guest) *towards rr: wd st to stands' rail: rdn 2f out and kpt on appr fnl f: nvr a factor* **14/1**

030/ **7** *nk* **Dado Mush**[488] 7784 8-8-11 **50**.......................................(p) MarcHalford 11 29
(Terry Clement) *towards rr tl sme late hdwy* **50/1**

001- **8** *5* **Monsieur Pontaven**[236] 5438 4-8-9 **53**............................ LMcNiff(5) 2 20
(Robin Bastiman) *dwlt: a towards rr* **33/1**

400- **9** *1¾* **Plenilune (IRE)**[140] 7646 6-8-7 **46**................................. FrannyNorton 12 —
(Mel Brittain) *a towards rr* **25/1**

450- **10** *8* **Spahi (FR)**[168] 7284 5-8-8 **52**... SeanLevey(5) 10 —
(David O'Meara) *in tch: hdwy to chse ldrs 3f out: sn rdn and wknd over 2f out* **11/4**[1]

0/0- **11** *3½* **Mujahope**[256] 4795 6-8-8 **47**......................................(v) PatrickMathers 4 —
(Colin Teague) *dwlt: t.k.h and sn chsng ldrs: rdn along over 3f out and sn wknd* **50/1**

00-0 **12** *19* **Scintillating (IRE)**[67] 517 4-8-7 **46** oh1........................ TomEaves 5 —
(Ray Peacock) *prom: rdn along 1/2-way: sn wknd* **66/1**

1m 43.54s (-0.16) **Going Correction** 0.0s/f (Stan) **12** Ran SP% **122.3**
Speed ratings (Par 101): **100,98,97,95,91 86,85,80,79,71 67,48**
toteswingers:1&2 £7.90, 2&3 £6.70, 1&3 £6.80 CSF £27.11 CT £108.15 TOTE £3.50: £1.10, £3.50, £1.90; EX 33.70.
Owner Darren & Annaley Yates **Bred** M Kerr-Dineen **Trained** Westow, N Yorks

FOCUS
Low-grade fare, though it was at least soundly run, the field finishing well strung out. The winner is rated to the form of last year's win here.
T/Plt: £477.30 to a £1 stake. Pool of £46,004.96 - 70.36 winning units. T/Qpdt: £20.50 to a £1 stake. Pool of £4,612.00 - 167.34 winning units. JR

1368 WOLVERHAMPTON (A.W) (L-H)
Tuesday, April 19

OFFICIAL GOING: Standard
Wind: Almost nil Weather: Fine

1469 GOT THE FEELING? GET TO LADBROKES H'CAP — 5f 20y(P)
5:45 (5:45) (Class 6) (0-65,64) 4-Y-0+ **£1,706** (£503; £252) **Stalls** Low

Form RPR

3040 **1** **Francis Albert**[10] 1247 5-8-3 **53** oh1 ow3.................(p) JosephYoung(7) 5 57
(Michael Mullineaux) *w ldr: led 4f out: hdd 1/2-way: chsd ldr: rdn ins fnl f: r.o to ld post* **7/1**

0-50 **2** *shd* **Miss Firefly**[10] 1248 6-8-12 **55**.. J-PGuillambert 1 59
(Ron Hodges) *led 1f: chsd ldr tl led again 1/2-way: rdn: carried hd high and edgd rt over 1f out: hdd post* **9/2**[3]

05- **3** *1¼* **Schoolboy Champ**[129] 7841 4-9-7 **64**.............................. StephenCraine 4 63
(Patrick Morris) *hld up: hdwy over 1f out: sn rdn: r.o* **11/2**

4065 **4** *hd* **Fear Nothing**[20] 1034 4-9-2 **64**....................................(b) LeeTopliss(5) 6 62
(Ian McInnes) *chsd ldrs: rdn 1/2-way: r.o* **3/1**[2]

3006 **5** *nse* **Rightcar**[20] 1043 4-8-7 **50** oh5..................................(b) RobbieFitzpatrick 3 48
(Peter Grayson) *s.i.s: sn pushed along in rr: r.o ins fnl f: nt rch ldrs* **25/1**

000- **6** *2¼* **Canadian Danehill (IRE)**[157] 7446 9-9-0 **57**..................... TomQueally 2 47
(Robert Cowell) *s.i.s: sn prom: rdn 1/2-way: no ex ins fnl f* **11/4**[1]

530- **7** *6* **Gracie's Games**[175] 7154 5-8-6 **54**..........................(v) AdamBeschizza(5) 7 23
(Richard Price) *sn outpcd* **9/1**

62.00 secs (-0.30) **Going Correction** -0.075s/f (Stan) **7** Ran SP% **111.6**
Speed ratings (Par 101): **99,98,96,96,96 92,83**
toteswingers:1&2:£5.90, 2&3:£4.60, 1&3:£6.70 CSF £36.24 CT £181.95 TOTE £16.80: £6.30, £2.50; EX 36.20.
Owner Michael Mullineaux **Bred** R S And Mrs S H Kitching **Trained** Alpraham, Cheshire

FOCUS
A good pace for this tricky little 0-65 sprint, but the front pair were always 1-2. Weak form, the winner 4lb wrong.

1470 LADBROKES.COM H'CAP — 1m 5f 194y(P)
6:15 (6:15) (Class 4) (0-85,85) 4-Y-0+ **£3,399** (£1,011; £505; £252) **Stalls** Low

Form RPR

/221 **1** **Accumulate**[25] 965 8-8-5 **66** oh1.. JoeFanning 6 78
(Bill Moore) *chsd ldr 3f: remained handy: pushed along over 3f out: rdn to ld wl ins fnl f: styd on* **11/2**[3]

44-0 **2** *1¼* **Crocus Rose**[17] 1105 5-9-3 **78**.. JimmyQuinn 9 88
(Harry Dunlop) *hld up: hdwy over 4f out: rdn to ld over 1f out: hdd and unable qck wl ins fnl f* **5/1**[2]

-500 **3** *3* **Denton (NZ)**[17] 1097 8-9-10 **85**.......................................(t) SteveDrowne 3 91
(Jeremy Gask) *hld up: hdwy u.p over 1f out: nt trble ldrs* **10/1**

101- **4** *1½* **Never Can Tell (IRE)**[207] 6331 4-9-3 **80**..................... JamieSpencer 10 84
(Jamie Osborne) *led: rdn: edgd rt and hdd over 1f out: no ex ins fnl f* **13/2**

1513 **5** *2* **Gunslinger (FR)**[14] 1156 6-8-12 **73**.................................. PatCosgrave 4 74
(Michael Scudamore) *s.i.s: hld up: rdn over 2f out: r.o ins fnl f: nvr nrr* **22/1**

454- **6** *3½* **Proud Times (USA)**[45] 7698 5-9-9 **84**................................ TedDurcan 7 80
(Alan Swinbank) *prom: chsd ldr 11f out tl rdn wl over 1f out: wknd ins fnl f* **6/1**

122- **7** *nse* **First Fandango**[32] 6437 4-9-2 **79**...............................(vt) StevieDonohoe 2 75
(Tim Vaughan) *chsd ldrs: pushed along over 3f out: wknd ins fnl f* **7/2**[1]

1246 **8** *4* **Dart**[39] 838 7-8-5 **69**.. DeclanCannon(3) 5 60
(John Mackie) *s.i.s: hld up: hdwy over 3f out: rdn and wknd over 2f out* **25/1**

00-4 **9** *¾* **Yahrab (IRE)**[11] 1215 6-9-7 **82**... DavidNolan 8 71
(Declan Carroll) *prom: rdn over 2f out: wknd over 1f out* **20/1**

31-2 **10** *11* **Cozy Tiger (USA)**[48] 32 6-9-1 **76**....................................... TomQueally 1 50
(Willie Musson) *hld up: rdn over 3f out: sn wknd* **10/1**

3m 0.85s (-5.15) **Going Correction** -0.075s/f (Stan)
WFA 4 from 5yo+ 2lb **10** Ran SP% **113.0**
Speed ratings (Par 105): **111,110,108,107,106 104,104,102,101,95**
toteswingers:1&2:£5.50, 2&3:£14.10, 1&3:£5.80 CSF £31.03 CT £265.26 TOTE £5.00: £1.20, £3.80, £4.50; EX 34.30.
Owner C W Moore **Bred** Raymond Cowie **Trained** Ledsham, Cheshire

FOCUS
A competitive contest for this staying handicap. The winner is clearly improving despite his age, and this was a clear personal best.

1471 PUNCHESTOWN LIVE ON ATR SKY 415 (S) STKS — 5f 216y(P)
6:45 (6:46) (Class 6) 3-Y-0+ **£1,535** (£453; £226) **Stalls** Low

Form RPR

140 **1** **Steelcut**[12] 1204 7-9-11 67..(p) PatCosgrave 2 78
(David Evans) *a.p: chsd ldr 2f out: rdn to ld 1f out: styd on u.p* **12/1**

-125 **2** *¾* **Orpenindeed (IRE)**[31] 914 8-9-11 75.............................(t) AdamKirby 3 76
(Frank Sheridan) *led: rdn and hdd 1f out: styd on* **11/8**[1]

6233 **3** *1¾* **Cavitie**[10] 1248 5-9-2 58..(p) LouisBeuzelin(3) 7 64
(Andrew Reid) *prom: racd keenly: rdn over 1f out: styd on* **8/1**

4-60 **4** *7* **Rainy Night**[10] 1239 5-9-5 67...(p) LiamKeniry 4 42
(Reg Hollinshead) *chsd ldr over 2f: rdn over 2f out: wknd over 1f out* **9/2**[3]

3131 **5** *1* **Bonnie Prince Blue**[7] 1289 8-9-11 72............................(b) TomQueally 5 44
(James Given) *prom: chsd ldr over 3f out tl rdn 2f out: wknd over 1f out* **5/2**[2]

3-00 **6** *1¼* **Yungaburra (IRE)**[20] 1034 7-9-2 63.....................(t) AndrewHeffernan(3) 6 34
(David C Griffiths) *s.i.s: hld up: rdn and wknd over 1f out* **28/1**

1m 13.93s (-1.07) **Going Correction** -0.075s/f (Stan)
WFA 3 from 5yo+ 11lb **6** Ran SP% **111.1**
Speed ratings (Par 101): **104,103,100,91,90 88**
toteswingers:1&2 £4.30, 2&3 £2.50, 1&3 £6.20 CSF £28.65 TOTE £13.70: £4.60, £1.10; EX 45.50.The winner was bought in for 4,250gns.
Owner Shropshire Wolves 3 **Bred** Mrs B Skinner **Trained** Pandy, Monmouths

FOCUS
A modest seller with the favourite and fifth disappointing. The form is rated around the winner.

1472 LADBROKES MOBILE H'CAP — 7f 32y(P)
7:15 (7:15) (Class 6) (0-60,60) 3-Y-0 **£1,706** (£503; £252) **Stalls** High

Form RPR

5-36 **1** **Spirit Of Oakdale (IRE)**[46] 760 3-9-3 **56**.......................(v[1]) AdamKirby 1 63
(Walter Swinburn) *pushed along early: led 1f: chsd ldrs: rdn to ld over 1f out: hung rt ins fnl f: styd on* **5/1**[1]

625- **2** *1¼* **Empress Charlotte**[136] 7691 3-9-6 **59**........................... JamieSpencer 12 62+
(Michael Bell) *hld up: hdwy on outer over 1f out: rdn and r.o ins fnl f: nt rch wnr* **5/1**[1]

2105 **3** *1¾* **Titan Diamond (IRE)**[32] 887 3-8-12 **58**................... RachealKneller(7) 5 57
(Mark Usher) *mid-div: hdwy 1/2-way: rdn over 1f out: styd on same pce ins fnl f* **8/1**

000- **4** *hd* **Climaxfortackle (IRE)**[222] 5882 3-9-7 **60**................. RobbieFitzpatrick 3 58
(Derek Shaw) *mid-div: hdwy over 2f out: rdn over 1f out: styd on same pce ins fnl f* **12/1**

-155 **5** *1½* **Princess Gail**[18] 1082 3-9-4 **57**...................................... GrahamGibbons 8 51
(Mark Brisbourne) *led 6f out: rdn and hdd over 1f out: nt clr run and no ex ins fnl f* **15/2**

56-1 **6** *2* **Onlyfoalsandhorses (IRE)**[25] 967 3-8-12 **56**............ RyanPowell(5) 6 45+
(J S Moore) *hld up: swtchd lft and hdwy over 1f out: nt trble ldrs* **13/2**[2]

440- **7** *½* **Sarangoo**[222] 5874 3-9-7 **60**.. JimmyQuinn 4 47
(Malcolm Saunders) *hld up: hdwy over 1f out: no imp ins fnl f* **33/1**

060- **8** *3* **Cadmium Loch**[179] 7065 3-9-2 **55**..................................... RussKennemore 7 34
(Reg Hollinshead) *hmpd sn after s: in rr: rdn over 1f out: nvr on terms* **22/1**

563 **9** *½* **Misere**[35] 855 3-9-4 **57**.. StephenCraine 2 35
(Kevin Ryan) *mid-div: nt clr run over 2f out: sn rdn: wknd over 1f out* **7/1**[3]

00-3 **10** *3½* **Chillie Peppar**[15] 1132 3-9-4 **57**.................................. KirstyMilczarek 9 25
(George Prodromou) *sn chsng ldrs: rdn over 2f out: wknd ins fnl f* **12/1**

0-66 **11** *13* **Encore View**[14] 1149 3-9-2 **60**...(t) RyanClark(5) 10 —
(Nick Littmoden) *jnd ldr 6f out tl rdn over 2f out: wknd wl over 1f out* **15/2**

1m 30.01s (0.41) **Going Correction** -0.075s/f (Stan) **11** Ran SP% **116.5**
Speed ratings (Par 96): **94,92,90,90,88 86,85,82,81,77 62**
toteswingers:1&2 £5.80, 2&3 £6.90, 1&3 £4.40 CSF £28.65 CT £201.37 TOTE £5.10: £1.50, £1.30, £3.30; EX 32.50.
Owner Tops **Bred** Denis McDonnell **Trained** Aldbury, Herts

FOCUS
A good pace for this 0-60 7f handicap. Modest form, rated around the third and fourth.

1473 PUNCHESTOWN LIVE ON ATR VIRGIN 534 H'CAP — 2m 119y(P)
7:45 (7:46) (Class 6) (0-60,56) 4-Y-0+ £1,706 (£503; £252) Stalls Low

Form				RPR
3012	1		**Six Of Clubs**[21] 1032 5-8-13 **52**.....(b) JakePayne(7) 3 (Bill Turner) *a.p: led over 1f out: sn rdn: all out* 11/4[1]	60
4-31	2	*nse*	**Blackstone Vegas**[10] 1253 5-9-10 **56**..... RobbieFitzpatrick 7 (Derek Shaw) *hld up: hdwy over 1f out: swtchd lft ins fnl f: r.o wl: jst failed* 6/1[3]	64+
6605	3	*1 ½*	**Miles Of Sunshine**[13] 1181 6-9-5 **51**..... J-PGuillambert 4 (Ron Hodges) *led 1f: chsd ldrs: rdn and ev ch over 1f out: styd on same pce ins fnl f* 28/1	57
05-0	4	*1*	**Pocket Too**[8] 33 8-9-6 **52**.....(p) AdamKirby 6 (Matthew Salaman) *sn pushed along in rr: hdwy u.p fr over 1f out: nvr nrr* 20/1	57
-362	5	*½*	**Dot's Delight**[11] 1218 7-9-3 **49**.....(t) SilvestreDeSousa 10 (Mark Rimell) *s.i.s: hld up: hdwy over 1f out: nt rch ldrs* 7/2[2]	53
-045	6	*2 ¾*	**Spiritonthemount (USA)**[7] 1297 6-9-1 **47**.....(b) WilliamCarson 8 (Peter Hiatt) *pushed along in rr early: hdwy to chse ldr 14f out: led 12f out: clr 10f out: drvn along over 6f out: hdd and no ex over 1f out* 10/1	48
0-05	7	*14*	**Primera Rossa**[74] 419 5-8-13 **45**..... LiamKeniry 5 (J S Moore) *mid-div: rdn over 4f out: wknd wl over 1f out* 20/1	29
63-0	8	*3 ½*	**Barra Raider**[95] 173 4-8-8 **47**..... JamesSullivan(3) 12 (Roger Fisher) *hld up: rdn over 3f out: nvr on terms* 33/1	27
2-50	9	*3 ½*	**Mystified (IRE)**[62] 560 8-9-6 **52**.....(tp) TomEaves 9 (Roger Fisher) *led after 1f: hdd 12f out: chsd ldr tl over 4f out: rdn and wknd over 3f out* 17/2	28
-400	10	*shd*	**Indefinite Hope (ITY)**[4] 1374 4-9-4 **54**.....(t) JamesDoyle 11 (Frank Sheridan) *prom: chsd ldr over 4f out: rdn over 2f out: sn wknd* 10/1	30
00-	11	*6*	**Court Princess**[300] 3324 8-9-6 **55**..... AndrewHeffernan(3) 1 (Richard Price) *hld up: a in rr: wknd over 3f out* 25/1	23

3m 38.9s (-2.90) **Going Correction** -0.075s/f (Stan)
WFA 4 from 5yo+ 4lb **11 Ran SP% 111.6**
Speed ratings (Par 101): **103,102,102,101,101 100,93,92,90,90 87**
toteswingers:1&2 £2.50, 2&3 £41.40, 1&3 £26.60 CSF £16.41 CT £362.93 TOTE £3.50: £1.50, £2.60, £9.20; EX 17.70.
Owner Gongolfin **Bred** R V Young **Trained** Sigwells, Somerset

FOCUS
A good test was set for this ordinary staying handicap, and the time was fair for the grade. The winner's best form since he was a 2yo.

1474 WOLVERHAMPTON-RACECOURSE.CO.UK MAIDEN FILLIES' STKS 1f 103y(P)
8:15 (8:16) (Class 5) 3-Y-0+ £1,813 (£539; £269; £134) Stalls Low

Form				RPR
5-	1		**Sacred Shield**[201] 6512 3-8-9 0..... TomQueally 1 (Sir Henry Cecil) *chsd ldr: led ins fnl f: rdn out* 10/11[1]	64+
0060	2	*2 ½*	**Sweet Possession (USA)**[70] 451 5-9-7 44.....(p) JamesSullivan(3) 2 (Pat Eddery) *led: rdn over 1f out: hdd and unable qck ins fnl f* 66/1	62
3	3	*1 ½*	**Redhotdoc**[10] 1252 7-9-10 0..... JoeFanning 10 (Bill Moore) *prom: rdn over 2f out: styd on same pce ins fnl f* 14/1	59
	4	*3 ¼*	**Tiger Tess** 3-8-9 0..... SilvestreDeSousa 7 (Jonathan Portman) *s.i.s: hld up: r.o ins fnl f: nvr nrr* 18/1	49+
4	5	*¾*	**Dark Spirit (IRE)**[14] 1146 3-8-9 0..... RobertHavlin 3 (Tim Pitt) *prom: rdn over 2f out: wknd over 1f out* 7/1[3]	47
	6	*1 ¼*	**Ash Cloud (IRE)** 3-8-9 0..... RichardKingscote 4 (Tom Dascombe) *hld up: rdn over 3f out: n.d* 11/2[2]	45+
3	7	*1*	**Lady of Burgundy**[11] 1220 5-9-10 0..... LiamKeniry 8 (Mark Usher) *hld up: hdwy over 2f out: edgd lft and wknd over 1f out* 16/1	46
/	8	*2 ¼*	**Dancing Primo**[17] 5-9-10 0..... GrahamGibbons 6 (Mark Brisbourne) *chsd ldrs: rdn over 2f out: wknd over 1f out* 80/1	41
6/	9	*3 ¼*	**Napoleons Mistress (IRE)**[36] 6389 4-9-10 0..... JamieSpencer 9 (Nicky Henderson) *hld up: rdn and wknd over 2f out* 12/1	34
03	10	*3 ¼*	**Sienna Blue**[8] 1277 3-8-9 0..... JimmyQuinn 5 (Malcolm Saunders) *prom: pushed along 1/2-way: wknd over 2f out* 16/1	24

2m 0.58s (-1.12) **Going Correction** -0.075s/f (Stan)
WFA 3 from 4yo+ 15lb **10 Ran SP% 114.4**
Speed ratings (Par 100): **101,98,97,94,93 92,91,89,87,84**
toteswingers:1&2 £19.20, 2&3 £53.80, 1&3 £5.10 CSF £80.93 TOTE £1.90: £1.10, £4.30, £2.00; EX 43.90.
Owner K Abdulla **Bred** Juddmonte Farms Ltd **Trained** Newmarket, Suffolk

FOCUS
A weak maiden for fillies. Shaky form with the runner-up the key.
Sienna Blue Official explanation: jockey said trainer filly stopped quickly

1475 PLAY ROULETTE AT LADBROKES.COM CLASSIFIED STKS 1m 1f 103y(P)
8:45 (8:45) (Class 5) 3-Y-0 £2,266 (£674; £337; £168) Stalls Low

Form				RPR
4510	1		**Bertie Blu Boy**[3] 1392 3-9-0 67..... SilvestreDeSousa 4 (Paul Green) *chsd ldr: rdn over 3f out: styd on u.p to ld wl ins fnl f* 7/2[3]	72
043	2	*hd*	**Barnum (USA)**[31] 909 3-9-0 70..... JoeFanning 5 (Mark Johnston) *prom: qcknd to ld over 4f out: rdn over 1f out: hdd wl ins fnl f* 5/2[1]	71
003-	3	*¾*	**Cunning Act**[197] 6634 3-9-0 69..... StephenCraine 3 (Jonathan Portman) *hld up: rdn over 2f out: hdwy over 1f out: r.o* 7/2[3]	70
3233	4	*¾*	**Colebrooke**[13] 1189 3-9-0 67..... RoystonFfrench 1 (Mark Johnston) *led: hdd over 4f out: rdn over 2f out: styd on same pce ins fnl f* 10/3[2]	68
205-	5	*4 ½*	**Retreat Content (IRE)**[200] 6542 3-9-0 69.....(b[1]) JamieSpencer 2 (Jamie Osborne) *chsd ldrs: rdn over 2f out: wknd over 1f out* 8/1	59

2m 3.09s (1.39) **Going Correction** -0.075s/f (Stan) **5 Ran SP% 107.2**
Speed ratings (Par 98): **90,89,89,88,84**
CSF £11.86 TOTE £6.10: £4.40, £1.10; EX 10.90.
Owner B & B Hygiene Limited **Bred** H Bourchier **Trained** Lydiate, Merseyside

FOCUS
A small turnout but a very tight classified contest where all five runners were only separated by 3lbs on official ratings. A muddling affair until the pace increased in the back straight. A length personal best from the winner.
T/Plt: £211.10 to a £1 stake. Pool of £61,462.52 - 212.50 winning units. T/Qpdt: £14.20 to a £1 stake. Pool of £7,753.63 - 403.10 winning units. CR

EPSOM (L-H)
Wednesday, April 20

OFFICIAL GOING: Derby course - good (good to firm in places); sprint course - good to firm (good in places)
Rail dolled out up to 8yds from 1m to winning post adding circa 10yds to races on round course
Wind: Moderate across Weather: Sunny

1476 INVESTEC ASSET MANAGEMENT H'CAP — 5f
2:00 (2:00) (Class 3) (0-95,93) 4-Y-0+
£7,477 (£2,239; £1,119; £560; £279; £140) Stalls High

Form				RPR
0520	1		**Falasteen (IRE)**[4] 1395 4-8-13 **85**..... JamieSpencer 5 (David Nicholls) *mde virtually all: edgd rt ins fnl 2f: drvn and styd on strly ins fnl f* 20/1	98
01-3	2	*1 ¾*	**Beat The Bell**[14] 1166 6-9-2 **88**..... GrahamGibbons 1 (David Barron) *chsd ldrs: drvn over 2f out: hdwy over 1f out: styd on to chse wnr ins fnl f but no imp* 8/1[3]	95+
350	3	*1 ¾*	**Cape Royal**[16] 1140 11-8-7 **79** oh4.....(bt) RichardKingscote 13 (Milton Bradley) *pressed ldrs: chsd wnr 2f out: no imp over 1f out and outpcd into 3rd ins fnl f* 20/1	79
136-	4	*½*	**Piazza San Pietro**[227] 5787 5-9-0 **86**..... NeilCallan 9 (Andrew Haynes) *sn in tch and drvn along: hdwy over 1f out: kpt on ins fnl f but no imp on ldng trio* 14/1	85
3211	5	*3 ¼*	**Best Trip (IRE)**[13] 1197 4-8-8 **80**..... FrannyNorton 11 (Richard Guest) *w wnr to 1/2-way: wknd ins fnl f* 10/1	67
660-	6	*¾*	**Skylla**[194] 6706 4-9-0 **86**..... PaulHanagan 14 (Richard Fahey) *in tch: pushed along and sme hdwy 2f out: wknd appr fnl f* 15/2[2]	70
036-	7	*nse*	**Indian Trail**[215] 6140 11-8-8 **80**.....(v) DaneO'Neill 10 (David Nicholls) *sn pushed along styd on ins fnl f: nvr a threat* 14/1	64
0101	8	*1*	**Breathless Kiss (USA)**[14] 1166 4-9-7 **93**.....(b) KierenFallon 4 (Kevin Ryan) *outpcd in rr: sme late hdwy* 15/2[2]	73
2602	9	*1 ¼*	**Silaah**[25] 989 7-9-6 **92**.....(p) AdrianNicholls 2 (David Nicholls) *in tch on outside: rdn 2f out: sn hung lft: wknd ins fnl f* 8/1[3]	68
0-00	10	*1*	**Fratellino**[17] 1111 4-9-7 **93**..... JamesDoyle 6 (Alan McCabe) *outpcd* 10/1	65
2233	11	*¾*	**Sir Geoffrey (IRE)**[13] 1200 5-8-13 **85**.....(b) IanMongan 7 (David Nicholls) *pressed ldrs over 3f* 16/1	55
020-	12	*3 ½*	**Archers Road (IRE)**[186] 6918 4-9-7 **93**..... RyanMoore 12 (David Barron) *broke wl: sn outpcd* 4/1[1]	50+
600-	13	*hd*	**Bertoliver**[221] 5967 7-9-0 **86**..... JackMitchell 8 (Stuart Williams) *pressed ldrs over 3f* 22/1	42
500-	14	*2*	**Ghostwing**[205] 6429 4-9-1 **87**.....(v) ChrisCatlin 3 (John Gallagher) *outpcd fr 1/2-way* 66/1	36

54.25 secs (-1.45) **Going Correction** -0.10s/f (Good) **14 Ran SP% 118.5**
Speed ratings (Par 107): **107,104,101,100,95 94,94,92,90,88 87,82,81,78**
toteswingers:1&2: £26.90, 2&3: £62.30, 1&3: £128.50 CSF £163.74 CT £3324.59 TOTE £19.40: £4.80, £3.20, £5.10; EX 218.50 TRIFECTA Not won..
Owner Dr Marwan Koukash **Bred** Mrs Anne Marie Burns **Trained** Sessay, N Yorks

FOCUS
A typically good competitive sprint over this downhill track and a number were sweating in the paddock beforehand. Last year's third and sixth were again taking part, and the veteran 2007 winner was also in the line-up. The front running winner recorded a slight personal bedst, but form over this C&D is rarely reliable.

NOTEBOOK
Falasteen(IRE), who was 2lb better off with Breathless Kiss compared with their recent Beverley running, had been well beaten since when looking wayward. However, he had won over 6f on his only previous visit here and clearly likes the place, as he blasted from the stalls and got across well to the stands' rail from his low draw. In front from halfway, he never looked like being caught and, although he will go up for this, connections are sure to have the 'Dash' back here in mind for him now, with possibly Chester in between. (op 18-1)
Beat The Bell ◆ handles a sharp track well but this was his first run here. He had finished just behind the winner at Beverley last time and did well to come from out of the pack and chase his old rival home, especially as he raced from the lowest draw. (op 11-1 tchd 15-2)
Cape Royal is a veteran now but won this in 2007 and scored here last August. He again ran well from his high draw, and his record over C&D is now 3-14 plus seven placings. (op 22-1)
Piazza San Pietro was progressive last season, winning six times, but was 4lb above his last winning mark. He ran well on this first try here and should come on for the outing. (op 16-1)
Best Trip(IRE), who had gained all his wins at Kempton on Polytrack, had only raced twice on turf and never over as short as this. He showed good early speed from his decent draw, but could not sustain it. (op 7-1)
Skylla, a dual juvenile winner who had not scored since, had a bit to find with the runner-up on last season's form and ran reasonably from a good draw on this return to action. (tchd 8-1)
Indian Trail, the winner's stable companion, had not won since June 2009 but that was here, and he finished third in this in 2009. He ran well on this comeback, considering he was out the back early, and the 6f handicap at the Derby meeting could be on the agenda again. (op 12-1)
Breathless Kiss(USA) ◆, a five-time 5f winner, was a narrow scorer on her seasonal debut with the first two here close behind. Out the back early, she ran on well late and batter can be expected back on a more conventional track. Her rider reported the filly was unsuited by the track. Official explanation: jockey said filly did not handle the track (op 8-1 tchd 7-1)
Silaah, arguably better at six and 7f, had been on the go through the winter and also went to Meydan, but had posted a good effort over this trip on his return. He did not perform too badly from his low draw. (op 13-2)
Archers Road(IRE) won first time out last season and was sent off favourite despite the fact this was his first run here. He tracked the pace but was already struggling when rather carried back by a weakening rival. His rider reported that the gelding was denied a clear run. Official explanation: jockey said gelding was denied a clear run (op 9-2)
Bertoliver likes this track, being a winner and twice placed in four previous starts including finishing third in this last season. However, this was his seasonal debut and his wins have all come after a recent start, so it was no surprise he faded out of things. He will be a different proposition if returning for the Dash. (op 25-1 tchd 20-1)

1477 INVESTEC GREAT METROPOLITAN H'CAP — 1m 4f 10y
2:35 (2:38) (Class 3) (0-95,94) 4-Y-0+
£9,346 (£2,799; £1,399; £700; £349; £175) Stalls Centre

Form				RPR
365-	1		**Sunny Game**[179] 7084 4-8-9 **82**..... JamieSpencer 6 (Michael Bell) *trckd ldrs: led over 2f out: pushed along ins fnl f: comf* 3/1[1]	100+

226- **2** *hd* **Rock A Doodle Doo (IRE)**[319] 2758 4-8-11 **84**............. PaulHanagan 3 99+
(William Jarvis) *hld up in rr: hdwy and nt clr run over 2f out: hdwy on outside sn after and styng on whn hmpd and swtchd rt over 1f out: str run ins fnl f to press for 2nd cl home: no ch w wnr: fin 3rd: plcd 2n* **10/1**

011- **3** *2 1/4* **Harlestone Times (IRE)**[204] 6437 4-9-2 **89**...................... TedDurcan 13 103+
(John Dunlop) *hld up in rr: hdwy and n.m.r over 2f out: hdwy sn after: rdn and hung lft over 1f out: chsd wnr 1f out: kpt on but no imp: fin 2nd: plcd 3rd* **8/1**[3]

110- **4** *2 3/4* **Trovare (USA)**[243] 5273 4-8-9 **82**..................................... JimCrowley 12 91
(Amanda Perrett) *chsd ldrs: drvn to chal over 2f out: outpcd by wnr over 1f out: lost 2nd ins fnl f and styd on same pce* **12/1**

114- **5** *2* **Zigato**[228] 5747 4-9-0 **87**.. WilliamBuick 2 93
(John Gosden) *trckd ldrs: pushed along over 2f out: styd on same pce* **11/2**[2]

211- **6** *3* **Dynamic Drive (IRE)**[185] 6957 4-8-12 **85**........................ AdamKirby 11 86
(Walter Swinburn) *in rr: hdwy 4f out: chsd ldrs 2f out: wknd over 1f out* **10/1**

120- **7** *hd* **Kings Troop**[68] 7084 5-8-12 **84**... RyanMoore 4 85
(Alan King) *hld up in rr: n.m.r over 2f out: edgd rt and hdwy over 1f out: kpt on ins fnl f but nvr any ch* **8/1**[3]

5544 **8** *3/4* **Hawaana (IRE)**[18] 1097 6-8-7 **82**................................ DeclanCannon(3) 1 81
(Gay Kelleway) *in rr: n.m.r over 2f out: sme prog ins fnl f* **20/1**

32-2 **9** *3/4* **Dahaam**[90] 235 4-8-9 **82**.. MartinLane 10 80
(David Simcock) *in rr: hdwy fr 4f out: chsd ldrs ins fnl 3f: wknd over 1f out* **16/1**

225- **10** *7* **Snoqualmie Star**[202] 6506 4-9-2 **89**................................(b) DaneO'Neill 5 79
(David Elsworth) *towards rr: hdwy on ins fr 3f out: nt clr run appr fnl 2f: no ch after* **12/1**

11-0 **11** *8* **Licence To Till (USA)**[39] 846 4-9-7 **94**.......................... KierenFallon 7 68
(Mark Johnston) *chsd ldr: led 3f out: hdd over 2f out: sn btn* **25/1**

10-0 **12** *16* **Missionaire (USA)**[18] 1102 4-8-10 **83**................................(p) NeilCallan 8 32
(Tony Carroll) *led tl hdd 3f out: wknd rapidly* **50/1**

010- **13** *32* **Mister Angry (IRE)**[185] 6971 4-9-5 **92**............................ FrankieDettori 9 —
(Mark Johnston) *in rr: dropped away qckly ins fnl 3f: virtually p.u fnl 2f* **14/1**

2m 39.15s (0.25) **Going Correction** +0.025s/f (Good)
WFA 4 from 5yo+ 1lb 13 Ran SP% **119.3**
Speed ratings (Par 107): **100,98,98,96,95 93,93,92,92,87 82,71,50**
toteswingers: 1&2 £8.40, 1&3 £7.70, 2&3 £10.40 CSF £32.63 CT £223.37 TOTE £4.40: £1.60, £3.70, £2.70; EX 40.50 Trifecta £267.40 Pool: £791.50 - 2.19 winning units..
Owner Tsega Horses **Bred** Tsega Breeding Limited **Trained** Newmarket, Suffolk

FOCUS
The ground on the round track was slightly slower than the sprint course, riding good, good to firm in places. A decent renewal of this long-established handicap but the pace did not appear that quick and, as is often the case here, there were hard-luck stories. The front six are all progressive 4yos and this was a good return from the winner.

NOTEBOOK
Sunny Game is a 1m2f winner on good ground, whose five previous outings had all been on Flat tracks. Making his seasonal debut, he was well backed and swept through to lead in the straight before scoring in ready fashion. He will go up for this, but the impression was he has improved since last year and could well follow up. (op 7-2 tchd 5-2)

Rock A Doodle Doo(IRE) ◆, a three-time Polytrack winner early last year and placed at up to 1m6f on turf, had not run since June but was clearly ready for this reappearance. He came from the back but was hampered by the drifting Harlestone Times, which cost him second place, and he was awarded that position by the Stewards. He looks capable of building on this. (tchd 12-1)

Harlestone Times(IRE) improved to win successive handicaps at 1m2f and this trip on varying ground last September but was 10lb higher on his first start since. He came from the back of the field to chase home the winner, but in doing so drifted down the camber, squeezing up Rock A Doodle Doo. This resulted in him being relegated to third. (op 7-1 tchd 13-2)

Trovare(USA), a progressive three-time winner at up to 1m5f on fast ground, was racing off 5lb higher than for his last success on this seasonal return. He travelled well in the wake of the leaders for a long way before fading, and is another who can do better with this behind him.

Zigato recorded successive wins at up to 1m6f on soft ground and Polytrack last season, but had the cheekpieces left off for this reappearance. Looking as if the run would bring him on, he ran reasonably despite wandering about and not looking happy on the camber in the straight. (tchd 5-1)

Dynamic Drive(IRE), a dual winner in a week at up to 1m5f on good and easy ground last September, was another who drifted under pressure and might prefer more give in the ground. (op 14-1)

Kings Troop, a dual C&D winner last season on good and easy ground, was 9lb higher but was fit from jumping. However, his rider let him drift back from a decent early pitch, and when he asked his mount for a run, encountered trouble, first being leant on by Dynamic Drive and then being short of room. He is better than this effort suggests and a more positive ride would be in his favour. His rider confirmed that the gelding was denied a clear run. Official explanation: jockey said gelding was denied a clear run

1478 INVESTEC DERBY TRIAL (CONDITIONS RACE) 1m 2f 18y
3:10 (3:11) (Class 2) 3-Y-0 **£18,693** (£5,598; £2,799; £1,401; £699) **Stalls** Low

Form RPR

0- **1** **Slumber**[204] 6442 3-8-13 0.. MichaelHills 3 96
(B W Hills) *hld up in tch: hdwy 3f out: edgd lft and led wl over 2f out: c clr over 1f: out: easily* **7/1**

1-53 **2** *3 1/2* **Borug (USA)**[48] 753 3-8-13 93....................................(p) FrankieDettori 1 89
(Saeed Bin Suroor) *in rr but in tch: hdwy fr 3f out: chsd wnr ins fnl 2f: nvr any ch but wl clr of 3rd* **5/2**[3]

32-6 **3** *4* **Planet Waves (IRE)**[14] 1175 3-8-13 77......................... PhilipRobinson 5 81
(Clive Brittain) *s.i.s: sn rcvrd and chsd ldr after 2f to 5f out: outpcd fr 3f out: styd on again for mod 3rd ins fnl f* **16/1**

2-11 **4** *3 3/4* **Musawama (IRE)**[13] 1194 3-8-13 81................................... RichardHills 4 74
(John Gosden) *led tl hdd wl over 2f out: sn no ch w wnr: wknd ins fnl 2f* **15/8**[1]

215- **5** *7* **Weapon Of Choice (IRE)**[184] 6982 3-8-13 87...........(t) JamieSpencer 2 60
(David Simcock) *in tch: trckd ldr 5f out: one pce whn hmpd wl over 2f out: no ch after* **9/4**[2]

2m 8.98s (-0.72) **Going Correction** +0.025s/f (Good) **5** Ran SP% **112.5**
Speed ratings (Par 104): **103,100,97,94,88**
CSF £25.04 TOTE £8.00: £3.10, £1.80; EX 30.50.
Owner K Abdulla **Bred** Millsec Limited **Trained** Lambourn, Berks

FOCUS
Probably the best recent winners of this Derby trial were the subsequent Arlington Million winners Storming Home and Debussy. This year's line-up looked unlikely to make any impact on the betting for the big race in June. The favourite disappointed and the form looks a bit limited.

NOTEBOOK
Slumber, the least experienced runner, stepped up considerably on his debut last season to score with something in hand, despite running rather green. He looks a decent prospect and, although he needs to improve considerably again to rate a credible contender in the Derby itself, this was still highly encouraging in beating a 93-rated runner with relative ease. He might go for the Chester Vase now. (op 8-1 tchd 9-1)

Borug(USA) who improved for the fitting of cheekpieces and switch to synthetics, set the standard here but could do no more than follow the winner home having been held up. It is questionable whether he is worth his 93 rating on turf though. (op 4-1)

Planet Waves(IRE), a fairly exposed performer at shorter trips and rated just 77, stayed on for third over this longer trip and might possibly be the best guide to the level. (tchd 20-1)

Musawama(IRE) made the running but faded tamely in the straight once passed by the winner. He came into this off the back of two wins on Polytrack and might not have been suited by the fast ground and undulating course. (op 11-10 tchd 2-1)

Weapon Of Choice(IRE) tracked the pace but was another to back out of things quite quickly. His best form has been when the ground was softer than good and this surface was quite different. His rider reported that the colt was unsuited by the going. Official explanation: jockey said colt was unsuited by the good (good to firm in places) ground (op 3-1)

1479 INVESTEC CITY AND SUBURBAN STKS (H'CAP) 1m 2f 18y
3:45 (3:48) (Class 2) (0-105,99) 4-Y-0+
£21,808 (£6,531; £3,265; £1,634; £815; £409) **Stalls** Low

Form RPR

340- **1** **Spanish Duke (IRE)**[179] 7100 4-9-6 **95**............................. EddieAhern 5 110+
(John Dunlop) *t.k.h: hld up in mid-div: hdwy on bit over 2f out: qcknd smartly to ld over 1f out: in n.d after: easily* **14/1**

015- **2** *1* **Resurge (IRE)**[179] 7100 6-9-5 **94**... IanMongan 2 105
(Stuart Kittow) *chsd ldrs: drvn to ld over 2f out: hdd over 1f out: sn no ch w wnr but kpt on wl for 2nd* **16/1**

56-4 **3** *4* **Ramona Chase**[18] 1102 6-8-6 **81**..........................(t) RobbieFitzpatrick 13 84
(Michael Attwater) *in rr: hdwy and nt clr run 3f out: sn hrd drvn: styd on wl ins fnl f to take 3rd cl home but no ch w ldng duo* **12/1**

321- **4** *1/2* **Opera Gal (IRE)**[207] 6355 4-9-4 **93**................................ DavidProbert 11 95
(Andrew Balding) *chsd ldrs: rdn and ev ch over 2f out: sn outpcd by ldng duo and lost 3rd cl home* **6/1**[2]

111- **5** *1* **Beachfire**[265] 4504 4-9-8 **97**...(b[1]) WilliamBuick 3 97
(John Gosden) *hld up in rr: pushed along and nt clr run 3f out: edging lft and hdwy 2f out: drvn and styd on ins fnl f but nvr gng pce to rch ldrs* **9/2**[1]

040- **6** *nk* **Shavansky**[165] 7350 7-9-4 **93**... JamesMillman 6 92
(Rod Millman) *s.i.s: in rr: rdn and hdwy on outside over 2f out: kpt on ins fnl f but nvr any ch* **20/1**

6016 **7** *4 1/2* **Georgebernardshaw (IRE)**[39] 846 6-9-1 **90**........... JamieSpencer 14 80
(David Simcock) *sn led: hdd over 2f out: wknd over 1f out* **25/1**

-320 **8** *3 3/4* **Tartan Gigha (IRE)**[18] 1094 6-9-10 **99**............................ KierenFallon 7 82
(Mark Johnston) *in rr: sme hdwy towards outside over 3f out: nvr rchd ldrs and no ch fnl 2f* **9/1**

21-1 **9** *1 1/2* **Ingleby Spirit**[15] 1154 4-9-4 **93**...................................... PaulHanagan 12 73
(Richard Fahey) *chsd ldrs: rdn over 3f out: wkng whn hmpd ins fnl 2f* **8/1**

220- **10** *9* **Sirvino**[165] 7350 6-9-8 **97**... GrahamGibbons 9 59
(David Barron) *in tch: rdn 3f out: btn sn after* **13/2**[3]

00-0 **11** *17* **Gaily Noble (IRE)**[18] 1102 5-8-10 **85**............................... JimCrowley 8 —
(Andrew Haynes) *chsd ldrs: rdn over 3f out: wknd qckly over 2f out* **33/1**

5102 **12** *10* **King Olav (UAE)**[11] 1238 6-9-2 **91**.. NeilCallan 1 —
(Tony Carroll) *in rr: rdn and sme hdwy towards outside over 4f out: nvr rchd ldrs and sn wknd* **50/1**

20-2 **13** *4* **Sand Skier**[27] 1011 4-9-1 **90**.. FrankieDettori 10 —
(Mark Johnston) *s.i.s: sn chsng ldrs: wknd qckly over 3f out* **9/2**[1]

2m 7.50s (-2.20) **Going Correction** +0.025s/f (Good) 13 Ran SP% **118.8**
Speed ratings (Par 109): **109,108,105,104,103 103,99,96,95,88 74,66,63**
toteswingers: 1&2 £25.10, 1&3 £30.80, 2&3 £29.00 CSF £209.55 CT £2760.55 TOTE £17.40: £4.60, £4.70, £4.20; EX 245.90 TRIFECTA Not won..
Owner Windflower Overseas Holdings Inc **Bred** Windflower Overseas Holdings Inc **Trained** Arundel, W Sussex

FOCUS
This good, competitive handicap usually falls to either a battle-hardened handicapper or a relatively unexposed sort with Group-race potential. The time was good, being 1.48secs faster than the earlier Derby Trial. The winner impressed and should do better, and the level is set around the second.

NOTEBOOK
Spanish Duke(IRE) ◆ scored in emphatic fashion, having travelled strongly throughout. He had previously seemed suited by some cut in the ground but had handled fast ground and the track at Brighton, so there was reason to hope he would cope with conditions here. He was keen under restraint early, but followed the runner-up through on the inside before switching to the outside as that rival went through a gap on the rail. It was soon clear he was travelling best and he powered past when asked, although the second was not stopping. He is likely to have a mark in the low-100s once reassessed, so Listed and Group races are likely to be on the agenda sooner rather than later. (op 20-1)

Resurge(IRE) took his record over C&D to 2-4, including two seconds. He travelled well in the wake of the leaders and took the gap next to the rail early in the straight. He looked briefly as if he might win before the winner loomed alongside. He might prefer more ease in the ground, but looks sure to win races again this season. (tchd 18-1)

Ramona Chase's only win since 2007 was over C&D last September and he ran well again, staying on steadily up the straight having been at the back turning in. (op 14-1 tchd 16-1)

Opera Gal(IRE), a dual winner at around this trip on fast and easy ground, was 8lb higher than for her win last September. Making her seasonal debut, she ran well enough before fading and should come on for the outing. (op 8-1)

Beachfire was lightly raced but progressive last season, winning four of five starts, with his trademark a strong, late finish. Wearing a visor for the first time on this seasonal debut but 6lb above his last winning mark, he was held up as usual but did not get a clear run early in the straight before staying on past beaten rivals. He can do better than this and it is debatable whether the headgear was of any help. This was his first run left-handed on turf and the feeling is this track did not play entirely to his strengths. (op 7-2 tchd 10-3)

Shavansky had gained all his turf wins at this trip on fast ground and ran an encouraging race on this reappearance, staying on well in the straight. (op 16-1)

Georgebernardshaw(IRE), for whom last month's 1m2f Polytrack win was his first since 2008, ran well enough from the front but seems best with more cut in the ground.

Tartan Gigha(IRE), a dual winner over the extended mile here at the Derby meeting (his only two previous starts on the track), had yet to prove he stayed this far. He never got competitive but will surely be seen to better effect if returning here in six weeks' time in his bid for a hat-trick. (op 7-1)

Ingleby Spirit had won successive races over this trip on fast and easy ground, one on his seasonal return earlier this month, but he was 7lb higher and dropped away in the straight, having raced up with the pace. (op 10-1)

Gaily Noble(IRE)'s rider reported the gelding stopped quickly. Official explanation: jockey said gelding stopped quickly (op 25-1)

Sand Skier was the disappointment of the race. Well-backed although he had not won since his juvenile days, he looked reasonably handicapped but lost his place at halfway. (op 13-2)

1480 INVESTEC SPECIALIST BANK MAIDEN STKS — 1m 114y
4:20 (4:20) (Class 5) 3-4-Y-0 — **£3,238** (£963; £481; £240) **Stalls** Low

Form — RPR

50- **1** **Barney Rebel (IRE)**[214] 6200 3-8-11 0 .... MichaelHills 5 76+
(B W Hills) *trckd ldrs: gd hdwy 2f out: drvn and qckdn ins fnl f: led cl home* **11/8**[1]

00- **2** *nk* **Carousel**[172] 7231 3-8-6 0 .... RichardKingscote 1 70
(Ralph Beckett) *led: rdn and kpt on wl whn chal fr ins fnl 2f: hdd and outpcd cl home* **11/2**

20-5 **3** *1 1/2* **Calaf**[13] 1203 3-8-11 75 .... JamieSpencer 3 73
(Jane Chapple-Hyam) *plld hrd and wnt rt after s: chsd ldr 7f out: drvn to chal ins fnl 2f: one pce ins fnl f* **3/1**[2]

5- **4** *8* **Danish Pastry**[167] 7312 3-8-6 0 .... WilliamBuick 4 49
(John Gosden) *carried rt s: sn rcvrd and in tch: drvn to cl on ldrs 3f out: nvr on terms and wknd fr 2f out* **9/2**[3]

5 *3 3/4* **Dakar (GER)** 3-8-11 0 .... IanMongan 2 45
(Pat Phelan) *in rr but in tch: sme hdwy 3f out: nvr on terms and wknd 2f out* **20/1**

0 **6** *2 1/2* **Daliana**[15] 1146 3-8-6 0 .... MartinLane 6 34
(Michael Bell) *plld hrd early and settled in rr: sme prog 3f out: sn wknd* **20/1**

1m 50.09s (3.99) **Going Correction** +0.025s/f (Good) **6** Ran SP% **110.2**
Speed ratings (Par 103): **83,82,81,74,70 68**
toteswingers: 1&2 £2.30, 1&3 £2.00, 2&3 £1.90 CSF £9.08 TOTE £2.30: £1.10, £2.30; EX 9.90.
Owner Rebel Racing **Bred** Marston Stud And Fleming Thoroughbreds **Trained** Lambourn, Berks

FOCUS
An ordinary maiden whose best recent winner was probably the subsequently useful hurdler Bothy. The early pace was steady and it turned into something of a three-furlong sprint. The form, which has been rated around the third, is a bit dubious.
Calaf Official explanation: jockey said colt hung right and was unsteerable

1481 INVESTEC INVESTMENTS H'CAP — 1m 114y
4:50 (4:50) (Class 5) (0-75,75) 3-Y-0 — **£3,238** (£963; £481; £240) **Stalls** Low

Form — RPR

05-2 **1** **Baqaat (USA)**[26] 959 3-9-3 **71** .... RichardHills 2 78+
(Ed Dunlop) *trckd ldr: drvn along 3f out: chal 2f out: led appr fnl f: edgd lft sn after: styd on wl and kpt finding ex cl home* **11/4**[1]

350- **2** *1/2* **Barathea Dancer (IRE)**[154] 7481 3-9-6 **74** .... JackMitchell 1 80
(Roger Teal) *chsd ldrs: drvn over 2f out: styd on wl u.p thrght ins fnl f but a jst hld by wnr* **11/2**[3]

10-4 **3** *nse* **Diplomasi**[93] 193 3-8-11 **65** .... PhilipRobinson 4 71+
(Clive Brittain) *chsd ldrs tl outpcd 4f out and wd into st over 3f out: styd on wl fr over 1f out: kpt on to press for 2nd cl home but a hld by wnr* **14/1**

21 **4** *1* **Greenflash**[14] 1179 3-9-7 **75** .... RichardHughes 5 78+
(Richard Hannon) *led: pushed along whn chal fr 2f out: hdd appr fnl f: styd on same pce fnl 120yds* **4/1**[2]

240- **5** *1* **High On The Hog (IRE)**[181] 7035 3-8-13 **67** .... NeilCallan 10 68
(John Dunlop) *hld up in rr: hdwy over 3f out: styd on fnl 2f: kpt on cl home but nt rch ldrs* **17/2**

-222 **6** *3* **Uncle Dermot (IRE)**[14] 1179 3-9-2 **70** .... DaneO'Neill 9 64
(Brendan Powell) *t.k.h in rr: hdwy over 2f out: styd on ins fnl f but nvr gng pce to get into contention* **10/1**

045- **7** *9* **Face Value**[175] 7163 3-9-4 **72** .... MartinDwyer 7 45
(Brian Meehan) *s.i.s pushed along over 4f out: a in rr* **8/1**

2-62 **8** *3 3/4* **Sottovoce**[61] 600 3-9-0 **68** .... RyanMoore 8 33
(Simon Dow) *chsd ldrs tl wknd over 4f out: rn wd bnd over 3f out* **15/2**

0-20 **9** *3/4* **Tymismoni (IRE)**[56] 655 3-8-0 **61** oh4 .... NathanAlison(7) 3 24
(Brett Johnson) *plld hrd in rr: lost tch fnl 3f* **40/1**

6265 **10** *53* **Aloneinthestreet (USA)**[14] 1191 3-8-13 **67** .... KierenFallon 6 —
(Mark Johnston) *rdn and lost tch over 4f out: t.o* **16/1**

1m 46.98s (0.88) **Going Correction** +0.025s/f (Good) **10** Ran SP% **119.5**
Speed ratings (Par 98): **97,96,96,95,94 92,84,80,80,32**
toteswingers:1&2: £3.90, 2&3: £15.20, 1&3: £11.30 CSF £18.47 CT £165.32 TOTE £4.20: £1.90, £1.70, £5.00; EX 23.90 Trifecta £375.10 Pool: £608.31 - 1.20 winning units..
Owner Hamdan Al Maktoum **Bred** Shadwell Estate Co Ltd **Trained** Newmarket, Suffolk

FOCUS
A fair handicap that was run at a sound gallop, with the time more than 3secs faster than the preceding maiden. A decent handicap for the grade with a clear personal best from the winner.
T/Jkpt: Not won. T/Plt: £3,240.70 to a £1 stake. Pool of £92,117.36 - 20.75 winning tickets.
T/Qpdt: £155.20 to a £1 stake. Pool of £6,481.86 - 30.90 winning tickets. ST

1330 KEMPTON (A.W) (R-H)
Wednesday, April 20

OFFICIAL GOING: Standard
Wind: Moderate, across (towards stands) Weather: Fine but cloudy, warm

1482 RACING AT SKYSPORTS.COM CLASSIFIED CLAIMING STKS — 6f (P)
6:20 (6:20) (Class 6) 3-Y-0 — **£1,748** (£516; £258) **Stalls** Low

Form — RPR

221- **1** **Magic Cross**[139] 7666 3-8-3 66 .... AdamBeschizza(5) 2 62
(Philip McBride) *trckd ldng pair: prog to go 2nd 2f out and sn clsd on ldr: rdn and styd on wl to ld last 100yds* **5/2**[2]

442 **2** *3/4* **Reachtothestars (USA)**[26] 964 3-8-8 58 .... (t) JamieSpencer 5 60
(Noel Quinlan) *led at gd clip: gng strly and more than 2 l clr over 2f out: rdn and pressed 1f out: hdd last 100yds: nt qckn* **3/1**[3]

0-05 **3** *2 1/2* **Brave Battle**[6] 1334 3-8-10 68 .... (b[1]) KieranO'Neill(5) 4 59
(Richard Hannon) *chsd ldr: rdn and no imp over 2f out: sn lost 2nd: one pce after* **6/1**

41-6 **4** *3 1/4* **Chilledtothebone**[19] 1074 3-8-10 67 .... (v) KierenFallon 3 43
(Linda Stubbs) *v sluggishly away: had to work hrd to rcvr and dispute 3rd 1/2-way: drvn over 2f out: nt qckn and sn btn* **13/8**[1]

0453 **5** *19* **Magical Star**[8] 1280 3-7-11 50 .... HannahNunn(7) 1 —
(Mark Rimmer) *dwlt: mostly in last: wl bhd over 2f out: t.o* **33/1**

1m 11.88s (-1.22) **Going Correction** -0.20s/f (Stan) **5** Ran SP% **108.9**
Speed ratings (Par 96): **100,99,95,91,66**
CSF £10.04 TOTE £2.70: £1.40, £2.00; EX 8.80.
Owner P J McBride **Bred** J W P Clark **Trained** Newmarket, Suffolk

FOCUS
A modest contest run at a fast pace. The runner-up is the best guide to the level.

1483 FREE ENTRY FOR BETDAQ MEMBERS H'CAP — 6f (P)
6:50 (6:50) (Class 5) (0-70,69) 3-Y-0 — **£1,565** (£1,565; £357) **Stalls** Low

Form — RPR

26-1 **1** **Apollo D'Negro (IRE)**[16] 1131 3-9-4 **69** .... JohnFahy(3) 6 75
(Clive Cox) *chsd ldng trio: rdn to chal wl over 1f out and upsides: narrowly hdd ins fnl f and edgd lft: rallied to dead-heat last stride* **9/2**[2]

045- **1** *dht* **Captain Noble (IRE)**[144] 7595 3-9-4 **66** .... FergusSweeney 3 72
(Peter Makin) *trckd ldr: rdn to dispute ld over 1f out: narrow advantage fnl f and edgd lft: jnd post* **6/1**[3]

26-0 **3** *2* **In Babylon (GER)**[17] 1108 3-9-2 **64** .... (t) TomQueally 1 63+
(Tom Dascombe) *hld up in 7th: prog 2f out: styd on to take 3rd ins fnl f: unable to chal* **10/1**

335- **4** *3/4* **Regal Bullet (IRE)**[126] 7871 3-8-13 **61** ow1 .... AdamKirby 2 58
(Dean Ivory) *led: hdd and nt qckn over 1f out: lost 3rd ins fnl f* **25/1**

4211 **5** *1 1/2* **Rambo Will**[13] 1193 3-9-4 **66** .... DavidProbert 5 58
(J R Jenkins) *chsd ldng pair: rdn over 2f out: steadily outpcd fr over 1f out* **6/1**[3]

230- **6** *2 3/4* **Whitecrest**[160] 7400 3-9-5 **67** .... FrannyNorton 7 50
(John Spearing) *chsd ldng quartet: rdn over 2f out: steadily wknd over 1f out* **20/1**

-563 **7** *1 1/4* **Saucy Buck (IRE)**[23] 1019 3-9-5 **67** .... JamieGoldstein 10 46
(Ralph Smith) *hld up in last trio: shuffled along over 2f out: modest late prog: nvr nr ldrs* **40/1**

06-2 **8** *3 1/4* **Delira (IRE)**[15] 1149 3-9-2 **64** .... KierenFallon 9 33
(Jonathan Portman) *racd wd in midfield: rdn over 2f out: no prog over 1f out: wknd* **8/1**

41- **9** *1/2* **Guided Missile (IRE)**[144] 7595 3-9-7 **69** .... JimmyFortune 4 36
(Andrew Balding) *s.i.s: a wl in rr: rdn and no prog over 2f out* **15/8**[1]

36-5 **10** *2 1/2* **Snow Ridge**[16] 1131 3-9-5 **67** .... SebSanders 11 26
(Andrew Haynes) *dwlt: mostly last and nvr gng wl: nvr a factor* **40/1**

160- **11** *1* **Miss Dutee**[224] 5863 3-9-0 **62** .... PatDobbs 8 18
(Richard Hannon) *chsd ldrs in 6th: rdn over 2f out: sn wknd* **50/1**

1m 12.39s (-0.71) **Going Correction** -0.20s/f (Stan) **11** Ran SP% **117.2**
Speed ratings (Par 98): **96,96,93,92,90 86,85,80,80,76 75**WIN: Apollo D'Negro £2.60 Captain Noble: £5.50 PL: A £1.30, CN £2.40, IB £5.10 EX: A/CN £20.20 CN/AN £18.70 CSF: A/CN £14.83 CN/A £15.62 TRI: A/CN/In Babylon £131.60 CN/A/IB £136.78 toteswingers: A&C £5.80, A&3 £11.70, C&3 £6.10, £0.027, £OwnerFour Seasons Racing Ltd Bred Trifecta £Roger Macnair Trained Ogbourne Maisey, Wilts.
Owner Gwyn Powell and Peter Ridgers **Bred** Patrick Cummins **Trained** Lambourn, Berks

FOCUS
An interesting sprint handicap confined to 3yos, in which few got competitive and two came clear in the closing stages. The judge couldn't split them at the line. The form is limited by the proximity of the fourth.
Saucy Buck(IRE) Official explanation: jockey said, regarding running and riding, that his orders were to tuck in from a wide draw and hold on to the gelding, but it broke slowly, was outpaced early, ran on but became tired closing stages.

1484 BETDAQ.COM EXCHANGE PRICE MULTIPLES MEDIAN AUCTION MAIDEN STKS — 1m 3f (P)
7:20 (7:20) (Class 6) 3-Y-0 — **£1,748** (£516; £258) **Stalls** Low

Form — RPR

0- **1** **Cry Fury**[187] 6883 3-9-3 0 .... SteveDrowne 1 86+
(Roger Charlton) *hld up in 5th: prog 4f out to chse ldr over 3f out: drvn and clsd to ld wl over 1f out: sn clr: swvd bdly lft 100yds out: jst hld on* **4/1**[2]

0-4 **2** *shd* **Greyfriars Drummer**[8] 1298 3-9-3 0 .... KierenFallon 2 85+
(Mark Johnston) *chsd ldr 1f: mostly 3rd after: pushed along fr 1/2-way: outpcd and drvn over 2f out: styd on to go 2nd ins fnl f: clsd on wnr fin: jst failed* **11/1**[3]

3 **3** *7* **Agiaal (USA)**[13] 1203 3-9-3 0 .... RichardHills 10 73
(John Gosden) *dwlt: rcvrd to trck ldr after 1f: led 5f out: drew more than 2 l clr over 2f out and gng strly: rdn and hdd wl over 1f out: fdd tamely* **4/7**[1]

030- **4** *2 1/2* **Hollow Tree**[180] 7059 3-9-3 73 .... JimmyFortune 4 68
(Andrew Balding) *led to 5f out: dropped to 4th and struggling 3f out: one pce after* **12/1**

05- **5** *1* **Swift Blade (IRE)**[193] 6742 3-9-3 0 .... JimCrowley 9 66
(William Knight) *hld up in 8th: prog to go 5th over 3f out: outpcd and no imp on ldrs over 2f out* **12/1**

3 **6** *1 1/2* **Clarion Call**[25] 983 3-9-3 0 .... TomQueally 5 64
(Eve Johnson Houghton) *trckd ldng trio to over 4f out: sn pushed along: outpcd 3f out: no imp after* **14/1**

0 **7** *1* **Take A Spin**[7] 1311 3-9-3 0 .... ChrisCatlin 8 62
(Paul Cole) *chsd ldrs in 6th: pushed along 1/2-way: no prog 4f out: sn wl outpcd: plugged on* **33/1**

00 **8** *27* **May Contain Nuts**[9] 1271 3-9-3 0 .... FergusSweeney 7 —
(Brendan Powell) *hld up last: nvr a factor: wknd 3f out: t.o* **66/1**

0 **9** *20* **Mundesley**[9] 1277 3-9-3 0 .... (t) RichardKingscote 3 —
(Tom Dascombe) *nvr bttr than 7th: last fr 1/2-way: sn wknd and eased: wl t.o* **66/1**

2m 18.88s (-3.02) **Going Correction** -0.20s/f (Stan) **9** Ran SP% **120.0**
Speed ratings (Par 96): **102,101,96,95,94 93,92,72,58**
toteswingers: 1&2 £5.00, 1&3 £1.10, 2&3 £3.60 CSF £48.13 TOTE £5.20: £1.50, £2.50, £1.10; EX 39.30 Trifecta £102.40 Pool: £8716.39 - 62.93 winning units..
Owner K Abdulla **Bred** Juddmonte Farms Ltd **Trained** Beckhampton, Wilts

FOCUS
A dramatic finish to this maiden with plenty to like about the front pair, although the form level is a bit fluid.

1485 LAY BACK AND WIN AT BETDAQ.COM H'CAP — 1m 3f (P)
7:50 (7:51) (Class 4) (0-80,80) 3-Y-0 — **£4,129** (£1,228; £614; £306) **Stalls** Low

Form — RPR

251- **1** **Parlour Games**[175] 7178 3-9-6 **79** .... AhmedAjtebi 4 87+
(Mahmood Al Zarooni) *hld up in 6th: plenty to do whn rdn over 2f out and lugging rt: prog wl over 1f out: wnt 2nd and clsd ins fnl f: led last 50yds* **13/5**[1]

1223 **2** *1 1/4* **School For Scandal (IRE)**[14] 1168 3-9-5 **78** .... (b) GregFairley 6 84
(Mark Johnston) *led after 2f: sn clr: 6 l up 4f out: rdn 2f out: tired but stl 3 l ahd 1f out: collared last 50yds* **10/1**

223- **3** *1/2* **El Mansour (USA)**[205] 6414 3-9-4 **77** .... AdamKirby 1 82
(Clive Cox) *led 2f: chsd clr ldr after: drvn 3f out: grad clsd over 1f out but lost 2nd last 100yds* **9/2**

1- **4** 1 3/4 **Brown Panther**[160] 7400 3-9-0 **73** .... RichardKingscote 3 75
(Tom Dascombe) *t.k.h early: chsd ldng pair: hrd rdn over 2f out: lost 3rd over 1f out: plugged on* **11/4**[2]

1216 **5** 5 **Malice Or Mischief (IRE)**[17] 1113 3-9-7 **80** .... NeilCallan 2 73
(Tony Carroll) *chsd ldng trio: rdn wl over 2f out: lost 4th and wknd over 1f out* **22/1**

3-11 **6** 7 **Songjiang**[56] 650 3-9-6 **79** .... WilliamBuick 5 59
(John Gosden) *n.m.r s: hld up last: rdn 3f out: no prog: eased ins fnl f* **4/1**[3]

33-1 **7** 1 3/4 **Odin (IRE)**[97] 140 3-9-5 **78** .... DaneO'Neill 7 55
(David Elsworth) *settled in 5th: first one u.p wl over 3f out: wl btn over 2f out* **9/1**

2m 19.0s (-2.90) **Going Correction** -0.20s/f (Stan) **7** Ran SP% **116.1**
Speed ratings (Par 100): **102,101,100,99,95 90,89**
CSF £29.40 TOTE £4.00: £2.20, £2.50; EX 31.00.
Owner Godolphin **Bred** Darley **Trained** Newmarket, Suffolk

FOCUS
There was a good pace on here and this looked a reasonable race for the grade. The form is rated on the positive side.

1486 BETDAQ MOBILE APPS H'CAP (LONDON MILE QUALIFIER) 1m (P)
8:20 (8:20) (Class 6) (0-60,60) 4-Y-O+ **£1,748** (£516; £258) **Stalls** Low

Form RPR

0600 **1** **Teen Ager (FR)**[14] 1177 7-8-6 **48** .... JohnFahy(3) 7 56
(Paul Burgoyne) *slowest away: settled wl in rr: gd prog fr 2f out: c through to chal ins fnl f: edgd rt but sustained effrt to ld last 100yds* **16/1**

0524 **2** 1/2 **Diddums**[5] 1357 5-8-0 **46** .... KatiaScallan(7) 2 52
(Alastair Lidderdale) *s.i.s: hld up in rr: prog on inner 2f out: rdn to ld 1f out: hdd and no ex last 100yds* **10/1**

3030 **3** 3/4 **Rainsborough**[6] 1333 4-9-2 **55** ....(e) JimCrowley 3 60
(Peter Hedger) *hld up in tch: gng strly bhd ldrs over 2f out: effrt to ld jst over 1f out: sn hdd and nt qckn* **15/2**[3]

5100 **4** nk **Join Up**[21] 1052 5-9-3 **59** .... KierenFox(3) 4 63
(Mark Brisbourne) *t.k.h: trckd ldng pair: lost pl and nt clr run 2f out: got through and rdn to chal 1f out: nt qckn* **10/1**

/10- **5** 3 **My Flame**[312] 2965 6-9-0 **53** .... FergusSweeney 13 50
(J R Jenkins) *racd wd: prom: rdn to chal and nrly upsides over 1f out: wknd ins fnl f* **33/1**

515 **6** shd **Spinning Ridge (IRE)**[9] 1276 6-9-7 **60** ....(b) DavidProbert 12 57
(Ronald Harris) *hld up towards rr: effrt over 2f out on outer: cl enough over 1f out but edging lft: fdd* **8/1**

00-1 **7** 1 1/4 **Bubbly Braveheart (IRE)**[7] 1308 4-9-6 **59** .... IanMongan 10 53
(Pat Phelan) *mde most: drvn over 2f out: hdd jst over 1f out: wknd ins fnl f* **3/1**[1]

00-0 **8** 3 **Motty's Gift**[14] 1177 4-9-0 **53** ....(v) AdamKirby 8 40
(Walter Swinburn) *wl in rr: u.p fr 1/2-way: struggling after and nvr on terms* **16/1**

5204 **9** nk **Christmas Coming**[14] 1184 4-9-4 **57** ....(t) NeilCallan 1 43
(Tony Carroll) *t.k.h: trckd ldng pair: stl cl up over 1f out: wknd ins fnl f* **8/1**

2625 **10** 2 1/2 **Clearing House**[6] 1333 6-9-7 **60** .... KirstyMilczarek 11 41
(John Ryan) *pressed ldr: upsides fr 1/2-way to wl over 1f out: wknd rapidly sn after* **6/1**[2]

5310 **11** hd **Guildenstern (IRE)**[14] 1177 9-8-11 **50** .... KierenFallon 5 30
(Michael Squance) *n.m.r after 1f in midfield: shkn up and lost pl over 2f out: sn btn* **11/1**

000 **P** **Jonny Ebeneezer**[14] 1177 12-9-3 **56** ....(be) JamesDoyle 6 —
(David Flood) *in tch: wknd 3f out: lost action and p.u 2f out* **33/1**

1m 39.69s (-0.11) **Going Correction** -0.20s/f (Stan) **12** Ran SP% **117.4**
Speed ratings (Par 101): **92,91,90,90,87 87,86,83,82,80 80,—**
toteswingers:1&2 £33.40, 2&3 £13.30, 1&3 £43.00 CSF £165.72 CT £1317.50 TOTE £24.80: £7.30, £5.60, £3.40; EX 245.00 Trifecta £548.20 Pool: £2000.54 - 2.70 winning units..
Owner L Tomlin **Bred** Haras De Beauvoir **Trained** Shepton Montague, Somerset
■ Stewards' Enquiry : Kirsty Milczarek two-day ban: careless riding (May 4-5)

FOCUS
A competitive heat which didn't seem to be run at a strong gallop early, but the leaders appeared to kick on for home too early and that played into the hands of the hold up horses. The form is modest but straightforward.

1487 RACING AT SKYSPORTS H'CAP 1m 4f (P)
8:50 (8:53) (Class 6) (0-60,60) 3-Y-O **£1,748** (£516; £258) **Stalls** Centre

Form RPR

00-2 **1** **Watered Silk**[7] 1312 3-8-12 **51** .... PatDobbs 5 58+
(Marcus Tregoning) *reluctant to enter stalls: hld up in 5th: pushed along and effrt over 2f out: rdn and clsd to ld 1f out: forged clr* **8/11**[1]

5441 **2** 3 **Gower Rules (IRE)**[7] 1312 3-9-4 **57** 6ex................ RichardKingscote 2 59
(John Bridger) *led 1f: sn settled in 3rd: chsd ldr wl over 2f out: clsd to ld over 1f out: hdd and outpcd 1f out* **11/2**[2]

060- **3** nse **Waterborne**[198] 6634 3-9-2 **60** .... KieranO'Neill(5) 3 62
(Roger Charlton) *trckd ldrs: pushed along over 3f out: tried to mount a chal over 1f out: kpt on but wl outpcd ins fnl f* **7/1**[3]

-000 **4** 5 **Neighbourhood (USA)**[23] 1018 3-9-1 **54** .... GregFairley 7 48
(Mark Johnston) *settled in 5th: u.p fr 1/2-way: sn dropped to last: plugged on fr over 2f out* **33/1**

-006 **5** 1 **Westhaven (IRE)**[61] 591 3-8-11 **50** ....(b[1]) DaneO'Neill 4 42
(David Elsworth) *s.v.s: in tch in last pair: rdn 3f out: hanging bdly rt over 2f out and nt keen: no ch after* **14/1**

050 **6** 4 **Harry Lime**[12] 1211 3-9-7 **60** .... KierenFallon 8 46
(Mark Johnston) *trckd ldr after 2f: led 3f out and kicked on: drvn 2f out: wknd rapidly and hdd over 1f out* **7/1**[3]

0046 **7** 37 **Ocean's Dream Day (IRE)**[16] 1134 3-8-13 **52**........(p) KirstyMilczarek 1 —
(John Ryan) *led after 1f and set decent pce: hdd & wknd rapidly 3f out: t.o* **20/1**

2m 34.15s (-0.35) **Going Correction** -0.20s/f (Stan) **7** Ran SP% **112.7**
Speed ratings (Par 96): **93,91,90,87,86 84,59**
toteswingers:1&2 £1.80, 2&3 £2.80, 1&3 £1.30 CSF £4.96 CT £15.26 TOTE £2.10: £1.90, £1.10; EX 4.80 Trifecta £22.60 Pool: £323.47 - 10.56 winning units..
Owner Mr And Mrs A E Pakenham **Bred** Mr & Mrs A E Pakenham **Trained** Lambourn, Berks

FOCUS
A moderate handicap but the winner looks to have more to offer.

1488 REWARDS4RACING.COM H'CAP 7f (P)
9:20 (9:22) (Class 5) (0-75,75) 4-Y-O+ **£2,417** (£713; £357) **Stalls** Low

Form RPR

544- **1** **Perfect Point (IRE)**[247] 5150 4-9-2 **70** .... AdamKirby 3 82+
(Walter Swinburn) *trckd ldrs: edgd lft but prog to go 2nd over 1f out: drvn to ld ins fnl f: styd on wl* **3/1**[1]

-021 **2** 1 1/2 **Maze (IRE)**[14] 1178 6-9-7 **75** .... NeilCallan 6 83
(Tony Carroll) *racd freely: led: edgd lft fr 2f out: hdd and no ex ins fnl f* **7/1**[3]

50-1 **3** 1/2 **Rondeau (GR)**[11] 1232 6-9-6 **74** .... GeorgeBaker 12 81
(Patrick Chamings) *dropped in fr wd draw: hld up and sn in 6th: effrt over 2f out: styd on to take 3rd ins fnl f* **8/1**

1431 **4** 2 1/4 **West Leake (IRE)**[14] 1177 5-8-12 **66** .... LiamKeniry 8 67
(Paul Burgoyne) *dwlt: t.k.h and sn trckd ldrs: drvn and effrt 2f out: nt qckn over 1f out: fdd* **7/1**[3]

-003 **5** shd **Ongoodform (IRE)**[35] 867 4-9-7 **75** .... LiamJones 4 75
(Paul D'Arcy) *dwlt: sn chsd ldr: rdn over 2f out: lost 2nd and fdd over 1f out* **4/1**[2]

0-40 **6** 3/4 **Exceedingly Bold**[42] 806 4-9-1 **69** ....(t) DaneO'Neill 10 67
(Jo Crowley) *hld up in 8th: rdn and effrt on outer over 2f out: plugged on but nvr gng pce to threaten* **7/1**[3]

1-01 **7** 4 1/2 **Cativo Cavallino**[22] 1026 8-8-10 **67** .... NataliaGemelova(3) 7 53
(John E Long) *chsd ldng pair: drvn over 2f out: sn lost pl and btn* **12/1**

24/3 **8** 2 1/4 **Viking Dancer**[50] 720 4-9-2 **70** .... JimmyFortune 9 50
(Andrew Balding) *racd wd: chsd ldrs: lost pl and struggling 1/2-way: wl btn over 2f out* **10/1**

0-00 **9** shd **Advertise**[9] 1269 5-9-4 **72** .... EddieCreighton 2 52
(Joseph Tuite) *a in same pl and nvr on terms: no prog 2f out* **33/1**

-000 **10** 2 1/4 **Ensnare**[14] 1177 6-8-11 **65** .... StevieDonohoe 1 39
(Noel Quinlan) *outpcd and a last* **40/1**

1m 24.72s (-1.28) **Going Correction** -0.20s/f (Stan) **10** Ran SP% **115.8**
Speed ratings (Par 103): **99,97,96,94,94 93,88,85,85,82**
toteswingers:1&2 £7.10, 2&3 £4.60, 1&3 £6.10 CSF £24.15 CT £155.91 TOTE £4.00: £2.10, £2.60, £4.10; EX 35.10 Trifecta £341.80 Part won. Pool of £461.95 - 0.91 winning units..
Owner Second Circle **Bred** Joseph Rogers **Trained** Aldbury, Herts

FOCUS
Not many got into this, but the winner is unexposed and looks the type to go in again. The runner-up and fourth help set the level.
T/Plt: £139.40 to a £1 stake. Pool of £50,492.57 - 264.33 winning tickets. T/Qpdt: £21.20 to a £1 stake. Pool of £5,459.30 - 190.50 winning tickets. JN

[1209] NEWCASTLE (L-H)
Wednesday, April 20

OFFICIAL GOING: Good to firm (firm in places; 8.0)
Wind: light 1/2 behind Weather: fine and sunny

1489 EUROPEAN BREEDERS' FUND NOVICE STKS 5f
5:05 (5:06) (Class 4) 2-Y-O **£4,144** (£1,233; £616) **Stalls** High

Form RPR

1 **1** **Lily's Angel (IRE)**[14] 1165 2-8-11 0................ TonyHamilton 4 87
(Richard Fahey) *hld up: trckd ldng pair: hdwy on ins to chal over 1f out: led 1f out: rdn and hld on* **7/4**[1]

2 **2** nk **Stonefield Flyer**[19] 1071 2-9-0 0................ PaulMulrennan 5 89
(Keith Dalgleish) *taken v early to post and led to s: led: hdd 1f out: kpt on wl: no ex towards fin* **3/1**[2]

1 **3** 8 **Marford Missile (IRE)**[12] 1209 2-8-13 0................ RossAtkinson(3) 3 62
(Tom Dascombe) *chsd ldrs: rdn and hung lft over 2f out: wknd over 1f out* **17/2**[3]

60.16 secs (-0.94) **Going Correction** -0.25s/f (Firm) **3** Ran SP% **71.9**
Speed ratings (Par 94): **97,96,83**
CSF £2.78 TOTE £1.50; EX 2.70.
Owner Middleham Park Racing XLVIII **Bred** N And Mrs N Nugent **Trained** Musley Bank, N Yorks
■ Tony Hamilton's first winner since returning from injury.

FOCUS
This had looked a decent contest considering it contained three previous winners, but it was dealt a disappointing blow when two runners came out during the morning. There was another twist when the favourite Hamza got really upset in the stalls and was withdrawn (7/4, deduct 35p in the £). Had he run, using the second-placed horse as a guide, he should have won. A cautious view of the form has been taken.

NOTEBOOK
Lily's Angel(IRE) had won on debut from a race-fit stablemate, so looked of obvious interest. She was getting weight from the runner-up here despite being a previous winner, and her next race might be a Listed contes in May at York. (op 9-4)
Stonefield Flyer got to the lead soon after the start and showed a good attitude under pressure once joined, but was unable to hold off the persistent challenge of Lily's Angel. Keith Dalgleish's horse, who was taken to the start very early, ought to have no trouble getting his head in front soon considering this effort. (op 7-2)
Marford Missile(IRE) showed a bit of pace to make a successful debut over C&D, but could stay with Stonefield Flyer as he blazed off in front, and was beaten before things got interesting. (op 10-1 tchd 11-1)

1490 LA TAXIS H'CAP 1m 2f 32y
5:35 (5:35) (Class 4) (0-85,84) 4-Y-O+ **£2,719** (£809; £404; £202) **Stalls** Low

Form RPR

0/ **1** **Desert Romance (IRE)**[225] 5845 5-9-7 **84**................ SilvestreDeSousa 1 97
(David O'Meara) *mde all: rdn over 2f out: styd on gamely ins fnl f* **15/2**

100- **2** 1 3/4 **Line Of Duty (IRE)**[195] 6698 4-9-6 **83**................ RobertWinston 4 92
(Alan Swinbank) *trckd wnr: chal over 3f out: sn rdn: kpt on same pce ins fnl f* **7/2**[2]

450- **3** 2 3/4 **Munsarim (IRE)**[182] 7012 4-8-11 **77**................ MichaelO'Connell(3) 2 81
(Keith Dalgleish) *trckd ldrs: effrt over 3f out: one pce* **4/1**[3]

63-3 **4** nse **The Galloping Shoe**[18] 1098 6-9-6 **83**................ TonyCulhane 5 86
(Alistair Whillans) *s.i.s: sn nudgled along detached in last: hrd drvn 5f out: hdwy 3f out: kpt on ins fnl f* **7/2**[2]

532- **5** 17 **Desert Vision**[160] 7414 7-8-12 **78**................(vt) JamesSullivan(3) 6 47
(Michael Easterby) *chsd ldrs: drvn over 3f out: lost pl over 2f out: eased* **10/1**

10-0 **6** 13 **Mainland (USA)**[18] 1097 5-8-9 **72**................ PaulMulrennan 3 15
(Tracy Waggott) *dwlt: hld up: hdwy over 4f out: drvn 3f out: wknd 2f out: sn heavily eased* **11/4**[1]

2m 8.50s (-3.40) **Going Correction** -0.20s/f (Firm) **6** Ran SP% **112.0**
Speed ratings (Par 105): **105,103,101,101,87 77**
toteswingers:1&2 £5.10, 2&3 £3.10, 1&3 £8.70 CSF £33.27 TOTE £9.70: £2.60, £1.40; EX 44.20.
Owner R G Fell **Bred** Gainsborough Stud Management Ltd **Trained** Nawton, N Yorks

FOCUS
The top four in the weights didn't appear to have much in hand on the handicapper, so this form may not turn out to be strong. The front pair were always 1-2 and Silvestre De Sousa deserves plenty of credit for dictating a pace to suit his mount. A personal best from the ex-Irish winner.

Mainland(USA) Official explanation: jockey said gelding never travelled

1491 COOPERS MARQUEES H'CAP 1m 4f 93y
6:05 (6:06) (Class 5) (0-70,68) 4-Y-0+ **£2,331** (£693; £346; £173) **Stalls** Low

Form RPR
44-0 **1** **Capable Guest (IRE)**[99] 118 9-8-10 **56**.............................. TomEaves 4 64
(George Moore) *hld up in mid-div: effrt on ins over 3f out: led over 1f out: styd on strly* **14/1**

45-3 **2** *2 ¼* **Hail Tiberius**[17] 1107 4-9-7 **68**.............................. DuranFentiman 6 72
(Tim Walford) *t.k.h in rr: hdwy over 4f out: styd on to take 2nd last 75yds* **3/1**[1]

46-0 **3** *½* **Law To Himself (IRE)**[18] 1099 4-9-7 **68**.................... RobertWinston 1 72
(Alan Swinbank) *trckd ldrs: t.k.h: drvn and hmpd 3f out: sn led: hdd over 1f out: kpt on same pce* **11/2**[3]

-020 **4** *½* **Lady Norlela**[7] 1305 5-8-4 **57**.............................. ShaneBKelly(7) 3 60
(Brian Rothwell) *in rr: hdwy on ins 3f out: sn chsng ldrs: one pce fnl 2f* **22/1**

455 **5** *1 ½* **General Duke's**[11] 1243 4-9-1 **62**..............................(t) PhillipMakin 8 62
(Kevin Ryan) *chsd ldrs: drvn and hmpd over 3f out: one pce fnl 2f* **8/1**

45-6 **6** *nk* **Heart Of Dubai (USA)**[15] 1153 6-8-7 **53** oh3..............(p) KellyHarrison 9 53
(Micky Hammond) *hld up in rr: hdwy on inner over 2f out: plld wd 1f out: kpt on* **16/1**

10-0 **7** *nse* **Dean Iarracht (IRE)**[17] 1107 5-9-3 **63**..............................(p) DavidAllan 2 63
(Tracy Waggott) *dwlt: in rr: pushed along over 4f out: kpt on fnl 2f* **8/1**

50-0 **8** *2 ¾* **Simple Jim (FR)**[17] 1107 7-8-9 **55**.............................. SilvestreDeSousa 7 50
(David O'Meara) *hld up in rr: sme hdwy on outside over 2f out: kpt on fnl f: nvr a factor* **4/1**[2]

004- **9** *2 ¼* **Hurlingham**[172] 7228 7-9-4 **64**..............................(b) PaulMulrennan 5 56
(Michael Easterby) *trckd ldrs: t.k.h: wknd over 1f out* **16/1**

0-06 **10** *4 ½* **Valdan (IRE)**[11] 1243 7-8-13 **62**..............................(t) AndrewHeffernan(3) 11 47
(Maurice Barnes) *swtchd lft after s: led: hdd over 2f out: lost pl over 1f out: bhd whn eased nr fin* **16/1**

11 *10* **Tropenfeuer (FR)**[200] 4-8-13 **60**.............................. PaddyAspell 10 27
(James Moffatt) *chsd ldrs: drvn over 3f out: lost pl over 2f out: bhd whn heavily eased clsng stages* **40/1**

2m 43.23s (-2.37) **Going Correction** -0.20s/f (Firm)
WFA 4 from 5yo+ 1lb **11** Ran SP% **113.7**
Speed ratings (Par 103): **99,97,97,96,95 95,95,93,92,89 82**
toteswingers:1&2 £12.50, 2&3 £3.50, 1&3 £17.10 CSF £53.95 CT £264.66 TOTE £12.10: £5.50, £1.50, £1.30; EX 31.40.
Owner Bentons Racing **Bred** Mountarmstrong Stud **Trained** Middleham Moor, N Yorks

FOCUS
An ordinary-looking handicap run at a moderate gallop early. Probably just ordinary form.
Dean Iarracht(IRE) Official explanation: jockey said gelding was slowly away
Hurlingham Official explanation: jockey said gelding ran too free

1492 SPORTPOOL.CO.UK MAIDEN STKS 1m 2f 32y
6:35 (6:37) (Class 5) 3-Y-0+ **£2,331** (£693; £346; £173) **Stalls** Low

Form RPR
53- **1** **Danadana (IRE)**[190] 6827 3-8-10 0.............................. J-PGuillambert 1 87+
(Luca Cumani) *trckd ldrs: wnt 2nd over 3f out: chal over 1f out: led last 150yds: pushed out* **15/8**[2]

2 **2** *½* **Munbaher (IRE)**[15] 1151 3-8-10 0.............................. TadhgO'Shea 3 84+
(Mark Johnston) *led: qcknd over 3f out: jnd over 1f out: hdd and no ex ins fnl f* **8/11**[1]

3 *13* **Harvey's Hope**[30] 5-9-13 0.............................. DavidAllan 7 61
(Keith Reveley) *s.s: hld up in last: hdwy on ins 3f out: wnt modest 3rd 2f out: kpt on* **20/1**

6 **4** *3 ½* **Khalashan (FR)**[6] 1328 5-9-13 0.............................. TonyHamilton 4 54
(Peter Niven) *s.s: towards rr: pushed along over 4f out: kpt on fnl 2f: nvr on terms* **80/1**

356- **5** *1 ¾* **Taste The Victory (USA)**[305] 3208 4-9-13 72.............. RobertWinston 6 51
(Alan Swinbank) *trckd ldrs: drvn over 3f out: wknd ins fnl f* **9/1**[3]

0 **6** *2* **Silvers Spirit**[12] 1210 5-9-8 0.............................. PaulMulrennan 8 42
(Keith Reveley) *stdd s: hld up in rr: pushed along over 4f out: nvr on terms* **50/1**

5 **7** *9* **Lure of The Night (IRE)**[12] 1212 4-9-13 0.............................. TomEaves 5 29
(Brian Rothwell) *chsd ldrs: lost pl over 2f out: sn bhd* **40/1**

2m 11.6s (-0.30) **Going Correction** -0.20s/f (Firm)
WFA 3 from 4yo+ 17lb **7** Ran SP% **113.1**
Speed ratings (Par 103): **93,92,82,79,78 76,69**
toteswingers:1&2: £1.02, 2&3: £3.50, 1&3: £4.80 CSF £3.47 TOTE £4.40: £1.60, £1.10; EX 3.80.

Owner Sheikh Mohammed Obaid Al Maktoum **Bred** Darley **Trained** Newmarket, Suffolk

FOCUS
It's unlikely too many superstars were hidden away in this field, but the two fancied runners streaked away from the remainder and look above average. The winner is probably a bit better than the bare form.

1493 SENDRIG CONSTRUCTION H'CAP 5f
7:05 (7:06) (Class 6) (0-60,60) 4-Y-0+ **£1,683** (£501; £250; £125) **Stalls** High

Form RPR
2452 **1** **We'll Deal Again**[7] 1307 4-9-5 **58**..............................(b) PaulMulrennan 3 71
(Michael Easterby) *trckd ldrs: led over 2f out: hdd 1f out: rdr dropped whip ins fnl f: kpt on to ld last 50yds* **4/1**[2]

04- **2** *½* **Time Medicean**[193] 6741 5-9-6 **59**.............................. TonyCulhane 11 70
(Paul Midgley) *trckd ldrs: led appr fnl f: sn rdn and edgd lft: hdd and no ex wl ins fnl f* **5/4**[1]

20-3 **3** *3 ½* **Choc'A'Moca (IRE)**[13] 1204 4-8-13 **57**..............................(v) NeilFarley(5) 1 56
(Declan Carroll) *racd wd: led tl over 2f out: wknd ins fnl f* **10/1**

-506 **4** *nse* **Rio's Girl**[21] 1034 4-9-0 **56**..............................(p) AmyRyan(3) 10 54
(Kevin Ryan) *dwlt: sn chsng ldrs: edgd lft 2f out: kpt on ins fnl f* **15/2**[3]

3300 **5** *1 ¾* **Galpin Junior (USA)**[12] 1213 5-9-1 **54**.............................. TomEaves 9 46
(Ruth Carr) *chsd ldrs: wknd over 1f out* **10/1**

0300 **6** *¾* **Tyrannosaurus Rex (IRE)**[12] 1213 7-8-8 **47** oh1 ow1 RobertWinston 8 36
(Derek Shaw) *prom: outpcd over 2f out: kpt on ins fnl f* **14/1**

00-0 **7** *½* **Lady Lube Rye (IRE)**[12] 1213 4-8-8 **47**.............................. DuranFentiman 6 35
(Noel Wilson) *chsd ldrs: drvn over 2f out: wknd over 1f out* **33/1**

15-0 **8** *2 ¼* **Talent Scout (IRE)**[107] 26 5-9-3 **56**.............................. DanielTudhope 5 36
(Tim Walford) *a in rr* **25/1**

30-0 **9** *1 ¾* **King Of Swords (IRE)**[21] 1034 7-9-7 **60**..............(p) SilvestreDeSousa 7 33
(Nigel Tinkler) *hld up in rr: nvr nr ldrs* **16/1**

420- **10** *4* **Tongalooma**[295] 3534 5-9-0 **53**..............................(p) PaddyAspell 4 —
(James Moffatt) *s.s: a bhd in last* **33/1**

59.67 secs (-1.43) **Going Correction** -0.25s/f (Firm) **10** Ran SP% **116.7**
Speed ratings (Par 101): **101,100,94,94,91 90,89,86,83,76**
toteswingers:1&2 £2.20, 2&3 £6.20, 1&3 £4.30 CSF £9.16 CT £45.01 TOTE £5.30: £1.60, £1.30, £2.40; EX 13.20.
Owner K Wreglesworth **Bred** K Wreglesworth **Trained** Sheriff Hutton, N Yorks

FOCUS
A low-grade but reasonably competitive sprint in which hardly any got involved. The winner looks the best guide to the form.
Galpin Junior(USA) Official explanation: jockey said gelding was unsuited by the good to firm (firm in places) ground

1494 NORTH SEA LOGISTICS H'CAP 6f
7:35 (7:35) (Class 6) (0-65,65) 3-Y-O **£1,683** (£501; £250; £125) **Stalls** High

Form RPR
-631 **1** **Trading**[7] 1303 3-9-3 **61** 6ex.............................. DuranFentiman 11 68
(Tim Easterby) *racd alone at first stands' side: chsd ldrs: led over 1f out: kpt on wl ins fnl f* **9/4**[1]

53-3 **2** *1 ¼* **Piccoluck**[11] 1249 3-9-7 **65**.............................. PaulMulrennan 7 68
(Deborah Sanderson) *stmbld s: sn chsng ldrs: outpcd over 3f out: hdwy over 2f out: chsd wnr over 1f out: styd on same pce ins fnl f* **10/1**

036- **3** *1 ¾* **Roman Ruler (IRE)**[214] 6184 3-9-1 **59**.............................. PhillipMakin 10 58
(Chris Fairhurst) *led tl over 1f out: kpt on same pce* **10/1**

011- **4** *1* **Pitkin**[159] 7423 3-9-3 **64**.............................. JamesSullivan(3) 3 60
(Michael Easterby) *t.k.h on outside: towards rr whn swtchd rt to r towards stands' side over 4f out: styd on fnl 2f: nt rch ldrs* **5/1**[2]

5 *2 ¾* **Green Warrior**[180] 7074 3-9-7 **65**.............................. SilvestreDeSousa 1 54
(Ann Duffield) *racd wd towards far side: w ldrs: wknd over 1f out* **13/2**[3]

-445 **6** *nk* **Bachelor Knight (IRE)**[26] 964 3-9-2 **65**..............(p) LeeTopliss(5) 9 53
(Ollie Pears) *chsd ldrs: wknd over 1f out* **14/1**

66-0 **7** *1 ¼* **Monel**[19] 1074 3-8-9 **53**.............................. AndrewMullen 5 37
(Jim Goldie) *t.k.h in mid-div: lost pl over 1f out* **14/1**

60-0 **8** *½* **Commander Veejay**[7] 1303 3-8-1 **52** oh5 ow1..........(p) ShaneBKelly(7) 4 35
(Brian Rothwell) *mid-div: outpcd and lost pl 3f out: kpt on ins fnl f* **80/1**

06-0 **9** *3 ½* **Mr Khan**[19] 1074 3-8-8 **52**.............................. DavidAllan 2 26
(Linda Perratt) *chsd ldrs: wknd over 1f out* **14/1**

3-23 **10** *3 ¾* **Lady Platinum Club**[11] 1246 3-9-6 **64**..............................(p) TomEaves 8 27
(Geoffrey Oldroyd) *chsd ldrs: lost pl over 2f out* **12/1**

1030 **11** *11* **Alfraamsey**[5] 1359 3-9-1 **59**..............................(v) SamHitchcott 6 —
(Mick Channon) *s.i.s: in rr and sn drvn along: bhd fnl 2f: eased ins fnl f* **14/1**

1m 13.41s (-1.19) **Going Correction** -0.25s/f (Firm) **11** Ran SP% **114.5**
Speed ratings (Par 96): **97,95,93,91,88 87,85,85,80,75 60**
toteswingers: 1&2 £7.20, 1&3 £6.90, 2&3 £13.00 CSF £24.95 CT £187.41 TOTE £2.40: £1.20, £2.50, £2.90; EX 20.20.
Owner Habton Farms **Bred** Major And Mrs R B Kennard **Trained** Great Habton, N Yorks

FOCUS
It wasn't a surprise to see Duran Fentiman make plenty of use of Trading down the stands' side over this trip after winning over 7f last time. The winner is the best guide.

1495 FREEBETTING.CO.UK H'CAP 1m 3y(S)
8:05 (8:05) (Class 6) (0-60,60) 3-Y-O **£1,683** (£501; £250; £125) **Stalls** High

Form RPR
00-4 **1** **Vetvey (IRE)**[14] 1169 3-9-0 **53**.............................. SilvestreDeSousa 10 63+
(Mark Johnston) *led stands' side rail: qcknd over 3f out: wnt 3 l clr ins fnl f: eased towards fin* **9/2**[3]

300- **2** *1 ½* **Downtown Boy (IRE)**[184] 6978 3-8-11 **50**.................... AndrewMullen 6 53
(Tom Tate) *dwlt: drvn and hdwy over 3f out: wnt 2nd 1f out: styd on same pce* **9/2**[3]

00-5 **3** *nk* **Byron Bear (IRE)**[19] 1074 3-8-12 **51**.............................. TonyCulhane 8 54+
(Paul Midgley) *t.k.h in rr: hdwy and nt clr run over 2f out: styd on to go 3rd 100yds out: kpt on same pce* **10/1**

2P-0 **4** *2 ½* **Chadford**[14] 1169 3-9-1 **54**..............................(p) DuranFentiman 3 50
(Tim Walford) *chsd ldrs: wknd ins fnl f* **33/1**

006- **5** *½* **One Of Twins**[210] 6293 3-8-7 **49**.............................. JamesSullivan(3) 7 44
(Michael Easterby) *in rr div: effrt and n.m.r over 2f out: edgd lft and kpt on same pce ins fnl f* **20/1**

000- **6** *2 ¾* **Dysios (IRE)**[144] 7595 3-9-7 **60**.............................. J-PGuillambert 2 49
(Luca Cumani) *trckd ldrs on outer: drvn over 2f out: wkng whn bmpd ins fnl f* **7/2**[2]

000- **7** *1 ¼* **Playful Girl (IRE)**[177] 7118 3-8-10 **49**.............................. DavidAllan 4 35
(Tim Easterby) *in rr: drvn: outpcd and lost pl over 3f out: kpt on ins fnl f* **28/1**

332 **8** *3* **Crown Ridge (IRE)**[7] 1303 3-9-6 **59**.............................. SamHitchcott 1 38
(Mick Channon) *s.s: hdwy to trck ldrs after 2f: drvn over 2f out: wknd over 1f out* **9/4**[1]

000- **9** *nse* **Newzflash**[182] 7016 3-8-8 **47**.............................. BarryMcHugh 5 26
(Ollie Pears) *trckd ldrs: t.k.h: lost pl over 1f out* **25/1**

00-0 **10** *2 ¼* **May Burnett (IRE)**[18] 1096 3-8-8 **47**..............................(t) TomEaves 9 21
(Brian Rothwell) *chsd ldrs: wknd 2f out* **50/1**

1m 41.72s (-1.68) **Going Correction** -0.25s/f (Firm) **10** Ran SP% **115.4**
Speed ratings (Par 96): **98,96,96,93,93 90,89,86,86,83**
toteswingers:1&2 £3.30, 2&3 £4.10, 1&3 £4.10 CSF £23.07 CT £191.87 TOTE £5.10: £1.70, £2.20, £5.90; EX 23.70.
Owner Brian Yeardley **Bred** Gestut Sohrenhof **Trained** Middleham Moor, N Yorks

FOCUS
An open-looking but weak handicap. The winner was value for double the actual margin.
Crown Ridge(IRE) Official explanation: jockey said gelding missed the break
T/Plt: £37.60 to a £1 stake. Pool of £46,898.61 - 909.05 winning tickets. T/Qpdt: £3.70 to a £1 stake. Pool of £5,819.83 - 1,143.78 winning tickets. WG

[1462]SOUTHWELL (L-H)
Wednesday, April 20

OFFICIAL GOING: Standard
Wind: Virtually nil Weather: Fione, dry and warm

1496 GOT THE FEELING GET TO LADBROKES MAIDEN STKS 1m (F)
2:10 (2:14) (Class 5) 3-Y-0+ **£2,388** (£705; £352) **Stalls** Low

Form RPR
0- **1** **Little Black Book (IRE)**[214] 6200 3-8-13 0.................. DarryllHolland 10 81
(Gerard Butler) *cl up on outer: effrt to chal 3f out: led over 2f out: rdn clr over 1f out: edgd rt and kpt on ins fnl f* **12/1**[3]

0-60 **2** *3 ¾* **All Right Now**[33] [893] 4-9-13 46 ..... AndreaAtzeni 1 76
(Derek Haydn Jones) *a.p: hdwy on inner 3f out: rdn and ev ch 2f out: drvn and kpt on same pce ins fnl f* **100/1**

2 **3** *3 ½* **Firebeam**[17] [1108] 3-8-13 0 ..... LiamJones 7 64
(William Haggas) *led: rdn along 3f out: hdd over 2f out: sn drvn and btn* **1/3**[1]

0-4 **4** *4 ½* **Spartan Spirit (IRE)**[21] [1047] 3-8-13 0 ..... SteveDrowne 6 54+
(Hughie Morrison) *chsd ldrs: rdn along 3f out: sn one pce* **14/1**

232 **5** *6* **Striking The Wind (USA)**[6] [1328] 3-8-13 0 ..... JoeFanning 3 40
(Mark Johnston) *chsd ldrs: rdn along over 3f out: sn outpcd* **7/2**[2]

6 *nk* **Robemaker** 3-8-13 0 ..... NickyMackay 13 39
(John Gosden) *s.i.s and in rr: hdwy 1/2-way: rdn 3f out: plugged on fnl 2f: nvr nr ldrs* **12/1**[3]

3- **7** *2* **Rio's Rosanna (IRE)**[242] [5303] 4-9-8 0 ..... MichaelStainton 9 34
(Richard Whitaker) *midfield: rdn along 1/2-way: nvr a factor* **33/1**

8 *8* **Vibration** 3-8-13 0 ..... TravisBlock 2 16
(Hughie Morrison) *s.i.s: a in rr* **66/1**

0- **9** *5* **Al Raqi**[254] [4899] 3-8-13 0 ..... RoystonFfrench 8 —
(Bryan Smart) *in tch: rdn along over 3f out: sn wknd* **66/1**

0/ **10** *3 ¼* **Carsington**[19] [2447] 7-9-8 0 ..... MickyFenton 12 —
(Lucinda Featherstone) *in rr and sn rdn along: outpcd bef 1/2-way: bhd fnl 3f* **100/1**

- **11** *1 ¾* **Blonde Maite** 5-9-13 0 ..... JimmyQuinn 11 —
(Roy Bowring) *v s.i.s: a in rr: bhd fnl 3f* **100/1**

12 *6* **Captain Slow** 4-9-13 0 ..... BarryMcHugh 4 —
(Julie Camacho) *s.i.s: a in rr: bhd fnl 3f* **100/1**

1m 41.9s (-1.80) **Going Correction** +0.075s/f (Slow) **12** Ran SP% **129.2**
WFA 3 from 4yo+ 14lb
Speed ratings (Par 103): **112,108,104,100,94 93,91,83,78,75 73,67**
CSF £837.60 TOTE £17.00: £2.90, £15.00, £1.10; EX 937.30.
Owner A D Spence **Bred** Rabbah Bloodstock Limited **Trained** Newmarket, Suffolk
■ Stewards' Enquiry : Andrea Atzeni caution: used whip down shoulder in the forehand.

FOCUS
This looked stronger than the vast majority of Southwell maidens, but it produced a real head-scratcher of a result for most punters. The runner-up will prove the key to the form.
Blonde Maite Official explanation: jockey said gelding was slowly away

1497 LADBROKES.COM H'CAP (DIV I) 7f (F)
2:45 (2:45) (Class 6) (0-55,61) 4-Y-O+ **£1,364** (£403; £201) **Stalls** Low

Form RPR

6535 **1** **Jonnie Skull (IRE)**[21] [1045] 5-8-11 50 .....(vt) LukeMorris 10 60
(Phil McEntee) *chsd ldr: cl up 3f out: effrt 2f out and ev ch: sn rdn and sltly outpcd: drvn and styd on strly ins fnl f to ld last 75yds* **7/1**[2]

3-10 **2** *¾* **Exceedingly Good (IRE)**[33] [893] 5-8-7 53 ..... LeonnaMayor(7) 8 61
(Roy Bowring) *hld up: smooth hdwy 1/2-way: led over 2f out: pushed clr over 1f out: sn rdn: hdd and no ex last 75yds* **11/1**

64-1 **3** *3 ½* **Dashwood**[6] [1336] 4-9-8 61 6ex ..... WilliamCarson 11 60
(Giles Bravery) *trckd ldrs: effrt and cl up 3f out: sn rdn and one pce fnl 2f* **4/7**[1]

6345 **4** *2 ¼* **Itsthursdayalready**[11] [1247] 4-9-2 55 ..... ShaneKelly 9 47
(Mark Brisbourne) *s.i.s and bhd: hdwy wl over 2f out: sn rdn and styd on appr fnl f: nrst fin* **10/1**

0-56 **5** *2 ¾* **Stonecrabstomorrow (IRE)**[35] [874] 8-8-2 46 oh1(e1) JemmaMarshall(5) 2 31
(Michael Attwater) *towards rr: hdwy 3f out: rdn over 2f out: sn no imp* **28/1**

2030 **6** *2 ½* **Street Crime**[9] [1273] 6-8-2 48 ..... JakePayne(7) 4 26
(Ron Hodges) *chsd ldrs on inner: rdn along 3f out: sn wknd* **16/1**

004- **7** *3 ¼* **Russian Brigadier**[177] [7131] 4-8-7 46 oh1 ..... JoeFanning 7 16
(Mel Brittain) *chsd ldng pair: rdn along over 3f out: sn wknd* **25/1**

00-0 **8** *5* **Charity Fair**[11] [1248] 4-8-4 46 oh1 ..... NataliaGemelova(3) 3 —
(Ron Barr) *s.i.s: a in rr* **66/1**

-060 **9** *9* **Fools Gold**[28] [950] 6-8-7 46 ..... AndreaAtzeni 6 —
(Richard Guest) *led: rdn along 3f out: hdd over 2f out and sn wknd* **9/1**[3]

1m 31.48s (1.18) **Going Correction** +0.075s/f (Slow) **9** Ran SP% **118.2**
Speed ratings (Par 101): **96,95,91,88,85 82,78,73,62**
toteswingers: 1&2 £3.70, 1&3 £1.60, 2&3 £3.00 CSF £79.95 CT £111.11 TOTE £6.30: £1.50, £2.30, £1.30; EX 46.00.
Owner Eventmaker Racehorses **Bred** Canice Farrell Jnr **Trained** Newmarket, Suffolk

FOCUS
A moderate handicap and a comprehensive defeat for another odds-on favourite. the slower of the two divisions. The winner is up a length or so on his recent Polytrack form.
Itsthursdayalready Official explanation: jockey said gelding was slowly away
Fools Gold Official explanation: jockey said gelding stopped quickly

1498 LADBROKES.COM H'CAP (DIV II) 7f (F)
3:20 (3:20) (Class 6) (0-55,55) 4-Y-O+ **£1,364** (£403; £201) **Stalls** Low

Form RPR

3253 **1** **Bold Diva**[6] [1336] 6-8-13 52 .....(v) LukeMorris 3 63
(Tony Carroll) *dwlt: hld up in tch: hdwy 3f out: chal 2f out: rdn to ld over 1f out: drvn out* **3/1**[1]

3022 **2** *2 ¼* **Meydan Style (USA)**[30] [933] 5-8-8 47 ..... JoeFanning 2 52
(Bruce Hellier) *trckd ldrs: hdwy 3f out: chal over 2f out: sn rdn and ev ch tl drvn and one pce appr fnl f* **10/3**[2]

000- **3** *1 ½* **Tamino (IRE)**[229] [5714] 8-8-9 48 ..... AndreaAtzeni 8 49
(Mark Brisbourne) *led: rdn along 3f out: drvn wl over 1f out: sn hdd and one pce* **12/1**

4030 **4** *1 ¼* **Norcroft**[14] [1177] 9-8-0 46 .....(p) DanielHarris(7) 7 36
(Christine Dunnett) *towards rr: hdwy over 2f out: sn rdn and n.d: fin 5th: plcd 4th* **9/1**[3]

6606 **5** *¾* **Duplicity**[6] [1331] 4-8-13 55 .....(e1) RobertLButler(3) 6 43
(Richard Guest) *s.i.s and bhd: wd st: rdn 2f out: sme late hdwy: fin 6th: plcd 5th* **22/1**

00-0 **6** *7* **Plenilune (IRE)**[1] [1468] 6-8-7 46 ..... JimmyQuinn 5 15
(Mel Brittain) *chsd ldrs: rdn along over 3f out: sn wknd: fin 7th: plcd 6th* **12/1**

-002 **7** *1 ½* **Wotatomboy**[36] [856] 5-8-7 46 oh1 .....(v) MichaelStainton 9 —
(Richard Whitaker) *cl up: rdn along 3f out: sn wknd: fin 8th: plcd 7th* **10/1**

00-0 **8** *2 ¼* **Craicattack (IRE)**[106] [37] 4-8-6 52 .....(p) DarylByrne(7) 4 —
(Sharon Watt) *cl up: rdn along over 3f out: sn wknd: fin 9th: plcd 8th* **40/1**

600- **9** *82* **Marsh's Gift**[160] [7406] 4-8-7 46 oh1 .....(p) LeeNewman 1 —
(Colin Teague) *s.i.s: a bhd: t.o and eased fnl 3f: fin 10th: plcd 9th* **50/1**

2553 **10** *3* **Olympic Dream**[43] [798] 5-9-1 54 .....(p) DarryllHolland 10 47
(Michael Herrington) *chsd ldrs on outer: rdn along over 2f out: sn drvn and one pce: fin 4th, 2 ¼l, 1 1/2l, 3l: disq &plcd last: rdr failed to weigh in* **10/3**[2]

1m 30.77s (0.47) **Going Correction** +0.075s/f (Slow) **10** Ran SP% **114.4**
Speed ratings (Par 101): **100,97,95,90,90 82,80,77,—,92**
toteswingers: 1&2 £1.40, 1&3 £16.60, 2&3 £12.50 CSF £12.55 CT £104.02 TOTE £4.60: £1.70, £1.50, £2.90; EX 13.00.
Owner Mrs P Izamis **Bred** Peter Balding **Trained** Cropthorne, Worcs
■ Stewards' Enquiry : Darryll Holland three-day ban: careless riding (May 4-6)

FOCUS
Another weak handicap, though the winning time was 0.71 seconds faster than the first division. The winner found a bit on her recent form.

1499 LADBROKES MOBILE FILLIES' H'CAP 1m (F)
3:55 (3:55) (Class 4) (0-80,80) 4-Y-O+ **£2,914** (£867; £433; £216) **Stalls** Low

Form RPR

501- **1** **Maristar (USA)**[201] [6543] 4-9-3 76 ..... DarryllHolland 2 89
(Gerard Butler) *trckd ldrs: hdwy 3f out: chal 2f out: rdn to ld appr fnl f: kpt on* **2/1**[1]

100- **2** *2 ¾* **Bianca De Medici**[159] [7421] 4-9-0 73 ..... SteveDrowne 4 80
(Hughie Morrison) *cl up: rdn to ld over 2f out: drvn and hdd appr fnl f: edgd rt and kpt on same pce ins fnl f* **7/2**[3]

42-6 **3** *8* **Mozayada (USA)**[11] [1245] 7-9-1 74 ..... JoeFanning 3 63
(Mel Brittain) *led: rdn along 3f out: hdd over 2f out and sn one pce* **9/2**

4546 **4** *¾* **Amary (IRE)**[5] [1373] 4-8-7 66 oh2 .....(p) BarryMcHugh 5 53
(John Harris) *in tch: rdn along 1/2-way: nvr a factor* **12/1**

20-4 **5** *14* **Gracious Melange**[30] [932] 4-9-7 80 ..... JimmyQuinn 1 51
(Marco Botti) *dwlt: sn trcking ldrs: effrt 3f out: sn rdn and wknd* **11/4**[2]

1m 42.22s (-1.48) **Going Correction** +0.075s/f (Slow) **5** Ran SP% **108.1**
Speed ratings (Par 102): **110,107,99,98,84**
CSF £8.86 TOTE £4.60: £1.10, £2.30; EX 7.30.
Owner M V Deegan **Bred** Barnett Enterprises **Trained** Newmarket, Suffolk

FOCUS
A tight little fillies' handicap in which the pace was ordinary. The winner is progressing on the AW.
Gracious Melange Official explanation: trainer's rep said, regarding running, that the filly was unsuited by the fibresand surface.

1500 PLAY ROULETTE AT LADBROKES.COM (S) STKS 1m (F)
4:30 (4:31) (Class 6) 3-Y-O **£1,706** (£503; £252) **Stalls** Low

Form RPR

3415 **1** **Sofias Number One (USA)**[27] [951] 3-9-2 67 ..... AndreaAtzeni 3 63
(Michael Wigham) *chsd ldng pair and sn pushed along: hdwy on outer 3f out: chal 2f out: rdn to ld and hung lft over 1f out: drvn out* **4/9**[1]

6-03 **2** *5* **Back For Tea (IRE)**[8] [1285] 3-8-11 47 ..... WilliamCarson 2 46
(Phil McEntee) *led: rdn along and jnd wl over 2f out: drvn and hdd over 1f out: kpt on same pce u.p ins fnl f* **9/1**[3]

00-0 **3** *2 ¼* **Fire N'Brimstone**[47] [760] 3-8-11 49 ..... FrankieMcDonald 4 41
(Mouse Hamilton-Fairley) *chsd ldr: hdwy and cl up wl over 2f out: sn rdn and ch tl drvn wl over 1f out and sn one pce* **25/1**

4 *45* **Lady Of Killough** 3-8-7 0 ow1 ..... MickyFenton 1 —
(Stef Higgins) *s.i.s: sn rdn along and outrpced in rr: wl bhd fr 1/2-way* **11/4**[2]

1m 46.62s (2.92) **Going Correction** +0.075s/f (Slow) **4** Ran SP% **109.8**
Speed ratings (Par 96): **88,83,80,35**
CSF £5.29 TOTE £1.50; EX 4.40.The winner was bought by R. Bowring for 3,500gns.
Owner D Hassan **Bred** Rosecrest Farm Llc **Trained** Newmarket, Suffolk
■ Stewards' Enquiry : Andrea Atzeni caution: careless riding.

FOCUS
A very moderate seller seller, the winner making hard work of beating poor rivals.

1501 FOLLOW @ATTHERACES ON TWITTER (S) STKS 5f (F)
5:00 (5:00) (Class 6) 3-Y-O+ **£1,706** (£503; £252) **Stalls** High

Form RPR

[illegible] **1** [illegible] [illegible] .....(b) [illegible]
(Ronald Harris) *cl up: led after 1f: rdn and qcknd clr wl over 1f out: kpt on wl towards fin* **2/1**[1]

26 **2** *1 ¼* **Clear Ice (IRE)**[8] [1287] 4-9-2 59 .....(b) RobertLButler(3) 5 62
(Richard Guest) *trckd ldng pair: swtchd lft and rdn wl over 1f out: sn chsng wnr: kpt on towards fin* **11/2**

4001 **3** *1 ¾* **Efistorm**[9] [1274] 10-9-10 67 ..... KirstyMilczarek 2 60
(Conor Dore) *chsd ldrs: rdn along and sltly outpcd wl over 1f out: styd on u.p ins fnl f* **11/4**[3]

0304 **4** *1* **Ridley Didley (IRE)**[21] [1034] 6-9-5 62 ..... LeeNewman 6 52
(Noel Wilson) *led 1f: cl up: rdn along over 2f out: sn drvn and grad wknd* **5/2**[2]

000- **5** *4 ½* **Kalahari Desert (IRE)**[180] [7052] 4-9-5 50 ..... MichaelStainton 1 35
(Richard Whitaker) *a in rr: rdn along 1/2-way: sn outpcd* **25/1**

0500 **6** *nse* **Ronnie Howe**[1] [1464] 7-8-12 43 .....(bt) LeonnaMayor(7) 4 35
(Roy Bowring) *bhd: rdn along 1/2-way: nvr a factor* **66/1**

60.12 secs (0.42) **Going Correction** +0.10s/f (Slow) **6** Ran SP% **109.3**
Speed ratings (Par 101): **100,98,95,93,86 86**
toteswingers:1&2: £1.60, 2&3: £1.50, 1&3: £1.90 CSF £12.69 TOTE £2.40: £1.40, £1.20; EX 8.10.There was no bid for the winner.
Owner P Nurcombe **Bred** C A Cyzer **Trained** Earlswood, Monmouths

FOCUS
An ordinary sprint seller with early speed all-important. The winner is the most reliable guide to the form.

1502 VISIT AT THE RACES ON FACEBOOK H'CAP 1m 4f (F)
5:30 (5:31) (Class 6) (0-60,60) 3-Y-O **£1,706** (£503; £252) **Stalls** Low

Form RPR

00-6 **1** **Ivanov (IRE)**[23] [1018] 3-8-7 46 oh1 ..... MickyFenton 7 63
(Willie Musson) *sn outpcd and bhd: rdn along after 3f: hdwy to chse ldng pair over 3f out: styd on u.p fnl 2f: led ins fnl f: kpt on strly* **25/1**

00-0 **2** *5* **Captain Bellamy (USA)**[7] [1312] 3-9-2 55 ..... TravisBlock 3 64
(Hughie Morrison) *slt ld at str pce: rdn wl over 3f out: drvn 2f out: edgd rt over 1f out: hdd and no ex ins fnl f* **9/2**[3]

6-22 **3** *6* **Trojan Touch (USA)**[19] [1082] 3-8-8 47 .....(b) WilliamCarson 6 46
(Chris Dwyer) *cl up: disp ld at str pce after 3f: rdn wl over 3f out: drvn 2f out: wknd over 1f out* **9/4**[2]

-214 **4** *49* **Investment World (IRE)**[7] [1312] 3-9-7 60 ..... JoeFanning 1 —
(Mark Johnston) *chsd clr ldng duo: rdn along 5f out: sn outpcd and bhd* **10/11**[1]

0-05 5 12 **Generous Genella**[16] 1134 3-8-9 **48** .... JimmyQuinn 4 —
(Julia Feilden) *chsd clr ldng duo: rdn along 1/2-way: sn outpcd and wl bhd fnl 4f* **20/1**

2m 42.87s (1.87) **Going Correction** +0.075s/f (Slow) **5** Ran SP% **109.9**
Speed ratings (Par 96): **96,92,88,56,48**
CSF £123.80 TOTE £16.40: £3.70, £2.00; EX 74.10.
Owner The Philosophers **Bred** Compagnia Generale S R L **Trained** Newmarket, Suffolk
■ Stewards' Enquiry : Jimmy Quinn caution: used whip down shoulder in the forehand.

FOCUS
A nonsense of a contest with the second and third going off very fast, and the form can be taken with a large pinch of salt. The race has not been rated positively.
Ivanov(IRE) Official explanation: trainer said, regarding apparent improvement in form, the race was run to suit the gelding, very fast early on as it stays well.
Investment World(IRE) Official explanation: jockey said colt never travelled
Generous Genella Official explanation: jockey said filly stopped quick

1503 ATTHERACES.COM EXCLUSIVE HUGH TAYLOR TIPPING H'CAP 5f (F)
6:00 (6:00) (Class 5) (0-70,64) 3-Y-O+ **£1,942** (£578; £288; £144) **Stalls** High

Form RPR
1406 1 **Shawkantango**[12] 1213 4-9-9 **64** .... (v) DaleSwift(5) 6 74
(Derek Shaw) *chsd ldrs: hdwy over 1f out: rdn and qcknd to ld ins fnl f* **11/4**[1]

0600 2 1 ¼ **Dancing Freddy (IRE)**[1] 1463 4-9-9 **62** .... (p) RobertLButler(3) 3 68
(Richard Guest) *a.p: effrt to chal over 2f out: rdn and ev ch over 1f out: sn drvn and kpt on same pce ins fnl f* **11/1**

4332 3 ¾ **Decider (USA)**[9] 1274 8-9-13 **63** .... (p) LukeMorris 4 66
(Ronald Harris) *mde most: rdn wl over 1f out: drvn and hdd ins fnl f: one pce* **7/2**[2]

3141 4 1 **Ace Master**[35] 868 3-9-0 **60** .... JimmyQuinn 7 55
(Roy Bowring) *dwlt and in rr: rdn along 2f out: styd on u.p ins fnl f: nrst fin* **7/2**[2]

0020 5 ¾ **Fashion Icon (USA)**[4] 1411 5-9-7 **62** .... (b) SeanLevey(5) 5 59
(David O'Meara) *prom: rdn along over 2f out: sn drvn and one pce fr over 1f out* **8/1**[3]

0-15 6 3 ¼ **Tsar Bomba (USA)**[62] 571 4-9-13 **63** .... LeeNewman 2 48
(David Barron) *dwlt: sn chsng ldrs on outer: hdwy 2f out: rdn wl over 1f out: wknd ent fnl f* **7/2**[2]

60.17 secs (0.47) **Going Correction** +0.10s/f (Slow)
WFA 3 from 4yo+ 10lb **6** Ran SP% **112.8**
Speed ratings (Par 103): **100,98,96,95,94 88**
toteswingers:1&2: £8.50, 2&3 £8.10, 1&3 £2.50 CSF £32.10 TOTE £3.40: £2.10, £3.50; EX 30.40.
Owner Mrs Lyndsey Shaw **Bred** Derek Shaw **Trained** Sproxton, Leics

FOCUS
An ordinary sprint handicap. The leaders went off fast but the winning time was fractionally slower than the seller. The winner completed a four-timer over C&D and the runner-up was back to form.
T/Plt: £11.50 to a £1 stake. Pool of £40,812.82 - 2,578.91 winning tickets. T/Qpdt: £5.50 to a £1 stake. Pool of £2,426.32 - 322.50 winning tickets. JR

1280 FOLKESTONE (R-H)
Thursday, April 21

OFFICIAL GOING: Good to firm (firm in places; watered; 8.8)
Wind: virtually nil Weather: very hot and sunny

1504 DUKE OF CUMBERLAND AND OLD NEPTUNE MEDIAN AUCTION MAIDEN STKS 5f
2:00 (2:00) (Class 5) 3-Y-O **£2,388** (£705; £352) **Stalls** High

Form RPR
420- 1 **Stone Of Folca**[244] 5276 3-9-3 **101** .... LukeMorris 1 73+
(John Best) *mounted on crse: pushed rt and stdd s: t.k.h: trckd ldr: pushed along to chal ent fnl f: edgd rt and led ins fnl f: cleverly* **1/8**[1]

4322 2 ½ **Welsh Inlet (IRE)**[16] 1145 3-8-12 **65** .... CathyGannon 2 66
(John Bridger) *wnt rt s: led: rdn and edgd rt jst over 1f out: hdd ins fnl f: kpt on same pce after* **6/1**[2]

3 10 **Starbust (IRE)** 3-9-3 0 .... PaulDoe 4 35
(Jim Best) *dwlt: reminders after 1f: rdn and wknd wl over 1f out: wnt modest 3rd ins fnl f* **50/1**[3]

0-00 4 2 ¼ **Pharoh Jake**[36] 863 3-8-12 **46** .... RyanPowell(5) 3 27
(John Bridger) *stdd s: chsd ldrs on outer: rdn 2f out: wknd qckly over 1f out* **100/1**

60.45 secs (0.45) **Going Correction** -0.025s/f (Good) **4** Ran SP% **106.1**
Speed ratings (Par 98): **95,94,78,74**
CSF £1.20 TOTE £1.10; EX 1.40.
Owner Folkestone Racecourse Owners Group **Bred** D R Botterill **Trained** Hucking, Kent

FOCUS
The attendance of the winner ensured this was a seriously uncompetitive sprint maiden. The runner-up looks the best guide.

1505 E.B.F. MCCLOUD FAMILY AFFAIR MAIDEN STKS 5f
2:30 (2:32) (Class 5) 2-Y-O **£3,173** (£944; £471; £235) **Stalls** High

Form RPR
1 **Gatepost (IRE)** 2-9-3 0 .... JamieSpencer 8 87+
(Mick Channon) *hld up in tch: smooth hdwy to press ldr wl over 1f out: rdn to ld over 1f out: sn in command and clr ins fnl f: eased towards fin: comf* **15/8**[2]

2 2 ¼ **Bayleyf (IRE)** 2-9-3 0 .... LukeMorris 4 76
(John Best) *restless in stalls: stdd s: t.k.h: hld up in tch: rdn and hdwy 2f out: rn green and hung rt ins fnl f: styd on to go 2nd fnl 75yds: no threat to wnr* **16/1**

32 3 ½ **Choice Of Remark (IRE)**[15] 1185 2-9-3 0 .... CathyGannon 1 74
(David Evans) *broke fast: led: clr 1/2-way: rdn and pressed wl over 1f out: sn hdd: styd on same pce and no threat to wnr fnl f: lost 2nd fnl 75yds* **7/1**

4 4 **Karuga** 2-8-12 0 .... RyanMoore 2 55
(Richard Hannon) *chsd ldr tl edgd rt whn rdn wl over 1f out: wknd u.p ent fnl f: fdd fnl 100yds* **6/1**[3]

6 5 ¾ **Night Angel (IRE)**[22] 1042 2-8-12 0 .... JamesMillman 9 52
(Rod Millman) *sn pushed along towards rr: lost tch 2f out: no ch but plugged on ins fnl f* **20/1**

3 6 5 **Chillie Billie**[8] 1316 2-9-3 0 .... KierenFallon 5 43
(Phil McEntee) *in tch on outer: rdn and pushed sltly rt wl over 1f out: sn fnd little and btn over 1f out: wl btn and nt pushed fnl f* **6/4**[1]

4 7 2 **Si Sealy (IRE)**[12] 1235 2-8-10 0 .... MatthewCosham(7) 7 32
(David Evans) *in tch towards rr: rdn and struggling over 2f out: sn wknd* **66/1**

8 *nse* **Fromthestables Com (IRE)** 2-9-3 0 .... SebSanders 3 32
(J W Hills) *in tch on outer: rdn and struggling over 2f out: lost tch wl over 1f out* **66/1**

9 4 **Samasana (IRE)** 2-8-12 0 .... JamesDoyle 6 12
(Ian Wood) *restless in stalls: wnt rt s and slowly away: a bhd: lost tch 2f out: t.o* **20/1**

60.12 secs (0.12) **Going Correction** -0.025s/f (Good) **9** Ran SP% **120.0**
Speed ratings (Par 92): **98,94,93,87,86 78,74,74,68**
toteswingers:1&2:£5.90, 1&3:£3.50, 2&3:£7.40 CSF £30.89 TOTE £3.90: £1.40, £2.80, £1.80; EX 42.50 Trifecta £223.80 Pool: £692.86 - 2.29 winning units..
Owner Dr Marwan Koukash **Bred** Michael Doyle **Trained** West Ilsley, Berks

FOCUS
Previous experience in juvenile maidens at this early stage of the season is no doubt an advantage, but eight winners of this event in the past ten years had been newcomers.

NOTEBOOK
Gatepost(IRE) ◆, well backed, ran out a comfortable winner, keeping up the good start of the trainer's juveniles this season, and looks set for better things. Another furlong should not pose him a problem this season, but he clearly has plenty of dash and looks well up to winning a novice event. (op 3-1)
Bayleyf(IRE) ◆ was reported by his trainer beforehand to be buzzy at home and he duly took a keen hold after jumping out. There was a good deal to like about the way he finished once the penny dropped, though, and there is every reason to think he will score next time out. (tchd 14-1 tchd 25-1 in a place and 20-1 in places)
Choice Of Remark(IRE) had been placed on his two previous outings, going down narrowly at Nottingham 15 days earlier, and so he is a decent guide for the form. (op 15-2)
Karuga was a market drifter on her racecourse debut and, despite knowing her job early, she proved too green under pressure to do herself full justice. Improvement can be expected for the run. (op 7-1 tchd 15-2 in a place)
Chillie Billie, well backed, just set the standard on his promising debut third at Newmarket eight days earlier. He was in trouble passing 2f out here, however, and Fallon eased him off inside the final furlong. Perhaps the run came too soon. (op 5-4 tchd 11-10 and 13-8)

1506 STERLINGSERVICE.CO.UK CHAUFFEUR H'CAP 6f
3:00 (3:01) (Class 4) (0-85,77) 4-Y-O+ **£3,238** (£963; £481; £240) **Stalls** High

Form RPR
01-0 1 **Victorian Bounty**[17] 1140 6-9-7 **77** .... MickyFenton 1 85
(Stef Higgins) *chsd ldr: rdn along and clsd over 2f out: led wl over 1f out: kpt on wl fnl f: rdn out* **5/2**[1]

0-60 2 *nk* **Rum King (USA)**[3] 1444 4-8-11 **72** .... KieranO'Neill(5) 4 79
(Richard Hannon) *taken down early: sn chsng ldrs: rdn and clsd over 2f out: ev ch u.p over 1f out: r.o but a hld fnl f* **5/1**

4165 3 3 ½ **Sherjawy (IRE)**[8] 1309 7-8-10 **66** .... KirstyMilczarek 3 62
(Zoe Davison) *sn outpcd and pushed along in 4th: clsd u.p jst over 2f out: swtchd rt and chsd ldrs over 1f out: chsd ldng pair 1f out: wknd fnl 150yds* **13/2**

00-0 4 ¾ **Rough Rock (IRE)**[18] 1109 6-8-11 **72** .... AdamBeschizza(5) 2 65
(Chris Dwyer) *wl off the pce in last: rdn and effrt over 2f out: drvn and hdwy over 1f out: no prog ent fnl f: wl btn fnl 150yds* **3/1**[3]

5455 5 1 ¾ **Billy Red**[6] 1371 7-9-2 **72** .... (b) FergusSweeney 6 60
(J R Jenkins) *led: hdd and rdn wl over 1f out: sn struggling: wknd jst over 1f out* **11/4**[2]

1m 13.3s (0.60) **Going Correction** -0.025s/f (Good) **5** Ran SP% **110.2**
Speed ratings (Par 105): **95,94,89,88,86**
CSF £14.82 TOTE £3.10: £1.40, £2.30; EX 10.70.
Owner David Gilbert **Bred** Mrs P D Gray And H Farr **Trained** Lambourn, Berks

FOCUS
This ordinary sprint handicap was run at a sound pace and the first pair dominated nearing the furlong marker. The winner is rated close to his previous winning mark.

1507 PLAY BLACKJACK AT TOTESPORT.COM H'CAP 5f
3:30 (3:30) (Class 4) (0-80,78) 4-Y-O+ **£3,412** (£1,007; £504) **Stalls** High

Form RPR
6455 1 **Liberty Lady (IRE)**[10] 1279 4-9-5 **76** .... JamesDoyle 5 87
(Des Donovan) *chsd ldr: rdn to ld over 1f out: r.o wl fnl f* **5/2**[1]

0-00 2 2 **Rocker**[17] 1140 7-8-13 **70** .... RyanMoore 3 74
(Gary Moore) *chsd ldrs: rdn and hdwy wl over 1f out: chsd wnr and drvn ins fnl f: no imp* **3/1**[2]

05-0 3 2 **Diamond Johnny G (USA)**[6] 1371 4-9-5 **76** .... (t) EddieCreighton 4 73
(Edward Creighton) *taken down early: dwlt: sn outpcd in last: rdn 3f out: hdwy over 1f out: styd on to snatch 3rd on line: nvr trbld ldrs* **25/1**

20-2 4 *nse* **Magical Speedfit (IRE)**[9] 1281 6-9-0 **74** .... SimonPearce(3) 1 70
(George Margarson) *hld up in last pair: hdwy wl over 1f: rdn and no prog 1f out: wl hld after* **9/2**[3]

2021 5 2 **Black Baccara**[9] 1281 4-8-10 **67** 6ex .... (be) KierenFallon 2 56
(Phil McEntee) *led: rdn and hdd over 1f out: fnd little u.p: wknd 1f out* **5/1**

5003 U **Grudge**[8] 1309 6-8-9 **66** .... (be) KirstyMilczarek 7 —
(Conor Dore) *taken down early: rrd and uns rdr as stalls opened: tk no part* **9/2**[3]

59.23 secs (-0.77) **Going Correction** -0.025s/f (Good) **6** Ran SP% **110.4**
Speed ratings (Par 105): **105,101,98,98,95** —
toteswingers:1&2:£2.10, 1&3:£6.80, 2&3:£8.40 CSF £9.89 TOTE £2.60: £1.70, £2.20; EX 12.50.
Owner Mark Jones **Bred** Chris Giblett **Trained** Newmarket, Suffolk

FOCUS
A moderate sprint handicap, run at a solid pace. The winner is generally progressive on turf.

1508 PLAY ROULETTE AT TOTESPORT.COM H'CAP 1m 1f 149y
4:00 (4:00) (Class 6) (0-60,59) 4-Y-O+ **£1,706** (£503; £252) **Stalls** Centre

Form RPR
00-0 1 **Mister Bit (IRE)**[43] 814 4-9-7 **59** .... (b[1]) LukeMorris 6 70
(John Best) *chsd ldr tl over 2f out: rdn to chse ldr again wl over 1f out: led ins fnl f: kpt on to forge clr fnl 100yds* **10/1**

5100 2 2 ½ **Miss Bounty**[28] 957 6-8-13 **54** .... (v[1]) MatthewDavies(3) 7 60
(Jim Boyle) *taken down early: in tch: pushed along to chse ldr over 2f out: led wl over 1f out: hdd and fnd little ins fnl f: btn fnl 100yds* **9/2**

5054 3 3 **Thundering Home**[12] 1233 4-9-3 **55** .... (p) RobbieFitzpatrick 3 54
(Michael Attwater) *dwlt: bhd: rdn over 3f out: c wd ent st: kpt on to go 3rd fnl 100yds: nvr gng pce to chal ldrs* **4/1**[3]

-323 4 ¾ **Sunset Boulevard (IRE)**[49] 553 8-9-2 **54** .... (b) PaulDoe 5 52
(Jim Best) *stdd after s: hld up in last pair: rdn and effrt over 2f out: chsd ldng pair and hung rt fr over 1f out: no imp* **7/2**[2]

0-60 **5** 3/4 **Final Try**[15] [1184] 4-8-0 **45**.......... NathanAlison(7) 2 41
(Paddy Butler) *t.k.h: chsd ldrs: rdn and unable qck jst over 2f out: styng on one pce and wl hld whn carried lft fnl f* **50/1**

-546 **6** 1 1/4 **Derby Desire (IRE)**[6] [1353] 7-8-7 **48**.......... SophieDoyle(3) 1 42
(Des Donovan) *broke wl: sn stdd and racd in last trio: rdn and no hdwy jst over 2f out: wl btn whn nt clr run and swtchd lft wl ins fnl f* **3/1**[1]

-000 **7** 18 **Vezere (USA)**[84] [317] 4-9-3 **55**.......... SebSanders 4 26
(Simon Dow) *led tl rdn and hdd wl over 1f out: sn wknd: virtually p.u ins fnl f: t.o* **5/1**

2m 4.34s (-0.56) **Going Correction** -0.025s/f (Good) **7** Ran SP% **113.1**
Speed ratings (Par 101): **101,99,96,96,95 94,80**
toteswingers:1&2:8.80, 2&3, 5.50, 1&3:7.10 CSF £52.76 TOTE £13.10: £5.80, £3.80; EX 51.20.
Owner H J Jarvis **Bred** John Best **Trained** Hucking, Kent
■ Stewards' Enquiry : Paul Doe two-day ban: careless riding (May 5-6)

FOCUS
A weak handicap. It was run at a decent tempo, but still few got seriously involved from off the pace. The winner is rated back to his early form.

1509 PLAY POKER AT TSPOKER.COM H'CAP — 1m 4f
4:30 (4:30) (Class 5) (0-75,74) 4-Y-O+ **£2,388** (£705; £352) **Stalls** High

Form | RPR

445- **1** **Rockfella**[194] [6754] 5-9-3 **70**.......... KierenFallon 4 77
(Denis Coakley) *chsd ldr: rdn to ld 2f out: drvn over 1f out: kpt on wl fnl f* **11/8**[1]

-203 **2** 1 1/4 **Trachonitis (IRE)**[30] [938] 7-9-1 **68**.......... AdrianMcCarthy 3 73
(J R Jenkins) *hld up in last: hdwy to chse ldrs and nt clr run over 1f out: sn swtchd rt: chsd wnr ins fnl f: one pce and hld fnl 100yds* **22/1**

46-0 **3** 2 **On Terms (USA)**[92] [209] 5-9-7 **74**.......... SebSanders 6 76
(Simon Dow) *led: rdn and hdd 2f out: unable qck and sltly hmpd over 1f out: kpt on same pce fnl f* **7/2**[3]

0222 **4** 2 1/2 **Sunset Place**[23] [1025] 4-8-9 **63**..........(p) RobertHavlin 5 61
(Jonathan Geake) *chsd ldrs: effrt to chal ent st: ev ch: drvn and nt qckn over 1f out: wknd fnl f* **12/1**

016- **5** 32 **Sircozy (IRE)**[24] [4694] 5-9-6 **73**..........(p) RyanMoore 2 —
(Gary Moore) *hld up in tch: rdn and struggling over 3f out: sn lost tch: virtually p.u ent fnl f: t.o* **9/4**[2]

2m 39.43s (-1.47) **Going Correction** -0.025s/f (Good)
WFA 4 from 5yo+ 1lb **5** Ran SP% **107.1**
Speed ratings (Par 103): **103,102,100,99,77**
CSF £25.41 TOTE £2.00: £1.10, £5.40; EX 24.00.
Owner L M A Hurley **Bred** Ascagnano S P A **Trained** West Ilsley, Berks

FOCUS
Unsurprisingly with On Terms in attendance this tight handicap was run at a solid pace and the form makes sense, with the winner looking the best guide.
Sircozy(IRE) Official explanation: trainer said gelding was unsuited by the track and the good to firm (firm in places) ground
T/Plt: £171.70 to a £1 stake. Pool:£50,463.16 - 214.44 winning tickets T/Qpdt: £67.70 to a £1 stake. Pool:£4,987.16 - 54.45 winning tickets SP

1510 - 1512a (Foreign Racing) - See Raceform Interactive

1231 SAINT-CLOUD (L-H)
Thursday, April 21

OFFICIAL GOING: Turf: good

1513a PRIX PENELOPE (GROUP 3) (3YO FILLIES) (TURF) — 1m 2f 110y
1:50 (12:00) 3-Y-O **£34,482** (£13,793; £10,344; £6,896; £3,448)

RPR

1 **Don't Hurry Me (IRE)**[33] [918] 3-9-0 0.......... IoritzMendizabal 3 107
(J-C Rouget, France) *sent st to ld: rdn early in st: began flashing tail: sn wnt clr: r.o wl: nvr chal: comf* **8/5**[1]

2 1 1/2 **Pirika (IRE)**[168] 3-9-0 0.......... Pierre-CharlesBoudot 2 104
(A Fabre, France) *settled 3rd on rail: rdn 2f out: wnt 2nd 1 1/2f out: chsd ldr home: a hld* **11/2**

[illegible] [illegible] (FR) [illegible] (b) [illegible]
(C Baillet, France) *settled 2nd: rdn early in st: hung away fr whip: styd on fnl f: jst hld 3rd on line* **5/1**[3]

4 hd **Pagera (FR)**[45] 3-9-0 0.......... StephanePasquier 5 98
(Y Fouin, France) *settled at rr of field: moved 4th bef st: sn rdn: styd on to narrowly miss 3rd* **43/10**[2]

5 3/4 **Venise Jelois (FR)**[11] 3-9-0 0.......... OlivierPeslier 4 96
(Robert Collet, France) *racd in 4th tl bef st whn dropped to bk of field: rdn 2f out: no ex: styd on fnl f* **9/1**

2m 17.2s (-2.40) **5** Ran SP% **99.4**
WIN (incl 1 euro stake) : 2.60. PLACES: 1.60, 2.10. SF: 6.90.
Owner Jean-Francois Gribomont **Bred** G Rollain **Trained** Pau, France

NOTEBOOK
Don't Hurry Me(IRE) made all the running and won comfortably, although she did flash her tail in the closing stages. She'll head for the Prix de Diane next.
Pirika(IRE) stayed on well under a sympathetic ride and should come on a good bit for her reappearance.

1071 MUSSELBURGH (R-H)
Saturday, April 23

OFFICIAL GOING: Good changing to good to soft (good in places) after race 4 (3.40)
Wind: Virtually nil Weather: Overcast and raining

1514 RACING UK H'CAP (QUALIFIER FOR THE BETFAIR BONUS SCOTTISH RACING SPRINT FINAL) — 5f
1:55 (1:55) (Class 6) (0-65,65) 3-Y-O **£2,590** (£770; £385; £192) **Stalls** High

Form | RPR

500- **1** **Mr Mo Jo**[197] [6705] 3-9-3 **61**.......... DuranFentiman 4 69
(Lawrence Mullaney) *qckly away: mde all: rdn over 1f out: kpt on wl fnl f* **16/1**

025- **2** 1 1/4 **Rothesay Chancer**[178] [7174] 3-8-10 **57**.......... GaryBartley(3) 2 61
(Jim Goldie) *hld up in tch: hdwy on outer 2f out: rdn to chal and ch over 1f out: sn drvn and kpt on fnl f* **9/2**

4416 **3** 3/4 **Misty Morn**[10] [1306] 3-8-13 **57**.......... SilvestreDeSousa 5 58
(Alan Brown) *chsd ldrs: hdwy wl over 1f out: sn rdn and kpt on same pce fnl f* **7/2**[2]

6462 **4** 3/4 **Johnny Hancocks (IRE)**[16] [1193] 3-9-7 **65**.......... RoystonFfrench 1 63
(Linda Stubbs) *cl up: effrt 2f out: rdn over 1f out and ev ch tl no ex last 100yds* **3/1**[1]

240- **5** 3 1/4 **Saxonette**[183] [7050] 3-9-4 **62**.......... TonyHamilton 7 49
(Linda Perratt) *trckd ldrs: effrt whn n.m.r 2f out: sn rdn and n.d* **5/1**

5-42 **6** nk **Dr Red Eye**[39] [855] 3-9-2 **63**.......... TjadeCollier(3) 3 49
(David Nicholls) *chsd ldrs: rdn along 1/2-way: sn btn* **4/1**[3]

0-46 **7** 1/2 **Georgian Silver**[24] [1040] 3-7-12 **47**.......... NeilFarley(5) 6 31
(George Foster) *a towards rr* **10/1**

61.60 secs (1.20) **Going Correction** +0.15s/f (Good) **7** Ran SP% **117.0**
Speed ratings (Par 96): **96,94,92,91,86 85,85**
toteswingers: 1&2 £18.40, 1&3 £15.90, 2&3 £3.20. CSF £88.40 TOTE £22.10: £9.50, £2.90; EX 144.60.
Owner D A Flavell **Bred** D A Flavell **Trained** Great Habton, N Yorks

FOCUS
The ground was officially given as good, with a GoingStick reading of 5.9, and they were kicking the top off during this sprint handicap. The winner is rated around the placed horses.
Mr Mo Jo Official explanation: trainer said, regarding apparent improvement in form, that it was the gelding's first run for him and felt that it had benefited from a change of scenery.

1515 EUROPEAN BREEDERS' FUND MAIDEN STKS — 5f
2:30 (2:30) (Class 4) 2-Y-O **£5,180** (£1,541; £770; £384) **Stalls** High

Form | RPR

2 **1** **Alejandro (IRE)**[16] [1199] 2-9-3 0.......... PaulHanagan 3 82
(Richard Fahey) *mde most: rdn wl over 1f out: drvn ins fnl f: styd on gamely towards fin* **1/1**[1]

3 **2** 3 3/4 **Almond Branches**[16] [1199] 2-8-12 0.......... TomEaves 2 64+
(George Moore) *prom: hdwy to chal over 2f out: rdn wl over 1f out and ev ch tl drvn and wknd ins fnl f* **11/1**

3 1 1/2 **Blue Shoes (IRE)** 2-8-12 0.......... DavidAllan 7 58+
(Tim Easterby) *chsd ldrs: rdn and hmpd over 1f out: swtchd lft and kpt on wl fnl f* **16/1**

4 shd **Mr Majeika (IRE)** 2-9-3 0.......... PatDobbs 5 63
(Richard Hannon) *trckd ldrs: effrt 2f out: sn swtchd rt and rdn over 1f out: kpt on same pce* **3/1**[2]

5 **5** 1 3/4 **Kodiac King (IRE)**[16] [1199] 2-9-3 0.......... PhillipMakin 6 56
(Kevin Ryan) *cl up: rdn and sltly outpcd 1 1/2f out: sn swtchd rt and drvn: wknd fnl f* **10/1**

6 1/2 **Drummoyne (USA)** 2-9-3 0.......... SilvestreDeSousa 1 55+
(Mark Johnston) *wnt bdly rt s: sn outpcd and bhd: hdwy 2f out: kpt on fnl f* **8/1**[3]

7 4 1/2 **Lady Of Edge** 2-8-12 0.......... AndrewMullen 8 33
(Keith Dalgleish) *s.i.s: sn outpcd and a bhd* **33/1**

8 3 3/4 **Lucky Mark (IRE)** 2-9-3 0.......... RoystonFfrench 4 25+
(George Foster) *rrd s and lost several l: hdwy and in tch 1/2-way: sn rdn and wknd* **20/1**

62.45 secs (2.05) **Going Correction** +0.20s/f (Good) **8** Ran SP% **117.1**
Speed ratings (Par 94): **91,85,82,82,79 78,71,65**
toteswingers: 1&2 £13.80, 1&3 £4.80, 2&3 £13.40. CSF £14.50 TOTE £1.80: £1.10, £2.30, £3.40; EX 6.70 Trifecta £34.30 Pool: £441.47 - 9.51 winning units..
Owner F L F S Ltd **Bred** Yeomanstown Stud **Trained** Musley Bank, N Yorks
■ Stewards' Enquiry : Phillip Makin one-day ban: careless riding (May 7)

FOCUS
A fair maiden on paper with the winner rated close to his debut form.

NOTEBOOK
Alejandro(IRE) was fairly weak in the betting, but his debut second, where he had Almond Branches and Kodiac King well behind, gave him an outstanding chance, and he eventually justified favouritism. It wasn't easy for much of the race but he was nicely on top at the finish and he's now earned a crack at a little novice race somewhere. (op 4-5)
Almond Branches made the winner work but still only finished a length closer to him than she had done at Ripon on her debut. She has the ability to win a little maiden. (tchd 10-1)
Blue Shoes(IRE) shaped with promise on her debut. A late foal, she ran into a bit of trouble when Kodiac King crossed in front of her a furlong and a half out, but she kept on well to mark the frame and is entitled to go a lot closer next time.
Mr Majeika(IRE) is out of a mare who was bred to stay well, so it's probably fair to assume he'll improve for another furlong in time. (op 9-2)
Kodiac King(IRE) looked more professional this time and finished closer to the winner than he did on his debut. Official explanation: jockey said colt hung right throughout (op 12-1)
Drummoyne(USA), who holds a Phoenix Stakes entry, was coltish beforehand, very green in the race itself and has more to offer than he showed here. He'll appreciate another furlong as well. (op 17-2 tchd 9-1)
Lucky Mark(IRE) Official explanation: jockey said gelding reared as stalls opened

1516 RACING UK SHOWING THE BEST RACECOURSES H'CAP — 1m 1f
3:05 (3:05) (Class 2) (0-100,90) 3-Y-O
£12,462 (£3,732; £1,866; £934; £466; £234) **Stalls** Low

Form | RPR

311- **1** **Glen's Diamond**[238] [5525] 3-9-7 **90**.......... PaulHanagan 3 102+
(Richard Fahey) *hld up in rr: pushed along 3f out: hdwy on inner 2f out: swtchd lft and rdn to chal ins fnl f: styd on strly to ld last 100yds* **6/4**[1]

22-1 **2** 1 1/4 **Calypso Magic (IRE)**[22] [1076] 3-9-0 **83**.......... FrederikTylicki 5 92
(Howard Johnson) *set stdy pce: qcknd over 3f out: rdn over 2f out: drvn over 1f out: hdd and no ex last 100yds* **6/1**[3]

01- **3** 6 **Rastaban**[185] [7010] 3-8-8 **77**.......... LiamJones 6 73
(William Haggas) *chsd ldr: rdn along wl over 2f out: chal and ev ch wl over 1f out tl drvn and wknd ent fnl f* **4/1**[2]

0-36 **4** 3/4 **Malthouse (GER)**[16] [1202] 3-9-2 **85**.......... SilvestreDeSousa 2 79
(Mark Johnston) *trckd ldng pair: hdwy to chal 3f out: rdn over 2f out and ev ch tl drvn and wknd ent fnl f* **15/2**

06-2 **5** 6 **Muhandis (IRE)**[16] [1203] 3-8-13 **82**.......... TadhgO'Shea 1 63
(Ed Dunlop) *dwlt and hld up in rr: sme hdwy over 3f out: rdn wl over 2f out and sn btn* **4/1**[2]

051- **6** 7 **Kalleidoscope**[238] [5509] 3-8-10 **79**.......... SamHitchcott 4 45
(Mick Channon) *chsd ldrs: rdn along over 3f out: sn btn* **12/1**

1m 55.12s (1.22) **Going Correction** +0.25s/f (Good) **6** Ran SP% **113.7**
Speed ratings (Par 104): **104,102,97,96,91 85**
toteswingers: 1&2 £3.90, 1&3 £1.80, 2&3 £7.10. CSF £11.35 TOTE £2.10: £1.20, £2.70; EX 11.70.
Owner S & G Clayton **Bred** Doverlane Finance Ltd **Trained** Musley Bank, N Yorks

FOCUS
A decent handicap but the top-weight weighed in 10lb below the ceiling for the race and the early pace wasn't hectic. The level is a bit fluid but the winner impressed.

NOTEBOOK

Glen's Diamond ◆ won despite not having the race run to suit or handling the track particularly well, and he looks a 3-y-o going places. Bred to appreciate this step up in trip, he could have done with a stronger all-round pace, but he showed his class to overcome that and won a shade cleverly in the end. Another furlong will be to his benefit and he can win again. There's a valuable handicap over 1m4f here on Derby Day that will be considered. (tchd 13-8 and 7-4 in a place)

Calypso Magic(IRE) was allowed to do his own thing out in front, just as he had when taking his maiden over this C&D last time, and his jockey saved a bit for the straight. The favourite was made to work hard to get by him, but another rise in the weights won't do him any good. (op 11-2 tchd 13-2)

Rastaban had his chance in the straight but the first two saw their races out better. This was only his third-ever run and he can do better with softer ground possibly in his favour. (op 10-3 tchd 9-2 in a place)

Malthouse(GER) ran a better race than at Ripon without suggesting that he's on a mark he's about to exploit any time soon. (op 10-1)

Muhandis(IRE), who didn't look the most straightforward at Ripon, struggled to get competitive from off the pace. (op 11-2)

Kalleidoscope may do better when reverting to front-running tactics. (op 14-1)

1517 MUSSELBURGH GOLD CUP H'CAP — 1m 6f

3:40 (3:40) (Class 4) (0-85,85) 4-Y-O+

£12,462 (£3,732; £1,866; £934; £466; £234) **Stalls** Low

Form				RPR
145-	**1**		**High Office**[171] 7292 5-9-2 **84** .... LeeTopliss(5) 8 (Richard Fahey) *hld up in tch: hdwy on inner over 3f out: chsd ldr 2f out: sn swtchd lft and rdn to chal: led ins fnl f: drvn and kpt on wl towards fin* **18/1**	98
020-	**2**	*1 ¼*	**Becausewecan (USA)**[169] 7337 5-9-3 **80** .... JoeFanning 4 (Mark Johnston) *led: clr 1/2-way: rdn along 3f out: jnd and drvn wl over 1f out: hdd and no ex ins fnl f* **11/1**	92
120-	**3**	*7*	**Beat The Rush**[196] 6754 4-9-6 **85** .... BarryMcHugh 6 (Julie Camacho) *chsd ldng pair: hdwy over 3f out: rdn along over 2f out: sn drvn and kpt on same pce* **7/1**[3]	87
360-	**4**	*¾*	**Dazzling Light (UAE)**[189] 6926 6-9-0 **80** .... GaryBartley(3) 2 (Jim Goldie) *hld up in rr: hdwy on inner 3f out: rdn over 2f out: swtchd lft and drvn over 1f out: kpt on ins fnl f: nrst fin* **14/1**	81
00-0	**5**	*nk*	**European Dream (IRE)**[49] 180 8-9-4 **81** .... (p) PaulHanagan 7 (Richard Fahey) *midfield: hdwy over 3f out: rdn along over 2f out: sn drvn and one pce* **12/1**	82
62-1	**6**	*1 ¼*	**Ubi Ace**[14] 1243 5-9-2 **79** .... GrahamGibbons 11 (Tim Walford) *trckd ldrs: effrt on outer 4f out: rdn along over 3f out: drvn over 2f out: sn no imp* **11/2**[1]	78
050-	**7**	*nk*	**Wells Lyrical (IRE)**[224] 5940 6-9-3 **80** .... TomEaves 1 (Bryan Smart) *chsd ldr: rdn along over 4f out: drvn over 3f out and grad wknd* **14/1**	79
40-3	**8**	*1 ¼*	**Nave (USA)**[9] 1325 4-9-6 **85** .... GregFairley 9 (Mark Johnston) *in tch: effrt over 3f out: sn rdn along and no imp* **13/2**[2]	82
41-6	**9**	*3 ¾*	**Tres Coronas (IRE)**[21] 1097 4-9-5 **84** .... PhillipMakin 10 (David Barron) *hld up in rr: sme hdwy 3f out: sn rdn and nvr a factor* **8/1**	76
524-	**10**	*6*	**Gordonsville**[343] 2126 8-9-8 **85** .... DanielTudhope 13 (Jim Goldie) *stdd s: hld up in rr: sme hdwy over 4f out: nvr a factor* **12/1**	68
02-1	**11**	*11*	**Deauville Post (FR)**[24] 1046 4-9-2 **81** .... PatDobbs 12 (Richard Hannon) *trckd ldrs: pushed along over 3f out: sn rdn and wknd* **8/1**	49
532-	**12**	*5*	**Boston Blue**[207] 6448 4-9-4 **83** .... RoystonFfrench 3 (Tim Etherington) *hld up: a in rr* **12/1**	44
0514	**13**	*1 ½*	**Record Breaker (IRE)**[11] 1291 7-9-4 **81** .... (b) SilvestreDeSousa 14 (Mark Johnston) *in tch: rdn along 4f out: sn wknd* **11/1**	40
66-0	**14**	*9*	**Overrule (USA)**[18] 1154 7-9-3 **85** .... SeanLevey(5) 5 (Brian Ellison) *a in rr: wl bhd fnl 4f* **50/1**	31

3m 7.55s (2.25) **Going Correction** +0.30s/f (Good)
WFA 4 from 5yo+ 2lb **14** Ran SP% **123.7**
Speed ratings (Par 105): **105,104,100,99,99 98,98,98,95,92 86,83,82,77**
toteswingers: 1&2 £53.30, 1&3 £46.30, 2&3 £27.10. CSF £209.21 CT £1542.82 TOTE £30.90: £8.00, £2.70, £3.80; EX 428.30 TRIFECTA Not won..
Owner R A Fahey **Bred** Genesis Green Stud Ltd **Trained** Musley Bank, N Yorks

FOCUS
The going was changed to good to soft, good in places before this race. Not too many got into it as Becausewecan took them along at a pace to suit himself and it proved difficult to come from too far back. The runner-up sets the level rated to last season's form.
Deauville Post(FR) Official explanation: jockey said colt was unsuited by the good to soft (good in places) ground

1518 SCOTTISH RACING CONDITIONS STKS — 5f

4:15 (4:15) (Class 2) 3-Y-O+

£12,462 (£3,732; £1,866; £934; £466; £234) **Stalls** High

Form				RPR
44-3	**1**		**Hamish McGonagall**[14] 1242 6-8-12 107 .... DavidAllan 7 (Tim Easterby) *mde all: rdn wl over 1f out: drvn and edgd rt ins fnl f: kpt on strly* **11/10**[1]	111
55-2	**2**	*2*	**Waffle (IRE)**[20] 1111 5-8-12 100 .... SilvestreDeSousa 3 (David Barron) *trckd ldrs whn hmpd and lost pl after 1f: hdwy to trck ldrs and nt clr run 2f out: rdn to chal over 1f out and ev ch tl drvn and one pce ins fnl f* **9/4**[2]	104
64-0	**3**	*4*	**Fitz Flyer (IRE)**[21] 1093 5-8-12 94 .... TomEaves 6 (Bryan Smart) *chsd ldrs whn n.m.r on inner after 1f: rdn and hdwy wl over 1f out: kpt on ins fnl f: nrst fin* **18/1**	89
231-	**4**	*½*	**Elnawin**[281] 4105 5-9-5 104 .... PatDobbs 5 (Richard Hannon) *chsd ldrs whn n.m.r: hmpd and lost pl after 1f: rdn wl over 1f out: kpt on ins fnl f* **9/2**[3]	95
00-0	**5**	*2 ¼*	**Striking Spirit**[8] 1366 6-8-12 96 .... AndrewMullen 1 (David Nicholls) *cl up: rdn along over 2f out: sn drvn and wknd* **20/1**	80
4-00	**6**	*nk*	**Masta Plasta (IRE)**[65] 582 8-9-5 98 .... FrannyNorton 2 (David Nicholls) *cl up on outer: rdn along over 2f out: sn wknd* **18/1**	85
110-	**7**	*21*	**Burning Thread (IRE)**[227] 5851 4-9-12 97 .... RoystonFfrench 4 (Tim Etherington) *dwlt and hmpd s: a bhd* **50/1**	—

60.88 secs (0.48) **Going Correction** +0.35s/f (Good) **7** Ran SP% **113.8**
Speed ratings (Par 109): **110,106,100,99,96 95,61**
toteswingers: 1&2 £1.02, 1&3 £7.40, 2&3 £6.40. CSF £3.70 TOTE £2.10: £1.10, £1.80; EX 3.60.
Owner Reality Partnerships I **Bred** J P Coggan And Whitsbury Manor Stud **Trained** Great Habton, N Yorks

FOCUS
A fair conditions race with the first two basically to form.

NOTEBOOK

Hamish McGonagall, who ran well at Thirsk over 6f on his reappearance but is much more at home over a sharp 5f, as expected, bounced out quickly and, with the rail to help, set out to make every yard. He was briefly challenged by Waffle (carried same weight but rated 7lb lower) in the closing stages but he soon saw him off and won pretty comfortably in the end to register his fourth C&D win from six starts. He did no more than he was entitled to, but he will head for the Duke of York Stakes next while at the top of his game. (op 5-4)

Waffle(IRE) was an eyecatcher at Doncaster last time, but that race came over 6f. He had no trouble going the pace back down in trip, but was hampered early and couldn't get by the track specialist winner when brought with his challenge. It was a fair effort at the weights and, while it's slightly disconcerting that he's now finished second on five occasions and only has a maiden win to his name, he appeals as the type to run above himself in a big field sprint, where he'll get to weave his way through. (tchd 7-4)

Fitz Flyer(IRE), representing the stable successful in this race the previous two years, was the lowest-rated horse in the field and overcame some scrimmaging early on to run on for third. It was a sound effort in the circumstances. (op 20-1 tchd 16-1)

Elnawin, who has gone well fresh in the past, needs quick ground to be seen at his best so the softening conditions were not in his favour. (op 11-2 tchd 6-1)

Striking Spirit, who lost his action at Newbury, was second in this race last year, but he paid for trying to match strides with the winner this time and couldn't repeat that feat. (op 16-1)

Masta Plasta(IRE) showed precious little out in Dubai and faced no easy task at these weights. (op 16-1)

Burning Thread(IRE), who has had back problems and had to give weight all round, struggled throughout.

1519 SCOTTISH RACING H'CAP (QUALIFIER FOR THE BETFAIR BONUS SCOTTISH RACING STAYERS FINAL) — 1m 6f

4:45 (4:45) (Class 6) (0-60,58) 4-Y-O+ **£2,590** (£770; £385; £192) **Stalls** Low

Form				RPR
53-0	**1**		**Oddsmaker (IRE)**[24] 1036 10-9-6 **58** .... (t) PaulHanagan 2 (Maurice Barnes) *mde all: 4 l clr 1/2-way: rdn and qcknd wl clr over 3f out: styd on strly* **3/1**[1]	66
0/0-	**2**	*5*	**Oh Landino (GER)**[22] 3709 6-8-7 **45** .... AndrewMullen 4 (Jim Goldie) *a.p: chsd wnr fr over 3f out: drvn over 2f out: kpt on but no imp on wnr fnl f* **16/1**	46
00-0	**3**	*4 ½*	**Three White Socks (IRE)**[15] 1210 4-8-5 **45** .... SilvestreDeSousa 7 (Brian Ellison) *hld up in rr: hdwy over 3f out: rdn over 2f out: styd on fr over 1f out: nrst fin* **17/2**	40
004-	**4**	*6*	**Maid Of Meft**[178] 7176 4-9-3 **57** .... FrederikTylicki 8 (Linda Perratt) *hld up in rr: hdwy over 3f out: rdn wl over 2f out: kpt on appr fnl f: nvr nr ldrs* **11/1**	43
460-	**5**	*1 ½*	**Thescottishsoldier**[19] 3948 4-8-2 **45** .... JamesSullivan(3) 3 (Alistair Whillans) *in tch on inner: hdwy to chse ldng pair 3f out: drvn over 2f out and sn btn* **16/1**	29
000-	**6**	*8*	**Petella**[178] 7181 5-9-5 **57** .... TomEaves 10 (George Moore) *hld up in rr: hdwy over 3f out: sn rdn along and n.d* **7/2**[2]	30
54-0	**7**	*1*	**Ballade De La Mer**[64] 598 5-8-7 **45** .... (p) LeeNewman 6 (George Foster) *hld up in midfield: effrt over 4f out: sn rdn and nvr a factor* **7/1**	17
4-35	**8**	*nk*	**Leaving Alone (USA)**[10] 1305 4-9-0 **54** .... TonyHamilton 5 (Edwin Tuer) *chsd ldrs: rdn along over 3f out: drvn wl over 2f out and sn wknd* **4/1**[3]	25
03-	**9**	*11*	**Front Rank (IRE)**[27] 5364 11-8-7 **45** .... DuranFentiman 9 (Dianne Sayer) *chsd ldrs on outer: rdn along 5f out: sn wknd* **14/1**	—
26/0	**10**	*3 ¼*	**Michevious Spirit (IRE)**[10] 1305 4-8-7 **47** ow2 .... BarryMcHugh 1 (David Thompson) *prom: chsd wnr after 5f: rdn along over 3f out and sn wknd* **40/1**	—

3m 13.07s (7.77) **Going Correction** +0.60s/f (Yiel)
WFA 4 from 5yo+ 2lb **10** Ran SP% **119.5**
Speed ratings (Par 101): **101,98,95,92,91 86,86,85,79,77**
toteswingers: 1&2 £31.60, 1&3 £3.10, 2&3 £12.40. CSF £54.39 CT £378.18 TOTE £3.40: £2.10, £5.00, £2.10; EX 51.60 Trifecta £111.60 Pool: £316.80 - 2.10 winning units..
Owner M Barnes **Bred** Margaret Conlon **Trained** Farlam, Cumbria

FOCUS
A moderate handicap in which the winner is rated to last year's form.

1520 TURFTV H'CAP (QUALIFIER FOR THE BETFAIR BONUS SCOTTISH RACING MILE FINAL) — 1m

5:15 (5:16) (Class 6) (0-65,65) 4-Y-O+ **£2,590** (£770; £385; £192) **Stalls** High

Form				RPR
-522	**1**		**Ravi River (IRE)**[15] 1216 7-9-5 **63** .... SilvestreDeSousa 9 (Brian Ellison) *hld up in midfield: stdy hdwy over 2f out: swtchd lft and rdn to chse ldrs over 1f out: led jst ins fnl f and styd on wl* **2/1**[1]	74
0-03	**2**	*2*	**Amno Dancer (IRE)**[22] 1077 4-8-12 **56** .... LeeNewman 6 (David Barron) *trckd ldrs: hdwy 3f out and sn cl up: rdn to ld wl over 1f out: drvn and hdd jst ins fnl f: sn edgd lft and one pce* **11/2**[3]	62
305-	**3**	*4 ½*	**Casino Night**[175] 7228 6-9-6 **64** .... SamHitchcott 12 (Barry Murtagh) *cl up on outer: led over 3f out: rdn over 2f out: drvn and hdd over 1f out: sn one pce* **16/1**	60
30-4	**4**	*7*	**Royal Straight**[22] 1072 6-9-2 **65** .... LeeTopliss(5) 11 (Linda Perratt) *midfield: hdwy to chse ldrs 3f out: rdn over 2f out: drvn and wknd over 1f out* **14/1**	45
50-0	**5**	*6*	**Paradise Spectre**[15] 1221 4-9-4 **62** .... AndrewElliott 2 (Mrs K Burke) *towards rr: sme hdwy wl over 2f out: sn rdn and nvr nr ldrs* **14/1**	28
/00-	**6**	*6*	**Brisbane (IRE)**[62] 5819 4-8-13 **57** .... TonyHamilton 3 (Dianne Sayer) *chsd ldrs: rdn along 3f out: sn wknd* **40/1**	—
0350	**7**	*10*	**Mr Emirati (USA)**[7] 1394 4-9-0 **58** .... TomEaves 8 (Bryan Smart) *towards rr: hdwy on outer over 3f out: rdn and in tch over 2f out: sn drvn: hung rt and wknd* **33/1**	—
024-	**8**	*¾*	**Call Of Duty (IRE)**[205] 6492 6-9-7 **65** .... DuranFentiman 1 (Dianne Sayer) *cl up: led after 2f: rdn along and hdd over 3f out: grad wknd* **8/1**	—
03-0	**9**	*15*	**Bahamian Kid**[22] 1077 6-9-1 **59** .... PhillipMakin 4 (George Foster) *led 2f: cl up tl rdn along and wknd over 3f out* **33/1**	—
146-	**10**	*4 ½*	**Cold Quest (USA)**[222] 6026 7-8-8 **55** .... BillyCray(3) 5 (Linda Perratt) *s.i.s: a bhd* **10/1**	—
6/35	**11**	*7*	**The Gillie**[29] 971 4-8-13 **57** .... PaulHanagan 7 (Richard Fahey) *a in rr: bhd fr 1/2-way* **5/1**[2]	—
660-	**12**	*1 ¼*	**Glenluji**[219] 6108 6-9-4 **62** .... DanielTudhope 10 (Jim Goldie) *s.i.s: a bhd* **12/1**	—

1m 46.05s (4.85) **Going Correction** +0.65s/f (Yiel) **12** Ran SP% **120.8**
Speed ratings (Par 101): **101,99,94,87,81 75,65,64,49,45 38,37**
toteswingers: 1&2 £2.10, 1&3 £22.50, 2&3 £18.90. CSF £12.52 CT £145.18 TOTE £3.30: £1.80, £2.40, £3.90; EX 9.80 Trifecta £136.30 Part won. Pool: £184.22 - 0.10 winning units..
Owner Koo's Racing Club **Bred** Gainsborough Stud Management Ltd **Trained** Norton, N Yorks

FOCUS
A modest handicap in which the winner is rated to last year's spring form but not a race to be too positive about.
The Gillie Official explanation: jockey said gelding never travelled
T/Plt: £100.60 to a £1 stake. Pool:£46,821.01 - 339.67 winning tickets. T/Qpdt: £33.40 to a £1 stake. Pool:£3,099.04 - 68.60 winning tickets. JR

1185 NOTTINGHAM (L-H)

Saturday, April 23

OFFICIAL GOING: Good to firm (7.7)
All races on outer course.
Wind: Nil Weather: Overcast

1521 CALVERTS CARPETS YORK FILLIES' H'CAP — 5f 13y
5:30 (5:33) (Class 5) (0-75,75) 3-Y-O — **£4,209** (£1,252; £625; £312) **Stalls** High

Form					RPR
3302	1		**Sugar Beet**[23] 1062 3-9-2 **70** DavidProbert 6 (Ronald Harris) *hld up in tch: rdn to ld 1f out: r.o wl* **6/1**		77
-122	2	2 1/4	**Palais Glide**[38] 864 3-9-2 **75** KieranO'Neill(5) 5 (Richard Hannon) *unruly in stalls: dwlt: sn drvn along in rr: swtchd lft and hdwy over 1f out: edgd lft and styd on to go 2nd wl ins fnl f: nt trble wnr* **5/2**[1]		74
15-4	3	1 1/2	**Tro Nesa (IRE)**[22] 1079 3-9-7 **75** SebSanders 3 (Ann Duffield) *prom: sn drvn along: styd on same pce ins fnl f* **10/1**		69
16-3	4	nse	**Nine Before Ten (IRE)**[12] 1275 3-9-6 **74** (b[1]) PaulMulrennan 4 (Deborah Sanderson) *unruly in stalls: led: rdn and hdd over 1f out: no ex ins fnl f* **11/2**[3]		67
56-5	5	3/4	**Acclamatory**[94] 208 3-8-4 **63** RyanClark(5) 1 (Stuart Williams) *s.i.s: outpcd: r.o ins fnl f: nvr nrr* **9/1**		54
630-	6	nk	**Aurivorous**[232] 5720 3-8-13 **67** RussKennemore 8 (Anabel K Murphy) *chsd ldrs: led over 1f out: sn rdn: hung lft and hdd: no ex* **40/1**		57
-136	7	7	**Grandmas Dream**[19] 1141 3-9-7 **75** PaulDoe 7 (Jim Best) *chsd ldrs: rdn 1/2-way: wknd and eased fnl f* **4/1**[2]		39
0-15	8	5	**Winniepeg**[18] 1149 3-8-5 **62** JohnFahy(3) 2 (Clive Cox) *wnt lft s: sn prom: rdn over 3f out: edgd rt and wknd 2f out* **11/2**[3]		—

60.62 secs (-0.38) **Going Correction** -0.20s/f (Firm) **8** Ran SP% **115.2**
Speed ratings (Par 95): **95,91,89,88,87 87,76,68**
toteswingers: 1&2 £4.10, 1&3 £10.50, 2&3 £4.10. CSF £21.59 CT £148.14 TOTE £8.00: £2.30, £1.30, £2.30; EX 25.40.
Owner Ridge House Stables Ltd **Bred** Coln Valley Stud **Trained** Earlswood, Monmouths
FOCUS
A modest fillies' handicap run at a decent pace. The field all stayed stands' side. The winner is rated to her best juvenile form and the race might work out.
Acclamatory Official explanation: jockey said filly was outpaced
Aurivorous Official explanation: jockey said filly hung left
Winniepeg Official explanation: jockey said filly lost its action

1522 CALVERTS CARPETS YORK MAIDEN STKS — 5f 13y
6:00 (6:01) (Class 5) 2-Y-O — **£2,266** (£674; £337; £168) **Stalls** High

Form					RPR
4	1		**Ortea**[15] 1209 2-9-3 0 CathyGannon 9 (David Evans) *mde all: rdn and edgd lft over 1f out: r.o wl* **11/2**[2]		78+
	2	4 1/2	**Royal Purse** 2-8-12 0 TomMcLaughlin 8 (David Evans) *prom: rdn 1/2-way: hung lft over 1f out: styd on same pce fnl f* **25/1**		57
	3	1 3/4	**Bluebells Are Blue (IRE)** 2-9-3 0 FergusSweeney 5 (Eve Johnson Houghton) *s.i.s: sn chsng ldrs: rdn over 1f out: styd on same pce* **8/1**		55
	4	1	**Perfecto Tiempo (IRE)** 2-9-3 0 DavidProbert 6 (Ronald Harris) *s.i.s: sn pushed along in rr: styd on fr over 1f out: nt trble ldrs* **25/1**		52
	5	1/2	**Aljosan** 2-8-5 0 MatthewCosham(7) 3 (David Evans) *chsd ldrs: rdn 1/2-way: wknd fnl f* **20/1**		45
5	6	hd	**Jimmy The Lollipop (IRE)**[21] 1095 2-9-3 0 PaulMulrennan 4 (Kevin Ryan) *chsd wnr: rdn and ev ch over 1f out: wknd fnl f* **1/1**[1]		49+
0	7	1 3/4	**Outlaw Torn (IRE)**[21] 1095 2-9-3 0 JamesDoyle 2 (Alan McCabe) *dwlt: outpcd: sme hdwy 2f out: sn rdn and wknd* **8/1**		43
	8	1/2	**Red Socks (IRE)** 2-9-3 0 ChrisCatlin 7 (Gay Kelleway) *s.i.s: outpcd* **6/1**[3]		43+

61.96 secs (0.96) **Going Correction** -0.20s/f (Firm) **8** Ran SP% **114.3**
Speed ratings (Par 92): **84,76,74,72,71 71,68,67**
toteswingers: 1&2 £38.10, 1&3 £5.50, 2&3 £32.00. CSF £126.84 TOTE £5.40: £1.50, £9.00, £1.30; EX 47.40.
Owner Phil Slater **Bred** Bearstone Stud **Trained** Pandy, Monmouths
FOCUS
Probably no more than a fair a maiden in all likelihood with the field well bunched for much of the way. The action was again stands' side.
NOTEBOOK
Ortea ◆ had clearly come on a good deal for his debut when probably in need of the race, stretching clear in good style inside the last and never better than at the finish to win by a margin that seemed unlikely for a long way. He'll be suited by 6f before long and looks to have a bit about him physically, so should improve again. (op 7-1)
Royal Purse a half-sister to several winners out of an unraced half-sister to the top mile Where Or When, made an encouraging debut, never threatening to better her finishing position as she ran green but starting to get the hang of things as the race went on. She'll improve. (op 20-1 tchd 28-1)
Bluebells Are Blue(IRE), the first foal of a 7f winner, also shaped well first time up, travelling comfortably enough to halfway then keeping on. He should do better next time. (tchd 7-1)
Perfecto Tiempo(IRE), the second foal of an unraced mare, plugged on through beaten horses for fourth without ever looking as good as that position suggests and isn't going to be of much interest until sent over further. (tchd 28-1)
Aljosan, a half-sister to the 2010 2yo 5f winner Pick A Little, may have been disadvantaged by racing wide of the rest towards the centre and left the impression anyway the run was just needed. (op 16-1)
Jimmy The Lollipop(IRE) had shaped well in the Brocklesby but didn't make the expected progress under these quicker conditions, beaten approaching the last and eased late on. He's got scope to progress and shouldn't be written down yet. Official explanation: jockey said colt never travelled (op 11-10 tchd 10-11)
Outlaw Torn(IRE) Official explanation: jockey said colt hung left
Red Socks(IRE), who cost £26,000 earlier this year, was soon on the back foot after a slow start but showed signs the penny was dropping late on despite finishing last and is entitled to improve. (op 5-1 tchd 13-2)

1523 CALVERTS CARPETS YORK LTD H'CAP — 5f 13y
6:30 (6:31) (Class 6) (0-65,67) 4-Y-O+ — **£1,780** (£529; £264; £132) **Stalls** High

Form					RPR
6440	1		**Athwaab**[9] 1336 4-8-0 **51** oh3 CharlesBishop(7) 1 (Noel Quinlan) *chsd ldrs: led 3f out: rdn and edgd rt ins fnl f: r.o* **10/1**		68
600-	2	3 1/4	**Musical Bridge**[178] 7169 5-9-0 **65** ShaneBKelly(7) 11 (Lisa Williamson) *mid-div: sn pushed along: hdwy 1/2-way: rdn to chse wnr over 1f out: no imp ins fnl f* **8/1**		70
2314	3	nk	**Yankee Storm**[16] 1196 6-9-0 **58** (b) JimmyQuinn 10 (Tom Keddy) *dwlt: outpcd: hdwy over 1f out: r.o: nt rch ldrs* **3/1**[1]		62
40-4	4	2 1/4	**Lees Anthem**[7] 1411 4-9-4 **62** PatrickMathers 2 (Colin Teague) *prom: rdn 1/2-way: wknd ins fnl f* **8/1**		58
0623	5	1 3/4	**Silver Wind**[12] 1267 6-9-9 **67** (b) SebSanders 5 (Alan McCabe) *prom: rdn 1/2-way: wknd ins fnl f* **9/2**[2]		57
0150	6	1 1/4	**Triskaidekaphobia**[17] 1182 8-8-7 **51** oh2 (t) FrankieMcDonald 8 (Paul Fitzsimons) *led 2f: sn pushed along: wknd fnl f* **16/1**		36
00-6	7	2 1/4	**Canadian Danehill (IRE)**[4] 1469 9-8-13 **57** (p) TomQueally 3 (Robert Cowell) *chsd ldrs: rdn over 1f out: wknd fnl f* **12/1**		34
600-	8	1/2	**Gertmegalush (IRE)**[191] 6879 4-9-6 **64** StevieDonohoe 6 (John Harris) *s.i.s: outpcd: nvr nrr* **14/1**		39
5364	9	1 1/2	**Thoughtsofstardom**[11] 1283 8-8-7 **51** oh2 ChrisCatlin 4 (Phil McEntee) *chsd ldrs tl rdn 1/2-way: sn wknd* **14/1**		21
531-	10	1 1/2	**Crimson Queen**[141] 7684 4-9-0 **58** PaulMulrennan 9 (Roy Brotherton) *mid-div: sme hdwy 1/2-way: wknd wl over 1f out* **13/2**[3]		22
/0-0	11	13	**Excellent Vision**[17] 1171 4-9-5 **63** RichardKingscote 7 (Milton Bradley) *unruly in stalls: s.i.s: outpcd* **25/1**		—

59.79 secs (-1.21) **Going Correction** -0.20s/f (Firm) **11** Ran SP% **118.6**
Speed ratings (Par 101): **101,95,95,91,88 86,83,82,80,77 56**
toteswingers: 1&2 £22.90, 1&3 £7.20, 2&3 £5.10. CSF £88.39 CT £307.94 TOTE £13.50: £4.40, £4.30, £1.30; EX 75.40.
Owner Mrs Lynn McGregor **Bred** Shadwell Estate Co Ltd **Trained** Newmarket, Suffolk
FOCUS
A run-of-the-mill handicap contested mostly be exposed runners coming off a run on the all weather. The pace was good, the action again on the rail, but few ever got into it all the same. The level is a bit fluid and the winner could be rated higher.
Triskaidekaphobia Official explanation: jockey said gelding was slow away

1524 CALVERTS CARPETS AND FLOORING YORK H'CAP — 1m 75y
7:00 (7:01) (Class 6) (0-65,65) 3-Y-O — **£1,942** (£578; £288; £144) **Stalls** Centre

Form					RPR
45-0	1		**Zamina (IRE)**[14] 1251 3-9-4 **62** JamesDoyle 3 (Sylvester Kirk) *hld up: hdwy over 2f out: r.o to ld wl ins fnl f: readily* **11/2**[3]		70+
05-0	2	1 3/4	**Looksmart**[25] 1022 3-8-13 **62** KieranO'Neill(5) 5 (Richard Hannon) *led: hdd 7f out: led again 6f out: clr 2f out: sn rdn: hdd and unable qck wl ins fnl f* **13/2**		66
410-	3	2	**Tapis Libre**[187] 6978 3-9-7 **65** PaulMulrennan 7 (Michael Easterby) *chsd ldr: led 7f out to 6f out: chsd ldr: rdn over 2f out: no ex wl ins fnl f* **8/1**		64
00-0	4	5	**Lemon Drop Red (USA)**[25] 1022 3-9-6 **64** TomMcLaughlin 8 (Ed Dunlop) *hld up: rdn over 3f out: hdwy over 2f out: no imp fnl f* **13/8**[1]		52
06-5	5	2 1/2	**Rational Act (IRE)**[17] 1169 3-9-2 **60** RobertWinston 1 (Tim Easterby) *plld hrd and prom: rdn over 2f out: wknd fnl f* **4/1**[2]		42
0-00	6	9	**Gothic Chick**[22] 1082 3-8-11 **55** (p) TomQueally 4 (Alan McCabe) *s.i.s: sn prom: rdn and wknd over 2f out* **28/1**		16
000	7	3	**Savinien**[14] 1236 3-8-7 **51** oh4 (v[1]) CathyGannon 2 (David Evans) *s.s: hdwy 7f out: rdn and wknd over 2f out* **18/1**		—
0-03	8	15	**Melbury**[59] 655 3-8-8 **52** JimmyQuinn 6 (Michael Squance) *prom: lost pl 6f out: rdn and wknd over 3f out: t.o* **10/1**		—

1m 46.32s (0.72) **Going Correction** 0.0s/f (Good) **8** Ran SP% **115.7**
Speed ratings (Par 96): **96,94,92,87,84 75,72,57**
toteswingers: 1&2 £5.00, 1&3 £3.70, 2&3 £8.00. CSF £41.28 CT £287.00 TOTE £5.80: £2.40, £2.30, £3.10; EX 60.10.
Owner N Pickett & S Kirk **Bred** Churchtown Bloodstock **Trained** Upper Lambourn, Berks
FOCUS
A modest handicap essentially well run despite some early traffic problems, but all the same a race of limited interest looking forward. The third is rated basically to form.

1525 CALVERTS CARPETS YORK MEDIAN AUCTION MAIDEN STKS — 1m 2f 50y
7:30 (7:31) (Class 6) 3-Y-O — **£1,942** (£578; £288; £144) **Stalls** Low

Form					RPR
2-3	1		**Aldedash (USA)**[12] 1271 3-9-3 0 TomQueally 2 (Sir Henry Cecil) *mde all: shkn up over 2f out: clr over 1f out: in command fnl f: eased nr fin* **4/11**[1]		75+
	2	1	**Baltic Light (USA)** 3-8-12 0 IanMongan 3 (Sir Henry Cecil) *hld up in tch: outpcd over 2f out: rallied and hung lft over 1f out: r.o to go 2nd wl ins fnl f: no ch w wnr* **8/1**[3]		65+
64-3	3	1	**Major Domo (FR)**[17] 1173 3-9-3 71 LukeMorris 4 (Harry Dunlop) *trckd wnr: shkn up over 3f out: rdn over 2f out: styd on: lost 2nd wl ins fnl f* **4/1**[2]		68
660-	4	19	**My Elliemay**[288] 3861 3-8-12 0 CathyGannon 1 (David Evans) *prom: racd keenly: pushed along over 4f out: rdn and wknd over 2f out* **28/1**		25

2m 14.3s (2.60) **Going Correction** 0.0s/f (Good) **4** Ran SP% **107.9**
Speed ratings (Par 96): **89,88,87,72**
CSF £3.86 TOTE £1.70; EX 2.00.
Owner Axom (XXVII) **Bred** Morgan's Ford Farm **Trained** Newmarket, Suffolk
FOCUS
Probably fair form from the winner with his stable-companion shaping well in second. The pace was fair and the third sets the level.

1526 CALVERTS CARPETS YORK H'CAP — 1m 2f 50y
8:00 (8:00) (Class 6) (0-65,65) 3-Y-O — **£1,780** (£529; £264; £132) **Stalls** Low

Form					RPR
14-1	1		**Amistress**[17] 1189 3-9-3 **61** CathyGannon 4 (Eve Johnson Houghton) *a.p: rdn to chse ldr over 2f out: styd on to ld wl ins fnl f: eased nr fin* **13/8**[1]		68
4224	2	nk	**Echos Of Motivator**[11] 1300 3-9-7 **65** (p) LukeMorris 1 (Ronald Harris) *s.i.s: hld up: rdn over 3f out: r.o wl ins fnl f: nt quite get up* **10/1**		71
40-6	3	1/2	**Subramaniam**[10] 1312 3-9-2 **60** PaulMulrennan 9 (James Given) *led: rdn over 1f out: hdd and no ex wl ins fnl f:* **13/2**[3]		65?

600- **4** 1 3/4 **King Kurt (IRE)**[187] 6979 3-9-6 **64** StevieDonohoe 10 66
(Kevin Ryan) *chsd ldr tl rdn over 2f out: no ex ins fnl f* **12/1**

014- **5** 4 **Rosa Midnight (USA)**[224] 5961 3-9-5 **63** HayleyTurner 3 57
(Michael Bell) *chsd ldrs: rdn over 2f out: sn outpcd: styd on ins fnl f* **9/2**[2]

55-6 **6** 1 1/2 **Eduardo**[17] 1169 3-8-8 **55** MichaelO'Connell(3) 5 46
(Jedd O'Keeffe) *chsd ldrs: rdn over 2f out: sn hung lft and outpcd: n.d after* **8/1**

0040 **7** 2 1/4 **Varlak**[26] 1018 3-8-5 **52** SophieDoyle(3) 2 38
(Des Donovan) *s.i.s: hld up: bhd whn hung lft over 2f out: nvr nrr* **28/1**

000- **8** 1 1/4 **Market Maker (IRE)**[187] 6979 3-8-13 **57** RobertWinston 6 41
(Tim Easterby) *hld up: sme hdwy over 3f out: sn rdn and wknd* **14/1**

1333 **9** 2 1/2 **Better Self**[30] 951 3-9-4 **65** RichardEvans(3) 8 44
(David Evans) *hld up: racd keenly: nvr on terms* **12/1**

504- **10** 9 **Carver County (IRE)**[134] 7801 3-8-4 **53** oh6 ow2 RyanClark(5) 7 14
(Mandy Rowland) *s.i.s: hld up: a in rr: bhd fnl 3f* **66/1**

2m 13.23s (1.53) **Going Correction** 0.0s/f (Good) **10** Ran SP% **116.8**
Speed ratings (Par 96): **93,92,92,90,87 86,84,83,81,74**
toteswingers: 1&2 £2.50, 1&3 £2.60, 2&3 £10.70. CSF £19.44 CT £86.96 TOTE £2.10: £1.20, £3.00, £1.90; EX 19.90.
Owner Mrs P Robeson **Bred** Southcourt Stud **Trained** Blewbury, Oxon
■ Stewards' Enquiry : Ryan Clark two-day ban: weighed in 2lb heavy (May 7 & 9)

FOCUS
A modest handicap run at just a steady pace and it proved difficult to come from behind as things turned out, so the runner-up deserves some credit. This form looks ordinary.
T/Plt: £243.00 to a £1 stake. Pool:£40,435.35 - 121.46 winning tickets. T/Qpdt: £37.40 to a £1 stake. Pool:£4,081.49 - 80.60 winning tickets. CR

SANDOWN (R-H)
Saturday, April 23

OFFICIAL GOING: Flat & hurdle courses - good (good to firm in places; flat 8.1, hdl 7.8) chase course - good to firm (good in places; 8.4)
Other races under the rules of jumps racing. Home bend at outermost configuration adding 8yds to race distances.
Wind: Almost nil Weather: Sunny, warm

1527 BET365 MILE (GROUP 2) 1m 14y
3:45 (3:49) (Class 1) 4-Y-O+ **£45,416** (£17,216; £8,616; £4,296; £2,152) **Stalls** Low

Form RPR

153- **1** **Dick Turpin (IRE)**[202] 6611 4-9-0 124 RichardHughes 1 110+
(Richard Hannon) *trckd ldng pair: crusied through to ld wl over 1f out: sn jnd: shkn up and qcknd smartly to assert fnl f* **8/13**[1]

211- **2** 2 1/4 **Cityscape**[204] 6529 5-9-0 119 SteveDrowne 5 105+
(Roger Charlton) *hld up in last pair: prog on outer to join wnr over 1f out: styd on but readily outpcd fnl f* **5/1**[3]

010- **3** 1 1/4 **Dream Eater (IRE)**[132] 7853 6-9-0 116 (t) JimmyFortune 4 102
(Andrew Balding) *hld up in last pair: no move tl ldrs already gone over 1f out: tk 3rd fnl f and styd on: no ch* **12/1**

234- **4** 1/2 **Music Show (IRE)**[203] 6561 4-8-11 118 RyanMoore 3 97
(Mick Channon) *trckd ldr to jst over 2f out: readily outpcd over 1f out: kpt on* **4/1**[2]

65-0 **5** 1 3/4 **Highland Knight (IRE)**[21] 1092 4-9-0 87 (t) LiamKeniry 2 96
(Andrew Balding) *led to wl over 1f out: sn outpcd* **66/1**

1m 41.92s (-1.38) **Going Correction** +0.10s/f (Good) **5** Ran SP% **107.8**
Speed ratings (Par 115): **110,107,106,106,104**
CSF £3.89 TOTE £1.60: £1.10, £3.10; EX 4.30.
Owner John Manley **Bred** John McEnery **Trained** East Everleigh, Wilts

FOCUS
A smaller field than usual for this Group 2 event, but plenty of class on show including two Group 1 winners. Having taken five of the previous seven runnings with Hurricane Alan (twice), Paco Boy (twice) and Major Cadeaux, Richard Hannon had dominated this contest in recent years. He improved his record courtesy of Dick Turpin. The winner might have improved, although the time was nothing special.

NOTEBOOK
Dick Turpin(IRE) ◆ boasted smart form at the very highest level last season, including finishing runner-up in the English and French Guineas and St James's Palace, plus his richly deserved success in the Group 1 Prix Jean Prat. Bidding to provide Richard Hannon with a fourth consecutive win in this race, the only question was whether this surface would be suitable as he had never won on ground officially described as faster than good and he hung late on when runner-up in last year's 2000 Guineas (Good to firm). Any such worries were emphatically dispelled, however, as he travelled like a dream behind the leaders. If anything he may have hit the front soon enough when the pace-setter dropped away inside the last 2f. The runner-up was produced on his outside at the same time, but one could not helped but be impressed by the way he quickened away from that rival when asked, and he is going to be a serious rival to all in the big mile races this season, including his stable-companion Canford Cliffs, whom he might meet in the Lockinge. (op 4-6 tchd 8-11)
Cityscape was a progressive sort in a light campaign last year, culminating in his impressive success in the Group 3 Joel Stakes at Newmarket. This was another step up in grade and the ground was also a potential issue as he only managed to beat one horse home in Sea The Stars' 2000 Guineas - the only time he had previously encountered ground officially described as faster than good. He was only given the go-ahead to run here after Roger Charlton walked the course and his charge rewarded him with a solid effort in defeat. Held up last early, he was switched to the wide outside 2f out and eyeballed the favourite for a few strides, but the winner then produced another gear. There is no doubt Cityscape is up to this class, not least when he gets easier conditions, and he may take the winner on again in the Lockinge. (tchd 11-2)
Dream Eater(IRE), runner-up to Paco Boy in this race two years ago, raced keenly at the back of the field early and could only produce a limited response when asked for his final effort. He is now 0-21 at Group level. (op 10-1 tchd 8-1)
Music Show(IRE), who chased home Goldikova in the Prix Rothschild and enjoyed her finest hour when landing the Group 1 Falmouth Stakes at Newmarket last summer, was disappointing. The fast ground here was very much in her favour and she saw plenty of daylight on the outside of the pacemaker early, but Ryan Moore wasn't happy on her soon after turning in and it was only her class that kept her in contention for so long. Although she had won first time out in each of her first two seasons, her trainer expected her to come on for the run, so it's much too early to be giving up on her.
Highland Knight(IRE), in as pacemaker for Dream Eater, set by no means a breakneck gallop and helps explain why the outsider wasn't beaten that far at the line. (op 50-1, tchd 100-1 in a place)

1528 BET365 GORDON RICHARDS STKS (GROUP 3) 1m 2f 7y
4:20 (4:20) (Class 1) 4-Y-O+
£28,385 (£10,760; £5,385; £2,685; £1,345; £675) **Stalls** Low

Form RPR

22-2 **1** **Kings Gambit (SAF)**[16] 1201 7-9-0 110 JamieSpencer 5 110
(Tom Tate) *mde all and set str pce: clr after 4f: c bk to rivals over 2f out u.p: battled on really wl fnl f: jst hld on* **5/1**

346- **2** *shd* **Black Spirit (USA)**[217] 6219 4-9-0 107 (t) LukeMorris 4 110
(Clive Cox) *hld up in 4th: prog to chse wnr jst over 2f out: drvn over 1f out: chal fnl f: jst hld* **16/1**

64-1 **3** 2 1/4 **Shamali**[21] 1100 6-9-0 100 EddieAhern 2 105
(William Haggas) *chsd wnr to jst over 2f out: nt qckn and lost pl: kpt on again fnl f* **7/1**

110- **4** 2 1/4 **Nouriya**[202] 6613 4-8-11 106 RyanMoore 1 101+
(Sir Michael Stoute) *hld up in 5th: effrt on inner over 2f out: chal over 1f out disputing 2nd: hld whn short of room 100yds out and eased* **9/2**[3]

353- **5** 1 3/4 **Viscount Nelson (USA)**[294] 3693 4-9-0 114 CO'Donoghue 3 97
(A P O'Brien, Ire) *chsd ldng pair: pushed along over 4f out: lost pl over 2f out: no hdwy over 1f out and btn after* **15/8**[1]

111- **6** 2 1/2 **Afsare**[310] 3104 4-9-0 113 KierenFallon 6 92
(Luca Cumani) *hld up in last: effrt on outer over 2f out: rdn and no prog wl over 1f out: wknd* **10/3**[2]

2m 8.01s (-2.49) **Going Correction** +0.10s/f (Good) **6** Ran SP% **111.1**
Speed ratings (Par 113): **113,112,111,109,107 105**
CSF £68.32 TOTE £5.90: £2.70, £4.70; EX 45.20.
Owner Mrs Fitri Hay **Bred** Danika Stud **Trained** Tadcaster, N Yorks

FOCUS
A race won by the likes of Indian Skimmer and Singspiel in the past, this year's renewal contained no previous European Group winners (Kings Gambit was a dual Grade 1 winner in South Africa), although it did feature a couple of unexposed and progressive 4-y-os. Sir Michael Stoute had totally dominated this race in recent years. While there may not have been any superstars on show this time, this race will be remembered for one of the bravest performances put up by any horse on the Flat in recent years. The form looks ordinary for the grade with the third and fourth the best guides.

NOTEBOOK
Kings Gambit(SAF) had been placed in his last six starts, including in Group company, but he was only 1-17 since leaving South Africa. However, being a horse that likes to go from the front and with race-fitness on his side, Jamie Spencer set his stall out right from the start, setting a strong pace and establishing a clear advantage by halfway. He was predictably challenged on all sides once into the home straight, but he refused to give in, repelling all challengers under strong pressure and just managing to see his race out with nothing to spare. He richly deserved this, but may take a little while to get over it. (op 9-2)
Black Spirit(USA), returning from 217 days off, managed to make the frame at Group level in France after winning a hot 1m handicap off 97 here last July. Nothing was going better than him after turning in, but he hit a flat spot when first put under pressure, although he was closing right in on the winner at the line. He can land a Pattern race on this evidence. (op 12-1)
Shamali was having only his 11th start at the age of six and had upwards of 7lb to find with his five rivals, but at least he had an edge in fitness having recently won a Listed race on the Kempton Polytrack on his return from ten months off. He led the chasing group for much of the way before looking likely to drop out 2f from home, but he then got his second wind and was staying on again in the latter stages. Hopefully he will enjoy a longer campaign this season than he did last. (tchd 15-2)
Nouriya, bidding to give her trainer his fourth consecutive victory in the race, was a most progressive filly last season, although she just found the step up to Group 1 company beyond her when seventh of 11 in the Prix de l'Opera on her final outing. Although off the bridle a fair way out, she kept on up the inside rail over the last 2f but looked to have run her race when slightly hampered by the winner well inside the last furlong. She can win a Group race, most likely back against her own sex. (op 11-2)
Viscount Nelson(USA), the highest-rated runner in the field, was last seen finishing third of five behind Twice Over in the Eclipse over C&D last July, but he was just about the first beaten here and he is not going to be an easy horse to place. (op 11-4)
Afsare, having only his fifth start, hadn't been seen since narrowly winning the Listed Hampton Court Stakes at Royal Ascot due to a minor setback. Full of himself beforehand, he was inclined to race in snatches once under way and a brief effort on the wide outside inside the last 2f came to nothing. He was entitled to need this and there should be much better to come from him with this outing under his belt. (op 5-2)

1529 POKER AT BET365.COM H'CAP 1m 14y
4:50 (4:56) (Class 2) (0-105,101) 4-Y-O+
£12,462 (£3,732; £1,866; £934; £466; £234) **Stalls** Low

Form RPR

000- **1** **Wannabe King**[175] 7233 5-9-1 **95** (b[1]) TedDurcan 7 104
(David Lanigan) *trckd ldrs in 5th: plld out and effrt over 2f out: hd to one side but narrow ld over 1f out: hrd pressed after: jst hld on* **14/1**

2-25 **2** *nse* **Guest Book (IRE)**[7] 1410 4-8-2 **85** LouisBeuzelin(3) 15 94
(Mark Johnston) *trckd ldng trio: clsd to chal and upsides wl over 1f out: pressed wnr after: jst failed* **16/1**

210- **3** 1/2 **Julienas (IRE)**[182] 7100 4-8-12 **92** AdamKirby 12 100+
(Walter Swinburn) *settled towards rr: rdn over 2f out: prog wl over 1f out: styd on wl fnl f to take 3rd last strides* **8/1**[3]

025- **4** *nk* **Dunn'o (IRE)**[220] 6089 6-9-0 **94** PhilipRobinson 5 101
(Clive Cox) *taken down early: led at str pce: hrd pressed over 2f out: hdd over 1f out: battled on wl and nrly upsides ins fnl f: no ex last 100yds* **15/2**[2]

6412 **5** 3/4 **Benandonner (USA)**[17] 1172 8-8-7 **87** MartinLane 6 92
(Mike Murphy) *chsd ldr to over 2f out: lost pl but styd cl up: styd on fnl f but unable to chal* **22/1**

40-2 **6** 1 1/4 **Hacienda (IRE)**[14] 1240 4-8-12 **92** KierenFallon 4 95
(Mark Johnston) *trckd ldng pair: rdn on inner over 2f out: nt qckn and hld over 1f out: kpt on* **7/1**[1]

304- **7** 3 1/2 **Directorship**[175] 7233 5-8-6 **86** JimCrowley 10 81+
(Patrick Chamings) *dwlt: hld up in last trio: rdn on outer wl over 2f out: kpt on fr over 1f out: n.d* **8/1**[3]

00-4 **8** 1 **Axiom**[21] 1094 7-9-7 **101** NeilCallan 11 93
(Ed Walker) *trckd ldrs in 7th: drvn and effrt 2f out: no imp over 1f out: wknd fnl f* **28/1**

21-0 **9** 1 1/2 **Gunner Lindley (IRE)**[21] 1094 4-8-13 **93** MichaelHills 16 82
(B W Hills) *hld up in last trio: rdn and no real prog over 2f out* **14/1**

50-0 **10** 1/2 **Fremont (IRE)**[21] 1094 4-8-12 **92** RichardHughes 9 80
(Richard Hannon) *hld up towards rr: rdn over 2f out: no imp over 1f out: fdd* **10/1**

510- **11** ½ **Treble Jig (USA)**[289] 3824 4-8-8 **88**.................................... RyanMoore 3 74
(Sir Michael Stoute) *dwlt: a towards rr: rdn and no prog over 2f out* **8/1**[3]

233- **12** ½ **Invincible Soul (IRE)**[268] 4504 4-9-3 **97**.......................... EddieAhern 14 82+
(Richard Hannon) *hld up in 12th: shuffled along over 2f out: no prog and nvr nr ldrs* **16/1**

11-0 **13** 1¾ **Suited And Booted (IRE)**[7] 1406 4-9-2 **96**.................. JimmyFortune 8 77
(Richard Hannon) *chsd ldrs in 6th: rdn 3f out: steadily wknd fnl 2f* **16/1**

61-2 **14** 1 **Dance And Dance (IRE)**[21] 1092 5-8-11 **96**......... AdamBeschizza(5) 17 75
(Edward Vaughan) *v.s.a and racd awkwardly early: sn t.k.h and hld up in last pair: effrt on inner over 2f out: sn wknd and eased* **10/1**

-040 **15** 11 **Ezdeyaad (USA)**[14] 1240 7-8-8 **88**.................................. JackMitchell 1 42
(Ed Walker) *taken down early: nt that wl away: n.m.r on inner after 1f: chsd ldrs in 8th 1/2-way: wknd 2f out: eased: t.o* **50/1**

1m 42.13s (-1.17) **Going Correction** +0.10s/f (Good) **15** Ran SP% **116.5**
Speed ratings (Par 109): **109,108,108,108,107 106,102,101,100,99 99,98,96,95,84**
toteswingers:1&2:£55.80, 1&3:£29.90, 2&3:£34.80 CSF £189.16 CT £1433.43 TOTE £17.80: £6.00, £5.60, £3.60; EX 491.10 TRIFECTA Not won..
Owner Saif Ali & Saeed H Altayer **Bred** Chippenham Lodge Stud Ltd **Trained** Newmarket, Suffolk

FOCUS
A red-hot handicap run at an unrelenting pace, but predictably reduced to 15 runners when Huygens refused to enter the stalls (8/1, deduct 10p in the £ under R4). The winner's best effort since his 3yo days, with the solid fourth helping set the standard.

NOTEBOOK
Wannabe King was having his first start since October and had proved a disappointment since racking up a hat-trick in August 2009, but connections reached for the blinkers and the result was spectacular. In midfield early, he came through to just about hit the front over a furlong out and proved very brave in a driving finish. The usual question now arises with a horse like him as to whether the headgear will work a second time.
Guest Book(IRE), still relatively lightly raced, had given the impression he needs a return to further in his previous starts, but this strongly run mile was fine and he could hardly have done much more without winning. He deserves to add to his solitary previous victory.
Julienas(IRE), a lightly raced gelding, was returning from six months off but he won first time out last year. Well backed, he took too long in responding to pressure and by the time he eventually clicked into gear it was just too late. He should win again before too long. (op 14-1)
Dunn'o(IRE), who can go well fresh, hadn't managed a win in his 13 previous starts but he had a great record at this track (3-7 including this race two years ago) and had only once finished unplaced here. Soon able to establish his favourite position out in front, he rallied in typically game fashion once headed and lost no caste in defeat. (op 8-1)
Benandonner(USA), beaten at 4-6 in a four-runner Polytrack claimer last time, was always handy and kept going for longer than might have been expected. His last three wins have come on Polytrack, but he still has what it takes to be successful on turf. (op 25-1 tchd 20-1)
Hacienda(IRE), an encouraging second over an inadequate 7f on his Thirsk reappearance (first start since being gelded), was always in a good position and seemed to have no excuses. (op 6-1, tchd 15-2 in a place)
Directorship, returning from 175 days off, emerges with a lot of credit as he came from a long way back and was forced to go very wide in order to get a run. He ran some cracking races in defeat last season including two narrow defeats over this C&D, but the one worry is that his only win (also over C&D) in 16 starts was in July 2009. (op 11-1)
Axiom, a very respectable fourth in the Lincoln on his reappearance and first start for the yard, ran creditably under top weight but could have done without the ground firming up. (tchd 33-1)
Treble Jig(USA) is still unexposed and hadn't been seen since running poorly at Newmarket last July (first try on ground officially described as faster than good). He never figured and these conditions were probably not to his liking either. (op 7-1)
Dance And Dance(IRE) was very slowly away and then pulled like a train when back in touch with the rest of the field. It's probably best to put a line through this. (op 9-1)

1530 CASINO AT BET365.COM FLAT V JUMP JOCKEYS H'CAP 1m 14y
5:20 (5:30) (Class 4) (0-80,78) 4-Y-0+ **£4,533** (£1,348; £674; £336) **Stalls** Low

Form RPR

-452 **1** **Edgewater (IRE)**[12] 1269 4-11-1 **75**.................................... RyanMoore 8 83
(John Akehurst) *hld up in midfield: rdn and prog over 2f out to ld over 1f out: jnd 150yds out: plld out ex* **7/2**[1]

00-1 **2** ½ **Uncle Fred**[19] 1138 6-11-4 **78**... APMcCoy 13 85
(Patrick Chamings) [illegible] *brought w wl-timed chal and upsides 150yds out: nt qckn* **4/1**[2]

224- **3** 1¼ **Beaumont's Party (IRE)**[195] 6780 4-11-2 **76**............ RichardJohnson 7 80
(Andrew Balding) *trckd ldng pair: clsd to chal 2f out: nt qckn over 1f out: one pce after* **9/2**[3]

105- **4** nse **Beaver Patrol (IRE)**[175] 7238 9-11-3 **77**..................(v) AidanColeman 12 81
(Eve Johnson Houghton) *led after 1f and sn clr: c bk to field and hdd over 1f out: one pce after* **16/1**

153- **5** 5 **Super Duplex**[174] 7255 4-10-7 **67**.................................... JimmyFortune 2 60
(Pat Phelan) *chsd ldng trio: tried to cl to chal 2f out: lost pl and outpcd over 1f out: fdd* **8/1**

0-41 **6** 1½ **Silent Oasis**[23] 1058 5-10-10 **70**.. NeilCallan 3 59
(Brendan Powell) *s.s: hld up in last trio: effrt but hanging over 2f out: stuck on fnl f: no ch* **8/1**

0 **7** hd **Inef (IRE)**[93] 226 4-11-1 **75**.. LeightonAspell 4 64
(Laura Mongan) *hld up in rr: effrt on inner over 2f out: outpcd sn after: n.d* **40/1**

060- **8** 2¼ **Swift Chap**[215] 6260 5-10-10 **70**.. JimCrowley 10 53
(Rod Millman) *chsd ldrs but nvr on terms: no imp 2f out: fdd* **12/1**

130- **9** 2½ **Mr Udagawa**[180] 7125 5-10-4 **64** oh1........................... TimmyMurphy 14 42
(Bernard Llewellyn) *led 1f: chsd ldr to 2f out: wknd* **40/1**

0210 **10** 1¼ **Dubai Miracle (USA)**[5] 1443 4-11-3 **77**....................(t) PaulMoloney 6 52
(Laura Young) *a towards rr: rdn and no prog wl over 2f out* **20/1**

6043 **11** 1¾ **Gallantry**[25] 1021 9-10-12 **72**.. RichardHughes 5 43
(Michael Squance) *settled midfield: shkn up 3f out: no prog 2f out: wknd* **25/1**

1454 **12** 1 **Lastkingofscotland (IRE)**[11] 1296 5-11-1 **75**..............(b) KierenFallon 9 43
(Conor Dore) *a in rr: struggling over 2f out* **17/2**

1m 44.71s (1.41) **Going Correction** +0.10s/f (Good) **12** Ran SP% **120.2**
Speed ratings (Par 105): **96,95,94,94,89 87,87,85,82,81 79,78**
toteswingers:1&2:£4.40, 1&3:£4.60, 2&3:£5.50 CSF £16.79 CT £64.39 TOTE £5.00: £1.80, £1.90, £2.20; EX 15.70 Trifecta £45.90 Pool: £677.72 - 10.92 winning units..
Owner One More Bid Partnership **Bred** R Ahamad & P Scott **Trained** Epsom, Surrey

FOCUS
They didn't seem to go a great pace in this (the winning time was 2.58 seconds slower than the preceding 86-105 handicap) and few got into it, but it provided a thrilling finish between two masters of their respective trades. The winner was close to his early 3yo form.
T/Jkpt: Not won. T/Plt: £4,388.40 to a £1 stake. Pool:£148,185.88 - 24.65 winning tickets T/Qpdt: £42.90 to a £1 stake. Pool:£12,989.24 - 223.60 winning tickets JN

1531 - 1532a (Foreign Racing) - See Raceform Interactive

CORK (R-H)
Saturday, April 23

OFFICIAL GOING: Good (good to firm in places on round course; watered)

1533a CORK STKS (LISTED RACE) 6f
3:35 (3:35) 3-Y-0+ **£22,413** (£6,551; £3,103; £1,034)

RPR

1 **Inxile (IRE)**[7] 1420 6-9-10 ....(p) AdrianNicholls 10 109+
(David Nicholls) *dwlt sltly leaving stalls: sn led and mde virtually all: pushed along fr 2f out: qcknd clr ins fnl f: kpt on wl* **10/11**[1]

2 3 **Katla (IRE)**[27] 1006 3-8-10 103... WJLee 1 93
(J F Grogan, Ire) *trckd ldrs: 4th 1/2-way: hdwy to chal over 1f out: rdn and no imp on wnr ins fnl f: kpt on same pce* **9/1**

3 nk **Dawn Eclipse (IRE)**[155] 7513 6-9-4 85.............................. BACurtis 11 92
(T G McCourt, Ire) *chsd ldrs on stands' side: 6th 1/2-way: 5th u.p 1f out: kpt on fnl f wout troubling wnr* **66/1**

4 hd **Santo Padre (IRE)**[209] 6390 7-9-7 106................................ PJSmullen 2 94
(David Marnane, Ire) *settled towards rr: swtchd rt and hdwy fr over 2f out: 3rd and chal fr over 1f out: no imp u.p ins fnl f* **14/1**

5 hd **Knock Stars (IRE)**[7] 1420 3-8-7 97... PBBeggy 8 88
(Patrick Martin, Ire) *trckd ldrs: wnt 2nd over 2f out: rdn and no imp in 4th 1f out: kpt on one pce* **13/2**[3]

6 hd **Moonreach (IRE)**[22] 1088 4-9-7 94...................................... SHJames 5 93
(James J Hartnett, Ire) *towards rr: sme hdwy to chse ldrs 2f out: 7th 1f out: kpt on one pce* **16/1**

7 nk **Snaefell (IRE)**[7] 1420 7-9-12 108...(p) JMurtagh 3 97
(M Halford, Ire) *in rr of mid-div on outer: niggled along bef 1/2-way: 8th over 1f out: kpt on one pce* **12/1**

8 2½ **Rock Jock (IRE)**[44] 825 4-9-7 103.................................... PShanahan 7 84
(Tracey Collins, Ire) *prom: 2nd 1/2-way: drvn along and dropped to 6th over 1f out: no ex* **14/1**

9 5½ **Luisant**[20] 1118 8-9-10 109... FMBerry 4 70
(J A Nash, Ire) *slowly away and a towards rr: no imp fr wl over 1f out: eased whn btn fnl f* **6/1**[2]

10 2½ **Whipless (IRE)**[7] 1422 3-8-10 97.. KJManning 6 56
(J S Bolger, Ire) *a bhd* **25/1**

11 3 **Rodrigo De Torres**[238] 5526 4-9-7 102.......................... DPMcDonogh 9 49
(James J Hartnett, Ire) *prom early: dropped towards rr 2f out: no ex* **25/1**

1m 10.69s (-1.91)
WFA 3 from 4yo+ 11lb **11** Ran SP% **126.1**
CSF £11.07 TOTE £1.90: £1.10, £2.00, £13.30; DF 11.30.
Owner D Nicholls **Bred** Denis And Mrs Teresa Bergin **Trained** Sessay, N Yorks

FOCUS
The third and sixth limit the form and the winner did not have to match his previous effort to win.

NOTEBOOK
Inxile(IRE) followed up his easy success in the Woodlands Stakes at Naas last month. Racing prominently without trailblazing, Adrian Nicholls was able to keep a good bit in the tank. It did appear as though he was in for a serious challenge over a furlong out but when his rider got more serious with him inside the last he really opened up and put some daylight between himself and the remainder in a few strides. In its way it was even more impressive than the Naas performance, and he looks set to take in the Greenlands Stakes at the Curragh in a few weeks. (op 9/10)
Katla(IRE) was dropping back to this trip having seemingly failed to stay in the 1,000 Guineas Trial at Leopardstown, and she may well come on a bit more for this effort as well. Tracking the leaders towards the far side, she threw down what appeared to be a serious challenge over a furlong out but as soon as the winner quickened again she was left in his wake. (op 10/1)
Dawn Eclipse(IRE) should have struggled here off a mark of 85 but put in a career-best effort and looks likely to get a bit of a rise. She showed a fair bit of speed from her stands' side draw and kept going inside the last without managing to get on terms.
Santo Padre(IRE) had an unfavourable far-side draw but improved nicely from mid-division to throw down a challenge a furlong or so out before running out of steam close home. He should come on for this and there should be plenty to look forward to this season on this evidence.
Knock Stars(IRE) didn't manage to get any closer to Inxile than she managed when runner-up to him at Naas the previous week. She broke well and raced quite prominently. looked the most likely to challenge 2f out, but couldn't sustain it inside the last. (op 9/1 tchd 6/1)
Snaefell(IRE) never travelled. (op 11/1)
Luisant reared up leaving the stalls and didn't handle the quick ground. Official explanation: jockey said gelding reared up on leaving stalls, changed legs in running and did not handle today's ground (op 11/2 tchd 13/2)

1534 - 1537a (Foreign Racing) - See Raceform Interactive

1514 MUSSELBURGH (R-H)
Sunday, April 24

OFFICIAL GOING: Good (good to soft in places; 6.2)
Bottom bend moved in 3m to provide fresh ground but impact on distances not quantified.
Wind: Light, across Weather: Fine and dry

1538 TOTEJACKPOT CLASSIFIED (S) STKS 1m 1f
2:30 (2:30) (Class 6) 3-Y-0+ **£1,942** (£578; £288; £144) **Stalls** Low

Form RPR

466- **1** **Bolodenka (IRE)**[223] 6029 9-9-10 73............................... PaulHanagan 3 75
(Richard Fahey) *trckd ldr: hdwy to chal 2f out: rdn to ld jst over 1f out and sn hung rt: drvn out* **2/1**[1]

3033 **2** 1 **Cloudy Bay (USA)**[13] 1278 4-9-10 80.........................(p) SeanLevey(5) 1 78
(Mrs K Burke) *led: qcknd clr: rdn and jnd 2f out: drvn and hdd jst over 1f out: sn n.m.r on inner and swtchd lft ins fnl f: kpt on* **5/2**[2]

050- **3** 7 **Cry Alot Boy**[365] 1512 8-9-10 70...................................(t) PatCosgrave 4 58
(Kevin Morgan) *dwlt: sn in tch: effrt over 3f out and sn rdn along: drvn 2f out: kpt on to take 3rd ins fnl f* **3/1**[3]

322- **4** 2 **Birkside**[310] 3166 8-9-10 60.. PhillipMakin 5 53
(Linda Perratt) *dwlt: sn trcking ldrs: hdwy to chse ldng pair 3f out: sn rdn and one pce* **13/2**

3503 **5** 38 **Elusive Fame (USA)**[12] 1292 5-9-5 53..........................(b) JasonHart(7) 6 —
(Mark Johnston) *chsd ldng pair: rdn along over 4f out: sn wknd* **9/1**

1m 55.51s (1.61) **Going Correction** +0.325s/f (Good) **5** Ran SP% **110.2**
Speed ratings (Par 101): **105,104,97,96,62**
toteswingers: 1&2 £3.00 CSF £7.30 TOTE £2.40: £1.10, £1.80; EX 6.60.There was no bid for the winner.
Owner Aidan J Ryan **Bred** Kildaragh Stud **Trained** Musley Bank, N Yorks
■ Stewards' Enquiry : Paul Hanagan caution: careless riding.

FOCUS
This only concerned two runners, but they both ran to a fair level.

1539 TOTEPOOL FLEXI BETTING H'CAP 5f
3:05 (3:05) (Class 4) (0-85,85) 4-Y-0+ **£4,857** (£1,445; £722; £360) **Stalls** High

Form RPR
00-4 **1** **Mon Brav**[23] [1073] 4-8-6 **75** SeanLevey(5) 4 89
(Brian Ellison) *hld up in tch: swtchd outside and gd hdwy wl over 1f out: rdn to ld jst ins fnl f: kpt on wl* **15/2**
00-3 **2** *1* **Oldjoesaid**[23] [1073] 7-9-1 **79** PhillipMakin 12 89
(Kevin Ryan) *dwlt: sn in tch on inner: effrt and n.m.r over 1f out: rdn and styd on strly ins fnl f* **7/2**[1]
-060 **3** *1 ¾* **Chosen One (IRE)**[8] [1411] 6-8-0 **67** JamesSullivan(3) 8 71+
(Ruth Carr) *in tch: hdwy whn nt clr run over 1f out: swtchd lft and rdn ent fnl f: fin strly* **16/1**
06-1 **4** *¾* **Le Toreador**[57] [701] 6-9-2 **80** (p) SilvestreDeSousa 13 81
(Kevin Ryan) *led: rdn over 1f out: drvn: edgd rt and hdd jst ins fnl f: wknd last 100yds* **6/1**[3]
22-1 **5** *½* **Nadeen (IRE)**[23] [1073] 4-9-4 **82** RobertWinston 1 82
(Michael Smith) *stdd s and hld up in rr: swtchd rt and hdwy 2f out: rdn to chse ldrs over 1f out: sn drvn and one pce* **4/1**[2]
0-61 **6** *1* **Taurus Twins**[20] [1140] 5-8-11 **78** (b) BillyCray(3) 3 74
(Richard Price) *prom: rdn 2f out: drvn over 1f out and grad wknd* **7/1**
354- **7** *2 ½* **The Nifty Fox**[170] [7326] 7-9-6 **84** DavidAllan 7 71+
(Tim Easterby) *hld up towards rr: hdwy 2f out: nt clr run over 1f out: sn swtchd lft and no imp after* **11/1**
2102 **8** *4* **Apache Ridge (IRE)**[25] [1037] 5-8-8 **72** (p) PaulMulrennan 10 45
(Keith Dalgleish) *a towards rr* **16/1**
620- **9** *3 ¼* **Pavershooz**[162] [7443] 6-9-7 **85** DuranFentiman 9 46
(Noel Wilson) *cl up: rdn along 2f out: wknd over 1f out* **8/1**
15-0 **10** *3 ½* **Lesley's Choice**[23] [1073] 5-8-8 **72** (b) FrederikTylicki 5 20
(Linda Perratt) *cl up: rdn 2f out: sn wknd* **33/1**
30-0 **11** *3 ½* **Ignatieff (IRE)**[23] [1073] 4-8-6 **77** KristinStubbs(7) 6 13
(Linda Stubbs) *midfield: rdn along bef 1/2-way: sn wknd* **25/1**

60.59 secs (0.19) **Going Correction** +0.175s/f (Good) 11 Ran SP% 118.8
Speed ratings (Par 105): **105,103,100,99,98 97,93,86,81,75 70**
toteswingers: 1&2 £7.10, 1&3 £17.20, 2&3 £17.00 CSF £34.25 CT £423.25 TOTE £10.30: £3.60, £1.80, £5.10; EX 40.00.
Owner Koo's Racing Club **Bred** J D Graham **Trained** Norton, N Yorks

FOCUS
A fair sprint handicap. They raced middle to stands' side and there was no sign of a draw bias.
Nadeen(IRE) Official explanation: jockey said gelding finished distressed
Pavershooz Official explanation: jockey said gelding was coughing post-race

1540 TOTEPOOL A BETTER WAY TO BET MAIDEN STKS 7f 30y
3:40 (3:41) (Class 5) 3-Y-0+ **£2,590** (£770; £385; £192) **Stalls** Low

Form RPR
3-3 **1** **Hunza Dancer (IRE)**[24] [1060] 3-8-10 0 RobertHavlin 7 74+
(John Gosden) *trckd ldrs: hdwy 3f out: led 2f out: rdn over 1f out: edgd rt ins fnl f: kpt on* **5/6**[1]
03- **2** *2* **Cape Classic (IRE)**[158] [7479] 3-9-1 0 PaulHanagan 1 75+
(William Haggas) *trckd ldrs: hdwy over 2f out: n.m.r and swtchd lft 1 1/2f out: rdn to chse wnr ins fnl f: styng on whn n.m.r and swtchd lft last 100yds: no ex after* **5/2**[2]
0- **3** *2 ¾* **Intiqaal (IRE)**[220] [6124] 4-10-0 0 TadhgO'Shea 6 71
(Ed Dunlop) *hld up towards rr: hdwy wl over 2f out: rdn to chse wnr and edgd rt over 1f out: kpt on same pce* **5/1**[3]
0-00 **4** *4* **Eilean Eeve**[16] [1213] 5-9-6 **40** (p) JamesSullivan(3) 3 55?
(George Foster) *led: rdn along 3f out: drvn and hdd 2f out: sn edgd rt and wknd* **100/1**
0 **5** *3* **The Nifty Duchess**[15] [1246] 3-8-10 0 DavidAllan 4 42
(Tim Easterby) *sn rdn along and rn green in rr: sme hdwy fnl 2f: n.d* **25/1**
6 *4* **Isdaal** 4-9-9 0 PatCosgrave 8 36
(Kevin Morgan) *dwlt: a in rr* **33/1**
0 **7** *½* **Donnaconna (CAN)**[10] [1338] 3-9-1 0 SilvestreDeSousa 2 35
(Mark Johnston) *chsd ldng pair: green and rdn along 1/2-way: drvn and wknd over 2f out* **12/1**
0 **8** *5* **Friday Night Lad (IRE)**[16] [1210] 4-10-0 0 RobertWinston 5 26
(Alan Swinbank) *chsd ldr: cl up 3f out: rdn and edgd lft 2f out: wknd qckly* **33/1**

1m 31.46s (2.46) **Going Correction** +0.325s/f (Good)
WFA 3 from 4yo+ 13lb 8 Ran SP% 118.2
Speed ratings (Par 103): **98,95,92,88,84 80,79,73**
toteswingers: 1&2 £1.20, 1&3 £2.10, 2&3 £2.10 CSF £3.15 TOTE £1.70: £1.02, £1.20, £2.20; EX 3.40.
Owner B E Nielsen **Bred** Barronstown Stud **Trained** Newmarket, Suffolk
■ Stewards' Enquiry : Robert Havlin caution: careless riding.

FOCUS
The proximity of the 40-rated Eilean Eeve, who was sweating, limits the bare form, but the front three all look fair types. The form is rated around the front pair.

1541 ENTER THE FLAT TOTETENTOFOLLOW H'CAP 7f 30y
4:10 (4:10) (Class 3) (0-95,92) 4-Y-0+ **£7,771** (£2,312; £1,155; £577) **Stalls** Low

Form RPR
03-0 **1** **Nasri**[21] [1111] 5-9-5 **90** AdrianNicholls 11 104
(David Nicholls) *mde all: rdn over 2f out: jnd and drvn over 1f out: kpt on gamely towards fin* **4/1**[1]
3320 **2** *hd* **Sioux Rising (IRE)**[35] [923] 5-8-12 **83** TonyHamilton 12 96
(Richard Fahey) *trckd ldng pair: hdwy 3f out: chal 2f out: sn rdn: drvn and styd on wl fnl f: jst hld* **9/1**[3]
01-3 **3** *4* **Malcheek (IRE)**[43] [844] 9-8-13 **84** DavidAllan 9 86
(Tim Easterby) *trckd ldrs: hdwy over 2f out: rdn to chse ldng pair over 1f out: kpt on same pce fnl f* **4/1**[1]
6-10 **4** *¾* **Bowmaker**[15] [1240] 4-9-0 **85** SilvestreDeSousa 4 85
(Mark Johnston) *chsd wnr: rdn along over 3f out: drvn wl over 1f out: grad wknd* **16/1**
-660 **5** *½* **Dubai Dynamo**[21] [1110] 6-8-6 **77** TomEaves 6 76
(Ruth Carr) *midfield: hdwy on outer to chse ldrs over 2f out: sn rdn and no imp appr fnl f* **9/2**[2]
5P0- **6** *shd* **Silver Rime (FR)**[176] [7227] 6-9-1 **86** PhillipMakin 5 85
(Linda Perratt) *towards rr: hdwy 3f out: rdn over 2f out: kpt on same pce* **20/1**
366- **7** *2 ½* **High Resolution**[176] [7227] 4-8-4 **78** JamesSullivan(3) 10 70
(Linda Perratt) *towards rr: sme hdwy wl over 2f out: sn rdn and n.d* **40/1**
401- **8** *2* **Space War**[186] [7012] 4-9-0 **92** DavidSimmonson(7) 7 78
(Michael Easterby) *trckd ldrs: effrt on outer over 3f out: rdn wl over 2f out: grad wknd* **20/1**
-000 **9** *3 ¼* **Mo Mhuirnin (IRE)**[35] [923] 5-8-9 **80** PaulHanagan 2 58
(Richard Fahey) *plld hrd: rn wd bnd over 4f out: a in rr* **10/1**
000- **10** *½* **Esoterica (IRE)**[218] [6178] 8-8-12 **86** GaryBartley(3) 1 62
(Jim Goldie) *a towards rr* **20/1**
520- **11** *½* **Sooraah**[206] [6509] 4-9-2 **87** JoeFanning 3 62
(William Haggas) *dwlt: t.k.h and sn in midfield: rdn along wl over 2f out: sn btn* **4/1**[1]

1m 29.92s (0.92) **Going Correction** +0.325s/f (Good) 11 Ran SP% 119.9
Speed ratings (Par 107): **107,106,102,101,100 100,97,95,91,91 90**
toteswingers: 1&2 £9.30, 1&3 £3.70, 2&3 £8.50 CSF £39.03 CT £141.72 TOTE £6.60: £2.00, £3.50, £2.60; EX 56.90.
Owner Dab Hand Racing **Bred** Lady Hardy **Trained** Sessay, N Yorks

FOCUS
There was an advantage to prominent racers.

NOTEBOOK
Nasri made just about all of the running, a good ride from Adrian Nicholls to get the lead from stall 11. The winner had shaped nicely over 6f on his recent debut for this yard and just managed to see out the longer trip. It might be that he'll prove best back over sprint distances. (op 9-2)
Sioux Rising(IRE) again came up short in a battle and her losing run dates back to 2009, although she doesn't look to do much wrong under pressure. Strictly on form this was a useful performance, though she was always well placed. (op 11-1)
Malcheek(IRE) had improved significantly on the AW lately and was rated 17lb lower on turf. He can be keen when not dominating, and that was the case this time, so perhaps a more forward ride would have helped, for although he was drawn in nine, the front two were out even wider. This was a good effort in the circumstances, especially as he'd have preferred better ground. (tchd 9-2)
Bowmaker has lacked consistency but this was a respectable showing. (op 20-1)
Dubai Dynamo could not get seriously involved and probably would have preferred quicker ground. (op 5-1)
Silver Rime(FR) shaped nicely after a 176-day break. (op 16-1 tchd 22-1)
Mo Mhuirnin(IRE) Official explanation: jockey said mare ran too free
Sooraah was too keen on her first run of the season. (op 9-2)

1542 BET TOTEPOOL AT TOTESPORT.COM MAIDEN STKS 1m 4f 100y
4:40 (4:41) (Class 5) 3-Y-0+ **£2,590** (£770; £385; £192) **Stalls** Low

Form RPR
3 **1** **Eternal Heart (IRE)**[19] [1151] 3-8-8 0 JoeFanning 1 84+
(Mark Johnston) *mde all: rdn along wl over 2f out: sn jnd and drvn over 1f out: kpt on gamely* **3/1**[2]
00 **2** *3 ¾* **Camporosso**[8] [1407] 3-8-8 0 SilvestreDeSousa 2 78
(Mark Johnston) *chsd ldrs: hdwy 3f out: rdn over 2f out: kpt on u.p to take 2nd ins fnl f* **20/1**
20- **3** *1* **Cobbs Quay**[204] [6560] 3-8-8 0 PhilipRobinson 8 76
(John Gosden) *t.k.h: cl up on outer: sltly hmpd and rn wd home turn: sn chal and ev ch tl rdn: hung rt and btn over 1f out* **4/7**[1]
4 *9* **Jonny Delta**[15] 4-9-10 0 GaryBartley(3) 7 65
(Jim Goldie) *dwlt and hld up in rr: sme hdwy on inner 3f out: sn rdn and nvr nr ldrs* **6/1**[3]
6 **5** *11* **Abernethy (IRE)**[23] [1076] 3-8-8 0 PaulMulrennan 4 45
(Linda Perratt) *in tch: hdwy to chse ldrs over 3f out: rdn wl over 2f out and sn btn* **50/1**
2-3 **6** *2 ½* **Stetson**[44] [836] 5-10-0 0 RobertWinston 6 44
(Alan Swinbank) *in tch: effrt over 4f out: rdn along over 3f out: sn btn* **14/1**
40- **7** *½* **A Southside Boy (GER)**[204] [6566] 3-8-8 0 BarryMcHugh 3 41
(Jim Goldie) *chsd ldr: rdn along 1/2-way: sn wknd* **66/1**
6 **8** *29* **Amtired**[8] [1386] 5-10-0 0 TomEaves 5 —
(Brian Ellison) *led 3f: prom tl rdn along 5f out and sn wknd* **50/1**

2m 47.28s (5.28) **Going Correction** +0.325s/f (Good)
WFA 3 from 4yo 20lb 4 from 5yo 1lb 8 Ran SP% 119.8
Speed ratings (Par 103): **95,92,91,85,78 76,76,57**
toteswingers: 1&2 £9.40, 1&3 £1.10, 2&3 £7.40 CSF £56.89 TOTE £3.60: £1.30, £4.40, £1.10; EX 42.80.
Owner Mrs Joan Keaney **Bred** Mrs Joan Keaney **Trained** Middleham Moor, N Yorks

FOCUS
An interesting maiden and it looks worth taking a positive view of this form.

1543 BET TOTEPOOL ON 0800 221 221 EASTER H'CAP 7f 30y
5:10 (5:11) (Class 5) (0-75,72) 3-Y-0 **£2,590** (£770; £385; £192) **Stalls** Low

Form RPR
04-0 **1** **Ventura Sands (IRE)**[18] [1169] 3-9-0 **65** PaulHanagan 5 72
(Richard Fahey) *hld up in rr: hdwy 1/2-way: chal 2f out: rdn to ld jst over 1f out: drvn ins fnl f: jst hld on* **5/2**[2]
36-0 **2** *shd* **Iceblast**[15] [1246] 3-9-7 **72** GrahamGibbons 3 81+
(Michael Easterby) *trckd ldrs: hdwy over 2f out: effrt and cl up whn hmpd on inner ent fnl f: swtchd lft and rdn: styd on strly: jst failed* **13/2**[3]
-636 **3** *2 ¼* **Dolly Parton (IRE)**[6] [1439] 3-9-3 **68** (p) AdrianNicholls 6 69
(David Nicholls) *hld up towards rr: hdwy over 2f out: rdn wl over 1f out: kpt on ins fnl f nrst fin* **14/1**
0-41 **4** *nk* **Vetvey (IRE)**[4] [1495] 3-8-8 **59** 6ex SilvestreDeSousa 1 59
(Mark Johnston) *trckd ldr: tk cl order 3f out: rdn to ld over 2f out: drvn and hdd over 1f out: sn hung rt and one pce* **2/1**[1]
332- **5** *5* **Sabratha (IRE)**[176] [7223] 3-9-1 **66** TonyHamilton 4 53
(Linda Perratt) *hld up towards rr: hdwy 2f out: sn rdn and no imp appr fnl f* **9/1**
1326 **6** *1 ¾* **Eilean Mor**[10] [1329] 3-9-0 **65** TomEaves 7 47
(Bryan Smart) *in tch: effrt 3f out: sn rdn and n.d* **9/1**
610- **7** *2* **Country Waltz**[181] [7116] 3-8-12 **63** FrederikTylicki 8 40
(Linda Perratt) *led: rdn 3f out: sn hdd: hld whn hmpd on inner ent fnl f: wknd after* **20/1**
-046 **8** *16* **Jambo Bibi (IRE)**[65] [601] 3-8-7 **58** (b) JoeFanning 2 —
(Bruce Hellier) *dwlt: hdwy to chse ldrs 1/2-way: rdn along wl over 2f out and sn wknd* **20/1**
00-0 **9** *8* **Coracle**[8] [1392] 3-8-4 **58** ow1 TjadeCollier(3) 9 —
(David Nicholls) *plld hrd cl up on outer whn rn wd bnd after 2f and on home turn: sn wknd* **25/1**

1m 32.6s (3.60) **Going Correction** +0.325s/f (Good) 9 Ran SP% 115.3
Speed ratings (Par 98): **92,91,89,88,83 81,78,60,51**
toteswingers: 1&2 £4.10, 1&3 £5.50, 2&3 £9.00 CSF £18.49 CT £188.38 TOTE £4.00: £1.90, £1.90, £2.20; EX 19.20.
Owner Keith Denham **Bred** J Jamgotchian **Trained** Musley Bank, N Yorks
■ Stewards' Enquiry : Silvestre De Sousa three-day ban: careless riding (May 9-11)

FOCUS
A modest contest run at a good pace, though the time was quite a bit slower than the two earlier 7f races. That's not a total surprise considering the relative quality of each race and that the ground was presumably cutting up as the meeting progressed.

1544 BET TOTEPOOL ON ALL UK RACING H'CAP — 5f
5:40 (5:41) (Class 6) (0-60,60) 4-Y-0+ **£1,942** (£578; £288; £144) **Stalls** High

Form — RPR

00-0 **1** **Silvanus (IRE)**[25] 1034 6-9-7 **60** .... PaulHanagan 4 — 71
(Paul Midgley) *hld up: hdwy over 2f out: rdn to chal 1f out: drvn and kpt on wl to ld last 75yds* **11/2**[3]

15-3 **2** *nk* **Senate Majority**[8] 1411 4-9-7 **60** .... DavidAllan 7 — 70
(Tim Easterby) *prom: hdwy to ld 2f out: rdn and edgd rt over 1f out: drvn ent fnl f: hdd and no ex last 75yds* **2/1**[1]

455- **3** *2 3/4* **Sharp Bullet (IRE)**[132] 7860 5-8-13 **52** ....(p) JoeFanning 5 — 52
(Bruce Hellier) *cl up: rdn 2f out: drvn and ev ch whn hmpd over 1f out: sn one pce* **10/1**

326- **4** *2 1/2* **Dower Glen**[136] 7783 4-8-11 **50** ....(b) PaulMulrennan 6 — 41
(Keith Dalgleish) *hld up: hdwy wl over 1f out: sn rdn and kpt on ins fnl f: n.d* **7/1**

666- **5** *1 1/4* **Tournedos (IRE)**[214] 6299 9-8-13 **55** ....(b) JamesSullivan(3) 8 — 42
(Ruth Carr) *chsd ldrs: rdn 2f out: sn wknd* **22/1**

5502 **6** *1 1/4* **Cheveyo (IRE)**[5] 1464 5-8-2 **46** .... NeilFarley(5) 3 — 28
(Patrick Morris) *chsd ldrs on outer: rdn along 2f out: drvn and wknd over 1f out* **9/2**[2]

1 **7** *1 1/4* **Odd Ball (IRE)**[16] 1217 4-9-3 **56** .... StephenCraine 9 — 34
(Patrick Morris) *rrd s and slowly away: a in rr* **6/1**

5-00 **8** *10* **Ya Boy Sir (IRE)**[11] 1307 4-9-2 **55** ....(b[1]) LeeNewman 1 — —
(Noel Wilson) *qckly away and led: rdn along and hdd 2f out: sn wknd* **14/1**

62.47 secs (2.07) **Going Correction** +0.175s/f (Good) **8** Ran SP% **113.8**
Speed ratings (Par 101): **90,89,85,81,79 77,75,59**
toteswingers: 1&2 £3.30, 1&3 £12.50, 2&3 £5.30. totesuper7: Win: Not won; Place £88.50 CSF £16.76 CT £106.05 TOTE £6.00: £2.30, £1.30, £3.00; EX 10.80.
Owner Colin Alton **Bred** Barronstown Stud And Mrs T Stack **Trained** Westow, N Yorks

FOCUS
A moderate sprint.
T/Plt: £15.50 to a £1 stake. Pool: £46,800.65 2,203.13 T/Qpdt: £4.20 to a £1 stake. Pool £3,441.15. 597.15 winning tickets. JR

1527 SANDOWN (R-H)
Sunday, April 24

OFFICIAL GOING: Good (rnd 7.9; spr 8.1)
Home bend at outermost configuration adding 8yds to races on round course.
Wind: Almost nil Weather: Sunny, warm

1545 BET365 H'CAP — 5f 6y
2:10 (2:10) (Class 2) (0-105,99) 3-Y-0
£11,028 (£3,302; £1,651; £826; £412; £207) **Stalls** Low

Form — RPR

312- **1** **Night Carnation**[183] 7080 3-9-7 **99** .... JimmyFortune 1 — 113+
(Andrew Balding) *trckd ldrs on inner: plld out and smooth prog 2f out: shkn up to ld 1f out: pushed clr: comf* **7/2**[2]

141- **2** *2* **Ahtoug**[191] 6900 3-8-13 **91** .... AhmedAjtebi 3 — 98+
(Mahmood Al Zarooni) *prom: led 1/2-way: rdn and hdd 1f out: hld whn hit rail sn after: kpt on* **15/8**[1]

-365 **3** *3* **Bathwick Bear (IRE)**[11] 1322 3-9-3 **98** .... RichardEvans(3) 6 — 94
(David Evans) *pushed along in last pair 1/2-way: kpt on u.p to take 3rd jst over 1f out: n.d* **9/1**

130- **4** *2 1/4* **Julius Geezer (IRE)**[219] 6141 3-9-5 **97** .... JimCrowley 2 — 85
(Tom Dascombe) *led to 1/2-way: wknd over 1f out* **10/1**

600- **5** *1* **Belle Bayardo (IRE)**[129] 7891 3-9-1 **93** .... DavidProbert 7 — 77
(Ronald Harris) *s.i.s: rdn in last pair 1/2-way: sn outpcd: no ch after* **33/1**

50-2 **6** *1 1/2* **Roman Dancer (IRE)**[20] 1141 3-8-3 **81** oh3 ow1 .... ChrisCatlin 5 — 60
(John Gallagher) *racd wd: struggling to stay in tch w ldrs fr 1/2-way: sn btn* **11/2**

30-0 **7** *5* **Ballista (IRE)**[15] 1241 3-9-1 **93** .... SebSanders 4 — 54
(Tom Dascombe) *pressed ldrs 3f: sn wknd* **5/1**[3]

60.70 secs (-0.90) **Going Correction** -0.075s/f (Good) **7** Ran SP% **111.1**
Speed ratings (Par 104): **104,100,96,92,90 88,80**
toteswingers: 1&2 £1.30, 1&3 £4.00, 2&3 £3.00 CSF £9.86 TOTE £3.70: £2.20, £1.30; EX 9.60.
Owner George Strawbridge **Bred** George Strawbridge **Trained** Kingsclere, Hants

FOCUS
Following 5mm of rain overnight the going was given as good on both courses, and the jockeys thought it was riding on the slow side. A decent class handicap, albeit the top-weight weighed in 6lb below the ceiling. The winner looked Group class and the form is rated loosely around the third.

NOTEBOOK
Night Carnation ◆ finished second in a Listed race on her final start last year, and saw her mark rise 20lb as a result. She didn't look to face an easy task on her reappearance, but the way she won suggests she's thrived over the winter and connections have a pattern-race performer on their hands. Travelling strongly on the rail in behind the leader, she quickened up well once switched, and her rider hardly had to get that serious with her. She has the potential to make up into a smart sprinter this term, and she'll probably go for a 6f Listed race for fillies at Haydock next. Her trainer believes she needs a bit of cut to be seen at her best. (op 10-3)
Ahtoug, racing up with the pace one off the rail, came clear of the rest but had no chance with the impressive winner. He'll go up in the ratings now despite losing, but should be up to defying a rise. (op 2-1 tchd 5-2)
Bathwick Bear(IRE) might have been at a disadvantage racing wide of the rail for a significant portion of the race and, considering this trip is probably on the short side for him nowadays, this was a solid effort on his reappearance. (op 8-1 tchd 15-2)
Julius Geezer(IRE), who sweated up beforehand, made the running next to the far-side rail, which might have been an advantage, but he weakened in the manner of a horse who needed the outing. He won the Lily Agnes last year and his style of running suits that track, so he'll be interesting if he returns to Chester and bags a favourable draw. (tchd 9-1)
Belle Bayardo(IRE), for whom the overnight rain was no good, cannot have the ground fast enough. He struggled a little with the early pace and is entitled to come on for this.
Roman Dancer(IRE), who ran well at Windsor last time, was 3lb out of the handicap here and his rider also put up 1lb overweight. Racing furthest away from the far rail for most of the race was probably no help to his chance. (op 7-1 tchd 9-2)
Ballista(IRE) was the better backed of the Dascombe two, but he raced three or four wide of the rail early and dropped out tamely. (op 9-2 tchd 11-2)

1546 CASINO AT BET365.COM CONDITIONS STKS — 1m 14y
2:45 (2:47) (Class 3) 3-Y-0 **£7,165** (£2,145; £1,072; £537) **Stalls** Low

Form — RPR

1- **1** **Naqshabban (USA)**[194] 6828 3-9-2 0 .... KierenFallon 4 — 98+
(Luca Cumani) *reluctant to enter stalls: hld up bhd ldng pair: drvn and clsd over 1f out: led last 150yds: r.o wl* **4/1**[3]

3- **2** *nk* **Joviality**[176] 7232 3-8-7 0 .... WilliamBuick 1 — 88+
(John Gosden) *pressed ldr: pushed into narrow ld 2f out: hdd and drvn last 150yds: r.o but hld nr fin* **5/4**[1]

142- **3** *3 1/4* **Nordic Spruce (USA)**[246] 5284 3-8-11 86 ....[1] TomQueally 5 — 85
(Sir Henry Cecil) *stdd s: hld up bhd ldng pair: effrt on outer 2f out: nt qckn and sn btn* **9/1**

23-1 **4** *1 1/4* **King Of Jazz (IRE)**[21] 1108 3-9-2 95 .... RichardHughes 3 — 87
(Richard Hannon) *racd freely: mde most: stdd pce 1/2-way: rdn and hdd 2f out: wknd and eased fnl f* **7/4**[2]

1m 44.4s (1.10) **Going Correction** +0.175s/f (Good) **4** Ran SP% **110.8**
Speed ratings (Par 102): **101,100,97,96**
CSF £9.71 TOTE £4.40.
Owner Sheikh Mohammed Obaid Al Maktoum **Bred** Darley **Trained** Newmarket, Suffolk

FOCUS
Home bend at outermost configuration adding 8yds to races on Round course. Just the four runners but an interesting conditions race. There wasn't much pace on early, though, and all bar Nordic Spruce raced pretty keenly. The form is rated around the third and the winner is the type to do a fair bit better.

NOTEBOOK
Naqshabban(USA) ◆, who was gelded over the winter, still looked green but Fallon got him rolling from over 1f out and he gradually wore down the favourite. There's more improvement to come from him and he'll be much better suited by a stronger all-round pace over this trip, as he's going to get 1m2f in time. The handicapper surely can't go mad on the back of this so a valuable handicap will surely be his short-term target, but the Listed Hampton Court Stakes at Royal Ascot is in the back of his trainer's mind (same connections won the race last year with Afsare). (tchd 7-2)
Joviality, who holds Oaks and Coronation Stakes entries, shaped with promise in her one start at two and again showed she has plenty of ability, despite once again showing signs of greenness. Expected to come on for this, she should have little difficulty winning a maiden if connections choose to go that way. (op 7-4)
Nordic Spruce(USA), wearing a hood for the first time, settled best of the four runners but couldn't make that tell in the closing stages. Her trainer's runners have been tending to need their reappearances and she should be straighter next time. (op 7-1)
King Of Jazz(IRE), stepping up in trip, raced freely in front and didn't get home. He is by Acclamation and his stamina for this distance remains in question. (op 13-8 tchd 15-8)

1547 BET365.COM ESHER CUP (H'CAP) — 1m 14y
3:20 (3:21) (Class 2) (0-100,96) 3-Y-0
£11,028 (£3,302; £1,651; £826; £412; £207) **Stalls** Low

Form — RPR

12- **1** **Tazahum (USA)**[197] 6733 3-9-3 **92** .... RichardHills 6 — 106+
(Sir Michael Stoute) *hld up in 6th: prog 3f out: shkn up to ld over 1f out: sn pressed: r.o wl fnl f* **11/4**[1]

321- **2** *3/4* **Captain Bertie (IRE)**[226] 5900 3-8-9 **84** ow2 .... MichaelHills 8 — 96
(B W Hills) *t.k.h early: hld up in tch: prog over 2f out: rdn to chal over 1f out: r.o but hld fnl f* **9/2**[3]

014- **3** *4* **Star Surprise**[188] 6982 3-9-1 **90** .... JamieSpencer 7 — 93
(Michael Bell) *racd wd early: pressed ldr: led 3f out: drvn and hdd over 1f out: fdd fnl f* **14/1**

110- **4** *3/4* **Treasury Devil (USA)**[203] 6610 3-9-7 **96** .... WilliamBuick 1 — 97
(John Gosden) *hld up in 7th: shkn up over 2f out: no real prog tl styd on fnl f: clsng on 3rd nr fin* **3/1**[2]

0444 **5** *3 1/2* **Sonoran Sands (IRE)**[15] 1234 3-9-1 **90** ....(p) LiamKeniry 5 — 83
(J S Moore) *mde most: styd alone on inner st and sn hdd: fdd fnl 2f* **22/1**

1 1 **6** *[illegible]* **John Biscuit (IRE)**[18] 1175 3-9-10 **95** .... JimmyFortune 9 — 70
(Andrew Balding) *stdd s: hld up in 8th: rdn wl over 2f out: no significant prog* **11/1**

1-11 **7** *1 1/4* **Indian Jack (IRE)**[18] 1175 3-8-13 **88** .... LukeMorris 4 — 70
(Alan Bailey) *chsd ldng trio: rdn 3f out: sn lost pl: wl btn fnl 2f* **7/1**

105- **8** *6* **Invincible Ridge (IRE)**[183] 7080 3-9-6 **95** .... RichardHughes 3 — 64
(Richard Hannon) *hld up last: shuffled along over 2f out: no prog and sn no ch* **12/1**

3113 **9** *8* **Kingscroft (IRE)**[10] 1326 3-8-8 **83** .... KierenFallon 2 — 33
(Mark Johnston) *chsd ldng pair: wknd rapidly wl over 2f out* **16/1**

1m 43.56s (0.26) **Going Correction** +0.175s/f (Good) **9** Ran SP% **115.3**
Speed ratings (Par 104): **105,104,100,99,96 92,91,85,77**
toteswingers: 1&2 £4.20, 1&3 £4.70, 2&3 £4.90 CSF £15.38 CT £145.21 TOTE £3.70: £1.30, £1.70, £4.10; EX 15.50 Trifecta £170.30 Pool: £929.90 - 4.04 winning units..
Owner Hamdan Al Maktoum **Bred** Shadwell Australia Ltd **Trained** Newmarket, Suffolk
■ Stewards' Enquiry : Michael Hills three-day ban: weighed in 2lb heavy (May 9-11)

FOCUS
A handicap which usually proves strong form, and no reason to believe this year's race won't work out. The form is rated around the third and could be a few pounds out either way. They came wide, some eight horse widths off the rail, up the straight, suggesting the ground was riding faster there.

NOTEBOOK
Tazahum(USA) is in the St James's Palace Stakes and, while he'll have to improve quite a bit to justify that entry, he won this handicap in the manner of a colt who will soon be competing in pattern company. The impression left was that he won with more in hand than the winning margin suggests, and this lightly raced son of Redoute's Choice is one to keep on side if, as expected, he steps up to Listed grade next time. Quicker ground will suit him better. (op 7-2 tchd 4-1)
Captain Bertie(IRE) is by Captain Rio so there was a bit of a stamina doubt beforehand, but he got the trip well, simply bumping into a well-handicapped rival. His jockey weighed in 2lb heavy, which in theory was the difference between victory and defeat, but in reality probably wasn't. He won his maiden at Chester and it wouldn't be a surprise to see him return there next month.
Star Surprise, up with the pace throughout, led the pack up the seemingly favoured strip of ground down the centre of the track and posted a solid effort in defeat behind two unexposed rivals. He seems to have a liking for this track. (tchd 16-1)
Treasury Devil(USA), who was expected to be better for the outing, wasn't happy on the ground, which had more give in it than had been expected by many. He's likely to stay further this year and can do better. (op 9-4 tchd 7-2)
Sonoran Sands(IRE), one of the more exposed runners in the line-up, raced nearest the far rail in the straight, which might well have been a disadvantage. (op 25-1 tchd 28-1)
John Biscuit(IRE) may not have been entirely happy on the ground, but remains lightly raced and open to improvement. (tchd 12-1)

Indian Jack(IRE), who is unbeaten on the AW but has yet to score on turf, is another who might not have been suited by the rain-softened ground. (op 15-2 tchd 8-1)

1548 BET365 CLASSIC TRIAL (GROUP 3) 1m 2f 7y

3:50 (3:51) (Class 1) 3-Y-O

£28,385 (£10,760; £5,385; £2,685; £1,345; £675) Stalls Low

Form				RPR
331-	1		**Genius Beast (USA)**[211] 6365 3-9-0 88 AhmedAjtebi 2 (Mahmood Al Zarooni) *trckd ldrs: rdn and effrt 2f out: clsd to ld 1f out: drvn clr* **8/1**	110+
42-2	2	2 1/4	**Measuring Time**[10] 1339 3-9-0 104 RichardHughes 8 (Richard Hannon) *hld up in last trio: prog wl over 2f out: drvn to chal over 1f out: nt qckn: wl hld fnl f* **9/2**[3]	105
66-1	3	1/2	**Auld Burns**[10] 1339 3-9-0 105 JamieSpencer 6 (Richard Hannon) *hld up last: gd prog fr 3f out to ld 2f out: hrd rdn and hdd 1f out: no ex* **4/1**[2]	104
11	4	4 1/2	**Barbican**[21] 1113 3-9-0 88 J-PGuillambert 3 (Alan Bailey) *t.k.h and sn restrained to rr: rdn and effrt 3f out: lft bhd 2f out: plugged on to take 4th fnl f* **10/1**	95
16-	5	3/4	**Masked Marvel**[197] 6737 3-9-0 85 WilliamBuick 1 (John Gosden) *pressed ldr after 1f: led 3f out to 2f out: steadily wknd* **11/1**	94
0-	6	4	**Jackaroo (IRE)**[250] 5190 3-9-0 95 RyanMoore 7 (A P O'Brien, Ire) *led 1f: trckd ldrs tl wknd wl over 1f out* **11/1**	86
41-4	7	10	**Specific Gravity (FR)**[11] 1320 3-9-0 97 TomQuealy 4 (Sir Henry Cecil) *trckd ldrs: shkn up and effrt 3f out: wknd rapidly 2f out* **8/1**	66
4-2	8	11	**Canna (IRE)**[22] 1096 3-9-0 0 MichaelHills 10 (B W Hills) *chsd ldrs: wknd rapidly wl over 2f out: t.o* **14/1**	44
13-1	9	1 3/4	**Dordogne (IRE)**[11] 1320 3-9-0 103 FrankieDettori 5 (Mark Johnston) *led after 1f to 3f out: wknd rapidly 2f out: t.o* **3/1**[1]	40

2m 11.39s (0.89) **Going Correction** +0.175s/f (Good) 9 Ran SP% **117.8**
Speed ratings (Par 108): **103,101,100,97,96 93,85,76,75**
toteswingers: 1&2 £7.70, 1&3 £2.40, 2&3 £9.60 CSF £44.81 TOTE £11.30: £3.00, £2.30, £1.80; EX 46.50 Trifecta £177.40 Pool: £1,177.14 - 4.91 winning units..
Owner Godolphin **Bred** Darley **Trained** Newmarket, Suffolk
■ Stewards' Enquiry : Ahmed Ajtebi one-day ban: used whip in incorrect place (May 9)

FOCUS
The last winner of the Classic Trial to go on and win the Derby at Epsom was Shahrastani in 1986, and this race made little more than a ripple in the ante-post market. That said it was a slightly better renewal than recent years, rated round the second and third. They spread right out in the straight and, just as in the Esher Cup, the fastest part of the track appeared to be three or four strips off the far rail.

NOTEBOOK
Genius Beast(USA) was only given the go-ahead to race once the surface had been deemed suitable (not too fast) for him and, given that that it was in reality riding just on the slow side, this performance in no way suggests doubts about him handling quick ground have been dismissed. Bred to be smart, out of an Irish Oaks winner, he got the job done nicely, albeit while all the time racing on what appeared to be the fastest strip of ground, and has the scope to improve further. The Dante is a possibility for him now, but that will take a lot more winning, and Bet365 were happy to go a best price 66-1 for the Derby afterwards.
Measuring Time reversed Newmarket form with stable companion Auld Burns. The pair have met three times now and there hasn't been a great deal between them on any occasion. He could now go for the Italian Derby. (tchd 5-1 in places)
Auld Burns is a gelding so, unlike his stablemate, is ineligible for the Italian Derby. He is clearly a smart sort, though, and he should be able to find success at pattern level. (op 5-1)
Barbican was taking a big step up in class but justified the decision with a solid effort in fourth, despite racing keenly early and apparently finding the ground on the slow side. He can do better again on a quicker surface. (op 12-1)
Masked Marvel failed to build on a promising debut here when well beaten in the Autumn Stakes on his final start at two, but this wasn't a bad reappearance effort considering he came into the race with a mark of just 85. He'll get another 2f and should come on for the run, but might have to have his sights lowered a little. (op 10-1 tchd 12-1)
Jackaroo(IRE) ran well for a long way but got tired and shaped like he needed the run. He should last longer next time. (op 14-1)
Specific Gravity(FR) was expected to build on his reappearance fourth behind Dordogne in the Feilden and give that one more of a race, but that form took a caning here, the pair of them running well below their Newmarket efforts. Perhaps the race came too soon for both of them.
Canna(IRE), the only maiden in the field, faced a stiff task and dropped right out from early in the straight. (op 16-1)
Dordogne(IRE) ran a shocker and presumably, like Specific Gravity, he found this race coming too soon after the Feilden. (tchd 11-4 and 7-2 in places)

1549 POKER AT BET365.COM MAIDEN FILLIES' STKS 1m 2f 7y

4:25 (4:27) (Class 5) 3-Y-O £3,238 (£963; £481; £240) Stalls Low

Form				RPR
3-	1		**Arizona Jewel**[187] 7000 3-9-0 0 TomQueally 7 (Sir Henry Cecil) *prom: led 6f out: pushed along and in command 2f out: rdn out fnl f* **4/1**[2]	87
	2	1 1/2	**Skip Along** 3-9-0 0 NeilCallan 11 (John Gosden) *settled in midfield: shkn up and prog jst over 2f out: styd on fnl f to take 2nd nr fin* **11/1**	84+
2	3	1/2	**Miss Aix**[16] 1210 3-9-0 0 JamieSpencer 3 (Michael Bell) *cl up: chsd wnr wl over 2f out: drvn and no imp wl over 1f out: kpt on but lost 2nd nr fin* **6/1**[3]	83
2-	4	2 1/4	**Always The Lady**[229] 5829 3-9-0 0 AdamKirby 2 (Clive Cox) *prom: chsd wnr 6f out to wl over 2f out: drvn and one pce after* **9/4**[1]	78
	5	1	**Moment Of Time** 3-9-0 0 JimmyFortune 9 (Andrew Balding) *s.s: hld up last: pushed along and stdy prog over 2f out: chalng for pl over 1f out: fdd fnl f: fair debut* **16/1**	76
	6	hd	**Zafarana** 3-9-0 0 EddieAhern 1 (Ed Dunlop) *hld up in rr: last 3f out: pushed along and styd on steadily fnl 2f: quite promising* **40/1**	76+
	7	1	**Crassula** 3-9-0 0 MarcHalford 12 (Terry Clement) *prom: rdn and losing pl whn n.m.r over 2f out: fdd* **200/1**	74
03-	8	3 1/4	**Fennica (USA)**[193] 6843 3-9-0 0 WilliamBuick 4 (John Gosden) *led 4f: stdd bhd ldrs: shkn up over 2f out: grad wknd* **14/1**	67
6-	9	1	**Rien Ne Vas Plus (IRE)**[176] 7232 3-9-0 0 RyanMoore 10 (Sir Michael Stoute) *hld up in rr: sme prog 3f out: hanging 2f out: sn wknd* **4/1**[2]	65
	10	hd	**Compassion** 3-9-0 0 HayleyTurner 6 (Michael Bell) *difficult to load into stalls: hld up in rr: shkn up and effrt 3f out: no prog 2f out: wknd* **33/1**	65
-	11	nk	**Buttonhole** 3-8-11 0 LouisBeuzelin(3) 8 (Sir Michael Stoute) *hld up wl in rr: pushed along and sme prog over 2f out: wknd wl over 1f out* **25/1**	64
	12	19	**Galicuix** 3-9-0 0 KierenFallon 5 (Luca Cumani) *prom early: lost pl sn after 1/2-way: wknd over 2f out: t.o* **25/1**	—

2m 14.14s (3.64) **Going Correction** +0.175s/f (Good) **12** Ran SP% **119.5**
Speed ratings (Par 95): **92,90,90,88,87 87,86,84,83,83 83,67**
toteswingers: 1&2 £9.20, 1&3 £5.20, 2&3 £9.30 CSF £45.46 TOTE £5.30: £1.80, £2.50, £2.10; EX 53.80 Trifecta £391.70 Pool: £714.59 - 1.35 winning units..
Owner K Abdulla **Bred** Juddmonte Farms Ltd **Trained** Newmarket, Suffolk

FOCUS
A good-looking maiden on paper, featuring a number of well-bred fillies from big stables, and probably form to be positive about. The time was only modest though and the form is rated around the third and fourth. The first and third came up the apparently faster, third strip off the far-side rail.

1550 BET365.COM H'CAP 1m 2f 7y

4:55 (5:00) (Class 3) (0-90,88) 3-Y-O

£7,165 (£2,145; £1,072; £537; £267; £134) Stalls Low

Form				RPR
221-	1		**Chain Lightning**[207] 6473 3-9-4 85 RichardHughes 10 (Richard Hannon) *trckd ldr to 1/2-way: styd cl up: effrt to ld jst over 2f out: drvn and pressed over 1f out: styd on wl* **5/1**	101
10-	2	1 1/4	**Dominant (IRE)**[204] 6560 3-9-7 88 NeilCallan 2 (Roger Varian) *hld up in tch: looking for room on inner fr 3f out: bdly hmpd jst over 2f out: plld out to take modest 4th over 1f out: styd on wl to go 2nd last 50yds: unlucky* **9/2**[3]	106+
21-2	3	3/4	**Glencadam Gold (IRE)**[10] 1344 3-9-6 87 (t) TomQueally 1 (Sir Henry Cecil) *s.s: hld up in last pair: prog on outer fr 3f out: rdn to chse wnr jst over 1f out and cl enough: wandered and nt qckn after: lost 2nd last 50yds* **2/1**[1]	99+
1-	4	1 3/4	**Samurai Sword**[275] 4346 3-9-4 85 AhmedAjtebi 7 (Mahmood Al Zarooni) *hld up in tch: rdn and prog to chse wnr 2f out and sn chalng: nt qckn and lost 2nd jst over 1f out: one pce* **9/4**[2]	94
641	5	7	**Manifestation**[60] 649 3-9-2 83 WilliamBuick 4 (John Gosden) *led: jnd 4f out: hdd whn bmpd jst over 2f out: sn wl outpcd: kpt on fnl f* **20/1**	78
0-11	6	3 3/4	**She Ain't A Saint**[36] 907 3-9-4 85 KierenFallon 8 (Jane Chapple-Hyam) *t.k.h: cl up: chsd ldr 1/2-way: upsides 4f out: hung rt and bmpd rival jst over 2f out: sn wknd* **16/1**	72
15	7	1 1/4	**Loch Fleet (IRE)**[29] 988 3-8-10 77 JimmyFortune 9 (Andrew Balding) *hld up in last pair: rdn 3f out: no prog and wl btn 2f out* **50/1**	62
110-	8	hd	**Buxfizz (USA)**[176] 7236 3-9-4 85 EddieAhern 6 (Robert Mills) *chsd ldrs: rdn over 3f out: sn struggling: wknd 2f out* **50/1**	69
5-1	9	3 1/2	**Carrick A Rede (IRE)**[53] 726 3-8-11 78 LukeMorris 3 (Clive Cox) *hld up in rr: rdn and struggling 3f out: sn no ch* **20/1**	55

2m 11.69s (1.19) **Going Correction** +0.175s/f (Good) **9** Ran SP% **118.3**
Speed ratings (Par 102): **102,101,100,99,93 90,89,89,86**
toteswingers: 1&2 £5.80, 1&3 £3.70, 2&3 £3.30 CSF £27.23 CT £59.40 TOTE £6.20: £2.00, £1.80, £1.40; EX 32.60 Trifecta £55.20 Pool: £1,182.24 - 15.83 winning units..
Owner Michael Pescod **Bred** Ecurie I M Fares **Trained** East Everleigh, Wilts

FOCUS
Normally a handicap with a bit of quality about it and the form usually works out well, but there's a suspicion that this might not have been the hottest of renewals That said, the time was good and the first four came clear, so the form has been rated positively.

NOTEBOOK
Chain Lightning enjoyed a clear run and held off the unlucky-in-running second a shade comfortably at the line. He shouldn't go up too much for this and has the potential to progress through the handicapping ranks. (op 9-2 tchd 7-1)
Dominant(IRE) ◆ was badly hampered as he went for an ambitious run towards the inside 2f out. His momentum was halted and it's to his credit that he closed the gap with the winner down to just over a length at the line. He would surely have won with a clear run and looks well up to taking something similar off an even higher mark. Official explanation: jockey said colt suffered interference in running (tchd 4-1)
Glencadam Gold(IRE), wearing a tongue-tie for the first time, came from off the pace and had the benefit of what had looked to be the fastest strip of ground up the straight, but he carried his head a little high, wandered about under pressure and didn't look the most resolute. He might be one to avoid at cramped odds. (op 9-4, tchd 5-2 in places)
Samurai Sword, representing a stable very much in form, had his chance approaching the final furlong but didn't quite see it out. He holds Group race entries over distances ranging from 1m to 1m4f and it remains to be seen what his ideal trip will turn out to be. (op 4-1)
Manifestation ◆ was struck into, presumably 2f out when he was involved in the incident in which the runner-up was hampered. He ran on again to take fifth after weakening out of contention for the places and, as a half-brother to Sergeant Cecil, has plenty of scope to improve as he's stepped up in distance. Official explanation: vet said colt had been struck into (op 14-1)
She Ain't A Saint got a bump from the winner, which caused her to edge right and hamper the runner-up on the rail at the 2f pole. She was beating a retreat at the time and wasn't obviously suited by the step up from a mile. (op 10-1)
T/Jkpt: £14,089.70 to a £1 stake. Pool: £19,844.67. 1.00 winning ticket. T/Plt: £116.60 to a £1 stake. Pool £80,534.12. 503.96 winning tickets. T/Qpdt: £11.70 to a £1 stake. Pool £5,867.91 368.76 winning tickets. JN

9001 LONGCHAMP (R-H)

Sunday, April 24

OFFICIAL GOING: Turf: good

1551a PRIX NOAILLES (GROUP 2) (3YO) (TURF) 1m 2f

1:30 (12:00) 3-Y-O £63,879 (£24,655; £11,767; £7,844; £3,922)

			RPR
1		**Grand Vent (IRE)**[21] 1124 3-9-2 0 MaximeGuyon 7 (A Fabre, France) *settled in 5th: rdn 1 1/2f out: qcknd wl to take ld 150yds out: r.o strly* **3/1**[1]	104+
2	1/2	**Durer (FR)**[38] 882 3-9-2 0 IoritzMendizabal 1 (J-C Rouget, France) *settled in 2nd: qcknd early in st to chal for ld gng easily 1f out: led briefly: rdn but unable to hold off eventual wnr fnl 100yds: r.o wl* **4/1**[2]	103+
3	shd	**Touz Price (FR)**[33] 3-9-2 0 FranckBlondel 8 (J-M Lefebvre, France) *settled 6th: rdn 1 1/2f out: qcknd wl: fin strly fnl 100yds: wnt 3rd on line* **20/1**	103
4	snk	**Little Storm (FR)**[36] 3-9-2 0 PhilippeSogorb 3 (C Ferland, France) *settled in 5th: dropped bk to 7th bef st: racd wd: qcknd wl ent fnl f on wd outside: fin strly: clst at fin* **8/1**	103+

5 *hd* **Genzy (FR)**[27] 3-9-2 0.................................. Christophe-PatriceLemaire 5 102
(J E Pease, France) *settled in rr: r.o wl fnl f: clst at fin* **5/1**[3]

6 *3/4* **Oppenort (IRE)**[33] 3-9-2 0.................................. ChristopheSoumillon 2 101
(M Delzangles, France) *settled 4th on rail: rdn to go 2nd 1f out: no ex fnl 100yds: styd on* **5/1**[3]

7 *nk* **Cayman Islands**[10] 3-9-2 0.................................. Pierre-CharlesBoudot 4 100?
(A Fabre, France) *sn led: rdn early in st: r.o: hdd 1f out: styd on fnl 100yds* **25/1**

8 *1 1/2* **Moonyr (FR)**[189] 3-9-2 0.................................. OlivierPeslier 6 97
(F Head, France) *settled 3rd: ev ch 1 1/2f out: nt qckn: styd on one pce* **4/1**[2]

2m 5.42s (1.42) **Going Correction** +0.40s/f (Good) **8** Ran SP% **118.1**
Speed ratings: **110,109,109,109,109 108,108,107**
WIN (incl 1 euro stake): 3.70 (Grand Vent coupled with Cayman Islands). PLACES: 1.70, 2.30, 4.30. DF: 12.70. SF: 18.80.
Owner Godolphin SNC **Bred** Darley **Trained** Chantilly, France

NOTEBOOK
Grand Vent(IRE), a half-brother to Bushman, took a while to pick up but finished well and can rate higher when faced with a stronger pace. The Prix Hocquart is next up for him.

1552a PRIX DE FONTAINEBLEAU (GROUP 3) (3YO COLTS) (TURF) 1m
2:40 (12:00) 3-Y-0 **£34,482** (£13,793; £10,344; £6,896; £3,448)

RPR

1 **Glaswegian**[20] 3-9-2 0.................................. StephanePasquier 6 109+
(P Bary, France) *racd midfield: rdn 1 1/2f out: swtchd towards outer: qckndwl 1f out: r.o strly fnl 100yds: grabbed ld 50yds out: r.o wl* **10/1**

2 *nk* **Rosanabad (FR)**[26] 3-9-2 0.................................. Christophe-PatriceLemaire 2 109+
(J-C Rouget, France) *settled towards rr: qcknd wl between horses 1f out: r.o wl fnl 100yds to go 2nd cl home* **9/2**[3]

3 *snk* **Tin Horse (IRE)**[203] [6610] 3-9-2 0.................................. ThierryJarnet 4 108
(D Guillemin, France) *racd 4th: pulling freely: hmpd 1f out: qcknd wl fnl 100yds to go 3rd fnl 25yds: r.o wl* **7/1**

4 *snk* **Barocci (JPN)**[24] [1070] 3-9-2 0.................................. ChristopheSoumillon 7 108
(E Lellouche, France) *settled midfield towards outer: qcknd wl to ld 150yds out: hdd 50yds out: r.o wl* **4/1**[2]

5 *snk* **Mister Iceman (FR)**[34] 3-9-2 0.................................. IoritzMendizabal 8 108
(D Smaga, France) *settled bhd ldrs: short of room 1f out: swtchd to rail: r.o wl fnl 100yds* **33/1**

6 *1/2* **Salto (IRE)**[175] [7265] 3-9-2 0.................................. OlivierPeslier 10 107
(F Head, France) *settled towards rr towards outer: rdn 1 1/2f out: ev ch ent fnl f: nt qckn: styd on* **2/1**[1]

7 *1* **Private Jet (FR)**[24] [1070] 3-9-2 0.................................. MaximeGuyon 1 104
(H-A Pantall, France) *racd midfield: short of room 1f out: dropped towards rr: styd on again fnl 100yds* **16/1**

8 *1 1/2* **Maiguri (IRE)**[175] [7265] 3-9-2 0.................................. JohanVictoire 5 101
(C Baillet, France) *racd midfield: short of room 1f out: had to be stdd: lost ch: styd on* **10/1**

9 *1/2* **Chopsoave (FR)**[36] 3-9-2 0.................................. AnthonyCrastus 11 100
(Mme C Dufreche, France) *settled 3rd: wnt 2nd ent fnl f: rdn and no ex: fdd* **50/1**

10 *1 1/2* **Temps Au Temps (IRE)**[24] [1070] 3-9-2 0.................................. GregoryBenoist 3 96
(M Delzangles, France) *settled midfield: no room 1f out and dropped towards rr: stdd whn no ch fnl 100yds* **20/1**

11 **Hung Parliament (FR)**[231] [5799] 3-9-2 0.................................. RichardKingscote 9 96
(Tom Dascombe) *cl up on wd outside: plld his way to ld after 1 1/2f: led tl hdd jst over 1f out: rdn: no ex: sn fdd* **11/1**

1m 39.69s (1.29) **Going Correction** +0.40s/f (Good) **11** Ran SP% **126.1**
Speed ratings: **109,108,108,108,108 107,106,105,104,103 103**
WIN (incl 1 euro stake): 10.00. PLACES: 3.00, 2.10, 3.20. DF: 19.00. SF: 36.60..
Owner K Abdulla **Bred** Juddmonte Farms **Trained** Chantilly, France

NOTEBOOK
Glaswegian produced a good turn of foot to come out on top in a bunch finish, and will now go for the Poule d'Essai des Poulains.
Hung Parliament(FR) pulled too hard off the steady early pace, and his trainer might drop him back in trip now.

1553a PRIX DE LA GROTTE (GROUP 3) (3YO FILLIES) (TURF) 1m
3:10 (12:00) 3-Y-0 **£34,482** (£13,793; £10,344; £6,896; £3,448)

RPR

1 **Golden Lilac (IRE)**[205] 3-9-0 0.................................. MaximeGuyon 5 109+
(A Fabre, France) *settled 4th: swtchd to outside 1f out: qcknd wl to ld 100yds out: r.o wl: comfortably* **11/4**[2]

2 *1 1/2* **Mixed Intention (IRE)**[38] [884] 3-9-0 0.................................. SylvainRuis 3 103+
(F Vermeulen, France) *settled towards rr: followed eventual wnr in st: hrd rdn 1f out: r.o wl to go 2nd cl home* **12/1**

3 *snk* **Whip And Win (FR)**[17] [1207] 3-9-0 0.................................. GregoryBenoist 1 103
(Robert Collet, France) *settled 3rd on rail: rdn early in st to go 2nd 1f out: r.o wl fnl 100yds* **8/1**

4 *1 1/2* **Espirita (FR)**[187] [7008] 3-9-0 0.................................. AnthonyCrastus 4 100
(E Lellouche, France) *settled in 2nd: qcknd to ld 1 1/2f out: hdd 100yds out: styd on wl* **11/8**[1]

5 *1 1/2* **Glorious Sight (IRE)**[14] [1264] 3-9-0 0.................................. SebastienMaillot 6 96+
(Robert Collet, France) *a towards rr: styd on fnl f* **14/1**

6 *3/4* **Albaraah (IRE)**[33] 3-9-0 0.................................. DavyBonilla 2 94
(F Head, France) *racd freely fr s and plld way to ld after 1f: hdd 1 1/2f out: nt qckn under hrd ride: fdd fnl f* **6/1**[3]

7 *6* **Doo Lang (USA)**[192] 3-9-0 0.................................. Christophe-PatriceLemaire 7 81
(J-C Rouget, France) *racd midfield on rail: rdn and no ex in st: fdd* **9/1**

1m 43.62s (5.22) **Going Correction** +0.40s/f (Good) **7** Ran SP% **118.5**
Speed ratings: **89,87,87,85,84 83,77**
WIN (incl 1 euro stake): 3.10. PLACES: 1.80, 5.00. SF : 37.90..
Owner Gestut Ammerland **Bred** Gestut Ammerland **Trained** Chantilly, France

NOTEBOOK
Golden Lilac(IRE) extended her unbeaten record in good style, quickening up to score with a bit in hand. The Poule d'Essai des Pouliches will be her next race.

1126 SAN SIRO (R-H)
Sunday, April 24

OFFICIAL GOING: Turf: good

1554a PREMIO AMBROSIANO (GROUP 3) (4YO+) (TURF) 1m 2f
4:55 (12:00) 4-Y-0+ **£34,482** (£15,172; £8,275; £4,137)

RPR

1 **Cima De Pluie**[14] 4-8-11 0.................................. DarioVargiu 3 104
(B Grizzetti, Italy) *in rr after 2f: prog ent fnl 3f: hrd rdn to chal ldr fnl f: got up on line to snatch win by shortest of margins* **31/4**

2 *nse* **Estejo (GER)**[168] [7373] 7-8-11 0.................................. PierantonioConvertino 2 104
(R Rohne, Germany) *in 4th for 6f: 3rd ent st: gd prog under confident ride to ld ent fnl 2f: rdn to go a l clr of eventual wnr ent fnl f: hrd rdn whn chal: jst failed to hold on* **11/4**[2]

3 *3* **Voila Ici (IRE)**[147] [7615] 6-8-11 0.................................. MircoDemuro 4 98
(Vittorio Caruso, Italy) *in rr: rdn to stay in tch last 3f: hung sltly rt in bhd horses ent fnl 2f: hrd rdn to stay on for 3rd: nvr clsr* **8/15**[1]

4 *3/4* **Altair Star (IRE)**[21] [1128] 4-8-11 0.................................. AStarke 5 97
(P Schiergen, Germany) *racd 5th for 4f: ct for pce ent st: hrd rdn fr 3f out: moved to chal on outer ent fnl 2f tl hung bdly rt in bhd ldrs: lost 3rd fnl 50yds* **43/10**[3]

5 *4* **Christian Love (ITY)**[14] 4-8-11 0.................................. LManiezzi 1 89
(R Menichetti, Italy) *settled 3rd to trck ldrs after 1f: rdn and in tch 3f out: led briefly u.str ride under 2f out: sn hdd and btn 1f out* **29/1**

6 *6* **Russian King (GER)**[77] [441] 5-8-11 0.................................. WGambarota 7 77
(R Rohne, Germany) *broke wl to ld after 1f: set stdy pce for 5f: hdd 2 1/2f out: sn btn* **11/4**[2]

7 *3 1/2* **Ordenstreuer (IRE)**[31] [1011] 5-8-11 0.................................. THellier 6 70
(H-W Hiller, Germany) *trckd ldr in 2nd: chal to ld briefly 2 1/2f out: sn one pce: fdd* **199/10**

2m 1.90s (-4.80) **7** Ran SP% **157.0**
WIN (incl. 1 euro stake): 8.73. PLACES: 3.29, 2.28. DF: 25.83.
Owner Scuderia Cocktail **Bred** Grundy Bloodstock **Trained** Italy

1434 REDCAR (L-H)
Monday, April 25

OFFICIAL GOING: Good to firm (good in places; watered; 8.8)
Wind: Virtually nil Weather: Fine and dry

1555 MARKET CROSS JEWELLERS FILLIES' H'CAP 5f
2:00 (2:01) (Class 5) (0-75,69) 4-Y-0+ **£3,950** (£1,175; £587; £293) **Stalls** High

Form RPR

240- **1** **Dispol Kylie (IRE)**[205] [6572] 5-8-12 **63**.................. MichaelO'Connell(3) 6 72
(Kate Walton) *hld up towards rr: hdwy 2f out: swtchd rt and rdn ent fnl f: qckndwl to ld last 50yds* **8/1**

24-1 **2** *1 3/4* **Dreamacha**[105] [113] 4-9-6 **68**.................................. JamesDoyle 7 71
(Stuart Williams) *trckd ldrs: swtchd rt and hdwy 2f out: rdn to ld ent fnl f: hdd and nt qckn last 50yds* **9/2**[2]

26-3 **3** *1* **Carrie's Magic**[16] [1239] 4-9-7 **69**..............................(b) GrahamGibbons 4 68
(David Barron) *cl up: rdn to ld wl over 1f out: drvn whn sltly hmpd and hdd ent fnl f: kpt on same pce* **3/1**[1]

12-0 **4** *1 1/2* **Oondiri (IRE)**[9] [1411] 4-9-1 **63**.................................. PaulHanagan 5 57
(Tim Easterby) *cl up: chal over 2f out: sn rdn and hung lft over 1f out: wknd fnl f* **11/2**[3]

1455 **5** *2* **Six Wives**[9] [1411] 4-8-13 **64**.................................. BillyCray(3) 9 51
(David Nicholls) *chsd ldrs: rdn along 2f out: sn edgd lft and one pce* **15/[illegible]**

-462 **6** *3/4* **Hypnosis**[59] [696] 8-9-2 **64**.................................. LeeNewman 8 48
(Noel Wilson) *s.i.s: a in rr* **10/1**

0205 **7** *nse* **Fashion Icon (USA)**[5] [1503] 5-8-11 **62**...............(b) NataliaGemelova(3) 2 46
(David O'Meara) *chsd ldrs: rdn along 1/2-way: sn wknd* **20/1**

200- **8** *shd* **Song Of Parkes**[293] [3751] 4-9-6 **68**.................................. RobertWinston 1 52
(Eric Alston) *chsd ldrs on outer: rdn along 2f out: sn wandered and btn* **11/2**[3]

40-0 **9** *2* **Nomoreblondes**[18] [1204] 7-9-6 **68**...............(p) MickyFenton 3 44
(Paul Midgley) *led: rdn 2f out: sn hdd & wknd qckly fnl f* **20/1**

59.43 secs (0.83) **Going Correction** +0.20s/f (Good) **9** Ran SP% **115.4**
Speed ratings (Par 100): **101,98,96,94,91 89,89,89,86**
toteswingers:1&2:£8.40, 1&3:£3.00, 2&3:£2.40 CSF £43.86 CT £131.66 TOTE £10.70: £3.10, £1.70, £1.50; EX 47.30.
Owner W B Imison **Bred** Century Farms **Trained** Middleham Moor, N Yorks

FOCUS
A fair sprint for fillies and no reason why the form wouldn't prove solid for the level with the placed horses pretty good yardsticks. They went pretty hard up front, the front two both coming from off the pace. The winner is probably the best guide.

1556 WIN A VIP DAY OUT @ REDCARRACING.CO.UK H'CAP 2m 4y
2:35 (2:35) (Class 6) (0-65,60) 4-Y-0+ **£1,619** (£481; £240; £120) **Stalls** Low

Form RPR

3-60 **1** **King In Waiting (IRE)**[20] [1153] 8-9-7 **55**...............(p) DanielTudhope 2 64
(David O'Meara) *mde all: sn clr: rdn wl over 2f out: kpt on strly* **4/1**[3]

260- **2** *3* **Bandanaman (IRE)**[244] [5119] 5-9-5 **60**.................. GarryWhillans(7) 3 65
(Alan Swinbank) *trckd ldrs: effrt over 3f out: swtchd rt and rdn 2f out: kpt on fnl f: nt rch wnr* **7/2**[2]

00-0 **3** *1/2* **They All Laughed**[27] [1032] 8-8-11 **45**...............(p) PhillipMakin 8 49
(Marjorie Fife) *hld up towards rr: hdwy on outer wl over 2f out: rdn and kpt on fnl f: nrst fin* **11/2**

2-03 **4** *nk* **Valantino Oyster (IRE)**[12] [1305] 4-9-3 **58**............... PatrickDonaghy(3) 7 62
(Ben Haslam) *hld up and bhd: hdwy on outer over 4f out: rdn wl over 2f out: sn drvn and kpt on same pce* **11/4**[1]

604- **5** *1/2* **Dan's Heir**[70] [7145] 9-9-2 **53**.................................. JamesSullivan(3) 1 57
(Wilf Storey) *hld up towards rr: hdwy over 3f out: rdn over 2f out: sn drvn and one pce* **7/1**

/3-0 **6** *1 1/4* **Across The Sea (USA)**[17] [1211] 4-9-5 **60**............ MichaelO'Connell(3) 5 62
(Geoffrey Harker) *chsd ldr: drvn wl over 2f out: grad wknd* **14/1**

546- **7** *24* **Perez (IRE)**[8] [5203] 9-8-11 **45**...............(vt) MickyFenton 4 18
(Wilf Storey) *in tch: rdn along over 4f out: sn outpcd and bhd* **20/1**

40-0 **8** *33* **Always Dixie (IRE)**[12] 1305 4-8-9 **47** RobertWinston 6 —
(Andrew Crook) *chsd ldng pair: rdn along over 4f out: sn wknd: bhd and eased fnl 2f* **25/1**

3m 33.66s (2.26) **Going Correction** +0.20s/f (Good)
WFA 4 from 5yo+ 4lb **8** Ran SP% **112.0**
Speed ratings (Par 101): **102,100,100,100,99 99,87,70**
toteswingers:1&2:£1.30, 1&3:£6.20, 2&3:£5.10 CSF £17.62 CT £74.86 TOTE £4.30: £2.40, £1.20, £1.40; EX 14.60.
Owner Akv Cladding Fabrications Ltd **Bred** Abergwaun Farms **Trained** Nawton, N Yorks

FOCUS
A modest staying event with the winner making all, and the next five horses finishing in a bit of a heap behind. The winner is rated back to the sort of form he was in this time last year.

1557 RACING UK ON SKY 432 (S) STKS 7f
3:10 (3:10) (Class 6) 3-Y-O+ **£1,619** (£481; £240; £120) **Stalls** High

Form RPR

1252 **1** **Orpenindeed (IRE)**[6] 1471 8-9-11 75 (t) JamesDoyle 5 84
(Frank Sheridan) *trckd ldrs: smooth hdwy to ld over 3f out: rdn clr wl over 1f out: easily* **1/1**[1]

6454 **2** *7* **Mini's Destination**[13] 1288 3-8-1 58 PaulHanagan 4 49
(John Holt) *in tch: hdwy to chse wnr over 2f out and sn rdn: drvn over 1f out and no imp* **11/1**

400- **3** *3 3/4* **Rub Of The Relic (IRE)**[280] 4196 6-9-5 59 (v) MickyFenton 6 49
(Paul Midgley) *towards rr: hdwy wl over 2f out: sn rdn and styd on to take 3rd ins fnl f* **7/1**[3]

5100 **4** *1* **Abriachan**[46] 820 4-9-11 67 PhillipMakin 2 52
(Noel Quinlan) *hld up in tch: hdwy 3f out: rdn to chse ldng pair and hung lft wl over 1f out: sn btn* **11/4**[2]

00-0 **5** *7* **Isle Of Ellis (IRE)**[7] 1439 4-8-12 38 (v[1]) ShaneBKelly(7) 10 27
(Ron Barr) *prom: rdn along 3f out: drvn and wknd 2f out* **80/1**

000- **6** *2 1/2* **Hettie Hubble**[217] 6261 5-9-0 46 FrederikTylicki 1 16
(David Thompson) *dwlt: sn chsng ldrs: rdn along 3f out: sn wknd* **25/1**

050- **7** *1 1/4* **Efidium**[259] 4897 13-9-0 47 DaleSwift(5) 7 17
(Suzzanne France) *a towards rr* **33/1**

05-0 **8** *1 1/2* **Karate Queen**[16] 1247 6-9-0 40 BarryMcHugh 11 —
(Ron Barr) *prom: rdn along wl over 2f out: sn wknd* **50/1**

306- **9** *1* **Kaua'i Girl**[165] 7412 3-8-1 57 DuranFentiman 3 —
(Ann Duffield) *sn led: pushed along and hdd over 3f out: rdn over 2f out: sn wknd* **10/1**

004- **10** *2 1/4* **Dream Express (IRE)**[168] 7380 6-9-2 49 JamesSullivan(3) 8 —
(David Thompson) *a in rr* **25/1**

P0/0 **11** *4* **Glencairn Star**[26] 1037 10-9-5 40 (p) KellyHarrison 9 —
(Frederick Watson) *a in rr: bhd fnl 3f* **100/1**

1m 26.28s (1.78) **Going Correction** +0.20s/f (Good)
WFA 3 from 4yo+ 13lb **11** Ran SP% **121.4**
Speed ratings (Par 101): **97,89,84,83,75 72,71,69,68,65 61**
toteswingers:1&2:£4.80, 1&3:£1.40, 2&3:£15.70 CSF £14.02 TOTE £1.80: £1.10, £2.60, £3.10; EX 14.00.The winner was bought in for 7,000gns.
Owner Frank Sheridan **Bred** A Pereira **Trained** Wolverhampton, W Midlands

FOCUS
A seller which lacked depth and it was a very one-sided affair with the field well strung out. The form is rated around the winner.

1558 BUY YOUR TICKETS ON-LINE @ REDCARRACING.CO.UK H'CAP 7f
3:45 (3:45) (Class 5) (0-70,69) 4-Y-O+ **£2,072** (£616; £308; £153) **Stalls** High

Form RPR

5-00 **1** **No Quarter (IRE)**[7] 1439 4-8-7 **55** oh1 FrannyNorton 4 64
(Tracy Waggott) *hld up in midfield: hdwy over 2f out: rdn to ld appr fnl f: styd on wl* **20/1**

565- **2** *1 1/4* **Muftarres (IRE)**[226] 5958 6-9-0 **62** MickyFenton 7 68
(Paul Midgley) *hld up in rr: gd hdwy on wd outside over 2f out: rdn and ev ch over 1f out: drvn and one pce ins fnl f* **14/1**

30-2 **3** *3/4* **High Rolling**[16] 1245 4-9-1 **63** RobertWinston 9 67
(Tim Easterby) *prom: effrt over 2f out: sn rdn and ev ch tl drvn: edgd rt and one pce fnl f* **7/2**[1]

/05- **4** *nk* **Dialogue**[221] 6117 5-9-2 **67** MichaelO'Connell(3) 1 70
(Geoffrey Harker) *dwlt and in rr: hdwy wl over 2f out: rdn to chse ldrs over 1f out: n.m.r ins fnl f: swtchd lft and kpt on towards fin* **10/1**

015- **5** *1 1/2* **Cross The Boss (IRE)**[61] 6935 4-8-13 **61** (t) PhillipMakin 2 60
(Ben Haslam) *in tch: hdwy to chse ldrs over 2f out: sn rdn and kpt on same pce appr fnl f* **10/1**

6-20 **6** *4* **Klynch**[12] 1307 5-8-6 **57** (b) JamesSullivan(3) 3 45
(Ruth Carr) *chsd ldrs: rdn along over 2f out: sn drvn and grad wknd* **10/1**

-016 **7** *1/2* **Powerful Pierre**[16] 1239 4-8-11 **64** (v) LeeTopliss(5) 10 51
(Ian McInnes) *midfield: rdn along and sltly outpcd over 2f out: kpt on u.p fr over 1f out* **14/1**

250- **8** *2 1/4* **Chambers (IRE)**[191] 6917 5-8-9 **57** DuranFentiman 12 38
(Eric Alston) *led: rdn along over 2f out: drvn over 1f out: hdd & wknd appr fnl f* **12/1**

400- **9** *3/4* **Transmit (IRE)**[193] 6879 4-9-3 **65** DavidAllan 6 43
(Tim Easterby) *chsd ldrs: rdn along 3f out: wknd 2f out* **10/1**

-100 **10** *1/2* **Northern Flyer (GER)**[20] 1150 5-9-2 **64** (p) CDHayes 11 41
(John Quinn) *midfield: effrt and sme hdwy 3f out: sn rdn and btn 2f out* **17/2**[3]

5421 **11** *4* **Fleetwoodsands (IRE)**[28] 1017 4-9-7 **69** (t) BarryMcHugh 14 35
(Ollie Pears) *t.k.h: cl up: rdn along 3f out: sn wknd* **9/1**

0R-5 **12** *11* **Just The Tonic**[16] 1244 4-9-3 **65** KellyHarrison 13 —
(Marjorie Fife) *chsd ldrs: rdn along 1/2-way: sn lost pl and bhd* **20/1**

610- **13** *14* **Sea Salt**[182] 7125 8-9-6 **68** PaulHanagan 8 —
(Ron Barr) *racd alone far side: cl up: rdn along 1/2-way: wknd qckly and bhd fnl 2f* **8/1**[2]

1m 25.48s (0.98) **Going Correction** +0.20s/f (Good) **13** Ran SP% **120.8**
Speed ratings (Par 103): **102,100,99,99,97 93,92,89,89,88 83,71,55**
toteswingers:1&2:£74.00, 1&3:£17.00, 2&3:£8.20 CSF £278.61 CT £1219.25 TOTE £33.90: £9.20, £6.80, £1.60; EX 309.50.
Owner Miss T Waggott **Bred** Mrs T V Ryan **Trained** Spennymoor, Co Durham

FOCUS
A modest handicap run at a sound pace. Improvement from the winner, with the form rated around the second.
Dialogue ◆ Official explanation: jockey said gelding was denied a clear run
Fleetwoodsands(IRE) Official explanation: jockey said gelding ran flat

1559 REDCAR RACECOURSE CONFERENCE & EVENTS VENUE MAIDEN STKS 1m 1f
4:20 (4:20) (Class 5) 3-Y-O+ **£2,072** (£616; £308; £153) **Stalls** Low

Form RPR

6- **1** **Piave (IRE)**[178] 7203 3-8-10 0 AshleyHamblett(3) 9 68
(Peter Chapple-Hyam) *trckd ldrs: hdwy 3f out: chal and rdn wl over 1f out: drvn ent fnl f: styd on to ld nr line* **13/8**[1]

0-42 **2** *shd* **Bajan Flash**[9] 1394 4-10-0 67 AdrianNicholls 6 70
(David Nicholls) *cl up: led after 2f: rdn over 2f out: drvn and edgd rt over 1f out: hdd nr line* **15/8**[2]

320- **3** *3/4* **Residence And Spa (IRE)**[219] 6174 3-8-13 73 DavidAllan 7 66
(Tim Easterby) *trckd ldrs: hdwy over 3f out: rdn and cl up 2f out: n.m.r and swtchd lft jst ins fnl f: drvn and kpt on* **7/2**[3]

4- **4** *1/2* **Sartingo (IRE)**[241] 5478 4-9-7 0 GarryWhillans(7) 4 68
(Alan Swinbank) *wnt rt s: hld up in tch: hdwy over 3f out: rdn to chal 2f out: ev ch over 1f out: drvn and one pce ins fnl f* **20/1**

5 *3 1/4* **Lemon Queen (IRE)**[64] 5-9-9 0 CDHayes 5 55
(John Quinn) *dwlt and hmpd s: bhd: hdwy 4f out: rdn to chse ldrs 2f out: kpt on same pce appr fnl f* **50/1**

63- **6** *2* **Royal Bonsai**[142] 7700 3-8-6 0 ShaneBKelly(7) 3 53
(John Quinn) *hld up towards rr: sme hdwy on inner 4f out: sn rdn and outpcd: kpt on u.p fnl f* **9/1**

0 **7** *9* **Molannarch**[17] 1212 5-9-9 0 TonyHamilton 1 31
(Keith Reveley) *a in rr* **66/1**

0/-0 **8** *1/2* **Into Mac**[40] 873 5-10-0 0 PaulMulrennan 2 35
(Neville Bycroft) *led 2f: prom tl rdn along 4f out and sn wknd* **66/1**

0- **9** *7* **Stella Marris**[241] 5487 4-9-9 0 PhillipMakin 8 33
(Christopher Wilson) *plld hrd: racd wd: cl up: chsd ldr and rdn along 3f out: drvn over 2f out: sn wknd* **66/1**

1m 56.02s (3.02) **Going Correction** +0.20s/f (Good)
WFA 3 from 4yo+ 15lb **9** Ran SP% **116.3**
Speed ratings (Par 103): **94,93,93,92,89 88,80,79,73**
toteswingers:1&2:£1.02, 1&3:£1.10, 2&3:£1.10 CSF £4.83 TOTE £2.50: £1.60, £1.02, £2.00; EX 5.50.
Owner Eledy Srl **Bred** John Dwan And Tony Lewis **Trained** Newmarket, Suffolk
■ Stewards' Enquiry : Ashley Hamblett eight-day ban: used whip with excessive frequency down shoulder in the forehand without giving colt time to respond (May 9-16)

FOCUS
No more than a fair maiden, the second and third both fairly exposed types. The winner didn't need to improve on his 2yo debut. The gallop was just a modest one and the race did not begin in earnest until the final 4f.

1560 JOHN SMITH'S REDCAR STRAIGHT-MILE CHAMPIONSHIP H'CAP (QUALIFIER) 1m
4:55 (4:55) (Class 4) (0-85,80) 4-Y-O+ **£2,590** (£770; £385; £192) **Stalls** High

Form RPR

326- **1** **Aquarian Spirit**[212] 6366 4-9-3 **76** PaulHanagan 1 84
(Richard Fahey) *led: rdn along and hdd 2f out: drvn to ld again over 1f out: kpt on gamely u.p towards fin* **7/2**[2]

0-42 **2** *1/2* **Just Bond (IRE)**[35] 932 9-9-7 **80** PaulMulrennan 3 87
(Geoffrey Oldroyd) *hld up towards rr: smooth hdwy on outer 2f out: chal over 1f out: shkn up and ev ch ins fnl f: no ex towards fin* **13/2**

20-4 **3** *1 1/2* **Imperial Djay (IRE)**[22] 1109 6-9-4 **77** FrannyNorton 4 81
(Ruth Carr) *t.k.h: chsd ldrs: rdn wl over 1f out: drvn and kpt on ins fnl f* **9/2**

005- **4** *nse* **Kensei (IRE)**[196] 6807 4-8-13 **72** DanielTudhope 6 75
(David O'Meara) *trckd wnr: hdwy to ld 2f out: sn rdn and hdd over 1f out: kpt on same pce* **9/4**[1]

0341 **5** *4* **The Which Doctor**[14] 1278 6-9-4 **80** (e) RobertLButler(3) 5 74
(Richard Guest) *dwlt and in rr: effrt over 2f out: sn rdn and n.d* **14/1**

30-1 **6** *1/2* **George Benjamin**[16] 1245 4-9-7 **80** AdrianNicholls 7 73
(David Nicholls) *trckd ldrs: rdn over 2f out: drvn and wknd over 1f out* **4/1**[3]

1m 38.56s (0.56) **Going Correction** +0.20s/f (Good) **6** Ran SP% **111.2**
Speed ratings (Par 105): **105,104,103,102,98 98**
toteswingers:1&2:£7.60, 1&3:£4.30, 2&3:£2.20 CSF £24.94 TOTE £5.40: £2.30, £3.00; EX 27.60.
Owner P S Cresswell & Mrs P A Morrison **Bred** Whitwell Bloodstock **Trained** Musley Bank, N Yorks

FOCUS
The best quality race on the card. The winner was able to dictate what was no more than a modest gallop until past halfway. The front three are rated close to their marks.

1561 FOLLOW REDCARRACING ON FACEBOOK & TWITTER H'CAP 5f
5:30 (5:30) (Class 6) (0-60,60) 3-Y-O **£1,619** (£481; £240; £120) **Stalls** High

Form RPR

000- **1** **Melodize**[187] 7017 3-8-13 **52** DanielTudhope 7 62
(David O'Meara) *a.p: effrt 2f out: rdn to ld 1 1/2f out: kpt on strly ins fnl f* **7/1**[3]

30-1 **2** *1 1/4* **Irish Boy (IRE)**[12] 1306 3-9-2 **55** DuranFentiman 6 60
(Noel Wilson) *hld up: hdwy on outer 2f out: rdn to chse wnr ent fnl f: drvn and no imp towards fin* **11/4**[1]

5422 **3** *2 3/4* **Tancred Spirit**[12] 1306 3-8-8 **47** (p) PaulHanagan 4 42
(Paul Midgley) *led: rdn along over 2f out: hdd 1 1/2f out: sn drvn and one pce* **11/4**[1]

2524 **4** *hd* **Spontaneity (IRE)**[12] 1306 3-9-4 **57** TomEaves 1 51
(Bryan Smart) *dwlt: sn trcking ldrs: hdwy on outer wl over 1f out: rdn and edgd rt ent fnl f: sn one pce* **8/1**

066 **5** *2* **Fawara**[10] 1369 3-8-4 **46** oh1 JamesSullivan(3) 2 33
(Ruth Carr) *cl up: rdn along 2f out: drvn and wknd over 1f out* **66/1**

350- **6** *3 1/4* **Novalist**[224] 6035 3-9-7 **60** LeeNewman 5 35
(Robin Bastiman) *cl up: rdn along 1/2-way: sn wknd* **28/1**

0-43 **7** *3 1/2* **Majestic Millie (IRE)**[12] 1306 3-8-5 **47** NataliaGemelova(3) 8 10
(David O'Meara) *t.k.h: prom on outer: rdn along 2f out: sn wknd* **7/1**[3]

526- **8** *3/4* **Wild Hysteria (IRE)**[178] 7211 3-9-5 **58** MickyFenton 3 18
(Tom Tate) *dwlt: in tch: rdn along over 2f out: sn wknd* **9/2**[2]

60.66 secs (2.06) **Going Correction** +0.20s/f (Good) **8** Ran SP% **112.6**
Speed ratings (Par 96): **91,89,84,84,81 75,70,69**
toteswingers:1&2:£4.40, 1&3:£5.90, 2&3:£3.10; Tote Super 7: Win: Not won. Place: £32.20 CSF £25.75 CT £65.20 TOTE £10.20: £3.60, £1.10, £1.50; EX 36.40.
Owner Mrs Lynne Lumley **Bred** Foursome Thoroughbreds **Trained** Nawton, N Yorks

FOCUS
A modest handicap but some positives about the front pair.
Wild Hysteria(IRE) Official explanation: jockey said gelding reared as stalls opened

The Form Book, Raceform Ltd, Compton, RG20 6NL

T/Plt: £51.30 to a £1 stake. Pool:£44,058.51 - 625.76 winning tickets T/Qpdt: £8.50 to a £1 stake. Pool:£2,559.51 - 221.60 winning tickets JR

WARWICK (L-H)
Monday, April 25

OFFICIAL GOING: Good to firm (firm in places)
Wind: Virtually nil Weather: Sunny

1562 BETFAIR'S IPHONE AND ANDROID APP H'CAP — 6f
2:25 (2:27) (Class 5) (0-75,74) 4-Y-0+ **£4,533** (£1,348; £674; £336) **Stalls** Low

Form RPR
6235 **1** **Silver Wind**[2] 1523 6-9-0 **67**..........(b) SebSanders 8 76
(Alan McCabe) *sn drvn to chse ldrs: led over 1f out: edgd lft u.p nr fin: rdn out* **11/1**
3120 **2** *½* **Ebraam (USA)**[9] 1395 8-9-4 **71**.......... LukeMorris 5 78
(Ronald Harris) *in rr: hdwy over 2f out: styd on u.p over 1f out: chsd wnr ins fnl f but a hld* **4/1**[1]
-542 **3** *1 ½* **Stevie Gee (IRE)**[14] 1267 7-9-6 **73**..........(b) RichardKingscote 6 76
(Ian Williams) *in tch: hdwy fr 2f out: styd on to take 3rd ins fnl f but no imp on ldng duo* **11/2**[2]
2310 **4** *hd* **Desert Strike**[9] 1395 5-8-12 **72**..........(p) NoraLooby(7) 10 74
(Alan McCabe) *s.i.s: in rr: nt clr run ins fnl 2f: edgd rt and hdwy appr fnl f: kpt on wl cl home* **22/1**
-025 **5** *1* **Secret Queen**[16] 1232 4-9-1 **68**.......... JimmyFortune 9 67
(Martin Hill) *slowly away: in rr: rdn over 2f out: hdwy ins fnl f: fin wl* **12/1**
3-00 **6** *1 ¼* **Comptonspirit**[7] 1444 7-9-7 **74**.......... J-PGuillambert 7 69
(Brian Baugh) *in rr: hdwy 2f out: styd on ins fnl f but nvr gng pce to trble ldrs* **28/1**
410- **7** *shd* **Aleqa**[219] 6197 4-9-6 **73**.......... TedDurcan 11 67
(Chris Wall) *in rr: pushed along 1/2-way: hdwy appr fnl f: kpt on but nvr a threat* **10/1**
3120 **8** *½* **Primo De Vida (IRE)**[65] 612 4-8-9 **69**..........(p) NathanAlison(7) 1 62
(Jim Boyle) *led tl hdd over 2f out: wknd ins fnl f* **7/1**[3]
6000 **9** *1* **Elhamri**[9] 1395 7-9-0 **70**.......... MartinHarley(3) 12 60
(Conor Dore) *plunged s: sn chsng ldrs: rdn 3f out: wknd ins fnl f* **16/1**
060- **10** *½* **Yurituni**[158] 7494 4-9-5 **72**..........(v[1]) CathyGannon 13 60
(Eve Johnson Houghton) *pressed ldr: led over 2f out: hdd over 1f out and sn btn* **16/1**
260- **11** *nk* **Make My Dream**[163] 7442 8-9-2 **69**.......... ChrisCatlin 14 56
(John Gallagher) *chsd ldrs: rdn 3f out: wknd over 1f out* **22/1**
201- **12** *1* **Sermons Mount (USA)**[228] 5875 5-9-0 **67**.......... TravisBlock 2 51
(Mouse Hamilton-Fairley) *chsd ldrs: rdn over 2f out: wknd over 1f out* **10/1**
/0-5 **13** *5* **Come On Safari (IRE)**[27] 1026 4-9-5 **72**.......... TadhgO'Shea 4 40
(Joseph Tuite) *early spd: sn bhd* **20/1**
6432 **14** *30* **Co Dependent (USA)**[12] 1314 5-9-3 **70**.......... FergusSweeney 3 —
(Jamie Osborne) *s.i.s: t.k.h: wknd 1/2-way: virtually p.u nr fin* **11/1**

1m 11.56s (-0.24) **Going Correction** +0.05s/f (Good) course record **14** Ran SP% **119.1**
Speed ratings (Par 103): **103,102,100,100,98 97,96,96,94,94 93,92,85,45**
toteswingers: 1&2 £4.60, 2&3 £2.90, 1&3 £10.20 CSF £51.05 CT £276.13 TOTE £13.20: £3.60, £1.40, £2.70; EX 68.40.
Owner Derek Buckley **Bred** W H R John And Partners **Trained** Averham Park, Notts

FOCUS
An ordinary sprint handicap which was strong run. The winner was seemingly back to last season's form.
Secret Queen Official explanation: jockey said filly fly-leapt leaving gates
Elhamri Official explanation: vet said gelding lost a front and hind shoe
Co Dependent(USA) Official explanation: jockey said gelding lost its action

1563 BUDBROOKE (S) STKS — 5f
3:00 (3:01) (Class 6) 2-Y-0 **£2,047** (£604; £302) **Stalls** Low

Form RPR
[illegible] **1** **Van Go Go** [illegible].......... RichardKingscote [illegible]
(Tom Dascombe) *trckd ldrs: led ins fnl 2f: shkn up and hung rt ins fnl f: comf* **4/6**[1]
2 *3 ½* **She's Cool Too (IRE)** 2-8-3 0.......... KierenFox(3) 1 48
(Bill Turner) *led: hdd ins fnl 2f: sn outpcd by wnr ins fnl f but kpt on to readily hold 2nd* **7/1**[3]
3 *½* **Miss Muga** 2-7-13 0.......... CharlesBishop(7) 7 47
(Mick Channon) *green andd towards rr: drvn and green over 2f out: hdwy over 1f out: styd on to take 3rd ins fnl f: kpt on but nt rch ldng duo* **12/1**
4 *12* **I'm Talking (IRE)** 2-8-6 0.......... CathyGannon 2 3
(David Evans) *chsd ldrs: rdn 3f out: wknd 1/2-way: no ch whn hung rt ins fnl f* **9/2**[2]
6 **5** *2* **Early Ambition**[26] 1049 2-8-3 0.......... AndrewHeffernan(3) 3 —
(Andrew Haynes) *pressed ldr: sn hanging rt: wd bnd ins fnl 3f and sn no ch: continued to hang rt ins fnl f* **33/1**
6 *5* **Frankie Valley** 2-8-11 0.......... LiamKeniry 6 —
(J S Moore) *sn outpcd* **11/1**

61.34 secs (1.74) **Going Correction** +0.05s/f (Good) **6** Ran SP% **109.6**
Speed ratings (Par 90): **88,82,81,62,59 51**
toteswingers:1&2 £2.40, 2&3 £13.50, 1&3 £3.70 CSF £5.61 TOTE £1.70: £1.20, £3.00; EX 5.40.The winner was bought in for 7,200gns.
Owner A Black **Bred** A Black **Trained** Malpas, Cheshire

FOCUS
The winner looks an above-average type by juvenile selling standards. The winner had the edge on experience and showed slightly improved form.

NOTEBOOK
Van Go Go came here after landing a Redcar maiden auction. She took this in straightforward fashion and this was a good bit of placing from her connections. (op 5-6 tchd 10-11)
She's Cool Too(IRE), a half-sister to, among others, triple 7f-1m Direct Reaction, was readily held by the winner but showed enough to suggest she can win an ordinary seller. (op 6-1 tchd 11-2)
Miss Muga plugged on for pressure without having the required pace and should be better for the run. (op 11-1 tchd 9-1)
I'm Talking(IRE), the first foal of a 1m winner, showed little but her stable's runners can improve significantly for their first run.

1564 NORTON LINDSEY CONDITIONS STKS — 7f 26y
3:35 (3:36) (Class 3) 4-Y-0+ **£6,670** (£1,984; £991; £495) **Stalls** Low

Form RPR
21-0 **1** **Fathsta (IRE)**[9] 1397 6-8-8 **102**.......... StevieDonohoe 5 83
(David Simcock) *in rr: hdwy 2f out: str run u.p ins fnl f: led last strides* **7/4**[1]
050- **2** *nk* **No Hubris (USA)**[170] 7348 4-9-4 **90**.......... JamieSpencer 1 92
(Paul Cole) *sn led: hrd pressed and u.str.p over 1f out: kpt slt advantage tl ct last strides* **13/2**
164- **3** *½* **Sir Bruno (FR)**[165] 7411 4-8-8 **73**..........(p) DavidProbert 2 81
(Bryn Palling) *chsd ldrs: drvn and str chal fr over 1f out: stl upsides tl outpcd fnl 30yds* **33/1**
0-00 **4** *¾* **Jack My Boy (IRE)**[23] 1093 4-8-8 **92**..........(b) CathyGannon 3 79
(David Evans) *chsd ldr: drvn to chal over 1f out and stl upsides ins fnl f: wknd fnl 50yds* **6/1**[3]
1/0- **5** *nse* **Beauchamp Yorker**[263] 4750 4-8-8 **90**.......... DaneO'Neill 4 79
(Henry Candy) *in tch: pushed along and outpcd over 2f out: styd on again appr fnl f: kpt on nr fin but nvr gng pce to rch ldrs* **15/8**[2]
10-0 **6** *6* **Mujood**[9] 1406 8-8-8 **87**..........(v) FergusSweeney 6 63
(Eve Johnson Houghton) *sn pushed along in rr: wknd over 2f out* **14/1**

1m 22.35s (-2.25) **Going Correction** -0.125s/f (Firm) **6** Ran SP% **108.4**
Speed ratings (Par 107): **107,106,106,105,105 98**
toteswingers: 1&2 £2.70, 2&3 £39.10, 1&3 £8.80 CSF £12.44 TOTE £1.90: £1.10, £5.00; EX 10.80.
Owner Dr Marwan Koukash **Bred** Brian Miller **Trained** Newmarket, Suffolk

FOCUS
Typically muddling conditions race form. The time was much quicker than the following maiden, but runner-up and third-placed finisher hold the form down. The winner was well off his best.

NOTEBOOK
Fathsta(IRE) had produced his career-best performance over 6f on soft ground on his final outing last year, and he'd made little impression under similar conditions to this in a Leicester Listed race on his reappearance. It's hard to know how much he had to step up on that performance, if at all. He challenged closest to the stands' rail, but it's difficult to know whether that made any difference. (op 6-4)
No Hubris(USA) would have been 22lb better off with the winner in a handicap. He had won first-time out both previous seasons he's raced, so an absence of 170 days was not a concern. (op 15-2)
Sir Bruno(FR), who had been off for 165 days, looked exposed as just fair, his highest turf RPR being just 77 coming into this, but he ran well. (op 25-1)
Jack My Boy(IRE) performed well short of his official mark of 92. (op 7-1)
Beauchamp Yorker had been off for 263 days and challenged further away from the stands' rail. He might be able to do better. (op 2-1 tchd 9-4)

1565 HAPPY 70TH BIRTHDAY GEOFF JOYCE MAIDEN STKS — 7f 26y
4:10 (4:15) (Class 5) 3-Y-0 **£2,590** (£770; £385; £192) **Stalls** Low

Form RPR
33-6 **1** **Sylvestris (IRE)**[16] 1234 3-8-12 **78**.......... JimCrowley 12 75
(Ralph Beckett) *led 1f: styd trcking ldr: drvn to ld again over 1f out: hung lft u.p: styd on wl cl home* **3/1**[1]
3 **2** *1 ¾* **Dark Isle**[16] 1236 3-9-3 0.......... SebSanders 1 75
(J W Hills) *w ldr: led after 1f: styd pressed by wnr: rdn over 2f out: hdd over 1f out: kpt on ins fnl f: one pce nr fin* **9/1**
625- **3** *nk* **Qenaa**[199] 6704 3-8-12 **85**.......... TadhgO'Shea 5 69
(Mark Johnston) *chsd ldrs: rdn over 2f out: styd on same pce ins fnl f* **11/2**[3]
0- **4** *2* **Uppercut**[241] 5465 3-9-3 0.......... FergusSweeney 10 69
(Stuart Kittow) *in rr: pushed along and hdwy over 2f out: styd on ins fnl f: nt rch ldrs* **100/1**
05- **5** *hd* **Promenadia**[187] 7010 3-8-12 0.......... SteveDrowne 11 63+
(Roger Charlton) *in tch: pushed along: green and outpcd over 2f out: styd on again ins fnl f* **8/1**
6 *½* **Stage Attraction (IRE)** 3-9-3 0.......... JimmyFortune 7 67+
(Andrew Balding) *s.i.s: in rr: stl bhd 2f out: hdwy appr fnl f: fin wl* **16/1**
6- **7** *1 ¾* **Logans Legend (IRE)**[149] 7595 3-9-3 0.......... MichaelHills 13 62+
(B W Hills) *chsd ldrs: pushed along and outpcd 2f out: styd on again ins fnl f* **4/1**[2]
00- **8** *1 ¼* **Ride The Wind**[185] 7058 3-8-12 0.......... TedDurcan 8 54
(Chris Wall) *towards rr: hdwy over 1f out: kpt on ins fnl f* **33/1**
9 *1 ¾* **Aaranyow (IRE)** 3-9-3 0.......... DavidProbert 2 54
(Bryn Palling) *in tch: chsd ldrs and rdn over 2f out: wknd ins fnl f* **50/1**
4 **10** *1 ½* **Casternova**[13] 1284 3-8-12 0.......... TravisBlock 6 45
(Hughie Morrison) *t.k.h: chsd ldrs to 2f out: wknd over 1f out* **25/1**
65-4 **11** *10* **Flodden (USA)**[11] 1328 3-9-3 **68**.......... JamieSpencer 4 23
(Paul Cole) *t.k.h: stdd s: a in rr* **13/2**
0- **12** *2 ½* **High Table (IRE)**[213] 6334 3-9-3 0..........(t) RichardKingscote 9 16
(Tom Dascombe) *sn bhd* **50/1**

1m 24.03s (-0.57) **Going Correction** -0.125s/f (Firm) **12** Ran SP% **112.4**
Speed ratings (Par 98): **98,96,95,93,93 92,90,89,87,85 74,71**
toteswingers:1&2 £1.40, 2&3 £19.70, 1&3 £2.10 CSF £27.82 TOTE £3.00: £1.20, £3.20, £2.90; EX 30.80.
Owner Mr and Mrs David Aykroyd **Bred** Patrick Cassidy **Trained** Kimpton, Hants

FOCUS
This looked no more than a fair maiden. It's doubtful if the form pair, the winner and third, ran to their best.
Flodden(USA) Official explanation: jockey said gelding reared as stalls opened

1566 HATTON H'CAP — 1m 22y
4:45 (4:46) (Class 6) (0-60,60) 3-Y-0 **£2,047** (£604; £302) **Stalls** Low

Form RPR
0-01 **1** **Beach Babe**[26] 1053 3-9-5 **58**.......... NickyMackay 3 66
(Jonathan Portman) *in tch: rdn 3f out: hdwy u.p over 1f out: chsd ldr ins fnl f: rdn to ld last strides* **11/1**
5-14 **2** *nk* **Avalon Bay**[20] 1149 3-9-7 **60**.......... DaneO'Neill 2 67
(Pat Eddery) *sn led: rdn 2f out: styd on wl ins fnl f: hdd last strides* **4/1**[3]
03-3 **3** *3 ½* **Miss Firefox**[84] 368 3-9-4 **57**.......... TedDurcan 12 59+
(Nicky Vaughan) *in tch tl dropped in rr over 3f out: hmpd and nt clr run over 2f out: drvn and hdwy over 1f out: styd on to take 3rd wl ins fnl f* **11/1**
30-0 **4** *1 ¾* **Alexs Rainbow (USA)**[54] 729 3-9-7 **60**.......... ChrisCatlin 4 55
(John Gallagher) *chsd ldrs: wnt 2nd over 2f out: sn rdn and no imp on ldr: wknd ins fnl f* **22/1**
000- **5** *nk* **Bumbling Bertie**[193] 6859 3-8-12 **51**.......... JimmyFortune 7 45
(Andrew Balding) *chsd ldrs: rdn over 2f out: wknd wl over 1f out* **7/2**[2]
503- **6** *¾* **Fire Crystal**[180] 7177 3-8-12 **54**.......... MartinHarley(3) 10 47
(Mick Channon) *chsd ldrs: rdn 3f out: wknd ins fnl 2f* **14/1**
3050 **7** *2 ¾* **Imperial Fong**[37] 909 3-8-13 **52**..........(p) LukeMorris 13 38
(Ronald Harris) *s.i.s: in rr: rdn and hdwy over 2f out: styd on but nt rch ldrs* **14/1**
-553 **8** *½* **Poetically**[10] 1369 3-8-13 **52**.......... EddieCreighton 15 37
(Joseph Tuite) *rdn along 1/2-way: nvr beyond mid-div* **33/1**
-000 **9** *½* **Heart Felt**[28] 1018 3-8-5 **47**..........(v[1]) AndrewHeffernan(3) 11 31
(Roy Brotherton) *chsd ldrs: hung rt and wd bnd 3f out: no ch after* **25/1**

000- **10** *1* **Waterford Star (IRE)**[160] 7470 3-9-4 **57** .... JoeFanning 1 39
(Mark Johnston) *rdn fr stalls: nt respond and sn wl bhd: continued u.p tl styd on fnl 2f but nvr any ch* **11/4**[1]

0005 **11** *½* **Bellabooiou**[59] 684 3-8-9 **48** ....(bt[1]) FergusSweeney 6 28
(David Pinder) *in rr: sme hdwy on ins 3f out: wknd 2f out* **66/1**

-635 **12** *3 ¼* **Luckbealadytonight (IRE)**[60] 668 3-8-12 **51** .... RoystonFfrench 9 24
(Mark Johnston) *chsd ldrs: rdn over 3f out: wknd sn after* **16/1**

-333 **13** *1 ¼* **Sleeping Brave**[10] 1354 3-9-2 **55** ....(b) StephenCraine 8 25
(Jim Boyle) *slowly away: rcvrd into mid-div over 3f out: sn rdn and wknd* **11/1**

000- **14** *1 ½* **Snapshott (IRE)**[236] 5667 3-8-7 **46** oh1 .... DavidProbert 14 13
(Ronald Harris) *bhd most of way* **50/1**

1m 40.65s (-0.35) **Going Correction** -0.125s/f (Firm) **14** Ran SP% **127.7**
Speed ratings (Par 96): **96,95,92,90,90 89,86,86,85,84 84,80,79,78**
CSF £55.74 CT £535.86 TOTE £9.70: £2.80, £2.70, £3.80; EX 41.20.
Owner Mrs R F Knipe **Bred** R F And S D Knipe **Trained** Compton, Berks

FOCUS
A modest handicap in which two runners pulled clear. Improvement from the first two, but unconvincing form.
Sleeping Brave Official explanation: jockey said gelding was slowly away

1567 WHITNASH H'CAP — 1m 2f 188y
5:20 (5:20) (Class 6) (0-60,60) 4-Y-O+ — **£2,047** (£604; £302) **Stalls** Low

Form — RPR

200- **1** **Laverre (IRE)**[219] 6212 4-9-7 **60** .... DaneO'Neill 11 68
(Lucy Wadham) *chsd ldrs: drvn to ld jst ins fnl f: sn strly chal but a doing enough* **11/4**[1]

6050 **2** *½* **Dilys Maud**[16] 1233 4-8-12 **51** ....(b) RobertHavlin 3 58
(Roger Ingram) *hld up in rr: gd hdwy and swtchd rt wl over 1f out: drvn to press wnr ins fnl f: styd on but a jst hld* **8/1**

-600 **3** *3 ¾* **Warrior Nation (FR)**[54] 733 5-8-7 **46** oh1 .... DavidProbert 10 46
(Adrian Chamberlain) *t.k.h: chsd ldrs: wnt 2nd 2f out: led over 1f out: hdd jst ins fnl f: styd on same pce* **16/1**

5-00 **4** *1* **Zagarock**[40] 862 4-8-7 **46** .... NeilChalmers 12 44
(Bryn Palling) *in rr: hdwy and rdn over 2f out: styd on same pce fr over 1f out* **9/1**

-300 **5** *hd* **Market Puzzle (IRE)**[10] 1374 4-8-9 **48** ....(b) TedDurcan 1 46
(Mark Brisbourne) *chsd ldrs: drvn to chal over 1f out: wknd ins fnl f* **9/2**[2]

5001 **6** *hd* **Gems**[21] 1135 4-8-8 **54** .... LucyKBarry[(7)] 7 51
(Peter Hiatt) *chsd ldrs: rdn and nt clr run over 1f out: swtchd lft and one pce* **11/2**[3]

0-00 **7** *7* **Mistress Shy**[19] 1173 4-8-7 **46** oh1 .... RoystonFfrench 4 30
(Robin Dickin) *sn led: rdn 3f out: hdd over 1f out and sn wknd* **40/1**

0-54 **8** *1 ¾* **Animator**[33] 944 6-9-1 **54** .... LukeMorris 15 35
(Martin Hill) *t.k.h in rr: pushed along and no prog fr over 2f out* **11/2**[3]

60-6 **9** *2* **Just Zak**[81] 399 6-8-11 **50** .... LiamKeniry 9 27
(Owen Brennan) *s.i.s: t.k.h: nvr beyond mid-div: wknd fr 3f out* **16/1**

0-00 **10** *3* **Scintillating (IRE)**[6] 1468 4-8-4 **46** oh1 ....(p) KierenFox[(3)] 5 17
(Ray Peacock) *t.k.h: chsd ldrs tl wknd qckly 2f out* **33/1**

666 **11** *nk* **Carrside Lady**[9] 1399 5-8-7 **46** oh1 ....(b[1]) FrankieMcDonald 2 17
(Owen Brennan) *t.k.h: chsd ldrs tl wknd fr 3f out* **33/1**

0456 **F** **Hill Of Clare (IRE)**[52] 769 9-8-5 **47** oh1 ow1 .... SophieDoyle[(3)] 8 —
(George Jones) *s.i.s: in rr: drvn: hdwy and in tch 1/2-way: wkng whn crossed: clipped heels and fell wl over 1f out* **40/1**

2m 19.27s (-1.83) **Going Correction** -0.125s/f (Firm) **12** Ran SP% **119.3**
Speed ratings (Par 101): **101,100,97,97,97 96,91,90,89,86 86,—**
toteswingers: 1&2 £7.20, 2&3 £19.00, 1&3 £22.80 CSF £24.85 CT £299.25 TOTE £4.10: £1.50, £2.50, £7.40; EX 28.20.
Owner Mr And Mrs A E Pakenham **Bred** Kilnamoragh Stud **Trained** Newmarket, Suffolk
■ Stewards' Enquiry : Robert Havlin six-day ban: careless riding (May 9 -14)

FOCUS
A moderate contest, and a bit muddling with the field closely bunched turning in. The third helps limit the standard.
T/Jkpt: Not won. T/Plt: £28.20 to a £1 stake. Pool of £45,685.64 - 1,180.89 winning tickets.
T/Qpdt: £14.60 to a £1 stake. Pool of £2,012.46 - 101.70 winning tickets. ST

YARMOUTH (L-H)
Monday, April 25

OFFICIAL GOING: Good to firm
Wind: Fresh behind Weather: Fine

1568 BET ON TOTEPLACEPOT AT TOTESPORT.COM MAIDEN STKS — 1m 3y
2:30 (2:33) (Class 5) 3-Y-O+ — **£2,460** (£732; £365; £182) **Stalls** High

Form — RPR

1 **Aomen (IRE)** 3-8-12 0 .... PatCosgrave 3 86
(James Fanshawe) *hld up in tch: led wl over 1f out: drvn out* **11/1**

2 *1* **Chat Room** 3-8-12 0 .... AhmedAjtebi 9 84
(Mahmood Al Zarooni) *chsd ldrs: outpcd over 2f out: hdwy over 1f out: sn chsng wnr: edgd lft ins fnl f: r.o* **4/1**[2]

3 *4* **El Wasmi** 3-8-12 0 .... PhilipRobinson 2 74
(Clive Brittain) *s.i.s: sn chsng ldrs: rdn and ev ch wl over 1f out: no ex ins fnl f* **6/1**

4 *hd* **Polperro (USA)** 3-8-12 0 ....[1] WilliamBuick 7 74+
(John Gosden) *hld up: rdn over 3f out: hdwy over 1f out: nt rch ldrs* **9/1**

2- **5** *½* **Amhran (IRE)**[264] 4695 3-8-12 0 .... MartinDwyer 11 73
(Brian Meehan) *led: rdn and hdd wl over 1f out: styd on same pce ins fnl f* **11/2**[3]

00- **6** *2 ¼* **Ferruccio (IRE)**[207] 6514 3-8-12 0 .... JackMitchell 8 67+
(James Fanshawe) *hld up: rdn over 2f out: hdwy over 1f out: nvr nrr* **80/1**

0- **7** *½* **Regal Salute**[177] 7231 3-8-8 0 ow1 .... DarryllHolland 4 62
(Jeremy Noseda) *chsd ldrs: rdn over 2f out: wknd over 1f out* **3/1**[1]

2 **8** *2 ½* **Deerslayer (USA)**[13] 1284 5-9-12 0 .... PaulDoe 16 64
(Jim Best) *chsd ldr: rdn over 2f out: wknd over 1f out* **16/1**

0 **9** *½* **Azurinta (IRE)**[18] 1203 3-8-0 0 .... IanBurns[(7)] 13 54
(Michael Bell) *prom: rdn and hung lft over 2f out: wknd over 1f out* **66/1**

4-0 **10** *¾* **Apparel (IRE)**[14] 1270 3-8-7 0 .... EddieAhern 15 52
(Ed Dunlop) *hld up: pushed along over 3f out: n.d* **16/1**

11 *1* **Labroc (IRE)** 3-8-12 0 .... LiamJones 14 55
(William Haggas) *hld up: rdn 1/2-way: a in rr* **66/1**

6 **12** *1* **Hamilton Hill**[61] 649 4-9-12 0 .... MarcHalford 10 56?
(Terry Clement) *dwlt: a in rr* **250/1**

6 **13** *1 ¼* **Native Colony**[14] 1271 3-8-12 0 .... NeilCallan 12 49
(Roger Varian) *s.i.s: hld up: rdn over 2f out: a in rr* **10/1**

0- **14** *nk* **Zaheeb**[200] 6689 3-8-12 0 .... AdrianMcCarthy 6 49
(Dave Morris) *hld up: a in rr* **200/1**

15 *8* **She Wolf** 3-8-7 0 .... HayleyTurner 1 24
(Michael Bell) *mid-div and rn green: lost pl over 5f out: bhd fr 1/2-way* **16/1**

16 *nk* **Phoenix City (USA)** 3-8-7 0 .... RichardMullen 5 24
(Michael Bell) *hld up: rdn and wknd over 3f out* **66/1**

1m 39.58s (-1.02) **Going Correction** -0.25s/f (Firm)
WFA 3 from 4yo+ 14lb **16** Ran SP% **126.3**
Speed ratings (Par 103): **95,94,90,89,89 87,86,84,83,82 81,80,79,79,71 70**
toteswingers:1&2:£13.40, 1&3:£19.60, 2&3:£4.50 CSF £56.96 TOTE £12.80: £4.40, £1.80, £2.70; EX 74.10 Trifecta £262.00 Part won. Pool £354.06 - 0.81 winning units..
Owner Dragon Gate **Bred** Allevamento Pian Di Neve Srl **Trained** Newmarket, Suffolk
■ Stewards' Enquiry : William Buick caution: used whip down shoulder in the forehand.

FOCUS
Lots of powerful connections represented here and some nicely bred sorts on show, so a good chance this race will throw up plenty of future winners. The front pair are potentially a bit above average.
Amhran(IRE) Official explanation: trainer said colt was unsuited by the good to firm ground

1569 FREE RACING POST FORM AT TOTESPORT.COM H'CAP — 1m 3y
3:05 (3:06) (Class 5) (0-75,75) 4-Y-O+ — **£2,331** (£693; £346; £173) **Stalls** High

Form — RPR

1302 **1** **Tewin Wood**[13] 1296 4-9-5 **73** .... LiamJones 6 81
(Alan Bailey) *led: hdd briefly ins fnl f: rdn out* **5/1**[3]

530- **2** *hd* **Mashatu**[189] 6984 4-9-0 **68** .... PatCosgrave 7 76
(James Fanshawe) *a.p: chsd wnr over 3f out: rdn over 1f out: led briefly ins fnl f: unable qck towards fin* **7/2**[1]

1214 **3** *¾* **But Beautiful (IRE)**[38] 889 4-9-0 **68** .... FrankieDettori 4 74
(Robert Mills) *chsd wnr over 4f: remained handy: rdn over 2f out: styd on same pce ins fnl f* **7/2**[1]

422- **4** *3* **Strike A Deal (IRE)**[203] 6622 4-8-10 **64** .... NeilCallan 5 63
(Chris Wall) *chsd ldrs: rdn over 1f out: no ex fnl f* **9/2**[2]

331- **5** *3 ¼* **Oh So Saucy**[209] 6444 7-9-7 **75** .... GeorgeBaker 3 66
(Chris Wall) *hld up: rdn over 2f out: nvr trbld ldrs* **9/2**[2]

3033 **6** *¾* **Petomic (IRE)**[9] 1398 6-8-9 **63** .... HayleyTurner 2 53
(Richard Guest) *dwlt: hld up: rdn and edgd lft over 2f out: n.d* **7/1**

440- **7** *7* **Rio Tinto**[276] 4341 4-9-4 **72** .... WilliamCarson 1 46
(Giles Bravery) *hld up: rdn over 3f out: sn lost tch* **20/1**

1m 37.97s (-2.63) **Going Correction** -0.25s/f (Firm) **7** Ran SP% **114.7**
Speed ratings (Par 103): **103,102,102,99,95 95,88**
toteswingers:1&2:£4.40, 1&3:£4.20, 2&3:£2.70 CSF £22.94 TOTE £5.90: £3.50, £2.20; EX 31.00.
Owner Denco Thermal Limited **Bred** Perle D'Or Partnership **Trained** Newmarket, Suffolk

FOCUS
An ordinary handicap. The winner carried over his recent polytrack improvement.

1570 BET ON TODAY'S FOOTBALL AT TOTESPORT.COM H'CAP — 7f 3y
3:40 (3:40) (Class 6) (0-65,64) 4-Y-O+ — **£1,683** (£501; £250; £125) **Stalls** High

Form — RPR

010- **1** **Batgirl**[189] 6992 4-9-7 **64** .... FrankieDettori 3 73+
(John Berry) *hld up in tch: racd keenly: rdn to ld wl ins fnl f: r.o* **4/1**[2]

040- **2** *1 ¼* **Oh So Spicy**[224] 6023 4-9-2 **59** .... GeorgeBaker 1 65
(Chris Wall) *trckd ldr: plld hrd: rdn and ev ch ins fnl f: unable qck towards fin* **13/2**

000- **3** *hd* **Bennelong**[182] 7128 5-9-3 **60** ....(b[1]) PaulDoe 4 65
(Jim Best) *dwlt: sn rcvrd to ld: rdn 2f out: hdd and unable qck wl ins fnl f* **7/1**

314- **4** *2 ¼* **Watch Chain (IRE)**[146] 7646 4-9-4 **61** .... NeilCallan 2 60
(Mark H Tompkins) *trckd ldrs: plld hrd: rdn over 1f out: styd on same pce ins fnl f* **6/1**

6250 **5** *shd* **Clearing House**[5] 1486 6-9-3 **60** .... KirstyMilczarek 5 59
(John Ryan) *hld up: hdwy u.p over 1f out: styd on same pce ins fnl f* **11/2**[3]

6642 **6** *1 ¾* **Crocodile Bay (IRE)**[14] 1276 8-8-9 **52** ....(e) KierenFallon 7 46
(Richard Guest) *hld up: rdn over 2f out: no imp fnl f* **3/1**[1]

0305 **7** *hd* **Norcroft**[5] 1498 9-8-0 **50** oh5 ....(p) DanielHarris[(7)] 6 43
(Christine Dunnett) *sn prom: rdn over 3f out: no ex fnl f* **22/1**

/60- **8** *8* **Jamarjo (IRE)**[343] 2189 4-8-11 **54** .... DarryllHolland 8 26
(Steve Gollings) *chsd ldrs: rdn whn n.m.r over 2f out: wknd over 1f out: eased ins fnl f* **16/1**

0610 **9** *9* **Vertumnus**[37] 912 4-8-1 **51** ....(b) RichardOld[(7)] 9 —
(Nick Littmoden) *hld up: bhd fnl 3f* **25/1**

1m 25.3s (-1.30) **Going Correction** -0.25s/f (Firm) **9** Ran SP% **114.6**
Speed ratings (Par 101): **97,95,95,92,92 90,90,81,71**
toteswingers:1&2:£4.30, 1&3:£6.70, 2&3:£9.40 CSF £29.92 CT £175.49 TOTE £4.80: £2.00, £2.40, £2.70; EX 23.40 Trifecta £309.60 Part won. Pool £418.48 - 0.20 winning units..
Owner Tony Fordham **Bred** Mrs M L Parry & P M Steele-Mortimer **Trained** Newmarket, Suffolk
■ Stewards' Enquiry : Paul Doe one-day ban: careless riding (May 9); three-day ban: used whip with excessive frequency without giving gelding time to respond down shoulder in the forehand (May 10-12)

FOCUS
A low-grade handicap but won in good style by the progressive Batgirl. the level is determined by the disappointing third.
Jamarjo(IRE) Official explanation: jockey said gelding lost its action

1571 ENTER THE FLAT TOTETENTOFOLLOW H'CAP — 7f 3y
4:15 (4:15) (Class 4) (0-85,83) 3-Y-O — **£4,144** (£1,233; £616; £307) **Stalls** High

Form — RPR

156- **1** **Biaraafa (IRE)**[191] 6920 3-8-9 **71** .... HayleyTurner 7 80
(Michael Bell) *racd towards stands' side: chsd ldr: edgd lft fr over 3f out: rdn to ld wl ins fnl f* **20/1**

431- **2** *¾* **Majestic Dream (IRE)**[184] 7085 3-9-4 **80** .... AdamKirby 4 87
(Walter Swinburn) *racd centre: chsd ldrs: led over 1f out: sn rdn: hdd wl ins fnl f* **4/1**[3]

12-2 **3** *2* **Tasfeya**[19] 1175 3-9-4 **80** .... RichardHills 3 81
(Mark Johnston) *led centre: overall ldr 5f out: rdn and hdd over 1f out: styd on same pce ins fnl f* **11/4**[1]

3-1 **4** *hd* **Sand Owl**[25] 1060 3-9-3 **79** .... WilliamBuick 5 80
(Peter Chapple-Hyam) *s.i.s: swtchd to r centre: hdwy over 2f out: rdn over 1f out: styd on* **11/4**[1]

1-60 **5** *3 ¼* **Ninita**[22] 1113 3-8-9 **76** ....(b[1]) AdamBeschizza[(5)] 1 68
(Mark Rimmer) *racd centre: prom: rdn over 2f out: styd on same pce appr fnl f* **33/1**

01-2 **6** *shd* **Double Dealer**[12] 1313 3-9-7 **83**.................................... AhmedAjtebi 2 75
(Mahmood Al Zarooni) *racd centre: chsd ldrs: rdn over 1f out: wknd ins fnl f* **7/2**[2]

151- **7** *11* **Speedfit Girl (IRE)**[217] 6259 3-8-11 **73**........................ PhilipRobinson 6 35
(George Margarson) *racd towards stands' side and overall ldr to over 5f out: remained handy tl wknd 2f out* **12/1**

1m 24.13s (-2.47) **Going Correction** -0.25s/f (Firm) **7** Ran SP% **111.0**
Speed ratings (Par 100): **104,103,100,100,96 96,84**
toteswingers:1&2:£11.60, 1&3:£8.70, 2&3:£1.90 CSF £91.72 TOTE £30.50: £6.60, £2.50; EX 109.00.
Owner R L W Frisby **Bred** Palm Tree Thoroughbreds **Trained** Newmarket, Suffolk

FOCUS
Quite a competive little handicap and the pace appeared sound, so no reason to think the form shouldn't stand up. A clear personal best from the winner.

1572 PLAY BLACKJACK AT TOTESPORT.COM MEDIAN AUCTION MAIDEN STKS 1m 2f 21y

4:50 (4:50) (Class 6) 3-5-Y-O **£1,813** (£539; £269; £134) **Stalls** Low

Form RPR

1 **Diamond Vision (IRE)** 3-8-10 0.. NeilCallan 8 80+
(Robert Mills) *sn led: clr fr over 2f out: rdn over 1f out: styd on wl* **10/1**

460- **2** *3 ½* **Circus Star (USA)**[176] 7248 3-8-10 70.............................. MartinDwyer 3 73
(Brian Meehan) *led early: chsd wnr: rdn over 3f out: hung lft over 1f out: styd on same pce* **4/1**[3]

2330 **3** *6* **Roman Flame**[9] 1400 3-8-2 63.................................... LouisBeuzelin(3) 4 56
(Michael Quinn) *prom: rdn to go 3rd 2f out: styd on same pce* **16/1**

0- **4** *6* **Divinite Green (IRE)**[192] 6883 3-8-10 0.......................... JackMitchell 9 49
(Peter Chapple-Hyam) *sn chsng ldrs: rdn over 3f out: wknd 2f out* **2/1**[1]

0-4 **5** *1* **Young Jackie**[39] 878 3-8-5 0.. HayleyTurner 1 42
(George Margarson) *chsd ldrs: rdn over 3f out: wknd 2f out* **11/1**

0 **6** *nk* **Mina's Boy**[12] 1311 3-8-10 0..(b[1]) EddieAhern 5 46
(Ed Dunlop) *s.i.s: in rr: wl bhd 3f out: styd on ins fnl f* **10/1**

7 *nk* **Speed Dancer** 3-8-10 0.. DarryllHolland 2 46
(James Eustace) *hld up: rdn over 4f out: wknd over 2f out* **16/1**

5 **8** *3 ¼* **Pearl Mountain (IRE)**[19] 1173 4-9-5 0...................... SimonPearce(3) 6 37
(Lydia Pearce) *prom: lost pl over 6f out: wknd over 3f out* **28/1**

9 *1* **Rose Willow (USA)** 3-8-5 0.. SaleemGolam 7 32
(John Gosden) *dwlt: a bhd* **7/2**[2]

2m 7.89s (-2.61) **Going Correction** -0.25s/f (Firm)
WFA 3 from 4yo 17lb **9** Ran SP% **117.3**
Speed ratings (Par 101): **100,97,92,87,86 86,86,83,82**
toteswingers:1&2:£10.80, 1&3:£18.60, 2&3:£10.90 CSF £50.62 TOTE £11.80: £3.20, £1.50, £4.20; EX 70.10 TRIFECTA Not won..
Owner Exors Of The Late T G Mills **Bred** Jerry O'Sullivan **Trained** Headley, Surrey

FOCUS
Hard to know what to make of this form as they finished strung out like 3m chasers, but the winner made a nice start. The race is loosely rated around the third.
Mina's Boy Official explanation: jockey said, regarding running and riding, that his orders were to put the colt into the race and get in travelling but, having been slowly away and outpaced, he was unable to carry out the instructions.

1573 PLAY ROULETTE AT TOTESPORT.COM H'CAP 1m 2f 21y

5:25 (5:25) (Class 5) (0-75,67) 4-Y-0+ **£2,331** (£693; £346) **Stalls** Low

Form RPR

0-66 **1** **Sharakti (IRE)**[11] 1324 4-9-4 **67**.............................. DeclanCannon(3) 3 73
(Alan McCabe) *led at stdy pce tl qcknd clr 6f out: rdn over 1f out: styd on gamely* **5/2**[3]

626- **2** *1 ¼* **Locum**[175] 7270 6-8-13 **59**.. NeilCallan 2 63
(Mark H Tompkins) *hld up in tch: rdn over 1f out: chsd wnr ins fnl f: styd on* **15/8**[2]

3316 **3** *1 ¾* **Nolecce**[20] 1150 4-9-2 **62**.. KierenFallon 1 62
(Richard Guest) *trckd wnr: rdn and hung lft 2f out: nt run on* **5/4**[1]

2m 13.36s (2.86) **Going Correction** -0.25s/f (Firm) **3** Ran SP% **107.8**
Speed ratings (Par 103): **78,77,75**
CSF £6.91 TOTE £3.00; EX 5.30.
Owner Mrs D L Sharp **Bred** John Foley **Trained** Averham Park, Notts

FOCUS
Three hold-up horses in opposition, so it was predicable the early tempo was going to be sedate as nobody wanted to lead. the form is rated negatively.
Nolecce Official explanation: jockey said gelding hung left

1574 PLAY POKER AT TSPOKER.COM H'CAP 1m 3f 101y

5:55 (5:55) (Class 6) (0-65,63) 3-Y-O **£1,683** (£501; £250; £125) **Stalls** Low

Form RPR

04-5 **1** **Fine Style (IRE)**[27] 1027 3-9-1 **57**..............................(v[1]) HayleyTurner 6 66
(Michael Bell) *chsd ldr tl led over 6f out: clr over 5f out: rdn out* **9/2**[2]

-441 **2** *2* **Crossword**[38] 898 3-9-6 **62**..(b) AdamKirby 4 68
(Marco Botti) *a.p: rdn to chse wnr 3f out: styd on u.p* **13/2**

3321 **3** *1 ½* **Polly Holder (IRE)**[10] 1354 3-8-11 **56**..........................(p) AmyBaker(3) 5 59
(Alan Bailey) *hld up: hdwy over 2f out: rdn over 1f out: styd on: nt rch ldrs* **9/1**

6364 **4** *1 ½* **Surprise (IRE)**[21] 1134 3-8-10 **57**.............................. AdamBeschizza(5) 1 57
(Mark Rimmer) *hld up: hdwy over 2f out: sn rdn: styd on* **18/1**

3144 **5** *1 ¼* **Ad Vitam (IRE)**[13] 1299 3-9-0 **63**..............................(t) LeonnaMayor(7) 3 61
(David C Griffiths) *s.s: hld up: hdwy over 2f out: sn rdn: no ex ins fnl f* **25/1**

06-3 **6** *1 ¼* **Sukhothai (USA)**[12] 1312 3-9-2 **58**.............................. TomQueally 2 54
(James Fanshawe) *hld up: hdwy over 3f out: rdn over 2f out: wknd fnl f* **11/2**[3]

40-3 **7** *43* **Jeu De Vivre (IRE)**[11] 1327 3-9-7 **63**.............................. KierenFallon 7 —
(Mark Johnston) *prom: chsd wnr over 3f out: sn rdn and wknd: t.o* **11/10**[1]

5-00 **8** *10* **Elegant Star (IRE)**[13] 1293 3-8-7 **49** oh4.................(p) AdrianMcCarthy 8 —
(Dave Morris) *sn led: hdd over 6f out: rdn and wknd over 3f out: t.o* **100/1**

2m 28.0s (-0.70) **Going Correction** -0.25s/f (Firm) **8** Ran SP% **114.6**
Speed ratings (Par 96): **92,90,89,88,87 86,55,48**
toteswingers:1&2:£3.10, 1&3:£5.40, 2&3:£7.60 CSF £33.69 CT £251.41 TOTE £5.50: £1.80, £1.10, £2.60; EX 31.30 Trifecta £149.30 Pool £389.40 - 1.93 winning units..
Owner Saif Ali & Saeed H Altayer **Bred** Hascombe And Valiant Studs **Trained** Newmarket, Suffolk

FOCUS
A low-grade handicap, but the time was fair and the form is rated on the positive side. The winner produced a stone personal best.
Jeu De Vivre(IRE) Official explanation: trainer had no explanation for the poor form shown
T/Plt: £1,705.70 to a £1 stake. Pool of £42,058.58 - 18.00 winning tickets. T/Qpdt: £120.40 to a £1 stake. Pool of £2,278.61 - 14.00 winning tickets. CR

[1128]COLOGNE (R-H)

Monday, April 25

OFFICIAL GOING: Turf: good

1575a SILBERNE PEITSCHE DER SAUREN FONDS-SERVICE AG (GROUP 3) (3YO+) (TURF) 6f 110y

3:40 (4:12) 3-Y-0+

£27,586 (£9,482; £4,741; £2,586; £1,724; £1,293)

RPR

1 **Amico Fritz (GER)**[191] 6949 5-9-6 0.............................. MaximeGuyon 1 109
(H-A Pantall, France) *broke fast to ld: hdd bef first turn: first to chal early in st: qcknd wl: led 1 1/2f out: hrd rdn to hold on by minimum margin on line fr persistent runner-up* **1/1**[1]

2 *nse* **Walero (GER)**[184] 5-9-6 0.. EPedroza 4 109
(Uwe Ostmann, Germany) *broke wl: tk ld bef first turn: set fast pce: r.o wl in st: hdd 1 1/2f out: rallied strly ins fnl f: only jst failed on line* **146/10**

3 *1 ¾* **Konig Concorde (GER)**[170] 7370 6-9-6 0.......................... DPorcu 3 104
(C Sprengel, Germany) *broke wl: settled in midfield: short of room in centre of trck in st: picked up wl ins fnl f* **31/5**[3]

4 *1 ¾* **Aslana (IRE)**[198] 6765 4-9-3 0.. AStarke 8 96
(P Schiergen, Germany) *broke wl: settled in prom position: sn rdn and chal in st: r.o wl fnl f* **31/10**[2]

5 *hd* **Golden Whip (GER)**[183] 4-9-3 0.. APietsch 6 95
(W Hickst, Germany) *settled bhd ldng gp: wnt 4th bef st: briefly flattered early in st: outpcd: unable qck fnl f* **155/10**

6 *nk* **Glad Sky**[170] 7370 5-9-6 0.. GeorgBocskai 5 97
(W Gulcher, Germany) *settled midfield: kpt changing legs down bkstretch: r.o in st through btn horses* **132/10**

7 *1 ½* **Murcielago (GER)**[15] 1263 4-9-6 0.............................. AHelfenbein 10 93
(M Keller, Germany) *a towards the rr: nvr a factor* **245/10**

8 *3 ½* **Smooth Operator (GER)**[170] 7370 5-9-6 0.......................... THellier 7 83
(Mario Hofer, Germany) *racd promly fr s: briefly threatened early in st: no ex fnl 2f* **68/10**

9 *3* **Run Directa (GER)**[184] 4-9-6 0.. SHellyn 2 74
(D Moser, Germany) *a the bkmarker: nvr figured in st* **40/1**

10 *1 ¼* **Nareion (GER)**[18] 5-9-6 0.. StefanieHofer 9 71
(W Baltromei, Germany) *a in rr: nvr figured* **33/1**

1m 17.84s (77.84) **10** Ran SP% **129.9**
WIN (incl. 10 euro stake): 20. PLACES: 12, 22, 18. SF: 268..
Owner Alexandre Pereira **Bred** A Pereira **Trained** France

NOTEBOOK
Amico Fritz(GER) had to work hard to hold off the persistent challenge of Walero, who had set a strong pace early, but this trip stretches his stamina a bit. He wasn't 100 per cent fit on his return from a six-month absence either, according to his trainer, and he'll now be aimed once again at the Golden Jubilee Stakes, a race in which he was fifth last year.

SHA TIN (R-H)

Monday, April 25

OFFICIAL GOING: Turf: good to firm

1576a BMW CHAMPIONS MILE (GROUP 1) (3YO+) (TURF) 1m

9:35 (12:00) 3-Y-0+

£564,822 (£218,001; £99,091; £56,151; £33,030; £19,818)

RPR

1 **Xtension (IRE)**[36] 4-9-0 0.. DarrenBeadman 7 119
(J Moore, Hong Kong) *settled in midfield: 8th and plld outside appr fnl 2f: rdn to ld ins fnl f: r.o* **10/1**

2 *½* **Lucky Nine (IRE)**[50] 4-9-0 0.. BrettPrebble 9 118
(C Fownes, Hong Kong) *a in first four: r.o fr 1 1/2f out: chal ldr ins fnl f: led appr fnl 100yds: hdd 50yds out: no ex* **31/10**[1]

3 *shd* **Musir (AUS)**[30] 1002 5-9-0 0.............................. ChristopheSoumillon 5 118
(M F De Kock, South Africa) *chsd ldng gp: rdn ins fnl 2f: 5th 1 1/2f out: styd on wl u.p ins fnl f* **12/1**

4 *nk* **Beauty Flash (NZ)**[30] 1000 6-9-0 0..............................(t) GeraldMosse 14 117
(A S Cruz, Hong Kong) *w ldrs: led after 2f: hdd appr fnl 100yds: kpt on* **31/5**

5 *½* **Sparkling Power (IRE)**[44] 4-9-0 0.............................. DwayneDunn 8 116
(A T Millard, Hong Kong) *settled in fnl 3rd of field: 10th ins fnl 2f: r.o appr fnl f: nrest at fin* **33/1**

6 *nk* **Presvis**[30] 1000 7-9-0 0.. RyanMoore 10 115
(Luca Cumani) *dwlt and settled in rr: hdwy on rail 2 1/2f out: 9th and rdn 2f out: styd on fnl f: nt pce to chal* **73/10**

7 *1 ¼* **Sight Winner (NZ)**[22] 8-9-0 0.. WMLai 3 112
(J Size, Hong Kong) *trckd ldrs in 3rd: disp 2nd 1 1/2f out: sn rdn and btn* **142/1**

8 *nk* **Let Me Fight (IRE)**[22] 4-9-0 0..(p) ZacPurton 12 112
(J Moore, Hong Kong) *hld up towards rr: 12th 2f out: styd on late: n.d* **65/1**

9 *shd* **Sunny King (IRE)**[30] 999 8-9-0 0.. ODoleuze 1 111
(J Moore, Hong Kong) *racd in 6th: rdn 1 1/2f out: kpt on at one pce* **44/1**

10 *1* **Thumbs Up (NZ)**[22] 7-9-0 0.. WCMarwing 13 109
(C Fownes, Hong Kong) *w.w towards rr: last 2f out: nvr in contention* **15/2**

11 *shd* **Royal Bench (IRE)**[30] 1000 4-9-0 0.............................. OlivierPeslier 2 109
(Robert Collet, France) *nvr beyond mid-div: hanging lft over 1 1/2f out: n.d* **11/2**[3]

12 *nk* **Brave Kid (AUS)**[22] 6-9-0 0.. DouglasWhyte 4 108
(J Size, Hong Kong) *settled in midfield: effrt on outside over 2 1/2f out: 7th and running on appr 2f out: short of room 1 1/2f out: nt qckn fnl f* **126/1**

13 *¾* **Able One (NZ)**[16] 9-9-0 0.. DamienOliver 6 107
(J Moore, Hong Kong) *sn led: hdd after 2f: 2nd and rdn ins fnl 2f and nt qckn: wknd fnl f* **22/1**

14 *nk* **Good Ba Ba (USA)**[50] 9-9-0 0..(t) JeffLloyd 11 106
(C W Chang, Hong Kong) *hld up: effrt 1 1/2f out: no imp on ldrs* **104/1**

1m 34.71s (0.01) **14** Ran SP% **122.4**
PARI-MUTUEL (all including HK$10 stake): WIN 42.00; PLACE 16.00, 16.50, 40.50; DF 82.50.
Owner Mr & Mrs Steven Lo Kit Sing **Bred** Paul McCartan **Trained** Hong Kong

FOCUS
The sectionals for each quarter were 25.30, 23.50, 23.64, 22.27, so an ordinary gallop and only around a length and a half separated the first six finishers. Not strong Group 1 form.
NOTEBOOK
Xtension(IRE) hadn't won since taking the Group 2 Vintage Stakes for Clive Cox, but he'd run a number of creditable races in top company both for his former trainer and since being sold. Making his sixth start in Hong Kong, the drop in trip didn't inconvenience him and, despite there being a sprint finish, he quickened well, staying on from further behind than the next three finishers.
Musir(AUS) was well placed, but he came under pressure after the winner and could never build up sufficient momentum. This was a fine run from a horse more accustomed to racing on synthetics, and perhaps he just needed the experience of racing on turf for the first time since 2009.
Presvis was dropped back to 1m for the first time since his maiden days instead of waiting for the upcoming QEII Cup (won in 2009) in the hope there might be more pace than in the longer distance event, and because Ryan Moore was available to ride. However, he was full of himself beforehand and Ryan Moore had to dismount at one stage to encourage him to go to post. In addition, the race itself was not run to suit. Settled last, he made progress against the inside rail turning into the straight and recorded the quickest third-quarter sectional, but he had to be switched off the fence once in line for the finish and, although never really blocked in his run, he found the leaders were not coming back to him and the line coming too soon.

1232 LINGFIELD (L-H)
Tuesday, April 26

OFFICIAL GOING: Standard
Wind: Moderate, against Weather: Fine

1577 LINGFIELD PARK OWNERS CLUB (S) STKS — 1m 4f (P)
2:30 (2:30) (Class 6) 4-Y-0+ — **£1,706** (£503; £252) **Stalls** Low

Form — RPR
0414 **1** **Relative Strength (IRE)**[23] 1107 6-9-5 70 (bt) JamesDoyle 3 — 76
(Frank Sheridan) *trckd ldrs: rousted along over 2f out: prog on inner wl over 1f out: drvn and kpt on to ld last 100yds* **3/1**[2]
-243 **2** ¾ **Eagle Nebula**[21] 1148 7-8-10 67 KierenFox(3) 5 — 69
(Brett Johnson) *hld up in last pair: prog on outer over 3f out: led over 2f out: edgd rt over 1f out: hdd and nt qckn last 100yds* **5/1**[3]
345- **3** 3½ **Robby Bobby**[132] 7884 6-8-13 63 IanMongan 2 — 63
(Laura Mongan) *trckd ldrs: rdn and outpcd in 5th 3f out: plugged on again fr over 1f out* **16/1**
/5-5 **4** *nse* **Bin End**[18] 1215 5-8-13 80 HayleyTurner 4 — 64
(Michael Bell) *led: set mod pce tl briefly hdd 7f out: rdn over 3f out: hdd over 2f out: cl up but hld whn squeezed out jst ins fnl f* **1/1**[1]
3401 **5** 3½ **Stand Guard**[32] 968 7-9-5 72 TomQueally 9 — 64
(Michael Squance) *hld up: swift move to ld briefly 7f out: pressed ldr to 2f out: wknd over 1f out* **8/1**
2260 **6** 12 **Force Group (IRE)**[39] 897 7-8-6 62 (b) RichardOld(7) 8 — 38
(Nick Littmoden) *t.k.h early: in tch: pushed along over 4f out: wknd over 3f out* **28/1**
154- **7** 70 **Emerald Glade (IRE)**[8] 6623 4-8-7 66 (p) ChrisCatlin 7 — —
(Milton Harris) *chsd ldr 5f: sn wknd rapidly and wl t.o* **20/1**
2m 34.65s (1.65) **Going Correction** +0.225s/f (Slow)
WFA 4 from 5yo+ 1lb — 7 Ran SP% **116.9**
Speed ratings (Par 101): **103,102,100,100,97 89,43**
toteswingers:1&2 £4.40, 2&3 £10.10, 1&3 £14.10 CSF £19.06 TOTE £3.00: £1.10, £3.00; EX 17.80.There was no bid for the winner. Bin End was claimed by F. J. Brennan for £6000.
Owner Frank Sheridan **Bred** Holborn Trust Co **Trained** Wolverhampton, W Midlands
■ Stewards' Enquiry : Kieren Fox caution: careless riding.
FOCUS
A fair seller but the favourite was disappointing. The form makes sense around the first three.

1578 LINGFIELD DERBY TRIAL COMING SOON CLAIMING STKS — 7f (P)
3:00 (3:01) (Class 6) 3-Y-O — **£1,706** (£503; £252) **Stalls** Low

Form — RPR
-551 **1** **Exchange**[12] 1323 3-8-10 65 LiamJones 6 — 63
(Chris Gordon) *hld up in last pair: effrt and swtchd wd 2f out: hanging over 1f out: pushed along and clsd to ld last 100yds: sn in command* **4/1**[3]
0-12 **2** 1¼ **New Latin (IRE)**[54] 739 3-9-5 72 JamesDoyle 3 — 69
(Frank Sheridan) *dwlt: hld up in 4th: prog on outer to ld wl over 1f out w hd high: hdd and nt qckn last 100yds* **11/8**[1]
400- **3** 8 **Lady On Top (IRE)**[157] 7520 3-8-0 48 ow2 FrankieMcDonald 7 — 28
(Nerys Dutfield) *trckd ldr: chal over 2f out: tight for room wl over 1f out: wknd* **33/1**
410- **4** 6 **Rudegirl (IRE)**[185] 7085 3-8-10 78 HayleyTurner 2 — 22
(Conor Dore) *led: rdn and hdd wl over 1f out: wknd v rapidly* **9/4**[2]
6- **5** 9 **Smart Performance**[276] 4363 3-8-8 0 HarryBentley(5) 1 — —
(Alan Jarvis) *in tch tl wknd qckly over 3f out: t.o* **7/1**
000- **6** 9 **Street Cred (IRE)**[157] 7527 3-7-12 10 (t) AdrianMcCarthy 5 — —
(Paul Burgoyne) *a in last pair: wknd 1/2-way: t.o* **150/1**
1m 26.81s (2.01) **Going Correction** +0.225s/f (Slow) — 6 Ran SP% **109.0**
Speed ratings (Par 96): **97,95,86,79,69 59**
CSF £9.35 TOTE £9.10: £3.60, £1.40; EX 12.40.
Owner Richard Venn **Bred** Southill Stud **Trained** Morestead, Hants
FOCUS
A poor race with only four serious contenders and a couple of those looked distinctly iffy. Only the front pair showed their form.
New Latin(IRE) Official explanation: jockey said gelding did not handle the final bend
Rudegirl(IRE) Official explanation: jockey said filly hung right throughout

1579 LADIES DAY AT LINGFIELD PARK 6TH MAY FILLIES' H'CAP — 7f (P)
3:30 (3:33) (Class 5) (0-70,70) 3-Y-O — **£2,388** (£705; £352) **Stalls** Low

Form — RPR
0-1 **1** **Amelia's Surprise**[25] 1084 3-9-7 **70** HayleyTurner 6 — 74+
(Michael Bell) *stdd s: hld up last: stl there over 1f out in tightly packed field: weaved through ins fnl f: drvn to ld last 50yds* **7/1**[3]
032- **2** *hd* **Hurricane Lady (IRE)**[164] 7448 3-9-3 **66** EddieAhern 3 — 69+
(Walter Swinburn) *stdd s: hld up wl in rr: prog on inner over 1f out: drvn to chal last 75yds: jst hld* **7/2**[2]
003- **3** ¾ **Be Amazing (IRE)**[222] 6118 3-9-5 **68** TedDurcan 8 — 69
(David Lanigan) *mde most: hrd pressed over 1f out: hdd and outpcd last 50yds* **7/1**[3]
00-1 **4** *hd* **Ellie In The Pink (IRE)**[21] 1149 3-8-8 **62** HarryBentley(5) 7 — 62+
(Alan Jarvis) *hld up towards rr: rdn on outer 2f out: prog fnl f: styd on and nrly snatched 3rd* **8/1**
-400 **5** *shd* **Bedibyes**[39] 887 3-8-0 **56** oh1 IanBurns(7) 10 — 56
(Richard Mitchell) *prom: urged along furiously fr over 2f out: trying to cl on ldrs 1f out: nt qckn last 100yds* **25/1**
060- **6** ½ **Abeer (USA)**[197] 6796 3-9-1 **64** RichardHills 2 — 63
(Ed Dunlop) *prom: wnt 2nd wl over 1f out: sn chalng: nt qckn ins fnl f: lost pls nr fin* **10/3**[1]
2434 **7** ½ **Spirit Of Grace**[54] 751 3-9-3 **66** JamesDoyle 1 — 63
(Alan McCabe) *hld up in rr: prog on inner 2f out: wnt 3rd 1f out and looked like chalng: sn rdn and fnd nil* **10/1**
200- **8** ¾ **Russian Ice**[174] 7296 3-8-8 **57** AdrianMcCarthy 5 — 52
(Dean Ivory) *hld up in midfield: pushed along over 1f out: kpt on but nvr impr position* **66/1**
300- **9** 2 **Atia**[224] 6052 3-8-13 **62** MartinDwyer 4 — 52
(Jonathan Portman) *cl up: shkn up to dispute 3rd jst over 1f out: nt qckn and hld whn short of room ins fnl f* **20/1**
060- **10** 6 **Emmeline Pankhurst (IRE)**[181] 7164 3-8-7 **56** oh1 JimmyQuinn 12 — 30
(Julia Feilden) *racd wd in rr: brief effrt over 2f out: sn wknd* **20/1**
000- **11** 18 **Rafella (IRE)**[197] 6809 3-9-7 **70** SebSanders 9 — —
(Simon Dow) *pressed ldr tl eased 2f out: virtually p.u: sddle slipped* **15/2**
1m 27.58s (2.78) **Going Correction** +0.225s/f (Slow) — 11 Ran SP% **117.1**
Speed ratings (Par 95): **93,92,91,91,91 91,90,89,87,80 59**
toteswingers:1&2 £6.80, 2&3 £3.10, 1&3 £8.40 CSF £30.14 CT £183.74 TOTE £6.20: £1.50, £1.10, £1.90; EX 27.60.
Owner R A Pegum **Bred** Cranford Stud **Trained** Newmarket, Suffolk
FOCUS
A modest fillies' handicap, but a few of these were entitled to improve for the switch from maidens into a handicap. The front pair both came from well off the pace, but the principals all finished in a heap and the time was 0.77 seconds slower than the claimer, so the form doesn't look anything special. The form is rated around the third and there's more to come from the winner.
Rafella(IRE) Official explanation: jockey said saddle slipped

1580 SUMMER EVENINGS AT LINGFIELD PARK MEDIAN AUCTION MAIDEN STKS — 1m (P)
4:00 (4:01) (Class 5) 3-Y-O — **£1,706** (£503; £252) **Stalls** High

Form — RPR
40- **1** **Chief Of Men**[210] 6436 3-9-3 0 EddieAhern 9 — 72
(Denis Coakley) *t.k.h early: hld up in tch: prog on outer to cl on ldrs 2f out: rdn to ld 1f out: kpt on wl* **9/2**[2]
0- **2** ¾ **Daddyow**[196] 6827 3-9-0 0 DeclanCannon(3) 6 — 70
(Bryn Palling) *settled in 7th: clsd on ldrs 2f out: nt clr run briefly over 1f out: swtchd ins and kpt on to chse wnr ins fnl f: a hld* **100/1**
3 **3** ½ **Poyle Punch**[20] 1179 3-9-3 0 GeorgeBaker 5 — 69
(Ralph Beckett) *trckd ldrs: led 2f out: drvn and hdd 1f out: nt qckn* **11/2**[3]
4 2½ **Suomi** 3-9-3 0 [1] PatCosgrave 4 — 63
(James Fanshawe) *settled in last trio: rchd 7th over 2f out but sn outpcd: shoved along and styd on to take 4th ins fnl f* **10/1**
26-0 **5** 2¼ **Lady Bridget**[21] 1151 3-8-12 70 MichaelHills 3 — 53
(B W Hills) *chsd ldrs: rdn and in tch over 2f out: wknd over 1f out* **14/1**
4-5 **6** *nk* **Shelovestobouggie**[15] 1270 3-8-12 0 TomQueally 12 — 53
(Sir Henry Cecil) *prom: trckd ldr over 4f out: led briefly jst over 2f out: wknd jst over 1f out* **9/2**[2]
322- **7** 4½ **Songsmith**[197] 6802 3-9-3 77 ChrisCatlin 1 — 47
(Lucy Wadham) *led to jst over 2f out: wknd qckly over 1f out* **6/4**[1]
00- **8** 2¼ **Disturbia (IRE)**[236] 5691 3-8-12 0 SebSanders 8 — 37
(J W Hills) *wl in rr: brief effrt 3f out: sn lost tch w ldrs* **100/1**
9 *nk* **Dare To Bare (IRE)** 3-9-3 0 TedDurcan 10 — 41
(Amanda Perrett) *rn green in last: wl bhd 3f out: sme late prog* **33/1**
10 10 **Bop Till Dawn (IRE)** 3-8-12 0 LiamKeniry 7 — 13
(Harry Dunlop) *dwlt: racd wd: a in rr: t.o* **66/1**
00 **11** 1 **Pippas Prodigy (IRE)**[22] 1139 3-8-12 0 EddieCreighton 2 — 11
(Edward Creighton) *chsd ldr to over 4f out: sn lost pl u.p: t.o* **250/1**
1m 39.72s (1.52) **Going Correction** +0.225s/f (Slow) — 11 Ran SP% **114.3**
Speed ratings (Par 98): **101,100,99,97,95 94,90,87,87,77 76**
toteswingers:1&2 £68.30, 2&3 £68.30, 1&3 £7.00 CSF £379.40 TOTE £5.00: £1.20, £14.20, £3.00; EX 273.30.
Owner Chris Van Hoorn **Bred** P C Hunt **Trained** West Ilsley, Berks
FOCUS
This didn't look a strong maiden, though a couple of winners should emerge from it. The winner is rated up a length on his 2yo form.
Bop Till Dawn(IRE) Official explanation: jockey said filly hung right

1581 MARRIOTT HOTEL & COUNTRY CLUB H'CAP — 6f (P)
4:30 (4:30) (Class 6) (0-65,65) 4-Y-O+ — **£2,729** (£806; £403) **Stalls** Low

Form — RPR
2333 **1** **Cavitie**[7] 1471 5-9-0 **58** (p) JamesDoyle 2 — 68
(Andrew Reid) *t.k.h: hld up bhd ldrs: stl gng strly whn effrt 2f out: led jst over 1f out: sn pressed: jst hld on* **5/1**[1]
140- **2** *nse* **Elsie's Orphan**[197] 6812 4-9-6 **64** LiamKeniry 11 — 74
(Patrick Chamings) *hld up in midfield: prog to press ldrs on outer 2f out: drvn to chal fnl f: upsides last strides: jst pipped* **8/1**
1-53 **3** 1½ **Anjomarba (IRE)**[83] 388 4-9-1 **62** KierenFox(3) 5 — 67
(Brett Johnson) *hld up in rr: prog on inner wl over 1f out: styd on to take 3rd ins fnl f: unable to chal* **11/1**
4616 **4** 1 **Speak The Truth (IRE)**[13] 1314 5-9-4 **62** (p) TomQueally 12 — 64
(Jim Boyle) *urged along on outer in rr 4f out: prog on wd outside to press ldrs over 2f out: lost grnd bnd after: kpt on same pce ins fnl f* **7/1**[3]
4262 **5** *hd* **Jimmy Ryan (IRE)**[20] 1182 10-8-13 **57** (t) J-PGuillambert 6 — 61
(Tim McCarthy) *t.k.h: hld up bhd ldrs: gng strly but nowhere to go and lost pl 2f out: hrd rdn and kpt on one pce ins fnl f* **12/1**
25-5 **6** 1½ **Durgan**[34] 947 5-9-0 **58** (p) SteveDrowne 4 — 55
(Linda Jewell) *disp ld after 1f: hdd jst over 1f out: wknd ins fnl f* **14/1**
0-00 **7** ¾ **Caldermud (IRE)**[19] 1196 4-9-7 **65** (t) IanMongan 1 — 59
(Olivia Maylam) *dwlt: sn drvn in last: struggling thrght: styd on ins fnl f* **33/1**
3-13 **8** ½ **Dream Number (IRE)**[14] 1281 4-9-4 **62** MartinDwyer 10 — 55
(William Muir) *hld up in last pair after n.m.r s: pushed along over 1f out: no real prog and nvr nr ldrs* **8/1**
U-14 **9** 1 **Boldinor**[20] 1171 8-9-4 **62** GeorgeBaker 7 — 51
(Martin Bosley) *disp ld after 1f to wl over 1f out: wknd* **8/1**
0 **10** 15 **Gala Spirit (IRE)**[19] 1196 4-9-7 **65** AndreaAtzeni 3 — —
(Michael Wigham) *led 1f: styd prom on inner tl wknd rapidly over 2f out: t.o* **15/2**

1020 **11** ½ **Far View (IRE)**[20] [1182] 4-9-1 **62**..........................(tp) MatthewDavies(3) 8 —
(George Baker) *prom: pressed ldng pair over 3f out to 2f out: wknd rapidly: t.o* **11/2**[2]

1m 12.93s (1.03) **Going Correction** +0.225s/f (Slow) **11** Ran SP% **115.3**
Speed ratings (Par 101): **102,101,99,98,98 96,95,94,93,73 72**
toteswingers:1&2 £9.80, 2&3 £32.40, 1&3 £17.90 CSF £43.70 CT £427.05 TOTE £5.70: £1.30, £3.50, £4.90; EX 51.90.
Owner A S Reid **Bred** A S Reid **Trained** Mill Hill, London NW7

FOCUS
A modest if competitive sprint handicap and a three-way battle for the early lead ensured the pace was sound. The winner is rated to his recent best.

1582 GREAT DEALS ON ANNUAL MEMBERSHIP H'CAP 1m 2f (P)
5:00 (5:01) (Class 6) (0-60,60) 4-Y-0+ **£2,047** (£604; £302) **Stalls** Low

Form RPR

5142 **1** **Ocean Of Peace (FR)**[13] [1308] 8-9-2 **55**.......................... HayleyTurner 6 62
(Martin Bosley) *settled in midfield: sme prog 3f out: drvn in 5th over 2f out: grad clsd ins fnl f: styd on to ld last strides* **9/2**[1]

310- **2** *nk* **Big Sur**[189] [7005] 5-9-5 **58**.......................... SteveDrowne 5 64
(Tom Keddy) *led: hung rt bnd after 1f: hanging rt rest of way: rdn and narrowly hdd over 2f out: kpt on to press ldr ins fnl f but racing awkwardly: nt qckn last strides* **13/2**[3]

630- **3** *nse* **Byrd In Hand (IRE)**[173] [7316] 4-8-11 **55**.......................... SeanLevey(5) 7 61
(John Bridger) *t.k.h: sn pressed ldr: rdn to take narrow ld over 2f out: idled in front: hdd last strides* **16/1**

50-2 **4** ½ **Musashi (IRE)**[22] [1135] 6-9-7 **60**.......................... IanMongan 13 65
(Laura Mongan) *sn trckd ldrs: rdn and nt qckn wl over 2f out: tried to cl again over 1f out: kpt on: nvr quite able to chal* **8/1**

20-3 **5** ¾ **Crystal Gale (IRE)**[109] [83] 4-9-0 **58**.......................... HarryBentley(5) 2 63
(William Knight) *settled towards rr: effrt on inner whn n.m.r over 2f out: 8th and plenty to do sn after: prog over 1f out: keeping on but hld whn n.m.r nr fin* **8/1**

3122 **6** 2½ **Mr Maximas**[15] [1273] 4-8-13 **55**..........................(tp) DeclanCannon(3) 9 54
(Bryn Palling) *cl up: rdn 3f out to chse ldrs: lost pl and btn over 1f out* **5/1**[2]

326 **7** ½ **King Kieren (IRE)**[31] [992] 6-9-7 **60**.......................... EddieAhern 4 58
(Linda Jewell) *prom: rdn 3f out: losing pl whn n.m.r on inner over 2f out: n.d after* **9/1**

5230 **8** 3½ **Lytham (IRE)**[13] [1310] 10-9-2 **55**.......................... SebSanders 11 46
(Tony Carroll) *dwlt: hld up in rr: scrubbed along on outer 3f out: no prog over 2f out: str reminders over 1f out: nvr involved* **9/1**

050- **9** 1 **Winning Show**[139] [7765] 7-9-0 **53**.......................... LiamKeniry 10 42
(Chris Gordon) *dwlt: hld up wl in rr: shkn up 3f out: nvr nr ldrs* **40/1**

6-33 **10** *hd* **I'Lldoit**[49] [797] 4-8-12 **58**.......................... DavidKenny(7) 1 46
(Michael Scudamore) *v awkward s and slowly away: sn in tch in last pair: drvn over 4f out: sn btn* **16/1**

0-00 **11** 1¼ **Integria**[12] [1333] 5-9-7 **60**..........................(t) TonyCulhane 3 46
(George Baker) *hld up in rr: outpcd and rdn 3f out: nvr on terms after* **33/1**

-500 **12** 2 **Majestueux (USA)**[34] [943] 4-9-4 **57**..........................(p) ChrisCatlin 12 39
(Mark Hoad) *racd wd in midfield: drvn to stay in tch w ldrs over 2f out: wknd qckly wl over 1f out* **33/1**

-000 **13** 7 **Officer Lily (USA)**[41] [862] 4-8-7 **49**.......................... KierenFox(3) 8 17
(John Best) *a towards rr: u.str.p over 4f out: t.o* **16/1**

2m 9.80s (3.20) **Going Correction** +0.225s/f (Slow) **13** Ran SP% **116.4**
Speed ratings (Par 101): **96,95,95,95,94 92,92,89,88,88 87,85,80**
toteswingers:1&2 £6.30, 2&3 £19.60, 1&3 £16.30 CSF £31.71 CT £430.72 TOTE £3.70: £1.10, £3.10, £6.50; EX 40.00.
Owner Mrs Jean M O'Connor **Bred** Raoul Rousset **Trained** Chalfont St Giles, Bucks

FOCUS
A moderate handicap in which they went no pace early and the first five finished in a heap. Those that raced handily were helped as a result. The winner's best figure in Britain.
Big Sur Official explanation: jockey said gelding hung right throughout
T/Jkpt: Not won. T/Plt: £116.10 to a £1 stake. Pool of £66,540.66 - 418.21 winning tickets. T/Qpdt: £40.90 to a £1 stake. Pool of £4,376.38 - 79.10 winning tickets. JN

1469 WOLVERHAMPTON (A.W) (L-H)
Tuesday, April 26

OFFICIAL GOING: Standard
Wind: Fresh against Weather: Overcast

1583 PUNCHESTOWN LIVE ON ATR VIRGIN 534 MAIDEN STKS 5f 20y(P)
5:45 (5:45) (Class 5) 2-Y-0 **£2,388** (£705; £352) **Stalls** Low

Form RPR

1 **Monnoyer** 2-9-3 0.......................... PaulHanagan 6 78+
(Jeremy Noseda) *a.p: shkn up 1/2-way: led and hung lft ins fnl f: r.o* **8/11**[1]

06 **2** 2¼ **Courtland King (IRE)**[7] [1451] 2-9-3 0..........................(t) AdamKirby 5 70
(David Evans) *chsd ldrs: rdn over 1f out: nt clr run ins fnl f: styd on same pce: wnt 2nd towards fin* **33/1**

3 ¾ **Lord Ali McJones** 2-9-3 0.......................... RichardKingscote 2 67
(Tom Dascombe) *chsd ldrs: led over 1f out: hdd and no ex ins fnl f: lost 2nd towards fin* **8/1**

4 2¾ **Wolfgang (IRE)** 2-9-3 0.......................... RichardHughes 3 57
(Richard Hannon) *mid-div: sn drvn along: kpt on to go 4th wl ins fnl f: nvr nrr* **7/2**[2]

5 ¾ **Complex** 2-8-12 0.......................... CathyGannon 9 50
(David Evans) *s.i.s: outpcd: r.o ins fnl f: nrst fin* **33/1**

0 **6** *nse* **Powerful Wind (IRE)**[11] [1360] 2-9-3 0.......................... LukeMorris 4 54
(Ronald Harris) *led over 3f: wknd ins fnl f* **28/1**

7 1¼ **Vinnie Jones** 2-9-3 0.......................... WilliamBuick 1 50+
(John Gosden) *s.i.s: outpcd* **15/2**[3]

8 11 **Jawim** 2-8-12 0.......................... TomMcLaughlin 7 —
(Malcolm Saunders) *s.i.s: outpcd* **66/1**

9 5 **Stans Deelyte** 2-8-12 0.......................... TomEaves 8 —
(Lisa Williamson) *w ldr to 1/2-way: wknd wl over 1f out* **80/1**

62.70 secs (0.40) **Going Correction** -0.10s/f (Stan) **9** Ran SP% **115.1**
Speed ratings (Par 92): **92,88,87,82,81 81,79,61,53**
toteswingers:1&2 £8.10, 2&3 £5.70, 1&3 £2.40 CSF £38.79 TOTE £1.80: £1.10, £5.80, £1.90; EX 33.50.
Owner Mrs S Roy, P Dixon & B Morton **Bred** David John Brown **Trained** Newmarket, Suffolk

FOCUS
This opening juvenile maiden proved to be a lively betting heat and the market got it spot on. the winner should progress from this fair start.

NOTEBOOK
Monnoyer ◆ justified strong support to make a winning debut. Jeremy Noseda has yet to really start firing this season, but he went to the trouble of booking the champion jockey for his debutant by Dutch Art and his experience in the saddle counted for plenty. He briefly looked in trouble 3f out, but the penny began to drop as he was angled out straightening for home and, despite running green inside the final furlong, he ultimately won comfortably. His Group 1 entry is still some way off being justified, but he ought to improve a bundle for the run and is potentially very useful. Hanagan was later complimentary about him and said the kickback was "pretty bad", which affected his mount from halfway. (op 11-8)
Courtland King(IRE)'s proximity at first glance drags down this form, but his previous experience was a notable advantage in this field and he is clearly going the right way. The switch to Polytrack obviously suited. (op 20-1)
Lord Ali McJones posted a pleasing debut display, holding every chance. He is entitled to improve and won't mind a stiffer test. (op 10-1 tchd 7-1)
Wolfgang(IRE), whose trainer has not quite hit the ground running with his juveniles, proved too green to do himself full justice on this initial outing. He ought to get closer next time. (op 9-4 tchd 4-1)
Vinnie Jones was the first juvenile from John Gosden's team to be out this year and his dam was a 2-y-o C&D winner. He fell out of the gates, however, and badly needed the experience. (op 13-2 tchd 8-1)

1584 GREAT OFFERS AT WOLVERHAMPTON-RACECOURSE.CO.UK H'CAP 5f 20y(P)
6:20 (6:20) (Class 4) (0-85,82) 4-Y-0+ **£3,238** (£963; £481; £240) **Stalls** Low

Form RPR

0522 **1** **Fair Passion**[13] [1309] 4-8-8 **69**.......................... DaneO'Neill 6 79
(Derek Shaw) *stdd and hmpd s: hld up: hdwy over 1f out: hung lft ins fnl f: r.o to ld nr fin* **9/2**[2]

1021 **2** *nk* **Island Legend (IRE)**[19] [1196] 5-9-5 **80**..........................(p) RichardKingscote 4 89
(Milton Bradley) *chsd ldrs: led 1f out: sn rdn and hung lft: hdd nr fin* **9/2**[2]

5124 **3** ½ **Kylladdie**[27] [1048] 4-8-11 **72**..........................(b) WilliamBuick 7 79
(Steve Gollings) *hld up: hdwy over 1f out: hung lft and r.o ins fnl f: nt rch ldrs* **11/2**[3]

00-0 **4** 1 **Living It Large (FR)**[32] [970] 4-9-5 **80**.......................... TonyHamilton 2 83
(Roger Fisher) *disp ld tl def advantage over 1f out: rdn and hdd 1f out: styd on same pce ins fnl f* **16/1**

1-15 **5** 1¼ **Mottley Crewe**[26] [1067] 4-8-12 **73**.......................... TomEaves 1 72
(Michael Dods) *chsd ldrs: rdn over 1f out: no ex ins fnl f* **6/1**

2062 **6** *hd* **Garstang**[11] [1371] 8-9-2 **77**..........................(b) PaulHanagan 5 76
(John Balding) *hld up in tch: plld hrd: swtchd lft over 1f out: hung lft and nt clr run ins fnl f: no ex* **7/2**[1]

6000 **7** ¾ **Methaaly (IRE)**[10] [1382] 8-8-6 **74**..........................(be) JosephYoung(7) 8 69
(Michael Mullineaux) *s.i.s: swtchd lft sn after s: outpcd: running on whn nt clr run ins fnl f: nvr on terms* **11/1**

220- **8** 7 **La Fortunata**[218] [6256] 4-9-7 **82**.......................... JoeFanning 3 52
(Mike Murphy) *disp ld over 3f: sn wknd* **13/2**

61.44 secs (-0.86) **Going Correction** -0.10s/f (Stan) **8** Ran SP% **115.8**
Speed ratings (Par 105): **102,101,100,99,97 96,95,84**
toteswingers:1&2 £6.00, 2&3 £4.20, 1&3 £5.30 CSF £25.39 CT £113.66 TOTE £8.40: £3.50, £1.10, £2.30; EX 26.90.
Owner Mike Conway **Bred** D R Tucker **Trained** Sproxton, Leics

FOCUS
A modest sprint handicap in which all bar one of these had previously won at the course, five of them over C&D, and it was wide open. The pace was strong and the winner is rated back to last winter's form.
Garstang Official explanation: jockey said gelding hung left-handed

1585 NAME A RACE TO ENHANCE YOUR BRAND (S) STKS 5f 216y(P)
6:50 (6:50) (Class 6) 3-Y-0 **£1,535** (£453; £226) **Stalls** Low

Form RPR

500- **1** **Pick A Little**[176] [7271] 3-9-4 64.......................... DaneO'Neill 4 66
(Ron Hodges) *mde all: rdn over 1f out: edgd rt ins fnl f: jst hld on* **5/1**[3]

00-1 **2** *hd* **Cootehill Lass (IRE)**[26] [1056] 3-8-10 60.......................... MichaelO'Connell(3) 2 60
(Geoffrey Harker) *dwlt: hdwy to chse wnr 5f out: rdn to chal over 1f out: sn hung lft: hung rt ins fnl f: r.o* **4/6**[1]

1421 **3** ½ **Eternal Youth (IRE)**[12] [1334] 3-9-4 67..........................(b) LukeMorris 3 64
(Ronald Harris) *trckd ldrs: rdn over 1f out: r.o* **15/8**[2]

0006 **4** 11 **Welsh Dresser (IRE)**[22] [1137] 3-8-7 36.......................... RobbieFitzpatrick 1 18
(Peter Grayson) *chsd wnr 1f: remained handy tl wknd over 2f out* **100/1**

1m 15.19s (0.19) **Going Correction** -0.10s/f (Stan) **4** Ran SP% **112.4**
Speed ratings (Par 96): **94,93,93,78**
CSF £9.40 TOTE £11.40; EX 15.70.There was no bid for the winner.
Owner K B Hodges **Bred** D R Tucker **Trained** Charlton Mackrell, Somerset
■ Stewards' Enquiry : Michael O'Connell three-day ban: used whip with excessive frequency (May 10-12)

FOCUS
A trappy 3-y-o seller. The winner is rated to his latter 2yo form.

1586 JOHN ALLEN 60TH BIRTHDAY CELEBRATION H'CAP 1m 5f 194y(P)
7:25 (7:26) (Class 6) (0-65,65) 4-Y-0+ **£1,706** (£503; £252) **Stalls** Low

Form RPR

2-10 **1** **Storm Hawk (IRE)**[21] [1148] 4-9-5 **62**..........................(p) WilliamBuick 10 70
(Pat Eddery) *chsd ldrs: led wl over 1f out: sn rdn and hung lft: jst hld on* **13/2**[3]

-312 **2** *hd* **Blackstone Vegas**[7] [1473] 5-9-1 **56**.......................... RobbieFitzpatrick 3 64
(Derek Shaw) *hld up: hdwy 7f out: rdn over 1f out: r.o* **9/4**[1]

5225 **3** 1 **Leyte Gulf (USA)**[25] [1080] 8-9-7 **62**.......................... DaneO'Neill 9 68
(Chris Bealby) *s.i.s: hld up: hdwy over 2f out: rdn over 1f out: styd on* **10/1**

3432 **4** *nse* **Hallstatt (IRE)**[21] [1156] 5-9-10 **65**..........................(t) PaulHanagan 5 71
(John Mackie) *hld up: hdwy over 4f out: rdn over 2f out: styd on u.p* **9/2**[2]

0-00 **5** 7 **Paint The Town Red**[64] [630] 6-8-5 **46** oh1..........................(p) LukeMorris 1 42
(Richard Guest) *chsd ldrs: rdn over 1f out: wknd ins fnl f* **20/1**

3021 **6** 2¾ **Money Money Money**[18] [1218] 5-9-9 **64**..........................(b) JamesMillman 8 57
(Rod Millman) *trckd ldr: racd keenly: led 3f out: rdn and hdd wl over 1f out: wknd ins fnl f* **13/2**[3]

6053 **7** 12 **Miles Of Sunshine**[7] [1473] 6-8-10 **51**.......................... RichardHughes 2 27
(Ron Hodges) *led: rdn and hdd 3f out: wknd wl over 1f out* **13/2**[3]

0622 **8** 5 **Plush**[25] [1081] 8-9-10 **65**.......................... RussKennemore 6 34
(Shaun Lycett) *s.s: hld up: a bhd* **11/1**

00-0 **9** *41* **Roxy Spirit (IRE)**[46] 836 4-8-0 **46** oh1 .... JamesSullivan(3) 7 —
(Michael Mullineaux) plld hrd and prom: stdd and lost pl over 10f out: rdn 7f out: wknd 5f out: t.o **150/1**

3m 2.87s (-3.13) **Going Correction** -0.10s/f (Stan)
WFA 4 from 5yo+ 2lb **9** Ran SP% **111.8**
Speed ratings (Par 101): **104,103,103,103,99 97,90,88,64**
toteswingers:1&2 £5.40, 2&3 £4.70, 1&3 £7.90 CSF £20.53 CT £142.17 TOTE £7.90: £2.20, £1.10, £3.10; EX 33.30.
Owner Storm Hawk Partnership **Bred** Rodger O'Dwyer **Trained** Nether Winchendon, Bucks

FOCUS
A moderate staying handicap and another race with plenty of course form on offer. There was something of an uneven pace on, but there were no obvious excuses. Ordinary but sound form, the winner back to his old best.

1587 PUNCHESTOWN LIVE ON ATR SKY 415 FILLIES' H'CAP 1m 141y(P)
8:00 (8:01) (Class 5) (0-70,69) 4-Y-O+ **£2,388** (£705; £352) **Stalls** Low

Form RPR
053- **1** **Nahab**[320] 2901 4-9-7 **69** .... TedDurcan 6 81+
(David Lanigan) hld up: hdwy over 1f out: r.o to ld nr fin **10/11**[1]
0602 **2** *1 1/4* **Sweet Possession (USA)**[7] 1474 5-8-4 **55** oh10..(p) JamesSullivan(3) 7 62
(Pat Eddery) led: clr 5f out: rdn 1f out: hdd nr fin **14/1**
5321 **3** *1/2* **Moresweets 'n Lace**[17] 1233 4-9-5 **67** .... GeorgeBaker 3 73
(Gary Moore) chsd ldrs: shkn up over 2f out: rdn and hung lft ins fnl f: r.o: wnt 3rd post **11/4**[2]
45-3 **4** *shd* **Scorn (USA)**[11] 1353 4-9-3 **65** .... RichardHughes 2 71
(Richard Hannon) chsd ldrs: rdn over 1f out: styd on: lost 3rd post **6/1**[3]
646- **5** *1 1/2* **Wood Fair**[186] 7055 4-8-4 **55** oh1 .... PatrickDonaghy(3) 4 57
(Mrs K Burke) hld up: rdn and hdwy over 1f out: styd on: nt rch ldrs **25/1**
330 **6** *1 1/4* **Hill Tribe**[14] 1292 4-9-6 **68** .... WilliamBuick 1 67
(Richard Guest) chsd ldr: rdn over 2f out: styd on same pce ins fnl f **14/1**

1m 51.34s (0.84) **Going Correction** -0.10s/f (Stan) **6** Ran SP% **110.5**
Speed ratings (Par 100): **92,90,90,90,89 87**
CSF £14.88 TOTE £1.70: £1.10, £5.60; EX 15.90.
Owner Saif Ali **Bred** Rabbah Bloodstock Limited **Trained** Newmarket, Suffolk

FOCUS
This modest fillies' handicap proved to be a funny race and the form is to be treated with caution, but there is no doubting the best horse prevailed. She is probably better than the bare form.

1588 STAY AT THE WOLVERHAMPTON HOLIDAY INN H'CAP 1m 1f 103y(P)
8:30 (8:30) (Class 6) (0-60,60) 3-Y-O **£1,706** (£503; £252) **Stalls** Low

Form RPR
3322 **1** **Little Jazz**[14] 1293 3-9-4 **60** .... AndrewHeffernan(3) 3 69
(Paul D'Arcy) chsd ldrs: rdn to ld ins fnl f: hung lft: styd on **4/1**[2]
000- **2** *hd* **Ishikawa (IRE)**[181] 7178 3-8-10 **49** .... FergusSweeney 6 58
(Alan King) hld up: plld hrd: hdwy over 2f out: rdn and hung lft fr over 1f out: r.o wl **8/1**
033- **3** *1 3/4* **Countrywide Flame**[137] 7813 3-9-5 **58** ....(p) PhillipMakin 2 63
(Kevin Ryan) led: rdn over 1f out: hdd and unable qck ins fnl f **15/2**
4454 **4** *8* **Lindo Erro**[17] 1251 3-8-13 **52** .... PaulHanagan 4 40
(John Mackie) chsd ldr: rdn over 2f out: wknd over 1f out **12/1**
05-0 **5** *6* **Bobby Dazzler (IRE)**[20] 1189 3-9-6 **59** .... JamesDoyle 5 35
(Sylvester Kirk) hld up in tch: rdn and wknd 3f out **18/1**
050- **6** *8* **Kaifi (IRE)**[240] 5558 3-8-7 **46** oh1 .... ChrisCatlin 7 —
(Clive Brittain) hld up: rdn over 3f out: sn wknd **11/1**
000- **7** *3/4* **Al Furat (USA)**[229] 5892 3-9-0 **53** ....(b[1]) TedDurcan 1 —
(David Lanigan) chsd ldrs: rdn over 3f out: wknd over 2f out **11/4**[1]
40-4 **8** *67* **Flinty**[11] 1354 3-9-0 **53** .... RichardHughes 8 —
(Richard Hannon) hld up: shkn up over 3f out: wknd and eased sn after: t.o **9/2**[3]

2m 1.14s (-0.56) **Going Correction** -0.10s/f (Stan) **8** Ran SP% **109.0**
Speed ratings (Par 96): **98,97,96,89,83 76,76,16**
CSF £32.14 CT £205.66 TOTE £5.30: £1.10, £3.20, £3.60; EX 40.20.
Owner K Snell **Bred** K Snell **Trained** Newmarket, Suffolk

FOCUS
A moderate 3-y-o handicap with some potential improvers lurking. Few landed a blow from off the pace and the principals came clear. The favourite disappointed and the third is the bset guide.
Flinty Official explanation: trainer's rep said colt had a breathing problem

1589 SPONSOR A RACE BY CALLING 01902 390000 MAIDEN STKS 5f 20y(P)
9:00 (9:03) (Class 5) 3-4-Y-O **£1,942** (£578; £288; £144) **Stalls** Low

Form RPR
306- **1** **Gottcher**[190] 6986 3-9-3 68 .... PhillipMakin 2 76
(David Barron) chsd ldr: led over 3f out: edgd rt and clr over 1f out: r.o **7/2**[2]
-066 **2** *4 1/2* **Lady Mango (IRE)**[32] 964 3-8-12 57 .... LukeMorris 11 55
(Ronald Harris) hld up: rdn and r.o ins fnl f: no ch w wnr **28/1**
-2 **3** *3/4* **Ginzan**[18] 1217 3-8-12 0 .... TomMcLaughlin 7 52
(Malcolm Saunders) mid-div: reminders over 3f out: hdwy 1/2-way: styd on **13/2**[3]
00- **4** *nse* **Speightowns Kid (USA)**[288] 3959 3-9-3 0 .... WilliamBuick 13 57
(Matthew Salaman) sn chsng ldrs: rdn over 1f out: styd on same pce ins fnl f **7/1**
02- **5** *shd* **Arrow Storm (USA)**[150] 7603 3-9-3 0 .... RichardKingscote 9 57
(Tom Dascombe) hld up: hdwy over 1f out: nt rch ldrs **11/4**[1]
6 **6** *1* **Colourbearer (IRE)**[7] 1459 4-9-13 0 .... DaneO'Neill 12 57
(Milton Bradley) s.i.s: hld up: hdwy over 1f out: nvr nrr **28/1**
2434 **7** *1/2* **Gorgeous Goblin (IRE)**[7] 1464 4-9-5 48 ....(vt) JamesSullivan(3) 6 50
(David C Griffiths) prom: rdn over 1f out: styd on same pce **9/1**
66-3 **8** *2 1/2* **Stravsambition**[25] 1084 3-8-12 62 .... GrahamGibbons 4 37
(Reg Hollinshead) chsd ldrs: rdn over 1f out: wknd ins fnl f **7/1**
9 *1 1/2* **Lucky Country (IRE)** 3-8-12 0 ....(t) RobertHavlin 1 32
(Jeremy Gask) hld up: hdwy over 1f out: wknd ins fnl f **12/1**
-006 **10** *1 1/2* **Renesmee (IRE)**[18] 1217 3-8-12 42 .... RobbieFitzpatrick 5 27
(Peter Grayson) sn pushed along in rr: bhd fr 1/2-way **125/1**
505 **11** *2* **Marvellous City (IRE)**[26] 1065 3-9-3 47 .... AdamKirby 8 24
(Mandy Rowland) led: hdd over 3f out: rdn 1/2-way: wknd over 1f out **28/1**

61.39 secs (-0.91) **Going Correction** -0.10s/f (Stan)
WFA 3 from 4yo 10lb **11** Ran SP% **116.1**
Speed ratings (Par 103): **103,95,94,94,94 92,91,87,85,83 79**
toteswingers:1&2 £19.50, 2&3 £14.90, 1&3 £6.40 CSF £102.66 TOTE £3.50: £1.20, £6.20, £2.80; EX 116.20.
Owner Twinacre Nurseries Ltd **Bred** Peter Webb **Trained** Maunby, N Yorks

FOCUS
A weak maiden but a clear-cut winner who looks improved. The time compared favourably with the earlier handicap.
T/Plt: £183.70 to a £1 stake. Pool of £50,278.65 - 199.80 winning tickets. T/Qpdt: £66.70 to a £1 stake. Pool of £5,039.72 - 55.90 winning tickets. CR

1568 YARMOUTH (L-H)
Tuesday, April 26

OFFICIAL GOING: Good to firm (8.0)
Wind: gusty, behind Weather: overcast, brighter spells, chilly

1590 WT WASTE SKIP HIRE MAIDEN AUCTION STKS 5f 43y
2:10 (2:10) (Class 6) 2-Y-O **£1,878** (£558; £279; £139) **Stalls** High

Form RPR
43 **1** **Mousie**[14] 1290 2-7-13 0 .... KieranO'Neill(5) 4 63
(Alan McCabe) mde all: rdn and wnt clr over 1f out: in n.d after: comf **11/1**
5 **2** *3 1/4* **Marie's Fantasy**[12] 1337 2-8-7 0 ow1 .... KierenFallon 6 58
(Gay Kelleway) in tch: trckd ldng pair over 2f out: rdn and effrt to chse clr wnr over 1f out: no imp and wl hld ins fnl f **1/1**[1]
3 **3** *3/4* **Xyzzy**[19] 1192 2-8-6 0 .... RoystonFfrench 3 54
(Linda Stubbs) bustled along leaving leaving stalls: chsd wnr: rdn and edgd lft 1/2-way: outpcd and lost 2nd over 1f out: 3rd and wl hld ins fnl f **5/1**[3]
4 *5* **Indian Lizzy** 2-8-4 0 .... NickyMackay 5 34
(Paul Cole) sn outpcd in last pair: wnt modest 4th ent fnl f: nvr on terms **7/2**[2]
6 **5** *1 3/4* **The Coulbeck Kid**[22] 1129 2-8-9 0 .... DavidProbert 1 33
(Des Donovan) chsd ldrs tl 1/2-way: sn edging lft and rdn: wknd wl over 1f out **33/1**
6 *15* **Masivo Man (IRE)** 2-8-6 0 .... AdamBeschizza(5) 2 —
(Chris Dwyer) s.i.s: a in rr: rdn and struggling whn hmpd ent fnl 2f: sn wknd: wl bhd and eased ins fnl f: t.o **8/1**

63.01 secs (0.31) **Going Correction** -0.15s/f (Firm) **6** Ran SP% **111.3**
Speed ratings (Par 90): **91,85,84,76,73 49**
toteswingers:1&2 £2.80, 2&3 £1.70, 1&3 £2.70 CSF £22.39 TOTE £21.20: £9.40, £1.10; EX 25.90.
Owner Lucky Heather **Bred** Llety Stud **Trained** Averham Park, Notts

FOCUS
A low-grade juvenile maiden. Improved form from the winner, with the race rated around the next two.

NOTEBOOK
Mousie, switching to turf after two frame placings on the AW, made virtually all the running for a smooth success. Quickly out of the stalls, she eased across to the stands' rail and, once there, was never headed. She was not hard-pressed to score, but this is not strong form. (op 14-1 tchd 10-1)
Marie's Fantasy, fifth in a Newmarket maiden on her only previous run, did little to boost that race. Backed beforehand, she broke adequately, racing close-up in fourth in the early stages, before attempting to make a challenge from halfway. Her response for pressure was disappointing, though, and she only just managed to grab second. (op 5-4)
Xyzzy, third of four at Kempton on her only previous run, probably did not have to improve to fill the same position here. She was second for much of the journey, but overtaken by the runner-up in the closing stages. (op 4-1)
Indian Lizzy, an inexpensively-bought newcomer form a family of sprinters, did not show enough to suggest she will soon be winning. (op 11-4)
The Coulbeck Kid, last of six on his only start before this, already looks exposed as very moderate. Sellers probably beckon. (op 40-1)
Masivo Man(IRE), a gelded newcomer, was slowly away and always struggling. (op 10-1 tchd 11-1)

1591 MATTHEW CLARK MEDIAN AUCTION MAIDEN STKS 6f 3y
2:40 (2:42) (Class 5) 3-4-Y-O **£2,525** (£751; £375; £187) **Stalls** High

Form RPR
00-4 **1** **Button Moon (IRE)**[13] 1317 3-8-12 82 ....(p) MartinLane 7 80+
(Ian Wood) a travelling wl: pressed ldr tl led wl over 3f out: nudged along and readily wnt clr over 1f out: v easily **10/11**[1]
2 *3 1/4* **Moone's My Name** 3-8-12 0 .... JimCrowley 3 70+
(Ralph Beckett) in tch on outer: effrt to chse wnr 2f out: rdn and outpcd by wnr over 1f out: kpt on for clr 2nd but no ch **7/4**[2]
00- **3** *4* **Pearl Blue (IRE)**[194] 6878 3-8-12 0 .... NeilCallan 4 57+
(Chris Wall) s.i.s: sn swtchd rt and hld up towards rr: rdn and hdwy 2f out: kpt on ins fnl f: no ch w wnr **12/1**[3]
5 **4** *3 1/4* **Miakora**[28] 1020 3-8-12 0 .... FrannyNorton 10 46
(Michael Quinn) dwlt: sn rcvrd and in tch in midfield: rdn and unable qck ent fnl 2f: modest 4th whn nt clr run and swtchd rt over 1f out: styd on same pce and no ch after **33/1**
5 *1 1/2* **West Side (IRE)** 3-9-3 0 ....(t) DarryllHolland 2 47+
(Jeremy Noseda) s.i.s: sn pushed along and rn green in rr: swtchd rt and hdwy over 1f out: styd on past btn horses ins fnl f: n.d **12/1**[3]
00- **6** *1 3/4* **Alspritza**[179] 7201 3-8-12 0 .... JackMitchell 1 36
(Chris Wall) hld up in tch: shkn up and effrt jst over 2f out: pressing for 3rd but no ch w wnr whn hld hd high and racd awkwardly over 1f out: wknd ins fnl f **100/1**
0 **7** *1 1/4* **Zanoubiatta (USA)**[21] 1146 3-8-12 0 .... KierenFallon 6 32
(Ed Dunlop) chsd ldrs: chsd wnr over 3f out: rdn and nt qckn over 2f out: wknd u.p over 1f out **14/1**
8 *4 1/2* **Zagalinis Speech** 3-8-12 0 .... DavidProbert 5 18
(J R Jenkins) hmpd s: t.k.h and hld up in midfield: rdn and struggling 3f out: hung lft and wknd over 2f out **100/1**
000- **9** *6* **Algurayn (IRE)**[169] 7378 3-9-3 60 .... KirstyMilczarek 9 —
(George Prodromou) led tl 3f out: sn struggling: wknd over 2f out: t.o **50/1**
00-0 **10** *13* **Mint Imperial (IRE)**[19] 1203 3-9-3 42 .... NickyMackay 11 —
(Amy Weaver) s.i.s: a bhd: eased fnl 100yds: t.o **100/1**
0-00 **11** *16* **Exceedingthestars**[11] 1358 4-9-9 32 .... WilliamCarson 8 —
(Michael Squance) taken down early: t.k.h: hld up in tch: lost pl 4f out: bhd and hung lft 2f out: eased ent fnl f: t.o **125/1**

1m 12.6s (-1.80) **Going Correction** -0.15s/f (Firm)
WFA 3 from 4yo 11lb **11** Ran SP% **119.5**
Speed ratings (Par 103): **106,101,96,92,90 87,86,80,72,54 33**
toteswingers: 1&2 £1.60, 1&3 £3.80, 2&3 £4.30 CSF £2.64 TOTE £1.80: £1.10, £1.40, £2.40; EX 4.10 Trifecta £19.10 Pool: £753.78 - 29.11 winning units. .
Owner Paddy Barrett **Bred** Ballylinch Stud **Trained** Upper Lambourn, Berks

FOCUS
Not a lot of obvious depth to this ordinary-looking maiden. The winner did not need to improve and was not far off her sales race form.

Exceedingthestars Official explanation: jockey said filly moved poorly

1592 GREAT YARMOUTH TOURISM INDUSTRY (S) STKS — 1m 2f 21y
3:10 (3:14) (Class 6) 3-4-Y-O **£1,683** (£501; £250; £125) **Stalls** Low

Form	Pos	Dist	Horse / Trainer / Comment	Jockey	RPR
445	**1**		**Song To The Moon (IRE)**[23] 1114 4-9-4 72 (b) (George Baker) *s.i.s: hld up in last pair: hdwy to chse ldng trio 3f out: effrt ent fnl 2f: rdn to ld over 1f out: sn in command: easily* **2/5**[1]	FrankieDettori 2	63
-032	**2**	*7*	**Back For Tea (IRE)**[6] 1500 3-8-6 47 (Phil McEntee) *t.k.h: chsd ldr tl led 4f out: rdn ent fnl 3f: hdd over 1f out: sn outpcd by wnr: kpt on for 2nd* **28/1**	WilliamCarson 1	51
0-00	**3**	*4½*	**Fawley Green**[15] 1267 4-9-9 67 (William Muir) *t.k.h: chsd ldng pair: wnt 2nd over 3f out: rdn and unable qck ent fnl 2f: wknd jst over 1f out* **8/1**[3]	KierenFallon 4	45
4225	**4**	*1*	**Not So Bright (USA)**[10] 1400 3-8-6 57 (v) (Des Donovan) *dwlt and pushed along early: racd in last pair: hdwy to chse ldng pair over 3f out: rdn and nt qckn 2f out: wknd jst over 1f out* **9/2**[2]	DavidProbert 3	43
00-0	**5**	*13*	**Rural Pursuits**[26] 1060 3-8-1 52 (Christine Dunnett) *led rdrless to s: in tch: rdn and struggling 4f out: wknd over 2f out: eased ins fnl f: t.o* **66/1**	NickyMackay 5	—
455-	**6**	*2½*	**Penderyn**[154] 7538 4-9-4 47 (Charles Smith) *led: clr 6f out tl rdn and hdd 4f out: wknd u.p 3f out: eased wl ins fnl f: t.o* **50/1**	MartinLane 6	—

2m 8.88s (-1.62) **Going Correction** -0.15s/f (Firm)
WFA 3 from 4yo 17lb **6** Ran SP% **107.6**
Speed ratings (Par 101): **100,94,90,90,79 77**
toteswingers:1&2 £2.30, 2&3 £3.00, 1&3 £1.70 CSF £14.44 TOTE £1.30: £1.10, £6.20; EX 7.80.The winner was bought in for 4,600gns.
Owner M Khan X2 **Bred** Michael Woodlock & Seamus Kennedy **Trained** Whitsbury, Hants

FOCUS
Few had obvious claims in this weak seller. The winner didn't need to run near her best.

1593 PLEASUREWOOD HILLS H'CAP — 1m 2f 21y
3:40 (3:40) (Class 5) (0-75,75) 3-Y-O **£2,331** (£693; £346; £173) **Stalls** Low

Form	Pos	Dist	Horse / Trainer / Comment	Jockey	RPR
14-2	**1**		**Ivan Vasilevich (IRE)**[97] 217 3-8-10 73 (Jane Chapple-Hyam) *chsd ldr: jnd ldr 5f out: led 2f out: rdn ent fnl f: r.o wl* **11/2**	LewisWalsh(7) 2	78
2334	**2**	*1¾*	**Black Pond (USA)**[13] 1311 3-9-4 74 (Mark Johnston) *led at stdy gallop: stdd 5f out: reminders and qcknd ent fnl 4f: drvn over 2f out: hdd over 1f out: kpt on same pce ins fnl f* **12/1**	KierenFallon 6	76
5-12	**3**	*nk*	**Sammy Alexander**[39] 890 3-9-2 72 (David Simcock) *stdd s: hld wl in tch in last pair: hdwy 4f out: pressed ldrs and drvn over 1f out: styd on same pce ins fnl f* **11/2**	MartinLane 5	73
622-	**4**	*shd*	**Cadore (IRE)**[208] 6514 3-9-5 75 (Peter Chapple-Hyam) *t.k.h early: in tch: effrt and nt clr run 2f out tl ent fnl f: kpt on u.p towards fin* **10/3**[2]	JackMitchell 4	76
432-	**5**	*1*	**Arabian Star (IRE)**[227] 5947 3-9-5 75 (Mick Channon) *stdd s: t.k.h: chsd ldrs: rdn and effrt on outer over 2f out: unable qck u.p over 1f out: styd on one pce ins fnl f* **11/4**[1]	SamHitchcott 1	74
0-14	**6**	*1¾*	**Dazzling Valentine**[10] 1392 3-9-2 75 (Alan Bailey) *stdd s: t.k.h: hld up in last pair: effrt on rail 3f out: outpcd wl over 1f out: one pce and n.d fnl f* **7/2**[3]	AmyBaker(3) 3	71

2m 11.17s (0.67) **Going Correction** -0.15s/f (Firm) **6** Ran SP% **110.4**
Speed ratings (Par 98): **91,89,89,89,88 87**
CSF £59.96 TOTE £3.80: £2.30, £4.40; EX 31.20.
Owner Chris Fahy **Bred** Liam Butler **Trained** Dalham, Suffolk

FOCUS
A fair handicap, with the top weight rated 75, which looked very competitive on paper. It was slowly run and the winner is rated in line with his latest effort.

1594 MATTHEW CLARK H'CAP — 7f 3y
4:10 (4:11) (Class 3) (0-95,95) 4-Y-O+ **£6,560** (£1,963; £981; £490; £244) **Stalls** High

Form	Pos	Dist	Horse / Trainer / Comment	Jockey	RPR
041-	**1**		**Excellent Guest**[214] 6321 4-8-13 87 (George Margarson) *chsd ldrs: wnt 2nd over 3f out: upsides ldr 2f out: rdn ent fnl f: led fnl 100yds: kpt on* **20/1**	PhilipRobinson 7	95
2521	**2**	*nk*	**Bawaardi (IRE)**[10] 1382 5-8-9 83 (Richard Fahey) *taken down early: racd in last trio: rdn along over 4f out: hdwy u.p over 1f out: styd on wl ins fnl f: pressing wnr cl home* **10/1**	FrederikTylicki 5	90+
26-0	**3**	*1¼*	**Seek The Fair Land**[108] 99 5-8-7 81 oh3 (b) (Jim Boyle) *led: rdn wl over 1f out: hdd fnl 100yds: wknd towards fin* **33/1**	NickyMackay 3	84
1/2-	**4**	*2*	**Asraab (IRE)**[258] 4963 4-9-4 92 (Saeed Bin Suroor) *in tch in midfield: rdn 3f out: edgd lft and no imp u.p over 1f out: kpt on fnl 100yds: nvr gng pce to threaten ldrs* **4/5**[1]	FrankieDettori 6	90
501-	**5**	*¾*	**Gouray Girl (IRE)**[185] 7097 4-9-7 95 (Walter Swinburn) *stdd s: hld up in last trio: hdwy in centre over 2f out: chsd ldng pair over 1f out: rdn: hung lft and unable qck 1f out: wknd* **9/1**	ShaneKelly 2	91
000-	**6**	*1½*	**Noble Citizen (USA)**[151] 7574 6-8-13 92 (David Simcock) *stdd s: in rr: hdwy and nt clr run 2f out: sn swtchd rt: no real hdwy after: nvr trbld ldrs* **16/1**	LauraPike(5) 9	84
210-	**7**	*6*	**Swiss Cross**[175] 7289 4-8-10 84 (v) (Gerard Butler) *plld hrd: chsd ldrs: rdn over 2f out: wknd wl over 1f out: eased ins fnl f* **8/1**[3]	NeilCallan 4	60
15-0	**8**	*7*	**Mata Keranjang (USA)**[24] 1092 4-9-0 88 (b) (Paul Cole) *chsd ldr tl over 3f out: hrd drvn and fnd nil over 2f out: wknd wl over 1f out: wl bhd and eased ins fnl f* **6/1**[2]	JamieSpencer 1	45

1m 24.25s (-2.35) **Going Correction** -0.15s/f (Firm) **8** Ran SP% **113.6**
Speed ratings (Par 107): **107,106,105,102,102 100,93,85**
toteswingers:1&2 £9.60, 2&3 £15.00, 1&3 £35.20 CSF £198.01 CT £6447.76 TOTE £23.20: £4.60, £2.10, £5.00; EX 98.00 TRIFECTA Not won. .
Owner John Guest Racing **Bred** John Guest Racing Ltd **Trained** Newmarket, Suffolk

FOCUS
Easily the most interesting event on the card and, although there was an odds-on favourite, several had sound form claims. Probably only ordinary form for the grade, but a personal best from the winner.

NOTEBOOK
Excellent Guest, 7lb higher than when winning at Ascot in September, made light of that rise on this seasonal reappearance. Always in the first three, he hit the front around the 1f pole and responded well to driving. This was a sound display, but the handicapper will surely take note. (op 16-1)
Bawaardi(IRE), up 3lb since taking an amateurs' handicap ten days earlier, seems a feasible marker for the form. Held up early on, he began to make progress at halfway and finished with a flourish. He is in good form, but may well edge up the ratings again after this. (op 15-2)
Seek The Fair Land was racing from 3lb out of the handicap and ran nicely given that fact. Quickly away and soon in front, he led until the winner swept past and battled on gamely thereafter. (op 28-1)
Asraab(IRE), 7lb higher than when a hampered second at Sandown in August 2010, was heavily-backed beforehand. He never appeared likely to collect, however, needing to be vigorously ridden by halfway and failing to quicken significantly when really pressed. He did stay on in the closing stages, but not nearly fast enough to give his supporters any realistic hope. (op Evens tchd 11-10 in places)
Gouray Girl(IRE) had been raised 7lb since scoring on her last start at Newbury 165 days earlier and that increase proved beyond her here. She may improve for this seasonal bow but, unless she does, life will be tough from her current mark. Official explanation: jockey said filly hung left (op 10-1)
Noble Citizen(USA), without a victory since 2008, never promised to end his losing sequence. In rear early on, he made only limited late progress. (op 20-1)
Swiss Cross Official explanation: jockey said gelding ran too free

1595 BBC RADIO NORFOLK H'CAP — 5f 43y
4:40 (4:40) (Class 5) (0-70,65) 3-Y-O **£2,331** (£693; £346; £173) **Stalls** High

Form	Pos	Dist	Horse / Trainer / Comment	Jockey	RPR
25-1	**1**		**Novabridge**[14] 1280 3-9-5 63 (b) (Andrew Haynes) *wnt lft s: blinkers c loose sn after s and rdr removed them after 100yds: rdn along towards rr: swtchd lft and hdwy u.p ent fnl f: str run fnl 100yds: led last stride* **3/1**[3]	KierenFallon 6	67
00-1	**2**	*shd*	**Paradise Place**[25] 1078 3-9-1 59 (Robert Cowell) *squeezed s and s.i.s: sn in tch: chsd ldr wl over 1f out: rdn and ev ch ent fnl f: led wl ins fnl f: hdd last stride* **2/1**[1]	FrankieDettori 5	63
4624	**3**	*¾*	**Johnny Hancocks (IRE)**[3] 1514 3-9-7 65 (Linda Stubbs) *led for 1f: chsd ldr tl led again 2f out: drvn over 1f out: hdd wl ins fnl f: no ex towards fin* **11/4**[2]	RoystonFfrench 2	66
6502	**4**	*1¾*	**Dangerous Illusion (IRE)**[14] 1280 3-8-7 51 oh6 (Michael Quinn) *chsd ldng pair: rdn and effrt wl over 1f out: styd on same pce ins fnl f* **20/1**	FrannyNorton 1	46
6510	**5**	*½*	**Pineapple Pete (IRE)**[13] 1306 3-8-12 63 (t) (Alan McCabe) *pushed lft s and s.i.s: bhd: effrt and edgd lft over 1f out: kpt on ins fnl f: nvr trbld ldrs* **10/1**	RyanTate(7) 3	56
65-2	**6**	*3½*	**My Love Fajer (IRE)**[26] 1065 3-9-7 65 (George Prodromou) *taken down early: chsd ldr tl led after 1f: hdd and drvn 2f out: wknd ins fnl f* **11/2**	KirstyMilczarek 7	45

62.38 secs (-0.32) **Going Correction** -0.15s/f (Firm) **6** Ran SP% **114.2**
Speed ratings (Par 98): **96,95,94,91,91 85**
toteswingers:1&2 £1.90, 2&3 £2.10, 1&3 £1.90 CSF £9.72 TOTE £3.90: £1.30, £1.80; EX 10.10.
Owner Dajam Ltd **Bred** Bishopswood Bloodstock & Trickledown Stud **Trained** Limpley Stoke, Bath

FOCUS
A low-grade handicap, in which the top weight was rated just 65. The exposed third helps with the standard.
Novabridge Official explanation: jockey said blinkers became loose due to combination of high wind and gelding stretching and the velcro attaching the equipment became loose, moving round and interfering with vision, he therefore removed them.

1596 TIME & TIDE MUSEUM H'CAP — 2m
5:10 (5:10) (Class 5) (0-70,70) 4-Y-O+ **£2,331** (£693; £346; £173) **Stalls** High

Form	Pos	Dist	Horse / Trainer / Comment	Jockey	RPR
24-3	**1**		**Not Til Monday (IRE)**[14] 1282 5-9-11 65 (v1) (J R Jenkins) *mde virtually all: pushed along and clr over 1f out: rdn and styd on wl fr over 1f out* **7/2**[2]	KierenFallon 1	75
12-3	**2**	*3¼*	**Motirani**[14] 1297 4-9-4 65 (Lydia Pearce) *in tch: rdn and effrt 4f out: chsd clr wnr u.p 2f out: sme hdwy ent fnl f: no hdwy and btn fnl 100yds* **8/1**	SimonPearce(3) 2	71
24-3	**3**	*2*	**Wester Ross (IRE)**[18] 33 7-9-2 56 (b) (James Eustace) *reminder sn after s: a in rr: sme hdwy 2f out: hung lft over 1f out: wnt 3rd ins fnl f: nvr trbld wnr* **9/2**[3]	MickyFenton 5	60
55-5	**4**	*2¾*	**Corr Point (IRE)**[21] 1148 4-9-12 70 (Jamie Osborne) *stdd s: t.k.h: chsd ldrs: rdn to chse clr wnr over 3f out tl 2f out: wknd ent fnl f* **7/4**[1]	NeilCallan 4	70
2205	**5**	*9*	**Pinsplitter (USA)**[7] 1461 4-8-5 54 (p) (Alan McCabe) *stdd s: hld up in last pair: rdn 4f out: swtchd rt and drvn 3f out: sn struggling: wl btn fnl 2f* **9/2**[3]	KieranO'Neill(5) 6	44
0-36	**6**	*7*	**Astroleo**[34] 373 5-8-0 47 oh2 (Mark H Tompkins) *w wnr for 2f: chsd wnr after tl over 3f out: wknd u.p over 2f out* **25/1**	CharlesEddery(7) 7	35

3m 28.53s (-3.87) **Going Correction** -0.15s/f (Firm)
WFA 4 from 5yo+ 4lb **6** Ran SP% **109.9**
Speed ratings (Par 103): **103,101,100,99,94 94**
toteswingers:1&2 £2.10, 2&3 £2.70, 1&3 £2.70. Tote Super 7: Win: not won. Place: Not won. CSF £28.57 TOTE £4.30: £2.70, £4.50; EX 19.40.
Owner The Three Honest Men **Bred** G J King **Trained** Royston, Herts

FOCUS
No superstars here, with the top weight rated 70, but few could be confidently discounted. A fair time for the grade and the winner's getting closer to his old form.
T/Plt: £90.40 to a £1 stake. Pool: of £45,316.43 - 365.66 winning tickets. T/Qpdt: £40.50 to a £1 stake. Pool of £2,827.56 - 51.55 winning tickets. SP

1551 LONGCHAMP (R-H)
Tuesday, April 26

OFFICIAL GOING: Turf: good

1597a PRIX DE LA MADELEINE (CONDITIONS) (3YO FILLIES) (TURF) — 1m 3f
1:50 (12:00) 3-Y-O **£12,500** (£5,000; £3,750; £2,500; £1,250)

Pos	Dist	Horse / Trainer	Jockey	RPR
1		**Testosterone (IRE)**[22] 3-8-9 0 (P Bary, France) **9/5**[1]	Christophe-PatriceLemaire 8	82
2	*5*	**Goldtara (FR)**[175] 3-9-2 0 (A Lyon, France) **31/1**	RaphaelMarchelli 3	80
3	*snk*	**Gagarina (IRE)** 3-9-2 0 (J-C Rouget, France) **2/1**[2]	IoritzMendizabal 2	80
4	*nk*	**Karsabruni (FR)** 3-8-13 0 (H-A Pantall, France) **9/1**	MaximeGuyon 6	76
5	*2*	**Elodie**[19] 3-9-2 0 (F Head, France) **4/1**[3]	DavyBonilla 10	76
6	*1½*	**Style Show (USA)**[26] 3-8-9 0 (Mme C Head-Maarek, France) **22/1**	JohanVictoire 5	66
7	*4*	**Keyed Up (FR)**[29] 3-8-13 0 (F Doumen, France) **13/1**	ThierryThulliez 7	63

8 3/4 **Kirocco (FR)** 3-8-9 0 ThomasHuet 9 57
(F Doumen, France) **64/1**
9 10 **Pray From Heaven (IRE)** 3-8-9 0 StephanePasquier 4 39
(Sandor Kovacs, Hungary) **42/1**
10 1 1/2 **Sizzle (FR)**[17] 1252 3-8-9 0 MickaelBarzalona 1 37
(Tom Dascombe) *sn prom: rdn early in st: wknd qckly in st* **55/1**
2m 18.48s (-1.42) **10** Ran SP% **119.3**
WIN (incl. 1 euro stake): 2.80. PLACES: 1.20, 3.70, 1.30. DF: 62.00. SF: 70.50.
Owner Louis Duquesne **Bred** S C E A La Poterie **Trained** Chantilly, France

ASCOT (R-H)
Wednesday, April 27

OFFICIAL GOING: Good to firm (good in places; str 9.0; rnd 8.7)
Wind: Moderate ahead Weather: Sunny

1598 ALDERMORE CONDITIONS STKS 5f
2:00 (2:03) (Class 2) 2-Y-O **£8,100** (£2,425; £1,212; £607) **Stalls** High

Form RPR
1 **1** **Miss Work Of Art**[28] 1042 2-8-10 0 PaulHanagan 1 91+
(Richard Fahey) *s.i.s: sn pushed along and cl up: trckd ldr 2f out: drvn to chal 1f out: led ins fnl f: asserted fnl 120yds: readily* **5/1**[2]
1 **2** 1 3/4 **Magic City (IRE)**[12] 1360 2-9-1 0 RichardHughes 3 90
(Richard Hannon) *sn led: pushed along ins fnl 2f: jnd 1f out: hdd ins fnl f: no ex fnl 75yds* **1/4**[1]
21 **3** 4 **Dawn Lightning**[18] 1235 2-8-6 0 RichardMullen 4 66
(Alan McCabe) *trckd ldr 3f: sn rdn: outpcd by ldng duo over 1f out* **25/1**[3]
4 3 3/4 **Ewell Place (IRE)** 2-8-11 0 EddieAhern 5 57+
(Robert Mills) *loose bef s: a in 4th pl but in tch: pushed along and green 2f out: sn edging rt: no ch after* **50/1**
60.51 secs (-0.69) **Going Correction** +0.15s/f (Good) **4** Ran SP% **102.5**
Speed ratings (Par 98): **105,102,95,89**
CSF £6.13 TOTE £4.20; EX 5.00.
Owner Mel Roberts & Ms Nicola Meese 1 **Bred** Newsells Park Stud **Trained** Musley Bank, N Yorks
■ The Penny Horse (12/1) was withdrawn after refusing to enter the stalls. Deduct 5p in the £ under R4.

FOCUS
Not many runners but an interesting contest, and the market strongly suggested it was going to be a one-horse affair. However, those who took short odds before the race and amazingly 1.02 on Betfair in running were in for a nasty surprise. The third is the key to the form. The winner is improving but Magic City is 10-16lb off a typical Norfolk winner at this stage.

NOTEBOOK
Miss Work Of Art ◆ looked impressive when successful at Lingfield in late March but wasn't given a lot of hope up against what looked a classy colt. She got away nicely although did need to be ridden for a few strides as the tempo increased, but she kept on powerfully and was well on top passing the line. The Fahey stable has been in great form recently, and this filly looks booked for a return to this course for the Royal meeting, but whether she is a Queen Mary or Albany type isn't clear quite yet. First port of call, however, will be the Listed Marygate Stakes at York's Dante meeting.
Magic City(IRE) created a big impression on his debut when winning with lots to spare at Newbury and was backed to the exclusion of his rivals here. Quickly away, he grabbed the rail and showed speed before finding little once joined. He reportedly returned home with sore shins and can be allowed another chance. (tchd 2-7 in places)
Dawn Lightning won an ordinary-looking Lingfield AW maiden after a promising start at Leicester behind an above average sort, but wasn't in the same league as the two here.
Ewell Place(IRE), a £22,000 yearling half-sister to useful Baby Houseman, faced a stiff task on his debut and didn't get his career off to a great start after spooking at the stalls, unshipping his rider and then bolting up and down the track for a while. Still allowed to take his chance despite his antics, he showed enough to suggest he's capable of winning a lesser contest.

1599 X FACTOR EBF STKS (CONDITIONS RACE) (FILLIES) 1m (R)
2:30 (2:32) (Class 3) 3-Y-O **£8,723** (£2,612; £1,306; £653; £326; £163) **Stalls** Low

Form RPR
40-0 **1** **Emma's Gift (IRE)**[18] 1234 3-8-7 92 AdamBeschizza(5) 5 88
(Julia Feilden) *in tch: pushed along 3f out: swtchd lft to outside over 2f out: styd on u.p ins fnl f to ld fnl 150yds: kpt on wl* **16/1**
1 **2** 3/4 **Metropolitain Miss (IRE)**[22] 1146 3-8-12 77 SamHitchcott 3 86
(Mick Channon) *sn trcking ldr: chal appr fnl 2f: hrd drvn to ld over 1f out: hdd and nt qckn fnl 150yds* **16/1**
120- **3** 2 1/4 **Flood Plain**[173] 7340 3-8-12 96 WilliamBuick 4 87+
(John Gosden) *hld up in rr: hdwy on ins 2f out: styng on strly whn hmpd jst ins fnl f: kpt on again cl home and fin wl to take 3rd but nt rcvr* **4/1**[2]
1 **4** 1 1/4 **Hezmah**[12] 1362 3-8-12 0 RichardHills 6 78
(John Gosden) *trckd ldrs: pushed along to chal over 2f out: drvn and stl upsides over 1f out: one pce whn edgd rt jst ins fnl f: wknd and lost 3rd cl home* **2/1**[1]
1 **5** 1 **Mystic Dream**[54] 775 3-9-1 0 MichaelHills 2 79
(B W Hills) *in tch: hdwy to chse ldrs over 2f out: sn edging rt and swtchd lft to outside: styd on same pce* **9/2**[3]
1 **6** 4 **Dubaianswer**[34] 952 3-8-12 82 AdamKirby 1 69
(Marco Botti) *sn led: jnd over 2f out: hdd over 1f out: wkng whn hmpd ins fnl f* **4/1**[2]
101- **7** 5 **Byrony (IRE)**[196] 6845 3-9-1 90 RichardHughes 7 58
(Richard Hannon) *a in last: lost tch fnl 3f* **17/2**
1m 41.43s (0.73) **Going Correction** +0.15s/f (Good) **7** Ran SP% **113.8**
Speed ratings (Par 99): **102,101,99,97,96 92,87**
toteswingers:1&2 £15.80, 2&3 £10.80, 1&3 £11.70 CSF £221.65 TOTE £17.80: £5.40, £6.10; EX 161.80.
Owner Mrs Emma Raffan **Bred** Mark Commins **Trained** Exning, Suffolk

FOCUS
It's probably fair to say that no big stars have emerged from this contest in recent times, so how strong this form will prove to be is debatable. This looked a slightly below-par renewal and the form is rated around the winner.

NOTEBOOK
Emma's Gift(IRE) made a reasonable return to action at Lingfield in early April, without suggesting she was going to win next time, so this has to go down as a surprising result even though she ran some good races as a juvenile on occasions, including at this course in the Albany Stakes last June. She could come back for the Listed Sandringham Handicap Stakes in June. (op 14-1)
Metropolitain Miss(IRE) was an unfancied 20-1 shot when winning at Kempton on her first outing (runner-up went off 33-1 and form hasn't been enhanced since), so seemingly improved greatly on that with a good run. However, it remains to be seen quite how good she can become.
Flood Plain ◆ ran well in two starts before finishing a disappointing last on a trip to Churchill Downs for the Breeders' Cup Juvenile Fillies Turf, where she had excuses. Holding a Group 1 Coronation Stakes entry, she was keeping on really well until her stablemate got in the way about 1f out, and it's certainly not difficult to argue that with a clear passage she would have won. (op 3-1)
Hezmah made a good start to her career when winning at Newbury in a newcomers' race recently after being well backed. Holding a Group 1 Coronation Stakes entry, she dwarfed most of her rivals and moved powerfully just behind the leaders, but swept slightly wide rounding the final bend, and after looking sure to play a part in the final outcome, she soon found little and ran a bit green. There should have more to come and she could be the best horse out of the race in the long-term. (op 9-4)
Mystic Dream won on her debut at Deauville on the Fibresand, but doesn't look the biggest and was readily held. (op 6-1)
Dubaianswer made a winning debut at Kempton but offered little here once joined in the lead. (op 11-2)
Byrony(IRE) enjoyed a fair amount of success at a juvenile from eight starts. Running under a penalty, she showed little at any stage. (op 8-1)

1600 BRITAIN'S GOT TALENT PARADISE STKS (LISTED RACE) 1m (S)
3:05 (3:05) (Class 1) 4-Y-O+ **£17,031** (£6,456; £3,231; £1,611; £807; £405) **Stalls** High

Form RPR
12-3 **1** **Side Glance**[11] 1397 4-9-0 106 JimmyFortune 1 119
(Andrew Balding) *hld up in tch: stdy hdwy fr 3f out: led wl over 1f out: pushed clr ins fnl f: easily* **10/3**[2]
0-11 **2** 6 **St Moritz (IRE)**[11] 1385 5-9-3 104 AdrianNicholls 3 108
(David Nicholls) *chsd ldr: rdn over 2f out and ev ch 2f out: chsd wnr over 1f out but nvr any ch: kpt on wl for clr 2nd* **8/1**
110- **3** 2 **Critical Moment (USA)**[250] 5274 4-9-0 108 MichaelHills 4 100
(B W Hills) *trckd ldrs: pushed along and outpcd over 2f out: styd on again ins fnl f to take 3rd fnl 50yds but no ch w ldng duo* **6/1**
25-1 **4** 1 **Eton Forever (IRE)**[25] 1092 4-9-0 103 NeilCallan 5 98
(Roger Varian) *trckd ldrs: rdn and hdwy over 2f out: nvr quite gng pce to chal: wknd ins fnl f* **11/4**[1]
54/- **5** nk **City Leader (IRE)**[535] 7313 6-9-0 111 MartinDwyer 6 97
(Brian Meehan) *in tch: drvn and hdwy to chse ldrs over 2f out: nvr quite on terms: outpcd appr fnl f* **16/1**
455- **6** 2 1/2 **Zacinto**[276] 4412 5-9-0 115 RyanMoore 8 92
(Sir Michael Stoute) *in rr: drvn along over 2f out: mod prog clsng stages* **4/1**[3]
040- **7** nk **Lord Zenith**[314] 3104 4-9-0 109 WilliamBuick 7 91
(Andrew Balding) *in tch: pushed along and outpcd over 3f out: wnt rt to far side of gp over 2f out: mod prog again cl home* **20/1**
140- **8** 1 1/4 **King Of Dixie (USA)**[291] 3888 7-9-0 108 JimCrowley 2 88
(William Knight) *sn led: hdd & wknd wl over 1f out* **12/1**
1m 39.6s (-1.00) **Going Correction** +0.15s/f (Good) **8** Ran SP% **113.5**
Speed ratings (Par 111): **111,105,103,102,101 99,98,97**
toteswingers:1&2 £4.90, 2&3 £5.00, 1&3 £4.70 CSF £29.44 TOTE £4.60: £1.50, £2.20, £2.00; EX 27.90 Trifecta £122.90 Pool: £932.16 - 5.61 winning units..
Owner Kingsclere Racing CLub **Bred** Kingsclere Stud **Trained** Kingsclere, Hants

FOCUS
There are positives and negatives to be taken from this race, in which the field soon made for the centre of the track. Side Glance impressed, but it's hard to think that much else ran its race. The form has been rated at something like face value.

NOTEBOOK
Side Glance, placed in a what looked a weaker Listed race recently over 7f, streaked right away from his rivals once in command and came home a clear winner. He had some good handicap form at Ascot in the past, so clearly loves the course, and one would imagine connections will try and find the right race for him at the Royal meeting if, indeed, there is a suitable one. He might stay 1m2f in time. (op 4-1 tchd 9-2 in places)
St Moritz(IRE) was defending an unbeaten record since joining this stable after winning both starts, including a Listed race on his previous outing. He also had some fair course form, but was the only runner under a penalty, and couldn't go with the winner once he took it up. Official explanation: jockey said gelding hung right
Critical Moment(USA) ◆, absent since August last year, appeared to get badly outpaced at about the mid-way point but kept on again and finished strongly. (op 7-1 tchd 15-2 in places)
Eton Forever(IRE), who made a striking return to the course when winning the Spring Mile at Doncaster in taking style, was a very useful and unexposed sort in a short career at three, and ran to about the level he should have done using official figures as a guide. (op 3-1 tchd 5-2 and 7-2 in places)
City Leader(IRE), having his first run since finishing down the field in an Italian Group 1 in November 2009, has a decent record at Ascot, including a win in the 2007 Royal Lodge. He never really got involved with any chance of winning on his return, or placing, but it was a sound comeback and he will surely be straighter next time. (tchd 20-1 in a place)
Zacinto was fairly disappointing as a 4-y-o apart from one decent effort at Royal Ascot, so it was interesting to see that connections were persevering with him. However, he did no better on his return to action and one would imagine that he'll either be shown the door soon or be gelded. (op 7-2 tchd 10-3 and 3-1 in places)
Lord Zenith, gelded since his last start, looks one to avoid on this evidence until showing a lot more. (op 16-1)
King Of Dixie(USA), who beat the heavily odds-on Cityscape in this last year, travelled really well for much of the early part of the race but stopped in a matter of strides once off the bridle. (op 10-1)

1601 TOTEPOOL SAGARO STKS (GROUP 3) 2m
3:40 (3:40) (Class 1) 4-Y-O+ **£34,062** (£12,912; £6,462; £3,222; £1,614; £810) **Stalls** Low

Form RPR
05-3 **1** **Askar Tau (FR)**[21] 1188 6-9-1 104 (v) GeorgeBaker 8 108
(Marcus Tregoning) *hld up in rr: stdy prog fr 5f out: pushed along and styd on wl to chse ldr ins fnl 2f: led appr fnl f: drvn ins fnl f: won gng away* **4/1**[3]
04-5 **2** 2 1/2 **Akmal**[21] 1188 5-9-1 106 RichardHills 1 105
(John Dunlop) *led: drvn over 2f out: hdd appr fnl f: sn outpcd but styd on wl to hold 2nd* **8/1**
12-2 **3** nk **Free Agent**[21] 1188 5-9-1 107 RichardHughes 6 105
(Richard Hannon) *chsd ldrs: lft in 2nd pl 10f out: rdn 4f out: lost 2nd ins fnl 2f: styd on u.p and pressed for 2nd fnl 120yds: nvr any ch w wnr and no ex nr fin* **7/2**[2]
42-1 **4** nk **The Betchworth Kid**[21] 1188 6-9-1 102 HayleyTurner 5 104
(Alan King) *s.i.s: in rr: drvn along 5f out: styd on u.p fr 2f out: nt clr run over 1f out: swtchd lft and styd on ins fnl f: kpt on cl home* **8/1**

031- **5** 2 3/4 **Aaim To Prosper (IRE)**[193] 6926 7-9-1 92.................... LouisBeuzelin 7 101
(Brian Meehan) *chsng ldrs whn carried wd 10f out: sn rcvrd tl lost position 4f out: hdwy again 3f out and chsd ldrs over 2f out: wknd u.p ins fnl f* **16/1**

260- **6** *hd* **Theology**[228] 5945 4-8-11 109.. WilliamBuick 3 101
(Jeremy Noseda) *in tch: chsd ldrs 9f out: outpcd 5f out: hdwy on outside over 2f out: sn drvn along and no imp on ldrs: wknd ins fnl f* **2/1**[1]

004- **P** **Rajik (IRE)**[228] 5976 6-9-1 113.. DPMcDonogh 4 —
(C F Swan, Ire) *chsd ldr tl wnt lame and p.u 10f out* **17/2**

3m 29.42s (0.42) **Going Correction** +0.15s/f (Good)
WFA 4 from 5yo+ 4lb **7** Ran SP% **114.2**
Speed ratings (Par 113): **104,102,102,102,101 100,—**
CSF £34.88 TOTE £6.10: £3.00, £3.80; EX 41.10 Trifecta £118.00 Pool: £1575.46 - 9.88 winning units..
Owner Nurlan Bizakov **Bred** Gestut Zoppenbroich & Aerial Bloodstock **Trained** Lambourn, Berks

FOCUS
The early gallop wasn't strong, but it steadily increased down the back straight. That said, the whole of the field that completed finished in pretty much a bunch. An ordinary renewal and the form is still a fair way shy of Cup standard.

NOTEBOOK
Askar Tau(FR), a place behind Akmal in this race last season, started his season well at Nottingham and looked likely to win until not finding a great deal. However, with that experience under his belt, George Baker knew his mount a lot better and got him to the front here at the right stage to win by a clear margin. When on song, he is a top stayer but things do need to fall right for him. He is about a 20-1 chance for the Ascot Gold Cup. (op 7-2)
Akmal, who was said to have needed the outing last time, had the run of the race and is fairly one dimensional in his tactics. He just falls short at this level currently and will always be susceptible to something with a finishing kick.
Free Agent reversed the form with the fourth here but was soundly held by the winner. (op 10-3)
The Betchworth Kid got the better of Free Agent at Nottingham three weeks previously (a race which also involved Askar Tau and Akmal) found this a different task altogether and couldn't confirm his superiority. (tchd 15-2 and 17-2)
Aaim To Prosper(IRE) ◆, the winner of last year's Cesarewitch, had run well on all previous starts at Ascot so could be given a chance despite being the outsider. However, he lost his position quite easily when the gallop was quickening, without being stretched, before keeping on. One would have liked to have seen more made of his obvious stamina. (op 20-1)
Theology definitely has the potential to progress into a stop stayer considering his best form at a 3-y-o, which included a respectable eighth in the St Leger, where he split Rewilding and Dandino. Gelded since his last start, this was disappointing considering all the positive comments made before the race about his well-being. (op 5-2 tchd 11-4)
Rajik(IRE) enjoyed a good spell last July/August and finished his season with an excellent fourth in the Irish St Leger. Behind Aaim To Prosper when they last met at this track in the 2010 Ascot Stakes, he was sitting behind the leader when something went amiss quite early. He has a suspected broken pastern. (op 9-1 tchd 8-1)

1602 CLEANEVENT PAVILION STKS (LISTED RACE) 6f
4:15 (4:15) (Class 1) 3-Y-O
£17,031 (£6,456; £3,231; £1,611; £807; £405) **Stalls** High

Form RPR

30-0 **1** **Perfect Tribute**[11] 1404 3-8-6 98.. LukeMorris 8 99
(Clive Cox) *t.k.h: trckd ldrs: hrd drvn and swtchd rt ins fnl f: str run u.p to ld last strides* **14/1**

14-0 **2** *nk* **Aneedah (IRE)**[11] 1404 3-8-6 94.. WilliamBuick 3 98
(John Gosden) *t.k.h: trckd ldr: chal over 2f out tl led over 1f: styd on wl u.p ins fnl f: hdd cl home* **16/1**

235- **3** 1/2 **Margot Did (IRE)**[208] 6530 3-8-6 108.............................. HayleyTurner 2 96+
(Michael Bell) *hld up towards rr: swtchd rt and hdwy over 1f out: styd on u.p fnl 120yds but nt quite gng pce of ldng duo clsng stages* **2/1**[1]

65-2 **4** 1/2 **Libranno**[13] 1341 3-9-4 112.. RichardHughes 6 107
(Richard Hannon) *led: rdn 2f out: hdd over 1f out: styd chalng tl outpcd fnl 50yds* **3/1**[2]

00-2 **5** 1 1/4 **Madany (IRE)**[14] 1317 3-8-7 90 ow1................................ RichardHills 1 92
(B W Hills) *chsd ldrs: chal 2f out: rdn over 1f out: outpcd ins fnl f* **3/1**[2]

106 **6** 1/2 **Murbeh (IRE)**[200] 6751 3-9-11 95 .... MartinDwyer 7 91
(Brian Meehan) *in tch: rdn over 2f out: chsd ldrs over 1f out but nvr gng pce to chal: one pce ins fnl f* **16/1**

160- **7** 3 1/4 **Marine Commando**[200] 6734 3-9-0 102.............................. PaulHanagan 9 87
(Richard Fahey) *s.i.s: in rr but in tch: rdn over 2f out: no imp on ldrs and wknd appr fnl f* **8/1**[3]

10-0 **8** 5 **Penny's Pearl (IRE)**[12] 1361 3-8-6 88...................... FrankieMcDonald 4 63
(Richard Hannon) *puuled hrd: stdd in rr: swtchd rt to outside and sme prog to chse ldrs 3f out: sn wknd* **40/1**

1m 12.19s (-2.21) **Going Correction** +0.15s/f (Good) **8** Ran SP% **115.3**
Speed ratings (Par 106): **120,119,118,118,116 115,111,104**
toteswingers:1&2 £13.30, 2&3 £7.50, 1&3 £4.40 CSF £208.46 TOTE £17.80: £2.60, £3.40, £1.30; EX 204.00 Trifecta £1000.20 Part won. Pool of £1351.72 - 0.80 winning units..
Owner Mildmay Racing & D H Caslon **Bred** Mildmay Bloodstock **Trained** Lambourn, Berks

FOCUS
A strong-looking contest, but the form has not been rated too postively with the winner basically to last year's C&D form. The time was a new course record.

NOTEBOOK
Perfect Tribute finished in front of Aneedah in the Fred Darling (7f), both well beaten after running freely, and did so again, albeit in different circumstances. The Clive Cox-trained runner settled much better this time and was produced with a well-timed run to beat the runner-up close to the line. As long as she can be settled in her races, she can win at a slightly higher level. (op 12-1 tchd 16-1 in places)
Aneedah(IRE) ◆ was far too free in the Fred Darling too make any impact, but she too raced more kindly this time and seemed sure to win when hitting the front about 1f out. From that point, she didn't do a great deal wrong and was merely mugged close to the line. (tchd 14-1)
Margot Did(IRE) held her form well as a juvenile in some classy contests, and finished her season with a fair performance in the Group 1 Cheveley Park Stakes. Runner-up on both her previous starts at this course, she has a Group 1 Golden Jubilee entry so is clearly though capable of holding her own in top sprints this season, and although this run didn't suggest she was up to that level yet, she did show more than enough to say she had trained on. (op 5-2)
Libranno made a really encouraging return to action recently behind Guineas bound Native Khan, so that horse's supporters were looking for a good run from the Richard Hannon-trained runner. Back down to 6f, he showed plenty of dash but wasn't able to quicken again as the field closed in, so it's debatable what positives supporters of the Ed Dunlop Classic contender can draw from this result. (op 2-1)
Madany(IRE), whose rider put up 1lb of overweight, appeared a little unlucky in a valuable contest at Newmarket earlier this month (the fourth horse in that race, Button Moon, won the previous day) but didn't appear to have any excuses this time. (op 5-1)

Penny's Pearl(IRE) Official explanation: jockey said filly ran too free

1603 ASCOT RACECOURSE H'CAP 1m (S)
4:50 (4:50) (Class 4) (0-85,85) 4-Y-0+ **£6,476** (£1,927; £963; £481) **Stalls** High

Form RPR

110- **1** **Nelson's Bounty**[229] 5917 4-9-3 81.................................. TonyCulhane 5 94+
(Paul D'Arcy) *in tch: hdwy over 2f out: led over 1f out: drvn and styd on strly ins fnl f* **14/1**

26-1 **2** 1/2 **Lord Aeryn (IRE)**[24] 1109 4-9-6 84.................................. PaulHanagan 2 94
(Richard Fahey) *in rr: gd hdwy over 2f out: hrd drvn and styd on to chse wnr ins fnl f: kpt on wl but a hld* **5/1**[2]

3-05 **3** 1 **First Post (IRE)**[23] 1138 4-9-0 78................................ AndreaAtzeni 11 86
(Derek Haydn Jones) *trckd ldrs: rdn and ev ch appr fnl 2f: one pce ins fnl f* **20/1**

-633 **4** 1/2 **Standpoint**[27] 1061 5-8-13 77.. LiamKeniry 19 84
(Reg Hollinshead) *in tch: hdwy fr 2f out: styd on ins fnl f but nvr quite gng pce to rch ldng trio* **16/1**

-252 **5** 3/4 **Guest Book (IRE)**[4] 1529 4-9-0 85................................ DarylByrne(7) 3 90
(Mark Johnston) *chsd ldrs: drvn to ld 2f out: hdd over 1f out: kpt on same pce ins fnl f* **9/2**[1]

10-0 **6** 1 1/4 **Another Try (IRE)**[24] 1110 6-8-8 77........................... HarryBentley(5) 14 79
(Alan Jarvis) *mde most tl hdd 2f out: wknd ins fnl f* **25/1**

060- **7** 3/4 **Huzzah (IRE)**[189] 7012 6-9-2 80.. MichaelHills 10 81
(B W Hills) *in rr: rdn over 2f out: drvn and styd on ins fnl f: fin wl* **10/1**[3]

056- **8** *nk* **Tartan Trip**[208] 6534 4-9-5 83.. JimmyFortune 18 83
(Andrew Balding) *in tch: chsd ldrs 3f out: kpt on same pce ins fnl f* **10/1**[3]

620- **9** *hd* **Sohcahtoa (IRE)**[191] 6990 5-8-9 78.............................. SeanLevey(5) 12 77
(Robert Mills) *in tch tl outpcd 2f out: styd on again ins fnl f* **10/1**[3]

5214 **10** 7 **Baylini**[16] 1269 7-8-10 77.. SophieDoyle(3) 13 60
(Jamie Osborne) *in rr tl styd on ins fnl f* **12/1**

113 **11** *hd* **Rezwaan**[16] 1269 4-8-13 77..(be) RyanMoore 1 60
(Gary Moore) *in rr: hdwy over 2f out: nvr rchd ldrs: wknd over 1f out* **11/1**

12 1/2 **Butler (IRE)**[367] 1562 4-9-0 78...................................... J-PGuillambert 7 62
(Luca Cumani) *chsd ldrs 6f: eased whn btn ins fnl f* **20/1**

23-1 **13** 2 1/4 **Willow Dancer (IRE)**[20] 1198 7-8-13 77.......................(p) AdamKirby 15 53
(Walter Swinburn) *chsd ldrs 5f* **16/1**

540- **14** 1/2 **Satwa Laird**[199] 6780 5-9-5 83...................................... FrankieDettori 4 68
(Ed Dunlop) *in rr: hdwy over 2f out: nvr quite rchd ldrs: wknd appr fnl f: eased whn no ch* **10/1**[3]

026- **15** *nse* **Kings Bayonet**[198] 6805 4-9-1 79...................................... HayleyTurner 8 54
(Alan King) *s.i.s: nvr beyond mid-div* **33/1**

0-03 **16** 1 1/2 **Academy Blues (USA)**[8] 1467 6-9-7 85...................... AdrianNicholls 17 57
(David Nicholls) *s.i.s: t.k.h: nvr beyond mid-div and bhd fnl 2f* **25/1**

00-6 **17** 7 **Roodle**[25] 1103 4-9-5 83...(p) CathyGannon 16 39
(Eve Johnson Houghton) *pressed ldrs to 1/2-way: wknd 2f out* **33/1**

022- **18** 5 **Duster**[154] 7560 4-9-5 83.. SteveDrowne 6 27
(Hughie Morrison) *chsd ldrs 5f* **20/1**

1m 41.06s (0.46) **Going Correction** +0.15s/f (Good) **18** Ran SP% **133.5**
Speed ratings (Par 105): **103,102,101,101,100 99,98,97,97,90 90,90,87,87,87 85,78,73**
CSF £81.25 CT £1498.45 TOTE £16.50: £3.30, £2.30, £4.60, £5.00; EX 88.30 Trifecta £1637.30 Part won. Pool of £2212.69 - 0.50 winning units..
Owner The Newmarket Pirates **Bred** Slatch Farm Stud **Trained** Newmarket, Suffolk

FOCUS
This was the most competitive race on the card, with 18 horses charging down the home straight at a good gallop. The front pair are progressive and the standard is sound.
First Post(IRE) Official explanation: jockey said gelding hung left
T/Jkpt: Not won. T/Plt: £7,943.20 to a £1 stake. Pool of £103,914.84 - 9.55 winning tickets.
T/Qpdt: £80.10 to a £1 stake. Pool of £11,687.50 - 107.94 winning tickets. ST

1482 KEMPTON (A.W) (R-H)
Wednesday, April 27

OFFICIAL GOING: Standard
Wind: Strong, half against Weather: Sunny

1604 BETDAQ.COM EXCHANGE PRICE MULTIPLES H'CAP 1m (P)
5:50 (5:51) (Class 6) (0-60,60) 4-Y-0+ **£1,748** (£516; £258) **Stalls** Low

Form RPR

-300 **1** **Hecton Lad (USA)**[35] 944 4-8-8 47..................................(b1) LukeMorris 9 65
(John Best) *pressed ldr: led 3f out: edgd lft u.p fr over 1f out: sn drew clr* **8/1**

30-2 **2** 5 **Kanace**[111] 70 4-8-13 52.. StevieDonohoe 1 59
(Noel Quinlan) *prom: trckd ldng pair over 4f out: chsd wnr over 2f out: drvn and no imp over 1f out: lost grnd after* **9/2**[2]

-314 **3** 1 3/4 **Madame Boot (FR)**[13] 1333 4-9-7 60.............................. SteveDrowne 7 62
(Peter Makin) *chsd ldng pair to over 4f out: styd handy: rdn whn bmpd and veered lft 2f out: plugged on to take 3rd ins fnl f* **13/2**

0303 **4** 1/2 **Rainsborough**[7] 1486 4-9-2 55...............................(ve1) JimCrowley 4 56
(Peter Hedger) *hld up in midfield: trckd ldng trio 1/2-way: gng wl enough over 2f out: rdn to chse ldng pair wl over 1f out: no imp* **6/1**[3]

5156 **5** 2 **Spinning Ridge (IRE)**[7] 1486 6-9-7 60........................(b) DavidProbert 3 57
(Ronald Harris) *dwlt: hld up towards rr: prog to go 6th 1/2-way: effrt and squeezed through 2f out: no imp over 1f out: fdd* **7/2**[1]

5242 **6** 1 1/2 **Diddums**[7] 1486 5-8-1 47.. KatiaScallan(7) 10 40
(Alastair Lidderdale) *hld up in last trio: sme prog over 2f out: nt on terms w ldrs over 1f out: wknd last 100yds* **13/2**

0544 **7** *nk* **Novastasia (IRE)**[8] 1468 5-8-7 46.................................(b) LiamJones 6 39
(Dean Ivory) *nvr bttr than midfield: struggling fr 3f out and sn wl off the pce: kpt on late* **16/1**

5054 **8** 1/2 **Evey P (IRE)**[13] 1331 4-8-5 51.................................. LeonnaMayor(7) 2 42
(Gary Brown) *s.i.s: hld up in rr: effrt and sme prog over 2f out: no ch over 1f out: fdd* **18/1**

00-0 **9** 14 **Sunrise Lyric (IRE)**[105] 128 4-9-0 60...................... DuilioDaSilva(7) 12 19
(Paul Cole) *hld up on terms w ldrs: struggling sn after 1/2-way: t.o* **33/1**

02-4 **10** 8 **Jeremiah (IRE)**[79] 449 5-9-3 56...................................... KirstyMilczarek 13 —
(Laura Young) *chsd ldrs 3f: sn rdn and wknd: t.o* **14/1**

065 **11** *shd* **Tinkerbell Will**[23] 1133 4-8-12 51.................................. SamHitchcott 5 —
(John E Long) *drvn in midfield after 2f: nvr a factor: t.o* **66/1**

50-5 **12** 3 **Warm Memories**[84] 389 4-9-7 60.............................(e1) GeorgeBaker 11 —
(Simon Dow) *led at str pce to 3f out: wknd rapidly: t.o* **20/1**

1m 38.34s (-1.46) **Going Correction** -0.025s/f (Stan) **12** Ran SP% **119.5**
Speed ratings (Par 101): **106,101,99,98,96 95,94,94,80,72 72,69**
toteswingers: 1&2 £9.40, 1&3 £8.70, 2&3 £11.00. CSF £43.52 CT £257.00 TOTE £6.70: £4.50, £1.60, £1.20; EX 67.10.
Owner H J Jarvis **Bred** R D Daniels Jr & C B Daniels **Trained** Hucking, Kent

FOCUS
A low-grade opener featuring plenty of in-form horses that despite lacking any obvious front runner was run at a fair gallop. Even so, little got into it from behind. The time was good for the grade and the winner was nuch improved in the blinkers.
Tinkerbell Will Official explanation: jockey said filly never travelled

1605 FREE ENTRY FOR BETDAQ MEMBERS MAIDEN STKS (DIV I) 1m (P)
6:20 (6:21) (Class 5) 3-Y-0+ £2,417 (£713; £357) Stalls Low

Form RPR
5 **1** **Sure Route**[12] 1362 3-8-9 0 RichardHughes 4 77
(Richard Hannon) *led 2f: sn dropped to 4th: effrt 2f out: squeezed through to ld jst over 1f out: edgd lft fnl f: hld on wl* **3/1**[2]

2 *hd* **Cala Santanyi** 3-8-9 0 NeilCallan 2 76+
(Gerard Butler) *settled in midfield: 8th 1/2-way: pushed along and prog wl over 1f out: r.o to join wnr ins fnl f: nt qckn nr fin* **14/1**

3 *hd* **Dare To Dance (IRE)** 3-9-0 0 GeorgeBaker 13 81+
(Jeremy Noseda) *settled in last trio and wl off the pce: pushed along on outer over 2f out: gd prog after: styd on wl to take 3rd and cl on ldng pair nr fin* **20/1**

4 *2 ¼* **Abbraccio** 3-9-0 0 TomQueally 11 75+
(James Fanshawe) *pushed along in midfield: 7th 1/2-way: shkn up 2f out: styd on after but nt as qckly as sme who were bhd him: tk 4th wl ins fnl f* **8/1**

0 **5** *1* **Montegonian (USA)**[11] 1408 3-8-7 0 KatiaScallan(7) 10 73
(Marcus Tregoning) *pressed ldrs: effrt to chal 2f out: wknd jst over 1f out* **66/1**

6 *nse* **Mashaaref** 3-9-0 0 RichardHills 3 73+
(Roger Varian) *trckd ldrs: wnt 2nd 5f out: poised to chal over 2f out: shkn up and upsides over 1f out: fdd fnl f* **5/4**[1]

7 *1 ½* **Shamacam** 3-9-0 0 RyanMoore 14 69+
(Sir Michael Stoute) *wl in rr: urged along 3f out: sme prog fr 2f out: kpt on but no threat* **16/1**

4 **8** *½* **Serial Sinner (IRE)**[16] 1270 3-8-9 0 WilliamBuick 5 63
(Paul Cole) *led after 2f: kicked on over 2f out: hdd & wknd jst over 1f out* **15/2**[3]

0- **9** *nse* **Glass Mountain (IRE)**[205] 6626 3-9-0 0 PatCosgrave 6 68
(James Fanshawe) *chsd ldrs: cl 5th and rdn over 2f out: no imp jst over 1f out: fdd* **33/1**

/ **10** *3 ½* **Media Hype** 4-10-0 0 J-PGuillambert 7 64+
(Luca Cumani) *rn green and sn last: modest prog over 2f out to rch 10th over 1f out: no hdwy after* **80/1**

11 *9* **Rachael's Ruby**[32] 4-9-6 0 JohnFahy(3) 9 37
(Roger Teal) *s.s: a wl in rr: nvr a factor: t.o* **100/1**

12 *1 ¾* **Price Of Retrieval** 4-10-0 0 JackMitchell 12 38
(Peter Chapple-Hyam) *a towards rr: pushed along in 9th sn after 1/2-way: wknd over 2f out: t.o* **100/1**

13 *4* **Korithi** 3-8-9 0 SteveDrowne 1 19
(Roger Charlton) *trckd ldrs to over 2f out: wknd rapidly: t.o* **40/1**

14 *10* **Greeley House** 3-9-0 0 TedDurcan 8 —
(Chris Wall) *s.i.s: a towards rr and nvr gng wl: wknd over 2f out: t.o* **100/1**

1m 39.34s (-0.46) **Going Correction** -0.025s/f (Stan) **14** Ran SP% **120.7**
WFA 3 from 4yo 14lb
Speed ratings (Par 103): **101,100,100,98,97 97,95,95,95,91 82,81,77,67**
toteswingers: 1&2 £6.20, 1&3 £6.70. 2&3 £9.80 CSF £42.52 TOTE £5.90: £1.60, £4.70, £3.80; EX 62.60.
Owner Malih Lahej Al Basti **Bred** Malih L Al Basti **Trained** East Everleigh, Wilts

FOCUS
Plenty of newcomers or unexposed sorts in an interesting maiden run at a decent gallop for the type of race. The standard was not as good as division II and it was 17lb slower. The form is rated around the race averages.
Mashaaref Official explanation: jockey said colt was coltish

1606 FREE ENTRY FOR BETDAQ MEMBERS MAIDEN STKS (DIV II) 1m (P)
6:50 (6:56) (Class 5) 3-Y-0+ £2,417 (£713; £357) Stalls Low

Form RPR
5-3 **1** **Dream Achieved**[14] 1321 3-9-0 0 MichaelHills 5 91
(B W Hills) *mde all: pushed along 2f out: a in command after: rdn out fnl f* **11/5**[2]

2-2 **2** *1 ¼* **Afkar (IRE)**[14] 1315 3-9-0 0 PhilipRobinson 7 88
(Clive Brittain) *chsd wnr after 2f: shkn up 2f out: styd on but a readily hld fnl f* **2/1**[1]

3 *5* **Naasef** 4-10-0 0 RichardHills 4 81
(John Dunlop) *t.k.h: trckd ldng pair after 2f: cl enough 2f out: steadily lost grnd after* **3/1**[3]

4 *7* **Thistle Bird** 3-8-9 0 SteveDrowne 9 56+
(Roger Charlton) *racd wd: chsd ldrs: pushed along and wl outpcd fr over 3f out: kpt on again fnl f to take 4th last strides* **66/1**

0 **5** *nk* **Dunseverick (IRE)**[14] 1315 3-9-0 0 TedDurcan 12 60+
(David Lanigan) *settled off the pce in midfield: prog to go 5th 2f out but nowhere nr ldrs: kpt on* **20/1**

00- **6** *½* **Moonlight Mystery**[179] 7232 3-8-9 0 JackMitchell 3 54
(Chris Wall) *wl in tch: chsd ldng trio 1/2-way: clr of rest but nt on terms over 2f out: fdd and lost 2 pls nr fin* **50/1**

0- **7** *3 ¼* **Evergreen Forest (IRE)**[222] 6149 3-9-0 0 JimmyFortune 10 51
(Alastair Lidderdale) *a towards rr: shkn up sn after 1/2-way: no real prog* **66/1**

8 *½* **Llewellyn** 3-9-0 0[1] PatCosgrave 11 50
(James Fanshawe) *rn green and a towards rr: urged along fr 1/2-way: nvr on terms* **14/1**

9 *2* **Hertford Street** 3-9-0 0 FergusSweeney 8 45
(Peter Makin) *s.i.s: rchd midfield after 3f: 6th 1/2-way: wknd over 2f out* **80/1**

0 **10** *nk* **Hector The Brave (IRE)**[61] 684 4-10-0 0 SamHitchcott 6 49
(John E Long) *chsd wnr 2f: wandering sn after: wknd 3f out: sn wl bhd* **100/1**

11 *½* **New Hampshire (USA)** 3-9-0 0 WilliamBuick 2 44+
(John Gosden) *reluctant to enter stalls: rn v green and sn detached in last: nvr a factor* **14/1**

12 *14* **Poyle Todream** 3-9-0 0 JimCrowley 13 —
(Ralph Beckett) *s.s: a in last pair: wknd 3f out: t.o* **33/1**

1m 38.46s (-1.34) **Going Correction** -0.025s/f (Stan) **12** Ran SP% **117.8**
WFA 3 from 4yo 14lb
Speed ratings (Par 103): **105,103,98,91,91 90,87,87,85,84 84,70**
toteswingers: 1&2 £1.50, 1&3 £1.80, 2&3 £2.30. CSF £6.64 TOTE £4.50: £2.10, £1.10, £1.50; EX 7.50.
Owner K Abdulla **Bred** Millsec Limited **Trained** Lambourn, Berks

FOCUS
The second division of the maiden and a better race, but not much strength in depth, with the first three clear in the betting dominating the race and nothing else promising to get into contention. The pace was once again a decent one and the form looks sound.

1607 LAY BACK AND WIN AT BETDAQ.COM MAIDEN FILLIES' STKS 6f (P)
7:20 (7:23) (Class 5) 3-Y-0 £2,417 (£713; £357) Stalls Low

Form RPR
32 **1** **Flashbang**[13] 1343 3-9-0 0 JamieSpencer 12 82
(Paul Cole) *mde all: shifted lft 2f out: rdn and styd on wl over 1f out* **11/4**[1]

52- **2** *2 ½* **Psychic's Dream**[145] 7681 3-9-0 0 AdamKirby 6 74
(Marco Botti) *prom: rdn to chse wnr 2f out: styd on but no imp fnl f* **6/1**[2]

3- **3** *1 ¾* **Bless You**[184] 7123 3-9-0 0 FergusSweeney 8 68
(Henry Candy) *chsd wnr to 2f out: rdn and one pce after* **11/4**[1]

4 *1* **Gladys' Gal** 3-9-0 0 NeilCallan 5 65+
(Roger Varian) *hld up in tch: shkn up to go 4th 2f out: one pce and no imp after* **16/1**

30- **5** *1* **Abergeldie (USA)**[222] 6155 3-9-0 0 JimmyFortune 9 62+
(Andrew Balding) *towards rr and wd bnd 4f out: outpcd over 2f out: brought to nr side and styd on fr over 1f out: n.d* **10/1**[3]

0- **6** *nk* **All Honesty**[181] 7185 3-9-0 0 JimCrowley 1 61
(William Knight) *chsd ldrs: shkn up and outpcd over 2f out: kpt on again fnl f* **20/1**

5- **7** *2 ¼* **Dusty Bluebells (IRE)**[247] 5372 3-9-0 0 LukeMorris 4 53+
(J S Moore) *dwlt: rn green in rr: nvr a factor: styd on fnl f* **20/1**

40- **8** *nk* **Pearl Opera**[238] 5657 3-9-0 0 CathyGannon 2 52
(Denis Coakley) *chsd ldrs: shkn up and steadily outpcd over 2f out: wknd fnl f* **20/1**

9 *hd* **Heliograph** 3-8-7 0 AntiocoMurgia(7) 11 52+
(Mahmood Al Zarooni) *sltly hmpd over 4f out and wd bnd sn after: effrt on wd outside over 3f out: no hdwy 2f out: fdd* **10/1**[3]

0 **10** *2* **Pinch Of Posh (IRE)**[12] 1362 3-9-0 0 ChrisCatlin 7 45
(Paul Cole) *in tch in midfield: wknd fr 2f out* **14/1**

00- **11** *2 ¾* **No Refraction (IRE)**[209] 6497 3-8-9 0 LeeNewnes(5) 10 37
(Mark Usher) *a wl in rr: shkn up and btn over 2f out* **100/1**

0 **12** *36* **Canashito**[22] 1155 3-9-0 0 MichaelHills 3 —
(B W Hills) *in tch: hanging and eased over 2f out: virtually p.u: sddle slipped* **16/1**

1m 12.82s (-0.28) **Going Correction** -0.025s/f (Stan) **12** Ran SP% **119.5**
Speed ratings (Par 95): **100,96,94,93,91 91,88,87,87,84 81,33**
toteswingers: 1&2 £3.30, 1&3 £1.90, 2&3 £3.10. CSF £18.32 TOTE £3.00: £1.10, £2.90, £1.80; EX 18.90.
Owner A H Robinson **Bred** D J Weston **Trained** Whatcombe, Oxon

FOCUS
A fair maiden in all probability that went the way of the horse with the best form, who was able to dictate a stop-start gallop. She will probably improve again. The time was only modest.
Abergeldie(USA) Official explanation: jockey said, regarding running and riding, that his orders were to obtain a good early position and do his best, he was unable to secure a prominent position, due to the eventual winner overtaking him on the outside and he had to wait for a gap in the straight; trainer confirmed but, in his view, the filly has sufficient speed for 6f but would not rule out a step up to 7f.
Dusty Bluebells(IRE) Official explanation: jockey said filly suffered interference in running
Canashito Official explanation: jockey said saddle slipped

1608 BETDAQ MOBILE APPS H'CAP 1m 3f (P)
7:50 (7:50) (Class 5) (0-70,70) 4-Y-0+ £2,417 (£713; £357) Stalls Low

Form RPR
3-33 **1** **Kames Park (IRE)**[97] 232 9-9-2 68 RobertLButler(3) 2 76
(Richard Guest) *stdd s: hld up and last after 4f: stl there over 2f out but gng wl: cajoled along and prog on wd outside after: clsd to ld narrowly last 50yds* **20/1**

4520 **2** *hd* **Lisahane Bog**[35] 949 4-9-7 70 (ve) NeilCallan 1 77
(Peter Hedger) *hld up in 8th: looking for room over 2f out: hrd rdn and prog over 1f out: c to chal last 100yds: jst denied* **20/1**

200- **3** *hd* **On The Feather**[177] 7275 5-8-11 60 JamesMillman 11 67
(Rod Millman) *trckd ldng pair: led 2f out: drvn and kpt on fnl f: hdd last 50yds* **50/1**

300- **4** *1* **Now What**[198] 6816 4-9-1 64 JimCrowley 7 69
(Jonathan Portman) *trckd ldng pair: chal 2f out: pressed ldr 1f out: nt qckn after* **16/1**

-463 **5** *½* **Waahej**[19] 1222 5-8-12 61 ChrisCatlin 6 66
(Peter Hiatt) *hld up in rr: looking for room 2f out: gd prog ent fnl f: trying to cl whn nt clr run and lost momentum 100yds out* **12/1**

12-0 **6** *1 ¼* **Room For A View**[13] 1333 4-9-1 64 (p) TedDurcan 12 66
(Marcus Tregoning) *racd wd: chsd ldrs disputing 5th: rdn over 2f out: nt qckn over 1f out: kpt on same pce* **8/1**

211- **7** *½* **Jovial (IRE)**[184] 7117 4-8-13 65 JohnFahy(3) 3 66
(Denis Coakley) *trckd ldrs disputing 5th: effrt to chal wl over 1f out and nrly upsides: fdd ins fnl f* **4/1**[1]

6311 **8** *1* **Beau Fighter**[36] 938 6-9-4 67 (p) RyanMoore 8 66
(Gary Moore) *chsd ldrs disputing 5th: cl enough and rdn over 1f out: fdd fnl f* **9/2**[2]

005- **9** *hd* **Jinto**[154] 7562 4-8-11 60 DaneO'Neill 4 59
(David Elsworth) *s.s: hld up wl in rr: darted ins and prog 2f out: chsng ldrs over 1f out: wknd ins fnl f* **8/1**

-033 **10** *1 ¾* **Saviour Sand (IRE)**[40] 885 7-8-13 62 (t) CathyGannon 13 58
(Olivia Maylam) *pressed ldr: led briefly jst over 2f out: wknd jst over 1f out* **14/1**

-005 **11** *2* **Clear Sailing**[21] 1174 8-9-3 66 StevieDonohoe 10 58
(Noel Quinlan) *s.s: last tl modest prog 7f out: rdn and struggling in rr 2f out* **20/1**

03-0 **12** *½* **Monkton Vale (IRE)**[25] 1098 4-9-7 70 PaulHanagan 5 61
(Richard Fahey) *hld up in last quartet: swtchd ins and effrt 2f out: sn no prog and btn: wknd* **7/1**[3]

53-4 **13** *4* **Roanstar**[21] 1173 4-9-7 70 JimmyFortune 14 54
(Andrew Balding) *led: awkward bnd 8f out: hdd jst over 2f out: wknd rapidly over 1f out* **15/2**

2m 21.52s (-0.38) **Going Correction** -0.025s/f (Stan) **13** Ran SP% **121.2**
Speed ratings (Par 103): **100,99,99,98,98 97,97,96,96,95 93,93,90**
toteswingers: 1&2 £17.90, 1&3 £104.90, 2&3 £104.90. CSF £360.66 CT £17949.04 TOTE £29.40: £6.60, £4.50, £24.30; EX 118.10.
Owner Miss Vicki Shaw **Bred** Pat Beirne **Trained** Stainforth, S Yorks

FOCUS
A run-of-the mill handicap run at a decent pace overall, for it slackened in the middle and many horses still held a chance approaching the last. The form makes sense at face value.

Waahej Official explanation: jockey said gelding was denied a clear run

1609 SUMMER SERIES STARTS JUNE 1ST H'CAP 1m 3f (P)

8:20 (8:21) (Class 5) (0-75,74) 3-Y-O **£2,417** (£713; £357) **Stalls** Low

Form RPR

0-43 **1** **Diplomasi**[7] 1481 3-8-12 **65**................ PhilipRobinson 3 70
(Clive Brittain) *hld up in midfield: prog 2f out: sustained effrt to ld narrowly last 100yds: styd on* **5/1**[3]

13-2 **2** *nk* **My Vindication (USA)**[9] 1446 3-9-6 **73**................ RyanMoore 2 77
(Richard Hannon) *t.k.h: trckd ldr to over 3f out: effrt to ld 2f out: hrd rdn and hdd last 100yds: kpt on* **4/1**[2]

601- **3** *1 1/2* **Run On Ruby (FR)**[161] 7479 3-9-6 **73**................ TedDurcan 7 75+
(David Lanigan) *hld up last: rdn and effrt on outer 2f out: prog fnl f: styd on to take 3rd nr fin* **7/2**[1]

600- **4** *nse* **Achalas (IRE)**[186] 7099 3-8-9 **62**................ LukeMorris 1 64
(Heather Main) *trckd ldrs: lost pl sltly 4f out: drvn and nt qckn wl over 1f out: styd on again ins fnl f* **8/1**

36-0 **5** *hd* **Plattsburgh (USA)**[13] 1327 3-8-8 **68**................ AntiocoMurgia(7) 9 69
(Mahmood Al Zarooni) *led to 2f out: cl enough 1f out: nt qckn* **9/1**

04-5 **6** *2* **Valley Tiger**[15] 1299 3-8-9 **62**................ MartinDwyer 6 61
(William Muir) *s.i.s: hld up in rr: prog to trck ldrs 2f out: cl enough over 1f out: reminder and nt qckn: fdd and eased* **8/1**

241- **7** *nk* **Lexington Bay (IRE)**[148] 7644 3-9-6 **73**................ PaulHanagan 8 70
(Richard Fahey) *in tch on outer: rdn and prog over 3f out: nt qckn 2f out: fdd* **7/1**

40-2 **8** *3/4* **History Girl (IRE)**[15] 1285 3-8-10 **63**................ TomQueally 4 59
(Sir Henry Cecil) *hld up in last pair: shkn up and no prog over 2f out: nvr on terms after* **14/1**

053- **9** *nk* **Magical Flower**[219] 6247 3-9-2 **74**................ HarryBentley(5) 5 69
(William Knight) *trckd ldng pair: wnt 2nd over 3f out to over 2f out: sn wknd* **14/1**

2m 22.19s (0.29) **Going Correction** -0.025s/f (Stan) **9** Ran SP% **116.9**
Speed ratings (Par 98): **97,96,95,95,95 94,93,93,93**
toteswingers: 1&2 £3.90, 1&3 £2.70, 2&3 £4.40. CSF £25.69 CT £79.45 TOTE £5.00: £1.60, £1.40, £2.10; EX 23.30.
Owner C E Brittain **Bred** Ercan Dogan **Trained** Newmarket, Suffolk

FOCUS
An ordinary handicap run at a steady pace and more a test of finishing speed than stamina.Muddling form, and it's doubtful if the winner had to improve.

1610 PEPPA PIG AT KEMPTON ON MONDAY H'CAP 7f (P)

8:50 (8:50) (Class 4) (0-85,85) 4-Y-O+ **£4,129** (£1,228; £614; £153; £153) **Stalls** Low

Form RPR

-523 **1** **Tevez**[18] 1245 6-8-12 **76**................ CathyGannon 4 84
(Des Donovan) *bmpd s: settled in last trio: rdn and prog fr jst over 2f out: sustained effrt fnl f to ld last 75yds* **11/1**

152- **2** *1/2* **Hot Spark**[242] 5524 4-9-5 **83**................(t) DaneO'Neill 1 90
(John Akehurst) *chsd clr ldng trio: rdn to cl grad fr 2f out: kpt on same pce fnl f to take 2nd* **7/1**

1214 **3** *hd* **Majuro (IRE)**[8] 1467 7-9-4 **85**................(t) RobertLButler(3) 2 91
(Richard Guest) *w ldr and clr of rest: unable to keep tabs over 2f out: lost 2nd ins fnl f but plugged on* **11/1**

2151 **4** *nk* **Thunderball**[34] 956 5-8-11 **82**................(b) LeonnaMayor(7) 8 87
(David Nicholls) *mde most but pressed tl drew clr over 2f out: edgd lft after: stl def advantage ent fnl f: hdd & wknd last 75yds* **8/1**

003- **4** *dht* **Santefisio**[154] 7560 5-9-5 **83**................ WilliamBuick 11 88+
(Peter Makin) *dwlt: off the pce in last trio: shkn up over 2f out: no prog tl jst over 1f out: r.o fnl f: nrst fin* **13/2**[3]

10-6 **6** *1* **Sakhee's Pearl**[48] 822 5-9-0 **78**................(b) IanMongan 7 80
(Jo Crowley) *t.k.h: hld up in midfield: rdn and nt qckn over 2f out: kpt on same pce after: nvr gng to chal* **15/2**

321- **7** *3/4* **Avon Lady**[230] 5896 4-8-13 **77**................ PatCosgrave 12 77
(James Fanshawe) *hld up towards rr: shkn up over 2f out: kpt on fr over 1f out: nvr threatened* **5/1**[2]

106- **8** *4 1/2* **Master Mylo (IRE)**[184] 7114 4-9-0 **78**................ JimCrowley 5 66
(Dean Ivory) *sltly restless in stalls: nvr beyond midfield: rdn on inner 2f out: wknd fnl f* **16/1**

026- **9** *1 1/4* **Whispering Spirit (IRE)**[131] 7915 5-9-2 **80**................ PaulHanagan 6 65
(Ann Duffield) *chsd ldrs tl wknd jst over 2f out* **25/1**

-422 **10** *3/4* **Sunshine Always (IRE)**[20] 1198 5-8-3 **72**................ JemmaMarshall(5) 9 55
(Michael Attwater) *chsd ldrs: rdn over 2f out: sn wknd* **14/1**

0-15 **11** *3 1/4* **Caprio (IRE)**[21] 1178 6-8-12 **79**................ MatthewDavies(3) 3 53
(Jim Boyle) *a in last trio: shkn up and no prog over 2f out* **33/1**

4-53 **12** *6* **Street Power (USA)**[34] 956 6-9-4 **82**................(b1) SteveDrowne 10 40
(Jeremy Gask) *t.k.h: hld up on outer: rdn and no rspnse over 2f out: eased whn no ch over 1f out* **9/2**[1]

1m 25.25s (-0.75) **Going Correction** -0.025s/f (Stan) **12** Ran SP% **119.6**
Speed ratings (Par 105): **103,102,102,101,101 100,99,94,93,92 88,81**
toteswingers: 1&2 £23.30, 1&3 £60.80, 2&3 £23.80. CSF £86.76 CT £626.00 TOTE £12.30: £3.70, £2.60, £4.80; EX 186.80.
Owner River Racing **Bred** P A And Mrs D G Sakal **Trained** Newmarket, Suffolk

FOCUS
A well-run handicap with the two recognised front-runners setting a strong gallop and ensuring no hiding place for any of the runners. The first two recorded small personal bests.
Majuro(IRE) Official explanation: jockey said gelding hung badly left
Street Power(USA) Official explanation: jockey said gelding stopped quickly

1611 FAMILY FUN HERE ON MONDAY CLASSIFIED STKS 7f (P)

9:20 (9:24) (Class 5) 3-Y-O **£2,417** (£713; £357) **Stalls** Low

Form RPR

553- **1** **Elusivity (IRE)**[177] 7272 3-9-0 69................ MartinDwyer 4 74
(Brian Meehan) *led 2f: trckd ldr: led again over 1f out: hrd pressed fnl f: jst hld on* **14/1**

61-2 **2** *nse* **Classic Voice (IRE)**[11] 1400 3-9-0 70................ GeorgeBaker 2 74
(Hugo Palmer) *trckd ldrs: effrt wl over 1f out: rdn and clsd fnl f: jst failed* **3/1**[2]

653- **3** *nk* **Red Marling (IRE)**[179] 7224 3-8-7 69................ MatthewLawson(7) 11 73
(B W Hills) *led after 2f: rdn and hdd over 1f out: battled on wl fnl f but lost 2nd last strides* **10/1**

230- **4** *2 1/4* **Uptown Guy (USA)**[222] 6138 3-9-0 70................ RyanMoore 12 67+
(William Haggas) *hld up in rr: effrt on inner 2f out: kpt on same pce: n.d* **9/4**[1]

500- **5** *hd* **Mawjoodah**[186] 7098 3-9-0 70................ PhilipRobinson 5 67
(Clive Brittain) *wl in tch: rdn and effrt 2f out: nt qckn and no imp on ldrs after* **20/1**

00-4 **6** *1 1/2* **Arctic Mirage**[23] 1131 3-9-0 68................ LiamKeniry 1 63
(Michael Blanshard) *mostly in midfield: shkn up over 2f out: sn outpcd: no imp after* **25/1**

26-5 **7** *1 1/4* **Battle Of Britain**[14] 1315 3-9-0 69................(t) WilliamCarson 9 59
(Giles Bravery) *chsd ldrs: rdn over 2f out: steadily fdd* **16/1**

-431 **8** *1 3/4* **Storm Tide**[56] 729 3-9-0 70................ MartinLane 7 54
(Rae Guest) *racd awkwardly in rr after 2f: nvr on terms: modest late prog* **13/2**[3]

-204 **9** *1/2* **Cold Secret**[49] 811 3-9-0 70................ DaneO'Neill 6 53
(David Elsworth) *hld up in rr: shkn up over 2f out: no prog and sn btn* **20/1**

0-33 **10** *1 1/4* **Philharmonic Hall**[13] 1329 3-9-0 65................(p) PaulHanagan 8 50
(Richard Fahey) *nvr bttr than midfield: rdn over 2f out: sn btn* **12/1**

55-0 **11** *2* **Holcombe Boy**[40] 887 3-9-0 67................ StevieDonohoe 13 44
(Noel Quinlan) *s.i.s: mostly last: nvr a factor* **10/1**

1m 26.04s (0.04) **Going Correction** -0.025s/f (Stan) **11** Ran SP% **120.9**
Speed ratings (Par 98): **98,97,97,95,94 93,91,89,89,87 85**
toteswingers: 1&2 £8.70, 1&3 £48.90, 2&3 £5.40. CSF £55.98 TOTE £20.30: £6.30, £2.00, £2.10; EX 65.80.
Owner Mrs P Good **Bred** J Costello **Trained** Manton, Wilts

FOCUS
Potentially a more informative contest than its ordinary rating band dictates, as many races of this type are at this time of year. The pace seemed fair. The form is rated around the second and third.
T/Plt: £148.80 to a £1 stake. Pool of £52,834.11 - 259.13 winning tickets. T/Qpdt: £24.10 to a £1 stake. Pool of £5,471.33 - 167.80 winning tickets. JN

1489 NEWCASTLE (L-H)

Wednesday, April 27

OFFICIAL GOING: Good to firm (firm in places; 8.1)
Wind: Light 1/2 behind Weather: Fine and sunny

1612 FREEBETTING.CO.UK APPRENTICE H'CAP 6f

5:10 (5:10) (Class 6) (0-65,64) 4-Y-O+ **£1,683** (£501; £250; £125) **Stalls** High

Form RPR

400- **1** **Arch Walker (IRE)**[183] 7144 4-9-0 **60**................ GarryWhillans(3) 9 70
(Jedd O'Keeffe) *racd stands' side: chsd ldrs: led that gp over 2f out: edgd lft and chal 1f out: kpt on to ld post* **22/1**

4505 **2** *nse* **Beckermet (IRE)**[37] 928 9-8-8 **54**................ ShaneBKelly(3) 2 64
(Ruth Carr) *s.s: last of 3 far side: hdwy to ld that gp and overall ldr over 2f out: edgd rt over 1f out: sn jnd: hdd post* **12/1**

5-61 **3** *1* **Electioneer (USA)**[43] 857 4-9-7 **64**................ LeeTopliss 10 71+
(Michael Easterby) *edgd rt after s: racd stands' side: chsd ldrs: outpcd over 2f out: styd on wl ins fnl f* **11/10**[1]

06-0 **4** *1 1/2* **Baybshambles (IRE)**[20] 1204 7-8-11 **57**................ RosieJessop(3) 12 59
(Ron Barr) *racd stands' side: chsd ldrs: kpt on same pce appr fnl f* **11/1**[3]

244- **5** *1 1/2* **Secret City (IRE)**[217] 6295 5-9-1 **58**................(b) NeilFarley 1 55
(Robin Bastiman) *led gp of 3 far side: hdd over 2f out: kpt on same pce appr fnl f* **11/1**[3]

3-00 **6** *nk* **Sweet Mirasol (IRE)**[16] 1276 4-8-4 **50**................(t) NathanAlison(3) 15 46
(Mandy Rowland) *racd stands' side: chsd ldrs: outpcd over 2f out: kpt on fnl f* **22/1**

0-00 **7** *1* **Pearly Wey**[11] 1411 8-9-0 **57**................ AdamCarter 14 50
(Ian McInnes) *racd stands' side: in rr: kpt on fnl 2f: nvr a factor* **28/1**

000- **8** *2* **Blown It (USA)**[179] 7239 5-9-1 **58**................ TobyAtkinson 7 44
(Jim Goldie) *racd stands' side: outpcd and in rr: kpt on fnl 2f: nvr on terms* **16/1**

-660 **9** *3 1/4* **Cheery Cat (USA)**[42] 874 7-8-11 **54**................(v) DeclanCannon 13 30
(John Balding) *racd stands' side: in rr div: hdwy over 2f out: eased fnl f* **12/1**

50-0 **10** *2 1/4* **Quaestor (IRE)**[14] 1307 4-8-7 **55**................ DanielHarris(5) 4 24
(Andrew Crook) *chsd ldr far side: wknd 2f out* **50/1**

123- **11** *2 1/4* **Hot Rod Mamma (IRE)**[204] 6644 4-8-3 **51**................ CharlesBishop(5) 8 13
(Dianne Sayer) *led stands' side gp: hdd over 2f out: sn wknd* **10/1**[2]

-523 **12** *3* **Espy**[18] 1247 6-8-11 **59**................ DavidSimmonson(5) 3 11
(Ian McInnes) *dwlt: swtchd rt after s: racd stands' side: a in rr* **25/1**

000- **13** *17* **Sea Rover (IRE)**[235] 5760 7-8-8 **54**................ JohnCavanagh(3) 5 —
(Mel Brittain) *racd stands' side: w ldr: wknd over 2f out: eased whn bhd fnl f* **33/1**

40-0 **U** **Viking Warrior (IRE)**[22] 1150 4-9-1 **63**................ EdmondLinehan(5) 11 —
(Michael Dods) *racd stands' side: trckd ldrs: clipped heels and uns rdr after 150yds* **12/1**

1m 14.23s (-0.37) **Going Correction** -0.175s/f (Firm) **14** Ran SP% **123.2**
Speed ratings (Par 101): **95,94,93,91,89 89,87,85,80,77 74,70,48,—**
toteswingers: 1&2 £43.10, 1&3 £12.80, 2&3 £6.90. CSF £254.20 CT £563.08 TOTE £39.20: £8.20, £2.90, £1.60; EX 330.70.
Owner A Walker **Bred** T Hirschfeld **Trained** Middleham Moor, N Yorks
■ Stewards' Enquiry : Lee Topliss seven-day ban: used whip with excessive frequency (May 11-17); one-day ban: careless riding (May 18)

FOCUS
A modest sprint handicap in which the field split into two. Ultimately, the front pair, who raced in separate groups to begin, ended up centre-to-far side. A small personal best from the winner, with the second rated to his late 2009 form.

1613 SWARLANDSELFSTORAGE.CO.UK H'CAP 1m (R)

5:40 (5:40) (Class 6) (0-65,65) 4-Y-O+ **£2,331** (£693; £346; £173) **Stalls** Low

Form RPR

0-64 **1** **Fazza**[18] 1245 4-9-1 **59**................ TonyHamilton 9 67
(Edwin Tuer) *trckd ldrs: led over 1f out: hotly chal ins fnl f: all out* **13/2**[3]

45-0 **2** *shd* **Violent Velocity (IRE)**[28] 1035 8-8-12 **63**................ ShaneBKelly(7) 4 71
(John Quinn) *sn prom: effrt over 2f out: upsides ins fnl f: jst failed* **7/1**

-025 **3** *nse* **Classic Descent**[12] 1373 6-8-12 **56**................(bt) TomEaves 2 64
(Ruth Carr) *s.s: hdwy on ins 3f out: nt clr run over 1f out: chal ins fnl f: r.o* **16/1**

030- **4** *2 1/2* **Seldom (IRE)**[223] 6117 5-9-3 **61**................ FrannyNorton 3 63
(Mel Brittain) *chsd ldr: effrt on ins over 2f out: one pce fnl f* **12/1**

6-32 **5** *1 1/2* **Border Owl (IRE)**[21] 1190 6-9-0 **63**................ TobyAtkinson(5) 10 62
(Peter Salmon) *mid-div: effrt on outside over 2f out: chsng ldrs over 1f out: kpt on one pce* **4/1**[1]

10-6 **6** *1 3/4* **Twisted**[13] 1052 5-9-5 **63**................(b) GrahamGibbons 8 58
(Michael Easterby) *led: hdd over 1f out: sn wknd* **18/1**

1621 **7** *hd* **Mr Chocolate Drop (IRE)**[21] 1190 7-8-12 **56**................(t) JimmyQuinn 12 50
(Mandy Rowland) *stdd and swtchd lft after s: hld up in rr: effrt over 2f out: kpt on fnl f: nvr a threat* **13/2**[3]

3141 **8** *½* **Barton Bounty**[12] 1374 4-9-1 **59**....(b) PhillipMakin 1 52
(Peter Niven) *dwlt: hld up in rr: nt clr run over 2f out: kpt on fnl f: nvr rchd ldrs* **8/1**

55-4 **9** *2¾* **Ra Junior (USA)**[26] 1077 5-9-0 **58**.... MickyFenton 5 45
(Paul Midgley) *in rr: sn drvn along: nvr on terms* **9/2**[2]

-202 **10** *1* **White Deer (USA)**[21] 1164 7-9-4 **65**....(v) MichaelO'Connell(3) 7 50
(Geoffrey Harker) *chsd ldrs: wknd over 1f out* **11/1**

1m 43.52s (-1.78) **Going Correction** -0.175s/f (Firm) **10** Ran SP% **115.6**
Speed ratings (Par 101): **101,100,100,98,96 95,94,94,91,90**
toteswingers: 1&2 £9.60, 1&3 £12.60, 2&3 £18.40. CSF £51.00 CT £715.44 TOTE £8.70: £2.50, £3.60, £6.20; EX 89.20.
Owner E Tuer **Bred** D R Tucker **Trained** Great Smeaton, N Yorks

FOCUS
A thrilling finish to this moderate handicap. The winner is rated close to his old turf best.
Ra Junior(USA) Official explanation: trainer had no explanation for the poor form shown

1614 STP CONSTRUCTION CLAIMING STKS — 1m 3y(S)
6:10 (6:10) (Class 6) 3-Y-O+ **£1,683** (£501; £250; £125) **Stalls** High

Form RPR
-540 **1** **Fremen (USA)**[11] 1382 11-9-5 77.... PaulQuinn 6 82
(David Nicholls) *led: hung rt: qcknd over 2f out: styd on strly fnl f* **6/1**[2]

300- **2** *3¾* **Albaqaa**[291] 3921 6-9-11 98.... TonyHamilton 5 80
(Richard Fahey) *hld up: t.k.h: trckd ldrs: wnt 2nd over 2f out: rdn over 1f out: hung rt and no imp* **4/9**[1]

-444 **3** *2½* **Bold Marc (IRE)**[12] 1373 9-9-5 62.... AndrewElliott 4 68
(Mrs K Burke) *w wnr: kpt on one pce fnl 2f* **11/1**

40-0 **4** *6* **Handsome Falcon**[37] 932 7-9-1 73.... LeeTopliss(5) 2 55
(Ollie Pears) *hld up: effrt 3f out: rdn and wknd 2f out* **7/1**[3]

0-20 **5** *3¾* **Just Five (IRE)**[24] 1110 5-9-1 78.... GerardGalligan(7) 1 49
(Michael Dods) *w ldrs: wknd over 1f out* **16/1**

00-0 **6** *42* **Pengula (IRE)**[19] 1211 4-8-9 34.... TjadeCollier(3) 3 —
(Robert Johnson) *trckd ldrs: t.k.h: rdn and lost pl 4f out: sn bhd: t.o* **150/1**

1m 40.51s (-2.89) **Going Correction** -0.175s/f (Firm) **6** Ran SP% **110.9**
Speed ratings (Par 101): **107,103,100,94,91 49**
toteswingers: 1&2 £1.60, 1&3 £3.10, 2&3 £1.10. CSF £8.93 TOTE £4.40: £1.50, £1.10; EX 12.40.Albaqaa was claimed by Noel Quinlan for £13,000.
Owner Middleham Park Racing XXXV C King A Seed **Bred** Flaxman Holdings Ltd **Trained** Sessay, N Yorks

FOCUS
Only the front two mattered from 2f out in this fair claimer. The favourite disappointed and the third limits the form.

1615 SPORTPOOL.CO.UK H'CAP — 1m 2f 32y
6:40 (6:42) (Class 6) (0-60,60) 4-Y-O+ **£1,683** (£501; £250; £125) **Stalls** Low

Form RPR
53-6 **1** **Miss Blink**[26] 1077 4-8-9 **48**.... LeeNewman 9 60+
(Robin Bastiman) *chsd ldrs: edgd lft over 2f out: led appr fnl f: styd on wl* **9/1**

046- **2** *3* **Media Stars**[10] 6298 6-8-12 **51**.... TonyHamilton 12 57
(Robert Johnson) *w ldr: led over 5f out: hdd appr fnl f: no ex* **50/1**

0-00 **3** *nk* **Star Addition**[11] 1394 5-8-13 **52**.... RobertWinston 3 57
(Eric Alston) *trckd ldrs: t.k.h: hmpd after 1f: drvn over 3f out: kpt on same pce appr fnl f* **9/1**

0-42 **4** *hd* **Eijaaz (IRE)**[14] 1305 10-9-3 **59**....(p) MichaelO'Connell(3) 11 64
(Geoffrey Harker) *s.i.s: hld up in rr: stdy hdwy over 2f out: chsd ldrs 1f out: kpt on same pce* **11/2**[2]

50-0 **5** *1¼* **Weetfromthechaff**[14] 1305 6-8-11 **50**....(t) AndrewMullen 4 53
(Maurice Barnes) *chsd ldrs: hmpd 2f out: kpt on one pce* **14/1**

200- **6** *1¼* **Tropical Duke (IRE)**[194] 6890 5-8-13 **59**.... ShaneBKelly(7) 5 61+
(Ron Barr) *in rr: hdwy on ins 3f out: chsng ldrs over 1f out: one pce* **16/1**

7 *shd* **Suprise Vendor (IRE)**[37] 6785 5-9-0 **60**.... GarryWhillans(7) 1 60
(Stuart Coltherd) *mid-div: effrt over 2f out: kpt on one pce* **25/1**

0-45 **8** *nk* **Lucayan Dancer**[36] 939 11-9-0 **53**.... PaulQuinn 15 52
(David Nicholls) *in rr-div: hdwy on ins 3f out: kpt on fnl f* **16/1**

50-0 **9** *1¾* **Petrocelli**[10] 1216 4-8-10 **54**.... LeeTopliss(5) 2 50
(Wilf Storey) *in rr: kpt on fnl 3f: nvr nr ldrs* **20/1**

3205 **10** *8* **Verluga (IRE)**[11] 1394 4-9-2 **55**....(b) DuranFentiman 10 35
(Tim Easterby) *in tch: drvn 3f out: wknd over 1f out* **12/1**

4-32 **11** *1* **Marino Prince (FR)**[12] 1374 6-8-11 **50**.... MickyFenton 8 28
(Paul Midgley) *s.i.s: sme hdwy over 4f out: lost pl over 2f out* **6/1**[3]

/0-4 **12** *5* **Brasingaman Eric**[13] 1324 4-9-0 **53**.... TomEaves 6 21
(George Moore) *chsd ldrs: wkng whn hmpd over 2f out* **5/1**[1]

0-00 **13** *8* **Plenilune (IRE)**[7] 1498 6-8-7 **46**....(p) FrannyNorton 16 —
(Mel Brittain) *led tl over 5f out: wkng whn hmpd 2f out: eased clsng stages* **28/1**

0-00 **14** *12* **Stardust Dancer**[65] 634 4-8-6 **48**.... DeclanCannon(3) 17 —
(Paul Green) *s.i.s: sme hdwy over 4f out: drvn over 3f out: sn lost pl* **40/1**

/350 **15** *5* **The Gillie**[4] 1520 4-9-4 **57**.... FrederikTylicki 7 —
(Richard Fahey) *s.i.s: in rr and drvn over 4f out: bhd fnl 3f* **12/1**

-000 **16** *½* **Politbureau**[13] 1324 4-9-6 **59**.... PaulMulrennan 13 —
(Michael Easterby) *chsd ldrs: lost pl 3f out: sn bhd* **20/1**

2m 11.59s (-0.31) **Going Correction** -0.175s/f (Firm) **16** Ran SP% **121.4**
Speed ratings (Par 101): **94,91,91,90 89,89,88,87,81 80,76,69,60,56 55**
toteswingers: 1&2 £116.60, 1&3 £11.00, 2&3 £143.90. CSF £421.77 CT £4131.98 TOTE £13.10: £3.00, £9.60, £2.80, £1.50; EX 617.80.
Owner A Reed **Bred** Anthony Reed **Trained** Cowthorpe, N Yorks

FOCUS
A weak handicap, but it was competitive for the class. The winner improved and should do better still.
Stardust Dancer Official explanation: jockey said gelding never travelled

1616 LA TAXIS MAIDEN FILLIES' STKS — 1m 4f 93y
7:10 (7:10) (Class 5) 3-4-Y-O **£2,331** (£693; £346; £173) **Stalls** Low

Form RPR
04-2 **1** **Highest**[12] 1364 3-8-7 80.... NickyMackay 5 69+
(John Gosden) *mde all: qcknd over 3f out: styd on u.p fnl 2f: unchal* **1/3**[1]

2 *2* **Body Language (IRE)** 3-8-8 0 ow1.... PaulMulrennan 2 67+
(Ann Duffield) *in tch: effrt over 3f out: styd on to go 2nd over 2f out: kpt on wl fnl f* **33/1**

5-00 **3** *5* **Donna Elvira**[13] 1324 4-9-12 62.... TonyHamilton 1 60
(Edwin Tuer) *drvn early to chse wnr: regained 2nd over 3f out: one pce* **20/1**[3]

4 **4** *12* **Chapter Five**[19] 1211 4-9-12 0.... TomEaves 3 41
(Keith Reveley) *dwlt: hld up in rr: hdwy 4f out: lost pl over 2f out: eased nr fin* **28/1**

043- **5** *69* **Malacca Straits**[214] 6353 3-8-7 73.... RobertWinston 4 —
(B W Hills) *trckd ldrs: wnt 2nd 5f out: drvn over 3f out: sn lost pl: bhd whn eased fnl f: virtually p.u: wl t.o* **7/2**[2]

2m 42.98s (-2.62) **Going Correction** -0.175s/f (Firm)
WFA 3 from 4yo 20lb **5** Ran SP% **108.4**
Speed ratings (Par 100): **101,99,96,88,42**
CSF £15.93 TOTE £1.20: £1.10, £4.10; EX 6.20.
Owner Denford Stud **Bred** Belgrave Bloodstock **Trained** Newmarket, Suffolk

FOCUS
An uncompetitive fillies' maiden, with the second favourite not running her race. The winner didn't need to match her Newbury form.
Malacca Straits Official explanation: trainer had no explanation for the poor form shown

1617 GOSFORTH DECORATING & BUILDING SERVICES H'CAP — 1m 4f 93y
7:40 (7:40) (Class 6) (0-60,55) 4-Y-O+ **£1,683** (£501; £250; £125) **Stalls** Low

Form RPR
6-62 **1** **Tenhoo**[8] 1461 5-8-11 **52**.... NathanAlison(7) 7 68+
(Eric Alston) *t.k.h in mid-div: effrt and swtchd rt over 2f out: led over 1f out: sn rdn clr: rdn rt out* **5/4**[1]

060- **2** *2* **Falcun**[75] 5971 4-8-12 **47**.... FrederikTylicki 1 62+
(Micky Hammond) *dwlt: hld up in rr: hdwy on ins 3f out: wnt 2nd 1f out: kpt on: no imp* **16/1**

006- **3** *4½* **Grey Command (USA)**[216] 6306 6-9-0 **48**.... RobertWinston 2 54
(Mel Brittain) *chsd ldrs: drvn over 3f out: swtchd rt 2f out: wnt 3rd 1f out: one pce* **8/1**

550- **4** *4½* **Dechiper (IRE)**[4] 5687 9-8-11 **45**.... TonyHamilton 8 44
(Robert Johnson) *sn trcking ldrs: led briefly 2f out: edgd lft 1f out: one pce* **10/1**

00-6 **5** *nk* **Classic Contours (USA)**[24] 1039 5-9-6 **54**....(t) PaulMulrennan 5 52
(Tracy Waggott) *led: hdd 2f out: one pce whn n.m.r 1f out* **13/2**[3]

00-0 **6** *¾* **Dimashq**[14] 1305 9-8-11 **45**.... MickyFenton 3 42
(Paul Midgley) *hld up in rr: hdwy and nt clr run over 2f out: one pce whn sltly hmpd 1f out* **14/1**

0-25 **7** *4½* **Why So Serious**[29] 1028 5-9-2 **55**.... TobyAtkinson(5) 9 45
(Peter Salmon) *in rr: reminders and hdwy over 6f out: rdn 3f out: lost pl over 1f out* **33/1**

6/0- **8** *3* **Fossgate**[237] 5687 10-9-4 **52**.... AndrewElliott 4 37
(James Bethell) *trckd ldrs: t.k.h: drvn 4f out: wknd over 1f out* **20/1**

040- **9** *35* **Nayessence**[144] 7704 5-9-2 **50**....(t) GrahamGibbons 6 —
(Michael Easterby) *w ldr: t.k.h: wknd qckly 2f out: sn bhd: virtually p.u: wl t.o* **5/1**[2]

2m 43.5s (-2.10) **Going Correction** -0.175s/f (Firm)
WFA 4 from 5yo+ 1lb **9** Ran SP% **114.9**
Speed ratings (Par 101): **100,98,95,92,92 91,88,86,63**
toteswingers: 1&2 £6.00, 1&3 £3.20, 2&3 £17.90. CSF £24.47 CT £118.59 TOTE £1.70: £1.02, £6.30, £4.10; EX 21.30.
Owner Edges Farm Racing Stables Ltd **Bred** A G Antoniades **Trained** Longton, Lancs

FOCUS
A moderate handicap, rated around the winner, with a promising effort from the second.
Nayessence Official explanation: vet said gelding finished distressed

1618 SENDRIG CONSTRUCTION H'CAP — 6f
8:10 (8:10) (Class 4) (0-85,85) 4-Y-O+ **£3,497** (£1,040; £520; £259) **Stalls** High

Form RPR
60-1 **1** **King Of Eden (IRE)**[24] 1110 5-9-3 **81**.... DavidAllan 7 94
(Eric Alston) *dwlt: hld up in rr: hdwy over 2f out: led jst ins fnl f: sn pushed clr: readily* **9/4**[1]

21-5 **2** *3* **Grissom (IRE)**[20] 1205 5-9-0 **78**.... DuranFentiman 1 81
(Tim Easterby) *in rr: hdwy over 2f out: chsd wnr ins fnl f: no imp* **8/1**

4-34 **3** *½* **Marvellous Value (IRE)**[20] 1200 6-9-0 **78**.... FrederikTylicki 4 79
(Michael Dods) *w ldrs: led over 3f out: hdd jst ins fnl f: kpt on same pce* **4/1**[2]

3310 **4** *3* **Hinton Admiral**[18] 1245 7-8-8 **72**.... TomEaves 6 64
(Keith Dalgleish) *s.i.s: hdwy over 2f out: kpt on same pce* **14/1**

10-0 **5** *1¼* **Ghost (IRE)**[9] 1438 4-8-11 **82**.... PNolan(7) 3 70
(David Nicholls) *w ldrs on outside: hung lft over 2f out: kpt on fnl f* **33/1**

00-3 **6** *2¾* **Invincible Lad (IRE)**[20] 1205 7-8-12 **79**.... MichaelO'Connell(3) 5 58
(David Nicholls) *w ldrs: wknd 1f out* **15/2**[3]

00-0 **7** *2¼* **Prince Of Vasa (IRE)**[9] 1438 4-9-1 **79**.... RobertWinston 10 51
(Michael Smith) *v free to post: chsd ldrs: hung lft and outpcd over 2f out: no threat after* **18/1**

0-02 **8** *4* **Solar Spirit (IRE)**[9] 1438 6-9-0 **78**.... PaulMulrennan 8 37
(Tracy Waggott) *t.k.h: led tl over 3f out: wknd over 1f out* **4/1**[2]

040- **9** *9* **Eternal Instinct**[220] 6221 4-8-8 **72**.... AndrewMullen 9 —
(Jim Goldie) *in rr: lost pl over 2f out: sn bhd* **22/1**

1m 13.84s (-0.76) **Going Correction** -0.175s/f (Firm) **9** Ran SP% **112.9**
Speed ratings (Par 105): **98,94,93,89,87 84,81,75,63**
toteswingers: 1&2 £5.80, 1&3 £2.50, 2&3 £7.10. CSF £20.57 CT £67.40 TOTE £2.40: £1.10, £3.10, £2.90; EX 15.60.
Owner The Grumpy Old Geezers **Bred** Gainsborough Stud Management Ltd **Trained** Longton, Lancs

FOCUS
A fair sprint handicap and a progressive winner. The runner-up ran pretty much to form.
Prince Of Vasa(IRE) Official explanation: jockey said gelding ran too free to post
Solar Spirit(IRE) Official explanation: jockey said gelding ran too free
T/Plt: £84.60 to a £1 stake. Pool of £43,798.77 - 377.80 winning tickets. T/Qpdt: £6.80 to a £1 stake. Pool of £4,567.44 - 495.80 winning tickets. WG

1455 PONTEFRACT (L-H)
Wednesday, April 27

OFFICIAL GOING: Good to firm (8.4)
Wind: nil Weather: Sunny

1619 EUROPEAN BREEDERS' FUND WILLIAM HILL MAIDEN STKS — 5f
2:20 (2:20) (Class 4) 2-Y-O **£4,533** (£1,348; £674; £336) **Stalls** Low

Form RPR
3 **1** **Sweet Chilli (IRE)**[11] 1414 2-8-12 0.... GrahamGibbons 7 80+
(David Barron) *qckly away: sn led: rdn clr wl over 1f out: easily* **5/2**[2]

2 *3½* **Bling King** 2-9-3 0.... SebSanders 3 72
(Eve Johnson Houghton) *sltly hmpd s: in tch 1/2-way: hdwy over 2f out: rdn to chse wnr ins fnl f: no imp* **14/1**

534 **3** *1½* **Sabusa (IRE)**[14] 1316 2-9-3 0.... DarryllHolland 1 67
(Alan McCabe) *wnt bdly rt s: sn chsng ldng pair: rdn to chse wnr wl over 1f out: drvn and one pce appr fnl f* **7/1**[3]

4 **4** *5* **Safari Storm (USA)**[16] 1268 2-9-3 0....(t) ShaneKelly 5 49
(Brian Meehan) *trckd ldrs: effrt 2f out and sn rdn: drvn and edgd lft over 1f out: sn no imp* **2/1**[1]

5 *1 1/4* **Superplex** 2-9-3 0.... CDHayes 4 45+
(John Quinn) *sltly hmpd s: towards rr tl styd on fr over 1f out: nrst fin* **20/1**

3 **6** *1 3/4* **Nellie Pickersgill**[21] 1165 2-8-12 0.... DavidAllan 9 33
(Tim Easterby) *cl up: rdn wl over 1f out: grad wknd* **16/1**

7 *hd* **Kool Henry (IRE)** 2-9-3 0.... DanielTudhope 6 37
(David O'Meara) *cl up on outer: rdn along wl over 1f out: wknd appr fnl f* **14/1**

8 *6* **Nameitwhatyoulike** 2-9-0 0.... JamesSullivan(3) 8 16
(Michael Easterby) *a in rr: outpcd and bhd fr 1/2-way* **66/1**

9 *2 1/4* **Brimstone Hill (IRE)** 2-9-3 0.... RobertWinston 2 8
(B W Hills) *sltly hmpd s: a in rr* **8/1**

63.55 secs (0.25) **Going Correction** -0.10s/f (Good) **9** Ran SP% **111.0**
Speed ratings (Par 94): **94,88,86,78,76 73,72,63,59**
toteswingers:1&2 £5.60, 2&3 £7.00, 1&3 £2.60 CSF £34.89 TOTE £3.20: £1.70, £3.80, £2.00; EX 39.10.
Owner T D Barron **Bred** Hyperion Bloodstock **Trained** Maunby, N Yorks

FOCUS
On a sunny afternoon the ground was described as good to firm all around with a Goingstick reading of 8.4. A solid tempo for this maiden and, not for the first time at this track, it proved hard to come off the pace. The third has been rated to his Newmarket run.

NOTEBOOK
Sweet Chilli(IRE) came clear here in very pleasing fashion and can go on from this pleasing performance. Third on her debut, she has plenty of natural of speed and there are more races to be won with her. (op 11-4 tchd 3-1)
Bling King tracked the leaders before coming through for second. He should continue to improve and will get further in due course. A similar maiden will be well within his grasp. (op 12-1)
Sabusa(IRE), the most experienced runner in the line-up, again showed he is not devoid of ability. It will be a surprise if a maiden doesn't come his way, however he is vulnerable to anything above average. (op 13-2)
Safari Storm(USA), who was wearing a tongue-tie for the first time, couldn't build on his first run. (tchd 7-4)
Superplex caught the eye staying on nicely and will be sharper for this outing. (op 22-1)
Brimstone Hill(IRE) was always behind after a slow start. (op 9-1 tchd 10-1)

1620 GALA CORAL MAIDEN STKS — 1m 2f 6y
2:55 (2:56) (Class 5) 3-Y-0 — **£2,422** (£715; £357) **Stalls** Low

Form — RPR

0-42 **1** **Greyfriars Drummer**[7] 1484 3-9-3 0.... JoeFanning 2 87+
(Mark Johnston) *cl up on inner: led after 1 1/2f: rdn clr wl over 1f out: unchal* **11/4**[1]

36- **2** *7* **Matilda's Waltz**[181] 7198 3-8-12 0.... RichardKingscote 3 63
(Ralph Beckett) *trckd ldng pair: hdwy to chse wnr 2f out: sn rdn and one pce* **11/4**[1]

0- **3** *hd* **Circus Act**[175] 7303 3-9-3 0.... AhmedAjtebi 6 68
(Mahmood Al Zarooni) *hld up: hdwy on outer 4f out: rdn to chse ldrs over 2f out: drvn and sn one pce* **4/1**[2]

0- **4** *3/4* **Apticanti (USA)**[292] 3871 3-8-12 0.... RobertWinston 9 61+
(B W Hills) *in rr and green: effrt and pushed along 3f out: rdn 2f out: kpt on ins fnl f: nrst fin* **12/1**

00- **5** *4* **Geminus (IRE)**[194] 6894 3-9-3 0.... PaulMulrennan 7 58?
(Jedd O'Keeffe) *chsd ldrs: rdn along 4f out: drvn over 2f out and sn wknd* **100/1**

4- **6** *1* **Around The Clock (USA)**[154] 7559 3-9-3 0.... PatDobbs 5 56
(Amanda Perrett) *in tch: effrt over 4f out: sn rdn along and btn* **13/2**[3]

0-4 **7** *1* **Ugo (USA)**[16] 1271 3-9-3 0.... DaneO'Neill 4 54
(Heather Main) *led 1 1/2f: cl up rdn along 3f out: drvn over 2f out and sn wknd* **7/1**

8 *86* **Mir Hy (USA)** 3-9-3 0.... ChrisCatlin 1 —
(Clive Brittain) *s.i.s: green: sn rdn along and in rr: t.o fnl 4f* **22/1**

2m 12.89s (-0.81) **Going Correction** -0.10s/f (Good) **8** Ran SP% **112.2**
Speed ratings (Par 98): **90,93,93,92,89 88,87,19**
toteswingers:1&2 £1.90, 2&3 £3.30, 1&3 £4.20 CSF £9.82 TOTE £3.40: £1.10, £1.10, £3.20; EX 11.30.
Owner Greyfriars UK Ltd **Bred** Mrs Mary Taylor **Trained** Middleham Moor, N Yorks

FOCUS
A maiden that has thrown up useful winners in the past and this year's line-up looked interesting, but, that said, a few of them were coming back from a break. It was run at a sound pace, and again the first two raced up with the pace throughout.

1621 BETFRED.COM H'CAP — 1m 4y
3:30 (3:30) (Class 5) (0-75,78) 4-Y-0+ — **£2,422** (£715; £357) **Stalls** Low

Form — RPR

0-00 **1** **Hail Promenader (IRE)**[11] 1402 5-9-5 **73**.... RobertWinston 3 85
(B W Hills) *in tch: pushed along over 3f out: rdn 2f out: hdwy on inner 1 1/2f out: drvn to chse ldr ins fnl f: styd on to ld nr line* **10/3**[2]

50-1 **2** *shd* **Cono Zur (FR)**[11] 1394 4-9-1 **72**.... JamesSullivan(3) 4 83
(Ruth Carr) *led: rdn clr 2f out: drvn ins fnl f: hdd and no ex nr line* **9/2**[3]

430- **3** *2 1/2* **Mingun Bell (USA)**[203] 6677 4-9-5 **73**.... SebSanders 7 78
(Ed de Giles) *chsd ldng pair on outer: effrt over 2f out: sn rdn: drvn over 1f out: kpt on ins fnl f* **9/1**

-101 **4** *3 1/2* **Count Bertoni (IRE)**[8] 1460 4-9-10 **78** 6ex.... DanielTudhope 5 75
(David O'Meara) *trckd ldr: effrt 3f out: rdn over 2f out: sn drvn and wknd over 1f out* **9/4**[1]

1230 **5** *1/2* **Ours (IRE)**[27] 1061 8-9-7 **75**....(p) BarryMcHugh 1 71
(John Harris) *dwlt and in rr: hdwy on outer 2f out: rdn and styng on whn hmpd and swtchd lft over 1f out: fin wl* **15/2**

0-00 **6** *hd* **Aussie Blue (IRE)**[8] 1460 7-8-7 **66**.... DanielleMcCreery(5) 2 62
(Richard Whitaker) *hld up towards rr: hdwy over 2f out: swtchd rt to outer and rdn over 1f out: kpt on same pce* **14/1**

2-04 **7** *2 1/4* **Strike Force**[19] 1222 7-9-1 **69**....(t) DavidAllan 6 59
(Clifford Lines) *a towards rr* **12/1**

0-20 **8** *38* **Forzarzi (IRE)**[16] 1273 7-8-8 **62** oh12 ow1....(p) PaulMulrennan 8 —
(Hugh McWilliams) *chsd ldrs: rdn along wl over 2f out: sn wknd and eased* **40/1**

1m 44.43s (-1.47) **Going Correction** -0.10s/f (Good) **8** Ran SP% **110.6**
Speed ratings (Par 103): **103,102,100,96,96 96,93,55**
toteswingers:1&2 £2.70, 2&3 £4.70, 1&3 £7.20 CSF £17.42 CT £115.22 TOTE £4.70: £1.20, £1.90, £3.00; EX 22.80.
Owner B W Hills **Bred** Rathbarry Stud **Trained** Lambourn, Berks
■ Stewards' Enquiry : Danielle McCreery one-day ban: careless riding (May 11)

FOCUS
With two last-time-out winners and plenty of C&D form, this was a competitive 61-75 handicap in which the first four home raced prominently throughout. The winner is possibly better than the bare form.

1622 LADBROKES.COM FILLIES' H'CAP — 1m 2f 6y
4:05 (4:07) (Class 3) (0-90,86) 3-Y-0+
£6,449 (£1,931; £965; £483; £241; £121) **Stalls** Low

Form — RPR

5152 **1** **Snow Dancer (IRE)**[25] 1098 7-9-4 **79**.... JamesSullivan(3) 2 87+
(Hugh McWilliams) *hld up in rr: hdwy whn hmpd 2f out: swtchd wd and rdn over 1f out: str run ins fnl f to ld nr fin* **12/1**

31-2 **2** *1/2* **Hawaafez**[21] 1168 3-8-7 **82**.... TadhgO'Shea 6 86
(Marcus Tregoning) *trckd ldrs: hdwy 3f out: cl up 2f out: sn rdn and led ent fnl f: sn drvn and edgd lft: hdd and no ex nr fin* **5/6**[1]

013- **3** *3/4* **Antigua Sunrise (IRE)**[214] 6361 5-9-1 **80**.... GeorgeChaloner(7) 3 86+
(Richard Fahey) *trckd ldrs: hdwy on inner and n.m.r over 2f out: effrt and nt clr run over 1f out: swtchd rt and rdn ent fnl f: kpt on* **6/1**[2]

130- **4** *3/4* **Sea Of Galilee**[180] 7206 4-9-12 **84**.... DaneO'Neill 4 88
(Henry Candy) *led: rdn over 2f out: drvn over 1f out: hdd ent fnl f: one pce* **12/1**

31- **5** *nse* **Dubai Bounty**[269] 4619 4-9-10 **82**....(p) DarryllHolland 1 86
(Gerard Butler) *trckd ldrs: hdwy over 2f out: rdn and ch over 1f out: drvn and one pce ins fnl f* **6/1**[2]

31-0 **6** *7* **Fun Affair (USA)**[25] 1104 4-10-0 **86**.... RobertHavlin 7 76
(John Gosden) *hld up in rr: hdwy on outer 3f out: rdn and edgd lft 2f out: sn btn* **9/1**[3]

60-0 **7** *8* **Bollin Dolly**[11] 1388 8-9-5 **77**.... DavidAllan 8 51
(Tim Easterby) *in tch on outer: rdn along wl over 2f out: sn wknd* **28/1**

5-03 **8** *21* **Viewing**[11] 1388 4-9-2 **74**.... PaulMulrennan 5 —
(James Given) *cl up: rdn along over 2f out: sn wknd: bhd and eased ins fnl f* **20/1**

2m 11.7s (-2.00) **Going Correction** -0.10s/f (Good)
WFA 3 from 4yo+ 17lb **8** Ran SP% **116.7**
Speed ratings (Par 104): **104,103,103,102,102 96,90,73**
toteswingers:1&2 £3.30, 2&3 £2.60, 1&3 £6.20 CSF £23.06 CT £72.72 TOTE £13.10: £2.50, £1.40, £1.10; EX 38.10.
Owner Mrs L Wohlers **Bred** Liam Queally **Trained** Pilling, Lancs

FOCUS
A fillies' handicap for horses rated 71-90 handicap with the top weight 4lb below the ceiling rating. It was run at a very generous pace and the winner was last turning for home. The form is rated around the third, with the winner better than ever.

NOTEBOOK
Snow Dancer(IRE), who appears to relish this track, did well considering she was hampered turning for home as well. Clearly in good heart at present, she should remain competitive but it will require a career best to follow up next time.
Hawaafez appeared to have no excuses here. Doing nothing quickly, she was one of the first off the bridle and taking up her Oaks entry looks highly unlikely now. A step up in trip will see her in a better light though, and she can still win races but the handicapper has got her about right. (tchd 10-11 after early Evens in places)
Antigua Sunrise(IRE), coming from a yard firing in the winners, ran a cracker on her first run back after a break, especially as she had to be switched having been short of room on the rail early in the straight, and another productive season awaits this game mare. (op 8-1)
Sea Of Galilee will be better for the race. (op 14-1 tchd 11-1)
Viewing needs to come down in the weights before she can make her mark for this yard. (op 22-1)

1623 SPORTINGBET.COM H'CAP — 1m 4f 8y
4:40 (4:40) (Class 5) (0-75,66) 3-Y-0 — **£2,422** (£715; £357) **Stalls** Low

Form — RPR

00-5 **1** **Dark Dune (IRE)**[13] 1327 3-9-1 **60**.... DavidAllan 5 71
(Tim Easterby) *cl up: led after 1 1/2f: rdn 2f out: drvn over 1f out: kpt on gamely u.p ins fnl f* **12/1**

5-12 **2** *hd* **Pretty Diamond (IRE)**[9] 1442 3-9-5 **64**.... GregFairley 2 75
(Mark Johnston) *led 1 1/2f: trckd wnr: effrt 2f out: sn rdn and edgd lft over 1f out: drvn and kpt on ins fnl f: jst hld* **4/6**[1]

-065 **3** *5* **Bradbury (IRE)**[21] 1189 3-9-2 **61**....(p) DarryllHolland 4 64
(James Bethell) *in rr: rdn along and outpcd 4f out: kpt on u.p fnl 2f: n.d* **9/1**

-625 **4** *1* **Dew Reward (IRE)**[14] 1312 3-9-2 **61**.... SebSanders 1 62
(Eve Johnson Houghton) *trckd ldrs on inner: hdwy to chse ldng pair over 2f out: rdn wl over 1f out: sn drvn and one pce* **8/1**[3]

30-5 **5** *13* **Madison Square (USA)**[11] 1415 3-9-7 **66**.... AhmedAjtebi 3 46
(Mahmood Al Zarooni) *trckd ldrs: effrt over 3f out: rdn 2f out: sn btn* **4/1**[2]

2m 38.78s (-2.02) **Going Correction** -0.10s/f (Good) **5** Ran SP% **108.8**
Speed ratings (Par 98): **102,101,98,97,89**
CSF £20.62 TOTE £14.70: £3.90, £1.10; EX 23.90.
Owner Miss Betty Duxbury **Bred** P Turley **Trained** Great Habton, N Yorks

FOCUS
A handicap open to horses rated 61-75 but the top weight was rated 9lb below the ceiling rating. It was run at a sound pace and not for the first time on this card the winner made all the running. The form might not hold up but the winner and runner-up have been rated as running a personal bests.

1624 TOTESPORT.COM H'CAP — 6f
5:15 (5:16) (Class 5) (0-75,75) 3-Y-0 — **£2,422** (£715; £357) **Stalls** Low

Form — RPR

2426 **1** **Close To The Edge (IRE)**[82] 422 3-8-8 **62**.... ShaneKelly 8 68
(Alan McCabe) *cl up: rdn to ld over 1f out: sn hung rt: hdd and wandered ins fnl f: drvn and kpt on to ld nr fin* **16/1**

431- **2** *1/2* **Jibaal (IRE)**[194] 6902 3-9-4 **72**.... TadhgO'Shea 5 76
(Mark Johnston) *led: rdn 2f out: hdd over 1f out: drvn and rallied to ld ins fnl f: hdd and no ex nr fin* **5/1**[2]

05-2 **3** *hd* **Thirteen Shivers**[16] 1275 3-9-1 **72**.... JamesSullivan(3) 10 76
(Michael Easterby) *chsd ldrs: hdwy wl over 1f out: sn rdn and swtchd rt ins fnl f: kpt on wl towards fin* **15/2**

301- **4** *1 3/4* **Normandy Maid**[201] 6705 3-8-11 **72**.... LauraBarry(7) 1 70
(Richard Fahey) *chsd ldrs on inner: rdn wl over 1f out: kpt on same pce ins fnl f: n.m.r and swtchd rt nr fin* **17/2**

520- **5** *1/2* **Silken Thoughts**[222] 6163 3-8-13 **67**.... DarryllHolland 11 64+
(John Berry) *towards rr: hdwy 2f out: rdn over 1f out: kpt on wl ins fnl f: nrst fin* **6/1**[3]

35-0 **6** *3 1/4* **Mariners Lodge (USA)**[11] 1409 3-9-7 **75**.... AhmedAjtebi 7 61
(Mahmood Al Zarooni) *towards rr: hdwy on outer 2f out: sn rdn and kpt on ins fnl f: nt rch ldrs* **11/4**[1]

44-5 **7** *1 1/2* **Suddenly Susan (IRE)**[22] 1155 3-8-8 **65**.... BillyCray(3) 3 46
(David Nicholls) *chsd ldrs: rdn along 2f out: sn wknd* **7/1**

605- **8** 1/2 **Grazeon Again (IRE)**[217] 6294 3-8-7 **61** oh1 CDHayes 6 41
(John Quinn) *a towards rr* **22/1**
55-0 **9** *nk* **Icy Blue**[24] 1108 3-8-10 **69** DanielleMcCreery(5) 9 48
(Richard Whitaker) *s.i.s: a in rr* **20/1**
005- **10** *nse* **Mister Ben Vereen**[199] 6778 3-8-11 **65** SebSanders 4 44
(Eve Johnson Houghton) *in tch: rdn along over 2f out: sn wknd* **16/1**
1m 17.12s (0.22) **Going Correction** -0.10s/f (Good) **10** Ran SP% **113.3**
Speed ratings (Par 98): **94,93,93,90,90 85,83,83,82,82**
toteswingers:1&2 £14.70, 2&3 £4.90, 1&3 £11.60 CSF £91.51 CT £673.89 TOTE £19.90: £5.10, £1.70, £3.80; EX 129.40.
Owner Charles Wentworth **Bred** Martin Francis **Trained** Averham Park, Notts

FOCUS
A wide open 61-75 handicap run at a sound pace and yet again the first two home were the first two throughout. The winner is rated back to her debut form.
Icy Blue Official explanation: jockey said gelding missed the break
T/Plt: £14.00 to a £1 stake. Pool of £45,715.67 - 2,382.59 winning tickets. T/Qpdt: £7.30 to a £1 stake. Pool of £3,686.97 - 369.60 winning tickets. JR

1448 BATH (L-H)
Thursday, April 28

OFFICIAL GOING: Firm (10.4)
Wind: Moderate across Weather: Sunny

1625 NEW JAGUAR XJ FROM 0% FINANCE H'CAP 1m 5y
2:10 (2:10) (Class 6) (0-55,55) 4-Y-O+ **£1,780** (£529; £264; £132) **Stalls** Low

Form RPR
1314 **1** **Grey Boy (GER)**[36] 943 10-8-8 **54** GeorgeDowning(7) 11 61
(Tony Carroll) *stdd s: hld up in rr: hdwy over 2f out: pushed along to ld ins fnl f: kpt on wl* **9/2**[1]
00-0 **2** 1/2 **Goose Green (IRE)**[18] 810 7-8-13 **52** JimCrowley 2 58
(Ron Hodges) *chsd ldrs: rdn 3f out: styd on fnl f to take 2nd cl home but a jst hld by wnr* **11/1**
00-6 **3** 1/2 **Fitz**[29] 1045 5-9-0 **53** ow2 AdamKirby 8 57
(Matthew Salaman) *in tch: hrd drvn 3f out: styd on fr over 1f out: kpt on clsng stages to take 3rd last strides but nt quite rch ldng duo* **7/1**
5550 **4** *hd* **Aggbag**[36] 950 7-8-7 **46** MartinDwyer 1 50
(Tony Carroll) *chsd ldrs: rdn over 2f out: led over 1f out: hdd ins fnl f: lost two pls cl home* **13/2**
4606 **5** 2 **Fedora (IRE)**[13] 1374 5-9-0 **53** (t) CathyGannon 9 52
(Olivia Maylam) *t.k.h: stdd towards rr: hdwy and rdn over 2f out: styd on fnl f but nvr a threat* **7/1**
0505 **6** 3 1/4 **Escardo (GER)**[13] 1374 8-8-1 **47** oh1 ow1 (p) JoshBaudains(7) 10 39
(David Bridgwater) *w ldr: chal 4f out: slt ld over 2f out: hdd over 1f out: wknd fnl f* **18/1**
145- **7** 10 **Gee Major**[237] 5711 4-9-2 **55** NeilChalmers 7 24
(Nicky Vaughan) *slt ld: jnd 4f out tl hdd over 2f out: sn wknd* **5/1**[2]
50-0 **8** *nk* **Miss Tenacious**[13] 1374 4-8-0 **46** oh1 (b[1]) JakePayne(7) 5 14
(Ron Hodges) *t.k.h: towards rr most of way* **66/1**
0060 **9** 1 3/4 **Jiggalong**[40] 911 5-8-2 **48** oh1 ow2 LewisWalsh(7) 4 12
(Mrs D Thomas) *bhd most of way* **25/1**
0546 **10** 17 **Haulit**[22] 1184 5-8-12 **51** RichardHughes 6 —
(Gary Moore) *in rr: sme hdwy on outside over 3f out: nvr rchd ldrs: sn wknd: eased whn no ch fnl f* **11/2**[3]
300- **11** 8 **Coolella (IRE)**[208] 6579 4-8-13 **52** LukeMorris 3 —
(John Weymes) *sn bhd: eased whn no ch fnl f* **9/1**
1m 40.66s (-0.14) **Going Correction** -0.025s/f (Good) **11** Ran SP% **117.5**
Speed ratings (Par 101): **99,98,98,97,95 92,82,82,80,63 55**
toteswingers:1&2:£10.30, 1&3:£8.10, 2&3:£10.30 CSF £54.41 CT £351.21 TOTE £4.40: £2.10, £4.30, £3.40; EX 50.90 Trifecta £242.70 Part won. Pool: £328.04 - 0.89 winning units..
Owner Paul Downing **Bred** J Potempa **Trained** Cropthorne, Worcs

FOCUS
A weak handicap, though Gee Major and Escardo made sure it was run at a strong pace. The winner was close to his recent AW form.

1626 GRANGEJAGUAR.CO.UK CLASSIFIED STKS 1m 5y
2:40 (2:41) (Class 5) 3-Y-O **£2,456** (£725; £362) **Stalls** Low

Form RPR
4-50 **1** **Silverware (USA)**[10] 1446 3-9-0 73 RichardHughes 4 75
(Richard Hannon) *sn led: t.k.h: jnd fr 4f out: pushed along over 2f out: asserted over 1f out: kpt on wl* **9/2**[2]
200- **2** 1 1/2 **Sahafh (USA)**[210] 6511 3-9-0 73 FrankieDettori 3 72
(Saeed Bin Suroor) *t.k.h: chsd ldrs: pushed along and outpcd over 2f out: rdn and styd on again fnl f to take 2nd last strides but no ch w wnr* **5/1**[3]
23-0 **3** *nk* **Galloping Queen (IRE)**[12] 1415 3-8-11 72 (v[1]) MartinHarley(3) 5 71
(Mick Channon) *chsd wnr: upsides fr 4f out tl rdn 2f out: outpcd fnl f: btn whn hung lft fnl 120yds: lost 2nd last strides* **12/1**
04-4 **4** 2 1/2 **Firstknight**[24] 1141 3-9-0 74 AdamKirby 6 66
(Marco Botti) *t.k.h: hld up in rr: sme hdwy on outside over 2f out and sn rdn: no imp on ldng trio and no ch fnl f* **7/2**[1]
00-4 **5** 3 1/4 **L'Hermitage (IRE)**[15] 1315 3-9-0 73 (b[1]) MartinDwyer 2 58
(Brian Meehan) *s.i.s: in rr: hrd drvn over 2f out and no imp on ldrs: wknd over 1f out* **9/2**[2]
401- **6** 3 1/4 **Opera Dancer**[202] 6712 3-9-0 75 JimmyFortune 7 51
(Sylvester Kirk) *chsd ldrs: rdn 3f out: wknd ins fnl 2f* **11/2**
03-0 **7** 50 **Green Pearl (IRE)**[10] 1446 3-9-0 72 JimCrowley 1 —
(Ralph Beckett) *t.k.h: chsd ldrs tl wknd qckly 3f out: virtually p.u fnl 2f* **11/2**
1m 40.05s (-0.75) **Going Correction** -0.025s/f (Good) **7** Ran SP% **113.7**
Speed ratings (Par 98): **102,100,100,97,94 91,41**
toteswingers:1&2:£6.80, 1&3:£7.40, 2&3:£6.50 CSF £26.65 TOTE £6.90: £3.10, £2.80; EX 32.00.
Owner Mrs J Wood **Bred** Alliand Equine **Trained** East Everleigh, Wilts

FOCUS
Just 3lb covered the seven runners in this tight little classified event featuring only one previous winner. Again the tempo was solid and nothing got into it from off the pace. A length personal best from the winner.

1627 NEW JAGUAR XF DIESEL IN SHOWROOM SHORTLY H'CAP 5f 11y
3:10 (3:10) (Class 6) (0-60,62) 4-Y-O+ **£1,683** (£501; £250; £125) **Stalls** Centre

Form RPR
3323 **1** **Decider (USA)**[8] 1503 8-8-12 **50** (b) LukeMorris 4 61
(Ronald Harris) *mde all: hrd rdn fr over 1f out: hld on wl cl home* **4/1**[3]
52-1 **2** 3/4 **Rebecca Romero**[22] 1182 4-9-2 **54** (v) RichardHughes 8 62
(Denis Coakley) *t.k.h: hld up in rr but in tch: hdwy on outside 2f out: rdn and qcknd to chse wnr ins fnl f: kpt on wl but a hld* **15/8**[1]
4204 **3** 1 **The Tatling (IRE)**[9] 1453 14-9-6 **58** RichardKingscote 1 62
(Milton Bradley) *trckd ldrs: chsd wnr 1/2-way: no imp 2f out: one pce and lost 2nd fnl 120yds* **8/1**
1031 **4** 1 **Welcome Approach**[9] 1453 8-9-2 **54** 6ex JimmyQuinn 5 55
(John Weymes) *in tch: rdn and styd on same pce fnl 2f* **7/2**[2]
30-3 **5** *nk* **Bateleur**[9] 1453 7-9-0 **59** CharlesBishop(7) 3 59
(Mick Channon) *s.i.s: sn in tch: sme hdwy on ins 2f out: styd on same pce fnl f* **4/1**[3]
6-60 **6** 6 **Dancing Again**[29] 1041 5-8-2 **45** HarryBentley(5) 9 23
(Eric Wheeler) *outpcd most of way* **33/1**
-600 **7** 5 **Boga (IRE)**[9] 1453 4-8-3 **48** JakePayne(7) 6 —
(Ron Hodges) *chse wnr to 1/2-way: sn wknd* **25/1**
61.36 secs (-1.14) **Going Correction** -0.20s/f (Firm) **7** Ran SP% **114.9**
Speed ratings (Par 101): **101,99,98,96,96 86,78**
toteswingers:1&2:£2.30, 1&3:£4.10, 2&3:£4.50 CSF £12.08 CT £55.90 TOTE £5.30: £2.70, £1.30; EX 14.60 Trifecta £142.40 Pool: £429.37 - 2.23 winning units..
Owner Robert Bailey **Bred** Green Willow Farms **Trained** Earlswood, Monmouths

FOCUS
A moderate sprint handicap featuring some old favourites and no shortage of recent form with five of the seven runners having run within the previous nine days. Modest form, rated around the third.

1628 E.B.F./ALL MAKES & MODELS SERVICED FROM £149 MEDIAN AUCTION MAIDEN STKS 5f 11y
3:40 (3:41) (Class 5) 2-Y-O **£3,173** (£944; £471; £235) **Stalls** Centre

Form RPR
0 **1** **B Fifty Two (IRE)**[13] 1360 2-9-3 0 SebSanders 2 80
(J W Hills) *trckd ldrs: pushed along to chse ldr over 1f out: drvn and styd on to ld fnl 120yds: readily* **3/1**[2]
2 2 1/4 **Excavator** 2-9-3 0 SteveDrowne 7 72
(Roger Charlton) *sn led: pushed along 2f out: hdd and outpcd fnl 120yds but kpt on for clr 2nd* **10/3**[3]
3 2 1/2 **Verbeeck** 2-9-3 0 RichardMullen 1 63+
(Ed McMahon) *slowly away and sn drvn along in rr: hdwy 2f out: styng on whn hung lft ins fnl f: green after and no imp on ldng duo fnl 120yds* **9/4**[1]
4 2 1/4 **Selinda** 2-8-9 0 MartinHarley(3) 5 49
(Mick Channon) *sn chsng ldr: rdn over 2f out: lost 2nd over 1f out: sn btn* **10/1**
4 **5** *nse* **Choisirez (IRE)**[22] 1185 2-8-12 0 CathyGannon 4 49
(David Evans) *chsd ldrs: rdn 3f out: wknd fr 2f out* **7/2**
0 **6** 3 3/4 **Jettie**[29] 1049 2-8-12 0 TomMcLaughlin 3 36
(David Evans) *s.i.s: sn rdn: a outpcd* **33/1**
62.32 secs (-0.18) **Going Correction** -0.20s/f (Firm) **6** Ran SP% **113.1**
Speed ratings (Par 92): **93,89,85,81,81 75**
toteswingers:1&2:£2.60, 1&3:£2.00, 2&3:£2.20 CSF £13.57 TOTE £4.70: £3.40, £3.10; EX 20.40.
Owner Gary And Linnet Woodward **Bred** Mull Enterprises Ltd **Trained** Upper Lambourn, Berks

FOCUS
An ordinary median auction maiden.

NOTEBOOK
B Fifty Two(IRE) ran green when well beaten on his Newbury debut in the race won by Magic City, but the experience was obviously beneficial. Well backed, he quickened up nicely to hit the front a furlong out and won going away. He should win more races and is likely to be aimed at a novice event next. (op 6-1)
Excavator, a £25,000 gelding, showed decent speed for a long way until cut down by the winner's turn of foot. This was an encouraging debut as he is bred to need further on the dam's side of his pedigree. (op 11-4 tchd 7-2)
Verbeeck, a £34,000 colt out of a three-time winner at up to 7f, was popular to make a winning debut but he missed the break and then ran green. He managed to put in an effort over a furlong out, but then ran green again and the experience seemed to be much needed. (op 7-4 tchd 13-8)
Selinda, a half-sister to the winning sprinter Alfraamsey, was full of herself beforehand and twice dumped her rider in the paddock. She ran fast until weakening a furlong out and may need more time. (tchd 12-1)
Choisirez(IRE), a running-on fourth of seven on her Nottingham debut, was off the bridle at halfway before making a little late headway and looks in need of 6f already. (op 4-1 tchd 9-2)

1629 USED JAGUAR XF FROM £19,990 MAIDEN FILLIES' STKS 5f 161y
4:10 (4:10) (Class 4) 3-Y-O+ **£3,238** (£963; £481; £240) **Stalls** Centre

Form RPR
6 **1** **Vicona (IRE)**[13] 1362 3-8-12 0 FrankieDettori 3 70
(Paul Cole) *trckd ldrs: drvn to chse ldr 2f out: slt ld and edgd lft over 1f out but sn jnd: rdn to assert fnl 120yds: kpt on wl* **8/11**[1]
2 1/2 **Rohlindi** 3-8-12 0 LukeMorris 1 68
(Clive Cox) *s.i.s: sn rcvrd to chse ldrs: chal 2f out: upsides whn pushed lft over 1f out: str chal ins fnl f: outpcd fnl 120yds* **7/2**[2]
0562 **3** 4 **Dancing Tara**[9] 1449 3-8-12 49 TomMcLaughlin 6 55
(David Evans) *led: rdn and jnd 2f out: hdd over 1f out and pushed lft: sn wknd* **8/1**
0- **4** 1 1/4 **Silent Fright (USA)**[349] 2074 3-8-5 0 DuilioDaSilva(7) 5 51
(Paul Cole) *s.i.s: in rr and t.k.h: hdwy 2f out: nvr gng pce to rch ldrs and styd on same pce fnl f* **7/1**[3]
5 9 **Lady Rumba** 3-8-12 0 FergusSweeney 7 21
(John O'Shea) *sn outpcd* **25/1**
4- **6** 4 1/2 **Vivre La Secret**[364] 1632 3-8-5 0 JakePayne(7) 2 —
(Bill Turner) *chsd ldr to 1/2-way: sn wknd* **33/1**
7 7 **Dorothy's Dream (IRE)** 3-8-12 0 RobertHavlin 4 —
(John O'Shea) *s.i.s: sn outpcd* **33/1**
1m 11.23s (0.03) **Going Correction** -0.20s/f (Firm) **7** Ran SP% **113.5**
Speed ratings (Par 102): **91,90,85,83,71 65,56**
toteswingers:1&2:£2.20, 1&3:£2.10, 2&3:£2.50 CSF £3.39 TOTE £1.80: £1.10, £2.30; EX 6.60.
Owner Denford Stud **Bred** Snig Elevage **Trained** Whatcombe, Oxon

FOCUS
Not much strength in depth in this fillies' maiden. Little form to go in and the race has been rated around the third initially.

1630 BUY JAGUAR XK CONVERTIBLE FOR THE SUMMER FILLIES' H'CAP 5f 161y
4:40 (4:40) (Class 5) (0-70,70) 3-Y-O+ **£2,456** (£725; £362) **Stalls** Centre

Form RPR
-105 **1** **Dualagi**[77] 487 7-9-9 **61** GeorgeBaker 4 68
(Martin Bosley) *in rr but wl in tch: hdwy 2f out: drvn to ld jst ins fnl 2f: r.o wl* **11/2**

00-0 **2** *1* **Talamahana**[9] 1453 6-8-9 **54**..(b) SeanPalmer(7) 5 58
(Andrew Haynes) *sn drvn along: outpcd 3f out: hdwy 2f out: styd on fnl f and tk 2nd cl home but no ch w wnr* **20/1**

002- **3** *1 ½* **Volcanic Dust (IRE)**[189] 7040 3-9-7 **70**..................... RichardKingscote 3 66
(Milton Bradley) *trckd ldr: chal 3f out: led sn after: rdn 2f out: hdd jst ins fnl f: sn outpcd by wnr: lost 2nd cl home* **11/2**

005- **4** *1* **Adventure Story**[205] 6656 4-9-13 **65**............................ FergusSweeney 6 61
(Peter Makin) *s.i.s: in rr: hdwy on outside fr 3f out: chsd ldrs over 1f out but no imp and styd on same pce* **4/1**[3]

000- **5** *14* **Yes We Can**[162] 7483 4-9-10 **62**.. SteveDrowne 1 12
(Jeremy Gask) *sn led: jnd 3f out: hdd sn after: rdn over 2f out: wknd ins fnl 2f* **9/4**[1]

516- **6** *2 ½* **Dubai Affair**[237] 5725 3-9-7 **70**... LukeMorris 2 —
(Ronald Harris) *trckd ldr: t.k.h: chal 3f out to 2f out: wknd qckly wl over 1f out* **3/1**[2]

1m 11.83s (0.63) **Going Correction** -0.20s/f (Firm)
WFA 3 from 4yo+ 11lb **6** Ran SP% **111.3**
Speed ratings (Par 100): **87,85,83,82,63 60**
toteswingers:1&2:£9.50, 1&3:£2.90, 2&3:£8.10 CSF £87.34 CT £613.11 TOTE £7.20: £3.10, £9.70; EX 40.20 Trifecta £253.70 Pool: £411.40 - 1.20 winning units..
Owner Inca Financial Services **Bred** B Burrough **Trained** Chalfont St Giles, Bucks

FOCUS
A modest fillies' handicap. The winner's best form since mid-2008, with the second basically to form.

1631 NEW JAGUAR XKR-S IN SHOWROOM SHORTLY H'CAP 1m 5f 22y
5:10 (5:10) (Class 6) (0-65,65) 4-Y-0+ **£2,331** (£693; £346; £173) **Stalls** High

Form RPR

2224 **1** **Sunset Place**[7] 1509 4-9-5 **63**...(p) RobertHavlin 4 71+
(Jonathan Geake) *hld up in rr: hdwy on ins over 3f out: swtchd rt to outside 2f out: shkn up and qckn fnl f to ld fnl 30yds: comf* **5/1**

420- **2** *1* **Dove Cottage (IRE)**[228] 5991 9-8-10 **53**..................... FergusSweeney 6 58
(Stuart Kittow) *led: rdn ins fnl 3f: hdd ins fnl 2f: n.m.r on ins and rallied to ld fnl 150yds: hdd and outpcd fnl 30yds* **13/2**

05-3 **3** *shd* **Annelko**[9] 1454 4-8-6 **50** oh2... NeilChalmers 3 55
(Andrew Haynes) *chsd ldr: rdn to ld ins fnl 2f: hdd fnl 150yds: styd on to dispute one pce 2nd cl home* **8/1**

00-6 **4** *9* **Shy**[16] 1291 6-9-3 **60**.. JamesMillman 2 52
(Rod Millman) *chsd ldrs: rdn 3f out: wknd fr 2f out* **10/3**[2]

-243 **5** *1 ¼* **Minder**[15] 1310 5-8-8 **51**..(tp) RichardKingscote 1 41
(Jonathan Portman) *chsd ldrs: rdn 3f out: wknd 2f out* **9/2**[3]

/60- **6** *4 ½* **Peaceful Soul (USA)**[365] 1627 4-9-7 **65**...................... RichardMullen 5 48
(David Lanigan) *in rr: rdn over 3f out: little rspnse and sn wknd* **11/4**[1]

2m 51.11s (-0.89) **Going Correction** -0.025s/f (Good)
WFA 4 from 5yo+ 1lb **6** Ran SP% **109.0**
Speed ratings (Par 101): **101,100,100,94,94 91**
toteswingers:1&2:£3.50, 1&3:£5.90, 2&3:£2.80. Tote Super 7: Win: Not won. Place: Not won. CSF £33.66 TOTE £5.00: £2.60, £2.80; EX 39.30.
Owner Jag Racing 1 **Bred** London Thoroughbred Services Ltd **Trained** Marlborough, Wilts

FOCUS
A modest handicap although the pace wasn't bad. The form is rated around the third.
T/Plt: £494.70 to a £1 stake. Pool:£53,646.29 - 79.16 winning tickets T/Qpdt: £75.20 to a £1 stake. Pool:£4,210.29 - 41.40 winning tickets ST

1353 **BRIGHTON** (L-H)
Thursday, April 28

OFFICIAL GOING: Good to firm (watered; 8.9)
All races on the inner.
Wind: Fresh, half behind Weather: Overcast

1632 BRITISH STALLION STUDS SUPPORTING BRITISH RACING EBF MAIDEN STKS 5f 59y
5:05 (5:52) (Class 5) 2-Y-0 **£3,173** (£944; £471; £235) **Stalls** Low

Form RPR

0 **1** **Red Hearts (IRE)**[10] 1441 2-8-7 0............................ AdamBeschizza(5) 1 71
(Julia Feilden) *chsd ldng pair: drvn to ld wl over 1f out: hld on wl fnl f* **12/1**[3]

6 **2** *½* **Pitt Rivers**[13] 1360 2-9-3 0.. SamHitchcott 3 74
(Mick Channon) *sn outpcd and rdn along in rr: styd on wl fr over 1f out: tk 2nd nr fin* **11/8**[2]

3 *½* **Pius Parker (IRE)** 2-9-3 0... NeilCallan 4 72
(John Gallagher) *racd in 4th: hdwy on rail over 1f out: pressed ldrs ent fnl f: kpt on* **14/1**

52 **4** *1* **Always Ends Well (IRE)**[9] 1455 2-8-12 0......................... JoeFanning 2 64
(Mark Johnston) *led tl wl over 1f out: no ex fnl f* **1/1**[1]

45 **5** *10* **First Rebellion**[12] 1396 2-9-3 0....................................... EddieCreighton 5 33
(Joseph Tuite) *chsd ldr 2f: sn rdn and outpcd: n.d fnl 2f* **33/1**

62.11 secs (-0.19) **Going Correction** -0.20s/f (Firm) **5** Ran SP% **109.4**
Speed ratings (Par 92): **93,92,91,89,73**
CSF £28.94 TOTE £15.00; EX 41.10.
Owner R J Creese **Bred** Tally-Ho Stud **Trained** Exning, Suffolk

FOCUS
An ordinary juvenile maiden.

NOTEBOOK
Red Hearts(IRE) improved massively on her debut effort at Windsor and ran out a game winner. Julia Feilden's filly is out of a 2-y-o winner at this trip and had clearly come on a bundle for her initial experience ten days earlier. She is entitled to improve again and ought to get another furlong this year, but life will be tougher from now on. (op 14-1)
Pitt Rivers, whose stable has dominated this race in the past decade, would have won had he not again fluffed the start. He was in front just past the finish and should be winning when reverting to a more-galloping circuit, providing he learns to jump properly.
Pius Parker(IRE), whose stable does well here, turned in a nice debut display and should prove sharper next time out.
Always Ends Well(IRE) set the clear standard on her close third at Pontefract last time, but she did look vulnerable to anything with ability and her finishing effort was laboured on the quick ground. She will probably struggle to land a maiden. Official explanation: jockey said filly hung right-handed (op 11-10 tchd 5-6 in places)

1633 DGH RECRUITMENT H'CAP 6f 209y
5:35 (6:12) (Class 6) (0-55,55) 4-Y-0+ **£1,780** (£529; £264; £132) **Stalls** Low

Form RPR

0130 **1** **Fortunate Bid (IRE)**[35] 957 5-8-13 **55**.....................(p) JamesSullivan(3) 1 63
(Linda Stubbs) *in tch in 5th: effrt over 2f out: drvn to ld 1f out: carried hd high: fnd enough: all out* **4/1**[2]

0-54 **2** *nk* **Giulietta Da Vinci**[71] 561 4-8-12 **51**...........................(b[1]) HayleyTurner 9 58
(Steve Woodman) *towards rr: rdn and styd on wl fnl 2f: wnt 2nd and clsng at fin: jst hld* **11/2**

0020 **3** *½* **Wotatomboy**[8] 1498 5-8-7 **46** oh1..................................(b[1]) ChrisCatlin 10 52
(Richard Whitaker) *disp ld: led over 2f out tl 1f out: kpt on* **14/1**

0046 **4** *2* **Sirjosh**[25] 984 5-9-2 **55**.. NeilCallan 7 55
(Des Donovan) *dwlt: towards rr: drvn along over 2f out: styd on fnl f* **9/2**[3]

65-0 **5** *2 ¼* **Abhainn (IRE)**[112] 70 5-8-7 **46**... DavidProbert 11 40
(Bryn Palling) *towards rr: rdn 3f out: sme late hdwy* **4/1**[2]

0540 **6** *nk* **Evey P (IRE)**[1] 1604 4-8-12 **51**... LiamKeniry 2 45
(Gary Brown) *chsd ldrs: hrd rdn 3f out: wknd 2f out* **10/1**

0455 **7** *2 ½* **Sonny G (IRE)**[22] 1184 4-9-2 **55**... MartinLane 4 42
(John Best) *disp ld tl over 2f out: sn wknd* **7/2**[1]

-460 **8** *2 ¼* **Mogok Ruby**[13] 1357 7-8-10 **49**..(p) DaneO'Neill 8 30
(Brett Johnson) *w ldrs tl wknd over 2f out* **25/1**

6060 **9** *18* **Crazy Parachute**[29] 1045 4-8-7 **49**.......................(e[1]) RossAtkinson(3) 5 —
(Gary Moore) *s.s: sn in midfield and t.k.h: wknd 3f out* **14/1**

056 **10** *39* **Lady Freda**[13] 1358 5-8-7 **46** oh1.................................. RussKennemore 12 —
(Alan Coogan) *dwlt: a bhd: t.o fnl 2f* **33/1**

1m 22.0s (-1.10) **Going Correction** -0.20s/f (Firm) **10** Ran SP% **125.0**
Speed ratings (Par 101): **98,97,97,94,92 91,89,86,65,21**
toteswingers:1&2:£4.80, 1&3:£12.20, 2&3:£20.40 CSF £28.57 CT £298.87 TOTE £3.60: £1.20, £2.70, £5.90; EX 26.20 Trifecta £269.70 Pool: £2,442.39 - 6.70 winning units..
Owner Jason Button **Bred** E O'Leary **Trained** Norton, N Yorks
■ Stewards' Enquiry : Hayley Turner one-day ban: used whip with excessive frequency (May 12)

FOCUS
This low-grade sprint handicap was even weakened by the late withdrawal of last year's winner My Flame (7/2JF, lost a shoe, deduct 20p in the £ under R4). Sound if limited form.
Lady Freda Official explanation: jockey said mare hung right and was unsuited by the track

1634 JUICE FM H'CAP 6f 209y
6:05 (6:38) (Class 5) (0-75,75) 4-Y-0+ **£2,331** (£693; £346; £173) **Stalls** Low

Form RPR

03-2 **1** **Mandhooma**[13] 1357 5-8-7 **61**... ChrisCatlin 1 66
(Peter Hiatt) *hld up in 5th: rdn to ld over 1f out: hld on gamely fnl 100yds* **85/40**[1]

2401 **2** *hd* **Buxton**[13] 1356 7-9-6 **74**...(t) MartinLane 3 79+
(Roger Ingram) *stdd s: hld up in rr: swtchd wd and hdwy over 1f out: styd on wl fnl f: clsng at fin* **9/2**

3632 **3** *nk* **Could It Be Magic**[20] 1221 4-9-1 **72**.........................(b) JamesSullivan(3) 6 76
(Bill Turner) *chsd ldrs: drvn to chal over 1f out: kpt on* **4/1**[3]

06-3 **4** *2* **Kingswinford (IRE)**[29] 1037 5-9-4 **75**........................ RichardEvans(3) 5 74
(David Evans) *cl up: wnt 2nd after 2f: rdn over 2f out: one pce fnl f* **3/1**[2]

0123 **5** *4 ½* **Dvinsky (USA)**[15] 1314 10-8-12 **66**...(v) PaulDoe 2 52
(Michael Squance) *chsd ldr 2f: hrd rdn over 2f out: wknd 1f out* **8/1**

20-6 **6** *2* **Desert Falls**[63] 673 5-8-2 **61** oh2............................ JemmaMarshall(5) 4 42
(Richard Whitaker) *led tl over 1f out: hld whn n.m.r ent fnl f* **14/1**

1m 21.55s (-1.55) **Going Correction** -0.20s/f (Firm) **6** Ran SP% **113.0**
Speed ratings (Par 103): **100,99,99,97,92 89**
toteswingers:1&2:£1.30, 1&3:£2.00, 2&3:£2.90 CSF £12.20 TOTE £4.10: £2.00, £2.20; EX 10.50.
Owner P W Hiatt **Bred** Shadwell Estate Company Limited **Trained** Hook Norton, Oxon
■ Stewards' Enquiry : Richard Evans one-day ban: careless riding (May 12)

FOCUS
This modest handicap was run at an average pace and there was a tight three-way finish. Straightforward form with the third setting the standard and the winner better than ever.
Kingswinford(IRE) Official explanation: jockey said gelding hung right

1635 NEW BRASSERIE ITALIAN MARINA SQUARE H'CAP 1m 3f 196y
6:35 (7:03) (Class 6) (0-60,60) 4-Y-0+ **£1,780** (£529; £264; £132) **Stalls** High

Form RPR

5022 **1** **Filun**[15] 1310 6-8-9 **48**... LiamKeniry 3 56+
(Anthony Middleton) *a gng wl: hld up in 5th: cruised into contention 2f out: led 1f out: nvr c off bit* **3/1**[1]

0030 **2** *1 ¾* **Vinces**[15] 1310 7-8-13 **52**.. HayleyTurner 5 57
(Tim McCarthy) *prom: led wl over 1f out: hdd and no ch w cantering wnr 1f out* **13/2**

4160 **3** *¾* **Barbirolli**[15] 1310 9-8-2 **46**... LauraPike(5) 1 50
(William Stone) *s.s: hld up in rr: hdwy in centre 2f out: chal over 1f out: nt gng pce of wnr fnl f* **10/1**

231/ **4** *7* **Shesha Bear**[629] 4744 6-9-7 **60**.. StephenCraine 4 53
(Jonathan Portman) *stdd s: sn trcking ldrs: led over 2f out tl wl over 1f out: sn outpcd* **17/2**

-050 **5** *2 ¼* **Primera Rossa**[9] 1473 5-8-7 **46** oh1...............................(b[1]) SamHitchcott 7 35
(J S Moore) *prom 2f: stdd bk into midfield: outpcd and btn over 3f out* **20/1**

6-20 **6** *6* **Mayfair's Future**[78] 466 6-8-10 **49**...................................(p) DarryllHolland 8 29
(J R Jenkins) *led 1f: pressed ldr: led over 4f out tl over 2f out: sn wknd* **15/2**

630- **7** *2 ¼* **Yourgolftravel Com**[27] 6934 6-9-5 **58**.......................................(t) NeilCallan 6 34
(David Pipe) *stdd s: towards rr: rdn and n.d fnl 3f* **5/1**[3]

00-6 **8** *1 ¾* **Cossack Prince**[20] 223 6-9-0 **53**... IanMongan 9 26
(Laura Mongan) *led after 1f tl over 4f out: wknd over 2f out* **9/2**[2]

53-0 **9** *5* **Hibba (USA)**[111] 79 4-9-6 **60**.. MartinLane 2 25
(Mouse Hamilton-Fairley) *mid-div: wknd over 3f out: no ch fnl 2f* **16/1**

2m 32.75s (0.05) **Going Correction** -0.20s/f (Firm)
WFA 4 from 5yo+ 1lb **9** Ran SP% **115.2**
Speed ratings (Par 101): **91,89,89,84,83 79,77,76,73**
toteswingers:1&2:£2.20, 1&3:£3.50, 2&3:£8.60 CSF £22.69 CT £172.32 TOTE £3.20: £1.10, £3.00, £3.90; EX 20.40 Trifecta £101.40 Pool: £2,824.16 - 20.60 winning units..
Owner R J Matthews **Bred** Azienda Agricola Francesca **Trained** Granborough, Bucks

FOCUS
A weak handicap, run at a sound pace. The first three came clear and the winner looked value for more. The next two ran to their recent best.

1636 21ST JUNE TAKE THAT SUMMER MUSIC NIGHT H'CAP 1m 1f 209y
7:05 (7:31) (Class 6) (0-65,63) 4-Y-0+ £1,780 (£529; £264; £132) Stalls High

Form				RPR
0-2	1		**Timocracy**[9] 1454 6-9-7 **63** StevieDonohoe 3 (Andrew Haynes) *mde all: hrd rdn over 2f out: hld on gamely* **5/4**[1]	72
1002	2	nk	**Miss Bounty**[7] 1508 6-8-9 **54** (v) MatthewDavies(3) 1 (Jim Boyle) *chsd ldrs: drvn to chal thrght fnl f: kpt on: jst hld* **9/1**	62
-034	3	4	**Evident Pride (USA)**[34] 965 8-9-2 **58** IanMongan 2 (Brett Johnson) *chsd wnr: hrd rdn 2f out: no ex fnl f* **13/2**[3]	58
0-24	4	4	**Musashi (IRE)**[2] 1582 6-8-11 **60** CharlotteJenner(7) 5 (Laura Mongan) *t.k.h in rr early: wnt 4th after 3f: wknd 2f out* **15/2**	52
5003	5	8	**Jasmin Rai**[22] 1190 4-8-9 **51** DavidProbert 6 (Des Donovan) *in tch tl wknd over 2f out* **13/2**[3]	27
16-4	6	4 ½	**Lady Lam**[13] 1353 5-9-7 **63** (t) LiamKeniry 4 (Sylvester Kirk) *hld up in rr pair: rdn 3f out: sn struggling* **4/1**[2]	30

2m 1.52s (-2.08) **Going Correction** -0.20s/f (Firm) 6 Ran SP% 112.9
Speed ratings (Par 101): **100,99,96,93,86 83**
toteswingers:1&2:£4.00, 1&3:£3.60, 2&3:£12.10 CSF £13.61 TOTE £2.20: £1.60, £2.30; EX 10.10.
Owner Miss C Berry **Bred** Gainsborough Stud Management Ltd **Trained** Limpley Stoke, Bath

FOCUS
This moderate handicap was run at a fair pace and it was another race where three dominated in the home straight. The winner sets the standard and is rated back to his best.
Lady Lam Official explanation: jockey said mare never travelled

1637 2FOR1 TICKETS 9TH & 17TH MAY H'CAP 7f 214y
7:35 (7:51) (Class 5) (0-70,69) 4-Y-0+ £2,331 (£693; £346; £173) Stalls Low

Form				RPR
2301	1		**Princess Lexi (IRE)**[13] 1355 4-9-0 **62** StevieDonohoe 5 (Ian Williams) *pressed ldr: led 2f out: jnd on both sides fnl f: gamely* **2/1**[1]	71
1143	2	¾	**Eastern Gift**[13] 1355 6-9-7 **69** NeilCallan 3 (Gay Kelleway) *hld up in 4th: effrt 2f out: jnd wnr 1f out: str chal fnl f: nt qckn nr fin* **3/1**[2]	76
-300	3	½	**Regal Rave (USA)**[14] 1333 4-8-13 **61** DaneO'Neill 1 (Mouse Hamilton-Fairley) *bhd: hrd rdn and hdwy fr 2f out: jnd ldrs on rail ent fnl f: one pce fnl 50yds* **17/2**	67
6026	4	4 ½	**Prince Of Thebes (IRE)**[14] 1333 10-8-12 **60** PaulDoe 2 (Michael Attwater) *rdn to ld: hdd 2f out: wknd over 1f out* **11/2**	56
0043	5	5	**Aviso (GER)**[17] 1276 7-9-0 **62** MartinLane 4 (David Evans) *plld hrd in 3rd early: pushed along 4f out: wknd 2f out* **10/3**[3]	46

1m 33.8s (-2.20) **Going Correction** -0.20s/f (Firm) 5 Ran SP% 107.3
Speed ratings (Par 103): **103,102,101,97,92**
CSF £7.74 TOTE £3.10: £1.50, £1.50; EX 6.30.
Owner Dr Marwan Koukash **Bred** Epona Bloodstock Ltd And P A Byrne **Trained** Portway, Worcs

FOCUS
A fairly tight little handicap and there was a driving finish. The winner confirmed lateat form with the runner-up.

1638 TAKE THAT EXPERIENCE HERE 21ST JUNE H'CAP 5f 59y
8:05 (8:08) (Class 5) (0-70,70) 4-Y-0+ £2,331 (£693; £346; £173) Stalls Low

Form				RPR
100-	1		**The Jailer**[193] 6956 8-8-3 **57** RyanPowell(5) 2 (John O'Shea) *mde all: rdn and hung rt bdly to stands' rail fr 2f out: hld on wl fnl f* **3/1**[3]	65
-002	2	1	**Rocker**[7] 1507 7-9-2 **70** HarryBentley(5) 4 (Gary Moore) *cl up: led far side trio wl over 1f out: kpt on: a hld by wnr on other side of crse* **5/4**[1]	75
1653	3	1	**Sherjawy (IRE)**[7] 1506 7-9-3 **66** KirstyMilczarek 5 (Zoe Davison) *chsd wnr tl wl over 1f out: one pce* **11/4**[2]	67
2440	4	½	**Radiator Rooney (IRE)**[29] 1034 8-8-4 **56** oh4 LouisBeuzelin(3) 3 (Patrick Morris) *in tch in 4th: effrt 2f out: one pce fnl f* **8/1**	55

61.20 secs (-1.10) **Going Correction** -0.20s/f (Firm) 4 Ran SP% 107.2
Speed ratings (Par 103): **100,98,96,96**
CSF £7.12 TOTE £3.60; EX 6.30.
Owner Pete Smith Car Sales **Bred** D R Tucker **Trained** Elton, Gloucs

FOCUS
An open little sprint handicap and the form makes sense. The winner is rated similarly to last year's winning debut.
T/Plt: £111.50 to a £1 stake. Pool:£55,732.73 - 364.70 winning tickets T/Qpdt: £4.20 to a £1 stake. Pool:£6,357.61 - 1,096.69 winning tickets LM

1639 - 1647a (Foreign Racing) - See Raceform Interactive

1382 DONCASTER (L-H)
Friday, April 29

OFFICIAL GOING: Straight course - good to firm; round course - good (good to firm in places; watered; 8.5)
Wind: Moderate half behind Weather: Dry with sunny periods

1648 EARL OF DONCASTER MAIDEN FILLIES' STKS 1m (S)
2:30 (2:32) (Class 4) 3-Y-0+ £4,079 (£1,214; £606; £303) Stalls High

Form				RPR
6-6	1		**Adaria**[13] 1393 3-8-12 0 RobbieFitzpatrick 5 (David C Griffiths) *trckd ldr: swtchd lft and effrt 3f out: sn pushed along: rdn wl over 1f out: styd on ins fnl f to ld last 75yds* **9/2**[3]	71+
540-	2	¾	**Royal Hush**[228] 6034 3-8-12 69 PhillipMakin 3 (Kevin Ryan) *qckly away and led: pushed clr wl over 2f out: shkn up wl over 1f out: rdn and hung lft ins fnl f: hdd and no ex last 75yds* **1/1**[1]	69+
	3	7	**Bella Montagna** 3-8-12 0 JamieSpencer 4 (John Quinn) *s.i.s: in tch in rr: hdwy 1/2-way: rdn along over 2f out: kpt on same pce* **15/8**[2]	52
	4	nk	**Tasman Tiger**[176] 4-9-12 0 KellyHarrison 2 (Kate Walton) *chsd ldr: rdn along 3f out: wknd fnl 2f* **20/1**	55?

1m 38.24s (-1.06) **Going Correction** -0.35s/f (Firm)
WFA 3 from 4yo 14lb 4 Ran SP% 107.7
Speed ratings (Par 102): **91,90,83,82**
CSF £9.53 TOTE £6.00; EX 10.00.
Owner P Sutherland J Adlam G Noble **Bred** Floors Farming And Christopher J Heath **Trained** Bawtry, S Yorks

FOCUS
A weak fillies' maiden. The favourite rather threw it away and the winner is rated a length off her 2yo mark.

1649 WEDDING BELLES AND FORMAL ATTIRE H'CAP 7f
3:00 (3:01) (Class 5) (0-70,70) 4-Y-0+ £2,388 (£705; £352) Stalls High

Form				RPR
556-	1		**Music Festival (USA)**[181] 7225 4-8-11 **60** JoeFanning 7 (Jim Goldie) *trckd ldrs: hdwy to ld 2f out: rdn over 1f out: kpt on wl fnl f* **3/1**[1]	71+
000-	2	1 ¼	**Sairaam (IRE)**[161] 7501 5-8-13 **62** RobbieFitzpatrick 3 (Charles Smith) *racd wd: sn led: hdd after 1 1/2f and cl up: effrt over 2f out: sn rdn and ev ch tl drvn: edgd lft and no ex wl ins fnl f* **8/1**	69
1664	3	1 ¼	**Flying Applause**[18] 1276 6-8-9 **58** (bt) JimmyQuinn 4 (Roy Bowring) *dwlt: sn cl up: led on stands' rail after 1 1/2f: rdn along 3f out: hdd 2f out and sn drvn: edgd lft and kpt on same pce fnl f* **7/2**[2]	62
300-	4	4	**Tobrata**[164] 7473 5-8-9 **58** RobertWinston 6 (Mel Brittain) *chsd ldrs: rdn along over 2f out: sn one pce* **14/1**	51
040-	5	1 ¾	**Hayek**[192] 7006 4-8-7 **56** DavidAllan 2 (Tim Easterby) *towards rr: hdwy and in tch 1/2-way: sn rdn along and n.d* **4/1**[3]	44
21-0	6	6	**Little Pete (IRE)**[26] 1109 6-9-7 **70** PatrickMathers 1 (Ian McInnes) *in tch: rdn along 3f out: sn drvn and n.d* **8/1**	42
1346	7	5	**Peadar Miguel**[13] 1398 4-9-6 **69** AdamKirby 8 (Noel Quinlan) *hld up: a in rr: rdn along and outpcd fr wl over 2f out* **5/1**	28

1m 24.04s (-2.26) **Going Correction** -0.35s/f (Firm) 7 Ran SP% 112.8
Speed ratings (Par 103): **98,96,95,90,88 81,76**
toteswingers:1&2:£5.10, 1&3:£2.10, 2&3:£4.80 CSF £26.35 CT £85.70 TOTE £3.50: £2.20, £3.50; EX 26.50 Trifecta £54.70 Pool: £582.15 - 7.86 winning units..
Owner W M Johnstone **Bred** Gainsborough Farm Llc **Trained** Uplawmoor, E Renfrews

FOCUS
An ordinary handicap but it looked fairly competitive on paper. The winner has improved this year and may do better again.

1650 BETFAIR'S WILL THEY MARRY FURLONG H'CAP 5f
3:35 (3:35) (Class 3) (0-90,86) 3-Y-0 £6,141 (£1,813; £907) Stalls High

Form				RPR
160-	1		**Azzurra Du Caprio (IRE)**[207] 6619 3-9-0 **79** PJMcDonald 1 (Ben Haslam) *cl up on outer: effrt 2f out: rdn to chal over 1f out: led ins fnl f: r.o wl* **17/2**	87
000-	2	1 ¾	**Bold Bidder**[210] 6530 3-9-7 **86** PhillipMakin 4 (Kevin Ryan) *trckd ldrs: cl up 1/2-way: led wl over 1f out: sn rdn: drvn and hdd jst ins fnl f: kpt on* **5/1**[3]	88
044-	3	nse	**Major Muscari (IRE)**[186] 7127 3-9-1 **80** PaulMulrennan 6 (Geoffrey Oldroyd) *hld up in tch: hdwy and n.m.r 2f out: swtchd lft and rdn ent fnl f: kpt on wl towards fin* **9/1**	82
10-3	4	1 ¼	**Boundaries**[20] 1241 3-9-4 **83** (v) TomEaves 5 (Tim Easterby) *cl up: effrt to dispute ld over 2f out and ev ch tl rdn and one pce over 1f out* **5/1**[3]	81
01-0	5	nk	**Berberana (IRE)**[20] 1241 3-9-2 **81** DavidAllan 3 (Tim Easterby) *led: jnd and rdn 1/2-way: hdd wl over 1f out: sn drvn and grad wknd* **7/2**[2]	77
021-	6	¾	**Look Who's Kool**[210] 6520 3-9-2 **81** GrahamGibbons 2 (Ed McMahon) *hld up in tch: hdwy 2f out: rdn wl over 1f out: no imp* **7/1**	75
40-2	7	4 ½	**Defence Council (IRE)**[13] 1391 3-8-11 **76** RobertWinston 7 (Mel Brittain) *chsd ldrs: effrt 1/2-way: sn rdn and wknd wl over 1f out* **10/3**[1]	54

58.49 secs (-2.01) **Going Correction** -0.35s/f (Firm) 7 Ran SP% 111.7
Speed ratings (Par 102): **102,99,99,97,96 95,88**
toteswingers:1&2:£9.40, 1&3:£13.80, 2&3:£10.90 CSF £47.54 TOTE £12.90: £4.70, £2.50; EX 60.50.
Owner Blue Lion Racing IX **Bred** Glending Bloodstock **Trained** Middleham Moor, N Yorks

FOCUS
Not a bad little sprint handicap. The form's rated through the second and third, with a 6lb best from the winner.

NOTEBOOK
Azzurra Du Caprio(IRE), dropping back to 5f for the first time since she won her maiden almost a year ago, challenged widest of all and stayed on well to score. Where she raced was possibly an advantage, but clearly the drop in trip and return to fast ground was very much in her favour. She goes for a 6f fillies' handicap at Ripon next. (op 11-1 tchd 8-1)
Bold Bidder, highly tried in the second half of her juvenile campaign and last seen bringing up the rear in the Cheveley Park Stakes, was back in more realistic company and posted a sound effort on her reappearance. She should be up to winning something similar. (op 13-2)
Major Muscari(IRE) looked a little unlucky not to finish closer. Travelling well in behind horses and waiting for a gap from 2f out to the furlong pole, he took a while to pick up once in the clear but eventually stayed on well and only narrowly failed to take second. It was a good debut for his new stable and a stiffer track might help. (op 8-1)
Boundaries showed pace nearer the stands' rail, but couldn't sustain it. Returning to a sharper track should suit him. (op 7-2)
Berberana(IRE) might need softer ground to be seen at her best. (op 4-1)
Look Who's Kool was weak in the market and looked to need this reappearance. (op 13-2 tchd 6-1)
Defence Council(IRE) was possibly at a disadvantage racing next to the stands' side rail. His connections could offer no explanation for his poor performance. Official explanation: trainer's rep had no explanation for the poor form shown (op 7-2 tchd 3-1)

1651 BALLOONS AWAY ROYAL WEDDING H'CAP 1m 4f
4:10 (4:10) (Class 4) (0-80,80) 4-Y-0+ £3,753 (£1,108; £554) Stalls Low

Form				RPR
500-	1		**Bullet Man (USA)**[156] 7548 6-8-12 **71** (t) FrederikTylicki 7 (Paul Webber) *hld up in rr: stdy hdwy 4f out: swtchd rt and rdn to chse ldr wl over 2f out: styd on to ld ent fnl f: drvn out* **5/1**[3]	84
160-	2	2 ¾	**Incendo**[208] 5991 5-9-7 **80** (t) PatCosgrave 6 (James Fanshawe) *hld up: smooth hdwy 5f out: trckd ldng pair over 3f out: led on bit over 2f out: shkn up wl over 1f out: rdn and hdd ent fnl f: sn one pce* **9/2**[2]	89
5360	3	6	**Bedouin Bay**[27] 1098 4-8-13 **78** (v[1]) KieranO'Neill(5) 4 (Alan McCabe) *cl up: effrt 3f out and ev ch: rdn wl over 1f out: sn one pce* **14/1**	77
120-	4	8	**Fourth Generation (IRE)**[215] 6397 4-9-4 **78** RobertWinston 5 (Alan Swinbank) *trckd ldrs: effrt over 3f out: rdn whn sltly hmpd over 2f out: sn outpcd* **5/1**[3]	64
34-3	5	6	**Patavium (IRE)**[20] 1243 8-8-8 **70** JamesSullivan(3) 8 (Edwin Tuer) *hld up: a towards rr* **7/1**	47

1-23 **6** *14* **Archie Rice (USA)**[12] 315 5-8-9 **68** TomEaves 3 22
(Tom Keddy) *chsd ldng pair on inner: rdn along over 4f out: drvn over 3f out and sn wknd* **6/1**

-212 **7** *nse* **Red Kestrel (USA)**[15] 1325 6-9-3 **76** PhillipMakin 1 30
(Kevin Ryan) *led: rdn along 4f out: drvn and hdd wl over 2f out: sn wknd* **11/4**[1]

2m 32.0s (-2.90) **Going Correction** -0.10s/f (Good)
WFA 4 from 5yo+ 1lb **7 Ran SP% 111.6**
Speed ratings (Par 105): **105,103,99,93,89 80,80**
toteswingers:1&2:£5.10, 1&3:£9.00, 2&3:£8.50 CSF £26.16 CT £286.53 TOTE £6.30: £2.60, £3.60; EX 32.10 Trifecta £480.30 Part won. Pool: £649.17 - 0.65 winning units..
Owner Kevin Bailey & Clark Watson **Bred** Stillmeadow Farm Llc **Trained** Mollington, Oxon
■ Stewards' Enquiry : Frederik Tylicki one-day ban: careless riding (May 13)

FOCUS
A fair race, and as a result of Bedouin Bay taking on Red Kestrel out in front and the pair kicking for home plenty soon enough, it was set up for a pair of horses ridden with more patience. A slightly positive view has been taken of the front pair, who finished clear.

1652 ZESTBARANDGRILL.COM H'CAP — 1m 2f 60y
4:45 (4:45) (Class 4) (0-85,83) 3-Y-0 **£4,094** (£1,209; £604) **Stalls** Low

Form RPR

33-1 **1** **Halfsin (IRE)**[24] 1151 3-9-7 **83** AdamKirby 3 92
(Marco Botti) *trckd ldng pair: hdwy 3f out: chal wl over 1f out: rdn to take fractional ld jst ins fnl f: sn drvn and edgd lft: jst hld on* **1/2**[1]

01-6 **2** *nse* **Oasis Storm**[23] 1168 3-8-13 **75** FrederikTylicki 4 84
(Michael Dods) *trckd ldr: hdwy and cl up 5f out: led over 3f out: rdn and jnd over 1f out: hdd jst ins fnl f: drvn and rallied gamely: jst hld* **6/1**[2]

1236 **3** *16* **George Woolf**[13] 1392 3-8-12 **74** RobertWinston 2 52
(Alan McCabe) *in rr: rdn along and outpcd 1/2-way: plugged on to take remote 3rd ins fnl 2f* **6/1**[2]

1133 **4** *32* **Baharat (IRE)**[18] 1272 3-8-13 **75** RobbieFitzpatrick 5 —
(Richard Guest) *set str pce: pushed along over 4f out: hdd over 3f out and sn wknd* **6/1**[2]

2m 7.91s (-1.49) **Going Correction** -0.10s/f (Good) **4 Ran SP% 109.5**
Speed ratings (Par 100): **101,100,88,62**
CSF £4.02 TOTE £1.60; EX 4.20.
Owner Giuliano Manfredini **Bred** Glending Bloodstock **Trained** Newmarket, Suffolk

FOCUS
Just the four runners, but the first two had a real battle inside the last and little separated them on the line. They were well clear and were the only pair to run their races.

1653 MOSS PROPERTIES WAKEFIELD H'CAP — 1m (R)
5:20 (5:22) (Class 4) (0-85,76) 3-Y-0 **£4,094** (£1,209; £604) **Stalls** Low

Form RPR

2152 **1** **Bosambo**[11] 1437 3-9-5 **74** RobertWinston 4 85+
(Alan Swinbank) *hld up in rr: smooth hdwy on wd outside 3f out: led on bit over 1f out: rdn clr fnl f* **5/4**[1]

01-0 **2** *4* **Another Citizen (IRE)**[24] 1152 3-9-7 **76** DavidAllan 6 78
(Tim Easterby) *trckd ldrs: hdwy on outer over 4f out: sn cl up: led wl over 2f out: rdn wl over 1f out: hdd appr fnl f and sn one pce* **9/2**[3]

16-1 **3** *1½* **Lady Gar Gar**[15] 1329 3-9-0 **69** SilvestreDeSousa 3 68
(Geoffrey Oldroyd) *chsd ldr: effrt 4f out: rdn to chal 3f out and ev ch tl drvn wl over 1f out and sn one pce* **5/2**[2]

64-0 **4** *2½* **Tarantella Lady**[22] 1203 3-9-1 **70** TomEaves 1 63
(George Moore) *led: rdn along 4f out: drvn: edgd lft and hdd wl over 2f out: sn wknd* **11/1**

3215 **5** *1¾* **City Legend**[15] 1329 3-8-12 **72** KieranO'Neill(5) 2 61
(Alan McCabe) *trckd ldrs on inner: hdwy and cl up 4f out: rdn 3f out: wknd 2f out* **8/1**

1m 38.97s (-0.73) **Going Correction** -0.10s/f (Good) **5 Ran SP% 110.6**
Speed ratings (Par 100): **99,95,93,91,89**
CSF £7.31 TOTE £2.30: £1.60, £3.10; EX 6.40.
Owner Guy Reed **Bred** Theakston Stud **Trained** Melsonby, N Yorks
■ Stewards' Enquiry : Kieran O'Neill caution: used whip with excessive frequency.

FOCUS
The top-weight was rated 9lb below ceiling for the race so this wasn't quite as good a contest as the conditions suggested. That said, the winner is progressing nicely.
T/Plt: £942.80 to a £1 stake. Pool:£78,461.14 - 60.75 winning tickets T/Qpdt: £47.70 to a £1 stake. Pool:£6,300.20 - 97.55 winning tickets JR

1395 LEICESTER (R-H)
Friday, April 29

OFFICIAL GOING: Good to firm (good in places; watered; 8.6)
A scheduled 1m4f handicap was void as no declarations were received following a Horsemen's Group boycott. The maiden was divided as a result.
Wind: Fresh against Weather: Fine

1654 LADBROKES.COM WALCOTE MAIDEN STKS (DIV I) — 7f 9y
2:10 (2:11) (Class 5) 3-4-Y-0 **£1,942** (£578; £288; £144) **Stalls** High

Form RPR

5- **1** **Great Acclaim**[279] 4379 3-8-12 0 [1] PatCosgrave 6 66+
(James Fanshawe) *trckd ldrs: led and hung rt fr over 1f out: rdn out* **11/4**[2]

\- **2** *2* **Hitman Hatton** 4-9-11 0 DaneO'Neill 2 63
(Lucinda Featherstone) *dwlt: rdn 1/2-way: hdwy over 1f out: wnt 2nd ins fnl f: nt rch wnr* **40/1**

5- **3** *1¼* **Frozen Over**[192] 6995 3-8-12 0 FergusSweeney 1 55
(Stuart Kittow) *plld hrd: led 1f: chsd ldr: led again 2f out: rdn and hdd over 1f out: styd on same pce ins fnl f* **16/1**[3]

00-4 **4** *3* **Tiberius Claudius (IRE)**[26] 1108 3-8-12 77 TomQueally 4 47
(George Margarson) *led 6f out: rdn and hdd 2f out: nt clr run over 1f out: wknd ins fnl f* **5/4**[1]

5 *¾* **Chlodan** 4-9-11 0 BarryMcHugh 5 50
(Ollie Pears) *s.i.s: rdn over 2f out: styd on ins fnl f: nvr trbld ldrs* **20/1**

540- **6** *1¾* **Catalinas Diamond (IRE)**[279] 4356 3-8-7 83 RobertHavlin 3 35
(Pat Murphy) *chsd ldrs: rdn over 2f out: wknd over 1f out* **11/4**[2]

1m 26.79s (0.59) **Going Correction** +0.025s/f (Good)
WFA 3 from 4yo 13lb **6 Ran SP% 110.9**
Speed ratings (Par 103): **97,94,93,89,89 87**
toteswingers:1&2:£8.10, 1&3:£5.10, 2&3:£9.60 CSF £73.06 TOTE £3.80: £2.40, £4.80; EX 46.80.
Owner Norman Brunskill **Bred** Mr & Mrs A E Pakenham **Trained** Newmarket, Suffolk
■ Stewards' Enquiry : Pat Cosgrave caution: careless riding.

FOCUS
Both divisions of this maiden looked weak affairs, but the time was 1.11 seconds quicker than the other leg. Hard to pin down the form, which is rated conservatively.
Tiberius Claudius(IRE) Official explanation: jockey said gelding was unsuited by the good to firm (good in places) ground
Chlodan Official explanation: jockey said gelding ran green

1655 LADBROKES.COM WALCOTE MAIDEN STKS (DIV II) — 7f 9y
2:40 (2:40) (Class 5) 3-4-Y-0 **£1,942** (£578; £288; £144) **Stalls** High

Form RPR

40- **1** **Iron Step**[190] 7036 3-8-12 0 LukeMorris 2 65+
(Nicky Vaughan) *led 3f: chsd ldr: led again 2f out: sn rdn: styd on* **4/1**[3]

00- **2** *1¾* **Storm Runner (IRE)**[182] 7201 3-8-9 0 AshleyHamblett(3) 1 58
(George Margarson) *s.i.s: hld up: rdn 1/2-way: hdwy over 1f out: r.o to go 2nd wl ins fnl f: nt trble wnr* **8/1**

3 *nk* **Let's Dance (IRE)** 3-8-7 0 RichardKingscote 4 52+
(Tom Dascombe) *hld up in tch: rdn over 2f out: styd on* **5/2**[2]

0-40 **4** *3* **Chik's Dream**[44] 873 4-9-11 0 AndreaAtzeni 3 54
(Derek Haydn Jones) *chsd ldr tl led 4f out: rdn and hdd 2f out: no ex ins fnl f* **25/1**

05- **5** *1* **Arctic Cat (IRE)**[299] 3705 3-8-12 0 JimCrowley 6 46
(William Knight) *prom: rdn and ev ch 2f out: no ex fnl f* **9/4**[1]

4- **6** *2¼* **Griffin Point (IRE)**[214] 6420 4-9-6 0 MartinDwyer 5 40
(William Muir) *plld hrd and prom: rdn and ev ch 2f out: wknd fnl f* **9/2**

1m 27.9s (1.70) **Going Correction** +0.025s/f (Good)
WFA 3 from 4yo 13lb **6 Ran SP% 112.5**
Speed ratings (Par 103): **91,89,88,85,84 81**
toteswingers:1&2:£3.60, 1&3:£1.70, 2&3:£5.10 CSF £33.97 TOTE £5.30: £2.50, £6.00; EX 32.00.
Owner Andrew Tinkler **Bred** Brook Stud Bloodstock Ltd **Trained** Helshaw Grange, Shropshire

FOCUS
The time was 1.11 seconds slower than the modest-looking first division and this looks extremely limited form. The front pair had shown little previously.
Griffin Point(IRE) Official explanation: jockey said filly ran too free

1656 LADBROKESCASINO.COM H'CAP — 5f 218y
3:15 (3:15) (Class 4) (0-80,80) 4-Y-0+ **£3,238** (£963; £481; £240) **Stalls** High

Form RPR

1412 **1** **Norville (IRE)**[35] 961 4-9-5 **78** (b) CathyGannon 1 94
(David Evans) *chsd ldr: rdn to ld 2f out: styd on gamely* **9/2**[2]

04-0 **2** *½* **Flowing Cape (IRE)**[13] 1397 6-9-6 **79** GeorgeBaker 5 93
(Reg Hollinshead) *mid-div: hdwy 1/2-way: chsd wnr over 1f out: sn rdn and ev ch: nt qckn towards fin* **3/1**[1]

11-0 **3** *6* **Galatian**[25] 1140 4-9-4 **77** JamesMillman 6 72
(Rod Millman) *mid-div: pushed along over 2f out: styd on to go 3rd ins fnl f: nvr trbld ldrs* **8/1**

/0-0 **4** *nk* **Sumbe (USA)**[21] 1221 5-8-9 **68** AndreaAtzeni 8 62
(Michael Wigham) *sn outpcd: rdn 1/2-way: kpt on ins fnl f: nvr trbld ldrs* **20/1**

0433 **5** *shd* **Absa Lutte (IRE)**[14] 1371 8-8-9 **68** (bt) PaulHanagan 7 62
(Michael Mullineaux) *hld up: rdn over 2f out: hdwy over 1f out: no ex fnl f* **13/2**

2351 **6** *1¼* **Silver Wind**[4] 1562 6-9-0 **73** 6ex (b) SebSanders 3 63
(Alan McCabe) *chsd ldr: rdn and hung lft over 1f out: wknd fnl f* **5/1**[3]

-602 **7** *3* **Rum King (USA)**[8] 1506 4-8-13 **72** (p) DaneO'Neill 9 52
(Richard Hannon) *hld up: rdn over 2f out: nvr on terms* **7/1**

600- **8** *1¼* **Peter Island (FR)**[200] 6798 8-9-7 **80** (v) ChrisCatlin 2 56
(John Gallagher) *led 4f: wknd fnl f* **9/1**

0060 **9** *6* **Divertimenti (IRE)**[22] 1200 7-9-4 **77** (b) RussKennemore 4 34
(Roy Bowring) *chsd ldrs: rdn over 2f out: wknd wl over 1f out* **25/1**

1m 12.3s (-0.70) **Going Correction** +0.025s/f (Good) **9 Ran SP% 115.4**
Speed ratings (Par 105): **105,104,96,95,95 94,90,88,80**
toteswingers:1&2:£2.10, 1&3:£8.20, 2&3:£12.30 CSF £18.40 CT £104.98 TOTE £6.70: £2.00, £1.30, £2.10; EX 22.90.
Owner Raymond N R Auld **Bred** R N Auld **Trained** Pandy, Monmouths

FOCUS
A fair sprint handicap run at a strong pace. The first pair clear and the winner continues to progress.

1657 EBF NOSELEY MAIDEN FILLIES' STKS — 5f 2y
3:50 (3:50) (Class 5) 2-Y-0 **£3,238** (£963; £481; £240) **Stalls** High

Form RPR

3 **1** **Pyman's Theory (IRE)**[10] 1455 2-9-0 0 RichardKingscote 5 84
(Tom Dascombe) *chsd ldr: led over 1f out: r.o wl* **6/4**[1]

4 **2** *5* **Dark Ages (IRE)**[15] 1337 2-9-0 0 TomQueally 6 66
(Noel Quinlan) *led over 3f: no ex ins fnl f* **7/2**[3]

4 **3** *1¾* **Reina Sofia**[13] 1396 2-9-0 0 LukeMorris 3 60
(Tony Carroll) *chsd ldrs: rdn 1/2-way: styd on same pce appr fnl f* **16/1**

4 *½* **Fanoos** 2-9-0 0 RichardHills 2 58+
(John Gosden) *s.i.s: hdwy 1/2-way: wknd fnl f* **2/1**[2]

5 *1¾* **Iceni Girl** 2-9-0 0 WilliamBuick 7 56+
(John Gosden) *s.s: rn green and outpcd: styd on ins fnl f: nvr nrr* **10/1**

6 *3½* **Unforgiving (IRE)** 2-9-0 0 SebSanders 4 39
(Alan McCabe) *sn pushed along in rr: wknd over 1f out* **28/1**

61.67 secs (1.67) **Going Correction** +0.025s/f (Good) **6 Ran SP% 114.0**
Speed ratings (Par 89): **87,79,76,75,72 67**
toteswingers:1&2:£1.70, 1&3:£2.60, 2&3:£6.00 CSF £7.40 TOTE £2.30: £1.10, £2.00; EX 8.10.
Owner M Owen & M Williams **Bred** T Whitehead **Trained** Malpas, Cheshire

FOCUS
This looked a reasonable fillies' maiden and they went a good pace.

NOTEBOOK
Pyman's Theory(IRE) ◆ confirmed the promise she showed when third at Pontefract on her first start, finding plenty after travelling well. Heavily punted on her debut, she was once again strongly supported in the market, evidently being a well-regarded filly, and has come on plenty from that initial outing. She could now head to Chester for the Lily Agnes, a race her stable won last year, and her natural speed means she'll hold strong claims granted a low draw. (op 15-8 after early 9-4 in a place tchd 11-8)
Dark Ages(IRE) showed loads of pace but only helped set the race up for the above-average winner. She was fourth on her debut in a Newmarket fillies' maiden, but that probably wasn't a strong contest. (op 11-4)
Reina Sofia probably improved on the form she showed in a lesser race over C&D on her debut. (op 14-1)
Fanoos was a rare 2-y-o runner this early in the season for John Gosden, who admittedly happened to have another runner in the race, and she's an April foal, but she is bred to be speedy. She finished well held, but moved nicely until around halfway and can do better. (tchd 11-4)

Iceni Girl missed the break and ran green. (op 12-1)

1658 LADBROKES.COM KIMCOTE H'CAP — 1m 1f 218y
4:25 (4:28) (Class 5) (0-70,69) 4-Y-O+ — **£1,942** (£578; £288; £144) **Stalls** Low

Form				RPR
3-10	1		**Destiny Of A Diva**[95] 287 4-9-7 **69** ... GeorgeBaker 2 (Reg Hollinshead) *hld up: swtchd lft over 2f out: hdwy to ld over 1f out: sn rdn: styd on* **16/1**	78+
2-01	2	½	**Hong Kong Island (IRE)**[10] 1461 4-9-4 **66** ... PaulHanagan 5 (Micky Hammond) *led at stdy pce after 1f: qcknd over 3f out: rdn and hdd over 1f out: styd on* **8/11**[1]	74
132-	3	nse	**Kenyan Cat**[184] 7184 4-9-3 **65** ... TedDurcan 4 (Ed McMahon) *led 1f: chsd ldr to 7f out: remained handy: rdn over 1f out: styd on* **4/1**[2]	73
00-0	4	3 ¼	**Arashi**[26] 1107 5-9-1 **63** ... (p) DaneO'Neill 7 (Lucinda Featherstone) *hld up: rdn over 2f out: hdwy over 1f out: styd on: nt trble ldrs* **7/1**[3]	65
24-0	5	hd	**Aegean Destiny**[15] 1324 4-8-11 **62** ... DeclanCannon(3) 3 (John Mackie) *prom: rdn over 1f out: no ex ins fnl f* **10/1**	63
00-1	6	3 ¼	**Rowan Lodge (IRE)**[23] 1164 9-9-4 **66** ... (b) LiamKeniry 1 (Ollie Pears) *chsd ldrs: rdn over 2f out: btn over 1f out* **20/1**	61
050-	7	2 ¼	**Bidable**[182] 7214 7-9-6 **68** ... RichardKingscote 6 (Bryn Palling) *plld hrd and sn prom: trckd ldr 7f out: rdn over 2f out: wknd over 1f out: eased ins fnl f* **25/1**	58

2m 11.45s (3.55) **Going Correction** +0.025s/f (Good) 7 Ran SP% **114.0**
Speed ratings (Par 103): **86,85,85,82,82 80,78**
toteswingers:1&2:£3.10, 1&3:£4.20, 2&3:£1.30 CSF £28.29 TOTE £20.60: £5.00, £1.40; EX 38.00.
Owner M A Massarella **Bred** M Massarella **Trained** Upper Longdon, Staffs

FOCUS
The pace was steady and the time was 2.61 seconds slower than the following four-runner 3-y-o handicap. Muddling form, not rated too positively.
Hong Kong Island(IRE) Official explanation: jockey said gelding hung left throughout
Bidable Official explanation: jockey said mare ran too free

1659 LADBROKES.COM CLASSIFIED STKS — 1m 1f 218y
5:00 (5:00) (Class 5) 3-Y-O — **£1,942** (£578; £288; £144) **Stalls** Low

Form				RPR
2-24	1		**Lady Rosamunde**[24] 1151 3-9-0 70 ... TadhgO'Shea 2 (Marcus Tregoning) *s.i.s: hld up: hdwy over 2f out: rdn to ld over 1f out: styd on* **5/2**[3]	78
01-	2	1	**Midas Moment**[167] 7447 3-9-0 70 ... MartinDwyer 3 (William Muir) *chsd ldr: led over 2f out: rdn: edgd lft and hdd over 1f out: styd on* **15/8**[2]	76
P-13	3	7	**Moonlight Rhapsody (IRE)**[23] 1170 3-9-0 68 ... MichaelHills 1 (B W Hills) *led: rdn: hung lft and hdd over 2f out: wknd over 1f out* **7/4**[1]	62
56-1	4	6	**Red Zeus (IRE)**[25] 1132 3-9-0 67 ... LiamKeniry 4 (J S Moore) *hld up in tch: rdn over 3f out: wknd over 2f out* **9/1**	50

2m 8.84s (0.94) **Going Correction** +0.025s/f (Good) 4 Ran SP% **109.7**
Speed ratings (Par 98): **97,96,90,85**
CSF £7.60 TOTE £1.90; EX 9.00.
Owner Mr And Mrs A E Pakenham **Bred** Mr & Mrs A E Pakenham **Trained** Lambourn, Berks

FOCUS
The time was 2.61 seconds quicker than the modestly run older-horse Class 5 handicap earlier on the card, suggesting Moonlight Rhapsody set a fair gallop. It's hard to build too much enthusiasm for this form though with the favourite disappointing;
Moonlight Rhapsody(IRE) Official explanation: jockey said filly hung left

1660 LADBROKES.COM SOUTH CROXTON H'CAP — 1m 3f 183y
() (Class 4) (0-85,) 3-Y-O — £

T/Plt: £263.30 to a £1 stake. Pool:£57,311.23 - 158.86 winning tickets T/Qpdt: £21.70 to a £1 stake. Pool:£5,174.92 - 176.00 winning tickets CR

1661 - 1662a (Foreign Racing) - See Raceform Interactive

1375 DUNDALK (A.W) (L-H)
Friday, April 29

OFFICIAL GOING: Standard

1663a I105-107FM 3YO H'CAP — 7f (P)
7:30 (7:31) (47-70,70) 3-Y-O — **£4,758** (£1,103; £482; £275)

			RPR
1		**Cheers Buddy (IRE)**[191] 7026 3-9-4 67 ... JPO'Brien(3) 4 (Paul Hennessy, Ire) *settled in rr of mid-div: 12th ent st: hdwy on outer fr 2f out: styd on strly to ld clsng stages* **14/1**	74
2	nk	**Devonelli (IRE)**[21] 1224 3-9-3 70 ... CPHoban(7) 8 (M Halford, Ire) *towards rr: 13th ent st: rdn on outer and hdwy fr 2f out: kpt on wl fnl f wout quite matching wnr to go 2nd clsng stages* **12/1**	76
3	½	**Trans City (IRE)**[35] 975 3-9-9 69 ... JMurtagh 13 (G M Lyons, Ire) *a.p: 2nd 1/2-way: rdn to ld under 2f out: sn strly pressed and jnd 1f out: no ex and hdd clsng stages* **9/2**[1]	74
4	hd	**Extra Steps (IRE)**[14] 1376 3-9-0 67 ... RPWhelan(7) 6 (Paul Cashman, Ire) *mid-div: 8th 1/2-way: hdwy u.p to chal fr over 1f out: no ex wl ins fnl f* **9/2**[1]	71
5	1	**Brookley Lady (IRE)**[19] 1258 3-9-1 64 ... ShaneFoley(3) 3 (Seamus G O'Donnell, Ire) *mid-div: wnt 6th 2f out: gd hdwy between horses to dispute 1f out: hdd wl ins fnl f: no ex* **16/1**	65
6	shd	**Words Of Wisdom (IRE)**[12] 1424 3-9-6 66 ... PBBeggy 5 (Edward Lynam, Ire) *in rr of mid-div on inner: 10th 1/2-way: hdwy fr 2f out: nt clrest of runs fr over 1f out: kpt on one pce* **10/1**	69
7	1	**Fellisha (IRE)**[19] 1258 3-8-12 58 ... WMLordan 2 (Andrew Heffernan, Ire) *chsd ldrs: 6th 1/2-way: rdn 2f out: no imp fr 1f out: kpt on one pce* **14/1**	56
8	¾	**Cinarosa (IRE)**[35] 975 3-9-6 69 ... BACurtis(3) 1 (Francis Ennis, Ire) *led early: 3rd on inner 1/2-way: rdn and no imp fr 1 1/2f out: no ex ins fnl f* **15/2**[3]	65
9	1 ½	**Music On D Waters (IRE)**[14] 1377 3-8-4 50 oh3 ... (b[1]) MCHussey 9 (Peter Casey, Ire) *nvr a factor* **40/1**	42
10	1 ¾	**Blue Cannon (IRE)**[260] 5013 3-9-0 70 ... SamanthaBell(10) 7 (Kevin Prendergast, Ire) *nvr a factor* **16/1**	58
11	1	**Big Bad Lily (IRE)**[14] 1376 3-8-9 55 ... (p) CO'Donoghue 10 (Augustine Leahy, Ire) *trckd ldrs: 5th 1/2-way: rdn to go 3rd 2f out: no imp u.p ins fnl f: checked clsng stages and eased* **8/1**	52
12	1 ¾	**Abbeyshrule (IRE)**[215] 6399 3-7-11 50 oh2 ... (p) DarrenEdwardEgan(7) 11 (Paul W Flynn, Ire) *mid-div: 7th 1/2-way: no ex fr under 2f out* **22/1**	30
13	1 ¼	**Vetvey (IRE)**[5] 1543 3-9-5 65 ... GregFairley 12 (Mark Johnston) *led after 1f: strly pressed early st: hdd under 2f out: no imp whn hmpd 1f out: wknd* **5/1**[2]	42
14	nk	**Oakwood Princess (IRE)**[24] 1158 3-9-5 65 ... (b[1]) KLatham 14 (W McCreery, Ire) *s.i.s: hdwy to trck ldrs on outer: 4th 1/2-way: rdn early st: no ex fr over 1f out: wknd* **14/1**	41

1m 26.19s (86.19) 14 Ran SP% **131.2**
CSF £187.51 CT £923.30 TOTE £9.90: £2.50, £5.20, £1.02; DF 213.90.
Owner Martin Lanney **Bred** Jaykayenn Syndicate **Trained** Rathvawn, Co Kilkenny
■ Stewards' Enquiry : Shane Foley advice: careless riding

FOCUS
Quite a story here as Paul Hennessy, Ireland's leading greyhound trainer over the last decade, saw his first runner on the track emerge victorious.

NOTEBOOK
Cheers Buddy(IRE) had been with Tony Mullins but Hennessy assumed the training duties for the current campaign and he managed to rekindle the gelding's enthusiasm after ending last season in awful form, finishing 15th of 18 in a moderate 50-80 1m handicap at Navan on his final start.\n heaped praise on jockey Joseph O'Brien after the race and he was right to do so. Holding up his mount towards the rear for most of the contest, O'Brien edged towards the outside after entering the home straight and he needed to be at his strongest to collar Devonelli in the closing stages.
Devonelli(IRE) was unlucky not to open her account. Like the winner, she was held up in rear by Conor Hoban and made an almost identical move to the winner down the outside after turning for home. She looked a likely winner after passing Trans City inside the final furlong but Cheers Buddy had more momentum on her outside and narrowly prevailed. (op 10/1)
Trans City(IRE) was well backed on his first start in a handicap and hit the front at the 2f pole after travelling sweetly towards the head of affairs. But when Johnny Murtagh went to win his race, the response wasn't good enough and he was swallowed up inside the final furlong. (op 9/2 tchd 5/1)
Extra Steps(IRE) looked a potential danger 1f out when staying on down the outside but that run petered out in the closing stages. (op 11/2 tchd 6/1)
Brookley Lady(IRE) cut through the pack to dispute the lead passing the 1f pole but had nothing in reserve once headed.
Words Of Wisdom(IRE) seemed to be coming with a dangerous looking challenge when slightly short of room over 1f out. (op 10/1 tchd 11/1)
Cinarosa(IRE) was another who didn't enjoy the clearest of passages and is worth consideration in a similar contest as she is still unexposed. (op 7/1)

1664 - 1670a (Foreign Racing) - See Raceform Interactive

1648 DONCASTER (L-H)
Saturday, April 30

OFFICIAL GOING: Good to firm (good in places on round course; watered; 8.7)
Wind: Fresh half behind Weather: Fine and dry

1671 CROWNHOTEL-BAWTRY.CO.UK APPRENTICE H'CAP — 1m 2f 60y
5:35 (5:35) (Class 4) (0-85,84) 4-Y-O+ — **£3,885** (£1,156; £577; £288) **Stalls** Low

Form				RPR
60-1	1		**Frontline Phantom (IRE)**[28] 1099 4-8-7 **70** oh4 ... MatthewLawson 6 (Mrs K Burke) *trckd ldrs: hdwy to trck ldr after 3f: cl up 1/2-way: led wl over 3f out: jnd and rdn wl over 1f out: drvn and edgd lft ins fnl f: kpt on gamely towards fin* **7/4**[1]	77+
-661	2	¾	**Sharakti (IRE)**[5] 1573 4-8-10 **73** 6ex ... GarryWhillans 7 (Alan McCabe) *hld up in tch: hdwy 1/2-way: effrt 3f out and sn cl up: rdn to chal over 2f out: drvn and ev ch whn edgd lft ins fnl f and no ex last 75yds* **4/1**[2]	78
20-3	3	1	**Veiled Applause**[28] 1097 8-9-6 **83** ... ShaneBKelly 3 (John Quinn) *hld up in tch: stdy hdwy on inner 3f out: rdn to chse ldng pair ent fnl f: kpt on same pce* **9/2**[3]	86
32-5	4	1 ¼	**Desert Vision**[10] 1490 7-8-7 **75** ... (bt) DavidSimmonson(5) 1 (Michael Easterby) *trckd ldrs: hdwy 4f out: rdn to chse ldng pair 3f out: drvn and one pce appr fnl f* **20/1**	76
25-0	5	10	**Elmfield Giant (USA)**[21] 1243 4-8-8 **74** ... GeorgeChaloner(3) 4 (Richard Fahey) *chsd ldrs: pushed along wl over 3f out: sn rdn and outpcd fr over 2f out* **13/2**	56
2102	6	nk	**Kidlat**[24] 1183 6-9-0 **84** ... AlexOwen(7) 5 (Alan Bailey) *in tch: hdwy on wd outside 1/2-way and sn cl up: rdn along 4f out: sn wknd* **8/1**	65
5010	7	12	**El Dececy (USA)**[27] 1109 7-8-12 **75** ... (p) MatthewCosham 2 (John Balding) *led: rdn along and jnd over 4f out: hdd over 3f out: sn wknd* **22/1**	34

2m 8.65s (-0.75) **Going Correction** +0.05s/f (Good) 7 Ran SP% **108.1**
Speed ratings (Par 105): **105,104,103,102,94 94,84**
toteswingers:1&2:£2.30, 1&3:£1.10, 2&3:£2.60 CSF £7.73 TOTE £2.30: £1.20, £2.60; EX 9.60.
Owner Frontline Bathrooms **Bred** Joe Rogers **Trained** Middleham Moor, North Yorks

FOCUS
Not really a bonafide 0-85 with all but two of the runners rated 75 or less but it was run at a fair gallop considering the size of the field and the winner continues his upward curve. The third helps with the standard.
El Dececy(USA) Official explanation: jockey said gelding hung right throughout

1672 ONE CALL INSURANCE MAIDEN STKS — 6f
6:05 (6:05) (Class 5) 3-4-Y-O — **£2,914** (£867; £433; £216) **Stalls** High

Form				RPR
4	1		**Bahia Emerald (IRE)**[15] 1358 3-8-10 0 ... DarryllHolland 6 (Jeremy Noseda) *dwlt and in rr whn swvd bdly lft and hmpd rival ins first f: swtchd wd and hdwy 1/2-way: str run to ld over 1f out and sn hung bdly rt: rn green: put hd in air and wandered ins fnl f: kpt on* **11/4**[2]	63+
4-	2	1 ¼	**Spinatrix**[175] 7345 3-8-10 0 ... FrederikTylicki 4 (Michael Dods) *trckd ldrs: swtchd lft and effrt wl over 2f out: rdn wl over 1f out: kpt on ins fnl f* **11/10**[1]	55
00-	3	½	**Loose Quality (USA)**[213] 6465 3-9-1 0 ... FrannyNorton 5 (Tom Tate) *trckd ldrs: hdwy 1/2-way: cl up 2f out: sn rdn and ev ch whn n.m.r over 1f out: sn drvn and kpt on same pce* **13/2**[3]	58
4340	4	1 ¼	**Gorgeous Goblin (IRE)**[4] 1589 4-9-2 47 ... (vt) AdamBeschizza(5) 1 (David C Griffiths) *wnt lft s: towards rr whn bdly hmpd ins first f: hdwy on outer 1/2-way: rdn to ld 2f out: edgd rt and n.m.r whn hdd over 1f out: kpt on same pce* **18/1**	52
	5	¾	**Magic Rhythm** 3-8-10 0 ... AndrewElliott 3 (Mrs K Burke) *prom: effrt and cl up 1/2-way: rdn along and hld whn n.m.r over 1f out: one pce after* **10/1**	47
30	6	1 ¼	**Hootys Agogo**[22] 1217 3-9-1 0 ... DavidNolan 2 (Declan Carroll) *led: pushed along 1/2-way: sn rdn and hdd 2f out: grad wknd* **12/1**	48

1m 12.34s (-1.26) **Going Correction** -0.325s/f (Firm)
WFA 3 from 4yo 11lb 6 Ran SP% **109.7**
Speed ratings (Par 103): **95,93,92,91,90 88**
toteswingers:1&2:£1.10, 1&3:£4.40, 2&3:£1.50 CSF £5.85 TOTE £3.70: £2.40, £1.10; EX 4.90.
Owner Cheveley Park Stud **Bred** Corduff Stud **Trained** Newmarket, Suffolk

FOCUS
A two-horse race according to the betting and they duly filled the first two places but not in the order suggested at the end of a muddling affair not without incident. For all the best horse won, the form has a suspect look to it. It should ensure a modest mark for the winner, who is capable of better.

1673 FRENCHGATE SHOPPING CENTRE MAIDEN STKS — 5f
6:40 (6:41) (Class 5) 2-Y-O **£2,914** (£867; £433; £216) **Stalls** High

Form RPR
3 **1** **Forevertheoptimist (IRE)**[22] [1209] 2-9-3 0 .... TomEaves 1 88+
(Linda Stubbs) *cl up on outer: hdwy to chal wl over 1f out: rdn ent fnl f: sn led: kpt on wl towards fin* **7/2**[1]
2 *1* **Bannock (IRE)** 2-9-3 0 .... SilvestreDeSousa 3 84+
(Mark Johnston) *cl up: led 1/2-way: jnd and rdn wl over 1f out: drvn ent fnl f: sn hdd and kpt on same pce last 100yds* **7/1**[2]
5 **3** *1 1/4* **Misty Conquest (IRE)**[12] [1441] 2-8-12 0 .... RichardKingscote 2 75+
(Tom Dascombe) *a.p: effrt and cl up 2f out: sn rdn and ch tl drvn appr fnl f and kpt on same pce* **7/2**[1]
0 **4** *5* **Adranian (IRE)**[28] [1095] 2-9-3 0 .... CathyGannon 6 62
(David Evans) *in rr and sn rdn along: n.d* **8/1**[3]
4 **5** *3 3/4* **Springleaf (IRE)**[11] [1455] 2-8-12 0 .... TonyHamilton 5 43
(Richard Fahey) *trckd ldrs on inner: effrt 1/2-way: sn rdn along and wknd wl over 1f out* **7/2**[1]
0 **6** *1/2* **J J Leary (IRE)**[14] [1383] 2-9-3 0 .... AndrewMullen 4 47
(David Nicholls) *led: rdn along and hdd 1/2-way: sn wknd* **7/2**[1]
58.99 secs (-1.51) **Going Correction** -0.325s/f (Firm) **6** Ran SP% **112.5**
Speed ratings (Par 92): **99,97,95,87,81 80**
toteswingers:1&2:£2.30, 1&3:£1.90, 2&3:£4.60 CSF £28.30 TOTE £4.20: £1.50, £5.00; EX 13.10.
Owner G & T Bloodstock **Bred** Peter & Hugh McCutcheon **Trained** Norton, N Yorks

FOCUS
No more than a fair maiden in all probability with none of those with experience having shown great promise on their debuts.

NOTEBOOK
Forevertheoptimist(IRE) stepped up on his first run at Newcastle with a much more professional display despite missing the break slightly, soon travelling strongly up with the pace and always looking to have things in control from 2f out, value for more than the winning margin. He looks to have some scope about him and, being a late foal, seems sure to continue improving. (op 11-4 tchd 4-1 and 9-2 in places)
Bannock(IRE), a half-brother to some winners in Australia out of a UAE Oaks winner, ran a promising first race considering he was colty beforehand, soon to the fore and going down fighting for all the winner always looked to have the upper hand. He knew his job well once racing so might not improve quite as much as expected. (op 11-2)
Misty Conquest(IRE) stepped up on her debut Windsor form, albeit unable to match strides with the first two late on, but she'll have to improve as much again if she's going to win a maiden next time. (tchd 3-1)
Adranian(IRE) was the first off the bridle but to his credit stayed on and looks one that might improve again as he gains experience and, perhaps more importantly, steps up to 6f. (op 9-1 tchd 12-1)
Springleaf(IRE) disappointed after an encouraging debut albeit over a stiffer 5f than this. (op 9-2 tchd 3-1)
J J Leary(IRE) came in for some support but is possibly still in need of more time given how little he'd shown on his debut. (op 9-2 tchd 10-3)

1674 TRY TOTEQUICKPICK IF YOU'RE FEELING LUCKY CONDITIONS STKS — 7f
7:10 (7:12) (Class 3) 3-Y-O **£5,607** (£1,679; £839) **Stalls** High

Form RPR
164- **1** **Trade Storm**[235] [5831] 3-9-0 97 .... DarryllHolland 1 87+
(John Gallagher) *dwlt: trckd ldng pair: hdwy 2f out: swtchd lft over 1f out: rdn and qcknd to ld ent fnl f: styd on strly* **5/2**[2]
16-3 **2** *1 3/4* **Azrael**[14] [1384] 3-9-0 95 .... JamesDoyle 4 82
(Alan McCabe) *trckd ldr: hdwy 1/2-way: pushed along to ld wl over 2f out: rdn wl over 1f out: drvn and hdd ent fnl f: sn one pce* **1/3**[1]
3132 **3** *7* **Mazovian (USA)**[22] [1219] 3-8-7 66 .... DavidKenny(7) 2 63?
(Michael Chapman) *led: rdn along over 3f out: hdd over 2f out: drvn and wknd over 1f out* **18/1**[3]
1m 23.98s (-2.32) **Going Correction** -0.325s/f (Firm) **3** Ran SP% **108.9**
Speed ratings (Par 102): **100,98,90**
CSF £3.98 TOTE £3.50; EX 3.20.
Owner Universal Racing **Bred** G T Lucas **Trained** Chastleton, Oxon

FOCUS
A poor turnout for a minor event won by the useful Rodrigo De Torres last year, and a tactical affair with the outsider closer up for along way than he was entitled to be on account of just a fair gallop. The favourite disappointed and the third limits the form.

NOTEBOOK
Trade Storm was reported to have been in need of the race but it didn't look that way as he sat in the favourite's slipstream prior to unleasing the much better turn of foot, clear when inclined to edge to his right and pull up inside the last. Sixth in the Gimcrack last year, he's probably improved over the winter but still looks only on the fringe of Listed class right now, though the King Charles II Stakes at Newmarket, his next intended outing, should reveal more. (op 7-4)
Azrael, whose official rating of 95 looks on the high side, had no business starting at odds of 1-3 down in trip and given the winner was officially rated 2lb his superior, and he was made to look one-paced after dictating but failing to make the best use of his proven stamina. Connections might rue making a pig's ear of the tactics here. (op 8-13 tchd 4-6 in places)
Mazovian(USA) finished where he was entitled to on his turf debut and went well enough for a long way to think he'll be effective on it back in his rightful grade. (op 16-1)

1675 MERCEDES BENZ OF SOUTH YORKSHIRE H'CAP — 6f
7:45 (7:45) (Class 3) (0-90,90) 4-Y-O+ **£5,828** (£1,734; £866; £432) **Stalls** High

Form RPR
030- **1** **Enderby Spirit (GR)**[175] [7351] 5-9-7 90 .... TomEaves 6 97
(Bryan Smart) *trckd ldrs centre: hdwy wl over 1f out: rdn and styd on strly ins fnl f to ld last 50yds* **8/1**
2400 **2** *hd* **Star Rover (IRE)**[24] [1186] 4-9-6 89 .... CathyGannon 14 95
(David Evans) *racd towards stands' rail: chsd ldrs: hdwy 2f out: rdn over 1f out: drvn and kpt on strly ins fnl f: jst hld* **16/1**
31-5 **3** *1* **Whozthecat (IRE)**[24] [1166] 4-9-1 89 .... NeilFarley(5) 2 92
(Declan Carroll) *cl up centre: hdwy to ld over 2f out: rdn and hung bdly lft ent fnl f: hdd and no ex last 50yds* **9/1**
0-22 **4** *hd* **Internationaldebut (IRE)**[11] [1457] 6-9-5 88 .... TonyCulhane 8 90
(Paul Midgley) *hld up: hdwy 2f out: rdn over 1f out: kpt on strly ins fnl f: nrst fin* **5/1**[1]
213- **5** *nk* **Diman Waters (IRE)**[252] [5309] 4-8-13 82 .... PatCosgrave 4 83
(Eric Alston) *rrd and dwlt s: sn chsng ldrs centre: hdwy to chal and ev ch 2f out: rdn wl over 1f out and ev ch tl drvn and one pce ent fnl f* **17/2**
-541 **6** *4 1/2* **Cape Vale (IRE)**[23] [1200] 6-9-6 89 .... AdrianNicholls 11 76
(David Nicholls) *racd towards stands' rail: led: rdn along 1/2-way: hdd over 2f out and grad wknd* **15/2**
156- **7** *3/4* **Desert Poppy (IRE)**[212] [6509] 4-9-5 88 .... DaneO'Neill 7 73
(Walter Swinburn) *nvr bttr than midfield* **11/2**[2]
00-0 **8** *nk* **Hotham**[27] [1111] 8-9-6 89 .... BarryMcHugh 12 73
(Noel Wilson) *in tch towards stands' rail: rdn along over 2f out: sn btn* **33/1**
0-60 **9** *3* **Tabaret**[11] [1457] 8-9-1 84 .... TonyHamilton 1 58
(Richard Whitaker) *racd wd: cl up: rdn over 2f out: sn drvn and wknd* **14/1**
00-2 **10** *1* **Medici Time**[23] [1205] 6-8-13 82 ....(v) GrahamGibbons 5 53
(Tim Easterby) *in tch centre: effrt 1/2-way: sn rdn and n.d* **7/1**[3]
51-0 **11** *1 1/4* **Haajes**[11] [1457] 7-9-3 86 .... MickyFenton 13 53
(Paul Midgley) *in tch towards stands' rail: rdn along wl over 2f out: n.d* **33/1**
04-4 **12** *2 1/2* **We Have A Dream**[23] [1197] 6-9-1 84 .... SilvestreDeSousa 3 43
(William Muir) *a towards rr* **14/1**
000- **13** *5* **Gap Princess (IRE)**[204] [6721] 7-8-12 88 .... JordanNason(7) 10 31
(Geoffrey Harker) *v.s.a: a bhd* **25/1**
1m 10.47s (-3.13) **Going Correction** -0.325s/f (Firm) **13** Ran SP% **116.9**
Speed ratings (Par 107): **107,106,105,105,104 98,97,97,93,92 90,87,80**
toteswingers:1&2:£36.20, 1&3:£10.70, 2&3:£35.90 CSF £123.82 CT £1212.31 TOTE £9.70: £2.80, £3.00, £4.20; EX 164.40.
Owner Mrs Patricia Brown **Bred** Stavloi Th Nanou S A **Trained** Hambleton, N Yorks
■ Stewards' Enquiry : Cathy Gannon caution: used whip with excessive frequency.

FOCUS
A competitive and open sprint handicap in which the field raced wide across the track with the action taking place centre to far side in the closing stages. The pace was good. The principals were rated in line with this year's best.

NOTEBOOK
Enderby Spirit(GR) ended a losing streak stretching back to July 2009 but he had a good chance off just 90 here with his yard's sprinters in good form considering he was still being campaigned at Listed level at the end of 2010. He's clearly not in need of the headgear he ended last season in and should remain competitive after a small rise in the weights, with this trip probably suiting him better nowadays than 5f. (op 15-2)
Star Rover(IRE) hadn't had much chance in better company than this the last twice but back in a handicap on what is probably his ideal ground he showed he's still a force to be reckoned with at this level, albeit spoiling his effort by drifting left across the track. (tchd 18-1)
Whozthecat(IRE) ◆ ran a fine race, showing fine speed and looking the likely winner for much of the way only to throw away his chance when drifting badly left inside the last as his stamina ran out. He's worth looking out for next time back at 5f. Official explanation: jockey said gelding hung left (op 11-1 tchd 12-1)
Internationaldebut(IRE) gave his running once again but couldn't get going until too late on this sharper track and will be ideally suited by a return to 7f. (op 9-2)
Diman Waters(IRE) ◆ held his form well last year and travelled strongly enough for a long way here before finding either lack of a recent run or 6f catching him out to suggest he might even have come back an improved sprinter this year. He improved a good deal for his reappearance last season and is worth looking out for next time, not least back at 5f. (op 11-1 tchd 8-1)
Cape Vale(IRE) couldn't get his own way in front on this occasion but wasn't knocked about when beaten. (op 13-2 tchd 8-1)
Desert Poppy(IRE) ended 2010 on something of a low note and found little on her reappearance having travelled smoothly for a long way. (op 6-1)
Tabaret couldn't repeat last year's success off a similar mark but shaped a fair bit better than the result suggests, only really fading inside the last as if he might still be in need of the run.
Medici Time never really promised to build on his encouraging comeback. (op 8-1 tchd 6-1)
Gap Princess(IRE) ruined all chance by starting very slowly. (op 40-1)

1676 HAGUEPRINT.COM H'CAP — 1m 6f 132y
8:15 (8:16) (Class 4) (0-85,85) 4-Y-O+ **£5,245** (£1,560; £780; £389) **Stalls** Low

Form RPR
531- **1** **Old Hundred (IRE)**[227] [6084] 4-9-4 79 ....(v) PatCosgrave 8 90+
(James Fanshawe) *hld up in tch: hdwy over 3f out: chsd ldr 2f out: rdn to ld 1f out: drvn out* **5/2**[1]
0-30 **2** *1 1/4* **Nave (USA)**[7] [1517] 4-9-10 85 .... SilvestreDeSousa 5 93
(Mark Johnston) *trckd ldr: led 3f out: rdn 2 l clr 2f out: drvn and hdd 1f out: kpt on same pce* **11/4**[2]
2333 **3** *5* **Layla's Dancer**[22] [1223] 4-8-12 73 .... JamesDoyle 4 75
(Tony Carroll) *chsd ldng pair: hdwy 3f out: rdn over 2f out: drvn and one pce fr over 1f out* **13/2**
-551 **4** *1 1/4* **King's Counsel (IRE)**[17] [1305] 5-8-6 64 ow1 ....(v) GrahamGibbons 1 64
(David O'Meara) *led: rdn along over 4f out: hdd 3f out: sn drvn and wknd wl over 1f out* **9/2**[3]
4-44 **5** *3* **Russian George (IRE)**[23] [948] 5-9-9 81 .... DarryllHolland 2 77
(Steve Gollings) *hld up in rr: effrt 4f out: rdn along wl over 2f out: n.d* **8/1**
6 *1* **Viva Colonia (IRE)**[38] 6-9-3 75 .... DanielTudhope 6 70
(David O'Meara) *hld up: effrt 4f out: sn rdn along and n.d* **16/1**
312- **7** *shd* **Rosewin (IRE)**[130] [7957] 5-8-9 70 .... JamesSullivan(3) 7 65
(Ollie Pears) *in tch: pushed along 5f out: rdn wl over 3f out: n.d* **10/1**
3m 7.84s (0.44) **Going Correction** +0.05s/f (Good)
WFA 4 from 5yo+ 3lb **7** Ran SP% **112.8**
Speed ratings (Par 105): **100,99,96,96,94 93,93**
toteswingers:1&2:£2.10, 1&3:£3.80, 2&3:£3.10 CSF £9.36 CT £37.52 TOTE £3.30: £2.70, £2.20; EX 13.50.
Owner Lael Stable **Bred** Lael Stables **Trained** Newmarket, Suffolk

FOCUS
A fair staying handicap to end proceedings, but one at just a fair gallop despite the field being well strung out and those held right up never got competitive. the winner is on the up and the form is rated at something like face value.
Layla's Dancer Official explanation: jockey said gelding hung left

T/Plt: £174.20 to a £1 stake. Pool:£48,889.49 - 204.77 winning tickets T/Qpdt: £104.00 to a £1 stake. Pool:£4,303.26 - 30.60 winning tickets JR

GOODWOOD (R-H)

Saturday, April 30

OFFICIAL GOING: Straight course - good; round course - good to firm

First 2f of 1m course dolled out 6yds increasing distances on that course by 12yds.

Wind: Fresh, half behind Weather: Fine

1677 TOTESPORT.COM E B F DAISY WARWICK FILLIES' STKS (LISTED RACE) 1m 4f

2:15 (2:15) (Class 1) 4-Y-0+ **£17,778** (£6,723; £3,360; £1,680) Stalls High

Form				RPR
150-	1		**Gertrude Bell**[317] 3101 4-8-12 103 .... NickyMackay 10	108
			(John Gosden) *trckd ldng pair to 5f out: styd handy: effrt to chse ldr over 2f out: drvn to ld jst over 1f out: battled on strly to hold on* **7/2**[2]	
041-	2	hd	**Polly's Mark (IRE)**[218] 6320 5-9-2 106 .... AdamKirby 6	111
			(Clive Cox) *led 1f: trckd ldr: led again over 3f out: drvn and hdd jst over 1f out: fought on wl: jst hld* **5/2**[1]	
02-3	3	3 ½	**Pink Symphony**[28] 1100 4-8-12 105 .... StevieDonohoe 3	102
			(Paul Cole) *trckd ldng trio: wnt 3rd 5f out: effrt to chal on inner and w ldr over 3f out: lost 2nd over 2f out: steadily outpcd* **6/1**	
526-	4	hd	**Roxy Flyer (IRE)**[184] 7189 4-8-12 91 .... PatDobbs 5	102
			(Amanda Perrett) *settled in 5th: effrt whn n.m.r briefly wl over 2f out: rdn and cl enough 2f out: steadily outpcd* **4/1**[3]	
50-6	5	8	**Totally Ours**[28] 1104 4-8-12 95 .... JimCrowley 2	89
			(William Muir) *hld up in last trio: effrt over 3f out: outpcd but pressing for a pl over 1f out: wknd rapidly fnl f* **16/1**	
60-0	6	½	**Gallic Star (IRE)**[71] 607 4-8-12 103 .... ChrisCatlin 4	88
			(Mick Channon) *hld up in last trio: rdn over 2f out: no prog and sn btn* **8/1**	
-622	7	¾	**Resentful Angel**[28] 1100 6-8-13 92 .... LiamKeniry 8	87
			(Pat Eddery) *settled in last trio: shkn up 4f out: no prog whn hanging bdly rt fnl 2f* **10/1**	
6-03	8	22	**On Terms (USA)**[9] 1509 5-8-13 74 .... HayleyTurner 9	52
			(Simon Dow) *drvn to ld after 1f: rdn 1/2-way: hdd & wknd over 3f out: t.o* **40/1**	

2m 34.76s (-3.64) **Going Correction** -0.025s/f (Good)
WFA 4 from 5yo+ 1lb **8** Ran SP% **113.6**
Speed ratings (Par 108): **111,110,108,108,103 102,102,87**
toteswingers:1&2:£1.90, 1&3:£4.20, 2&3:£2.60 CSF £12.51 TOTE £4.80: £1.50, £1.30, £1.50; EX 15.00 Trifecta £34.20 Pool: £722.25 - 15.62 winning units..
Owner Ms Rachel D S Hood **Bred** Ms Rachel Hood **Trained** Newmarket, Suffolk

FOCUS

The pace seemed to slow at around halfway and consequently a forward ride was advantageous. Still, this seemed a decent fillies' Listed event and the form looks reliable enough, with the 'right' types dominating. The winner is up 4lb on her Oaks run.

NOTEBOOK

Gertrude Bell had been absent since disappointing in the Ribblesdale. She didn't handle the top bend on the run back towards the straight all that well and still looked a bit rusty under pressure, but she had been sensibly placed throughout by Nicky Mackay, and she showed a willing attitude. The impression was there will be significant improvement to come from Gertrude Bell, whose absence totalled 317 days, and she will be up to competing in Group races this year. (op 9-2 tchd 5-1)

Polly's Mark(IRE) is a game filly and she battled on well when joined by the winner, having been ideally placed throughout by Adam Kirby. There should to be more to come. (op 9-4)

Pink Symphony was the pick of the weights - she had 2lb in hand over the winner and runner-up on official figures - and she had the benefit of race-fitness over that pair, but she was unproven at this trip and was one-paced under pressure. (op 9-2)

Roxy Flyer(IRE) came into the race rated just 91 and had been off for six months. Both her wins have been gained at Goodwood, so the track probably helped. (op 5-1)

Totally Ours dropped out of contention quite quickly on her first try over a trip this far. (op 14-1 tchd 18-1)

Gallic Star(IRE) briefly looked threatening early in the straight but failed to pick up. (tchd 15-2)

Resentful Angel struggled badly with the track in the straight, hanging right. (op 11-1)

1678 BET ON THE GUINEAS WITH TOTEPOOL E B F MAIDEN STKS 5f

2:50 (2:51) (Class 5) 2-Y-0 **£3,561** (£1,059; £529; £264) Stalls High

Form				RPR
	1		**Foxtrot India (IRE)** 2-9-3 0 .... JimCrowley 2	83
			(Peter Winkworth) *slowest away: gd spd to rcvr and press ldng pair after 1f: upsides after tl drvn to ld 1f out: hld on* **14/1**	
	2	hd	**North Star Boy (IRE)** 2-9-3 0 .... PatDobbs 1	82
			(Richard Hannon) *w ldr: narrow ld 1/2-way to 1f out: rdn and rallied last 100yds: jst hld* **11/10**[1]	
	3	3 ¼	**Noor Zabeel (USA)** 2-9-3 0 .... ChrisCatlin 3	71+
			(Mick Channon) *led to 1/2-way: shkn up and nt qckn: kpt on same pce fnl f* **13/2**[3]	
	4	1	**Backtrade (IRE)** 2-9-3 0 .... DavidProbert 5	67
			(Andrew Balding) *settled in last pair: prog after 2f: cl up bhd ldng pair over 1f out: hanging and fdd* **8/1**	
	5	1 ½	**Evervescent (IRE)** 2-9-3 0 .... LiamKeniry 7	62
			(J S Moore) *settled in last pair: outpcd fr 2f out: shkn up over 1f out: no prog* **28/1**	
	6	shd	**Roman Soldier (IRE)** 2-9-3 0 .... ShaneKelly 8	61
			(Jeremy Noseda) *trckd ldrs and quite keen: outpcd fr 2f out: n.d after* **3/1**[2]	
	7	4 ½	**Main Focus (USA)** 2-9-3 0 .... NickyMackay 4	45
			(John Gosden) *racd on outer: chsd ldrs but rn green: wknd rapidly over 1f out* **11/1**	

58.70 secs (0.30) **Going Correction** -0.225s/f (Firm) **7** Ran SP% **115.5**
Speed ratings (Par 92): **88,87,82,80,78 78,71**
toteswingers:1&2:£8.40, 1&3:£14.60, 2&3:£2.90 CSF £30.76 TOTE £9.80: £2.70, £1.30; EX 35.00.
Owner Foxtrot Racing Partnership V **Bred** Edmond Kent **Trained** Chiddingfold, Surrey

FOCUS

A field of newcomers, but it looked a reasonable maiden that should produce winners. They raced towards the stands' side, but the rail was not an advantage.

NOTEBOOK

Foxtrot India(IRE) started slowly but quickly recovered and travelled well before knuckling down for pressure. A 20,000euros April foal, he's a brother to 5f-1m winner Kirsty's Boy and looks a useful type. (op 12-1)

North Star Boy(IRE), a 57,000gns March foal, looked a sharp type in the paddock and according to connections had gone "well enough" in a recent gallop with Windsor winner Lord Ofthe Shadows. He seemed well educated but just missed out. There should be a similar race in him. (op 10-11 tchd 6-5 and 5-4 in places)

Noor Zabeel(USA), who was warm in paddock, soon moved to the stands' rail. He lacked the finishing speed of the front two but was keeping on at the finish. This 50,000gns purchase is a May foal and can do better. (op 7-1 tched 15-2 in places)

Backtrade(IRE), a 37,000euros half-brother to, among others, dual 6f winner Shaard, out of a useful triple 6f winner at two, is a March foal. He was green in the preliminaries and in the race itself, missing the break and being inclined to hang under pressure. There should be more to come, provided he goes the right way. (op 11-1 tchd 12-1)

Evervescent(IRE), a February foal, only cost 3,500euros and is already gelded, but he's one to keep in mind. He looked a bit backward, still holding on to his winter coat, and he was never competitive after missing the break, but he has the scope to improve. (op 25-1)

Roman Soldier(IRE), an 80,000euros purchase, is a January foal and holds a Phoenix Stakes entry, but he didn't show much. (op 4-1 tchd 9-2)

Main Focus(USA) ruined his chance by hanging right, running as though the experience was badly needed. (op 12-1 tchd 10-1)

1679 TOTESCOOP6 H'CAP 1m 6f

3:30 (3:30) (Class 2) (0-105,102) 4-Y-0+ **£19,428** (£5,781; £2,889; £1,443) Stalls Low

Form				RPR
3/	1		**Investissement**[407] 6978 5-9-3 95 .... NickyMackay 6	105
			(John Gosden) *prom: trckd ldng pair 5f out: clsd to ld over 2f out: drvn and pressed fnl f: hld on wl* **16/1**	
23-2	2	½	**Moyenne Corniche**[27] 1112 6-9-5 97 .... GeorgeBaker 4	106
			(Brian Ellison) *hld up towards rr: stdy prog over 3f out: wnt 2nd over 1f out but hanging: drvn to chal fnl f: nt qckn* **11/2**[3]	
603-	3	2 ¼	**Simenon (IRE)**[175] 7350 4-9-3 97 .... DavidProbert 2	103
			(Andrew Balding) *disp ld 5f: pressed ldr after: led 5f out: rdn and hdd over 2f out: lost 2nd over 1f out: fdd ins fnl f* **3/1**[1]	
/30-	4	nk	**Petara Bay (IRE)**[315] 3191 7-9-10 102 .... JimCrowley 3	107
			(Robert Mills) *hld up in last pair: pushed along over 3f out: drvn and sme prog over 2f out: n.m.r briefly over 1f out: styd on wl last 150yds: nrly snatched 3rd* **7/1**	
120/	5	2 ½	**Harry Tricker**[49] 6061 7-8-11 89 .... (p) FergusSweeney 10	91
			(Gary Moore) *trckd ldrs in 5th: rdn 3f out: tried to cl 2f out: edging rt and nt qckn over 1f out: fdd* **20/1**	
030-	6	½	**Dazinski**[196] 6926 5-8-7 85 .... EddieAhern 1	86
			(Mark H Tompkins) *trckd ldrs in 6th: rdn on inner 3f out: no imp 2f out: wl hld after* **12/1**	
150-	7	10	**Very Good Day (FR)**[277] 4456 4-9-4 98 .... ChrisCatlin 8	85
			(Mick Channon) *stdd s: hld up last to 1/2-way: effrt 4f out: no prog 3f out: wl btn after* **7/1**	
1163	8	7	**Exemplary**[14] 1412 4-8-10 90 .... GregFairley 12	67
			(Mark Johnston) *disp ld: narrow advantage after 5f tl hdd 5f out: wknd over 3f out: sn bhd* **12/1**	
50-2	9	46	**Montparnasse (IRE)**[14] 1412 4-8-7 87 .... StevieDonohoe 9	—
			(Kevin Ryan) *taken down early and free to post: hld up in rr: wknd over 4f out: wl t.o and eased* **4/1**[2]	
0-1	10	10	**Battleoftrafalgar**[28] 1105 4-8-5 85 .... (b) TadhgO'Shea 7	—
			(Michael Attwater) *sn pushed up to chse ldng pair: wknd 5f out: wl t.o and eased* **16/1**	

2m 59.78s (-3.82) **Going Correction** -0.025s/f (Good)
WFA 4 from 5yo+ 2lb **10** Ran SP% **117.3**
Speed ratings (Par 109): **109,108,107,107,105 105,99,95,69,63**
toteswingers:1&2:£14.20, 1&3:£12.80, 2&3:£2.40 CSF £102.20 CT £343.29 TOTE £18.10: £4.50, £2.40, £1.50; EX 126.40 Trifecta £666.50 Part won. Pool: £900.73 - 0.40 winning units..
Owner R J H Geffen **Bred** Wertheimer Et Frere **Trained** Newmarket, Suffolk

FOCUS

A reasonable staying event and the pace was good, resulting in a time only 0.48 seconds above standard. The winner was on a fair mark on his French form and posted a small personal best.

NOTEBOOK

Investissement was useful on the Flat when trained by Andre Fabre in 2009, but he showed little in two starts over hurdles for Evan Williams in 2010 and was last seen pulling up in that year's Triumph Hurdle, after which it was reported he had a breathing problem and been very coltish. Following that he reportedly broke his pelvis on the gallops, but he's now a gelding and defied a lengthy break on his debut for John Gosden, further advertising the forwardness of the stable's older horses after Gertrude Bell also overcame an absence earlier on this card. An Irish St Leger entry suggested connections had high hopes for him and he could go on from this, although he'll be a prime candidate to bounce if turned out again quickly.

Moyenne Corniche looked the winner when travelling best early in the straight, but he was inclined to hang right once under pressure, not handling the track and a slap with the whip down his right shoulder not correcting him, and it soon became apparent he was held by the winner. (tchd 6-1)

Simenon(IRE) hasn't won since 2009, but this was a promising enough performance after 175 days off the track. (op 5-2)

Petara Bay(IRE) was slightly short of room towards the inside rail with over a furlong to run, but he was under strong pressure at the time and basically took too long to get going. He was keeping on well at the finish, though, and should be better for this first run in 315 days. (op 8-1)

Harry Tricker was tailed off in a novice chase the previous month, but this was an encouraging first start on the Flat since 2008. He has won twice at Goodwood, so the track obviously suited. (op 14-1)

Very Good Day(FR) didn't progress as expected after finishing a close third in a Listed race here on his 2010 (ran below form when subsequently landing a maiden), but he has plenty of size and looks to have filled out nicely. However, he moved to post as though the ground was plenty fast enough for him. He might be worth another chance. (op 17-2)

Montparnasse(IRE) shaped nicely on his return at Ripon, but he couldn't build on that and something may have been amiss. Official explanation: jockey said gelding moved poorly behind latter stages (op 9-2)

Battleoftrafalgar Official explanation: jockey said colt lost its action; trainer said colt lost a front shoe

1680 TOTEQUICKPICK H'CAP 5f

4:00 (4:00) (Class 3) (0-95,92) 4-Y-0+ **£9,714** (£2,890; £1,444; £721) Stalls High

Form				RPR
1-00	1		**Humidor (IRE)**[24] 1166 4-8-13 87 .... (t) MatthewDavies(3) 7	101
			(George Baker) *fractious gng out on to crse: chsd ldrs: clsd to ld over 1f out: hung rt u.p: kpt on wl* **15/2**	
324-	2	¾	**Addictive Dream (IRE)**[231] 5966 4-9-2 87 .... AdamKirby 2	98
			(Walter Swinburn) *chsd ldrs in 5th and racd on outer: clsd to chal wl over 1f out and edgd lft: pressed wnr after: carried rt fnl f: nt qckn* **7/2**[1]	
44-3	3	1 ½	**Captain Carey**[15] 1366 5-9-7 92 .... TomMcLaughlin 4	98
			(Malcolm Saunders) *wl off the pce in 9th early: prog on wd outside fr 1/2-way: chsd ldng pair 1f out: one pce and no imp after* **9/2**[2]	
020-	4	2 ½	**Favourite Girl (IRE)**[189] 7079 5-9-7 92 .... (v) DuranFentiman 8	89
			(Tim Easterby) *racd towards nr side: led to over 1f out: steadily fdd* **12/1**	
320-	5	hd	**Desert Phantom (USA)**[217] 6364 5-9-7 92 .... EddieAhern 1	88
			(David Simcock) *off the pce on wd outside early: effrt and in tch 1/2-way: outpcd and drvn over 1f out: no prog after* **10/1**	

-100 **6** *2 ¼* **Arganil (USA)**[24] 1166 6-9-4 **89**.................................(b) StevieDonohoe 6 77
(Kevin Ryan) *bdly outpcd in last: hanging rt fr 1/2-way: taken to outer and passed wkng rivals fnl f* **14/1**

00-1 **7** *¾* **Magical Macey (USA)**[15] 1371 4-8-11 **82**........................ ShaneKelly 10 67
(David Barron) *chsd ldng pair to 2f out: sn wknd* **10/1**

000- **8** *4 ½* **Judge 'n Jury**[181] 7254 7-9-6 **91**.....................................(t) DavidProbert 5 60
(Ronald Harris) *chsd ldng trio: shkn up and trying to mount a chal whn squeezed out wl over 1f out: wknd qckly: sddle slipped* **9/1**

/00- **9** *¾* **Mattamia (IRE)**[344] 2280 5-9-3 **88**................................. JamesMillman 9 55
(Rod Millman) *in tch: lost pl and rdn 1/2-way: sn struggling in rr: b.b.v* **20/1**

00-0 **10** *½* **Bertoliver**[10] 1476 7-8-13 **84**.. JackMitchell 12 49
(Stuart Williams) *pressed ldr to 1/2-way: sn lost pl u.p* **20/1**

110- **11** *1 ¾* **Kanaf (IRE)**[218] 6319 4-9-5 **90**.. TadhgO'Shea 3 48
(Ed Dunlop) *s.i.s: bdly outpcd in last pair: no imp over 1f out: keeping on whn stuck bhd rivals last 150yds* **6/1**[3]

56.29 secs (-2.11) **Going Correction** -0.225s/f (Firm) **11** Ran SP% **118.5**
Speed ratings (Par 107): **107,105,103,99,99 95,94,87,85,85 82**
toteswingers:1&2:£10.30, 1&3:£7.30, 2&3:£3.60 CSF £34.17 CT £134.36 TOTE £10.50: £2.90, £1.80, £2.20; EX 49.40.

Owner M Khan X2 **Bred** Yeomanstown Stud **Trained** Whitsbury, Hants

■ Stewards' Enquiry : Matthew Davies three-day ban: careless riding (May 15-17)

FOCUS
A competitive sprint handicap run at a strong pace and the time was extremely fast - just 0.28 seconds outside the track record. The front pair are progressive and a positive view has been taken of the form.

NOTEBOOK
Humidor(IRE), fitted with a tongue-tie for the first time, played up beforehand but was fine in the race itself, other than edging slightly right under pressure, and gamely improved his record at the course to 2-2, recording a career best in the process. His connections suggested he'll come back to Goodwood at some stage seeing as he handles the track so well and he could find more improvement. (op 8-1)

Addictive Dream(IRE) was well backed but looked as though this first run since last September would bring him on. He was inclined to hang left when first produced with is challenge, rather than knuckling down, and he was held when carried right by the winner. The impression is he has the ability to rate quite a bit higher, but one would like to see him look more determined under pressure in future. Both his wins to date have been gained on Polytrack and perhaps that surface suits best. (op 5-1)

Captain Carey ran okay without really building on the form of his Newbury comeback. He'll be third off the layoff next time. (op 5-1 tchd 11-2)

Favourite Girl(IRE) raced more towards the stands' rail than the front three, showing good speed throughout. She should come on for this first run in 189 days. (tchd 14-1)

Desert Phantom(USA) had been off for 217 days and has done all of his winning on much easier ground than this. (op 11-1 tchd 12-1)

Judge 'n Jury Official explanation: jockey said saddle slipped and the gelding was unsuited by the good ground on straight course

Mattamia(IRE) Official explanation: trainer said gelding bled

Kanaf(IRE) is at least two places better than his finishing position indicates. He was soon out the back and not travelling following a slow start, but he was keeping on in the closing stages without being given anything like a hard ride before getting stuck in behind two with nothing to offer. There was no obvious attempt to switch him around those runners and he was allowed to coast home inside the final furlong. (op 5-1)

1681 TOTEPOOL E B F CONQUEROR STKS (LISTED RACE) 1m

4:35 (4:35) (Class 1) 3-Y-0+

£17,031 (£6,456; £3,231; £1,611; £807; £405) **Stalls** Low

Form RPR

110- **1** **Seta**[210] 6561 4-9-7 107.. J-PGuillambert 1 107+
(Luca Cumani) *trckd ldng pair: nipped through on inner to ld over 2f out and sn qcknd clr: r.o wl* **10/3**[2]

120- **2** *3 ¾* **Anna Salai (USA)**[316] 3143 4-9-7 111.............................. AhmedAjtebi 2 98
(Mahmood Al Zarooni) *trckd ldng trio: ran on outer to take 2nd over 1f out but wnr already flown: no imp* **6/5**[1]

14-2 **3** *½* **Off Chance**[14] 1385 5-9-7 100.. DuranFentiman 7 97+
(Tim Easterby) *hld up in 6th: taken to outer and effrt 2f out: hrd rdn to take 3rd fnl f: kpt on to press runner-up nr fin* **5/1**[3]

63-3 **4** *¾* **Maid In Heaven (IRE)**[28] 1104 4-9-7 92........................... ShaneKelly 4 95
(Walter Swinburn) *led to over 2f out: sn outpcd and btn* **17/2**

156- **5** *2* **Conciliatory**[210] 6556 4-9-7 79...................................... DavidProbert 6 90?
(Rae Guest) *trckd ldr to over 2f out: wknd wl over 1f out* **40/1**

024- **6** *¾* **First City**[217] 6351 5-9-7 101.. EddieAhern 5 89
(David Simcock) *stdd s: t.k.h: hld up in 5th: sltly impeded on inner 3f out: no prog 2f out: sn wknd* **11/1**

604- **7** *8* **Fleeting Echo**[189] 7097 4-9-7 92.. PatDobbs 3 70
(Richard Hannon) *stdd s: hld up last: pushed along and in tch over 2f out: wknd qckly wl over 1f out* **16/1**

1m 37.35s (-2.55) **Going Correction** -0.025s/f (Good) **7** Ran SP% **112.4**
Speed ratings (Par 111): **111,107,106,106,104 103,95**
toteswingers:1&2:£1.30, 1&3:£3.30, 2&3:£2.20 CSF £7.43 TOTE £4.80: £2.80, £1.10; EX 7.90.

Owner Miss Sarah J Leigh **Bred** Sarah J Leigh And Robin S Leigh **Trained** Newmarket, Suffolk

■ Stewards' Enquiry : J-P Guillambert caution: careless riding.

FOCUS
They didn't go that quick and the fourth and fifth-placed finishers limit the form. The winner didn't need to improve, with the second not at her best.

NOTEBOOK
Seta created a nice impression on her reappearance. She was a three-time winner last year, including twice at this level, but struggled in the Sun Chariot when last seen. However, a tall filly, she's entitled to be filling her frame now and has probably returned a stronger type. She raced enthusiastically and was still able to draw clear when asked, despite the pace not being conducive to a big performance, and she should be competitive when upped to Group level. (op 5-2 tchd 9-4)

Anna Salai(USA) was runner-up in the Irish 1,000 Guineas on her debut for this yard, but had been off since disappointing in the Coronation Stakes next time. She was entitled to need this, but even so she was someway below the pick of her form and didn't strike as a filly who will be up to returning to the top level anytime soon. (op 13-8 tchd 11-10 and 7-4 in places)

Off Chance is at her best off a strong pace, so this performance can be upgraded. (op 11-2 tchd 6-1)

Maid In Heaven(IRE) set just an ordinary pace and looks flattered. (op 10-1 tchd 8-1)

Conciliatory had an official mark of just 79, but she was reported to have been unsuited by testing ground when last seen in 2010 and has probably returned a slightly improved filly. (op 33-1)

First City had been off for 217 days and was too keen. (op 9-1)

1682 TRY THE TOTEQUICKPICK IF YOU'RE FEELING LUCKY MEDIAN AUCTION MAIDEN STKS 7f

5:10 (5:12) (Class 5) 3-Y-0 **£3,238** (£963; £481; £240) **Stalls** Low

Form RPR

42-6 **1** **Yojimbo (IRE)**[23] 1203 3-9-3 79..(v[1]) ChrisCatlin 3 78
(Mick Channon) *trckd ldr to 3f out: sn dropped to 4th: renewed effrt over 1f out: drvn to ld last 150yds: kpt on* **6/1**

5-5 **2** *½* **Tinaheely (IRE)**[37] 952 3-8-12 0.................................... HayleyTurner 6 72
(Jonathan Portman) *led: rdn and jinked lft over 2f out: sn hrd pressed: kpt on wl u.p: hdd last 150yds: jst hld* **20/1**

04- **3** *1 ¼* **King Ferdinand**[203] 6748 3-9-3 0.................................... DavidProbert 7 73
(Andrew Balding) *trckd ldrs: prog on outer to chal 2f out: upsides and edgd lft over 1f out: nt qckn after* **9/2**[2]

30-3 **4** *1 ½* **With Hindsight (IRE)**[27] 1108 3-9-3 77........................ AdamKirby 11 69
(Clive Cox) *hld up towards rr: looking for room 3f out: prog to chse ldrs over 1f out: rdn and nt qckn after* **6/1**

3- **5** *2 ¼* **Perfect Cracker**[294] 3915 3-9-0 0.................................... JohnFahy(3) 12 63
(Clive Cox) *racd wd: hld up towards rr: effrt over 2f out: sn drvn: fdd over 1f out* **7/2**[1]

0- **6** *3 ½* **Art Thief**[183] 7201 3-9-3 0.. LiamKeniry 4 54
(Sylvester Kirk) *hld up towards rr: looking for room 3f out: wl outpcd 2f out: shkn up and no ch after* **20/1**

0 **7** *nse* **The Guru Of Gloom (IRE)**[16] 1338 3-9-3 0.................. GeorgeBaker 5 54
(William Muir) *trckd ldng pair: wnt 2nd 3f out: chal and upsides 2f out: wknd rapidly over 1f out* **15/2**

0- **8** *1 ¼* **Justice Walk (IRE)**[208] 6634 3-9-3 0................................ EddieAhern 2 55
(Paul Fitzsimons) *hld up in rr: squeezed out 4f out and dropped to last of main gp: pushed along and n.d after* **28/1**

56- **9** *5* **Yashila (IRE)**[245] 5527 3-8-12 0... PatDobbs 1 32
(Richard Hannon) *sn trckd ldrs on inner: shkn up over 2f out: wknd qckly* **5/1**[3]

024- **10** *3 ¼* **Fists And Stones**[233] 5886 3-9-0 77........................... MartinHarley(3) 9 28
(Mick Channon) *hld up in rr: shkn up and no prog over 2f out: sn no ch* **11/1**

00- **11** *dist* **Impulse Dancer**[334] 2594 3-8-9 0.................................. KierenFox(3) 8 —
(John Bridger) *sn t.o: virtually p.u 1/2-way: lame* **100/1**

1m 26.42s (-0.48) **Going Correction** -0.025s/f (Good) **11** Ran SP% **119.7**
Speed ratings (Par 98): **101,100,99,97,94 90,90,89,83,79 —**
toteswingers:1&2:£15.60, 1&3:£6.30, 2&3:£19.90 CSF £123.79 TOTE £7.20: £2.10, £6.20, £2.00; EX 149.40.

Owner Jon and Julia Aisbitt **Bred** Peter Kelly And Ms Wendy Daly **Trained** West Ilsley, Berks

FOCUS
Ordinary-looking form. The first pair both showed improvemed form but were mostly 1-2 throughout, so there are doubts.

Impulse Dancer Official explanation: vet said filly was lame right-hind

1683 TRY THE TOTEQUICKPICK ON ALL TOTEPOOL BETS H'CAP 1m 1f 192y

5:40 (5:44) (Class 5) (0-70,70) 3-Y-0 **£3,238** (£963; £481; £240) **Stalls** Low

Form RPR

000- **1** **Four Nations (USA)**[239] 5724 3-9-2 **65**........................... JimCrowley 18 78+
(Amanda Perrett) *forced to r wd towards rr: only 12th over 4f out: looking for room gng wl 3f out: swtchd outside and drvn 2f out: prog over 1f out: str run to ld last strides* **12/1**

045- **2** *nk* **Star Commander**[208] 6635 3-9-5 **68**.............................. GeorgeBaker 6 80
(Mark H Tompkins) *wl in tch in abt 7th: prog to trck ldrs over 2f out: drvn and r.o to ld ins fnl f: hdd last strides* **14/1**

000- **3** *1 ¼* **Grumeti**[205] 6689 3-9-2 **65**... HayleyTurner 9 75
(Michael Bell) *trckd ldng trio: rdn over 2f out: clsd u.str.p over 1f out: jnd ldr ins fnl f: no ex last 100yds* **5/2**[1]

564- **4** *2* **Experimentalist**[185] 7164 3-9-7 **70**................................. SteveDrowne 4 76
(Hughie Morrison) *settled in abt 9th: prog 3f out: drvn to chse ldrs over 1f out: kpt on same pce to take 4th nr fin* **14/1**

50-2 **5** *½* **Iron Green (FR)**[18] 1299 3-9-0 **63**.................................. EddieAhern 10 68
(Heather Main) *led: rdn over 2f out: hdd & wknd ins fnl f* **10/1**

5-01 **6** *½* **Zamina (IRE)**[7] 1524 3-9-4 **67**... LiamKeniry 14 71+
(Sylvester Kirk) *hld up in abt 10th: gng strly 3f out: prog sn after: hanging and nt qckn over 1f out: kpt on one pce after* **15/2**[2]

41-2 **7** *1 ½* **Unknown Rebel (IRE)**[16] 1327 3-9-2 **65**..................... StevieDonohoe 7 66
(Kevin Ryan) *trckd ldng pair: wnt 2nd over 3f out: wknd over 1f out* **9/1**[3]

000- **8** *3* **Fleeting Tiger**[195] 6953 3-8-7 **56** oh4................................ ChrisCatlin 1 51
(John Dunlop) *settled wl in rr: effrt on inner 3f out: plugged on fnl 2f: nvr on terms* **18/1**

-321 **9** *10* **Tagansky**[72] 579 3-9-7 **70**... JackMitchell 15 45
(Simon Dow) *t.k.h: racd wd in abt 8th: effrt over 3f out: wknd 2f out* **16/1**

00-6 **10** *1 ¼* **Smart George (IRE)**[31] 1053 3-8-6 **58**............................. JohnFahy(3) 5 30
(Clive Cox) *prom: pushed along by 1/2-way: struggling to hold pl over 3f out: wknd over 2f out* **14/1**

040- **11** *1 ¼* **Tileyf (IRE)**[200] 6831 3-9-7 **70**.. AdamKirby 17 40
(Clive Cox) *rousted along early: a in rr: drvn in 14th over 4f out: no ch after* **16/1**

06-6 **12** *½* **Corvette**[19] 1270 3-9-2 **65**.. FergusSweeney 13 34
(J R Jenkins) *trckd ldrs in 6th: rdn over 2f out: sn wknd* **33/1**

0432 **13** *2 ½* **Barnum (USA)**[11] 1475 3-9-6 **69**.................................... GregFairley 11 33
(Mark Johnston) *sn wl in rr: u.p and wl bhd 4f out: brief effrt on outer 3f out: sn wknd* **9/1**[3]

2053 **14** *24* **Indian Wish (USA)**[18] 1284 3-8-8 **57**..........................(t) NickyMackay 12 —
(Tim McCarthy) *chsd ldr to over 3f out: wknd rapidly: t.o* **40/1**

00-0 **15** *1 ¾* **Dune Island**[106] 158 3-8-4 **56** oh10.................................. KierenFox(3) 2 —
(John Bridger) *a wl in rr: already struggling whn rn wd bnd 5f out: t.o* **100/1**

060- **16** *32* **Maratib (USA)**[283] 4263 3-9-4 **67**...............................(b[1]) TadhgO'Shea 3 —
(David Lanigan) *sn off the pce in last pair: nvr a factor: t.o* **16/1**

000- **17** *dist* **Ponte Di Rosa**[210] 6563 3-8-10 **64**.............................. HarryBentley(5) 16 —
(Jonathan Portman) *sn dropped to last and t.o: hacked rnd ms bhd: sddle slipped* **33/1**

2m 7.86s (-0.14) **Going Correction** -0.025s/f (Good) **17** Ran SP% **129.3**
Speed ratings (Par 98): **99,98,97,96,95 95,94,91,83,82 81,81,79,60,58 33,—**
toteswingers:1&2:£37.80, 1&3:£8.30, 2&3:£11.30 CSF £175.93 CT £569.24 TOTE £16.60: £3.30, £4.20, £1.80, £4.00; EX 259.30.

Owner George Materna **Bred** Kirsten Rausing **Trained** Pulborough, W Sussex

FOCUS
A host of potential improvers lined up - the first four were all up in trip for their handicap debuts - and this is good form for the grade. They seemed to go a fair gallop and the time was relatively good.

Four Nations(USA) ◆ Official explanation: trainer said, regarding apparent improvement in form, that since being gelded after its last run, it has matured and become stronger over the break.
Maratib(USA) Official explanation: jockey said gelding never travelled
Ponte Di Rosa Official explanation: jockey said saddle slipped
T/Plt: £32.80 to a £1 stake. Pool:£76,120.72 - 1,693.85 winning tickets T/Qpdt: £11.70 to a £1 stake. Pool:£3,601.99 - 226.90 winning tickets JN

1337 NEWMARKET (R-H)
Saturday, April 30

OFFICIAL GOING: Good to firm (good in places; 8.8)
Stands' side course used. Stalls on stands' side except for 2000 Gns and Jockey Club Stakes which were in the centre.
Wind: Fresh, half against Weather: Dry, breezy

1684 QIPCO SPONSORS BRITISH CHAMPIONS SERIES SUFFOLK H'CAP — 1m 1f
2:00 (2:00) (Class 2) 3-Y-0+
£27,416 (£8,210; £4,105; £2,054; £1,025; £514) **Stalls** High

Form — RPR

011- **1** **Green Destiny (IRE)**[187] 7121 4-8-11 **87** .... MichaelHills 10 107+
(William Haggas) *lw: racd in centre gp: hld up in tch: hdwy and nt clr run ent fnl 2f: gd hdwy between horses to chse ldr 1f out: sn led: flashed tail u.p but r.o strly: readily* **13/2**[2]

00-4 **2** 3 ¾ **Proponent (IRE)**[14] 1406 7-9-5 **95** .... FrankieDettori 14 106
(Roger Charlton) *racd in centre gp: hld up in tch: rdn and hdwy 2f out: led over 1f out: hdd jst ins fnl f: nt pce of wnr but kpt on for clr 2nd: 2nd of 16 in gp* **11/2**[1]

0-04 **3** 2 ¼ **Breakheart (IRE)**[14] 1387 4-9-0 **90** .... JMurtagh 11 96+
(Michael Dods) *restless in stalls: racd in centre gp: in tch: rdn and outpcd over 2f out: rallied ent fnl f: styd on wl to snatch 3rd last strides: 3rd of 16 in gp* **7/1**[3]

00-1 **4** hd **Kay Gee Be (IRE)**[19] 1269 7-8-10 **86** .... PaulHanagan 6 92
(Richard Fahey) *racd in centre gp: mde most tl over 1f out: styd on same pce fnl f: 4th of 16 in gp* **8/1**

14-3 **5** ¾ **Ellemujie**[26] 1138 6-8-7 **83** .... LukeMorris 4 87
(Dean Ivory) *racd in centre gp: in tch: rdn and effrt wl over 2f out: hrd drvn and chsd ldrs over 1f out: styd on same pce fnl f: 5th of 16 in gp* **33/1**

46-0 **6** ¾ **Chapter And Verse (IRE)**[28] 1100 5-8-12 **88** .... TonyCulhane 5 91
(Mike Murphy) *racd in centre gp: hld up in tch: hdwy to press ldrs and rdn over 1f out: wknd ins fnl f: 6th of 16 in gp* **20/1**

0-20 **7** 1 ½ **Sand Skier**[10] 1479 4-8-12 **88** .... RichardHills 1 87
(Mark Johnston) *lw: racd in centre gp: chsd ldrs: rdn over 2f out: wknd over 1f out: 7th of 16 in gp* **20/1**

4-50 **8** 1 ¾ **Cumulus Nimbus**[14] 1403 4-9-9 **99** .... RichardHughes 9 95
(Richard Hannon) *racd in centre gp: taken down early: stdd s: hld up in tch in rr: rdn and effrt over 2f out: no hdwy over 1f out: 8th of 16 in gp* **28/1**

6220 **9** hd **Buaiteoir (FR)**[27] 1109 5-8-5 **84** .... AndrewHeffernan(3) 12 79
(Paul D'Arcy) *racd in centre gp: hld up in tch in rr: hdwy over 2f out: rdn over 1f out: no ex and wknd ins fnl f: 9th of 16 in gp* **28/1**

01-0 **10** ¾ **Brick Red**[14] 1406 4-9-3 **93** .... JimmyFortune 2 86
(Andrew Balding) *racd in centre gp: t.k.h: hld up in tch: rdn and unable qck over 2f out: drvn and no hdwy wl over 1f out: 10th of 16 in gp* **11/1**

415- **11** ¾ **Colour Scheme (IRE)**[154] 7591 4-8-10 **86** .... (t) MartinDwyer 18 78
(Brian Meehan) *racd in last of stands' side trio: stdd s: hld up in rr: hdwy 3f out: rdn and no hdwy over 1f out: no ch w overall ldrs fnl f: 1st of 3 in gp* **25/1**

24-3 **12** ¾ **Beaumont's Party (IRE)**[7] 1530 4-7-9 **76** .... KieranO'Neill(5) 19 66
(Andrew Balding) *lw: racd stands' side trio: led that gp and chsd ldrs overall: rdn and struggling over 2f out: wknd over 1f out: 2nd of 3 in gp* **12/1**

036- **13** 2 **Viva Vettori**[154] 7593 7-8-8 **84** .... (p) WilliamBuick 3 70
(David Elsworth) *racd in centre gp: trckd ldrs gng wl: ev ch 2f out: rdn and fnd little over 1f out: fdd fnl f:11th of 16 in gp* **16/1**

320- **14** ½ **Greylami (IRE)**[154] 7591 6-9-1 **96** .... SeanLevey(5) 13 81+
(Robert Mills) *racd in centre gp: hld up in tch towards rr: rdn and effrt over 2f out: sn struggling: wl baten ent fnl f: 12th of 16 in gp* **50/1**

3200 **15** 12 **Tartan Gigha (IRE)**[10] 1479 6-9-6 **96** .... JoeFanning 17 54
(Mark Johnston) *racd in stands' side trio: chsd ldrs overall tl wknd wl over 1f out: eased ins fnl f: 3rd of 3 in gp* **16/1**

3/4- **16** 1 ½ **Namecheck (GER)**[364] 1702 4-9-7 **97** .... MickaelBarzalona 7 52
(Mahmood Al Zarooni) *on toes: swtg: racd in centre gp: chsd ldrs: rdn 3f out: racd awkwardly and struggling over 2f out: wl btn and eased fnl f: t.o: 13th of 16 in gp* **16/1**

340- **17** 11 **Sandor**[189] 7100 5-9-5 **95** .... (v) RyanMoore 16 26
(Peter Makin) *racd in centre gp: shkn up 3f out: rdn and no hdwy 2f out: no ch fr wl over 1f out: t.o: 14th of 16 in gp* **12/1**

-043 **18** 2 ½ **Tiger Reigns**[25] 1154 5-9-10 **100** .... TomEaves 15 25
(Michael Dods) *racd in centre gp: rdn and struggling over 2f out: sn wknd: eased ins fnl f: t.o: 15th of 16 in gp* **50/1**

200- **19** dist **Vainglory (USA)**[182] 7233 7-9-2 **92** .... MartinLane 8 —
(David Simcock) *racd in centre gp: in tch tl wknd qckly wl over 1f out: eased fr over 1f out: virtually p.u ins fnl f: wl t.o: 16th of 16 in gp* **50/1**

1m 52.27s (0.57) **Going Correction** +0.30s/f (Good) **19** Ran SP% **122.8**
Speed ratings (Par 109): **109,105,103,103,102 102,100,99,99,98 97,97,95,94,84 82,73,70,—**
toteswingers: 1&2 £7.60, 1&3 £8.80, 2&3 £10.20. CSF £36.39 CT £262.33 TOTE £7.10: £2.00, £2.10, £2.40, £2.10; EX 36.40 Trifecta £247.70 Pool: £3,020.11 - 9.02 winning units..
Owner Saleh Al Homaizi & Imad Al Sagar **Bred** Mubkera Syndicate **Trained** Newmarket, Suffolk

FOCUS
The winning rider in the first described the ground as "quick", and said that there was a gusty side wind. The time for the opener was around four seconds slower than standard. This was a valuable and competitive handicap, and the form should prove sound. The unexposed winner impressed and has more to offer. Three of the runners raced detached from the others down the stands' rail, with the main body in a bunch in the centre-to-far side of the track.

NOTEBOOK
Green Destiny(IRE), who had just three races under his belt, was much less exposed than most. Last seen winning a Leicester handicap six months ago, he was 5lb higher here but has reportedly thrived in the spring. Quickening up in fine style to lead and easily pulling clear, he rates a smart prospect who may well be capable of making his mark in Group 3/Listed company. His trainer had been worried about this ground beforehand and although the gelding handled it well, he won't be asked to run on a sound surface too often. (tchd 6-1)

Proponent(IRE) caught the eye finishing fourth in the Spring Cup, a position he also filled in the Newbury race three years ago before going on to take this event. Now 5lb higher than when successful in 2008, he tracked the pacesetting Kay Gee Be before being pulled out to lead and momentarily appeared in command, but the winner quickly cut him down. There was no disgrace in coming up short against a lightly raced and progressive opponent, but he remains fairly hard to win with after just two victories - both on the Rowley Mile - in his last 27 starts. (op 13-2)
Breakheart(IRE) is reportedly a stuffy horse and difficult to get fit. Making his third appearance of the month, he was slow to break but was staying on determinedly at the end and snatched third place near the line. A return to 1m2f should suit. (op 8-1 tchd 13-2)
Kay Gee Be(IRE)'s Windsor form has been boosted by a subsequent win for runner-up Edgewater. He made much of the running in the main group and stuck on for fourth. (op 15-2)
Ellemujie is commendably consistent and he ran another solid race. A suitable target is likely to be the 1m2f handicap here at the end of the month, a race he won last year. (op 28-1)
Chapter And Verse(IRE) travelled strongly towards the far side of the group but was not able to quicken up. He is currently rated 8lb lower on turf than on the AW and is more than capable of landing a decent handicap on this surface.
Sand Skier ran no sort of race when joint favourite for the City and Suburban at Epsom and this was better, but he was on the retreat going into the Dip. (op 25-1)
Cumulus Nimbus, back in trip after finding himself outclassed in the John Porter Stakes, made modest late gains without being given too hard a time. He seems likely to continue to prove hard to place.
Colour Scheme(IRE) did best of the three to race on the stands' side, albeit finishing only 11th. He is still one to keep on the right side. (op 20-1)
Tartan Gigha(IRE), last year's winner, was another who had no realistic chance racing on the stands' side. He is well handicapped, 4lb below his last winning mark. (op 14-1)
Namecheck(GER), off the track since this fixture a year ago, weakened with over a furlong to run and was eased right off.
Sandor had some decent form in big-field handicaps last term but was well beaten on this seasonal return.
Vainglory(USA) Official explanation: jockey said horse lost its action

1685 QIPCO JOCKEY CLUB STKS (GROUP 2) — 1m 4f
2:30 (2:31) (Class 1) 4-Y-0+
£45,416 (£17,216; £8,616; £4,296; £2,152; £1,080) **Stalls** Centre

Form — RPR

00-1 **1** **Dandino**[14] 1416 4-8-11 113 .... PaulMulrennan 5 117
(James Given) *sltly on toes: chsd ldr: rdn to ld ent fnl 3f: hdd ins fnl f: rallied gamely to ld again on line* **7/4**[1]

003/ **2** nse **Native Ruler**[631] 4760 5-8-12 97 .... TomQueally 1 117
(Sir Henry Cecil) *h.d.w: t.k.h early: chsd ldrs: ev ch 3f out: rdn jst over 2f out: led ins fnl f: hdd on line* **18/1**

60-1 **3** 4 **Indian Days**[14] 1403 6-9-1 114 .... PaulHanagan 4 114
(James Given) *stdd s: hld up in tch: hdwy to press ldrs 3f out wknd u.p 1f out* **13/2**

130- **4** 2 ½ **Campanologist (USA)**[179] 7291 6-8-12 116 .... FrankieDettori 3 107
(Saeed Bin Suroor) *hld up in tch: rdn and effrt over 2f out: 4th and one pce fr wl over 1f out* **9/2**[3]

11-4 **5** 3 ½ **Laaheb**[35] 1001 5-8-12 115 .... RichardHills 2 101
(Roger Varian) *chsd ldrs: ev ch 3f out: wknd 2f out* **5/2**[2]

53-3 **6** 22 **Monitor Closely (IRE)**[23] 1201 5-8-12 106 .... RyanMoore 6 87
(Michael Bell) *led tl 3f out: wknd qckly jst over 2f out: eased fnl f: t.o* **12/1**

2m 33.7s (1.70) **Going Correction** +0.30s/f (Good)
WFA 4 from 5yo+ 1lb **6** Ran SP% **109.4**
Speed ratings (Par 115): **106,105,103,101,99 84**
toteswingers: 1&2 £7.00, 1&3 £2.20, 2&3 £6.80. CSF £30.14 TOTE £2.50: £1.80, £4.80; EX 33.10.
Owner Elite Racing Club **Bred** Elite Racing Club **Trained** Willoughton, Lincs

FOCUS
The Jockey Club Stakes has often been the starting point for some of the previous season's Classic heroes, with the St Leger winners Millenary (2001) and Sixties Icon (2007) successful within the past ten years, while the subsequent Arc winner Marienbard took this in 2002. Andre Fabre twice made successful raids with Shirocco (2006) and Getaway (2008), but there was no international challenge this time and only one 4-y-o took part. Favourites had dominated recent runnings with the market leader successful five times in the previous seven years. The pace was a fair one thanks to Monitor Closely and the six runners raced in a tight group down the centre of the track down the long home straight. It provided a stirring finish between the front pair and even after the line no-one was quite sure who had won. Dandino improved again and Native Ruler produced a big step up.

NOTEBOOK
Dandino improved a total of 36lb last season, starting off by winning a Redcar maiden and ending the campaign taking on the best in the St Leger and Japan Cup, if well held in both. His recent easy success in a Ripon conditions event (a race that took little winning) at least showed that he had returned fit and well and this performance strongly suggests that he has improved again. Content to get an early lead from Monitor Closely, he was one of the first off the bridle but his ability to battle has never been in doubt. Having been involved in a protracted duel with the runner-up throughout the last quarter-mile, he started to hang under pressure and looked to be getting the worse of it in the last half-furlong, but one last thrust up the hill enabled him to snatch the race by the narrowest of margins. He already looks a much more mature horse this year and will get another chance to test his mettle at the top level in the Coronation Cup. (op 2-1)
Native Ruler, whose participation in this was in doubt due to the ground, was making only his sixth appearance having not been since August 2009 and he didn't seem to stay in his only previous try at the trip. Allowed to take his chance, he loomed up passing the 3f pole, battled very hard under pressure, and looked to have done just enough on the run to the line, but he was up against a dogged rival who would just not go away and he had the prize snatched from him in the very last stride. This was a magnificent piece of training and he hardly deserved to lose, but although connections believe he will be sharper for the run he may need a little time to get over it. (op 16-1 tchd 20-1)
Indian Days, the winner's stablemate, was conceding weight to his four rivals on account of his victory in the Group 2 International Bosphorus Cup at Veliefendi last September, but he had already shown that he was as good as ever this season with his battling win in the John Porter. Having been given a patient ride, he saw plenty of daylight towards the far side of the group in the straight and was off the bridle at the same time as the winner, but he kept staying on for a very creditable third. Likely to be given another crack at Group 1 company, he could well chalk up a win at that level abroad. he may take on stablemate Dandino in the Coronation Cup. (op 7-1)
Campanologist(USA), successful three times on the international stage last year, including twice at Group 1 level, was racing for the first time since finishing 16th in the Melbourne Cup and looked likely to be better for it, but he has a decent record fresh, so a bit better might have been expected. He appeared to get a bit outpaced around a quarter of a mile out and could then only plug on at the same pace. He will no doubt be on his travels again this term. (tchd 5-1)
Laaheb improved throughout last season for Michael Jarvis culminating in a pair of Group 3 successes over this trip, and there was little wrong with his fourth behind Rewilding in the Dubai Sheema Classic on his return, but having been prominent early he found disappointingly little under pressure. His trainer felt that this may have come a bit too soon after Dubai and that he wouldn't be risked on quick ground like this too often. (op 9-4)

Monitor Closely(IRE) hasn't been at his best in an abbreviated career since finishing a close third in the 2009 St Leger and, having made the early running, he put up little resistance once headed 3f from home.

1686 QIPCO 2000 GUINEAS (203RD RUNNING) (GROUP 1) (ENTIRE COLTS & FILLIES) 1m

3:10 (3:14) (Class 1) 3-Y-O

£198,695 (£75,320; £37,695; £18,795; £9,415; £4,725) **Stalls** Centre

Form RPR

11-1 **1** **Frankel**[14] 1405 3-9-0 126 .... TomQueally 1 133+
(Sir Henry Cecil) *warm: lw: sn led and clr: at least 10 lengths clr 1/2-way: rdn jst over 1f out: idling but kpt on fnl f: rdn out: unchal: impressive* **1/2**[1]

0-11 **2** *6* **Dubawi Gold**[21] 1234 3-9-0 101 .... RichardHughes 5 119
(Richard Hannon) *lw: stdd s: hld up towards rr: hdwy 1/2-way: disputing modest 2nd and hung lft 2f out: chsd clr wnr over 1f out: kpt on but no threat to wnr* **33/1**

14-1 **3** *½* **Native Khan (FR)**[16] 1341 3-9-0 111 .... OlivierPeslier 11 118
(Ed Dunlop) *sltly on toes: hld up off the pce in midfield: rdn and hdwy over 3f out: chsd clr wnr wl over 2f out tl over 1f out: kpt on but no threat to wnr* **16/1**

245- **4** *11* **Slim Shadey**[217] 6347 3-9-0 101 .... LukeMorris 6 93
(J S Moore) *lw: racd off the pce in midfield: rdn and sme hdwy whn hung rt over 2f out: wnt modest 4th jst ins fnl f: n.d* **200/1**

11- **5** *½* **Fury**[210] 6560 3-9-0 103 .... JMurtagh 4 92
(William Haggas) *w'like: cl cpld: racd off the pce in midfield: rdn and no real hdwy whn hung rt over 2f out: n.d* **12/1**

41-2 **6** *5* **Happy Today (USA)**[17] 1320 3-9-0 102 .... MartinDwyer 7 80
(Brian Meehan) *sltyl on toes: s.i.s: bhd: sme hdwy over 2f out: n.d* **100/1**

111- **7** *3* **Pathfork (USA)**[231] 5975 3-9-0 120 .... (t) FMBerry 2 73
(Mrs John Harrington, Ire) *lengthy: athletic: lw: prom in main gp: rdn and no hdwy 1/2-way: no ch fnl 2f* **8/1**[2]

14-2 **8** *½* **Rerouted (USA)**[17] 1318 3-9-0 110 .... (b[1]) MichaelHills 13 72
(B W Hills) *lw: chsd wnr for 2f: rdn 3f out: no hdwy and no ch after: wknd over 2f out* **66/1**

12- **9** *1 ¼* **Loving Spirit**[197] 6884 3-9-0 98 .... RobertHavlin 8 69
(James Toller) *hld up in midfield: rdn and short-lived effrt wl over 2f out: wl bhd after* **66/1**

211- **10** *8* **Casamento (IRE)**[189] 7081 3-9-0 119 .... FrankieDettori 10 51
(Mahmood Al Zarooni) *lw: chsd clr wnr after 2f: rdn and no hdwy over 3f out: lost pl and wl btn over 2f out: t.o* **11/1**[3]

21- **11** *2* **Roderic O'Connor (IRE)**[181] 7265 3-9-0 119 .... RyanMoore 3 46
(A P O'Brien, Ire) *nt grwn: prom in main gp: rdn and struggling over 3f out: wl bhd fnl 2f: t.o* **8/1**[2]

116- **12** *14* **Saamidd**[196] 6924 3-9-0 115 .... (t) MickaelBarzalona 9 —
(Saeed Bin Suroor) *a in rr: nvr on terms: t.o fnl 2f: eased ins fnl f: fin lame* **22/1**

410- **13** *11* **Broox (IRE)**[180] 7277 3-9-0 112 .... WilliamBuick 12 —
(E J O'Neill, France) *cmpt: sltly on toes: awkward leaving stalls: sme hdwy into midfield 5f out: wknd over 3f out: t.o and eased fr over 1f out* **100/1**

1m 37.3s (-1.30) **Going Correction** +0.30s/f (Good) **13** Ran SP% **123.5**
Speed ratings (Par 112): **118,112,111,100,100 95,92,91,90,82 80,66,55**
toteswingers: 1&2 £8.40, 1&3 £4.40, 2&3 £35.70. CSF £34.53 CT £179.45 TOTE £1.40: £1.02, £7.10, £3.70; EX 28.20 Trifecta £238.10 Pool: £20,537.50 - 63.81 winning units..
Owner K Abdulla **Bred** Juddmonte Farms Ltd **Trained** Newmarket, Suffolk
■ Tom Queally's first Classic winner and Henry Cecil's 25th. The shortest priced 2000 Guineas winner since Colombo (2/7) in 1934.

FOCUS

This looked an up-to-scratch renewal of the season's first Classic, featuring an outstanding unbeaten Dewhurst and Greenham winner, colts successful in the Group 1 National Stakes, Racing Post Trophy and Criterium International last year, as well as the winner of the Craven Stakes. There were three notable absentees, though, in Dream Ahead (rated the equal of Frankel at two by the official handicappers), Wootton Bassett and Dubai Prince, and the field was the smallest since Mark Of Esteem beat 12 rivals in 1996. Frankel put up probably the best Guineas-winning performance since RPRs started, the form rated around the second and third in line with average Guineas placed form which puts Frankel somewhere between 131 and 136.

NOTEBOOK

Frankel produced an extraordinary performance, crushing his field in a manner rarely seen in a Classic. His outside draw had been a slight worry for a colt with a tendency to race keenly, and he was on the opposite flank to his pacemaker Rerouted, but he was taught to work in front in a recent gallop and it quickly became apparent that he would be making his own running. Displaying his long, raking stride down the centre of the track, he was a good 10 lengths at halfway with none of the others remotely able to lay up with him. He had the race won there unless something dramatic happened, and Tom Queally kept him up to his work in the last furlong and a half as he started to tire slightly or perhaps idle. The winning margin has been bettered only by Tudor Minstrel, who won by eight lengths in 1947, and while some of his opponents were clearly below par he is plainly an exceptional racehorse. Henry Cecil, on target in the 2,000 Guineas for the first time since enjoying back-to-back wins with Bolkonski and Wollow in the mid-1970s, initially suggested the Dante Stakes next in order to gauge his potential stamina for the Derby, but Epsom was later virtually ruled out in favour of staying at a mile for now in the St James's Palace. He possesses astonishing speed, and the Ascot race should be his for the taking, with older stars such as Goldikova and Canford Cliffs waiting to take him on at the trip later in the season. Unfortunately connections ruled out dropping him back to 6f in the July Cup, even though there is surely no sprinter around that could live with him. (op 4-7 tchd 8-13 in places)

Dubawi Gold may have finished a remote second but still deserves bags of credit for this effort. A dual Listed winner on the Lingfield Polytrack this spring, he is settling much better this year and, with nine previous races, was the most experienced colt in the line-up. Getting the better of a tussle with Native Khan for second, he turned around form with that horse and with Casamento from last autumn's Racing Post Trophy. His jockey thought he would have won easily without Frankel in the field, and he will go to the Curragh for the Irish Guineas.

Native Khan(FR), without the suspended Kieren Fallon, ran a solid race and finished 11 lengths clear of the fourth horse. The Craven winner was well at home on the quick ground and looks as solid a guide as any to this form. A tough, smart colt, he has further big races in him provided he avoids Frankel, of course. The Derby and the Prix du Jockey Club are possibilities for him, with Epsom the preferred option of his trainer. (op 18-1 tchd 20-1)

Slim Shadey had not been seen since finishing last of five to Frankel in the Royal Lodge. With the same owner and same sire as the 2007 winner Cockney Rebel, he was beaten further by Frankel here but ran a thoroughly creditable race and saw out the mile well. He is another Irish Guineas possible.

Fury was never seen with a chance of a first-three finish but was staying on well at the end. This winner of a valuable sales race at the back-end, he missed a planned run in the Free Handicap because of a foot problem, which didn't help his preparation. The fast ground suited and he may stay a bit further. (op 16-1)

Happy Today(USA)'s Feilden Stakes conqueror Dordogne let down the form badly in the Sandown Classic Trial. Running here rather than in the Newmarket Stakes, Brian Meehan's colt was never a factor but is a smart performer who should get 1m2f.

Pathfork(USA), the National Stakes winner at two, wore a tongue-tie for the first time. He surrendered his unbeaten record, coming under pressure at halfway and never posing any sort of threat to the winner, although he was disputing a remote third at one stage. He may go for the Irish Guineas. (op 7-1)

Rerouted(USA), runner-up in the Free Handicap and tried in blinkers for the first time, was acting as pacemaker for Frankel but could only match strides with him for around a furlong. In the circumstances his final position of eighth was perfectly respectable.

Loving Spirit was unexposed, finishing runner-up in the Houghton Stakes on the second of his two appearances last year, and had reportedly pleased in his work. He might have preferred easier ground and was never seen with a chance.

Casamento(IRE) had Native Khan fourth and Dubawi Gold back in ninth when winning the Racing Post Trophy for Michael Halford. Regarded as more of a Derby horse than a Guineas type by connections, he ran here in preference to the Dante. Frankie Dettori soon had him chasing Frankel but the colt's efforts told after five furlongs and he was well beaten when Dettori eased him up in the latter stages. (op 12-1)

Roderic O'Connor(IRE)'s stable regularly has more than one candidate for the Guineas but this one was their sole representative this year. Runner-up to Frankel in the Dewhurst before landing the Group 1 Criterium International at Saint-Cloud in testing ground, he came here without a previous run in common with O'Brien's five winners of this race. He was prominent early, but couldn't lay up, and finished well back. The ground was too quick for him and this was not his running. (op 9-1)

Saamidd was on a recovery mission after flopping behind Frankel in the Dewhurst, having become stirred up in the preliminaries. Equipped with a tongue-tie, he behaved better here but after a slow start he was never in the hunt. He reportedly returned lame and is likely to be out of action for some time. (op 25-1 tchd 20-1)

Broox(IRE) was slowly away before racing too keenly, eventually dropping right away. His didn't stay.

1687 PEARL BLOODSTOCK PALACE HOUSE STKS (GROUP 3) 5f

3:45 (3:46) (Class 1) 3-Y-O+

£28,385 (£10,760; £4,035; £4,035; £1,345; £675) **Stalls** High

Form RPR

411- **1** **Tangerine Trees**[212] 6508 6-9-0 103 .... (v) TomEaves 3 110
(Bryan Smart) *mde all: rdn appr fnl f: styd on strly* **18/1**

0002 **2** *½* **Rain Delayed (IRE)**[15] 1366 5-9-0 103 .... JMurtagh 10 108+
(Michael Dods) *lw: in rr: stl plenty to do over 1f out: rdn and rapid hdwy ins fnl f: fin fast to take 2nd last strides but nt rch wnr* **16/1**

125- **3** *shd* **Jonny Mudball**[224] 6177 5-9-0 104 .... (t) SebSanders 11 108
(Tom Dascombe) *chsd ldrs: rdn 2f out: kpt on wl fnl f but no imp on wnr* **8/1**[3]

61-0 **3** *dht* **Sole Power**[35] 996 4-9-0 117 .... WMLordan 5 108
(Edward Lynam, Ire) *lw: chsd ldrs: rdn ins fnl 2f: kpt on but nvr gng pce to rch wnr ins fnl f* **8/1**[3]

160- **5** *nk* **Borderlescott**[238] 5744 9-9-0 112 .... NeilCallan 15 107
(Robin Bastiman) *early spd: rdn and outpcd 2f out: styd on again ins fnl f: gng on cl home* **14/1**

12 **6** *½* **Lisselan Diva (IRE)**[29] 1122 5-8-11 95 .... WilliamsSaraiva 13 102
(Mme J Bidgood, France) *a chsng ldrs: rdn 2f out: kpt on same pce ins fnl f* **66/1**

1010 **7** *hd* **Breathless Kiss (USA)**[10] 1476 4-8-11 93 .... (b) JimmyFortune 4 101
(Kevin Ryan) *s.i.s: in rr and rdn 1/2-way: hdwy 2f out: chsd ldrs u.p appr fnl f: kpt on same pce cl home* **50/1**

501 **8** *½* **Evens And Odds (IRE)**[21] 1242 7-9-0 104 .... WilliamCarson 7 103
(David Nicholls) *broke wl: rdn and outpcd after 2f: styd on again fnl f: kpt on cl home* **20/1**

0145 **9** *hd* **Prohibit**[35] 996 6-9-0 112 .... (p) FrankieDettori 14 102
(Robert Cowell) *n.m.r and awkward s: in rr: hdwy over 1f out: kpt on ins fnl f but nvr gng pce to get into contention* **8/1**[3]

1212 **10** *hd* **Iver Bridge Lad**[16] 1340 4-9-0 106 .... (b) JimmyQuinn 12 101
(John Ryan) *in tch: rdn 2f out: styd on same pce ins fnl f* **6/1**[2]

230- **11** *½* **Group Therapy**[224] 6194 6-9-0 105 .... RyanMoore 8 99
(David Barron) *stdd s: t.k.h towards rr: hdwy fr 2f out to chse ldrs 1f out: no imp and sn one pce* **9/1**

016- **12** *1* **Arctic Feeling (IRE)**[203] 6734 3-8-4 102 .... PaulHanagan 6 96
(Richard Fahey) *t.k.h in rr: rdn and sme hdwy ins fnl 2f: nvr gng pce to get into contention* **20/1**

311- **13** *2 ¾* **Astrophysical Jet**[224] 6194 4-9-0 110 .... GrahamGibbons 9 86
(Ed McMahon) [illegible] **11/1**[1]

000- **14** *1 ¼* **Mister Hughie (IRE)**[203] 6735 4-9-0 105 .... TomQueally 1 80
(Tim Easterby) *spd to 1/2-way* **25/1**

6024 **15** *19* **Secret Asset (IRE)**[15] 1366 6-9-0 95 .... RichardHughes 2 —
(Jane Chapple-Hyam) *early spd: wknd 2f out: eased fnl f* **50/1**

59.70 secs (0.60) **Going Correction** +0.30s/f (Good)
WFA 3 from 4yo+ 10lb **15** Ran SP% **120.9**
Speed ratings (Par 113): **107,106,106,106,105 104,104,103,103,103 102,100,96,94,63**toteswingers: 1&2 £60.10, 1& Jonny Mudball £14.90, 1& Sole Power £19.20, 2& JM £12.90, 2& SP £17.10. PLACES: £6.00, £5.40, JM £1.70, SP £1.80. TRIFECTA: TT, RD & JM £2,420.70, TT, RD & SP £2,178.60. CSF £259.36 TOTE £21.60; EX 339.70 TRIFECTA27 Owner.

FOCUS

The first domestic Group sprint of the season and a competitive affair, with two previous Group 1 winners taking part. Although 3-y-os have a decent record in the race and had taken it three times in the previous five years, there was only one representative from the Classic generation this time. They went a typically scorching pace, resulting in another all-the way winner, but only around 4l covered the first 12 horses at the line. The winner carried over last year's progress but the principals are much of a muchness.

NOTEBOOK

Tangerine Trees, representing the same trainer/jockey combination that took this race with Captain Gerrard three years ago, was making his Group-race debut after seven months off, but he was a most progressive sprinter last season, winning five of his seven starts, culminating in a Listed success and he also scored first time out. He only knows how to run one way and duly blitzed his rivals from the start, but although he was being closed down up the hill he never looked like being caught. He will be aimed at the King's Stand and may take in the Temple Stakes first. (op 16-1)

Rain Delayed(IRE) ran his best race for some time in a Newbury handicap last time, but he had failed to make the frame in four previous tries at this level. Held up at the back of the field early, he finished with a real flourish up the hill and deserves a lot of credit as the other principals all raced handily. He should be up to winning another Listed race at least. (op 14-1)

Sole Power, a creditable fourth in this last year, officially had upwards off 5lb in hand of his rivals after his shock 100-1 win in last season's Nunthorpe, but he ran poorly in his only outing since when 14th of 16 in the Al Quoz Sprint at Meydan last month. His trainer expected him to come on for this run, so this was also an encouraging performance from him. (op 10-1)

Jonny Mudball, having his first try both in Pattern company and over the minimum trip, was handy early and ran on again after seemingly getting a little outpaced inside the last 2f. His trainer had warned that he might not be 100 per cent for this, so this will have delighted his connections. (op 10-1)

Borderlescott, third and second in the last two runnings of this when making his seasonal reappearance, stayed on towards the nearside late on. He is apparently harder to get fit as he gets older, so yet another Group-race sprint success this season can hardly be ruled out. (op 12-1)

Lisselan Diva(IRE), a very useful sprinter in France since the cheekpieces were applied last summer, was without them here and also had question marks against her on this quick ground, though her trainer didn't seem too concerned. As it turned out she ran with a lot of credit having been handy early and she should be able to win a Listed race when conditions are more in her favour.

Breathless Kiss(USA), making her Group-race debut, ran creditably considering she had plenty to find on official ratings.

Evens And Odds(IRE) came into this in form after his Thirsk success, but his four wins since he was a 2-y-o had come over 6f and he was only here because there was nothing else for him. Not surprisingly, he was doing all his best work late and he should be able to win a Pattern race back over an extra furlong, possibly overseas. (op 16-1)

Astrophysical Jet improved throughout last season ending with a couple of Group 3 successes over this trip, for which she carried a 3lb penalty here. She made a successful racecourse debut at two, but needed her first start last season, so her absence since September was a concern and she dropped away here as though needing it, though connections were more inclined to blame the ground. Official explanation: jockey said filly was unsuited by the good to firm (good in places) ground (op 3-1, tchd 10-3 in places)

Secret Asset(IRE) Official explanation: jockey said gelding moved poorly

1688 QATAR BLOODSTOCK H'CAP 6f

4:20 (4:22) (Class 2) (0-100,100) 3-Y-O £12,952 (£3,854; £1,926; £962) Stalls High

Form RPR

1- **1** **Seal Rock**^{175} [7346] 3-8-6 **85** .... DaneO'Neill 2 94+
(Henry Candy) *str: lw: hld up in midfield: hdwy over 3f out: chsd ldr and edgd lft ent fnl 2f: rdn to ld 1f out: r.o wl* **9/2**^{1}

313- **2** 1 ¾ **Coeus**^{311} [3327] 3-8-8 **87** .... SebSanders 12 91
(Sir Mark Prescott Bt) *lengthy: lw: led: rdn ent fnl 2f: hdd 1f out: kpt on same pce fnl f* **6/1**^{3}

05-6 **3** *hd* **Remotelinx (IRE)**^{17} [1322] 3-8-8 **87** .... MichaelHills 8 90
(J W Hills) *lw: stdd s: hld up in rr: swtchd rt over 2f out: hdwy jst over 1f out: kpt on wl fnl 150yds* **16/1**

100- **4** 1 ¼ **Forjatt (IRE)**^{210} [6568] 3-9-7 **100** .... FrankieDettori 7 99
(Roger Varian) *lw: in tch towards rr: hdwy and nt clr run over 1f out: swtchd rt ins fnl f: styd on fnl 100yds* **7/1**

11-2 **5** *1* **Bunce (IRE)**^{32} [1023] 3-8-0 **84** .... KieranO'Neill(5) 1 80
(Richard Hannon) *in tch towards rr: rdn along and hdwy 3f out: kpt on same pce fnl f* **16/1**

210- **6** *nk* **Cadeaux Pearl**^{255} [5221] 3-8-6 **88** .... BillyCray(3) 16 83
(David Nicholls) *trckd ldrs: swtchd rt wl over 1f out: pressed ldr and rdn over 1f out: wknd ins fnl f* **20/1**

144- **7** 1 ¾ **Cloud Rock**^{199} [6850] 3-8-6 **85** .... MartinDwyer 9 77+
(Peter Chapple-Hyam) *in tch: effrt and rdn over 2f out: styng on same pce and hld whn nt clr run ins fnl f* **20/1**

10-0 **8** 2 ½ **Mutajare (IRE)**^{25} [1152] 3-8-3 **82** .... JoeFanning 15 63
(Mark Johnston) *lw: towards rr: nt clr run and swtchd lft over 2f out: no imp fr over 1f out* **40/1**

14L- **9** *nk* **Regal Approval**^{224} [6191] 3-8-2 **81** oh1 .... JimmyQuinn 3 61
(Hughie Morrison) *in tch: rdn and effrt to chse ldr whn wandered u.p 2f out: wknd over 1f out* **17/2**

11-4 **10** 4 ½ **Indian Ballad (IRE)**^{17} [1322] 3-8-7 **86** .... GrahamGibbons 5 58+
(Ed McMahon) *chsd ldrs: rdn and struggling jst over 2f out: wknd over 1f out* **13/2**

2-30 **11** *nk* **Breedj (IRE)**^{14} [1404] 3-9-2 **95** .... PhilipRobinson 11 60
(Clive Brittain) *taken down early: chsd ldr tl ent fnl 2f: sn wknd* **20/1**

22-1 **12** 2 ¾ **Commended**^{17} [1315] 3-8-6 **85** .... WilliamBuick 4 41
(B W Hills) *lw: in tch: rdn and losing pl over 3f out: wl bhd over 1f out* **11/2**^{2}

400- **13** 1 ¾ **Primo Lady**^{260} [5036] 3-8-8 **87** .... MickaelBarzalona 14 38
(Gay Kelleway) *restless in stalls: s.i.s: a bhd* **16/1**

1m 13.04s (0.84) **Going Correction** +0.30s/f (Good) **13** Ran SP% **118.6**
Speed ratings (Par 104): **106,103,103,101,100 100,97,94,93,87 87,83,81**
toteswingers: 1&2 £7.30, 1&3 £15.90, 1&3 £25.00. CSF £28.63 CT £414.12 TOTE £5.50: £2.20, £2.50, £5.90; EX 26.60 Trifecta £717.20 Pool: £1,744.75 - 1.80 winning units..

Owner P A Deal **Bred** Mrs A D Bourne **Trained** Kingston Warren, Oxon

FOCUS

A decent handicap for 3yos, likely to have a bearing on similar events in the coming weeks. They raced in one group near the stands' side. There are one or two doubts over the form, but the winner is unexposed and will surely do better.

NOTEBOOK

Seal Rock made a winning debut on the last day of the turf season at Doncaster and made it two from two on this handicap debut. After travelling well he picked up nicely to get on top in the final furlong. He will have found the ground plenty quick enough and looks a nice prospect for a yard which does so well with its sprinters. Similar events back here next month and at York in June looks obvious targets for this likeable gelding. (op 5-1 tchd 11-2)

Coeus ◆ had not been seen out since last June and was running on turf for the first time. He had the rail to race against and showed bright pace, only relinquishing his advantage at the furlong pole and keeping on to secure second. The handicapper may well raise him for this, but he holds four entries over Thursday and Friday of next week so it seems likely that he will be out for one of those before his new mark kicks in. (tchd 11-2)

Remotelinx(IRE) caught the eye at the Craven meeting and confirmed that promise with another nice effort, running on down the outside from the rear of the field. (tchd 20-1)

Forjatt(IRE) ◆ has been gelded since a 2yo campaign which included a second to Wootton Bassett. He ran a promising race on this seasonal return, finishing nicely after meeting trouble, and gives the impression he will be worth a try over 7f. Frankie Dettori reported that his mount had been denied a clear run. Official explanation: jockey said gelding was denied a clear run (op 8-1 tchd 13-2)

Bunce(IRE) ran a sound race on this return to turf and appears to act on most types of ground. (op 12-1)

Cadeaux Pearl, who was free to post, ran well for a long way near the fence and is the type that his new yard should do well with. (op 14-1)

Cloud Rock performed creditably without the drop in trip necessarily being what he wanted.

Regal Approval dropped away after threatening briefly to play a hand in the finish. Jimmy Quinn reported that the gelding had lost his action. Official explanation: jockey said gelding lost its action (op 9-1 tchd 8-1)

Indian Ballad(IRE), fourth over C&D from this mark last time, was just starting to feel the pinch but attempting to rally when he was short of room. Graham Gibbons confirmed that the gelding had been denied a clear run. Official explanation: jockey said gelding was denied a clear run (op 9-1)

Breedj(IRE), who chased the pace, was already struggling when she was squeezed out. She had been put up 13lb for her run in the Fred Darling at Newbury and may be tricky to place. (op 16-1)

Commended, winner of a maiden at the Craven meeting, could not lead and was disappointing dropped back in trip. (op 9-2)

1689 MAKFI NEWMARKET STKS (LISTED RACE) 1m 2f

4:55 (4:55) (Class 1) 3-Y-O

£22,708 (£8,608; £4,308; £2,148; £1,076; £540) Stalls High

Form RPR

5-1 **1** **Ocean War**^{17} [1321] 3-8-12 0 .... MickaelBarzalona 2 108+
(Mahmood Al Zarooni) *lw: stdd s: hld up in last pair: hdwy over 2f out: edgd rt and led over 1f out: in command whn faltered ins fnl f: sn rcvrd and pushed out* **4/1**^{2}

11-1 **2** 2 ¼ **Cai Shen (IRE)**^{15} [1365] 3-8-12 101 .... RichardHughes 4 104+
(Richard Hannon) *lw: stdd s: hld up in last pair: hdwy 3f out: short of room over 2f out: chsd wnr over 1f out: styd on same pce fnl f* **4/1**^{2}

10-4 **3** *nk* **Treasury Devil (USA)**^{6} [1547] 3-8-12 96 .... WilliamBuick 1 103
(John Gosden) *lw: in tch: hdwy on far side 3f out: rdn and chsd ldng pair 1f out: kpt on but nvr gng pce to threaten wnr* **5/1**

33-1 **4** *5* **Discoteca**^{26} [1139] 3-8-12 85 .... JimmyFortune 6 93
(Andrew Balding) *led: rdn over 3f out: hdd and drvn over 2f out: wknd ent fnl f* **14/1**

13-4 **5** 1 ½ **Namibian (IRE)**^{16} [1339] 3-8-12 100 .... JoeFanning 7 90
(Mark Johnston) *chsd ldr: rdn to ld over 2f out: edgd rt u.p and hdd over 1f out: wknd ent fnl f* **9/2**^{3}

3-2 **6** ½ **Hamlool (IRE)**^{21} [1234] 3-8-12 0 .... PhilipRobinson 5 89
(Clive Brittain) *str: gd bodied: lw: chsd ldrs: rdn and unable qck 3f out: wknd wl over 1f out* **3/1**^{1}

4-20 **7** *24* **Canna (IRE)**^{6} [1548] 3-8-12 0 .... MichaelHills 3 41
(B W Hills) *chsd ldrs tl lost pl qckly ent fnl 3f: wl bhd fnl 2f: t.o* **28/1**

2m 7.08s (1.28) **Going Correction** +0.30s/f (Good) **7** Ran SP% **110.0**
Speed ratings (Par 106): **106,104,103,99,98 98,79**
toteswingers: 1&2 £2.90, 1&3 £4.00, 2&3 £4.70. CSF £18.66 TOTE £5.20: £2.80, £2.00; EX 19.80.

Owner Godolphin **Bred** Newsells Park Stud Limited **Trained** Newmarket, Suffolk

FOCUS

Although nominally a Derby Trial, the Newmarket Stakes has produced more horses that have made the frame at Epsom within the past 20 yards rather than winners, with Presenting (1995), Beat All (1999) and Beat Hollow (2000) all successful here before going on to finish third in the Derby. Recent winners have fared less well, however, with only four of the previous ten horses successful in this managing to win another race. Again the field started off down the centre of the track, but ended up closer to the far rail as the race progressed. Although the pace looked steady, the front pair came from the back of the field. Nice progress from the winner, but ordinary Listed form.

NOTEBOOK

Ocean War came into this still very much an unknown quantity having been successful in a C&D maiden at the Craven meeting, and the third horse (the only one to have raced) has since franked the form. Having been brought wide with his effort to lead over a furlong from home, he still looked green once in front, hanging and carrying his head a little high, so there is every reason to believe he still has a great deal more to offer. He holds entries in the King Edward VII Stakes, Eclipse and Derby, for which he remains a top-priced 33-1. (op 9-2 tchd 7-2)

Cai Shen(IRE), bidding for a four-timer on this step up in grade, was given a skilful ride when making a successful reappearance from a couple of nice prospects at Newbury a fortnight earlier. Given another patient ride, he made his move at around the same time as the winner and was briefly short of room around 2f from home, but it did not affect his chances of winning. This ground may have been a bit quicker than ideal. (op 7-2)

Treasury Devil(USA), taking a step up in trip after finishing fourth off 96 in the Esher Cup six days earlier, had his chance towards the far side of the track but couldn't quicken and and he too may have found the ground faster than he cares for. (tchd 11-2)

Discoteca, from the stable that took this last year, was taking a step up in class after bolting up in a Windsor maiden on his reappearance, but he had up to 16lb to find with a few of these on official ratings. He attempted to make all, but was cut down around a quarter of a mile from home and then started to hang. Hopefully, his handicap mark won't be affected by this and he can still find opportunities at a more realistic level. (op 11-1 tchd 10-1)

Namibian(IRE) met trouble in running when fourth in a valuable sales race over C&D on his return, but he had no such excuses here and this looks about as good as he is. (op 4-1)

Hamlool(IRE) was beaten half a length by the 2,000 Guineas runner-up Dubawi Gold on the Lingfield Polytrack last time, but he was off the bridle and going nowhere passing the 2f pole. (op 7-2)

Canna(IRE) ran poorly in the Classical Trial at Sandown six days earlier and was comprehensively outclassed again here. (tchd 33-1)

1690 QIPCO SUPPORTS RACING WELFARE H'CAP 1m

5:25 (5:26) (Class 2) (0-105,93) 3-Y-O £12,952 (£3,854; £1,926; £962) Stalls High

Form RPR

400- **1** **Bahceli (IRE)**^{233} [5880] 3-9-1 **87** .... RichardHughes 1 100
(Richard Hannon) *stdd s: hld up in last pair: rdn and hdwy over 2f out: ev ch u.p ent fnl f: led and edgd lft ins fnl f: kpt on wl* **16/1**

10-1 **2** *hd* **Sikeeb (IRE)**^{15} [1361] 3-9-7 **93** .... PhilipRobinson 3 105
(Clive Brittain) *in tch: rdn and effrt ent fnl 2f: ev ch fnl f: jst hld towards fin* **3/1**^{1}

332- **3** 1 ½ **Zain Shamardal (IRE)**^{187} [7112] 3-8-10 **82** .... MartinDwyer 8 91
(Brian Meehan) *in tch: rdn and effrt over 2f out: drvn to ld 1f out: sn hdd: wknd towards fin* **3/1**^{1}

2221 **4** 1 ¼ **Crown Counsel (IRE)**^{23} [1203] 3-8-11 **83** .... JoeFanning 2 89
(Mark Johnston) *chsd ldrs: ev ch over 2f out tl jst ins fnl f: wknd fnl 100yds* **4/1**^{2}

510- **5** *shd* **Mubtadi**^{224} [6200] 3-8-11 **83** .... MartinLane 7 89+
(David Simcock) *in tch: effrt and hanging lft over 2f out: hdwy to chse ldrs u.p over 1f out: kpt on but nvr gng pce to threaten ldrs* **12/1**

10-3 **6** *4* **Well Sharp**^{27} [1113] 3-8-10 **82** .... PaulHanagan 6 83+
(Michael Dods) *t.k.h: w ldr tl led 3f out: sn rdn: hdd 1f out: wkng whn short of room ins fnl f* **8/1**

321- **7** *2* **Twice Bitten**^{185} [7163] 3-8-5 **77** .... AdrianMcCarthy 4 69
(James Toller) *in tch: rdn and lost pl 3f out: no threat to ldrs fnl 2f* **16/1**

12- **8** *8* **Darej (USA)**^{238} [5751] 3-8-12 **84** .... RichardHills 5 66
(William Haggas) *led tl 3f out: sn rdn: wknd over 1f out: eased ins fnl f* **13/2**^{3}

1m 40.2s (1.60) **Going Correction** +0.30s/f (Good) **8** Ran SP% **113.9**
Speed ratings (Par 104): **104,103,102,101,100 96,94,86**
toteswingers: 1&2 £8.70, 1&3 £6.50, 2&3 £2.30. CSF £63.32 CT £188.93 TOTE £16.00: £4.00, £1.10, £1.70; EX 62.30 Trifecta £713.10 Pool: £1,098.61 - 1.14 winning units..

Owner Middleham Park Racing II **Bred** Dr Mariann And Richard Klay **Trained** East Everleigh, Wilts

FOCUS

This handicap can go to a very decent sort, with Notnowcato (2005) and Dunelight (2006) both taking this before going on to much better things. Six of the eight runners were making their handicap debuts and although the winning time was nearly three seconds slower than the Guineas, the race should produce winners.

NOTEBOOK

Bahceli(IRE) started off last season on a high, but ended it by being beaten a long way in two ultra-valuable sales races at York and Doncaster won by Wootton Bassett. Gelded since last season, he was up 1 1/2f in trip for this return but although sent off a decent price, was by no means unbacked. Held up early, he was under pressure a fair way out but responded well to hit the front over a furlong from home and, despite hanging to his left, was always doing just enough. He obviously goes well fresh and there are no specific plans for him. (op 25-1)

Sikeeb(IRE) was up 7lb for his successful return in a 7f handicap at Newbury earlier this month. He didn't seem to do a lot when first coming off the bridle here, but eventually responded, only just failing to get up, and may need a step up to 1m now. His rider reported that he had hung left. Official explanation: jockey said colt hung left (tchd 10-3)

Zain Shamardal(IRE) showed ability in all three starts at two, though he was a beaten favourite on the last two occasions. Another to run on again after seemingly being tapped for toe, he was only seen off in the very latter stages and, with the outing under his belt, can surely break his duck before too long. (tchd 11-4)

Crown Counsel(IRE), winner of a Ripon maiden on his turf debut earlier this month from which those in behind have run in ten races since but none has won, had every chance and was in front coming to the last furlong, but he didn't get home. (op 9-2)

Mubtadi probably had excuses when well beaten in a valuable sales race here on his most recent outing last September. He looked more likely to finish last when off the bridle at the back of the field at halfway, but made some late progress against the nearside rail and is entitled to come on for this first start in 224 days. (op 14-1)

Well Sharp didn't seem to get home over 1m2f on his Doncaster reappearance despite a soft lead. He had every chance here back down in trip, but had run his race when hampered by the runner-up a furlong from home.

Twice Bitten showed progressive form when switched to Polytrack last autumn culminating in a narrow Kempton success. Gelded since last seen, he lost his place after halfway and reportedly didn't handle the ground. A return to the all-weather may be in order. Official explanation: jockey said gelding was unsuited by the good to firm (good in places) ground

Darej(USA) came into this unexposed having won a weak Yarmouth maiden and finishing second of three in a Kempton conditions event last season, but he dropped out very tamely after making the early running on this return and now has questions to answer. (op 11-2 tchd 5-1)

T/Jkpt: Not won. T/Plt: £137.60 to a £1 stake. Pool: £193,337.17 - 1,025.02 winning tickets. T/Qpdt: £36.90 to a £1 stake. Pool: £8,234.12 - 164.92 winning tickets. SP

1239 THIRSK (L-H)

Saturday, April 30

OFFICIAL GOING: Good (8.4)

Wind: Fresh 1/2 against Weather: Fine and sunny but breezy

1691 TOTEPLACEPOT MAIDEN AUCTION STKS — 5f

1:50 (1:50) (Class 5) 2-Y-O — **£2,914** (£867; £433; £216) **Stalls** High

Form — RPR

56 **1** **Profile Star (IRE)**[14] [1383] 2-9-3 0 .... LeeNewman 9 — 78+
(David Barron) *mde all: drifted lft fr over 1f out: hld on wl towards fin* **11/2**

2 *1/2* **Amadeus Denton (IRE)** 2-9-3 0 .... FrederikTylicki 3 — 76+
(Michael Dods) *chsd ldrs: chal over 1f out: carried lft: no ex clsng stages* **16/1**

4 **3** *3* **Fayr Fall (IRE)**[12] [1434] 2-9-3 0 .... DavidAllan 5 — 65
(Tim Easterby) *chsd ldrs: swtchd lft 2f out: kpt on same pce* **5/1**[3]

4 *2* **Auntie Joy** 2-8-9 0 .... JamesSullivan(3) 16 — 53+
(Michael Easterby) *bhd: hdwy 2f out: styd on ins fnl f* **50/1**

5 *nse* **Rent Free** 2-9-3 0 .... SilvestreDeSousa 11 — 59
(Nigel Tinkler) *chsd ldrs: hmpd 2f out: kpt on same pce fnl 2f* **28/1**

6 *1/2* **Farang Kondiew** 2-8-12 0 .... NeilFarley(5) 7 — 56
(Declan Carroll) *dwlt: in rr: styd on fnl 2f: nvr nr ldrs* **3/1**[1]

7 *1 3/4* **See Clearly** 2-8-10 0 ow3 .... LanceBetts(5) 8 — 48
(Tim Easterby) *s.s: bhd tl styd on fnl 2f* **66/1**

6 **8** *shd* **Xinbama (IRE)**[14] [1396] 2-9-0 0 .... PatrickHills(3) 13 — 50
(J W Hills) *chsd ldrs: wknd 2f out* **14/1**

5 **9** *2 1/4* **Aljosan**[7] [1522] 2-8-12 0 .... CathyGannon 15 — 36
(David Evans) *mid-div: sn pushed along: hung lft over 2f out: sn wknd* **[illegible]**

10 *3 1/2* **Lady Gadfly** 2-8-12 0 .... PJMcDonald 6 — 24
(Micky Hammond) *in rr: sme hdwy 2f out: nvr on terms* **100/1**

11 *1 1/2* **Dolly Danca** 2-8-12 0 .... MickyFenton 4 — 18
(Paul Midgley) *w wnr: wkng whn hmpd 2f out* **66/1**

632 **12** *2 1/4* **Triggerlo**[14] [1396] 2-9-3 0 .... SamHitchcott 12 — 15
(Mick Channon) *chsd ldrs: wknd over 1f out* **4/1**[2]

0 **13** *1/2* **Nameitwhatyoulike**[3] [1619] 2-9-3 0 .... DavidNolan 1 — 14
(Michael Easterby) *dwlt: outpcd and a bhd* **100/1**

6220 **14** *nse* **Umph (IRE)**[14] [1383] 2-9-3 0 .... PatCosgrave 14 — 13
(David Evans) *chsd ldrs: wknd 2f out* **11/1**

6 **15** *1/2* **Witty Buck**[19] [1268] 2-9-3 0 .... RobertWinston 10 — 12
(Alan McCabe) *in rr: sn drvn along: nvr on terms* **33/1**

61.62 secs (2.02) **Going Correction** +0.40s/f (Good) **15** Ran SP% **119.6**

Speed ratings (Par 92): **99,98,93,90,90 89,86,86,82,77 74,71,70,70,69**

toteswingers: 1&2 £11.70, 1&3 £7.80, 2&3 £22.00. CSF £86.03 TOTE £6.00: £2.00, £5.10, £2.20; EX 69.60.

Owner Profile Storage Ltd **Bred** Knocklong House Stud **Trained** Maunby, N Yorks

■ Stewards' Enquiry : Lee Newman three-day ban: careless riding (May 15-17)

FOCUS

A lot of these had no previous experience, so it is not easy to judge how good a contest this was. All of the runners headed towards the stands' side early, but the first three home ended up close to the far side.

NOTEBOOK

Profile Star(IRE) had been progressing and won this after attracting market support, despite edging across the course in the final furlong. He had to survive a stewards' inquiry but the result was probably right on the day. (op 8-1)

Amadeus Denton(IRE) looks an early type on breeding and appeared a little unlucky considering he was carried across the track by the winner. The pair came clear so he must have the ability to win something similar. (op 14-1)

Fayr Fall(IRE) had shown promise when a 16-1 fourth in a maiden auction event at Redcar, and built on that with a staying-on effort here. (tchd 9-2 and 11-2)

Auntie Joy ◆ was allowed to get into it nice and slowly and ran an eyecatching race. Her pedigree suggests she'll be better over a bit further and she is a nice prospect. (op 40-1)

Rent Free is bred to be pacey and showed quite a bit of ability. His cause wasn't helped by being slightly hampered by the winner as he started to shift left, but he wouldn't have won. (op 33-1)

Farang Kondiew ◆, an 11,000gns Selkirk colt, looked to be green in behind and is sure to come on for the experience. He can win races. (op 10-3 tchd 7-2)

Triggerlo had shown steady improvement with each outing, so this was a long way below what he'd shown previously. Official explanation: trainer's rep had no explanation for the poor form shown (op 3-1 tchd 11-4)

Umph(IRE) Official explanation: trainer's rep had no explanation for the poor form shown

1692 TOTESWINGER FLEXI BETTING MAIDEN STKS — 1m 4f

2:25 (2:29) (Class 5) 3-Y-O+ — **£2,914** (£867; £433; £216) **Stalls** Low

Form — RPR

1 **The Fun Crusher** 3-8-8 0 .... RobertWinston 2 — 81+
(Tim Easterby) *s.i.s: hdwy over 3f out: styd on to ld appr fnl f: drvn out* **33/1**

626- **2** *1/2* **Kadoodd (IRE)**[182] [7236] 3-8-8 77 .... SamHitchcott 6 — 78
(Mick Channon) *s.i.s: hdwy over 3f out: chsng ldrs over 2f out: styd on to take 2nd last 50yds* **15/2**

32-4 **3** *1 1/2* **King Of The Celts (IRE)**[23] [1203] 3-8-8 76 .... DavidAllan 1 — 76
(Tim Easterby) *trckd ldrs: chal over 1f out: kpt on same pce* **3/1**[2]

-323 **4** *2 1/2* **Dressing Room (USA)**[12] [1445] 3-8-8 73 ....(v) SilvestreDeSousa 11 — 72
(Mark Johnston) *led: hdd appr fnl f: wknd last 150yds* **5/1**[3]

5 **5** *6* **Cape Princess**[15] [1364] 3-8-3 0 .... CathyGannon 8 — 57
(Michael Bell) *chsd ldrs: lost pl over 1f out* **13/2**

6 *1/2* **Aeneid**[105] 6-10-0 0 .... DavidNolan 9 — 63
(Declan Carroll) *s.i.s: hdwy 7f out: chsng ldrs over 2f out: wknd over 1f out* **40/1**

06-4 **7** *4 1/2* **Judicious**[22] [1212] 4-9-10 0 .... MichaelO'Connell(3) 10 — 56
(Geoffrey Harker) *hld up in rr: nvr on terms* **40/1**

33- **8** *3 1/2* **Estourah (IRE)**[189] [7099] 3-8-8 0 .... TedDurcan 14 — 48
(Saeed Bin Suroor) *trckd ldrs: drvn over 3f out: wknd 2f out* **13/8**[1]

5-6 **9** *8* **Garth Mountain**[22] [1212] 4-9-10 0 .... RichardEvans(3) 13 — 38
(David Evans) *mid-div: drvn 6f out: lost pl over 4f out* **50/1**

00-0 **10** *18* **Benamy Boy**[53] [800] 5-10-0 38 .... FrannyNorton 12 — —
(Neville Bycroft) *in rr: bhd fnl 7f: t.o fnl 3f* **200/1**

0-4 **11** *16* **Big Zaf**[17] [1304] 3-8-8 0 .... MickyFenton 7 — —
(Paul Midgley) *mid-div: lost pl over 5f out: t.o over 3f out* **200/1**

2m 39.14s (2.94) **Going Correction** +0.40s/f (Good)

WFA 3 from 4yo 20lb 4 from 5yo+ 1lb **11** Ran SP% **115.6**

Speed ratings (Par 103): **106,105,104,103,99 98,95,93,88,76 65**

toteswingers: 1&2: £30.10, 1&3: £18.60, 2&3: £4.50 CSF £253.67 TOTE £35.70: £8.80, £2.50, £1.20; EX 354.80.

Owner Jim McGrath **Bred** Worksop Manor Stud **Trained** Great Habton, N Yorks

■ Stewards' Enquiry : Sam Hitchcott one-day ban: used whip in incorrect place (May 15)

FOCUS

A fairly big field but only a handful could be seriously fancied. The early pace didn't look frenetic but two that got behind played a part in the finish. Ordinary form judged around the third and fourth.

Judicious Official explanation: jockey said gelding ran too free

Estourah(IRE) Official explanation: trainer's rep had no explanation for thr poor form shown

1693 TOTEEXACTA FLEXI BETTING MAIDEN STKS — 7f

3:00 (3:03) (Class 4) 3-Y-O — **£4,533** (£1,348; £674; £336) **Stalls** Low

Form — RPR

624- **1** **Lamasaas (USA)**[197] [6882] 3-9-3 80 .... RobertWinston 10 — 71
(B W Hills) *trckd ldrs: drvn to ld appr fnl f: rdn out* **4/6**[1]

0 **2** *3/4* **Maxamillion Bounty**[21] [1246] 3-9-3 0 .... TonyHamilton 9 — 69
(Michael Dods) *chsd ldr: upsides and hung lft over 1f out: kpt on same pce* **66/1**

6-4 **3** *2 1/4* **Prince Of Passion (CAN)**[29] [1084] 3-9-3 0 .... FrederikTylicki 5 — 63
(Michael Dods) *led: hdd appr fnl f: fdd* **16/1**

4 *2* **Thatcherite (IRE)** 3-9-3 0 .... BarryMcHugh 4 — 58
(Neville Bycroft) *mid-div: hdwy to chse ldrs over 2f out: one pce* **100/1**

5 *nk* **Singzak** 3-9-0 0 .... JamesSullivan(3) 3 — 61+
(Michael Easterby) *mid-div: lost pl over 2f out: hmpd appr fnl f: styd on* **66/1**

5 **6** *1/2* **Full Pelt (USA)**[12] [1436] 3-9-3 0 .... RichardKingscote 7 — 55
(Tom Dascombe) *mid-div: hdwy over 3f out: edgd rt over 1f out: one pce* **14/1**

0- **7** *1* **Uncle Bryn**[210] [6569] 3-9-3 0 .... AdrianNicholls 13 — 53
(John Quinn) *chsd ldrs: fdd over 1f out* **50/1**

0- **8** *hd* **Henrys Gift (IRE)**[255] [5196] 3-9-0 0 .... PatrickDonaghy(3) 12 — 52
(Michael Dods) *in rr-div: kpt on fnl 2f: hmpd nr fin: nvr on terms* **66/1**

[illegible]

(Declan Carroll) *s.i.s: in rr: sme hdwy on ins whn nt clr run over 1f out: nvr a factor* **100/1**

10 *3/4* **Orbit The Moon (IRE)** 3-9-3 0 .... DavidAllan 6 — 47+
(Michael Dods) *mid-div: lost pl and hmpd over 1f out* **20/1**

0-2 **11** *nk* **Auto Mac**[12] [1436] 3-9-3 0 .... FrannyNorton 8 — 51
(Neville Bycroft) *chsd ldrs: rdn 3f out: wknd over 1f out* **6/1**[2]

0 **12** *3* **Joe Rocco (IRE)**[23] [1203] 3-9-3 0 .... PJMcDonald 1 — 39
(Alan Swinbank) *a towards rr* **50/1**

13 *nk* **Shopping Oasis** 3-9-3 0 .... SilvestreDeSousa 14 — 38
(Mark Johnston) *swvd rt s: bhd and swtchd lft sn after s: a in rr* **12/1**[3]

1m 29.89s (2.69) **Going Correction** +0.40s/f (Good) **13** Ran SP% **109.7**

Speed ratings (Par 100): **100,99,96,94,93 93,92,92,90,90 89,86,85**

toteswingers: 1&2: £33.70, 1&3: £2.70, 2&3: £83.10 CSF £73.91 TOTE £1.60: £1.10, £11.00, £3.00; EX 63.80.

Owner Hamdan Al Maktoum **Bred** Dell Ridge Farm, D Ryan & K Donworth **Trained** Lambourn, Berks

■ Blink Of An Eye (8/1) was withdrawn after refusing to enter the stalls. Deduct 10p in the £ under R4.

■ Stewards' Enquiry : Richard Kingscote four-day ban: careless riding (May 15-18)

FOCUS

The betting market spoke volumes here as no-one was interested in anything other than the favourite. The winner probably didn't need to match his 2yo best and the form has been rated conservatively.

Singzak ◆ Official explanation: jockey said colt ran green

1694 TOTESPORT.COM THIRSK HUNT CUP (H'CAP) — 1m

3:35 (3:37) (Class 2) (0-100,98) 4-Y-O+ — **£12,952** (£3,854; £1,926; £962) **Stalls** Low

Form — RPR

10-4 **1** **Justonefortheroad**[28] [1092] 5-8-8 **90** .... LeeTopliss(5) 7 — 101
(Richard Fahey) *mid-div: effrt and swtchd outside over 2f out: r.o to ld ins fnl f: drvn out* **4/1**[2]

5111 **2** *1* **Snow Bay**[14] [1410] 5-9-1 **92** .... AdrianNicholls 1 — 100
(David Nicholls) *led: hdd and no ex nr fin* **11/2**[3]

01-0 **3** *1* **Space War**[6] [1541] 4-9-1 **92** .... DavidNolan 11 — 98
(Michael Easterby) *mid-div: hdwy over 2f out: kpt on wl fnl f* **40/1**

06-4 **4** *hd* **Dhaular Dhar (IRE)**[21] [1240] 9-8-12 **89** .... DanielTudhope 12 — 94
(Jim Goldie) *chsd ldrs: hung lft and kpt on same pce appr fnl f* **25/1**

0-04 **5** *3/4* **Osteopathic Remedy (IRE)**[11] [1457] 7-9-6 **97** .... FrederikTylicki 3 — 101
(Michael Dods) *chsd ldrs: effrt over 2f out: sn outpcd: kpt on wl fnl f* **16/1**

610- **6** *hd* **Pendragon (USA)**[210] 6562 8-8-9 **89** .... AmyRyan(3) 8 92+
(Brian Ellison) *hld up in rr: hdwy over 2f out: kpt on wl fnl f* **25/1**
0-60 **7** *hd* **Smarty Socks (IRE)**[14] 1410 7-8-11 **88** .... SilvestreDeSousa 14 91
(David O'Meara) *in rr: hdwy and swtchd outside 2f out: kpt on same pce fnl f* **11/1**
5-00 **8** *1 1/2* **Charlie Cool**[14] 1387 8-8-9 **89** .... (b) JamesSullivan(3) 15 88
(Ruth Carr) *in rr: hdwy 2f out: styd on ins fnl f* **25/1**
10-0 **9** *hd* **Oriental Scot**[28] 1092 4-8-13 **90** .... PJMcDonald 5 89
(William Jarvis) *mid-div: effrt over 3f out: one pce fnl 2f* **7/1**
0-26 **10** *2 1/4* **Hacienda (IRE)**[7] 1529 4-9-1 **92** .... RoystonFfrench 6 86
(Mark Johnston) *chsd ldrs: wknd appr fnl f* **7/2**[1]
50-0 **11** *hd* **Dream Lodge (IRE)**[28] 1094 7-9-1 **92** .... AndrewMullen 16 85
(David Nicholls) *mid-div: effrt over 2f out: nvr on terms* **33/1**
00-0 **12** *nk* **Kiwi Bay**[28] 1094 6-9-2 **93** .... DarryllHolland 9 85
(Michael Dods) *s.i.s: a in rr* **28/1**
4-00 **13** *2* **Our Joe Mac (IRE)**[28] 1094 4-9-1 **92** .... TonyHamilton 2 80
(Richard Fahey) *sn chsng ldrs: wknd over 1f out* **14/1**
00-3 **14** *3 1/4* **Balcarce Nov (ARG)**[14] 1385 6-9-7 **98** .... MickyFenton 4 78
(Tom Tate) *dwlt: mid-div: drvn over 3f out: lost pl over 1f out* **10/1**
66-0 **15** *7* **Collateral Damage (IRE)**[21] 1240 8-8-11 **88** .... (t) DavidAllan 10 52
(Tim Easterby) *rrd s: s.i.s: in rr: bhd fnl 2f* **25/1**

1m 41.47s (1.37) **Going Correction** +0.40s/f (Good) **15** Ran SP% **124.3**
Speed ratings (Par 109): **109,108,107,106,106 105,105,104,103,101 101,101,99,95,88**
toteswingers:1&2:£2.00, 1&3:£55.80, 2&3:£53.30 CSF £24.69 CT £814.92 TOTE £5.50: £2.20, £2.00, £13.30; EX 23.40 Trifecta £536.60 Part won. Pool: £725.20 - 0.60 winning units..
Owner The Pontoon Partnership **Bred** Wellsummers Farm & Hammarsfield B'Stock **Trained** Musley Bank, N Yorks

FOCUS
All of these handicappers came with some sort of claim and those who finished close up weren't separated by a great deal of distance. Straightforward, fair form.

NOTEBOOK
Justonefortheroad won on his side of the draw in the Spring Mile, but was comfortably beaten by Eton Forever. Well ridden here just off the speed, he was produced at the right time to get to the front and did just enough once there to hold on. This was the target, so there are no immediate plans for the future. (op 5-1 tchd 7-2)
Snow Bay was chasing a four-timer here and made a bold bid to collect that victory after making the early runnings. It was credit to the horse that he kept on to claim second. (tchd 6-1)
Space War won a Newmarket maiden for John Gosden on second start last year and signed off with another success at Ffos Las. Well beaten over 7f at Musselburgh when weak in the market on his debut for this yard, this was a promising performance from off the pace and he can be competitive in decent handicaps. (op 33-1)
Dhaular Dhar(IRE) finished behind Hacienda over the course last time, but readily reversed that form over 1f further. He has entry at Chester next week, a course he goes well over, and judged on this effort, he must go there with a chance. (op 28-1)
Osteopathic Remedy(IRE) is much higher in the weights now than he was when taking this race in 2010, so this was probably a decent effort.
Pendragon(USA) ◆ caught the eye with the way he finished through runners and will be interesting next time with this run under his belt, as he certainly knows how to win.
Hacienda(IRE) had every chance over 2f but weakened quickly thereafter. (op 11-2)
Balcarce Nov(ARG) wasn't beaten far when hampered in Listed company at Doncaster last time but has only scored once from 19 starts for his current trainer. Third in this last year, this was a long way below his best and it might be wise to ignore the run. Official explanation: jockey said horse never travelled
Collateral Damage(IRE) Official explanation: jockey said gelding reared at start and never travelled

1695 TOTETRIFECTA FLEXI BETTING H'CAP (DIV I) 7f
4:10 (4:10) (Class 4) (0-85,85) 4-Y-0+ **£4,209** (£1,252; £625; £312) **Stalls** Low

Form RPR
6605 **1** **Dubai Dynamo**[6] 1541 6-8-13 **77** .... PJMcDonald 8 88+
(Ruth Carr) *hmpd s: in rr: gd hdwy over 2f out: led over 1f out: styd on wl* **9/2**[2]
-310 **2** *1* **Everymanforhimself (IRE)**[84] 438 7-9-3 **84** .... (b) AmyRyan(3) 9 93
(Kevin Ryan) *wnt lft s: hld up in midfield: effrt on wd outside over 2f out: styd on to take 2nd ins fnl f* **8/1**
0-03 **3** *1 3/4* **Karaka Jack**[12] 1438 4-8-11 **75** .... AdrianNicholls 4 79
(David Nicholls) *led 1f: chsd ldrs: kpt on same pce fnl f* **3/1**[1]
10-0 **4** *3 1/4* **Illustrious Prince (IRE)**[23] 1205 4-8-12 **81** .... NeilFarley(5) 12 76
(Declan Carroll) *t.k.h: trckd ldrs on outer: hung rt bnd over 4f out: drvn 3f out: wknd appr fnl f* **14/1**
000- **5** *2* **Bond Fastrac**[282] 4288 4-8-11 **75** .... SilvestreDeSousa 11 65
(Geoffrey Oldroyd) *led after 1f: hdd over 1f out: sn wknd* **20/1**
002- **6** *nse* **Ginger Ted (IRE)**[183] 7207 4-9-2 **83** .... TjadeCollier(3) 2 73+
(Richard Guest) *stdd s: hld up in rr: r.o fnl 2f: nvr nr ldrs* **16/1**
0-04 **7** *1 1/2* **Arry's Orse**[12] 1438 4-9-4 **82** .... RoystonFfrench 3 68
(Bryan Smart) *trckd ldrs: t.k.h: chsd ldr over 2f out: wknd appr fnl f* **8/1**
00-4 **8** *3/4* **Northern Fling**[29] 1075 7-9-3 **84** .... GaryBartley(3) 6 68
(Jim Goldie) *in rr: kpt on fnl 2f: nvr on terms* **7/1**[3]
20-3 **9** *shd* **Summer Dancer (IRE)**[14] 1382 7-9-2 **80** .... MickyFenton 1 63
(Paul Midgley) *hld up in midfield: t.k.h: effrt over 2f out: nvr nr ldrs* **8/1**
002- **10** *7* **Reel Buddy Star**[240] 5685 6-9-7 **85** .... DanielTudhope 10 49
(George Moore) *chsd ldr: wknd over 2f out* **8/1**
1366 **11** *7* **Qadar (IRE)**[15] 1368 9-8-9 **73** .... (e) RobertWinston 5 19
(Alan McCabe) *s.i.s: a in rr: bhd fnl 2f* **33/1**
5/0- **12** *4 1/2* **Arabian Pride**[222] 6253 4-8-12 **76** .... TonyHamilton 7 —
(Keith Dalgleish) *wnt rt s: mid-div: lost pl over 2f out: sn bhd* **50/1**

1m 28.76s (1.56) **Going Correction** +0.40s/f (Good) **12** Ran SP% **122.3**
Speed ratings (Par 105): **107,105,103,100,97 97,96,95,95,87 79,73**
toteswingers:1&2:£9.30, 1&3:£3.90, 2&3:£24.10 CSF £41.17 CT £129.73 TOTE £4.30: £2.00, £2.70, £1.40; EX 48.30 Trifecta £176.90 Pool: £401.65 - 1.68 winning units..
Owner The Bottom Liners **Bred** T K & Mrs P A Knox **Trained** Huby, N Yorks

FOCUS
The first of the two divisions of this handicap was run at a slow early tempo (but recorded just the quicker time), meaning plenty were fighting for their heads in the back straight and round the bend. The first two had both come down in the weights and the winner may be able to defy a regulation rise.
Summer Dancer(IRE) Official explanation: jockey said gelding ran too free

1696 TOTETRIFECTA FLEXI BETTING H'CAP (DIV II) 7f
4:45 (4:46) (Class 4) (0-85,85) 4-Y-0+ **£4,209** (£1,252; £625; £312) **Stalls** Low

Form RPR
0-43 **1** **Imperial Djay (IRE)**[5] 1560 6-8-13 **77** .... PJMcDonald 8 92
(Ruth Carr) *stdd s: hld up in rr: smooth hdwy over 2f out: led on bit appr fnl f: shkn up and sn wnt clr* **5/1**[2]
-140 **2** *4* **Rio Cobolo (IRE)**[14] 1382 5-8-12 **76** .... AdrianNicholls 7 80
(David Nicholls) *led: hdd appr fnl f: kpt on same pce* **15/2**
/31- **3** *nk* **Amazing Star (IRE)**[217] 6366 6-8-7 **76** .... NeilFarley(5) 10 79
(Declan Carroll) *hld up in rr: stdy hdwy over 2f out: kpt on same pce fnl f* **12/1**
240- **4** *1* **Daring Dream (GER)**[182] 7227 6-8-8 **72** .... AndrewMullen 12 72
(Jim Goldie) *trckd ldr: kpt on same pce appr fnl f* **28/1**
04-0 **5** *hd* **Keys Of Cyprus**[14] 1410 9-9-2 **80** .... PaulQuinn 11 80
(David Nicholls) *hld up towards rr: hdwy on outside over 3f out: kpt on same pce fnl 2f* **10/1**
41- **6** *nk* **Pirate Coast**[302] 3635 4-8-10 **74** .... DavidAllan 4 73
(Tim Easterby) *chsd ldrs: effrt over 2f out: one pce over 1f out* **5/1**[2]
511- **7** *1 1/4* **Who's Shirl**[226] 6113 5-9-5 **83** .... KellyHarrison 2 79
(Chris Fairhurst) *hld up towards rr: kpt on fnl 2f: nvr a factor* **10/1**
40-0 **8** *3/4* **Legal Legacy**[31] 1035 5-8-11 **75** .... TonyHamilton 3 69
(Michael Dods) *hld up in mid field: effrt on ins over 2f out: edgd lft and wknd fnl f* **9/2**[1]
60-0 **9** *hd* **Champagne Style (USA)**[28] 1092 4-9-1 **82** .... RobertLButler(3) 6 78
(Richard Guest) *hld up in rr: sme hdwy on ins 2f out: nt clr run and swtchd rt ins fnl f: nvr a factor* **33/1**
3101 **10** *2* **Thrust Control (IRE)**[31] 1037 4-9-7 **85** .... SilvestreDeSousa 1 73
(Brian Ellison) *trckd ldrs: drvn 3f out: lost pl over 1f out* **11/2**[3]
4-00 **11** *2 3/4* **Aerodynamic (IRE)**[14] 1410 4-9-0 **81** .... JamesSullivan(3) 5 61
(Clive Mulhall) *in rr: rdn over 3f out: sn bhd* **16/1**

1m 29.32s (2.12) **Going Correction** +0.40s/f (Good) **11** Ran SP% **116.8**
Speed ratings (Par 105): **103,98,98,96,96 96,94,94,93,91 88**
toteswingers:1&2:£10.00, 1&3:£6.80, 2&3:£25.20 CSF £42.10 CT £429.31 TOTE £5.70: £2.10, £3.10, £3.90; EX 46.60 Trifecta £502.50 Part won. Pool: £679.07 - 0.90 winning units..
Owner Hollinbridge Partnership **Bred** D Veitch And Musagd Abo Salim **Trained** Huby, N Yorks

FOCUS
This looked a bit of a messy race, as a few of the runners appeared to find trouble in running in the final stages

1697 TOTEPOOL A BETTER WAY TO BET CLASSIFIED STKS 6f
5:15 (5:15) (Class 5) 3-Y-0 **£2,914** (£867; £433; £216) **Stalls** High

Form RPR
6-02 **1** **Iceblast**[6] 1543 3-8-11 72 .... JamesSullivan(3) 2 86
(Michael Easterby) *dwlt: in rr: hdwy to ld 2f out: rdn and drew clr ins fnl f* **7/2**[2]
441- **2** *3* **Jade**[219] 6301 3-9-0 72 .... SilvestreDeSousa 10 77
(Ollie Pears) *dwlt: jnd ldr after 2f: kpt on to take 2nd nr fin* **11/4**[1]
00-1 **3** *hd* **Golden Taurus (IRE)**[22] 1219 3-8-13 75 ow2 .... PatrickHills(3) 4 78
(J W Hills) *hld up in rr: stdy hdwy over 2f out: chsng ldrs over 1f out: kpt on same pce* **13/2**
03-1 **4** *2* **Another Wise Kid (IRE)**[31] 1038 3-9-0 72 .... MickyFenton 6 70
(Paul Midgley) *chsd ldrs: hung lft and wknd fnl f* **4/1**[3]
124- **5** *8* **Crimson Cloud**[144] 7739 3-8-7 75 .... LauraBarry(7) 8 44
(Richard Fahey) *led tl 2f out: hung lft and wknd appr fnl f: eased towards fin* **9/1**
4-66 **6** *4 1/2* **Bussa**[22] 1214 3-9-0 75 .... CathyGannon 3 30
(David Evans) *chsd ldrs: wknd over 1f out* **16/1**
66-0 **7** *9* **Blaze Of Thunder (IRE)**[25] 1152 3-9-0 74 .... PJMcDonald 9 —
(Alan Swinbank) *chsd ldrs: rdn and lost pl 2f out: eased whn bhd ins fnl f* **13/2**

1m 13.99s (1.29) **Going Correction** +0.40s/f (Good) **7** Ran SP% **111.4**
Speed ratings (Par 98): **107,103,102,100,89 83,71**
toteswingers:1&2:£2.50, 1&3:£2.70, 2&3:£5.50 CSF £12.83 TOTE £4.10: £2.00, £2.10; EX 11.20.
Owner B Padgett **Bred** A C M Spalding **Trained** Sheriff Hutton, N Yorks
■ Stewards' Enquiry : Patrick Hills three-day ban: weighed in 2lb heavy (May 15-17)

FOCUS
One got the impression that the leaders went off a bit too quickly considering where the winner came from. The form looks sound enough for the grade.

1698 TOTESPORT 0800 221 221 H'CAP 5f
5:45 (5:46) (Class 4) (0-80,80) 4-Y-0+ **£4,533** (£1,348; £674; £336) **Stalls** High

Form RPR
0-32 **1** **Oldjoesaid**[6] 1539 7-9-6 **79** .... BarryMcHugh 1 87
(Kevin Ryan) *mid-div on outer: hdwy over 2f out: led over 1f out: edgd rt: jst hld on* **7/2**[1]
40-0 **2** *hd* **Select Committee**[14] 1411 6-8-9 **73** .... (v) LeeTopliss(5) 15 81
(John Quinn) *sn chsng ldrs stands' side: upsides over 1f out: styd on wl ins fnl f: jst hld* **12/1**
36-0 **3** *1/2* **Indian Trail**[10] 1476 11-9-6 **79** .... (v) AdrianNicholls 13 85+
(David Nicholls) *in rr-div stands' side: gd hdwy and swtchd centre over 1f out: n.m.r ins fnl f: styd on wl towards fin* **17/2**[3]
203- **4** *1 1/4* **Secret Venue**[185] 7175 5-8-8 **67** .... PJMcDonald 4 68
(Jedd O'Keeffe) *chsd ldrs outer: kpt on same pce fnl f* **20/1**
5624 **5** *shd* **Green Manalishi**[15] 1371 10-9-2 **80** .... (p) JulieBurke(5) 3 81
(Kevin Ryan) *bmpd s: mid-div on outer: hdwy over 2f out: kpt on same pce appr fnl f* **16/1**
040- **6** *1/2* **Mullglen**[238] 5760 5-8-9 **68** .... KellyHarrison 10 67
(Tim Easterby) *dwlt: bhd: hdwy over 1f out: styng on at fin* **11/1**
25-0 **7** *hd* **Bronze Beau**[26] 1140 4-9-1 **77** .... (t) JamesSullivan(3) 14 75
(Linda Stubbs) *led overall on stands' side rail: hung lft and hdd over 1f out: kpt on same pce* **20/1**
6-14 **8** *3/4* **Le Toreador**[6] 1539 6-9-4 **80** .... (p) AmyRyan(3) 6 76
(Kevin Ryan) *chsd ldrs centre: upsides over 1f out: wknd jst ins fnl f* **8/1**[2]
3104 **9** *shd* **Desert Strike**[5] 1562 5-8-13 **72** .... (p) RobertWinston 11 67+
(Alan McCabe) *sn outpcd and in rr: kpt on fnl 2f: nvr on terms* **9/1**
520- **10** *1 1/2* **Lost In Paris (IRE)**[166] 7466 5-9-6 **79** .... (v) DavidAllan 8 69
(Tim Easterby) *w ldrs stands' side: crowded over 1f out: sn wknd* **14/1**
066- **11** *hd* **Tillys Tale**[243] 5600 4-8-9 **68** .... MickyFenton 2 57+
(Paul Midgley) *wnt rt s: w ldrs centre: hmpd whn wkng ins fnl f: eased* **22/1**
040- **12** *nk* **Mey Blossom**[204] 6723 6-9-6 **79** .... RussKennemore 7 67+
(Richard Whitaker) *in rr: sme hdwy 2f out: nt clr run over 1f out: nvr on terms* **16/1**
5-00 **13** *1/2* **Grand Stitch (USA)**[14] 1411 5-8-3 **67** .... (v) NeilFarley(5) 16 53
(Declan Carroll) *dwlt: racd stands' side: a in rr* **12/1**
06-2 **14** *3/4* **Bosun Breese**[14] 1411 6-9-3 **76** .... LeeNewman 9 60
(David Barron) *mid-div: drvn over 2f out: wknd over 1f out* **10/1**
0-54 **15** *5* **Go Nani Go**[26] 1140 5-9-6 **79** .... PatCosgrave 5 45
(Ed de Giles) *mid-div: lost pl 2f out: eased whn bhd* **11/1**

61.09 secs (1.49) **Going Correction** +0.40s/f (Good) **15** Ran SP% **127.3**
Speed ratings (Par 105): **104,103,102,100,100 99,99,98,98,95 95,95,94,93,85**
toteswingers:1&2:£8.30, 1&3:£10.00, 2&3:£38.00 CSF £47.32 CT £357.34 TOTE £5.60: £2.30, £4.50, £3.60; EX 77.30.
Owner Mrs Angie Bailey **Bred** Mrs R D Peacock **Trained** Hambleton, N Yorks

■ Stewards' Enquiry : Adrian Nicholls two-day ban: careless riding (May 15-16)

FOCUS
There had been a slight suspicion that low stalls could be fancied over the higher ones considering a couple of races earlier on the card, but despite the winner coming from one, the draw appeared to have little affect on the result. Ordinary sprint form in a relatively slow time.
Mey Blossom Official explanation: jockey said mare was denied a clear run
T/Plt: £272.40 to a £1 stake. Pool:£51,625.65 - 138.30 winning tickets T/Qpdt: £16.10 to a £1 stake. Pool:£3,626.08 - 166.30 winning tickets WG

1661 DUNDALK (A.W) (L-H)
Saturday, April 30

OFFICIAL GOING: Standard

1699a IRISH STALLION FARMS EUROPEAN BREEDERS FUND 2YO MEDIAN AUCTION MAIDEN 5f (P)
2:35 (2:37) 2-Y-O **£7,732** (£1,793; £784; £448)

RPR
1 **Naseem Sea (IRE)**[15] 1375 2-8-12 .... WJSupple 8 84
(P D Deegan, Ire) *chsd ldrs: 4th 1/2-way: impr to chal 2f out and sltly hmpd: rdn into narrow ld under 1f out: sn jnd: jst edgd ahd cl home* **7/1**
2 *nk* **Danziger (IRE)**[13] 1426 2-8-12 .... PJSmullen 2 83
(D K Weld, Ire) *chsd ldrs: 3rd 1/2-way: cl 4th and hmpd 2f out: rdn to chal 1f out: sn jnd ldr: no ex cl home* **7/2**[2]
3 *3* **Pea Shooter**[14] 1383 2-9-3 .... PhillipMakin 3 77
(Kevin Ryan) *sn led: chal 2f out: rdn and hdd under 1f out: no ex and kpt on same pce* **1/1**[1]
4 *4* **Hexagonal (IRE)**[15] 1375 2-9-3 .... GFCarroll 7 63
(Lee Smyth, Ire) *prom: 2nd 1/2-way: rn arnd 2f out: rdn in 4th and no ex 1 1/2f out: kpt on same pce* **10/1**
5 *1 ¾* **Greek Canyon (IRE)**[15] 1375 2-9-3 .... KLatham 6 56
(G M Lyons, Ire) *mid-div: 6th 1/2-way: rdn 2f out: no imp and kpt on one pce* **25/1**
6 *shd* **Homecoming Queen (IRE)** 2-8-12 .... CO'Donoghue 5 51
(A P O'Brien, Ire) *chsd ldrs early: sn outpcd: 5th 1/2-way: rdn in 7th 2f out: mod 6th 1f out: kpt on one pce* **4/1**[3]
7 *1 ½* **Yo Credo (IRE)**[13] 1426 2-8-12 .... SeamieHeffernan 4 46
(Irene J Monaghan, Ire) *mid-div: 7th 1/2-way: rdn into 5th and no imp 2f out: kpt on one pce* **50/1**
8 *4* **Beau Amadeus (IRE)** 2-9-3 .... CDHayes 9 36
(Adrian McGuinness, Ire) *slowly away: a towards rr* **25/1**
9 *¾* **Light Of Equuleus (IRE)** 2-8-9 .... BACurtis(3) 10 28
(T G McCourt, Ire) *in rr of mid-div thrght: nvr a factor* **33/1**
10 *1* **Doonard Prince (IRE)** 2-9-0 .... ShaneFoley(3) 12 30
(Miss Elizabeth Doyle, Ire) *a towards rr* **20/1**
57.62 secs (57.62) **10 Ran SP% 131.2**
CSF £34.07 TOTE £8.50: £2.20, £1.02, £1.10; DF 51.00.
Owner Jaber Abdullah **Bred** Shadwell Estate Company Limited **Trained** The Curragh, Co Kildare

NOTEBOOK
Naseem Sea(IRE) fulfilled the promise of her debut third to Ishvana (since second to a promising sort at Cork) by grinding out a narrow victory in what looked a decent maiden over the minimum trip. She did have to wait for the stewards to give the green light after some interference inside the final furlong, but it was no surprise to hear that there was no alteration to the outcome as it was more greenness than anything else that brought the first three home close together in the closing stages. (op 6/1)
Danziger(IRE) had ran well over this trip at the Curragh and Navan and this was another sound effort. There was nothing ungenuine about her effort either and despite some unfortunate figures now against her name, she just looks to have come up against better horses. She should open her account soon. (op 3/1)
Pea Shooter, runner-up on his Doncaster debut, was well supported to pay a winning visit. However, after making much of the running and looking the likeliest winner passing the 2f pole, the son of Piccolo had nothing more to give inside the final furlong and faded into third. (op 1/1 tchd 10/11)
Hexagonal(IRE) was just a head behind Naseem Sea on his debut earlier in the month and although she was further behind that rival here, it was another big effort from the cheaply bought son of One Cool Cat, who looks sure to pick up a maiden at some stage.
Greek Canyon(IRE) was a head further back and could benefit from a step up in trip. (op 20/1)
Homecoming Queen(IRE) came in for a flurry of support just before the off was a shade disappointing and looked one-paced in the home straight after settling well in the early stages. (op 7/1 tchd 8/1)

1704a DUNDALK STADIUM ON FACEBOOK 3YO MAIDEN 1m 2f 150y(P)
5:10 (5:13) 3-Y-O **£5,948** (£1,379; £603; £344)

RPR
1 **Smartcity (USA)**[20] 1260 3-9-5 .... CDHayes 8 79+
(Andrew Oliver, Ire) *chsd ldrs: 4th 1/2-way: 3rd 4f out: rdn 1 1/2f out: chal under 1f out: led last 100yds: kpt on wl* **5/1**[3]
2 *2* **Alayir (IRE)**[34] 1009 3-9-5 82 .... NGMcCullagh 9 76
(John M Oxx, Ire) *chsd ldr in 2nd: chal 2f out: rdn to take narrow ld 1f out: hdd fnl 100yds: no ex and kpt on same pce* **6/4**[1]
3 *hd* **Warrior Song (IRE)** 3-9-5 .... PJSmullen 1 75
(P D Deegan, Ire) *chsd ldrs: 6th 1/2-way: hdwy into 4th 3f out: rdn in 5th 2f out: 4th 1f out: kpt on same pce fnl f* **14/1**
4 *shd* **Takapour (IRE)**[27] 1120 3-9-2 .... ShaneFoley(3) 6 75
(M Halford, Ire) *mid-div: 8th 1/2-way: hdwy into 6th 2f out: rdn and nt clr run briefly in 5th 1f out: kpt on same pce fnl f* **12/1**
5 *¾* **Carrowbeg (IRE)**[14] 1415 3-9-5 .... PhillipMakin 10 74
(Mark Johnston) *led: chal 2f out: rdn and hdd 1f out: no ex ins fnl f* **15/2**
6 *11* **Amen (IRE)** 3-9-5 .... SeamieHeffernan 3 52
(A P O'Brien, Ire) *stmbld leaving stalls: chsd ldrs: 5th 1/2-way: rdn in 4th whn edgd lft and c across rival 2f out: lost action and eased* **10/3**[2]
7 *16* **De Vesci (IRE)**[20] 1260 3-9-5 .... KJManning 7 21
(J T Gorman, Ire) *chsd ldrs: 3rd 1/2-way: rdn in 5th 3f out: no ex ent st: wknd* **66/1**
8 *3* **Midnight Show (IRE)**[14] 1417 3-8-12 .... DJBenson(7) 4 —
(G M Lyons, Ire) *a towards rr: wknd 3f out* **33/1**
9 *¾* **El Gran Torino (IRE)**[20] 1260 3-9-5 .... KLatham 5 —
(G M Lyons, Ire) *mid-div: 7th 1/2-way: rdn 3f out: no imp whn hmpd 2f out: wknd* **14/1**
10 *1 ¼* **Campas Bay (IRE)**[141] 7822 3-9-5 .... (p) GFCarroll 2 —
(M Halford, Ire) *a towards rr: wknd 4f out* **33/1**
2m 16.64s (136.64) **10 Ran SP% 119.9**
CSF £13.14 TOTE £5.50: £1.30, £1.10, £3.40; DF 14.90.
Owner Peter Thomas **Bred** Airlie Stud **Trained** Caledon, Co Tyrone

■ Stewards' Enquiry : Seamie Heffernan three-day ban: careless riding (May 15, 17, 20)
C D Hayes caution: use of the whip

NOTEBOOK
Smartcity(USA) ◆ was sent off at 50-1 for a high-quality maiden won by Quest For Peace at Leopardstown on his debut but he ran a lot better than his starting price suggested and finished sixth of the 15 runners after shaping with plenty of promise. He wasn't anything near that price here with plenty of observers penning him into their notebooks after that debut effort. After settling in mid-division, Chris Hayes eased his mount to the outside on the home turn and he galloped on well for a decisive success. The further he went, the more impressive he looked and he looks sure to get 1m4f. The son of Smarty Jones could be a decent long-term prospect. (op 5/1 tchd 11/2)
Alayir(IRE) was strongly supported but he is becoming expensive to follow and looked devoid of a turn of foot in the closing stages here. Niall McCullagh, who was looking for a treble, gave his mount every chance of shedding his maiden tag, and hit the front passing the 2f pole but he was unable to fend off the winner and just held on for second. (op 6/4 tchd 11/8)
Warrior Song(IRE) ◆ made an eye-catching debut. A half-brother to King Of Rome, he looked likely to play a hand in the finish entering the final furlong but just ran out of steam and looks sure to come on a lot for the run. (op 12/1)
Takapour(IRE), in the second colours of the Aga Khan, stepped up considerably on his Curragh effort. (op 10/1)
Carrowbeg(IRE) travelled sweetly at the head of affairs but didn't appear to stay on his first try at 1m2f. (op 7/1)
Amen(IRE), a beautifully-bred son of Galileo, looked to be fighting a losing battle when colliding with El Gran Torino on his inside over 1f out. Both were eased down after and Seamus Heffernan was given a three-day ban by the stewards. (op 7/2 tchd 4/1)

1705a WWW.DUNDALKSTADIUM.COM RACE 1m 2f 150y(P)
5:40 (5:45) 4-Y-0+ **£7,435** (£1,724; £754; £431)

RPR
1 **Address Unknown**[243] 5619 4-9-2 108 .... (b) PJSmullen 1 92+
(D K Weld, Ire) *trckd ldr in 2nd: chal 2f out: rdn to ld 1f out: kpt on strly ins fnl f: clr clsng stages* **8/11**[1]
2 *3 ½* **Stephen's Green (USA)**[15] 1378 4-9-6 85 .... KJManning 4 87
(James M Ryan, Ire) *hld up in last: niggled along 3f out: 3rd 2f out: cl up 1 1/2f out: no ex ins fnl f: kpt on same pce to 2nd cl home* **6/1**[3]
3 *nk* **Bikini Babe (IRE)**[14] 1416 4-8-11 .... PhillipMakin 3 77+
(Mark Johnston) *led: rdn and chal 2f out: hdd 1f out: no ex ins fnl f: lost 2nd cl home* **5/2**[2]
4 *1 ¾* **Plum Sugar (IRE)**[169] 7434 4-8-11 86 .... CDHayes 2 74+
(P J Prendergast, Ire) *settled 3rd: rdn in cl 4th 2f out: no ex over 1f out: kpt on same pce* **12/1**
2m 16.15s (136.15) **4 Ran SP% 108.5**
CSF £5.48 TOTE £1.60; DF 2.90.
Owner K Abdulla **Bred** Juddmonte Farms Ltd **Trained** The Curragh, Co Kildare

NOTEBOOK
Address Unknown was entitled to win this and while he wasn't overly impressive in disposing of his three rivals, he did it quite well in the end after looking in a spot of bother passing the 2f pole. After opening his account in a 1m maiden at this track, the son of Oasis Dream went on to finish second to Midas Touch in the Derrinstown Derby Trial, so if he reproduced anything near as good as that effort, he was always going to prove hard to beat here. He doesn't look the most straightforward type and the race was delayed a few minutes as he was unruly in the stalls. But despite those antics, he broke well enough and was soon tracking the pacesetting Bikini Babe. Pat Smullen switched to the outside of his main rival after entering the home straight and after briefly looking in trouble; he found an extra gear inside the final furlong to win quite cosily. Connections remarked afterwards that a step up to 1m4f might be the next move. (op 4/6 tchd 8/13)
Stephen's Green(USA) was taking a big step up in grade after winning an ordinary-looking maiden at this venue a fortnight ago but proved himself to be an improving type and mounted a big challenge down the outside passing the 2f marker. A step into handicap company, where his original rating of 85 looks workable, could be next on his agenda. (op 9/1 tchd 10/1)
Bikini Babe(IRE) was a decent juvenile and ran well on her last appearance here when finishing third to Shimmering Moment last November. But she hasn't fired this term and after getting an easy lead throughout, folded tamely in the home straight. (op 2/1 tchd 11/4)
Plum Sugar(IRE) was rated 22lb inferior to the winner going into the race and it was no surprise to see her struggle at the business end of the race. (op 16/1 tchd 10/1)

1706a CROWNE PLAZA LEADING JOCKEY & TRAINER CHAMPIONSHIP 3YO H'CAP 1m 2f 150y(P)
6:10 (6:11) (50-80,80) 3-Y-O **£5,948** (£1,379; £603; £344)

RPR
1 **Lexi's Boy (IRE)**[75] 543 3-9-0 70 .... PhillipMakin 5 75
(Kevin Ryan) *mde all: chal 2f out: rdn and strly pressed ins fnl f: kpt on wl u.p* **15/2**
2 *¾* **Black Belt (IRE)**[29] 1089 3-9-2 72 .... PJSmullen 1 76
(Tracey Collins, Ire) *chsd ldrs: 3rd 1/2-way: rdn over 2f out: styd on into 2nd 1f out: sn strly pressed ldr: no ex cl home* **14/1**
3 *1* **Crystal Belle (IRE)**[22] 1227 3-9-5 78 .... ShaneFoley(3) 7 80
(Patrick Martin, Ire) *chsd ldrs: 4th 1/2-way: rdn 2f out: kpt on same pce fr over 1f out* **13/2**[3]
4 *¾* **Via Del Corso**[13] 1429 3-7-11 60 oh9 .... (t) DarrenEdwardEgan(7) 4 61
(Paul W Flynn, Ire) *hld up towards rr: hdwy into 6th 2f out: rdn in 5th and no imp 1f out: kpt on same pce fnl f* **16/1**
5 *hd* **Reasons Unknown (IRE)**[13] 1429 3-8-7 63 .... KLatham 6 63
(G M Lyons, Ire) *mid-div: 5th 1/2-way: rdn in 7th 2f out: kpt on same pce fr over 1f out* **6/1**[2]
6 *hd* **Haziyna (IRE)**[34] 1008 3-9-7 80 .... BACurtis(3) 8 80
(John M Oxx, Ire) *chsd ldr in 2nd: rdn in 3rd 1 1/2f out: no ex fnl f* **5/4**[1]
7 *2* **President Lincoln (USA)**[20] 1258 3-8-13 72 .... JPO'Brien(3) 9 68
(A P O'Brien, Ire) *hld up towards rr: no imp st: kpt on one pce* **6/1**[2]
8 *nk* **Watch The Birdie (IRE)**[34] 1008 3-8-8 69 .... SHJames(5) 3 64
(Kevin Prendergast, Ire) *mid-div: 7th 1/2-way: rdn into 5th 2f out: no ex over 1f out* **14/1**
9 *¾* **Dearest (IRE)**[41] 927 3-8-4 60 oh2 .... DMGrant 2 54
(John Joseph Murphy, Ire) *mid-div: rdn and dropped towards rr 3f out: no ex* **20/1**
2m 15.52s (135.52) **9 Ran SP% 122.1**
Daily Double: Not won. Pool of £560.00 carried over to Gorwan Park Sunday. CSF £111.10 CT £731.23 TOTE £6.80: £2.60, £3.00, £2.50; DF 23.40.
Owner Mrs Margaret Forsyth **Bred** R S Cockerill (farms) Ltd & Peter Dodd **Trained** Hambleton, N Yorks

NOTEBOOK
Lexi's Boy(IRE) made it a hat-trick of wins after making every yard of the running for Phillip Makin, who deserves credit for this front-running ride as he kept enough in reserve to hold off a plethora of challengers in the home straight. After breaking well, Makin made his intentions known early and sent Kevin Ryan's charge straight into the lead. He wasn't pressurised either and was allowed to saunter along at his own pace. There seemed to be plenty travelling well in behind turning for home but he kept finding and knew how to win. (op 6/1)
Black Belt(IRE) was never far away and looked as if he might creep past the winner on the inside passing the 1f pole. But Lexi's Boy proved a tough nut to crack and Pat Smullen had to settle for second. Still, this was a fine showing and the daughter of Big Bad Bob should be good enough to shed her maiden tag soon. (op 10/1)
Crystal Belle(IRE) is a model of consistency at this venue and ran her usual sound race. She travelled well into the straight and Shane Foley looked as if he had plenty in the tank when switching to the outside for a run after turning for home but she just stayed on at the one pace. (op 6/1)
Via Del Corso did best of those held up and could be of interest next time.
Reasons Unknown(IRE) stayed on well enough but never really looked like winning.
Haziyna(IRE) was far too keen in the early stages and refused to settle for Ben Curtis. That proved her undoing as she travelled best into the straight and looked a likely winner passing the 2f pole. As expected though, she ran out of petrol in the closing stages and was unable to follow up her impressive recent Leopardstown success. (op 15/8)
T/Jkpt: Not won. T/Plt: @91.00. Pool of @12,406.75 - 102 winning units. II

1700 - 1703a (Foreign Racing) - See Raceform Interactive

[1597] LONGCHAMP (R-H)
Saturday, April 30

OFFICIAL GOING: Turf: good

1707a PRIX DE BARBEVILLE - BEACHCOMBER HOTELS LE DINAROBIN *****LUXE (GROUP 3) (4YO+) (TURF) 1m 7f 110y
1:30 (12:00) 4-Y-0+ **£34,482** (£13,793; £10,344; £6,896; £3,448)

RPR
1 **Dunaden (FR)**[63] [705] 5-9-1 0 .... GregoryBenoist 7 111
(M Delzangles, France) *racd towards rr: swtchd wd early in st: qcknd wl to ld 1f out: r.o wl* **113/10**
2 *1* **Mashoor (FR)**[22] [1231] 4-8-13 0 .... MaximeGuyon 5 112
(A Fabre, France) *racd 2nd: rdn 1 1/2f out: led briefly 1f out: sn hdd: r.o wl ins fnl f to jst hold 2nd on line* **13/1**
3 *nse* **Kasbah Bliss (FR)**[22] [1231] 9-9-1 0 .... ThierryThulliez 9 110
(F Doumen, France) *racd towards rr: rdn 2f out: qcknd wl between horses ins fnl f: narrowly missed 2nd on line* **43/10**[2]
4 *nk* **Brigantin (USA)**[16] [1352] 4-9-1 0 .... FlavienPrat 3 114
(A Fabre, France) *racd midfield: rdn 2f out: qcknd wl 1f out: styd on wl fnl 100yds* **32/1**
5 *2* **Marinous (FR)**[35] [1001] 5-9-5 0 .... DavyBonilla 1 111
(F Head, France) *racd towards rr: rdn early in st to cl on ldrs: ev ch 1f out: no ex* **16/1**
6 *shd* **Americain (USA)**[22] [1231] 6-9-7 0 .... GeraldMosse 2 113
(A De Royer-Dupre, France) *racd in midfield: rdn 2f out: nt qckn: styd on clsng stages* **1/1**[1]
7 *snk* **Le Larron (IRE)**[22] [1231] 4-8-13 0 .... ChristopheSoumillon 8 109
(A De Royer-Dupre, France) *sn led and stl in front 1 1/2f out: rdn: hdd 1f out: no ex: styd on* **9/2**[3]
8 *2 1/2* **Los Cristianos (FR)**[22] [1231] 5-9-1 0 .... Christophe-PatriceLemaire 6 104
(A Couetil, France) *settled 4th: stl prom whn rdn 1 1/2f out: no ex: fdd* **18/1**
9 *2 1/2* **Foundation Filly**[42] 4-8-6 0 .... SylvainRuis 4 97
(F Doumen, France) *settled 3rd: bhd ldrs 2f out: hrd rdn: no ex: fdd* **67/1**

3m 21.47s (-0.03)
WFA 4 from 5yo+ 3lb **9** Ran SP% **118.0**
WIN (incl. 1 euro stake): 12.30. PLACES: 2.90, 3.30, 1.60. DF: 46.60. SF: 133.90.
Owner Pearl Bloodstock Ltd **Bred** Comte E Decazes **Trained** France

NOTEBOOK
Dunaden(FR) came from last to first to score and, although causing minor interefernce in doing so, was allowed to keep the race. This was his first start for his new trainer since leaving Richard Gibson, and he will go for the Prix Vicomtesse Vigier next.
Kasbah Bliss(FR) did not get the clearest of passages, having come from the back like the winner. He will be kept fresh for the Ascot Gold Cup.
Americain(USA), unlucky on his previous start, disappointed this time for no obvious reason.

1708a PRIX GANAY - PRIX AIR MAURITIUS (GROUP 1) (4YO+) (TURF) 1m 2f 110y
2:45 (12:00) 4-Y-0+ **£147,775** (£59,120; £29,560; £14,767; £7,396)

RPR
1 **Planteur (IRE)**[20] [1266] 4-9-2 0 .... ChristopheSoumillon 7 124+
(E Lellouche, France) *settled 5th: swtchd towards rail 1 1/2f out: qcknd between horses to take ld 1f out: r.o wl: comf* **1/1**[1]
2 *1* **Sarafina (FR)**[209] [6612] 4-8-13 0 .... Christophe-PatriceLemaire 6 118
(A De Royer-Dupre, France) *settled 4th: qcknd wl on outside 1 1/2f out: r.o strly fnl 100yds* **3/1**[2]
3 *1* **Cirrus Des Aigles (FR)**[42] [920] 5-9-2 0 .... FranckBlondel 4 119
(Mme C Barande-Barbe, France) *settled 3rd: rdn 1 1/2f out: r.o wl fnl f* **11/1**
4 *1/2* **Cape Blanco (IRE)**[35] [1002] 4-9-2 0 .... JamieSpencer 2 118
(A P O'Brien, Ire) *sn led: stl in front 1 1/2f out: hrd rdn: hdd 1f out: styd on clsng stages* **6/1**[3]
5 *nse* **Ley Hunter (USA)**[20] [1266] 4-9-2 0 .... MaximeGuyon 3 118
(A Fabre, France) *settled towards rr: rdn early in st: styd on wl fnl f* **8/1**
6 *snk* **Silver Pond (FR)**[20] [1266] 4-9-2 0 .... DavyBonilla 1 118
(C Laffon-Parias, France) *s.i.s: settled at rr: styd on wl fnl f* **11/1**
7 *15* **Pouvoir Absolu**[46] [860] 6-9-2 0 .... (b) AnthonyCrastus 5 88
(E Lellouche, France) *racd 2nd as pcemaker for eventual wnr: stl prom 1 1/2f out: eased fnl f* **38/1**

2m 7.29s (-2.91) **7** Ran SP% **119.6**
WIN (incl. 1 euro stake): 2.00 (Planteur and Pouvoir Absolu coupled). PLACES: 1.40, 2.00. SF: 5.90.
Owner Ecurie Wildenstein **Bred** Dayton Investments Ltd **Trained** Lamorlaye, France

FOCUS
A decent renewal of this traditionally informative Group 1 which has been won in recent years by the subsequent Prince of Wales's Stakes winners Vision d'Etat and Duke of Marmalade and it looks as though that race at Royal Ascot is the obvious destination for Planteur too who retained his unbeaten run readily at the conclusion of a race run at no more than a fair gallop despite the presence of an apparent pacemaker.

NOTEBOOK
Planteur(IRE) ◆ had run out a very cosy winner of the Prix D'Harcourt here last month when ridden by Christophe Soumillon for the first time and having Ley Hunter and Silver Pond behind, and he once again put those rivals to the sword as well as the more talented Sarafina and Cape Blanco by settling matters with an equally impressive turn of foot, the winning margin once again not reflecting his superiority on the day after having to extricate himself from a pocket early in the straight. Ascot with its short run-in looks ideal for one with his sit-and-pounce running style, and right now he looks to have very strong claims if brought over to the Royal meeting.
Sarafina(FR) quickly developed into a top-class filly last year, winning the Prix Saint-Alary and the Prix de Diane before finishing third to Midday in the Prix Vermeille and Workforce in the Arc, where she didn't get the best of runs. This trip is probably short enough for her nowadays at the very top level and she lost nothing in defeat behind a much-improved rival with slightly more guns at the trip, unable to match that one's turn of foot having been ideally placed entering the straight. She looks to have lost none of her ability and will be extremely hard to beat back at 1m4f next time.
Cirrus Des Aigles(FR) is a reliable performer albeit one not quite up to Group 1 standard, his reappearance second in the Prix Exbury when having Silver Pond just behind being a good indication of his standing among the older French horses. Though he ran well having every chance, like a couple of others behind he probably finished closer than he was entitled to on account of the gallop.
Cape Blanco(IRE) hadn't been seen to best effect in the Dubai World Cup on his return and wasn't at his best here either, his rider electing to head off the pacemaker and make the running but in doing so at the pace he did ended up playing more to the strengths of the winner than his own, readily outdone for a turn of speed. He might yet bounce back to his best away from heavily watered French ground but his Irish Champion Stakes win is starting to look something of a standout effort.
Ley Hunter(USA) is a bit better than this run suggests as he was always up against it spotting Planteur a couple of lengths into the straight and didn't get the best of runs while making his effort.
Silver Pond(FR) was also set a bit to so but was never helping his rider much by wanting to hang to his right.
Pouvoir Absolu proved a poor excuse for a pacemaker

1709a PRIX VANTEAUX - BEACHCOMBER HOTELS LE ROYAL PALM *****LUXE (GROUP 3) (3YO FILLIES) (TURF) 1m 1f 55y
3:15 (12:00) 3-Y-0 **£34,482** (£13,793; £10,344; £6,896; £3,448)

RPR
1 **Epic Love (IRE)**[18] 3-9-0 0 .... StephanePasquier 4 108
(P Bary, France) *settled 4th: rdn 1 1/2f out: qcknd wl to chse ldr ins fnl f: got up cl home* **3/1**[2]
2 *hd* **La Pernelle (IRE)**[32] 3-9-0 0 .... Christophe-PatriceLemaire 6 107
(Y De Nicolay, France) *settled in 2nd: rdn into ld 1f out: r.o wl: hdd cl home* **27/1**
3 *3/4* **Starformer (USA)**[16] 3-9-0 0 .... JohanVictoire 1 105
(Mme C Head-Maarek, France) *settled 3rd: rdn 1 1/2f out: picked up wl: r.o strly fnl 100yds* **4/1**[3]
4 *1/2* **Camelia Rose (FR)**[26] 3-9-0 0 .... IoritzMendizabal 5 104
(J-C Rouget, France) *led tl hdd 1f out: styd on fnl 100yds* **14/5**[1]
5 *1* **Finding Neverland (FR)**[186] 3-9-0 0 .... ThierryThulliez 7 102
(N Clement, France) *settled at rr: r.o wl fnl f* **20/1**
6 *nse* **Margravine (USA)**[11] 3-9-0 0 .... MaximeGuyon 3 102
(A Fabre, France) *racd towards rr: rdn 1 1/2f out: r.o fnl f* **9/1**
7 *1 1/2* **Putyball (USA)**[170] [7415] 3-9-0 0 .... GregoryBenoist 8 99
(X Nakkachdji, France) *settled 6th: rdn and no ex fnl f* **58/10**
8 *2 1/2* **La Mouche**[30] [1069] 3-9-0 0 .... AnthonyCrastus 2 93
(E Lellouche, France) *settled 5th: rdn 1 1/2f out: no ex: fdd fnl f* **15/2**

1m 56.11s (0.81) **8** Ran SP% **116.1**
WIN (incl. 1 euro stake): 4.00. PLACES: 1.80, 4.80, 2.20. DF: 33.20. SF: 57.50.
Owner James Richard Treptow **Bred** Round Hill Stud **Trained** Chantilly, France

NOTEBOOK
Epic Love(IRE) had to work hard to get past the long-time leader, and her trainer would like to go directly for the Prix de Diane.
La Pernelle(IRE), the owner's second-string, put up a brave effort and only just lost out.

HAMILTON (R-H)
Sunday, May 1

OFFICIAL GOING: Good (good to firm in places; 9.5)
Rail realignment around the loop increased distances on round course by about 8yds.
Wind: Fresh, across Weather: Hot, sunny

1710 TRY TOTEQUICKPICK ON TOTEPOOL BETS MAIDEN STKS 1m 65y
2:30 (2:30) (Class 5) 3-5-Y-0 **£3,238** (£963; £481; £240) Stalls Low

Form RPR
-242 1 **Honest Deal**[15] [1415] 3-9-1 75 .... PJMcDonald 5 79
(Alan Swinbank) *mde all: qcknd clr 2f out: readily* **2/5**[1]
2 *8* **Rio Park (IRE)** 3-9-1 0 .... TomEaves 2 61
(Bryan Smart) *hld up in tch: effrt over 2f out: chsd (clr) wnr appr fnl f: no imp* **6/1**[3]
00- 3 *2 3/4* **Ninth Parallel (USA)**[184] [7202] 3-9-1 0 .... FrannyNorton 4 54
(Ann Duffield) *prom: pushed along 1/2-way: effrt over 2f out: one pce fr over 1f out* **33/1**
0-3 4 *1/2* **Honest Buck**[23] [1210] 4-10-0 0 .... FrederikTylicki 1 56
(Kate Walton) *t.k.h: trckd ldrs: rdn: edgd rt and chsd wnr over 2f out to appr fnl f: no ex* **11/1**
0- 5 *3* **Walleyd (IRE)**[186] [7171] 4-9-7 0 .... RossSmith(7) 3 49
(Linda Perratt) *s.i.s: hld up: effrt over 3f out: no imp fr 2f out* **100/1**
042- 6 *4 1/2* **Sam Nombulist**[191] [7049] 3-9-1 74 .... RussKennemore 6 36
(Richard Whitaker) *t.k.h: sn prom on outside: rdn and drifted lft fr over 3f out: wknd wl over 1f out* **4/1**[2]
0-40 7 *2 1/4* **Machir Bay**[16] [1374] 4-10-0 41 .... TonyHamilton 8 34
(Keith Dalgleish) *trckd wnr to over 2f out: sn wknd* **33/1**
5 8 *6* **American Lover (FR)**[17] [1328] 4-9-9 0 .... PaddyAspell 9 —
(John Wainwright) *missed break: bhd: rdn over 3f out: sn btn* **50/1**
00/ 9 *2 1/2* **Wing N Prayer (IRE)**[577] [6408] 4-9-9 50 .... PatrickMathers 7 —
(Alan Berry) *hld up: rdn over 3f out: wknd fr 2f out* **80/1**

1m 45.89s (-2.51) **Going Correction** -0.325s/f (Firm)
WFA 3 from 4yo 13lb **9** Ran SP% **124.1**
Speed ratings (Par 103): **99,91,88,87,84 80,78,72,69**
toteswingers: 1&2 £1.90, 1&3 £6.80, 2&3 £13.00. CSF £4.02 TOTE £1.40: £1.02, £2.80, £5.90; EX 4.80.
Owner Guy Reed **Bred** G Reed **Trained** Melsonby, N Yorks

FOCUS
A weak maiden, lacking depth. The winner was entitled to score easily with his main form rival disappointing, but still clocked a decent time.

Sam Nombulist Official explanation: jockey said gelding hung left throughout

1711 BET TOTEPOOL ON THE GUINEAS TANGERINE TREES CONDITIONS STKS 5f 4y

3:05 (3:06) (Class 3) 3-Y-O **£7,771** (£2,312; £1,155; £577) **Stalls** High

Form RPR

005- **1** **Shoshoni Wind**[225] 6176 3-7-13 92 .... JulieBurke(5) 2 91
(Kevin Ryan) *mde all: shkn up over 1f out: kpt on strly fnl f* **7/2**[3]

24-5 **2** *2* **Cocktail Charlie**[22] 1241 3-8-9 94 .... DavidAllan 4 89
(Tim Easterby) *chsd wnr: effrt over 1f out: kpt on same pce ins fnl f* **11/8**[1]

223- **3** *1 1/4* **Crimson Knot (IRE)**[186] 7174 3-8-4 78 .... PatrickMathers 3 79
(Alan Berry) *trckd ldrs: rdn over 2f out: effrt over 1f out: kpt on same pce fnl f* **25/1**

113- **4** *9* **Excel Bolt**[318] 3100 3-9-0 102 .... TomEaves 1 57
(Bryan Smart) *t.k.h: cl up tl hung rt and wknd fr 2f out: fin lame* **6/4**[2]

58.20 secs (-1.80) **Going Correction** -0.30s/f (Firm) **4** Ran SP% **108.2**
Speed ratings (Par 103): **102,98,96,82**
CSF £8.73 TOTE £4.60; EX 9.40.
Owner Hambleton Racing Ltd XVI **Bred** Mrs A F Tullie **Trained** Hambleton, N Yorks

FOCUS
A small field, but a fascinating contest.

NOTEBOOK
Shoshoni Wind, fifth at Group 3 level over 6f as a juvenile and officially rated 92, made all and scored cosily. Quickly into her stride and soon racing up against the stands' rail, she upped the tempo after halfway and left the rest struggling. This appears her ideal trip and connections are contemplating another 5f conditions event at the Dante meeting. The alternative is seemingly a 6f Group 3 at the Curragh in early June. (op 11-2)
Cocktail Charlie, 5lb better off with Excel Bolt than when losing out by a short-head at Musselburgh in June 2010, could never get to grips with the winner. He chased her throughout but, when put under pressure, did not quicken enough to get alongside. (op 13-8 tchd 7-4)
Crimson Knot(IRE), third off 78 in a Musselburgh nursery last backend, puts the overall form of the race into perspective. Last at halfway, she plugged on unavailingly in the closing stages. (op 33-1)
Excel Bolt, third in the 2010 Norfolk Stakes but off since due to a bone chip in a knee, tried to match early strides with the first two. He began to drift right soon after halfway, however, as if he was feeling something. He reportedly finished lame and will probably need more time off now. Official explanation: vet said colt finished lame (op Evens)

1712 ALEX FERGUSSON MEMORIAL H'CAP 6f 5y

3:40 (3:41) (Class 5) (0-70,65) 4-Y-0+ **£2,914** (£867; £433; £216) **Stalls** High

Form RPR

0435 **1** **Toby Tyler**[16] 1368 5-9-2 61 ....(v) MickyFenton 5 70
(Paul Midgley) *sn drvn along towards rr in centre: hdwy over 1f out: led wl ins fnl f: r.o* **16/1**

6110 **2** *3/4* **Pelmanism**[22] 1239 4-9-1 63 ....(b) AmyRyan(3) 4 70+
(Kevin Ryan) *s.i.s centre: hdwy and prom 1/2-way: led and edgd rt over 1f out: hdd wl ins fnl f: r.o* **6/1**[3]

06-6 **3** *nk* **Two Turtle Doves (IRE)**[18] 1307 5-8-9 61 .... JosephYoung(7) 11 67
(Michael Mullineaux) *prom stands' side: rdn over 2f out: hdwy and ev ch ins fnl f: kpt on: hld nr fin* **12/1**

561- **4** *1 3/4* **Hellbender (IRE)**[192] 7047 5-8-13 63 .... DaleSwift(5) 9 63
(George Foster) *hld up stands' side: rdn over 2f out: r.o fnl f: nrst fin* **10/1**

11-0 **5** *2 1/2* **Henry Morgan**[22] 1239 4-9-5 64 .... TomEaves 10 56
(Bryan Smart) *prom stands' side: rdn over 2f out: no ex fnl f* **3/1**[1]

43-0 **6** *1 1/4* **Berbice (IRE)**[30] 1073 6-9-5 64 .... DavidAllan 3 52
(Linda Perratt) *prom centre tl rdn and no ex over 1f out* **12/1**

556- **7** *1/2* **Mandarin Spirit (IRE)**[186] 7175 11-9-6 65 ....(b) TonyHamilton 1 51
(Linda Perratt) *unruly bef s: led and sn clr: hdd over 1f out: sn btn* **33/1**

30-0 **8** *1* **Cheyenne Red (IRE)**[22] 1239 5-9-3 62 .... FrederikTylicki 7 45
(Michael Dods) *prom stands' side tl rdn and wknd appr fnl f* **4/1**[2]

543- **9** *1* **North Central (USA)**[191] 7056 4-8-13 61 .... GaryBartley(3) 8 41
(Jim Goldie) *midfield stands' side: rdn over 2f out: nvr able to chal* **13/2**

22-5 **10** *3 1/4* **Sandwith**[24] 1204 8-9-5 64 ....(v) LeeNewman 6 34
(George Foster) *in tch on outside of stands' side gp: rdn over 2f out: btn over 1f out* **14/1**

405- **11** *nse* **Distant Sun (USA)**[186] 7169 7-9-2 61 .... BarryMcHugh 2 30
(Linda Perratt) *hld up towards centre: pushed along 2f out: sn btn* **25/1**

1m 11.08s (-1.14) **Going Correction** -0.30s/f (Firm) **11** Ran SP% **110.4**
Speed ratings (Par 103): **95,94,93,91,87 86,85,84,82,78 78**
toteswingers: 1&2 £16.50, 1&3 £42.90, 2&3 £10.60. CSF £108.06 CT £1229.24 TOTE £21.10: £4.60, £3.20, £5.00; EX 169.20.
Owner Anthony D Copley **Bred** Whitsbury Manor Stud **Trained** Westow, N Yorks

FOCUS
A low-grade handicap in which the top weight was rated 65. The field split into two groups and went a decent pace. The winner is rated to his winter AW form.

1713 TOTEPOOL A BETTER WAY TO BET BUTTONHOOK H'CAP 1m 5f 9y

4:15 (4:15) (Class 3) (0-70,87) 4-Y-0+ **£7,771** (£2,312; £1,155; £577) **Stalls** Low

Form RPR

20-2 **1** **Becausewecan (USA)**[8] 1517 5-9-4 84 .... GregFairley 6 96+
(Mark Johnston) *mde all: qcknd clr over 3f out: rdn over 1f out: r.o wl: eased last 50yds* **11/4**[1]

50-2 **2** *3 1/2* **Royal Swain (IRE)**[32] 1036 5-9-0 80 .... PJMcDonald 3 85
(Alan Swinbank) *in tch: effrt over 3f out: chsd (clr) wnr over 1f out: no imp fnl f* **7/2**[2]

00-5 **3** *7* **Crackentorp**[26] 1154 6-9-7 87 .... GrahamGibbons 9 81
(Tim Easterby) *in tch: stdy hdwy 4f out: rdn and edgd rt over 2f out: sn no imp* **7/2**[2]

5140 **4** *1/2* **Record Breaker (IRE)**[8] 1517 7-9-0 80 ....(b) RoystonFfrench 1 74
(Mark Johnston) *sn chsng wnr: rdn over 3f out: lost 2nd over 1f out: wknd* **14/1**

0/0- **5** *2 1/2* **Bureaucrat**[47] 205 9-8-9 75 ....(p) FrederikTylicki 2 65
(Kate Walton) *hld up: drvn over 3f out: no imp fr 2f out* **20/1**

36-3 **6** *1/2* **Chookie Hamilton**[32] 1036 7-8-12 78 .... TomEaves 7 67
(Keith Dalgleish) *hld up in tch: effrt and rdn 3f out: nvr able to chal* **8/1**

0-05 **7** *3 3/4* **European Dream (IRE)**[8] 1517 8-9-0 80 .... TonyHamilton 8 63
(Richard Fahey) *hld up: rdn 1/2-way: sme hdwy and hung rt over 2f out: sn btn* **13/2**[3]

-060 **8** *24* **Valdan (IRE)**[11] 1491 7-7-11 68 oh10 ....(t) NeilFarley(5) 4 15
(Maurice Barnes) *slowly away: hld up: shortlived effrt over 3f out: sn btn: t.o* **66/1**

10-0 **9** *25* **Full Speed (GER)**[26] 1154 6-8-12 85 .... GarryWhillans(7) 5 —
(Alan Swinbank) *cl up: rdn 1/2-way: wknd over 3f out: t.o* **25/1**

2m 47.3s (-6.60) **Going Correction** -0.325s/f (Firm) **9** Ran SP% **112.3**
Speed ratings (Par 107): **107,104,100,100,98 98,96,81,65**
toteswingers: 1&2 £3.10, 1&3 £3.10, 2&3 £3.70. CSF £11.73 CT £32.70 TOTE £3.30: £1.10, £1.50, £2.20; EX 10.70.
Owner Douglas Livingston **Bred** Tony Holmes & Walter Zent **Trained** Middleham Moor, N Yorks

FOCUS
A decent handicap and on paper several appeared to have solid claims. it was well run in a decent time. The winner is rated back to his best.

NOTEBOOK
Becausewecan(USA) was 4lb higher than second at Musselburgh on his latest outing, but smoothly shrugged off that rise. Headed briefly at the outset, he soon took over in front and led for the remainder of the race. He had a healthy advantage turning for home and, although the second was closing in the final furlong, always had the upper hand. He clearly stays well and may handle a longer trip. (op 7-2)
Royal Swain(IRE), raised 3lb since his reappearance second at Catterick in March, probably ran close to the same level. Always in the first five, he went second 3f from home and tried hard to cut back the winner's lead. This was a solid effort. (op 4-1)
Crackentorp lined up bidding for his first win since 2008 and was far from disgraced. He too was in the leading quintet throughout and, while he never seriously threatened to collect, he plugged on gamely.
Record Breaker(IRE), 7lb higher than when scoring at Pontefract in early April, seems to need help with his mark. He chased the winner in mid-race, but was left well behind in the home straight. (op 12-1)
Bureaucrat, having his first Flat run for 470 days, was never in contention and has not scored in this discipline since 2008. (op 16-1)
Chookie Hamilton was 1lb lower than when third at Catterick last time out, but failed to take advantage of that small drop. The best position he held was fourth and he faded late on. (op 7-1)
European Dream(IRE)'s rider reported the gelding was never travelling. Official explanation: jockey said gelding never travelled (op 6-1 tchd 7-1)

1714 LIVE EQUINE ANATOMY HERE TODAY H'CAP 1m 65y

4:50 (4:52) (Class 5) (0-70,70) 4-Y-0+ **£2,914** (£867; £433; £216) **Stalls** Low

Form RPR

3-50 **1** **Euston Square**[30] 1075 5-9-7 70 .... FrederikTylicki 10 81
(Alistair Whillans) *in tch: hdwy to ld over 2f out: sn rdn and edgd rt: kpt on strly fnl f* **18/1**

32-4 **2** *2 1/2* **Spavento (IRE)**[13] 1440 5-8-7 56 oh1 .... DavidAllan 5 61
(Eric Alston) *in tch: rdn over 2f out: chsd wnr ins fnl f: r.o* **13/2**

6-03 **3** *hd* **Law To Himself (IRE)**[11] 1491 4-9-6 69 .... PJMcDonald 7 74+
(Alan Swinbank) *hld up: pushed along over 3f out: hdwy over 1f out: r.o wl fnl f* **5/1**[3]

315- **4** *1 1/2* **Key Breeze**[212] 6540 4-9-2 65 ....(t) TomEaves 3 66
(Kevin Ryan) *taken early to post: t.k.h: hld up: hdwy over 2f out: chsd wnr over 1f out to ins fnl f: no ex* **9/1**

3U3- **5** *1 1/2* **Botham (USA)**[183] 7230 7-8-8 57 .... AndrewMullen 12 55
(Jim Goldie) *hld up towards rr: drvn 3f out: kpt on fnl 2f: no imp* **16/1**

-422 **6** *3 3/4* **Bajan Flash**[6] 1559 4-9-4 67 ....(v) FrannyNorton 6 56
(David Nicholls) *t.k.h: cl up: effrt and chsd wnr fr over 2f out to over 1f out: sn btn* **11/4**[1]

506- **7** *1/2* **Mangham (IRE)**[120] 7988 6-9-5 68 .... LeeNewman 8 56
(George Foster) *hld up: hdwy on outside over 3f out: edgd rt and wknd over 1f out* **40/1**

0- **8** *nk* **Rosbertini**[205] 6710 5-8-7 56 oh1 .... BarryMcHugh 13 43
(Linda Perratt) *led tl hdd over 2f out: wknd over 1f out* **33/1**

3-02 **9** *3* **Swiftly Done (IRE)**[12] 1460 4-9-0 68 ....(b) NeilFarley(5) 1 48
(Declan Carroll) *s.i.s: hld up on ins: drvn along 3f out: btn over 1f out* **10/3**[2]

351- **10** *14* **Blue Noodles**[214] 6452 5-9-1 64 .... PaddyAspell 11 12
(John Wainwright) *prom tl rdn and wknd over 2f out* **11/1**

640- **11** *4 1/2* **Primo Way**[274] 4585 10-8-7 56 oh11 ....(be) PatrickMathers 9 —
(Donal Nolan) *cl up tl rdn and wknd over 3f out* **100/1**

1m 46.25s (-2.15) **Going Correction** -0.325s/f (Firm) **11** Ran SP% **115.6**
Speed ratings (Par 103): **97,94,94,92,91 87,87,86,83,69 65**
toteswingers: 1&2 £15.10, 1&3 £14.30, 2&3 £4.20. CSF £127.45 CT £693.28 TOTE £27.00: £5.30, £2.20, £1.80; EX 153.10.
Owner Granite City Racing **Bred** Juddmonte Farms Ltd **Trained** Newmill-On-Slitrig, Borders

FOCUS
Just a run-of-the-mill handicap, with the top weight rated 70, but it looked very competitive. The winner's best effort since he was a 3yo.

1715 CANCER RESEARCH CLAIMING STKS 6f 5y

5:25 (5:25) (Class 6) 4-6-Y-O **£2,047** (£604; £302) **Stalls** High

Form RPR

000- **1** **Saucy Brown (IRE)**[226] 6142 5-9-8 78 .... FrannyNorton 1 86
(David Nicholls) *t.k.h: trckd ldrs: swtchd lft and hdwy to ld over 1f out: drvn out fnl f* **7/2**[2]

2-05 **2** *1/2* **Esprit De Midas**[12] 1467 5-9-3 90 .... TomEaves 4 80
(Kevin Ryan) *chsd ldrs: outpcd over 3f out: rallied to chse wnr appr fnl f: r.o fin* **5/4**[1]

-000 **3** *4 1/2* **Mark Anthony (IRE)**[46] 870 4-8-12 70 ....(p) PJMcDonald 5 60
(Kevin Ryan) *sn w ldr: rdn and no ex appr fnl f* **11/1**

40-0 **4** *2 3/4* **Fol Hollow (IRE)**[25] 1166 6-9-1 88 .... PNolan(7) 2 62
(David Nicholls) *mde most to over 1f out: sn wknd* **4/1**[3]

0-0 **5** *1 1/4* **Go Go Green (IRE)**[30] 1073 5-8-7 77 .... GaryBartley(3) 3 46
(Jim Goldie) *hld up: rdn over 2f out: effrt over 1f out: btn fnl f* **5/1**

-600 **6** *1 3/4* **Areeg (IRE)**[32] 1038 4-7-11 42 ow1 .... VictorSantos(7) 6 34
(Alan Berry) *dwlt: bhd: effrt over 2f out: sn wknd* **100/1**

1m 10.63s (-1.57) **Going Correction** -0.30s/f (Firm) **6** Ran SP% **112.7**
Speed ratings: **98,97,91,87,86 83**
toteswingers: 1&2 £1.40, 1&3 £5.00, 2&3 £2.50. CSF £8.38 TOTE £5.90: £2.00, £1.90; EX 10.20.Esprit De Midas was claimed by Dandy Nicholls for £15,000.
Owner D Nicholls **Bred** Churchtown House Stud **Trained** Sessay, N Yorks

FOCUS
Not much encouraging recent form on offer in this small-field claimer, and it's doubtful how literally this can be taken. The poor sixth wasn't beaten far.

1716 RACING UK ON SKY 432 H'CAP 5f 4y

5:55 (5:55) (Class 6) (0-60,60) 4-Y-0+ **£2,047** (£604; £302) **Stalls** High

Form RPR

5064 **1** **Rio's Girl**[11] 1493 4-9-2 55 ....(p) TomEaves 1 64
(Kevin Ryan) *cl up: rdn to ld over 1f out: hld on wl fnl f* **7/2**[2]

55-3 **2** *hd* **Sharp Bullet (IRE)**[7] 1544 5-8-13 52 ....(p) RoystonFfrench 6 60
(Bruce Hellier) *in tch: effrt over 2f out: styd on wl fnl f* **11/2**[3]

3-14 **3** *hd* **Ballarina**[23] 1213 5-9-7 60 .... DavidAllan 8 68
(Eric Alston) *racd towards stands' side away fr main gp: led to over 1f out: kpt on fnl f: hld towards fin* **9/4**[1]

-306 **4** *2 1/4* **Dispol Grand (IRE)**[22] 1247 5-9-2 55 .... MickyFenton 10 54
(Paul Midgley) *hld up: hdwy over 1f out: kpt on fnl f: no imp* **6/1**

26-4 **5** *shd* **Dower Glen**[7] 1544 4-8-4 50 .... ShirleyTeasdale(7) 9 49
(Keith Dalgleish) *hld up: hdwy over 1f out: no imp fnl f* **14/1**

056- **6** 6 **Sumay Buoy (IRE)**[191] 7052 4-8-9 **48** AndrewMullen 5 26+
(Jean McGregor) *hmpd s and after 1f: bhd: rdn whn nt clr run over 1f out: nvr on terms* **50/1**

6500 **7** 2 ½ **Royal Blade (IRE)**[13] 1439 4-8-9 **48** FrannyNorton 3 17
(Alan Berry) *in tch: drvn 1/2-way: wknd over 1f out* **16/1**

0401 **8** 1 **Francis Albert**[12] 1469 5-8-10 **56** (p) JosephYoung(7) 7 21
(Michael Mullineaux) *cl up tl rdn and wknd over 1f out* **10/1**

060- **9** 1 **Midget**[208] 6656 4-8-11 **55** NeilFarley(5) 2 16
(Declan Carroll) *prom on outside: rdn after 2f: wknd fr 2f out* **8/1**

59.26 secs (-0.74) **Going Correction** -0.30s/f (Firm) **9** Ran SP% **117.4**

Speed ratings (Par 101): **93,92,92,88,88 79,75,73,71**

toteswingers: 1&2 £4.80, 1&3 £3.00, 2&3 £3.40. totesuper7: WIN: Not won. PLACE: £224.30 - 2 winning units. CSF £23.60 CT £52.57 TOTE £4.80: £1.60, £2.00, £1.40; EX 33.50.

Owner Tracey Gaunt & David Gibbons **Bred** Hellwood Stud Farm **Trained** Hambleton, N Yorks

FOCUS

A weak finale with the top weight rated 60. The winner is rated back to her best.

Sumay Buoy(IRE) Official explanation: jockey said gelding was denied a clear run

T/Plt: £225.20 to a £1 stake. Pool:£48,649.18 - 157.66 winning tickets. T/Qpdt: £42.60 to a £1 stake. Pool:£3,797.89 - 65.89 winning tickets. RY

1684 NEWMARKET (R-H)

Sunday, May 1

OFFICIAL GOING: Good to firm (8.9)

Stands' side course used with stalls on stands' side except for first race and 1000 Gns.

Wind: Strong, 1/2 against Weather: Sunny and breezy

1717 QIPCO SPONSORS BRITISH CHAMPIONS SERIES H'CAP 1m 4f

2:05 (2:05) (Class 2) (0-105,102) 4-Y-O+

£24,924 (£7,464; £3,732; £1,868; £932; £468) **Stalls** Centre

Form RPR

21-4 **1** **Times Up**[28] 1112 5-9-10 **102** RichardHughes 2 113
(John Dunlop) *t.k.h early: hld up in tch: hdwy to chse ldrs 3f out: rdn and effrt wl over 1f out: ev ch and drvn 1f out: sustained chal to ld last stride* **8/1**

212- **2** shd **Sharaayeen**[211] 6565 4-9-1 **93** RichardHills 4 104+
(B W Hills) *hld up in tch towards rr: smooth hdwy to trck ldrs 3f out: swtchd rt and qcknd to ld over 1f out: kpt on wl u.p fnl f tl hdd last stride* **9/2**[1]

615- **3** 2 ¼ **Life And Soul (IRE)**[198] 6889 4-9-0 **92** NeilCallan 6 99
(Amanda Perrett) *t.k.h: hld up wl in tch: hdwy to join ldrs 3f out: rdn wl over 1f out: outpcd by ldng pair 1f out: kpt on same pce after* **11/2**[2]

130- **4** 4 **The Fonz**[204] 6736 5-9-0 **92** RyanMoore 8 93
(Sir Michael Stoute) *hld up in tch: pushed along 3f out: hdwy and rdn ent fnl 2f: hung rt and outpcd by ldng trio over 1f out: one pce and no threat to ldrs fnl f* **7/1**[3]

54-5 **5** 1 **Nanton (USA)**[28] 1112 9-9-10 **102** DanielTudhope 3 101
(Jim Goldie) *stdd s: hld up in rr: hdwy whn pushed rt and hmpd 2f out: styd on same pce and no imp fr over 1f out* **33/1**

2-21 **6** 2 ¼ **Fox Hunt (IRE)**[44] 900 4-9-3 **95** (b) JoeFanning 12 90
(Mark Johnston) *t.k.h: chsd ldrs tl wnt 2nd 5f out: led 3f out: sn rdn: hdd over 1f out: sn btn: wknd fnl f* **11/2**[2]

25-6 **7** ¾ **Mr Willis**[29] 1100 5-8-11 **89** RobertHavlin 5 83
(Terry Clement) *stdd s: hld up in tch towards rr: hdwy to chse ldrs and rdn over 2f out: wknd wl over 1f out* **40/1**

100- **8** 7 **Yorgunnabelucky (USA)**[64] 5949 5-9-0 **92** (p) FrankieDettori 11 75
(Mark Johnston) *in tch in midfield: rdn and short-lived effrt ent fnl 2f: sn btn: no ch and eased ins fnl f* **20/1**

/14- **9** 10 **Coin Of The Realm (IRE)**[330] 2747 6-9-3 **95** GeorgeBaker 9 62
(Gary Moore) *stdd s: hld up in tch in last trio: rdn and wknd 2f out: wl bhd and eased ins fnl f* **16/1**

-111 **10** 5 **Sweet Origin**[39] 948 4-8-11 **89** AdamKirby 15 48
(Marco Botti) *t.k.h: chsd ldrs: hdwy and ev ch 3f out: wandered u.p 2f out: sn wknd: wl bhd and eased fnl f: t.o* **8/1**

534- **11** 4 **Perpetually (IRE)**[344] 2317 5-8-9 **87** MichaelHills 1 40
(Mark Johnston) *led for 2f: chsd ldr tl 5f out: wknd wl over 2f out: wl bhd over 1f out: eased ins fnl f: t.o* **16/1**

000- **12** 32 **Chiberta King**[198] 6889 5-9-2 **94** JimmyFortune 14 —
(Andrew Balding) *awkward leaving stalls and slowly away: rcvrd to ld after 2f: hdd 3f out: dropped out qckly ent fnl 2f: t.o and eased fnl f* **8/1**

2m 36.46s (4.46) **Going Correction** +0.45s/f (Yiel) **12** Ran SP% **116.7**

Speed ratings (Par 109): **103,102,101,98,98 96,96,91,84,81 78,57**

toteswingers: 1&2 £5.60, 1&3 £9.40, 2&3 £5.60. CSF £42.28 CT £217.86 TOTE £9.40: £3.20, £1.70, £1.60; EX 43.20 Trifecta £382.00 Pool: £1,177.21 - 2.28 winning units..

Owner Mrs I H Stewart-Brown & M J Meacock **Bred** I Stewart-Brown And M Meacock **Trained** Arundel, W Sussex

FOCUS

The going had quickened up overnight to just good to firm from good to firm, good in places, and the final mile had been watered with 6mm of water applied. The clerk of the course thought the head wind they faced was stronger than on Saturday. The day started off with a really competitive middle-distance handicap. The pace seemed to be fair despite a few taking a grip in behind, but the winning time was pretty slow. However, the form looks good for the grade and is rated positively.

NOTEBOOK

Times Up narrowly prevailed under a strong drive. He had looked a little disappointing on his return considering his starting odds, but that was easy to ignore after what he did on his first outing the previous year, and he returned to his best with a solid performance under top weight. He had verdicts over plenty he faced again here (he also loves both tracks at Newmarket) so it's safe to assume that he could operate at a slightly higher level if the opportunity arises. The Duke of Edinburgh Handicap at Royal Ascot is the target as long as the ground remains quick, although he will need to defy a stiff mark. (op 15-2 tchd 7-1)

Sharaayeen ◆ was tucked in towards the rear, but he came with what looked a well-timed effort before rivals rallied around him. He showed a good attitude on his first outing since October and is worthy of respect in similar contests this season. A drop in trip won't be against him. (tchd 5-1)

Life And Soul(IRE) ◆, for whom there was a lot of money, even allowing for the horses that were withdrawn, and he justified that support with a good performance. Always moving powerfully, his jockey seemed keen to hang on to his mount for as long as possible before stretching on. That may not have helped his chance of winning as one got the impression that he could have been even more dangerous had he gone on when going to the front moving well. That said, it was a fine effort on the back of a layoff and he can be fancied to go well next time. He, unlike the second, may stay further judged on this. (op 6-1)

The Fonz looks a nice handicapper to own as he can be raced in all the decent handicaps at around this distance with a good chance. This was a fair return to action after a winter break, after taking a grip in midfield, and he will no doubt be a bit sharper next time. (op 8-1)

Nanton(USA) showed absolutely nothing in the Doncaster Shield on his first start of the season (one place but 38l behind Times Up), so this looked better. The handicapper does seem to have his measure but he will no doubt give his all wherever he goes when conditions suit. (tchd 40-1 in a place)

Fox Hunt(IRE) quickly developed into a very useful sort last season and carried a similar level of form over the winter on the AW, including a 5l victory on the Fibresand at Deauville. Back on turf, he raced handily but had nothing more left when the tempo lifted and was one paced. (op 9-2)

Mr Willis, having his first run at this distance and returning to turf for the first time since last July, was given a patient ride in order to get home, and although he was well beaten the run wasn't without promise.

Sweet Origin, 11lb higher than last time, had looked really good on the AW and the big question he needed to answer was if he could replicate that form back on turf. Quickly away, he raced a bit keenly just in behind before dropping out disappointingly quickly once the petrol ran out. It could be that he is a much better horse on Polytrack than grass (the trainer said before the race he felt the ground might be too quick here) but she should be allowed another chance to confirm that impression before conclusions are drawn. (op 10-1)

Chiberta King, back down to a fair mark and runner-up in this race in 2010, didn't break quickly but was soon able to dominate in front. It looked as though he set fair fractions, nothing too fast, so it was worrying that he faded rapidly once he'd seemingly given his all. Official explanation: jockey said gelding had no more to give

1718 QATAR BLOODSTOCK DAHLIA STKS (GROUP 3) 1m 1f

2:35 (2:37) (Class 1) 4-Y-O+

£28,385 (£10,760; £5,385; £2,685; £1,345; £675) **Stalls** High

Form RPR

153- **1** **I'm A Dreamer (IRE)**[218] 6346 4-8-12 97 WilliamBuick 7 115
(David Simcock) *hld up in tch towards rr: hdwy over 2f out: rdn and qcknd to ld over 1f out: clr jst ins fnl f: r.o strly: readily* **10/1**

024- **2** 4 ½ **Sea Of Heartbreak (IRE)**[198] 6886 4-8-12 103 SteveDrowne 11 105
(Roger Charlton) *stdd s: hld up in tch in rr: nt clr run wl over 2f out: hdwy and nt clr run over 1f out: swtchd rt over 1f out: chsd clr wnr ins fnl f: r.o: no ch w wnr* **16/1**

025- **3** 2 ½ **Chachamaidee (IRE)**[253] 5305 4-8-12 105 TomQueally 3 100
(Sir Henry Cecil) *stdd s: sn in tch in midfield: hdwy to ld 3f out: rdn over 2f out: hdd over 1f out: nt qckn w wnr and btn 1f out: lost 2nd and wknd ins fnl f* **9/1**[3]

124- **4** 1 **Field Day (IRE)**[210] 6613 4-8-12 109 (t) MartinDwyer 9 97
(Brian Meehan) *t.k.h: hld up in tch in midfield: rdn and unable qck jst over 2f out: edgd rt over 1f out: no ch but kpt on on fnl f* **5/1**[1]

112- **5** ¾ **Mirror Lake**[232] 5951 4-8-12 108 JimCrowley 5 96
(Amanda Perrett) *t.k.h: in tch: hdwy to join ldrs 3f out: rdn and wandered u.p wl over 1f out: wknd ent fnl f* **5/1**[1]

310- **6** 1 ¼ **Eleanora Duse (IRE)**[197] 6928 4-9-3 113 RyanMoore 6 98
(Sir Michael Stoute) *in tch: rdn and unable qck ent fnl 3f: edgd rt and wknd over 1f out* **5/1**[1]

524- **7** 1 ¼ **Contredanse (IRE)**[197] 6950 4-8-12 110 FrankieDettori 8 90
(Luca Cumani) *chsd ldrs: ev ch and rdn wl over 2f out: wknd u.p over 1f out* **5/1**[1]

060- **8** 5 **Crystal Gal (IRE)**[182] 7259 4-8-12 99 PaulHanagan 2 79
(Lucy Wadham) *t.k.h: w ldr: rdn 3f out: sn struggling: wknd wl over 1f out* **20/1**

51-3 **9** nk **Pachattack (USA)**[36] 991 5-8-12 106 (p) NeilCallan 1 78
(Gerard Butler) *led and racd alone on stands' rail: rdn and hdd 3f out: wknd u.p over 1f out* **6/1**[2]

35-0 **10** ½ **Saphira's Fire (IRE)**[29] 1100 6-8-12 100 Christophe-PatriceLemaire 4 77
(William Muir) *in tch towards rr: rdn and btn ent fnl 2f: wl btn over 1f out* **20/1**

6004 **11** 11 **Kinky Afro (IRE)**[29] 1104 4-8-12 95 RichardHughes 10 53
(J S Moore) *hld up in tch: rdn 3f out: wknd 2f out: wl bhd and eased ins fnl f: t.o* **40/1**

1m 52.78s (1.08) **Going Correction** +0.45s/f (Yiel) **11** Ran SP% **117.9**

Speed ratings (Par 113): **113,109,106,105,105 104,103,98,98,97 88**

toteswingers: 1&2 £23.80, 1&3 £16.20, 2&3 £24.10. CSF £153.81 TOTE £12.50: £2.90, £4.90, £4.00; EX 181.00 TRIFECTA Not won..

Owner St Albans Bloodstock LLP **Bred** Sean Murphy **Trained** Newmarket, Suffolk

FOCUS

This Group 3 for older fillies has been dominated in recent years by Sir Michael Stoute, who had saddled the previous four winners, comprising the subsequent Group 1 winner Echelon plus solid Group 2 performers Heaven Sent (twice) and Strawberrydaiquiri. The first two are possibly flattered by the margins but both look to have improved from last year.

NOTEBOOK

I'm A Dreamer(IRE) ◆ won her first three starts last season but was held when stepped up into Listed company, including behind today's third and fourth at Ascot. However, she was open to improvement after just five runs and had clearly progressed as she swept around the outside of her rivals after being held up at the back. She soon had the race in safe keeping and looks a capable of scoring at an even higher level with the Windsor Forest at Royal Ascot looking a suitable next step, and possibly the Nassau Stakes later on, as the plan is to step her up in distance. (op 11-1 tchd 12-1)

Sea Of Heartbreak(IRE) ◆, a progressive handicapper last season who stays 1m4f but is well suited by 1m2f, was having just her second try at this level. Like the winner she was open to further progress and like that rival she was held up at the back early. She made her move first, but tried to come through her field and did not get the clearest of passages. That said, she would not have beaten the winner but looks up to scoring at this level, possibly over a little further.

Chachamaidee(IRE), a Listed winner on fast ground last season but held in Group races, was having her first try beyond 1m. She slightly missed the break but was soon prominent and quite keen early on. In the circumstances she did well to finish as close as she did, being the only one of the first four to race up with the pace. (op 8-1)

Field Day(IRE), who was progressive in the first half of 2010, beating Chachamaidee in an Ascot Listed race, put up fair efforts on soft ground in France afterwards, including the Prix de l'Opera. Settled out the back early, she ran on late and can be expected to come on for the outing. (op 7-1)

Mirror Lake, a three-time winner last summer at 1m2f including at Listed level and Group 3 placed afterwards, was another who raced close to the pace and gradually faded up the hill. The run should bring her on and a step back up in trip will help her. (op 11-2)

Eleanora Duse(IRE), whose trainer had won the last four runnings of this, had the highest official rating in what looked a competitive heat. She went off as one of four co-favourites but never really got competitive, only passing beaten rivals late on. (tchd 9-2)

Contredanse(IRE), who won her first three races in 2010 - all on a sound surface - graduating from handicaps to take the Italian Oaks, had followed that with fair efforts in Group 1s subsequently. She raced with the leaders but was a little keen and had nothing in reserve for the latter stages. (op 9-2 tchd 11-2)

Crystal Gal(IRE), whose best efforts for Kevin Prendergast were places in Listed and Group 3 company at 7f on soft ground, was bought for 150,000gns in the autumn but was too keen early on this debut for new connections. (tchd 18-1)

Pachattack(USA), dropping in trip, made the early running but was left isolated when switching to the rail before halfway and was beaten a fair way from home. (op 13-2 tchd 11-2)

Saphira's Fire(IRE), who is reportedly in-foal, has not found her form so far this season. (op 22-1 tchd 25-1)

Kinky Afro(IRE), who ran well on her return from Dubai last time, travelled well enough but dropped away tamely. (op 50-1)

1719 QIPCO 1000 GUINEAS (GROUP 1) (FILLIES) 1m
3:15 (3:18) (Class 1) 3-Y-O

£213,739 (£81,022; £40,549; £20,218; £10,127; £5,082) **Stalls** Centre

Form RPR

211- **1** **Blue Bunting (USA)**[183] 7235 3-9-0 **99**........................ FrankieDettori 16 116+
(Mahmood Al Zarooni) *towards rr: rdn 1/2-way: styd on and hdwy wl over 1f out: chsd ldng pair on stands' rail 1f out: str run to ld wl ins fnl f: gng away at fin* **16/1**

35-5 **2** *3/4* **Together (IRE)**[17] 1339 3-9-0 **110**.................................. CO'Donoghue 4 114
(A P O'Brien, Ire) *hld up towards rr: hdwy on far side 3f out: rdn to ld wl over 1f out: drvn ent fnl f: kpt on wl tl hdd and no ex wl ins fnl f* **33/1**

43-3 **3** *1 1/4* **Maqaasid**[18] 1319 3-9-0 **105**... RichardHills 3 111+
(John Gosden) *hld up towards rr: hdwy to chse ldrs gng wl and nt clr run jst over 2f out: swtchd rt and chsd ldr over 1f out: ev ch u.p ins fnl f: wknd towards fin* **22/1**

42- **4** *3 1/4* **Nova Hawk**[31] 1069 3-9-0 **108**...............................(t) StephanePasquier 7 103
(Rod Collet, France) *t.k.h: hld up in tch in midfield: effrt and switching lft 2f out: chsd ldng trio ent fnl f: no imp u.p after* **25/1**

32-1 **5** *hd* **Barefoot Lady (IRE)**[18] 1319 3-9-0 **104**......................... PaulHanagan 8 106+
(Richard Fahey) *in tch: rdn and unable qck 3f out: outpcd over 2f out: rallied u.p and edging rt over 1f out: no ch but styd on steadily fnl f* **16/1**

11- **6** *nk* **Havant**[212] 6528 3-9-0 **105**... RyanMoore 5 102
(Sir Michael Stoute) *t.k.h: hld up towards rr: switching rt to far side of field and hdwy ent fnl 2f: styd on steadily ins fnl f: nvr trbld ldrs* **13/2**[3]

4-1 **7** *3 3/4* **Moonlight Cloud**[24] 1207 3-9-0 **113**...................................... DavyBonilla 9 94+
(F Head, France) *hld up in rr: gd hdwy over 3f out: rdn to ld 2f out: sn hung lft u.p and hdd: 3rd and btn jst over 1f out: wknd fnl f* **9/2**[1]

111- **8** *1 1/2* **Hooray**[212] 6530 3-9-0 **116**.. SebSanders 13 90
(Sir Mark Prescott Bt) *led: rdn and hrd pressed over 2f out: hdd 2f out: edgd lft u.p and wknd over 1f out* **9/1**

153- **9** *nk* **I Love Me**[197] 6927 3-9-0 **103**.. JimmyFortune 6 90+
(Andrew Balding) *t.k.h: hld up in midfield: hdwy to press ldrs gng wl 3f out: rdn and unable qck over 2f out: hmpd wl over 1f out: edgd rt and wknd over 1f out* **10/1**

2-20 **10** *2 3/4* **Elshabakiya (IRE)**[18] 1319 3-9-0 **95**.......................... PhilipRobinson 14 83
(Clive Brittain) *chsd ldr: ev ch 3f out: edgd rt u.p wl over 1f out: sn wknd* **50/1**

211- **11** *3 3/4* **Misty For Me (IRE)**[210] 6609 3-9-0 **113**............................... PJSmullen 2 75
(A P O'Brien, Ire) *chsd ldrs: rdn and struggling 3f out: wknd 2f out: wl btn fnl f* **9/1**

31-0 **12** *1/2* **Cape Dollar (IRE)**[15] 1404 3-9-0 **105**........................... RichardMullen 10 73
(Sir Michael Stoute) *t.k.h: chsd ldrs: rdn and unable qck over 2f out: wkng whn hmpd 2f out* **40/1**

10-1 **13** *3* **The Shrew**[18] 1313 3-9-0 **86**.. WilliamBuick 18 67
(John Gosden) *t.k.h: hld up in tch: effrt to chse ldrs and rdn 3f out: sn struggling: wknd over 2f out* **66/1**

21-4 **14** *3 1/2* **Show Rainbow**[18] 1319 3-9-0 **98**.. NeilCallan 11 58
(Mick Channon) *in tch: effrt to chse ldrs and rdn wl over 2f out: wknd wl over 1f out* **100/1**

0-1 **15** *3 1/4* **Empowering (IRE)**[35] 1006 3-9-0 **103**................................ JPO'Brien 15 51
(A P O'Brien, Ire) *chsd ldrs: rdn and struggling 3f out: wkng whn edgd lft and hmpd 2f out* **25/1**

01- **16** *1 1/2* **Make A Dance (USA)**[183] 7231 3-9-0 **86**......................... MichaelHills 12 48
(B W Hills) *a in rr: rdn and struggling 1/2-way: wl bhd fnl 2f* **16/1**

212- **17** *nse* **Laughing Lashes (USA)**[245] 5570 3-9-0 **112**...................... FMBerry 17 47
(Mrs John Harrington, Ire) *chsd ldrs tl rdn and lost pl over 3f out: wl bhd fnl 2f* **18/1**

116- **18** *37* **Memory (IRE)**[245] 5570 3-9-0 **111**.................................. RichardHughes 1 —
(Richard Hannon) *rel to r and immediately t.o* **6/1**[2]

1m 39.27s (0.67) **Going Correction** +0.45s/f (Yiel) **18** Ran SP% **119.7**
Speed ratings (Par 110): **114,113,112,108,108 108,104,103,102,99 96,95,92,89,85 84,84,47**
toteswingers: [illegible] TOTE £17.00: £5.00, £7.20, £8.30; EX 503.00 TRIFECTA Not won..
Owner Godolphin **Bred** B M Kelley **Trained** Newmarket, Suffolk

■ Mahmood Al Zarooni's first British Classic winner.

■ Stewards' Enquiry : C O'Donoghue two-day ban: used whip with excessive frequency (May 15-16)

FOCUS

The second Classic of the season and a big field for what looked a strong but fairly open renewal, with the majority of last season's leading juvenile fillies taking their chance, including the winners of the Lowther and Cheveley Park, Moyglare and Marcel Boussac, Albany and Cherry Hinton and the Queen Mary and Rockfel, but Fillies' Mile winner White Moonstone, a leading fancy for Godolphin, missed the race after a setback. Unfortunately, it proved something of an unsatisfactory race. The race was dominated by relative outsiders, with the first three coming clear, although the form is rated up to scratch for the race, with the runner-up the best guide. Immortal Verse (66/1) was withdrawn after giving trouble in the stalls. No R4 deduction.

NOTEBOOK

Blue Bunting(USA) ◆ had progressed from maiden company to win a Listed race over C&D last autumn but was up in grade and having her first try on fast ground here. Held up out of the wind early, she made her effort nearest the stands' rail and, as her stamina kicked in up the hill, she was able to reel in the leaders and get up near the line. She is regarded as an Oaks filly and that will be her next port of call in an attempt to emulate the same owner's Kazzia, who did the double in 2002. She was top priced at 9-2 for the Epsom Classic following this. (op 25-1 tchd 33-1 in places)

Together(IRE) had solid juvenile form, not being beaten far in the Moyglare and narrowly held by the winner's stable companion in the Fillies' Mile. However, she had been to the Breeders' Cup in between being beaten in two valuable sales races here since and was the longest priced of the stable's trio of runners. She moved into the lead going really well but despite keeping on under pressure was unable to resist the late surge of the winner. She is likely to renew rivalry in the Oaks and her pedigree suggests the trip will not be beyond her. (op 40-1)

Maqaasid, the winner of the Queen Mary on her second start last year but beaten by Hooray in the Lowther and Cheveley Park afterwards, had finished third in the Nell Gwyn to Barefoot Lady and there were doubts raised about her staying this trip. However, she travelled really well into the race and kept on under pressure up the middle of the track. Her rider believes the round mile at Ascot in the Coronation Stakes will be in her favour and that is her next target. (tchd 25-1)

Nova Hawk, a winner and placed at Listed level at this trip but all of whose form was on very soft ground, ran really well on this faster surface stepped up in grade. Her rider felt her inexperience of a straight track cost her, and she should win good races this season back in her homeland. (op 33-1)

Barefoot Lady(IRE) was a very useful juvenile but stepped up on that form when winning the Nell Gwyn over 7f here, and was supplemented for this for £30,000. Up again in trip and grade she ran well, chasing the leaders throughout and, despite being pushed along some way out, kept on when others cried enough. She could run in the Musidora Stakes. (tchd 14-1)

Havant ◆, unbeaten in two starts including a Group 3 over 7f here, was up in trip and had to prove she handled fast going, although her sire and siblings handled it well enough. She stayed on steadily from the back and, although she was deposed as favourite for the Oaks after this, could well be a more potent force in that race as her stable has yet to hit top gear and the longer trip should be in her favour. (op 6-1 tchd 7-1 and 8-1 in places)

Moonlight Cloud, an easy winner of the Prix Imprudence on her return to action, was up in trip and having her first try on fast ground. The Maisons-Laffitte race has proved a good guide to this in the past, and when she came through to challenge over 2f out it looked as if she might win. However, she was soon under pressure and weakened over a furlong from home with her rider letting her come home in her own time once her chance had gone. It appeared she may have been asked for her effort too soon, but Davy Bonilla and Freddie Head blamed the delay at the start for her below-par performance, the filly being kept waiting in the stalls, and she can surely bounce back. (op 11-2)

Hooray improved in the second half of last season to win three Group races, including the Lowther and Cheveley Park, making all each time. There was a question over whether her style of racing would enable her to get this far and she was not helped by having to race into a pretty strong breeze. In the circumstances she did not fare badly but one suspects that we might see her back at shorter trips in future. (op 8-1 tchd 15-2)

I Love Me, a surprise winner of a sales race over 7f here on her debut, had improved to finish a close third in the Rockfel (behind Cape Dollar) from a poor draw. She looked open to improvement and was noted moving up menacingly into contention at a round the halfway point. However, she drifted across a couple of her rivals and could not go with the leaders running down the hill before gradually fading. (op 12-1)

Elshabakiya(IRE) came into this a maiden but was only narrowly beaten on her first three starts, including by Maqaasid on her debut and by 2,000 Guineas runner-up Dubawi Gold on her return. She chased the leader early but couldn't sustain her effort and was reportedly unsuited by the fast ground. Official explanation: jockey said filly was unsuited by the good to firm ground (op 66-1)

Misty For Me(IRE), the winner of the Moyglare and the Marcel Boussac last season, looked just about the form pick on that. She moved on to the heels of the leaders at around the halfway mark but, when the race began in earnest, she was soon struggling. (op 8-1 tchd 10-1 in places)

Cape Dollar(IRE), the winner of the Rockfel over 7f on easy ground last autumn, is suited by fast going but finished well beaten on her return at Newbury. She tracked the leaders early but was already struggling when short of room and she may struggle this season as she does not look up to this class and will have to carry a Group 2 penalty in lower-grade contests. (tchd 50-1 in places)

The Shrew, the winner of a handicap at this trip on Polytrack, had lots to find at this level. She raced just behind the pace early but was done with at the top of the hill. (op 80-1)

Show Rainbow, who was not beaten far when fourth in the Nell Gwyn, raced in the leading group until dropping away under pressure.

Empowering(IRE), who took a Guineas trial at Leopardstown, was another who raced in the leading group until dropping away under pressure. (tchd 28-1)

Make A Dance(USA) had a lot to find on the bare form of her 7f maiden win here in October, but she did attract some market support earlier in the week. However, she was one of the first under pressure and her rider reported the filly was unsuited by the ground. Official explanation: jockey said filly was unsuited by the good to firm ground (tchd 20-1 in places)

Laughing Lashes(USA), whose form was closely linked in with Misty For Me, was disappointing on this seasonal debut, dropping away after racing prominently early. (op 20-1 tchd 25-1 in places)

Memory(IRE), well supported in the days leading up to the race, was reluctant to race and left the stalls so slowly that she had no chance and was tailed off. She had a tendency to be slowly away last season so will have intensive schooling to try to alleviate the problem and might now run in the French 1,000 Guineas. Official explanation: jockey said filly was reluctant to race (op 5-1)

1720 AL RAYAN H'CAP 6f
3:50 (3:53) (Class 2) 4-Y-O+

£24,924 (£7,464; £3,732; £1,868; £932; £468) **Stalls** High

Form RPR

001- **1** **Pastoral Player**[193] 7014 4-9-1 **96**................................. SteveDrowne 9 109+
(Hughie Morrison) *s.i.s: in rr: stdy hdwy towards far side of gp 2f out: qcknd to ld fnl 150yds: drvn and in command fnl 100yds: readily* **12/1**[3]

-000 **2** *2* **Fratellino**[11] 1476 4-8-9 **90**..(t) JamesDoyle 1 96
(Alan McCabe) *pressed ldrs: chal ins fnl 2f: narrow ld 1f out: hdd fnl 150yds: sn outpcd by wnr but hld on wl for 2nd* **40/1**

2-26 **3** *nk* **Docofthebay (IRE)**[29] 1094 7-9-0 **95**............................(b) IanMongan 23 100
(David Nicholls) *chsd ldrs: rdn over 2f out: styd on wl fnl f to take 3rd cl home but no ch w wnr* **12/1**[3]

[illegible] **4** [illegible] [illegible]
(Jim Goldie) *hld up in rr: gd hdwy ins fnl 2f: nt clr run over 1f out and jst ins fnl f: rallied wl fnl 100yds: fin strly to take 4th on line* **8/1**[1]

-006 **5** *hd* **Wildcat Wizard (USA)**[12] 1457 5-8-9 **90**.......................... NeilCallan 22 94
(David Nicholls) *in tch: hdwy 2f out: styd on wl u.p ins fnl f: fin wl* **22/1**

10-0 **6** *nse* **Hamoody (USA)**[25] 1166 7-8-1 **85**................................. BillyCray(3) 15 89
(David Nicholls) *s.i.s: in rr: hdwy 2f out: rdn and styd on wl fnl f: gng on cl home* **33/1**

6020 **7** *1/2* **Silaah**[11] 1476 7-8-10 **91**..(p) AdrianNicholls 10 94
(David Nicholls) *w ldr: led after 2f: rdn over 2f out: narrowly hdd 1f out: stl 3rd tl lost four pls cl home* **16/1**

30-0 **8** *1 1/2* **Johannes (IRE)**[28] 1111 8-9-0 **95**................................... PaulHanagan 3 93+
(Richard Fahey) *in tch: hdwy whn n.m.r over 1f out: r.o again ins fnl f: nt rch ldrs* **16/1**

10-0 **9** *1/2* **Colonel Mak**[28] 1111 4-8-13 **99**...................................... LMcNiff(5) 13 95
(David Barron) *in rr: rdn and hdwy fr 2f out: kpt on ins fnl f: nt rch ldrs* **20/1**

0-06 **10** *shd* **Prime Defender**[17] 1340 7-9-10 **105**............................. SebSanders 12 101
(B W Hills) *pressed ldrs: rdn over 2f out: one pce fnl f: wknd nr fin* **14/1**

4033 **11** *hd* **Lui Rei (ITY)**[15] 1420 5-9-5 **100**................................. FrankieDettori 14 101+
(Robert Cowell) *in rr: hdwy over 1f out: styng on whn nt clr run fnl 120yds: nt rcvr* **16/1**

040- **12** *nse* **Tiddliwinks**[225] 6175 5-8-13 **94**..................................... PhillipMakin 5 89+
(Kevin Ryan) *pressed ldrs: rdn and upsides over 1f out: wknd fnl 120yds* **8/1**[1]

050- **13** *1* **Swilly Ferry (USA)**[204] 6752 4-9-5 **100**........................ MichaelHills 25 92
(B W Hills) *in tch: chsd ldrs over 2f out: wknd ins fnl f* **18/1**

060- **14** *nk* **Fireback**[233] 5911 4-8-8 **89**.. DavidProbert 8 80
(Andrew Balding) *chsd ldrs: rdn 3f out: wknd ins fnl f* **11/2**[1]

0440 **15** *1 1/4* **Five Star Junior (USA)**[16] 1366 5-8-8 **92**............ JamesSullivan(3) 24 79
(Linda Stubbs) *in rr tl pushed along and sme hdwy fnl f: nvr gng pce to rch ldrs* **40/1**

3143 **16** *3/4* **Clear Praise (USA)**[24] 1197 4-8-1 **82**............................. NickyMackay 7 67
(Simon Dow) *in tch: chsd ldrs fr 2f out: wkng whn n.m.r fnl 100yds* **20/1**

050- **17** *1/2* **Novellen Lad (IRE)**[216] 6429 6-8-6 **87**.......................... JamieMackay 6 70+
(Willie Musson) *in rr: hdwy on far side of gp over 1f out: styd on but nvr any ch of rching ldrs* **16/1**

0-00 **18** *nse* **Rocket Rob (IRE)**[25] 1166 5-8-4 **85**........................... AdrianMcCarthy 4 68
(Willie Musson) *chsd ldrs towards far side of gp: wknd fnl f* **66/1**

04-0 **19** *1* **Baldemar**[24] 1197 6-8-4 **85**.. JimmyQuinn 27 65
(Richard Fahey) *chsd ldrs over 3f* **33/1**

-034 **20** 2 1/2 **Barney McGrew (IRE)**[72] 602 8-9-5 **100**........................ RyanMoore 18 72
(Michael Dods) *in tch tl rdn and wknd 2f out* **14/1**

600- **21** 2 1/4 **Citrus Star (USA)**[198] 6888 4-9-6 **101**............................ GeorgeBaker 11 65
(Chris Wall) *in tch: stl in tch whn hmpd and wknd over 1f out* **25/1**

-004 **22** 3/4 **Jack My Boy (IRE)**[6] 1564 4-8-11 **92**........................(b) JimmyFortune 26 54
(David Evans) *chsd ldrs 4f* **16/1**

06-1 **23** 10 **Curtains**[37] 961 4-8-7 **88**.. JoeFanning 19 —
(Simon Dow) *early spd: wknd qckly 1/2-way* **20/1**

113- **24** 1 1/2 **Drawnfromthepast (IRE)**[193] 7014 6-9-0 **95**.................. MartinDwyer 2 —
(Ed Walker) *led 2f: sn wknd* **25/1**

1m 13.83s (1.63) **Going Correction** +0.45s/f (Yiel) **24** Ran SP% **132.5**
Speed ratings (Par 109): **107,104,103,103,103 103,102,100,100,100 99,99,98,97,96 95,94,94,93,89 86,85,72,70**
toteswingers: 1&2 not won, 1&3 £61.60, 2&3 not won. CSF £447.17 CT £5890.83 TOTE £13.10: £3.40, £10.90, £3.90, £2.30; EX 1923.80 Trifecta £1467.00 Part won. Pool: £1,982.53 - 0.20 winning units..
Owner The Pursuits Partnership **Bred** Whitsbury Manor Stud & Pigeon House Stud **Trained** East Ilsley, Berks

FOCUS
A huge field of classy handicappers hurtled down the straight 6f and the pace was unsurprisingly strong. There were a few hard-luck stories in behind but the winner looks on the upgrade. The form looks solid despite the lack of obvious improvers.

NOTEBOOK
Pastoral Player ◆, who was said to have needed this run, made the perfect start to his career when winning on his racecourse debut but took a while to collect another victory, although most of the efforts in between were consistent at a good level. Racing off 4lb higher than when winning on his last start of 2010 – a victory at Ffos Las, he showed that he is a sprinter of some potential with a taking display here. The only query hanging over him is whether he is best caught fairly fresh as if you remove his win in Wales last year, he won first time out, finished a good second over C&D after a 166-day absence, and won here after 192 days off the track. If a long break isn't vital, the winner looks a strong contender for something like the Wokingham Handicap later in the year, but connections said afterwards they feel he is Listed class so he might be tried at that level next. (op 11-1)
Fratellino looked on a decent mark and put up his best display of the year with a tongue-tie added for the first time. He didn't get home as strongly as the winner after holding every chance, but rallied.
Docofthebay(IRE) must be a great horse to own as he is so versatile. This was his first try at 6f and he didn't disappoint with a staying-on effort. Not bad for a horse who once finished second to Pipedreamer in a Cambridgeshire. (op 16-1)
Hawkeyethenoo(IRE), the winner the previous season off a 15lb lower mark, met all sorts of problems while making his bid and would have been closer with a clear passage. Official explanation: jockey said gelding was denied a clear run (tchd 15-2)
Wildcat Wizard(USA) ◆, without the blinkers that he tried last time, caught the eye with the way he finished after being dropped out and looks primed for success soon. (op 20-1)
Hamoody(USA) ◆ ran well on his return and again here and he is one to keep an eye on for any return trip to Goodwood, a course he has done well at in the past.
Silaah ◆, who was reported to have hung left, showed a ton of speed and is one to keep in mind when returned to a sharper, speed-favouring track. Official explanation: jockey said gelding hung left
Johannes(IRE) ◆ looked a bit unlucky not to finish closer after getting in behind a wall of horses. He looks nicely weighted currently and can be given another chance.
Lui Rei(ITY) came in for market support but found trouble in the latter stages when staying on. (op 20-1)
Tiddliwinks moved up going well, looking sure to play a part in the finish but weakened in the final stages. He should be straighter next time and is fairly handicapped.
Drawnfromthepast(IRE) Official explanation: jockey said gelding lost its action

1721 MAKFI FUTURE STARS MAIDEN STKS 5f
4:25 (4:26) (Class 3) 2-Y-O **£7,447** (£2,216; £1,107; £553) **Stalls** High

Form RPR

3 **1** **Commissar**[16] 1360 2-9-3 0.. JimmyFortune 5 92+
(Paul Cole) *mde all: rdn and drew clr over 1f out r.o strly: easily* **7/2**[2]

2 **2** 5 **Tell Dad**[18] 1316 2-9-3 0... RichardHughes 8 74
(Richard Hannon) *in tch: shkn up and effrt wl over 1f out: rdn to chse clr wnr 1f out: no imp: eased towards fin* **13/8**[1]

3 hd **Come On Blue Chip (IRE)** 2-9-3 0.............................. TonyCulhane 1 73+
(Paul D'Arcy) *stdd and dropped in bhd s: hld up in last trio: pushed along and hdwy over 1f out: styd on steadily fnl f: pressing for 2nd cl home: no ch w wnr* **40/1**

5 **4** 2 **Liebesziel**[15] 1383 2-9-3 0.. NeilCallan 4 69
(Alan McCabe) *in tch: rdn and unable qck over 1f out: clipped heels and stmbld jst over 1f out: no ch w wnr and styd on same pce ins fnl f* **20/1**

5 **5** nk **Chunky Diamond (IRE)**[16] 1360 2-9-3 0........................ JackMitchell 2 65
(Peter Chapple-Hyam) *t.k.h: chsd ldrs: wnt 2nd 1/2-way: rdn and pressing wnr wl over 1f out: sn unable qck: wkng and edgd lft jst over 1f out: fdd ins fnl f* **9/1**

6 nk **Mizbah** 2-9-3 0... FrankieDettori 7 64+
(Saeed Bin Suroor) *dwlt and short of room sn after s: a in rr: rdn and m green wl over 1f out: no ch but plugged on fnl f* **8/1**[3]

7 shd **Democretes** 2-9-3 0.. TomQueally 9 64
(Richard Hannon) *wnt early to s and s.i.s: hld up in rr: rdn and hdwy jst over 2f out: wknd over 1f out* **9/1**

8 11 **Red Aggressor (IRE)** 2-9-3 0..................................... PhilipRobinson 3 24
(Clive Brittain) *racd freely: chsd wnr tl 1/2-way: sn lost pl: bhd and m green over 1f out* **20/1**

61.68 secs (2.58) **Going Correction** +0.45s/f (Yiel) **8** Ran SP% **103.4**
Speed ratings (Par 97): **97,89,88,85,85 84,84,66**
toteswingers: 1&2 £1.50, 1&3 £16.30, 2&3 £13.40. CSF £7.44 TOTE £3.50: £1.30, £1.10, £6.50; EX 8.70 Trifecta £686.70 Part won. Pool: £928.02 - 0.84 winning units..
Owner C Shiacolas **Bred** R A Instone **Trained** Whatcombe, Oxon
■ Rio Grande (11/2) was withdrawn after proving unruly in the stalls. Deduct 15p in the 3 under R4.

FOCUS
Plenty of good horses have won this race in the past and this year's winner looks well up to the standard you'd like to see.

NOTEBOOK
Commissar ◆, whose trainer said he was very disappointed with his debut effort at Newbury but expected considerable improvement, showed good speed from the outset and destroyed his rivals when quickening clear. Obviously well regarded, he looks sure to head to Royal Ascot, but which race is uncertain as although he has the speed for 5f, one would imagine he'll have little problems with 6f - connections seemed to be leaning towards the Norfolk. On a separate note, the Newbury race he ran in is starting to work out nicely, so that is a contest worth following. (op 5-1)
Tell Dad showed plenty on his debut when coming up against some race-fit rivals in a conditions event so this was a shade disappointing as he never looked like giving the winner too many problems. He has a bit to prove now, although no doubt he'll win a maiden without too much trouble. (op 6-4, tchd 7-4 in places)
Come On Blue Chip(IRE), who in another stride would have been second, made a good start to his career. Already gelded, he looks sure to stay further considering the way he finished.
Liebesziel shaped nicely last time when 80-1 and went well here until clipping heels (he also didn't seem to handle the Dip). A return to a flatter track will help. (op 22-1)
Chunky Diamond(IRE), two places behind the winner at Newbury, showed up early but faded out of contention. (op 15-2)
Mizbah didn't have a sexy pedigree for a powerful stable and wasn't that fancied judged on the betting, so he may have needed this. He was green and will surely be a bit better than he showed. (op 17-2 tchd 9-1 and 10-1 in places)
Democretes looked the second string on jockey bookings and also raced a bit green close to the stands' rail. He will definitely come on for this. (op 8-1 tchd 10-1)

1722 TWEENHILLS PRETTY POLLY STKS (LISTED RACE) 1m 2f
5:00 (5:00) (Class 1) 3-Y-O
£22,708 (£8,608; £4,308; £2,148; £1,076; £540) **Stalls** High

Form RPR

122 **1** **Dorcas Lane**[28] 1113 3-8-12 87... PaulHanagan 6 103
(Lucy Wadham) *chsd ldrs: pushed along and hdwy to ld 2f out: styd on wl fnl f: rdn out* **9/2**[3]

41- **2** 2 **Charleston Lady**[188] 7113 3-8-12 80................................. JimCrowley 2 99
(Ralph Beckett) *hld up in last pair: rdn and effrt wl over 1f out: chsd wnr 1f out: kpt on u.p but a hld* **5/1**

2-1 **3** 2 **Izzi Top**[20] 1270 3-8-12 84... WilliamBuick 7 95
(John Gosden) *chsd ldrs: rdn to chse wnr wl over 1f out: unable qck u.p over 1f out: styd on same pce fnl f* **3/1**[2]

1- **4** 1/2 **Primevere (IRE)**[200] 6844 3-8-12 83.................................. SteveDrowne 4 94
(Roger Charlton) *hld up wl in tch: rdn and effrt wl over 1f out: no imp jst over 1f out: one pce and wl hld fnl f* **15/8**[1]

45-0 **5** 8 **Nabah**[29] 1096 3-8-12 93.. PhilipRobinson 5 78
(Clive Brittain) *chsd ldr tl rdn to ld over 2f out: hdd 2f out: wknd and edgd rt over 1f out* **8/1**

3-5 **6** 2 3/4 **Hidden Valley**[16] 1363 3-8-12 0.. JimmyFortune 1 73
(Andrew Balding) *stdd s: hld up in last pair: rdn 3f out: no prog: no ch and nt pushed out fr over 1f out* **16/1**

03-2 **7** 10 **Cinta**[22] 1251 3-8-12 73.. MichaelHills 8 53
(Marco Botti) *led tl rdn and hdd over 2f out: wknd wl over 1f out: wl bhd and eased ins fnl f* **25/1**

2m 9.47s (3.67) **Going Correction** +0.45s/f (Yiel) **7** Ran SP% **115.5**
Speed ratings (Par 107): **103,101,99,99,93 90,82**
toteswingers: 1&2 £3.80, 1&3 £2.70, 2&3 £3.20. CSF £27.52 TOTE £4.70: £2.20, £2.90; EX 29.30 Trifecta £60.80 Pool: £1,227.46 - 14.92 winning units..
Owner Richard S Keeley **Bred** Elms Stud Co Ltd **Trained** Newmarket, Suffolk

FOCUS
Apart from Ouija Board winning this in 2004 on her way to Classic glory, this hasn't been a particularly good race for producing fillies that are competitive at a higher grade on a regular basis, in fact most recent winners haven't won another contest. This race is rated slightly below average for the contest.

NOTEBOOK
Dorcas Lane started her career this year with a 50-1 success and has made good progress since, which has now resulted in a valuable Listed victory. One would imagine she'll continue to run at this level and possibly a bit higher, and it's not difficult so see her take up her engagement in the Ribblesdale at Royal Ascot, as she races as though she'll get 1m4f. (op 4-1)
Charleston Lady made a pleasing comeback. She had only had a 1m Polytrack maiden under her belt but stepped up on that over this extra distance. Ralph Beckett certainly knows how to handle a decent filly and it will be interesting to see how she is campaigned considering she has Oaks and Ribblesdale entries. (op 13-2)
Izzi Top looked to have Classic pretensions (she was entered in the 1000 Guineas), but any notion that she is capable of operating at Group 1 level were surely dispelled in this. The form of the maiden she won at Windsor hadn't been working out, and she appeared to have every chance here. (op 11-4 tchd 5-2 and 10-3 in places)
Primevere(IRE) ◆, a nice-looking type, travelled strongly in behind for a lot of the race and can be given another chance on easier ground as she reportedly returned home with sore shins. She appears to be well regarded and can prove much better than she showed here. (op 2-1 tchd 9-4 and 5-2 in places)
Nabah raced up with the leaders early but found only the one pace from around the furlong marker. Beaten just over 3l by the 1000 Guineas winner as a juvenile, she could do with a confidence-building win in a maiden before trying this grade again. (op 10-1, tchd 11-1 in places)

1723 QIPCO SUPPORTING RACING WELFARE H'CAP 1m 2f
5:35 (5:36) (Class 2) (0-100,91) 3-Y-O
£12,462 (£3,732; £1,866; £934; £466; £234) **Stalls** High

Form RPR

110- **1** **Buthelezi (USA)**[213] 6505 3-9-7 **91**................................. WilliamBuick 2 102
(John Gosden) *stdd s: swtchd lft to r alone on stands' rail and wnt prom after 2f: led 3f out: kpt on u.p fnl f: all out* **5/1**

114 **2** 1/2 **Barbican**[7] 1548 3-9-4 **88**... AdamKirby 4 98
(Alan Bailey) *chsd ldrs: drvn and ev ch fr over 1f out: pressed wnr thrght fnl f: no ex and hld towards fin* **9/4**[1]

14-6 **3** 3 **Bridle Belle**[15] 1384 3-9-0 **84**... PaulHanagan 7 88
(Richard Fahey) *t.k.h: in tch: lost pl and rdn 3f out: drvn and rallied over 1f out: kpt on wl ins fnl f to go 3rd nr fin* **11/1**

50-3 **4** nk **Sergeant Ablett (IRE)**[17] 1344 3-9-6 **90**........................ PaulMulrennan 1 93
(James Given) *stdd s: hld up in tch: hdwy to chse ldrs 4f out: drvn and ev ch over 1f out: wknd ins fnl f* **9/2**[3]

-111 **5** nse **Art History (IRE)**[17] 1344 3-9-3 **87**.................................. FrankieDettori 5 90
(Mark Johnston) *chsd ldr: chsd wnr and hung lft u.p over 2f out: styd on same pce fr over 1f out* **5/2**[2]

50-1 **6** 1 1/4 **Barney Rebel (IRE)**[11] 1480 3-8-12 **82**............................ MichaelHills 3 83
(B W Hills) *stdd s: t.k.h: hld up in tch in rr: hdwy and effrt in centre over 2f out: no imp over 1f out: kpt on same pce fnl f* **12/1**

41-0 **7** 44 **Golden Hinde**[17] 1344 3-8-12 **82**...................................... JoeFanning 6 —
(Mark Johnston) *led tl 3f out: sn lost pl: t.o and virtually p.u ins fnl f* **25/1**

2m 9.30s (3.50) **Going Correction** +0.45s/f (Yiel) **7** Ran SP% **114.1**
Speed ratings (Par 105): **104,103,101,100,100 99,64**
toteswingers: 1&2 £2.90, 1&3 £8.70, 2&3 £3.60. CSF £16.61 TOTE £6.10: £3.00, £1.70; EX 11.10.
Owner H R H Princess Haya Of Jordan **Bred** Dr John A Chandler **Trained** Newmarket, Suffolk

FOCUS
A good, competitive handicap despite the relatively small field. The time was fractionally faster than the preceding Listed race and looks worth being positive about.

NOTEBOOK

Buthelezi(USA) is reportedly not straightforward, but he managed to win twice last season before disappointing in a first-time eyeshield and on soft ground on his final start. He was taken to race nearer the stands' rail than the rest and showed ahead over 2f out. He looked to be headed briefly soon after but responded to pressure and battled on well to hold off the favourite. Whatever his quirks he has plenty of ability and will not have to improve much to be contesting Pattern races. His trainer is considering the Listed Fairway Stakes over C&D at the end of the month. (op 13-2)

Barbican, who beat the winner of the previous fillies' Listed race - admittedly getting weight - before finishing fourth in the Sandown Classic Trial, was running here before being reassessed. He again appeared to run his race, getting the better of the fifth before battling with the winner up the hill. He did wander about under pressure and this ground might have been faster than ideal. (op 11-4)

Bridle Belle ◆ was stepping up in trip and had to prove this fast ground suits. She ran well, though, staying on up the hill to grab the minor placing. She can win a decent race against her own sex. (op 8-1)

Sergeant Ablett(IRE), who was 4lb better off for a length-and-a-half beating by Art History over C&D earlier in the month, ran pretty close to that form with his old rival. Held up early this time, he came through to challenge around 2f out before fading up the hill. (op 11-2)

Art History(IRE), whose trainer had won this in two of the previous four years, was bidding for a four-timer but was 5lb higher and, after having every chance 2f out, had nothing in reserve for the climb to the line. (op 9-4 tchd 2-1)

Barney Rebel(IRE), the winner of an ordinary Epsom maiden, looked high enough in the weights for this handicap debut. He was very keen under restraint early and, after ending up on the outside of his field, never landed a blow. (op 9-1)

T/Jkpt: Not won. T/Plt: £2,715.70 to a £1 stake. Pool:£202,118.00 - 54.33 winning tickets T/Qpdt: £236.00 to a £1 stake. Pool:£12,312.02 - 38.60 winning tickets SP

SALISBURY (R-H)

Sunday, May 1

OFFICIAL GOING: Firm (good to firm in places); last 4 furlongs - good to firm (firm in places)

False rail between 6f and 2f positioned up to 12ft off permanent far side rail.

Wind: Quite stiff across Weather: Overcast but warm

1724 BET ON TOTEPLACEPOT AT TOTESPORT.COM MAIDEN STKS 6f

1:50 (1:51) (Class 5) 3-Y-0+ **£2,914** (£867; £433; £216) **Stalls** Low

Form RPR

0-3 **1** **L'Ami Louis (IRE)**[18] [1315] 3-9-0 0 .... DaneO'Neill 15 89+
(Henry Candy) *mde all: rdn whn hrd pressed fr 2f out: kpt on wl to hold on gamely thrght fnl f: drvn out* **11/10**[1]

- **2** *nk* **Foxtrot Hotel (IRE)** 3-9-0 0 .... LukeMorris 6 88+
(Peter Winkworth) *trckd ldrs: chal 2f out: sn rdn: kpt on wl: ev ch thrght fnl f: hld nr fin* **20/1**

333- **3** *3 ½* **Miss Mediator (USA)**[296] [3858] 3-8-9 74 .... PatDobbs 14 72
(Richard Hannon) *mid-div: rdn to chse ldng pair 2f out: styd on but nt gng pce to get on terms* **11/4**[2]

0- **4** *5* **Allumeuse (USA)**[234] [5892] 3-8-9 0 .... LiamKeniry 12 56
(Andrew Balding) *mid-div: swtchd lft 3f out: sn rdn: styd on same pce fnl 2f* **10/1**

5 *4 ½* **Dead Cool** 3-8-9 0 .... HayleyTurner 4 41+
(Hughie Morrison) *s.i.s: towards rr: styd on fnl f: nvr a factor* **11/1**

00- **6** *nk* **Piccolete**[202] [6796] 3-8-9 0 .... FrankieMcDonald 5 40+
(Richard Hannon) *towards rr of mid-div: short of room over 2f out: styd on fnl f: nvr a factor* **40/1**

- **7** *1 ¼* **Diamond Run** 3-8-10 0 ow1 .... DarryllHolland 11 37
(J W Hills) *sme late prog whn swtchd lft but mainly towards rr* **28/1**

00- **8** *½* **Camberley Two**[190] [7099] 3-9-0 0 .... ChrisCatlin 10 40
(Roger Charlton) *trckd wnr: rdn over 3f out: grad fdd fr 2f out* **25/1**

9 *nk* **Ippios** 3-9-0 0 .... J-PGuillambert 9 39
(Luca Cumani) *trckd ldrs: rdn 3f out: wknd fnl f* **8/1**[3]

000- **10** *nk* **One Cool Chick**[202] [6811] 3-8-9 45 .... CathyGannon 13 33
(John Bridger) *trckd ldrs: rdn 3f out: wknd 2f out* **100/1**

0- **11** *2 ¾* **Madame Kintyre**[322] [3000] 3-8-11 0 ow2 .... JamesMillman 2 26
(Rod Millman) *chsd ldrs tl wknd over 2f out* **80/1**

12 *12* **Beggers Belief** 3-9-0 0 .... EddieCreighton 7 —
(Eric Wheeler) *s.i.s: a struggling in rr* **100/1**

1m 11.09s (-3.71) **Going Correction** -0.525s/f (Hard) course record **12** Ran SP% **120.8**

Speed ratings (Par 103): **103,102,97,91,85 84,83,82,82,81 78,62**

toteswingers: 1&2 £9.10, 1&3 £1.10, 2&3 £9.70. CSF £32.24 TOTE £2.40: £1.50, £3.20, £1.60; EX 31.30.

Owner First Of Many Partnership **Bred** J M Carroll **Trained** Kingston Warren, Oxon

FOCUS

False rail between 6f and 2f positioned up to 12ft off permanent far side rail. The ground was pretty quick and they broke the course record in the opener, the winner dipping nearly two seconds inside the standard. A strong tailwind was a contributory factor to the quick times. This maiden lacked strength in depth, but the first two came clear of the 74-rated third so their form looks decent. The third is rated 10lb off her 2yo level.

Diamond Run Official explanation: jockey said filly was free to post

Madame Kintyre Official explanation: trainer said filly had been struck into

1725 BET ON GUINEAS AT TOTESPORT.COM H'CAP 6f 212y

2:20 (2:21) (Class 3) (0-95,94) 3-Y-0 **£7,512** (£2,235; £1,117; £557) **Stalls** Low

Form RPR

50-0 **1** **Chilworth Lad**[18] [1322] 3-9-4 94 .... MartinHarley(3) 12 101
(Mick Channon) *mid-div: swtchd lft 3f out: sn pushed along and hdwy: rdn over 1f out: r.o wl to ld ins fnl f: readily* **14/1**

034- **2** *1* **Perfect Mission**[213] [6514] 3-7-13 75 oh2 .... SimonPearce(3) 11 79
(Andrew Balding) *trckd ldr: rdn to ld over 1f out: hdd ins fnl f: kpt on but no ex* **20/1**

10-5 **3** *¾* **Cruiser**[18] [1317] 3-8-12 85 .... LukeMorris 8 87
(William Muir) *mid-div: swtchd lft and rdn 2f out: r.o ins fnl f: wnt 3rd towards fin* **9/2**[1]

32-1 **4** *¾* **Yair Hill (IRE)**[19] [1284] 3-8-7 80 .... TedDurcan 3 80
(John Dunlop) *in tch: rdn over 2f out: nt pce to chal: styd on ins fnl f* **9/2**[1]

10-4 **5** *shd* **Norse Blues**[16] [1361] 3-8-7 80 .... LiamKeniry 13 80
(Sylvester Kirk) *trckd ldrs: rdn over 2f out: kpt on same pce fnl f* **5/1**[2]

1052 **6** *1 ¼* **Fred Willetts (IRE)**[15] [1384] 3-9-0 87 .... (v) PatCosgrave 2 84
(David Evans) *trckd ldr: rdn 2f out: sn swtchd rt: kpt on tl fdd fnl 75yds* **8/1**

1224 **7** *nk* **Dasho**[18] [1313] 3-8-6 79 .... HayleyTurner 4 75
(Olivia Maylam) *led: rdn and hdd over 1f out: fdd fnl 75yds* **14/1**

000- **8** *nk* **Major Conquest (IRE)**[225] [6191] 3-8-10 83 ow1 .... DarryllHolland 10 78
(J W Hills) *hld up towards rr: rdn over 2f out: no imp tl styd on fnl 120yds* **20/1**

25-2 **9** *nk* **Avonmore Star**[18] [1322] 3-9-7 94 .... DaneO'Neill 9 88
(Richard Hannon) *hld up towards rr: swtchd lft 3f out: sn rdn: little imp* **7/1**[3]

00-4 **10** *6* **Orientalist**[17] [1326] 3-9-0 87 .... CathyGannon 7 65
(Eve Johnson Houghton) *mid-div: rdn over 3f out: wknd 2f out* **16/1**

610- **11** *1 ½* **Sister Red (IRE)**[212] [6528] 3-8-8 81 .... PatDobbs 5 55
(Richard Hannon) *hld up towards rr: rdn over 2f out: wknd over 1f out* **12/1**

15-4 **12** *2 ¾* **Conducting**[36] [990] 3-8-12 85 .... (b[1]) EddieCreighton 1 52
(Brian Meehan) *in tch: rdn over 3f out: wknd over 2f out* **22/1**

1m 24.91s (-3.69) **Going Correction** -0.525s/f (Hard) course record **12** Ran SP% **117.4**

Speed ratings (Par 103): **102,100,100,99,99 97,97,96,96,89 88,84**

toteswingers: 1&2 £23.30, 1&3 £17.10, 2&3 £22.90. CSF £266.61 CT £1465.59 TOTE £19.40: £5.30, £8.20, £2.40; EX 282.90.

Owner 7Rus **Bred** Phil Jen Racing **Trained** West Ilsley, Berks

FOCUS

A decent 3yo handicap in which they finished in a bit of a heap. They didn't appear to go off that quickly, but it still produced another course record, emphasising how fast conditions were. The winner is rated back to his 2yo best, with improvement from the second.

NOTEBOOK

Chilworth Lad was fourth in a pair of Group 2 races at two and made a satisfactory reappearance in a 6f handicap at the Craven meeting when five places behind Avonmore Star. The extra furlong was to his liking and he won a shade comfortably in the end, but a rise for this may make things tough. (op 20-1)

Perfect Mission was in the frame in a couple of maidens last term. He was up with the pace throughout on this handicap debut, leading for a brief spell until the winner pounced, and this was a good run from 2lb out of the weights. (op 16-1)

Cruiser ran pleasingly in a sales race at Newmarket and this was his handicap debut back up in trip. He took a little time to find full stride but was running on at the line once switched. His sole win so far came in soft ground. (tchd 5-1)

Yair Hill(IRE)'s official mark was untouched after his easy all-the-way maiden win at Folkestone. He was unable to replicate those tactics but did stick on for fourth without entirely convincing that he is straightforward. (op 5-1 tchd 4-1)

Norse Blues is settling better this year. He finished his race off in good style and might be ready for a step up to a mile. Official explanation: vet said colt lost a right-hind shoe (op 6-1 tchd 13-2)

Fred Willetts(IRE) was prominent against the fence for much of the trip and remains in decent form. (op 17-2)

Dasho, who was sent to post early for this turf debut, made a lot of the running. (tchd 12-1)

Major Conquest(IRE) has been gelded since his last appearance in September and the tongue-tie was left off. He made eyecatching late headway and it will be interesting to see if he builds on this. Official explanation: jockey said gelding ran too free (tchd 22-1)

Avonmore Star could not confirm his Newmarket superiority over Chilworth Lad on 2lb worse terms, with the longer trip finding him out. (op 15-2 tchd 13-2)

1726 BET TOTEPOOL AT TOTESPORT.COM FILLIES' CONDITIONS STKS 5f

2:55 (2:55) (Class 3) 2-Y-0 **£6,605** (£1,965; £982; £490) **Stalls** Low

Form RPR

1 **1** **Cockney Fire**[15] [1396] 2-8-9 0 .... CathyGannon 2 80
(David Evans) *trckd ldr: shkn up to take v narrow advantage over 1f out: kpt on wl fnl f: pushed out to hold on* **10/11**[1]

1 **2** *nk* **Dijarvo**[32] [1049] 2-8-9 0 .... LukeMorris 3 79
(Tony Carroll) *trckd ldrs: rdn upsides over 1f out: ev ch througout fnl f: kpt on* **4/1**[3]

3 *3 ¼* **Esentepe (IRE)** 2-8-6 0 .... DaneO'Neill 4 67+
(Richard Hannon) *little slowly away: chsd ldng trio: rdn over 2f out: kpt on fr over 1f out but nt gng pce to get on terms* **9/4**[2]

P **4** *6* **En Ete**[15] [1396] 2-8-2 0 .... JakePayne(7) 1 46
(Bill Turner) *led tl over 1f out: sn wknd* **20/1**

59.93 secs (-1.07) **Going Correction** -0.525s/f (Hard) **4** Ran SP% **107.9**

Speed ratings (Par 94): **87,86,81,71**

CSF £4.84 TOTE £2.30; EX 3.90.

Owner G Amey & P D Evans **Bred** G E Amey **Trained** Pandy, Monmouths

FOCUS

Just a fair conditions event, run quicker than standard.

NOTEBOOK

Cockney Fire escaped a penalty for her debut win at Leicester. She hung to her left after taking a slender lead but knuckled down well to repel the runner-up slightly more easily than the margin suggests. She may not turn out as good as Dingle View, who won this for the Evans yard 12 months ago, but she should win more races. (tchd Evens)

Dijarvo, like the winner, made a winning debut in maiden auction company, in her case on the Wolverhampton Polytrack. The placed horses have been beaten in selling company since, so the form isn't strong, but she ran a good race here and went down fighting. (op 9-2 tchd 5-1)

Esentepe(IRE)'s yard won this event five times in the previous dozen years, including with smart juveniles Presto Vento, Gilded and Cake, and this one holds an entry in the Weatherbys Super Sprint which Presto Vento won in 2002. A little green on this debut, she wasn't given a hard time when held by the front pair, but there is improvement in her. She is bred to need further than this. (op 2-1)

En Ete was pulled up after losing her action on her debut in Cockney Fire's Leicester race. She showed pace here but again hung her right, and faded to finish a well beaten last. (tchd 16-1)

1727 BET ON TODAY'S FOOTBALL AT TOTESPORT.COM H'CAP 1m 1f 198y

3:30 (3:30) (Class 4) (0-85,82) 3-Y-0 **£4,662** (£1,387; £693; £346) **Stalls** Low

Form RPR

31- **1** **Boogie Shoes**[162] [7530] 3-9-7 82 .... AndreaAtzeni 6 93+
(Roger Varian) *trckd ldr: led over 3f out: rdn clr fnl f: comf* **4/1**[2]

413- **2** *2 ¾* **Whiplash Willie**[165] [7481] 3-9-4 79 .... LiamKeniry 1 81
(Andrew Balding) *trckd ldr: rdn to chse wnr fr 2f out: kpt on but no ch w wnr fnl f* **4/1**[2]

0-11 **3** *½* **Tijori (IRE)**[72] [594] 3-8-12 73 .... PatDobbs 7 74
(Richard Hannon) *in tch: rdn to dispute 2nd over 2f out: kpt on same pce fnl f* **17/2**

4 *nse* **Deorai (IRE)**[244] [5616] 3-9-7 82 .... DaneO'Neill 3 83
(Jo Crowley) *hld up: hdwy over 2f out: sn rdn: chal for 3rd ent fnl f: kpt on same pce* **9/1**

521- **5** *1 ¼* **Mattoral**[183] [7242] 3-9-2 77 .... FergusSweeney 2 75
(Peter Makin) *in tch: rdn over 2f out: kpt on but nt pce to chal* **5/1**[3]

51- **6** *2 ¼* **Masaraat (FR)**[244] [5583] 3-9-0 75 .... TadhgO'Shea 5 69
(John Dunlop) *hld up: rdn over 2f out: nt gng pce to get on terms* **3/1**[1]

6-43 **7** *3 ½* **Ibsaar**[18] [1313] 3-9-2 77 .... LiamJones 4 64
(William Haggas) *racd keenly: led tl rdn over 3f out: wknd ent fnl f* **6/1**

2m 8.70s (-1.20) **Going Correction** -0.10s/f (Good) **7** Ran SP% **116.5**

Speed ratings (Par 101): **100,97,97,97,96 94,91**

toteswingers: 1&2 £2.70, 1&3 £3.60, 1&3 £9.00. CSF £21.00 TOTE £4.70: £3.80, £1.40; EX 15.30.

Owner A D Spence **Bred** Haydock Park Stud **Trained** Newmarket, Suffolk

FOCUS
This handicap has been won by some progressive types in recent years, among them Snoqualmie Boy and Spanish Duke. Winners should come out of this year's edition, in which none of the runners had tackled this far before. The pace was relatively steady. The form is rated around the third to fifth and the winner was value for a bit extra.

1728 GET LIVE FOOTBALL STATS AT TOTESPORT.COM MAIDEN STKS 1m 4f
4:05 (4:06) (Class 5) 3-Y-O £2,914 (£867; £433; £216) **Stalls** High

Form RPR
04-3 **1** **Reflect (IRE)**[15] 1407 3-9-3 81 PatDobbs 4 80
(Richard Hannon) *disp ld tl over 6f out: trckd ldr: led 2f out: immediately strly pressed and rdn: edgd rt sn after: hld on: all out* **1/3**[1]
0-0 **2** *nk* **Sirius Superstar**[15] 1407 3-9-3 0 LiamKeniry 1 79
(Andrew Balding) *trckd ldng pair: rdn for str chal fr 2f out: ev ch thrght fnl f: kpt on wl: hld nring fin* **4/1**[2]
0 **3** *15* **Refusal**[20] 1271 3-9-0 0 SophieDoyle(3) 2 55
(Andrew Reid) *disp ld tl clr ldr over 6f out: rdn whn hdd 2f out: wknd fnl f* **33/1**
00- **4** *11* **Golestan Palace (IRE)**[179] 7302 3-9-3 0 J-PGuillambert 5 37
(Ed Walker) *in last pair but in tch: nudged along over 5f out: rdn over 3f out: wknd wl over 1f out* **14/1**[3]
5 *1 ½* **Band Of Thunder** 3-9-3 0 NeilChalmers 3 35
(Andrew Balding) *s.i.s: in last pair but in tch: pushed along over 5f out: rdn over 3f out: wknd wl over 1f out* **14/1**[3]

2m 36.06s (-1.94) **Going Correction** -0.10s/f (Good) **5** Ran SP% **111.3**
Speed ratings (Par 99): **102,101,91,84,83**
CSF £2.08 TOTE £1.30: £1.02, £3.10; EX 2.20.
Owner Mrs J Wood **Bred** D Harron & J G Davis **Trained** East Everleigh, Wilts

FOCUS
A weak maiden in which only three ever got involved. The pace slowed appreciably on the turn into the straight. Muddling form with the runner-up much closer to the winner than he had been at Newbury.

1729 BET ON SNOOKER AT TOTESPORT.COM H'CAP 1m 6f 21y
4:40 (4:40) (Class 3) (0-95,91) 4-Y-O+ £7,512 (£2,235; £1,117; £557)

Form RPR
4-16 **1** **Momkinzain (USA)**[16] 1367 4-8-7 75 SamHitchcott 6 84
(Mick Channon) *hld up: rdn over 3f out: hdwy over 2f out: drifted lft over 1f out: led jst ins fnl f: styd on wl* **8/1**[3]
44-3 **2** *1* **Aurorian (IRE)**[29] 1105 5-9-0 84 PatrickHills(3) 8 92
(Richard Hannon) *hld up in tch: hdwy over 3f out: led over 2f out: sn rdn and drifted lft: hdd jst ins fnl f: no ex* **8/1**[3]
5 **3** *2 ¾* **English Summer**[15] 1412 4-9-8 90 SilvestreDeSousa 5 94
(Mark Johnston) *led for 4f: trckd ldr: led over 3f out: sn rdn: hdd over 2f out: styd on same pce fnl 2f* **11/4**[1]
100- **4** *2 ½* **Rajeh (IRE)**[197] 6423 8-9-5 86 CathyGannon 2 87
(John Spearing) *trckd ldrs: rdn over 3f out: styd on same pce fnl 2f* **25/1**
222- **5** *½* **Cosimo de Medici**[142] 7815 4-8-9 77 HayleyTurner 4 77
(Hughie Morrison) *hld up: pushed along briefly on bnd over 6f out: rdn over 3f out: sme late prog: nvr a factor* **5/1**[2]
113- **6** *1 ¾* **Colloquial**[267] 4817 10-9-10 91 (v) FergusSweeney 3 89
(Henry Candy) *trckd ldrs: led after 4f: rdn and hdd over 3f out: kpt chsng ldrs tl wknd ins fnl f* **8/1**[3]
3-06 **7** *nk* **Sherman McCoy**[36] 994 5-9-2 83 JamesMillman 7 80
(Rod Millman) *trckd ldrs: rdn 3f out: sn btn* **17/2**
02-3 **8** *3* **Albeed**[16] 1367 4-8-6 74 TedDurcan 10 67
(John Dunlop) *hld up in tch: hdwy over 3f out: effrt over 2f out: wknd ins fnl f* **5/1**[2]
31-0 **9** *14* **Sula Two**[16] 1367 4-8-7 75 LukeMorris 1 48
(Ron Hodges) *trckd ldrs: rdn over 3f out: wknd 2f out* **10/1**

3m 3.32s (-4.08) **Going Correction** -0.10s/f (Good)
WFA 4 from 5yo+ 1lb **9** Ran SP% **116.8**
Speed ratings (Par 107): **107,106,104,103,103 102,101,100,92**
toteswingers: 1&2 £12.40, 1&3 £4.50, 2&3 £4.40. CSF £70.81 CT £222.39 TOTE £10.70: £2.90, £2.60, £1.90; EX 90.40.
Owner Jaber Abdullah **Bred** Berkshire Stud **Trained** West Ilsley, Berks

FOCUS
A fair staying handicap run at an ordinary pace. The winner is rated back to his maiden best.

NOTEBOOK
Momkinzain(USA) came from the rear of the field and although he drifted to his left as he was brought with his challenge, perhaps in response to the runner-up who was doing the same, he won well enough in the end. He turned around Newbury form with the disappointing Albeed and this was his first victory on turf. (op 10-1)
Aurorian(IRE) travelled well into contention, but edged to his left when coming under pressure and was outpointed by the winner. He is currently 4lb above his last winning mark and this ground might have been a shade quick for him. (op 17-2 tchd 10-1)
English Summer was always to the fore and stuck on well enough for third. He has no problem with fast ground and, having run only seven times so far, can improve. (op 3-1)
Rajeh(IRE), last seen in the autumn over hurdles, was keen early on and plugged on at the same pace at the business end. (tchd 28-1)
Cosimo de Medici was runner-up on sand four times in a row when last seen before Christmas. Without the regular tongue tie, he didn't handle the bend into the straight too well but made modest late progress. (op 11-2 tchd 9-2)
Colloquial should improve for this first outing since August, but he's currently 2lb above his highest winning mark. (tchd 17-2)

1730 BET ON LIVE SPORT AT TOTESPORT.COM LADY RIDERS' H'CAP 6f 212y
5:15 (5:18) (Class 6) (0-65,65) 4-Y-O+ £1,873 (£581; £290; £145) **Stalls** Low

Form RPR
0-60 **1** **Cape Kimberley**[25] 1171 4-9-7 58 MissCHJones(7) 10 67
(Tony Newcombe) *sweating: trckd ldrs: pushed along for str run ins fnl f: led fnl stride* **14/1**
-002 **2** *shd* **George Baker (IRE)**[38] 957 4-9-13 57 MissSBrotherton 13 66
(George Baker) *in tch: hdwy 3f out: rdn over 1f out: led jst ins fnl f: ct fnl stride* **7/2**[1]
120- **3** *¾* **Witchry**[221] 6284 9-10-2 63 MissLMasterton(3) 9 70
(Tony Newcombe) *led: rdn whn hdd jst ins fnl f: kpt on but no ex* **20/1**
6630 **4** *4* **Nubar Boy**[64] 698 4-10-3 61 MrsEEvans 8 57
(David Evans) *towards rr: rdn whn swtchd lft wl over 1f out: kpt on wl fnl f: nrst fin* **10/1**
6-00 **5** *1 ¼* **Batchworth Blaise**[72] 589 8-9-0 51 oh2 MissCNosworthy(7) 15 44
(Eric Wheeler) *s.i.s: in rr: hdwy into midfield over 2f out: sn rdn: styd on fnl f* **12/1**
6-22 **6** *nk* **Grand Piano (IRE)**[46] 863 4-10-0 65 MissEMelbourn(7) 3 57
(Andrew Balding) *chsd ldr: rdn 2f out: sn one pce* **10/1**
360- **7** *¾* **Emiratesdotcom**[154] 7614 5-9-11 60 MissSBradley(5) 1 50+
(Milton Bradley) *t.k.h in mid-div: rdn 2f out: no imp* **14/1**
-060 **8** *¾* **Little Perisher**[20] 1276 4-9-11 55 MissZoeLilly 5 43
(Karen George) *chsd ldrs: rdn whn swtchd lft over 2f out: one pce after* **33/1**
1510 **9** *1* **Crystallize**[16] 1357 5-10-3 61 MissEJJones 4 46
(Andrew Haynes) *mid-div: effrt over 2f out: one pce fnl f* **14/1**
006- **10** *2 ¾* **King Columbo (IRE)**[165] 7491 6-9-7 58 MissSBirkett(7) 7 36
(Julia Feilden) *chsd ldrs: rdn over 2f out: wknd fnl f* **8/1**[3]
3324 **11** *nse* **Dichoh**[44] 885 8-9-9 58 (v) MissHayleyMoore(5) 11 35
(Michael Madgwick) *mid-div: pushed along over 3f out: nvr any imp* **9/2**[2]
3204 **12** *3 ½* **Tuscan King**[12] 1448 4-9-10 54 (tp) MissIsabelTompsett 16 22
(Bernard Llewellyn) *a towards rr* **17/2**
060- **13** *1 ¾* **Charlie Delta**[177] 7332 8-9-8 57 (b) MissJessicaLodge(5) 14 20
(John O'Shea) *hld up in mid-div: rdn over 2f out: wknd over 1f out* **16/1**
41-0 **14** *10* **Spinning Spirit (IRE)**[25] 1171 4-10-1 64 MissHDavies(5) 6 —
(Milton Bradley) *chsd ldrs: rdn over 2f out: sn wknd* **20/1**

1m 26.05s (-2.55) **Going Correction** -0.525s/f (Hard) **14** Ran SP% **126.3**
Speed ratings (Par 101): **95,94,94,89,88 87,86,85,84,81 81,77,75,64**
toteswingers: 1&2 £12.90, 1&3 £41.60, 2&3 £12.20. CSF £63.97 CT £1030.52 TOTE £14.30: £4.00, £2.10, £5.00; EX 115.60.
Owner J R Salter **Bred** Heather Raw **Trained** Yarnscombe, Devon

FOCUS
A moderate handicap for lady amateurs, and not form to treat too seriously. The principals were always towards the fore and the winner is rated to last year's turf best.
Grand Piano(IRE) Official explanation: jockey said saddle slipped
T/Plt: £45.80 to a £1 stake. Pool:£46,659.41 - 743.07 winning tickets. T/Qpdt: £10.20 to a £1 stake. Pool:£2,263.28 - 164.10 winning tickets. TM

1731 - 1737a (Foreign Racing) - See Raceform Interactive

1431 CAPANNELLE (R-H)
Sunday, May 1

OFFICIAL GOING: Turf: soft

1738a PREMIO REGINA ELENA (GROUP 3) (3YO FILLIES) (TURF) 1m
4:05 (12:00) 3-Y-O £73,275 (£32,241; £17,586; £8,793)

RPR
1 **Stay Alive (IRE)**[196] 6975 3-8-11 0 DarioVargiu 4 104
(B Grizzetti, Italy) *settled midfield for 3f: in tch bhd ldng gp ent st: swtchd rt between horses 2 1/2f out: led 2f out: rdn out fnl 300yds to a stay in command* **59/10**
2 *2* **Adamantina**[21] 3-8-11 0 MircoDemuro 12 99
(Vittorio Caruso, Italy) *broke wl on outer to r midfield after 1f: hdwy ent st to chal ldrs: hrd rdn over 2f out: same pce fnl f: nvr trbld wnr* **11/10**[1]
3 *snk* **Good Karma (ITY)**[189] 3-8-11 0 FabioBranca 7 99
(S Botti, Italy) *broke wl and trckd ldrs in 5th tl ent st: rdn 3f out: mde gd prog to ld briefly 2 1/2f out: hdd 2f out: styd on under hrd ride but ct cl home for 2nd* **29/10**[2]
4 *2* **Senza Rete (IRE)**[28] 3-8-11 0 PierantonioConvertino 17 94
(M Gasparini, Italy) *hld up in rr on outer for 4f: gd prog on wd outside 3 1/2f out to move win a few l of ldng gp: rdn 2 1/2f out and sn fnd wanting: one pce fnl 1 1/2f* **67/10**
5 *2* **Oeuvre D'Art (IRE)**[274] 3-8-11 0 StefanoLandi 10 90
(B Grizzetti, Italy) *midfield ent st: rdn to stay in tch 3 1/2f out: sn one pce* **97/10**
6 *3* **Malagenia (IRE)**[217] 3-8-11 0 CristianDemuro 14 83
(L Riccardi, Italy) *slowly away and in rr for 4 1/2f: hrd rdn fr 3f out to pass wkng horses* **97/10**
7 *2* **Coco Demure (IRE)**[147] 3-8-11 0 CFiocchi 5 78
(A Candi, Italy) *midfield on inner tl ent st: ct for pce 3 1/2f out: hrd rdn and one pce* **29/1**
8 *3* **Ksenia (ITY)**[28] 3-8-11 0 LManiezzi 16 71
(R Menichetti, Italy) *hld up nr rr on outer tl ent st: effrt 3f out: sn no ex* **45/1**
9 *2 ½* **Cookies (IRE)**[28] 3-8-11 0 MEsposito 11 66
(E Botti, Italy) *slowly away and in rr after 1f: last and ct for pce 3 1/2f out: nvr figured* **51/1**
10 *1* **Extra (ITY)** 3-8-11 0 GBietolini 6 63
(L Riccardi, Italy) *broke wl to trck ldrs in 3rd tl ent st: led briefly 3f out: hrd rdn 2 1/2f out: btn over 2f out: eased fnl f* **68/1**
11 *2* **Bezique**[21] 3-8-11 0 MKolmarkaj 13 59
(M Gasparini, Italy) *slowly away: rdn to gain position midfield: outpcd and struggling over 3f out* **23/5**[3]
12 *4* **Kagera**[14] 1432 3-8-11 0 CColombi 1 50
(B Grizzetti, Italy) *broke wl to trck ldrs in 2nd tl ent st: w ldr and ev ch 3f out: sn wknd and eased ent fnl 2f* **97/10**
13 *7* **Itasip (IRE)**[21] 3-8-11 0 UmbertoRispoli 8 33
(B Grizzetti, Italy) *in rr gp: rdn and one pce fr 3f out* **34/1**
14 *3* **Speculante (FR)**[28] 3-8-11 0 MarcoMonteriso 3 27
(M Massimi Jr, Italy) *trckd ldrs in 4th tl ent st: ct for pce 3f out: hmpd bdly by fading horses 2 1/2f out when already btn* **99/1**
15 *6* **Sacidevi (IRE)** 3-8-11 0 (b) APolli 2 13
(F Trappolini, Italy) *broke wl to ld after 1f: three l clr ent st: sn one pce and eased over 3f out* **94/1**

1m 39.6s (-0.20) **15** Ran SP% **160.4**
WIN (incl. 1 euro stake): 6.89. PLACES: 1.78, 1.28, 1.48. DF: 18.92.
Owner Scuderia Vittadini **Bred** Grundy Bloodstock S R L **Trained** Italy

NOTEBOOK
Stay Alive(IRE) travelled well into contention, tracking the leaders as the pace quickened, and went on at the quarter-mile pole. She reversed last season's form with today's runner-up, and is expected to be better when tackling a sound surface.

FRANKFURT (L-H)
Sunday, May 1

OFFICIAL GOING: Turf: good

1739a FRUHJAHRS-PREIS DES BANKHAUSES METZLER - STADTRAT ALBERT VON METZLER-RENNEN (GROUP 3) (3YO) (TURF) 1m 2f
3:40 (4:01) 3-Y-0

£27,586 (£9,482; £4,741; £2,586; £1,724; £1,293)

RPR

1 **Earl Of Tinsdal (GER)** 3-9-2 0 .... EPedroza 4 110
(A Wohler, Germany) *broke fast to ld: set solid pce: r.o wl u.p in st to hold off all chals* **3/1[3]**

2 ½ **Saltas (GER)** 3-9-2 0 .... AStarke 5 109
(P Schiergen, Germany) *a.p: settled cl bhd ldr: sn chal in st: r.o wl fnl f* **5/2[2]**

3 1 ½ **Mawingo (GER)**[245] 3-9-2 0 .... ADeVries 1 106
(J Hirschberger, Germany) *broke wl: settled 3rd on inner: swtchd to middle of trck in st: r.o wl wout threatening first two* **6/4[1]**

4 2 ½ **Salut (GER)** 3-9-2 0 .... AGoritz 3 101
(P Schiergen, Germany) *settled towards rr: r.o wl in st but nvr threatened first three* **164/10**

5 6 **World Star (GER)** 3-9-2 0 .... SylvainRuis 2 89
(W Hickst, Germany) *setted midfield on inner: sn rdn in st: nvr threatened* **67/10**

6 3 ½ **Victorian Number (FR)**[45] 882 3-9-2 0 .... ThomasHuet 6 82
(E J O'Neill, France) *settled midfield: flattered briefly in st: sn fdd* **102/10**

7 28 **Fly The Stars (GER)**[196] 6972 3-9-2 0 .... APietsch 7 26
(W Hickst, Germany) *broke away to outside rail at s: nrly unseating rdr: rejnd field at first turn only to shy away again towards outside rail at first turn: hrd rdn to rejoin field in st: clsd on ldr but sn wknd qckly* **77/10**

2m 8.41s (-0.16) **7** Ran SP% **132.7**
WIN (incl. 10 euro stake): 40. PLACES: 12, 12 SF: 94.
Owner Sunrace Stables **Bred** Hannes K Gutschow **Trained** Germany

1513 SAINT-CLOUD (L-H)
Sunday, May 1

OFFICIAL GOING: Turf: good

1740a PRIX DU MUGUET (GROUP 2) (4YO+) (TURF) 1m
2:45 (12:00) 4-Y-0+ **£63,879** (£24,655; £11,767; £7,844; £3,922)

RPR

1 **Rajsaman (FR)**[36] 1000 4-8-11 0 .... (b[1]) ThierryJarnet 3 118
(F Head, France) *settled midfield: qcknd wl 1 1/2f out: chal for ld ent fnl 100yds: tk ld 50yds out: r.o wl: comf* **11/1**

2 1 **Byword**[231] 6015 5-9-4 0 .... MaximeGuyon 10 122
(A Fabre, France) *settled in 2nd: qcknd wl into ld 1f out: r.o wl: hdd 50yds out: r.o wl to hold 2nd on line* **13/8[1]**

3 snk **Sehrezad (IRE)**[175] 7372 6-9-1 0 .... IoritzMendizabal 5 119
(Andreas Lowe, Germany) *a.p in 3rd: rdn 2f out: rallied wl and r.o wl fnl f: narrowly missed 2nd on line* **20/1**

4 2 **Skins Game**[28] 1125 5-8-11 0 .... ChristopheSoumillon 7 110
(J-C Rouget, France) *v s.i.s: qcknd wl 1f out: fin strly: nrest at fin* **5/1[3]**

5 nk **Polytechnicien (USA)**[17] 1342 5-8-11 0 .... OlivierPeslier 1 110
(A Fabre, France) *settled midfield: rdn 1 1/2f out: styd on on fnl f* **3/1[2]**

6 ½ **Kingsfort (USA)**[80] 503 4-8-11 0 .... ThierryThulliez 8 109
(Saeed Bin Suroor) *sn led: stl in front 1f out but sn chal: no ex: styd on* **11/1**

7 2 **Shamalgan (FR)**[21] 4-8-11 0 .... TLukasek 4 104
(A Savujev, Czech Republic) *w.w towards rr: styd on on wd outside fnl f* **20/1**

8 shd **Silverside (USA)**[28] 1125 5-8-11 0 .... JulienGrosjean 6 104
(F Sanchez, France) *sn prom: ev ch in st: sn fdd* **28/1**

9 ¾ **Rostrum (FR)**[28] 1125 4-8-11 0 .... MickaelBarzalona 9 102
(A Fabre, France) *slowly away: w.w towards rr: nt qckn in st: nvr figured* **15/2**

10 15 **Chilpa (FR)**[10] 4-8-9 0 ow1 .... FrankieLeroy 2 66
(P Capelle, France) *in rr fr s: nvr figured in st* **100/1**

1m 38.3s (-9.20) **10** Ran SP% **121.5**
WIN (incl. 1 euro stake): 8.50. PLACES: 2.30, 1.50, 3.10. DF: 11.20. SF: 26.50.
Owner Saeed Nasser Al Romaithi **Bred** Hh The Aga Khan Studs Sc **Trained** France

NOTEBOOK

Rajsaman(FR), wearing blinkers for the first time, won this in good style. He has no immediate entries but could win again if the blinkers work as well next time.
Byword, last year's winner, had a penalty to carry and ran well on this return, but could not hold the winner in the closing stages. He is likely to go for the Prix D'Ispahan next.
Kingsfort(USA) made the running but faded quickly once headed entering the last furlong.

1741 - 1743a (Foreign Racing) - See Raceform Interactive

1576 SHA TIN (R-H)
Sunday, May 1

OFFICIAL GOING: Turf: good

1742a AUDEMARS PIGUET QE II CUP (GROUP 1) (TURF) 1m 2f
9:35 (12:00) 3-Y-0+

£658,959 (£254,335; £115,606; £66,061; £37,985; £23,121)

RPR

1 **Ambitious Dragon (NZ)**[42] 5-9-0 0 .... (b) DouglasWhyte 12 120
(A T Millard, Hong Kong) *settled midfield on rail: 8th and plld wd over 2f out: qcknd 1 1/2f out to ld w 110yds to go: eased cl home* **13/10[1]**

2 ¾ **California Memory (USA)**[63] 5-9-0 0 .... MChadwick 11 118+
(A S Cruz, Hong Kong) *w.w in rr: hdwy 2f out: r.o wl: tk 2nd cl home: nrest at fin* **26/5[3]**

3 nk **Mighty High (FR)**[42] 5-9-0 0 .... WCMarwing 13 117
(J Moore, Hong Kong) *trckd ldr: led 2f out: hdd fnl 110yds: no ex: lost 2nd cl home* **31/1**

4 ½ **Irian (GER)**[28] 5-9-0 0 .... BrettPrebble 8 116+
(J Moore, Hong Kong) *hld up in fnl 3rd of field: mde grnd over 2f out: r.o u.p to take 4th on line: nvr nrr* **22/5[2]**

5 nk **Viva Pataca**[28] 9-9-0 0 .... DarrenBeadman 9 116
(J Moore, Hong Kong) *chsd ldng quartet: 3rd ins fnl f: unable qck* **19/1**

6 ¾ **River Jetez (SAF)**[36] 1000 8-8-10 0 .... BernardFayd'Herbe 2 110
(M F De Kock, South Africa) *pushed along to chse ldng gp but squeezed out first bnd: racd in midfield: pushed along 3 1/2f out: styd on ins fnl 2f: nt pce to chal* **44/5**

7 ¾ **Sapelli (NZ)**[14] 6-9-0 0 .... ZacPurton 4 113
(J Size, Hong Kong) *racd in 3rd: nt qckn fnl f* **113/1**

8 nk **Gitano Hernando**[36] 1002 5-9-0 0 .... DamienOliver 6 112
(H J Brown, South Africa) *towards rr: prog on rail over 2f out: nt qckn fnl f: n.d* **42/1**

9 ¾ **Mr Medici (IRE)**[28] 6-9-0 0 .... GeraldMosse 14 111
(L Ho, Hong Kong) *trckd ldng gp: rdn and no imp fnl 2f* **70/1**

10 1 **Packing Winner (NZ)**[63] 9-9-0 0 .... ODoleuze 7 109
(L Ho, Hong Kong) *led: hdd 2f out: wknd fnl f* **114/1**

11 ½ **Wigmore Hall (IRE)**[36] 1000 4-9-0 0 .... JamieSpencer 10 108
(Michael Bell) *settled towards rr: rdn and no imp fnl 2f* **9/1**

12 nk **Destined For Glory (IRE)**[22] 4-9-0 0 .... JeffLloyd 1 107
(J Moore, Hong Kong) *nvr in contention* **11/1**

13 1 ¼ **Semos (FR)**[42] 4-9-0 0 .... PStrydom 3 105
(D E Ferraris, Hong Kong) *chsd ldrs: rdn and wknd fr 2f out* **99/1**

14 1 ½ **King Dancer (IRE)**[36] 1001 5-9-0 0 .... (b) BrettDoyle 5 102
(S Woods, Hong Kong) *a bhd* **68/1**

2m 2.23s (0.83) **14** Ran SP% **122.7**
PARI-MUTUEL (all including HK$10 stake): WIN 23.00; PLACE 11.50, 19.00, 59.00; DF 75.50.
Owner Johnson Lam Pui Hung **Bred** E P Lowry **Trained** Hong Kong

NOTEBOOK

Ambitious Dragon(NZ), who became the first horse since Vengeance Of Rain in 2005 to add this to the Hong Kong Derby victory, had improved out of all recognition in Hong Kong this season with six wins from seven starts, stepping up in distance on his previous two starts, which included vcitories in the Mercedes-Benz HK Classic Cup and in the HK Derby – form that was boosted in the International Mile by Xtension. Held up, as one would have expected, he showed a great attitude and change of gear to win in the style of a fast-improving Group 1 performer. It will be fascinating to see how he is campaigned because he beat this decent field with something to spare.
California Memory(USA) is quite a small grey who came with a strong finish to win the HK Gold Cup on his first run at 2,000m in Hong Kong – raced as Portus Blendium in France. Another confirmed come-from-behind performer, he stuck to his task well but wasn't quite in the same league as Ambitious Dragon.
Mighty High(FR), who finished behind California Memory in the HK Gold Cup, raced prominently and kept on trying all the way to the line to gain a deserved place. He is far from being a star in Hong Kong but is a soild performer.
Irian(GER) reportedly got on his toes pre-race and was replated (lost that plate in run) when 6th behind California Memory in the Citibank HK Gold Cup, came with his customary late flourish but wasn't up to troubling the winner in the final sprint.
Viva Pataca, the highest money winner in Hong Kong, with earnings of almost HK$82 million, had not finished better than fourth in five starts this season but is still more than capable of making his presence felt, as he showed two starts back when 4th to California Memory in the HK Gold Cup despite a medial quarter crack. His record in this race over past four years reads 1321, and even at the age of nine, he still posted an honourable effort after holding every chance.
River Jetez(SAF), trained by Mike de Kock, looking for his third victory in this race, appeared to get knocked about a little in midpack, so may have become unsettled. Her jockey managed to get her back to hold some sort of chance turning in, but she didn't get home as well as some others. There was a suggestion from her jockey afterwards that she may not have been in a great mood.
Gitano Hernando, who ran respectably in the World Cup without looking a strong candidate for success, had five starts on the turf for one win and two placings, and a fourth to Twice Over in the Newmarket Champion Stakes, but had never raced right-handed. Said to have been working nicely since arriving, he was held up but never got involved. The rider said afterwards that he could be the type for the Melbourne Cup later in the year.
Wigmore Hall(IRE) looked unlucky when third behind Presvis in the Dubai Duty Free (River Jetez a place in front) after finishing in front of the Luca Cumani-trained runner on his previous outing, but didn't look to have any excuse here and just ran flat. He is likely to come home although a race in Singapore might come under consideration.

1323 BEVERLEY (R-H)
Monday, May 2

OFFICIAL GOING: Good to firm (firm in places in back straight)

Bottom bend at narrowest configuration.

Wind: Fresh behind Weather: Fine, dry and blustery

1744 TURFTV MEDIAN AUCTION MAIDEN STKS 5f
2:20 (2:22) (Class 6) 2-Y-0 **£1,683** (£501; £250; £125) **Stalls** Low

Form RPR

1 **Cravat** 2-9-3 0 .... SilvestreDeSousa 7 74+
(Mark Johnston) *cl up: rdn 2f out: drvn and kpt on ent fnl f to ld last 100yds* **11/2[3]**

5 2 ¾ **Superplex**[5] 1619 2-9-3 0 .... PaulHanagan 8 71
(John Quinn) *led: rdn wl over 1f out: drvn ent fnl f: hdd and no ex last 100yds* **10/3[2]**

3 2 ¼ **Tight Lipped (IRE)** 2-9-3 0 .... RichardMullen 6 63
(David Brown) *chsd ldrs: rdn along over 2f out: kpt on same pce appr fnl f* **6/1**

0 4 1 ½ **First Fast Now (IRE)**[16] 1414 2-8-12 0 .... PaulMulrennan 2 53
(Nigel Tinkler) *chsd ldrs: rdn along over 2f out: rdn wl over 1f out: sn one pce* **16/1**

5 ½ **Basantee** 2-8-12 0 .... RichardKingscote 4 51+
(Tom Dascombe) *towards rr: pushed along 1/2-way: sme late hdwy* **11/2[3]**

6 1 ¾ **Maria Medecis (IRE)** 2-8-12 0 .... PhillipMakin 5 45
(Ann Duffield) *in tch: rdn along over 2f out: sn no imp* **9/1**

7 6 **Master Bond** 2-9-3 0 .... TomEaves 1 41+
(Bryan Smart) *s.i.s and bhd: swtchd lft and hdwy on outer to chse ldrs over 2f out: sn rdn and wknd* **3/1[1]**

0 8 3 ½ **Bertie Dancing (IRE)**[26] 1165 2-9-3 0 .... BarryMcHugh 3 16
(Nigel Tinkler) *dwlt: a in rr* **20/1**

61.57 secs (-1.93) **Going Correction** -0.425s/f (Firm) **8** Ran SP% **113.8**
Speed ratings (Par 91): **98,96,93,90,90 87,77,72**
toteswingers: 1&2 £1.90, 1&3 £2.00, 2&3 £3.20. CSF £23.92 TOTE £5.90: £2.60, £1.10, £1.60; EX 15.40.

Owner Sheikh Hamdan Bin Mohammed Al Maktoum **Bred** Darley **Trained** Middleham Moor, N Yorks

FOCUS
An ordinary maiden and the level is fluid, but a pleasing start from the winner.

NOTEBOOK
Cravat, a March foal, half-brother to, among others, useful 6f 2-y-o winner Cedarberg, seemed well enough educated and showed a good attitude to make a winning start. He looks the type to progress. (old market op 6-1 new market op 5-1)

Superplex showed ability on his debut at Pontefract and built on that with a solid performance. He faced competition for the lead but still kept on well and should soon be winning. (new market op 4-1 tchd 3-1)

Tight Lipped(IRE), a March foal 17,000gns half-brother to, among others, 1m-1m1f winner Moyoko, should improve. (new market op 11-2)

First Fast Now(IRE) has learnt from her debut at Ripon and should come on again. (old market op 14-1 new market op 14-1)

Basantee, a £12,000 March foal, half-sister to multiple sprint winner Gentle Guru, ran as though in need of the experience. (new market op 13-2)

Master Bond, an April foal, is not that big but looked fit and well. He seemed fancied but missed the break and was never really going well enough. (new market tchd 7-2)

1745 MAYDAY RACEDAY H'CAP — 5f
2:50 (2:51) (Class 5) (0-75,75) 3-Y-O — **£2,298** (£684; £341; £170) **Stalls** Low

Form — RPR

3-14 **1** **Another Wise Kid (IRE)**[2] 1697 3-9-4 **72** MickyFenton 5 — 77
(Paul Midgley) *towards rr: pushed along 1/2-way: hdwy over 1f out: sn rdn and styd on strly ins fnl f to ld nr fin* **13/2**[2]

3122 **2** ¾ **Rhal (IRE)**[23] 1249 3-9-1 **69** TomEaves 2 — 71
(Bryan Smart) *led: rdn clr over 1f out: edgd lft ent fnl f: drvn and hung lft ins fnl 100yds: hdd and no ex nr fin* **8/1**

241- **3** hd **Shesastar**[177] 7347 3-9-0 **68** SilvestreDeSousa 1 — 69
(David Barron) *dwlt: sn in tch on inner: hdwy to chse ldrs 1/2-way: rdn over 1f out: drvn and kpt on ins fnl f* **7/2**[1]

5105 **4** 1 ¾ **Pineapple Pete (IRE)**[6] 1595 3-8-2 **63** (t) NoraLooby(7) 11 — 58
(Alan McCabe) *sn outpcd and bhd: swtchd rt 1/2-way: hdwy on inner 2f out: rdn and n.m.r ent fnl f: kpt on wl towards fin* **20/1**

620- **5** hd **Sea Flower (IRE)**[254] 5301 3-9-0 **68** DavidAllan 4 — 62
(Tim Easterby) *chsd ldr: rdn wl over 1f out: drvn and wknd ent fnl f* **9/1**

0-00 **6** hd **Boundless Spirit**[16] 1391 3-9-3 **71** (t) PaulQuinn 10 — 65
(David Nicholls) *s.i.s and bhd: rdn along 1/2-way: hdwy over 1f out: kpt on ins fnl f: nrst fin* **12/1**

4060 **7** nse **Insolenceofoffice (IRE)**[24] 1214 3-9-2 **75** (p) SeanLevey(5) 3 — 68
(Andrew Crook) *chsd ldng pair: rdn along 2f out: drvn appr fnl f: sn wknd* **28/1**

1323 **8** ¾ **Mazovian (USA)**[2] 1674 3-8-12 **66** KellyHarrison 8 — 57
(Michael Chapman) *chsd ldrs: rdn along 2f out: sn wknd* **18/1**

642- **9** 2 ½ **Surely This Time (IRE)**[256] 5239 3-9-2 **70** PhillipMakin 6 — 52
(Kevin Ryan) *wnt lft s: sn chsng ldrs: rdn along 2f out: drvn over 1f out: sn wknd* **7/1**[3]

2114 **10** hd **Fantasy Fry**[13] 1452 3-9-7 **75** RichardKingscote 9 — 56
(Tom Dascombe) *a towards rr* **22/1**

00-1 **11** nse **Melodize**[7] 1561 3-8-7 **58** 6ex PaulHanagan 7 — 42
(David O'Meara) *hmpd s: midfield: rdn along over 2f out: sn btn* **7/2**[1]

60.84 secs (-2.66) **Going Correction** -0.425s/f (Firm) **11** Ran SP% **116.9**
Speed ratings (Par 99): **104,102,102,99,99 99,98,97,93,93 93**
toteswingers: 1&2 £2.40, 1&3 £8.70, 2&3 £10.30. CSF £55.63 CT £212.68 TOTE £8.00: £2.60, £1.90, £2.10; EX 40.10.

Owner Michael Ng **Bred** Paul Kavanagh **Trained** Westow, N Yorks

■ Stewards' Enquiry : Tom Eaves caution: careless riding.

FOCUS
A modest 3-y-o sprint handicap rated through the fourth to his latest mark.

Surely This Time(IRE) Official explanation: jockey said gelding hung left final 2f

1746 BEVERLEY ROTARY CLUB H'CAP — 1m 1f 207y
3:20 (3:20) (Class 4) (0-80,78) 4-Y-O+ — **£4,144** (£1,233; £616; £307) **Stalls** Low

Form — RPR

5355 **1** **Danderek**[16] 1390 5-9-5 **76** PaulHanagan 7 — 84
(Richard Fahey) *trckd ldr: hdwy to ld wl over 2f out: rdn clr wl over 1f out: drvn ent fnl f: hld on wl* **4/1**[1]

2-03 **2** nk **Zaplamation (IRE)**[18] 1324 6-8-6 **68** SeanLevey(5) 3 — 76
(John Quinn) *hld up: hdwy wl over 2f out: swtchd lft and rdn over 1f out: styd on wl fnl f* **9/2**[2]

-161 **3** 1 ¾ **Prince Apollo**[17] 1353 6-9-5 **76** (t) DarryllHolland 8 — 80
(Gerard Butler) *midfield: hdwy 4f out: rdn to chse ldrs 2f out and sn edgd rt: drvn and kpt on fnl f* **4/1**[1]

22-2 **4** 2 ¼ **Saint Thomas (IRE)**[24] 1223 4-9-7 **78** GrahamGibbons 4 — 78
(John Mackie) *trckd ldng pair: effrt over 2f out: rdn to chse wnr wl over 1f out: sn drvn and kpt on same pce* **5/1**[3]

322- **5** 1 **Silvery Moon (IRE)**[210] 6624 4-8-13 **70** DavidAllan 1 — 68
(Tim Easterby) *in rr: hdwy 3f out: rdn along 2f out: kpt on appr fnl f: nt rch ldrs* **6/1**

0-40 **6** 11 **Yahrab (IRE)**[13] 1470 6-9-7 **78** (b) DavidNolan 10 — 54
(Declan Carroll) *led: rdn along over 3f out: hdd wl over 2f out and sn wknd* **16/1**

000- **7** 5 **King Fingal (IRE)**[29] 6677 6-9-5 **76** TomEaves 11 — 42
(John Quinn) *trckd ldrs: hdwy 4f out: rdn along 3f out: sn drvn and btn* **9/1**

0 **8** 12 **Strong Knight**[16] 1390 4-9-0 **71** DanielTudhope 6 — 13
(Tim Walford) *in rr: wd st to stands' rail: sn rdn and nvr a factor* **40/1**

1540 **9** 2 ¾ **Lingfield Bound (IRE)**[33] 1046 4-9-3 **74** PhillipMakin 2 — —
(John Best) *chsd ldrs: hdwy 1/2-way: rdn along 3f out and sn wknd* **18/1**

2m 3.40s (-3.60) **Going Correction** -0.425s/f (Firm) **9** Ran SP% **112.7**
Speed ratings (Par 105): **97,96,95,93,92 83,79,70,68**
toteswingers: 1&2 £1.30, 1&3 £3.50, 2&3 £6.30 CSF £21.37 CT £74.78 TOTE £3.30: £1.10, £1.80, £2.10; EX 21.00.

Owner B Buckley D Rowlands & D Keenan **Bred** Mrs Maureen Buckley **Trained** Musley Bank, N Yorks

■ Stewards' Enquiry : Sean Levey one-day ban: used whip in incorrect place (May 16)

FOCUS
An ordinary handicap rated around the third and fourth.

Strong Knight Official explanation: jockey said gelding hung left in straight

Lingfield Bound(IRE) Official explanation: trainer's rep said colt was unsuited by the good to firm (firm in places) ground

1747 GARDEN FETE IN THE COURSE ENCLOSURE H'CAP — 1m 100y
3:50 (3:50) (Class 4) (0-85,84) 4-Y-O+ — **£4,209** (£1,252; £625; £312) **Stalls** Low

Form — RPR

0-12 **1** **Cono Zur (FR)**[5] 1621 4-8-6 **72** JamesSullivan(3) 5 — 81
(Ruth Carr) *mde all: rdn wl over 1f out: edgd lft and kpt on wl fnl f* **3/1**[1]

0-60 **2** 1 ¾ **Doctor Zhivago**[16] 1387 4-9-7 **84** AdrianNicholls 2 — 89
(David Nicholls) *in tch: hdwy 4f out: rdn to chse ldrs over 2f out: drvn and kpt on same pce fnl f* **9/2**[2]

2433 **3** nk **Elijah Pepper (USA)**[31] 1075 6-8-13 **76** GrahamGibbons 6 — 80
(David Barron) *sn trcking wnr: effrt over 2f out: rdn wl over 1f out: drvn and one pce fnl f* **13/2**

60-0 **4** 2 ¼ **Fibs And Flannel**[29] 1110 4-8-9 **72** DavidAllan 7 — 71
(Tim Easterby) *hld up: hdwy over 2f out: rdn to chse ldrs over 1f out: sn drvn and no imp fnl f* **6/1**[3]

400- **5** 3 ½ **Sunnyside Tom (IRE)**[177] 7352 7-9-3 **80** PaulHanagan 9 — 71
(Richard Fahey) *hld up: hdwy over 2f out: rdn wl over 1f out: sn no imp* **13/2**

50-0 **6** 1 **Shadowtime**[16] 1410 6-9-2 **79** PatrickMathers 8 — 67
(Colin Teague) *chsd ldrs: rdn along over 2f out: drvn and wknd over 1f out* **12/1**

100- **7** 2 ½ **En Fuego**[203] 6805 4-8-13 **76** SilvestreDeSousa 4 — 59
(Geoffrey Harker) *in tch: rdn along on inner wl over 2f out: sn wknd* **25/1**

0-00 **8** nk **Barren Brook**[16] 1410 4-8-9 **79** DavidSimmonson(7) 3 — 61
(Michael Easterby) *a in rr* **25/1**

00-0 **9** 6 **Spying**[16] 1410 4-9-0 **77** PaulMulrennan 1 — 45
(Ann Duffield) *chsd ldrs on inner: rdn along wl over 2f out: wknd wl over 1f out* **6/1**[3]

1m 43.89s (-3.71) **Going Correction** -0.425s/f (Firm) **9** Ran SP% **113.8**
Speed ratings (Par 105): **101,99,98,96,93 92,89,89,83**
toteswingers: 1&2 £2.60, 1&3 £2.20, 2&3 £13.10 CSF £16.03 CT £79.25 TOTE £3.40: £1.30, £2.20, £2.10.

Owner Ruth Carr Racing **Bred** Jean-Pierre-Joseph Dubois **Trained** Huby, N Yorks

FOCUS
A fair handicap, although it paid to race prominently and the first two set the standard.

En Fuego Official explanation: jockey said gelding hung right

1748 YORKSHIRE RACING SUMMER FESTIVAL IN JULY H'CAP — 7f 100y
4:20 (4:20) (Class 5) (0-75,73) 4-Y-O+ — **£2,298** (£684; £341; £170) **Stalls** Low

Form — RPR

00-0 **1** **My Gacho (IRE)**[29] 1109 9-9-7 **73** (v) AdrianNicholls 2 — 80
(David Nicholls) *mde all: rdn wl over 1f out: drvn and edgd lft ins fnl f: hld on wl* **9/2**[3]

0-04 **2** ¾ **Handsome Falcon**[5] 1614 7-9-2 **73** (p) LeeTopliss(5) 3 — 78
(Ollie Pears) *trckd ldrs: effrt on inner and n.m.r over 2f out: swtchd lft and rdn to chse wnr wl over 1f out: drvn ent fnl f: kpt on wl towards fionish* **15/2**

0160 **3** ¾ **Powerful Pierre**[7] 1558 4-8-12 **64** (p) BarryMcHugh 1 — 67
(Ian McInnes) *hld up in tch: hdwy on inner wl over 1f out: rdn and n.m.r ins fnl f: drvn and kpt on towards fin* **9/1**

5-02 **4** shd **Violent Velocity (IRE)**[5] 1613 8-8-4 **63** ShaneBKelly(7) 7 — 66
(John Quinn) *hld up: hdwy wl over 2f out: rdn to chse ldrs over 1f out: drvn ins fnl f: kpt on* **3/1**[1]

00-0 **5** 4 ½ **Rock 'N' Royal**[23] 1245 4-9-4 **70** PaulHanagan 6 — 62
(Richard Fahey) *trckd ldrs: hdwy on outer 1/2-way: rdn over 2f out: drvn over 1f out: sn wknd* **9/2**[3]

001- **6** hd **Burns Night**[269] 4796 5-9-4 **70** SilvestreDeSousa 4 — 61
(Geoffrey Harker) *hld up in rr: hdwy 2f out: rdn over 1f out: no imp* **9/1**

30-4 **7** ¾ **Seldom (IRE)**[5] 1613 5-8-9 **61** DavidAllan 5 — 50
(Mel Brittain) *cl up: rdn along over 2f out: sn drvn and wknd wl over 1f out* **4/1**[2]

1m 31.37s (-2.43) **Going Correction** -0.425s/f (Firm) **7** Ran SP% **113.1**
Speed ratings (Par 103): **96,95,94,94,89 88,87**
toteswingers: 1&2 £20.30, 1&3 £7.20, 2&3 £14.80 CSF £36.33 TOTE £4.60: £2.30, £5.20; EX 49.90.

Owner Grant Mercer **Bred** Mount Coote Stud **Trained** Sessay, N Yorks

FOCUS
A modest handicap run in a time was 0.88 seconds quicker than the following Class 6 event for 3-y-os. The third sets a reasonable standard.

1749 WHITE RABBIT H'CAP — 7f 100y
4:50 (4:52) (Class 6) (0-65,65) 3-Y-O — **£1,683** (£501; £250; £125) **Stalls** Low

Form — RPR

30-4 **1** **Coax**[34] 1031 3-9-7 **65** SilvestreDeSousa 12 — 70+
(Mark Johnston) *cl up: effrt over 2f out: rdn over 1f out: led appr fnl f: drvn out* **7/2**[1]

00-0 **2** nk **Alensgrove (IRE)**[23] 1246 3-9-1 **59** MickyFenton 2 — 63+
(Paul Midgley) *towards rr: pushed along on outer over 2f out: rdn wl over 1f out: str run ent fnl f: drvn and edgd rt towards fin: jst failed* **20/1**

060- **3** hd **Valeo Si Vales (IRE)**[299] 3785 3-9-3 **61** PhillipMakin 9 — 64
(Jamie Osborne) *trckd ldrs: hdwy over 2f out: rdn to chse ldng pair over 1f out: drvn and kpt on wl fnl f* **5/1**[2]

6-55 **4** 1 ¼ **Rational Act (IRE)**[9] 1524 3-8-13 **57** DavidAllan 3 — 57
(Tim Easterby) *led: rdn along over 2f out: drvn wl over 1f out: hdd appr fnl f: kpt on same pce* **11/2**[3]

400- **5** 1 ½ **Millies Folly**[180] 7296 3-9-5 **63** DavidNolan 8 — 60
(Declan Carroll) *towards rr: hdwy over 2f out: rdn wl over 1f out: kpt on same pce fnl f* **11/1**

1-52 **6** 3 **Roman Strait**[94] 335 3-9-6 **64** PaulHanagan 10 — 53
(Michael Blanshard) *hld up: hdwy 3f out: rdn to chse ldrs 2f out: drvn over 1f out and sn no imp* **11/2**[3]

050- **7** 1 ½ **Say A Prayer**[261] 5099 3-8-9 **53** FrederikTylicki 4 — 38
(Tim Easterby) *chsd ldrs on inner: rdn along wl over 2f out: grad wknd* **12/1**

0-63 **8** 3 ¾ **Twennyshortkid**[19] 1303 3-8-7 **51** oh1 BarryMcHugh 7 — 27
(Paul Midgley) *in tch: effrt over 3f out: rdn over 2f out: sn drvn and btn* **6/1**

00-0 **9** nk **Sleights Boy (IRE)**[18] 1331 3-8-9 **53** PatrickMathers 1 — 28
(Ian McInnes) *chsd ldrs: rdn along wl over 2f out: sn wknd* **40/1**

03-0 **10** 6 **Inca Chief**[14] 1437 3-9-1 **59** (t) PaulMulrennan 5 — 19
(Ann Duffield) *in tch on inner: pushed along over 3f out: rdn wl over 2f out and sn wknd* **14/1**

55-0 **11** *40* **Oldmeldrum (IRE)**[33] 1038 3-9-5 **63**............................ DarryllHolland 6 —
(Peter Salmon) *rrd s and slowly away: a bhd: eased fnl 2f* **12/1**

1m 32.25s (-1.55) **Going Correction** -0.425s/f (Firm) **11** Ran SP% **121.5**
Speed ratings (Par 97): **91,90,90,89,87 83,82,77,77,70 24**
toteswingers: 1&2 £15.30, 1&3 £5.40, 2&3 £24.60 CSF £81.86 CT £365.54 TOTE £5.40: £1.30, £6.60, £2.40; EX 104.80.
Owner Sheikh Hamdan Bin Mohammed Al Maktoum **Bred** Darley **Trained** Middleham Moor, N Yorks

FOCUS
A modest 3-y-o handicap run at a good pace and, despite the winner possibly being advantaged by making the running, the form looks sound overall.
Inca Chief Official explanation: trainer said gelding had a breathing problem
Oldmeldrum(IRE) Official explanation: jockey said filly was slowly away; trainer said filly was unsuited by the good to firm (firm in places) ground
T/Plt: £112.30 to a £1 stake. Pool:£50,540.70 - 328.33 winning tickets. T/Qpdt: £30.30 to a £1 stake. Pool:£32,979.99 - 72.70 winning tickets. JR

CHEPSTOW (L-H)

Monday, May 2

OFFICIAL GOING: Good to firm (watered; 8.1)
Wind: Strong half across, partially behind in relation to straight. Weather: Sunny

1750 GRAND PIER WESTON-SUPER-MARE H'CAP — 1m 4f 23y
2:15 (2:15) (Class 6) (0-65,71) 4-Y-O+ — £1,683 (£501; £250; £125) Stalls Low

Form — RPR

20-1 **1** **Boa**[16] 1398 6-9-3 **61**............................ DavidProbert 6 — 70
(Reg Hollinshead) *mid-div: hdwy 3f out: sn rdn: led ent fnl f: hld on: all out* **7/2**[1]

000- **2** *shd* **Marju King (IRE)**[217] 6427 5-9-4 **62**............................ TomMcLaughlin 2 — 69
(Stuart Kittow) *hld up towards rr: hdwy fr 4f out: rdn to chse ldrs over 2f out: str run fnl 120yds: jst failed* **12/1**

- **3** *1 1/2* **Rajnagan (IRE)**[172] 7-8-11 **58**............................(t) JohnFahy(3) 8 — 63
(Paul Webber) *towards rr of midfield: hdwy fr 4f out: rdn to ld over 2f out: hdd ent fnl f: kpt on same pce* **14/1**

000- **4** *3 1/4* **Outland (IRE)**[194] 7011 5-8-10 **54**............................ AdrianMcCarthy 14 — 53
(J R Jenkins) *trckd ldrs: led 4f out: sn rdn: hdd over 2f out: kpt on same pce* **20/1**

350- **5** *4* **Dancing Storm**[197] 6959 8-9-3 **61**............................ GeorgeBaker 3 — 54
(Stuart Kittow) *mid-div: rdn over 3f out: one pce fnl 2f* **11/2**[3]

46-5 **6** *1 3/4* **James Pollard (IRE)**[15] 1107 6-9-4 **62**............................(t) JimmyQuinn 1 — 52
(Bernard Llewellyn) *slowly away: towards rr of midfield: rdn and sme imp 3f out: one pce fnl 2f* **9/2**[2]

1306 **7** *5* **Carr Hall (IRE)**[19] 1308 8-8-12 **59**............................ MartinHarley(3) 15 — 41
(Tony Carroll) *hld up towards rr: pushed along and hdwy over 3f out: nvr threatened ldrs: wknd fnl f* **9/2**[2]

-004 **8** *1 1/4* **Zagarock**[7] 1567 4-8-7 **51** oh5............................ NeilChalmers 12 — 31
(Bryn Palling) *broke wl: restrained bk into mid-div: wknd over 2f out* **12/1**

40-5 **9** *3/4* **Bussell Along (IRE)**[42] 930 5-8-0 **51** oh6............(t) RachealKneller(7) 11 — 30
(Pam Ford) *trckd ldrs: rdn 3f out: wknd fnl f* **66/1**

-340 **10** *9* **Soundbyte**[54] 808 6-9-3 **61**............................ TadhgO'Shea 10 — 26
(John Gallagher) *in tch tl wknd 3f out* **17/2**

000- **11** *1 1/4* **Nobbys Girl**[207] 6699 6-8-4 **51** oh6............................ KierenFox(3) 4 — 14
(Ronald Harris) *trckd ldr: rdn over 5f out: wknd over 3f out* **50/1**

4-50 **12** *3 1/2* **Darfour**[23] 1233 7-8-2 **51** oh6............................(t) RyanPowell(5) 5 — —
(Martin Hill) *sddle slipped over 8f out: a towards rr* **40/1**

000- **13** *3/4* **Arakette (IRE)**[192] 7069 4-8-2 **51** oh6.................... DanielleMcCreery(5) 7 — —
(Paul Burgoyne) *led tl 4f out: sn rdn: wknd over 2f out* **80/1**

2m 36.69s (-2.31) **Going Correction** -0.125s/f (Firm) **13** Ran SP% **118.4**
Speed ratings (Par 101): **102,101,100,98,96 94,91,90,90,84 83,81,80**
toteswingers:1&2:£4.30, 1&3:£11.20, 2&3:£20.10 CSF £45.23 CT £531.64 TOTE £4.30: £1.70, £3.80, £5.40; EX 45.70.
Owner Geoff Lloyd **Bred** R Hollinshead **Trained** Upper Longdon, Staffs

FOCUS
Run-of-the-mill fare, although the pace was sound enough in the main and there's no reason the form won't prove solid for the level with the front three pulling clear. The race is rated through the runner-up to the balance of his form.
Darfour Official explanation: jockey said saddle slipped

1751 GRAND PIER WESTON-SUPER-MARE MAIDEN STKS — 1m 2f 36y
2:45 (2:46) (Class 5) 3-Y-O+ — £2,590 (£770; £385; £192) Stalls Low

Form — RPR

0- **1** **Gold Mine**[207] 6689 3-8-12 0............................(t) DavidProbert 5 — 73
(Andrew Balding) *trckd ldr: rdn to ld jst ins 2f out: styd on wl: asserting nr fin: rdn out* **11/2**

00- **2** *3/4* **Brezza Di Mare (IRE)**[207] 6689 3-8-9 0.................... LouisBeuzelin(3) 2 — 71
(Brian Meehan) *led: rdn 3f out: hdd jst ins 2f out: kpt pressing wnr: hld nring fin* **4/1**[2]

00- **3** *2* **Deceptive**[191] 7094 3-8-7 0............................ JimmyQuinn 7 — 62+
(Roger Charlton) *trckd ldrs tl lost pl on bnd over 6f out: rdn 4f out: hdwy 3f out: wnt 3rd 2f out: styd on fnl f* **9/2**[3]

00/ **4** *8* **Lion Road (USA)**[564] 6789 5-9-10 0............................ MartinHarley(3) 1 — 52
(Alan King) *trckd ldrs: rdn over 3f out: sn one pce: fdd fnl f* **11/1**

0 **5** *shd* **Nuzool (IRE)**[18] 1338 3-8-12 0............................ TadhgO'Shea 9 — 51
(John Dunlop) *trckd ldrs: rdn over 3f out: sn one pce: fdd fnl f* **7/2**[1]

00- **6** *3* **Tidal Run**[232] 5985 3-8-7 0............................ SaleemGolam 4 — 40
(Mick Channon) *trckd ldrs: rdn over 3f out: wknd 2f out* **15/2**

7 *30* **Elby**[160] 4-9-10 0............................ JohnFahy(3) 6 — —
(Eve Johnson Houghton) *little slowly away: a towards rr: t.o fr over 2f out* **33/1**

8 *81* **Ellies Girl (IRE)** 3-8-10 0 ow3............................ TomMcLaughlin 8 — —
(Ronald Harris) *dwlt: a last: lost tch fr 4f out: t.o* **12/1**

0- **S** **Blue Mamba**[310] 3437 4-9-8 0............................ RussKennemore 3 — —
(Reg Hollinshead) *hld up: in tch in 6th whn slipped up ent st wl over 4f out* **7/1**

2m 8.13s (-2.47) **Going Correction** -0.125s/f (Firm)
WFA 3 from 4yo+ 15lb **9** Ran SP% **119.0**
Speed ratings (Par 103): **104,103,101,95,95 92,68,4,—**
toteswingers:1&2:£5.00, 1&3:£6.40, 2&3:£4.70 CSF £28.73 TOTE £8.60: £2.40, £2.00, £2.20; EX 33.50.
Owner Sir Gordon Brunton **Bred** Sir Gordon Brunton **Trained** Kingsclere, Hants

FOCUS
The bare form of this maiden is almost certainly nothing out of the ordinary, although it did contain a few lightly raced raced sorts who are likely to improve as they gain experience and the time was good.

1752 PREMIER FOOD COURTS LTD VETERANS' H'CAP — 5f 16y
3:15 (3:15) (Class 5) (0-75,73) 6-Y-O+ — £2,331 (£693; £346; £173) Stalls High

Form — RPR

11-6 **1** **Wooden King (IRE)**[14] 1444 6-9-0 **66**............................ TomMcLaughlin 5 — 73
(Malcolm Saunders) *a.p: rdn to ld over 1f out: hld on: all out* **9/2**[2]

140- **2** *shd* **Matterofact (IRE)**[216] 6440 8-9-3 **72**............................ MartinHarley(3) 10 — 79
(Malcolm Saunders) *in tch: hdwy over 2f out: rdn and str run ent fnl f: edgd lft: kpt on: jst hld* **16/1**

050- **3** *1/2* **Triple Dream**[145] 7754 6-8-11 **66**............................(tp) SimonPearce(3) 11 — 71
(Milton Bradley) *led: rdn and hdd over 1f out: keeping on in cl 3rd whn short of room nring fin* **12/1**

3-60 **4** *2 1/2* **Atlantic Beach**[14] 1444 6-9-7 **73**............................ JimmyQuinn 9 — 69
(Milton Bradley) *chsd ldrs: rdn 3f out: kpt on same pce fnl 2f* **7/1**

401 **5** *1/2* **Steelcut**[13] 1471 7-9-2 **71**............................(p) JohnFahy(3) 4 — 65
(David Evans) *chsd ldrs: rdn over 2f out: kpt on same pce* **7/1**

6425 **6** *nk* **Even Bolder**[21] 1267 8-9-4 **73**............................ KierenFox(3) 6 — 66
(Eric Wheeler) *towards rr: swtchd rt over 1f out: kpt on but nt pce to trble ldrs* **6/1**[3]

023- **7** *2* **First In Command (IRE)**[15] 1425 6-9-2 **68**..................(t) TadhgO'Shea 2 — 54
(Daniel Mark Loughnane, Ire) *s.i.s: towards rr: nvr gng pce to get involved* **10/3**[1]

000- **8** *1 3/4* **Hoh Hoh Hoh**[219] 6374 9-9-4 **70**............................ GeorgeBaker 7 — 50
(Richard Price) *chsd ldrs: rdn over 2f out: wknd fnl f* **12/1**

4240 **9** *6* **Misaro (GER)**[13] 1453 10-8-7 **59** oh4............................(b) DavidProbert 8 — 17
(Ronald Harris) *sn struggling in rr: eased whn btn over 1f out* **14/1**

40-4 **10** *1/2* **Desperate Dan**[21] 1274 10-9-7 **73**............................(v) NeilChalmers 3 — 29
(Andrew Haynes) *chsd ldrs tl wknd over 2f out* **18/1**

58.47 secs (-0.83) **Going Correction** -0.125s/f (Firm) **10** Ran SP% **113.7**
Speed ratings: **101,100,100,96,95 94,91,88,79,78**
toteswingers:1&2:£12.00, 1&3:£13.00, 2&3:£36.60 CSF £71.61 CT £820.98 TOTE £5.50: £1.10, £5.30, £4.40; EX 48.30.
Owner Pat Hancock **Bred** Terence E Connelly **Trained** Green Ore, Somerset

FOCUS
Fair form in a sprint confined to horses aged six and over. The first and third set the gallop in a race where the runner-up was only the one who threatened to get into it from off the pace. The runner-up sets the standard.
First In Command(IRE) Official explanation: vet said gelding bled from the nose
Misaro(GER) Official explanation: jockey said gelding was unsuited by the good to firm ground

1753 FESTIVAL RACING H'CAP — 6f 16y
3:45 (3:48) (Class 6) (0-65,69) 3-Y-O — £1,683 (£501; £250; £125) Stalls High

Form — RPR

550- **1** **Swendab (IRE)**[205] 6740 3-9-0 **63**............................ RyanPowell(5) 7 — 67
(John O'Shea) *a.p: rdn 3f out: r.o to ld ins fnl f: rdn out* **14/1**

364- **2** *nk* **Shes Rosie**[224] 6258 3-9-5 **63**............................ RussKennemore 9 — 66
(John O'Shea) *a.p: rdn over 2f out: edgd lft and led ent fnl f: hdd fnl 120yds: no ex* **14/1**

544- **3** *3/4* **St Oswald**[282] 4379 3-9-5 **63**............................ GeorgeBaker 2 — 64+
(Roger Charlton) *mid-div: pushed along over 3f out: hdwy over 2f out: sn rdn: kpt on ins fnl f but nvr quite getting there* **15/8**[1]

-330 **4** *hd* **Quadra Hop (IRE)**[83] 452 3-9-0 **58**............................(t) DavidProbert 8 — 58
(Bryn Palling) *led: rdn over 2f out: hdd ent fnl f: kpt on but no ex* **16/1**

5-11 **5** *1 1/4* **Novabridge**[6] 1595 3-9-11 **69** 6ex............................(b) SaleemGolam 11 — 65
(Andrew Haynes) *mid-div: pushed along and hdwy over 3f out: sn rdn: kpt on same pce fnl 2f* **13/2**[2]

5243 **6** *hd* **Scommettitrice (IRE)**[31] 1078 3-8-9 **53**....................(b) NeilChalmers 12 — 48
(Ronald Harris) *chsd ldrs: outpcd over 2f out: kpt on ins fnl f* **9/1**

5254 **7** *nk* **Local Diktator**[32] 1064 3-8-13 **60**............................(t) KierenFox(3) 13 — 54
(Ronald Harris) *mid-div: hung bdly lft over 4f out: sn on far side rails and run: kpt on ins fnl f* **20/1**

-000 **8** *2* **Crazy In Love**[68] 655 3-8-7 **51** oh4............................(v[1]) JimmyQuinn 5 — 39
(Olivia Maylam) *mid-div: rdn over 2f out: nvr any imp* **50/1**

000- **9** *1 3/4* **Silca Conegliano (IRE)**[171] 7418 3-8-13 **60**............ MartinHarley(3) 10 — 42
(Mick Channon) *chsd ldrs: rdn over 2f out: fdd ent fnl f* **25/1**

5-0 **10** *1* **Teriyaki (IRE)**[17] 1376 3-9-7 **65**............................ TadhgO'Shea 3 — 44
(Daniel Mark Loughnane, Ire) *hmpd over 4f out: a towards rr* **16/1**

-60 **11** *2* **Excellence (IRE)**[13] 1449 3-8-7 **51** oh4............................ JamieMackay 14 — 24
(Karen George) *sn pushed along: a towards rr* **80/1**

263 **12** *3/4* **Sailing North (USA)**[13] 1449 3-9-6 **64**............................ TomMcLaughlin 4 — 34
(Ronald Harris) *chsd ldrs: rdn over 2f out: sn wknd* **12/1**

0453 **13** *1 3/4* **Three Scoops**[38] 967 3-8-4 **51** oh2............................(tp) BillyCray(3) 1 — 16
(Dominic Ffrench Davis) *mid-div tl wknd over 2f out* **7/1**[3]

0000 **14** *1/2* **Five Cool Kats (IRE)**[34] 1022 3-8-4 **51** oh1............................ JohnFahy(3) 6 — 14
(Paul Burgoyne) *s.i.s: sn pushed along: a towards rr* **25/1**

1m 11.95s (-0.05) **Going Correction** -0.125s/f (Firm) **14** Ran SP% **119.1**
Speed ratings (Par 97): **95,94,93,93,91 91,91,88,86,84 82,81,78,78**
toteswingers:1&2:£49.50, 1&3:£9.10, 2&3:£10.30 CSF £183.77 CT £553.76 TOTE £25.50: £5.20, £5.30, £1.80; EX 200.80.
Owner The Cross Racing Club & Patrick Brady **Bred** P Brady **Trained** Elton, Gloucs

FOCUS
Just a run-of-the-mill handicap, the majority a lot more exposed than many who contest 3-y-o handicaps at this time of year. The main action unfolded towards the centre, most of the principals up with the pace throughout. The third can do better having come from off the pace.
Three Scoops Official explanation: jockey said filly never travelled

1754 SJH MACHINERY KUBOTA DEALER H'CAP — 1m 14y
4:15 (4:16) (Class 4) (0-80,78) 3-Y-O — £3,885 (£1,156; £577; £288) Stalls High

Form — RPR

2165 **1** **Malice Or Mischief (IRE)**[12] 1485 3-9-2 **75**.................... DavidProbert 4 — 81
(Tony Carroll) *trckd ldrs: led jst over 2f out: kpt on wl fnl f: rdn out* **7/2**[3]

625- **2** *2 1/4* **Shewalksinbeauty (IRE)**[237] 5830 3-9-4 **77**............................ GeorgeBaker 1 — 77
(Richard Hannon) *hld up in cl 5th: pushed along and hdwy over 1f out: rdn to dispute 2nd ent fnl f: kpt on same pce* **4/1**

50-1 **3** *nse* **Great Shot**[37] 993 3-9-5 **78**............................ TravisBlock 2 — 78
(Sylvester Kirk) *trckd ldrs: rdn over 2f out: disp 2nd ent fnl f: kpt on same pce* **2/1**[1]

524- **4** *4 1/2* **Sinfonico (IRE)**[155] 7610 3-9-4 **77**............................ JimmyQuinn 5 — 67
(Richard Hannon) *racd keenly: led: rdn over 2f out: hdd jst over 2f out: fdd ent fnl f* **10/3**[2]

0-00 5 ¾ **Royal Opera**[14] 1446 3-9-2 **75** .... JamesMillman 3 63
(Rod Millman) *w ldr: rdn over 2f out: fdd ent fnl f* **8/1**
1m 34.44s (-1.76) **Going Correction** -0.125s/f (Firm) 5 Ran SP% **109.7**
Speed ratings (Par 101): **103,100,100,96,95**
CSF £17.09 TOTE £3.30: £1.30, £3.40; EX 11.60.
Owner Bill Adams **Bred** Kilnamoragh Stud **Trained** Cropthorne, Worcs

FOCUS
A small field and the fact a fairly exposed sort was able to run out a ready winner doesn't say a great deal for the overall form. The pace was on the steady side in the first half of the race, but the overall time was reasonable and the form looks sound but limited.

1755 LINDLEY CATERING FIRST CHOICE FOR CONFERENCES H'CAP 7f 16y
4:45 (4:47) (Class 5) (0-70,69) 4-Y-0+ **£2,331** (£693; £346; £173) **Stalls** High

Form RPR
50-0 1 **Bidable**[3] 1658 7-9-3 **68** .... DeclanCannon(3) 9 76
(Bryn Palling) *bmpd leaving stalls: towards rr: sn pushed along: hdwy 3f out: sn rdn: led jst ins fnl f: r.o wl* **8/1**
020 2 1¼ **Valmina**[19] 1314 4-8-12 **60** ....(t) JimmyQuinn 1 64
(Tony Carroll) *hld up towards rr: stdy hdwy fr over 2f out: rdn over 1f out: r.o and ch ent fnl f: no ex towards fin* **9/1**
0111 3 ¾ **Angelena Ballerina (IRE)**[26] 1184 4-9-3 **65** ....(v) TadhgO'Shea 6 67
(Karen George) *towards rr: sn pushed along: rdn and hdwy 2f out: kpt on ins fnl f* **11/2**[3]
000- 4 nk **You've Been Mowed**[208] 6671 5-8-9 **62** .... RyanClark(5) 11 63
(Richard Price) *racd alone on stands' side for most of way: mid-div: hdwy over 2f out: sn rdn: led over 1f out: hdd ins fnl f: no ex* **7/2**[1]
P0-0 5 2 **Polar Annie**[14] 1444 6-9-2 **64** .... TomMcLaughlin 4 60
(Malcolm Saunders) *chsd ldrs: rdn over 2f out: kpt on same pce* **16/1**
0-60 6 2 **Belle Park**[21] 1273 4-8-4 **55** oh3 .... SimonPearce(3) 5 46
(Karen George) *mid-div: rdn wl over 2f out: kpt on same pce fnl f* **16/1**
260- 7 hd **Lutine Charlie (IRE)**[185] 7205 4-9-3 **68** ....(p) KierenFox(3) 8 58
(Ronald Harris) *led: rdn over 2f out: hung rt and hdd over 1f out: fdd ins fnl f* **10/1**
4/30 8 2¾ **Viking Dancer**[12] 1488 4-9-3 **65** .... DavidProbert 2 48
(Andrew Balding) *in tch: rdn over 2f out: wknd over 1f out* **5/1**[2]
504- 9 nse **Hobson**[175] 7376 6-9-4 **69** .... JohnFahy(3) 3 52
(Eve Johnson Houghton) *mid-div: hdwy 3f out: sn rdn to chse ldrs: wknd ent fnl f* **5/1**[2]
6/56 10 4 **Lilyannabanana**[60] 747 4-8-4 **55** .... RossAtkinson(3) 10 27
(David Evans) *wnt rt s: in tch tl rdn over 3f out: sn towards rr* **33/1**
000- 11 6 **Marie Cuddy (IRE)**[168] 7461 4-8-7 **55** oh3 .... JamieMackay 7 —
(Karen George) *prom for over 4f: sn wknd* **40/1**
1m 22.3s (-0.90) **Going Correction** -0.125s/f (Firm) 11 Ran SP% **118.3**
Speed ratings (Par 103): **100,98,97,97,95 92,92,89,89,84 77**
toteswingers:1&2:£11.30, 1&3:£7.90, 2&3:£5.60 CSF £78.50 CT £441.27 TOTE £10.10: £2.70, £3.60, £2.10; EX 87.80.
Owner Flying Eight Partnership **Bred** W D Hodge **Trained** Tredodridge, Vale Of Glamorgan

FOCUS
An ordinary handicap to conclude proceedings but the form looks sound rated around the placed horses.
Lutine Charlie(IRE) Official explanation: jockey said gelding hung right-handed
T/Plt: £626.00 to a £1 stake. Pool:£50,600.42 - 59.00 winning tickets T/Qpdt: £92.30 to a £1 stake. Pool:£3,280.75 - 26.30 winning tickets TM

1604 KEMPTON (A.W) (R-H)
Monday, May 2

OFFICIAL GOING: Standard
Wind: Breezy, across Weather: Sunny

1756 CALVERTS CARPETS YORK LTD H'CAP 1m 2f (P)
2:00 (2:00) (Class 6) (0-65,65) 4-Y-0+ **£1,748** (£516; £258) **Stalls** Low

Form RPR
00-1 1 **Addikt (IRE)**[40] 944 6-9-0 **65** .... DavidKenny(7) 4 73+
(Michael Scudamore) *t.k.h: in tch: effrt and drvn 2f out: kpt on fnl f: led nr fin* **4/1**[1]
01-0 2 ½ **Mountrath**[73] 248 4-9-4 **62** ....(v) RyanMoore 7 69
(Gary Moore) *t.k.h: led at ordinary gallop: rdn over 1f out: kpt on fnl f: hdd nr fin* **14/1**
1530 3 nk **Visions Of Johanna (USA)**[16] 1390 6-9-7 **65** .... JamieSpencer 6 71
(Ian Williams) *t.k.h: trckd ldrs: effrt and ev ch over 1f out: kpt on fnl f: hld nr fin* **13/2**[3]
21-0 4 2¼ **Majestic Bright**[18] 1330 4-9-5 **63** .... KirstyMilczarek 10 65+
(Luca Cumani) *in tch: drvn and outpcd over 2f out: styd on u.p fnl f: nt gng pce to chal* **8/1**
-432 5 ¾ **Aldo**[17] 1373 4-9-6 **64** ....(t) JamesDoyle 13 64
(Alastair Lidderdale) *racd wd: cl up: drvn and hung lft over 2f out: kpt on same pce* **15/2**
-452 6 1¼ **Crinan Classic**[18] 1333 4-8-12 **56** .... LukeMorris 11 54
(Clive Cox) *t.k.h: trckd ldrs: drvn and outpcd over 2f out: n.d after* **11/1**
6-46 7 nk **Lady Lam**[4] 1636 5-9-5 **63** ....(t) RichardHughes 9 60+
(Sylvester Kirk) *hld up: rdn 2f out: kpt on fnl f: nvr able to chal* **10/1**
0-U6 8 nk **Holden Eagle**[47] 862 6-9-1 **59** .... SteveDrowne 8 55
(Tony Newcombe) *hld up: rdn over 2f out: sme late hdwy: nvr on terms* **5/1**[2]
5302 9 4½ **Serious Drinking (USA)**[33] 1052 5-9-6 **64** ....(t) ShaneKelly 5 51
(Walter Swinburn) *hld up in midfield: effrt 2f out: wknd fnl f* **9/1**
114 10 2 **Lunar River (FR)**[39] 954 8-8-10 **61** ....(t) NathanAlison(7) 3 44
(David Pinder) *s.i.s: bhd: struggling over 2f out: sn btn* **14/1**
0330 11 6 **Saviour Sand (IRE)**[5] 1608 7-8-13 **62** ....(t) KylieManser(5) 1 33
(Olivia Maylam) *midfield: hmpd and lost pl 4f out: sn struggling* **40/1**
2m 7.95s (-0.05) **Going Correction** -0.025s/f (Stan) 11 Ran SP% **116.1**
Speed ratings (Par 101): **99,98,98,96,95 94,94,94,90,89 84**
toteswingers: 1&2 £28.00, 1&3 £6.50, 2&3 £19.20. CSF £60.60 CT £358.13 TOTE £5.60: £1.80, £7.20, £3.00; EX 92.00.
Owner Good Breed Limited **Bred** Deerpark Stud **Trained** Bromsash, Herefordshire

FOCUS
A modest handicap run at an ordinary pace and, with so little rain about recently, there looked to be plenty of dust flying about once they got under way. It paid to be handy and the form is rated around the placed horses.
Lunar River(FR) Official explanation: jockey said mare was slowly away and ran flat

1757 EUROPEAN BREEDERS' FUND MAIDEN STKS 5f (P)
2:30 (2:30) (Class 5) 2-Y-O **£3,330** (£991; £495; £247) **Stalls** Low

Form RPR
1 **Boomerang Bob (IRE)** 2-9-3 0 .... SebSanders 1 78+
(J W Hills) *prom: effrt over 1f out: qcknd to ld ins fnl f: pushed out: comf* **7/1**[3]
0 2 1¼ **Red Socks (IRE)**[9] 1522 2-9-3 0 .... NeilCallan 2 73
(Gay Kelleway) *t.k.h: cl up: effrt and ev ch over 1f out: chsd wnr ins fnl f: r.o* **7/1**[3]
42 3 2 **Copper Falls**[13] 1451 2-8-12 0 .... JimmyFortune 5 61
(Brendan Powell) *led: rdn over 1f out: hdd ins fnl f: kpt on same pce* **3/1**[1]
6 4 4 **Marygold**[14] 1441 2-8-12 0 .... GregFairley 8 47
(John Akehurst) *prom: drvn and outpcd over 2f out: rallied fnl f: nt pce to chal* **7/1**[3]
5 ¾ **Minal** 2-9-3 0 .... RichardHughes 9 49
(Richard Hannon) *wnt lft s: sn pushed along and green: prom on outside tl wknd over 1f out* **3/1**[1]
6 ¾ **Otto The Great** 2-9-3 0 .... ShaneKelly 4 46+
(Walter Swinburn) *missed break: bhd and outpcd: sme late hdwy: bttr for r* **4/1**[2]
7 8 **Compton Monarch** 2-9-3 0 .... JamesDoyle 7 17
(Hans Adielsson) *prom: drvn and outpcd over 2f out: n.d after* **12/1**
8 ½ **Arbeejay** 2-8-12 0 .... RobertHavlin 6 11
(Paul Burgoyne) *missed break: bhd and outpcd: no ch fr 1/2-way* **50/1**
60.88 secs (0.38) **Going Correction** -0.025s/f (Stan) 8 Ran SP% **117.2**
Speed ratings (Par 93): **95,93,89,83,82 81,68,67**
toteswingers: 1&2 £10.80, 1&3 £4.40, 2&3 £5.30. CSF £56.03 TOTE £5.90: £1.40, £2.50, £1.40; EX 73.00.
Owner R J Tufft **Bred** Dean Harron & Ederidge Ltd **Trained** Upper Lambourn, Berks

FOCUS
Probably an ordinary juvenile maiden and a few of these proved green, but the winner may be above average. The draw played its part with stall 1 beating stall 2 but the form is rated slightly better than average for the race.

NOTEBOOK
Boomerang Bob(IRE), a 30,000 euros half-brother to a Listed winner in France, had apparently been working well with the stable's recent Bath winner B Fifty Two and he travelled well behind the leaders from the plum draw. He briefly ran green over a furlong out, but was soon gathered together to put in a sustained run against the inside rail. This was a fair effort to outbattle a couple of rivals with previous experience and he should be able to add to this. He is likely to reappear in a 5f novice stakes later on this month. (op 13-2)
Red Socks(IRE) improved a great deal from his Nottingham debut when last of eight especially as he was keen enough early. He should be able to find an ordinary maiden. (op 8-1)
Copper Falls was the most streetwise in the field having already shown plenty of ability in her first two starts. She tried to make her experience count under a positive ride, but she didn't get home and will remain vulnerable to more progressive types. (op 5-2)
Marygold, a fair sixth of 14 on her Windsor debut, plugged on to take fourth but may not have achieved much. She may be one for handicaps much further down the line. (op 8-1)
Minal, a half-brother to the stable's five-time winner (including on Polytrack) Avon River, who ran later on this card, found the combination of greenness and the outside stall too much of a burden to overcome.
Otto The Great, a half-brother to five winners at up to 1m4f including the useful Expensive, attracted plenty of market support but he fell out of the stalls and that was that. He has obviously shown something at home so is one to watch. (op 7-1)

1758 FAMILY FUN WITH PEPPA PIG H'CAP 5f (P)
3:00 (3:00) (Class 4) (0-85,85) 3-Y-O **£4,129** (£1,228; £614; £306) **Stalls** Low

Form RPR
2-12 1 **Quality Art (USA)**[13] 1452 3-8-11 **75** .... RyanMoore 5 95+
(Gary Moore) *mde all: qcknd clr over 1f out: shkn up and kpt on strly fnl f* **2/1**[1]
260- 2 4 **Swiss Dream**[177] 7347 3-9-2 **80** .... JimmyFortune 8 85
(David Elsworth) *cl up: rdn over 1f out: kpt on fnl f: no ch w wnr* **7/1**
0-1 3 1½ **Fair Value (IRE)**[34] 1020 3-8-12 **76** ow1 .... SebSanders 6 76+
(Simon Dow) *dwlt: hld up: hdwy on outside 1/2-way: effrt over 1f out: kpt on same pce fnl f* **7/2**[2]
1222 4 2½ **Palais Glide**[9] 1521 3-8-11 **75** .... RichardHughes 2 66
(Richard Hannon) *dwlt: hld up: hdwy 1/2-way: rdn and no imp over 1f out* **4/1**[3]
600- 5 1¼ **Scarlet Rocks (IRE)**[210] 6636 3-9-0 **78** .... JamesDoyle 4 65
(David Evans) *t.k.h: cl up tl rdn and wknd over 1f out* **20/1**
15-0 6 1½ **Barbieri (IRE)**[23] 1241 3-9-7 **85** .... NeilCallan 1 68
(Jeremy Gask) *in tch on ins: n.m.r briefly 2f out: sn rdn and btn* **13/2**
0-00 7 6 **Watts Up Son**[16] 1391 3-8-7 **76** ....(t) NeilFarley(5) 3 36
(Declan Carroll) *sn towards rr: struggling after 2f: n.d after* **14/1**
59.17 secs (-1.33) **Going Correction** -0.025s/f (Stan) 7 Ran SP% **112.8**
Speed ratings (Par 101): **109,102,100,96,94 91,82**
toteswingers: 1&2 £2.40, 1&3 £2.60, 2&3 £8.00. CSF £16.23 CT £45.17 TOTE £3.20: £1.80, £4.80; EX 16.00.
Owner R A Green **Bred** Farfellow Farms & Darley Stud Management **Trained** Lower Beeding, W Sussex

FOCUS
They went a blistering pace in this and the winner was very impressive. He recorded a clear persoan best and the runner-up sets the level.

1759 CALVERTS CARPETS MAIDEN STKS 1m (P)
3:30 (3:32) (Class 4) 3-Y-O **£4,129** (£1,228; £614; £306) **Stalls** Low

Form RPR
44- 1 **Dimension**[212] 6569 3-9-3 0 .... RyanMoore 2 90+
(James Fanshawe) *trckd ldrs: rdn to ld over 1f out: drew clr fnl f: readily* **11/4**[2]
3 2 4 **Danehill Dante (IRE)**[16] 1408 3-9-3 0 .... RichardHughes 13 80
(Richard Hannon) *cl up: rdn and rn green over 3f out: led over 2f out to over 1f out: edgd lft and kpt on same pce fnl f* **4/6**[1]
3 ½ **Maali (IRE)** 3-9-3 0 .... PhilipRobinson 12 79
(Clive Brittain) *hld up on outside: hdwy 3f out: kpt on fnl f: nrst fin* **33/1**
4 ½ **Coco Rouge (IRE)** 3-8-12 0 .... ShaneKelly 3 73
(Walter Swinburn) *midfield on ins: effrt and in tch 2f out: kpt on same pce fnl f* **20/1**
05 5 ½ **Montegonian (USA)**[5] 1605 3-8-10 0 .... KatiaScallan(7) 9 76
(Marcus Tregoning) *hld up in midfield: effrt and shkn up over 2f out: no imp fnl f* **25/1**
6 6 2 **Robemaker**[12] 1496 3-9-3 0 .... RobertHavlin 14 72
(John Gosden) *hld up: shkn up and stdy hdwy 2f out: nvr nr ldrs* **20/1**

43 **7** *hd* **Prime Mover**[18] 1328 3-9-3 0.. JimCrowley 6 71
(Ed Dunlop) *plld hrd in midfield: rdn over 2f out: sn no imp* **14/1**
8 *1/2* **Amber Heights** 3-8-12 0.. JimmyFortune 10 65
(David Pinder) *prom: effrt over 2f out: wknd fnl f* **66/1**
9 *2 1/4* **Artisan** 3-9-3 0.. JamesDoyle 5 65
(Willie Musson) *hld up: shkn up over 2f out: nvr able to chal* **50/1**
10 *2* **Dansette** 3-8-12 0.. FrannyNorton 8 55
(Jim Boyle) *s.i.s: bhd: rdn over 2f out: nvr on terms* **33/1**
5- **11** *3/4* **Watercourse (IRE)**[200] 6874 3-9-3 0.. NeilCallan 7 58
(Roger Varian) *hld up: shkn up over 2f out: nvr nr ldrs* **12/1**[3]
12 *3/4* **Rave (IRE)** 3-9-3 0.. SebSanders 4 56
(J W Hills) *s.s: a bhd* **40/1**
13 *1 1/4* **Habsburg** 3-9-3 0.. GregFairley 1 53
(Paul Fitzsimons) *led to over 2f out: sn rdn and wknd* **66/1**
14 *9* **What About Now** 3-8-12 0.. JamieSpencer 11 27
(J W Hills) *cl up tl hung rt and wknd over 2f out* **66/1**

1m 40.05s (0.25) **Going Correction** -0.025s/f (Stan) **14** Ran SP% **129.1**
Speed ratings (Par 101): **97,93,92,92,91 89,89,88,86,84 83,83,81,72**
toteswingers: 1&2 £1.10, 1&3 £27.40, 2&3 £15.10. CSF £4.80 TOTE £3.10: £1.10, £1.10, £9.50; EX 6.60.
Owner Cheveley Park Stud **Bred** Cheveley Park Stud Ltd **Trained** Newmarket, Suffolk

FOCUS
They bet 12-1 bar two and the market leaders filled the first two places, though this was probably a fair maiden of its type and the race should produce winners. The level is rather fluid, with the fifth to the previous week's C&D form the best guide.

1760 KEMPTON.CO.UK JUBILEE H'CAP (LONDON MILE QUALIFIER) 1m (P)
4:00 (4:01) (Class 3) (0-90,89) 4-Y-0+
£6,418 (£1,922; £961; £481; £240; £120) **Stalls** Low

Form RPR
3-00 **1** **Merchant Of Medici**[16] 1406 4-8-10 **78**.. NeilCallan 4 91
(William Muir) *hld up towards rr: rdn 3f out: hdwy to ld over 1f out: kpt on wl fnl f* **14/1**
41-6 **2** *1 1/2* **All Action (USA)**[16] 1402 4-9-3 **85**.. IanMongan 3 94+
(Sir Henry Cecil) *s.i.s: bhd and sn pushed along: drvn and swtchd lft over 2f out: carried lft 2f out: kpt on wl fnl f: tk 2nd cl home* **7/2**[1]
5-05 **3** *hd* **Highland Knight (IRE)**[9] 1527 4-9-5 **87**.. (t) JimmyFortune 5 96+
(Andrew Balding) *led 1f: prom: rdn and edgd lft over 2f out: effrt and ev ch over 1f out: kpt on fnl f: lost 2nd cl home* **8/1**
055- **4** *1 1/4* **Huygens**[233] 5970 4-9-7 **89**.. JamieSpencer 10 95
(Denis Coakley) *midfield: effrt and swtiched lft over 2f out: hdwy wl over 1f out: kpt on same pce fnl f* **9/2**[2]
040- **5** *1/2* **Dukes Art**[284] 4306 5-9-1 **83**.. RobertHavlin 7 88
(James Toller) *hld up in midfield: effrt whn nt clr run over 2f out: hdwy over 1f out: kpt on same pce fnl f* **33/1**
0-00 **6** *2* **Shamir**[37] 991 4-9-4 **86**.. FrannyNorton 1 86
(Jo Crowley) *in tch: rdn along over 3f out: kpt on same pce fnl 2f* **14/1**
400- **7** *1/2* **Big Noise**[199] 6888 7-9-5 **87**.. JimCrowley 12 86
(Dr Jon Scargill) *hld up: hdwy and rdn whn carried lft 2f out: kpt on fnl f: nvr able to chal* **25/1**
143- **8** *3/4* **Call To Reason (IRE)**[184] 7238 4-9-4 **86**.. RyanMoore 8 84+
(Jeremy Noseda) *hld up: effrt over 2f out: edgd lft over 1f out: sn no ex* **11/2**[3]
0000 **9** *1* **The Scorching Wind (IRE)**[38] 963 5-8-12 **80**.......(t) PhilipRobinson 13 75
(Stuart Williams) *prom: rdn over 2f out: effrt and ev ch over 1f out: wknd fnl f* **25/1**
204- **10** *2 1/2* **Watch Amigo (IRE)**[226] 6204 5-9-4 **86**.. ShaneKelly 11 75
(Walter Swinburn) *hld up: pushed along over 2f out: nvr able to chal* **14/1**
4-04 **11** *hd* **Space Station**[32] 1061 5-9-1 **83**.. (b) SebSanders 9 72
(Simon Dow) *hld up: rdn over 2f out: nvr rchd ldrs* **14/1**
-111 **12** *8* **Resuscitator (USA)**[79] 528 4-8-10 **78** (v) RoystonFfrench 14 49
(Heather Main) *led after 1f and sn clr: hdd over 1f out: sn btn* **10/1**
0400 **13** *1 1/4* **Greyfriarschorista**[16] 1406 4-9-5 **87**.. GregFairley 6 55
(Mark Johnston) *cl up: drvn 3f out: wknd over 1f out* **14/1**
1002 **14** *7* **Avon River**[30] 1103 4-9-3 **85**.. RichardHughes 2 37
(Richard Hannon) *cl up tl rdn and wknd over 1f out* **12/1**

1m 37.56s (-2.24) **Going Correction** -0.025s/f (Stan) **14** Ran SP% **124.4**
Speed ratings (Par 107): **110,108,108,107,106 104,104,103,102,99 99,91,90,83**
toteswingers: 1&2 £17.70, 1&3 £36.50, 2&3 £5.10. CSF £63.34 CT £354.29 TOTE £24.60: £6.00, £2.00, £3.70; EX 107.50.
Owner S Jones & R Haim **Bred** Cheveley Park Stud Ltd **Trained** Lambourn, Berks

FOCUS
They went very fast early in this competitive handicap, too fast as it turned out as the first three at halfway, namely Resuscitator, Avon River and Greyfriarschorista, were tailed off at the line. This set the race up for the closers and the winning time was 2.49 seconds faster than the maiden. The runner-up is rated to his best, backed up by the fourth and fifth.

NOTEBOOK
Merchant Of Medici was at a more realistic level here, but was yet to win beyond 7f and the way this race was run would have exposed any chinks in his stamina. He answered those questions emphatically, however, quickening up on the inside after the intersection and winning in clear-cut fashion. Connections believe he has a decent handicap in him and the final of this series would come under consideration.

All Action(USA) was making his all-weather debut and racing over shorter than 1m2f for the first time, but circumstances conspired against him here. Having given his rivals a start, he was then carried wide in the home straight by Call To Reason and ended up against the stands' rail. He finished strongly, but the winner had got first run and a step back up in trip looks needed. (op 5-1)

Highland Knight(IRE), who acted as a pacemaker for Dream Eater in a Sandown Group 2 last time, came into this 1-1 on Polytrack and deserves credit for this as he chased the strong pace early before being allowed to drop back into mid-division, but he was produced again to hold every chance. Official explanation: jockey said gelding hung left throughout (tchd 9-1)

Huygens was racing for the first time in 233 days, though he did win over C&D on his reappearance last season. He was running on inside the last furlong and still looks capable of winning off this sort of mark. (op 6-1)

Dukes Art ◆, not seen since last July and gelded in the meantime, made an encouraging comeback especially as he was short of room passing the 2f pole. He is one to watch.

Shamir, who had valid excuses for both defeats this year, came into this 2-4 over C&D and this was another solid effort.

Big Noise has won first time out before and was another to run on late having been carried over to the stands' rail, but he has only scored once in his last 18 starts. (op 33-1)

Call To Reason(IRE) Official explanation: jockey said filly hung left

1761 BRITISH BIG BAND 22.06.11 H'CAP 2m (P)
4:30 (4:31) (Class 5) (0-75,74) 4-Y-0+ **£2,417** (£713; £357) **Stalls** Low

Form RPR
23-1 **1** **Seaside Sizzler**[26] 1174 4-9-5 **71**.. (bt) JimCrowley 3 84
(Ralph Beckett) *w ldr: led and drifted lft to stands' rail fr 2f out: clr fnl f: eased towards fin* **7/2**[2]
3122 **2** *7* **Blackstone Vegas**[6] 1586 5-8-10 **59**.. RobbieFitzpatrick 8 63+
(Derek Shaw) *hld up: outpcd whn pce qcknd over 3f out: rallied 2f out: styd on to take 2nd nr fin: no ch w wnr* **13/2**
3-25 **3** *nk* **High On A Hill (IRE)**[17] 1367 4-9-8 **74**.. RichardHughes 4 78
(Sylvester Kirk) *chsd ldrs: rdn and wnt 2nd 2f out: drifted lft to stands' rail: one pce fnl f: lost 2nd cl home* **10/3**[1]
/620 **4** *4* **Kavaloti (IRE)**[27] 1148 7-9-5 **68**.. (be) RyanMoore 1 67
(Gary Moore) *set stdy pce: rdn 3f out: hdd over 2f out: sn outpcd* **6/1**[3]
35/2 **5** *9* **Mac Federal (IRE)**[26] 1181 9-8-6 **58**.. SophieDoyle(3) 5 46
(Sheena West) *hld up in tch: outpcd whn n.m.r wl over 2f out: n.d after* **7/1**
4310 **6** *3/4* **Squad**[29] 1107 5-9-6 **69**.. (v) SebSanders 6 56
(Simon Dow) *hld up in tch: effrt over 3f out: edgd rt and wknd fr 2f out* **16/1**
5135 **7** *16* **Gunslinger (FR)**[13] 1470 6-9-10 **73**.. JimmyFortune 7 41
(Michael Scudamore) *hld up: drvn over 3f out: sn btn: t.o* **10/1**
-102 **8** *19* **Coda Agency**[27] 1148 8-9-7 **70**.. NeilCallan 9 15
(David Arbuthnot) *in tch: rdn over 4f out: wknd over 3f out: t.o* **7/1**
4050 **9** *20* **Harrys**[19] 1311 4-7-9 **54** oh9.. (p) KatiaScallan(7) 2 —
(Michael Squance) *t.k.h: trckd ldrs: lost pl 4f out: sn struggling: t.o* **100/1**

3m 28.89s (-1.21) **Going Correction** -0.025s/f (Stan)
WFA 4 from 5yo+ 3lb **9** Ran SP% **113.9**
Speed ratings (Par 103): **102,98,98,96,91 91,83,73,63**
toteswingers: 1&2 £4.20, 1&3 £2.60, 2&3 £3.80. CSF £26.14 CT £80.94 TOTE £4.00: £1.80, £3.40, £1.60; EX 19.60.
Owner I J Heseltine **Bred** Redmyre Bloodstock And S Hillen **Trained** Kimpton, Hants

FOCUS
Unlike many 2m handicaps here, the pace was a solid one with the result that they finished spread out all over Sunbury and a few were in danger of being lapped. The first three all raced prominently and the runner-up looks the best guide.

1762 PETER ANDRE 06.07.11 FILLIES' H'CAP 6f (P)
5:00 (5:01) (Class 4) (0-85,85) 4-Y-0+ **£4,129** (£1,228; £614; £306) **Stalls** Low

Form RPR
-450 **1** **Ray Of Joy**[68] 651 5-9-5 **83**.. RichardHughes 1 89
(J R Jenkins) *w ldr: led over 1f out: pushed out fnl f* **4/1**[2]
150- **2** *3/4* **Cloud's End**[257] 5205 4-9-0 **78**.. JimCrowley 6 82
(Robert Cowell) *led tl rdn and hdd over 1f out: kpt on ins fnl f* **7/2**[1]
40/6 **3** *3/4* **Quaroma**[25] 1197 6-9-2 **80**.. JimmyFortune 7 81
(Peter Hedger) *trckd ldrs: effrt over 1f out: kpt on same pce fnl f* **13/2**[3]
1122 **4** *nk* **Ivory Silk**[16] 1395 6-9-7 **85**.. RyanMoore 4 85+
(Jeremy Gask) *hld up in last: effrt and hdwy over 1f out: kpt on fnl f: nvr able to chal* **7/2**[1]
400- **5** *nk* **Chaussini**[289] 4145 4-8-13 **77**.. NeilCallan 2 76
(James Toller) *t.k.h: trckd ldrs: effrt and shkn up appr fnl f: sn no ex* **13/2**[3]
-233 **6** *1* **Diapason (IRE)**[74] 577 5-8-10 **74**.. (t) RichardSmith 5 70
(Tom Dascombe) *hld up in tch: drvn and effrt over 1f out: no imp fnl f* **15/2**
640- **7** *16* **Boogie Waltzer**[193] 7041 4-8-8 **72**.. (t) WilliamCarson 3 17
(Stuart Williams) *in tch: outpcd 1/2-way: wknd wl over 1f out: t.o* **8/1**

1m 12.87s (-0.23) **Going Correction** -0.025s/f (Stan) **7** Ran SP% **114.0**
Speed ratings (Par 102): **100,99,98,97,97 95,74**
toteswingers: 1&2 £2.00, 1&3 £4.50, 2&3 £5.80. CSF £18.24 TOTE £6.30: £4.70, £3.70; EX 25.00.
Owner Robin Stevens **Bred** D R Tucker **Trained** Royston, Herts

FOCUS
A fair fillies' sprint handicap, but it was crucial to race handily as the first two were at the sharp end throughout. The winner is the best guide to the level.
T/Plt: £56.90 to a £1 stake. Pool:£58,878.92 - 755.00 winning tickets. T/Qpdt: £9.00 to a £1 stake. Pool:£3,211.53 - 264.05 winning tickets. RY

1562 WARWICK (L-H)
Monday, May 2
OFFICIAL GOING: Good to firm (firm in places; 9.0)
Wind: Fresh against Weather: Fine

1763 JOIN TODAY AT REWARDS4RACING.COM APPRENTICE H'CAP 1m 22y
2:10 (2:11) (Class 6) (0-60,60) 4-Y-0+ **£2,047** (£604; £302) **Stalls** Low

Form RPR
5504 **1** **Aggbag**[4] 1625 7-8-8 **46**.. AdamBeschizza 7 53
(Tony Carroll) *s.i.s: hld up: hdwy over 2f out: rdn to ld over 1f out: r.o* **3/1**[1]
06-5 **2** *1* **Hathaway (IRE)**[21] 1273 4-9-2 **54**.. DaleSwift 4 59
(Mark Brisbourne) *dwlt: hld up: hdwy over 1f out: sn rdn: r.o* **6/1**
3141 **3** *1 1/4* **Grey Boy (GER)**[4] 1625 10-9-3 **60** 6ex.. GeorgeDowning(5) 6 62
(Tony Carroll) *hld up: hdwy and swtchd rt over 1f out: r.o* **7/2**[2]
5056 **4** *1 3/4* **Escardo (GER)**[4] 1625 8-8-0 **45**.. (p) JoshBaudains(7) 8 43
(David Bridgwater) *prom: chsd ldr 1/2-way: led wl 2f out: hdd over 1f out: styd on same pce ins fnl f* **10/1**
131- **5** *1* **Swansea Jack**[187] 7161 4-9-7 **59**.. (t) RyanClark 2 55
(Stuart Williams) *racd keenly: led to 3f: no ex ins fnl f* **9/2**[3]
1004 **6** *3/4* **Join Up**[12] 1486 5-9-2 **59**.. ThomasBrown(5) 1 53
(Mark Brisbourne) *chsd ldr 3f: remained handy: rdn over 1f out: no ex fnl f* **7/1**
2402 **7** *6* **Lily Wood**[23] 1248 5-8-9 **52**.. (p) AlexEdwards(5) 5 32
(James Unett) *trckd ldrs: racd keenly: rdn over 2f out: wknd over 1f out* **11/1**
-000 **8** *1 1/2* **Mistress Shy**[7] 1567 4-8-2 **45**.. JackDuern(5) 3 22
(Robin Dickin) *prom: led 3f out: hdd 2f out: sn wknd* **50/1**

1m 40.82s (-0.18) **Going Correction** 0.0s/f (Good) **8** Ran SP% **111.6**
Speed ratings (Par 101): **100,99,97,96,95 94,88,86**
toteswingers: 1&2 £3.50, 1&3 £2.50, 2&3 £13.70. CSF £20.24 CT £62.61 TOTE £4.40: £1.70, £2.10, £1.10; EX 25.20.
Owner Dennis & Andy Deacon **Bred** D R Tucker **Trained** Cropthorne, Worcs

FOCUS
A typically low-grade apprentice handicap rated around the first three.

1764 WARWICK FOR WEDDINGS H'CAP 5f
2:40 (2:40) (Class 6) (0-60,60) 3-Y-O **£2,047** (£604; £302) **Stalls** Low

Form RPR

0-12 **1** **Irish Boy (IRE)**[7] 1561 3-9-2 **55** DuranFentiman 7 62
(Noel Wilson) *chsd ldrs: rdn to ld and hung lft fr over 1f out: r.o* **5/2**[1]

0-12 **2** ½ **Paradise Place**[6] 1595 3-9-6 **59** PatCosgrave 6 64
(Robert Cowell) *hld up: hdwy and swtchd lft 2f out: sn rdn: chsd wnr ins fnl f: r.o* **5/2**[1]

00-4 **3** ¾ **Cara Carmela**[39] 953 3-8-9 **48** JackMitchell 4 50
(Stuart Williams) *plld hrd and prom: rdn over 1f out: r.o* **11/1**

325 **4** 1½ **Ladydolly**[13] 1465 3-9-1 **57** (p) AndrewHeffernan(3) 5 54
(Roy Brotherton) *led: rdn and hdd over 1f out: styd on same pce ins fnl f* **16/1**

0-45 **5** 2 **Chester Deelyte (IRE)**[20] 1294 3-8-7 **46** ChrisCatlin 8 36
(Lisa Williamson) *chsd ldr: rdn and ev ch over 1f out: wknd ins fnl f* **40/1**

60-0 **6** 2¾ **Miss Dutee**[12] 1483 3-9-7 **60** PatDobbs 2 40
(Richard Hannon) *prom 3f* **10/1**

5533 **7** 1½ **Pickled Pumpkin**[73] 595 3-8-10 **54** AdamBeschizza(5) 3 28
(Olivia Maylam) *s.i.s: sn pushed along and a in rr* **7/1**[3]

06-1 **8** 1¼ **Dreams Of Glory**[20] 1294 3-8-13 **52** HayleyTurner 9 22
(Ron Hodges) *sn pushed along in rr: bhd fr 1/2-way* **5/1**[2]

62.29 secs (2.69) **Going Correction** +0.375s/f (Good) **8 Ran SP% 112.1**
Speed ratings (Par 97): **93,92,91,88,85 81,78,76**
toteswingers: 1&2 £1.10, 1&3 £11.10, 2&3 £8.60. CSF £8.03 CT £53.66 TOTE £3.50: £2.20, £1.10, £4.40; EX 6.00.
Owner Annwell Inn Syndicate **Bred** Seamus McMullan **Trained** Sandhutton, N Yorks

FOCUS
Quite a competitive sprint handicap but the time was moderate and not a race to be too positive about.
Pickled Pumpkin Official explanation: jockey said gelding lost its action

1765 EUROPEAN BREEDERS' FUND PRIMROSE MAIDEN FILLIES' STKS 5f
3:10 (3:12) (Class 5) 2-Y-O **£3,626** (£1,079; £539; £269) **Stalls** Low

Form RPR

1 **Vocational (USA)** 2-9-0 0 JoeFanning 7 75+
(Mark Johnston) *mde virtually all: rdn over 1f out: r.o* **10/3**[2]

2 ½ **Nayarra (IRE)** 2-9-0 0 ChrisCatlin 2 73+
(Mick Channon) *chsd ldrs: rdn over 1f out: r.o* **6/4**[1]

3 **3** 1¾ **Worth**[13] 1451 2-9-0 0 MartinDwyer 8 67
(Brian Meehan) *chsd ldrs: rdn over 1f out: styd on same pce ins fnl f* **5/1**[3]

4 **4** hd **Kyllasie**[30] 1101 2-8-11 0 PatrickHills(3) 5 66
(Richard Hannon) *s.i.s: hdwy 2f out: sn rdn: styd on same pce ins fnl f* **7/1**

3 **5** 1 **Summathisnthat**[16] 1396 2-9-0 0 AndreaAtzeni 3 63
(Des Donovan) *hld up: rdn over 1f out: nvr trbld ldrs* **7/1**

6 **6** 4½ **Bella Ponte**[28] 1136 2-9-0 0 PatCosgrave 1 46
(John Gallagher) *s.i.s: sn chsng wnr: rdn over 1f out: wknd ins fnl f* **25/1**

7 5 **Purple Angel** 2-9-0 0 NickyMackay 6 28
(Jonathan Portman) *s.i.s: outpcd* **20/1**

61.75 secs (2.15) **Going Correction** +0.375s/f (Good) **7 Ran SP% 113.4**
Speed ratings (Par 90): **97,96,93,93,91 84,76**
toteswingers: 1&2 £1.20, 1&3 £1.60, 2&3 £3.30. CSF £8.59 TOTE £4.50: £3.40, £2.40; EX 8.70.
Owner Sheikh Hamdan Bin Mohammed Al Maktoum **Bred** Darley **Trained** Middleham Moor, N Yorks

FOCUS
Probably a decent fillies' juvenile contest and the form is rated positively.

NOTEBOOK
Vocational(USA) ◆ is bred to be speedy (dam won Cheveley Park, sire often produces precocious types) and the fact she holds an engagement in this week's Lily Agnes suggests she's held in high regard. She clearly knew her job, soon bagging the lead, and really ground it out well in the straight. There should be more to come and she deserves a rise in grade now. (op 7-2 tchd 3-1)
Nayarra(IRE), bred to stay further, clearly has some speed also and she was backed into favouritism. She had her chance, keeping on well, but never really looked the winner. Normal progress should see her going one better. (op 9-4)
Worth probably improved on her Bath debut effort, bumping into a couple of fair types. She looks ready for a slightly stiffer test now and can win an ordinary maiden. (op 4-1 tchd 7-2)
Kyllasie, only fourth when 4/11 for her Kempton debut (didn't get best of runs), wasn't the best away, but did keep on showed improved form. (op 15-2 tchd 13-2)
Summathisnthat never got involved, failing to improve on her debut effort. (op 6-1 tchd 15-2)

1766 QUANTUM MANUFACTURING FILLIES' H'CAP 7f 26y
3:40 (3:44) (Class 5) (0-70,67) 3-Y-O+ **£2,266** (£674; £337; £168) **Stalls** Low

Form RPR

340- **1** **Treasure Way**[215] 6479 4-9-12 **63** RobertWinston 8 72
(Patrick Chamings) *chsd ldrs: led and edgd lft 2f out: rdn out* **7/2**[1]

2-30 **2** ½ **Gemma's Delight (IRE)**[13] 1464 4-9-4 **55** (p) LiamJones 4 62
(James Unett) *plld hrd and prom: rdn to chse wnr and hung lft over 1f out: ev ch ins fnl f: unable qck nr fin* **11/2**[2]

144 **3** 2½ **Caelis**[16] 1400 3-9-0 **63** (b[1]) RichardThomas 6 59
(Ralph Beckett) *sn outpcd: hdwy over 1f out: nt rch ldrs* **7/2**[1]

31-0 **4** 2¼ **Crimson Queen**[9] 1523 4-9-4 **58** AndrewHeffernan(3) 5 52
(Roy Brotherton) *led 5f: sn rdn: no ex ins fnl f* **12/1**

60-5 **5** 2¼ **Merrjanah**[32] 1060 3-9-3 **66** ChrisCatlin 3 50
(Clive Brittain) *w ldr: rdn and ev ch over 2f out: wknd fnl f* **7/1**[3]

55-0 **6** hd **Madame Excelerate**[16] 1394 4-10-0 **65** PatCosgrave 9 53
(Mark Brisbourne) *hld up in tch: rdn over 2f out: wknd over 1f out* **8/1**

6245 **7** 7 **Loves Theme (IRE)**[17] 1359 3-9-4 **67** SamHitchcott 7 39
(Alan Bailey) *sn drvn along and a in rr: wknd over 1f out* **16/1**

2553 **8** 14 **Timpanist (USA)**[28] 1133 4-9-12 **63** HayleyTurner 1 —
(Simon Dow) *prom: hmpd 1/2-way: wknd 2f out: eased* **11/2**[2]

1m 24.34s (-0.26) **Going Correction** 0.0s/f (Good)
WFA 3 from 4yo 12lb **8 Ran SP% 112.4**
Speed ratings (Par 100): **101,100,97,95,92 92,84,68**
toteswingers: 1&2 £2.40, 1&3 £1.70, 2&3 £3.40. CSF £20.64 CT £55.23 TOTE £4.50: £2.10, £1.10, £2.30; EX 23.20.
Owner Mrs Alexandra J Chandris **Bred** Queenway S A **Trained** Baughurst, Hants

FOCUS
A moderate fillies' handicap rated through the runner-up to her best.

1767 JOIN TODAY AT REWARDS4RACING.COM MEDIAN AUCTION MAIDEN FILLIES' STKS 1m 22y
4:10 (4:14) (Class 5) 3-5-Y-O **£2,266** (£674; £337; £168) **Stalls** Low

Form RPR

1 **Foxley (IRE)** 3-8-12 0 MartinDwyer 5 68
(Brian Meehan) *led 1f: chsd ldr tl led 3f out: rdn and hung lft ins fnl f: jst hld on* **7/1**[2]

6- **2** shd **Zafaraan**[203] 6804 3-8-12 0 JackMitchell 3 67
(Peter Chapple-Hyam) *a.p: chsd wnr over 2f out: rdn over 1f out: ev ch ins fnl f: r.o* **10/11**[1]

- **3** 4½ **Oneiric** 3-8-12 0 RichardThomas 8 57
(Ralph Beckett) *unruly bhd stalls: s.i.s: hld up: hdwy over 1f out: styd on same pce ins fnl f* **15/2**[3]

4 9 **Hygrove Welshlady (IRE)** 3-8-9 0 PatrickHills(3) 4 36
(J W Hills) *s.i.s: hld up: rdn over 2f out: nvr on terms* **12/1**

05 **5** hd **Graceful Spirit**[16] 1399 4-9-11 0 AndreaAtzeni 7 39
(Des Donovan) *chsd ldrs: rdn over 1f out: wknd over 1f out* **40/1**

6 12 **La Belle Au Bois (IRE)**[24] 5-9-11 0 JoeFanning 1 11
(Nick Lampard) *s.i.s: rcvrd to ld 7f out: hdd 3f out: wknd over 1f out* **16/1**

1m 41.58s (0.58) **Going Correction** 0.0s/f (Good)
WFA 3 from 4yo+ 13lb **6 Ran SP% 92.7**
Speed ratings (Par 100): **97,96,92,83,83 71**
toteswingers: 1&2 £1.10, 1&3 £2.90, 2&3 £1.20. CSF £9.21 TOTE £6.80: £3.20, £1.10; EX 10.00.
Owner Ladyswood Stud **Bred** Ladyswood Stud **Trained** Manton, Wilts

FOCUS
The front pair drew clear in what was a fairly weak fillies' maiden.

1768 1707 BUILDING H'CAP 1m 22y
4:40 (4:49) (Class 5) (0-70,70) 3-Y-O **£2,266** (£674; £337; £168) **Stalls** Low

Form RPR

46-6 **1** **Sergeant Troy (IRE)**[14] 1446 3-9-4 **67** SteveDrowne 6 77+
(Roger Charlton) *hld up: hdwy over 2f out: rdn to ld 1f out: edgd lft: r.o: eased towards fin* **5/6**[1]

4246 **2** 2 **Imaginary World (IRE)**[18] 1327 3-9-5 **68** (b[1]) RobertWinston 5 73
(Alan McCabe) *a.p: chsd ldr over 3f out: shkn up to ld over 1f out: sn rdn and hdd: styd on same pce ins fnl f* **9/1**

5101 **3** 4 **Bertie Blu Boy**[13] 1475 3-9-4 **67** PatCosgrave 1 63
(Paul Green) *led: rdn and hdd over 1f out: wknd ins fnl f* **7/1**[3]

0431 **4** 1¼ **Beautiful Lando (FR)**[26] 1176 3-8-12 **61** (v) FrankieMcDonald 3 54
(Heather Main) *s.i.s: sn prom: rdn over 1f out: wknd fnl f* **8/1**

644- **5** 1¾ **Countess Ellen (IRE)**[235] 5895 3-9-7 **70** NickyMackay 7 59+
(Gerard Butler) *chsd ldrs: carried wd bnd over 3f out: nt rcvr* **8/1**

06-0 **6** 10 **No Larking (IRE)**[14] 1446 3-9-2 **65** (b[1]) FergusSweeney 2 31
(Henry Candy) *trckd ldr: plld hrd: hung rt over 3f out: sn bhd* **13/2**[2]

1m 40.21s (-0.79) **Going Correction** 0.0s/f (Good) **6 Ran SP% 112.6**
Speed ratings (Par 99): **103,101,97,95,94 84**
toteswingers: 1&2 £3.70, 1&3 £2.20, 2&3 £8.50. CSF £9.32 TOTE £1.80: £1.20, £3.50; EX 9.90.
Owner Michael Pescod **Bred** Dr Peter Harms **Trained** Beckhampton, Wilts
■ Stewards' Enquiry : Nicky Mackay Fine: £140. Breach of Rule (D)49. Failed to report poor performance fully.

FOCUS
A modest handicap with the runner-up rated as having run a narrow personal-best.
Countess Ellen(IRE) Official explanation: jockey said, regarding tender riding in home straight, the filly had been carried wide on bend, suffering interference and appeared to lose its action on the good to firm ground, hung slightly left up the straight and felt it best to ride sympathetically to the line.
No Larking(IRE) Official explanation: jockey said gelding ran too free and hung right on the bend

1769 RACING UK H'CAP 1m 2f 188y
5:10 (5:16) (Class 6) (0-60,59) 3-Y-O **£2,388** (£705; £352) **Stalls** Low

Form RPR

54-4 **1** **Anton Dolin (IRE)**[26] 1189 3-9-7 **59** ChrisCatlin 1 68+
(John Dunlop) *chsd ldrs: rdn to ld and hung lft fr over 1f out: styd on* **10/3**[1]

230- **2** nk **Dr Darcey**[137] 7888 3-9-5 **57** PatDobbs 10 65
(Richard Hannon) *led: rdn and hdd over 1f out: stl ev ch ins fnl f: hmpd towards fin: styd on* **8/1**

0-44 **3** 2½ **Spartan Spirit (IRE)**[12] 1496 3-9-0 **52** SteveDrowne 5 56+
(Hughie Morrison) *s.i.s: hld up: hdwy over 1f out: hung lft and styd on: nt rch ldrs* **7/2**[2]

612- **4** 1 **Salvationist**[195] 7004 3-9-3 **58** LouisBeuzelin(3) 15 60+
(John Dunlop) *stdd s: hld up: hdwy over 1f out: nvr trbld ldrs* **14/1**

560- **5** 1¼ **Castlemorris King**[195] 7004 3-9-1 **53** JackMitchell 7 53+
(Peter Chapple-Hyam) *hld up: hdwy u.p over 2f out: no imp fr over 1f out* **11/2**[3]

0226 **6** 2 **The Absent Mare**[20] 1299 3-8-12 **50** (t) AndreaAtzeni 14 46
(Frank Sheridan) *hld up in tch: rdn over 2f out: wknd fnl f* **16/1**

3213 **7** 1¼ **Polly Holder (IRE)**[7] 1574 3-8-11 **56** (p) NatashaEaton(7) 17 50
(Alan Bailey) *prom: rdn over 3f out: wknd over 1f out* **8/1**

460- **8** nk **Oliver's Gold**[137] 7888 3-9-7 **59** JoeFanning 2 52
(Amanda Perrett) *hld up: rdn over 2f out: nvr on terms* **10/1**

566 **9** 2¾ **Sing Alana Sing**[28] 1132 3-8-0 **45** (t) JakePayne(7) 3 33
(Bill Turner) *hld up in tch: rdn over 2f out: sn wknd* **50/1**

000- **10** 1¼ **Arctic Reach**[136] 7916 3-8-5 **50** DavidKenny(7) 12 36
(Brendan Powell) *hld up: hdwy 4f out: rdn and hung lft over 2f out: sn wknd* **25/1**

0-50 **11** 5 **Phoenix Fantasy (IRE)**[19] 1312 3-9-3 **55** NickyMackay 6 32
(Jonathan Portman) *chsd ldrs: rdn over 2f out: wknd over 1f out* **50/1**

2306 **12** 2 **Jane's Legacy**[20] 1300 3-8-7 **52** JackDuern(7) 13 25
(Reg Hollinshead) *s.i.s: hld up: rdn over 2f out: n.d* **50/1**

60-0 **13** 15 **Dancing Cavalier (IRE)**[20] 1300 3-8-12 **50** RobertWinston 9 —
(Reg Hollinshead) *plld hrd and prom: chsd ldr over 5f out tl rdn over 2f out: wknd over 1f out* **18/1**

2m 21.43s (0.33) **Going Correction** 0.0s/f (Good) **13 Ran SP% 119.5**
Speed ratings (Par 97): **98,97,95,95,94 92,91,91,89,88 85,83,72**
toteswingers: 1&2 £10.50, 1&3 £2.90, 2&3 £5.90. totesuper7: WIN: Not won. PLACE: £60.20 - 6 winning units. CSF £29.65 CT £98.90 TOTE £3.60: £1.10, £3.80, £1.70; EX 35.30.Chilworth Lass (No 9) was withdrawn. Price at time of withdrawal 40-1. Rule 4 does not apply.
Owner Windflower Overseas Holdings Inc **Bred** Windflower Overseas Holdings Inc **Trained** Arundel, W Sussex
■ Stewards' Enquiry : Chris Catlin one-day ban: careless riding (May 16)

FOCUS
This wasn't as competitive as the field-size suggested it may be but the first five are either improving or have had relatively few chances.
Spartan Spirit(IRE) Official explanation: jockey said saddle slipped; vet said colt returned lame
T/Plt: £6.50 to a £1 stake. Pool:£34,961.28 - 3,899.98 winning tickets. T/Qpdt: £4.30 to a £1 stake. Pool:£2,188.21- 371.89 winning tickets. CR

[1441] WINDSOR (R-H)

Monday, May 2

OFFICIAL GOING: Good to firm (8.8)
Stands' rail dolled out 6yds at 6f down to 2f at winning post. Top bend dolled out 3yds which added 14yds to races of 1m and over.
Wind: Brisk across Weather: sunny

1770 BETFAIR RACING EXCELLENCE APPRENTICE TRAINING SERIES H'CAP 6f
2:25 (2:26) (Class 6) (0-65,63) 4-Y-0+ **£1,706** (£503; £252) **Stalls** Low

Form RPR
6040 **1** **Memphis Man**[20] 1287 8-8-10 **52**.............................. MatthewCosham 6 61
(David Evans) *in tch: hdwy over 1f out: rdn and styd on to ld fnl 50yds: styd on wl* **11/1**
-533 **2** *1 ¼* **Anjomarba (IRE)**[6] 1581 4-8-13 **62**......................... AccursioRomeo(7) 7 67
(Brett Johnson) *s.i.s: in rr: hdwy fr 2f out: chal ins fnl f and slt ld fnl 120yds: hdd and outpcd fnl 50yds* **3/1**[1]
0522 **3** *½* **Libertino (IRE)**[18] 1331 4-8-8 **55**................................ CharlesBishop(5) 9 58
(Tony Carroll) *chsd ldrs: chal fr 2f out tl slt ld over 1f out: hdd fnl 120yds: no ex* **9/2**[2]
003- **4** *hd* **C'Mon You Irons (IRE)**[152] 7655 6-9-6 **62**................... AntiocoMurgia 3 65
(Mark Hoad) *led tl hdd over 1f out: styd on same pce ins fnl f* **15/2**
2426 **5** *¾* **Diddums**[5] 1604 5-8-10 **57**..(p) LeonnaMayor(5) 10 57
(Alastair Lidderdale) *s.i.s: in rr: hdwy over 1f out: styd on fnl f: nvr gng pce to rch ldrs* **5/1**[3]
0335 **6** *2* **Rich And Reckless**[60] 747 4-8-13 **62**..........................(vt[1]) TimClark(7) 1 56
(Tobias B P Coles) *s.i.s: sn rcvrd to press ldrs: wknd appr fnl f* **12/1**
0 **7** *hd* **Do More Business (IRE)**[23] 1232 4-8-13 **58**................ LucyKBarry(3) 4 51
(Pat Phelan) *chsd ldrs: ev ch fr 2f out tl wknd fnl f* **10/1**
0026 **8** *2 ¼* **Gwilym (GER)**[21] 1267 8-9-7 **63**.................................. MatthewLawson 2 49
(Derek Haydn Jones) *pressed ldrs: ev ch 2f out: wknd over 1f out* **6/1**
-450 **9** *3* **Kate Skate**[33] 1034 4-9-4 **63**....................................... NatashaEaton(3) 11 40
(Gay Kelleway) *sn in tch on outside: rdn over 2f out: sn wknd* **20/1**

1m 15.75s (2.75) **Going Correction** +0.125s/f (Good) **9** Ran SP% **115.8**
Speed ratings (Par 101): **86,84,83,83,82 79,79,76,72**
toteswingers: 1&2 £4.90, 1&3 £5.30, 2&3 £2.50. CSF £44.24 CT £174.36 TOTE £7.90: £2.20, £1.30, £2.20; EX 37.50 TRIFECTA Not won..
Owner Mrs I M Folkes **Bred** R T And Mrs Watson **Trained** Pandy, Monmouths
■ Stewards' Enquiry : Accursio Romeo seven-day ban: used whip in the forehand in contravention of rules (May 18,20,23,25,27,30,Jun 1)

FOCUS
A moderate sprint handicap, run at no more than an average pace and rated through the runner-up.

1771 IT DOESN'T GET BETTER THAN BARBADOS H'CAP 6f
2:55 (2:57) (Class 4) (0-80,84) 4-Y-0+ **£3,753** (£1,108; £554) **Stalls** Low

Form RPR
4121 **1** **Norville (IRE)**[3] 1656 4-9-13 **84** 6ex..............................(b) CathyGannon 1 98
(David Evans) *in tch: nt clr run ins fnl 2f: drvn and qcknd 1f out: str chal fnl 120yds: led fnl 50yds: jst hld on* **5/1**[3]
-013 **2** *shd* **New Leyf (IRE)**[29] 1109 5-9-7 **78**..................................... WilliamBuick 3 91+
(Jeremy Gask) *hld up in rr but in tch: pushed along 2f out: hdwy and nt clr run over 1f out: rapid hdwy fnl 120yds: fin fast: jst failed* **4/1**[1]
4112 **3** *1* **Collect Art (IRE)**[17] 1355 4-8-11 **68**............................. StevieDonohoe 6 78
(Andrew Haynes) *pressed ldrs: upsides 2f out: drvn and slt ld 1f out: jnd fnl 120yds: hdd and outpcd fnl 50yds* **13/2**
50-5 **4** *1 ½* **Seamus Shindig**[14] 1444 9-8-11 **73**................................ AmyScott(5) 2 78
(Henry Candy) *in rr: hdwy 2f out: styd on to dispute cl 2nd ins fnl f: no imp fnl 120yds: one pce cl home* **10/1**
410- **5** *½* **Baby Dottie**[148] 7719 4-9-1 **72**... IanMongan 7 76
(Pat Phelan) *pressed ldrs: ev ch 2f out: wknd u.p ins fnl f* **14/1**
0-06 **6** *1 ¼* **Another Try (IRE)**[5] 1603 6-9-3 **77**......................... MatthewDavies(3) 12 77
(Alan Jarvis) *pressed ldrs: ev ch 2f out: wknd ins fnl f* **13/2**
3-40 **7** *shd* **The Wee Chief (IRE)**[14] 1444 5-8-5 **67**...................... KieranO'Neill(5) 11 66
(Jimmy Fox) *in rr: hdwy to chse ldrs ins fnl 2f: hung rt and wknd fnl f* **12/1**
55-3 **8** *1 ½* **Getcarter**[30] 1103 5-9-4 **75**... DaneO'Neill 5 69
(Richard Hannon) *s.i.s: in rr: hdwy on outside and n.m.r over 2f out: chsd ldrs sn after: wknd appr fnl f* **9/2**[2]
5025 **9** *hd* **Desert Icon (IRE)**[86] 435 5-8-5 **69**............................... AliceHaynes(7) 9 63
(David Simcock) *t.k.h in rr: hdwy to chse ldrs on outside 2f out: wknd over 1f out* **20/1**
-616 **10** *¾* **Taurus Twins**[8] 1539 5-9-7 **78**....................................(b) WilliamCarson 8 69
(Richard Price) *led tl hdd & wknd 1f out* **20/1**
013- **11** *9* **Bathwick Xaara**[203] 6812 4-8-11 **68**........................... StephenCraine 4 31
(Jonathan Portman) *chsd ldrs 4f* **28/1**

1m 12.98s (-0.02) **Going Correction** +0.125s/f (Good) **11** Ran SP% **116.4**
Speed ratings (Par 105): **105,104,103,101,100 99,99,97,96,95 83**
toteswingers: 1&2 £3.70, 1&3 £4.30, 2&3 £4.20. CSF £24.26 CT £152.35 TOTE £5.40: £1.50, £1.10, £2.90; EX 23.20 Trifecta £115.40 Pool: £616.19 - 3.95 winning units..
Owner Raymond N R Auld **Bred** R N Auld **Trained** Pandy, Monmouths

FOCUS
A modest sprint handicap, run a solid enough pace and the form looks sound, rated through the third.

1772 COMPLETE CARIBBEAN CLASSIC H'CAP 1m 2f 7y
3:25 (3:38) (Class 4) (0-85,84) 4-Y-0+ **£4,079** (£1,214; £606; £303) **Stalls** High

Form RPR
01-0 **1** **Warlu Way**[16] 1402 4-9-0 **77**... TedDurcan 9 87+
(John Dunlop) *trckd ldrs: pushed along over 2f out: swtchd lft and qcknd to chse ldr fnl 120yds: styd on strly to ld nr fin* **9/1**
231- **2** *nk* **Shallow Bay**[189] 7111 4-9-7 **84**.. AdamKirby 11 93+
(Walter Swinburn) *led: rdn and qcknd fr 2f out: kpt on wl fnl f tl hdd and outpcd nr fin* **3/1**[1]
14-0 **3** *2* **Tinshu (IRE)**[16] 1402 5-9-6 **83**.. DaneO'Neill 10 88
(Derek Haydn Jones) *in tch: hdwy 2f out: chsd ldr and rdn 2f out: no imp and outpcd into 3rd fnl 120yds* **7/2**[2]
4113 **4** *1* **Edgeworth (IRE)**[13] 1450 5-8-10 **73**..........................(tp) CathyGannon 3 76
(Brendan Powell) *chsd ldrs tl rdn and outpcd over 2f out: styd on again u.p fnl f but nvr gng pce to get into contention* **9/1**
131- **5** *hd* **Aurora Sky (IRE)**[144] 7778 5-8-12 **75**......................... StevieDonohoe 1 78
(John Akehurst) *in rr: rdn and hdwy over 2f out: styd on ins fnl f but nvr gng pce to rch ldrs* **20/1**
33-0 **6** *3* **Effigy**[13] 1460 7-8-5 **73**.. AmyScott(5) 4 70
(Henry Candy) *hld up in rr: pushed along over 2f out: mod prog fnl 2f* **16/1**
114- **7** *¾* **True To Form (IRE)**[95] 6573 4-8-10 **73**......................... TonyCulhane 6 68
(George Baker) *in rr: dropped off pce 3f out: mod prog again fr over 1f out* **12/1**
1- **8** *2 ¼* **Constant Craving**[203] 6815 4-8-10 **73**............................... LukeMorris 7 64
(Clive Cox) *chsd ldr: rdn 3f out: wknd fr 2f out* **9/2**[3]
030- **9** *7* **Silverglas (IRE)**[196] 6990 5-8-12 **75**............................... WilliamBuick 5 52
(William Knight) *chsd ldrs: rdn 3f out: wknd qckly over 2f out* **9/1**

2m 7.78s (-0.92) **Going Correction** +0.075s/f (Good) **9** Ran SP% **113.7**
Speed ratings (Par 105): **106,105,104,103,103 100,100,98,92**
toteswingers: 1&2 £6.90, 1&3 £6.80, 2&3 £3.00. CSF £35.64 CT £113.62 TOTE £9.70: £3.30, £1.50, £1.70; EX 40.90 Trifecta £219.10 Pool: £799.50 - 2.70 winning units..
Owner The Earl Cadogan **Bred** The Earl Cadogan **Trained** Arundel, W Sussex

FOCUS
A fair handicap, run at an uneven pace and it was a disadvantage to race from off the pace. The first two are unexposed and the third is a solid marker for the form.
True To Form(IRE) Official explanation: jockey said gelding moved poorly throughout
Constant Craving Official explanation: jockey said filly was unsuited by the good to firm ground
Silverglas(IRE) Official explanation: jockey said gelding was unsuited by the good to firm ground

1773 MANGO BAY CLASSIC H'CAP 1m 67y
3:55 (4:05) (Class 3) (0-90,87) 3-Y-0 **£6,670** (£1,984; £991; £495) **Stalls** Low

Form RPR
234- **1** **Harry Luck (IRE)**[267] 4856 3-8-11 **77**............................... DaneO'Neill 5 83+
(Henry Candy) *in tch: rdn and outpcd over 2f out: rdn: hdwy and swtchd lft over 1f out: str run to ld fnl 100yds: won gng away* **10/3**[2]
13-2 **2** *1 ¼* **Islesman**[119] 27 3-8-12 **78**... LukeMorris 1 81
(Heather Main) *chsd ldrs tl rdn and outpcd 3f out: drvn and gd hdwy over 1f out: str chal and upsides ins fnl f tl outpcd by wnr fnl 100yds* **8/1**
61-1 **3** *½* **The Tichborne (IRE)**[114] 101 3-9-7 **87**.............................. AdamKirby 3 89
(Roger Teal) *chsd ldr: drvn to ld 2f out: jnd and u.p ins fnl f: outpcd into 3rd fnl 100yds* **5/1**[3]
213- **4** *3 ¾* **Marzante (USA)**[233] 5969 3-8-12 **78**.............................. WilliamBuick 2 71
(Roger Charlton) *hld up in rr and t.k.h: hdwy 3f out to chse ldrs 2f out: rdn: hung lft and wknd qckly wl over 1f out* **2/1**[1]
00-4 **5** *1 ¾* **Persian Herald**[30] 1106 3-8-13 **79**............................... CathyGannon 4 68
(William Muir) *t.k.h in rr: rdn and hdwy on outside over 2f out: nvr quite rchd ldrs and wknd over 1f out* **11/1**
1-4 **6** *1* **Cheque Book**[52] 841 3-9-1 **81**.. MichaelHills 6 68
(B W Hills) *led tl hdd & wknd 2f out* **5/1**[3]

1m 44.79s (0.09) **Going Correction** +0.075s/f (Good) **6** Ran SP% **109.2**
Speed ratings (Par 103): **102,100,100,96,94 93**
toteswingers: 1&2 £4.00, 1&3 £3.10, 2&3 £3.70. CSF £26.91 TOTE £3.40: £2.20, £3.30; EX 12.00.
Owner Six Too Many **Bred** Muirhill Bloodstock Ltd **Trained** Kingston Warren, Oxon
■ Stewards' Enquiry : Adam Kirby two-day ban: careless riding (May 16-17)

FOCUS
A fair 3-y-o handicap, run at a sound pace and there was a tight three-way finish. There are doubts over the form but the winner looks the best guide.

NOTEBOOK
Harry Luck(IRE) made the frame in each of his three runs as a juvenile, which included his first two outings here, and he gamely opened his account on this seasonal return. He took time to pick up, perhaps feeling the quick ground somewhat, but the longer trip was more up his street. In good hands, he is said by his trainer to have matured now and is expected to rate a bit higher this year. (tchd 11-4)
Islesman was back up in trip and again found one too good back on turf, but still turned in a career-best effort. This lightly raced son of Oratorio fully deserves to go one better again. (op 7-1)
The Tichborne(IRE) was bidding for a hat-trick after a 114-day break and making his turf debut. Easy to back, he ran a solid race in defeat and still looks capable of improving. (op 11-2 tchd 6-1)
Marzante(USA) showed promise in three outings last year and was well backed for his return. He looked as though he was coming with a winning challenge in the home straight, but hung under maximum pressure and it's a fair bet he was feeling the fast surface. (op 9-4)
Persian Herald proved keen early and that looked to cost him after he made a promising move in the centre of the home straight. There could be another race in him before long back over 7f. Official explanation: jockey said colt hung left (op 9-1)

1774 THINK HOLIDAY. BOOK HAYES & JARVIS MEDIAN AUCTION MAIDEN STKS 1m 67y
4:25 (4:32) (Class 5) 3-4-Y-0 **£2,388** (£705; £352) **Stalls** Low

Form RPR
4 **1** **England Rules (IRE)**[18] 1338 3-9-1 0.......................... WilliamBuick 12 79+
(Jeremy Noseda) *trckd ldrs: pushed along and hdwy over 2f out: rdn and edgd rt appr f: drvn to chal ins fnl f: r.o strly to ld fnl 120yds: in command clsng stages* **11/10**[1]
3-42 **2** *½* **Whistle On By**[37] 993 3-9-1 75.. MichaelHills 8 78
(B W Hills) *chsd ldrs: drvn to chal 2f out: led wl over 1f out: jnd ins fnl f: hdd and outpcd fnl 120yds* **4/1**[2]
3 *3* **Kleitomachos (IRE)** 3-9-1 0.. AdamKirby 6 71+
(Stuart Kittow) *s.i.s: in rr: pushed along over 2f out: styd on wl to take 3rd wl ins fnl f but nvr gng pce to rch ldng duo* **33/1**
40- **4** *2* **Norse Wing**[193] 7034 3-8-10 0..................................... StevieDonohoe 3 62
(Ralph Beckett) *chsd ldrs: rdn and swtchd lft 2f out: wknd fnl f* **20/1**
06- **5** *hd* **Adone (IRE)**[234] 5916 3-8-12 0...................................... JalonSamuel(3) 4 66
(Sir Michael Stoute) *sn chsng ldr: led 5f out: rdn and jnd again 3f out: hdd over 2f out but styd upsides tl wknd appr fnl f* **7/1**
0-0 **6** *¾* **Joe Strummer (IRE)**[20] 1298 3-9-1 0................................. MartinLane 1 64
(Michael Bell) *mid-div: rdn over 4f out: styd on same pce fnl 2f* **25/1**
0- **7** *1 ½* **Hoofprintinthesnow**[216] 6442 3-9-1 0............................... LukeMorris 9 61
(Amanda Perrett) *in rr: sme prog fnl 2f* **16/1**
620- **8** *3 ¼* **Hard Bargain (IRE)**[236] 5865 3-9-1 72........................... CathyGannon 10 53
(Denis Coakley) *led tl hdd 5f out: led again 3f out: jnd 2f out: hdd & wknd wl over 1f out* **6/1**[3]
9 *½* **Bravo King (IRE)** 3-9-1 0... PaulDoe 5 52
(Jim Best) *s.i.s: in rr: rdn and sme prog ins fnl 3f: sn wknd* **33/1**
0 **10** *5* **Ambala**[21] 1270 3-8-10 0.. TedDurcan 7 36
(Chris Wall) *in rr: brief effrt 3f out: sn wknd* **33/1**
60 **11** *2 ¼* **Hamilton Hill**[7] 1568 4-10-0 0....................................... MarcHalford 11 36
(Terry Clement) *green: a in rr* **50/1**

0- 12 *nk* **Librettela**[228] 6102 3-8-12 0 .... MatthewDavies(3) 13 35
(Alan Jarvis) *chsd ldrs: awkward bnd 6f out: wknd 4f out* **100/1**

1m 45.42s (0.72) **Going Correction** +0.075s/f (Good)
WFA 3 from 4yo 13lb **12** Ran SP% **120.7**
Speed ratings (Par 103): **99,98,95,93,93 92,91,87,87,82 80,79**
toteswingers: 1&2 £1.90, 1&3 £28.50, 2&3 £26.80. CSF £5.05 TOTE £2.10: £1.10, £1.80, £11.60; EX 5.40 Trifecta £287.90 Pool: £712.12 - 1.83 winning units..
Owner Mrs Susan Roy **Bred** Mrs T V Ryan **Trained** Newmarket, Suffolk

FOCUS
A modest maiden where the first pair came clear and the form looks relatively sound.
Hard Bargain(IRE) Official explanation: jockey said gelding was unsuited by the good to firm ground

1775 DISCOVERY BAY BY REX RESORTS H'CAP 1m 3f 135y
4:55 (4:55) (Class 4) (0-85,80) 4-Y-0+ **£4,079** (£1,214; £606; £303) **Stalls** High

Form RPR
20-5 **1** **Mons Calpe (IRE)**[18] 1325 5-8-4 **68**............................(p) KieranO'Neill(5) 7 76
(Paul Cole) *sn led: rdn and hdd over 2f out: n.m.r on inner sn after: rdn and rallied to ld again over 1f out: pushed out clsng stages* **5/1**

031- **2** *1 3/4* **Loden**[201] 6846 4-9-1 **74**.. KirstyMilczarek 3 79+
(Luca Cumani) *hld up in rr: hdwy on outside 3f out: swtchd rt to ins over 1f out: drvn and stdy on to take 2nd nr fin but nt rch wnr* **5/2**[1]

165- **3** *1 1/4* **Goldtrek (USA)**[236] 5858 4-9-4 **77**..................................... WilliamBuick 2 80
(Roger Charlton) *hld up in tch: drvn and qcknd to chal 3f out: led sn after: rdn and hung rt ins fnl 2f: hdd 1f out: sn no ch w wnr: lost 2nd nr fin* **10/3**[2]

4312 **4** *3/4* **Where's Susie**[30] 962 6-9-1 **74**.. RobertHavlin 4 76
(Michael Madgwick) *chsd ldrs: rdn to dispute 2nd 4f out tl over 2f out: wknd fnl f* **6/1**

3333 **5** *nk* **Layla's Dancer**[2] 1676 4-9-0 **73**... LukeMorris 1 74
(Tony Carroll) *chsd wnr: rdn 3f out: styd on same pce u.p fnl 2f* **9/2**[3]

60- **6** *22* **Shalambar (IRE)**[38] 6990 5-8-12 **71**.................................... TedDurcan 5 52
(Tony Carroll) *slowly away: a in rr: eased fnl 2f* **16/1**

6-40 **7** *36* **Langley**[30] 1105 4-9-7 **80**... DaneO'Neill 6 —
(Pat Murphy) *chsd ldrs tl wknd over 2f out: eased* **12/1**

2m 27.79s (-1.71) **Going Correction** +0.075s/f (Good) **7** Ran SP% **114.4**
Speed ratings (Par 105): **108,106,106,105,105 90,66**
toteswingers: 1&2 £4.10, 1&3 £4.20, 2&3 £2.60. CSF £17.93 TOTE £7.40: £3.90, £1.90; EX 18.10.
Owner H R H Sultan Ahmad Shah **Bred** Swettenham Stud **Trained** Whatcombe, Oxon

FOCUS
A fairly tight-looking handicap a but the time was fairly decent and the winner looks the best guide to the level.

1776 HAPPY RETIREMENT RUSSELL KNIGHT H'CAP 5f 10y
5:25 (5:25) (Class 5) (0-70,68) 3-Y-0 **£2,388** (£705; £352) **Stalls** Low

Form RPR
444- **1** **Best Be Careful (IRE)**[185] 7211 3-9-0 **61**............................ DaneO'Neill 4 66
(Mark Usher) *chsd ldrs: drvn to ld appr fnl f: drvn out* **7/1**

3222 **2** *nk* **Welsh Inlet (IRE)**[11] 1504 3-9-4 **65**................................... LukeMorris 2 69
(John Bridger) *chsd ldrs: outpcd 2f out: rallied u.p: swtchd to stands' rail and styd on u.p fnl 120yds: tk 2nd last strides: nt rch wnr* **6/1**[2]

30-6 **3** *shd* **Whitecrest**[12] 1483 3-9-4 **65**... FrannyNorton 3 69
(John Spearing) *chsd ldrs: rdn and outpcd over 1f out: rallied ins fnl f to press wnr fnl 50yds: a jst hld: lost 2nd last strides* **10/1**

-113 **4** *1 1/4* **Dorothy's Dancing (IRE)**[25] 1193 3-8-12 **59**...............(p) WilliamBuick 7 59
(Gary Moore) *stdd to trck ldrs: edgd lft: drvn and qcknd to chal jst ins fnl f: no ex and wknd clsng stages* **3/1**[1]

2003 **5** *1* **Majestic Ridge (IRE)**[17] 1359 3-8-9 **56**........................(v) CathyGannon 5 52
(David Evans) *sn led: rdn 1/2-way: hdd appr fnl f: wknd fnl 120yds* **8/1**

150- **6** *1 3/4* **Sensational Love (IRE)**[171] 7423 3-9-7 **68**....................... RobertHavlin 6 58
(Robert Mills) *slowly away: drvn and styd on fr over 1f out: nt rch ldrs* **8/1**

422 **7** *6* **Reachtothestars (USA)**[12] 1482 3-9-1 **62**........................(t) AdamKirby 1 30
(Noel Quinlan) *chsd ldrs: btn whn hmpd on rails appr fnl f* **15/2**

32-4 **8** *1* **Stunning In Purple (IRE)**[17] 1359 3-9-7 **68**................ StevieDonohoe 9 32
(Andrew Haynes) *outpcd most of way* **13/2**[3]

1224 **9** *2 1/2* **Kassaab**[23] 1249 3-9-1 **62**...(b) TedDurcan 8 17
(Jeremy Gask) *spd to 1/2-way* **10/1**

61.63 secs (1.33) **Going Correction** +0.125s/f (Good) **9** Ran SP% **117.3**
Speed ratings (Par 99): **94,93,93,91,89 86,77,75,71**
toteswingers: 1&2 £6.50, 1&3 £15.50, 2&3 £15.20. CSF £49.31 CT £423.93 TOTE £8.20: £2.50, £2.20, £1.90; EX 73.20 Trifecta £488.50 Part won. Pool: £660.12 - 0.86 winning units..
Owner Mrs Jill Pellett **Bred** M Phelan **Trained** Upper Lambourn, Berks

FOCUS
A moderate sprint handicap with the runner-up rated to recent form.
Majestic Ridge(IRE) Official explanation: jockey said gelding ran too free
Reachtothestars(USA) Official explanation: jockey said colt suffered interference in running
T/Jkpt: Not won. T/Plt: £61.50 to a £1 stake. Pool:£73,613.07 - 873.49 winning tickets. T/Qpdt: £10.70 to a £1 stake. Pool:£4,686.97 - 323.85 winning tickets. ST

1115 CURRAGH (R-H)
Monday, May 2

OFFICIAL GOING: Good to firm

1779a STARSPANGLEDBANNER EUROPEAN BREEDERS FUND ATHASI STKS (GROUP 3) (F&M) 7f
3:20 (3:22) 3-Y-0+ **£40,625** (£11,875; £5,625; £1,875)

RPR
1 **Emiyna (USA)**[24] 1224 3-8-11 .... JMurtagh 7 106+
(John M Oxx, Ire) *hld up in rr: gd hdwy fr 2f out: chal 1f out: sn led: kpt on u.p: strly pressed and jst hld on cl home* **5/2**[1]

2 *shd* **Lolly For Dolly (IRE)**[29] 1118 4-9-12 108........................(b) WMLordan 3 113
(T Stack, Ire) *trckd ldrs: 5th 1/2-way: hdwy to chal over 1f out: kpt on wl u.p ins fnl f: jst failed* **7/2**[2]

3 *4* **Seeharn (IRE)**[36] 1006 3-8-11 99.. DPMcDonogh 9 97
(Kevin Prendergast, Ire) *trckd ldrs in 3rd: hdwy to ld jst under 2f out: strly pressed and hdd early fnl f: sn no ex* **5/1**[3]

4 *1* **Intapeace (IRE)**[230] 6068 4-9-9 96.......................................(p) BACurtis 2 96
(Francis Ennis, Ire) *chsd ldrs on far rail: 4th 1/2-way: drvn along under 2f out: no imp fr 1f out: kpt on one pce* **22/1**

5 *3* **Claiomh Solais (IRE)**[22] 1260 3-8-11 .... KJManning 6 84
(J S Bolger, Ire) *hld up towards rr: pushed along over 2f out: 8th over 1f out: kpt on ins fnl f wout threatening* **12/1**

6 *3 1/2* **Look At Me (IRE)**[213] 6528 3-8-11 .... CO'Donoghue 8 90
(A P O'Brien, Ire) *trckd ldrs: 6th 1/2-way: pushed along and no ex fr over 1f out: eased whn btn ins fnl f (showing signs of coming into season post-r)* **7/2**[2]

7 *5* **Enchanted Evening (IRE)**[24] 1225 5-9-9 92....................(b) PJSmullen 4 65
(D K Weld, Ire) *trckd ldr in 2nd: rdn over 2f out: no ex over 1f out: sn wknd* **14/1**

8 *1 1/4* **Headford View (IRE)**[246] 5571 7-9-9 93...........................(p) PShanahan 5 62
(James Halpin, Ire) *a towards rr: pushed along and no ex fr under 2f out* **50/1**

9 *2* **Duchess Of Foxland (IRE)**[232] 6007 4-9-9 101 .... FMBerry 1 56
(Mark L Fagan, Ire) *led: strly pressed over 2f out: sn hdd & wknd* **11/1**

1m 25.64s (-5.16)
WFA 3 from 4yo+ 12lb **9** Ran SP% **118.7**
CSF £11.68 TOTE £2.90: £1.50, £1.02, £1.70; DF 13.80.
Owner H H Aga Khan **Bred** H H Aga Khan's Studs Sc **Trained** Curragh, Co Kildare

NOTEBOOK
Emiyna(USA) ◆, winner of a maiden over this trip at Dundalk last month having raced only once last season, was up against some older and more experienced rivals here and, after being held up at the back of the field, she began to close travelling well under two furlongs out. She edged ahead early in the final furlong and had to be kept up to her work to hold on in a tight finish. The time was just a fraction quicker than that clocked in the previous race, the Tetrarch Stakes. Trainer John Oxx said of the winner: "We've always liked her and she will take her chance in the Irish 1,000 Guineas back here in three weeks time. There is plenty of stamina on her dam's side but she has a lot of speed and probably won't get further than a mile." (op 7/2 tchd 9/4)
Lolly For Dolly(IRE) was on a Group 3 hat-trick here having won the Park Express Stakes and the Gladness Stakes at the course this season. She only just failed to achieve it, sticking to her task well under pressure after tracking the leaders and beginning her challenge over a furlong out. Considering the ground was much quicker than ideal it was a highly creditable effort. (op 10/3)
Seeharn(IRE), twice a winner, once at Listed level, over 6f here last year, had finished fifth in the 1,000 Guineas Trial at Leopardstown on her reappearance. She was always in the front rank and went into the lead two furlongs out before having no more to offer when tackled and headed by the winner. (op 13/2)
Intapeace(IRE) had not raced since September and the 96-rated mare performed creditably, although unable to make much impression on the principals after coming under pressure soon after the two-furlong marker. (op 22/1 tchd 25/1)
Claiomh Solais(IRE), a maiden dropping down in trip having been placed on her first two starts over 1m and 1m2f, appeared to be getting nowhere when driven along well over two furlongs out, but she did stay on through the final furlong without posing any sort of threat. (op 14/1)
Look At Me(IRE), runner-up to Havant in a Group 3 at Newmarket in October after winning a maiden over this trip on her debut at Fairyhouse, was eased inside the final furlong when her chance had gone and was reported to be showing signs of coming in season. Official explanation: vet said mare was showing signs of being in season post-race (op 5/2)

1781a HIGH CHAPARRAL EUROPEAN BREEDERS FUND MOORESBRIDGE STKS (GROUP 3) 1m 2f
4:20 (4:24) 4-Y-0+ **£40,625** (£11,875; £5,625; £1,875)

RPR
1 **So You Think (NZ)**[181] 7291 5-9-6 126...................... SeamieHeffernan 4 128+
(A P O'Brien, Ire) *trckd ldrs in 3rd: clsr ent st: hdwy to ld under 2f out: sn asserted: styd on strly fnl f: easily* **2/13**[1]

2 *10* **Bob Le Beau (IRE)**[177] 7358 4-9-1 103.................................... FMBerry 2 102
(Mrs John Harrington, Ire) *chsd ldr in 2nd: clsr ent st: hdwy to ld briefly 2f out: hdd and sn no ch w wnr: kpt on same pce* **9/1**[2]

3 *2* **Mid Mon Lady (IRE)**[43] 924 6-8-12 100...........................(b) CDHayes 1 95+
(H Rogers, Ire) *towards rr: 5th 1/2-way: sme hdwy into 4th 2f out: wnt mod 3rd 1f out: kpt on one pce* **33/1**

4 *3/4* **Termagant (IRE)**[43] 924 4-8-12 105 .... DPMcDonogh 3 94+
(Kevin Prendergast, Ire) *chsd ldrs: 4th 1/2-way: 5th 2f out: no imp fr over 1f out* **14/1**[3]

5 *nk* **Cashelgar (IRE)**[18] 1351 5-9-1 105.. PJSmullen 6 96+
(D K Weld, Ire) *a towards rr: pushed along 2f out: no imp fr over 1f out* **20/1**

6 *9* **Windsor Palace (IRE)**[148] 7753 6-9-1 97 .... JPO'Brien 5 81
(A P O'Brien, Ire) *led: 6 l clr after 1/2-way: reduced ld ent st: strly pressed and hdd 2f out: no ex fr over 1f out* **25/1**

2m 12.83s (-1.47) **6** Ran SP% **114.9**
CSF £2.40 TOTE £1.10: £1.02, £2.20; DF 2.70.
Owner Smith/Magnier/Tabor/Dato Tan/Tunku Yahaya **Bred** M J Moran & Piper Farm Ltd **Trained** Ballydoyle, Co Tipperary

NOTEBOOK
So You Think(NZ) ◆, one of the finest middle-distance performers in Australian racing history, got his northern hemisphere career off to a simple, fuss-free start. Having amassed an exceptional record in Australia, the dual Cox Plate winner was running for the first time since a lack of stamina proved his undoing in the Melbourne Cup, in which he nevertheless managed to finish a fine third only three days after romping to a fifth Group 1 success in the Mackinnon Stakes. Returning to the scene of his Curragh racecourse gallop last month, the 5-y-o, masculine and muscular, dominated the race as he had dominated the paddock, travelling with ease under Seamie Heffernan before quickening smartly to put upwards of ten lengths between himself and his rivals. Aidan O'Brien made absolutely clear after the race that his new recruit has not been given a hard time and it will be an enormous shock if he does not strip considerably fitter when he returns to this venue later in the month for a fascinating showdown with Investec Derby and Prix de l'Arc de Triomphe hero Workforce in the Tattersalls Gold Cup. Given So You Think's exceptional record over 1m2f, he ought to have too much pace for Sir Michael Stoute's 1m4f specialist, but beyond that contest it is only guesswork as to where he will then head. Quite clearly all the world's major races will be available to him and he will be a warm order wherever he goes, but it was still bizarre in the extreme for Paddy Power to slash him to 5-2 from 6-1 for the King George VI and Queen Elizabeth II Stakes following a 2-13 victory that, in itself, told us little new. (op 1/6 tchd 1/7)
Bob Le Beau(IRE) spent most of the race splitting So You Think and the latter's pacemaker Windsor Palace, confirmed himself to be a genuine Listed-class animal with a commendable second. (op 11/1)
Mid Mon Lady(IRE) flopped on her seasonal return, but despite running slightly better on this quicker ground, she did not achieve a great deal. On the evidence of this and last season, she is flattered to hold an official rating of 100. (op 25/1)
Termagant(IRE), triumphant in the 2009 Moyglare Stud Stakes, has raced only three times since but it is hard to argue that she has done anything other than regress in those three runs. She could now become very hard to place.
Cashelgar(IRE) is another horse who looks to be a long way off what he once was. (op 16/1)
Windsor Palace(IRE)'s role here was to set the pace for So You Think and he executed that job perfectly.

1777 - 1778a, 1780, 1782 - 1783a (Foreign Racing) - See Raceform Interactive

1646 CHANTILLY (R-H)

Monday, May 2

OFFICIAL GOING: Turf: good

1784a PRIX ALLEZ FRANCE (GROUP 3) (4YO+ FILLIES & MARES) (TURF) 1m 2f

2:55 (12:00) 4-Y-0+ £34,482 (£13,793; £10,344; £6,896; £3,448)

RPR

1 **Announce**[212] 6591 4-9-0 0 MaximeGuyon 9 115
(A Fabre, France) *settled in 3rd: rdn and qcknd wl 1f out: r.o strly to ld 50yds out* **11/2**[3]

2 *1* **Shamanova (IRE)**[212] 6591 4-8-9 0 Christophe-PatriceLemaire 4 108
(A De Royer-Dupre, France) *settled towards rr on rail: bhd horses and short of room 1 1/2f out: qcknd wl through horses 1f out: r.o strly fnl 100yds: clst at fin* **58/10**

3 *snk* **Rock My Soul (IRE)**[25] 1208 5-8-7 0 MickaelBarzalona 10 106
(A Fabre, France) *settled in 3rd: rdn 1 1/2f out on outer: grabbed ld 1f out: r.o wl: hdd 50yds out: r.o: lost 2nd cl home* **18/1**

4 *snk* **One Clever Cat (IRE)**[25] 1208 5-8-7 0 FlavienPrat 5 105
(T Clout, France) *settled in rr: gd prog on outer 1 1/2f out: r.o wl fnl f: clst at fin* **3/1**[1]

5 *1* **Kartica**[26] 4-8-10 0 ow1 OlivierPeslier 6 106
(P Demercastel, France) *settled in 2nd: rdn and led briefly 1 1/2f out: hdd and no ex 1f out: styd on* **11/1**

6 *1* **Belle Masquee (IRE)**[25] 1208 4-8-7 0 (b) GregoryBenoist 8 101
(D Smaga, France) *settled in midfield: rdn 1 1/2f out: nt qckn: styd on fnl f* **12/1**

7 *shd* **Toi Et Moi (IRE)**[215] 6486 4-8-7 0 StephanePasquier 3 101
(P Bary, France) *w.w towards rr: styd on fr 1f out* **15/1**

8 *2* **Akarlina (FR)**[22] 1266 5-9-0 0 ThierryThulliez 7 104
(N Clement, France) *sn led: hdd 1 1/2f out: no ex fnl f: grad fdd* **7/2**[2]

9 *3* **Roche Ambeau (FR)**[160] 7546 4-8-7 0 AnthonyCrastus 2 91
(E Lellouche, France) *racd in midfield pulling freely: dropped bk towards rr bef st: hrd rdn 1 1/2f out: no ex: fdd* **23/1**

10 *5* **Katsya (FR)**[26] 4-8-7 0 JohanVictoire 1 81
(J E Pease, France) *settled bhd ldrs: rdn 2f out: no ex: grad fdd* **15/1**

2m 0.50s (-4.30) **10** Ran SP% **115.3**

WIN (incl. 1 euro stake): 4.80 (Announce coupled with Rock My Soul). PLACES: 2.90, 2.40, 3.90. DF: 13.40. SF: 25.00.

Owner K Abdulla **Bred** Juddmonte Farms **Trained** Chantilly, France

NOTEBOOK

Announce hadn't run since disappointing at Longchamp last October, but had always looked the type to make a better 4-y-o, and she showed a decent turn of foot to collect. There's more to come and she should make her mark at Group 1 level this term.

Shamanova(IRE) was probably unfortunate not to get even closer to the winner, coming from a poor position to take a never-nearer second. She needs further than this, and is another winning in waiting.

Rock My Soul(IRE), a stablemate to the winner, ran as well as could have been expected.

One Clever Cat(IRE), a winner at Maisons-Laffitte on her reapperance, never got close enough to challenge.

1625 BATH (L-H)

Tuesday, May 3

OFFICIAL GOING: Firm (10.9)

Wind: Brisk across Weather: Sunny spells

1785 HSBC MAIDEN AUCTION STKS 5f 11y

2:30 (2:31) (Class 5) 2-Y-0 £2,456 (£725; £362) Stalls Centre

Form RPR

2 1 **Signifer (IRE)**[18] 1360 2-8-12 0 MartinHarley(3) 3 83+
(Mick Channon) *mde all: t.k.h and hung rt and awkward bnd over 3f out: shkn up ins fnl f: comf* **2/5**[1]

5 2 *1* **Dream Whisperer**[33] 1055 2-8-3 0 BillyCray(3) 2 70
(Dominic Ffrench Davis) *chsd wnr thrght: rdn over 2f out: styd on ins fnl f but a comf hld* **20/1**

0 3 *2* **Steady The Buffs**[19] 1337 2-8-8 0 LukeMorris 5 65
(Hugo Palmer) *chsd ldng duo: hrd rdn 2f out: no imp fr over 1f out* **40/1**

2 4 *4* **That's Dangerous**[28] 1143 2-8-13 0 SteveDrowne 4 55
(Roger Charlton) *in rr: pushed along and no prog fr 1/2-way: tk modest 4th nr fin* **10/3**[2]

5 *1/2* **Shout For Joy (IRE)** 2-8-9 0 ow1 RichardHughes 1 49
(Richard Hannon) *racd in 4th: pushed along and swtchd rt to outside 2f out: no imp: sn wknd: lost mod 4th nr fin* **10/1**[3]

61.20 secs (-1.30) **Going Correction** -0.225s/f (Firm) 5 Ran SP% **110.8**

Speed ratings (Par 93): **101,99,96,89,89**

CSF £10.61 TOTE £1.50: £1.10, £5.80; EX 10.80.

Owner Insignia Racing (Roundel) **Bred** Maurice Burns **Trained** West Ilsley, Berks

FOCUS

With no rain at the track for four weeks it was very fast ground here, and a brisk following wind up the straight suggested times were likely to be on the fast side. That was borne out by the time of the first, with the juveniles running close to the standard and producing the best time of the three races over the trip. The form is not totally convincing but the winner can do better.

NOTEBOOK

Signifer(IRE), who had finished second to Magic City at Newbury on his debut, with a subsequent winner back in third. He jumped out and made all, but did not pull away from the runner-up as might have been expected. That might have been down to the fast ground but he scored well enough and should be able to win again. He might go to Royal Ascot, possibly for the Windsor Castle, after another run. (op 1-2)

Dream Whisperer finished fifth on her debut in a contest from which the first two had won since, and she built on that by giving the winner a good race. She certainly looks capable of winning.

Steady The Buffs stepped up on her debut as she chased the pace throughout and responded to pressure, but the first two were too strong.

That's Dangerous, who made a promising debut on the Kempton Polytrack, unseated his rider before going into the stalls and was always out the back. It appeared he was unable to stretch out on the fast ground. (tchd 3-1 and 7-2)

Shout For Joy(IRE), the first foal of a winning miler and making her debut, was always struggling to go the pace and wandered under pressure. She was subsequently found to be lame on her off-fore. Official explanation: vet said filly returned lame right-fore (op 11-1 tchd 12-1)

1786 BATH CHRONICLE (S) STKS 5f 11y

3:00 (3:00) (Class 6) 2-Y-0 £1,683 (£501; £250; £125) Stalls Centre

Form RPR

053 1 **Middleton Flyer (IRE)**[15] 1434 2-8-6 0 CathyGannon 5 64
(David Evans) *trckd ldr: led 3f out: drvn and styd on strly ins fnl f* **4/5**[1]

3 2 *1 1/2* **Miss Muga**[8] 1563 2-7-13 0 CharlesBishop(7) 3 58
(Mick Channon) *chsd ldrs in 3rd: rdn: hung rt and outpcd over 2f out: drvn and styd on again appr fnl f: kpt on to take 2nd fnl 100yds but no ch w wnr* **5/1**[3]

30 3 *1 1/2* **Mrs Mop (IRE)**[15] 1441 2-8-1 0 KieranO'Neill(5) 2 53
(Richard Hannon) *chsd wnr 3f out: rdn and no imp fr 2f out: one pce and lost 2nd fnl 100yds* **4/1**[2]

4 *4* **Jaci Uzzi (IRE)** 2-8-6 0 LukeMorris 7 38
(David Evans) *s.i.s: in rr: drvn along 3f out: sme prog fnl f* **8/1**

5 5 *9* **She's Reel Dusty**[31] 1101 2-7-13 0 JakePayne(7) 6 5
(Bill Turner) *s.i.s: in rr: hung rt 3f out and no ch after* **20/1**

0 6 *6* **Foolscap (IRE)**[22] 1268 2-8-8 0 (b[1]) MatthewDavies(3) 4 —
(Jim Boyle) *led tl hung rt and hdd 3f out: continued to hang and no ch after* **40/1**

61.98 secs (-0.52) **Going Correction** -0.225s/f (Firm) 6 Ran SP% **110.5**

Speed ratings (Par 91): **95,92,90,83,69 59**

Tote Swingers: 1&2 £1.50, 1&3 £1.50, 2&3 £2.00 CSF £5.05 TOTE £1.60: £1.40, £1.40; EX 5.30.The winner was bought in for 11,500gns.

Owner 24 - 7 / Gap Personnel **Bred** Maurice Burns **Trained** Pandy, Monmouths

■ Stewards' Enquiry : Jake Payne two-day ban: used whip with excessive frequency (May 17-18)

FOCUS

David Evans and Mick Channon trained the two previous winners of this seller and both had runners this time, and their runners filled the first two places. The experienced winner looks the best guide.

NOTEBOOK

Middleton Flyer(IRE), the most experienced in the field and dropping in grade, was rather left in front when Foolscap drifted but did the rest in straightforward fashion. Her trainer went to 11,500gns to retain her, and she is probably the sort who can win a nursery later in the season. (op 5-6 tchd 10-11)

Miss Muga built on her debut effort, staying on but making no impression on the winner in the last furlong. (op 9-2)

Mrs Mop(IRE) showed good pace before tiring and connections believe she will need further in time. (op 5-1)

Jaci Uzzi(IRE), the winner's stablemate and the only debutante, missed the break on this debut and was outpaced but was noted keeping on well late on. (tchd 9-1)

She's Reel Dusty was back on heels when the stalls opened and was always struggling. (op 16-1)

Foolscap(IRE), wearing blinkers for the first time, made the early running but drifted out into the middle of the track around halfway and proved virtually unrideable. Official explanation: jockey said colt hung badly right (op 28-1)

1787 BATH TOURISM PLUS H'CAP 5f 11y

3:30 (3:30) (Class 6) (0-65,61) 4-Y-0+ £1,683 (£501; £250; £125) Stalls Centre

Form RPR

0-35 1 **Bateleur**[5] 1627 7-9-2 **59** MartinHarley(3) 6 66
(Mick Channon) *s.i.s: in rr: hdwy on ins 2f out: rdn to ld over 1f out: r.o wl fnl 120yds* **11/2**[3]

4401 2 *1 1/4* **Athwaab**[10] 1523 4-8-13 **60** CharlesBishop(7) 2 62
(Noel Quinlan) *trckd ldr: led over 2f out: sn rdn: hdd over 1f out: sn no ch w wnr: edgd rt fr ins fnl f and kpt on to hold 2nd* **15/8**[1]

0052 3 *1/2* **Metropolitan Chief**[14] 1453 7-8-3 **48** DanielleMcCreery(5) 4 48+
(Paul Burgoyne) *in rr hdwy: nt clr run and swtchd sharply rt ins fnl 2f: continued to go rt: styd on ins fnl f to take 3rd nr fin: nt rch ldng duo* **9/1**

640- 4 *1* **The Name Is Frank**[190] 7125 6-9-7 **61** (t) FergusSweeney 1 58
(Mark Gillard) *chsd ldrs: rdn and one pce 3rd ins fnl f: one pce into 4th nr fin* **10/1**

0600 5 *1/2* **Little Perisher**[2] 1730 4-9-1 **55** (b[1]) DarryllHolland 7 50
(Karen George) *sn rdn in rr: sme prog on outer whn carried rt fr ins fnl 2f: kpt on cl home but nvr any ch* **17/2**

4404 6 *shd* **Radiator Rooney (IRE)**[5] 1638 8-8-12 **52** RichardHughes 3 46
(Patrick Morris) *chsd ldrs: hung rt fnl f and styd on same pce* **9/2**[2]

0411 7 *16* **Spic 'n Span**[13] 1501 6-9-2 **56** (b) LukeMorris 5 —
(Ronald Harris) *v keen to post: led tl hdd over 2f out: btn whn bmpd ins fnl 2f* **6/1**

61.39 secs (-1.11) **Going Correction** -0.225s/f (Firm) 7 Ran SP% **112.3**

Speed ratings (Par 101): **99,97,96,94,93 93,68**

Tote Swingers: 1&2 £3.40, 1&3 £9.30, 2&3 £5.70 CSF £15.65 TOTE £3.40: £3.60, £1.70; EX 17.00.

Owner Dave and Gill Hedley **Bred** G Hedley & Mike Channon Bloodstock Limited **Trained** West Ilsley, Berks

FOCUS

A moderate sprint handicap with the runner-up to her latest for the best guide.

Little Perisher Official explanation: jockey said gelding suffered interference in running

Radiator Rooney(IRE) Official explanation: jockey said gelding hung right

Spic 'n Span Official explanation: jockey said gelding was struck into

1788 WESTERN DAILY PRESS H'CAP 2m 1f 34y

4:05 (4:05) (Class 4) (0-85,80) 4-Y-0+ £3,885 (£1,156; £577) Stalls Centre

Form RPR

12-5 1 **Saborido (USA)**[15] 1443 5-9-2 **75** PatDobbs 2 79+
(Amanda Perrett) *trckd ldng duo: wnt 2nd 3f out: shkn up to chal appr fnl f: pushed along to ld fnl 150yds: easily* **1/2**[1]

01-4 2 *3 1/2* **Never Can Tell (IRE)**[14] 1470 4-9-1 **80** SophieDoyle(3) 3 80
(Jamie Osborne) *disp ld tl def advantage 10f out: pushed along 2f out: hdd and hung lft fnl 150yds: sn btn* **5/2**[2]

500- 3 *64* **Baddam**[259] 4467 9-9-5 **78** IanMongan 1 —
(Ian Williams) *slt ld tl hdd 10f out: drvn along to chse ldr fr 1m out: lost 2nd 3f out: wknd qckly 2f out: virtually p.u fnl f* **15/2**[3]

3m 44.71s (-7.19) **Going Correction** -0.225s/f (Firm)

WFA 4 from 5yo+ 3lb 3 Ran SP% **107.0**

Speed ratings (Par 105): **107,105,75**

CSF £2.01 TOTE £1.40; EX 1.60.

Owner Tracey, Cotton, James, Slade **Bred** R D Hubbard And R Masterson **Trained** Pulborough, W Sussex

FOCUS
A small field for this stayers' handicap and the winner did not need to run to his best to score.

1789 200 YEARS OF RACING AT LANSDOWN FILLIES' H'CAP 1m 5y
4:35 (4:35) (Class 5) (0-75,74) 4-Y-O+ **£2,331** (£693; £346; £173) **Stalls** Low

Form RPR
421 **1** **Saddlers Bend (IRE)**[19] 1330 5-9-1 **71**.................. MatthewDavies(3) 5 78
(George Baker) *hld up in rr but in tch: hdwy on outside fr 2f out: str run u.p to chal fnl 120yds: led last stride* **9/2**
-602 **2** *nse* **Dr Wintringham (IRE)**[14] 1448 5-9-4 **71**...................... DarryllHolland 2 78
(Karen George) *t.k.h: trckd ldrs: rdn and outpcd over 1f out: rallied ins fnl f and str chal fnl 120yds: slt advantage fnl 50yds: hdd last stride* **10/3**[3]
50-6 **3** *nk* **Jewelled**[22] 1269 5-9-3 **70**.. RichardHughes 6 76
(Lady Herries) *hld up in tch: hdwy 3f out: pressed ldrs 2f out: chal appr fnl f: led fnl 120yds: hdd and nt qckn fnl 50yds* **11/4**[2]
43-0 **4** *1 1/4* **Commerce**[118] 54 4-8-13 **66**...................................... HayleyTurner 1 69
(Simon Dow) *led: rdn whn jnd fr 3f out: kpt slt advantage fr over 1f out tl hdd fnl 120yds: wknd nr fin* **8/1**
210- **5** *2 3/4* **Tap Dance Way (IRE)**[202] 6852 4-9-4 **71**........................ JimCrowley 4 68
(Patrick Chamings) *trckd ldr: chal fr 3f out: rdn 2f out and stl upsides: wknd ins fnl f* **2/1**[1]

1m 39.63s (-1.17) **Going Correction** -0.225s/f (Firm) **5** Ran SP% **112.4**
Speed ratings (Par 100): **96,95,95,94,91**
CSF £19.72 TOTE £5.30: £3.50, £2.10; EX 12.90.
Owner Mrs Christine Cone **Bred** J F Tuthill **Trained** Whitsbury, Hants

FOCUS
A competitive fillies' handicap despite the relatively small field and all five were still in with a winning chance inside the last 2f. The form is a bit muddling and is limited by the proximity of the fourth.

1790 BATH ABBEY H'CAP 1m 5y
5:10 (5:10) (Class 6) (0-60,60) 3-Y-O **£1,683** (£501; £250; £125) **Stalls** Low

Form RPR
03-6 **1** **Fire Crystal**[8] 1566 3-8-12 **54**.. MartinHarley(3) 4 58+
(Mick Channon) *trckd ldrs: wnt 2nd on ins 5f out: led 2f out: drvn over 1f out: hld on wl thrght fnl f* **7/2**[3]
05-5 **2** *nk* **Areef (IRE)**[21] 1288 3-8-13 **52**.. HayleyTurner 5 55+
(Michael Bell) *in rr: hdwy fr 3f out: chsd wnr over 1f out: styd on u.p fnl 120yds but a jst hld* **11/8**[1]
5-05 **3** *1 1/4* **Out Of The Storm**[35] 1022 3-9-5 **58**.................................. LukeMorris 6 58
(Simon Dow) *in rr: drvn along over 2f out: hdwy appr fnl f: kpt on u.p cl home but no imp on ldng duo* **9/2**
3320 **4** *3 1/2* **Crown Ridge (IRE)**[13] 1495 3-9-0 **60**........................ CharlesBishop(7) 3 52
(Mick Channon) *trckd ldrs: rdn and effrt fr 3f out: nvr gng pce to chal and wknd fnl f* **3/1**[2]
0050 **5** *2 3/4* **Bellaboolou**[8] 1566 3-8-9 **48**.................................(b) FergusSweeney 1 34
(David Pinder) *led: rdn 3f out: hdd 2f out: hung lft and wknd qckly fnl f* **33/1**
00-6 **6** *38* **Street Cred (IRE)**[7] 1578 3-8-7 **46** oh1.........................(t) CathyGannon 2 —
(Paul Burgoyne) *chsd ldrs tl wnt wd bnd 5f out: wknd fr 3f out: virtually p.u fnl f* **50/1**

1m 40.85s (0.05) **Going Correction** -0.225s/f (Firm) **6** Ran SP% **112.4**
Speed ratings (Par 97): **90,89,88,84,82 44**
Tote Swingers: 1&2 £2.30, 1&3 £2.10, 2&3 £1.90. Tote Super 7: Win: Not won. Place: £24.90. CSF £8.79 CT £20.17 TOTE £6.80: £2.80, £1.10; EX 9.10.
Owner M Channon **Bred** Mike Channon Bloodstock Ltd **Trained** West Ilsley, Berks

FOCUS
A moderate handicap which few came into in decent form. It resulted in a third winner on the day for Mick Channon and his rider Michael Harley. The form is best rated through the third.
Crown Ridge(IRE) Official explanation: jockey said gelding hit its head on stalls
T/Plt: £15.10 to a £1 stake. Pool:£40,462.31 - 1,951.30 winning tickets. T/Qpdt: £8.40 to a £1 stake. Pool:£2,242.07 - 196.10 winning tickets. ST

1301 CATTERICK (L-H)
Tuesday, May 3
OFFICIAL GOING: Good to firm (9.1)
Wind: moderate 1/2 behind Weather: fine and sunny

1791 XTREMEADVENTURESUK.COM MAIDEN AUCTION STKS 5f
6:00 (6:00) (Class 6) 2-Y-O **£1,706** (£503; £252) **Stalls** Low

Form RPR
1 **Judas Jo (FR)** 2-8-8 0.. RoystonFfrench 7 72+
(Gay Kelleway) *drvn to chse ldrs: plld outside 2f out: styd on to ld last 100yds* **15/2**
5 **2** *1 3/4* **Oneniteinheaven (IRE)**[14] 1455 2-8-7 0 ow1.............. AdrianNicholls 5 64
(Ann Duffield) *w ldrs: led after 2f: hdd and no ex ins fnl f* **9/2**[3]
3 *1 1/4* **Miss Rosie** 2-8-6 0.. GregFairley 8 61+
(Mark Johnston) *w ldrs: drvn over 2f out: edgd lft and styd on same pce ins fnl f* **2/1**[1]
6 **4** *nk* **Mebsuta (IRE)**[17] 1414 2-8-10 0.. PhillipMakin 2 61
(Kevin Ryan) *dwlt: drvn to chse ldrs: kpt on same pce appr fnl f* **3/1**[2]
5 *2 1/2* **Yearbook** 2-8-8 0.. RobbieFitzpatrick 3 50+
(Tim Easterby) *dwlt: drvn and outpcd over 2f out: hdwy over 1f out: kpt on same pce: nvr rchd ldrs* **12/1**
0 **6** *6* **Imperial Weapon (IRE)**[15] 1441 2-8-6 0........................ FrannyNorton 1 27
(John Spearing) *v free to post: w ldrs: wknd ins fnl f* **25/1**
7 *1* **Come To Mind** 2-8-9 0.. PatrickMathers 4 26
(Alan Berry) *s.v.s: nvr on terms* **80/1**
8 *17* **Musical Valley** 2-8-9 0..(t) RichardKingscote 6 —
(Tom Dascombe) *led 2f: wknd over 1f out: heavily eased: t.o* **8/1**

59.47 secs (-0.33) **Going Correction** -0.10s/f (Good) **8** Ran SP% **112.2**
Speed ratings (Par 91): **98,95,93,92,88 79,77,50**
toteswingers:1&2 £4.60, 2&3 £2.80, 1&3 £3.20 CSF £39.48 TOTE £14.00: £2.70, £1.10, £2.10; EX 18.10.
Owner Panther Racing Ltd **Bred** Ashbrittle Stud **Trained** Exning, Suffolk

FOCUS
A modest auction maiden with those that had run before only setting the bar low. The winner and third might do better.

NOTEBOOK
Judas Jo(FR), the first foal of a 7f winner in Germany out of a half-sister to the high-class German middle-distance scorer Catella, attracted some money beforehand and ultimately ran out a more convincing winner than looked likely for some way, or the winning margin suggests, taking time to get herself organised on this tricky track but finishing to very good effect. She's sure to do better and will be suited by 6f and maybe 7f before long. (op 13-2)
Oneniteinheaven(IRE) looked to have learnt from her debut at Pontefract and lasted longer on this sharper track, albeit probably in a weaker race, and whether she'll improve much more has to be open to doubt. (op 8-1)
Miss Rosie, the second foal of a sprint winner in the US, shaped better than the result, arguably second best on the day, and should improve, never looking comfortable on the track as she constantly wanted to hang to the left so making it difficult for her jockey to ride her out. (op 15-8)
Mebsuta(IRE) looked to just about set the standard on form but, rather as on her debut, she found things happening a bit too quickly for her and remains capable of better again over a stiffer 5f or 6f. (tchd 10-3)
Yearbook whose dam won at 6f and whose previous foals include the fairly useful sprinter Day By Day, is sure to do better. Soon on the back foot after missing the break here, she made promising headway before either a lack of a previous run or that effort told. This trip looks fine for now. (op 9-1)
Imperial Weapon(IRE) showed more than she did at Ripon on her debut but looks destined for sellers sooner rather than later. (op 22-1)
Come To Mind lost all chance with a very slow start and all in all was too green to do herself justice.
Musical Valley, quite a late foal and a very cheap purchase, showed pace to halfway but dropped away alarmingly quickly equipped with a tongue-tie. (op 9-1)

1792 CRABBIES ALCOHOLIC GINGER BEER CLAIMING STKS 1m 3f 214y
6:30 (6:30) (Class 6) 4-Y-O+ **£1,706** (£503; £252) **Stalls** Low

Form RPR
556- **1** **Hel's Angel (IRE)**[209] 6677 5-9-8 72................................ PaulHanagan 3 78
(Ann Duffield) *mde all: qcknd over 4f out: kpt on u.p fnl 2f: all out* **10/3**[2]
-424 **2** *nse* **Eijaaz (IRE)**[6] 1615 10-8-9 59..................................(p) SilvestreDeSousa 4 65
(Geoffrey Harker) *dwlt: hld up in rr: effrt over 2f out: styd on to chal last 100yds: jst hld* **7/2**[3]
4141 **3** *1 3/4* **Relative Strength (IRE)**[7] 1577 6-8-7 70...............(bt) RoystonFfrench 1 60
(Frank Sheridan) *trckd ldrs: drvn over 3f out: kpt on same pce appr fnl f* **10/11**[1]
3415 **4** *14* **The Which Doctor**[8] 1560 6-9-1 80.........................(e) RobertLButler(3) 5 49
(Richard Guest) *hld up in rr: t.k.h: drvn over 3f out: hung lft over 2f out: wknd over 1f out* **9/1**
000- **5** *20* **I Feel Fine**[348] 2085 8-8-7 40 ow1..................................... AndrewElliott 2 —
(Alan Kirtley) *trckd ldrs: drvn 4f out: lost pl over 2f out: sn bhd: t.o* **150/1**

2m 36.14s (-2.76) **Going Correction** -0.10s/f (Good) **5** Ran SP% **108.3**
Speed ratings (Par 101): **105,104,103,94,81**
CSF £14.49 TOTE £3.90: £1.50, £1.60; EX 11.90.Relative Strength was claimed by Ms Jennie Candlish for £5000.
Owner Mrs H Baines & Middleham Park Racing VII **Bred** S White **Trained** Constable Burton, N Yorks

FOCUS
An uncompetitive claimer run at just a fair gallop with the runner-up to recent handicap form the best guide.

1793 BOOK RACEDAY HOSPITALITY ON 01748 810165 H'CAP 7f
7:00 (7:00) (Class 4) (0-80,80) 4-Y-O+ **£4,209** (£1,252; £625; £312) **Stalls** Centre

Form RPR
30-3 **1** **Mujaadel (USA)**[24] 1244 6-8-13 **75**.....................(p) MichaelO'Connell(3) 3 86
(David Nicholls) *chsd ldrs: swtchd rt over 1f out: styd on to ld jst ins fnl f: drew clr clsng stages: readily* **4/1**[2]
0-16 **2** *3 1/2* **George Benjamin**[8] 1560 4-9-7 **80**................................. AdrianNicholls 9 82
(David Nicholls) *chsd ldr: led over 2f out: hdd jst ins fnl f: no ex* **10/3**[1]
11-0 **3** *1* **Not My Choice (IRE)**[30] 1110 6-8-11 **70**................(t) RobbieFitzpatrick 1 69
(David C Griffiths) *chsd ldrs: kpt on same pce appr fnl f* **10/1**
0U-1 **4** *nk* **Khandaq (USA)**[18] 1368 4-9-4 **77**.................................. PaulMulrennan 6 78+
(Keith Dalgleish) *dwlt: sn chsng ldrs: kpt on same pce ins fnl f* **11/2**[3]
00-2 **5** *3 1/4* **Mandalay King (IRE)**[24] 1239 6-8-9 **68**........................ PhillipMakin 8 57
(Marjorie Fife) *hld up in rr: hdwy over 2f out: kpt on same pce: nvr trbld ldrs* **17/2**
-006 **6** *1/2* **Ryedane (IRE)**[17] 1382 9-8-9 **68**..(b) DavidAllan 5 56
(Tim Easterby) *s.i.s: t.k.h in rr: drvn over 3f out: hdwy on ins over 2f out: nvr nr ldrs* **22/1**
0653 **7** *1 1/2* **Mastership (IRE)**[30] 1110 7-9-7 **80**...............................(p) PaulHanagan 10 64
(John Quinn) *hld up in rr: hdwy over 3f out: sn drvn: nvr a factor* **11/2**[3]
-060 **8** *1/2* **Raleigh Quay (IRE)**[14] 1460 4-8-10 **69**........................ FrederikTylicki 7 52
(Micky Hammond) *s.i.s: in rr: sme hdwy over 1f out: nt clr run ins fnl f: sticking on at fin* **16/1**
000- **9** *hd* **Mr Wolf**[182] 7283 10-9-2 **75**..(p) TonyHamilton 4 57
(John Quinn) *led: hdd over 2f out: wknd ins fnl f* **40/1**
-030 **10** *5* **Night Trade (IRE)**[17] 1382 4-9-5 **78**.....................(p) SilvestreDeSousa 11 46
(Deborah Sanderson) *chsd ldrs: drvn over 3f out: hung lft and wknd over 1f out* **9/1**

1m 25.33s (-1.67) **Going Correction** -0.10s/f (Good) **10** Ran SP% **116.1**
Speed ratings (Par 105): **105,101,99,99,95 95,93,92,92,87**
toteswingers:1&2 £4.00, 2&3 £5.30, 1&3 £6.20 CSF £17.67 CT £126.79 TOTE £4.10: £1.30, £1.10, £5.00; EX 19.60.
Owner W R B Racing 49 **Bred** Lawrence Goichman **Trained** Sessay, N Yorks

FOCUS
A fair handicap run at a decent gallop, but it wasn't easy to come from off the pace. The form looks reliable though, with those in the frame behind the winner close to their best.
Night Trade(IRE) Official explanation: jockey said filly hung left

1794 THANK YOU CHRIS GRANT SENIOR H'CAP 1m 7f 177y
7:30 (7:30) (Class 6) (0-65,60) 4-Y-O+ **£1,706** (£503; £252) **Stalls** Centre

Form RPR
5-66 **1** **Heart Of Dubai (USA)**[13] 1491 6-9-1 **51**......................(p) KellyHarrison 6 60
(Micky Hammond) *t.k.h in rr: hdwy 3f out: swtchd lft 2f out: sn chsng ldrs: styd on to ld last 100yds* **9/1**
0-03 **2** *1/2* **They All Laughed**[8] 1556 8-8-9 **45**................................(p) PhillipMakin 5 53
(Marjorie Fife) *hld up in rr: hdwy 7f out: led over 2f out: hdd and no ex ins fnl f* **7/2**[2]
400- **3** *1* **Sendali (FR)**[10] 7181 7-9-0 **50**.. PaulHanagan 8 57
(Chris Grant) *mid-div: hdwy to chse ldrs 7f out: drvn over 3f out: upsides 1f out: kpt on same pce* **9/2**
0-05 **4** *7* **Ultimate Quest (IRE)**[14] 1458 6-8-12 **55**...................(b) DavidKenny(7) 3 54
(Michael Chapman) *chsd ldrs: wknd 1f out* **14/1**
60-2 **5** *2 1/4* **Bandanaman (IRE)**[8] 1556 5-9-10 **60**.............................. PJMcDonald 7 56
(Alan Swinbank) *trckd ldrs: drvn 3f out: wknd 1f out* **11/4**[1]
0456 **6** *3 1/4* **Spiritonthemount (USA)**[14] 1473 6-8-10 **46**.............(b) WilliamCarson 4 38
(Peter Hiatt) *s.i.s: sn chsng ldrs: drvn over 4f out: lost pl over 2f out* **14/1**
5-00 **7** *6* **Drop The Hammer**[20] 1305 5-9-5 **55**.......................(b) SilvestreDeSousa 1 40
(David O'Meara) *led: hdd over 2f out: wknd qckly 1f out* **4/1**[3]

The Form Book, Raceform Ltd, Compton, RG20 6NL

000/ **8** *26* **Endeavor**[37] 4019 6-8-9 **45**........ DuranFentiman 2 —
(Dianne Sayer) *s.i.s: drvn 6f out: bhd fnl 3f: t.o* **66/1**

3m 31.71s (-0.29) **Going Correction** -0.10s/f (Good) **8** Ran SP% **111.9**
Speed ratings (Par 101): **96,95,95,91,90 89,86,73**
toteswingers:1&2 £4.70, 2&3 £3.40, 1&3 £4.60 CSF £38.79 CT £159.96 TOTE £9.30: £2.70, £1.50, £2.40; EX 28.50.
Owner M D Hammond **Bred** Sez Who Thoroughbreds **Trained** Middleham Moor, N Yorks
■ Stewards' Enquiry : Kelly Harrison caution: used whip down shoulder in the forehand.

FOCUS
Low-grade stuff, but the pace looked reasonable and the winner was able to come from off it. The form is rated through the third to his mark in the race last year.

1795 CATTERICKBRIDGE.CO.UK MAIDEN STKS 7f
8:00 (8:02) (Class 5) 3-Y-O+ **£2,072** (£616; £308; £153) **Stalls** Centre

Form RPR
-300 **1** **Dazeen**[14] 1463 4-9-12 62........ TonyCulhane 6 70
(Paul Midgley) *chsd ldrs: led over 1f out: hrd rdn and edgd rt ins fnl f: styd on* **7/2**[2]
2 *2 ½* **Burning Stone (USA)**[323] 4-9-7 0........ AdamBeschizza(5) 7 63
(Gay Kelleway) *hld up: effrt on outside 3f out: sn chsng ldrs: rdn over 1f out: edgd lft and styd on to take 2nd last 100yds: no imp* **6/5**[1]
600- **3** *2 ¾* **Stilettoesinthemud (IRE)**[201] 6866 3-8-9 62........ PaulMulrennan 5 47
(James Given) *led tl over 4f out: upsides over 2f out: kpt on same pce ins fnl f* **13/2**[3]
4 *1 ¼* **Wicked Streak (IRE)**[16] 6-9-12 0........ FrederikTylicki 2 52
(Micky Hammond) *s.i.s: in rr: sme hdwy over 2f out: styd on ins fnl f* **33/1**
66-0 **5** *¾* **Spread Boy (IRE)**[109] 171 4-9-12 50........ PatrickMathers 4 50
(Alan Berry) *sn chsng ldrs: one pce fnl 2f* **33/1**
6 *shd* **Ollianna (IRE)** 3-8-9 0........ RichardKingscote 1 41
(Tom Dascombe) *w ldr: led over 4f out: hdd over 1f out: wknd ins fnl f* **7/1**
5 **7** *3* **Lemon Queen (IRE)**[8] 1559 5-9-7 0........ PaulHanagan 8 37
(John Quinn) *in rr: hdwy over 3f out: chsng ldrs 2f out: wknd ins fnl f* **15/2**
8 *17* **Toffee Nose** 4-9-12 0........ BarryMcHugh 3 —
(Ron Barr) *s.s: in rr: bhd fnl 2f: t.o* **33/1**

1m 27.33s (0.33) **Going Correction** -0.10s/f (Good)
WFA 3 from 4yo+ 12lb **8** Ran SP% **114.1**
Speed ratings (Par 103): **94,91,88,86,85 84,81,61**
toteswingers:1&2 £1.10, 2&3 £3.20, 1&3 £4.20 CSF £7.95 TOTE £8.20: £1.02, £1.90, £1.30; EX 9.50.
Owner Darren & Annaley Yates **Bred** Bond Thoroughbred Corporation **Trained** Westow, N Yorks

FOCUS
Modest fare, as the fact that one so exposed and with an official rating of 62 was able to win so readily suggests. The pace was just fair, picking up entering the straight and the winner sets the level rated to last year's level.

1796 DON'T MISS TOTESPORT SATURDAY 28TH MAY H'CAP 5f
8:30 (8:31) (Class 5) (0-70,69) 4-Y-O+ **£2,183** (£644; £322) **Stalls** Low

Form RPR
5-00 **1** **Kyzer Chief**[25] 1213 6-8-1 **56**........ ShaneBKelly(7) 2 63
(Ron Barr) *w ldrs: led after 2f: kpt on wl clsng stages* **15/2**
305- **2** *½* **Patch Patch**[272] 4703 4-9-1 **66**........ TjadeCollier(3) 1 71
(Michael Dods) *hood removed v late: dwlt: sn w ldrs: upsides 1f out: no ex clsng stages* **9/1**
6002 **3** *1* **Dancing Freddy (IRE)**[13] 1503 4-9-4 **69**........(p) RobertLButler(3) 5 71
(Richard Guest) *chsd ldrs: kpt on same pce ins fnl f* **11/1**
-051 **4** *½* **Mandurah (IRE)**[17] 1411 7-9-7 **69**........ AdrianNicholls 6 69
(David Nicholls) *led 2f: sn hrd drvn: kpt on one pce appr fnl f* **13/8**[1]
4626 **5** *1* **Hypnosis**[8] 1555 8-9-2 **64**........ LeeNewman 7 60
(Noel Wilson) *v reluctant to go to s: hood removed v late: wnt rt s: sn chsng ldrs: one pce fnl 2f* **11/2**[3]
6321 **6** *4 ½* **Spirit Of Coniston**[14] 1464 8-8-10 **58**........ TonyCulhane 4 38
(Paul Midgley) *lost pl over 3f out: hung lft over 1f out: eased nr fin* **7/2**[2]
344- **7** *2* **Wicked Wilma (IRE)**[182] 7281 7-9-1 **63**........ PatrickMathers 8 36
(Alan Berry) *bmpd s: chsd ldr: outpcd over 2f out: sn btn* **14/1**

59.10 secs (-0.70) **Going Correction** -0.10s/f (Good) **7** Ran SP% **112.5**
Speed ratings (Par 103): **101,100,98,97,96 89,85**
toteswingers:1&2 £10.30, 2&3 £5.30, 1&3 £10.70 CSF £67.74 CT £734.33 TOTE £13.10: £5.90, £1.50, EX 52.70.
Owner R E Barr **Bred** Mrs H F Mahr **Trained** Seamer, N Yorks

FOCUS
A modest finale in which the main action took place towards the far rail. The first two set the level.
T/Plt: £224.20 to a £1 stake. Pool £47,609.18 - 154.95 winning tickets. T/Qpdt: £68.70 to a £1 stake. Pool of £4,774.19 - 51.40 winning tickets. WG

1612 NEWCASTLE (L-H)
Tuesday, May 3

OFFICIAL GOING: Good to firm (watered, 7.8)
Bend at 12f moved out a yard and bend into straight moved in 2yds.
Wind: Slight, half behind Weather: Cloudy, bright

1797 EUROPEAN BREEDERS' FUND MEDIAN AUCTION MAIDEN STKS 5f
2:10 (2:12) (Class 5) 2-Y-O **£3,238** (£963; £481; £240) **Stalls** High

Form RPR
22 **1** **Stonefield Flyer**[13] 1489 2-9-3 0........ PaulMulrennan 1 90
(Keith Dalgleish) *taken early to post: sn swtchd to stands' rail: t.k.h: mde all: qcknd clr appr fnl f: readily* **15/8**[1]
4 **2** *6* **Choisan (IRE)**[17] 1383 2-9-3 0........ DavidAllan 6 68
(Tim Easterby) *chsd wnr thrght: rdn 2f out: kpt on same pce appr fnl f* **2/1**[2]
3 *1 ¼* **Moonville (IRE)** 2-9-3 0........ PaulHanagan 3 64
(Richard Fahey) *in tch: rn green and outpcd after 2f: hdwy over 1f out: no imp fnl f* **5/1**[3]
32 **4** *1 ½* **Almond Branches**[10] 1515 2-8-12 0........ PJMcDonald 2 54
(George Moore) *chsd ldrs: rdn over 2f out: no ex over 1f out* **6/1**
5 *5* **Indepub** 2-9-3 0........ PhillipMakin 5 41+
(Kevin Ryan) *s.i.s: bhd: outpcd 1/2-way: sme late hdwy: nvr on terms* **20/1**
6 *5* **Just Like Heaven (IRE)** 2-9-3 0........ DuranFentiman 4 23
(Tim Easterby) *s.i.s: bhd and rdn along 1/2-way: nvr on terms* **33/1**
7 *2* **Celestial Dawn** 2-8-12 0........ GrahamGibbons 7 10
(John Weymes) *bhd and sn outpcd: struggling 1/2-way: sn btn* **33/1**

60.21 secs (-0.89) **Going Correction** -0.30s/f (Firm) **7** Ran SP% **109.7**
Speed ratings (Par 93): **95,85,83,81,73 65,61**
Tote Swingers: 1&2 £2.20, 2&3 £1.80 CSF £5.34 TOTE £2.50: £1.40, £1.80; EX 5.30.
Owner G R Leckie **Bred** Ian Crawford And Gordon Leckie **Trained** Carluke, South Lanarkshire

FOCUS
The going was good to firm on a watered track. Three of the runners had achieved fair form in this decent maiden but the winner put in an impressive front-running performance to hammer his rivals. The winner is rated below previous form so the winner could go higher.

NOTEBOOK
Stonefield Flyer was a bit green and unruly before finishing second at 14-1 on debut and stepped up on that form when splitting two previous winners in a three-runner novice event over C&D last time. This strong form contender was very quickly away and never in any danger under a freewheeling ride. He looks very speedy and should go on to better things. (op 9-4 tched 11-4 in places early)
Choisan(IRE) showed promise when a strong finishing fourth on debut at Doncaster last month but he couldn't get close enough to threaten the emphatic winner here. However, this was fair effort behind a potentially useful type and there should be more to come from this sprint bred 2-y-o whose sales price shot up to 18,000euros last year. (op 9-4)
Moonville(IRE), a first foal of an Irish 6f winner, ran green but shaped well in a decent event on debut. This was an encouraging start by a £22,000 colt who holds some entries in valuable sales races later on. (op 7-2)
Almond Branches ran respectably faced with a bit to find on form. She has finished in the frame in all three of her runs but has a consistent rather than progressive profile. (tchd 7-1)
Indepub looked inexperienced but did some late work from a long way back thrown into a tough race on debut. He should improve for the run and is related to a clutch of sprint winners, including the owner's prolific 5f-6f handicapper Brut. (op 16-1)

1798 FREEBETTING.CO.UK H'CAP 1m 4f 93y
2:40 (2:40) (Class 5) (0-70,70) 4-Y-O+ **£2,266** (£674; £337; £168) **Stalls** Low

Form RPR
2-60 **1** **Houston Dynimo (IRE)**[24] 1243 6-8-13 **62**........ PaulMulrennan 1 71
(Nicky Richards) *mde all: qcknd 3f out: rdn and kpt on wl fnl f* **6/1**[3]
60/0 **2** *1 ¼* **Dar Es Salaam**[24] 1243 7-8-11 **65**........ DaleSwift(5) 5 72
(Brian Ellison) *hld up in tch: effrt over 2f out: hdwy to chse wnr 1f out: r.o fnl f* **14/1**
342- **3** *2 ¼* **Bollin Judith**[185] 7226 5-9-5 **68**........(t) DavidAllan 7 72
(Tim Easterby) *prom: effrt and drvn over 3f out: kpt on same pce over 1f out* **5/1**[2]
5-32 **4** *½* **Hail Tiberius**[13] 1491 4-9-7 **70**........ DuranFentiman 2 73
(Tim Walford) *t.k.h: chsd ldrs: wnt 2nd over 3f out: rdn over 2f out: nt qckn over 1f out* **7/2**[1]
0-00 **5** *3* **Dean Iarracht (IRE)**[13] 1491 5-8-12 **61**........(p) RobertWinston 8 59
(Tracy Waggott) *missed break: hld up ins: rdn over 2f out: hdwy appr fnl f: nvr able to chal* **15/2**
0600 **6** *nk* **Valdan (IRE)**[2] 1713 7-8-9 **58**........(t) PaulHanagan 6 56
(Maurice Barnes) *hld up in tch: rdn over 2f out: sn no imp* **14/1**
4-01 **7** *3 ¾* **Capable Guest (IRE)**[13] 1491 9-8-13 **62**........ PJMcDonald 10 54
(George Moore) *hld up: rdn 4f out: no imp fnl 2f* **7/1**
005- **8** *4* **Beneath**[148] 7726 4-8-11 **60**........ PhillipMakin 9 45
(Kevin Ryan) *hld up: pushed along 3f out: nvr on terms* **10/1**
3-06 **9** *28* **Across The Sea (USA)**[8] 1556 4-8-11 **60**........ SilvestreDeSousa 4 —
(Geoffrey Harker) *chsd wnr tl wknd qckly over 3f out: eased whn no ch fnl f: fin lame* **13/2**

2m 42.26s (-3.34) **Going Correction** -0.30s/f (Firm) **9** Ran SP% **113.2**
Speed ratings (Par 103): **99,98,96,96,94 94,91,88,70**
Tote Swingers: 1&2 £31.30, 1&3 £6.70, 2&3 £20.70 CSF £83.30 CT £447.84 TOTE £8.70: £2.60, £8.60, £2.20; EX 148.10 Trifecta £258.20 Part won. Pool: £348.94 - 0.70 winning units..
Owner Mark Barnard & Richard Helliwell **Bred** Sweetmans Bloodstock **Trained** Greystoke, Cumbria

FOCUS
A minor middle-distance handicap. It was run at a steady pace and the winner made all. The form looks messy with the fourth the best guide for now.
Across The Sea(USA) Official explanation: vet said gelding finished lame right-fore

1799 SWARLANDSELFSTORAGE.CO.UK MAIDEN FILLIES' STKS 1m 2f 32y
3:10 (3:10) (Class 5) 3-Y-O+ **£2,266** (£674; £337; £168) **Stalls** Low

Form RPR
420- **1** **Pandoro De Lago (IRE)**[248] 5509 3-8-8 75........ PaulHanagan 8 76+
(Richard Fahey) *mde all: qcknd clr over 2f out: eased ins fnl f* **11/10**[1]
2 *7* **Brook Star (IRE)** 3-8-8 0........ FrederikTylicki 1 50
(Michael Dods) *chsd wnr: rdn over 3f out: plugged on fnl 2f: no imp* **5/1**[3]
00-0 **3** *½* **Lady Of The Knight (IRE)**[74] 600 3-8-5 25........(p) JamesSullivan(3) 4 49?
(Hugh McWilliams) *hld up in tch: rdn 3f out: no imp fnl 2f* **150/1**
6- **4** *1* **Alemaratiya**[188] 7164 3-8-8 0........ MartinLane 7 47
(David Simcock) *prom: effrt and rdn 3f out: kpt on same pce* **10/3**[2]
06 **5** *3 ¼* **Silvers Spirit**[13] 1492 5-9-9 0........ TonyCulhane 2 42
(Keith Reveley) *hld up: rdn over 3f out: nvr able to chal* **20/1**
6 *4* **Woolamaloo** 3-8-8 0........ DavidAllan 3 33
(Tim Easterby) *dwlt: hld up: rdn over 3f out: sn btn* **7/1**
00 **7** *¾* **Molannarch**[8] 1559 5-9-9 0........ TonyHamilton 6 31
(Keith Reveley) *hld up in tch: rdn over 3f out: wknd 2f out* **33/1**
0 **8** *2 ¾* **Poosie Nansie (IRE)**[25] 1210 4-9-4 0........(p) DaleSwift(5) 5 27
(George Foster) *trckd ldrs: drvn over 3f out: wknd fnl 2f* **100/1**

2m 14.91s (3.01) **Going Correction** -0.30s/f (Firm)
WFA 3 from 4yo+ 15lb **8** Ran SP% **109.2**
Speed ratings (Par 100): **75,69,69,68,65 62,61,59**
Tote Swingers: 1&2 £2.50, 1&3 £15.40, 2&3 £12.90 CSF £6.17 TOTE £2.00: £1.40, £1.30, £11.40; EX 6.60 Trifecta £97.30 Pool: £867.82 - 6.60 winning units..
Owner Sir Robert Ogden **Bred** Stratford Place Stud & Watership Down Stud **Trained** Musley Bank, N Yorks

FOCUS
A weak fillies' maiden with the winner close to last season's level and the third a dubious improver.

1800 SPORTPOOL.CO.UK H'CAP 7f
3:45 (3:45) (Class 5) (0-75,75) 4-Y-O+ **£2,266** (£674; £337; £168) **Stalls** High

Form RPR
0-0 **1** **Vito Volterra (IRE)**[61] 744 4-8-11 **70**........ SeanLevey(5) 2 77
(Michael Smith) *mde all: clr 1/2-way: rdn and hld on wl fnl f* **15/2**
0-15 **2** *½* **Ezra Church (IRE)**[24] 1245 4-9-4 **72**........ LeeNewman 4 78
(David Barron) *chsd wnr thrght: rdn and outpcd 2f out: kpt on u.p fnl f* **5/2**[1]
0211 **3** *¾* **Frequency**[15] 1439 4-9-4 **72**........(b) JoeFanning 7 76
(Keith Dalgleish) *hld up in tch: stdy hdwy to dispute 2nd over 2f out: rdn over 1f out: kpt on fnl f: hld nr fin* **7/2**[2]
16-0 **4** *2* **Feel The Heat**[26] 1200 4-9-7 **75**........ TomEaves 5 74
(Bryan Smart) *prom: drvn and outpcd over 2f out: kpt on fnl f: nt pce to chal* **5/1**[3]
650- **5** *9* **Whispered Times (USA)**[198] 6963 4-9-5 **73**........ RobertWinston 3 47
(Tracy Waggott) *dwlt: hld up: rdn over 2f out: hung lft and sn wknd* **6/1**
44-0 **6** *6* **Salerosa (IRE)**[24] 1245 6-8-13 **67**........(p) PaulMulrennan 6 25
(Ann Duffield) *hld up: drvn over 2f out: sn btn* **16/1**

56-5 **7** 1 ¼ **Taste The Victory (USA)**[13] 1492 4-9-0 **68**.................... PJMcDonald 1 23
(Alan Swinbank) *prom: drvn and outpcd 1/2-way: btn fnl 2f* **6/1**
1m 25.92s (-1.88) **Going Correction** -0.30s/f (Firm) 7 Ran SP% **113.7**
Speed ratings (Par 103): **103,102,101,99,89 82,80**
Tote Swingers: 1&2 £6.60, 1&3 £6.40, 2&3 £3.30 CSF £26.30 TOTE £11.80: £5.20, £2.90; EX 34.20.
Owner Ace Racing **Bred** O McElroy **Trained** Kirkheaton, Northumberland

FOCUS
Several of the runners had something to prove in this handicap and the form does not look particularly strong.
Vito Volterra(IRE) Official explanation: trainer had no explanation for the apparent improvement in form

1801 SENDRIG CONSTRUCTION H'CAP 1m 3y(S)
4:15 (4:16) (Class 5) (0-70,70) 3-Y-O **£2,266** (£674; £337; £168) **Stalls** High

Form RPR
10-3 **1** **Tapis Libre**[10] 1524 3-8-13 **65**.................... JamesSullivan(3) 8 71+
(Michael Easterby) *trckd ldrs: rdn over 2f out: led over 1f out: kpt on wl fnl f* **9/2**[3]
56-5 **2** 1 ¼ **Adlington**[17] 1392 3-9-7 **70**.................... PaulHanagan 6 73
(Richard Fahey) *led tl hdd over 1f out: kpt on ins fnl f* **11/4**[1]
32-5 **3** ¾ **Sabratha (IRE)**[9] 1543 3-9-3 **66**.................... TonyHamilton 3 67
(Linda Perratt) *stdd in tch: effrt over 2f out: chsd ldrs over 1f out: kpt on same pce ins fnl f* **12/1**
00-0 **4** 5 **Deep Applause**[27] 1189 3-9-1 **64**.................... TomEaves 1 54
(Michael Dods) *hld up: stdy hdwy over 2f out: rdn over 1f out: kpt on fnl f: nvr able to chal* **15/2**
3052 **5** 8 **Lough Corrib (USA)**[18] 1369 3-8-7 **56**....................(p) PaulMulrennan 2 27
(Kevin Ryan) *cl up: rdn over 2f out: sn wknd* **10/1**
46-0 **6** 3 **Fimias (IRE)**[27] 1168 3-9-2 **65**.................... SilvestreDeSousa 4 29
(Geoffrey Harker) *prom on outside: rdn over 3f out: wknd over 2f out* **16/1**
40-0 **7** 3 ¼ **Regimental (IRE)**[17] 1392 3-9-5 **68**.................... SebSanders 7 25
(Ann Duffield) *trckd ldrs: lost pl over 3f out: sn btn* **3/1**[2]
036- **8** 18 **Kalkan Bay**[182] 7280 3-9-7 **70**.................... PJMcDonald 5 —
(Jedd O'Keeffe) *uns rdr and loose bef s: cl up tl rdn and wknd over 3f out: t.o* **16/1**
1m 40.41s (-2.99) **Going Correction** -0.30s/f (Firm) **8** Ran SP% **110.2**
Speed ratings (Par 99): **102,100,100,95,87 84,80,62**
Tote Swingers: 1&2 £3.40, 1&3 £5.00, 2&3 £5.70 CSF £15.96 CT £127.11 TOTE £6.40: £2.30, £1.10, £2.10; EX 14.50 Trifecta £73.70 Pool: £655.00 - 6.57 winning units..
Owner Carpet Kings Syndicate **Bred** Sedgecroft Stud **Trained** Sheriff Hutton, N Yorks

FOCUS
They went a fairly steady pace in this handicap but the first three pulled clear. The winner looks an improver and the second recorded a slight personal-best.
Lough Corrib(USA) Official explanation: jockey said gelding hung right-handed final 3f
Regimental(IRE) Official explanation: jockey said gelding never travelled

1802 STP CONSTRUCTION H'CAP 6f
4:45 (4:45) (Class 5) (0-70,70) 3-Y-O **£2,266** (£674; £337; £168) **Stalls** High

Form RPR
0-04 **1** **Barkston Ash**[15] 1437 3-8-7 **56** oh1.................... DuranFentiman 8 69
(Eric Alston) *trckd ldrs: led 1/2-way: forged clr fnl f* **10/1**
11-4 **2** 3 **Pitkin**[13] 1494 3-9-1 **64**.................... PaulMulrennan 4 67+
(Michael Easterby) *hld up in midfield on outside: effrt whn nt clr run briefly over 2f out: chsd wnr over 1f out: r.o* **9/2**[2]
3-32 **3** 3 ¾ **Piccoluck**[13] 1494 3-8-11 **65**.................... LanceBetts(5) 10 56
(Deborah Sanderson) *midfield: effrt over 2f out: kpt on same pce appr fnl f* **9/4**[1]
40-5 **4** 3 ¼ **Saxonette**[10] 1514 3-8-11 **60**.................... BarryMcHugh 2 41+
(Linda Perratt) *dwlt: bhd: hdwy on wd outside over 2f out: kpt on fnl f: nvr able to chal* **40/1**
5-00 **5** *hd* **Anddante (IRE)**[15] 1437 3-8-13 **62**....................(b[1]) DavidAllan 11 42
(Tim Easterby) *dwlt: bhd: rdn 1/2-way: hdwy u.p over 1f out: nvr able to chal* **6/1**[3]
0-61 **6** 3 ¾ **Meandmyshadow**[19] 1323 3-8-11 **60**....................(p) SilvestreDeSousa 7 28
(Alan Brown) *led to 1/2-way: cl up tl rdn and wknd ent fnl f* **18/1**
10-0 **7** 1 **Country Waltz**[9] 1543 3-9-0 **63**.................... FrederikTylicki 9 28
(Linda Perratt) *prom: rdn over 2f out: sn wknd* **12/1**
6-54 **8** 4 **Sergeant Suzie**[25] 1214 3-9-0 **70**.................... ShaneBKelly(7) 3 22
(Michael Dods) *hld up: rdn over 2f out: nvr on terms* **16/1**
2-31 **9** 5 **Roodee Queen**[18] 1369 3-9-4 **67**.................... StephenCraine 1 —
(Patrick Morris) *cl up tl rdn and wknd fr 2f out* **33/1**
36-3 **10** 3 ¼ **Roman Ruler (IRE)**[13] 1494 3-8-8 **57**.................... JoeFanning 6 —
(Chris Fairhurst) *midfield: struggling 1/2-way: sn btn* **7/1**
24-0 **11** 3 ¾ **Brave Dream**[25] 1214 3-9-7 **70**.................... TomEaves 5 —
(Kevin Ryan) *cl up tl rdn and wknd over 2f out* **12/1**
1m 13.12s (-1.48) **Going Correction** -0.30s/f (Firm) 11 Ran SP% **116.7**
Speed ratings (Par 99): **97,93,88,83,83 78,77,71,65,60 55**
Tote Swingers: 1&2 £11.60, 1&3 £6.20, 2&3 £3.20 CSF £54.20 CT £141.11 TOTE £12.00: £2.70, £3.60, £1.10; EX 88.70 Trifecta £327.90 Part won. Pool: £443.15 - 0.68 winning units..
Owner The Selebians **Bred** Jonathan Shack **Trained** Longton, Lancs

FOCUS
A fairly competitive sprint handicap. The field all shifted towards the near side and a 10-1 winner surged clear against the stands' side rail. He is rated to near his juvenile best.

1803 LA TAXIS H'CAP 7f
5:20 (5:21) (Class 6) (0-60,60) 4-Y-O+ **£1,619** (£481; £240; £120) **Stalls** High

Form RPR
0-00 **1** **Tombellini (IRE)**[17] 1398 4-8-13 **52**.................... AndrewMullen 4 64
(David Nicholls) *mde all (and overall ldr) far side: qcknd clr 2f out: kpt on strly fnl f: shied cl home: 1st of 8 in gp* **22/1**
-542 **2** 4 ½ **Convince (USA)**[68] 674 10-9-0 **56**.................... AndrewHeffernan(3) 3 56
(Kevin M Prendergast) *prom far side: effrt over 2f out: chsd (clr) wnr ins fnl f: r.o: 2nd of 8 in gp* **10/1**[3]
20-0 **3** ¾ **Broctune Papa Gio**[25] 1216 4-8-10 **49**.................... FrederikTylicki 8 47
(Keith Reveley) *prom: effrt and chsd (clr) wnr over 1f out: no imp and lost 2nd ins fnl f: 3rd of 8 in gp* **4/1**[1]
00-0 **4** ¾ **Shunkawakhan (IRE)**[32] 1077 8-8-7 **46** oh1....................(p) BarryMcHugh 7 42
(Linda Perratt) *hld up far side: hdwy over 2f out: kpt on ins fnl f: no imp: 4th of 8 in gp* **28/1**
05/5 **5** 2 ¼ **Mrs E**[22] 1277 4-9-0 **53**.................... PaulMulrennan 13 43
(Michael Easterby) *trckd stands' side ldrs: effrt and led that gp 2f out: kpt on fnl f: no ch w far side gp: 1st of 6 in gp* **14/1**
2435 **6** ¾ **Ubenkor (IRE)**[49] 854 6-9-6 **59**.................... TonyCulhane 16 47
(Michael Herrington) *prom stands' side: pushed along over 2f out: hdwy and ev ch that gp ins fnl f: edgd lft: one pce: 2nd of 6 in gp* **5/1**[2]
0 **7** 4 **Drive Home (USA)**[34] 1038 4-9-7 **60**.................... LeeNewman 10 37
(Noel Wilson) *hld up in tch far side: outpcd over 2f out: sn n.d: 5th of 8 in gp* **16/1**
000- **8** ¾ **Balance On Time (IRE)**[185] 7229 5-8-7 **46** oh1.................... JoeFanning 2 28
(Linda Perratt) *s.i.s: bhd far side: sme hdwy over 1f out: nvr rchd ldrs: 6th of 8 in gp* **25/1**
3-00 **9** 2 ½ **Bahamian Kid**[10] 1520 6-8-11 **55**....................(v) DaleSwift(5) 1 23
(George Foster) *trckd far side ldrs tl rdn and wknd fr over 2f out: 7th of 8 in gp* **25/1**
400- **10** 1 **Reset To Fit**[200] 6896 4-9-2 **55**.................... RobertWinston 6 20
(Eric Alston) *cl up far side tl rdn and wknd over 2f out: last of 8 in gp* **11/1**
0555 **11** 6 **Carnival Dream**[67] 690 6-8-7 **46**.................... TomEaves 9 —
(Hugh McWilliams) *swtchd rt s and cl up stands' side gp tl rdn and wknd over 2f out: 3rd of 6 in gp* **10/1**[3]
315- **12** ½ **Adam De Beaulieu (USA)**[137] 7912 4-9-6 **59**.............(t) PJMcDonald 12 —
(Ben Haslam) *led stands' side gp to over 2f out: rdn and wknd wl over 1f out: 4th of 6 in gp* **4/1**[1]
00-0 **13** 7 **Du Plessis**[15] 1439 4-8-10 **49**.................... DanielTudhope 11 —
(Brian Ellison) *prom stands' side: rdn 1/2-way: wknd over 2f out: 5th of 6 in gp* **14/1**
0/00 **14** 7 **Glencairn Star**[8] 1557 10-8-7 **46** oh1.................... KellyHarrison 15 —
(Frederick Watson) *bhd stands' side: struggling 3f out: sn btn: last of 6 in gp* **66/1**
1m 26.32s (-1.48) **Going Correction** -0.30s/f (Firm) **14** Ran SP% **119.4**
Speed ratings (Par 101): **101,95,95,94,91 90,86,85,82,81 74,73,65,57**
Tote Swingers: 1&2 £19.20, 1&3 £18.30, 2&3 £4.90 CSF £216.13 CT £1076.71 TOTE £19.60: £6.00, £3.20, £1.70; EX 153.60 Trifecta £342.30 Part won. Pool: £462.56 - 0.20 winning units. .
Owner W R B Racing 52 **Bred** Mr And Mrs P & S Martin **Trained** Sessay, N Yorks

FOCUS
An ordinary handicap. They split into two groups and the first four all raced against the far rail. The form is rated close to face value.
Tombellini(IRE) Official explanation: trainer said, regarding apparent improvement in form, that the gelding benefited from the drop back in trip.
Ubenkor(IRE) Official explanation: trainer's rep said gelding had a breathing problem
T/Jkpt: Not won. T/Plt: £119.30 to a £1 stake. Pool:£62,763.27 - 384.00 winning tickets. T/Qpdt: £7.80 to a £1 stake. Pool:£4,421.81 - 418.42 winning tickets. RY

L'ANCRESSE
Monday, May 2

OFFICIAL GOING: Good to firm
Meeting abandoned after race 2; conditions unsafe.
Wind: Strong, half against Weather: Rain

1804a BOB FROOME MEMORIAL H'CAP 6f
2:30 (2:30) 3-Y-O+ **£1,800** (£750; £450)

RPR
1 **Kersivay**[24] 1213 5-9-10 ....(v) RichardEvans 2 66
(David J Evans, Jersey)
2 3 ½ **Unlimited**[24] 1221 9-10-12 .... PHolley 4 71
(Tony Carroll)
R **Fast Freddie**[7] 7-10-3 7ex.................... MarkLawson 6 —
(Mrs A Corson, Jersey)
1m 18.0s (78.00) **3** Ran
.
Owner Mrs I M Folkes **Bred** Brook Stud Bloodstock Ltd **Trained** Jersey

1805a JACKSONS (C.I.) LIMITED H'CAP 1m
3:05 (3:05) 3-Y-O+ **£1,800** (£750; £450)

RPR
1 **I Confess**[20] 1295 6-10-12 .... RichardEvans 2 —
(David J Evans, Jersey)
2 3 **Superduper**[7] 6-10-8 7ex.................... RobertKirk 6 —
(Mrs A Malzard, Jersey)
3 7 **Christmas Coming**[12] 1486 4-9-13 .... PHolley 5 —
(Tony Carroll)
P **Crianza**[7] 1743 5-9-8 7ex.................... EmmettStack 3 —
(Mrs J L Le Brocq, Jersey)
1m 47.0s (107.00) **4** Ran
.
Owner J E Abbey **Bred** Gestut Sohrenhof **Trained** Pandy, Monmouths

CHESTER (L-H)
Wednesday, May 4

OFFICIAL GOING: Good to firm (8.1)
No false rail bur rail realignment increased 5f race by 12yds, 10f &12f by 25yds and Chester Cup by 50yds.
Wind: Light, across Weather: Sunny

1806 MANOR HOUSE STABLES LILY AGNES CONDITIONS STKS 5f 16y
1:45 (1:46) (Class 2) 2-Y-O
£9,969 (£2,985; £1,492; £747; £372; £187) **Stalls** Low

Form RPR
11 **1** **Lily's Angel (IRE)**[14] 1489 2-8-10 0.................... PaulHanagan 2 89+
(Richard Fahey) *w'like: str: missed break: in rr: hdwy over 2f out: r.o to ld fnl 150yds: wl on top at fin* **7/4**[1]
13 **2** 1 ¾ **Marford Missile (IRE)**[14] 1489 2-8-12 0.................... JimCrowley 7 84
(Tom Dascombe) *w'like: dwlt: sn outpcd: hdwy over 3f out: sn chsd ldrs: chalng ins fnl f: nt gng pce of wnr towards fin* **40/1**
12 **3** ½ **Redair (IRE)**[32] 1095 2-8-10 0.................... CathyGannon 3 80
(David Evans) *w ldr: rdn and chalng ins fnl f: kpt on same pce fnl 75yds* **7/2**[2]
323 **4** *shd* **Choice Of Remark (IRE)**[13] 1505 2-8-12 0.................... KierenFallon 1 82
(David Evans) *led: rdn over 1f out: hdd fnl 150yds: no ex towards fin* **7/2**[2]
31 **5** 1 **He's So Cool (IRE)**[32] 1095 2-9-1 0.................... KierenFox 5 81+
(Bill Turner) *leggy: missed break: struggled to handle trck: missed break: outpcd and bhd: c wd ent st wl over 1f out: hdwy ins fnl f: fin strly: nt gng pce to chal* **7/1**[3]

211 **6** *2* **Van Go Go**[9] 1563 2-8-7 0 .... RichardKingscote 8 66
(Tom Dascombe) *w'like: gd spd w ldrs and racd 4 wd: rdn over 1f out: wknd fnl 150yds* **16/1**

02 **7** *½* **Beau Mistral (IRE)**[18] 1414 2-8-7 0 .... JamesSullivan 10 64
(Paul Green) *cmpt: wnt rt s: racd keenly: towards rr: hdwy to chse ldrs over 3f out: wknd ins fnl f* **22/1**

431 **8** *12* **Mousie**[8] 1590 2-8-7 0 .... KieranO'Neill 9 21
(Alan McCabe) *leggy: racd on wd outer in midfield: effrt to chse ldrs 3f out: sn u.p and lost pl: wknd over 1f out* **33/1**

1 **9** *1 ¾* **Jawking**[32] 1101 2-9-1 0 .... NeilCallan 4 22
(David Evans) *wnt rt s: prom and racd 3 wd: lost pl 3f out: outpcd 2f out: bhd over 1f out* **28/1**

61.02 secs (0.02) **Going Correction** -0.025s/f (Good) **9** Ran SP% **112.4**
Speed ratings (Par 99): **98,95,94,94,92 89,88,69,66**
toteswingers:1&2 £7.40, 2&3 £10.30, 1&3 £1.40 CSF £89.37 TOTE £2.60: £1.40, £6.00, £1.50; EX 82.50 Trifecta £401.30 Pool: £1401.13 - 2.58 winning units..
Owner Middleham Park Racing XLVIII **Bred** N And Mrs N Nugent **Trained** Musley Bank, N Yorks
■ Stewards' Enquiry : Paul Hanagan two-day ban; careless riding (18th, 19th May)

FOCUS
This looked a prety weak running of the Lily Agnes and the pace was overly strong. The third and sixth help to set the level.

NOTEBOOK
Lily's Angel(IRE) was immediately out the back after missing the break, but was in the right place considering how the race unfolded and was cleverly ridden by Paul Hanagan, hugging the inside rail for as long as possible. Once in the straight she was further helped by the leaders edging off the fence and nipped through to win convincingly, although it was slightly disconcerting to see her flash her tail a couple of times late on. She had also bucked her rider off prior to being loaded into the stalls. She cost only £8,000 but has been well placed to land all three of her starts so far. It would be unwise to get carried away, though, as she's likely to face stiffer competition before long. Plus it was interesting to hear Richard Fahey say afterwards, judged on homework, she hadn't looked quite as good as the stable's recent Ascot winner Miss Work Of Art. She may now head to Beverley for the Hilary Needler. (op 15-8 tchd 13-8 and 2-1 in places)
Marford Missile(IRE) was behind Lily's Angel in a novice event last time and looked the second string from his stable, who was sponsoring the race for the third year in succession. He raced off the pace, although not as far back as the winner and was a bit keen. Despite that, he kept on well for second. (op 33-1)
Redair(IRE), runner-up to He's So Cool in the Brocklesby, fared best of those who raced on the pace, despite being stuck two wide throughout and being unable to dominate. He can rate higher. (op 4-1 tchd 9-2 in a place)
Choice Of Remark(IRE) was well drawn and led against the inside rail, showing good speed, but was kept honest throughout and ruined his chance by edging right under pressure. Official explanation: jockey said colt hung right handed throughout (op 5-1)
He's So Cool(IRE) ◆, who had Redair behind in second when winning the Brocklesby last time, ran a noteworthy race. He missed the break and was being pushed along in last approaching the turn into straight before going extremely wide. It was a surprise to see him finish so close in the circumstances and he was probably at least the second best horse on the day. (op 5-1)
Van Go Go, a shorter price than her stablemate in second, paid for going off fast and wide. (op 12-1 tchd 18-1)

1807 WEATHERBYS BANK CHESHIRE OAKS (FOR THE ROBERT SANGSTER MEMORIAL CUP) (LISTED RACE) (FILLIES) 1m 3f 79y

2:20 (2:20) (Class 1) 3-Y-O

£17,031 (£6,456; £3,231; £1,611; £807; £405) **Stalls** Low

Form RPR

2- **1** **Wonder Of Wonders (USA)**[6] 1645 3-8-12 0 .... RyanMoore 8 103+
(A P O'Brien, Ire) *lengthy: scope: lw: hld up in midfield: pushed along over 3f out and looked ill at ease on trck: hdwy 2f out: wnt 2nd over 1f out: rn to ld fnl 110yds: pushed out and stretched clr towards fin* **6/5**[1]

23 **2** *2 ¾* **Blaise Chorus (IRE)**[47] 901 3-8-12 0 .... MichaelHills 1 93
(B W Hills) *led: kicked abt 4 l clr 2f out: rdn ins fnl f: hdd fnl 110yds: nt gng pce of wnr and wl hld towards fin* **16/1**

034- **3** *3 ½* **Fork Handles**[221] 6348 3-8-12 98 .... JamieSpencer 3 87
(Mick Channon) *hld up: hdwy over 1f out: styd on to take 3rd wl ins fnl f: nt gng pce to trble front 2* **7/1**[3]

30-6 **4** *½* **Musharakaat (IRE)**[21] 1320 3-8-12 95 .... RichardHills 7 86
(Ed Dunlop) *hld up in midfield: plld out and hdwy over 1f out: sn chsd ldrs but no imp [illegible] ins fnl f* **14/1**

134- **5** *3 ½* **Jaaryah (IRE)**[193] 7085 3-8-12 89 .... FrankieDettori 6 80
(Roger Varian) *lw: chsd ldrs: u.p 2f out: sn outpcd: bmpd whn btn ins fnl f* **8/1**

60- **6** *1* **Bilidn**[289] 4203 3-8-12 0 .... PhilipRobinson 9 78
(Clive Brittain) *hld up in rr: outpcd over 2f out: rdn over 1f out: kpt on steadily ins fnl f: nvr able to get on terms w ldrs* **100/1**

2-4 **7** *hd* **Sunday Bess (JPN)**[19] 1364 3-8-12 0 .... RichardKingscote 4 78+
(Tom Dascombe) *lw: stdd s: hld up in rr: outpcd over 2f out: rdn over 1f out: kpt on steadily ins fnl f: nvr able to get on terms w ldrs* **20/1**

431- **8** *3* **Encore Une Annee**[180] 7325 3-8-12 77 .... JimCrowley 5 72
(Ralph Beckett) *chsd ldrs: pushed along over 3f out: rdn and wknd over 1f out* **14/1**

210- **9** *1* **Midnight Caller**[236] 5910 3-8-12 87 .... WilliamBuick 2 70
(John Gosden) *chsd ldr: pushed along 3f out: outpcd by ldr 2f out: lost 2nd over 1f out: wknd ins fnl f* **9/2**[2]

2m 24.81s (0.01) **Going Correction** -0.025s/f (Good) **9** Ran SP% **112.2**
Speed ratings (Par 104): **105,103,100,100,97 96,96,94,93**
toteswingers:1&2 £5.70, 2&3 £10.00, 1&3 £1.10 CSF £22.67 TOTE £2.20: £1.10, £3.10, £1.40; EX 21.50 Trifecta £144.20 Pool: £953.99 - 4.89 winning units..
Owner M Tabor, D Smith & Mrs John Magnier **Bred** Liberty Bloodstock **Trained** Ballydoyle, Co Tipperary

FOCUS
A race that can prove a worthwhile Oaks trial. The most obvious recent example is the 2007 running when Light Shift defeated All My Loving (trained by Aidan O'Brien) into second before that pair finished first and third respectively at Epsom. The pace, set by the runner-up, seemed to slow at about halfway. This looked a decent renewal and the winner has been rated positively.

NOTEBOOK
Wonder Of Wonders(USA) ◆ gave the runner-up, who had enjoyed the run of the race, about a 5l start when taking little while to get into full stride, but she was nicely on top in plenty of time. Perhaps the best way of assessing just what she achieved is to ignore the well-ridden Blaise Chorus, and there was upwards of over 6l back to the remainder. She was still green when winning a slowly run maiden at Tipperary only six days earlier, notably carrying her head high in the closing stages, a trait she'd also exhibited on her two starts prior, but she already looks to have grown up plenty, going about her business in a more professional manner under pressure. A big, scopey filly, it's fair to say her main asset is stamina rather than speed, but Ryan Moore described her as good-moving, well-balanced type and says she'll have no trouble handling Epsom. Wonder Of Wonders is out of 2004 Oaks runner-up All Too Beautiful, who's a sister to Galileo and half-sister to Sea The Stars, and there's more to come, especially off a stronger pace. It's possible she'll come unstuck against a speedier type, but it will be a surprise if she finishes outside the first three at Epsom on June 3. (op 11-8 tchd 11-10)
Blaise Chorus(IRE), runner-up in a couple of maidens prior to this, on the Lingfield Polytrack and Deauville Fibresand, is flattered by the result as she very much had the run of the race, though this was a good first start on turf. (op 20-1)
Fork Handles was too far back considering how the race unfolded and came wide into the straight. This was her first start since finishing fourth in the Fillies' Mile, so she might be capable of better. (op 8-1 tchd 13-2)
Musharakaat(IRE), last year's May Hill third, had been well beaten in the Feilden Stakes at Newmarket on her return and fared little better. (tchd 12-1)
Jaaryah(IRE) was officially rated only 89 and did not find the required improvement. (tchd 7-1)
Bilidn had been well beaten in two 6f maidens last year. Her trainer doesn't shy away from a challenge, though, and this was a big step up. (op 66-1)
Sunday Bess(JPN) should be better suited by a more galloping track. (tchd 25-1)
Encore Une Annee Official explanation: jockey said filly shied away from rival on final bend
Midnight Caller had been absent since failing to beat a rival in the May Hill and again ran poorly. (op 4-1 tchd 7-2)

1808 TOTESPORT.COM CHESTER CUP (HERITAGE H'CAP) 2m 2f 147y

2:55 (2:56) (Class 2) 4-Y-O+

£62,310 (£18,660; £9,330; £4,670; £2,330; £1,170) **Stalls** High

Form RPR

/10- **1** **Overturn (IRE)**[18] 5220 7-8-13 99 .... EddieAhern 1 106
(Donald McCain) *lw: mde all: pushed along 3f out: kicked clr over 1f out: r.o wl and a in command* **11/2**[2]

241- **2** *1 ¾* **Tastahil (IRE)**[200] 6929 7-9-11 111 .... RichardHills 3 116
(B W Hills) *chsd wnr: pushed along whn abt 2 l down 3f out: outpcd by wnr over 1f out: kpt on ins fnl f but a hld* **8/1**

014- **3** *2 ¼* **Mystery Star (IRE)**[166] 7507 6-8-10 96 .... NeilCallan 16 99
(Mark H Tompkins) *midfield: hdwy 3f out: rdn and styd on over 2f out: wnt 3rd over 1f out: edgd rt ins fnl f: nt rch front 2* **50/1**

00-1 **4** *¾* **Mount Athos (IRE)**[19] 1381 4-8-11 101 .... JamieSpencer 19 103+
(David Wachman, Ire) *lw: hld up: hdwy on wd outside 3f out: styd on towards fin: nt rch ldrs* **9/1**

0- **5** *nk* **Admiral Barry (IRE)**[200] 6926 6-8-12 98 .... JMurtagh 4 99
(Eoin Griffin, Ire) *lw: midfield: effrt over 3f out: chsd ldrs and styd on ins fnl f: unable to chal* **15/2**[3]

4/2- **6** *nse* **Blue Bajan (IRE)**[445] 266 9-9-0 100 .... DanielTudhope 6 101+
(David O'Meara) *hld up: u.p over 2f out: hdwy over 1f out: styd on ins fnl f: gng on at fin but nt gng pce to chal ldrs* **28/1**

50-2 **7** *nse* **Icon Dream (IRE)**[18] 1416 4-8-9 99 .... JimCrowley 15 100
(David Simcock) *hld up: hdwy over 2f out: styd on ins fnl f: nt trble ldrs* **25/1**

062- **8** *2 ¾* **Darley Sun (IRE)**[212] 6621 5-9-1 101 .... FrankieDettori 13 100
(Saeed Bin Suroor) *racd keenly: chsd ldrs: tk false step on bnd after 2f: pushed along over 3f out: outpcd by front 2 over 2f out: wknd ins fnl f* **14/1**

03-0 **9** *2* **Plymouth Rock (IRE)**[32] 1102 5-8-8 97 .... (v) JohnFahy[(3)] 11 93+
(Jeremy Noseda) *hld up in rr: keeping on steadily whn swtchd rt ins fnl f: nvr able to trble ldrs* **16/1**

0601 **10** *2 ¾* **Montaff**[18] 1412 5-9-0 100 .... SamHitchcott 10 93
(Mick Channon) *racd keenly: hld up: hdwy u.p over 2f out: chsd ldrs but no imp over 1f out: wknd ins fnl f* **22/1**

030- **11** *4 ½* **Swingkeel (IRE)**[26] 6926 6-8-11 97 .... JimmyFortune 17 85
(Nigel Twiston-Davies) *midfield: rdn over 3f out: n.d* **33/1**

20-2 **12** *1* **Red Cadeaux**[32] 1102 5-9-3 103 .... RyanMoore 5 94
(Ed Dunlop) *lw: chsd ldrs: rdn and no imp over 2f out: wknd and eased ins fnl f* **5/1**[1]

30-4 **13** *4 ½* **Halla San**[18] 1412 9-8-11 97 .... PaulHanagan 14 79
(Richard Fahey) *hld up: u.p 3f out: nvr on terms* **25/1**

15-3 **14** *1* **Dirar (IRE)**[47] 667 6-9-7 107 .... WMLordan 12 88
(Gordon Elliott, Ire) *midfield: rdn over 3f out: wknd over 2f out* **14/1**

/10- **15** *hd* **Mamlook (IRE)**[27] 3447 7-9-0 100 .... RichardHughes 9 81
(David Pipe) *chsd ldrs tl rdn and wknd 2f out* **14/1**

320- **16** *18* **La Vecchia Scuola (IRE)**[50] 7350 7-8-12 98 .... WilliamBuick 2 59
(Jim Goldie) *handy in chsng gp: rdn and wknd 3f out* **50/1**

636- **17** *14* **Sentry Duty (FR)**[27] 6926 9-9-2 102 .... MichaelHills 8 47
(Nicky Henderson) *midfield: hdwy over 5f out: handy in chsng gp tl wknd qckly over 3f out: t.o over 2f out* **33/1**

3m 59.39s (-5.41) **Going Correction** -0.025s/f (Good) course record
WFA 4 from 5yo+ 4lb **17** Ran SP% **118.9**
Speed ratings (Par 109): **110,109,108,108,107 107,107,106,105,104 102,102,100,100,99 92,86**
CSF £41.69 CT £2000.40 TOTE £4.80: £1.90, £2.50, £8.40, £2.70; EX 45.40 Trifecta £2483.50 Part won. Pool £3356.12 - 0.75 winning units..
Owner T G Leslie **Bred** Pendley Farm **Trained** Cholmondeley, Cheshire

FOCUS
This year's Chester Cup was set up perfectly for Overturn and the first pair were always 1-2 in a race surprisingly light on incident. Setting fractions to suit allowed the winner to record a time only half a second outside the course record. He could rate higher based on his hurdles form.

NOTEBOOK
Overturn(IRE) was drawn one and faced no pressure whatsoever for the lead around a track that favours speed. He was fit from hurdling and defied a 6lb higher mark than when winning last year's Northumberland Plate. He looked in trouble when under strong pressure inside the final half-mile, but he had plenty left and responded well. Connections suggested afterwards that he could bid to follow up last season's success in the Northumberland Plate (could do likewise in the Galway Hurdle), but a hefty weight rise is likely to scupper him at Newcastle. (op 9-2)
Tastahil(IRE) needed to be ridden along early to make the most of stall three, but he soon travelled well in a good position. This was a fine effort off a mark 3lb higher than when a head second to Mamlook in last year's race. (op 15-2)
Mystery Star(IRE) did well to get to the rail from stall 16, but the pace of the race meant he was unable to challenge the front two.
Mount Athos(IRE) ◆ looked one to follow when winning nicely on his debut for this yard over 1m4f at Dundalk on his reappearance, but stall 17 gave him little hope. Dropped in well off the modest pace, he was asked to challenge widest of all around the bend into the straight and did well to finish so close. He's likely to prove better than a handicapper in due course.
Admiral Barry(IRE) didn't make use of his favourable draw and had no chance. (op 9-1)
Blue Bajan(IRE) had been off for over a year. He was entitled to need this but was keeping on at the finish.
Icon Dream(IRE) was another dropped in well off the pace from a wide draw and had little hope. (op 33-1)
Red Cadeaux, 8lb higher than when unlucky in this last year, was ridden along to recover from a sluggish start, and though better placed than many, was still some way off the winner and found nothing for serious pressure. (op 6-1)

Mamlook(IRE), 4lb higher than when winning this last year, wasn't as poorly placed as some but ran flat.

1809 STELLAR GROUP H'CAP — 5f 16y

3:30 (3:33) (Class 2) (0-105,105) 4£14,193 (£4,248; £2,124; £1,062; £528) **Stalls** Low

Form — RPR

00-1 **1** **Doctor Parkes**[16] 1438 5-8-5 **89**........ PaulHanagan 7 100
(Eric Alston) *midfield: hdwy over 1f out: r.o ins fnl f to ld towards fin* **10/1**

21-6 **2** *1* **Captain Dunne (IRE)**[28] 1186 6-9-6 **104**........ DavidAllan 9 111
(Tim Easterby) *lw: chsd ldrs: rdn to ld over 1f out: edgd lft ins fnl f: worn down towards fin* **16/1**

000- **3** *1 1/4* **Masamah (IRE)**[207] 6752 5-9-2 **100**........ JamieSpencer 13 103+
(Kevin Ryan) *chsd ldrs: effrt 2f out: ev ch over 1f out: nt qckn ins fnl f* **14/1**

00-4 **4** *1/2* **Confessional**[28] 1166 4-8-8 **92**........(e) RobertWinston 12 93+
(Tim Easterby) *towards rr: pushed along over 2f out: gd prog ins fnl f: gng on at fin* **25/1**

20-0 **5** *2 1/4* **Noverre To Go (IRE)**[19] 1366 5-8-11 **95**........(t) NeilCallan 3 88
(Tom Dascombe) *chsd ldrs: effrt over 1f out: kpt on same pce ins fnl f* **14/1**

5201 **6** *nk* **Falasteen (IRE)**[14] 1476 4-8-8 **92**........ AdrianNicholls 4 84+
(David Nicholls) *wnt rt s: hld up: kpt on ins fnl f: nt gng pce to trble ldrs* **9/2**[1]

100- **7** *1 1/2* **Blue Jack**[213] 6608 6-9-7 **105**........(v) RichardKingscote 6 91+
(Tom Dascombe) *lw: bmpd s: bhd: hdwy on inner over 1f out: styd on ins fnl f: nt rch ldrs* **9/2**[1]

00-0 **8** *hd* **Moorhouse Lad**[19] 1366 8-8-11 **95**........ TomEaves 1 80
(Bryan Smart) *led: rdn and hdd over 1f out: wknd wl ins fnl f* **8/1**[3]

1-32 **9** *1 1/4* **Beat The Bell**[14] 1476 6-8-7 **91** ow1........ GrahamGibbons 11 72
(David Barron) *in tch: lost pl wl over 1f out: sn wl outpcd* **11/1**

20-0 **10** *1/2* **Archers Road (IRE)**[14] 1476 4-8-9 **93**........ SamHitchcott 10 72
(David Barron) *awkward s: towards rr and sn struggling: nvr on terms* **40/1**

0-00 **11** *1 1/4* **Green Park (IRE)**[15] 1457 8-8-2 **91**........(b) NeilFarley(5) 2 66
(Declan Carroll) *sn pushed along to chse ldrs: rdn over 1f out: wknd ins fnl f* **10/1**

0100 **12** *1* **Breathless Kiss (USA)**[4] 1687 4-8-9 **93**........(b) KierenFallon 5 64+
(Kevin Ryan) *hmpd s: a outpcd and bhd* **6/1**[2]

534- **13** *1/2* **Fathom Five (IRE)**[200] 6918 7-8-7 **91**........ AndrewMullen 8 60
(David Nicholls) *bit bkwd: gd spd w ldr: rdn and wknd over 1f out* **16/1**

59.73 secs (-1.27) **Going Correction** -0.025s/f (Good) **13** Ran SP% **119.7**
Speed ratings (Par 109): **109,107,105,104,101 100,98,97,95,95 93,91,90**
toteswingers:1&2 £67.90, 2&3 £31.50, 1&3 £28.90 CSF £160.37 CT £2317.44 TOTE £10.30: £2.80, £4.10, £3.80; EX 230.20 Trifecta £1490.20 Part won. Pool £2013.86 - 0.20 winning units..

Owner Joseph Heler **Bred** Joseph Heler **Trained** Longton, Lancs

FOCUS

No horse drawn higher than eight had made the top three in this sprint handicap for the last 12 years, but that stat was broken this time with the runner-up and third-placed finisher posted out wide. The pace was predictably quick. The winner looks better than ever but the first pair are the only ones to show their form.

NOTEBOOK

Doctor Parkes, up 5lb for winning over 6f on his reappearance, had no trouble with the drop in trip and was defying a rating 10lb higher rating than when winning a 3-y-o handicap at this meeting two years ago. He won decisively and can continue to improve. The Wokingham and Stewards' Cup were mentioned as possible targets. (op 11-1 tchd 8-1)

Captain Dunne(IRE) was well ridden by David Allan, managing to get a handy position from stall nine without forfeiting too much ground. This was a smart performance off a mark of 104. (op 14-1)

Masamah(IRE), 10lb higher than when making all in this last year from stall three, was unable to dominate and was stuck wide from the widest gate, so this rates a highly creditable effort. (op 20-1 tchd 12-1)

Confessional was dropped in from stall 12 but still had to challenge wide. This was a respectable performance. (op 33-1)

Noverre To Go(IRE) ◆ showed surprisingly good speed to be well placed just off the leaders for much of the journey, but he still became outpaced in the straight. He should be spot-on for a return to 6f next time. (op 22-1)

Falasteen(IRE) has an issue with the stalls. That wasn't apparent when he made all at Epsom last time, but in his two runs prior he'd blown the start, and this time he didn't help himself by going right when the gates opened. (tchd 4-1 and 5-1)

Blue Jack won first time out last season and also has a C&D Listed success to his name, but his chance was ruined when he was hampered by Falasteen on leaving the stalls. Official explanation: jockey said gelding was hampered at start (op 5-1 tchd 6-1 in a place)

Breathless Kiss(USA) lost her chance when hampered on leaving the gates. She was 7lb lower than in future. Official explanation: jockey said filly was hampered at start and hung right throughout

1810 MERSEYRAIL MAIDEN STKS — 1m 2f 75y

4:05 (4:06) (Class 4) 3-Y-O **£6,152** (£1,830; £914; £456) **Stalls** High

Form — RPR

3-3 **1** **Colombian (IRE)**[18] 1409 3-9-3 0........ WilliamBuick 6 97+
(John Gosden) *lw: trckd ldrs: hmpd on bnd under 3f out: wnt 2nd 2f out: chalng over 1f out: led ins fnl f: r.o and wl on top towards fin* **1/1**[1]

5-4 **2** *2* **Tanfeeth**[18] 1408 3-9-3 0........ RichardHills 3 93+
(Ed Dunlop) *lw: prom: led 4f out: rdn whn pressed over 1f out: hdd ins fnl f: wl hld and nt gng pce of wnr towards fin* **9/4**[2]

0 **3** *10* **Change The Subject (USA)**[18] 1408 3-9-3 0........ IanMongan 8 74
(Sir Henry Cecil) *lw: in tch: chalng 3f out: outpcd by front 2 over 1f out: n.d after* **8/1**[3]

6 **4** *3 1/2* **Planetoid (IRE)**[16] 1445 3-9-3 0........ TedDurcan 5 66+
(David Lanigan) *unf: bhd: got unbalanced on bnd wl over 7f out: rn green: hdwy over 1f out: kpt on to take 4th ins fnl f: nt pce to get competitive* **33/1**

62- **5** *1 1/4* **Layla's King**[161] 7558 3-9-3 0........ KierenFallon 7 64
(Jane Chapple-Hyam) *trckd ldrs: chalng over 3f out: got unbalanced on bnd under 3f out: sn outpcd: n.d after* **14/1**

6 **6** *2* **Ash Cloud (IRE)**[15] 1474 3-8-12 0........ RichardKingscote 2 55
(Tom Dascombe) *w'like: led: hdd 4f out: wknd over 2f out* **50/1**

0- **7** *1* **Ari Gold (IRE)**[257] 5263 3-9-3 0........(p) JimCrowley 1 58
(Tom Dascombe) *hld up in midfield: rdn and btn over 2f out* **33/1**

8 *15* **Leah's Angel (IRE)** 3-8-5 0........ JosephYoung(7) 4 23
(Michael Mullineaux) *lw: nvr gng wl and a bhd* **100/1**

3 **9** *3 3/4* **El Wasmi**[9] 1568 3-9-3 0........ PhilipRobinson 9 20+
(Clive Brittain) *w'like: str: in tch: stmbld on bnd and lost pl wl over 7f out: sn pushed along towards rr: lost tch over 2f out* **17/2**

2m 10.06s (-1.14) **Going Correction** -0.025s/f (Good) **9** Ran SP% **117.9**
Speed ratings (Par 101): **107,105,97,94,93 92,91,79,76**
CSF £3.37 TOTE £2.00: £1.20, £1.30, £2.20; EX 4.30 Trifecta £14.00 Pool: £1574.34 - 82.84 winning units..

Owner H R H Princess Haya Of Jordan **Bred** Smythson **Trained** Newmarket, Suffolk

FOCUS

Last season's running didn't work out that well, but this maiden often produces smart types, the most recent example being the 2009 edition when Harbinger defeated subsequent Ebor runner-up Changingoftheguard, while Daraahem won in 2008 before taking the following year's Chester Cup. This edition looked up to scratch with the first pair clear and showing improved form.

El Wasmi Official explanation: jockey said colt did not handle track

1811 WARE INVESTMENT AND BRIDGING4U H'CAP — 1m 4f 66y

4:40 (4:47) (Class 3) (0-95,85) 3-Y-O **£9,066** (£2,697; £1,348; £673) **Stalls** Low

Form — RPR

1-4 **1** **Brown Panther**[14] 1485 3-8-9 **73**........ RichardKingscote 1 84+
(Tom Dascombe) *str: racd keenly: led after: hdd after 2f: remained prom: rdn and nt qckn w ldrs over 1f out: r.o towards fin to ld fnl stride* **5/1**[3]

6-1 **2** *nk* **Fadhaa (IRE)**[22] 1298 3-8-13 **77**........ RichardHills 2 86+
(B W Hills) *lw: midfield: hdwy 5f out: led 1f out: continually pressed ins fnl f: hdd fnl stride* **11/8**[1]

100- **3** *1/2* **Colour Vision (FR)**[214] 6555 3-9-3 **81**........ JoeFanning 4 89
(Mark Johnston) *lw: led for 1f: remained prom: moved upsides 2f out: sn led: rdn and hdd 1f out: continued to chal ins fnl f: hld fnl strides* **14/1**

516- **4** *3 3/4* **Time To Work (IRE)**[198] 6982 3-9-6 **84**........ JimmyFortune 6 86
(Andrew Balding) *trckd ldrs: rdn over 1f out: one pce ins fnl f* **8/1**

41-4 **5** *2 1/2* **Argocat (IRE)**[19] 1365 3-9-7 **85**........ JamieSpencer 3 83
(Paul Cole) *hld up bhd: rdn over 1f out: plugged on at one pce and no imp on ldrs ins fnl f* **9/2**[2]

4211 **6** *1/2* **Gottany O'S**[21] 1304 3-9-6 **84**........ SamHitchcott 8 81
(Mick Channon) *racd keenly: hld up: pushed along over 2f out: plugged on at one pce and no imp on ldrs ins fnl f* **6/1**

2-63 **7** *3 3/4* **Planet Waves (IRE)**[14] 1478 3-9-7 **85**........ PhilipRobinson 5 76
(Clive Brittain) *racd keenly: prom: led after 2f: rdn and hdd under 2f out: sn wknd* **18/1**

41 **8** *8* **Gawaarib (USA)**[28] 1173 3-9-0 **78**........(b) TadhgO'Shea 7 56
(John Gosden) *niggled along towards rr early: forced wd on bnd after 4f: wl adrift over 2f out* **18/1**

2m 37.05s (-1.45) **Going Correction** -0.025s/f (Good) **8** Ran SP% **119.5**
Speed ratings (Par 103): **108,107,107,104,103 102,100,95**
toteswingers:1&2 £2.60, 2&3 £7.00, 1&3 £10.70 CSF £12.92 CT £93.49 TOTE £5.90: £1.70, £1.30, £3.20; EX 15.30 Trifecta £128.60 Pool: £1855.66 - 10.67 winning units..

Owner Owen Promotions Limited **Bred** Owen Promotions Ltd **Trained** Malpas, Cheshire

FOCUS

Regularly a decent 3-y-o handicap and it rates as such again. The first two should do better than the bare form.

NOTEBOOK

Brown Panther ◆ won despite finding a bit of trouble around a track that was probably not ideal. A big, scopey sort who is likely to come into his own around a galloping circuit, he was well placed for much of the journey but was short of room early in the straight and had to be switched. There was no immediate acceleration when in the clear, but he did well to sustain a challenge that saw him get up in the final strides. He's expected to stay further and can rate a lot higher. (op 9-2)

Fadhaa(IRE) failed only narrowly to follow up his reappearance win in a Wolverhampton maiden and has started off in handicaps on a good mark. (op 2-1)

Colour Vision(FR) was reported to have lost his action when last seen at Epsom in October. This was a promising return, finishing close up behind two well-handicapped looking rivals, and he was clear of the remainder. (op 10-1)

Time To Work(IRE) can be expected to come on for this first run in 198 days. (op 15-2 tchd 9-1)

Argocat(IRE) didn't improve significantly for the step up in trip. (op 8-1)

Gottany O'S was on a hat-trick after a couple of wins in minor company, but this was his handicap debut and he doesn't seem to be on a good mark. (op 11-2 tchd 13-2)

T/Jkpt: £5,632.10 to a £1 stake. Pool of £133,981.89 -16.89 winning tickets. T/Plt: 69.60 to a £1 stake. Pool of £148,257.50 - 1,554.71 winning tickets T/Qpdt: £34.70 to a £1 stake. Pool of £6,847.32 - 145.80 winning tickets. DO

1496 SOUTHWELL (L-H)

Wednesday, May 4

OFFICIAL GOING: Standard

Wind: Light half against Weather: Fine and dry

1812 LADBROKESBINGO.COM MEDIAN AUCTION MAIDEN STKS — 7f (F)

2:10 (2:18) (Class 6) 3-4-Y-O **£1,706** (£503; £252) **Stalls** Low

Form — RPR

32 **1** **York Glory (USA)**[64] 721 3-8-9 0........ PhillipMakin 7 79
(Kevin Ryan) *trckd ldrs on outer: smooth hdwy 3f out: cl up 2f out: rdn over 1f out: led ins fnl f: drvn and kpt on wl last 100yds* **8/13**[1]

-426 **2** *nk* **Dr Red Eye**[11] 1514 3-8-6 61........ BillyCray(3) 2 78
(David Nicholls) *cl up on inner: led after 2f: rdn over 2f out and sn jnd: drvn over 1f out: hdd ins fnl f: no ex last 50yds* **12/1**

630- **3** *8* **El Maachi**[244] 5676 3-8-6 71........ MickyFenton(3) 11 57
(Jim Best) *prom: rdn along 3f out: drvn and one pce fnl 2f* **8/1**[3]

0-53 **4** *2 1/2* **Calaf**[14] 1480 3-8-9 74........ SilvestreDeSousa 4 50
(Jane Chapple-Hyam) *chsd ldrs: rdn along 1/2-way: drvn wl over 2f out and sn one pce* **3/1**[2]

0-00 **5** *1 1/2* **Coracle**[10] 1543 3-8-6 57........ TjadeCollier(3) 8 46
(David Nicholls) *towards rr: rdn along and hdwy 3f out: kpt on one pce u.p fnl 2f: nvr nr ldrs* **50/1**

\- **6** *1 1/2* **Cuckney Bear** 3-8-9 0........ RichardMullen 12 42
(Ed McMahon) *dwlt and towards rr: hdwy 3f out: kpt on same pce fnl 2f: nvr nr ldrs* **25/1**

04- **7** *1 3/4* **Kian's Delight**[214] 6566 3-8-8 0 ow2........ MichaelO'Connell(3) 6 39
(Jedd O'Keeffe) *s.i.s: a towards rr* **25/1**

8 *3 1/4* **Tootie Flutie** 3-8-4 0........ FrannyNorton 3 23
(Richard Whitaker) *dwlt: nvr bttr than midfield* **100/1**

006- **9** *15* **Cannon Bolt (IRE)**[198] 6980 3-8-9 48........ LeeNewman 5 —
(Robin Bastiman) *a in rr* **80/1**

00-0 **10** *3/4* **Terrys Flutter**[35] 1044 3-7-13 40........(b1) RyanPowell(5) 10 —
(Mark Allen) *led 2f: cl up: rdn along 3f out: sn hung rt and wknd qckly* **150/1**

11 *6* **On The Lash (IRE)** 3-8-9 0........ PJMcDonald 1 —
(Alan Swinbank) *a in rr* **33/1**

1m 29.84s (-0.46) **Going Correction** +0.125s/f (Slow) **11** Ran SP% **121.2**
Speed ratings (Par 101): **107,106,97,94,92 91,89,85,68,67 60**
toteswingers:1&2 £3.50, 2&3 £5.80, 1&3 £2.80 CSF £10.29 TOTE £1.70: £1.20, £2.30, £2.10; EX 10.30.

Owner Salman Rashed **Bred** Paget Bloodstock & Horse France **Trained** Hambleton, N Yorks

The Form Book, Raceform Ltd, Compton, RG20 6NL

FOCUS
Varying levels of ability in this older-horse maiden and an uncompetitive race with only four considered in the market. They dominated the race, although in effect only two mattered in the straight. Only the front pair showed their form.
Terrys Flutter Official explanation: jockey said filly hung left

1813 LADBROKESPOKER.COM MAIDEN STKS — 5f (F)
2:45 (2:51) (Class 5) 3-Y-0+ — **£2,388** (£705; £352) **Stalls** High

Form — RPR

4262 **1** **Beautiful Day**[15] 1465 3-9-1 65 .... PhillipMakin 12 — 68
(Kevin Ryan) *wnt sltly lft s: trckd ldrs: hdwy 2f out: rdn to ld jst over 1f out: drvn and edgd lft ins fnl f: kpt on wl* **7/1**

2 ¾ **Triviality (IRE)** 3-9-1 0 .... FergusSweeney 2 — 66+
(Jamie Osborne) *dwlt and sltly hmpd s: in tch: hdwy 2f out: rdn wl over 1f out: ev ch ins fnl f: edgd rt and no ex last 50yds* **33/1**

42-2 **3** *hd* **Bertiewhittle**[25] 1246 3-9-1 72 .... LeeNewman 6 — 65+
(David Barron) *stmbld s: in tch: rdn along and sltly outpcd 1/2-way: gd hdwy over 1f out: drvn and kpt on ins fnl f: n.m.r towards fin* **13/8**[1]

-23 **4** 3 ¾ **Ginzan**[8] 1589 3-8-10 0 .... TomMcLaughlin 11 — 47
(Malcolm Saunders) *sltly hmpd s: sn cl up: rdn to ld 2f out: drvn and hdd jst over 1f out: wknd ins fnl f* **9/1**

23/ **5** 3 **Moorhouse Girl**[605] 5693 4-9-0 0 .... DaleSwift(5) 8 — 40
(George Foster) *cl up: rdn and ev ch 2f out: sn edgd lft and wknd over 1f out* **5/1**[2]

02 **6** 1 ¾ **Mecca's Team**[35] 1038 3-8-10 0 .... FrederikTylicki 13 — 29
(Michael Dods) *led: pushed along and hdd 2f out: sn rdn and grad wknd* **13/2**[3]

00-0 **7** 3 ¾ **Chardonnay Star (IRE)**[16] 1439 4-8-12 36 ....(v) DanielleMooney(7) 1 — 20
(Colin Teague) *sn outpcd and a in rr* **150/1**

5-56 **8** ½ **Durgan**[8] 1581 5-9-10 58 ....(p) SteveDrowne 7 — 23
(Linda Jewell) *dwlt: sn outpcd and a in rr* **16/1**

06 **9** ¾ **Bird Dog**[95] 347 5-9-5 0 .... AdamBeschizza(5) 3 — 20
(Phil McEntee) *dwlt and sltly hmpd s: in tch and sn rdn along: outpcd and rr fr 1/2-way* **150/1**

6 **10** 2 ¾ **Chipofftheoldblock**[26] 1220 3-8-10 0 .... RoystonFfrench 5 — —
(Bruce Hellier) *in tch: rdn along over 2f out: sn wknd* **66/1**

60.66 secs (0.96) **Going Correction** +0.175s/f (Slow)
WFA 3 from 4yo+ 9lb — **10** Ran SP% **102.2**
Speed ratings (Par 103): **99,97,97,91,86 83,77,77,75,71**
toteswingers:1&2 £18.90, 2&3 £10.40, 1&3 £2.30 CSF £159.92 TOTE £6.80: £1.60, £5.30, £1.20; EX 126.20.
Owner Guy Reed **Bred** G Reed **Trained** Hambleton, N Yorks

FOCUS
Another modest maiden in which they appeared to go too fast early, as two of the first three came from well back. The form is rated around the winner.

1814 LADBROKESCASINO.COM H'CAP — 1m (F)
3:20 (3:21) (Class 6) (0-65,65) 4-Y-0+ — **£1,706** (£503; £252) **Stalls** Low

Form — RPR

0-04 **1** **Koo And The Gang (IRE)**[15] 1463 4-9-1 59 .... SilvestreDeSousa 8 — 77
(Brian Ellison) *trckd ldrs: hdwy 3f out: chal 2f out: rdn to ld ent fnl f: drvn out* **7/2**[2]

-602 **2** 1 ¾ **All Right Now**[14] 1496 4-9-7 65 .... AndreaAtzeni 2 — 79
(Derek Haydn Jones) *trckd ldr: led 3f out: jnd and rdn wl over 1f out: drvn: edgd lft and hdd ent fnl f: no ex last 100yds* **3/1**[1]

4603 **3** 8 **Eastern Hills**[15] 1463 6-8-12 56 ....(p) ShaneKelly 5 — 52
(Alan McCabe) *chsd ldrs on inner: hdwy over 2f out: rdn to chse ldng pair wl over 1f out: sn drvn and kpt on same pce* **12/1**

5056 **4** ½ **General Tufto**[15] 1461 6-9-4 62 ....(b) MartinLane 4 — 56
(Charles Smith) *sn rdn along and outpcd in rr: hdwy wl over 1f out: styd on strly ins fnl f: nrst fin* **12/1**

00-3 **5** 1 ½ **Rub Of The Relic (IRE)**[9] 1557 6-9-1 59 ....(v) MickyFenton 14 — 50
(Paul Midgley) *racd wd: midfield: rdn and hdwy 2f out: sn drvn and no imp fr wl over 1f out* **28/1**

/10- **6** *hd* **Hit The Switch**[463] 298 5-9-4 62 .... StephenCraine 9 — 53
(Patrick Morris) *chsd ldrs: rdn wl over 2f out: [illegible]* **25/1**

2531 **7** *nk* **Bold Diva**[14] 1498 6-8-13 57 ....(v) LukeMorris 12 — 47
(Tony Carroll) *in tch: hdwy to chse ldrs 3f out: rdn over 2f out: sn drvn and wknd* **10/1**

4303 **8** 2 ¼ **Buzz Bird**[15] 1468 4-8-10 54 .... PhillipMakin 10 — 39
(David Barron) *midfield: effrt 3f out: sn rdn and no hdwy* **8/1**[3]

4214 **9** ½ **Positivity**[49] 870 5-8-11 60 ....(p) AdamCarter(5) 6 — 44
(Bryan Smart) *in tch on inner: effrt and sme hdwy 3f out: sn rdn and btn 2f out* **9/1**

503- **10** 1 **Betteras Bertie**[191] 7128 8-8-13 57 .... FrannyNorton 13 — 38
(Neville Bycroft) *towards rr: sme hdwy over 3f out: rdn and wknd over 2f out* **12/1**

2255 **11** 3 ½ **Kipchak (IRE)**[19] 1372 6-9-6 64 ....(v[1]) HayleyTurner 7 — 37
(Conor Dore) *led: rdn along and hdd 3f out: sn drvn and wknd* **16/1**

4213 **12** 4 ½ **Nevada Desert (IRE)**[54] 837 11-8-13 57 .... ChrisCatlin 1 — 20
(Richard Whitaker) *a in rr* **16/1**

0-62 **13** 4 ½ **Play The Blues (IRE)**[30] 1133 4-9-2 65 .... RyanPowell(5) 11 — 17
(Mark Allen) *rrd s and s.i.s: a bhd* **66/1**

/666 **14** 8 **Final Tune (IRE)**[23] 1273 8-8-9 53 ....(vt[1]) JimmyQuinn 3 — —
(Mandy Rowland) *s.i.s: a bhd* **16/1**

1m 42.5s (-1.20) **Going Correction** +0.125s/f (Slow) — **14** Ran SP% **126.9**
Speed ratings (Par 101): **111,109,101,100,99 99,98,96,96,95 91,87,82,74**
toteswingers:1&2 £4.70, 2&3 £20.40, 1&3 £20.00 CSF £15.05 CT £124.27 TOTE £3.40: £1.40, £2.50, £3.10; EX 3.80.
Owner Koo's Racing Club **Bred** Vincent Howley **Trained** Norton, N Yorks

FOCUS
A modest but pretty competitive handicap in which it paid to race close to the pace. It produced something of a music-related finish. The first pair came clear and the winner is rated better than ever.
Play The Blues(IRE) Official explanation: jockey said filly missed the break

1815 VISIT ATTHERACES.COM/PUNCHESTOWN H'CAP (DIV I) — 6f (F)
3:55 (3:58) (Class 6) (0-55,55) 4-Y-0+ — **£1,364** (£403; £201) **Stalls** Low

Form — RPR

5004 **1** **Boy The Bell**[27] 1204 4-9-2 55 .... SilvestreDeSousa 9 — 64
(Brian Ellison) *cl up: led wl over 2f out: rdn and hdd 1f out: drvn and rallied last 100yds to ld on line* **1/1**[1]

-102 **2** *shd* **Exceedingly Good (IRE)**[14] 1497 5-8-9 55 .... LeonnaMayor(7) 7 — 64
(Roy Bowring) *trckd ldng pair: hdwy 2f out: rdn to ld 1f out: slt advantage tl hdd nr line* **4/1**[2]

400- **3** 2 ½ **Eeny Mac (IRE)**[172] 6076 4-8-7 46 oh1 .... FrannyNorton 2 — 47
(Neville Bycroft) *prom: effrt over 2f out: swtchd lft and rdn wl over 1f out and ev ch tl drvn and one pce ent fnl f* **17/2**

00-3 **4** ½ **Tamino (IRE)**[14] 1498 8-8-8 47 .... AndreaAtzeni 10 — 46
(Mark Brisbourne) *sn led: rdn and hdd wl over 1f out: drvn and one pce fr over 1f out* **13/2**[3]

6100 **5** 2 ¼ **Vertumnus**[9] 1570 4-8-12 51 ....(b) KellyHarrison 1 — 43
(Nick Littmoden) *in tch: effrt over 2f out: sn rdn and edgd lft wl over 1f out: sn swtchd rt and drvn: one pce* **25/1**

5606 **6** ½ **Flow Chart (IRE)**[70] 654 4-8-7 46 oh1 ....(b) RobbieFitzpatrick 4 — 37
(Peter Grayson) *towards rr: sme hdwy 2f out: sn rdn and no imp ins fnl f* **100/1**

4400 **7** *nk* **Charles Parnell (IRE)**[79] 544 8-9-2 55 .... ChrisCatlin 3 — 45
(Simon Griffiths) *s.i.s and in rr: wd st: hdwy over 2f out: sn rdn and no imp* **8/1**

000- **8** 11 **Hopeshedoes (USA)**[271] 4791 4-8-11 50 .... SteveDrowne 11 — —
(Linda Jewell) *a in rr* **33/1**

6-0 **9** *nk* **Mission Impossible**[15] 1464 6-8-13 52 .... PatrickMathers 5 — —
(Colin Teague) *a towards rr* **66/1**

-0U0 **10** 6 **Cinderella**[20] 1331 4-8-4 46 oh1 .... SimonPearce(3) 6 — —
(Lucinda Featherstone) *sn outpcd: a in rr* **66/1**

1m 17.29s (0.79) **Going Correction** +0.125s/f (Slow) — **10** Ran SP% **115.7**
Speed ratings (Par 101): **99,98,95,94,91 91,90,76,75,67**
toteswingers:1&2 £2.50, 2&3 £4.50, 1&3 £2.90 CSF £4.84 CT £21.76 TOTE £2.40: £1.20, £1.10, £2.80; EX 6.80.
Owner L S Keys **Bred** D J P Turner **Trained** Norton, N Yorks

FOCUS
The first division of this moderate sprint handicap in which the first four held those placed throughout. It was quicker than division II and the form is sound enough.
Hopeshedoes(USA) Official explanation: jockey said filly moved poorly throughout

1816 GOT THE FEELING GET TO LADBROKES FILLIES' H'CAP — 5f (F)
4:30 (4:30) (Class 4) (0-80,75) 4-Y-0+ — **£2,914** (£867; £433; £216) **Stalls** High

Form — RPR

66-0 **1** **Tillys Tale**[4] 1698 4-9-6 68 .... MickyFenton 2 — 77
(Paul Midgley) *qckly away: mde all: rdn and qcknd clr over 1f out: kpt on strly* **14/1**

6-33 **2** 3 **Carrie's Magic**[9] 1555 4-9-7 69 ....(b) LeeNewman 4 — 67
(David Barron) *trckd ldrs: pushed along 1/2-way: rdn wl over 1f out: drvn and kpt on same pce ins fnl f* **9/4**[1]

5221 **3** 1 ¼ **Fair Passion**[8] 1584 4-9-13 75 6ex .... DaneO'Neill 5 — 69
(Derek Shaw) *trckd ldrs: hdwy 2f out: rdn to chse wnr over 1f out: sn drvn and one pce* **5/2**[2]

4366 **4** 1 ¼ **Caramelita**[36] 1024 4-9-3 65 ....(v[1]) DavidProbert 1 — 54
(J R Jenkins) *chsd ldng pair: rdn along over 2f out: drvn wl over 1f out and sn btn* **13/2**

600- **5** 3 ¾ **Cloth Ears**[147] 7754 5-8-7 60 .... AdamBeschizza(5) 6 — 36
(Phil McEntee) *cl up: rdn along over 2f out: grad wknd* **28/1**

40-2 **6** 3 **Matterofact (IRE)**[2] 1752 8-9-4 66 .... TomMcLaughlin 3 — 31
(Malcolm Saunders) *in tch: hdwy on outer 1/2-way: rdn along wl over 1f out: sn btn* **11/4**[3]

61.77 secs (2.07) **Going Correction** +0.175s/f (Slow) — **6** Ran SP% **109.5**
Speed ratings (Par 102): **90,85,83,81,75 70**
toteswingers:1&2 £4.10, 2&3 £1.40, 1&3 £4.40 CSF £43.45 TOTE £17.20: £10.00, £1.30; EX 51.90.
Owner Mrs M Hills **Bred** M & S Hills **Trained** Westow, N Yorks

FOCUS
A small field for this fillies' sprint. Modest form, rated around the winner.

1817 ATTHERACES.COM EXCLUSIVE GARY O'BRIEN TIPPING H'CAP — 1m 6f (F)
5:05 (5:05) (Class 5) (0-75,75) 4-Y-0+ — **£2,266** (£674; £337; £168) **Stalls** Low

Form — RPR

2242 **1** **Calculating (IRE)**[22] 1291 7-8-11 67 .... LeeNewnes(5) 2 — 75
(Mark Usher) *trckd ldrs: hdwy on inner over 3f out: cl up 2f out and sn rdn: drvn and edgd rt 1f out: led ent fnl f: kpt on* **6/1**

[illegible] **2** ¾ [illegible]
(Kevin Ryan) *chsd ldng pair: effrt to chse ldr 4f out: rdn to chal over 2f out: led wl over 1f out: drvn and hdd ent fnl f: kpt on* **13/2**

2452 **3** 3 ½ **First Rock (IRE)**[15] 1466 5-8-9 60 .... PJMcDonald 1 — 62
(Alan Swinbank) *led 1f: cl up on inner tl led again over 5f out: rdn 3f out: drvn and hdd wl over 1f out: hld whn n.m.r and swtchd lft 1f out: one pce* **3/1**[2]

1161 **4** 1 **Irish Jugger (USA)**[15] 1466 4-9-4 70 .... JamesMillman 4 — 71
(Rod Millman) *hld up in rr: hdwy over 5f out: effrt on outer and cl up 3f out: rdn over 2f out: sn drvn and one pce* **11/4**[1]

14-6 **5** 1 ¾ **Gaselee (USA)**[47] 894 5-9-10 75 .... MartinLane 3 — 73
(Rae Guest) *cl up: led after 1f: rdn along over 5f out: sn hdd & wknd over 3f out* **11/1**

140- **6** 18 **Simonside**[166] 6926 8-9-4 69 .... SilvestreDeSousa 5 — 57
(Brian Ellison) *hld up: pushed along in rr over 5f out: rdn along over 3f out: sn wknd* **7/2**[3]

3m 10.96s (2.66) **Going Correction** +0.125s/f (Slow)
WFA 4 from 5yo+ 1lb — **6** Ran SP% **109.8**
Speed ratings (Par 103): **97,96,94,94,93 82**
toteswingers:1&2 £3.90, 2&3 £3.70, 1&3 £2.50 CSF £40.69 TOTE £5.90: £1.90, £3.60; EX 24.40.
Owner Brian Rogan **Bred** Darley **Trained** Upper Lambourn, Berks
■ Stewards' Enquiry : Lee Newnes one-day ban; careless riding (18th May)

FOCUS
An ordinary handicap. The winner showed his best form since last summer.

1818 VISIT ATTHERACES.COM/PUNCHESTOWN H'CAP (DIV II) — 6f (F)
5:40 (5:42) (Class 6) (0-55,55) 4-Y-0+ — **£1,364** (£403; £201) **Stalls** Low

Form — RPR

3454 **1** **Itsthursdayalready**[14] 1497 4-9-2 55 .... ShaneKelly 9 — 67
(Mark Brisbourne) *chsd ldrs: gd hdwy to ld 2f out: rdn clr over 1f out: kpt on* **11/4**[1]

3403 **2** 4 **Kheley (IRE)**[15] 1464 5-8-12 51 .... LiamJones 7 — 50
(Mark Brisbourne) *towards rr: hdwy 1/2-way: rdn to chse ldrs 2f out: drvn to chse wnr over 1f out: sn no imp* **6/1**

60-0 **3** ¾ **Jamarjo (IRE)**[9] 1570 4-9-1 54 ....(p) MartinLane 5 — 51
(Steve Gollings) *outpcd and wl bhd: rdn 1/2-way: hdwy wl over 1f out: str run appr fnl f: tk 3rd on line* **12/1**

0222 **4** *nse* **Meydan Style (USA)**[14] 1498 5-8-9 48 .... RoystonFfrench 4 — 45
(Bruce Hellier) *dwlt and sltly hmpd s: towards rr and rdn along 1/2-way: hdwy 2f out: drvn over 1f out: kpt on: nrst fin* **5/1**[3]

/0-0 **5** *hd* **Mujahope**[15] 1468 6-8-7 **46** oh1 ....(v) PatrickMathers 1 42
(Colin Teague) *dwlt: sn in tch on inner: rdn to chse ldng pair wl over 1f out: sn drvn and one pce: lost 3rd wl ins fnl f* **40/1**

036- **6** *5* **Call The Law (IRE)**[278] 4559 5-8-11 **50** .... MickyFenton 2 30
(Pam Sly) *chsd ldng pair: rdn along and ch over 2f out: sn drvn and wknd* **8/1**

5006 **7** *1 ¼* **Ronnie Howe**[14] 1501 7-8-1 **47** oh1 ow1 ....(b) LeonnaMayor(7) 10 23
(Roy Bowring) *cl up: led 1/2-way: rdn and hdd 2f out: sn wknd* **33/1**

6-03 **8** *4* **Tenancy (IRE)**[26] 1213 7-9-2 **55** ....(b) ChrisCatlin 6 18
(Shaun Harris) *led: hdd 1/2-way: sn rdn and wknd 2f out* **5/1**[3]

0601 **9** *5* **Novay Essjay (IRE)**[25] 1248 4-8-13 **52** ....(b) LukeMorris 3 —
(Alan Juckes) *in tch: rdn along 1/2-way: sn drvn and btn* **9/2**[2]

1m 18.6s (2.10) **Going Correction** +0.125s/f (Slow) **9** Ran SP% **116.7**
Speed ratings (Par 101): **91,85,84,84,84 77,76,70,64**
toteswingers:1&2 £4.70, 2&3 £9.70, 1&3 £9.30 CSF £19.87 CT £170.73 TOTE £4.70: £2.10, £1.30, £6.80; EX 15.30.
Owner Wayne Hennessey **Bred** St Clare Hall Stud **Trained** Great Ness, Shropshire
■ Stewards' Enquiry : Patrick Mathers four-day ban: used whip with excessive frequency (May 18-21)

FOCUS
The second division of this moderate sprint was run 1.31secs slower than the first leg. Weak form, which shouldn't be taken literally.

1819 FOLLOW @ATTHERACES ON TWITTER H'CAP 1m 3f (F)
6:15 (6:15) (Class 5) (0-70,70) 3-Y-O **£2,266** (£674; £337; £168) **Stalls** Low

Form RPR

4554 **1** **Freedom Flyer (IRE)**[37] 1018 3-8-11 **60** .... SilvestreDeSousa 7 68
(Brian Ellison) *trckd ldrs: hdwy and cl up 1/2-way: led 3f out: jnd and rdn 2f out: drvn over 1f out and ch tl and kpt on wl ins fnl f* **5/1**[3]

62-4 **2** *1 ¼* **Elfine (IRE)**[30] 1139 3-9-7 **70** .... DaneO'Neill 2 76
(Harry Dunlop) *trckd ldrs: hdwy over 3f out: rdn 2f out: drvn to chse wnr appr fnl f and ch tl no ex last 100yds* **11/1**

-121 **3** *5* **Jack's Revenge (IRE)**[64] 716 3-8-12 **61** ....(p) TonyCulhane 4 58
(George Baker) *hld up in tch: pushed along over 3f out: rdn to chal over 2f out and ev ch tl drvn and one pce appr fnl f* **11/4**[1]

546- **4** *½* **Divine Rule (IRE)**[212] 6634 3-9-3 **66** .... SteveDrowne 1 62
(Hughie Morrison) *trckd ldr: cl up on inner: 3f out: rdn and ch 2f out: drvn and wknd appr fnl f* **7/2**[2]

0-61 **5** *3 ¾* **Runaway Tiger (IRE)**[71] 643 3-9-0 **63** .... LiamJones 6 52
(Paul D'Arcy) *dwlt and in rr: hdwy on wd outside over 3f out: rdn to chal over 2f out and ev ch tl drvn and wknd over 1f out* **5/1**[3]

00-0 **6** *7* **Sum Satisfaction**[23] 1271 3-9-1 **64** .... MartinLane 3 41
(Dominic Ffrench Davis) *led: rdn along and hdd 3f out: sn wknd* **12/1**

00-0 **7** *8* **Waterford Star (IRE)**[9] 1566 3-8-8 **57** ....(b[1]) GregFairley 5 19
(Mark Johnston) *towards rr and sn rdn along: lost pl after 3f and bhd after* **12/1**

2414 **8** *6* **Goal (IRE)**[33] 1082 3-8-13 **62** .... RobbieFitzpatrick 8 14
(Richard Guest) *hld up in rr: effrt and sme hdwy over 3f out: sn rdn and wknd* **9/1**

2m 29.12s (1.12) **Going Correction** +0.125s/f (Slow) **8** Ran SP% **115.9**
Speed ratings (Par 99): **100,99,95,95,92 87,81,77**
toteswingers:1&2 £10.40, 2&3 £4.10, 1&3 £3.60. Tote Super 7: Win: Not won. Place: Not won. CSF £58.23 CT £181.23 TOTE £4.50: £1.20, £4.20, £1.70; EX 54.10.
Owner L S Keys **Bred** Rabbah Bloodstock Limited **Trained** Norton, N Yorks

FOCUS
A modest handicap and quite a test for 3-y-os. The first two were clear and the winner showed clear improvement.
Waterford Star(IRE) Official explanation: jockey said gelding was never travelling
T/Plt: £72.20 to a £1 stake. Pool of £42,447.69 - 429.17 winning tickets. T/Qpdt: £45.00 to a £1 stake. Pool of £2,478.13 - 40.70 winning tickets. JR

1806 CHESTER (L-H)
Thursday, May 5

OFFICIAL GOING: Good to firm (8.2)
Rail out 4yds from 4f to top of home straight leaving a 3yd drop in at 1.5f marker. 5f increased by 15yds, 6, 7f, & 10f by 28yds and 12f by 40yds.
Wind: Light to moderate, behind Weather: Overcast

1820 BOODLES DIAMOND ETERNITY H'CAP 7f 122y
1:45 (1:49) (Class 2) (0-100,90) 3-Y£8,193 (£4,248; £2,124; £1,062; £528) **Stalls** Low

Form RPR

2214 **1** **Crown Counsel (IRE)**[5] 1690 3-9-0 **83** .... FrankieDettori 4 91
(Mark Johnston) *lw: trckd ldrs: rdn to take 2nd over 1f out: r.o to ld ins fnl f: pushed out and in control towards fin* **5/1**[2]

0526 **2** *1* **Fred Willetts (IRE)**[4] 1725 3-9-4 **87** ....(v) JimmyFortune 5 92
(David Evans) *led: rdn over 1f out: hdd ins fnl f: continued to chal: hld towards fin* **16/1**

21-2 **3** *1 ½* **Captain Bertie (IRE)**[11] 1547 3-8-13 **82** .... MichaelHills 1 83
(B W Hills) *lw: chsd ldrs: chalng 3f out: rdn and nt qckn over 1f out: kpt on same pce ins fnl f and wl hld by front 2* **1/2**[1]

1130 **4** *1 ¾* **Kingscroft (IRE)**[11] 1547 3-9-0 **83** .... JoeFanning 2 80
(Mark Johnston) *midfield: hdwy 3f out: chsd ldrs over 2f out: lugged lft and one pce ins fnl f* **25/1**

15-5 **5** *2 ¾* **Weapon Of Choice (IRE)**[15] 1478 3-9-4 **87** .... JamieSpencer 3 77
(David Simcock) *hld up: rdn over 1f out: kpt on ins fnl f: nvr able to chal* **16/1**

04-1 **6** *2* **Belle Royale (IRE)**[21] 1326 3-9-6 **89** .... RyanMoore 6 74
(Mark Brisbourne) *missed break: bhd: past btn horses ins fnl f: nvr able to get on terms w ldrs* **11/1**[3]

30-0 **7** *2* **Shafgaan**[22] 1317 3-9-7 **90** .... PhilipRobinson 9 70
(Clive Brittain) *wnt rt s: midfield: clsd and in tch w ldrs 3f out: outpcd over 2f out: wl btn ins fnl f* **20/1**

1334 **8** *6* **Baharat (IRE)**[6] 1652 3-8-7 **76** oh1 ....(v) JohnEgan 8 41
(Richard Guest) *niggled along towards rr: u.p in midfield over 2f out but no imp on ldrs: wknd over 1f out* **50/1**

121- **9** *25* **First Class Favour (IRE)**[201] 6920 3-9-4 **87** .... DavidAllan 7 —
(Tim Easterby) *racd keenly: w ldr: u.p and wknd over 2f out: eased whn wl btn over 1f out: t.o* **20/1**

1m 33.55s (-0.25) **Going Correction** +0.05s/f (Good) **9** Ran SP% **118.8**
Speed ratings (Par 105): **103,102,100,98,96 94,92,86,61**
toteswingers:1&2: £6.40, 2&3: £4.00, 1&3: £1.80 CSF £74.08 CT £107.24 TOTE £6.20: £1.40, £3.20, £1.10; EX 84.20 Trifecta £151.20 Pool: £1714.47 - 8.39 winning units..
Owner Sheikh Hamdan Bin Mohammed Al Maktoum **Bred** Gerrardstown House Stud **Trained** Middleham Moor, N Yorks

FOCUS
Officials at the course applied 4mm of water after racing the previous day, and the going was given as good to firm. The gallop looked to be strong. The form is rated around the runner-up and may not prove that reliable.

NOTEBOOK
Crown Counsel(IRE) didn't start his career until February this year, and was making a quick reappearance after running at Newmarket the previous weekend. Settled in just behind the leaders, Frankie Dettori produced his mount to win inside the final furlong and the pair won in good style. (op 11-2 tched 6-1 in places)
Fred Willetts(IRE), another making a quick reappearance, won three races on the AW in January, and is on a lower mark on turf, so it was no surprise to see him go well. He kept on really well considering he helped to share the early work, and is the type to win around this track in the future at 6f or 7f. (tchd 14-1)
Captain Bertie(IRE), one of the least exposed in the line-up and officially 8lb well in after his good effort at Sandown, got backed off the boards leading up to the off. He wasn't the quickest away and made his bid about three-wide heading round the last bend, after needing to be pushed into a prominent position. He found disappointingly little when push came to shove and, although it's possible that he'd prefer easier ground, connections suggested this run came a bit too soon after his previous performance. (op 8-13 tchd 4-6 in a place)
Kingscroft(IRE) has already had quite a bit of racing this year, with plenty of success on Polytrack, but had seen his mark rise from 68. Already behind a couple he faced here since returning to turf, he moved well in midfield but didn't have a change of gear when those around him quickened and was ultimately done for pace. (op 20-1)
Weapon Of Choice(IRE) finished a disappointing last of five in the Derby Trial at Epsom recently. Taking quite a drop in trip, he got caught flat-footed turning in before keeping on. (tchd 20-1)
Belle Royale(IRE) took plenty of racing as a juvenile and returned to the track this year in good heart when taking a race at Beverley at odds of 16-1. She had two wins and a second from four starts at this course last year, but fell out of the stalls this time and didn't have any chance to get back into contention. It looked as though she flew home late on but it was probably more a case of horses around her tiring. (op 10-1)

1821 BETFAIR HUXLEY STKS (FOR THE TRADESMAN'S CUP) (GROUP 3) 1m 2f 75y
2:20 (2:21) (Class 1) 4-Y-O+ **£28,385** (£10,760; £5,385; £2,685; £1,345) **Stalls** High

Form RPR

0/1- **1** **Await The Dawn (USA)**[243] 5772 4-9-3 120 .... RyanMoore 5 125+
(A P O'Brien, Ire) *str: racd in 2nd pl: moved upsides gng wl 2f out: led over 1f out: edgd rt ins fnl f and stormed clr: impressive* **8/11**[1]

313- **2** *4 ½* **Distant Memories (IRE)**[215] 6592 5-9-0 114 .... JamieSpencer 3 113
(Tom Tate) *lw: led: rdn over 2f out: sn jnd: hdd over 1f out: no ch w wnr ins fnl f* **6/1**[2]

11-6 **3** *½* **Forte Dei Marmi**[21] 1342 5-9-0 111 .... FrankieDettori 4 112+
(Luca Cumani) *hld up: niggled along over 3f out: rdn to take 3rd over 1f out: kpt on ins fnl f: unable to chal* **15/2**

10-3 **4** *2 ½* **Critical Moment (USA)**[8] 1600 4-9-0 108 .... MichaelHills 1 107
(B W Hills) *lw: chsd ldrs: pushed along over 3f out: rdn over 1f out: wknd ins fnl f* **8/1**

10-3 **5** *1 ½* **Dream Eater (IRE)**[12] 1527 6-9-0 116 ....(t) JimmyFortune 6 104
(Andrew Balding) *missed break: bhd: niggled along over 3f out: nvr able to get on terms w ldrs* **7/1**[3]

2m 8.54s (-2.66) **Going Correction** +0.05s/f (Good) **5** Ran SP% **107.6**
Speed ratings (Par 113): **116,112,112,110,108**
toteswingers:1&2: £3.00, 2&3: £3.70, 1&3: £2.90 CSF £5.16 TOTE £1.70: £1.10, £2.50; EX 5.10.

Owner M Tabor & Mrs John Magnier **Bred** Juddmonte Farms Inc **Trained** Ballydoyle, Co Tipperary

FOCUS
This was right up to the standard you would hope to see for a race of this nature and it produced a classy-looking winner in a time quicker than RP standard. The form is rated around the runner-up and the fourth, and the winner should hold his own in better races.

NOTEBOOK
Await The Dawn(USA) ◆ looked really good on his final start last season, demolishing South Easter 9l in a Group 3 at Leopardstown on his final start of 2010. The only runner carrying a penalty, and the highest-rated on official figures, he was given an intelligent ride and won going away. He is definitely capable of Group 2 success at the very least, so one would imagine it'll depend on what happens with stablemate So You Think as to which Royal Ascot race he may head for. Given that the former Australian star is already a proven top-class operator, one would imagine that the Hardwicke Stakes will be Await The Dawn's target next month, all things being equal. He would also be an intriguing deputy for the Coronation Cup at Epsom should any of his higher-rated stablemates not take their chance in that. (op 4-5 after 10-11 in places)
Distant Memories(IRE) has developed into a solid performer at this type of level and is a mainly consistent sort. Probably at his best with some ease in the ground (he only ran here after the trainer declared the ground to be suitable), he led the field and his jockey dictated a quick early gallop before slowing it down. He then tried to get away again when he made his bid for success, but had no chance of living with the winner once he swept past. (tchd 11-2 and 13-2)
Forte Dei Marmi ◆ showed nothing when stepped out of handicaps and into Group-company for the first time at Newmarket, but presumably something wasn't right there, as he ran miles below expectations. This was a bit better after racing keenly under restraint and hopefully he can progress from this. (tchd 7-1)
Critical Moment(USA) made a highly satisfactory comeback at Ascot in a Listed contest, which had presumably teed him up for this race. A dual winner as a 3-y-o, he ran badly in the Chester Vase at this meeting last year (trip was too far) and didn't show a great deal in this. (tchd 9-1)
Dream Eater(IRE) has plenty of ability and has run many decent races at a high level, as was the case of his previous start behind the exciting Dick Turpin, but he was chasing an illusive first win in Group company. Connections were testing out a new distance with him here, but they won't have learned a great deal because Dream Eater exited the stalls really slowly and had no realistic chance from that point. (op 13-2)

1822 MBNA CHESTER VASE (GROUP 3) 1m 4f 66y
2:55 (2:55) (Class 1) 3-Y-O **£28,385** (£10,760; £5,385; £2,685; £1,345) **Stalls** Low

Form RPR

3- **1** **Treasure Beach**[222] 6347 3-8-12 105 .... RyanMoore 2 111+
(A P O'Brien, Ire) *lw: racd keenly: trckd ldrs: nt clr run over 1f out: rdn and qcknd to ld ins fnl f: r.o gamely whn pressed: a doing enough towards fin* **7/2**[3]

22-1 **2** *hd* **Nathaniel (IRE)**[19] 1389 3-8-12 91 .... WilliamBuick 5 110+
(John Gosden) *lw: chsd ldr: pushed along 3f out: rdn and chalng thrght fnl f: r.o but a looked hld towards fin* **6/4**[1]

0-1 **3** *3* **Slumber**[15] 1478 3-8-12 101 .... MichaelHills 3 105
(B W Hills) *lw: hld up: effrt wl over 1f out: nt qckn and hung lft ins fnl f: tk 3rd towards fin but nvr a match for front pair* **5/2**[2]

1-10 **4** *½* **Sadler's Risk (IRE)**[21] 1339 3-8-12 95 .... JoeFanning 4 104?
(Mark Johnston) *led: rdn and hdd ins fnl f: no ex fnl 50yds* **6/1**

04-0 **5** *4 ½* **Madawi**[21] 1339 3-8-12 93 .... PhilipRobinson 1 96
(Clive Brittain) *hld up: pushed along and outpcd over 2f out: sn lft bhd* **20/1**

2m 39.1s (0.60) **Going Correction** +0.05s/f (Good) 5 Ran SP% **109.8**
Speed ratings (Par 109): **104,103,101,101,98**
CSF £9.18 TOTE £4.10: £1.80, £1.30; EX 6.30.
Owner D Smith, Mrs J Magnier, M Tabor **Bred** Ashley House Stud **Trained** Ballydoyle, Co Tipperary

FOCUS
It's probably fair to say that this race hasn't really produced an obvious Derby contender for some time. 2009 winner Golden Sword was a respectable fifth to Sea The Stars when going off at odds of 25-1 for the Classic, Doctor Fremantle, an 11-2 shot, finished sixth to New Approach, while Soldier Of Fortune (14-1) was fifth to Authorized. Last year's winner Ted Spread was a disappointment at Epsom, even though he started a relatively unfancied 28-1 shot. This year's renewal didn't look to contain any obvious types for Epsom, but that is not to say there wasn't a potential Classic winner lurking. It looked a slightly below-standard edition, with the winner rated up 4lb on his 2yo form.

NOTEBOOK
Treasure Beach was kept fairly low key in the early part of his juvenile career, winning a Galway handicap on his third start off a mark of 84 before being beaten in another one at Listowel at short odds. He was allowed to take his chance against Frankel on his final outing at two, but like so many others, he was simply blown away. With a long break behind him, this was a decent performance after sitting behind the pace, and connections will no doubt be pleased to collect a Group 3 prize with him so early in the season. One would imagine that he isn't going to be as good as the likes of stablemates Seville and possibly Marksmanship, but he will no doubt feature in plenty of big races (he has lots of entries) and will hold his own. (tchd 4-1)
Nathaniel(IRE) was the lowest-rated of these on official figures, which was surprising considering he is the horse that has got closest in any race to the phenomenon that is Frankel. His juvenile form had all worked out fantastically and he didn't break sweat when winning on his 3-y-o comeback at the prohibitive odds of 1-20. A little warm here, he lacked the pace of the winner, but definitely confirmed he is a horse with a big future if continuing his progress. Chester didn't seem to play to his strengths, as he needed plenty of pressure to maintain his place towards the head of affairs, but he kept on and appeared to be gaining again on Treasure Beach in the final stages. Obviously Epsom will be a big temptation, although the trainer appeared to indicate later that Nathaniel would miss the Derby, but he looks every inch a potential St Leger winner so it might be better for the horse if he ran in the King Edward VII Stakes next en route to some staying events later on. John Gosden saddled the runner-up in the aforementioned race last year, Arctic Cosmos. (op 13-8 tchd 11-8 and 7-4 in a place)
Slumber finished down the field in a Newmarket maiden on his only start at two but really came to life when streaking away with the Derby Trial at Epsom from a 93-rated rival. This was another step up in class and he ran nicely without being quite good enough - he reportedly got on the wrong leg turning in and the runner-up came across him late on. He is still improving and can be given another chance at this level. (op 2-1tchd 11-4 in a place)
Sadler's Risk(IRE) made quite an impression when winning at Leicester but was a shade disappointing when tried in the valuable 3-y-o Trophy at Newmarket last time - form had received a boost with the run of Together in the 1,000 Guineas. He was quick to take control once it became clear his rivals didn't want to make the running, but found only the one pace when the race took shape down the home straight. (op 9-1)
Madawi didn't look an obvious candidate to win here despite going up in trip, and failed to make any impression. (op 18-1)

1823 IRISH STALLION FARMS E B F MAIDEN STKS — 5f 16y
3:30 (3:30) (Class 3) 2-Y-O **£7,771** (£2,312; £1,155; £577) **Stalls** Low

Form RPR

1 **Gabrial (IRE)** 2-9-3 0 .... PaulHanagan 6 82+
(Richard Fahey) *w'like: scope: lengthy: in tch: effrt to chal over 1f out: led ins fnl f: sn edgd lft: r.o wl and in command after* **5/2**[1]

3 **2** *2 ½* **Sea Odyssey (IRE)**[31] 1136 2-9-3 0 .... MichaelHills 10 72
(B W Hills) *lengthy: wnt lft and bmpd s: chsd ldrs: ev ch over 1f out: nt qckn ins fnl f: kpt on to take 2nd towards fin but no ch w wnr* **5/2**[1]

3 **3** *nk* **Lord Ali McJones**[9] 1583 2-9-3 0 .... RichardKingscote 2 71
(Tom Dascombe) *w'like: a.p: led over 2f out: rdn and hdd ins fnl f: one pce towards fin* **4/1**[2]

062 **4** *hd* **Courtland King (IRE)**[9] 1583 2-9-3 0 .... KierenFallon 12 70+
(David Evans) *pushed along and outpcd towards rr: hdwy on outer over 1f out: r.o ins fnl f: nrst fin* **11/1**[3]

5 *hd* **Nearly A Gift (IRE)** 2-8-12 0 .... DuranFentiman 1 64+
(Tim Easterby) *w'like: leggy: pushed along towards rr: hdwy 3f out: sn chsd ldrs: nt clr run and swtchd rt over 1f out: sn sltly outpcd by ldrs: styd on towards fin* **22/1**

6 *3* **Gin Twist** 2-8-12 0 .... RussKennemore 3 54
(Tom Dascombe) *w'like: midfield: plld off rail 2f out: one pce and no imp ins fnl f* **14/1**

7 *1* **Peters Pursuit (IRE)** 2-9-3 0 .... TonyHamilton 4 55+
(Richard Fahey) *w'like: dwlt: outpcd and bhd: kpt on ins fnl f: nvr gng pce to be competitive* **11/1**[3]

8 *3 ¼* **Ferdy (IRE)** 2-9-0 0 .... JamesSullivan(3) 5 43
(Paul Green) *w'like: missed break: a outpcd and bhd* **33/1**

9 *1 ¾* **Chester Aristocrat** 2-9-3 0 .... GrahamGibbons 9 37
(Eric Alston) *leggy: bmpd s: rn green: chsd ldrs: wknd wl over 1f out* **28/1**

0 **10** *1* **Stans Deelyte**[9] 1583 2-8-12 0 .... TomEaves 7 28
(Lisa Williamson) *led: hdd over 2f out: wknd ins fnl f: sn edgd rt whn wl btn* **150/1**

11 *10* **Gabrial's Girl (IRE)** 2-8-12 0 .... JamieSpencer 11 —
(Gay Kelleway) *leggy: stmbld s: towards rr: wl outpcd 3f out: wl bhd after* **25/1**

61.61 secs (0.61) **Going Correction** +0.05s/f (Good) 11 Ran SP% **115.7**
Speed ratings (Par 97): **97,93,92,92,91 87,85,80,77,75 59**
toteswingers:1&2: £2.00, 2&3: £3.00, 1&3: £2.90 CSF £7.75 TOTE £3.60: £1.30, £1.30, £2.00; EX 9.70 Trifecta £25.20 Pool: £1312.67 - 38.53 winning units..
Owner Dr Marwan Koukash **Bred** B Kennedy **Trained** Musley Bank, N Yorks

FOCUS
A few decent horses have taken this maiden down the years, but that last three winners have only won a single race between them since their victory here, and Metal Soldier, the 2009 victor, hasn't made the course since. One of the best previous winners of this was Dark Angel. Retired after his 2-y-o career, he had two runners in this race and they finished first and second. The form has been rated at the top end of the race averages and Gabrial should rate higher.

NOTEBOOK
Gabrial(IRE) ◆, who was well backed on this debut, was noticeably sweating (he is said to be an on-his-toes type at home) beforehand. He has lots of size about him and the further he went, the better he looked. His dam came into her own over 1m2f at three, and his sales price rise to £46,000 last year, so he had obviously been showing plenty. It would be a surprise if he wasn't capable of winning again this season, and a race at Beverley next was suggested. (op 11-4 tchd 3-1)
Sea Odyssey(IRE) showed plenty of speed on his debut at Windsor in a race that is working out, and came from a stable with a good record in this contest. Always to the fore, he at least ran as well as he had done on debut and gives the form a solid look. (op 3-1 tchd 7-2)
Lord Ali McJones ◆ rallied really well and ought to be winning something soon. (op 7-2 tched 9-2 in a place)
Courtland King(IRE) was the most experienced in the field and had finished in front of Lord Ali McJones and Stans Deelyte last time on Polytrack, but he was drawn wide here and failed to make any impression until the race was over. (tchd 10-1 and 12-1)
Nearly A Gift(IRE) ◆ looked to have the best of the draw on her first outing but couldn't make use of it after taking a while to get going. However, once this big sort had found her feet, she kept on in a most pleasing fashion and should continue to improve the longer the season goes on. (op 20-1)
Gin Twist, a £60,000 yearling with sprinters in her pedigree, looked the stable second-string on jockey bookings and didn't appear as big as some in the field. She would have finished closer had she not got stuck behind the weakening Chester Aristocrat at the wrong time. (tchd 12-1)
Peters Pursuit(IRE), the first foal of a maiden half-sister to Paco Boy, saw his sales price almost halve to 22,000gns when reoffered as a yearling, but this effort wasn't without promise, as he looked green early before staying on well. (op 14-1)
Ferdy(IRE) was another to look clueless early before the penny dropped late on. He should be much straighter for this. (tchd 28-1)

1824 TIMES+ H'CAP — 1m 2f 75y
4:05 (4:05) (Class 2) (0-105,96) 4-Y-0+ **£14,193** (£4,248; £2,124; £1,062; £528) **Stalls** High

Form RPR

350- **1** **Jutland**[222] 6355 4-9-1 90 .... JoeFanning 1 98+
(Mark Johnston) *lw: prom: pushed along over 2f out: r.o to ld ins fnl f: wl in command towards fin* **6/1**[3]

11-5 **2** *1 ¼* **Beachfire**[15] 1479 4-9-7 96 .... WilliamBuick 3 101+
(John Gosden) *s.i.s: hld up: pushed along and hdwy over 4f out: rdn to chal 4 wd over 2f out: kpt on to take 2nd towards fin: nt gng pce of wnr* **15/8**[1]

1026 **3** *1* **Kidlat**[5] 1671 6-8-9 84 .... RyanMoore 6 87
(Alan Bailey) *lw: led: pressed over 2f out: rdn over 1f out: hdd ins fnl f: kpt on same pce towards fin* **16/1**

0160 **4** *1* **Georgebernardshaw (IRE)**[15] 1479 6-8-12 87 .... JamieSpencer 2 88
(David Simcock) *in tch: u.p and outpcd 2f out: styd on towards fin: nt gng pce to trble ldrs* **9/1**

1521 **5** *shd* **Snow Dancer (IRE)**[8] 1622 7-8-7 85 6ex .... JamesSullivan(3) 8 86
(Hugh McWilliams) *lw: hld up: rdn and hdwy over 1f out: styd on ins fnl f: nt quite gng pce to get to ldrs* **7/1**

050- **6** *¾* **Classic Colori (IRE)**[203] 6877 4-9-3 92 .... RichardKingscote 7 91
(Tom Dascombe) *hld up: u.p over 1f out: kpt on ins fnl f: unable to chal* **14/1**

4-26 **7** *1* **Changing The Guard**[19] 1387 5-8-10 85 .... PaulHanagan 4 82
(Richard Fahey) *trckd ldrs: pushed along to chal 3 wd over 2f out: rdn over 1f out: fdd ins fnl f* **11/2**[2]

060- **8** *2* **Thin Red Line (IRE)**[180] 7350 5-9-1 90 .... TomEaves 5 83
(Michael Dods) *midfield: hdwy 6f out: sn prom: chalng 2 wd over 2f out: rdn over 1f out: wknd ins fnl f* **7/1**

2m 11.75s (0.55) **Going Correction** +0.05s/f (Good) 8 Ran SP% **112.0**
Speed ratings (Par 109): **103,102,101,100,100 99,98,97**
toteswingers:1&2: £3.20, 2&3: £7.70, 1&3: £12.50 CSF £16.93 CT £167.64 TOTE £8.10: £2.60, £1.10, £4.40; EX 20.50 Trifecta £277.80 Pool: £1655.75 - 4.41 winning units..
Owner Sheikh Hamdan Bin Mohammed Al Maktoum **Bred** Darley **Trained** Middleham Moor, N Yorks

FOCUS
Not an easy race to assess, as plenty of these had a minus or two to overcome to win. The winning time was the slowest of the three races run over this distance on the day.

NOTEBOOK
Jutland, absent since running really badly over C&D last September, didn't look obviously well treated, but he took this in good style after travelling strongly just off the speed. He has an entry at York on the 11th for another handicap, so one would imagine there is every chance he'll go there next. (op 7-1)
Beachfire didn't run too badly on his seasonal debut when tried in blinkers, but it was noticeable that they were removed for this run. Dropped 1lb since Epsom, he needed pushing along soon after exiting the stalls, but was soon on an even keel and ran up to his best after sweeping wide off the final bend. (op 9-4 tched 5-2 in a place)
Kidlat was interesting with Ryan Moore taking over from an inexperienced, albeit promising, apprentice, and the horse appeared to run his race.
Georgebernardshaw(IRE), who can lead, is tumbling down the ratings from a high of 110, but only ran a fair race in this. He is one to watch out for if returned to the course later in the year (considering his connections) off what is becoming a good mark. (op 11-1)
Snow Dancer(IRE), raised 6lb for beating a short-priced 3-y-o at Pontefract on her previous outing, sat in rear and kept on from that position up the home straight. (tchd 6-1)
Classic Colori(IRE) ◆ could easily be given a chance on his best form, but he had looked to have become a bit unpredictable in 2010, and backing him came with risks. Settled in rear, he got outpaced before keeping on, and he is worth a second look next time with this run under his belt. (op 12-1 tchd 16-1)
Changing The Guard had gone quite a few runs since his last success, and faded once his chance had gone. (op 5-1 tchd 6-1)
Thin Red Line(IRE) doesn't have the most impressive form figures, but that is not to say that he isn't a consistent horse. A winner over C&D on his seasonal debut last year, his first run for Michael Dods, who took this race in 2010 with Sweet Lightning, he moved with menace towards the head of affairs but found little once his jockey asked for maximum effort at the top of the home straight. (op 11-2 tchd 15-2)

1825 B&M RETAIL H'CAP — 6f 18y
4:35 (4:36) (Class 3) (0-90,89) 3-Y-O **£9,066** (£2,697; £1,348; £673) **Stalls** Low

Form RPR

50-2 **1** **Lexi's Hero (IRE)**[30] 1152 3-9-7 89 .... JamieSpencer 6 98+
(Kevin Ryan) *lw: mde all: kicked on over 1f out: r.o wl: in command ins fnl f* **4/1**[2]

2 *1 ¾* **Jamesie (IRE)**[27] 1227 3-8-12 80 .... CO'Donoghue 10 83
(David Marnane, Ire) *midfield: hdwy 2f out: styd on ins fnl f: tk 2nd towards fin: no imp on wnr* **16/1**

0-34 **3** *½* **Boundaries**[6] 1650 3-9-1 83 .... (v) TomEaves 9 84+
(Tim Easterby) *lw: hld up: hdwy over 3f out: lft in 2nd pl 2f out: rdn and outpcd by wnr over 1f out: styd on u.p ins fnl f: lost 2nd towards fin* **18/1**

5-21 **4** *3 ½* **Oneladyowner**[31] 1141 3-8-10 78 .... RyanMoore 3 79+
(David Brown) *lw: chsd ldrs: nt clr run and hmpd 2f out: lost grnd: prog ins fnl f: styd on towards fin* **6/1**[3]

23-3 **5** *½* **Crimson Knot (IRE)**[4] 1711 3-8-10 78 .... PatrickMathers 1 67
(Alan Berry) *midfield: rdn and hdwy over 1f out: styd on ins fnl f: one pce fnl 75yds* **10/1**

113- **6** *1 ¾* **Whipphound**[127] 8002 3-8-10 78 .... GrahamGibbons 8 61
(Mark Brisbourne) *n.m.r and hmpd s: pushed along towards rr: rdn and hdwy over 1f out: kpt on ins fnl f: one pce fnl 100yds: unable to get to ldrs* **33/1**

252- **7** *1 3/4* **No Poppy (IRE)**[180] 7347 3-8-12 **80** DuranFentiman 12 57
(Tim Easterby) *missed break: outpcd: kpt on ins fnl f: nt gng pce to get competitve* **25/1**

152- **8** *nk* **Robert The Painter (IRE)**[213] 6619 3-9-3 **85** PaulHanagan 4 61+
(Richard Fahey) *lw: midfield: sn pushed along: nt clr run on outer wl over 1f out: n.d after* **11/4**[1]

040- **9** *1 1/4* **Orchid Street (USA)**[208] 6745 3-8-9 **77** (p) MickyFenton 5 49
(Ann Duffield) *dwlt: towards rr: nvr able to get on terms* **40/1**

000- **10** *1/2* **Serena's Pride**[180] 7347 3-8-12 **80** JimmyFortune 2 51
(Alan Jarvis) *trckd ldrs: hmpd 2f out: sn lost pl: wknd ins fnl f* **11/1**

130- **11** *6* **Jack Smudge**[140] 7891 3-9-6 **88** PaulMulrennan 11 40+
(James Given) *prom: bdly hmpd 2f out and lost pl: n.d after and bhd ins fnl f* **20/1**

312- **12** *3 1/2* **Steps (IRE)**[126] 8020 3-8-12 **80** NeilCallan 7 20+
(Roger Varian) *lw: prom: ev ch whn stmbld 2f out: lost grnd and nt rcvr: eased ins fnl f* **9/1**

0-54 **13** *16* **Satin Love (USA)**[30] 1152 3-8-11 **79** (v[1]) KierenFallon 13 —
(Mark Johnston) *restless in stalls: completely missed break: a bhd: eased ins fnl f* **22/1**

1m 14.42s (0.62) **Going Correction** +0.05s/f (Good) 13 Ran SP% **117.9**
Speed ratings (Par 103): **97,94,94,89,88 86,84,83,81,81 73,68,47**
toteswingers:1&2: £18.40, 2&3: £46.20, 1&3: £19.20 CSF £60.00 CT £1041.74 TOTE £4.70: £2.10, £4.40, £5.30; EX 92.30 Trifecta £821.60 Part won. Pool of £1110.37 - 0.68 winning units..

Owner Dr Marwan Koukash **Bred** T J Pabst **Trained** Hambleton, N Yorks

FOCUS
A really competitive handicap for 3-y-o sprinters, in which the pace looked sound, but something of a messy race. There may still be more to come from the winner.

NOTEBOOK
Lexi's Hero(IRE), up 3lb for a good return effort at Pontefract, had previous course experience and made full use of a decent draw. Jamie Spencer made sure the gallop was strong and he kept just enough in hand to hold on. The Reg Griffin Memorial Trophy on the June 12 is being targeted. (op 10-3 tchd 9-2)
Jamesie(IRE) warmed up for this with a run at Dundalk in a race that had produced a couple of winners already. He kept on nicely inside the final furlong, catching Lexi's Hero with every stride. (tchd 14-1)
Boundaries had run well in a couple of 5f contests this season and was defending a 1-1 record at this course. Not the best away, he made good ground to get involved before halfway and clearly loves it around the turns of Chester. (op 20-1 tchd 22-1)
Oneladyowner is related to some good horses and had already proved himself quite capable with two wins from four starts. Up 5lb for his success last time, he was going nicely chasing the leaders when he became one of a few hampered by Steps, who lost his footing on the final bend. The David Brown-trained horse can easily be given another chance. (op 7-1 tchd 5-1)
Crimson Knot(IRE) doesn't know how to run badly but didn't take full advantage of her stall 1 position, although she would probably have gone too fast had she taken on Lexi's Hero. (op 11-1)
Whipphound, a dual winner at Wolverhampton, made good late ground and should find races on turf. (op 50-1)
Robert The Painter(IRE) finished a place behind Jack Smudge on his final start at two, but wasn't exposed and looked capable of finding more improvement. A nice, big sort, he met trouble in running when attempting to make ground and is better than his final position suggests. (op 7-2)
Serena's Pride was one of the chief sufferers when Steps lost his footing. Official explanation: jockey said filly suffered interference in running (op 14-1)
Jack Smudge Official explanation: jockey said colt suffered interference in running
Steps(IRE) Official explanation: jockey said colt slipped on final bend

1826 INVESTEC STRUCTURED PRODUCTS H'CAP 1m 2f 75y
5:10 (5:11) (Class 3) (0-90,89) 4-Y-0+ **£9,066** (£2,697; £1,348; £673) **Stalls** High

Form RPR

-03 **1** **Granny McPhee**[83] 515 5-8-11 **79** LiamJones 8 86
(Alan Bailey) *hld up in midfield: rdn and hdwy to chse ldrs over 1f out: r.o ins fnl f: led fnl stride in driving fin* **12/1**

1-60 **2** *shd* **Tres Coronas (IRE)**[12] 1517 4-9-1 **83** GrahamGibbons 3 90
(David Barron) *hld up: hdwy over 3f out: rdn over 1f out: hung lft ins fnl f: r.o and jst lost out in driving fin* **8/1**[2]

42-0 **3** *nk* **Bahamian Music (IRE)**[21] 1325 4-8-12 **80** PaulHanagan 10 86
(Richard Fahey) *lw: trckd ldr: rdn to chal over 1f out: led narrowly ins fnl f: hdd fnl stride* **14/1**

100- **4** *1 1/4* **Inspirina (IRE)**[199] 6990 7-8-12 **80** TonyHamilton 4 84
(Richard Ford) *led: rdn over 1f out: hdd narrowly ins fnl f: no ex fnl strides* **20/1**

20-3 **5** *3* **One Scoop Or Two**[19] 1390 5-8-10 **78** RussKennemore 13 76
(Reg Hollinshead) *trckd ldrs: rdn over 1f out: one pce ins fnl f* **16/1**

/0-2 **6** *3/4* **Nibani (IRE)**[24] 1271 4-9-0 **82** RyanMoore 1 78+
(Sir Michael Stoute) *lw: bustled along early: midfield: looked ill at ease on trck: one pce and no imp fnl f* **11/10**[1]

-255 **7** *nk* **Norman Orpen (IRE)**[33] 1092 4-9-0 **89** LewisWalsh(7) 9 84
(Jane Chapple-Hyam) *s.i.s: hmpd sn after s: rdn over 1f out: kpt on ins fnl f: no imp on ldrs* **10/1**[3]

000- **8** *2* **Marjury Daw (IRE)**[148] 7756 5-9-3 **85** PaulMulrennan 11 76
(James Given) *hld up: pushed along over 2f out: nvr able to get on terms* **40/1**

0-00 **9** *1* **Speed Dating**[19] 1387 5-9-2 **84** (b) JamieSpencer 14 73
(John Quinn) *hld up in rr: pushed along over 2f out: nvr able to get on terms* **16/1**

03/1 **10** *9* **Ivory Jazz**[29] 1172 4-9-5 **87** JohnEgan 2 58
(Richard Guest) *prom: rdn over 2f out: sn wknd* **14/1**

-411 **11** *40* **Strong Vigilance (IRE)**[35] 1066 4-8-7 **75** WilliamBuick 6 —
(Michael Bell) *midfield tl wknd over 3f out: t.o* **10/1**[3]

2m 11.25s (0.05) **Going Correction** +0.05s/f (Good) 11 Ran SP% **116.9**
Speed ratings (Par 107): **105,104,104,103,101 100,100,98,98,90 58**
toteswingers:1&2: £25.40, 2&3: £16.90, 1&3: £25.40 CSF £104.00 CT £1367.21 TOTE £13.50: £2.80, £2.40, £4.40; EX 119.30 Trifecta £897.70 Part won. Pool of £1213.17 - 0.40 winning units..

Owner Middleham Park Racing XXVI & Alan Bailey **Bred** Sugar Puss Corporation **Trained** Newmarket, Suffolk

FOCUS
A solid-looking handicap, with established handicappers taking on a well-fancied, unexposed horse from a big stable. The pace looked uneven, which probably helped produce a tight finish. Sound form, with the winner and third basically to their best.

NOTEBOOK
Granny McPhee has a good record at this course and enhanced that further with a narrow success. Towards the rear early, travelling keenly, she showed plenty of guts to hang on as three horses came close together in the final strides. She was declared to run again the following day. (op 14-1)
Tres Coronas(IRE), unsuccessfully tried over 1m6f last time, came with a strong, late burst to almost thread a winning surge between horses. His jockey needed to get out quickly with about 2f to go from an inside sit, and the combination were a little unlucky not to win considering margin of defeat. (tchd 9-1)
Bahamian Music(IRE) hit the front late on and looked the likely winner, but she wasn't able to hold the late thrust of the first two home. (op 16-1)
Inspirina(IRE), having his first run since October, has a fairly good record at Chester and ran a blinder until steadily worn down inside the final furlong.
One Scoop Or Two caught the eye on his return to the track this season at Haydock, and didn't run too badly here despite being well held. (op 14-1)
Nibani(IRE) was of obvious interest on his handicap debut for such powerful connections, especially with the best of the draw. Once with Dante, Derby and Irish Derby entries, he was pushed along on leaving the stalls and Ryan Moore never happy, indeed the horse never looked like winning. He might be better than this (the tight track may not have suited) and can be given another chance, as his stable don't seem to be firing on all cylinders at the moment. (op 6-4 tchd Evens)
Ivory Jazz caused a bit of a shock when winning a claimer for Dean Ivory on his previous start after a 624-day absence. Claimed by Richard Guest after that win for £6,000, the horse was going keenly close up when slipping rounding the bend with a circuit to go. That incident didn't lose him much ground but wouldn't have helped either. Official explanation: jockey said gelding slipped on viaduct bend (op 11-1)
Strong Vigilance(IRE) was chasing a hat-trick after two wins at Wolverhampton in the February and March, but never looked like claiming that third victory and was eased. (op 8-1)
T/Jkpt: £7983.10 to a £1 stake. Pool of £11117.10 - 0.50 winning units. T/Plt: £9.40 to a £1 stake. Pool of £122,995.53 - 9,468.24 winning tickets. T/Qpdt: £6.40 to a £1 stake. Pool of £4,863.88 - 558.30 winning tickets. DO

FFOS LAS (L-H)
Thursday, May 5

OFFICIAL GOING: Good to firm (8.6)
Wind: Light half-behind Weather: Rain clearing after the first race

1827 EUROPEAN BREEDERS' FUND MAIDEN STKS 5f
4:55 (4:59) (Class 5) 2-Y-O **£3,238** (£963; £481; £240) **Stalls** High

Form RPR

4 **1** **Mr Majeika (IRE)**[12] 1515 2-9-3 0 PatDobbs 5 77
(Richard Hannon) *chsd ldrs: rdn 3f out: hung lft 1/2-way: styd on to ld nr fin* **5/2**[2]

0 **2** *1/2* **Meloneras**[20] 1360 2-8-12 0 JamesMillman 6 70
(Rod Millman) *chsd ldr: rdn and hung lft over 1f out: lft in ld ins fnl f: hdd nr fin* **12/1**

3 *7* **Es Que Love (IRE)** 2-9-3 0 RoystonFfrench 4 70+
(Mark Johnston) *sn led: hung lft fr over 1f out: swvd lft ins fnl f: sn hdd and nt rcvr* **8/11**[1]

0 **4** *3* **Abercandy (IRE)**[23] 1290 2-8-12 0 CathyGannon 1 34
(David Evans) *sn outpcd* **33/1**

3 **5** *hd* **Bluebells Are Blue (IRE)**[12] 1522 2-9-3 0 FergusSweeney 2 38
(Eve Johnson Houghton) *sn outpcd* **7/1**[3]

6 *3 1/4* **Captain Baldwin** 2-9-3 0 MartinLane 3 26
(David Evans) *sn outpcd* **25/1**

7 *56* **Bajan Hero** 2-9-3 0 JamesDoyle 7 —
(David Evans) *s.s: bucked and kicked on leaving stalls: sn t.o* **25/1**

57.06 secs (-1.24) **Going Correction** -0.30s/f (Firm) 7 Ran SP% **117.3**
Speed ratings (Par 93): **90,89,78,73,72 67,—**
Tote Swingers: 1&2 £4.50, 1&3 £1.20, 2&3 £3.10 CSF £30.58 TOTE £3.40: £2.50, £10.90; EX 28.20.

Owner Dougie McKay **Bred** Barouche Stud (ire) Ltd **Trained** East Everleigh, Wilts

FOCUS
There was some rain in the afternoon ahead of the meeting but the times were still on the quick side with course records falling all evening. Little strength in depth to this maiden in all probability, and not an easy event to rate, but a race full of incident all the same. The third can rate higher.

NOTEBOOK
Mr Majeika(IRE) had shown only a modest level of form at Musselburgh first time up but almost certainly left that behind as runners from this yard tend to do, though he was something of a fortunate winner in that the eventual third clearly had his measure when throwing the race away when swerving badly left, and it took all the trip to master the second (who was well beaten on her debut). He'll be suited by 6f but doesn't look up to winning another a minor event any time soon. (tchd 9-4 and 11-4)
Meloneras left her Newbury debut form behind with an always-prominent display against the rail, looking the likely winner once left in front but just unable to hang on. Being out of a German 1m2f winner, she's bred to get further in time. (op 14-1)
Es Que Love(IRE), a colt by Clodovil out of a mare that won at around 1m in France, looked all set to make a winning debut when hanging violently left and ending up on the far rail, and was eased when beaten. He'd been on his toes beforehand, so clearly has a quirk or two, but for a long way the money that came for him didn't look misplaced and he's good enough to gain consolation if keeping straight next time. Official explanation: jockey said saddle slipped (op 10-11, tchd Evens in places)
Abercandy(IRE) was soon outpaced and never a threat (op 40-1 tchd 28-1)
Bluebells Are Blue(IRE) might have been expected to have stepped up on his Nottingham debut but showed none of the dash he displayed there. (op 15-2)
Bajan Hero appeared to have a major problem with his tack on leaving the stalls and virtually took no part as he hung badly left from the stalls.

1828 GLYN ABBEY CLAIMING STKS 1m (R)
5:25 (5:25) (Class 6) 3-Y-O+ **£2,047** (£604; £302) **Stalls** Low

Form RPR

0020 **1** **Avon River**[3] 1760 4-9-10 85 (b) PatDobbs 3 73
(Richard Hannon) *led 7f out: rdn over 1f out: r.o* **4/1**[3]

5401 **2** *1/2* **Fremen (USA)**[8] 1614 11-9-6 77 AdrianNicholls 6 68
(David Nicholls) *hmpd sn after s: chsd ldrs: nt clr run over 2f out: rdn over 1f out: r.o* **11/4**[2]

0-00 **3** *1 1/4* **Camerooney**[19] 1410 8-9-7 88 DaleSwift(5) 8 71
(Brian Ellison) *led 1f: chsd wnr: rdn over 3f out: hung lft over 2f out: styd on same pce ins fnl f* **7/4**[1]

00-2 **4** *1/2* **Uphold**[24] 1278 4-9-7 88 (b) SophieDoyle(3) 9 68
(Jamie Osborne) *swtchd lft sn after s: prom: rdn over 3f out: hung lft fnl 2f: styd on* **11/2**

213 **5** *2* **So Is She (IRE)**[63] 739 3-7-12 66 (p) AmyBaker(3) 1 51
(Alan Bailey) *hmpd sn after s: hld up: rdn over 2f out: styd on fr over 1f out: nvr trbld ldrs* **14/1**

05-5 **6** *2* **Mister Fantastic**[16] 1454 5-9-4 47 JamesDoyle 4 53
(Dai Burchell) *hmpd sn after s: hld up: pushed along 1/2-way: nvr on terms* **66/1**

The Form Book, Raceform Ltd, Compton, RG20 6NL

3330 **7** *5* **Better Self**[12] 1526 3-8-0 62................................ CathyGannon 7 34
(David Evans) *hld up: rdn over 3f out: n.d* **18/1**

60-0 **8** *15* **Charlie Delta**[4] 1730 8-9-5 57.................................(v) WilliamCarson 5 —
(John O'Shea) *s.i.s: a in rr: rdn over 3f out: sn lost tch* **66/1**

1m 37.29s (-3.71) **Going Correction** -0.30s/f (Firm)
WFA 3 from 4yo+ 13lb 8 Ran SP% **113.3**
Speed ratings (Par 101): **104,103,102,101,99 97,92,77**
Tote Swingers: 1&2 £2.50, 1&3 £3.40, 2&3 £2.80 CSF £15.14 TOTE £4.60: £3.10, £1.10, £1.60; EX 18.60.
Owner Jim Horgan **Bred** Poulton Stud **Trained** East Everleigh, Wilts

FOCUS
An uncompetitive claimer run at a no more than a fair gallop. It was a reasonable race of its type on the figures but the form has been rated fairly negatively.

1829 TANNERS CHAMPAGNE H'CAP 1m 2f (R)
6:00 (6:00) (Class 4) (0-80,80) 4-Y-O+ **£4,144** (£1,233; £616; £307) **Stalls** Low

Form RPR

0403 **1** **Pelham Crescent (IRE)**[55] 835 8-8-12 74.............. DeclanCannon(3) 7 82
(Bryn Palling) *s.i.s and hmpd s: hld up: hdwy over 1f out: r.o u.p to ld wl ins fnl f* **9/1**

144- **2** *3/4* **Shabak Hom (IRE)**[268] 4923 4-8-12 71.............................. MartinLane 8 78
(David Simcock) *hld up: plld hrd: hdwy over 2f out: led wl over 1f out: rdn and hdd wl ins fnl f* **15/2**

10-6 **3** *nk* **Grams And Ounces**[19] 1390 4-9-2 75........................ CathyGannon 2 81
(Amy Weaver) *a.p: rdn and ev ch over 1f out: styd on same pce wl ins fnl f* **5/1**[2]

22-0 **4** *4 1/2* **Rock The Stars (IRE)**[19] 1402 4-8-11 70 ow1................. SebSanders 3 67
(J W Hills) *chsd ldrs: rdn over 2f out: wknd ins fnl f* **5/2**[1]

5440 **5** *1 1/4* **Hawaana (IRE)**[15] 1477 6-9-2 80............................ AdamBeschizza(5) 9 74
(Gay Kelleway) *s.i.s: hld up: rdn over 2f out: styd on ins fnl f: nvr nrr* **11/2**[3]

1620 **6** *1* **Pertuis (IRE)**[19] 1402 5-9-0 73.............................. JamesDoyle 1 65
(Harry Dunlop) *prom: chsd ldr 1/2-way: led over 2f out: rdn and hdd wl over 1f out: wknd ins fnl f* **11/2**[3]

2-24 **7** *1/2* **Resplendent Light**[36] 1046 6-8-12 71....................(tp) RoystonFfrench 6 62
(Bernard Llewellyn) *chsd ldr to 1/2-way: sn pushed along: rdn 3f out: sn hung lft: wknd over 1f out* **10/1**

00-0 **8** *6* **Aspectus (IRE)**[24] 1269 8-9-4 80............................... SophieDoyle(3) 4 59
(Jamie Osborne) *led over 7f: wknd over 1f out* **14/1**

30-0 **9** *2 1/4* **Mr Udagawa**[12] 1530 5-8-2 66 oh4................................ LauraPike(5) 5 41
(Bernard Llewellyn) *s.i.s: a in rr: wknd 2f out* **25/1**

2m 4.85s (-4.55) **Going Correction** -0.30s/f (Firm) 9 Ran SP% **117.4**
Speed ratings (Par 105): **102,101,101,97,96 95,95,90,88**
Tote Swingers: 1&2 £11.00, 1&3 £19.40, 2&3 £14.40 CSF £75.61 CT £379.47 TOTE £16.70: £4.50, £4.60, £2.70; EX 50.20.
Owner Wayne Devine **Bred** Cathal M Ryan **Trained** Tredodridge, Vale Of Glamorgan

FOCUS
An ordinary handicap in which despite the early pace seeming only steady the first two still managed to come from the back. The winner is rated to last year's best.

1830 TANNERS CLARET H'CAP 6f
6:30 (6:30) (Class 5) (0-75,75) 3-Y-O **£2,331** (£693; £346; £173) **Stalls** High

Form RPR

-232 **1** **Shostakovich (IRE)**[20] 1359 3-9-3 71.........................(tp) JamesDoyle 5 73
(Sylvester Kirk) *mde all: rdn over 1f out: jst hld on* **2/1**[1]

5-15 **2** *hd* **Ceffyl Gwell**[33] 1106 3-9-7 75.. PatDobbs 2 76
(Richard Hannon) *chsd ldrs: nt clr run over 2f out: rdn to chse wnr fnl f: edgd lft: r.o* **5/2**[3]

0-42 **3** *5* **Cristaliyev**[31] 1131 3-8-8 62.. FergusSweeney 1 47
(Jim Boyle) *w wnr tl rdn and edgd lft over 1f out: no ex ins fnl f* **4/1**

40-3 **4** *31* **Bajan Bear**[19] 1400 3-8-13 67... WilliamCarson 3 —
(Michael Blanshard) *hld up in tch: pushed along over 3f out: cl 4th whn bdly hmpd over 2f out: nt rcvr* **9/4**[2]

68.12 secs (-1.88) **Going Correction** -0.30s/f (Firm) 4 Ran SP% **112.7**
Speed ratings (Par 99): **98,97,91,49**
CSF £7.53 TOTE £3.90; EX 7.30.
Owner F J Stephens **Bred** Marchwood Aggregates **Trained** Upper Lambourn, Berks
■ Stewards' Enquiry : Pat Dobbs seven-day ban: careless riding (May 19-21,23-26)

FOCUS
An uncompetitive affair rendered made even more so when one of the runners was impeded badly and crashed into the rails. Only the first pair showed their form.

1831 TANNERS BURGUNDY FILLIES' H'CAP 6f
7:05 (7:05) (Class 5) (0-75,75) 4-Y-O+ **£2,331** (£693; £346; £173) **Stalls** High

Form RPR

00-1 **1** **The Jailer**[7] 1638 8-8-4 63 6ex.....................................(p) RyanPowell(5) 4 67
(John O'Shea) *mde all: rdn over 1f out: styd on* **11/2**[3]

66-4 **2** *1 1/4* **Suzy Alexander**[21] 1330 4-8-3 62.................................... LauraPike(5) 1 62
(David Simcock) *s.i.s: hdwy 1/2-way: rdn to chse wnr over 1f out: edgd rt: styd on* **5/1**[2]

23-0 **3** *1/2* **Supreme Spirit (IRE)**[19] 1411 4-9-7 75......................... AdrianNicholls 3 73
(David Nicholls) *s.i.s: rcvrd to chse wnr 5f out: rdn over 1f out: styd on* **8/15**[1]

0600 **4** *hd* **Chinese Democracy (USA)**[62] 763 4-8-3 57............ CathyGannon 5 55
(Dai Burchell) *hld up in tch: rdn over 1f out: styd on: nt pce to chal* **14/1**

0-02 **5** *8* **Talamahana**[7] 1630 6-7-13 56 oh3...................................(v) AmyBaker(3) 2 28
(Andrew Haynes) *chsd ldrs: rdn over 3f out: wknd 2f out* **16/1**

67.80 secs (-2.20) **Going Correction** -0.30s/f (Firm) 5 Ran SP% **109.8**
Speed ratings (Par 100): **100,98,97,97,86**
CSF £30.68 TOTE £11.20: £2.40, £1.10; EX 25.50.
Owner Pete Smith Car Sales **Bred** D R Tucker **Trained** Elton, Gloucs

FOCUS
Quite a weak affair with the favourite disappointing and the winner made all against the rail.

1832 TANNERS WINES H'CAP 1m (R)
7:40 (7:40) (Class 4) (0-85,85) 4-Y-O+ **£4,144** (£1,233; £616; £307) **Stalls** Low

Form RPR

-153 **1** **Zebrano**[19] 1410 5-9-0 78..(b) JamesDoyle 3 88+
(Andrew Haynes) *hld up: pushed along and swtchd rt over 2f out: sn rdn: r.o to ld wl ins fnl f: readily* **2/1**[1]

136- **2** *1* **Tariq Too**[200] 6963 4-8-11 75... MartinLane 5 82+
(David Simcock) *s.i.s: hld up: hdwy over 2f out: rdn to ld wl ins fnl f: sn hdd and unable qck* **4/1**[3]

00-4 **3** *2* **Guilded Warrior**[31] 1138 8-9-7 85.............................. FergusSweeney 6 87
(Stuart Kittow) *led: rdn over 1f out: hdd wl ins fnl f* **6/1**

3021 **4** *nk* **Tewin Wood**[10] 1569 4-8-12 79 6ex................................... AmyBaker(3) 1 81
(Alan Bailey) *chsd ldr: rdn over 2f out: ev ch ins fnl f: styd on same pce* **9/1**

-132 **5** *3/4* **Yes Chef**[31] 1138 4-8-9 73.. JamesMillman 8 73
(Rod Millman) *hld up in tch: rdn over 1f out: hung lft: styd on same pce ins fnl f* **3/1**[2]

05-4 **6** *1 1/4* **Beaver Patrol (IRE)**[12] 1530 9-8-13 77.......................(v) CathyGannon 4 74
(Eve Johnson Houghton) *trckd ldrs: racd keenly: rdn and hung lft over 2f out: no ex fnl f* **8/1**

1m 37.12s (-3.88) **Going Correction** -0.30s/f (Firm) 6 Ran SP% **113.7**
Speed ratings (Par 105): **104,103,101,100,99 98**
Tote Swingers: 1&2 £1.30, 1&3 £2.20, 2&3 £3.20 CSF £10.55 CT £39.41 TOTE £3.60: £1.70, £3.40; EX 10.20.
Owner Caloona Racing **Bred** P R Attwater **Trained** Limpley Stoke, Bath

FOCUS
A fairly useful handicap run at a decent clip with the complexion of the race changing well inside the last as the course record set earlier by Avon River tumbled. The fourth sets the standard and the first pair are capable of better.

1833 THREE CLIFFS CLOTHING H'CAP 1m 6f (R)
8:10 (8:11) (Class 6) (0-60,60) 4-Y-O+ **£2,047** (£604; £302) **Stalls** Low

Form RPR

5-33 **1** **Annelko**[7] 1631 4-8-8 48.. MartinLane 4 58
(Andrew Haynes) *mde all: rdn over 1f out: styd on gamely: edgd lft nr fin* **4/1**[2]

000/ **2** *2 3/4* **Bocciani (GER)**[9] 6248 6-8-11 55................................. DaleSwift(5) 8 61
(Brian Ellison) *a.p: chsd wnr over 4f out: rdn over 2f out: styd on same pce fr over 1f out* **8/13**[1]

00-0 **3** *1 1/4* **Court Princess**[16] 1473 8-8-10 49.............................. JamesDoyle 3 53
(Richard Price) *hld up: hdwy over 3f out: rdn over 1f out: styd on same pce* **25/1**

14-0 **4** *8* **Mustajed**[32] 1107 10-9-7 60.. JamesMillman 7 53
(Rod Millman) *hld up: rdn over 3f out: mod late prog: nvr on terms* **7/1**[3]

0600 **5** *5* **Jiggalong**[7] 1625 5-8-4 46 oh1.................................. SophieDoyle(3) 1 32
(Mrs D Thomas) *trckd ldrs: racd keenly: n.m.r over 4f out: rdn over 2f out: wknd over 1f out* **33/1**

3260 **6** *26* **King Kieren (IRE)**[9] 1582 6-9-4 60.......................... AshleyHamblett(3) 6 10
(Linda Jewell) *hld up: pushed along 6f out: wknd 3f out: t.o* **10/1**

2-04 **7** *22* **Olivino (GER)**[84] 419 10-8-7 46 oh1.......................(p) RoystonFfrench 5 —
(Bernard Llewellyn) *chsd wnr tl rdn 5f out: wknd 3f out: t.o* **16/1**

3m 0.93s (-2.87) **Going Correction** -0.30s/f (Firm)
WFA 4 from 5yo+ 1lb 7 Ran SP% **116.2**
Speed ratings (Par 101): **96,94,93,89,86 71,58**
Tote Swingers: 1&2 £1.30, 1&3 £18.40, 2&3 £8.70 CSF £7.03 CT £51.27 TOTE £6.80: £3.70, £1.20; EX 9.60.
Owner David Prosser **Bred** Paul Wyatt Ranby Hall **Trained** Limpley Stoke, Bath

FOCUS
A modest finale run at a reasonable gallop overall, but the winner looks one that might progress kept to staying trips. The form is rated around him but may not hold up.
Jiggalong Official explanation: jockey said mare hung right
King Kieren(IRE) Official explanation: jockey said gelding never travelled
Olivino(GER) Official explanation: vet said gelding lost a hind shoe
T/Plt: £107.50 to a £1 stake. Pool of £35,400.07 - 240.18 winning tickets. T/Qpdt: £31.50 to a £1 stake. Pool of £4,172.60 - 97.80 winning tickets. CR

1677 GOODWOOD (R-H)
Thursday, May 5

OFFICIAL GOING: Good to firm (8.8)
First 2f of 1m course dolled out 6yds increasing distances on that course by 12yds.
Wind: light, across Weather: dry, overcast, but sun trying to break through

1834 32RED STKS (H'CAP) 1m 1f
2:05 (2:07) (Class 3) (0-90,89) 3-Y-O+ **£6,799** (£2,023; £1,011; £505) **Stalls** Low

Form RPR

336- **1** **Jehanbux (USA)**[217] 6505 3-8-11 86........................... RichardHughes 4 95+
(Richard Hannon) *t.k.h: chsd clr ldr: rdn and effrt ent fnl 2f: hdwy jst over 1f out: rdn hands and heels and r.o wl to ld ins fnl f: wl in command towards fin* **11/4**[1]

100- **2** *1 1/4* **Constant Contact**[301] 3824 4-10-0 89............................. DavidProbert 6 95
(Andrew Balding) *broke wl: led at stdy gallop and allowed to go clr: rdn wl over 1f out: hdd ins fnl f: sn outpcd by wnr: kpt on* **4/1**[2]

556- **3** *1 1/2* **Moynahan (USA)**[223] 6318 6-9-13 88............................ ChrisCatlin 2 91
(Paul Cole) *t.k.h: hld up in midfield: effrt and rdn to chse ldng pair 2f out: outpcd over 1f out: kpt on again ins fnl f: nt gng pce to threaten ldng pair* **4/1**[2]

3-42 **4** *4 1/2* **Potentiale (IRE)**[16] 1450 7-8-11 75 oh1.....................(p) PatrickHills(3) 5 68
(J W Hills) *stdd s: hld up and unable qck over 3f out: drvn and outpcd 2f out: 4th and wl hld ins fnl f* **13/2**[3]

430- **5** *nk* **First Cat**[187] 7233 4-9-2 82.. KieranO'Neill(5) 8 74
(Richard Hannon) *stdd s: t.k.h: hld up in rr: effrt and rdn over 2f out: edging rt and no imp ent fnl f: pressing for 4th but wl hld ins fnl f* **13/2**[3]

00-0 **6** *3 3/4* **Kavachi (IRE)**[19] 1382 8-9-4 79.................................... GeorgeBaker 3 63
(Gary Moore) *stdd after s: hld up in last pair: travelling wl but nt clr run on inner 3f out: swtchd lft and stl nt clr run over 2f out tl wl over 1f out: rdn and fnd little over 1f out: no ch ins fnl f* **12/1**

0-06 **7** *1 1/2* **Mujood**[10] 1564 8-9-9 87...(v) JohnFahy(3) 1 68
(Eve Johnson Houghton) *reluctant to s and led down fnl 5f: s.i.s: a towards rr: rdn over 4f out: hrd drvn and no rspnse 3f out: wl btn fnl 2f* **9/1**

1m 56.52s (0.22) **Going Correction** +0.025s/f (Good)
WFA 3 from 4yo+ 14lb 7 Ran SP% **111.0**
Speed ratings (Par 107): **100,98,97,93,93 89,88**
toteswingers:1&2 £3.00, 2&3 £3.70, 1&3: £2.90 CSF £12.96 CT £40.22 TOTE £2.80: £1.60, £2.40; EX 13.90 Trifecta £61.50 Pool: £475.80 - 5.68 winning units..
Owner K N Dhunjibhoy, V B Shirke, B M Desai **Bred** Brereton C Jones **Trained** East Everleigh, Wilts

FOCUS
The first 2f of the 1m course were dolled out six yards. Following this race, winning rider Richard Hughes described the ground as firm on the round course. The early pace was just steady and it paid to race prominently with the front pair always 1-2. The winner didn't need to improve much.

NOTEBOOK

Jehanbux(USA) stalked the leader throughout and won with a bit in hand under a confident ride. He was the only 3-y-o in the field, but showed he has trained on well and also proved he didn't need headgear (wore blinkers when last seen) on this first run for 217 days. Things are going to get tougher and he won't always get such a kind trip, but he's smartly bred and has evidently progressed into a very useful type. He's expected to stay 1m2f. (op 9-4)

Constant Contact, who's now a gelding, couldn't make the most of a particularly soft lead, but has been off since last July. (op 11-2)

Moynahan(USA) raced enthusiastically off the pace and was always held by the front in the closing stages, although he kept on reasonably well on his first start for 223 days. He usually needs his first run back. (op 5-1 tchd 11-2)

Potentiale(IRE) had a race-fitness advantage over the front three, but this company was a bit hot for him. (op 11-2)

First Cat, who looked the stable second string on his first start for 187 days, raced well off the modest pace after a sluggish start and carried his head to one side as usual. (op 6-1)

1835 EBF GOODWOOD MAIDEN STKS 6f

2:40 (2:41) (Class 5) 2-Y-O **£2,914** (£867; £433; £216) **Stalls** High

Form				RPR
	1		**Crown Dependency (IRE)** 2-9-3 0 ... RichardHughes 3 (Richard Hannon) *pushed along briefly leaving stalls: hld up in tch: swtchd rt and jnd ldrs on bit wl over 1f out: shkn up to ld jst over 1f out: rdn and qcknd clr fnl 75yds: eased towards fin* **4/1**[3]	85+
4	2	2 1/4	**Ewell Place (IRE)**[8] 1598 2-9-3 0 ... EddieAhern 7 (Robert Mills) *t.k.h: chsd ldrs: rdn and ev ch over 1f out tl unable qck w wnr and brushed aside fnl 75yds* **3/1**[1]	76
	3	2	**Airborne Again (IRE)** 2-9-3 0 ... DaneO'Neill 8 (Richard Hannon) *pressed ldr: rdn and ev ch over 1f out: outpcd by ldng pair and btn ent fnl f: kpt on same pce after* **10/1**	71+
6	4	3/4	**Drummoyne (USA)**[12] 1515 2-9-3 0 ... GregFairley 4 (Mark Johnston) *led: rdn 2f out: hdd jst over 1f out: outpcd and btn ent fnl f: kpt on same pce after* **7/2**[2]	68
0	5	1	**Arabian Falcon**[20] 1360 2-9-3 0 ... MartinDwyer 2 (Brian Meehan) *s.i.s: pushed along and outpcd in last pair: sme hdwy and switching rt over 1f out: styd on ins fnl f but nvr gng pce to trble ldrs* **7/2**[2]	66+
	6	8	**Dovils Date** 2-9-3 0 ... TomMcLaughlin 1 (Rod Millman) *sn chsng ldrs on outer: pushed along after 2f out: wknd ent fnl 2f: wl bhd ins fnl f* **40/1**	41
	7	hd	**Blank Czech (IRE)** 2-9-3 0 ... JimCrowley 5 (Amanda Perrett) *v.s.a: a outpcd in rr* **8/1**	40
	8	2	**Fresteem** 2-9-3 0 ... PatCosgrave 6 (Luke Dace) *chsd ldrs tl jst over 2f out: sn wknd: wl bhd ins fnl f* **66/1**	34

1m 12.5s (0.30) **Going Correction** +0.025s/f (Good) **8** Ran SP% **113.6**

Speed ratings (Par 93): **99,96,93,92,91 80,80,77**

toteswingers:1&2: £2.80, 2&3: £5.40, 1&3 £5.40 CSF £16.20 TOTE £5.70: £1.70, £2.00, £5.00; EX 18.30.

Owner Coriolan Links Partnership Iii **Bred** Top Row Partnership **Trained** East Everleigh, Wilts

FOCUS

The first 6f 2-y-o race in Britain this year. The winner impressed but the depth of the race is hard to quantify yet.

NOTEBOOK

Crown Dependency(IRE) ◆ is a £65,000 February foal. He was relatively weak in the market, perhaps owing to the stable having suffered a few reversals with their juveniles in recent weeks, but under a patient ride he absolutely tanked along throughout. He has apparently been a bit keen at home, hence the waiting tactics, and Richard Hughes had to take a pull on a number of occasions. Such was the horse's enthusiasm there was a question mark over what he would find when asked, but once let go he didn't require serious pressure to readily see off the well-backed Ewell Place, who had the benefit of a previous run.The bare form might not amount to a great deal in the context of Royal Ascot juveniles, but the impression is Crown Dependency could prove up to such a standard - he looked as though the run would bring him on and a strongly run race is likely to see him in an even better light. He's expected to prove equally effective over 5f, though may now go for the Woodcote over this trip at Epsom on Derby day. (op 11-4)

Ewell Place(IRE) got loose ahead of his debut, when he finished last of four at Ascot, but the market suggested a lot better was expected this time. He duly posted an improved effort, but ran into a potentially well above-average sort. (op 8-1)

Airborne Again(IRE), a 40,000gns January foal, out of a Listed-placed 5f winner, showed speed and should be better for the run. (op 11-1)

Drummoyne(USA) got warm beforehand and failed to build sufficiently on his Musselburgh debut. (tchd 3-1)

Arabian Falcon, a well-held eighth in a red-hot Newbury maiden on debut, didn't improve as one might have expected, starting slowly and finding only the one pace for pressure. (op 11-4)

Blank Czech(IRE) ◆ was free and green to the start, and he looked clueless in the race itself. Having needed a blanket for stalls entry, he missed the break and was always well out the back. He can do significantly better in time. (tchd 15-2)

1836 ROYAL SUSSEX REGIMENT MAIDEN STKS 1m

3:15 (3:16) (Class 5) 3-Y-O+ **£2,590** (£770; £385; £192) **Stalls** Low

Form				RPR
62-	1		**Dubai Queen (USA)**[189] 7185 3-8-9 0 ... J-PGuillambert 3 (Luca Cumani) *t.k.h early: chsd ldrs: 3rd and rdn wl over 1f out: hdwy and chsd ldr 1f out: qcknd to ld ins fnl f: in command and idling after: pushed out* **15/8**[1]	84+
54-	2	1	**Trojan Nights (USA)**[189] 7186 3-9-0 0 ... EddieAhern 6 (William Haggas) *led: rdn and fnd ex over 1f out: hdd ins fnl f: kpt on but readily hld after* **8/1**[3]	87
33	3	2 1/4	**Agiaal (USA)**[15] 1484 3-9-0 0 ... RichardHills 12 (John Gosden) *chsd ldr: rdn and effrt jst over 2f out: drvn and unable qck over 1f out: 3rd and one pce fnl f* **2/1**[2]	81
5-	4	2	**Al Janadeirya**[356] 2088 3-8-9 0 ... TedDurcan 1 (David Lanigan) *in tch in midfield: rdn and effrt ent fnl 2f: no imp on ldng trio over 1f out: wnt 4th ins fnl f* **20/1**	72
0	5	1 3/4	**Junoob**[19] 1409 3-9-0 0 ... TadhgO'Shea 13 (John Dunlop) *dwlt: bmpd and swtchd rt s: early reminder: in tch towards rr: rdn and rn green over 2f out: swtchd lft to outer 2f out: hdwy and edging rt ent fnl f: r.o strly fnl 150yds: nvr trbld ldrs* **50/1**	73+
4-	6	shd	**Sleek Gold**[169] 7479 3-8-9 0 ... MartinDwyer 2 (Brian Meehan) *t.k.h: chsd ldrs: rdn and unable qck ent fnl 2f: wknd u.p over 1f out* **14/1**	68
56-	7	2	**Paperetto**[183] 7294 3-8-9 0 ... SeanLevey(5) 15 (Robert Mills) *wnt rt and bmpd s: swtchd rt after s: hld up towards rr on inner: stdy hdwy over 3f out: pushed along and effrt over 1f out: sn no imp and wl hld ins fnl f* **66/1**	68
-	8	1/2	**Another Whisper (IRE)** 3-8-10 0 ow1 ... RichardHughes 7 (Richard Hannon) *in tch in midfield: rdn along and effrt 2f out: unable qck and btn over 1f out: pushed along and n.d ins fnl f* **14/1**	63
6-0	9	1/2	**Red Inca**[19] 1409 3-9-0 0 ... ShaneKelly 9 (Brian Meehan) *in tch: rdn and effrt over 2f out: no prog u.p wl over 1f out: wknd over 1f out* **12/1**	66
00-	10	1/2	**Illandrane (IRE)**[215] 6559 3-8-9 0 ... TomMcLaughlin 8 (Ed Dunlop) *t.k.h: hld up in tch in midfield: rdn and wknd 2f out* **16/1**	60
00-	11	4 1/2	**Guards Chapel**[194] 7094 3-8-7 0 ... TalibHussain(7) 5 (Luca Cumani) *stdd s: hld up in rr: pushed along and no real hdwy over 2f out: styd on past btn horses fr over 1f out: n.d* **50/1**	54
0	12	hd	**Duchess Of Magenta (IRE)**[20] 1362 3-8-4 0 ... AmyScott(5) 4 (Eve Johnson Houghton) *hld up in midfield: rdn and struggling over 2f out: wknd over 2f out* **100/1**	49
3-0	13	4 1/2	**Ringstead Bay (FR)**[19] 1408 3-9-0 0 ... JimCrowley 11 (Ralph Beckett) *hld up in last quartet: rdn and no hdwy over 2f out: n.d* **33/1**	43
0	14	10	**Dare To Bare (IRE)**[9] 1580 3-9-0 0 ... JimmyQuinn 10 (Amanda Perrett) *stdd s: hld up in midfield on outer: lost pl and dropped to rr 4f out: rdn and wknd 3f out: eased wl ins fnl f: t.o* **100/1**	—
00-	15	hd	**Hurricane Spear**[245] 5676 3-8-11 0 ... RossAtkinson(3) 16 (Gary Moore) *t.k.h: hld up in last quartet: rdn and struggling over 3f out: wl bhd fnl 2f: eased wl ins fnl f: t.o* **100/1**	—

1m 40.8s (0.90) **Going Correction** +0.025s/f (Good) **15** Ran SP% **122.2**

Speed ratings (Par 103): **96,95,92,90,89 88,86,86,85,85 80,80,76,66,66**

toteswingers:1&2: £4.80, 2&3: £3.90, 1&3: £1.60 CSF £17.12 TOTE £2.70: £1.20, £2.90, £1.40; EX 23.20.

Owner Sheikh Mohammed Obaid Al Maktoum **Bred** Darley **Trained** Newmarket, Suffolk

FOCUS

Only two of these were seriously backed (the winner and third-placed finisher), but there were plenty of interesting types on show. The pace was steady, meaning it paid to race prominently, and the time was 1.77 seconds slower than the later Class 4 fillies' handicap. The form has been rated on the positive side.

Another Whisper(IRE) Official explanation: jockey said, regarding running and riding, that his orders were to jump out, ride a race and do his best, when he let the filly down inside the final 2f it was feeling the ground and was unable to extend.

1837 GOLF AT GOODWOOD FILLIES' STKS (H'CAP) 1m

3:50 (3:53) (Class 4) (0-85,85) 3-Y-O **£4,209** (£1,252; £625; £312) **Stalls** Low

Form				RPR
01-5	1		**Beatrice Aurore (IRE)**[32] 1113 3-8-13 **77** ... TedDurcan 3 (John Dunlop) *in tch towards rr: hdwy on inner 3f out: trckd ldrs and swtchd lft wl over 1f out: rdn to ld and edgd rt ins fnl f: sn in command: readily* **4/1**[2]	101+
212-	2	2	**Askaud (IRE)**[251] 5490 3-8-13 **77** ... IanMongan 1 (David Nicholls) *restless in stalls: s.i.s: in tch in last trio: switche to outer and gd hdwy over 2f out: edging rt but led 2f out: hdd and swtchd lft ins fnl f: no ch w wnr but kpt on for clr 2nd* **13/2**	89
12	3	7	**Metropolitain Miss (IRE)**[8] 1599 3-8-13 **77** ... SamHitchcott 11 (Mick Channon) *in tch: chsd ldrs 1/2-way: rdn and pressing ldrs whn hung rt and hld hd high ent 2f out: nt qckn and btn over 1f out: plugged on to go modest 3rd nr fin* **7/2**[1]	73
210-	4	nk	**Submission**[201] 6927 3-9-1 **79** ... J-PGuillambert 8 (Luca Cumani) *in tch: shuffled bk towards rr over 3f out: nt clr run and lost tch w ldrs ent fnl 2f: poor 7th and nudged along over 1f out: continued to be tenderly handled but kpt on ins fnl f to press for 3rd at fin* **6/1**	75
10-	5	1/2	**Catfish (IRE)**[285] 4356 3-9-6 **84** ... MartinDwyer 2 (Brian Meehan) *t.k.h: chsd ldrs: chsd ldr 3f out: rdn wl over 1f out: 3rd and btn 1f out: wknd ins fnl f: lost 2 pls wl ins fnl f* **14/1**	78
22-1	6	7	**Desert Shine (IRE)**[63] 751 3-8-11 **75** ... HayleyTurner 4 (Michael Bell) *in tch: effrt and rdn 3f out: struggling and short of room 2f out: wknd u.p wl over 1f out: no ch ins fnl f* **13/2**	53
0-50	7	1/2	**Miss Boops (IRE)**[21] 1335 3-8-8 **72** ... LiamKeniry 5 (Zoe Davison) *awkward leaving stalls: hld up in rr: rdn and lost tch ent fnl 2f: no ch fr over 1f out* **100/1**	49
61	8	2 1/4	**Absolute Princess**[44] 937 3-8-6 **73** ... BillyCray(3) 7 (David Nicholls) *chsd ldr tl 3f out: sn struggling: wkng whn short of room and hmpd over 2f out: sn bhd* **33/1**	45
1	9	nk	**Deity**[21] 1343 3-9-7 **85** ... ShaneKelly 6 (Jeremy Noseda) *dwlt: sn pushed along and rcvrd to ld after 1f: t.k.h after: rdn and hdd 2f out: wknd over 1f out: fdd ins fnl f* **5/1**[3]	56
206-	10	2	**Whoateallthepius (IRE)**[219] 6445 3-8-11 **75** ... LukeMorris 10 (Dean Ivory) *stdd s: t.k.h: hld up in rr: rdn and struggling over 3f out: wl bhd fnl 2f* **40/1**	42
10-	11	36	**Golden Delicious**[194] 7098 3-9-5 **83** ... SteveDrowne 12 (Hughie Morrison) *chsd ldrs: rdn and btn 3f out: sn lost pl: bhd and hanging rt 2f out: t.o and eased fr over 1f out* **16/1**	—

1m 39.03s (-0.87) **Going Correction** +0.025s/f (Good) **11** Ran SP% **118.8**

Speed ratings (Par 98): **105,103,96,95,95 88,87,85,85,83 47**

toteswingers:1&2: £5.70, 2&3: £5.80, 1&3: £3.50 CSF £30.36 CT £102.36 TOTE £5.40: £2.20, £2.20, £1.10; EX 34.70.

Owner Benny Andersson **Bred** Chess Racing Ab **Trained** Arundel, W Sussex

FOCUS

The time was 1.77 seconds quicker than the earlier maiden, but that race was slowly run. A few of these were keen and the field were still well bunched turning into the straight, suggesting the pace was just ordinary, yet the front two pulled a long way clear. They were the only ones to show their form, with the winner impressive and the second stepping up.

Deity Official explanation: jockey said filly ran flat

1838 FEDERATION OF BLOODSTOCK AGENTS STKS (H'CAP) 6f

4:25 (4:26) (Class 5) (0-70,70) 4-Y-O+ **£2,590** (£770; £385; £192) **Stalls** High

Form				RPR
6/62	1		**Mymumsaysimthebest**[17] 1444 6-9-7 **70** ... GeorgeBaker 8 (Gary Moore) *wnt rt s: racd in midfield: hdwy over 2f out: effrt to chal over 1f out: rdn to ld ins fnl f: kpt on wl: rdn out* **9/2**[2]	86+
1123	2	3/4	**Collect Art (IRE)**[3] 1771 4-9-5 **68** ... StevieDonohoe 4 (Andrew Haynes) *w ldrs: led jst over 2f out: rdn 2f out: hrd pressed over 1f out: hdd and kpt on same pce ins fnl f* **11/4**[1]	82
60-0	3	2 3/4	**Emiratesdotcom**[4] 1730 5-8-11 **60** ... LukeMorris 10 (Milton Bradley) *racd off the pce in midfield: rdn over 3f out: hdwy on stands' rail over 1f out: chsd ldng pair ins fnl f: no imp* **8/1**	65
-253	4	3 3/4	**Hand Painted**[17] 1444 5-9-3 **66** ... (p) TravisBlock 6 (Peter Makin) *hmpd s and slowly away: bhd: hdwy in centre wl over 1f out: rdn and no hdwy 1f out: wnt 4th wl ins fnl f* **7/1**[3]	59
4555	5	3/4	**Six Wives**[10] 1555 4-8-12 **64** ... BillyCray(3) 12 (David Nicholls) *led tl rdn and hdd jst over 2f out: wknd u.p ent fnl f: lost 4th wl ins fnl f* **14/1**	55

1200 **6** *nk* **Primo De Vida (IRE)**[10] 1562 4-8-13 **69**..................(p) NathanAlison(7) 9 59
(Jim Boyle) *in tch: rdn and effrt over 2f out: no prog over 1f out: no threat to ldrs ins fnl f* **16/1**

010- **7** *1/2* **Spiritual Art**[12] 6199 5-9-3 **66**.......................... PatCosgrave 7 54
(Luke Dace) *short of room and hmpd s: bhd: styd on ins fnl f: nvr trbld ldrs* **20/1**

1226 **8** *1* **Rio Royale (IRE)**[26] 1232 5-9-1 **64**..................(p) JimCrowley 14 49
(Amanda Perrett) *in tch: rdn and unable qck whn n.m.r ent fnl 2f: wknd over 1f out* **8/1**

44-5 **9** *1 1/2* **Doc Hay (USA)**[22] 1314 4-9-4 **67**..........................(t) ChrisCatlin 3 47
(Paul Cole) *chsd ldrs: rdn and unable qck ent fnl 2f: wknd ent fnl f: hung rt after* **10/1**

-405 **10** *2 1/4* **Highland Harvest**[62] 763 7-9-4 **67**..........................(t) IanMongan 2 40
(Jamie Poulton) *hld up in last trio: hdwy jst over 2f out: no prog whn carried lft by loose horse jst over 1f out: no ch ins fnl f* **25/1**

120- **11** *2* **Towy Boy (IRE)**[127] 8005 6-9-0 **63**..........................(bt) RichardHughes 1 29
(Ian Wood) *bhd: hdwy ent fnl 2f: shkn up and no hdwy ent fnl f: wknd ins fnl f* **20/1**

0200 **12** *39* **Far View (IRE)**[9] 1581 4-8-10 **62**..........................(tp) MatthewDavies(3) 5 —
(George Baker) *sn pressing ldrs: wknd 1/2-way: t.o and virtually p.u ins fnl f* **25/1**

005- **U** **Dusty Spirit**[314] 3400 4-9-1 **67**..........................(t) KierenFox(3) 13 —
(Bill Turner) *uns rdr sn after s* **33/1**

1m 10.98s (-1.22) **Going Correction** +0.025s/f (Good) **13** Ran SP% **121.4**
Speed ratings (Par 103): **109,108,104,99,98 97,97,95,93,90 88,36,—**
toteswingers:1&2: £4.40, 2&3: £6.70, 1&3: £9.10 CSF £16.09 CT £102.80 TOTE £5.00: £1.60, £1.40, £2.50; EX 16.40.
Owner Mrs M J George **Bred** Bearstone Stud **Trained** Lower Beeding, W Sussex

FOCUS
They raced towards the stands' side, but the winner was not against the rail and there has yet to be any sign of a major bias on the straight track at Goodwood this year. This was an ordinary sprint handicap, but the first pair were clear and the form looks reasonable for the grade.
Towy Boy(IRE) Official explanation: jockey said gelding was unsuited by the good to firm ground

1839 JUNE 17TH EVENING RACING STKS (H'CAP) 2m
5:00 (5:00) (Class 5) (0-70,70) 4-Y-0+ **£2,590** (£770; £385; £192) **Stalls** High

Form RPR

344- **1** **Spice Fair**[232] 6084 4-9-4 **67**.......................... RichardHughes 2 73
(Mark Usher) *t.k.h: hld up in last trio: hdwy gng wl and switching rt over 2f out: swtchd lft over 1f out: chsng ldrs and swtchd rt ins fnl f: qcknd to ld fnl 75yds: drvn and hld on cl home* **15/2**[3]

2-21 **2** *shd* **Mohanad (IRE)**[12] 1148 5-9-2 **67**.......................... HarryBentley(5) 13 73
(Sheena West) *in tch in midfield: hdwy 3f out: rdn to chal over 1f out: led ins fnl f: hdd fnl 75yds: rallied towards fin: jst hld* **7/2**[1]

1021 **3** *1/2* **My Valley (IRE)**[23] 1282 9-9-8 **68**.......................... IanMongan 5 74
(Pat Phelan) *chsd ldrs: rdn and ev ch 2f out: led over 1f out tl ins fnl f: no ex towards fin* **8/1**

0-34 **4** *1 1/4* **Marcus Antonius**[23] 1282 4-8-9 **58**.......................... PatCosgrave 10 62
(Jim Boyle) *chsd ldr tl 11f out: styd prom in main gp: rdn 3f out ev ch over 1f out: no ex and btn fnl 100yds* **13/2**[2]

54-2 **5** *hd* **Stormy Morning**[23] 1282 5-9-5 **65**..........................(p) LiamKeniry 7 69
(J S Moore) *in tch in midfield: rdn and effrt wl over 2f out: kpt on tl no imp ins fnl f* **9/1**

2241 **6** *1/2* **Sunset Place**[7] 1631 4-9-4 **67** 6ex..........................(p) RobertHavlin 1 70
(Jonathan Geake) *stdd s: hld up in last pair: hdwy on inner 3f out: nt clr run and hmpd jst over 2f out: rallied and swtchd lft over 1f out: kpt on: nt rch ldrs* **8/1**

/03- **7** *2 3/4* **American Spin**[435] 688 7-9-10 **70**.......................... ShaneKelly 4 70
(Luke Dace) *led tl 10f out: rdn and clsd on ldr over 3f out: led 3f out: hdd over 1f out: styd pressing ldrs tl wknd ins fnl f* **14/1**

45-3 **8** *hd* **Robby Bobby**[9] 1577 6-9-0 **60**.......................... JimCrowley 8 60
(Laura Mongan) *racd off the pce towards rr: effrt and rdn on outer wl over 2f out: styd on same pce and no imp ent fnl f* **12/1**

4-16 **9** *2 3/4* **Kadouchski (FR)**[17] 1148 7-8-1 **54**.......................... HannahNunn(7) 12 50
(John Berry) *s.i.s: a towards rr: effrt and in tch over 2f out: edging rt and no hdwy wl over 1f out* **16/1**

66-2 **10** *1 1/4* **Ned Ludd (IRE)**[44] 563 8-8-11 **57**..........................(p) EddieAhern 11 52
(Jonathan Portman) *racd in midfield: lost pl and dropped towards rr over 5f out: rdn and effrt on outer wl over 2f out: no hdwy* **10/1**

60-0 **11** *9* **Double Fortune**[43] 943 4-8-7 **56**..........................(b) LukeMorris 9 40
(Jamie Poulton) *t.k.h: chsd ldrs: led 10f out: clr 6f out tl hdd and rdn 3f out: wknd qckly over 1f out eased ins fnl f* **20/1**

620- **12** *2 3/4* **Happy Fleet**[176] 7388 8-8-10 **56**.......................... DaneO'Neill 3 41
(Roger Curtis) *in tch in midfield: rdn and strugging ent fnl 2f: sn wknd: wl bhd and eased ins fnl f* **33/1**

2-53 **13** *16* **L'Homme De Nuit (GER)**[10] 955 7-9-4 **64**..................(p) SteveDrowne 6 26
(Jim Best) *a bhd: lost tch and virtually p.u fr 2f out: t.o* **22/1**

3m 39.42s (10.42) **Going Correction** +0.025s/f (Good)
WFA 4 from 5yo+ 3lb **13** Ran SP% **120.9**
Speed ratings (Par 103): **74,73,73,73,72 72,71,71,69,69 64,63,55**
toteswingers:1&2: £6.50, 2&3: £7.10, 1&3: £15.40 CSF £33.39 CT £223.23 TOTE £8.90: £3.00, £2.20, £2.50; EX 35.00.
Owner Saxon House Racing **Bred** Mrs D Hughes **Trained** Upper Lambourn, Berks

FOCUS
A time over 17 seconds above standard suggests this was far from a severe stamina test. There was a bunch finish and the winner didn't need to match his best.
L'Homme De Nuit(GER) Official explanation: jockey said gelding had a breathing problem

1840 THREE FRIDAY NIGHTS MAIDEN STKS 1m 4f
5:30 (5:32) (Class 5) 3-Y-0+ **£2,590** (£770; £385; £192) **Stalls** High

Form RPR

1 **Action Front (USA)** 3-8-9 0.......................... EddieAhern 3 83+
(Amanda Perrett) *led: sn hdd and chsd ldrs after: rdn to ld and edgd lft 2f out: clr ent fnl f: kpt on: wl: eased towards fin* **16/1**

0- **2** *1 1/4* **Thubiaan (USA)**[202] 6883 3-8-9 0.......................... RichardHills 9 79+
(William Haggas) *hld up towards rr: hdwy on outer 3f out: chsng ldrs u.p 2f out: lft disputing 2nd over 1f out: one pce and no imp ins fnl f* **2/1**[1]

0- **3** *nk* **Starlight Walk**[187] 7231 3-8-4 0.......................... HayleyTurner 6 73
(Roger Charlton) *chsd ldrs: rdn and n.m.r ent fnl 2f: sn swtchd rt and lft disputing 2nd over 1f out: kpt on same pce fnl f* **8/1**

4 *6* **Lidar (FR)**[38] 6-10-0 0.......................... DaneO'Neill 4 71
(Alan King) *t.k.h: in tch: rdn and effrt over 3f out: outpcd and struggling ent fnl 2f: lft 5th and wl hld over 1f out: wnt 4th ins fnl f* **10/1**

00-2 **5** *2* **High Samana**[19] 1399 3-8-9 78.......................... JimCrowley 1 65
(Ralph Beckett) *sn led: hdd and rdn 2f out: btn whn lft 4th over 1f out: wknd fnl f* **5/2**[2]

4 **6** *1/2* **Star Alliance (IRE)**[19] 1399 3-8-9 0.......................... ShaneKelly 10 65
(John Dunlop) *s.i.s: hld up in last pair: rdn and effrt on inner 3f out: no real hdwy: plugged on* **16/1**

7 *5* **Minkie Moon (IRE)** 3-8-9 0.......................... MartinDwyer 5 57
(Amanda Perrett) *s.i.s and bustled along early: a in rr: rdn and no hdwy 3f out: no dnager but plugged on fnl f* **33/1**

8 *16* **Bad Sir Brian (IRE)**[48] 6-10-0 0.......................... IanMongan 2 33
(Nick Gifford) *hld up towards rr: rdn and effrt on inner over 3f out: sn struggling: wl bhd fnl 2f: t.o* **66/1**

000- **9** *nk* **Rio Prince**[207] 6781 4-10-0 45.......................... NeilChalmers 11 33
(John Bridger) *t.k.h: chsd ldrs early: steadily lost pl: rdn and wknd ent fnl 3f: wl bhd 2f out: t.o* **250/1**

002 **P** **Camporosso**[11] 1542 3-8-9 0.......................... GregFairley 7 —
(Mark Johnston) *sn chsng ldr: rdn and ev ch ent fnl 2f: unable qck and disputing 2nd whn lost action and p.u over 1f out: fatally injured* **9/2**[3]

2m 37.42s (-0.98) **Going Correction** +0.025s/f (Good)
WFA 3 from 4yo+ 19lb **10** Ran SP% **116.9**
Speed ratings (Par 103): **104,103,102,98,97 97,93,83,83,—**
toteswingers:1&2: £10.40, 2&3: £5.60, 1&3: £20.9. Tote Super 7: Win: Not won. Place: Not won. CSF £48.43 TOTE £22.70: £4.20, £1.90, £2.50; EX 72.00.
Owner K Abdulla **Bred** Juddmonte Farms Inc **Trained** Pulborough, W Sussex

FOCUS
Probably an ordinary maiden, but not much to go on and it has been rated around the race averages. A nice start from the winner.
Bad Sir Brian(IRE) Official explanation: jockey said gelding suffered interference in runing
T/Plt: £16.30 to a £1 stake. Pool of £56,343.34 - 2,517.25 winning tickets. T/Qpdt: £5.40 to a £1 stake Pool of £4,210.76 - 572.05 w. tckts SP 1841a (Foreign Racing) - See Raceform Int.

1707 LONGCHAMP (R-H)
Thursday, May 5

OFFICIAL GOING: Turf: good

1842a PRIX D'HEDOUVILLE (GROUP 3) (4YO+) (TURF) 1m 4f
2:55 (12:00) 4-Y-0+ **£34,482** (£13,793; £10,344; £6,896; £3,448)

RPR

1 **Ivory Land (FR)**[21] 1352 4-8-11 0.......................... ChristopheSoumillon 1 114+
(A De Royer-Dupre, France) *led after 1f: stl in front 1 1/2f out whn rdn: qcknd wl: r.o wl fnl 100yds: a in command* **6/5**[1]

2 *3/4* **Zack Hall (FR)**[200] 6974 4-8-9 0.................. Christophe-PatriceLemaire 5 111
(M Delzangles, France) *settled 5th: qcknd wl towards outside 1 1/2f out: wnt 2nd 1f out: r.o wl fnl 100yds* **78/10**

3 *3/4* **Watar (IRE)**[21] 1352 6-8-11 0.......................... DavyBonilla 6 112
(F Head, France) *settled towards rr: swtchd to outside early in st: qcknd wl 1f out: r.o wl wout threatening first two ins fnl 50yds* **11/2**[3]

4 *nk* **Lucas Cranach (GER)**[180] 7369 4-8-9 0..........................(b) EFrank 2 109
(S Smrczek, Germany) *s.i.s: rdn to go 3rd on settling: drooped bk to rr early in st: looked btn: hrd rdn: picked up wl 1f out: fin strly* **14/1**

5 *1 1/2* **Wiener Walzer (GER)**[25] 1266 5-8-11 0.......................... MaximeGuyon 7 109
(A Fabre, France) *settled midfield: ev ch 1 1/2f out: rdn but no no ex: styd on fnl f* **9/2**[2]

6 *3/4* **Celtic Celeb (IRE)**[25] 1266 4-9-4 0.......................... ThierryThulliez 3 115
(F Doumen, France) *initially led then settled 2nd after 1f: ev ch 1 1/2f out: rdn but no ex fr 1f out: styd on* **6/1**

7 *1* **Karatoya (IRE)**[21] 1352 4-8-9 0.......................... AnthonyCrastus 8 104
(E Lellouche, France) *settled in rr: prog bef st to go 4th: rdn 1 1/2f out: no ex ins fnl f: dropped bk to rr of field* **14/1**

2m 36.7s (6.30) **7** Ran SP% **118.0**
WIN (incl 1 euro stake): 2.20. PLACES: 1.20, 1.90, 1.50. DF: 9.90. SF: 15.80.
Owner Eduardo Fierro **Bred** Suc. Z Hakam **Trained** Chantilly, France

NOTEBOOK
Ivory Land(FR), three times a winner in Listed company, recorded his first win at Group level, picking up well and winning in the style of a potential smart stayer. He's already placed over 1m7f, and remains capable of adding success at a higher level.
Zack Hall(FR) was going on close home, posting an improved effort.
Watar(IRE) is a solid performer at this sort of level and the way he ran very much suggested he'll be suited by a return to further.
Wiener Walzer(GER) was again disappointing, and Andre Fabre doesn't yet look to have worked his magic on the 5-y-o.
Celtic Celeb(IRE) ◆ is a potentially top-class stayer, as his placed form over 1m7f from last season shows. For the second time this season he was running over an inadequate trip, and for a hold-up horse with a turn of foot, making the early running was never going to suit. He wasn't discredited and will show his class once stepped back up to a staying distance.

1598 ASCOT (R-H)
Friday, May 6

OFFICIAL GOING: Good to firm (straight: stands 9.9, centre 9.3, far 9.7; rnd 8.5)
Rail movement increased 10f &12f races by 12yds and 2m race by 16yds.
Wind: Brisk behind Weather: Sunny

1843 T & R GROUP H'CAP 1m (S)
5:20 (5:21) (Class 4) (0-85,85) 3-Y-0 **£5,180** (£1,541; £770; £384) **Stalls** Centre

Form RPR

1-4 **1** **Samurai Sword**[12] 1550 3-9-7 **85**.......................... AhmedAjtebi 7 101+
(Mahmood Al Zarooni) *hld up in rr: nt clr run fr 2f out: qcknd and squeezed between horses appr 1f out: led ins fnl f: styng on strly whn rdn and hung rt fnl 75yds* **2/1**[1]

5-41 **2** *1* **Tropical Beat**[28] 1210 3-9-0 **78**.......................... WilliamBuick 6 88
(John Gosden) *t.k.h: in tch: rdn along 1/2-way and sn outpcd: rallied u.p fr 2f out: styd on wl fnl f to press ldrs: nt pce of wnr clsng stages but kpt on wl to take 2nd last strides* **7/2**[2]

326- **3** *shd* **Above All**[192] 7150 3-8-9 **73**.......................... TadhgO'Shea 12 83
(William Haggas) *sn narrow ldr: rdn over 2f out: hdd ins fnl f: styd on wl but nt pce of wnr: ct for 2nd last strides* **25/1**

0-21 **4** *2 1/4* **Obsession (IRE)**[83] 520 3-8-11 **75**..........................(v) TomQueally 4 80
(Jeremy Noseda) *in rr: gd hdwy fr 2f out: pressed ldrs 1f out: kpt on same pce ins fnl f* **14/1**

216- **5** *2* **Mama Lulu (USA)**216 6563 3-8-11 **75**........................(v) HayleyTurner 10 75
(Michael Bell) *in rr: nt clr run: rdn and swtchd lft fr 2f out: kpt on fnl f but nt rch ldrs* **20/1**

364- **6** *½* **Buckland (IRE)**197 7036 3-9-3 **81**.................................. MartinDwyer 3 80
(Brian Meehan) *chsd ldrs: rdn and ev ch 2f out: wknd ins fnl f* **33/1**

0-11 **7** *¾* **Buzz Law (IRE)**18 1437 3-8-11 **75**........................ AndrewElliott 9 73
(Mrs K Burke) *in tch: rdn over 2f out: sme prog over 1f out: nvr gng pce to chal and wknd ins fnl f* **9/2**3

024- **8** *9* **Silenzio**142 7873 3-8-10 **74**.. PatDobbs 5 51
(Richard Hannon) *pressed ldrs: ev ch 2f out: wkng whn hmpd 1f out* **50/1**

1-51 **9** *9* **Soweto Star (IRE)**18 1446 3-9-2 **80**................................. LukeMorris 2 36
(John Best) *towards rr: drvn and hdwy to chse ldrs over 2f out: wknd qckly over 1f out* **12/1**

-116 **10** *2¾* **She Ain't A Saint**12 1550 3-9-7 **85**................................. PatCosgrave 11 35
(Jane Chapple-Hyam) *chsd ldrs over 5f* **20/1**

10-0 **11** *½* **Custom House (IRE)**30 1175 3-9-2 **80**........................ RichardHughes 1 29
(Richard Hannon) *pressed ldrs tl wknd qckly fr 2 out* **40/1**

3211 **12** *1¼* **Ana Emarati (USA)**38 1031 3-9-2 **80**................................ EddieAhern 8 26
(Ed Dunlop) *in rr: pushed along 1/2-way: sme prog into mid-div: nvr rchd ldrs and sn wknd* **20/1**

1m 40.02s (-0.58) **Going Correction** -0.05s/f (Good) **12** Ran SP% **113.6**
Speed ratings (Par 101): **100,99,98,96,94 94,93,84,75,72 72,70**
Tote Swingers: 1&2 £2.40, 1&3 £13.70, 2&3 £19.00 CSF £7.15 CT £128.94 TOTE £2.50: £1.20, £2.30, £8.00; EX 10.50.

Owner Godolphin **Bred** Darley **Trained** Newmarket, Suffolk

■ Stewards' Enquiry : Ahmed Ajtebi caution: careless riding.

FOCUS
The going was good to firm on a watered track. A decent handicap. They raced up the centre and the favourite scored in good style under a confident hold-up ride. The form looks strong for the grade, containing lots of unexposed types. The winner looks better than the bare form and looks one to follow.

Soweto Star(IRE) Official explanation: vet said colt lost both front shoes

1844 TRANSFORMERS & RECTIFIERS LTD 60TH ANNIVERSARY H'CAP 7f
5:50 (5:52) (Class 2) 3-Y-O **£25,904** (£7,708; £3,852; £1,924) **Stalls** Centre

Form RPR

116- **1** **Winter's Night (IRE)**195 7098 3-8-4 **87**............................ LukeMorris 2 95+
(Clive Cox) *hld up in tch: hdwy over 2f out: sn rdn: led 1f out: kpt on wl: edgd lft clsng stages: readily* **9/1**

-111 **2** *1¼* **Acclamazing (IRE)**23 1322 3-9-1 **98**................................(t) AdamKirby 7 105+
(Marco Botti) *hld up trcking ldrs: hdwy between horses whn persistently denied clr run wl over 1f out: swtchd rt and styd on wl fnl f: tk 2nd cl home but no imp on wnr* **5/2**1

40-5 **3** *hd* **Toolain (IRE)**23 1320 3-9-7 **104**... NeilCallan 8 108
(Roger Varian) *trckd ldr: drvn to chal fr 2f out: one pce ins fnl f and hld whn crossed clsng stages* **7/1**

13-2 **4** *¾* **Coeus**6 1688 3-8-4 **87**.. HayleyTurner 1 89
(Sir Mark Prescott Bt) *trckd ldrs: drvn to chal 2f out: led and hung lft u.p over 1f out: hdd sn after: styd on same pce* **4/1**3

24-1 **5** *2¾* **Florestans Match**31 1155 3-7-10 **84**.......................... HarryBentley(5) 3 79
(Ralph Beckett) *fly-jmpd s: sn chsng ldrs: rdn over 2f out: wknd ins fnl f* **11/2**

000- **6** *5* **Idiom (IRE)**224 6317 3-8-0 **83**... AndreaAtzeni 6 64
(David Simcock) *stdd in rr: rdn along 3f out: wknd fr 2f out* **50/1**

1-34 **7** *1* **Vanguard Dream**20 1405 3-8-12 **95**............................ RichardHughes 4 73
(Richard Hannon) *led tl hdd over 1f out: btn whn n.m.r sn after* **7/2**2

1m 26.37s (-0.83) **Going Correction** -0.05s/f (Good) **7** Ran SP% **110.6**
Speed ratings (Par 105): **107,105,105,104,101 95,94**
Tote Swingers: 1&2 £3.70, 1&3 £5.90, 2&3 £3.60 CSF £29.75 CT £159.85 TOTE £7.10: £3.60, £1.50; EX 27.20.

Owner J T Thomas **Bred** J T And Mrs Thomas **Trained** Lambourn, Berks

FOCUS
A hot handicap for 3-y-os. The pace appeared steady early but the time was inside the standard. Improved form from the first two.

NOTEBOOK
Winter's Night(IRE) had a 195-day absence to shrug off on the fastest ground she has encountered but her trainer reported that she had done well over the winter and this filly resumed with a gutsy effort to defy a mark 15lb higher than when a nursery winner here last year. She has quite a bit of scope for further progress and should be able to win more races. (op 10-1)
Acclamazing(IRE) has been relentlessly progressive in five starts since last July and completed a four-timer in good style over 6f at Newmarket last month. He was 9lb higher here but the steady pace was against him and he ran into repeated traffic problems before coming up a bit short in an attempt to make it five wins in a row on this return to 7f. He could get back in the groove if getting a bit of luck and a stronger pace next time. Official explanation: jockey said gelding was denied a clear run (op 9-4 tchd 11-4 and 3-1 in a place)
Toolain(IRE) won a C&D Listed event last July and was not far off that form when fifth in the Feilden Stakes on his return at Newmarket last month. The drop in trip looked a positive on this first skirmish in a handicap and he gave it a good try off mark 104. (op 15-2 tchd 9-1)
Coeus improved on his 2-y-o AW form when runner-up in a fast-ground Newmarket handicap last week on turf debut. This speedily bred gelding was well treated with his mark due to go up 2lb, but he was a bit keen off the slow gallop and his finishing effort probably suffered as a result. (op 7-2 tchd 3-1 and 9-2 in a place)
Florestans Match was a bit awkward at the start and couldn't find an effective response after seeing plenty of daylight on the outside. (op 9-2)
Vanguard Dream, fourth behind superstar Frankel in the Greenham, had the run of the race back in much more suitable company but was readily picked off before dropping away. Official explanation: jockey said colt felt wrong behind (op 5-1)

1845 FREIXENET MAIDEN FILLIES' STKS 1m 2f
6:25 (6:27) (Class 4) 3-Y-O+ **£5,828** (£1,734; £866; £432) **Stalls** Low

Form RPR

4 **1** **Creme Anglaise**21 1363 3-8-12 0.............................. HayleyTurner 4 82
(Michael Bell) *trckd ldr: pushed along 2f out: styd on wl fnl f to ld fnl 100yds* **9/1**

23-3 **2** *1¼* **Rainbow Springs**20 1393 3-8-12 105........................ WilliamBuick 3 79
(John Gosden) *led: pushed along over 2f out: kpt on tl edgd lft and hdd fnl 100yds: one pce* **1/1**1

3 *½* **Floral Beauty** 3-8-9 0.. LouisBeuzelin(3) 9 78+
(Sir Michael Stoute) *in rr: hdwy and wd bnd ins fnl 3f: swtchd rt ins fnl 2f and green: hdwy over 1f out: hung rt and stl green: styd on wl to cl on 2nd cl home but nt rch wnr* **25/1**

30- **4** *2¼* **Parvana (IRE)**188 7235 3-8-12 0.................................. EddieAhern 2 74
(William Haggas) *trckd ldng duo: pushed along over 2f out: kpt on same pce fnl f* **11/4**2

56 **5** *¾* **Trend Line (IRE)**21 1363 3-8-12 0.................................... NeilCallan 5 72
(Peter Chapple-Hyam) *chsd ldrs: rdn and one pce over 2f out: kpt on again fnl f* **20/1**

4- **6** *2¼* **Marie Rose**170 7478 3-8-12 0.................................. MartinDwyer 7 68
(Brian Meehan) *chsd ldrs: rdn: green and hung rt wl over 2f out: no ch after* **8/1**3

7 *2¼* **Satwa Sunrise (FR)** 4-9-13 0.................................... RichardHughes 10 64
(Ed Dunlop) *wl in tch w ldrs on ins: hung rt and green over 2f out: btn whn squeezed for room wl over 1f out* **33/1**

5- **8** *1¼* **Bint Nas (IRE)**211 6688 3-8-9 0................................ MartinHarley(3) 6 61
(Mick Channon) *in rr: shkn up whn pushed lft over 2f out: nvr in contention* **25/1**

0- **9** *¾* **Blazing Field**219 6468 3-8-12 0.. LukeMorris 1 59
(Clive Cox) *green and sn pushed along in mid-div: styd midfield but green: wknd ins fnl 3f* **66/1**

0 **10** *1¼* **Formal Dining (USA)**21 1363 3-8-12 0........................... TomQueally 8 57
(Edward Vaughan) *s.i.s: in rr: nt clr run and green over 2f out: no ch after* **66/1**

2m 7.88s (0.88) **Going Correction** +0.10s/f (Good)
WFA 3 from 4yo 15lb **10** Ran SP% **116.2**
Speed ratings (Par 102): **100,99,98,96,96 94,92,91,91,90**
Tote Swingers: 1&2:£1.50, 1&3:£14.70, 2&3:£10.40 CSF £17.51 TOTE £8.70: £2.10, £1.10, £3.60; EX 14.60.

Owner Mrs G Rowland-Clark **Bred** Newsells Park Stud **Trained** Newmarket, Suffolk

■ Stewards' Enquiry : Hayley Turner one-day ban: used whip in incorrect place (May 20)

FOCUS
Much of the interest in this fillies' event revolved around the Group 1-placed favourite who was trying to get back on track, but she was foiled in her bid to make all and was again a long way off her 2yo best. The form is rated round the winner and fifth.

Formal Dining(USA) Official explanation: jockey said filly was denied a clear run

1846 T & R TEST EQUIPMENT LTD MAIDEN FILLIES' STKS 5f
7:00 (7:01) (Class 3) 2-Y-O **£6,476** (£1,927; £963; £481) **Stalls** Centre

Form RPR

3 **1** **Guru Girl**22 1337 2-9-0 0.. AndrewElliott 5 72
(Mrs K Burke) *pressed ldrs: slt ld ins fnl 2f: strly pressed thrght fnl f: edgd lft u.p cl home: all out* **3/1**1

2 *nse* **Toffee Tart** 2-9-0 0... SebSanders 4 72+
(J W Hills) *uns rdr to post: s.i.s and pushed along: hdwy over 2f out: chalng whn wandered rt and lft appr fnl f: sn chalng and styd upsides: jst failed* **16/1**

3 *hd* **Represent (IRE)** 2-8-11 0.. MartinHarley(3) 7 72+
(Mick Channon) *s.i.s: in rr: hdwy and nt clr run 2f out: swtchd rt to outside over 1f out: green and hung rt sn after but str run ins fnl f: fin fast: jst failed* **10/3**2

4 *hd* **My Lucky Liz (IRE)** 2-9-0 0... NeilCallan 10 70+
(David Simcock) *pressed ldrs: rdn and outpcd 2f out: r.o again ins fnl f and gng on cl home whn carried lft* **15/2**

5 *4½* **Starfly (IRE)** 2-9-0 0.. WilliamBuick 6 54
(Jeremy Noseda) *trckd ldrs: drvn 1/2-way and kpt on wl tl wknd fnl 150yds* **11/2**

43 **6** *¾* **Reina Sofia**7 1657 2-9-0 0.. LukeMorris 2 51
(Tony Carroll) *slt ld tl hdd ins fnl 2f: wknd fnl f* **14/1**

4 **6** *dht* **Karuga**15 1505 2-9-0 0.. RichardHughes 9 51+
(Richard Hannon) *in rr: pushed along and hdwy over 1f out: nvr gng pce to rch ldrs: should improve* **5/1**3

8 *1¼* **Miss Astragal (IRE)** 2-9-0 0... PatDobbs 8 47
(Richard Hannon) *in rr: shkn up: hung rt and green ins fnl 2f: no further prog* **22/1**

9 *¾* **First Of February (IRE)** 2-9-0 0...................................... PatCosgrave 1 44
(Jim Boyle) *wnt rt s: sn rcvrd to press ldrs: wknd fnl f* **66/1**

10 *8* **River Nova** 2-9-0 0.. KierenFallon 3 15
(Alan Jarvis) *spd to 1/2-way* **14/1**

61.54 secs (0.34) **Going Correction** -0.05s/f (Good) **10** Ran SP% **117.0**
Speed ratings (Par 94): **89,88,88,88,81 79,79,77,76,63**
Tote Swingers: 1&2:£12.30, 1&3:£4.90, 2&3:£17.50 CSF £52.60 TOTE £4.40: £1.60, £3.30, £1.80; EX 71.20.

Owner D Redvers & Mrs E Burke **Bred** Redmyre Bs & Trinity Gate Bs **Trained** Middleham Moor, North Yorks

FOCUS
An interesting fillies' maiden, featuring mostly debutantes so not an easy race to rate. There was a thrilling finish involving four runners spread across the track and one the experienced runners prevailed.

NOTEBOOK
Guru Girl was always thereabouts when 25-1 third in a Newmarket fillies' maiden on debut. She set a fair standard on that form and battled bravely under a prominent ride to hold on in a four-way finish. She looks a willing sort with scope for further improvement and while her sire is an influence for speed, she also has winners at 6f-1m5f on her dam's side. (op 7-2)
Toffee Tart, a cheaply bought yearling out of a mare who won at 6f (as 2-y-o) to 1m, unseated her rider on the way to the start but that didn't stop her running a huge race at a biggish price on debut for a yard which has been quick out of the blocks with its juveniles this year.
Represent(IRE) ◆ could be the one to take out of the race because she travelled smoothly into contention after a slow start and finished well after being forced to switch to the far side. Her dam is a prolific source of winners, mainly by stouter sires over further, but this daughter of Exceed And Excel has plenty of speed and should not have much trouble gaining compensation for this slightly unfortunate debut run. (op 9-2)
My Lucky Liz(IRE), the first 2-y-o runner of the year for the yard, travelled well for a long before fighting her way into the firing line on debut. Described as "an early type" by her trainer in a recent stable tour, this was a very encouraging start by a filly who has speed on both sides of her pedigree. (op 8-1)
Starfly(IRE) shaped well on debut but couldn't match the finishing speed of the leading bunch. She has plenty going for her on pedigree as a half-sister to five winners in France, including 2-y-o 6f Listed winner Mytographie, and should improve on this debut run. (op 7-2)
Karuga was never going the pace in a bid to build on her debut fourth at Folkestone, but she is closely related to two 5f-7f winners and should improve with time and distance. (tchd 13-2)

1847 TRANSFORMERS & RECTIFIERS LTD H'CAP 2m
7:35 (7:35) (Class 3) (0-90,87) 4-Y-O+
£7,477 (£2,239; £1,119; £560; £279; £140) **Stalls** Low

Form RPR

14-5 **1** **Zigato**16 1477 4-9-6 **86**.. WilliamBuick 4 98+
(John Gosden) *hld up in rr: nudged along 5f out: stl plenty to do whn swtchd lft to outside wl over 2f out: drvn and qcknd wl over 1f out to ld ins fnl f: sn clr: comf* **15/8**1

101- **2** *1 ¾* **Ermyn Lodge**^{223} 6352 5-9-7 **84**......(v) IanMongan 13 91
(Pat Phelan) *led after 4f: rdn fr 3f out: styd on gamely whn strly chal fr 2f out: hdd ins fnl f and sn outpcd by wnr but stuck on wl to hold 2nd* **6/1**^{2}

2134 **3** *½* **Parhelion**^{21} 1367 4-8-13 **79**...... DaneO'Neill 8 85
(Derek Haydn Jones) *stdd in rr: gd prog fr 6f out: drvn and qcknd to chal 2f out and stl upsides 1f out: outpcd by wnr ins fnl f and one pce into 3rd cl home* **16/1**

0 **4** *nse* **Kayef (GER)**^{20} 1412 4-8-9 **82**...... DavidKenny$^{(7)}$ 2 88
(Michael Scudamore) *s.i.s: in rr: hdwy on outside 5f out: drvn to chse ldrs over 2f out: styd on ins fnl f: kpt on cl home* **33/1**

431- **5** *4* **Salontyre (GER)**^{23} 2923 5-8-5 **68** oh3......(p) DavidProbert 10 69
(Bernard Llewellyn) *sn in tch: rdn to chse ldrs fr 3f out: no imp and one pce fnl 2f* **9/1**^{3}

010- **6** *2* **Cat O' Nine Tails**^{229} 6224 4-8-12 **78**...... KierenFallon 5 78
(Mark Johnston) *in tch: chsd ldrs fr 6f out: pushed along and kpt on 2f out: sltly checked wl over 1f out and one pce: kpt on again cl home* **12/1**

604- **7** *1 ¼* **Bow To No One (IRE)**^{24} 7612 5-9-2 **79**...... NeilCallan 11 78
(Alan Jarvis) *in rr: hdwy on outside 5f out: chsd ldrs and styng on whn hmpd over 1f out: nt rcvr and wknd* **12/1**

10-0 **8** *10* **My Arch**^{20} 1412 9-9-10 **87**...... BarryMcHugh 1 72
(Ollie Pears) *hdwy to trck ldrs whn hmpd and dropped to rr 12f out: styd in rr: sme prog on outside 3f out: kpt on past btn horses fnl f* **16/1**

202- **9** *3 ¼* **Comedy Act**^{41} 7061 4-9-7 **87**...... SebSanders 12 68
(Philip Hobbs) *chsd ldrs: rdn 3f out: stl wl there whn hmpd wl over 1f out and sn btn: eased* **16/1**

1325 **10** *1* **Muzo (USA)**^{34} 1105 5-9-0 **77**...... AndreaAtzeni 6 57
(Chris Dwyer) *led 4f: styd chsng ldrs: rdn and one pce whn n.m.r and wknd wl over 1f out* **16/1**

0/0- **11** *9* **Gee Dee Nen**^{26} 4467 8-9-5 **82**......(v) GeorgeBaker 3 51
(Gary Moore) *chsd ldrs tl wknd 3f out* **11/1**

26/2 **12** *9* **Advisor (FR)**^{18} 1443 5-9-5 **82**...... RichardHughes 7 41
(Michael Bell) *in tch to 1/2-way: no ch after* **9/1**^{3}

3m 27.62s (-1.38) **Going Correction** +0.10s/f (Good)
WFA 4 from 5yo+ 3lb **12** Ran SP% **119.3**
Speed ratings (Par 107): **107,106,105,105,103 102,102,97,95,95 90,86**
Tote Swingers: 1&2 £2.00, 1&3 £21.10, 2&3 £15.40 CSF £12.40 CT £142.56 TOTE £2.40: £1.30, £2.50, £6.30; EX 15.50.
Owner Lady Bamford & Ms Rachel D S Hood **Bred** Lady Bamford **Trained** Newmarket, Suffolk

FOCUS
A good 2m handicap which didn't look that strong run. The first four finished clear of the rest and the winner looks very progressive at this trip.

NOTEBOOK
Zigato was heavily backed and produced a sweeping run out wide to win from a very unpromising position. This progressive half-brother to Sariska won back-to-back events on Polytrack and soft turf last summer and has hit a personal best on this first try at 2m on the fastest ground he has raced on. There may be quite a bit more to come from him and he could be a major player in big staying handicaps this summer. (op 5-2 tchd 11-4)
Ermyn Lodge gradually adopted a front-running role and battled bravely on this commendable return from 223 days off. He was a very game front-running winner of three 2m handicaps last season and looks poised for further success this time round. (op 5-1 tchd 4-1)
Parhelion had found life tough in two starts since winning a five-runner 1m6f handicap off 4lb lower at Southwell in March but this reliable type bounced back with a big run off a career-high mark.
Kayef(GER), a hurdle winner in February and ex-French 1m2f winner, didn't shine in cheekpieces last month but he did well to work his way into the frame from a long way back without the headgear this time. (tchd 40-1)
Salontyre(GER) has developed into a fairly useful hurdler. He ran respectably switched back to the Flat without transferring his improvement back to this sphere. (op 11-1)
Bow To No One(IRE) Official explanation: jockey said mare suffered interference in running
My Arch Official explanation: jockey said gelding suffered interference in running
Advisor(FR) has lost his way as a hurdler. He made a pleasing Flat return at Windsor last month but produced a limited response before dropping away stepped up to 2m for the first time. Official explanation: jockey said gelding was unsuited by the good to firm ground and lost an off-hind shoe (op 15-2)

1848 FRED COWLEY MBE CONDITIONS STKS 5f
8:10 (8:10) (Class 3) 3-Y-O+ **£9,714** (£2,890; £1,444; £721) **Stalls** Centre

Form RPR

31-4 **1** **Elnawin**^{13} 1518 5-9-7 102...... RichardHughes 5 110
(Richard Hannon) *trckd ldr in main gp: drvn over 2f out: styd on grimly thrght fnl f to ld last strides* **13/2**^{3}

21-1 **2** *hd* **Noble Storm (USA)**^{21} 1366 5-9-9 108...... GrahamGibbons 6 111
(Ed McMahon) *led main gp: pushed along and qcknd into overall ld over 2f out: styd on wl whn hrd drvn fnl f: hdd last strides* **8/11**^{1}

4020 **3** *½* **Monsieur Joe (IRE)**^{41} 996 4-9-4 112......(v) EddieAhern 7 104
(Walter Swinburn) *in tch: rdn and outpcd 1/2-way: hdwy over 1f out: chsd ldring duo ins fnl f but no imp* **4/1**^{2}

/00- **4** *3 ¾* **Taajub (IRE)**^{196} 7073 4-9-4 100...... TadhgO'Shea 2 91
(William Haggas) *in tch: drvn and hdwy to chse ldrs ins fnl 2f: nvr gng pce to chal and wknd ins fnl f* **8/1**

34-0 **5** *¾* **Rowe Park**^{41} 989 8-9-4 99......(p) IanMongan 1 88
(Linda Jewell) *slowly away: in rr and detached 1/2-way: styd on thrght fnl f but nvr any ch of rching ldrs* **16/1**

36-0 **6** *4* **Above Limits (IRE)**^{20} 1420 4-8-13 93...... NeilCallan 3 69
(David Simcock) *racd alone and overall ldr tl hdd over 2f out: wknd over 1f out* **25/1**

59.26 secs (-1.94) **Going Correction** -0.05s/f (Good) **6** Ran SP% **112.1**
Speed ratings (Par 107): **107,106,105,99,98 92**
Tote Swingers: 1&2:£1.80, 1&3:£2.80, 2&3:£1.10 CSF £11.75 TOTE £6.70: £1.80, £1.40; EX 11.60.
Owner Noodles Racing **Bred** D R Tucker **Trained** East Everleigh, Wilts

FOCUS
The hot favourite was caught close home in this conditions event. The form is rated around the winner who is at least as good as ever.

NOTEBOOK
Elnawin snapped a lengthy losing run faced with a gilt-edged opportunity at Newmarket last July on his final run of 2010. He had excuses when below-par on his reappearance and bounced back with huge run to reel in the leading form contender. This enthusiastic traveller was a Group 3 winner as a juvenile and this victory is probably not far off his peak efforts. (op 7-1 tchd 6-1)
Noble Storm(USA) ended 2010 with a comfortable odds-on win in a conditions race at Southwell and then blitzed his rivals when winning a Newbury handicap off 102 on his comeback last month. Ridden prominently, he gave it a good shot conceding weight all round but was just mugged by a revived rival in his bid to improve his strike-rate to 8-25. (op 4-5 tchd 5-6)
Monsieur Joe(IRE) won a 5f York handicap off 97 last August and put in a couple of fine efforts in defeat at Meydan. This King's Stand entered gelding had decent claims on official figures and produced his trademark fast finishing effort but couldn't quite land a blow on the front pair. (op 7-2)
Taajub(IRE) ran respectably back from a break, but was ultimately well held. Last season was something of a non-event for this former Gimcrack and Cornwallis runner-up and he still has a little bit to prove. (op 11-1 tchd 15-2)
Rowe Park had something to find and was never competitive after a slow start. Official explanation: jockey said gelding missed the break
T/Plt: £17.90 to a £1 stake. Pool £59,974.63 - 2,437.93 winning tickets. T/Qpdt: £4.40 to a £1 stake. Pool £5,274.70 - 870.30 winning tickets. ST

1820 CHESTER (L-H)
Friday, May 6

OFFICIAL GOING: Good to firm (8.2)
Rail out 6yds from 6f to top of home straight leaving a 6yd drop in at 1.5f marker.5f races inc. by 17yd, 7f-10.5f by 28yds,12f by 42yds, 13f by 89yds.
Wind: Moderate, half-behind Weather: Cloudy

1849 LAYLA HOTEL EARL GROSVENOR H'CAP 7f 122y
1:45 (1:45) (Class 2) (0-105,102) 4Y0+ **£15,770** (£4,720; £2,360; £1,180; £587) **Stalls** Low

Form RPR

0-30 **1** **Kyllachy Star**^{34} 1092 5-8-13 **94**...... PaulHanagan 12 102
(Richard Fahey) *hld up in midfield: hdwy and swtchd rt over 1f out: r.o ins fnl f: led fnl strides* **6/1**^{2}

2-02 **2** *hd* **Pintura**^{20} 1406 4-8-12 **93**...... JamieSpencer 5 101
(David Simcock) *chsd ldrs: effrt over 2f out: rdn to ld over 1f out: pressed wl ins fnl f: hdd fnl strides* **4/1**^{1}

1103 **3** *1* **Lowther**^{20} 1406 6-9-7 **102**......(be) JimmyFortune 15 107
(Alan Bailey) *in rr: rdn and hdwy over 1f out: hung lft and r.o strly ins fnl f: gng on at fin* **6/1**^{2}

100- **4** *1 ½* **My Kingdom (IRE)**^{181} 7348 5-8-10 **91**...... JimCrowley 6 92+
(David Nicholls) *midfield: hdwy over 3f out: swtchd lft over 1f out: sn chalng: no ex towards fin* **11/1**

40-1 **5** *1* **Lucky Numbers (IRE)**^{29} 1205 5-8-8 **89**...... RyanMoore 3 88
(Paul Green) *chsd ldrs: rdn over 1f out: kpt on u.p ins fnl f: one pce fnl 100yds* **8/1**^{3}

12-0 **6** *½* **Amethyst Dawn (IRE)**^{20} 1410 5-8-7 **88**...... DavidAllan 2 86
(Tim Easterby) *midfield: pushed along over 2f out: hdwy over 1f out: styd on ins fnl f: nt pce to get to ldrs* **10/1**

060- **7** *2* **Marine Boy (IRE)**^{338} 2657 5-8-11 **92**......(t) RichardKingscote 8 87
(Tom Dascombe) *stdd s: hld up: rdn whn nt clr run over 1f out: hdwy whn nt clr again ins fnl f: kpt on: nt trble ldrs* **16/1**

6-00 **8** *1 ¼* **Collateral Damage (IRE)**^{6} 1694 8-8-7 **88**......(t) JohnEgan 9 77
(Tim Easterby) *hld up: rdn over 2f out: nt clr run ins fnl f: kpt on u.p: eased whn no imp fnl 75yds* **28/1**

0-00 **9** *1* **San Cassiano (IRE)**^{20} 1410 4-8-6 **87**...... FrannyNorton 16 74
(Ruth Carr) *midfield: pushed along 2f out: n.m.r whn no imp ins fnl f: nvr a danger* **40/1**

00-0 **10** *2 ½* **Glenridding**^{27} 1240 7-8-5 **86**......(p) JoeFanning 7 67
(James Given) *bustled along to ld: rdn and hdd over 1f out: edgd rt whn wkng ins fnl f* **25/1**

5403 **11** *1 ½* **Captain Ramius (IRE)**^{28} 1228 5-8-6 **87**...... RichardMullen 14 64+
(Kevin Ryan) *hld up: nt clr run and hmpd over 2f out: u.p over 1f out: nvr on terms* **16/1**

40-1 **12** *4 ½* **Joseph Henry**^{27} 1240 9-8-11 **92**...... AdrianNicholls 10 68
(David Nicholls) *chsd ldr: rdn over 2f out: lost 2nd over 1f out: wknd and eased ins fnl f* **12/1**

1110 **13** *13* **Syrian**^{34} 1102 4-8-9 **90**...... CathyGannon 4 23
(David Evans) *s.v.s: a bhd: nvr on terms* **28/1**

04-0 **14** *70* **Maundy Money**^{28} 1228 8-9-0 **95**...... CO'Donoghue 1 —
(David Marnane, Ire) *in tch: rdn over 3f out: wknd qckly wl over 2f out: t.o: lame* **10/1**

1m 33.96s (0.16) **Going Correction** +0.10s/f (Good) **14** Ran SP% **118.8**
Speed ratings (Par 109): **104,103,102,101,100 99,97,96,95,93 91,87,74,4**
Tote Swingers: 1&2 £3.10, 1&3 £7.70, 2&3 £5.20 CSF £28.51 CT £156.78 TOTE £7.00: £2.30, £2.00, £3.00; EX 24.70 Trifecta £79.50 Pool: £1,854.89 - 17.25 winning units..
Owner Dr Marwan Koukash **Bred** John James **Trained** Musley Bank, N Yorks

FOCUS
The rail was moved out by four yards from the 6f marker round to the home straight. Between 4-5mm of water had been put on the track on Thursday night, but riders involved in the opener thought conditions were much the same as the previous day. A good, competitive handicap, run at a sound pace, with leaders Glenridding and Joseph Henry swallowed up in the straight. The winner and third both overcame high draws. Dr Marwan Koukash sponsored the race and was rewarded with the 1-2 and the fourth from his three runners. The front pair recored small personal bests.

NOTEBOOK
Kyllachy Star had work to do if he was to defy stall 12 and Hanagan was pushing away in about sixth place entering the straight, but his mount responded well once pulled out to get up near the line. A second winner of this race for the Fahey yard in the last three runnings, he has never been out of the frame in five appearances at Chester now. (op 8-1 tchd 11-2)
Pintura went up 3lb to a career-high mark after finishing second in the Spring Cup at Newbury. He ran another solid race, getting to the front in the straight but just failing to hold off the winner. He confirmed Spring Cup form with Lowther on slightly worse terms, though. (tchd 9-2 in places)
Lowther was dropped in from stall 15 and still only had three behind him entering the short straight, but stormed through the final furlong and would have troubled the first two with a bit further to run. Representing the yard successful in this event 12 months ago, he is capable of landing a big handicap on turf. (op 9-1)
My Kingdom(IRE) had not been seen for six months and this was only his second start since he was sold out of Hughie Morrison's yard. Carrying the first Koukash colours, he had his chance after being switched inside but could not quite quicken up. His wins have come on easier ground and this was a sound effort. (op 12-1)
Lucky Numbers(IRE) had what seemed a favourable draw and the recent Ripon winner ran a creditable race off this 4lb higher mark. His stamina for this longer trip was waning late on. (op 15-2 tchd 7-1)
Amethyst Dawn(IRE), drawn in two, did not get away to the best of starts and was unable to adopt her favoured front-running style. This game mare was keeping on after encountering trouble and will be paying her way again this season. (op 8-1)
Marine Boy(IRE) remains without a win since his debut success in August 2008 but is edging down the weights and did not shape badly. Official explanation: jockey said gelding was denied a clear run (op 20-1)
Collateral Damage(IRE) was 2lb badly in and was not discredited after meeting trouble.
San Cassiano(IRE) was trapped wide from his outside draw.
Joseph Henry Official explanation: jockey said gelding hung left
Syrian Official explanation: jockey said gelding missed the break

Maundy Money had the plum draw but, after tracking the pace on the inner, racing a little keenly, he was going backwards from the three pole. His turf wins have come on easier ground. Official explanation: vet said gelding finished lame right-hind

1850 ADDLESHAW GODDARD DEE STKS (GROUP 3) 1m 2f 75y
2:20 (2:20) (Class 1) 3-Y-O
£28,385 (£10,760; £5,385; £2,685; £1,345; £675) **Stalls** High

Form RPR
11-1 **1** **Glen's Diamond**[13] [1516] 3-8-12 98 PaulHanagan 3 107+
(Richard Fahey) *trckd ldrs: effrt on outer 2f out: led 1f out: sn edgd lft: r.o wl: in command towards fin* **2/1**[1]
5-2 **2** *2 1/4* **Maqaraat (IRE)**[23] [1321] 3-8-12 0 RichardHills 2 102
(B W Hills) *sn led: edgd off rail 7f out: pushed along 3f out: rdn and hdd 1f out: kpt on u.p ins fnl f: nt pce of wnr fnl 100yds* **5/2**[2]
3-15 **3** *nse* **Tinkertown (IRE)**[27] [1234] 3-8-12 99 JamieSpencer 1 102
(Paul Cole) *hld up: niggled along 5f out: rdn to go pce over 2f out: hdwy over 1f out: sn chalng: kpt on u.p: nt pce of wnr fnl 100yds* **11/1**
5-1 **4** *1/2* **Laajooj (IRE)**[20] [1408] 3-8-12 85 FrankieDettori 6 101
(Mahmood Al Zarooni) *trckd ldrs: wnt 2nd 7f out: chalng 3 out: rdn and stl ev ch over 1f out: kpt on same pce fnl 100yds* **5/1**
44-4 **5** *2 1/2* **The Paddyman (IRE)**[23] [1318] 3-8-12 106 RyanMoore 4 97
(William Haggas) *broke wl: led early: chsd ldr tl n.m.r briefly 7f out: rdn and stl cl up whn n.m.r 1f out: n.d after: eased fnl 75yds* **4/1**[3]
6 *9* **Tlaad (USA)** 3-8-12 0 PhilipRobinson 5 78
(Clive Brittain) *bhd: niggled along over 4f out: outpcd and wl adrift wl over 1f out* **40/1**

2m 11.24s (0.04) **Going Correction** +0.125s/f (Good) **6** Ran SP% **109.3**
Speed ratings (Par 109): **108,106,106,105,103 96**
Tote Swingers: 1&2 £1.70, 1&3 £3.50, 2&3 £3.60 CSF £6.84 TOTE £2.80: £1.70, £1.80; EX 6.20.
Owner S & G Clayton **Bred** Doverlane Finance Ltd **Trained** Musley Bank, N Yorks

FOCUS
No chance of any of these emulating Dee Stakes winners Oath and Kris Kin and going on to take the Derby, as none of the six holds an entry at Epsom. Most recent winners have failed to build on their victories, but Gitano Hernando, narrowly beaten two years ago, has gone on to win in Grade 1 company in the USA. This looked a slightly below-par renewal but the winner is progressing.

NOTEBOOK
Glen's Diamond was a taking winner of a handicap off 90 at Musselburgh first time out and, raised 8lb for that, looked well worth a try in this sort of company. His in-form trainer was concerned about both the quick ground and the turning track, but his charge handled both and ran on strongly down the outside to win most decisively. The step up in trip suited but he will be seen to even greater effect at 1m4f plus. Fahey has no immediate plans for him, but holds him in high regard and mentioned the Melbourne Cup as a long-term aim. As a gelding the winner is ineligible for the Derby and the St Leger, but there is no doubt that he is a bright prospect about whom more will be heard. (op 9-4 tchd 11-4 in places)
Maqaraat(IRE) had had his second to Ocean War at the Craven meeting boosted when the winner took a Listed race next time. The grey dictated the pace and, although unable to fend off Glen's Diamond, just held on for second. He saw out the longer trip well and is likely to bid for a maiden win before moving back up in class. (op 9-4)
Tinkertown(IRE) was outpaced in fifth at one stage but got involved in the straight and missed out on second spot on the nod. This was a creditable return to turf and he stayed the longer trip well enough. (op 14-1)
Laajooj(IRE) improved to issue a challenge to the leader in the straight, but was unable to get his head in front. The longer trip just found him out and he gave the impression that he may prefer slightly easier ground. (op 4-1)
The Paddyman(IRE) set the standard with a BHA rating of 106 but had his stamina to prove, not having tackled further than 7f previously. The Free Handicap fourth, who had to be reined back early on after running up the heels of the leader, was held when tightened up again late on. He is likely to prove hard to place successfully. (op 9-2)
Tlaad(USA) was coltish and green in the preliminaries and his inexperience was evident in the race as he missed the break and brought up the rear throughout. A half-brother to Group 3 winner Queen's Best, out of a mare who won the Nell Gwyn, he has been spoken well of by his trainer but has much to prove if he is to justify his Dante and St James's Palace Stakes entries. (op 28-1)

1851 BOODLES DIAMOND ORMONDE STKS (GROUP 3) 1m 5f 89y
2:55 (2:55) (Class 1) 4-Y-O+ **£36,900** (£13,988; £7,000; £3,490; £1,748) **Stalls** Low

Form RPR
/6-3 **1** **St Nicholas Abbey (IRE)**[33] [1119] 4-9-0 115 RyanMoore 2 124+
(A P O'Brien, Ire) *hld up: impr to take 2nd over 3f out: led over 1f out: qcknd clr ins fnl f: impressive* **11/8**[2]
50-4 **2** *9* **Allied Powers (IRE)**[20] [1403] 6-9-0 111 JamieSpencer 4 111
(Michael Bell) *hld up in last pl: effrt to chse ldrs over 2f out: rdn and nt qckn over 1f out: kpt on to take 2nd fnl 110yds: no ch w wnr* **8/1**[3]
011- **3** *1 1/2* **Harris Tweed**[218] [6506] 4-9-0 112 LiamJones 1 108
(William Haggas) *racd keenly: led: stdd tempo after 4f: increased pce 3f out: rdn whn hdd and jinked rt over 1f out: sn outpcd by wnr: lost 2nd fnl 110yds: no ex* **1/1**[1]
-110 **4** *11* **Fanditha (IRE)**[34] [1104] 5-8-11 88 PaulHanagan 3 89
(Mick Channon) *chsd ldrs: lost pl and n.m.r briefly over 3f out: outpcd over 2f out: lost tch fnl f* **50/1**
360- **5** *15* **Chink Of Light**[283] [4461] 4-9-0 97 (v) JimmyFortune 5 69
(Andrew Balding) *pressed ldr: lost 2nd over 3f out: wknd over 2f out* **25/1**

2m 52.27s (-0.53) **Going Correction** +0.125s/f (Good) **5** Ran SP% **109.0**
Speed ratings (Par 113): **107,101,100,93,84**
CSF £11.83 TOTE £2.20: £1.30, £2.90; EX 9.70.
Owner D Smith, Mrs J Magnier, M Tabor **Bred** Barton Bloodstock & Villiers Synd **Trained** Ballydoyle, Co Tipperary

FOCUS
They went a stop-start pace but the time was respectable. St Nicholas Abbey impressed and is clearly back, but the next pair were not at their best.

NOTEBOOK
St Nicholas Abbey(IRE) could well follow in the footsteps of Harbinger, who took this a year ago before going on to Group 1 glory. Last year's beaten Guineas favourite had much to prove after his disappointing return in a Listed race at the Curragh, but he was up more than 3f in trip here and racing on very different ground. Settling well, he went after the winner in the straight before powering clear to win going away by an increasingly wide margin. He has a wide range of options, with the Coronation Cup favoured at this stage, a race in which his connections' Macarthur was third three years ago after winning this. However connections also have several other leading older horses to juggle, among them So You Think, Fame And Glory and Await The Dawn, and it will be interesting to see where St Nicholas Abbey ranks among them. Wherever he goes St Nicholas Abbey will deserve respect, as this was only the sixth race of his life and there is improvement to come. (tchd 5-4 and 6-4 in places)
Allied Powers(IRE) won a handicap at this fixture three years ago. He made a satisfactory comeback in the John Porter and stepped up on that with a solid effort, coming through for second without being able to threaten the winner. He prefers much easier ground and is likely to head for France and the Grand Prix de Chantilly, which he won last year, followed by a crack at Saint-Cloud's Grand Prix at the end of June. (op 13-2)
Harris Tweed had a fine season at three, culminating in a pair of Listed wins from the front here and at Newmarket. Pestered for the lead by Chink Of Light and not really settling, he slowed down the tempo with a lap to run when getting his way in front, before trying to wind things up again. He wandered under pressure in the straight and had no answers at all to St Nicholas Abbey. This was a little disappointing but it would be unwise to write him off. (op 11-8 tchd 6-4 in places)
Fanditha(IRE) was up against it in this company and had not run over this far. She was predictably well beaten, and the search for black type goes on. (op 28-1)
Chink Of Light was third in last season's Chester Vase but had been well beaten in two subsequent races. Not seen since Glorious Goodwood, he took Harris Tweed on for the lead through the early parts and was on the retreat before the straight. (op 16-1)

1852 VICTOR CHANDLER H'CAP 5f 16y
3:30 (3:30) (Class 2) (0-105,99) 3-£10,193 (£4,248; £2,124; £1,062; £528) **Stalls** Low

Form RPR
41-2 **1** **Ahtoug**[12] [1545] 3-8-13 **91** FrankieDettori 5 100+
(Mahmood Al Zarooni) *dwlt: n.m.r and hmpd s: swtchd rt and hdwy over 1f out: str run ins fnl f to ld towards fin* **7/4**[1]
00-2 **2** *3/4* **Bold Bidder**[7] [1650] 3-8-8 **86** FrannyNorton 3 88
(Kevin Ryan) *led: rdn over 1f out: hdd towards fin* **6/1**
00-4 **3** *1* **Jamesway (IRE)**[27] [1241] 3-8-11 **89** PaulHanagan 2 88
(Richard Fahey) *chsd ldrs: rdn to take 2nd 1f out: unable to get to ldr: lost 2nd wl ins fnl f: kpt on* **9/2**[3]
150- **4** *1/2* **Mappin Time (IRE)**[216] [6568] 3-9-0 **92** DavidAllan 6 89
(Tim Easterby) *chsd ldrs: rdn ins fnl f: styd on same pce* **25/1**
00-3 **5** *3/4* **Face The Problem (IRE)**[30] [1186] 3-9-7 **99** MichaelHills 1 93
(B W Hills) *missed break: hld up: hdwy over 1f out: kpt on ins fnl f: nt pce to get to ldrs* **3/1**[2]
0-00 **6** *2* **Ballista (IRE)**[12] [1545] 3-9-1 **93** RichardKingscote 8 80
(Tom Dascombe) *gd spd to r w ldr tl rdn over 1f out: sn lost 2nd: wknd fnl 110yds* **28/1**
00-5 **7** *1* **Scarlet Rocks (IRE)**[4] [1758] 3-8-2 **80** oh2 CathyGannon 4 64
(David Evans) *wnt rt s: towards rr: rdn over 1f out: nvr able to get on terms* **20/1**
30-4 **8** *3 1/4* **Julius Geezer (IRE)**[12] [1545] 3-9-5 **97** JimCrowley 7 69
(Tom Dascombe) *in tch: rdn 2f out: sn wknd* **16/1**

60.89 secs (-0.11) **Going Correction** +0.125s/f (Good) **8** Ran SP% **111.8**
Speed ratings (Par 105): **105,103,102,101,100 97,95,90**
Tote Swingers: 1&2 £2.90, 1&3 £2.40, 2&3 £4.30 CSF £12.02 CT £38.82 TOTE £2.60: £1.10, £1.90, £1.70; EX 15.30 Trifecta £54.70 Pool: £919.55 - 12.42 winning units..
Owner Godolphin **Bred** Darley **Trained** Newmarket, Suffolk

FOCUS
A decent sprint handicap run at a strong pace. The winner should do better again and the next three seem fairly exposed.

NOTEBOOK
Ahtoug ultimately ran out a cosy winner. Things looked bleak as he missed the kick and found himself trapped wide in rear, but after straightening up virtually last he delivered a strong run down the outside to lead close home. Racing off the same mark as when runner-up at Sandown, and 3lb well in, he is developing into a smart sprinter, but things will be tougher for him once he is reassessed for this. He should have no trouble with 6f. (op 9-4 tchd 5-2 in places)
Bold Bidder was running off the same mark as when second on her seasonal debut. Making the best part of the running, she went for home in the straight but Ahtoug nabbed her close home. She goes well on fast ground. (op 15-2)
Jamesway(IRE) ran a solid race out of stall two and looks a decent marker to this form. (op 5-1 tchd 7-2)
Mappin Time(IRE), still minus the headgear he wore at two, was always in a similar position and did little wrong. Both look held off their current marks. (op 33-1)
Face The Problem(IRE) was drawn in one but missed the kick and could never really get involved. Currently rated 99, like a number of these he isn't going to be easy to place. (op 9-4)
Ballista(IRE), behind Ahtoug at Sandown, showed bright speed from the outside stall but weakened inside the last. He is set to be eased in the handicap now. (op 25-1 tchd 33-1)
Scarlet Rocks(IRE) Official explanation: jockey said filly jumped right out of stalls and hung right throughout
Julius Geezer(IRE), last year's Lily Agnes winner and fourth in the Sandown race, was never really a factor. He is set to be eased in the handicap now. (op 12-1)

1853 HIGHSTREETVOUCHERS.COM MAIDEN FILLIES' STKS 7f 2y
4:05 (4:07) (Class 4) 3-Y-O **£6,152** (£1,830; £914; £456) **Stalls** Low

Form RPR
330- **1** **Layla Jamil (IRE)**[239] [5882] 3-9-0 75 JamieSpencer 4 81
(Mick Channon) *mde all: rdn and qcknd away over 1f out: r.o wl and a in command fnl f* **7/1**
3- **2** *1 3/4* **Elmaam**[188] [7231] 3-9-0 0 RichardHills 1 81+
(William Haggas) *s.s: hld up: nt clr run over 2f out: hdwy over 1f out: styd on ins fnl f: tk 2nd post: nt rch wnr* **5/2**[1]
2 **3** *nse* **Cala Santanyi**[9] [1605] 3-9-0 0 FrankieDettori 11 76
(Gerard Butler) *hld up: hdwy over 3f out: wnt 2nd ins fnl f: styd on: nvr able to get to wnr: lost 2nd post* **9/2**[3]
2 **4** *3 3/4* **Cheherazad (IRE)**[21] [1362] 3-9-0 0 JimmyFortune 10 66
(Paul Cole) *chsd wnr: chalng 3f out: rdn and lost 2nd ins fnl f: no ex fnl 100yds* **7/2**[2]
0- **5** *1 1/2* **I Hate To Lose (USA)**[219] [6451] 3-9-0 0 RyanMoore 12 62
(Philip McBride) *hld up: hdwy 2f out: kpt on ins fnl f: nvr able to chal* **18/1**
0- **6** *hd* **My Ruby (IRE)**[361] [1972] 3-9-0 0 FrannyNorton 8 61
(Jim Best) *towards rr: rdn over 1f out: hdwy ins fnl f: nt pce to get to ldrs* **33/1**
4-4 **7** *2* **Heatherbird**[22] [1343] 3-9-0 0 JimCrowley 5 56+
(William Jarvis) *led to s: slowly away: racd keenly: hld up: nt clr run wl over 1f out: nvr able to get on terms* **7/1**
435- **8** *2* **Winged Valkyrie (IRE)**[232] [6118] 3-9-0 76 MichaelHills 2 50
(B W Hills) *midfield: outpcd over 2f out: nvr a danger* **9/1**
6-30 **9** *nse* **Stravsambition**[10] [1589] 3-9-0 62 RichardKingscote 3 50
(Reg Hollinshead) *racd keenly: trckd ldrs: rdn over 2f out: nt qckn over 1f out: wknd fnl f* **80/1**
10 *3* **Anathena** 3-9-0 0 RussKennemore 9 42
(Reg Hollinshead) *midfield: hdwy over 4f out: chalng 3f out: wknd over 1f out* **80/1**
00-4 **11** *1 3/4* **Bailadeira**[23] [1302] 3-8-11 60 MichaelO'Connell(3) 7 38
(Tim Etherington) *prom: rdn 2f out: wknd ins fnl f* **100/1**
20- **12** *7* **Azzoom (IRE)**[245] [5719] 3-9-0 0 PhilipRobinson 6 19
(Clive Brittain) *in tch: pushed along over 3f out: wknd over 1f out* **16/1**

1m 28.18s (1.68) **Going Correction** +0.125s/f (Good) **12** Ran SP% **121.5**
Speed ratings (Par 98): **95,93,92,88,86 86,84,82,82,78 76,68**
Tote Swingers: 1&2 £5.00, 1&3 £6.90, 2&3 £3.20 CSF £25.34 TOTE £8.00: £2.40, £1.70, £1.90; EX 28.50 Trifecta £111.40 Pool: £1,263.17 - 8.38 winning units..
Owner Dr Marwan Koukash **Bred** Patrick Gleeson **Trained** West Ilsley, Berks

FOCUS
Winners at an ordinary level should emerge from this maiden, the best winner of which in the past decade was Chic, successful in 2003. Fair form, which has been rated slightly on the positive side.

1854 BOXES AND PACKAGING H'CAP 7f 2y
4:40 (4:42) (Class 4) (0-85,90) 4-Y-O+ **£6,152** (£1,830; £914; £456) **Stalls** Low

Form RPR

-431 **1** **Imperial Djay (IRE)**[6] 1696 6-9-5 **83** 6ex.......................... FrannyNorton 11 93
(Ruth Carr) *towards rr: niggled along over 4f out: rdn and hdwy over 1f out: r.o ins fnl f: got up to ld post* **8/1**[2]

1211 **2** *nse* **Norville (IRE)**[4] 1771 4-9-12 **90** 12ex..............................(b) CathyGannon 4 100
(David Evans) *chsd ldrs: rdn over 1f out: hung lft and r.o to ld wl ins fnl f: hdd post* **8/1**[2]

10-0 **3** *3/4* **Swiss Cross**[10] 1594 4-9-6 **84**......................................(t) FrankieDettori 13 92
(Gerard Butler) *hld up: hdwy over 3f out: rdn to chse ldrs over 1f out: styd on to chal ins fnl f: hld fnl strides* **20/1**

2143 **4** *nk* **Majuro (IRE)**[9] 1610 7-9-1 **79**...(t) JohnEgan 12 86
(Richard Guest) *midfield: hdwy 3f out: rdn to ld over 1f out: hdd ins fnl f: no ex fnl strides* **20/1**

3202 **5** *1 3/4* **Sioux Rising (IRE)**[12] 1541 5-9-5 **83**............................... PaulHanagan 3 85+
(Richard Fahey) *chsd ldrs: n.m.r and hmpd 2f out: sn lost pl: prog over 1f out: one pce fnl 75yds* **3/1**[1]

3102 **6** *1 1/4* **Everymanforhimself (IRE)**[6] 1695 7-9-6 **84**...........(b) JimmyFortune 10 83
(Kevin Ryan) *in tch: rdn 2f out: kpt on ins fnl f: unable to trble ldrs* **12/1**

0422 **7** *shd* **Mr Macattack**[27] 1244 6-9-1 **79**................................(t) RichardKingscote 9 78
(Tom Dascombe) *hld up: rdn and hdwy on outer 2f out: kpt on ins fnl f: nvr able to chal* **16/1**

1-33 **8** *1/2* **Malcheek (IRE)**[12] 1541 9-9-6 **84**.. DavidAllan 8 81
(Tim Easterby) *chsd ldrs: rdn to chal under 2f out: nt qckn ent fnl f: no ex fnl 110yds* **14/1**

1514 **9** *1* **Thunderball**[9] 1610 5-9-1 **82**...............................(b) MichaelO'Connell[(3)] 6 77
(David Nicholls) *w ldr: led 3f out: rdn and hdd over 1f out: wknd fnl 100yds* **14/1**

0- **10** *1/2* **Bashir Biyoum Zain (IRE)**[35] 1088 4-9-4 **82**............... RichardMullen 1 75+
(Amy Weaver) *in tch: nt clr run 2f out and lost pl: plugged on at one pce and no imp fnl f* **9/1**[3]

2-25 **11** *3/4* **Shifting Star (IRE)**[20] 1395 6-9-7 **85**................................ RyanMoore 14 76
(Walter Swinburn) *stdd s: hld up: nvr able to get ton terms* **20/1**

-020 **12** *5* **Solar Spirit (IRE)**[9] 1618 6-9-4 **82**................................... KellyHarrison 2 60+
(Tracy Waggott) *awkward s and slowly away: hld up: n.m.r and hmpd after 1f: n.m.r and hmpd again 2f out: nvr on terms* **25/1**

000- **13** *15* **Invincible Force (IRE)**[188] 7243 7-9-7 **85**.................(b) JamieSpencer 5 22
(Paul Green) *led: hdd 3f out: handy in 4th whn n.m.r and hmpd 2f out: sn lost pl: eased whn btn over 1f out* **12/1**

116- **14** *4* **Moretta Blanche**[293] 4145 4-9-5 **83**................................... JimCrowley 7 9
(Ralph Beckett) *missed break: a bhd: nvr on terms* **8/1**[2]

1m 26.83s (0.33) **Going Correction** +0.125s/f (Good) **14** Ran SP% **121.1**
Speed ratings (Par 105): **103,102,102,101,99 98,98,97,96,95 95,89,72,67**
Tote Swingers: 1&2 £6.10, 1&3 £29.80, 2&3 £25.80 CSF £66.79 CT £1284.39 TOTE £9.20: £3.20, £2.70, £5.10; EX 61.50 Trifecta £875.50.
Owner Hollinbridge Partnership **Bred** D Veitch And Musagd Abo Salim **Trained** Huby, N Yorks

FOCUS
The second running of this handicap produced a competitive race, and decent form for the grade, but it was quite a messy race. The winner confirmed his Thirsk form with the second improving again.
Moretta Blanche Official explanation: jockey said filly missed the break

1855 CRUISE NIGHTSPOT H'CAP 1m 4f 66y
5:10 (5:12) (Class 4) (0-85,85) 4-Y-O+ **£6,152** (£1,830; £914; £456) **Stalls** Low

Form RPR

-120 **1** **Lovers Causeway (USA)**[34] 1102 4-8-11 **75**..............(v[1]) JoeFanning 10 84
(Mark Johnston) *mde all: rdn over 1f out: pressed ins fnl f: plld out more towards fin* **12/1**

[illegible] **2** [illegible] **Sir Boss (IRE)**[11] [illegible] 6-9-7 **89**.. LiamJones 5 91
(Michael Mullineaux) *hld up: hdwy over 3f out: wnt 2nd over 1f out: chalng ins fnl f: nt qckn and hld fnl 5o yds* **10/1**

2-20 **3** *2 1/4* **Dahaam**[16] 1477 4-9-1 **79**.. JamieSpencer 4 81
(David Simcock) *midfield: rdn and hdwy over 2f out: styd on ins fnl f: nt rch front 2* **5/1**[2]

031 **4** *hd* **Granny McPhee**[1] 1826 5-9-0 **85** 6ex.......................... NatashaEaton[(7)] 9 87
(Alan Bailey) *s.i.s: hld up: hdwy over 4f out: prom over 3f out: effrt 2f out: styd on same pce ins fnl f* **8/1**

14-5 **5** *hd* **Captain John Nixon**[34] 1102 4-9-7 **85**............................... RyanMoore 11 87
(Pat Eddery) *chsd ldr tl rdn and nt qckn over 1f out: styd on same pce ins fnl f* **6/1**[3]

66-2 **6** *hd* **Oriental Cavalier**[20] 1390 5-8-11 **75**..............................(v) PaulHanagan 1 76
(Mark Buckley) *chsd ldrs: rdn over 2f out: kpt on same pce ins fnl f* **7/2**[1]

1121 **7** *1 1/2* **Carter**[77] 597 5-8-13 **82**... RyanClark[(5)] 6 81
(Ian Williams) *midfield: pushed along and outpcd over 2f out: kpt on ins fnl f: no imp* **10/1**

11-6 **8** *1* **Dynamic Drive (IRE)**[16] 1477 4-9-5 **83**.............................. JimCrowley 7 80
(Walter Swinburn) *hld up: rdn over 1f out: kpt on ins fnl f: nt trble ldrs* **5/1**[2]

4145 **9** *6* **Straversjoy**[67] 715 4-8-7 **71** oh6.................................. RussKennemore 2 59
(Reg Hollinshead) *racd keenly: chsd ldrs: pushed along 3f out: wknd over 2f out* **50/1**

03-0 **10** *3/4* **Destinys Dream (IRE)**[20] 1387 6-9-7 **85**......................... KellyHarrison 3 72
(Tracy Waggott) *hld up: rdn over 1f out: nvr on terms w ldrs* **12/1**

2230 **11** *5* **Brouhaha**[18] 1443 7-8-10 **74**.. RichardKingscote 8 53
(Tom Dascombe) *in tch: rdn and wknd over 2f out* **33/1**

2m 38.5s **Going Correction** +0.125s/f (Good) **11** Ran SP% **119.4**
Speed ratings (Par 105): **109,107,106,106,105 105,104,104,100,99 96**
Tote Swingers: 1&2 £17.70, 1&3 £8.40, 2&3 £9.40 CSF £128.28 CT £687.88 TOTE £15.50: £4.00, £2.60, £2.40; EX 177.70 Trifecta £833.90 Part won. Pool: £1,127.01 - 0.61 winning units..
Owner Crone Stud Farms Ltd **Bred** Skara Glen Stables **Trained** Middleham Moor, N Yorks

FOCUS
An interesting handicap for the grade. The winner was well in on his Polytrack efforts and this was his first turf form.
T/Jkpt: Not won. T/Plt: £64.10 to a £1 stake. Pool of £129,944 - 1,478.41 winning tickets. T/Qpdt: £18.70 to a £1 stake. Pool of £6,505.00 - 256.15 winning tickets. DO

1710 HAMILTON (R-H)
Friday, May 6

OFFICIAL GOING: Good (good to soft in places; 8.3)
Rail realignment around the loop added 8yds to distances on round course.
Wind: Breezy, half behind Weather: Cloudy

1856 DANNY BOY APPRENTICE RIDERS' H'CAP (QUALIFIER FOR THE BETFAIR BONUS SCOTTISH RACING SPRINT) 5f 4y
6:00 (6:06) (Class 6) (0-65,65) 4-Y-O+ **£2,729** (£806; £403) **Stalls** High

Form RPR

1000 **1** **Sharp Shoes**[20] 1411 4-9-2 **62**.......................................(p) LauraBarry[(5)] 4 72
(Ann Duffield) *mde all: rdn over 1f out: hld on wl fnl f* **8/1**

6-45 **2** *1 1/2* **Dower Glen**[5] 1716 4-8-2 **50**..................................(v) ShirleyTeasdale[(7)] 8 54
(Keith Dalgleish) *walked to post: trckd ldrs: effrt and edgd rt over 1f out: styd on to go 2nd nr fin: nt rch wnr* **14/1**

100- **3** *nk* **Arriva La Diva**[191] 7175 5-9-1 **61**.................................. RossSmith[(5)] 5 64
(Linda Perratt) *w wnr: rdn over 1f out: one pce ins fnl f: lost 2nd nr fin* **50/1**

5000 **4** *1 1/4* **Royal Blade (IRE)**[5] 1716 4-8-0 **48**......................... DanielleMooney[(7)] 11 47
(Alan Berry) *prom: rdn and hung rt wl over 1f out: kpt on ins fnl f* **50/1**

2-50 **5** *3/4* **Sandwith**[5] 1712 8-9-9 **64**...(v) GarryWhillans 12 60
(George Foster) *bhd tl hdwy over 1f out: kpt on fnl f: nrst fin* **9/1**

00-2 **6** *1/2* **Musical Bridge**[13] 1523 5-9-10 **65**... DarylByrne 9 59
(Lisa Williamson) *in tch: drvn and outpcd 1/2-way: r.o fnl f: no imp* **13/2**[3]

1121 **7** *nk* **Straboe (USA)**[46] 934 5-8-11 **57**.................................(v) NoelGarbutt[(5)] 1 50
(Stuart Williams) *hld up in midfield on outside: pushed along 1/2-way: kpt on fnl f: nvr able to chal* **11/4**[1]

3410 **8** *hd* **Ingleby Star (IRE)**[20] 1411 6-9-7 **65**..................(p) EdmondLinehan[(3)] 10 57
(Ian McInnes) *unruly in paddock: towards rr: sme hdwy over 1f out: nvr on terms* **6/1**[2]

0-00 **9** *1* **King Of Swords (IRE)**[16] 1493 7-9-0 **58**.......................(p) NoraLooby[(3)] 7 47
(Nigel Tinkler) *in tch: rdn over 2f out: no ex over 1f out* **33/1**

3216 **10** *hd* **Spirit Of Coniston**[3] 1796 8-8-12 **58**..................... DavidSimmonson[(5)] 3 46
(Paul Midgley) *towards rr and sn pushed along: nvr able to chal* **11/1**

0-20 **11** *1/2* **Lake Chini (IRE)**[46] 928 9-9-7 **65**............................(b) GeorgeChaloner[(3)] 6 51
(Michael Easterby) *s.i.s: bhd and sn pushed along: nvr on terms* **18/1**

66-5 **12** *1/2* **Tournedos (IRE)**[12] 1544 9-9-0 **55**.................................(b) ShaneBKelly 2 39
(Ruth Carr) *in tch tl rdn and wknd over 1f out* **8/1**

05-0 **13** *1* **Distant Sun (USA)**[5] 1712 7-8-13 **61**..................... CherylArmstrong[(7)] 13 42
(Linda Perratt) *s.i.s: nvr on terms* **20/1**

59.39 secs (-0.61) **Going Correction** -0.075s/f (Good) **13** Ran SP% **118.4**
Speed ratings (Par 101): **101,98,98,96,94 94,93,93,91,91 90,89,88**
Tote Swingers: 1&2 £22.00, 1&3 £46.30, 2&3 £64.50 CSF £109.76 CT £5145.78 TOTE £11.30: £3.80, £4.90, £12.20; EX 138.20.
Owner T P McMahon and D McMahon **Bred** Mrs Mary Rowlands **Trained** Constable Burton, N Yorks

■ Stewards' Enquiry : Noel Garbutt three-day ban: careless riding (21-23 May)

FOCUS
One of the few places in Britain that has had some rain recently and 14.5mm fell in the preceding 36 hours. An ordinary apprentices' 0-65 sprint handicap, run at a decent pace, just under a second outside the standard, but very few got into it. The winner is rated close to his AW best.
Spirit Of Coniston Official explanation: jockey said gelding hung left throughout

1857 FLYING WITHOUT WINGS H'CAP (QUALIFIER FOR THE BETFAIR BONUS SCOTTISH RACING MILE FINAL) 1m 65y
6:35 (6:36) (Class 6) (0-65,64) 4-Y-O+ **£2,590** (£770; £385; £192) **Stalls** Low

Form RPR

4443 **1** **Bold Marc (IRE)**[9] 1614 9-9-0 **62**....................................... SeanLevey[(5)] 5 72
(Mrs K Burke) *prom: hdwy to ld over 2f out: pushed out fnl f* **4/1**[1]

05-3 **2** *1/2* **Casino Night**[13] 1520 6-9-2 **64**.. DaleSwift[(5)] 11 73
(Barry Murtagh) *led to over 2f out: sn drvn: rallied: kpt on fnl f but a hld* **4/1**[1]

65-2 **3** *5* **Muftarres (IRE)**[11] 1558 6-9-5 **62**...................................... MickyFenton 2 60
(Paul Midgley) *hld up in midfield: stdy hdwy over 3f out: rdn and edgd rt 2f out: sn no imp* **9/2**[2]

0253 **4** *1/2* **Classic Descent**[9] 1613 6-8-10 **56**............................(bt) JamesSullivan[(3)] 3 52
(Ruth Carr) *s.i.s: hld up: hdwy over 2f out: edgd rt wl over 1f out: sn no imp* **6/1**[3]

00-6 **5** *3 3/4* **Hettie Hubble**[11] 1557 5-8-2 **50** oh4..................................(v[1]) JulieBurke[(5)] 10 38
(David Thompson) *in tch: rdn over 2f out: wknd over 1f out* **50/1**

60-0 **6** *2 1/4* **Glenluji**[13] 1520 6-9-5 **62**.. DanielTudhope 8 45
(Jim Goldie) *hld up: pushed along over 2f out: nvr able to chal* **20/1**

00-0 **7** *1 3/4* **Carlitos Spirit (IRE)**[31] 1150 7-9-1 **63**...........................(v) LeeTopliss[(5)] 1 42
(Ian McInnes) *trckd ldrs tl rdn and wknd fr 2f out* **7/1**

160- **8** *1 1/4* **Smarty Sam (USA)**[280] 4546 4-9-7 **64**................................... PJMcDonald 9 40
(Alan Swinbank) *midfield: outpcd over 3f out: wknd fnl 2f* **9/1**

0-44 **9** *8* **Lady Excel (IRE)**[78] 580 5-8-10 **60**.................................. ShaneBKelly[(7)] 4 17
(Brian Rothwell) *bhd: rdn over 3f out: sn btn* **25/1**

0-0 **10** *1 3/4* **Rosbertini**[5] 1714 5-8-12 **55**... FrederikTylicki 6 —
(Linda Perratt) *prom: rdn over 3f out: wknd over 2f out* **11/1**

3-35 **11** *10* **King Bertolini (IRE)**[84] 509 4-8-13 **56**........................ PatrickMathers 7 —
(Alan Berry) *towards rr: drvn 1/2-way: btn over 2f out* **66/1**

1m 47.27s (-1.13) **Going Correction** -0.075s/f (Good) **11** Ran SP% **115.4**
Speed ratings (Par 101): **102,101,96,96,92 90,88,87,79,77 67**
Tote Swingers: 1&2 £4.80, 1&3 £4.80, 2&3 £3.80 CSF £18.70 CT £75.52 TOTE £4.70: £1.50, £2.00, £1.60; EX 22.60.
Owner Aricabeau Racing Limited **Bred** Eamon D Delany **Trained** Middleham Moor, North Yorks

FOCUS
A fair handicap run at a steady pace and the market proved a good guide, with the three principals filling the frame. The form looks solid with the first pair clear.

1858 WHISKEY IN THE JAR H'CAP (QUALIFIER FOR THE BETFAIR BONUS SCOTTISH RACING STAYERS FINAL) 1m 3f 16y
7:05 (7:05) (Class 6) (0-65,63) 3-Y-O **£2,590** (£770; £385; £192) **Stalls** High

Form RPR

33-3 **1** **Countrywide Flame**[10] 1588 3-8-11 **58**...........................(p) JulieBurke[(5)] 2 72+
(Kevin Ryan) *enterprisingly rdn: mde all: clr 1/2-way: kpt on strly: eased fnl 75yds: unchal* **4/1**[2]

600- **2** *3 3/4* **Silver Tigress**[193] 7118 3-8-4 **46**... PatrickMathers 8 51
(George Moore) *hld up and bhd: hdwy over 2f out: chsd (clr) wnr ins fnl f: no imp* **16/1**

4-51 3 1 **Fine Style (IRE)**11 1574 3-9-7 63 6ex............................(v) MickyFenton 3 66
(Michael Bell) *dwlt: sn pushed along and chsd wnr after 2f: effrt and rdn over 2f out* **10/11**1

45-5 4 5 **Operateur (IRE)**24 1300 3-9-7 63.................................... PJMcDonald 7 57
(Ben Haslam) *hld up towards rr: drvn and outpcd over 3f out: styd on fnl f: nvr able to chal* **10/1**3

00-0 5 2 1/4 **Playful Girl (IRE)**16 1495 3-8-2 47.................................... AmyRyan(3) 5 37
(Tim Easterby) *towards rr: outpcd over 4f out: sme late hdwy: nvr on terms* **22/1**

006- 6 2 1/4 **Smart Violetta (IRE)**235 6036 3-8-0 45..........................(t) JamesSullivan(3) 4 31
(Ann Duffield) *bhd: hdwy on outside over 3f out: sn rdn and btn fnl 2f* **18/1**

046- 7 30 **Arashone**226 6294 3-8-8 50.. FrederikTylicki 1 —
(John Weymes) *in tch: pushed along 1/2-way: wknd over 3f out: t.o* **33/1**

00-0 8 3 3/4 **Allez Leulah (IRE)**25 1270 3-9-2 58.................................. GregFairley 6 —
(Mark Johnston) *in tch tl wknd over 3f out: t.o* **10/1**3

000- 9 15 **Sandpipers Dream**252 5498 3-8-10 52....................... DanielTudhope 9 —
(Tim Walford) *cl up tl lost pl 1/2-way: sn struggling: t.o* **25/1**

2m 23.71s (-1.89) **Going Correction** -0.075s/f (Good) 9 Ran SP% **112.8**
Speed ratings (Par 97): **103,100,99,95,94 92,70,68,57**
Tote Swingers: 1&2 £14.10, 1&3 £1.10, 2&3 £7.50 CSF £60.46 CT £102.87 TOTE £4.90: £1.10, £4.50, £1.10; EX 101.70.
Owner Countrywide Racing **Bred** Michael Clarke **Trained** Hambleton, N Yorks

FOCUS
A modest 0-65 handicap run at a modest pace and very few got into it. Pretty weak form but the winner looks much improved.

1859 WORLD OF GOOD H'CAP 1m 1f 36y
7:40 (7:41) (Class 4) (0-80,78) 4-Y-0+ **£4,857** (£1,445; £722; £360) **Stalls** Low

Form RPR

0033 1 **Gala Casino Star (IRE)**17 1461 6-8-7 69........................ LeeTopliss(5) 1 79
(Richard Fahey) *hld up: pushed along over 3f out: hdwy over 1f out: led and hung lft ins fnl f: r.o wl* **9/4**1

66-0 2 1 1/4 **High Resolution**12 1541 4-9-4 78.............................. JamesSullivan(3) 5 85
(Linda Perratt) *hld up: gd hdwy on outside to ld appr fnl f: hdd and blkd ins fnl f: one pce* **8/1**

50-3 3 4 **Munsarim (IRE)**16 1490 4-9-5 76...................................... MickyFenton 4 74
(Keith Dalgleish) *in tch: hdwy to ld over 2f out: hung rt: hdd appr fnl f: sn outpcd* **5/1**3

20-0 4 3/4 **Lord Raglan (IRE)**34 1097 4-9-0 76................................ SeanLevey(5) 7 73
(Mrs K Burke) *cl up: chal over 2f out: sn rdn: no ex over 1f out* **9/2**2

66-4 5 1 3/4 **I'm Super Too (IRE)**24 1292 4-9-1 72............................. PJMcDonald 6 65
(Alan Swinbank) *prom: effrt over 2f out: wknd over 1f out* **13/2**

00-5 6 4 **Sennockian Storm (USA)**36 1058 4-8-10 67................... GregFairley 2 51
(Mark Johnston) *t.k.h: in tch tl rdn and wknd fr 2f out* **15/2**

00-0 7 3/4 **Scarab (IRE)**34 1099 6-8-10 67................................(p) DanielTudhope 8 49
(Tim Walford) *t.k.h: led tl hdd over 2f out: sn wknd* **20/1**

0-00 8 2 **Antoniola (IRE)**20 1390 4-9-0 71..............................(be1) FrederikTylicki 3 54
(Tim Easterby) *hld up on ins: drvn 3f out: sn btn* **14/1**

1m 57.79s (-1.91) **Going Correction** -0.075s/f (Good) 8 Ran SP% **113.3**
Speed ratings (Par 105): **105,103,100,99,98 94,93,92**
Tote Swingers: 1&2 £5.70, 1&3 £8.60, 2&3 £3.70 CSF £20.64 CT £80.54 TOTE £3.00: £1.02, £4.60, £2.60; EX 14.30.
Owner The Friar Tuck Racing Club **Bred** Glashare House Stud **Trained** Musley Bank, N Yorks

FOCUS
A well-contested handicap run at a decent pace, with those coming off it faring best. The form looks solid with the improved first two clear, the winner showing his best form since late last year.

1860 COCKLES AND MUSSELS MAIDEN STKS 6f 5y
8:15 (8:15) (Class 5) 3-Y-0+ **£2,590** (£770; £385; £192) **Stalls** Centre

Form RPR

54- 1 **Louis The Pious**219 6465 3-9-3 0.................................... FrederikTylicki 9 76+
(Kevin Ryan) *trckd ldrs: hdwy to ld 2f out: edgd rt: rdn and styd on wl fnl f* **9/5**2

3- 2 hd **Diablo Dancer**364 1879 3-8-12 0.................................. DanielTudhope 6 70+
(Tim Walford) *s.i.s: bhd: hdwy whn nt clr run and swtchd lft wl over 1f out: sn chsng wnr: kpt on wl fnl f: jst hld* **7/1**3

232- 3 4 1/2 **Royal Liaison**293 4124 3-8-12 72.................................... MickyFenton 1 56
(Michael Bell) *t.k.h: prom: smooth hdwy on outside and ev ch wl over 1f out: sn rdn and nt qckn fnl f* **11/10**1

40-6 4 2 1/2 **Prince Titus (IRE)**110 182 3-9-0 58........................ JamesSullivan(3) 8 53
(Linda Stubbs) *t.k.h: cl up: ev ch and rdn 1/2-way: no ex over 1f out* **16/1**

0-0 5 1 1/2 **Vintage Grape (IRE)**17 1459 3-8-12 0............................. GregFairley 2 43
(Eric Alston) *led tl rdn and hdd 2f out: sn no ex* **40/1**

00 6 1 3/4 **Friday Night Lad (IRE)**12 1540 4-9-13 0........................ PJMcDonald 7 46
(Alan Swinbank) *towards rr: drvn along 1/2-way: nvr able to chal* **40/1**

05 7 nk **The Nifty Duchess**12 1540 3-8-7 0.............................. LeeTopliss(5) 5 37
(Tim Easterby) *dwlt: towards rr: pushed along 1/2-way: nvr on terms* **20/1**

60-P 8 1 1/2 **Blind Stag (IRE)**23 1303 3-8-12 56................................ JulieBurke(5) 4 37
(David Thompson) *cl up: rdn and ev ch 2f out: sn wknd* **33/1**

06- 9 4 1/2 **Face East (USA)**218 6488 3-9-3 0............................ PatrickMathers 10 22
(Alan Berry) *dwlt: bhd: rdn 1/2-way: sn struggling* **100/1**

1m 12.35s (0.15) **Going Correction** -0.075s/f (Good)
WFA 3 from 4yo 10lb 9 Ran SP% **115.3**
Speed ratings (Par 103): **96,95,89,86,84 82,81,79,73**
Tote Swingers: 1&2 £3.00, 2&3 £1.02 CSF £13.84 TOTE £2.90: £1.02, £2.00, £1.30; EX 7.40.
Owner F Gillespie **Bred** Ashbrittle Stud **Trained** Hambleton, N Yorks

FOCUS
Plenty of dead wood among those who contested this weak 6f maiden, which was run at only a fair pace, but the front two drew clear. The favourite disappointed but the winner produced a clear best. They came up the centre of the track before fanning out.

1861 TO WIN JUST ONCE H'CAP 6f 5y
8:45 (8:46) (Class 5) (0-70,68) 4-Y-0+ **£3,412** (£1,007; £504) **Stalls** Centre

Form RPR

-206 1 **Klynch**11 1558 5-8-7 57..(b) JamesSullivan(3) 2 70
(Ruth Carr) *dwlt: hld up in tch: hdwy and edgd rt over 1f out: led ins fnl f: r.o wl* **10/1**

1102 2 1 3/4 **Pelmanism**5 1712 4-9-2 63...(b) PJMcDonald 5 70
(Kevin Ryan) *cl up: led over 2f out: rdn: edgd rt and hdd ins fnl f: kpt on same pce* **5/4**1

3-06 3 nk **Berbice (IRE)**5 1712 6-8-12 64.................................... DaleSwift(5) 6 70
(Linda Perratt) *dwlt: t.k.h: hld up: hdwy over 1f out: disp 2nd ins fnl f: hld nr fin* **8/1**

00-1 4 4 **Arch Walker (IRE)**9 1612 4-8-13 60............................... FrederikTylicki 3 53
(Jedd O'Keeffe) *trckd ldrs: drvn and outpcd over 2f out: no imp fnl f* **7/2**2

000- 5 2 1/2 **Autocracy**277 4649 4-8-10 57.. MickyFenton 4 42
(Eric Alston) *led to over 2f out: sn rdn: wknd ent fnl f* **15/2**

40-0 6 3/4 **Northern Bolt**27 1239 6-9-2 68...................................(b) LeeTopliss(5) 1 51
(Ian McInnes) *sn drvn and cl up: rdn over 2f out: wknd wl over 1f out* **7/1**3

-000 7 4 1/2 **Pearly Wey**9 1612 8-8-10 57...................................... PatrickMathers 7 25
(Ian McInnes) *hld up in tch: drvn 1/2-way: wknd fnl 2f* **33/1**

1m 11.76s (-0.44) **Going Correction** -0.075s/f (Good) 7 Ran SP% **114.1**
Speed ratings (Par 103): **99,96,96,90,87 86,80**
Tote Swingers: 1&2 £3.30, 1&3 £5.60, 2&3 £3.50 CSF £22.98 TOTE £7.70: £3.20, £1.10; EX 28.50.
Owner Douglas Renton **Bred** J C S Wilson Bloodstock **Trained** Huby, N Yorks

FOCUS
Not the most competitive 0-70 handicap, but it was run at a true pace. The form is rated around the second.
Klynch Official explanation: trainer's rep said, regarding apparent improvement in form, that the gelding was better suited by the softer ground.
T/Plt: £64.00 to a £1 stake. Pool of £38,501.90 - 438.90 winning tickets. T/Qpdt: £2.40 to a £1 stake. Pool of £3,566.15 - 1,064.85 winning tickets. RY

1577 LINGFIELD (L-H)
Friday, May 6

OFFICIAL GOING: Turf: good to firm (round course 8.8; straight course 8.9) all weather: standard
Wind: light, behind Weather: warm and sunny

1862 LINGFIELDPARK.CO.UK CLASSIFIED STKS 1m 2f
1:35 (1:35) (Class 5) 3-Y-O **£2,661** (£785; £393) **Stalls** Low

Form RPR

32-5 1 **Arabian Star (IRE)**10 1593 3-8-11 75........................... MartinHarley(3) 5 83
(Mick Channon) *dwlt: hdwy to ld after 1f: mde rest: clr 6f out tl over 3f out: drvn ent fnl 2f: hrd pressed fr over 1f out: battled on v gamely fnl f: all out* **7/2**3

51- 2 shd **Haylaman (IRE)**217 6542 3-9-0 74.............................. TomMcLaughlin 3 83
(Ed Dunlop) *chsd ldng pair: rdn to chse wnr 3f out: upsides wnr over 1f out: r.o u.p fnl f: a jst hld* **13/2**

1 3 6 **Libritish**98 344 3-9-0 75.. AdamKirby 2 71
(Marco Botti) *hld up in tch in last pair: rdn and effrt wl over 2f out: chsd ldng pair 2f out: hung lft and no hdwy over 1f out: wknd fnl f* **11/4**2

01-0 4 2 1/2 **Orange Ace**20 1384 3-9-0 75.. EddieAhern 4 66
(Paul Cole) *led for 1f: chsd wnr after: rdn and clsd on wnr 4f out: rdn and unable qck 3f out: wknd u.p over 1f out:* **9/2**

152- 5 1 3/4 **Lucy Limelites**200 6978 3-9-0 73.................................. SteveDrowne 1 62+
(Roger Charlton) *broke wl: stdd and hld up in tch in last: t.k.h: racd awkwardly on downhill run over 3f out: rdn and effrt towards centre 3f out: no prog 2f out: wl btn over 1f out* **9/4**1

2m 11.12s (0.62) **Going Correction** -0.25s/f (Firm) 5 Ran SP% **111.2**
Speed ratings (Par 99): **87,86,82,80,78**
CSF £24.42 TOTE £4.50: £1.40, £3.50; EX 18.40.
Owner Jackie & George Smith **Bred** G A E And J Smith Bloodstock Ltd **Trained** West Ilsley, Berks

FOCUS
These classified stakes are often trappy, and there was little to separate the front pair at the line. Muddling form, rated around the winner.

1863 EUROPEAN BREEDERS' FUND MAIDEN STKS 5f
2:05 (2:05) (Class 5) 2-Y-O **£3,343** (£987; £493) **Stalls** High

Form RPR

0 1 **Tioman Legend**21 1360 2-9-3 0.................................... SteveDrowne 3 86+
(Roger Charlton) *stdd s: t.k.h: sn chsng ldrs: jnd wnr over 2f out: pushed ahd over 1f out: sn clr: eased wl ins fnl f: easily* **8/11**1

02 2 5 **Red Socks (IRE)**4 1757 2-9-3 0.. NeilCallan 2 65
(Gay Kelleway) *led: rdn and hdd over 1f out: sn no ch w wnr: kpt on fnl f* **5/2**2

2 3 1 **Royal Purse**13 1522 2-8-12 0.. PatCosgrave 4 56
(David Evans) *chsd ldrs: rdn 1/2-way: outpcd and btn over 1f out: battling for modest 3rd fnl f* **9/1**3

4 nse **Denton Dancer** 2-9-3 0.. LukeMorris 1 61
(James Eustace) *chsd ldr tl over 2f out: sn rdn and unable qck: wknd over 1f out: battling for modest 3rd fnl f* **9/1**3

5 14 **Lady Cresta (IRE)** 2-8-12 0.. DavidProbert 5 5
(Ronald Harris) *dwlt: sn pushed along in rr: lost tch 1/2-way: t.o* **40/1**

57.96 secs (-0.24) **Going Correction** -0.25s/f (Firm) 5 Ran SP% **108.9**
Speed ratings (Par 93): **91,83,81,81,58**
CSF £2.67 TOTE £1.80: £1.10, £1.50; EX 3.10.
Owner H R H Sultan Ahmad Shah **Bred** Times Of Wigan Ltd **Trained** Beckhampton, Wilts

FOCUS
An uncompetitive juvenile maiden. The easy winner paid another compliment to the Magic City form and looks useful.

NOTEBOOK
Tioman Legend had shaped with promise in a good maiden at Newbury on debut and found this much easier. Although racing a few off the favoured stands' rail, he was much the best horse in the field and readily drew clear having taken it up over 1f out. There should be more to come as he goes up to 6f, and he could be even better on a slower surface. (op 5-6 tchd 10-11 in places)
Red Socks(IRE), runner-up at Kempton earlier in the week, was quick to bag the rail and held every chance, but the winner was far too good. (op 11-4 tchd 3-1)
Royal Purse probably ran to a similar level as she had done on debut. (op 8-1)
Denton Dancer, bred to want a little further, made a satisfactory debut and should improve. (tchd 17-2 10-1 in a place)
Lady Cresta(IRE), a half-sister to three winners, including smart 5f 2-y-o Jewel In The Sand, looked clueless on this racecourse debut, never leaving last and finishing well adrift. Official explanation: jockey said filly was unsuited by the good to firm ground (op 28-1)

1864 WILL & LYNSEY'S WEDDING DAY H'CAP 5f
2:40 (2:40) (Class 4) (0-85,85) 4-Y-O+ **£3,238** (£963; £481; £240) **Stalls** High

Form RPR

4551 1 **Liberty Lady (IRE)**15 1507 4-9-4 82................................ JamesDoyle 2 93
(Des Donovan) *broke wl and crossed to chse ldrs towards stands' side: rdn over 1f out: kpt on wl u.p ins fnl f to ld last stride* **8/1**

132- 2 shd **Admirable Duchess**226 6284 4-8-7 71........................... EddieAhern 10 82
(Dominic Ffrench Davis) *led: rdn over 1f out: kpt on fnl f: hdd last stride* **7/2**1

00-0 3 1/2 **Solemn**30 1166 6-9-2 80..(b) LiamKeniry 9 89
(Milton Bradley) *chsd ldr: rdn over 1f out: drvn ent fnl f: ev ch ins fnl f: unable qck fnl 75yds* **15/2**

5-33 **4** *1 1/2* **Ajjaadd (USA)**[32] 1140 5-8-8 **72**........................ SteveDrowne 8 76
(Ted Powell) *hld up in midfield: nt clr run over 1f out: swtchd lft and hdwy ent fnl f: no imp fnl 75yds* **6/1**

36-4 **5** *1/2* **Piazza San Pietro**[16] 1476 5-9-7 **85**........................ RobertHavlin 4 87
(Andrew Haynes) *racd in midfield: hdwy on outer ent fnl 2f: chsd ldrs and drvn ent fnl f: styd on same pce fnl 150yds* **11/2**[3]

0022 **6** *1 3/4* **Rocker**[8] 1638 7-8-2 **71** oh1........................ HarryBentley(5) 7 67
(Gary Moore) *towards rr: hdwy and edging lft fr 2f out: no imp ent fnl f* **4/1**[2]

60-0 **7** *1 3/4* **Make My Dream**[11] 1562 8-8-7 **71** oh2........................ TadhgO'Shea 6 60
(John Gallagher) *racd in midfield: rdn and unable qck 2f out: styng on same pce and hld whn sltly hmpd 1f out* **16/1**

1534 **8** *shd* **Estonia**[23] 1309 4-8-7 **71** oh6........................ LukeMorris 3 60
(Michael Squance) *stdd s: a in rr: rdn and no hdwy 2f out: nvr trbld ldrs* **25/1**

5-03 **9** *2 1/2* **Diamond Johnny G (USA)**[15] 1507 4-8-10 **74**........(t) EddieCreighton 5 54
(Edward Creighton) *taken down early: stmbld s and slowly away: a bhd* **28/1**

610- **10** *3/4* **Night Affair**[256] 5368 5-8-12 **76**........................ NeilCallan 1 53
(David Arbuthnot) *chsd ldrs: rdn 2f out: styng on same pce and looking btn whn hmpd 1f out: eased after* **14/1**

56.32 secs (-1.88) **Going Correction** -0.25s/f (Firm) **10** Ran SP% **114.6**
Speed ratings (Par 105): **105,104,104,101,100 98,95,95,91,89**
Tote Swingers: 1&2 £5.50, 1&3 £15.10, 2&3 £13.10 CSF £35.49 CT £224.36 TOTE £8.50: £2.30, £1.60, £2.20; EX 52.50 Trifecta £327.10 Part won. Pool: £442.16 - 0.10 winning units..
Owner Mark Jones **Bred** Chris Giblett **Trained** Newmarket, Suffolk
■ Stewards' Enquiry : Robert Havlin one-day ban: careless riding (May 20)
Neil Callan one-day ban: careless riding (May 20)

FOCUS
An open sprint handicap in which it paid to race near the stands' rail. The first three were always to the fore and the winner produced a length personal best.
Estonia Official explanation: trainer said filly was unsuited by the good to firm ground
Diamond Johnny G(USA) Official explanation: jockey said gelding stumbled leaving stalls

1865 HEART'S FEEL GOOD FRIDAY MAIDEN STKS 7f
3:15 (3:15) (Class 5) 3-Y-O **£2,661** (£785; £393) **Stalls** High

Form RPR

0622 **1** **Hugely Exciting**[22] 1329 3-9-3 73........................(p) LiamKeniry 6 73
(J S Moore) *in tch: swtchd lft and effrt wl over 1f out: rdn to chal over 1f out: led 1f out: kpt on u.p: forged ahd fnl 100yds* **11/4**[2]

40 **2** *1 3/4* **Rafaaf (IRE)**[23] 1317 3-9-3 0........................ AndreaAtzeni 2 68
(Robert Eddery) *stdd s: hld up towards rr: hdwy on outer to chse ldrs over 1f out: rdn and pressed wnr 1f out: btn fnl 100yds: wknd towards fin* **9/4**[1]

0- **3** *nk* **Full Footage**[246] 5691 3-8-12 0........................ SteveDrowne 3 62
(Roger Charlton) *chsd ldr tl pushed ahd 2f out: drvn and hdd 1f out: kpt on same pce ins fnl f* **9/2**

4 *3/4* **Tortilla (IRE)** 3-8-12 0........................ JamesDoyle 7 60
(Des Donovan) *in tch: effrt to chse ldng trio over 1f out: kpt on same pce ins fnl f* **16/1**

0 **5** *3 1/4* **Lightning Spirit**[21] 1362 3-8-12 0........................ StevieDonohoe 4 52+
(Gary Moore) *bhd: rdn and sme hdwy over 1f out: no threat to ldrs but kpt on fnl f* **7/2**[3]

40 **6** *1 3/4* **Casternova**[11] 1565 3-8-12 0........................ TravisBlock 10 47+
(Hughie Morrison) *t.k.h: hld up in tch: chsd ldrs: rdn and struggling whn nt clr run 2f out: swtchd lft and no hdwy over 1f out* **25/1**

7 *1/2* **Joyful Sound (IRE)** 3-9-3 0........................ RobertHavlin 9 51+
(Andrew Haynes) *dwlt: in tch towards rr: rdn and struggling ent fnl 2f: sn btn* **14/1**

60 **8** *1 1/2* **Elite Syncopations**[37] 1053 3-8-12 0........................ FergusSweeney 1 42
(Andrew Haynes) *broke wl: led and sn crossed to r on stands' rail: hdd and rdn 2f out: wknd qckly over 1f out: fdd fnl f* **66/1**

9 *7* **A B Celebration** 3-8-12 0........................ NeilChalmers 5 23
(John Bridger) *s.i.s: rdn and struggling over 2f out: sn lost tch* **66/1**

1m 22.44s (-0.86) **Going Correction** -0.25s/f (Firm) **9** Ran SP% **117.2**
Speed ratings (Par 99): **94,92,91,90,87 85,84,82,74**
Tote Swingers: 1&2 £1.10, 1&3 £4.90, 2&3 £2.80 CSF £9.45 TOTE £3.50: £1.30, £1.10, £2.00; EX 9.50 Trifecta £28.20 Pool: £501.38 - 13.14 winning units..
Owner The Insurance Boys **Bred** Snowdrop Stud Co Limited **Trained** Upper Lambourn, Berks

FOCUS
A modest 3-y-o maiden, rated around the winner. Little got involved.

1866 LADIES DAY H'CAP (LADY AMATEUR RIDERS) 7f
3:50 (3:50) (Class 5) (0-75,74) 4-Y-O+ **£2,571** (£790; £395) **Stalls** High

Form RPR

2342 **1** **April Fool**[21] 1356 7-10-5 **72**........................(b) MissIsabelTompsett 6 85
(David Evans) *broke fast and crossed to r on stands' rail: mde all: wl clr 1/2-way: edgd lft whn rdn fr over 1f out: kpt on: unchal* **5/2**[1]

0135 **2** *3 3/4* **Perfect Ch'I (IRE)**[22] 1330 4-10-3 **70**........................ MissGAndrews 9 73
(Ian Wood) *chsd clr wnr thrght: rdn and effrt wl over 1f out: edgd lft and no imp fnl f* **3/1**[2]

3660 **3** *3/4* **Qadar (IRE)**[6] 1695 9-10-6 **73**........................(p) MissEJJones 5 74
(Alan McCabe) *taken down early: t.k.h: chsd ldng pair: rdn and edgd lft fr over 1f out: kpt on same pce* **11/1**

0-24 **4** *3 1/4* **Magical Speedfit (IRE)**[15] 1507 6-10-0 **74**........ MissKMargarson(7) 8 66
(George Margarson) *chsd ldng trio in centre: pushed along and no hdwy 2f out: wl btn fnl f* **9/1**

06-0 **5** *2 1/4* **King Columbo (IRE)**[5] 1730 6-9-0 **60** oh2........................ MissSBirkett(7) 2 46
(Julia Feilden) *taken down early: racd wl off the pce in midfield: rdn wl over 1f out: nvr trbld ldrs* **14/1**

2630 **6** *5* **Shaded Edge**[37] 1045 7-9-7 **60** oh4........................ MissSBrotherton 1 33
(David Arbuthnot) *aced wl off the pce in midfield: pushed along and struggling 1/2-way: nvr on terms* **11/2**[3]

6500 **7** *8* **Realt Na Mara (IRE)**[20] 1382 8-9-8 **68**........................ MissNDumelow(7) 4 19
(Hughie Morrison) *a outpcd in last trio: lost tch and no ch fr 1/2-way* **14/1**

30-0 **8** *1/2* **Rock With You**[21] 1353 4-9-4 **64**........................ MissLWilliams(7) 7 14
(Pat Phelan) *a wl bhd: lost tch 1/2-way* **20/1**

-000 **9** *1 3/4* **Advertise**[16] 1488 5-9-10 **68**........................ MissHayleyMoore(5) 3 13
(Joseph Tuite) *s.i.s: a wl bhd: lost tch 1/2-way* **9/1**

1m 20.91s (-2.39) **Going Correction** -0.25s/f (Firm) **9** Ran SP% **115.4**
Speed ratings (Par 103): **103,98,97,94,91 85,76,76,74**
Tote Swingers: 1&2 £2.90, 1&3 £6.90, 2&3 £7.30 CSF £9.99 CT £68.14 TOTE £3.40: £1.70, £1.70, £3.30; EX 8.10 TRIFECTA Pool: £375.54 - 5.48 winning units..
Owner Mrs E Evans **Bred** Miss B Swire **Trained** Pandy, Monmouths
■ Stewards' Enquiry : Miss Hayley Moore caution: used whip when out of contention

FOCUS
Plenty of pace on for this lady riders' handicap. A clear personal best from the winner with the level set around the third.

1867 HEART'S FEEL GOOD FRIDAY H'CAP (DIV I) 1m (P)
4:25 (4:25) (Class 5) (0-70,75) 4-Y-O+ **£2,320** (£685; £342) **Stalls** High

Form RPR

53-1 **1** **Nahab**[10] 1587 4-9-12 **75** 6ex........................ TedDurcan 10 90+
(David Lanigan) *bhd: smooth hdwy on outer over 1f out: led on bit jst ins fnl f: sn in command and idling fnl 100yds: pushed out: easily* **13/8**[1]

4-56 **2** *1 3/4* **Tilsworth Glenboy**[31] 1144 4-8-12 **61**........................ StephenCraine 3 65
(J R Jenkins) *dwlt: hld up in tch towards rr: hdwy on inner jst over 2f out: chsd ldrs and drvn 1f out: kpt on but no ch w wnr: snatched 2nd on post* **14/1**

3251 **3** *nse* **Sasheen**[22] 1333 4-9-4 **67**........................(p) SteveDrowne 8 71
(Jeremy Gask) *chsd ldr: drvn to ld wl over 1f out: hdd jst ins fnl f: one pce and no ch w wnr after: lost 2nd on post* **6/1**[2]

3412 **4** *1* **The Big Haerth (IRE)**[27] 1232 5-9-4 **70**........................(t) RichardEvans(3) 9 72
(David Evans) *in tch: pushed along ent fnl 2f: rdn and hdwy over 1f out: kpt on ins fnl f: no ch w wnr* **6/1**[2]

604- **5** *1 1/4* **Beat Up**[163] 7562 5-8-12 **61**........................ NeilChalmers 4 60
(Patrick Chamings) *chsd ldrs: swtchd off of rail and rdn over 1f out: kpt on same pce fnl f* **8/1**

61-5 **6** *nk* **Leelu**[31] 1147 5-9-3 **66**........................ LiamKeniry 7 64
(David Arbuthnot) *taken down early: chsd ldrs: drvn and unable qck over 1f out: one pce and btn fnl f* **8/1**

6U2- **7** *nse* **Emeebee**[187] 7255 5-9-5 **68**........................[1] StevieDonohoe 5 66
(Willie Musson) *bhd: rdn along over 2f out: sme hdwy on inner jst over 1f out: swtchd rt ins fnl f: nvr trbld ldrs* **15/2**

0/00 **8** *1* **Focail Eile**[50] 881 6-9-2 **65**........................ J-PGuillambert 6 61
(Noel Quinlan) *in tch: rdn and lost pl over 2f out: rdn and styd on same pce fr over 1f out: swtchd rt ins fnl f* **7/1**[3]

5406 **9** *12* **Pytheas (USA)**[86] 472 4-9-3 **66**........................(b[1]) JamesDoyle 1 34
(Michael Attwater) *sn led: drvn and hdd wl over 1f out: wknd over 1f out: wl bhd and eased ins fnl f* **40/1**

1m 39.58s (1.38) **Going Correction** +0.25s/f (Slow) **9** Ran SP% **122.3**
Speed ratings (Par 103): **103,101,101,100,98 98,98,97,85**
Tote Swingers: 1&2 £6.60, 1&3 £2.70, 2&3 £13.70 CSF £29.92 CT £120.87 TOTE £2.50: £1.40, £3.10, £2.80; EX 33.40 Trifecta £422.90 Part won. Pool: £571.55 - 0.99 winning units..
Owner Saif Ali **Bred** Rabbah Bloodstock Limited **Trained** Newmarket, Suffolk

FOCUS
The bare form is ordinary, rated around the second and third, but the winner impressed and has more to offer.

1868 HEART'S FEEL GOOD FRIDAY H'CAP (DIV II) 1m (P)
5:00 (5:02) (Class 5) (0-70,70) 4-Y-O+ **£2,320** (£685; £342) **Stalls** High

Form RPR

4314 **1** **West Leake (IRE)**[16] 1488 5-9-3 **66**........................ LiamKeniry 3 74
(Paul Burgoyne) *t.k.h: hld up in tch: rdn and effrt to chse ldr ent fnl f: chal ins fnl f: kpt on to ld towards fin* **11/2**

1100 **2** *hd* **Ede's Dot Com (IRE)**[63] 765 7-8-12 **61**........................ IanMongan 6 68
(Pat Phelan) *chsd ldrs: wnt 2nd 5f out tl led jst over 2f out: drvn over 1f out: had pressed ins fnl f: kpt on tl hdd and no ex towards fin* **9/1**

-504 **3** *1/2* **Salient**[27] 1232 7-9-4 **67**........................(v[1]) TedDurcan 4 73
(Michael Attwater) *in tch: hdwy on inner 2f out: pressed ldrs and hrd drvn ins fnl f: kpt on same pce towards fin* **6/1**

52-6 **4** *1/2* **Striding Edge (IRE)**[29] 1198 5-9-4 **67**........................ JamesDoyle 2 72
(Hans Adielsson) *in tch in midfield: rdn and unable qck over 2f out: swtchd rt over 1f out: styd on wl fnl f: nt rch ldrs* **9/2**[2]

-205 **5** *3 1/4* **Charlie Smirke (USA)**[49] 885 5-9-6 **69**........................(bt) GeorgeBaker 8 66
(Gary Moore) *in tch: hdwy to trck ldng pair 3f out: rdn and fnd nil ent fnl f: sn btn: wknd ins fnl f* **5/1**[3]

106- **6** *5* **Ashkalara**[207] 6807 4-9-2 **65**........................ KirstyMilczarek 10 51
(Stuart Howe) *led: rdn and hdd jst over 2f out: wknd u.p over 1f out* **11/1**

0400 **7** *1 1/4* **Diplomatic (IRE)**[17] 1460 6-9-3 **66**........................ WilliamCarson 7 49
(Michael Squance) *s.i.s: a towards rr: rdn over 4f out: wknd u.p wl over 1f out* **12/1**

0000 **8** *nk* **Ensnare**[16] 1488 6-8-13 **62**........................ StevieDonohoe 9 44
(Noel Quinlan) *a towards rr: rdn and wknd 2f out: sn bhd* **25/1**

3153 **9** *hd* **Chief Exec**[38] 1026 9-9-7 **70**........................ SteveDrowne 5 54
(Jeremy Gask) *s.i.s: bhd: stl plenty to do and nt clr run wl over 1f out: swtchd lft and drvn over 1f out: no hdwy: n.d* **7/2**[1]

1m 39.93s (1.73) **Going Correction** +0.25s/f (Slow) **9** Ran SP% **116.6**
Speed ratings (Par 103): **101,100,100,99,96 91,90,90,89**
Tote Swingers: 1&2 £6.00, 1&3 £6.10, 2&3 £9.80 CSF £54.39 CT £308.63 TOTE £4.90: £1.50, £4.20, £2.70; EX 64.00 Trifecta £280.60 Part won. Pool: £280.60 - 0.44 winning units..
Owner L Tomlin **Bred** Rathbarry Stud **Trained** Shepton Montague, Somerset
■ Stewards' Enquiry : James Doyle two-day ban: careless riding (May 20-21)

FOCUS
This looked more competitive than the second division and it produced a tight finish. Ordinary form, set around the runner-up.
Chief Exec Official explanation: jockey said gelding was unsuited by the kickback

1869 LINGFIELD PARK OWNERS CLUB H'CAP 7f (P)
5:35 (5:38) (Class 5) (0-70,69) 3-Y-O **£2,661** (£785; £393) **Stalls** Low

Form RPR

50-3 **1** **Twinkled**[35] 1082 3-8-6 **61**........................ IanBurns(7) 3 69
(Michael Bell) *led: sn hdd: chsd ldr tl led again over 2f out: styd on wl fnl f* **15/2**

00-2 **2** *1 1/2* **Court Applause (IRE)**[37] 1047 3-9-1 **63**........................ GeorgeBaker 6 67
(William Muir) *t.k.h: hld up in midfield: hdwy over 2f out: rdn and hung lft over 1f out: chsd wnr ins fnl f: no imp fnl 100yds* **9/4**[1]

4314 **3** *1/2* **Beautiful Lando (FR)**[4] 1768 3-8-13 **61**................(v) FrankieMcDonald 7 63
(Heather Main) *dwlt: hdwy into midfield over 3f out: rdn and hanging lft over 1f out: swtchd rt ins fnl f: r.o to go 3rd towards fin: nt rch ldrs* **7/1**

430- **4** *3/4* **Royal Reverie**[231] 6162 3-9-7 **69**........................ LiamKeniry 4 69
(Walter Swinburn) *chsd ldrs: wnt 2nd over 2f out tl 2f out: rdn to chse wnr again over 1f out tl ins fnl f: wknd fnl 75yds* **16/1**

6-03 **5** *5* **In Babylon (GER)**[16] 1483 3-9-2 **64**........................(t) SteveDrowne 2 51
(Tom Dascombe) *mounted on crse: chsd ldrs: rdn to chse ldr 2f out tl over 1f out: drvn and btn 1f out: wknd fnl f* **10/1**

-244 **6** *nk* **Midnight Trader (IRE)**[30] 1176 3-9-4 **66**........................ TonyCulhane 8 52
(Paul D'Arcy) *stdd after s: hld up wl bhd in last: c v wd bnd 2f out: and pushed along: styd on fnl f: n.d* **3/1**[2]

03-3 **7** *2* **Be Amazing (IRE)**[10] 1579 3-9-6 **68**................................(p) TedDurcan 9 49
(David Lanigan) *racd wl off the pce in last trio: sme hdwy over 2f out: rdn and struggling ent fnl 2f: sn wl btn* **11/2**[3]

00-0 **8** *10* **Complicate**[42] 966 3-8-4 **55** oh10..............................(p) SophieDoyle(3) 5 —
(Andrew Reid) *s.i.s: sn rdn along and a struggling in rr: lost tch ent fnl 2f* **100/1**

2355 **9** *59* **Bodie**[58] 801 3-8-12 **60**...(b) FergusSweeney 1 —
(Pam Sly) *sn led and racd freely: hdd over 2f out: sn dropped out: wl bhd and eased fr over 1f out: t.o* **12/1**

1m 26.34s (1.54) **Going Correction** +0.25s/f (Slow) **9** Ran SP% **119.1**
Speed ratings (Par 99): **101,99,98,97,92 91,89,78,10**
Tote Swingers: 1&2 £5.50, 1&3 £9.00, 2&3 £4.00. Tote Super 7: Win: Not won. Place: £1,283.10. CSF £25.57 CT £128.64 TOTE £10.40: £3.10, £1.60, £2.40; EX 35.30 Trifecta £179.80 Part won. Pool: £243.02 - 0.10 winning units..
Owner D W & L Y Payne **Bred** D W And L Y Payne And Barton Stud **Trained** Newmarket, Suffolk

FOCUS
Few got into this but the form looks sound enough.
Royal Reverie Official explanation: vet said gelding lost right-hind shoe
Bodie Official explanation: trainer said gelding had a breathing problem
T/Plt: £18.00 to a £1 stake. Pool of £38,017.00 - 1,541.21 winning tickets. T/Qpdt: £4.80 to a £1 stake. Pool of £3,784.00 - 580.20 winning tickets. SP

[1521] NOTTINGHAM (L-H)
Friday, May 6

OFFICIAL GOING: Good to firm (good in places; 7.7)
All races on outer course.
Wind: Light against Weather: Cloudy with sunny spells

1870 DICK'S FINAL FLING MEDIAN AUCTION MAIDEN FILLIES' STKS 5f 13y
1:55 (1:58) (Class 5) 2-Y-O **£2,525** (£751; £375; £187) **Stalls** Centre

Form RPR

1 **Dozy (IRE)** 2-9-0 0.. PhillipMakin 7 76+
(Kevin Ryan) *s.i.s: sn chsng ldr: swtchd lft 2f out: rdn to ld over 1f out: r.o* **5/2**[2]

65 **2** *1 ½* **Night Angel (IRE)**[15] 1505 2-9-0 0..........................(b[1]) JamesMillman 6 71
(Rod Millman) *led: rdn and hdd over 1f out: styd on same pce ins fnl f* **15/2**

3 *11* **Fairy Moss (IRE)** 2-9-0 0.. PatDobbs 3 31
(Richard Hannon) *dwlt: outpcd: styd on to go mod 3rd post* **4/1**[3]

4 *shd* **J Cunningham** 2-9-0 0.. DaneO'Neill 8 31
(Mark Usher) *prom: swtchd lft 1/2-way: rdn and wknd over 1f out* **15/2**

0 **5** *shd* **Samasana (IRE)**[15] 1505 2-9-0 0.. MartinLane 5 30
(Ian Wood) *prom: rdn 1/2-way: wknd over 1f out* **28/1**

6 *4 ½* **Perfect Day (IRE)** 2-9-0 0....................................... SilvestreDeSousa 2 14
(Paul Cole) *chsd ldrs: rdn over 3f out: wknd 1/2-way* **9/4**[1]

61.92 secs (0.92) **Going Correction** +0.10s/f (Good) **6** Ran SP% **106.3**
Speed ratings (Par 90): **96,93,76,75,75 68**
CSF £18.43 TOTE £2.50: £1.80, £3.70; EX 17.40.
Owner D Redvers & J H & S M Wall **Bred** Mountarmstrong Stud **Trained** Hambleton, N Yorks

FOCUS
This didn't look a strong fillies' maidens and the front two pulled a long way clear, which given the runner-up had shown only modest form in two previous starts, suggests the rest are no great shakes at this stage of their careers. The winner has been rated on the positive side.

NOTEBOOK
Dozy(IRE) was far more professional in the way she went about her job than most of her fellow newcomers and, having tracked the leader up the stands' rail, picked her rival off approaching the final furlong and went away, although she did tend to edge to her right, across the runner-up's path, and her jockey even struck Night Angel's nose with his whip at one point, which clearly wouldn't have helped that rival's chance. That said, the best filly probably won on the day, and she has a pedigree that suggests she'll stay further, so this was a very good start and connections think she could be Royal Ascot material, but her next start, which may be the Hilary Needler at Beverley, will tell us plenty more. (op 13-8)
Night Angel(IRE) had shown only ordinary form in two previous runs and her sales price was one of the cheapest of these runners, but she posted an improved effort in the first-time blinkers, making the running up the stands' rail and keeping on well despite being slightly impeded once headed. (op 13-2 tchd 8-1)
Fairy Moss(IRE) dwelt from the stalls and it took a while for the penny to drop but she shaped like she'd improve plenty for the experience. (op 5-1)
J Cunningham was too green to do herself justice. (op 14-1 tchd 7-1)
Perfect Day(IRE) was beaten a long way out and this was a poor effort. (op 3-1)

1871 BDN CONSTRUCTION H'CAP 1m 2f 50y
2:30 (2:30) (Class 6) (0-60,66) 4-Y-0+ **£1,813** (£539; £269; £134) **Stalls** Low

Form RPR

00-1 **1** **Laverre (IRE)**[11] 1567 4-9-13 **66** 6ex.................................. DaneO'Neill 5 74+
(Lucy Wadham) *chsd ldrs: pushed along over 4f out: rdn to ld over 1f out: styd on* **11/8**[1]

0466 **2** *1 ½* **Professor John (IRE)**[17] 1454 4-9-7 **60**............................ MartinLane 4 63
(Ian Wood) *chsd ldr over 3f: remained handy: pushed along over 3f out: led over 2f out: rdn and hdd over 1f out: styd on same pce ins fnl f* **12/1**

3005 **3** *hd* **Market Puzzle (IRE)**[11] 1567 4-8-9 **48**...............................(b) ShaneKelly 3 51
(Mark Brisbourne) *broke wl: stdd and lost pl after 1f: hld up: hdwy over 2f out: rdn over 1f out: r.o* **11/2**[3]

3554 **4** *1 ¾* **Moment Of Clarity**[27] 1253 9-8-7 **46** oh1.........................(p) ChrisCatlin 8 46
(Shaun Harris) *led: rdn and hdd over 2f out: no ex ins fnl f* **22/1**

-250 **5** *7* **Why So Serious**[9] 1617 5-8-11 **55**........................ TobyAtkinson(5) 1 41
(Peter Salmon) *s.i.s: hdwy 7f out: rdn over 3f out: wknd over 2f out* **50/1**

0-00 **6** *½* **Dragon Slayer (IRE)**[34] 1099 9-9-2 **58**...................... RobertLButler(3) 9 43
(John Harris) *s.i.s: hld up: hdwy over 3f out: hung lft and wknd over 2f out* **14/1**

150- **7** *4 ½* **Pattern Mark**[196] 7068 5-9-2 **55**.. BarryMcHugh 6 31
(Ollie Pears) *prom: racd keenly: chsd ldr over 6f out: rdn over 3f out: wknd over 2f out* **3/1**[2]

050- **8** *5* **Filibuster**[276] 4679 4-8-13 **52**.. JackMitchell 2 18
(Chris Wall) *dwlt: a in rr: bhd fnl 3f* **10/1**

2m 13.79s (2.09) **Going Correction** -0.15s/f (Firm) **8** Ran SP% **112.2**
Speed ratings (Par 101): **85,83,83,82,76 76,72,68**
Tote Swingers: 1&2 £1.30, 2&3 £1.60 CSF £19.13 CT £69.76 TOTE £2.30: £1.70, £3.20, £1.60; EX 15.90.
Owner Mr And Mrs A E Pakenham **Bred** Kilnamoragh Stud **Trained** Newmarket, Suffolk

FOCUS
A moderate handicap and the early pace was very steady, so the form isn't strong although the winner can do better. The race has been rated fairly negatively.

1872 IDEAGEN H'CAP 1m 6f 15y
3:05 (3:06) (Class 5) (0-75,70) 3-Y-O **£2,525** (£751; £375; £187) **Stalls** Low

Form RPR

-031 **1** **Szabo's Destiny**[17] 1456 3-9-6 **69**................................ PaulMulrennan 7 74
(James Given) *led over 3f: chsd ldr tl led again 5f out: rdn over 1f out: styd on gamely* **4/1**[2]

00-3 **2** *½* **Veloce (IRE)**[20] 1399 3-8-12 **61**.. ShaneKelly 1 65+
(John Dunlop) *hld up: rdn over 3f out: swtchd rt over 2f out: edgd lft and r.o u.p ins fnl f: nt rch wnr* **5/2**[1]

2-35 **3** *shd* **Bow River Arch (USA)**[25] 1272 3-9-7 **70**.......................... SebSanders 3 74
(Jeremy Noseda) *a.p: chsd wnr 2f out: sn rdn: styd on: lost 2nd post* **4/1**[2]

3-06 **4** *2* **Cuban Piece (IRE)**[18] 1442 3-8-10 **62**...................(p) RossAtkinson(3) 5 63
(Tom Dascombe) *hld up: hdwy 10f out: rdn over 2f out: styd on same pce ins fnl f* **11/1**[3]

460 **5** *1* **Ocean's Dream Day (IRE)**[16] 1487 3-7-11 **51** oh3...(p) RyanPowell(5) 2 51
(John Ryan) *hld up: hdwy u.p over 1f out: no ex ins fnl f* **50/1**

5-45 **6** *14* **Blade Pirate**[124] 10 3-7-11 **51** oh2.........................(e) RosieJessop(5) 6 31
(John Ryan) *chsd wnr tl led over 10f out: hdd 5f out: chsd wnr tl rdn 2f out: sn wknd* **66/1**

0-11 **P** **Birdwatcher (IRE)**[24] 1300 3-9-5 **68**................................ KierenFallon 4 —
(Mark Johnston) *s.s: bhd and drvn along: t.o whn p.u 10f out: lame* **5/2**[1]

3m 5.37s (-1.93) **Going Correction** -0.15s/f (Firm) **7** Ran SP% **108.9**
Speed ratings (Par 99): **99,98,98,97,96 88,—**
Tote Swingers: 1&2 £1.30, 2&3 £1.60 CSF £13.00 TOTE £5.50: £4.30, £2.20; EX 11.50.
Owner Danethorpe Racing Partnership **Bred** Limestone And Tara Studs **Trained** Willoughton, Lincs

FOCUS
Modest form, weakened by the favourite not runnning her race. The winner has improved.
Birdwatcher(IRE) Official explanation: vet said gelding pulled up lame

1873 BDN CONSTRUCTION MAIDEN FILLIES' STKS 1m 75y
3:40 (3:41) (Class 5) 3-Y-O **£2,525** (£751; £375; £187) **Stalls** Centre

Form RPR

655- **1** **Traffic Sister (USA)**[223] 6348 3-9-0 90.............................. ChrisCatlin 1 83
(J S Moore) *mde virtually all: rdn over 1f out: styd on wl* **5/1**[3]

230- **2** *2 ¼* **Our Gal**[188] 7232 3-9-0 70.. DaneO'Neill 4 78
(Noel Quinlan) *a.p: rdn over 2f out: chsd wnr over 1f out: no imp ins fnl f* **10/1**

424- **3** *3 ¼* **Saskia's Dream**[188] 7231 3-8-7 74.................................. LewisWalsh(7) 3 70
(Jane Chapple-Hyam) *led early: chsd wnr tl rdn over 1f out: wknd ins fnl f* **14/1**

4 *nk* **Sedaine** 3-9-0 0.. RichardThomas 10 70+
(Ralph Beckett) *s.i.s: hld up: r.o ins fnl f: nvr nrr* **33/1**

3 **5** *hd* **Misrepresent (USA)**[21] 1362 3-9-0 0.............................. NickyMackay 2 69
(John Gosden) *prom: rdn over 2f out: wknd ins fnl f* **13/8**[1]

3 **6** *2* **To The Spring**[22] 1343 3-9-0 0.. KierenFallon 6 65
(William Haggas) *chsd ldrs: rdn over 2f out: wkng whn hung lft fnl f* **3/1**[2]

40 **7** *2 ¾* **Serial Sinner (IRE)**[9] 1605 3-9-0 0.................................. ShaneKelly 8 58
(Paul Cole) *mid-div: hdwy 1/2-way: rdn over 2f out: wknd over 1f out* **20/1**

8 *1 ¾* **Street Secret (USA)** 3-9-0 0.. JackMitchell 5 54+
(Roger Varian) *s.i.s: hld up: nvr on terms* **14/1**

06 **9** *½* **Daliana**[16] 1480 3-9-0 0... SaleemGolam 11 53
(Michael Bell) *hld up: n.d* **150/1**

00 **10** *8* **Azurinta (IRE)**[11] 1568 3-9-0 0.. JamieMackay 9 35
(Michael Bell) *hld up: a in rr* **150/1**

11 *6* **Hint Of Silver (IRE)** 3-9-0 0.. MartinLane 7 21
(Andrew Haynes) *s.i.s: a in rr* **125/1**

1m 45.66s (0.06) **Going Correction** -0.15s/f (Firm) **11** Ran SP% **112.0**
Speed ratings (Par 96): **93,90,87,87,87 85,82,80,80,72 66**
Tote Swingers: 1&2 £7.70, 1&3 £8.70, 2&3 £17.70 CSF £49.25 TOTE £5.40: £1.70, £4.30, £9.30; EX 66.30.
Owner Mrs Fitri Hay **Bred** Frank Penn & John R Penn **Trained** Upper Lambourn, Berks
■ Stewards' Enquiry : Jamie Mackay one-day ban: used whip down shoulder in the forehand (May 20)

FOCUS
Little depth to this maiden and they were quite well strung out from the outset. The winner went some way to confirming last year's Group form, with the race rated around the second and third.
Misrepresent(USA) Official explanation: jockey said filly never travelled

1874 TOTESPORT.COM H'CAP 1m 2f 50y
4:15 (4:15) (Class 5) (0-75,75) 4-Y-0+ **£2,525** (£751; £375; £187) **Stalls** Low

Form RPR

0-11 **1** **Frontline Phantom (IRE)**[6] 1671 4-8-5 **66**............ MatthewLawson(7) 5 77
(Mrs K Burke) *chsd ldr: rdn to ld ins fnl f: edgd rt: r.o* **8/11**[1]

5-26 **2** *¾* **Hydrant**[34] 1098 5-8-13 **72**.. TobyAtkinson(5) 4 81
(Peter Salmon) *led: rdn and edgd lft 2f out: hdd ins fnl f: styd on* **10/1**[3]

2632 **3** *4 ½* **The Winged Assasin (USA)**[36] 1066 5-8-10 **69**......(t) KieranO'Neill(5) 2 69
(Shaun Lycett) *s.i.s: hld up: hdwy over 3f out: rdn over 1f out: edgd rt and wknd ins fnl f* **22/1**

1163 **4** *shd* **Hits Only Jude (IRE)**[17] 1462 8-8-5 **64**..........................(b) NeilFarley(5) 6 64
(Declan Carroll) *hld up: hdwy over 3f out: rdn over 2f out: styd on same pce appr fnl f* **25/1**

5-05 **5** *1 ½* **Elmfield Giant (USA)**[6] 1671 4-9-6 **74**.............................. DavidNolan 3 71
(Richard Fahey) *chsd ldrs: rdn over 2f out: sn wknd* **16/1**

120- **6** *nse* **Destiny Blue (IRE)**[197] 7042 4-9-6 **74**.............................. PhillipMakin 7 71+
(Jamie Osborne) *s.i.s: hld up: hdwy over 3f out: hmpd 2f out: sn rdn: wknd over 1f out* **11/4**[2]

2520 **7** *½* **The Lock Master (IRE)**[34] 1098 4-9-7 **75**.......................... ChrisCatlin 1 71
(Michael Appleby) *s.i.s: heeadway over 8f out: rdn and wknd over 2f out* **20/1**

2m 11.86s (0.16) **Going Correction** -0.15s/f (Firm) **7** Ran SP% **112.5**
Speed ratings (Par 103): **93,92,88,88,87 87,87**
Tote Swingers: 1&2 £2.90, 1&3 £2.80, 2&3 £11.70 CSF £8.76 TOTE £2.00: £2.00, £3.00; EX 9.40.
Owner Frontline Bathrooms **Bred** Joe Rogers **Trained** Middleham Moor, North Yorks
■ Stewards' Enquiry : Toby Atkinson two-day ban: careless riding (May 20-21)

FOCUS
Ordinary form with the first pair clear. The winner was 7lb well in but probably showed his form.

1875 BET TOTEPOOL AT TOTESPORT.COM APPRENTICE H'CAP 6f 15y
4:50 (4:50) (Class 6) (0-60,60) 4-Y-0+ **£1,176** (£1,176; £269; £134) **Stalls** Centre

Form RPR
5-50 **1** **Fathey (IRE)**[101] [289] 5-8-4 **46** oh1 .... MatthewLawson(3) 9 55
(Charles Smith) *chsd ldrs: rdn and hung lft fr 1/2-way: led over 1f out: jnd on post* **14/1**
5351 **1** *dht* **Jonnie Skull (IRE)**[16] [1497] 5-8-2 **46** oh1 .... (vt) TobyAtkinson(5) 4 55
(Phil McEntee) *edgd lft s: sn chsng ldrs: reminders over 2f out: chal ins fnl f: r.o to join wnr post* **6/1**
5223 **3** *1 1/4* **Libertino (IRE)**[4] [1770] 4-8-11 **55** .... GeorgeDowning(5) 8 60
(Tony Carroll) *sn pushed along and prom: bmpd 4f out: rdn over 1f out: styd on: wnt 3rd post* **9/2**
1022 **4** *nk* **Exceedingly Good (IRE)**[2] [1815] 5-8-11 **55** .... LeonnaMayor(5) 7 59
(Roy Bowring) *s.i.s: hld up: hdwy and n.m.r over 2f out: ev ch ins fnl f: hung lft and no ex: lost 3rd post* **3/1**[1]
1040 **5** *1 1/4* **Dancing Welcome**[69] [698] 5-9-4 **57** .... (b) AdamCarter 6 59
(Milton Bradley) *sn pushed along and prom: bmpd 4f out: rdn over 1f out: styng on same pce whn n.m.r wl ins fnl f* **4/1**[3]
00-3 **6** *3/4* **Bennelong**[11] [1570] 5-9-7 **60** .... (b) KieranO'Neill 2 58
(Jim Best) *chsd ldr: rdn over 2f out: no ex ins fnl f* **7/2**[2]
0060 **7** *4* **Ronnie Howe**[2] [1818] 7-8-4 **46** oh1 .... (b) JamesRogers(3) 5 31
(Roy Bowring) *led: rdn and hdd over 1f out: wknd ins fnl f* **25/1**
6-00 **8** *14* **Edge End**[71] [662] 7-8-4 **46** oh1 .... (v) NathanAlison(3) 3 —
(Lisa Williamson) *dwlt: bhd fr 1/2-way* **150/1**
4-00 **9** *1 1/4* **Boxer Shorts**[72] [652] 5-8-3 **47** oh1 ow1 .... JosephYoung(5) 1 —
(Michael Mullineaux) *s.i.s: bhd fr 1/2-way* **66/1**

1m 15.24s (0.34) **Going Correction** +0.10s/f (Good) **9** Ran SP% **112.4**
Speed ratings (Par 101): **101,101,99,98,97 96,90,72,70**
Win: Fathey £5.30 Jonnie Skull £4.30. Place: F £5.30 JS £3.50 Libertino £2.00. Ex: F,JS £45.81 JS,F £40.22. Tricast: F,JS,L £221.98 JS,F,L £206.00. Tote Swingers: F&JS £7.90, F&L £5.60, JS&L £2.70 .
Owner Eventmaker Racehorses **Bred** Canice Farrell Jnr **Trained** Newmarket, Suffolk
Owner Rob Lewin **Bred** Rathasker Stud **Trained** Temple Bruer, Lincs

FOCUS
A dead-heat in this poor event in which most of them ply their trade on the all-weather nowadays. The form has been rated around the third.
T/Plt: £218.00 to a £1 stake. Pool of £33,205.00 - 111.19 winning tickets. T/Qpdt: £29.50 to a £1 stake. Pool of £2,474.00 - 62.00 winning tickets. CR

1410 RIPON (R-H)
Friday, May 6

OFFICIAL GOING: Good to firm (9.0)
Rail on bend from back straight to home straight bend out 6m adding 11yds to distances on round course.
Wind: Virtually nil Weather: Fine and dry

1876 ISIS MAIDEN AUCTION STKS 5f
5:40 (5:42) (Class 5) 2-Y-O **£2,590** (£770; £385; £192) **Stalls** High

Form RPR
1 **Chevanah (IRE)** 2-8-6 0 .... SilvestreDeSousa 6 66
(Ann Duffield) *trckd ldng pair: hdwy wl over 1f out: swtchd rt and rdn to chal jst ins fnl f: styd on wl to ld nr fin* **11/1**
3 **2** *nk* **Blue Shoes (IRE)**[13] [1515] 2-8-6 0 .... DuranFentiman 1 65
(Tim Easterby) *sn led: rdn along wl over 1f out: drvn ent fnl f: hdd and no ex towards fin* **9/2**[3]
223 **3** *3/4* **One Kool Dude**[20] [1383] 2-8-12 0 .... TonyHamilton 5 68
(Richard Fahey) *a cl up: rdn 2f out: drvn and ev ch ent fnl f: one pce last 100yds* **4/5**[1]
4 *3 3/4* **Excelette (IRE)** 2-8-13 0 .... TomEaves 2 56
(Bryan Smart) *chsd ldrs on outer: effrt 2f out: sn rdn: edgd rt and no imp* **7/2**[2]
5 *4 1/2* **Maria Anna (IRE)** 2-8-7 0 .... PaulMulrennan 3 34+
(Ann Duffield) *wnt lft s: a outpcd in rr* **12/1**
6 *5* **Metal Dealer (IRE)** 2-8-7 0 .... BillyCray(3) 4 19
(George Foster) *s.i.s and hmpd s: a bhd* **40/1**

59.57 secs (-1.13) **Going Correction** -0.175s/f (Firm) **6** Ran SP% **114.4**
Speed ratings (Par 93): **102,101,100,94,87 79**
Tote Swingers: 1&2 £3.00, 1&3 £2.30, 2&3 £2.10 CSF £59.65 TOTE £14.00: £4.30, £1.80; EX 74.70.
Owner D Mac A'Bhaird **Bred** Donal Mac A Bhaird **Trained** Constable Burton, N Yorks

FOCUS
Just a fair maiden, rated around the third and the race averages.

NOTEBOOK
Chevanah(IRE), a daughter of Chevalier, has a bit about her physically and can be expected to go on from this, not least as the experience is sure to sharpen her up, a little on and off the bridle but picking up well once she really grasped what was required. She'll be suited by 6f. (op 12-1 tchd 10-1)
Blue Shoes(IRE) duly stepped up on her Musselburgh third, showing bright speed, and a similar event should come her way before long. (op 5-1)
One Kool Dude will pick up a race at some point, but he's starting to look a little exposed already, having no obvious excuses here. (op 8-11 tchd 10-11)
Excelette(IRE), a daughter of Exceed And Excel, must have been showing something at home judged on her position in the betting and can be expected to do better next time, moving up threateningly but running green off the bridle (edged right). (op 4-1 tchd 10-3)
Maria Anna(IRE), a stablemate of the winner, is quite speedily bred but was too green to do herself justice, though hinting at ability by the finish without being subjected to a hard time. She'll do better in due course. (op 22-1)
Metal Dealer(IRE) didn't shape with any immediate promise, slowly away and always behind. (op 50-1)

1877 SIS PICTURE SERVICES (S) STKS 1m 1f 170y
6:10 (6:10) (Class 6) 3-4-Y-O **£1,942** (£578; £288) **Stalls** Low

Form RPR
-333 **1** **Bernisdale**[20] [1413] 3-8-4 54 .... RoystonFfrench 5 58
(George Moore) *mde all: rdn over 2f out: drvn appr fnl f: hld on gamely* **9/1**[3]
451 **2** *1/2* **Song To The Moon (IRE)**[10] [1592] 4-9-7 72 .... (p) MatthewDavies(3) 1 62
(George Baker) *propped and s.i.s and lost several l s: stdy hdwy and in tch 1/2-way: effrt and cl up 3f out: rdn to chse wnr over 2f out: drvn and hung rt ent fnl f: nt go past towards fin* **2/7**[1]
26-5 **3** *8* **Hartforth**[18] [1437] 3-8-9 67 .... (b) PaulMulrennan 2 45
(James Bethell) *chsd wnr: rdn along 3f out: sn drvn and btn* **9/2**[2]

2m 4.75s (-0.65) **Going Correction** -0.175s/f (Firm)
WFA 3 from 4yo 15lb **3** Ran SP% **105.9**
Speed ratings (Par 101): **95,94,88**
CSF £12.79 TOTE £6.60; EX 10.10.There was no bid for the winner.
Owner Evelyn Duchess Of Sutherland **Bred** Evelyn Duchess Of Sutherland **Trained** Middleham Moor, N Yorks

FOCUS
A weak race even by selling standards, this didn't take much winning.

1878 WEST MOOR STUD H'CAP 6f
6:45 (6:46) (Class 4) (0-85,85) 4-Y-O+ **£4,533** (£1,348; £674; £336) **Stalls** High

Form RPR
0-25 **1** **Discanti (IRE)**[17] [1457] 6-9-7 **85** .... (t) DuranFentiman 14 94
(Tim Easterby) *trckd ldrs: hdwy on stands' rail over 2f out: rdn to chse ldr over 1f out: styd on u.p ins fnl f to ld nr fin* **11/2**[2]
0-00 **2** *hd* **Legal Eagle (IRE)**[20] [1395] 6-8-6 **77** .... (p) DuilioDaSilva(7) 10 85
(Paul Green) *cl up: led 1/2-way: rdn pushed clr wl over 1f out: rdn ins fnl f: hdd and no ex nr fin* **10/1**
011- **3** *3/4* **Caranbola**[251] [5513] 5-8-8 **72** .... RobertWinston 3 78
(Mel Brittain) *swtchd rt s to r towards far rail: hdwy 1/2-way: rdn to chse ldrs over 1f out: kpt on* **16/1**
00-6 **4** *3/4* **Feeling Fresh (IRE)**[24] [1296] 6-8-7 **71** oh1 .... JamieMackay 6 74
(Paul Green) *dwlt and in rr: hdwy and nt clr run 2f out: swtchd rt and rdn wl over 1f out: kpt on strly fnl f: nrest at fin* **40/1**
2-15 **5** *1* **Nadeen (IRE)**[12] [1539] 4-9-4 **82** .... SilvestreDeSousa 2 82
(Michael Smith) *dwlt and towards rr: hdwy 2f out: sn rdn and kpt on ins fnl f: nrst fin* **5/1**[1]
001- **6** *2 1/4* **Sunrise Safari (IRE)**[200] [6987] 8-9-3 **81** .... (v) TonyHamilton 4 74
(Richard Fahey) *chsd ldrs: rdn along wl over 2f out: sn one pce* **11/1**
045- **7** *1/2* **Walvis Bay (IRE)**[189] [7212] 4-9-4 **82** .... AndrewMullen 1 73
(Tom Tate) *swtchd to r towards far rail: cl up 1/2-way: sn hdd and rdn: edgd lft and grad wknd* **7/1**
00-6 **8** *1* **Jobe (USA)**[29] [1200] 5-9-2 **80** .... (p) PhillipMakin 12 68
(Kevin Ryan) *hld up: effrt over 2f out: sn rdn and n.d* **17/2**
1111 **9** *1/2* **Dickie Le Davoir**[20] [1395] 7-9-1 **82** .... (b) RobertLButler(3) 11 68
(Richard Guest) *sn outpcd and a in rr* **13/2**[3]
U-00 **10** *1 1/2* **Red Cape (FR)**[18] [1438] 8-9-1 **79** .... TomEaves 5 61
(Ruth Carr) *led to 1/2-way: sn rdn along and wknd wl over 1f out* **14/1**
140- **11** *2* **Captain Scooby**[200] [6981] 5-8-9 **73** .... PaulMulrennan 13 48
(Richard Whitaker) *in tch: rdn along 1/2-way: sn btn* **25/1**
2330 **12** *1 1/2* **Sir Geoffrey (IRE)**[16] [1476] 5-9-1 **82** .... (b) BillyCray(3) 7 52
(David Nicholls) *chsd ldrs: rdn along wl over 2f out: sn wknd* **16/1**
20-0 **13** *6* **Di Stefano**[29] [1205] 4-8-10 **74** .... AdrianNicholls 8 25
(David Nicholls) *chsd ldrs: rdn along wl over 2f out: sn wknd* **11/1**
36-3 **14** *1 1/2* **Lady Florence**[11] [1356] 6-8-3 **74** .... JakePayne(7) 9 20
(David C Griffiths) *in tch: rdn along 1/2-way: sn wknd* **66/1**

1m 11.14s (-1.86) **Going Correction** -0.175s/f (Firm) **14** Ran SP% **120.4**
Speed ratings (Par 105): **105,104,103,102,101 98,97,96,95,93 91,89,81,79**
Tote Swingers: 1&2 £10.80, 1&3 £14.60, 2&3 £56.30 CSF £58.94 CT £859.73 TOTE £6.60: £2.80, £4.00, £5.40; EX 76.30.
Owner The Lapin Blanc Racing Partnership **Bred** Glending Bloodstock **Trained** Great Habton, N Yorks

FOCUS
A fairly useful sprint, and straightforward form for the grade. A couple went over to the far rail, including the third, which suggests there wasn't much between the sides, though it did pay to race handily. The first three all up there throughout, the fourth doing particularly well under the circumstances.
Jobe(USA) Official explanation: jockey said gelding hung right
Sir Geoffrey(IRE) Official explanation: jockey said gelding was unsuited by the good to firm ground

1879 SIS OB SERVICES H'CAP 1m 1f 170y
7:15 (7:16) (Class 3) (0-90,88) 4-Y-O+ **£7,569** (£2,265; £1,132; £566; £282) **Stalls** Low

Form RPR
51-1 **1** **Prince Of Johanne (IRE)**[20] [1200] 5-9-4 **85** .... (p) RobertWinston 4 93
(Tom Tate) *hld up in tch: hdwy over 3f out: trckd ldrs over 2f out: rdn to chal ent fnl f: sn led: drvn out* **4/1**[2]
00-0 **2** *nk* **Pleasant Day (IRE)**[34] [1092] 4-9-6 **87** .... TonyHamilton 2 95
(Richard Fahey) *hld up in rr: hdwy on outer over 2f out: rdn over 1f out: kpt on wl fnl f* **8/1**
00-1 **3** *1 1/4* **Granston (IRE)**[22] [1325] 10-9-7 **88** .... PhilipRobinson 1 93
(James Bethell) *trckd ldrs: hdwy over 3f out: cl up 2f out: led over 1f out: hdd and rdn ins fnl f: wknd fnl 100yds* **13/2**
305- **4** *1 3/4* **Dolphin Rock**[188] [7227] 4-8-13 **80** .... PhillipMakin 3 81
(David Barron) *trckd ldrs on inner: swtchd lft and rdn 2f out: drvn whn edgd rt ins fnl f: one pce* **11/4**[1]
10-5 **5** *1 1/2* **Jonny Lesters Hair (IRE)**[34] [1098] 6-9-1 **82** .... DuranFentiman 8 80
(Tim Easterby) *tk keen: hold chsd ldrs: hdwy and cl up 1/2-way: rdn to chal 3f out: drvn and slt ld wl over 1f out: hdd appr fnl f: hld whn n.m.r ins fnl f* **5/1**[3]
0332 **6** *1/2* **Cloudy Bay (USA)**[12] [1538] 4-8-13 **80** .... (p) PaulMulrennan 6 77
(Mrs K Burke) *chsd ldr: rdn along 3f out: drvn 2f out and grad wknd* **11/1**
52 **7** *1* **White Diamond**[20] [1388] 4-8-7 **74** .... TomEaves 7 69
(Malcolm Jefferson) *led: rdn along 3f out and sn jnd: drvn and hdd 2f out: hld whn n.m.r ins fnl f* **8/1**
4614 **8** *13* **Ahlawy (IRE)**[28] [1223] 8-9-0 **81** .... (bt) SilvestreDeSousa 5 49
(Frank Sheridan) *dwlt: a in rr* **18/1**

2m 2.27s (-3.13) **Going Correction** -0.175s/f (Firm) **8** Ran SP% **112.5**
Speed ratings (Par 107): **105,104,103,102,101 100,99,89**
Tote Swingers: 1&2 £7.20, 1&3 £5.10, 2&3 £9.90 CSF £34.37 CT £200.61 TOTE £6.00: £2.20, £2.00, £2.30; EX 42.20.
Owner David Storey **Bred** T J Rooney And Corduff Stud **Trained** Tadcaster, N Yorks

FOCUS
A fair handicap. It often pays to race handily on the round course here but the opposite proved the case on this occasion, the front two both coming from off the pace. The winner is rated better than ever.

NOTEBOOK
Prince Of Johanne(IRE) hasn't always looked the most straightforward, but is hard to fault at present, winning for the third start running here. He shouldn't go up too much more for this so is likely to be competitive again next time. (op 7-2)
Pleasant Day(IRE), runner-up in a Group 3 as a juvenile, shaped well on just his second start for Richard Fahey and shouldn't be long in taking advantage of this mark, running on strongly at the finish, the step up in trip clearly suiting. (op 10-1 tchd 15-2)
Granston(IRE) is as good as ever at the age of ten, travelling well enough for a long way to suggest his 4lb rise for Beverley may not prove beyond him. (op 6-1)

Dolphin Rock enjoyed a good first season for David Barron and the strength behind him in the market suggests shrewd connections believe there may be more to come from him this time round. He wasn't ridden as prominently as is often the case here and probably deserves another chance. (op 10-3 tchd 7-2)

Jonny Lesters Hair(IRE) has been a bit too keen for his own good on both starts this year, but has certainly shown enough to suggest he retains ability. (op 11-2 tchd 9-2)

Cloudy Bay(USA) has been allotted a stiff opening handicap mark on this evidence. (op 12-1 tchd 10-1)

White Diamond wasn't able to dominate as she had at Doncaster and faded.

1880 SIS LIVE MAIDEN STKS — 6f
7:50 (7:50) (Class 5) 3-Y-O — **£2,590** (£770; £385; £192) **Stalls** High

Form — RPR

332- **1** **Elusive Prince**[203] 6899 3-9-3 78 .... LeeNewman 5 — 84+
(David Barron) *prom stands' side: cl up 1/2-way: led over 2f out: rdn clr appr fnl f: kpt on strly* **9/2**[3]

64-4 **2** *4 1/2* **Moral Issue**[18] 1436 3-9-0 75 .... PatrickDonaghy(3) 9 — 69
(Jedd O'Keeffe) *prom stands' side: rdn along over 2f out: drvn over 1f out: styd on ins fnl f: 2nd of 9 in gp* **17/2**

0 **3** *1 1/4* **Alive And Kicking**[17] 1459 3-9-3 0 .... PhilipRobinson 10 — 65+
(James Bethell) *dwlt: sn chsng ldrs stands' side: n.m.r and swtchd rt 2f out: sn rdn and kpt on ins fnl f: nrst fin: 3rd of 9 in gp* **6/1**

50-0 **4** *1 1/4* **Decadence**[20] 1393 3-8-12 50 .... RobertWinston 4 — 56
(Eric Alston) *chsd ldng pair far side: rdn along over 2f out: hdwy to ld that gp over 1f out: kpt on 1st of 3 in gp* **22/1**

6-30 **5** *hd* **Roman Ruler (IRE)**[3] 1802 3-9-3 57 .... PhillipMakin 1 — 61
(Chris Fairhurst) *led far side gp: cl up 1/2-way: sn rdn and wknd wl over 1f out: 2nd of 3 in gp* **20/1**

6 *nk* **Imperator Augustus (IRE)**[161] 7587 3-9-3 82 .... PaulMulrennan 7 — 60
(Patrick Holmes) *trckd ldrs stands' side: hdwy to chse ldr 1/2-way: rdn over 2f out: drvn and wknd appr fnl f: 4th of 9 in gp* **22/1**

60- **7** *1 1/4* **Ryedale Dancer (IRE)**[265] 5092 3-8-12 0 .... DuranFentiman 6 — 51
(Tim Easterby) *racd stands' side: a midfield: 5th of 9 in gp* **50/1**

2-23 **8** *1* **Mother Jones**[18] 1436 3-8-12 75 .... TomEaves 11 — 47
(Bryan Smart) *overall ldr stands' side: rdn along 1/2-way: hdd over 2f out: sn drvn and wknd: hld whn n.m.r ins fnl f: 6th of 9 in gp* **11/4**[1]

9 *nk* **Love For Love**[26] 1258 3-8-12 59 .... SilvestreDeSousa 3 — 46
(David O'Meara) *racd far side: cl up: rdn along 1/2-way: sn wknd: last of 3 in gp* **9/1**

10 *1 1/4* **Beechcraft Baron (IRE)** 3-9-0 0 .... GilmarPereira(3) 2 — 47
(William Haggas) *dwlt and swtchd lft s: a in rr stands' side: 7th of 9 in gp* **33/1**

2- **11** *3 1/4* **Pearl Storm (IRE)**[314] 3439 3-9-3 0 .... LiamJones 12 — 37
(William Haggas) *s.i.s: a in rr stands' side: 8th of 9 in gp* **4/1**[2]

12 *22* **Ingenti** 3-8-12 0 .... PaddyAspell 8 — —
(Christopher Wilson) *s.i.s: a in rr stands' side: last of 9 in gp* **80/1**

1m 11.5s (-1.50) **Going Correction** -0.175s/f (Firm) — **12** Ran SP% **119.3**
Speed ratings (Par 99): **103,97,95,93,93 93,91,90,89,87 83,54**
Tote Swingers: 1&2 £9.40, 1&3 £6.10, 2&3 £11.10 CSF £38.89 TOTE £5.30: £2.30, £3.10, £2.10; EX 58.20.

Owner Bridge Extraction Systems Ltd **Bred** Usk Valley Stud **Trained** Maunby, N Yorks

FOCUS
Not a strong maiden overall, the proximity of some lowly-rated runners holding the form down. The winner is rated up 4lb on his 2yo best with the fifth the key to the form.

Imperator Augustus(IRE) Official explanation: jockey said gelding hung left throughout

Pearl Storm(IRE) Official explanation: trainer's rep had no explanation for the poor form shown

Ingenti Official explanation: jockey said filly had a breathing problem

1881 SIS FIRST FOR FOOTBALL DATA H'CAP — 2m
8:25 (8:25) (Class 5) (0-70,70) 4-Y-O+ — **£2,590** (£770; £385; £192) **Stalls** High

Form — RPR

00-6 **1** **Petella**[13] 1519 5-8-9 **55** .... TomEaves 8 — 68
(George Moore) *hld up in tch: smooth hdwy over 4f out: led on bit over 2f out: rdn clr over 1f out: styd on strly* **4/1**[2]

-350 **2** *6* **Leaving Alone (USA)**[13] 1519 4-8-5 **54** .... (p) AdrianNicholls 4 — 59
(Edwin Tuer) *hld up in rr: hdwy over 4f out and sn pushed along: swtchd outside and rdn over 2f out: drvn to chse wnr over 1f out: no imp fnl f* **6/1**[3]

5-01 **3** *2 3/4* **Spruzzo**[17] 1458 5-9-0 **60** .... KellyHarrison 6 — 62
(Chris Fairhurst) *led 2f: cl up: led over 7f out: rdn along and qcknd clr 4f out: hdd over 2f out: sn drvn and kpt on same pce* **6/1**[3]

06-3 **4** *hd* **Grey Command (USA)**[9] 1617 6-8-5 **51** oh3 .... AndrewMullen 9 — 53
(Mel Brittain) *prom: rdn along over 3f out: drvn over 2f out: kpt on same pce* **16/1**

-601 **5** *1* **King In Waiting (IRE)**[11] 1556 8-9-1 **61** 6ex .... (p) SilvestreDeSousa 5 — 62
(David O'Meara) *prom: led after 2f: pushed along and hdd over 7f out: rdn and outpcd 3f out: swtchd lft and drvn over 2f out: plugged on* **13/8**[1]

21-0 **6** *9* **Jackday (IRE)**[27] 1243 6-9-10 **70** .... (p) DuranFentiman 1 — 60
(Tim Easterby) *hld up: a bhd* **8/1**

0-46 **7** *2 1/2* **Terenzium (IRE)**[17] 1458 9-8-9 **55** .... (p) PaulMulrennan 7 — 42
(Micky Hammond) *hld up towards rr: sme hdwy over 5f out: rdn 4f out: sn no imp* **14/1**

/5-0 **8** *15* **Tayarat (IRE)**[26] 1036 6-8-9 **55** .... (bt) RoystonFfrench 3 — 24
(Michael Chapman) *dwlt and reminders s: sn chsng ldrs: rdn along over 4f out: sn wknd and bhd* **40/1**

56-0 **9** *15* **Smarties Party**[8] 407 8-8-5 **54** .... PatrickDonaghy(3) 2 — —
(Clive Mulhall) *a towards rr: outpcd and bhd fnl 4f* **40/1**

3m 29.53s (-2.27) **Going Correction** -0.175s/f (Firm)
WFA 4 from 5yo+ 3lb — **9** Ran SP% **115.2**
Speed ratings (Par 103): **98,95,93,93,93 88,87,79,72**
Tote Swingers: 1&2 £5.10, 1&3 £7.10, 2&3 £2.20 CSF £28.18 CT £140.20 TOTE £4.90: £1.10, £2.50, £2.10; EX 29.70.

Owner A Crute & Partners **Bred** C And Mrs Wilson **Trained** Middleham Moor, N Yorks

FOCUS
A modest staying event, though it was at least soundly run, the winner hacking up. The favourite disappointed and the form is rated around the placed horses for now.

T/Plt: £1,402.50 to a £1 stake. Pool of £39,155.00 - 20.38 winning tickets. T/Qpdt: £54.90 to a £1 stake Pool of £4,819.00 - 64.90 w. tckts JR 1882a (Foreign Racing) - See Raceform Int.

1843 ASCOT (R-H)
Saturday, May 7

OFFICIAL GOING: Good to firm (good in places; stands' side 9.7, centre 9.3, far side 9.2; round 8.5)
Rail movement increased 10 &12f races by 12yds.
Wind: Moderate across Weather: low cloud

1883 JOHN DOYLE BUCKHOUNDS STKS (LISTED RACE) — 1m 4f
2:20 (2:20) (Class 1) 4-Y-O+ — **£17,031** (£6,456; £3,231; £1,611; £807; £405) **Stalls** Low

Form — RPR

/11- **1** **Alainmaar (FR)**[364] 1911 5-8-12 112 .... RichardHills 5 — 117
(Roger Varian) *trckd ldr: led over 2f out: pushed clr ins fnl f: easily* **11/8**[1]

4-13 **2** *6* **Shamali**[14] 1528 6-9-1 105 .... JimmyFortune 2 — 110
(William Haggas) *racd in 4th tl hdwy into 3rd 5f out: styd on u.p to chse wnr over 1f out but nvr any ch: hld on wl for 2nd* **7/2**[3]

11-5 **3** *1 1/4* **Verdant**[21] 1403 4-8-12 103 .... RyanMoore 1 — 105
(Sir Michael Stoute) *hld up in rr: pushed along over 3f out: swtchd lft to outside wl over 2f out: styd on fr over 1f out but nvr gng to rch 2nd and nvr any ch w wnr* **2/1**[2]

50-5 **4** *1* **World Heritage**[23] 1342 5-8-12 105 .... AndreaAtzeni 6 — 104?
(Robert Eddery) *led: rdn and hdd over 2f out: outpcd by wnr sn after and lost 2nd over 1f out: styd on same pce* **20/1**

0000 **5** *13* **Big Creek (IRE)**[42] 991 4-8-12 94 .... (p) JamesDoyle 3 — 83
(J S Moore) *t.k.h: chsd ldrs in 3rd to 5f out: wknd fr 3f out* **33/1**

0-0 **6** *6* **Full Steam**[120] 92 4-8-7 90 .... HayleyTurner 4 — 68
(Ed Dunlop) *in rr but in tch: rdn over 3f out: sn wknd* **20/1**

2m 32.28s (-0.22) **Going Correction** +0.25s/f (Good) — **6** Ran SP% **110.1**
Speed ratings (Par 111): **110,106,105,104,95 91**
toteswingers:1&2 £1.10, 2&3 £1.80, 1&3 £1.10 CSF £6.20 TOTE £2.10: £1.70, £1.70; EX 5.20.

Owner Hamdan Al Maktoum **Bred** Fares Stables Ltd **Trained** Newmarket, Suffolk

FOCUS
Following 4.5mm of rain overnight and during the morning the going was given as good to firm, good in places (GoingStick: Stands' side 9.7, Centre 9.3, Far side 9.2; Round 8.9). The rail was positioned 4yds in from the maximum width on the Round course from around the 1m2f start to the home straight, increasing distances by approximately 16yds over 2m and by 12yds over 1m2f and 1m4f. Richard Hills described the ground as "just on the quick side of good".A decent little Listed race, and the winner is likely to be able to compete successfully at a higher level this year. It is worth being positive about the form.

NOTEBOOK
Alainmaar(FR) looked a progressive sort prior to sustaining a hairline fracture to a pastern a year ago, and this performance suggests he's lost none of his ability during his time off the track. He stayed on strongly to win comfortably and, while favoured by the weights in this contest, looks fully capable of taking the step up to Group company now. Having now shown he acts round here it wouldn't be a surprise to see him return for the Hardwicke at the Royal meeting. (op 6-5 tchd 11-10)

Shamali didn't face an easy task giving weight all round, but he has a good record at this track and his trainer believed the longer trip would suit him well. He ran a solid race, without the extra distance looking a huge plus, and probably a strongly run 1m2f is ideal for him. (tchd 4-1)

Verdant ran poorly on his reappearance at Newbury but was expected to strip fitter here. This was another sub-par performance, though, and his stable just hasn't hit top form yet. (op 5-2 tchd 11-4)

World Heritage, who made the running, didn't run at all badly, but is still below the level he showed for Pascal Bary in France. (op 22-1 tchd 16-1)

Big Creek(IRE) sweated up between his hind legs beforehand. (op 40-1)

Full Steam, who was debuting for a new stable having previously been trained by Andre Fabre, was outclassed. (op 16-1 tchd 14-1)

1884 BOVIS HOMES FILLIES' H'CAP — 1m (S)
2:50 (2:53) (Class 2) 3-Y-O+ — **£29,142** (£8,671; £4,333; £2,164) **Stalls** Centre

Form — RPR

51-4 **1** **Law Of The Range**[34] 1114 4-8-11 **82** .... SebSanders 4 — 94
(Marco Botti) *pressed ldrs tl def advantage over 2f out: sn drvn and qcknd over 1f out: jnd ins fnl f and hrd pressed but kpt finding and hld on gamely clsng stages* **12/1**

20-0 **2** *nk* **Sooraah**[13] 1541 4-8-11 **87** .... HarryBentley(5) 10 — 98
(William Haggas) *hld up in tch: smooth hdwy fr 2f out: drvn and qcknd ins fnl f and sn upsides: stl chalng tl outpcd by wnr clsng stages* **10/1**

200- **3** *nk* **Fontley**[224] 6346 4-9-10 **95** .... DarryllHolland 5 — 105
(Eve Johnson Houghton) *hld up in rr: rdn and rapid hdwy appr fnl f to qckn and chal wnr: stl upsides tl outpcd clsng stages* **25/1**

00-2 **4** *11* **Bianca De Medici**[17] 1499 4-8-2 **73** .... HayleyTurner 14 — 58
(Hughie Morrison) *slt ld tl hdd over 2f out: styd pressing ldrs tl outpcd by ldng trio appr fnl f* **10/1**

2120 **5** *nk* **Avonrose**[21] 1406 4-8-1 **77** .... NeilFarley(5) 11 — 61
(Derek Shaw) *chsd ldrs: rdn: hung rt and easily outpcd over 1f out* **20/1**

3-34 **6** *1 1/2* **Maid In Heaven (IRE)**[7] 1681 4-9-7 **92** .... JimCrowley 12 — 73
(Walter Swinburn) *in rr: stl plenty to do 2f out: drvn and styd on wl ins fnl f but nvr any ch* **6/1**[2]

3- **7** *3/4* **Bea Remembered**[202] 6970 4-9-10 **95** .... MartinDwyer 6 — 74
(Brian Meehan) *bmpd s: in rr: hdwy 2f: nvr rchd ldrs and one pce ins fnl f* **25/1**

42-0 **8** *nk* **Bahati (IRE)**[35] 1104 4-9-7 **92** .... JimmyFortune 7 — 70
(Jonathan Portman) *wnt rt s: sn chsng ldrs: rdn and hung rt over 1f out: sn btn* **12/1**

221- **9** *1 3/4* **Entitled**[184] 7310 4-8-8 **79** .... RyanMoore 13 — 53
(Sir Michael Stoute) *in tch: chsd ldrs 2f out: no imp: wknd ins fnl f* **7/2**[1]

350- **10** *2 1/4* **Kalahaag (IRE)**[217] 6559 3-7-7 **82** .... KieranO'Neill(5) 1 — 48
(Richard Hannon) *in rr: sme hdwy and in tch over 2f out: nvr rchd ldrs and btn over 1f out* **11/1**

50-0 **11** *1/2* **Lily Again**[24] 1319 3-8-11 **95** .... MichaelHills 3 — 60
(Paul Cole) *in tch: sme hdwy fr 3f out: nvr gng pce to chal and wknd wl over 1f out* **14/1**

01-0 **12** *2 3/4* **Celebrity**[22] 1361 3-8-1 **85** .... FrankieMcDonald 9 — 44
(Richard Hannon) *nvr beyond mid-div* **20/1**

21-5 **13** *7* **Oceanway (USA)**[42] 990 3-8-0 **87** .... LouisBeuzelin(3) 8 — 30
(Mark Johnston) *pressed ldrs over 4f: sn btn* **14/1**

212- **14** *nk* **Frances Stuart (IRE)**[301] [3918] 4-8-7 **78**........................ DavidProbert 2 23
(Andrew Balding) *pressed ldrs 5f* **15/2**[3]

1m 40.69s (0.09) **Going Correction** +0.10s/f (Good)
WFA 3 from 4yo 13lb **14** Ran SP% **120.7**
Speed ratings (Par 96): **103,102,102,91,91 89,88,88,86,84 84,81,74,74**
toteswingers:1&2:£28.30, 2&3:£67.60, 1&3:£41.20 CSF £120.32 CT £2999.34 TOTE £14.50: £4.10, £4.40, £9.00; EX 155.40 TRIFECTA Not won..
Owner Christopher McHale **Bred** Brookside Breeders Club **Trained** Newmarket, Suffolk

FOCUS
They came up the centre of the track and three came clear in this fillies' handicap and provided a thrilling finish. They have been rated positively but none of the others showed their form.

NOTEBOOK
Law Of The Range raced prominently throughout and gradually pulled away from the rest from the 2f pole, but she got lonely out in front and when the second and third closed her down it looked to be game over. She rallied once joined, though, and the impression left was that she was value for further than the winning margin indicates. She has shown this tenacity on more than one occasion in the past, and it will stand her in good stead as she steps up in class. Apparently she wouldn't want the ground any quicker than this. (op 9-1)
Sooraah was too keen and proved disappointing at Musselburgh on her reappearance, but she holds a Windsor Forest entry, suggesting her connections think she's a bit better than her current mark might suggest. She settled better this time and came through to challenge going well. She quickened when asked, too, but the winner just found more close home. She can probably win a similar race even after a rise in the weights.
Fontley, apart from the runner-up, was the only other filly in the line-up who holds a Windsor Forest entry. She faced no easy task under top weight but picked up well from off the pace to join the first two in the battle for the line. She lacked the previous run the first two had had, and can be expected to come on for this (won second time out previous two seasons).
Bianca De Medici looked fairly handicapped on the best of her AW efforts, and ran a fair race to finish fourth, but she was still 11 lengths back from the first three. (op 12-1)
Avonrose, another with plenty of AW form to her name, ran a lot better than she did at Newbury on her return to the turf. (tchd 16-1)
Maid In Heaven(IRE) looks held off her current mark and probably needs easing a pound or two. (op 8-1)
Bea Remembered, debuting for her new stable, is entitled to come on for this, although she's another who looks high enough in the weights at present. (tchd 22-1)
Entitled had every chance if good enough, but was another fancied horse from the Stoute stable to fail to run to her best. (tchd 9-2)

1885 TOTESPORT VICTORIA CUP (H'CAP) 7f
3:25 (3:29) (Class 2) 4-Y-0+
£52,963 (£15,861; £7,930; £3,969; £1,980; £994) **Stalls** Centre

Form RPR
00-4 **1** **Hawkeyethenoo (IRE)**[6] [1720] 5-8-7 **96**........................ GaryBartley(3) 7 110
(Jim Goldie) *hld up in tch: smooth hdwy and squeezed between horses 2f out: drvn to ld 1f out: kpt on strly* **15/2**[2]
0-30 **2** *2 1/2* **Manassas (IRE)**[21] [1406] 6-8-7 **93**.................... MartinDwyer 3 100
(Brian Meehan) *chsd ldrs: str chal fr 2f out and upsides u.p 1f out: nt gng pce of wnr ins fnl f but hld on wl for 2nd* **25/1**
3-01 **3** *3/4* **Nasri**[13] [1541] 5-8-8 **97**.................................... MichaelO'Connell(3) 4 102
(David Nicholls) *disp ld tl def advantage over 2f out: sn hrd drvn: hdd 1f out: kpt on same pce ins fnl f* **20/1**
0-26 **4** *2 1/4* **Brae Hill (IRE)**[21] [1406] 5-8-7 **98**..................................... LeeTopliss(5) 15 97+
(Richard Fahey) *in rr: drvn and hdwy over 1f out: styd on wl fnl f: nt rch ldrs* **9/1**[3]
01-1 **5** *nse* **Horseradish**[34] [1111] 4-9-0 **100**.. HayleyTurner 1 99
(Michael Bell) *pressed ldrs: rdn over 2f out: ev ch over 1f out: wknd ins fnl f* **5/1**[1]
1-01 **6** *nk* **Fathsta (IRE)**[12] [1564] 6-9-0 **100**... SebSanders 9 98
(David Simcock) *pressed ldrs: ev ch 2f out: outpcd ins fnl f* **20/1**
115/ **7** *hd* **Shamandar (FR)**[582] [6449] 4-9-0 **100**.............................. MichaelHills 10 97+
(William Haggas) *in rr: hdwy fr 2f out: styd on fnl f: nt rch ldrs* **20/1**
06-0 **8** *1 1/4* **Parisian Pyramid (IRE)**[34] [1111] 5-8-8 **94**..................... CathyGannon 6 88
(Kevin Ryan) *in tch: rdn and kpt on ins fnl f: nt rch ldrs* **33/1**
00-6 **9** *1/2* **Noble Citizen (USA)**[11] [1594] 6-8-6 **92**.......................(be) MartinLane 26 85+
(David Simcock) *in rr: rapid hdwy 2f out: styd on ins fnl f: nt rch ldrs* **33/1**
41-1 **10** *hd* **Excellent Guest**[11] [1594] 4-8-2 **91**................................ SimonPearce(3) 5 83
(George Margarson) *disp ld tl over 2f out: wknd ins fnl f* **12/1**
01-5 **11** *1 1/2* **Gouray Girl (IRE)**[11] [1594] 4-8-9 **95**............................ DarryllHolland 18 83
(Walter Swinburn) *in tch: drvn and kpt on fr over 1f out: nt rch ldrs* **33/1**
520- **12** *1 3/4* **Zero Money (IRE)**[204] [6888] 5-7-13 **90**.......................... KieranO'Neill(5) 8 73
(Roger Charlton) *in tch: rdn over 2f out: kpt on ins fnl f: nt trble ldrs* **16/1**
00-5 **13** *1/2* **Advanced**[34] [1111] 8-8-1 **90** ow1.. AmyRyan(3) 12 72
(Kevin Ryan) *chsd ldrs: rdn 3f out: one pce fnl 2f* **16/1**
000- **14** *2 1/4* **Mon Cadeaux**[232] [6147] 4-8-9 **95**................................... DavidProbert 11 71
(Andrew Balding) *disp ld tl over 2f out: wknd appr fnl f* **50/1**
-110 **15** *nk* **Bravo Echo**[21] [1406] 5-8-2 **91** ow1...................................... KierenFox(3) 2 66
(Michael Attwater) *sn drvn along: styd on ins fnl f: nvr rchd ldrs* **33/1**
1033 **16** *1 1/4* **Lowther**[1] [1849] 6-9-2 **102**......................................(be) GrahamGibbons 14 74
(Alan Bailey) *chsd ldrs: rdn and no imp over 2f out: wknd over 1f out* **16/1**
40-0 **17** *1 1/4* **Himalya (IRE)**[23] [1340] 5-9-10 **110**.................................... RyanMoore 22 78
(Jeremy Noseda) *slowly away: in rr: pushed along and sme hdwy 2f out: rchd ldrs* **20/1**
03-4 **18** *nk* **Douze Points (IRE)**[21] [1410] 5-7-12 **89**...................(p) HarryBentley(5) 19 57
(Ed de Giles) *nvr bttr than mid-div* **25/1**
00-0 **19** *3/4* **Rulesn'regulations**[56] [848] 5-8-5 **96**.......................... AdamBeschizza(5) 24 62
(Matthew Salaman) *chsd ldrs: wknd 2f out* **33/1**
400- **20** *1 1/4* **Sunraider (IRE)**[224] [6363] 4-8-0 **93** ow2................. MatthewLawson(7) 17 55
(B W Hills) *in tch: rdn 3f out: wknd 2f out* **50/1**
03-4 **21** *1/2* **Lutine Bell**[34] [1111] 4-8-6 **92**......................................(b) GregFairley 27 53
(Mike Murphy) *chsd ldrs over 4f* **20/1**
6-44 **22** *shd* **Dhaular Dhar (IRE)**[7] [1694] 9-8-3 **89**........................ AndrewMullen 20 50
(Jim Goldie) *spd over 3f* **40/1**
6-04 **23** *1 1/4* **Castles In The Air**[28] [1242] 6-9-1 **101**......................... FrederikTylicki 16 58
(Richard Fahey) *disputed ld tl over 2f out: sn btn* **20/1**
-000 **24** *5* **Oasis Dancer**[72] [678] 4-9-1 **101**..................................... JimCrowley 21 45
(Ralph Beckett) *chsd ldrs over 4f* **40/1**
0-00 **25** *2 1/2* **Al Muheer (IRE)**[21] [1406] 6-7-12 **89**.............................(v) NeilFarley(5) 25 26
(David Nicholls) *chsd ldrs over 4f* **16/1**
65-0 **26** *1 3/4* **Corporal Maddox**[31] [1186] 4-9-0 **100**............................. RichardHills 23 32
(Jamie Osborne) *bhd fr 1/2-way* **80/1**
-000 **27** *3 3/4* **Golden Desert (IRE)**[79] [587] 7-8-13 **99**......................... JimmyFortune 28 21
(Robert Mills) *a in rr* **33/1**
65-0 **28** *2 1/2* **Layla's Hero (IRE)**[34] [1111] 4-8-4 **90**........................ FrankieMcDonald 13 —
(David Nicholls) *bhd fr 1/2-way* **33/1**

1m 26.49s (-0.71) **Going Correction** +0.10s/f (Good) **28** Ran SP% **136.5**
Speed ratings (Par 109): **112,109,108,105,105 105,105,103,103,102 101,99,98,96,95 94,92,92,91,90 89,89,88,82,79 77,73,7**
toteswingers: 1&2:£25.00, 2&3:£340.10, 1&3:£67.00 CSF £184.74 CT £3676.02 TOTE £7.40: £1.80, £9.00, £9.90, £2.70; EX 288.90 Trifecta £11808.00 Pool: £56,072.99 - 3.39 winning units..
Owner Johnnie Delta Racing **Bred** S Leigh & R Leigh & Islandmore Stud **Trained** Uplawmoor, E Renfrews

FOCUS
A typically competitive Victoria Cup. They merged into one group up the centre for most of the race before fanning out 2f out, and the principals came to the fore towards the far side. Low draws dominated. A clear personal best from the winner with the next two solid guides.

NOTEBOOK
Hawkeyethenoo(IRE) didn't get the best of luck when a running-on fourth over 6f at Newmarket on his reappearance and, while this was a step up in trip (last ran over further than 6f back in July 2009), he did win over 7.5f at Beverley as a 3-y-o, and the way he finishes his races suggested the return to this distance wouldn't inconvenience him. Running off the same mark as at Newmarket, he quickened up well from off the pace to win quite comfortably, and a rise in the weights shouldn't prevent him from being a big player in similar races later in the season. It looks likely that he'll be dropped back to 6f for the Wokingham next. (op 8-1, tchd 9-1 in places)
Manassas(IRE) hadn't run well here in the past but he'd put in a couple of solid efforts in defeat this season and came here in form. He ran close to his best in defeat, but a likely rise will not make things any easier.
Nasri, put up 7lb for winning at Musselburgh, was always up with the pace towards the far side and ran a solid race. He could probably be just as effective back over 6f.
Brae Hill(IRE) gets credit as he raced away from where the race developed on the far side, but stayed on strongly to get into the frame. Like the runner-up, he came here on the back of good efforts in similarly competitive 1m handicaps. (op 12-1)
Horseradish didn't look harshly treated off just 4lb higher than when successful on his reappearance over 6f at Doncaster but, having travelled well, he didn't see this seventh furlong out as well here. Easier ground suits him best, but a return to 6f is probably key, and he'll still hold strong claims in the Wokingham. (op 7-1)
Fathsta(IRE) didn't get home and is probably at his best over 6f or an easy 7f.
Shamandar(FR), returning from a lengthy absence, shaped with a good deal of promise and can be expected to come on quite a bit for this. She was last seen running in Group 1 company at two, and her Windsor Forest entry suggests connections haven't entirely given up hope she retains pattern-race ability.
Parisian Pyramid(IRE) showed pace for a long way, but he's a sprinter really and will be suited by a drop back in trip. (tchd 40-1)
Noble Citizen(USA) ◆, drawn near the stands' side, raced on the outer of the pack throughout and produced a strong run to try to get into contention as the principals, racing on the far side, drew clear. He faced an impossible task as it turned out, but ran a lot better than his finishing position suggests. Placed in two tough handicaps over this C&D last season off similar marks to this, he could well have a hand to play in the Buckingham Palace Stakes at the Royal meeting granted more luck with the draw.
Golden Desert(IRE) Official explanation: jockey said gelding never travelled and hung right-handed

1886 MCGEE GROUP MAIDEN STKS 5f
4:00 (4:01) (Class 3) 2-Y-O
£7,771 (£2,312; £1,155; £577) **Stalls** Centre

Form RPR
2 **1** **North Star Boy (IRE)**[7] [1678] 2-9-3 0................................ RyanMoore 6 83+
(Richard Hannon) *in tch: pushed along 1/2-way: str run to ld ins fnl f: styd on to go clr nr fin* **8/11**[1]
2 *1 1/2* **Lethal Force (IRE)** 2-9-3 0.. JamesDoyle 7 78
(Clive Cox) *wnt lft s: sn rcvrd and pressed ldrs 1/2-way: chal 1f out: kpt on ins fnl f but nt gng pce of wnr cl home* **33/1**
2 **3** *nk* **Bayleyf (IRE)**[16] [1505] 2-9-3 0.. LukeMorris 3 77
(John Best) *trckd ldrs: slt ld ins fnl 2f: hdd ins fnl f: kpt on same pce* **3/1**[2]
4 *3/4* **Caledonian Spring (IRE)** 2-9-3 0.............................. DarryllHolland 2 74+
(Paul D'Arcy) *in tch: hdwy and nt clr run ins fnl 2f: rdn and styd on wl ins fnl f nt rch ldng trio* **8/1**[3]
5 *2 1/4* **Dissent (IRE)** 2-9-3 0.. SebSanders 1 66
(Gerard Butler) *pressed ldrs: ev ch over 1f out: outpcd ins fnl f* **12/1**
6 *4* **Charles The Great (IRE)** 2-9-3 0................................... JimmyFortune 4 51
(Andrew Balding) *in tch: rdn along 1/2-way: wknd appr fnl f* **33/1**
54 **7** *hd* **Liebesziel**[6] [1721] 2-8-12 0... KieranO'Neill(5) 5 51
(Alan McCabe) *slt ld tl hdd insde fnl 2f: wknd over 1f out* **28/1**

61.36 secs (0.16) **Going Correction** +0.10s/f (Good) **7** Ran SP% **111.0**
Speed ratings (Par 97): **97,94,94,92,89 82,82**
toteswingers 1&2:£6.10, 2&3:£5.30, 1&3:£1.10 CSF £32.18 TOTE £1.90: £1.40, £4.20; EX 22.80 Trifecta £35.90 Pool: £1,17.20 - 24.23 winning units..
Owner Robert Tyrrell **Bred** Hascombe And Valiant Studs **Trained** East Everleigh, Wilts

FOCUS
It's questionable how strong a maiden this was, but the time was good and the form has been rated on the positive side.

NOTEBOOK
North Star Boy(IRE) put up no more than a workmanlike effort to win, but he looks the type that will improve further for racing, and another furlong should suit him. He's a possible for the Coventry but his stable has plenty of ammunition in this division. (op 5-6 after Evens in a place, tchd 10-11)
Lethal Force(IRE), a half-brother to modest triple 7f scorer Army Of Stars, was unfancied but showed up well the whole way and ran a pleasing race on his debut. His stable is in good form. (op 20-1)
Bayleyf(IRE) showed ability despite being green on his debut at Folkestone, but it's doubtful he stepped up considerably on that effort here. (tchd 5-2)
Caledonian Spring(IRE) was tightened up for room around a furlong out and might have finished a bit closer with a clearer run. He's fully entitled to come for his debut. (op 10-1)
Dissent(IRE), who is out of a mare who was a Group 2 winning sprinter at two, is another entitled to benefit from this debut effort. (op 11-1 tchd 14-1)
Charles The Great(IRE) is bred to improve as he steps up in trip. (op 25-1)

1887 D'ARENBERG H'CAP 1m 4f
4:35 (4:35) (Class 3) (0-95,93) 4-Y-O+ **£8,418** (£2,505; £1,251; £625) **Stalls** Low

Form RPR
26-3 **1** **Rock A Doodle Doo (IRE)**[17] [1477] 4-9-3 **89**................. MartinDwyer 8 101+
(William Jarvis) *hld up in rr: gd hdwy between horses fr 2f out: qcknd appr fnl f: str run u.p to ld fnl 100yds: won gng away* **9/2**[2]
101- **2** *3/4* **Blissful Moment (USA)**[234] [6074] 4-9-5 **91**...................... RyanMoore 9 102+
(Sir Michael Stoute) *chsd ldrs: drvn and styd on to ld appr fnl f: hdd fnl 100yds: kpt on: nt gng pce of wnr* **11/2**[3]
16-2 **3** *1 3/4* **Udabaa (IRE)**[21] [1402] 4-8-10 **82**...................................... RichardHills 11 90
(Marcus Tregoning) *chsd ldrs: rdn 3f out: hmpd ins fnl 2f: styd on again to take 3rd ins fnl f* **4/1**[1]

146- **4** *hd* **Zuider Zee (GER)**[239] 5908 4-9-4 **90** NickyMackay 3 100+
(John Gosden) *in tch: lost position 4f out: hdwy over 2f out: styng on whn hmpd over: kpt on again cl home: nt rcvr* **8/1**

10-5 **5** *1¼* **Cashpoint**[21] 1402 6-8-5 **82** KieranO'Neill(5) 10 88
(Anthony Middleton) *disp ld 3f: styd chsng ldr: slt ld u.p 2f out: hdd appr fnl f: wknd nr fin* **16/1**

400- **6** *1¼* **Berling (IRE)**[260] 5273 4-9-2 **88** JimmyFortune 7 99+
(John Dunlop) *in rr: str run on outside fr 2f out: styng on to press ldrs and ev ch whn veered bdly lft to stands' side ins fnl f:* **8/1**

01-2 **7** *½* **Dansili Dancer**[42] 991 9-9-7 **93** AdamKirby 2 96
(Clive Cox) *in tch: chsd ldrs fr 2f out and wl there fnl f tl wknd fnl 120yds* **8/1**

1-00 **8** *2¾* **Licence To Till (USA)**[17] 1477 4-9-4 **90** GregFairley 6 89
(Mark Johnston) *drvn to disp ld and def advantage 9f out: rdn 3f out: hdd 2f out: wknd appr fnl f* **33/1**

10-0 **9** *¾* **Mister Angry (IRE)**[17] 1477 4-9-6 **92** DarryllHolland 1 90
(Mark Johnston) *chsd ldrs: rdn along 3f out: wknd fr 2f out* **33/1**

116- **10** *½* **Sparkling Smile (IRE)**[225] 6320 4-9-6 **92** DavidProbert 12 89
(David Lanigan) *in rr: hdwy to chse ldrs 4f out: wknd over 2f out* **16/1**

1211 **11** *2½* **Beaubrav**[28] 1238 5-8-9 **81** (t) JimCrowley 4 74
(Michael Madgwick) *rdn 3f out: a in rr* **16/1**

111- **12** *1* **Spensley (IRE)**[160] 7612 5-8-10 **82** HayleyTurner 5 73
(James Fanshawe) *hld up in rr: sme hdwy on ins fr 4f out: kpt on into mid-div on rail over 2f out: nvr nr ldrs and sn wknd* **9/1**

2m 33.15s (0.65) **Going Correction** +0.25s/f (Good) **12** Ran SP% **120.4**
Speed ratings (Par 107): **107,106,105,105,104 103,103,101,100,100 98,98**
toteswingers 1&2:£4.00, 2&3:£6.10, 1&3:£3.10 CSF £30.06 CT £107.88 TOTE £5.50: £2.20, £2.50, £2.00; EX 32.10 Trifecta £60.30 Pool: £1,459.66 - 17.89 winning units..
Owner The Doodle Doo Partnership **Bred** Mrs A S O'Brien And Lars Pearson **Trained** Newmarket, Suffolk

FOCUS
This looked a decent handicap on paper and the winner is better than the margin of success suggests. The first four were all unexposed or progressive and this is strong form, rated on the positive side.

NOTEBOOK
Rock A Doodle Doo(IRE) ◆, held up in rear, was bumped 2f out and squeezed for room approaching the furlong marker, but he bravely went through the gap and eventually ran down Blissful Moment inside the last. He can't go up too much for this and will remain of interest in similar company, and the bigger the field and stronger the pace the better he will look. The Ebor is in the back of connections' mind for later in the season, but nearer to hand the Duke of Edinburgh Handicap, back over this C&D, is likely to be on his agenda. (op 5-1)
Blissful Moment(USA) came with a strong run down the outside to look the winner entering the final furlong, but he was run down by the winner well inside the last. A galloping companion of Carlton House, it was a good effort given his stable's other representatives haven't appeared to be shining. (op 7-1)
Udabaa(IRE), who found Modun too good at Newbury on his reappearance, got squeezed up between two rivals just inside the final 2f and again just inside the final furlong. He kept on afterwards, though, and again showed enough to suggest a race like this can be won with him. (op 9-2)
Zuider Zee(GER) shaped well on his reappearance despite being hampered a furlong out. He stays further than this and will be of interest when reverting to a longer trip. (op 11-1)
Cashpoint, behind Udabaa when fifth in the Newbury handicap won by Modun on his reappearance, couldn't reverse that form but still ran a solid race from towards the front.
Berling(IRE) won at Newbury last May despite veering badly when in front, but he threw any chance he had away with a similar manoeuvre this time. He was running on down the outside to dispute third when he suddenly veered left across to the stands' rail. Clearly, for all that he is talented, he is pretty quirky. Official explanation: jockey said colt veered left inside final furlong (op 17-2 tchd 9-1)
Dansili Dancer, second in a Group 3 on Polytrack last time, isn't as good on turf, but it was still a little disappointing to see him run such an average race off what looked a fair mark. (tchd 7-1 and 17-2)

1888 ALFRED FRANKS & BARTLETT SUNGLASSES H'CAP 6f
5:10 (5:10) (Class 3) (0-95,95) 4-Y-0+ **£8,418** (£2,505; £1,251; £625) **Stalls** Centre

Form RPR

234- **1** **Imperial Guest**[204] 6888 5-9-3 **94** AshleyHamblett(3) 11 104
(George Margarson) *trckd ldrs: drvn to ld and edgd rt appr fnl f: hld on wl* **12/1**

230- **2** *nk* **Deacon Blues**[225] 6319 4-9-7 **95** HayleyTurner 5 106+
(James Fanshawe) *hld up in tch: nt clr run fr 2f out: swtchd lft appr fnl f: str run fnl 120yds: fin wl: nt quite get up* **8/1**[3]

241- **3** *hd* **Edinburgh Knight (IRE)**[130] 7993 4-9-1 **89** TonyCulhane 2 98
(Paul D'Arcy) *trckd ldrs and hdwy 2f out to chal thrght fnl f: no ex clsng stages and lost 2nd last strides* **8/1**[3]

66-5 **4** *1½* **Yer Woman (IRE)**[35] 1104 4-8-9 **88** KieranO'Neill(5) 9 92
(Richard Hannon) *in rr: hdwy 2f out: styd on u.p on rails fnl f: nt rch ldng trio* **28/1**

0-05 **5** *¾* **Striking Spirit**[14] 1518 6-9-6 **94** AndrewMullen 8 96
(David Nicholls) *mde most tl hdd appr fnl f: wknd fnl 50yds* **14/1**

00-0 **6** *1* **Ghostwing**[17] 1476 4-8-11 **85** (b) FergusSweeney 15 83
(John Gallagher) *s.i.s: in rr: nt clr run fr 2f out: swtchd rt and hdwy fnl f: styd on wl clsng stages but nt gng pce to rch ldrs* **66/1**

52-1 **7** *1* **Chiefdom Prince (IRE)**[18] 1459 4-8-13 **87** RyanMoore 3 88+
(Sir Michael Stoute) *pressed ldrs: stl wl there but drvn whn hmpd appr fnl f: nt rcvr* **11/2**[2]

212- **8** *nk* **Dungannon**[225] 6319 4-9-2 **90** JimmyFortune 6 84+
(Andrew Balding) *trckd ldrs: nt clr run 2f out: styng on whn bdly hmpd appr fnl f: nt rcvr* **10/1**

45-1 **9** *1* **Son Of The Cat (USA)**[28] 1237 5-9-0 **93** (t) AdamBeschizza(5) 17 84+
(Brian Gubby) *in rr: drvn along 1/2-way: styd on ins fnl f: nt rch ldrs* **20/1**

0-45 **10** *shd* **Mac Gille Eoin**[30] 1197 7-8-12 **86** DarryllHolland 1 77
(John Gallagher) *chsd ldrs: rdn over 2f out and outpcd: n.d after* **33/1**

050- **11** *½* **Kingsgate Choice (IRE)**[238] 5966 4-9-0 **88** LukeMorris 19 77
(John Best) *in rr: rdn 1/2-way: styd on ins fnl f: nvr a threat* **28/1**

4002 **12** *1½* **Star Rover (IRE)**[7] 1675 4-9-3 **91** CathyGannon 20 75
(David Evans) *chsd ldrs over 3f* **16/1**

0-00 **13** *½* **Joe Packet**[34] 1111 4-9-5 **93** JimCrowley 12 76
(Jonathan Portman) *in tch: rdn 3f out: no ch fnl 2f* **18/1**

40-3 **14** *1½* **Crown Choice**[18] 1457 6-9-6 **94** AdamKirby 7 72
(Walter Swinburn) *outpcd most of way* **9/2**[1]

111- **15** *2½* **Kuanyao (IRE)**[231] 6198 5-9-5 **93** SebSanders 16 63
(Peter Makin) *chsd ldrs: wkng and no ch whn n.m.r ins fnl f* **9/1**

230- **16** *1½* **Secret Witness**[197] 7060 5-9-7 **95** (b) TomMcLaughlin 4 60
(Ronald Harris) *pressed ldrs 4f* **16/1**

30-6 **17** *hd* **Sohraab**[22] 1366 7-8-12 **86** ChrisCatlin 13 50
(Hughie Morrison) *chsd ldrs over 3f* **33/1**

266- **18** *6* **Barons Spy (IRE)**[199] 7014 10-8-2 **81** HarryBentley(5) 14 26
(Richard Price) *spd to 1/2-way* **100/1**

1m 13.91s (-0.49) **Going Correction** +0.10s/f (Good) **18** Ran SP% **126.3**
Speed ratings (Par 107): **107,106,106,104,103 102,100,100,98,98 98,96,95,93,90 88,87,79**
toteswingers: 1&2:£20.20, 2&3:£14.40, 1&3:£13.00 CSF £101.01 CT £861.01 TOTE £12.60: £2.80, £2.50, £2.60, £7.30; EX 120.90 Trifecta £1307.60 Part won. Pool: £1,767.09 - 0.10 winning units..
Owner John Guest Racing **Bred** John Guest Racing Ltd **Trained** Newmarket, Suffolk
■ Stewards' Enquiry : Ashley Hamblett two-day ban: careless riding (May 21,23)

FOCUS
Following the Victoria Cup, where those drawn low were favoured, the field edged over to race towards the far-side rail in this sprint handicap. Things got a bit messy. The winner carried on his 2010 progress.

NOTEBOOK
Imperial Guest picked up well when asked to go on and just held off the late challenge of the top weight. He has a liking for this track and, although his three good efforts in defeat here last year came over 7f, he showed here that he's equally if not more effective over the sprinters' distance. Presumably the Wokingham will be the target now. (op 16-1)
Deacon Blues ◆ travelled well in behind and was brought with a late run which came up just a little short. A progressive 3-y-o last year, he appears to be still on the upgrade judged by this reappearance effort, and he has the style of running that suits these big-field sprint handicaps. He's one to keep in mind for a similar contest. (op 15-2)
Edinburgh Knight(IRE) had a good draw and looked fairly handicapped judged on his last win on the all-weather. He ran well. Official explanation: vet said gelding lost a right-fore shoe (op 12-1 tchd 15-2)
Yer Woman(IRE), back in trip, came from off the pace on the far side, which was the place to be. She won't mind stepping up to 7f. (op 25-1)
Striking Spirit made the running up the centre of the track before drifting over to the far side. He looks to be steadily regaining his form.
Ghostwing given a very patient ride out the back, got going all too late, but showed enough to suggest he might have a race in him off this mark if things drop right. He carries his head high and isn't straightforward, though.
Chiefdom Prince(IRE) had a good draw and showed early pace but dropped out quite tamely after being squeezed up approaching the final furlong. His stable really doesn't look to be at the top of its game at the moment. Official explanation: jockey said colt suffered interference in running (op 5-1 tchd 13-2)
Dungannon was staying on when badly hampered next to the rail approaching the furlong marker. He was in the process of running a sound race on his reappearance and is entitled to come on for the outing. Official explanation: jockey said gelding suffered interference in running
Son Of The Cat(USA), poorly drawn, did quite well as he challenged widest of all. He's run well over this C&D before and, although fairly high in the handicap now, isn't one to write off.
Crown Choice was in trouble some way out and proved disappointing. He hadn't run particularly well here on his previous two tries and perhaps the track just isn't to his liking. (op 11-2)
T/Jkpt: Not Won. T/Plt: £453.00. to a £1 stake. Pool of £158,570.52 - 255.48 winning units. T/Qpdt: £32.40 to a £1 stake. Pool of £11,127.33 - 253.55 winning units. ST

1389 HAYDOCK (L-H)
Saturday, May 7

OFFICIAL GOING: Flat course - good (good to firm in places) changing to good (good to soft in places) after race 1 (2.00); jumps course - good (good to soft in places)
All races on outer home straight and distances on round course reduced by 6yds.
Wind: Light, half-behind Weather: Overcast with rain before racing

1889 TOTEPLACEPOT SPRING TROPHY STKS (LISTED RACE) 7f
2:00 (2:02) (Class 1) 3-Y-O+
£17,031 (£6,456; £3,231; £1,611; £807; £405) **Stalls** Low

Form RPR

542- **1** **Beacon Lodge (IRE)**[294] 4166 6-9-7 109 PhilipRobinson 2 114
(Clive Cox) *racd keenly: a.p: n.m.r briefly jst under 2f out: led over 1f out: asserted wl ins fnl f: r.o wl* **4/1**[2]

110- **2** *2* **Kakatosi**[224] 6349 4-9-7 103 LiamKeniry 7 109
(Andrew Balding) *a.p: effrt to chal over 1f out: nt qckn wl ins fnl f: wl hld cl home* **9/2**[3]

10-2 **3** *¾* **Redford (IRE)**[28] 1242 6-9-7 111 TedDurcan 3 107
(David Nicholls) *hld up: effrt to chse ldrs over 1f out: wnt 3rd ins fnl f: kpt on but unable to mount serious chal* **15/8**[1]

-344 **4** *2¼* **Duff (IRE)**[21] 1397 8-9-7 103 (b) ShaneKelly 4 101
(Edward Lynam, Ire) *led: rdn and carried hd high 2f out: hdd over 1f out: wknd fnl 100yds* **5/1**

0-50 **5** *8* **Lovelace**[21] 1397 7-9-7 104 AdrianNicholls 8 79
(David Nicholls) *missed break: bhd: u.p 2 out: nvr able to get on terms* **6/1**

133- **6** *3¾* **Folly Bridge**[247] 5694 4-9-2 93 SteveDrowne 6 64
(Roger Charlton) *in tch: pushed along 3f out: rdn 2f out: wknd over 1f out* **16/1**

1m 26.96s (-3.94) **6** Ran SP% **109.8**
toteswingers: 1&2 £4.60, 1&3 £2.90, 2&3 £3.60. CSF £20.89 TOTE £5.00: £2.80, £2.60; EX 23.60 Trifecta £69.30 Pool: £740.00 - 7.89 winning units..
Owner Mr And Mrs P Hargreaves **Bred** Mrs Bill O'Neill **Trained** Lambourn, Berks

FOCUS
All races on outer home straight and distances on Round course reduced by 6yds. This was well run and the form looks sound. Beacon Lodge was close to his 2009 level.

NOTEBOOK
Beacon Lodge(IRE), winner of the race in 2009, again came out on top, forcing his way between runners, having already been bumped, just inside the final 2f and staying on strongly for the in-form Clive Cox. He was only allowed to take his chance because the rain arrived in time, and he's always one to consider at Listed/minor Group 3 level when conditions are in his favour. (op 9-2)
Kakatosi travelled strongly and stayed on once headed, making a pleasing reappearance. A progressive 7f handicapper last season, winning four times, he looks well worth a try at 6f on run style and breeding, and should improve on this first outing in 224 days. (op 5-1)
Redford(IRE) reappeared with a satisfactory effort over 6f behind a stablemate at Thirsk and was understandably made favourite, but he lacked the pace to seriously challenge on the day, and will be seen to better effect back in a bigger field, although whether he's likely to get that now with a rating of 111 remains to be seen. (op 7-4)
Duff(IRE) is a regular in this type of race, but he hasn't won since October 2009, and was always likely to leave himself vulnerable in blasting off. (op 13-2)
Lovelace, last year's winner, was always on the backfoot having blown the start, and can be given another chance. (op 13-2)

Folly Bridge, with the lowest BHA rating of these by some way, never threatened to get involved and will do better back in handicaps. (op 12-1)

1890 TRY TOTEQUICKPICK IF YOU'RE FEELING LUCKY MAIDEN STKS 6f

2:30 (2:31) (Class 5) 2-Y-O **£2,914** (£867; £433; £216) **Stalls** High

Form	Pos	Dist	Horse / Trainer / Comment	Jockey	RPR
	1		**Mabroor (USA)** 2-9-3 0 (Mark Johnston) *in tch: rdn over 3f out: prog and swtchd rt jst ins fnl f: r.o to ld fnl 100yds: sn edgd lft and won a shade comf* **7/2**[2]	SilvestreDeSousa 4	87+
	2	3/4	**Brocklebank (IRE)** 2-9-3 0 (Kevin Ryan) *prom: pushed along and nt qckn 2f out: r.o to chal ins fnl f: hld cl home* **16/1**	PaulMulrennan 6	85+
	3	3 1/4	**Ballesteros** 2-9-3 0 (Brian Meehan) *trckd ldrs: wnt 2nd over 2f out: rdn to ld 1f out: hdd fnl 100yds: no ex fnl 50yds* **7/1**	ShaneKelly 3	75+
	4	6	**Banksy** 2-9-3 0 (John Gosden) *led: rdn and hdd 1f out: wknd fnl 100yds* **7/1**	RobertHavlin 11	57+
	5	2 1/2	**Fiction Or Fact (IRE)** 2-9-3 0 (Kevin Ryan) *dwlt: towards rr: u.p and swtchd rt over 2f out: hdwy to chse clr front quartet over 1f out: no imp* **11/1**	FrannyNorton 7	53+
	6	3 1/2	**Echoes Of Joy** 2-9-3 0 (David Evans) *dwlt: rn green: bhd: kpt on modly fnl f: nvr a danger* **33/1**	PatCosgrave 9	39
	7	2 1/4	**Special Boy (IRE)** 2-9-3 0 (Saeed Bin Suroor) *midfield: pushed along over 2f out: btn over 1f out* **3/1**[1]	TedDurcan 2	32
	8	5	**Lexi's Prince (IRE)** 2-9-3 0 (Tom Dascombe) *missed break: rn green and bhd: u.p over 2f out: nvr a threat* **13/2**[3]	RichardKingscote 8	17
0	9	2 1/2	**Cotes Du Rhone (IRE)**[25] 1290 2-8-12 0 (David Evans) *dwlt: a bhd* **50/1**	SeanLevey(5) 5	10
	10	11	**Pint Size** 2-9-3 0 (David Nicholls) *dwlt: sn pushed along in midfield: wknd over 1f out: eased whn btn ins fnl f* **11/1**	AdrianNicholls 1	—
5	11	1 1/2	**Egyptian Cross**[29] 1209 2-9-3 0 (John Weymes) *prom: pushed along over 2f out: sn wknd: eased whn btn ins fnl f* **33/1**	J-PGuillambert 10	—

1m 15.24s (1.44) **Going Correction** +0.10s/f (Good) **11** Ran SP% **115.9**
Speed ratings (Par 93): **92,91,86,78,75 70,67,61,57,43 41**
toteswingers: 1&2 £14.40, 1&3 £5.30, 2&3 £25.60. CSF £56.32 TOTE £5.20: £2.00, £5.00, £2.40; EX 76.40.
Owner Hamdan Al Maktoum **Bred** Falcon Wood Partners **Trained** Middleham Moor, N Yorks

FOCUS

Probably just an ordinary juvenile maiden, but the race should produce winners. The field was well spaced out and the form could be rated higher.

NOTEBOOK

Mabroor(USA), whose price increased to $300,000 as a yearling, is a half-brother to two winners in the US. He needed to be kept up to his work early, but became stronger as the race progressed and, once switched towards the rail, he really hit overdrive. As with so many juveniles from this yard, he's expected to come on appreciably, especially once encountering a sounder surface, and it'll be interesting to see where he heads next. (op 5-1)

Brocklebank(IRE), whose dam was a fairly useful sprinter, looked the apparent Kevin-Ryan second string, but was well away and soon prominent. He looked beaten with 2f to run, but really started to stay on strongly. This was a nice start and he should go one better.

Ballesteros, whose dam is related to smart sprinter Chief Editor, comes from a yard whose juveniles often benefit markedly from a run, and this one's inexperience was evident late on. He showed a good bit of ability, though, and should improve, with him likely to be effective at 5f at this stage. (op 9-2)

Banksy, who cost £70,000 as a 2-y-o, showed plenty of pace before tiring late on. He's likely to appreciate quicker ground and should improve for his leading yard. (op 5-1)

Fiction Or Fact(IRE), half-brother to several winners, including one over 5f as a 2-y-o, appeared to find it all a bit overwhelming early, but he was noted keeping on nicely under a hands and heels ride, and should improve considerably.

Echoes Of Joy has plenty of stamina in his pedigree, the dam being a 2m winner including over hurdles, related to Classic Cliché and My Emma, and he was badly in need of this experience. Already gelded, he's likely to have learned a lot, and can win once granted a stiffer test, possibly in nurseries. (op 28-1)

Special Boy(IRE), by a speedy sire but with plenty of stamina on his dam's side, didn't offer much, and needs to improve markedly before he's winning. (op 5-1)

Lexi's Prince(IRE) is related to numerous winners at up to 1m2f, but has plenty of speed in his pedigree. He blew his chance with a slow start and fully deserves another shot. (op 15-2 tchd 8-1 in a place)

1891 BET TOTEPOOL AT TOTESPORT.COM CONDITIONS STKS 6f

4:10 (4:12) (Class 2) 3-Y-O+ **£12,462** (£3,732; £1,866; £934; £466) **Stalls** High

Form	Pos	Dist	Horse / Trainer / Comment	Jockey	RPR
34-0	1		**Bated Breath**[35] 1093 4-9-0 107 (Roger Charlton) *a.p on outer: led under 2f out: rdn over 1f out: edgd lft and r.o ins fnl f: a doing enough whn pressed* **9/4**[2]	SteveDrowne 1	112+
20-0	2	1/2	**Society Rock (IRE)**[23] 1340 4-9-0 115 (James Fanshawe) *hld up in rr: effrt to chse wnr over 1f out: chalng ins fnl f but a looked hld* **11/4**[3]	PatCosgrave 2	110
60-6	3	1	**Royal Rock**[35] 1093 7-9-0 103 (Chris Wall) *hld up: effrt to chse ldrs over 1f out: styd on same pce wl ins fnl f* **15/2**	TedDurcan 4	107
122-	4	6	**Victoire De Lyphar (IRE)**[231] 6177 4-9-0 103 (David Nicholls) *racd keenly: led: rdn and hdd under 2f out: wknd ins fnl f* **9/5**[1]	AdrianNicholls 6	88
0/0-	5	18	**Tamagin (USA)**[386] 1353 8-9-0 108 (Lydia Pearce) *w ldr tl pushed along and wknd over 2f out: lost tch fnl f: t.o* **28/1**	(p) StevieDonohoe 5	—

1m 12.33s (-1.47) **Going Correction** +0.10s/f (Good) **5** Ran SP% **108.4**
Speed ratings (Par 109): **111,110,109,101,77**
toteswinger: 1&2 £5.30. CSF £8.48 TOTE £2.60: £1.30, £1.50; EX 7.50.
Owner K Abdulla **Bred** Juddmonte Farms Ltd **Trained** Beckhampton, Wilts

FOCUS

Good form for the grade, rated around the runner-up.

NOTEBOOK

Bated Breath endured a nightmare run on his reappearance at Doncaster, but trouble in running was never likely to be a problem in this small field and, having travelled strongly through the early part of the race, he went on inside the final 2f and stayed on for a workmanlike success. He saw plenty of daylight, which probably wouldn't have been ideal, and can improve on this bare form returned to a more competitive heat. This was only his seventh start and he's expected to be a Group-class sprinter come the end of the season. (tchd 2-1)

Society Rock(IRE), last season's 50-1 Golden Jubilee runner-up, hasn't matched that form since and was disappointing on his return when doing too much on his way to post. Held up early, he was a touch keen, and didn't respond immediately when asked, but stayed on nicely to bustle up the winner and perhaps a return to Ascot will see him recapture his best form. (tchd 3-1)

Royal Rock will have been suited by the little cut in the ground and he ran his best race since winning at Ascot back in October 2009. This type of race probably presents him with his best chance of winning these days, and he was probably unfortunate to bump into a couple of younger, up-and-coming sorts. (tchd 7-1)

Victoire De Lyphar(IRE) was most progressive when joining Dandy Nicholls last year, winning a valuable 3-y-o sprint at York and finishing runner-up in the Ayr Gold Cup on his final start. Expected to progress on to Group-race honours this year, he seemed fit enough and bagged the early lead against the rail, but always looked to be over-racing and ultimately had little left in reserve. Although disappointing, this should have taken the fizz out of him, and a return to quicker ground can help in future. He was reported to have hung left-handed. Official explanation: jockey said gelding hung left-handed (op 15-8 tchd 9-4)

Tamagin(USA), returning from 386 days off on this debut for a new yard, would have been a player on his old form, but dropped right out and, although he probably needed it, it remains to be seen how much ability he retains. (op 25-1)

1892 BET TOTEPOOL ON 0800 221 221 H'CAP 1m 2f 95y

5:20 (5:20) (Class 4) (0-85,85) 4-Y-O+ **£5,180** (£1,541; £770; £384) **Stalls** Low

Form	Pos	Dist	Horse / Trainer / Comment	Jockey	RPR
11-4	1		**Bourne**[21] 1402 5-9-5 **83** (Luca Cumani) *in tch: effrt to chal over 1f out: led ent fnl f: r.o: in command fnl 100yds* **8/11**[1]	J-PGuillambert 4	91+
644-	2	3/4	**Onyx Of Arabia (IRE)**[198] 7042 4-8-7 **71** (Brian Meehan) *rrd s: hld up in rr: rdn over 1f out: hdwy ins fnl f: styd on to take 2nd towards fin: nt gng pce to chal wnr* **25/1**	(b) ShaneKelly 9	77
003-	3	hd	**The Only Key**[221] 6447 5-8-10 **81** (Jane Chapple-Hyam) *a.p: rdn to ld 2f out: hdd ent fnl f: styd on same pce towards fin* **7/2**[2]	LewisWalsh(7) 7	87
513-	4	1 1/4	**Leader Of The Land (IRE)**[234] 6074 4-9-5 **83** (David Lanigan) *prom: effrt to chal over 2f out: stl ev ch 1f out: nt qckn fnl 75yds* **8/1**[3]	TedDurcan 6	86
1340	5	1	**Porgy**[21] 1412 6-8-12 **81** (David Simcock) *hld up: impr to chal over 2f out: one pce ins fnl f* **18/1**	LauraPike(5) 8	82
54-0	6	hd	**Tartan Gunna**[21] 1410 5-9-7 **85** (Mark Johnston) *hld up: rdn over 1f out: kpt on ins fnl f: nvr able to chal* **17/2**	PhilipRobinson 2	86
403-	7	3/4	**Quanah Parker (IRE)**[143] 7878 5-8-8 **72** oh1 ow1 (Richard Whitaker) *plld hrd: in tch: rdn and outpcd 2f out: no imp on ldrs after* **33/1**	RobertHavlin 1	71
33-3	8	2 1/4	**Azimuth (USA)**[18] 1460 4-8-9 **73** (Ann Duffield) *led: rdn and hdd 2f out: wknd fnl f* **14/1**	FrannyNorton 3	68

2m 15.6s (-0.40) **Going Correction** +0.10s/f (Good) **8** Ran SP% **120.5**
Speed ratings (Par 105): **105,104,104,103,102 102,101,99**
toteswingers: 1&2 £5.90, 1&3 £1.80, 2&3 £12.30. CSF £26.86 CT £51.17 TOTE £1.70: £1.10, £3.30, £1.50; EX 19.50.
Owner Aston House Stud **Bred** Aston House Stud **Trained** Newmarket, Suffolk

FOCUS

A fairly ordinary handicap, run at a steady gallop. Bourne can be rated better than bare form, with the next two close to their marks.

T/Plt: £1,375.30 to a £1 stake. Pool of £91,565.41 - 48.60 winning tickets. T/Qpdt: £175.30 to a £1 stake. Pool of £5,486.05 - 23.15 winning tickets. DO

1862 LINGFIELD (L-H)

Saturday, May 7

OFFICIAL GOING: Good to firm (8.6)

Wind: medium, behind Weather: dry, warm

1893 TOTESPORT 0800 221 221 CHARTWELL FILLIES' STKS (GROUP 3) (TURF) 7f

2:10 (2:10) (Class 1) 3-Y-O+

£28,385 (£10,760; £5,385; £2,685; £1,345; £675) **Stalls** High

Form	Pos	Dist	Horse / Trainer / Comment	Jockey	RPR
0-01	1		**Perfect Tribute**[10] 1602 3-8-5 98 (Clive Cox) *restless in stalls: chsd ldrs: rdn and outpcd 1/2-way: rallied u.p and swtchd lft over 1f out: edgd lft u.p: led ins fnl f: r.o wl: eased towards fin* **12/1**	LukeMorris 7	110
33-1	2	1 3/4	**Flambeau**[21] 1397 4-9-3 107 (Henry Candy) *lw: led: rdn 2f out: hdd ins fnl f: no ex and btn fnl 75yds* **8/11**[1]	DaneO'Neill 6	110
103-	3	1 3/4	**Pyrrha**[281] 4540 5-9-3 105 (Chris Wall) *chsd ldrs: rdn to chse ldr and edgd rt wl over 1f out: unable qck ent fnl f: kpt on same pce after* **12/1**	NeilCallan 3	106
311-	4	1	**Tropical Paradise (IRE)**[251] 5554 5-9-3 108 (Peter Winkworth) *racd in midfield: rdn over 2f out: hdwy u.p to chse ldng trio jst over 1f out: no ex and btn 1f out: one pce after* **10/1**[3]	IanMongan 2	102
211-	5	1/2	**Dever Dream**[204] 6887 4-9-3 105 (William Haggas) *lw: stdd and swtchd rt s: hld up wl bhd: stl plenty to do whn swtchd rt bhd rival wl over 1f out: swtchd lft and nudged along over 1f out: kpt on ins fnl f: nvr on terms* **9/2**[2]	EddieAhern 4	101+
11-3	6	2 3/4	**Eucharist (IRE)**[21] 1404 3-8-5 100 (Richard Hannon) *racd in midfield: rdn ent fnl 3f: struggling u.p over 2f out: n.d after* **10/1**[3]	JoeFanning 9	90
400-	7	6	**Sonning Rose (IRE)**[203] 6927 3-8-5 95 (Mick Channon) *stdd s and sn swtchd rt: a in rr: no ch fnl 2f* **50/1**	SamHitchcott 1	73
4/5-	8	3/4	**Green Dandy (IRE)**[16] 4-9-3 100 (E J O'Neill, France) *chsd ldr tl wl over 1f out: one pce whn short of room and hmpd sn after: lost pl and wl btn after* **25/1**	FrankieDettori 5	75

1m 20.05s (-3.25) **Going Correction** -0.175s/f (Firm) course record
WFA 3 from 4yo+ 12lb **8** Ran SP% **115.5**
Speed ratings (Par 110): **111,109,107,105,105 102,95,94**
toteswingers:1&2 £3.30, 2&3 £2.60, 1&3:£14.90 CSF £21.51 TOTE £13.00: £2.40, £1.20, £3.00; EX 25.90 Trifecta £355.70 Pool: £884.45 - 1.84 winning units..
Owner Mildmay Racing & D H Caslon **Bred** Mildmay Bloodstock **Trained** Lambourn, Berks
■ Stewards' Enquiry : Luke Morris one-day ban: careless riding (May 21); 2nd incident, two-day ban: careless riding (May 23-24)

FOCUS
There was 2mm of rain overnight and a further millimetre in the morning, but the ground was still on the fast side. The straight course was at its full width. Jockeys confirmed it was quick going, and there were reports after the Oaks trial that the round course was a bit patchy. There was a medium wind following the runners up the straight. This Group 3 was won in 2006 by Echelon, whose numerous triumphs afterwards included a Group 1, and in 2008 Sabana Perdida, who followed up in the Windsor Forest at Royal Ascot. The third from last season's race, Reggane, later won the Grade 1 in E P Taylor Stakes in Canada. The form of this latest running looks strong, with the pace was good and the 'right' horses chasing home a rapidly improving winner, and the course record was lowered by 0.13 seconds. The slight tailwind will have helped the quick time, though, and it paid to race prominently.

NOTEBOOK
Perfect Tribute ◆ became the first 3-y-o to win this since 2004. Having needed all of 6f when landing an Ascot Listed race on her previous start, the step up in trip helped her on this return to Group 3 company. She had been too keen in the Fred Darling when racing at the same level over 7f on her reappearance, but this time she was under pressure well over 3f out. However, she had been well placed and responded gamely to pressure, as so many tend to for the increasingly effective Luke Morris. A daughter of the impressive Dubawi, this was only the winner's sixth start and there's no telling how far she can progress. One to keep on side. (op 11-1)
Flambeau impressed when winning a Listed race over this trip at Leicester on her reappearance, and the form has worked out nicely. However, she's a filly with a lot more speed than stamina and didn't stay as well in this stronger company, her stride shortening inside the final furlong after leading at a good clip against the near rail. She got warm beforehand, but did the same before her return. It's possible this came a little bit soon after such a big performance (only three-week break), but she looks a sprinter. (op 4-5 tchd 5-6)
Pyrrha made all in this race on her reappearance last year, but the competition was tougher 12 months on. She was stuck a bit wide of the rail and was one-paced, but kept on. (op 10-1)
Tropical Paradise(IRE) ran as though in need of the outing. Her latest three wins have been gained at Goodwood, including at this level when last seen in August. (op 9-1 tchd 8-1)
Dever Dream ◆, returning from a 204-day break, was given an awfully negative ride by Eddie Ahern. Admittedly, a wide draw didn't help, but the third and fourth-placed finishers were berthed even lower and her record suggests it's not essential that she's held up well off the pace. She had little chance considering how the race unfolded, but despite her unpromising position the jockey took a long time to get serious and then found trouble over a furlong out. There should be better to come. (op 7-1)
Eucharist(IRE) was well below the form she showed in the Fred Darling on her reappearance. (op 11-1)

1894 TOTEPOOL OAKS TRIAL STKS (LISTED RACE) (TURF) 1m 3f 106y
2:40 (2:43) (Class 1) 3-Y-O

£22,708 (£8,608; £4,308; £2,148; £1,076; £540) **Stalls** High

Form				RPR
1-1	**1**		**Zain Al Boldan**[25] [1286] 3-8-12 78 SamHitchcott 5 (Mick Channon) *stdd s: hld up towards rr: gd hdwy over 3f out: led over 2f out: sn rdn and qcknd clr: r.o strly: v easily* **5/1**	105+
4-1	**2**	6	**Field Of Miracles (IRE)**[23] [1332] 3-8-12 82 WilliamBuick 1 (John Gosden) *swtg: pushed along leaving stalls: led after 1f: rn wd bnd ent st: edging bk to inner after: hdd and rdn over 2f out: sn outpcd by wnr and wl hld fnl 2f: kpt on for clr 2nd* **9/4**[1]	93
65-0	**3**	3 ½	**Date With Destiny (IRE)**[23] [1339] 3-8-12 94 RichardHughes 8 (Richard Hannon) *stdd s: hld up in last: hdwy on outer 3f out: rdn ent fnl 2f: wnt modest 3rd over 1f out: no imp after* **4/1**[3]	87
0-2	**4**	2 ¾	**Galivant (IRE)**[23] [1332] 3-8-12 0 FrankieDettori 7 (J W Hills) *chsd ldng trio: rdn and unable qck wl over 2f out: one pce u.p and wl hld fnl 2f* **12/1**	82
-211	**5**	¾	**Saint Helena (IRE)**[21] [1401] 3-8-12 72 ChrisCatlin 2 (Harry Dunlop) *led for 1f: chsd ldrs after: pushed along and struggling on downhill run 4f out: drvn and outpcd wl over 2f out: one pce and wl btn fnl 2f* **20/1**	81
2-4	**6**	1	**Always The Lady**[13] [1549] 3-8-12 0 AdamKirby 9 (Clive Cox) *lw: chsd ldr after 1f out: rdn and unable qck wl over 2f out: drvn and btn ent fnl 2f* **7/2**[2]	79
4-	**7**	nse	**Al Mayasah (IRE)**[207] [6825] 3-8-12 0 TomQueally 3 (David Simcock) *str: stdd s: hld up in last trio: swtchd rt and effrt ent fnl 2f: sn rdn and no prog: n.d* **25/1**	79
-111	**8**	13	**Palm Pilot (IRE)**[38] [1051] 3-8-12 79 EddieAhern 6 (Ed Dunlop) *lw: in tch in midfield: lost pl qckly ent st: lost tch over 2f out: eased ins fnl f* **12/1**	64
50-2	**9**	½	**Barathea Dancer (IRE)**[17] [1481] 3-8-12 76 JohnFahy 4 (Roger Teal) *broke wl: grad stdd bk towards rr: dropped to last and struggling on downhill run 4f out: lost tch u.p 3f out: eased ins fnl f* **16/1**	56

2m 29.66s (-1.84) **Going Correction** -0.175s/f (Firm) **9** Ran SP% **119.5**
Speed ratings (Par 107): **99,94,92,90,89 88,88,79,78**
toteswingers:1&2 £3.10, 2&3 £3.50, 1&3 £4.70 CSF £17.31 TOTE £5.80: £1.90, £1.40, £2.00; EX 20.20 Trifecta £120.80 Pool: £684.44 - 4.19 winning units..
Owner Jaber Abdullah **Bred** Tweenhills & R & L Warner Bloodstock **Trained** West Ilsley, Berks

FOCUS
Last year's running had little influence on the Oaks, but the 2009 winner Midday finished second at Epsom, while 2008 runner-up Look Here went one better in the main event. The last filly to win this race and follow up in the Epsom Oaks was Ramruma in 1999. This looked a weak edition beforehand, with the highest RPR on offer just 90, and that was achieved by Date With Destiny over 7f at as a 2-y-o. The winner did it well and the time was similar to the colts in the Derby Trial, but this is well off Oaks form.

NOTEBOOK
Zain Al Boldan travelled well and handled the track beautifully before striding away without having to be seriously asked, but it's questionable what she achieved. The time was a respectable 0.16 seconds slower than the following Derby Trial, but the runner-up, Field Of Miracles, earned an RPR of only 76 when winning a maiden last time and looks thoroughly awkward, while the third-placed finisher, the aforementioned Date With Destiny, did not handle the track, and the fourth, Galivant, is still a maiden. The winner was taking her record to 3-3, but her profile before this was hardly that of a serious Oaks contender. She won her maiden at Brighton and returned with a narrow handicap win off just 73 over only two rivals at lowly Folkestone. It's clear she's taken a fair step forward, but she was the only runner to do so. Not that tall, she's a chunky type and her ability to cope with this course bodes well for her Epsom prospects, but she doesn't appeal at around the 14-1 mark. (op 9-1)
Field Of Miracles(IRE), just as when winning a weak 1m4f Kempton maiden on her reappearance, carried her head high for much of the way, despite a noseband again being fitted, and she was a bit keen. She had also got rather lathered up beforehand. However, she had the run of the race and picked up some black type. (op 3-1)
Date With Destiny(IRE) looked unsuited by the track and her connections felt she didn't see out the trip, even though this wasn't a severe stamina test. The only progeny of the ill-fated George Washington, she earned important back type. (op 7-2 tchd 10-3 and 9-2)
Galivant(IRE), runner-up to Field Of Miracles on her return, couldn't reverse form. (op 9-1)
Saint Helena(IRE), who played up beforehand (rider had to dismount and jog her to post), was well held. (op 14-1)
Always The Lady got warm beforehand and didn't do much for the form of recent Sandown maiden winner and Musidora entrant Arizona Jewel, having finished fourth behind that rival in a Sandown maiden two weeks earlier. (op 5-1)
Palm Pilot(IRE) was reported to have been unsuited by the quick ground and the extra distance. Official explanation: jockey said filly was unsuited by the good to firm ground and longer trip (op 10-1)

1895 TOTESPORT.COM DERBY TRIAL STKS (GROUP 3) (C&G) (TURF) 1m 3f 106y
3:10 (3:11) (Class 1) 3-Y-O

£34,062 (£12,912; £6,462; £3,222; £1,614; £810) **Stalls** High

Form				RPR
3-10	**1**		**Dordogne (IRE)**[13] [1548] 3-8-12 103 NeilCallan 2 (Mark Johnston) *swtg: mde all: rdn and fnd ex over 2f out: edgd sltly lft u.p ins fnl f: a holding on* **10/1**	104
12	**2**	½	**Hurricane Higgins (IRE)**[51] [882] 3-8-12 88 JoeFanning 7 (Mark Johnston) *lengthy: scope: lw: in tch: shkn up: effrt and hanging lft fr 3f out: chsd wnr and hung bdly lft to rail over 1f out: nt clr run and swtchd rt wl ins fnl f: kpt on to press wnr cl home* **2/1**[2]	105+
2-22	**3**	6	**Measuring Time**[13] [1548] 3-8-12 105 RichardHughes 6 (Richard Hannon) *lw: mostly chsd wnr: rdn to chal briefly 3f out: uanable to qckn w wnr and drvn over 2f out: 3rd and wkng whn sltly hmpd over 1f out* **5/4**[1]	93
-532	**4**	½	**Borug (USA)**[17] [1478] 3-8-12 93 (p) FrankieDettori 5 (Saeed Bin Suroor) *hld up in tch: rdn and short-lived effrt over 2f out: 4th and no hdwy fr over 1f out* **11/1**	92
5-1	**5**	9	**Laughing Jack**[26] [1271] 3-8-12 84 EddieAhern 3 (Ed Dunlop) *t.k.h: chsd ldrs: rdn and dropped out qckly wl over 2f out: wl bhd fnl 2f* **8/1**[3]	77
1-	**6**	6	**Marhaba Malyoon (IRE)**[222] [6414] 3-8-12 78 WilliamBuick 4 (David Simcock) *hld up in tch in last: rdn and no prog jst over 2f out: wl bhd 2f: eased ins fnl f* **16/1**	67

2m 29.5s (-2.00) **Going Correction** -0.175s/f (Firm) **6** Ran SP% **112.2**
Speed ratings (Par 109): **100,99,95,94,88 84**
toteswingers:1&2: £4.80, 2&3:£1.10, 1&3:£2.40 CSF £30.42 TOTE £11.30: £3.70, £2.10; EX 25.20.
Owner Sheikh Hamdan Bin Mohammed Al Maktoum **Bred** Mr & Mrs G Middlebrook **Trained** Middleham Moor, N Yorks

FOCUS
The last winner of this trial to win the Derby was High-Rise in 1998, although Aqaleem, successful in 2007, went on to finish third at Epsom. Two years ago this went to Age Of Aquarius who made no impression in the Derby and didn't actually win again, but he was later twice runner-up in Group 1 company, including in the Ascot Gold Cup. This didn't look a strong contest, but the runner-up can rate a lot higher if going the right way. The winner is rated up 3lb with his stablemate a bigger improver. The time was 0.16 seconds quicker than the earlier Oaks Trial won by Zain Al Boldan.

NOTEBOOK
Dordogne(IRE) was apparently unsuited by ground softer than an official description of 'good' when last of all in the Sandown Classic Trial on his previous start. Before that the Singspiel colt had won the Feilden Stakes on his reappearance and this was a game performance. He is, though, flattered as stable companion Hurricane Higgins would have won by open lengths had he not continually hung left in the straight. Official explanation: trainer said, regarding apparent improvement in form, that the colt was better suited by the good to firm ground (op 7-1)

Hurricane Higgins(IRE) is a fine, big type who was far from guaranteed to handle the track, so it was a surprise to see him take his chance here, although in fairness he had been due to contest the Sandown Classic Trial, only to miss the race owing to a reported rash. He handled the downhill run around the final bend surprisingly well, but could not keep straight in the closing stages, perhaps feeling the lively ground. A grandson of Montjeu, whose progeny can be quirky, it's not a given than he'll go the right way mentally, but he has the potential to be high class if doing so. The King Edward VII at Royal Ascot was mentioned as a possible target. (op 15-8)

Measuring Time was a fair way back in third. He seemed to run a bit flat after a couple of tough races. (op 15-8)

Borug(USA) provided further evidence that the Epsom Derby Trial counted for little this year - he had finished runner-up in that race last time. (tchd 10-1)

Laughing Jack didn't confirm the promise of his recent Windsor maiden win. Official explanation: jockey said colt ran too free (op 9-1 tchd 15-2)

1896 WEATHERBYS BLOODSTOCK INSURANCE CONDITIONS STKS (TURF) 1m 2f
3:45 (3:45) (Class 3) 4-Y-O+ **£9,066** (£2,697; £1,348) **Stalls** Low

Form				RPR
126-	**1**		**Jet Away**[211] [6720] 4-8-12 105 TomQueally 2 (Sir Henry Cecil) *lw: stdd s: t.k.h: hld up in 3rd: hdwy on inner to chal 3f out: rdn to ld wl over 1f out: r.o wl to draw clr ins fnl f: comf* **3/1**[3]	114
200-	**2**	3 ¼	**Sri Putra**[146] [7854] 5-8-12 114 NeilCallan 1 (Roger Varian) *chsd ldr: rdn over 2f out: ev ch over 1f out: nt pce of wnr and btn ins fnl f* **10/11**[1]	110
131/	**3**	5	**Passion For Gold (USA)**[539] [7404] 4-8-12 116 FrankieDettori 3 (Saeed Bin Suroor) *lw: led: rn wd of bnd ent st: rdn over 2f out: hdd over 1f out: wknd jst ins fnl f: eased fnl 100yds* **5/2**[2]	102

2m 9.12s (-1.38) **Going Correction** -0.175s/f (Firm) **3** Ran SP% **106.0**
Speed ratings (Par 107): **98,95,91**
CSF £6.03 TOTE £3.90; EX 10.00.
Owner K Abdulla **Bred** Juddmonte Farms Ltd **Trained** Newmarket, Suffolk

FOCUS
Only three runners and they were all reappearing for the first time this season. The form is a bit muddling as it's doubtful if the second and third were at their best.

NOTEBOOK
Jet Away ◆ put up a performance of a Group 1 horse, if the result is taken literally, but it's rarely wise to go overboard about conditions-race form. Whatever the case, the winner clearly posted a smart effort. He was a bit keen early, but it was nothing to be worried about and he picked up well, appreciating the quick ground. This was only his sixth start and entries in both the Prince of Wales's and Hardwicke Stakes at Royal Ascot indicate his connections have high hopes for him. (op 9-4)

Sri Putra won the Group 3 Earl of Sefton on his reappearance in 2010, so better could have been expected, although time may show he faced a tough task. (op Evens)

Passion For Gold(USA), absent since winning the Group 1 Criterium de Saint-Cloud on heavy going in November 2009, may not have appreciated ground this quick (trainer said beforehand the colt would not like it too firm), especially for his return, and he understandably wasn't given a hard time once held. Provided he comes out of this well, he could do a lot better. (op 3-1 tchd 9-4 and 10-3 in places)

1897 BET ON TODAY'S FOOTBALL AT TOTESPORT.COM MAIDEN STKS (TURF) — 1m 2f

4:20 (4:21) (Class 5) 3-Y-O+ — **£3,070** (£906; £453) **Stalls** Low

Form — RPR

044- **1** **Audacious**[213] 6676 3-8-11 **86**........................ RichardHughes 5 — 83+
(Sir Michael Stoute) *mde all: jnd over 2f out: pushed along and fnd ex ent fnl 2f: in command and pushed out fnl f: eased towards fin: comf* **1/1**[1]

3 **2** *1* **Laashak (USA)**[23] 1338 3-8-11 **0**........................ TadhgO'Shea 4 — 78+
(Sir Michael Stoute) *chsd wnr thrght: rdn to chal over 2f out: drvn and unable qck wl over 1f out: styd on same pce ins fnl f* **6/4**[2]

3 *9* **Notabadlad** 4-9-12 **0**........................ NeilCallan 3 — 64?
(Simon Dow) *unf: angular: s.i.s: sn chsng ldng pair and t.k.h: rdn and unable qck jst over 2f out: wknd wl over 1f out: eased ins fnl f* **12/1**

4 *8* **Sciampin** 3-8-6 **0**........................ TobyAtkinson(5) 2 — 44+
(Marco Botti) *w'like: bit bkwd: stdd s: t.k.h: hld up in last pair: struggling 5f out: lost tch and rn wd bnd over 3f out* **7/1**[3]

5 *5* **Kindlelight Soleil (FR)**[85] 4-9-12 **0**........................ IanMongan 1 — 35+
(Nick Littmoden) *w'like: a in last pair: struggling in 4th on downhill run 4f out: lost tch and rn wd bnd over 3f out* **40/1**

2m 13.35s (2.85) **Going Correction** -0.175s/f (Firm)
WFA 3 from 4yo 15lb — **5** Ran SP% **112.6**
Speed ratings (Par 103): **81,80,73,66,62**
CSF £2.85 TOTE £1.60: £1.30, £1.10; EX 2.90.
Owner The Queen **Bred** The Queen **Trained** Newmarket, Suffolk

FOCUS
An uncompetitive maiden, but the Stoute pair pulled clear and look potentially useful. The third will ultimately set the level.

1898 MORE LIVE FOOTBALL AT TOTESPORT.COM H'CAP (TURF) — 7f

4:55 (4:56) (Class 4) (0-85,84) 4-Y-O+ — **£5,828** (£1,734; £866; £432) **Stalls** High

Form — RPR

1- **1** **Free For All (IRE)**[390] 1257 4-9-5 **82**........................ RichardHughes 12 — 94
(Sylvester Kirk) *mde all: rdn and qcknd clr over 1f out: in command but hung lft across to far rail ins fnl f: r.o wl* **10/1**

-104 **2** *3 1/2* **Bowmaker**[13] 1541 4-9-6 **83**........................ JoeFanning 13 — 85
(Mark Johnston) *chsd wnr for 2f: in tch after: effrt on stands' rail to chse clr wnr over 1f out: one pce and no imp fnl f* **9/2**[2]

00-0 **3** *1 1/4* **Nezami (IRE)**[44] 956 6-8-13 **76**........................ AndreaAtzeni 9 — 75+
(John Akehurst) *hld up towards rr: switching lft and effrt 2f out: pressing for placings but no ch w wnr ins fnl f: kpt on* **10/1**

004- **4** *2 1/4* **Aye Aye Digby (IRE)**[251] 5551 6-9-7 **84**........................ EddieAhern 1 — 77
(Patrick Chamings) *broke wl and sn crossed to r towards stands' rail: chsd wnr after 2f tl unable qck u.p over 1f out: wknd ins fnl f* **16/1**

6-03 **5** *3/4* **Seek The Fair Land**[11] 1594 5-9-4 **81**........................(b) FrankieDettori 6 — 72
(Jim Boyle) *in tch: rdn and effrt wl over 1f out: drvn and outpcd over 1f out: wknd ins fnl f* **10/3**[1]

-052 **6** *2 1/2* **Den's Gift (IRE)**[21] 1382 7-8-12 **82**........................(b) LucyKBarry(7) 10 — 66
(Clive Cox) *racd in midfield: rdn and struggling ent fnl 3f: no ch but styd on past btn horses ins fnl f* **9/2**[2]

4012 **7** *3 1/2* **Buxton**[9] 1634 7-8-12 **75**........................(t) MartinLane 11 — 50
(Roger Ingram) *stdd s: hld up towards rr: hdwy on outer 1/2-way: rdn over 2f out: wknd wl over 1f out: wl btn ins fnl f* **10/1**

03-1 **8** *1 3/4* **Leadenhall Lass (IRE)**[32] 1147 5-8-2 **70** oh1........ JemmaMarshall(5) 7 — 40
(Pat Phelan) *bhd: effrt whn stmbld over 2f out: no real hdwy after: n.d* **28/1**

130- **9** *4 1/2* **Red Yarn**[242] 5838 4-8-10 **73**........................(b) WilliamBuick 4 — 31
(Gary Moore) *chsd ldrs: drvn and fnd nil ent fnl 2f: wknd wl over 1f out: wl bhd and eased ins fnl f* **20/1**

036- **10** *2 3/4* **Slugger O'Toole**[198] 7047 6-8-10 **73**........................ WilliamCarson 3 — 23
(Stuart Williams) *racd alone in centre: a towards rr: rdn and btn jst over 2f out: wl bhd and eased ins fnl f* **25/1**

4121 **11** *1/2* **Wilfred Pickles (IRE)**[42] [illegible] [illegible]........................ DaneO'Neill [illegible] — [illegible]
(Jo Crowley) *hld up in midfield: hdwy 3f out: rdn and fnd nil ent fnl 2f: wknd qckly wl over 1f out: wl bhd and eased ins fnl f* **7/1**[3]

000- **12** *26* **Aldermoor (USA)**[182] 7352 5-8-11 **74**........................ MickyFenton 2 — —
(Stuart Williams) *stdd s: hld up in rr: lost tch over 2f out: virtually p.u ins fnl f: t.o* **33/1**

1m 21.06s (-2.24) **Going Correction** -0.175s/f (Firm) — **12** Ran SP% **120.1**
Speed ratings (Par 105): **105,101,99,97,96 93,89,87,82,79 78,48**
toteswingers:1&2 £10.70, 2&3 £11.50, 1&3 £20.40 CSF £52.92 CT £474.49 TOTE £11.60: £2.90, £2.40, £4.30; EX 69.70.
Owner J C Smith **Bred** Miss A R Byrne **Trained** Upper Lambourn, Berks

FOCUS
The ground was quick, the near rail seemed to offer a bit of an advantage and there was a slight following wind, so the winner might be flattered. He was well on top though and produced a clear personal best.
Leadenhall Lass(IRE) Official explanation: jockey said mare was not suited by the track
T/Plt: £48.50 to a £1 stake. Pool of £63,880.63 - 959.97 winning tickets. T/Qpdt: £28.50 to a £1 stake. Pool of £2,685.49 - 69.50 winning tickets. SP

1870 NOTTINGHAM (L-H)

Saturday, May 7

OFFICIAL GOING: Good to firm (7.5)
All races on outer course.
Wind: Virtually nil Weather: Sunny periods

1899 BOX CLEVER DISPLAY H'CAP — 5f 13y

1:50 (1:50) (Class 5) (0-75,76) 4-Y-O+ — **£1,470** (£1,470; £337; £168) **Stalls** High

Form — RPR

4335 **1** **Absa Lutte (IRE)**[8] 1656 8-8-13 **67**........................(t) KierenFallon 2 — 73
(Michael Mullineaux) *dwlt: hld up in tch: hdwy on outer 2f out: rdn to chse ldrs over 1f out: drvn ins fnl f: kpt on to join ldr on line* **11/2**

022- **1** *dht* **Bilash**[209] 6773 4-8-12 **66**........................ TonyCulhane 8 — 72
(Reg Hollinshead) *dwlt: hld up towards rr: swtchd lft and hdwy over 1f out: sn rdn: qcknd to ld wl ins fnl f: jnd on line* **11/1**

60-0 **3** *nk* **Yurituni**[12] 1562 4-8-11 **70**........................(v) AmyScott(5) 3 — 75
(Eve Johnson Houghton) *chsd ldng pair: rdn and edgd rt 2f out: n.m.r and swtchd lft over 1f out: kpt on wl u.p ins fnl f* **13/2**

0215 **4** *nk* **Black Baccara**[16] 1507 4-8-9 **63**........................(be) JamieSpencer 1 — 67
(Phil McEntee) *led: rdn and edgd rt over 1f out: drvn and hdd wl ins fnl f: no ex* **10/1**

-604 **5** *3/4* **Atlantic Beach**[5] 1752 6-9-5 **73**........................(p) PatDobbs 6 — 74
(Milton Bradley) *cl up: rdn wl over 1f out: one pce ins fnl f* **9/2**[3]

000- **6** *4* **Micky Mac (IRE)**[191] 7193 7-8-7 **61** oh1........................ PatrickMathers 5 — 48
(Colin Teague) *chsd ldrs: rdn along whn n.m.r and swtchd lft wl over 1f out: sn wknd* **50/1**

0-02 **7** *1 3/4* **Select Committee**[7] 1698 6-9-8 **76**........................(v) PaulHanagan 7 — 56
(John Quinn) *hld up: effrt and n.m.r 2f out: nvr a factor* **3/1**[1]

03-4 **8** *3 1/4* **Secret Venue**[7] 1698 5-8-13 **67**........................ TonyHamilton 4 — 36
(Jedd O'Keeffe) *hld up towards rr: effrt 2f out: n.m.r and squeezed out wl over 1f out: bhd after* **7/2**[2]

59.77 secs (-1.23) **Going Correction** -0.15s/f (Firm) — **8** Ran SP% **113.5**
Speed ratings (Par 103): **103,103,102,102,100 94,91,86**WIN: Absa Lutte £4.80, Bilash £6.70 PL: AL £2.90 B £3.10 EX: AL/B £41.20, b/al £29.40 CSF: AL/B £30.94, B/AL £34.41 TRI: AL/B/Yuritini £201.03, B/AL/Y £215.45 toteswingers: AL&B ££25.00, AL&3 £4.20, B&3 Not won. CSF £34.41 CT £215.45, £2.50; EX 41.2027 Trifecta £0Owner D & D Coatings Ltd Bred.
Owner M Pyle & Mrs T Pyle **Bred** M Pyle & Mrs T Pyle **Trained** Upper Longdon, Staffs
■ This dead-heat followed the one in the last race at the track the previous day.
■ Stewards' Enquiry : Amy Scott one-day ban: careless riding (May 21); 2nd incident two-day ban: careless riding (May 23-24)

FOCUS
Not a particularly strong sprint in all probability, with the field smaller than usually contests these races, while a few of the market leaders ran well below expectations. Modest form, taken at face value.

1900 CRABBIE'S ALCOHOLIC GINGER BEER MEDIAN AUCTION MAIDEN STKS — 6f 15y

2:25 (2:26) (Class 5) 3-Y-O — **£2,266** (£674; £337; £168) **Stalls** High

Form — RPR

5- **1** **Dickie's Lad (IRE)**[205] 6878 3-9-3 **0**........................(t) PhillipMakin 8 — 88
(Kevin Ryan) *wnt bdly lft s: mde all: rdn clr wl over 1f out: kpt on strly* **7/4**[2]

56-3 **2** *14* **Abadejo**[67] 721 3-9-3 **66**........................ PaulHanagan 7 — 43
(J R Jenkins) *hmpd s: chsd ldrs: hdwy to chse wnr over 1f out: sn drvn and no imp* **4/1**[3]

5 **3** *3/4* **Waterbury Girl**[18] 1449 3-8-9 **0**........................ DeclanCannon(3) 1 — 36
(Bryn Palling) *chsd ldrs: rdn along and outpcd 1/2-way: styd on u.p appr fnl f: tk 3rd nr line* **12/1**

3- **4** *1/2* **Circuitous**[143] 7871 3-9-3 **0**........................ JamieSpencer 5 — 39
(Paul Cole) *bdly hmpd and almost uns rdr s: sn prom: rdn along 2f out: drvn over 1f out and sn one pce* **6/4**[1]

5 *5* **Crabbies Ginger** 3-9-3 **0**........................ TomEaves 3 — 23
(Lisa Williamson) *sltly hmpd s: in tch: rdn along wl over 2f out: sn wknd* **20/1**

0 **6** *1/2* **Lucky Cap**[19] 1436 3-9-3 **0**........................ BarryMcHugh 4 — 22
(Paul Midgley) *sltly hmpd s: in tch: rdn along wl over 2f out: sn wknd* **66/1**

0 **7** *19* **Zagalinis Speech**[11] 1591 3-8-5 **0**........................ DannyBrock(7) 6 — —
(J R Jenkins) *hmpd s: in tch: rdn along and lost pl bef 1/2-way: sn bhd* **66/1**

1m 12.81s (-2.09) **Going Correction** -0.15s/f (Firm) — **7** Ran SP% **111.8**
Speed ratings (Par 99): **107,88,87,86,80 79,54**
toteswingers:1&2 £1.80, 2&3 £8.30, 1&3 £7.10 CSF £8.70 TOTE £2.80: £1.40, £2.00; EX 9.90.
Owner Duddy, McNulty & Duncan **Bred** Ballyhane Stud **Trained** Hambleton, N Yorks

FOCUS
A most one-sided maiden, the impressive Dickie's Lad scoring by 14l. Hard form to rate with his market rival disappointing, but the time was good.

1901 WEATHERBYS BLOODSTOCK INSURANCE H'CAP — 1m 6f 15y

2:55 (2:59) (Class 4) (0-85,82) 4-Y-O+ — **£5,180** (£1,541; £770; £384) **Stalls** Low

Form — RPR

126- **1** **Bollin Greta**[177] 7410 6-9-1 **72**........................(t) DavidAllan 1 — 81
(Tim Easterby) *hld up towards rr: smooth hdwy 4f out: led over 2f out: rdn wl over 1f out: drvn ins fnl f: kpt on wl* **6/1**[3]

4324 **2** *1/2* **Hallstatt (IRE)**[11] 1586 5-8-8 **65**........................(t) PaulHanagan 5 — 73
(John Mackie) *hld up in tch: hdwy over [illegible]f out: cl up 3f out: rdn to chse wnr wl over 1f out: drvn and ch ent fnl f: no ex last 100yds* **9/4**[2]

300- **3** *2 3/4* **Wild Desert (FR)**[14] 5286 6-9-6 **77**........................ JamieSpencer 3 — 81
(Charlie Longsdon) *led 1f: trckd ldng pair: hdwy 5f out: led 3f out: rdn over 2f out and sn hdd: drvn and one pce fr over 1f out* **9/1**

455- **4** *2 3/4* **Daylami Dreams**[249] 5646 7-8-10 **67**........................ BarryMcHugh 2 — 67
(John Harris) *bolted and galloped rdrless for a circ bef s: in tch: rdn along over 4f out: drvn 3f out: kpt on same pce fnl 2f* **20/1**

043- **5** *9* **Shernando**[294] 4153 4-9-10 **82**........................ KierenFallon 6 — 70
(Mark Johnston) *dwlt: sn disputing ld tl led after 5f: rdn along over 4f out: hdd and drvn 3f out: sn wknd* **7/4**[1]

0 **6** *21* **Emrani (USA)**[35] 1105 4-9-8 **80**........................(b1) PhillipMakin 4 — 38
(Donald McCain) *t.k.h: cl up tl slt ld after 1f: hdd after 5f: chsd ldr tl rdn along over 4f out: sn wknd* **6/1**[3]

3m 3.44s (-3.86) **Going Correction** -0.15s/f (Firm)
WFA 4 from 5yo+ 1lb — **6** Ran SP% **110.5**
Speed ratings (Par 105): **105,104,103,101,96 84**
toteswingers:1&2:£1.70, 2&3:£4.90, 1&3:£3.40 CSF £19.26 TOTE £5.10: £2.10, £1.80; EX 20.50.
Owner Sir Neil Westbrook **Bred** Sir Neil & Exors Of Late Lady Westbrook **Trained** Great Habton, N Yorks

FOCUS
A fair staying event. It was set up for those coming from behind, the leaders going off too hard after taking each other on. The form makes sense.

1902 WEATHERBYS BLOODSTOCK INSURANCE KILVINGTON FILLIES' STKS (LISTED RACE) — 6f 15y

3:30 (3:34) (Class 1) 3-Y-O+

£17,031 (£6,456; £3,231; £1,611; £807; £405) **Stalls** High

Form — RPR

56-0 **1** **Bounty Box**[23] 1340 5-9-3 **102**........................ GeorgeBaker 5 — 102
(Chris Wall) *qckly away: mde all: rdn and edgd lft ins fnl f: kpt on wl* **3/1**[2]

10-3 **2** *3/4* **Khor Sheed**[24] 1317 3-8-7 **104**........................ KierenFallon 8 — 99
(Luca Cumani) *trckd ldrs: effrt 2f out: rdn to chal ent fnl f: ev ch tl drvn and nt qckn last 50yds* **11/4**[1]

10- **3** *1 1/4* **Poppy Seed**[238] 5952 4-9-3 **86**........................ PatDobbs 9 — 96
(Richard Hannon) *trckd ldrs on inner: effrt wl over 1f out: sn rdn: edgd lft and kpt on same pce ins fnl f* **28/1**

0-20 **4** *1/2* **Capercaillie (USA)**[22] 1366 4-9-3 **85**........................ PaulHanagan 7 — 94
(Clive Cox) *cl up: rdn 2f out: drvn over 1f out: one pce ins fnl f* **16/1**

135- **5** *1* **Dubai Media (CAN)**[219] 6509 4-9-3 84 .... JamieSpencer 10 94+
(Ed Dunlop) *dwlt: hld up in rr: swtchd rt to inner and gd hdwy over 1f out: chsd ldrs ins fnl f: eased towards fin* **10/1**

005- **6** *hd* **Beyond Desire**[204] 6887 4-9-3 95 .... TomEaves 2 91
(Roger Varian) *stmbld s and towards rr: hdwy 1/2-way: rdn to chse ldrs 2f out: drvn over 1f out and kpt on same pce* **6/1**[3]

4-20 **7** *1 3/4* **Glas Burn**[21] 1404 3-8-7 93 .... DavidAllan 11 82
(Jonathan Portman) *towards rr: hdwy 1/2-way: rdn over 2f out and n.d* **33/1**

1214 **8** *1* **Anne Of Kiev (IRE)**[23] 1340 6-9-7 102 ....(t) RoystonFfrench 4 86
(Jeremy Gask) *towards rr: effrt and n.m.r 2f out: sn rdn and n.d* **6/1**[3]

60-5 **9** *4 1/2* **Mortitia**[21] 1404 3-8-7 98 .... EddieCreighton 1 64
(Brian Meehan) *s.i.s: a in rr* **20/1**

16-0 **10** *8* **Tallahasse (IRE)**[21] 1404 3-8-7 90 .... PJMcDonald 6 39
(Alan Swinbank) *chsd ldrs on outer: rdn along over 2f out: sn wknd* **18/1**

6-10 **11** *5* **Curtains**[6] 1720 4-9-3 88 .... RichardMullen 3 26
(Simon Dow) *dwlt: a towards rr* **25/1**

1m 12.14s (-2.76) **Going Correction** -0.15s/f (Firm) **11** Ran SP% **115.5**
WFA 3 from 4yo+ 10lb
Speed ratings (Par 108): **112,111,109,108,107 107,104,103,97,86 80**
toteswingers:1&2:£2.90, 2&3:£1.10, 1&3:£29.90 CSF £10.79 TOTE £3.70: £1.70, £1.20, £7.20; EX 15.40.
Owner John E Sims **Bred** Farmers Hill Stud **Trained** Newmarket, Suffolk

FOCUS
Only three rated over 100 in a fillies' Listed race that lacked depth, although two of the three did at least come to the fore and the form looks up to scratch for the race. Not that many threatened to get into it and the winner was able to dictate.

NOTEBOOK
Bounty Box had led for a long way in the Abernant and duly came right back to her best with that outing behind her, always holding the runner-up inside the last. She'll always be a force to be reckoned with in Listed/minor Pattern races involving her own sex. (op 11-4 tchd 5-2, 10-3 in places)
Khor Sheed ran up to her best but was never quite able to muster the speed to get upsides the winner. It should only be a matter of time before she picks up a similar event at 6f/7f, the latter trip one which should suit her well this year. (op 2-1 tchd 3-1)
Poppy Seed had made no impact pitched in at this level on her final start last year, but that was on soft ground and she showed she is up to this class back under firmer conditions. She has raced only at 6f so far but goes through her races as though 5f will suit and is still lightly raced for a 4yo, this being only her seventh start. (op 33-1 tchd 25-1)
Capercaillie(USA) returned to form back over 6f, but was well placed up with the pace and will need to take her form up a notch to go close in this grade. Official explanation: jockey said filly hung left throughout (op 18-1 tchd 14-1)
Dubai Media(CAN) hasn't really looked back since joining this yard and is likely to make more of an impact at this level another day, ending up with a lot to do the way things unfolded and keeping on without being unduly knocked about, Jamie Spencer even standing up in the saddle late on. Official explanation: jockey said filly was denied a clear run (op 18-1 tchd 20-1)
Beyond Desire rather lost her way after winning a Listed event on her reappearance last year, so it remains to be seen if she goes on from this, but the way she travelled for much of the way does suggest her ability remains intact. Best at sprint trips, she's been kept to good going or firmer so far. (op 15-2)
Anne Of Kiev(IRE) had showed she's just as good on turf as AW when finishing in front of Bounty Box in the Abernant, so might have been expected to do a lot better. (op 11-2 tchd 5-1)

1903 WEATHERBYS BANK H'CAP — 1m 2f 50y
4:05 (4:05) (Class 3) (0-90,87) 3-Y-O **£8,418** (£2,505; £1,251; £625) **Stalls** Low

Form RPR

21- **1** **Badeel (USA)**[206] 6843 3-9-7 87 .... JamieSpencer 5 102+
(Saeed Bin Suroor) *mde all: qcknd clr wl over 2f out: hung rt over 1f out: shkn up and styd on strly fnl f: eased nr fin* **4/1**

1 **2** *3* **Mezyaad (USA)**[21] 1399 3-9-0 80 .... JackMitchell 2 82
(Roger Varian) *hld up in rr: hdwy 4f out: effrt over 2f out: rdn to chse wnr over 1f out: drvn and kpt on same pce ins fnl f* **5/2**[1]

31-0 **3** *shd* **Qushchi**[24] 1319 3-9-3 83 .... PaulHanagan 4 85
(William Jarvis) *chsd ldng pair: effrt 3f out: rdn over 2f out: drvn 1f out: kpt on same pce* **7/2**[3]

114- **4** *3 3/4* **Sky Falcon (USA)**[238] 5969 3-8-12 78 .... KierenFallon 1 73
(Mark Johnston) *chsd wnr: rdn along 4f out: drvn wl over 2f out and sn wknd* **13/2**

210- **5** *1* **Profondo Rosso (IRE)**[219] 6505 3-9-2 82 .... RichardMullen 3 75
(Sir Michael Stoute) *s.i.s: sn in tch: effrt 4f out: rdn along over 3f out: drvn and outpcd over 2f out* **3/1**[2]

2m 11.63s (-0.07) **Going Correction** -0.15s/f (Firm) **5** Ran SP% **109.1**
Speed ratings (Par 103): **94,91,91,88,87**
CSF £14.00 TOTE £4.00: £2.60, £1.10; EX 9.70.
Owner Godolphin **Bred** Shadwell Farm LLC **Trained** Newmarket, Suffolk

FOCUS
This looked an interesting race beforehand, with some powerful yards represented by some progressive-looking types, so it's a race to take a positive view about. The form is rated around the fourth and fifth and the winer was value for double the margin.

NOTEBOOK
Badeel(USA) made light of a mark of 87 on his handicap bow and just third start in all. Ths son of El Prado had things sewn up a long way out, pulling further clear despite still showing signs of inexperience once finally shaken up and being value for more like double his winning margin. Epsom may come a bit soon for this Derby entry, and he wouldn't be a certain stayer either, but it's unlikely to be too long before he is making his mark at a higher level. (op 7-2)
Mezyaad(USA) probably didn't improve much on the form of his Leicester win but time may show he faced an impossible task with the winner and he remains the type to do better before long. He was a bit outpaced early in the straight but kept on well at the finish. He'll be suited by further. (op 3-1)
Qushchi had found it tough in the Nell Gwyn on her reappearance and was back on the up here, seemingly coping well enough with the 3f longer trip. She is another lightly raced sort who we may not have seen the best of yet.
Sky Falcon(USA) largely went the right way at two, winning twice over 7f, and ran as though a return to shorter may suit ideally on his return, having nothing left at the finish having gone keenly enough through the first half of the race. (op 6-1 tchd 7-1)
Profondo Rosso(IRE) didn't always look entirely straightforward as a juvenile, despite a maiden win, and this certainly raised a few doubts as to whether he will progress as so many from the yard do. He'll have a bit to prove next time. (tchd 10-3)

1904 MAKE MINE A CRABBIE'S H'CAP — 1m 75y
4:40 (4:40) (Class 5) (0-75,72) 3-Y-O **£2,266** (£674; £337; £168) **Stalls** Centre

Form RPR

32-0 **1** **Good Boy Jackson**[36] 1074 3-9-0 65 .... PhillipMakin 1 79
(Kevin Ryan) *dwlt: sn pushed along on inner to ld after 100yds: rdn along 3f out: drvn over 1f out: kpt on gamely u.p ins fnl f* **8/1**

43-3 **2** *1* **Chosen Character (IRE)**[19] 1437 3-9-6 71 ....(vt[1]) RichardKingscote 5 82
(Tom Dascombe) *t.k.h: chsd ldng pair: hdwy to chse wnr after 3f: rdn over 2f out: drvn to chal over 1f out: ev ch tl edgd lft ins fnl f and no ex last 75yds* **3/1**[2]

05-1 **3** *1* **Certral**[33] 1137 3-8-5 59 ow1 .... PaulPickard(3) 2 69
(Brian Ellison) *hld up in rr: hdwy on inner over 3f out: rdn to chal wl over 1f out and ev ch tl drvn: n.m.r and one pce ins fnl f* **6/1**[3]

55-3 **4** *6* **Number Theory**[21] 1392 3-9-1 71 .... JamesRogers(5) 6 66
(John Holt) *hld up in tch: hdwy on outer 1/2-way: rdn along to chse ldrs 3f out: drvn and wknd wl over 1f out* **3/1**[2]

1-22 **5** *shd* **Classic Voice (IRE)**[10] 1611 3-9-7 72 .... GeorgeBaker 3 67
(Hugo Palmer) *trckd wnr: cl up 1/2-way: rdn along over 2f out: wknd wl over 1f out* **15/8**[1]

1m 44.96s (-0.64) **Going Correction** -0.15s/f (Firm) **5** Ran SP% **110.2**
Speed ratings (Par 99): **97,96,95,89,88**
CSF £31.40 TOTE £4.80: £4.00, £1.80; EX 38.00.
Owner The C H F Partnership **Bred** The C H F Partnership **Trained** Hambleton, N Yorks

FOCUS
A small field for this ordinary handicap, but sound form with the first three clear in a decent time.

1905 SPIFFINGLY REFRESHING ALCOHOLIC CRABBIE'S GINGER BEER APPRENTICE H'CAP — 1m 75y
5:15 (5:15) (Class 6) (0-60,60) 4-Y-O+ **£1,780** (£529; £264; £132) **Stalls** Centre

Form RPR

0022 **1** **George Baker (IRE)**[6] 1730 4-8-13 57 .... DavidKenny(5) 10 69
(George Baker) *hld up in tch: hdwy 3f out: rdn to chse ldr over 1f out: drvn and styd on ins fnl f to ld last 50yds* **11/4**[1]

6210 **2** *3/4* **Mr Chocolate Drop (IRE)**[10] 1613 7-8-11 55 ....(t) NathanAlison(5) 12 65
(Mandy Rowland) *dwlt and stdd s: hld up in rr: hdwy on inner 3f out: led 2f out and sn rdn clr: drvn ins fnl f: hdd and no ex last 50yds* **8/1**

1413 **3** *3 3/4* **Grey Boy (GER)**[5] 1763 10-8-11 57 .... GeorgeDowning(7) 6 59
(Tony Carroll) *hld up in midfield: hdwy over 3f out: rdn 2f out and ev ch tl drvn and one pce appr fnl f* **4/1**[2]

6-52 **4** *3/4* **Hathaway (IRE)**[5] 1763 4-8-10 54 .... ShaneBKelly(5) 9 54
(Mark Brisbourne) *midfield: effrt 3f out: rdn wl over 1f out: kpt on ins fnl f: nrst fin* **5/1**[3]

4-06 **5** *1 3/4* **Kheskianto (IRE)**[31] 1164 5-8-2 48 ow1 ....(bt) LeonnaMayor(7) 3 44
(Michael Chapman) *chsd ldrs: rdn along 3f out: drvn 2f out: kpt on same pce* **40/1**

0046 **6** *1 1/2* **Join Up**[5] 1763 5-9-6 59 .... RossAtkinson 4 51
(Mark Brisbourne) *towards rr: hdwy 3f out: rdn 2f out: kpt on ins fnl f: nrst fin* **12/1**

0-55 **7** *2* **Bajan Pride**[31] 1164 7-9-0 60 .... DavidSimmonson(7) 13 48
(Paul Midgley) *cl up: led over 3f out: rdn and hdd over 2f out: sn wknd* **28/1**

6022 **8** *2* **Sweet Possession (USA)**[11] 1587 5-9-0 58 ....(p) RachealKneller(5) 11 41
(Pat Eddery) *cl up: led after 2f: rdn along 4f out: sn hdd & wknd 2f out* **10/1**

0-00 **9** *3/4* **Sunrise Lyric (IRE)**[10] 1604 4-9-0 58 .... DuilioDaSilva(5) 1 40
(Paul Cole) *towards rr: effrt and sme hdwy 3f out: sn rdn and btn* **22/1**

5-05 **10** *10* **Abhainn (IRE)**[9] 1633 5-8-7 46 oh1 .... DeclanCannon 2 —
(Bryn Palling) *chsd ldrs: rdn along over 3f out: sn wknd* **14/1**

45-0 **11** *14* **Gee Major**[9] 1625 4-8-13 55 .... JulieBurke(3) 8 —
(Nicky Vaughan) *led 2f: prom tl rdn along over 3f out and sn wknd* **8/1**

/606 **12** *10* **Crystal Bridge**[26] 1274 4-8-0 46 oh1 ....(b) NoelGarbutt(7) 5 —
(Bill Moore) *chsd ldrs: rdn along over 3f out: sn wknd* **100/1**

1m 45.27s (-0.33) **Going Correction** -0.15s/f (Firm) **12** Ran SP% **120.2**
Speed ratings (Par 101): **95,94,90,89,88 86,84,82,81,71 57,47**
toteswingers:1&2 £4.10, 2&3 £9.40, 1&3 £3.30 CSF £25.03 CT £91.37 TOTE £3.40: £1.70, £2.50, £1.30; EX 31.00.
Owner George Baker & Partners **Bred** Mull Enterprises Ltd **Trained** Whitsbury, Hants
■ Stewards' Enquiry : Nathan Alison two-day ban: used whip with excessive frequency (May 21,23)

FOCUS
A modest apprentice event to conclude proceedings. They went hard up front, setting it up for those coming from behind. The winner is rated up a length on his latest form.
Abhainn(IRE) Official explanation: jockey said gelding never travelled
T/Plt: £183.50 to a £1 stake. Pool of £35,617.62 - 141.65 winning tickets. T/Qpdt: £15.50 to a £1 stake. Pool of £2,220.90 - 105.90 winning tickets. JR

1691 THIRSK (L-H)
Saturday, May 7

OFFICIAL GOING: Good (8.0)
Wind: Light 1/2 against Weather: Overcast, light rain after race 1

1906 TURFTV.CO.UK (S) STKS — 6f
6:00 (6:02) (Class 6) 3-Y-O+ **£2,914** (£867; £433; £216) **Stalls** High

Form RPR

6363 **1** **Dolly Parton (IRE)**[13] 1543 3-8-5 68 ....(p) AdrianNicholls 2 62
(David Nicholls) *led: edgd rt after 1f: hdd 3f out: led over 1f out: hld on towards fin* **11/4**[1]

0003 **2** *hd* **Mark Anthony (IRE)**[6] 1715 4-9-6 70 ....(p) PaulMulrennan 3 69
(Kevin Ryan) *chsd wnr: swtchd rt after 1f: led 3f out: hdd over 1f out: no ex clsng stages* **3/1**[2]

0-60 **3** *1 1/4* **Excusez Moi (USA)**[95] 376 9-9-6 75 .... PJMcDonald 5 65
(Ruth Carr) *dwlt: mid-div: hdwy over 2f out: chal ins fnl f: no ex* **11/2**

1315 **4** *3 3/4* **Bonnie Prince Blue**[18] 1471 8-9-6 75 ....(b) DaleSwift(5) 4 58
(Ian McInnes) *mid-div on outside: outpcd and lost pl 3f out: hdwy 2f out: kpt on* **9/2**[3]

500- **5** *1/2* **Newbury Street**[193] 7148 4-9-6 62 .... AndrewElliott 8 52
(Patrick Holmes) *chsd ldrs: hmpd after 1f: outpcd and hung lft over 2f out: chsng ldrs over 1f out: kpt on same pce* **16/1**

04-0 **6** *1 3/4* **Russian Brigadier**[17] 1497 4-9-6 38 .... RobertWinston 11 46?
(Mel Brittain) *hmpd after 1f: outpcd and sn in rr: styd on fnl 2f: nvr nr ldrs* **33/1**

0-00 **7** *3* **Chardonnay Star (IRE)**[3] 1813 4-9-1 36 ....(v) PatrickMathers 10 31
(Colin Teague) *sn outpcd and bhd: nvr on terms* **100/1**

06-0 **8** *2 3/4* **Kaua'i Girl**[12] 1557 3-8-2 54 ....(v[1]) JamesSullivan(3) 9 20
(Ann Duffield) *chsd ldrs: wknd 2f out* **18/1**

0-66 **9** *29* **Desert Falls**[9] 1634 5-9-6 59 .... TonyHamilton 6 —
(Richard Whitaker) *chsd ldrs: hmpd after 1f: wknd over 1f out: heavily eased: t.o* **8/1**

40-0 **10** *7* **Wolds Agent**[23] 1329 3-8-10 52........(be) DavidAllan 1 —
(Tim Easterby) *racd wd: sn outpcd and in rr: bhd fnl 2f: heavily eased: t.o* **50/1**

1m 13.15s (0.45) **Going Correction** +0.075s/f (Good)
WFA 3 from 4yo+ 10lb **10** Ran SP% **113.4**
Speed ratings (Par 101): **100,99,98,93,92 90,86,82,43,34**
toteswingers: 1&2 £3.10, 1&3 £3.70, 2&3 £4.40. CSF £10.67 TOTE £3.80: £1.60, £1.70, £2.00; EX 12.90.There was no bid for the winner.
Owner David Nicholls & I Glenton **Bred** Ian W Glenton **Trained** Sessay, N Yorks

FOCUS
A typical seller with a wide range of abilities on show. The action took place on the stand rail and concerned only the first two from a long way out, the pace strong. The winner didn't need to match her latest form.
Desert Falls Official explanation: jockey said gelding lost its action

1907 DICK PEACOCK SPRINT H'CAP 6f
6:30 (6:32) (Class 5) (0-75,74) 4-Y-0+ **£2,914** (£867; £433; £216) **Stalls** High

Form RPR
60-0 **1** **River Falcon**[30] 1200 11-9-5 72........ DanielTudhope 6 83
(Jim Goldie) *racd exclusively far side: towards rr: hdwy over 2f out: styd on to ld last 100yds* **16/1**

262 **2** *1* **Clear Ice (IRE)**[17] 1501 4-8-2 60 oh2........(b) DanielleMcCreery(5) 4 68
(Richard Guest) *overall ldr towards far side: edgd rt over 1f out: hdd and no ex ins fnl f* **33/1**

1040 **3** *2 1/4* **Desert Strike**[7] 1698 5-9-5 72........(p) RobertWinston 17 73
(Alan McCabe) *led stands' side gp 1f: chsd ldrs: styd on to take 2nd that side ins fnl f* **9/1**

4521 **4** *1* **We'll Deal Again**[17] 1493 4-8-11 64........(b) PaulMulrennan 16 62
(Michael Easterby) *racd stands' side: chsd ldrs: hung lft over 1f out: kpt on same pce* **9/2**[2]

0603 **5** *2* **Chosen One (IRE)**[13] 1539 6-8-11 67........ JamesSullivan(3) 10 58
(Ruth Carr) *racd stands' side: chsd ldrs: kpt on same pce appr fnl f* **7/2**[1]

10-0 **6** *hd* **Sea Salt**[12] 1558 8-8-10 68........ DaleSwift(5) 1 59
(Ron Barr) *racd excsluevly far side: chsd ldr: one pce fnl 2f* **33/1**

040- **7** *1 3/4* **Belinsky (IRE)**[213] 6679 4-8-12 65........ RoystonFfrench 15 50
(Mark Campion) *chsd ldrs stands' side: kpt on same pce over 1f out* **33/1**

-016 **8** *1/2* **Sir Nod**[30] 1205 9-9-7 74........ PaulHanagan 5 57
(Julie Camacho) *racd far side: chsd overall ldr: wknd over 1f out* **11/1**

0-25 **9** *1/2* **Mandalay King (IRE)**[4] 1793 6-9-1 68........ PJMcDonald 7 50
(Marjorie Fife) *s.s: racd stands' side: in rr tl kpt on fnl 2f: nvr nr ldrs* **9/1**

40-6 **10** *1* **Mullglen**[7] 1698 5-9-1 68........ DavidAllan 13 47
(Tim Easterby) *chsd ldrs stands' side on outer: hung lft and wknd over 1f out* **8/1**[3]

5300 **11** *nk* **Ace Of Spies (IRE)**[25] 1296 6-9-3 70........ KirstyMilczarek 9 48
(Conor Dore) *racd stands' side on outer: prom: drvn over 2f out: sn outpcd* **28/1**

2300 **12** *1* **Incomparable**[21] 1411 6-9-2 72........(bt) BillyCray(3) 3 46
(David Nicholls) *s.i.s: racd far side: outpcd and in rr* **20/1**

005- **13** *3/4* **Bossy Kitty**[205] 6879 4-8-8 61........ SilvestreDeSousa 2 33
(Nigel Tinkler) *racd far side: chsd ldrs: wknd over 1f out* **22/1**

0023 **14** *nk* **Dancing Freddy (IRE)**[4] 1796 4-8-13 69........(p) RobertLButler(3) 12 40
(Richard Guest) *gave problems in stalls: swvd rt s: racd stands' side: hdwy to ld that side after 1f: wknd appr fnl f* **12/1**

00-0 **15** *8* **Sea Rover (IRE)**[10] 1612 7-8-7 60 oh10........ AdrianNicholls 14 —
(Mel Brittain) *s.i.s: racd stands' side: a bhd* **50/1**

666- **16** *nk* **Leonid Glow**[267] 5054 6-9-7 74........ TomEaves 8 —
(Michael Dods) *swtchd rt s: in rr stands' side: bhd fnl 2f* **14/1**

1m 12.61s (-0.09) **Going Correction** +0.075s/f (Good) **16** Ran SP% **123.4**
Speed ratings (Par 103): **103,101,98,97,94 94,92,91,90,89 89,87,86,86,75 75**
toteswingers: 1&2 £81.60, 1&3 £16.30, 2&3 £62.90. CSF £478.20 CT £5184.86 TOTE £12.80: £3.10, £6.80, £2.50, £1.80; EX 362.60.
Owner The Reluctant Suitor's **Bred** Manor Farm Packers Ltd **Trained** Uplawmoor, E Renfrews

FOCUS
An open sprint handicap in which the runners ended up spread all across the track after stalls 1-6 had initially split and raced down the centre. The pace seemed good, dictated by the runner-up. Straightforward form.
We'll Deal Again Official explanation: jockey said gelding hung left throughout
Mullglen Official explanation: jockey said gelding hung left

1908 GT GROUP H'CAP 1m 4f
7:00 (7:00) (Class 4) (0-80,78) 4-Y-0+ **£6,476** (£1,927; £963; £481) **Stalls** Low

Form RPR
330- **1** **George Adamson (IRE)**[210] 6754 5-9-1 72........ PJMcDonald 7 83+
(Alan Swinbank) *hld up in rr: hdwy 5f out: led 2f out: edgd lft: drvn out* **7/1**[3]

3-1 **2** *1 1/4* **Lady Chaparral**[29] 1211 4-9-1 72........ TomEaves 10 80
(George Moore) *led after 1f: hung rt and wd bnd over 8f out: hdd 2f out: kpt on fnl f* **9/2**[1]

210- **3** *nk* **Maneki Neko (IRE)**[244] 5790 9-9-0 71........ TonyHamilton 3 79
(Edwin Tuer) *trckd ldrs: swtchd rt over 1f out: styd on fnl f* **14/1**

625- **4** *6* **Beat The Shower**[186] 7284 5-8-12 69........ DavidAllan 5 67
(Peter Niven) *in rr: effrt over 3f out: kpt on: nvr rchd ldrs* **7/1**[3]

110- **5** *1/2* **The Caped Crusader (IRE)**[210] 6753 4-9-4 75........ BarryMcHugh 8 73
(Ollie Pears) *t.k.h: trckd ldrs: wknd over 1f out* **9/2**[1]

041- **6** *3 1/4* **Penangdouble O One**[199] 7022 4-9-1 72........(t) StevieDonohoe 11 64
(Ralph Beckett) *mid-div: drvn 7f out: outpcd over 3f out: kpt on fnl f* **11/2**[2]

00-0 **7** *4 1/2* **Green Lightning (IRE)**[23] 1325 4-9-7 78........(b) RoystonFfrench 2 63
(Mark Johnston) *led 1f: chsd ldrs: drvn over 3f out: wknd 2f out* **9/1**

4154 **8** *1 1/2* **The Which Doctor**[4] 1792 6-9-4 78........ RobertLButler(3) 4 61
(Richard Guest) *sn w ldr: wknd 2f out* **33/1**

030- **9** *7* **Kingsdale Orion (IRE)**[298] 3974 7-9-0 76........ DaleSwift(5) 9 48
(Brian Ellison) *s.s: detached in rr: sme hdwy over 2f out: nvr on terms* **9/1**

/00- **10** *1 1/2* **Dzesmin (POL)**[385] 1398 9-9-1 72........ SilvestreDeSousa 6 41
(David O'Meara) *mid-div: drvn over 4f out: lost pl over 2f out* **16/1**

/23- **11** *63* **Daredevil Dan**[41] 1427 5-8-11 68........ PaulHanagan 1 —
(Tina Jackson) *detached in rr: bhd fnl 6f: t.o 4f out: virtually p.u* **28/1**

2m 36.73s (0.53) **Going Correction** +0.075s/f (Good) **11** Ran SP% **115.7**
Speed ratings (Par 105): **101,100,99,95,95 93,90,89,84,83 41**
toteswingers: 1&2 £5.40, 1&3 £11.30, 2&3 £9.10. CSF £37.85 CT £431.83 TOTE £10.10: £2.40, £1.60, £5.20; EX 40.50.
Owner Mrs S Sanbrook **Bred** Miss O O'Connor & Stephanie Von Schilcher **Trained** Melsonby, N Yorks

FOCUS
A fair handicap run at a reasonable gallop with the field soon well strung out. Only the first three showed their form, finishing clear. The winner can probably do better.
Daredevil Dan Official explanation: jockey said gelding moved poorly throughout

1909 CALVERTS CARPETS H'CAP 1m
7:30 (7:30) (Class 5) (0-75,81) 4-Y-0+ **£2,914** (£867; £433; £216) **Stalls** Low

Form RPR
-641 **1** **Fazza**[10] 1613 4-8-8 62........ TonyHamilton 15 74
(Edwin Tuer) *fast away fr outside draw and crossed over: chsd ldr: chal over 1f out: styd on to ld clsng stages* **14/1**

24-0 **2** *1/2* **Call Of Duty (IRE)**[14] 1520 6-8-10 64........ DuranFentiman 18 75
(Dianne Sayer) *fast away fr outside draw: led and crossed over: jnd over 1f out: hdd and no ex last 75yds* **33/1**

0-31 **3** *5* **Mujaadel (USA)**[4] 1793 6-9-10 81 6ex........(p) MichaelO'Connell(3) 13 80+
(David Nicholls) *in rr: gd hdwy on outside over 2f out: edgd lft over 1f out: kpt on same pce* **5/1**[1]

5221 **4** *hd* **Ravi River (IRE)**[14] 1520 7-9-1 69........ SilvestreDeSousa 11 68+
(Brian Ellison) *mid-div: hdwy over 2f out: kpt on wl fnl f* **5/1**[1]

66-4 **5** *3/4* **Rosbay (IRE)**[35] 1099 7-9-1 69........ DavidAllan 3 66+
(Tim Easterby) *s.i.s: bhd: gd hdwy 2f out: styng on wl at fin* **7/1**[2]

3104 **6** *6* **Trans Sonic**[21] 1382 8-9-1 74........(b) SeanLevey(5) 5 57
(David O'Meara) *s.i.s: drvn along to chse ldrs after 2f: outpcd over 2f out: no threat after* **11/1**

00-4 **7** *1/2* **Tobrata**[8] 1649 5-8-7 61 oh3........ RoystonFfrench 8 43
(Mel Brittain) *in rr: hdwy over 2f out: nvr nr ldrs* **66/1**

126- **8** *1* **Emeralds Spirit (IRE)**[197] 7056 4-8-10 64 ow2........ PhillipMakin 2 44
(John Weymes) *chsd ldrs: drvn over 2f out: one pce* **28/1**

/05- **9** *1* **More Than Many (USA)**[266] 5071 5-9-2 70........ PaulHanagan 16 48
(Richard Fahey) *s.i.s: in rr: sme hdwy on outside 2f out: nvr nr ldrs* **5/1**[1]

200- **10** *shd* **Fifty Moore**[215] 6624 4-8-13 67........ AndrewElliott 12 44
(Jedd O'Keeffe) *hld up towards rr: kpt on fnl 2f: nvr a factor* **66/1**

0-00 **11** *3/4* **Legal Legacy**[7] 1696 5-9-5 73........ TomEaves 1 49
(Michael Dods) *s.s: sme hdwy and n.m.r 2f out: nvr a factor* **11/1**

25-6 **12** *4 1/2* **Apache Warrior**[29] 1210 4-8-13 67........ PJMcDonald 14 32
(George Moore) *mid-div: drvn over 2f out: nvr a factor* **33/1**

306 **13** *3 3/4* **Hill Tribe**[11] 1587 4-8-7 64........(p) TjadeCollier(3) 7 21
(Richard Guest) *chsd ldrs: drvn over 4f out: wknd over 2f out* **33/1**

105- **14** *nk* **Red Scintilla**[220] 6461 4-9-2 70........ PaulMulrennan 10 26
(Nigel Tinkler) *t.k.h: in tch: outpcd over 2f out: sn wknd* **50/1**

0-60 **15** *1* **Baltimore Jack (IRE)**[23] 1324 7-8-10 67........ JamesSullivan(3) 6 21
(G P Kelly) *in rr: hdwy on ins over 2f out* **40/1**

50-0 **16** *1 3/4* **Chambers (IRE)**[12] 1558 5-8-2 61 oh4........ NeilFarley(5) 17 —
(Eric Alston) *chsd ldrs: wnt 3rd over 3f out: lost pl over 1f out* **28/1**

2-63 **17** *4 1/2* **Mozayada (USA)**[17] 1499 7-8-8 62 oh3 ow1........ RobertWinston 4 —
(Mel Brittain) *hdwy to chse ldrs after 1f: wknd fnl 2f* **22/1**

400- **18** *14* **Our Boy Barrington (IRE)**[212] 6692 4-9-2 70........ AdrianNicholls 9 —
(David Nicholls) *s.s: a detached in last: eased over 1f out: t.o* **10/1**[3]

1m 39.99s (-0.11) **Going Correction** +0.075s/f (Good) **18** Ran SP% **122.4**
Speed ratings (Par 103): **103,102,97,97,96 90,90,89,88,87 87,82,78,78,77 75,71,57**
toteswingers: 1&2 £71.10, 1&3 £13.00, 2&3 £91.80. CSF £422.13 CT £1688.75 TOTE £10.20: £3.50, £6.60, £1.90, £1.40; EX 932.90.
Owner E Tuer **Bred** D R Tucker **Trained** Great Smeaton, N Yorks

FOCUS
A run-of-the mill handicap but something of an odd one with most of those drawn towards the inside not electing to make the best of use of their draws and thereby allowing a couple drawn wide to get well clear and dominate throughout.

1910 SOLDIERS CHARITY MAIDEN STKS 1m
8:00 (8:03) (Class 5) 3-Y-0+ **£4,209** (£1,252; £625; £312) **Stalls** Low

Form RPR
00-2 **1** **Carousel**[17] 1480 3-8-8 70........ StevieDonohoe 11 73
(Ralph Beckett) *hmpd s: w ldr: clr 2nd over 3f out: kpt on to chal over 1f out: led last 75yds: all out* **7/2**[2]

23 **2** *nk* **War Poet**[21] 1386 4-9-12 0........ DanielTudhope 4 80+
(David O'Meara) *hld up: hdwy and modest 4th over 3f out: styd on wl fnl f: tk 2nd nr fin: jst hld* **3/1**[1]

026- **3** *1* **Quite Sparky**[292] 4197 4-9-12 70........ SilvestreDeSousa 0 78
(David O'Meara) *hmpd s: led: drvn clr over 3f out: jnd over 1f out: hdd and no ex ins fnl f* **3/1**[1]

0 **4** *1* **Muffin McLeay (IRE)**[34] 1108 3-8-13 0........ LeeNewman 7 73
(David Barron) *wnt rt s: chsd ldrs: mod 3rd over 1f out: upsides over 1f out: kpt on same pce* **7/1**[3]

4-4 **5** *14* **Sartingo (IRE)**[12] 1559 4-9-12 0........ PJMcDonald 5 44
(Alan Swinbank) *mid-div: outpcd over 3f out: no ch after* **7/1**[3]

6 *3 1/2* **Le Chat D'Or** 3-8-13 0........ BarryMcHugh 1 32
(Neville Bycroft) *s.s: nvr a factor* **28/1**

-0 **7** *4* **Situation Vacant**[29] 1210 4-9-12 0........ RoystonFfrench 6 26
(Mark Johnston) *sn chsng ldrs: reminders over 4f out: lost pl over 3f out* **33/1**

0 **8** *3/4* **Penang Pacific**[35] 1096 3-8-13 0........ RobertWinston 8 22
(Alan McCabe) *hmpd s: chsd ldrs on outer: outpcd: hung lft and lost pl over 3f out* **12/1**

000- **9** *2* **Be My Spy**[227] 6293 3-8-5 30........ BillyCray(3) 10 —
(Peter Salmon) *hmpd s: a in rr* **100/1**

10 *1 1/4* **Hard Rok (IRE)** 3-8-13 0........ TonyHamilton 2 —
(Richard Whitaker) *s.i.s: nvr on terms* **28/1**

1m 41.55s (1.45) **Going Correction** +0.075s/f (Good)
WFA 3 from 4yo 13lb **10** Ran SP% **115.7**
Speed ratings (Par 103): **95,94,93,92,78 75,71,70,68,67**
toteswingers: 1&2 £2.90, 1&3 £4.40, 2&3 £2.70. CSF £13.90 TOTE £3.20: £1.60, £1.50, £1.10; EX 12.00.
Owner Prince Of Wales And Duchess Of Cornwall **Bred** The Prince Of Wales & The Duchess Of Cornwall **Trained** Kimpton, Hants

FOCUS
A modest maiden and little of interest behind the first five. Once again, the early leader was able to build a sizeable advantage. The third is the key to the form.
Penang Pacific Official explanation: jockey said gelding hung left throughout

1911 THIRSK RACES AGAIN NEXT SATURDAY H'CAP 7f
8:30 (8:34) (Class 6) (0-55,58) 4-Y-0+ **£2,590** (£770; £385; £192) **Stalls** Low

Form RPR
00-0 **1** **Dhhamaan (IRE)**[50] 893 6-9-2 53........(b) PJMcDonald 14 65
(Ruth Carr) *fast away fr outside draw and crossed over to ld: drvn clr over 2f out: jst hld on* **25/1**

506- **2** *hd* **Silly Gilly (IRE)**[194] 7125 7-8-11 53........ DaleSwift(5) 1 64
(Ron Barr) *trckd ldrs: wnt 3rd over 3f out: chsd wnr over 1f out: r.o: jst hld* **14/1**

5052 **3** 5 **Beckermet (IRE)**[10] 1612 9-8-13 57 ShaneBKelly(7) 12 55
(Ruth Carr) *swvd rt s: bhd: hdwy on outside over 2f out: kpt on same pce fnl f* **7/2**[1]

-001 **4** 3 1/4 **Tombellini (IRE)**[4] 1803 4-9-4 58 6ex MichaelO'Connell(3) 9 47
(David Nicholls) *chsd wnr: wknd fnl f* **7/2**[1]

040- **5** 1 1/4 **Thinking**[227] 6295 4-9-4 55 RobertWinston 7 40
(Tim Easterby) *mid-div: effrt over 2f out: kpt on: nvr nr ldrs* **25/1**

506- **6** 1 1/4 **Maxi Moo (IRE)**[202] 6966 4-9-1 52 SilvestreDeSousa 13 34
(Geoffrey Harker) *s.i.s: in rr tl kpt on fnl 2f* **25/1**

1301 **7** 1 **Fortunate Bid (IRE)**[9] 1633 5-9-3 57 (p) JamesSullivan(3) 10 36
(Linda Stubbs) *in rr: kpt on fnl 2f: nvr on terms* **8/1**[2]

3500 **8** nk **Mr Emirati (USA)**[14] 1520 4-9-4 55 (p) TomEaves 3 33
(Bryan Smart) *in rr: hung rt over 1f out: styd on ins fnl f* **50/1**

0-22 **9** nk **Kanace**[10] 1604 4-9-2 53 (p) StevieDonohoe 4 31
(Noel Quinlan) *in tch: effrt over 2f out: sn btn* **8/1**[2]

00-5 **10** 2 1/2 **Bahamian Jazz (IRE)**[24] 1307 4-9-4 55 LeeNewman 8 26
(Robin Bastiman) *mid-div: drvn over 3f out: lost pl over 2f out* **16/1**

10-5 **11** 3 1/4 **My Flame**[17] 1486 6-9-4 55 PaulHanagan 11 17
(J R Jenkins) *chsd ldrs: hung lft 2f out: sn wknd* **10/1**[3]

6066 **12** 1 **Duplicity**[17] 1498 4-9-1 55 (t) RobertLButler(3) 6 14
(Richard Guest) *mid-div: effrt over 2f out: nvr a factor* **33/1**

050- **13** 6 **Celtic Step**[220] 6462 7-9-2 53 PaulMulrennan 5 —
(Alan Kirtley) *a towards rr: bhd fnl 2f* **40/1**

1m 27.87s (0.67) **Going Correction** +0.075s/f (Good) **13 Ran SP% 107.2**
Speed ratings (Par 101): **99,98,93,89,87 86,85,85,84,81 78,76,70**
toteswingers: 1&2 £53.20, 1&3 £6.80, 2&3 £7.90. CSF £258.56 CT £1185.97 TOTE £27.20: £6.60, £2.60, £1.70; EX 295.20.
Owner S B Clark **Bred** D Veitch And Musagd Abo Salim **Trained** Huby, N Yorks

FOCUS
A low-grade affair to end proceedings, with the winner another on the night to benefit from an enterprising ride from a wide draw. He is rated to his best form in the last couple of years.
T/Plt: £97.70 to a £1 stake. Pool of £60,115.14 - 448.94 winning tickets. T/Qpdt: £26.70 to a £1 stake. Pool of £4,399.22 - 121.50 winning tickets. WG

1763 WARWICK (L-H)
Saturday, May 7

OFFICIAL GOING: Good to firm (8.0)
Wind: Light across Weather: Overcast

1912 HA-HA CLUB @ WARWICK JUNE 17TH H'CAP 6f
5:45 (5:47) (Class 6) (0-65,65) 4-Y-0+ **£2,072** (£616; £231; £231) **Stalls** Low

Form RPR
4542 **1** **Steel City Boy (IRE)**[18] 1463 8-8-7 51 oh3 KellyHarrison 9 62
(Garry Woodward) *mde all: rdn and edgd rt over 1f out: r.o* **8/1**

00-0 **2** 3 **Defector (IRE)**[79] 577 5-9-7 65 FrankieMcDonald 3 66
(David Bourton) *a.p: rdn to chse wnr over 1f out: edgd rt and no imp ins fnl f* **25/1**

300- **3** 1 1/2 **Volito**[247] 5698 5-9-5 63 RussKennemore 2 60
(Anabel K Murphy) *s.i.s: hdwy over 4f out: rdn 1/2-way: no ex ins fnl f* **7/1**[2]

005- **3** dht **Euroquip Boy (IRE)**[346] 2441 4-8-11 55 EddieCreighton 1 52
(Michael Scudamore) *chsd ldrs: rdn 1/2-way: styd on same pce fnl f* **10/1**

0401 **5** hd **Memphis Man**[5] 1770 8-8-1 52 MatthewCosham(7) 4 48
(David Evans) *hld up: hdwy over 1f out: r.o: nt rch ldrs* **11/2**[1]

-140 **6** shd **Boldinor**[11] 1581 8-8-12 61 LeeNewnes(5) 6 57
(Martin Bosley) *prom: rdn over 1f out: styd on* **9/1**

0314 **7** 3/4 **Welcome Approach**[9] 1627 8-8-12 56 JimmyQuinn 8 49
(John Weymes) *mid-div: lost pl over 3f out: hdwy u.p fnl f: nt trble ldrs* **11/2**[1]

0115 **8** 2 3/4 **Loyal Royal (IRE)**[18] 1453 8-9-2 60 (bt) LiamKeniry 10 44
(Milton Bradley) *hld up: plld hrd: hdwy over 2f out: rdn and n.m.r over 1f out: eased whn btn ins fnl f* **14/1**

234- **9** 2 1/2 **Millden**[192] 7166 4-8-13 60 KierenFox(3) 11 36
(Milton Bradley) *in rr and rdn 1/2-way: n.d* **20/1**

0360 **10** 1/2 **Valentino Swing (IRE)**[72] 664 8-8-7 51 NeilChalmers 13 26
(Michael Appleby) *s.s: hdwy over 3f out: rdn and edgd rt over 1f out: sn wknd* **28/1**

3050 **11** 5 **Fantasy Fighter (IRE)**[52] 867 6-8-4 51 JohnFahy(3) 5 10
(John Quinn) *chsd ldrs: rdn over 2f out: wknd over 1f out* **15/2**[3]

220- **12** 1/2 **Bermondsey Bob (IRE)**[194] 7125 5-9-4 62 SamHitchcott 12 19
(John Spearing) *s.i.s: hdwy over 4f out: rdn 1/2-way: wknd over 1f out* **7/1**[2]

1m 12.38s (0.58) **Going Correction** +0.075s/f (Good) **12 Ran SP% 116.5**
Speed ratings (Par 101): **99,95,93,93,92 92,91,87,84,83 77,76**toteswingers: 1&2 £38.10, 1& Volito £7.80, 1& Euroquip Boy £8.20, 2&V £12.20, 2&EB £23.50. PLACES: £2.10, £8.70, V £1.90, EB £2.60. TRICAST: Steel City Boy, Defector & Volito £744.44. SCB, D & EB £1,020.75. CSF £193.37 TOTE £8.20; EX 393.20 TR27 Owner.

FOCUS
After 2mm of overnight rain, plus a further 3mm during the morning, underfoot conditions were officially good to firm. The GoingStick reading was 8.0. A modest handicap, rated around the winner's recent AW form.
Volito Official explanation: jockey said gelding hung right

1913 PSA PEUGEOT CITROEN LONG SERVICE MAIDEN AUCTION STKS 5f 110y
6:15 (6:16) (Class 5) 2-Y-0 **£3,070** (£906; £453) **Stalls** Low

Form RPR
3234 **1** **Choice Of Remark (IRE)**[3] 1806 2-8-6 0 MatthewCosham(7) 4 74+
(David Evans) *mde all: rdn over 1f out: edgd lft ins fnl f: r.o: eased nr fin* **4/7**[1]

0 **2** 2 **Fromthestables Com (IRE)**[16] 1505 2-8-10 0 PatrickHills(3) 2 65
(J W Hills) *chsd wnr: rdn over 1f out: styd on same pce ins fnl f: wnt 2nd post* **33/1**

3 hd **Grand Gold** 2-8-10 0 MartinHarley(3) 3 65+
(Mick Channon) *s.i.s: rn green and outpcd: r.o ins fnl f: wnt 3rd post: nt rch ldrs* **11/1**

4 hd **Dixie's Dream (IRE)** 2-8-13 0 PatDobbs 1 64+
(Richard Hannon) *chsd wnr: rdn and ev ch jst ins fnl f: no ex: lost 2 pls nr fin* **7/2**[2]

6 **5** 5 **Manderston**[25] 1290 2-8-9 0 KierenFallon 5 44
(Mark Johnston) *chsd ldrs: reminder and hung rt over 3f out: rdn over 1f out: wknd and eased ins fnl f* **9/1**[3]

68.45 secs (2.55) **Going Correction** +0.075s/f (Good) **5 Ran SP% 107.2**
Speed ratings (Par 93): **86,83,83,82,76**
CSF £18.73 TOTE £1.70: £1.40, £2.40; EX 8.20.
Owner Nick Shutts **Bred** K Molloy **Trained** Pandy, Monmouths

FOCUS
Just one runner had a serious form claim in this juvenile maiden, but he was opposed by two nicely-bred newcomers. The race averages set the level.

NOTEBOOK
Choice Of Remark(IRE), fourth in the Lily Agnes at Chester three days earlier, made virtually all the running and notched a workmanlike success. He broke quickly and was soon in front but, after negotiating the home turn at the head of affairs, wandered slightly when put under pressure. He was well on top at the finish, but whether he will improve for this is open to question. (op 4-6)
Fromthestables Com(IRE), almost 12 lengths behind Choice Of Remark on his only previous run, had clearly made progress since. He still looked green here, though, despite responding well to late driving, and more improvement is possible. Official explanation: jockey said colt ran green
Grand Gold, a first-time-out half-brother to the fairly useful Buddy Holly, was comprehensively outpaced in the first half of the race. He knuckled down well in the final furlong, however, but showed enough promise to suggest he can land a maiden. (op 14-1 tchd 10-1)
Dixie's Dream(IRE), a newcomer from a decent sprinting family, ran as if this run was needed. He showed good early pace, racing in second at halfway and briefly challenged the winner, but faded in the closing stages. (op 11-4, tchd 4-1 in places)
Manderston, well beaten when slowly away on his Southwell debut, seemed not to handle the dogleg turn into the home straight. He made up some ground when drifting out and reaching the stands' rail, but then tired and dropped away tamely. (tchd 8-1)

1914 JOHN AND JENNY WEDDING DAY H'CAP 1m 6f 213y
6:45 (6:45) (Class 5) (0-75,73) 4-Y-0+ **£2,914** (£867; £433; £216) **Stalls** Low

Form RPR
360- **1** **Rare Ruby (IRE)**[197] 7061 7-9-6 69 TomQueally 4 77
(Jennie Candlish) *hld up: hdwy over 2f out: led over 1f out: sn rdn: edgd lft ins fnl f: styd on wl* **11/4**[2]

365- **2** 3 **My Mate Max**[211] 6715 6-9-10 73 (p) GrahamGibbons 2 77
(Reg Hollinshead) *pushed along to ld: rdn over 2f out: hdd over 1f out: styd on same pce ins fnl f* **11/4**[2]

4-25 **3** 3/4 **Stormy Morning**[2] 1839 5-9-2 65 (p) LiamKeniry 5 68
(J S Moore) *prom: chsd ldr 12f out: rdn over 2f out: styd on same pce fnl f* **5/2**[1]

202- **4** 3/4 **Raktiman (IRE)**[209] 6774 4-9-4 69 RichardKingscote 1 71
(Tom Dascombe) *racd keenly: trckd ldr 3f: remained handy: rdn over 2f out: no ex ins fnl f* **8/1**

-404 **5** 49 **Dubara Reef (IRE)**[24] 1305 4-9-3 68 (p) SteveDrowne 3 —
(Paul Green) *hld up: pushed along over 7f out: bhd fnl 3f: t.o* **11/2**[3]

3m 20.75s (1.75) **Going Correction** +0.075s/f (Good)
WFA 4 from 5yo+ 2lb **5 Ran SP% 108.4**
Speed ratings (Par 103): **98,96,96,95,69**
CSF £10.26 TOTE £3.00: £2.00, £1.60; EX 10.10.
Owner Mrs Judith Ratcliff **Bred** Robert And Michelle Dore **Trained** Basford Green, Staffs

FOCUS
No more than a run-of-the-mill handicap, but competitive on paper. Ther first two had both slipped to fair marks.
Dubara Reef(IRE) Official explanation: jockey said gelding never travelled

1915 EUROPEAN BREEDERS' FUND MAIDEN FILLIES' STKS 1m 2f 188y
7:15 (7:18) (Class 5) 3-Y-0+ **£3,561** (£1,059; £529; £264) **Stalls** Low

Form RPR
2-4 **1** **Baisse**[21] 1393 3-8-11 0 TomQueally 4 79+
(Sir Henry Cecil) *chsd ldr tl led over 2f out: shkn up over 1f out: r.o wl* **5/4**[1]

2 3 1/2 **Light Blow (USA)** 3-8-11 0 IanMongan 1 72+
(Sir Henry Cecil) *dwlt: hld up and rn green in rr: hdwy 4f out: rdn over 2f out: styd on same pce but wnt 2nd ins fnl f* **7/2**[3]

020- **3** 3/4 **Mia Madonna**[201] 6979 3-8-11 72 MartinDwyer 6 71
(Brian Meehan) *hld up in tch: rdn over 1f out: no ex ins fnl f* **8/1**

64- **4** 1/2 **Alfouzy**[206] 6843 3-8-11 0 NeilCallan 2 70
(Roger Varian) *chsd ldrs: rdn over 2f out: no ex ins fnl f* **9/4**[2]

/0 **5** 19 **Dancing Primo**[18] 1474 5-10-0 0 GrahamGibbons 3 36
(Mark Brisbourne) *led: rdn and hdd over 2f out: wknd over 1f out* **40/1**

2m 19.23s (-1.87) **Going Correction** +0.075s/f (Good)
WFA 3 from 5yo 17lb **5 Ran SP% 111.0**
Speed ratings (Par 100): **109,106,105,105,91**
toteswinger: 1&2 £4.80. CSF £6.09 TOTE £2.20: £1.30, £1.80; EX 5.10.
Owner G Schoenigh **Bred** Elsdon Farms **Trained** Newmarket, Suffolk

FOCUS
Quite an interesting fillies' maiden, despite the low turnout, and they went a decent pace. The bare form is only ordinary judged around the third.

1916 BAM CONSTRUCTION H'CAP 7f 26y
7:45 (7:46) (Class 4) (0-85,81) 3-Y-0 **£5,180** (£1,541; £770; £384) **Stalls** Low

Form RPR
02-1 **1** **Freckenham (IRE)**[22] 1358 3-9-2 76 HayleyTurner 5 81
(Michael Bell) *mde all: set stdy pce tl qcknd over 2f out: drvn out* **4/1**[3]

2155 **2** nk **City Legend**[8] 1653 3-8-8 71 (bt) MartinHarley(3) 2 75
(Alan McCabe) *chsd ldrs: rdn over 1f out: r.o: wnt 2nd nr fin* **16/1**

13-3 **3** nk **Nawaashi**[30] 1202 3-9-4 78 TadhgO'Shea 3 81
(Mark Johnston) *chsd wnr: rdn over 1f out: r.o: lost 2nd nr fin* **5/2**[1]

13-1 **4** 1/2 **Rossetti**[23] 1335 3-9-7 81 PatCosgrave 6 83+
(James Fanshawe) *hld up: rdn over 2f out: r.o wl ins fnl f: nt rch ldrs* **3/1**[2]

005- **5** nk **My Son Max**[205] 6870 3-9-6 80 PatDobbs 1 81+
(Richard Hannon) *hld up in tch: rdn over 1f out: r.o* **7/1**

11-3 **6** hd **Tamareen (IRE)**[23] 1335 3-9-1 75 (t) RichardHills 8 75
(Ed Dunlop) *chsd ldrs: rdn: nt clr run and swtchd lft over 1f out: r.o* **9/2**

13-5 **7** 14 **Wolf Slayer**[18] 1452 3-8-11 71 RichardKingscote 4 34
(Tom Dascombe) *hld up: wknd over 2f out* **33/1**

1m 25.61s (1.01) **Going Correction** +0.075s/f (Good) **7 Ran SP% 113.1**
Speed ratings (Par 101): **97,96,96,95,95 95,79**
toteswingers: 1&2 £5.50, 1&3 £2.90, 2&3 £9.80. CSF £59.55 CT £188.73 TOTE £4.70: £1.90, £7.80; EX 84.20 TRIFECTA Not won..
Owner Sheikh Marwan Al Maktoum **Bred** Darley **Trained** Newmarket, Suffolk

FOCUS
A decent handicap in which few could be confidently discounted. It was a muddling race though and it's doubtful if the form will prove reliable.

1917 OFFICIAL AFTERPARTY AT KOKO'S NIGHTCLUB LEAMINGTON H'CAP 7f 26y
8:15 (8:16) (Class 5) (0-75,78) 4-Y-0+ **£2,914** (£867; £433; £216) **Stalls** Low

Form RPR
3421 **1** **April Fool**[1] 1866 7-9-3 78 6ex (b) MatthewCosham(7) 2 87
(David Evans) *chsd ldr tl led over 5f out: rdn and hung lft fr over 1f out: r.o* **7/2**[2]

64-3 **2** *1* **Sir Bruno (FR)**[12] 1564 4-9-7 **75**.....................(p) DavidProbert 9 82+
(Bryn Palling) *a.p: rdn over 2f out: hung lft and r.o to go 2nd wl ins fnl f: nt rch wnr* **3/1**[1]

3516 **3** *1* **Silver Wind**[8] 1656 6-9-4 **72**.....................(b) NeilCallan 4 76
(Alan McCabe) *led: hdd over 5f out: chsd wnr: rdn over 1f out: hung lft ins fnl f: styd on same pce* **8/1**[3]

6-34 **4** *3* **Kingswinford (IRE)**[9] 1634 5-9-4 **75**..................... RichardEvans(3) 7 71
(David Evans) *chsd ldrs: rdn over 1f out: eased whn btn ins fnl f* **11/1**

213- **5** *2* **Lord Of The Dance (IRE)**[147] 7842 5-9-4 **72**............ GrahamGibbons 3 63
(Mark Brisbourne) *prom: rdn over 1f out: wknd ins fnl f* **14/1**

3-21 **6** *1/2* **Mandhooma**[9] 1634 5-8-9 **63**..................... ChrisCatlin 8 52+
(Peter Hiatt) *hld up: hmpd wl over 2f out: n.d* **10/1**

0202 **7** *nk* **Valmina**[5] 1755 4-8-7 **61** oh1.....................(t) JimmyQuinn 10 49
(Tony Carroll) *hld up: plld hrd: edgd lft wl over 2f out: nvr on terms* **8/1**[3]

1325 **8** *1 3/4* **Needwood Ridge**[29] 1222 4-8-13 **67**.....................(t) JamesDoyle 5 51
(Frank Sheridan) *s.i.s: plld hrd and sn prom: rdn over 2f out: wknd over 1f out* **8/1**[3]

3132 **9** *14* **Copperwood**[22] 1368 6-9-0 **68**..................... LiamKeniry 6 14+
(Michael Blanshard) *hood removed late: s.s: hld up: racd keenly: bdly hmpd wl over 2f out: eased* **17/2**

1m 24.49s (-0.11) **Going Correction** +0.075s/f (Good) 9 Ran SP% **115.2**
Speed ratings (Par 103): **103,101,100,97,95 94,94,92,76**
toteswingers: 1&2 £1.60, 1&3 £4.70, 2&3 £8.40. CSF £14.40 CT £77.48 TOTE £3.80: £1.60, £1.50, £2.60; EX 16.80 Trifecta £40.60 Pool: £111.95 - 2.04 winning units..
Owner Mrs E Evans **Bred** Miss B Swire **Trained** Pandy, Monmouths

FOCUS
Plenty could be fancied in this competitive 61-75 handicap. The winner followed up his win the day before with an effort of similar standard.
T/Plt: £182.40 to a £1 stake. Pool of £40,748.49 - 163.00 winning tickets. T/Qpdt: £25.70 to a £1 stake. Pool of £3,995.40 - 114.80 winning tickets. CR

1738 CAPANNELLE (R-H)
Saturday, May 7

OFFICIAL GOING: Turf: good

1918a PREMIO CARLO D'ALESSIO (GROUP 3) (4YO+) (TURF) 1m 4f
1:50 (12:00) 4-Y-0+ £34,482 (£15,172; £8,275; £4,137)

RPR

1 **Jakkalberry (IRE)**[146] 7851 5-8-9 0..................... FabioBranca 2 120+
(E Botti, Italy) *settled in 5th for 4f: stdy prog to move 3rd into fnl turn: eased to front 3f out and sn 3 l clr: rdn to go 4 l clr 2f out: 6 l clr ent fnl f: eased fnl 100yds: comf* **20/75**[1]

2 *6* **Lord Chaparral (IRE)**[27] 4-8-9 0..................... MircoDemuro 3 110
(R Brogi, Italy) *trckd ldrs: in tch in 4th ent st: sltly ct for pce 4f out: rdn 3f out to enter battle for 2nd: gained upper hand fnl 100yds: nvr trbld wnr* **4/1**[2]

3 *3/4* **Frankenstein (ITY)**[195] 4-8-11 0..................... DarioVargiu 4 111
(B Grizzetti, Italy) *settled in rr for 5f: trckd eventual wnr 4f out: sn battling only for 2nd wout pce to stay w ldr: lost 2nd fnl 100yds* **11/2**[3]

4 *4* **Permesso**[27] 6-8-9 0..................... CristianDemuro 6 103
(G Pucciatti, Italy) *hld up nr rr tl ent st: rdn and sme prog on outer 3f out: sn one pce* **107/10**

5 *2 1/2* **Sopran Prince (IRE)**[96] 371 5-8-9 0..................... SSulas 5 99
(M Mercalli, Italy) *led for 4f: settled to trck ldr tl st: rdn 4f out and outpcd: sn btn* **177/10**

6 *4* **Trovajoli (ITY)**[174] 4-8-9 0..................... StefanoLandi 1 92
(F & L Camici, Italy) *wnt rt at s to r alone on rail for 2f: led after 4f: rdn and lost ld 3f out: sn no ex* **55/1**

2m 28.1s (0.90) 6 Ran SP% **130.0**
WIN (incl. 1 euro stake): 1.26. PLACES: 1.12, 1.61. DF: 2.06.
Owner Effevi **Bred** Azienda Agricola Allevamento Deni **Trained** Italy

1919a PREMIO TUDINI (GROUP 3) (3YO+) (TURF) 6f
2:55 (12:00) 3-Y-0+ £34,482 (£15,172; £8,275; £4,137)

RPR

1 **Spirit Quartz (IRE)**[41] 3-8-6 0..................... CFiocchi 9 105
(D Grilli, Italy) *broke wl to share ld after 1f: rdn ent fnl 2 1/2f to ld by 1 l: chal by eventual 2nd on inner 2f out: hrd rdn fnl f to hold on on line* **19/2**

2 *hd* **Dagda Mor (ITY)**[13] 4-9-1 0..................... FabioBranca 11 103
(S Botti, Italy) *broke wl to share ld after 1f: ct for pce 2 1/2f out: rallied u.str ride fnl 200yds to almost get up fnl strides* **224/10**

3 *2* **Charming Woman (IRE)**[20] 1432 4-8-11 0..................... MircoDemuro 8 93
(Vittorio Caruso, Italy) *settled in mid-div for 2f: prog to trck ldng pair 3f out: hrd-rdn 2f out and little imp: styd on one pce fnl f* **8/5**[1]

4 *1 3/4* **Lipfix (ITY)**[64] 3-8-5 0..................... MEsposito 2 91
(V di Napoli, Italy) *settled in rr on rail after 1f: n.m.r whn looking for run 3f out: styd on wl fnl 2f whn gap eventually c* **208/10**

5 *3 1/2* **Rebecca Rolfe**[20] 1432 5-8-11 0..................... MKolmarkaj 5 76
(M Gasparini, Italy) *mid-div for 3f: ct for pce and sltly hmpd 2 1/2f out: one pce fnl 2f* **71/10**

6 *3/4* **Le Vie Infinite (IRE)**[20] 4-9-1 0..................... GBietolini 13 78
(R Brogi, Italy) *nr rr for 3f: prog whn swtchd rt 2 1/2f out: rdn and styd on one pce fnl 2f* **152/10**

7 *2 1/2* **El Suacillo (IRE)**[293] 4185 4-9-1 0..................... StefanoLandi 1 70
(D Camuffo, Italy) *on rail and in tch for 3f: ev ch 2 1/2f out: sn hrd rdn and no ex ent fnl 2f* **44/1**

8 *nk* **Rosendhal (IRE)**[13] 4-9-5 0.....................(b) MarcoMonteriso 7 73
(A Renzoni, Italy) *in rr: nvr figured* **13/2**[3]

9 *nk* **Farrel (IRE)**[13] 6-9-1 0..................... DarioVargiu 10 68
(B Grizzetti, Italy) *mid-div: ct for pce 3f out: eased fnl f* **19/5**[2]

10 *3* **Thinking Robins (IRE)**[174] 7459 8-9-1 0.....................(b) SGuerrieri 15 58
(Ottavio Di Paolo, Italy) *racd alone in centre of trck: struggled fnl 3f to stay in tch: sn fdd* **99/1**

11 *2* **Madda's Force (ITY)**[20] 1432 5-8-11 0..................... MPasquale 14 48
(R Betti, Italy) *in tch w ldrs: outpcd 3f out: sn btn* **219/10**

12 *hd* **Jakor (ITY)**[13] 5-9-5 0..................... UmbertoRispoli 3 55
(M Marcialis, Italy) *trckd ldrs for 2 1/2f: rdn 3f out: n.d* **9/1**

13 *5* **Diglett (IRE)**[13] 5-9-1 0..................... GMarcelli 6 35
(P Riccioni, Italy) *in rr: nvr figured* **51/1**

14 *nse* **Questi Amori (IRE)**[182] 7370 4-9-1 0..................... SSulas 4 35
(M Guarnieri, Italy) *in rr: nvr figured* **97/10**

68.10 secs (-2.20)
WFA 3 from 4yo+ 10lb 14 Ran SP% **138.4**
PARI-MUTUEL (all including 1 euro stakes): WIN 10.53; PLACE 3.43, 7.04, 1.62; DF 359.10.
Owner Devis Grilli **Bred** Ballygallon Stud Limited **Trained** Italy

1920a DERBY ITALIANO (GROUP 2) (3YO COLTS & FILLIES) (TURF) 1m 3f
4:50 (12:00) 3-Y-0 £318,965 (£140,344; £76,551; £38,275)

RPR

1 **Crackerjack King (IRE)**[37] 3-9-2 0..................... FabioBranca 2 112+
(S Botti, Italy) *settled in 6th on rail after 2f: cut for pce at 3f marker: prog between horses 2 1/2f out: rdn to ld 2f out: chal briefly on outer 1 1/2f out: rdn out fnl f to hold command: comf* **6/4**[1]

2 *2* **Cazals (IRE)**[34] 1127 3-9-2 0..................... UmbertoRispoli 1 108
(B Grizzetti, Italy) *slowly away and forced to take up postion in rr on inner: prog 3f out whn swtchd wd: chal ldr and ev ch 2f out: styd on under hrd ride fnl f* **6/1**[3]

3 *2 1/2* **Danedream (GER)**[27] 3-8-13 0..................... AStarke 5 101
(P Schiergen, Germany) *mid-diivision tl ent st: rdn to trck ldrs on outer 3f out: styd on under v hrd ride fnl 2f to grab 3rd fnl 100yds* **15/2**

4 *2 1/4* **Sneak A Peek (ITY)**[21] 3-9-2 0..................... SSulas 13 101
(S Botti, Italy) *broke wl: led: set stdy pce for 6f: rdn and 1 l ld 3f out: hdd 2f out and sn one pce* **111/10**

5 *10* **Doquet (IRE)**[20] 1431 3-9-2 0..................... CColombi 10 82
(B Grizzetti, Italy) *broke wl: stdd to r nr rr after 1f: prog under hrd ride under 2f out: sn one pce* **99/1**

6 *10* **Figli Fanesi (IRE)**[20] 3-9-2 0..................... MircoDemuro 7 64
(Vittorio Caruso, Italy) *settled in 5th tl ent st: produced 3f out to chal ldr briefly: sn hrd rdn and fdd qckly* **11/5**[2]

7 *2 1/2* **Bacchelli**[20] 3-9-2 0..................... GBietolini 4 59
(S Botti, Italy) *trckd ldrs in 3rd for 7f: rdn to stay in tch 3 1/2f out: btn 2 1/2f out* **247/10**

8 *3 1/2* **Plushenko (IRE)**[20] 3-9-2 0..................... CristianDemuro 8 53
(L Riccardi, Italy) *trckd ldr in 2nd for 7f: rdn 4f out: sn one pce: btn 3f out* **26/1**

9 *3* **Lake Drop (USA)**[21] 3-9-2 0..................... MEsposito 12 48
(S Botti, Italy) *in rr: struggling and stl last 4f out: nvr figured* **106/10**

10 *2* **Fairyhall**[37] 3-9-2 0..................... DarioVargiu 6 44
(B Grizzetti, Italy) *settled bhd ldrs in 4th tl ent st: rdn to keep position 3 1/2f out: sn btn and eased fnl f* **167/10**

11 *12* **Kephas (IRE)**[150] 3-9-2 0.....................(b) MKolmarkaj 9 22
(F Iovine, Italy) *mid-div on outer for 7f: rdn 4f out sn no ex* **93/1**

12 *14* **Ekasin**[34] 1127 3-9-2 0..................... MarcoMonteriso 11 —
(Marco Botti) *plld hrd in mid-div for 3f: in tch ent st: sn rdn and fdd rapidly* **26/1**

2m 15.8s (135.80) 12 Ran SP% **133.2**
PARI-MUTUEL (all including 1 euro stakes): WIN 2.50; PLACE 1.44, 2.02, 2.24; DF 13.50.
Owner Effevi **Bred** Azienda Agricola Al Deni S R L **Trained** Italy

NOTEBOOK
Crackerjack King(IRE), a half-brother to 2007 winner Awelmarduk, as well as Jakkalberry who won a Group 3 on this card, maintained his unbeaten record on this step up in trip. He won with a fair bit in hand and could be set to dominate the top middle-distances in his homeland this year.
Cazals(IRE) was unlucky not to get closer, taking up a poor posiiton having been slowly away. He was no match for the winner, but had the rest well enough beaten.
Danedream(GER), the only filly in the field, had the form to run well and stayed on under strong pressure.
Figli Fanesi(IRE) was disappointing, considering he had won well over C&D on his reappearance.
Ekasin was second to today's runner-up Cazals last time but disappointed here.

1882 CHURCHILL DOWNS (L-H)
Saturday, May 7

OFFICIAL GOING: Dirt: fast; turf: firm

1921a 137TH KENTUCKY DERBY PRESENTED BY YUM! BRANDS (GRADE 1) (3YO) (DIRT) 1m 2f (D)
11:24 (11:31) 3-Y-0 £905,000 (£256,410; £128,205; £64,102; £38,461)

RPR

1 **Animal Kingdom (USA)**[42] 3-9-0 0.....................(b) JRVelazquez 16 126+
(H Graham Motion, U.S.A) **209/10**

2 *2 3/4* **Nehro (USA)**[21] 3-9-0 0..................... CNakatani 18 120+
(Steven Asmussen, U.S.A) **17/2**[3]

3 *nk* **Mucho Macho Man (USA)**[42] 3-9-0 0..................... RMaragh 13 119
(Kathy Ritvo, U.S.A) **93/10**

4 *3/4* **Shackleford (USA)**[34] 1123 3-9-0 0..................... JLCastanon 14 117
(Dale Romans, U.S.A) **231/10**

5 *1 3/4* **Master Of Hounds (USA)**[42] 998 3-9-0 0..................... GKGomez 11 114+
(A P O'Brien, Ire) **168/10**

6 *nse* **Santiva (USA)**[21] 3-9-0 0..................... SXBridgmohan 12 113
(Eddie Kenneally, U.S.A) **35/1**

7 *nse* **Brilliant Speed (USA)**[21] 3-9-0 0..................... JRosario 2 113
(Thomas Albertrani, U.S.A) **28/1**

8 *2* **Dialed In (USA)**[34] 1123 3-9-0 0..................... JRLeparoux 8 113+
(Nicholas Zito, U.S.A) **26/5**[1]

9 *nk* **Pants On Fire (USA)**[42] 3-9-0 0..................... RosieNapravnik 7 109+
(Kelly Breen, U.S.A) **81/10**[2]

10 *2 3/4* **Twice The Appeal (USA)**[40] 3-9-0 0.....................(b) CHBorel 3 103
(Jeff Bonde, U.S.A) **119/10**

11 *nk* **Soldat (USA)**[34] 1123 3-9-0 0..................... AGarcia 17 103
(Kiaran McLaughlin, U.S.A) **119/10**

12 *1 1/2* **Stay Thirsty (USA)**[34] 1123 3-9-0 0..................... RADominguez 4 100
(Todd Pletcher, U.S.A) **172/10**

13 *3 1/4* **Derby Kitten (USA)**[14] 3-9-0 0.....................(b) JJCastellano 9 93
(Michael J Maker, U.S.A) **36/1**

14 *1 1/4* **Decisive Moment (USA)**[42] 3-9-0 0..................... KDClark 5 91
(Juan D Arias, U.S.A) **39/1**

15 *1* **Archarcharch (USA)**[21] 3-9-0 0.....................(b) JKCourt 1 89+
(William H Fires, U.S.A) **125/10**

16 *1* **Midnight Interlude (USA)**[27] 3-9-0 0.....................(b) VEspinoza 15 87
(Bob Baffert, U.S.A) **96/10**

17 ½ **Twinspired (USA)**[21] 3-9-0 0 .... MESmith 10 86
(Michael J Maker, U.S.A) **33/1**

18 3¾ **Watch Me Go (USA)**[28] 3-9-0 0 .... (b) RBejarano 19 78
(Kathleen O'Connell, U.S.A) **34/1**

19 ½ **Comma To The Top (USA)**[27] 3-9-0 0 .... (b) PValenzuela 6 77+
(Peter Miller, U.S.A) **36/1**

2m 2.04s (0.85) **19** Ran SP% **119.5**

PARI-MUTUEL (all including $2 stakes): WIN 43.80; PLACE (1-2) 19.60, 8.80; SHOW (1-2-3) 13.00, 6.40, 7.00; SF 329.80.

Owner Team Valor International **Bred** Team Valor **Trained** USA

FOCUS

Last year's champion 2yo male, Uncle Mo, failed to make the line-up and not a single member of the field had recorded a time usually expected of a major contender in their final prep run. The race itself was unsatisfactory. The sectionals for each quarter were 23.24, 48.63, 1.13.40, 1.37.49. Compare that to the last time there was a dry track for the Derby - the 2008 running won by Big Brown - when the field went 23.30, 47.04, 1.11.14, 1.36.56. Consequently, it rode a bit more like a turf race than is often the case.

NOTEBOOK

Animal Kingdom(USA), who's bred for grass on both sides of his pedigree, had never previously raced on dirt. The winner's final trial came on Polytrack and his finishing effort was too quick for a bunch of rivals who, put simply, are slow by the usual standard of the US Classic division. Fifth-placed Master Of Hounds also has a mainly turf pedigree and had never previously tried dirt. Considering the lack of quality on show, and that this was a not typical test of a dirt runner, there have to reservations about the worth of the form. However, Animal Kingdom's victory was still well earned, one that could only be achieved by handling the surface, and it would be wrong to underplay the impressive change of pace he showed to move from a modest mid-division sit, into a serious challenging position around the final bend. If he faces much the same calibre of opposition in the Preakness come May 21 then he could take another step towards the coveted Triple Crown, a feat last achieved by Affirmed in 1978.

Nehro(USA) had a wide trip from stall 19, but for most of the journey he wasn't actually much further out than the winner, who started from gate 16. He committed before Animal Kingdom, leading into the straight, but that was understandable considering the lack of pace and that he's bred to stay, and he just lacked the winner's speed in the closing stages. This was his third consecutive second placing (only has maiden win to his name) and his attitude is questionable, not least because he carried his head at an angle down the back straight, and it might be that blinkers will be the making of him, while a stronger-run race should also help.

Mucho Macho Man(USA) was better placed than the winner leaving the back straight, but lacked that one's finished speed.

Shackleford(USA) set a furious gallop before only just being caught by Dialed In when contesting the Florida Derby last time, and he was able to dictate the pace to suit on this occasion, but he didn't stay.

Master Of Hounds(USA) earned his shot with a second-place finish in the UAE Derby, but he had never tried this surface and didn't work over the Churchill Downs dirt before the race. He only arrived on the Tuesday before the race and reportedly wasn't even schooled in the stalls. Theoretically he was conceding a huge advantage to his opponents and it was a preparation hard to fathom from a trainer who usually leaves so little to chance with his runners in Europe. The horse ran a blinder in the circumstances. He broke okay, but lacked tactical pace, soon being poorly placed, and he couldn't quicken sufficiently leaving the back straight. There was much to like about his finishing kick, though, and considering he should have learnt plenty, he'll be worth another try on the surface in something like the Preakness and/or the Belmont Stakes. Garrett Gomez said he's looking forward to riding him in the latter contest.

Santiva(USA) wasn't good enough.

Brilliant Speed(USA) is better than he showed. He started from stall two, but ended up having to circle much of the field after being dropped in soon after the start and was wide into the straight. A stronger-run race would have suited better.

Dialed In(USA), a confirmed hold-up performer, was undone by the lack of early pace, but even so this was a seriously ill-judged ride from Julien Leparoux. He had his mount in a detached last, showing no obvious urgency to move even a little closer than usual considering how the race was unfolding, and hardly seemed to go for his mount until he approached the straight. The horse only had two rivals behind once in line for the finish and did well to get so close. He emerged from the race with some credit, but his rider did not.

Pants On Fire(USA) was said to have bled quite badly.

Archarcharch(USA) was pulled up lame and will reportedly require surgery after suffering a lateral condylar fracture.

Comma To The Top(USA) was also said to have picked up an ankle injury.

1740 SAINT-CLOUD (L-H)

Saturday, May 7

OFFICIAL GOING: Turf: good to soft

1922a PRIX CLEOPATRE (GROUP 3) (3YO FILLIES) (TURF) 1m 2f 110y

4:35 (12:00) 3-Y-0 **£34,482** (£13,793; £10,344; £6,896; £3,448)

RPR

1 **Galikova (FR)**[29] 3-8-9 0 .... OlivierPeslier 5 114+
(F Head, France) *sn 2nd bhd pcemaker: cruised into ld 2f out: r.o wl: nvr threatened: easily* **13/10**[1]

2 3 **Adventure Seeker (FR)**[27] 1264 3-8-9 0 .... ChristopheSoumillon 4 106
(A De Royer-Dupre, France) *settled towards rr: gd prog early in st: wnt 2nd 1 1/2f out: r.o wl but no threat to wnr* **6/1**[3]

3 2 **Wavering (IRE)**[18] 3-8-9 0 .... Pierre-CharlesBoudot 1 102+
(A Fabre, France) *in rr fr s: racing freely: on outside early in st: rdn and swtchd towards rail 2f out: picked up and fin wl fnl f* **13/2**

4 2 **Jehannedarc (IRE)**[27] 3-8-9 0 .... Christophe-PatriceLemaire 8 98
(A De Royer-Dupre, France) *settled towards rr: rdn 1 1/2f out: styd on wl fnl f* **21/1**

5 hd **Bernieres (IRE)**[46] 3-8-9 0 .... GregoryBenoist 2 98
(Mme Pia Brandt, France) *settled in midfield: rdn but nt qckn 1 1/2f out: styd on fnl f* **13/1**

6 2 **Pirika (IRE)**[16] 1513 3-8-9 0 .... MaximeGuyon 7 94
(A Fabre, France) *settled 3rd: rdn but no ex fr 2f out* **14/5**[2]

7 8 **Venise Jelois (FR)**[8] 1669 3-8-9 0 .... ThierryJarnet 3 78
(Robert Collet, France) *settled 5th: rdn early in st: no ex: fdd* **31/1**

8 10 **Polemique (IRE)**[33] 3-8-9 0 .... MickaelBarzalona 6 59
(F Head, France) *set gd pce for eventual wnr: hdd 2f out: sn dropped away* **34/1**

2m 8.00s (-11.60) **8** Ran SP% **115.1**

WIN (incl. 1 euro stake): 2.10 (Galikova coupled with Polemique). PLACES: 1.10, 1.50, 1.70. DF: 6.20. SF: 9.30.

Owner Wertheimer & Frere **Bred** Wertheimer & Frere **Trained** France

NOTEBOOK

Galikova(FR) ◆, a half-sister to wonder filly Goldikova, won tidily on her reappearance and stamped herself as a potential top-notcher with this impressive display. Soon tracking the pacemaker, she readily went to the front under Peslier, and drew clear with the minimum of fuss. Improving all the time, she looks a leading contender for Diane, which she'll be well fancied to take en route to better things.

Adventure Seeker(FR) stayed on without posing a serious threat to the impressive winner.

Wavering(IRE) ran as though there'll be more to come once settling better. She had won at Longchamp on her reappearance and can be rated better than the bare form.

1923a PRIX GREFFULHE (GROUP 2) (3YO COLTS & FILLIES) (TURF) 1m 2f

5:35 (12:00) 3-Y-0 **£63,879** (£24,655; £11,767; £7,844; £3,922)

RPR

1 **Pour Moi (IRE)**[27] 1265 3-9-2 0 .... MickaelBarzalona 8 118+
(A Fabre, France) *bk of the field tl st: qcknd wl on outside 2f out: grabbed ld 150yds out: r.o wl: comf* **123/10**

2 1½ **Bubble Chic (FR)**[18] 9001 3-9-2 0 .... GeraldMosse 1 114
(G Botti, Italy) *settled in 2nd: wnt 3rd in bk st: qcknd wl 2f out: slipped through on rail to take ld 1 1/2f out: hdd 150yds out: r.o wl* **10/1**[3]

3 1 **Vadamar (FR)**[34] 1124 3-9-2 0 .... Christophe-PatriceLemaire 5 112
(A De Royer-Dupre, France) *initially 2nd bhd pcemaker: dropped bk to 3rd bef st: rdn early in st: wnt 3rd 1 1/2f out: styd on wl fnl f wout threatening two ldrs* **4/5**[1]

4 3 **Dildar (IRE)**[27] 3-9-2 0 .... ThierryJarnet 2 106
(A De Royer-Dupre, France) *set gd pce for favourite: hdd 1 1/2f out: styd on gamely fnl f* **22/1**

5 hd **Questioning (IRE)**[23] 1339 3-9-2 0 .... MaximeGuyon 9 106
(John Gosden) *settled towards rr: rdn and styd on wl fnl 2f* **11/1**

6 8 **Lustre (FR)**[34] 1124 3-9-2 0 .... ChristopheSoumillon 4 90
(Y De Nicolay, France) *settled 4th: rdn early in st: fnd nthing: sn wknd* **13/1**

7 nk **Saint Desir**[27] 3-9-2 0 .... AnthonyCrastus 7 89
(E Lellouche, France) *racd in midfield: rdn early in st: fnd nthing: wknd* **11/2**[2]

8 8 **Maxios**[27] 1265 3-9-2 0 .... StephanePasquier 3 73
(J E Pease, France) *settled 5th: rdn early in st: no ex: sn wknd* **11/1**

9 8 **Berigny (FR)**[16] 3-9-2 0 .... SamuelFargeat 6 57
(E Lellouche, France) *settled 3rd on outer: wnt 2nd bef st: sn rdn: wknd qckly* **31/1**

2m 3.02s (-12.98) **9** Ran SP% **118.8**

WIN (incl. 1 euro stake): 13.30. PLACES: 2.40, 1.90, 1.20. DF: 37.30. SF: 79.70.

Owner Mrs J Magnier, D Smith & M Tabor **Bred** Lynch Bages Ltd **Trained** Chantilly, France

NOTEBOOK

Pour Moi(IRE), who may well have needed his reappearance run at Longchamp, posted a performance that highlighted him as a serious Jockey Club contender. Brought wide with his challenge, he quickened in the style on a very smart performer, winning with plenty in hand, and also has races such as the Grand Prix de Paris and Arc on his agenda, according to Andre Fabre.

Bubble Chic(FR) boasted some smart juvenile form and he's run well enough on both starts at three to suggest he's trained on well. He lacked the class of the winner, but is probably capable of winning at this level.

Vadamar(FR) came into this with something of a reputation, connections talking of him as a possible Epsom horse, but he was made to look rather paceless, keeping on late having been readily outpaced. He clearly needs 1m4f, and could be one for the Grand Prix de Paris, although it remains to be seen whether he's up to that level.

Dildar(IRE) kept on well having been used as a pacemaker.

Questioning(IRE) never threatened to get into it and doesn't look up to this level.

Maxios has now disappointed on both starts this season, and doesn't look to have trained on.

1924 - 1926a (Foreign Racing) - See Raceform Interactive

1256 LEOPARDSTOWN (L-H)

Sunday, May 8

OFFICIAL GOING: Good

1927a DERRINSTOWN STUD DERBY TRIAL STKS (GROUP 2) 1m 2f

4:15 (4:15) 3-Y-0 **£53,232** (£15,560; £7,370; £2,456)

RPR

1 **Recital (FR)**[28] 1259 3-9-4 114 .... KierenFallon 3 118+
(A P O'Brien, Ire) *trckd ldrs in 3rd: hdwy into 2nd 3f out: impr to ld under 2f out: pushed out and hung lft fr over 1f out: kpt on* **1/2**[1]

2 1½ **Memphis Tennessee (IRE)**[170] 7509 3-9-1 94 .... JPO'Brien 5 109
(A P O'Brien, Ire) *chsd ldr in 2nd: 3rd 3f out: rdn over 2f out: 2nd 1f out: no imp on ldr: kpt on same pce* **25/1**

3 1½ **Regent Street (IRE)**[28] 1259 3-9-1 106 .... (b[1]) SeamieHeffernan 4 106
(A P O'Brien, Ire) *led: rdn and chal 2f out: sn hdd: no ex over 1f out: kpt on same pce* **12/1**

4 1¾ **Best Hello**[42] 1009 3-9-1 .... WJSupple 7 103
(P D Deegan, Ire) *chsd ldrs: 4th 1/2-way: rdn and no imp ent st: kpt on same pce* **20/1**

5 3½ **Zanughan (IRE)**[21] 1430 3-9-1 .... (t) JMurtagh 6 96
(John M Oxx, Ire) *a in rr: pushed along and trailing 1/2-way: kpt on one pce st* **9/2**[2]

6 nk **Rich Tapestry (IRE)**[28] 1259 3-9-1 104 .... (b[1]) PJSmullen 2 95
(D K Weld, Ire) *hld up in 6th: rdn into 5th 2f out: no imp and kpt on one pce* **14/1**

7 9 **Giant Step (IRE)**[15] 1537 3-9-1 .... WMLordan 1 77
(David Wachman, Ire) *settled bhd ldrs: 5th 1/2-way: rdn and no imp ent st: wknd* **9/1**[3]

2m 4.09s (-4.11) **Going Correction** 0.0s/f (Good) **7** Ran SP% **117.8**

Speed ratings: **116,114,113,112,109 109,101**

CSF £18.64 TOTE £1.50: £1.20, £5.30; DF 16.70.

Owner Mrs John Magnier **Bred** Mme Renee Geffroy & Caragh Bloodstock **Trained** Ballydoyle, Co Tipperary

FOCUS

A ninth win in this Derby trial for Aidan O'Brien but a renewal produced more questions than answers with odds-on favourite Recital leading home stablemates Memphis Tennessee and Regent Street. The bare form of this race is nothing exceptional and the time was 1.09 secs slower than standard on quick ground. The form is rated around the winner and third.

NOTEBOOK

Recital(FR) went to the front 2f out and the result was never really in doubt but he carried his head high - he was very keen when held up here in the Ballysax Stakes in which he ran third last month - and on this occasion he repeatedly hung left towards the rail after taking the lead. He doesn't lack ability but he looks a tricky ride and, while connections appeared pleased with his performance, it remains to be seen whether the Derby and Epsom and all that the race and occasion entail will suit him. If he does handle the track it would be no surprise to see his challenge being delivered late. (op 1/2 tchd 4/9)

Memphis Tennessee(IRE), rated 94 and 20lb inferior to the winner, who was conceding 3lb to him, won a 1m maiden at Dundalk late last season. He raced in second place and was being pushed along 4f out before dropping to third 3f out. He regained second spot entering the final furlong and kept on without troubling the winner.

Regent Street(IRE), one length in front of Recital when making the running and finishing second in the Ballysax Stakes over the same course and trip last month, was blinkered for the first time to sharpen him in his pacemaking role. He led until 2f out and kept on when headed. Like the runner-up, he will have no problem going 1m4f. (op 10/1)

Best Hello, a 33-1 shot when beating the Ballydoyle-trained Apache in a maiden on his debut over this course and trip, acquitted himself well here. An Irish Derby entry, he was always handy and stayed on quite well after being ridden along and making little impression turning for home. (op 16/1)

Zanughan(IRE), winner of a 1m2f maiden on yielding ground at Navan last month, was behind and outpaced before staying on from 2f out. He will be well suited by 1m4f but at quite what level of competition remains to be seen. (op 11/2)

Rich Tapestry(IRE), only a short head behind Recital in the Ballysax, was blinkered for the first time but was unable to pose any sort of threat over the last 2f. (op 14/1 tchd 16/1)

1928a DERRINSTOWN STUD 1,000 GUINEAS TRIAL (GROUP 3) (FILLIES) 1m
4:45 (4:48) 3-Y-O **£35,021** (£10,237; £4,849; £1,616)

RPR

1 **Ballybacka Lady (IRE)**30 1225 3-9-0 93 FMBerry 8 104
(P A Fahy, Ire) *disp early: sn 2nd: rdn to ld 2f out: kpt on strly fr over 1f out* **33/1**

2 1 ¾ **Sapphire Pendant (IRE)**15 1535 3-9-0 WMLordan 6 100
(David Wachman, Ire) *mid-div: 6th 1/2-way: rdn into 5th 2f out: 4th 1f out: kpt on to go 2nd ins fnl f: nt rch wnr* **4/1**3

3 ¾ **Dance Secretary (IRE)**6 1783 3-9-0 JMurtagh 10 98
(John M Oxx, Ire) *chsd ldrs: 4th 1/2-way: rdn 2f out: styd on into 2nd 1f out: no ex ins fnl f: kpt on same pce* **8/1**

4 1 ¾ **Handassa**209 6819 3-9-0 DPMcDonogh 7 94+
(Kevin Prendergast, Ire) *hld up towards rr: rdn in 8th 2f out: 7th 1f out: kpt on same pce ins fnl f* **11/4**1

5 shd **Zaminast**285 4464 3-9-0 PJSmullen 2 94
(D K Weld, Ire) *settled bhd ldrs: 5th 1/2-way: rdn in 6th 2f out: kpt on one pce in 5th fr 1f out* **7/2**2

6 2 **Radharcnafarraige (IRE)**42 1006 3-9-0 100 KJManning 5 90
(J S Bolger, Ire) *mid-div: 7th 1/2-way: rdn and no imp 2f out: kpt on one pce* **12/1**

7 ¾ **Hurricane Havoc (IRE)**42 1006 3-9-0 94 (p) RPWhelan 3 87
(J S Bolger, Ire) *towards rr for most: nvr a factor* **14/1**

8 1 **Face Reality (USA)**30 1225 3-9-0 93 CO'Donoghue 9 85
(David Marnane, Ire) *chsd ldrs: 3rd 1/2-way: rdn 2f out: 2nd and no imp 1 1/2f out: 3rd 1f out: wknd ins fnl f* **14/1**

9 4 **Gemstone (IRE)**21 1428 3-9-0 102 (p) SeamieHeffernan 1 76
(A P O'Brien, Ire) *sn led: rdn and hdd 2f out: no ex in 4th 1 1/2f out: wknd over 1f out* **11/2**

1m 39.76s (-1.44) **Going Correction** 0.0s/f (Good) 9 Ran SP% **119.4**
Speed ratings: **107,105,104,102,102 100,99,98,94**
CSF £166.04 TOTE £22.90: £4.40, £1.70, £2.70; DF 441.50.
Owner Mrs P Corcoran **Bred** Sean O'Keeffe **Trained** Leighlinbridge, Co Carlow

FOCUS

A surprise outcome to this Guineas Trial. Improved form from the winner in beating some unexposed types.

NOTEBOOK

Ballybacka Lady(IRE) recorded her second career win. She had lost valuable ground leaving the stalls in her previous start on the AW at Dundalk but loaded in last here certainly helped her cause. She travelled well tracking the leader Gemstone, who set a decent clip, and when they straightened for home she took over after passing the 2f pole and kept on well. The Etihad Airways Irish 1,000 Guineas is next and she's entitled to take her chance on this performance.

Sapphire Pendant(IRE) ◆ was fancied to supplement her Cork maiden win in April. Her rider said after that it took her a while to get going when the race unfolded, so she should be sharper with this pleasing run behind her after keeping on well in the final furlong to take the runner-up berth.

Dance Secretary(IRE) couldn't raise her game enough to get to the winner when she took over. (op 8/1 tchd 7/1)

Handassa was sent off favourite but the runaway Curragh back-end juvenile winner last season wasn't helped when she jumped and landed in the middle of the road shortly after the start. Her rider said she was struggling after that off the pace and did well in the circumstances to reach the frame. She should be better for this comeback run and might be more at home with a slight ease. (op 4/1)

Zaminast, a half-sister to Famous Name who won the finale, showed her inexperience when the race unfolded into the straight and according to her rider "the experience will do her the world of good". Official explanation: trainer said filly did not enjoy a clear run in the home straight (op 11/4)

1930a AMETHYST STKS (GROUP 3) 1m
5:45 (5:45) 3-Y-O+ **£32,219** (£9,418; £4,461; £1,487)

RPR

1 **Famous Name**28 1257 6-9-12 117 PJSmullen 4 123+
(D K Weld, Ire) *settled 3rd: impr ent st: led under 2f out: clr over 1f out: easily* **1/6**1

2 7 **Across The Rhine (USA)**35 1118 5-9-9 105 PShanahan 5 102
(Tracey Collins, Ire) *hld up towards rr: rdn in 5th 2f out: 3rd 1f out: kpt on into 2nd ins fnl f: no ch w wnr* **12/1**2

3 nk **Fighting Brave (USA)**10 1642 4-9-9 96 (p) WMLordan 1 101
(David Wachman, Ire) *chsd ldrs: 4th 1/2-way: rdn and no imp ent st: kpt on same pce fr over 1f out: 3rd cl home* **16/1**3

4 hd **Separate Ways (IRE)**10 1642 6-9-9 99 (b) CO'Donoghue 3 101
(David Marnane, Ire) *hld up towards rr: rdn 3f out: sme late hdwy in 5th 1f out: kpt on same pce ins fnl f* **20/1**

5 nk **Barack (IRE)**28 1257 5-9-9 103 (bt) DPMcDonogh 6 100
(Francis Ennis, Ire) *led: jnd and disp after 3f: rdn and hdd under 2f out: no ex over 1f out: kpt on same pce* **12/1**2

6 13 **Libano (IRE)**28 1257 5-9-9 98 SMGorey 2 70
(D K Weld, Ire) *chsd ldr in 2nd: impr to dispute after 3f: rdn in 2nd 2f out: sn no ex and wknd over 1f out* **20/1**

1m 38.92s (-2.28) **Going Correction** 0.0s/f (Good) 6 Ran SP% **116.5**
Speed ratings: **111,104,103,103,103 90**
Daily Double: Not Won. Pool of 2,480.00 carried forward to Roscommon on Monday 9th May. Pick Six: Not won. Pool of 35,686.65 carried over to 15th May. CSF £3.99 TOTE £1.10: £1.10, £1.90; DF 4.30.
Owner K Abdulla **Bred** Juddmonte Farms Ltd **Trained** The Curragh, Co Kildare

FOCUS

As the market suggested, this was a one-horse race and so it proved. Famous Name rates a personal best and the form makes sense.

NOTEBOOK

Famous Name bolted up to bring his career-winning tally to 12 and remarkably his eighth win at this venue. Stablemate Libano and Barack raced at the head of affairs setting a good gallop from the outset before the long odds-on favourite moved closer to take over under 2f from home and went on to win with the minimum of fuss. Described as "a proper horse and a joy to train" by his trainer, the Tattersalls Gold Cup was mentioned as a possible target but should So You Think and Workforce both turn up in that, a rethink could be on the cards indicated Dermot Weld.The target coming into this campaign was a first Group 1 success and the Champion Stakes at Leopardstown when he might get his favoured easier ground in September could be a possible target later in the season. (op 1/6 tchd 1/7)

Across The Rhine(USA) came from well back to take second and showed his preference for a decent surface in the process. He had enjoyed a successful campaign in Dubai, winning a 7f handicap off a mark of 104 in February on good ground, and this was more encouraging for connections.

Fighting Brave(USA), runner-up in a 7f conditions race at Tipperary (good-firm) last month, ran another decent race.

Separate Ways(IRE) closed from the rear to stay on in the straight without looking a threat.

Barack(IRE) finished closer to the winner when they met here last month but after setting a strong pace he had no more to offer in the straight.

T/Jkpt: @30,352.50 to a £1 stake. Pool of 40,470.00 - 1 winning unit. T/Plt: @360.70. Pool of @26,865.41 - 55.847 winning units. II

1929a (Foreign Racing) - See Raceform Interactive

1575 COLOGNE (R-H)
Sunday, May 8

OFFICIAL GOING: Turf: good

1931a GERLING-PREIS (GROUP 2) (4YO+) (TURF) 1m 4f
4:15 (4:40) 4-Y-O+
£34,482 (£13,362; £5,603; £3,448; £2,155; £1,293)

RPR

1 **Scalo**224 6410 4-9-6 0 FrankieDettori 1 116
(A Wohler, Germany) *hld up in rr on ins rail: cruised arnd fnl turn: swtchd to outside: qcknd wl to take ld 150yds out: r.o wl: comf* **2/5**1

2 ¾ **Sir Lando**24 1352 4-9-0 0 EddieAhern 7 109
(Wido Neuroth, Norway) *hld up towards rr: chal for ld early in st: r.o wl: tk 2nd ins fnl f but no match for wnr* **109/10**

3 2 **Val Mondo (GER)**238 6011 4-9-0 0 AHelfenbein 4 106
(Uwe Ostmann, Germany) *settled in 2nd: trckd ldr into fnl turn: chal early in st: led 2f out: r.o wl: hdd 150yds out: lost 2nd cl home* **44/5**3

4 1 ¼ **Night Magic (GER)**203 6977 5-9-3 0 ADeVries 3 107
(W Figge, Germany) *racd 3rd: t.k.h: fnd traffic problems early in st: got clr in centre of trck 1 1/2f out: r.o but fnd nthing ex fnl 150yds* **5/2**2

5 3 ½ **Lamool (GER)**30 1231 4-9-0 0 JohanVictoire 2 98
(Mario Hofer, Germany) *sent st to ld: set solid pce: hdd 2f out: styd on one pce* **206/10**

6 ¾ **Lagalp (GER)**210 6790 4-8-10 0 AStarke 5 93
(P Schiergen, Germany) *a towards rr: nvr figured* **193/10**

7 21 **Derwisch (IRE)**197 7102 5-9-0 0 ASuborics 6 64
(Andreas Lowe, Germany) *a towards rr: nvr a factor* **212/10**

2m 29.22s (-3.68) 7 Ran SP% 122.7
WIN (incl. 10 euro stake): 14. PLACES: 10, 14, 13. SF: 103.
Owner Gestut Ittlingen **Bred** Gestut Hof Ittlingen **Trained** Germany

1632 BRIGHTON (L-H)
Monday, May 9

OFFICIAL GOING: Good to firm (good in places; 8.1)
Rail dolled out 2metres from 4.5f to 2f adding 6yds to all distances.
Wind: Fresh, against Weather: Sunny

1932 HARDINGS CATERING MAIDEN AUCTION STKS 5f 59y
2:10 (2:10) (Class 5) 2-Y-O **£2,331** (£693; £346; £173) Stalls Low

Form RPR

03 1 **Steady The Buffs**6 1785 2-8-3 0 AdamBeschizza(5) 3 68
(Hugo Palmer) *chsd ldr: led over 2f out: hung lft: drvn out* **4/1**2

0 2 ½ **Rooknrasbryripple**21 1441 2-8-8 0 FrankieMcDonald 1 66
(Mick Channon) *in tch disputing 4th: effrt 2f out: drvn to press wnr ins fnl f: kpt on: a hld* **12/1**

3 2 ¾ **Shere Khan** 2-9-0 0 RichardHughes 4 65+
(Richard Hannon) *colty: s.s: bhd: hdwy and edgd rt over 1f out: edgd lft and r.o to take 3rd fnl 100yds* **8/13**1

4 4 ½ **Multi Blessing**34 1143 2-8-5 0 HarryBentley(5) 6 58
(Alan Jarvis) *led tl over 2f out: pressed wnr tl no ex ins fnl f* **40/1**

5 1 **I Dream Of Genie** 2-8-8 0 JimmyQuinn 5 53
(Peter Winkworth) *t.k.h: chsd ldng pair tl outpcd fnl 2f* **14/1**

54 6 9 **Sea Poet**20 1451 2-8-8 0 JohnFahy(3) 2 27
(Andrew Haynes) *s.i.s: sn t.k.h and in tch disputing 4th: plld outside and mod effrt over 2f out: sn wknd* **8/1**3

63.50 secs (1.20) **Going Correction** -0.025s/f (Good) 6 Ran SP% **109.8**
Speed ratings (Par 93): **89,88,83,83,81 67**
toteswingers: 1&2 £4.60, 1&3 £1.20, 2&3 £3.00 CSF £44.02 TOTE £3.40: £1.40, £7.00; EX 40.10.
Owner Rascals Racing **Bred** Longview Stud & Bloodstock Ltd **Trained** Newmarket, Suffolk
■ Hugo Palmer's first winner.

FOCUS

A pretty weak juvenile maiden, run at a brisk pace. The winner just needed to reproduce her form to score.

NOTEBOOK

Steady The Buffs made it third time lucky with a game effort, handing her rookie trainer a first ever winner. Her previous experience, along with a 5lb claiming rider, proved a winning advantage but she still looked somewhat green when asked to win the race. She ought to get a bit further down the line, but this looks very much her sort of trip at present. (op 11-4)

Rooknrasbryripple dropped right out after showing speed on her debut at Windsor 21 days earlier and proved easy to back here. She picked up nicely when asked for an effort, though, and was closing on the more-experienced winner all the way to the line. There ought to be something similar for her in the coming weeks. (op 11-1 tchd 10-1)

Shere Khan ◆, half-brother to a 5f juvenile winner for his stable last year, was well backed earlier in the day and, despite fully advertising his inexperience in the parade ring, was also heavily supported on track. He was never a serious factor after a tardy start, but finished nicely enough and ought to go close next time. (op 5-6, tchd evens in places)

Multi Blessing performed miles below market expectations on his debut at Kempton last month and his supporters failed to materialise here. He once again showed speed before hanging left under pressure and needs more time. (op 25-1)

1933 VIESSMANN QUALITY MATTERS CLASSIFIED STKS — 6f 209y

2:40 (2:43) (Class 6) 3-Y-0+ — **£1,619** (£481; £240; £120) **Stalls** Low

Form — RPR

-000 **1** **Integria**[13] [1582] 5-9-8 55 ....(bt) TonyCulhane 16 — 74
(George Baker) *in tch: led over 2f out: drvn clr over 1f out: comf* **15/2**

5-00 **2** *4 ½* **Interakt**[51] [906] 4-9-3 55 ....(b[1]) HarryBentley(5) 15 — 62
(Joseph Tuite) *mid-div: hdwy 3f out: chsd wnr fnl 2f: no imp* **11/2**[2]

4542 **3** *2* **Mini's Destination**[14] [1557] 3-8-10 55 .... JimmyQuinn 3 — 52
(John Holt) *mid-div: sme hdwy and hrd rdn 2f out: styd on to take 3rd ins fnl f* **13/2**[3]

-003 **4** *2 ¼* **Set To Go**[24] [1357] 4-9-8 47 ....(b) ChrisCatlin 4 — 50
(Tor Sturgis) *w ldrs tl outpcd fnl 2f* **5/1**[1]

000- **5** *2* **Easydoesit (IRE)**[195] [7152] 3-8-7 50 .... JohnFahy(3) 13 — 41
(Des Donovan) *towards rr: hrd rdn and styd on fnl 2f: nvr nrr* **5/1**[1]

304 **6** *1* **Ereka (IRE)**[33] [1179] 3-8-10 55 .... FrankieMcDonald 7 — 38
(Murty McGrath) *s.i.s: towards rr: rdn and sme hdwy 2f out: no further prog* **12/1**

0000 **7** *shd* **Crazy In Love**[7] [1753] 3-8-5 47 ....(v) LauraPike(5) 12 — 38
(Olivia Maylam) *mid-div: drvn along and no hdwy fnl 3f* **33/1**

60-0 **8** *nk* **Emmeline Pankhurst (IRE)**[13] [1579] 3-8-5 55 ...(b[1]) AdamBeschizza(5) 5 — 37
(Julia Feilden) *s.s and early reminder: bhd: rdn and styd on fnl 3f: nt trble ldrs* **8/1**

6-00 **8** *dht* **Blazing Apostle (IRE)**[39] [1060] 3-8-3 47 .... DanielHarris(7) 2 — 37
(Christine Dunnett) *dwlt: bhd: rdn 3f out: sme hdwy fnl 2f* **125/1**

00-6 **10** *12* **Deveze (IRE)**[20] [1465] 3-8-10 45 ....(p) KirstyMilczarek 9 — —
(Dean Ivory) *led tl over 2f out: sn wknd* **40/1**

600/ **11** *2 ½* **Madhal**[508] [7787] 5-9-3 43 .... LeeNewnes(5) 11 — —
(Matthew Salaman) *prom 4f* **33/1**

5530 **12** *5* **Poetically**[14] [1566] 3-8-10 50 .... MartinLane 14 — —
(Joseph Tuite) *mid-div tl wknd 3f out: sn bhd* **25/1**

0505 **13** *nk* **Bellaboolou**[6] [1790] 3-8-10 46 ....(bt) HayleyTurner 8 — —
(David Pinder) *chsd ldrs over 3f* **28/1**

0065 **14** *hd* **Clonusker (IRE)**[35] [1137] 3-8-11 45 ow1 ....(p) NeilCallan 1 — —
(Linda Jewell) *in tch: rdn 3f out: sn wknd* **80/1**

000- **15** *30* **Southern Breeze**[306] [3788] 4-9-8 52 ....(t) RichardHughes 10 — —
(Sylvester Kirk) *prom over 3f: bhd whn virtually p.u 1f out* **20/1**

1m 22.48s (-0.62) **Going Correction** -0.025s/f (Good)
WFA 3 from 4yo+ 12lb — **15 Ran SP% 115.0**
Speed ratings (Par 101): **102,96,94,92,89 88,88,88,88,74 71,65,65,65,30**
toteswingers: 1&2 £9.00, 1&3 £10.50, 2&3 £7.00 CSF £42.03 TOTE £10.90: £3.50, £1.30, £2.20; EX 38.30 Trifecta £229.10 Pool: £368.50 - 1.19 winning units..
Owner Mrs Natalie Heath **Bred** Littleton Stud **Trained** Whitsbury, Hants

FOCUS
A weak classified event and not a race to be too positive about. There was a solid pace on.
Southern Breeze Official explanation: jockey said gelding lost action

1934 CITY CABS MAIDEN STKS — 7f 214y

3:10 (3:10) (Class 5) 3-Y-0+ — **£2,266** (£674; £337; £168) **Stalls** Low

Form — RPR

6-25 **1** **Muhandis (IRE)**[16] [1516] 3-9-0 80 .... RichardHills 4 — 79
(Ed Dunlop) *chsd ldr: led over 5f out: hrd rdn and jnd over 1f out: drvn ahd again fnl 100yds* **4/7**[1]

5- **2** *2* **Emilio Largo**[361] [2048] 3-9-0 0 .... JimmyQuinn 5 — 74+
(Sir Henry Cecil) *racd freely early: led over 1f: trckd ldr after tl rdn level over 1f out: nt qckn fnl 100yds* **2/1**[2]

5- **3** *10* **Dililah**[166] [7558] 3-8-4 0 .... HarryBentley(5) 6 — 46
(William Knight) *wnt rt s: in tch disputing 3rd tl outpcd fnl 2f* **14/1**[3]

00- **4** *2 ¼* **Mokalif**[215] [6676] 3-9-0 0 .... HayleyTurner 2 — 46
(Michael Bell) *sn rdn along and bhd: wnt modest 4th fnl 50yds* **22/1**

00-0 **5** *1* **Disturbia (IRE)**[13] [1580] 3-8-9 46 .... MartinLane 3 — 39
(J W Hills) *in tch disputing 3rd tl wknd 2f out* **66/1**

1m 35.78s (-0.22) **Going Correction** -0.025s/f (Good)
WFA 3 from 4yo 13lb — **5 Ran SP% 109.5**
Speed ratings (Par 103): **100,98,88,85,84**
toteswinger: 1&2 £1.90 CSF £1.90 TOTE £1.80: £1.10, £1.20; EX 1.80.
Owner Hamdan Al Maktoum **Bred** Shadwell Estate Co Ltd **Trained** Newmarket, Suffolk

FOCUS
A weakish maiden, rated around the winner who ran to his Ripon level.

1935 DIGIBET H'CAP — 1m 3f 196y

3:40 (3:41) (Class 5) (0-75,75) 4-Y-0+ — **£2,331** (£693; £346; £173) **Stalls** High

Form — RPR

011- **1** **Milnagavie**[224] [6424] 4-9-7 75 .... RichardHughes 1 — 85
(Richard Hannon) *chsd ldr: rdn 4f out: led over 2f out: edgd lft: rdn out* **13/8**[2]

2152 **2** *2 ¾* **Wily Fox**[24] [1353] 4-9-1 69 .... SebSanders 3 — 74
(James Eustace) *led tl over 2f out: nt qckn fnl f* **5/2**[3]

33-0 **3** *7* **Kerchak (USA)**[21] [1443] 4-9-6 74 .... JimCrowley 4 — 68
(William Jarvis) *in tch in 4th: effrt over 2f out: wknd wl over 1f out* **6/4**[1]

400- **4** *6* **Brave Enough (USA)**[9] [2906] 4-8-7 61 oh2 .... FrankieMcDonald 2 — 45
(Roger Curtis) *chsd ldng pair: rdn 4f out: wknd 2f out* **50/1**

2m 30.76s (-1.94) **Going Correction** -0.025s/f (Good) — **4 Ran SP% 108.6**
Speed ratings (Par 103): **105,103,98,94**
CSF £5.97 TOTE £2.50; EX 3.70.
Owner Mrs R Ablett **Bred** Darley **Trained** East Everleigh, Wilts

FOCUS
A tight handicap, run at a sound pace. The winner progressed but this was a fairly weak race.

1936 TAKE THAT EXPERIENCE HERE 21ST JUNE H'CAP — 1m 1f 209y

4:10 (4:10) (Class 5) (0-70,69) 4-Y-0+ — **£2,266** (£674; £337; £168) **Stalls** High

Form — RPR

0022 **1** **Miss Bounty**[11] [1636] 6-8-4 57 ....(v) HarryBentley(5) 2 — 66
(Jim Boyle) *chsd ldr: led over 2f out: rdn out* **9/2**[2]

0-21 **2** *1* **Timocracy**[11] [1636] 6-9-5 67 .... StevieDonohoe 5 — 74
(Andrew Haynes) *led: hdd and hrd rdn over 2f out: kpt on gamely* **6/5**[1]

2312 **3** *1 ½* **Lilli Palmer (IRE)**[24] [1354] 4-8-7 55 .... MartinLane 1 — 59
(Mike Murphy) *chsd ldng pair: hrd rdn 2f out: one pce fnl f* **6/1**

1432 **4** *1 ½* **Eastern Gift**[11] [1637] 6-9-7 69 .... NeilCallan 4 — 70
(Gay Kelleway) *hld up in 4th: effrt 2f out: one pce* **5/1**[3]

2055 **5** *57* **Ocean Countess (IRE)**[46] [957] 5-8-7 60 .... AdamBeschizza(5) 3 — —
(Tony Carroll) *hld up in rr: hdwy whn hmpd on rail over 4f out: sn drvn along: wknd and virtually p.u 2f out* **13/2**

2m 4.66s (1.06) **Going Correction** -0.025s/f (Good) — **5 Ran SP% 107.9**
Speed ratings (Par 103): **94,93,92,90,45**
CSF £10.02 TOTE £3.70: £2.00, £1.40; EX 11.80.
Owner Friends Of The Samson Centre Partnership **Bred** J M Beever **Trained** Epsom, Surrey

FOCUS
A moderate handicap, but not bad form for the class. The winner reversed latest form with the runner-up.
Ocean Countess(IRE) Official explanation: vet said mare finished distressed

1937 PARTY ON THE HILL HERE 27TH MAY H'CAP — 5f 213y

4:40 (4:40) (Class 4) (0-85,85) 4-Y-0+ — **£3,238** (£963; £481; £240) **Stalls** Low

Form — RPR

6-45 **1** **Piazza San Pietro**[3] [1864] 5-9-7 85 .... NeilCallan 3 — 95
(Andrew Haynes) *hld up in 4th: trckd ldrs 2f out: led 1f out: rdn out* **6/4**[1]

-244 **2** *1 ¼* **Magical Speedfit (IRE)**[3] [1866] 6-8-7 74 .... SimonPearce(3) 1 — 80
(George Margarson) *hld up and bhd: promising hdwy whn nt clr run on rail fr 2f out: swtchd rt and chsd wnr fnl f: a hld* **11/2**[3]

0212 **3** *1 ¼* **Maze (IRE)**[19] [1488] 6-8-13 77 .... SebSanders 4 — 79
(Tony Carroll) *chsd ldr: led wl over 1f out: hdd and one pce ent fnl f* **5/2**[2]

00-6 **4** *3 ½* **Kyllachy Storm**[20] [1453] 7-8-2 71 oh12 .... HarryBentley(5) 6 — 62
(Ron Hodges) *in tch in 5th: effrt on outer over 2f out: no imp* **18/1**

6533 **5** *1* **Sherjawy (IRE)**[11] [1638] 7-8-7 71 oh7 .... KirstyMilczarek 4 — 59
(Zoe Davison) *chsd ldng pair: rdn over 2f out: wknd over 1f out* **18/1**

00-0 **6** *2 ½* **Peter Island (FR)**[10] [1656] 8-9-1 79 ....(v) ChrisCatlin 5 — 59
(John Gallagher) *led tl wl over 1f out: sn wknd* **6/1**

69.25 secs (-0.95) **Going Correction** -0.025s/f (Good) — **6 Ran SP% 108.8**
Speed ratings (Par 105): **105,103,101,97,95 92**
toteswingers: 1&2 £2.00, 2&3 £1.60, 1&3 £1.50 CSF £9.52 TOTE £1.90: £1.02, £3.50; EX 8.50.
Owner K Corke **Bred** T E Pocock **Trained** Limpley Stoke, Bath

FOCUS
A competitive sprint handicap and unsurprisingly it was run at a frantic pace. A length personal best from the winner with the second to his mark.

1938 BRASSERIE ITALIAN MARINA SQUARE H'CAP — 5f 59y

5:10 (5:10) (Class 6) (0-60,60) 4-Y-0+ — **£1,619** (£481; £240; £120) **Stalls** Low

Form — RPR

4012 **1** **Athwaab**[6] [1787] 4-9-0 60 .... CharlesBishop(7) 3 — 71
(Noel Quinlan) *mde all: in control fnl f: rdn out* **6/4**[1]

00-0 **2** *2 ¾* **Imaginary Diva**[30] [1248] 5-8-10 49 .... TomQueally 2 — 50
(George Margarson) *hld up: effrt on outer over 2f out: drvn to chse wnr over 1f out: no imp* **3/1**[2]

-502 **3** *1* **Miss Firefly**[20] [1469] 6-9-4 57 .... GeorgeBaker 1 — 55
(Ron Hodges) *hld up: rdn to chse ldrs over 1f out: one pce* **3/1**[2]

6000 **4** *2* **Boga (IRE)**[11] [1627] 4-8-2 46 oh1 .... HarryBentley(5) 4 — 37
(Ron Hodges) *chsd wnr: hrd rdn 2f out: wknd fnl f* **20/1**

3400 **5** *4 ½* **Wanchai Whisper**[23] [1411] 4-9-4 57 ....(p) WilliamCarson 5 — 32
(Mark Rimmer) *stmbld sltly s: sn chsng ldrs: wknd over 1f out* **9/2**[3]

62.05 secs (-0.25) **Going Correction** -0.025s/f (Good) — **5 Ran SP% 112.9**
Speed ratings (Par 101): **101,96,95,91,84**
CSF £6.53 TOTE £3.30: £1.30, £2.00; EX 8.60.
Owner Mrs Lynn McGregor **Bred** Shadwell Estate Co Ltd **Trained** Newmarket, Suffolk

FOCUS
This low-grade sprint was a fillies' handicap in all but name. Weak form, rated through the winner who was still a few pounds off her 3yo best.
T/Plt: £48.40 to a £1 stake. Pool: £46,042.72. 693.84 winning tickets. T/Qpdt: £7.40 to a £1 stake. Pool: £3,997.58. 398.79 winning tickets. LM

1555 REDCAR (L-H)

Monday, May 9

OFFICIAL GOING: Good to firm (good in places; 9.1)
Wind: Moderate, behind Weather: Sunny and dry, but breezy

1939 BUY YOUR TICKETS ON-LINE @ REDCARRACING.CO.UK MEDIAN AUCTION MAIDEN STKS — 5f

2:20 (2:21) (Class 6) 2-Y-0 — **£1,706** (£503; £252) **Stalls** High

Form — RPR

2 **1** **Bannock (IRE)**[9] [1673] 2-9-3 0 .... JoeFanning 5 — 84+
(Mark Johnston) *mde all: pushed clr over 1f out: easily* **2/7**[1]

0 **2** *4 ½* **Arcticality (IRE)**[23] [1414] 2-8-12 0 .... PaulHanagan 6 — 60
(Richard Fahey) *a chsng wnr: rdn along 2f out: drvn over 1f out: kpt on same pce* **6/1**[2]

6 **3** *1* **Made In The Shade**[38] [1071] 2-8-12 0 .... FrederikTylicki 7 — 56
(Paul Midgley) *dwlt: sn cl up on outer: effrt 2f out and sn rdn: drvn and one pce fr over 1f out* **25/1**

4 *shd* **Phoenix Clubs (IRE)** 2-8-12 0 .... BarryMcHugh 3 — 56+
(Paul Midgley) *in tch: green and pushed along 2f out: rdn and wandered over 1f out: kpt on ins fnl f: nrst fin* **40/1**

5 *½* **Galilee Chapel (IRE)** 2-9-3 0 .... TomEaves 1 — 59
(Howard Johnson) *wnt lft s: sn chsng ldrs: rdn and cl up 2f out: wknd over 1f out* **16/1**

6 *2* **Neil's Pride** 2-8-12 0 .... TonyHamilton 2 — 47
(Richard Fahey) *s.i.s: a in rr* **14/1**[3]

7 *3 ¾* **Musical Strike** 2-9-0 0 .... RobertLButler(3) 4 — 38
(Shaun Harris) *in tch: rdn along and outpcd fr 1/2-way* **80/1**

58.41 secs (-0.19) **Going Correction** -0.175s/f (Firm) — **7 Ran SP% 112.1**
Speed ratings (Par 91): **94,86,85,85,84 81,75**
toteswingers: 1&2 £1.02, 1&3 £3.10, 2&3 £6.30 CSF £2.30 TOTE £1.30: £1.02, £2.20; EX 2.10.

Owner Sheikh Hamdan Bin Mohammed Al Maktoum **Bred** Darley **Trained** Middleham Moor, N Yorks

FOCUS

An uncompetitive juvenile maiden that was won in good style by the favourite who set a fair level on his debut form. The runner-up is only rated to plating level.

NOTEBOOK

Bannock(IRE) stood out on his debut effort when second at Doncaster. Quickly away, he began to pull clear from 1f out, and won in the style of a horse who will prove just as effective at 6f, making him a possible contender for the Woodcote Stakes at Epsom on Derby Day. (op 2-5 tchd 4-9 in places)

Articality(IRE), although not the biggest, stepped up on her initial effort and should appreciate 6f. (op 11-2 tchd 7-1)

Made In The Shade had clearly learned from her debut and was another doing her best work late. (op 20-1)

Phoenix Clubs(IRE) was only a cheap purchase but shaped like there's more to come. (op 33-1)

Galilee Chapel(IRE), who's already gelded, went left out of the stalls but did show some ability before fading late on.

Neil's Pride, whose dam was a winner at up to 1m6f, was never going the pace and should fare better later in the season once tackling nurseries at 7f and beyond. (tchd 16-1)

1940 ENJOY THE HOSPITALITY AT REDCAR RACECOURSE (S) STKS 5f

2:50 (2:53) (Class 6) 3-Y-0+ **£1,706** (£503; £252) **Stalls** High

Form RPR

0-00 **1** **Nomoreblondes**[14] 1555 7-9-7 65 ....(v[1]) PJMcDonald 6 72
(Paul Midgley) *chsd ldr: hdwy 2f out: rdn to ld over 1f out: kpt on fnl f* **9/2**[3]

003U **2** *2 ½* **Grudge**[18] 1507 6-9-12 67 ....(b) TomEaves 2 68
(Conor Dore) *chsd ldng pair: hdwy 2f out: rdn to chse wnr ent fnl f: sn drvn and no imp* **9/2**[3]

3044 **3** *2 ½* **Ridley Didley (IRE)**[19] 1501 6-9-12 60 .... AdrianNicholls 1 59
(Noel Wilson) *led: rdn along 2f out: drvn and hdd over 1f out: wknd fnl f* **3/1**[2]

05-2 **4** *½* **Patch Patch**[6] 1796 4-9-12 66 ....(p) FrederikTylicki 7 57
(Michael Dods) *dwlt sltly: in tch tl niggled along and outpcd after 2f: sn rdn: n.d* **9/4**[1]

4345 **5** *1 ½* **William Wainwright (IRE)**[21] 1439 3-9-3 50 ....(t) PaulHanagan 4 48
(Ann Duffield) *s.i.s: a in rr* **10/1**

000- **6** *9* **Hitches Dubai (BRZ)**[238] 6040 6-9-9 61 .... MichaelO'Connell[(3)] 5 19
(Geoffrey Harker) *sn outpcd and a in rr* **11/1**

57.28 secs (-1.32) **Going Correction** -0.175s/f (Firm)
WFA 3 from 4yo+ 9lb **6** Ran SP% **109.6**
Speed ratings (Par 101): **103,99,95,94,91 77**
toteswingers: 1&2 £4.70, 1&3 £2.30, 2&3 £2.30 CSF £23.28 TOTE £8.70: £4.30, £3.10; EX 21.20.There was no bid for the winner.
Owner Anthony D Copley **Bred** P John And Redmyre Bloodstock **Trained** Westow, N Yorks

FOCUS

Few got into this. There are doubts over the form but the winner is rated to something like her best in the visor.

1941 VOLTIGEUR 2 COURSE SPECIAL MENU £10.95 MAIDEN FILLIES' STKS 6f

3:20 (3:20) (Class 5) 3-Y-0+ **£2,266** (£674; £337; £168) **Stalls** High

Form RPR

632- **1** **Lady Kildare (IRE)**[189] 7269 3-8-9 70 .... PatrickDonaghy[(3)] 4 59
(Jedd O'Keeffe) *cl up: rdn to chal 2f out: led wl over 1f out: drvn and kpt on fnl f* **4/1**[3]

0- **2** *1 ¼* **Dream Dream Dream (IRE)**[206] 6905 4-9-5 50.... AndrewHeffernan[(3)] 6 58
(Kevin M Prendergast) *led: rdn along and edgd lft 2f out: sn drvn and hdd: kpt on u.p fnl f* **33/1**

06-0 **3** *hd* **Cool In The Shade**[34] 1155 3-8-12 47 .... BarryMcHugh 5 54
(Paul Midgley) *chsd ldng pair: effrt over 2f out: sn rdn and n.m.r: swtchd rt and drvn wl over 1f out: kpt on ins fnl f* **50/1**

3404 **4** *¾* **Gorgeous Goblin (IRE)**[9] 1672 4-9-8 52 ....(vt) TomEaves 8 55
(David C Griffiths) *trckd ldrs: edgd lft 1/2-way: effrt over 2f out: rdn and stmbld sltly wl over 1f out: sn drvn and ch over 1f out: hung lft and wknd ins fnl f* **14/1**

4-2 **5** *½* **Spinatrix**[9] 1672 3-8-12 0 .... FrederikTylicki 7 50
(Michael Dods) *trckd ldrs: effrt over 2f out: sn rdn and one pce* **7/2**[2]

23- **6** *6* **Pantella (IRE)**[203] 6986 3-8-12 0 .... PhillipMakin 1 31
(Kevin Ryan) *s.i.s and bhd: hdwy to chse ldrs 1/2-way: rdn over 2f out: sn btn* **8/11**[1]

0- **7** *17* **Dorden**[179] 7406 4-9-1 0 .... PNolan[(7)] 3 —
(Noel Wilson) *dwlt: a in rr* **100/1**

8 *6* **Noels Princess** 4-9-8 0 .... DanielTudhope 2 —
(David O'Meara) *cl up on outer: rdn along and hung bdly lft 1/2-way: bit slipped through mouth: sn bhd* **20/1**

1m 10.82s (-0.98) **Going Correction** -0.175s/f (Firm)
WFA 3 from 4yo 10lb **8** Ran SP% **117.4**
Speed ratings (Par 100): **99,97,97,96,95 87,64,56**
toteswingers: 1&2 £20.60, 1&3 £44.90, 2&3 £44.90 CSF £115.40 TOTE £4.20: £1.50, £7.60, £10.90; EX 150.40.
Owner The Fatalists **Bred** Glending Bloodstock **Trained** Middleham Moor, N Yorks

FOCUS

A typically weak 3-y-o plus sprint maiden that was thrown open when odds-on favourite Pantella blew the start. The form amounts to little, with the placed horses rated 50 and 47 respectively. The winner did not need to match her previous best.

Noels Princess Official explanation: jockey said bit slipped through filly's mouth

1942 REDCAR RACECOURSE WEDDING AND CONFERENCE VENUE H'CAP 7f

3:50 (3:51) (Class 4) (0-85,85) 3-Y-0+ **£2,914** (£867; £433; £216) **Stalls** High

Form RPR

153- **1** **Cathedral Spires**[233] 6184 3-8-10 **79** .... PaulHanagan 3 86
(Howard Johnson) *trckd ldrs: hdwy 3f out: rdn to chal and edgd rt 2f out: sn led: drvn out* **5/2**[1]

02-0 **2** *1 ¾* **Reel Buddy Star**[9] 1695 6-10-0 **85** .... PJMcDonald 6 91
(George Moore) *trckd ldrs early: sn stdd and hld up towards rr: hdwy over 2f out: rdn over 1f out: kpt on u.p ins fnl f* **9/1**

1402 **3** *nk* **Rio Cobolo (IRE)**[9] 1696 5-9-5 **76** .... AdrianNicholls 9 81
(David Nicholls) *trckd ldng pair: effrt and n.m.r 2f out: sn swtchd lft and rdn wl over 1f out: drvn and kpt on same pce fnl f* **6/1**[3]

-152 **4** *1 ¼* **Ezra Church (IRE)**[6] 1800 4-9-1 **72** ....(p) LeeNewman 7 74
(David Barron) *towards rr: hdwy 1/2-way: sn pushed along: rdn to chse ldrs and n.m.r 2f out: sn drvn and one pce* **7/2**[2]

0-30 **5** *¾* **Summer Dancer (IRE)**[9] 1695 7-9-9 **80** .... PhillipMakin 8 80
(Paul Midgley) *wnt lft s: hld up in rr: hdwy over 2f out: rdn wl over 1f out: kpt on ins fnl f: nrst fin* **17/2**

00-0 **5** *dht* **En Fuego**[7] 1747 4-9-2 **76** .... MichaelO'Connell[(3)] 1 76
(Geoffrey Harker) *in tch: hdwy on outer and cl up 1/2-way: rdn along over 2f out: grad wknd* **33/1**

140- **7** *nk* **Polish World (USA)**[240] 5964 7-9-4 **75** .... BarryMcHugh 2 74
(Paul Midgley) *led: rdn along 3f out: drvn 2f out and sn hdd: grad wknd* **14/1**

0-05 **8** *7* **Ghost (IRE)**[12] 1618 4-9-0 **78** .... PNolan[(7)] 4 58
(David Nicholls) *t.k.h: sn prom: rdn along 3f out: sn wknd* **16/1**

0-2 **9** *½* **Frognal (IRE)**[40] 1035 5-9-1 **75** .... JamesSullivan[(3)] 11 54
(Ruth Carr) *towards rr: effrt over 2f out: sn rdn and n.d* **13/2**

1m 22.27s (-2.23) **Going Correction** -0.175s/f (Firm)
WFA 3 from 4yo+ 12lb **9** Ran SP% **114.4**
Speed ratings (Par 105): **105,103,102,101,100 100,100,92,91**
toteswingers: 1&2 £4.90, 2&3 £6.90, 1&3 £2.90 CSF £25.69 CT £122.54 TOTE £2.90: £1.10, £3.40, £2.40; EX 27.20.
Owner Transcend Bloodstock LLP **Bred** D Curran **Trained** Billy Row, Co Durham
■ Stewards' Enquiry : Lee Newman caution; used whip excessive frequency

FOCUS

An ordinary handicap, but the winner is generally progressive and the form is sound enough.

Polish World(USA) Official explanation: jockey said gelding hung right

1943 WIN A VIP DAY @ REDCARRACING.CO.UK CLAIMING STKS 6f

4:20 (4:20) (Class 6) 3-Y-0+ **£1,706** (£503; £252) **Stalls** High

Form RPR

1010 **1** **Thrust Control (IRE)**[9] 1696 4-9-5 85 .... DaleSwift[(5)] 2 79
(Brian Ellison) *cl up: chal 2f out: sn rdn and led 1 1/2f out: drvn out* **1/1**[1]

0-00 **2** *nk* **Prince Of Vasa (IRE)**[12] 1618 4-9-1 75 .... SeanLevey[(5)] 5 74
(Michael Smith) *slt ld: rdn 2f out: drvn and hdd 1 1/2f out: kpt on u.p fnl f tl no ex towards fin* **6/1**[3]

4216 **3** *2* **Dark Lane**[21] 1438 5-9-8 80 .... PaulHanagan 6 70
(Richard Fahey) *chsd ldng pair: rdn over 2f out: drvn over 1f out: kpt on ins fnl f* **11/8**[2]

0-05 **4** *8* **Isle Of Ellis (IRE)**[14] 1557 4-8-10 38 ....(v) ShaneBKelly[(7)] 1 39
(Ron Barr) *in tch: rdn along over 2f out: sn outpcd and bhd* **66/1**

/000 **5** *3 ¾* **Glencairn Star**[6] 1803 10-9-4 37 ....(v[1]) DuranFentiman 8 28
(Frederick Watson) *in tch: rdn along wl over 2f out: sn outpcd and bhd* **100/1**

69.98 secs (-1.82) **Going Correction** -0.175s/f (Firm) **5** Ran SP% **108.9**
Speed ratings (Par 101): **105,104,101,91,86**
toteswinger: 1&2 £5.60 CSF £7.41 TOTE £2.20: £1.70, £4.80; EX 7.40.The winner was claimed by Mr David Tate for £12,000.
Owner Koo's Racing Club **Bred** Rathasker Stud **Trained** Norton, N Yorks

FOCUS

A trappy claimer, and weakish form with the third below par. The winner did not need to match his best.

1944 RACING UK ON CHANNEL 432 H'CAP 1m 1f

4:50 (4:53) (Class 5) (0-70,70) 3-Y-0 **£2,266** (£674; £337; £168) **Stalls** Low

Form RPR

504- **1** **Ollon (USA)**[199] 7066 3-9-3 **66** .... PaulHanagan 4 69
(Richard Fahey) *trckd ldng pair: hdwy and cl up 1/2-way: rdn wl over 2f out: drvn to take slt ld 1 1/2f out: edgd lft ins fnl f: hld on wl* **6/4**[1]

60-0 **2** *nk* **Rapturous Applause**[33] 1169 3-8-11 **60** .... FrederikTylicki 3 62
(Micky Hammond) *led: jnd and rdn 3f out: drvn and hdd 1 1/2f out: kpt on gamely fnl f* **25/1**

1445 **3** *nk* **Ad Vitam (IRE)**[14] 1574 3-8-9 **61** ....(t) MichaelO'Connell[(3)] 1 62
(David C Griffiths) *hld up towards rr: gd hdwy on inner 3f out: rdn to chse ldng pair 2f out: drvn over 1f out: kpt on ins fnl f* **15/2**[3]

4-06 **4** *1* **Pintrada**[23] 1415 3-9-4 **67** .... GrahamGibbons 6 66
(James Bethell) *trckd ldrs: hdwy over 3f out: rdn 2f out: drvn appr fnl f: kpt on same pce* **5/2**[2]

05-2 **5** *9* **Pinotage**[23] 1413 3-8-4 **56** oh1 .... JamesSullivan[(3)] 2 35
(Richard Whitaker) *chsd ldr: rdn along 4f out: sn wknd* **9/1**

000- **6** *1 ½* **Last Destination (IRE)**[203] 6978 3-9-5 **68** .... JoeFanning 8 44
(Nigel Tinkler) *hld up in rr: hdwy over 4f out: in tch 3f out: sn rdn and wknd fnl 2f* **28/1**

252- **7** *3 ½* **Baby Driver**[238] 6027 3-8-12 **61** .... TomEaves 5 29
(Howard Johnson) *t.k.h: racd wd: a towards rr: bhd fnl 3f* **16/1**

1m 55.8s (2.80) **Going Correction** -0.175s/f (Firm) **7** Ran SP% **103.5**
Speed ratings (Par 99): **80,79,79,78,70 69,66**
toteswingers: 1&2 £6.30, 2&3 £2.70, 1&3 £12.30 CSF £32.08 CT £153.10 TOTE £2.50: £1.80, £8.80; EX 19.00.
Owner Keep Racing **Bred** William Patterson & James Glenn **Trained** Musley Bank, N Yorks
■ Copper Canyon (6/1) was withdrawn after refusing to enter the stalls. Deduct 10p in the £ under R4.

FOCUS

The rain had set in quite heavily by the time of this low-grade 3-y-o handicap, and the visibility wasn't the best. The winner's best effort since his 2yo debut.

1945 JOHN SMITH'S REDCAR STRAIGHT-MILE CHAMPIONSHIP (H'CAP) (QUALIFIER) 1m

5:20 (5:24) (Class 6) (0-60,59) 3-Y-0 **£1,706** (£503; £252) **Stalls** High

Form RPR

4140 **1** **Vetvey (IRE)**[10] 1663 3-9-7 **59** .... JoeFanning 6 70
(Mark Johnston) *mde all: rdn clr 2f out: drvn ins fnl f: kpt on* **7/1**

060- **2** *1 ¾* **Inca Blue**[196] 7124 3-9-0 **52** .... DavidAllan 2 59
(Tim Easterby) *trckd ldrs: hdwy 3f out: rdn to chse wnr 2f out: sn drvn and edgd rt: no imp fnl f* **10/1**

06-5 **3** *nk* **One Of Twins**[19] 1495 3-8-6 **47** .... JamesSullivan[(3)] 1 53
(Michael Easterby) *in tch on outer: hdwy over 2f out: rdn to chse ldng pair over 1f out: drvn and kpt on same pce ins fnl f* **18/1**

0-00 **4** *3 ½* **Commander Veejay**[19] 1494 3-8-4 **45** ....(p) AndrewHeffernan[(3)] 4 43
(Brian Rothwell) *midfield: pushed along 3f out: rdn 2f out: styd on u.p appr fnl f: nrst fin* **66/1**

5-52 **5** *hd* **Areef (IRE)**[6] 1790 3-8-7 **52** ....(v[1]) IanBurns[(7)] 11 50
(Michael Bell) *a.p: chsd wnr 1/2-way: rdn 2f out: sn drvn and grad wknd* **9/2**[3]

00-2 **6** *1 ¾* **Downtown Boy (IRE)**[19] 1495 3-8-12 **50** .... AndrewMullen 8 44
(Tom Tate) *trckd ldrs: hdwy 3f out: rdn whn nt much 2f out: sn drvn and grad wknd* **15/2**

000- **7** *½* **Dashing Eddie (IRE)**[177] 7452 3-9-0 **52** .... PhillipMakin 12 45
(Kevin Ryan) *in tch: effrt to chse ldrs 3f out and sn rdn: drvn over 2f out and sn btn* **4/1**[2]

P-04 **8** *10* **Chadford**[19] 1495 3-9-0 **52** ....(p) GrahamGibbons 5 22
(Tim Walford) *nvr bttr than midfield* **16/1**

000- 9 2 3/4 **Hal Of A Lover**[214] 6695 3-9-5 **57** DanielTudhope 14 20
(David O'Meara) *in tch on outer: rdn along 3f out: sn wknd* **28/1**
60-0 10 1/2 **Go**[32] 1203 3-9-3 **55** FrederikTylicki 7 17
(Micky Hammond) *a towards rr: bhd fnl 3f* **40/1**
00-6 11 hd **Fully Armed (IRE)**[30] 1236 3-8-7 **45** (t) FrannyNorton 9 —
(Rae Guest) *s.i.s: a in rr* **28/1**
0-53 12 14 **Byron Bear (IRE)**[19] 1495 3-8-13 **51** PaulHanagan 13 —
(Paul Midgley) *in tch on wd outside: effrt over 3f out: sn rdn and wknd over 2f out* **3/1**[1]
030- 13 4 **Spin A Wish**[180] 7395 3-9-3 **55** TonyHamilton 3 —
(Richard Whitaker) *prom: rdn along 1/2-way: sn wknd* **66/1**
1m 37.42s (-0.58) **Going Correction** -0.175s/f (Firm) **13** Ran SP% **120.0**
Speed ratings (Par 97): **95,93,92,89,89 87,87,77,74,73 73,59,55**
toteswingers: 1&2 £11.90, 2&3 £15.50, 1&3 £21.90; totesuper7: Win: Not won; Place: Not won CSF £72.60 CT £1216.34 TOTE £7.80: £2.90, £4.80, £7.10; EX 89.80.
Owner Brian Yeardley **Bred** Gestut Sohrenhof **Trained** Middleham Moor, N Yorks
■ Stewards' Enquiry : Ian Burns caution; careless riding

FOCUS
An open-looking handicap. Moderate form, but the first three improved to pull clear.
Byron Bear(IRE) Official explanation: jockey said gelding ran to free
T/Plt: £80.60 to a £1 stake. Pool: £44,266.30. 400.46 winning tickets. T/Qpdt: £47.90 to a £1 stake. Pool: £3,445.91. 53.20 winning tickets. JR

1770 WINDSOR (R-H)
Monday, May 9

OFFICIAL GOING: Good (7.6)
Stands' rail dolled out 6yds at 6f down to 2f at winning post. Top bend dolled out 3yd which added 14yds to races of 1m and over.
Wind: Fresh, across Weather: Fine, warm

1946 SPORTINGBET.COM MAIDEN FILLES' STKS 5f 10y
5:40 (5:41) (Class 4) 2-Y-O £3,432 (£1,021; £510; £254) Stalls Low

Form RPR
1 **Angels Will Fall (IRE)** 2-9-0 0 RobertWinston 2 86+
(B W Hills) *trckd ldrs: gng easily but looking for a gap fr 1/2-way: barged through jst over 1f out to ld ins fnl f: sn clr: quite impressive* **9/4**[1]
2 3 3/4 **Glee** 2-9-0 0 RichardHughes 3 73
(Richard Hannon) *nt quickest away but sn led: shkn up 1f out: hdd and comf outpcd ins fnl f* **5/2**[2]
3 3 1/4 **Rougini (IRE)** 2-9-0 0 AndrewElliott 6 61
(Mrs K Burke) *sn prom: rdn 2f out: wl outpcd fnl f* **16/1**
4 2 **Balm** 2-9-0 0 RyanMoore 5 54+
(Richard Hannon) *dwlt: in tch: shkn up whn bmpd jst over 1f out: immediately outpcd* **11/2**
5 1 3/4 **Sweet Ovation** 2-9-0 0 LiamKeniry 8 48
(Mark Usher) *sltly awkward s: last early: effrt on outer 1/2-way: sing to fade whn sltly impeded in knock-on effect jst over 1f out* **18/1**
0 6 3/4 **Ida Inkley (IRE)**[21] 1441 2-9-0 0 EddieAhern 4 46
(Jonathan Portman) *pressed ldr to over 1f out: sing to lose pl whn bmpd by wnr sn after* **33/1**
6 7 2 **Gin Twist**[4] 1823 2-9-0 0 RichardKingscote 1 38
(Tom Dascombe) *chsd ldrs on inner: shkn up 2f out: wknd jst over 1f out* **9/2**[3]
8 4 **Mount McLeod (IRE)** 2-9-0 0 FergusSweeney 7 23
(Jamie Osborne) *dwlt: in tch in rr: rdn 2f out: wknd over 1f out* **16/1**
61.04 secs (0.74) **Going Correction** -0.075s/f (Good) **8** Ran SP% **112.9**
Speed ratings (Par 95): **91,85,79,76,73 72,69,63**
toteswingers: 1&2 £3.30, 1&3 £14.90, 2&3 £5.60 CSF £7.85 TOTE £4.80: £1.50, £1.20, £3.30; EX 10.00 Trifecta £97.70 Pool: £12,256.68 - 92.77 winning units..
Owner Mrs E O'Leary **Bred** Islanmore Stud **Trained** Lambourn, Berks
■ Stewards' Enquiry : Robert Winston three-day ban: careless riding (May 23 to 25)

FOCUS
This maiden was won last year by Rimth, winner of the Fred Darling this season. This was an impressive start from Angels Will Fall and the form has been rated positively, at the top end of the race averages.

NOTEBOOK
Angels Will Fall(IRE) ◆ won this in the manner of a Royal Ascot filly. There was plenty of money around for the Barry Hills-trained debutante, who had apparently been pleasing at home, and she looks smart. She had to wait for a gap when apparently full of running in the straight, but Robert Winston was patient for as long as possible, before forcing his mount between rivals a furlong out. This daughter of Acclamation produced an impressive change of pace to draw clear in a matter of strides. A 90,000gns February foal, she's out of a triple sprint winner, including at Listed level, and clearly has bags of speed. She will apparently be considered for the Albany Stakes and the Queen Mary, and may not run again beforehand. (op 5-2 tchd 11-4)
Glee ◆, a 42,000gns March foal, was the better fancied of the Hannon pair and showed speed, but the winner was too good. She's a half-sister to useful sprinter Dark Mischief and should win soon. (op 15-8 tchd 11-4)
Rougini(IRE), a 6,000euros February foal, showed up well for a fair way. Time will probably show she bumped into at least one well above-average filly. (op 20-1)
Balm's dam won a 6f maiden here on debut, but this experience was needed. Not best away from the stalls, she was held and not being given a hard time when bumped around a furlong out. (op 6-1 tchd 5-1)
Sweet Ovation was another who was held when getting bumped in the closing stages, but she showed ability and should come on plenty. (op 16-1 tchd 20-1)
Ida Inkley(IRE) knew a lot more than when well beaten over C&D on her debut three weeks earlier, this time showing good speed before fading. (op 40-1)
Gin Twist did not build on the form she showed on her debut at Chester four days earlier. (op 11-2 tchd 4-1)
Mount McLeod(IRE) looked clueless and should improve on this initial effort. (op 20-1)

1947 SIS LIVE H'CAP 1m 2f 7y
6:10 (6:11) (Class 5) (0-75,73) 3-Y-O £2,266 (£674; £337; £168) Stalls High

Form RPR
31- 1 **Fine Threads**[191] 7223 3-9-5 **71** RobertWinston 10 83
(B W Hills) *dwlt: sn trckd ldrs in 6th: rdn and prog over 2f out: led over 1f out: drvn out and styd on wl* **14/1**
501- 2 1 3/4 **Mountain Range (IRE)**[210] 6809 3-9-3 **72** LouisBeuzelin(3) 8 80+
(John Dunlop) *hld up in last pair: prog fr 3f out: drvn to cl over 1f out: disp 2nd fnl f: no imp on wnr* **15/2**
0-1 3 shd **Little Black Book (IRE)**[19] 1496 3-9-7 **73** DarrylHolland 12 81
(Gerard Butler) *led 1f: trckd ldr: led again over 3f out: drvn and hdd over 1f out: kpt on same pce* **4/1**[2]
362- 4 2 3/4 **Levantera (IRE)**[222] 6471 3-9-6 **72** LukeMorris 9 75
(Clive Cox) *pressed ldrs: effrt on outer 3f out: drvn and cl enough wl over 1f out: nt qckn* **25/1**
624- 5 1 **Puttingonthestyle (IRE)**[201] 7020 3-9-7 **73** RichardHughes 3 74
(Richard Hannon) *trckd ldrs: nt clr run over 2f out: drvn and edgd lft over 1f out: nt qckn and no imp* **11/4**[1]
-113 6 nk **Tijori (IRE)**[8] 1727 3-9-7 **73** RyanMoore 1 73
(Richard Hannon) *pushed along early but sn in last quartet: urged along and no prog over 3f out: sme late hdwy: n.d* **11/1**
655- 7 1 **Undulant Way**[200] 7036 3-9-1 **67** PatDobbs 5 65
(Amanda Perrett) *sed slowest of all: hld up in last pair: stl last 3f out: taken to outer and pushed along over 2f out: kpt on steadily* **20/1**
02-3 8 1 3/4 **Praxios**[27] 1298 3-9-6 **72** KierenFallon 4 69
(Luca Cumani) *s.s: mostly in last quartet: reminder 4f out: nvr threatened ldrs: sme prog over 1f out* **9/2**[3]
630- 9 3/4 **Red Mercury (IRE)**[193] 7186 3-9-4 **70** FergusSweeney 2 63
(Alan King) *hld up in midfield: nt clr run briefly wl over 2f out: pushed along and no prog wl over 1f out: fdd* **33/1**
2145 10 4 1/2 **Brilliant Barca**[21] 1442 3-8-10 **62** SamHitchcott 11 46
(Mick Channon) *prom: drvn to try to chal wl over 2f out: wknd rapidly wl over 1f out* **16/1**
230- 11 3 1/2 **Jaridh (USA)**[196] 7112 3-9-7 **73** FrankieDettori 7 50
(Saeed Bin Suroor) *led after 1f to over 3f out: wknd quite qckly over 2f out* **12/1**
024- 12 13 **Sylas Ings**[162] 7609 3-9-7 **73** IanMongan 6 24
(Pat Phelan) *nvr beyond midfield: rdn 4f out: wknd 3f out: t.o* **50/1**
2m 8.11s (-0.59) **Going Correction** -0.075s/f (Good) **12** Ran SP% **118.7**
Speed ratings (Par 99): **99,97,97,95,94 94,93,92,91,87 85,74**
toteswingers: 1&2 £37.50, 1&3 £6.10, 2&3 £4.30 CSF £110.89 CT £507.23 TOTE £11.80: £2.80, £2.70, £2.20; EX 63.20 Trifecta £3195.10 Pool: £4,317.80 - 0.50 winning units..
Owner Lady Bamford **Bred** Lady Bamford **Trained** Lambourn, Berks

FOCUS
Potentially good form for the grade. The winner is rated a up a stone on his 2yo runs, the second up 7lb and the next four close to their marks.

1948 SPORTINGBET.COM STKS (REGISTERED AS THE ROYAL WINDSOR STAKES) (LISTED RACE) 1m 67y
6:40 (6:40) (Class 1) 3-Y-O+
£17,031 (£6,456; £3,231; £1,611; £807; £405) Stalls Low

Form RPR
2-31 1 **Side Glance**[12] 1600 4-9-6 113 JimmyFortune 1 119
(Andrew Balding) *t.k.h: hld up in 5th: plenty to do 3f out: rdn and prog on outer 2f out: styd on wl to ld last 100yds: won gng away* **4/6**[1]
25-2 2 1 1/4 **The Cheka (IRE)**[36] 1118 5-9-2 108 KierenFallon 2 112
(Eve Johnson Houghton) *trckd ldng pair: effrt to ld 2f out: drvn over 1f out: hdd and outpcd last 100yds* **7/2**[2]
25-4 3 2 1/4 **Penitent**[37] 1100 5-9-6 111 RichardHughes 7 111
(William Haggas) *hld up in 4th: shkn up and nt qckn over 2f out: kpt on one pce u.p to take 3rd nr fin* **6/1**[3]
16-6 4 nk **The Rectifier (USA)**[23] 1385 4-9-2 104 MickyFenton 3 106
(Jim Boyle) *pushed up to ld: rdn and hdd 2f out: steadily outpcd* **33/1**
0-16 5 8 **Dunelight (IRE)**[23] 1397 8-9-6 105 (v) AdamKirby 5 92
(Clive Cox) *chsd ldr to over 2f out: wknd qckly over 1f out* **14/1**
1-60 6 18 **Spirit Of Sharjah (IRE)**[23] 1397 6-9-6 97 FrankieDettori 4 64
(Julia Feilden) *hld up in last: shkn up and no prog over 2f out: eased over 1f out: wl t.o* **20/1**
1m 42.24s (-2.46) **Going Correction** -0.075s/f (Good) **6** Ran SP% **110.9**
Speed ratings (Par 111): **109,107,105,105,97 79**
toteswingers: 1&2 £2.40, 1&3 £1.10, 2&3 £1.10 CSF £3.15 TOTE £2.10: £1.50, £1.50; EX 3.80.
Owner Kingsclere Racing CLub **Bred** Kingsclere Stud **Trained** Kingsclere, Hants

FOCUS
A couple of these like to front run, so the pace was predictably quick. Side Glance confirmed the merit of his Ascot win with an above-average effort for the grade.

NOTEBOOK
Side Glance showed he remains progressive. There was a danger this would come too soon after an impressive success at the same level at Ascot only 12 days earlier, but that wasn't the case and he's a tough sort. The good gallop helped as a few rivals got a slight start on him and he responded willingly to strong pressure. According to connections, a sound surface and a conventional track are important to the gelding and he apparently has options in Canada and Germany. Considering he acts so well at Ascot (course form figures 1321) it's a shame there probably isn't a suitable race for him at the Royal meeting, although there is the option of the Hunt Cup off a lofty rating. After all, being a gelding it's not essential that he contests pattern races. (op 10-11)
The Cheka(IRE), who missed an engagement two days earlier having spread a plate, seemed to run close to his best but was just unable to contain the improving winner.
Penitent is probably best watched until racing on ground with soft in the description. (op 9-2)
The Rectifier(USA) was allowed to dominate, but probably couldn't get much of a breather in. He ran well. (op 25-1)
Dunelight(IRE), who was second in this race in 2008, had a tough task at the weights under his penalty. (tchd 16-1)
Spirit Of Sharjah(IRE) is better over 7f and he was heavily eased once his chance had passed. Apparently he could run at York on Thursday. (op 18-1)

1949 VESTRA WEALTH PRIVATE CLIENT H'CAP 1m 67y
7:10 (7:11) (Class 5) (0-70,70) 3-Y-O £2,266 (£674; £337; £168) Stalls Low

Form RPR
11-5 1 **Ree's Rascal (IRE)**[25] 1335 3-9-4 **67** PatCosgrave 4 80
(Jim Boyle) *trckd ldrs gng strly: squeezed through over 1f out and sn led: rdn clr fnl f* **10/1**
610- 2 4 1/2 **Screenprint**[273] 4911 3-9-6 **69** (t) JamieSpencer 14 72
(Michael Bell) *led: drvn and hdd over 1f out: kpt on but wl outpcd* **14/1**
-666 3 1 1/4 **Bussa**[9] 1697 3-9-4 **70** RichardEvans(3) 10 70
(David Evans) *in tch: prog on outer 3f out: rdn to chal wl over 1f out: one pce after* **50/1**
03-1 4 1/2 **Konstantin (IRE)**[23] 1400 3-9-7 **70** HayleyTurner 5 69
(Marcus Tregoning) *prom on inner: hrd rdn over 2f out: one pce over 1f out* **4/1**[2]
53-1 5 1 1/4 **Franciscan**[23] 1392 3-9-7 **70** KierenFallon 13 66
(Luca Cumani) *trckd ldrs: rdn and hld whn nudged by rival over 1f out: fdd* **7/2**[1]
3210 6 hd **Tagansky**[9] 1683 3-9-5 **68** NeilCallan 8 64
(Simon Dow) *trckd ldrs: rdn over 2f out: nt qckn and fdd over 1f out* **16/1**
632- 7 2 1/4 **Pandorica**[211] 6770 3-9-7 **70** LukeMorris 1 60
(Clive Cox) *taken down early and free to post: t.k.h in rr: n.m.r after 1f: rchd midfield 1/2-way: no hdwy 2f out: kpt on* **12/1**

00-2 **8** *1 3/4* **Pivot Bridge**[33] [1191] 3-9-2 **65** .... RobertWinston 2 51
(B W Hills) *dwlt: hld up in rr and n.m.r after 1f: rdn and prog over 2f out: no imp and hld whn nudged by rival over 1f out: wknd* **9/2**[3]

02-5 **9** *1 1/2* **Arrow Storm (USA)**[13] [1589] 3-9-7 **70** .... RichardKingscote 6 53
(Tom Dascombe) *hld up in last trio: shkn up briefly over 1f out and no prog: nvr a factor* **20/1**

222- **10** *1 1/2* **Choose The Moment**[247] [5755] 3-9-4 **67** .... EddieAhern 12 63+
(Eve Johnson Houghton) *chsd ldr: jst sing to lose pl whn nudged by wnr over 1f out: wknd and eased* **16/1**

35-4 **11** *1* **Hawk Moth (IRE)**[33] [1191] 3-9-2 **65** .... SamHitchcott 11 42
(John Spearing) *slowest away: t.k.h in last pair: prog on outer 3f out: in tch 2f out: wknd* **20/1**

-142 **12** *7* **Avalon Bay**[14] [1566] 3-9-2 **65** .... DaneO'Neill 9 26
(Pat Eddery) *settled in rr: rdn and prog on outer fr 3f out: no hdwy wl over 1f out: wknd qckly and eased* **15/2**

00-0 **13** *13* **Ponte Di Rosa**[9] [1683] 3-9-1 **64** .... JimCrowley 7 —
(Jonathan Portman) *sn last: wknd 3f out: eased: t.o* **66/1**

1m 44.98s (0.28) **Going Correction** -0.075s/f (Good) **13** Ran SP% **120.4**
Speed ratings (Par 99): **95,90,89,88,87 87,85,83,81,80 79,72,59**
toteswingers: 1&2 £20.00, 1&3 £63.90, 2&3 £64.50 CSF £137.58 CT £6723.89 TOTE £11.10: £2.40, £4.00, £12.20; EX 149.00 Trifecta £1848.10 Pool: £3,496.47 - 1.40 winning units..
Owner Walter Hayford **Bred** Pier House Stud **Trained** Epsom, Surrey
■ Stewards' Enquiry : Pat Cosgrave two-day ban: careless riding (May 23 and 24)

FOCUS
Quite a rough race. The form is modest but some of these might be capable of better. Improvement from the first two.
Bussa Official explanation: jockey said gelding hung right
Pandorica Official explanation: jockey said filly suffered interference in running

1950 VESTRAWEALTH.COM MEDIAN AUCTION MAIDEN STKS 1m 2f 7y
7:40 (7:40) (Class 5) 3-5-Y-O **£2,266** (£674; £337; £168) **Stalls** High

Form RPR

4 **1** **Alkimos (IRE)**[26] [1321] 3-8-13 0 .... KierenFallon 1 95+
(Luca Cumani) *prom: chsd ldr over 2f out: drvn to ld jst over 1f out: styd on wl to assert ins fnl f* **4/6**[1]

5 **2** *1 1/2* **Moment Of Time**[15] [1549] 3-8-10 0 ow2 .... JimmyFortune 13 89+
(Andrew Balding) *led: drvn and hdd jst over 1f out: drew rt away fr rest but hld by wnr fnl f* **3/1**[2]

0- **3** *9* **Knightly Escapade**[221] [6504] 3-8-13 0 .... DaneO'Neill 10 74
(John Dunlop) *dwlt: sn trckd ldrs: wl outpcd fr 2f out: shkn up to win battle for 3rd fnl f: possible improver* **20/1**

22-3 **4** *1* **Loyaliste (FR)**[34] [1144] 4-10-0 71 .... RichardHughes 12 73
(Richard Hannon) *mostly chsd ldr to over 2f out: sn wl outpcd: shkn up and lost battle for 3rd fnl f* **14/1**

03-4 **5** *4* **Glyn Ceiriog**[39] [1060] 3-8-9 0 ow1 .... TedDurcan 4 60
(George Baker) *trckd ldrs: shuffled along and outpcd fr 2f out: possible improver* **8/1**[3]

22-2 **6** *nk* **Woop Woop (IRE)**[124] [51] 3-8-8 72 .... MickyFenton 11 58
(Stef Higgins) *hld up wl in rr: promising hdwy on wd outside 3f out: shuffled along and wl outpcd fnl 2f* **25/1**

30- **7** *1* **Sugar Hiccup (IRE)**[199] [7057] 3-8-8 0 .... LukeMorris 5 56
(Clive Cox) *dwlt: nvr bttr than midfield: rdn over 2f out: sn outpcd and btn* **66/1**

5- **8** *2* **Cyber Star**[202] [7001] 3-8-8 0 .... PatCosgrave 2 52
(James Fanshawe) *trckd ldrs: rdn 3f out: lost pl over 2f out: steadily fdd* **25/1**

56- **9** *nk* **Toymaker**[251] [5623] 4-10-0 0 .... MartinLane 8 58
(Rae Guest) *dwlt: hld up in last trio: nudged along over 2f out: nvr involved: possible improver* **100/1**

0- **10** *1/2* **Amoya (GER)**[198] 4-9-9 80 .... (t) RyanMoore 7 52
(Philip McBride) *plld hrd in rr: stl keen whn promising hdwy on outer 3f out: suddenly wknd and eased 2f out* **20/1**

50 **11** *1* **I'm A Celebrity**[26] [1311] 3-8-13 0 .... AdamKirby 9 54
(Marco Botti) *hld up wl in rr: pushed along and reminder 3f out: no prog and hld together after* **100/1**

06 **12** *2* **Mina's Boy**[14] [1572] 3-8-13 0 .... TomMcLaughlin 6 50
(Ed Dunlop) *[illegible] 4f out: struggling after* **100/1**

2m 8.10s (-0.60) **Going Correction** -0.075s/f (Good)
WFA 3 from 4yo 15lb **12** Ran SP% **124.4**
Speed ratings (Par 103): **99,97,90,89,86 86,85,83,83,83 82,80**
toteswingers: 1&2 £1.20, 1&3 £6.50, 2&3 £30.10 CSF £2.65 TOTE £1.70: £1.10, £1.80, £4.70; EX 5.40 Trifecta £49.40 Pool: £662.84 - 9.92 winning units..
Owner Leonidas Marinopoulos **Bred** C O'Brien B McGarvey & D Everard **Trained** Newmarket, Suffolk

FOCUS
The time was almost identical to the earlier Class 5 handicap for 3-y-os, but the pace was muddling. Despite that, a couple of runners, who both look above average, pulled clear. The form is set around the fourth.
Amoya(GER) Official explanation: jockey said filly ran too freely

1951 VESTRA WEALTH MANAGEMENT H'CAP 1m 3f 135y
8:10 (8:10) (Class 5) (0-75,74) 3-Y-O **£2,266** (£674; £337; £168) **Stalls** High

Form RPR

-431 **1** **Dubai Glory**[21] [1442] 3-8-11 **64** .... JamesDoyle 6 73
(Sheena West) *mostly trckd ldr: led 3f out and kicked on: hrd pressed and drifted lft fnl f: hld on* **6/1**[2]

2242 **2** *hd* **Echos Of Motivator**[16] [1526] 3-8-13 **66** .... (p) DavidProbert 8 75
(Ronald Harris) *hld up towards rr: prog 3f out: drvn to chse wnr wl over 1f out: str chal and drifted lft fnl f: nt qckn last strides* **14/1**

03-3 **3** *4 1/2* **Cunning Act**[20] [1475] 3-9-2 **69** .... KierenFallon 4 72+
(Jonathan Portman) *s.i.s: hld up in last pair: effrt 3f out: keeping on but no ch whn squeezed out 1f out: drvn and styd on to snatch 3rd post* **12/1**

321- **4** *nse* **Slight Advantage (IRE)**[222] [6471] 3-9-6 **73** .... LukeMorris 3 74
(Clive Cox) *prom: pushed along 4f out: nt qckn and outpcd 2f out: kpt on u.p* **8/1**

05-5 **5** *1 1/2* **Swift Blade (IRE)**[19] [1484] 3-9-3 **70** .... JimCrowley 10 68
(William Knight) *t.k.h: hld up in tch: effrt on outer 3f out: wandered u.p fr 2f out: one pce* **25/1**

30-3 **6** *1 3/4* **Sixty Roses (IRE)**[35] [1134] 3-9-0 **67** .... EddieAhern 1 62
(John Dunlop) *trckd ldrs: rdn wl over 2f out: steadily outpcd fnl 2f* **6/1**[2]

3-22 **7** *2 1/2* **Standout**[33] [1189] 3-9-5 **72** .... RichardHughes 5 63
(Richard Hannon) *trckd ldrs: rdn to chse wnr over 2f out to wl over 1f out: wknd* **9/2**[1]

40-1 **8** *1* **Romeo Montague**[27] [1299] 3-9-0 **67** .... TomMcLaughlin 2 56+
(Ed Dunlop) *s.s: hld up last: brought wd 3f out and sme prog: hung bdly lft fnl 2f and wknd* **6/1**[2]

605- **9** *5* **Blue Dazzler (IRE)**[210] [6809] 3-9-1 **68** .... PatDobbs 9 49
(Amanda Perrett) *hld up in last trio: rdn and no prog over 2f out: sn btn* **11/1**

6-53 **10** *5* **September Draw (USA)**[21] [1442] 3-8-9 **62** .... RyanMoore 7 34
(Richard Hannon) *led to 3f out: sn wknd* **16/1**

01-3 **11** *3 3/4* **Run On Ruby (FR)**[12] [1609] 3-9-7 **74** .... TedDurcan 11 40
(David Lanigan) *trckd ldrs: rdn wl over 2f out: wknd rapidly wl over 1f out: eased fnl f* **7/1**[3]

2m 29.04s (-0.46) **Going Correction** -0.075s/f (Good) **11** Ran SP% **117.1**
Speed ratings (Par 99): **98,97,94,94,93 92,91,90,87,83 81**
toteswingers: 1&2 £14.40, 1&3 £9.60, 2&3 £38.30 CSF £86.35 CT £979.69 TOTE £7.70: £2.10, £4.50, £3.90; EX 82.70 TRIFECTA Not won..
Owner The Affordable (2) Partnership **Bred** Hascombe And Valiant Studs **Trained** Falmer, E Sussex

FOCUS
A modest handicap, but the front two showed themselves ahead of their current marks, pulling clear. The winner showed his latest improvement to be no fluke.
Romeo Montague Official explanation: jockey said gelding hung badly right
T/Jkpt: £54,543.80 to a £1 stake. Pool: £76,822.35. 1.00 winning ticket. T/Plt: £433.50 to a £1 stake. Pool: £97,005.02. 163.33 winning tickets. T/Qpdt: £131.70 to a £1 stake. Pool: £6,113.98. 34.35 winning tickets. JN

1583 WOLVERHAMPTON (A.W) (L-H)
Monday, May 9

OFFICIAL GOING: Standard
Wind: Fresh, half-behind Weather: Overcast

1952 32REDBET.COM H'CAP (DIV I) 7f 32y(P)
1:30 (1:30) (Class 6) (0-60,60) 3-Y-O **£1,364** (£403; £201) **Stalls** High

Form RPR

60-0 **1** **Cadmium Loch**[20] [1472] 3-9-0 **53** .... RussKennemore 2 61
(Reg Hollinshead) *led: hdd over 5f out: led again 1/2-way: rdn over 1f out: r.o* **33/1**

602- **2** *1 3/4* **Whitby Jet (IRE)**[236] [6081] 3-9-5 **58** .... ShaneKelly 6 62+
(Edward Vaughan) *s.i.s: hld up: hdwy over 2f out: r.o to go 2nd towards fin: nt trble wnr* **9/2**[1]

00-0 **3** *1/2* **Cathcart Castle**[119] [109] 3-9-1 **57** .... MartinHarley(3) 1 59
(Mick Channon) *a.p: chsd ldr over 2f out: rdn over 1f out: styd on same pce wl ins fnl f: lost 2nd towards fin* **6/1**[2]

00-4 **4** *1 1/4* **Climaxfortackle (IRE)**[20] [1472] 3-9-7 **60** .... RobbieFitzpatrick 8 59
(Derek Shaw) *a.p: rdn over 1f out: styd on same pce ins fnl f* **8/1**

00-1 **5** *3 1/2* **Invigilator**[25] [1331] 3-9-5 **58** .... LukeMorris 5 48
(Harry Dunlop) *chsd ldrs: rdn over 2f out: wknd fnl f* **9/2**[1]

1555 **6** *3* **Princess Gail**[20] [1472] 3-9-2 **55** .... TomMcLaughlin 9 36
(Mark Brisbourne) *hld up: rdn over 2f out: r.o ins fnl f: nvr nrr* **6/1**[2]

2054 **7** *1/2* **Lennoxwood (IRE)**[44] [987] 3-8-13 **52** .... (v[1]) DaneO'Neill 11 32
(Mark Usher) *s.i.s: hld up: rdn over 1f out: nvr on terms* **6/1**[2]

4530 **8** *hd* **Three Scoops**[7] [1753] 3-8-10 **49** .... JamesDoyle 3 29
(Dominic Ffrench Davis) *chsd ldr tl led over 5f out: hdd 1/2-way: rdn over 2f out: wknd fnl f* **14/1**

60-0 **9** *1 1/2* **Tahitian Princess (IRE)**[27] [1299] 3-8-10 **49** .... PaulMulrennan 7 25
(Ann Duffield) *chsd ldrs: rdn over 2f out: sn wknd* **20/1**

00-1 **10** *2* **Century Dancer**[45] [966] 3-8-11 **55** .... RyanPowell(5) 10 25
(Tor Sturgis) *s.i.s: a in rr* **7/1**[3]

540- **11** *2 1/2* **Miskin Diamond (IRE)**[255] [5465] 3-8-10 **52** .... DeclanCannon(3) 4 15
(Bryn Palling) *sn prom: rdn 1/2-way: wknd over 2f out* **12/1**

1m 30.17s (0.57) **Going Correction** -0.025s/f (Stan) **11** Ran SP% **124.9**
Speed ratings (Par 97): **95,93,92,91,87 83,83,82,81,78 75**
toteswingers: 1&2 £36.10, 1&3 £54.40, 2&3 £9.50 CSF £186.96 CT £1075.67 TOTE £45.60: £18.00, £1.60, £3.30; EX 225.20.
Owner M Johnson **Bred** R Hollinshead And M Johnson **Trained** Upper Longdon, Staffs

FOCUS
A couple of unexposed performers in a moderate handicap. The gallop was an ordinary one and the winner ended up towards the centre late on. A fairly sound standard with a clear personal best from the winner.
Cadmium Loch Official explanation: trainer said regarding apparent improvement in form gelding was a late to mature and had been given the Monty Roberts rug to help settle him in the stalls.

1953 32REDBET.COM H'CAP (DIV II) 7f 32y(P)
2:00 (2:00) (Class 6) (0-60,59) 3-Y-O **£1,364** (£403; £201) **Stalls** High

Form RPR

030 **1** **Sienna Blue**[20] [1474] 3-9-6 **58** .... CathyGannon 5 68+
(Malcolm Saunders) *a.p: rdnch over 2f out: chsd ldr fnl f: r.o u.p to ld nr fin* **9/2**[2]

5630 **2** *shd* **Misere**[20] [1472] 3-9-3 **55** .... PaulMulrennan 1 65+
(Kevin Ryan) *led: clr whn rdn and hung rt fr over 1f out: hdd nr fin* **6/1**[3]

1053 **3** *5* **Titan Diamond (IRE)**[20] [1472] 3-8-13 **58** .... RachealKneller(7) 7 54
(Mark Usher) *hld up: hdwy over 1f out: no ex ins fnl f* **10/3**[1]

005- **4** *hd* **Sandtail (IRE)**[200] [7034] 3-9-7 **59** .... DaneO'Neill 10 54
(J W Hills) *hld up: hdwy 3f out: rdn over 1f out: hung lft and styd on same pce fnl f* **6/1**[3]

365- **5** *6* **Robber Stone**[130] [8012] 3-9-0 **55** .... MartinHarley(3) 3 34
(Mick Channon) *chsd ldrs: rdn over 1f out: wknd fnl f* **9/2**[2]

0000 **6** *1 1/4* **Five Cool Kats (IRE)**[7] [1753] 3-8-12 **50** .... LukeMorris 8 26
(Paul Burgoyne) *s.i.s: bhd tl styd on ins fnl f: nvr nrr* **33/1**

000- **7** *1/2* **Look For Love**[185] [7325] 3-9-0 **52** .... RussKennemore 2 27
(Reg Hollinshead) *hld up: rdn 1/2-way: sme hdwy over 1f out: sn wknd* **14/1**

-030 **8** *1* **Melbury**[16] [1524] 3-9-0 **52** .... ShaneKelly 9 24
(Michael Squance) *s.i.s: sn pushed along in rr: sme hdwy over 2f out: sn wknd* **14/1**

0-06 **9** *2 1/2* **High Class Lady**[44] [987] 3-9-3 **55** .... AdamKirby 6 20
(Walter Swinburn) *chsd ldr: rdn 1/2-way: wknd over 1f out* **12/1**

560 **10** *3 3/4* **Kaminski Kabs**[39] [1065] 3-8-6 **49** .... DanielleMcCreery(5) 4 —
(Phil McEntee) *prom: hung rt 1/2-way: wknd 2f out* **50/1**

1m 30.74s (1.14) **Going Correction** -0.025s/f (Stan) **10** Ran SP% **113.9**
Speed ratings (Par 97): **92,91,86,85,79 77,77,75,73,68**
toteswingers: 1&2 £7.20, 1&3 £3.50, 2&3 £3.40 CSF £30.90 CT £102.66 TOTE £5.50: £1.50, £2.60, £1.40; EX 54.80.
Owner M S Saunders **Bred** Raymond Cowie **Trained** Green Ore, Somerset

FOCUS
Division two of a moderate handicap. It was the weaker division and the time was slower. The gallop was no more than fair to the home turn and the gambled-on winner came down the centre in the straight. The first pair were clear and can do better.

Misere Official explanation: jockey said filly hung right-handed throughout

1954 32RED CLAIMING STKS — 5f 20y(P)
2:30 (2:30) (Class 6) 2-Y-O — £1,706 (£503; £252) Stalls Low

Form — RPR

2116 **1** **Van Go Go**[5] [1806] 2-8-9 0 .... RichardKingscote 4 — 67
(Tom Dascombe) *mde all: shkn up to go clr fnl f: easily* — 2/5[1]

530 **2** 3 ¾ **Aquasulis (IRE)**[21] [1434] 2-8-5 0 .... CathyGannon 6 — 49
(David Evans) *sn pushed along and prom: rdn over 1f out: hung lft and styd on to chse wnr ins fnl f: no imp* — 9/1[3]

4 **3** nk **Selinda**[11] [1628] 2-8-5 0 ow1 .... MartinHarley(3) 5 — 50
(Mick Channon) *s.i.s: hld up: hdwy over 1f out: styd on same pce ins fnl f* — 7/1[2]

2 **4** 3 ½ **She's Cool Too (IRE)**[14] [1563] 2-8-3 0 .... KierenFox(3) 2 — 36
(Bill Turner) *chsd wnr: rdn over 1f out: hung rt and wknd ins fnl f* — 7/1[2]

06 **5** 6 **Foolscap (IRE)**[6] [1786] 2-8-0 0 .... NathanAlison(7) 3 — 15
(Jim Boyle) *plld hrd and prom: rdn and wknd over 1f out* — 40/1

65 **6** 3 ¾ **Early Ambition**[14] [1563] 2-8-1 0 ow2 .... AmyRyan(3) 8 — —
(Andrew Haynes) *prom: rdn 1/2-way: wknd wl over 1f out* — 66/1

6 **7** hd **Masivo Man (IRE)**[13] [1590] 2-8-8 0 .... (v[1]) LukeMorris 1 — —
(Chris Dwyer) *s.i.s: hld up: shkn up 1/2-way: sn wknd* — 33/1

63.20 secs (0.90) **Going Correction** -0.025s/f (Stan) — 7 Ran SP% **113.3**
Speed ratings (Par 91): **91,85,84,78,69 63,63**
toteswingers: 1&2 £2.40, 1&3 £1.50, 2&3 £3.40 CSF £4.81 TOTE £1.40: £1.10, £4.00; EX 6.10.The winner was claimed by Paul J. Dixon for £12,000.
Owner A Black **Bred** A Black **Trained** Malpas, Cheshire

FOCUS
As the market suggested, this was an uncompetitive claimer. The gallop was a reasonable one and the winner came down the centre in the straight. She lookd a useful type fro this grade.

NOTEBOOK
Van Go Go, who wasn't disgraced in the Lily Agnes at Chester last week, didn't have to improve too much to win with plenty in hand in this lesser grade returned to Polytrack. She's a speedy type who should be able to win again in this company. (tchd 1-2 in places)
Aquasulis(IRE) had been well beaten after hanging on firm ground last time, but finished much closer to the winner returned to Polytrack. She should be suited by the step up to 6f and is the type to win a small race for this yard. (op 8-1 tchd 7-1)
Selinda, a half-sister to Polytrack and turf winner Alfraamsey, stepped up on the form shown on turf on her debut, but while she clearly has her limitations she should be able to pick up a low-grade event in the coming months. (op 12-1)
She's Cool Too(IRE) had hinted at ability behind the Van Go Go on her debut at Warwick, but although matching strides with that one to the home turn finished further behind that rival this time. She's probably worth another chance in lesser company. (op 8-1)

1955 32RED CASINO CLAIMING STKS — 5f 20y(P)
3:00 (3:00) (Class 6) 3-Y-O+ — £1,706 (£503; £252) Stalls Low

Form — RPR

015 **1** **Steelcut**[7] [1752] 7-9-4 74 .... (p) CathyGannon 1 — 77
(David Evans) *hld up: hdwy over 1f out: rdn to ld ins fnl f: jst hld on* — 9/2[3]

1243 **2** hd **Kylladdie**[13] [1584] 4-9-8 73 .... (b) WilliamBuick 3 — 80
(Steve Gollings) *hld up: hdwy over 1f out: rdn: hung lft and r.o wl ins fnl f: jst failed* — 3/1[2]

3231 **3** 1 ¾ **Decider (USA)**[11] [1627] 8-9-2 62 .... (b) LukeMorris 8 — 68
(Ronald Harris) *sn led: clr 3f out: rdn: hung lft and hdd ins fnl f: no ex* — 11/1

-026 **4** 1 ½ **Jigajig**[23] [1411] 4-9-3 70 .... (p) AmyRyan(3) 7 — 67
(Kevin Ryan) *chsd ldr: rdn over 1f out: no ex ins fnl f* — 15/2

0000 **5** nk **Elhamri**[14] [1562] 7-9-1 74 .... MartinHarley(3) 2 — 64
(Conor Dore) *chsd ldrs: rdn over 1f out: styd on same pce fnl f* — 20/1

6245 **6** nk **Green Manalishi**[9] [1698] 10-9-10 84 .... (p) PaulMulrennan 5 — 68
(Kevin Ryan) *prom: rdn over 1f out: btn whn hmpd ins fnl f* — 15/8[1]

44-6 **7** 2 ¾ **Angelo Poliziano**[32] [1204] 5-9-1 68 .... (v) RosieJessop(5) 6 — 55
(Ann Duffield) *s.s: rdn over 1f out: n.d* — 12/1

61.89 secs (-0.41) **Going Correction** -0.025s/f (Stan) — 7 Ran SP% **110.5**
Speed ratings (Par 101): **102,101,98,96,96 95,91**
toteswingers: 1&2 £2.20, 1&3 £5.40, 2&3 £3.00 CSF £17.10 TOTE £4.60: £3.10, £1.40; EX 24.90.
Owner Shropshire Wolves 3 **Bred** Mrs B Skinner **Trained** Pandy, Monmouths

FOCUS
Exposed performers and the useful market leader disappointed, but still a fair race of its type. The gallop was a decent one and the winner raced centre-to-far-side in the straight. The first three basically ran to form.

1956 32RED.COM H'CAP — 1m 5f 194y(P)
3:30 (3:30) (Class 6) (0-65,65) 4-Y-O+ — £1,706 (£503; £252) Stalls Low

Form — RPR

3440 **1** **Profit's Reality (IRE)**[40] [1046] 9-9-7 **65** .... KierenFox(3) 5 — 76
(Michael Attwater) *hld up: hdwy over 5f out: rdn over 1f out: styd on to ld nr fin* — 20/1

-101 **2** nk **Storm Hawk (IRE)**[13] [1586] 4-9-9 **65** .... (p) WilliamBuick 6 — 76
(Pat Eddery) *chsd ldrs: led wl over 1f out: sn rdn: hdd nr fin* — 15/8[1]

3412 **3** 2 **Broughtons Paradis (IRE)**[24] [1372] 5-9-5 **60** .... AndreaAtzeni 7 — 68
(Willie Musson) *hld up: hdwy over 3f out: rdn over 1f out: styd on* — 11/2[3]

2/0- **4** 1 ¼ **Kings Maiden (IRE)**[388] [1207] 8-9-2 **60** .... AmyRyan(3) 4 — 66
(James Moffatt) *s.i.s: hld up: hdwy over 2f out: rdn over 1f out: styd on: nt rch ldrs* — 16/1

0-04 **5** 4 ½ **Colonel Sherman (USA)**[24] [1372] 6-9-2 **57** .... (t) RussKennemore 2 — 57
(Philip Kirby) *led: clr 8f out: rdn and hdd wl over 1f out: wknd fnl f* — 9/1

2253 **6** 5 **Leyte Gulf (USA)**[13] [1586] 8-9-7 **62** .... DaneO'Neill 3 — 55
(Chris Bealby) *s.s: hld up: hdwy over 2f out: wknd over 1f out: eased ins fnl f* — 3/1[2]

33-4 **7** ¾ **Dr Finley (IRE)**[14] [1016] 4-9-7 **63** .... (p) MickyFenton 9 — 55
(Lydia Pearce) *hld up: n.d* — 16/1

2215 **8** 3 **Kingaroo (IRE)**[20] [1466] 5-9-5 **63** .... BillyCray(3) 10 — 50
(Garry Woodward) *chsd ldr 3f: remained handy: rdn over 3f out: wknd over 2f out* — 16/1

13-4 **9** 3 ¼ **Dandarrell**[88] [496] 4-9-0 **56** .... PaulMulrennan 1 — 39
(Julie Camacho) *prom: chsd ldr 11f out: rdn over 3f out: wknd over 1f out* — 16/1

60-6 **10** 16 **Peaceful Soul (USA)**[11] [1631] 4-9-6 **62** .... RichardMullen 8 — 23
(David Lanigan) *mid-div: rdn and lost pl 6f out: bhd fnl 4f: t.o* — 16/1

3m 3.96s (-2.04) **Going Correction** -0.025s/f (Stan)
WFA 4 from 5yo+ 1lb — 10 Ran SP% **119.3**
Speed ratings (Par 101): **104,103,102,101,99 96,96,94,92,83**
toteswingers: 1&2 £10.90, 1&3 £17.00, 2&3 £3.40 CSF £59.17 CT £251.73 TOTE £25.60: £5.60, £1.10, £1.40; EX 49.90.
Owner Roger Milner & Charles Bamford **Bred** Michael Munnelly **Trained** Epsom, Surrey

FOCUS
A modest handicap run in a fair time for the grade. The winner came down the centre in the straight and is rated up 3lb on recent form.

1957 32REDPOKER.COM MAIDEN AUCTION FILLIES' STKS — 5f 20y(P)
4:00 (4:00) (Class 5) 2-Y-O — £2,388 (£705; £352) Stalls Low

Form — RPR

33 **1** **Xyzzy**[13] [1590] 2-8-7 0 .... RoystonFfrench 7 — 70
(Linda Stubbs) *chsd ldr tl led 1/2-way: rdn out* — 7/1[2]

2 ¾ **Blodwen Abbey** 2-8-9 0 .... LiamJones 9 — 69
(James Unett) *a.p: rdn to chse wnr and hung rt fr over 1f out: r.o* — 20/1

0 **3** 4 ½ **Economic Crisis (IRE)**[21] [1434] 2-8-6 0 .... PatrickMathers 4 — 50
(Alan Berry) *s.i.s: outpcd: hdwy 1/2-way: rdn over 1f out: styd on* — 33/1

4 **4** 1 ¾ **Bojangle (IRE)**[27] [1290] 2-8-4 0 .... BillyCray(3) 8 — 45
(Dominic Ffrench Davis) *mid-div: pushed along over 3f out: hdwy over 1f out: no ex ins fnl f* — 9/1

0 **5** ½ **Vieira Da Silva (IRE)**[23] [1414] 2-8-9 0 .... MartinHarley(3) 6 — 48
(Mick Channon) *chsd ldrs: rdn over 1f out: no ex fnl f* — 7/1[2]

6 5 **Silvas Romana (IRE)** 2-8-0 0 .... KieranO'Neill(5) 2 — 23
(Mark Brisbourne) *dwlt: outpcd: hung lft over 1f out: r.o ins fnl f: nvr nrr* — 16/1

7 ½ **Bitter Lemon** 2-8-1 0 .... AmyRyan(3) 10 — 22
(Kevin Ryan) *s.s: hdwy 1/2-way: wknd over 1f out* — 8/1[3]

8 1 ¾ **Compton Shuttle (IRE)** 2-8-10 0 .... JamesDoyle 3 — 20
(Hans Adielsson) *sn outpcd* — 20/1

9 1 ½ **Fanrouge (IRE)** 2-8-8 0 .... CathyGannon 1 — 13
(Malcolm Saunders) *sn pushed along in rr: nvr on terms* — 12/1

25 **10** 1 ¼ **Launch On Line**[23] [1414] 2-8-4 0 .... KierenFox(3) 5 — 7
(Bill Turner) *led to 1/2-way: rdn over 1f out: wknd fnl f* — 5/4[1]

62.58 secs (0.28) **Going Correction** -0.025s/f (Stan) — 10 Ran SP% **116.6**
Speed ratings (Par 90): **96,94,87,84,84 76,75,72,70,68**
toteswingers: 1&2 £13.00, 2&3 £45.30, 1&3 £17.80 CSF £137.67 TOTE £10.10: £3.30, £8.60, £9.20; EX 136.20.
Owner Facts & Figures **Bred** Low Ground Stud **Trained** Norton, N Yorks

FOCUS
The market leader proved very disappointing and this was no more than a modest fillies' maiden. The gallop was reasonable and the first two pulled clear. The winner, who showed improved form, was another to race down the centre.

NOTEBOOK
Xyzzy is a steadily progressive sort who took advantage of the below-par run of the market leader and turned in her best effort to get off the mark at the third attempt. She's clearly speedy, but things will be tougher until the nursery season begins. (op 11-2)
Blodwen Abbey ◆, a half-sister to very useful triple Polytrack winner Dark Prospect, has a bit more size than the majority of this field and shaped with a fair bit of promise, despite her obvious greenness on this debut. She'll be suited by the step up to 6f and should win a race. Official explanation: jockey said filly hung right (op 16-1)
Economic Crisis(IRE), a sparely made filly who was well beaten on firm ground on her debut but who shaped with more promise on this all-weather debut. A step up to 6f may suit better, but she's likely to remain vulnerable in this grade. (op 28-1)
Bojangle(IRE) bettered the form of her Fibresand debut. She'll be of more interest once the nursery season gets underway. (op 17-2 tchd 10-1)
Vieira Da Silva(IRE) attracted plenty of support but, although she showed ability on this all-weather debut, she again underlined her vulnerability in this type of event. (op 14-1)
Launch On Line was very well supported but dropped away tamely early in the straight back on Polytrack and was again a long way below the form she showed on her debut. She looks one to have reservations about. Official explanation: jockey said filly never picked up in the home straight (op 7-4)

1958 CONNOLLY'S RED MILLS HORSE FEEDS FILLIES' H'CAP — 1m 141y(P)
4:30 (4:30) (Class 5) (0-70,70) 3-Y-O — £2,388 (£705; £352) Stalls Low

Form — RPR

005- **1** **Dragonera**[207] [6873] 3-9-5 **68** .... PaulMulrennan 11 — 77
(Ed Dunlop) *hld up: hdwy over 2f out: led and hung rt fr over 1f out: r.o* — 7/1[3]

256- **2** 3 ¼ **Silver Show (IRE)**[236] [6071] 3-8-13 **65** .... MartinHarley(3) 12 — 66
(Mick Channon) *led 1f: chsd ldr tl led again 3f out: rdn and hdd over 1f out: hmpd ins fnl f: styd on same pce* — 12/1

-011 **3** nse **Beach Babe**[14] [1566] 3-9-2 **65** .... NickyMackay 10 — 66
(Jonathan Portman) *a.p: rdn and hung rt over 2f out: hmpd ins fnl f: styd on same pce* — 9/2[1]

005- **4** ½ **Lady Barastar (IRE)**[211] [6770] 3-9-1 **64** .... ShaneKelly 8 — 64
(Walter Swinburn) *s.i.s: sn pushed along in rr: hdwy u.p over 1f out: r.o: nt rch ldrs* — 9/1

5153 **5** nk **Crystal Sky (IRE)**[27] [1286] 3-9-1 **64** .... JamesDoyle 4 — 63+
(Andrew Haynes) *prom: rdn over 2f out: styd on same pce fr over 1f out* — 5/1[2]

44-5 **6** 2 ¼ **Countess Ellen (IRE)**[7] [1768] 3-9-7 **70** .... WilliamBuick 9 — 67+
(Gerard Butler) *hld up: hdwy 3f out: rdn and swtchd lft over 1f out: styng on same pce whn nt clr run ins fnl f* — 5/1[2]

006- **7** ½ **Formidable Girl (USA)**[234] [6161] 3-8-13 **62** .... JackMitchell 6 — 55
(Kevin Ryan) *hld up: hdwy u.p over 1f out: nvr nrr* — 16/1

00-0 **8** nk **Scarborough Lily**[124] [52] 3-8-7 **56** oh4 .... CathyGannon 5 — 48+
(Edward Vaughan) *mid-div: lost pl 3f out: n.d after* — 16/1

055- **9** 2 **Arctic Maiden**[173] [7484] 3-9-0 **63** .... JamieMackay 13 — 51
(Willie Musson) *hld up: nt clr run wl over 1f out: nvr nr to chal* — 33/1

36-0 **10** ½ **Eyes On**[23] [1400] 3-8-6 **60** .... TobyAtkinson(5) 7 — 46
(Philip McBride) *s.i.s: rdn over 2f out: a in rr* — 16/1

6-16 **11** shd **Onlyfoalsandhorses (IRE)**[20] [1472] 3-8-2 **56** .... RyanPowell(5) 3 — 42
(J S Moore) *chsd ldrs: rdn over 2f out: wkng whn hung lft over 1f out* — 16/1

555- **12** 1 ¼ **Miss Villefranche**[232] [6222] 3-9-3 **66** .... (v[1]) SaleemGolam 1 — 49
(Michael Bell) *chsd ldrs: rdn over 2f out: wknd over 1f out* — 11/1

05-5 **13** 12 **Lady Deanie (IRE)**[33] [1179] 3-8-9 **58** .... DavidProbert 2 — 14
(Bryn Palling) *led over 7f out: hdd 3f out: sn rdn: wknd 2f out* — 20/1

1m 50.58s (0.08) **Going Correction** -0.025s/f (Stan) — 13 Ran SP% **121.3**
Speed ratings (Par 96): **98,95,95,94,94 92,91,91,89,89 89,88,77**
toteswingers: 1&2 £17.00, 2&3 £7.40, 1&3 £17.00 CSF £89.80 CT £338.24 TOTE £8.10: £3.30, £4.40, £1.90; EX 118.60.
Owner J Weatherby, Champneys **Bred** Preston Lodge Stud **Trained** Newmarket, Suffolk
■ Stewards' Enquiry : William Buick one-day ban: careless riding (May 23)

FOCUS
Several unexposed sorts in a modest fillies' handicap. The gallop was only fair and the winner edged towards the far side in the straight. A big personal best from the winner with the third probably the best guide.
Beach Babe Official explanation: jockey said filly suffered interference in running

Scarborough Lily Official explanation: jockey said filly clipped heels on the bend

1959 32REDBINGO.COM AMATEUR RIDERS' H'CAP 1m 4f 50y(P)
5:00 (5:00) (Class 6) (0-55,54) 4-Y-O+ **£1,648** (£507; £253) **Stalls** Low

Form RPR
3222 **1** **Wrecking Crew (IRE)**[45] [969] 7-10-4 **51** MrsDBamonte[(7)] 8 60
(Rod Millman) *s.i.s: hld up: plld hrd: hdwy 8f out: led 2f out: gng clr whn rdr dropped whip wl over 1f out: styd on* **7/2**[1]
-450 **2** *1 1/4* **Amical Risks (FR)**[36] [1107] 7-10-7 **54** MissVCoates[(7)] 2 61
(Ollie Pears) *hld up: hdwy over 2f out: chsd wnr ins fnl f: r.o* **7/2**[1]
4356 **3** *5* **Private Equity (IRE)**[26] [1310] 5-10-12 **52** MissSBrotherton 12 51
(William Jarvis) *hld up: hdwy 7f out: styd on same pce appr fnl f* **4/1**[2]
4440 **4** *1 3/4* **Laura Land**[30] [1253] 5-10-5 **50** MissBeckyBrisbourne[(5)] 9 46
(Mark Brisbourne) *chsd ldrs: rdn over 1f out: wknd fnl f* **7/1**[3]
0615 **5** *nk* **Acropolis (IRE)**[31] [1218] 10-10-4 **51** MrCCarroll[(7)] 5 47
(Tony Carroll) *hld up: racd keenly: hmpd over 7f out: r.o ins fnl f: nvr trbld ldrs* **17/2**
05/6 **6** *hd* **Graycliffe (IRE)**[18] [1253] 5-10-7 **50** MrJHamer[(3)] 10 45
(Patrick Morris) *chsd ldr tl led over 6f out: hdd 2f out: wknd ins fnl f* **33/1**
062/ **7** *2 1/2* **Top Achiever (IRE)**[11] [4710] 10-10-7 **52** (p) MrBJPoste[(5)] 6 43
(Bill Moore) *chsd ldrs: rdn and ev ch over 2f out: wknd over 1f out* **12/1**
6-40 **8** *8* **Herecomethegirls**[54] [862] 5-10-13 **53** (p) MissEJJones 4 32
(Olivia Maylam) *hld up: hdwy over 3f out: wknd over 2f out* **16/1**
00-3 **9** *3/4* **Talk Of Saafend (IRE)**[21] [1440] 6-10-11 **54** MissECSayer[(3)] 3 31
(Dianne Sayer) *prom: rdn over 2f out: sn wknd* **16/1**
5-04 **10** *2 1/2* **Pocket Too**[20] [1473] 8-10-6 **51** (b) MrJBanks[(5)] 7 24
(Matthew Salaman) *led: hdd over 6f out: rdn 4f out: wknd 3f out* **8/1**

2m 43.92s (2.82) **Going Correction** -0.025s/f (Stan) **10** Ran SP% **121.0**
Speed ratings (Par 101): **89,88,84,83,83 83,81,76,75,74**
toteswingers: 1&2 £4.60, 2&3 £3.50, 1&3 £4.50 CSF £16.34 CT £52.28 TOTE £3.20: £1.10, £2.00, £2.00; EX 27.40.
Owner Perry Bamonte **Bred** Ben Clarke **Trained** Kentisbeare, Devon
■ Donna Bamonte's first winner under rules.

FOCUS
A moderate handicap run at a steady gallop and one in which the market leaders came to the fore. The first two pulled clear and the winner edged towards the far rail late on. Unconvincing form, rated around the front pair.
T/Plt: £235.50 to a £1 stake. Pool: £43,031.41. 133.35 winning tickets. T/Qpdt: £33.00 to a £1 stake. Pool £4,618.74. 103.30 winning tickets. CR

1964 - (Foreign Racing) - See Raceform Interactive

1784 CHANTILLY (R-H)
Monday, May 9

OFFICIAL GOING: Turf: good

1965a PRIX DE GUICHE (GROUP 3) (3YO COLTS) (TURF) 1m 1f
2:55 (12:00) 3-Y-O **£34,482** (£13,793; £10,344; £6,896; £3,448)

RPR
1 **Absolutly Yes (FR)**[25] 3-9-2 0 FabienLefebvre 4 106
(Y-M Porzier, France) *settled 3rd: rdn 2f out: chal for ld 1f out: led 150yds out: r.o wl* **76/10**
2 *1* **Nobel Winner (FR)**[36] [1124] 3-9-2 0 MaximeGuyon 8 104
(J-M Beguigne, France) *settled towards rr: prog to 5th ent st: rdn 2f out: swtchd to outer: qcknd wl fnl f: wnt 2nd fnl 50yds* **83/10**
3 *3/4* **Ch'Tio Bilote (FR)**[11] 3-9-2 0 ChristopheSoumillon 5 102
(J-P Gallorini, France) *settled 4th: rdn 2f out: r.o: wnt 3rd ins fnl 50yds* **13/2**[3]
4 *3* **Inoubliable**[31] 3-9-2 0 Pierre-CharlesBoudot 6 96
(A Fabre, France) *sn wnt 2nd bhd pcemaker: rdn to ld 1 1/2f out: hdd 1f out: broke down bdly 50yds out but managed to stay uprt and fin* **9/10**[1]
5 *1/2* **Staros (IRE)**[29] [1265] 3-9-2 0 JohanVictoire 3 95
(E Lellouche, France) *settled 5th: rdn 2f out: no ex* **43/10**[2]
6 *6* **O'Kelly Hammer (IRE)**[15] 3-9-2 0 MickaelBarzalona 2 82
(A Fabre, France) *slowly away: rdn to set pce for favourite Inoubliable: [illegible]* **[illegible]**
7 *15* **Balbrown (FR)**[15] 3-9-2 0 GeraldMosse 7 51
(A Savujev, Czech Republic) *settled at rr: rdn early in st: fnd nthing: wknd qckly: t.o* **23/1**

1m 49.1s (-2.00) **7** Ran SP% **117.6**
WIN (incl. 1 euro stake): 8.60. PLACES: 3.50, 2.80, 2.70. DF: 31.30. SF: 59.40.
Owner Paul Sebag **Bred** Mme C Niederhauser Dietrich **Trained** France

NOTEBOOK
Absolutly Yes(FR), from a good family, gave his sire a first Pattern winner in this trial for the Prix du Jockey-Club. He will probably return here for the colt's classic next.
Inoubliable was sent off favourite but was weakening when he broke down badly and was subsequently put down.

1744 BEVERLEY (R-H)
Tuesday, May 10

OFFICIAL GOING: Good to firm (9.2)
Rail around bottom bend at narrowest configuration.
Wind: fresh 1/2 against Weather: overcast, breezy

1966 TURFTV BETTING SHOP SERVICE MAIDEN STKS 5f
2:00 (2:02) (Class 5) 2-Y-O **£2,422** (£715; £357) **Stalls** Low

Form RPR
1 **Caspar Netscher** 2-9-3 0 RobertWinston 1 85+
(Alan McCabe) *dwlt: hdwy on ins whn nt clr run and swtchd lft 2f out: chsd ldr appr fnl f: led jst ins fnl f: drew clr* **10/3**[3]
2 *2 1/4* **Last Bid** 2-8-12 0 DavidAllan 2 72+
(Tim Easterby) *s.i.s: hdwy over 1f out: styd on to chse wnr last 75yds* **25/1**
3 *nse* **Fulbright** 2-9-3 0 JoeFanning 3 77+
(Mark Johnston) *chsd ldrs: outpcd over 2f out: n.m.r and swtchd lft over 1f out: kpt on wl ins fnl f* **11/4**[2]
4 *2 1/4* **Whisky Bravo** 2-9-3 0 PhillipMakin 7 69
(David Brown) *s.i.s: hdwy on wd outside over 1f out: kpt on same pce* **16/1**
52 **5** *1 1/4* **Superplex**[8] [1744] 2-9-3 0 PaulHanagan 8 64
(John Quinn) *wnt lft s: chsd ldrs: hung lft over 1f out: wknd last 150yds* **9/4**[1]
6 *3 3/4* **Valley Of Hope** 2-9-3 0 TonyHamilton 9 51
(Richard Fahey) *wnt lft s: hdwy on outer to ld after 1f: clr 2f out: wknd and hdd jst ins fnl f* **13/2**
0 **7** *5* **Johnny Cavagin**[24] [1383] 2-9-0 0 (t) RobertLButler[(3)] 4 33
(Richard Guest) *chsd ldrs: hung rt 2f out: sn wknd* **66/1**
4 **8** *nk* **Mad For Fun (IRE)**[22] [1435] 2-8-12 0 MickyFenton 6 27
(Paul Midgley) *s.s: a bhd* **40/1**
9 *2 3/4* **Beechey's Beauty** 2-9-3 0 TomEaves 5 22
(Ann Duffield) *led 1f: chsd ldrs: lost pl over 1f out* **14/1**

63.55 secs (0.05) **Going Correction** -0.10s/f (Good) **9** Ran SP% **114.2**
Speed ratings (Par 93): **95,91,91,87,85 79,71,71,66**
Tote Swingers: 1&2 £7.80, 1&3 £1.20, 2&3 £16.10 CSF £80.30 TOTE £3.70: £1.30, £4.40, £1.50; EX 84.30.
Owner Charles Wentworth **Bred** Meon Valley Stud **Trained** Averham Park, Notts

FOCUS
They went a good pace and the first four home were all newcomers, so the race should produce winners. The winner looks useful.

NOTEBOOK
Caspar Netscher, a 65,000gns 2-y-o and a half-brother to a winning sprinter, was available at 20-1 when betting opened, so someone obviously knew something. Held up early, he had to be angled off the rail over 1f out, but fairly took off when in the clear and won with some authority. This May foal can only continue to improve and he may return here for the Brian Yeardley later this month before a possible crack at the Windsor Castle or Norfolk. (op 7-2 tchd 11-4)
Last Bid ◆ is a half-sister to a couple of winning sprinters, but she only fetched 800gns as a yearling so this performance suggests that connections may have picked up a bargain. She was very slowly away, but did some pleasing late work to snatch the runner-up spot, and a similar race should come her way with the experience under her belt. (tchd 20-1)
Fulbright, a 52,000gns foal and a half-brother to seven winners, including the Pattern-class sprinters Baltic King and Domingues, looked in need of the experience, but he kept on well after having much room to play with over 1f out. (op 5-2)
Whisky Bravo ◆, a half-brother to five winners over trips ranging from 5f-1m4f, was another to finish well after blowing the start and gives the impression he will appreciate another furlong. (op 20-1)
Superplex was only caught close home after trying to make all over C&D eight days earlier, but he could never get to the front this time and was reported to have hung left throughout. He rates the benchmark. Official explanation: jockey said colt hung left throughout (op 5-2 tchd 11-4)
Valley Of Hope, an £8,500 half-brother to a winning sprinter, showed plenty of early speed until the winner cut him down inside the final furlong, and he may appreciate an easier track. (op 11-2)

1967 FANTASTIC PRIZES AT LUCKY IN LOVE (S) STKS 5f
2:30 (2:33) (Class 6) 3-Y-O **£1,661** (£494; £247; £123) **Stalls** Low

Form RPR
-616 **1** **Meandmyshadow**[7] [1802] 3-8-11 **60** (p) GrahamGibbons 1 58
(Alan Brown) *chsd ldr: styd on fnl f: led clsng stages* **4/1**[3]
6243 **2** *nk* **Johnny Hancocks (IRE)**[14] [1595] 3-8-11 **65** TomEaves 5 57
(Linda Stubbs) *led: clr over 2f out: hdd towards fin* **11/8**[1]
36 **3** *1 1/4* **Poppy's Rocket (IRE)**[96] [396] 3-8-6 0 KellyHarrison 4 47
(Marjorie Fife) *dwlt: hdwy 2f out: wnt 3rd 1f out: kpt on* **20/1**
0-00 **4** *3* **Sleights Boy (IRE)**[8] [1749] 3-8-11 **53** PatrickMathers 3 41
(Ian McInnes) *chsd ldrs: kpt on same pce over 1f out* **40/1**
50-6 **5** *6* **Novalist**[15] [1561] 3-8-11 **57** LeeNewman 7 20
(Robin Bastiman) *chsd ldrs: wknd over 1f out* **20/1**
6004 **6** *3* **Running Water**[26] [1323] 3-8-3 **49** JamesSullivan[(3)] 9 —
(Hugh McWilliams) *in rr: lost pl over 1f out* **20/1**
400- **7** *3 1/2* **Clipthorne**[218] [6619] 3-8-6 **70** (p) PaulHanagan 6 —
(Ollie Pears) *dwlt: sn detached in rr: nvr on terms* **11/4**[2]
02-0 **8** *4 1/2* **Bigalo's Laura B (IRE)**[27] [1303] 3-8-7 **52** ow1 (e) RoystonFfrench 2 —
(G P Kelly) *chsd ldrs: hung lft and wknd 2f out* **33/1**
26-0 **9** *2 1/2* **Wild Hysteria (IRE)**[15] [1561] 3-8-11 **57** MickyFenton 8 —
(Tom Tate) *chsd ldrs on outside: sn given reminders: hung rt and lost pl 2f out: sn bhd and eased* **12/1**

63.53 secs (0.03) **Going Correction** -0.10s/f (Good) **9** Ran SP% **116.1**
Speed ratings (Par 97): **95,94,92,87,78 73,67,60,56**
Tote Swingers: 1&2 £1.10, 1&3 £12.50, 2&3 £9.90 CSF £9.26 TOTE £7.90: £2.00, £1.10, £4.00; EX 13.00.No bid for the winner.
Owner G Morrill **Bred** M J Dawson **Trained** Yedingham, N Yorks

FOCUS
A weak seller and very few got into it. The winner stepped up slightly on his recent C&D win.
Bigalo's Laura B(IRE) Official explanation: jockey said filly hung left

1968 ANNIE OXTOBY MEMORIAL H'CAP 5f
3:00 (3:02) (Class 5) (0-75,74) 4-Y-O+ **£2,298** (£684; £341; £170) **Stalls** Low

Form RPR
12-0 **1** **Highland Warrior**[39] [1073] 12-9-2 **69** MickyFenton 5 78
(Paul Midgley) *dwlt: hdwy over 1f out: styd on to ld last 75yds* **20/1**
2622 **2** *3/4* **Clear Ice (IRE)**[3] [1907] 4-8-2 **60** oh2 (b) DanielleMcCreery[(5)] 8 66
(Richard Guest) *w ldrs: chal ins fnl f: no ex* **13/2**[3]
120- **3** *nk* **Red Roar (IRE)**[193] [7207] 4-8-12 **65** PaulHanagan 10 70+
(Alan Berry) *in rr: hdwy on outer over 1f out: styd on ins fnl f* **12/1**
0654 **4** *3/4* **Fear Nothing**[21] [1469] 4-8-10 **63** (b) TomEaves 4 65
(Ian McInnes) *mid-div: hdwy over 1f out: kpt on ins fnl f* **16/1**
-006 **5** *nk* **Comptonspirit**[15] [1562] 7-9-5 **72** GrahamGibbons 7 73
(Brian Baugh) *chsd ldr: led appr fnl f: hdd ins fnl f: fdd* **12/1**
40-0 **6** *1* **Captain Scooby**[4] [1878] 5-9-6 **73** TonyHamilton 2 74+
(Richard Whitaker) *mid-div: outpcd over 3f out: hdwy on inner and nt clr run over 1f out: kpt on ins fnl f* **8/1**
11-3 **7** *1 1/2* **Caranbola**[4] [1878] 5-9-5 **72** RobertWinston 6 64
(Mel Brittain) *drvn to chse ldrs: nt clr run over 1f out: wknd jst ins fnl f* **15/8**[1]
5112 **8** *shd* **Lucky Art (USA)**[28] [1287] 5-8-5 **61** JamesSullivan[(3)] 1 53
(Ruth Carr) *led: hdd appr fnl f: sn wknd* **10/3**[2]
00-0 **9** *3/4* **Gertmegalush (IRE)**[17] [1523] 4-8-9 **62** BarryMcHugh 11 54+
(John Harris) *dwlt: a in rr on outer* **33/1**
00-0 **10** *3/4* **Kakapuka**[24] [1395] 4-9-7 **74** (v[1]) RussKennemore 9 60
(Anabel K Murphy) *in rr: effrt and hung lft over 1f out: n.m.r jst ins fnl f: nvr on terms* **33/1**
0-44 **11** *1* **Lees Anthem**[17] [1523] 4-8-9 **62** PatrickMathers 3 45
(Colin Teague) *chsd ldrs: wknd over 1f out* **12/1**

62.62 secs (-0.88) **Going Correction** -0.10s/f (Good) **11** Ran SP% **121.9**
Speed ratings (Par 103): **103,101,101,100,99 98,95,95,94,93 91**
Tote Swingers: 1&2 £49.40, 1&3 £49.40, 2&3 £19.70 CSF £147.53 TOTE £33.50: £7.00, £2.10, £3.10; EX 246.40.
Owner R Wardlaw **Bred** Rowcliffe Stud **Trained** Westow, N Yorks

FOCUS
A competitive sprint handicap and there was no hanging about, but the leaders may have gone off too quick and set it up for the closers. The winning time was 0.91 seconds faster than the seller. The winner is rated to his best form of the last couple of years.

Captain Scooby Official explanation: jockey said gelding was denied a clear run
Gertmegalush(IRE) Official explanation: jockey said gelding was denied a clear run
Kakapuka Official explanation: jockey said colt hung left throughout
Lees Anthem Official explanation: jockey said gelding was denied a clear run

1969 BEVERLEY MIDDLE DISTANCE SERIES H'CAP — 1m 4f 16y
3:30 (3:30) (Class 6) (0-60,66) 3-Y-O — **£2,590** (£770; £385; £192) **Stalls** Low

Form — RPR
0-41 **1** **Dance For Livvy (IRE)**[43] 1018 3-9-1 **57** .... PatrickDonaghy(3) 1 — 63
(Ben Haslam) *trckd ldrs: drvn over 3f out: led jst ins fnl f: all out* **10/3**[2]
3644 **2** *shd* **Surprise (IRE)**[15] 1574 3-9-2 **55** .... PaulHanagan 6 — 61
(Mark Rimmer) *trckd ldrs: lft in ld after 3f: hdd jst ins fnl f: rallied: jst hld* **11/2**
000- **3** *1 ¾* **Mayan Flight (IRE)**[250] 5682 3-8-12 **51** .... TonyHamilton 2 — 54
(Richard Whitaker) *hld up: effrt 3f out: styd on same pce fnl f* **20/1**
00-0 **4** *2 ½* **Market Maker (IRE)**[17] 1526 3-9-0 **53** .... DavidAllan 3 — 52
(Tim Easterby) *led: rn v wd, hdd and lost pl bnd after 3f: sme hdwy over 2f out: edgd lft over 1f out: one pce* **11/1**
06-3 **5** *1 ¼* **Goodmanyourself**[28] 1293 3-8-7 **46** .... MickyFenton 4 — 43
(Paul Midgley) *rrd s: in rr: effrt on outside over 2f out: kpt on fnl f* **5/1**[3]
000- **6** *3 ¼* **Tigerino (IRE)**[230] 6300 3-8-7 **46** oh1 .... KellyHarrison 5 — 38
(Chris Fairhurst) *hld up: jnd ldr after 3f: drvn over 3f out: wknd 2f out* **16/1**
5541 **7** *½* **Freedom Flyer (IRE)**[6] 1819 3-9-8 **66** 6ex .... DaleSwift(5) 7 — 57
(Brian Ellison) *chsd ldrs: drvn over 3f out: hung rt: lost pl over 1f out* **7/4**[1]
000- **8** *13* **Caledonia Prince**[238] 6053 3-8-7 **46** oh1 .... GrahamGibbons 8 — 24
(Pat Murphy) *sn chsng ldrs: carried v wd and lost pl bnd after 3f: hdwy over 5f out: lost pl 3f out: eased whn bhd* **25/1**

2m 37.84s (-1.96) **Going Correction** -0.275s/f (Firm) **8 Ran SP% 114.3**
Speed ratings (Par 97): **95,94,93,92,91 89,88,80**
Tote Swingers: 1&2 £7.60, 1&3 £25.80, 2&3 £29.40 CSF £21.99 CT £312.91 TOTE £3.80: £2.30, £1.70, £6.20; EX 23.70.
Owner Mark James **Bred** Lynn Lodge Stud **Trained** Middleham Moor, N Yorks

FOCUS
A modest handicap and a messy race with Market Maker trying to run out on the stable bend. The time was fair for the grade and the form has been rated through the runner-up.

1970 HAPPY 65TH BIRTHDAY GRAHAM ROBERTS H'CAP — 1m 100y
4:00 (4:00) (Class 4) (0-85,85) 4-Y-O+ — **£4,144** (£1,233; £616; £307) **Stalls** Low

Form — RPR
-422 **1** **Just Bond (IRE)**[15] 1560 9-9-3 **81** .... TomEaves 6 — 89
(Geoffrey Oldroyd) *hld up in rr: hdwy on ins over 2f out: nt clr run: burst through to ld last 75yds: hld on wl* **7/1**
2P-0 **2** *½* **Cheers For Thea (IRE)**[37] 1114 6-9-2 **85** ....(bt) LanceBetts(5) 9 — 92
(Tim Easterby) *swtchd rt after s: hld up in rr: smooth hdwy on outer over 2f out: chal jst ins fnl f: no ex towards fin* **25/1**
26-1 **3** *1 ¼* **Aquarian Spirit**[15] 1560 4-9-0 **78** .... PaulHanagan 2 — 82+
(Richard Fahey) *led: drvn 3f out: hdd jst ins fnl f: kpt on same pce* **15/8**[1]
-001 **4** *3* **Hail Promenader (IRE)**[13] 1621 5-9-1 **79** .... RobertWinston 1 — 76
(B W Hills) *dwlt: sn trcking ldrs: effrt 3f out: nt clr run: swtchd lft 1f out: kpt on one pce* **4/1**[2]
100- **5** *¾* **Ailsa Craig (IRE)**[200] 7062 5-8-13 **77** .... TonyHamilton 7 — 72
(Edwin Tuer) *trckd ldrs: wknd fnl f* **12/1**
4333 **6** *1 ¼* **Elijah Pepper (USA)**[8] 1747 6-8-12 **76** .... GrahamGibbons 4 — 68
(David Barron) *w ldrs: drvn 3f out: wknd fnl f* **9/2**[3]
-042 **7** *4 ½* **Handsome Falcon**[8] 1748 7-8-4 **71** oh1 ....(p) JamesSullivan(3) 5 — 53
(Ollie Pears) *rrd s: sn trcking ldrs and keen on outer: effrt over 3f out: lost pl over 1f out* **9/1**
0-06 **8** *hd* **Shadowtime**[8] 1747 6-9-1 **79** .... PatrickMathers 3 — 61
(Colin Teague) *dwlt: hld up in midfield: hdwy to trck ldrs 5f out: wknd over 1f out* **16/1**

1m 44.21s (-3.39) **Going Correction** -0.275s/f (Firm) **8 Ran SP% 112.9**
Speed ratings (Par 105): **105,104,103,100,99 98,93,93**
Tote Swingers: 1&2 £67.50, 1&3 £4.40, 2&3 £5.90 CSF £149.28 CT £457.65 TOTE £7.10: £1.80, £3.60, £1.10; EX 120.90.
Owner R C Bond **Bred** Schwindibode Ag **Trained** Brawby, N Yorks

FOCUS
A decent handicap which was strong run. The form should stand up with the winner rated to his best of the last couple of years and the second back to her bset too.

1971 NEW NOSEBAG CAFETERIA MAIDEN STKS — 7f 100y
4:30 (4:31) (Class 5) 3-Y-O — **£2,298** (£684; £341; £170) **Stalls** Low

Form — RPR
4- **1** **Taqaat (USA)**[213] 6743 3-9-3 0 .... TadhgO'Shea 1 — 79
(Mark Johnston) *mde all: drvn over 2f out: edgd lft over 1f out: styd on wl fnl f* **5/2**[2]
0 **2** *1 ¼* **Orbit The Moon (IRE)**[10] 1693 3-9-0 0 ....(t) SeanLevey(3) 3 — 76
(Michael Dods) *trckd ldrs: drvn 3f out: kpt on to chal jst ins fnl f: kpt on same pce* **12/1**
036- **3** *nk* **Power Punch (IRE)**[262] 5294 3-9-3 75 .... RobertWinston 4 — 75
(B W Hills) *w ldr: t.k.h: effrt over 2f out: hung rt: kpt on same pce fnl f* **4/5**[1]
4 *2 ¼* **Maharanee (USA)** 3-8-12 0 .... PhillipMakin 2 — 65
(Ann Duffield) *sn trcking ldrs: drvn over 2f out: one pce over 1f out* **8/1**[3]
00-4 **5** *7* **Gud Day (IRE)**[32] 1210 3-9-3 0 .... DanielTudhope 6 — 52
(Deborah Sanderson) *wnt lft s: hld up in rr: drvn over 3f out: wknd 2f out* **14/1**
000- **6** *2 ½* **Illawalla**[223] 6458 3-9-0 40 .... JamesSullivan(3) 5 — 46?
(Hugh McWilliams) *hld up in rr: drvn over 3f out: lost pl over 1f out* **100/1**

1m 34.14s (0.34) **Going Correction** -0.275s/f (Firm) **6 Ran SP% 110.6**
Speed ratings (Par 99): **87,85,85,82,74 71**
Tote Swingers: 1&2 £6.50, 1&3 £1.02, 2&3 £16.50 CSF £28.97 TOTE £3.80: £1.30, £6.00; EX 37.20.
Owner Hamdan Al Maktoum **Bred** Shadwell Farm LLC **Trained** Middleham Moor, N Yorks

FOCUS
An uncompetitive maiden, run at a modest pace, and little to get excited about. The form does make sense.

1972 BEST UK RACECOURSES ON TURFTV H'CAP — 1m 1f 207y
5:00 (5:00) (Class 5) (0-70,70) 3-Y-O — **£2,298** (£512; £512; £170) **Stalls** Low

Form — RPR
1-20 **1** **Unknown Rebel (IRE)**[10] 1683 3-9-2 **65** .... PhillipMakin 8 — 75
(Kevin Ryan) *trckd ldr: lft in ld 4f out: drvn clr over 1f out: styd on wl* **3/1**[1]
00-4 **2** *2* **Kodicil (IRE)**[26] 1327 3-8-7 **56** oh1 .... GrahamGibbons 7 — 62+
(Tim Walford) *chsd ldrs: carried wd 4f out: chsd wnr 3f out: styd on same pce appr fnl f* **10/1**
0-04 **2** *dht* **Lemon Drop Red (USA)**[17] 1524 3-8-13 **62** .... TomMcLaughlin 3 — 68
(Ed Dunlop) *s.i.s: hld up in rr: effrt 3f out: styd on wl fnl f* **8/1**
0-30 **4** *¾* **Jeu De Vivre (IRE)**[15] 1574 3-9-0 **63** .... JoeFanning 4 — 68
(Mark Johnston) *hld up in rr: t.k.h: effrt over 3f out: kpt on same pce appr fnl f* **13/2**
20-3 **5** *6* **Residence And Spa (IRE)**[15] 1559 3-9-7 **70** .... DavidAllan 1 — 63
(Tim Easterby) *stmbld s: drvn and sme hdwy over 6f out: lost pl 2f out* **15/2**
65-0 **6** *1 ¼* **Smart Step**[34] 1189 3-8-12 **61** .... RoystonFfrench 6 — 51
(Mark Johnston) *in tch: hdwy to chse ldrs 3f out: wknd over 1f out* **10/1**
40-4 **7** *6* **Al Andalyya (USA)**[22] 1446 3-9-6 **69** .... TadhgO'Shea 2 — 47
(David Lanigan) *s.i.s: t.k.h towards rr: hdwy to chse ldrs over 3f out: hung rt and lost pl over 2f out* **11/2**[3]
0-63 **8** *66* **Subramaniam**[17] 1526 3-8-11 **60** .... PaulMulrennan 9 — —
(James Given) *led: hung bdly lft: rn wd and hdd 4f out: lost pl: bhd and wd over 2f out: heavily eased: virtually p.u* **4/1**[2]

2m 4.42s (-2.58) **Going Correction** -0.275s/f (Firm) **8 Ran SP% 114.8**
Speed ratings (Par 99): **99,97,97,96,92 91,86,33**Place: Lemon Drop Red £3.30 Kodicil £4.00. Exacta: Unknown Rebel,LDR £13.81 UR,K £18.30 CSF: UR,LDR £13.81 UR,K £16.92. Tricast UR,LDR,K £106.07, UR,K,LDR £108.79. Tote Swingers: 1&2 £3.20, 1&3 £4.80, 2&3 £33.70. TOTE £4.60: £1.60 Trifecta £027 Owner D Reilly & Mrs C Reilly.

FOCUS
An ordinary handicap and the form may be dubious with a few of these appearing to not handle the track/ground. A clear personal best from the winner to confirm form with the second and fourth.
Residence And Spa(IRE) Official explanation: jockey said gelding stumbled on leaving stalls
Subramaniam Official explanation: jockey said colt hung left throughout
T/Plt: £189.50 to a £1 stake. Pool: £50,286.41. 193.62 winning tickets. T/Qpdt: £49.00 to a £1 stake. Pool: £2,895.15. 334.80 winning tickets. WG

1812 SOUTHWELL (L-H)
Tuesday, May 10

OFFICIAL GOING: Standard
Wind: Light across Weather: Cloudy

1973 SAFETY PROBLEMS SOLUTIONS H'CAP — 2m (F)
5:30 (5:30) (Class 6) (0-60,58) 4-Y-O+ — **£1,706** (£503; £252) **Stalls** Low

Form — RPR
0-03 **1** **Three White Socks (IRE)**[17] 1519 4-8-5 **45** .... PaulPickard(3) 8 — 56+
(Brian Ellison) *trckd ldng pair: hdwy over 3f out: rdn to ld wl over 1f out: sn clr: styd on wl* **7/2**[3]
4-53 **2** *5* **Trojan Gift (USA)**[28] 1291 4-9-7 **58** .... BarryMcHugh 4 — 63
(Julie Camacho) *hld up in tch: hdwy 4f out: wd st: sn rdn: chsd wnr appr fnl f: sn drvn and no imp* **5/2**[1]
0033 **3** *3 ¼* **Bold Adventure**[21] 1466 7-9-5 **53** .... StevieDonohoe 1 — 54
(Willie Musson) *hld up in tch: hdwy 4f out: wd st and sn chsng ldrs: rdn wl over 1f out: kpt on same pce* **9/2**
0121 **4** *5* **Six Of Clubs**[21] 1473 5-9-0 **55** ....(b) JakePayne(7) 2 — 50+
(Bill Turner) *t.k.h: trckd ldng pair on inner: led 5f out and sn clr: rdn 3f out: hdd & wknd wl over 1f out* **3/1**[2]
16-6 **5** *¾* **Court Wing (IRE)**[28] 1297 5-9-0 **51** .... SimonPearce(3) 5 — 45
(Richard Price) *trckd ldr: effrt over 4f out: rdn along over 3f out: sn drvn and outpcd* **16/1**
3625 **6** *4 ½* **Dot's Delight**[21] 1473 7-9-0 **48** .... PJMcDonald 7 — 37
(Mark Rimell) *hld up towards rr: effrt over 4f out: sn rdn along and nvr a factor* **11/1**
00-0 **7** *51* **Nobbys Girl**[8] 1750 6-8-11 **45** .... LukeMorris 3 — —
(Ronald Harris) *led: rdn along over 5f out: sn hdd & wknd qckly: t.o fnl 2f* **66/1**
000- **8** *7* **The Mighty Mod (USA)**[186] 7330 4-8-1 **45** .... LeonnaMayor(7) 6 — —
(Michael Chapman) *a in rr: outpcd over 4f out: t.o fnl 2f* **50/1**

3m 45.54s (0.04) **Going Correction** +0.025s/f (Slow)
WFA 4 from 5yo+ 3lb **8 Ran SP% 111.6**
Speed ratings (Par 101): **100,97,95,93,93 90,65,61**
Tote Swingers: 1&2 £3.60, 1&3 £4.20, 2&3 £3.70 CSF £12.04 CT £37.45 TOTE £5.00: £1.90, £1.90, £2.10; EX 17.30.
Owner Racing Management & Training Ltd **Bred** Hippodromos Y Caballos S A **Trained** Norton, N Yorks

FOCUS
A moderate handicap in which a moderate gallop (resulting in a slow time) increased leaving the back straight. The winner raced centre to far side in the straight. The bare form is limited but the winner has more to offer.
Nobbys Girl Official explanation: jockey said mare had no more to give

1974 SEVEN 7 SEVEN ACCOUNTANCY MEDIAN AUCTION MAIDEN STKS — 1m (F)
6:00 (6:00) (Class 6) 3-5-Y-O — **£1,706** (£503; £252) **Stalls** Low

Form — RPR
1 **William Haigh (IRE)** 3-9-0 0 .... PJMcDonald 6 — 74
(Alan Swinbank) *trckd ldrs: hdwy on outer 1/2-way: led 3f out: rdn 2f out: hdd over 1f out: drvn and rallied ins fnl f to ld last 50yds* **6/1**[3]
0 **2** *½* **Hab Reeh**[27] 1321 3-9-0 0 ....(t) PhilipRobinson 7 — 73
(Clive Brittain) *prom: effrt on inner over 2f out: rdn to ld over 1f out: drvn ins fnl f: hdd and no ex last 50yds* **16/1**
232- **3** *2* **Frosty Friday**[144] 7907 3-8-9 64 .... AdrianNicholls 4 — 63
(J R Jenkins) *chsd ldrs on wd outside: rdn along 1/2-way: wd st and drvn over 2f out: kpt on u.p: nrst fin* **7/1**
442 **4** *2 ¼* **McCool Bannanas**[29] 1277 3-9-0 64 .... ShaneKelly 5 — 63
(James Unett) *sn led: rdn along and hdd 3f out: drvn over 2f out and grad wknd* **17/2**
5 *1 ¼* **Zennor**[561] 7071 4-9-8 0 .... RichardKingscote 10 — 58
(Tom Dascombe) *prom: effrt 3f out: rdn over 2f out: drvn wl over 1f out and sn one pce* **5/2**[1]
00- **6** *12* **Kambis**[172] 7503 3-8-7 0 .... TalibHussain(7) 9 — 33
(Luca Cumani) *s.i.s: a in rr* **16/1**
000- **7** *2 ¾* **Damascus Symphony**[206] 6920 3-8-6 59 .... SimonPearce(3) 1 — 21
(James Bethell) *in tch on inner: rdn along 1/2-way: sn outpcd* **33/1**
8 *2 ¾* **Money Bridge**[12] 4-9-8 0 .... LeeTopliss(5) 8 — 23
(Derek Shaw) *dwlt: a in rr: bhd fnl 3f* **9/1**
9 *5* **Tobetall**[14] 4-9-8 0 .... BarryMcHugh 3 — —
(Malcolm Jefferson) *dwlt: a in rr: bhd fnl 3f* **100/1**

5 **10** *36* **Faith And Hope (IRE)**^{79} [624] 3-8-9 0..........................(t) LukeMorris 2 —
(James Fanshawe) *chsd ldrs: rdn along 1/2-way: sn drvn and wknd qckly: bhd and eased fr wl over 1f out* **7/2**^{2}

1m 44.19s (0.49) **Going Correction** +0.025s/f (Slow)
WFA 3 from 4yo 13lb **10** Ran SP% **113.8**
Speed ratings (Par 101): **98,97,95,93,92 80,77,74,69,33**
Tote Swingers: 1&2 £16.60, 1&3 £8.00, 2&3 £14.60 CSF £94.22 TOTE £9.80: £2.50, £3.50, £2.00; EX 72.30.
Owner Shropshire Wolves II **Bred** Mrs C L Weld **Trained** Melsonby, N Yorks

FOCUS
The proximity of the 64-rated third and fourth confirms this is just ordinary form, but the first two should be able to better these bare facts in due course. The gallop was a reasonable one and the winner came down the centre in the straight.
Faith And Hope(IRE) Official explanation: jockey said filly would not face the kickback

1975 LOUGHBOROUGH GRAMMAR SCHOOL F '48 (S) STKS 6f (F)
6:30 (6:30) (Class 6) 3-Y-O **£1,706** (£503; £252) Stalls Low

Form RPR
004- **1** **Paper Dreams (IRE)**^{190} [7269] 3-8-7 62..........................(p) PaulHanagan 3 59
(Kevin Ryan) *chsd ldr: rdn 2f out: drvn to ld jst ins fnl f: kpt on* **11/4**^{1}

-331 **2** *2* **Jay Jays Joy**^{28} [1293] 3-9-3 58..........................(b) LeeNewman 2 62
(David Barron) *dwlt: sn chsng ldrs: hdwy 1/2-way: rdn 2f out: drvn over 1f out: styd on ins fnl f: nrst fin* **11/4**^{1}

4140 **3** *1 1/2* **Goal (IRE)**^{6} [1819] 3-8-9 62..........................(bt^{1}) RobertLButler$^{(3)}$ 1 52
(Richard Guest) *led: qcknd clr bef 1/2-way: rdn 2f out: drvn over 1f out: hdd jst ins fnl f: sn wknd* **7/2**^{2}

4353 **4** *1/2* **Winning Draw (IRE)**^{22} [1439] 3-8-7 55..........................(p) MickyFenton 6 46
(Paul Midgley) *stdd and swtchd lft s: bhd: rdn over 2f out: kpt on appr fnl f: nrst fin* **5/1**^{3}

2540 **5** *3 1/2* **Local Diktator**^{8} [1753] 3-9-3 60..........................(t) LukeMorris 4 44
(Ronald Harris) *towards rr: hdwy on inner wl over 2f out: sn rdn and no imp* **7/1**

0460 **6** *7* **Jambo Bibi (IRE)**^{16} [1543] 3-8-7 56..........................(b) RichardKingscote 5 12
(Bruce Hellier) *chsd ldng pair: rdn along bef 1/2-way: sn wknd* **14/1**

1m 17.22s (0.72) **Going Correction** +0.025s/f (Slow) **6** Ran SP% **111.4**
Speed ratings (Par 97): **96,93,91,90,86 77**
Tote Swingers: 1&2 £1.40, 1&3 £3.70, 2&3 £2.80 CSF £10.33 TOTE £4.20: £1.80, £1.80; EX 11.60.No bid for the winner.
Owner Opus Industrial Services Partnership **Bred** J Joyce **Trained** Hambleton, N Yorks

FOCUS
No more than a modest seller. The pace was sound and the winner came down the centre in the straight. She is rated to her maiden form.
Local Diktator Official explanation: jockey said colt hung badly left on bend

1976 A&G PLASTERING CONTRACTORS CLASSIFIED CLAIMING STKS 1m (F)
7:00 (7:01) (Class 6) 3-Y-O+ **£1,706** (£503; £252) Stalls Low

Form RPR
66-1 **1** **Bolodenka (IRE)**^{16} [1538] 9-9-7 69.......................... PaulHanagan 1 78
(Richard Fahey) *trckd ldr: led over 3f out: sn clr: rdn out* **11/8**^{2}

2435 **2** *17* **Faithful Ruler (USA)**^{21} [1448] 7-9-4 74..........................(p) LukeMorris 4 48
(Ronald Harris) *dwlt and reminders s: chsd ldng pair and rdn along bef 1/2-way: hdwy to chse wnr over 2f out: sn drvn and no imp: eased fnl f* **5/6**^{1}

400- **3** *16* **Kathindi (IRE)**^{203} [7003] 4-8-9 55.......................... LeonnaMayor$^{(7)}$ 3 —
(Michael Chapman) *in rr: sme hdwy over 2f out: tk remote 3rd appr fnl f* **66/1**

10-4 **4** *12* **Rudegirl (IRE)**^{14} [1578] 3-8-9 75..........................(p) HayleyTurner 2 —
(Conor Dore) *led: rdn along 1/2-way: hdd over 3f out and sn wknd* **10/1**^{3}

1m 42.94s (-0.76) **Going Correction** +0.025s/f (Slow)
WFA 3 from 4yo+ 13lb **4** Ran SP% **107.2**
Speed ratings (Par 101): **104,87,71,59**
CSF £2.82 TOTE £2.40; EX 3.00.
Owner Aidan J Ryan **Bred** Kildaragh Stud **Trained** Musley Bank, N Yorks
■ Stewards' Enquiry : Paul Hanagan caution: used whip when clearly winning

FOCUS
With the favourite underperforming this was a very one-sided race but, although the gallop seemed no more than fair, it was run over a second quicker than the maiden over the same trip an hour earlier. The winner came down the centre and is rated to last season's form.
Faithful Ruler(USA) Official explanation: jockey said gelding never travelled

1977 SHARPLINE DECORATORS H'CAP 1m 3f (F)
7:30 (7:30) (Class 4) (0-80,80) 4-Y-O+ **£3,561** (£1,059; £529; £264) Stalls Low

Form RPR
3110 **1** **Beau Fighter**^{13} [1608] 6-8-5 67..........................(p) SeanLevey$^{(3)}$ 9 79
(Gary Moore) *a.p: hdwy on outer and cl up 4f out: led wl over 2f out and sn rdn clr: edgd rt and kpt on u.p fnl f* **7/2**^{1}

5200 **2** *2 1/2* **The Lock Master (IRE)**^{4} [1874] 4-9-5 78.......................... NeilChalmers 1 85
(Michael Appleby) *s.i.s and bhd: hdwy and wl st: rdn to chse ldrs wl over 1f out: drvn and hung lft ent fnl f: kpt on: nt rch wnr* **5/1**^{2}

45-0 **3** *3/4* **Persian Peril**^{28} [1291] 7-8-10 69.......................... PJMcDonald 3 75
(Alan Swinbank) *hld up in tch: hdwy 4f out: rdn to chse ldrs over 2f out: drvn and keeping on whn n.m.r ent fnl f: sn one pce* **7/1**

210 **4** *3 3/4* **Cobo Bay**^{60} [835] 6-9-7 80..........................(b) HayleyTurner 4 79
(Conor Dore) *led: rdn along 4f out: hdd wl over 2f out: sn drvn and kpt on same pce* **7/2**^{1}

2032 **5** *1/2* **Trachonitis (IRE)**^{19} [1509] 7-8-11 70.......................... PaulHanagan 6 68
(J R Jenkins) *trckd ldrs: smooth hdwy over 3f out: chsd ldng pair wl over 2f out: sn rdn and btn over 1f out* **13/2**^{3}

124/ **6** *2 1/2* **John Forbes**^{457} [7170] 9-8-10 72.......................... PaulPickard$^{(3)}$ 7 66
(Brian Ellison) *towards rr: rdn along 3f out: sme late hdwy* **14/1**

5343 **7** *7* **Camps Bay (USA)**^{41} [1046] 7-8-13 72.......................... KirstyMilczarek 5 53
(Conor Dore) *hld up in tch: hdwy to chse ldrs over 4f out: rdn along over 3f out: sn wknd* **8/1**

5230 **8** *hd* **Jungle Bay**^{69} [725] 4-8-12 71.......................... JimmyQuinn 8 52
(Jane Chapple-Hyam) *prom: rdn along over 3f out: sn drvn and wknd* **11/1**

05-0 **9** *8* **Urban Space**^{40} [1061] 5-8-7 69.......................... MartinHarley$^{(3)}$ 2 35
(Conor Dore) *chsd ldrs on inner: rdn along over 4f out and sn wknd* **50/1**

2m 26.69s (-1.31) **Going Correction** +0.025s/f (Slow) **9** Ran SP% **115.0**
Speed ratings (Par 105): **105,103,102,99,99 97,92,92,86**
Tote Swingers: 1&2 £4.70, 1&3 £8.90, 2&3 £11.70 CSF £20.86 CT £115.30 TOTE £4.40: £2.30, £1.40, £3.20; EX 34.30.
Owner The Hillians **Bred** Mrs P G Kingston **Trained** Lower Beeding, W Sussex
■ Stewards' Enquiry : Neil Chalmers one-day ban: careless riding (May 24)

FOCUS
Mainly exposed performers in a fair handicap. The gallop was an ordinary one to 3f out and the winner was another to come down the centre. He is rated back to his best old form.

Jungle Bay Official explanation: jockey said colt had no more to give

1978 TAGPLUS SAFETY & IMAGE AT WORK H'CAP 1m (F)
8:00 (8:01) (Class 5) (0-70,70) 4-Y-O+ **£2,388** (£705; £352) Stalls Low

Form RPR
-325 **1** **Border Owl (IRE)**^{13} [1613] 6-8-13 62.......................... PaulHanagan 2 70
(Peter Salmon) *trckd ldng pair: hdwy and cl up 1/2-way: led wl over 2f out: rdn over 1f out: kpt on: dismntd after line - lame* **7/4**^{1}

5035 **2** *1 3/4* **Elusive Fame (USA)**^{16} [1538] 5-8-13 69..........................(b) JasonHart$^{(7)}$ 3 73
(Mark Johnston) *trckd ldrs on inner: hdwy 3f out: rdn to chse wnr over 1f out: edgd rt and kpt on same pce fnl f* **4/1**^{3}

4303 **3** *3 3/4* **Gordy Bee (USA)**^{16} [1058] 5-8-7 56..........................(be) RobbieFitzpatrick 1 51
(Richard Guest) *sn led: rdn along over 3f out: hdd wl over 2f out: sn drvn and kpt on same pce* **7/1**

-503 **4** *1 3/4* **Miss Bootylishes**^{88} [508] 6-9-4 70.......................... AmyBaker$^{(3)}$ 6 61
(Paul Burgoyne) *hld up: hdwy on inner 3f out: rdn to chse ldrs 2f out: sn drvn and no imp* **7/1**

055- **5** *hd* **Mudhish (IRE)**^{288} [4438] 6-9-1 64..........................(b) PhilipRobinson 4 55
(Clive Brittain) *t.k.h: in tch: effrt to chse ldrs 3f out: rdn over 2f out and sn wknd* **3/1**^{2}

0-5 **6** *28* **Gracelightening**^{88} [516] 4-8-7 56 oh1.......................... RichardKingscote 7 —
(Bruce Hellier) *chsd ldr on outer: pushed along 5f out: rdn 4f out and sn wknd: bhd and eased fnl 2f* **25/1**

1m 43.68s (-0.02) **Going Correction** +0.025s/f (Slow) **6** Ran SP% **110.2**
Speed ratings (Par 103): **101,99,95,93,93 65**
Tote Swingers: 1&2 £1.10, 1&3 £4.40, 2&3 £7.40 CSF £8.68 TOTE £2.40: £1.70, £1.80; EX 8.70.
Owner Viscount Environmental **Bred** Gainsborough Stud Management Ltd **Trained** Kirk Deighton, West Yorks

FOCUS
A modest handicap run at just an ordinary gallop. The winner continued the trend of coming down the centre in the straight. He's rated to something like last year's form.

1979 UCD SHOPFITTING H'CAP 7f (F)
8:30 (8:32) (Class 6) (0-60,65) 4-Y-O+ **£1,706** (£503; £252) Stalls Low

Form RPR
-041 **1** **Koo And The Gang (IRE)**^{6} [1814] 4-9-9 65 6ex.......................... PaulPickard$^{(3)}$ 8 77+
(Brian Ellison) *trckd ldr: led 3f out and sn rdn clr: kpt on strly fnl f* **4/5**^{1}

0-03 **2** *3 1/2* **Jamarjo (IRE)**^{6} [1818] 4-8-13 52..........................(b^{1}) MartinLane 7 55
(Steve Gollings) *towards rr and sn rdn along: hdwy 2f out: styd on strly appr fnl f: nrst fin* **16/1**

2466 **3** *2* **Elusive Warrior (USA)**^{28} [1292] 8-8-12 58..........................(p) NoraLooby$^{(7)}$ 5 55
(Alan McCabe) *led: rdn along and hdd 3f out: drvn and edgd rt ent fnl f: lost 2nd last 100yds* **11/1**

5365 **4** *2 1/2* **Tomintoul Star**^{21} [1468] 5-8-9 51..........................(b) JamesSullivan$^{(3)}$ 2 41
(Ruth Carr) *trckd ldrs: hdwy to chse ldng pair wl over 2f out: drvn wl over 1f out and sn one pce* **13/2**^{3}

4-65 **5** *2 3/4* **Vogarth**^{105} [290] 7-8-0 46 oh1..........................(b) LeonnaMayor$^{(7)}$ 9 29
(Michael Chapman) *chsd ldrs: rdn along wl over 2f out: wknd wl over 1f out* **50/1**

2224 **6** *3 3/4* **Meydan Style (USA)**^{6} [1818] 5-8-9 48.......................... RoystonFfrench 10 21
(Bruce Hellier) *in tch on outer: hdwy 3f out: rdn over 2f out and sn no imp* **12/1**

6060 **7** *2* **Moon Lightning (IRE)**^{63} [800] 5-8-7 46 oh1.......................... PaulHanagan 3 13
(Tina Jackson) *in rr: wd st: sn rdn and no hdwy* **22/1**

556- **8** *5* **Deferto Delphi**^{234} [6186] 4-9-7 60.......................... PJMcDonald 1 14
(Barry Murtagh) *in tch on inner: rdn along 1/2-way: sn wknd* **66/1**

2223 **9** *2 1/2* **Gold Story**^{28} [1283] 4-9-6 59..........................(e^{1}) TonyCulhane 4 —
(George Baker) *in tch: rdn along 1/2-way: sn wknd* **11/2**^{2}

000- **10** *10* **Cookie Galore**^{270} [5055] 4-9-0 53.......................... RobbieFitzpatrick 6 —
(John Harris) *dwlt: a towards rr* **66/1**

1m 29.85s (-0.45) **Going Correction** +0.025s/f (Slow) **10** Ran SP% **115.5**
Speed ratings (Par 101): **103,99,96,93,90 86,84,78,75,64**
Tote Swingers: 1&2 £7.80, 1&3 £5.30, 2&3 £21.20 CSF £15.70 CT £86.75 TOTE £1.50: £1.10, £2.20, £2.20; EX 15.60.
Owner Koo's Racing Club **Bred** Vincent Howley **Trained** Norton, N Yorks

FOCUS
A modest handicap that went to the progressive and well-backed market leader. The gallop was fair and the winner raced centre to far side in the straight. The time was good for the grade.
T/Plt: £191.30 to a £1 stake. Pool: £52,758. 191.30 winning tickets. T/Qpdt: £27.10 to a £1 stake. Pool: £4,769. 130.10 winning tickets. JR

1912 WARWICK (L-H)
Tuesday, May 10

OFFICIAL GOING: Good (good to firm in places; 7.5)
Wind: Light behind Weather: Cloudy with sunny spells

1980 JOIN TODAY AT REWARDS4RACING.COM H'CAP 6f
2:10 (2:11) (Class 6) (0-65,65) 3-Y-O **£2,047** (£604; £302) Stalls Low

Form RPR
-041 **1** **Barkston Ash**^{7} [1802] 3-9-3 61 6ex.......................... DuranFentiman 14 72+
(Eric Alston) *chsd ldrs: led over 2f out: rdn out* **4/1**^{2}

4261 **2** *2* **Close To The Edge (IRE)**^{13} [1624] 3-9-7 65.......................... ShaneKelly 15 70
(Alan McCabe) *unruly in stalls: dwlt: hdwy over 2f out: rdn to chse wnr over 1f out: r.o* **8/1**

00-0 **3** *2 1/4* **Atia**^{14} [1579] 3-9-2 60.......................... JimmyFortune 7 57+
(Jonathan Portman) *mid-div: swtchd lft over 4f out: hdwy u.p over 1f out: r.o: nt rch ldrs* **25/1**

060 **4** *1 1/2* **Shaunas Spirit (IRE)**^{29} [1270] 3-8-7 51 oh2.......................... JimmyQuinn 5 44
(Dean Ivory) *in rr: hdwy u.p fr over 1f out: nrst fin* **100/1**

14 **5** *1/2* **Royal Bajan (USA)**^{28} [1294] 3-9-2 60.......................... PaulMulrennan 11 51
(James Given) *led over 3f: rdn over 1f out: styd on same pce* **15/2**^{3}

5623 **6** *nk* **Dancing Tara**^{12} [1629] 3-8-10 54.......................... GregFairley 10 44
(David Evans) *mid-div: hdwy 1/2-way: sn rdn: styd on same pce fr over 1f out* **16/1**

-006 **7** *hd* **Gothic Chick**^{17} [1524] 3-8-4 51 oh2..........................(p) JohnFahy$^{(3)}$ 12 40
(Alan McCabe) *sn pushed along in rr: styd on u.p fr over 1f out: nvr nrr* **50/1**

53-2 **8** *1 3/4* **Crucis Abbey (IRE)**^{39} [1084] 3-9-4 62.......................... JamieSpencer 3 46
(James Unett) *chsd ldrs: rdn over 2f out: wknd fnl f* **7/2**^{1}

0000 **9** *1 1/2* **Ajaafa**^{25} [1359] 3-8-13 57.......................... NeilChalmers 9 36
(Michael Appleby) *prom: rdn over 2f out: wknd fnl f* **50/1**

0662 **10** *3/4* **Lady Mango (IRE)**^{14} [1589] 3-8-13 57.......................... LukeMorris 1 34
(Ronald Harris) *prom: rdn over 3f out: wknd over 1f out* **14/1**

3304 **11** *hd* **Quadra Hop (IRE)**[8] 1753 3-9-0 **58**.................................(t) DavidProbert 2 34
(Bryn Palling) *s.i.s: sn chsng ldrs: rdn 2f out: wknd fnl f* **8/1**

540- **12** *nse* **Loved To Bits**[187] 7313 3-9-2 **60**.................................. FergusSweeney 8 36
(Peter Makin) *s.i.s: a in rr* **20/1**

0300 **13** *½* **Alfraamsey**[20] 1494 3-8-9 **56**.. MartinHarley(3) 16 30
(Mick Channon) *sn pushed along and a in rr* **28/1**

0035 **14** *¾* **Majestic Ridge (IRE)**[8] 1776 3-8-12 **56**....................(v) CathyGannon 17 28
(David Evans) *s.i.s: hdwy over 4f out: rdn over 2f out: sn wknd* **20/1**

6-55 **15** *8* **Acclamatory**[17] 1521 3-9-4 **62**.. JamesDoyle 13 8
(Stuart Williams) *prom: rdn 1/2-way: wknd over 2f out* **14/1**

1m 11.84s (0.04) **Going Correction** -0.05s/f (Good) **15** Ran SP% **117.2**
Speed ratings (Par 97): **97,94,91,89,88 88,88,85,83,82 82,82,81,80,70**
Tote Swingers: 1&2 £5.30, 1&3 £21.50, 2&3 £30.80 CSF £31.85 CT £724.01 TOTE £4.90: £3.10, £3.80, £11.00; EX 24.20.

Owner The Selebians **Bred** Jonathan Shack **Trained** Longton, Lancs

FOCUS
A modest sprint handicap but, as at recent meetings, the rail in the straight proved the place to be. The winner is rated back to his 2yo best.
Majestic Ridge(IRE) Official explanation: jockey said gelding lost an off-fore shoe

1981 EUROPEAN BREEDERS' FUND MAIDEN FILLIES' STKS 5f 110y
2:40 (2:40) (Class 5) 2-Y-O **£3,626** (£1,079; £539; £269) **Stalls** Low

Form RPR

1 **Sajwah (IRE)** 2-9-0 0.. RichardHills 1 81+
(B W Hills) *trckd ldrs: rdn to chse ldr and hung lft over 1f out: led wl ins fnl f: eased nr fin* **5/2**[2]

4 **2** *¾* **Supreme Quest**[22] 1441 2-9-0 0...................................... SteveDrowne 5 78
(Roger Charlton) *led: rdn and hdd wl ins fnl f* **5/2**[2]

3 **3** *¾* **Esentepe (IRE)**[9] 1726 2-9-0 0.. RyanMoore 3 76
(Richard Hannon) *chsd ldr tl rdn and edgd lft over 1f out: styd on same pce ins fnl f* **9/4**[1]

4 *4 ½* **Naseem Alyasmeen (IRE)** 2-8-11 0......................... MartinHarley(3) 7 64+
(Mick Channon) *dwlt: hdwy over 3f out: rdn over 2f out: wknd fnl f* **33/1**

5 *4 ½* **Nimiety** 2-9-0 0.. GregFairley 2 46
(Mark Johnston) *chsd ldrs: rdn over 3f out: wknd over 1f out* **20/1**

6 *nk* **Ivor's Princess** 2-9-0 0... JamesMillman 4 45
(Rod Millman) *s.i.s: outpcd: r.o ins fnl f* **50/1**

6 **7** *12* **Stormin Gordon (IRE)**[21] 1455 2-9-0 0.......................... NeilChalmers 6 —
(Michael Appleby) *chsd ldrs: rdn over 2f out: wknd wl over 1f out* **9/2**[3]

66.12 secs (0.22) **Going Correction** -0.05s/f (Good) **7** Ran SP% **115.8**
Speed ratings (Par 90): **96,95,94,88,82 81,65**
Tote Swingers: 1&2 £2.40, 1&3 £1.60, 2&3 £1.80 CSF £9.30 TOTE £2.60: £1.50, £1.90; EX 11.60.

Owner Hamdan Al Maktoum **Bred** Shadwell Estate Company Limited **Trained** Lambourn, Berks

FOCUS
An ordinary juvenile fillies' event in previous seasons, but a number of major yards were represented. the second and third will dictate the level of the form.

NOTEBOOK
Sajwah(IRE) ◆ made a nice start to her career in beating two more experienced rivals. She had to battle, but found extra and should know more next time. She will appreciate further in future and her trainer, who said she had done all her work on a synthetic surface, hopes she might make up into a Royal Ascot filly, with the Albany rather than the Queen Mary the possible target. (op 2-1 tchd 15-8)
Supreme Quest built on her debut fourth in a maiden auction and, having got to the rail in the straight, looked likely to prevail. However, she eventually had to give best but looks capable of getting off the mark if going on from this. (op 7-2 tchd 4-1)
Esentepe(IRE), another who is bred to need further, was being niggled virtually throughout to hold her prominent pitch. She kept plugging away and was not beaten far, so can do better over longer trips in due course. (op 11-4, tchd 3-1 in places)
Naseem Alyasmeen(IRE) has a middle-distance pedigree and, having missed the break, did well to finish as close as she did on this debut.
Nimiety, yet another who will appreciate further in time, chased the pace early before fading. (op 14-1)
Ivor's Princess, a half-sister to four-time winning juvenile Rosina Grey, was outpaced early on this debut before getting the hang of things and running on late. She should be better with this under her belt.
Stormin Gordon(IRE), whose price collapsed from 33/1 to as low as 2/1 before drifting in the run up to the race, was close up early but her supporters knew their fate early in the straight, as she came under pressure and dropped away to finish last. Official explanation: jockey said filly lost its action (op 11-2 tchd 6-1)

1982 RACING UK HORSERACING IN YOUR HOME H'CAP 5f
3:10 (3:10) (Class 5) (0-70,68) 4-Y-O+ **£2,388** (£705; £352) **Stalls** Low

Form RPR

0-00 **1** **Make My Dream**[4] 1864 8-9-7 **68**.. ChrisCatlin 3 76
(John Gallagher) *hld up: hdwy 2f out: rdn to ld wl ins fnl f: r.o* **5/1**[3]

50-3 **2** *nk* **Triple Dream**[8] 1752 6-9-5 **66**...(tp) LukeMorris 1 73
(Milton Bradley) *chsd ldrs: rdn over 1f out: led ins fnl f: sn hdd: r.o* **3/1**[2]

0212 **3** *2 ¼* **Island Legend (IRE)**[14] 1584 5-9-3 **64**.................(p) RichardKingscote 6 64
(Milton Bradley) *led: rdn whn hung rt and hdd ins fnl f: styd on same pce* **11/8**[1]

4010 **4** *shd* **Francis Albert**[9] 1716 5-8-2 **56**..................................(b) JosephYoung(7) 4 55
(Michael Mullineaux) *chsd ldr tl rdn over 1f out: no ex ins fnl f* **20/1**

-351 **5** *3* **Bateleur**[7] 1787 7-9-1 **65** 6ex.. MartinHarley(3) 2 53
(Mick Channon) *hld up: hdwy 2f out: rdn over 1f out: wknd ins fnl f* **7/1**

510- **6** *14* **Wreningham**[208] 6880 6-9-1 **62**.. WilliamCarson 7 —
(Stuart Williams) *stdd s: hld up: nt clr run 2f out: sn wknd* **10/1**

60.29 secs (0.69) **Going Correction** -0.05s/f (Good) **6** Ran SP% **110.1**
Speed ratings (Par 103): **92,91,87,87,82 60**
Tote Swingers: 1&2 £2.10, 1&3 £2.40, 2&3 £1.60 CSF £19.45 TOTE £5.70: £3.30, £3.00; EX 11.30.

Owner Mark Benton **Bred** The Valentines **Trained** Chastleton, Oxon

FOCUS
A tightly knit sprint handicap that produced a good finish. The time was modest compared with the earlier races over slightly longer trips. Modest form.

1983 BEST OF WARWICK H'CAP 1m 22y
3:40 (3:41) (Class 4) (0-85,85) 3-Y-O **£4,079** (£1,214; £606; £303) **Stalls** Low

Form RPR

0-1 **1** **Ektibaas**[26] 1328 3-8-12 **76**... SebSanders 3 88
(B W Hills) *led 7f out: rdn over 1f out: styd on wl* **5/1**[2]

212- **2** *2 ¼* **Sagramor**[208] 6870 3-9-7 **85**... SteveDrowne 9 92
(Hughie Morrison) *hld up: hdwy over 2f out: rdn to chse wnr fnl f: styd on* **4/1**[1]

154- **3** *1 ¾* **Whaileyy (IRE)**[242] 5901 3-9-5 **83**.. RyanMoore 5 86
(Sir Michael Stoute) *led 1f: chsd wnr: rdn over 1f out: styd on same pce ins fnl f* **5/1**[2]

352- **4** *1 ¼* **Prophet In A Dream**[197] 7116 3-8-9 **73**........................... JamieSpencer 7 73
(Mick Channon) *hld up: plld hrd: hdwy over 1f out: sn rdn: nt rch ldrs* **9/1**[3]

2-23 **5** *½* **Tasfeya**[15] 1571 3-9-2 **80**... RichardHills 8 79
(Mark Johnston) *trckd ldrs: rdn over 2f out: no ex fnl f* **4/1**[1]

031- **6** *4 ½* **Mr Perceptive (IRE)**[272] 4962 3-9-1 **79**................................ PatDobbs 6 68
(Richard Hannon) *prom: lost pl over 6f out: wknd over 2f out* **16/1**

312- **7** *3 ¾* **Dunhoy (IRE)**[144] 7916 3-9-0 **78**... AdamKirby 4 58
(Stef Higgins) *hld up in tch: rdn over 2f out: hung lft and wknd over 1f out* **10/1**

4-31 **8** *13* **Cheylesmore (IRE)**[110] 228 3-8-7 **71** oh1.................(t) WilliamCarson 2 21
(Stuart Williams) *plld hrd: trckd ldrs: rdn over 2f out: wknd wl over 1f out* **28/1**

1m 41.19s (0.19) **Going Correction** +0.025s/f (Good) **8** Ran SP% **101.8**
Speed ratings (Par 101): **100,97,96,94,94 89,86,73**
Tote Swingers: 1&2 £3.80, 1&3 £5.20, 2&3 £2.20 CSF £19.83 CT £73.39 TOTE £3.90: £1.30, £2.10, £1.60; EX 20.00.

Owner Hamdan Al Maktoum **Bred** Shadwell Estate Company Limited **Trained** Lambourn, Berks
■ Aciano was withdrawn after losing a front shoe (8/1, deduct 10p in the £.)

FOCUS
Few got into this 3-y-o handicap. The unexposed winner is rated up 10lb, with the second to his best.

1984 WARWICK RACECOURSE MAIDEN STKS (DIV I) 7f 26y
4:10 (4:15) (Class 5) 3-Y-O+ **£2,388** (£705; £352) **Stalls** Low

Form RPR

425- **1** **Fityaan**[229] 6301 3-9-0 78... RichardHills 7 81+
(B W Hills) *a.p: trckd ldr over 5f out: shkn up to ld over 1f out: comf* **5/6**[1]

0-4 **2** *½* **Uppercut**[15] 1565 3-9-0 0... FergusSweeney 2 79+
(Stuart Kittow) *a.p: swtchd rt 2f out: rdn to chse wnr ins fnl f: r.o* **7/1**[3]

404- **3** *6* **Proper Charlie**[235] 6145 3-9-0 72.................................... JamieSpencer 1 63
(William Knight) *led: rdn and hdd over 1f out: wknd ins fnl f* **5/2**[2]

0-0 **4** *1 ¾* **Kalendar Girl (IRE)**[47] 952 3-8-9 0................................ JamieMackay 8 53
(Willie Musson) *prom: outpcd over 2f out: styd on ins fnl f* **20/1**

5 *nk* **Brio** 3-9-0 0.. JamesDoyle 12 57
(Alan McCabe) *hld up in tch: rdn over 2f out: wknd over 1f out* **50/1**

6 *6* **Hawridge Song** 3-9-0 0... JamesMillman 9 41
(Rod Millman) *s.i.s: hld up: styd on ins fnl f: nvr nrr* **25/1**

6P- **7** *1* **Muroona (IRE)**[228] 6323 3-8-9 0... GregFairley 5 34
(Mark Johnston) *prom: rdn over 2f out: wknd over 1f out* **14/1**

8 *½* **Ondeafears (IRE)**[203] 4-9-7 0... JimmyQuinn 3 36
(Stuart Howe) *s.i.s: hld up: nvr on terms* **150/1**

66 **9** *1 ¼* **Colourbearer (IRE)**[14] 1589 4-9-12 0............................... LiamKeniry 11 38
(Milton Bradley) *chsd ldrs: rdn over 2f out: wknd over 1f out* **40/1**

10 *hd* **Gambatte** 4-9-7 0... DavidProbert 4 32
(Tony Carroll) *s.i.s: hld up: sme hdwy over 2f out: sn rdn and wknd* **80/1**

0 **11** *¾* **Elby**[8] 1751 4-9-12 0.. CathyGannon 13 35
(Eve Johnson Houghton) *s.i.s: a in rr* **100/1**

12 *9* **Voodoo Queen** 3-8-9 0.. ChrisCatlin 10 —
(Christopher Kellett) *s.i.s: a in rr: bhd fr 1/2-way* **100/1**

0-3 **13** *8* **Chillianwallah**[43] 1015 3-9-0 0.. MartinDwyer 6 —
(James Unett) *s.i.s: sn mid-div: wknd 3f out* **50/1**

1m 25.06s (0.46) **Going Correction** +0.025s/f (Good)
WFA 3 from 4yo 12lb **13** Ran SP% **121.1**
Speed ratings (Par 103): **98,97,90,88,88 81,80,79,78,78 77,66,57**
Tote Swingers: 1&2 £2.30, 1&3 £1.40, 2&3 £2.90 CSF £7.40 TOTE £2.10: £1.20, £1.90, £1.10; EX 8.60.

Owner Hamdan Al Maktoum **Bred** Usk Valley Stud **Trained** Lambourn, Berks

FOCUS
A fair maiden judged on the marks of those with ratings. The market concerned just four.

1985 WARWICK RACECOURSE MAIDEN STKS (DIV II) 7f 26y
4:40 (4:45) (Class 5) 3-Y-O+ **£2,388** (£705; £352) **Stalls** Low

Form RPR

2- **1** **Anoint**[185] 7346 3-9-0 0.. RyanMoore 6 82+
(William Haggas) *half-rrd s: sn prom: pushed along over 4f out: chsd ldr over 1f out: rdn to ld wl ins fnl f* **4/6**[1]

0- **2** *1 ¼* **Vizean (IRE)**[230] 6293 3-8-9 0.. RichardMullen 4 74
(Ed McMahon) *led: racd keenly: clr over 1f out: hdd wl ins fnl f* **50/1**

05- **3** *2 ¾* **Another For Joe**[200] 7049 3-9-0 0.................................... DaneO'Neill 10 72
(Ian Williams) *hld up: hdwy over 1f out: r.o: nt trble ldrs* **20/1**

05 **4** *½* **Dunseverick (IRE)**[13] 1606 3-9-0 0.................................. ChrisCatlin 5 70+
(David Lanigan) *s.i.s: hld up: hdwy over 1f out: nrst fin* **14/1**[3]

54- **5** *¾* **Musnad (USA)**[222] 6504 3-9-0 0...................................... RichardHills 9 68
(B W Hills) *hld up in tch: rdn over 2f out: no ex fnl f* **2/1**[2]

6 *1 ¾* **Coupland Lass (IRE)** 3-8-9 0... JackMitchell 2 59
(Willie Musson) *s.i.s: bhd: rdn and swtchd rt over 1f out: styd on ins fnl f: nvr nrr* **66/1**

/0 **7** *4* **Media Hype**[13] 1605 4-9-12 0.. J-PGuillambert 11 57
(Luca Cumani) *s.i.s: hld up: pushed along 1/2-way: styd on ins fnl f: nvr on terms* **16/1**

50 **8** *2 ¼* **Ellielusive (IRE)**[24] 1393 4-9-7 0.................................... GeorgeBaker 12 46
(Mark Brisbourne) *chsd ldrs tl rdn and wknd over 1f out* **200/1**

0 **9** *1 ¼* **Hertford Street**[13] 1606 3-9-0 0.................................... FergusSweeney 8 43
(Peter Makin) *mid-div: wknd over 2f out* **100/1**

0000 **10** *shd* **Heart Felt**[15] 1566 3-8-6 45..................................(b[1]) AndrewHeffernan(3) 3 38
(Roy Brotherton) *chsd ldr tl rdn over 2f out: wknd over 1f out* **200/1**

-0 **11** *4 ½* **Polly McGinty**[25] 1362 3-8-6 0...................................... DeclanCannon(3) 1 26
(Nicky Vaughan) *chsd ldrs tl rdn and wknd over 1f out* **100/1**

1m 25.13s (0.53) **Going Correction** +0.025s/f (Good)
WFA 3 from 4yo 12lb **11** Ran SP% **117.1**
Speed ratings (Par 103): **97,95,92,91,91 89,84,81,80,80 75**
Tote Swingers: 1&2 £11.60, 1&3 £4.50, 2&3 £50.50 CSF £60.55 TOTE £1.50: £1.10, £7.10, £3.50; EX 53.20.

Owner Cheveley Park Stud **Bred** Cheveley Park Stud Ltd **Trained** Newmarket, Suffolk

FOCUS
A fair maiden.

1986 JOIN TODAY AT REWARDS4RACING.COM FILLIES' H'CAP 7f 26y
5:10 (5:14) (Class 5) (0-70,70) 3-Y-O **£2,266** (£674; £337; £168) **Stalls** Low

Form RPR

4340 **1** **Spirit Of Grace**[14] 1579 3-9-2 **65**...................................... JamesDoyle 14 70
(Alan McCabe) *w ldr: led over 2f out: rdn ins fnl f: jst hld on* **33/1**

0-14 **2** *nk* **Ellie In The Pink (IRE)**[14] 1579 3-8-8 **62**.................... HarryBentley(5) 9 66
(Alan Jarvis) *chsd ldrs: rdn and n.m.r over 1f out: r.o* **14/1**

30-5 **3** *nse* **Abergeldie (USA)**[13] 1607 3-9-2 **65**............................... JimmyFortune 8 69
(Andrew Balding) *s.i.s: racd keenly and sn prom: rdn over 1f out: r.o u.p* **11/2**[2]

0-1 **4** *hd* **Here To Eternity (USA)**[36] 1133 3-9-5 **68**...................... JackMitchell 13 71+
(Peter Chapple-Hyam) *hld up: hld up: hdwy over 1f out: nt clr run and swtchd lft sn after: r.o* **16/1**

00-0 **5** *2 ½* **Russian Ice**[14] 1579 3-8-7 **56** oh1.............................. AdrianMcCarthy 11 52
(Dean Ivory) *prom: rdn over 2f out: styd on same pce ins fnl f* **50/1**

0-04 **6** *½* **Alexs Rainbow (USA)**[15] 1566 3-8-10 **59**.......................... ChrisCatlin 3 54
(John Gallagher) *hld up: hdwy over 1f out: nt rch ldrs* **18/1**

32-2 **7** *hd* **Hurricane Lady (IRE)**[14] 1579 3-9-5 **68**......................... AdamKirby 10 62
(Walter Swinburn) *hld up in tch: rdn over 2f out: no ex fnl f* **7/1**[3]

4310 **8** *½* **Storm Tide**[13] 1611 3-9-4 **70**.. MartinHarley(3) 12 63
(Rae Guest) *s.i.s: hld up: hdwy over 2f out: rdn over 1f out: hmpd sn after: no ex ins fnl f* **16/1**

5-02 **9** *¾* **Looksmart**[17] 1524 3-9-0 **63**.. RyanMoore 1 54
(Richard Hannon) *sn pushed along into mid-div: rdn over 1f out: no ex ins fnl f* **4/1**[1]

6-20 **10** *2* **Delira (IRE)**[20] 1483 3-9-1 **64**... CathyGannon 4 50
(Jonathan Portman) *hld up: rdn over 1f out: nvr trbld ldrs* **14/1**

326- **11** *hd* **Blue Maisey**[152] 7780 3-9-5 **68**.. JimmyQuinn 6 53
(Sam Davison) *hld up: rdn over 3f out: n.d* **66/1**

25-2 **12** *¾* **Empress Charlotte**[21] 1472 3-8-13 **62**.............................. JamieSpencer 7 45
(Michael Bell) *hld up: rdn and swtchd rt 2f out: swtchd lft over 1f out: eased whn btn ins fnl f* **11/2**[2]

-202 **13** *¾* **Finefrenzyrolling (IRE)**[32] 1220 3-9-0 **63**....................... AndrewElliott 2 44
(Mrs K Burke) *sn led: rdn and hdd over 2f out: wknd ins fnl f* **7/1**[3]

30U- **14** *½* **Red Lite (IRE)**[232] 6259 3-9-3 **66**.................................... EddieCreighton 5 46
(Brian Meehan) *s.i.s and sn pushed along: a in rr* **22/1**

1m 25.66s (1.06) **Going Correction** +0.025s/f (Good) **14** Ran SP% **116.9**
Speed ratings (Par 96): **94,93,93,93,90 89,89,89,88,86 85,84,84,83**
Tote Swingers: 1&2 £108.60, 1&3 £37.10, 2&3 £12.20 CSF £422.53 CT £3005.59 TOTE £49.70: £11.90, £6.10, £1.60; EX 418.70.

Owner Placida Racing **Bred** Tarworth Bloodstock & Genesis Green Stud **Trained** Averham Park, Notts

FOCUS
A modest but competitive fillies' handicap run over half a second slower than the preceding divisions of the maiden. It resulted in a close finish in a somewhat messy contest and a surprise result.

1987 BEST HORSE RACING ON SKY CHANNEL 432 H'CAP — 1m 2f 188y
5:40 (5:41) (Class 6) (0-55,55) 4-Y-O+ — **£2,047** (£604; £302) **Stalls** Low

Form — RPR

2300 **1** **Lytham (IRE)**[14] 1582 10-9-3 **54**....................................... AdamKirby 15 62
(Tony Carroll) *hld up: hdwy over 5f out: led over 1f out: drvn out* **14/1**

46-5 **2** *½* **Wood Fair**[14] 1587 4-8-12 **54**... HarryBentley(5) 17 61+
(Mrs K Burke) *s.i.s: hld up: hdwy over 1f out: r.o: nt rch wnr* **11/2**[1]

05- **3** *hd* **Transfer**[150] 7825 6-8-11 **48**... JamesDoyle 10 55
(Richard Price) *hld up in tch: racd keenly: rdn over 1f out: styd on* **9/1**

0-00 **4** *2 ½* **Tt's Dream**[48] 943 4-8-13 **50**..(b[1]) SteveDrowne 16 52
(Alastair Lidderdale) *hld up: hdwy over 4f out: rdn over 1f out: edgd rt ins fnl f: styd on same pce* **33/1**

026- **5** *1 ½* **Belle Boleyn**[197] 7117 4-9-4 **55**.. GeorgeBaker 12 55
(Chris Wall) *chsd ldrs: rdn over 2f out: styd on same pce appr fnl f* **17/2**[3]

-256 **6** *hd* **Kathleen Kennet**[40] 1068 11-8-10 **47**................................ LiamKeniry 7 47
(Jonathan Geake) *chsd ldr: led over 2f out: rdn and hdd over 1f out: no ex ins fnl f* **35/1**

6-30 **7** *nk* **Crazy Bold (GER)**[19] 773 8-8-11 **48**.............................. DavidProbert 14 47
(Tony Carroll) *s.i.s: hld up: styd on fr over 1f out: nvr nrr* **16/1**

3-50 **8** *nse* **Peaceful Means (IRE)**[2] 526 8-8-13 **55**....................... RyanPowell(5) 5 54
(Evan Williams) *hld up: hdwy over 1f out: nt rch ldrs* **12/1**

4006 **9** *1 ¼* **Art Scholar (IRE)**[25] 1357 4-9-1 **52**................................. ChrisCatlin 3 49
(Michael Appleby) *led 1f: chsd ldrs tl rdn and wknd over 1f out* **25/1**

4420 **10** *¾* **Iguacu**[48] 943 7-9-0 **51**..(p) DaneO'Neill 2 47
(George Baker) *dwlt: hld up: nvr on terms* **13/2**[2]

1603 **11** *½* **Barbirolli**[12] 1635 9-8-5 **47**.. LauraPike(5) 1 42
(William Stone) *hld up: rdn over 2f out: nvr on terms* **9/1**

0543 **12** *¾* **Thundering Home**[19] 1508 4-9-2 **53**........................(p) RobbieFitzpatrick 8 46
(Michael Attwater) *s.i.s: a in rr* **12/1**

5000 **13** *3 ¼* **King Of Connacht**[21] 1454 8-8-11 **48**......................(b[1]) CathyGannon 13 36
(Mark Wellings) *prom: rdn over 2f out: wknd over 1f out* **50/1**

0016 **14** *3 ½* **Gems**[15] 1567 4-8-10 **54**.. LucyKBarry(7) 9 36
(Peter Hiatt) *led after 1f: rdn and hdd over 2f out: wknd over 1f out* **10/1**

400- **15** *5* **Sanctum**[156] 7716 5-8-12 **49**... AdrianMcCarthy 6 22
(Dr Jon Scargill) *mid-div: rdn over 6f out: wknd over 3f out* **16/1**

240- **16** *11* **Trecase**[208] 6865 4-9-4 **55**.. SebSanders 4 10
(Tony Carroll) *prom tl rdn and wknd over 2f out* **20/1**

000/ **17** *3 ¾* **Lord Wheathill**[559] 7121 4-8-10 **50**.......................... AndrewHeffernan(3) 11 —
(Lisa Williamson) *plld hrd and prom: wknd over 3f out* **66/1**

2m 20.96s (-0.14) **Going Correction** +0.025s/f (Good) **17** Ran SP% **121.0**
Speed ratings (Par 101): **101,100,100,98,97 97,97,97,96,95 95,94,92,89,86 78,75**
Tote Swingers: 1&2 £20.00, 1&3 £32.70, 2&3 £14.60; totesuper7: Win: Not won; Place: Not won CSF £81.71 CT £750.87 TOTE £15.80: £4.20, £2.30, £3.70, £6.20; EX 72.60.

Owner Morgan, Clarke & Parris **Bred** Mrs A S O'Brien And Lars Pearson **Trained** Cropthorne, Worcs

FOCUS
A very moderate handicap but only 8lb covered the entire field on official ratings.

T/Jkpt: £4,733.30 to a £1 stake. Pool: £10,000. 1.50 winning tickets. T/Plt: £35.00 to a £1 stake. Pool: £49,030.73. 1,022.57 winning tickets. T/Qpdt: £9.60 to a £1 stake. Pool: £3,959.45. 302.54 winning tickets. CR

1590 YARMOUTH (L-H)
Tuesday, May 10

OFFICIAL GOING: Good to firm (8.0)
Wind: fresh, against Weather: sunny, warm breezy

1988 SWIFT TAXIS 300 300 MAIDEN STKS — 6f 3y
2:20 (2:20) (Class 5) 2-Y-0 — **£2,266** (£674; £337; £168) **Stalls** High

Form — RPR

1 **Samminder (IRE)** 2-9-3 0.. WilliamBuick 6 84+
(Peter Chapple-Hyam) *in tch in last trio: hdwy over 2f out: chsd ldr and drew clr of field over 1f out: shkn up to chal ent fnl f: pushed ahd ins fnl f: readily drew clr fnl 75yds: comf* **1/1**[1]

2 *2 ¾* **Pickled Pelican (IRE)** 2-9-3 0... JimCrowley 2 76+
(William Haggas) *trckd ldng pair: hdwy to ld gng wl ent fnl 2f: rdn and drew clr w wnr over 1f out: hdd ins fnl f: outpcd by wnr fnl 75yds: kpt on* **7/2**[2]

3 *3 ¼* **Rock Canyon (IRE)** 2-9-3 0.. EddieAhern 4 66+
(Robert Mills) *in tch: rdn along 3f out: switching lft and sme hdwy wl over 1f out: outpcd by ldng pair over 1f out: wnt 3rd 1f out: kpt on but no threat to ldrs fnl f* **20/1**

32 **4** *6* **Dougie Boy**[28] 1290 2-9-0 0.. KierenFox(3) 7 48
(Bill Turner) *restless in stalls: bhd: rdn and struggling over 3f out: effrt u.p and switching lft 2f out: plugged on to go modest 4th wl ins fnl f: n.d* **8/1**

6 **5** *½* **Topcoat (IRE)**[33] 1199 2-9-3 0.. KierenFallon 3 47
(Mark Johnston) *led: hdd ent fnl 2f: sn rdn: unable qck and struggling whn short of room over 1f out: sn wknd: wl btn fnl f* **5/1**[3]

5 **6** *8* **Darnathean**[28] 1290 2-9-3 0..(b[1]) NeilCallan 5 23
(Paul D'Arcy) *pressed ldr tl 2f out: sn rdn and struggling whn hmpd and snatched up over 1f out: no ch after: wknd fnl f* **12/1**

7 *10* **Flatford Mill** 2-9-3 0.. RussellPrice 1 —
(Patrick Gilligan) *taken down early: dwlt: sn bustked along and rcvrd to in midfield: wknd qckly ent fnl 2f: t.o ins fnl f* **100/1**

1m 15.74s (1.34) **Going Correction** -0.025s/f (Good) **7** Ran SP% **113.4**
Speed ratings (Par 93): **90,86,82,74,73 62,49**
Tote Swingers: 1&2 £2.00, 1&3 £7.40, 2&3 £13.60 CSF £4.62 TOTE £1.50: £1.20, £2.30; EX 5.60.

Owner Ziad A Galadari **Bred** Galadari Sons Stud Company Limited **Trained** Newmarket, Suffolk

FOCUS
Little worthwhile form, but it a clutch of potentially-interesting newcomers. The winner impressed and the form has been given a chance through him.

NOTEBOOK
Samminder(IRE), a newcomer whose dam won five times at sprint trips, registered a highly encouraging victory. Well-backed in the morning, he was always cruising in the race and, once asked to quicken approaching the final furlong, eased clear. He will surely score again in better class and, although his trainer played down Royal Ascot plans, he did call this colt 'a nice horse'. (tchd 6-5)
Pickled Pelican(IRE), another newcomer, is from a decent family of precocious types and did more than enough to suggest he can collect in the near future. He was not the quickest away, but had got to the front between the 2f and 1f poles, and beat all bar the winner decisively. (op 4-1)
Rock Canyon(IRE), a first-time-out brother to a 1m6f winner, performed as might have been expected on his pedigree. He broke fairly well, but was outpaced in mid-race before staying on towards to the finish. He will have no problems with a longer trip. (op 22-1)
Dougie Boy, beaten 8l when second at Southwell last time out, was comprehensively outpaced in the early stages. He responded well to driving, though, and came home in good style. (op 7-1)
Topcoat(IRE), sixth of eight at Ripon on his only previous start, showed early speed. He hung right and faded dramatically, however, once overtaken. (op 6-1)
Darnathean, fitted with blinkers after a modest debut run in a visor, was another to exhibit pace leaving the stalls. He too dropped away tamely in closing stages, however, and wasn't helped by being slightly impeded. (op 10-1 tchd 9-1)
Flatford Mill, a newcomer with smart winners in his pedigree, looked very green. Slowly away, he made some ground in mid-race, but then stopped quite quickly.

1989 RACING WELFARE H'CAP — 6f 3y
[illegible] ([illegible]) (Class 6) (0-50,50) 4-Y-O+ — **£1,619** (£481; £240; £120) **Stalls** High

Form — RPR

0-00 **1** **Miss Polly Plum**[25] 1357 4-8-7 **46** oh1..........................(p) AndreaAtzeni 5 63
(Chris Dwyer) *chsd ldr: led over 2f out: rdn and drew clr over 1f out: in command and wandered u.p 1f out: kpt on: rdn out* **25/1**

3446 **2** *2 ½* **This Ones For Eddy**[52] 906 6-8-11 **50**............................. NeilCallan 11 59
(John Balding) *in tch: rdn wl over 1f out: hdwy u.p to chse clr wnr ent fnl f: kpt on but no theat to wnr* **4/1**[2]

3511 **3** *1 ½* **Jonnie Skull (IRE)**[4] 1875 5-8-8 **47** oh1 ow1.............(vt) KierenFallon 10 52
(Phil McEntee) *led: rdn and hdd over 2f out: edgd lft and nt qckn w wnr over 1f out: 3rd and one pce fnl f* **9/4**[1]

4015 **4** *1* **Memphis Man**[3] 1912 8-8-6 **52**.......................... MatthewCosham(7) 4 53
(David Evans) *taken down early: hld up towards rr: rdn and hdwy wl over 1f out: swtchd rt over 1f out: styd on fnl f: nvr trbld ldrs* **5/1**[3]

-000 **5** *2 ¾* **Avec Moi**[28] 1287 4-8-0 **46** oh1................................... DanielHarris(7) 8 39
(Christine Dunnett) *chsd ldrs and sn bustled along: rdn over 2f out: outpcd by wnr but stl ev ch of 2nd over 1f out: wknd fnl f* **100/1**

401- **6** *2* **Hollow Jo**[442] 658 11-8-11 **50**... DarryllHolland 12 36
(J R Jenkins) *hld up in last trio: swtchd rt and effrt wl over 1f out: n.d* **12/1**

60-0 **7** *½* **Rileys Crane**[52] 912 4-8-12 **51**.................................(p) SaleemGolam 14 36
(Christine Dunnett) *towards rr: rdn and struggling over 2f out: hung lft u.p over 1f out: no ch after* **66/1**

340- **8** *1 ¼* **Angel Of Fashion (IRE)**[235] 6168 4-9-0 **58**............ AdamBeschizza(5) 2 39
(Peter Charalambous) *stdd s: hld up in rr: effrt ent fnl 2f in centre: no hdwy u.p over 1f out: wknd ent fnl f* **15/2**

663- **9** *1 ¼* **Croeso Mawr**[302] 3952 5-9-0 **53**.. EddieAhern 1 30
(John Spearing) *a in rr: rdn and sme hdwy over 2f out: no prog and wl btn over 1f out* **12/1**

36-6 **10** *½* **Call The Law (IRE)**[6] 1818 5-8-7 **53** ow3...................... ChristyMews(7) 9 28
(Pam Sly) *in tch in midfield: pushed along and unable qck ent fnl 2f: wknd over 1f out: fdd fnl f* **16/1**

2000 **11** *3* **Young Simon**[41] 1041 4-9-4 **57**......................................(v) TomQueally 15 22
(George Margarson) *in tch: rdn and fnd nil over 2f out: wknd wl over 1f out: sn bhd* **14/1**

1m 14.0s (-0.40) **Going Correction** -0.025s/f (Good) **11** Ran SP% **113.5**
Speed ratings (Par 101): **101,97,95,94,90 88,87,85,84,83 79**
Tote Swingers: 1&2 £23.80, 1&3 £11.90, 2&3 £2.90 CSF £117.99 CT £322.09 TOTE £48.30: £8.30, £1.10, £1.70; EX 200.60 TRIFECTA Not won..

Owner Mrs J Hughes & Miss C Hughes **Bred** Brookfield Stud & Partners **Trained** Burrough Green, Cambs

FOCUS
A weak handicap made less competitive by a raft of non-runners. Surprise improvement from the winner, who could rate higher at face value.
Miss Polly Plum Official explanation: trainer said, regarding apparent improvement in form, that the filly is very inconsistent.
Croeso Mawr Official explanation: jockey said mare lost its action

1990 WEATHERBYS BANK H'CAP — 7f 3y
3:20 (3:22) (Class 5) (0-75,75) 4-Y-0+ — **£2,266** (£674; £337; £168) **Stalls** High

Form — RPR

14-4 **1** **Watch Chain (IRE)**[15] 1570 4-8-7 **61** .... KierenFallon 7 — 72
(Mark H Tompkins) *hld up in tch in rr: gd hdwy wl over 1f out: rdn to chse ldr ent fnl f: pushed ahd ins fnl f: r.o wl* — **12/1**

30-2 **2** ¾ **Mashatu**[15] 1569 4-9-2 **70** .... PatCosgrave 3 — 79
(James Fanshawe) *chsd ldrs: rdn and effrot 2f out: led wl over 1f out: drvn ent fnl f: hdd ins fnl f: kpt on for clr 2nd but readily hld by wnr* — **9/4**[1]

0035 **3** 3¼ **Ongoodform (IRE)**[20] 1488 4-9-7 **75** .... NeilCallan 8 — 75
(Paul D'Arcy) *led main gp and chsd overall ldr: rdn ent fnl 2f: unable qck u.p over 1f out: outpcd by ldng pair and btn ins fnl f: hld on for 3rd cl home* — **3/1**[2]

0-04 **4** nk **Rough Rock (IRE)**[19] 1506 6-9-2 **70** .... TomQueally 5 — 69
(Chris Dwyer) *stdd s: hld up in rr: effrt and hdwy over 1f out: drvn ent fnl f: no ch w ldng pair but kpt on to press for 3rd cl home* — **12/1**

10-0 **5** 1¾ **Aleqa**[15] 1562 4-9-4 **72** .... TedDurcan 1 — 67
(Chris Wall) *hld up in tch: hdwy ent fnl 2f: chsd ldrs and drvn over 1f out: outpcd 1f out: one pce and wl hld ins fnl f* — **15/2**

4540 **6** 1¾ **Lastkingofscotland (IRE)**[17] 1530 5-9-6 **74** ....(b) HayleyTurner 4 — 64
(Conor Dore) *t.k.h: hld up in tch: rdn wl over 1f out: sn btn* — **10/1**

1030 **7** 3½ **Hip Hip Hooray**[75] 666 5-8-9 **63** .... FrankieMcDonald 2 — 43
(Luke Dace) *awkward leaving stalls and slowly away: bhd: hdwy into midfield after 2f: rdn and struggling over 2f out: wl btn over 1f out* — **25/1**

00-2 **8** 1¾ **Sairaam (IRE)**[11] 1649 5-8-9 **63** .... KirstyMilczarek 9 — 39
(Charles Smith) *overall ldr and racd alone on stands' rail: shkn up over 2f out: rdn and hung lft 2f out: sn hdd & wknd* — **5/1**[3]

1m 26.7s (0.10) **Going Correction** -0.025s/f (Good) — **8** Ran SP% **112.5**
Speed ratings (Par 103): **98,97,93,93,91 89,85,83**
Tote Swingers: 1&2 £3.30, 1&3 £6.40, 2&3 £2.30 CSF £38.11 CT £104.14 TOTE £16.20: £3.80, £1.10, £1.30; EX 43.90 Trifecta £291.10 Pool: £472.15 - 1.20 winning units..
Owner Raceworld **Bred** Miss S Von Schilcher **Trained** Newmarket, Suffolk

FOCUS
Just a run-of-the-mill handicap, with the top weight rated 75, and all bar one (Sairaam) raced up the centre of the track. Improved form from the first two, who were clear.

1991 LINDLEY VENUE CATERING MEDIAN AUCTION MAIDEN STKS — 1m 2f 21y
3:50 (3:52) (Class 6) 3-Y-O — **£1,619** (£481; £240; £120) **Stalls** Low

Form — RPR

62- **1** **Blue Destination**[195] 7172 3-9-3 0 .... NeilCallan 1 — 87+
(Philip McBride) *chsd ldrs: trcking ldrs and waiting for gap on inner fr over 2f out: squeezed through and rdn to ld over 1f out: styd on strlyand drew fnl f: readily* — **5/6**[1]

25-2 **2** 3¼ **Zakon (IRE)**[28] 1298 3-9-3 74 .... EddieAhern 3 — 79
(Denis Coakley) *chsd ldr: ev ch 2f out: rdn over 1f out: edging lft and outpcd by wnr ins fnl f: kpt on* — **5/1**[3]

45-2 **3** 2¼ **Star Commander**[10] 1683 3-9-3 72 .... KierenFallon 6 — 74
(Mark H Tompkins) *chsd ldrs: rdn over 2f out: pressed ldrs 2f out: unable qck u.p over 1f out: plugged on same pce fnl f* — **3/1**[2]

0-4 **4** 1½ **Divinite Green (IRE)**[15] 1572 3-9-3 0 .... DarryllHolland 8 — 72+
(Peter Chapple-Hyam) *led: rdn 2f out: hdd over 1f out: unable qck whn short of room and snatched up sn after: one pce and no threat to ldrs after* — **20/1**

40- **5** 12 **Newby Lodge (IRE)**[200] 7049 3-8-12 0 .... JimCrowley 5 — 42
(William Haggas) *stdd s: hld up in last trio: hdwy and tagged onto bk of ldng gp 4f out: nt clr run on inner over 3f out: tl swtchd rt ent fnl 2f: sn shkn up and fnd little: no ch wl over 1f out* — **12/1**

0 **6** ¾ **Speed Dancer**[15] 1572 3-9-3 0 .... TomQueally 4 — 46
(James Eustace) *in tch in midfield: rdn and outpcd over 3f out: no ch w ldrs fnl 2f* — **40/1**

7 12 **Sit Tight** 3-9-3 0 .... TedDurcan 9 — 22
(Chris Wall) *dwlt: rn green: in tch in midfield: rdn and struggling over 3f out: wknd over 2f out: eased ins fnl f: t.o* — **40/1**

8 24 **Fairest Isle (IRE)** 3-8-12 0 ....(t) WilliamBuick 7 — —
(James Fanshawe) *v.s.a: a bhd: lost tch wl over 2f out: virtually p.u fnl f: t.o* — **16/1**

0 **9** 8 **Who Loves Ya Baby**[27] 1315 3-8-12 0 .... AdamBeschizza(5) 2 — —
(Peter Charalambous) *s.i.s: sn rdn along and a in rr: lost tch over 3f out: t.o and virtually p.u fnl f* — **66/1**

2m 7.09s (-3.41) **Going Correction** -0.20s/f (Firm) — **9** Ran SP% **120.9**
Speed ratings (Par 97): **105,102,100,99,89 89,79,60,54**
Tote Swingers: 1&2 £23.80, 1&3 £11.90, 2&3 £2.90 CSF £5.74 TOTE £2.30: £1.30, £1.70, £1.10; EX 7.00 Trifecta £17.90 Pool: £949.43 - 39.22 winning units..
Owner The Honorable Earle I Mack **Bred** Kirtlington Stud Ltd **Trained** Newmarket, Suffolk

FOCUS
Not a bad maiden, featuring some solid form contenders and a clutch of well-bred newcomers. The form is rated around the second and third and the winner can do better.
Divinite Green(IRE) Official explanation: jockey said colt suffered interference in running
Newby Lodge(IRE) Official explanation: jockey said filly was slowly away

1992 WEATHERBYS BLOODSTOCK INSURANCE FILLIES' H'CAP — 1m 2f 21y
4:20 (4:22) (Class 4) (0-80,80) 4-Y-0+ — **£4,079** (£1,214; £606; £303) **Stalls** Low

Form — RPR

11-4 **1** **Piano**[24] 1390 4-9-7 **80** .... WilliamBuick 8 — 95+
(John Gosden) *hld up in tch: smooth hdwy on outer 2f out: pushed to ld 1f out: pushed out and readily drew clr ins fnl f: easily* — **5/4**[1]

1 **2** 3¼ **Satwa Pearl**[47] 1011 5-9-4 **77** .... KierenFallon 1 — 83
(Ed Dunlop) *v.s.a: clsd and in tch over 7f out: effrt and switching rt 2f out: styd on to go 2nd ins fnl f: no ch w wnr* — **13/2**[3]

23-5 **3** 1¾ **Countess Comet (IRE)**[24] 1388 4-9-6 **79** .... JimCrowley 5 — 82
(Ralph Beckett) *led: rdn ent fnl 2f: hdd 1f out: sn outpcd by wnr and btn: lost 2nd ins fnl f* — **11/1**

430- **4** 1 **Ela Gorrie Mou**[297] 4137 5-8-9 **73** .... AdamBeschizza(5) 3 — 74
(Peter Charalambous) *t.k.h: in tch: rdn and effrt jst over 2f out: drvn and unable qck 1f out: one pce and no threat to wnr ins fnl f* — **11/1**

41-0 **5** 1¼ **Snow Magic (IRE)**[37] 1114 4-9-2 **75** .... PatCosgrave 7 — 74
(James Fanshawe) *s.i.s: hld up in tch: rdn and effrt to press ldrs over 1f out: drvn and unable qck 1f out: wknd ins fnl f* — **9/1**

2-21 **6** 4 **Shamardal Phantom (IRE)**[92] 448 4-8-11 **70** .... TomQueally 2 — 61
(David Simcock) *chsd ldrs: nt clr run on inner over 2f out tl wl over 1f out: unable qck u.p over 1f out: sn btn* — **3/1**[2]

2225 **7** 4½ **The Blue Dog (IRE)**[26] 1324 4-8-4 **66** oh1 ....(b) LouisBeuzelin(3) 9 — 48
(Mark Rimmer) *t.k.h: sn chsng ldr: rdn jst over 2f out: wkng u.p whn n.m.r over 1f out: bhd fnl f: eased towards fin* — **25/1**

2m 6.95s (-3.55) **Going Correction** -0.20s/f (Firm) — **7** Ran SP% **113.3**
Speed ratings (Par 102): **106,103,102,101,100 97,93**
Tote Swingers: 1&2 £3.30, 1&3 £6.40, 2&3 £2.30 CSF £9.88 CT £60.29 TOTE £1.90: £1.10, £2.70; EX 6.50 Trifecta £56.20 Pool: £782.17 - 10.29 winning units..
Owner Cheveley Park Stud **Bred** Cheveley Park Stud Ltd **Trained** Newmarket, Suffolk

FOCUS
A competitive fillies' handicap in which, on paper, few could be confidently discounted. The winner looks destined for better and the second ran as well as ever on her British debut.

1993 LINDLEY CATERING H'CAP — 1m 2f 21y
4:50 (4:51) (Class 6) (0-60,60) 4-Y-0+ — **£1,619** (£481; £240; £120) **Stalls** Low

Form — RPR

2130 **1** **Sail Home**[38] 1099 4-9-2 **60** .... AdamBeschizza(5) 12 — 72
(Julia Feilden) *mde all: rdn over 2f out: drew clr 2f out: drvn ins fnl f: pressed towards fin: a jst holding on* — **9/2**[2]

05-0 **2** hd **Nurai**[15] 292 4-8-12 **51** .... NeilCallan 11 — 62
(Paul D'Arcy) *s.i.s: sn pushed along in rr: stdy hdwy fr 3f out: rdn to chse clr wnr over 1f out: kpt on wl fnl f: pressing wnr cl home: nt quite get up* — **9/1**

000- **3** 7 **Chantilly Dancer (IRE)**[201] 7037 5-8-4 **46** oh1 .... LouisBeuzelin(3) 3 — 44
(Michael Quinn) *s.i.s: bhd: hdwy over 4f out: rdn ent fnl 2f: wnt modest 3rd 1f out: no imp after* — **18/1**

-005 **4** 2¾ **Paint The Town Red**[14] 1586 6-8-7 **46** oh1 ....(p) TedDurcan 13 — 38
(Richard Guest) *dwlt: t.k.h: hld up in tch in midfield on outer: rdn and no real prog ent fnl 2f: no ch but plugged on to go modest 4th towards fin* — **15/2**

-206 **5** ½ **Mayfair's Future**[12] 1635 6-8-9 **48** ....(p) DarryllHolland 8 — 39
(J R Jenkins) *chsd ldrs: rdn and disputing 2nd over 2f out: outpcd by wnr 2f out: lost 2nd and wl btn over 1f out: wknd ins fnl f* — **7/1**

0-00 **6** 1¼ **Alhudhud (USA)**[61] 819 5-8-7 **46** oh1 .... AndreaAtzeni 4 — 35
(Kevin Morgan) *chsd ldrs: rdn and unable qck on inner over 3f out: wknd ent fnl 2f* — **14/1**

5544 **7** nk **Moment Of Clarity**[4] 1871 9-8-0 **46** oh1 ....(p) NathanAlison(7) 5 — 34
(Shaun Harris) *t.k.h: hld up in tch in midfield: swtchd rt and hdwy over 3f out: disputing 2nd and outpcd by wnr 2f out: wknd over 1f out* — **6/1**[3]

660/ **8** 1½ **Ajara Boy**[570] 6858 4-8-7 **46** oh1 .... FrankieMcDonald 7 — 33
(Luke Dace) *t.k.h: hld up in midfield: rdn and struggling over 2f out: sn btn: no ch fnl 2f* — **33/1**

00-6 **9** 4½ **Guga (IRE)**[34] 1190 5-9-2 **55** ....(p) TomQueally 14 — 31
(John Mackie) *t.k.h: w wnr tl rdn and fnd little over 2f out: sn wknd* — **3/1**[1]

/00- **10** 6 **Carlcol Girl**[251] 5656 4-8-4 **46** oh1 ....(v) KierenFox(3) 10 — —
(Christine Dunnett) *hld up in last trio: effrt on outer and rdn 4f out: wknd over 2f out: sn wl bhd* — **80/1**

603- **11** ½ **Renege The Joker**[15] 5565 8-8-0 **46** oh1 .... NoelGarbutt(7) 6 — —
(Sean Regan) *s.i.s: a bhd: rdn and lost tch qckly over 2f out: eased ins fnl f* — **33/1**

0-00 **12** 2½ **Motty's Gift**[20] 1486 4-8-11 **50** .... EddieAhern 9 — —
(Walter Swinburn) *chsd ldrs: rdn and wknd over 2f out: no ch fnl 2f: eased ins fnl f* — **10/1**

2m 8.01s (-2.49) **Going Correction** -0.20s/f (Firm) — **12** Ran SP% **119.9**
Speed ratings (Par 101): **101,100,95,93,92 91,91,90,86,81 81,79**
Tote Swingers: 1&2 £7.20, 1&3 £23.20, 2&3 £38.30 CSF £44.88 CT £676.10 TOTE £5.30: £1.50, £4.30, £9.40; EX 42.10 Trifecta £265.10 Part won. Pool: £358.37 - 0.30 winning units..
Owner Hoofbeats Racing Club **Bred** Juddmonte Farms Ltd **Trained** Exning, Suffolk

FOCUS
A low-grade affair and half the field were 1lb out of the handicap. The first pair were clear but the form is rated a bit cautiously.

1994 THELINDLEYGROUP.COM H'CAP — 1m 6f 17y
5:20 (5:20) (Class 5) (0-75,74) 4-Y-0+ — **£2,266** (£674; £337; £168) **Stalls** Low

Form — RPR

22-2 **1** **Sancho Panza**[37] 1107 4-8-6 **61** .... AdamBeschizza(5) 2 — 72
(Julia Feilden) *hld up in tch: hdwy to chse clr ldr wl over 3f out: rdn to chal ent fnl 2f: led over 1f out: pushed clr fnl f: comf* — **15/8**[2]

01-6 **2** 7 **Alubari**[26] 1325 4-9-6 **70** .... JimCrowley 4 — 71+
(David Simcock) *plld hrd: hld up in last: sddle moved forward and hdwy to ld 9f out: sn clr: rdn and pressed ent fnl 2f: hdd over 1f out: drvn and btn jst ins fnl f* — **9/2**[3]

323- **3** 5 **Sheila's Castle**[53] 7422 7-8-6 **62** .... DavidKenny(7) 5 — 56
(Sean Regan) *chsd ldr tl 9f out: rdn 4f out: hung lft and outpcd over 3f out: no ch fnl 2f* — **6/1**

120- **4** 50 **Tobernea (IRE)**[207] 6895 4-9-10 **74** .... KierenFallon 3 — —
(Mark Johnston) *awkward leaving stalls: led tl 9f out: chsd ldr after: rdn 5f out: dropped to last 4f out: sn lost tch: virtually p.u fnl f: t.o* — **11/8**[1]

3m 4.83s (-2.77) **Going Correction** -0.20s/f (Firm)
WFA 4 from 7yo 1lb — **4** Ran SP% **109.4**
Speed ratings (Par 103): **99,95,92,63**
CSF £9.88 TOTE £2.50; EX 8.80.
Owner Carol Bushnell & Partners **Bred** Harts Farm Stud **Trained** Exning, Suffolk

FOCUS
A modest handicap, with the top weight rated 74, but it looked open on paper. The winner had little to beat but has been progressing.
Alubari Official explanation: jockey said gelding slipped
Tobernea(IRE) Official explanation: jockey said gelding never travelled
T/Plt: £26.70 to a £1 stake. Pool: £58,796.81. 1,605.29 winning tickets. T/Qpdt: £9.60 to a £1 stake. Pool: £3,959.45. 302.54 winning tickets. SP

1756 KEMPTON (A.W) (R-H)
Wednesday, May 11

OFFICIAL GOING: Standard
Wind: Moderate across Weather: Early evening sun

1995 FREE ENTRY FOR BETDAQ MEMBERS H'CAP — 7f (P)
6:20 (6:20) (Class 6) (0-65,65) 4-Y-0+ — **£1,706** (£503; £252) **Stalls** Low

Form — RPR

640- **1** **Saturn Way (GR)**[189] 7298 5-9-4 **62** .... GeorgeBaker 8 — 74
(Patrick Chamings) *trckd ldrs: rdn 2f out: slt ld 1f out: drvn and styd on wl clsng stages* — **4/1**[1]

1143 **2** *¾* **Katmai River (IRE)**[26] 1368 4-9-3 **61**..............................(v) LiamKeniry 11 71
(Mark Usher) *chsd ldrs: drvn to chal wl over 1f out and stl ev ch ins fnl f: nt pce of wnr fnl 50yds* **13/2**[2]

130- **3** *2¼* **Foxtrot Alpha (IRE)**[218] 6656 5-9-4 **62**.............................. LukeMorris 10 66
(Peter Winkworth) *trckd ldr: slt ld 3f out: rdn 2f out and strly chal sn after: narrowly hdd 1f out: outpcd by ldng duo fnl 120yds* **11/1**

0-63 **4** *hd* **Fitz**[13] 1625 5-9-1 **59**.............................. TedDurcan 3 62+
(Matthew Salaman) *in rr: hdwy over 3f out: drvn over 2f out: styd on fnl f but nvr gng pce to rch ldng duo* **8/1**[3]

4425 **5** *1¼* **Kai Mook**[26] 1357 4-8-12 **59**..............................(t) KierenFox(3) 9 59
(Roger Ingram) *in rr: drvn along over 2f out: hdwy over 1f out: kpt on fnl f: nt rch ldrs* **20/1**

460- **6** *1* **Poor Prince**[164] 7614 4-8-13 **62**.............................. KieranO'Neill(5) 1 59
(Jeremy Gask) *t.k.h: led: narrowly hdd 3f out: wknd over 1f out* **11/1**

1565 **7** *½* **Spinning Ridge (IRE)**[14] 1604 6-9-1 **59**..............................(b) DavidProbert 7 55
(Ronald Harris) *wnt rt s: in rr: swtchd lft wl over 2f out: hdwy over 1f out: styd on fnl f: nvr any ch* **8/1**[3]

/114 **8** *½* **Stoneacre Gareth (IRE)**[63] 810 7-9-2 **60**.............................. AdamKirby 2 55
(K F Clutterbuck) *chsd ldrs: rdn 3f out: wknd fr 2f out* **4/1**[1]

2505 **9** *½* **Clearing House**[16] 1570 6-8-7 **58**.............................. BradleyBosley(7) 12 51+
(John Ryan) *in rr: sme hdwy on ins over 2f out: nvr rchd ldrs* **16/1**

-000 **10** *¾* **Caldermud (IRE)**[15] 1581 4-9-4 **62**..............................(t) IanMongan 13 53
(Olivia Maylam) *in rr: drvn and sme prog fr over 1f out* **40/1**

5033 **11** *5* **Onceaponatime (IRE)**[28] 1314 6-9-7 **65**..............................(b) CathyGannon 4 43
(Michael Squance) *t.k.h: hmpd wl over 2f out: a in rr* **14/1**

3064 **12** *¾* **Army Of Stars (IRE)**[29] 1295 5-9-2 **65**..............................(p) RyanClark(5) 14 41
(Michael Blake) *chsd ldrs 5f* **25/1**

-000 **13** *3* **Dingaan (IRE)**[88] 521 8-9-4 **62**.............................. RobbieFitzpatrick 6 30
(Peter Grayson) *a towards rr* **40/1**

1-00 **14** *nk* **Bishopbriggs (USA)**[26] 1368 6-9-4 **62**.............................. ChrisCatlin 5 29
(K F Clutterbuck) *in tch 5f* **40/1**

1m 25.75s (-0.25) **Going Correction** -0.075s/f (Stan) **14** Ran SP% **120.7**
Speed ratings (Par 101): **98,97,94,94,92 91,91,90,90,89 83,82,79,78**
toteswingers: 1&2 £4.20, 1&3 £12.90, 2&3 £9.90. CSF £27.48 CT £264.88 TOTE £5.60: £2.20, £2.50, £2.20; EX 47.10 Trifecta £122.80 Pool: £2,607.39 - 15.70 winning units..
Owner Mrs Alexandra J Chandris **Bred** Queensway S A **Trained** Baughurst, Hants
■ Stewards' Enquiry : David Probert two-day ban: careless riding (May 25-26)

FOCUS
They went just a fair pace in this ordinary handicap and nothing got into it from behind.
Stoneacre Gareth(IRE) Official explanation: jockey said gelding had no more to give

1996 BETDAQ MOBILE APPS MEDIAN AUCTION MAIDEN FILLIES' STKS 6f (P)

6:50 (6:50) (Class 5) 2-Y-O **£2,388** (£705; £352) **Stalls** Low

Form RPR

0 **1** **Red Larkspur (IRE)**[23] 1441 2-9-0 0.............................. DaneO'Neill 7 76+
(Roger Teal) *mde all: pushed along and qcknd clr fr 2f out: unchal* **13/2**[3]

2 *2½* **Costa Del Fortune (IRE)** 2-9-0 0.............................. RichardHughes 3 69+
(Richard Hannon) *racd in 3rd and drvn along fr 1/2-way: chsd wnr 1f out: kpt on but nvr any ch* **11/8**[1]

3 *hd* **Red Mischief (IRE)** 2-8-11 0.............................. JohnFahy(3) 8 68
(Harry Dunlop) *chsd wnr: rdn and flashed tail 2f out: styd on but nvr any ch: lost 2nd 1f out: kpt on same pce* **16/1**

4 *1¾* **Quick Bite (IRE)** 2-9-0 0.............................. LukeMorris 6 63
(Hugo Palmer) *chsd ldrs in 4th thrght: rdn 2f out: kpt on same pce fnl f* **14/1**

5 *1½* **Good Clodora (IRE)** 2-9-0 0.............................. ShaneKelly 2 58
(Brian Meehan) *a chsng ldrs in 5th: drvn and styd on fr over 2f out but nvr gng pce to rch ldrs* **7/1**

6 *¾* **Greatest Dancer (IRE)** 2-9-0 0.............................. FergusSweeney 4 56+
(Jamie Osborne) *towards rr but in tch: pushed along over 2f out: styd on but nvr gng pce to get into contention* **9/1**

7 *nse* **Flosse** 2-9-0 0.............................. J-PGuillambert 5 56+
(Ed Walker) *s.i.s: rdn along and green in rr: styd on fr 2f out but nvr gng pce to get into contention* **25/1**

8 *3¾* **Schmooze (IRE)** 2-9-0 0.............................. AdamKirby 1 10
(Marco Botti) *slowly away: green and a outpcd in rr* **5/1**[2]

1m 13.76s (0.66) **Going Correction** -0.075s/f (Stan) **8** Ran SP% **111.0**
Speed ratings (Par 90): **92,88,88,86,84 83,83,78**
toteswingers: 1&2 £2.10, 1&3 £19.10, 2&3 £7.40. CSF £14.91 TOTE £7.20: £1.90, £1.20, £4.20; EX 21.20 Trifecta £290.00 Pool: £3,527.27 - 9.00 winning units..
Owner The Gracenote Partnership **Bred** Wardstown Stud Ltd **Trained** Ashtead, Surrey

FOCUS
Seven of the eight runners were debutantes in this fillies' maiden and it went to the experienced runner who made all. Very guessy form but the winner stepped up massively.

NOTEBOOK
Red Larkspur(IRE) showed speed before fading into a 10l ninth of 14 in an ordinary 5f Windsor maiden on debut, but this time she didn't stop and ran her inexperienced rivals into gradual submission. It is hard to know how to rate the form but it was a professional display by this Red Clubs filly who is the second foal of a 7f 2-y-o winner. (op 15-2 tchd 6-1)
Costa Del Fortune(IRE) was pushed along at an early stage and could never get to grips with the winner. This was a bit disappointing from the hot favourite but she should have learned a lot and this 50,000gns second foal of a 2-y-o 6f Listed winner should improve next time. (op 13-8 tchd 7-4)
Red Mischief(IRE) was always in the leading trio on this encouraging first run. She cost just 1,500gns but is a half-sister to prolific 5f winner Guto. (op 14-1)
Quick Bite(IRE), a 29,000euros March foal, showed a bit of promise staying on late on debut.
Good Clodora(IRE), a £48,000 half-sister to smart sprinter Ruby Rocket, couldn't pick up when things got serious but she should be sharper and more streetwise on her second start. (op 13-2)
Schmooze(IRE) was prominent in the betting but she ran green after a slow start and was always outpaced on debut. Official explanation: jockey said filly ran green (op 4-1)

1997 BETDAQ.COM EXCHANGE PRICE MULTIPLES H'CAP 1m 4f (P)

7:20 (7:20) (Class 6) (0-65,65) 3-Y-O **£1,706** (£503; £252) **Stalls** Centre

Form RPR

00-4 **1** **Achalas (IRE)**[14] 1609 3-9-5 **63**.............................. EddieAhern 12 71+
(Heather Main) *in tch: racd on outside: drvn along whn pce qckns over 3f out: hdwy over 2f out: chsd ldr wl over 1f out: led fnl 120yds: readily* **9/2**[2]

4412 **2** *1* **Gower Rules (IRE)**[21] 1487 3-8-13 **60**.............................. SeanLevey(3) 4 66
(John Bridger) *sn led: qcknd 3 l clr ins fnl 3f: stl clr wl over 1f out: hdd and no ex fnl 120yds but kpt on wl to hold on for 2nd* **9/1**

600- **3** *nk* **Peira**[179] 7448 3-9-3 **61**.............................. JimmyQuinn 10 67+
(Jane Chapple-Hyam) *trckd ldrs tl n.m.r and checked over 2f out: drvn and qcknd 2f out and chsng wnr sn after: jnd for 2nd over 1f out: kpt on same pce into 3rd ins fnl f* **14/1**

000- **4** *6* **Ministry**[203] 7020 3-9-2 **60**.............................. LukeMorris 1 56
(John Best) *towards rr but stl in tch: hdwy: nt clr run and swtchd lft wl over 2f out: styd on fr over 1f out to take 4th ins fnl f but nvr gng pce to rch ldng trio* **8/1**

0-00 **5** *2¾* **Short Takes (USA)**[23] 1445 3-9-5 **63**.............................. SaleemGolam 2 55
(John Gosden) *chsd ldrs: drvn along fr 5f out: styd wl there tl wknd wl over 1f out* **15/2**[3]

60-3 **6** *¾* **Waterborne**[21] 1487 3-9-5 **63**.............................. TedDurcan 7 53
(Roger Charlton) *racd towards outside and chsd ldrs: pushed along fr 4f out and effrt over 2f out: nvr quite on terms and wknd over 1f out* **7/2**[1]

6-33 **7** *1½* **Warrant**[91] 469 3-9-4 **62**.............................. ShaneKelly 13 50
(Jane Chapple-Hyam) *towards rr: pushed along and hung rt wl over 2f out: sme prog fnl f but nvr any ch* **14/1**

50-0 **8** *3* **Viking Rose (IRE)**[30] 1270 3-9-4 **62**.............................. SebSanders 8 45
(James Eustace) *racd towards outside: sme prog fr 2f out but nvr anywhere nr ldrs* **25/1**

-535 **9** *1¼* **Laffraaj (IRE)**[28] 1311 3-9-6 **64**..............................(v) ChrisCatlin 3 45
(Pat Eddery) *chsd ldrs: rdn and hung rt ins fnl 3f: wknd ins fnl 2f* **20/1**

4030 **10** *10* **Anna Fontenail**[54] 898 3-9-2 **60**.............................. JamesMillman 14 25
(Rod Millman) *taken down early: s.i.s: t.k.h: a in rr* **16/1**

14-5 **11** *1¾* **Rosa Midnight (USA)**[18] 1526 3-9-0 **63**.............................. HarryBentley(5) 5 25
(Michael Bell) *sn chsng ldr: rdn 3f out: wknd rapidly appr fnl 2f* **8/1**

0-03 **12** *19* **Valdaw**[42] 1053 3-9-3 **61**.............................. EddieCreighton 9 —
(Joseph Tuite) *rdn 1/2-way: a in rr* **25/1**

030- **13** *2* **Fastada (IRE)**[209] 6875 3-9-6 **64**.............................. CathyGannon 11 —
(Jonathan Portman) *rdn most of way: a bhd* **25/1**

2m 33.62s (-0.88) **Going Correction** -0.075s/f (Stan) **13** Ran SP% **119.9**
Speed ratings (Par 97): **99,98,98,94,92 91,90,88,87,81 80,67,66**
toteswingers: 1&2 £8.20, 1&3 £11.50, 2&3 £26.10. CSF £42.46 CT £516.67 TOTE £5.90: £2.40, £3.00, £6.60; EX 58.00 TRIFECTA Not won..
Owner Highnote Thoroughbreds **Bred** Stonethorn Stud Farms Ltd **Trained** Kingston Lisle, Oxon

FOCUS
A modest handicap for 3-y-os. The first three pulled clear and the winner did well to reel in the long-time leader.
Valdaw Official explanation: jockey said colt lost its action
Fastada(IRE) Official explanation: jockey said filly did not face the kickback

1998 LAY BACK AND WIN AT BETDAQ.COM MEDIAN AUCTION MAIDEN STKS 1m 4f (P)

7:50 (7:51) (Class 6) 3-4-Y-O **£1,706** (£503; £252) **Stalls** Centre

Form RPR

24- **1** **Mulaqen**[192] 7248 3-8-9 0.............................. TadhgO'Shea 7 83+
(Marcus Tregoning) *trckd ldrs: led over 2f out: sn rdn and hung rt: styd on u.p thrght fnl f: kpt on all out cl home* **3/1**[2]

2 *¾* **Keys (IRE)**[130] 4-10-0 0.............................. TedDurcan 10 84+
(Roger Charlton) *hld up in tch: drvn and hdwy to go 2nd 2f out: styd on thrght fnl f but nvr gng pce to rch wnr* **8/15**[1]

044- **3** *8* **Kyllachy Spirit**[242] 5954 3-8-9 73.............................. ShaneKelly 4 69
(William Knight) *jnd ldr 9f out: led 6f out: rdn 3f out: hdd over 2f out: sn no ch w ldng duo* **11/1**[3]

36 **4** *2¾* **Clarion Call**[21] 1484 3-8-9 0.............................. CathyGannon 6 65
(Eve Johnson Houghton) *t.k.h and chsd ldrs: rdn 3f out: no ch w ldng trio fnl 2f but clrly 4th best* **14/1**

50 **5** *9* **Pearl Mountain (IRE)**[16] 1572 4-9-6 0.............................. SimonPearce(3) 8 47
(Lydia Pearce) *in tch: rdn: effrt and hung rt ins fnl 3f: sn btn* **50/1**

6 *1* **Mr Pyramus** 3-8-9 0.............................. EddieAhern 9 49
(Jonathan Portman) *in rr: rn wd and green bnd 4f out: nvr anywhere nr ldrs* **33/1**

7 *1* **Reveal The Light**[90] 4-9-9 0.............................. KirstyMilczarek 5 44
(Garry Woodward) *slowly away: in rr: drvn and mod prog 4f out: nvr nr ldrs and sn wknd* **66/1**

0- **8** *3* **Ocean Treasure (IRE)**[146] 7887 4-9-9 0.............................. LiamKeniry 2 39
(Edward Vaughan) *chsd ldrs: lost position 6f out: sme prog on ins bnd 3f out: green: hung lft and wknd sn after* **50/1**

0 **9** *4* **Rachael's Ruby**[14] 1605 4-9-6 0.............................. JohnFahy(3) 1 33
(Roger Teal) *led tl hdd 6f out: wknd qckly 3f out* **66/1**

0 **10** *78* **Ellies Girl (IRE)**[9] 1761 [illegible].............................. LukeMorris 3 —
(Ronald Harris) *s.i.s: t.k.h: a wl bhd: t.o* **66/1**

2m 33.56s (-0.94) **Going Correction** -0.075s/f (Stan)
WFA 3 from 4yo 19lb **10** Ran SP% **116.6**
Speed ratings (Par 101): **100,99,94,92,86 85,85,83,80,28**
toteswingers: 1&2 £1.20, 1&3 £2.20, 2&3 £2.70. CSF £4.83 TOTE £4.50: £1.30, £1.10, £2.10; EX 7.10 Trifecta £21.80 Pool: £6,039.53 - 204.41 winning units..
Owner Hamdan Al Maktoum **Bred** Stowell Hill Ltd **Trained** Lambourn, Berks
■ Stewards' Enquiry : Tadhg O'Shea one-day ban: used whip in incorrect place (May 25)

FOCUS
There was little strength in depth in this maiden. The two market leaders finished a long way clear but not in the order the market suggested they would.
Mr Pyramus Official explanation: jockey said gelding was slowly away
Ellies Girl(IRE) Official explanation: jockey said filly hung badly left

1999 BRITISH BIG BAND 22.06.11 CLAIMING STKS 1m (P)

8:20 (8:20) (Class 6) 3-Y-O **£1,706** (£503; £252) **Stalls** Low

Form RPR

1 **Merton Lady** 3-8-4 0.............................. LukeMorris 9 65+
(Peter Winkworth) *hld up in rr: smooth hdwy on ins over 2f out to ld on bit wl over 1f out: v easily* **9/2**[3]

135 **2** *2¾* **So Is She (IRE)**[6] 1828 3-8-10 66..............................(p) CathyGannon 3 61
(Alan Bailey) *led: rdn 2f out: hdd wl over 1f out: sn no ch w wnr but kpt on wl for clr 2nd* **11/8**[1]

0-00 **3** *4* **Custom House (IRE)**[5] 1843 3-9-9 80.............................. RichardHughes 8 65
(Richard Hannon) *trckd ldr: pushed along to chal insde fnl 3f: nvr quite upsides and btn over 1f out: eased whn wl hld clsng stages* **7/4**[2]

00-0 **4** *3* **Arctic Reach**[9] 1769 3-8-11 50.............................. AndreaAtzeni 4 46
(Brendan Powell) *chsd ldrs: rdn 3f out: no ch w ldng trio fnl 2f* **25/1**

6-05 **5** *8* **Senor Tibor (USA)**[26] 1369 3-8-11 51..............................(v) EddieCreighton 5 28
(Edward Creighton) *awkward leaving stalls and sn drvn to get in tch: rdn again 4f out: no ch fnl 3f* **66/1**

0-00 **6** *1¾* **Dune Island**[11] 1683 3-9-1 45.............................. SeanLevey(3) 7 31
(John Bridger) *chsd ldrs tl wknd 3f out* **100/1**

-500 **7** *11* **Miss Boops (IRE)**[6] 1837 3-9-4 72.............................. LiamKeniry 10 —
(Zoe Davison) *chsd ldrs tl wd and wknd 3f out* **16/1**

1m 39.46s (-0.34) **Going Correction** -0.075s/f (Stan) **7** Ran SP% **108.9**
Speed ratings (Par 97): **98,95,91,88,80 78,67**
toteswingers: 1&2 £1.90, 1&3 £2.50, 2&3 £1.10. CSF £10.05 TOTE £4.60: £2.10, £1.20; EX 11.10 Trifecta £49.40 Pool: £350.73 - 5.25 winning units..Merton Lady was claimed by Mr T A Jones for £3,.000.

Owner P Winkworth **Bred** Peter Winkworth **Trained** Chiddingfold, Surrey

FOCUS

A newcomer put in a smooth display to power clear from the market leaders in this claimer.

2000 PETER ANDRE 06.07.11 H'CAP — 1m (P)

8:50 (8:50) (Class 4) (0-85,85) 4-Y-0+ **£4,079** (£1,214; £606; £303) **Stalls** Low

Form / RPR

461- **1** **Point North (IRE)**[196] 7183 4-9-2 **80** ....(t) WilliamBuick 9 95+
(Jeremy Noseda) *t.k.h: hld up in tch: shkn up and qcknd over 1f out to ld jst ins fnl f: sn in command: easily* **2/1**[1]

56-0 **2** 1 ½ **Tartan Trip**[14] 1603 4-9-5 **83** ....(v) DavidProbert 11 89
(Andrew Balding) *in rr but in tch: hdwy 2f out: styd on wl appr fnl f: tk 2nd cl home but nvr any ch w easy wnr* **11/2**[2]

00-6 **3** nk **Gobama**[22] 1467 4-9-5 **83** .... SebSanders 12 89
(J W Hills) *trckd ldrs: drvn and qcknd to chse wnr ins fnl f but nvr any ch: ct for 2nd cl home* **16/1**

5231 **4** nk **Tevez**[14] 1610 6-9-1 **79** .... CathyGannon 8 84
(Des Donovan) *in rr: hdwy on outer fr 2f out: styd on wl fnl f and kpt on wl clsng stages but nvr any ch w wnr* **10/1**

3-31 **5** 2 **Tiradito (USA)**[29] 1296 4-9-5 **83** ....(p) AdamKirby 7 83
(Marco Botti) *chsd ldrs: rdn over 2f out: styd wl there tl outpcd fnl f* **11/1**

0-00 **6** shd **Gaily Noble (IRE)**[21] 1479 5-9-3 **81** .... FergusSweeney 13 81
(Andrew Haynes) *chsd ldr: rdn over 2f out: wknd ins fnl f* **16/1**

1110 **7** 1 **Resuscitator (USA)**[9] 1760 4-9-0 **78** ....(v) EddieAhern 10 76
(Heather Main) *led tl hdd jst ins fnl f: sn btn* **16/1**

2-13 **8** shd **Chilli Green**[80] 623 4-9-5 **83** .... DaneO'Neill 14 80
(John Akehurst) *chsd ldrs: rdn ins fnl 2f: wknd fnl f* **15/2**[3]

6040 **9** ½ **Pegasus Again (USA)**[74] 703 6-8-12 **79** .... SeanLevey(3) 6 75+
(Robert Mills) *hld up in rr: continually nt clr run thrght fnl 2f: nt rcvr* **25/1**

2060 **10** 1 ½ **Titan Triumph**[22] 1460 7-8-13 **82** ....(t) HarryBentley(5) 5 75
(William Knight) *chsd ldrs: rdn appr fnl 2f: wknd jst ins fnl f* **20/1**

1121 **11** ½ **Almahaza (IRE)**[22] 1467 7-9-3 **81** .... NeilChalmers 4 72+
(Adrian Chamberlain) *in rr: hdwy fr 2f out: nt clr run over 1f out and again whn effrt ins fnl f: no ch after* **25/1**

-304 **12** hd **Red Somerset (USA)**[39] 1103 8-9-5 **83** .... MartinLane 2 74
(Mike Murphy) *in rr: rdn and sme prog over 1f out but nvr gng pce to get beyond mid-div* **14/1**

0-30 **13** 5 **Icelandic**[22] 1467 9-9-7 **85** ....(t) JamesDoyle 3 64
(Frank Sheridan) *bhd most of way* **25/1**

1m 38.19s (-1.61) **Going Correction** -0.075s/f (Stan) **13** Ran SP% **118.5**
Speed ratings (Par 105): **105,103,103,102,100 100,99,99,97 97,97,92**
toteswingers: 1&2 £2.80, 1&3 £33.70, 2&3 £17.40. CSF £10.95 CT £131.51 TOTE £2.60: £2.50, £1.90, £4.10; EX 18.90 Trifecta £172.80 Part won. Pool: £233.53 - 0.10 winning units..

Owner Sir Robert Ogden **Bred** Barronstown Stud **Trained** Newmarket, Suffolk

FOCUS

A decent handicap in which the well-backed favourite was an impressive winner from off the steady pace.

Resuscitator(USA) Official explanation: vet said gelding lost a left-fore shoe

Pegasus Again(USA) Official explanation: jockey said, regarding running and riding, that his orders were to ride a patient race as the gelding has had breathing problems and the trainer was keen to get it relaxed and to finish, adding that in the home straight he encountered traffic problems and never got a clear run.

Almahaza(IRE) Official explanation: jockey said gelding was denied a clear run

2001 REWARDS4RACING.COM H'CAP — 6f (P)

9:20 (9:20) (Class 5) (0-70,70) 4-Y-0+ **£2,388** (£705; £352) **Stalls** Low

Form / RPR

4-13 **1** **Dashwood**[21] 1497 4-9-0 **63** ....(t) WilliamCarson 4 76+
(Giles Bravery) *n.m.r sn after s: chsd ldrs: drvn to ld appr fnl f: rdn out* **6/4**[1]

-400 **2** 2 ¼ **The Wee Chief (IRE)**[9] 1771 5-9-4 **67** ....(t) PatDobbs 2 73
(Jimmy Fox) *stdd s: hld up in tch: travelling wl fr 2f out: rdn to chse wnr ins fnl f but hd high and sn fnd no ex* **11/2**[3]

660- **3** 1 ¼ **Dies Solis**[231] 6295 4-8-10 **59** .... WilliamBuick 1 61
(Jeremy Gask) *drvn to ld: rdn 2f out: hdd appr fnl f: kpt on same pce* **4/1**[2]

156- **4** ½ **Katy's Secret**[161] 7656 4-8-10 **59** .... LukeMorris 7 59
(William Jarvis) *in rr: hdwy and swtchd rt ins fnl 2f: styd on same pce u.p fnl f* **25/1**

155- **5** nk **Paphos**[146] 7892 4-8-9 **63** ....(v) RyanClark(5) 11 62
(Stuart Williams) *in rr: hdwy 2f out: styd on fnl f: one pce cl home* **8/1**

00-0 **6** 2 **Knightfire (IRE)**[28] 1314 4-9-2 **65** .... ShaneKelly 8 58
(Walter Swinburn) *in rr: drvn along fr 2f out: nvr gng pce to get into contention* **16/1**

0006 **7** 1 ¼ **Vhujon (IRE)**[30] 1276 6-8-11 **60** .... RobbieFitzpatrick 9 49
(Peter Grayson) *in rr: faltered bnd 3f out: mod late prog* **50/1**

00 **8** shd **Gala Spirit (IRE)**[15] 1581 4-8-13 **62** .... AndreaAtzeni 5 51
(Michael Wigham) *chsd ldrs tl wknd appr fnl f* **33/1**

4455 **9** 3 ½ **Bold Ring**[56] 865 5-8-8 **57** .... EddieCreighton 3 35
(Edward Creighton) *chsd ldrs tl wknd ins fnl 2f* **40/1**

1235 **10** ¾ **Dvinsky (USA)**[13] 1634 10-9-7 **70** ....(b) AdamKirby 6 45
(Michael Squance) *n.m.r sn after s: chsd ldrs 4f* **10/1**

1m 12.37s (-0.73) **Going Correction** -0.075s/f (Stan) **10** Ran SP% **112.7**
Speed ratings (Par 103): **101,98,96,95,95 92,90,90,86,85**
toteswingers: 1&2 £2.90, 1&3 £2.70, 2&3 £3.90. CSF £9.04 CT £26.64 TOTE £2.80: £1.80, £2.80, £1.10; EX 10.50 Trifecta £63.70 Pool: £310.80 - 3.61 winning units..

Owner Macattack, William Lea Screed & Form IT **Bred** Darley **Trained** Cowlinge, Suffolk

FOCUS

A minor sprint handicap run at a fair pace.

Dvinsky(USA) Official explanation: jockey said gelding hung right

T/Plt: £27.50 to a £1 stake. Pool:£57,548.79 - 1,524.76 winning tickets. T/Qpdt: £10.80 to a £1 stake. Pool:£4,726.32 - 322.30 winning tickets. ST

YORK (L-H)

Wednesday, May 11

OFFICIAL GOING: Good (7.3)

Wind: Moderate 1/2 against Weather: Fine and sunny

2002 INFINITY TYRES STKS (H'CAP) — 1m 2f 88y

1:30 (1:31) (Class 2) (0-100,99) 4-Y-0+ **£12,952** (£3,854; £1,926; £962) **Stalls** Low

Form / RPR

4/1- **1** **Pekan Star**[209] 6876 4-8-7 **85** .... NeilCallan 17 97+
(Roger Varian) *trckd ldrs: hmpd 3f out: effrt over 2f out: r.o to ld ins fnl f: kpt on wl* **13/2**[2]

422- **2** 1 ¼ **Right Step**[165] 7591 4-8-11 **94** .... HarryBentley(5) 5 104
(Alan Jarvis) *lw: trckd ldrs: chal over 2f out: led and edgd rt over 1f out: hdd ins fnl f: no ex* **20/1**

0041 **3** 1 ¾ **Arlequin**[25] 1387 4-9-0 **92** .... PhilipRobinson 1 98
(James Bethell) *swtg: chsd ldrs: hmpd and swtchd lft 3f out: upsides over 1f out: kpt on same pce* **14/1**

1042 **4** 2 **Suits Me**[25] 1410 8-8-11 **89** .... DarryllHolland 4 91
(David Barron) *trckd ldrs: led over 2f out: hdd and carried rt over 1f out: kpt on same pce* **14/1**

40-6 **5** 1 ½ **Shavansky**[21] 1479 7-8-13 **91** .... JimmyFortune 16 90
(Rod Millman) *in rr: hdwy on wd outside over 4f out: chsng ldrs whn sltly hmpd over 1f out: kpt on same pce* **25/1**

1-10 **6** 1 ¾ **Ingleby Spirit**[21] 1479 4-8-8 **93** .... LauraBarry(7) 13 89+
(Richard Fahey) *lw: hld up in rr: hdwy and swtchd outside over 2f out: styd on wl fnl f* **33/1**

15-2 **7** 2 ¼ **Resurge (IRE)**[21] 1479 6-9-7 **99** .... IanMongan 12 90
(Stuart Kittow) *swtg: s.i.s: in rr: styd on fnl 2f: nt rch ldrs* **20/1**

116- **8** 1 ½ **Taqleed (IRE)**[221] 6562 4-9-3 **95** .... RichardHills 20 83
(John Gosden) *hld up in rr: hdwy over 2f out: kpt on one pce nvr nr ldrs* **11/2**[1]

0/1 **9** shd **Desert Romance (IRE)**[21] 1490 5-8-11 **89** .... DanielTudhope 15 77
(David O'Meara) *w ldrs: wknd 2f out* **40/1**

12-3 **10** 2 ¼ **Northside Prince (IRE)**[25] 1387 5-8-9 **87** .... PJMcDonald 19 70+
(Alan Swinbank) *in rr: sme hdwy over 2f out: nt clr run: nvr on terms* **16/1**

5-10 **11** nk **Nice Style (IRE)**[46] 991 6-9-5 **97** .... SteveDrowne 6 80
(Jeremy Gask) *s.i.s: sme hdwy over 2f out: nvr nr ldrs* **40/1**

0-05 **12** ½ **Itlaaq**[25] 1387 5-8-12 **90** .... PaulMulrennan 18 72
(Michael Easterby) *in rr: sme hdwy over 4f out: nvr nr ldrs* **33/1**

20-1 **13** ¾ **Bonfire Knight**[39] 1098 4-8-13 **91** .... TomEaves 7 71
(John Quinn) *chsd ldrs: lost pl 3f out* **12/1**

10-0 **14** shd **Treble Jig (USA)**[18] 1529 4-8-10 **88** .... RyanMoore 10 68
(Sir Michael Stoute) *lw: chsd ldrs: drvn over 3f out: lost pl over 2f out* **14/1**

20-0 **15** 2 ¼ **Sirvino**[21] 1479 6-9-3 **95** .... GrahamGibbons 2 71
(David Barron) *hld up in rr: sme hdwy 2f out: nvr on terms* **16/1**

100- **16** 1 ¾ **Gold Rules**[256] 5511 4-8-4 **89** .... DavidSimmonson(7) 3 61
(Michael Easterby) *mid-div: hmpd after 1f: no threat after* **66/1**

0-02 **17** hd **Pleasant Day (IRE)**[5] 1879 4-8-9 **87** .... PaulHanagan 14 59
(Richard Fahey) *in rr: drvn over 3f out: nvr a factor* **8/1**[3]

400- **18** 4 ½ **Caldercruix (USA)**[214] 6749 4-8-9 **87** .... JamieSpencer 8 50
(Tom Tate) *led: hdd over 2f out: sn wknd: eased ins fnl f* **40/1**

-200 **19** 2 ¼ **Sand Skier**[11] 1684 4-8-8 **86** .... KierenFallon 9 44
(Mark Johnston) *t.k.h in mid-div: drvn over 3f out: sn lost pl* **16/1**

14- **20** 2 ¾ **Diescentric (USA)**[363] 2045 4-8-12 **90** .... TomQueally 11 43
(Sir Henry Cecil) *lw: trckd ldrs: effrt 3f out: sn wknd* **11/1**

2m 8.73s (-3.77) **Going Correction** -0.075s/f (Good) **20** Ran SP% **121.6**
Speed ratings (Par 109): **112,111,109,108,106 105,103,102,102,100 100,99,99,99,97 96,95,92,90,88**
toteswingers: 1&2 £46.00, 1&3 £19.30, 2&3 £55.70. CSF £137.65 CT £1774.90 TOTE £7.10: £2.30, £4.60, £2.90, £3.40; EX 173.60 TRIFECTA Not won..

Owner H R H Sultan Ahmad Shah **Bred** Ecurie Les Monceaux **Trained** Newmarket, Suffolk

FOCUS

A typically hot handicap, as you would expect, and they took no prisoners early. The field came up the centre in the straight. The winner is rated up 6lb, but there are doubts over how many showed their form.

NOTEBOOK

Pekan Star has obviously been very hard to train with his three efforts to date (including this one) coming over a period of 621 days, but the form of his Nottingham maiden win last October has received several boosts since and he looked fit. There was one slightly anxious moment after a furlong when his rider briefly lost his left iron, but apart from that everything went smoothly and he quickened up impressively to hit the front inside the last furlong and win going away. There are no specific plans for him and connections will wait to see what the handicapper does. Also it's hoped he comes out of this race in one piece, but all being well he looks just the type for a big handicap at Royal Ascot such as the Wolferton or Duke Of Edinburgh. (op 6-1)

Right Step ran some fine races in defeat last year, but he was returning to the track off another new career-high mark despite being without a win since his second start at two. Having travelled well behind the leaders, he was in front over a furlong out but then proved no match for the winner. He was unfortunate to bump into an unexposed sort here, and the likelihood is that he will be put up again. (op 25-1)

Arlequin, put up 6lb for last month's Doncaster success, was always up there and had every chance 2f out before being unable to quicken. He has probably run right up to his best. (tchd 12-1)

Suits Me, put up 6lb for last month's Doncaster success, was always up there and had every chance 2f out before being unable to quicken. He has probably run right up to his best.

Shavansky, not disgraced in the City And Suburban on his reappearance, looked dangerous when moving up to challenge coming to the last furlong, but his effort then flattened out. (op 33-1)

Ingleby Spirit was well held off this career-high mark in the City And Suburban and Paul Hanagan desert him in favour of Pleasant Day. Given plenty to do, he ran on well after being switched right over 2f out, but had far too much ground to make up.

Resurge(IRE) was hoisted up 5lb for finishing second in the City And Suburban when he had four of today's rivals behind him, but he could make little impression from the middle of the field here. (op 18-1)

Taqleed(IRE), last seen finishing sixth in the Cambridgeshire in October, was allowed to take his chance this time but it was always going to be difficult for him from the outside stall. Held up last early, a brief effort after turning into the straight came to nothing but he still remains capable of a lot more than he was able to show here. (op 6-1)

Northside Prince(IRE) Official explanation: jockey said gelding was denied a clear run

Treble Jig(USA) showed nothing on his Sandown return, but he won second time out in each of his previous two seasons, so better might have been expected. He was handy enough early, but then lost his place after turning in and there was no way back. (op 12-1)

Diescentric(USA) showed he could go well fresh when winning the Wood Ditton on his debut in April of last year, so his absence since the following month wasn't a great concern, but as it turned out he ran a shocker. He was expected to perform a lot better than this so it looks a case of back to the drawing board. (op 10-1)

2003 DOWNLOAD THE BLUE SQUARE IPHONE APP STKS (H'CAP) — 7f

2:00 (2:01) (Class 2) (0-100,97) 3-Y-0 **£12,952** (£3,854; £1,926; £962) **Stalls** Low

Form / RPR

14-2 **1** **Common Touch (IRE)**[27] 1326 3-8-7 **83** .... FrederikTylicki 4 91+
(Richard Fahey) *athletic: leggy: t.k.h towards rr: hdwy over 2f out: chal over 1f out: styd on to ld ins fnl f: kpt on wl towards fin* **11/2**

00-6 **2** 1 ¼ **Chiswick Bey (IRE)**[36] 1152 3-9-0 **90** .... PaulHanagan 7 95
(Richard Fahey) *trckd ldrs: effrt over 2f out: upsides over 1f out: styd on same pce last 75yds* **5/1**[3]

-021 **3** ¾ **Iceblast**[11] 1697 3-8-4 **83** oh3 .... JamesSullivan(3) 6 86
(Michael Easterby) *hld up: effrt and sltly outpcd over 2f out: hdwy over 1f out: styd on same pce fnl f* **9/2**[2]

05-0 **4** 3/4 **Invincible Ridge (IRE)**[17] 1547 3-9-5 **95** RyanMoore 1 96
(Richard Hannon) *trckd ldrs: led over 2f out: hdd last 100yds: edgd lft and fdd* **13/2**

4445 **5** 7 **Sonoran Sands (IRE)**[17] 1547 3-8-11 **87** (b[1]) LiamKeniry 2 69
(J S Moore) *led: hdd over 2f out: sn lost pl* **7/1**

10-3 **6** 7 **Shropshire (IRE)**[25] 1405 3-9-7 **97** RobertWinston 3 60
(B W Hills) *dwlt: hld up: effrt and edgd lft over 3f out: upsides over 2f out: sn wknd: eased nr fin* **15/8**[1]

1m 23.88s (-1.42) **Going Correction** -0.075s/f (Good) **6** Ran SP% **110.8**
Speed ratings (Par 105): **105,103,102,101,93 85**
toteswingers: 1&2 £3.20, 1&3 £2.50, 2&3 £4.20. CSF £31.30 TOTE £7.20: £2.40, £3.00; EX 14.40.
Owner Nicholas Wrigley & Kevin Hart **Bred** Overbury Stallions Ltd And D Boocock **Trained** Musley Bank, N Yorks

FOCUS
A smaller field than normal for this good-quality handicap and it produced a 1-2 for trainer Richard Fahey. Again the runners came down the centre of the track in the straight. It was well run and the form is rated on the positive side.

NOTEBOOK
Common Touch(IRE) was 3lb higher than when narrowly beaten on his Beverley return, but was deserted by Paul Hanagan in favour of Chiswick Bey. However, it was clear from some way out that he was travelling better than his stable companion and, once the gun was put to his head, he found plenty. This was only his fourth start, so further progress is very likely. (op 13-2 tchd 5-1)
Chiswick Bey(IRE) was much more streetwise than the winner, which may have been the reason for the stable jockey choosing him, and he had shaped as though this step up to 7f would suit following his Pontefract reappearance. He had every chance and certainly the trip didn't beat him, but he was up against a much more progressive rival. (op 9-2)
Iceblast was 3lb wrong here, which meant he was 11lb higher than when easily winning a Thirsk classified event last month. He took a little time to pick up when first coming under pressure 2f from home, and the way he then stayed on suggests that 1m might suit him even better now.
Invincible Ridge(IRE) didn't run very well off this mark on his Sandown reappearance, but this was better and having held every chance he wasn't seen off until well inside the last furlong. He lacks the scope of a few of these, though. (op 9-1 tchd 10-1)
Sonoran Sands(IRE), having his eighth start of the year, had first-time blinkers replacing the cheekpieces but he raced plenty freely out in front and had run himself into the ground before the 2f pole. (op 8-1)
Shropshire(IRE), making his handicap debut after finishing 10l behind Frankel in the Greenham, was travelling well when brought to challenge on the far side of the group over 2f from home, but was on the retreat almost as soon as he arrived. This was too bad to be true. (op 7-4 tchd 2-1)

2004 TATTERSALLS MUSIDORA STKS (GROUP 3) (FILLIES) 1m 2f 88y
2:30 (2:31) (Class 1) 3-Y-O **£36,900** (£13,988; £7,000; £3,490; £1,748) **Stalls** Low

Form RPR

3-2 **1** **Joviality**[17] 1546 3-8-12 0 WilliamBuick 3 108
(John Gosden) *lw: dwlt: hld up: stdy hdwy over 3f out: styd on to ld 1f out: hld on nr fin* **5/1**[3]

2-15 **2** hd **Barefoot Lady (IRE)**[10] 1719 3-8-12 104 PaulHanagan 2 108
(Richard Fahey) *t.k.h early: trckd ldrs: pushed along over 5f out: styd on to ld over 1f out: sn hdd: rallied ins fnl f: jst hld* **9/4**[2]

40- **3** 9 **Whey Sauce (JPN)**[193] 7235 3-8-12 0 JackMitchell 1 90?
(Peter Chapple-Hyam) *trckd ldrs: drvn over 2f out: sn outpcd: kpt on to take modest 3rd nr fin* **25/1**

3-1 **4** hd **Arizona Jewel**[17] 1549 3-8-12 0 TomQueally 4 90
(Sir Henry Cecil) *lw: trckd ldr: led over 2f out: hdd over 1f out: sn wknd* **11/8**[1]

5 hd **Amazing Beauty (IRE)**[33] 1230 3-8-12 0 RyanMoore 5 89
(A P O'Brien, Ire) *w'like: led: qcknd over 4f out: hdd over 2f out: wknd over 1f out* **11/2**

2m 10.6s (-1.90) **Going Correction** -0.075s/f (Good) **5** Ran SP% **108.8**
Speed ratings (Par 106): **104,103,96,96,96**
CSF £16.14 TOTE £5.40: £2.50, £1.50; EX 12.50.
Owner H R H Princess Haya Of Jordan **Bred** Highclere Stud And Floors Farming **Trained** Newmarket, Suffolk

FOCUS
It's highly unlikely any of these will run in the Oaks, let alone have a serious a chance. The pace seemed just modest before being wound up early in the straight, and the final time was 1.87 seconds slower than earlier Class 2 older horse handicap. Only five runners and the front two finished well clear, so hard to know exactly what to make of the form, but it was probably just fair for the grade. This was not a severe test of stamina.

NOTEBOOK
Joviality has plenty of size and won despite looking green and probably still being a bit on the weak side. She displayed good speed to move into a challenging position early in the straight and briefly looked set to win well, but she got stuck in a protracted duel with the far more battle-hardened Barefoot Lady. Once under maximum pressure, she was inclined to carry her head just a touch high on occasions, but that was most likely down to immaturity and she did well to get the better of Richard Fahey's filly. By Cape Cross, out of a 1m-winning Night Shift mare, it is doubtful she'll stay much further and she's likely to be aimed at the French Oaks, which is run over only a few more yards. She will need to progress significantly to have serious claims, though, and while that's possible, the suspicion is she'll find it tough going at this stage of her development. Her stamina for a stronger-run race will also have to proven. (op 11-2)
Barefoot Lady(IRE) was worth a try in this considering all she did was stay on when winning the Nell Gwyn and finishing fifth in the Guineas, and her dam won over 1m2f. It's hard to argue she didn't get the trip, although she didn't help herself by racing a bit too enthusiastically through the opening stages. Paul Hanagan suggested afterwards the filly will get further and will be suited by a bigger field and a stronger pace. (op 2-1)
Whey Sauce(JPN) had a stiff task for a twice-raced maiden, not least because she was the only filly who hadn't had a run this year, but she performed creditably, picking up some valuable black type in the process. She can win a minor race before stepping back up in class. (op 33-1)
Arizona Jewel disappointed. There's a theory that she benefited from racing on a favourable strip of ground when winning a decent Sandown maiden over this trip on her reappearance and she struggled badly on this rise in class. It might be that she'll prove herself a smart filly in due course and an excuse came to light when she was later found to have been heavily in season. (op 7-4)
Amazing Beauty(IRE) found this a lot tougher than the Dundalk maiden she won her reappearance. Her stable have a more realistic Oaks contender in the shape of Wonder Of Wonders, although supporters of that filly might have liked to see this one fare at least a little better. (op 5-1 tchd 9-2)

2005 DUKE OF YORK BLUE SQUARE STKS (GROUP 2) 6f
3:00 (3:00) (Class 1) 3-Y-O+
£56,770 (£21,520; £10,770; £5,370; £2,690; £1,350) **Stalls** High

Form RPR

140- **1** **Delegator**[186] 7364 5-9-7 112 FrankieDettori 9 117+
(Saeed Bin Suroor) *lw: hld up: stdy hdwy stands' side 2f out: r.o wl to ld towards fin* **5/1**[1]

64-5 **2** 1/2 **Regal Parade**[38] 1118 7-9-7 119 AdrianNicholls 12 115
(David Nicholls) *in rr: hdwy stands' side over 2f out: led ins fnl f: hdd and no ex nr fin* **13/2**[2]

40-0 **3** 1/2 **Tiddliwinks**[10] 1720 5-9-7 94 PhillipMakin 8 114
(Kevin Ryan) *trckd ldrs: n.m.r 2f out: kpt on wl ins fnl f* **40/1**

-554 **4** 1/2 **Hitchens (IRE)**[39] 1093 6-9-7 102 GrahamGibbons 13 112
(David Barron) *hld up in mid-div: stdy hdwy over 2f out: upsides ins fnl f: no ex* **14/1**

00-0 **5** 1 **Triple Aspect (IRE)**[46] 996 5-9-7 107 RyanMoore 10 109
(William Haggas) *mid-div: effrt over 2f out: nt clr run over 1f out: edgd rt: styd on wl last 150yds* **12/1**

223- **6** 1/2 **Dalghar (FR)**[191] 7278 5-9-7 113 JimmyFortune 7 107
(Andrew Balding) *wnt lft s: trckd ldrs: upsides over 1f out: kpt on same pce ins fnl f* **7/1**[3]

42-1 **7** 2 **Genki (IRE)**[27] 1340 7-9-7 111 (v) SteveDrowne 5 101+
(Roger Charlton) *mid-div: drvn over 2f out: kpt on fnl f: nvr a threat* **17/2**

4-31 **8** hd **Hamish McGonagall**[18] 1518 6-9-7 107 DavidAllan 2 100
(Tim Easterby) *w ldr: kpt on same pce appr fnl f* **20/1**

261- **9** 1 1/4 **Markab**[249] 5744 8-9-12 118 PatCosgrave 4 101
(Henry Candy) *lw: led: hdd ins fnl f: fdd fnl 75yds* **10/1**

31-5 **10** 2 **Ladies Are Forever**[28] 1319 3-8-8 103 TomEaves 11 84
(Geoffrey Oldroyd) *sn chsng ldrs: wknd over 1f out* **20/1**

-060 **11** nk **Prime Defender**[10] 1720 7-9-7 105 RobertWinston 3 89
(B W Hills) *lw: chsd ldrs: sn drvn along: one pce over 1f out: eased nr fin* **25/1**

0022 **12** 2 **Rain Delayed (IRE)**[11] 1687 5-9-7 105 JMurtagh 1 82
(Michael Dods) *in rr: sme hdwy 2f out: hung rt: nvr a factor* **12/1**

61-5 **13** 2 **Inler (IRE)**[27] 1340 4-9-7 106 MartinDwyer 14 76
(Brian Meehan) *trckd ldrs: wknd over 1f out* **11/1**

520- **14** 5 **Rose Blossom**[220] 6608 4-9-4 106 PaulHanagan 6 57
(Richard Fahey) *dwlt and hmpd s: sn in mid-div: lost pl over 1f out: eased clsng stages* **9/1**

1m 10.18s (-1.72) **Going Correction** -0.075s/f (Good)
WFA 3 from 4yo+ 10lb **14** Ran SP% **118.3**
Speed ratings (Par 115): **108,107,106,106,104 104,101,101,99,96 96,93,91,84**
toteswingers:1&2:£8.10, 1&3:£34.40, 2&3:£78.00 CSF £33.23 TOTE £5.60: £2.50, £3.00, £9.80; EX 40.50 Trifecta £1945.40 Part won. Pool: £2,629.02 - 0.20 winning units..
Owner Godolphin **Bred** Mrs P Good **Trained** Newmarket, Suffolk

FOCUS
The bare form looks ordinary for the level, although that said, it might be dangerous to underestimate third-placed Tiddliwinks, who although officially rated just 94 coming into the race, seemingly improved significantly. The winner is rated to last year's form at face value. The action unfolded middle to stands' side, and those caught widest (closest to the far rail) struggled to get involved.

NOTEBOOK
Delegator has twice finished runner-up over 1m in Group 1 company, including to Sea The Stars in the Guineas in 2009, but he's a strong-travelling type and coped well with this first try over a sprint trip. He moved powerfully under a confident, patient ride and picked up well when produced with his chance closest to the stands' rail. His connections said he was only around 85% ready, but this was the third season in a row in which he has made a successful reappearance, so it would be wrong to assume he will improve for the run. That said, he's fully entitled to progress as he gains experience of sprinting. The Golden Jubilee at Royal Ascot is the obvious next target, although that will probably require a bit more. He's a general 10-1 shot. (op 13-2 tchd 7-1)
Regal Parade appreciates a bit of give in the ground, but he probably got a bit bogged down on heavy going at the Curragh on his reappearance. This was a significant step back in the right direction, if still a little shy of his best form, and his long-term aim is the Prix Maurice De Gheest, a race he won last year. (tchd 6-1)
Tiddliwinks stepped up a good deal on his previous turf efforts. His career-best RPR on grass coming into the race was just 99, although he does have a 107 to his name on Polytrack and it seems he bettered that level. In fairness, he's not always had things go his way on turf but is a strong traveller (moved well for long way on reappearance until getting tired) and may now be maturing as a 5-y-o. He's well entered, suggesting his connections have high hopes for him this year. (op 50-1)
Hitchens(IRE) travelled well for a long way and kept on for pressure. He wasn't quite good enough, but is probably a bit better than his current official mark of 102 indicates. (op 16-1)
Triple Aspect(IRE) didn't get the clearest of runs but was not unlucky. He's not quite up to this level and tends to need the leaders to go too quick. (op 16-1)
Dalghar(FR) ◆, having his first start since leaving Alain De Royer-Dupre, shaped better than the result suggests. He has won when fresh in the past, but this time gave the impression the run (his first for 191 days) was needed, fading late having travelled almost as well as the winner. The 20-1 generally available for the Golden Jubilee is fair. (tchd 15-2)
Genki(IRE), winner of the Abernant on his reappearance, might be a bit better than he showed as he was caught more towards the far side than those who finished in front of him. (op 13-2)
Hamish McGonagall has won here three times, but all of those victories were over 5f and he has yet to win at this distance. (op 18-1)
Markab, having his first start since winning last year's Sprint Cup at Haydock, had a 5lb penalty to contend with and was expected to need the run. That proved the case as, after making the running he faded. (op 8-1)
Prime Defender remains winless since his surprise success in this last year, although he was caught more towards the far side than most.
Rose Blossom offered little on her first start for 220 days, although she was short of room at the start.

2006 COUNTRYWIDE FREIGHT STKS (H'CAP) 1m 4f
3:35 (3:36) (Class 4) (0-85,90) 4-Y-O+ **£7,123** (£2,119; £1,059; £529) **Stalls** Centre

Form RPR

00-2 **1** **Line Of Duty (IRE)**[21] 1490 4-9-7 **85** PJMcDonald 19 94
(Alan Swinbank) *mid-div: hdwy over 5f out: led racing stands' side over 1f out: edgd lft: drvn out* **28/1**

2-16 **2** 1 1/4 **Ubi Ace**[18] 1517 5-9-1 **79** GrahamGibbons 13 86
(Tim Walford) *lw: trckd ldrs: led 3f out: hdd over 1f out: styd on same pce* **20/1**

3-34 **3** nse **The Galloping Shoe**[21] 1490 6-9-4 **82** SteveDrowne 5 89
(Alistair Whillans) *in rr-div: drvn over 4f out: hdwy and n.m.r over 2f out: egded rt and styd on to take 3rd wl ins fnl f* **25/1**

604- **4** 1 3/4 **Hayzoom**[225] 6448 4-9-2 **80** JimmyFortune 14 85
(Peter Chapple-Hyam) *mid-div: drvn over 4f out: kpt on wl fnl 2f: hmpd ins fnl f* **14/1**

13-3 **5** nk **Antigua Sunrise (IRE)**[14] 1622 5-9-3 **81** PaulHanagan 15 85
(Richard Fahey) *w ldrs: chal 3f out: kpt on same pce fnl f: fdd towards fin* **8/1**[3]

20-3 **6** nk **Satwa Moon (USA)**[25] 1402 5-9-6 **84** FrankieDettori 7 87
(Ed Dunlop) *in tch: drvn over 3f out: kpt on one pce* **6/1**[1]

4-54 **7** 1 1/4 **Arizona John (IRE)**[27] 1325 6-9-3 **81** PhillipMakin 17 82+
(John Mackie) *s.i.s: in rr: styd on wl fnl 2f: nrst fin* **28/1**

000/ **8** nk **Gifted Leader (USA)**[32] 6995 6-9-1 **79** (v) KierenFallon 4 81
(Ian Williams) *mid-div: drvn over 4f out: hdwy on ins to chse ldrs over 2f out: one pce* **8/1**[3]

-602 **9** *1 ½* **Doctor Zhivago**[9] 1747 4-9-6 **84** AdrianNicholls 8 82
(David Nicholls) *chsd ldrs: drvn 6f out: one pce fnl 3f* **20/1**

113- **10** *hd* **Kathleen Frances**[214] 6754 4-9-0 **78** TomQueally 11 76+
(Mark H Tompkins) *lw: t.k.h in midfield: hdwy to join ldrs over 2f out: wknd over 1f out* **8/1**[3]

50-2 **11** *2 ¾* **Embsay Crag**[25] 1387 5-9-2 **80** PaulMulrennan 20 74
(Kate Walton) *hood removed late: dwlt and swtchd lft s: in rr: bhd 3f out: sme hdwy over 1f out: nvr on terms* **25/1**

003- **12** *½* **Daaweitza**[158] 7698 8-9-0 **78** TomEaves 1 71
(Brian Ellison) *chsd ldrs: lost pl over 1f out* **66/1**

0-21 **13** *3 ¼* **Becausewecan (USA)**[10] 1713 5-9-12 **90** 6ex GregFairley 3 78
(Mark Johnston) *led: hdd 3f out: sn wknd* **15/2**[2]

0-33 **14** *¾* **Veiled Applause**[11] 1671 8-8-12 **83** ShaneBKelly(7) 12 69
(John Quinn) *lw: trckd ldrs: wknd over 2f out* **25/1**

1201 **15** *1 ¾* **Lovers Causeway (USA)**[5] 1855 4-9-3 **81** 6ex (v) JoeFanning 2 65
(Mark Johnston) *lw: dwlt: sn chsng ldrs: lost pl over 1f out* **9/1**

50-0 **16** *2 ½* **Red Courtier**[25] 1402 4-9-0 **78** WilliamBuick 9 58
(Paul Cole) *in rr: rdn and lost pl over 3f out: sn bhd* **10/1**

20-0 **17** *20* **Kings Troop**[21] 1477 5-9-6 **84** RyanMoore 18 32
(Alan King) *in rr: wl bhd fnl 3f: t.o* **16/1**

3-00 **P** **Destinys Dream (IRE)**[5] 1855 6-9-7 **85** KellyHarrison 6 —
(Tracy Waggott) *hld up towards rr: p.u over 3f out: fatally injured* **50/1**

2m 31.98s (-1.22) **Going Correction** -0.075s/f (Good) **18** Ran SP% **122.4**
Speed ratings (Par 105): **101,100,100,98,98 98,97,97,96,96 94,94,92,91,90 88,75,—**
toteswingers:1&2:£101.90, 1&3:£96.20, 2&3:£96.20 CSF £487.13 CT £13302.22 TOTE £41.60: £6.40, £4.50, £6.70, £3.60; EX 1051.00 TRIFECTA Not won..
Owner J N Swinbank **Bred** Olive O'Connor And Raymond Gaffney **Trained** Melsonby, N Yorks
■ Stewards' Enquiry : Steve Drowne caution: careless riding.

FOCUS
Another competitive handicap in which they went a fair pace, but it was by no means breakneck. They came centre-to-stands' side in the straight. Ordinary form for the track and grade, with the fifth a pretty sound guide.
Kathleen Frances Official explanation: jockey said filly ran too free
Embsay Crag Official explanation: jockey said that although he was slightly slow in removing blindfold, the gelding usually breaks quickly but hesitated
Kings Troop Official explanation: jockey said gelding was upset in stalls and never travelled

2007 BET AT BLUESQ.COM E B F NOVICE STKS 5f
4:10 (4:11) (Class 3) 2-Y-O **£7,447** (£2,216; £1,107; £553) **Stalls** High

Form RPR

1 **1** **Gatepost (IRE)**[20] 1505 2-9-5 0 JamieSpencer 9 98+
(Mick Channon) *leggy: athletic: wnt lft s: sn outpcd: hdwy and swtchd lft over 1f out: r.o to ld ins fnl f: r.o strly* **7/2**[2]

1 **2** *2 ½* **Hamza (IRE)**[40] 1071 2-9-5 0 PhillipMakin 1 89
(Kevin Ryan) *w'like: swtchd rt s: led over 1f: led over 2f out: hdd and no ex ins fnl f* **11/2**

1 **3** *2* **Ponty Acclaim (IRE)**[25] 1414 2-8-11 0 DuranFentiman 2 74
(Tim Easterby) *w'like: scope: dwlt: sn chsng ldrs: upsides 1f out: kpt on same pce* **8/1**

1 **4** *1* **Monnoyer**[15] 1583 2-9-5 0 FrankieDettori 7 78
(Jeremy Noseda) *w'like: athletic: chsd ldrs: drvn over 2f out: edgd rt and kpt on same pce fnl f* **2/1**[1]

21 **5** *½* **Alejandro (IRE)**[18] 1515 2-9-5 0 PaulHanagan 5 81+
(Richard Fahey) *w'like: hmpd s: trckd ldrs: bmpd after 1f: hmpd over 1f out: n.m.r and kpt on towards fin* **9/2**[3]

1 **6** *shd* **Cravat**[9] 1744 2-9-2 0 JoeFanning 4 73
(Mark Johnston) *str: lw: hmpd s: chsd ldrs: hmpd after 1f: one pce appr fnl f* **20/1**

7 *2* **Rio Grande** 2-9-0 0 RyanMoore 8 67+
(Jeremy Noseda) *w'like: scope: dwlt: in rr: hung lft over 1f out: nvr on terms* **16/1**

8 *5* **Dicky Mint** 2-8-11 0 JamesSullivan(3) 6 46
(Michael Easterby) *w'like: dwlt: outpcd and bhd: sme late hdwy* **100/1**

00 **9** *1 ¼* **Nameitwhatyoulike**[11] 1691 2-8-7 0 DavidSimmonson(7) 3 42
(Michael Easterby) *w'like: outpcd and lost pl after 1f: sn bhd* **150/1**

561 **10** *½* **Profile Star (IRE)**[11] 1691 2-9-2 0 (b1) LeeNewman 10 42
(David Barron) *str: chsd ldrs: edgd lft and led over 3f out: hdd over 2f out: lost pl over 1f out* **25/1**

59.23 secs (-0.07) **Going Correction** -0.075s/f (Good) **10** Ran SP% **116.4**
Speed ratings (Par 97): **97,93,89,88,87 87,84,76,74,73**
toteswingers:1&2:£5.10, 1&3:£6.30, 2&3:£8.60 CSF £22.41 TOTE £5.30: £2.40, £1.70, £2.50; EX 26.10 Trifecta £148.30 Pool: £1,857.80 - 9.27 winning units..
Owner Dr Marwan Koukash **Bred** Michael Doyle **Trained** West Ilsley, Berks
■ Stewards' Enquiry : Phillip Makin two-day ban: careless riding (May 25-26)
Frankie Dettori one-day ban: careless riding (May 25)

FOCUS
A hot novice event featuring seven previous winners and they went an unrelenting pace, resulting in a fast time. The form could be rated even higher and the winner looks a ready-made Norfolk Stakes type, provided he improves for this.

NOTEBOOK
Gatepost(IRE) had been successful in an ordinary Folkestone maiden on his debut that has since produced a winner, but he did win that race with some authority. Weak in the market, he came together with Rio Grande exiting the stalls, but that may have been a help as he then wasn't involved in the battle for the early lead. Switched left over a furlong from home, he quickened past his rivals in the manner of a decent horse and may now head for the Coventry. (op 5-2)
Hamza(IRE), impressive winner of a Musselburgh maiden on his debut from which the second and fifth have won since, took turns in front at various stages and battled on well even after the winner swept past. There should be more decent prizes in him. (op 5-1 tchd 9-2)
Ponty Acclaim(IRE) did it nicely when making a successful debut in a Ripon maiden last month that has since produced a winner. Well backed, she was never far away and kept on all the way to the line. There is a decent race in her back in fillies-only company. (op 12-1)
Monnoyer, winner of a modest Wolverhampton maiden on his debut, was always being taken along a stride quicker than he wanted and he could never land an effective blow. A step up to 6f looks needed. (op 11-4)
Alejandro(IRE) can be rated quite a bit closer as he was squeezed out after a furlong or so and then had no room to play with at all between the 2f and 1f poles. He deserves to gain compensation and add to his Musselburgh success. (op 5-1 tchd 4-1)
Cravat won nicely on his Beverley debut, but the form was let down by the runner-up at the same track the previous day and he was firmly put in his place after holding every chance here. (tchd 22-1)
Rio Grande ◆, a 180,000euros half-brother to a 1m1f Polytrack winner, gave himself plenty to do after colliding with the winner exiting the stalls, but he eventually stayed on nicely without being by any means knocked about. It was no disgrace to finish behind six previous winners on this racecourse debut, and he is likely to need much further than this on breeding. (op 14-1)

2008 THERIPLEYCOLLECTION.COM STKS (H'CAP) 1m 2f 88y
4:45 (4:45) (Class 4) (0-85,85) 3-Y-O **£6,476** (£1,927; £963; £481) **Stalls** Low

Form RPR

22-1 **1** **Sud Pacifique (IRE)**[39] 1096 3-9-7 **85** RyanMoore 13 95+
(Jeremy Noseda) *lw: hld up in rr: hdwy 3f out: edgd rt and chal 2f out: led over 1f out: hld on towards fin* **3/1**[1]

01-2 **2** *nk* **Mica Mika (IRE)**[28] 1304 3-9-1 **79** PaulHanagan 4 89
(Richard Fahey) *led: edgd rt and jnd 2f out: hdd over 1f out: kpt on wl: no ex nr fin* **16/1**

01- **3** *2 ¾* **Rain Mac**[236] 6159 3-9-7 **85** WilliamBuick 2 89+
(John Gosden) *lw: s.i.s: hld up in rr: hdwy on ins over 2f out: sn chsng ldrs: kpt on same pce fnl f* **5/1**[3]

51-0 **4** *hd* **El Torbellino (IRE)**[25] 1384 3-8-11 **75** DanielTudhope 9 79
(David O'Meara) *chsd ldrs: outpcd over 2f out: kpt on wl fnl f* **33/1**

431- **5** *nk* **Defence Of Duress (IRE)**[209] 6873 3-9-3 **81** JamieSpencer 1 84
(Tom Tate) *trckd ldr: t.k.h early: drvn 3f out: sn outpcd and hung rt: styd on fnl f* **9/2**[2]

53-2 **6** *3 ¾* **Discovery Bay**[25] 1408 3-9-4 **82** SteveDrowne 6 78
(Roger Charlton) *mid-div: hdwy 6f out: drvn and hmpd over 2f out: sn wknd* **6/1**

31- **7** *nk* **Rutland Boy**[165] 7602 3-8-13 **77** FrankieDettori 10 72+
(Ed Dunlop) *lw: dwlt: hld up in rr: effrt over 2f out: wknd over 1f out* **9/1**

052- **8** *½* **Barwick**[243] 5900 3-9-0 **78** NeilCallan 5 72
(Mark H Tompkins) *swtg: s.i.s: hdwy 5f out: chsng ldrs over 2f out: edgd lft and wknd over 1f out* **14/1**

014- **9** *1 ¼* **Bloodsweatandtears**[263] 5310 3-9-4 **82** JimCrowley 8 73
(William Knight) *mid-div: effrt 3f out: wknd 2f out* **20/1**

0-31 **10** *4 ½* **Tapis Libre**[8] 1801 3-8-4 **71** 6ex JamesSullivan(3) 11 53
(Michael Easterby) *trckd ldrs: t.k.h: drvn 3f out: sn wknd* **16/1**

152- **11** *½* **Raucous Behaviour (USA)**[217] 6670 3-9-2 **80** GregFairley 3 61
(Mark Johnston) *drvn to chse ldrs: lost pl over 1f out* **16/1**

314- **12** *53* **Rutterkin (USA)**[258] 5452 3-8-3 **74** VictorSantos(7) 12 —
(Alan Berry) *hld up in rr: hdwy on outside over 4f out: sn lost pl and wl bhd: t.o* **80/1**

2m 11.31s (-1.19) **Going Correction** -0.075s/f (Good) **12** Ran SP% **117.4**
Speed ratings (Par 101): **101,100,98,98,98 95,94,94,93,89 89,47**
toteswingers: 1&2 £8.70, 1&3 £4.30, 2&3 £12.80. CSF £53.35 CT £236.43 TOTE £3.70: £1.70, £2.70, £2.20; EX 46.00 Trifecta £89.60 Pool: £1,419.44 - 11.72 winning units..
Owner Sir Robert Ogden **Bred** Eduard Mordukhovitch **Trained** Newmarket, Suffolk

FOCUS
There was always a good chance this would be the slowest of the three races over this trip considering it was being compared with an older-horse handicap and the Musidora, and so it proved, but even so, the time seems to confirm the visual impression that they didn't go that quick. The form is rated on the positive side.
Defence Of Duress(IRE) Official explanation: jockey said colt hung right
T/Jkpt: Not won. T/Plt: £2,923.40 to a £1 stake. Pool:£182,016.70 - 45.45 winning tickets T/Qpdt: £190.00 to a £1 stake. Pool:£11,121.65 - 43.30 winning tickets WG

1417 NAAS (L-H)
Wednesday, May 11
OFFICIAL GOING: Good to firm (watered)

2012a IRISH STALLION FARMS EUROPEAN BREEDERS FUND BLUE WIND STKS (GROUP 3) (F&M) 1m 2f
7:00 (7:00) 3-Y-O+ **£43,426** (£12,693; £6,012; £2,004)

RPR

1 **Banimpire (IRE)**[10] 1734 3-8-12 104 KJManning 7 107+
(J S Bolger, Ire) *trckd ldrs in 4th: smooth hdwy to chal early st: led 2f out: rdn and kpt on wl fr over 1f out: comf* **5/2**[2]

2 *¾* **Spin (IRE)**[24] 1428 3-8-9 95 WMLordan 3 100
(A P O'Brien, Ire) *led early: hdd after 2f and settled in 3rd: pushed along and dropped to 6th 2f out: rallied fr over 1f out: kpt on wl to go 2nd ins fnl f: nt rch wnr* **16/1**

3 *¾* **Mid Mon Lady (IRE)**[9] 1781 6-9-9 98 (b) FMBerry 6 98
(H Rogers, Ire) *towards rr: sme hdwy on outer early st: 5th over 1f out: kpt on same pce u.p fnl f* **25/1**

4 *1 ¼* **Luxurious (IRE)**[213] 6784 3-8-9 89 DavidMcCabe 8 96
(A P O'Brien, Ire) *led after 2f: jnd appr st: hdd 2f out: 3rd and no imp u.p 1f out: kpt on one pce* **25/1**

5 *¾* **Vivacious Vivienne (IRE)**[10] 1734 5-9-9 98 CDHayes 9 94
(Donal Kinsella, Ire) *chsd ldrs: 6th 1/2-way: drvn along to chal on outer over 2f out: no imp on wnr in 2nd 1f out: no ex fnl f* **8/1**

6 *½* **Mesariya (IRE)**[45] 1003 3-8-10 ow1 JMurtagh 5 94
(John M Oxx, Ire) *trckd ldrs in 5th: pushed along over 2f out: no ex fr over 1f out* **6/4**[1]

7 *shd* **Why (IRE)**[24] 1428 3-8-9 94 CO'Donoghue 11 93
(A P O'Brien, Ire) *hld up in rr: nvr a factor: swtchd rt 2f out: kpt on same pce on outer fnl f* **16/1**

8 *2* **Cilium (IRE)**[38] 1119 5-9-9 95 WJSupple 2 89
(Jeffrey Ian Mulhern, Ire) *trckd ldr in 2nd: hdwy to dispute appr st: hdd 2f out: sn no ex and wknd fr over 1f out* **20/1**

9 *1 ¼* **Eirnin (IRE)**[52] 926 3-8-9 84 PJSmullen 4 86
(A P O'Brien, Ire) *nvr a factor: no ex fr 2f out* **25/1**

10 *17* **Asheerah**[24] 1428 3-8-9 99 DPMcDonogh 1 64
(Kevin Prendergast, Ire) *racd freely on inner in mid-div: rdn and no ex fr 2f out: eased whn btn 1f out* **7/1**[3]

2m 13.18s (-2.42)
WFA 3 from 4yo+ 15lb **10** Ran SP% **120.2**
CSF £40.20 TOTE £3.30: £1.02, £7.00, £3.10; DF 62.20.
Owner Mrs J S Bolger **Bred** Kilcarn Stud **Trained** Coolcullen, Co Carlow
■ Stewards' Enquiry : F M Berry severe caution: careless riding

FOCUS
The pace was a steady one and the winner was always well placed. It has been rated around the third to her best.

NOTEBOOK

Banimpire(IRE) completed a hat-trick in good style following victories in the Group 3 Ballysax Stakes at Leopardstown, in which Recital finished third, and the Listed Victor McCalmont Stakes at Gowran Park. The pace was only ordinary but it mattered little to the winner who was always handy behind the leaders before going to the front 2f out. She warmed to her task up the hill and kept on well. According to trainer Jim Bolger, the Etihad Airways Irish 1,000 Guineas on May 22 followed by the Darley Irish Oaks in July is the plan for the winner. Epsom is not on her schedule.
Spin(IRE) holds an Investec Oaks entry and she gave every indication here that she will appreciate going 1m4f. She led early and remained close up, going second under pressure over 1f out and staying on in the closing stages.
Mid Mon Lady(IRE) made progress from behind in the straight, going third over 1f out and running on under pressure. (op 20/1)
Luxurious(IRE), another Investec Oaks entry, was having her first run of the season. In front after going 1 1/2f, she was joined at halfway and disputed the lead until headed 2f out from where she kept on without finding much. (op 33/1)
Vivacious Vivienne(IRE), a 98-rated 5-y-o and a five-time winner, twice over 1m4f, would have appreciated more pace in the race and ran a decent race in the circumstances. She tracked the leaders from halfway and went second 2f out before failing to quicken.
Mesariya(IRE), who won a Leopardstown maiden nicely, found precious little when gathered together to try and challenge under 2f out. (op 7/4 tchd 11/8)
Asheerah was eased when beaten after making the running. Held up, she was struggling early in the straight and was eased when any chance of being involved had gone. The quick ground might not have suited her. (op 11/2)

2099 - 2011a, 2013 - 2015a (Foreign Racing) - See Raceform Interactive

1717 NEWMARKET (R-H)

Thursday, May 12

OFFICIAL GOING: Good to firm (good in places)

Stands' side track used with stalls on far side.

Wind: Light behind Weather: Cloudy

2016 HOMESTORE AND SAFEPAC "HANDS AND HEELS" APPRENTICE SERIES H'CAP (RACING EXCELLENCE INITIATIVE) — 6f

5:45 (5:45) (Class 5) (0-75,75) 4-Y-0+ **£2,590** (£770; £385; £192) **Stalls** Low

Form RPR

1232 **1** **Collect Art (IRE)**[7] 1838 4-9-0 **68** ...... LucyKBarry 9 79+
(Andrew Haynes) *sn chsng ldr: led over 1f out: pushed out* **11/8**[1]

0353 **2** *2 1/4* **Ongoodform (IRE)**[2] 1990 4-9-2 **75** ...... ChristopherGraham(5) 1 79
(Paul D'Arcy) *a.p: shkn up over 1f out: styd on: wnt 2nd wl ins fnl f* **4/1**[2]

2113 **3** *nk* **Frequency**[9] 1800 4-9-4 **72** ......(b) EdmondLinehan 7 75
(Keith Dalgleish) *chsd ldrs: pushed along over 1f out: styd on smae pce ins fnl f* **13/2**[3]

0250 **4** *3/4* **Desert Icon (IRE)**[10] 1771 5-8-12 **69** ...... AliceHaynes(3) 13 70
(David Simcock) *s.s: hld up: hdwy over 1f out: wnt 4th towards fin: nvr nrr* **16/1**

5400 **5** *1/2* **Simple Rhythm**[31] 1267 5-8-2 **61** oh4 ......(p) BradleyBosley(5) 5 60
(John Ryan) *led over 4f: no ex ins fnl f* **50/1**

6-63 **6** *2 3/4* **Two Turtle Doves (IRE)**[11] 1712 5-8-4 **61** ...... JosephYoung(3) 6 51
(Michael Mullineaux) *prom: pushed along over 2f out: styd on same pce appr fnl f* **10/1**

4-12 **7** *nk* **Dreamacha**[17] 1555 4-8-13 **70** ...... NoelGarbutt(3) 2 59
(Stuart Williams) *dwlt: sn pushed along in rr: styd on fr over 1f out: nvr nrr* **7/1**

400- **8** *1* **Shaws Diamond (USA)**[236] 6210 5-8-4 **61** oh1 ...... LeonnaMayor(3) 8 47
(Derek Shaw) *hld up: styd on ins fnl f: nvr on terms* **33/1**

000- **9** *4* **Captainrisk (IRE)**[331] 3062 5-8-8 **65** ...... DanielHarris(3) 10 38
(Christine Dunnett) *prom: pushed along over 2f out: wknd over 1f out* **100/1**

2024 **10** *3/4* **Spin Again (IRE)**[34] 1221 6-8-12 **69** ...... GeorgeDowning(3) 12 40
(Mark Wellings) *prom: pushed along over 3f out: wknd over 2f out* **20/1**

00-0 **11** *1 1/4* **Zowington**[24] 1444 9-8-9 **68** ......(v) CarolineKelly(5) 3 35
(Stuart Williams) *s.s: a in rr* **33/1**

1m 10.96s (-1.24) **Going Correction** -0.125s/f (Firm) 11 Ran SP% 116.5
Speed ratings (Par 100): **100,100,99,98,97 94,93,92,87,86 84**
toteswingers:1&2:£3.20, 2&3:£4.90, 1&3:£3.00 CSF £6.19 CT £26.98 TOTE £2.60: £1.60, £1.80, £2.10; EX 8.30 Trifecta £18.50 Pool: £6276.21 - 249.99 winning units..
Owner Athos Racing **Bred** Pier House Stud **Trained** Limpley Stoke, Bath

FOCUS
An ordinary sprint to open proceedings, the field sticking to the far rail and those prominent throughout favoured, partly helped by a strong tailwind. The winner probably only had to run to his Goodwood level.

2017 CHASSIS CAB DAF MAIDEN AUCTION STKS — 6f

6:15 (6:25) (Class 5) 2-Y-0 **£3,238** (£963; £481; £240) **Stalls** Low

Form RPR

53 **1** **Misty Conquest (IRE)**[12] 1673 2-7-13 0 ...... HarryBentley(5) 3 79+
(Tom Dascombe) *mde all: shkn up and hung lft over 1f out: r.o* **11/10**[1]

2 *4* **Pride And Joy (IRE)** 2-9-1 0 ...... FergusSweeney 7 78
(Jamie Osborne) *w wnr tl rdn over 1f out: styd on same pce* **14/1**

3 *3 1/2* **Majestic Zafeen** 2-8-8 0 ...... SamHitchcott 6 61
(Mick Channon) *chsd ldrs: rdn over 2f out: styd on same pce fr over 1f out: wnt 3rd wl ins fnl f* **5/1**[2]

4 *1 1/4* **Tidal's Baby** 2-8-11 0 ...... RichardMullen 1 60
(Noel Quinlan) *chsd ldrs: rdn over 1f out: wknd ins fnl f* **25/1**

5 *2 1/4* **Sheila's Buddy** 2-8-9 0 ...... LiamKeniry 5 51
(J S Moore) *s.i.s: outpcd: styd on fr over 1f out: nvr nrr* **33/1**

6 *nk* **Finley Connolly (IRE)** 2-9-3 0 ...... RobertWinston 4 58
(Brian Meehan) *chsd ldrs tl wknd over 2f out: t.o* **7/1**[3]

7 *20* **Milwr** 2-8-9 0 ...... DarryllHolland 8 —
(Chris Dwyer) *mid-div: rn green and sn drvn along: hung lft and wknd over 2f out* **9/1**

8 *22* **Hiding In The Open (IRE)** 2-9-1 0 ...... WilliamBuick 9 —
(Brian Meehan) *dwlt: outpcd: t.o* **11/1**

1m 12.72s (0.52) **Going Correction** -0.125s/f (Firm) 8 Ran SP% 108.6
Speed ratings (Par 93): **91,85,81,79,76 75,49,19**
toteswingers:1&2:£4.60, 2&3:£9.20, 1&3:£1.50 CSF £16.50 TOTE £2.10: £1.10, £3.80, £1.90; EX 17.40 Trifecta £117.30 Pool: £4827.48 - 30.43 winning units..
Owner Deva Racing Mujadil Partnership **Bred** Polish Belle Partnership **Trained** Malpas, Cheshire
■ Sister Guru (25/1, unruly in stalls) & Eagle Of Rome (12/1, ref to ent stalls) were withdrawn. R4 deduction, 5p in the £.

FOCUS
Probably no more than an average maiden auction contest after two horses were withdrawn at the start. The winning time was 1.76sec slower than the opener.

NOTEBOOK

Misty Conquest(IRE) was well backed to break her maiden tag at the third time of asking (the second at Doncaster last time had given the form a boost since) and she put her experience to good use, always just about having things in control and drawing clear inside the last. She'll need to improve again to win a novice or conditions race, but is at least going the right way. (op 2-1after early 9-4 and 5-2 in places)
Pride And Joy(IRE), a Dark Angel half-brother to a couple of useful winners in Ireland, shaped well on his debut despite having proved troublesome to load, matching the winner for a long way until either lack of experience or a recent run told up the hill. (op 12-1 tchd 16-1)
Majestic Zafeen also proved troublesome to load and looked far from the finished article in the race too, never travelling comfortably while looking inexperienced but for all that still seeing her race out well. Her pedigree is largely all speed and she's sure to improve. (op 13-2)
Tidal's Baby is out of a mare that won at 1m4f but he showed plenty of speed on debut, almost upsides the first two running into the Dip but unable to see his race out. He'll improve too, and market support next time would be significant. (op 16-1)
Sheila's Buddy, who's already been gelded, is a half-brother to 1m4f winner Sheila's Bond and looks in need of a longer trip already, soon run off his feet. (op 16-1)
Finley Connolly(IRE), whose dam won at 1m, shaped better then the result suggests, running green throughout and not given a hard time as he seemed caught out by the Dip. Newcomers from his yard tend to need their first experience and he might well improve substantially next time. Official explanation: jockey said colt ran green (op 13-2 tchd 8-1)

2018 C H LINDSEY & SON RENEWABLE ENERGY FILLIES H'CAP — 1m

6:50 (6:53) (Class 5) (0-75,75) 3-Y-0 **£2,590** (£770; £385; £192) **Stalls** Low

Form RPR

021- **1** **Cloud Illusions (USA)**[132] 8030 3-9-7 **75** ...... KierenFallon 10 83+
(Heather Main) *hld up: hdwy 1/2-way: led over 2f out: hung rt over 1f out: rdn out* **10/1**

2462 **2** *3/4* **Imaginary World (IRE)**[10] 1768 3-9-0 **68** ......(b) RobertWinston 3 77+
(Alan McCabe) *s.s: hld up: hdwy: nt clr run and swtchd lft over 1f out: r.o to go 2nd wl ins fnl f: nt rch wnr* **8/1**

3-31 **3** *3 1/2* **Hunza Dancer (IRE)**[18] 1540 3-9-7 **75** ...... WilliamBuick 6 73
(John Gosden) *mid-div: pushed along over 3f out: hdwy over 2f out: styd on same pce ins fnl f* **5/2**[1]

53-0 **4** *nk* **Monicalew**[27] 1364 3-8-13 **67** ...... AdamKirby 2 65
(Walter Swinburn) *hld up in tch: rdn over 2f out: styd on same pce ins fnl f* **14/1**

00-5 **5** *3 1/2* **Mawjoodah**[15] 1611 3-9-2 **70** ...... PhilipRobinson 8 59
(Clive Brittain) *hld up: plld hrd: hdwy over 3f out: rdn over 1f out: wknd ins fnl f* **12/1**

-146 **6** *nk* **Dazzling Valentine**[16] 1593 3-9-6 **74** ...... SamHitchcott 9 63
(Alan Bailey) *sn pushed along in mid-div: outpcd over 2f out: styd on ins fnl f* **11/1**

214 **7** *1 1/2* **Greenflash**[22] 1481 3-9-7 **75** ...... PatDobbs 5 60
(Richard Hannon) *led over 3f: rdn over 2f out: wknd ins fnl f* **13/2**[3]

23-4 **8** *4 1/2* **Gay Gallivanter**[38] 1133 3-9-2 **70** ...... PatCosgrave 1 45
(Michael Quinn) *chsd ldrs tl rdn and wknd over 1f out* **40/1**

656- **9** *1 3/4* **Spade**[189] 7311 3-9-1 **69** ...... DarryllHolland 11 40
(David Elsworth) *s.i.s: hld up: hdwy over 2f out: wknd over 1f out* **6/1**[2]

3-03 **10** *2 3/4* **Galloping Queen (IRE)**[14] 1626 3-9-1 **72** ......(v) MartinHarley(3) 4 37
(Mick Channon) *prom tl wknd 2f out* **17/2**

566- **11** *2* **Grecian Goddess (IRE)**[197] 7163 3-9-0 **68** ...... StevieDonohoe 7 28
(John Ryan) *prom 5f* **28/1**

-605 **12** *5* **Ninita**[17] 1571 3-9-6 **74** ......(b) SteveDrowne 12 23
(Mark Rimmer) *sn prom: led over 4f out: hdd over 2f out: wknd over 1f out* **25/1**

1m 37.85s (-0.75) **Going Correction** -0.125s/f (Firm) 12 Ran SP% 119.3
Speed ratings (Par 99): **98,97,93,93,89 89,88,83,81,79 77,72**
toteswingers:1&2:£16.50, 2&3:£6.80, 1&3:£6.50 CSF £86.70 CT £269.85 TOTE £8.30: £1.90, £2.90, £1.30; EX 61.90 Trifecta £462.90 Pool: £4128.89 - 6.60 winning units..
Owner Norman Brunskill & Wetumpka Racing **Bred** John C Oxley **Trained** Kingston Lisle, Oxon

FOCUS
An ordinary fillies' handicap in which the field raced mid to far side and there was little between the runners until well past halfway. Not many showed their form and the first pair were clear. The third and fourth were close to their maiden form with the rest rated 10lb+ off.

2019 SIMON GIBSON MAIDEN STKS — 1m 2f

7:25 (7:25) (Class 5) 3-Y-0 **£3,238** (£963; £481; £240) **Stalls** Low

Form RPR

3- **1** **Lyric Street (IRE)**[195] 7203 3-9-3 0 ...... KierenFallon 1 86+
(Luca Cumani) *w ldr tl rdn to ld over 2f out: hung rt ins fnl f: styd on: hung lft nr fin* **8/13**[1]

2 *1 1/2* **Wild Coco (GER)** 3-8-12 0 ...... TomQueally 5 78+
(Sir Henry Cecil) *s.i.s and stmbld s: hld up: racd keenly: hdwy over 2f out: rdn over 1f out: styd on to go 2nd wl ins fnl f: nt rch wnr* **14/1**

54- **3** *3/4* **Muqtarrib (IRE)**[201] 7099 3-9-3 0 ...... RichardHills 3 82
(Brian Meehan) *a.p: rdn to chse wnr over 1f out tl styd on same pce wl ins fnl f* **8/1**

35 **4** *7* **Informed Award**[31] 1271 3-9-3 0 ...... WilliamBuick 2 68
(John Gosden) *led: rdn and hdd over 2f out: wknd ins fnl f* **15/2**[3]

062- **5** *3 1/4* **Malanos (IRE)**[195] 7203 3-9-3 79 ...... AdamKirby 4 61
(David Elsworth) *prom: rdn over 2f out: sn hung rt and wknd* **7/1**[2]

0- **6** *2 1/4* **Striking Veil (USA)**[213] 6803 3-8-12 0 ...... RichardMullen 8 52
(Sir Michael Stoute) *hld up: rdn over 3f out: nt clr run and wknd over 2f out* **25/1**

7 *2* **Hursley Hope (IRE)** 3-8-12 0 ...... DarryllHolland 9 48
(David Elsworth) *s.i.s: a in rr* **50/1**

8 *1 3/4* **Arkaim** 3-9-3 0 ...... J-PGuillambert 10 49
(Ed Walker) *chsd ldrs tl rdn and wknd over 2f out* **100/1**

9 *nk* **Ravindra** 3-9-3 0 ...... IanMongan 6 48
(Sir Henry Cecil) *hld up: rdn over 3f out: wknd over 2f out* **14/1**

2m 3.49s (-2.31) **Going Correction** -0.125s/f (Firm) 9 Ran SP% 117.4
Speed ratings (Par 99): **104,102,102,96,94 92,90,89,88**
toteswingers:1&2:£4.10, 2&3:£3.00, 1&3:£3.30 CSF £11.57 TOTE £1.80: £1.10, £1.80, £2.50; EX 8.30 Trifecta £38.90 Pool: £6493.39 - 123.37 winning units..
Owner The Honorable Earle I Mack **Bred** Gestut Wittekindshof **Trained** Newmarket, Suffolk

FOCUS
Usually a good maiden and no reason to doubt that this renewal will be much different, with several promising unexposed types from top yards pitched against each other. The first three were clear and the form could be worth more.

2020 ORBITAL FOOD MACHINERY H'CAP — 7f

8:00 (8:00) (Class 3) (0-95,87) 4-Y-0+ **£7,771** (£2,312; £1,155; £577) **Stalls** Low

Form RPR

020- **1** **Decent Fella (IRE)**[209] 6888 5-9-5 **85** ......(v) LiamKeniry 7 95
(Andrew Balding) *chsd ldrs: led over 1f out: drvn out* **6/1**[2]

614- **2** *1 ¼* **Red Gulch**[201] 7092 4-9-3 **83** .... J-PGuillambert 8 90
(Ed Walker) *chsd ldrs: rdn over 2f out: ev ch wl over 1f out: styd on same pce towards fin* **25/1**

521- **3** *nk* **Primaeval**[201] 7092 5-9-6 **86** .... (v) HayleyTurner 3 92+
(James Fanshawe) *hld up: hdwy and n.m.r over 1f out: rdn and hung lft ins fnl f: r.o* **3/1**[1]

20-2 **4** *1 ¼* **Masai Moon**[23] 1467 7-9-7 **87** .... JamesMillman 1 90
(Rod Millman) *chsd ldr tl led 3f out: rdn and hdd over 1f out: edgd lft and styd on same pce ins fnl f* **15/2**[3]

1/0- **5** *1 ½* **Bronze Prince**[230] 6321 4-9-7 **87** .... WilliamBuick 2 86+
(John Gosden) *trckd ldrs: shkn up over 1f out: styd on same pce ins fnl f* **6/1**[2]

4220 **6** *½* **Mr Macattack**[6] 1854 6-8-6 **79** .... (t) BenWilliams(7) 10 76+
(Tom Dascombe) *dwlt: bhd: r.o ins fnl f: nvr nrr* **25/1**

364- **7** *½* **Greensward**[194] 7238 5-9-7 **87** .... KierenFallon 6 83
(Brian Meehan) *hld up: hdwy over 3f out: rdn over 1f out: no ex ins fnl f* **9/1**

54-0 **8** *nse* **Linnens Star (IRE)**[40] 1092 4-9-6 **86** .... JimCrowley 4 82
(Ralph Beckett) *chsd ldrs: rdn over 2f out: sn ev ch: hung lft and no ex ins fnl f* **15/2**[3]

03-4 **9** *¾* **Santefisio**[15] 1610 5-9-3 **83** .... SteveDrowne 9 77
(Peter Makin) *hld up: rdn over 2f out: no imp ins fnl f* **6/1**[2]

0214 **10** *1* **Tewin Wood**[7] 1832 4-8-10 **76** .... LiamJones 11 67
(Alan Bailey) *led 4f: wknd over 1f out* **12/1**

1m 24.34s (-1.06) **Going Correction** -0.125s/f (Firm) **10** Ran SP% **116.8**
Speed ratings (Par 107): **101,99,99,97,96 95,94,94,94,92**
toteswingers:1&2:£31.30, 2&3:£20.20, 1&3:£4.80 CSF £141.58 CT £532.81 TOTE £5.20: £2.30, £4.40, £1.50; EX 157.60 Trifecta £236.60 Part won. Pool of £319.85 - 0.97 winning units..

Owner One Carat Partnership **Bred** Michael Dalton **Trained** Kingsclere, Hants

FOCUS
A useful handicap but one run at something of a steady pace and the form may well be muddling. The fourth helps with the level.

NOTEBOOK
Decent Fella(IRE) ◆ never really delivered for this yard last year after arriving from Ireland with a tall reputation, but it might well be a different story this year after an impressive reappearance, tanking along for the most part and well on top at the line. He ran his best race last year at 1m, but didn't look here as if he would be out of place back at 6f, though looking ahead to next month the Buckingham Palace Handicap would be an obvious immediate target. (op 8-1)

Red Gulch always had the winner in his sights but was never travelling quite as well as that horse. Nevertheless he stuck on well and looks to have resumed where he left off in 2010, still on an upward curve. (op 20-1)

Primaeval shouldn't be long in getting back to winning ways as he's clearly as good on turf as he is on all-weather despite only finishing third here, that ostensibly as a consequence of being poorly placed on the rail when the race was developing well to his left in front of him. He might be the type best off a strong pace but remains the type that has more handicaps in him. (op 7-2 tchd 11-4)

Masai Moon ran respectably, albeit well placed throughout, from what looks a hard enough mark. Official explanation: jockey said gelding hung left throughout (op 8-1 tchd 7-1)

Bronze Prince shaped as if he retains all his ability on only his second run since winning his sole start as a two-year-old when with Godolphin, keeping on well nicely under a considerate ride. He's not resumed on a bad mark, and probably has more to come over 1m. (op 7-2)

Mr Macattack did reasonably well to finish as close as he did after blowing the start but his overall profile isn't a persuasive one and it might not be too wise to take too much from this. (op 33-1)

Linnens Star(IRE) looked like a horse racing at the wrong trip. He'll be suited by a return to 1m, maybe more. (op 9-1 tchd 10-1)

Santefisio was a shade disappointing but this race wasn't really run to suit his stalking style. (op 7-1 tchd 11-2)

2021 EAST ANGLIAN DAILY TIMES H'CAP 1m 2f
8:30 (8:32) (Class 5) (0-75,75) 4-Y-O+ **£2,590** (£770; £385; £192) **Stalls** Low

Form RPR

500- **1** **Chain Of Events**[190] 7293 4-8-13 **67** .... HayleyTurner 3 78
(Neil King) *chsd ldrs: led wl over 1f out: rdn clr ins fnl f* **7/1**[3]

2-53 **2** *3 ½* **Laconicos (IRE)**[33] 1233 9-8-3 **62** .... (t) LauraPike(5) 9 66
(William Stone) *chsd ldrs: rdn over 2f out: styd on* **9/2**[1]

36-0 **3** *½* **Rosco Flyer (IRE)**[26] 1402 5-9-7 **75** .... DarryllHolland 2 78
(Roger Teal) *mid-div: hdwy over 2f out: sn rdn: styd on* **6/1**[2]

5130 **4** *3 ¼* **Classically (IRE)**[24] 1443 5-9-6 **74** .... SteveDrowne 10 71
(Peter Hedger) *hld up: hdwy over 2f out: rdn over 1f out: no ex ins fnl f* **10/1**

5400 **5** *1 ¼* **Negotiation (IRE)**[66] 790 5-9-1 **69** .... PatCosgrave 6 63
(Michael Quinn) *s.i.s and sn pushed along: hdwy to ld over 8f out: rdn and hdd over 1f out: wknd ins fnl f* **16/1**

0-65 **6** *6* **Royal Defence (IRE)**[26] 1398 5-8-5 **62** .... LouisBeuzelin(3) 4 44
(Michael Quinn) *hld up: rdn over 3f out: nvr on terms* **25/1**

22-5 **7** *¾* **Inpursuitoffreedom**[55] 889 4-9-2 **70** .... KierenFallon 1 51
(Philip McBride) *hld up: shkn up over 2f out: nvr nr to chal* **9/2**[1]

/065 **8** *3 ½* **Ajdaad (USA)**[55] 894 4-9-4 **72** .... RobertWinston 5 46
(Alan McCabe) *led: hdd over 8f out: chsd ldr: rdn over 2f out: wknd ins fnl f* **15/2**

05-0 **9** *3 ¼* **Jinto**[15] 1608 4-8-4 **61** oh2 .... DeclanCannon(3) 7 28
(David Elsworth) *mid-div: rdn 1/2-way: wknd over 2f out* **8/1**

30-3 **10** *49* **Highland Park (IRE)**[52] 930 4-9-2 **70** .... AndreaAtzeni 11 —
(Michael Wigham) *hld up in tch: rdn 1/2-way: wknd over 3f out: t.o* **8/1**

2m 4.96s (-0.84) **Going Correction** -0.125s/f (Firm) **10** Ran SP% **116.0**
Speed ratings (Par 103): **98,95,94,92,91 86,85,83,80,41**
toteswingers:1&2:£2.90, 2&3:£8.10, 1&3:£10.80 CSF £38.32 CT £201.94 TOTE £7.40: £2.60, £1.50, £1.50; EX 48.10 TRIFECTA Not won..

Owner P J Edwards **Bred** Bishop Wilton Stud **Trained** Newmarket, Suffolk

FOCUS
An ordinary handicap to end proceedings, run at a fair gallop but in a relatively modest time. The winner had the run of things and is rated back to his turf mark.

Highland Park(IRE) Official explanation: jockey said gelding never travelled

T/Plt: £37.10 to a £1 stake. Pool of £54,077.77 - 1,063.99 winning tickets. T/Qpdt: £20.80 to a £1 stake. Pool of £4,727.81- 167.90 winning tickets. CR

1724 SALISBURY (R-H)
Thursday, May 12

OFFICIAL GOING: Good to firm (8.6)
Rail up to 20ft off permanent far side rail between 6f and winning post.
Wind: fresh half across Weather: cloudy with sunny periods

2022 BRITISH STALLION STUDS SUPPORTING BRITISH RACING E B F FILLIES' H'CAP 1m 1f 198y
2:10 (2:10) (Class 4) (0-85,76) 3-Y-O **£5,504** (£1,637; £818; £408) **Stalls** Low

Form RPR

00-0 **1** **Miss Topsy Turvy (IRE)**[27] 1364 3-8-4 **59** oh1 ow2 .... ChrisCatlin 5 68+
(John Dunlop) *rrd leaving stalls: in last pair: rdn and sltly outpcd 3f out: stdy prog over 1f out: str run ins fnl f: drifted rt: led nring fin* **11/2**[2]

5-1 **2** *¾* **Sacred Shield**[23] 1474 3-9-0 **69** .... EddieAhern 3 77
(Sir Henry Cecil) *sn led: hdd over 4f out: trckd ldrs: rdn over 2f out: sn swtchd lft: led jst ins fnl f: kpt on but no ex whn hdd nr fin* **11/8**[1]

651- **3** *¾* **Istishaara (USA)**[225] 6468 3-9-7 **76** .... TadhgO'Shea 7 82
(John Dunlop) *hld up: hdwy over 3f out: sn rdn to chal: ev ch tl no ex wl ins fnl f: 3rd and hld whn carried sltly rt towards fin* **15/2**

021- **4** *¾* **Reem Star**[157] 7723 3-9-3 **72** .... GeorgeBaker 2 77
(Ed Dunlop) *cl up in 5th: rdn whn outpcd 3f out: styng on ins fnl f whn short of room nr fin* **10/1**

4-11 **5** *¾* **Amistress**[19] 1526 3-8-10 **65** .... CathyGannon 4 68
(Eve Johnson Houghton) *prom: rdn over 2f out: tk narrow advantage wl over 1f out: hdd jst ins fnl f: no ex* **6/1**[3]

6311 **6** *2* **Apache Glory (USA)**[55] 890 3-9-2 **71** .... RichardHughes 6 70
(Richard Hannon) *trckd ldrs: pushed along to ld and qckn pce over 4f out: rdn and hrd pressed fr over 2f out: narrowly hdd wl over 1f out: kpt on w ev ch tl no ex fnl 100yds* **8/1**

201- **7** *2* **Fly By White (IRE)**[210] 6859 3-9-5 **74** .... PatDobbs 1 69
(Richard Hannon) *racd freely: trckd ldrs: rdn over 3f out: kpt chsng ldrs tl fdd ins fnl f* **14/1**

2m 10.55s (0.65) **Going Correction** +0.05s/f (Good) **7** Ran SP% **110.4**
Speed ratings (Par 98): **99,98,97,97,96 95,93**
toteswingers:1&2:£2.10, 2&3:£1.80, 1&3:£5.50 CSF £12.56 TOTE £8.00: £4.00, £1.50; EX 19.10.

Owner Windflower Overseas Holdings Inc **Bred** Windflower Overseas **Trained** Arundel, W Sussex

■ Stewards' Enquiry : Chris Catlin two-day ban: careless riding (May 26-27)

FOCUS
Plenty of these had claims, so this looked a decent race, but the pace was uneven and the result may not be completely reliable. The form is rated through the fifth and the first two have more to offer.

Miss Topsy Turvy(IRE) ◆ Official explanation: trainer said, regarding apparent improvement in form, that the filly was big and backward but has matured.

2023 WHITSBURY MANOR STUD MAIDEN STKS 5f
2:40 (2:40) (Class 5) 2-Y-O **£2,914** (£867; £433; £216) **Stalls** Centre

Form RPR

3 **1** **Airborne Again (IRE)**[7] 1835 2-9-3 0 .... RichardHughes 5 80+
(Richard Hannon) *mde all: shkn up over 1f out: clr jst ins fnl f: edgd lft: r.o wl: readily* **1/1**[1]

2 *1 ½* **Marcus Augustus (IRE)** 2-9-3 0 .... PatDobbs 3 74+
(Richard Hannon) *trckd ldrs: rdn over 2f out: swtchd lft to squeeze through gap ent fnl f: kpt on to snatch 2nd fnl stride* **12/1**

62 **3** *shd* **Pitt Rivers**[14] 1632 2-9-3 0 .... ChrisCatlin 6 74
(Mick Channon) *pressed wnr: rdn 2f out: kpt on but hld ent fnl f: lost 2nd fnl stride* **5/2**[2]

4 *1 ¾* **Tina's Spirit (IRE)** 2-8-12 0 .... DaneO'Neill 4 63+
(Richard Hannon) *s.i.s: outpcd in rr: styd on wl ins fnl f: wnt 4th fnl strides: nrst fin* **14/1**

5 *nk* **Singalat** 2-9-3 0 .... CathyGannon 9 67
(David Evans) *s.i.s: sn chsng ldrs: rdn over 3f out: disputing cl 3rd whn carried lft ent fnl f: kpt on same pce: lost 3rd fnl stride* **33/1**

6 *2 ½* **Red Art (IRE)** 2-9-3 0 .... MichaelHills 7 60+
(B W Hills) *s.i.s: sn trcking ldrs: rdn to dispute cl 3rd 2f out: keeping on at same pce whn squeezed out ent fnl f: nt rcvr* **7/1**[3]

7 *1 ¼* **Zigazag (IRE)** 2-9-3 0 .... JamesDoyle 2 53
(David Evans) *sn pushed along in tch: rdn over 3f out: wknd ent fnl f* **33/1**

62.79 secs (1.79) **Going Correction** +0.05s/f (Good) **7** Ran SP% **111.3**
Speed ratings (Par 93): **87,84,84,81,81 77,75**
toteswingers:1&2 £3.40, 2&3 £4.20, 1&3 £1.10 CSF £14.03 TOTE £1.50: £1.10, £6.10; EX 14.50.

Owner Kennet Valley Thoroughbreds II **Bred** Jnp Bloodstock Ltd **Trained** East Everleigh, Wilts

FOCUS
Some decent performers have won this down the years and the form of this season's contest looks straightforward, with some eyecatching performers in behind.

NOTEBOOK
Airborne Again(IRE), dropping in trip, showed plenty of speed and ability on his debut and got away quickly again before doing just enough to hold on. One would imagine he could cope with going up in distance again, but he does hold an entry in the Weatherbys Super Sprint in July. (tchd 5-6, 11-10 in places and 5-4 in a place)

Marcus Augustus(IRE) ◆, a 32,000gn half-brother to a fair Irish performer, looked the stable's second string on jockey bookings and ran a blinder despite being green. He seems sure to improve and may be better than the winner in time. (op 14-1 tchd 16-1)

Pitt Rivers was the most experienced runner in the field and appeared to run his race. This is about has good as he is. (op 11-4)

Tina's Spirit(IRE) ◆, a half-sister to the smart juvenile of 2008 Luck Money (Group 2 placed) among other winners, didn't look to have a clue what was going on early but picked up strongly inside the final furlong to catch the eye. As long as she improves mentally for this, she ought to go even closer next time. (tchd 12-1)

Singalat was hard ridden for a lot of the contest and can probably do a bit better with this effort under his belt. Official explanation: jockey said gelding was hampered a furlong out (op 28-1)

Red Art(IRE), who cost £50,000 last year, was keeping on at the one pace when hampered in the final stages. He may have been a bit closer but not by much. (tchd 10-1)

2024 DUTTON GREGORY CLASSIFIED CLAIMING STKS 6f 212y
3:10 (3:10) (Class 5) 3-Y-O **£2,428** (£722; £361; £180) **Stalls** Centre

Form RPR

5511 **1** **Exchange**[16] 1578 3-9-0 66 .... LiamJones 2 62
(Chris Gordon) *stdd s: trckd ldrs: pushed along whn swtchd lft over 1f out: str run ins fnl f: led fnl 30yds* **11/4**[3]

04-5 **2** *1/2* **Danceyourselfdizzy (IRE)**[47] 987 3-9-0 63............. RichardHughes 3 61
(Richard Hannon) *prom: rdn to ld 2f out: sn hrd pressed: kpt on but no ex whn hdd fnl 30yds* **7/2**

00-1 **3** *1 1/4* **Pick A Little**[16] 1585 3-8-8 68.. DaneO'Neill 4 52
(Ron Hodges) *racd keenly: trckd ldrs: rdn for str chal 2f out: kpt on tl no ex fnl 100yds* **5/2**[2]

5310 **4** *6* **Silly Billy (IRE)**[28] 1335 3-9-2 75...................................... JamesDoyle 1 43
(Sylvester Kirk) *led: rdn and hdd 2f out: sn edgd lft and hld: fdd ins fnl f* **2/1**[1]

1m 31.24s (2.64) **Going Correction** +0.05s/f (Good) **4** Ran SP% **110.8**
Speed ratings (Par 99): **86,85,84,77**
CSF £12.08 TOTE £6.20; EX 11.20.Exchange was claimed by M. P. Gibbens for £10,000.
Owner Richard Venn **Bred** Southill Stud **Trained** Morestead, Hants

FOCUS
All of these could be given a chance, but the race became tactical, as one would have imagined for a small field. Weak form, rated through the first pair.
Silly Billy(IRE) Official explanation: jockey said gelding hung left-handed

2025 ST JOHN AMBULANCE CHARITY RACEDAY H'CAP 6f
3:45 (3:45) (Class 5) (0-75,75) 3-Y-O **£2,428** (£722; £361; £180) **Stalls** Low

Form RPR
622- **1** **Sluggsy Morant**[190] 7301 3-9-3 71...................................... DaneO'Neill 9 81+
(Henry Candy) *travelled wl bhd ldrs: qcknd up to ld jst ins fnl f: readily* **3/1**[1]

-526 **2** *3/4* **Roman Strait**[10] 1749 3-8-10 64.. LukeMorris 8 71+
(Michael Blanshard) *hld up: nt clr run and snatched up 2f out: hdwy over 1f out: styd on strly fnl f: wnt 2nd towards fin: fin wl but nvr gng to catch wnr* **22/1**

6-11 **3** *1/2* **Apollo D'Negro (IRE)**[22] 1483 3-9-4 75......................... JohnFahy(3) 10 77
(Clive Cox) *trckd ldrs: rdn to ld over 1f out: hdd fnl 140yds: no ex whn lost 2nd nr fin* **9/2**[3]

1- **4** *1 1/2* **Echo Ridge (IRE)**[165] 7608 3-9-7 75................................ GeorgeBaker 3 72
(Ralph Beckett) *trckd ldrs: rdn 2f out: kpt on but nt gng pce to mount chal* **4/1**[2]

61 **5** *2 1/2* **Vicona (IRE)**[14] 1629 3-8-13 67.. MichaelHills 11 56
(Paul Cole) *wnt lft s: sn prom: led over 3f out: rdn and hdd over 1f out: fading whn hung rt ins fnl f* **7/1**

00-0 **6** *1/2* **One Cool Chick**[11] 1724 3-8-2 61 oh16......................... RyanPowell(5) 1 49?
(John Bridger) *rrd leaving stalls: mid-div on far rails: rdn whn swtchd lft to centre 2f out: nvr any imp* **100/1**

2436 **7** *2 1/4* **Fairy Tales**[27] 1359 3-8-7 61 oh3...................................... CathyGannon 2 41
(John Bridger) *a towards rr* **66/1**

60-1 **8** *nk* **Native Picture (IRE)**[27] 1359 3-9-6 74......................... RichardHughes 7 53
(Richard Hannon) *trckd ldrs: rdn over 2f out: nt gng pce to chal: wkng whn hmpd on rails ins fnl f* **9/2**[3]

060- **9** *5* **Goodwood Treasure**[226] 6435 3-9-1 69........................... EddieAhern 4 32
(John Dunlop) *led tl over 3f out: wknd 2f out* **10/1**

060- **10** *1/2* **Putin (IRE)**[206] 6988 3-8-10 64.. AndreaAtzeni 5 26
(Derek Haydn Jones) *t.k.h in tch: rdn whn swtchd lft 2f out: wkng whn hmpd over 1f out* **20/1**

1m 15.75s (0.95) **Going Correction** +0.05s/f (Good) **10** Ran SP% **114.5**
Speed ratings (Par 99): **95,94,93,91,88 87,84,83,77,76**
toteswingers:1&2:£12.00, 2&3:£10.80, 1&3:£4.30 CSF £73.26 CT £260.94 TOTE £3.70: £1.20, £5.90, £1.80; EX 74.20.
Owner Henry Candy & Partners II **Bred** A B Barraclough **Trained** Kingston Warren, Oxon
■ Stewards' Enquiry : John Fahy one-day ban: careless riding (May 26)

FOCUS
A competitive handicap run at a good pace. The front pair both looked a bit better than bare form.

2026 BRIDGEND HOTEL ISLAY MAIDEN FILLIES' STKS 1m 1f 198y
4:20 (4:21) (Class 5) 3-Y-O+ **£2,914** (£867; £433; £216) **Stalls** Low

Form RPR
33 **1** **Tasheyaat**[27] 1364 3-8-12 0.. TadhgO'Shea 4 83
(B W Hills) *mid-div: pushed along over 4f out: rdn and hdwy 3f out: styd on to ld over 1f out: hld on: all out* **6/4**[1]

6- **2** *shd* **Hairstyle**[214] 6770 3-8-12 0.. ShaneKelly 2 83
(Sir Michael Stoute) [illegible]
out: kpt on ins fnl f: jst hld **16/1**

0 **3** *4 1/2* **Dawn Gale (IRE)**[27] 1364 3-8-12 0.................................. TravisBlock 8 74+
(Hughie Morrison) *led for 1f: trckd ldrs: rdn whn outpcd 3f out: 7th 1f out: styd on wl ins fnl f: wnt 3rd nr fin* **100/1**

6 **4** *1* **Zafarana**[18] 1549 3-8-12 0.. EddieAhern 9 72
(Ed Dunlop) *trckd ldrs: rdn 3f out: disputing 1 l 2nd whn hmpd 2f out: kpt on same pce after* **10/3**[2]

6-3 **5** *hd* **Crystal Etoile**[31] 1270 3-8-9 0................................... LouisBeuzelin(3) 5 72
(Sir Michael Stoute) *trckd ldrs: led over 3f out: sn rdn: egded rt over 2f out: hdd over 1f out: fdd ins fnl f* **13/2**[3]

0-2 **6** *1* **Lunar Phase (IRE)**[31] 1270 3-8-12 0................................ LukeMorris 11 70
(Clive Cox) *led after 1f: rdn and hdd over 3f out: kpt on same pce tl fdd fnl 100yds* **10/3**[2]

7 *1 1/4* **Gosbeck** 3-8-12 0.. DaneO'Neill 6 67
(Henry Candy) *towards rr: rdn over 3f out: nvr any real imp* **25/1**

8 *1* **Funny Enough** 3-8-12 0.. MichaelHills 1 65
(George Baker) *hld up towards rr: pushed along and hdwy over 3f out: chsd ldrs 2f out: wknd ins fnl f* **66/1**

9 *3 1/2* **Ace Serve** 3-8-12 0.. JackMitchell 10 58
(Roger Varian) *s.i.s: kpt wd and hdwy to trck ldrs after 2f: rdn over 3f out: edgd rt and fdd fnl 2f* **40/1**

0 **10** *8* **Galicuix**[18] 1549 3-8-12 0.. KirstyMilczarek 3 42
(Luca Cumani) *s.i.s: a towards rr* **66/1**

2m 11.46s (1.56) **Going Correction** +0.05s/f (Good) **10** Ran SP% **115.6**
Speed ratings (Par 100): **95,94,91,90,90 89,88,87,84,78**
toteswingers:1&2:£5.90, 2&3:£51.60, 1&3:£30.60 CSF £28.24 TOTE £2.50: £1.20, £4.40, £19.40; EX 25.90.
Owner Hamdan Al Maktoum **Bred** Shadwell Estate Company Limited **Trained** Lambourn, Berks

FOCUS
A tricky-looking maiden to sort out, as it contained plenty of high-profile stables with nicely bred fillies. However, two finished well clear. They are probably up to the race averages.

2027 AXMINSTER CARPETS RACING EXCELLENCE APPRENTICE H'CAP (WHIPS SHALL BE CARRIED BUT NOT USED) 6f 212y
4:55 (4:55) (Class 5) (0-70,68) 4-Y-O+ **£2,428** (£722; £361; £180) **Stalls** Centre

Form RPR
0221 **1** **George Baker (IRE)**[5] 1905 4-8-9 63 6ex................. CharlesBishop(5) 2 74+
(George Baker) *in tch: hdwy to chal over 2f out: led over 1f out: sn clr: comf* **11/8**[1]

0-50 **2** *3* **Come On Safari (IRE)**[17] 1562 4-9-0 68.....................(b[1]) LukeRowe(5) 5 71
(Joseph Tuite) *awkard leaving stalls and stdd: bhd: pushed along over 1f out: styd on wl whn swtchd lft ent fnl f: snatched 2nd fnl stride: nvr any ch w wnr* **33/1**

4265 **3** *hd* **Diddums**[10] 1770 5-8-3 57.. KatiaScallan(5) 11 59
(Alastair Lidderdale) *hld up towards rr: hdwy over 2f out: sn pushed along: styd on ins fnl f: wnt 2nd briefly fnl 50yds* **16/1**

455- **4** *nk* **Night Sky**[206] 6992 4-8-11 60... DuilioDaSilva 6 61
(Peter Makin) *hld up in last pair: pushed along and hdwy 2f out: swtchd lft and styd on ins fnl f* **14/1**

00-4 **5** *1 1/4* **You've Been Mowed**[10] 1755 5-8-8 62.......................... IanBurns(5) 10 60
(Richard Price) *chsd ldrs: kpt on same pce fnl 2f* **15/2**[3]

014 **6** *nk* **French Art**[26] 1394 6-9-3 66.......................................(p) ShaneBKelly 9 63
(Nigel Tinkler) *mid-div: hdwy over 3f out: led over 2f out tl over 1f out: no ex ins fnl f* **9/2**[2]

0435 **7** *8* **Aviso (GER)**[14] 1637 7-8-5 61.................................... KevinLundie(7) 3 36
(David Evans) *chsd ldrs: ev ch 2f out tl over 1f out: wknd ins fnl f* **16/1**

0-05 **8** *2* **Polar Annie**[10] 1755 6-8-12 64.. JakePayne(3) 7 34
(Malcolm Saunders) *chsd ldrs: ev ch 3f out tl wknd wl over 1f out* **12/1**

5100 **9** *2 3/4* **Crystallize**[11] 1730 5-8-7 61... SeanPalmer(5) 8 24
(Andrew Haynes) *mid-div tl wknd wl over 1f out* **33/1**

0255 **10** *5* **Secret Queen**[17] 1562 4-9-5 68............................. MatthewLawson 4 17
(Martin Hill) *prom: led 3f out: hdd over 2f out: sn wknd* **11/1**

-520 **11** *6* **Freddie's Girl (USA)**[35] 1196 4-8-8 64...................... JohnLawson(7) 12 —
(Seamus Durack) *mid-div tl wknd 2f out* **28/1**

60-0 **12** *32* **Lutine Charlie (IRE)**[10] 1755 4-9-0 68.......................(p) LewisWalsh(5) 1 —
(Ronald Harris) *led tl 3f out: sn wknd: t.o* **16/1**

1m 28.32s (-0.28) **Going Correction** +0.05s/f (Good) **12** Ran SP% **121.7**
Speed ratings (Par 103): **103,99,99,99,97 97,88,85,82,76 70,33**
toteswingers:1&2: £18.70, 2&3:£77.40, 1&3:£6.80. Tote super 7: Win: Not won. Place: £325.80. CSF £67.30 CT £554.45 TOTE £1.90: £1.10, £11.80, £6.50; EX 65.00.
Owner George Baker & Partners **Bred** Mull Enterprises Ltd **Trained** Whitsbury, Hants

FOCUS
A modest event but the market proved a good guide. The placed form looks weak.
T/Plt: £77.10 to a £1 stake. Pool of £39,675.30 - 375.64 winning tickets. T/Qpdt: £29.50 to a £1 stake. Pool of £1,862.00 - 46.60 winning tickets TM

2002 YORK (L-H)
Thursday, May 12

OFFICIAL GOING: Good (7.4)

2028 TOTEPOOL STKS (H'CAP) 5f
1:30 (1:30) (Class 2) (0-105,105) 4-Y-O+ **£12,952** (£3,854; £1,926; £962) **Stalls** High

Form RPR
25-3 **1** **Ancient Cross**[33] 1240 7-8-5 89................................(t) GrahamGibbons 9 99
(Michael Easterby) *dwlt: sn in midfield: swtchd rt and hdwy 1/2-way: rdn to chal over 1f out: led ins fnl f: kpt on wl* **10/1**

2016 **2** *1/2* **Falasteen (IRE)**[8] 1809 4-8-8 92...................................... JamieSpencer 8 100
(David Nicholls) *led: pushed along and hdd 2f out: sn rdn and rallied to ld briefly ent fnl f: sn hdd and no ex towards fin* **15/2**[3]

420- **3** *nk* **Racy**[327] 3218 4-8-4 88.. SilvestreDeSousa 16 95+
(Kevin Ryan) *lw: towards rr: hdwy 2f out: swtchd rt and rdn over 1f out: styd on wl ins fnl f* **12/1**

00-0 **4** *1 3/4* **Judge 'n Jury**[12] 1680 7-8-7 91...................................(t) JoeFanning 11 92
(Ronald Harris) *cl up: led 2f out: rdn and hdd enering fnl f: sn drvn and one pce* **14/1**

204- **5** *1/2* **Secret Millionaire (IRE)**[193] 7254 4-8-2 89............ JamesSullivan(3) 12 88
(Patrick Morris) *chsd ldrs: hdwy 2f out: rdn and n.m.r over 1f out: kpt on ins fnl f* **25/1**

50-0 **6** *nk* **Duchess Dora (IRE)**[36] 1166 4-7-11 86...................... KieranO'Neill(5) 3 84
(John Quinn) *cl up: rdn along 2f out: drvn over 1f out: grad wknd* **6/1**[2]

0-00 **7** *shd* **Johannes (IRE)**[11] 1720 8-8-11 95................................ PaulHanagan 19 92+
(Richard Fahey) *dwlt and in rr: hdwy wl over 1f out: swtchd lft and rdn* [illegible] *kpt on: first fin* **5/1**[1]

000- **8** *1 1/2* **Swiss Franc**[364] 2054 6-8-11 95...................................... KierenFallon 18 87
(David Elsworth) *chsd ldrs: rdn along 2f out: n.m.r over 1f out: sn wknd* **25/1**

4-03 **9** *1/2* **Fitz Flyer (IRE)**[19] 1518 5-8-8 92...................................... TomEaves 2 82
(Bryan Smart) *b.hind: lw: cl up on outer: rdn along 2f out: grad wknd* **22/1**

00-0 **10** *nse* **Blue Jack**[8] 1809 6-9-7 105....................................(v) RichardKingscote 1 95
(Tom Dascombe) *lw: s.i.s: hdwy towards outer over 2f out: sn rdn and nt rch ldrs* **9/1**

235/ **11** *3/4* **Befortyfour**[664] 4059 6-8-11 95.. TomQueally 5 82
(Noel Quinlan) *chsd ldrs: hdwy and cl over 2f out: sn rdn and wknd over 1f out* **50/1**

0340 **12** *1 1/4* **Barney McGrew (IRE)**[11] 1720 8-9-2 100.......................... JMurtagh 13 97+
(Michael Dods) *lw: hld up in rr: n.m.r over 1f out: swtchd lft and n.m.r ins fnl f: nvr a factor* **16/1**

60-6 **13** *hd* **Skylla**[22] 1476 4-7-11 86 oh2.. NeilFarley(5) 10 68
(Richard Fahey) *b: prom: rdn along over 2f out: sn wknd* **14/1**

130- **14** *3/4* **Hazelrigg (IRE)**[208] 6918 6-8-4 88...........................(be) DuranFentiman 17 67
(Tim Easterby) *towards rr fr 1/2-way* **20/1**

010- **15** *1 1/2* **Foxy Music**[229] 6364 7-7-10 87...................................... NathanAlison(7) 14 61
(Eric Alston) *chsd ldrs on stands' rail: pushed along whn n.m.r 2f out: rdn and wkng whn n.m.r wl over 1f out* **25/1**

-600 **16** *1 1/2* **Tabaret**[12] 1675 8-8-2 86 oh4.. PaulQuinn 15 55
(Richard Whitaker) *chsd ldrs: rdn along 1/2-way: sn wknd* **33/1**

0200 **17** *hd* **Solar Spirit (IRE)**[6] 1854 6-8-2 86 oh4............................ FrannyNorton 6 54
(Tracy Waggott) *a towards rr* **40/1**

32-0 **18** *12* **Courageous (IRE)**[27] 1366 5-8-8 92.................................. AdrianNicholls 4 —
(David Nicholls) *chsd ldrs: rdn along 1/2-way: sn wknd: bhd and eased ins fnl f* **14/1**

57.97 secs (-1.33) **Going Correction** -0.025s/f (Good) **18** Ran SP% **123.4**
Speed ratings (Par 109): **109,108,107,104,104 103,103,101,100,100 99,97,96,95,93 90,90,71**
toteswingers:1&2: £12.20, 2&3:£14.80, 1&3:£16.20 CSF £74.15 CT £957.20 TOTE £10.40: £2.70, £2.10, £2.50, £4.40; EX 80.80 Trifecta £378.00 Pool: £2196.50 - 4.30 winning units..
Owner Pete Bown & Backup Technology **Bred** Darley **Trained** Sheriff Hutton, N Yorks

FOCUS
A competitive sprint. Unsurprisingly the place to be was against the stands' rail. It was a respectable winning time considering the wind coming across the track. The majority of riders were afterwards complimentary about the ground and claimed it hadn't dried out that much, if at all. Improved form from the first two.

NOTEBOOK

Ancient Cross came into this with a consistent profile, but has been called some names in the past due to his moderate strike-rate. He showed a resolute attitude when running as well as ever off this career-high mark on his return at Thirsk last month, and dropping back 2f in trip proved right up his street. No doubt bagging the near rail was a big help, but he travelled beautifully and there was no faulting his attitude when asked to get on top. Providing he maintains his current mood he could be set for bigger and better prizes this term. (op 14-1)

Falasteen(IRE), who posted a career-best effort when making all at Epsom on his penultimate outing, was much better away from the gates again here and ran a bold race from the front. This track suits his style and is no doubt capable of defying this mark when on a going day. (op 7-1)

Racy ◆ was having his first outing since disappointing on his final start for Sir Michael Stoute last summer and he had been gelded. There was money for him, but he was keen to post and eased back out again. Racing on the near side, with a clear passage he may well have made a winning return and looks to have improved a deal from three to four. His next outing will reveal more, but he appeals as one to firmly keep on side. (op 11-1 tchd 10-1)

Judge 'n Jury, 8lb lower than when fifth in this race last year, turned in a much-improved effort under a positive ride and looks to be on his way back.

Secret Millionaire(IRE) was making his seasonal debut and ran a blinder. There should be a deal of improvement in him for the outing. (op 33-1)

Duchess Dora(IRE) was fancied to improve on the level of her seasonal return last month, when racing from a poor draw, but again fared moderately on that front. She saw plenty of daylight, but still turned in a more encouraging effort and an end to her losing run looks immanent. (op 15-2 tchd 8-1 in a place)

Johannes(IRE) caught the eye on his second run back at Newmarket 11 days earlier and was on the same mark as when winning this last year (not won since). He was also highest drawn so it wasn't surprising to see him being backed. The breaks didn't come for him against the stands' rail after he wasn't the best away, however, and he was another who must be rated better than the bare form. (tchd 9-2 and 11-2 in places)

Swiss Franc was having his first outing since running with encouragement in this race last season. He too endured a luckless passage and would have been a deal closer had the gaps arrived, so is definitely one to bear in mind next time. Official explanation: jockey said gelding hung right (op 22-1)

Blue Jack wasn't disgraced considering he was slowly away and drawn worst of all. (tchd 8-1)

Barney McGrew(IRE) ◆'s run is best forgotten. He had no luck at all but caught the eye finishing with plenty in the tank. He looked in terrific shape beforehand and is one to keep in mind. Official explanation: jockey said, regarding running and riding, that his orders were to drop the gelding in early and settle as it has a tendency not to get home, it was slightly outpaced early and was denied a clear run latterly. (tchd 14-1)

2029 TOTESPORT.COM MIDDLETON STKS (GROUP 2) (F&M) 1m 2f 88y

2:00 (2:01) (Class 1) 4-Y-0+

£56,770 (£21,520; £10,770; £5,370; £2,690; £1,350) **Stalls** Low

Form RPR

112- **1** **Midday**[188] 7343 5-9-3 121 .... TomQueally 4 123
(Sir Henry Cecil) *lw: trckd ldrs: hdwy 3f out: rdn to chal wl over 1f out: led ent fnl f: kpt on wl* **11/10**[1]

121- **2** *2* **Sajjhaa**[215] 6765 4-8-12 109 .... FrankieDettori 7 115
(Saeed Bin Suroor) *led: shkn up and qcknd 3f out: rdn along over 2f out: jnd wl over 1f out: drvn and hdd ent fnl f: kpt on same pce towards fin* **7/1**

121- **3** *4* **Timepiece**[194] 7237 4-8-12 111 .... IanMongan 3 107
(Sir Henry Cecil) *t.k.h: chsd ldng pair: rdn along 3f out: drvn wl over 1f out and sn one pce* **6/1**[3]

34-4 **4** *2 ¾* **Music Show (IRE)**[19] 1527 4-8-12 116 .... JamieSpencer 1 102
(Mick Channon) *trckd ldrs: hdwy over 3f out: rdn over 2f out: sn no imp* **5/1**[2]

050- **5** *2 ¼* **Brushing**[208] 6928 5-8-12 102 .... KierenFallon 5 98
(Mark H Tompkins) *hld up: effrt 3f out: sn rdn along and n.d* **66/1**

10-4 **6** *1* **Nouriya**[19] 1528 4-8-12 106 .... RyanMoore 6 96
(Sir Michael Stoute) *prom: chsd ldr 1/2-way: rdn along 3f out: sn wknd* **14/1**

24-4 **7** *10* **Field Day (IRE)**[11] 1718 4-8-12 109 .... (t) MartinDwyer 8 77
(Brian Meehan) *lw: hld up: a towards rr* **16/1**

112- **8** *7* **Myplacelater**[208] 6928 4-8-12 110 .... PaulHanagan 2 63
(David Elsworth) *a in rr* **16/1**

2m 10.05s (-2.45) **Going Correction** -0.025s/f (Good) **8** Ran SP% **111.0**
Speed ratings (Par 115): **108,106,103,101,99 98,90,84**
toteswingers:1&2:£2.30, 2&3:£6.00, 1&3:£2.50 CSF £8.71 TOTE £1.80: £1.10, £1.60, £2.30; EX 6.20 Trifecta £30.60 Pool: £2242.17 - 54.09 winning units..

Owner K Abdulla **Bred** Juddmonte Farms Ltd **Trained** Newmarket, Suffolk

FOCUS

A good fillies' Group 2. Midday was close to her best in defying a penalty.

NOTEBOOK

Midday was runner-up in this 12 months ago. However, she developed into a really top filly last term, winning the Nassau for the second successive year, the Yorkshire Oaks and Prix Vermeille, she also narrowly failed to retain her title in the Breeders' Cup Filly & Mare Turf. She came through to challenge the leader over 2f out, but had to fight to wear that rival down before getting on top inside the last. She should figure in many of the same races she did last season, but might go for the Coronation Cup first. (op 6-4)

Sajjhaa won her maiden at this trip on her debut but her subsequent Listed and Group 3 wins were at 1m. She was fractious in the paddock and had to be loaded using a blanket, but in the race she did nothing wrong. Frankie Dettori set the pace but gave his mount a breather on the home turn before getting across to the stands' rail. She was still going best over 2f out and the filly responded well when asked, and it was no disgrace to give best to a top older mare. She will be aimed at the Windsor Forest Stakes at Royal Ascot. (op 6-1)

Timepiece did not appear to get 1m4f and finally found her feet at 1m-1m2f later last season. Stepping up in grade, she was a little keen early and, after appearing to have every chance, was left behind by the first two in the closing stages. (op 9-2)

Music Show(IRE) ran consistently well against the top 3-y-o fillies last season and posted a fair return at Sandown. Stepping up in trip, she was close enough early in the straight but could only keep on at the one speed, and has to prove she stays this far. (tchd 11-2)

Brushing, who progressed from handicaps to win a Listed race over 1m4f here in August. She ran with credit on this step up in grade, although the drop back in trip did not play to her strengths.

Nouriya, a dual Listed winner at around this trip last season but held in Group company, was close up early but faded and does not look up to this grade. (op 12-1)

Field Day(IRE) progressed to win a 1m Listed race and finish in the frame in Group company on all three subsequent starts. She had to prove she stays this far but disappointed as she was never close enough to land a blow. (tchd 18-1)

Myplacelater, making her reappearance, was always out the back and never got involved. (op 11-1)

2030 TOTESPORT DANTE STKS (GROUP 2) 1m 2f 88y

2:30 (2:32) (Class 1) 3-Y-0

£85,155 (£32,280; £16,155; £8,055; £4,035; £2,025) **Stalls** Low

Form RPR

21- **1** **Carlton House (USA)**[201] 7099 3-9-0 102 .... RyanMoore 6 115+
(Sir Michael Stoute) *lw: t.k.h early: trckd ldrs: effrt over 2f out: rdn to chal wl over 1f out: led ent fnl f: kpt on strly* **11/4**[3]

2- **2** *1 ½* **Seville (GER)**[201] 7081 3-9-0 0 .... ChristopheSoumillon 2 112
(A P O'Brien, Ire) *trckd ldr: hdwy and cl up over 3f out: led over 2f out: jnd and rdn wl over 1f out: hdd ent fnl f: sn edgd lft and one pce towards fin* **5/4**[1]

120- **3** *2 ½* **Pisco Sour (USA)**[193] 7265 3-9-0 98 .... JimmyFortune 1 107
(Hughie Morrison) *led: rdn and qcknd over 3f out: hdd over 2f out: drvn and wknd appr fnl f* **40/1**

1 **4** *3 ¼* **World Domination (USA)**[26] 1407 3-9-0 96 .... TomQueally 3 101
(Sir Henry Cecil) *t.k.h early: trckd ldng pair: hdwy over 3f out: rdn and ch over 2f out: sn drvn and wknd* **5/2**[2]

3-14 **5** *2 ¾* **Ashva (USA)**[26] 1384 3-9-0 79 .... JMurtagh 5 95?
(Michael Dods) *lengthy: hld up in rr: effrt over 3f out: sn rdn along and outpcd* **100/1**

21-3 **6** *1 ¾* **Yaseer (IRE)**[28] 1341 3-9-0 104 .... RichardHills 4 92
(Marcus Tregoning) *hld up in rr: effrt 3f out: sn rdn and outpcd* **12/1**

2m 13.49s (0.99) **Going Correction** -0.025s/f (Good) **6** Ran SP% **110.8**
Speed ratings (Par 111): **95,93,91,89,87 85**
toteswingers:1&2:£1.20, 2&3:£6.30, 1&3:£8.90 CSF £6.40 TOTE £3.20: £1.70, £1.30; EX 6.80.

Owner The Queen **Bred** Darley **Trained** Newmarket, Suffolk

FOCUS

The leading Derby trial and an intriguing clash. It was a messy affair, however, with a slow winning time as a result. The first two still came clear, though, and the winner should take the beating at Epsom. The form is rated loosely around the third, with the first two unable to show their true dominance over the rest.

NOTEBOOK

Carlton House(USA) gave Sir Michael Stoute his sixth winner of the race. With his yard's horses not running up to their usual high standards at this stage of the season he had a little to prove, despite reportedly pleasing in his home work. He showed signs of inexperience in the preliminaries and got himself a touch warm, before proving somewhat reluctant to load into the stalls. He then proved keen in the early stages, but got better as the race went on and came to the leaders in the home straight in the style of a proper horse. The manner in which he went through the gap when asked to get on top was very pleasing and he got the better of his battle with the runner-up without Moore going for the whip. He was nicely on top at the finish, advertising his versatility regards underfoot conditions, and looks nailed on to improve for the experience. His dam's side of the pedigree allays any fears over him getting the extra distance at Epsom and it was no surprise that he shot to the head of the Derby betting. He was cut to as short as 6-4, which does look skinny, but was a general 2-1 shot and William Hill went biggest at 5-2 (soon mopped up). Connections later reported they expect him to come on a deal as he had taken time to come to himself, and he will arrive on the first Saturday of June attempting to become the first Derby winner for a Monarch since Minoru won for King Edward VII in 1909. His ability to handle that different track must be taken on trust, but he's in the right hands and it's not easy to see anything improving past him there. (op 9-4)

Seville(GER) was the form pick after his second in the Group 1 Racing Post Trophy on his final start at two, and was well backed in the lead up to this race. Connections also booked top French jockey Christophe Soumillon (previously 3-14 for them) with their seemingly preferred choice of rider committing to Carlton House. The colt raced close up early and it looked 3f out as he bagged the rail as though he was the one to be on. However, he drifted when put under maximum pressure, not doing the winner any favours, and was comfortably held at the finish. Not for the first time his head carriage was a little awkward when it really mattered and he was later eased to as big as 8-1 for the Derby. His breeding strongly suggests the longer trip there will be in his favour and he wouldn't be without total hope of reversing form with the winner, although that rival is open to greater improvement. His stablemate, last weekend's Derrinstown winner Recital, was promoted past him in the betting, but connections confirmed he will now renew rivalry at Epsom. (op 13-8 tchd 7-4 in a place)

Pisco Sour(USA) was having his first outing since trailing in behind 2,000 Guineas flop Roderic O'Connor on heavy ground in the Group 1 Criterium International last October. He was allowed to dictate as he pleased and was perfectly placed as the dash developed. While unable to go with the first pair late on, he stuck on creditably and no doubt posted a career-best effort for the step up in trip. He has to rate as flattered at this stage, but he could be capable of making his mark in Group company this year and his trainer wasn't ruling out running him at Epsom. His performance there will reveal more as to his true potential, though it's nigh on impossible to see him reversing this form.

World Domination(USA) had gone some way to justifying his lofty reputation when an impressive winner on his debut at Newbury last month. Once it became apparent his Classic-winning stablemate Frankel was going to bypass the Derby, he was then promoted to favouritism in the ante-post betting at a general 4-1. Henry Cecil originally thought of taking in the Lingfield Derby trial, but came here after his colt bruised a foot as it gave him more time. He was uneasy in the market, perhaps owing to doubts about his experience and the lack of once-raced maiden winners on the roll of honour. He too proved green in the paddock and took a keen hold off the steady gallop. He also had to race on the outer after straitening for home, thus getting no cover, and was beaten 2f out. This ends his Derby hopes, but it would be folly to write him off on the back of this and his trainer clearly thinks highly of him. The King Edward VII Stakes over 1m4f at Royal Ascot is now his likely target and he deserves another chance. (op 11-4 tchd 3-1 in a place)

Ashva(USA) was predictably outclassed. However, he looked to enjoy being more patiently ridden and is one to keep an eye on back in handicaps.

Yaseer(IRE), slammed by the winner on his debut last year, had won his final outing at two and looked sure to enjoy a stiffer test when a decent third in the Craven on his return last month. He ran no sort of race, though, and didn't look comfortable in the home straight. Something presumably went amiss. (op 11-1)

2031 TOTESPORT 0800 221 221 HAMBLETON H'CAP (LISTED RACE) 1m

3:00 (3:03) (Class 1) (0-110,109) 4-Y-0+**£17,778** (£6,723; £3,360; £1,680) **Stalls** Low

Form RPR

-112 **1** **St Moritz (IRE)**[15] 1600 5-9-2 **104** .... AdrianNicholls 8 112
(David Nicholls) *lw: hld up: stdy hdwy 1/2-way: cl up on outer over 2f out: led wl over 1f out: sn edgd rt and rdn: drvn ins fnl f and kpt on gamely* **15/2**[2]

060- **2** *hd* **Mont Agel**[215] 6749 4-8-7 **95** oh1 .... HayleyTurner 7 102
(Michael Bell) *lw: hld up in midfield: hdwy over 2f out: rdn to chse ldrs over 1f out: drvn to chal ent fnl f and ev ch tl nt qckn towards fin* **12/1**

1-20 **3** *nk* **Dance And Dance (IRE)**[19] 1529 5-8-8 **96** .... SilvestreDeSousa 6 103
(Edward Vaughan) *lw: s.i.s and bhd: stdy hdwy on outer 3f out: rdn over 1f out: drvn and ev ch ins fnl f: no ex towards fin* **9/1**[3]

-022 **4** *¾* **Pintura**[6] 1849 4-8-7 **95** oh2 .... JamieSpencer 2 102+
(David Simcock) *lw: trckd ldrs: effrt and n.m.r over 2f out: hmpd over 1f out: swtchd lft and rdn ent fnl f: kpt on wl towards fin* **4/1**[1]

4-23 **5** *½* **Off Chance**[12] [1681] 5-8-12 **100**.................................... DuranFentiman 15 104+
(Tim Easterby) *hld up towards rr: hdwy 3f out: swtchd outside and rdn over 1f out: styd on ins fnl f: nrst fin* **14/1**

0-41 **6** *½* **Justonefortheroad**[12] [1694] 5-8-7 **95**.............................. PaulHanagan 19 98+
(Richard Fahey) *hld up on outer: effrt and n.m.r 2f out: rdn and hdwy over 1f out: kpt on ins fnl f: nrst fin* **15/2**[2]

023- **7** *1* **Balducci**[194] [7234] 4-9-0 **102**.. JimmyFortune 12 102
(Andrew Balding) *a.p: effrt 3f out: sn rdn along and wknd over 1f out* **14/1**

4325 **8** *nse* **Fareer**[26] [1385] 5-9-7 **109**.. RichardHills 10 112+
(Ed Dunlop) *hld up in rr: effrt and nt clr run wl over 2f out: swtchd lft over 1f out: styd on strly ins fnl f: nrest fnish* **16/1**

0-01 **9** *nk* **Light From Mars**[26] [1406] 6-8-13 **101**.............................. TomEaves 16 100
(David Nicholls) *led: rdn along wl over 2f out: drvn and hdd wl over 1f out: wknd appr fnl f* **10/1**

60-0 **10** *hd* **Crystal Gal (IRE)**[11] [1718] 4-8-11 **99**.................................. RyanMoore 9 98
(Lucy Wadham) *nvr bttr than midfield* **16/1**

-606 **11** *2* **Spirit Of Sharjah (IRE)**[3] [1948] 6-8-9 **97**......................... JoeFanning 11 91
(Julia Feilden) *nvr bttr than midfield* **33/1**

00-1 **12** *1 ¼* **Wannabe King**[19] [1529] 5-8-10 **98**...................................(b) TedDurcan 17 90+
(David Lanigan) *hld up in rr: n.m.r 2f out: swtchd lft and sme hdwy appr fnl f: nvr a factor* **14/1**

30-P **13** *½* **Capital Attraction (USA)**[26] [1406] 4-8-12 **100**.................. TomQueally 1 90
(Sir Henry Cecil) *lw: chsd ldrs: hdwy and cl up 3f out: sn rdn and wknd over 1f out* **33/1**

360- **14** *nk* **Party Doctor**[268] [5188] 4-8-8 **96**.. KierenFallon 18 86
(Tom Dascombe) *trckd ldng pair: rdn along 3f out: wknd over 2f out* **25/1**

0-65 **15** *1* **Totally Ours**[12] [1677] 4-8-7 **95** oh1.................................. MartinLane 13 82
(William Muir) *lw: a towards rr* **66/1**

10-0 **16** *hd* **Harrison George (IRE)**[40] [1094] 6-9-6 **108**..................... TonyHamilton 5 95
(Richard Fahey) *b: midfield: pushed along over 3f out: sn rdn and n.d* **28/1**

-045 **17** *½* **Osteopathic Remedy (IRE)**[12] [1694] 7-8-9 **97**................. SeanLevey 14 83
(Michael Dods) *chsd ldrs: rdn along 3f out: sn drvn and wknd* **28/1**

520- **18** *2 ½* **Mass Rally (IRE)**[209] [6888] 4-8-9 **97**.............................. FrederikTylicki 4 77
(Michael Dods) *blind removed late and slowly away: a in rr* **25/1**

1m 37.23s (-1.57) **Going Correction** -0.025s/f (Good) **18** Ran SP% **124.0**
Speed ratings (Par 111): **106,105,105,104,104 103,102,102,102,102 100,98,98,98,97 96,96,93**
toteswingers:1&2:£20.80, 2&3:£24.50, 1&3:£7.00 CSF £88.02 CT £839.96 TOTE £8.60: £2.40, £3.60, £2.20, £1.60; EX 143.60 Trifecta £1909.10 Pool: £3715.15 - 1.44 winning units..
Owner Billy Hughes **Bred** Newsells Park Stud **Trained** Sessay, N Yorks
■ Stewards' Enquiry : Adrian Nicholls two-day ban: careless riding (May 26-27)
Hayley Turner five-day ban:used whip with excessive frequency (May 26-30)

FOCUS
A high-class and competitive handicap which was run under the standard time and produced a good finish. However, there were several hard-luck stories as the runners congregated close to the stands' rail in the straight. Most of the field were exposed and it's doubtful the winner had to improve much.

NOTEBOOK
St Moritz(IRE), who progressed from handicaps to win a Listed race earlier this season, was racing off his highest-ever mark in a handicap. Held up early, he made good ground early in the straight to join the leaders and, after getting to the front over 2f out and moving to the rail, he ran on with utmost gameness to resist the challengers on his outside. The Royal Hunt Cup is reportedly off his agenda and future plans remain fluid. (op 7-1 tchd 8-1 in places)
Mont Agel had not won since taking a juvenile maiden in October 2009 but had raced mostly in pattern company since. He had a bit to find with some of these on last year's course form, but was given a good ride and looked the most likely winner entering the final furlong, only to find the winner too resolute. He can win a good race if able to repeat this form. (op 14-1 tchd 16-1)
Dance And Dance(IRE) looked an improved performer before not finding things going his way at Sandown last time when missing the break and racing too keenly. Racing off 6lb above his last winning mark, he again blew the start but got into a challenging position and did not shirk the issue. The tendency to start slowly needs to be overcome if his improvement is to continue. (tchd 8-1)
Pintura came into this in good form despite two narrow defeats of late, and was well enough placed early on. However, he rather got carried back and blocked as Balducci weakened and had to switch before running on again. He deserves better luck. (op 5-1)
Off Chance, well suited by 1m and fast ground, had been racing in Listed company of late and was 1lb worse off with today's winner for a half-length beating at Doncaster. She was ponied to the start but ran well considering she was held up at the back, then had to come more towards the centre of the track than most in the closing stages. (op 16-1)
Justonefortheroad won the Thirsk Hunt Cup off 5lb lower and a turning mile was ideal. Held up from his wide draw, he had nowhere to go when needing a run early in the straight and finished well when the gaps opened. He can be rated better than the bare form. (op 7-1)
Balducci showed up for a long way and the outing should bring him on with future targets in mind. (op 12-1)
Fareer, the winner of this race in 2010 off 7lb lower, had not scored since but had been running consistently at Meydan. Racing without the visor he has been wearing recently, he was another held up at the back and could not get a clear run until it was far too late. Official explanation: jockey said gelding was denied a clear run (op 20-1)
Wannabe King was out the back alongside Fareer and this run has to be forgotten as he got no run in the home straight. Official explanation: jockey said gelding was denied a clear run (op 12-1)
Mass Rally(IRE), having his first run for a new yard, missed the break after his hood was removed late, which spoilt his chance. Official explanation: jockey said he was unable to remove the blindfold at the first attempt due to it being stuck. (op 28-1)

2032 IRISH STALLION FARMS E B F SPRINT CONDITIONS STKS 5f
3:35 (3:36) (Class 2) 3-Y-O **£12,952** (£3,854; £1,926; £962) **Stalls** High

Form RPR

12-1 **1** **Night Carnation**[18] [1545] 3-8-11 108.............................. JimmyFortune 1 99+
(Andrew Balding) *lw: trckd ldrs: hdwy 2f out: rdn to chal over 1f out: drvn to ld ins fnl f: kpt on* **4/6**[1]

52-3 **2** *½* **Move In Time**[41] [1122] 3-9-2 102.............................. TomEaves 7 102+
(Bryan Smart) *in tch: hdwy 1/2-way: rdn to ld over 1f out: drvn and hdd ins fnl f: kpt on* **12/1**

530- **3** *hd* **The Thrill Is Gone**[215] [6734] 3-8-11 98.............................. RyanMoore 8 96
(Mick Channon) *hld up: swtchd lft and hdwy 2f out: sn rdn and kpt on wl ins fnl f* **18/1**

35-3 **4** *nk* **Margot Did (IRE)**[15] [1602] 3-8-11 106.............................. HayleyTurner 6 95+
(Michael Bell) *lw: in tch whn hmpd after 1f: in rr and swtchd lft 1/2-way: sn rdn and styd on strly fnl f: nrst fin: sddle slipped* **5/2**[2]

05-1 **5** *1 ½* **Shoshoni Wind**[11] [1711] 3-8-11 92.............................. PhillipMakin 3 90
(Kevin Ryan) *b.hind: cl up: rdn along 2f out: sn drvn and kpt on same pce* **10/1**[3]

250- **6** *1 ½* **Waking Warrior**[299] [4138] 3-9-2 87.............................. PaulMulrennan 9 89
(Kevin Ryan) *in rr and rdn along 1/2-way: kpt on appr fnl f: n.d* **66/1**

-111 **7** *¾* **Lord Avon**[23] [1452] 3-9-2 89.............................. KierenFox 2 87
(Bill Turner) *cl up: led after 1 1/2f: rdn over 2f out: drvn and hdd over 1f out: sn wknd* **28/1**

03 **8** *8* **Take Root**[34] [1217] 3-9-2 0.............................. RussKennemore 4 58
(Reg Hollinshead) *sn outpcd and bhd fr 1/2-way* **200/1**

58.99 secs (-0.31) **Going Correction** -0.025s/f (Good) **8** Ran SP% **116.0**
Speed ratings (Par 105): **101,100,99,99,97 94,93,80**
toteswingers:1&2:£2.80, 2&3:£7.20, 1&3:£3.50 CSF £11.16 TOTE £1.80: £1.10, £2.00, £2.00; EX 10.30 Trifecta £56.50 Pool: £2090.40 - 27.34 winning units..
Owner George Strawbridge **Bred** George Strawbridge **Trained** Kingsclere, Hants
■ Stewards' Enquiry : Kieren Fox one-day ban: careless riding (May 26)

FOCUS
Unsurprisingly there was no hanging about in this decent conditions event and towards the stands' side again saw all of the action. The form looks solid and the winner, although some way off her Sandown figure, is still a potential Group figure.

NOTEBOOK
Night Carnation showed she had wintered well when impressively defying top weight in what is traditionally a strong 3-y-o sprint handicap at Sandown on her seasonal return 18 days earlier. The second that day had since won readily at Chester and, well suited by the race conditions here, she attracted heavy support. She followed up by just doing enough and deserves credit as she was drawn on the outside. At Sandown last time she did carry her head somewhat high once asked for her effort and did so again. That could have been down to the quicker ground as she is said to prefer some cut, but one would want to see her correcting that as the season develops. This highly regarded filly looks well worth her place in Pattern company and returning to a slightly stiffer track should prove ideal. (op 4-5 tchd 5-6)
Move In Time returned with a solid effort in Listed company against his elders in France 41 days earlier and was back on quicker ground. He was again positively ridden and made the winner fight for her prize. Although not simple to place off his mark of 102, he is the type his trainer tends to excel with and certainly deserves to add to his tally. (op 16-1)
The Thrill Is Gone ◆ often ran well in Listed/Group company after winning her maiden last year, but had something to find with the first pair at the weights. She ran better than the bare form, having to switch wide for her challenge, and has obviously trained on from two to three. She too deserves to find another race and her turn is not looking far off again. (op 20-1 tchd 16-1)
Margot Did(IRE) showed she had trained on fine with a close third over 6f at Ascot on her comeback 15 days previously and was the danger to the winner at these weights. She was unlucky to get a bump early, causing her to lose balance, and also had to come wide with her effort. She unsurprisingly finished with a flourish and was somewhat unlucky, but she has become a difficult horse to win with. (tchd 11-4)
Shoshoni Wind ran right up to her best when making all at Hamilton on her return 11 days earlier, but this was a lot tougher. She raced against the stands' rail and, while lacking the raw speed of the principals, posted a decent effort in defeat. Connections expect her to progress further as she matures and stepping back up in trip may prove ideal later in the season. (tchd 9-1)
Waking Warrior ◆, rated 87, was Kevin Ryan's second string and having his first outing since failing to fire in the Super Sprint last July. He was never a threat, but kept on steadily towards the finish and should improve plenty. Another furlong should be to his liking this year and he could well go in next time if eased in class.

2033 STRATFORD PLACE STUD FOR ROYAL ASCOT 2YO'S E B F MAIDEN STKS 6f
4:10 (4:10) (Class 3) 2-Y-O **£7,447** (£2,216; £1,107; £553) **Stalls** High

Form RPR

3 **1** **Noor Zabeel (USA)**[12] [1678] 2-9-3 0.............................. RyanMoore 5 86
(Mick Channon) *w'like: str: mde all: rdn and styd on wl ins fnl f* **7/2**[1]

0 **2** *2* **Apostle (IRE)**[26] [1396] 2-9-3 0.............................. JamieSpencer 2 80
(Michael Bell) *str: bit bkwd: mid-div: hdwy on wd outside over 2f out: rdn and hung bdly rt jst ins fnl f: kpt on same pce* **12/1**

3 *1* **Tortoni (IRE)** 2-9-3 0.............................. PhillipMakin 12 77
(Kevin Ryan) *leggy: scope: dwlt: hld up in rr: hdwy stands' side over 2f out: rdn and hung lft over 1f out: kpt on same pce* **12/1**

4 *3 ¼* **Overpowered** 2-9-3 0.............................. JimmyFortune 6 67
(Paul Cole) *leggy: scope: dwlt: sn chsng ldrs: wknd fnl 150yds* **10/1**

5 *3 ¼* **Barolo Top (IRE)** 2-9-3 0.............................. RichardKingscote 1 58+
(Tom Dascombe) *cls cpld: sn outpcd and in rr: hdwy and swtchd rt over 1f out: gng on wl at fin* **18/1**

6 *1* **Bop It** 2-9-3 0.............................. TomEaves 3 55
(Bryan Smart) *b.hind: sn w ldrs: wkng whn hmpd and swtchd lft jst ins fnl f* **16/1**

3 **7** *½* **Come On Blue Chip (IRE)**[11] [1721] 2-9-3 0.............................. TonyCulhane 9 53
(Paul D'Arcy) *w ldrs stands' side: outpcd 2f out: kpt on ins fnl f* **5/1**[2]

8 *1 ¼* **Hadrians Rule (IRE)** 2-9-3 0.............................. DavidAllan 11 49
(Tim Easterby) *w'like: bit bkwd: s.v.s: gd hdwy over 2f out: fdd ins fnl f: promising* **5/1**[2]

9 *2 ½* **Moon Trip** 2-9-3 0.............................. JoeFanning 8 42+
(Mark Johnston) *lengthy: bit bkwd: chsd ldrs: wknd over 1f out* **9/1**

10 *1 ¾* **Giorgio's Dragon (IRE)** 2-9-3 0.............................. PaulHanagan 4 37
(Richard Fahey) *chsd ldrs: wknd over 1f out* **11/2**[3]

0 **11** *2 ¼* **Art Dzeko**[41] [1071] 2-9-3 0.............................. DuranFentiman 7 30
(Tim Easterby) *lengthy: scope: chsd ldrs: lost pl over 1f out* **25/1**

1m 12.75s (0.85) **Going Correction** -0.025s/f (Good) **11** Ran SP% **120.4**
Speed ratings (Par 97): **93,90,89,84,80 79,78,76,73,71 68**
toteswingers:1&2:£7.30, 2&3:£19.60, 1&3:£12.50 CSF £48.70 TOTE £3.90: £1.30, £4.20, £4.20; EX 51.50 Trifecta £873.40 Part won..
Owner Jaber Abdullah **Bred** Stephen D Peskoff **Trained** West Ilsley, Berks

FOCUS
Usually a decent juvenile maiden and the form looks sound enough.

NOTEBOOK
Noor Zabeel(USA) lacked the finishing speed of the front two on his debut but was keeping on at the finish. The runner-up in that contest had won since and this 50,000gns purchase had clearly learnt a lot from that experience, as he was always up with the pace before asserting over a furlong out. The trainer thinks he needs further and is looking at the Newmarket July meeting rather than Royal Ascot for him. (op 10-3)
Apostle(IRE), who cost £60,000 and was a strong favourite for his debut, showed nothing then but had clearly benefited from the experience and ran much better. He wandered under rather strong pressure but should be able to win races if going on from this. (tchd 14-1)
Tortoni(IRE) ◆, out of a high-class French sprinter and related to Zipping and Last Tycoon, made an encouraging debut, travelling well until fading late on. He looks sure to improve for the outing.
Overpowered ◆, a first foal by a sprinter who is bred to stay further on the dam's side, was another to perform well on this debut. He should also win races before long.
Barolo Top(IRE), a 50,000gns half-brother to Kingsgate Prince and Captain Ramius, was backed but could not go the early gallop. He was doing his best work late and should be more streetwise next time. (op 33-1 tchd 16-1)
Bop It, closely rated to the speedy trio Ladies Are Forever, Hoof It and Forever's Girl, showed he had inherited the family pace and helped make the running. He showed in front over 2f out but was on the retreat when done no favours by the runner-up. He should find easier opportunities and a drop back to 5f should hold no fears. (op 14-1)

Come On Blue Chip(IRE), a half-brother to winners at 7f and 1m6f by a juvenile winner, had posted a promising effort on his debut and showed up early. However, he was on the retreat over 2f from home and needs a drop in grade. (tchd 11-2)
Hadrians Rule(IRE) ◆, a 32,000gns second foal from the family of Flanders, is evidently well regarded but badly missed the break and was well detached for much of the way. He shaped well in the circumstances and looks capable of much better. Official explanation: jockey said colt missed the break (op 15-2)
Giorgio's Dragon(IRE) showed early pace but could not sustain it. (tchd 6-1)

2034 INVESTEC STKS (H'CAP) 2m 2f
4:45 (4:45) (Class 4) (0-80,80) 4-Y-O+ **£6,476** (£1,927; £963; £481) **Stalls** Low

Form RPR
01-5 **1** **Dark Ranger**[19] [1144] 5-8-7 **62**.......... SeanLevey(3) 2 73
(Tim Pitt) *mid-div: hdwy over 3f out: led over 2f out: forged clr ins fnl f* **28/1**
1222 **2** *2 ¼* **Blackstone Vegas**[10] [1761] 5-8-7 **59** oh1.......... RobbieFitzpatrick 10 68
(Derek Shaw) *hld up in rr: gd hdwy on outer 3f out: styd on to take 2nd last 75yds* **20/1**
251- **3** *3 ¾* **Hawridge Star (IRE)**[195] [7208] 9-9-9 **75**.......... RyanMoore 11 79
(Stuart Kittow) *bhd: hdwy 3f out: wnt 2nd over 1f out: styd on same pce* **8/1**
6-13 **4** *1 ¼* **Descaro (USA)**[23] [1458] 5-9-8 **74**.......... SilvestreDeSousa 5 77
(David O'Meara) *trckd ldrs: rdn and hung lft over 2f out: kpt on same pce* **8/1**
411- **5** *4* **Lady Bluesky**[27] [7226] 8-9-1 **67**.......... PaulMulrennan 14 66
(Alistair Whillans) *mid-div: effrt over 3f out: kpt on wl ins fnl f* **16/1**
4-32 **6** *½* **Night Orbit**[23] [1458] 7-8-7 **59**.......... GregFairley 6 57
(Julia Feilden) *in rr: drvn 5f out: styd on fnl 2f* **14/1**
22-1 **7** *½* **Warne's Way (IRE)**[27] [1367] 8-9-7 **73**..........(b) KierenFallon 13 71
(Brendan Powell) *trckd ldrs: upsides 7f out: led over 4f out: hdd over 2f out: wknd rapidly fnl 150yds* **7/1**[3]
32-0 **8** *2* **Boston Blue**[19] [1517] 4-9-5 **80**..........(v) DaleSwift(5) 4 75
(Tim Etherington) *led 2f: w ldr: ev ch tl wknd over 1f out* **16/1**
230/ **9** *4* **Counting House (IRE)**[28] [6210] 8-8-13 **65**.......... JimmyFortune 16 56
(Jim Old) *s.i.s: hdwy 8f out: wknd over 2f out* **8/1**
3-12 **10** *½* **Blackmore**[37] [1153] 4-9-5 **75**.......... PaulHanagan 17 65
(Julia Feilden) *dwlt: sn in tch: effrt 3f out: hung rt and sn wknd* **4/1**[1]
2505 **11** *1 ¼* **Why So Serious**[6] [1871] 5-8-4 **59** oh7.......... BillyCray(3) 1 48
(Peter Salmon) *bhd: drvn and sme hdwy over 5f out: nvr a factor* **100/1**
125- **12** *nk* **Blazing Desert**[194] [5940] 7-9-8 **74**.......... TomEaves 8 63+
(John Quinn) *in tch: t.k.h: trcaking ldrs over 3f out: wknd 2f out* **28/1**
6 **13** *nk* **Viva Colonia (IRE)**[12] [1676] 6-9-6 **72**.......... DanielTudhope 15 60
(David O'Meara) *trckd ldrs: upsides over 3f out: lost pl 2f out* **50/1**
606- **14** *¾* **Hollins**[28] [5492] 7-9-11 **77**.......... FrederikTylicki 9 65
(Micky Hammond) *lw: in tch: drvn over 3f out: sn lost pl* **11/2**[2]
40-6 **15** *shd* **Simonside**[8] [1817] 8-9-8 **74**.......... DavidAllan 12 61
(Brian Ellison) *bhd: hdwy over 7f out: lost pl 3f out* **16/1**
12-0 **16** *nk* **Rosewin (IRE)**[12] [1676] 5-8-12 **67**.......... JamesSullivan(3) 18 54
(Ollie Pears) *trckd ldrs: t.k.h: upsides 7f out: wknd 3f out* **40/1**
0-20 **17** *48* **Nemo Spirit (IRE)**[27] [1367] 6-9-12 **78**..........(vt) RichardKingscote 3 —
(Tom Dascombe) *led after 2f: reminders sn after s: drvn 7f out: styd alone far side and hdd over 4f out: bhd and heavily eased 2f out: wl t.o* **25/1**

3m 55.08s (-3.12) **Going Correction** -0.025s/f (Good)
WFA 4 from 5yo+ 4lb **17** Ran SP% **126.4**
Speed ratings (Par 105): **105,104,102,101,100 99,99,98,96,96 96,95,95,95,95 95,74**
CSF £499.05 CT £4855.64 TOTE £46.90: £7.20, £3.80, £2.70, £2.50; EX 997.50 Trifecta £1654.90 Part won. Pool of £2236.42 - 0.30 winning units..
Owner Recycled Products Limited **Bred** Thomas G N Burrage **Trained** Norton, N Yorks

FOCUS
A modest but competitive staying handicap. There was a sound enough pace on and many chances in the home straight. The form makes sense.
Warne's Way(IRE) Official explanation: jockey said gelding had no more to give
Blackmore Official explanation: jockey said gelding hung right throughout
T/Jkpt: £4,062.80 to a £1 stake. Pool of £20,028.00- 3.50 winning tickets. T/Plt: £20.40 to a £1 stake. Pool of £189,973.53 - 6,775.51 winning tickets. T/Qpdt: £5.70 to a £1 stake. Pool of £9,356.46 - 1,194.67 winning tickets. JR

2035 - 2041a (Foreign Racing) - See Raceform Interactive

1856 HAMILTON (R-H)
Friday, May 13

OFFICIAL GOING: Good (good to soft in places)
Rail realignment around the loop added 8yds to distances on round course.

2042 BRITISH STALLION STUDS SUPPPORTING BRITISH RACING E B F MAIDEN STKS 5f 4y
5:50 (5:51) (Class 5) 2-Y-O **£3,238** (£963; £481; £240) **Stalls** High

Form RPR
1 **Bapak Chinta (USA)** 2-9-0 0.......... PhillipMakin 5 91+
(Kevin Ryan) *mde all: pushed along and qcknd clr fnl f: readily* **1/2**[1]
2 *3* **Frederick Engels** 2-8-11 0.......... DeclanCannon(3) 2 76+
(David Brown) *dwlt: t.k.h: sn pressing wnr: effrt over 1f out: kpt on same pce fnl f* **7/1**[3]
3 *3 ¾* **Joshua The First** 2-8-11 0.......... JamesSullivan(3) 4 62
(Keith Dalgleish) *green in preliminaries: sn drvn and outpcd: struggling 1/2-way: sme late hdwy: nvr on terms* **16/1**
3 **4** *½* **Devlin**[42] [1071] 2-9-3 0.......... TonyHamilton 1 63
(Richard Fahey) *cl up: rdn over 2f out: wknd wl over 1f out* **11/4**[2]

61.40 secs (1.40) **Going Correction** +0.20s/f (Good) **4** Ran SP% **111.7**
Speed ratings (Par 93): **96,91,85,84**
CSF £4.87 TOTE £1.80; EX 4.70.
Owner T A Rahman **Bred** E T Buckley, S Varney & A O'Donnell **Trained** Hambleton, N Yorks

FOCUS
An interesting juvenile sprint maiden with only one of the four having previous experience. It was run at a sound pace and it could prove a decent race despite the paucity of runners. The winner impressed and can rate higher.

NOTEBOOK
Bapak Chinta(USA), a $46,000 breeze-up purchase, was well backed for his debut. Bounced out and allowed to bowl along against the rail, he made virtually all the running and looked very professional. The yard have done well with their better two-year-olds first time out and this laid-back individual will come on for the run. Royal Ascot may be on the cards. (op 4-5)
Frederick Engels was the biggest of the quartet and the most athletic-looking in the paddock. He missed the break and but he stuck to the task willingly. Given that he probably bumped into a useful sort, this half-brother to useful Colonel Mak - who took a couple of runs to get used to things - looks very capable of winning races. (op 9-1)
Joshua The First, a tall, rangy type, was the greenest of the bunch. He was labouring early on but once the penny dropped, he stayed on nicely. He still has plenty to learn but the feeling is he will progress. (tchd 18-1)
Devlin was the one with previous experience and was relatively easy in the market. He contested the lead from his outside draw until he was the first to come under pressure inside the final 2f. This stiffer track didn't appear to suit him but he was a little disappointing nonetheless. (op 15-8, tchd 3-1 in a place)

2043 WILLIAMHILL.COM H'CAP 6f 5y
6:20 (6:23) (Class 4) (0-85,85) 3-Y-O **£5,180** (£1,541; £770; £384) **Stalls** High

Form RPR
21 **1** **Clara Zetkin**[25] [1436] 3-8-8 **75**.......... DeclanCannon(3) 6 75
(David Brown) *hld up in tch: hdwy on outside 2f out: led ins fnl f: hld on wl* **10/3**[3]
1-40 **2** *nk* **Indian Ballad (IRE)**[13] [1688] 3-9-7 **85**.......... GrahamGibbons 1 84
(Ed McMahon) *cl up: rdn to ld over 1f out: hdd ins fnl f: rallied: jst hld* **3/1**[2]
31-0 **3** *½* **Indieslad**[34] [1241] 3-9-0 **78**.......... PhillipMakin 4 76
(Ann Duffield) *trckd ldrs: effrt over 2f out: rdn and ev ch over 1f out: kpt on fnl f: hld nr fin* **4/1**
40-3 **4** *1 ¾* **My Single Malt (IRE)**[38] [1152] 3-9-1 **79**.......... RoystonFfrench 5 71
(Tom Tate) *trckd ldrs: rdn along over 2f out: kpt on same pce fnl f* **7/4**[1]
0- **5** *3 ½* **Cruise Tothelimit (IRE)**[231] [6325] 3-8-12 **76**.......... StephenCraine 8 57
(Patrick Morris) *taken early to post: t.k.h: led to over 1f out: sn btn* **25/1**

1m 14.06s (1.86) **Going Correction** +0.25s/f (Good) **5** Ran SP% **108.3**
Speed ratings (Par 101): **95,94,93,91,86**
CSF £13.04 TOTE £3.90: £3.10, £1.90; EX 10.70.
Owner Norton Common Farm Racing **Bred** Howard Barton Stud **Trained** Averham Park, Notts
■ Stewards' Enquiry : Graham Gibbons caution: used whip with excessive frequency.

FOCUS
A sparse field for this competitive handicap, which was run over four seconds slower than standard, although it looked a truly-run race.

2044 WILLIAM HILL BRAVEHEART H'CAP (LISTED RACE) 1m 4f 17y
6:55 (6:55) (Class 1) (0-110,109) 4-Y-O **£26,667** (£10,084; £5,040; £2,520) **Stalls** Low

Form RPR
0-20 **1** **Red Cadeaux**[9] [1808] 5-9-4 **103**.......... TomMcLaughlin 1 111
(Ed Dunlop) *in tch: effrt and drvn over 2f out: no imp tl hdwy appr fnl f: styd on to ld wl ins fnl f: kpt on* **6/1**
10-1 **2** *1 ¼* **Cracking Lass (IRE)**[40] [1112] 4-8-10 **95**.......... TonyHamilton 5 101
(Richard Fahey) *hld up on outside: effrt over 3f out: kpt on fnl f: wnt 2nd nr fin: nt rch wnr* **15/2**
3-22 **3** *nse* **Moyenne Corniche**[13] [1679] 6-9-1 **100**.......... PhillipMakin 4 106
(Brian Ellison) *t.k.h: trckd ldrs: effrt and led over 1f out: hdd wl ins fnl f: r.o* **9/2**[3]
-216 **4** *shd* **Fox Hunt (IRE)**[12] [1717] 4-8-10 **95**..........(b) GregFairley 6 101
(Mark Johnston) *trckd ldrs: drvn along over 2f out: styd on ins fnl f* **7/2**[1]
12- **5** *1* **Merchant Of Dubai**[383] [1560] 6-9-2 **101**.......... DanielTudhope 3 105
(Jim Goldie) *led 4f: cl up: led and rdn over 3f out: hdd over 1f out: kpt on same pce fnl f* **4/1**[2]
50-1 **6** *3 ¼* **Jutland**[8] [1824] 4-8-10 **93** 3ex.......... JoeFanning 7 94
(Mark Johnston) *trckd ldrs: drvn and outpcd 2f out: edgd rt and sn no imp* **15/2**
534- **7** *½* **Saptapadi (IRE)**[251] [5749] 5-9-10 **109**.......... GrahamGibbons 8 107
(Brian Ellison) *stdd s: hld up: rdn over 3f out: sn no imp* **11/1**
-033 **8** *40* **Bikini Babe (IRE)**[13] [1705] 4-8-13 **98**..........(b[1]) RoystonFfrench 2 —
(Mark Johnston) *cl up: led after 4f: hdd whn hmpd 3f out: sn struggling: t.o* **25/1**
366- **9** *9* **Shahwardi (FR)**[229] [6389] 5-9-4 **103**.......... TravisBlock 9 —
(Jeremy Gask) *hld up: rdn over 2f out: sn btn: t.o* **33/1**

2m 36.55s (-2.05) **Going Correction** +0.125s/f (Good) **9** Ran SP% **113.3**
Speed ratings (Par 111): **111,110,110,110,109 107,106,80,74**
toteswingers:1&2:£9.80, 1&3:£7.40, 2&3:£5.20 CSF £49.23 CT £220.10 TOTE £7.40: £3.10, £3.60, £1.70; EX 64.50.
Owner R J Arculli **Bred** Foursome Thoroughbreds **Trained** Newmarket, Suffolk
■ Stewards' Enquiry : Phillip Makin two-day ban: careless riding (May 27-28); caution: used whip down shoulder in the forehand
Tom McLaughlin one-day ban: careless riding (May 27)

FOCUS
There were plenty in contention with 2f to run but it was a race of changing fortunes inside the final 300 yards.

NOTEBOOK
Red Cadeaux got the split at the right time. On the rail and looking boxed in with 2f to run, he was angled out around Merchant Of Dubai and the stiff hill clearly helped him. Stamina is his forte and he got a proper test here. He won going away and a little more easily than the margin would suggest. (op 11-2)
Cracking Lass(IRE) was closely matched with Moyenne Corniche on Doncaster running and the handicapper had it spot on. She produced a career-best effort here, coming with a withering late run and only just failing. She looks progressive. (op 8-1)
Moyenne Corniche was the first to make his move, having tracked Merchant Of Dubai, but he hit the front too soon and idled. He is a frustrating sort, as he has a string of near misses to his name and just one maiden victory. This was another very good effort, though. (op 11-2)
Fox Hunt(IRE) was well backed and was another who caught the eye. He travelled well and came with a withering run but ran out of time. He looks exposed off this current mark in this sort of company, however. (op 9-2 tchd 3-1)
Merchant Of Dubai, who travelled really strongly throughout on his first start for over a year, looked to have poached a winning lead, but faded with a furlong to run. This was his first run for his new yard and he will come on a lot for the run. (op 3-1, tchd 9-2 in a place)
Saptapadi(IRE), placed in Group 2/3 company for Sir Michael Stoute last year, travelled sweetly on his first run for Brian Ellison, but this was a tough task off a mark of 109 after 229 days off and there will be other days for him. This was a fine effort in the circumstances. (op 12-1 tchd 14-1)
Bikini Babe(IRE) didn't appear at ease with first-time blinkers. She pulled hard and raced prominently before fading. (tchd 22-1)

2045 WILLIAM HILL THE HOME OF BETTING MAIDEN STKS 1m 1f 36y
7:25 (7:26) (Class 5) 3-Y-O+ **£2,914** (£867; £433; £216) **Stalls** Low

Form RPR
22- **1** **Little Rocky**[199] [7152] 3-8-13 0.......... MartinLane 8 78+
(David Simcock) *hld up on outside: smooth hdwy over 3f out: led gng wl over 1f out: qckd clr fnl f: comf* **8/15**[1]
4- **2** *3 ½* **Abdicate (IRE)**[258] [5509] 3-8-8 0.......... TonyHamilton 1 59+
(Richard Fahey) *trckd ldrs: effrt and ev ch over 1f out: kpt on fnl f: nt pce of wnr* **7/2**[2]
3- **3** *1 ¼* **Al Burkaan (IRE)**[346] [2630] 3-8-13 0.......... TomMcLaughlin 4 61
(Ed Dunlop) *t.k.h: chsd ldr: led over 2f to 1f out: sn one pce* **8/1**[3]

4 1 1/2 **Amaze** 3-8-13 0 .... PhillipMakin 5 58
(Brian Ellison) *prom: lost pl 1/2-way: rdn and rallied over 1f out: kpt on: nvr able to chal* **33/1**

0-5 5 1 3/4 **Walleyd (IRE)**[12] 1710 4-9-6 0 .... RossSmith(7) 2 56?
(Linda Perratt) *hld up in midfield: effrt over 2f out: sn rdn: outpcd over 1f out* **100/1**

4 6 1 **Jonny Delta**[19] 1542 4-9-10 0 .... GaryBartley(3) 10 54
(Jim Goldie) *hld up in tch on outside: outpcd over 2f out: n.d after* **14/1**

- 7 nk **Chickini (IRE)**[29] 6-9-8 0 .... DanielTudhope 6 48
(Simon Waugh) *t.k.h: hld up: hdwy over 2f out: sn no imp* **100/1**

8 2 3/4 **Bunacurry**[59] 6-9-6 0 .... GarryWhillans(7) 9 47
(Barry Murtagh) *s.i.s: hld up: struggling 1/2-way: sme late hdwy: nvr on terms* **125/1**

0 9 15 **Ellemental**[40] 1108 3-8-5 0 .... SeanLevey(3) 3 —
(Mrs K Burke) *trckd ldrs tl rdn and wknd fr over 2f out* **25/1**

00 10 2 3/4 **Donnaconna (CAN)**[19] 1540 3-8-13 0 .... JoeFanning 7 —
(Mark Johnston) *led to over 2f out: sn rdn and wknd* **33/1**

2m 2.45s (2.75) **Going Correction** +0.125s/f (Good)
WFA 3 from 4yo+ 14lb **10** Ran SP% **117.7**
Speed ratings (Par 103): **92,88,87,86,84 84,83,81,67,65**
toteswingers:1&2:£1.60, 1&3:£2.40, 2&3:£2.60 CSF £2.51 TOTE £1.60: £1.02, £1.60, £2.30; EX 4.20.
Owner C J Murfitt **Bred** C J Murfitt **Trained** Newmarket, Suffolk

FOCUS
A lot of dead wood in this maiden, which was run at a relatively sluggish pace.
Ellemental Official explanation: jockey said filly finished distressed

2046 NVT & COMMVAULT FIRST DASH CHARITY H'CAP 1m 65y
8:00 (8:00) (Class 5) (0-75,76) 4-Y-0+ **£3,070** (£906; £453) **Stalls** Low

Form RPR

006- 1 **Take It To The Max**[196] 7205 4-9-6 **72** .... TonyHamilton 6 82
(Richard Fahey) *prom: smooth hdwy to ld over 2f out: rdn over 1f out: hld on wl fnl f* **11/8**[1]

0-53 2 3/4 **Dabbers Ridge (IRE)**[37] 1164 9-9-3 **72** .... GaryBartley(3) 5 80
(Ian McInnes) *hld up: effrt over 2f out: no imp tl swtchd lft and styd on strly fnl f: tk 2nd last stride* **33/1**

5-32 3 nse **Casino Night**[7] 1857 6-8-7 **64** .... NeilFarley(5) 2 72
(Barry Murtagh) *trckd ldrs: effrt over 2f out: kpt on fnl f: hld nr fin* **11/2**[3]

-501 4 3/4 **Euston Square**[12] 1714 5-9-10 **76** 6ex .... RoystonFfrench 4 82
(Alistair Whillans) *hld up in tch: effrt over 2f out: kpt on same pce ins fnl f* **11/1**

44-2 5 shd **Shabak Hom (IRE)**[8] 1829 4-9-5 **71** .... MartinLane 3 77
(David Simcock) *s.i.s: hld up on ins: effrt over 2f out: kpt on same pce fnl f* **7/1**

4431 6 2 1/2 **Bold Marc (IRE)**[7] 1857 9-8-13 **68** 6ex .... SeanLevey(3) 8 68
(Mrs K Burke) *prom: effrt over 2f out: kpt on same pce over 1f out* **8/1**

/0-0 7 20 **Arabian Pride**[13] 1695 4-9-7 **73** .... JoeFanning 1 27
(Keith Dalgleish) *led at decent gallop: sn hrd pressed: hdd over 2f out: sn wknd: t.o* **80/1**

4-02 8 nk **Call Of Duty (IRE)**[6] 1909 6-8-9 **64** .... JamesSullivan(3) 10 17
(Dianne Sayer) *disp ld: rdn over 3f out: wknd over 2f out: t.o* **9/2**[2]

15-4 9 1 **Key Breeze**[12] 1714 4-8-13 **65** .... (t) PhillipMakin 9 16
(Kevin Ryan) *s.i.s: hld up: shortlived effrt 3f out: edgd rt and sn btn* **12/1**

40-0 10 1 3/4 **Eternal Instinct**[16] 1618 4-9-3 **69** .... DanielTudhope 7 16
(Jim Goldie) *hld up in midfield on outside: struggling over 2f out: sn btn: t.o* **80/1**

1m 49.7s (1.30) **Going Correction** +0.125s/f (Good) **10** Ran SP% **120.7**
Speed ratings (Par 103): **98,97,97,96,96 93,73,73,72,70**
toteswingers:1&2:£16.30, 1&3:£4.90, 2&3:£22.00 CSF £60.82 CT £211.63 TOTE £2.60: £1.50, £5.10, £1.80; EX 59.30.
Owner Mrs Phillipa Davies **Bred** Whatton Manor Stud **Trained** Musley Bank, N Yorks

FOCUS
A tight handicap run at only a fair pace. They finished in a heap.

2047 RACING UK ON SKY CHANNEL 432 (S) H'CAP 6f 5y
8:30 (8:33) (Class 6) (0-60,57) 3-5-Y-O **£2,047** (£604; £302) **Stalls** High

Form RPR

000- 1 **Blues Jazz**[217] 6710 5-8-11 **47** .... GarryWhillans(7) 1 61
(Ian Semple) *sn bhd: gd hdwy to ld 1f out: sn clr* **16/1**

-000 2 2 1/4 **Chardonnay Star (IRE)**[6] 1906 4-9-2 **45** .... (v) PatrickMathers 7 52
(Colin Teague) *bhd and sn outpcd: gd hdwy over 1f out: chsd wnr ins fnl f: r.o* **100/1**

050- 3 3 1/2 **Ballinargh Boy**[230] 6365 3-8-11 **55** .... NeilFarley(5) 10 48
(Robert Wylie) *in tch: effrt over 2f out: hung lft over 1f out: styd on fnl f: tk 3rd cl home* **11/2**[3]

-452 4 hd **Dower Glen**[7] 1856 4-9-1 **49** .... (v) JulieBurke(5) 8 44
(Keith Dalgleish) *slt ld tl hdd 1f out: kpt on same pce* **3/1**[1]

0-00 5 1 1/2 **Tahitian Princess (IRE)**[4] 1952 3-8-3 **49** .... LauraBarry(7) 9 37
(Ann Duffield) *trckd ldrs: rdn over 2f out: nt qckn over 1f out* **15/2**

3354 6 3 3/4 **Neytiri**[25] 1439 3-8-8 **50** .... (b) JamesSullivan(3) 4 26
(Linda Stubbs) *towards rr: rdn and edgd lft over 2f out: sn no imp* **8/1**

0352 7 hd **Elusive Fame (USA)**[3] 1978 5-9-0 **50** .... (b) JasonHart(7) 5 28
(Mark Johnston) *in tch: sn drvn and outpcd: rallied over 1f out: no imp* **4/1**[2]

00-6 8 1 1/4 **Brisbane (IRE)**[20] 1520 4-9-7 **50** .... (bt[1]) TonyHamilton 12 24
(Dianne Sayer) *w ldr tl rdn and wknd 2f out* **12/1**

6006 9 4 **Areeg (IRE)**[12] 1715 4-8-9 **45** .... VictorSantos(7) 6 6
(Alan Berry) *missed break: bhd: hdwy after 2f: rdn and wknd 2f out* **80/1**

54-0 10 1/2 **Whatyouwoodwishfor (USA)**[125] 98 5-9-11 **57**(b) RobertLButler(3) 3 17
(Richard Guest) *spd on outside tl edgd lft and wknd 2f out* **14/1**

3455 11 7 **William Wainwright (IRE)**[4] 1940 3-8-11 **50** .... StephenCraine 13 —
(Ann Duffield) *in tch tl rdn and wknd over 2f out* **6/1**

1m 13.71s (1.51) **Going Correction** +0.20s/f (Good)
WFA 3 from 4yo+ 10lb **11** Ran SP% **120.0**
Speed ratings (Par 101): **97,94,89,89,87 82,81,80,74,74 64**
toteswingers:1&2:£126.10, 1&3:£19.70, 2&3:£94.10 CSF £953.86 CT £9687.88 TOTE £18.50: £5.50, £8.50, £2.50; EX 500.80.There was no bid for the winner.
Owner Robert Reid **Bred** David Sugars And Bob Parker **Trained** Carluke, S Lanarks
■ A winner for Ian Semple with his first runner since coming out of retirement.

FOCUS
Calling this a run-of-the-mill seller would be too kind, but it was run at a decent pace.
Blues Jazz Official explanation: trainer said, regarding apparent improvement in form, that this was the gelding's first run for him and had been in great form at home.

2048 JIM GRAY MEMORIAL H'CAP 5f 4y
9:00 (9:04) (Class 5) (0-75,75) 4-Y-0+ **£3,238** (£963; £481; £240) **Stalls** High

Form RPR

0001 1 **Sharp Shoes**[7] 1856 4-8-1 **62** .... (p) LauraBarry(7) 6 72
(Ann Duffield) *w ldrs: rdn over 1f out: led ins fnl f: jst hld on* **7/2**[2]

4100 2 shd **Ingleby Star (IRE)**[7] 1856 6-8-8 **65** .... (p) GaryBartley(3) 11 74
(Ian McInnes) *in tch: effrt and hdwy over 1f out: rdn and chal wl ins fnl f: jst hld* **11/1**

5-00 3 1 3/4 **Lesley's Choice**[19] 1539 5-9-1 **69** .... (b) PhillipMakin 8 72
(Linda Perratt) *led: rdn 2f out: hdd ins fnl f: kpt on same pce* **13/2**[3]

44-0 4 1 1/4 **Wicked Wilma (IRE)**[10] 1796 7-8-9 **63** .... PatrickMathers 5 62
(Alan Berry) *midfield: effrt and hdwy over 1f out: no imp fnl f* **33/1**

0-00 5 2 **Ignatieff (IRE)**[19] 1539 4-9-4 **75** .... JamesSullivan(3) 4 66
(Linda Stubbs) *prom tl rdn and nt qckn over 1f out* **22/1**

43-0 6 1/2 **North Central (USA)**[12] 1712 4-8-2 **61** .... NeilFarley(5) 7 51
(Jim Goldie) *s.i.s: bhd and outpcd: hdwy fnl f: nvr able to chal* **10/1**

5-32 7 nk **Sharp Bullet (IRE)**[12] 1716 5-7-11 **56** oh5 .... (p) JulieBurke(5) 10 44
(Bruce Hellier) *prom: drvn over 2f out: wknd wl over 1f out* **7/1**

6222 8 3/4 **Clear Ice (IRE)**[3] 1968 4-7-13 **58** .... (b) DanielleMcCreery(5) 1 44
(Richard Guest) *cl up in centre tl rdn and wknd over 1f out* **3/1**[1]

003- 9 hd **Bahamian Ballet**[218] 6700 9-9-1 **69** .... GrahamGibbons 9 54
(Ed McMahon) *in tch: rdn and outpcd 2f out: n.d after* **14/1**

5-3 10 2 1/4 **Schoolboy Champ**[24] 1469 4-8-9 **63** .... JoeFanning 3 40
(Patrick Morris) *s.i.s: bhd and outpcd: rdn over 2f out: nvr on terms* **12/1**

56-0 11 1 **Mandarin Spirit (IRE)**[12] 1712 11-8-11 **65** .... (b) TonyHamilton 2 38
(Linda Perratt) *bhd and outpcd: rdn over 2f out: nvr on terms* **18/1**

60.59 secs (0.59) **Going Correction** +0.20s/f (Good) **11** Ran SP% **117.4**
Speed ratings (Par 103): **103,102,100,98,94 94,93,92,92,88 86**
toteswingers:1&2:£10.30, 1&3:£4.80, 2&3:£13.70 CSF £41.96 CT £246.98 TOTE £4.70: £2.40, £5.00, £1.90; EX 53.60.
Owner T P McMahon and D McMahon **Bred** Mrs Mary Rowlands **Trained** Constable Burton, N Yorks

FOCUS
An ordinary handicap run at a decent pace with an exciting finish.
T/Plt: £205.50 to a £1 stake. Pool:£46,723.26 - 165.90 winning tickets T/Qpdt: £63.90 to a £1 stake. Pool:£4,060.20 - 47.00 winning tickets RY

1402 NEWBURY (L-H)
Friday, May 13

OFFICIAL GOING: Good to firm (good in places; 7.3)
Rail moved out from 7f to 5f increasing distances on round course by 32metres.
Wind: Moderate ahead Weather: Overcast

2049 RAMSAY HEALTH CARE MAIDEN STKS 6f 8y
1:40 (1:41) (Class 4) 2-Y-O **£3,885** (£1,156; £577; £288) **Stalls** Centre

Form RPR

1 **Wise Venture (IRE)** 2-9-3 0 .... JimCrowley 6 85
(Alan Jarvis) *trckd ldrs: pushed along over 2f out: str run fnl f: edgd rt nr fin: led last strides* **40/1**

2 nse **Poole Harbour (IRE)** 2-9-3 0 .... JimmyFortune 11 85
(Richard Hannon) *chsd ldrs: rdn to ld appr fnl f: drvn: kpt on and edgd lft fnl 75yds: hdd last strides* **15/2**

3 shd **Trumpet Major (IRE)** 2-9-3 0 .... RichardHughes 5 85+
(Richard Hannon) *chsd ldrs: pushed along 2f out: drvn and qcknd ins fnl f: styd on strly cl home: nt quite get to ldng duo* **15/8**[1]

4 2 **St Barths** 2-9-3 0 .... RichardHills 3 83+
(Brian Meehan) *hld up in rr: smooth hdwy fr 2f out: styng on wl whn nt clr run appr fnl f: gd prog again ins fnl f whn hmpd fnl 75yds: nt rcvr* **14/1**

5 nk **Forest Row** 2-9-3 0 .... LukeMorris 4 78+
(Clive Cox) *s.i.s: hdwy 3f out: hung rt 2f out: styd on wl fnl f: green and edgd lft along but kpt on wl* **3/1**[2]

0 6 1/2 **Main Focus (USA)**[13] 1678 2-9-3 0 .... NickyMackay 2 76
(John Gosden) *led after 1f: rdn and hung rt fr 2f out: hdd appr fnl f: wknd fnl 150yds* **14/1**

7 1 3/4 **All Nighter (IRE)** 2-9-0 0 .... LouisBeuzelin(3) 9 71
(Brian Meehan) *chsd ldrs: ev ch over 1f out: wknd ins fnl f* **66/1**

8 4 **Jacob Cats** 2-9-3 0 .... EddieAhern 12 59+
(Richard Hannon) *led 1f: pressed ldrs: rdn over 2f out: wknd appr fnl f* **22/1**

9 nk **Space Raider (AUS)** 2-9-3 0 .... WilliamCarson 1 58
(B W Hills) *s.i.s: in rr: hdwy 3f out: wknd ins fnl 2f* **100/1**

10 7 **Verge (IRE)** 2-8-12 0 .... StevieDonohoe 8 32
(Edward Vaughan) *in rr: sme late prog* **100/1**

11 nk **Mister Musicmaster** 2-9-3 0 .... JamesMillman 14 36
(Rod Millman) *chsd ldrs 4f* **100/1**

0 12 1 **Bajan Hero**[8] 1827 2-8-12 0 .... MatthewCosham(5) 15 33
(David Evans) *racd along stands' side over 3f and w ldrs: wknd 2f out* **100/1**

13 1/2 **Zammy** 2-8-10 0 .... MatthewLawson(7) 10 32
(B W Hills) *in rr: hdwy 3f out: wknd 2f out* **40/1**

14 2 **Macdonald Mor (IRE)** 2-9-3 0 .... FrankieDettori 13 26
(Paul Cole) *in tch: hdwy to trck ldrs 3f out: wl there tl wknd qckly over 1f out: eased whn no ch* **11/2**[3]

15 1/2 **Native Hedgerow (IRE)** 2-9-3 0 .... DaneO'Neill 7 24
(Peter Hedger) *s.i.s: a in rr* **100/1**

1m 13.71s (0.71) **Going Correction** 0.0s/f (Good) **15** Ran SP% **115.9**
Speed ratings (Par 95): **95,94,94,92,91 91,88,83,83,73 73,71,71,68,67**
toteswingers:1&2:£16.00, 1&3:£11.90, 2&3:£5.80 CSF £301.28 TOTE £48.70: £4.70, £2.50, £1.50; EX 557.30.
Owner Allen B Pope & Jarvis Associates **Bred** Joe Rogers **Trained** Twyford, Bucks

FOCUS
The going was good to firm (good in places). The rails were moved out from 7f to 5f, and the round course was 32m longer than the measured distances. A hot 2-y-o maiden. Richard Hannon has won this race, or a division of it, in each of the last four years, but two of his candidates were just denied by a 40-1 shot in a tight three-way-photo in this renewal.

NOTEBOOK
Wise Venture(IRE) raced out wide towards the far side but made steady progress and showed a good attitude to fight his way to the front in a very tight finish. Out of a 1m winner in Italy, he cost just 8,000gns as a foal and was unfancied for this debut, but he has probably achieved useful form in overhauling two rivals who were prominent in the market. He should go on to better things and is bred to stay quite a bit further than this in time. (op 33-1, tchd 100-1 in places)

Poole Harbour(IRE) has been the subject of good reports and he travelled smoothly into the lead at the furlong marker but was just worn down close home. This was a highly promising start by an Elusive City colt whose sales price rocketed to £70,000 last year. He should have no trouble emulating his brother who was a 5f 2-y-o winner, and looks a useful prospect. (op 5-1)
Trumpet Major(IRE) was Richard Hughes's pick of the stable trio. He showed signs of inexperience when the pace lifted but finished well and was just denied. By the same sire as Dick Turpin and out of an unraced half-sister to eight winners in Germany and Italy, he looks another very promising juvenile for a top yard. (tchd 9-4)
St Barths ran into plenty of traffic problems but did really well to finish just behind the leading trio on his first run. He is an early foal who cost £40,000 last year and has speed on both sides of his pedigree. (op 10-1)
Forest Row, a subject of strong support, took a while to get the hang of things after as slow start before finishing well from some way back. He is a 30,000gns half-brother to top-class 9f/10f performer Presvis and was described as "quite exciting" in a stable tour. (op 7-2 tchd 4-1)
Main Focus(USA) was too green to do himself justice on debut but this brother to 7f/1m Polytrack winner Signal Fire and half-brother to 1m4f Group 3 winner Exhibit One, put in a more fluent display on this much improved second run.
All Nighter(IRE), a 14,000gns gelded first foal of a 1m-1m1f winner, showed a plenty of pace and ability on debut for a yard whose youngsters usually improve for a run. (op 100-1)
Jacob Cats showed up well for a long way before fading in the closing stages. He is a half-brother to very useful winners Island Sound, Fair Trade and Serge Lifar (at 1m-1m4f), but he also seems to have inherited quite a bit of speed from his sire Dutch Art. (op 20-1)

2050 SWETTENHAM STUD FILLIES' TRIAL STKS (LISTED RACE) 1m 2f 6y
2:10 (2:12) (Class 1) 3-Y-O

£17,031 (£6,456; £3,231; £1,611; £807; £405) **Stalls** Low

Form				RPR
2-13	1		**Izzi Top**[12] 1722 3-8-12 84 ... DaneO'Neill 2	103+
			(John Gosden) *hld up in rr but in tch: gd hdwy over 2f out: drvn and qcknd to take narrow ld jst ins fnl f: hld on wl clsng stages* **8/1**	
2-1	2	*hd*	**Dancing Rain (IRE)**[28] 1364 3-8-12 86 ... EddieAhern 8	103+
			(William Haggas) *t.k.h: sn trcking ldr: rdn to take narrow ld appr fnl 2f: hdd jst ins fnl f: styd pressing wnr but no ex clsng stages* **7/2**[2]	
001-	3	*3*	**Rumh (GER)**[197] 7198 3-8-12 90 ... FrankieDettori 6	97
			(Saeed Bin Suroor) *sn led: rdn 3f out: hdd appr fnl f 2f: outpcd by ldng duo fnl f* **4/1**[3]	
3	4	*½*	**Stella Point (IRE)**[28] 1363 3-8-12 0 ... RichardHughes 4	96
			(Mick Channon) *in rr but in tch: hdwy fr 3f out: drvn and kpt on fnl f to cl on 3rd but no ch w ldng duo* **3/1**[1]	
21-	5	*3 ½*	**Devastation**[203] 7057 3-8-12 85 ... NickyMackay 3	89
			(John Gosden) *chsd ldrs: rdn to chal over 2f out: wknd appr fnl f* **7/1**	
210-	6	*hd*	**Secret Love (IRE)**[223] 6559 3-8-12 88 ... JimmyFortune 1	89
			(Mikael Magnusson) *s.i.s: in rr: rdn and sme hdwy 2f out: nvr gng pce to get into contention* **10/1**	
201-	7	*1 ¾*	**Mohedian Lady (IRE)**[206] 7001 3-8-12 88 ... J-PGuillambert 7	85
			(Luca Cumani) *in rr: rdn and wknd over 2f out* **8/1**	
42-	8	*3 ¾*	**Miss Diagnosis (IRE)**[191] 7303 3-8-12 0 ... JimCrowley 9	78
			(Ralph Beckett) *t.k.h: chsd ldrs tl wknd over 2f out* **22/1**	

2m 6.94s (-1.86) **Going Correction** 0.0s/f (Good) 8 Ran SP% **115.4**
Speed ratings (Par 104): **107,106,104,104,101 101,99,96**
toteswingers:1&2:£4.40, 1&3:£5.80, 2&3:£4.90 CSF £36.50 TOTE £8.60: £2.20, £1.80, £1.70; EX 23.50 Trifecta £95.10 Pool: £599.01 - 4.66 winning units..
Owner Helena Springfield Ltd **Bred** Meon Valley Stud **Trained** Newmarket, Suffolk

FOCUS
Eswarah became the Oaks heroine after winning this race in 2005 but other than that it hasn't been a great guide to Epsom in recent years. This looked an interesting renewal though, involving a number of unexposed types with plenty of untapped potential for middle-distances. The pace was very steady but the first two pulled clear of the rest. The time was almost four seconds slower than standard.

NOTEBOOK
Izzi Top appeared to have every chance when third in a 1m2f Listed race last time, but she quickly got back in the groove, showing a good turn of foot and willing attitude in this race that developed into a sprint. This unexposed filly is out of a Prix de l'Opera winner and still has plenty of scope for further progress. Connections will consider an Oaks bid for her but the step up in trip is not certain to suit and she didn't look entirely comfortable on the undulations at Newmarket two runs back. (op 10-1 tchd 7-1)
Dancing Rain(IRE), a £200,000 sister to useful 7f-1m2f performer, fulfilled the promise of her 2-y-o soft-ground second with a ready defeat of a subsequent long odds-on maiden winner in a 1m2f fast-ground maiden here last month. Prominent in the market for this step up to Listed company, she took a fierce hold early on but gradually settled and did well to keep battling in a duel with the other breakaway runner. She remains capable of better and will be suited by chasing a stronger pace. (op 3-1 tchd 4-1)
Rumh(GER), an easy front-running winner of a Wolverhampton maiden when last seen in October, had the run of things under another positive ride in this steadily run race but this scopey filly couldn't hang in there on comeback from 197 days off. (tchd 5-1)
Stella Point(IRE), a £150,000 Pivotal filly who holds a stack of big-race entries, was well backed to improve on her 11-1 third in a C&D fillies' maiden last month, but she couldn't land a blow faced with quite a bit to find against some more experienced rivals. However, this still represents a step forward from a lightly raced type who is clearly thought capable of better. (op 7-2, tchd 9-2 in a place)
Devastation made a promising move early in the straight before her effort petered out. Her trainer has reported that she has been slow to come to hand this year and this filly who is by a top-notch stallion out of a brilliant miler, should improve next time. (op 13-2 tchd 5-1)
Secret Love(IRE) was a market springer but couldn't work her way into a dangerous position. (op 20-1)
Mohedian Lady(IRE) compromised her chance by taking a keen hold out wide. (op 7-1)

2051 SCOPE CHARITY H'CAP 1m 2f 6y
2:40 (2:42) (Class 5) (0-70,70) 4-Y-O+ **£2,590** (£770; £385; £192) **Stalls** Low

Form				RPR
	1		**Mauritino (GER)**[25] 7-9-5 68 ... JimCrowley 13	79+
			(Jonjo O'Neill) *hld up in rr: reminder over 3f out: stl plenty to do 2f out: smooth hdwy over 1f out: quicked wl fnl 120yds under hand riding to ld cl home: cosily* **8/1**[3]	
3213	2	*1*	**Moresweets 'n Lace**[17] 1587 4-9-4 67 ... RichardHughes 15	74
			(Gary Moore) *chsd ldrs: drvn to chal 1f out: styd on u.p to ld fnl 120yds: hdd cl home* **7/1**[2]	
5-04	3	*½*	**Morning Chief (IRE)**[24] 1450 4-9-4 67 ...(bt[1]) LukeMorris 4	73
			(Clive Cox) *led at mod pce: drvn and qcknd fr over 2f out: jnd 1f out: hdd fnl 120yds:* **14/1**	
2143	4	*½*	**But Beautiful (IRE)**[18] 1569 4-9-6 69 ... FrankieDettori 6	74
			(Robert Mills) *sn trcking ldrs: rdn 2f out: ev ch appr fnl f: one pce fnl 120yds* **7/2**[1]	
1421	5	*½*	**Ocean Of Peace (FR)**[17] 1582 8-8-6 58 ... MartinHarley(3) 12	62
			(Martin Bosley) *trckd ldr: drvn to chal fr 2f out: no ex fnl 120yds* **14/1**	
540-	6	*shd*	**Golden Prospect**[51] 6860 7-8-8 57 ... FrankieMcDonald 11	61
			(Paul Fitzsimons) *in rr: hdwy fr 2f out: styd on wl thrght fnl f: gng on cl home* **33/1**	
500-	7	*2*	**Bold Cross (IRE)**[223] 6581 8-8-12 66 ... MatthewCosham(5) 3	66
			(Edward Bevan) *s.i.s: in rr: t.k.h: hdwy 3f out: chsd ldrs 2f out: one pce appr fnl f* **12/1**	
030/	8	*shd*	**Phonic (IRE)**[579] 6697 4-9-7 70 ... JimmyFortune 14	70
			(John Dunlop) *in rr: hdwy over 2f out: kpt on fnl f: nt rch ldrs* **9/1**	
1002	9	*¾*	**Ede's Dot Com (IRE)**[7] 1868 7-8-7 61 ... JemmaMarshall(5) 1	59
			(Pat Phelan) *s.i.s: in rr: rdn along and sme hdwy fr over 2f out: kpt on but nt rch ldrs* **20/1**	
030/	10	*4 ½*	**Burza**[606] 5940 5-9-5 68 ... EddieAhern 2	57
			(John Mackie) *chsd ldrs: rdn 3f out: wknd fr 2f out: eased whn no ch ins fnl f* **10/1**	
603	11	*8*	**Roe Valley (IRE)**[51] 945 4-9-0 63 ... StevieDonohoe 16	36
			(Linda Jewell) *chsd ldrs over 6f* **66/1**	
6/6-	12	*nse*	**Regional Counsel**[381] 282 7-9-1 67 ...(t) LouisBeuzelin(3) 9	40
			(Alex Hales) *t.k.h: towards rr: sme prog 3f out: sn wknd* **33/1**	
051-	13	*8*	**One Hit Wonder**[211] 6862 4-9-2 65 ... NickyMackay 10	22
			(Mouse Hamilton-Fairley) *t.k.h: racd towards outside: wknd fr 3f out* **14/1**	
5202	14	*7*	**Lisahane Bog**[16] 1608 4-9-0 63 ...(v) DaneO'Neill 8	—
			(Peter Hedger) *s.i.s: sme prog into mid-div 4f: in tch and rdn over 2f out: sn wknd* **14/1**	
-020	15	*¾*	**Buddy Holly**[24] 1461 6-9-2 65 ... AndreaAtzeni 5	—
			(Robert Eddery) *in rr: hdwy on ins fr 3f out: nvr quite rchd ldrs and wknd 2f out* **9/1**	

2m 9.73s (0.93) **Going Correction** 0.0s/f (Good) 15 Ran SP% **121.4**
Speed ratings (Par 103): **96,95,94,94,94 93,92,92,91,88 81,81,75,69,69**
toteswingers:1&2:£6.50, 1&3:£13.30, 2&3:£34.40 CSF £61.05 CT £787.54 TOTE £7.90: £2.60, £2.20, £4.30; EX 36.60.
Owner P A Byrne **Bred** Werner Klein **Trained** Cheltenham, Gloucs

FOCUS
An ordinary handicap for the track. The pace was very steady for a long way and the performance of the winner can be marked up because he came from a long way back.
One Hit Wonder Official explanation: jockey said gelding ran too free

2052 SCOPE H'CAP 1m 3f 5y
3:10 (3:10) (Class 4) (0-85,85) 3-Y-O **£3,885** (£1,156; £577; £288) **Stalls** Low

Form				RPR
021-	1		**Census (IRE)**[208] 6953 3-9-7 85 ... RichardHughes 8	98
			(Richard Hannon) *trckd ldr: pushed along to ld wl over 1f out: shkn up and qcknd clr fnl 150yds: easily* **11/4**[1]	
1-	2	*2 ½*	**Seelo (USA)**[239] 6127 3-8-13 77 ... NickyMackay 6	85+
			(John Gosden) *hld up in rr: rdn 3f out: hung lft and green over 2f out: stl hanging lft over 1f out: styd on to go 2nd ins fnl f and kpt on but nvr any ch w wnr* **3/1**[2]	
0-21	3	*1 ¾*	**Viking Storm**[31] 1285 3-8-13 77 ... DaneO'Neill 5	82
			(Harry Dunlop) *in rr: hdwy on outside fr 2f out: styd on fnl f to take 3rd fnl 120yds but no imp on ldng duo* **11/2**	
23-3	4	*1*	**El Mansour (USA)**[23] 1485 3-9-0 78 ... LukeMorris 1	81
			(Clive Cox) *disp 2nd: t.k.h: rdn to chal over 2f out: pushed lft over 1f out: one pce whn swtchd rt ins fnl f* **6/1**	
22-4	5	*shd*	**Cadore (IRE)**[17] 1593 3-8-11 75 ... JackMitchell 4	78
			(Peter Chapple-Hyam) *chsd ldrs: rdn and effrt over 2f out: nvr quite on terms and styd on same pce ins fnl f* **11/1**	
0-45	6	*5*	**L'Hermitage (IRE)**[15] 1626 3-8-8 72 ... EddieCreighton 2	66
			(Brian Meehan) *s.i.s: sn rcvrd and in tch: drvn along fr 6f out: wknd over 2f out* **40/1**	
1	7	*½*	**Diamond Vision (IRE)**[18] 1572 3-9-1 79 ... JimCrowley 3	72
			(Robert Mills) *led: rdn 2f out: hdd wl over 1f out: edgd lft and wknd jst ins fnl f* **4/1**[3]	

2m 22.5s (1.30) **Going Correction** 0.0s/f (Good) 7 Ran SP% 112.1
Speed ratings (Par 101): **95,93,91,91,91 87,87**
toteswingers:1&2:£4.40, 1&3:£2.40, 2&3:£4.90 CSF £10.80 CT £40.06 TOTE £3.40: £2.30, £2.20; EX 13.30.
Owner Highclere Thoroughbred Racing (Beeswing) **Bred** Brian Williamson **Trained** East Everleigh, Wilts
■ Stewards' Enquiry : Jim Crowley £290 fine: breach of rule (D)41.1 (unwilling to take the mount because the prizemoney for the race was below the Horsemen's Tariff)

FOCUS
Some interesting prospects lined up for this competitive handicap. The pace was steady but the winner produced an impressive display and looks a very progressive type.
Diamond Vision(IRE) Official explanation: vet said gelding had been struck into behind

2053 SCOPE CHARITY FILLIES' CONDITIONS STKS 5f 34y
3:45 (3:45) (Class 3) 2-Y-O **£4,673** (£1,399; £699) **Stalls** Centre

Form				RPR
1	1		**Best Terms**[25] 1441 2-8-10 0 ... RichardHughes 2	93+
			(Richard Hannon) *mde all: jnd appr fnl f but remained travelling on bit tl shkn up to assert fnl 120yds: sn clr: v easily* **1/4**[1]	
12	2	*2*	**Dijarvo**[12] 1726 2-8-10 0 ... LukeMorris 5	84
			(Tony Carroll) *s.i.s: racd in 3rd tl chsd wnr 2f out: drvn: edgd lft and qcknd to press wnr appr fnl f: easily outpcd fnl 120yds but wl clr of 3rd* **10/3**[2]	
45	3	*8*	**Choisirez (IRE)**[15] 1628 2-8-10 0 ... JimCrowley 4	55
			(David Evans) *trckd wnr to 2f out: wknd fnl f* **33/1**[3]	

62.40 secs (1.00) **Going Correction** 0.0s/f (Good) 3 Ran SP% **106.0**
Speed ratings (Par 94): **92,88,76**
CSF £1.35 TOTE £1.20; EX 1.30.
Owner R Barnett **Bred** W And R Barnett Ltd **Trained** East Everleigh, Wilts

FOCUS
The hot favourite did the job in effortless style to give Richard Hannon a third consecutive win in this small-field fillies' conditions event.

NOTEBOOK
Best Terms was sent off favourite and finished clear with a gambled-on market rival when winning a 14-runner Windsor fillies' maiden auction on debut. The fourth and fifth had upheld that form, and she set the standard against her two rivals here. Always travelling very smoothly, she quickly settled matters when asked a question before coasting to victory. She is a half-sister to two useful 1m2f winners, but this Exceed And Excel filly has a lot of speed and is rated as Royal Ascot material by her trainer who has plenty of candidates for that meeting. (op 3-10, tchd 1-3 in places)
Dijarvo didn't achieve much when making a winning debut at Wolverhampton in March but she took a marked step forward when going close behind unbeaten/odds-on Cockney Fire in a Salisbury class fillies' conditions event and backed that up with another fair effort behind a potentially smart type. She will face much less demanding assignments. (tchd 3-1)

Choisirez(IRE) ran respectably thrown in to the deep end on her third start. She seems to be getting the hang of things and is a Choisir filly who is out of a French 7f/1m winner. (op 25-1)

2054 WHITMAN HOWARD INVESTMENT BANK CARNARVON STKS (LISTED RACE) 6f 8y

4:20 (4:20) (Class 1) 3-Y-O

£17,031 (£6,456; £3,231; £1,611; £807; £405) **Stalls** Centre

Form RPR

33-5 **1** **Elzaam (AUS)**[30] 1318 3-9-0 107 .... RichardHills 7 117
(Roger Varian) *n.m.r s: stdd in rr: hdwy on outside fr 2f out: led wl over 1f out: drvn clr: easily* **10/3**[2]

54-3 **2** *6* **Cape To Rio (IRE)**[30] 1322 3-9-0 99 .... JimmyFortune 2 98
(Richard Hannon) *trckd ldrs: styd on to chse wnr fnl f but nvr any ch* **20/1**

24-3 **3** *2 ½* **Dinkum Diamond (IRE)**[29] 1340 3-9-3 106 .... DaneO'Neill 4 93
(Henry Candy) *stdd s: in tch: nt clr run fr 2f out tl drvn and hdwy 1f out: styd on to take 3rd fnl f and clsng on runner-up but no ch w wnr* **1/1**[1]

01-6 **4** *1* **Sweet Cecily (IRE)**[30] 1319 3-8-12 100 .... RichardHughes 9 85
(Richard Hannon) *chsd ldrs: pushed along and one pce 2f out: kpt on again ins fnl f* **10/1**

23-0 **5** *1 ¾* **Darajaat (USA)**[27] 1404 3-8-9 99 .... LukeMorris 1 76
(Marcus Tregoning) *led tl hdd wl over 1f out: wknd ins fnl f* **13/2**[3]

120- **6** *2* **Pabusar**[216] 6734 3-9-0 104 .... JimCrowley 6 75
(Ralph Beckett) *nor much room after s: in tch: riddwn 2f out: wknd ins fnl f* **10/1**

0-41 **7** *3* **Button Moon (IRE)**[17] 1591 3-8-9 82 ....(p) StevieDonohoe 8 60
(Ian Wood) *chsd ldrs: rdn 2f out: wknd fnl f* **25/1**

623- **8** *nk* **Admirable Spirit**[244] 5965 3-8-9 86 .... EddieAhern 3 59
(Richard Hannon) *in tch tl outpcd fnl 2f* **66/1**

3653 **9** *4 ½* **Bathwick Bear (IRE)**[19] 1545 3-9-3 96 .... RichardEvans 5 53
(David Evans) *n.m.r after s: pressed ldrs tl wknd 2f out* **50/1**

1m 11.68s (-1.32) **Going Correction** 0.0s/f (Good) **9** Ran SP% **116.7**
Speed ratings (Par 107): **108,100,96,95,93 90,86,85,79**
toteswingers:1&2:£6.70, 1&3:£2.10, 2&3:£4.20 CSF £68.15 TOTE £3.60: £1.20, £3.10, £1.10; EX 40.90.

Owner Hamdan Al Maktoum **Bred** Kia Ora Stud **Trained** Newmarket, Suffolk

FOCUS

Six of the runners were rated between 99 and 107 in this Listed event. The winner blew the race apart with a blistering move inside the final two furlongs and the favourite didn't get any luck in-running.

NOTEBOOK

Elzaam(AUS) had leading claims on his defeat by a nose in last season's Coventry Stakes. The return to sprinting looked a good move after a non-staying effort in a visor in the 7f Free Handicap at Newmarket last month, and he put in a devastating display to storm clear. Some of his rivals did run into some trouble while he got a clear run nearest the rail, but it is hard to get away from the impressive nature of this win, from a lightly raced 3-y-o who has form on fast and slow ground. He should have a bright future as a sprinter and could be stepped up to Group 1 company in the Golden Jubilee at Royal Ascot next time. (op 11-4 tchd 5-2)

Cape To Rio(IRE) had something to find on official figures but did well to snatch second from out of the pack. (op 14-1)

Dinkum Diamond(IRE) showed smart form as a 2-y-o, going close in a Group 2 at Doncaster after acquitting himself well against his seniors in the Nunthorpe. His close third in a Listed event at Newmarket on reappearance proved that he is at least as good at this trip and he was heavily backed to defy a penalty. However, he found plenty of trouble buried away in the middle of the pack and the winner had blasted clear by the time he got out. (op 6-4)

Sweet Cecily(IRE) looked short of gears when she needed them. She is a likeable type but her form may have levelled out after nine runs. (tchd 9-1)

Darajaat(USA) finished ahead of three of these when third in the 5f Cornwallis at Ascot last year and failed to get home in a Group 3 over 7f here last month. She got a fairly comfortable lead in her bid to bounce back but had no response when the winner unleashed his turn of foot and then lost a couple of places close home. (op 15-2)

2055 SCOPE APPRENTICE H'CAP 1m 4f 5y

4:55 (4:56) (Class 5) (0-75,75) 4-Y-O+ **£2,590** (£770; £385; £192) **Stalls** Low

Form RPR

053- **1** [illegible] (IRE)[205] 7011 [illegible] .... [illegible]
(William Knight) *stdd s: hld up in rr: stdy hdwy over 2f out: led wl over 1f out: sn wl clr: v easily* **4/1**[1]

603- **2** *8* **Eastern Magic**[198] 7184 4-8-6 65 .... JackDuern(5) 9 68
(Reg Hollinshead) *chsd ldrs: pushed along fr 3f out: styd on fnl f to take 2nd cl home but nvr any ch w v easy wnr* **20/1**

63-0 **3** *½* **Cornish Beau (IRE)**[24] 1461 4-9-0 68 .... CharlesEddery 2 70
(Mark H Tompkins) *led tl narrowly hdd 3f out: styd pressing ldr and stl upsides ins fnl 2f: one pce fnl f but kpt on to retake 2nd fnl 120yds: no ex and one pce into 3rd cl home* **20/1**

1024 **4** *nk* **Zafranagar (IRE)**[24] 1461 6-8-5 64 .... GeorgeDowning(5) 7 66
(Tony Carroll) *chsd ldrs: slt ld fr 3f out tl hdd wl over 1f out: styd on same pce* **9/2**[2]

3-40 **5** *4 ½* **Roanstar**[16] 1608 4-8-8 67 .... ThomasBrown(5) 12 62
(Andrew Balding) *stdd in rr s: stl bhd 3f out: drvn over 2f out: styd on but nvr any ch* **9/1**

31/4 **6** *1* **Shesha Bear**[15] 1635 6-8-2 61 oh1 .... IanBurns(5) 4 54
(Jonathan Portman) *in tch: rdn and sme hdwy fr 2f out: nvr rchd ldrs* **25/1**

434- **7** *½* **Dynamic Idol (USA)**[302] 4062 4-9-7 75 .... MatthewLawson 1 67
(Mikael Magnusson) *t.k.h: in tch: rdn and effrt fr 3f out: nvr gng pce to rch ldrs: no ch fnl 2f* **10/1**

6424 **8** *2* **Maslak (IRE)**[34] 1243 7-8-8 67 .... CharlesBishop(5) 6 56
(Peter Hiatt) *chsd ldr: rdn over 3f out: wknd 2f out* **5/1**[3]

0-34 **9** *8* **Blue Spartan (IRE)**[25] 1443 6-9-7 75 .... DavidKenny 10 51
(Rod Millman) *in rr: sme hdwy on outer 3f out: nvr any ch and sn wknd* **8/1**

103- **10** *3* **On Khee**[168] 6872 4-9-2 75 .... JacobMoore(5) 3 47
(Hughie Morrison) *in tch tl rdn and wknd qckly over 2f out* **9/2**[2]

2m 34.42s (-1.08) **Going Correction** 0.0s/f (Good) **10** Ran SP% **116.6**
Speed ratings (Par 103): **103,97,97,97,94 93,93,91,86,84**
toteswingers:1&2:£11.80, 1&3:£18.60, 2&3:£22.40 CSF £86.45 CT £1429.89 TOTE £3.60: £1.30, £5.50, £5.50; EX 79.60.

Owner The Pro-Claimers **Bred** D Couper Snr **Trained** Patching, W Sussex

FOCUS

A minor handicap in which there was a runaway winner under a very confident ride.

Shesha Bear Official explanation: jockey said mare was struck into

T/Plt: £16.20 to a £1 stake. Pool:£51,777.61 - 2,319.61 winning tickets T/Qpdt: £6.80 to a £1 stake. Pool:£2,518.28 - 272.15 winning ticket ST

[1797]NEWCASTLE (L-H)

Friday, May 13

OFFICIAL GOING: Good to firm (good in places; watered; 7.7)

All rails around back of course moved in 2yds to provide fresh ground.

Wind: Fresh half against Weather: fine

2056 LA TAXIS NOVICE STKS 6f

5:40 (5:41) (Class 4) 2-Y-O **£3,238** (£963; £481; £240) **Stalls** Centre

Form RPR

315 **1** **He's So Cool (IRE)**[9] 1806 2-9-2 .... KierenFox(3) 4 84
(Bill Turner) *mde all: rdn over 1f out: kpt on* **6/4**[2]

2 *4* **Travis County (IRE)** 2-9-0 .... SilvestreDeSousa 3 67
(Brian Ellison) *trckd ldr: t.k.h early: rdn over 2f out: edgd lft: kpt on ins fnl f: no ch w wnr* **20/1**[3]

3 *20* **Priestley's Reward (IRE)** 2-8-11 .... PatrickDonaghy(3) 2 7+
(Mrs K Burke) *slowly away: sn chsd along in rr: a bhd* **33/1**

31 **4** *7* **Forevertheoptimist (IRE)**[13] 1673 2-9-5 .... PaulMulrennan 1 —
(Linda Stubbs) *trckd ldr: rdn over 3f out: wknd qckly* **4/6**[1]

1m 17.68s (3.08) **Going Correction** 0.0s/f (Good) **4** Ran SP% **107.7**
CSF £19.33 TOTE £2.30; EX 15.10.

Owner E A Brook **Bred** Crone Stud Farms Ltd **Trained** Sigwells, Somerset

FOCUS

Good to firm ground, with some good patches and the stalls were in the centre. This looked a two-horse race on paper but with the heavily backed Forevertheoptimist bombing out completely it provided a straightforward task.

NOTEBOOK

He's So Cool(IRE) benefited from the poor run of the favourite to supplement his Brocklesby success. Stepping up to 6f for the first time, he made the running down the middle of the track and, once his main market rival dropped away, he didn't really have to be asked any serious questions to see off newcomer Travis County. While the winner did it well and the longer trip proved no issue, the form amounts to very little and the time was over five seconds above standard. (op 11-10)

Travis County(IRE) produced a very encouraging debut despite not yet having reached his second birthday. He is related to winners and looks connections will surely be very pleased with this sound first effort. (op 12-1)

Priestley's Reward(IRE) blew the start and was never a factor so needs to improve considerably for the experience. (op 14-1)

Forevertheoptimist(IRE) was rearing up in the gates but broke on terms. He came under pressure over 2f out and quickly dropped away. This was clearly not his running. Official explanation: trainer said, regarding running, that the gelding got upset in the stalls and never travelled. (op 6-5)

2057 DIGIBET.COM H'CAP 1m 3y(S)

6:10 (6:16) (Class 6) (0-60,60) 4-Y-O+ **£1,813** (£539; £269; £134) **Stalls** Centre

Form RPR

2-42 **1** **Spavento (IRE)**[12] 1714 5-9-2 55 .... AndrewElliott 9 66
(Eric Alston) *chsd ldrs: hdwy to chal over 1f out: drvn to ld narrowly ins fnl f: hld on all out* **9/1**

-001 **2** *hd* **Dazakhee**[24] 1468 4-9-7 60 .... ChrisCatlin 7 71
(Paul Midgley) *dwlt: hld up: smooth hdwy over 2f out: led on bit over 1f out: sn rdn: hdd jst ins fnl f: kpt on: jst failed* **8/1**[3]

15-5 **3** *7* **Cross The Boss (IRE)**[18] 1558 4-9-7 60 ....(t) PJMcDonald 12 54
(Ben Haslam) *trckd ldrs: rdn over 3f out: ev ch 2f out: wknd ins fnl f* **10/1**

506- **4** *5* **Sinatramania**[278] 4867 4-9-0 53 .... KellyHarrison 6 36
(Tracy Waggott) *midfield: rdn over 3f out: kpt on one pce: wnt 4th nr fin: n.d* **20/1**

46-2 **5** *1 ¾* **Media Stars**[16] 1615 6-8-9 51 ....(p) PatrickDonaghy(3) 10 30
(Robert Johnson) *s.i.s: led after 1f: rdn whn hdd over 1f out: wknd ins fnl f* **33/1**

06-6 **6** *1 ¾* **Maxi Moo (IRE)**[6] 1911 4-8-13 52 .... SilvestreDeSousa 2 27
(Geoffrey Harker) *hld up: rdn wl over 3f out: no imp tl kpt on ins fnl f: n.d* **11/8**[1]

-440 **7** *½* **Lady Excel (IRE)**[7] 1857 5-9-7 60 .... FrederikTylicki 3 34
(Brian Rothwell) [illegible] **100/1**

0-00 **8** *2* **Rosbertini**[7] 1857 5-9-2 55 .... BarryMcHugh 11 24
(Linda Perratt) *hld up: rdn over 3f out: no imp* **100/1**

-001 **9** *4* **No Quarter (IRE)**[18] 1558 4-9-0 60 .... ShaneBKelly(7) 16 20
(Tracy Waggott) *dwlt: hld up: swtchd lft after 2f out: rdn over 3f out: no imp* **14/1**

-032 **10** *¾* **Amno Dancer (IRE)**[20] 1520 4-9-0 58 .... LMcNiff(5) 8 16
(David Barron) *in tch: rdn over 3f out: wknd over 2f out* **7/1**[2]

1002 **11** *2 ¾* **On The Cusp (IRE)**[24] 1468 4-8-10 52 ....(p) JohnFahy(3) 5 —
(Richard Guest) *led for 1f: pushed along and lost pl over 4f out: wknd over 2f out* **22/1**

0014 **12** *17* **Tombellini (IRE)**[6] 1911 4-9-5 58 6ex .... PaulMulrennan 4 —
(David Nicholls) *prom: rdn over 3f out: wknd over 2f out* **12/1**

43-1 **13** *19* **Master Leon**[122] 122 4-9-2 60 ....(p) AdamCarter(5) 13 —
(Bryan Smart) *sn pushed along more towards stands' side: bhd fnl 3f* **12/1**

50-0 **14** *4 ½* **Celtic Step**[6] 1911 7-9-0 53 .... RussKennemore 14 —
(Alan Kirtley) *sn pushed along to keep in tch towards stands' side: bhd 1/2-way* **66/1**

1m 43.95s (0.55) **Going Correction** 0.0s/f (Good) **14** Ran SP% **122.4**
Speed ratings (Par 101): **97,96,89,84,83 81,80,78,74,74 71,54,35,30**
toteswingers:1&2:£6.40, 1&3:£12.70, 2&3:£13.10 CSF £76.48 CT £747.90 TOTE £8.40: £2.70, £2.00, £4.40; EX 45.20.

Owner Whitehills Racing Syndicate **Bred** E Prosser, J Singh, & N & E Kent **Trained** Longton, Lancs

FOCUS

A weak handicap in which a huge gamble on Maxi Moo went pear-shaped in no uncertain terms.

Maxi Moo(IRE) Official explanation: jockey said gelding hung right-handed

Tombellini(IRE) Official explanation: jockey said gelding ran flat

2058 SPORTPOOL.CO.UK MEDIAN AUCTION MAIDEN STKS 1m 2f 32y

6:45 (6:47) (Class 5) 3-Y-O **£2,525** (£751; £375; £187) **Stalls** Low

Form RPR

1 **Gusting** 3-9-3 0 .... ChrisCatlin 9 90+
(Mahmood Al Zarooni) *hld up: t.k.h early: gd hdwy on inner over 2f out: rdn over 1f out: led ins fnl f: sn clr* **10/1**

00-2 **2** *6* **Lady Chloe**[25] 1440 3-8-12 60 .... RussKennemore 7 73
(Philip Kirby) *w ldr: led 3f out: rdn whn hdd ins fnl f: no ch w wnr* **12/1**

3 *3* **Emperor Of Rome (IRE)** 3-9-3 0 .... FrederikTylicki 1 72+
(Michael Dods) *s.i.s: sn chsd clr ldng pair: rdn wl over 3f out: kpt on one pce* **20/1**

4 9 **Autobahn** 3-8-10 0 AntiocoMurgia(7) 3 75+
(Mahmood Al Zarooni) *dwlt: sn trckd clr ldng pair: hdwy over 2f out: 2nd wnt hung bdly rt over 1f out: wknd ins fnl f* **6/4[1]**

3342 5 4 **Black Pond (USA)**[17] 1593 3-9-3 74 (b1) SilvestreDeSousa 10 46
(Mark Johnston) *led: rdn whn hdd 3f out: sn wknd* **3/1[2]**

036- 6 7 **Blake Dean**[234] 6268 3-9-3 65 PaulMulrennan 12 32
(Ben Haslam) *hld up: pushed along over 3f out: kpt on ins fnl f: n.d* **40/1**

7 1 **Indycisive** 3-9-0 0 PaulPickard(3) 4 30
(Simon West) *midfield: rdn over 3f out: no imp* **25/1**

00-5 8 1 **Geminus (IRE)**[16] 1620 3-9-0 62 PatrickDonaghy(3) 6 28
(Jedd O'Keeffe) *midfield: rdn over 4f out and sn lost pl: last over 2f out: kpt on ins fnl f* **33/1**

65 9 4 ½ **Abernethy (IRE)**[19] 1542 3-9-3 0 BarryMcHugh 11 19
(Linda Perratt) *hld up: rdn over 3f out: brief hdwy over 2f out: wknd over 1f out* **100/1**

0-3 10 44 **Georgey Girl**[45] 1027 3-8-12 0 PJMcDonald 5 —
(Alan Swinbank) *midfield: rdn over 3f out: sn wknd: t.o* **10/3[3]**

2m 13.89s (1.99) **Going Correction** +0.30s/f (Good) **10** Ran SP% **119.8**
Speed ratings (Par 99): **104,99,96,89,86 80,80,79,75,40**
toteswingers:1&2:£8.10, 1&3:£12.80, 2&3:£25.90 CSF £114.45 TOTE £9.20: £2.20, £2.70, £4.80; EX 75.00.

Owner Godolphin **Bred** Darley **Trained** Newmarket, Suffolk

FOCUS
A few interesting types in here but it's hard to know what to make of the form with 74-rated Black Pond well beaten in fifth yet 60-rated Lady Chloe appearing to run really well in second.
Georgey Girl Official explanation: jockey said filly never travelled

2059 CHIN UP CHARITY H'CAP 1m 2f 32y
7:15 (7:16) (Class 4) (0-80,80) 4-Y-0+ **£3,885** (£1,156; £577; £288) **Stalls** Low

Form RPR

6-45 1 **Rosbay (IRE)**[6] 1909 7-8-10 69 DuranFentiman 4 78
(Tim Easterby) *in tch on inner: hdwy over 1f out: led jst ins fnl f: rdn out* **4/1[2]**

-032 2 2 **Zaplamation (IRE)**[11] 1746 6-8-2 68 ShaneBKelly(7) 3 73
(John Quinn) *s.i.s: sn t.k.h in midfield on inner: hdwy over 1f out: rdn and kpt on wl ins fnl f* **3/1[1]**

3-00 3 1 ¾ **Monkton Vale (IRE)**[16] 1608 4-8-9 68 (b) BarryMcHugh 7 70
(Richard Fahey) *led after 1f: set stdy pce: rdn over 1f out: hdd jst ins fnl f: no ex* **12/1**

2-0 4 ½ **So Bazaar (IRE)**[44] 1035 4-8-8 67 PJMcDonald 2 68
(Alan Swinbank) *led for 1f: trckd ldr: rdn over 1f out: kpt on one pce* **11/1**

1-0 5 ½ **Hakuna Matata**[34] 1244 4-8-12 71 SilvestreDeSousa 12 71
(Brian Ellison) *t.k.h early: midfield on outer: rdn over 3f out: kpt on ins fnl f* **8/1**

0-44 6 ½ **Royal Straight**[20] 1520 6-8-7 66 oh3 ChrisCatlin 8 65+
(Linda Perratt) *t.k.h: hld up in tch: pushed along over 1f out: kpt on ins fnl f: n.d* **25/1**

3-00 7 nk **Sharp Sovereign (USA)**[24] 1461 5-8-9 68 LeeNewman 5 66
(David Barron) *trckd ldrs: rdn over 2f out: no ex ins fnl f* **28/1**

22-4 8 2 **Birkside**[19] 1538 8-8-4 66 oh6 AmyRyan(3) 1 60
(Linda Perratt) *hld up in midfield: sltly short of room over 1f out: sn pushed along: no imp* **25/1**

6-00 9 1 ¼ **Overrule (USA)**[20] 1517 7-9-4 80 PaulPickard(3) 6 71
(Brian Ellison) *hld up: rdn over 2f out: kpt on ins fnl f: nvr threatened* **33/1**

0-31 10 ½ **Tribal Myth (IRE)**[29] 1324 4-8-7 66 PaulMulrennan 10 56
(Kevin Ryan) *trckd ldr: rdn 3f out: wknd ins fnl f* **11/2[3]**

432- 11 3 ¼ **Tayacoba (CAN)**[235] 6244 4-8-10 72 PatrickDonaghy(3) 11 56
(Martin Todhunter) *slowly away: hld up: rdn over 2f out: no imp* **66/1**

301- 12 ¾ **Best Prospect (IRE)**[55] 7228 9-9-4 77 (vt) FrederikTylicki 9 59
(Michael Dods) *hld up: rdn over 2f out: no imp* **15/2**

2m 15.18s (3.28) **Going Correction** +0.30s/f (Good) **12** Ran SP% **114.9**
Speed ratings (Par 105): **98,96,95,94,94 93,93,91,90,90 87,87**
toteswingers:1&2:£5.80, 1&3:£10.20, 2&3:£19.20 CSF £14.84 CT £130.55 TOTE £5.90: £1.90, £1.20, £4.20; EX 19.80.

Owner Richard Taylor & Philip Hebdon **Bred** Alan Dargan **Trained** Great Habton, N Yorks

FOCUS
A competitive handicap.
Royal Straight Official explanation: jockey said gelding was denied a clear run

2060 NORTH SEA LOGISTICS H'CAP 2m 19y
7:50 (7:51) (Class 5) (0-70,68) 4-Y-0+ **£2,525** (£751; £375; £187) **Stalls** Low

Form RPR

42-3 1 **Bollin Judith**[10] 1798 5-9-10 68 (t) DavidAllan 6 84
(Tim Easterby) *trckd ldng pair: hdwy 3f out: led over 2f out: rdn clr over 1f out: kpt on* **5/2[2]**

0-61 2 5 **Petella**[7] 1881 5-8-10 61 6ex ShaneBKelly(7) 9 71+
(George Moore) *hld up in midfield: stl plenty to do over 2f out: sn rdn: kpt on wl: wnt 2nd appr fnl 1f: no ch w wnr* **13/8[1]**

04-4 3 6 **Maid Of Meft**[20] 1519 4-8-8 55 FrederikTylicki 1 58
(Linda Perratt) *hld up: rdn over 2f out: kpt on wl ins fnl f: wnt 3rd nr fin* **16/1**

50-4 4 1 **Dechiper (IRE)**[16] 1617 9-8-5 49 oh4 SilvestreDeSousa 5 51
(Robert Johnson) *prom: chal 3f out: sn rdn: one pce: lost 3rd nr fin* **16/1**

3-54 5 nk **Tower**[26] 393 4-8-5 55 (p) JohnFahy(3) 10 57
(Chris Grant) *led: rdn whn hdd over 2f out: one pce* **10/1**

6006 6 hd **Valdan (IRE)**[10] 1798 7-9-0 58 (t) PJMcDonald 2 59
(Maurice Barnes) *hld up: rdn over 2f out: kpt on ins fnl f: n.d* **40/1**

544/ 7 nk **Westlin' Winds (IRE)**[50] 6027 5-9-4 65 PaulPickard(3) 3 66
(Brian Ellison) *hld up in rr: rdn over 2f out: kpt on ins fnl f: nvr threatened* **7/1[3]**

226- 8 ¾ **Into The Light**[17] 6829 6-9-5 63 RussKennemore 7 63
(Philip Kirby) *in tch: rdn over 3f out: sn one pce: no ex ins fnl f* **40/1**

055- 9 2 ¾ **Napoletano (ITY)**[55] 7199 5-8-7 51 oh1 ow2 AndrewElliott 8 48
(Robert Johnson) *midfield: rdn over 3f out: wknd over 1f out* **100/1**

-032 10 6 **They All Laughed**[10] 1794 8-8-5 49 oh4 (p) ChrisCatlin 4 39
(Marjorie Fife) *hld up: rdn over 3f out: a in rr* **10/1**

3m 42.79s (3.39) **Going Correction** +0.30s/f (Good)
WFA 4 from 5yo+ 3lb **10** Ran SP% **115.0**
Speed ratings (Par 103): **103,100,97,97,96 96,96,96,94,91**
toteswingers:1&2:£1.60, 1&3:£9.50, 2&3:£8.10 CSF £6.74 CT £49.32 TOTE £3.40: £1.10, £2.10, £4.60; EX 6.70.

Owner Sir Neil Westbrook **Bred** Sir Neil & Exors Of Late Lady Westbrook **Trained** Great Habton, N Yorks

FOCUS
Just an ordinary staying handicap but it had two outstanding candidate.

2061 COOPERS MARQUEES H'CAP 7f
8:20 (8:23) (Class 3) (0-95,90) 4-Y-0+ **£5,504** (£1,637; £818; £408) **Stalls** Centre

Form RPR

5212 1 **Bawaardi (IRE)**[17] 1594 5-9-3 86 PaulHanagan 12 95
(Richard Fahey) *chsd ldrs: rdn over 2f out: led fnl 100yds: kpt on wl* **9/1**

6051 2 1 **Dubai Dynamo**[13] 1695 6-9-0 83 PJMcDonald 3 89
(Ruth Carr) *w ldr: led over 2f out: rdn 2f out: hdd fnl 100yds: kpt on* **11/2[3]**

P0-6 3 ½ **Silver Rime (FR)**[19] 1541 6-9-3 86 PaulMulrennan 7 91
(Linda Perratt) *trckd ldrs: rdn over 2f out: kpt on ins fnl f* **22/1**

00-0 4 ¾ **Leviathan**[27] 1406 4-9-4 87 FrederikTylicki 10 90
(Tony Newcombe) *dwlt: hld up: rdn over 2f out: hdwy over 1f out: kpt on ins fnl f: nrst fin* **3/1[1]**

0-11 5 hd **King Of Eden (IRE)**[16] 1618 5-9-5 88 DavidAllan 13 90
(Eric Alston) *midfield: rdn over 2f out: kpt on ins fnl f* **13/2**

0132 6 hd **New Leyf (IRE)**[11] 1771 5-8-9 78 SilvestreDeSousa 8 80
(Jeremy Gask) *t.k.h in midfield: rdn over 2f out: kpt on ins fnl f* **5/1[2]**

4-05 7 1 ¼ **Keys Of Cyprus**[13] 1696 9-8-11 80 AdrianNicholls 11 78
(David Nicholls) *hld up: rdn over 2f out: kpt on ins fnl f: n.d* **20/1**

200- 8 ½ **The Osteopath (IRE)**[237] 6178 8-9-1 87 PatrickDonaghy(3) 1 84
(Michael Dods) *hld up in midfield: rdn over 2f out: kpt on: nvr threatened* **33/1**

036- 9 2 ¾ **Ginger Jack**[229] 6391 4-9-7 90 PaulQuinn 5 80
(Geoffrey Harker) *led: hdd over 2f out: sn rdn: wknd over 1f out* **28/1**

30-5 10 2 ½ **Zomerlust**[34] 1240 9-9-4 87 (v) TomEaves 6 70
(John Quinn) *midfield: rdn over 2f out: wknd over 1f out* **50/1**

30-5 11 ½ **Magic Cat**[40] 1110 5-8-13 82 AndrewElliott 9 64
(Mrs K Burke) *hld up: rdn over 2f out: sn no imp* **9/1**

-313 12 8 **Mujaadel (USA)**[6] 1909 6-8-10 82 6ex ow1 (p) MichaelO'Connell(3) 2 42
(David Nicholls) *in tch: rdn over 2f out: wknd over 1f out* **10/1**

1m 27.31s (-0.49) **Going Correction** 0.0s/f (Good) **12** Ran SP% **116.9**
Speed ratings (Par 107): **107,105,105,104,104 103,102,101,98,95 95,86**
toteswingers:1&2:£12.70, 1&3:£47.50, 2&3:£24.60 CSF £53.41 CT £1078.99 TOTE £9.80: £3.20, £3.00, £5.00; EX 61.20.

Owner The Matthewman One Partnership **Bred** Millsec Limited **Trained** Musley Bank, N Yorks

FOCUS
With top-weight Ginger Jack rated 5lb below the ceiling for this grade, this was perhaps not the strongest of Class 3 handicaps.

NOTEBOOK
Bawaardi(IRE), despite racing off a career-high mark, continued his excellent recent form by staying on strongly to get the better of Dubai Dynamo inside the final furlong. This 5-y-o still looks to be improving and, given the form of the stable, it would be unwise to think he couldn't cope with another rise in the weights. (op 14-1)

Dubai Dynamo ◆, who won this race off a 6lb higher mark last year, very nearly followed up and lost nothing in defeat. He is clearly back in the groove now, which coincides with the return to form of his stable, and he looks one to keep a close eye on. (op 13-2 tchd 8-1)

Silver Rime(FR) travelled well in behind the speed before staying on well to finish close up. This was a major step forward on his reappearance run. (op 33-1)

Leviathan looked a little isolated as he tried to make headway up the near side but he never really looked like landing a blow on those who raced centre-field. The strong market support throughout the day suggests connections were expecting a bold bid and it may be that things didn't pan out. (op 2-1 tchd 15-8)

King Of Eden(IRE) ran well again but he found another 7lb rise against the strongest opposition he has faced so far just too much. (op 15-2 tchd 6-1)

New Leyf(IRE), for whom there appeared to be no excuses, couldn't never land a blow on the principals but kept on well enough. He is probably better suited by a slightly easier test at this trip. (op 7-1)

2062 FREEBETTING.CO.UK FILLIES' H'CAP 5f
8:50 (8:50) (Class 5) (0-70,70) 3-Y-0+ **£2,525** (£751; £375; £187) **Stalls** Centre

Form RPR

601- 1 **Foreign Rhythm (IRE)**[208] 6965 6-8-11 62 ShaneBKelly(7) 9 71
(Ron Barr) *hld up: rdn over 2f out: hdwy over 1f out: led ins fnl f: kpt on* **9/1**

40-1 2 ½ **Dispol Kylie (IRE)**[18] 1555 5-9-9 70 MichaelO'Connell(3) 8 77
(Kate Walton) *in tch: rdn over 1f out: kpt on wl ins fnl f* **4/1[3]**

00-3 3 1 ½ **Arriva La Diva**[7] 1856 5-9-3 61 DavidAllan 7 63
(Linda Perratt) *led narrowly: rdn over 2f out: hdd ins fnl f: no ex* **10/1**

-332 4 ¾ **Carrie's Magic**[9] 1816 4-9-6 69 (b) LMcNiff(5) 1 68+
(David Barron) *racd alone far side: w ldrs: rdn over 1f out: no ex fnl 100yds* **5/1**

4343 5 1 ¾ **These Dreams**[52] 936 3-8-3 56 oh4 SilvestreDeSousa 3 45
(Richard Guest) *hld up: rdn over 2f out: kpt on one pce ins fnl f: nvr threatened* **25/1**

20-3 6 shd **Red Roar (IRE)**[3] 1968 4-9-7 65 PaulHanagan 5 57
(Alan Berry) *trckd ldrs: t.k.h early: rdn over 2f out: no ex ins fnl f* **10/3[1]**

1222 7 3 ¾ **Rhal (IRE)**[11] 1745 3-9-2 69 (p) TomEaves 6 44
(Bryan Smart) *w ldr: rdn over 2f out: wknd ins fnl f* **7/2[2]**

406- 8 5 **Hansomis (IRE)**[236] 6221 7-8-13 57 (b) FrederikTylicki 2 18
(Bruce Mactaggart) *hld up: rdn along bef 1/2-way: a towards rr* **12/1**

400- 9 21 **Tabiet**[225] 6492 4-8-12 56 oh1 LeeNewman 4 —
(Linda Perratt) *hld up: rdn over 2f out: sn wknd: bhd over 1f out* **16/1**

61.58 secs (0.48) **Going Correction** 0.0s/f (Good)
WFA 3 from 4yo+ 9lb **9** Ran SP% **118.5**
Speed ratings (Par 100): **96,95,92,91,88 88,82,74,41**
toteswingers:1&2:£6.10, 1&3:£11.60, 2&3:£10.50 CSF £46.14 CT £306.41 TOTE £18.40: £4.40, £1.40, £1.60; EX 58.00.

Owner P Cartmell **Bred** Yeomanstown Stud **Trained** Seamer, N Yorks

FOCUS
Just an ordinary fillies' sprint handicap to close and once again the action unfolded down middle of the track.

T/Plt: £346.00 to a £1 stake. Pool:£56,396.07 - 118.96 winning tickets T/Qpdt: £52.80 to a £1 stake. Pool:£6,233.05 - 87.20 winning tickets AS

2016 NEWMARKET (R-H)

Friday, May 13

OFFICIAL GOING: Good to firm (8.1)

Stands' side track used with stalls on stands' side except for 2.50 centre.

Wind: Fresh across Weather: Cloudy with sunny spells

2063 LLOYDS TSB FINANCIAL MARKETS E B F MAIDEN FILLIES' STKS — 6f

1:50 (1:50) (Class 4) 2-Y-O **£4,533** (£1,348; £674; £336) **Stalls** High

Form RPR

2 **1** **Royal Blush**[29] 1337 2-9-0 0.. NeilCallan 1 75
(Paul Cole) *w ldr tl led over 4f out: rdn over 1f out: r.o* **4/6**[1]

2 ¾ **Lemon Rock** 2-9-0 0.. AdamKirby 4 73+
(Noel Quinlan) *a.p: swtchd rt over 2f out: rdn to chse wnr over 1f out: r.o* **7/2**[2]

3 2 **Fairyinthewind (IRE)** 2-9-0 0.. TonyCulhane 3 67
(Paul D'Arcy) *led: hdd over 4f out: chsd wnr tl rdn over 1f out: styd on same pce ins fnl f* **14/1**

4 4 ½ **Midas Medusa (FR)** 2-9-0 0.. PatDobbs 2 53
(Richard Hannon) *dwlt and swvd rt s: sn in tch: rdn and hmpd over 2f out: wknd over 1f out* **4/1**[3]

1m 13.43s (1.23) **Going Correction** -0.05s/f (Good) **4 Ran SP% 108.9**
Speed ratings (Par 92): **89,88,85,79**
CSF £3.34 TOTE £1.50; EX 3.60.

Owner Denford Stud **Bred** Denford Stud Ltd **Trained** Whatcombe, Oxon

FOCUS

An interesting little maiden, featuring one with solid form up against three interesting newcomers. They only seemed to go steady in the early stages.

NOTEBOOK

Royal Blush, who was a most encouraging second in a maiden here at the Craven Meeting (from which two of those behind have gone in since), justified the odds. However, she had to work hard to hold on after crossing to the rail 2f from home and that previous experience probably made all the difference. (op 4-5 tchd 8-13)

Lemon Rock ◆, a 32,000gns half-sister to two winners at up to 1m including one in Listed company, appeared to be highly regarded by connections and there was plenty of money for her. Content to track the pace early, she was angled out 2f from home and made sure the odds-on favourite was never able to take things easy. She looks a nice prospect and would be fancied to reverse the form with the winner were they to meet again. (op 3-1)

Fairyinthewind(IRE), a 15,000euros half-sister to a winning juvenile sprinter, showed good speed for a long way but the way she held her head suggested the experience was very much needed and she can only improve. (op 10-1 tchd 16-1)

Midas Medusa(FR) swerved right exiting the stalls, was the first of the quartet off the bridle, and took a bump from the runner-up 2f out when seemingly held. This 190,000euros sister to the multiple winning sprinter (including in Listed company) Mister Hughie is surely capable of much better. (op 9-2 tchd 11-2)

2064 LLOYDS TSB COMMERCIAL H'CAP — 1m

2:20 (2:20) (Class 5) (0-75,75) 3-Y-O **£2,590** (£770; £385; £192) **Stalls** High

Form RPR

40-1 **1** **Iron Step**[14] 1655 3-9-4 **72**.. JamesDoyle 2 78+
(Nicky Vaughan) *chsd ldrs: rdn over 2f out: led wl ins fnl f: r.o* **12/1**

53-1 **2** ½ **Elusivity (IRE)**[16] 1611 3-9-5 **73**.. ShaneKelly 9 78
(Brian Meehan) *led: rdn over 1f out: hdd wl ins fnl f: styd on* **7/1**[3]

406- **3** ¾ **May Be Some Time**[248] 5830 3-8-9 **63**.. LiamKeniry 7 66
(Stuart Kittow) *prom: pushed along 1/2-way: outpcd over 2f out: rallied over 1f out: r.o* **33/1**

-214 **4** ½ **Obsession (IRE)**[7] 1843 3-9-7 **75**..(v) DarryllHolland 8 77+
(Jeremy Noseda) *hld up in tch: hld up: pushed along over 3f out: sn outpcd: swtchd rt over 1f out: r.o wl ins fnl f: nt rch ldrs* **2/1**[1]

1 **5** ½ **Protractor (IRE)**[56] 888 3-9-7 **75**.. RobertWinston 4 76
(B W Hills) *chsd ldr: rdn over 2f out: styd on same pce fnl f* **7/1**[3]

00-6 **6** 1 **Ferruccio (IRE)**[18] 1568 3-9-0 **68**..(t) PatCosgrave 10 67
(James Fanshawe) *s.i.s: hld up: hdwy over 2f out: rdn over 1f out: styd on same pce fnl f* **8/1**

2226 **7** nk **Uncle Dermot (IRE)**[23] 1481 3-9-0 **68**.. FergusSweeney [illegible] [illegible]
(Brendan Powell) *s.i.s: hdwy over 4f out: rdn over 2f out: no ex ins fnl f* **20/1**

000- **8** 10 **Korngold**[203] 7058 3-8-8 **62**.. TedDurcan 1 37
(John Dunlop) *dwlt: hld up: rdn over 3f out: a in rr* **9/2**[2]

000- **9** 1 ½ **Warden Bond**[184] 7386 3-8-2 **61** oh1.. LauraPike(5) 5 33
(William Stone) *mid-div: rdn and n.m.r 1/2-way: sn lost pl: wknd over 2f out* **66/1**

3220 **10** 1 ¾ **Hackett (IRE)**[45] 1022 3-8-8 **62**.. DavidProbert 11 30
(Michael Quinn) *chsd ldrs: rdn over 2f out: wkng whn hung rt sn after* **20/1**

6-46 **11** 1 ¾ **Focail Maith**[30] 1313 3-9-6 **74**.. AdamKirby 6 38
(Noel Quinlan) *hld up: rdn and wknd 3f out* **16/1**

1m 38.33s (-0.27) **Going Correction** -0.05s/f (Good) **11 Ran SP% 115.2**
Speed ratings (Par 99): **99,98,97,97,96 95,95,85,83,82 80**
toteswingers:1&2:£24.40, 1&3:£89.50, 2&3:£53.90 CSF £87.49 CT £2721.93 TOTE £15.20: £2.80, £1.90, £6.40; EX 91.40.

Owner Andrew Tinkler **Bred** Brook Stud Bloodstock Ltd **Trained** Helshaw Grange, Shropshire

FOCUS

As modest a handicap as you are likely to get on the Rowley Mile and very few ever got into it.

Focail Maith Official explanation: trainer said gelding was unsuited by the track

2065 LLOYDS TSB COMMERCIAL FINANCE MAIDEN FILLIES' STKS — 1m 4f

2:50 (2:52) (Class 5) 3-Y-O **£3,238** (£963; £481; £240) **Stalls** Centre

Form RPR

2 **1** **Skip Along**[19] 1549 3-9-0 0.. DarryllHolland 8 88
(John Gosden) *led after 1f: hdd over 5f out: led again over 3f out: drvn out* **1/3**[1]

0 **2** nk **Crassula**[19] 1549 3-9-0 0.. PatDobbs 2 87
(Terry Clement) *a.p: rdn to chse wnr over 1f out: r.o* **16/1**

53-0 **3** 7 **Magical Flower**[16] 1609 3-8-9 72.. HarryBentley(5) 7 75
(William Knight) *led 1f: chsd wnr tl led again over 5f out: hdd over 3f out: rdn and ev ch wl over 1f out: wknd fnl f* **16/1**

0- **4** 7 **Spectacle**[195] 7231 3-9-0 0.. RichardMullen 6 64
(Sir Michael Stoute) *s.i.s: sn prom: rdn over 4f out: sn hung rt: wknd over 2f out* **11/1**[3]

4- **5** 1 ¼ **Schism**[259] 5489 3-9-0 0.. FergusSweeney 9 62
(Henry Candy) *s.s: hdwy 1/2-way: rdn and wknd over 2f out* **11/2**[2]

0 **6** 7 **Compassion**[19] 1549 3-9-0 0.. TedDurcan 1 51
(Michael Bell) *hld up: a in rr: rdn and wknd over 2f out* **16/1**

04- **7** 3 ¼ **Astromagick**[221] 6618 3-8-9 0.. AshleyMorgan(5) 5 46
(Mark H Tompkins) *hld up: a in rr: wknd over 2f out* **33/1**

0-0 **8** 30 **Supreme Seductress (IRE)**[28] 1363 3-9-0 0.. RobertWinston 3 —
(B W Hills) *prom: rdn over 3f out: sn wknd: t.o* **20/1**

2m 30.35s (-1.65) **Going Correction** -0.05s/f (Good) **8 Ran SP% 124.1**
Speed ratings (Par 96): **103,102,98,93,92 87,85,65**
toteswingers:1&2:£2.00, 1&3:£4.20, 2&3:£53.70 CSF £9.92 TOTE £1.30: £1.02, £4.40, £5.20; EX 9.70.

Owner Mrs J Magnier, D Smith & M Tabor **Bred** Biddestone Stud **Trained** Newmarket, Suffolk

FOCUS

An uncompetitive fillies' maiden, though several of these were bred to improve for the longer trip. They finished well spread out.

Supreme Seductress(IRE) Official explanation: trainer said filly was unsuited by the good to firm ground

2066 LLOYDS TSB FOR THE JOURNEY H'CAP — 1m 2f

3:25 (3:25) (Class 3) (0-90,89) 4-Y-O+ **£7,447** (£2,216; £1,107; £553) **Stalls** High

Form RPR

11- **1** **Vita Nova (IRE)**[266] 5259 4-9-5 **87**.. IanMongan 7 106
(Sir Henry Cecil) *w ldr tl led over 7f out: hdd over 5f out: led again over 3f out: rdn clr fr over 1f out* **11/4**[1]

60-2 **2** 6 **Incendo**[14] 1651 5-8-13 **81**..(t) PatCosgrave 5 88
(James Fanshawe) *s.i.s: hld up: hdwy over 1f out: chsd wnr fnl f: no imp* **12/1**

31-2 **3** 1 **Shallow Bay**[11] 1772 4-9-2 **84**.. AdamKirby 10 89
(Walter Swinburn) *chsd ldrs: rdn over 1f out: styd on same pce* **9/2**[2]

21-0 **4** ¾ **Significant Move**[27] 1402 4-8-9 **77**.. LiamKeniry 12 81
(Stuart Kittow) *hld up: hdwy over 2f out: hmpd over 1f out: r.o: nt trble ldrs* **11/1**

12-3 **5** 1 ½ **Lunar Victory (USA)**[41] 1102 4-9-5 **87**.. RichardMullen 2 88
(John Gosden) *chsd ldrs: rdn over 2f out: wknd fnl f: b.b.v* **5/1**[3]

-053 **6** 1 ½ **First Post (IRE)**[16] 1603 4-8-12 **80**.. RobertWinston 3 78
(Derek Haydn Jones) *hld up in tch: rdn over 2f out: hung lft and wknd over 1f out* **12/1**

6-43 **7** nk **Ramona Chase**[23] 1479 6-8-12 **80**..(t) RobbieFitzpatrick 4 77
(Michael Attwater) *s.i.s: hld up: r.o ins fnl f: nvr nrr* **16/1**

4-35 **8** ½ **Ellemujie**[13] 1684 6-9-0 **82**.. ShaneKelly 8 78
(Dean Ivory) *hld up: rdn over 1f out: styd on fnl f: nt trble ldrs* **12/1**

310- **9** nk **Aktia (IRE)**[237] 6199 4-9-5 **87**.. KirstyMilczarek 1 82
(Luca Cumani) *hld up: rdn over 2f out: nvr on terms* **20/1**

25-0 **10** 1 **Snoqualmie Star**[23] 1477 4-9-0 **87**..(b) HarryBentley(5) 9 80
(David Elsworth) *led: hdd over 7f out: led again over 5f out: hdd over 3f out: sn rdn: edgd lft and wknd over 1f out* **12/1**

5-60 **11** 1 ¼ **Mr Willis**[12] 1717 5-9-7 **89**.. PatDobbs 11 80
(Terry Clement) *hld up in tch: rdn over 3f out: wknd over 2f out* **33/1**

12 4 ½ **Tindaro (FR)**[222] 4-9-7 **89**.. TedDurcan 6 71
(Paul Webber) *hld up: hdwy over 3f out: wknd over 1f out* **20/1**

2m 2.22s (-3.58) **Going Correction** -0.05s/f (Good) **12 Ran SP% 119.0**
Speed ratings (Par 107): **112,107,106,105,104 103,103,102,102,101 100,97**
toteswingers:1&2:£16.00, 1&3:£2.90, 2&3:£2.30 CSF £36.68 CT £147.87 TOTE £2.90: £2.00, £4.30, £2.40; EX 31.40.

Owner H E Sheikh Sultan Bin Khalifa Al Nahyan **Bred** Paget Bloodstock **Trained** Newmarket, Suffolk

FOCUS

A decent handicap and the winner looks a league or two above this level.

NOTEBOOK

Vita Nova(IRE) ◆ had won both of her starts over 1m4f last term, but was reappearing after 266 days off. Always up with the pace, she forged right away when leading on her own inside the last 2f and just went further and further clear. She holds entries in the Hardwicke and Pretty Polly, but although that sort of level would be a huge leap from this company, she does look capable of winning a Listed race at least. This ground was probably quicker than ideal for her and the return to further wouldn't bother her at all. (op 7-2 tchd 4-1)

Incendo has plenty of ability but is a renowned hard ride, hence all the headgear. Slow to break, he didn't have much room to play with between Shallow Bay and the stands' rail over a furlong out, but he was very much second-best on merit. (tchd 14-1 in places)

Shallow Bay was 3lb well in compared to his revised mark following his promising return at Windsor earlier this month and he ran well for a long way here, but life isn't going to get any easier for him in the short term. (tchd 4-1)

Significant Move was entitled to need the run on his debut for the yard at Newbury last month and he finished with quite a flourish here after becoming short of room over a furlong out, but he may need easier ground to show his best. (op 16-1)

Lunar Victory(USA) had run two excellent races on Polytrack since winning his maiden at Goodwood last August and he had every chance out in the centre of the track 2f from home, but he didn't get up the hill. It transpired that he had bled. Official explanation: trainer's rep said colt bled from the nose (op 4-1)

First Post(IRE) continued his return to form with an excellent effort at Ascot last time, but a 2lb rise for that left him 6lb above his last winning mark. He was close enough 3f from home, but then hung away to his left under strong pressure and was well beaten when racing awkwardly a furlong out. Official explanation: jockey said gelding hung left (op 14-1 tchd 16-1)

Aktia(IRE) was reported to have hung left. Official explanation: jockey said filly hung left (op 18-1)

Tindaro(FR) was reported to have been unsuited by the going. Official explanation: trainer said gelding was unsuited by the good to firm ground (op 16-1 tchd 14-1)

2067 LLOYDS TSB FINANCIAL MARKETS H'CAP — 6f

4:00 (4:00) (Class 3) (0-95,95) 3-Y-O **£7,447** (£2,216; £1,107; £553) **Stalls** High

Form RPR

1-1 **1** **Seal Rock**[13] 1688 3-9-4 **92**.. FergusSweeney 5 102+
(Henry Candy) *traked ldrs: swtchd rt over 2f out: rdn to ld and edgd lft ins fnl f: r.o* **4/9**[1]

01-0 **2** ¾ **El Viento (FR)**[34] 1241 3-8-12 **86**..(b) TedDurcan 2 92
(Richard Fahey) *led: rdn over 1f out: edgd rt and hdd ins fnl f: r.o* **11/1**

10-6 **3** 3 ¾ **Cadeaux Pearl**[13] 1688 3-8-10 **87**.. BillyCray(3) 4 81
(David Nicholls) *chsd ldr: rdn and ev ch over 1f out: wknd wl ins fnl f* **8/1**[3]

5-63 **4** 7 **Remotelinx (IRE)**[13] 1688 3-9-0 **88**.. DarryllHolland 1 59
(J W Hills) *trckd ldrs: shkn up over 2f out: wknd over 1f out* **9/2**[2]

1m 10.86s (-1.34) **Going Correction** -0.05s/f (Good) **4 Ran SP% 106.9**
Speed ratings (Par 103): **106,105,100,90**
CSF £5.72 TOTE £1.30; EX 3.90.

Owner P A Deal **Bred** Mrs A D Bourne **Trained** Kingston Warren, Oxon

FOCUS

A small but select field and three of the four runners met in a C&D handicap on 2000 Guineas day.

NOTEBOOK

Seal Rock had both Cadeaux Pearl and Remotelinx behind him when winning here a fortnight earlier and was put up 7lb for that. Sent off at very short odds to maintain his unbeaten record, he wasn't in a great position in a pocket early and had to be angled out to the centre of the track over 2f from home. He maintained his effort to hit the front inside the final furlong, however, and although the margin was narrow he was always going to win once in the clear. This ground looked plenty quick enough for him and the William Hill Trophy at York on June 11 may be his next port of call. (tchd 2-5)

El Viento(FR) never got into the race on his Thirsk reappearance, but both wins as a juvenile were in blinkers and they were back on here. He made a bold bid to make all and fought back well when the winner headed him, but although he will win more races he doesn't have the scope of the favourite. (op 9-1)

Cadeaux Pearl had an 8lb pull for a beating off just over 4l by Seal Rock over C&D earlier this month and he seemed to run his race with few excuses. (op 7-1)

Remotelinx(IRE) enjoyed a 6lb pull with Seal Rock for a 2l beating here last time, but was the first of the quartet off the bridle and was beaten further here. He was reported to have hung right. Official explanation: jockey said gelding hung right (op 11-2)

2068 LLOYDS TSB COMMERCIAL MAIDEN STKS — 1m

4:35 (4:36) (Class 5) 3-Y-O — **£3,238** (£963; £481; £240) **Stalls** High

Form — RPR

32-3 **1** **Zain Shamardal (IRE)**[13] 1690 3-9-3 83 ShaneKelly 8 — 93
(Brian Meehan) *chsd ldrs: led over 3f out: drvn out* **8/15**[1]

0 **2** *2 ¼* **Rave (IRE)**[11] 1759 3-9-0 0 PatrickHills(3) 9 — 88
(J W Hills) *s.i.s: hld up: racd keenly: hdwy over 5f out: rdn and ev ch fr over 1f out tl no ex wl ins fnl f* **66/1**

3 *1 ½* **Night And Dance (IRE)** 3-8-12 0 IanMongan 16 — 79+
(Sir Henry Cecil) *dwlt: hld up: swtchd rt and hdwy over 2f out: rdn over 1f out: styd on same pce fnl f* **8/1**[3]

36- **4** *6* **Muzdahi (USA)**[294] 4346 3-9-3 0 TedDurcan 7 — 71+
(John Dunlop) *chsd ldrs: rdn over 2f out: wknd over 1f out* **11/1**

-320 **5** *1* **Rojo Boy**[29] 1339 3-9-3 80 (b) AdamKirby 14 — 68
(David Elsworth) *prom: rdn over 2f out: wknd over 1f out* **14/1**

6 *4 ½* **Maricopa** 3-9-3 0 RichardMullen 13 — 58
(Mahmood Al Zarooni) *s.i.s: sn prom: rdn and wknd over 2f out* **7/1**[2]

00- **7** *3* **Cotton Grass**[195] 7232 3-8-7 0 AshleyMorgan(5) 1 — 46
(Mark H Tompkins) *hld up: rdn over 3f out: n.d* **66/1**

4-6 **8** *1* **Around The Clock (USA)**[16] 1620 3-9-3 0 DarryllHolland 6 — 49
(Amanda Perrett) *led over 4f: sn rdn: wknd wl over 1f out* **20/1**

0- **9** *2* **Akrias (USA)**[191] 7303 3-9-3 0 KirstyMilczarek 10 — 44
(Luca Cumani) *hld up: rdn over 3f out: wknd over 2f out* **33/1**

10 *½* **Dresden (IRE)** 3-8-10 0 TalibHussain(7) 15 — 43
(Luca Cumani) *dwlt: a in rr* **50/1**

0-0 **11** *12* **Zaheeb**[18] 1568 3-9-3 0 AdrianMcCarthy 11 — —
(Dave Morris) *mid-div: rdn and lost pl 1/2-way: sn bhd: t.o* **150/1**

40- **12** *31* **Dancerella**[214] 6804 3-8-12 0 LiamKeniry 5 — —
(David Elsworth) *hld up: bhd fr 1/2-way: t.o* **66/1**

00 **13** *11* **Who Loves Ya Baby**[3] 1991 3-9-3 0 (v[1]) RobertWinston 3 — —
(Peter Charalambous) *w ldrs tl rdn 1/2-way: sn wknd: t.o* **150/1**

1m 36.93s (-1.67) **Going Correction** -0.05s/f (Good) **13** Ran SP% **119.3**
Speed ratings (Par 99): **106,103,102,96,95 90,87,86,84,84 72,41,30**
toteswingers:1&2:£23.30, 1&3:£1.50, 2&3:£124.20 CSF £79.83 TOTE £1.70: £1.02, £8.60, £2.60; EX 64.80.

Owner Jaber Abdullah **Bred** Kevin & Meta Cullen **Trained** Manton, Wilts

FOCUS

This maiden has been won by some decent types in recent years with the 2010 Royal Hunt Cup winner Invisible Man taking it two years ago, whilst last year's victor Afsare also went on to win at Royal Ascot. Punters only wanted to know one horse.

2069 LLOYDS TSB COMMERCIAL FINANCE H'CAP — 5f

5:10 (5:10) (Class 4) (0-85,83) 4-Y-O+ — **£4,533** (£1,348; £674; £336) **Stalls** High

Form — RPR

0-03 **1** **Solemn**[7] 1864 6-9-4 **80** (b) LiamKeniry 6 — 90
(Milton Bradley) *chsd ldr: rdn to ld ins fnl f: r.o* **4/1**[2]

0403 **2** *1* **Desert Strike**[6] 1907 5-8-10 **72** (p) RobertWinston 7 — 78
(Alan McCabe) *hld up in tch: rdn and hung rt over 1f out: r.o ins fnl f: wnt 2nd nr fin: nt rch wnr* **7/2**[1]

000- **3** *¾* **Osiris Way**[227] 6446 9-9-6 **82** TedDurcan 8 — 86
(Patrick Chamings) *chsd ldrs: rdn to ld and hung rt over 1f out: hdd and unable qck ins fnl f: lost 2nd towards fin* **4/1**[2]

0-00 **4** *1 ¼* **Bertoliver**[13] 1680 7-9-7 **83** JamesDoyle 4 — 82
(Stuart Williams) *led: rdn and hdd over 1f out: no ex ins fnl f* **14/1**

0-00 **5** *¾* **Fantasy Explorer**[49] 961 8-9-0 **76** JimmyQuinn 5 — 73
(John Quinn) *chsd ldrs: nt clr run over 1f out: styd on same pce ins fnl f* **8/1**

1-50 **6** *½* **Brandywell Boy (IRE)**[118] 178 8-8-4 **69** oh1 BillyCray(3) 2 — 64
(Dominic Ffrench Davis) *chsd ldrs: rdn 1/2-way: styd on same pce fr over 1f out* **20/1**

4555 **7** *1 ¾* **Billy Red**[22] 1506 7-8-8 **70** (b) FergusSweeney 1 — 58
(J R Jenkins) *chsd ldrs: rdn 1/2-way: wknd over 1f out* **10/1**

610- **8** *6* **Brynfa Boy**[275] 4961 5-9-0 **76** TonyCulhane 3 — 43
(Paul D'Arcy) *s.i.s: a in rr* **9/2**[3]

58.68 secs (-0.42) **Going Correction** -0.05s/f (Good) **8** Ran SP% **112.0**
Speed ratings (Par 105): **101,99,98,96,95 94,91,81**
toteswingers:1&2:£23.30, 1&3:£1.50, 2&3:£124.20 CSF £17.62 CT £57.58 TOTE £6.70: £1.70, £1.10, £1.80; EX 20.30.

Owner E A Hayward **Bred** Cheveley Park Stud Ltd **Trained** Sedbury, Gloucs

FOCUS

A fair sprint handicap run at a strong early pace.

T/Plt: £34.90 to a £1 stake. Pool:£41,491.90 - 867.64 winning tickets T/Qpdt: £2.70 to a£1 stake. Pool:£3,606.21 - 958.90 winning tickets CR

[2028] YORK (L-H)

Friday, May 13

OFFICIAL GOING: Good to firm (good in places; 7.7)

Rail moved out 3m from 9f to entrance to straight adding 20yds to races of 1m and further.

Wind: Fresh across Weather: Cloudy - sunny periods

2070 LANGLEYS SOLICITORS E B F SHIROCCO FILLIES' STKS (REGISTERED AS MARYGATE FILLIES STAKES) (LISTED) — 5f

1:30 (1:31) (Class 1) 2-Y-O — **£17,778** (£6,723; £3,360; £1,680) **Stalls** High

Form — RPR

11 **1** **Miss Work Of Art**[16] 1598 2-8-12 0 PaulHanagan 7 — 97+
(Richard Fahey) *chsd ldrs: pushed along and hdwy 2f out: rdn to chal over 1f out: led ent fnl f: edgd lft and kpt on* **6/5**[1]

1 **2** *1* **Vocational (USA)**[11] 1765 2-8-12 0 JoeFanning 6 — 93
(Mark Johnston) *led: jnd and rdn wl over 1f out: drvn and hdd ent fnl f: kpt on* **7/1**[3]

2 **3** *nk* **Bubbly Ballerina**[48] 982 2-8-12 0 RyanMoore 5 — 92
(Alan Bailey) *a cl up: rdn 2f out: drvn and kpt on wl fnl f* **9/1**

31 **4** *shd* **Sweet Chilli (IRE)**[16] 1619 2-8-12 0 GrahamGibbons 4 — 92+
(David Barron) *trckd ldrs: swtchd rt and rdn 2f out: sltly outpcd over 1f out: styd on wl fnl f* **5/1**[2]

31 **5** *1* **Pyman's Theory (IRE)**[14] 1657 2-8-12 0 RichardKingscote 1 — 88
(Tom Dascombe) *dwlt: hdwy on outer and in tch 3f out: effrt to chse ldrs 2f out: rdn and edgd lft over 1f out: sn one pce* **5/1**[2]

01 **6** *3* **Red Hearts (IRE)**[15] 1632 2-8-12 0 AdamBeschizza 9 — 77
(Julia Feilden) *towards rr: rdn along 1/2-way: sme late hdwy* **66/1**

7 *2 ½* **How Sweet It Is (IRE)** 2-8-12 0 TomQueally 3 — 68
(James Bethell) *dwlt: sn rdn along and a towards rr* **66/1**

41 **8** *¾* **Princess Banu**[29] 1337 2-8-12 0 ChrisCatlin 8 — 65
(Mick Channon) *chsd ldr: rdn along 1/2-way: sn wknd* **12/1**

123 **9** *7* **Redair (IRE)**[9] 1806 2-8-12 0 CathyGannon 10 — 39
(David Evans) *dwlt: in rr and sn rdn along: outpcd fr 1/2-way* **20/1**

58.70 secs (-0.60) **Going Correction** -0.10s/f (Good) **9** Ran SP% **116.7**
Speed ratings (Par 98): **100,98,97,97,96 91,87,86,74**
toteswingers:1&2:£3.00, 1&3:£2.90, 2&3:£7.60 CSF £10.34 TOTE £1.90: £1.10, £2.00, £2.70; EX 6.00 Trifecta £59.50 Pool: £1,465.58 - 18.20 winning units..

Owner Mel Roberts and Ms Nicola Meese **Bred** Newsells Park Stud **Trained** Musley Bank, N Yorks

FOCUS

The rail had been moved out 3m from the 1m1f pole to the entrance to the home straight, adding 20 yards to race distances of over 1m. Paul Hanagan, successful in the first two races, confirmed that the ground had dried out slightly since the previous day. First run in 2005, this has gone to some decent filies in its short history, the pick of them being 2009 scorer Misheer, who won the Cherry Hinton Stakes and was runner-up in the Cheveley Park. It has had a positive bearing on the Queen Mary Stakes at Royal Ascot, with Misheer and 2008 winner Langs Lash both finishing second there, and Gilded taking both races in 2006. This event is likely to assume greater significance early in the season now that the Hilary Needler Trophy at Beverley has lost its Listed status. This edition looked up to scratch on paper, with seven of the eight fillies to have run already winners, six of them last time out. The pace was strong and the time was just under a second outside the standard.

NOTEBOOK

Miss Work Of Art, one of two unbeaten contenders, made it three from three with another taking performance. A daughter of promising first-season sire Dutch Art, she was the form pick on her defeat of the very useful colt Magic City at Ascot but was surprisingly easy to back. Chasing the pace close to the rail, she had to work a bit to get on top but showed a most willing attitude to assert. She is sure to appreciate a step up to 6f and her owner favours aiming her at the Cherry Hinton, rather than go to Ascot for either the Albany Stakes over that trip or the Queen Mary. She will be worthy of repect wherever she goes, but will need to improve on the bare form of this victory. (op 8-11 tchd 4-6)

Vocational(USA) went left leaving the stalls but then showed blistering pace down the centre, only succumbing to the favourite inside the last. Out of a Cheveley Park winner, she should get 6f in time but may be best kept to the minimum trip for the time being. (op 8-1)

Bubbly Ballerina took a bump from the runner-up leaving the stalls but it didn't stop her from helping force the pace. A pacey filly who had been runner-up to Redair on her only previous start, on Polytrack back in March, she will have no problem winning a maiden. (op 12-1 tchd 14-1 and 16-1 in a place)

Sweet Chilli(IRE) made virtually all at Pontefract but could not get to the front here. She was outpaced by the leaders at one point but was staying on well near the line, suggesting a return to a stiffer track or a step up to 6f may suit. (op 10-1)

Pyman's Theory(IRE) was not best away but ran creditably from the widest draw. Unable to find a change of gear inside the last, she ought to get 6f. (op 13-2)

Red Hearts(IRE) found things happening too quickly and was never really involved, but can win again back in easier grade. Her rider was unable to claim his 5lb allowance. (op 100-1)

How Sweet It Is(IRE), a sister to last season's Listed 2yo scorer Sweet Cecily, was a bit slow to break and never a factor. This was a tough ask on her debut. (op 100-1)

Princess Banu showed early pace before fading on this rise in grade. (op 14-1 tchd 16-1)

Redair(IRE), placed both in the Brocklesby and behind a stablemate of Miss Work Of Art in the Lily Agnes, was always trailing after a tardy start.

2071 SPORTINGBET.COM JORVIK STKS (H'CAP) — 1m 4f

2:00 (2:03) (Class 2) (0-105,99) 4-Y-O+ **£25,904** (£7,708; £3,852; £1,924) **Stalls** Centre

Form — RPR

310- **1** **Tepmokea (IRE)**[188] 7350 5-9-1 **90** PaulHanagan 12 — 101
(Richard Fahey) *trckd ldrs whn hmpd and lost pl after 3f: hdwy and wd st to chse ldrs stands' side: effrt to ld over 2f out: rdn over 1f out: kpt on strly fnl f* **9/1**

32-6 **2** *1 ¼* **Averroes (IRE)**[41] 1102 4-9-1 **90** PhilipRobinson 17 — 99
(Clive Cox) *t.k.h: trckd ldrs: wd st and hdwy to chse ldng pair stands' side 3f out: rdn 2f out: drvn to chse wnr appr fnl f: kpt on* **17/2**[3]

111- **3** *nk* **Kansai Spirit (IRE)**[251] 5743 5-9-9 **98** WilliamBuick 2 — 107
(John Gosden) *hld up in midfield: hdwy 4f out: rdn to chse ldrs centre 2f out: drvn and kpt on fnl f* **10/1**

00-6 **4** *1* **Deauville Flyer**[27] 1412 5-9-2 **91** KierenFallon 1 — 98+
(Tim Easterby) *hld up and bhd: styd towards far rail st: swtchd rt to join centre gp and hdwy over 3f out: rdn to chse ldrs 2f out: drvn and kpt on fnl f: nrst fin* **12/1**

0-22 **5** *1 ¼* **Royal Swain (IRE)**[12] 1713 5-8-5 **80** JimmyQuinn 7 — 85
(Alan Swinbank) *in tch whn hmpd after 3f and towards rr: hdwy in centre over 3f out: rdn to chse ldrs wl over 1f out: drvn and kpt on ins fnl f: nrst fin* **10/1**

62-3 **6** ½ **Bowdler's Magic**[48] 994 4-8-12 87 .... GregFairley 11 91
(Mark Johnston) *hld up and bhd: styd far side st and gd hdwy 3f out: rdn over 2f out: kpt on fnl f: nrst fin* **25/1**

120- **7** ½ **Hanoverian Baron**[245] 5908 6-9-3 92 .... SteveDrowne 9 95
(Tony Newcombe) *hld up towards rr: c wd st to chse ldrs stands' side: rdn over 2f out: drvn and edgd lft over 1f out: one pce* **8/1**[2]

53 **8** *shd* **English Summer**[12] 1729 4-9-1 90 .... RoystonFfrench 3 93
(Mark Johnston) *trckd ldrs on inner: styd far side rail in st: rdn along over 3f out: drvn and plugged on fnl 2f* **20/1**

30-4 **9** ½ **The Fonz**[12] 1717 5-9-3 92 .... RyanMoore 5 94+
(Sir Michael Stoute) *in tch whn hmpd and lost pl after 3f: towards rr tl hdwy and in tch centre over 2f out: sn rdn and no imp fr wl over 1f out* **7/2**[1]

60-4 **10** 2¾ **Dazzling Light (UAE)**[20] 1517 6-8-0 80 .... NeilFarley(5) 14 78
(Jim Goldie) *t.k.h: trckd ldrs tl led after 1 1/2f: pushed clr 5f out: c wd st to stands' rail and sn rdn: drvn and hdd over 2f out: sn wknd* **20/1**

0-53 **11** 1½ **Crackentorp**[12] 1713 6-8-12 87 .... (v[1]) GrahamGibbons 13 83
(Tim Easterby) *chsd ldrs: prom in centre 4f out: sn rdn and wknd over 2f out* **18/1**

320- **12** *nk* **Chilly Filly (IRE)**[216] 6736 5-9-3 92 .... PaulMulrennan 10 87
(James Given) *prom: rdn along centre over 4f out: wknd wl over 2f out* **33/1**

311- **13** 2¼ **Awsaal**[356] 2323 4-9-10 99 .... TadhgO'Shea 4 91
(John Dunlop) *hld up towards rr: wd st and hdwy to chse ldrs stands' rail over 3f out: sn rdn and wknd* **10/1**

0-20 **14** 9 **Montparnasse (IRE)**[13] 1679 4-8-12 87 .... JamieSpencer 15 64
(Kevin Ryan) *prom: rdn along in centre over 4f out: sn wknd* **20/1**

2010 **15** 14 **Lovers Causeway (USA)**[2] 2006 4-8-6 81 6ex .... (v) JoeFanning 8 36
(Mark Johnston) *led 1 1/2f: prom: styd far side st: rdn along 4f out and sn wknd* **20/1**

152- **16** 2¼ **Mataaleb**[289] 4470 4-9-2 91 .... TomQueally 16 42
(Lydia Pearce) *towards rr: wd st and sme hdwy on stands' rail over 4f out: sn rdn and wknd* **20/1**

2m 32.18s (-1.02) **Going Correction** +0.15s/f (Good) **16** Ran SP% **124.7**
Speed ratings (Par 109): **109,108,107,107,106 106,105,105,105,103 102,102,100,94,85 84**
toteswingers:1&2:£12.80, 1&3:£16.00, 2&3:£19.40 CSF £75.69 CT £799.90 TOTE £10.70: £3.00, £2.30, £3.10, £2.30; EX 92.90 Trifecta £847.50 Pool: £2,003.83 - 1.74 winning units..
Owner Keep Racing **Bred** J H A Baggen **Trained** Musley Bank, N Yorks

FOCUS
A valuable and competitive handicap, run as the Jorvik Stakes since 2007. There was a difference of opinion amongst the jockeys as the field entered the home straight, with only six horses, including the first two home, opting to take the stands' rail route which had looked favoured on the meeting's first two days. Three runners stayed on the far rail and at the three-furlong pole the field was spread across the course. The form has a slightly dubious look to it as a result, but this is a race which should certainly produce winners.

NOTEBOOK
Tepmokea(IRE)'s jockey seemed in two minds at first whether to take him to the stands' side, but having got the rail the gelding stayed on deteminedly. An admirably consistent and hardy individual who was slightly hampered early on, he is currently operating on a career-high mark but may have more improvement to offer and should continue to pay his way. (op 11-1 tchd 17-2)
Averroes(IRE) had been a beaten favourite in the Rosebery at Kempton but returned to form back on turf. He may have been a little flattered by racing down the stands' side, but this was still a solid effort. However, he has now been held from this mark on his last five starts. (op 9-1 tchd 11-1)
Kansai Spirit(IRE) was hampered in some early scrimmaging. He ran on well down the centre of the track, running a thoroughly creditable race off a 6lb higher mark than when winning at Haydock on his last appearance of 2010. He won't mind a return to 1m6f and is capable of holding his own in Listed company. (op 7-1)
Deauville Flyer, held up from the inside stall, improved down the centre of the track to have every chance. A winner over C&D at this fixture a year ago, beating The Fonz by a short head, he will appreciate a return to further but the handicapper is not going to make it easy for him.
Royal Swain(IRE) was running off the same mark as when second at Hamilton and was a pound well in, but the horse who beat him there, Becausewecan, disappointed at York on Wednesday. He was staying on to good effect late on and a handicap should come his way. (op 9-1)
Bowdler's Magic, another with form over further, did best of the three who stayed on the inside rail, staying on quite well at the end. (op 22-1)
Hanoverian Baron, last year's winner, was 9lb higher this time round. Sticking to the stands' side he was never quite able to get in a blow at the leaders on this seasonal bow but remains relatively unexposed at this distance. (tchd 15-2)
English Summer, who was coming back in trip, was second of the three who opted to remain on the far side in the home straight. (op 25-1)
The Fonz, successful over C&D last August, was another chief sufferer in the early chain reaction and found himself just two from the back turning in. He stayed on well down the centre until his effort fizzled out inside the last, and is worth another chance. (op 15-2)
Crackentorp, runner-up in this 12 months ago, raced keenly in the first-time visor behind the leaders and did not get home. He remains without a win since his 3yo days. (op 16-1)
Awsaal looked a smart prospect when winning at Haydock a year ago but reportedly fractured a knee shortly afterwards. Resuming off an 11lb higher mark, he was disappointing, but he may have needed it and a Hardwicke Stakes entry shows the regard in which he's held. (op 8-1)
Lovers Causeway(USA) was a pound well in on this second run at the meeting, but he quickly lost his lead and trailed home well beaten. (op 16-1)
Mataaleb, who had not run since being beaten on the nod at Glorious Goodwood, will be suited by some easier ground. (tchd 18-1)

2072 EMIRATES AIRLINE YORKSHIRE CUP (GROUP 2) 1m 6f
2:30 (2:38) (Class 1) 4-Y-0+

£79,478 (£30,128; £15,078; £7,518; £3,766; £1,890) **Stalls** Low

Form RPR
410- **1** **Duncan**[222] 6612 6-9-2 119 .... WilliamBuick 7 117
(John Gosden) *mde all: raced wd for 4f: wd st to stands' rail: qcknd over 3f out: jnd and rdn 2f out: drvn ins fnl f: styd on wl towards fin* **11/4**[2]

/2-6 **2** ½ **Blue Bajan (IRE)**[9] 1808 9-8-13 100 .... DanielTudhope 4 113
(David O'Meara) *hld up in tch: hdwy wl over 2f out: rdn to chal 1f out: sn drvn and ev ch tl no ex towards fin* **25/1**

503- **3** ½ **Manighar (FR)**[181] 7458 5-8-13 114 .... KierenFallon 2 112
(Luca Cumani) *trckd ldrs: hdwy 3f out: rdn to chal over 2f out and ev ch tl drvn and one pce fnl f* **7/1**

03/2 **4** *nk* **Native Ruler**[13] 1685 5-8-13 112 .... TomQueally 8 112
(Sir Henry Cecil) *hld up in tch: hdwy over 3f out: effrt and n.m.r wl over 1f out: sn rdn: swtchd lft and drvn ins fnl f: kpt on same pce* **5/2**[1]

603- **5** 2½ **Buxted (IRE)**[209] 6929 5-8-13 102 .... JoeFanning 6 108
(Robert Mills) *trckd wnr: rdn along and outpcd over 3f out: drvn and plugged on u.p appr fnl f* **33/1**

5-31 **6** 1 **Askar Tau (FR)**[16] 1601 6-8-13 106 .... (v) GeorgeBaker 1 107
(Marcus Tregoning) *hld up in tch: hdwy 3f out: rdn 2f out: sn drvn and one pce* **5/1**[3]

2-23 **7** 9 **Free Agent**[16] 1601 5-8-13 106 .... (p) RyanMoore 9 94
(Richard Hannon) *dwlt: a in rr* **15/2**

240- **8** 10 **Electrolyser (IRE)**[245] 5909 6-8-13 111 .... PhilipRobinson 5 80
(Clive Cox) *trckd wnr on inner: effrt and cl up 3f out: sn rdn and wknd* **10/1**

2m 58.33s (-1.87) **Going Correction** +0.15s/f (Good) **8** Ran SP% **112.0**
Speed ratings (Par 115): **111,110,110,110,108 108,103,97**
toteswingers:1&2:£11.30, 1&3:£4.00, 2&3:£13.60 CSF £62.14 TOTE £3.10: £1.50, £3.80, £2.10; EX 58.50 Trifecta £448.10 Pool: £1,913.75 - 3.16 winning units..
Owner Normandie Stud Ltd **Bred** Normandie Stud Ltd **Trained** Newmarket, Suffolk
■ Stewards' Enquiry : William Buick one-day ban: careless riding (May 27)

FOCUS
The staying division currently lacks a standout performer and the bare form of this year's Doncaster Cup is weak for the level, with the 9-y-o runner-up rated just 100, but a few of these can do better, including the winner. The pace, set by Duncan for much of the way, seemed just ordinary, although a time only 0.33 seconds above standard shows this was a true enough test of stamina. Once again, the unsatisfactory nature of this track was evident when all of the runners made their respective bids towards the stands' rail in the straight.

NOTEBOOK
Duncan ◆'s trainer said beforehand that this race had been the plan all winter for his charge, who had been gelded since finishing well down the field in last season's Arc, and it was a plan well executed. He was nicely ridden by William Buick, being kept wide of his rivals early on and leading when joining the main group, and he was first to grab the stands' rail in the straight. Once under maximum pressure, he responded in willing fashion and was always doing enough. This form amounts to little in the context of the Gold Cup and much more will be required if he's to have a major say at Royal Ascot, so the first thought was to write off his chances. However, he's actually one to consider, indeed the standout 20-1 with William Hill is too big, especially if a top-class stayer fails to emerge. Already a Group 2 winner over 1m4f, at last year's Royal meeting he was a fine second to Harbinger in the Hardwicke, and he's also won a Listed race at the course. This was his first start over a trip this far and he can surely progress when he tackles even further seeing as he's a half-brother to Doncaster Cup (2m2f) winner Samuel, and it was encouraging to hear that Buick had trouble pulling him up. His connections expect this run to have taken the freshness out of him, which will make him amenable to more patient tactics if need be, so there are plenty of positives. (op 3-1)
Blue Bajan(IRE) made a promising return from a lengthy absence when sixth in the Chester Cup (off 100) on his debut for this yard and this was a decent effort. He fared best of those held up and filled the same position as in the 2009 running. (op 20-1)
Manighar(FR), returning from a six-month break, was produced with every chance but he's a horse with a knee action and didn't convince that he let himself down on the quick going. He can do better when there is give in the ground. (op 5-1 tchd 9-2)
Native Ruler was a prime candidate to bounce after a close second in the Jockey Club Stakes on his return from a lengthy absence last month, but he ran respectably on this step up in trip. His connections felt he's better than he showed as he's long-striding horse and the way the race unfolded didn't allow him to lengthen as well as he can. (op 7-2)
Buxted(IRE) showed a knee action and was one-paced under pressure on his return from a 209-day break. (op 25-1)
Askar Tau(FR) couldn't repeat the form he showed when winning the Sagaro Stakes 16 days earlier and maybe this came too soon. He did, though, confirm form with the disappointing Free Agent, whose slow start was a bit disconcerting. (op 9-2)
Free Agent, whose slow start was a bit disconcerting, was a disappointment. (op 10-1 tchd 7-1)
Electrolyser(IRE) Official explanation: jockey said horse hung right

2073 SPORTINGBET.COM FILLIES' STKS (REGISTERED AS THE MICHAEL SEELY MEMORIAL STAKES) (LISTED RACE) 1m
3:00 (3:05) (Class 1) 3-Y-0

£22,708 (£8,608; £4,308; £2,148; £1,076; £540) **Stalls** Low

Form RPR
136- **1** **Theyskens' Theory (USA)**[189] 7342 3-9-3 108 .... MartinDwyer 9 105+
(Brian Meehan) *trckd ldr: cl up 4f out: led wl over 2f out: pushed clr whn edgd lft and stmbld sltly jst ins fnl f: easily* **15/8**[1]

3-61 **2** 3¼ **Sylvestris (IRE)**[18] 1565 3-8-12 80 .... RichardKingscote 3 92
(Ralph Beckett) *led: pushed along over 3f out: rdn and hdd wl over 2f out: sn drvn and kpt on same pce fnl f* **16/1**

45-1 **3** 2¼ **Wrekin Sunset**[27] 1393 3-8-12 78 .... AndrewElliott 7 87
(Mrs K Burke) *trckd ldrs on outer: effrt over 3f out: rdn to chse ldrs 2f out: [illegible]* **25/1**

1-4 **4** ½ **Primevere (IRE)**[12] 1722 3-8-12 83 .... SteveDrowne 10 86
(Roger Charlton) *hld up towards rr: hdwy over 3f out: rdn over 2f out: drvn over 1f out: kpt on same pce* **4/1**[3]

0-01 **5** *nse* **Emma's Gift (IRE)**[16] 1599 3-8-12 95 .... AdamBeschizza 6 86
(Julia Feilden) *hld up in rr: hdwy on outer wl over 2f out: rdn wl over 1f out and sn no imp* **8/1**

6-61 **6** 1 **Adaria**[14] 1648 3-8-12 69 .... HayleyTurner 2 83
(David C Griffiths) *chsd ldrs: rdn along wl over 2f out: sn one pce* **66/1**

20-3 **7** 4 **Flood Plain**[16] 1599 3-8-12 96 .... WilliamBuick 4 74
(John Gosden) *trckd ldrs: hdwy over 3f out: rdn to chse ldrs over 2f out: drvn wl over 1f out and sn wknd* **9/4**[2]

15 **8** 16 **Mystic Dream**[16] 1599 3-8-12 0 .... MichaelHills 5 55
(B W Hills) *dwlt: reminders and sn keen in tch: pushed along over 4f out: rdn over 3f out: sn outpcd and bhd fnl 2f* **14/1**

1m 38.14s (-0.66) **Going Correction** +0.15s/f (Good) **8** Ran SP% **114.6**
Speed ratings (Par 104): **109,105,103,103,102 101,97,81**
toteswingers:1&2:£5.30, 1&3:£10.50, 2&3:£13.10 CSF £33.51 TOTE £2.60: £1.30, £3.70, £5.40; EX 33.50 Trifecta £439.00 Pool: £1,934.11 - 3.26 winning units..
Owner Andrew Rosen **Bred** Ar Enterprises Llc **Trained** Manton, Wilts

FOCUS
Not much strength in depth to this fillies' Listed event. They raced middle to stands' side in the straight.

NOTEBOOK
Theyskens' Theory(USA) was a class apart, readily defying a 5lb penalty on her first start since finishing sixth in last year's Breeders' Cup Juvenile Fillies. It's fair to stay the winner was fully entitled to take this with ease considering she had 23lb in hand over the runner-up on official figures, but there was still much to like about the performance and her connections expect her to improve plenty for the run. The aim now is the Coronation Stakes as Royal Ascot and while that will be a lot tougher, she has clearly trained on well. (op 2-1 tchd 11-4)
Sylvestris(IRE), off the mark in a 7f Warwick maiden on her previous start, picked up some valuable black type with a career-best performance.
Wrekin Sunset was the only runner who was taken directly against the stands' rail in the straight and she kept on well, but this was tougher than the Haydock maiden she won on her reappearance. (op 18-1 tchd 16-1)
Primevere(IRE), fourth in the 1m2f Pretty Polly at Newmarket on her reappearance, was a bit one-paced on this drop in trip. (op 7-2)
Emma's Gift(IRE), whose jockey couldn't claim his usual 5lb, failed to build on her success in an Ascot conditions race and that form is not working out at all. She did, though, confirm placings with Flood Plain. (op 10-1)

Flood Plain disappointed and was further behind Emma's Gift than she had been at Ascot. Official explanation: jockey said filly was unsuited by the good to firm (good in places) ground (op 5-2 tchd 15-8)

2074 RALPH RAPER MEMORIAL STKS (H'CAP) 5f

3:35 (3:38) (Class 4) (0-80,80) 3-Y-O £6,476 (£1,927; £963; £481) Stalls High

Form RPR

5-23 **1** **Thirteen Shivers**[16] 1624 3-9-0 **73** DavidNolan 4 85
(Michael Easterby) *cl up centre: effrt 2f out: rdn to ld over 1f out: edgd lft and kpt on wl fnl f* **16/1**

100- **2** 1 **Apace (IRE)**[223] 6559 3-9-4 **77** RyanMoore 6 86
(Sir Michael Stoute) *towards rr: hdwy 2f out and sn rdn: styd on wl u.p fnl f* **10/1**

60-2 **3** ½ **Swiss Dream**[11] 1758 3-9-7 **80** KierenFallon 3 87
(David Elsworth) *racd towards centre: led: rdn along 2f out: hdd over 1f out: kpt on same pce fnl f* **11/1**

333- **4** nk **Eland Ally**[211] 6878 3-8-12 **71** MickyFenton 16 77
(Tom Tate) *racd towards stands' rail: in tch: hdwy 2f out: sn rdn and kpt on ins fnl f* **12/1**

-121 **5** nk **Mr Optimistic**[27] 1391 3-9-7 **80** PaulHanagan 19 85+
(Richard Fahey) *racd towards stands' rail: in tch: hdwy 2f out: n.m.r and rdn over 1f out: kpt on ins fnl f: nrst fin* **6/1**[1]

621- **6** nk **Manoori (IRE)**[193] 7268 3-9-0 **73** GeorgeBaker 20 77+
(Chris Wall) *chsd ldrs stands' rail: effrt and nt clr run wl over 1f out: sn swtchd lft and rdn: kpt on fnl f* **7/1**[3]

06-1 **7** ½ **Gottcher**[17] 1589 3-9-2 **75** LeeNewman 13 77
(David Barron) *led stands' side gp: cl up and ev ch 2f out: sn rdn and grad wknd* **13/2**[2]

-321 **8** nk **Barnet Fair**[93] 465 3-9-4 **80** RobertLButler(3) 9 81+
(Richard Guest) *v.s.a and bhd: rdn along and hdwy 1/2-way: kpt on u.p fnl f: nrst fin* **18/1**

22-3 **9** 1¾ **Millyluvstobouggie**[24] 1452 3-9-3 **76** PhilipRobinson 12 71
(Clive Cox) *cl up towards stands' rail: effrt and ev ch 2f out: sn rdn and grad wknd appr fnl f* **7/1**[3]

1100 **10** shd **Sacrosanctus**[27] 1391 3-9-6 **79** TomQueally 2 73
(David Nicholls) *cl up towards centre: rdn along 2f out: grad wknd* **28/1**

13-0 **11** ½ **Captain Kolo (IRE)**[27] 1391 3-9-3 **76** DuranFentiman 14 68
(Tim Easterby) *racd nr stands' rail: chsd ldrs: rdn along wl over 2f out: edgd lft and grad wknd* **20/1**

45-0 **12** 2½ **Style And Panache (IRE)**[27] 1391 3-9-2 **75** CathyGannon 17 58
(David Evans) *sn rdn along and outpcd: a in rr stands' side* **33/1**

0-20 **13** 7 **Defence Council (IRE)**[14] 1650 3-9-3 **76** AdrianNicholls 1 34
(Mel Brittain) *cl up on wd outside: rdn along over 2f out: sn wknd* **33/1**

120- **14** ¾ **Diamond Vine (IRE)**[188] 7347 3-9-5 **78** (p) TadhgO'Shea 15 34
(Ronald Harris) *a in rr* **33/1**

0600 **15** nk **Insolenceofoffice (IRE)**[11] 1745 3-9-2 **75** (p) HayleyTurner 10 29
(Andrew Crook) *outpcd and bhd fr 1/2-way* **40/1**

24-1 **16** 2 **Oh So Kool**[117] 182 3-9-1 **74** (t) WilliamBuick 5 21
(Stuart Williams) *chsd ldrs centre: rdn along over 2f out: sn drvn and wknd* **20/1**

2114 **17** 2 **Mandy's Hero**[93] 465 3-8-13 **72** (p) JamieSpencer 18 12
(Ian Williams) *stmbld s: a towards rr* **14/1**

120- **18** ½ **Bellemere**[238] 6139 3-8-4 **70** DavidSimmonson(7) 11 —
(Michael Easterby) *a towards rr: bhd fr 1/2-way* **66/1**

1-05 **19** 7 **Berberana (IRE)**[14] 1650 3-9-7 **80** DavidAllan 8 —
(Tim Easterby) *in tch centre: rdn along 1/2-way: sn wknd* **16/1**

59.16 secs (-0.14) **Going Correction** -0.10s/f (Good) **19 Ran SP% 127.2**
Speed ratings (Par 101): **97,95,94,94,93 93,92,91,89,88 88,84,72,71,71 68,64,64,52**
toteswingers:1&2:£53.60, 1&3:£55.90, 2&3:£15.70 CSF £157.10 CT £1142.57 TOTE £23.20: £3.70, £3.00, £2.90, £4.00; EX 304.20 Trifecta £1095.90 Part won. Pool: £1,480.97 - 0.20 winning units..

Owner Keith Wreglesworth & Andre Fordham **Bred** Cheveley Park Stud Ltd **Trained** Sheriff Hutton, N Yorks

FOCUS

Rain began to fall heavily prior to this race, but did not have much time to get into the ground by this stage. This was the fifth running of this handicap, which has gone to some speedy types like Morinqua and Hamish McGonagall. It was a decent race for the grade and should have a bearing on similar 3yo sprints to come. Not many were able to get involved and low numbers came out on top, with the main action taking place centre to far side.

Defence Council(IRE) Official explanation: jockey said colt hung right

Mandy's Hero Official explanation: jockey said gelding stumbled start

Berberana(IRE) Official explanation: jockey said filly was upset in stalls and never travelled

2075 SPORTINGBET.COM STKS (H'CAP) 6f

4:10 (4:12) (Class 2) (0-105,105) 4-Y-O+ £12,952 (£3,854; £1,926; £962) Stalls High

Form RPR

21- **1** **Hoof It**[202] 7079 4-9-1 **99** KierenFallon 8 111+
(Michael Easterby) *trckd ldrs centre: smooth hdwy over 1f out: rdn and qcknd to lead ent fnl f: pushed out* **7/1**[3]

1-15 **2** 1 **Horseradish**[6] 1885 4-9-2 **100** HayleyTurner 7 109
(Michael Bell) *hld up in tch: effrt and nt clr run wl over 1f out: swtchd lft and rdn ent fnl f: sn chsng wnr: drvn and nt qckn towards fin* **4/1**[1]

00-3 **3** ½ **Our Jonathan**[40] 1111 4-8-10 **94** JamieSpencer 3 101
(Kevin Ryan) *hld up in rr: hdwy and nt clr run wl over 1f out: swtchd lft and rdn ent fnl f: fin strly* **5/1**[2]

-263 **4** nk **Docofthebay (IRE)**[12] 1720 7-8-11 **95** (b) TomQueally 14 101
(David Nicholls) *hld up towards rr: hdwy wl over 1f out: n.m.r and swtchd rt ent fnl f sn rdn and kpt on wl: nrst fin* **12/1**

42-0 **5** nk **Midnight Martini**[37] 1166 4-8-8 **92** (t) DavidAllan 12 97
(Tim Easterby) *led: rdn along 2f out: drvn over 1f out: hdd ent fnl f: wknd towards fin* **28/1**

00-6 **6** 1¼ **Damika (IRE)**[34] 1242 8-8-11 **95** SebSanders 16 96
(Richard Whitaker) *in tch towards stands' rail: effrt and n.m.r 2f out: swtchd rt and rdn over 1f out: kpt on wl fnl f: nrst fin* **33/1**

5-20 **7** ½ **Medicean Man**[40] 1111 5-8-10 **94** (b) SteveDrowne 5 93
(Jeremy Gask) *hld up in rr: effrt 2f out and sn rdn: nt clr run wl over 1f out and again ent fnl f: swtchd lft and kpt on wl towards fin* **14/1**

140- **8** ½ **Cheveton**[188] 7351 7-8-8 **97** DaleSwift(5) 11 95
(Richard Price) *cl up: rdn to dispute ld wl over 1f out: sn drvn and grad wknd* **40/1**

53-0 **9** nse **Irish Heartbeat (IRE)**[41] 1094 6-8-12 **96** PaulHanagan 9 94
(Richard Fahey) *prom: effrt and ch 2f out: sn rdn and wknd over 1f out* **8/1**

50-0 **10** shd **Tajneed (IRE)**[41] 1093 8-8-13 **100** MichaelO'Connell(3) 10 97
(David Nicholls) *cl up centre: chal over 2f out: sn rdn and grad wknd appr fnl f* **33/1**

30-1 **11** 1 **Enderby Spirit (GR)**[13] 1675 5-8-9 **93** TomEaves 17 87
(Bryan Smart) *prom: rdn along 2f out: drvn and wkng whn n.m.r ent fnl f* **14/1**

0020 **12** 3½ **Star Rover (IRE)**[6] 1888 4-8-7 **91** CathyGannon 6 74
(David Evans) *chsd ldrs: centre: rdn along 2f out: drvn: edgd lft and wknd over 1f out* **33/1**

00-0 **13** nse **Mister Hughie (IRE)**[13] 1687 4-9-7 **105** DuranFentiman 13 88
(Tim Easterby) *in tch nr stands' rail: rdn along 1/2-way: sn wknd* **40/1**

4101 **14** 2 **Flipando (IRE)**[24] 1457 10-9-0 **98** LeeNewman 15 74
(David Barron) *in tch towards stands' rail: rdn along 1/2-way: sn wknd* **33/1**

005- **15** hd **Kaldoun Kingdom (IRE)**[188] 7351 6-8-11 **102** GeorgeChaloner(7) 2 78
(Richard Fahey) *cl up on outer: rdn along over 2f out: wknd wl over 1f out* **22/1**

41-3 **16** ½ **Edinburgh Knight (IRE)**[6] 1888 4-8-2 **89** AndrewHeffernan(3) 20 63
(Paul D'Arcy) *dwlt: sn chsng ldrs nr stands' rail: rdn along wl over 2f out: sn wknd* **8/1**

05-0 **17** 3½ **Tombi (USA)**[24] 1457 7-8-7 **91** PaulQuinn 1 54
(Geoffrey Harker) *cl up on wd outside: rdn along over 2f out: sn wknd* **66/1**

200- **18** 2½ **Sonny Red (IRE)**[217] 6708 7-8-8 **92** AndrewMullen 18 47
(David Nicholls) *prom nr stands' rail: rdn along over 2f out: sn wknd* **50/1**

50-0 **19** ½ **Swilly Ferry (USA)**[12] 1720 4-9-2 **100** MichaelHills 19 53
(B W Hills) *chsd ldrs stands' rail: rdn along 1/2-way: sn wknd* **25/1**

50-0 **20** 1 **Desert Creek (IRE)**[62] 844 5-8-6 **90** AdrianNicholls 4 40
(David Nicholls) *dwlt: a bhd* **40/1**

69.81 secs (-2.09) **Going Correction** -0.10s/f (Good) **20 Ran SP% 126.6**
Speed ratings (Par 109): **109,107,107,106,106 104,103,103,103,103 101,97,96,94,94 93,88,85,84,83**
toteswingers:1&2:£5.50, 1&3:£9.00, 2&3:£6.10 CSF £30.88 CT £160.67 TOTE £6.00: £1.70, £1.60, £1.60, £2.60; EX 23.00 Trifecta £80.50 Pool: £3,495.20 - 32.09 winning units..

Owner A Chandler & L Westwood **Bred** Bond Thoroughbred Corporation **Trained** Sheriff Hutton, N Yorks

■ Stewards' Enquiry : Cathy Gannon one-day ban: used whip down shoulder in the forehand (May 27)

FOCUS

A competitive sprint. They raced middle to stands' side and main action unfolded up the centre of the track, with the first three finishers drawn in single figures. It was the only race on the card run in a time under standard, despite there being a heavy shower earlier in the afternoon.

NOTEBOOK

Hoof It ◆ won in taking fashion and looks every inch a Group horse in the making. He hadn't run for 202 days, but had been a non-runner twice already this season, so has been on the go for a while, and he had no trouble defying the absence. After winning his maiden over this trip, his next four victories were all gained over 5f, the latest at Doncaster last October off 5lb lower, but he was well suited by the step back up in trip, defeating mainly race-fit rivals with more authority than the margins indicate. A scopey type, it's no surprise he's progressed so well from three to four and there should be a lot more to come. He's reportedly going to be aimed at the Wokingham (provided he's not rated above 110 according to connections) before stepping up to pattern company and he's likely to be hugely popular at Royal Ascot, justifiably so. (op 6-1)

Horseradish, fifth in the Victoria Cup six days earlier, ran a fine race against the well-handicapped winner. He had to wait for a clear run, but was not unlucky. (op 9-2 tchd 9-1 in a place)

Our Jonathan, given more to do than the front two, finished well, proving just unable to reverse earlier Doncaster form with Horseradish. His last success came in a Group2 as a juvenile, but he can win off this sort of mark. (op 9-2 tchd 11-2)

Docofthebay(IRE) didn't get the clearest of runs but he was really going on at the line. He's worth persevering with at this trip and might win a similar race when the leaders go too quick.

Midnight Martini raced more towards the stands' side than the principals through the early stages but she plugged on and this was a respectable effort. (op 33-1)

Damika(IRE) had to be switched just as he was trying to stay on and he got going a bit too late, but this was a promising performance nonetheless. (tchd 40-1)

Medicean Man, with blinkers back on, got too far behind to be seriously competitive but he was yet another who finished well. (op 16-1 tchd 18-1)

Edinburgh Knight(IRE) was 2lb well in and this was a disappointing performance. (op 9-1 tchd 10-1 in a place)

2076 CONSTANT SECURITY STKS (H'CAP) 1m 4f

4:45 (4:46) (Class 4) (0-80,81) 3-Y-O £6,476 (£1,927; £963; £481) Stalls Centre

Form RPR

4-62 **1** **Communicator**[25] 1445 3-9-5 **78** HayleyTurner 8 93
(Michael Bell) *trckd ldng pair: hdwy over 2f out: rdn to ld over 1f out: drvn and edgd rt ins fnl f: kpt on wl* **13/2**[2]

2-1 **2** 1¼ **Ittirad (USA)**[35] 1212 3-9-7 **80** NeilCallan 5 93+
(Roger Varian) *hld up in tch: hdwy over 3f out: rdn to chal wl over 1f out and ev ch tl drvn and no ex wl ins fnl f* **15/8**[1]

41-0 **3** 2¼ **Lexington Bay (IRE)**[16] 1609 3-8-13 **72** PaulHanagan 14 81
(Richard Fahey) *chsd ldrs: wd st and hdwy 3f out: rdn and ch whn hung bdly lft over 1f out: drvn and one pce after* **20/1**

5-1 **4** nk **Sandusky**[30] 1311 3-9-5 **78** AhmedAjtebi 4 87
(Mahmood Al Zarooni) *hld up in midfield: stdy hdwy on inner 3f out: rdn to chse ldrs wl over 1f out: drvn and edgd lft ent fnl f: sn one pce* **8/1**[3]

60-2 **5** 7 **Circus Star (USA)**[18] 1572 3-8-12 **71** MartinDwyer 11 68
(Brian Meehan) *led: rdn along over 4f out: hdd 3f out: sn drvn and grad wknd* **20/1**

0-51 **6** nk **Dark Dune (IRE)**[16] 1623 3-8-7 **66** (e[1]) DavidAllan 12 63
(Tim Easterby) *trckd ldr: cl up over 4f out: led 3f out: rdn 2f out: sn drvn and hdd: grad wknd* **16/1**

40-1 **7** 5 **First Battalion (IRE)**[32] 1272 3-9-3 **76** RyanMoore 7 65
(Sir Michael Stoute) *hld up in rr: hdwy 3f out: rdn along over 2f out: n.d* **9/1**

21-5 **8** 1¼ **Mattoral**[12] 1727 3-9-4 **77** SebSanders 3 64
(Peter Makin) *a towards rr* **25/1**

22-1 **9** nk **Bouggatti**[29] 1327 3-8-8 **67** KierenFallon 2 53
(William Jarvis) *in tch: hdwy to chse ldrs 1/2-way: wd st: rdn along over 3f out: sn drvn and wknd* **9/1**

01- **10** 6 **Pink Diva (IRE)**[232] 6305 3-9-2 **75** JamieSpencer 1 52
(Tom Tate) *hld up: a in rr* **16/1**

2-31 **11** 9 **Aldedash (USA)**[20] 1525 3-9-4 **77** TomQueally 15 39
(Sir Henry Cecil) *hld up in midfield: effrt and sme hdwy over 3f out: sn rdn and wknd* **14/1**

3-22 **12** ½ **Prince Freddie**[24] 1456 3-8-11 **70** SteveDrowne 6 32
(Philip Kirby) *in rr: sme hdwy 4f out: sn rdn and wknd* **20/1**

3-22 **13** *8* **Rasam Aldaar**[37] [1173] 3-8-13 **72**.................................... SamHitchcott 16 21
(Mick Channon) *trckd ldrs on outer: hdcway to chse ldng pair 1/2-way: rdn along 4f out: sn wknd* **33/1**

2m 33.98s (0.78) **Going Correction** +0.15s/f (Good) **13** Ran SP% **118.7**
Speed ratings (Par 101): **103,102,100,100,95 95,92,91,91,87 81,80,75**
toteswingers:1&2:£5.20, 1&3:£23.40, 2&3:£11.40. Totesuper 7: Win: Not won. Place: Not won CSF £17.22 CT £238.88 TOTE £7.30: £2.60, £1.60, £4.10; EX 26.40 Trifecta £522.30 Pool: £1,517.36 - 2.14 winning units..
Owner Lady Davis **Bred** Lady Davis **Trained** Newmarket, Suffolk

FOCUS
A strong 3-y-o handicap for the class, but the early pace was steady and those still held up by the time they reached the straight had no chance.
T/Jkpt: Not won. T/Plt: £176.30 to a £1 stake. Pool:£201,772.97 - 835.38 winning tickets T/Qpdt: £51.60 to a £1 stake. Pool:£9,406.91 - 134.90 winning tickets JR

2077 - 2090a (Foreign Racing) - See Raceform Interactive

1671 DONCASTER (L-H)

Saturday, May 14

OFFICIAL GOING: Good (good to firm in places; 7.6)
Wind: Fresh against Weather: Cloudy with sunny periods

2091 CONSTRUCTION INDEX APPRENTICE H'CAP — 1m 4f
6:00 (6:00) (Class 5) (0-70,68) 4-Y-O+ **£3,070** (£906; £453) **Stalls** Low

Form RPR

-621 **1** **Tenhoo**[17] [1617] 5-8-8 **60**.. NathanAlison(5) 4 78+
(Eric Alston) *hld up in rr: smooth hdwy over 3f out: trckd ldrs whn n.m.r 2f out: effrt and hmpd over 1f out: rdn and styd on strly to ld ins fnl f: sn clr* **9/2**[2]

0/02 **2** *5* **Dar Es Salaam**[11] [1798] 7-9-4 **68**.. DaleSwift(3) 9 75
(Brian Ellison) *trckd ldrs: hdwy and cl up over 3f out: rdn to ld over 2f out and sn edgd lft: drvn and hung lft over 1f out: hdd ins fnl f: one pce* **10/3**[1]

0-35 **3** *2 1/4* **Crystal Gale (IRE)**[18] [1582] 4-8-11 **61**.......................... HarryBentley(3) 1 64
(William Knight) *trckd ldng pair on inner: hdwy 3f out: 2f out: n.m.r over 1f out: kpt on same pce: u.p fnl f* **10/1**

4-05 **4** *nk* **Aegean Destiny**[15] [1658] 4-8-13 **60**................................ DeclanCannon 2 63
(John Mackie) *hld up: hdwy 4f out: rdn along to chse ldrs over 2f out: drvn and kpt on same pce appr fnl f* **8/1**

625- **5** *3/4* **Parc Des Princes (USA)**[64] [3559] 5-9-1 **67**........... EdmondLinehan(5) 8 68
(Nicky Richards) *hld up in rr: hdwy on outer over 3f out: rdn along 2f out: plugged on same pce u.p fnl f* **20/1**

-003 **6** *1/2* **Donna Elvira**[17] [1616] 4-9-1 **62**... AmyRyan 6 63
(Edwin Tuer) *hld up: hdwy over 3f out: chsd ldrs over 2f out: sn rdn and kpt on same pce* **8/1**

045/ **7** *3/4* **Bajan Parkes**[560] [7170] 8-9-1 **67**................................ ShaneBKelly(5) 10 66
(John Quinn) *hld uip in rr: hdwy on inner 3f out: swtchd rt and rdn 2f out: kpt on: nvr nr ldrs* **20/1**

0-11 **8** *2 3/4* **Boa**[12] [1750] 6-8-12 **66**.. JackDuern(7) 5 61
(Reg Hollinshead) *trckd ldrs: hdwy over 3f out: rdn and ch 2f out: sn edgd lft and wknd appr fnl f* **13/2**[3]

5514 **9** *4* **King's Counsel (IRE)**[14] [1676] 5-9-2 **63**.........................(v) SeanLevey 11 52
(David O'Meara) *sn led: rdn along over 3f out: hdd jst over 2f out: sn drvn: edgd lft and wknd over 1f out* **7/1**

130- **10** *1* **Golden Future**[223] [6187] 8-8-1 **55**.................................... LauraBarry(7) 12 42
(Peter Niven) *chsd ldrs on outer: rdn along 4f out: wknd 3f out* **33/1**

4430 **11** *2 3/4* **Eton Fable (IRE)**[35] [1243] 6-8-13 **60**.......................(p) AndrewHeffernan 3 43
(Colin Teague) *chsd ldr: rdn along 4f out: sn wknd* **33/1**

2055 **12** *20* **Pinsplitter (USA)**[18] [1596] 4-8-2 **54** oh4.........................(p) NoraLooby(5) 7 —
(Alan McCabe) *s.i.s: a bhd* **25/1**

2m 32.44s (-2.46) **Going Correction** -0.075s/f (Good) **12** Ran SP% **117.7**
Speed ratings (Par 103): **105,101,100,99,99 99,98,96,94,93 91,78**
Tote Swingers: 1&2 £2.20, 1&3 £10.00, 2&3 £11.00 CSF £10.14 CT £141.20 TOTE £5.20: [illegible], [illegible], [illegible]; EX 19.90 Trifecta £158.80 Pool: £852.23 - 3.97 winning units..
Owner Edges Farm Racing Stables Ltd **Bred** A G Antoniades **Trained** Longton, Lancs

FOCUS
Just a modest apprentice event.
Pinsplitter(USA) Official explanation: jockey said gelding missed the break

2092 MULTIFAB METALS ENGINEERING & FABRICATION H'CAP — 1m (R)
6:35 (6:37) (Class 4) (0-85,80) 3-Y-O **£5,180** (£1,541; £770; £384) **Stalls** Low

Form RPR

30-6 **1** **Shamdarley (IRE)**[41] [1108] 3-8-10 **69**............................ FrederikTylicki 9 83+
(Michael Dods) *hld up in rr: smooth hdwy over 3f out: cl up on bit 2f out: led 1 1/2f out: rdn clr and hung rt ins fnl f: kpt on wl towards fin* **5/1**[3]

0-00 **2** *1 1/2* **Mutajare (IRE)**[14] [1688] 3-9-6 **79**................................. TadhgO'Shea 2 86+
(Mark Johnston) *trckd ldng pair on inner: effrt 3f out: rdn along 2f out and sn n.m.r: nt clr run and swtchd rt over 1f out: rdn to chse wnr ins fnl f: no imp towards fin* **16/1**

2421 **3** *4* **Honest Deal**[13] [1710] 3-9-5 **78**... PJMcDonald 3 76
(Alan Swinbank) *t.k.h: trckd ldrs: smooth hdwy 3f out: led 2f out: sn rdn and hdd 1 1/2f out: drvn and one pce ent fnl f* **7/4**[1]

4-01 **4** *3/4* **Ventura Sands (IRE)**[20] [1543] 3-8-12 **71**.......................... PaulHanagan 5 67
(Richard Fahey) *in tch: hdwy to trck ldrs over 3f out: rdn along and sltly outpcd over 2f out: kpt on u.p fnl f* **9/2**[2]

1-02 **5** *4* **Another Citizen (IRE)**[15] [1653] 3-9-3 **76**..................... DuranFentiman 8 63
(Tim Easterby) *hld up in rr: effrt 3f out: rdn along over 2f out: kpt on appr fnl f: nvr nr ldrs* **9/1**

3-21 **6** *2 3/4* **Roninski (IRE)**[29] [1370] 3-9-2 **75**.. TomEaves 1 56
(Bryan Smart) *led: rdn along 3f out: drvn and hdd 2f out: grad wknd* **15/2**

411- **7** *1 3/4* **Rock Ace (IRE)**[277] [4935] 3-9-7 **80**.......................... SilvestreDeSousa 6 57
(Deborah Sanderson) *hld up: hdwy on outer over 3f out: rdn over 2f out: sn wknd* **14/1**

3340 **8** *1 3/4* **Baharat (IRE)**[9] [1820] 3-9-0 **73**..(v) JohnEgan 7 46
(Richard Guest) *hld up: hdwy on inner over 3f out: rdn to chse ldrs over 2f out: sn drvn and wknd* **40/1**

51-6 **9** *5* **Kalleidoscope**[21] [1516] 3-9-4 **77**...................................... SamHitchcott 4 38
(Mick Channon) *cl up: rdn along over 3f out: drvn and wknd 2f out* **14/1**

1m 39.81s (0.11) **Going Correction** -0.075s/f (Good) **9** Ran SP% **114.6**
Speed ratings (Par 101): **96,94,90,89,85 83,81,79,74**
Tote Swingers: 1&2 £15.40, 1&3 £2.40, 2&3 £7.80 CSF £79.47 CT £193.42 TOTE £7.30: £2.60, £3.90, £1.10; EX 125.00 Trifecta £747.40 Pool: £5,757.12 - 5.70 winning units..
Owner Andrew Tinkler **Bred** D Veitch & R O'Brien **Trained** Denton, Co Durham

FOCUS
Quite a competitive race of its type and almost certainly form to view positively, the leading pair deserve credit for pulling clear off what was just a modest gallop.

2093 BEAVER84 HIRE & SALES MAIDEN AUCTION STKS — 5f
7:05 (7:10) (Class 5) 2-Y-O **£3,070** (£906; £453) **Stalls** High

Form RPR

2 **1** **Amadeus Denton (IRE)**[14] [1691] 2-8-9 0........................ FrederikTylicki 2 76
(Michael Dods) *cl up: led wl over 1f out: shkn up 1f out: rdn and hdd ins fnl f: rallied to ld on line* **30/100**[1]

2 *shd* **Artists Corner** 2-8-6 0.. BarryMcHugh 5 73+
(Richard Fahey) *uns rdr and bolted bef s: sn pushed along to chse ldrs: rdn 2f out: drvn over 1f out: styd on to chal ent fnl f: ev ch whn n.m.r and no ex towards fin: uns rdr after line* **20/1**

3 *nse* **Kohala (IRE)** 2-8-5 0 ow1.. RoystonFfrench 1 71+
(David Barron) *dwlt and in rr: hdwy 2f out: swtchd outside and str run to chal ent fnl f: rdn to ld last 100yds: sn edgd rt: hdd and no ex nr line* **25/1**

4 **4** *13* **Red Tyke (IRE)**[38] [1165] 2-8-11 0... TomEaves 6 31
(John Quinn) *in tch: rdn along over 2f out: n.d* **18/1**[3]

5 **5** *1* **Yearbook**[11] [1791] 2-8-4 0... DuranFentiman 3 20
(Tim Easterby) *cl up: rdn 2f out: drvn and wknd over 1f out* **20/1**

52 **6** *nse* **Oneniteinheaven (IRE)**[11] [1791] 2-8-4 0......................... PaulHanagan 4 20
(Ann Duffield) *led: rdn along 2f out: sn hdd & wknd* **5/1**[2]

61.04 secs (0.54) **Going Correction** -0.075s/f (Good) **6** Ran SP% **112.2**
Speed ratings (Par 93): **92,91,91,70,69 69**
Tote Swingers: 1&2 £1.20, 1&3 £3.40, 2&3 £17.60 CSF £10.16 TOTE £1.60: £1.40, £5.30; EX 12.20.
Owner Denton Hall Racing Ltd **Bred** Shane Moroney **Trained** Denton, Co Durham

FOCUS
Not the easiest race to assess, the short-priced favourite scrambling home from a pair of newcomers who weren't fancied judged on the betting.

NOTEBOOK
Amadeus Denton(IRE) made a bit of a meal of landing the short odds but did travel powerfully for a long way and could still go on to better things. He was a first juvenile winner of the season for a yard which ended a bit of a barren spell with two winners on the card. (op 8-15 tchd 8-13 in places)
Artists Corner, a daughter of promising first-season sire Dutch Art, gave problems before the start, but it's hard to knock her effort. She knuckled down well and is entitled to improve. (op 14-1)
Kohala(IRE)'s yard has made a bright start with juveniles and this one should be adding to their tally before long. She was weak in the betting, was green early but quickened in good style before again showing signs of inexperience near the finish. She'll improve. (op 16-1)
Red Tyke(IRE) is unlikely to be of any interest until his sights are lowered. (op 16-1)
Oneniteinheaven(IRE)'s performance suggested the form of the race she contested at Catterick probably isn't up to much and was particularly disappointing here. (op 4-1)

2094 GILKS FENCING MEDIAN AUCTION MAIDEN STKS — 6f
7:40 (7:42) (Class 5) 3-4-Y-O **£3,070** (£906; £453) **Stalls** High

Form RPR

5 **1** **Main Beach**[120] [171] 4-9-13 0..................................(t) StevieDonohoe 7 74+
(Tobias B P Coles) *dwlt and hmpd s: bhd: hdwy after 2f: swtchd wd and str run fr over 1f out: rdn to ld ins fnl f: edgd lft and kpt on* **16/1**

05 **2** *nk* **Daisyclipper**[25] [1459] 3-8-12 0...................................... PaulHanagan 1 65+
(Ann Duffield) *towards rr: hdwy over 2f out: swtchd outside and rdn over 1f out: ev ch ins fnl f: no ex towards fin* **16/1**

2-23 **3** *3/4* **Bertiewhittle**[10] [1813] 3-9-3 72... LeeNewman 2 67+
(David Barron) *cl up: rdn 2f out: led over 1f out: drvn and hdd ins fnl f: kpt on* **5/2**[2]

0-0 **4** *1 1/4* **Glass Mountain (IRE)**[17] [1605] 3-9-3 0............................ PatCosgrave 5 63+
(James Fanshawe) *trckd ldrs: effrt and nt clr run 2f out and again over 1f out: swtchd lft and rdn ent fnl f: kpt on same pce* **12/1**

32 **5** *1 1/4* **Dark Isle**[19] [1565] 3-9-3 0.. SebSanders 9 59
(J W Hills) *led: rdn along 2f out: drvn and hdd over 1f out: kpt on same pce* **2/1**[1]

4044 **6** *nse* **Gorgeous Goblin (IRE)**[5] [1941] 4-9-3 52.....................(vt) HarryBentley(5) 3 57
[illegible] *trckd ldrs: hdwy 2f out: [illegible] and wknd ent fnl f* **25/1**

6- **7** *2 1/4* **Crabbies Gold (IRE)**[236] [6240] 3-9-3 0............................... TomEaves 12 52
(Lisa Williamson) *in tch on inner: pushed along and outpcd 1/2-way: swtchd lft and sme hdwy 2f out: no imp* **50/1**

3-2 **8** *5* **Diablo Dancer**[8] [1860] 3-8-12 0................................. GrahamGibbons 4 31
(Tim Walford) *cl up: rdn along over 2f out: wkng whn n.m.r wl over 1f out* **4/1**[3]

\- **9** *hd* **Ivory Trilogy (IRE)** 3-8-12 0.. DaleSwift(5) 10 35
(Tim Etherington) *in tch: pushed along bef 1/2-way: sn outpcd* **40/1**

10 *nse* **Yougoigo** 3-9-3 0... PaulMulrennan 6 35
(Marjorie Fife) *dwlt and wnt rt s: a in rr* **66/1**

11 *2* **Crew Cut (IRE)** 3-9-3 0... SilvestreDeSousa 8 29
(Jeremy Gask) *cl up: rdn along over 2f out: drvn and wkng whn n.m.r wl over 1f out* **14/1**

0 **12** *17* **This Is Us (IRE)**[26] [1436] 3-8-12 0................................ DuranFentiman 11 —
(Eric Alston) *v.s.a: a wl bhd* **40/1**

1m 13.56s (-0.04) **Going Correction** -0.075s/f (Good)
WFA 3 from 4yo 10lb **12** Ran SP% **120.2**
Speed ratings (Par 103): **97,96,95,93,92 92,89,82,82,82 79,56**
Tote Swingers: 1&2 £55.60, 1&3 £11.00, 2&3 £8.60 CSF £238.15 TOTE £19.00: £5.70, £6.30, £1.60; EX 527.20 TRIFECTA Not won..
Owner Mrs R Coles **Bred** Miss J Chaplin **Trained** Newmarket, Suffolk

FOCUS
A fair sprint maiden, the 72-rated third the obvious guide to the form.
This Is Us(IRE) Official explanation: jockey said filly missed the break

2095 CMEC H'CAP — 6f
8:10 (8:14) (Class 4) (0-80,81) 4-Y-O+ **£3,885** (£1,156; £577; £288) **Stalls** High

Form RPR

5163 **1** **Silver Wind**[7] [1917] 6-8-13 **72**.........................(b) RobertWinston 18 84
(Alan McCabe) *hld up stands' side: hdwy 2f out: swtchd lft and rdn over 1f out: led ins fnl f: rdn out* **16/1**

02-5 **2** *1 1/2* **Jarrow (IRE)**[26] [1438] 4-9-3 **76**...................................... AdrianNicholls 9 83
(David Nicholls) *dwlt and swtchd rt s: towards rr stands' side: swtchd lft and gd hdwy 2f out: rdn to ld over 1f out: drvn and hdd ins fnl f: kpt on* **12/1**[3]

2321 **3** *1/2* **Collect Art (IRE)**[2] [2016] 4-8-11 **70**................................ StevieDonohoe 5 76+
(Andrew Haynes) *trckd ldrs far side: hdwy over 2f out: rdn to ld that gp as gps merged over 1f out: kpt on ins fnl f* **7/2**[1]

2-0 **4** 1 ¼ **Poppanan (USA)**65 822 5-9-1 79 AdamBeschizza(5) 14 81
(Simon Dow) in tch stands' side: hdwy and cl up 2f out: sn rdn and ev ch tl drvn and one pce ent fnl f 22/1

00-5 **5** ¾ **Bond Fastrac**14 1695 4-9-2 75 (p) SilvestreDeSousa 20 74
(Geoffrey Oldroyd) in tch stands' side: swtchd lft and hdwy wl over 1f out: sn rdn and kpt on ins fnl f: nrst fin 14/1

0100 **6** nk **El Dececy (USA)**14 1671 7-8-12 71 (p) GrahamGibbons 15 69
(John Balding) overall ldr stands' side: rdn along over 2f out: drvn and hdd over 1f out: grad wknd 50/1

56-1 **7** ¾ **Music Festival (USA)**15 1649 4-8-7 66 oh2 JoeFanning 17 62
(Jim Goldie) prom stands' side: rdn along over 2f out: drvn and wknd appr fnl f 8/1²

00-5 **8** shd **One Way Or Another (AUS)**114 226 8-9-6 79 SebSanders 7 75
(Jeremy Gask) chsd ldrs far side: rdn along over 2f out: grad wknd 16/1

5423 **9** ½ **Stevie Gee (IRE)**19 1562 7-8-9 73 (v) RyanClark(5) 2 67
(Ian Williams) cl up far side: rdn along 2f out: drvn and kpt on same pce fr over 1f out 16/1

0-60 **10** 2 ¾ **Jobe (USA)**8 1878 5-9-4 77 (b¹) PhillipMakin 11 62
(Kevin Ryan) dwlt and swtchd rt s: towards rr stands' side: sme hdwy fnl 2f: n.d 20/1

00-4 **11** nk **Elusive Sue (USA)**35 1244 4-9-0 73 PaulHanagan 3 57
(Richard Fahey) chsd ldrs far side: rdn along over 2f out: sn wknd 16/1

0-54 **12** ½ **Seamus Shindig**12 1771 9-8-8 72 AmyScott(5) 12 55
(Henry Candy) in tch far side: hdwy and cl up 2f out: sn rdn and wknd 16/1

6-24 **13** ½ **Fishforcompliments**110 285 7-9-0 80 LauraBarry(7) 10 61
(Richard Fahey) chsd ldrs far side: rdn along over 2f out: sn wknd 20/1

1434 **14** nk **Majuro (IRE)**8 1854 7-9-8 81 (t) JohnEgan 4 61
(Richard Guest) chsd ldrs far side: rdn along over 2f out: sn wknd 8/1²

-000 **15** ½ **Red Cape (FR)**8 1878 8-9-1 77 JamesSullivan(3) 13 55
(Ruth Carr) cl up stands' side: rdn along over 2f out: sn wknd 16/1

1-52 **16** ¾ **Grissom (IRE)**17 1618 5-9-5 78 DuranFentiman 16 54
(Tim Easterby) cl up stands' side: rdn along over 2f out: sn wknd 8/1²

0000 **17** nk **Methaaly (IRE)**18 1584 8-8-3 69 JosephYoung(7) 8 44
(Michael Mullineaux) a towards rr far side 33/1

026- **18** 19 **Quasi Congaree (GER)**135 8016 5-9-5 78 (t) LeeNewman 19 —
(Ian Wood) chsd ldrs stands' side: rdn along 1/2-way: sn lost pl and bhd 33/1

1132 **19** 28 **Alpha Tauri (USA)**25 1462 5-9-1 77 (t) RobertLButler(3) 1 —
(Richard Guest) led far side: rdn along 1/2-way: sn hdd & wknd: bhd and eased fnl 2f 33/1

1m 12.35s (-1.25) **Going Correction** -0.075s/f (Good) **19** Ran SP% **129.9**
Speed ratings (Par 105): **105,103,102,100,99 99,98,98,97,93 93,92,92,91,91 90,89,64,40**
Tote Swingers: 1&2 £80.10, 1&3 £21.90, 2&3 £15.90 CSF £189.49 CT £864.25 TOTE £23.40: £5.20, £4.10, £1.10, £6.80; EX 472.70 Trifecta £566.10 Part won. Pool: £765.12 - 0.50 winning units..
Owner Derek Buckley **Bred** W H R John And Partners **Trained** Averham Park, Notts

FOCUS
A competitive sprint and no reason why the form won't hold up. There was a pretty even split from the stalls, nine going far side and ten stands' side. There didn't appear to be much between the groups for a long way but six of the first seven home raced stand's side.
Alpha Tauri(USA) Official explanation: jockey said gelding lost its action

2096 PTL OCCUPATIONAL HYGIENE ASBESTOS MANAGEMENT H'CAP 7f
8:40 (8:40) (Class 4) (0-85,82) 3-Y-O **£5,180** (£1,541; £770; £384) **Stalls** High

Form RPR

106- **1** **The Mellor Fella**203 7085 3-9-3 78 PaulHanagan 4 87
(Richard Fahey) hld up towards rr: hdwy wl over 2f out: rdn to ld jst over 1f out: kpt on strly 13/2

52-1 **2** 3 **Maverik**36 1214 3-9-3 78 FrederikTylicki 7 79
(Michael Dods) cl up: led 2f out: sn rdn and hdd jst over 1f out: drvn and one pce ins fnl f 4/1³

000- **3** ¾ **Dubai Celebration**189 7347 3-8-11 75 PatrickDonaghy(3) 6 74
(Jedd O'Keeffe) hld up in tch: hdwy to chse ldrs over 2f out: effrt and n.m.r wl over 1f out: sn swtchd rt and rdn: kpt on ins fnl f 20/1

1521 **4** 2 **Bosambo**15 1653 3-9-7 82 PJMcDonald 5 76
(Alan Swinbank) trckd ldrs: hdwy 3f out: chsd ldr 2f out: sn rdn and wknd appr fnl f 7/4¹

5-43 **5** 1 **Tro Nesa (IRE)**21 1521 3-8-13 74 PhillipMakin 1 65
(Ann Duffield) dwlt and rr tl styd on fnl 2f: n.d 16/1

230- **6** 1 **Maggie Mey (IRE)**203 7085 3-8-11 72 DuranFentiman 3 60
(David O'Meara) cl up on outer: rdn over 2f out: sn drvn and wknd wl over 1f out 14/1

-12 **7** 5 **Falmouth Bay (USA)**72 750 3-9-6 81 SilvestreDeSousa 8 56
(Mark Johnston) led 1 1/2f: cl up on inner tl led again 1/2-way: rdn and hdd 2f out: sn wknd 3/1²

36-0 **8** 15 **Kalkan Bay**11 1801 3-8-9 70 (b) PaulMulrennan 2 —
(Jedd O'Keeffe) wnt lft s: chsd ldrs tl led after 1 1/2f: pushed along and hdd 1/2-way: sn rdn and wknd 2f out: eased 40/1

1m 26.93s (0.63) **Going Correction** -0.075s/f (Good) **8** Ran SP% **114.4**
Speed ratings (Par 101): **93,89,88,86,85 84,78,61**
Tote Swingers: 1&2 £7.10, 1&3 £18.70, 2&3 £6.90 CSF £32.68 CT £492.19 TOTE £8.50: £2.90, £2.10, £5.40; EX 41.40 TRIFECTA Part won. Pool: £218.80 - 0.40 winning units..
Owner Mr & Mrs G Calder **Bred** Mr & Mrs G Calder **Trained** Musley Bank, N Yorks

FOCUS
Just a fair handicap.
T/Plt: £181.10 to a £1 stake. Pool:£80,867.24 - 393.90 winning tickets T/Qpdt: £55.10 to a £1 stake. Pool:£5,488.74 - 122.62 winning tickets JR

2049 NEWBURY (L-H)
Saturday, May 14

OFFICIAL GOING: Good to firm (7.6)
Rail movement between 8f and 5f increased distances on round course by 16m.
Wind: Moderate ahead Weather: Overcast

2097 BET ON THE CUP FINAL AT TOTESPORT.COM MAIDEN STKS (DIV I) 1m 2f 6y
1:25 (1:25) (Class 4) 3-Y-O **£4,857** (£1,445; £722; £360) **Stalls** Low

Form RPR

5 **1** **Fiorente (IRE)**28 1407 3-9-3 0 RyanMoore 1 93+
(Sir Michael Stoute) lw: trckd ldrs: led jst ins fnl 2f: pushed clr fnl f: comf 8/11¹

3- **2** 3 ¾ **No Heretic**238 6196 3-9-3 0 JamieSpencer 10 82
(Paul Cole) lw: racd towards outside: hdwy over 3f out: led sn after: grad edgd lft to get far rails 2f out and hdd sn after: styd chalng tl over 1f out: kpt on but readily outpcd fnl f: hld on wl for 2nd 4/1²

30- **3** hd **Unex Renoir**226 6504 3-9-3 0 MichaelHills 6 82
(John Gosden) in tch drvn along 3f out: hdwy 2f out: styd on to dispute 2nd ins fnl 2f: sn no ch w wnr: one pce into 3rd clsng stages 9/1³

4 2 ¼ **Incitement** 3-9-3 0 KierenFallon 8 78+
(Ed Dunlop) w'like: scope: str: in rr: rdn and hdwy between horses over 2f out: hrd drvn and kpt on fnl f but nvr any ch w ldng trio 20/1

5 hd **Run Rabbit Run** 3-9-3 0 NeilCallan 5 77
(Roger Varian) lengthy: scope: in rr: hdwy over 3f out: sn pushed along and green: kpt on same pce fnl 2f 12/1

6 3 ¼ **The Cash Generator (IRE)** 3-9-3 0 JamieGoldstein 11 71
(Ralph Smith) unf: s.i.s: t.k.h in rr: hdwy on inner over 2f out: kpt on ins fnl f but nvr a threat 66/1

0 **7** 1 ½ **Crimson Knight**28 1408 3-9-0 0 LouisBeuzelin(3) 4 68
(Brian Meehan) w'like: chsd ldrs: hrd drvn over 3f out: btn fnl 2f 40/1

8 2 ¼ **Searing Heat (USA)** 3-9-3 0 TomQueally 12 63+
(Sir Henry Cecil) w'like: str: racd on outer: drvn along 5f out: nvr gng pce to rch ldrs and no ch fnl 2f 10/1

0 **9** 4 ½ **Dansette**12 1759 3-8-12 0 StephenCraine 3 49
(Jim Boyle) w'like: led tl hdd 3f out: wknd 2f out 66/1

40- **10** 2 ¼ **Novel Dancer**219 6689 3-9-3 0 RichardHughes 9 50
(Richard Hannon) chsd ldrs: chal over 3f out tl hung lft and wknd qckly 2f out 20/1

11 25 **Talbot Green** 3-9-3 0 DavidProbert 7 —
(William Muir) str: in tch: rdn: green: hung bdly lft and wknd 3f out: t.o 100/1

2m 6.82s (-1.98) **Going Correction** -0.025s/f (Good) **11** Ran SP% **120.6**
Speed ratings (Par 101): **106,103,102,101,100 98,97,95,91,89 69**
toteswingers:1&2:£2.10, 1&3:£3.60, 2&3:£3.90 CSF £3.56 TOTE £2.00: £1.10, £1.60, £2.70; EX 4.40 Trifecta £23.20 Pool: £969.59 - 30.90 winning units..
Owner Ballymacoll Stud **Bred** Ballymacoll Stud Farm Ltd **Trained** Newmarket, Suffolk

FOCUS
The riders thought it was quick ground, but safe with a good covering of grass, and there was a strong headwind. This maiden has not thrown up any stars in recent years and the chances are that this first division was just an ordinary race of its type for the track, although the winner was quite impressive and it was the quickest of the three C&D races. The form has been rated positively and has been rated on the positive side.
No Heretic ◆ Official explanation: jockey said colt hung left-handed

2098 JLT ASTON PARK STKS (LISTED RACE) 1m 5f 61y
2:00 (2:00) (Class 1) 4-Y-O+
£17,031 (£6,456; £3,231; £1,611; £807; £405) **Stalls** Low

Form RPR

-446 **1** **Drunken Sailor (IRE)**65 826 6-8-12 110 (b) KierenFallon 6 118
(Luca Cumani) lw: hld up in rr but in tch: stdy hdwy between horses 2f out: led over 1f out: gng clr whn hung rt ins fnl f: readily 4/1³

41-2 **2** 7 **Polly's Mark (IRE)**14 1677 5-8-10 106 LukeMorris 7 106
(Clive Cox) in tch: rdn and styd on to chse ldr over 2f out: chsd wnr but no ch whn hung rt fnl f: jst hld on for 2nd 6/4¹

4-52 **3** nk **Akmal**17 1601 5-8-12 105 RichardHills 1 108
(John Dunlop) led: pushed along 2f out: hdd over 1f out: styd disputing 2nd ins fnl f tl cl home but no ch w wnr 10/3²

652- **4** ¾ **Ship's Biscuit**226 6506 4-8-7 99 RyanMoore 5 101
(Sir Michael Stoute) s.i.s and drvn along: in rr and detached 7f out: hdwy fr 3f out: hd to one side and hung lft whn styng on to chse ldrs ins fnl 2f: edgd lft again and fnd no ex ins fnl f 11/2

330- **5** 7 **Western Pearl**198 7189 4-8-7 95 JamieSpencer 3 91
(William Knight) chsd ldr tl rdn over 2f out: sn btn 16/1

65-4 **6** 1 ¼ **Apprimus (IRE)**38 1188 5-8-12 99 AdamKirby 2 94
(Marco Botti) lw: chsd ldrs: rdn 3f out: wknd over 2f out 16/1

2m 47.91s (-4.09) **Going Correction** -0.025s/f (Good) **6** Ran SP% **110.2**
Speed ratings (Par 111): **111,106,106,106,101 100**
toteswingers:1&2:£2.10, 1&3:£2.60, 2&3:£1.90 CSF £10.06 TOTE £4.10: £2.00, £1.40; EX 9.70.
Owner Samanda Racing & Tony Bloom **Bred** Cyril Kiernan **Trained** Newmarket, Suffolk

FOCUS
Ordinary Listed form, but the pace was solid despite the small field and the time was inside the standard. The form is rated around the winner who looked better than ever.

NOTEBOOK
Drunken Sailor(IRE) got a good tow into the race and, when getting in the clear at the cutaway, he quickened away for a comfortable victory. He drifted to his right through the final furlong and ended up near the stands' rail, with the rest of the field following him to a certain extent. Having his first run in Britain since winning at Glorious Goodwood last summer, he had failed to fire in three runs in Dubai earlier this year but did not really settle off the modest pace he encountered in those races. He is quirky and was in front sooner than his rider wished here, but didn't look like idling once in front. He just missed the cut in last year's Melbourne Cup and that race could be the target again. Paddy Power offer 20/1. (op 3-1)
Polly's Mark(IRE) is a genuine and consistent mare and she ran her race in second, but the ground may have been a shade quick for her. There will be plenty of opportunities for her, including another crack at the Lancashire Oaks at Haydock in July, in which she was second last year. (op 2-1)
Akmal, down in trip after finishing second in the Sagaro at Ascot, \bAkmal\p set a good pace, but he was left standing when the winner quickened to the front and lost second too late on. Likeable though he is, he remains vulnerable to anything with a turn of foot. (op 4-1 tchd 3-1)
Ship's Biscuit was detached in last at one stage before closing in the straight. Not given a hard time when held, she is likely to come into her own later in the season with the Park Hill Stakes a long-term target. (op 9-2 tchd 6-1)
Western Pearl had something to find in this company and was in trouble with 3f to run. Slightly easier ground may suit her. (op 14-1 tchd 12-1)
Apprimus(IRE) dropped away when the race developed and is going to prove hard to place. Adam Kirby reported that he was unsuited by the ground. Official explanation: jockey said gelding was unsuited by the good to firm ground (tchd 20-1)

2099 BERRY BROS & RUDD MAGNUM H'CAP 6f 8y
2:35 (2:35) (Class 2) (0-100,97) 4-Y-O+
£7,477 (£2,239; £1,119; £560; £279; £140) **Stalls** Centre

Form RPR

50-0 **1** **Novellen Lad (IRE)**13 1720 6-8-10 86 KierenFallon 16 97
(Willie Musson) s.i.s: in rr: swtchd lft and hdwy over 2f out: pushed rt sn after: drvn to ld appr fnl f: sn hrd drvn: hld on wl 16/1

114- **2** hd **Mac's Power (IRE)**189 7351 5-9-7 97 (t) PatCosgrave 13 108
(James Fanshawe) lw: hld up in rr: gd hdwy between horses fr 2f out to chal 1f out: styd pressing wnr thrght fnl f: no ex clsng stages 13/2²

30-0 **3** *1 1/2* **Secret Witness**[7] 1888 5-9-3 **93**........(b) TomMcLaughlin 17 99
(Ronald Harris) *in rr: hdwy and rdn 2f out: sn nt clr run: r.o ins fnl f: gng on cl home* **22/1**

24-2 **4** *1 1/4* **Addictive Dream (IRE)**[14] 1680 4-9-1 **91**........ RyanMoore 10 93
(Walter Swinburn) *lw: in tch: hdwy fr 2f out: styd on ins fnl nt pce to rch ldrs* **9/2**[1]

5-10 **5** *3/4* **Son Of The Cat (USA)**[7] 1888 5-8-12 **93**........(t) AdamBeschizza(5) 1 93
(Brian Gubby) *chsd ldrs: ev ch and edgd rt fr 2f out: styd on same pce ins fnl f* **14/1**

5/3- **6** *1 1/4* **Dorback**[386] 1499 4-9-0 **90**........ JamieSpencer 11 86+
(Henry Candy) *in rr: nt clr run on stands' side fr over 2f out and wnt steadily lft to outer and r.o fnl f: nt rch ldrs* **9/1**

410- **7** *nk* **Oil Strike**[232] 6319 4-9-0 **90**........ LukeMorris 12 85
(Peter Winkworth) *in tch: pushed along and styng on whn n.m.r over 1f out: kpt on again fnl f* **8/1**[3]

0-00 **8** *hd* **Judd Street**[25] 1457 9-9-2 **92**........(b) CathyGannon 8 86
(Eve Johnson Houghton) *chsd ldrs: rdn over 2f out: outpcd ins fnl f* **40/1**

0-60 **9** *shd* **Sohraab**[7] 1888 7-8-8 **84**........ MartinDwyer 15 82+
(Hughie Morrison) *in rr: nt clr run on stands' side 2f out: styng on whn hmpd again ins fnl f: kpt on again cl home* **16/1**

13-0 **10** *2 3/4* **Drawnfromthepast (IRE)**[13] 1720 6-9-4 **94**........ NeilCallan 4 79
(Ed Walker) *disp ld: rdn and stl ev ch 2f out: wknd* **50/1**

50-0 **11** *nse* **Kingsgate Choice (IRE)**[7] 1888 4-8-8 **87**........ KierenFox(3) 19 72
(John Best) *lw: in rr: rdn along 1/2-way: hdwy over 2f out: chsd ldrs over 1f: wknd ins fnl f* **20/1**

6-54 **12** *1* **Yer Woman (IRE)**[7] 1888 4-8-7 **88**........ KieranO'Neill(5) 3 70
(Richard Hannon) *in tch: rdn 1/2-way: nvr gng pce to rch ldrs* **18/1**

100- **13** *1/2* **Summerinthecity (IRE)**[204] 7060 4-9-1 **91**........ TomQueally 7 71
(Ed de Giles) *pressed ldrs: slt ld over 2f out: hdd appr fnl f: wknd ins fnl f* **33/1**

04-0 **14** *1* **Fleeting Echo**[14] 1681 4-9-2 **92**........ RichardHughes 18 69
(Richard Hannon) *in rr on stands' side: hdwy whn nt clr run over 1f out: clr run again ins fnl f: nt rcvr* **14/1**

05-1 **15** *4 1/2* **Baby Strange**[50] 970 7-9-3 **93**........ JimCrowley 5 55
(Derek Shaw) *in tch: chsd ldrs over 2f out: one pce whn hmpd sn after: sn btn* **16/1**

510- **16** *10* **R Woody**[189] 7351 4-9-3 **93**........ GeorgeBaker 6 —
(Dean Ivory) *mde most tl hdd over 2f out: sn wknd: eased fnl f* **11/1**

040- **17** *2 1/4* **Olynard (IRE)**[216] 6776 5-8-12 **88**........ RoystonFfrench 9 —
(Dr Richard Newland) *lw: chsd ldrs to 1/2-way: sn wknd* **25/1**

00-1 **18** *3 3/4* **Spanish Bounty**[26] 1444 6-8-11 **87**........ EddieAhern 2 —
(Jonathan Portman) *chsd ldrs to 1/2-way: sn wknd* **12/1**

1m 12.54s (-0.46) **Going Correction** -0.025s/f (Good) **18** Ran SP% **125.2**
Speed ratings (Par 109): **102,101,99,98,97 95,95,94,94,90 90,89,88,87,81 68,65,60**
toteswingers:1&2:£39.50, 1&3:£102.90, 2&3:£33.60 CSF £109.31 CT £1434.79 TOTE £21.10: £4.90, £2.20, £6.30, £1.60; EX 109.31 Trifecta £1564.20 Part won. Pool: £2,113.89 - 0.10 winning units..
Owner Johnson & Broughton **Bred** Mrs Chris Harrington **Trained** Newmarket, Suffolk

FOCUS
There was plenty of trouble in this competitive big-field sprint. The pace did not appear particularly quick but the first three home all came from the back of the field. Sound form, the winner rated back to his best.

NOTEBOOK
Novellen Lad(IRE) was last to leave the stalls and Kieren Fallon took him right round the field to find a clear passage before bringing him back over to his right. The gelding stuck his neck out well to hold the runner-up on only his second start since leaving Eric Alston. Fast ground suits, and races like the Wokingham and Stewards' Cup will be considered. (op 12-1)
Mac's Power(IRE) burst through to have every chance but the winner proved the tougher in the last half-furlong. He was 7lb higher than when scoring at Doncaster in the autumn and this was a good effort on ground which was quicker than he's prefer. He too could run in the Wokingham. (op 6-1 tchd 11-2)
Secret Witness met trouble towards the stands' side and ran on when in the clear, too late to have an impact on the first two. Currently 18lb higher than when last winning, he has been placed no fewer than ten times since last getting his head in front and is largely consistent. (op 20-1)
Addictive Dream(IRE), back up to 6f, came with his run on the far side of the bunch, away from trouble, and had no obvious excuse. He is useful and consistent. (op 6-1)
Son Of The Cat(USA) was one of a pair who raced a little way apart from the main body of the field for the first part of the race. He was always prominent and was only run out of the frame late on. (op 16-1)
Dorback ◆ put in an eyecatching run, making steady headway from the rear after being switched. This was his first start in over a year, having reportedly incurred a fracture, and he should be kept in mind. (tchd 15-2)
Oil Strike ran with credit on this return to action, travelling well when momentarily stopped in his run. Official explanation: jockey said gelding was denied a clear run (op 11-1)
Judd Street, who's on a decent mark now, ran respectably with blinkers replacing the usual visor. (op 33-1)
Sohraab was hampered before running on when it was all over and is nicely handicapped now, a pound below his last winning mark. (op 28-1)
Fleeting Echo, back at sprint distances, got no run near the stands' side and this effort can be ignored. Official explanation: jockey said filly was denied a clear run
Baby Strange, a winner on Polytrack last time, was in trouble after the winner edged across him. Official explanation: jockey said gelding suffered interference in running (tchd 14-1)
Spanish Bounty, the other of the low-drawn pair who were a little isolated, finsihed last off a 12lb higher mark than when winning at Windsor. (op 10-1)

2100 TOTESPORT.COM LONDON GOLD CUP (H'CAP) 1m 2f 6y
3:10 (3:10) (Class 2) (0-105,98) 3-Y-O

£18,693 (£5,598; £2,799; £1,401; £699; £351) **Stalls** Low

Form RPR

51-2 **1** **Al Kazeem**[29] 1365 3-9-4 **95**........ SteveDrowne 1 109
(Roger Charlton) *lw: mde all: qcknd clr 2f out: in command fnl f: readily* **9/2**[3]

41-4 **2** *1 1/4* **Labarinto**[30] 1344 3-8-10 **87**........ RyanMoore 6 98+
(Sir Michael Stoute) *lw: s.i.s: in tch: rdn and hdwy 2f out: chsd wnr over 1f out: kpt on but a comf hld fnl f* **7/2**[2]

31-0 **3** *1 1/2* **Fulgur**[31] 1320 3-8-7 **83** ow1........ KierenFallon 9 92+
(Luca Cumani) *t.k.h in last: swtchd rt to centre over 2f out: str run ent fnl f: drifted lft: r.o: nrst fin* **13/2**

01-3 **4** *2* **Rastaban**[21] 1516 3-8-0 **77**........ CathyGannon 8 81
(William Haggas) *trckd ldrs: rdn wl over 2f out: chsd wnr briefly wl over 1f out: edgd lft: kpt on same pce fnl f* **22/1**

10-2 **5** *1* **Dominant (IRE)**[20] 1550 3-9-3 **94**........ NeilCallan 7 96+
(Roger Varian) *in tch: trckd ldrs over 3f out: effrt over 2f out: kpt on same pce* **13/8**[1]

10-0 **6** *hd* **State Opera**[30] 1339 3-8-9 **86**........ RichardHills 5 88
(Mark Johnston) *sn trcking ldrs: rdn over 2f out: kpt on same pce* **25/1**

25-2 **7** *1 1/2* **General Synod**[28] 1409 3-8-7 **83** ow1........ JamieSpencer 2 83
(Richard Hannon) *disp for 2f: trckd wnr tl rdn over 2f out: wknd fnl f* **10/1**

0-45 **8** *1/2* **Norse Blues**[13] 1725 3-8-3 **80**........ DavidProbert 4 78
(Sylvester Kirk) *t.k.h early: hld up bhd ldrs: rdn over 2f out: sn outpcd: n.d* **33/1**

2m 9.02s (0.22) **Going Correction** -0.025s/f (Good) **8** Ran SP% **112.1**
Speed ratings (Par 105): **98,97,95,94,93 93,92,91**
toteswingers:1&2:£2.80, 1&3:£4.70, 2&3:£3.60 CSF £19.61 CT £99.41 TOTE £4.90: £1.80, £1.40, £1.70; EX 20.30 Trifecta £69.30 Pool: £1,351.62 - 14.43 winning units..
Owner D J Deer **Bred** D J And Mrs Deer **Trained** Beckhampton, Wilts

FOCUS
This handicap has proved a hot race in recent years and, while this year's edition attracted a smaller field than usual, it should still produce winners in decent company. Horses of the calibre of last year's runner-up Monterosso, Regal Flush and Maraahel have all been beaten in this before progressing into Group performers, while last year's scorer Green Moon went on to win in Listed company. Unfortunately this was a falsely run race, the winner dictating and turning it into something of a sprint, and the form is not the most solid, although it has still been rated on the positive side. The time was six seconds slower than standard.

NOTEBOOK
Al Kazeem was kicked on by Steve Drowne at the two pole and ran on strongly. While he had the run of things here, he improved on what he showed in a slowly-run conditions race here last month and looks a nice prospect. Well at home on quick ground, he is entered in the King Edward VII Stakes and should have further progress in him at 1m4f, but apparently is more likely to be kept to this trip at Ascot in the Hampton Court Stakes. (op 11-2)
Labarinto came from out of the bunch to chase home the winner and continues on the upgrade. He has no problem with fast ground but his one win came in soft so he wouldn't mind an ease in underfoot conditions. (op 4-1)
Fulgur ◆ was held up in last place, racing keenly again. He ran on strongly down the outside in the latter stages for third and has a good deal more to offer granted a true gallop over this trip, or even over 1m4f. Easier ground may play to his strengths too. (op 6-1)
Rastaban, third to subsequent Dee Stakes winner Glen's Diamond at Musselburgh, was up a furlong but this wasn't a true test at the trip. This was a solid run in the circumstances. (op 20-1)
Dominant(IRE), raised 6lb after his luckless second at Sandown, couldn't quicken up when it was demanded of him but is worth another chance. (op 6-4 tchd 11-8)
State Opera had finished last in two valuable sales races since winning on his debut at two. He ran a bit better on this first start in a handicap but still has plenty to prove. (op 33-1)
General Synod might not have stayed on this handicap debut and remains a maiden. (op 8-1)
Norse Blues failed to settle through the early parts on this step up in trip. (tchd 40-1)

2101 JLT LOCKINGE STKS (GROUP 1) 1m (S)
3:45 (3:45) (Class 1) 4-Y-O+

£99,347 (£37,660; £18,847; £9,397; £4,707; £2,362) **Stalls** Centre

Form RPR

111- **1** **Canford Cliffs (IRE)**[290] 4469 4-9-0 127........ RichardHughes 4 126+
(Richard Hannon) *lw: hld up in tch: smooth hdwy between horses fr 2f out to take narrow ld 1f out: shkn up ins fnl f: drvn and qcknd readily clr fnl 120yds: comf* **4/5**[1]

131- **2** *1 1/4* **Worthadd (IRE)**[20] 4-9-0 116........ MircoDemuro 7 123
(Vittorio Caruso, Italy) *led: jnd 5f out: qcknd readily fr 2f out: hdd 1f out: styd w wnr tl outpcd fnl 120yds but clrly 2nd best* **25/1**

20-4 **3** *2 3/4* **Premio Loco (USA)**[49] 997 7-9-0 119........ GeorgeBaker 5 117
(Chris Wall) *lw: t.k.h: hld up in rr but in tch: hdwy and edgd rt over 1f out: drvn and styd on to take 3rd fnl 120yds but nvr any ch w ldng duo* **33/1**

53-1 **4** *2* **Dick Turpin (IRE)**[21] 1527 4-9-0 124........ RyanMoore 8 112
(Richard Hannon) *trckd ldrs: pushed along and nt much daylight whn bmpd over 1f out: outpcd ins fnl f and wknd fnl 120yds* **11/4**[2]

31-3 **5** *1/2* **Red Jazz (USA)**[49] 997 4-9-0 120........ MichaelHills 1 111
(B W Hills) *pressed ldr tl rdn appr fnl 2f: sn one pce: wknd ins fnl f* **14/1**

1-10 **6** *3 1/4* **Twice Over**[49] 1002 6-9-0 125........ TomQueally 10 104
(Sir Henry Cecil) *pressed ldr fr 5f out tl rdn over 2f out: wknd over 1f out* **7/1**[3]

510- **7** *33* **Balthazaar's Gift (IRE)**[210] 6949 8-9-0 111........ PhilipRobinson 6 —
(Clive Cox) *tk keem hold: a in last: lost tch fr 1/2-way: t.o* **66/1**

1m 36.52s (-3.18) **Going Correction** -0.025s/f (Good) **7** Ran SP% **109.7**
Speed ratings (Par 117): **114,112,110,108,107 104,71**
toteswingers:1&2:£5.90, 1&3:£6.30, 2&3:£22.80 CSF £24.18 TOTE £1.90: £1.30, £6.10; FX 24.10 Trifecta £[illegible] Pool: £[illegible] - [illegible] winning units..
Owner The Heffer Syndicate, M Tabor & D Smith **Bred** S And S Hubbard Rodwell **Trained** East Everleigh, Wilts

FOCUS
The best edition of the Lockinge Stakes for some time, with three proven Group 1 performers in opposition. It was run at an ordinary pace and the time was just under a second outside the standard. Richard Hannon landed the race with Paco Boy 12 months ago and the champion trainer was double handed here with the two principal contenders. Canford Cliffs did not need to be at his best with Dick Turpin and Twice Over below par. Worthadd probably improved.

NOTEBOOK
Canford Cliffs(IRE) was beaten on his first two starts last season but proceeded to rack up a Group 1 hat-trick in the Irish Guineas, the St James's Palace and the Sussex Stakes, before an unsatisfactory scope ruled him out of the Queen Elizabeth II Stakes. Returning to action a stronger individual, he settled well in midfield, shadowing his stablemate, and cruised up to the leader with a furlong to go. He took a little time to subdue the runner-up, but was pulling away at the finish for a comfortable victory. The bare form is nothing special, with his two principal rivals below par, but it was a thoroughly pleasing reappearance and there is considerable improvement to come from him with the run under his belt. He is all class and his turn of foot will make him a threat to everything in the top mile races this term, with the Queen Anne Stakes at Ascot his next target. He is likely to be taken on there by Goldikova, who narrowly beat Paco Boy in the Queen Anne last year. Further down the line Frankel could lie in wait too. (tchd 5-6 and 10-11 in places)
Worthadd(IRE) is a prolific winner in his native Italy and had been beaten just once in eight starts since his raceourse debut, when tackling this grade for the first time at San Siro last autumn. This represented much his biggest test to date and he ran really well from the front, racing keenly while carrying his head a little low. Let down approaching the furlong pole, he battled on well but was comfortably held by the favourite late on. A versatile sort, effective at 7f-1m3f, he has plenty of form in soft conditions and this was his first run on fast ground. The Prix Jacques le Marois at Deauville could be next for him. (op 22-1 tchd 20-1)
Premio Loco(USA) came through from the rear for third without ever troubling the first two. Also third to Canford Cliffs in the Sussex on his one previous attempt in this grade, this admirable gelding has plenty of options back at a lower level, among them the Diomed Stakes at Epsom and the John O'Gaunt Stakes at Haydock. There are more races to be won with him. (tchd 40-1)
Dick Turpin(IRE) beat Canford Cliffs in the Greenham here last spring and again when they were second and third in the 2000 Guineas. He had a race fitness advantage over his old rival too, having won the Group 2 Sandown Mile last month, but Richard Hughes was adamant that Canford Cliffs is the better horse. Already under pressure in midfield when he was short of room over a furlong from home, Dick Turpin was not done any favours by the fast ground and will appreciate a bit of cut underfoot. His Prix Jean Prat win at Chantilly last summer came in easy ground. He could return to France later this month for the Prix d'Ispahan at Longchamp, where Goldikova may be in opposition. Official explanation: jockey said colt was unsuited by the good to firm ground (op 3-1 tchd 5-2)

Red Jazz(USA), third in a Group 2 at Meydan on his reappearance, had been third in the Queen Elizabeth II in the autumn, but while he ran respectably he is perhaps not quite up to this level. That Ascot run was a career-best effort, but 7f may still be his optimum trip. (op 16-1)
Twice Over pressed Worthadd for the lead near the rail but failed to pick up when coming off the bridle. This was his first run at a mile since he his close third to Virtual in this race two years ago, and he has proved himself a top-notch performer at 1m2f since then. Following his lacklustre effort in a most unsatisfactory Dubai World Cup he has to prove his well-being, but it would be folly to write him off. (op 13-2 tchd 6-1)
Balthazaar's Gift(IRE), having only his second run at a mile, dropped right away to finish a long last. He has now been beaten on all 15 starts in the top grade. Philip Robinson reported his mount hung right-handed. Official explanation: jockey said horse hung right-handed

2102 HEADS & ALL THREADS 25TH ANNIVERSARY FILLIES' H'CAP 7f (S)
4:20 (4:20) (Class 4) (0-85,85) 3-Y-O £5,180 (£1,541; £770; £384) **Stalls** Centre

Form RPR
50-5 **1** **Rhythm Of Light**[28] 1384 3-8-13 **77** RichardKingscote 15 91+
(Tom Dascombe) *racd stands' side: hld up in last pair: making smooth hdwy whn hmpd over 1f out: r.o wl to ld wl ins fnl f: readily* **20/1**
51 **2** *1* **Sure Route**[17] 1605 3-8-12 **76** RichardHughes 2 87
(Richard Hannon) *lw: racd centre: trckd ldrs rdn whn swtchd rt over 1f out: led ins fnl f: sn hdd: kpt on but no ex* **9/1**
21- **3** *3* **Blanche Dubawi (IRE)**[211] 6892 3-9-2 **80** TomQueally 3 83
(Noel Quinlan) *str: racd centre: rrd leaving stalls: hld up towards rr: hdwy over 2f out: rdn to ld over 1f out: hdd ins fnl f: no ex* **7/1**[3]
56-1 **4** *½* **Biaraafa (IRE)**[19] 1571 3-8-13 **77** JamieSpencer 14 79
(Michael Bell) *lw: racd stands' side: hld up towards rr: swtchd to stands' side rails over 2f out: hdwy wl over 1f out: sn rdn: kpt on ins fnl f: fin wl* **11/2**[2]
00-0 **5** *½* **Primo Lady**[14] 1688 3-9-5 **83** DavidProbert 4 83
(Gay Kelleway) *racd centre: chsd ldrs rdn whn sltly outpcd over 2f out: kpt on ins fnl f* **40/1**
321 **6** *2 ¼* **Flashbang**[17] 1607 3-9-0 **78** KierenFallon 19 72
(Paul Cole) *racd stands' side: wnt rt s: sn chsng ldr: chal 2f out: rdn whn veered lft jst over 1f out: continued to hang lft and one pce fnl f* **4/1**[1]
10-5 **7** *shd* **Catfish (IRE)**[9] 1837 3-9-1 **82** LouisBeuzelin(3) 7 76
(Brian Meehan) *led centre gp: overall ldr 2f out: rdn and hdd over 1f out: kpt on same pce* **10/1**
41-3 **8** *¾* **Camache Queen (IRE)**[40] 1141 3-8-13 **77** CathyGannon 16 69
(Denis Coakley) *racd stands' side: chsd ldrs: rdn over 2f out: one pce fnl f* **18/1**
40-3 **9** *¾* **Obiter Dicta**[25] 1459 3-8-8 **72** FrankieMcDonald 1 62+
(Henry Candy) *racd centre: chsd ldrs: rdn over 2f out: styng on at the same pce in 7th whn hmpd ins fnl f* **18/1**
3-14 **10** *nse* **Sand Owl**[19] 1571 3-9-1 **79** RyanMoore 5 69+
(Peter Chapple-Hyam) *lw: racd centre: mid-div: hdwy 2f out: sn pushed along to chse ldrs: bdly hmpd ent fnl f: eased whn no ch after* **8/1**
41- **11** *½* **Herminella**[171] 7550 3-8-8 **72** LukeMorris 8 60
(William Muir) *racd centre: chsd ldrs: rdn over 2f out: fdd jst over 1f out* **33/1**
442- **12** *½* **Golden Tempest (IRE)**[199] 7165 3-9-1 **82** JohnFahy(3) 10 69
(Walter Swinburn) *racd centre: chsd ldrs: rdn 2f out: wkng whn sltly hmpd ent fnl f* **14/1**
1-46 **13** *14* **Cheque Book**[12] 1773 3-9-0 **78** MichaelHills 17 27
(B W Hills) *racd stands' side: mid-div tl wknd 2f out* **25/1**
01-6 **14** *½* **Opera Dancer**[16] 1626 3-8-3 **72** AdamBeschizza(5) 13 20
(Sylvester Kirk) *racd centre: a towards rr* **25/1**
015- **15** *2* **My Delirium**[173] 7534 3-9-7 **85** JimCrowley 18 28
(Ralph Beckett) *racd stands' side: chsd ldrs: rdn over 2f out: sn wknd* **20/1**
10-0 **16** *14* **Shim Sham (IRE)**[31] 1317 3-9-7 **85** (b[1]) MartinDwyer 20 —
(Brian Meehan) *led stands' side gp and overall ldr tl 2f out: wknd qckly* **14/1**

1m 25.55s (-0.15) **Going Correction** -0.025s/f (Good) 16 Ran SP% **124.5**
Speed ratings (Par 98): **99,97,94,93,93 90,90,89,88,88 88,87,71,71,68 52**
toteswingers:1&2:£34.40, 1&3:£45.00, 2&3:£9.60 CSF £181.27 CT £1467.83 TOTE £22.80: £4.40, £2.50, £2.00, £1.80; EX 394.40 TRIFECTA Not won..
Owner Lowe Silver Deal **Bred** Hermes Services Ltd **Trained** Malpas, Cheshire
■ Stewards' Enquiry : Richard Hughes one-day ban: careless riding (May 28)

FOCUS
This handicap was won in 2006 by Red Evie, who went on to take the Lockinge a year later. This was a competitive renewal containing a number of unexposed fillies. They soon split into two groups, with seven fillies racing on the stands' side, before the groups merged in the latter stages. Decent form, the winner rated up a stone.
Camache Queen(IRE) Official explanation: jockey said filly hung right-handed

2103 MORE LIVE FOOTBALL BETTING AT TOTESPORT.COM MAIDEN STKS 7f (S)
4:55 (4:55) (Class 5) 3-Y-O £3,885 (£1,156; £577; £288) **Stalls** Centre

Form RPR
2 **1** *shd* **Moone's My Name**[18] 1591 3-8-12 0 JimCrowley 17 75
(Ralph Beckett) *wnt rt s: sn chsng ldrs: chsd wnr ins fnl f: drvn to take slt ld fnl 120yds: hdd fnl strides* **6/1**[3]
4 **2** *¾* **Rougette**[29] 1362 3-8-12 0 MichaelHills 7 73
(B W Hills) *lw: chsd ldrs: rdn 2f out: styd on ins fnl f: kpt on to take 3rd nr fin but nt rch ldng duo* **9/2**[2]
3 *¾* **Dreams Of Dawn** 3-9-3 0 CathyGannon 19 76
(Mick Channon) *w'like: chsd ldrs: rdn: green and hung lft ins fnl f: rallied and styd on again clsng stages* **28/1**
25-3 **4** *1* **Qenaa**[19] 1565 3-8-12 85 RichardHills 15 68
(Mark Johnston) *led tl hdd appr fnl f: stl chsng ldrs whn squeezed out and wknd fnl 100yds* **9/1**
00 **5** *1 ¾* **The Guru Of Gloom (IRE)**[14] 1682 3-9-3 0 SteveDrowne 9 69
(William Muir) *sn mid-div: rdn along over 2f out: styd on fnl f: nt rch ldrs* **33/1**
0- **6** *1 ¼* **Heezararity**[228] 6443 3-9-3 0 AdamKirby 11 65
(Stuart Kittow) *chsd ldrs: rdn over 2f out: outpcd fnl f* **40/1**
7 *½* **Shahzan (IRE)** 3-9-3 0 NeilCallan 2 64
(Roger Varian) *leggy: unf: t.k.h: in rr: hdwy into mid-div over 3f out: drvn to chse ldrs 2f out: wknd fnl f* **9/1**
0-0 **8** *1 ¼* **Evergreen Forest (IRE)**[17] 1606 3-9-0 0 SophieDoyle(3) 16 60
(Alastair Lidderdale) *pressed ldrs: wknd ins fnl 2f* **66/1**
0- **9** *2 ¼* **Swing Door (IRE)**[189] 7346 3-8-12 0 EddieAhern 4 49
(B W Hills) *in rr: pushed along and styd on fnl 2f: nt rch ldrs* **33/1**
0 **10** *hd* **Habsburg**[12] 1759 3-9-3 0 FrankieMcDonald 12 54
(Paul Fitzsimons) *w'like: chsd ldrs tl wknd 2f out* **100/1**
11 *¾* **Desert Chieftain** 3-9-3 0 KierenFallon 14 52
(Luca Cumani) *w'like: str: s.i.s: in rr: hdwy into mid-div 1/2-way: wknd fr 2f out* **16/1**
24-0 **12** *1 ¾* **Fists And Stones**[14] 1682 3-9-3 75 RichardHughes 1 47
(Mick Channon) *in rr: hdwy and in tch over 2f out: sn wknd* **16/1**
0- **13** *5* **Ollywood**[274] 5033 3-9-3 0 LukeMorris 5 34
(Tony Carroll) *towards rr most of way* **100/1**
14 *2 ¼* **Fluctuation (IRE)** 3-9-3 0 LiamJones 13 28
(William Haggas) *str: a in rr* **20/1**
0-0 **15** *nk* **Justice Walk (IRE)**[14] 1682 3-9-3 0 JamieSpencer 18 27
(Paul Fitzsimons) *str: bmpd s: a towards rr* **40/1**
0 **16** *7* **Poyle Todream**[17] 1606 3-9-3 0 GeorgeBaker 8 —
(Ralph Beckett) *pressed ldrs 4f* **50/1**
4 **D** **Quadrant (IRE)**[28] 1409 3-9-3 0 MartinDwyer 20 81+
(Brian Meehan) *lw: pressed ldrs: rdn to take narrow ld appr fnl f: jst hdd fnl 120yds: rallied wl to ld again last strides: fin 1st, shd: subs disq* **13/8**[1]

1m 26.76s (1.06) **Going Correction** -0.025s/f (Good) 17 Ran SP% **126.7**
Speed ratings (Par 99): **91,91,90,89,87 85,85,83,81,80 79,77,72,69,69 61,92**
toteswingers:1&2:£4.90, 1&3:£3.10, 2&3:£6.00 CSF £10.53 TOTE £2.50: £1.20, £2.40, £2.00; EX 17.30 Trifecta £22.80 Pool: £837.92 - 27.09 winning units..
Owner McDonagh Murphy And Nixon **Bred** Baroness Bloodstock & Tweenhills Stud **Trained** Kimpton, Hants

FOCUS
Not much depth to this maiden despite the large field. It was run in a time just over a second slower than the earlier fillies' handicap.
Dreams Of Dawn Official explanation: jockey said gelding hung left-handed

2104 BET ON THE CUP FINAL AT TOTESPORT.COM MAIDEN STKS (DIV II) 1m 2f 6y
5:30 (5:30) (Class 4) 3-Y-O £4,857 (£1,445; £722; £360) **Stalls** Low

Form RPR
0- **1** **Spifer (IRE)**[199] 7178 3-9-3 0 KierenFallon 4 76+
(Luca Cumani) *bit bkwd: trckd ldr: rdn to ld 2f out: immediately hrd pressed: kpt on gamely u.str.p fnl f: all out: hld on* **11/4**[2]
2 *nse* **End Or Beginning** 3-9-3 0 JamieSpencer 6 75+
(Paul Cole) *w'like: s.i.s: sn rcvrd to ld: rdn whn narrowly hdd 2f out: rallied gamely thrght fnl f: jst hld* **2/1**[1]
0- **3** *¾* **Warneford**[228] 6442 3-9-3 0 MartinDwyer 12 73
(Brian Meehan) *lw: trckd ldrs: jnd ldrs 3f out tl rdn 2f out: kpt on ins fnl f* **11/4**[2]
0-0 **4** *8* **Like A Boy**[40] 1139 3-9-3 0 SteveDrowne 10 57
(Peter Makin) *lw: trckd ldrs: rdn over 2f out: nt pce to threaten: no ex fnl f* **12/1**
5 *7* **Gilt (USA)** 3-8-12 0 JimCrowley 1 38
(Ed Dunlop) *w'like: bit bkwd: s.i.s: hld up bhd ldrs: effrt 3f out: wl hld fr 2f out* **6/1**[3]
6 *2 ¼* **Springtime Melody (FR)** 3-9-3 0 FrankieMcDonald 5 39
(David Bourton) *w'like: s.i.s: hld up bhd ldrs: effrt 3f out: wl hld fr 2f out* **25/1**

2m 11.9s (3.10) **Going Correction** -0.025s/f (Good) 6 Ran SP% **112.5**
Speed ratings (Par 101): **86,85,85,78,73 71**
toteswingers:1&2:£1.70, 1&3:£1.80, 2&3:£1.60 CSF £8.73 TOTE £4.00: £1.70, £2.00; EX 8.30 Trifecta £24.80 Pool: £55.92 - 16.51 winning units..
Owner Scuderia Rencati Srl **Bred** Tullamaine Castle Stud **Trained** Newmarket, Suffolk
■ Stewards' Enquiry : Jamie Spencer caution: used whip down shoulder in the forehand.

FOCUS
With half the declared runners taken out, this lost much of its interest, and the form is only fair. It was run in a time more than five seconds slower than the first division. The form is rated slightly negatively around the fourth.
T/Jkpt: Not won. T/Plt: £27.20 to a £1 stake. Pool:£154,451.31 - 4,144.69 winning tickets T/Qpdt: £14.30 to a £1 stake. Pool:£7,998.83 - 411.11 winning tickets TM

2063 NEWMARKET (R-H)
Saturday, May 14

OFFICIAL GOING: Good to firm
Stands' side track used. Stalls on stands' side except 2.50 &3.25 centre.
Wind: Strong, half behind Weather: Cloudy

2105 STOBART BIOMASS H'CAP 1m
1:45 (1:45) (Class 3) (0-95,93) 4-Y-O+ £8,418 (£2,505; £1,251; £625) **Stalls** High

Form RPR
4125 **1** **Benandonner (USA)**[21] 1529 8-9-1 **87** MartinLane 5 95
(Mike Murphy) *pressed ldrs: drvn and nt qckn over 2f out: looked hld after: rallied strly fnl f: styd on wl to ld post* **16/1**
63-6 **2** *hd* **Arabian Spirit**[28] 1410 6-9-0 **86** PaulHanagan 11 94+
(Richard Fahey) *hld up wl in rr: gd prog over 2f out: squeezed through over 1f out: drvn to ld jst ins fnl f: styd on: hdd post* **12/1**
-003 **3** *nse* **Camerooney**[9] 1828 8-8-10 **85** (p) PaulPickard(3) 4 92
(Brian Ellison) *led main gp in centre and on terms w ldr: stl upsides and drvn 1f out: pressed ldr after: jst hld nr fin* **20/1**
10-1 **4** *1 ¾* **Nelson's Bounty**[17] 1603 4-9-0 **86** TonyCulhane 10 89
(Paul D'Arcy) *settled towards rr: rdn and prog on outer over 2f out: clsd on ldrs fnl f: one pce last 100yds* **13/2**[3]
6334 **5** *nk* **Standpoint**[17] 1603 5-8-7 **79** oh1 ChrisCatlin 12 82
(Reg Hollinshead) *mid-div: rdn over 2f out: clsd on ldrs over 1f out: kpt on same pce fnl f* **33/1**
0400 **6** *¾* **Ezdeyaad (USA)**[21] 1529 7-9-0 **86** JackMitchell 14 87
(Ed Walker) *taken down early: racd alone against nr side rail early: led: edgd rt over 2f out: hdd & wknd jst ins fnl f* **80/1**
36-0 **7** *nk* **Viva Vettori**[14] 1684 7-8-11 **83** WilliamBuick 3 83+
(David Elsworth) *s.s: wl adrift in last early and given time to rcvr: sme prog 3f out: rdn and kpt on fnl 2f: nrst fin* **8/1**
4-03 **8** *nk* **Tinshu (IRE)**[12] 1772 5-8-11 **83** AndreaAtzeni 9 83
(Derek Haydn Jones) *in tch in midfield: drvn wl over 2f out: clsd on ldrs over 1f out: wknd last 150yds* **20/1**
-000 **9** *5* **San Cassiano (IRE)**[8] 1849 4-8-13 **85** SebSanders 2 73
(Ruth Carr) *prom on outer: drvn over 2f out: cl enough jst over 1f out: wknd fnl f* **16/1**
11-5 **10** *6* **Nazreef**[28] 1406 4-9-1 **87** (t) TravisBlock 13 61
(Hughie Morrison) *restless stalls: a towards rr: rdn and no prog over 2f out: bhd over 1f out* **5/1**[2]
/0-5 **11** *6* **Beauchamp Yorker**[19] 1564 4-9-4 **90** DaneO'Neill 6 51
(Henry Candy) *s.i.s: sn prom on outer: rdn over 3f out: wknd over 2f out: t.o* **11/1**

122- **12** *2 ½* **Con Artist (IRE)**[282] 4757 4-9-7 **93** .... FrankieDettori 8 48
(Saeed Bin Suroor) *trckd ldrs: rdn over 2f out: wknd rapidly wl over 1f out: eased: t.o* **7/2**[1]

15-0 **13** *½* **Signor Verdi**[28] 1406 4-9-0 **86** .... ShaneKelly 7 40
(Brian Meehan) *dwlt: a in rr: bhd fnl 3f: t.o* **7/1**

1m 36.45s (-2.15) **Going Correction** -0.075s/f (Good) **13** Ran SP% **117.3**
Speed ratings (Par 107): **107,106,106,105,104 103,103,103,98,92 86,83,83**
toteswingers:1&2:£37.90, 1&3:£49.90, 2&3:£39.40 CSF £184.12 CT £3961.77 TOTE £18.10: £4.40, £3.10, £4.40; EX 168.40.

Owner Phil Woods **Bred** Gainsborough Farm Llc **Trained** Westoning, Beds

FOCUS
Despite showers and watering a strong crosswind had dried the ground out to good to firm all over. A good handicap that has been won by some tough milers such as Plum Pudding and Ace Of Hearts in recent years. This looked a competitive contest once again and it fell to another battle-hardened performer.

NOTEBOOK
Benandonner(USA) had not won on turf for nearly two years but is effective on fast ground and was well handicapped on his old form. He built on a decent effort on his previous start and, despite being short of room in the Dip, once in the clear he found extra for pressure to nose ahead near the line.

Arabian Spirit had gained all his wins on flat and/or turning tracks but was 11lb above his last winning mark here. He was delivered with what looked a winning run but could not put the race to bed up the hill and was caught near the line. A return to a flatter track might enable him to gain compensation. (op 11-1)

Camerooney, a multiple winner at 7f who acts on fast ground, also ran well in the Cambridgeshire over further. Back to his last winning mark, he put up another game performance and was only just run out of it. He deserves to win a similar contest before long. (tchd 18-1)

Nelson's Bounty was progressive last season and stepped up again on his return at Ascot. Racing off 5lb higher and up in class, he race more towards the centre of the track than most and did pretty well in the circumstances. (tchd 11-2)

Standpoint had not won for two years but was handicapped to finish close to Nelson's Bounty and ran pretty much to form with that gelding. (op 25-1)

Ezdeyaad(USA), a three-time winner at around this time last season, was 4lb below his last winning mark and performed well having been in the firing line throughout. (op 66-1)

Viva Vettori had run well several times in similar races here and caught the eye staying on after badly missing the break (something confirmed by his rider). However, he has never won on turf but did indicate that is stable is starting to find some form. Official explanation: jockey said horse was slowly away (op 12-1)

Tinshu(IRE) had shown most of her form and gained all her wins at 1m2f but was dropping in trip and did not run badly until fading late on. (op 16-1)

Nazreef was never travelling that well and disappointed. He did have an excuse though, as he panicked and tried to get under the stalls which probably upset him. (tchd 11-2)

Con Artist(IRE) was never travelling that well and also disappointed, finishing up well beaten. (op 3-1 tchd 4-1 in a place)

2106 STOBART GROUP KING CHARLES II STKS (LISTED RACE) 7f
2:15 (2:15) (Class 1) 3-Y-O

£17,031 (£6,456; £3,231; £1,611; £807; £405) **Stalls** High

Form RPR

212- **1** **Codemaster**[224] 6568 3-9-0 96 .... DaneO'Neill 4 115+
(Henry Candy) *hld up in 3rd of centre gp quartet: rdn 2f out: clsd qckly to ld jst over 1f out: edgd lft but r.o wl* **7/2**[3]

53-0 **2** *2* **I Love Me**[13] 1719 3-8-9 103 .... JimmyFortune 3 103
(Andrew Balding) *led centre gp quartet: rdn to ld wl over 1f out: edgd lft and hdd jst over 1f out: styd on but readily outpcd* **11/10**[1]

31-6 **3** *2 ¼* **Masaya**[31] 1317 3-8-9 98 .... ChrisCatlin 5 97
(Clive Brittain) *led nr side pair and clr overall ldr: hdd wl over 1f out: outpcd* **16/1**

64-1 **4** *1 ¼* **Trade Storm**[14] 1674 3-9-0 98 .... DarryllHolland 1 98
(John Gallagher) *hld up last of centre gp quartet: rdn over 2f out: nt qckn over 1f out: hanging lft fnl f* **12/1**

0-03 **5** *½* **Utley (USA)**[31] 1318 3-9-0 110 .... WilliamBuick 2 97
(John Gosden) *trckd ldr in centre: rdn over 2f out: no prog over 1f out: fdd* **3/1**[2]

21- **6** *½* **March On Beetroot**[150] 7880 3-9-0 75 .... RichardMullen 6 95
(Robert Cowell) *hld up bhd ldr on nr side: nvr on terms: shkn up and no prog over 2f out* **28/1**

1m 22.18s (-3.22) **Going Correction** -0.075s/f (Good) **6** Ran SP% **111.9**
Speed ratings (Par 107): **115,112,110,108,108 107**
CSF £7.72 TOTE £4.40: £2.00, £1.40; EX 8.10.

Owner Pearl Bloodstock Ltd **Bred** J Byrne And Partners **Trained** Kingston Warren, Oxon

FOCUS
This Listed race has been a good guide to the Jersey Stakes with Jeremy and Tariq following up at the royal meeting and Fokine finishing runner-up. This did not look the strongest renewal but there were a couple of interesting and unexposed types in the line-up.

NOTEBOOK
Codemaster ◆, who won his maiden on the July course before finishing runner-up in the Redcar Two-Year-Old Trophy, was making his seasonal return. Having his first try at 7f and without having previously encountered fast ground, he looked in trouble when ridden well over 2f out but kept finding for pressure and proved much the strongest up the hill, breaking the track record in the process. He looks a decent prospect and the Jersey Stakes is a logical target now. (op 3-1)

I Love Me, who won a sales race over C&D on her racecourse debut and travelled well in the 1000 Guineas until appearing not to stay, was sent off favourite on this drop in grade. She made the running up the centre and it looked in the Dip as if she might prevail, but her market rival was too strong up the climb to the line. Connections might consider dropping her back to 6f, as there are likely to be more opportunities against her own sex. (op 7-4 tchd 15-8 in places)

Masaya, the winner of a sales race over C&D on soft, had looked less effective on fast going. She made the running nearer the stands' rail but had no more to offer when the market leaders challenged. (op 14-1)

Trade Storm gained both his wins on fast ground at around this trip but was held in a Listed and Group race in between and he failed to cope with this better company again here. He might be better off back in handicaps or conditions races. His rider reported that the colt hung left. Official explanation: jockey said colt hung left (tchd 11-1)

Utley(USA), held in Group company after winning his maiden on soft ground, ran well in the Free Handicap over C&D on fast going and was top rated. He will not find things easy off his current rating on this evidence. (op 5-2 tchd 10-3)

March On Beetroot, both of whose runs before Christmas were on Polytrack, was taking a big step up in grade on this turf debut. Rated just 75, he did not fare too badly considering he was keen early but has probably blown his handicap mark as a result of finishing as close as he did. (op 16-1)

2107 EDDIE STOBART STKS (H'CAP) 1m 6f
2:50 (2:50) (Class 2) (0-105,100) 4-Y-O+

£27,416 (£8,210; £4,105; £2,054; £1,025; £514) **Stalls** Centre

Form RPR

00-0 **1** **Yorgunnabelucky (USA)**[13] 1717 5-9-1 **91** .... (p) JoeFanning 2 101
(Mark Johnston) *mostly pressed ldr: rdn to ld 2f out: hld on wl u.p fnl f* **33/1**

225- **2** *½* **Tactician**[246] 5908 4-9-3 **94** .... HayleyTurner 5 103
(Michael Bell) *trckd ldrs: clsd 4f out: rdn to chse wnr wl over 1f out: no imp ent fnl f: styd on nr fin* **9/2**[1]

10-4 **3** *¾* **Trovare (USA)**[24] 1477 4-8-5 **82** .... JimmyQuinn 12 90
(Amanda Perrett) *hld up bhd ldrs: rdn and nt qckn over 2f out: sn outpcd: rallied fnl f to take 3rd nr fin* **8/1**[3]

00-0 **4** *½* **Chiberta King**[13] 1717 5-9-0 **90** .... (p) JimmyFortune 9 97
(Andrew Balding) *led: hrd rdn and hdd 2f out: one pce after* **14/1**

-302 **5** *3 ¼* **Nave (USA)**[14] 1676 4-8-11 **88** .... GregFairley 3 91
(Mark Johnston) *pressed ldng pair to over 2f out: sn outpcd: kpt on same pce after* **20/1**

0023 **6** *¾* **Tominator**[35] 1238 4-9-0 **91** .... TonyCulhane 10 93
(Reg Hollinshead) *stdd s: hld up in last pair: stl gng wl enough whn bmpd wl over 2f out: styd on fr over 1f out: unable to threaten* **33/1**

45-1 **7** *nk* **High Office**[21] 1517 5-9-0 **90** .... TedDurcan 1 91
(Richard Fahey) *trckd ldrs: rdn 3f out: outpcd over 2f out: no imp over 1f out* **8/1**[3]

42-4 **8** *½* **Abergavenny**[9] 1098 4-8-4 **84** .... PaulPickard(3) 11 85+
(Brian Ellison) *hld up towards rr: stl gng wl whn bmpd wl over 2f out: hung rt and kpt on fr over 1f out: n.d* **9/2**[1]

4-55 **9** *nk* **Nanton (USA)**[13] 1717 9-9-10 **100** .... DanielTudhope 4 100
(Jim Goldie) *stdd s: hld up in last pair: swtchd outside and effrt over 2f out: kpt on after: nvr gng pce to threaten* **14/1**

0-11 **10** *20* **Cosmic Sun**[42] 1102 5-9-5 **95** .... PaulHanagan 14 67
(Richard Fahey) *hld up in rr: rdn and no prog 3f out: sn wknd: t.o* **11/2**[2]

20-0 **11** *4* **La Vecchia Scuola (IRE)**[10] 1808 7-9-6 **96** .... WilliamBuick 6 63
(Jim Goldie) *hld up in rr: rdn over 3f out and no prog: sn wl btn: t.o* **20/1**

211- **12** *19* **Kazbow (IRE)**[323] 3398 5-9-0 **90** .... J-PGuillambert 8 —
(Luca Cumani) *trckd ldrs tl wknd over 3f out: eased: t.o* **10/1**

115- **13** *2 ¼* **Herostatus**[155] 7823 4-9-2 **93** .... (b) FrankieDettori 13 —
(Mark Johnston) *hld up on outer towards rr: rdn over 3f out: hung rt and wknd wl over 2f out: t.o* **14/1**

2m 55.36s (-1.64) **Going Correction** -0.075s/f (Good)
WFA 4 from 5yo+ 1lb **13** Ran SP% **118.5**
Speed ratings (Par 109): **101,100,100,100,98 97,97,97,97,85 83,72,71**
toteswingers:1&2:£38.10, 1&3:£64.00, 2&3:£10.00 CSF £169.04 CT £1332.83 TOTE £36.00: £8.50, £1.90, £3.10; EX 303.30 Trifecta £3974.90 Pool: £61,951.73 - 11.53 winning units..

Owner Mrs S J Brookhouse **Bred** March Thoroughbreds **Trained** Middleham Moor, N Yorks

FOCUS
Decent prize-money produced a competitive field for this stayers' handicap.

NOTEBOOK
Yorgunnabelucky(USA), well suited by good/fast ground, had been held off higher marks since scoring last August and finished well beaten on his return here earlier in the month after a spell over hurdles with Alan King. Back with his former trainer, he came through to lead around 2f from home and battled on well to hold challenges on both sides. Connections might now be thinking in terms of the Ebor later in the season.

Tactician ran well in handicaps at this trip on fast ground last season but was up 8lb following those efforts. Making his seasonal debut, he was produced to challenge two furlongs out and, although he kept on, was always being held by the winner. The outing should bring him on. (op 11-2 tchd 6-1)

Trovare(USA), a three-time winner last season including twice on the July Course, ran well at Epsom on his return and the second and fifth had won subsequently. He tracked the pace throughout and was going as well as any three furlongs out, but his rivals seemed to get away from him soon after and, although he stayed on, he never looked like getting there.

Chiberta King, whose trainer had saddled the last two winners of the race, gained his last success in the race in 2010. Wearing first-time cheekpieces, he made the running and kept going under pressure to post his best effort for a while, just being run out of the paces. This meeting seems to bring out the best in him. (tchd 16-1)

Nave(USA), on the upgrade, had a lot to find with High Office on Musselburgh form but reversed those placings having been in the leading group throughout. A slight drop in grade might enable him to return to winning form. (op 16-1)

Tominator had been showing decent form on the AW over the winter and early spring but had been given a short break since. Up in distance, he stayed on steadily from the back despite having got involved in a barging match with the favourite. (op 40-1)

High Office had been steadily progressive and looked to have improved again when winning on his first try at this trip at Musselburgh. However, all his wins had been on flat tracks and he did not look so effective on this undulating course. (tchd 15-2)

Abergavenny, a dual winner at 1m2f for Mark Johnston last season, was sold for 32,000gns and had won twice over hurdles recently for new connections. Racing off 9lb above his last winning mark, he was short of room and had a barging match with Tominator when trying to make his move and never figured thereafter. (op 5-1 tchd 4-1 and 11-2 in places)

Nanton(USA), whose good efforts in Group races and being placed in two Cambridgeshires had scuppered his chances in handicaps, did gain his last win over this trip. Gradually dropping in the weights, he was doing his best work late on but needs more help from the handicapper to be competitive again.

Cosmic Sun has taken well to the AW this year but his turf mark is 6lb higher. Nevertheless, this run was somewhat disappointing and his rider reported that the gelding was never travelling. Official explanation: jockey said gelding never travelled (op 6-1 tchd 5-1)

La Vecchia Scuola(IRE)'s rider reported that the mare was unsuited by the going. Official explanation: trainer's rep said mare was unsuited by the good to firm ground (op 25-1)

2108 EDDIE STOBART CHILLED H'CAP 1m 4f
3:25 (3:25) (Class 3) (0-95,95) 3-Y-O **£8,418** (£2,505; £1,251; £625) **Stalls** Centre

Form RPR

1-23 **1** **Glencadam Gold (IRE)**[20] 1550 3-9-1 **89** .... IanMongan 5 102+
(Sir Henry Cecil) *hld up in last pair: smooth prog to ld over 2f out: sn in command: idled sltly and shkn up fnl f* **2/1**[2]

1-22 **2** *2 ¼* **Hawaafez**[17] 1622 3-8-11 **85** .... TadhgO'Shea 3 92
(Marcus Tregoning) *led: rdn and hdd over 2f out: no ch w wnr after: kpt on* **7/2**[3]

51-1 **3** *2 ½* **Parlour Games**[24] 1485 3-8-11 **85** .... AhmedAjtebi 8 89
(Mahmood Al Zarooni) *hld up in last pair: prog over 3f out: rdn and nt qckn wl over 2f out: hld after: eased fnl 75yds* **15/8**[1]

1-45 **4** *6* **Argocat (IRE)**[10] 1811 3-8-9 **83** .... ChrisCatlin 4 76
(Paul Cole) *t.k.h: trckd ldng pair: wnt 2nd 5f out to over 3f out: sn wknd* **8/1**

60-0 **5** *1* **Stentorian (IRE)**[35] 1234 3-9-7 **95** .... FrankieDettori 7 87?
(Mark Johnston) *chsd ldr to 5f out: dropped to last and struggling over 3f out: sn bhd* **12/1**

2m 30.66s (-1.34) **Going Correction** -0.075s/f (Good) **5** Ran SP% **109.1**
Speed ratings (Par 103): **101,99,97,93,93**
CSF £9.10 TOTE £3.10: £1.90, £2.00; EX 8.80.
Owner Angus Dundee Distillers plc **Bred** Roalso Ltd **Trained** Newmarket, Suffolk

FOCUS
Another good class handicap despite the three non-runners.

NOTEBOOK
Glencadam Gold(IRE), with the tongue-tie he wore last time left off, travelled well into the race and put this to bed when going on and quickly opening up a lead 2f out. He carried his head high in the closing stages, something he has done before, but kept running and the longer trip seemed to suit. The King George V Handicap at Ascot could be on the agenda now. (tchd 9-4)
Hawaafez does not have much in the way of a change of pace and was sensibly sent off in front on this step up in distance. She kept trying when headed and might end up racing over even further before the end of the season. (op 3-1)
Parlour Games, an AW winner on his return to action, was sent off favourite despite the fact that he had never before encountered fast going. He came to deliver his challenge over 2f out but quickly came under pressure and had no more to offer. The ground rather than a lack of stamina might have been the problem. (op 2-1 tchd 7-4)
Argocat(IRE), whose only win was here, has struggled a bit on fast ground this season and did so again. He is dropping in the weights but will need to improve to be competitive. (op 9-1)
Stentorian(IRE) has lost his way this year after a good juvenile season and was the first beaten. (tchd 10-1)

2109 ELITEDREAMBEDDING.COM NOVICE STKS 6f
4:00 (4:00) (Class 4) 2-Y-O **£4,533** (£1,348; £674; £336) **Stalls** High

Form RPR

01 **1** **B Fifty Two (IRE)**[16] 1628 2-9-2 0 .... SebSanders 4 84
(J W Hills) *cl up: jnd ldr 1/2-way: drvn to ld jst over 1f out: hld on wl last 100yds* **7/1**[3]

1 **2** *hd* **Lilbourne Lad (IRE)**[28] 1383 2-9-5 0 .... PatDobbs 7 86
(Richard Hannon) *mde most: shkn up over 1f out: sn hdd: styd on fnl f: a jst hld* **4/6**[1]

22 **3** *1 1/2* **Tell Dad**[13] 1721 2-9-0 0 .... JMurtagh 5 77
(Richard Hannon) *restless stalls: dwlt: hld up in 5th: plld out and prog to chse ldng pair 2f out: edgd rt over 1f out: kpt on but nvr able to chal* **5/2**[2]

4 *3 3/4* **Casa Bex** 2-9-0 0 .... DaneO'Neill 6 65
(Philip McBride) *v difficult to load into stalls: dwlt: in tch in rr: promising effrt 2f out: rn green and sn outpcd* **33/1**

51 **5** *2* **Snowed In (IRE)**[39] 1143 2-9-2 0 .... LiamKeniry 3 61
(J S Moore) *pressed ldr to 1/2-way: easily outpcd fnl 2f* **50/1**

6 *7* **Manomine** 2-9-0 0 .... ChrisCatlin 1 38
(Clive Brittain) *spd on outer over 3f: wknd qckly* **20/1**

7 *2* **Ooi Long** 2-9-0 0 .... (t) MarcHalford 2 32
(Mark Rimmer) *dwlt: a in last pair: wknd over 2f out* **66/1**

1m 11.78s (-0.42) **Going Correction** -0.075s/f (Good) **7** Ran SP% **112.2**
Speed ratings (Par 95): **99,98,96,91,89 79,77**
toteswingers:1&2:£1.50, 1&3:£1.70, 2&3:£1.30 CSF £11.92 TOTE £8.20: £2.50, £1.10; EX 8.20.
Owner Gary And Linnet Woodward **Bred** Mull Enterprises Ltd **Trained** Upper Lambourn, Berks
■ Stewards' Enquiry : Pat Dobbs caution: used whip down shoulder in the forehand.

FOCUS
This novice stakes traditionally has a single-figure field but has thrown up some decent horses, the best being subsequent Group 1 winner Red Clubs. Three previous winners and three newcomers featured in this seven-runner line-up but none of the latter group were supported in the market and they bet 20-1 bar three.

NOTEBOOK
B Fifty Two(IRE) built on his debut behind Magic City to take a small Bath maiden auction next time. Never far away here, he got to the front in the Dip and showed real tenacity to hold off the renewed challenge of the favourite. He has no fancy entries but his attitude should enable him to win more races. (op 13-2 tchd 15-2)
Lilbourne Lad(IRE) made a winning debut at Doncaster but the form has not worked out that well, although the longer trip was expected to be in his favour. He made the running and battled back when headed and he looks more the sort for sales races rather than Group races at this stage. (op 8-11 tchd 4-5)
Tell Dad, runner-up on both his starts over 5f here, tracked the pace early and looked to be going well enough when switched out to challenge. However, he soon came under pressure once in the clear and the response was less than expected. (op 11-4 tchd 9-4)
Casa Bex, from a family of winners at 7f-1m1f, proved difficult to load into the stalls on this debut but ran reasonably well and should be better for the experience. (op 16-1)
Snowed In(IRE) put his experience to good use to win a Polytrack maiden on his second outing but, after being up with the pace early on this turf debut, dropped away quite quickly from the quarter-mile pole. (op 33-1)

2110 SOUTHEND AIRPORT PERFECT FLYING CONDITIONS STKS 1m
4:35 (4:35) (Class 3) 3-Y-O **£8,418** (£2,505; £1,251) **Stalls** High

Form RPR

12-0 **1** **Neebras (IRE)**[31] 1317 3-8-12 110 .... FrankieDettori 2 111+
(Mahmood Al Zarooni) *taken steadily to post to ld of others: cl up: led 3f out: pushed along and drew rt away fr 2f out: heavily eased last 150yds* **4/6**[1]

-153 **2** *7* **Tinkertown (IRE)**[8] 1850 3-8-12 99 .... ChrisCatlin 1 91
(Paul Cole) *on terms to 1/2-way: sn rdn and struggling: plugged on to take remote 2nd last 100yds* **5/2**[2]

6-32 **3** *1 1/2* **Azrael**[14] 1674 3-8-12 93 .... JamesDoyle 3 88
(Alan McCabe) *led: rdn and hdd 3f out: no ch w wnr after: lost remote 2nd last 100yds* **9/2**[3]

1m 35.29s (-3.31) **Going Correction** -0.075s/f (Good) **3** Ran SP% **106.7**
Speed ratings (Par 103): **113,106,104**
CSF £2.55 TOTE £1.50; EX 1.90.
Owner Godolphin **Bred** Michael E Wates **Trained** Newmarket, Suffolk

FOCUS
A small field conditions stakes but the three previous winners all went on to contest the Hampton Court Stakes at Royal Ascot and all subsequently won or were placed at Listed level. The time was over a second faster than the opening handicap.

NOTEBOOK
Neebras(IRE), who was keen to post when well beaten on his return here last month, was the clear best on official ratings based on his juvenile form. He was taken very steadily to post this time though and that did the trick, as he was always travelling well before settling the issue quickly with 2f to go and coming right away. He has an entry in the St James's Palace Stakes, but the hustle and bustle at the royal meeting might have a negative effect so connections may opt for easier targets. (tchd 8-13 and 8-11)
Tinkertown(IRE) had some decent form at up to 1m2f but was dropping in trip and grade. He was the first under pressure and, although he stayed on again, was not in the same league as the winner. A return to further should be in his favour. (op 9-4 tchd 11-4)
Azrael had a lot to find on the ratings but made the running and did as well as could be expected in comparison with the runner-up. A drop back to 7f might suit. (op 5-1 tchd 11-2)

2111 EDDIE SPOTTERS H'CAP 7f
5:10 (5:10) (Class 4) (0-80,80) 4-Y-O+ **£5,180** (£1,541; £770; £384) **Stalls** High

Form RPR

1-03 **1** **Galatian**[15] 1656 4-9-3 **76** .... JamesMillman 7 88
(Rod Millman) *led: rdn and hdd 2f out: rallied gamely fnl f to ld again last 100yds* **8/1**

21-6 **2** *1/2* **Kingsdine (IRE)**[40] 1138 4-9-4 **77** .... TomMcLaughlin 12 88
(Malcolm Saunders) *trckd ldr: led 2f out gng strly: rdn over 1f out: hdd and nt qckn last 100yds* **4/1**[2]

444- **3** *3 1/4* **Suffolk Punch (IRE)**[134] 8033 4-9-6 **79** .... JimmyFortune 4 82
(Andrew Balding) *pressed ldng pair: rdn and nt qckn over 2f out: one pce and wl hld fr over 1f out* **10/3**[1]

06-0 **4** *3/4* **Master Mylo (IRE)**[17] 1610 4-9-5 **78** .... ShaneKelly 9 79
(Dean Ivory) *taken down early: trckd ldrs: rdn and outpcd 2f out: one pce after* **16/1**

116- **5** *1 1/2* **Fantasy Gladiator**[143] 7970 5-9-7 **80** .... (p) JimmyQuinn 6 77
(Robert Cowell) *awkward s and slowly away: hld up in last trio: rdn over 2f out: limited prog over 1f out: n.d* **11/2**[3]

2123 **6** *hd* **Jake The Snake (IRE)**[38] 1172 10-9-1 **74** .... IanMongan 11 70
(Tony Carroll) *hld up in last pair: rdn over 2f out: one pce and no imp on ldrs* **8/1**

0-04 **7** *4* **Sumbe (USA)**[15] 1656 5-8-7 **66** .... AndreaAtzeni 5 51
(Michael Wigham) *chsd ldrs: rdn over 2f out: steadily wknd* **9/1**

2124 **8** *12* **The Happy Hammer (IRE)**[49] 995 5-8-13 **72** .... ChrisCatlin 8 25
(Eugene Stanford) *restless stalls: t.k.h: hld up in last pair: wknd over 2f out: t.o* **7/1**

400- **9** *5* **Boogie Diva**[238] 6198 4-9-4 **77** .... DarryllHolland 3 16
(George Margarson) *in tch: rdn 3f out: sn btn: t.o* **10/1**

1m 24.02s (-1.38) **Going Correction** -0.075s/f (Good) **9** Ran SP% **118.2**
Speed ratings (Par 105): **104,103,99,98,97 96,92,78,72**
toteswingers:1&2:£9.40, 1&3:£5.60, 2&3:£3.90. Totesuper 7: Win: Not won. Place: £47.40 CSF £41.02 CT £130.81 TOTE £9.40: £2.70, £1.60, £1.70; EX 41.20.
Owner Tarka Racing **Bred** Mrs B A Matthews **Trained** Kentisbeare, Devon

FOCUS
A fair handicap run 1.86secs slower than the record-breaking Listed race earlier on the card and nothing got involved from off the pace.
Fantasy Gladiator Official explanation: jockey said gelding was slowly away
Sumbe(USA) Official explanation: trainer said gelding was unsuited by the good to firm ground
The Happy Hammer(IRE) Official explanation: trainer said gelding was unsuited by the good to firm ground
Boogie Diva Official explanation: trainer said filly was unsuited by the good to firm ground
T/Plt: £473.90 to a £1 stake. Pool:£98,463.32 - 151.65 winning tickets T/Qpdt: £22.10 to a £1 stake. Pool:£5,745.18 - 191.60 winning tickets JN

1906 THIRSK (L-H)
Saturday, May 14

OFFICIAL GOING: Good (9.0)
Wind: Strong, half behind Weather: Cloudy

2112 MARION GIBSON BROWN MEMORIAL H'CAP (DIV I) 1m
1:35 (1:36) (Class 4) (0-85,85) 4-Y-O+ **£4,209** (£1,252; £625; £312) **Stalls** Low

Form RPR

05-4 **1** **Kensei (IRE)**[19] 1560 4-8-8 **72** .... SilvestreDeSousa 10 82+
(David O'Meara) *prom: hdwy on ins to ld over 1f out: drew clr fnl f: eased towards fin* **7/2**[1]

0-40 **2** *2 1/2* **Northern Fling**[14] 1695 7-9-1 **82** .... GaryBartley(3) 1 84
(Jim Goldie) *hld up towards rr: hdwy over 2f out: styd on to go 2nd nr fin: no ch w wnr* **10/1**

5-00 **3** *3/4* **Sir George (IRE)**[28] 1410 6-9-7 **85** .... BarryMcHugh 4 85
(Ollie Pears) *midfield: hdwy and ev ch over 1f out: kpt on same pce fnl f: lost 2nd nr fin* **6/1**[3]

21-0 **4** *1 3/4* **Cara's Request (AUS)**[41] 1110 6-8-13 **84** .... PNolan(7) 2 80
(David Nicholls) *led: qckn 3f out: hdd over 1f out: kpt on same pce* **16/1**

-000 **5** *1/2* **Barren Brook**[12] 1747 4-8-12 **76** .... PaulMulrennan 3 71
(Michael Easterby) *s.i.s: hld up: stdy hdwy 2f out: kpt on fnl f: nvr nr to chal* **22/1**

126- **6** *6* **Xilerator (IRE)**[144] 7955 4-9-6 **84** .... AdrianNicholls 8 65
(David Nicholls) *plld hrd: trckd ldrs: rdn over 2f out: wknd over 1f out* **10/1**

-545 **7** *1 1/4* **Vanilla Rum**[36] 1221 4-8-4 **71** oh1 .... DeclanCannon(3) 9 49
(John Mackie) *hld up: rdn over 2f out: nvr able to chal* **28/1**

60-0 **8** *nk* **Lucky Windmill**[42] 1098 4-9-2 **80** .... PJMcDonald 11 58
(Alan Swinbank) *hld up: rdn over 2f out: nvr rchd ldrs* **7/1**

2-54 **9** *1/2* **Desert Vision**[14] 1671 7-8-9 **73** .... (vt) GrahamGibbons 6 50
(Michael Easterby) *in tch: rdn over 2f out: sn wknd* **8/1**

-121 **10** *6* **Cono Zur (FR)**[12] 1747 4-8-10 **77** .... JamesSullivan(3) 5 40
(Ruth Carr) *chsd ldr: rdn and wknd over 2f out* **4/1**[2]

001- **11** *1/2* **Bond City (IRE)**[204] 7063 9-8-10 **79** .... DanielleMcCreery(5) 7 41
(Geoffrey Oldroyd) *hld up on outside: struggling 3f out: sn wknd* **22/1**

1m 39.34s (-0.76) **Going Correction** +0.05s/f (Good) **11** Ran SP% **116.3**
Speed ratings (Par 105): **105,102,101,100,99 93,92,91,91,85 84**
Tote Swingers: 1&2 £11.80, 1&3 £7.20, 2&3 £11.30 CSF £37.48 CT £208.46 TOTE £4.50: £1.40, £4.40, £2.00; EX 51.90.
Owner Archibald Nichol **Bred** Paget Bloodstock Ltd **Trained** Nawton, N Yorks

FOCUS
A fair handicap which was run at a decent pace thanks to Cara's Request.
Cono Zur(FR) Official explanation: jockey said gelding ran flat

2113 BRITISH STALLION STUDS SUPPORTING BRITISH RACING E B F MAIDEN FILLIES' STKS 5f
2:05 (2:11) (Class 4) 2-Y-O **£4,533** (£1,348; £674; £336) **Stalls** High

Form RPR

1 **Lexington Spirit (IRE)** 2-9-0 0 .... TonyHamilton 10 73+
(Richard Fahey) *prom: a gng wl: smooth hdwy to ld over 1f out: qcknd clr ins fnl f: readily* **6/1**[3]

04 **2** *2 1/2* **Red Shadow**[28] 1414 2-9-0 0 .... SilvestreDeSousa 3 59
(Alan Brown) *unruly bef s: w ldrs: ev ch and hung lft over 1f out: kpt on fnl f: nt gng pce of wnr* **9/1**

3 ¾ **Rhianna Brianna (IRE)** 2-8-11 0 JamesSullivan(3) 11 56
(Michael Easterby) *missed break: bhd: hdwy and hung lft over 1f out: kpt on wl fnl f: nrst fin* **25/1**

36 4 shd **Nellie Pickersgill**[17] 1619 2-9-0 0 DuranFentiman 4 56
(Tim Easterby) *cl up: effrt and ev ch over 1f out: kpt on same pce fnl f* **14/1**

5 ½ **Chorister Girl** 2-9-0 0 PaulMulrennan 14 54
(Howard Johnson) *in tch: drvn over 2f out: edgd lft over 1f out: kpt on fnl f* **6/1**[3]

0 6 shd **Dolly Danca**[14] 1691 2-9-0 0 MickyFenton 12 54
(Paul Midgley) *mde most tl hdd over 1f out: kpt on same pce fnl f* **40/1**

0 7 1¼ **Headstight (IRE)**[38] 1165 2-9-0 0 BarryMcHugh 9 49
(Paul Midgley) *in tch: rdn over 2f out: edgd lft and kpt on same pce fnl f* **28/1**

8 nse **Zaffy (IRE)** 2-9-0 0 DavidAllan 16 49
(Tim Easterby) *missed break: bhd and rdn along: kpt on fnl f: nvr nrr* **4/1**[1]

9 hd **Busy Bimbo (IRE)** 2-9-0 0 PatrickMathers 13 48
(Alan Berry) *s.i.s: bhd and sn pushed along: no imp tl kpt on fnl f: nrst fin* **33/1**

10 hd **Justine Time (IRE)** 2-9-0 0 LeeNewman 6 47
(David Barron) *prom tl rdn and outpcd fr 2f out* **14/1**

11 1½ **Elegant Flight** 2-8-11 0 MatthewDavies(3) 2 42
(Alan Jarvis) *cl up on outside: rdn and hung lft over 1f out: sn wknd* **22/1**

12 3¼ **Come Hither** 2-9-0 0 GrahamGibbons 1 30
(Michael Easterby) *missed break and swvd bdly lft s: bhd and rdn along: nvr on terms* **40/1**

5 13 ¾ **Maria Anna (IRE)**[8] 1876 2-9-0 0 PhillipMakin 5 27
(Ann Duffield) *towards rr: drvn along 1/2-way: nvr on terms* **12/1**

14 3¼ **Lady Victory (IRE)** 2-9-0 0 SamHitchcott 8 15
(Mick Channon) *dwlt: sn pushed along towards rr: nvr on terms* **9/2**[2]

15 1¾ **Roger Sez (IRE)** 2-9-0 0 RobertWinston 7 8
(Tim Easterby) *towards rr: bhd and rn green over 2f out: sn btn* **16/1**

16 5 **Isolde's Return** 2-9-0 0 PJMcDonald 15 —
(George Moore) *missed break: bhd and sn struggling: no ch fr 1/2-way* **40/1**

60.54 secs (0.94) **Going Correction** -0.175s/f (Firm) **16** Ran SP% **125.6**
Speed ratings (Par 92): **85,81,79,79,78 78,76,76,76,75 73,68,67,61,59 51**
Tote Swingers: 1&2 £6.10, 1&3 £42.60, 2&3 £64.50 CSF £56.68 TOTE £7.50: £3.00, £3.30, £12.80; EX 72.20.
Owner Middleham Park Racing XXXIV **Bred** Kildaragh Stud **Trained** Musley Bank, N Yorks

FOCUS
A couple of these fillies proved very awkward in the preliminaries, but this may not have been a bad race of its type as three of the newcomers attracted good market support so were obviously fancied.

NOTEBOOK
Lexington Spirit(IRE) ◆, a £26,000 half-sister to a 7f winner in France, was travelling like a winner from some way out and showed a nice turn of foot to lead entering the last furlong. She won so easily that her rider was able to admire himself on the big screen and the filly looks capable of going on to rather better things. (op 11-2)
Red Shadow, despite being one of the most experienced in the field, proved a real handful beforehand, unshipping her rider twice and running loose. However, she showed a lot of speed once under way and can win a race like this providing her temperament doesn't get the better of her. (op 7-1)
Rhianna Brianna(IRE), a half-sister to a dual winner at up to an extended 1m, finished with a real flourish from off the pace and normal improvement should win her a maiden. Official explanation: jockey said filly hung left (op 22-1)
Nellie Pickersgill was disappointing at Pontefract last time after her encouraging Beverley debut and ran rather better here having been handy from the off, but she will remain vulnerable to less exposed types. (op 12-1)
Chorister Girl, out of a dual winner over 6f-7f, was one of the newcomers to attract market support and she ran well until hanging away to her left inside the last furlong. She obviously has ability. Official explanation: jockey said filly hung left (op 11-1)
Dolly Danca showed early speed before fading over C&D last month and lasted longer in front this time. A small race on a quick track may come her way. (op 50-1)
Zaffy(IRE), a £28,000 filly out of a half-sister to two winners at up to 1m2f, was well supported but she fell out of stalls and gave the leaders a huge advantage. However, the way she stayed on up the stands' rail suggested that she does possess ability. (op 8-1)
Elegant Flight, out of a 7f juvenile winner, was another to prove awkward before the start, but she ran better than it may have seemed as she showed good speed despite being rather marooned out in the centre of the track. This May foal can do better. (op 25-1 tchd 16-1)
Lady Victory(IRE), a £37,000 half-sister to last year's Brocklesby winner Chiswick Bey, was another well backed but she was always struggling and proved disappointing. (op 6-1 tchd 4-1)
Roger Sez(IRE) Official explanation: jockey said filly hung left

2114 WHITBY MAIDEN STKS 1m 4f
2:40 (2:43) (Class 5) 3-Y-O+ **£2,914** (£867; £433; £216) **Stalls** Low

Form RPR

0-6 1 **Ardlui (IRE)**[28] 1407 3-8-9 0 FergusSweeney 8 92+
(Henry Candy) *trckd ldrs: led 2f out: rdn clr: comf* **11/10**[1]

3-0 2 7 **Rio's Rosanna (IRE)**[24] 1496 4-9-9 0 RussKennemore 4 78
(Richard Whitaker) *midfield: hdwy over 3f out: rdn over 2f out: wnt 2nd over 1f out: kpt on to pull clr rest: no ch w wnr* **28/1**

3 8 **Tricksofthetrade (IRE)**[18] 5-10-0 0 PJMcDonald 10 70
(Alan Swinbank) *slowly away: sn pushed along into midfield: hdwy to chse ldrs 3f out: sn rdn: kpt on to take 3rd ins fnl f* **11/2**

4- 4 1¼ **Unex Picasso**[192] 7303 3-8-9 0 PhillipMakin 9 66
(William Haggas) *s.i.s: led after 1f: rdn whn hdd 2f out: wknd ins fnl f* **11/4**[2]

2 5 2½ **Body Language (IRE)**[17] 1616 3-8-4 0 SilvestreDeSousa 14 57
(Ann Duffield) *trckd ldrs: pushed along over 4f out: wnt 2nd over 3f out: rdn over 2f out: wknd over 1f out* **4/1**[3]

5- 6 8 **Rosie Raymond**[409] 1067 6-9-9 0 RobbieFitzpatrick 6 46
(Charles Smith) *hld up: sme hdwy over 3f out: one pce: n.d* **100/1**

50 7 hd **Lure of The Night (IRE)**[24] 1492 4-9-11 0 SeanLevey(3) 12 51
(Brian Rothwell) *in tch: rdn over 3f out: wknd fnl 2f* **150/1**

3 8 ½ **Harvey's Hope**[24] 1492 5-10-0 0 TonyHamilton 1 50
(Keith Reveley) *hld up: pushed along over 4f out: no imp* **33/1**

05 9 26 **Serenader**[28] 1386 4-9-11 0 NataliaGemelova(3) 11 —
(David O'Meara) *midfield: pushed along over 5f out: wknd over 3f out* **100/1**

0 10 9 **Perfect Deal**[58] 878 4-10-0 0 DavidNolan 5 —
(Michael Easterby) *dwlt: hld up: a towards rr* **150/1**

00 11 31 **Poosie Nansie (IRE)**[11] 1799 4-9-4 0 (p) DaleSwift(5) 2 —
(George Foster) *hld up: reminders over 7f out: sn bhd* **200/1**

/-00 12 13 **Into Mac**[19] 1559 5-10-0 0 PaulMulrennan 7 —
(Neville Bycroft) *led for 1f: trckd ldrs: rdn over 4f out: wknd over 3f out* **100/1**

3 13 3¾ **The Snorer**[31] 1304 3-8-9 0 GrahamGibbons 13 —
(John Holt) *prom: rdn over 4f out: wknd qckly: t.o* **66/1**

2m 35.41s (-0.79) **Going Correction** +0.05s/f (Good)
WFA 3 from 4yo+ 19lb **13** Ran SP% **122.3**
Speed ratings (Par 103): **104,99,94,93,91 86,86,85,68,62 41,33,30**
Tote Swingers: 1&2 £15.70, 1&3 £3.60, 2&3 £38.50 CSF £42.79 TOTE £1.30: £6.10, £2.10; EX 62.90.
Owner Thomas Barr **Bred** Sunderland Holdings Ltd **Trained** Kingston Warren, Oxon
■ Stewards' Enquiry : Sean Levey caution: eased gelding approaching line.

FOCUS
A very uncompetitive maiden with only four holding any sort of chance according to the betting.

2115 MARION GIBSON BROWN MEMORIAL H'CAP (DIV II) 1m
3:15 (3:17) (Class 4) (0-85,84) 4-Y-O+ **£4,209** (£1,252; £625; £312) **Stalls** Low

Form RPR

00-6 1 **Extraterrestrial**[41] 1110 7-9-6 **83** FrederikTylicki 5 96+
(Richard Fahey) *in tch: smooth hdwy to ld over 1f out: rdn clr fnl f: eased towards fin* **7/4**[1]

-030 2 4½ **Academy Blues (USA)**[17] 1603 6-9-7 **84** AdrianNicholls 3 84
(David Nicholls) *t.k.h: trckd ldrs: effrt and hung rt over 1f out: chsd (clr) wnr ins fnl f: no imp* **15/2**

0-00 3 ¾ **Champagne Style (USA)**[14] 1696 4-8-13 **79** RobertLButler(3) 7 77
(Richard Guest) *hld up: effrt and swtchd rt wl over 1f out: edgd lft and kpt on fnl f: nrst fin* **20/1**

121- 4 ½ **Dream Win**[259] 5533 5-8-9 **75** SeanLevey(3) 1 72
(Brian Ellison) *cl up: led and rdn over 2f out: hdd over 1f out: kpt on same pce fnl f* **4/1**[2]

40-4 5 4 **Daring Dream (GER)**[14] 1696 6-8-9 **72** AndrewMullen 9 60
(Jim Goldie) *racd wd 3f: cl up: rdn over 2f out: edgd lft and wknd over 1f out* **11/2**[3]

-000 6 3¼ **Aerodynamic (IRE)**[14] 1696 4-9-0 **77** PaulMulrennan 8 57
(Clive Mulhall) *bhd: struggling over 3f out: sme late hdwy: nvr on terms* **28/1**

6-60 7 nk **Chosen Forever**[100] 405 6-8-8 **71** TomEaves 10 51
(Geoffrey Oldroyd) *hld up: struggling 3f out: nvr on terms* **12/1**

-031 8 ½ **Mountain Cat (IRE)**[36] 1222 7-9-2 **79** RobertWinston 4 57
(Mrs K Burke) *led to over 2f out: no ex whn hmpd over 1f out: sn btn* **9/1**

500- 9 3 **Without Prejudice (USA)**[211] 6888 6-9-7 **84** GrahamGibbons 2 56
(Michael Easterby) *s.i.s: bhd: drvn 3f out: sn btn* **22/1**

1m 40.21s (0.11) **Going Correction** +0.05s/f (Good) **9** Ran SP% **113.8**
Speed ratings (Par 105): **101,96,95,95,91 88,87,87,84**
Tote Swingers: 1&2 £3.90, 1&3 £10.60, 2&3 £8.50 CSF £14.74 CT £192.57 TOTE £2.10: £1.10, £2.30, £3.40; EX 13.40.
Owner G J Paver **Bred** Lostford Manor Stud **Trained** Musley Bank, N Yorks

FOCUS
The winning time was 0.87 seconds slower than the first division, but it produced just as emphatic a winner.
Mountain Cat(IRE) Official explanation: trainer said gelding had a breathing problem

2116 STONEACRE FORD H'CAP 6f
3:50 (3:52) (Class 3) (0-90,89) 4-Y-O+ **£6,476** (£1,927; £963; £481) **Stalls** High

Form RPR

0-41 1 **Mon Brav**[20] 1539 4-8-10 **81** SeanLevey(3) 2 91+
(Brian Ellison) *racd far side: trckd ldrs: led over 1f out and overall ldr: sn edgd rt: drvn and hld on wl towards fin* **10/1**

0-50 2 ¾ **Advanced**[7] 1885 8-9-3 **88** (p) AmyRyan(3) 15 96
(Kevin Ryan) *prom stands' side: rdn over 2f out: led gp 1f out: kpt on wl ins fnl f: 1st of 8 in gp* **13/2**[1]

-224 3 ½ **Internationaldebut (IRE)**[14] 1675 6-9-6 **88** (p) MickyFenton 12 94
(Paul Midgley) *racd stands' side: chsd ldrs: rdn over 2f out: kpt on ins fnl f: 2nd of 8 in gp* **7/1**[2]

40-0 4 shd **Ursula (IRE)**[41] 1109 5-8-8 **76** AndrewElliott 17 82
(Mrs K Burke) *racd stands' side: hld up in tch: rdn and hdwy over 1f out: kpt on ins fnl f: 3rd of 8 in gp* **16/1**

1006 5 shd **Arganil (USA)**[14] 1680 6-9-5 **87** (b) PhillipMakin 6 93
(Kevin Ryan) *racd far side: s.i.s: sn chsd along in rr: hdwy over 1f out: kpt on wl ins fnl f: 2nd of 8 in gp* **20/1**

6-20 6 1¼ **Bosun Breese**[14] 1698 6-8-8 **76** LeeNewman 4 78
(David Barron) *prom on far side: rdn over 1f out: kpt on ins fnl f: 3rd of 8 in gp* **40/1**

1-53 7 nk **Whozthecat (IRE)**[14] 1675 4-9-2 **89** (b[1]) NeilFarley(5) 14 90
(Declan Carroll) *led stands' side and overall ldr: rdn over 2f out: edgd lft over 1f out: sn hdd: no ex ins fnl f: 4th of 8 in gp* **7/1**[2]

110- 8 nk **Amenable (IRE)**[239] 6142 4-9-7 **89** AndrewMullen 5 89
(David Nicholls) *sn led far side: rdn whn hdd over 1f out: no ex ins fnl f: 4th of 8 in gp* **25/1**

0-01 9 nk **River Falcon**[7] 1907 11-8-7 **78** MartinHarley(3) 9 77
(Jim Goldie) *racd far side: hld up in tch: rdn over 2f out: kpt on ins fnl f: 5th of 8 in gp* **14/1**

0-05 10 1½ **Rash Judgement**[35] 1242 6-9-7 **89** RobertWinston 8 83
(Eric Alston) *racd far side: hld up in tch: hdwy over 2f out: ev ch over 1f out: wknd fnl 100yds: 6th of 8 in gp* **25/1**

02-6 11 1¼ **Ginger Ted (IRE)**[14] 1695 4-9-1 **83** (p) RobbieFitzpatrick 16 73
(Richard Guest) *racd stands' side: hld up: rdn over 2 out: one pce: 5th of 8 in gp* **18/1**

-251 12 1½ **Discanti (IRE)**[8] 1878 6-9-6 **88** (t) DuranFentiman 3 73
(Tim Easterby) *racd far side: trckd ldrs: rdn over 2f out: wknd over 1f out: 7th of 8 in gp* **12/1**

200- 13 ¾ **Roker Park (IRE)**[239] 6142 6-9-0 **82** SilvestreDeSousa 10 65
(David O'Meara) *chsd ldrs stands' side: wknd over 1f out: 6th of 8 in gp* **15/2**[3]

0-06 14 2¾ **Hamoody (USA)**[13] 1720 7-9-3 **85** AdrianNicholls 11 59
(David Nicholls) *chsd ldrs stands' side: wknd over 1f out: 7th of 8 in gp* **7/1**[2]

000- 15 1½ **Bonnie Charlie**[217] 6749 5-9-0 **85** MichaelO'Connell(3) 1 54
(David Nicholls) *racd far side: hld up in tch: wknd over 1f out: last of 8 in gp* **12/1**

0-00 16 2¼ **Earlsmedic**[95] 455 6-8-7 **75** oh1 (v) WilliamCarson 13 37
(Stuart Williams) *towards rr stands' side: rdn over 3f out: wknd over 1f out* **80/1**

1m 10.51s (-2.19) **Going Correction** -0.175s/f (Firm) **16** Ran SP% **121.0**
Speed ratings (Par 107): **107,106,105,105,105 103,103,102,102,100 98,96,95,91,89 86**
Tote Swingers: 1&2 £17.30, 1&3 £17.00, 2&3 £11.10 CSF £68.94 TOTE £13.30: £2.70, £1.30, £2.80, £4.80; EX 88.80.

Owner Koo's Racing Club **Bred** J D Graham **Trained** Norton, N Yorks
■ Stewards' Enquiry : Sean Levey three-day ban: used whip with excessive frequency (May 28-30)

FOCUS
There was a sharp shower before this race. A competitive sprint handicap and the field split into two equal groups of eight. Those that raced towards the nearside had a marginal advantage, as although the winner was draw low he hung over towards the nearside late on.

NOTEBOOK
Mon Brav came into this 1-1 at the track and was up 6lb after making a successful debut for the yard from a subsequent winner at Musselburgh last month. Having been sent to the front of the far-side group over 1f out, he then hung away to his right under pressure but was always doing more than enough. He seems to have thrived for the change of scenery. (tchd 11-1)
Advanced was always close to the pace towards the nearside and led that group a furlong out, but he could never get to the winner. He is currently rated 26lb below his peak, but is on a losing run of 20. (op 9-1)
Internationaldebut(IRE) came into this on a losing run of 26 and had cheekpieces on for the first time. He was doing all his best work late towards the nearside and this was another good effort, but despite his length of time without a win he is 6lb higher than at the start of the season. (op 8-1)
Ursula(IRE) ◆ finished with quite a flourish against the nearside rail and is becoming much better handicapped. (op 22-1)
Arganil(USA), rated 20lb lower than in his prime, stayed on to emerge second-best of the far-side group but he hasn't scored on turf since September 2008. (op 33-1)
Bosun Breese, who ran poorly here last time, performed better here as he was never far away against the far rail, but he does look a bit better over the minimum trip. (op 33-1)
Whozthecat(IRE), 1-1 at Thirsk before this, had blinkers on for the first time and showed plenty of early speed in the nearside group, but he didn't get home. Official explanation: jockey said gelding hung left (op 13-2)
Amenable(IRE), not seen since running poorly in last year's Ayr Bronze Cup, ran well for a long way in the far-side group and can be expected to benefit from the outing.
Hamoody(USA) Official explanation: jockey said gelding hung left

2117 GREEN FARM HEALTH H'CAP 5f
4:25 (4:25) (Class 2) (0-100,99) 4-Y-0+ **£9,714** (£2,890; £1,444; £721) **Stalls** High

Form RPR
300- **1** **Singeur (IRE)**[204] 7060 4-9-0 **92** .... LeeNewman 9 101
(Robin Bastiman) *hld up: hdwy stands' rail appr fnl f: styd on wl to ld nr fin* **14/1**
0200 **2** ½ **Silaah**[13] 1720 7-8-12 **90** .... (p) AdrianNicholls 12 97
(David Nicholls) *t.k.h: led: rdn and hung lft over 1f out: edgd rt u.p ins fnl f: kpt on: hdd nr fin* **5/2**[1]
-320 **3** 1 **Beat The Bell**[10] 1809 6-8-12 **90** .... GrahamGibbons 6 94
(David Barron) *prom: rdn over 2f out: styd on ins fnl f* **9/2**[2]
20-4 **4** nk **Favourite Girl (IRE)**[14] 1680 5-8-13 **91** .... (v) DavidAllan 5 94
(Tim Easterby) *w ldrs: rdn 2f out: kpt on same pce ins fnl f* **5/1**[3]
0330 **5** ½ **Lui Rei (ITY)**[13] 1720 5-9-7 **99** .... RobertWinston 8 100+
(Robert Cowell) *stdd s: hld up: effrt and swtchd rt over 1f out: styd on fnl f: nrst fin* **15/2**
-006 **6** ½ **Masta Plasta (IRE)**[21] 1518 8-9-4 **96** .... PaulQuinn 4 95
(David Nicholls) *w ldrs tl rdn and no ex ins fnl f* **20/1**
-321 **7** ½ **Oldjoesaid**[14] 1698 7-8-7 **85** oh2 .... BarryMcHugh 1 82
(Kevin Ryan) *trckd ldrs: rdn 2f out: nt qckn over 1f out* **7/1**
0-15 **8** 2½ **Lucky Numbers (IRE)**[8] 1849 5-8-8 **89** .... JamesSullivan(3) 3 77
(Paul Green) *in tch: drvn and outpcd 2f out: n.d after* **12/1**
-000 **9** 1½ **Green Park (IRE)**[10] 1809 8-8-6 **89** .... (b) NeilFarley(5) 2 72
(Declan Carroll) *dwlt: bhd and rdn along 1/2-way: nvr on terms* **33/1**
0-00 **10** ½ **Archers Road (IRE)**[10] 1809 4-9-0 **92** .... SamHitchcott 10 73
(David Barron) *prom tl rdn and wknd over 1f out* **20/1**
0-00 **11** 6 **Hotham**[14] 1675 8-8-9 **87** .... PaulMulrennan 7 46
(Noel Wilson) *prom: drvn along 1/2-way: wknd fr 2f out* **28/1**
59.26 secs (-0.34) **Going Correction** -0.025s/f (Good) **11** Ran SP% **118.0**
Speed ratings (Par 109): **101,100,98,98,97 96,95,91,89,88 78**
Tote Swingers: 1&2 £12.90, 1&3 £16.10, 2&3 £3.10 CSF £47.04 CT £194.49 TOTE £22.80: £4.90, £1.80, £2.00; EX 80.90.
Owner Ms M Austerfield **Bred** Patrick Cassidy **Trained** Cowthorpe, N Yorks

FOCUS
The rain continued to come down in the lead up to this race. A decent sprint handicap in which they stayed close to the nearside rail.

NOTEBOOK
Singeur(IRE) had been off since October and hadn't won since he was a juvenile though he apparently has suffered from foot problems, but the handicapper had at least shown him some mercy. He was switched off out the back early, but he was probably helped a good deal by the runner-up hanging away to his left as it left him with a yawning gap against the nearside rail, and he took advantage to hit the front inside the last furlong. A rise back up the weights is inevitable, but with his confidence now restored it wouldn't be a surprise to see him back this up. (op 16-1)
Silaah showed plenty of speed when a close seventh in a hot handicap at Newmarket earlier this month and arguably should have won this. Having shown his usual early pace again here, he hung away to his left from well over a furlong out and that left him vulnerable to the winner's late burst against the rail. (op 11-4 tchd 10-3)
Beat The Bell ◆ was undone by the draw at Chester last time and this was more like it. He was running on well inside the last furlong and looks more than capable of winning a decent sprint handicap this season. (op 5-1)
Favourite Girl(IRE), all the better for last month's Goodwood reappearance effort, was always up there and, although she was carried out to her left by the hanging Silaah from over a furlong out, her chance of winning wasn't affected. She should be winning again before long. (op 13-2)
Lui Rei(ITY) ◆ hasn't won since coming to Britain last summer, but he ran much better than his finishing position would suggest at Newmarket last time. He was the main eye-catcher here too, making up plenty of late ground from off the pace without being by any means knocked about. He is one to watch very closely. (op 7-1)
Masta Plasta(IRE) ran fast for a long way, but he hasn't won a handicap since July 2008. (op 16-1 tchd 22-1)
Oldjoesaid was 2lb wrong, which meant he was 6lb higher than when winning over C&D a fortnight earlier. He didn't run badly under the circumstances as he was forced to race on the outside of the field from his low draw. (op 13-2)
Archers Road(IRE) Official explanation: jockey said gelding stopped very quickly final furlong

2118 FILEY H'CAP 5f
5:00 (5:00) (Class 4) (0-85,85) 4-Y-0+ **£4,533** (£1,348; £674; £336) **Stalls** High

Form RPR
-140 **1** **Le Toreador**[14] 1698 6-9-0 **78** .... (p) PhillipMakin 15 86
(Kevin Ryan) *trckd ldrs: effrt over 1f out: styd on wl u.p to ld towards fin* **15/2**[2]
663- **2** shd **Strike Up The Band**[208] 6981 8-9-3 **84** .... MichaelO'Connell(3) 17 92
(David Nicholls) *led: rdn over 1f out: edgd lft ins fnl f: kpt on: hdd towards fin* **12/1**
20-0 **3** ¾ **Lost In Paris (IRE)**[14] 1698 5-9-0 **78** .... GrahamGibbons 4 83+
(Tim Easterby) *midfield: rdn 1/2-way: effrt over 1f out: styd on ins fnl f: nrst fin* **18/1**
54-0 **4** 1 **The Nifty Fox**[20] 1539 7-9-5 **83** .... DavidAllan 11 85
(Tim Easterby) *midfield: effrt and pushed along 2f out: styd on fnl f: nrst fin* **14/1**
0-10 **5** ½ **Magical Macey (USA)**[14] 1680 4-9-4 **82** .... (b) LeeNewman 5 82
(David Barron) *cl up: rdn over 2f out: kpt on same ins pce fnl f* **14/1**
13-5 **6** nk **Diman Waters (IRE)**[14] 1675 4-9-4 **82** .... (b[1]) RobertWinston 12 81
(Eric Alston) *in tch: effrt and rdn 2f out: edgd lft over 1f out: kpt on same pce fnl f* **7/2**[1]
3503 **7** 1 **Cape Royal**[24] 1476 11-8-9 **76** .... (bt) MartinHarley(3) 14 71
(Milton Bradley) *cl up tl rdn and nt qckn fnl f* **14/1**
064- **8** 3 **Master Rooney (IRE)**[352] 2465 5-9-6 **84** .... PaulMulrennan 7 68
(Bryan Smart) *dwlt: bhd: shkn up and sme hdwy over 1f out: nvr nr ldrs* **16/1**
1-00 **9** ½ **Haajes**[14] 1675 7-9-7 **85** .... MickyFenton 10 68
(Paul Midgley) *hld up: pushed along over 2f out: nvr able to chal* **25/1**
1110 **10** 1 **Dickie Le Davoir**[8] 1878 7-9-1 **82** .... (b) RobertLButler(3) 13 61
(Richard Guest) *dwlt: bhd: effrt on outside 2f out: nvr rchd ldrs* **14/1**
20-0 **11** nse **Pavershooz**[20] 1539 6-9-6 **84** .... AndrewElliott 9 63
(Noel Wilson) *midfield: hung lft and shkn up over 1f out: sn outpcd* **28/1**
-002 **12** 1 **Legal Eagle (IRE)**[8] 1878 6-8-8 **79** .... (p) DuilioDaSilva(7) 8 54
(Paul Green) *midfield on outside: rdn 1/2-way: btn over 1f out* **10/1**[3]
6-03 **13** 3 **Indian Trail**[14] 1698 11-9-4 **82** .... (v) AdrianNicholls 3 46
(David Nicholls) *towards rr: struggling 1/2-way: nvr on terms* **15/2**[2]
020- **14** 4 **Bedloe's Island (IRE)**[199] 7180 6-8-4 **71** oh1 .... JamesSullivan(3) 2 21
(Neville Bycroft) *rdr slow to remove blindfold and s.s: nvr on terms* **16/1**
15-1 **15** 3¼ **Stratton Banker (IRE)**[122] 125 4-8-11 **75** .... WilliamCarson 1 13
(Stuart Williams) *hld up on outside: struggling 2f out: sn btn* **10/1**[3]
58.79 secs (-0.81) **Going Correction** -0.025s/f (Good) **15** Ran SP% **122.6**
Speed ratings (Par 105): **105,104,103,102,101 100,99,94,93,91 91,90,85,79,73**
Tote Swingers: 1&2 £17.00, 1&3 £47.80, 2&3 £77.50 CSF £95.72 CT £1613.78 TOTE £9.40: £3.30, £3.70, £8.40; EX 77.20.
Owner Guy Reed **Bred** G Reed **Trained** Hambleton, N Yorks

FOCUS
A fair sprint handicap in which the whole field raced towards the nearside of the track. It proved crucial to race handily as nothing was able to get into it from off the pace.

2119 SANDS END H'CAP 1m
5:35 (3:36) (Class 6) (0-65,65) 3-Y-0 **£2,590** (£770; £385; £192) **Stalls** Low

Form RPR
026- **1** **Hernando Torres**[196] 7224 3-9-0 **58** .... GrahamGibbons 5 68
(Michael Easterby) *hld up towards rr: pushed along 1/2-way: gd hdwy 2f out: led ent fnl f: sn clr: readily* **9/1**
05-0 **2** 2½ **White Fusion**[28] 1415 3-8-11 **55** .... PaulMulrennan 4 59
(Howard Johnson) *hld up: hdwy on outside over 2f out: chsd (clr) wnr wl ins fnl f: no imp* **25/1**
000- **3** ¾ **Oetzi**[212] 6875 3-9-1 **62** .... MatthewDavies(3) 13 64
(Alan Jarvis) *trckd ldrs: effrt over 2f out: kpt on u.p fnl f* **12/1**
-330 **4** 3¾ **Philharmonic Hall**[17] 1611 3-9-7 **65** .... (b[1]) TonyHamilton 12 58
(Richard Fahey) *cl up: rdn and ev ch over 2f out: no ex fnl f* **17/2**
-005 **5** 1¼ **Coracle**[10] 1812 3-8-4 **55** .... LeonnaMayor(7) 1 46
(David Nicholls) *in tch: effrt on ins wl over 1f out: no imp fnl f* **33/1**
060- **6** nk **Illustrious Forest**[239] 6159 3-8-13 **60** .... JamesSullivan(3) 10 50
(John Mackie) *t.k.h: prom: rdn 3f out: edgd lft and no imp over 1f out* **20/1**
3-61 **7** ½ **Fire Crystal**[11] 1790 3-8-10 **57** .... MartinHarley(3) 9 46
(Mick Channon) *trckd ldrs: effrt over 2f out: wknd ent fnl f* **13/2**[2]
4-56 **8** 2¼ **Valley Tiger**[17] 1609 3-9-3 **61** .... PhillipMakin 2 44
(William Muir) *s.i.s: t.k.h: hld up: pushed along whn n.m.r 2f out: nvr rchd ldrs* **12/1**
13-0 **9** 1 **Reason To Believe (IRE)**[38] 1169 3-9-4 **65** .... PatrickDonaghy(3) 7 46
(Ben Haslam) *fly-jmpd s: hld up on outside: rdn 3f out: nvr able to chal* **14/1**
6311 **10** nk **Trading**[24] 1494 3-9-7 **65** .... DavidAllan 11 49
(Tim Easterby) *led: rdn over 2f out: hdd ent fnl f: wknd* **3/1**[1]
4-50 **11** 1¼ **Suddenly Susan (IRE)**[17] 1624 3-9-4 **62** .... (p) AdrianNicholls 3 40
(David Nicholls) *t.k.h in midfield: rdn over 2f out: btn over 1f out* **10/1**
0-02 **12** 20 **Rapturous Applause**[5] 1944 3-9-2 **60** .... KellyHarrison 6 —
(Micky Hammond) *midfield: rdn over 3f out: wknd over 2f out: t.o* **8/1**[3]
000- **13** 3¼ **Tommy Tiger**[189] 7345 3-8-12 **56** .... MickyFenton 8 —
(Stuart Williams) *hld up on outside: rdn and struggling over 3f out: eased whn btn fnl 2f* **16/1**
1m 43.11s (3.01) **Going Correction** +0.325s/f (Good) **13** Ran SP% **118.5**
Speed ratings (Par 97): **97,94,93,90,88 88,87,85,84,84 83,63,59**
Tote Swingers: 1&2 £36.20, 1&3 £26.10, 2&3 £34.80 CSF £218.45 CT £278.96 TOTE £15.10: £3.70, £8.50, £4.50; EX 359.10.
Owner N W A Bannister **Bred** Mrs J A Chapman & Mrs Shelley Dwyer **Trained** Sheriff Hutton, N Yorks

FOCUS
A modest handicap and this was a race set up for the closers.
Reason To Believe(IRE) Official explanation: jockey said gelding reared as stalls opened
Suddenly Susan(IRE) Official explanation: jockey said filly ran too free
T/Plt: £78.90 to a £1 stake. Pool:£55,841.43 - 516.15 winning tickets T/Qpdt: £15.50 to a £1 stake. Pool:£2,988.76 - 142.20 winning tickets RY

1876 RIPON (R-H)
Sunday, May 15

OFFICIAL GOING: Good
Rail on bend from back straight to home straight moved out 6m adding 11yds to races on round course.
Wind: Light half behind Weather: Showers & sunny periods

2120 SIS LIVE MAIDEN STKS 6f
2:10 (2:10) (Class 5) 2-Y-0 **£2,590** (£770; £385; £192) **Stalls** High

Form RPR
1 **Piece By Piece** 2-9-3 0 .... GrahamGibbons 2 76
(Tim Easterby) *dwlt and swtchd lft s: in rr: hdwy 1/2-way: pushed along to chse ldrs wl over 1f out: chal ent fnl f: kpt on to ld nr fin* **16/1**
3 **2** nse **Grand Gold**[8] 1913 2-9-0 0 .... MartinHarley(3) 1 76
(Mick Channon) *trckd ldrs: hdwy on outer over 2f out: rdn to ld wl over 1f out: jnd and drvn ins fnl f: hdd nr fin* **3/1**[1]

04 **3** *5* **Adranian (IRE)**[15] 1673 2-9-3 0....................................(v[1]) CathyGannon 6 61
(David Evans) *cl up: rdn and ev ch 2f out: sn drvn and kpt on same pce ent fnl f* **5/1**[3]

4 *nk* **Maastricht (IRE)** 2-9-3 0.. JoeFanning 8 60
(Mark Johnston) *trckd ldrs on inner: hdwy over 2f out: rdn and ch wl over 1f out: drvn and one pce ent fnl f* **10/3**[2]

6 **5** *4* **Maria Medecis (IRE)**[13] 1744 2-8-12 0.................... SilvestreDeSousa 4 43
(Ann Duffield) *prom: rdn along over 2f out: drvn and wknd over 1f out* **11/1**

6 *1* **Arrowroot** 2-9-3 0.. DuranFentiman 9 45
(Tim Easterby) *s.i.s and bhd tl styd on wl appr fnl f: nrst fin* **20/1**

6 **7** *1 3/4* **Metal Dealer (IRE)**[9] 1876 2-9-3 0.............................. PaulMulrennan 10 40
(George Foster) *led: pushed along 1/2-way: rdn over 2f out: hdd wl over 1f out and sn wknd* **80/1**

8 *1/2* **Regal Acclaim (IRE)** 2-9-3 0.. RobertWinston 7 38
(Tim Easterby) *chsd ldrs: rdn along over 2f out: sn wknd* **7/1**

5 **9** *hd* **Indepub**[12] 1797 2-9-3 0... PhillipMakin 5 40
(Kevin Ryan) *dwlt: in tch: rdn along over 2f out and sn wknd* **7/1**

10 *28* **King Laertis (IRE)** 2-9-3 0... PJMcDonald 3 —
(Ben Haslam) *s.i.s: sn outpcd and wl bhd fr 1/2-way* **28/1**

1m 13.0s **Going Correction** -0.30s/f (Firm) **10** Ran SP% **113.4**
Speed ratings (Par 93): **88,87,81,80,75 74,71,71,70,33**
Tote Swingers: 1&2 £7.30, 1&3 £5.00, 2&3 £3.20 CSF £61.11 TOTE £18.40: £4.20, £1.40, £1.90; EX 57.00 TRIFECTA Not won..
Owner J Musgrave **Bred** M J Dawson **Trained** Great Habton, N Yorks

FOCUS
Rain all morning resulted in the going being changed to good before the first race and the jockeys confirmed the description as accurate. There were a couple of newcomers with interesting breeding in this maiden. The first pair finished clear.

NOTEBOOK
Piece By Piece, a cheaply bought debutant, overcame inexperience to score narrowly. A half-brother to a triple 5f winner, he missed the break but gradually picked up ground and came to get the better of the more experienced favourite near the line. He looks capable of going on from this. (op 14-1)
Grand Gold, a half-brother to the fairly useful Buddy Holly, had shown promise on his debut and was sent off favourite. He came to take the lead over a furlong out only to lose out by a fraction. He was clear of the rest and a similar race should enable him to get off the mark. (op 9-4)
Adranian(IRE) had shown moderate form at 5f on a sound surface but was backed having been fitted with a first-time visor. He put up an improved effort but could not go with the principals in the last furlong. (op 6-1 tchd 9-2)
Maastricht(IRE), a 30,000gns colt out of a very useful mare and whose trainer had supplied the winner of this race three times in the preceding ten years, showed up well for most of the way but could not find extra under pressure. He looks as if he will be suited by longer trips sooner rather than later. (op 4-1 tchd 5-1)
Maria Medecis(IRE), from the family of Soviet Line and Quay Line, had been well held on her debut but was in the process of running a better race when done no favours by the placed horses around 2f from home.
Arrowroot ◆, the first foal of a 2-y-o debut winner over 6f, caught the eye running on late on this debut, having been totally outpaced in the first half of the race. He should come on a lot for the experience. (op 16-1)

2121 ALL STEELS TRADING SUPPORTING WOODEN SPOON CHARITY (S) STKS 6f

2:40 (2:41) (Class 6) 2-Y-0 **£2,590** (£770; £385; £192) **Stalls** High

Form RPR

32 **1** **Miss Muga**[12] 1786 2-8-2 .... CharlesBishop(7) 3 62
(Mick Channon) *cl up: led wl over 2f out: rdn clr over 1f out: kpt on* **11/4**[2]

23 **2** *1 1/2* **Royal Purse**[5] 1863 2-8-9 .... CathyGannon 6 57
(David Evans) *trckd ldrs: swtchd rt and hdwy 2f out: rdn to chse wnr over 1f out: drvn ins fnl f and no imp towards fin* **9/4**[1]

65 **3** *2 1/2* **Manderston**[8] 1913 2-9-0 .... JoeFanning 4 55
(Mark Johnston) *sn led: rdn along 1/2-way: sn hdd and drvn: kpt on same pce* **13/2**

1 **4** *17* **Spiders Of Spring (IRE)**[27] 1435 2-9-5 .... TonyHamilton 1 9
(Richard Fahey) *chsd ldrs: rdn along 1/2-way: sn drvn and outpcd* **10/3**[3]

0 **5** *1 1/4* **Punchie**[26] 1455 2-8-9 ....(b[1]) DuranFentiman 2 —
(Tim Easterby) *dwlt: a bhd* **20/1**

6 *10* **Mister Tancred** 2-8-11 .... MichaelO'Connell(3) 5 —
(David Nicholls) *lse bfre strt: s.i.s: a wl bhd* **8/1**

1m 13.35s (0.35) **Going Correction** -0.30s/f (Firm) **6** Ran SP% **109.7**
Speed ratings (Par 91): **85,83,79,57,55 42**
Tote Swingers: 1&2 £1.20, 1&3 £3.40, 2&3 £1.40 CSF £8.91 TOTE £2.90: £1.40, £2.10; EX 7.70.There was no bid for the winner.Royal Purse was claimed by Claes Bjorling for £6,000.
Owner R Bastian **Bred** R Bastian **Trained** West Ilsley, Berks

FOCUS
A seller in which several of the runners had reasonable form for the level. The time was 0.35sec slower than the preceding maiden.

NOTEBOOK
Miss Muga, placed in two sellers, both under this jockey over 5f, appeared suited by the step up in trip and handled the undulations better than her rivals to get off the mark. There was no bid afterwards but she might even be up to winning a small nursery later in the season. (tchd 10-3)
Royal Purse, a half-sister to several winners from the family of Where Or When, had been placed in fillies' maidens at 5f and was dropping in grade. She could not hold her pitch on the rail and had to be switched out to challenge, but could not reduce the winner's advantage in the last furlong. She was subsequently claimed. (op 5-2 tchd 2-1)
Manderston had shown very moderate form in two starts but, dropped in grade, he set off at a good pace but could not sustain it. (op 10-1)
Spiders Of Spring(IRE), related to multiple winners, had made all to win a seller on fast ground at Redcar on his debut. Carrying a 5lb penalty for that, he was disappointing, being beaten at around halfway. The undulating track and/or the rain-softened ground might have been against him. (op 3-1 tchd 5-2)
Mister Tancred, a gelded second foal of a half-sister to Tancred Times amongst others, was making his debut but reared and unseated his rider on the way to the start before running loose. He was unable to go the early pace but did make ground at the halfway mark before fading. He has some ability. (op 15-2 tchd 9-1)

2122 C. B. HUTCHINSON MEMORIAL CHALLENGE CUP (FILLIES' H'CAP) 6f

3:10 (3:10) (Class 3) (0-95,88) 3-Y-0 **£7,254** (£2,171; £1,085; £406; £406) **Stalls** High

Form RPR

320- **1** **Pepper Lane**[231] 6394 4-9-0 **74**.. DanielTudhope 2 93
(David O'Meara) *qckly away: mde all: clr 1/2-way: rdn over 1f out: kpt on strly* **10/1**

41-2 **2** *3 1/2* **Jade**[15] 1697 3-8-2 **72**.. SilvestreDeSousa 8 77
(Ollie Pears) *hld up in tch: hdwy over 3f out: effrt 2f out: rdn over 1f out: chsd wnr ins fnl f: no imp* **7/4**[1]

60-1 **3** *1* **Azzurra Du Caprio (IRE)**[16] 1650 3-9-0 **84**...................... PJMcDonald 9 85
(Ben Haslam) *trckd ldrs: hdwy over 2f out: rdn wl over 1f out: drvn and kpt on same pce ins fnl f* **5/1**[2]

300- **4** *1/2* **Misplaced Fortune**[204] 7079 6-9-13 **87**.............................. JoeFanning 4 90
(Nigel Tinkler) *trckd ldrs: hdwy on outer and cl up halfgway: rdn over 2f out: kpt on same pce* **13/2**[3]

4501 **4** *dht* **Ray Of Joy**[13] 1762 5-9-8 **82**... StephenCraine 1 85
(J R Jenkins) *chsd wnr: rdn along over 2f out: drvn over 1f out: kpt on same pce* **11/1**

40-0 **6** *1/2* **Mey Blossom**[15] 1698 6-9-5 **79**... TonyHamilton 6 80
(Richard Whitaker) *hld up: swtchd outside and hdwy over 2f out: sn rdn and one pce appr fnl f* **25/1**

064- **7** *2* **Kerrys Requiem (IRE)**[260] 5521 5-9-4 **81**.......................... SeanLevey(3) 7 76
(Tim Pitt) *hld up: a towards rr* **12/1**

621- **8** *3/4* **Black Annis Bower**[193] 7301 3-8-0 **73**...................... JamesSullivan(3) 10 62
(Michael Easterby) *prom: pushed along bef 1/2-way: rdn and wknd wl over 2f out* **20/1**

00-0 **9** *shd* **Gap Princess (IRE)**[15] 1675 7-9-11 **88**.................. MichaelO'Connell(3) 5 80
(Geoffrey Harker) *dwlt: a bhd* **33/1**

50-2 **10** *30* **Cloud's End**[13] 1762 4-9-4 **78**.. EddieAhern 3 —
(Robert Cowell) *a in rr: outpcd and wl bhd fr 1/2-way: lost action and eased fnl 2f* **17/2**

1m 10.93s (-2.07) **Going Correction** -0.30s/f (Firm)
WFA 3 from 4yo+ 10lb **10** Ran SP% **113.6**
Speed ratings (Par 104): **101,96,95,94,94 93,91,90,89,49**
Tote Swingers: 1&2 £4.70, 1&3 £14.20, 2&3 £1.20 CSF £26.49 CT £101.92 TOTE £13.60: £3.30, £1.30, £1.40; EX 39.30 Trifecta £249.70 Pool: £558.52 - 1.14 winning units..
Owner Mrs Lynne Lumley & K Nicholson **Bred** Conor J C Parsons & Brian M Parsons **Trained** Nawton, N Yorks

FOCUS
A decent fillies' handicap run over two seconds faster than the two earlier juvenile races and effectively won at the start.

NOTEBOOK
Pepper Lane ◆, making her seasonal reappearance, absolutely pinged the gates and the advantage she gained enabled her to get across to the rail from her outside stall. She found extra to go clear when asked and won with a bit in hand despite her rider reporting she blew up over a furlong out. She seems to have strengthened up since last year and could be worth following. (op 11-1 tchd 12-1)
Jade had run well on her return and was a strong favourite. She tracked the pace early but had to work quite hard to get into second place, and by the time she did so the race was over. She might need a stiffer test. (op 2-1 tchd 9-4 in a place)
Azzurra Du Caprio(IRE) just got the better of a blanket finish for the minor placing. She would have preferred the rain to have stayed away but she did not look totally happy on the track. She was running off a career-high mark and may not have finished improving. (op 11-2 tchd 9-2)
Misplaced Fortune, whose last success was in this race last season, had two previous runs on that occasion but was making her reappearance this time. She did pretty well but, 10lb above her last winning mark, she needs the handicapper to give her a little more leeway but her consistency limits his options. (op 15-2)
Ray Of Joy has been running well on the all-weather but her sole turf win was on easy ground so the rain might have helped her chance. She ran her race and just managed to share a place the frame. (op 15-2)
Mey Blossom, stepping up from 5f, could not lie up early but did get into the battle for places late on. She seems ideally suited by a stiffer finish. (op 22-1 tchd 20-1)
Cloud's End reportedly lost her action and later scoped dirty. Official explanation: jockey said filly lost its action; trainer's rep said filly scoped dirty (op 8-1 tchd 9-1)

2123 RIPON, YORKSHIRE'S GARDEN RACECOURSE H'CAP 1m

3:40 (3:40) (Class 2) (0-105,95) 4-Y-0+

£11,215 (£3,358; £1,679; £840; £419; £210) **Stalls** Low

Form RPR

0-14 **1** **Kay Gee Be (IRE)**[15] 1684 7-8-12 **86**.............................. TonyHamilton 1 97
(Richard Fahey) *trckd ldrs: hdwy wl over 2f out: swtchd lft and rdn to chse ldr over 1f out: sn led: drvn ins fnl f and hld on wl* **10/3**[1]

0512 **2** *1/2* **Dubai Dynamo**[2] 2061 6-8-9 **83**... PhillipMakin 9 93+
(Ruth Carr) *dwlt and in rr: hdwy 3f out: str run on outer fr wl over 1f out: chal ins fnl f and ev ch tl drvn and no ex last 50yds* **5/1**[3]

1112 **3** *1 1/4* **Snow Bay**[14] 1694 5-9-6 **94**.. FrannyNorton 6 100
(David Nicholls) *led 1f: chsd ldr tl led again wl over 2f out: sn rdn: drvn and hdd appr fnl f: kpt on same pce* **6/1**

-000 **4** *1 3/4* **Charlie Cool**[15] 1694 8-9-0 **88**...................................(b) RobertWinston 4 90
(Ruth Carr) *hld up in rr: gd hdwy wl over 2f out: rdn wl over 1f out: kpt on wl fnl f: nrst fin* **8/1**

260- **5** *hd* **Mr Rainbow**[269] 5242 5-9-1 **89**.. PJMcDonald 5 90
(Alan Swinbank) *in tch: hdwy to chse ldrs 3f out: rdn 2f out: drvn and one pce fnl f* **33/1**

311- **6** *nse* **Sarrsar**[226] 6534 4-9-7 **95**.. TedDurcan 10 96
(Saeed Bin Suroor) *trckd ldrs: effrt over 2f out and sn rdn: drvn and kpt on same pce appr fnl f* **4/1**[2]

0-00 **7** *2* **Kiwi Bay**[15] 1694 6-9-3 **91**.. TomEaves 3 88
(Michael Dods) *hld up in rr: sme hdwy over 2f out: sn rdn and n.d* **20/1**

1-03 **8** *2* **Space War**[15] 1694 4-9-1 **92**...................................... JamesSullivan(3) 12 84
(Michael Easterby) *led after 1f: rdn along 3f out: sn hdd and grad wknd* **16/1**

0-00 **9** *1 1/4* **Dream Lodge (IRE)**[15] 1694 7-8-13 **90**................. MichaelO'Connell(3) 8 79
(David Nicholls) *hld up: a towards rr* **33/1**

4000 **10** *4 1/2* **Greyfriarschorista**[13] 1760 4-8-10 **84**............................(v[1]) JoeFanning 11 63
(Mark Johnston) *prom: rdn along over 3f out: wknd wl over 2f out* **18/1**

2-06 **11** *1 1/2* **Amethyst Dawn (IRE)**[9] 1849 5-8-13 **87**...................... DuranFentiman 13 62
(Tim Easterby) *chsd ldrs: rdn along over 3f out: sn wknd* **20/1**

-000 **12** *1 3/4* **Collateral Damage (IRE)**[9] 1849 8-8-11 **85**................. KellyHarrison 2 56
(Tim Easterby) *in tch: hdwy 4f out: rdn along over 3f out and sn wknd* **22/1**

1m 38.58s (-2.82) **Going Correction** -0.125s/f (Firm) **12** Ran SP% **116.0**
Speed ratings (Par 109): **109,108,106,105,104 104,102,100,99,95 93,91**
Tote Swingers: 1&2 £2.80, 1&3 £3.00, 2&3 £5.30 CSF £17.64 CT £95.21 TOTE £5.40: £2.40, £1.30, £2.20; EX 26.60 Trifecta £44.60 Pool: £558.52 - 9.25 winning units..
Owner G H Leatham & M A Leatham **Bred** Pursuit Of Truth Syndicate **Trained** Musley Bank, N Yorks

FOCUS
A good handicap despite the fact that the top weight was 10lb below the race ceiling.

NOTEBOOK
Kay Gee Be(IRE), bought out of William Jarvis's stable for 27,000gns last autumn, has paid more than half of that back with two wins in three starts. He was unable to get the early lead but tucked in behind the pacesetters and was noted going well over 3f out. He got the gap when the third went on and once hitting the front found enough to resist the runner-up's late effort. He could be worth taking to Royal Ascot for the Hunt Cup, providing he gets into the race, but alternatively the July meeting at Newmarket might provide a suitable opportunity. (op 7-2 tchd 4-1)

Dubai Dynamo ◆, stepping up in trip, was held up at the back before coming with a sweeping run down the outside. This was a good effort and he remains in fine form with scope to win again, as he is well treated compared with this time last year. (op 11-2 tchd 9-2)
Snow Bay tried to make the running but was taken on for the lead. He got back in front around 2f from home but had nothing in reserve once challenged by the winner. (op 9-2)
Charlie Cool, a stable companion of the runner-up, got closer to Snow Bay than at Thirsk and, as his last two wins came here, is one to bear in mind if returning later in the month. (op 14-1)
Mr Rainbow is lightly raced but made an encouraging comeback on this step back up in trip. He would have appreciated the morning rain and should be better for the outing. (op 40-1)
Sarrsar, another lightly raced performer making his seasonal reappearance, was dropping in trip and could not go the pace early in the straight before staying on. A return to further next time should see him in a better light. His rider reported that the gelding hung right. Official explanation: jockey said gelding hung right (op 7-2)
Space War won the battle for the early lead but paid for his exertions in the last 2f. (op 12-1)

2124 MIDDLEHAM TRAINERS ASSOCIATION H'CAP — 1m 1f 170y
4:10 (4:11) (Class 4) (0-85,85) 4-Y-0+ — **£4,533** (£1,348; £674; £336) Stalls Low

Form — RPR
0 **1** **Butler (IRE)**[18] 1603 4-8-11 **75** .... J-PGuillambert 6 — 83
(Luca Cumani) *hld up: effrt 3f out and sn rdn along: swtchd to outer and drvn over 1f out: styd on u.p to chal ins fnl f and sn edgd rt: kpt on to ld nr fin* **12/1**
6612 **2** ½ **Sharakti (IRE)**[15] 1671 4-8-10 **74** .... RobertWinston 2 — 81
(Alan McCabe) *chsd clr ldr: gd hdwy 3f out: led wl over 1f out and sn edgd rt: drvn and edgd lft ins fnl f: hdd and no ex towards fin* **13/2**
40-0 **3** ¾ **City Of The Kings (IRE)**[29] 1410 6-9-6 **84** .... SilvestreDeSousa 4 — 89
(Geoffrey Harker) *stdd s and hld up in rr: hdwy over 2f out: rdn to chse ldrs over 1f out: swtchd rt and drvn ins fnl f: ev ch tl no ex nr fin* **10/1**
1613 **4** 2¼ **Prince Apollo**[13] 1746 6-8-12 **76** ....(t) DarryllHolland 5 — 77
(Gerard Butler) *in tch: hdwy to chse ldng pair wl over 2f out: drvn over 1f out: kpt on to ld jst ins fnl f: sn hung rt: hdd & wknd last 100yds* **9/2**[2]
0-55 **5** 2 **Jonny Lesters Hair (IRE)**[9] 1879 6-8-12 **81** .... LanceBetts(5) 8 — 78
(Tim Easterby) *led and sn clr: rdn over 2f out: hdd wl over 1f out: swtchd lft and drvn to rally ent fnl f and ev ch tl edgd rt and wknd last 100yds* **5/1**[3]
02-0 **6** 2¼ **Ejteyaaz**[43] 1097 4-9-3 **81** .... TonyHamilton 7 — 73
(Richard Fahey) *hld up: effrt and sme hdwy over 2f out: sn rdn and n.d* **10/1**
60-2 **7** 2¼ **Oneofapear (IRE)**[43] 1097 5-9-7 **85** .... PJMcDonald 1 — 88+
(Alan Swinbank) *in tch: hdwy and pushed along 3f out: rdn to chse ldrs over 1f out: styng on whn hmpd ins fnl f: nt rcvr* **4/1**[1]
0-00 **8** 3¼ **Full Speed (GER)**[14] 1713 6-8-9 **80** .... GarryWhillans(7) 10 — 61
(Alan Swinbank) *a towards rr* **50/1**
1531 **9** 16 **Zebrano**[10] 1832 5-9-5 **83** ....(b) JamesDoyle 3 — 31
(Andrew Haynes) *s.i.s: a bhd* **5/1**[3]
000- **10** 25 **Gumnd (IRE)**[197] 7228 4-8-12 **76** .... PhilipRobinson 9 — —
(James Bethell) *chsd ldng pair: rdn along 4f out: sn wknd* **14/1**
2m 2.69s (-2.71) **Going Correction** -0.125s/f (Firm) — **10 Ran SP% 119.4**
Speed ratings (Par 105): **105,104,104,102,100 98,97,94,81,61**
Tote Swingers: 1&2 £12.50, 1&3 £26.90, 2&3 £15.40 CSF £89.93 CT £823.58 TOTE £13.80: £4.20, £1.80, £3.40; EX 131.00 TRIFECTA Not won..
Owner W Bellew **Bred** Darley **Trained** Newmarket, Suffolk

FOCUS
A competitive handicap in which the early leader went off at a rate of knots and, as the pace collapsed, there was scrimmaging in the closing stages.
Oneofapear(IRE) Official explanation: jockey said gelding suffered interference in running
Zebrano Official explanation: jockey said gelding bucked several times on leaving stalls
Gumnd(IRE) Official explanation: jockey said gelding lost its action

2125 GOTTOHAVEDIAMONDS.COM MAIDEN STKS — 1m 1f
4:40 (4:41) (Class 5) 3-Y-0 — **£2,590** (£770; £385; £192) Stalls High

Form — RPR
54-2 **1** **Trojan Nights (USA)**[10] 1836 3-9-3 80 .... EddieAhern 7 — 82+
(William Haggas) *trckd ldr: smooth hdwy to ld over 2f out: pushed clr over 1f out* **2/7**[1]
2 3¼ **Sir Francis Drake** 3-9-3 0 .... AhmedAjtebi 5 — 75+
(Mahmood Al Zarooni) *chsd ldrs: green and pushed along 1/2-way: rdn over 2f out: styd on wl to chse wnr ins fnl f* **9/2**[2]
2 **3** 6 **Rio Park (IRE)**[14] 1710 3-9-3 0 .... TomEaves 2 — 62
(Bryan Smart) *trckd ldrs: rdn along 3f out: plugged on fnl 2f: tk 3rd ins fnl f* **9/1**[3]
0 **4** 1¼ **Love For Love**[9] 1880 3-8-12 55 .... SilvestreDeSousa 4 — 54
(David O'Meara) *led: rdn along 3f out: hdd over 2f out: sn wknd* **22/1**
00 **5** 13 **Joe Rocco (IRE)**[15] 1693 3-8-10 0 .... GarryWhillans(7) 8 — 31
(Alan Swinbank) *midfield: rdn along over 3f out: nvr a factor* **80/1**
0- **6** nk **Margot De Medici (FR)**[258] 5595 3-8-12 0 .... FrederikTylicki 3 — 25
(Micky Hammond) *in tch: rdn along over 3f out: nvr a factor* **66/1**
5 **7** 6 **Singzak**[15] 1693 3-8-10 0 .... DavidSimmonson(7) 1 — 17
(Michael Easterby) *a bhd* **14/1**
8 22 **Eastward Ho** 3-9-0 0 .... BillyCray(3) 9 — —
(Jason Ward) *s.i.s: a in rr: bhd fr 1/2-way* **66/1**
6 **9** 22 **Excuse Me**[54] 937 3-9-3 0 .... PJMcDonald 6 — —
(Alan Swinbank) *s.i.s: a in rr: bhd fr 1/2-way* **33/1**
1m 53.38s (-1.32) **Going Correction** -0.125s/f (Firm) — **9 Ran SP% 124.1**
Speed ratings (Par 99): **100,97,91,90,79 78,73,53,34**
Tote Swingers: 1&2 £1.60, 1&3 £2.00, 2&3 £2.10 CSF £2.29 TOTE £1.30: £1.02, £1.20, £2.50; EX 2.40 Trifecta £9.80 Pool: £867.47 - 65.34 winning units..
Owner Mohamed Obaida **Bred** Rabbah Bloodstock Llc **Trained** Newmarket, Suffolk

FOCUS
An uncompetitive maiden but featuring a couple of well-bred sorts from major stables.

2126 TOTESWINGER H'CAP — 5f
5:10 (5:11) (Class 5) (0-70,75) 4-Y-0+ — **£2,590** (£770; £385; £192) Stalls High

Form — RPR
4-60 **1** **Angelo Poliziano**[6] 1955 5-9-5 **68** ....(p) SilvestreDeSousa 4 — 79
(Ann Duffield) *in tch: hdwy 1/2-way: rdn to ld wl over 1f out: sn edgd lft and kpt on strly* **10/1**
6-04 **2** 1¾ **Baybshambles (IRE)**[18] 1612 7-8-7 **56** .... BarryMcHugh 8 — 61
(Ron Barr) *hld up: hdwy 2f out: nt clr run and swtchd rt over 1f out: kpt on to chse wnr ins fnl f: sn no imp* **7/1**
6-01 **3** 1 **Tillys Tale**[11] 1816 4-9-12 **75** .... MickyFenton 12 — 76
(Paul Midgley) *cl up: rdn along 2f out: drvn over 1f out: kpt on same pce fnl f* **11/1**
5-32 **4** ¾ **Senate Majority**[21] 1544 4-9-1 **64** .... GrahamGibbons 11 — 62+
(Tim Easterby) *trckd ldrs on stands' rail: effrt and n.m.r wl over 1f out: rdn and nt clr run appr fnl f: swtchd lft and kpt on: nrst fin* **7/2**[1]
-440 **5** ¾ **Lees Anthem**[5] 1968 4-8-13 **62** .... PatrickMathers 1 — 58
(Colin Teague) *towards rr: hdwy on outer 2f out: sn rdn and kpt on same pce appr fnl f* **16/1**
0-32 **6** ¾ **Triple Dream**[5] 1982 6-9-5 **68** ....(tp) TedDurcan 6 — 61+
(Milton Bradley) *trckd ldrs: pushed along 1/2-way: rdn and styng on whn nt clr run ins fnl f: one pce after* **13/2**[3]
-001 **7** ¾ **Kyzer Chief**[12] 1796 6-8-4 **60** .... ShaneBKelly(7) 3 — 50
(Ron Barr) *prom: rdn along 2f out: hld whn n.m.r and swtchd rt over 1f out: wknd* **14/1**
-000 **8** hd **King Of Swords (IRE)**[9] 1856 7-8-8 **57** ....(p) AndrewElliott 10 — 47
(Nigel Tinkler) *chsd ldrs: rdn along 1/2-way: sn wknd* **28/1**
0514 **9** 1¾ **Mandurah (IRE)**[12] 1796 7-9-3 **69** .... MichaelO'Connell(3) 5 — 52
(David Nicholls) *a towards rr* **7/1**
0641 **10** 1¾ **Rio's Girl**[14] 1716 4-8-9 **58** ....(b[1]) PhillipMakin 9 — 35
(Kevin Ryan) *led: rdn along 2f out: drvn and hdd wl over 1f out: hld whn hmpd and wknd appr fnl f* **5/1**[2]
0-60 **11** 3 **Canadian Danehill (IRE)**[22] 1523 9-8-7 **56** oh1 ....(p) CathyGannon 2 — 22
(Robert Cowell) *a towards rr* **28/1**
-030 **12** 8 **Tenancy (IRE)**[11] 1818 7-8-7 **59** .... BillyCray(3) 7 — —
(Shaun Harris) *in tch: rdn along 1/2-way: sn wknd* **33/1**
58.82 secs (-1.88) **Going Correction** -0.30s/f (Firm) — **12 Ran SP% 117.0**
Speed ratings (Par 103): **103,100,98,97,96 95,93,93,90,87 83,70**
Tote Swingers: 1&2 £10.30, 1&3 £9.90, 2&3 £14.20 . Totesuper 7: Win: Not won. Place: £92.40 - 13 winning units. CSF £75.89 CT £802.74 TOTE £14.90: £4.10, £2.20, £3.30; EX 102.20 Trifecta £404.30 Part won. Pool: £546.43 - 0.54 winning units..
Owner Middleham Park Racing XXVIII **Bred** Bumble Bs, C Liesack & Mrs S Nicholls **Trained** Constable Burton, N Yorks

FOCUS
A modest but tightly knit sprint handicap.
Kyzer Chief Official explanation: jockey said gelding hung right inside final furlong
Rio's Girl Official explanation: jockey said filly lost its action
T/Jkpt: Not won. T/Plt: £26.70 to a £1 stake. Pool:£82,833.88 - 2,262.75 winning tickets T/Qpdt: £16.00 to a £1 stake. Pool:£5,149.52 - 237.74 winning tickets JR

2127 - 2133a (Foreign Racing) - See Raceform Interactive

1918 CAPANNELLE (R-H)
Sunday, May 15

OFFICIAL GOING: Turf: soft

2134a PREMIO PRESIDENTE DELLA REPUBBLICA GBI RACING (GROUP 1) (4YO+) (TURF) — 1m 2f
4:40 (5:00) 4-Y-0+ — **£116,379** (£51,206; £27,931; £13,965)

RPR
1 **Estejo (GER)**[21] 1554 7-9-2 0 .... UmbertoRispoli 5 — 112
(R Rohne, Germany) *stdd s to trck ldrs in 3rd: wnt 4th 3f out: moved lft fr bhd ldng trio 2f out: hrd rdn to ld 1f out: styd on wl to hold chalr comf fnl f* **7/2**[2]
2 1½ **Voila Ici (IRE)**[21] 1554 6-9-2 0 .... MircoDemuro 9 — 109
(Vittorio Caruso, Italy) *midfield for 6f: 7th ent st: rdn and gd prog fr 3f out to move 3rd fr 2f out: chal eventual wnr 1f out and ev ch: one pce fnl f* **4/1**[3]
3 nk **Quiza Quiza Quiza**[119] 5-8-13 0 .... GMarcelli 8 — 105
(L Riccardi, Italy) *slowly away and nr rr tl 3f out: hrd rdn on inner 2 1/2f out: swtchd lft to outer: wnt 5th 1f out: styd on wl fnl f to go cl for 2nd on line* **30/1**
4 2 **Cima De Pluie**[21] 1554 4-9-2 0 .... DarioVargiu 2 — 104
(B Grizzetti, Italy) *settled midfield for 6f: ct for pce 3f out: hrd rdn fr 2f out: one pce and nvr trbld ldrs* **97/10**
5 ½ **Branderburgo (IRE)**[35] 4-9-2 0 .... GBietolini 4 — 103
(L Riccardi, Italy) *trckd ldrs in 2nd for 6f: led 2 1/2f out: hrd rdn 1 1/2f out: chal and passed by eventual wnr 1f out: sn one pce* **22/5**
6 6 **Russian King (GER)**[21] 1554 5-9-2 0 .... WGambarota 3 — 91
(R Rohne, Germany) *broke wl to ld after 100yds: set gd pce: rdn 4f out: chal 3f out: hdd 2 1/2f out and sn btn* **7/2**[2]
7 ¾ **Zazou (GER)**[42] 1128 4-9-2 0 ....(b) TomQueally 1 — 90
(Mario Hofer, Germany) *trckd eventual wnr in 4th for 6f: rdn and 3rd 3f out: ev ch whn chal ldr 2f out: hrd rdn and sn btn* **1/1**[1]
8 6 **Lord Chaparral (IRE)**[8] 1918 4-9-2 0 .... FabioBranca 7 — 78
(R Brogi, Italy) *nr rr: nvr figured* **77/10**
9 4 **Freemusic (IRE)**[14] 7-9-2 0 .... CristianDemuro 6 — 70
(L Riccardi, Italy) *v.s.a and a in rr* **201/10**
2m 0.60s (-2.70) — **9 Ran SP% 161.8**
WIN (incl. 1 euro stake): 4.53 (coupled with Russian King). PLACES: 1.91, 1.62, 3.66; DF 9.18.
Owner Giovanne Martone **Bred** Gestut Schallern **Trained** Germany

NOTEBOOK
Estejo(GER) landed the second Group 1 success of his career with a 11/2-length defeat of old rival Voila Ici. He is trained in Germany by Ralf Rohne but has raced there only once, with all but five of his 24 career starts having been in Italy, where his owner is based.\n\x\x The seven-year-old's previous Group 1 success came in the 2008 Premio Roma.\n
Voila Ici(IRE) got within a head of the winner a furlong out, he could not quicken. He looked to be almost back to his best, having taken time to come to himself this year.
Zazou(GER) had his chance early in the straight but dropped away quite quickly in the last 2f and finished seventh of nine.

2135 - (Foreign Racing) - See Raceform Interactive

1841 LONGCHAMP (R-H)
Sunday, May 15

OFFICIAL GOING: Turf: good

2136a PRIX HOCQUART (GROUP 2) (3YO) (TURF) — 1m 3f
1:30 (12:00) 3-Y-0 — **£63,879** (£24,655; £11,767; £7,844; £3,922)

RPR
1 **Prairie Star (FR)**[35] 1265 3-9-2 0 .... ChristopheSoumillon 4 — 112+
(E Lellouche, France) *settled in 2nd: qcknd wl 2f out: tk ld 1 1/2f out: r.o wl: hrd rdn fnl 100yds: jst hld on* **11/4**[2]
2 nse **Grand Vent (IRE)**[21] 1551 3-9-2 0 .... MickaelBarzalona 5 — 112+
(A Fabre, France) *in rr fr s: swtchd to outside early in st: rdn and qcknd wl 1 1/2f out: chal for ld 100yds out: r.o strly: failed narrowly* **11/4**[2]
3 1½ **Genius Beast (USA)**[21] 1548 3-9-2 0 .... FrankieDettori 3 — 109
(Mahmood Al Zarooni) *sent to ld sn after s: rdn 2f out: hdd 1 1/2f out: r.o wl fnl f* **7/4**[1]

4 *1* **Barentin (USA)**[26] 9001 3-9-2 0.................. Christophe-PatriceLemaire 1 107
(J-C Rouget, France) *settled 4th: rdn 2f out: ev ch 1f out: nt qckn: styd on wl* **5/1**[3]
5 *3* **Lindenthaler (GER)**[28] 1433 3-9-2 0....................................... AStarke 2 102
(P Schiergen, Germany) *settled 3rd on rail: rdn 2f out: nt qckn: styd on fnl f* **20/1**

2m 17.27s (-2.63) **Going Correction** +0.05s/f (Good) **5** Ran SP% **111.1**
Speed ratings: **111,110,109,109,106**
WIN (incl 1 euro stake): 2.70. PLACES: 1.40, 1.50. SF: 8.30.
Owner Ecurie Wildenstein **Bred** Dayton Investments Ltd **Trained** Lamorlaye, France

FOCUS
Yet another small field in France for a decent Group race this season, where it really was almost impossible to pick between the main contenders. The pace seemed a fair one, although the first four weren't covered by too many lengths. The form is rated around the third.

NOTEBOOK
Prairie Star(FR) had plenty of experience at Group level and boasted some decent form. He managed to finish in front of Pour Moi last time in the Prix La Force, when his trainer reportedly said his colt would need the run, so with normal progression, he looked the one to beat. Travelling stylishly on the heels of the leader, possibly a bit too keen, he looked all set to win in good style, but there was no searing change of foot and he made a meal of winning a race he looked like taking clearly at one stage. Plans probably include the Prix Du Jockey Club next (stablemate Planteur finished runner-up in that last year) but, judged on this performance, the 1m4f Grand Prix De Paris looks a more sensible target. Hopefully the performance of Prairie Star here will help to convince Andre Fabre/Coolmore to send Pour Moi over for the Epsom Derby. It also gives another huge boost to the Jean-Claude Rouget-trained Baraan, who must be very good to have beaten at least two potential Group 1 horses.
Grand Vent(IRE) has been running well and set a decent standard. However, with only just over 3l covered the eight runners in the Prix Noailles, and a strict line on his meeting with Vadamar (well beaten by Pour Moi last time) in the Prix Francois Mathet suggested he had something to find with the winner. Positioned in last, he came with a nice run on the outside of the field but wasn't able to force his head in front. In contrast to the winner, this or a bit shorter looks to be his trip, and one would imagine he'll head to Chantilly next unless connections feel they have stronger candidates.
Genius Beast(USA)'s rider did exactly the right thing, because there did look a worry that the horse lacked a change of gear. The pair went a fair and even gallop, trying to stretch the field, but weren't able to grind out a victory. It was far from a bad performance, and maybe he'll develop in a St Leger type in the long term.
Barentin(USA) ran for respected connections but looked to have plenty to find, so the fact he finished close up after holding every chance bodes well for him. He looks capable of picking up a good race.
Lindenthaler(GER) came here rather than staying in Germany. There seemed little fluke about the way he took the Dr Busch Memorial last time (raced prominently before quickening) from a decent field, and poor horses don't win that contest. Although a few lengths off the first four, he ran nicely and will command respect wherever he goes.

2137a POULE D'ESSAI DES POULICHES (GROUP 1) (3YO FILLIES) (TURF) 1m
2:08 (12:00) 3-Y-0 **£221,663** (£88,681; £44,340; £22,150; £11,094)

RPR
1 **Golden Lilac (IRE)**[21] 1553 3-9-0 0................................ OlivierPeslier 6 116+
(A Fabre, France) *t.k.h in 2nd: rdn to ld 1 1/2f out: sn clr: r.o wl: comf* **5/2**[1]
2 *3* **Glorious Sight (IRE)**[21] 1553 3-9-0 0........................ SebastienMaillot 2 109
(Robert Collet, France) *led: stl in front 2f out: chal and hdd 1 1/2f out: r.o wl* **33/1**
3 *1/2* **Wild Wind (GER)**[14] 1734 3-9-0 0..................................... RyanMoore 1 108
(A P O'Brien, Ire) *settled 3rd: rdn and qcknd wl 1 1/2f out: r.o wl fnl f* **16/1**
4 *3/4* **Nova Hawk**[14] 1719 3-9-0 0... ThierryThulliez 3 106
(Rod Collet, France) *settled midfield on rail: gd prog 1 1/2f out: r.o wl fnl f: clst at fin* **10/1**
5 *nk* **Sharnberry**[29] 1404 3-9-0 0... KierenFallon 8 105
(Ed Dunlop) *a.p: ev ch 1 1/2f out: nt qckn: styd on fnl f* **16/1**
6 *shd* **Espirita (FR)**[21] 1553 3-9-0 0................................ AnthonyCrastus 15 105
(E Lellouche, France) *towards rr: rdn 2f out: r.o wl fnl f* **16/1**
7 *1* **Mixed Intention (IRE)**[21] 1553 3-9-0 0........................... SylvainRuis 4 103
(F Vermeulen, France) *settled 6th: rdn 2f out: styd on wl fnl f* **22/1**
8 *snk* **Maqaasid**[14] 1719 3-9-0 0... RichardHills 14 102+
(John Gosden) *settled towards rr: rdn 2f out: r.o* **15/2**[3]
9 *3/4* **Rimth**[29] 1101 3-9-0 0 ChristopheSoumillon 7 101
(Paul Cole) *sn prom on outer: rdn 1 1/2f out: no ex* **15/2**[3]
10 *1 1/2* **Miss Liberty (FR)**[17] 1646 3-9-0 0............................. GregoryBenoist 5 97
(Mme Pia Brandt, France) *racd towards rr: rdn but no ex in st* **66/1**
11 *shd* **Immortal Verse (IRE)**[41] 3-9-0 0............. Christophe-PatriceLemaire 12 97
(Robert Collet, France) *w.w in rr: rdn but no ex in st: fdd* **25/1**
12 *3/4* **Nova Step**[38] 1207 3-9-0 0.............................. Francois-XavierBertras 10 95
(F Rohaut, France) *midfield tl st: rdn but no ex in st* **50/1**
13 *snk* **Helleborine**[38] 1207 3-9-0 0.................................. StephanePasquier 11 95
(Mme C Head-Maarek, France) *w.w towards rr: rdn but no ex in st* **5/1**[2]
14 *2 1/2* **Mambia**[38] 1207 3-9-0 0... IoritzMendizabal 9 89
(J-C Rouget, France) *towards rr: nvr figured in st* **33/1**
15 *nk* **Etive (USA)**[16] 1668 3-9-0 0... FabriceVeron 13 89
(H-A Pantall, France) *a towards rr: nvr figured in st* **33/1**
16 *3/4* **Zoowraa**[204] 7098 3-9-0 0... FrankieDettori 16 87
(Mahmood Al Zarooni) *a towards rr: rdn early in st: sn wknd* **10/1**

1m 39.31s (0.91) **Going Correction** +0.05s/f (Good) **16** Ran SP% **125.1**
Speed ratings: **97,94,93,92,92 92,91,91,90,88 88,88,87,85,85 84**
WIN (incl 1 euro stake): 2.50. PLACES: 1.50, 6.80, 5.60. DF: 67.60. SF: 110.30..
Owner Gestut Ammerland **Bred** Gestut Ammerland **Trained** Chantilly, France

FOCUS
This is a tricky contest to work out for future races as the winner was clear-cut and classy, but the runner-up was seemingly in the contest to do pace-making duties for a more-fancied stablemate. Also, it paid to race handy as nothing held up, by design or circumstance, made much of an impact when it mattered. The fourth is rated around the fourth and sixth.

NOTEBOOK
Golden Lilac(IRE) is a hugely talented filly and looks set to dominate her division this season. She took a good grip under 'substitute' rider Olivier Peslier (Maxime Guyon missed the ride due to suspension) close to the leader before simply powering clear once asked to win. Quite what she beat on the day is debatable but there is no denying she has a big engine at her disposal if her enthusiasm remains harnessed. The Prix De Diane will probably be on her agenda.
Glorious Sight(IRE) was apparently the pacemaker for Immortal Verse and is the slight problem, as although she is at least a Listed-class performer, not many could have predicted she was going to be good enough to place in a classic, although she wasn't beaten far by the winner last time in the Prix De La Grotte. It remains to be seen whether she can repeat this effort in the future.
Wild Wind(GER) had run well on both her previous outings this season without winning, and kept on here after settling close up. Her effort gives supporters of the progressive Banimpire a nice boost, as she finished a neck behind that rival last time.
Nova Hawk, the Newmarket 1000 Guineas fourth, reversed form with Maqaasid after settling nicely in midfield before keeping on up the inside rail at the one pace.
Sharnberry reversed recent Dubai Duty Free (Fred Darling) form with Rimth. Ed Dunlop's filly is on the upgrade.
Espirita(FR) did the best of those that had to be dropped in from a wide stall and is certainly well worth giving another chance to with a kinder draw. She started favourite for the Prix De La Grotte last time, so is clearly held in some regard.
Mixed Intention(IRE), the runner-up in the Prix de la Grotte, looked the one with a bit of a hard-luck story, as her jockey was penned in by Soumillon down the home straight when it looked like he wanted to get out. It's impossible to know how much that affected her chance, because once she had the gaps, she came home at the one pace.
Maqaasid, third in the 1000 Guineas at Newmarket, had a wide stall to exit from and was forced to drop in behind a wall of horses. She did not run too badly in the circumstances.
Rimth recovered quite quickly after appearing to be tripped by Sharnberry early. She got caught one paced when the tempo quickened, but it's not easy to say whether she stayed or not, because she wasn't fading.
Immortal Verse(IRE), the runner-up's shorter-priced stablemate, got crowded out early on and was forced to drop in behind. She stayed in that position until the home straight and looked to be travelling strongly, but she was never going to make the ground up from her starting position and is probably a lot better than her final position suggests.
Helleborine didn't run too badly on her seasonal debut but there wasn't a lot in this effort to suggest she is anywhere her juvenile form yet.
Zoowraa, another with a poor draw to overcome, never got into contention but this has to rate as a little disappointing.

2138a PRIX DE SAINT-GEORGES (GROUP 3) (3YO+) (TURF) 5f (S)
2:45 (12:00) 3-Y-0+ **£34,482** (£13,793; £10,344; £6,896; £3,448)

RPR
1 **Inxile (IRE)**[22] 1533 6-9-0 0.......................................(p) AdrianNicholls 3 111
(David Nicholls) *sn prom bhd ldr: hrd rdn fnl f: got up on line* **2/1**[1]
2 *nse* **Captain Dunne (IRE)**[11] 1809 6-9-0 0................................ DavidAllan 7 111
(Tim Easterby) *sn led: ct on line* **14/1**
3 *shd* **Split Trois (FR)**[17] 1646 3-8-8 0................. Christophe-PatriceLemaire 5 110
(Y De Nicolay, France) *w.w: qcknd wl on outside 1 1/2f out: r.o strly: narrowly failed* **33/1**
4 *snk* **Prohibit**[15] 1687 6-9-2 0...(p) FrankieDettori 2 112
(Robert Cowell) *hld up towards rr: str run up rail fnl 1 1/2f: fin wl* **8/1**[3]
5 *shd* **Mar Adentro (FR)**[17] 1647 5-9-2 0...................(p) ChristopheSoumillon 1 112
(R Chotard, France) *w.w: gd prog 1 1/2f out: fin strly* **10/1**
6 *3/4* **Piccadilly Filly (IRE)**[50] 996 4-8-13 0...................... EddieCreighton 12 106
(Edward Creighton) *qckly away in centre of trck: 3rd 1f out: no ex ins fnl f: r.o* **12/1**
7 *3/4* **Fred Lalloupet**[17] 1647 4-9-0 0....................................... OlivierPeslier 10 104
(D Smaga, France) *racd midfield: no ex fnl f* **28/1**
8 *hd* **Sabratah**[27] 3-8-2 0.. FabriceVeron 11 97
(H-A Pantall, France) *racd bhd ldrs fr s: stl prom 1f out: no ex: fdd* **16/1**
9 *1* **Kagura (USA)**[44] 1122 3-8-2 0.................................. MickaelBarzalona 13 93
(G Henrot, France) *towards rr: rdn 1 1/2f out: no ex* **33/1**
10 *hd* **Bluster (FR)**[17] 1647 5-9-2 0....................................... IoritzMendizabal 4 101
(Robert Collet, France) *racd towards rr: rdn but no ex fnl 2f* **16/1**
11 *2* **Jonny Mudball**[15] 1687 5-9-2 0... SebSanders 6 94
(Tom Dascombe) *prom tl 2f out: fdd* **4/1**[2]

55.92 secs (-0.38) **Going Correction** +0.25s/f (Good)
WFA 3 from 4yo+ 9lb **11** Ran SP% **109.0**
Speed ratings: **113,112,112,112,112 111,109,109,108,107 104**
WIN (incl 1 euro stake): 3.10. PLACES: 1.70, 5.80, 3.70. DF: 35.00. SF: 37.10..
Owner Mrs Jackie Love & David Nicholls **Bred** Denis And Mrs Teresa Bergin **Trained** Sessay, N Yorks

FOCUS
Fast and furious stuff.

NOTEBOOK
Inxile(IRE) avenged his demotion in this race back in 2009. He has pace aplenty and goes on virtually any surface, but even he couldn't live with the second as he strode on. Adrian Nicholls kept pushing away and success looked unlikely at one stage about a furlong out, but the horse rallied under pressure and got in front right on the line. He must be a great horse to own as he takes his travelling well and rarely runs poorly. This was a first win at this level for the horse (he has six Listed race victories), but considering how open the sprinting division is, he could easily be good enough to take something even better.
Captain Dunne(IRE) pinged out of the stalls and set a good pace once getting to the front. Second in a Chester handicap last time when giving the winner weight, he looked set to collect the prize heading into the final furlong but found challengers appearing from all directions in behind, and lost out narrowly to another British-trained runner. If heading to the Epsom 'Dash' handicap, a race he has run well in before, he'll take some catching, especially with a fair draw.
Split Trois(FR), a 3-y-o filly taking on her elders, got behind at one point and carried her tail quite high at times, but hit top gear late on while threading through rivals.
Prohibit reversed Palace House form with Jonny Mudball quite comfortably. He looked a lost cause as he lost positions, but Dettori kept pushing away and the pair came home strongly. The horse looks more than capable of winning at this level or higher when things fall right.
Mar Adentro(FR) hadn't shone since finishing third in last season's Prix De L'Abbaye, so this was a lot better.
Piccadilly Filly(IRE) showed early speed but couldn't live with the runner-up as he strode on. However, she stuck to her task well and wasn't beaten far.
Fred Lalloupet looked to suffer some traffic problems and is definitely better than his seventh place implies.
Bluster(FR) seemingly didn't have a lot of room when his jockey wanted to come with his effort inside the final furlong and is better than the bare result indicates.
Jonny Mudball didn't seem to have any obvious excuses except for missing the kick a bit leaving the stalls. It is possible that a quick 5f is not what he wants.

2139a POULE D'ESSAI DES POULAINS (GROUP 1) (3YO COLTS) (TURF) 1m
3:25 (12:00) 3-Y-0 **£221,663** (£88,681; £44,340; £22,150; £11,094)

RPR
1 **Tin Horse (IRE)**[21] 1552 3-9-2 0...................................... ThierryJarnet 1 117+
(D Guillemin, France) *trckd ldrs on rail: rdn 2f out: qcknd wl to chal for ld 1f out: tk ld 150yds out: r.o wl: comf* **10/1**
2 *2* **Havane Smoker**[38] 1206 3-9-2 0.............................. IoritzMendizabal 11 112
(J-C Rouget, France) *settled in 2nd: qcknd wl to chal for ld 1 1/2f out: led briefly 1f out: hdd 150yds out: r.o wl: jst hld 2nd on line* **18/1**
3 *shd* **Venomous**[33] 3-9-2 0.. FlavienPrat 6 112
(T Clout, France) *towards rr fr s: swtchd to outer 1 1/2f out: qcknd wl ins fnl f: narrowly missed 2nd on line* **66/1**
4 *1 1/2* **Temps Au Temps (IRE)**[21] 1552 3-9-2 0................. GregoryBenoist 15 108
(M Delzangles, France) *in rr tl st: qcknd wl on outside fnl f: fin strly* **66/1**
5 *snk* **Wootton Bassett**[224] 6610 3-9-2 0................................ PaulHanagan 14 108
(Richard Fahey) *broke wl and sn crossed to rail: led tl hdd 1f out: no ex* **11/8**[1]

6 snk **Barocci (JPN)**[21] 1552 3-9-2 0 ChristopheSoumillon 12 107
(E Lellouche, France) *towards rr tl st: proged in centre of trck: r.o fnl f* **12/1**

7 snk **Imperial Rome (IRE)**[13] 1778 3-9-2 0 RyanMoore 5 107
(David Wachman, Ire) *settled midfield: rdn 1 1/2f out: no ex: styd on* **14/1**

8 nk **Glaswegian**[21] 1552 3-9-2 0 StephanePasquier 4 106
(P Bary, France) *settled in 4th fr s: rdn 2f out: nt qckn: styd on* **17/2**[3]

9 ¾ **Salto (IRE)**[21] 1552 3-9-2 0 OlivierPeslier 3 105
(F Head, France) *racd bhd ldrs: threatened briefly 2f out: rdn but no ex fnl f* **9/1**

10 ¾ **Maiguri (IRE)**[21] 1552 3-9-2 0 GeraldMosse 9 103
(C Baillet, France) *racd towards rr: rdn 1 1/2f out but nt qckn: fdd* **22/1**

11 6 **Surfrider (IRE)**[38] 1206 3-9-2 0 Christophe-PatriceLemaire 8 88
(E Libaud, France) *settled bhd ldng gp: rdn but nt qckn in st: fdd* **14/1**

12 2 **Modern History (IRE)**[16] 1668 3-9-2 0 FrankieDettori 13 84
(A Fabre, France) *sn prom: ev ch early in st: rdn and sn wknd* **7/1**[2]

13 2 **Hung Parliament (FR)**[21] 1552 3-9-2 0 DavyBonilla 7 79
(Tom Dascombe) *nvr figured* **40/1**

14 ¾ **Midsummer Fair (USA)**[31] 1338 3-9-2 0 MickaelBarzalona 2 77
(Mahmood Al Zarooni) *settled midfield on rail: rdn and sn wknd early in st* **16/1**

1m 36.33s (-2.07) **Going Correction** +0.05s/f (Good) **14** Ran SP% **126.2**
Speed ratings: **112,110,109,108,108 108,107,107,106,106 100,98,96,95**
WIN (incl 1 euro stake): 7.80 (Tin Horse and Temps au Temps coupled). PLACES: 2.40, 7.80, 6.30. DF: 117.10. SF: 225.70..

Owner Marquesa De Moratalla **Bred** Marquesa De Moratalla **Trained** France
■ The first Group 1 winner for Didier Guillermin.

FOCUS
This had a far weaker look to it than the English 2000 Guineas and connections/supporters of Frankel won't be having too many sleepless nights that France holds a serious 3-y-o challenger to him. The gallop set by the leader looked fair, although plenty in behind were pulling for their heads, and unlike the Pouliches earlier on the card, horses did get involved from off the pace. The winning time was much quicker than the Pouliches. The Prix De Fontainebleau has provided the winner in seven of the last nine years (four of them were beaten in the trial), and that proved to be the key again. The standard is rated around the sixth, seventh and eighth.

NOTEBOOK
Tin Horse(IRE) improved past Glaswegian, who won the Prix De Fontainebleau, to claim victory. He'd been unlucky as a 2-y-o in the Prix Jean-Luc Lagardere, where he finished behind the favourite for this, but had more than enough good form to be a contender, although some of it had come over trips of five and 6f. There was a brief moment in the home straight when it looked as though he might meet trouble in running, but, luckily for his supporters, the gaps appeared and he came home strongly. He has a St James' Palace entry, one connections appear keen to take up, but surely isn't good enough to trouble an on-song Frankel.

Havane Smoker has always been well regarded and returned to his best with a solid performance. Beaten a narrow margin by Surfrider in Prix Djebel, he proved that form to be all wrong by readily reversing placings. He is on the upgrade and can be a leading player in Prix Du Jockey Club if aimed that way. However, the Jersey Stakes was also mentioned.

Venomous ran a blinder for a horse having his first outing in Group company, and with no obvious form claims. His jockey took a while to find space, but he came home strongly towards the centre of the course when in the clear. It remains to be seen if he is flattered by this effort and, of course, his run helps to give the form a modest look.

Temps Au Temps(IRE), tenth in the Prix De Fontainebleau, was one of the biggest eyecatchers, as although he had to drop in from a wide draw, he was going strongly at the top of the home straight in rear before passing all but three rivals.

Wootton Bassett, who finished in front of the winner last year in the Prix Jean-Luc Lagardere, had been the subject of some good recent reports, and as the only Group 1 winner in the field, he was rightly made favourite. He was handed a poor draw here but was able to get across quite easily to the front, and Paul Hanagan dictated matters while there - reports afterward suggest the plan to lead was formulated after seeing the Pouliches earlier on the card, where those on the speed dominated. The rider quickened the tempo on turning in but couldn't get away from the chasing pack and gave the impression that he didn't get home. Of course, he is entitled to another try at the trip in case the run was needed (he was the only runner in field that hadn't raced at least once this year), and then a far clearer opinion can be formed, but the temptation at the moment is to say he'll probably be most effective at the highest level over shorter than 1m. He was fine after the race and connections thought he went off too quick.

Barocci(JPN), fourth in the Prix De Fontainebleau, looked to get caught out by the quickening pace while being held up (he also got in behind a few horses), but came home well in the final stages. Beautifully bred, being by Japanese superstar Deep Impact, out of a 1m2f Listed winning daughter of Giant's Causeway, he will surely be of much more interest over further and he looks a likely type for the Prix Du Jockey Club.

Imperial Rome(IRE) had won his last three starts, a couple of minor events over 1m on Polytrack and a Listed race at the Curragh over 7f on quick turf. Ryan Moore took over but the horse looked one paced under pressure and not good enough.

Glaswegian was on the face of it disappointing, considering he'd beaten a few of these last time, but he looks to have plenty of size about him, and has the potential to be better the more he strengthens up.

Salto(IRE) looked worst affected by a lack of space. Olivier Peslier was desperate for room on a number of occasions in the final 2f and found every gap close on him until it was too late. It is difficult to say he may have won with any conviction, but he would have had every chance of placing had he been able to get a run when the jockey wanted to go.

Modern History(IRE), a half-brother to Favourable Terms, who was high-class over 1m-1m2f (including Group 1) for Sir Michael Stoute, showed promise on his only 2-y-o start but won both of his outings this year, defeating Glaswegian (albeit getting 4lb) in minor company over C&D before taking a Toulouse Listed race. Representing a trainer who had won this five times, including last year, he looked to pull too hard under Dettori close up in the early stages, and wasn't given a hard time once it was clear the jockey had accepted his mount was beat. It would be surprising if this was his true form.

Hung Parliament(FR) is British trained but all four starts since his debut had come in France. He pulled too hard in Prix De Fontainebleau on his return and did so again here at the rear of the field. Davy Bonilla accepted defeat quickly once the horse came off the bridle, so presumably the horse had nothing more to give. He is a fine, big sort, capable of winning a decent race, but he'll either need to race more prominently in the future or always hope that he will have a strong pace to sit off.

Midsummer Fair(USA), who was supplemented for this, found this a bridge too after winning the Wood Ditton on his only previous outing.

[1785] BATH (L-H)
Monday, May 16

OFFICIAL GOING: Firm (good to firm in places; 9.4)
Wind: Brisk ahead Weather: Overcast

2140 SIS LIVE H'CAP — 2m 1f 34y
2:00 (2:00) (Class 6) (0-65,65) 4-Y-O+ **£1,619** (£481; £240; £120) **Stalls** Centre

Form				RPR
4566	1		**Spiritonthemount (USA)**[13] 1794 6-8-5 **46** oh1 (b) ChrisCatlin 10 (Peter Hiatt) *rdn fr stalls and sn led: drvn 7f out: 6 l clr 5f out: drvn fnl 3f: hld on wl* **7/1**[3]	54
0530	2	2	**Miles Of Sunshine**[20] 1586 6-8-10 **51** SamHitchcott 3 (Ron Hodges) *hld up in rr: drvn and rapid hdwy over 3f out: chsd wnr wl over 1f out: kpt on but a wl hld* **14/1**	57
021-	3	3 ¼	**Aaman (IRE)**[212] 6921 5-9-10 **65** EddieAhern 8 (Bernard Llewellyn) *chsd wnr: rdn 3f out: styd on but nvr on terms: lost 2nd wl over 1f out* **11/4**[2]	67
330-	4	1	**Spinning Waters**[37] 6272 5-8-2 **46** oh1 SimonPearce(3) 6 (Dai Burchell) *in rr: pushed along over 4f out: styd on fnl 2f: nt rch ldrs* **5/2**[1]	47
5-60	5	hd	**Garth Mountain**[16] 1692 4-9-3 **60** CathyGannon 7 (David Evans) *chsd ldrs: rdn over 3f out: one pce fnl 2f* **8/1**	61
2356	6	14	**Prince Charlemagne (IRE)**[40] 1181 8-8-12 **58** MatthewCosham(5) 9 (Dr Jeremy Naylor) *in rr but in tch: hdwy 5f out: wd bnd 3f out and sn wknd* **20/1**	42
6003	7	2 ½	**Warrior Nation (FR)**[21] 1567 5-8-5 **46** oh1 DavidProbert 1 (Adrian Chamberlain) *chsd ldrs: rdn over 3f out: wknd over 2f out* **16/1**	27
0505	8	15	**Primera Rossa**[18] 1635 5-8-0 **46** oh1 (b) RyanPowell(5) 5 (J S Moore) *chsd ldrs: wknd 3f out: hung rt over 2f out* **33/1**	—
4133	9	13	**Noah Jameel**[33] 1308 9-9-4 **59** DaneO'Neill 2 (Tony Newcombe) *in tch: rdn and wknd 3f out: t.o* **7/1**[3]	—
060/	10	54	**Galandora**[53] 6857 11-8-2 **46** oh1 (t) AmyBaker(3) 4 (Dr Jeremy Naylor) *slowly away: a in rr: t.o fr 1/2-way* **100/1**	—

3m 49.52s (-2.38) **Going Correction** -0.10s/f (Good)
WFA 4 from 5yo+ 2lb **10** Ran SP% **112.6**
Speed ratings (Par 101): **101,100,98,98,97 91,90,83,77,51**
toteswingers:1&2:£9.70, 1&3:£4.40, 2&3:£7.70 CSF £93.69 CT £331.57 TOTE £8.50: £2.50, £3.30, £2.10; EX 58.50 Trifecta £139.20 Pool: £233.37 - 1.24 winning units..
Owner Bob Coles **Bred** Ivy Dell Stud, Llc **Trained** Hook Norton, Oxon

FOCUS
There was a strong head wind in the straight, which would only have led to the ground drying further. It was changed to firm, good to firm in places before the opener. A low-grade staying handicap, and weak form with half the field out of the handicap.
Noah Jameel Official explanation: vet said gelding finished lame and bled from the nose

2141 LINDLEY CATERING MEDIAN AUCTION MAIDEN STKS — 5f 11y
2:30 (2:31) (Class 6) 3-4-Y-O **£1,619** (£481; £240; £120) **Stalls** Centre

Form				RPR
0-5	1		**Black Cadillac (IRE)**[37] 1236 3-9-0 0 (v[1]) DavidProbert 3 (Andrew Balding) *s.i.s: in rr: hdwy on inner fr 2f out: styd on u.p to ld fnl 50yds* **6/1**	63
254	2	¾	**Ladydolly**[14] 1764 3-8-6 55 AndrewHeffernan(3) 8 (Roy Brotherton) *slt ld: rdn fr ins fnl 2f: kpt narrow advantage tl hdd and no ex fnl 50yds* **12/1**	55
3-4	3	½	**Circuitous**[9] 1900 3-9-0 0 ChrisCatlin 7 (Paul Cole) *chsd ldrs: drvn to chal fr 2f out: styd on fnl f but nt pce of ldng duo clsng stages* **3/1**[1]	58
	4	¾	**Howyadoingnotsobad (IRE)** 3-8-11 0 RossAtkinson(3) 5 (Karen George) *s.i.s: sn in tch: hdwy over 2f out: pressed ldrs ins fnl f: styd on same pce cl home* **20/1**	56
00-0	5	shd	**Silca Conegliano (IRE)**[14] 1753 3-8-6 57 MartinHarley(3) 6 (Mick Channon) *in rr: rdn 3f out: styd on u.pover 1f out: r.o wl clsng stages: nt rch ldrs* **9/1**	50
5	6	1 ½	**Lady Rumba**[18] 1629 3-8-4 0 RyanPowell(5) 1 (John O'Shea) *sn chsng ldrs: pushed along 2f out on ins: outpcd over 1f out: styd on again clsng stages* **33/1**	45
6236	7	nk	**Dancing Tara**[6] 1980 3-8-9 54 CathyGannon 2 (David Evans) *w ldr: stl ev ch over 1f out: wknd ins fnl f* **11/2**[3]	44
0350	8	1	**Majestic Ridge (IRE)**[6] 1980 3-9-0 56 TomMcLaughlin 10 (David Evans) *wnt rt s: in rr but in tch: hdwy on outside over 1f out: rdn and kpt on fnl f but nvr in contention* **6/1**	45
2-0	9	shd	**Pearl Storm (IRE)**[10] 1880 3-9-0 0 EddieAhern 4 (William Haggas) *chsd ldrs: pushed along and nt clr run over 1f out: stl there whn bmpd sn after: sn btn* **7/2**[2]	45
00-6	10	3 ¼	**Alspritza**[20] 1591 3-8-9 45 NickyMackay 9 (Chris Wall) *chsd ldrs: rdn over 2f out: hung lft and wknd over 1f out* **50/1**	28
0	11	2 ¾	**Dorothy's Dream (IRE)**[18] 1629 3-8-9 0 RobertHavlin 11 (John O'Shea) *s.i.s: outpcd* **40/1**	18

63.85 secs (1.35) **Going Correction** +0.25s/f (Good) **11** Ran SP% **121.0**
Speed ratings (Par 101): **99,97,97,95,95 93,92,91,91,85 81**
toteswingers:1&2:£13.90, 1&3:£5.80, 2&3:£4.70 CSF £74.54 TOTE £8.50: £2.10, £3.30, £1.60; EX 77.50 Trifecta £78.40 Pool: £184.56 - 1.74 winning units..
Owner N Botica **Bred** John Foley & Miss Ann Aungier **Trained** Kingsclere, Hants

FOCUS
A typically weak 3-y-o plus sprint maiden.

2142 M.J. CHURCH H'CAP — 5f 161y
3:00 (3:02) (Class 5) (0-70,70) 4-Y-O+ **£2,266** (£674; £337; £168) **Stalls** Centre

Form				RPR
0-64	1		**Kyllachy Storm**[7] 1937 7-8-5 **59** HarryBentley(5) 8 (Ron Hodges) *chsd ldrs: led over 1f out: pushed along and styd on strly fnl f* **6/1**[3]	73
1-61	2	2 ¼	**Wooden King (IRE)**[14] 1752 6-9-7 **70** TomMcLaughlin 12 (Malcolm Saunders) *chsd ldrs towards outside: drvn to chse wnr 1f out: no imp but hld on wl for 2nd* **9/2**[1]	77
20-3	3	nk	**Witchry**[15] 1730 9-9-0 **63** DaneO'Neill 9 (Tony Newcombe) *in tch: hdwy on outside and hrd drvn over 1f out: styd on ins fnl f to press for 2nd but no ch w wnr* **6/1**[3]	69
22-1	4	2	**Bilash**[9] 1899 4-9-5 **68** JimCrowley 4 (Reg Hollinshead) *stdd s and racd wl in tch: rdn over 1f out and kpt on same pce* **8/1**	67

-025 **5** *hd* **Talamahana**[11] 1831 6-8-7 **56** oh2 (v) ChrisCatlin 5 55
(Andrew Haynes) *in rr: pushed along over 2f out: styd on towards outside over 1f out: kpt on cl home but nvr gng pce to rch ldrs* **33/1**

40-4 **6** *shd* **The Name Is Frank**[13] 1787 6-8-12 **61** (t) EddieAhern 1 59
(Mark Gillard) *sn led: rdn 2f out: hdd over 1f out and sn wknd* **11/2**[2]

01-0 **7** *hd* **Sermons Mount (USA)**[21] 1562 5-9-4 **67** TravisBlock 11 65
(Mouse Hamilton-Fairley) *in rr: hdwy towards outside over 1f out: kpt on: nt rch ldrs* **9/1**

05-U **8** *7* **Dusty Spirit**[11] 1838 4-8-11 **67** (t) JakePayne(7) 7 42
(Bill Turner) *chsd ldrs: rdn 1/2-way: wknd wl over 1f out* **28/1**

00-0 **9** *½* **Hoh Hoh Hoh**[14] 1752 9-9-4 **67** SebSanders 10 40
(Richard Price) *in rr: sme hdwy on outside 2f out: nvr rchd ldrs and sn wknd* **20/1**

3515 **10** *4 ½* **Bateleur**[6] 1982 7-8-10 **62** MartinHarley(3) 6 20
(Mick Channon) *s.i.s: sn rcvrd into mid-div: wknd ins fnl 2f* **11/2**[2]

0-00 **11** *nk* **Excellent Vision**[23] 1523 4-8-11 **60** CathyGannon 3 17
(Milton Bradley) *chsd ldrs over 3f* **50/1**

34-0 **12** *3 ¼* **Millden**[9] 1912 4-8-9 **58** NickyMackay 2 —
(Milton Bradley) *chsd ldrs to 1/2-way* **25/1**

1m 12.25s (1.05) **Going Correction** +0.25s/f (Good) **12** Ran SP% **115.6**
Speed ratings (Par 103): **103,100,99,96,96 96,96,86,86,80 79,75**
toteswingers:1&2:£6.00, 1&3:£6.50, 2&3:£4.90 CSF £30.16 CT £169.75 TOTE £7.30: £2.10, £1.50, £2.60; EX 38.80 Trifecta £304.90 Pool: £453.27 - 1.10 winning units..
Owner Mrs Angela Hart **Bred** Sir Eric Parker **Trained** Charlton Mackrell, Somerset

FOCUS
A modest sprint handicap but the form is sound enough. The winner's best effort since his third in this race last year.
Excellent Vision Official explanation: jockey said gelding had no more to give

2143 BRITISH STALLION STUDS E B F / SIS LIVE MAIDEN STKS 5f 161y
3:30 (3:30) (Class 5) 2-Y-0 **£3,173** (£944; £471; £235) **Stalls** Centre

Form RPR

1 **Percy Jackson** 2-9-3 0 EddieAhern 5 80+
(Denis Coakley) *in tch: trckd ldrs and hdwy 2f out: led wl over 1f out: pushed clr: easily* **2/1**[1]

6 **2** *2 ¼* **Otto The Great**[14] 1757 2-9-3 0 ShaneKelly 7 73
(Walter Swinburn) *trckd ldrs: chsd wnr appr fnl f and kpt on but a easily hld* **7/1**

60 **3** *1 ½* **Xinbama (IRE)**[16] 1691 2-9-3 0 SebSanders 2 68
(J W Hills) *pressed ldrs: drvn to chal 2f out: outpcd by ldng duo fnl f* **12/1**

4 *2* **Armiger** 2-9-3 0 MartinDwyer 9 61
(William Muir) *broke wl: sn outpcd: swtchd lft to ins fr 2f out and kpt on fnl f but nt pce of ldng trio* **33/1**

0624 **5** *6* **Courtland King (IRE)**[11] 1823 2-9-3 0 CathyGannon 1 41
(David Evans) *slt ld: rdn and hung rt fr 2f out: hdd & wknd wl over 1f out* **3/1**[3]

6 *½* **Faraway** 2-9-3 0 ChrisCatlin 8 40
(William Haggas) *a outpcd* **14/1**

33 **7** *1* **Lord Ali McJones**[11] 1823 2-9-3 0 JimCrowley 6 36
(Tom Dascombe) *chsd ldrs on outside: wknd u.p fr 2f out* **11/4**[2]

0 **8** *7* **Jawim**[20] 1583 2-8-12 0 TomMcLaughlin 4 —
(Malcolm Saunders) *spd 3f* **100/1**

1m 13.85s (2.65) **Going Correction** +0.25s/f (Good) **8** Ran SP% **115.8**
Speed ratings (Par 93): **92,89,87,84,76 75,74,65**
toteswingers:1&2:£3.50, 1&3:£5.80, 2&3:£8.00 CSF £17.28 TOTE £3.20: £1.30, £2.80, £2.60; EX 15.90 Trifecta £108.00 Pool: £421.97 - 2.89 winning units..
Owner Count Calypso Racing **Bred** Clive Dennett **Trained** West Ilsley, Berks

FOCUS
An interesting juvenile maiden. Not much form to go on but this probably be towards the weaker end of the averages.

NOTEBOOK
Percy Jackson was a first runner, and winner, for Derby-winning sire Sir Percy. Very well backed, he was given a nice introductory ride by Eddie Ahern, and readily asserted without being given an overly hard time. He looks a decent prospect and, while there are no specific plans, he'll definitely appreciate further in time. (op 7-2)
Otto The Great had clearly learned a good deal from his debut run, travelling nicely and picking up well, but the winner was just too good. (op 8-1)
Xinbama(IRE) ran his best race yet and will be of interest in nurseries later in the season. (op 14-1)
Armiger is related to numerous winners, but mainly over further, and he very much looked in need of this initial experience.
Courtland King(IRE) had all the experience, but looked vulnerable against several less exposed types, and was readily brushed aside. (tchd 11-4)
Faraway was soon outpaced, but should improve. (op 11-1)
Lord Ali McJones was disappointing, failing to reproduce anything like the form shown in two previous starts having been out wide. (op 2-1 tchd 3-1)

2144 MRS GLYNIS TAYLOR BIRTHDAY H'CAP 1m 5y
4:00 (4:00) (Class 5) (0-70,70) 4-Y-0+ **£2,266** (£674; £337; £168) **Stalls** Low

Form RPR

0-63 **1** **Jewelled**[13] 1789 5-9-7 **70** SebSanders 7 77
(Lady Herries) *hld up in rr: hdwy on outside over 2f out: drvn and styd on wl to ld clsng stages* **2/1**[1]

1113 **2** *¾* **Angelena Ballerina (IRE)**[14] 1755 4-9-2 **65** (v) KirstyMilczarek 4 70
(Karen George) *t.k.h: trckd ldr: drvn to chal over 2f out: slt ld 1f out: repeatedly pressed tl hdd and no ex clsng stages* **6/1**

0-00 **3** *½* **Mr Udagawa**[11] 1829 5-8-11 **60** (p) DavidProbert 1 64
(Bernard Llewellyn) *led: jnd over 2f out: narrowly hdd 1f out: styd chalng tl one pce fnl 30yds* **20/1**

0-02 **4** *1 ¾* **Goose Green (IRE)**[18] 1625 7-8-2 **56** oh3 HarryBentley(5) 6 56
(Ron Hodges) *chsd ldrs: rdn to chal ins fnl 2f: wknd ins fnl f* **11/2**[3]

30-0 **5** *1* **Yourgolftravel Com**[18] 1635 6-8-7 **56** oh1 (bt[1]) ChrisCatlin 2 54
(David Pipe) *stdd s: t.k.h in rr: rdn over 2f out: prog u.p ins fnl f but nt rch ldrs* **20/1**

255- **6** *¾* **Catchanova (IRE)**[210] 6991 4-9-0 **63** EddieAhern 5 59
(Eve Johnson Houghton) *stdd in rr but in tch: rdn over 2f out and no imp on ldrs* **5/2**[2]

3003 **7** *1* **Regal Rave (USA)**[18] 1637 4-8-11 **60** DaneO'Neill 3 54
(Mouse Hamilton-Fairley) *t.k.h: chsd ldrs: rdn over 2f out: btn sn after* **6/1**

1m 44.47s (3.67) **Going Correction** -0.10s/f (Good) **7** Ran SP% **115.4**
Speed ratings (Par 103): **77,76,75,74,73 72,71**
toteswingers:1&2:£3.40, 1&3:£8.60, 2&3:£11.60 CSF £14.92 TOTE £3.40: £2.00, £3.10; EX 15.80.
Owner Seymour Bloodstock (uk) Ltd **Bred** Wyck Hall Stud Ltd **Trained** Patching, W Sussex

FOCUS
The early pace was very steady for this 1m handicap. Slightly muddling form, rated around the runner-up.

2145 LINDLEY CATERING FILLIES' H'CAP 1m 5f 22y
4:30 (4:30) (Class 5) (0-70,70) 4-Y-0+ **£2,266** (£674; £337; £168) **Stalls** High

Form RPR

0-11 **1** **Laverre (IRE)**[10] 1871 4-9-7 **70** DaneO'Neill 7 76
(Lucy Wadham) *racd in 4th tl hdwy 3f out: pushed along to chse ldr appr fnl 2f: chal fr 1f out tl led fnl 100yds: drvn out* **8/15**[1]

0160 **2** *nk* **Gems**[6] 1987 4-8-7 **56** oh2 ChrisCatlin 3 61
(Peter Hiatt) *led: t.k.h: hrd rdn fr over 1f out and sn jnd: kpt slt advantage tl hdd and no ex fnl 100yds* **12/1**

01-4 **3** *2* **Leitzu (IRE)**[40] 1167 4-8-8 **64** CharlesBishop(7) 2 67
(Mick Channon) *rrd leaving stalls: bhd but in tch: swtchd rt to outside over 1f out and styd on to take 3rd ins fnl f but imp on ldng duo* **7/1**[3]

0216 **4** *¾* **Money Money Money**[20] 1586 5-9-0 **63** (b) JamesMillman 5 64
(Rod Millman) *t.k.h: chsd to 3f out: sn rdn: styd on same pce fr over 1f out* **5/1**[2]

3-00 **5** *2 ½* **Hibba (USA)**[18] 1635 4-8-4 **56** oh4 SimonPearce(3) 4 53
(Mouse Hamilton-Fairley) *in rr: pushed along 3f out: sme prog sn after: nvr rchd ldrs and btn over 1f out* **50/1**

0-00 **6** *¾* **Double Fortune**[11] 1839 4-8-8 **57** oh1 ow1 (p) RobertHavlin 1 53
(Jamie Poulton) *chsd ldrs: wnt 2nd u.p 3f out tl over 2f out: wknd ins fnl f* **20/1**

2m 54.58s (2.58) **Going Correction** -0.10s/f (Good) **6** Ran SP% **108.8**
Speed ratings (Par 100): **88,87,86,86,84 84**
toteswingers:1&2:£2.00, 1&3:£1.90, 2&3:£4.60 CSF £7.56 TOTE £2.00: £1.40, £5.90; EX 7.20.
Owner Mr And Mrs A E Pakenham **Bred** Kilnamoragh Stud **Trained** Newmarket, Suffolk

FOCUS
There wasn't much pace on early in this middle-distance handicap, and it probably wasn't a thorough test at the distance. Moderate form, rated slightly negatively.

2146 DIGIBET.COM H'CAP 1m 2f 46y
5:00 (5:00) (Class 5) (0-75,74) 3-Y-0 **£2,266** (£674; £337; £168) **Stalls** Low

Form RPR

05-5 **1** **Canaveral**[28] 1445 3-9-0 **67** MartinDwyer 4 75
(Brian Meehan) *trckd ldr: drvn fr 3f out: hung lft u.p over 1f out sn chalng: led fnl 150yds: won gng away* **13/8**[1]

3234 **2** *1 ¼* **Dressing Room (USA)**[16] 1692 3-9-6 **73** (v) RoystonFfrench 6 78
(Mark Johnston) *led: rdn over 1f out: hdd fnl 150yds: no ex* **4/1**[3]

-016 **3** *1* **Zamina (IRE)**[16] 1683 3-9-0 **67** TravisBlock 3 70
(Sylvester Kirk) *in rr but in tch tl rdn and outpcd 3f out: styd on again over 1f out: tk 3rd cl home but no imp on ldng duo* **3/1**[2]

40-5 **4** *hd* **High On The Hog (IRE)**[26] 1481 3-8-13 **66** EddieAhern 7 69
(John Dunlop) *in rr but in tch: hdwy over 2f out and sn trcking ldng duo: outpcd appr fnl f: lost 3rd cl home* **3/1**[2]

6254 **5** *1 ¼* **Dew Reward (IRE)**[19] 1623 3-8-4 **60** SimonPearce(3) 1 60
(Eve Johnson Houghton) *chsd ldrs rdn over 2f out: no imp and styd on same pce* **12/1**

2m 10.99s (-0.01) **Going Correction** -0.10s/f (Good) **5** Ran SP% **115.8**
Speed ratings (Par 99): **96,95,94,94,93**
Totesuper 7: Win: Not won. Place: Not won CSF £9.06 TOTE £3.20: £1.02, £2.20; EX 7.30.
Owner Manton Racing Partnership **Bred** Heather Raw **Trained** Manton, Wilts

FOCUS
Few made appeal in this moderate 3-y-o handicap. The winner reversed Windsor form with the runner-up, and the form seems pretty sound.
Canaveral Official explanation: trainer's rep said, regarding apparent improvement in form, that the gelding did not act previously around Windsor but was much more relaxed having been fitted with a drop noseband.
T/Plt: £57.30 to a £1 stake. Pool:£52,004.96 - 661.79 winning tickets T/Qpdt: £11.30 to a £1 stake. Pool:£3,533.96 - 230.40 winning tickets ST

1654 LEICESTER (R-H)
Monday, May 16

OFFICIAL GOING: Good to firm (good in places; 8.0)
Wind: Medium, across Weather: sunny

2147 LADBROKES.COM JOHN FERNELEY H'CAP 7f 9y
6:10 (6:10) (Class 4) (0-80,80) 3-Y-0 **£3,238** (£963; £481; £240) **Stalls** High

Form RPR

50-1 **1** **Lightning Cloud (IRE)**[34] 1288 3-9-2 **75** PhillipMakin 2 87+
(Kevin Ryan) *t.k.h: hld up in midfield: shkn up to ld over 1f out: rdn ent fnl f: fnd ex whn pressed fnl 100yds: r.o wl: rdn out* **13/8**[1]

1552 **2** *1* **City Legend**[9] 1916 3-8-13 **72** (bt) RobertWinston 4 79
(Alan McCabe) *sn pushed along in last trio: rdn and effrt towards centre over 2f out: styd on u.p to press wnr fnl 100yds: no ex and hld readily hld towards fin* **15/2**

05-5 **3** *1* **My Son Max**[9] 1916 3-9-7 **80** PatDobbs 3 84
(Richard Hannon) *stdd s: hld up in last trio: rdn over 2f out: hdwy on stands' rail over 1f out: chsd wnr ent fnl f tl ins fnl f: one pce fnl 100yds* **15/2**

53-3 **4** *3 ¼* **Red Marling (IRE)**[19] 1611 3-8-5 **71** MatthewLawson(7) 6 66
(B W Hills) *led: rdn 2f out: hdd over 1f out: wknd ins fnl f* **7/1**[3]

321 **5** *1 ¾* **Shostakovich (IRE)**[11] 1830 3-8-13 **72** (tp) JamesDoyle 9 63
(Sylvester Kirk) *chsd ldr tl wl over 1f out: nt qckning: hung rt and racing awkwardly whn hmpd over 1f out: n.d fnl f* **5/1**[2]

1124 **6** *8* **May's Boy**[32] 1335 3-8-9 **73** (p) LeeNewnes(5) 5 42
(Mark Usher) *chsd ldrs: rdn jst over 2f out: wknd qckly wl over 1f out: wl bhd fnl f* **8/1**

14 **7** *6* **National Hope (IRE)**[73] 764 3-9-0 **73** TonyCulhane 1 26
(George Baker) *stdd and awkward leaving stalls: t.k.h: hld up in last trio: pushed along 1/2-way: effrt u.p over 2f out: wknd wl over 1f out: wl btn and eased ins fnl f* **10/1**

1m 24.65s (-1.55) **Going Correction** -0.175s/f (Firm) **7** Ran SP% **111.0**
Speed ratings (Par 101): **101,99,98,95,93 83,77**
toteswingers: 1&2 £4.70, 1&3 £5.10, 2&3 £7.00 CSF £13.48 CT £66.76 TOTE £2.10: £1.10, £2.50.
Owner Hambleton Racing Ltd XVIII **Bred** John Cullinan **Trained** Hambleton, N Yorks

FOCUS
The going was good to firm, good in places. An ordinary handicap run at a fair pace. The well-backed favourite was value for a bit more than the winning margin implies and should be able to win more races. The second and third set the standard.
Shostakovich(IRE) Official explanation: jockey said colt hung right

May's Boy Official explanation: jockey said colt never travelled

2148 BRITISH STALLION STUDS E B F LADBROKES.COM MAIDEN STKS 5f 2y

6:40 (6:40) (Class 4) 2-Y-O **£4,338** (£1,291; £645; £322) **Stalls** High

Form RPR

1 **Arnold Lane (IRE)** 2-9-3 0 SamHitchcott 6 83+
(Mick Channon) *s.i.s: in tch towards rr: hdwy 1/2-way: pushed along to ld wl over 1f out: edgd rt fnl f: r.o wl* **15/2**[3]

0 2 1 ¼ **Red Aggressor (IRE)**[15] 1721 2-9-3 0 PhilipRobinson 2 78
(Clive Brittain) *chsd ldrs: rdn to chse wnr over 2f out: pressed wnr ins fnl f: no ex and btn fnl 75yds* **40/1**

3 3 2 **Shere Khan**[7] 1932 2-9-3 0 PatDobbs 4 71
(Richard Hannon) *dwlt: sn in tch in midfield: nt clr run ent fnl 2f: rdn over 1f out: no threat to ldng pair but kpt on fnl f: wnt 3rd towards fin* **10/1**

3 4 nk **Crowning Star (IRE)**[44] 1095 2-9-3 0 LukeMorris 3 70
(J S Moore) *s.i.s: sn pushed along: rdn and hdwy on outer ent fnl 2f: chsd ldng pair ent fnl f: no imp: wknd fnl 100yds* **2/1**[2]

5 2 **Alabanda (IRE)** 2-8-12 0 DavidAllan 7 58
(Tim Easterby) *in tch in midfield: shuffled bk towards rr 1/2-way: swtchd lft and sme hdwy over 1f out: kpt on fnl f but no ch w ldrs* **20/1**

32 6 2 **Sea Odyssey (IRE)**[11] 1823 2-9-3 0 MichaelHills 5 56
(B W Hills) *w ldr tl led after 2f: hdd and rdn wl over 1f out: btn ent fnl f: fdd* **6/4**[1]

524 7 2 ¼ **Always Ends Well (IRE)**[18] 1632 2-8-12 0 GregFairley 1 42
(Mark Johnston) *led for 2f: pressed ldr tl 2f out: wknd over 1f out: wl btn fnl f* **16/1**

5343 8 3 ¾ **Sabusa (IRE)**[19] 1619 2-9-3 0 (b[1]) JamesDoyle 8 34
(Alan McCabe) *chsd ldrs: rdn over 2f out: wkng and towards rr whn hung rt and hmpd wl over 1f out: wl btn fnl f* **40/1**

3 9 ½ **Pius Parker (IRE)**[18] 1632 2-9-3 0 TadhgO'Shea 9 32
(John Gallagher) *s.i.s: sn niggled towards rr: rdn and no hdwy ent fnl 2f: hung rt and wl btn ent fnl f* **28/1**

59.80 secs (-0.20) **Going Correction** -0.175s/f (Firm) 9 Ran SP% **113.2**
Speed ratings (Par 95): **94,92,88,88,85 81,78,72,71**
toteswingers: 1&2 £23.80, 1&3 £14.30, 2&3 £77.80 CSF £259.24 TOTE £11.40: £2.70, £12.10, £4.40; EX 178.90.
Owner Nick & Olga Dhandsa & John & Zoe Webster **Bred** Lynn Lodge Stud **Trained** West Ilsley, Berks

FOCUS
A decent maiden, as it often is. The market leaders finished fourth and sixth but there was plenty to like about the performance of a winning newcomer, who looks a likely improver.

NOTEBOOK
Arnold Lane(IRE) had a fair target to aim at on debut but he was sent off third favourite and powered through from off the pace to win with a bit in hand. The negative from a form point of view is that the favourite was disappointing and the second was a big price, but this was still a very pleasing debut by a colt who cost 60,000euros as a yearling and is out of an unraced half-sister to several winners, including Zoning who was smart at up to 1m. (op 9-2)
Red Aggressor(IRE) raced freely before dropping out on his Newmarket debut, but he settled better and looked a lot more streetwise in this much improved second run. This 20,000gns colt has plenty of speed in his pedigree and should go close in a similar race next time.
Shere Khan looked inexperienced when unable to deliver at odds-on in a Brighton maiden last week, but it was interesting that he was turned out quickly and he stayed on steadily behind the front pair. He should be able emulate his half-brother Roches Des Vents who was a 5f 2-y-o winner for the stable at around this time last year. (op 12-1 tchd 9-1)
Crowning Star(IRE) was a promising 12-1 third in the Brocklesby on debut, form which was boosted by the winner dominating a novice stakes last week and the second finishing placed in the Lily Agnes. He had decent form claims and made a promising move out widest of all before his effort flattened out. (op 5-2 after early 3-1 in places)
Alabanda(IRE) looked inexperienced but shaped with promise on debut. She is a sister to 6f 2-y-o winner Camache Queen and is out of a triple 6f-7f winner. (tchd 22-1)
Sea Odyssey(IRE) had strong claims on his placed efforts in decent maidens at Windsor and Chester. He was well backed and adopted a prominent position but didn't find much when the closers loomed up. (op 15-8 after early 2-1 and 9-4 in places)
Sabusa(IRE) was reported to have hung right. Official explanation: jockey said colt hung right (op 33-1)

2149 LADBROKES.COM JAMES WARD (S) STKS 1m 60y

7:10 (7:10) (Class 6) 3-Y-O+ **£1,619** (£481; £240; £120) **Stalls** Low

Form RPR

4012 1 **Fremen (USA)**[11] 1828 11-9-12 77 PaulQuinn 5 78+
(David Nicholls) *chsd ldr tl led after 2f: mde rest: pushed along and readily asserted over 1f out: nudged along fnl f: easily* **8/11**[1]

03-0 2 3 ¼ **Fault**[134] 9 5-9-7 64 (t) TomQueally 1 65
(Stef Higgins) *t.k.h: chsd ldrs: drvn and effrt to chse wnr ent fnl 2f: readily brushed aside over 1f out: plugged on same pce fnl f* **7/1**[2]

6400 3 1 ¾ **Kenswick**[54] 950 4-9-2 46 (v) FrannyNorton 8 56
(Pat Eddery) *stdd s: hld up towards rr: rdn and hdwy on inner 2f out: kpt on u.p fnl f: no ch w wnr* **16/1**

-205 4 ½ **Just Five (IRE)**[19] 1614 5-9-4 75 PatrickDonaghy[(3)] 11 60
(Michael Dods) *chsd ldr: rdn over 2f out: outpcd u.p wl over 1f out: one pce and wl hld fnl f* **12/1**[3]

0035 5 ¾ **Jasmin Rai**[18] 1636 4-9-2 50 LukeMorris 12 53
(Des Donovan) *stdd s and swtchd rt after s: hld up in rr: stl plenty to do and effrt on inner 2f out: drvn and styd on same pce fr over 1f out* **33/1**

-003 6 4 ½ **Fawley Green**[20] 1592 4-9-7 60 (v[1]) DarryllHolland 2 48
(William Muir) *dwlt: sn t.k.h and hdwy to r in midfield: rdn and no hdwy wl over 2f out: wknd 2f out* **25/1**

6-30 7 3 ½ **Lady Florence**[10] 1878 6-9-2 72 JamesDoyle 7 35
(David C Griffiths) *led for 2f: chsd wnr tl ent fnl 2f: wknd u.p wl over 1f out: wl btn fnl f* **14/1**

0464 8 ¾ **Sirjosh**[18] 1633 5-9-7 54 AndreaAtzeni 3 38
(Des Donovan) *in tch in midfield: rdn and struggling 3f out: wknd 2f out: wl bhd fnl f* **33/1**

-550 9 1 ¾ **Bajan Pride**[9] 1905 7-9-7 58 (p) MickyFenton 6 34
(Paul Midgley) *a towards rr: rdn and btn wl over 2f out: wl bhd fnl f* **50/1**

0000 10 7 **Advertise**[10] 1866 5-9-7 65 EddieCreighton 4 18
(Joseph Tuite) *stdd s: t.k.h: hld up in rr: effrt on outer ent fnl 3f: sn btn: wl bhd and eased ins fnl f: t.o* **40/1**

06 11 23 **The Blind Side (IRE)**[33] 1302 3-8-9 0 NeilChalmers 10 —
(Michael Appleby) *wnt lft s: a in rr: lost tch over 2f out* **150/1**

1m 44.31s (-0.79) **Going Correction** -0.025s/f (Good) 11 Ran SP% **105.4**
WFA 3 from 4yo+ 12lb
Speed ratings (Par 101): **102,98,97,96,95 91,87,87,85,55 78**
toteswingers: 1&2 £1.10, 1&3 £4.90, 2&3 £6.60 CSF £4.00 TOTE £2.20: £1.20, £1.20, £5.20; EX 5.50.There was no bid for the winner. Just Five was claimed by Mr Alan D Crombie for £7,000.
Owner Middleham Park Racing XXXV C King A Seed **Bred** Flaxman Holdings Ltd **Trained** Sessay, N Yorks
■ Unlimited (8/1) was withdrawn after proving unruly in the stalls. R4 applies, deduct 10p in the £.

FOCUS
Quite a few had something to prove or find in this seller, and the heavily backed favourite ran out a clear-cut winner. He didn't need to match his recent best.

2150 LADBROKES.COM G.D. GILES H'CAP 1m 1f 218y

7:40 (7:40) (Class 4) (0-80,79) 4-Y-O+ **£3,238** (£963; £481; £240) **Stalls** Low

Form RPR

3-06 1 **Effigy**[14] 1772 7-8-8 71 AmyScott[(5)] 8 77
(Henry Candy) *hld up in tch: swtchd lft and effrt 2f out: rdn to chal ent fnl f: led ins fnl f: hld on wl* **6/1**

240- 2 ½ **Wiggy Smith**[230] 6447 12-9-5 77 FergusSweeney 4 82
(Henry Candy) *hld up wl off the pce in last pair: clsd and in tch 5f out: rdn and effrt wl over 1f out: hdwy to press ldrs 1f out: ev ch fnl 100yds: kpt on but hld towards fin* **4/1**[1]

0-00 3 ½ **Bollin Dolly**[19] 1622 8-9-2 74 DavidAllan 1 78
(Tim Easterby) *t.k.h: led for 2f: chsd ldr after tl led again 3f out: sn rdn: hdd ins fnl f: kpt on same pce after* **5/1**[3]

-466 4 ½ **The Cayterers**[28] 1443 9-9-4 79 MichaelO'Connell[(3)] 5 82
(Tony Carroll) *in tch in midfield: hdwy on inner 3f out: swtchd lft over 1f out: chsng ldrs but nvr enough room thrght fnl f: swtchd rt and kpt on cl home: unable to chal* **5/1**[3]

-651 5 1 **Understory (USA)**[41] 1144 4-9-4 76 TomQueally 9 77
(Tim McCarthy) *chsd ldrs: ev ch 3f out: rdn ent fnl 2f: stl ev ch 1f wknd ins fnl f* **11/1**

045- 6 11 **Supa Seeker (USA)**[222] 6677 5-8-10 68 LukeMorris 10 47
(Tony Carroll) *s.i.s: racd in midfield: rdn and effrt ent fnl 3f: wknd 2f out: wl bhd fnl f* **9/2**[2]

10-0 7 7 **Ancient Greece**[28] 1443 4-9-0 72 TonyCulhane 3 37
(George Baker) *sn bhd: detached last and losing tch 5f out: n.d after* **11/1**

315- 8 2 ¼ **Aspro Mavro (IRE)**[18] 1780 5-9-5 77 (b[1]) DarryllHolland 7 38
(Jim Best) *chsd ldr tl led after 2f: hdd 3f out: wknd qckly over 2f out: eased ins fnl f* **10/1**

2m 6.22s (-1.68) **Going Correction** -0.025s/f (Good) 8 Ran SP% **111.6**
Speed ratings (Par 105): **105,104,104,103,103 94,88,86**
toteswingers: 1&2 £5.20, 1&3 £4.70, 2&3 £5.10 CSF £28.66 CT £125.29 TOTE £8.70: £1.10, £2.10, £2.50; EX 17.70.
Owner Henry Candy **Bred** The Earl Cadogan **Trained** Kingston Warren, Oxon

FOCUS
A fair handicap. The first five finished in a bunch and were clear of the rest. Ordinary form for the grade, rated around the runner-up.
Aspro Mavro(IRE) Official explanation: trainer's rep said gelding was unsuited by the good to firm (good in places) ground

2151 LADBROKES.COM SARTORIUS MAIDEN STKS 5f 218y

8:10 (8:13) (Class 5) 3-Y-O **£2,388** (£705; £352) **Stalls** High

Form RPR

0- 1 **Amazing Amoray (IRE)**[334] 3087 3-9-3 0 PhillipMakin 7 87
(David Barron) *t.k.h: chsd ldrs: hdwy to ld over 1f out: edgd lft u.p 1f out: r.o strly and drew clr fnl 150yds: readily* **9/1**

32- 2 3 ¾ **Formal Demand**[304] 4110 3-9-3 0 JamieSpencer 5 75+
(Edward Vaughan) *stdd s: t.k.h: hld up towards rr: hdwy into midfield 1/2-way: hdwy to chse wnr over 1f out: rdn ent fnl f: outpcd by wnr ins fnl f: kpt on for clr 2nd* **4/1**[2]

6-0 3 2 ½ **Logans Legend (IRE)**[21] 1565 3-9-3 0 MichaelHills 13 67
(B W Hills) *chsd ldrs: rdn wl over 1f out: unable qck over 1f out: chsd ldng pair fnl f: no imp* **4/1**[2]

5 4 2 ¾ **West Side (IRE)**[20] 1591 3-9-3 0 (t) DarryllHolland 12 58+
(Jeremy Noseda) *s.i.s: bhd: rn green and hung rt 1/2-way: hdwy wl over 1f out: running on whn swtchd rt ins fnl f: gng on wl fin: nvr trbld ldrs* **12/1**

5 ½ **Izzy The Ozzy (IRE)** 3-8-7 0 LMcNiff[(5)] 14 52+
(David Barron) *stdd s: wl bhd: pushed along ent fnl 2f: hdwy over 1f out: r.o wl ins fnl f: gng on wl fin: nvr trbld ldrs* **33/1**

0-32 6 ½ **Alpha Delta Whisky**[42] 1130 3-9-3 72 TadhgO'Shea 11 55
(John Gallagher) *racd keenly: w ldr: ev ch and rdn ent fnl 2f: btn jst over 1f out: wknd ins fnl f* **10/1**

7 1 ¼ **Ragda** 3-8-12 0 TomQueally 6 46
(Jeremy Noseda) *s.i.s: racd off the pce towards rr: rdn along and rn green 1/2-way: sme hdwy over 1f out: nvr trbld ldrs* **7/1**[3]

00-2 8 2 ½ **Mixed Emotions (IRE)**[31] 1358 3-8-12 71 PatDobbs 1 38
(Richard Hannon) *t.k.h: chsd ldrs: rdn ent fnl 2f: wknd qckly over 1f out: fdd fnl f* **11/4**[1]

6 9 1 ¼ **Ollianna (IRE)**[13] 1795 3-8-12 0 RobertWinston 10 34
(Tom Dascombe) *racd freely: led: rdn 2f out: hdd over 1f out: wknd qckly jst over 1f out: fdd fnl f* **22/1**

4- 10 2 ¾ **Crabbies Bay**[334] 3072 3-8-12 0 TomEaves 3 25
(Lisa Williamson) *racd in midfield: rdn and lost pl 3f out: bhd and no ch whn nt clr run and hmpd over 1f out* **100/1**

00 11 1 ¼ **Zanoubiatta (USA)**[20] 1591 3-8-7 0 HarryBentley[(5)] 2 21
(Ed Dunlop) *in tch: rdn and struggling wl over 2f out: wknd 2f out: wl btn whn hung rt over 1f out* **33/1**

12 7 **Tigerbill** 3-9-3 0 LukeMorris 9 —
(Nicky Vaughan) *s.i.s: a outpcd towards rr: stuggling bdly fr 1/2-way* **66/1**

1m 11.47s (-1.53) **Going Correction** -0.175s/f (Firm) 12 Ran SP% **118.7**
Speed ratings (Par 99): **103,98,94,91,90 89,88,84,83,79 77,68**
toteswingers: 1&2 £7.30, 1&3 £6.30, 2&3 £3.00 CSF £43.43 TOTE £11.40: £3.60, £1.10, £1.90; EX 56.60.
Owner Raymond Miquel **Bred** Marie & Mossy Fahy **Trained** Maunby, N Yorks

FOCUS
A reasonable maiden. The winner was quite impressive and there were gaps between each of the first four home. The level is initially set around the third.
Mixed Emotions(IRE) Official explanation: jockey said filly ran too free

2152 LADBROKES.COM HENRY ALKEN H'CAP 1m 3f 183y

8:40 (8:41) (Class 5) (0-70,70) 3-Y-O **£2,266** (£674; £337; £168) **Stalls** Low

Form RPR

041 1 **Caravan Rolls On**[87] 591 3-9-5 68 JackMitchell 4 79+
(Peter Chapple-Hyam) *dwlt: in tch in midfield: rdn and effrt 3f out: hdwy 2f out: pressed ldrs ent fnl f: led ins fnl f: in command and idling fnl 50yds* **3/1**[1]

000 2 2 **May Contain Nuts**[26] 1484 3-8-11 60 FergusSweeney 5 65
(Brendan Powell) *chsd ldrs: rdn and unable qck ent fnl 3f: rallied to press ldrs ent fnl f: chsd wnr and kpt on same pce fnl 100yds* **40/1**

-431 **3** 1 1/4 **Diplomasi**[19] 1609 3-9-6 **69**.. PhilipRobinson 1 72
(Clive Brittain) *dwlt: t.k.h: sn rcvrd to chse ldrs: swtchd lft and rdn 2f out: pressed ldrs u.p 1f out: no ex and outpcd fnl 100yds* **9/2**[3]

0-40 **4** *shd* **Ugo (USA)**[19] 1620 3-9-7 **70**.. LukeMorris 3 73
(Heather Main) *chsd ldr: rdn and ev ch over 2f out: hrd drvn ent fnl f: no ex and btn fnl 100yds* **14/1**

3-31 **5** 3/4 **Countrywide Flame**[10] 1858 3-9-3 **66**.............................(p) PhillipMakin 2 68
(Kevin Ryan) *led: jnd over 2f out: hrd drvn over 1f out: hdd ins fnl f: wknd fnl 100yds* **7/2**[2]

56-4 **6** 1/2 **Mojolika**[27] 1456 3-9-2 **65**...(e[1]) DavidAllan 8 66
(Tim Easterby) *towards rr: rdn and effrt over 2f out: no real hdwy tl kpt on ins fnl f: nvr gng pce to rch ldrs* **5/1**

00-3 **7** *nk* **C P Joe (IRE)**[34] 1299 3-8-8 **57**.. FrannyNorton 9 59+
(Paul Green) *t.k.h: hld up in rr: effrt on inner and rdn over 2f out: drvn and kpt on fr over 1f out: nvr gng pce to rch ldrs* **10/1**

50-4 **8** 4 **Breton Star**[28] 1442 3-8-11 **60**... MartinLane 7 54
(David Simcock) *a last trio: rdn and struggling 4f out: plugged on same pce fnl 2f: nvr trbld ldrs* **14/1**

6-05 **9** 8 **Lady Bridget**[20] 1580 3-9-5 **68**.. MichaelHills 6 50
(B W Hills) *in tch in midfield: rdn and unable qck ent fnl 3f: wknd 2f out: sn bhd* **18/1**

2m 33.57s (-0.33) **Going Correction** -0.025s/f (Good) **9 Ran SP% 112.2**
Speed ratings (Par 99): **100,98,97,97,97 96,96,94,88**
toteswingers: 1&2 £28.30, 1&3 £2.20, 2&3 £48.50 CSF £112.99 CT £528.64 TOTE £3.10: £1.80, £6.80, £2.90; EX 151.40.
Owner Paul Hancock **Bred** Miss K Rausing **Trained** Newmarket, Suffolk

FOCUS
Three-last-time-out winners lined up in this middle-distance handicap. The pace was steady and there was not much separating the first seven, but the winner is an improver who was making it two wins from four starts. The third is a fair guide to the form.
T/Plt: £148.20 to a £1 stake. Pool: £60,189.90. 296.42 winning tickets. T/Qpdt: £16.80 to a £1 stake. Pool: £5,438.34. 238.53 winning tickets. SP

1946 WINDSOR (R-H)
Monday, May 16

OFFICIAL GOING: Good to firm (good in places; 8.6)
Stands' rail dolled out 6yds at 6f down to 2f at winning post. Top bend dolled out 3yd which added 14yds to races of 1m and over.
Wind: Fresh, half behind Weather: Fine

2153 SPORTINGBET.COM BRITISH STALLION STUDS E B F MAIDEN FILLIES' STKS 5f 10y
6:00 (6:02) (Class 5) 2-Y-O **£3,302** (£982; £491; £245) **Stalls** Low

Form RPR

5 **1** **Starfly (IRE)**[10] 1846 2-9-0 0.. RyanMoore 2 76+
(Jeremy Noseda) *mde virtually all against nr side rail: hrd pressed ins fnl f: drvn out* **9/2**[2]

2 *nk* **Diamond Finesse (IRE)** 2-9-0 0................................. JimmyFortune 6 75+
(Ed Dunlop) *in tch at rr of main gp: prog nr side 2f out: chsd wnr jst ins fnl f: str chal after: jst hld nr fin* **14/1**

3 2 1/2 **Miss Lahar** 2-8-11 0.. MartinHarley(3) 1 66
(Mick Channon) *trckd ldrs: hanging lft fr 2f out: sn nt qckn: styd on fnl f to take 3rd last strides* **15/2**[3]

4 **4** 1/2 **Balm**[7] 1946 2-9-0 0.. RichardHughes 9 65
(Richard Hannon) *chsd wnr tl jst ins fnl f: pushed along and lost 3rd last strides* **8/1**

5 1 3/4 **Leenavesta (USA)** 2-8-9 0...................................... KieranO'Neill(5) 8 58
(Richard Hannon) *chsd ldrs: outpcd fr 2f out: kpt on same pce fr over 1f out* **40/1**

4 **6** 3/4 **My Lucky Liz (IRE)**[10] 1846 2-9-0 0.............................. WilliamBuick 3 56
(David Simcock) *trckd ldrs: lost pl 2f out and n.m.r sn after: kpt on fnl f: n.d* **1/1**[1]

7 1 **Luv U Forever** 2-9-0 0... NeilCallan 13 52
(Pat Murphy) *nt that wl away: t.k.h and rn green: sn on outer to chse ldrs over 3f out: wknd jst over 1f out* **100/1**

8 2 3/4 **Roedean (IRE)** 2-9-0 0.. ShaneKelly 15 42+
(Richard Hannon) *s.v.s: virtually t.o in last early: pushed along and styd on steadily fr over 1f out* **33/1**

9 3/4 **Arabian Flight** 2-9-0 0... TomMcLaughlin 10 39
(Ed Dunlop) *hld up in tch in rr of main gp: effrt on outer 1/2-way: wknd over 1f out* **66/1**

10 1 1/4 **Premature** 2-8-9 0.. AdamBeschizza(5) 4 34
(Dean Ivory) *snatched up on inner wl over 3f out and dropped off the pce: effrt towards outer 2f out: sn wknd* **80/1**

06 **11** 3/4 **Jettie**[18] 1628 2-9-0 0... CathyGannon 14 32
(David Evans) *spd 3f: bmpd wl over 1f out: wknd* **150/1**

12 *hd* **Bertorella (IRE)** 2-9-0 0.. JimCrowley 5 31
(Ralph Beckett) *s.s: outpcd in last pair and a bhd* **20/1**

13 1 **Calusa Bay (IRE)** 2-9-0 0.. IanMongan 11 27
(Pat Phelan) *sn struggling and lost tch: a bhd* **80/1**

0 **14** 5 **First Of February (IRE)**[10] 1846 2-9-0 0....................... PatCosgrave 12 9
(Jim Boyle) *spd 3f: losing pl whn n.m.r wl over 1f out: wknd rapidly* **50/1**

60.43 secs (0.13) **Going Correction** -0.175s/f (Firm) **14 Ran SP% 115.4**
Speed ratings (Par 90): **91,90,86,85,82 81,80,75,74,72 71,71,69,61**
toteswingers: 1&2 £20.00, 1&3 £5.90, 2&3 £16.90 CSF £57.89 TOTE £5.80: £1.80, £3.10, £2.30; EX 60.50 Trifecta £231.40 Pool: £2,815.35 - 9.00 winning units..
Owner Highclere Thoroughbred Racing - Starter **Bred** Patrick F Kelly **Trained** Newmarket, Suffolk

FOCUS
A dry night and day at a track that has seen up to 21mm of water applied since the last meeting. The stands' rail was dolled out 6yds at the 6f pole, 2yds at the winning post, while the top bend was dolled out 3yds from its normal configuration, adding 14yds to distances of 1m and above.\n\x\x This is a race usually won by one that has gone on to show very useful or smart form, but this looked an ordinary renewal and one that didn't take as much winning as seemed likely with the short-priced market leader disappointing. The time was decent though and the form has been given a chance. The gallop was a reasonable one and the winning rider described the ground as good to firm.

NOTEBOOK
Starfly(IRE) had the run of the race against the inside rail and showed improved form and a pleasing attitude to get off the mark to reverse debut placings with the below-par market leader. She should have no problems with 6f and, although things were in her favour, she may be capable of better. (tchd 11-2)
Diamond Finesse(IRE) ◆, a £45,000 yearling and half-sister to three winners from 6f-1m, was relatively easy in the market but shaped with plenty of promise on this racecourse debut. She will be suited by the step up to 6f and should be able to win a similar event.
Miss Lahar has several winners from sprint to middle distances in her pedigree and who shaped well without being unduly knocked about for a yard whose juveniles have been in good form. She should be suited by 6f. (op 7-1 tchd 6-1)
Balm stepped up on the moderate level of form shown on her debut over this course and distance. She wasn't at all knocked about in the closing stages and, while she is likely to remain vulnerable in this grade, she looks the type that should fare better in nurseries. (op 7-1)
Leenavesta(USA) wasn't disgraced on this racecourse debut and is entitled to improve for the experience. She will be of more interest when qualified for a nursery mark. (op 50-1 tchd 33-1)
My Lucky Liz(IRE) showed fair form when over four lengths in front of today's winner at Ascot on their respective debuts but failed by a long chalk to confirm those placings at this sharper course. The step up to 6f should suit much better and she is worth another chance. (op 11-10 tchd 5-4)
Roedean(IRE), who cost 50,000gns and is the second foal of a half-sister to a couple of smart types, showed ability after a slow start and she should do better with this experience behind her when upped to 6f and beyond. (op 28-1)

2154 WEATHERBYS PRIVATE BANK CONDITIONS STKS 5f 10y
6:30 (6:30) (Class 3) 2-Y-O **£5,828** (£1,734; £866; £432) **Stalls** Low

Form RPR

21 **1** **Bannock (IRE)**[7] 1939 2-8-11 0..................................... JoeFanning 5 90
(Mark Johnston) *mde virtually all: rdn 2 l clr over 1f out: styd on wl* **8/1**[3]

12 **2** *nk* **Magic City (IRE)**[19] 1598 2-9-0 0............................ RichardHughes 2 93
(Richard Hannon) *stdd s: hld up in last pair: stl there wl over 1f out: shkn up and prog to chse wnr jst ins fnl f: rdn and r.o to cl gap nr fin: nvr gng to get there* **2/5**[1]

21 **3** 1 3/4 **Signifer (IRE)**[13] 1785 2-8-8 0.................................. MartinHarley(3) 6 83
(Mick Channon) *plld hrd: hld up bhd ldrs: chsd wnr wl over 1f out tl jst ins fnl f: one pce* **9/1**

1 **4** *shd* **Foxtrot India (IRE)**[16] 1678 2-9-0 0............................... JimCrowley 3 85
(Peter Winkworth) *dwlt: hld up in last pair: effrt towards outer 2f out: kpt on same pce fr over 1f out* **6/1**[2]

0531 **5** 3 **Middleton Flyer (IRE)**[13] 1786 2-8-6 0.......................... CathyGannon 1 66
(David Evans) *chsd ldrs: lost pl whn squeezed out over 1f out: wknd* **125/1**

41 **6** *shd* **Ortea**[23] 1522 2-9-0 0.. PatCosgrave 7 74
(David Evans) *chsd ldrs: rdn 1/2-way: wknd over 1f out* **50/1**

031 **7** 3 3/4 **Steady The Buffs**[7] 1932 2-8-2 0 ow1.................... AdamBeschizza(5) 4 54
(Hugo Palmer) *w wnr to 2f out: wknd qckly* **66/1**

59.96 secs (-0.34) **Going Correction** -0.175s/f (Firm) **7 Ran SP% 111.1**
Speed ratings (Par 97): **95,94,91,91,86 86,80**
toteswingers: 1&2 £5.50, 1&3 £25.80, 2&3 £11.50 CSF £11.12 TOTE £5.90: £2.30, £1.40; EX 16.60.
Owner Sheikh Hamdan Bin Mohammed Al Maktoum **Bred** Darley **Trained** Middleham Moor, N Yorks

FOCUS
Several smart sorts have won this race this century and, although the very short-priced favourite was turned over, this still looked a decent-quality conditions event in which every one of the seven was a previous winner. The gallop was only fair and the first two pulled a couple of lengths clear. The form is rated slightly positively but is likely to be anchored by the fifth.

NOTEBOOK
Bannock(IRE) ◆ is a progressive sort who was easy in the market but turned in his best effort after enjoying the run of the race and after getting first run on the favourite (who was conceding 3lb). He's the sort physically to make further progress, he should have no problems with 6f in due course and will be well worth his place if sent to Royal Ascot. (op 15-2)
Magic City(IRE) ◆, who reportedly returned home with sore shins after getting turned over at prohibitive odds at Ascot, was again chinned at odds-on after racing keenly (ridden with more restrain than on first two starts) but almost certainly ran as well as he ever has done after conceding 3lb to a progressive winner who got first run. He should be equally effective over 6f and he's well worth another chance to make amends. He may now go for the National Stakes. (op 4-9, tchd 1-2 in places)
Signifer(IRE) is a progressive individual who ran as well as he ever has done after racing with the choke out in the first half of the race and who got closer to the runner-up than on their respective debuts at Newbury last month. He should be better suited by 6f and there may be more to come. (op 10-1)
Foxtrot India(IRE) created a favourable impression on his debut when accounting for two subsequent winners and duly bettered that effort in this much stronger company. He's the type to win more races. (op 13-2)
Middleton Flyer(IRE), the most experience member in this field, looked to have a fair bit to find in this company but shaped a bit better than the bare result suggests after encountering trouble at a crucial stage. There will be easier opportunities than this one. (op 100-1)
Ortea found this much tougher than when winning an ordinary maiden on his previous start at Nottingham. He'll be of more interest once the nursery season begins.
Steady The Buffs, whose rider posted 1lb of overweight, had her limitations firmly exposed in this grade.

2155 SPORTINGBET.COM CLAIMING STKS 6f
7:00 (7:00) (Class 6) 3-Y-O+ **£1,619** (£481; £240; £120) **Stalls** Low

Form RPR

6304 **1** **Nubar Boy**[15] 1730 4-9-3 60.......................................(v) PatCosgrave 2 69
(David Evans) *trckd ldrs: wnt 2nd against rail 1/2-way: gap opened and drvn to ld jst over 1f out: hld on* **12/1**[3]

4211 **2** *nk* **April Fool**[9] 1917 7-9-2 82.......................................(b) RichardEvans(3) 6 70
(David Evans) *led: rdn over 2f out: hung lft off rail over 1f out: sn hdd: tried to rally fnl f but nt qckn last 100yds* **8/13**[1]

0-21 **3** 2 1/4 **Indian Shuffle (IRE)**[27] 1449 3-9-1 70............................ JoeFanning 9 66
(Jonathan Portman) *prom on outer: rdn over 2f out: nt qckn over 1f out: one pce* **12/1**[3]

5-30 **4** 1/2 **Getcarter**[14] 1771 5-9-10 73...................................... RichardHughes 5 66
(Richard Hannon) *stdd s: hld up in 9th and off the pce: rdn 2f out: kpt on fr over 1f out: nvr rchd ldrs* **11/4**[2]

4-6 **5** 1 **Griffin Point (IRE)**[17] 1655 4-8-12 0.............................. NeilCallan 7 51
(William Muir) *chsd ldr to 1/2-way: steadily fdd over 1f out* **40/1**

000 **6** 1 1/4 **Sunrise Lyric (IRE)**[9] 1905 4-8-4 55......................... DuilioDaSilva(7) 11 46
(Paul Cole) *stdd s: settled in last pair and wl off the pce: rdn 2f out: kpt on fr over 1f out: no ch* **40/1**

44-0 **7** *hd* **Bahkov (IRE)**[47] 1045 5-8-12 49.................................... KierenFox(3) 4 49
(Eric Wheeler) *stdd s: settled in last pair and wl off the pce: rdn 2f out: kpt on fr over 1f out: no ch* **80/1**

044- **8** 1 **Doctor Hilary**[166] 7656 9-9-0 60...................................(v) JimCrowley 8 45
(Mark Hoad) *prom tl wknd over 1f out* **20/1**

00-4 **9** 3/4 **Prince Namid**[47] 1045 9-9-0 59..................................... WilliamCarson 1 43
(Jonathen de Giles) *nvr bttr than midfield: u.p by 1/2-way and struggling: n.d* **25/1**

400- **10** 1 **Mollyow (IRE)**[203] 7124 3-8-3 56.................................(v[1]) DavidProbert 10 36
(Bryn Palling) *nvr on terms w ldrs: u.p fr 1/2-way: struggling after* **66/1**

03-4 **11** *6* **Brave Tiger (IRE)**[39] 1193 3-8-5 53....................(tp) AdamBeschizza(5) 3 —
(Hugo Palmer) *chsd ldrs: u.p and outpcd bef 1/2-way: sn wknd* **50/1**
1m 12.66s (-0.34) **Going Correction** -0.175s/f (Firm)
WFA 3 from 4yo+ 9lb **11** Ran SP% **122.1**
Speed ratings (Par 101): **95,94,91,90,89 87,87,86,85,84 76**
toteswingers: 1&2 £5.80, 1&3 £14.00, 2&3 £2.70 CSF £20.04 TOTE £13.80: £2.60, £1.10, £1.90; EX 33.60 Trifecta £152.40 Pool: £5,020.19 - 24.37 winning units..
Owner Phil Slater **Bred** Low Ground Stud **Trained** Pandy, Monmouths

FOCUS
Not the most competitive of claimers and one that didn't take as much winning as seemed likely beforehand with the two market leaders disappointing to varying degrees. The winner probably only had to run to his AW winter form. The gallop was sound and the winner was another to race right up with the pace against the stands' rail in a race where those held up were at a disadvantage.

2156 ROYAL WINDSOR RACING CLUB H'CAP 1m 3f 135y
7:30 (7:30) (Class 4) (0-80,78) 4-Y-0+ **£3,561** (£1,059; £529; £264) **Stalls High**

Form RPR
260- **1** **Dance Tempo**[242] 6115 4-9-5 77.. SteveDrowne 8 90
(Hughie Morrison) *trckd ldng pair: clsd to ld wl over 1f out: sn drvn clr* **9/2**[2]
4031 **2** *4 1/2* **Pelham Crescent (IRE)**[11] 1829 8-9-3 78................ DeclanCannon(3) 1 83
(Bryn Palling) *dwlt: hld up last: prog over 2f out: hrd rdn to chse wnr jst over 1f out: no imp* **13/2**
5-00 **3** *1* **Urban Space**[6] 1977 5-9-0 72.. JimCrowley 6 75
(Conor Dore) *trckd ldrs: drvn on outer over 2f out: nt qckn wl over 1f out: one pce after* **20/1**
0-51 **4** *3/4* **Mons Calpe (IRE)**[14] 1775 5-9-2 74................................(p) RyanMoore 9 76
(Paul Cole) *led and nt pressed: hrd rdn and nt qckn 2f out: sn hdd and btn* **5/2**[1]
31-5 **5** *1 3/4* **Aurora Sky (IRE)**[14] 1772 5-9-3 75.............................. RichardHughes 7 74
(John Akehurst) *t.k.h: trckd ldr: moved up to chal 2f out: sn nt qckn and btn* **5/1**[3]
60-3 **6** *1 3/4* **Meglio Ancora**[28] 1443 4-9-0 72... JoeFanning 2 68
(Jonathan Portman) *trckd ldrs: rdn towards outer over 2f out: nt qckn wl over 1f out: fdd* **15/2**
50-1 **7** *4* **Gloucester**[33] 531 8-9-2 74... PatCosgrave 5 63
(Michael Scudamore) *hld up in last pair: crept clsr over 2f out: shkn up and no rspnse wl over 1f out: wknd* **10/1**
-331 **8** *11* **Admirable Duque (IRE)**[65] 849 5-9-5 77.......................(p) NeilCallan 3 48
(Dominic Ffrench Davis) *dwlt: sn trckd ldrs: shkn up over 2f out: wknd qckly over 1f out: eased* **8/1**
2m 29.6s (0.10) **Going Correction** +0.15s/f (Good) **8** Ran SP% **113.5**
Speed ratings (Par 105): **105,102,101,100,99 98,95,88**
toteswingers: 1&2 £4.80, 1&3 £16.40, 2&3 £41.30 CSF £33.05 CT £524.37 TOTE £6.30: £3.80, £2.50, £4.10; EX 44.90 Trifecta £569.80 Pool: £2,695.35 - 3.50 winning units..
Owner A N Solomons **Bred** H H L Bloodstock **Trained** East Ilsley, Berks

FOCUS
Mainly exposed sorts in just a fair handicap. The gallop was an ordinary one until the pace increased with over a quarter of a mile to run. The winner impressed and the form is rated around the second and fourth.

2157 SPIFFING CRABBIE'S ALCOHOLIC GINGER BEER MAIDEN FILLIES' STKS 1m 67y
8:00 (8:02) (Class 5) 3-Y-0+ **£2,266** (£674; £337; £168) **Stalls Low**

Form RPR
- **1** **Nahrain** 3-8-12 0.. NeilCallan 2 94+
(Roger Varian) *trckd ldrs in 5th: prog over 3f out: rdn to ld over 1f out: styd on wl: in command last 100yds* **11/2**
2 *1 1/4* **Paoletta (USA)** 3-8-12 0.. FrankieDettori 1 91+
(Mahmood Al Zarooni) *mde most: rdn and hdd over 1f out: tried to respond but hld last 100yds* **9/1**
5- **3** *3 3/4* **Regal Heiress**[291] 4508 3-8-12 0..................................... RyanMoore 8 82
(Sir Michael Stoute) *trckd ldrs in 6th: effrt over 2f out: chsd ldng pair over 1f out: styd on but no imp* **3/1**[2]
4 *4 1/2* **Flaunter (USA)** 3-8-12 0.. AhmedAjtebi 12 72+
(Mahmood Al Zarooni) *dwlt and stdd s: hld up wl in rr: effrt on wd outside 3f out: rn green but styd on fnl 2f to take 4th nr fin* **25/1**
4 **5** *1* **Coco Rouge (IRE)**[14] 1759 3-8-12 0................................ ShaneKelly 5 69
(Walter Swinburn) *s.i.s: sn trckd ldng pair to over 2f out: readily outpcd after* **16/1**
6-2 **6** *2 1/4* **Zafaraan**[14] 1767 3-8-12 0... WilliamBuick 11 64
(Peter Chapple-Hyam) *pressed ldr: led briefly after 2f: lost 2nd over 2f out and sn outpcd: wknd fnl f* **14/1**
7 *3* **Perilously (USA)** 3-8-12 0.. RichardHughes 6 57+
(Jeremy Noseda) *dwlt: sn in tch in midfield: shkn up in 7th 3f out: sn outpcd* **9/4**[1]
2 **8** *1 1/2* **Inklet**[30] 1393 3-8-12 0.. SebSanders 7 54
(Marco Botti) *mostly trckd ldng trio: rdn on outer wl over 2f out: sn wknd* **9/2**[3]
0 **9** *3* **Satwa Sunrise (FR)**[10] 1845 4-9-10 0........................... GeorgeBaker 13 50
(Ed Dunlop) *hld up towards rr and racd wd bnd 6f out to 5f out: shuffled along and steadily lost grnd fnl 3f* **40/1**
0 **10** *2* **What About Now**[14] 1759 3-8-12 0................................ SteveDrowne 14 42
(J W Hills) *hld up and a wl in rr: no prog over 2f out* **100/1**
0- **11** *1/2* **Unbeatable**[173] 7559 3-8-12 0....................................... JimCrowley 3 41
(William Knight) *s.i.s: hld up in rr: no prog over 2f out: wknd* **125/1**
00 **12** *nk* **Formal Dining (USA)**[10] 1845 3-8-12 0.......................... PatCosgrave 9 40
(Edward Vaughan) *s.s: hld up wl in rr: shkn up and wknd 3f out* **125/1**
5-3 **13** *2 1/4* **Dililah**[7] 1934 3-8-5 0.. LukeRowe(7) 4 35
(William Knight) *v.s.a: detached in last: virtually t.o 1/2-way: nudged along and lost no further grnd* **100/1**
1m 44.37s (-0.33) **Going Correction** +0.15s/f (Good)
WFA 3 from 4yo 12lb **13** Ran SP% **121.7**
Speed ratings (Par 100): **107,105,102,97,96 94,91,89,86,84 84,83,81**
toteswingers: 1&2 £13.60, 1&3 £7.40, 2&3 £4.00 CSF £54.17 TOTE £7.90: £2.60, £3.10, £1.80; EX 72.30 Trifecta £190.50 Pool: £643.63 - 2.50 winning units..
Owner Sheikh Ahmed Al Maktoum **Bred** Darley **Trained** Newmarket, Suffolk

FOCUS
A race that threw up subsequent multiple Listed/minor Group winner Strawberrydaiquiri (also Group 1-placed) in 2009 and one that has also been won by several very useful sorts in the last ten years. Although the early gallop was a fairly sedate one (again suiting those up with the pace), the first two pulled clear and both look decent prospects in a race that should throw up winners. The form is rated around the top end of the averages.

2158 TICKETS FOR TROOPS H'CAP 5f 10y
8:30 (8:36) (Class 4) (0-85,85) 3-Y-0 **£4,079** (£1,214; £606; £303) **Stalls Low**

Form RPR
-121 **1** **Quality Art (USA)**[14] 1758 3-9-7 85................................ RyanMoore 8 92
(Gary Moore) *mde all and sn crossed to nr side rail: pushed along to assert over 1f out: rdn out nr fin* **8/13**[1]
5-00 **2** *1* **Style And Panache (IRE)**[3] 2074 3-8-11 75.................. PatCosgrave 6 78
(David Evans) *chsd ldrs in 5th: effrt 2f out: rdn and styd on fr over 1f out to take 2nd nr fin* **20/1**
0-50 **3** *shd* **Scarlet Rocks (IRE)**[10] 1852 3-8-11 75......................... CathyGannon 4 78
(David Evans) *chsd ldrs: drvn 2f out: kpt on same pce fnl f: nvr able to chal* **14/1**
0-13 **4** *1 1/4* **Fair Value (IRE)**[14] 1758 3-8-11 75.................................... NeilCallan 7 74
(Simon Dow) *chsd wnr: drvn to chal 2f out: lft bhd over 1f out: lost 2 pls nr fin* **7/1**[3]
22-0 **5** *7* **Khaleeji**[32] 1335 3-8-13 77.. SebSanders 1 50
(J W Hills) *sn wl outpcd in last and pushed along: nvr a factor: kpt on nr fin* **14/1**
0-00 **6** *nse* **Penny's Pearl (IRE)**[19] 1602 3-9-7 85......................... RichardHughes 2 58
(Richard Hannon) *sn wl off the pce in 6th: pushed along 2f out: no real prog* **5/1**[2]
21-6 **7** *2 1/4* **Look Who's Kool**[17] 1650 3-9-3 81............................ GrahamGibbons 3 46
(Ed McMahon) *chsd ldrs: u.p 2f out: wknd over 1f out* **12/1**
59.24 secs (-1.06) **Going Correction** -0.175s/f (Firm) **7** Ran SP% **116.9**
Speed ratings (Par 101): **101,99,99,97,86 85,82**
toteswingers: 1&2 £7.60, 1&3 £4.70, 2&3 £13.50 CSF £17.13 CT £102.76 TOTE £1.40: £1.10, £10.50; EX 23.70 Trifecta £112.50 Pool: £628.43 - 4.13 winning units..
Owner R A Green **Bred** Farfellow Farms & Darley Stud Management **Trained** Lower Beeding, W Sussex

FOCUS
Not the strongest of handicaps, but a decent gallop and a progressive winner. The first four finished clear and the first home was another to race against the stands' rail in sprints on the card. He is rated similar to his latest Kempton form.
T/Plt: £101.40 to a £1 stake. Pool: £67,419.36. 485.08 winning tickets. T/Qpdt: £16.80 to a £1 stake Pool: £6,194.80. 272.07 winning tickets. JN

[1952] WOLVERHAMPTON (A.W) (L-H)
Monday, May 16

OFFICIAL GOING: Standard
Wind: Fresh behind Weather: Overcast

2159 GREAT OFFERS AT WOLVERHAMPTON-RACECOURSE.CO.UK AMATEUR RIDERS' CLASSIFIED CLAIMING STKS 1m 4f 50y(P)
1:40 (1:40) (Class 6) 4-Y-0+ **£1,648** (£507; £253) **Stalls Low**

Form RPR
4015 **1** **Stand Guard**[20] 1577 7-9-11 70... MrJBanks(5) 3 73
(Michael Squance) *chsd ldrs: pushed along over 2f out: rdn to ld wl ins fnl f: r.o* **9/1**
0/0- **2** *1 1/2* **Alaghiraar (IRE)**[8] 25 7-9-11 67.......(v[1]) MissPernillaHermansson(3) 11 69
(Richard Ford) *a.p: chsd ldr 4f out: led 2f out: rdn and hung lft over 1f out: hdd and unable qck wl ins fnl f* **66/1**
-331 **3** *1 3/4* **Kames Park (IRE)**[19] 1608 9-10-10 71................. MissSBrotherton 10 76
(Richard Guest) *s.i.s: hld up: hdwy over 2f out: hung lft and r.o ins fnl f: nt rch ldrs* **5/1**[3]
1043 **4** *1* **William's Way**[49] 1016 9-10-5 70.................................(t) MrCMartin(3) 8 73
(Ian Wood) *hld up: rdn over 3f out: hdwy over 1f out: styd on* **6/1**
3430 **5** *hd* **Camps Bay (USA)**[6] 1977 7-10-1 72......................... BrendanPowell(5) 9 70
(Conor Dore) *hld up: rdn over 2f out: r.o ins fnl f: nvr nrr* **12/1**
3030 **6** *4* **Bavarica**[28] 1443 9-10-5 67... MissSBirkett(7) 12 70
(Julia Feilden) *s.i.s: hld up: hdwy over 3f out: wknd fnl f* **20/1**
2160 **7** *1/2* **Bentley**[74] 744 7-10-5 71.. MrFMitchell(5) 7 67
(Brian Baugh) *chsd ldrs: rdn over 3f out: wknd fnl f* **40/1**
-240 **8** *3* **Resplendent Light**[11] 1829 6-10-4 69...............(t) MissIsabelTompsett 2 56
(Bernard Llewellyn) *mid-div: hdwy over 7f out: rdn over 2f out: wknd over 1f out* **9/2**[2]
254- **9** *1 1/4* **River Ardeche**[254] 5757 6-10-4 73.................................(t) MrSWalker 6 54
(Ben Haslam) *led: rdn and hdd 2f out: wknd fnl f* **7/2**[1]
062- **10** *11* **Saloon (USA)**[359] 2343 7-10-1 75.........................(p) MissAZetterholm(5) 4 39
(Jane Chapple-Hyam) *chsd ldr 8f: wknd over 2f out* **15/2**
600- **11** *10* **Boo**[61] 4932 9-10-1 69...(v) MissCHJones(5) 1 23
(James Unett) *dwlt: a in rr: hmpd over 6f out: lost tch fnl 5f: t.o* **50/1**
0/ **U** **Exotic Dream (FR)**[159] 5-10-6 68................................... MissEJJones 5 —
(Ronald Harris) *hld up in tch: racd keenly: stmbld and uns rdr over 6f out* **33/1**
2m 39.3s (-1.80) **Going Correction** -0.175s/f (Stan) **12** Ran SP% **114.4**
Speed ratings (Par 101): **99,98,96,96,96 93,93,91,90,82 76,—**
toteswingers:1&2:£59.60, 2&3:£50.20, 1&3:£9.20 CSF £506.80 TOTE £13.80: £3.60, £19.80, £2.10; EX 1634.70.Stand Guard was claimed by Noel P. Quinlan for £6,000.
Owner The Circle Bloodstock I Limited **Bred** Juddmonte Farms Ltd **Trained** Newmarket, Suffolk

FOCUS
A moderate contest and the pace was ordinary. The form is rated around the winner and third.

2160 STAY AT THE WOLVERHAMPTON HOLIDAY INN MAIDEN AUCTION STKS 5f 20y(P)
2:10 (2:11) (Class 6) 2-Y-0 **£2,266** (£674; £337; £168) **Stalls Low**

Form RPR
43 **1** **Fayr Fall (IRE)**[16] 1691 2-8-9 0.................................... DuranFentiman 4 69+
(Tim Easterby) *mde all: shkn up over 1f out: edgd lft ins fnl f: r.o* **5/6**[1]
4 **2** *1/2* **Auntie Joy**[16] 1691 2-8-1 0.. JamesSullivan(3) 1 62
(Michael Easterby) *a.p: rdn to chse wnr 2f out: r.o* **11/4**[2]
0 **3** *2* **Monumental Man**[30] 1396 2-9-1 0.................................... LiamJones 3 66
(James Unett) *sn outpcd: hdwy 1/2-way: rdn over 1f out: styng on same pce whn hung lft ins fnl f* **22/1**
5 **4** *2 3/4* **Complex**[20] 1583 2-8-10 0.. RichardMullen 8 51
(David Evans) *sn outpcd: hdwy over 1f out: rdn and hung lft fnl f: nt trble ldrs* **12/1**[3]

44 **5** *1 ¾* **Bojangle (IRE)**[7] 1957 2-8-8 0 ow1 .... JamesDoyle 7 43
(Dominic Ffrench Davis) *prom: outpcd 1/2-way: n.d after* **14/1**

4 **6** *½* **Perfecto Tiempo (IRE)**[23] 1522 2-8-12 0 .... LukeMorris 6 45
(Ronald Harris) *prom: rdn and hung rt 1/2-way: wknd over 1f out* **14/1**

7 *6* **Very First Blade** 2-8-9 0 .... GrahamGibbons 5 20
(Mark Brisbourne) *w ldrs tl rdn and hung rt fr over 3f out: wknd 1/2-way* **20/1**

8 *2 ½* **Peering** 2-8-10 0 ow1 .... DarryllHolland 2 12
(Nick Littmoden) *chsd wnr tl rdn over 2f out: wknd over 1f out* **22/1**

62.37 secs (0.07) **Going Correction** -0.175s/f (Stan) **8** Ran SP% **115.7**
Speed ratings (Par 91): **92,91,88,83,80 80,70,66**
toteswingers:1&2:£1.70, 1&3:£6.20, 2&3:£7.80 CSF £3.08 TOTE £1.90: £1.02, £1.40, £6.20; EX 4.10.
Owner Reality Partnerships **Bred** M Sinanan **Trained** Great Habton, N Yorks

FOCUS
An ordinary maiden auction and the market only concerned the front pair, who franked the Thirsk form. The level is a bit guessy given the modest time.

NOTEBOOK
Fayr Fall(IRE) had 2l to spare over Auntie Joy on his second outing at Thirsk last month and made every yard to confirm the form, but was all out to do so. He is likely to find things much harder from now on. (op 5-4 tchd 11-8)
Auntie Joy was making her racecourse debut when behind Fayr Fall at Thirsk and showed the benefit of that by getting much closer here. She may have done even better had she not made her final effort tight against the dreaded inside rail, but the way she was having to be niggled along to keep in touch in the early stages suggests she may need the extra furlong now. (tchd 5-2 and 3-1)
Monumental Man stepped up plenty from his Leicester debut and was again doing his best work late. A small race can come his way.
Complex ran an identical race to her debut over C&D last month, getting outpaced early before finishing well. There seems to be some ability there. (op 11-1)
Bojangle(IRE) never got into it and is becoming exposed. (op 12-1)
Perfecto Tiempo(IRE) can be forgiven this to a degree as he hung extremely wide off the final bend. (op 12-1 tchd 16-1)

2161 GOT THE FEELING - GO TO LADBROKES H'CAP (DIV I) 5f 216y(P)
2:40 (2:40) (Class 6) (0-55,55) 4-Y-0+ **£1,364** (£403; £201) **Stalls** Low

Form RPR
-330 **1** **Avonlini**[37] 1247 5-8-12 **50** .... JackMitchell 7 58
(Brian Baugh) *led 1f: chsd ldr: rdn to ld ins fnl f: r.o* **5/1**[3]

2233 **2** *¾* **Libertino (IRE)**[10] 1875 4-9-3 **55** .... LukeMorris 3 61
(Tony Carroll) *chsd ldrs: rdn over 2f out: r.o* **7/2**[2]

6643 **3** *½* **Flying Applause**[17] 1649 6-9-1 **53** ....(bt) RussKennemore 2 57
(Roy Bowring) *chsd ldrs: drvn along over 2f out: r.o* **3/1**[1]

000- **4** *hd* **Ghost Dancer**[222] 6672 7-8-12 **50** ....(p) LiamKeniry 5 54+
(Milton Bradley) *hld up: nt clr run wl over 1f out: rdn and r.o ins fnl f: nt rch ldrs* **33/1**

4046 **5** *hd* **Radiator Rooney (IRE)**[13] 1787 8-8-13 **51** .... JamieSpencer 13 54+
(Patrick Morris) *hld up: r.o ins fnl f: nvr nrr* **13/2**

-000 **6** *hd* **Avontuur (FR)**[40] 1164 9-8-11 **52** ....(b) JamesSullivan(3) 6 54
(Ruth Carr) *led 5f out: rdn over 1f out: hdd ins fnl f: no ex towards fin* **9/1**

4020 **7** *1* **Lily Wood**[14] 1763 5-9-0 **52** ....(p) LiamJones 9 51
(James Unett) *mid-div: hdwy over 1f out: sn rdn: r.o* **13/2**

440 **8** *1 ¼* **Rightcar Dominic**[115] 250 6-8-8 **46** oh1 .... RobbieFitzpatrick 1 41
(Peter Grayson) *s.i.s: sn drvn along to go prom: rdn over 2f out: styd on* **66/1**

1005 **9** *3 ½* **Vertumnus**[12] 1815 4-8-10 **48** ....(b) KellyHarrison 12 32
(Nick Littmoden) *s.i.s: hld up: rdn over 1f out: nvr on terms* **25/1**

0004 **10** *¾* **Boga (IRE)**[7] 1938 4-8-8 **46** oh1 .... MartinLane 4 28
(Ron Hodges) *prom: rdn over 2f out: wknd fnl f* **40/1**

4-00 **11** *9* **Suhayl Star (IRE)**[117] 210 7-8-8 **46** oh1 .... JimmyQuinn 10 —
(Paul Burgoyne) *chsd ldrs: rdn over 2f out: wkng whn hmpd sn after* **16/1**

604 **12** *2 ½* **Hesindamood**[49] 1015 4-8-11 **49** .... SaleemGolam 11 —
(Joanne Priest) *sn pushed along in rr: bhd fr 1/2-way* **50/1**

1m 14.1s (-0.90) **Going Correction** -0.175s/f (Stan) **12** Ran SP% **119.1**
Speed ratings (Par 101): **99,98,97,97,96 96,95,93,88,87 75,72**
toteswingers:1&2:£4.90, 1&3:£4.30, 2&3:£3.00 CSF £22.12 CT £63.43 TOTE £7.50: £2.00, £1.30, £1.80; EX 30.70.
Owner J H Chrimes **Bred** J H Chrimes **Trained** Audley, Staffs

FOCUS
A moderate sprint handicap and not many got into it. Sound if limited form. The winner reversed March running with the third.

2162 GOT THE FEELING - GO TO LADBROKES H'CAP (DIV II) 5f 216y(P)
3:10 (3:11) (Class 6) (0-55,55) 4-Y-0+ **£1,364** (£403; £201) **Stalls** Low

Form RPR
360- **1** **Charlietoo**[248] 5927 5-8-8 **46** oh1 ....(p) LukeMorris 9 56
(Edward Bevan) *a.p: rdn over 2f out: r.o to ld wl ins fnl f* **16/1**

1000 **2** *1 ¾* **Almaty Express**[56] 933 9-9-3 **55** ....(b) DarryllHolland 7 59
(John Weymes) *led: rdn and hdd wl ins fnl f* **12/1**

4032 **3** *¾* **Kheley (IRE)**[12] 1818 5-8-7 **50** .... JamesRogers(5) 3 52
(Mark Brisbourne) *chsd ldrs: rdn over 2f out: r.o* **5/1**[2]

2400 **4** *nk* **Misaro (GER)**[14] 1752 10-9-1 **53** ....(b) GregFairley 1 54
(Ronald Harris) *chsd ldrs: rdn over 2f out: r.o* **10/1**

0-6 **5** *1 ¼* **Sopran Nad (ITY)**[130] 69 7-8-8 **46** oh1 ....(t) SilvestreDeSousa 2 43+
(Frank Sheridan) *hld up: r.o wl ins fnl f: nt rch ldrs* **10/3**[1]

0-44 **6** *hd* **Avoncreek**[37] 1248 7-8-8 **46** .... KellyHarrison 11 42
(Brian Baugh) *hld up: hdwy over 1f out: r.o: nrst fin* **11/1**

6530 **7** *½* **Errigal Lad**[69] 793 6-8-12 **50** .... FergusSweeney 12 45+
(Garry Woodward) *hld up and bhd: stl last turning for home: r.o wl ins fnl f: too much to do* **8/1**[3]

1604 **8** *1 ¼* **Figaro Flyer (IRE)**[47] 1043 8-9-0 **52** .... JimmyQuinn 13 43
(Michael Squance) *mid-div: rdn over 1f out: nvr trbld ldrs* **16/1**

-006 **9** *1* **Sweet Mirasol (IRE)**[19] 1612 4-8-4 **49** ....(t) NathanAlison(7) 5 37
(Mandy Rowland) *mid-div: rdn and outpcd over 2f out: n.d after* **12/1**

5026 **10** *2* **Cheveyo (IRE)**[22] 1544 5-8-10 **48** ....(v) JamieSpencer 10 29
(Patrick Morris) *hld up: rdn ins fnl f: n.d* **10/1**

-005 **11** *shd* **What Katie Did (IRE)**[95] 482 6-8-9 **47** oh1 ow1 ....(p) LiamKeniry 4 28
(Milton Bradley) *chsd ldrs: rdn over 2f out: wknd over 1f out* **14/1**

000/ **12** *15* **Wee Buns**[770] 1152 6-9-0 **52** .... RichardThomas 8 —
(Paul Burgoyne) *chsd ldrs: rdn over 2f out: sn wknd* **50/1**

500- **R** **Erfaan (USA)**[206] 7064 4-8-12 **50** ....(v[1]) BarryMcHugh 6 —
(Julie Camacho) *c out of stalls but ref to r* **20/1**

1m 14.17s (-0.83) **Going Correction** -0.175s/f (Stan) **13** Ran SP% **117.9**
Speed ratings (Par 101): **98,95,94,94,92 92,91,90,88,86 85,65,—**
toteswingers:1&2:£13.60, 1&3:£8.10, 2&3:£7.30 CSF £193.24 CT £1140.84 TOTE £17.90: £4.90, £3.20, £1.80; EX 217.80.
Owner E G Bevan **Bred** Longdon Stud Ltd **Trained** Ullingswick, H'fords

FOCUS
As in the first division, it was crucial to race up with the pace. The winning time was 7/100ths of a second slower than the first leg. The form is sound enough.
Errigal Lad Official explanation: jockey said gelding hung right-handed
Cheveyo(IRE) Official explanation: jockey said gelding hung right-handed throughout
Erfaan(USA) Official explanation: trainer's rep said gelding would not face the first time visor

2163 SPONSOR A RACE BY CALLING 01902 390000 H'CAP 5f 216y(P)
3:40 (3:42) (Class 6) (0-60,60) 3-Y-0 **£1,706** (£503; £252) **Stalls** Low

Form RPR
1333 **1** **Juarla (IRE)**[34] 1294 3-9-7 **60** .... LukeMorris 1 69
(Ronald Harris) *w ldrs: led over 3f out: rdn over 1f out: styd on* **11/2**[2]

0-44 **2** *½* **Climaxfortackle (IRE)**[7] 1952 3-9-7 **60** .... RobbieFitzpatrick 7 67+
(Derek Shaw) *s.i.s: hld up: hdwy over 1f out: rdn and hung rt ins fnl f: r.o* **12/1**

-300 **3** *2* **Stravsambition**[10] 1853 3-9-7 **60** .... GrahamGibbons 5 61
(Reg Hollinshead) *a.p: rdn to chse wnr over 1f out: styd on same pce ins fnl f* **20/1**

1414 **4** *nk* **Ace Master**[26] 1503 3-9-7 **60** .... JimmyQuinn 2 60
(Roy Bowring) *led 5f out: hdd over 3f out: rdn over 1f out: r.o* **7/1**[3]

2436 **5** *½* **Scommettitrice (IRE)**[14] 1753 3-9-0 **53** ....(b) GregFairley 11 51
(Ronald Harris) *mid-div: rdn over 2f out: swtchd lft and r.o ins fnl f: nt rch ldrs* **16/1**

6302 **6** *hd* **Misere**[7] 1953 3-9-2 **55** .... PhillipMakin 4 53
(Kevin Ryan) *chsd ldrs: rdn over 2f out: styd on u.p* **5/4**[1]

000- **7** *nk* **Alluring Star**[192] 7335 3-9-0 **53** .... DavidNolan 13 50
(Michael Easterby) *hld up: r.o ins fnl f: nrst fin* **25/1**

-554 **8** *1 ½* **Rational Act (IRE)**[14] 1749 3-9-4 **57** .... DuranFentiman 8 49
(Tim Easterby) *led 1f: chsd ldrs: rdn over 1f out: styd on same pce fnl f* **7/1**[3]

-660 **9** *1 ¼* **Encore View**[27] 1472 3-9-5 **58** ....(t) DarryllHolland 12 46
(Nick Littmoden) *hld up: hdwy over 2f out: sn rdn: wknd fnl f* **28/1**

604- **10** *2 ¼* **Ted's Brother (IRE)**[195] 7280 3-9-4 **60** .... RobertLButler(3) 3 41
(Richard Guest) *hld up: in rr whn hmpd over 2f out: nvr on terms* **25/1**

5-43 **11** *2* **Look Twice**[112] 274 3-9-5 **58** .... LiamJones 9 32
(Alex Hales) *prom: rdn over 2f out: wknd wl over 1f out* **25/1**

5330 **12** *8* **Pickled Pumpkin**[14] 1764 3-9-1 **54** .... JackMitchell 6 —
(Olivia Maylam) *s.i.s: a in rr: rdn over 2f out: sn wknd* **22/1**

1m 14.57s (-0.43) **Going Correction** -0.175s/f (Stan) **12** Ran SP% **122.5**
Speed ratings (Par 97): **95,94,91,91,90 90,89,87,86,83 80,69**
toteswingers:1&2:£13.40, 1&3:£9.70, 2&3:£20.70 CSF £63.12 CT £1267.09 TOTE £4.50: £1.20, £3.40, £4.60; EX 76.80.
Owner Robert & Nina Bailey **Bred** D And Mrs D Veitch **Trained** Earlswood, Monmouths
■ Stewards' Enquiry : Robbie Fitzpatrick caution: careless riding.

FOCUS
A moderate 3-y-o handicap and the winning time was just under half a second slower than both divisions of the older-horse handicap over the same trip. The winner is rated back to his best.

2164 LADBROKES.COM H'CAP 5f 20y(P)
4:10 (4:10) (Class 6) (0-60,60) 4-Y-0+ **£1,706** (£503; £252) **Stalls** Low

Form RPR
-040 **1** **First Blade**[74] 743 5-9-7 **60** ....(b) PaulQuinn 1 68
(Roy Bowring) *chsd ldrs: rdn to ld ins fnl f: r.o* **8/1**

2043 **2** *hd* **The Tatling (IRE)**[18] 1627 14-9-7 **60** .... LiamKeniry 2 67
(Milton Bradley) *hld up: hdwy 2f out: shkn up ins fnl f: r.o* **13/2**

-331 **3** *hd* **Sparking**[59] 892 4-9-3 **56** .... GrahamGibbons 4 63
(David Barron) *chsd ldrs: rdn and hung rt over 1f out: r.o* **5/2**[1]

1506 **4** *2 ¼* **Triskaidekaphobia**[23] 1523 8-9-3 **56** ....(t) FrankieMcDonald 7 54
(Paul Fitzsimons) *led: rdn and hdd ins fnl f: styd on same pce* **12/1**

0065 **5** *1 ¾* **Rightcar**[27] 1469 4-8-9 **48** ....(b) RobbieFitzpatrick 9 40
(Peter Grayson) *sn outpcd: rdn 1/2-way: r.o ins fnl f: nrst fin* **28/1**

0645 **6** *½* **Shakespeares Excel**[27] 1464 4-8-9 **48** ow1 .... JamieSpencer 10 38
(Derek Shaw) *hld up: hdwy over 1f out: r.o: nt trble ldrs* **7/2**[2]

2235 **7** *3* **Attrition**[34] 1287 4-9-2 **58** ....(p) SophieDoyle(3) 11 38
(Andrew Reid) *w ldrs tl rdn 2f out: wknd fnl f* **11/2**[3]

0104 **8** *3 ¾* **Francis Albert**[6] 1982 5-8-10 **56** ....(be) JosephYoung(7) 6 [illegible]
(Michael Mullineaux) *chsd ldrs tl wknd over 1f out* **12/1**

10 **9** *4 ½* **Odd Ball (IRE)**[22] 1544 4-9-3 **56** .... StephenCraine 13 —
(Patrick Morris) *s.s: outpcd* **16/1**

050- **10** *3 ¼* **Ishipink**[329] 3255 4-8-7 **46** .... MartinLane 5 —
(Ron Hodges) *hmpd s: sn prom: wknd 2f out* **40/1**

60.97 secs (-1.33) **Going Correction** -0.175s/f (Stan) **10** Ran SP% **117.8**
Speed ratings (Par 101): **103,102,102,98,95 95,90,84,77,71**
toteswingers:1&2:£10.30, 1&3:£5.40, 2&3:£4.00 CSF £59.81 CT £158.81 TOTE £6.30: £2.10, £1.80, £1.60; EX 67.00.
Owner S R Bowring **Bred** S R Bowring **Trained** Edwinstowe, Notts
■ Stewards' Enquiry : Frankie McDonald one-day ban: failed to ride to draw (May 30)
Paul Quinn caution: careless riding

FOCUS
Another moderate sprint handicap. Straightforward form.

2165 LADBROKES MOBILE H'CAP 7f 32y(P)
4:40 (4:41) (Class 5) (0-70,70) 4-Y-0+ **£2,266** (£674; £337; £168) **Stalls** High

Form RPR
3331 **1** **Cavitie**[20] 1581 5-8-13 **62** ....(p) DarryllHolland 6 73
(Andrew Reid) *led early: chsd ldrs: rdn to ld 1f out: r.o* **12/1**

66-4 **2** *nk* **Tamasou (IRE)**[31] 1368 6-9-4 **67** .... RichardMullen 4 77
(Ed McMahon) *chsd ldrs: led over 1f out: sn rdn and hdd: r.o* **5/2**[1]

-024 **3** *1 ½* **Khajaaly (IRE)**[58] 915 4-9-5 **68** .... JimmyQuinn 1 74
(Julia Feilden) *hld up: hdwy over 2f out: rdn over 1f out: styd on same pce ins fnl f* **13/2**[3]

0-03 **4** *½* **Devil You Know (IRE)**[35] 1274 5-9-4 **67** ....(t) GrahamGibbons 7 72
(Michael Easterby) *chsd ldrs: rdn and ev ch over 1f out: styd on same pce ins fnl f* **14/1**

5512 **5** *1 ¼* **Polemica (IRE)**[35] 1279 5-9-0 **63** ....(bt) SilvestreDeSousa 8 65
(Frank Sheridan) *hld up in tch: rdn over 2f out: styd on same pce fnl f* **7/2**[2]

00-0 **6** *hd* **Shaws Diamond (USA)**[4] 2016 5-8-11 **60** .... MartinLane 11 61
(Derek Shaw) *in rr: pushed along over 5f out: r.o ins fnl f: nvr nrr* **12/1**

4000 **7** *1 ¼* **Justcallmehandsome**[47] 1052 9-8-8 **60** ....(v) BillyCray(3) 3 58
(Dominic Ffrench Davis) *hld up: r.o ins fnl f: nvr nrr* **16/1**

2550 **8** *2* **Kipchak (IRE)**[12] 1814 6-8-13 **62** ....(v) HayleyTurner 10 54
(Conor Dore) *chsd ldr: rdn over 2f out: ev ch over 1f out: wknd ins fnl f* **20/1**

1-03 **9** *4* **Not My Choice (IRE)**[13] 1793 6-9-7 **70** ....(t) RobbieFitzpatrick 5 52
(David C Griffiths) *sn pushed along to ld: rdn and hdd over 1f out: wknd fnl f* **8/1**

200- **10** 5 **Gazboolou**[151] 7889 7-8-12 **66** JamesRogers(5) 12 34
(David Pinder) *a in rr* **14/1**
106- **11** 1 ¼ **Gracie's Gift (IRE)**[161] 7730 9-8-11 **63** (p) RobertLButler(3) 9 —
(Richard Guest) *s.i.s: a in rr* **25/1**
1-06 **12** ½ **Little Pete (IRE)**[17] 1649 6-9-4 **67** PatrickMathers 2 —
(Ian McInnes) *prom: lost pl 4f out: sn rdn and hung rt: wknd over 2f out* **40/1**

1m 27.89s (-1.71) **Going Correction** -0.175s/f (Stan) 12 Ran SP% **120.9**
Speed ratings (Par 103): **102,101,99,99,97 97,96,94,89,83 82,81**
toteswingers:1&2:£9.40, 1&3:£7.30, 2&3:£4.20 CSF £42.04 CT £226.76 TOTE £16.30: £4.70, £1.10, £3.00; EX 75.60.
Owner A S Reid **Bred** A S Reid **Trained** Mill Hill, London NW7

FOCUS
An ordinary handicap, but a strong pace with Not My Choice and Kipchak duelling for the early lead and running themselves into the ground in the process. Sound form.

2166 PLAY ROULETTE AT LADBROKES.COM H'CAP 1m 1f 103y(P)
5:10 (5:10) (Class 6) (0-60,60) 3-Y-O £1,619 (£481; £240; £120) Stalls Low

Form RPR
00-2 **1** **Ishikawa (IRE)**[20] 1588 3-9-0 **53** FergusSweeney 11 60+
(Alan King) *hld up: hdwy over 2f out: rdn to ld and edgd rt ins fnl f: r.o* **9/4**[1]
6-36 **2** ½ **Sukhothai (USA)**[21] 1574 3-9-5 **58** JackMitchell 4 64
(James Fanshawe) *chsd ldrs: rdn over 2f out: ev ch 1f out: r.o* **12/1**
000- **3** nk **Mystic Edge**[198] 7231 3-9-5 **58** HayleyTurner 5 63
(Michael Bell) *a.p: rdn to ld 1f out: sn hdd: r.o* **17/2**
2266 **4** 1 ¼ **The Absent Mare**[14] 1769 3-8-9 **48** (bt[1]) SilvestreDeSousa 9 51+
(Frank Sheridan) *hld up: hdwy over 1f out: r.o: nt rch ldrs* **12/1**
6-53 **5** ¾ **One Of Twins**[7] 1945 3-8-5 **47** JamesSullivan(3) 7 48
(Michael Easterby) *prom: drvn along 7f out: rdn over 2f out: styd on same pce ins fnl f* **12/1**
650 **6** 1 **Beauchamp Zest**[31] 1364 3-9-7 **60** (t) MartinLane 1 59
(Hans Adielsson) *chsd ldrs: rdn over 1f out: sn ev ch: no ex ins fnl f* **25/1**
60-2 **7** 2 ½ **Inca Blue**[7] 1945 3-8-13 **52** DuranFentiman 2 46
(Tim Easterby) *led: rdn and hdd over 2f out: no ex fnl f* **6/1**[3]
5-66 **8** 1 **Eduardo**[23] 1526 3-9-4 **60** PatrickDonaghy(3) 12 52
(Jedd O'Keeffe) *chsd ldrs: led over 2f out: rdn and hdd 1f out: wknd ins fnl f* **25/1**
00-5 **9** 4 ½ **Bumbling Bertie**[21] 1566 3-8-11 **50** (v[1]) LiamKeniry 8 32
(Andrew Balding) *chsd ldr: rdn and ev ch over 2f out: wknd over 1f out* **12/1**
400- **10** 2 **Soldiers Point**[191] 7346 3-9-2 **55** JamieSpencer 10 33
(Jane Chapple-Hyam) *hld up: rdn 3f out: a in rr* **9/2**[2]
0-00 **11** 12 **Dancing Cavalier (IRE)**[14] 1769 3-8-7 **46** oh1 GrahamGibbons 3 —
(Reg Hollinshead) *s.s: a bhd* **28/1**
060- **12** 53 **Miss T**[213] 6894 3-9-0 **53** PaulMulrennan 6 —
(James Given) *hld up: bhd fnl 5f: t.o* **50/1**

2m 0.23s (-1.47) **Going Correction** -0.175s/f (Stan) 12 Ran SP% **117.6**
Speed ratings (Par 97): **99,98,98,97,96 95,93,92,88,86 76,28**
toteswingers:1&2:£7.70, 1&3:£6.60, 2&3:£17.20 CSF £29.72 CT £199.34 TOTE £3.30: £1.10, £3.70, £3.90; EX 37.90.
Owner Alan King **Bred** Ken Carroll **Trained** Barbury Castle, Wilts

FOCUS
A modest 3-y-o handicap and several were still in with every chance a furlong out. Probably sound form, the fourth helping with the level.
Dancing Cavalier(IRE) Official explanation: jockey said gelding was slowly away
Miss T Official explanation: jockey said filly never travelled and hung left-handed
T/Plt: £39.50 to a £1 stake. Pool:£51,799.73 - 957.22 winning tickets T/Qpdt: £14.30 to a £1 stake. Pool:£3,726.37 - 191.80 winning tickets CR

1932 BRIGHTON (L-H)
Tuesday, May 17

OFFICIAL GOING: Good to firm (8.5)
Rail dolled out 2m from 4.5f to 2f increasing distances by 6yds.
Wind: Fresh, half-against. Weather: Fine

2167 SUMMER MUSIC NIGHT HERE 21ST JUNE H'CAP 5f 59y
2:20 (2:21) (Class 5) (0-70,70) 4-Y-O+ £2,266 (£674; £337; £168) Stalls Low

Form RPR
0226 **1** **Rocker**[11] 1864 7-9-7 **70** (b) RyanMoore 3 78
(Gary Moore) *stdd in rr: plld wd and hdwy fr over 1f out: drvn to ld ins fnl f* **5/4**[1]
5550 **2** 1 ¼ **Billy Red**[4] 2069 7-9-7 **70** (b) FergusSweeney 5 74
(J R Jenkins) *sn led: hrd rdn and hdd ins fnl f: one pce* **7/2**[2]
5023 **3** ½ **Miss Firefly**[8] 1938 6-8-3 **57** HarryBentley(5) 6 59
(Ron Hodges) *reluctant to go to post: broke wl: pressed ldr: hrd rdn 2f out: one pce ins fnl f* **6/1**[3]
4050 **4** ½ **Highland Harvest**[12] 1838 7-9-2 **65** RobertHavlin 1 66
(Jamie Poulton) *in tch in 5th: effrt 2f out: one pce ins fnl f* **16/1**
603- **5** ¾ **Maryolini**[193] 7334 6-8-7 **56** JimmyQuinn 4 54
(Tom Keddy) *broke wl: stdd bk into 4th: effrt 2f out: no ex fnl f* **7/1**
0-11 **6** 2 ½ **The Jailer**[12] 1831 8-8-12 **66** (p) RyanPowell(5) 2 55
(John O'Shea) *chsd ldng pair: rdn over 2f out: wknd fnl f: eased whn btn fnl 75yds* **6/1**[3]

62.59 secs (0.29) **Going Correction** +0.05s/f (Good) 6 Ran SP% **113.6**
Speed ratings (Par 103): **99,97,96,95,94 90**
toteswingers:1&2: £1.70, 2&3: £3.80, 1&3: £2.30 CSF £5.96 TOTE £1.80: £1.20, £2.60; EX 7.00.

Owner Sir Eric Parker **Bred** Sir Eric Parker **Trained** Lower Beeding, W Sussex

FOCUS
The going was good to firm on a watered track. They went a fair pace in this sprint handicap involving five C&D winners. The heavily backed favourite swooped late and there was not much separating the first five. The winner is rated back to something like his best.

2168 WEATHERBYS BLOODSTOCK INSURANCE MAIDEN STKS 5f 213y
2:50 (2:51) (Class 5) 3-Y-O+ £2,266 (£674; £337; £168) Stalls Low

Form RPR
20 **1** **Deerslayer (USA)**[22] 1568 5-9-10 PaulDoe 3 73
(Jim Best) *mde all: hung bdly rt and hrd rdn fr over 2f out: bmpd runner-up jst ins fnl f: drvn out* **6/1**[2]
00-5 **2** 1 ½ **Chaussini**[15] 1762 4-9-5 76 RyanMoore 1 65
(James Toller) *t.k.h in 2nd: effrt and carried bdly rt fr over 2f out: bmpd and squeezed on stands' rail by wnr jst ins fnl f: swtchd lft: nt qckn* **1/5**[1]
5- **3** 11 **Secret Lake**[204] 7119 3-8-7 AshleyHamblett(3) 4 26
(George Margarson) *reluctant to load: cl up tl wknd 2f out* **14/1**[3]
60-4 **4** 1 **Make My Mark (IRE)**[28] 1449 3-8-10 49 MartinLane 2 23
(John Gallagher) *cl up: hmpd after 1f: wknd 2f out* **40/1**

1m 11.42s (1.22) **Going Correction** +0.05s/f (Good)
WFA 3 from 4yo+ 9lb 4 Ran SP% **106.7**
Speed ratings (Par 103): **93,91,76,75**
CSF £7.87 TOTE £4.80; EX 8.10.
Owner M&R Refurbishments Ltd **Bred** Bjorn Nielsen **Trained** Lewes, E Sussex
■ Stewards' Enquiry : Paul Doe three-day ban: careless riding (May 31,Jun 1-2); four-day ban: used whip with excessive frequency some down shoulder in the forehand (Jun 6-9)

FOCUS
A small-field maiden. The hot odds-on favourite was turned over by a wayward front-runner who survived a long stewards' enquiry. Weak form, and shaky.

2169 DIGIBET.COM H'CAP 6f 209y
3:20 (3:20) (Class 3) (0-90,87) 4-Y-O+ £5,180 (£1,541; £770; £384) Stalls Low

Form RPR
0-03 **1** **Swiss Cross**[11] 1854 4-9-7 **87** (t) DarryllHolland 2 100
(Gerard Butler) *w ldr: led after 1f: rdn clr ins fnl f* **2/1**[1]
5-46 **2** 2 ½ **Beaver Patrol (IRE)**[12] 1832 9-8-10 **76** (v) TomQueally 3 82
(Eve Johnson Houghton) *led 1f: chsd wnr: rdn and lost pl ins fnl 2f: rallied to regain 2nd ins fnl f* **11/2**[3]
2442 **3** 1 ½ **Magical Speedfit (IRE)**[8] 1937 6-8-2 **73** RyanPowell(5) 4 75
(George Margarson) *chsd ldrs: rdn to chal ins fnl 2f: one pce* **8/1**
0-06 **4** 1 **Ghostwing**[10] 1888 4-9-4 **84** (v) FergusSweeney 6 83
(John Gallagher) *sn pushed along in 5th: effrt over 2f out: hung lft and no ex ins fnl f* **7/1**
04-4 **5** 4 ½ **Aye Aye Digby (IRE)**[10] 1898 6-9-4 **84** RyanMoore 5 71
(Patrick Chamings) *chsd ldng pair: rdn to chal ins fnl f: wknd 1f out* **11/4**[2]
0120 **6** 3 ½ **Buxton**[10] 1898 7-8-9 **75** (t) MartinLane 7 53
(Roger Ingram) *hld up in rr: brief effrt 2f out: hung lft and wknd over 1f out* **10/1**
-150 **7** 3 ½ **Caprio (IRE)**[20] 1610 6-8-11 **77** NickyMackay 1 45
(Jim Boyle) *towards rr: hdwy in centre to press ldrs over 2f out: wknd over 1f out: eased whn no ch fnl 75yds* **25/1**

1m 22.19s (-0.91) **Going Correction** +0.05s/f (Good) 7 Ran SP% **111.9**
Speed ratings (Par 107): **107,104,102,101,96 92,88**
toteswingers:1&2: £2.80, 2&3: £7.30, 1&3: £3.50 CSF £12.84 TOTE £2.30: £1.70, £2.30; EX 13.90.
Owner A D Spence **Bred** Lordship Stud **Trained** Newmarket, Suffolk

FOCUS
A decent handicap in which the field shifted towards the stands' side in the straight. The pace was strong but the first two both raced prominently. The winner rates better than ever.

NOTEBOOK
Swiss Cross hit a new personal best with headgear left off when a close third from a bad draw in a competitive 7f Chester handicap last time. He had strong claims off 3lb higher in this weaker race and produced a dynamic front-running performance to win with quite a bit in hand. He can throw in the odd disappointment and will face another fair rise after this, but there could be more improvement to come from this tactically adaptable 4-y-o. (op 5-2 tchd 11-4 in a place)
Beaver Patrol(IRE) is not the horse he was but he ended a long losing run off 1lb lower over this C&D last September and put in a creditable and enthusiastic display under a prominent ride on this third run back from a break. (op 6-1 tchd 5-1)
Magical Speedfit(IRE) was the subject of a hard-luck story here last time and is a four-time winner at this track, but all of his victories have been at around 5f and his promising effort flattened out in the closing stages stepped back up to 7f. (op 7-1)
Ghostwing can look moody at times and doesn't have a great conversion rate, but he was an eye-catching sixth of 18 in a useful 6f Ascot handicap last time and backed that up with a fair effort up the centre of the track back at 7f. (op 11-2 tchd 15-2)
Aye Aye Digby(IRE) attracted support but couldn't improve on his 7l fourth at Lingfield on his reappearance. He has a bit to prove but a return to slower ground could help reignite him. (op 10-3)

2170 WEATHERBYS BETTRENDS.CO.UK H'CAP 1m 3f 196y
3:50 (3:54) (Class 5) (0-70,70) 4-Y-O+ £2,266 (£674; £337; £168) Stalls High

Form RPR
4-04 **1** **Penang Cinta**[28] 1454 8-8-8 **57** CathyGannon 2 66
(David Evans) *trckd ldr: drvn to chal whn carried lft to far rail by wnr ins fnl f: got up fnl 30yds* **9/2**[3]
214- **2** shd **Celestial Girl**[216] 6846 4-9-6 **69** ChrisCatlin 5 78
(Hughie Morrison) *in tch: led over 2f out: strly chal and hung bdly lft fnl f: hdd fnl 30yds* **2/1**[2]
1-62 **3** 15 **Alubari**[7] 1994 4-9-7 **70** JamieSpencer 1 55
(David Simcock) *led tl over 2f out: wknd wl over 1f out* **1/1**[1]
50-6 **4** ½ **Agapanthus (GER)**[42] 1156 6-9-4 **67** TomQueally 4 51
(Barney Curley) *stdd s: hdwy to chse ldrs after 3f: pushed along over 3f out: wknd wl over 1f out* **16/1**
-000 **5** 21 **The Wonga Coup (IRE)**[38] 1233 4-8-2 **56** oh4 JemmaMarshall(5) 3 —
(Pat Phelan) *in tch: styd alone far side st: hrd rdn and wknd 2f out* **40/1**

2m 34.33s (1.63) **Going Correction** +0.05s/f (Good) 5 Ran SP% **109.8**
Speed ratings (Par 103): **96,95,85,85,71**
CSF £13.83 TOTE £5.00: £2.50, £1.10; EX 9.50.
Owner Trevor Gallienne **Bred** Mrs A K H Ooi **Trained** Pandy, Monmouths
■ Stewards' Enquiry : Chris Catlin two-day ban: careless riding (May 31-Jun 1)

FOCUS
There was a very tight finish between the breakaway front pair who shifted from the stands' rail to the far side in this middle-distance handicap. The first two came a long way clear and the others didn't run their races.

2171 TAKE THAT EXPERIENCE HERE 21ST JUNE H'CAP 7f 214y
4:20 (4:20) (Class 6) (0-60,61) 4-Y-O+ £1,619 (£481; £240; £120) Stalls Low

Form RPR
0001 **1** **Integria**[8] 1933 5-9-8 **61** 6ex (bt) TonyCulhane 6 69
(George Baker) *bhd: rdn over 3f out: hdwy 2f out: drvn to chal fnl f: got up fnl strides* **9/4**[1]
054- **2** hd **Phluke**[181] 7487 10-9-4 **57** CathyGannon 3 64
(Eve Johnson Houghton) *led: hrd rdn and kpt on wl fnl f: hdd fnl strides* **11/1**
2300 **3** 2 ¼ **Indian Violet (IRE)**[74] 765 5-9-7 **60** JamieGoldstein 7 62
(Ralph Smith) *t.k.h: chsd ldrs: effrt over 2f out: nt qckn fnl f* **18/1**
-024 **4** 3 ¾ **Goose Green (IRE)**[1] 2144 7-9-0 **53** JimCrowley 2 46
(Ron Hodges) *chsd ldrs: hrd rdn 2f out: wknd 1f out* **9/2**[3]
5041 **5** nse **Aggbag**[15] 1763 7-8-4 **48** AdamBeschizza(5) 8 41
(Tony Carroll) *bhd: sme hdwy and rdn over 2f out: nvr able to chal* **3/1**[2]
3001 **6** 2 **St Ignatius**[32] 1357 4-8-12 **54** (p) SeanLevey(3) 9 43
(Michael Appleby) *pressed ldr: hrd rdn over 2f out: sn wknd* **13/2**

440- 7 6 **Prince Valentine**[208] 7038 10-8-2 **46** oh1..................(p) HarryBentley(5) 4 21
(Gary Moore) *chsd ldrs tl hrd rdn and wknd 2f out* **20/1**
0-00 8 2 **Fly By Nelly**[117] 225 5-8-11 **50**.. ChrisCatlin 5 20
(Mark Hoad) *towards rr: pushed along over 3f out: wknd 2f out* **16/1**
1m 36.18s (0.18) **Going Correction** +0.05s/f (Good) **8** Ran SP% **111.5**
Speed ratings (Par 101): **101,100,98,94,94 92,86,84**
toteswingers:1&2: £5.30, 2&3: £21.80, 1&3: £6.10 CSF £26.62 CT £346.96 TOTE £2.40: £1.10, £2.90, £4.10; EX 27.10 Trifecta £348.30 Part won. Pool £470.68 - 0.92 winning units..
Owner Mrs Natalie Heath **Bred** Littleton Stud **Trained** Whitsbury, Hants
■ Stewards' Enquiry : Tony Culhane one-day ban: used whip with excessive frequency without giving gelding time to respond (May 31)

FOCUS
An ordinary handicap in which the first two pulled clear. The form is rated around the second.

2172 PARTY ON THE HILL HERE 27TH MAY H'CAP 6f 209y
4:50 (4:50) (Class 6) (0-60,60) 3-Y-O **£1,619** (£481; £240; £120) **Stalls** Low

Form RPR
0-06 1 **Miss Dutee**[15] 1764 3-8-13 **57**.. KieranO'Neill(5) 5 64
(Richard Hannon) *stdd s: bhd: gd hdwy 2f out: led on stands' rail ent fnl f: hung lft: rdn clr* **12/1**
-200 2 2 1/2 **Tymismoni (IRE)**[27] 1481 3-9-0 **56**...............................(v) KierenFox(3) 9 56
(Brett Johnson) *chsd ldrs: effrt over 2f out: nt qckn fnl f* **7/1[2]**
0-03 3 shd **Cathcart Castle**[8] 1952 3-9-1 **57**.................................... MartinHarley(3) 8 57
(Mick Channon) *mid-div: rdn over 2f out: r.o fr over 1f out: nrst fin* **7/4[1]**
00-3 4 1/2 **Lady On Top (IRE)**[21] 1578 3-8-9 **48**.............................. FrankieMcDonald 2 46
(Nerys Dutfield) *w ldrs: led 2f out tl ent fnl f: one pce* **25/1**
4-00 5 shd **Talkative Guest (IRE)**[38] 1251 3-9-4 **60**................. AshleyHamblett(3) 3 58
(George Margarson) *mid-div: rdn and hdwy over 1f out: styd on same pce ins fnl f* **15/2[3]**
0050 6 1 1/4 **Ability Girl**[33] 1331 3-8-12 **51**... NickyMackay 4 46
(Chris Wall) *mid-div: effrt and nt clr rn over 1f out: no imp whn n.m.r ins fnl f* **16/1**
0-60 7 nk **Salesiano**[42] 1149 3-9-5 **58**... FergusSweeney 11 52
(Peter Makin) *w ldrs tl wknd over 1f out* **18/1**
3330 8 1 1/4 **Sleeping Brave**[22] 1566 3-8-9 **55**..............................(p) NathanAlison(7) 1 46
(Jim Boyle) *s.s: bhd: rdn and sme hdwy over 1f out: nt trble ldrs* **8/1**
0000 9 hd **Ajaafa**[7] 1980 3-9-1 **57**... SeanLevey(3) 10 47
(Michael Appleby) *in tch: nt clr run over 2f out: swtchd lft: rdn and n.m.r over 1f out: sn wknd* **20/1**
-456 10 4 1/2 **Blade Pirate**[11] 1872 3-8-1 **47**.................................(p) BradleyBosley(7) 12 25
(John Ryan) *mde most tl wknd 2f out* **16/1**
53-6 11 1/2 **Koha (USA)**[132] 44 3-8-10 **49**... KirstyMilczarek 7 26
(Dean Ivory) *in tch: rdn whn squeezed for room over 1f out: n.d after* **8/1**
000- 12 11 **Maxiyow (IRE)**[321] 3562 3-8-4 **46** oh1......................... DeclanCannon(3) 6 —
(Bryn Palling) *dwlt: a towards rr: no ch fnl 2f* **40/1**
1m 24.26s (1.16) **Going Correction** +0.05s/f (Good) **12** Ran SP% **118.6**
Speed ratings (Par 97): **95,92,92,91,91 89,89,88,87,82 82,69**
toteswingers:1&2: £16.60, 2&3: £4.00, 1&3: £7.00 CSF £91.64 CT £221.77 TOTE £17.50: £5.00, £1.60, £1.30; EX 60.90 Trifecta £330.70 Pool £597.48 - 1.33 winning units..
Owner Tollputt Racing **Bred** N Poole And A Franklin **Trained** East Everleigh, Wilts

FOCUS
A weak handicap. Most of the runners were struggling for form and 11 of them were still maidens. It was a messy affair and quite a few found trouble. The form is rated around the second and third.
Talkative Guest(IRE) Official explanation: trainer said filly did not handle the track
Ability Girl Official explanation: jockey said filly was denied a clear run
Sleeping Brave Official explanation: jockey said gelding was slowly away
Koha(USA) Official explanation: jockey said filly suffered interference 1f out
T/Plt: £125.50 to a £1 stake. Pool of £45,916.11. 266.93 winning tickets. T/Qpdt: £10.90 to a £1 stake. Pool of £3,975.39. 269.45 winning tickets LM

1995 KEMPTON (A.W) (R-H)
Tuesday, May 17

OFFICIAL GOING: Standard
Wind: Moderate, across. Weather: light showers

2173 REWARDS4RACING.COM MEDIAN AUCTION MAIDEN STKS 5f (P)
6:00 (6:01) (Class 6) 2-Y-O **£1,706** (£503; £252) **Stalls** Low

Form RPR
06 1 **Powerful Wind (IRE)**[21] 1583 2-9-3 0................................. LukeMorris 6 76
(Ronald Harris) *broke wl: mde all and sn crossed to rail: rdn and clr ent fnl f: kpt on: rdn out* **33/1**
4 2 1 3/4 **Banksy**[10] 1890 2-9-3 0... WilliamBuick 5 70
(John Gosden) *hmpd s: chsd ldrs: wnt 2nd 1/2-way: rdn and nt qckn w wnr jst over 1f out: styd on same pce fnl f* **10/11[1]**
3 1/2 **Red Alpha (IRE)** 2-9-3 0.. RyanMoore 4 68+
(Jeremy Noseda) *hmpd s: bhd: rdn 3f out: hdwy jst over 1f out: kpt on wl fnl f: nt rch ldrs* **4/1[3]**
022 4 2 **Red Socks (IRE)**[11] 1863 2-9-3 0...................................... JimmyQuinn 3 64
(Gay Kelleway) *s.i.s and short of room sn after s: sn rdn along: hdwy over 1f out: kpt on fnl f: nt rch ldrs* **3/1[2]**
35 5 nk **Summathisnthat**[15] 1765 2-8-12 0...................................... JamesDoyle 1 55
(Des Donovan) *chsd wnr tl 1/2-way: rdn and unable qck wl over 1f out: kpt on same pce and wl hld fnl f* **10/1**
0 6 3 **River Nova**[11] 1846 2-8-12 0... MartinLane 2 44
(Alan Jarvis) *in tch in midfield: rdn and struggling over 2f out: bhd fr over 1f out* **50/1**
61.54 secs (1.04) **Going Correction** +0.025s/f (Slow) **6** Ran SP% **111.4**
Speed ratings (Par 91): **92,89,88,85,84 79**
Tote Swingers:1&2:£6.90, 2&3:£1.10, 1&3:£7.60 CSF £63.86 TOTE £43.90: £17.40, £1.10; EX 115.40.
Owner Anthony Cooke **Bred** Miss Ciara Doyle **Trained** Earlswood, Monmouths

FOCUS
An uncompetitive event and one run at an ordinary gallop. The winner raced just off the inside rail throughout and this form is probably no better than modest. The winner may rate higher.

NOTEBOOK
Powerful Wind(IRE) raced with the choke out but stepped up a fair bit on his previous efforts to get off the mark over a course-and-distance that suits his prominent style of racing. He may do better when the nursery season begins. (op 25-1)
Banksy, well backed before the start, was down in trip and stepped up on his debut (turf) form but it was still disappointing he couldn't take care of a rival who had only previously shown moderate form. The return to 6f may help but he's likely to remain vulnerable in this grade. (op 6-4)
Red Alpha(IRE) ◆ was too green to do himself justice over a trip that looked on the sharp side but he showed ability on this debut. This Redcar Two-Year-Old Trophy entry runs and is bred to be suited by 6f on a more galloping track and he should be able to win an ordinary race. Official explanation: jockey said colt was hampered at start (op 7-2)
Red Socks(IRE), a market drifter, looked likely to be a good guide to the worth of this form but disappointed after dwelling and being checked at the start. He's better than this but is another that is likely to remain vulnerable in this company. Official explanation: jockey said colt was slowly away and never travelled (op 9-4 tchd 10-3)
Summathisnthat should be seen to better effect in ordinary nurseries in due course. (op 9-1)
River Nova didn't show enough on this all-weather debut to suggest she's of much short-term interest. (op 40-1)

2174 IRISH NIGHT AT KEMPTON 03.08.11 MEDIAN AUCTION MAIDEN STKS 7f (P)
6:30 (6:31) (Class 6) 3-Y-O **£1,706** (£503; £252) **Stalls** Low

Form RPR
33 1 **Poyle Punch**[21] 1580 3-9-3 0... JimCrowley 10 77
(Ralph Beckett) *chsd ldr: rdn and ev ch ent fnl 2f: drvn to ld 1f out: kpt on wl u.p* **11/2[2]**
03- 2 1/2 **Set Me Free (IRE)**[297] 4392 3-8-10 0........................... TalibHussain(7) 3 75+
(Luca Cumani) *in tch: swtchd rt and rdn ent fnl 2f: chsd ldrs ent fnl f: kpt on to chse wnr fnl 75yds: styd on wl fin* **10/1**
02- 3 nk **Top Diktat**[170] 7609 3-9-3 0.. RyanMoore 8 74
(Sir Michael Stoute) *chsd ldrs: rdn and effrt to press ldrs ent fnl 2f: unable qck and sltly outpcd over 1f out: kpt on again u.p ins fnl f: wnt 3rd wl ins fnl f* **6/4[1]**
0- 4 1/2 **Starbound (IRE)**[192] 7345 3-8-12 0............................... JamieSpencer 7 68
(William Haggas) *led for 2f: chsd ldrs after: effrt on inner 2f out: chsd wnr u.p ins fnl f: kpt on same pce: lost 2 pls fnl 75yds* **15/2**
5 1 3/4 **Arabian Heights** 3-9-3 0.. SebSanders 4 68+
(Sir Mark Prescott Bt) *hld up towards rr: rdn and effrt on inner jst over 2f out: kpt on steadily fnl f: nt rch ldrs* **13/2[3]**
0 6 1/2 **Amber Heights**[15] 1759 3-8-12 0.................................... JimmyFortune 13 62
(David Pinder) *led after 2f: pushed along wl over 1f out: hdd 1f out: wknd fnl 100yds* **14/1**
06- 7 1/2 **Coin Box**[214] 6894 3-8-12 0... WilliamBuick 6 61
(Mahmood Al Zarooni) *broke wl: t.k.h: grad stdd and hld up in tch in tch in midfield: rdn and effrt ent fnl 2f: kpt on u.p fnl f: nt pce to rch ldrs* **11/2[2]**
8 3 3/4 **Carpentras** 3-8-12 0.. LiamKeniry 2 51
(Dr Jon Scargill) *hld up in midfield: effrt on inner and rdn ent fnl f: no hdwy over 1f out: wl hld and kpt on same pce fnl f* **66/1**
56 9 3 1/4 **Full Pelt (USA)**[17] 1693 3-9-3 0.................................... RichardSmith 11 47
(Tom Dascombe) *stdd s: hld up on outer: rdn and effrt over 2f out: sn edgd lft and no hdwy* **66/1**
10 nse **Haafhd Decent (IRE)** 3-8-12 0.. DarryllHolland 9 42
(Karen George) *in tch in midfield: rdn and unable qck over 2f out: struggling whn edgd lft jst over 2f out: no ch fr over 1f out* **66/1**
0-0 11 1 1/2 **Librettela**[15] 1774 3-9-3 0... MartinLane 12 43
(Alan Jarvis) *s.i.s: a towards rr: rdn and struggling wl over 2f out: wl btn fnl 2f* **100/1**
0- 12 2 **Broken Belle (IRE)**[363] 2223 3-8-12 0................................... PatDobbs 5 32
(J W Hills) *stdd s: plld hrd: short of room sn after s: hld up in midfield: rdn and wknd qckly jst over 2f out* **66/1**
0- 13 3 1/2 **Go On The Badger**[153] 7879 3-8-12 0............................ RobertHavlin 14 23
(James Toller) *hld up in last trio: rdn and struggling wl over 2f out: wl bhd fnl 2f* **66/1**
14 8 **Circus Master** 3-9-3 0.. LukeMorris 1 —
(James Eustace) *s.i.s: rn green and a in rr: lost tch over 2f out* **40/1**
1m 28.44s (2.44) **Going Correction** +0.025s/f (Slow) **14** Ran SP% **122.5**
Speed ratings (Par 97): **87,86,86,85,83 82,82,78,74,74 72,70,66,57**
Tote Swingers:1&2:£9.40, 2&3:£3.70, 1&3:£3.20 CSF £59.71 TOTE £7.60: £1.30, £2.70, £1.30; EX 59.50.
Owner Cecil And Miss Alison Wiggins **Bred** Cecil And Miss Alison Wiggins **Trained** Kimpton, Hants

FOCUS
No more than a fair maiden and a steady pace to 2f out but the first seven finished clear and this race should throw up winners at an ordinary level. Improved form from the first three. The winner came down the centre in the straight and those held up were at a disadvantage.

2175 FREE ENTRY FOR BETDAQ MEMBERS MEDIAN AUCTION MAIDEN FILLIES' STKS 1m 3f (P)
7:00 (7:05) (Class 5) 3-Y-O **£2,388** (£705; £352) **Stalls** Low

Form RPR
2 1 **Baltic Light (USA)**[24] 1525 3-9-0 0................................... TomQueally 6 79
(Sir Henry Cecil) *dwlt: in tch in midfield: hdwy to trck ldng pair over 3f out: rdn to ld over 1f out: kpt on wl and forged ahd ins fnl f: wl in command at fin* **5/4[1]**
3-56 2 2 1/2 **Hidden Valley**[16] 1722 3-9-0 73... JimmyFortune 7 74
(Andrew Balding) *chsd ldr: rdn over 2f out: drvn and chsd wnr 1f out: styd on same pce fnl f: nt pushed whn btn fnl 50yds* **13/8[2]**
0 3 2 1/2 **Rose Willow (USA)**[22] 1572 3-9-0 0.................................. WilliamBuick 3 70
(John Gosden) *led: rdn over 2f out: hdd over 1f out: drvn ent fnl f: wknd fnl 100yds* **10/1[3]**
4 4 2 1/2 **Hygrove Welshlady (IRE)**[15] 1767 3-9-0 0........................ SebSanders 5 65
(J W Hills) *hld up in last trio: hdwy over 3f out: outpcd by ldrs over 2f out: wnt modest 4th wl over 1f out: no imp after* **25/1**
4 5 8 **Tiger Tess**[28] 1474 3-9-0 0... JimCrowley 1 51
(Jonathan Portman) *t.k.h: chsd ldrs: rdn and unable qck over 2f out: sn wknd: no ch over 1f out* **12/1**
5-3 6 3 3/4 **Heavenly Music (IRE)**[129] 95 3-9-0 0.................................. LiamKeniry 4 44
(Sylvester Kirk) *hld up in last trio: rdn and struggling whn hung bdly lft over 2f out: wl btn after: eased wl ins fnl f* **10/1[3]**
7 8 **Morgana** 3-9-0 0... StephenCraine 2 29
(Jonathan Portman) *v.s.a: in tch in rr after 1f: rdn and lost tch qckly over 2f out* **66/1**
00 8 16 **April Belle**[36] 1270 3-9-0 0... LukeMorris 8 —
(Tim McCarthy) *chsd ldrs: rdn and lost pl 5f out: last and lost tch 3f out: t.o fnl f* **100/1**
2m 23.23s (1.33) **Going Correction** +0.025s/f (Slow) **8** Ran SP% **114.7**
Speed ratings (Par 96): **96,94,92,90,84 82,76,64**
CSF £3.45 TOTE £2.50: £1.20, £1.02, £2.60; EX 4.30.
Owner Gestut Ammerland **Bred** Gestut Ammerland **Trained** Newmarket, Suffolk

FOCUS
An uncompetitive maiden and one run at just a moderate gallop to the home straight. The winner came down the centre and the first four finished clear. Modest form with the winner rated up 10lb.

Heavenly Music(IRE) Official explanation: jockey said filly hung both ways

2176 BETDAQ.COM EXCHANGE PRICE MULTIPLES FILLIES' H'CAP 1m 4f (P)
7:30 (7:30) (Class 5) (0-70,68) 4-Y-0+ £2,388 (£705; £352) Stalls Centre

Form RPR
012- 1 **Danvilla**[186] 7422 4-9-4 66 WilliamCarson 7 74+
(Paul Webber) *chsd ldr: jnd ldr 4f out: led over 2f out: rdn wl over 1f out: drvn and hld on wl fnl f* **11/8**[1]
00-3 2 ¾ **On The Feather**[20] 1608 5-9-0 62 JamesMillman 1 69
(Rod Millman) *hld up in tch in midfield: hdwy 2f out: rdn to chse wnr 1f out: kpt on but a hld fnl f* **10/1**
05-6 3 ¾ **Perfect Vision**[54] 954 4-9-0 62 LukeMorris 3 68
(Clive Cox) *chsd ldrs: rdn 3f out: drvn and chsd wnr over 1f out tl 1f out: styd on same pce u.p fnl 100yds* **9/1**
-225 4 1 ½ **Mediterranean Sea (IRE)**[98] 457 5-9-4 66 RyanMoore 5 69
(J R Jenkins) *hld up in tch in rr: rdn and effrt ent fnl 2f: hdwy u.p ent fnl f: no imp fnl 100yds* **17/2**
-24P 5 1 **Beauchamp Xiara**[69] 813 5-9-3 65 JamesDoyle 6 67
(Hans Adielsson) *hld up in tch in rr: rdn and effrt on inner wl over 1f out: no imp ins fnl f* **25/1**
00-4 6 hd **Now What**[20] 1608 4-9-3 65 JimCrowley 2 66
(Jonathan Portman) *chsd ldrs: rdn and n.m.r over 2f out: keeping on same pce and n.m.r again jst over 1f out: no imp fnl f* **8/1**
1252 7 ½ **Stargazing (IRE)**[39] 1222 5-9-0 62 AndreaAtzeni 4 63
(Marco Botti) *stdd s: hld up in tch in midfield: swtchd lft over 2f out: drvn and unable qck over 1f out: one pce and hld fnl f* **5/1**[2]
0-43 8 3 ¼ **Goodlukin Lucy**[75] 742 4-9-6 68 DaneO'Neill 8 63
(Pat Eddery) *sn led: rdn and hdd over 2f out: wkng u.p whn sltly hmpd jst ins fnl f: eased wl ins fnl f* **13/2**[3]

2m 33.64s (-0.86) **Going Correction** +0.025s/f (Slow) 8 Ran SP% **116.7**
Speed ratings (Par 100): **103,102,102,101,100 100,99,97**
Tote Swingers:1&2:£7.90, 2&3:£15.90, 1&3:£3.70 CSF £17.06 CT £93.69 TOTE £2.80: £1.50, £2.70, £3.50; EX 27.50.
Owner Shully Liebermann **Bred** Minster Stud **Trained** Mollington, Oxon

FOCUS
A modest handicap run at just a moderate gallop. The winner came down the centre in the straight and recorded a small personal best.

2177 RACING AT SKYSPORTS.COM CLAIMING STKS 6f (P)
8:00 (8:01) (Class 6) 3-Y-0 £1,706 (£503; £252) Stalls Low

Form RPR
2450 1 **Loves Theme (IRE)**[15] 1766 3-8-2 64 (b) CathyGannon 1 63
(Alan Bailey) *in tch: swtchd rt and effrt u.p wl over 1f out: hrd drvn to chse ldr 1f out: kpt on to ld fnl 75yds: drvn out* **9/2**[3]
-310 2 ½ **Roodee Queen**[14] 1802 3-8-4 65 PaulHanagan 2 64
(Patrick Morris) *chsd ldrs: rdn to ld over 1f out: hrd drvn 1f out: hdd and no ex fnl 75yds* **3/1**[1]
5405 3 3 **Local Diktator**[7] 1975 3-8-9 60 (p) LukeMorris 3 59
(Ronald Harris) *stdd s: hld up in last trio: rdn and effrt towards inner 2f out: hrd drvn over 1f out: styd on u.p to go 3rd fnl 50yds: no threat to ldng pair* **9/1**
2464 4 ¾ **Fifth In Line (IRE)**[33] 1334 3-8-2 62 JimmyQuinn 4 50
(David Flood) *awkward leaving stalls: t.k.h: chsd ldrs: jnd ldr over 2f out: drvn over 1f out: hrd drvn 1f out: wknd ins fnl f* **9/1**
0533 5 1 **Titan Diamond (IRE)**[8] 1953 3-8-0 58 RachealKneller(7) 6 51
(Mark Usher) *bhd: pushed along over 2f out: styd on steadily ins fnl f: nvr trbld ldrs* **4/1**[2]
220 6 nse **Reachtothestars (USA)**[15] 1776 3-8-8 60 AdamBeschizza(5) 9 57
(Noel Quinlan) *broke fast: led and crossed to r towards rail: rdn over 2f out: drvn and hdd over 1f out: wknd ins fnl f* **6/1**
0-60 7 1 ¾ **Deveze (IRE)**[8] 1933 3-8-2 45 (p) KirstyMilczarek 10 41
(Dean Ivory) *chsd ldrs: rdn and unable qck ent fnl 2f: wknd u.p jst over 1f out* **40/1**
605 8 ½ **Add Lib**[32] 1358 3-8-2 46 DavidProbert 5 39
(Matthew Salaman) *t.k.h: hld up in tch: rdn and outpcd over 2f out: styd on same pce and no threat to ldrs fnl 2f* **50/1**
3046 9 1 ¼ **Ereka (IRE)**[8] 1933 3-7-13 55 RyanPowell(5) 7 37
(Murty McGrath) *s.i.s: a in rr: rdn and no hdwy wl over 2f out: nvr trbld ldrs* **12/1**
0-0 10 ¾ **Queens Troop**[33] 1343 3-8-12 0 DarryllHolland 8 43
(Dean Ivory) *fly j. leaving stalls and s.i.s: a in rr: rdn over 2f out: no prog and wl hld whn hung rt over 1f out* **14/1**

1m 12.76s (-0.34) **Going Correction** +0.025s/f (Slow) 10 Ran SP% **116.2**
Speed ratings (Par 97): **103,102,98,97,96 95,93,92,91,90**
Tote Swingers:1&2:£3.40, 2&3:£6.80, 1&3:£10.00 CSF £18.32 TOTE £6.90: £2.10, £1.60, £3.30; EX 23.50.
Owner Raymond Gomersall **Bred** Deer Forest Stud **Trained** Newmarket, Suffolk
■ Stewards' Enquiry : Adam Beschizza one-day ban: failed to ride to draw (May 31)

FOCUS
A modest claimer in which the gallop was sound. The winner raced against the inside rail late on and the first two pulled clear. It;s hard to be positive about this form.
Queens Troop Official explanation: jockey said filly was slowly away

2178 SKYSPORTS.COM RACING H'CAP (LONDON MILE QUALIFIER) 1m (P)
8:30 (8:30) (Class 4) (0-80,80) 4-Y-0+ £4,079 (£1,214; £606; £303) Stalls Low

Form RPR
03-3 1 **Tarooq (USA)**[31] 1394 5-8-11 70 PaulHanagan 5 78
(Richard Fahey) *led for 2f: chsd ldrs after: rdn wl over 1f out: led ins fnl f: sn hdd: kpt on gamely to ld again last strides* **7/2**[1]
2314 2 hd **Tevez**[6] 2000 6-9-6 79 CathyGannon 10 86
(Des Donovan) *v.s.a: bhd: rdn over 2f out: hdwy 2f out: str run to chse ldrs and swtchd rt ent fnl f: drvn to ld fnl 75yds: hdd last strides* **11/1**
005- 3 1 ½ **Gallant Eagle (IRE)**[209] 7012 4-9-7 80 PatCosgrave 8 84
(Ed de Giles) *t.k.h: chsd ldrs: wnt 2nd over 4f out: rdn to chal 2f out: drvn ahd over 1f out: hdd ins fnl f: kpt on same pce fnl 100yds* **10/1**[3]
45-5 4 hd **Spa's Dancer (IRE)**[35] 1296 4-9-5 78 SebSanders 9 82+
(J W Hills) *stdd after s: t.k.h: hld up in midfield: rdn and effrt jst over 2f out: hung lft and styd on same pce fnl f* **11/1**
3-10 5 ¾ **Willow Dancer (IRE)**[20] 1603 7-9-4 77 (p) ShaneKelly 12 79
(Walter Swinburn) *chsd ldrs: led after 2f: jnd and rdn ent fnl 2f: hdd over 1f out: stl ev ch tl wknd ins fnl f* **14/1**
505- 6 ½ **Mishrif (USA)**[204] 7115 5-9-1 74 StephenCraine 1 75
(J R Jenkins) *hld up in tch towards rr: hmpd 4f out: rdn and hdwy wl over 1f out: no imp fnl 150yds* **40/1**
0430 7 nk **Gallantry**[24] 1530 9-8-11 70 JimmyQuinn 2 70
(Michael Squance) *in tch in midfield on inner: rdn jst over 2f out: unable qck u.p over 1f out: one pce and hld fnl f* **66/1**
0-12 8 ¾ **Uncle Fred**[24] 1530 6-9-7 80 JimCrowley 3 78
(Patrick Chamings) *stdd s: hld up in rr: effrt on inner 2f out: styd on same pce and no imp ins fnl f* **10/1**[3]
/00- 9 1 ¼ **Botanist**[229] 6510 4-9-6 79 RyanMoore 6 74
(Sir Michael Stoute) *stdd after s: t.k.h: hld up in midfield: dropped towards rr 4f out: rdn and effrt over 2f out: kpt on same pce and no imp over 1f out* **9/2**[2]
44-1 10 ¾ **Perfect Point (IRE)**[27] 1488 4-9-3 76 LukeMorris 4 70
(Walter Swinburn) *chsd ldrs: rdn over 2f out: unable qck u.p over 1f out: wknd 1f out* **7/2**[1]
6022 11 2 ¾ **All Right Now**[13] 1814 4-8-11 70 DaneO'Neill 7 57
(Derek Haydn Jones) *chsd ldrs: rdn and unable qck over 2f out: edgd rt and wknd wl over 1f out* **12/1**
5003 12 12 **Hereford Boy**[40] 1198 7-8-13 72 RobertHavlin 11 —
(Dean Ivory) *stdd after s: hld up towards rr on outer: rdn and effrt ent fnl 2f: no prog and btn 2f out: eased ins fnl f* **25/1**

1m 38.93s (-0.87) **Going Correction** +0.025s/f (Slow) 12 Ran SP% **119.6**
Speed ratings (Par 105): **105,104,103,103,102 101,101,100,99,98 96,84**
Tote Swingers:1&2:£3.90, 2&3:£29.80, 1&3:£13.50 CSF £43.35 CT £365.46 TOTE £3.70: £1.20, £4.30, £6.90; EX 38.70.
Owner Y Nasib **Bred** Kirsten Rausing **Trained** Musley Bank, N Yorks

FOCUS
A fair handicap run at just an ordinary gallop to the home straight. The winner was another to race down the centre in the closing stages, and is rated back to his maiden best.

2179 PETER ANDRE 06.07.11 H'CAP 6f (P)
9:00 (9:01) (Class 5) (0-75,75) 4-Y-0+ £2,388 (£705; £176; £176) Stalls Low

Form RPR
2432 1 **Kylladdie**[8] 1955 4-9-5 73 (b) JamieSpencer 2 84+
(Steve Gollings) *chsd ldr for 2f: in tch after: hdwy to join ldr on bit wl over 1f out: led over 1f out and sn rdn clr: r.o wl: comf* **2/1**[1]
6451 2 3 **Italian Tom (IRE)**[34] 1314 4-9-3 71 LukeMorris 5 72
(Ronald Harris) *in tch: rdn 2f out: hdwy u.p over 1f out: drvn and kpt on to go 2nd towards fin: no ch w wnr* **8/1**[3]
0330 3 ½ **Onceaponatime (IRE)**[6] 1995 6-8-11 65 (b) PaulHanagan 1 65
(Michael Squance) *taken down early: bhd: rdn and hdwy over 1f out: styd on u.p fnl f: no ch w wnr* **8/1**[3]
40-0 3 dht **Boogie Waltzer**[15] 1762 4-8-11 70 (t) RyanClark(5) 3 70
(Stuart Williams) *mounted on crse: hld up towards rr: hdwy on inner over 2f out: chsd clr wnr jst over 1f out: no imp and wl hld fnl f: lost 2nd towards fin* **25/1**
164- 5 ¾ **Micky P**[194] 7320 4-8-13 67 (t) WilliamCarson 6 64+
(Stuart Williams) *bhd: rdn 3f out: stl last wl over 1f out: hdwy ent fnl f: styd on u.p: n.d* **12/1**
0062 6 1 **Pipers Piping (IRE)**[59] 904 5-8-5 66 LauraSimpson(7) 10 60
(Michael Squance) *chsd ldrs: pushed along and effrt to chse ldr jst over 2f out tl wl over 1f out: sn outpcd: wknd ent fnl f* **16/1**
2521 7 1 ¼ **Orpenindeed (IRE)**[22] 1557 8-9-7 75 (t) JamesDoyle 9 65
(Frank Sheridan) *sprawled as stalls opened and slowly away: rcvrd and in tch after 2f: rdn and unable qck 2f out: drvn and no hdwy over 1f out* **3/1**[2]
-640 8 ½ **Starwatch**[86] 625 4-8-6 63 SeanLevey(3) 12 52
(John Bridger) *racd freely: chsd ldrs: wnt 2nd 4f out tl jst over 2f out: wknd u.p over 1f out* **20/1**
1006 9 hd **Bookiesindex Boy**[40] 1196 7-9-6 74 (t) StephenCraine 8 62
(J R Jenkins) *hld up in tch in midfield: shkn up and fnd nil over 1f out: n.d fnl f* **40/1**
544- 10 nk **Kinigi (IRE)**[157] 7841 5-9-4 72 (b) DavidProbert 7 59
(Ronald Harris) *led: rdn and hdd over 1f out: wknd 1f out: fdd fnl f* **20/1**
1150 11 1 **Loyal Royal (IRE)**[10] 1912 8-9-1 69 (bt) LiamKeniry 4 53
(Milton Bradley) *stdd s: hld up in rr: effrt on inner ent fnl 2f: no prog over 1f out: n.d fnl f* **20/1**
000- 12 3 ½ **Tubby Isaacs**[229] 6501 7-9-5 73 JimCrowley 11 46
(Dean Ivory) *taken down early: stdd s: t.k.h: in tch on outer: wknd qckly 2f out: bhd fnl f* **8/1**[3]

1m 12.53s (-0.57) **Going Correction** +0.025s/f (Slow) 12 Ran SP% **125.8**
Speed ratings (Par 103): **104,100,99,99,98 97,95,94,94,94 92,88**
Tote Swingers:1&2:£4.90, 2&BW:£16.40, 1&BW:£9.60, 2&O:£2.90, 1&O:£2.20 CSF £18.56 CT £57.74 TOTE £2.60: £1.10, £1.10; EX 12.20 TRIFECTA PL: Boogie Waltzer £6.40, Onceuponatime £1.60.
Owner P S Walter **Bred** Horizon Bloodstock Limited **Trained** Scamblesby, Lincs

FOCUS
Exposed performers in a fair handicap. The gallop was a reasonable one and the winner edged towards the far rail in the closing stages. He produced a 4lb personal best.
Orpenindeed(IRE) Official explanation: jockey said gelding was slowly away having anticipated the start
Starwatch Official explanation: jockey said gelding ran too freely early
T/Plt: £32.60 to a £1 stake. Pool of £56,144.17. 1,253.98 winning tickets T/Qpdt: £14.40 to a £1 stake. Pool of £5,434.23. 278.65 winning tickets SP

1899 NOTTINGHAM (L-H)
Tuesday, May 17

OFFICIAL GOING: Good to firm (8.4)
Outer course used and rail realignment increased distances on round course by 7yds.
Wind: Fresh, against. Weather: Overcast

2180 MAGNERS GOLD H'CAP 6f 15y
2:00 (2:09) (Class 5) (0-75,75) 3-Y-0 £2,266 (£674; £337; £168) Stalls High

Form RPR
2224 1 **Palais Glide**[15] 1758 3-9-7 75 RichardHughes 8 82
(Richard Hannon) *racd centre tl gps merged over 2f out: prom: rdn to ld ins fnl f: r.o* **9/1**
321 2 ½ **York Glory (USA)**[13] 1812 3-9-5 73 PhillipMakin 1 78+
(Kevin Ryan) *racd centre tl gps merged over 2f out: sn pushed along and prom: led overall over 2f out: hung rt: hdd and unable qck ins fnl f* **7/2**[1]
5546 3 1 **Restless Bay (IRE)**[31] 1391 3-9-7 75 (v) GeorgeBaker 7 77
(Reg Hollinshead) *racd centre tl gps merged over 2f out: s.i.s: hld up: hdwy over 1f out: sn rdn: no ex towards fin* **20/1**

1054 **4** ½ **Pineapple Pete (IRE)**[15] 1745 3-8-8 **62**..................(t) RobertWinston 14 62
(Alan McCabe) *racd stands' side: hld up in tch: edgd lft over 2f out: rdn over 1f out: r.o* **9/1**
41 **5** *shd* **Bahia Emerald (IRE)**[17] 1672 3-8-9 **63**........................... WilliamBuick 6 63
(Jeremy Noseda) *racd centre tl gps merged over 2f out: hld up: hdwy over 2f out: rdn over 1f out: styd on same pce ins fnl f* **4/1**[2]
0-34 **6** *nk* **Bajan Bear**[12] 1830 3-8-13 **67**... LiamKeniry 13 66
(Michael Blanshard) *chsd ldr stands' side: edgd lft over 2f out: rdn over 1f out: styd on same pce ins fnl f* **11/1**
46-2 **7** *2* **Da Ponte**[47] 1064 3-9-7 **75**... ShaneKelly 5 68
(Walter Swinburn) *racd centre tl gps merged over 2f out: prom: rdn over 1f out: no ex ins fnl f* **9/1**
00-3 **8** *2 ½* **Loose Quality (USA)**[17] 1672 3-8-7 **61** oh1................. FrannyNorton 11 46+
(Tom Tate) *racd centre tl gps merged over 2f out: hld up: racd keenly: rdn over 1f out: nvr trbld ldrs* **12/1**
3230 **9** *hd* **Mazovian (USA)**[15] 1745 3-8-10 **64**........................ SilvestreDeSousa 4 48
(Michael Chapman) *racd centre tl gps merged over 2f out: chsd ldrs: rdn 1/2-way: wknd over 1f out* **33/1**
016- **10** *2 ¼* **Rowan Spirit (IRE)**[158] 7803 3-9-6 **74**........................ GrahamGibbons 9 51
(Mark Brisbourne) *racd centre tl gps merged over 2f out: chsd ldrs: rdn 1/2-way: wknd over 1f out* **33/1**
221- **11** *2 ½* **Celtic Sixpence (IRE)**[219] 6778 3-9-7 **75**...................... PaulHanagan 3 44
(Noel Quinlan) *racd centre tl gps merged over 2f out: led that gp and overall ldr over 3f out tl hdd over 2f out: wknd over 1f out* **8/1**[3]
-006 **12** *nk* **Boundless Spirit**[15] 1745 3-9-1 **69**...................................(t) PaulQuinn 12 37
(David Nicholls) *led stands' side: rdn and edgd lft over 2f out: wknd over 1f out* **16/1**
13-6 **13** *1 ¼* **Pippa's Gift**[124] 140 3-9-4 **72**... MartinDwyer 10 36
(William Muir) *racd centre tl gps merged 1/2-way: hld up: wknd and eased over 1f out* **25/1**

1m 14.74s (-0.16) **Going Correction** -0.125s/f (Firm) **13** Ran SP% **119.7**
Speed ratings (Par 99): **96,95,94,93,93 92,90,86,86,83 80,79,78**
Tote Swingers:1&2:£8.10, 2&3:£17.10, 1&3:£26.40 CSF £38.82 CT £642.10 TOTE £11.50: £2.40, £2.40, £6.40; EX 51.90.
Owner Guy Reed **Bred** Theakston Stud **Trained** East Everleigh, Wilts

FOCUS
A fair but competitive 3-y-o sprint handicap. The form looks sound. The majority raced up the centre of the track before converging around 2f out.
Celtic Sixpence(IRE) Official explanation: jockey said filly hung right
Pippa's Gift Official explanation: trainer's rep said colt was unsuited by the good to firm ground

2181 BRITISH STALLION STUDS SUPPORTING BRITISH RACING E B F MAIDEN STKS 6f 15y
2:30 (2:37) (Class 5) 2-Y-O **£3,238** (£963; £481; £240) **Stalls** High

Form RPR
1 **Eureka (IRE)** 2-9-3 0... RichardHughes 8 83+
(Richard Hannon) *sn trcking ldrs: rdn and hung lft ins fnl f: r.o to ld post* **16/1**
2 *nse* **Burwaaz** 2-9-3 0.. RichardHills 6 83+
(Ed Dunlop) *plld hrd and prom: rdn to ld wl ins fnl f: hdd post* **17/2**
4 **3** *shd* **Caledonian Spring (IRE)**[10] 1886 2-9-3 0...................... KierenFallon 5 83
(Paul D'Arcy) *led: rdn and hdd wl ins fnl f* **5/2**[2]
4 *4 ½* **Universal (IRE)** 2-9-3 0.. FrankieDettori 4 70
(Mahmood Al Zarooni) *hld up in tch: effrt over 1f out: wknd ins fnl f* **6/4**[1]
0 **5** *¾* **Brimstone Hill (IRE)**[20] 1619 2-9-3 0............................. MichaelHills 12 67
(B W Hills) *prom: rdn over 1f out: wknd fnl f* **50/1**
6 *5* **One New Cat (IRE)** 2-9-3 0....................................... TomMcLaughlin 7 52
(Ed Dunlop) *s.i.s and hmpd s: nvr trbld ldrs* **50/1**
2 **7** *1* **Bling King**[20] 1619 2-9-3 0.. SebSanders 11 49
(Eve Johnson Houghton) *hld up: hdwy over 2f out: wknd over 1f out* **13/2**[3]
8 *hd* **Yammos (IRE)** 2-9-3 0... SamHitchcott 9 49
(Mick Channon) *s.s: hdwy over 3f out: rdn and wknd over 1f out* **33/1**
9 *1 ½* **Dishy Guru** 2-9-3 0... LiamKeniry 1 44
(Michael Blanshard) *unruly in stalls: dwlt: outpcd* **100/1**
10 *1 ½* **Hyperlink (IRE)** 2-9-3 0.. JoeFanning 10 40
(Mark Johnston) *chsd ldrs: nt clr run 2f out: sn hung lft and wknd* **12/1**
11 *8* **Lucifers Shadow (IRE)** 2-9-3 0.. JamesDoyle 2 22
(Sylvester Kirk) *chsd ldrs: rdn over 2f out: wknd over 1f out* **66/1**

1m 15.43s (0.53) **Going Correction** -0.125s/f (Firm) **11** Ran SP% **115.4**
Speed ratings (Par 93): **91,90,90,84,83 77,75,75,73,71 63**
Tote Swingers:1&2:£19.10, 2&3:£14.00, 1&3:£3.60 CSF £138.15 TOTE £13.20: £4.60, £3.20, £1.60; EX 135.50.
Owner Noodles Racing **Bred** Jerry Murphy **Trained** East Everleigh, Wilts

FOCUS
Very few with any previous experience in this juvenile maiden but some major stables were represented and it resulted in a close finish. The time was 0.69secs slower than the opener. The first three came clear and the third helps with the level.

NOTEBOOK
Eureka(IRE), a £20,000 half-brother to a middle-distance Flat and jumping winner, was relatively unfancied on this debut considering his connections. However, he travelled well in behind the leaders and despite running green found enough to get to the front near the line. He looks open to further improvement but the Royal meeting will probably come too soon.
Burwaaz, a half-brother to a dual sprint juvenile winner out of a 6f Listed scorer; was quite keen early before being switched to challenge entering the final furlong. He also showed signs of inexperience and was just denied, but his winning turn should not be long delayed. (op 8-1 tchd 10-1)
Caledonian Spring(IRE) had more experience than the first two, showing promise when not getting the best of runs in an Ascot maiden on his debut. He made much of the running and responded when challenged on both sides, but just lost out. He was clear of the rest and can win races. (tchd 9-4 and 11-4)
Universal(IRE), a 160,000euros second foal of a half-sister to Seazun, was a well-backed favourite, possibly in response to the rumour that he was the yard's Coventry Stakes colt. He had his chance but was under pressure inside the last 2f and faded late on. He can do better but at this stage does not look a Royal Ascot contender. (op 7-4 tchd 2-1)
Brimstone Hill(IRE) was hampered and was always behind in the maiden in which Bling King was runner-up on his debut and reversed placings with his old rival.
Bling King showed promise in a 5f Pontefract maiden that is not really working out and did not help his chance by getting a bit worked up beforehand. (tchd 6-1 and 7-1)
Hyperlink(IRE) Official explanation: jockey said colt ran green

2182 CORONA H'CAP 5f 13y
3:00 (3:00) (Class 6) (0-65,65) 4-Y-O+ **£1,619** (£481; £240; £120) **Stalls** High

Form RPR
260- **1** **Baby Queen (IRE)**[287] 4672 5-8-11 **55**......................... J-PGuillambert 7 67
(Brian Baugh) *mde all: clr 1/2-way: pushed out* **8/1**
2154 **2** *2 ¼* **Black Baccara**[10] 1899 4-9-5 **63**...................................(be) KierenFallon 5 67
(Phil McEntee) *a.p: swtchd lft over 2f out: rdn to chse wnr fnl f: no imp* **3/1**[2]
060- **3** *1 ½* **Liberty Ship**[169] 7628 6-9-1 **59**...(b) ShaneKelly 2 58
(Mark Buckley) *chsd wnr: rdn over 1f out: styd on same pce fnl f* **16/1**
05-0 **4** *nk* **Bossy Kitty**[10] 1907 4-9-1 **59**...................................... SilvestreDeSousa 8 56
(Nigel Tinkler) *chsd ldrs: rdn over 1f out: swtchd lft ins fnl f: styd on same pce* **7/2**[3]
0-01 **5** *¾* **Silvanus (IRE)**[23] 1544 6-9-7 **65**.. PaulHanagan 1 60
(Paul Midgley) *hld up: sme hdwy over 1f out: no ex fnl f* **13/2**
33-5 **6** *2* **Bouncy Bouncy (IRE)**[39] 1213 4-8-11 **55**.....................(t) HayleyTurner 6 43
(Michael Bell) *hld up: rdn over 1f out: wknd ins fnl f* **11/4**[1]
30-0 **7** *5* **Gracie's Games**[28] 1469 5-8-5 **54**............................(v) TobyAtkinson(5) 3 24
(Richard Price) *sn outpcd* **22/1**

60.22 secs (-0.78) **Going Correction** -0.125s/f (Firm) **7** Ran SP% **108.6**
Speed ratings (Par 101): **101,97,95,94,93 90,82**
Tote Swingers:1&2:£3.30, 2&3:£9.70, 1&3:£13.10 CSF £28.93 CT £333.53 TOTE £13.60: £4.50, £1.90; EX 34.40.
Owner G B Hignett **Bred** Gainsborough Stud Management Ltd **Trained** Audley, Staffs

FOCUS
A modest sprint handicap with not much between the runners on the ratings. The winner is rated pretty much back to her best.
Bouncy Bouncy(IRE) Official explanation: trainer's rep said filly was unsuited by the good to firm ground

2183 RACINGUK.COM H'CAP 2m 9y
3:30 (3:30) (Class 5) (0-75,74) 4-Y-O+ **£2,266** (£674; £337; £168) **Stalls** Low

Form RPR
4-31 **1** **Not Til Monday (IRE)**[21] 1596 5-9-5 **70**........................(v) KierenFallon 5 78
(J R Jenkins) *led: rdn and hdd over 2f out: rallied to ld wl ins fnl f* **7/4**[1]
60-1 **2** *hd* **Rare Ruby (IRE)**[10] 1914 7-9-9 **74**.. JoeFanning 1 82
(Jennie Candlish) *chsd wnr 2f: remained handy: wnt 2nd again 4f out: led over 2f out: rdn and edgd lft fr over 1f out: hdd wl ins fnl f* **15/8**[2]
111- **3** *6* **Andorn (GER)**[13] 5687 7-9-5 **70**............................... RussKennemore 3 71
(Philip Kirby) *hld up: hdwy over 3f out: sn rdn: styd on same pce appr fnl f* **9/2**[3]
200- **4** *9* **Arab League (IRE)**[207] 7061 6-9-9 **74**........................... WilliamCarson 2 64
(Richard Price) *chsd ldrs: rdn 5f out: wknd over 1f out: eased* **7/1**
55-4 **5** *14* **Daylami Dreams**[10] 1901 7-9-0 **65**.. BarryMcHugh 4 38
(John Harris) *chsd wnr after 2f tl rdn 4f out: wknd over 2f out* **14/1**

3m 28.99s (-1.31) **Going Correction** -0.125s/f (Firm) **5** Ran SP% **108.5**
Speed ratings (Par 103): **98,97,94,90,83**
CSF £5.18 TOTE £2.40: £1.70, £1.50; EX 5.60.
Owner The Three Honest Men **Bred** G J King **Trained** Royston, Herts

FOCUS
A small field for this ordinary stayers' handicap and the order hardly changed for three-quarters of the trip, but only two mattered in the last 3f. Modest form.

2184 CAFFREYS FILLIES' H'CAP 1m 2f 50y
4:00 (4:00) (Class 4) (0-80,77) 3-Y-O **£4,079** (£1,214; £606; £303) **Stalls** Low

Form RPR
51-6 **1** **Masaraat (FR)**[16] 1727 3-9-4 **74**.. TadhgO'Shea 3 81+
(John Dunlop) *hld up: swtchd rt 2f out: hdwy over 1f out: rdn and hung lft ins fnl f: r.o to ld nr fin* **7/2**[2]
5-21 **2** *hd* **Baqaat (USA)**[27] 1481 3-9-5 **75**.. RichardHills 2 81
(Ed Dunlop) *led 2f: chsd ldr tl led again over 4f out: rdn over 1f out: hdd nr fin* **9/4**[1]
1- **3** *nk* **Janicellaine (IRE)**[229] 6511 3-9-7 **77**................................ MichaelHills 5 82
(B W Hills) *s.i.s: hld up: plld hrd: hdwy to ld 8f out: hdd over 4f out: outpcd over 3f out: rallied to chse ldr 2f out: r.o* **5/1**[3]
15- **4** *3 ¼* **Beyeh (IRE)**[270] 5257 3-9-5 **75**....................................... PhilipRobinson 4 74
(Clive Brittain) *chsd ldrs: rdn over 2f out: no ex ins fnl f* **12/1**
5-12 **5** *5* **Elvira Delight (IRE)**[92] 543 3-9-0 **70**............................ FrankieDettori 1 59
(Jeremy Noseda) *chsd ldrs: rdn over 2f out: wknd and eased fnl f* **9/4**[1]

2m 14.09s (2.99) **Going Correction** -0.125s/f (Firm) **5** Ran SP% **108.1**
Speed ratings (Par 98): **83,82,82,80,76**
CSF £11.29 TOTE £4.80: £3.20, £1.10; EX 10.70.
Owner Hamdan Al Maktoum **Bred** Shadwell Estate Co Ltd **Trained** Arundel, W Sussex

FOCUS
Not many runners but the whole field were covered by 7lb in this fillies' handicap. It resulted in another close finish and the form is a bit muddling, but has been given a chance.

2185 FAMILY FUN DAY SUNDAY 29TH MAY MAIDEN STKS 1m 75y
4:30 (4:31) (Class 5) 3-Y-O **£2,266** (£674; £337; £168) **Stalls** Centre

Form RPR
6 **1** **Mashaaref**[20] 1605 3-9-3 0.. RichardHills 6 87+
(Roger Varian) *trckd ldrs: rdn to ld and hung lft fr over 1f out: jst hld on* **9/4**[2]
3 **2** *hd* **Maali (IRE)**[15] 1759 3-9-3 0.. PhilipRobinson 11 88+
(Clive Brittain) *prom: rdn over 3f out: hmpd 2f out: rallied fnl f: r.o* **5/1**[3]
4- **3** *2 ¼* **Burj Hatta (USA)**[325] 3452 3-9-3 0................................. FrankieDettori 5 81
(Saeed Bin Suroor) *led: rdn and hdd over 1f out: no ex ins fnl f* **7/4**[1]
5-0 **4** *1 ¼* **Watercourse (IRE)**[15] 1759 3-9-3 0...................................... NeilCallan 9 78+
(Roger Varian) *mid-div: pushed along 3f out: r.o ins fnl f: nt trble ldrs* **33/1**
24-3 **5** *1* **Saskia's Dream**[11] 1873 3-8-12 74..................................... KierenFallon 3 71
(Jane Chapple-Hyam) *chsd ldr: rdn and ev ch over 2f out: no ex fnl f* **12/1**
4 **6** *1 ½* **Dervisher (IRE)**[31] 1415 3-9-3 0.. IanMongan 12 73
(Sir Henry Cecil) *chsd ldrs: rdn and hung lft 2f out: no ex fnl f* **11/1**
7 *2* **Covert Desire** 3-9-3 0... AhmedAjtebi 4 68+
(Mahmood Al Zarooni) *s.s: bhd: hdwy over 2f out: r.o: nt rch ldrs* **10/1**
-6 **8** *4 ½* **Cuckney Bear**[13] 1812 3-9-3 0.. RichardMullen 15 58
(Ed McMahon) *mid-div: pushed along over 3f out: sn wknd* **100/1**
9 *hd* **Highland Colori (IRE)** 3-9-3 0... DavidProbert 14 57
(Tom Dascombe) *s.i.s: hld up: nvr on terms* **50/1**
3 **10** *6* **Bella Montagna**[18] 1648 3-8-12 0.. TomEaves 1 38
(John Quinn) *mid-div: rdn and wknd over 2f out* **40/1**
11 *2 ¼* **Totally Trusted** 3-8-9 0... BillyCray(3) 7 33
(David Nicholls) *s.i.s: outpcd* **100/1**
0 **12** *2 ¾* **Hint Of Silver (IRE)**[11] 1873 3-8-12 0........................... StevieDonohoe 10 27
(Andrew Haynes) *sn outpcd* **150/1**
13 *1 ¾* **En Pointe** 3-8-12 0.. FrederikTylicki 2 23
(James Given) *sn outpcd* **150/1**

14 *11* **Dream Of Wunders** 3-8-12 0 .... PaulMulrennan 13 —
(James Given) *chsd ldrs: pushed along 1/2-way: wknd over 2f out* **80/1**

1m 44.62s (-0.98) **Going Correction** -0.125s/f (Firm) **14** Ran SP% **120.8**
Speed ratings (Par 99): **99,98,96,95,94 92,90,86,86,80 77,75,73,62**
Tote Swingers:1&2:£3.90, 2&3:£3.60, 1&3:£2.30 CSF £13.90 TOTE £3.20: £1.30, £2.10, £1.10; EX 20.90.
Owner Hamdan Al Maktoum **Bred** Shadwell Estate Company Limited **Trained** Newmarket, Suffolk

FOCUS
Not many of these 3-y-os had much racecourse experience but there was plenty of interest with a number of the top Newmarket yards having runners, and they filled the placings. The form is rated on the positive side.
Dervisher(IRE) Official explanation: jockey said gelding hung badly left closing stages

2186 REWARDS4RACING.COM CLASSIFIED STKS 1m 75y
5:00 (5:01) (Class 6) 3-Y-O **£1,619** (£481; £240; £120) **Stalls** Centre

Form RPR
23-2 **1** **Abidhabidubai**[34] 1302 3-9-0 65 .... TomEaves 4 73
(John Quinn) *chsd ldrs: led over 1f out: rdn out* **15/2**
4262 **2** *hd* **Dr Red Eye**[13] 1812 3-8-11 65 .... BillyCray(3) 5 72
(David Nicholls) *led: rdn and hdd over 1f out: styd on* **5/1**[3]
3221 **3** *1 3/4* **Little Jazz**[21] 1588 3-8-11 65 .... AndrewHeffernan(3) 2 68
(Paul D'Arcy) *hld up: hmpd 4f out: hdwy over 2f out: sn rdn: styd on* **6/1**
60-6 **4** *4 1/2* **Abeer (USA)**[21] 1579 3-9-0 64 .... RichardHills 8 58
(Ed Dunlop) *trckd ldrs: rdn over 2f out: wknd fnl f* **4/1**[2]
-323 **5** *hd* **Piccoluck**[14] 1802 3-9-0 65 .... (t) SilvestreDeSousa 7 58
(Deborah Sanderson) *hld up: hdwy over 2f out: rdn and hung lft over 1f out: wknd fnl f* **3/1**[1]
6-50 **6** *3 1/2* **Snow Ridge**[27] 1483 3-9-0 63 .... (v[1]) StevieDonohoe 1 49
(Andrew Haynes) *hld up in tch: swtchd rt 4f out: hdwy over 2f out: wknd over 1f out* **9/1**
405- **7** *2* **Cuban Quality (USA)**[257] 5675 3-9-0 64 .... (v) RobertWinston 10 45
(Tom Dascombe) *hld up: rdn over 2f out: nvr on terms* **11/1**
1450 **8** *8* **Brilliant Barca**[8] 1947 3-9-0 62 .... (v[1]) SamHitchcott 6 26
(Mick Channon) *prom: rdn over 3f out: wknd 2f out* **15/2**
-000 **9** *2 1/2* **Blazing Apostle (IRE)**[8] 1933 3-8-7 47 .... DanielHarris(7) 3 21
(Christine Dunnett) *chsd ldrs: rdn over 3f out: wknd over 2f out* **150/1**

1m 44.9s (-0.70) **Going Correction** -0.125s/f (Firm) **9** Ran SP% **118.5**
Speed ratings (Par 97): **98,97,96,91,91 87,85,77,75**
Tote Swingers:1&2:£7.90, 2&3:£5.20, 1&3:£5.10 CSF £46.01 TOTE £8.40: £1.90, £2.80, £2.40; EX 33.20.
Owner Nigel S Cooper **Bred** Brightwalton Stud **Trained** Settrington, N Yorks
■ Stewards' Enquiry : Billy Cray two-day ban: used whip with excessive frequency (May 31-Jun 1)

FOCUS
A very tight classified stakes with just 3lb covering all of the runners but one. The time was only 0.28secs slower than the preceding maiden. An 8lb personal best from the winner.
T/Jkpt: Not won. T/Plt: £61.90 to a £1 stake. Pool £59,803.49. 704.27 winning tickets. T/Qpdt: £8.20 to a £1 stake. Pool £2,648.12. 237.67 winning tickets. CR

1834 GOODWOOD (R-H)
Wednesday, May 18

OFFICIAL GOING: Good (good to firm in places on round course)
First 2f of mile course dolled out 5yds. Lower bend out 6yds from 6f to 2f up the straight and distances on round course increased by circa 12yds.
Wind: Moderate, half against Weather: Overcast

2187 IRISH STALLION FARMS E B F MAIDEN FILLIES' STKS 6f
2:00 (2:02) (Class 5) 2-Y-O **£3,238** (£963; £481; £240) **Stalls** High

Form RPR
2 **1** **Glee**[9] 1946 2-9-0 0 .... RichardHughes 3 75
(Richard Hannon) *str: lw: trckd ldr to 1/2-way: shkn up 2f out in 3rd: looked in trble over 1f out: rdn and picked up fnl f to ld nr fin* **4/9**[1]
2 *1/2* **Falls Of Lora (IRE)** 2-9-0 0 .... FrankieDettori 4 74
(Mahmood Al Zarooni) *tall: athletic: dwlt: sn rcvrd and prom: trckd ldr 1/2-way: chal 2f out: green but edgd ahd fnl f: hdd nr fin* **4/1**[2]
64 **3** *1/2* **Marygold**[16] 1757 2-9-0 0 .... JoeFanning 5 72
(John Akehurst) *w'like: leggy: led: hanging rt whn chal 2f out: hdd fnl f: stl nrly upsides 100yds out: nt qckn* **40/1**
5 **4** *1 1/4* **Iceni Girl**[19] 1657 2-9-0 0 .... WilliamBuick 6 68
(John Gosden) *w'like: gd bodied: chsd ldng trio: pushed along 1/2-way: nvr able to chal but kpt on steadily fnl 2f* **7/1**[3]
5 *1* **Lolita Lebron (IRE)** 2-9-0 0 .... PatDobbs 1 65+
(Richard Hannon) *w'like: on toes: difficult to load into stalls: in tch in 5th: pushed along 1/2-way: no imp 2f out: kpt on steadily ins fnl f* **25/1**
6 *6* **Single Girl (IRE)** 2-9-0 0 .... JimCrowley 7 47+
(Jonathan Portman) *leggy: a in last pair: ill at ease downhill to 1/2-way: bhd after: pushed along and lost little further grnd* **80/1**
7 *1* **Thefillyfromsutton** 2-8-9 0 .... JemmaMarshall(5) 2 44
(Pat Phelan) *leggy: dwlt: outpcd in last: nvr on terms but lost no grnd fr 1/2-way* **100/1**

1m 14.02s (1.82) **Going Correction** +0.125s/f (Good) **7** Ran SP% **110.3**
Speed ratings (Par 90): **92,91,90,89,87 79,78**
toteswingers:1&2: £1.10, 2&3: £7.20, 1&3: £4.30 CSF £2.23 TOTE £1.50: £1.10, £2.00; EX 2.60.
Owner Mrs J Wood **Bred** Jeremy Green And Sons **Trained** East Everleigh, Wilts

FOCUS
Leading 2-y-o trainer Richard Hannon has farmed this fillies' maiden, winning it for the past three seasons and five times in the past decade, including with subsequent Albany and Cherry Hinton winner Memory in 2010. His winner in 2009, Elusive Wave, was afterwards sold to race in France and went on to land the French 1000 Guineas at three. The form looks a bit below what might be expected at the track, but there are some potential improvers.

NOTEBOOK
Glee proved all the rage to continue the stable's dominance and she duly did the business, but made awfully hard work of landing the odds. She was not the best away on her debut at Windsor nine days earlier (still led), but broke a lot more professionally and soon bagged the rail. However, it was clear around 2f out she was in some trouble and Richard Hughes had to get really serious with her to pick up. Having the rail was in her favour, though, and to her credit she was doing her best work towards the finish over this extra furlong. She ultimately won cosily but it was not a surprise that her trainer later dismissed a trip to Royal Ascot, and she is likely to come into her own over a stiffer test before long, although there is not a lot for her in the short term. (op 1-2, tchd 4-7 in places)
Falls Of Lora(IRE) ◆, a second juvenile runner this term for her trainer, is bred to come into her own over a longer trip in due course. Therefore this has to rate as a promising debut display as she was only picked off by the winner near the business end and looks certain to improve for the experience.
Marygold, who got a bit warm, was having her third outing and was the most experienced runner in this line up. That proved very much to her advantage as she pinged out to lead and only tired inside the closing stages. It was no doubt an improved effort for the extra furlong, but her two previous runs marked her down as moderate and she does hold down the form somewhat.
Iceni Girl fluffed the start on her debut at Leicester last month and ran distinctly green. Although better away this time, she still proved too inexperienced to land a serious blow and ought to improve again a deal for the run. John Gosden is now 0-8 with juveniles this year. (op 15-2 tchd 8-1)
Lolita Lebron(IRE) is a half-sister to a dual 5f winner, including at two, and didn't go unbacked. She proved restless in the stalls, but broke well enough and left the clear impression that she would sharpen up for the initial outing. (tchd 20-1)

2188 PAUL SPENCER 50TH BIRTHDAY STKS (H'CAP) 1m 1f
2:35 (2:36) (Class 4) (0-85,83) 3-Y-O
£4,050 (£1,212; £606; £303; £151; £76) **Stalls** Low

Form RPR
01-3 **1** **Club Oceanic**[42] 1175 3-9-6 82 .... (p) FrankieDettori 1 93+
(Jeremy Noseda) *lw: sltly awkward s: settled to trck ldng trio: smooth prog over 2f out to ld over 1f out: sn pressed and rdn: r.o wl whn strly chal last 150yds* **9/4**[1]
-412 **2** *hd* **Tropical Beat**[12] 1843 3-9-5 81 .... WilliamBuick 4 91+
(John Gosden) *sn in 5th: pushed along bef 1/2-way: prog on outer over 2f out: drvn to chal 1f out: upsides w hd high 100yds out: r.o but outbattled* **9/4**[1]
520- **3** *3 3/4* **Mutayaser**[210] 7020 3-9-1 77 .... RichardHills 5 80+
(Sir Michael Stoute) *hld up in 6th: stdy prog over 2f out: rdn to chal and nrly upsides ent fnl f: squeezed out last 100yds* **11/1**
0-45 **4** *2* **Persian Herald**[16] 1773 3-9-2 78 .... JimCrowley 6 75
(William Muir) *stdd s: hld up last and wl off the pce: rdn 2f out: kpt on fr over 1f out: no ch* **66/1**
0-41 **5** *1/2* **Coax**[16] 1749 3-8-7 69 oh1 .... JoeFanning 3 65
(Mark Johnston) *led at decent pce: hdd over 1f out: wknd ins fnl f* **15/2**[3]
50-0 **6** *1 1/2* **Kalahaag (IRE)**[11] 1884 3-9-6 82 .... RichardHughes 7 75
(Richard Hannon) *trckd ldr after 1f to over 2f out: jst pushed along and steadily lost grnd* **12/1**
12-2 **7** *8* **Askaud (IRE)**[13] 1837 3-9-7 83 .... TomQueally 2 58
(David Nicholls) *trckd ldr 1f: rdn to go 2nd again briefly over 2f out: hanging rt and sn in trble: wknd qckly over 1f out* **4/1**[2]

1m 56.37s (0.07) **Going Correction** +0.125s/f (Good) **7** Ran SP% **110.8**
Speed ratings (Par 101): **104,103,100,98,98 96,89**
toteswingers:1&2: £1.80, 2&3: £3.70, 1&3: £4.50 CSF £6.79 TOTE £3.60: £1.90, £1.70; EX 8.60.
Owner Sir Robert Ogden **Bred** Card Bloodstock **Trained** Newmarket, Suffolk

FOCUS
A fair 3-y-o handicap, run at a solid pace. The form should work out with the joint favourites coming clear. The form looks sound rated through the fourth.
Askaud(IRE) Official explanation: jockey said filly hung right

2189 CASCO HEIGHT OF FASHION STKS (LISTED RACE) (FILLIES) 1m 1f 192y
3:10 (3:11) (Class 1) 3-Y-O **£17,778** (£6,723; £3,360; £1,680) **Stalls** Low

Form RPR
1-51 **1** **Beatrice Aurore (IRE)**[13] 1837 3-9-0 91 .... TedDurcan 1 99+
(John Dunlop) *sn restrained bhd ldng pair: pushed along and effrt 2f out: clsd to ld jst ins fnl f: sn in command: readily* **2/1**[1]
4-21 **2** *1 1/2* **Highest**[21] 1616 3-9-0 80 .... FrankieDettori 5 96
(John Gosden) *led to 7f out: led again over 4f out: rdn 2f out: hdd and outpcd jst ins fnl f* **6/1**
1 **3** *1 1/2* **Imperial Pippin (USA)**[33] 1363 3-9-0 0 .... WilliamBuick 3 93
(John Gosden) *trckd ldng pair: shkn up over 2f out: wandering and nt qckn over 1f out: kpt on* **7/2**[3]
13-5 **4** *1 1/4* **Poplin**[34] 1344 3-9-0 87 .... KierenFallon 6 91+
(Luca Cumani) *settled in last: pushed along and wl off the pce 3f out: prog on outer and cl enough 2f out: one pce after* **5/2**[2]
5-03 **5** *1 1/4* **Date With Destiny (IRE)**[11] 1894 3-9-0 92 .... RichardHughes 2 88
(Richard Hannon) *sn pressed ldr: led 7f out to over 4f out: drvn over 2f out: edging rt and wknd jst over 1f out* **9/1**
4-16 **6** *4* **Belle Royale (IRE)**[13] 1820 3-9-0 89 .... FrannyNorton 7 80
(Mark Brisbourne) *on toes: a in last trio: rdn and no prog 3f out: no ch fnl 2f* **25/1**
123 **7** *5* **Metropolitain Miss (IRE)**[13] 1837 3-9-0 93 .... SamHitchcott 4 70
(Mick Channon) *on toes: t.k.h early: hld up in 5th: hrd rdn 3f out: no prog: wknd 2f out* **33/1**

2m 7.63s (-0.37) **Going Correction** +0.125s/f (Good) **7** Ran SP% **115.2**
Speed ratings (Par 104): **106,104,103,102,101 98,94**
toteswingers:1&2: £2.90, 2&3: £2.20, 1&3: £2.90 CSF £14.93 TOTE £3.20: £1.60, £2.40; EX 14.40.
Owner Benny Andersson **Bred** Chess Racing Ab **Trained** Arundel, W Sussex

FOCUS
Formerly known as the Lupe Stakes, this fillies' Listed event has something of a mixed history as an Oaks trial. However, 2000 winner Love Divine went on to success at Epsom and last year's winner, Snow Fairy, landed both the Oaks and Irish Oaks on her next two outings, before signing off with two Group 1 wins in the Far East. The 2009 winner Moneycantbuymelove also went on to land the Listed Sandringham Handicap at Royal Ascot, and in 2008 Michita failed to fire at Epsom, but won the Group 2 Ribblesdale on her next outing. All things considered the race can be rated a cut above its current status and it was an interesting bunch in attendance this season, although only two held entries for the Oaks. While they didn't crawl, it was run at something of an uneven pace and it paid to race handily. The form is ordinary for the grade but still looks solid, rated around the fourth and fifth.

NOTEBOOK
Beatrice Aurore(IRE), who looked very fit beforehand, was hiked up a stone for a taking success in a fillies' handicap over 1m on her debut at this venue 13 days earlier and proved very popular despite this representing a much stiffer task. She had also flopped on her comeback at Doncaster when trying this trip for the first time in March. She confirmed herself to be a fast-improving filly with a ready success to follow up, though, and relished racing more handily at this distance. While further progression is obviously required for her to have a say at Epsom next month, she appeals as the type to improve again and looks well worth her place there. The extra distance is also likely to pose her no real problems with plenty of stamina on the dam's side of her pedigree, and her ability to handle undulating tracks is already proven. A general 50-1 shot beforehand, she was cut to 20-1 in most ante-post lists, with some going as short as 16-1. (op 15-8 tchd 7-4, 9-4, 5-2 and 13-8 in a place)
Highest ◆ was dropping back in trip after shedding her maiden tag at the fourth attempt over 1m4f last month and unsurprisingly helped to force the pace. She took it up 3f out and made a bold bid, but the winner outpaced her where it mattered. She has plenty of scope, will probably enjoy reverting to a more galloping track over further, and should be given respect if taking up her entry in the Ribblesdale at Royal Ascot as is expected.

Imperial Pippin(USA) looked a filly with a bright future when winning on her belated debut over this trip at Newbury last month, and was seemingly the first string from her yard being the choice of stable jockey William Buick. She had her chance, but her inexperience told as things got serious in the home straight and she didn't look totally at home on this contrasting track. As this was just her second outing it would be folly to write her off and she too is an intended runner in the Ribblesdale next month, where she could also go well. Her trainer later said she had missed a bit of work beforehand and wasn't in love with this track. However, she is not as obviously bred to get 1m4f like Highest. (op 4-1, tchd 3-1 and 9-2 in places)

Poplin won her maiden at this course last year and was expected to come on plenty for her comeback effort upped to 1m2f in a handicap at Newmarket last month. Well backed, she got herself warm beforehand and was restrained in rear. That wasn't an advantage as the race developed and, despite closing in the home straight, she lacked the required gear change to seriously challenge. A more positive ride over this trip looks required (bred to get further) and she could prove up to Listed class later on this term, as easier ground may be what she wants. (op 7-2)

Date With Destiny(IRE), the only other Epsom entrant, was third in the Lingfield Oaks Trial 11-days previously and got ridden a lot more positively on this drop back in distance. A little keen early, she felt the pinch 3f out and was well beaten. She rates the best guide for the from and will be tricky to place form now on. (tchd 8-1)

Metropolitain Miss(IRE), who looked very fit, was comfortably held. (op 25-1)

2190 RUK SUSSEX STAYERS STKS (H'CAP) 2m

3:45 (3:45) (Class 4) (0-85,85) 4-Y-O+ **£4,209** (£1,252; £625; £312) **Stalls** Low

Form RPR

22-5 **1** **Cosimo de Medici**[17] 1729 4-8-13 **76**..........(t) RichardHughes 8 83
(Hughie Morrison) *lw: taken down early: hld up in last pair: pushed along and prog over 4f out: wnt 3rd 3f out: clsd on tiring ldr w runner-up over 1f out: led last 100yds: rdn out* **11/4**[2]

2-51 **2** *nk* **Saborido (USA)**[15] 1788 5-9-4 **79**.......... PatDobbs 2 86
(Amanda Perrett) *mostly chsd clr ldr: def 2nd over 4f out and rdn in pursuit: clsd over 1f out: chal ins fnl f: jst outpcd* **5/1**[3]

30-6 **3** *3* **Dazinski**[18] 1679 5-9-9 **84**.......... KierenFallon 4 87
(Mark H Tompkins) *settled in last pair: nvr looked to be gng that wl: u.p in 5th 4f out and no prog: styd on fnl 2f: tk 3rd last strides* **2/1**[1]

-060 **4** *3/4* **Sherman McCoy**[17] 1729 5-9-6 **81**.......... JamesMillman 3 83
(Rod Millman) *mostly chsd ldng pair: shoved along 6f out: no imp and lost 3rd 3f out: plugged on* **7/1**

116- **5** *hd* **Alsadaa (USA)**[148] 7612 8-9-10 **85**.......... JimCrowley 6 87
(Laura Mongan) *racd freely: led and sn clr: abt 15 l up 1/2-way: stl clr whn rdn over 2f out: tired over 1f out: swamped last 100yds* **13/2**

031- **6** *24* **Miss Miracle**[22] 3312 4-8-12 **75**..........(p) DavidProbert 7 48
(Jonjo O'Neill) *in tch in chsng gp: rdn over 4f out: wknd 3f out: t.o* **22/1**

7 *52* **Psi (USA)**[7] 6-9-2 **77**..........(b) TomQueally 1 —
(Gary Moore) *in tch in chsng gp tl rdn and wknd 5f out: wl t.o* **16/1**

3m 28.95s (-0.05) **Going Correction** +0.125s/f (Good) **7** Ran SP% **112.7**
WFA 4 from 5yo+ 2lb
Speed ratings (Par 105): **105,104,103,102,102 90,64**
toteswingers:1&2: £2.90, 2&3: £2.50, 1&3: £1.90 CSF £16.35 CT £31.72 TOTE £3.50: £2.10, £1.80; EX 16.80.
Owner Bevan, Doyle & Lawrence **Bred** Shortgrove Manor Stud **Trained** East Ilsley, Berks

FOCUS
This modest staying handicap proved a messy race and that is reflected in the form, with the third the best guide.

2191 IBA COCKED HAT STKS (LISTED RACE) (C&G) 1m 3f

4:20 (4:20) (Class 1) 3-Y-O **£17,031** (£6,456; £3,231; £1,611; £807) **Stalls** High

Form RPR

16-5 **1** **Masked Marvel**[24] 1548 3-9-0 **95**.......... WilliamBuick 2 111
(John Gosden) *lw: covered up bhd ldrs: effrt 2f out: shkn up to ld jst over 1f out: r.o wl: comf* **13/2**[3]

3-45 **2** *3* **Namibian (IRE)**[18] 1689 3-9-0 **100**.......... JoeFanning 1 106
(Mark Johnston) *lw: disp 2nd early: dropped to 4th 4f out: rousted along on outer 3f out: styd on to ld wl over 1f out to jst over 1f out: outpcd* **8/1**

13-5 **3** *2 1/2* **Picture Editor**[32] 1405 3-9-0 **99**.......... TomQueally 5 101
(Sir Henry Cecil) *mostly trckd ldr: led over 2f out: rdn and hdd wl over 1f out: nt qckn and outpcd* **9/2**[2]

6-13 **4** *4* **Auld Burns**[24] 1548 3-9-0 **101**.......... RichardHughes 3 94
(Richard Hannon) *hld up in last: nvr appeared to be gng that wl fr 1/2-way: shkn up over 2f out: wl outpcd fr over 1f out* **2/1**[1]

21-1 **5** *3 3/4* **Badeel (USA)**[11] 1903 3-9-0 **96**.......... FrankieDettori 4 87
(Saeed Bin Suroor) *lengthy: attr: lw: led at mod pce: hdd over 2f out: wknd over 1f out* **2/1**[1]

2m 25.55s (-0.95) **Going Correction** +0.125s/f (Good) **5** Ran SP% **109.3**
Speed ratings (Par 107): **108,105,104,101,98**
CSF £49.13 TOTE £6.90: £3.80, £4.20; EX 49.80.
Owner B E Nielsen **Bred** Newsells Park Stud **Trained** Newmarket, Suffolk

FOCUS
It seems a long time ago that this Listed contest was considered a prominent Derby trial and not since Troy scored in 1979 has it produced a winner in the big one. Subsequent Group 1 winner Rewilding did the race no harm when finishing third at Epsom last year, but the form of this season's renewal is a bit below par and unlikely to have a serious bearing on next month's Classic.

NOTEBOOK
Masked Marvel was well beaten in the Group 3 Sandown Classic Trial on his 3-y-o return last month, but was still officially raised 10lb for that display. Despite that rise he was the lowest of these on BHA ratings and was as big as 66-1 in the ante-post betting for the Derby. He showed his true colours, though, with a ready success and the extra furlong proved right up his street. The manner in which he came through horses when asked to win the race was pleasing and he was well on top at the finish. It was the quickest ground he had encountered and so proves his versatility on that front, and there is every reason to think he will improve again for 1m4f. He was cut to a general 25-1 shot for Epsom and his trainer later reported that while he thinks Carlton House will win, his colt is an intended runner as it looks wide open for the places. (op 11-2 tchd 7-1)

Namibian(IRE), not entered in the Derby, showed his previous Newmarket effort to be wrong and made a bold bid under a positive ride, hitting the front nearing the furlong marker. The winner went away from him near the finish and, while he remains open to some improvement, this could be as far as he wants to go. (op 17-2 tchd 10-1)

Picture Editor was running on his own merits back up in trip having been deployed as pacemaker for stablemate Frankel in the Greenham on his comeback last month. One of the second favourites for the Derby last year before his defeat in the Zetland Stakes, this test seemed sure to suit him but he proved easy to back and took a keen hold to post. He held every chance, but lacked any sort of gear change and didn't overly impress with his head carriage under maximum pressure. An even stiffer test may suit now, but he does have a little to prove. (op 4-1 tchd 3-1)

Auld Burns had finished in front of the first pair when showing the benefit of a gelding operation on his two previous outings this year. Ridden to get the extra furlong, he was taken to the inside for his challenge 2f out but ultimately failed to get home. This track may not have suited, but he is not going to prove simple to place from here on. (op 11-4 tchd 15-8 and 3-1 in places)

Badeel(USA) made an impressive winning reappearance when up to 1m2f in a handicap off 87 11 days earlier. Very well backed, he again set out to make all under Frankie Dettori for the first time, who has few peers when it comes to front-running. However, his stride shortened dramatically as the field closed up 3f out and dropped away tamely. The run presumably came too soon. (op 15-8, tchd 9-4 in places)

2192 GOLDRING SECURITY SERVICES MAIDEN FILLIES' STKS 7f

4:55 (4:56) (Class 5) 3-Y-O

£2,803 (£839; £419; £210; £104; £52) **Stalls** Low

Form RPR

0 **1** **Doricemay (IRE)**[33] 1362 3-9-0 0.......... PatDobbs 11 76
(Clive Cox) *pressed ldr: narrow ld 2f out: rdn and kpt on wl ins fnl f* **12/1**

2 *1/2* **Mundana (IRE)** 3-9-0 0.......... KierenFallon 7 75+
(Luca Cumani) *tall: athletic: attr: lw: s.s: hld up wl in rr: stdy prog on outer 3f out: shkn up over 1f out: styd on ins fnl f to take 2nd nr fin* **9/4**[1]

64- **3** *hd* **Panoptic**[246] 6058 3-9-0 0..........[1] TomQueally 13 74
(Sir Henry Cecil) *w'like: tall: lw: trckd ldrs: smooth prog to chal 2f out: rdn and upsides over 1f out: nt qckn ins fnl f* **11/2**

33-3 **4** *3/4* **Miss Mediator (USA)**[17] 1724 3-9-0 74.......... RichardHughes 10 72
(Richard Hannon) *on toes: led: rdn and hdd 2f out: tried to respond but one pce ins fnl f* **4/1**[3]

5 *shd* **Brinmore** 3-9-0 0.......... JoeFanning 9 72+
(William Knight) *w'like: bit bkwd: str: dwlt: hld up in last trio: sme prog on outer over 2f out: nudged along and styd on takingly over 1f out: nrst fin* **66/1**

0-6 **6** *2 1/2* **My Ruby (IRE)**[12] 1853 3-9-0 0.......... PaulDoe 4 65+
(Jim Best) *lw: t.k.h: hld up disputing 6th: lost pl and dropped in rr over 2f out: shkn up and styd on again fr over 1f out* **10/1**

04- **7** *3/4* **Dualite (IRE)**[286] 4753 3-9-0 0.......... SamHitchcott 15 63
(John Dunlop) *w'like: hld up in midfield: shkn up and effrt 2f out: no prog over 1f out: fdd ins fnl f* **40/1**

0-5 **8** *4* **I Hate To Lose (USA)**[12] 1853 3-9-0 0.......... FrankieDettori 14 52
(Philip McBride) *trckd ldrs in 4th: shkn up and cl enough 2f out: lost pl over 1f out: wknd and eased* **7/2**[2]

00- **9** *3 3/4* **Jody Bear**[162] 7733 3-9-0 0.......... JackMitchell 5 42
(Jonathan Portman) *fit: sn trckd ldng pair on inner: shkn up and wknd over 2f out* **66/1**

0-6 **10** *1* **All Honesty**[21] 1607 3-9-0 0.......... JimCrowley 6 39+
(William Knight) *unf: t.k.h: hld up in 5th: shkn up over 2f out: hanging and wknd wl over 1f out* **16/1**

00- **11** *2 3/4* **Notify**[230] 6498 3-9-0 0.......... DavidProbert 1 32
(Patrick Chamings) *leggy: on toes: hld up towards rr on inner: wknd over 2f out* **100/1**

0 **12** *hd* **A B Celebration**[12] 1865 3-8-9 0.......... RyanClark(5) 3 31
(John Bridger) *leggy: hld up last: reminder over 3f out: sn lost tch and bhd: keeping on at fin* **200/1**

00- **13** *13* **Dixie Land Band**[202] 7198 3-9-0 0.......... RichardThomas 8 —
(Paul Burgoyne) *bit bkwd: b.hind: in tch tl wknd rapidly wl over 2f out: sn bhd: t.o* **100/1**

1m 29.97s (3.07) **Going Correction** +0.125s/f (Good) **13** Ran SP% **118.9**
Speed ratings (Par 96): **87,86,86,85,85 82,81,76,72,71 68,68,53**
toteswingers:1&2:£8.10, 2&3:£5.40, 1&3:£10.10 CSF £39.16 TOTE £15.60: £4.00, £1.80, £2.20; EX 55.20.
Owner Dennis Shaw **Bred** Barouche Stud Ireland Ltd **Trained** Lambourn, Berks

FOCUS
They went a sound enough pace in this maiden for 3-y-o fillies and, rated around the 74-rated fourth, it looked a fair event.

2193 TURFTV.CO.UK APPRENTICE STKS (H'CAP) 5f

5:30 (5:30) (Class 6) (0-65,66) 4-Y-O+ **£2,266** (£674; £337; £168) **Stalls** High

Form RPR

5555 **1** **Six Wives**[13] 1838 4-9-0 **62**.......... LeonnaMayor(5) 1 70
(David Nicholls) *ducked as stalls opened: hld up in 5th: smooth prog on outer fr 1/2-way: led over 1f out and taken to nr side rail: rdn ins fnl f: a holding on* **7/2**[2]

5335 **2** *1/2* **Sherjawy (IRE)**[9] 1937 7-9-4 **64**.......... MatthewLawson(3) 4 70
(Zoe Davison) *chsd ldrs in 4th: pushed along fr 1/2-way: rdn and effrt to chse wnr 1f out: styd on: a hld* **9/1**

6303 **3** *3/4* **Commandingpresence (USA)**[42] 1182 5-8-7 **50**.......... RyanClark 6 53
(John Bridger) *trckd ldng pair against rail: drvn 2f out: kpt on ins fnl f: nvr able to chal* **9/1**

4005 **4** *2 3/4* **Simple Rhythm**[6] 2016 5-8-7 **57**..........(p) BradleyBosley(7) 2 50
(John Ryan) *pressed ldr: upsides 2f out: bmpd along and steadily fdd* **7/2**[2]

0121 **5** *nse* **Athwaab**[9] 1938 4-9-4 **66** 6ex.......... CharlesBishop(5) 3 59
(Noel Quinlan) *racd against rail: led: rdn 2f out: hdd over 1f out: steadily fdd* **9/4**[1]

1542 **6** *2 1/2* **Black Baccara**[1] 2182 4-9-6 **63**..........(be) TobyAtkinson 5 47
(Phil McEntee) *s.s: a in last and nvr on terms* **9/2**[3]

60.00 secs (1.60) **Going Correction** +0.125s/f (Good) **6** Ran SP% **113.4**
Speed ratings (Par 101): **92,91,90,85,85 81**
toteswingers:1&2: £4.00, 2&3:£6.90, 1&3:£5.30 CSF £33.25 TOTE £4.10: £3.00, £3.80; EX 30.60.
Owner Sexy Six Partnership **Bred** Cheveley Park Stud Ltd **Trained** Sessay, N Yorks
■ Stewards' Enquiry : Ryan Clark caution: used whip with excessive frequency.

FOCUS
A moderate sprint handicap, confined to apprentice riders. All bar one of the six runners were fillies and there was a decent pace on, so the form appears straightforward.
Black Baccara Official explanation: jockey said filly missed the break
T/Plt: £190.90 to a £1 stake. Pool of £62,912.74 - 240.50 winning tickets. T/Qpdt: £121.50 to a £1 stake. Pool of £2,975.46 - 18.12 winning tickets. JN

2173 KEMPTON (A.W) (R-H)

Wednesday, May 18

OFFICIAL GOING: Standard
Wind: Moderate behind Weather: Overcast

2194 FREE ENTRY FOR BETDAQ MEMBERS MAIDEN AUCTION STKS 6f (P)

2:10 (2:10) (Class 6) 2-Y-O **£1,706** (£503; £252) **Stalls** Low

Form RPR

1 **Norse Gold** 2-8-9 0.......... DaneO'Neill 6 79+
(David Elsworth) *hld up in rr but in tch: stdy hdwy to trck ldr over 1f out: qcknd to ld fnl 150yds: easily* **9/1**

02 **2** *2 ¾* **Rooknrasbryripple**[9] 1932 2-8-5 0 MartinHarley(3) 7 68
(Mick Channon) *trckd ldr: led 2f out: rdn over 1f out: hdd and outpcd fnl 150yds but stl clr of 3rd* **9/2**[2]

55 **3** *3* **Latte**[30] 1434 2-8-9 0 TomEaves 8 60
(Linda Stubbs) *trckd ldrs: pushed along over 1f out: styd on one pce ins fnl f and no ch w ldng duo* **7/2**[1]

4 **4** *1 ½* **Indian Lizzy**[22] 1590 2-8-4 0 SilvestreDeSousa 4 51
(Paul Cole) *led tl hdd 2f out: wknd ins fnl f* **9/1**

02 **5** *½* **Fromthestables Com (IRE)**[11] 1913 2-8-12 0 PatrickHills(3) 5 60
(J W Hills) *chsd ldrs: rdn along fr 1/2-way: wknd over 1f out* **9/2**[2]

6 *¾* **Chater Garden (IRE)** 2-8-10 0 HarryBentley(5) 3 58
(Alan Jarvis) *chsd ldrs: pushed along 2f out: wknd appr fnl f* **11/1**

7 *nk* **Hamble** 2-9-1 0 RyanMoore 1 57+
(William Haggas) *outpcd* **11/2**[3]

8 *14* **Intomist (IRE)** 2-8-13 0 StephenCraine 9 13
(Jim Boyle) *wnt lft s: slowly away: a bhd* **8/1**

9 *3* **Hollywood All Star (IRE)** 2-8-11 0 MartinDwyer 10 2
(William Muir) *hmpd s: slowly away: racd wd: a in rr* **25/1**

1m 13.45s (0.35) **Going Correction** -0.075s/f (Stan) **9** Ran SP% **117.3**
Speed ratings (Par 91): **94,90,86,84,83 82,82,63,59**
toteswingers:1&2: £9.20, 2&3: £5.00, 1&3: £6.80 CSF £50.02 TOTE £15.20: £3.90, £1.70, £1.20; EX 65.50.
Owner D R C Elsworth **Bred** D R C Elsworth **Trained** Newmarket, Suffolk

FOCUS
Although several of these had previous experience, none of the runners in this maiden auction had raced on sand before. In the end a newcomer beat four more experienced rivals. He can rate higher with the third helping to set the level.

NOTEBOOK
Norse Gold, who twice went through the ring unsold for relatively small amounts, is a half-brother to a couple of minor winners out of a 1m2f scorer. He tracked the pace before picking up strongly when asked and ran down the leader late on to win going away. He clearly knew his job but should appreciate further in time. (op 10-1)
Rooknrasbryripple improved on her debut when a good second in a similar race at Brighton. She travelled well and fought off her challengers to assert, but could not respond to the winner's late surge. (op 7-2)
Latte showed moderate form in two starts in April but was backed in to favourite. He travelled comfortably but could not pick up as well as the winner in the last furlong and a half. (op 5-1)
Indian Lizzy, from a family of sprinters, had been well beaten on her debut in a similar event. She ran better from the front but was seen off quite comfortably in the closing stages. (op 10-1)
Fromthestables Com(IRE) improved on his debut to finish closer to the winner than he had on his debut at Warwick second time. However, he was pushed along from an early stage to hold his place and was unable to land a meaningful blow. (op 11-2)
Chater Garden(IRE), a £9,000 half-brother to Miss Zooter and other winners at 5f-1m, showed good pace on this debut before fading. (op 14-1)
Hamble, a 9,000gns half-brother to five winners at 6f-1m2f, was outpaced early on before staying on late. The experience should be of benefit next time. (op 4-1)

2195 BETDAQ.COM EXCHANGE PRICE MULTIPLES CLAIMING STKS 1m 3f (P)
2:45 (2:45) (Class 6) 3-4-Y-O £1,706 (£503; £252) Stalls Low

Form RPR
0-02 **1** **Humor Me Rene (USA)**[25] 879 4-9-2 67 MatthewDavies(3) 2 66
(George Baker) *racd in cl 4th tl hdwy to cl on ldrs and rdn 3f out: chsd ldr and 3 l down fr 2f out: styd on u.p ins fnl f: carried lft slosing stages and led last strides* **11/4**[2]

3335 **2** *shd* **Layla's Dancer**[16] 1775 4-9-12 72 NeilCallan 5 73
(Tony Carroll) *led: stdd pce 7f out: qckn again fr 3f out and 3 l clr 2f out: hrd drvn ins fnl f: edgd lft clsng stages and hdd last strides* **4/6**[1]

5-05 **3** *5* **Bobby Dazzler (IRE)**[22] 1588 3-8-6 56 CathyGannon 4 59
(Sylvester Kirk) *chsd ldr: t.k.h whn pce slackened 7f out: rdn 3f out: lost 2nd 2f out: no ch w ldng duo sn after* **10/1**

34 **4** *17* **Lean Machine**[37] 1278 4-9-9 64 (p) LukeMorris 3 30
(Ronald Harris) *chsd ldrs in 3rd: rdn 3f out: wknd wl over 2f out* **6/1**[3]

5 *36* **Sally Anne** 3-8-3 0 NickyMackay 6 —
(John Holt) *slowly away: rdn to stay in tch after 3f: a in last: t.o fnl 3f* **50/1**

2m 22.64s (0.74) **Going Correction** -0.075s/f (Stan)
WFA 3 from 4yo 15lb **5** Ran SP% **112.0**
Speed ratings (Par 101): **94,93,90,77,51**
CSF £5.10 TOTE £3.60: £1.40, £1.10; EX 5.50.Bobby Dazzler was claimed by Mr J. J. Best for £5000.
Owner M Khan X2 **Bred** Adrian P Hamman Jr Et Al **Trained** Whitsbury, Hants

FOCUS
A modest claimer but a good finish between the market leaders, although neither ran to their best.

2196 LAY BACK AND WIN AT BETDAQ.COM H'CAP (DIV I) 1m (P)
3:20 (3:22) (Class 6) (0-65,65) 3-Y-O £1,706 (£503; £252) Stalls Low

Form RPR
506- **1** **Robin Hoods Bay**[157] 7843 3-9-6 64 NeilCallan 9 81+
(Edward Vaughan) *in rr: gd hdwy ins fnl 3f: chsd ldr ins fnl 2f: led 1f out: sn pushed clr: easily* **5/1**[2]

1-20 **2** *4* **Snow Trooper**[58] 931 3-9-4 62 MartinDwyer 5 67
(Dean Ivory) *in rr: drvn and hdwy over 2f out: styd on wl fnl f to take 2nd nr fin but nvr any ch w easy wnr* **11/1**

03-2 **3** *½* **Matavia Bay (IRE)**[32] 1392 3-9-1 64 HarryBentley(5) 1 68+
(Alan Jarvis) *disp ld tl def advantage 5f out: wnt 4 l clr ins fnl 3f: rdn 2f out: hdd 1f out: sn no ch w wnr and lost 2nd nr fin* **7/2**[1]

40-0 **4** *3 ½* **Pearl Opera**[21] 1607 3-9-0 58 ShaneKelly 7 54
(Denis Coakley) *in rr: hdwy over 2f out: styd on to take one pce 4th clsng stages* **25/1**

4-52 **5** *nk* **Danceyourselfdizzy (IRE)**[6] 2024 3-9-5 63 RyanMoore 4 58
(Richard Hannon) *chsd ldrs: drvn along 3f out: styd on to take one pce 3rd 1f out: wknd ins fnl f* **7/1**[3]

56-2 **6** *4* **Silver Show (IRE)**[9] 1958 3-9-4 65 MartinHarley(3) 6 51
(Mick Channon) *chsd ldrs: rdn 3f out: wknd appr fnl f* **7/1**[3]

46-4 **7** *2 ½* **Divine Rule (IRE)**[14] 1819 3-9-7 65 JimmyFortune 3 45
(Hughie Morrison) *chsd ldrs: rdn over 2f out: wknd over 1f out* **7/2**[1]

6-60 **8** *1 ¾* **Corvette**[18] 1683 3-9-5 63 StephenCraine 11 39
(J R Jenkins) *broke wl: sn towards rr: sme hdwy towards outside into mid-div 4f out: mod prog clsng stages* **50/1**

060- **9** *nk* **Drummer Boy**[238] 6279 3-8-13 57 LukeMorris 12 33
(Peter Winkworth) *chsd ldrs: wnt 2nd 3f out to 2f out: sn btn* **20/1**

000- **10** *½* **Rasteau (IRE)**[230] 6504 3-8-8 52 oh1 ow1 SteveDrowne 8 26
(Tom Keddy) *in tch: rdn along 1/2-way: styd mid-div tl wknd over 2f out* **33/1**

-160 **11** *18* **Onlyfoalsandhorses (IRE)**[9] 1958 3-8-7 56 (p) RyanPowell(5) 2 —
(J S Moore) *slt ld tl hdd 5f out: hung rt and wknd over 2f out* **33/1**

01-4 **12** *2 ¾* **Slumbering Sioux**[50] 1022 3-9-4 62 AdamKirby 10 —
(Harry Dunlop) *sn chsng ldrs: wknd u.p over 3f out* **12/1**

1m 39.52s (-0.28) **Going Correction** -0.075s/f (Stan) **12** Ran SP% **118.6**
Speed ratings (Par 97): **98,94,94,90,89 85,83,81,81,80 62,59**
toteswingers:1&2 £17.10, 2&3 £6.30, 1&3 £7.80 CSF £54.85 CT £222.13 TOTE £8.40: £2.50, £3.60, £1.70; EX 73.60.
Owner A M Pickering **Bred** Palm Tree Thoroughbreds **Trained** Newmarket, Suffolk

FOCUS
The first leg of this modest handicap was run in an ordinary time, but the winner was clear-cut and three of the first four were at the back turning in. The placed horses set the standard.
Robin Hoods Bay Official explanation: trainer said, regarding apparent improvement in form, that it had been gelded over the winter and was better suited by the longer trip.
Slumbering Sioux Official explanation: jockey said filly stopped quickly

2197 LAY BACK AND WIN AT BETDAQ.COM H'CAP (DIV II) 1m (P)
3:55 (3:55) (Class 6) (0-65,65) 3-Y-O £1,706 (£503; £252) Stalls Low

Form RPR
00-6 **1** **Dysios (IRE)**[28] 1495 3-9-0 58 J-PGuillambert 11 79+
(Luca Cumani) *pressed ldr: chal 3f out: led sn after: pushed clr over 1f out: sn clr: eased clsng stages* **11/2**[3]

02-2 **2** *6* **Whitby Jet (IRE)**[9] 1952 3-9-0 58 ShaneKelly 7 64
(Edward Vaughan) *in rr: rdn and hdwy over 2f out: styd on fnl f to take 2nd fnl 75yds but nvr any ch w eased wnr* **9/2**[2]

30-3 **3** *1 ¼* **El Maachi**[14] 1812 3-9-7 65 RobbieFitzpatrick 10 68
(Jim Best) *led: jnd over 3f out: hdd sn after: styd chsng wnr but no ch fr 2f out: one pce into 3rd fnl 75yds* **25/1**

043- **4** *nk* **Ice Nelly (IRE)**[183] 7470 3-9-4 62 JimmyFortune 8 64+
(Hughie Morrison) *in tch: nt clr run and lost position wl over 2f out: drvn and styd on fr over 1f out: kpt on same pce clsng stages* **8/1**

-361 **5** *2* **Spirit Of Oakdale (IRE)**[29] 1472 3-9-4 62 (v) AdamKirby 4 60
(Walter Swinburn) *chsd ldrs: rdn in 3rd fr 3f out: no imp over 2f out: wknd jst ins fnl f* **8/1**

44-3 **6** *1* **St Oswald**[16] 1753 3-9-5 63 SteveDrowne 6 59
(Roger Charlton) *s.i.s: in rr: drvn along ins fnl 3f: styd on fr over 1f out: gng on clsng stages but nvr any ch* **15/8**[1]

3300 **7** *½* **Sleeping Brave**[1] 2172 3-8-4 55 (p) NathanAlison(7) 1 49
(Jim Boyle) *slowly away: in rr: rdn over 2f out: styd on ins fnl f but nvr any ch* **50/1**

1420 **8** *shd* **Avalon Bay**[9] 1949 3-9-7 65 DaneO'Neill 2 59
(Pat Eddery) *broke wl: n.m.r on ins and lost position 4f out: nt clr run and swtchd rt on inner over 2f out: styd on same pce* **13/2**

6350 **9** *3 ¼* **Luckbealadytonight (IRE)**[23] 1566 3-8-7 51 oh3 SilvestreDeSousa 9 38
(Mark Johnston) *chsd ldr to 1/2-way: wknd 2f out* **25/1**

-053 **10** *2 ¼* **Out Of The Storm**[15] 1790 3-8-13 57 SebSanders 12 39
(Simon Dow) *in tch: rdn 3f out: wknd 2f out* **25/1**

1m 39.59s (-0.21) **Going Correction** -0.075s/f (Stan) **10** Ran SP% **117.4**
Speed ratings (Par 97): **98,92,90,90,88 87,86,86,83,81**
toteswingers :1&2:£4.00, 2&3:£38.60, 1&3:£47.80 CSF £29.43 CT £575.45 TOTE £8.30: £2.70, £1.80, £8.10; EX 41.40.
Owner Leonidas Marinopoulos **Bred** Fin A Co S R L **Trained** Newmarket, Suffolk

FOCUS
The second division of this handicap was run fractionally slower than the first, but this time the principals were close to the pace turning for home. The winner recorded a personal best with the runner-up to his recent mark.
Dysios(IRE) ◆ Official explanation: trainer's rep said, regarding apparent improvement in form, that it had been gelded since its last run and was more settled in the preliminaries.
St Oswald Official explanation: jockey said gelding reared as stalls opened
Sleeping Brave Official explanation: jockey said gelding was slowly away

2198 BETDAQ MOBILE APPS FILLIES' H'CAP 1m (P)
4:30 (4:31) (Class 5) (0-70,70) 4-Y-O+ £2,388 (£705; £352) Stalls Low

Form RPR
2-52 **1** **Wishformore (IRE)**[33] 1370 4-8-4 58 (p) RyanPowell(5) 3 65
(J S Moore) *chsd ldrs: rdn to go 2nd over 2f out: styd on u.p fnl f to ld fnl 50yds: kpt on wl* **9/1**

0220 **2** *¾* **Sweet Possession (USA)**[11] 1905 5-8-4 56 (p) JamesSullivan(3) 8 61
(Pat Eddery) *led: travelling ok 2f out: rdn fnl f: hdd and no ex fnl 50yds* **7/1**

4255 **3** *¾* **Kai Mook**[7] 1995 4-8-10 59 (t) CathyGannon 7 62+
(Roger Ingram) *hld up in rr: rdn over 2f out: hdwy over 1f out: styd on to dispute 2nd fnl 120yds: no ex clsng stages* **6/1**

5-06 **4** *4* **Madame Excelerate**[16] 1766 4-9-0 63 TomMcLaughlin 9 57
(Mark Brisbourne) *sn chsng ldrs: rdn over 2f out: hung rt and no imp fnl f* **11/2**[3]

3123 **5** *1 ¾* **Lilli Palmer (IRE)**[9] 1936 4-8-2 56 oh1 JulieBurke(5) 1 46
(Mike Murphy) *in rr: rdn over 2f out: mod prog fnl f* **5/2**[1]

5034 **6** *7* **Miss Bootylishes**[8] 1978 6-9-4 70 AmyBaker(3) 6 44
(Paul Burgoyne) *chsd ldr tl over 2f out: wknd over 1f out* **16/1**

6134 **7** *½* **Very Well Red**[32] 1388 8-8-9 58 WilliamCarson 2 31
(Peter Hiatt) *in tch: rdn over 3f out: no ch fnl 2f* **11/4**[2]

003/ **8** *5* **Appointment**[329] 5429 6-8-7 56 oh5 JamieGoldstein 5 17
(Ralph Smith) *rdn along towards outside 1/2-way: bhd fnl 3f* **25/1**

00-0 **9** *16* **Arakette (IRE)**[16] 1750 4-8-7 56 oh11 LukeMorris 4 —
(Paul Burgoyne) *a in rr* **66/1**

1m 39.31s (-0.49) **Going Correction** -0.075s/f (Stan) **9** Ran SP% **118.6**
Speed ratings (Par 100): **99,98,97,93,91 84,84,79,63**
toteswingers:1&2:£9.50, 2&3:£6.40, 1&3:£8.90 CSF £72.21 CT £415.83 TOTE £19.90: £2.90, £3.20, £1.30; EX 65.50.
Owner J S Moore **Bred** Tally-Ho Stud **Trained** Upper Lambourn, Berks
■ Stewards' Enquiry : James Sullivan three-day ban: careless riding (Jun 1,2,6)

FOCUS
This fillies' handicap was run 0.21secs faster than the quicker of the two divisions of the handicap earlier in the afternoon. Despite that it is best rated on the negative side.

2199 SERVICE DESK INSTITUTE H'CAP 6f (P)
5:05 (5:06) (Class 4) (0-85,85) 3-Y-O £4,079 (£1,214; £606; £303) Stalls Low

Form RPR
1- **1** **Instance**[210] 7021 3-8-12 76 RyanMoore 5 84+
(Jeremy Noseda) *s.i.s: t.k.h: rdn and hdwy fr 2f out: str run ins fnl f to ld fnl 120yds: edgd rt: readily* **9/4**[2]

233- **2** *¾* **Dozy Joe**[146] 7975 3-9-7 85 NeilCallan 3 91
(Ian Wood) *chsd ldrs: led wl over 1f out: hdd and outpcd fnl 120yds* **11/1**

4-10 **3** *2* **Green Apple**[44] 1141 3-8-9 73 SteveDrowne 7 73
(Peter Makin) *chsd ldrs: rdn and ev ch over 1f out: outpcd by ldng duo ins fnl f* **25/1**

133- **4** *nk* **Local Singer (IRE)**[263] 5537 3-8-13 **80** .... LouisBeuzelin(3) 2 80
(Malcolm Saunders) *sn chsd ldrs: rdn 2f out: styd on fnl f: nvr quite gng pce to chal: eased clsng stages* **20/1**

0-1 **5** *nk* **Munaaseb**[39] 1236 3-9-5 **83** .... RichardHills 6 81
(Ed Dunlop) *t.k.h: trckd ldrs: n.m.r over 2f out: drvn over 1f out: styd on same pce ins fnl f* **7/4**[1]

0-26 **6** *1 3/4* **Roman Dancer (IRE)**[24] 1545 3-8-13 **77** .... ChrisCatlin 4 69
(John Gallagher) *sn led: hdd wl over 1f out: wknd ins fnl f* **33/1**

611- **7** *1/2* **Cinderkamp**[216] 6868 3-8-12 **76** .... ShaneKelly 11 66+
(Edward Vaughan) *s.i.s: in rr: drvn over 2f out: hdwy appr fnl f: kpt on wl clsng stages but nvr a threat* **12/1**

126- **8** *3/4* **Forty Proof (IRE)**[139] 8020 3-8-12 **83** .... LukeRowe(7) 1 71+
(William Knight) *s.i.s: in rr: shkn up over 2f out: kpt on ins fnl f but nvr gng pce to get into contention* **25/1**

1-25 **9** *1/2* **Bunce (IRE)**[18] 1688 3-9-5 **83** .... JimmyFortune 9 69
(Richard Hannon) *in rr: pushed along and sme hdwy whn rdr dropped rein ins fnl f and no further prog* **10/1**[3]

015- **10** *2 3/4* **Silver Alliance**[312] 3887 3-8-12 **76** .... AdamKirby 12 54
(Walter Swinburn) *chsd ldrs: wknd wl over 1f out* **14/1**

1140 **11** *5* **Fantasy Fry**[16] 1745 3-8-13 **77** .... RichardSmith 8 39
(Tom Dascombe) *chsd ldrs: wknd over 2f out: eased whn no ch ins fnl f* **40/1**

1m 12.36s (-0.74) **Going Correction** -0.075s/f (Stan) 11 Ran SP% **116.8**
Speed ratings (Par 101): **101,100,97,96,96 94,93,92,91,88 81**
toteswingers:1&2:£3.90, 2&3:£37.50, 1&3:£14.50 CSF £24.71 CT £495.75 TOTE £3.30: £1.10, £3.20, £8.80; EX 20.90.
Owner The Hon William Vestey **Bred** T R G Vestey **Trained** Newmarket, Suffolk
■ Stewards' Enquiry : Louis Beuzelin ten-day ban: failed to ride out for 3rd (Jun 1-4,6-11)

FOCUS
A decent 3-y-o sprint handicap and a winner of some potential. The form is rated around those in the frame behind the winner.
Cinderkamp Official explanation: jockey said colt suffered interference in running

2200 BETDAQ.COM EVERY WEDNESDAY AT KEMPTON PARK CLASSIFIED STKS 7f (P)

5:40 (5:40) (Class 5) 3-Y-O **£2,388** (£705; £352) **Stalls** Low

Form RPR

24-4 **1** **Sinfonico (IRE)**[16] 1754 3-9-0 75 .... RyanMoore 6 91
(Richard Hannon) *hld up in rr: rdn and hdwy fr 2f out: str run over 1f out to ld ins fnl f: pushed clr: readily* **5/1**[2]

-152 **2** *2 1/4* **Ceffyl Gwell**[13] 1830 3-8-9 75 .... KieranO'Neill(5) 9 85
(Richard Hannon) *chsd ldrs: led over 2f out: hdd ins fnl f: sn no ch w wnr but hld on wl for 2nd* **6/1**[3]

1- **3** *3 1/2* **Watneya**[215] 6893 3-9-0 74 .... LiamJones 2 76
(William Haggas) *s.i.s: in rr: in tch 1/2-way: rdn over 2f out: styd on ins fnl f to take 3rd clsng stages but no imp on ldng duo* **6/1**[3]

12-3 **4** *1/2* **Queen Of Cash (IRE)**[44] 1131 3-9-0 72 .... JimmyFortune 1 74
(Hughie Morrison) *chsd ldrs: rdn over 2f out: one pce ins fnl f* **8/1**

1 **5** *nk* **El Djebena (IRE)**[135] 20 3-9-0 75 .... SebSanders 4 73+
(Sir Mark Prescott Bt) *s.i.s: in rr and hmpd sn after s: plenty to do whn drvn and hdwy over 2f out: styd on over 1f out but nvr rchd ldrs: one pce ins fnl f* **7/2**[1]

13 **6** *1 1/4* **Hoover**[63] 864 3-9-0 75 .... StephenCraine 10 70
(Jim Boyle) *in rr and rdn: swtchd rt and hdwy over 1f out: styd on ins fnl f: nvr a threat* **25/1**

133 **7** *3/4* **Christmas Aria (IRE)**[46] 1106 3-9-0 74 .... NeilCallan 7 68
(Simon Dow) *chsd ldrs: rdn over 2f out: wknd ins fnl f* **11/1**

-540 **8** *1/2* **Satin Love (USA)**[13] 1825 3-9-0 75 ....(v) SilvestreDeSousa 5 67
(Mark Johnston) *led tl hdd over 2f out: styd chsng ldrs tl wknd ins fnl f* **8/1**

0-13 **9** *3 1/4* **Golden Taurus (IRE)**[18] 1697 3-9-0 74 .... MichaelHills 3 58
(J W Hills) *sn chsng ldrs: rdn over 2f out: wknd over 1f out* **8/1**

5443 **10** *1 1/2* **Toms River Tess (IRE)**[50] 1023 3-9-0 72 .... CathyGannon 8 54
(Zoe Davison) *t.k.h: chsd ldrs: wknd 2f out* **33/1**

20-0 **11** *28* **Azzoom (IRE)**[12] 1853 3-9-0 70 .... PhilipRobinson 11 —
(Clive Brittain) *s.i.s: hung lft on outer and wd bnd 3f out: sn wknd: eased whn no ch* **33/1**

1m 25.33s (-0.67) **Going Correction** -0.075s/f (Stan) 11 Ran SP% **110.9**
Speed ratings (Par 99): **100,97,93,92,92 91,90,89,85,84 52**
toteswingers:1&2 £5.30, 2&3 £7.60, 1&3 £6.50 CSF £34.85 TOTE £6.90: £2.10, £1.90, £2.10; EX 28.50.
Owner White Beech Farm **Bred** P Doyle Bloodstock & J K Thoroughbred **Trained** East Everleigh, Wilts

FOCUS
A fair and tightly knit classified stakes with just 5lb between the field on official ratings. The winner looked a considerable improver with the placed horses and fifth also progressing.

2201 REWARDS4RACING.COM H'CAP 7f (P)

6:15 (6:16) (Class 6) (0-65,65) 4-Y-O+ **£1,706** (£503; £252) **Stalls** Low

Form RPR

320- **1** **Woolston Ferry (IRE)**[186] 7439 5-8-13 **62** .... JamesRogers(5) 1 71
(David Pinder) *s.i.s: sn in tch: drvn and hdwy to ld jst ins fnl 2f: drvn out ins fnl f* **20/1**

0-03 **2** *3/4* **Emiratesdotcom**[13] 1838 5-9-4 **62** .... LukeMorris 8 69+
(Milton Bradley) *in rr: rdn: hdwy and nt clr run over 1f out: swtchd lft sn after and str run ins fnl f: tk 2nd nr fin but nt rch wnr* **9/1**[3]

45-3 **3** *hd* **Eager To Bow (IRE)**[42] 1177 5-9-6 **64** .... TedDurcan 11 70
(Patrick Chamings) *swtchd rt s: in tch 3f out: rdn over 2f out: hdwy and ev ch appr fnl f: chsd wnr sn after and no imp: lost 2nd nr fin* **11/4**[1]

230- **4** *1/2* **Meia Noite**[211] 7006 4-9-2 **60** .... GeorgeBaker 6 65+
(Chris Wall) *chsd ldrs: drvn and ev ch fr ins fnl 2f: no ex ins fnl f* **9/1**[3]

622- **5** *1/2* **Suzhou**[154] 7874 4-9-2 **60** ....(v) CathyGannon 10 64
(Denis Coakley) *hld up in rr: awward bnd 3f out: hdwy: nt clr run and swtchd rt over 1f out: str run fnl f: fin wl* **10/1**

6001 **6** *nk* **Teen Ager (FR)**[28] 1486 7-8-7 **51** oh1 .... JimmyQuinn 13 54
(Paul Burgoyne) *hld up in rr: hdwy fr 3f out to chse ldrs 2f out: ev ch over 1f out: no ex ins fnl f* **12/1**

1432 **7** *nk* **Katmai River (IRE)**[7] 1995 4-9-3 **61** ....(v) SteveDrowne 12 63
(Mark Usher) *chsd ldrs: rdn over 2f out: ev ch fr over 1f out tl ins fnl f: outpcd fnl 50yds* **3/1**[2]

-216 **8** *1/2* **Mandhooma**[11] 1917 5-9-5 **63** .... ChrisCatlin 3 64
(Peter Hiatt) *chsd ldrs: rdn over 2f out: ev ch over 1f out: wknd ins fnl f* **12/1**

3356 **9** *1 3/4* **Rich And Reckless**[16] 1770 4-9-1 **59** ....(vt) TomMcLaughlin 7 55
(Tobias B P Coles) *chsd ldr tl over 2f out: btn sn after* **25/1**

3034 **10** *hd* **Rainsborough**[21] 1604 4-8-10 **54** ....(ve) DaneO'Neill 9 50
(Peter Hedger) *chsd ldrs: rdn over 2f out: wknd ins fnl f* **10/1**

00-0 **11** *3/4* **Captainrisk (IRE)**[6] 2016 5-9-0 **65** .... DanielHarris(7) 2 58
(Christine Dunnett) *sn led: hdd jst ins fnl 2f: wknd ins fnl f* **50/1**

4004 **12** *2* **Cut And Thrust (IRE)**[53] 984 5-9-2 **60** .... AdamKirby 4 48
(Mark Wellings) *rdn over 2f out: a outpcd* **20/1**

1m 25.87s (-0.13) **Going Correction** -0.075s/f (Stan) 12 Ran SP% **120.6**
Speed ratings (Par 101): **97,96,95,95,94 94,94,93,91,91 90,88**
toteswingers:1&2:£32.40, 2&3:£2.00, 1&3:£20.80. Totes Super 7: Win: Not won. Place: Not won. CSF £185.64 CT £670.11 TOTE £28.40: £9.60, £2.50, £1.80; EX 238.20.
Owner Ms L Burns **Bred** Tim Taylor **Trained** Kingston Lisle, Oxon

FOCUS
This moderate contest was run 0.54 secs slower than the preceding classified stakes and there were a number in line over a furlong out. The form looks straightforward and sound rated aroudn those in the frame behind the surprise winner.
T/Jkpt: £116,559.70 to a £1 stake. Pool of £492,506.09 - 3.00 winning tickets. T/Plt: £160.90 to a £1 stake. Pool of £58,832.42 - 266.77 winning tickets. T/Qpdt: £67.30 to a £1 stake. Pool of £3,269.21 - 35.90 winning tickets. ST

1893 LINGFIELD (L-H)

Wednesday, May 18

OFFICIAL GOING: Turf course - good to firm (good in places; 8.8) all-weather - standard
Wind: fresh, half behind Weather: overcast

2202 LINGFIELD PARK OWNERS CLUB H'CAP (TURF) 1m 3f 106y

2:25 (2:26) (Class 6) (0-60,60) 4-Y-O+ **£1,706** (£503; £252) **Stalls** High

Form RPR

0221 **1** **Filun**[20] 1635 6-9-3 **56** .... LiamKeniry 1 63+
(Anthony Middleton) *t.k.h: chsd ldr: cruised upside ldr over 2f out: led over 1f out: shkn up and qcknd ent fnl f: pushed along and in command after: comf* **10/11**[1]

00-4 **2** *1 1/2* **Kayaan**[32] 1398 4-9-7 **60** .... MickyFenton 6 65
(Pam Sly) *stdd s: t.k.h: hld up in tch: effrt on inner ent fnl 2f: sn ev ch: unable qck w wnr ent fnl f: kpt on same pce ins fnl f* **5/2**[2]

-460 **3** *1/2* **Lady Lam**[16] 1756 5-9-6 **59** ....(t) TravisBlock 4 63
(Sylvester Kirk) *t.k.h early: chsd ldrs: rdn and ev ch 2f out: drvn and unable qck w wnr ent fnl f: kpt on same pce after* **11/2**[3]

00-0 **4** *11* **The Chester Giant**[48] 1063 4-8-2 **46** oh1 .... KieranO'Neill(5) 2 31
(Patrick Morris) *dwlt: sn led and set stdy gallop: rdn jst over 3f out: hdd and drvn over 1f out: wknd ent fnl f* **66/1**

60/0 **5** *17* **Ajara Boy**[8] 1993 4-8-7 **46** oh1 .... JimmyQuinn 5 —
(Luke Dace) *in tch in rr: rdn and lost tch 3f out: eased ins fnl f* **25/1**

-600 **P** **Dawson Creek (IRE)**[69] 819 7-8-7 **49** oh1 ow3 .... KierenFox(3) 3 —
(Mark Hoad) *in tch tl eased and p.u 6f out: sddle slipped* **14/1**

2m 39.79s (8.29) **Going Correction** +0.225s/f (Good) 6 Ran SP% **108.3**
Speed ratings (Par 101): **78,76,76,68,56** —
toteswingers:1&2: £1.40, 2&3: £1.10, 1&3: £1.50 CSF £3.05 TOTE £1.70: £1.10, £1.90; EX 3.70.
Owner R J Matthews **Bred** Azienda Agricola Francesca **Trained** Granborough, Bucks

FOCUS
The ground on the turf course appeared to be riding nearer good than good to firm. A weak race with three of the runners well out of the weights. The pace was very steady, resulting in a dash up the home straight, and the time was nearly 13secs outside the standard. Not form to treat too seriously with the third the best guide.
Dawson Creek(IRE) Official explanation: jockey said saddle slipped

2203 LINGFIELD MARRIOTT HOTEL & COUNTRY CLUB MAIDEN STKS (TURF) 1m 3f 106y

3:00 (3:00) (Class 5) 3-Y-O+ **£2,388** (£705; £352) **Stalls** High

Form RPR

23-4 **1** **Tiger Webb**[30] 1445 3-8-11 78 .... IanMongan 3 88+
(Sir Henry Cecil) *stdd after s: hld up in last pair: hdwy to press ldr over 3f out: led jst over 3f out: sn pushed clr and in n.d after: eased fnl 75yds* **2/1**[1]

2 *5* **Favorite Girl (GER)** 3-8-7 0 ow1 .... EddieAhern 4 71
(Sir Henry Cecil) *s.i.s: hld up in last pair: rdn and effrt 3f out: chsd clr wnr 2f out: no imp tl clsd on eased wnr fnl 75yds* **11/2**[3]

0-3 **3** *6* **Circus Act**[21] 1620 3-8-11 0 .... RichardMullen 2 65
(Mahmood Al Zarooni) *t.k.h: chsd ldng pair: outpcd by wnr jst over 3f out: wnt modest 2nd 3f out tl 2f out: 3rd and wl btn after* **10/3**[2]

0 **4** *5* **Minkie Moon (IRE)**[13] 1840 3-8-11 0 .... PatCosgrave 1 56
(Amanda Perrett) *led: jnd over 3f out: hdd jst over 3f out: sn struggling u.p: 4th and wl btn fnl 2f* **33/1**

22 **5** *30* **Rainy Champion (USA)**[32] 1386 3-8-11 0 ....(p) DarryllHolland 5 —
(Gerard Butler) *chsd ldr tl over 3f out: sn lost pl on downhill run: rdn and lost tch 3f out: t.o and eased ins fnl f* **2/1**[1]

2m 33.76s (2.26) **Going Correction** +0.225s/f (Good) 5 Ran SP% **108.1**
Speed ratings (Par 103): **100,96,92,88,66**
CSF £12.67 TOTE £3.50: £1.80, £3.10; EX 9.40.
Owner R A H Evans **Bred** Meon Valley Stud **Trained** Newmarket, Suffolk

FOCUS
Just a fair maiden, run in a modest time but still six seconds quicker than the slowly run 46-60 handicap. With one of the joint favourites very disappointing, the form is not too solid. Henry Cecil had a 1-2. The third and fifth were disappointing although the winner improved for the trip.
Rainy Champion(USA) Official explanation: jockey said gelding did not handle the bend and lost its action

2204 FOREST ROW FILLIES' H'CAP (TURF) 1m 2f

3:35 (3:35) (Class 5) (0-70,70) 4-Y-O+ **£2,388** (£705; £352) **Stalls** Low

Form RPR

2132 **1** **Moresweets 'n Lace**[5] 2051 4-9-4 **67** .... GeorgeBaker 3 73+
(Gary Moore) *chsd ldrs: nt clr run over 3f out tl 2f out: swtchd rt and shkn up to chse ldng pair wl over 1f out: drvn to chal ins fnl f: r.o wl to ld last strides* **2/1**[2]

32-3 **2** *shd* **Kenyan Cat**[19] 1658 4-9-4 **67** .... RichardMullen 1 72
(Ed McMahon) *t.k.h: hld up in tch in last trio: nt clr run 3f out: sn swtchd rt and rdn: chsd ldr 2f out: drvn and ev ch fr over 1f out: kpt on wl* **15/8**[1]

3-04 **3** *shd* **Commerce**[15] 1789 4-9-1 **64** .... HayleyTurner 7 69
(Simon Dow) *led for 1f: chsd ldr after: pushed ahd again over 2f out: hrd pressed and rdn over 1f out: kpt on wl u.p tl hdd and lost 2 pls last strides* **11/1**

-216 **4** *6* **Shamardal Phantom (IRE)**[8] 1992 4-9-7 **70** .... MartinLane 4 63
(David Simcock) *stdd s: t.k.h: hld up in last pair: rdn and hdwy on outer 3f out: press ldrs but wanting to hang rt u.p wl over 1f out: wknd 1f out* **5/1**[3]

10-0 **5** ½ **Spiritual Art**[13] 1838 5-9-3 **66** PatCosgrave 5 58
(Luke Dace) *wl in tch: rdn and effrt to chse ldrs wl over 2f out: wknd u.p ent fnl f* **15/2**

3-15 **6** 2 **Adoyen Spice**[82] 687 4-9-0 **63** TonyCulhane 2 51
(Mike Murphy) *stdd s: t.k.h: hld up in rr: effrt and rdn ent fnl 3f: no real hdwy: btn 2f out* **18/1**

500- **7** 3 **Pursestrings**[29] 7570 4-8-7 **56** oh10 (t) FergusSweeney 6 38
(Laura Mongan) *dwlt: led after 1f: rdn and hdd over 2f out: wknd u.p wl over 1f out* **100/1**

2m 12.63s (2.13) **Going Correction** +0.225s/f (Good) **7** Ran SP% **111.1**
Speed ratings (Par 100): **100,99,99,95,94 93,90**
CSF £5.76 CT £27.40 TOTE £3.10: £1.70, £1.80; EX 6.00 Trifecta £34.10 Pool: £606.25 - 13.15 winning units..
Owner Darrell Hinds **Bred** Jeremy Hinds **Trained** Lower Beeding, W Sussex

FOCUS
A modest handicap for fillies and mares, run at an ordinary pace, which produced a tight three-way finish. The third sets the standard.

2205 TANDRIDGE CLASSIFIED (S) STKS 6f (P)
4:10 (4:11) (Class 6) 3-Y-O+ **£1,706** (£503; £252) **Stalls** Low

Form RPR

3304 **1** **Athaakeel (IRE)**[37] 1279 5-9-5 61 (b) KirstyMilczarek 1 68
(Ronald Harris) *dwlt: swtchd rt sn after s: hdwy on outer to chse ldrs over 3f out: rdn 2f out: drvn ent fnl f: led fnl 75yds: kpt on wl* **4/1**[3]

2350 **2** nk **Dvinsky (USA)**[7] 2001 10-9-11 70 (b) JimmyQuinn 5 73
(Michael Squance) *sn rdn along to chse ldr: ev ch ent fnl 2f: hrd drvn over 1f out: led ins fnl f: hdd fnl 75yds: kpt on but a jst hld* **13/2**

0005 **3** 2 **Elhamri**[9] 1955 7-9-11 74 HayleyTurner 7 67
(Conor Dore) *wl in tch: rdn and outpcd wl over 1f out: drvn over 1f out: rallied u.p fnl f: nt gng pce to rch ldng pair* **2/1**[1]

2003 **4** 1 **Waterloo Dock**[49] 1044 6-9-11 68 (b) PatCosgrave 2 63
(Michael Quinn) *led: rdn ent fnl 2f: hdd ins fnl f: wknd fnl 75yds* **3/1**[2]

3154 **5** 1½ **Bonnie Prince Blue**[11] 1906 8-9-11 73 (b) TomEaves 3 59
(Ian McInnes) *stdd s: hld up in tch: rdn and outpcd ent fnl 2f: no threat to ldrs after: plugged on ins fnl f* **4/1**[3]

00-0 **6** 4 **Rio Sands**[76] 752 6-9-5 45 MickyFenton 6 40
(Richard Whitaker) *stdd after s: hld up in tch in rr: struggling ent fnl 2f: wl btn over 1f out* **50/1**

1m 12.64s (0.74) **Going Correction** +0.15s/f (Slow) **6** Ran SP% **113.6**
Speed ratings (Par 101): **101,100,97,96,94 89**
CSF £29.46 TOTE £8.50: £3.50, £2.20; EX 36.00.There was no bid for the winner.
Owner Drag Star On Swan **Bred** Shadwell Estate Company Limited **Trained** Earlswood, Monmouths

FOCUS
This classified seller was a fair race for the grade, but several of these did not arrive in the best of the form. The form is rated around the first two.
Rio Sands Official explanation: jockey said gelding banged its head on the stalls

2206 STARBOROUGH CLAIMING STKS 7f (P)
4:45 (4:45) (Class 6) 3-Y-O+ **£1,706** (£503; £252) **Stalls** Low

Form RPR

2211 **1** **I Confess**[16] 1805 6-8-13 70 (b) MatthewCosham(5) 1 69
(David Evans) *led for 1f: chsd ldr after: clsd on ldr 2f out: pushed along over 1f out: led ins fnl f: r.o wl* **4/1**[2]

5406 **2** 1½ **Lastkingofscotland (IRE)**[8] 1990 5-9-8 74 (b) HayleyTurner 9 69
(Conor Dore) *chsd ldrs: wnt 3rd 4f out: clsd on ldr 2f out: drvn ent fnl f: chsd wnr wl ins fnl f: no imp* **4/1**[2]

1643 **3** 1 **Rubenstar (IRE)**[36] 1295 8-9-3 72 LiamKeniry 8 61
(Patrick Morris) *stdd s: t.k.h: hld up in last trio: hdwy ent fnl 2f: rdn ins fnl f: styd on same pce fnl 150yds* **13/2**[3]

0036 **4** nk **Fawley Green**[2] 2149 4-9-7 60 (v) MartinDwyer 4 64
(William Muir) *led after 1f: clr over 1f out: c bk to field 2f out: drvn ent fnl f: hdd ins fnl f: wknd fnl 75yds* **25/1**

R-52 **5** 1¼ **Stefanki (IRE)**[69] 822 4-9-12 82 TonyCulhane 5 66
(George Baker) *hld up in last trio: shkn up and effrt whn wd bnd 2f out: sn drvn: kpt on ins fnl f: nvr able to chal* **10/11**[1]

3100 **6** nk **Guildenstern (IRE)**[28] 1486 9-9-3 49 JimmyQuinn 10 56
(Michael Squance) *racd in midfield: pushed along over 4f out: drvn 2f out: styd on same pce u.p ins fnl f* **50/1**

50-0 **7** 5 **Arachnophobia (IRE)**[36] 1296 5-9-2 74 RobertHavlin 3 42
(Martin Bosley) *w ldrs for over 1f: sn pushed along and steadily lost pl: u.p in midfield over 3f out: wknd and bhd wl over 1f out* **16/1**

8 21 **Ossie Ardiles (IRE)** 3-8-8 0 NeilChalmers 11 —
(Michael Appleby) *s.i.s: a bhd: rdn over 2f out: lost tch wl over 1f out: t.o* **40/1**

1m 25.55s (0.75) **Going Correction** +0.15s/f (Slow)
WFA 3 from 4yo+ 11lb **8** Ran SP% **119.8**
Speed ratings (Par 101): **101,99,98,97,96 96,90,66**
Swingers:1&2:£3.30, 2&3:£4.40, 1&3:£2.00 CSF £21.17 TOTE £3.90: £1.10, £1.30, £1.50; EX 16.40 Trifecta £41.10 Pool: £664.11 - 11.93 winning units..
Owner J E Abbey **Bred** Gestut Sohrenhof **Trained** Pandy, Monmouths

FOCUS
A fair claimer run at a brisk pace but the proximity of the sixth limits the form.

2207 LINGFIELDPARK.CO.UK H'CAP 1m (P)
5:20 (5:20) (Class 5) (0-75,75) 4-Y-O+ **£2,388** (£705; £352) **Stalls** High

Form RPR

-423 **1** **Sunset Kitty (USA)**[34] 1330 4-9-3 **74** JohnFahy(3) 2 84
(Walter Swinburn) *chsd ldrs: wnt 3rd 2f out: rdn and effrt on rail over 1f out: drvn to ld fnl 100yds: r.o wl* **13/2**[3]

0-00 **2** 1 **Aspectus (IRE)**[13] 1829 8-9-6 **74** (p) FergusSweeney 8 82
(Jamie Osborne) *led after 1f: rdn wl over 1f out: hdd and one pce fnl 100yds* **16/1**

2-64 **3** 2 **Striding Edge (IRE)**[12] 1868 5-8-13 **67** JamesDoyle 3 70
(Hans Adielsson) *hld up in midfield: rdn and effrt on inner wl over 1f out: kpt on to go 2nd wl ins fnl f: nvr gng pce to rch ldrs* **7/1**

2055 **4** ¾ **Charlie Smirke (USA)**[12] 1868 5-8-13 **67** (bt) RichardMullen 7 68
(Gary Moore) *hld up in midfield: rdn and effrt over 1f out: styd on fnl f to snatch 4th last strides: nvr a threat to ldrs* **20/1**

500- **5** hd **Prince Of Sorrento**[281] 4929 4-9-2 **70** IanMongan 1 71
(John Akehurst) *chsd ldrs: wnt 2nd wl over 3f out: rdn ent fnl 2f: unable qck u.p over 1f out: wknd ins fnl f* **16/1**

2124 **6** 2½ **Al Aqabah (IRE)**[43] 1147 6-9-0 **73** (b) AdamBeschizza(5) 12 68
(Brian Gubby) *dwlt: bhd early: hdwy to chse ldrs 1/2-way: rdn and unable qck jst over 2f out: one pce and no threat to ldrs fr over 1f out* **7/1**

260- **7** 2 **Aultcharn (FR)**[215] 6904 4-9-7 **75** MartinDwyer 5 66
(Brian Meehan) *led for 1f: chsd ldr tl wl over 3f out: rdn jst over 2f out: btn over 1f out: wknd ins fnl f* **6/1**[2]

4220 **8** 1¾ **Sunshine Always (IRE)**[21] 1610 5-9-1 **72** KierenFox(3) 6 59
(Michael Attwater) *stdd s: hld up in rr: rdn and effrt wl over 1f out: stl plenty to do whn sltly hmpd ent fnl f: no prog after* **6/1**[2]

-010 **9** 1¾ **Cativo Cavallino**[28] 1488 8-8-9 **66** NataliaGemelova(3) 4 49
(John E Long) *midfield early: dropped in rr over 6f out: swtchd to outer over 4f out: rdn and effrt over 3f out: wd and wknd bnd 2f out* **16/1**

4124 **10** 8 **The Big Haerth (IRE)**[12] 1867 5-9-2 **70** (p) PatCosgrave 10 34
(David Evans) *t.k.h: hld up in tch towards rr: rdn and no hdwy over 2f out: wl bhd and eased ins fnl f* **13/2**[3]

3141 **11** 1 **West Leake (IRE)**[12] 1868 5-9-0 **68** LiamKeniry 11 30
(Paul Burgoyne) *t.k.h: hld up towards rr: rdn and no hdwy over 2f out: bhd and wd bnd 2f out: wl btn and eased ins fnl f* **5/1**[1]

1m 37.77s (-0.43) **Going Correction** +0.15s/f (Slow) **11** Ran SP% **119.3**
Speed ratings (Par 103): **108,107,105,104,104 101,99,97,96,88 87**
toteswingers:1&2:£25.90, 2&3:£28.30, 1&3:£9.80 CSF £106.79 CT £770.58 TOTE £5.40: £1.60, £5.10, £2.40; EX 216.10 TRIFECTA Not won..There was no bid for the winner.
Owner Cool Cats **Bred** Mckee Stables Inc **Trained** Aldbury, Herts

FOCUS
Nothing got involved from the rear in this modest handicap. The form looks a little muddling with few getting involved.
West Leake(IRE) Official explanation: jockey said gelding ran flat
T/Plt: £76.80 to a £1 stake. Pool of £57,564.54 - 546.57 winning tickets. T/Qpdt: £30.70 to a £1 stake Pool of £3,516.34 84.60 w. tckts SP 2208 - 2212a (Foreign Racing) - See RI

1889

HAYDOCK (L-H)
Thursday, May 19

OFFICIAL GOING: Good (7.0)
All races on outer home straight and distances on round course increased by 5yds.
Wind: Light, half-against Weather: Fine

2213 SPORTECH RACING H'CAP 1m 2f 95y
1:50 (1:51) (Class 5) (0-75,74) 4-Y-O+ **£2,266** (£674; £337; £168) **Stalls** Centre

Form RPR

031 **1** **Mcbirney (USA)**[34] 1372 4-9-2 **72** AndrewHeffernan(3) 14 85+
(Paul D'Arcy) *hld up: rdn and hdwy over 2f out: wnt 2nd over 1f out: sn chalng: styd on to ld wl ins fnl f* **14/1**

4540 **2** ¾ **Amazing Blue Sky**[44] 1156 5-8-4 **60** JamesSullivan(3) 12 71
(Ruth Carr) *led: rdn over 2f out: hdd wl ins fnl f: styd on but hld after* **20/1**

03-0 **3** 3 **Quanah Parker (IRE)**[12] 1892 5-9-3 **70** NeilCallan 2 75
(Richard Whitaker) *chsd ldrs: wnt 2nd over 3f out: rdn over 2f out: lost 2nd over 1f out: nt qckn ins fnl f: no imp on front pair fnl 100yds* **12/1**

10-5 **4** ¾ **The Caped Crusader (IRE)**[12] 1908 4-9-7 **74** BarryMcHugh 11 78
(Ollie Pears) *hld up in midfield: pushed along over 3f out: rdn and stdy hdwy over 2f out: styd on to chse ldrs over 1f out: kpt on ins fnl f: nt pce to chal ldrs* **6/1**[2]

44-2 **5** shd **Onyx Of Arabia (IRE)**[12] 1892 4-9-5 **72** (b) MartinDwyer 17 76+
(Brian Meehan) *in rr: rdn and hdwy 2f out: styd on ins fnl f: nt pce to rch ldrs* **5/1**[1]

-033 **6** 2¼ **Law To Himself (IRE)**[18] 1714 4-9-2 **69** PJMcDonald 7 68
(Alan Swinbank) *in tch: rdn over 2f out: styd on same pce ins fnl f* **6/1**[2]

5303 **7** 3¼ **Visions Of Johanna (USA)**[17] 1756 6-8-13 **66** JamieSpencer 5 59
(Ian Williams) *chsd ldrs: rdn over 2f out: one pce fnl f* **15/2**[3]

6546 **8** 5 **Striker Torres (IRE)**[41] 1222 5-9-3 **70** GrahamGibbons 3 54
(Geoffrey Oldroyd) *s.s: racd keenly: hld up: rdn and stdy hdwy over 2f out: one pce fnl f: nvr able to chal* **25/1**

1634 **9** 1 **Hits Only Jude (IRE)**[13] 1874 8-8-5 **63** (v) NeilFarley(5) 8 45
(Declan Carroll) *midfield: niggled along early: u.p over 3f out: nvr able to get on terms w ldrs* **20/1**

-324 **10** 2½ **Hail Tiberius**[16] 1798 4-9-2 **69** DuranFentiman 1 46
(Tim Walford) *chsd ldr: rdn over 3f out: sn lost 2nd: wknd over 1f out* **12/1**

5400 **11** 3 **Lingfield Bound (IRE)**[17] 1746 4-9-5 **72** LukeMorris 10 43
(John Best) *in tch: rdn wl over 2f out: sn btn: eased ins fnl f* **40/1**

0-06 **12** ¾ **Mainland (USA)**[29] 1490 5-9-4 **71** FrederikTylicki 6 41
(Tracy Waggott) *s.i.s: hld up: rdn over 2f out: no imp* **25/1**

3-64 **13** 2½ **High Five Society**[62] 897 7-9-0 **72** (b) RyanClark(5) 9 37
(Roy Bowring) *hld up: u.p over 2f out: nvr on terms* **40/1**

1-0 **14** 26 **Constant Craving**[17] 1772 4-9-4 **71** AdamKirby 13 —
(Clive Cox) *midfield: rdn over 3f out: sn wknd: eased whn wl btn fnl f: t.o* **8/1**

010- **15** 4 **Highland Love**[187] 6937 6-8-4 **60** oh2 PatrickDonaghy(3) 16 —
(Jedd O'Keeffe) *stdd s: hld up: u.p over 3f out: nvr on terms: eased whn wl btn fnl f: t.o* **100/1**

6-52 **L** **Wood Fair**[9] 1987 4-8-0 **60** oh6 MatthewLawson(7) 4 —
(Mrs K Burke) *styd in stalls: ref to r* **16/1**

2m 13.8s (-2.20) **Going Correction** -0.125s/f (Firm) **16** Ran SP% **119.1**
Speed ratings (Par 103): **103,102,100,99,99 97,94,90,90,88 85,85,83,62,59** —
toteswingers:1&2:£48.30, 1&3:£26.80, 2&3:£55.50 CSF £270.30 CT £3434.95 TOTE £13.40: £3.40, £4.30, £3.00, £1.60; EX 411.30 TRIFECTA Not won..
Owner D'Arcy & Saunders **Bred** Charles H Wacker **Trained** Newmarket, Suffolk

FOCUS
Something of a slow-motion finish to this modest but competitive handicap, the early pace set by runner-up Amazing Blue Sky being a decent one. The winner looks progressive, the third is rated close to his AW form and the fifth did well from a poor draw.

2214 SPORTECH PLC MAIDEN AUCTION STKS 6f
2:20 (2:22) (Class 5) 2-Y-O **£2,266** (£674; £337; £168) **Stalls** Centre

Form RPR

5 **1** **Evervescent (IRE)**[19] 1678 2-8-9 0 NeilCallan 2 77
(J S Moore) *chsd ldr: rdn to ld 1f out: hung lft ins fnl f: r.o* **5/1**

3 **2** 1½ **Tight Lipped (IRE)**[17] 1744 2-8-11 0 RichardMullen 11 74
(David Brown) *chsd ldrs: rdn and hung lft ins fnl f: styd on* **7/2**[2]

3 1¼ **Fortrose Academy (IRE)** 2-8-11 0 DavidProbert 7 71
(Andrew Balding) *dwlt: hdwy 1/2-way: rdn and swtchd rt over 1f out: styd on same pce ins fnl f* **14/1**

05 **4** ½ **Arabian Falcon**[14] 1835 2-9-2 0 MartinDwyer 1 74
(Brian Meehan) *led: rdn and hdd 1f out: no ex ins fnl f* **3/1**[1]

5 2¼ **Lupo D'Oro (IRE)** 2-8-13 0 LukeMorris 6 64
(John Best) *chsd ldrs: rdn and hung lft over 1f out: wknd ins fnl f* **10/1**

5 **6** *hd* **Fiction Or Fact (IRE)**[12] 1890 2-8-11 0 ... PhillipMakin 12 62+
(Kevin Ryan) *mid-div: rdn over 2f out: styd on ins fnl f: nt trble ldrs* **9/2**[3]
0 **7** *6* **Chester Aristocrat**[14] 1823 2-8-11 0 ... GrahamGibbons 5 44
(Eric Alston) *mid-div: rdn over 2f out: sn wknd* **33/1**
8 *2 3/4* **Lady Nickandy (IRE)** 2-8-4 0 ... AndrewMullen 14 28
(Alan McCabe) *sn pushed along in rr: nvr on terms* **28/1**
9 *4 1/2* **Spoken Words** 2-8-1 0 ... JamesSullivan(3) 10 15
(Hugh McWilliams) *mid-div: rdn and wknd over 2f out* **100/1**
06 **10** *2 3/4* **J J Leary (IRE)**[19] 1673 2-8-13 0 ...(v1) JamieSpencer 4 16
(David Nicholls) *w ldr over 3f: wknd 2f out* **14/1**
11 *1 3/4* **Dylan's Dream (IRE)** 2-8-4 0 ... DuranFentiman 3 —
(Tim Easterby) *mid-div: rdn 1/2-way: outpcd over 2f out* **16/1**
0 **12** *3 3/4* **Hiding In The Open (IRE)**[7] 2017 2-8-13 0 ... EddieCreighton 13 —
(Brian Meehan) *s.i.s: outpcd* **50/1**
13 *2 1/2* **Dr Irv** 2-8-8 0 ... MichaelO'Connell(3) 9 —
(Kate Walton) *s.s: outpcd* **100/1**

1m 17.63s (3.83) **Going Correction** +0.525s/f (Yiel) **13** Ran SP% **120.7**
Speed ratings (Par 93): **93,91,89,88,85 85,77,73,67,64 61,56,53**
toteswingers:1&2:£5.70, 1&3:£9.20, 2&3:£11.90 CSF £22.55 TOTE £7.00: £2.00, £1.70, £5.80; EX 29.80 Trifecta £293.20 Part won. Pool: £396.25 - 0.62 winning units..
Owner Ever Equine **Bred** Keogh Family **Trained** Upper Lambourn, Berks

FOCUS
Quite an open maiden auction. The main action unfolded towards the inside rail. The winner and second both look to be improving, although possibly not the strongest of races for the track.

NOTEBOOK
Evervescent(IRE), who needed the experience when fifth over 5f at Goodwood on his debut, relished every yard of the step up to 6f and responded well to pressure, despite hanging left on to the rail. He may take his chance at Royal Ascot, with the Coventry the likely aim, although he'll probably be doing no more than making up the numbers. (op 7-1)
Tight Lipped(IRE) travelled well and displayed a fair bit of speed, confirming the promise of his Beverley debut. He looks capable of winning an ordinary maiden. (tchd 10-3)
Fortrose Academy(IRE), related to several winners, was taken out because of fast ground on his intended Salisbury debut, and conditions here clearly suited better. He was green early, but made good headway to challenge for a place, and should come on plenty for the experience. (op 12-1)
Arabian Falcon was soon prominent over on the far rail, tracked by the winner, and posted his best effort to date, but was found wanting for speed in the closing stages. He's a likely type for nurseries. (op 7-2 tchd 4-1)
Lupo D'Oro(IRE), half-brother to a 6f juvenile winner, shaped with plenty of promise on this racecourse debut, travelling strongly until his lack of experience told. He should improve and can win a small maiden. (op 11-1 tchd 9-1)
Fiction Or Fact(IRE) built on his initial effort, appreciating the better ground, but still doesn't look up to winning over this trip. He could be one for 7f nurseries. (op 11-2 tchd 6-1 in places)
J J Leary(IRE) exerted too much energy early in the first-time visor. (op 12-1)

2215 BETDAQ THE BETTING EXCHANGE H'CAP (DIV I) 7f
2:50 (2:51) (Class 4) (0-80,80) 3-Y-O **£4,209** (£1,252; £625; £312) **Stalls** Low

Form RPR
3-32 **1** **Chosen Character (IRE)**[12] 1904 3-8-11 **70** ...(vt) RichardKingscote 9 86
(Tom Dascombe) *dwlt: bmpd s: rdn and hdwy under 2f out: led jst over 1f out: r.o wl to draw clr ins fnl f* **11/2**[2]
51- **2** *5* **Prince Of Burma (IRE)**[176] 7551 3-9-7 **80** ... WilliamBuick 2 83+
(John Gosden) *bhd: sn outpcd: rn wd on bnd wl over 5f out: u.p 4f out: hdwy over 2f out: sn travelling okay: chalng over 1f out tl outpcd by wnr fnl f* **9/2**[1]
551- **3** *1 3/4* **Reposer (IRE)**[216] 6899 3-9-7 **80** ... LukeMorris 10 78
(John Best) *dwlt: hld up: rdn and hdwy wl over 1f out: sn edgd lft: kpt on ins fnl f: no real imp on front 2* **20/1**
2-53 **4** *3* **Sabratha (IRE)**[16] 1801 3-8-4 **66** oh1 ... JamesSullivan(3) 1 56
(Linda Perratt) *hld up: hdwy over 2f out: led under 2f out: rdn and hdd jst over 1f out: one pce ins fnl f* **14/1**
5-1 **5** *1 1/4* **Youhavecontrol (IRE)**[40] 1246 3-9-1 **74** ... FrederikTylicki 4 73+
(Michael Dods) *midfield: stmbld jst bef bnd under 5f out: nt clr run fr over 2f out: sn lost pl: rdn over 1f out: styd on ins fnl f but had lost all ch* **9/2**[1]
0-05 **6** *4 1/2* **Stamp Duty (IRE)**[41] 1214 3-9-0 **73** ... BarryMcHugh 3 47
(Ollie Pears) *midfield: effrt over 2f out: chsd ldrs over 1f out: one pce ins fnl f* **50/1**
-534 **7** *2 1/4* **Calaf**[15] 1812 3-9-0 **73** ... TomQueally 5 11
(Jane Chapple-Hyam) *racd keenly: trckd ldrs: rdn to ld over 2f out: hdd under 2f out: wknd 1f out* **25/1**
3401 **8** *3 3/4* **Spirit Of Grace**[9] 1986 3-8-12 **71** 6ex ... RobertWinston 7 29
(Alan McCabe) *midfield: hdwy to chse ldrs 3f out: rdn over 1f out: sn wknd* **14/1**
13-6 **9** *1 1/2* **Whipphound**[14] 1825 3-9-4 **77** ... GrahamGibbons 11 31
(Mark Brisbourne) *racd keenly: prom: rdn over 2f out: n.m.r whn wkng over 1f out* **25/1**
441- **10** *nk* **Indian Emperor (IRE)**[189] 7408 3-9-3 **76** ... NeilCallan 12 29
(Roger Varian) *prom: rdn 2f out: wknd over 1f out* **10/1**[3]
34-2 **11** *2 3/4* **Perfect Mission**[18] 1725 3-9-4 **77** ... DavidProbert 6 23
(Andrew Balding) *in tch: rdn over 2f out: wknd over 1f out: eased whn btn ins fnl f* **9/2**[1]
3631 **12** *13* **Dolly Parton (IRE)**[12] 1906 3-8-9 **68** ...(p) AdrianNicholls 8 —
(David Nicholls) *led: rdn and hdd over 2f out: wknd over 1f out: eased whn wl btn ins fnl f* **16/1**

1m 29.08s (-1.82) **Going Correction** -0.125s/f (Firm) **12** Ran SP% **112.7**
Speed ratings (Par 101): **105,99,97,93,92 87,84,80,78,78 75,60**
toteswingers:1&2:£6.20, 1&3:£25.80, 2&3:£17.50 CSF £27.34 CT £460.55 TOTE £5.00: £1.50, £2.20, £6.60; EX 47.40 Trifecta £487.10 Part won. Pool: £658.27 - 0.20 winning units..
Owner Aykroyd And Sons Ltd **Bred** Moyglare Stud Farm Ltd **Trained** Malpas, Cheshire

FOCUS
The first division of a fairly ordinary handicap. They didn't dawdle early, and the race seemed to favour those coming from behind. The winning time was 0.92secs quicker than the second division and the first six came from the back.
Prince Of Burma(IRE) ◆ Official explanation: jockey said colt slipped leaving stalls
Youhavecontrol(IRE) Official explanation: jockey said gelding was denied a clear run
Whipphound Official explanation: jockey said gelding slipped on bend
Dolly Parton(IRE) Official explanation: jockey said filly had no more to give

2216 BETDAQ THE BETTING EXCHANGE H'CAP (DIV II) 7f
3:25 (3:26) (Class 4) (0-80,80) 3-Y-O **£4,209** (£1,252; £625; £312) **Stalls** Low

Form RPR
11 **1** **Sound Amigo (IRE)**[40] 1249 3-8-9 **68** ... BarryMcHugh 10 82+
(Ollie Pears) *a.p: rdn to ld wl ins fnl f: r.o* **9/1**
222- **2** *3/4* **Johnny Castle**[247] 6053 3-9-7 **80** ... WilliamBuick 6 92
(John Gosden) *led: rdn over 1f out: hdd wl ins fnl f* **4/1**[1]
1 **3** *nk* **Aanna Heneeih (IRE)**[61] 905 3-9-0 **73** ... NeilCallan 12 84+
(Ed Dunlop) *s.i.s: hld up: hdwy 3f out: rdn over 1f out: r.o* **9/1**
54-1 **4** *2* **Louis The Pious**[13] 1860 3-9-1 **74** ... PhillipMakin 3 80
(Kevin Ryan) *chsd ldrs: rdn and edgd lft over 1f out: styd on same pce fnl f* **13/2**
33-1 **5** *1 1/4* **Shadow Catcher**[36] 1302 3-8-13 **72** ... FrederikTylicki 9 75
(Michael Dods) *hld up: plld hrd: rdn over 2f out: styd on: nt trble ldrs* **16/1**
034- **6** *hd* **Orthodox Lad**[190] 7386 3-8-11 **70** ... LukeMorris 4 72
(John Best) *hld up: hdwy 1/2-way: rdn over 2f out: no ex ins fnl f* **25/1**
10- **7** *2* **Azameera (IRE)**[244] 6156 3-9-5 **78** ... AdamKirby 2 75
(Clive Cox) *trckd ldr: plld hrd: styd far side turning for home: rdn and ev ch over 2f out: wknd fnl f* **5/1**[3]
4425 **8** *2* **Dream Catcher (FR)**[33] 1391 3-9-2 **75** ... JamieSpencer 7 66
(David Nicholls) *chsd ldrs: rdn over 2f out: wknd wl over 1f out* **11/1**
1013 **9** *nse* **Bertie Blu Boy**[17] 1768 3-8-7 **66** oh2 ... FrannyNorton 11 57
(Paul Green) *hld up: rdn over 2f out: nvr on terms* **25/1**
1-42 **10** *8* **Pitkin**[16] 1802 3-8-7 **66** oh1 ... GrahamGibbons 8 35
(Michael Easterby) *plld hrd and prom: rdn and wknd wl over 1f out* **9/2**[2]
1-13 **11** *8* **Stirling Bridge**[113] 302 3-9-4 **77** ...(b) SteveDrowne 1 25
(William Jarvis) *hld up: hdwy over 2f out: hung lft and wknd over 1f out: eased fnl f* **12/1**

1m 30.0s (-0.90) **Going Correction** -0.125s/f (Firm) **11** Ran SP% **117.8**
Speed ratings (Par 101): **100,99,98,96,95 94,92,90,90,81 71**
toteswingers:1&2:£9.10, 1&3:£14.00, 2&3:£5.00 CSF £44.97 CT £342.51 TOTE £12.10: £4.00, £1.20, £3.60; EX 70.60 Trifecta £662.20 Part won. Pool: £894.99 - 0.30 winning units..
Owner Tom McManus **Bred** Sherbourne Lodge **Trained** Norton, N Yorks

FOCUS
The winning time wasn't as fast as the first division (0.92secs slower) but that's as a result of there being more of a pace on early in the previous contest. That said the form looks sound enough rated around the fourth, fifth and sixth.
Stirling Bridge Official explanation: jockey said gelding slipped on bend

2217 WIN £3 MILLION AT FOOTBALLPOOLS.COM H'CAP 1m
4:00 (4:01) (Class 3) (0-90,90) 4-Y-0+ **£7,447** (£2,216; £1,107; £553) **Stalls** Low

Form RPR
/20- **1** **Sam Sharp (USA)**[376] 1907 5-8-13 **82** ... RichardKingscote 10 94
(Ian Williams) *midfield: hdwy 2f out: effrt to chse ldr over 1f out: r.o to ld ins fnl f: wl in command fnl 75yds* **12/1**
6-02 **2** *2 1/4* **Tartan Trip**[8] 2000 4-9-0 **83** ...(v) DavidProbert 14 90
(Andrew Balding) *midfield: hdwy over 4f out: led 2f out: rdn and edgd lft over 1f out: hdd ins fnl f: nt pce of wnr fnl 75yds* **13/2**[1]
-000 **3** *1/2* **Our Joe Mac (IRE)**[19] 1694 4-9-1 **89** ...(p) LeeTopliss(5) 5 95
(Richard Fahey) *bmpd s: trckd ldrs: rdn to chal 2f out: nt qckn over 1f out: styd on same pce ins fnl f* **17/2**[3]
0004 **4** *1* **Charlie Cool**[4] 2123 8-9-5 **88** ...(b) RobertWinston 13 92
(Ruth Carr) *hld up in midfield: rdn and hdwy 2f out: kpt on to chse ldrs over 1f out: one pce fnl 50yds* **13/2**[1]
P-02 **5** *3 1/2* **Cheers For Thea (IRE)**[9] 1970 6-9-2 **85** ...(bt) DavidAllan 12 81+
(Tim Easterby) *in rr: rdn 2f out: hdwy over 1f out: styd on u.p but no imp on front 4 ins fnl f* **10/1**
-241 **6** *2 3/4* **She's A Character**[46] 1114 4-8-11 **80** ... FrederikTylicki 8 69
(Richard Fahey) *racd keenly in midfield: rdn and hdwy over 2f out: kpt on but no imp on ldrs fnl f* **9/1**
40-0 **7** *3/4* **Satwa Laird**[22] 1603 5-8-12 **81** ... NeilCallan 9 68
(Ed Dunlop) *hld up: hdwy 2f out: nt clr run for a stride whn no imp over 1f out: one pce fnl f* **14/1**
-260 **8** *1 3/4* **Hacienda (IRE)**[19] 1694 4-9-7 **90** ... JoeFanning 4 73
(Mark Johnston) *bmpd s: prom: led over 2f out: sn hdd: rdn over 1f out: wknd fnl f* **10/1**
3-40 **9** *1 3/4* **Douze Points (IRE)**[12] 1885 5-9-6 **89** ...(p) PhillipMakin 16 68
(Ed de Giles) *s.s: swtchd lft sn after s: hld up: rdn over 2f out: sme hdwy and hung lft u.p over 1f out: one pce and no imp fnl f* **12/1**
15-0 **10** *3 1/2* **Colour Scheme (IRE)**[19] 1684 4-9-3 **86** ...(t) MartinDwyer 3 57
(Brian Meehan) *bmpd s: trckd ldrs: chalng over 2f out: rdn over 1f out: wknd fnl f* **8/1**[2]
5-00 **11** *2* **Layla's Hero (IRE)**[12] 1885 4-9-4 **87** ... WilliamBuick 11 54
(David Nicholls) *hld up: rdn 3f out: no imp* **20/1**
000- **12** *1 3/4* **Celtic Change (IRE)**[216] 6904 7-9-0 **83** ...(tp) DuranFentiman 6 46
(Geoffrey Harker) *bmpd s: prom: rdn to chal over 2f out: wknd over 1f out* **50/1**
6-02 **13** *3/4* **High Resolution**[13] 1859 4-8-8 **80** ... JamesSullivan(3) 15 41
(Linda Perratt) *in rr: pushed along 3f out: nvr on terms* **25/1**
060- **14** *3/4* **Venutius**[203] 7187 4-9-4 **87** ... GrahamGibbons 7 46
(Ed McMahon) *in tch: pushed along and wknd 2f out* **12/1**
21-0 **15** *1 3/4* **South Cape**[33] 1406 8-9-6 **89** ...(p) TadhgO'Shea 2 44
(Gary Moore) *bhd: rdn over 2f out: nvr on terms* **20/1**
00-0 **16** *11* **Marjury Daw (IRE)**[14] 1826 5-8-12 **81** ... TomQueally 1 —
(James Given) *led: rdn and hdd over 2f out: wknd over 1f out* **33/1**

1m 41.41s (-1.49) **Going Correction** -0.125s/f (Firm) **16** Ran SP% **124.5**
Speed ratings (Par 107): **102,99,99,98,94 92,91,89,87,84 82,80,79,79,77 66**
toteswingers:1&2:£28.50, 1&3:£50.30, 2&3:£11.90 CSF £84.14 CT £747.62 TOTE £11.20: £4.60, £1.90, £2.40, £1.80; EX 140.10 TRIFECTA Not won..
Owner N Martin **Bred** Michael Cahan Thoroughbreds **Trained** Portway, Worcs

FOCUS
A wide-open handicap that was run at an even tempo. The placed horses set a reasonable level.

NOTEBOOK
Sam Sharp(USA), off for 376 days and making his debut for Ian Williams (ex-Henry Cecil), had a bit to prove on this return to 1m, but had speed enough to cope and stayed on strongest inside the final furlong. This was his first win in a handicap and it'll be interesting to see whether he can progress from this. The Hunt Cup was mentioned as a possible target, although it remains to be seen whether he'd have the pace for that, even if he did get in. (tchd 14-1)
Tartan Trip, off the same mark as when runner-up at Kempton, travelled well and went on inside the final 2f, but couldn't stay on as strongly as the winner. On this evidence he should be effective back at 7f. (op 8-1)
Our Joe Mac(IRE) left a string of disappointing efforts behind in the first-time cheekpieces. The slight ease in the straight would have suited him also and the way he travelled suggests he's up to winning off this sort of mark. (op 10-1)
Charlie Cool appears to be running into form and is on his last successful mark, so may be back winning soon. (op 7-1)
Cheers For Thea(IRE) was putting in some good late work, having got a little too far behind.
She's A Character, up 7lb in a better race, could never get close enough to challenge. (op 10-1)
Satwa Laird is on a decent mark, but needs to show more. (op 12-1)
Hacienda(IRE) looked vulnerable and was readily held. (op 11-1 tchd 12-1)
Douze Points(IRE) could never land a blow having been dropped in from his wide draw.
Colour Scheme(IRE) couldn't quicken for pressure and ultimately dropped away.

Layla's Hero(IRE) Official explanation: jockey said gelding had no more to give

2218 FOOTBALL POOLS MAIDEN STKS (DIV I) 1m 3f 200y
4:35 (4:36) (Class 5) 3-Y-0+ **£2,266** (£674; £337; £168) **Stalls** Centre

Form RPR

5 **1** **Midsummer Sun**[36] 1321 3-8-11 0 ..... TomQueally 10 86+
(Sir Henry Cecil) *trckd ldr: racd keenly: led over 2f out: rdn clr fnl f* **2/5**[1]

203- **2** *6* **Lady Amakhala**[238] 6302 3-8-6 71 ..... PJMcDonald 7 71
(George Moore) *a.p: rdn over 3f out: chsd wnr fnl f: styd on same pce* **25/1**

6-2 **3** *3 1/4* **Madrasa (IRE)**[33] 1389 3-8-11 0 ..... RichardMullen 6 71
(Ed McMahon) *led over 9f: sn rdn: wknd fnl f* **20/1**

4 **4** *4 1/2* **Sciampin**[12] 1897 3-8-4 0 ..... AntiocoMurgia(7) 2 64
(Marco Botti) *chsd ldrs: rdn over 2f out: wknd over 1f out* **66/1**

0- **5** *nk* **Tafaneen (USA)**[201] 7232 3-8-6 0 ..... TadhgO'Shea 5 58
(Roger Varian) *hld up: hdwy over 7f out: rdn over 3f out: wknd over 2f out* **7/1**[2]

6 **6** *3/4* **Golden City (IRE)**[34] 1364 3-8-7 0 ow1 ..... GrahamGibbons 3 58
(Chris Wall) *hld up: styd on appr fnl f: nvr nrr* **16/1**

46 **7** *1/2* **Star Alliance (IRE)**[14] 1840 3-8-11 0 ..... TedDurcan 9 61
(John Dunlop) *prom: rdn over 3f out: wknd over 2f out* **25/1**

8 *3/4* **Rishikesh** 3-8-11 0 ..... WilliamBuick 1 60
(Michael Bell) *s.i.s: hdwy to chse ldrs 10f out: rdn over 3f out: edgd lft and wknd over 1f out* **10/1**[3]

60 **9** *1 1/4* **Amtired**[25] 1542 5-9-9 0 ..... DaleSwift(5) 8 58?
(Brian Ellison) *hld up: rdn over 2f out: a in rr* **150/1**

10 *8* **Al Khawaneej** 3-8-11 0 ..... JamieSpencer 11 53
(Ed Dunlop) *s.s: rn green and a in rr* **20/1**

0 **11** *7* **Leah's Angel (IRE)**[15] 1810 3-8-6 0 ..... DuranFentiman 4 29
(Michael Mullineaux) *chsd ldrs: lost pl over 7f out: bhd fnl 3f* **100/1**

2m 33.84s (-0.16) **Going Correction** -0.125s/f (Firm)
WFA 3 from 5yo 17lb **11 Ran SP% 119.3**
Speed ratings (Par 103): **95,91,88,85,85 85,84,84,83,78 73**
toteswingers:1&2:£5.60, 1&3:£5.10, 2&3:£12.60 CSF £19.99 TOTE £1.60: £1.10, £4.90, £2.80; EX 19.40 Trifecta £93.00 Pool: £855.45 - 6.80 winning units..
Owner K Abdulla **Bred** Juddmonte Farms Ltd **Trained** Newmarket, Suffolk

FOCUS
The first of two uncompetitive maidens over the trip. The winner did not need to improve with the placed horses setting the standard.

2219 FOOTBALL POOLS MAIDEN STKS (DIV II) 1m 3f 200y
5:05 (5:07) (Class 5) 3-Y-0+ **£2,266** (£674; £337; £168) **Stalls** Centre

Form RPR

2 **1** **Solar Sky**[33] 1407 3-8-11 0 ..... TomQueally 1 86+
(Sir Henry Cecil) *a shade keen: trckd ldr: rdn and nt qckn over 1f out: carried lft ins fnl f: styd on to ld fnl 75yds: in control at fin* **2/13**[1]

2-40 **2** *2 1/4* **Sunday Bess (JPN)**[15] 1807 3-8-6 87 ..... RichardKingscote 10 80+
(Tom Dascombe) *led: rdn 2f out: wandered over 1f out: drifted lft ins fnl f: hdd and veered rt fnl 75yds: hld after* **5/1**[2]

4 **3** *5* **Lidar (FR)**[14] 1840 6-9-11 0 ..... MartinHarley(3) 4 75
(Alan King) *hld up in midfield: hdwy to chse ldrs 3f out: nt qckn u.p 2f out: kpt on to take 3rd towards fin: no ch w front 2* **20/1**

05 **4** *3/4* **Nuzool (IRE)**[17] 1751 3-8-11 0 ..... TadhgO'Shea 3 73
(John Dunlop) *midfield: hdwy to chse ldrs 3f out: one pce over 1f out* **18/1**[3]

33 **5** *1 3/4* **Redhotdoc**[30] 1474 7-9-9 0 ..... JoeFanning 11 66?
(Bill Moore) *in tch: effrt whn chsng ldrs over 2f out: one pce over 1f out* **25/1**

6 **6** *1 1/4* **Aeneid**[19] 1692 6-10-0 0 ..... DavidNolan 5 69
(Declan Carroll) *s.i.s: hld up in midfield: effrt to chse ldrs 3f out: no real imp: one pce over 1f out: wl btn fnl f* **40/1**

7 *18* **Ahwaak (USA)**[47] 1831 7-10-0 0 ..... SteveDrowne 2 40
(Alastair Lidderdale) *trckd ldrs: lost pl 6f out: bhd 5f out: plugged on to take poor 7th over 2f out* **100/1**

0- **8** *1 3/4* **Neptune Equester**[33] 6115 8-9-7 0 ..... JacobButterfield(7) 8 37
(Brian Ellison) *hld up: pushed along over 2f out: nvr on terms* **25/1**

64 **9** *10* **Khalashan (FR)**[29] 1492 5-10-0 0 ..... PhillipMakin 6 —
(Peter Niven) *hld upl: struggling over 4f out: nvr on terms* **100/1**

00- **10** *nk* **Bigern**[224] 6696 4-9-7 0 ..... JosephYoung(7) 7 —
(Michael Mullineaux) *plld hrd: prom: pushed along over 4f out: wknd over 3f out* **100/1**

2m 32.9s (-1.10) **Going Correction** -0.125s/f (Firm)
WFA 3 from 4yo+ 17lb **10 Ran SP% 126.4**
Speed ratings (Par 103): **98,96,93,92,91 90,78,77,70,70**
toteswingers:1&2:£1.30, 1&3:£2.80, 2&3:£3.50 CSF £1.64 TOTE £1.30: £1.02, £1.20, £2.90; EX 1.90 Trifecta £5.40 Pool: £937.19 - 127.04 winning units..
Owner Lordship Stud **Bred** Lordship Stud **Trained** Newmarket, Suffolk
■ Stewards' Enquiry : Richard Kingscote caution: careless riding.

FOCUS
This had appeared to be a straightforward task for Solar Sky, but he made very hard work of it. The first pair are rated below their best with the third to his Flat debut mark.

2220 LITTLEWOODSBINGO.COM H'CAP 1m 3f 200y
5:35 (5:35) (Class 4) (0-85,85) 4-Y-0+ **£5,828** (£1,734; £866; £432) **Stalls** Centre

Form RPR

400- **1** **Plaisterer**[202] 7206 6-9-7 85 ..... WilliamBuick 1 96
(Chris Wall) *broke wl: a.p: led wl over 2f out: r.o wl fnl f and in command: comf* **22/1**

031- **2** *1 1/2* **Kitty Wells**[148] 7963 4-9-2 80 ..... KirstyMilczarek 9 89+
(Luca Cumani) *s.i.s: bhd: rdn and hdwy whn nt clr run over 2f out: nt clr run and swtchd lft over 1f out: styd on to take 2nd wl ins fnl f: nt rch wnr* **8/1**[3]

20-0 **3** *2 1/4* **King Zeal (IRE)**[33] 1390 7-9-0 78 ..... RobertWinston 2 83
(Barry Leavy) *racd keenly in midield: hdwy 2f out: wnt 2nd wl over 1f out: sn rdn and no imp on wnr: lost 2nd wl ins fnl f: kpt on same pce* **25/1**

2-20 **4** *1/2* **Pittodrie Star (IRE)**[120] 209 4-8-11 75 ..... DavidProbert 10 79
(Andrew Balding) *midfield: rdn 2f out: hdwy over 1f out: styd on ins fnl f: one pce fnl 100yds* **33/1**

1-01 **5** *2* **Warlu Way**[17] 1772 4-9-4 82 ..... TedDurcan 8 86+
(John Dunlop) *hld up: nt clr run under 3f out: rdn 2f out: sn nt clr run and hmpd: styd on fnl f: nt rch ldrs* **8/1**[3]

-540 **6** *2* **Arizona John (IRE)**[8] 2006 6-9-0 81 ..... DeclanCannon(3) 6 79
(John Mackie) *hld up: hdwy into midfield 5f out: rdn and nt clr run over 2f out: kpt on ins fnl f: nt get to ldrs* **14/1**

430- **7** *1/2* **Union Island (IRE)**[93] 4619 5-8-12 79 ..... MartinHarley(3) 14 76
(Alan King) *sn dropped to midfield: pushed along over 3f out: effrt to chse ldrs over 2f out: one pce fnl f* **50/1**

425- **8** *2 1/4* **Issabella Gem (IRE)**[202] 7206 4-8-13 77 ..... PhilipRobinson 3 70
(Clive Cox) *s.i.s: racd keenly: hdwy into midfield after 3f: u.p and outpcd over 1f out* **10/1**

31 **9** *7* **Gogeo (IRE)**[33] 1386 4-9-7 85 ..... PJMcDonald 7 67
(Alan Swinbank) *hld up: struggling over 3f out: nvr on terms* **10/1**

03-3 **10** *nk* **The Only Key**[12] 1892 5-9-3 81 ..... TomQueally 4 63
(Jane Chapple-Hyam) *hld up: rdn and hdwy 2f out: no imp on ldrs over 1f out: eased whn btn ins fnl f* **10/1**

65-3 **11** *1* **Goldtrek (USA)**[17] 1775 4-8-13 77 ..... SteveDrowne 5 57
(Roger Charlton) *racd keenly: prom: rdn over 2f out: wknd over 1f out* **14/1**

005- **12** *3/4* **Pevensey (IRE)**[209] 7061 9-9-1 79 ..... GrahamGibbons 12 58
(David Barron) *s.i.s: towards rr: hdwy to go prom after 2f: rdn and wknd over 1f out* **25/1**

-203 **13** *2 3/4* **Dahaam**[13] 1855 4-9-0 78 ..... JamieSpencer 11 53
(David Simcock) *trckd ldrs: rdn 3f out: wknd 2f out* **10/1**

2/1- **14** *3/4* **Rock My World (IRE)**[260] 5665 4-8-13 77 ..... NeilCallan 13 50
(Roger Varian) *midfield: hdwy to chse ldrs 5f out: rdn and wkng whn n.m.r jst over 2f out* **3/1**[1]

3-12 **15** *hd* **Lady Chaparral**[12] 1908 4-8-10 74 ..... JoeFanning 15 47
(George Moore) *racd keenly: sn led: rdn and hdd wl over 2f out: sn wknd* **7/1**[2]

2m 31.89s (-2.11) **Going Correction** -0.125s/f (Firm) **15 Ran SP% 126.4**
Speed ratings (Par 105): **102,101,99,99,97 96,96,94,90,89 89,88,86,86,86**
toteswingers:1&2:£33.60, 1&3:£49.80, 2&3:£62.40. Totes Super 7: Win: Not won. Place: £511.30 CSF £188.38 CT £4452.34 TOTE £31.70: £6.30, £3.10, £12.30; EX 282.50 Trifecta £220.40 Part won. Pool: £297.87 - 0.50 winning units..
Owner David Andrews Plastering **Bred** Vogue Development Company (kent) Ltd **Trained** Newmarket, Suffolk
■ Stewards' Enquiry : David Probert two-day ban: careless riding (Jun 2,6)
Kirsty Milczarek one-day ban: careless riding (Jun 2)

FOCUS
A decent middle-distance handicap, although the pace was a fairly steady one. For the first time on the day, the field elected to come stands' side in the straight, and that led to trouble in running, with at least two of the runners having claims for being unlucky. The third and fourth ran close to their marks and set the level.
T/Jkpt: Not won. T/Plt: £94.60 to a £1 stake. Pool:£79,274.09 - 611.53 winning tickets T/Qpdt: £11.00 to a £1 stake. Pool:£5,696.95 - 383.09 winning tickets DO

2022 SALISBURY (R-H)
Thursday, May 19

OFFICIAL GOING: Good to firm (watered; 8.6)
Wind: virtually nil Weather: sunny

2221 BRITISH STALLION STUDS SUPPORTING BRITISH RACING E B F MAIDEN STKS 5f
6:00 (6:00) (Class 4) 2-Y-0 **£4,241** (£1,262; £630; £315) **Stalls** Low

Form RPR

1 **Sixx** 2-9-3 0 ..... KierenFallon 4 78+
(Richard Hannon) *mde virtually all: pushed along over 1f out: kpt on gamely: only pushed out to jst hold on* **10/1**[3]

2 *nse* **Right Result (IRE)** 2-9-3 0 ..... RichardHughes 3 78
(Richard Hannon) *sn trcking wnr: rdn 2f out: str chal thrght fnl f: jst hld* **2/5**[1]

3 *2 1/2* **Verse Of Love** 2-9-3 0 ..... CathyGannon 2 69+
(David Evans) *trckd ldrs pushed along over 3f out: rdn over 2f out: kpt on same pce* **28/1**

4 *1/2* **Light Burst (USA)** 2-9-3 0 ..... AhmedAjtebi 1 67
(Mahmood Al Zarooni) *stdd sn after s: trckd ldrs: rdn and rn green over 2f out: kpt on same pce* **7/2**[2]

62.45 secs (1.45) **Going Correction** 0.0s/f (Good) **4 Ran SP% 106.2**
Speed ratings (Par 95): **88,87,83,83**
CSF £14.82 TOTE £8.40; EX 10.00.
Owner Steve Lamb & Barry Bull **Bred** P And Mrs A G Venner **Trained** East Everleigh, Wilts

FOCUS
A maiden won by the subsequent Norfolk Stakes winner Approve last year but this renewal probably represents no more than fair form, with the pace just steady initially and the field finishing well bunched. The winner is value for a little more than the offical margin.

NOTEBOOK
Sixx, a colt by Royal Applause, seemed the lesser fancied of the stable's two runners judged by the betting but looked to know his job, getting across to the fence to make the running and then always looking likely to hold on under a largely educational ride. He's likely to improve but this form isn't easy to assess and his next race will reveal much more about him. (op 7-1)
Right Result(IRE)holds an entry in the Super Sprint and was sent off a very short-priced favourite but this son of Acclamation was always being worked harder than his stable-companion and perhaps wasn't quite as at ease on the fast ground, not looking to stride out with the same fluency in the closing stages. The betting suggested he was expected to win this and there's a fair chance he's better than this. (op 4-7)
Verse Of Love, who's a half-brother to the 5f winner Nabeeda, was a big outsider but never looked outclassed at any stage albeit never looking likely to finish any closer. (op 18-1 tchd 33-1)
Light Burst(USA)isn't as well bred as many from his yard but was far too green and in need of the experience to do himself justice, too keen early on and then carrying his head awkwardly through the race, nonetheless keeping going all the way to the line. He'll do better with this behind him stepped up to 6f. (op 3-1)

2222 POOLE SPEEDWAY H'CAP 6f
6:30 (6:30) (Class 6) (0-65,66) 4-Y-0+ **£1,942** (£578; £288; £144) **Stalls** Low

Form RPR

0154 **1** **Memphis Man**[9] 1989 8-8-9 57 ..... MatthewCosham(5) 7 66
(David Evans) *in tch: nt clr run over 2f out: sn swtchd lft and rdn: r.o wl to ld fnl 120yds: won gng away* **8/1**

0405 **2** *2* **Dancing Welcome**[13] 1875 5-8-12 55 .....(b) ChrisCatlin 1 58
(Milton Bradley) *trckd ldr: rdn 2f out: led over 1f out: hdd fnl 120yds: nt pce of wnr* **4/1**[2]

6005 **3** *1* **Little Perisher**[16] 1787 4-8-10 53 .....(b) RichardHughes 3 53
(Karen George) *trckd ldrs: rdn 2f out: kpt on ins fnl f* **7/1**

3041 **4** *1/2* **Nubar Boy**[3] 2155 4-9-6 66 6ex .....(v) RichardEvans(3) 5 64+
(David Evans) *v awkwardly away: sn in tch: travelling wl whn nt clr run jst over 2f out: sn swtchd rt and rdn: keeping on at same pce whn nt clrest of runs again fnl 120yds* **7/2**[1]

20-0 **5** 3 ¾ **Bermondsey Bob (IRE)**[12] 1912 5-9-4 **61** .... CathyGannon 4 47
(John Spearing) *led: rdn 2f out: hdd over 1f out: no ex ins fnl f* **8/1**

1406 **6** *nk* **Boldinor**[12] 1912 8-9-3 **60** .... GeorgeBaker 9 45
(Martin Bosley) *in last pair: effrt in centre over 2f out: sn one pce* **6/1**[3]

05-4 **7** 2 ½ **Adventure Story**[21] 1630 4-9-7 **64** .... FergusSweeney 8 41
(Peter Makin) *trckd ldr: rdn over 2f out: wknd ent fnl f* **17/2**

660- **8** *nk* **Bold Argument (IRE)**[234] 6421 8-8-10 **53** .... RobertHavlin 2 29
(Nerys Dutfield) *s.i.s: in last pair: rdn over 3f out: nvr any imp* **11/1**

20-0 **9** *11* **Madam Isshe**[59] 934 4-9-0 **57** .... WilliamCarson 6 —
(Malcolm Saunders) *in tch: rdn over 2f out: wknd ent fnl f* **16/1**

1m 14.65s (-0.15) **Going Correction** 0.0s/f (Good) **9** Ran SP% **116.0**
Speed ratings (Par 101): **101,98,97,96,91 90,87,87,72**
toteswingers:1&2:£6.50, 1&3:£12.10, 2&3:£5.30 CSF £40.21 CT £239.37 TOTE £7.00: £2.30, £1.30, £4.00; EX 26.20.
Owner Mrs I M Folkes **Bred** R T And Mrs Watson **Trained** Pandy, Monmouths

FOCUS
An ordinary sprint that didn't seem to favour either those held up or ridden prominently. The form is modest rated around the placed horses.
Nubar Boy Official explanation: jockey said gelding was denied a clear run

2223 BATHWICK TYRES ANDOVER MAIDEN FILLIES' STKS 6f
7:05 (7:05) (Class 5) 3-Y-0+ **£2,914** (£867; £433; £216) **Stalls** Low

Form RPR

5 **1** **Dead Cool**[18] 1724 3-8-12 0 .... KierenFallon 6 66
(Hughie Morrison) *in tch: pushed along and hdwy over 2f out: sn rdn to chal: led jst ins fnl f: r.o: rdn out* **3/1**[1]

40-6 **2** *nk* **Catalinas Diamond (IRE)**[20] 1654 3-8-12 79 .... RobertHavlin 8 65
(Pat Murphy) *hld up: hdwy whn nt clr run over 2f out: swtchd lft: sn rdn: kpt on to press wnr ins fnl f: hld towards fin* **15/2**

55- **3** ¾ **Ma Quillet**[239] 6286 3-8-12 0 .... FergusSweeney 5 63
(Henry Candy) *travelled wl trcking ldrs: rdn to ld over 1f out: hdd jst ins fnl f: edgd rt and no ex fnl 100yds* **4/1**[3]

0- **4** 1 ¼ **Adelina Patti**[322] 3590 3-8-12 0 .... JimCrowley 2 59
(Walter Swinburn) *trckd ldrs: nt clrest of runs bhd wall of horses over 2f out: sn rdn: styd on fnl f but nt pce to threaten* **4/1**[3]

0-0 **5** *nk* **Madame Kintyre**[18] 1724 3-8-12 0 .... JamesMillman 7 58
(Rod Millman) *w ldr: led 3f out: rdn and hdd over 1f out: no ex fnl 130yds* **28/1**

0- **6** ¾ **Burst Of Stardust**[266] 5441 3-8-12 0 .... CathyGannon 4 55
(Bryn Palling) *outpcd in rr after 1f: stdy prog fr over 1f out: styng on at fin* **40/1**

6 **7** 2 ¼ **Gennie**[44] 1146 3-8-12 0 .... RichardHughes 3 48
(Richard Hannon) *hld up in tch: rdn over 2f out: nt pce to get involved* **17/2**

0-20 **8** *8* **Mixed Emotions (IRE)**[3] 2151 3-8-7 71 .... KieranO'Neill(5) 1 22
(Richard Hannon) *racd keenly: led tl 3f out: sn rdn: wknd over 1f out* **7/2**[2]

1m 15.19s (0.39) **Going Correction** 0.0s/f (Good) **8** Ran SP% **115.4**
Speed ratings (Par 100): **97,96,95,93,93 92,89,78**
toteswingers:1&2:£4.70, 1&3:£4.00, 2&3:£6.80 CSF £26.41 TOTE £4.30: £1.80, £3.10, £1.10; EX 29.90.
Owner C E Trading & Crichel Farms Limited **Bred** Crichel Farms Ltd **Trained** East Ilsley, Berks

FOCUS
A modest sprint maiden and debateable whether the form deserves to be rated too highly, but it was at least run at a reasonable pace. The winner improved on her debut but the second does not look up to her current mark.

2224 BATHWICK TYRES H'CAP 1m 6f 21y
7:40 (7:40) (Class 4) (0-85,83) 4-Y-0+ **£4,209** (£1,252; £625; £312)

Form RPR

4-55 **1** **Captain John Nixon**[13] 1855 4-9-7 **83** .... ChrisCatlin 2 91
(Pat Eddery) *prom: led after 2f: rdn and hrd pressed fr wl over 2f out: battled on gamely fnl f: hld on: all out* **10/1**

24-5 **2** *hd* **Sunny Future (IRE)**[30] 1450 5-8-9 **71** .... LukeMorris 6 78
(Malcolm Saunders) *hld up: pushed along 5f out: rdn and hdwy over 2f out: nt clr run whn swtchd rt jst over 1f out: r.o strly: jst failed* **40/1**

3-30 **3** *shd* **Eshtyaaq**[31] 1443 4-8-5 **67** .... CathyGannon 9 74
(David Evans) *t.k.h: hld up: hdwy over 3f out: nt clrest of runs over 2f out tl over 1f out: styd on wl ins fnl f: jst hld* **25/1**

11-1 **4** *1* **Milnagavie**[10] 1935 4-9-5 **81** 6ex .... RichardHughes 5 86
(Richard Hannon) *trckd ldrs: rdn wl over 2f out: nvr quite upsides: styd on but no ex fnl 75yds* **7/1**[3]

105- **5** *nk* **Hawridge King**[202] 7208 9-8-10 **72** .... FergusSweeney 3 77
(Stuart Kittow) *in tch: jnd wnr on rails over 2f out: rdn over 1f out: styd on but no ex ins fnl f: lost 3 pls towards fin* **25/1**

-161 **6** 3 ¾ **Momkinzain (USA)**[18] 1729 4-9-4 **80** .... SamHitchcott 1 80
(Mick Channon) *hld up: hdwy 3f out: sn rdn to chse ldrs: fdd fnl f* **5/1**[2]

31-2 **7** *5* **Loden**[17] 1775 4-9-0 **76** .... KierenFallon 7 69
(Luca Cumani) *hld up: rdn over 2f out: swtchd lft over 1f out: nvr any imp* **4/5**[1]

1-60 **8** *8* **Dynamic Drive (IRE)**[13] 1855 4-9-5 **81** .... GeorgeBaker 4 62
(Walter Swinburn) *trckd ldrs: rdn to dispute cl 2nd 3f out: wknd wl over 1f out* **8/1**

311/ **9** *1* **Hibiki (IRE)**[16] 5509 7-9-1 **82** ....(p) KieranO'Neill(5) 10 62
(Sarah Humphrey) *in tch: pushed along over 4f out: effrt 3f out: wknd 2f out* **28/1**

431- **10** *25* **Drawn Gold**[326] 3475 7-8-4 **66** .... WilliamCarson 8 —
(Reg Hollinshead) *led for 2f: w wnr: rdn and ev ch 3f out: wknd 2f out: eased fnl f* **40/1**

3m 3.86s (-3.54) **Going Correction** 0.0s/f (Good) **10** Ran SP% **120.9**
Speed ratings (Par 105): **110,109,109,109,109 106,104,99,98,84**
toteswingers:1&2:£45.40, 1&3:£44.10, 2&3:£80.10 CSF £350.82 CT £9304.21 TOTE £12.60: £3.80, £6.00, £8.60; EX 307.30.
Owner Paul Dean **Bred** Patrick Eddery Ltd **Trained** Nether Winchendon, Bucks

FOCUS
A fairly useful handicap run at a decent gallop that provided a very tight finish, with arguably both the placed horses unlucky to different degrees. The form is not rated too positively around the winner and fourth.

2225 BATHWICK TYRES SALISBURY H'CAP 1m 4f
8:15 (8:17) (Class 6) (0-65,70) 3-Y-0 **£1,942** (£578; £288; £144) **Stalls** High

Form RPR

4311 **1** **Dubai Glory**[10] 1951 3-9-12 **70** 6ex .... JamesDoyle 6 77+
(Sheena West) *a.p: led over 3f out: sn rdn: styd on but drifted lft ins fnl f: a doing enough* **5/1**[3]

0-21 **2** ¾ **Watered Silk**[29] 1487 3-9-2 **60** .... ChrisCatlin 1 65+
(Marcus Tregoning) *trckd ldrs: nt clr run briefly 3f out and sn sltly outpcd: 5th ent fnl f: styd on wl: wnt 2nd nr fin* **2/1**[1]

00-0 **3** *nk* **Fleeting Tiger**[19] 1683 3-8-8 **52** .... JimCrowley 7 57
(John Dunlop) *trckd ldrs: rdn over 2f out: chsd wnr over 1f out: kpt on but a being hld: lost 2nd towards fin* **9/2**[2]

00-3 **4** 1 ½ **Deceptive**[17] 1751 3-9-4 **62** .... GeorgeBaker 9 65
(Roger Charlton) *trckd ldrs: rdn 3f out: styd on same pce fnl 2f: wnt 4th nr fin* **9/2**[2]

30-2 **5** 1 ¼ **Dr Darcey**[17] 1769 3-9-4 **62** .... RichardHughes 2 63
(Richard Hannon) *led tl over 3f out: sn rdn: chsd wnr tl over 1f out: fdd fnl 120yds* **9/2**[2]

4-00 **6** *4* **Apparel (IRE)**[24] 1568 3-9-6 **64** .... KierenFallon 8 58
(Ed Dunlop) *hld up in last trio: rdn 3f out: nt pce to threaten: fdd ins fnl f* **11/1**

0-06 **7** *nk* **Sum Satisfaction**[15] 1819 3-9-4 **62** .... LukeMorris 10 56
(Dominic Ffrench Davis) *fly-jmpd leaving stalls: racd keenly: hld up: rdn 3f out: nt pce to threaten: fdd ins fnl f* **33/1**

0-60 **8** *47* **Brandy Alexander**[87] 634 3-9-7 **65** ....(p) FergusSweeney 3 —
(Neil Mulholland) *hld up in last trio tl outpcd 3f out: t.o* **66/1**

2m 39.22s (1.22) **Going Correction** 0.0s/f (Good) **8** Ran SP% **117.3**
Speed ratings (Par 97): **95,94,94,93,92 89,89,58**
toteswingers:1&2:£3.60, 1&3:£2.40, 2&3:£3.30 CSF £15.89 CT £48.73 TOTE £5.80: £1.90, £1.90, £1.70; EX 17.10.
Owner The Affordable (2) Partnership **Bred** Hascombe And Valiant Studs **Trained** Falmer, E Sussex

FOCUS
An interesting race for the grade with several improvers up against each other and probably decent form for all it has the potential to be misleading after the pace was only steady. The fourth sets the level rated close to recent maiden form.

2226 BATHWICK TYRES BOURNEMOUTH CLASSIFIED STKS 1m 1f 198y
8:45 (8:46) (Class 5) 3-Y-0 **£2,428** (£722; £361; £180) **Stalls** Low

Form RPR

6663 **1** **Bussa**[10] 1949 3-9-0 70 .... CathyGannon 6 74
(David Evans) *wnt lft s: hld up last but in tch: hdwy 3f out: sn rdn: swtchd lft 2f out: str chal ins fnl f: won on nod* **16/1**

3-33 **2** *nse* **Cunning Act**[10] 1951 3-9-0 69 .... KierenFallon 4 74
(Jonathan Portman) *carried sltly lft s: led after 1f: rdn whn pressed fr over 2f out: hung lft fr over 1f out: kpt on: lost on nod* **3/1**[2]

64-4 **3** 3 ¾ **Experimentalist**[19] 1683 3-9-0 70 .... RichardHughes 2 67
(Hughie Morrison) *trckd ldr: rdn to chal 2f out: 1/2 l down and looking hld whn squeezed out ent fnl f: no ch after* **11/10**[1]

6-00 **4** *hd* **Red Inca**[14] 1836 3-8-11 68 .... LouisBeuzelin(3) 3 66
(Brian Meehan) *s.i.s: sn trcking ldrs: rdn 3f out: styd on fnl f: wnt 4th nring fin* **5/1**[3]

513 **5** 1 ½ **Tornado Force (IRE)**[59] 931 3-9-0 68 .... LukeMorris 1 63
(J S Moore) *led for 1f: trckd ldr: rdn wl over 2f out: styd on same pce fnl f* **13/2**

3-00 **6** *5* **Ringstead Bay (FR)**[14] 1836 3-9-0 65 .... JimCrowley 5 53
(Ralph Beckett) *hld up in tch: pushed along over 4f out: rdn 3f out: wknd ent fnl f* **16/1**

2m 10.9s (1.00) **Going Correction** 0.0s/f (Good) **6** Ran SP% **114.4**
Speed ratings (Par 99): **96,95,92,92,91 87**
toteswingers:1&2:£7.90, 1&3:£6.30, 2&3:£1.10 CSF £64.63 TOTE £15.70: £3.30, £1.60; EX 36.00.
Owner Nick Shutts **Bred** Natton House Thoroughbreds & Mark Woodall **Trained** Pandy, Monmouths

FOCUS
A modest classified event to end with, run at a steady pace. The fourth looks the best guide to the level.
Experimentalist Official explanation: jockey said gelding hung left-handed
T/Plt: £2,299.40 to a £1 stake. Pool:£45,043.28 - 14.30 winning tickets T/Qpdt: £109.80 to a £1 stake. Pool:£5,871.01 - 39.55 winning tickets TM

1545 SANDOWN (R-H)
Thursday, May 19

OFFICIAL GOING: Good (good to firm in places on round course; sprint 8.4, round 8.2)
Home bend at outermost configuration increasing distances on Round course by 8yds.
Wind: virtually nil Weather: bright and sunny

2227 PANMURE GORDON SMALL COMPANIES E B F MAIDEN FILLIES' STKS 5f 6y
5:50 (5:52) (Class 5) 2-Y-0 **£3,238** (£963; £481; £240) **Stalls** Low

Form RPR

1 **Charlotte Rosina** 2-8-11 0 .... JohnFahy(3) 2 79+
(Roger Teal) *in tch: pushed along and hdwy to press ldr and qcknd clr of field ent fnl f: led ins fnl f: kpt on wl: pushed out* **20/1**[3]

2 **2** *nk* **Nayarra (IRE)**[17] 1765 2-9-0 0 .... RyanMoore 3 78
(Mick Channon) *led: pushed along 2f out: qcknd clr w wnr ent fnl f: hdd ins fnl f: styd on same pce fnl 100yds* **2/5**[1]

3 *9* **Finalist** 2-9-0 0 .... JimmyQuinn 4 46+
(Dean Ivory) *s.i.s: sn rcvrd and in tch: rdn wl over 1f out: 4th and outpcd by ldng pair ent fnl f: wnt modest 3rd fnl 150yds* **100/1**

5 **4** 1 ½ **Sweet Ovation**[10] 1946 2-9-0 0 .... LiamKeniry 5 40
(Mark Usher) *pressed ldr: rdn 2f out: outpcd by ldng pair and btn ent fnl f: wl btn after* **33/1**

5 *1* **Princess Palmer** 2-9-0 0 .... DarryllHolland 6 37
(Lydia Pearce) *chsd ldrs: rdn ent fnl 2f: wknd over 1f out* **33/1**

6 *20* **Huma Bird** 2-9-0 0 .... FrankieDettori 7 —+
(Mahmood Al Zarooni) *wnt lft s: sn chsng ldrs: pressing ldrs and gng wl 2f out: veered bdly lft and lost pl wl over 1f out: nt rcvr and no ch after: hung rt and eased ins fnl f* **11/4**[2]

7 *7* **Leading Star** 2-9-0 0 .... IanMongan 1 —
(Michael Madgwick) *s.i.s: a outpcd in detached last: wl bhd fr 1/2-way: t.o* **66/1**

62.15 secs (0.55) **Going Correction** -0.025s/f (Good) **7** Ran SP% **111.2**
Speed ratings (Par 90): **94,93,79,76,75 43,31**
toteswingers:1&2:£1.90, 1&3:£7.80, 2&3:£4.40 CSF £28.35 TOTE £23.60: £5.90, £1.10; EX 31.60.
Owner Edward Hyde **Bred** Edward Hyde **Trained** Ashtead, Surrey

FOCUS
10mm of water was applied to the round course on Monday and 12mm was added to the sprint course the following day before 1mm of rain fell on Wednesday morning. The home bend was at its outermost configuration adding approximately 8yds to all distances on the round course. The going was eased slightly before the start of racing and the riders described the ground as close to the official description. The first two were clear and the form could prove reasonable.\n\x\x A race won last year by subsequent Queen Mary winner and 1000 Guineas third Maqaasid and one that has frequently been won by a smart type in the last ten years. However this race lacked much in the way of strength in depth and was rendered less competitive when the second favourite swerved her chance away passing the two furlong pole. The gallop was reasonable.

NOTEBOOK
Charlotte Rosina has plenty of sprinting blood in her pedigree and created a favourable impression to beat a more experienced rival on this racecourse debut. She has the physical scope to improve and she should be able to hold her own in slightly stronger company. (op 16-1)
Nayarra(IRE)'s promising debut run at Warwick had been franked when the winner there ran well in a Listed event at York last week and she looked the one to beat. However, although she failed to step up on that level, she again showed enough to suggest a similar event can be found, especially when upped to 6f. (op 4-9, tchd 1-2 in places and 8-15 in a place)
Finalist, who has plenty of winners from 5f-1m2f in her pedigree, showed ability at an ordinary at a moderate level. She should be suited by 6f and has physical scope but she is likely to remain vulnerable in this type of event. (tchd 80-1)
Sweet Ovation again had her limitations firmly exposed over this trip on a sound surface and her short-term future lies in low-grade nurseries. (tchd 40-1)
Princess Palmer only hinted at ability and her pedigree suggests she will fare better in ordinary handicaps over much further in due course.
Huma Bird, a well-bred sort who attracted support on this racecourse debut, raced with the choke out but threw her chance away when diving markedly left passing the 2f pole, before hanging back to the far side when her chance had clearly gone. She will be one to watch rather than bet on next time. (tchd 5-2)

2228 PANMURE GORDON CORPORATE FINANCE H'CAP — 1m 6f
6:20 (6:20) (Class 4) (0-85,82) 3-Y-O — **£4,079** (£1,214; £606; £303) **Stalls** Low

Form / RPR

31 **1** **Eternal Heart (IRE)**[25] 1542 3-9-7 **82**........ SilvestreDeSousa 7 — 89+
(Mark Johnston) *racd in midfield: pushed along 6f out: rdn and looked to be struggling whn hung rt 3f out: swtchd lft and hdwy to chse ldng pair over 1f out: styd on dourly u.p to ld fnl 75yds: won gng away at fin* **2/1**[1]

-212 **2** 1 ½ **Jacobs Son**[49] 1057 3-8-13 **77**........ SeanLevey(3) 4 — 82
(Robert Mills) *led and set str gallop: clr 12f out: rdn 2f out: drvn and kpt on wl fr over 1f out: hdd and no ex fnl 75yds* **11/1**

0-41 **3** 1 ¼ **Achalas (IRE)**[8] 1997 3-8-8 **69** 6ex........ EddieAhern 1 — 72
(Heather Main) *hld up off the pce towards rr: pushed along and hdwy 3f out: swtchd lft and rdn to chse ldr 2f out: hanging rt and nt qckning over 1f out: styd on same pce ins fnl f* **6/1**

0-32 **4** nk **Veloce (IRE)**[13] 1872 3-8-2 **63** oh1........ JimmyQuinn 3 — 66
(John Dunlop) *bhd: rdn and struggling in 6th over 3f out: kpt on u.p fr 2f out: wnt 4th ent fnl f: kpt on dourly to press for 3rd nr fin: nvr gng pce to rch ldrs* **9/2**[3]

30-4 **5** 6 **Hollow Tree**[29] 1484 3-8-11 **72**........ JimmyFortune 2 — 67
(Andrew Balding) *t.k.h: chsd ldng pair: clsd 3f out: rdn and unable qck over 2f out: wknd over 1f out* **10/1**

-114 **6** 6 **Musawama (IRE)**[29] 1478 3-9-5 **80**........ RichardHills 6 — 66
(John Gosden) *chsd ldr: rdn 3f out: hung rt and struggling ent fnl 2f: wknd over 1f out* **7/2**[2]

62-5 **7** 8 **Layla's King**[15] 1810 3-8-11 **72**........ ShaneKelly 5 — 47
(Jane Chapple-Hyam) *a in rr: rdn and no prog wl over 3f out: wl bhd fnl 2f* **16/1**

3m 3.68s (-0.82) **Going Correction** -0.025s/f (Good) — **7** Ran SP% **111.3**
Speed ratings (Par 101): **101,100,99,99,95 92,87**
toteswingers:1&2:£2.50, 1&3:£3.30, 2&3:£5.70 CSF £23.68 TOTE £2.60: £1.40, £4.80; EX 26.70.
Owner Mrs Joan Keaney **Bred** Mrs Joan Keaney **Trained** Middleham Moor, N Yorks

FOCUS
A useful handicap featuring a couple of unexposed sorts and one in which the gallop was soon sound. The runner-up looks the best guide to the worth of this form.
Jacobs Son Official explanation: vet said gelding returned lame left-fore

2229 PANMURE GORDON INSTITUTIONAL EQUITIES H'CAP — 1m 14y
6:55 (6:57) (Class 4) (0-85,80) 3-Y-O — **£4,079** (£1,214; £606; £303) **Stalls** Low

Form / RPR

121- **1** **Tullius (IRE)**[170] 7636 3-9-4 **77**........ IanMongan 1 — 88
(Peter Winkworth) *led for 1f: styd chsng ldrs: rdn to chse ldr jst over 2f out: drvn to 1f out: kpt on wl u.p fnl f* **16/1**

541- **2** ¾ **Charles Camoin (IRE)**[204] 7179 3-9-5 **78**........ LiamKeniry 5 — 87
(Sylvester Kirk) *t.k.h: chsd ldrs: rdn wl over 2f out: kpt on u.p to chse ldr jst ins fnl f: kpt on but nvr enough pce to rch wnr* **20/1**

040- **3** shd **Levitate**[209] 7058 3-8-11 **70**........ RyanMoore 12 — 79+
(Sir Michael Stoute) *stdd and swtchd rt after s: bhd in last pair: rdn 3f out: stl only 9th but hdwy on outer over 1f out: r.o wl ins fnl f: gng on wl and pressing for 2nd fin* **7/1**[3]

4622 **4** 1 ½ **Imaginary World (IRE)**[7] 2018 3-8-9 **68**........(b) FrankieDettori 8 — 74
(Alan McCabe) *hld up towards rr: hdwy and edging towards inner 3f out: chsng ldrs and swtchd lft over 1f out: disputing 2nd 1f out: no ex and btn fnl 75yds* **3/1**[1]

21-0 **5** 2 **Home Office**[34] 1361 3-9-5 **78**........ SilvestreDeSousa 4 — 79
(Mark Johnston) *chsd ldr tl led after 1f: clr 1/2-way: rdn ent fnl 2f: drvn and hdd 1f out: wknd fnl 100yds* **14/1**

1-51 **6** ¾ **Ree's Rascal (IRE)**[10] 1949 3-9-0 **73** 6ex........ PatCosgrave 9 — 72
(Jim Boyle) *hld up in tch towards rr: hdwy 3f out: rdn and sltly outpcd 2f out: plugged on again ins fnl f: nvr gng pce to chal ldrs* **9/2**[2]

61-0 **7** 2 ½ **Rasheed**[33] 1392 3-9-1 **74**........ RichardHills 10 — 68
(John Gosden) *chsd ldrs: wnt 2nd after 2f tl jst over 2f out: sn unable qck and losing pl wknd over 1f out* **10/1**

010- **8** shd **Aciano (IRE)**[229] 6560 3-9-4 **77**........ ShaneKelly 2 — 70
(Brian Meehan) *awkward leaving stalls and s.i.s: bhd: rdn and no prog wl over 2f out: hdwy ent fnl f: styd on ins fnl f: nvr trbld ldrs* **14/1**

25-2 **9** ½ **Shewalksinbeauty (IRE)**[17] 1754 3-9-4 **77**........ JimmyFortune 6 — 69
(Richard Hannon) *hld up in rr: hdwy and edging rt over 2f out: rdn and no hdwy 2f out: wknd ent fnl f* **16/1**

610- **10** ¾ **Kingarrick**[231] 6505 3-9-0 **76**........ JohnFahy(3) 11 — 66
(Eve Johnson Houghton) *in tch in midfield on outer: effrt to chse ldrs and drvn 2f out: btn over 1f out: wknd fnl f* **20/1**

40-1 **11** 3 ¼ **Chief Of Men**[23] 1580 3-9-4 **77**........ DarryllHolland 3 — 60
(Denis Coakley) *t.k.h: hld up in tch in midfield: racd awkwardly bnd 1/2-way: rdn and no hdwy on inner over 2f out: n.d fr over 1f out* **10/1**

3-22 **12** 12 **Islesman**[17] 1773 3-9-7 **80**........ EddieAhern 7 — 35
(Heather Main) *stdd s: t.k.h: sn in tch in midfield: rdn and btn over 2f out: bhd and eased ins fnl f* **9/1**

1m 44.08s (0.78) **Going Correction** -0.025s/f (Good) — **12** Ran SP% **118.5**
Speed ratings (Par 101): **95,94,94,92,90 89,87,87,86,86 82,70**
toteswingers:1&2:£62.10, 1&3:£35.80, 2&3:£31.60 CSF £300.18 CT £2463.31 TOTE £19.90: £5.60, £9.60, £1.10; EX 272.90.
Owner Kennet Valley Thoroughbreds VI **Bred** Sc Archi Romani **Trained** Chiddingfold, Surrey

FOCUS
Several winners and a few unexposed sorts in a fair three-year-old handicap that should throw up its share of winners. The form is a bit messy and the fourth is probably the best guide.
Aciano(IRE) Official explanation: jockey said gelding was slowly away
Islesman Official explanation: jockey said gelding suffered interference in running

2230 HARRY PANMURE GORDON MEMORIAL H'CAP — 1m 2f 7y
7:30 (7:30) (Class 4) (0-85,83) 3-Y-O — **£4,079** (£1,214; £606; £303) **Stalls** Low

Form / RPR

-364 **1** **Malthouse (GER)**[26] 1516 3-9-7 **83**........ SilvestreDeSousa 2 — 100+
(Mark Johnston) *chsd ldrs: rdn jst over 2f out: pressing ldrs whn squeezed out and lost pl 2f out: swtchd lft and rallied over 1f out: led jst ins fnl f: hld on wl fnl 100yds: rdn out* **5/1**[3]

51-2 **2** ½ **Haylaman (IRE)**[13] 1862 3-9-2 **78**........ FrankieDettori 8 — 93
(Ed Dunlop) *hld up in tch: rdn and effrt on outer ent fnl 2f: pressed wnr ins fnl f: kpt on wl but a hld* **10/3**[2]

0-13 **3** 2 ¾ **Little Black Book (IRE)**[10] 1947 3-8-13 **75**........ DarryllHolland 7 — 84
(Gerard Butler) *led tl over 8f out: chsd ldr after tl rdn to ld over 2f out: drvn over 1f out: hdd jst ins fnl f: no ex and btn fnl 100yds* **11/4**[1]

4-21 **4** 6 **Ivan Vasilevich (IRE)**[23] 1593 3-8-8 **77**........ LewisWalsh(7) 1 — 74
(Jane Chapple-Hyam) *in tch: pushed along and edging lft ent fnl 2f: no hdwy and btn over 1f out: n.d but plugged on same pce to go 4th wl ins fnl f* **7/1**

10-0 **5** 1 ¼ **Buxfizz (USA)**[25] 1550 3-9-3 **82**........ SeanLevey(3) 6 — 77
(Robert Mills) *w ldrs tl led over 8f out: rdn over 3f out: hdd and drvn over 2f out: styd pressing ldr tl wkng whn short of room jst ins fnl f: wknd fnl 150yds* **20/1**

05-0 **6** 2 ¾ **Misk Khitaam (USA)**[36] 1315 3-9-2 **78**........ RichardHills 5 — 67
(John Dunlop) *bhd: last and no hdwy whn rdn jst over 3f out: nvr a threat to ldrs* **11/1**

014- **7** 2 **Aldwick Bay (IRE)**[204] 7165 3-9-0 **76**........ RyanMoore 3 — 61
(Richard Hannon) *in tch on outer: rdn and fnd nil jst over 2f out: sn wknd* **9/1**

321- **8** 11 **Labore**[189] 7412 3-9-4 **80**........ JimmyFortune 4 — 43
(Marco Botti) *stdd s: hld up in tch: rdn and effrt ent fnl 2f: sn btn: wl bhd and eased ins fnl f* **8/1**

2m 10.56s (0.06) **Going Correction** -0.025s/f (Good) — **8** Ran SP% **113.1**
Speed ratings (Par 101): **98,97,95,90,89 87,85,77**
toteswingers:1&2:£5.80, 1&3:£1.60, 2&3:£3.40 CSF £21.54 CT £53.92 TOTE £4.30: £1.40, £2.30, £1.30; EX 24.00.
Owner Sheikh Hamdan Bin Mohammed Al Maktoum **Bred** Dr Chr Berglar **Trained** Middleham Moor, N Yorks

FOCUS
Several winners in another useful 3-y-o handicap. The gallop steadied after 2f and the first three pulled clear. The winner looks better than the bare form with the third setting the level.

2231 PANMURE GORDON LIVERPOOL MAIDEN STKS — 1m 2f 7y
8:05 (8:06) (Class 5) 3-4-Y-O — **£2,266** (£674; £337; £168) **Stalls** Low

Form / RPR

5-42 **1** **Tanfeeth**[15] 1810 3-8-12 **88**........ RichardHills 6 — 83+
(Ed Dunlop) *chsd ldr: led 2f out: rdn over 1f out: kpt on and a doing enough fnl f: eased nr fin* **4/11**[1]

2 1 ¾ **Almagest** 3-8-12 0........ NickyMackay 9 — 79+
(John Gosden) *s.i.s: towards rr: c wd and stdy prog fr over 3f out: rn green and edging rt fr 2f out: chsd wnr over 1f out: kpt edging rt and no hdwy fnl 100yds* **16/1**

0- **3** 1 **Monopolize**[176] 7558 3-8-12 0........ IanMongan 8 — 77
(Sir Henry Cecil) *chsd ldrs: rdn and effrt ent fnl 2f: chsd ldng pair ent fnl f: kpt on trying but kpt on same pce fnl 150yds* **7/1**[3]

00 **4** 4 **Dare To Bare (IRE)**[14] 1836 3-8-12 0........ RyanMoore 1 — 69
(Amanda Perrett) *led: jnd and rdn over 2f out: hdd 2f out: btn ent fnl f: wknd fnl 150yds* **50/1**

0- **5** 4 ½ **Elfaaten (USA)**[208] 7094 3-8-12 0........ DaneO'Neill 11 — 60
(Marcus Tregoning) *racd off the pce in midfield: rdn along and outpcd over 2f out: no threat to ldrs fr wl over 1f out* **33/1**

6 2 ½ **Tin Pan Alley** 3-8-12 0........ FrankieDettori 5 — 55
(Mahmood Al Zarooni) *s.i.s: sn rcvrd and in midfield after 1f: rdn and outpcd jst over 2f out: 5th and wl btn over 1f out* **13/2**[2]

4-6 **7** 1 ½ **Tanassuq (USA)**[35] 1343 3-8-7 0........ EddieAhern 7 — 47
(John Dunlop) *racd off the pce in midfield: pushed along and outpcd by ldrs jst over 2f out: nudged along and wl btn fr over 1f out* **20/1**

00- **8** 1 **Boston Court (IRE)**[222] 6748 3-8-12 0........ ShaneKelly 10 — 50
(Brian Meehan) *chsd ldrs: rdn and struggling over 2f out: wknd ent fnl 2f: wl btn over 1f out* **66/1**

9 1 **Bright Abbey** 3-8-12 0........ JimmyFortune 3 — 48
(Walter Swinburn) *s.i.s: a in rr: rdn and no prog over 3f out: nvr on terms* **40/1**

60 **10** 1 ½ **Native Colony**[24] 1568 3-8-12 0........ JackMitchell 12 — 45
(Roger Varian) *t.k.h: hld up in rr: rdn: rn green and edging rt wl over 2f out: wl btn whn nt clr run ins fnl f: nvr on terms* **20/1**

11 11 **Milton Hill**[111] 4-9-12 0........ LiamKeniry 2 — 23
(Dominic Ffrench Davis) *s.i.s: rn green and a in rr: lost tch and edging lft wl over 2f out: t.o* **100/1**

12 1 ¼ **Brunello** 3-8-12 0........ DarryllHolland 4 — 21
(Walter Swinburn) *s.i.s: a towards rr: shkn up and no hdwy over 2f out: wl bhd and eased ins fnl f: t.o* **40/1**

2m 12.43s (1.93) **Going Correction** -0.025s/f (Good)
WFA 3 from 4yo 14lb — **12** Ran SP% **126.8**
Speed ratings (Par 103): **91,89,88,85,82 80,78,78,77,76 67,66**
toteswingers:1&2:£3.60, 1&3:£2.40, 2&3:£3.30 CSF £8.74 TOTE £1.60: £1.02, £4.80, £1.60; EX 12.20.
Owner Hamdan Al Maktoum **Bred** Shadwell Estate Company Limited **Trained** Newmarket, Suffolk

FOCUS
The third running of a race taken last year by subsequent Listed/Group 3 winner Sajjhaa but this looked an ordinary maiden by Sandown standards, lacking anything in the way of strength, and one in which the gallop was an ordinary one. The fourth is probably the key to the form.

2232 PANMURE GORDON STOCKBROKING FILLIES' H'CAP 1m 1f
8:35 (8:37) (Class 5) (0-75,75) 3-Y-O+ **£2,590** (£770; £385; £192) **Stalls** Low

Form RPR

34-6 **1** **Miss Chicane**[40] [1251] 3-8-9 **69**.......... EddieAhern 5 78
(Walter Swinburn) *dwlt: sn bustled along and flashed tail: hld up in tch: hdwy on inner ent fnl 2f: nt clr run over 1f out: swtchd lft to chse ldrs and barged rival 1f out: rdn along hands and heels and r.o wl to ld fnl 75yds* **12/1**

00 **2** *1 1/4* **Inef (IRE)**[26] [1530] 4-9-11 **72**.......... IanMongan 8 80
(Laura Mongan) *in tch on outer: effrt and pressed ldrs over 2f out: edgd rt and rdn to chal 2f out: drvn to ld narrowly over 1f out: hdd and no ex fnl 75yds* **16/1**

500- **3** *3/4* **Golden Waters**[309] [4022] 4-9-3 **64**.......... LiamKeniry 10 70
(Eve Johnson Houghton) *chsd ldr tl led after 3f: hdd and rdn over 1f out: flashed tail u.p: styd on same pce ins fnl f* **25/1**

315- **4** *1* **Regal Kiss**[247] [6059] 3-9-0 **74**.......... SilvestreDeSousa 6 76
(Mark Johnston) *in tch in midfield: rdn and effrt over 2f out: keeping on and chsng ldrs whn pushed lft 1f out: kpt on u.p ins fnl f* **13/2**[2]

1 **5** *1 1/2* **Foxley (IRE)**[17] [1767] 3-8-9 **69**.......... ShaneKelly 1 68
(Brian Meehan) *led for 3f: styd pressing ldrs: rdn and unable qck whn n.m.r over 1f: one pce and hld fnl f* **7/1**[3]

1/0- **6** *2* **Qaraaba**[153] [7915] 4-10-0 **75**.......... FrankieDettori 2 71
(Seamus Durack) *stdd s: hld up in tch in rr: hdwy on outer ent fnl 2f: in tch and stl gng okay whn sltly hmpd ent fnl f: sn pushed along and fnd little: kpt on same pce after* **14/1**

/0-6 **7** *3/4* **Golden Aria (IRE)**[46] [1114] 4-10-0 **75**.......... JimmyFortune 9 70
(Richard Hannon) *t.k.h: chsd ldrs: rdn and pressing ldrs whn hmpd and lost pl jst over 2f out: keeping on same pce whn hmpd again over 1f out: hanging rt and no threat to ldrs fnl f* **25/1**

05-1 **8** *1 1/4* **Dragonera**[10] [1958] 3-9-0 **74** 6ex.......... RyanMoore 3 64+
(Ed Dunlop) *hld up wl in tch in midfield: shkn up ent fnl 2f: short of room and bdly hmpd wl over 1f out: dropped in rr and n.d after* **2/1**[1]

2-42 **9** *1/2* **Elfine (IRE)**[15] [1819] 3-9-0 **74**.......... DaneO'Neill 4 63
(Harry Dunlop) *t.k.h: chsd ldrs early: hld up wl in tch after 2f: rdn and lost pl ent fnl 2f: no threat to ldrs fr over 1f out* **8/1**

3011 **10** *hd* **Princess Lexi (IRE)**[21] [1637] 4-9-3 **64**.......... StevieDonohoe 11 56
(Ian Williams) *sn pushed along in last trio: rdn ent fnl 2f: swtchd rt to inner and sme hdwy whn barged rival 1f out: no imp after: nvr trbld ldrs* **8/1**

-416 **11** *1* **Silent Oasis**[26] [1530] 5-9-2 **70**.......... DavidKenny[(7)] 7 61
(Brendan Powell) *hld up in tch towards rr: swtchd to inner and effrt wl over 1f out: keeping on same pce and hld whn bdly hmpd 1f out: n.d after* **12/1**

1m 57.97s (2.27) **Going Correction** -0.025s/f (Good)
WFA 3 from 4yo+ 13lb **11** Ran SP% **117.0**
Speed ratings (Par 100): **88,86,86,85,84 82,81,80,80,79 78**
toteswingers:1&2:£79.10, 1&3:£57.90, 2&3:£44.30 CSF £187.59 CT £4685.70 TOTE £17.00: £3.40, £8.20, £7.10; EX 417.80.
Owner Flexible Friends **Bred** W And R Barnett Ltd **Trained** Aldbury, Herts

FOCUS
No more than a fair fillies' handicap but a rough race run at a muddling gallop. The market leader was badly hampered and consequently the race took less winning than seemed likely. The form looks unreliable.
Dragonera Official explanation: jockey said filly suffered interference in running
Princess Lexi(IRE) Official explanation: jockey said filly hung right
T/Plt: £926.20 to a £1 stake. Pool:£58,277.53 - 45.93 winning tickets T/Qpdt: £269.40 to a £1 stake. Pool:£5,788.93 - 15.90 winning tickets SP

1973 SOUTHWELL (L-H)
Thursday, May 19

OFFICIAL GOING: Standard
Wind: Light across Weather: Fine and dry

2233 SOUTHWELL H'CAP 7f (F)
2:10 (2:11) (Class 6) (0-55,55) 4-Y-O+ **£1,706** (£503; £252) **Stalls** Low

Form RPR

06-0 **1** **Blue Charm**[98] [490] 7-8-7 **49** ow1.......... GaryBartley[(3)] 2 56
(Ian McInnes) *s.i.s and towards rr: pushed along and hdwy 3f out: rdn to chse ldrs over 1f out: drvn and styd on ins fnl f: led last 100yds* **22/1**

60-1 **2** *1/2* **Charlietoo**[3] [2162] 5-8-9 **51** 6ex..........(p) KierenFox[(3)] 8 56+
(Edward Bevan) *in rr and rdn along 1/2-way: wd in st: rdn and hdwy on outer over 1f out: ev ch whn edgd lft ins fnl f: no ex towards fin* **4/1**[2]

0016 **3** *1/2* **St Ignatius**[2] [2171] 4-9-1 **54**..........(p) NeilChalmers 4 58
(Michael Appleby) *cl up: rdn to ld 1 1/2f out: drvn ins fnl f: hdd and no ex last 100yds* **7/2**[1]

5440 **4** *1 1/2* **Moment Of Clarity**[9] [1993] 9-8-4 **46** oh1..........(p) SimonPearce[(3)] 9 46
(Shaun Harris) *chsd ldng pair: rdn along 3f out: drvn wl over 1f out: kpt on u.p appr fnl f* **16/1**

40-5 **5** *1* **Thinking**[12] [1911] 4-9-1 **54**.......... TonyHamilton 5 51
(Tim Easterby) *chsd ldrs: rdn over 2f out: sn drvn and kpt on same pce* **9/2**[3]

0600 **6** *nk* **Moon Lightning (IRE)**[9] [1979] 5-8-8 **47** oh1 ow1.......... PaulMulrennan 11 43
(Tina Jackson) *chsd ldrs on outer: rdn along 3f out: drvn and kpt on same pce fr over 1f out* **25/1**

0564 **7** *2 1/2* **Escardo (GER)**[17] [1763] 8-8-0 **46** oh1..........(p) JoshBaudains[(7)] 3 36
(David Bridgwater) *towards rr: rdn along and sme hdwy on inner fnl 2f: n.d* **12/1**

00-3 **8** *nk* **Eeny Mac (IRE)**[15] [1815] 4-8-7 **46** oh1.......... KellyHarrison 1 35
(Neville Bycroft) *chsd ldrs on inner: rdn along over 2f out: sn btn* **7/1**

0-05 **9** *nk* **Mujahope**[15] [1818] 6-8-7 **46** oh1..........(v) RobbieFitzpatrick 10 34
(Colin Teague) *dwlt: nvr bttr than midfield* **50/1**

0203 **10** *3 1/2* **Wotatomboy**[21] [1633] 5-8-7 **46**..........(b) TomEaves 6 25
(Richard Whitaker) *led: rdn along over 2f out: hdd 1 1/2f out and sn wknd* **6/1**

0-00 **11** *3 1/4* **Quaestor (IRE)**[22] [1612] 4-9-2 **55**..........(p) AndrewElliott 7 25
(Andrew Crook) *a in rr* **28/1**

1m 31.17s (0.87) **Going Correction** +0.10s/f (Slow) **11** Ran SP% **114.4**
Speed ratings (Par 101): **99,98,97,96,95 94,91,91,91,87 83**
toteswingers:1&2:£17.90, 1&3:£15.10, 2&3:£2.80 CSF £102.24 CT £398.73 TOTE £17.60: £4.20, £1.20, £1.80; EX 123.70.
Owner J Morris **Bred** Mrs R Pease **Trained** Catwick, E Yorks

FOCUS
A moderate handicap and in-running punters got their fingers burnt, with the runner-up touching 1.05 and the third 1.06. The form is pretty limited with the placed horses to recent marks.

2234 BRITISH STALLION STUDS SUPPORTING BRITISH RACING E B F MAIDEN STKS 6f (F)
2:40 (2:40) (Class 5) 2-Y-O **£3,238** (£963; £481; £240) **Stalls** Low

Form RPR

5 **1** **Basantee**[17] [1744] 2-8-12 0.......... SebSanders 6 78+
(Tom Dascombe) *cl up on outer: led 2f out: sn rdn clr: easily* **11/8**[1]

2 *8* **Ingleby Angel (IRE)** 2-9-3 0.......... DanielTudhope 1 57
(David O'Meara) *trckd ldrs on inner: hdwy 2f out: rdn wl over 1f out: kpt on to take 2nd ins fnl f: no ch w wnr* **11/4**[2]

3 *nk* **Always Et Toujours** 2-9-3 0.......... GregFairley 2 56
(Mark Johnston) *led: rdn along 1/2-way: hdd 2f out and sn drvn: one pce and lost 2nd wl ins fnl f* **3/1**[3]

65 **4** *6* **The Coulbeck Kid**[23] [1590] 2-9-0 0.......... PaulPickard[(3)] 3 38
(Des Donovan) *cl up: effrt 3f out: rdn over 2f out: hung lft and wknd wl over 1f out* **33/1**

05 **5** *9* **Just Dixie**[36] [1301] 2-8-12 0.......... TomEaves 4 6
(John Weymes) *trckd ldrs: rdn along 1/2-way: sn wknd* **22/1**

6 *1/2* **Mr Mallo** 2-9-3 0.......... PaulMulrennan 7 10
(Richard Ford) *in tch: rdn along bef 1/2-way: sn outpcd and bhd* **11/1**

1m 17.99s (1.49) **Going Correction** +0.10s/f (Slow) **6** Ran SP% **109.4**
Speed ratings (Par 93): **94,83,82,74,62 62**
toteswingers:1&2:£1.70, 1&3:£1.70, 2&3:£1.90 CSF £5.06 TOTE £1.90: £1.20, £1.80; EX 3.50.
Owner The MHS 8X8 Partnership **Bred** R Phillips And Tweenhills Farm And Stud **Trained** Malpas, Cheshire

FOCUS
An uncompetitive maiden, but an impressive winner. The form is rated around race averages.

NOTEBOOK
Basantee, a creditable fifth of eight on her Beverley debut, looked completely different gear this time around and, having established the lead on her own passing the 2f pole, bounded away to win with any amount in hand. She may not have beaten much with a couple of newcomers chasing her home, but she could hardly have done this any easier. Connections believe she will relish a step up to 7f in due course. (op 6-5 tchd 6-4)
Ingleby Angel(IRE), a half-brother to a winning juvenile sprinter, attracted market support beforehand but the best he could do was stay on to win the battle for second at a respectful distance behind the filly. He is entitled to improve and should be able to win an ordinary maiden on this surface. (op 4-1)
Always Et Toujours, out of a juvenile winner over 7f, disputed the lead until getting totally outpaced over the last 2f. Market weakness beforehand suggested that the run might have been thought to be needed. (op 9-4 tchd 2-1)
The Coulbeck Kid, well beaten in two turf outings, showed up early but was seen off well before his ability to see out the extra furlong was tested. (op 25-1 tchd 40-1)

2235 MEMBERSHIP OF SOUTHWELL GOLF CLUB CLAIMING STKS 1m 4f (F)
3:15 (3:15) (Class 5) 3-Y-O+ **£2,388** (£705; £352) **Stalls** Low

Form RPR

1111 **1** **La Estrella (USA)**[51] [1030] 8-10-0 **86**.......... DaneO'Neill 5 88+
(Don Cantillon) *hld up: hdwy to trck ldrs 1/2-way: cl up 4f out: led 3f out: sn clr: easily* **1/4**[1]

0 **2** *5* **Host The Band**[38] [1271] 7-9-1 0.......... DavidKenny[(7)] 4 67
(Tony Newcombe) *trckd ldng pair: hdwy to chse wnr over 2f out: rdn wl over 1f out: kpt on: no ch w wnr* **66/1**

104 **3** *10* **Cobo Bay**[9] [1977] 6-10-0 **80**..........(b) SebSanders 2 57
(Conor Dore) *trckd ldr: led over 5f out: rdn along 4f out: hdd 3f out: sn drvn and outpcd* **5/1**[2]

30-0 **4** *1 3/4* **Crystal Celebre (IRE)**[31] [1443] 5-9-6 **69**.......... AmyScott[(5)] 6 51
(Henry Candy) *hld up in rr: sme hdwy over 3f out: sn rdn and nvr a factor* **9/1**[3]

5-22 **5** *2 1/4* **Dunaskin (IRE)**[130] [103] 11-9-6 **55**..........(b) RobertLButler[(3)] 1 45
(Richard Guest) *led: pushed along 1/2-way: sn hdd & wknd over 3f out* **25/1**

[illegible] **6** *[illegible]* **Paint The Town Red**[0] [illegible] [illegible]..........(p) RobbieFitzpatrick 3 42
(Richard Guest) *chsd ldrs: rdn along over 4f out: sn wknd* **66/1**

2m 41.62s (0.62) **Going Correction** +0.10s/f (Slow) **6** Ran SP% **113.5**
Speed ratings (Par 103): **101,97,91,89,88 87**
toteswingers:1&2:£9.10, 1&3:£1.20, 2&3:£12.40 CSF £33.50 TOTE £1.40: £1.02, £21.40; EX 21.40.
Owner Don Cantillon **Bred** Five Horses Ltd And Theatrical Syndicate **Trained** Newmarket, Suffolk

FOCUS
An uncompetitive claimer.

2236 SOUTHWELL GOLF CLUB LADY MEMBERS CLASSIFIED (S) STKS 7f (F)
3:50 (3:50) (Class 6) 3-Y-O **£1,706** (£503; £252) **Stalls** Low

Form RPR

1403 **1** **Goal (IRE)**[9] [1975] 3-8-12 **60**..........(t) SebSanders 5 68
(Richard Guest) *prom on outer: led wl over 2f out: sn rdn: drvn and edgd lft over 1f out: kpt on* **4/1**[3]

3312 **2** *3 1/4* **Jay Jays Joy**[9] [1975] 3-9-4 **58**..........(b) LeeNewman 4 65
(David Barron) *sn trcking ldrs: hdwy and cl up 4f out: rdn to ld briefly 3f out: sn hdd and drvn: kpt on same pce* **5/4**[1]

352 **3** *1* **So Is She (IRE)**[8] [1999] 3-9-4 **66**..........(p) LiamJones 3 63
(Alan Bailey) *led: rdn along and hdd 3f out: drvn 2f out: swtchd rt and kpt on same pce appr fnl f* **7/4**[2]

000- **4** *20* **Dreamweaving (IRE)**[217] [6878] 3-8-12 **45**..........(v[1]) TomEaves 2 —
(Nigel Tinkler) *chsd ldrs: rdn along 1/2-way: drvn and wknd wl over 2f out* **25/1**

46-0 **5** *11* **Arashone**[13] [1858] 3-8-12 **47**..........(p) PaulMulrennan 1 —
(John Weymes) *sn rdn along in rr: outpcd and bhd fr 1/2-way* **50/1**

1m 31.14s (0.84) **Going Correction** +0.10s/f (Slow) **5** Ran SP% **106.6**
Speed ratings (Par 97): **99,95,94,71,58**
CSF £8.88 TOTE £4.20: £2.20, £1.02; EX 8.50.The winner was bought in for 5,250gns.
Owner Willie McKay **Bred** A M F Persse **Trained** Stainforth, S Yorks

FOCUS
This moderate seller only ever concerned the three market leaders and none of them possess anything in the way of scope. The first two are rated to form.

2237 PLAY GOLF BEFORE RACING H'CAP 1m (F)
4:25 (4:26) (Class 6) (0-60,60) 4-Y-O+ **£1,706** (£503; £252) **Stalls** Low

Form RPR

2140 **1** **Positivity**[15] [1814] 5-9-6 **59**..........(p) TomEaves 12 73+
(Bryan Smart) *chsd ldrs: rdn along 3f out: cl up whn hmpd 2f out: led wl over 1f out: sn rdn and kpt on wl fnl f* **15/2**

0020 **2** 1 **On The Cusp (IRE)**6 2057 4-8-8 **52**...........................(p) JulieBurke(5) 14 62
(Richard Guest) *prom: hdwy on outer and cl up 3f out: rdn to ld and hung bdly lft 2f out: sn hdd and drvn: kpt on same pce fnl f* **9/2**1
10-6 **3** ½ **Hit The Switch**15 1814 5-9-7 **60**.................................(p) StephenCraine 3 69
(Patrick Morris) *midfield: hdwy 3f out: trckd ldrs whn hmpd 2f out: sn rdn and kpt on wl fnl f* **15/2**
5/66 **4** 1 **Graycliffe (IRE)**10 1959 5-8-11 **50**............................... DanielTudhope 10 57+
(Patrick Morris) *towards rr: hdwy wl over 2f out: sn rdn and kpt on wl appr fnl f: nrst fin* **14/1**
4663 **5** 1¼ **Elusive Warrior (USA)**9 1979 8-8-12 **58**...................(p) NoraLooby(7) 5 62
(Alan McCabe) *trckd ldrs: hdwy and cl up whn hmpd 2f out: sn rdn and kpt on same pce* **9/1**
3654 **6** 4 **Tomintoul Star**9 1979 5-8-12 **51**...............................(b) PaulMulrennan 9 46
(Ruth Carr) *led: rdn along 3f out: hdd and cl up whn hmpd 2f out: sn drvn and wknd* **5/1**2
-320 **7** 3½ **Marino Prince (FR)**22 1615 6-8-11 **50**............................ TonyCulhane 6 37
(Paul Midgley) *sn rdn along: a towards rr* **6/1**3
5000 **8** 2½ **Realt Na Mara (IRE)**13 1866 8-8-12 **56**.............. JemmaMarshall(5) 11 37
(Hughie Morrison) *reminders s and sn rdn along: a towards rr* **10/1**
000- **9** ½ **Denison Flyer**271 5303 4-8-7 **49**................................. PaulPickard(3) 8 29
(Lawrence Mullaney) *sn rdn along: a towards rr* **20/1**
-000 **10** 6 **Helpmeronda**70 819 5-8-7 **46** oh1.................................(b) LiamJones 2 —
(Ian Williams) *chsd ldrs: rdn along over 3f out: sn wknd* **20/1**
-330 **11** 7 **I'Lldoit**23 1582 4-8-11 **57**.. DavidKenny(7) 4 —
(Michael Scudamore) *dwlt: a in rr* **12/1**
0600 **12** 14 **Ronnie Howe**13 1875 7-8-7 **46** oh1.................................(b) PaulQuinn 7 —
(Roy Bowring) *cl up: rdn 3f out: sn wknd* **80/1**
4/50 **13** 3 **Velvet Band**69 839 4-8-11 **50**.................................(v1) TonyHamilton 13 —
(Richard Whitaker) *chsd ldrs: rdn along 1/2-way: sn wknd* **40/1**

1m 44.0s (0.30) **Going Correction** +0.10s/f (Slow) **13** Ran SP% **119.3**
Speed ratings (Par 101): **102,101,100,99,98 94,90,88,87,81 74,60,57**
toteswingers:1&2:£7.50, 1&3:£6.20, 2&3:£8.80 CSF £39.55 CT £276.15 TOTE £7.40: £2.00, £2.10, £2.10; EX 14.40.
Owner Mrs F Denniff **Bred** Mrs Fiona Denniff **Trained** Hambleton, N Yorks

FOCUS
A competitive handicap, if a modest one, and the leaders went off far too fast. There was a chain reaction coming to the last 2f when On The Cusp hung away to his left, hampering Tomintoul Star, Positivity, Elusive Warrior and Hit The Switch. Nevertheless, the form looks straightforward if moderate.

2238 GOLF AND RACING AT SOUTHWELL H'CAP 6f (F)
4:55 (4:56) (Class 6) (0-60,60) 4-Y-O+ £1,706 (£503; £252) Stalls Low

Form RPR
2220 **1** **Clear Ice (IRE)**6 2048 4-9-4 **60**.............................(b) RobertLButler(3) 11 73
(Richard Guest) *trckd ldng pair: hdwy 3f out: led wl over 1f out: rdn out* **9/2**2
4000 **2** 1¼ **Charles Parnell (IRE)**15 1815 8-8-7 **53**........................ LucyKBarry(7) 1 62
(Simon Griffiths) *s.i.s and bhd: gd hdwy on inner 2f out: sn rdn and styd on wl fnl f* **16/1**
4541 **3** 1 **Itsthursdayalready**15 1818 4-9-7 **60**......................... TomMcLaughlin 9 66
(Mark Brisbourne) *midfield: hdwy 3f out: wd st: rdn to chse ldrs wl over 1f out: kpt on same pce* **9/2**2
5421 **4** 1 **Steel City Boy (IRE)**12 1912 8-9-3 **59**................................ BillyCray(3) 5 62
(Garry Woodward) *led: rdn along over 2f out: drvn and hdd wl over 1f out: one pce* **3/1**1
-001 **5** 2 **Miss Polly Plum**9 1989 4-8-12 **51** 6ex........................(p) AndreaAtzeni 10 47
(Chris Dwyer) *cl up: rdn along 3f out: drvn 2f out: grad wknd* **8/1**
0-06 **6** 4 **Northern Bolt**13 1861 6-9-2 **58**....................................(b) GaryBartley(3) 2 41
(Ian McInnes) *bhd and sn rdn along: sme late hdwy* **8/1**
21-6 **7** ½ **Accamelia**72 798 5-9-5 **58**.. PaulMulrennan 8 40
(Chris Fairhurst) *chsd ldrs: rdn along and outpcd on outer 1/2-way: sme late hdwy* **13/2**3
604- **8** 1¼ **Ridgeway Sapphire**318 3727 4-8-7 **46**...................(v) RichardThomas 3 24
(Mark Usher) *chsd ldrs: rdn along 1/2-way: drvn over 2f out and sn wknd* **16/1**
65-0 **9** 7 **Real Diamond**36 1307 5-9-1 **54**.. TomEaves 12 —
(Ollie Pears) *chsd ldrs on outer: rdn along wl over 2f out: grad wknd* **16/1**
000- **10** 20 **Piste**243 6189 5-8-9 **48**.. TonyHamilton 6 —
(Tina Jackson) *chsd ldrs: rdn along 1/2-way: sn wknd* **40/1**

1m 17.52s (1.02) **Going Correction** +0.10s/f (Slow) **10** Ran SP% **117.0**
Speed ratings (Par 101): **97,95,94,92,90 84,84,82,73,46**
toteswingers:1&2:£14.10, 1&3:£6.20, 2&3:£11.40 CSF £73.85 CT £351.40 TOTE £4.00: £1.20, £8.00, £2.00; EX 91.10.
Owner Future Racing (Notts) Limited **Bred** Mrs Noelle Walsh **Trained** Stainforth, S Yorks

FOCUS
A moderate sprint handicap and most of the action took place centre-to-stands' side in the home straight. The winner is rated back to his best with the three in the frame not far off recent form.
Northern Bolt Official explanation: jockey said gelding resented the kickback

2239 DINE IN THE PANTRY H'CAP 1m 3f (F)
5:25 (5:25) (Class 6) (0-60,60) 3-Y-O £1,706 (£503; £252) Stalls Low

Form RPR
0-02 **1** **Captain Bellamy (USA)**29 1502 3-9-2 **55**.................... TravisBlock 4 64+
(Hughie Morrison) *prom: rdn along and sltly outpcd 3f out: hdwy over 2f out: led over 1f out: kpt on* **11/4**2
-564 **2** ¾ **Revolutionary**104 424 3-9-2 **58**................................... SophieDoyle(3) 9 62
(Jamie Osborne) *cl up: led 3f out: rdn over 2f out: drvn and hdd over 1f out: one pce ins fnl f* **11/1**
003 **3** ¾ **Pizzetti (IRE)**107 378 3-9-5 **58**...................................... SebSanders 2 61
(Sir Mark Prescott Bt) *sn rdn along on inner to chse ldrs: rn in snatches: hrd rdn 3f out: drvn fnl 2f kpt on same pce* **5/2**1
6-35 **4** ½ **Goodmanyourself**9 1969 3-8-7 **46**.............................. MickyFenton 1 48
(Paul Midgley) *sn led: rdn along 4f out: hdd 3f out: drvn and kpt on same pce fnl 2f* **12/1**
-223 **5** 8 **Trojan Touch (USA)**29 1502 3-8-8 **47**.......................(b) AndreaAtzeni 5 35
(Chris Dwyer) *chsd ldrs: rdn along 4f out: drvn fr wl over 2f out and no imp* **7/1**3
0-04 **6** 9 **Market Maker (IRE)**9 1969 3-9-0 **53**........................ TonyHamilton 8 25
(Tim Easterby) *chsd ldrs: rdn along over 4f out: sn wknd* **18/1**
00-3 **7** 1¾ **Mayan Flight (IRE)**9 1969 3-8-12 **51**............................. TomEaves 10 19
(Richard Whitaker) *a in rr* **9/1**
0-04 **8** 11 **Karmarouge (IRE)**33 1413 3-8-7 **46**.............................(t) LeeNewman 3 —
(Brian Rothwell) *a in rr* **40/1**
-630 **9** 27 **Subramaniam**9 1972 3-9-7 **60**...................................... PaulMulrennan 7 —
(James Given) *a in rr: bhd and eased fnl 3f* **8/1**

000- **10** 2½ **Blade**222 6743 3-8-13 **55**.. RossAtkinson(3) 6 —
(Mark Brisbourne) *a in rr: rdn along 1/2-way: sn outpcd and bhd* **66/1**

2m 30.0s (2.00) **Going Correction** +0.10s/f (Slow) **10** Ran SP% **114.1**
Speed ratings (Par 97): **96,95,94,94,88 82,80,72,53,51**
toteswingers:1&2:£9.10, 1&3:£3.00, 2&3:£7.50 CSF £32.46 CT £83.63 TOTE £4.60: £1.10, £3.30, £1.40; EX 31.80.
Owner A C Pickford & G J Parrott **Bred** Brereton C Jones **Trained** East Ilsley, Berks
■ Stewards' Enquiry : Ross Atkinson three-day ban: used whip with excessive frequency (Jun 26-7)

FOCUS
A slow-motion finish with the front four finishing in a heap, but they pulled miles clear of the others. This looks very modest form and is not a race to rate too positively.
T/Plt: £29.10 to a £1 stake. Pool:£49,268.00 - 1,232.04 winning tickets T/Qpdt: £11.30 to a £1 stake Pool:£3,318.28 - 215.90 w. tckts JR 2240a (Foreign Racing) - See Raceform Int.

2140 BATH (L-H)
Friday, May 20

OFFICIAL GOING: Firm (good to firm in places; 9.0)
Wind: Brisk ahead Weather: Overcast

2241 EVENING POST MEDIAN AUCTION MAIDEN FILLIES' STKS 5f 161y
2:10 (2:10) (Class 6) 2-Y-O £1,813 (£539; £269; £134) Stalls Centre

Form RPR
1 **Betty Fontaine (IRE)** 2-8-11 0............................... MatthewDavies(3) 1 70+
(Mick Channon) *in rr but wl in tch: swtchd rt to outside over 1f out: qcknd to ld fnl 140yds: sn in command: easily* **14/1**3
2 **2** 1¾ **Toffee Tart**14 1846 2-8-11 0.. PatrickHills(3) 4 64
(J W Hills) *s.i.s: sn in tch: hdwy on outside fr 2f out: pushed along and chsd wnr fr jst ins fnl f: no imp and styd on same pce to chse wnr fnl 30yds* **2/13**1
06 **3** 1½ **Ida Inkley (IRE)**11 1946 2-9-0 0....................................... CathyGannon 5 59
(Jonathan Portman) *led: rdn 2f out: hdd fnl 140yds: wknd into 3rd fnl 30yds* **25/1**
66 **4** 13 **Bella Ponte**18 1765 2-9-0 0.. ChrisCatlin 3 16
(John Gallagher) *in tch: rdn and effrt to chse ldrs fr 2f out: wknd wl over 1f out* **40/1**
0 **5** 3½ **Purple Angel**18 1765 2-9-0 0.. DavidProbert 6 5
(Jonathan Portman) *s.i.s: sn pressing ldr and ev ch 2f out: wknd wl over 1f out* **28/1**
05 **6** 5 **Vieira Da Silva (IRE)**11 1957 2-9-0 0........................... SamHitchcott 2 —
(Mick Channon) *chsd ldrs: hd to one side fr over 2f out and sn wknd* **12/1**2

1m 13.37s (2.17) **Going Correction** +0.10s/f (Good) **6** Ran SP% **110.7**
Speed ratings (Par 88): **89,86,84,67,62 56**
toteswingers:1&2:£1.60, 2&3:£2.60, 1&3:£7.30 CSF £16.91 TOTE £11.70: £4.50, £1.02; EX 20.20.
Owner Billy Parish **Bred** Tony And Mary McKiernan **Trained** West Ilsley, Berks

FOCUS
Despite 5mm of rain since the meeting here four days earlier, the ground remained firm, good to firm in places. This moderate fillies' maiden looked to be a penalty kick for the favourite, but not only did those who backed her at prohibitive odds catch a chill, those who backed her in running also suffered financially. The form looks fluid.

NOTEBOOK
Betty Fontaine(IRE) cost just 800euros as a yearling, is very small, and doesn't have a particularly attractive pedigree, but she produced a nice turn of foot once switched to the wide outside here and there seemed no fluke about this. Whatever she achieves now, her owners have themselves a real bargain. (tchd 16-1)
Toffee Tart ran a blinder when touched off by a nose on her Ascot debut, despite getting loose beforehand, and the form has been boosted with the fifth horse going in since. This looked an ideal opportunity for her, but she wasn't best away and then raced keenly on the outside of the field. She still had every chance, but made hard work of getting the better of the leader once under pressure and, whilst she was doing so, the winner swept past them both. She hit 1.01 in running and her rider has now gone 273 days and 41 rides without a winner. She was reported to have raced green. Official explanation: jockey said filly ran very green (op 2-11, tchd 1-5 in places)
Ida Inkley(IRE) hinted at ability on her second start and tried to make all. She lost the advantage after faltering inside the last furlong, but was third-best on the day. Still, this has to be regarded as another step forward.

2242 WESTERN DAILY PRESS H'CAP 1m 5y
2:40 (2:40) (Class 5) (0-70,67) 4-Y-O+ £2,525 (£751; £375; £187) Stalls Low

Form RPR
00-0 **1** **Bold Cross (IRE)**7 2051 8-9-6 **66**.................................... CathyGannon 3 73
(Edward Bevan) *t.k.h in 4th tl hdwy fr 4f out to chse ldr 3f out: drvn to chal fr over 1f out: led last stride* **6/4**1
4350 **2** nse **Aviso (GER)**8 2027 7-8-10 **61**................................. MatthewCosham(5) 4 68
(David Evans) *led: 4 l clr over 3f out: jnd over 1f out but kpt on dourly to hold slt ld tl hdd last stride* **6/1**3
520- **3** ½ **Fire King**211 7037 5-8-12 **58**...(p) MartinLane 1 64
(Andrew Haynes) *in rr: hdwy 3f out: drvn to chse ldng duo on outside fr over 1f out: styd on but nvr quite gng pce to chal* **17/2**
2513 **4** 4½ **Sasheen**14 1867 4-9-7 **67**...(p) RobertHavlin 5 63
(Jeremy Gask) *chsd ldrs in 3rd tl wknd into 4th over 1f out and no ch after* **5/2**2
402- **5** ¾ **Fifty Cents**350 2714 7-9-2 **62**... FergusSweeney 6 56
(Milton Harris) *t.k.h: hld up in rr: stl plenty to do ins fnl 3f: hdwy over 1f out: styd on ins fnl f but nvr any ch* **6/1**3
4060 **6** ½ **Pytheas (USA)**14 1867 4-8-13 **64**.........................(tp) JemmaMarshall(5) 2 57
(Michael Attwater) *chsd ldr to 3f out: rdn sn after: wknd ins fnl 2f* **20/1**

1m 41.2s (0.40) **Going Correction** 0.0s/f (Good) **6** Ran SP% **112.4**
Speed ratings (Par 103): **98,97,97,92,92 91**
toteswingers:1&2:£1.80, 2&3:£10.10, 1&3:£2.70 CSF £11.12 TOTE £2.30: £1.60, £2.80; EX 11.00.
Owner E G Bevan **Bred** M Hosokawa **Trained** Ullingswick, H'fords

FOCUS
An ordinary handicap, though the pace looked solid enough, and it provided a stirring finish. The form looks relatively sound.

2243 BRISTOL OBSERVER H'CAP 1m 5y
3:10 (3:10) (Class 6) (0-60,60) 3-Y-O £1,813 (£539; £269; £134) Stalls Low

Form RPR
666- **1** **Henrys Air**169 7666 3-8-13 **52**.................................... RobbieFitzpatrick 7 57
(David Bridgwater) *in tch: hdwy 3f out: led ins fnl 2f: sn drvn: styd on u.p thrght ins fnl f* **66/1**

05-0 **2** *nk* **Mister Ben Vereen**[23] 1624 3-9-7 **60**.............................. CathyGannon 3 67+
(Eve Johnson Houghton) *in tch: trcking ldrs but continually denied clr run fr over 2f out tl drvn and qcknd between horses ins fnl f: styd on wl clsng stages but nt rcvr* **12/1**

0-04 **3** *1 ¼* **Arctic Reach**[9] 1999 3-8-8 **47**..................................(p) FrankieMcDonald 8 48
(Brendan Powell) *chsd ldrs: awkward bnd ins fnl 5f: rdn fr over 3f out: stl chsng ldrs whn n.m.r and edgd lft ins fnl f: and one pce: styd on again to take 3rd clsng stages* **11/1**

-610 **4** *1 ¾* **Fire Crystal**[6] 2119 3-9-1 **57**.................................. MatthewDavies(3) 6 54+
(Mick Channon) *in tch: swtchd rt to outside then nt clr run over 2f out: pressed ldrs 1f out: wknd fnl 120yds* **11/4**[1]

4005 **5** *1* **Bedibyes**[24] 1579 3-8-10 **56**.................................. IanBurns(7) 9 51
(Richard Mitchell) *in rr: hdwy and swtchd rt to outside fr 3f out: chsd ldrs fr 2f out: wknd ins fnl f* **10/1**[3]

0-01 **6** *1 ½* **Cadmium Loch**[11] 1952 3-9-6 **59** 6ex.......................... RussKennemore 2 50
(Reg Hollinshead) *chsd ldrs on ins thrght: rdn over 2f out: wknd ins fnl f* **11/2**[2]

3-33 **7** *1* **Miss Firefox**[25] 1566 3-9-4 **57**.................................. SamHitchcott 4 46
(Nicky Vaughan) *led tl hdd ins fnl 2f: wknd 1f out* **11/4**[1]

00-0 **8** *1 ¼* **No Refraction (IRE)**[23] 1607 3-8-7 **46** oh1.................... DavidProbert 1 32
(Mark Usher) *in tch: hdwy 3f out: wknd ins fnl 2f* **11/1**

00-0 **9** *1 ¾* **Maxiyow (IRE)**[3] 2172 3-8-7 **46** oh1.............................. NeilChalmers 13 28
(Bryn Palling) *unruly stalls: in rr: swtchd rt then hung rt fr 2f out: sme prog ins fnl f* **66/1**

0550 **10** *1 ½* **Twilight Express (IRE)**[37] 1312 3-8-7 **46** oh1................ LiamKeniry 10 25
(Emma Lavelle) *chsd ldrs: awkward bnd ins fnl 5f: hung lft: n.m.r and wknd 2f out* **12/1**

250- **11** *7* **Kilk**[242] 6248 3-9-2 **55**.................................. FergusSweeney 11 17
(Tony Newcombe) *s.i.s: a in rr* **18/1**

1m 42.14s (1.34) **Going Correction** 0.0s/f (Good) 11 Ran SP% **118.1**
Speed ratings (Par 97): **93,92,91,89,88 87,86,84,83,81 74**
toteswingers:1&2:£48.30, 2&3:£11.10, 1&3:£48.30 CSF £728.07 CT £9077.98 TOTE £62.30: £10.40, £3.60, £3.50; EX 535.10.
Owner Alan A Wright **Bred** Miss J Hunt **Trained** Icomb, Gloucs

FOCUS
A poor handicap with only two of these having tasted success before and a few didn't take the home bend at all well. The third is the best guide to the form while the runner-up was unlucky and can be rated the winner.
Miss Firefox Official explanation: jockey said filly hung right-handed

2244 EVENING POST H'CAP 5f 161y
3:40 (3:40) (Class 4) (0-85,83) 4-Y-0+ **£4,533** (£1,348; £674; £336) **Stalls** Centre

Form RPR

3213 **1** **Collect Art (IRE)**[6] 2095 4-8-8 **70**.................................. MartinLane 1 78+
(Andrew Haynes) *trckd ldr: drvn to ld fr ins fnl 2f: pushed along and in command fnl 120yds* **5/4**[1]

4-02 **2** *1* **Flowing Cape (IRE)**[21] 1656 6-9-7 **83**.............................. ChrisCatlin 6 88
(Reg Hollinshead) *in rr but in tch: hdwy on outside over 2f out: styd on to dispute 2nd fnl f and jst hld that position cl home but nvr any imp on wnr* **9/2**[3]

1202 **3** *hd* **Ebraam (USA)**[25] 1562 8-8-12 **74**.............................. DavidProbert 5 78
(Ronald Harris) *in rr: rdn and hdwy over 1f out but nt clr run: squeezed between horses u.p ins fnl f to press for 2nd clsng stages but no imp on wnr* **7/2**[2]

-506 **4** *nse* **Brandywell Boy (IRE)**[7] 2069 8-8-4 **69** oh1...................... BillyCray(3) 7 73
(Dominic Ffrench Davis) *chsd ldrs on outside: ev ch fr 2f out: disp 2nd u.p fnl f and kpt on cl home but nvr gng pce of wnr* **22/1**

1-01 **5** *½* **Victorian Bounty**[29] 1506 6-9-3 **82**.............................. JohnFahy(3) 4 84
(Stef Higgins) *chsd ldrs: ev ch 2f out: disp 2nd ins fnl f but nvr any ch w wnr: one pce clsng stages* **11/1**

10-0 **6** *½* **Night Affair**[14] 1864 5-8-13 **75**.................................. CathyGannon 2 76
(David Arbuthnot) *trckd ldrs: drvn to dispute 2nd ins fnl f: nvr gng pce of wnr and fdd clsng stages* **10/1**

6045 **7** *6* **Atlantic Beach**[13] 1899 6-8-9 **71**..................................(p) LiamKeniry 3 52
(Milton Bradley) *led tl hdd ins fnl 2f: wknd appr fnl f* **16/1**

1m 11.04s (-0.16) **Going Correction** +0.10s/f (Good) 7 Ran SP% **112.5**
Speed ratings (Par 105): **105,103,103,103,102 102,94**
toteswingers:1&2:£1.10, 2&3:£1.80, 1&3:£1.70 CSF £6.89 TOTE £2.50: £1.50, £2.70; EX 9.00.
Owner Athos Racing **Bred** Pier House Stud **Trained** Limpley Stoke, Bath

FOCUS
A decent sprint handicap and, although the favourite did it well, there was little covering the next five home. The form makes sense with the third to his latest turf mark.

2245 D.J.M. SOLICITORS H'CAP 1m 2f 46y
4:10 (4:11) (Class 5) (0-70,69) 4-Y-0+ **£2,525** (£751; £375; £187) **Stalls** Low

Form RPR

310- **1** **Halyard (IRE)**[240] 6290 4-9-4 **69**..................................(v) JohnFahy(3) 4 76
(Walter Swinburn) *trckd ldrs: hdwy to chse ldr over 1f out: drvn to ld jst ins fnl f: styd on wl clsng stages* **7/2**[3]

-212 **2** *1* **Timocracy**[11] 1936 6-9-5 **67**.................................. SamHitchcott 3 72
(Andrew Haynes) *chsd ldr: hrd drvn fr 4f out: led u.p 2f out: hdd jst ins fnl f: no ex clsng stages* **5/4**[1]

2653 **3** *1 ½* **Diddums**[8] 2027 5-8-0 **55**.................................. KatiaScallan(7) 2 57
(Alastair Lidderdale) *s.i.s: racd in 4th tl plld hrd and wnt 3rd 5f out: outpcd into 4th over 2f out: styd on again fnl f to take one pce in 3rd clsng stages* **12/1**

1221 **4** *1 ½* **Duneen Dream (USA)**[31] 1454 6-8-11 **59**.......................... DavidProbert 5 58
(Nikki Evans) *led: drvn and hdd 2f out: hrd rdn and ev ch 1f out: wknd ins fnl f* **2/1**[2]

2m 10.16s (-0.84) **Going Correction** 0.0s/f (Good) 4 Ran SP% **107.7**
Speed ratings (Par 103): **103,102,101,99**
CSF £8.29 TOTE £6.50; EX 8.20.
Owner Hall Of Fame Partnership **Bred** Mount Coote Stud And M H Dixon **Trained** Aldbury, Herts

FOCUS
A modest handicap, run at an ordinary pace and the runner-up looks a fair guide to the level.

2246 DIGIBET.COM H'CAP 1m 3f 144y
4:40 (4:40) (Class 6) (0-60,63) 4-Y-0+ **£1,878** (£558; £279; £139) **Stalls** Low

Form RPR

0040 **1** **Zagarock**[18] 1750 4-8-9 **45**.................................. NeilChalmers 8 56
(Bryn Palling) *mde all: drvn along 7f out: jnd and hrd drvn over 3f out tl asserted fr 2f out: kpt on wl ins fnl f* **6/1**[3]

0-50 **2** *3* **Bussell Along (IRE)**[18] 1750 5-8-2 **45**.......................... RachealKneller(7) 7 50
(Pam Ford) *s.i.s: hld up in rr tl hdwy over 2f out: styd on to chse wnr fnl 150yds but nvr any ch* **14/1**

-331 **3** *3 ¼* **Annelko**[15] 1833 4-9-4 **54**.................................. MartinLane 4 54
(Andrew Haynes) *chsd wnr: hrd drvn fr 6f out: chal over 3f out and upsides tl shkn off fr 2f out: wknd over 1f out: lost 2nd fnl 150yds* **7/4**[2]

-041 **4** *½* **Penang Cinta**[3] 2170 8-9-10 **63** 6ex.......................... RichardEvans(3) 5 62
(David Evans) *chsd ldrs in 3rd: rdn 3f out and no ch w ldrs after but kpt on again clsng stages* **11/8**[1]

006- **5** *18* **Telescopic**[247] 6094 4-8-9 **45**.................................. FrankieMcDonald 1 13
(James Frost) *chsd ldrs tl hung rt and awkward bnd ins fnl 5f: no ch after* **40/1**

060- **6** *nk* **Kargarann (IRE)**[175] 7579 4-8-12 **48**.......................... SamHitchcott 2 16
(Seamus Durack) *s.i.s: sn rcvrd: wknd 4f out* **20/1**

520- **7** *55* **Flamestone**[401] 1305 7-8-6 **49**.................................. DavidKenny(7) 3 —
(Andrew Price) *in rr: sn rdn and nvr travelling: lost tch fr 4f out* **16/1**

2m 31.19s (0.59) **Going Correction** 0.0s/f (Good) 7 Ran SP% **112.5**
Speed ratings (Par 101): **98,96,93,93,81 81,44**
toteswingers:1&2:£6.10, 2&3:£4.30, 1&3:£1.80 CSF £77.65 CT £205.02 TOTE £5.40: £2.20, £5.70; EX 68.10.
Owner Flying Eight Partnership **Bred** Aiden Murphy **Trained** Tredodridge, Vale Of Glamorgan

FOCUS
A moderate handicap, but they went a good pace and finished spread out all over Lansdown Hill. A persoanl best from the winner but the form is not convincing.
T/Plt: £2,037.80 to a £1 stake. Pool of £42,013.10 - 15.05 winning tickets. T/Qpdt: £1,820.70 to a £1 stake. Pool of £3,444.61 - 1.40 winning tickets. ST

1791 CATTERICK (L-H)
Friday, May 20

OFFICIAL GOING: Good to firm (8.7)
Wind: Breezy, half against Weather: Sunny

2247 SUPPORT THE HOUSE THAT JACK BUILT APPRENTICE H'CAP 5f
6:20 (6:20) (Class 6) (0-60,60) 4-Y-0+ **£1,706** (£503; £252) **Stalls** Low

Form RPR

0443 **1** **Ridley Didley (IRE)**[11] 1940 6-9-4 **60**..........................(p) NeilFarley(3) 1 69
(Noel Wilson) *t.k.h early: mde all: pushed along over 1f out: hld on wl fnl f* **4/1**[2]

0041 **2** *½* **Boy The Bell**[16] 1815 4-9-6 **59**.................................. DaleSwift 4 66
(Brian Ellison) *dwlt: sn prom: rdn along and outpcd 1/2-way: rallied over 1f out: chsd wnr ins fnl f: r.o* **2/1**[1]

2160 **3** *1* **Spirit Of Coniston**[14] 1856 8-8-12 **56**.......................... DavidSimmonson(5) 5 59
(Paul Midgley) *cl up: rdn 1/2-way: kpt on same pce ins fnl f* **14/1**

6-50 **4** *1 ¾* **Tournedos (IRE)**[14] 1856 9-8-10 **54**..........................(b) LauraBarry(5) 2 51
(Ruth Carr) *hld up in tch: effrt over 1f out: kpt on ins fnl f* **11/1**

0010 **5** *¾* **Kyzer Chief**[5] 2126 6-9-2 **60**.................................. ShaneBKelly(5) 7 54
(Ron Barr) *cl up: rdn along 1/2-way: kpt on same pce fnl f* **7/1**[3]

0-33 **6** *2 ½* **Choc'A'Moca (IRE)**[30] 1493 4-9-0 **56**..........................(v) LMcNiff(3) 12 41
(Paul Midgley) *prom: outpcd 1/2-way: no imp fr over 1f out* **15/2**

6-60 **7** *shd* **Call The Law (IRE)**[10] 1989 5-8-3 **49**.......................... ChristyMews(7) 10 34
(Pam Sly) *bhd: pushed along 1/2-way: hdwy fnl f: nvr rchd ldrs* **20/1**

200- **8** *1* **Red River Boy**[244] 6206 6-8-10 **52**.............................. AdamCarter(3) 3 33
(Chris Fairhurst) *towards rr: rdn after 2f: no imp fnl 2f* **7/1**[3]

0/0- **9** *2 ¼* **Blue Rum (IRE)**[215] 6966 4-8-6 **50**.............................. LukeStrong(5) 11 23
(Alan Kirtley) *racd wd in rr: sn outpcd: nvr on terms* **33/1**

-000 **10** *3 ½* **Edge End**[14] 1875 7-8-3 **47** oh1 ow1.......................... MatthewLawson(5) 9 —
(Lisa Williamson) *s.i.s: bhd and sn drvn along: no ch fr 1/2-way* **100/1**

59.20 secs (-0.60) **Going Correction** -0.025s/f (Good) 10 Ran SP% **113.8**
Speed ratings (Par 101): **103,102,100,97,96 92,92,90,87,81**
toteswingers:1&2:£2.40, 2&3:£8.40, 1&3:£13.40 CSF £11.83 CT £98.51 TOTE £4.10: £1.20, £1.60, £3.40; EX 15.90.
Owner Frank Tobin & Nicola Wilson **Bred** Peter Molony **Trained** Sandhutton, N Yorks
■ Stewards' Enquiry : Matthew Lawson caution: used whip down shoulder in the forehand.

FOCUS
A low-grade apprentice handicap and the pace was fast and furious. The winner is rated to his reappearance form with the second close to his best.

2248 BRITISH STALLION STUDS SUPPORTING BRITISH RACING EBF MAIDEN FILLIES' STKS 5f
6:50 (6:51) (Class 5) 2-Y-O **£3,207** (£947; £473) **Stalls** Low

Form RPR

1 **On The Dark Side (IRE)** 2-9-0 0.................................. PhillipMakin 7 67+
(Kevin Ryan) *cl up gng wl: led over 1f out: rdn and kpt on fnl f: jst hld on* **15/8**[1]

2 *hd* **Slenningford** 2-9-0 0.................................. PaulMulrennan 2 63
(Ollie Pears) *led to over 1f out: ev ch and kpt on fnl f: jst hld* **6/1**[3]

03 **3** *nk* **Economic Crisis (IRE)**[11] 1957 2-9-0 0.......................... FrannyNorton 4 62
(Alan Berry) *prom: rdn 1/2-way: hdwy over 1f out: kpt on wl fnl f: jst hld* **10/1**

4 *3* **Arachis Bow** 2-8-11 0.................................. JamesSullivan(3) 1 51+
(Michael Easterby) *rn green and sn outpcd: hdwy over 1f out: shkn up and kpt on fnl f: nvr nrr* **12/1**

52 **5** *3 ½* **Marie's Fantasy**[24] 1590 2-9-0 0.............................. PaulHanagan 6 39
(Gay Kelleway) *trckd ldrs: edgd lft 1/2-way: sn drvn and outpcd: btn fnl f* **2/1**[2]

00 **6** *½* **Headstight (IRE)**[6] 2113 2-9-0 0.............................. PJMcDonald 3 37
(Paul Midgley) *w ldr: rdn 1/2-way: wknd fnl f* **8/1**

7 *4* **Hawaiian Freeze** 2-9-0 0.................................. AndrewMullen 5 22
(Richard Ford) *dwlt: bhd and a outpcd* **33/1**

61.14 secs (1.34) **Going Correction** -0.025s/f (Good) 7 Ran SP% **113.2**
Speed ratings (Par 90): **88,87,87,82,76 76,69**
toteswingers:1&2:£2.40, 2&3:£8.40, 1&3:£13.40 CSF £13.41 TOTE £2.10: £1.10, £3.30; EX 15.80.
Owner Mrs Angie Bailey **Bred** Thomas Foy **Trained** Hambleton, N Yorks

FOCUS
A maiden juvenile fillies' race and three almost in a line at the finish. The winner can do better with the third rated an improver over her previous efforts.

NOTEBOOK
On The Dark Side(IRE), a newcomer from a powerful stable with a good line to juvenile form, had the outside draw. She travelled much the best in the field but in the end had to be asked some serious questions. She will be much better suited by a step up to six and in time could prove useful. (op 9-4)
Slenningford, another newcomer, certainly knew her job and after taking the winner and one other along towards the middle she went down fighting. She looks a ready-made winner of a similar event. (op 8-1)
Economic Crisis(IRE), slowly away on her first two starts, proved difficult to load. Switched to race against the far-side rail at halfway she seemed to show much improved form but may have been flattered by her track position. (tchd 11-1)

Arachis Bow, from a speedy family this stable knows so well, stayed on in good style after getting outpaced. She is not very big but is sure to have learnt plenty. (op 16-1 tchd 18-1)
Marie's Fantasy, having her third start, struggled to keep up and was switched to the far rail at halfway. She has not progressed from her sound first run. Official explanation: jockey said filly never travelled (op 15-8 tchd 13-8)
Headstight(IRE) is all pace, but on her third start she again showed a tendency to hang left before dropping out in the final furlong. She may have to descend to claimers or sellers. (op 7-1 tchd 13-2)

2249 XTREMEADVENTURESUK.COM (S) STKS — 7f
7:20 (7:21) (Class 6) 3-4-Y-O — £1,706 (£503; £252) Stalls Centre

Form — RPR
-445 1 **Sinadinou**[41] 1246 3-8-8 65 ... AndrewMullen 4 — 57
(David Nicholls) *trckd ldrs: rdn to ld over 1f out: edgd rt ins fnl f: hld on wl* 5/2[1]
52-0 2 ½ **Baby Driver**[11] 1944 3-8-8 61 ... PaulMulrennan 6 — 55
(Howard Johnson) *cl up: led 2f out to over 1f out: rallied fnl f: hld nr fin* 9/1
-005 3 2 **Anddante (IRE)**[17] 1802 3-8-9 59 ow1 ...(e[1]) GrahamGibbons 8 — 51
(Tim Easterby) *trckd ldrs: hdwy to chal 2f out: hung lft: kpt on same pce fnl f* 10/3[2]
4500 4 1 **Kate Skate**[18] 1770 4-8-13 60 ... NatashaEaton(7) 7 — 52
(Gay Kelleway) *hld up: hdwy on ins whn nt clr run and swtchd rt over 1f out: r.o fnl f: nrst fin* 20/1
-054 5 ¾ **Isle Of Ellis (IRE)**[11] 1943 4-8-12 38 ...(v) ShaneBKelly(7) 1 — 49?
(Ron Barr) *midfield on ins: effrt over 2f out: no imp over 1f out* 33/1
3546 6 hd **Neytiri**[7] 2047 3-7-10 50 ...(p) KristinStubbs(7) 2 — 40
(Linda Stubbs) *hld up: hdwy 2f out: no imp ins fnl f* 12/1
-002 7 1¾ **Uddy Mac**[32] 1439 4-9-0 52 ...(b) PaulHanagan 11 — 39
(Neville Bycroft) *midfield on outside: rdn over 2f out: hdwy over 1f out: no imp fnl f* 8/1
6433 8 1¼ **Ever Roses**[31] 1465 3-8-3 51 ...(v) FrannyNorton 9 — 32
(Paul Midgley) *prom: effrt and drvn over 2f out: wknd fnl f* 12/1
0 9 6 **Serenata Mia**[49] 1076 4-8-11 0 ... SeanLevey(3) 5 — 19
(Michael Smith) *s.i.s: bhd: pushed along 1/2-way: nvr on terms* 50/1
00-5 10 ½ **Kalahari Desert (IRE)**[30] 1501 4-9-0 48 ... DanielleMcCreery(5) 10 — 23
(Richard Whitaker) *stmbld and nrly uns rdr s: bhd: rdn 3f out: nvr on terms* 28/1
00 11 2½ **Hey Up There (IRE)**[36] 1323 3-8-0 0 ... JamesSullivan(3) 12 — —
(Ruth Carr) *bhd: pushed along and rn wd bnd ent st: nvr on terms* 100/1
666- 12 2 **Saxby (IRE)**[275] 5211 4-9-5 59 ... SilvestreDeSousa 3 — —
(Geoffrey Harker) *led tl hdd over 2f out: wknd over 1f out: eased whn no ch fnl f* 11/2[3]

1m 26.86s (-0.14) **Going Correction** -0.15s/f (Firm)
WFA 3 from 4yo 11lb — 12 Ran SP% 117.6
Speed ratings (Par 101): **94,93,91,90,89 88,86,85,78,78 75,72**
toteswingers:1&2:£7.20, 2&3:£6.10, 1&3:£2.70 CSF £24.40 TOTE £3.50: £1.90, £3.10, £2.90; EX 37.50.There was no bid for the winner.
Owner Middleham Park Racing XLVII **Bred** Mickley Stud & Mrs M Landers **Trained** Sessay, N Yorks

FOCUS
Plenty of no hopers in this selling race and the form is rated negatively, with the proximity of the fifth making the form look dubious.
Kalahari Desert(IRE) Official explanation: jockey said gelding stumbled on leaving stalls
Saxby(IRE) Official explanation: jockey said gelding had no more to give

2250 DEREK JONES 60TH BIRTHDAY H'CAP — 5f
7:50 (7:50) (Class 4) (0-80,79) 3-Y-O+ — £4,209 (£1,252; £625; £312) Stalls Low

Form — RPR
5-00 1 **Bronze Beau**[20] 1698 4-9-6 76 ...(t) JamesSullivan(3) 6 — 88
(Linda Stubbs) *mde all: shkn up and qcknd clr fnl f: readily* 8/1
6160 2 2¾ **Taurus Twins**[18] 1771 5-9-10 77 ...(b) SilvestreDeSousa 9 — 79
(Richard Price) *chsd ldrs: drvn 1/2-way: kpt on fnl f: nt pce of wnr* 5/1[2]
-020 3 nk **Select Committee**[13] 1899 6-9-2 76 ...(v) ShaneBKelly(7) 2 — 77
(John Quinn) *trckd ldrs: effrt over 1f out: kpt on same pce fnl f* 7/1[3]
0066 4 ¾ **Ryedane (IRE)**[17] 1793 9-8-13 66 ...(b) PaulMulrennan 4 — 64
(Tim Easterby) *dwlt: bhd and outpcd: hdwy over 1f out: nvr able to chal* 7/1[3]
2456 5 2¼ **Green Manalishi**[11] 1955 10-9-7 79 ...(tp) ChrisDCogan(5) 8 — 69
(Kevin Ryan) *hld up in tch: effrt over 1f out: no imp* 9/1
00-0 6 2½ **Mr Wolf**[17] 1793 10-9-8 75 ...(p) PaulHanagan 1 — 56
(John Quinn) *cl up tl rdn and wknd over 1f out* 5/1[2]
4032 7 ½ **Desert Strike**[7] 2069 5-9-5 72 ...(p) RobertWinston 7 — 51
(Alan McCabe) *trckd ldrs: drvn 1/2-way: wknd over 1f out* 2/1[1]
6000 8 2¾ **Insolenceofoffice (IRE)**[7] 2074 3-8-8 72 ...(p) SeanLevey(3) 3 — 42
(Andrew Crook) *bhd and outpcd: struggling fr 1/2-way* 33/1

58.93 secs (-0.87) **Going Correction** -0.025s/f (Good)
WFA 3 from 4yo+ 8lb — 8 Ran SP% 115.7
Speed ratings (Par 105): **105,100,100,98,95 91,90,86**
toteswingers:1&2:£5.80, 2&3:£7.30, 1&3:£8.90 CSF £48.11 CT £298.22 TOTE £11.00: £2.60, £2.00, £2.00; EX 62.50.
Owner D Arundale **Bred** Meon Valley Stud **Trained** Norton, N Yorks

FOCUS
A competitive 5f dash but in the end very much a one-horse race. The winner is progressive and with the runner-up helps set the level.
Desert Strike Official explanation: jockey said gelding was unsuited by the track

2251 LESLIE PETCH H'CAP — 1m 3f 214y
8:20 (8:24) (Class 5) (0-75,74) 3-Y-O+ — £2,072 (£616; £308; £153) Stalls Low

Form — RPR
00-4 1 **King Kurt (IRE)**[27] 1526 3-7-13 62 ... SilvestreDeSousa 8 — 71+
(Kevin Ryan) *trckd ldr: led over 2f out: drvn and hung rt over 1f out: styd on wl fnl f* 2/1[1]
-601 2 1¼ **Houston Dynimo (IRE)**[17] 1798 6-9-7 67 ... PhillipMakin 2 — 74
(Nicky Richards) *trckd ldrs: hdwy and ev ch over 2f out: sn rdn: edgd rt over 1f out: kpt on same pce fnl f* 9/2[3]
262- 3 ½ **Maoi Chinn Tire (IRE)**[13] 6078 4-9-7 67 ... StephenCraine 4 — 73
(Jennie Candlish) *hld up in tch: hdwy to chse ldrs whn carried sltly rt over 1f out: rdn and kpt on same pce fnl f* 13/2
4-35 4 1 **Patavium (IRE)**[21] 1651 8-9-6 69 ... JamesSullivan(3) 5 — 74
(Edwin Tuer) *prom: hdwy and ev ch over 2f out: nt qckn fnl f* 14/1
56-1 5 8 **Hel's Angel (IRE)**[17] 1792 5-10-0 74 ... PaulHanagan 7 — 66
(Ann Duffield) *led to over 2f out: rdn and wknd over 1f out* 9/4[2]
-030 6 6 **Viewing**[23] 1622 4-9-13 73 ... PaulMulrennan 6 — 55
(James Given) *reluctant to enter stalls: hld up in tch: flashed tail repeatedly: hdwy over 2f out: wknd over 1f out* 28/1
-005 7 18 **Dean Iarracht (IRE)**[17] 1798 5-9-1 61 oh1 ...(v) FrannyNorton 3 — —
(Tracy Waggott) *missed break: hld up: rdn after 4f: lost tch fr 4f out* 12/1

2m 36.01s (-2.89) **Going Correction** -0.15s/f (Firm)
WFA 3 from 4yo+ 17lb — 7 Ran SP% 113.4
Speed ratings (Par 103): **103,102,101,101,95 91,79**
toteswingers:1&2:£3.00, 2&3:£4.40, 1&3:£3.00 CSF £11.28 CT £47.69 TOTE £2.30: £1.10, £3.50; EX 16.00.
Owner Matthew Taylor **Bred** Hong Kong Breeders Club **Trained** Hambleton, N Yorks
■ Stewards' Enquiry : Phillip Makin one-day ban: careless riding (Jun 6)
Silvestre De Sousa two-day ban: careless riding (Jun 6-7)

FOCUS
A strong pace and the first four ended up racing towards the stands' side rail. The form is ordinary rated around the second and fourth.
Viewing Official explanation: vet said filly was found to be in season

2252 ELLERY HILL RATING RELATED MAIDEN STKS — 7f
8:50 (8:52) (Class 6) 3-Y-O+ — £1,706 (£503; £252) Stalls Centre

Form — RPR
002- 1 **Mont Ras (IRE)**[323] 3587 4-9-11 62 ... SilvestreDeSousa 9 — 77
(David O'Meara) *prom: shkn up to ld over 1f out: rdn and edgd lft: styd on strly fnl f* 11/4[2]
3304 2 3 **Philharmonic Hall**[6] 2119 3-9-0 65 ...(v[1]) PaulHanagan 11 — 65
(Richard Fahey) *hld up: hdwy to chse wnr appr fnl f: kpt on: no imp* 5/2[1]
0-04 3 3 **Deep Applause**[17] 1801 3-8-11 61 ... SeanLevey(3) 4 — 57
(Michael Dods) *hld up in tch: rdn over 2f out: no imp over 1f out* 6/1
00-3 4 ¾ **Stilettoesinthemud (IRE)**[17] 1795 3-8-11 60 ... PaulMulrennan 3 — 52
(James Given) *cl up: rdn and ev ch over 2f out: kpt on same pce fr over 1f out* 20/1
00-5 5 ½ **Millies Folly**[18] 1749 3-8-11 62 ... BarryMcHugh 7 — 51
(Paul Midgley) *led tl rdn and hdd over 1f out: wknd ins fnl f* 8/1
30-3 6 2½ **Consistant**[50] 1064 3-9-0 65 ... GrahamGibbons 2 — 47
(Brian Baugh) *prom: rdn over 2f out: edgd lft and wknd over 1f out* 5/1[3]
600- 7 hd **Safari Guide**[233] 6462 5-9-6 52 ... DaleSwift(5) 1 — 50
(Kevin M Prendergast) *hld up: rdn over 2f out: wknd over 1f out* 20/1
5540 8 2 **Rational Act (IRE)**[4] 2163 3-8-11 57 ...(b[1]) JamesSullivan(3) 6 — 41
(Tim Easterby) *t.k.h: in tch: effrt on outside over 2f out: edgd lft and wknd appr fnl f* 12/1
360- 9 25 **Brian Sprout**[239] 6309 3-9-0 57 ... PhillipMakin 10 — —
(John Weymes) *plld hrd: bhd: lost tch after 3f: t.o* 50/1

1m 26.7s (-0.30) **Going Correction** -0.15s/f (Firm)
WFA 3 from 4yo+ 11lb — 9 Ran SP% 116.5
Speed ratings (Par 101): **95,91,88,87,86 83,83,81,52**
toteswingers:1&2:£2.20, 2&3:£3.20, 1&3:£4.20 CSF £9.90 TOTE £3.20: £1.10, £2.20, £2.20; EX 8.00.
Owner Colne Valley Racing **Bred** Patrick M Ryan **Trained** Nawton, N Yorks

FOCUS
A weak 0-65 rating related maiden race with just 3lb between the first five home on official figures. The placed horses set the level of the form.
T/Plt: £94.90 to a £1 stake. Pool of £42,850.09 - 329.48 winning tickets T/Qpdt: £43.50 to a £1 stake. Pool £3,200.56 - 54.40 winning tickets RY

2213 HAYDOCK (L-H)
Friday, May 20

OFFICIAL GOING: Good (7.2)
All races on outer home straight and distances on round course increased by 5yds.
Wind: against Weather: Overcast

2253 THE SCISSOR SISTERS LIVE ON 16TH JULY H'CAP — 1m 2f 95y
2:30 (2:30) (Class 5) (0-75,75) 3-Y-O — £2,590 (£770; £385; £192) Stalls Centre

Form — RPR
00-3 1 **Grumeti**[20] 1683 3-8-13 67 ... JamieSpencer 6 — 78+
(Michael Bell) *hld up: hdwy and swtchd lft over 2f out: sn rdn: led 1f out: sn edgd lft: r.o: a doing enough towards fin* 9/4[1]
-330 2 ¾ **The Bells O Peover**[36] 1339 3-9-4 72 ... SilvestreDeSousa 9 — 82
(Mark Johnston) *in rr: niggled along 7f out: nt travelling wl after: hdwy u.p over 2f out: hung lft whn proging ins fnl f: wnt 2nd towards fin: styd on wl* 9/1
-220 3 1 **Standout**[11] 1951 3-9-4 72 ... RichardHughes 7 — 80
(Richard Hannon) *midfield: hdwy 3f out: trckd ldr over 2f out: effrt whn n.m.r and bmpd over 1f out: sn swtchd lft and chalng: nt qckn fnl 50yds* 8/1[3]
331- 4 1¼ **Tenby Lady (USA)**[216] 6936 3-9-5 73 ... SebSanders 1 — 78+
(Sir Mark Prescott Bt) *broke wl: chsd ldr: led over 2f out: rdn and hdd 1f out: sn edgd lft: no ex fnl 75yds* 10/1
01- 5 6 **Man Of God (IRE)**[246] 6128 3-9-6 74 ... WilliamBuick 11 — 67
(John Gosden) *s.i.s: in rr: niggled along 4f out: styd on u.p over 1f out: nvr able to threaten ldrs* 3/1[2]
6-1 6 nk **Piave (IRE)**[25] 1559 3-9-4 75 ... AshleyHamblett(3) 5 — 67
(Peter Chapple-Hyam) *midfield: pushed along 3f out: outpcd over 2f out: kpt on fnl f: no imp on ldrs* 33/1
20-3 7 1¾ **Mia Madonna**[13] 1915 3-9-4 72 ... MartinDwyer 8 — 61
(Brian Meehan) *hld up: rdn and hdwy into midfield over 3f out: no imp on ldrs: one pce ins fnl f: eased whn no imp fnl 100yds* 20/1
300 8 3½ **Strewth (IRE)**[34] 1409 3-8-13 67 ... SteveDrowne 10 — 49
(John Best) *racd keenly: trckd ldrs tl rdn and wknd 2f out* 33/1
0-60 9 1¼ **Atlas Shrugged (IRE)**[34] 1407 3-9-0 68 ...(b[1]) LukeMorris 12 — 47
(Clive Cox) *sn led: rdn and hdd over 2f out: wknd over 1f out* 16/1
532 10 14 **Enriching (USA)**[62] 909 3-9-3 71 ... DaneO'Neill 4 — 22
(David Elsworth) *in tch: rdn and wknd over 2f out* 25/1
20-1 11 6 **Pandoro De Lago (IRE)**[17] 1799 3-9-7 75 ... PaulHanagan 3 — 14
(Richard Fahey) *led early: racd keenly: chsd ldrs: effrt over 2f out: wknd over 1f out: eased whn btn ins fnl f* 9/1

2m 13.73s (-2.27) **Going Correction** -0.25s/f (Firm) — 11 Ran SP% 116.3
Speed ratings (Par 99): **99,98,97,96,91 91,90,87,86,75 70**
CSF £21.88 CT £136.46 TOTE £2.80: £1.20, £3.00, £2.30; EX 20.00.
Owner Thurloe Thoroughbred XXVIII **Bred** Catridge Farm Stud Ltd **Trained** Newmarket, Suffolk
■ Stewards' Enquiry : Jamie Spencer one-day ban: careless riding (Jun 6)

FOCUS
Following a dry night the going was given as good, with a GoingStick reading of 7.2. The races were held on the old outer home straight, adding 5yds to the distances of the 1m, 1m 2f 100yds and 1m3f 200yds races. The first four came clear in this handicap and the form looks good and sound enough for the grade.

2254 BRITISH STALLION STUDS SUPPORTING BRITISH RACING E B F MAIDEN FILLIES' STKS — 6f

3:00 (3:02) (Class 5) 2-Y-O **£3,561** (£1,059; £529; £264) **Stalls** Centre

Form RPR

1 **Switcher (IRE)** 2-9-0 0 .... RichardKingscote 4 83+
(Tom Dascombe) *dwlt: hld up: pushed along and hdwy over 2f out: swtchd lft wl over 1f out: sn led: r.o wl and in command fnl 100yds* **17/2**

2 *3½* **Dare To Dream** 2-9-0 0 .... RichardHughes 2 73+
(Richard Hannon) *chsd ldrs: effrt and swtchd rt 2f out: chalng over 1f out: edgd lft ins fnl f: nt gng pce of wnr fnl 110yds* **4/1[2]**

3 *¾* **Vassaria (IRE)** 2-9-0 0 .... FrederikTylicki 7 70+
(Michael Dods) *prom: led 2f out: rdn and hdd over 1f out: styd on same pce ins fnl f* **16/1**

4 *5* **Sunrise Dance** 2-9-0 0 .... JimCrowley 5 55
(Alan Jarvis) *racd keenly toward rr: pushed along 4f out: kpt on fr over 1f out: nvr able to trble ldrs* **33/1**

2 5 *1½* **Blodwen Abbey**[11] [1957] 2-9-0 0 .... ShaneKelly 9 51
(James Unett) *led: hdd 2f out: sn rdn: wknd ins fnl f* **11/2[3]**

3 6 *1¾* **Represent (IRE)**[14] [1846] 2-8-11 0 .... MartinHarley(3) 6 46
(Mick Channon) *prom: pushed along over 2f out: wknd over 1f out* **6/5[1]**

7 *11* **She's Flawless (USA)** 2-9-0 0 .... MartinDwyer 3 13
(Brian Meehan) *dwlt: rn green towards rr: bmpd 4f out: wl outpcd fnl 2f: nvr on terms* **20/1**

8 *18* **Caterina** 2-9-0 0 .... DaneO'Neill 11 —
(Richard Hannon) *dwlt: hld up: u.p over 2f out: nvr a threat* **16/1**

9 *1* **Tooley Woods (IRE)** 2-9-0 0 .... PaulHanagan 8 —
(Tony Carroll) *prom: j. road over 5f out: lost pl 3f out: bhd fnl 2f* **25/1**

1m 16.49s (2.69) **Going Correction** +0.45s/f (Yiel) 9 Ran SP% **114.7**
Speed ratings (Par 90): **98,93,92,85,83 81,66,42,41**
toteswingers:1&2:£6.00, 2&3:£7.50, 1&3:£10.10 CSF £41.14 TOTE £8.30: £2.70, £1.60, £4.60; EX 49.80.
Owner The Whipper Partnership **Bred** Eugene McDermott **Trained** Malpas, Cheshire

FOCUS
Probably a decent enough maiden of its type, with the first three pulling clear. The form looks sluightly above average for the grade.

NOTEBOOK
Switcher(IRE) was a little slowly away, but travelled well in behind the pace and stayed on in a taking manner to win without her rider having to get too serious. She's a half-sister to the stable's Marine Boy, who was impressive in winning his maiden at Newbury first time up, but ultimately failed to go on as expected, so her connections will no doubt be hoping she progresses better. The Albany will no doubt come into consideration for her now but, in view of what happened with Marine Boy, it's possible her trainer will take things steadier with her. (op 14-1)
Dare To Dream is out of a mare who won the Musidora, but her sire is an influence for speed, and she showed enough on her debut here to suggest she'll be winning something similar soon. (op 5-1 tchd 7-2)
Vassaria(IRE), whose four siblings have all won at least once, showed speed for a long way. She'll get further in time and one would imagine that she can win one of these if building only slightly on this effort.
Sunrise Dance, a bit keen early, looked in need of the race experience-wise, and didn't shape badly in the circumstances. A half-sister to Serena's Pride, she should benefit from the outing. (op 20-1)
Blodwen Abbey, who had the benefit of a previous run, promised to be suited by the step up to 6f but in the event she dropped away after showing speed. (op 10-1 tchd 5-1)
Represent(IRE) dropped out tamely with over a furlong to run, and perhaps this easier ground didn't suit her as well as the fast surface she encountered at Ascot on her debut. (op 4-5 tchd 5-4)

2255 ROBINS & DAY PEUGEOT 508 CLASSIFIED STKS — 6f

3:30 (3:31) (Class 4) 3-Y-O **£4,533** (£1,348; £674; £336) **Stalls** Centre

Form RPR

01- 1 **Bassett Road (IRE)**[154] [7914] 3-8-11 80 .... RossAtkinson(3) 9 85+
(Tom Dascombe) *racd keenly: mde all: rdn and hung lft ins fnl f: r.o wl and a looked in control* **12/1**

401- 2 *1¾* **St Augustine (IRE)**[198] [7294] 3-9-0 80 .... LukeMorris 8 79
(John Best) *hld up: rdn and hdwy over 1f out: styd on and hung lft ins fnl f: wnt 2nd fnl 110yds: nt rch wnr* **12/1**

4L-0 3 *1¾* **Regal Approval**[20] [1688] 3-9-0 79 .... SteveDrowne 6 73
(Hughie Morrison) *in tch: wnt 2nd 2f out: rdn over 1f out: lost 2nd fnl 110yds: no ex towards fin: rn wout decalred tongue tie* **7/2[1]**

2240 4 *½* **Dasho**[19] [1725] 3-9-0 77 .... JamieSpencer 1 75+
(Olivia Maylam) *hld up: pushed along 2f out: n.m.r and snatched up wl over 1f out: sn swtchd rt: styd on to cl and hung lft ins fnl f: nt quite get to ldrs* **10/1**

516- 5 *1½* **Squires Gate (IRE)**[228] [6636] 3-9-0 77 .... MichaelHills 7 67
(B W Hills) *dwlt: hld up in rr: rdn and hdwy over 1f out: sn chsd ldrs: edgd lft ins fnl f: one pce fnl 100yds* **14/1**

422- 6 *2¾* **Chokidar (IRE)**[248] [6047] 3-9-0 77 .... PaulHanagan 2 58
(David Nicholls) *prom: rdn over 1f out: wknd ins fnl f* **4/1[2]**

00-0 7 *1* **Serena's Pride**[15] [1825] 3-9-0 80 .... RichardHughes 4 55
(Alan Jarvis) *racd keenly: trckd ldrs tl wknd tamely 1f out* **9/1**

52-0 8 *2½* **No Poppy (IRE)**[15] [1825] 3-9-0 80 ....(b) RobertWinston 5 47
(Tim Easterby) *racd keenly: trckd ldrs: effrt over 2f out: sn hung lft u.p: wknd over 1f out* **11/2**

010- 9 *11* **Days Of Summer (IRE)**[244] [6176] 3-9-0 79 .... JimCrowley 3 —
(Ralph Beckett) *hld up in tch: rdn 2f out: wknd over 1f out* **5/1[3]**

1m 15.95s (2.15) **Going Correction** +0.45s/f (Yiel) 9 Ran SP% **115.4**
Speed ratings (Par 101): **101,98,96,95,93 90,88,85,70**
toteswingers:1&2:£17.80, 2&3:£11.10, 1&3:£11.40 CSF £144.86 TOTE £16.90: £5.00, £3.00, £2.50; EX 122.80.
Owner Mrs Sam Dascombe **Bred** Michael Mullins **Trained** Malpas, Cheshire
■ Stewards' Enquiry : Richard Hughes caution: entered wrong stall.

FOCUS
Just 3lb separated the nine runners on the ratings. The winner looks an improver with those in the frame backing up the form to some extent.
Dasho Official explanation: jockey said gelding was denied a clear run
Serena's Pride Official explanation: jockey said filly ran too free early atages

2256 BETFRED THE BONUS KING H'CAP — 1m

4:00 (4:02) (Class 4) (0-85,84) 3-Y-O **£2,941** (£2,941; £674; £336) **Stalls** Low

Form RPR

333 1 **Agiaal (USA)**[15] [1836] 3-8-13 **76** .... WilliamBuick 3 86
(John Gosden) *racd keenly: in tch: lost pl over 5f out: hdwy 2f out: sn rdn: drew level 1f out: r.o gamely in duel ins fnl f* **4/1[2]**

214- 1 *dht* **Enthusing (IRE)**[214] [6989] 3-8-12 **75** .... DaneO'Neill 7 85
(David Elsworth) *a.p: led 2f out: sn rdn: jnd 1f out: r.o gamely in duel ins fnl f* **6/1**

100- 3 *5* **Cosmic Moon**[216] [6920] 3-8-10 **73** .... BarryMcHugh 9 72
(Richard Fahey) *midfield: hdwy over 4f out: effrt over 2f out: styd on same pce ins fnl f* **9/1**

6-61 4 *shd* **Sergeant Troy (IRE)**[18] [1768] 3-8-10 **73** .... SteveDrowne 4 71+
(Roger Charlton) *hld up: effrt whn nt clr run 2f out: impr and swtchd lft to chse ldrs over 1f out: no ex fnl 100yds* **7/4[1]**

1- 5 *1¼* **Manaaber (USA)**[195] [7345] 3-8-11 **74** .... TadhgO'Shea 1 69+
(B W Hills) *hld up: nt clr run fr over 2f out: continually denied a run: swtchd lft over 1f out to come arnd the field: no imp after* **9/2[3]**

42-6 6 *¾* **Sam Nombulist**[19] [1710] 3-8-11 **74** .... NeilCallan 5 68
(Richard Whitaker) *racd keenly in midfield: effrt 2f out: edgd lft over 1f out: one pce ins fnl f* **40/1**

1-50 7 *2½* **Oceanway (USA)**[13] [1884] 3-9-7 **84** .... SilvestreDeSousa 10 72
(Mark Johnston) *midfield: effrt over 3f out: nt clr run over 2f out: sn swtchd lft: denied a run over 1f out: one pce ins fnl f* **20/1**

-025 8 *3¾* **Another Citizen (IRE)**[6] [2092] 3-8-13 **76** .... RobertWinston 2 57
(Tim Easterby) *trckd ldrs: effrt to chal 2f out: wknd ins fnl f: eased whn btn fnl 100yds* **14/1**

545- 9 *9* **Enlightening (IRE)**[177] [7550] 3-8-12 **75** .... RichardHughes 6 43
(Richard Hannon) *led: hdd 2f out: wknd over 1f out* **22/1**

6 10 *nk* **Imperator Augustus (IRE)**[14] [1880] 3-8-12 **75** .... AndrewElliott 8 33
(Patrick Holmes) *prom tl rdn and wknd over 2f out* **66/1**

1m 44.11s (1.21) **Going Correction** -0.25s/f (Firm) **10** Ran SP% **118.5**
Speed ratings (Par 101): **83,83,78,77,76 75,73,69,60,60**
WIN: Agiaal £2.40 Enthusing £3.60 PL: A £1.10, E £2.30 Cosmic Moon £3.00. EX: A/E £19.40 E/A £15.40 CSF: A/E £13.78 E/A £14.82 TRI: A/E/Cosmic Moon £105.22 E/A/CM £111.32 toteswingers:A&E £5.1, A& £7.00, E&3 £7.50.
Owner Ben CM Wong **Bred** Paul Kavanagh **Trained** Newmarket, Suffolk
Owner Hamdan Al Maktoum **Bred** Shadwell Farm LLC **Trained** Newmarket, Suffolk

FOCUS
The field headed over to the stands' side rail in the straight and the judge couldn't split the first two as they crossed the line. A subsequent stewards' inquiry left the placings unaltered. The form makes sense overall and is rated at face value.
Manaaber(USA) ◆ Official explanation: jockey said filly was denied a clear run
Oceanway(USA) Official explanation: jockey said filly was denied a clear run

2257 NORTHERN RACING CLUB MAIDEN STKS (DIV I) — 1m 2f 95y

4:30 (4:33) (Class 5) 3-Y-O+ **£2,590** (£770; £385; £192) **Stalls** Centre

Form RPR

1 **Antarctic (IRE)** 3-9-0 0 .... WilliamBuick 2 75+
(John Gosden) *handy: rn green: lost pl and pushed along over 5f out: hdwy 2f out: led ins fnl f: r.o: on top cl home* **7/2[1]**

62- 2 *nk* **She's Got The Luck (IRE)**[228] [6618] 3-8-9 0 .... BarryMcHugh 11 70
(Richard Fahey) *prom: led over 4f out: rdn over 1f out: hdd ins fnl f: hld cl home* **9/2[2]**

62-5 3 *1¼* **Malanos (IRE)**[8] [2019] 3-9-0 79 .... DaneO'Neill 6 72
(David Elsworth) *prom: rdn to chal over 2f out: nt qckn fnl 75yds* **5/1[3]**

3 4 *hd* **Let's Dance (IRE)**[21] [1655] 3-8-9 0 .... RichardKingscote 8 67
(Tom Dascombe) *racd keenly: trckd ldrs: rdn over 2f out: nt qckn over 1f out: kpt on ins fnl f but nt pce of ldrs* **13/2**

5 *2¼* **Mill Mick**[41] 4-10-0 0 .... StephenCraine 10 67
(John Mackie) *midfield: hdwy over 2f out: chsd ldrs over 1f out: one pce ins fnl f* **125/1**

6 *½* **Momaris** 3-9-0 0 .... NeilCallan 12 66+
(Roger Varian) *hld up: pushed along over 4f out: hdwy 3f out: effrt to chse ldrs over 2f out: wknd over 1f out* **9/2[2]**

0- 7 *shd* **Diamond Bob**[233] [6474] 3-9-0 0 .... JimCrowley 13 66+
(Ed Dunlop) *hld up: rdn 2f out: hdwy and edgd lft over 1f out: one pce ins fnl f* **28/1**

8 *1* **Opera Box** 3-8-9 0 .... TadhgO'Shea 7 59
(Marcus Tregoning) *midfield: outpcd over 2f out: swtchd lft over 1f out: nvr on terms w ldrs* **20/1**

0- 9 *2¼* **Mancunian (IRE)**[191] [7385] 3-9-0 0 .... LukeMorris 1 59
(John Best) *midfield: lost pl over 5f out: u.p over 2f out: n.d after* **33/1**

0 10 *5* **Reveal The Light**[9] [1998] 4-9-9 0 .... SteveDrowne 14 44
(Garry Woodward) *trckd ldrs: rdn and wknd over 1f out: eased whn btn ins fnl f* **200/1**

4 11 *nk* **Tasman Tiger**[21] [1648] 4-9-9 0 .... KellyHarrison 9 44
(Kate Walton) *led: hdd over 4f out: pushed along over 2f out: wknd wl over 1f out* **40/1**

12 *7* **Daruband** 3-9-0 0 .... AhmedAjtebi 4 47+
(Mahmood Al Zarooni) *hld up: hdwy 3f out: chalng over 2f out: wknd over 1f out: eased whn btn ins fnl f* **7/1**

0 13 *nk* **Vibration**[30] [1496] 3-9-0 0 .... TravisBlock 5 34
(Hughie Morrison) *u.p over 3f out: a bhd* **66/1**

2m 16.95s (0.95) **Going Correction** -0.25s/f (Firm)
WFA 3 from 4yo 14lb **13** Ran SP% **117.5**
Speed ratings (Par 103): **86,85,84,84,82 82,82,81,79,75 75,69,69**
toteswingers:1&2:£4.50, 2&3:£4.70, 1&3:£5.40 CSF £17.82 TOTE £3.40: £1.40, £2.20, £2.10; EX 24.20.
Owner H R H Princess Haya Of Jordan **Bred** Wardstown Stud Ltd **Trained** Newmarket, Suffolk

FOCUS
This certainly looked the more open of the two divisions, and there were several in with a chance down the straight, where the field headed for the stands' rail. The form is rated loosely around the placed horses.

2258 TOM JONES LIVE ON 18TH JUNE MAIDEN STKS (DIV II) — 1m 2f 95y

5:00 (5:02) (Class 5) 3-Y-O+ **£2,590** (£770; £385; £192) **Stalls** Centre

Form RPR

2- 1 **Mijhaar**[225] [6689] 3-9-0 0 .... NeilCallan 12 97+
(Roger Varian) *broke wl: a.p: led over 4f out: hung lft over 1f out: r.o wl to draw clr ins fnl f: impressive* **4/5[1]**

2 *7* **Timeline** 3-9-0 0 .... AhmedAjtebi 2 87+
(Mahmood Al Zarooni) *trckd ldrs: chalng over 2f out: outpcd by wnr and no ch ins fnl f* **20/1**

4- **3** 2 3/4 **High Jinx (IRE)**[205] 7179 3-9-0 0 .... PatCosgrave 1 77+
(James Fanshawe) *trckd ldrs: rdn over 2f out: one pce over 1f out* **6/1**[3]

0 **4** 3 **Plimsoll Line (USA)**[34] 1408 3-9-0 0 .... JamieSpencer 4 71+
(Michael Bell) *hld up: swtchd lft 2f out: kpt on over 1f out: nvr trbld ldrs* **20/1**

20-3 **5** 2 **Cobbs Quay**[26] 1542 3-9-0 80 .... WilliamBuick 10 67
(John Gosden) *midfield: hdwy over 6f out: sn trckd ldrs: rdn over 3f out: one pce over 1f out* **4/1**[2]

6 1/2 **Diptimat** 3-8-7 0 .... (b[1]) AntiocoMurgia(7) 8 66
(Marco Botti) *midfield early: dropped in rr after 3f: u.p in midfield over 2f out: no imp* **100/1**

7 2 3/4 **Tanmawy (IRE)** 3-9-0 0 .... TadhgO'Shea 13 61
(Ed Dunlop) *in tch: lost pl after 2f: rdn in midfield over 2f out: no imp on ldrs: eased whn btn ins fnl f* **100/1**

5- **8** hd **Mafeteng**[221] 6803 3-8-9 0 .... RichardHughes 6 55
(John Dunlop) *hld up: hdwy into midfield 5f out: u.p over 2f out: outpcd after* **25/1**

9 4 1/2 **Midnight Oil** 3-9-0 0 .... J-PGuillambert 3 51+
(Luca Cumani) *midfield: rdn over 2f out: nvr able to trble ldrs* **33/1**

/05 **10** 4 **Dancing Primo**[13] 1915 5-9-9 0 .... LukeMorris 9 38
(Mark Brisbourne) *led: hdd over 4f out: rdn and wknd over 2f out* **250/1**

03 **11** 2 1/2 **Change The Subject (USA)**[16] 1810 3-9-0 0 .... TomQueally 7 38
(Sir Henry Cecil) *s.i.s: hdwy to chse ldrs over 6f out: edgd lft whn rdn and wkng 2f out* **12/1**

20 **12** nse **Sizzle (FR)**[24] 1597 3-8-9 0 .... RichardKingscote 11 33
(Tom Dascombe) *midfield: outpcd over 2f out: n.d* **40/1**

13 18 **Conesuala** 4-9-9 0 .... JimCrowley 5 —
(Alan Jarvis) *a bhd: lost tch over 1f out* **100/1**

2m 14.36s (-1.64) **Going Correction** -0.25s/f (Firm) **13** Ran SP% **119.7**
WFA 3 from 4yo+ 14lb
Speed ratings (Par 103): **96,90,88,85,84 83,81,81,77,74 72,72,58**
toteswingers:1&2:£4.50, 2&3:£12.80, 1&3:£2.80 CSF £25.99 TOTE £1.80: £1.10, £3.40, £2.60; EX 21.70.
Owner Sheikh Ahmed Al Maktoum **Bred** Darley **Trained** Newmarket, Suffolk

FOCUS
They didn't appear to go that quick early here but the pace picked up from some way out and the winning time compared very favourably with the first division, being 2.59sec quicker. Once again they came towards the stands' side in the straight. The winner looks smart and the next three should progress as well.
Change The Subject(USA) Official explanation: jockey said colt stumbled leaving stalls

2259 BETDAQ THE BETTING EXCHANGE APPRENTICE TRAINING SERIES H'CAP (RACING EXCELLENCE INITIATIVE) 1m 3f 200y
5:30 (5:31) (Class 5) (0-70,70) 4-Y-O+ **£2,590** (£770; £385; £192) **Stalls** Centre

Form RPR

6211 **1** **Tenhoo**[6] 2091 5-9-0 66 6ex .... NathanAlison(3) 7 76+
(Eric Alston) *hld up in midfield: hdwy over 3f out: swtchd rt over 2f out: sn nt clr run and hmpd: swtchd lft to chal jst after: r.o ins fnl f to ld fnl 75yds* **4/7**[1]

4045 **2** 1 1/4 **Dubara Reef (IRE)**[13] 1914 4-9-1 67 .... (p) DuilioDaSilva(3) 1 75
(Paul Green) *led: rdn over 3f out: pressed fnl f: hdd fnl 75yds: hld cl home* **16/1**

4502 **3** 6 **Amical Risks (FR)**[11] 1959 7-8-4 56 oh2 .... RosieJessop(3) 2 54
(Ollie Pears) *hld up: hdwy over 2f out: sn nt clr run: swtchd lft jst after: rdn and ch over 1f out: no ex fnl 100yds* **9/2**[2]

1450 **4** 2 3/4 **Straversjoy**[14] 1855 4-8-9 63 .... JackDuern(5) 4 57
(Reg Hollinshead) *trckd ldrs: wnt 2nd over 7f out: sn w ldr: pushed along over 2f out: wknd ins fnl f* **12/1**[3]

000- **5** 6 **Cluain Alainn (IRE)**[41] 2934 5-9-7 70 .... (vt[1]) RyanClark 5 54
(Ian Williams) *hld up: struggling over 4f out: nvr able to trble ldrs* **14/1**

6 8 **Amana (USA)**[334] 2194 7-8-12 64 .... JamesRogers(3) 8 36
(Mark Brisbourne) *in tch: rdn and wknd over 2f out* **25/1**

0-00 **7** 8 **Scarab (IRE)**[14] 1859 6-8-13 65 .... (p) AntiocoMurgia(3) 3 24
(Tim Walford) *prom tl rdn and wknd over 2f out* **25/1**

2m 34.19s (0.19) **Going Correction** -0.25s/f (Firm) **7** Ran SP% **109.8**
Speed ratings (Par 103): **89,88,84,82,78 73,67**
toteswingers:1&2:£3.20, 2&3:£3.50, 1&3:£1.30. Tote Super 7: Win: £4,579.80. Place: £67.60 CSF £10.61 CT £21.30 TOTE £1.80: £1.10, £4.30; EX 8.40.
Owner Edges Farm Racing Stables Ltd **Bred** A G Antoniades **Trained** Longton, Lancs
■ Stewards' Enquiry : Nathan Alison one-day ban: careless riding (Jun 6)
Duilio Da Silva three-day ban: careless riding (Jun 6-8)

FOCUS
This apprentices' handicap was all about whether the favourite could defy his 6lb penalty. The winner did not need to improve but the second ran a personal-best.
T/Jkpt: £4,228.90 to a £1 stake. Pool of £11,912.63 - 2.00 winning tickets. T/Plt: £142.40 to a £1 stake. Pool of £76,624.45 - 392.72 winning tickets. T/Qpdt: £13.80 to a £1 stake. Pool of £5,483.36 293.80 winning tickets. DO

1538 MUSSELBURGH (R-H)
Friday, May 20

OFFICIAL GOING: Sprint course - good (good to firm in places); round course - good to firm (6.2)
Wind: Fresh against Weather: Fine and dry - blustery

2260 EDINBURGH EVENING NEWS APPRENTICE H'CAP (QUALIFIER FOR BETFAIR BONUS SCOTTISH RACING MILE FINAL) 1m
6:30 (6:30) (Class 6) (0-65,65) 4-Y-O+ **£2,590** (£770; £385; £192) **Stalls** Low

Form RPR

0-00 **1** **Global**[31] 1461 5-9-4 62 .... PaulPickard 12 72
(Brian Ellison) *qckly away fr wd draw: mde all: rdn over 2f out: jnd and drvn over 1f out: kpt on gamely towards fin* **10/3**[1]

5-40 **2** 3/4 **Ra Junior (USA)**[23] 1613 5-8-13 57 .... MichaelO'Connell 8 65
(Paul Midgley) *chsd wnr: hdwy 2f out: rdn to chal over 1f out: ev ch tl drvn and no ex wl ins fnl f* **10/1**

-024 **3** 2 1/2 **Violent Velocity (IRE)**[18] 1748 8-9-4 65 .... LeeTopliss(3) 9 67+
(John Quinn) *towards rr: hdwy over 2f out: rdn wl over 1f out: styd on to chse ldng pair ins fnl f: no imp towards fin* **5/1**[2]

466- **4** 7 **Jewelled Dagger (IRE)**[23] 5436 7-9-4 65 .... HarryBentley(3) 11 51
(Jim Goldie) *chsd ldng pair: rdn along over 2f out: drvn wl over 1f out: kpt on same pce* **10/3**[1]

4400 **5** 1 3/4 **Lady Excel (IRE)**[7] 2057 5-8-13 57 .... PatrickDonaghy 1 39
(Brian Rothwell) *dwlt: sn in tch on inner: pushed along 3f out: rdn and styd on same pce fnl 2f* **40/1**

U3-5 **6** 1 1/4 **Botham (USA)**[19] 1714 7-8-6 55 .... NoraLooby(5) 6 34
(Jim Goldie) *hld up in rr: hdwy on inner over 2f out: sn rdn and kpt on appr fnl f* **14/1**

3306 **7** 1 3/4 **Noble Attitude**[31] 1468 5-8-7 51 oh6 .... DeclanCannon 7 26
(Richard Guest) *a towards rr* **33/1**

26-0 **8** nk **Emeralds Spirit (IRE)**[13] 1909 4-9-1 62 .... JulieBurke(3) 3 37
(John Weymes) *t.k.h: chsd ldrs: rdn along wl over 2f out: sn wknd* **8/1**[3]

431- **9** nk **Military Call**[271] 5337 4-9-0 63 .... GarryWhillans(5) 10 37
(Alistair Whillans) *a in rr* **9/1**

-350 **10** 3 **King Bertolini (IRE)**[14] 1857 4-8-1 52 .... DanielleMooney(7) 4 19
(Alan Berry) *s.i.s: a bhd* **80/1**

00-0 **11** 1/2 **Coolella (IRE)**[22] 1625 4-8-8 52 .... AmyRyan 5 18
(John Weymes) *chsd ldrs on outer: rdn along wl over 2f out: sn wknd* **28/1**

-000 **12** 4 **Ninth House (USA)**[63] 895 9-8-7 51 oh4 .... (b) AndrewHeffernan 2 —
(Ruth Carr) *t.k.h early: chsd ldrs: rdn along wl over 2f out: sn drvn and wknd* **14/1**

1m 40.98s (-0.22) **Going Correction** +0.025s/f (Good) **12** Ran SP% **116.4**
Speed ratings (Par 101): **102,101,98,91,90 88,87,86,86,83 82,78**
toteswingers:1&2:£6.70, 2&3:£12.10, 1&3:£4.40 CSF £36.44 CT £165.85 TOTE £3.80: £1.70, £2.60, £2.20; EX 39.70.
Owner Koo's Racing CLub III **Bred** Lt-Col And Mrs R Bromley Gardner **Trained** Norton, N Yorks

FOCUS
This moderate handicap for apprentice riders looked wide open, but the first pair dominated from the gates and had it to themselves. The winner is rated to last year's form with the second to his best for his current yard.

2261 BRITISH STALLION STUDS SUPPORTING BRITISH RACING E B F MAIDEN STKS 5f
7:00 (7:00) (Class 4) 2-Y-O **£5,180** (£1,541; £770; £384) **Stalls** High

Form RPR

3 **1** **Fulbright**[10] 1966 2-9-3 0 .... JoeFanning 6 89
(Mark Johnston) *led: rdn and jnd 1/2-way: hdd over 1f out: kpt on u.p to ld again jst ins fnl f: styd on strly* **11/5**[2]

2 4 **Exceedance** 2-9-3 0 .... TomEaves 7 75+
(Bryan Smart) *dwlt: t.k.h and sn trcking ldrs: smooth hdwy and cl up 1/2-way: qcknd wl to ld over 1f out: sn rn green and edgd rt: rdn and hdd jst ins fnl f: one pce* **2/1**[1]

32 **3** 1 1/2 **Blue Shoes (IRE)**[14] 1876 2-8-12 0 .... DavidAllan 8 64
(Tim Easterby) *chsd ldrs on inner: rdn along 2f out: sn edgd rt and drvn: kpt on same pce* **7/2**[3]

0 **4** 1 1/2 **Kool Henry (IRE)**[23] 1619 2-9-3 0 .... DanielTudhope 1 64
(David O'Meara) *in tch on outer: hdwy 2f out: sn rdn and kpt on same pce* **14/1**

6 **5** 1/2 **Valley Of Hope**[10] 1966 2-9-3 0 .... TonyHamilton 2 62
(Richard Fahey) *wnt lft s: towards rr: hdwy and n.m.r 2f out: effrt whn nt clr run and hmpd appr fnl f: swtchd lft and nt rcvr* **7/1**

6 **6** 3 1/4 **Sonko (IRE)**[44] 1185 2-8-8 0 ow1 .... LeeTopliss(5) 4 46
(Tim Pitt) *wnt rt s: cl up: rdn along 2f out: grad wknd* **33/1**

0 **7** 1 1/2 **Come To Mind**[17] 1791 2-8-13 0 ow1 .... SladeO'Hara(5) 3 46
(Alan Berry) *sltly hmpd s: sn in tch: rdn along 1/2-way: edgd lft 2f out and sn wknd* **100/1**

60.88 secs (0.48) **Going Correction** -0.175s/f (Firm) **7** Ran SP% **109.9**
Speed ratings (Par 95): **89,82,80,77,77 71,69**
toteswingers:1&2:£1.80, 2&3:£2.00, 1&3:£1.80 CSF £6.41 TOTE £2.20: £1.20, £2.70; EX 6.30.
Owner Sheikh Hamdan Bin Mohammed Al Maktoum **Bred** R F And S D Knipe **Trained** Middleham Moor, N Yorks

FOCUS
This ought to prove fair maiden form and the winner looks potentially Pattern class. The third sets the level backed up by the sixth.

NOTEBOOK
Fulbright ◆ looked to have come on nicely for his debut and raced professionally up front. However, as was the case first time out, he again hit something of a flat spot around halfway and appeared vulnerable to the runner-up. He had the benefit of the rail, though, and there was a lot to like about the way he responded to come clear at the finish. Bred to make his mark in Pattern-class sprints, he rates Royal Ascot material and the stiffer nature of that track ought to prove right up his street. (op 9-4 tchd 2-1)
Exceedance, by the same sire as Fulbright and from a family the trainer knows all about, proved very popular to make a winning debut. Full of himself beforehand and given a handler down at the start, he raced freely off the leaders early. He loomed up nearing 2f out going sweetly, but his inexperience told when the winner found extra and he was ultimately well held. Providing he goes forward for the run, which he is fully entitled to do, he ought to be hard to beat next time. (op 9-4 tchd 15-8)
Blue Shoes(IRE) has now been placed on each of her three outings and rates a solid benchmark. A stiffer test is likely to prove ideal for her. (op 5-2 tchd 4-1)
Kool Henry(IRE), who needed his debut last time, met some support and ran with more encouragement. He is entitled to come on again. (op 33-1)
Valley Of Hope was beaten around 8l by the winner on his debut. He went left at the start, bumping Come To Mind, and didn't get a great passage when trying to improve from off the pace. (op 13-2)

2262 CANACCORD GENUITY H'CAP 1m 6f
7:30 (7:30) (Class 4) (0-85,83) 4-Y-O+ **£6,476** (£1,927; £963; £481) **Stalls** Low

Form RPR

010- **1** **Hawk Mountain (UAE)**[216] 6926 6-9-5 81 .... FrederikTylicki 4 88
(John Quinn) *hld up: hdwy 3f out: chsd ldrs 2f out: sn rdn and styd on strly ent fnl f to ld last 75yds* **11/1**

53-1 **2** 1 1/4 **Peintre D'Argent (IRE)**[7] 2055 5-8-0 67 .... HarryBentley(5) 10 72
(William Knight) *hld up in rr: stdy hdwy over 4f out: chsd ldrs on outer over 2f out: led 1/2f out: sn rdn and edgd rt ent fnl f: hdd and no ex last 75yds* **1/1**[1]

24-0 **3** 1 **Gordonsville**[27] 1517 8-9-7 83 .... DanielTudhope 6 87
(Jim Goldie) *hld up towards rr: stdy hdwy over 6f out: cl up 4f out: effrt to chal 3f out and sn led: rdn 2f out: drvn and hdd 1 1/2f out: kpt on same pce fnl f* **16/1**

14-6 **4** 1/2 **Mason Hindmarsh**[35] 1036 4-8-1 66 .... AndrewHeffernan(3) 3 69
(Karen McLintock) *a.p: rdn along over 3f out: drvn and n.m.r over 1f out: kpt on same pce after* **100/1**

1163 **5** nk **French Hollow**[42] 1215 6-8-2 64 .... DuranFentiman 9 67
(Tim Fitzgerald) *hld up in rr: hdwy 3f out: rdn along over 2f out: kpt on appr fnl f: nrst fin* **33/1**

50-0 **6** 3/4 **Wells Lyrical (IRE)**[27] 1517 6-9-1 77 .... TomEaves 8 79
(Bryan Smart) *chsd ldr: rdn along 3f out: drvn 2f out and grad wknd* **9/2**[2]

10-6 **7** nk **Cat O' Nine Tails**[14] 1847 4-9-1 77 .... JoeFanning 2 78
(Mark Johnston) *led: rdn along 3f out: sn hdd and drvn: wknd appr fnl f* **7/1**[3]

/022 **8** ½ **Dar Es Salaam**[6] 2091 7-8-3 68 .... PaulPickard(3) 1 68
(Brian Ellison) *chsd ldrs on inner: rdn along 4f out: drvn 3f out and grad wknd* **17/2**

26-1 **9** 2¼ **Bollin Greta**[13] 1901 6-8-13 75 ....(t) DavidAllan 5 72
(Tim Easterby) *hld up in rr: effrt and sme hdwy over 3f out: sn rdn and nvr a factor* **18/1**

6-36 **10** 9 **Chookie Hamilton**[19] 1713 7-8-10 77 .... LeeTopliss(5) 7 62
(Keith Dalgleish) *trckd ldrs: hdwy 1/2-way: cl up over 4f out: rdn along 3f out: drvn over 2f out and sn wknd* **12/1**

3m 3.82s (-1.48) **Going Correction** +0.025s/f (Good) **10** Ran SP% **122.3**
Speed ratings (Par 105): **105,104,103,103,103 102,102,102,101,95**
CSF £23.51 CT £198.76 TOTE £14.20: £3.00, £1.10, £5.00; EX 38.20.
Owner Paul Morrison & Nick Luck **Bred** Darley **Trained** Settrington, N Yorks

FOCUS
An average handicap which was run at a sound gallop, but the majority still took a keen hold. The winner is rated back to his best with the third and fourth close to their marks.

2263 BERNARD HUNTER CRANE HIRE (S) STKS 5f
8:00 (8:00) (Class 6) 3-Y-O+ **£2,590** (£770; £385; £192) **Stalls** High

Form RPR
4524 **1** **Dower Glen**[7] 2047 4-8-12 50 ....(v) JoeFanning 3 58
(Keith Dalgleish) *led: rdn along 2f out and sn hdd: drvn and rallied to ld again ins fnl f: edgd rt and kpt on wl towards fin* **8/1**

-003 **2** ½ **Lesley's Choice**[7] 2048 5-9-3 69 ....(b) TomEaves 4 61
(Linda Perratt) *cl up: rdn to ld wl over 1f out: edgd lft and drvn ent fnl f: sn hdd and no ex towards fin* **3/1**[2]

0264 **3** 1½ **Jigajig**[11] 1955 4-9-0 70 .... AmyRyan(3) 7 56
(Kevin Ryan) *chsd ldng pair: effrt 2f out and sn n.m.r: swtchd rt and rdn over 1f out: kpt on u.p ins fnl f* **9/4**[1]

0-00 **4** 1½ **Di Stefano**[14] 1878 4-9-3 72 ....(v) AdrianNicholls 6 50
(David Nicholls) *prom: swtchd rt 2f out: sn rdn and kpt on same pce ins fnl f* **3/1**[2]

2-01 **5** 1 **Highland Warrior**[10] 1968 12-9-9 69 .... MickyFenton 5 53
(Paul Midgley) *chsd ldrs: effrt wl over 1f out: sn rdn and no imp* **5/1**[3]

6-00 **6** 1 **Mandarin Spirit (IRE)**[7] 2048 11-9-3 64 ....(b) TonyHamilton 1 43
(Linda Perratt) *swvd bdly rt s: a bhd* **25/1**

56-6 **7** 3 **Sumay Buoy (IRE)**[19] 1716 4-9-3 46 .... PaulQuinn 2 32
(Jean McGregor) *in tch: rdn along 2f out: sn drvn and wknd* **100/1**

60.25 secs (-0.15) **Going Correction** -0.175s/f (Firm) **7** Ran SP% **113.4**
Speed ratings (Par 101): **94,93,90,88,86 85,80**
.There was no bid for the winner. Lesley's Choice was claimed by Miss J Davis for £12,000.\n\x\x

Owner S Laffan **Bred** Emma Thorman & Trickledown Stud **Trained** Carluke, South Lanarkshire
■ Stewards' Enquiry : Amy Ryan two-day ban: careless riding (Jun 6-7)

FOCUS
A fairly tight seller, run at a brisk pace. The winner is rated back to his best.

2264 TURCAN CONNELL H'CAP 7f 30y
8:30 (8:31) (Class 5) (0-70,70) 3-Y-O **£3,885** (£1,156; £577; £288) **Stalls** Low

Form RPR
05-5 **1** **Fairlie Dinkum**[41] 1251 3-9-4 67 .... TomEaves 8 78
(Bryan Smart) *mde all: rdn along over 2f out: drvn wl over 1f out: styd on gamely ins fnl f* **6/1**[3]

202- **2** 2¼ **Nicola's Dream**[223] 6748 3-9-5 68 .... TonyHamilton 9 73
(Richard Fahey) *in tch: hdwy on outer over 3f out: rdn to chse ldng pair over 2f out: drvn and ch over 1f out: kpt on same pce ins fnl f* **13/2**

3-1 **3** nk **Materialism**[121] 212 3-9-7 70 .... JoeFanning 6 74
(Mark Johnston) *coltish in preliminaries: trckd ldng pair: hdwy to chse wnr 4f out: rdn wl over 2f out: drvn over 1f out and kpt on same pce* **7/4**[1]

3110 **4** 4 **Trading**[6] 2119 3-9-2 65 .... DuranFentiman 3 58
(Tim Easterby) *chsd wnr: rdn along 1/2-way: sn drvn and grad wknd* **9/2**[2]

066- **5** ¾ **Purkab**[244] 6174 3-8-10 59 .... DanielTudhope 1 50
(Jim Goldie) *dwlt and in rr: hdwy on inner wl over 2f out: sn rdn and kpt on appr fnl f: nrst fin* **9/1**

6310 **6** 1½ **Dolly Parton (IRE)**[1] 2215 3-9-5 68 ....(p) AdrianNicholls 2 55
(David Nicholls) [illegible] *and one hdwy wl over 2f out: sn rdn and no imp* **17/2**

446 **7** 1½ **Fleurie Lover (IRE)**[45] 1155 3-8-4 56 .... DeclanCannon(3) 4 39
(Richard Guest) *in tch: rdn along bef 1/2-way: sn wknd* **25/1**

6-43 **8** ½ **Prince Of Passion (CAN)**[20] 1693 3-9-6 69 .... FrederikTylicki 5 51
(Michael Dods) *in tch: rdn along over 4f out: sn outpcd* **9/1**

1m 29.76s (0.76) **Going Correction** +0.025s/f (Good) **8** Ran SP% **116.5**
Speed ratings (Par 99): **96,93,93,88,87 85,84,83**
toteswingers:1&2:£5.50, 2&3:£1.80, 1&3:£4.80 CSF £45.23 CT £96.63 TOTE £6.40: £2.70, £1.40, £1.20; EX 50.10.
Owner Minster Horseboxes **Bred** Lesley Winn And Reveley Farms **Trained** Hambleton, N Yorks

FOCUS
A modest 3-y-o handicap, run at a solid pace and the form looks fair. The form looks sound enough with the runner-up to his best juvenile form.

2265 WEIR PROPERTY MANAGEMENT H'CAP (A QUALIFIER FOR THE BETFAIR BONUS SCOTTISH RACING SPRINT FINAL) 5f
9:00 (9:01) (Class 6) (0-65,63) 3-Y-O **£2,590** (£770; £385; £192) **Stalls** High

Form RPR
25-2 **1** **Rothesay Chancer**[27] 1514 3-9-0 59 .... GaryBartley(3) 7 69
(Jim Goldie) *in tch: hdwy to chse ldrs 2f out: swtchd rt and rdn to chal ent fnl f: sn led and edgd lft: drvn out* **4/1**[2]

36-5 **2** 1 **Pizzarra**[135] 44 3-8-13 55 .... JoeFanning 6 61
(James Given) *led: rdn along 2f out: drvn over 1f out: edgd rt and hdd ins fnl f: no ex last 50yds* **9/1**

635- **3** ¾ **Fast Shot**[283] 4935 3-9-3 59 .... DavidAllan 3 62+
(Tim Easterby) *dwlt and towards rr: hdwy 1/2-way: rdn to chse ldrs over 1f out: kpt on ins fnl f* **8/1**

00-4 **4** nk **Speightowns Kid (USA)**[24] 1589 3-9-4 63 .... MichaelO'Connell(3) 2 65
(Matthew Salaman) *chsd ldrs: hdwy 2f out: rdn to chal over 1f out: drvn and ch whn hmpd ins fnl f: one pce after* **8/1**

3435 **5** ¾ **These Dreams**[7] 2062 3-8-7 52 .... DeclanCannon(3) 10 52
(Richard Guest) *chsd ldrs: effrt 2f out and ch whn n.m.r and drvn ent fnl f: one pce* **12/1**

0-P0 **6** ½ **Blind Stag (IRE)**[14] 1860 3-8-9 54 ....(p) PaulPickard(3) 13 52
(David Thompson) *towards rr: hdwy and swtchd rt 2f out: effrt and nt clr run over 1f out: swtchd rt and drvn ent fnl f: sn edgd rt and kpt on: nrst fin* **33/1**

-121 **7** 1 **Irish Boy (IRE)**[18] 1764 3-9-3 59 .... DuranFentiman 12 53+
(Noel Wilson) *midfield: rdn along over 2f out: sn drvn and n.d* **3/1**[1]

0-10 **8** 1 **Melodize**[18] 1745 3-9-3 59 .... DanielTudhope 8 50+
(David O'Meara) *midfield: effrt over 2f out: sn rdn and n.d* **7/1**[3]

0665 **9** 3¼ **Fawara**[25] 1561 3-8-0 45 .... AndrewHeffernan(3) 5 24
(Ruth Carr) *chsd ldrs on outer: rdn along 2f out: grad wknd* **66/1**

0-05 **10** ½ **Empress Royal**[44] 1187 3-9-6 62 .... FrederikTylicki 4 39
(Michael Dods) *prom: rdn along 2f out: sn drvn and wknd* **16/1**

5244 **11** 3¼ **Spontaneity (IRE)**[25] 1561 3-8-13 55 .... TomEaves 9 20
(Bryan Smart) *prom: rdn along 1/2-way: sn wknd* **12/1**

0-00 **12** 9 **Country Waltz**[17] 1802 3-9-5 61 .... TonyHamilton 1 —
(Linda Perratt) *chsd ldrs on outer: rdn along bef 1/2-way: sn wknd* **25/1**

06-0 **13** 12 **Face East (USA)**[14] 1860 3-8-5 47 ow2 .... AdrianNicholls 11 —
(Alan Berry) *s.i.s: a bhd* **100/1**

59.87 secs (-0.53) **Going Correction** -0.175s/f (Firm) **13** Ran SP% **120.3**
Speed ratings (Par 97): **97,95,94,93,92 91,90,88,83,82 77,62,43**
toteswingers:1&2:£7.80, 2&3:£13.60, 1&3:£8.10 CSF £39.45 CT £281.26 TOTE £4.60: £2.00, £3.30, £3.30; EX 36.80.
Owner Discovery Racing Club 2 **Bred** Mrs S R Kennedy **Trained** Uplawmoor, E Renfrews

FOCUS
A moderate and wide-open 3-y-o sprint handicap, run at a decent pace. The form could be worth a bit more with the first two slight improvers and the third to his juvenile mark.
Blind Stag(IRE) Official explanation: jockey said gelding hung right
T/Plt: £70.40 to a £1 stake. Pool of £50825.79 - 526.85 winning units. T/Qpdt: £25.80 to a £1 stake. Pool of £3515.96 - 100.84 winning units. JR

1988 YARMOUTH (L-H)
Friday, May 20

OFFICIAL GOING: Good to firm (7.9)
Back straight and bottom bend dolled out 3m increasing distances on round course by 15m.
Wind: fairly light, across Weather: bright and sunny

2266 NORFOLK NELSON MUSEUM MEDIAN AUCTION MAIDEN STKS 6f 3y
2:20 (2:21) (Class 6) 3-5-Y-O **£1,813** (£539; £269; £134) **Stalls** High

Form RPR
3- **1** **Mosaicist (IRE)**[248] 6058 3-8-12 0 .... KierenFallon 8 77+
(James Fanshawe) *t.k.h: hld up in tch: pushed along and hdwy 2f out: led ent fnl f: kpt on wl and a holding rival fnl 150yds* **2/1**[2]

2 shd **Outsmart** 3-9-3 0 .... FrankieDettori 2 81+
(Mahmood Al Zarooni) *stdd s: hld up in tch in rr: hdwy ent fnl 2f: rdn and ev ch over 1f out: hld hd high and a jst hld by wnr fnl 150yds* **5/1**[3]

0-55 **3** 3½ **Merrjanah**[18] 1766 3-8-12 64 .... PhilipRobinson 7 65
(Clive Brittain) *led: rdn jst over 2f out: hdd ent fnl f: outpcd by ldng pair jst ins fnl f: hld on for 3rd ins fnl f* **12/1**

0-3 **4** ½ **Intiqaal (IRE)**[26] 1540 4-9-12 0 ....(t) RichardHills 9 70
(Ed Dunlop) *chsd ldr: ev ch ent fnl 2f: rdn and unable qck 1f out: outpcd by ldng pair jst ins fnl f: kpt on same pce* **13/8**[1]

0 **5** 1½ **Beechcraft Baron (IRE)**[14] 1880 3-9-0 0 .... GilmarPereira(3) 5 64
(William Haggas) *t.k.h: chsd ldrs: rdn 2f out: outpcd by ldrs and u.p over 1f out: one pce and wl hld ins fnl f* **66/1**

3- **6** ½ **Celestyna**[239] 6309 3-8-5 0 ....[1] CharlesEddery(7) 1 57
(Sir Henry Cecil) *hld up in tch in midfield: rdn and fnd little 2f out: plugged on same pce and no threat to ldrs fr over 1f out* **12/1**

7 ½ **Ducal** 3-9-3 0 .... StevieDonohoe 3 60
(Sir Mark Prescott Bt) *s.i.s: sn nudged along in detached last: sme hdwy jst over 1f out: kpt on ins fnl f: nvr trbld ldrs* **16/1**

8 8 **Grayfriars** 3-9-3 0 .... JimmyQuinn 6 35
(J R Jenkins) *t.k.h: chsd ldrs tl lost pl qckly 3f out: bhd fnl 2f* **100/1**

56- **9** 7 **Polish Sunset**[156] 7880 3-9-3 0 .... RichardMullen 10 12
(Amy Weaver) *t.k.h: chsd ldrs: lost pl and unbalanced* [illegible] *tch: wl bhd and eased ins fnl f* **100/1**

1m 11.24s (-3.16) **Going Correction** -0.225s/f (Firm)
WFA 3 from 4yo 9lb **9** Ran SP% **112.8**
Speed ratings (Par 101): **112,111,107,106,104 103,103,92,83**
toteswingers:1&2:£2.40, 2&3:£8.60, 1&3:£3.70 CSF £12.16 TOTE £2.20: £1.10, £1.30, £3.90; EX 11.90 Trifecta £54.60 Pool: £404.83 - 5.48 winning units..
Owner Shooting Star Racing **Bred** Newberry Stud Company **Trained** Newmarket, Suffolk

FOCUS
The going was good to firm on a watered track. A decent maiden, A strong form contender and a Godolphin newcomer pulled clear, but the 64-rated third sets the standard and holds the form down at the same time.
Beechcraft Baron(IRE) Official explanation: vet said gelding lost a shoe

2267 AGRIPLANTSOLUTIONS.CO.UK (S) STKS 5f 43y
2:50 (2:50) (Class 6) 2-Y-O **£1,813** (£539; £269; £134) **Stalls** High

Form RPR
6 **1** **First Bid**[32] 1434 2-8-12 0 .... RichardMullen 1 68+
(Kevin Ryan) *dwlt: sn chsng ldrs: rdn ent fnl 2f: led over 1f out: gng clr whn rn green jst ins fnl f: rdn and drew wl clr fnl 150yds: comf* **2/5**[1]

43 **2** 3¾ **Selinda**[11] 1954 2-8-0 0 .... CharlesBishop(7) 5 49
(Mick Channon) *sn pushed along and chsng ldrs: rdn to ld 2f out: drvn and hdd over 1f out: nt gng pce of wnr and wl hld fnl 150yds* **9/2**[2]

24 **3** 1½ **She's Cool Too (IRE)**[11] 1954 2-8-4 0 ....(t) KierenFox(3) 2 44
(Bill Turner) *broke fast but rdr lost iron for 1f: w ldr tl wl over 1f out: wkng whn hung lft u.p 1f out: no ch w wnr after* **13/2**[3]

60 **4** 5 **Masivo Man (IRE)**[11] 1954 2-8-12 0 .... AndreaAtzeni 3 31
(Chris Dwyer) *led tl 2f out: rdn and struggling whn hung lft over 1f out: continued to hang lft and wknd ins fnl f* **66/1**

5 12 **Tumbleowtashoes** 2-8-12 0 .... KirstyMilczarek 4 —
(John Ryan) *taken down early: bhd: lost tch 1/2-way: t.o ins fnl f* **25/1**

63.79 secs (1.09) **Going Correction** -0.225s/f (Firm) **5** Ran SP% **108.3**
Speed ratings (Par 91): **82,76,73,65,46**
CSF £2.45 TOTE £1.40: £1.30, £1.60; EX 2.90.The winner was bought in for 5,800gns.
Owner J C Fretwell **Bred** J W Ford **Trained** Hambleton, N Yorks

FOCUS
A modest seller for 2-y-os but the winner scored decisively, although the time was moderate.

NOTEBOOK
First Bid was easy to back but showed up well for a long way when just over 4l sixth of ten in a Redcar maiden on debut, form which has been boosted by the winner, third and fourth all scoring since. Very heavily backed dropped into a seller, he took a while to seize control on the outside but eventually forged clear. (op 8-13 after early 4-6 and 8-11 in places)

Selinda had decent claims on her fourth behind subsequent Newmarket winner B Fifty Two on debut and a third in a claimer last time. She couldn't live with the winner but kept on quite well against the stands' rail on this third attempt. She clearly has her limitations but may be able to pick up a low-grade event in the coming months. (op 7-2)

She's Cool Too(IRE) got a bit closer to the runner-up than she did at Wolverhampton last time, but she has still not really built on her debut second in a Warwick seller. (op 6-1 tchd 5-1 and 7-1)

Masivo Man(IRE) finished a remote last in a maiden and claimer in two previous runs. He showed a bit more ridden positively this time but was still ultimately well beaten. (op 33-1)

Tumbleowtashoes who was ponied to post early, ran green before dropping out at a relatively early stage on debut. (op 14-1)

2268 DIGIBET.COM H'CAP — 1m 3y

3:20 (3:21) (Class 6) (0-60,67) 4-Y-0+ — £1,813 (£539; £269; £134) Stalls High

Form — RPR

6001 **1** **Cane Cat (IRE)**[58] 950 4-8-11 49 (t) LiamJones 11 — 54
(Tony Carroll) *dwlt and hmpd sn after s: bhd: rdn over 2f out: stl plenty to do but hdwy u.p over 1f out: wnt 4th 1f out: kpt on strly u.p to ld towards fin* **22/1**

0011 **2** ½ **Integria**[3] 2171 5-10-1 67 12ex (bt) TonyCulhane 10 — 71+
(George Baker) *s.i.s: bhd and sn rdn along: hdwy 1/2-way: drvn to ld over 1f out: clr but idling jst ins fnl f: drvn and fnd little fnl 150yds: hdd and hung lft towards fin* **7/2**[2]

130- **3** nk **Colinca's Lad (IRE)**[246] 6125 9-9-4 56 PhilipRobinson 6 — 59
(Peter Charalambous) *w ldr: rdn over 2f out: outpcd by ldr ent fnl f: rallied u.p ins fnl f: kpt on* **9/2**[3]

055 **4** 1 **Graceful Spirit**[18] 1767 4-8-7 45 AndreaAtzeni 4 — 46
(Des Donovan) *led: rdn 2f out: outpcd by ldr ent fnl f: kpt on same pce ins fnl f* **25/1**

660- **5** 1 **Hotfoot**[268] 5414 4-9-7 59 RichardMullen 3 — 57
(John Berry) *chsd ldrs: rdn over 2f out: drvn and outpcd over 1f out: kpt on again ins fnl f: nt pce to threaten ldrs* **22/1**

0466 **6** ¾ **Join Up**[13] 1905 5-9-3 55 TomMcLaughlin 8 — 52
(Mark Brisbourne) *t.k.h: hld up towards rr: swtchd rt and bmpd rival over 5f out: rdn and effrt 2f out: no imp u.p over 1f out: kpt on same pce ins fnl f* **10/1**

4133 **7** 5 **Grey Boy (GER)**[13] 1905 10-8-13 58 GeorgeDowning(7) 2 — 43
(Tony Carroll) *hld up in tch towards rr: rdn and effrt 2f out: no prog and n.d fr over 1f out* **11/2**

50-0 **8** hd **Filibuster**[14] 1871 4-8-11 49 TedDurcan 5 — 34
(Chris Wall) *hld up in tch in rr: rdn and struggling over 2f out: no ch w ldrs wl over 1f out: styd on past btn horses ins fnl f: n.d* **16/1**

0005 **9** 7 **Avec Moi**[10] 1989 4-8-0 45 DanielHarris(7) 7 — 14
(Christine Dunnett) *rdr removed blind late and s.i.s: hld up in tch: bmpd and pushed rt over 5f out: rdn and effrt over 2f out: wknd 2f out* **66/1**

0-00 **10** 1 **Rileys Crane**[10] 1989 4-8-13 51 (p) SaleemGolam 1 — 17
(Christine Dunnett) *in tch: struggling u.p and losing pl 1/2-way: bhd fnl 2f* **100/1**

3001 **11** ½ **Hecton Lad (USA)**[23] 1604 4-9-5 57 (b) FrankieDettori 12 — 22+
(John Best) *chsd ldrs: lost pl and unbalanced wl over 2f out: wl btn and eased 1f out* **5/2**[1]

1m 38.85s (-1.75) **Going Correction** -0.225s/f (Firm) — 11 Ran SP% 114.4
Speed ratings (Par 101): **99,98,98,97,96 95,90,90,83,82 81**
toteswingers:1&2:£11.80, 2&3:£3.30, 1&3:£19.10 CSF £92.02 CT £419.76 TOTE £18.00: £4.80, £1.40, £2.10; EX 74.30 Trifecta £481.00 Part won. Pool: £650.05 - 0.10 winning units..
Owner John W Egan **Bred** Mrs G P Booth And J Porteous **Trained** Cropthorne, Worcs
■ Stewards' Enquiry : Tony Culhane one-day ban: used whip with excessive frequency (Jun 6)

FOCUS
Three last-time-out winners lined-up in this ordinary handicap. The pace was quite quick early on but it slackened at around halfway. The form looks very limited with the third the best guide.

Filibuster Official explanation: jockey said gelding had no more to give

Hecton Lad(USA) Official explanation: trainer's rep said gelding was unsuited by the good to firm ground

2269 AVENUE PUBLIC HOUSE FILLIES' H'CAP — 1m 3y

3:50 (3:53) (Class 4) (0-85,85) 4-Y-0+ — £4,533 (£1,348; £505; £505) Stalls High

Form — RPR

511- **1** **Wallis**[175] 7573 4-9-3 81 KierenFallon 3 — 90+
(Luca Cumani) *t.k.h: mde virtually: set stdy gallop: qcknd jst over 2f out: rdn wl over 1f out: r.o wl and a holding rivals ins fnl f* **8/1**

163- **2** ½ **Babycakes (IRE)**[189] 7420 4-9-7 85 FrankieDettori 6 — 93
(Michael Bell) *stdd s: t.k.h: hld up in tch in rr: hdwy over 3f out: rdn to chal over 1f out: r.o u.p but a hld by wnr* **4/1**[3]

6120 **3** ¾ **Night Lily (IRE)**[34] 1406 5-9-2 80 LiamJones 1 — 86
(Paul D'Arcy) *stdd s: hld up in tch: rdn jst over 2f out: hdwy and drvn to chse ldng pair over 1f out: kpt on same pce ins fnl f* **9/4**[2]

30-4 **3** dht **Ela Gorrie Mou**[10] 1992 5-8-9 73 PhilipRobinson 5 — 79
(Peter Charalambous) *stdd s: t.k.h: hld up in tch in last: rdn and effrt over 1f out: kpt on ins fnl f: unable to chal* **14/1**

010- **5** 6 **Rosedale**[202] 7238 4-8-7 71 oh1 AdrianMcCarthy 4 — 63
(James Toller) *t.k.h: chsd ldrs: rdn over 2f out: wknd u.p over 1f out* **33/1**

3-11 **6** 1¼ **Nahab**[14] 1867 4-9-5 83 TedDurcan 7 — 72
(David Lanigan) *in tch: rdn and unable qck 2f out: wknd over 1f out* **7/4**[1]

145- **7** 3½ **Mazamorra (USA)**[189] 7420 4-9-2 80 AdamKirby 2 — 61
(Marco Botti) *pressed ldr tl 2f out: rdn and btn over 1f out: wknd ins fnl f* **20/1**

1m 38.39s (-2.21) **Going Correction** -0.225s/f (Firm) — 7 Ran SP% 112.6
Speed ratings (Par 102): **102,101,100,100,94 93,90**
toteswingers:1&2:£2.70, 2&Night Lily:£0.70, 1&Night Lily:£1.70, 2&Ela Gorrie Mou:£4.20, 1&Ela Gorrie Mou:£8.60 CSF £38.48 TOTE £5.50: £4.90, £2.10; EX 20.70.
Owner Fittocks Stud **Bred** Fittocks Stud **Trained** Newmarket, Suffolk

FOCUS
A decent fillies' handicap. The pace was steady but the first four pulled clear and the winner looks one to follow. The form looks fair with a couple of unexposed sorts dominating.

2270 BRYAN HAYLETT 80TH BIRTHDAY H'CAP — 7f 3y

4:20 (4:22) (Class 5) (0-70,70) 4-Y-0+ — £2,525 (£751; £375; £187) Stalls High

Form — RPR

10-1 **1** **Batgirl**[25] 1570 4-9-5 68 FrankieDettori 3 — 81+
(John Berry) *t.k.h: hld up in tch: swtchd lft and effrt wl over 1f out: rdn and r.o wl to ld fnl 75yds: gng away at fin* **5/2**[1]

13-5 **2** 1 **Lord Of The Dance (IRE)**[13] 1917 5-9-7 70 TomMcLaughlin 2 — 76
(Mark Brisbourne) *led at stdy gallop: rdn along and qcknd ent fnl 2f: drvn jst ins fnl f: hdd and no ex fnl 70yds* **17/2**

000- **3** 2 **Excellent Aim**[212] 7019 4-8-10 59 DarrylHolland 9 — 60
(George Margarson) *t.k.h: hld up in tch: hdwy to join ldrs 4f out: ev ch and rdn 2f out: racd awkwardly: nt qckn and hung lft over 1f out: styd on same pce ins fnl f* **16/1**

-044 **4** 1¾ **Rough Rock (IRE)**[10] 1990 6-9-2 70 AdamBeschizza(5) 4 — 66
(Chris Dwyer) *stdd after s: hld up in tch in rr: rdn and effrt over 1f out: drvn and kpt on same pce ins fnl f* **7/1**

40-2 **5** 3 **Oh So Spicy**[25] 1570 4-8-11 60 TedDurcan 7 — 48
(Chris Wall) *t.k.h: prom: rdn and unable qck 2f out: wknd u.p ent fnl f* **9/2**[2]

4-41 **6** ¾ **Watch Chain (IRE)**[10] 1990 4-9-4 67 6ex KierenFallon 1 — 53
(Mark H Tompkins) *hld up in tch: rdn and effrt 2f out: unable qck over 1f out: btn ent fnl f: wknd* **5/1**[3]

2020 **7** 1¼ **Valmina**[13] 1917 4-9-0 63 ow1 AdamKirby 5 — 45
(Tony Carroll) *in tch: hdwy to join ldrs 3f out: ev ch and rdn ent fnl 2f: wknd u.p ent fnl f* **16/1**

31-5 **8** 2 **Swansea Jack**[18] 1763 4-8-10 59 (t) WilliamCarson 6 — 36
(Stuart Williams) *stdd s: hld up in tch: effrt and rdn wl over 2f out: hanging lft and no prog over 2f out: bhd fr over 1f out* **6/1**

1m 26.35s (-0.25) **Going Correction** -0.225s/f (Firm) — 8 Ran SP% 112.5
Speed ratings (Par 103): **92,90,88,86,83 82,80,78**
toteswingers:1&2:£5.70, 2&3:£26.30, 1&3:£10.80 CSF £23.76 CT £276.41 TOTE £2.10: £1.20, £3.40, £6.30; EX 26.70 Trifecta £585.10 Part won. Pool of £790.76 - 0.62 winning units..
Owner Tony Fordham **Bred** Mrs M L Parry & P M Steele-Mortimer **Trained** Newmarket, Suffolk

FOCUS
A minor handicap. The pace was not very strong but the first two finished clear and the winner can be rated better than the bare form.

2271 NORFOLKBROADS.COM H'CAP — 1m 2f 21y

4:50 (4:53) (Class 6) (0-55,60) 4-Y-0+ — £1,813 (£539; £269; £134) Stalls Low

Form — RPR

3-61 **1** **Miss Blink**[23] 1615 4-9-1 54 LeeNewman 10 — 70
(Robin Bastiman) *chsd clr ldng pair: pushed along and clsd over 3f out: rdn to ld over 1f out: kpt on wl* **4/1**[3]

466- **2** 1¾ **Petsas Pleasure**[213] 6999 5-8-8 47 KierenFallon 4 — 59
(Ollie Pears) *hld up off the pce in midfield: stdy hdwy 3f out: pushed along and chsd ldng trio 2f out: rdn to chse wnr 1f out: so no imp ins fnl f* **7/2**[2]

030/ **3** 5 **Moonlight Fantasy (IRE)**[1068] 3089 8-8-13 52 TomMcLaughlin 5 — 54
(Lucinda Featherstone) *led and sn clr: rdn over 2f out: hdd over 1f out: btn 1f out and kpt on same pce ins fnl f* **40/1**

0053 **4** 5 **Market Puzzle (IRE)**[14] 1871 4-8-9 48 TedDurcan 9 — 40
(Mark Brisbourne) *hld up wl off the pce in last quartet: rdn and effrt 3f out: no hdwy and wl btn over 1f out: plugged on to go modest 4th ins fnl f* **10/1**

-650 **5** 1½ **Ocean Rosie (IRE)**[36] 1333 4-8-11 50 LiamJones 11 — 39
(Tony Carroll) *chsd ldr and clr of field: clsd on ldr 4f out: rdn and no imp ent fnl 2f: 4th and wl btn over 1f out* **33/1**

3001 **6** 1 **Lytham (IRE)**[10] 1987 10-9-7 60 6ex AdamKirby 8 — 47
(Tony Carroll) *prom in main gp: clsd on ldrs over 3f out: drvn and unable qck over 2f out: 5th and wl btn over 1f out* **10/1**

0000 **7** 2 **Officer Lily (USA)**[24] 1582 4-8-4 46 oh1 KierenFox(3) 2 — 29
(John Best) *stdd s: hld up wl bhd in last: rdn and effrt on outer wl over 2f out: no real prog: no ch wl over 1f out* **20/1**

0355 **8** nse **Jasmin Rai**[4] 2149 4-8-6 50 AdamBeschizza(5) 12 — 33
(Des Donovan) *stdd s: hld up in last pair: pushed along and effrt 4f out: drvn and no hdwy over 2f out: no ch wl over 1f out* **12/1**

600 **9** 2¾ **Hamilton Hill**[18] 1774 4-9-2 55 StevieDonohoe 6 — 32
(Terry Clement) *dwlt and rdn along early: racd wl off the pce in midfield: rdn and dropped in rr 4f out: no ch fnl 3f* **20/1**

5-02 **R** **Nurai**[10] 1993 4-8-12 51 DarrylHolland 1 — —
(Paul D'Arcy) *ref to r* **2/1**[1]

2m 9.00s (-1.50) **Going Correction** -0.125s/f (Firm) — 10 Ran SP% 116.3
Speed ratings (Par 101): **101,99,95,91,90 89,88,87,85,—**
toteswingers:1&2:£3.00, 2&3:£0.00, 1&3:£27.10 CSF £17.46 CT £485.81 TOTE £3.80: £1.40, £1.80, £14.40; EX 24.10 Trifecta £218.80 Pool: £706.67 - 2.39 winning units..
Owner A Reed **Bred** Anthony Reed **Trained** Cowthorpe, N Yorks

FOCUS
A low-grade handicap. They were quite well strung out in the early stages and it was a similar story at the end. The hot favourite refused to race when the stalls opened. The winner is on the upgrade but the form behind is weak.

Lytham(IRE) Official explanation: trainer's rep said gelding was unsuited by the good to firm ground

2272 YARMOUTH GREYHOUND STADIUM H'CAP — 1m 6f 17y

5:20 (5:21) (Class 6) (0-60,60) 4-Y-0+ — £1,813 (£539; £269; £134) Stalls High

Form — RPR

-000 **1** **Torran Sound**[31] 1458 4-8-13 52 KierenFallon 5 — 60+
(James Eustace) *dwlt: sn rdn along and rcvrd to ld after 1f: set stdy gallop: jnd and qcknd over 3f out: hdd 3f out: rdn and styd w ldr tl led again ins fnl f: styd on wl* **9/4**[1]

-366 **2** 1 **Astroleo**[24] 1596 5-8-7 46 oh1 NickyMackay 4 — 52
(Mark H Tompkins) *chsd ldrs: wnt 2nd 10f out: rdn to press ldr over 3f out: led 3f out: clr w wnr 2f out: drvn over 1f out: hdd ins fnl f: no ex fnl 100yds* **13/2**

044- **3** 7 **Royal Premier (IRE)**[239] 6306 8-8-11 50 TedDurcan 1 — 46
(Tom Keddy) *chsd ldrs: rdn and effrt 3f out: 3rd and btn over 1f out* **3/1**[2]

55-0 **4** 3½ **Yeomanry**[15] 8 6-8-8 47 SaleemGolam 9 — 38
(Ian Williams) *hld up in tch in last trio: hdwy on inner 4f out: drvn and no imp over 2f out: 4th and wl btn over 1f out* **17/2**

0/6- **5** 2 **Arctic Wings (IRE)**[14] 7181 7-9-0 60 GeorgeDowning(7) 2 — 48
(Tony Carroll) *in tch: rdn and struggling 3f out: 5th and no ch w ldrs fnl 2f* **7/2**[3]

000- **6** 46 **Fantastic Storm**[206] 7147 4-8-7 46 oh1 LeeNewman 8 — —
(Robin Bastiman) *bhd: rdn and short-lived effrt 4f out: lost tch 3f out: t.o and eased ins fnl f* **16/1**

-006 **7** 51 **Alhudhud (USA)**[10] 1993 5-8-7 46 oh1 AndreaAtzeni 7 — —
(Kevin Morgan) *led for 1f: chsd ldr tl 10f out: rdn and lost pl over 5f out: lost tch 3f out: virtually p.u fr over 1f out: wl t.o* **16/1**

3m 7.17s (-0.43) **Going Correction** -0.125s/f (Firm) — 7 Ran SP% 113.6
Speed ratings (Par 101): **96,95,91,89,88 62,32**
toteswingers:1&2: £3.40, 2&3:£5.90, 1&3:£1.50 CSF £17.22 CT £43.49 TOTE £1.90: £1.10, £6.20; EX 19.90 Trifecta £61.30 Pool: £396.08 - 4.78 winning units..
Owner The MacDougall Two **Bred** R E Crutchley **Trained** Newmarket, Suffolk

FOCUS
A weak handicap. Most of the runners were struggling for form or returning from an absence. The first two were always prominent and there was a big gap back to the rest. The runner-up to last year's form looks the best guide.

T/Plt: £152.90 to a £1 stake. Pool of £49,511.72 - 236.37 winning tickets. T/Qpdt: £47.30 to a £1 stake. Poo of £3,664.59 57.30 winning tickets SP

2273 - 2279a (Foreign Racing) - See Raceform Interactive

1849 CHESTER (L-H)

Saturday, May 21

OFFICIAL GOING: Good (good to firm in places; 7.9)

No drop in but rail movement increased 6f races by 21yds, 7f by 23yds, 10.5f by 28yds, 11.5f by 39yds and 13.5f by 41yds.

Wind: Fresh, half-against Weather: Overcast

2280 LAMB'S NAVY RUM H'CAP (DIV I) — 6f 18y

1:50 (1:50) (Class 5) (0-75,75) 4-Y-0+ **£3,723** (£1,108; £553; £276) **Stalls** Low

Form RPR

0151 **1** **Steelcut**[12] 1955 7-9-3 **71**....(p) CathyGannon 7 78
(David Evans) *hld up: rdn and hdwy over 1f out: led ins fnl f: r.o and edgd lft: a looked on top* **7/1**

140- **2** *½* **Jack Luey**[215] 6985 4-9-5 **73**.... DuranFentiman 10 78
(Lawrence Mullaney) *in tch: effrt over 2f out: chalng ins fnl f: r.o: hld cl home* **22/1**

0000 **3** *3¾* **Methaaly (IRE)**[7] 2095 8-8-6 **67**....(be) JosephYoung(7) 11 60
(Michael Mullineaux) *hld up: rdn over 1f out: hdwy ins fnl f: r.o towards fin: tk 3rd fnl stride: no imp on front pair* **33/1**

-302 **4** *nk* **Gemma's Delight (IRE)**[19] 1766 4-8-7 **61** oh3....(p) LiamJones 6 53
(James Unett) *racd keenly w ldrs 3 wd: led over 2f out: rdn over 1f out: hdd ins fnl f: no ex fnl 75yds* **8/1**

5-60 **5** *2½* **Cyflymder (IRE)**[35] 1382 5-8-11 **70**.... NeilFarley(5) 5 54
(Declan Carroll) *hld up: rdn over 1f out: nt clr run ent fnl f: kpt on after but n.d* **6/1**[2]

2525 **6** *½* **Northern Dare (IRE)**[50] 1073 7-9-6 **74**....(b) TonyHamilton 2 57
(Richard Fahey) *led narrowly: hdd over 2f out: rdn over 1f out: wknd ins fnl f* **6/1**[2]

4-04 **7** *2¼* **Wicked Wilma (IRE)**[8] 2048 7-8-7 **61**.... FrannyNorton 4 37
(Alan Berry) *trckd ldrs: rdn and n.m.r briefly 2f out: wknd ins fnl f* **8/1**

0-02 **8** *1¼* **Defector (IRE)**[14] 1912 5-8-12 **66**.... TonyCulhane 1 38
(David Bourton) *w ldr: pushed along over 2f out: rdn over 1f out: wknd ins fnl f* **13/2**[3]

1133 **9** *1* **Frequency**[9] 2016 4-9-4 **72**....(b) JoeFanning 3 40+
(Keith Dalgleish) *restless in stalls: midfield: nt clr run over 1f out: sn rdn: denied a run again sn after: eased whn no run ins fnl f: dropped away* **7/2**[1]

-20 **10** *2¾* **Frognal (IRE)**[12] 1942 5-9-7 **75**....(b) PJMcDonald 8 35
(Ruth Carr) *hld up: u.p over 1f out: nvr on terms* **12/1**

1m 15.43s (1.63) **Going Correction** +0.25s/f (Good) **10** Ran SP% **113.8**
Speed ratings (Par 103): **99,98,93,92,89 88,85,84,82,79**
toteswingers:1&2:£15.10, 2&3:£60.30, 1&3:£0.00 CSF £143.23 CT £2961.56 TOTE £8.90: £2.50, £5.60, £5.70; EX 231.90.
Owner Shropshire Wolves 3 **Bred** Mrs B Skinner **Trained** Pandy, Monmouths

FOCUS
A dry day with ground on the fast side of good. This was the first of four 6f races on the card so will be useful for time comparison purposes. A few of these came into this in good form but the form is ordinary rated through the winner.
Cyflymder(IRE) Official explanation: jockey said gelding was denied a clear run
Defector(IRE) Official explanation: jockey said gelding did not handle the bend
Frequency Official explanation: jockey said gelding was denied a clear run

2281 CRABBIE'S "SPIFFING" ALCOHOLIC GINGER BEER MAIDEN STKS — 6f 18y

2:25 (2:28) (Class 4) 3-Y-0 **£5,180** (£1,541; £770; £384) **Stalls** Low

Form RPR

04-3 **1** **King Ferdinand**[21] 1682 3-9-3 72.... DavidProbert 9 81+
(Andrew Balding) *s.i.s: bustled along early to get position: trckd ldrs 5f out: effrt whn nt clr run and snatched up over 1f out: sn swtchd lft: r.o ins fnl f and wanted to lugg rt: led towards fin* **7/2**[2]

[illegible] **2** *nk* [illegible] 3-9-3 [illegible] [illegible] 77+
(David Simcock) *led: rdn over 1f out: strly pressed: hdd towards fin* **10/1**

-233 **3** *1* **Bertiewhittle**[7] 2094 3-9-3 72.... JoeFanning 4 74+
(David Barron) *a.p: chalng over 2f out: rdn over 1f out: ev ch tl nt qckn fnl 50yds* **9/2**[3]

342- **4** *4½* **Question Times**[204] 7204 3-8-12 96.... JackMitchell 3 54
(Peter Chapple-Hyam) *in tch: effrt on outer 2f out: one pce ins fnl f* **4/5**[1]

0 **5** *¾* **Anathena**[15] 1853 3-8-12 0.... RussKennemore 5 52
(Reg Hollinshead) *hld up: pushed along over 2f out: nvr able to get on terms w ldrs* **28/1**

-00 **6** *2* **Bygones For Coins (IRE)**[32] 1459 3-8-12 0.... FrannyNorton 8 46
(Alan Berry) *racd keenly: hld up: pushed along over 2f out: swtchd lft over 1f out: nvr on terms* **80/1**

5 **7** *6* **Crabbies Ginger**[14] 1900 3-9-3 0.... PJMcDonald 2 31
(Lisa Williamson) *w ldr tl pushed along and lost pl over 2f out: sn wl btn: wl bhd over 1f out* **25/1**

1m 15.4s (1.60) **Going Correction** +0.25s/f (Good) **7** Ran SP% **113.6**
Speed ratings (Par 101): **99,98,97,91,90 87,79**
toteswingers:1&2:£6.90, 2&3:£12.50, 1&3:£2.40 CSF £34.90 TOTE £4.60: £2.20, £4.10; EX 42.60.
Owner Thurloe Thoroughbred XXVII **Bred** Farleigh Court Racing Partnership **Trained** Kingsclere, Hants

FOCUS
Not much depth to this maiden and, with 96-rated Question Times clearly running to no where near that mark, it's probably safe to assume the form is no more than fair, rated through the third.

2282 LAMBRINI ORIGINAL H'CAP — 1m 2f 75y

2:55 (2:55) (Class 4) (0-85,85) 4-Y-0+ **£5,180** (£1,156; £1,156; £384) **Stalls** High

Form RPR

4-30 **1** **Beaumont's Party (IRE)**[21] 1684 4-8-11 **75**.... DavidProbert 11 86+
(Andrew Balding) *trckd ldrs: effrt over 1f out: led jst ins fnl f: r.o wl to draw clr sn after* **13/2**[3]

6-26 **2** *3¾* **Oriental Cavalier**[15] 1855 5-8-10 **74**....(v) CathyGannon 1 78
(Mark Buckley) *midfield: rdn and hdwy over 1f out: styd on ins fnl f: disp 2nd post: no ch w wnr* **9/1**

0-35 **2** *dht* **One Scoop Or Two**[16] 1826 5-8-13 **77**.... RussKennemore 9 81
(Reg Hollinshead) *racd keenly: prom: rdn to ld over 1f out: edgd lft and hdd jst ins fnl f: outpcd by wnr sn after: jnd for 2nd post* **12/1**

4-06 **4** *¾* **Tartan Gunna**[14] 1892 5-9-5 **83**....(b) JoeFanning 6 85
(Mark Johnston) *midfield: rdn over 1f out: kpt on ins fnl f: nvr able to chal* **6/1**[2]

20-4 **5** *hd* **Fourth Generation (IRE)**[22] 1651 4-8-13 **77**.... PJMcDonald 7 79
(Alan Swinbank) *trckd ldrs: pushed along over 3f out: nt qckn over 1f out: kpt on same pce ins fnl f* **20/1**

00-4 **6** *¾* **Inspirina (IRE)**[16] 1826 7-9-2 **80**.... DarryllHolland 4 80
(Richard Ford) *led: stdd pce over 7f out: pushed along over 2f out: rdn and hdd over 1f out: no ex fnl 75yds* **15/2**

2-03 **7** *1½* **Bahamian Music (IRE)**[16] 1826 4-9-4 **82**.... TonyHamilton 3 79
(Richard Fahey) *hld up in rr: pushed along and outpcd over 2f out: nvr able to get on terms* **4/1**[1]

314 **8** *1* **Granny McPhee**[15] 1855 5-9-5 **83**.... LiamJones 5 78
(Alan Bailey) *hld up: hdwy into midfield over 3f out: no imp on ldrs: wknd over 1f out* **4/1**[1]

1604 **9** *nk* **Georgebernardshaw (IRE)**[16] 1824 6-9-7 **85**.... ShaneKelly 10 80
(David Simcock) *s.i.s: hld up: pushed along over 1f out: nvr on terms* **9/1**

0/ **10** *14* **Qeethaara (USA)**[355] 2612 7-9-0 **78**.... FrannyNorton 2 45
(Mark Brisbourne) *hld up: nvr able to get on terms: lost tch over 1f out* **40/1**

2m 10.8s (-0.40) **Going Correction** +0.25s/f (Good) **10** Ran SP% **114.3**
Speed ratings (Par 105): **115,112,112,111,111 110,109,108,108,97**PL: One Scoop or Two £3.10 Oriental Cavalier £3.30 EX: Beaumont's Party/OS £53.40, BP/OC £32.80 CSF: BM/OS £39.86 BP/OC £31.14 TRI: BP/OS/OC £350.37 BP/OC/OS £341.72. toteswingers:1&OS:£9.10, OS&OC:£15.80, 1&OC:£8.20 CSF £31.14 TOTE £7.80: £2.70; EX 53.4027 Trifecta £0Owner Thurloe Thoroughbreds XXV Bred.

FOCUS
A wide-open handicap run at a stop-start gallop, making it difficult for those that were held up to get in a blow. A personal best from the winner with the dead-heater setting the level.
Bahamian Music(IRE) Official explanation: jockey said filly stumbled on leaving stalls
Georgebernardshaw(IRE) Official explanation: jockey said gelding became upset in stalls

2283 TSINGTAO CHINESE BEER E B F MAIDEN STKS — 6f 18y

3:25 (3:28) (Class 4) 2-Y-O **£4,533** (£1,348; £674; £336) **Stalls** Low

Form RPR

3 **1** **Moonville (IRE)**[18] 1797 2-9-3 0.... TonyHamilton 10 75+
(Richard Fahey) *s.i.s: sn chsd ldr: led over 1f out: sn rdn: r.o wl and in command ins fnl f* **9/2**[2]

3 **2** *2¼* **Tortoni (IRE)**[9] 2033 2-9-3 0.... DarryllHolland 2 68+
(Kevin Ryan) *chsd ldrs: a niggled along: n.m.r over 2f out: nt qckn over 1f out: styd on to take 2nd fnl 100yds: no imp on wnr* **1/2**[1]

6 **3** *1¾* **Silvas Romana (IRE)**[12] 1957 2-8-12 0.... FrannyNorton 6 58
(Mark Brisbourne) *swtchd lft early: bhd: pushed along 3f out: styd on fnl 100yds: nrst fin: nvr gng pce to get competitive* **33/1**

00 **4** *nk* **Bajan Hero**[8] 2049 2-9-3 0.... IanMongan 4 62
(David Evans) *broke wl but racd awkwardly early and rdn: in tch: outpcd by ldrs over 1f out: no imp* **33/1**

03 **5** *nk* **Monumental Man**[5] 2160 2-9-3 0.... ShaneKelly 8 61
(James Unett) *led: rdn and hdd over 1f out: wknd fnl 75yds* **11/1**

043 **6** *4* **Adranian (IRE)**[6] 2120 2-9-3 0....(v) CathyGannon 5 49
(David Evans) *forced wd early: bhd: sn pushed along and outpcd: nvr on terms* **10/1**[3]

1m 16.49s (2.69) **Going Correction** +0.25s/f (Good) **6** Ran SP% **108.2**
Speed ratings (Par 95): **92,89,86,86,85 80**
toteswingers:1&2:£1.10, 2&3:£27.90, 1&3:£11.60 CSF £6.57 TOTE £5.10: £2.20, £1.10; EX 7.10.
Owner M Wynne **Bred** L K I Bloodstock & Diomed Bloodstock **Trained** Musley Bank, N Yorks

FOCUS
Not much depth to this maiden and Tortoni was backed as if defeat wasn't an option. However, he never looked happy on the track and proved no match for the winner. The form is muddling and is rated using the time and averages for now.

NOTEBOOK
Moonville(IRE) looks to have appreciated stepping up in trip after an encouraging debut over 5f and he left that debut form well behind with a really good display. He could be useful. (op 4-1 tchd 5-1)
Tortoni(IRE) was been niggled along from an early stage and didn't look happy at any point. He may have been beaten by the track, but equally he may just have met his match in terms of a talented rival, so it will be interesting to see how he gets on [illegible] Group 1 Phoenix Stakes entry suggests connections think he's a lot better than this. (op 10-11 tchd evens in a place)
Silvas Romana(IRE) ran with some promise, staying on up the inside having been some way off the pace early. She is already shaping like she needs a stiffer test of stamina. (op 28-1)
Bajan Hero got a bit outpaced before keeping on well. This was his best run so far and he looks an interesting one for nurseries. (op 25-1)
Adranian(IRE) Official explanation: jockey said colt never travelled

2284 CRABBIE'S "TICKETY BOO" ALCOHOLIC GINGER BEER H'CAP — 7f 2y

4:00 (4:01) (Class 2) (0-105,102) 4-Y-0+ **£12,952** (£3,854; £1,926; £962) **Stalls** Low

Form RPR

0-33 **1** **Our Jonathan**[8] 2075 4-9-0 **95**.... FrannyNorton 6 105+
(Kevin Ryan) *hld up: hdwy and swtchd rt over 1f out and c arnd the field: str run ins fnl f: led towards fin* **10/3**[1]

00-0 **2** *nk* **Mon Cadeaux**[14] 1885 4-8-12 **93**.... DavidProbert 11 102
(Andrew Balding) *in tch: nt clr run over 1f out: effrt and swtchd lft sn after: chalng ins fnl f: led fnl 100yds: hdd towards fin* **16/1**

0-30 **3** *1¼* **Balcarce Nov (ARG)**[21] 1694 6-9-1 **96**.... MickyFenton 3 102
(Tom Tate) *led: hdd over 5f out: remained prom: rdn to regain ld over 1f out: hdd fnl 100yds: kpt on but hld towards fin* **14/1**

2112 **4** *nk* **Norville (IRE)**[15] 1854 4-9-0 **95**....(b) CathyGannon 5 100
(David Evans) *prom: led over 5f out: rdn and hdd over 1f out: stl ev ch ins fnl f: styd on same pce fnl 75yds* **8/1**

0330 **5** *1* **Lowther**[14] 1885 6-9-7 **102**....(be) LiamJones 8 104
(Alan Bailey) *midfield: hdwy 3f out: hung lft whn chalng over 1f out: styd on same pce fnl 100yds* **8/1**

0-66 **6** *1* **Damika (IRE)**[8] 2075 8-8-13 **94**.... PJMcDonald 1 93
(Richard Whitaker) *prom: rdn over 1f out and stl ch: one pce fnl 100yds* **14/1**

-301 **7** *½* **Kyllachy Star**[15] 1849 5-9-2 **97**.... TonyHamilton 2 95
(Richard Fahey) *bmpd s: in tch: lost pl over 3f out: rdn over 1f out: no imp* **7/1**

-264 **8** *nse* **Brae Hill (IRE)**[14] 1885 5-9-3 **98**.... BarryMcHugh 12 96
(Richard Fahey) *in tch: rdn to chal over 1f out: one pce ins fnl f* **11/2**[3]

1010 **9** *2* **Flipando (IRE)**[8] 2075 10-9-3 **98**.... JackMitchell 9 91
(David Barron) *rrd s: hld up: hmpd 5f out: hdwy on outer 3f out: no imp on ldrs: outpcd and btn over 1f out* **25/1**

1430 **10** *16* **Brave Prospector**[37] 1340 6-9-7 **102**....(t) ShaneKelly 7 51+
(Jane Chapple-Hyam) *hld up: n.m.r 5f out: nvr able to get to terms: eased whn wl btn ins fnl f* **33/1**

112- 11 9 **Man Of Action (USA)**[315] 3886 4-9-1 **96**...................... DarryllHolland 10 21+
(Saeed Bin Suroor) *hld up: pushed along over 2f out: outpcd after* **9/2**[2]

1m 26.58s (0.08) **Going Correction** +0.25s/f (Good) **11** Ran SP% **117.4**
Speed ratings (Par 109): **109,108,107,106,105 104,104,103,101,83 73**
toteswingers:1&2:£6.40, 2&3:£70.60, 1&3:£26.60 CSF £59.54 CT £679.21 TOTE £4.40: £1.80, £5.40, £5.10; EX 82.20.
Owner Dr Marwan Koukash **Bred** W G M Turner **Trained** Hambleton, N Yorks

FOCUS
A competitive handicap, but the top pair were rated 3lb below the ceiling for this grade so it wasn't outstanding form. The form is rated around the placed horses.

NOTEBOOK
Our Jonathan stormed home down the outside to get up. His many supporters would have been concerned when he'd been hampered mid-race and his rider was forced to switch right around the field early in the straight. He picked up strongly to mow them down and make a winning debut over this trip. There were strong grounds for believing this 4-y-o was well handicapped on the pick of last season's efforts in Group company and it's pretty safe to say he's value for more than the official winning margin here. This trip could be the making of him. (op 9-2)
Mon Cadeaux has run a blinder in defeat, continuing the excellent form of his stable, and this was a huge improvement on his last couple of runs. He looks poised to strike soon. (op 20-1)
Balcarce Nov(ARG) helped make much of the running and battled on well once headed. He hasn't won for a while and is a bit hit and miss, but this was a good run. (op 12-1)
Norville(IRE) faded away in the closing stages, but this was his toughest assignement to date so he was not disgraced. (tchd 7-1)
Lowther wasn't disgraced, especially as this trip is on the sharp side for him. Official explanation: jockey said gelding hung left
Man Of Action(USA) was slowly away and never a factor. He's better than this. (op 4-1)

2285 CRABBIE'S "WIZARD" ALCOHOLIC GINGER BEER H'CAP 1m 5f 89y
4:35 (4:35) (Class 3) (0-90,89) 4-Y-O+ **£8,418** (£2,505; £1,251; £625) **Stalls** Low

Form RPR
530 1 **English Summer**[8] 2071 4-9-7 **89**.................................... FrannyNorton 6 97
(Mark Johnston) *chsd ldr tl over 7f out: remained prom: rdn to ld 1f out: r.o ins fnl f: a doing enough in driving fin* **11/2**[3]
102- 2 hd **Plato (JPN)**[236] 6423 4-9-2 **84**... IanMongan 9 92
(Sir Henry Cecil) *chsd ldrs: wnt 2nd over 7f out: big effrt to chal strly fr over 1f out: r.o ins fnl f: a looked hld* **6/1**
1212 3 1 **Sir Boss (IRE)**[15] 1855 6-9-4 **86**.. LiamJones 2 92
(Michael Mullineaux) *racd keenly: chsd ldrs: rdn and swtchd rt over 1f out: styd on towards fin* **11/2**[3]
2-36 4 ¾ **Bowdler's Magic**[8] 2071 4-9-5 **87**...................................... JoeFanning 4 92
(Mark Johnston) *in tch: rdn whn chsng ldrs over 1f out: nt qckn ins fnl f* **3/1**[1]
02-0 5 hd **Comedy Act**[15] 1847 4-9-3 **85**...............................(p) MickyFenton 1 90
(Philip Hobbs) *led: rdn and hdd 1f out: stl ev ch ins fnl f: no ex fnl 50yds* **14/1**
0-40 6 2½ **Dazzling Light (UAE)**[8] 2071 6-8-9 **77**.......................... JackMitchell 8 78+
(Jim Goldie) *hld up: pushed along over 2f out: kpt on u.p ins fnl f: nt trble ldrs* **5/1**[2]
3405 7 1 **Porgy**[14] 1892 6-8-12 **80**.. ShaneKelly 3 79+
(David Simcock) *s.i.s: hld up: pushed along over 1f out: nvr trbld ldrs* **12/1**
2211 8 ½ **Accumulate**[32] 1470 8-8-5 **73**.. BarryMcHugh 7 72+
(Bill Moore) *hld up: pushed along and outpcd over 2f out: no imp* **14/1**
110- 9 1¾ **Regal Park (IRE)**[211] 7061 4-9-5 **87**............................... CathyGannon 10 83+
(Marco Botti) *dwlt: hld up: pushed along over 2f out: nvr on terms* **8/1**
523- 10 1¾ **Bollin Felix**[65] 7173 7-9-5 **87**.. DuranFentiman 5 80+
(Tim Easterby) *midfield: pushed along over 2f out and outpcd: bhd ins fnl f* **25/1**

2m 56.21s (3.41) **Going Correction** +0.25s/f (Good) **10** Ran SP% **122.7**
Speed ratings (Par 107): **100,99,99,98,98 97,96,96,95,94**
toteswingers:1&2:£4.80, 2&3:£16.40, 1&3:£5.90 CSF £40.73 CT £195.97 TOTE £6.30: £2.20, £2.20, £1.80; EX 57.50.
Owner Dr Marwan Koukash **Bred** Juddmonte Farms Ltd **Trained** Middleham Moor, N Yorks

FOCUS
Just a steady gallop to this staying handicap and the form looks muddling, although it is taken at face value.

NOTEBOOK
English Summer was always travelling well just behind the leaders and he picked up well when the gap came up the inside before holding on gamely. This was slightly easier than the York race the winner was beaten 5l in last time and he travelled like a horse on really good terms with himself. There could still be more to come from this fellow given this was only his ninth career start. (op 8-1)
Plato(JPN), the other relatively unexposed runner in the line-up, stayed on strongly to push the winner all the way and this was a good effort. He could be another with more to offer this year. (op 11-2)
Sir Boss(IRE) was another to finish well and he remains a progressive type as he stays further so would have ideally needed a stronger pace over this trip. Official explanation: jockey said gelding was denied a clear run (op 9-2)
Bowdler's Magic ran another solid race in defeat, but he doesn't have any leeway off this sort of mark so needs things to drop just right. (op 9-2)
Dazzling Light(UAE) made some late headway he was never threatening the principals. The steady pace was all against him. (op 7-1)

2286 LAMB'S NAVY RUM H'CAP (DIV II) 6f 18y
5:10 (5:11) (Class 5) (0-75,75) 4-Y-O+ **£3,723** (£1,108; £553; £276) **Stalls** Low

Form RPR
5210 1 **Orpenindeed (IRE)**[4] 2179 8-9-7 **75**...............................(t) LiamJones 2 87
(Frank Sheridan) *led early: racd w ldr: rdn and str chal over 1f out: r.o to ld narrowly wl ins fnl f: jst prevailed in driving fin* **9/2**[1]
-030 2 shd **Not My Choice (IRE)**[5] 2165 6-9-2 **70**..............................(t) DavidNolan 1 81
(David C Griffiths) *bustled along s: sn led: rdn whn strly pressed over 1f out: hdd narrowly wl ins fnl f: r.o u.p: jst denied in driving fin* **5/1**[2]
-344 3 3½ **Kingswinford (IRE)**[14] 1917 5-9-3 **74**......................... RichardEvans(3) 7 73+
(David Evans) *midfield: rdn and hdwy 1f out: styd on ins fnl f: unable to trble front pair* **7/1**
0160 4 1½ **Sir Nod**[14] 1907 9-9-4 **72**.. BarryMcHugh 3 67
(Julie Camacho) *trckd ldrs: rdn over 1f out: one pce ins fnl f* **8/1**
0-36 5 ½ **Red Roar (IRE)**[8] 2062 4-8-12 **66**...................................... CathyGannon 5 59+
(Alan Berry) *hld up: styd on u.p ins fnl f: nvr able to trble ldrs* **8/1**
3351 6 nk **Absa Lutte (IRE)**[14] 1899 8-9-1 **69**.................................(t) DarryllHolland 8 61
(Michael Mullineaux) *hld up: hdwy 2f out: chsd ldrs over 1f out: one pce and no further imp ins fnl f* **13/2**[3]
5413 7 1½ **Itsthursdayalready**[2] 2238 4-8-7 **61** oh1......................... FrannyNorton 9 48
(Mark Brisbourne) *hld up: rdn over 1f out: no imp* **7/1**
000- 8 1½ **Arabian Pearl (IRE)**[203] 7238 5-9-5 **73**.........................(b) JackMitchell 11 56
(Peter Chapple-Hyam) *prom: pushed along over 2f out: wknd 1f out* **16/1**
0-06 9 1½ **Captain Scooby**[11] 1968 5-9-4 **72**.................................... TonyHamilton 6 50
(Richard Whitaker) *squeezed out s: a bhd* **9/1**
5-30 10 ½ **Schoolboy Champ**[8] 2048 4-8-6 **62**.................................... JoeFanning 4 38
(Patrick Morris) *trckd ldrs: pushed along over 2f out: sn wknd* **16/1**

1m 14.89s (1.09) **Going Correction** +0.25s/f (Good) **10** Ran SP% **117.2**
Speed ratings (Par 103): **102,101,97,95,94 94,92,90,88,87**
toteswingers:1&2:£3.20, 2&3:£6.20, 1&3:£4.50 CSF £26.89 CT £159.99 TOTE £5.50: £2.00, £2.70, £2.10; EX 28.20.
Owner Frank Sheridan **Bred** A Pereira **Trained** Wolverhampton, W Midlands

FOCUS
An ordinary event in which it proved impossible for the hold-up horses to get in a blow. The runner-up is rated to his autumn form.
Kingswinford(IRE) Official explanation: jockey said gelding suffered interference leaving stalls
Red Roar(IRE) Official explanation: jockey said filly suffered interference shortly after start
Itsthursdayalready Official explanation: jockey said gelding hung right in home straight

2287 CRABBIE'S "STEADY ON" ALCOHOLIC GINGER BEER H'CAP 1m 3f 79y
5:45 (5:45) (Class 4) (0-85,84) 3-Y-O **£5,180** (£1,541; £770; £384) **Stalls** Low

Form RPR
031- 1 **Swift Alhaarth (IRE)**[155] 7916 3-8-13 **76**........................... JoeFanning 4 87
(Mark Johnston) *racd keenly: mde all: rdn and r.o wl to draw clr ins fnl f: eased cl home* **15/2**
1-22 2 2¾ **Mica Mika (IRE)**[10] 2008 3-9-7 **84**................................... TonyHamilton 5 89
(Richard Fahey) *a.p: chalng 2 wd 3f out: rdn and nt qckn over 1f out: kpt on u.p but outpcd by wnr ins fnl f* **3/1**[2]
16-4 3 shd **Time To Work (IRE)**[17] 1811 3-9-7 **84**............................ DavidProbert 6 89
(Andrew Balding) *s.i.s: hld up in rr: hdwy 4f out: chalng 3 wd 3f out: u.p and nt qckn over 1f out: kpt on u.p ins fnl f* **7/2**[3]
2-41 4 6 **Baisse**[14] 1915 3-9-3 **80**... IanMongan 2 74
(Sir Henry Cecil) *hld up: hdwy over 3f out: chalng 4 wd 3f out: outpcd over 1f out: n.d after* **6/4**[1]
2-51 5 10 **Arabian Star (IRE)**[15] 1862 3-9-2 **79**............................ SamHitchcott 1 55
(Mick Channon) *prom: lost pl over 3f out: outpcd over 2f out: bhd ins fnl f* **13/2**

2m 28.27s (3.47) **Going Correction** +0.25s/f (Good) **5** Ran SP% **112.3**
Speed ratings (Par 101): **103,101,100,96,89**
CSF £30.04 TOTE £8.00: £3.90, £2.00; EX 32.60.
Owner Dr Marwan Koukash **Bred** Mrs Joan Murphy **Trained** Middleham Moor, N Yorks

FOCUS
A good little race but the form is muddling, with the third the best guide.
T/Plt: £1,873.00 to a £1 stake. Pool of £74,535.82 - 29.05 winning tickets. T/Qpdt: £55.30 to a £1 stake. Pool of £6,021.41 - 80.50 winning tickets. DO

2187 GOODWOOD (R-H)
Saturday, May 21

OFFICIAL GOING: Good to firm (good in places on straight course 8.0)
Lower bend dolled out 6yds from 6f to 2f up the straight increasing distances on round course by 12yds.
Wind: Moderate, half against Weather: Fine

2288 HAMPSHIRE SOCIETY STKS (H'CAP) 6f
2:15 (2:16) (Class 2) (0-105,100) 3-Y-O+
£12,462 (£3,732; £1,866; £934; £466; £234) **Stalls** High

Form RPR
0-30 1 **Crown Choice**[14] 1888 6-9-8 **94**.. AdamKirby 6 102+
(Walter Swinburn) *taken down early: hld up in last quartet: rdn and prog wl over 1f out: r.o to ld last 100yds: readily* **15/2**
100- 2 ¾ **Love Delta (USA)**[144] 7993 4-9-11 **97**............................... GregFairley 9 102
(Mark Johnston) *pressed ldr: rdn to chal and upsides fr over 1f out: kpt on ins fnl f but outpcd last 100yds* **28/1**
6-00 3 hd **Parisian Pyramid (IRE)**[14] 1885 5-9-7 **93**..................... StephenCraine 7 98
(Kevin Ryan) *w ldr: led 2f out: hrd pressed after: hdd and one pce last 100yds* **9/2**[2]
3-40 4 hd **Lutine Bell**[14] 1885 4-9-5 **91**...(b) MartinDwyer 12 95
(Mike Murphy) *fluffed s and lost abt 4 l: t.k.h and hld up in last pair: pushed along 2f out: prog over 1f out: drvn and r.o ins fnl f: gaining fin* **14/1**
3305 5 ½ **Lui Rei (ITY)**[7] 2117 5-9-13 **99**.. RichardMullen 1 101
(Robert Cowell) *hld up in last quartet: stdy prog fr 1/2-way to chse ldrs over 1f out: drvn to try to chal fnl f: one pce last 100yds* **9/1**
12-0 6 nk **Dungannon**[14] 1888 4-9-4 **90**... LiamKeniry 8 91
(Andrew Balding) *trckd ldrs: swtchd lft and effrt over 1f out: tried to cl on ldrs ins fnl f: nt qckn* **7/2**[1]
6060 7 nk **Spirit Of Sharjah (IRE)**[9] 2031 6-9-9 **95**........................ JimmyQuinn 11 95
(Julia Feilden) *mostly in midfield: rdn 2f out: styd on same pce ins fnl f: nvr able to chal* **22/1**
-016 8 1 **Fathsta (IRE)**[14] 1885 6-9-9 **100**....................................... LauraPike(5) 3 99+
(David Simcock) *taken down early: pressed ldrs: upsides 2f out: nt qckn 1f out: hld whn short of room and eased last 75yds* **10/1**
120- 9 2¼ **Slip Sliding Away (IRE)**[239] 6319 4-8-7 **82**.................. JohnFahy(3) 13 72
(Peter Hedger) *towards rr: drvn and no prog over 1f out: fdd* **8/1**
5-00 10 1½ **Corporal Maddox**[14] 1885 4-9-11 **97**................................. TomQueally 10 82
(Jamie Osborne) *chsd ldrs: rdn and no imp 2f out: wknd over 1f out* **33/1**
1026 11 2 **Everymanforhimself (IRE)**[15] 1854 7-9-2 **88**..............(b) WilliamBuick 4 70
(Kevin Ryan) *in tch in midfield: no prog 2f out: wknd and eased ins fnl f* **16/1**
511- 12 ¾ **Take Ten**[189] 7443 4-9-10 **96**... FrankieDettori 2 86+
(Mahmood Al Zarooni) *mde most to 2f out: wknd rapidly 1f out and heavily eased* **11/2**[3]
4-05 13 nk **Rowe Park**[15] 1848 8-9-13 **99**...(p) SteveDrowne 5 75
(Linda Jewell) *edgy in stalls: a in last quartet: eased whn no ch ins fnl f* **50/1**

1m 11.32s (-0.88) **Going Correction** +0.10s/f (Good) **13** Ran SP% **123.0**
Speed ratings (Par 109): **109,108,107,107,106 106,106,104,101,99 97,96,95**
toteswingers:1&2:£43.60, 2&3:£84.70, 1&3:£9.30 CSF £212.27 CT £1069.29 TOTE £10.20: £2.90, £7.40, £1.90; EX 280.40 TRIFECTA Not won..
Owner P W Harris **Bred** Howard Barton Stud **Trained** Aldbury, Herts

FOCUS
Racing began with competitive sprint handicap in which few could be confidently discounted and which might well offer significant clues for Royal Ascot. They all raced down the centre of the track and the form looks pretty solid.

NOTEBOOK

Crown Choice, whose four wins prior to this were all registered over 7f, came with a powerful late run to lift this prize. In midfield early on, he began to edge forward at halfway and was switched right to get a clear run just after the 2f pole. He quickened up nicely thereafter and appeared to win with a little in hand. Connections now plan to aim for the Wokingham Stakes and felt taking the gelding down early here may have helped. (op 9-1 tchd 10-1)

Love Delta(USA) lined up bidding for his first victory on turf and made a bold fist of it. Never too far off the pace, he was second 2f out and stayed on well even after the winner shot past. This was a sound first effort of 2011. (tchd 33-1)

Parisian Pyramid(IRE), successful in this event in 2010, showed again that he handles this course. Always prominent, and in front by halfway, he stuck to his guns all the way to the line. (op 6-1)

Lutine Bell, down the field when behind Fastha last time out, fluffed the start and lost a good deal of ground. He was therefore always playing catch-up, in a race not run at a breakneck gallop, so this has to go down as a commendable performance. (op 12-1)

Lui Rei(ITY) lined up looking for his first win since arriving from Italy in 2010 and, though he never looked likely to collect, ran well enough to suggest he is on a mark from which he can be competitive. He showed good speed from the outset, but was unable to quicken at the business end. (tchd 10-1)

Dungannon, badly hampered when eighth at Ascot on his only previous start this term, tried hard to get into a threatening position from halfway. His run petered out towards the finish, however, and he was a fraction disappointing. His jockey reported he would not let himself down on the ground and indicated that a softer surface would be an advantage. (tchd 4-1)

Spirit Of Sharjah(IRE) Official explanation: trainer said gelding bled from the nose

2289 BRIGHTON ARGUS STKS (H'CAP) 1m 4f

2:45 (2:47) (Class 2) (0-105,103) 4-Y-O+**£17,809** (£5,299; £2,648; £1,322) **Stalls** High

Form RPR

11-2 **1** **Harlestone Times (IRE)**[31] 1477 4-8-13 **95**....................... TedDurcan 8 106+
(John Dunlop) *settled wl in rr: prog on outer fr over 4f out: chsd ldr over 2f out: hrd rdn and styd on to ld last 100yds* **3/1**[2]

3025 **2** *3/4* **Nave (USA)**[7] 2107 4-8-5 **87**.................................... GregFairley 1 95
(Mark Johnston) *led: kicked on over 4f out: drvn 2f out: edgd lft and worn down last 100yds* **10/1**

1-52 **3** *2 1/4* **Beachfire**[16] 1824 4-9-2 **98**.................................... WilliamBuick 5 102
(John Gosden) *s.i.s: detached in last and cajoled along: effrt on outer fr 4f out: urged along and prog to chse ldng pair 2f out: hanging and nt qckn over 1f out: one pce after* **2/1**[1]

2426 **4** *3 1/4* **Halicarnassus (IRE)**[35] 1403 7-8-13 **98**.................. MartinHarley(3) 7 97
(Mick Channon) *chsd ldrs: lost pl 1/2-way: rdn 4f out: prog on inner and squeezed through to chse ldng trio 2f out: disp 3rd 1f out: wknd last 100yds* **20/1**

20-0 **5** *3/4* **Greylami (IRE)**[21] 1684 6-8-7 **92**........................ SeanLevey(3) 3 90
(Robert Mills) *t.k.h: hld up in midfield: tried to cl on ldrs fr 3f out: one pce and no imp 2f out* **20/1**

-500 **6** *3/4* **Cumulus Nimbus**[21] 1684 4-9-0 **96**........................ DaneO'Neill 9 92
(Richard Hannon) *s.i.s: wl off the pce in 10th: nt clr run 3f out: rdn and sme prog over 2f out: kpt on one pce* **16/1**

0-20 **7** *1/2* **Icon Dream (IRE)**[17] 1808 4-9-3 **99**........................ TomQueally 2 95
(David Simcock) *chsd ldrs early: lost pl and dropped to last trio 4f out: rdn and kpt on fr over 2f out: n.d* **8/1**[3]

034- **8** *6* **Classic Vintage (USA)**[175] 7350 5-8-11 **93**.................. MartinDwyer 6 79
(Amanda Perrett) *sn chsd ldrs: rdn in 5th over 3f out: wknd wl over 2f out* **9/1**

060- **9** *3 1/2* **Kid Charlemagne (IRE)**[267] 5492 8-8-5 **87**.................. TadhgO'Shea 4 67
(Warren Greatrex) *chsd ldng pair: rdn to go 2nd over 3f out to over 2f out: wknd qckly* **50/1**

0-00 **10** *5* **Mister Angry (IRE)**[14] 1887 4-8-6 **88**........................(b[1]) JimmyQuinn 11 60
(Mark Johnston) *chsd ldr to over 3f out: sn wknd* **20/1**

652- **11** *3 1/2* **Chock A Block (IRE)**[192] 7384 5-9-7 **103**.................. FrankieDettori 10 70
(Saeed Bin Suroor) *in tch: trckd ldrs 1/2-way: 4th over 4f out: wknd 3f out: eased* **11/1**

2m 35.73s (-2.67) **Going Correction** +0.025s/f (Good) **11** Ran SP% **119.0**
Speed ratings (Par 109): **109,108,107,104,104 103,103,99,97,93 91**
toteswingers:1&2:£7.90, 2&3:£5.80, 1&3:£1.30 CSF £31.58 CT £74.38 TOTE £3.40: £1.90, £1.40, £1.20; EX 39.70 Trifecta £74.40 Pool: £760.92 - 7.50 winning units..
Owner J L Dunlop **Bred** J L Dunlop **Trained** Arundel, W Sussex

FOCUS

A decent handicap, with the top weight rated 103, and plenty could be fancied. The winner recorded another personal best with the second helps set the level.

NOTEBOOK

Harlestone Times(IRE), successful over 1m2f here in September 2010, notched his second course victory with a game effort. Held up in midfield early on, he gradually worked his way forward in the home straight and hit the front inside the final furlong. He clearly stays this trip well and, judged on this evidence, may handle further. Connections already have half an eye on a crack at the Ebor. (op 11-4)

Nave(USA) 10lb higher than when successful over C&D in August 2010, made a bold bid to lead throughout. Fast away, he established a clear advantage by the home turn and kicked again after straightening up. He began to tire at the 1f pole, though, and could not respond when the winner edged past. (op 9-1)

Beachfire, 2lb higher than when second over 1m2f at Chester last time out, was slowly away. He tends to make a habit of that, but here he was perhaps five lengths adrift of the penultimate runner when last at the start of the home turn. He made significant late progress in the straight, racing wide of the rest, but never looked likely to get closer than his finishing position. (op 11-4)

Halicarnassus(IRE), runner-up off this mark in Dubai in February, was always in the first half-dozen. He failed to quicken in the closing stages, though, and this fantastic servant to connections seems now to be in slow but predictable decline.

Greylami(IRE), successful over 1m3f here in 2008, was never really in contention. Fifth was the closest he ever got and, while this was not a bad effort, his recent profile suggests he could do with a little more help from the handicapper. (tchd 22-1)

Cumulus Nimbus, stepping up in distance after a trio of fair runs this season, was given every chance to get the trip. He made some late progress after racing towards the rear for the first half of the journey, but it was not nearly enough to threaten the principals.

2290 ITWCP FESTIVAL STKS (LISTED RACE) 1m 1f 192y

3:20 (3:21) (Class 1) 4-Y-O+

£17,031 (£6,456; £3,231; £1,611; £807; £405) **Stalls** Low

Form RPR

4/-5 **1** **City Leader (IRE)**[24] 1600 6-8-12 110.......................... MartinDwyer 4 114
(Brian Meehan) *hld up last: prog on outer over 2f out: drvn to cl ins fnl f: narrow ld last 100yds: styd on wl* **16/1**

124- **2** *hd* **Class Is Class (IRE)**[266] 5539 5-8-12 111....................(v) WilliamBuick 5 113
(Sir Michael Stoute) *led 1f: restrained bhd ldrs after and keen: shkn up 3f out: clsd over 1f out: wandered u.p but chal and upsides ins fnl f: jst hld* **6/1**[3]

140- **3** *hd* **Principal Role (USA)**[218] 6886 4-8-7 103.......................... TomQueally 7 108
(Sir Henry Cecil) *prom: trckd ldr over 4f out: led over 2f out: drvn fnl f: hdd last 100yds: styd on* **12/1**

24-2 **4** *1 3/4* **Sea Of Heartbreak (IRE)**[20] 1718 4-8-7 103.................. SteveDrowne 2 105
(Roger Charlton) *trckd ldrs: gng strly whn prog to go 2nd briefly wl over 1f out: sn rdn and nt qckn* **9/1**

1-63 **5** *1 1/4* **Forte Dei Marmi**[16] 1821 5-8-12 111.................................. KierenFallon 8 107+
(Luca Cumani) *t.k.h: hld up in 6th: looking for room over 2f out: effrt whn nt clr run over 1f out: no real imp ins fnl f* **5/2**[1]

142- **6** *nse* **Prince Siegfried (FR)**[203] 7237 5-8-12 109.................. RichardMullen 3 107
(Saeed Bin Suroor) *led briefly after 1f: styd prom: shkn up and nt qckn on inner 2f out: one pce after* **12/1**

634- **7** *7* **Al Zir (USA)**[218] 6885 4-8-12 109......................................(t) FrankieDettori 1 93
(Saeed Bin Suroor) *s.i.s: led over 8f out: rdn and hdd over 2f out: wknd qckly over 1f out* **11/4**[2]

40-1 **8** *6* **Spanish Duke (IRE)**[31] 1479 4-8-12 105............................ TedDurcan 6 81
(John Dunlop) *s.i.s: hld up in last trio: effrt on outer over 2f out and in tch: ill at ease and wknd over 1f out* **13/2**

2m 6.63s (-1.37) **Going Correction** +0.025s/f (Good) **8** Ran SP% **114.1**
Speed ratings (Par 111): **106,105,105,104,103 103,97,92**
toteswingers:1&2:£14.20, 2&3:£12.60, 1&3:£23.00 CSF £107.37 TOTE £20.30: £3.80, £2.30, £4.40; EX 122.20 Trifecta £1053.90 Part won. Pool of £1424.27 - 0.44 winning units..
Owner Roldvale Ltd, Sangster Family & A K Collins **Bred** Swettenham Stud **Trained** Manton, Wilts
■ Stewards' Enquiry : Martin Dwyer caution: careless riding.
William Buick caution: used whip without giving gelding time to respond.

FOCUS

A fascinating Listed event, featuring established performers at this level and handicappers attempting to make the leap. Nobody seemed eager to go on at the outset, though, and the race was run at a stop-start pace. That suggests the form may not be entirely reliable, despite the runner-up being close to his best.

NOTEBOOK

City Leader(IRE), having only his second outing since missing all of 2010, came late to snatch the prize in a tight finish. Held up in last early on, he gradually made progress in the home straight and, racing wide of all the rest out towards the centre of the course, he quickened decisively to get his head in front in the closing stages. On the strength of this, he deserves a shot at another decent prize. (op 20-1)

Class Is Class(IRE), successful in this race in 2010 but returning from a 266-day layoff, led briefly after the start. Reined back quickly, however, he tended to run with the choke out afterwards as he took up a position in fourth. His early exertions probably counted against him inside the final furlong and, while he was far from disgraced, he failed to quicken close home. (op 9-2)

Principal Role(USA), a Listed winner against other fillies in 2010, ran a cracker tackling colts. She was always in the first three and battled gamely all the way to the line. She can surely win again at this level when reverting to a distaff-only contest. (tchd 14-1)

Sea Of Heartbreak(IRE), second in a fillies' and mares' Group 3 last time, seemed to run right up to her best. She too performed commendably, but how easy she will be to place this term remains to be seen. (tchd 17-2)

Forte Dei Marmi, third in a Group 3 at Chester 16 days earlier, was a little disappointing. Official ratings suggested he should have finished alongside Class Is Class, but he never really threatened to make the first three. (op 10-3 tchd 7-2 in places)

Prince Siegfried(FR), runner-up in a Newmarket Listed contest in October 2010, was prominent in the early stages after breaking quickly from the stalls. However, he was left behind in the closing stages when the principals got down to their three-way battle. Official explanation: trainer said gelding was unsuited by the good to firm ground (tchd 14-1)

Al Zir(USA), sixth in the 2010 Derby and fourth in a Group 3 last time out, was bitterly disappointing. He led after 1f and was still in front in the home straight. He soon dropped away when the pace quickened, however, and was ultimately comprehensively beaten. Official explanation: trainer said colt was unsuited by the good to firm ground (op 10-3 tchd 5-2)

Spanish Duke(IRE), a smooth winner off 95 in an Epsom handicap a month earlier, was never in contention. He had a bit to find on official ratings, but is surely better than he was able to show here. Official explanation: trainer said gelding was unsuited by the good to firm ground (op 6-1 tchd 5-1)

2291 E B F SUSSEX SOCIETY MAGAZINE MAIDEN STKS 6f

3:50 (3:50) (Class 4) 2-Y-O **£4,533** (£1,348; £674; £336) **Stalls** High

Form RPR

3 **1** **Trumpet Major (IRE)**[8] 2049 2-9-3 0 DaneO'Neill [illegible]
(Richard Hannon) *w ldr: led against rail 1/2-way: pushed along and drew clr over 1f out: eased last 75yds* **4/7**[1]

0 **2** *2 1/4* **Macdonald Mor (IRE)**[8] 2049 2-9-3 0............................ KierenFallon 10 76
(Paul Cole) *s.i.s: sn in tch: prog to join wnr over 2f out: upsides wl over 1f out: sn brushed aside* **6/1**[2]

3 *hd* **Right To Dream (IRE)** 2-9-3 0.. MartinDwyer 2 76
(Brian Meehan) *rn green but chsd ldrs: effrt over 2f out: wnt 3rd 1f out: styd on* **16/1**

4 *2 1/2* **Bronze Angel (IRE)** 2-9-3 0.. TedDurcan 3 68+
(Marcus Tregoning) *dwlt: mostly last tl shkn up and kpt on fr over 1f out: tk 4th nr fin* **20/1**

5 *hd* **Radiomarelli (USA)** 2-9-3 0.. SebSanders 5 68
(Ralph Beckett) *dwlt: rn green and pushed along in rr: nvr on terms: kpt on ins fnl f* **12/1**

6 *3/4* **Maroosh** 2-9-3 0.. WilliamBuick 1 65+
(Brian Meehan) *dwlt: settled in rr: effrt on wd outside 1/2-way: no prog over 1f out: fdd ins fnl f* **14/1**

7 *1/2* **Orders From Rome (IRE)** 2-9-3 0................................. TomQueally 4 64
(Eve Johnson Houghton) *hld up in tch: effrt over 2f out: chsd ldrs over 1f out: sn wknd* **20/1**

8 *1* **Hamis Al Bin (IRE)** 2-9-3 0.. GregFairley 6 61
(Mark Johnston) *led to 1/2-way: sn lost pl and btn* **10/1**[3]

9 *3 1/4* **Melting Pot** 2-9-3 0.. SteveDrowne 9 51
(Hugo Palmer) *t.k.h bhd ldrs: in tch 2f out: wknd qckly ins fnl f* **25/1**

1m 13.14s (0.94) **Going Correction** +0.10s/f (Good) **9** Ran SP% **120.6**
Speed ratings (Par 95): **97,94,93,90,90 89,88,87,82**
toteswingers:1&2:£2.90, 2&3:£10.60, 1&3:£4.40 CSF £4.54 TOTE £1.50: £1.10, £1.90, £2.50; EX 5.50.
Owner John Manley **Bred** John Cullinan **Trained** East Everleigh, Wilts

FOCUS

Three withdrawals took some of the shine off what was nevertheless an interesting juvenile event. The winner was value for further and looks a nice prospect.

NOTEBOOK

Trumpet Major(IRE), a strong-finishing third over this trip at Newbury on his only previous outing, won comfortably. Quickly away and able to grab a position close to the stands' rail, he was always travelling like the best horse and was eased markedly close home. The form is hard to evaluate, with only one of his rivals having had previous experience, but he should collect again at some stage. Connections believe he will continue to progress and suggested he may return to Goodwood for the Richmond Stakes, won by the yard's Dick Turpin, also a son of Arakan, in 2009. (tchd 8-13)

Macdonald Mor(IRE), third favourite but well beaten when behind Trumpet Major first time out, got a good deal closer on this occasion. Although the ease with which the winner scored has to be taken into account, the runner-up was always in the first three and, given that he showed pace throughout, ought to break his duck before too long. (op 8-1)

Right To Dream(IRE), a debutant half-brother to several winners, never held a better position that at the finish. Most debutants from his stable improve for a run, so it would be no surprise if he picks up one of these in the near future.

Bronze Angel(IRE), a £42,000 yearling purchase by a young sire making waves, was slowly away. He made up significant late ground, though, and seems likely to be more streetwise next time out.

Maroosh, whose dam won three times over 1m, ran as might be expected from his pedigree. Towards the rear early, he stayed on in the closing stages and will ultimately appreciate either a longer trip or a stiffer track.

Hamis Al Bin(IRE), a first-time-out half-brother to multiple winner Shakespearean, showed good early speed, trying to match strides with the winner. He faded late on, but should improve for the outing. (op 9-1)

Melting Pot Official explanation: jockey said colt ran too free

2292 SOUTHERN DAILY ECHO TAPSTER STKS (LISTED RACE) 1m 4f

4:25 (4:25) (Class 1) 4-Y-0+ **£17,778** (£6,723; £3,360; £1,680) **Stalls** High

Form				RPR
31/3	**1**		**Passion For Gold (USA)**[14] [1896] 4-9-0 109 .... FrankieDettori 4 (Saeed Bin Suroor) *mde virtually all: jnd over 4f out: rdn to assert over 1f out: clr and in n.d ins fnl f* **13/2**[3]	115
26-1	**2**	2 ½	**Jet Away**[14] [1896] 4-9-0 114 .... TomQueally 2 (Sir Henry Cecil) *t.k.h: hld up last: quick prog to join wnr over 4f out: rdn over 2f out: nt qckn over 1f out: jst hld on for 2nd* **4/6**[1]	111
2614	**3**	nk	**Steele Tango (USA)**[37] [1342] 6-9-0 114 .... TedDurcan 5 (Roger Teal) *hld up in 4th: dropped to last 1/2-way: pushed along and struggling over 3f out: styd on to take 3rd over 1f out: clsd on runner-up fin* **3/1**[2]	110
26-4	**4**	1 ¾	**Roxy Flyer (IRE)**[21] [1677] 4-8-9 98 .... JimmyQuinn 3 (Amanda Perrett) *trckd ldng pair: pushed along over 3f out: one pce u.p fnl 2f* **12/1**	102
353-	**5**	9	**Status Symbol (IRE)**[175] [7594] 6-9-0 102 .... (t) WilliamCarson 1 (Giles Bravery) *trckd wnr: upsides over 4f out to over 2f out: hanging and wknd qckly over 1f out* **25/1**	93

2m 37.93s (-0.47) **Going Correction** +0.025s/f (Good) **5** Ran SP% **109.9**
Speed ratings (Par 111): **102,100,100,98,92**
CSF £11.49 TOTE £5.80: £2.90, £1.50; EX 8.20.
Owner Godolphin **Bred** Mr And Mrs M Roy Jackson **Trained** Newmarket, Suffolk

FOCUS
A small field and, based on previous form, only the first three home had obvious chances. The form is muddling but the fourth limits things.

NOTEBOOK
Passion For Gold(USA), a six-length winner of a Saint-Cloud Group 1 in 2009 but only third behind Jet Away last time out, scored smoothly under a superb ride. He led from the start and, setting just a fair pace, established a clear advantage turning for home. Given a breather approaching 2f out, he was rousted along again with just over 1f left and quickened away smartly. This was a big step up on his seasonal bow, which was presumably badly needed, and he should be able to hold his own back in Group class from now on. Connections are considering a crack at Royal Ascot's Hardwicke Stakes and believe he will come on again after this victory. (op 11-2 tchd 5-1)

Jet Away, easy winner of a three-runner 1m2f Class 3 at Lingfield two weeks earlier when Passion For Gold was more than eight lengths adrift, could not confirm that form. Last in the early stages, he was pushed forward to take third early in the home straight and disputed the lead at the 3f pole. He failed to quicken when the winner did soon afterwards, and on this evidence, was flattered by his previous success. (op 5-6 tchd 4-7)

Steele Tango(USA), a 1m1f Group 3 winner in 2009 and successful off 112 in a 1m2f Dubai handicap in March, was held up to get this trip. Never closer than at the finish, he ran creditably without proving for certain that this distance suits him. (op 7-2)

Roxy Flyer(IRE), fourth in a fillies' and mares' Listed event here three weeks earlier, had a lot to find on official ratings and ran as well as could be expected. The best position she ever held was third. (op 9-1)

Status Symbol(IRE), third in this grade at Kempton in November 2010, chased the winner in the early stages, but was left well behind when the pace quickened. (op 16-1)

2293 HAMPSHIRE CHRONICLE STKS (H'CAP) 1m 3f

5:00 (5:01) (Class 5) (0-70,69) 3-Y-0 **£3,238** (£963; £481; £240) **Stalls** High

Form				RPR
4-41	**1**		**Anton Dolin (IRE)**[19] [1769] 3-9-3 65 .... TedDurcan 5 (John Dunlop) *led over 1f: trckd ldrs after: led 3f out gng wl: pressed over 2f out: drvn whn lft clr over 1f out: styd on wl* **2/1**[1]	75+
000-	**2**	3 ½	**Drumadoon (IRE)**[234] [6473] 3-8-2 55 oh4 .... RosieJessop(5) 3 (John Dunlop) *t.k.h: trckd ldng pair to 1/2-way: lost pl: hmpd in rr 3f out: drvn and prog 2f out: styd on to take 2nd nr fin* **20/1**	61+
0-10	**3**	hd	**Romeo Montague**[12] [1951] 3-9-5 67 .... KierenFallon 4 (Ed Dunlop) *dwlt: racd lazily in last early: prog on outer over 3f out: pressed wnr over 2f out: nrly upsides whn veered bdly lft over 1f out: threw away ch and lost 2nd nr fin* **5/2**[2]	71+
665-	**4**	1	**Memory Lane**[234] [6453] 3-9-6 68 .... SebSanders 6 (Sir Mark Prescott Bt) *trckd ldrs: hrd rdn and in tch over 2f out: outpcd after* **9/1**	70
0-00	**5**	½	**Emmeline Pankhurst (IRE)**[12] [1933] 3-8-7 55 oh3 .... JimmyQuinn 9 (Julia Feilden) *hld up in last trio: prog to trck ldrs over 2f out: rdn in 3rd over 1f out: outpcd after* **33/1**	56?
60-0	**6**	7	**Oliver's Gold**[19] [1769] 3-8-9 57 .... LiamKeniry 1 (Amanda Perrett) *hld up in last trio: shkn up 3f out: no prog 2f out: wknd ins fnl f* **9/1**	45
4122	**7**	8	**Gower Rules (IRE)**[10] [1997] 3-8-12 63 .... SeanLevey(3) 2 (John Bridger) *dwlt: pushed up to ld over 9f out: rdn 4f out: hdd & wknd 3f out* **6/1**[3]	37
5-55	**8**	31	**Swift Blade (IRE)**[12] [1951] 3-9-7 69 .... TomQueally 8 (William Knight) *racd wd early: trckd ldr after 2f to over 3f out: wknd rapidly: wl t.o* **15/2**	—

2m 28.46s (1.96) **Going Correction** +0.025s/f (Good) **8** Ran SP% **115.7**
Speed ratings (Par 99): **93,90,90,89,89 84,78,55**
toteswingers:1&2:£10.30, 2&3:£8.50, 1&3:£1.60 CSF £43.96 CT £105.23 TOTE £2.80: £1.60, £5.40, £1.40; EX 50.50.
Owner Windflower Overseas Holdings Inc **Bred** Windflower Overseas Holdings Inc **Trained** Arundel, W Sussex

FOCUS
A modest handicap, with the top weight rated just 69. the winner looks an improver with the third close to his all-weather mark.

2294 NEWSQUEST STKS (H'CAP) 5f

5:35 (5:35) (Class 5) (0-75,73) 3-Y-0 **£3,238** (£963; £481; £240) **Stalls** High

Form				RPR
30-3	**1**		**Perfect Pastime**[45] [1187] 3-9-7 73 .... TedDurcan 10 (Walter Swinburn) *trckd ldr against rail: plld out and effrt 1/2-way: hrd rdn over 1f out: r.o to ld last strides* **9/2**[2]	79
615	**2**	nk	**Vicona (IRE)**[9] [2025] 3-8-7 66 .... DuilioDaSilva(7) 4 (Paul Cole) *racd centre: led after 1f: hrd pressed over 1f out: hdd u.p last strides* **17/2**	71
0-63	**3**	shd	**Whitecrest**[19] [1776] 3-9-0 66 .... SebSanders 9 (John Spearing) *only one to r against nr side rail thrght: wl on terms w ldrs: hrd rdn over 1f out: styd on* **14/1**	70
2621	**4**	1 ½	**Beautiful Day**[17] [1813] 3-9-0 66 .... TomQueally 3 (Kevin Ryan) *w ldrs in centre: rdn over 1f out: one pce ins fnl f* **6/1**[3]	65
2222	**5**	nk	**Welsh Inlet (IRE)**[19] [1776] 3-9-0 66 .... MarcHalford 6 (John Bridger) *led 1f in centre: styd w ldr tl hanging and nt qckn over 1f out: one pce after* **11/1**	64
31-	**6**	¾	**Yasmeena (USA)**[267] [5466] 3-9-5 71 .... TadhgO'Shea 11 (B W Hills) *outpcd in last pair: shkn up 1/2-way: r.o fnl f: nrst fin* **11/4**[1]	66
35-4	**7**	nk	**Regal Bullet (IRE)**[31] [1483] 3-8-7 59 .... JimmyQuinn 2 (Dean Ivory) *racd centre: in tch: effrt 2f out: nt qckn and no imp fnl f* **9/1**	53
44-1	**8**	2 ½	**Best Be Careful (IRE)**[19] [1776] 3-8-11 63 .... LiamKeniry 7 (Mark Usher) *racd towards centre: wl on terms w ldrs tl wknd jst over 1f out* **6/1**[3]	48
0-06	**9**	4	**One Cool Chick**[9] [2025] 3-8-2 59 oh9 .... RyanPowell(5) 8 (John Bridger) *rrd s: wl in rr towards nr side: drvn and struggling 1/2-way* **25/1**	30
30-6	**10**	hd	**Aurivorous**[28] [1521] 3-8-13 65 .... GregFairley 1 (Anabel K Murphy) *racd centre: cl up bhd ldrs tl wknd over 1f out* **25/1**	35
50-6	**11**	2 ½	**Sensational Love (IRE)**[19] [1776] 3-8-12 67 .... SeanLevey(3) 5 (Robert Mills) *s.i.s: outpcd in last pair: rdn 1/2-way: no prog over 1f out: wknd* **16/1**	28

59.14 secs (0.74) **Going Correction** +0.10s/f (Good) **11** Ran SP% **122.5**
Speed ratings (Par 99): **98,97,97,94,94 93,92,88,82,82 78**
toteswingers:1&2:£8.30, 2&3:£14.50, 1&3:£11.90 CSF £44.69 CT £509.76 TOTE £6.40: £2.30, £2.80, £4.60; EX 56.30.
Owner Country Friends **Bred** Richard & Tina Levin **Trained** Aldbury, Herts

FOCUS
An ordinary finale, with the top weight rated 73, but it looked competitive on paper. They went a good gallop and the majority of the field stayed more or less 'in lane' after breaking from the stalls. The form is rated as average for the grade.

Sensational Love(IRE) Official explanation: jockey said filly reared as stalls opened

T/Plt: £49.50 to a £1 stake. Pool of £92,375.71 - 1,360.59 winning tickets. T/Qpdt: 10.80 to a £1 stake. Pool of £4,536.06 - 308.12 winning tickets. JN

2253 HAYDOCK (L-H)

Saturday, May 21

OFFICIAL GOING: 5f & 6f - good to firm (good in places; 8.7); 7f & further - good (7.7)

5f and 6f races run on new Inner home straight. Other races run on outer home straight and races on Round course increased by 13yds.

Wind: Fresh across Weather: Overcast, breezy

2295 BETFRED "BOTH TEAMS SCORE...GOALS GALORE!" H'CAP 1m 3f 200y

2:00 (2:00) (Class 3) (0-95,90) 3-Y-0

£9,969 (£2,985; £1,492; £747; £372; £187) **Stalls** Centre

Form				RPR
1-41	**1**		**Brown Panther**[17] [1811] 3-8-12 81 .... RichardKingscote 8 (Tom Dascombe) *hld up towards rr: smooth hdwy over 2f out: nt clr run: swtchd rt over 1f out: led last 100yds: v readily* **2/1**[1]	95+
4-31	**2**	1 ¾	**Reflect (IRE)**[20] [1728] 3-9-2 85 .... RyanMoore 1 (Richard Hannon) *w ldrs: led over 2f out: hdd and no ex ins fnl f* **13/2**[3]	93
1-03	**3**	nk	**Qushchi**[14] [1903] 3-9-0 83 .... JimCrowley 6 (William Jarvis) *hld up in rr: hdwy 3f out: chsng ldr over 1f out: styd on same pce* **20/1**	91
2116	**4**	4 ½	**Gottany O'S**[17] [1811] 3-8-12 81 .... TomEaves 5 (Mick Channon) *hld up in midfield: effrt 3f out: sn outpcd: kpt on fnl f* **20/1**	82
0-1	**5**	2	**Cry Fury**[31] [1484] 3-9-7 90 .... NeilCallan 7 (Roger Charlton) *t.k.h in midfield: effrt 3f out: wknd over 1f out* **11/2**[2]	88
-213	**6**	½	**Viking Storm**[8] [2052] 3-8-8 77 .... ChrisCatlin 4 (Harry Dunlop) *trckd ldrs: upsides over 3f out: wknd over 1f out* **12/1**	74
13-2	**7**	¾	**Whiplash Willie**[20] [1727] 3-8-8 80 .... SimonPearce(3) 3 (Andrew Balding) *s.i.s: hdwy on ins 6f out: chsng ldrs over 3f out: wknd over 1f out* **9/1**	76
014-	**8**	1 ¼	**Spyder**[179] [7536] 3-8-7 76 .... AndreaAtzeni 2 (Jane Chapple-Hyam) *led: hdd over 2f out: wknd over 1f out* **33/1**	70
-421	**9**	9	**Greyfriars Drummer**[24] [1620] 3-9-7 90 .... PaulHanagan 9 (Mark Johnston) *drvn to r upsides after 1f: lost pl over 2f out: sn bhd* **8/1**	69
02-4	**10**	4	**Wayward Glance**[35] [1407] 3-9-2 85 .... JamieSpencer 10 (Michael Bell) *mid-div: hdwy on outside over 4f out: upsides over 3f out: wknd 2f out: eased whn bhd* **11/2**[2]	58+

2m 30.77s (-3.23) **Going Correction** -0.275s/f (Firm) **10** Ran SP% **118.7**
Speed ratings (Par 103): **99,97,97,94,93 92,92,91,85,82**
toteswingers: 1&2 £6.40, 1&3 £17.00, 2&3 £44.30. CSF £15.06 CT £206.08 TOTE £2.90: £1.40, £2.20, £5.20; EX 19.80 Trifecta £357.10 Pool: £743.18 - 1.54 winning units..
Owner Owen Promotions Limited **Bred** Owen Promotions Ltd **Trained** Malpas, Cheshire

FOCUS
A dry night and the going on the new inner home straight was given as good to firm, good in places, with a GoingStick reading of 8.6, while the going on the round course was given as good, with a GoingStick reading of 7.7. Races over 7f plus used the outer home straight, adding 13 yards to the official distances. This had the look of a quality 3-y-o handicap, the form should work out and it's likely to throw up a few winners in the coming weeks.

The Form Book, Raceform Ltd, Compton, RG20 6NL

NOTEBOOK

Brown Panther ◆ had been raised 8lb for his Chester win, but he promised to be better suited to this more galloping track and that proved the case as he won easily, overcoming trouble in running. He led at Chester but was dropped in this time as his connections wanted him to learn something, and once he was switched out from behind runners he picked up in impressive style. Still a shade green, he's clearly a progressive colt and it wouldn't be a surprise to see him develop into a Pattern performer later in the season. Indeed, his rider mentioned the possibility of the German Derby after the race, but his trainer pointed the way to the King George V Handicap at Royal Ascot, although the colt would not want the ground too firm apparently. (op 11-4 tchd 7-2 in a place and 3-1 in places)

Reflect(IRE) made hard work of landing the odds at Salisbury last time but his previous third to World Domination at Newbury (narrowly in front of Wayward Glance there) gave him a good shout off a mark of 85. He travelled well through the race and had every chance and, while the winner had too much in hand at these weights, he showed enough to suggest he'll be winning again soon.

Qushchi, the only filly in the field, has improved her RPR on each start and this appears to have been another career-best effort. The extra 2f proved in her favour and she'll be of more interest when racing against her own sex again. (op 16-1)

Gottany O'S finished only slightly closer to Brown Panther than at Chester last time despite an 11lb pull in the weights, which underlines the winner's improvement.

Cry Fury was just a short head in front of Greyfriars Drummer when the pair finished first and second in a Kempton maiden last month, and the Johnston horse had since won his maiden easily at Pontefract. Meeting each other again on level weights, Cry Fury easily confirmed Kempton form despite racing keenly and hanging under pressure, as Greyfriars Drummer dropped out tamely early in the straight. (op 6-1)

Viking Storm, running off the same mark as when third at Newbury eight days earlier, ran a solid race in a tougher contest.

Whiplash Willie performed respectably on his reappearance and the step up to 1m4f looked likely to suit him judged on his pedigree (half-brother to a 2m winner). On this evidence he might need even further.

Wayward Glance looked interesting on his reappearance fourth (narrowly behind Reflect), but was awkward to load on his second start last year, and is out of a mare who was far from straightforward, so temperament issues are a concern. After heading to the stands' side in the straight, he wandered about under pressure and seemed to throw in the towel quickly. (op 9-2)

2296 BETFRED SILVER BOWL H'CAP 1m

2:30 (2:33) (Class 2) 3-Y-O

£37,386 (£11,196; £5,598; £2,802; £1,398; £702) **Stalls** Low

Form RPR

12-2 **1** **Sagramor**[11] 1983 3-8-2 **85** .... NickyMackay 15 98
(Hughie Morrison) *swtchd lft after s: hld up in mid-div: hdwy wd outside over 2f out: r.o to ld ins fnl f* **15/2**[3]

3-14 **2** *3/4* **King Of Jazz (IRE)**[27] 1546 3-8-10 **93** .... RyanMoore 5 104
(Richard Hannon) *trckd ldrs: led 2f out: hdd ins fnl f: no ex* **16/1**

16-1 **3** *nse* **Winter's Night (IRE)**[15] 1844 3-8-7 **90** .... JimCrowley 13 101
(Clive Cox) *hld up towards rr: effrt and nt clr run 2f out: gd hdwy appr fnl f: styd on wl* **9/1**

12-4 **4** *3 1/4* **Mariachi Man**[44] 1202 3-8-7 **90** .... DavidAllan 6 93
(Tim Easterby) *w ldrs: led after 2f: hdd 2f out: kpt on same pce* **14/1**

0-53 **5** *1* **Toolain (IRE)**[15] 1844 3-9-7 **104** .... NeilCallan 2 105
(Roger Varian) *led 2f: chsd ldrs: kpt on same pce over 1f out* **14/1**

21-1 **6** *1/2* **Polar Kite (IRE)**[44] 1202 3-8-4 **87** .... PaulHanagan 14 87
(Richard Fahey) *hld up in mid-div: effrt 3f out: kpt on same pce over 1f out: nvr rchd ldrs* **7/2**[1]

0-53 **7** *1/2* **Cruiser**[20] 1725 3-7-11 **85** .... KieranO'Neill(5) 10 84
(William Muir) *hld up in rr: styd far side in st: hdwy 3f out: one pce over 1f out* **14/1**

0-40 **8** *1 1/2* **Orientalist**[20] 1725 3-7-11 **85** ....(p) HarryBentley(5) 3 80
(Eve Johnson Houghton) *mid-div: chsng ldrs over 2f out: wknd fnl f* **50/1**

5262 **9** *nse* **Fred Willetts (IRE)**[16] 1820 3-8-2 **90** ....(v) MatthewCosham(5) 16 85+
(David Evans) *s.i.s: styd far side in st: hdwy to chse ldrs over 2f out: wknd over 1f out* **40/1**

0-12 **10** *1 3/4* **Sikeeb (IRE)**[21] 1690 3-9-0 **97** .... PhilipRobinson 9 88+
(Clive Brittain) *hld up in mid-div: styd far side in st: nt clr run over 2f out: wknd fnl f* **6/1**[2]

5-55 **11** *2 1/4* **Weapon Of Choice (IRE)**[16] 1820 3-8-2 **85** .... AndreaAtzeni 4 71+
(David Simcock) *in rr: styd far side in st: hdwy to chse ldrs over 1f out: sn wknd* **33/1**

10-5 **12** *hd* **Mubtadi**[21] 1690 3-8-0 **83** .... MartinLane 12 69+
(David Simcock) *chsd ldrs: styd far side in st: wknd over 1f out* **12/1**

-110 **13** *1 1/4* **Indian Jack (IRE)**[27] 1547 3-8-5 **88** .... BarryMcHugh 17 71
(Alan Bailey) *s.i.s: styd far side in st: hdwy 3f out: wkng whn nt clr run over 1f out* **25/1**

2141 **14** *hd* **Crown Counsel (IRE)**[16] 1820 3-8-5 **88** .... HayleyTurner 11 70
(Mark Johnston) *chsd ldrs: drvn over 3f out: wknd over 1f out* **11/1**

00-0 **15** *hd* **Sonning Rose (IRE)**[14] 1893 3-8-9 **92** .... ChrisCatlin 1 74
(Mick Channon) *s.i.s: mid-div: hdwy over 1f out: wknd over 1f out* **40/1**

14-3 **16** *7* **Star Surprise**[27] 1547 3-8-7 **90** .... JamieSpencer 8 56
(Michael Bell) *chsd ldrs: wkng whn nt clr run over 1f out: eased* **12/1**

30-3 **17** *nk* **Rigolleto (IRE)**[36] 1361 3-8-9 **92** .... TomEaves 7 57
(Mick Channon) *chsd ldrs: wknd over 1f out* **20/1**

1m 40.07s (-2.83) **Going Correction** -0.275s/f (Firm) course record **17** Ran **SP% 126.3**
Speed ratings (Par 105): **103,102,102,98,97 97,96,95,95,93 91,91,89,89,89 82,82**
toteswingers: 1&2 £33.30, 1&3 £17.00, 2&3 £26.10. CSF £117.00 CT £1157.60 TOTE £10.20: £2.30, £4.20, £2.90, £3.70; EX 211.80 Trifecta £1450.40 Part won. Pool of £1960.09 - 0.10 winning units..
Owner Melksham Craic **Bred** Melksham Craic **Trained** East Ilsley, Berks

FOCUS

A hot-looking 3-y-o handicap, the form of which normally works out well, and there's no reason to believe this year's race will be any different. It was a bit messy early, and there was some scrimmaging going into the first bend, and while the field headed to the stands' side early in the straight, they fanned out across the track with around 2f to go. The form looks sound rated around the third, fourth and fifth.

NOTEBOOK

Sagramor, who had shaped well on his return at Warwick, was drawn out wide and was a shade keen as his rider tried to get cover. He ended up racing wide around the turn and, while that may not have been to his advantage, the suspicion is that he ended up coming over to a favoured part of the track on the stands' side. Challenging nearest the rail, he saw his race out strongly and looks sure to relish the uphill finish at Ascot in the Britannia Stakes.

King Of Jazz(IRE) finished fourth of four in a cracking little conditions race at Sandown last time out, in which the Musidora winner finished second. Running in a handicap for the first time, he ran a fine race, albeit while edging towards the favoured stands' side up the straight. He tends to race keenly, so the quicker they go the better it is for him.

Winter's Night(IRE), one of two fillies in the race, had her stamina to prove on this step up to 1m, but she could be spotted travelling well in behind horses towards the stands' side with 2f to run and, although she got a bump or two, kept on well for third. She certainly wasn't beaten for lack of stamina. (op 10-1)

Mariachi Man, who took them along, headed towards the stands' side in the straight but ended up edging left more towards the centre. Softer ground might have suited him ideally, but it was still a good effort to reverse Ripon form with the well-fancied Polar Kite. (op 12-1)

Toolain(IRE), another who was prominent throughout, faced no easy task under top weight, and a 3lb pull was insufficient to turn Ascot form around with Winter's Night. (op 12-1)

Polar Kite(IRE) ◆ won on his return, his first start since being gelded, and he'd been targeted at this race ever since. He made obvious appeal off 6lb higher for a stable that must have had a number of options for this but was their sole representative. He struggled to settle in the early stages and as a result failed to pick up when the race got serious. He remains interesting for races such as the Britannia. (op 4-1 tchd 9-2 in places)

Cruiser's effort flattened out after he came through to challenge inside the last, and perhaps a strongly run 7f will see him at his best.

Orientalist put up an improved effort in the first-time cheekpieces, but there's no margin for error for him off his current mark. (op 40-1)

Fred Willetts(IRE) raced nearest the far-side rail up the straight, so his effort can probably be upgraded.

Sikeeb(IRE) finished second in a Newmarket handicap last time out, when Crown Counsel was fourth and Mubtadi was fifth. That form took a knock here, although the Clive Brittain-trained colt failed to settle early, which didn't help his cause. (op 15-2)

Mubtadi challenged away from the favoured stands' side in the straight. (op 11-1)

Crown Counsel(IRE) was 2lb well in at the weights and didn't appear to have such an obvious excuse.

Star Surprise Official explanation: jockey said colt had no more to give

2297 BETFRED.COM TEMPLE STKS (GROUP 2) 5f

3:00 (3:03) (Class 1) 3-Y-O+

£45,416 (£17,216; £8,616; £4,296; £2,152; £1,080) **Stalls** Centre

Form RPR

1-03 **1** **Sole Power**[21] 1687 4-9-4 114 .... KLatham 5 121
(Edward Lynam, Ire) *hld up in mid-div: hdwy and edgd rt 2f out: led 1f out: hld on wl* **8/1**[3]

436- **2** *3/4* **Kingsgate Native (IRE)**[160] 7852 6-9-4 115 .... RyanMoore 12 118
(Sir Michael Stoute) *hld up towards rr: hdwy and edgd lft 2f out: styd on to chse wnr ins fnl f: no ex* **7/2**[2]

4504 **3** *1/2* **Prohibit**[6] 2138 6-9-4 112 ....(p) JimCrowley 11 116
(Robert Cowell) *towards rr: hdwy 2f out: kpt on wl ins fnl f* **12/1**

60-5 **4** *3/4* **Borderlescott**[21] 1687 9-9-4 112 .... NeilCallan 1 114
(Robin Bastiman) *chsd ldrs: drvn over 2f out: chsd ldrs 1f out: styd on same pce* **10/1**

30-0 **5** *1* **Group Therapy**[21] 1687 6-9-4 105 .... JamieSpencer 8 110+
(David Barron) *s.s: in rr: swtchd stands' side over 1f out: fin wl* **20/1**

20-0 **6** *1/2* **Rose Blossom**[10] 2005 4-9-1 106 .... PaulHanagan 7 105
(Richard Fahey) *chsd ldrs: one pce appr fnl f* **14/1**

/10- **7** *1/2* **Overdose**[34] 6-9-4 0 .... ASuborics 6 106
(Jozef Roszival, Hungary) *w ldrs: kpt on same pce fnl f* **9/4**[1]

-310 **8** *1/2* **Hamish McGonagall**[10] 2005 6-9-4 107 .... DavidAllan 2 105
(Tim Easterby) *led 1f: w ldrs: edgd lft 1f out: kpt on same pce* **20/1**

20-1 **9** *shd* **Stone Of Folca**[30] 1504 3-8-10 101 .... FrederikTylicki 4 101
(John Best) *dwlt: hdwy over 2f out: kpt on fnl f* **33/1**

11-1 **10** *shd* **Tangerine Trees**[21] 1687 6-9-4 107 ....(v) TomEaves 9 104
(Bryan Smart) *w ldrs: led after 1f tl 1f out: sn wknd* **8/1**[3]

61-0 **11** *1 1/2* **Markab**[10] 2005 8-9-11 118 .... PatCosgrave 10 105
(Henry Candy) *racd alone stands' side: mid-div: lost pl over 1f out* **11/1**

113- **12** *2* **New Planet (IRE)**[253] 5907 3-8-10 105 .... MartinLane 3 88
(John Quinn) *s.i.s: sn outpcd and in rr* **25/1**

57.67 secs (-3.13) **Going Correction** -0.175s/f (Firm) course record
WFA 3 from 4yo+ 8lb **12** Ran **SP% 123.3**
Speed ratings (Par 115): **119,117,117,115,114 113,112,111,111,111 109,105**
toteswingers: 1&2 £5.00, 1&3 £18.60, 2&3 £10.60. CSF £35.81 TOTE £10.00: £3.10, £1.60, £4.20; EX 37.00 Trifecta £737.00 Pool: £3286.64 - 3.30 winning units..
Owner Mrs S Power **Bred** G Russell **Trained** Dunshaughlin, Co Meath

FOCUS

This Group 2 sprint looked up to standard on paper, with four individual Group 1 winners and, most interestingly of all, they were joined by Hungarian star sprinter Overdose, who was making his eagerly awaited debut in Britain. A strong pace looked assured and the race was run to suit those ridden more patiently. The form looks sound with the four immediately behind the winner close to their marks.

NOTEBOOK

Sole Power, last year's shock Nunthorpe winner, didn't run badly at Newmarket last time but a flat track suits him better, and his style of running was suited to the way this race was run. Held up off the pace and towards the stands' side, he came with a sustained late run to lead a furlong out and was always holding his challengers in the closing stages. His York win had looked a bit of a fluke but it's quite clear now that, given ideal conditions, he's a high-class sprinter and a repeat win in the Nunthorpe will be his major target this season. (op 9-1 tchd 15-2)

Kingsgate Native(IRE) has disappointed as often as he has delivered but he did win this race last year on his reappearance and looked to hold sound claims again. Ridden patiently, he challenged more towards the centre of the track than the winner and posted a sound effort in defeat. He won second time out in 2008 and 2009 and will once again hold claims at Royal Ascot, where the King's Stand is apparently the favoured option over the Golden Jubilee. (op 9-2)

Prohibit ran well in France just six days earlier but has shown in the past that he can back up quickly, and this race was run to suit him, as he likes to finish late and fast from off the pace. He has a fair record at Ascot and will no doubt take his chance in the King's Stand.

Borderlescott, placed in the last three runnings of this race, ran a satisfactory race at York on his reappearance and was fully entitled to have come on for that. He ran a sound race in fourth, especially as he was temporarily blinded and lost momentum after a furlong and a half when a blindfold used on Overdose for stalls entry (got caught in saddle when removed by Suborics) dislodged and flew back into his face! He might not go to Royal Ascot this year, as his connections are keen to simply find a race for him that he can win, and there should still be plenty of those judged by this effort.

Group Therapy stayed on up the stands' rail from a detached last place to take fifth. His last two wins have come at Ascot and Beverley and a stiffer finish suits him best.

Rose Blossom has recorded her four wins to date from the front, but leading this field was always going to be difficult. Settled in behind the pace, she ran well enough, but perhaps isn't quite up to this level and will be of more interest back against her own sex. (op 12-1)

Overdose, winner of 15 of his previous 16 starts, famously 'won' the voided Abbaye in 2008, and his career has been notable for a series of wide-margin victories, albeit against lesser opposition than he faced here. Having suffered a leg injury in 2009 that kept him off the track for more than a year, there remained a question as to whether he was quite as good as he was three years ago, although an easy win in course record time in a minor event in Germany on his reappearance this year gave some hope on that score. His only previous defeat came on his final start last year when he got stewed up beforehand, was reluctant to load and delayed the start by several minutes, but he was well behaved on this occasion. He was fast enough away and was in the front rank, although not in the lead, from early on, but he came under pressure some way out and never showed what his supporters had hoped he would. His connections blamed the quick ground, and it's true his form is largely in softer conditions, but he'll have to step up markedly on this performance if he's to have any say at Royal Ascot. (op 5-2 tchd 2-1)

Hamish McGonagall showed plenty of pace but, along with Tangerine Trees, simply ended up setting things up for a closer.
Stone Of Folca, one of two runners representing the Classic generation, which had provided 15 of the previous 40 winners, didn't look to hold strong claims on paper and finished well held. (op 40-1)
Markab, who raced alone on the stands' side for a portion of the race, faced a difficult task under his 7lb penalty for winning the Sprint Cup here last autumn, especially as 5f is too short for him. (op 9-1)

2298 BETFRED THE BONUS KING STKS (REGISTERED AS CECIL FRAIL STAKES) (LISTED RACE) (F&M) 6f
3:30 (3:34) (Class 1) 3-Y-0+
£17,031 (£6,456; £3,231; £1,611; £807; £405) **Stalls** Centre

Form RPR
2140 **1** **Anne Of Kiev (IRE)**[14] 1902 6-9-6 102 (t) PatCosgrave 15 107
(Jeremy Gask) *s.i.s: hdwy over 2f out: styd on wl to ld ins fnl f* **11/1**
35-5 **2** *2* **Dubai Media (CAN)**[14] 1902 4-9-2 86 TomMcLaughlin 7 97
(Ed Dunlop) *in rr: hdwy 2f out: styd on fnl f: tk 2nd on line* **12/1**
1-40 **3** *shd* **Show Rainbow**[20] 1719 3-8-7 98 ChrisCatlin 4 94
(Mick Channon) *w ldrs: led over 1f out: hdd and no ex ins fnl f* **18/1**
-200 **4** *1 ½* **Elshabakiya (IRE)**[20] 1719 3-8-7 95 PhilipRobinson 1 89
(Clive Brittain) *sn chsng ldrs: kpt on same pce fnl f* **8/1**
-204 **5** *shd* **Capercaillie (USA)**[14] 1902 4-9-2 87 PaulHanagan 14 91
(Clive Cox) *chsd ldrs: outpcd 2f out: styd on wl ins fnl f* **20/1**
2-05 **6** *½* **Midnight Martini**[8] 2075 4-9-2 91 (t) DavidAllan 13 90
(Tim Easterby) *in rr: hdwy 2f out: styd on wl fnl f* **7/1**[2]
21-3 **7** *1* **Hot Pursuits**[35] 1395 4-9-2 78 TravisBlock 6 86
(Hughie Morrison) *dwlt: mid-div: effrt over 2f out: kpt on same pce fnl f* **25/1**
1410 **8** *1 ¼* **Strictly Pink (IRE)**[38] 1319 3-8-7 79 HayleyTurner 9 80
(Alan Bailey) *in rr-div: hdwy over 2f out: edgd lft over 1f out: kpt on: nvr nr ldrs* **33/1**
0-3 **9** *½* **Poppy Seed**[14] 1902 4-9-2 88 RyanMoore 11 81
(Richard Hannon) *sn w ldrs: wknd over 1f out* **10/1**
4-02 **10** *nse* **Aneedah (IRE)**[24] 1602 3-8-7 97 NickyMackay 8 79
(John Gosden) *w ldrs: wknd fnl f* **4/1**[1]
500- **11** *1 ½* **Tweedy (IRE)**[8] 2078 4-9-2 98 KLatham 10 76
(Edward Lynam, Ire) *chsd ldrs: outpcd over 2f out: no threat after* **14/1**
31-1 **12** *nk* **Nimue (USA)**[51] 1061 4-9-2 83 JamieSpencer 17 75
(Paul Cole) *in rr: edgd lft over 1f out: kpt on ins fnl f: nvr a factor* **16/1**
5-15 **13** *4 ½* **Shoshoni Wind**[9] 2032 3-8-7 92 JulieBurke 5 58
(Kevin Ryan) *narrow ld: hdd over 1f out: sn lost pl: eased whn bhd* **16/1**
013- **14** *7* **Amitola (IRE)**[218] 6887 4-9-2 90 TomEaves 2 —
(David Barron) *racd towards far side: chsd ldrs: wknd 2f out: eased whn bhd* **16/1**
220- **15** *6* **Golden Destiny (IRE)**[218] 6887 5-9-2 105 (b) FergusSweeney 3 —
(Peter Makin) *s.i.s: sn trcking ldrs: wknd 2f out* **12/1**
221- **16** *11* **Russian Spirit**[196] 7351 5-9-6 98 NeilCallan 12 —
(Roger Varian) *w ldrs stands' side: rdn 2f out: sn wknd: heavily eased whn bhd* **15/2**[3]

1m 10.99s (-2.81) **Going Correction** -0.175s/f (Firm)
WFA 3 from 4yo+ 9lb **16 Ran SP% 129.3**
Speed ratings (Par 111): **109,106,106,104,104 103,102,100,99,99 97,97,91,81,73 59**
toteswingers: 1&2 £40.70, 1&3 £72.00, 2&3 £44.30. CSF £141.86 TOTE £13.20: £4.20, £4.30, £8.30; EX 274.60.
Owner P Bamford **Bred** Deerfield Farm **Trained** Sutton Veny, Wilts

FOCUS
This looked a competitive Listed race, if not that classy, but two of the three who were best in at the weights based on official ratings finished in the first three, including the winner. The form looks sound with the third and fourth close to their marks.

NOTEBOOK
Anne Of Kiev(IRE) wants proper fast ground on turf and apparently didn't handle the loose surface when behind three of these at Nottingham last time. She travelled well in behind horses here before being delivered inside the last, and although the majority of her wins have come on the AW, she is clearly just as effective on turf as on artificial surfaces. (op 12-1)
Dubai Media(CAN) had to be niggled along in the early stages but stayed on well to take second. She raced over further than this earlier in her career and the harder they go the better she looks over this trip. (tchd 11-1)
Show Rainbow, fourth in the Nell Gwyn on her reappearance but well beaten in the Guineas last time, coped well with the drop back in distance and posted a sound effort. (op 20-1)
Elshabakiya(IRE), another Guineas also-ran performed creditably on this drop in class and trip, especially as she was drawn in stall one and raced more or less widest of all throughout. (op 17-2 tchd 9-1)
Capercaillie(USA) deserves another try over further as she got going only inside the final furlong here. (op 22-1 tchd 25-1)
Midnight Martini, who appears to be in no man's land off her current mark, had the stands' rail to help in the closing stages. (tchd 13-2)
Hot Pursuits was stuck out wider and ran a decent race considering she was worst in at the weights, having come into the race rated only 78.
Aneedah(IRE) ran well at Ascot last time but this was very disappointing, as she hung left under pressure and dropped out tamely. (op 5-1)
Russian Spirit showed early speed but was eased down as though something might have been amiss. (op 8-1)

2299 BETFRED TEXT "FRED" TO 89660 H'CAP 6f
4:05 (4:06) (Class 4) (0-85,85) 4-Y-0+ **£5,180** (£1,541; £770; £384) **Stalls** Centre

Form RPR
1100 **1** **Dickie Le Davoir**[7] 2118 7-9-1 82 (b) RobertLButler(3) 14 93
(Richard Guest) *s.s: in rr: gd hdwy stands' side over 1f out: edgd lft and styd on wl to ld fnl 50yds* **20/1**
-033 **2** *nk* **Karaka Jack**[21] 1695 4-8-8 75 MichaelO'Connell(3) 2 85
(David Nicholls) *chsd ldr: led 1f out: hdd and no ex clsng stages* **4/1**[1]
126- **3** *½* **Sutton Veny (IRE)**[144] 7993 5-9-5 83 RyanMoore 3 91
(Jeremy Gask) *mid-div: hdwy 2f out: chal ins fnl f: no ex* **6/1**[3]
-000 **4** *nk* **Rocket Rob (IRE)**[20] 1720 5-9-4 82 StevieDonohoe 11 89
(Willie Musson) *in rr: hdwy 2f out: kpt on same pce ins fnl f* **12/1**
515- **5** *1 ¾* **Orpsie Boy (IRE)**[300] 4413 8-8-11 80 DaleSwift(5) 16 86+
(Ruth Carr) *dwlt: in rr: nt clr run over 1f out: styd on wl ins fnl f* **12/1**
-206 **6** *hd* **Bosun Breese**[7] 2116 6-8-11 75 TomEaves 6 76
(David Barron) *t.k.h: led tl 1f out: fdd ins fnl f* **14/1**
11-0 **7** *½* **Who's Shirl**[21] 1696 5-9-5 83 KellyHarrison 10 85+
(Chris Fairhurst) *wnt lft s: in rr: effrt and nt clr run and swtchd stands' side rail over 1f out: styd on ins fnl f* **9/1**
-030 **8** *2 ½* **Indian Trail**[7] 2118 11-9-3 81 (v) AndrewMullen 4 73
(David Nicholls) *chsd ldrs: wknd appr fnl f* **16/1**
-014 **9** *¾* **Tasmeem (IRE)**[51] 1067 4-9-0 78 JimCrowley 13 67
(David Nicholls) *mid-div: effrt over 2f out: nvr nr ldrs* **12/1**
-000 **10** *nk* **Haajes**[7] 2118 7-9-5 83 TonyCulhane 1 71
(Paul Midgley) *w ldrs: hung rt and wknd over 1f out* **33/1**
00-6 **11** *2* **Great Charm (IRE)**[51] 1067 6-8-13 77 PatCosgrave 12 59
(Eric Alston) *chsd ldrs: wknd over 1f out* **9/1**
600- **12** *½* **Haadeeth**[243] 6253 4-9-1 79 PaulHanagan 5 59
(Richard Fahey) *mid-div: effrt over 2f out: wknd over 1f out* **5/1**[2]
00-0 **13** *hd* **Invincible Force (IRE)**[15] 1854 7-9-7 85 HayleyTurner 8 65
(Paul Green) *sn chsng ldrs: wknd appr fnl f* **25/1**
6000 **14** *2 ½* **Tabaret**[9] 2028 8-9-3 81 (p) NeilCallan 9 53
(Richard Whitaker) *hmpd s: sn chsng ldrs: wknd over 1f out* **14/1**

1m 11.69s (-2.11) **Going Correction** -0.175s/f (Firm) **14 Ran SP% 124.8**
Speed ratings (Par 105): **105,104,103,103,101 100,100,96,95,95 92,92,91,88**
toteswingers: 1&2 £6.40, 1&3 £17.00, 2&3 £44.30. CSF £100.01 CT £578.20 TOTE £20.20: £4.50, £1.90, £2.00; EX 208.30.
Owner Future Racing (Notts) Limited **Bred** P And Mrs A G Venner **Trained** Stainforth, S Yorks

FOCUS
An open handicap but the form looks solid and should work out.
Who's Shirl Official explanation: jockey said mare was denied a clear run
Haajes Official explanation: jockey said gelding hung right
Great Charm(IRE) Official explanation: jockey said gelding was unsuited by the good to firm (good in places) ground

2300 BETFRED DENNIS DOOTSON 60TH BIRTHDAY H'CAP 7f
4:40 (4:41) (Class 4) (0-85,90) 4-Y-0+ **£5,180** (£1,541; £770; £384) **Stalls** Low

Form RPR
36-2 **1** **Tariq Too**[16] 1832 4-8-12 76 MartinLane 3 87
(David Simcock) *dwlt: effrt over 3f out: hung lft and led over 1f out: kpt on towards fin* **7/2**[2]
00-5 **2** *¾* **Sunnyside Tom (IRE)**[19] 1747 7-8-7 78 LauraBarry(7) 7 87
(Richard Fahey) *s.i.s: hdwy over 3f out: chal over 1f out: no ex wl ins fnl f* **16/1**
0-50 **3** *1 ¼* **Magic Cat**[8] 2061 5-9-4 82 AndrewElliott 10 88
(Mrs K Burke) *hld up in rr: hdwy over 2f out: edgd lft: kpt on same pce fnl f* **16/1**
20-1 **4** *1* **Decent Fella (IRE)**[9] 2020 5-9-12 90 (v) RyanMoore 4 93
(Andrew Balding) *dwlt: mid-div: hdwy over 2f out: kpt on same pce fnl f* **2/1**[1]
-035 **5** *3* **Seek The Fair Land**[14] 1898 5-9-2 80 (b) PatCosgrave 1 75+
(Jim Boyle) *chsd ldrs: led over 2f out: edgd rt: hdd over 1f out: kpt on same pce* **12/1**
0-00 **6** *5* **Glenridding**[15] 1849 7-9-1 84 (p) DaleSwift(5) 2 66
(James Given) *led 1f: w ldrs: wknd 2f out* **20/1**
1205 **7** *1 ¾* **Avonrose**[14] 1884 4-8-13 77 TomEaves 11 54
(Derek Shaw) *n.m.r sn after s: in rr: sme hdwy over 2f out: nvr on terms* **40/1**
2112 **8** *shd* **April Fool**[5] 2155 7-8-13 82 (b) MatthewCosham(5) 13 59
(David Evans) *wnt rt s: trckd ldrs: wknd over 2f out* **6/1**[3]
4-32 **9** *½* **Sir Bruno (FR)**[14] 1917 4-8-13 77 (p) TomMcLaughlin 9 52
(Bryn Palling) *prom: hmpd bnd after 1f: wknd 2f out* **8/1**
2163 **10** *1 ¾* **Dark Lane**[12] 1943 5-9-1 79 PaulHanagan 8 50
(Richard Fahey) *trckd ldrs: wknd over 2f out* **16/1**
0-01 **11** *nk* **My Gacho (IRE)**[19] 1748 9-8-10 77 MichaelO'Connell(3) 12 47
(David Nicholls) *led after 1f: hdd over 2f out: sn wknd* **20/1**
1350 **12** *7* **Ocean Legend (IRE)**[49] 1103 6-9-4 82 NeilCallan 14 44
(Tony Carroll) *carried rt s: trckd ldrs: edgd lft bnd after 1f: wknd 2f out: eased ins fnl f* **25/1**

1m 27.96s (-2.94) **Going Correction** -0.275s/f (Firm) **12 Ran SP% 122.1**
Speed ratings (Par 105): **105,104,102,101,98 92,90,90,89,87 87,79**
toteswingers: 1&2 £14.30, 2&3 £15.00, 2&3 £28.10. CSF £56.89 CT £825.30 TOTE £4.50: £1.70, £4.30, £3.90; EX 80.70.
Owner Saleh Al Homaizi & Imad Al Sagar **Bred** D R Botterill **Trained** Newmarket, Suffolk
■ Stewards' Enquiry : Neil Callan three-day ban: careless riding (Jun 6-8)

FOCUS
The first four, who were held up early, finished clear in this handicap and the action developed towards the middle of the track this time. The placed horses help set the level of the form.

2301 BETFRED BUNDLES H'CAP 1m
5:15 (5:16) (Class 4) (0-80,79) 4-Y-0+ **£5,180** (£1,541; £770; £384) **Stalls** Low

Form RPR
3001 **1** **Dazeen**[18] 1795 4-8-8 66 ow1 TonyCulhane 6 79
(Paul Midgley) *t.k.h in rr: nt clr run over 3f out and over 2f out: swtchd lft over 1f out: styd on strly to ld last 100yds* **16/1**
05-4 **2** *1 ¼* **Dolphin Rock**[15] 1879 4-9-7 79 TomEaves 1 89
(David Barron) *w ldrs: led 2f out: hdd and no ex ins fnl f* **13/2**[3]
-004 **3** *2 ¼* **Jordaura**[35] 1395 5-9-1 73 NeilCallan 7 78
(Tony Carroll) *mid-div: hdwy over 2f out: kpt on to take n.d 3rd nr line* **11/2**[2]
0-04 **4** *shd* **Fibs And Flannel**[19] 1747 4-8-13 71 DavidAllan 3 76
(Tim Easterby) *dwlt: sn chsng ldrs: kpt on same pce fnl 2f: tk 4th nr fin* **5/1**[1]
30-3 **5** *¾* **Mingun Bell (USA)**[24] 1621 4-9-1 73 PatCosgrave 5 76
(Ed de Giles) *s.i.s: t.k.h in midfield: chsng ldrs over 2f out: lost 2 pls nr fin* **14/1**
3345 **6** *¾* **Standpoint**[7] 2105 5-9-6 78 ChrisCatlin 9 79
(Reg Hollinshead) *w ldrs: styd on same pce fnl f* **13/2**[3]
56-2 **7** *1* **Frontline Girl (IRE)**[48] 1114 5-9-0 72 AndrewElliott 4 71
(Mrs K Burke) *in rr: hdwy on ins over 2f out: nvr nr ldrs* **9/1**
1210 **8** *2* **Cono Zur (FR)**[7] 2112 4-9-0 77 DaleSwift(5) 8 71
(Ruth Carr) *led tl 2f out: fdd fnl f* **12/1**
5 **9** *½* **Power Force (SAF)**[35] 1382 5-9-5 77 AndrewMullen 11 70
(Tom Tate) *chsd ldrs: drvn over 3f out: hung lft: one pce fnl 2f* **14/1**
6-11 **10** *2 ¾* **Bolodenka (IRE)**[11] 1976 9-9-3 75 PaulHanagan 13 62
(Richard Fahey) *in rr: nvr a factor* **7/1**
-050 **11** *1 ¼* **Keys Of Cyprus**[8] 2061 9-9-4 79 MichaelO'Connell(3) 12 63
(David Nicholls) *chsd ldrs: drvn over 3f out: grad wknd* **16/1**
-003 **12** *6* **Champagne Style (USA)**[7] 2115 4-9-4 79 RobertLButler(3) 2 49
(Richard Guest) *dwlt: hdwy on inner over 2f out: sn lost pl: eased towards fin* **14/1**
P-10 **13** *17* **African Cheetah**[35] 1390 5-9-5 77 (v[1]) StevieDonohoe 10 8
(Reg Hollinshead) *s.i.s: a in rr: bhd and eased over 1f out: t.o* **33/1**

3010 **14** *12* **Big Bay (USA)**63 908 5-9-2 **74** PhilipRobinson 14 —
(Jane Chapple-Hyam) *swtchd lft after s: sn chsng ldrs: drvn 4f out: lost pl over 2f out: sn bhd and eased: t.o* **20/1**

1m 41.83s (-1.07) **Going Correction** -0.275s/f (Firm) **14** Ran SP% **128.4**
Speed ratings (Par 105): **94,92,90,90,89 88,87,85,85,82 81,75,58,46**
toteswingers: 1&2 £31.20, 1&3 £30.10, 2&3 £5.50. CSF £124.25 CT £687.31 TOTE £30.90: £7.20, £2.60, £2.40; EX 224.50.
Owner Darren & Annaley Yates **Bred** Bond Thoroughbred Corporation **Trained** Westow, N Yorks

FOCUS
An ordinary handicap and, just like in the last race, the action developed a little away from the stands' rail. The winner recorded a personal best with the placed horses helping to set the level.
African Cheetah Official explanation: trainer's rep said horse had a breathing problem
T/Jkpt: Not won. T/Plt: £1,087.40 to a £1 stake. Pool of £154,107.12 - 103.45 winning tickets. T/Qpdt: £153.10 to a £1 stake. Pool of £6,850.35 - 33.10 winning tickets. WG

2202 LINGFIELD (L-H)
Saturday, May 21

OFFICIAL GOING: Turf course - good to firm (watered; 8.8); all-weather - standard
Wind: Fairly light, behind Weather: Sunny and warm

2302 BRITISH STALLION STUDS SUPPORTING BRITISH RACING E B F MAIDEN FILLIES' STKS (TURF) 6f
5:50 (5:52) (Class 5) 2-Y-O **£3,412** (£1,007; £504) **Stalls** High

Form RPR
0 **1** **Lady Victory (IRE)**7 2113 2-8-11 0 MartinHarley(3) 3 68+
(Mick Channon) *chsd ldr tl over 3f out: rdn over 2f out: drvn and swtchd lft 1f out: qcknd between horses ins fnl f to ld fnl 50yds: r.o wl* **15/2**

2 *½* **Cristal Gem** 2-9-0 0 WilliamBuick 2 67+
(Richard Hannon) *rn green: chsd ldrs: wnt 2nd over 3f out: rdn over 2f out: ev ch but rn green u.p over 1f out: unable qck wl ins fnl f: wnt 2nd on last strides* **6/4**1

3 **3** *hd* **Red Mischief (IRE)**10 1996 2-9-0 0 KirstyMilczarek 1 66
(Harry Dunlop) *led and sn crossed to r on stands' rail: travelling best 2f out: rdn over 1f out: flashed tail u.p: hdd and no ex fnl 75yds: lost 2nd last strides* **4/1**3

4 *5* **Colorful Notion (IRE)** 2-9-0 0 AdamKirby 4 51
(Marco Botti) *s.i.s: hmpd and pushed lft sn after s: steadily rcvrd and in tch over 3f out: rdn and unable qck ent fnl 2f: wknd 1f out: btn whn edgd rt ins fnl f* **15/8**2

5 *61* **Alice's Dancer (IRE)** 2-9-0 0 RichardMullen 5 —
(William Muir) *rrd over bkwards and galloped loose to s: dwlt: hung lft sn after s: last and struggling over 3f out: sn lost tch: wl t.o fnl 2f: eased ins fnl f* **16/1**

1m 10.79s (-0.41) **Going Correction** -0.20s/f (Firm) **5** Ran SP% **112.4**
Speed ratings (Par 90): **94,93,93,86,5**
CSF £19.78 TOTE £8.20: £2.70, £3.00; EX 14.70.
Owner Jaber Abdullah **Bred** Mrs Kay Egan **Trained** West Ilsley, Berks

FOCUS
Just an ordinary little fillies' maiden and the form looks limited.

NOTEBOOK
Lady Victory(IRE) stepped up markedly on what was a disappointing debut to get on top in the final 50 yards. The way Mick Channon's filly was backed on debut suggests connections thought she was capable of much better than she achieved that day but the experience wasn't lost on her and she showed a bright turn of foot to go through a gap in the final furlong and get off the mark at the second attempt. She is speedily bred, being a half-sister to Brocklesby winner Chiswick Bey, and she has a couple of big sprint race entries, so ought to be capable of going on from this. (op 13-2 tchd 6-1)
Cristal Gem ◆ was noticeably green throughout yet still managed to finish within half a length of the winner. With this under her belt she could be a formidable opponent next time. (tchd 13-8 tchd 7-4 in places)
Red Mischief(IRE), who ran well on her debut, led the field up the rail but was swamped close home. This was another good effort and, while she is clearly of only limited ability at this stage, she looks capable of winning a small maiden. (op 10-3)
Colorful Notion(IRE), whose stable's juveniles haven't really got going yet, was quite strong in the market but things went wrong from the outset when she was sluggish from the stalls. She showed some ability before beginning to struggle a couple of furlongs out and promises to fare much better next time. (op 7-2)
Alice's Dancer(IRE) Official explanation: jockey said filly went to the start loose and too free

2303 CRABBIE'S ALCOHOLIC GINGER BEER FILLIES' H'CAP (TURF) 6f
6:20 (6:20) (Class 5) (0-75,75) 4-Y-O+ **£3,070** (£906; £453) **Stalls** High

Form RPR
0-03 **1** **Yurituni**14 1899 4-9-0 **71** (v) PatrickHills(3) 2 80+
(Eve Johnson Houghton) *chsd ldr: led and swtchd rt to r on stands' rail: cruised clr on bit wl over 1f out: in n.d after: eased wl ins fnl f: v easily* **11/4**3

6-42 **2** *3¾* **Suzy Alexander**16 1831 4-8-3 **62** LauraPike(5) 3 55
(David Simcock) *chsd ldrs: hdwy to ld 4f out: rdn and nt pce of wnr 2f out: drvn and btn over 1f out: kpt on same pce fnl f* **13/8**2

00- **3** *1¼* **Basle**223 6772 4-9-2 **75** AdamBeschizza(5) 4 64
(Gay Kelleway) *chsd ldrs: hmpd and dropped to last but stl in tch after 1f: edging lft and rdn 3f out: drvn and outpcd by wnr 2f out: no ch after: kpt on same pce fnl f* **6/4**1

00-5 **4** *6* **Cloth Ears**17 1816 5-8-7 **61** oh4 KirstyMilczarek 1 31
(Phil McEntee) *led and crossed to r on stands' rail sn after s: hdd 4f out: edging lft and rdn over 2f out: wknd u.p wl over 1f out: wl bhd and eased fnl 50yds* **16/1**

69.74 secs (-1.46) **Going Correction** -0.20s/f (Firm) **4** Ran SP% **110.6**
Speed ratings (Par 100): **101,96,94,86**
CSF £7.76 TOTE £4.00; EX 5.20.
Owner Mrs R F Johnson Houghton **Bred** Jeremy Green And Sons **Trained** Blewbury, Oxon

FOCUS
A weak fillies' handicap and basically a one-horse race.
Cloth Ears Official explanation: trainer said mare was unsuited by the good to firm ground

2304 WHYTELEAFE TAVERN H'CAP (TURF) 5f
6:50 (6:50) (Class 5) (0-75,75) 3-Y-O+ **£3,070** (£906; £453) **Stalls** High

Form RPR
32-2 **1** **Admirable Duchess**15 1864 4-9-12 **75** WilliamBuick 7 89
(Dominic Ffrench Davis) *mde all: rdn wl over 1f out: kpt on gamely and a holding runner-up fnl f* **3/1**2

-612 **2** *¾* **Wooden King (IRE)**5 2142 6-9-7 **70** RichardMullen 9 81
(Malcolm Saunders) *chsd ldrs: swtchd lft ent fnl 2f: rdn to chse wnr ent fnl f: kpt on but hld fnl 100yds* **2/1**1

-334 **3** *1½* **Ajjaadd (USA)**15 1864 5-9-8 **71** J-PGuillambert 2 77
(Ted Powell) *racd in midfield: pushed along and effrt wl over 1f out: rdn ins fnl f: kpt on to go 3rd fnl 50yds: nt gng pce to rch ldng pair* **4/1**3

03U2 **4** *1¼* **Grudge**12 1940 6-9-3 **66** (b) AdamKirby 6 68
(Conor Dore) *taken down early: chsd ldrs but hung lft thrght: rdn and unable qck over 2f out: no hdwy and plugged on same pce fr over 1f out* **10/1**

-005 **5** *nk* **Ignatieff (IRE)**8 2048 4-9-9 **72** RobbieFitzpatrick 8 72
(Linda Stubbs) *chsd wnr: rdn 2f out: drvn and lost 2nd ent fnl f: wknd fnl 100yds* **10/1**

0260 **6** *shd* **Gwilym (GER)**19 1770 8-8-13 **62** MartinDwyer 1 62
(Derek Haydn Jones) *sn outpcd in last trio and pushed along: no imp tl styd on wl ins fnl f: nvr trbld ldrs* **14/1**

0-00 **7** *1¾* **Zowington**9 2016 9-9-3 **66** (v) WilliamCarson 3 60
(Stuart Williams) *s.i.s: a struggling to go pce in rr: u.p and no prog 3f out: modest hdwy fnl f: nvr on terms* **25/1**

0-26 **8** *hd* **Matterofact (IRE)**17 1816 8-9-9 **75** MartinHarley(3) 4 68
(Malcolm Saunders) *racd in midfield: pushed along and effrt wl over 1f out: fnd little and no prog ent fnl f: wknd fnl 150yds* **12/1**

5004 **9** *8* **Mister Green (FR)**36 1355 5-9-2 **65** (b) StephenCraine 5 29
(David Flood) *s.i.s: sn u.p and a outpcd in last* **33/1**

56.71 secs (-1.49) **Going Correction** -0.20s/f (Firm) **9** Ran SP% **117.7**
Speed ratings (Par 103): **103,101,99,97,96 96,93,93,80**
toteswingers: 1&2 £2.30, 1&3 £3.00, 2&3 £2.70. CSF £9.62 CT £23.92 TOTE £3.80: £1.60, £1.60, £1.40; EX 11.60.
Owner Exors of the Late Brian W Taylor **Bred** Whitsbury Manor Stud & Pigeon House Stud **Trained** Lambourn, Berks

FOCUS
A race in which it paid to be on or close to the pace. The runner-up is rated as having run to form.
Grudge Official explanation: jockey said gelding hung left throughout

2305 LINGFIELD PARK OWNERS CLUB (S) STKS 1m 4f (P)
7:25 (7:26) (Class 6) 3-Y-O **£1,706** (£503; £252) **Stalls** Low

Form RPR
-456 **1** **L'Hermitage (IRE)**8 2052 3-8-12 70 (p) MartinDwyer 2 68
(Brian Meehan) *in tch in last quartet: hdwy into midfield 6f out: rdn and swtchd to outer bnd 2f out: drvn and styd on to ld 1f out: sn clr and styd on strly* **11/4**2

6-42 **2** *5* **Arizona High**73 801 3-8-12 66 LiamKeniry 9 60
(Andrew Balding) *t.k.h: in tch: pushed along and effrt to press ldr 2f out: drvn and fnd little over 1f out: led narrowly jst over 1f out: sn hdd and nt pce of wnr: wl btn but hld on for 2nd fnl f* **13/8**1

2545 **3** *¾* **Dew Reward (IRE)**5 2146 3-8-12 58 SebSanders 5 59
(Eve Johnson Houghton) *chsd ldrs: rdn and effrt jst over 2f out: drvn and unable qck over 1f out: no ch w wnr and plugged on same pce fnl f* **7/2**3

356 **4** *¾* **Peachez**39 1298 3-8-7 57 (b) JimmyQuinn 3 53
(Marco Botti) *t.k.h: led after 1f: drvn 2f out: hdd jst over 1f out: outpcd and no ch w wnr ins fnl f: wknd fnl 100yds* **5/1**

-500 **5** *9* **Phoenix Fantasy (IRE)**19 1769 3-8-12 50 StephenCraine 8 43
(Jonathan Portman) *led for 1f: chsd ldr tl ent fnl 2f: sn struggling u.p: wknd over 1f out* **25/1**

000- **6** *½* **Xenophon**224 6742 3-8-9 48 LouisBeuzelin(3) 7 42
(Brendan Powell) *in tch in midfield: rdn and struggling over 2f out: wknd and wl btn over 1f out* **16/1**

0650 **7** *27* **Clonusker (IRE)**12 1933 3-8-5 44 (v1) DavidKenny(7) 6 —
(Linda Jewell) *t.k.h: racd in last trio: rdn and lost tch ent fnl 3f: t.o fnl 2f* **66/1**

6-6 **8** *8* **Milk Maid (IRE)**75 787 3-8-0 0 JakePayne(7) 4 —
(Bill Turner) *stdd after s: a in rr: pushed along over 8f out: rdn and lost tch over 4f out: t.o fnl 3f* **50/1**

0064 **9** *42* **Welsh Dresser (IRE)**25 1585 3-8-7 36 RobbieFitzpatrick 1 —
(Peter Grayson) *stdd s: a in rr: rdn and lost tch over 4f out: wl t.o fnl 3f* **66/1**

2m 35.28s (2.28) **Going Correction** +0.225s/f (Slow) **9** Ran SP% **118.3**
Speed ratings (Par 97): **101,97,97,96,90 90,72,67,39**
toteswingers: 1&2 £1.80, 1&3 £1.90, 2&3 £2.00. CSF £7.73 TOTE £3.80: £1.70, £1.30, £1.10; EX 8.70.The winner was bought in for 8,500gns. Arizona High was claimed by Mr A Crook for £6,000.
Owner Paul & Jenny Green **Bred** Paul Green **Trained** Manton, Wilts

FOCUS
Not a bad seller but not form to be positive about.

2306 VINES OF GATWICK MAIDEN STKS 1m (P)
7:55 (7:55) (Class 5) 3-Y-O+ **£3,070** (£906; £453) **Stalls** High

Form RPR
3- **1** **Skilful**196 7345 3-9-1 0 WilliamBuick 6 94+
(John Gosden) *mde all: styd wd tl crossed to rail 5f out: nudged along and readily drew clr over 1f out: in command after: v easily* **8/13**1

32- **2** *3* **Ajeeb (USA)**224 6742 3-8-10 0 AdamBeschizza(5) 4 82+
(David Simcock) *in tch: n.m.r briefly over 2f out: rdn and effrt to chse ldng trio 2f out: swtchd rt and hdwy u.p over 1f out: kpt on to go 2nd fnl 100yds: no ch w wnr* **17/2**

3 *2* **Escape To Glory (USA)** 3-9-1 0 J-PGuillambert 8 77
(Mikael Magnusson) *chsd ldng pair: rdn ent fnl 2f: chsd wnr ent fnl f: no imp and lost 2nd fnl f: kpt on* **33/1**

2-5 **4** *5* **Amhran (IRE)**26 1568 3-9-1 0 MartinDwyer 2 66
(Brian Meehan) *chsd wnr: rdn ent fnl 2f: outpcd by wnr and lost 2nd ent fnl f: fdd fnl 150yds* **9/2**2

4-0 **5** *¾* **Goodness**35 1415 3-8-12 0 LouisBeuzelin(3) 3 64
(Sir Michael Stoute) *chsd ldng trio: rdn and unable qck on inner ent fnl 2f: no threat to ldrs but plugged on fnl f* **7/1**3

6 *hd* **Stand To Reason (IRE)** 3-9-1 0 LiamKeniry 5 64+
(Mikael Magnusson) *s.i.s: towards rr: nt clr run 4f out: lost tch w ldrs over 2f out: pushed along and hdwy ent fnl f: gng on fin: nvr trbld ldrs* **33/1**

4 **7** *1¾* **Tortilla (IRE)**15 1865 3-8-7 0 MartinHarley(3) 12 55
(Des Donovan) *in tch: styd wd tl swtchd lft to join field over 6f out: rdn and struggling ent fnl 2f: wknd wl over 1f out* **20/1**

8 *1* **Satwa Ballerina** 3-8-10 0 AdrianMcCarthy 9 52
(Ed Dunlop) *hld up towards rr: rdn and struggling over 2f out: wl btn fnl 2f* **50/1**

5-4 **9** *4½* **Danish Pastry**31 1480 3-8-10 0 NickyMackay 11 42
(John Gosden) *towards rr: pushed along ent fnl 4f: rdn and no hdwy wl over 2f out: sn wknd: wl btn fnl 2f* **33/1**

6 **10** *3* **Isdaal**[27] 1540 4-9-8 0 RobbieFitzpatrick 7 38
(Kevin Morgan) *towards rr: rdn and struggling bdly wl over 2f out: wl btn fnl 2f* **100/1**

11 *2* **Kings Fortune** 3-9-1 0 RichardMullen 10 36
(Michael Bell) *s.i.s: a in rr: swtchd rt to outer and rdn 3f out: no hdwy: wl bhd fnl 2f* **50/1**

0- **12** *½* **Handel's Messiah (IRE)**[301] 4375 3-9-1 0 AdamKirby 1 34
(Michael Bell) *dwlt: a towards rr: rdn and struggling bdly wl over 2f out: wl bhd fnl 2f* **50/1**

1m 39.45s (1.25) **Going Correction** +0.225s/f (Slow)
WFA 3 from 4yo 12lb **12 Ran SP% 123.6**
Speed ratings (Par 103): **102,99,97,92,91 91,89,88,83,80 78,78**
toteswingers: 1&2 £2.50, 1&3 £12.00, 2&3 £49.90. CSF £6.70 TOTE £1.90: £1.10, £1.30, £8.30; EX 7.90.
Owner Mark Dixon & J L Rowsell **Bred** Ashbrittle Stud & M H Dixon **Trained** Newmarket, Suffolk

FOCUS
This was turned into a procession and, although the form looks fluid, it is worth taking a positive view.

2307 LINGFIELD PARK SUPPORTS THE NCYPE H'CAP 1m 2f (P)
8:30 (8:31) (Class 6) (0-60,60) 3-Y-O **£1,706** (£503; £252) **Stalls** Low

Form RPR

0065 **1** **Westhaven (IRE)**[31] 1487 3-8-9 **48** (b) NickyMackay 7 57
(David Elsworth) *dwlt: sn swtchd lft and pushed along to rcvr on inner: chsd ldrs after 2f: 3rd and rdn 2f out: drvn to chal 1f out: led ins fnl f: styd on strly to draw clr fnl 75yds* **12/1**

066- **2** *2* **Nutshell**[204] 7210 3-9-2 **55** JimmyQuinn 9 60
(Harry Dunlop) *dwlt: sn in tch in midfield: rdn and effrt to chse ldng trio 2f out: nt clr run 1f out: r.o u.p fnl 150yds to go 2nd nr fin* **25/1**

00-3 **3** *½* **Diverting**[119] 260 3-9-7 **60** MartinDwyer 2 64
(William Jarvis) *chsd ldr: rdn to chal 2f out: drvn to ld ent fnl f: hdd ins fnl f: no ex and btn fnl 75yds: lost 2nd nr fin* **9/4**[1]

5660 **4** *3* **Sing Alana Sing**[19] 1769 3-8-4 **46** oh1 (t) KierenFox[(3)] 1 44
(Bill Turner) *led: rdn and hrd pressed 2f out: drvn and hdd ent fnl f: wknd fnl 100yds* **40/1**

00-4 **5** *¾* **Golestan Palace (IRE)**[20] 1728 3-9-5 **58** J-PGuillambert 5 55
(Ed Walker) *t.k.h: in midfield tl stdd bk to rr but stl wl in tch over 8f out: rdn and hdwy jst over 2f out: styd on same pce fnl f* **8/1**

00-0 **6** *1 ½* **Hurricane Spear**[16] 1836 3-8-4 **46** oh1 SeanLevey[(3)] 6 40
(Gary Moore) *chsd ldrs: rdn: hld hd high and nt qckn bnd 2f out: one pce and no threat to ldrs after* **15/2**[3]

-250 **7** *¾* **Ippi N Tombi (IRE)**[81] 716 3-8-7 **46** oh1 KirstyMilczarek 10 38
(Phil McEntee) *in tch towards rr: hdwy into midfield over 5f out: n.m.r and shuffled bk over 2f out: rdn and tried to rally 2f out: no hdwy and n.d fr wl over 1f out* **25/1**

0530 **8** *4 ½* **Indian Wish (USA)**[21] 1683 3-9-6 **59** SebSanders 11 42
(Tim McCarthy) *hld up in tch in rr: rdn and lost tch w ldrs over 2f out: no ch fr wl over 1f out* **20/1**

-305 **9** *1* **Mountain Myst**[94] 564 3-9-7 **60** RichardMullen 4 41
(William Muir) *sn rdn along: in tch in midfield: dropped to rr over 4f out: struggling u.p 3f out: wl btn fnl 2f* **16/1**

0-00 **10** *6* **Scarborough Lily**[12] 1958 3-8-8 **52** AdamBeschizza[(5)] 12 21
(Edward Vaughan) *dwlt: stuck wd bnd over 8f out: in tch towards rr: effrt and n.m.r over 2f out: stl plenty to do whn racd awkwardly and wd bnd 2f out: no ch after* **4/1**[2]

0600 **11** *15* **Tegan (IRE)**[53] 1022 3-9-0 **53** WilliamBuick 3 —
(Richard Hannon) *chsd ldrs tl rdn and struggling over 2f out: sn lost pl: wl bhd and eased ins fnl f: t.o* **14/1**

0322 **12** *1 ¾* **Back For Tea (IRE)**[25] 1592 3-8-13 **52** WilliamCarson 8 —
(Phil McEntee) *t.k.h: in tch in midfield on outer: rdn and wknd over 2f out: wl bhd and eased ins fnl f: t.o* **8/1**

2m 9.52s (2.92) **Going Correction** +0.225s/f (Slow) **12 Ran SP% 119.9**
Speed ratings (Par 97): **97,95,95,92,92 90,90,86,85,81 69,67**
toteswingers: 1&2 £58.40, 1&3 £7.30, 2&3 £19.30. CSF £286.54 CT £925.74 TOTE £18.30: £5.70, £10.20, £1.60; EX 312.40.
Owner J C Smith **Bred** Littleton Stud **Trained** Newmarket, Suffolk

FOCUS
A weak race in which the pace was very steady, so not great form and not particularly solid.
Westhaven(IRE) Official explanation: trainer's rep said, regarding apparent improvement in form, that it had improved for being gelded and from getting into the race, having on occasion missed the break.
T/Plt: £12.00 to a £1 stake. Pool of £50,758.22 - 3,087.27 winning tickets. T/Qpdt: £2.60 to a £1 stake. Pool of £6,762.05 - 1,889.64 winning tickets. SP

2097 NEWBURY (L-H)
Saturday, May 21

OFFICIAL GOING: Good to firm (good in places; 7.0)
Rail realignment between 8f and 5f increased distances on round course by 11m.
Wind: Brisk ahead Weather: Early sun

2308 BETFAIR SUPPORTS ORACLE CANCER TRUST AMATEUR RIDERS' H'CAP 1m 2f 6y
6:05 (6:05) (Class 5) (0-70,69) 4-Y-O+ **£2,810** (£871; £435; £217) **Stalls** Low

Form RPR

-040 **1** **Strike Force**[24] 1621 7-10-7 **67** (t) MissALHutchinson[(5)] 11 77+
(Clifford Lines) *in rr: swtchd sharply rt to outside over 2f out: styd on wl fr over 1f out to ld ins fnl f: kpt on wl* **20/1**

0221 **2** *1 ½* **Miss Bounty**[12] 1936 6-10-1 **61** (v) MrFMitchell[(5)] 5 68
(Jim Boyle) *in tch: hdwy over 2f out: drvn to chal ins fnl f: kpt on: nt pce of wnr* **6/1**[2]

1140 **3** *½* **Lunar River (FR)**[19] 1756 8-10-5 **60** (t) MissEJJones 13 66
(David Pinder) *towards rr: hdwy over 3f out: drvn and ev ch fr over 1f out: no ex wl ins fnl f* **20/1**

5500 **4** *nk* **Bajan Pride**[5] 2149 7-9-12 **58** MissWGibson[(5)] 4 63
(Paul Midgley) *sn led: pushed along and styd on wl fr over 2f out: hdd ins fnl f: kpt on same pce* **28/1**

4230 **5** *shd* **Free Tussy (ARG)**[13] 1144 7-10-5 **65** (bt) MissHayleyMoore[(5)] 1 70+
(Gary Moore) *in tch: styd on far rail and rdn over 2f out: styd on fnl f but nt pce to rch ldng quartet* **16/1**

2234 **6** *3 ¼* **Kyle Of Bute**[52] 1052 5-10-6 **61** MissSBrotherton 10 60
(Brian Baugh) *in tch: hdwy 3f out: rdn and styd on same pce fr over 1f out* **5/1**[1]

-532 **7** *2* **Laconicos (IRE)**[9] 2021 9-10-0 **62** (t) MissCScott[(7)] 3 57
(William Stone) *chsd ldrs: wknd ins fnl 2f* **8/1**[3]

000- **8** *3 ½* **Northern Spy (USA)**[351] 2714 7-10-4 **64** MrJCoffill-Brown[(5)] 6 52
(Simon Dow) *t.k.h: chsd ldrs tl wknd fr 2f out* **18/1**

256- **9** *2* **Herschel (IRE)**[244] 4055 5-10-7 **69** MrLOswin[(7)] 7 53
(Gary Moore) *in rr: sme prog over 2f out: nvr rchd ldrs* **12/1**

4-04 **10** *3 ½* **Mustajed**[16] 1833 10-9-12 **58** (b) MrPMillman[(5)] 16 35
(Rod Millman) *stdd and swtchd lft s: wl bhd tl styd on fr over 2f out: nvr in contention* **8/1**[3]

4662 **11** *nk* **Professor John (IRE)**[15] 1871 4-10-2 **60** MrCMartin[(3)] 14 36
(Ian Wood) *in tch on outside tl wknd 2f out* **17/2**

0-35 **12** *¾* **Rub Of The Relic (IRE)**[17] 1814 6-9-9 **57** (v) MissHDukes[(7)] 9 32
(Paul Midgley) *racd on outside: nvr bttr than mid-div* **25/1**

04-5 **13** *4 ½* **Beat Up**[15] 1867 5-10-0 **60** MrNdeBoinville[(5)] 12 26
(Patrick Chamings) *in rr: rdn over 3f out: nvr beyond mid-div* **9/1**

-060 **14** *11* **It's Dubai Dolly**[94] 553 5-10-4 **59** MissZoeLilly 15 —
(Alastair Lidderdale) *chsd ldrs tl wknd 3f out* **14/1**

3244 **15** *8* **Idol Deputy (FR)**[36] 1374 5-9-7 **55** oh6 MrMTStanley[(7)] 2 —
(Mark Usher) *chsd ldr tl wknd over 2f out* **22/1**

2-40 **16** *3 ¾* **Jeremiah (IRE)**[24] 1604 5-10-5 **60** (b) MissGAndrews 8 —
(Laura Young) *chsd ldrs: wknd fr 3f out* **50/1**

2m 8.24s (-0.56) **Going Correction** -0.025s/f (Good) **16 Ran SP% 122.3**
Speed ratings (Par 103): **101,99,99,99,99 96,94,92,90,87 87,86,83,74,68 65**
toteswingers: 1&2 £26.20, 1&3 £56.40, 2&3 £29.80. CSF £126.83 CT £2474.36 TOTE £24.20: £6.30, £1.80, £6.10, £7.70; EX 292.70 TRIFECTA Not won..
Owner Miss A L Hutchinson **Bred** Cheveley Park Stud Ltd **Trained** Exning, Suffolk

FOCUS
The course was watered heavily on Monday and, although there was a dry and warm run up to the meeting, the clerk of the course left the going as good to firm, good in places as the track hadn't dried out as quickly as he feared it might. The rail was moved in from the 8f to the 5f and the course is 11m longer on the round course. A modest opener but one run at a sound gallop and suited those held up, with the placed horses setting the level.

2309 RELYON CLEANING NEWBURY MAIDEN AUCTION FILLIES' STKS 6f 8y
6:35 (6:37) (Class 5) 2-Y-O **£2,914** (£867; £433; £216) **Stalls** Centre

Form RPR

3 **1** **Poetic Dancer**[33] 1441 2-8-1 0 JohnFahy[(3)] 5 78
(Clive Cox) *w ldrs: drvn to take narrow ld 1f out: strly chal ins fnl f: pushed along and a jst doing enough* **7/1**

33 **2** *½* **Esentepe (IRE)**[11] 1981 2-8-11 0 DaneO'Neill 3 83
(Richard Hannon) *trckd ldrs: chal fr ins fnl 2f and stl upsides ins fnl f: kpt on but nt gng pce of wnr clsng stages* **12/1**

3 *3* **Blackdown Fair** 2-8-4 0 AndreaAtzeni 8 67
(Rod Millman) *chsd ldrs: rdn and outpcd 2f out: styd on again fnl f to take 3rd fnl 75yds but nvr gng pce to rch ldng duo* **100/1**

42 **4** *1 ¾* **Supreme Quest**[11] 1981 2-8-8 0 SteveDrowne 13 66
(Roger Charlton) *led: rdn 2f out: hdd 1f out: wknd ins fnl f* **7/2**[2]

5 *1* **Winter Hill** 2-8-4 0 RichardKingscote 15 64+
(Tom Dascombe) *s.i.s: hdwy 1/2-way: nt clr run fr over 2f out: kpt on fr over 1f out and styd on wl thrght fnl f but nt rch ldrs* **2/1**[1]

6 *1 ½* **Concordia Notte (IRE)** 2-8-3 0 AndrewHeffernan[(3)] 16 56
(Paul D'Arcy) *chsd ldrs: rdn over 2f out: wknd appr fnl f* **12/1**

7 *½* **Lady Gibraltar** 2-8-8 0 ow2 KierenFallon 11 57
(Alan Jarvis) *s.i.s: in rr: nt clr run and swtchd lft ins fnl 2f: styd on fnl f: nt rch ldrs* **20/1**

8 *nk* **Plym** 2-8-8 0 FrankieMcDonald 10 56+
(Richard Hannon) *s.i.s: outpcd in rr: drvn over 2f out: styd on wl fnl f: gng on clsng stages* **50/1**

9 *1* **Zain Princess (IRE)** 2-8-6 0 SaleemGolam 7 54+
(Gerard Butler) *broke wl: stdd towards rr: effrt whn hmpd ins fnl 2f: kpt on fnl f: gng on cl home* **66/1**

10 *½* **Cresta Star** 2-8-8 0 JimCrowley 12 51+
(Richard Hannon) *in rr: effrt whn hmpd ins fnl 2f: kpt on again fnl f* **28/1**

11 *shd* **Nude (IRE)** 2-7-13 0 KieranO'Neill[(5)] 14 47
(Sylvester Kirk) *sn chsng ldrs: rdn 1/2-way: wknd ins fnl 2f* **33/1**

0 **12** *1 ½* **Raspberry Fizz**[33] 1441 2-8-3 0 SimonPearce[(3)] 2 45
(Eve Johnson Houghton) *sn in tch: chsd ldrs 1/2-way: wknd fr 2f out* **25/1**

13 *¾* **Love Grows Wild (USA)** 2-8-8 0 HayleyTurner 9 44
(Michael Bell) *pressed ldrs over 3f* **13/2**[3]

14 *1 ½* **Dressed In Lace** 2-8-8 0 NeilChalmers 4 40
(Andrew Balding) *slowly away: drvn and sme prog 1/2-way: nvr rchd ldrs: hung lft and wknd 2f out* **25/1**

15 *¾* **Strictly Mine** 2-8-4 0 MartinLane 6 34
(Jonathan Portman) *slowly away: rdn and prog to get into mid-div 3f out: wknd ins fnl 2f* **50/1**

1m 14.13s (1.13) **Going Correction** +0.075s/f (Good) **15 Ran SP% 122.0**
Speed ratings (Par 90): **95,94,90,88,86 84,84,83,82,81 81,79,78,76,75**
toteswingers: 1&2 £17.50, 1&3 £168.70, 2&3 £106.10. CSF £79.63 TOTE £6.50: £2.50, £2.00, £20.30; EX 63.90 TRIFECTA Not won..
Owner The Laureates **Bred** Mrs Hugh Maitland-Jones **Trained** Lambourn, Berks

FOCUS
A race that has thrown up a few smart fillies in the last ten years but, although the first two pulled clear in the closing stages, this form has an ordinary feel to it. The pace was reasonable but those held up were at a disadvantage. The runner-up and fourth help set the level.

NOTEBOOK
Poetic Dancer ◆, who shaped well over 5f in a race that threw up numerous winners on her debut, duly turned in an improved effort upped in trip and showed a good attitude to get off the mark. She should have no problems with 7f in due course and can she's the type to win again. (op 11-2)
Esentepe(IRE), who has improved with every outing, turned in her best effort yet over this longer trip. She pulled clear of the remainder, should have no problems with 7f in due course and is sure to pick up a run-of-the-mill maiden on turf. (op 10-1)
Blackdown Fair was easy in the market but this cheaply bough half-sister to a 6f winner, showed a fair level of ability to chase home more experienced rivals on this racecourse debut. She should improve for this experience.
Supreme Quest, the most experienced in the field, looked to have decent claims over a trip that looked sure to suit but she didn't get home as well as the principals after enjoying the run of the race. On this showing the return to 5f may suit but she doesn't look one for maximum faith. (op 4-1 tchd 3-1)
Winter Hill ◆, out of a French 1m winner, attracted a good deal of support for this racecourse debut but could never land a blow after losing ground at the start and after meeting trouble. She's better than this and can make amends in ordinary company. (op 9-4 tchd 15-8)
Concordia Notte(IRE), out of a sister to a 6f winner, hinted at ability and should improve for the experience. (op 25-1)
Lady Gibraltar, a 17,000gns half-sister to very useful Akhenaten, who attempted to come from an unpromising position on this racecourse debut under 2lb of overweight and should prove better than this bare form. (op 16-1)
Plym, a 16,000gns half-sister to 7f Group 3 winner and 2000 Guineas third Frenchmans Bay, showed a modicum of ability after a tardy start on this racecourse debut.

Cresta Star, who has plenty of physical scope, should do a good deal better with time and over further. (op 20-1)

2310 BETFAIR SUPPORTS ORACLE CANCER TRUST H'CAP 1m 7y(R)
7:05 (7:07) (Class 4) (0-85,85) 4-Y-0+ **£5,180** (£1,541; £770; £384) **Stalls** Low

Form RPR
52-1 **1** **Boom And Bust (IRE)**[32] 1448 4-9-2 **80**........................ HayleyTurner 1 90+
(Marcus Tregoning) *mde all but pressed tl shkn up and qcknd appr fnl f: pushed along and r.o strly clsng stages: comf* **7/2**[1]
0201 **2** ½ **Avon River**[16] 1828 4-9-2 **85**........................ KieranO'Neill(5) 11 92
(Richard Hannon) *pressed wnr tl rdn 2f out: hung lft and outpcd fnl f* **18/1**
0-00 **3** 1 **Marajaa (IRE)**[35] 1406 9-9-5 **83**........................ JamieMackay 10 88+
(Willie Musson) *hld up in rr: hdwy 2f out: swtchd rt to outside over 1f out: rapid hdwy ins fnl f: fin wl but nt rch ldng duo* **14/1**
-001 **4** 2¼ **Merchant Of Medici**[19] 1760 4-9-4 **82**........................ JimCrowley 6 82
(William Muir) *s.i.s: in rr: hdwy 4f out: drvn to chse ldrs 2f out: no imp and one pce fnl f* **11/2**[2]
60-0 **5** 1¾ **Huzzah (IRE)**[24] 1603 6-9-2 **80**........................ RobertHavlin 4 76
(B W Hills) *chsd ldrs: rdn over 2f out: wknd fnl f* **13/2**[3]
4521 **6** 2¾ **Edgewater (IRE)**[28] 1530 4-9-0 **78**........................ DaneO'Neill 5 67
(John Akehurst) *chsd ldrs: rdn: hung lft and wknd fr 2f out* **15/2**
00-0 **7** 1¼ **Big Noise**[19] 1760 7-9-7 **85**........................ SteveDrowne 12 71
(Dr Jon Scargill) *in rr: rdn and hung lft fr 2f out: nvr gng pce to get into contention* **12/1**
0-06 **8** 6 **Kavachi (IRE)**[16] 1834 8-8-10 **77**........................ RossAtkinson(3) 9 50
(Gary Moore) *s.i.s: in rr: rdn over 2f out: a outpcd* **40/1**
200- **9** nk **Truism**[265] 5556 5-9-5 **83**........................ MartinLane 2 55
(Amanda Perrett) *chsd ldrs: rdn 3f out: wknd ins fnl 2f* **12/1**
2/1- **10** 20 **Poltergeist (IRE)**[347] 2841 4-9-4 **82**........................ KierenFallon 7 —
(William Haggas) *t.k.h early in tch: rdn 3f out: little rspnse: sn wknd: eased ins fnl f* **7/2**[1]

1m 37.66s (-1.04) **10** Ran SP% **114.7**
toteswingers: 1&2 £11.20, 1&3 £12.90, 2&3 £45.40. CSF £70.02 CT £805.62 TOTE £4.40: £1.70, £3.10, £4.70; EX 49.20 Trifecta £1405.70 Pool: £2,659.52 - 1.40 winning units..
Owner Jas Singh **Bred** Duncan A McGregor **Trained** Lambourn, Berks

FOCUS
Mainly exposed performers in a useful handicap. The gallop was no more than fair and this suited those right up with the pace.
Poltergeist(IRE) Official explanation: trainer's rep said gelding was unsuited by the good to firm (good in places) ground

2311 BATHWICK TYRES MAIDEN STKS 6f 8y
7:40 (7:41) (Class 5) 3-Y-0 **£3,238** (£963; £361; £361) **Stalls** Centre

Form RPR
-2 **1** **Foxtrot Hotel (IRE)**[20] 1724 3-9-3 0........................ JimCrowley 8 89+
(Peter Winkworth) *w ldrs and a gng wl: chal on bit fr 2f out: slt ld gng easily jst ins fnl f: given one tap and qcknd readily clr fnl 50yds* **4/9**[1]
0 **2** 1¼ **Ippios**[20] 1724 3-9-3 0........................ KierenFallon 9 80
(Luca Cumani) *pressed ldrs tl led appr fnl 2f but sn jnd by easy travelling wnr: narrowly hdd and rdn jst ins fnl f: styd on tl easily outpcd fnl 50yds* **5/1**[2]
22-0 **3** 7 **Choose The Moment**[12] 1949 3-8-12 66........................ FergusSweeney 2 53
(Eve Johnson Houghton) *pressed ldrs: rdn over 2f out and lft bhd over 1f out whn ldng duo qcknd but styd on again fnl f to share wl-hld 3rd* **6/1**[3]
00 **3** dht **Canashito**[24] 1607 3-8-12 0........................ SteveDrowne 3 53
(B W Hills) *narrow ldr tl hdd appr fnl 2f: lft bhd as ldng duo qcknd appr fnl f but kpt on to share wl-hld 3rd* **16/1**
0 **5** ¾ **Mistress Quick**[58] 952 3-8-12 0........................ DaneO'Neill 5 50
(Ben De Haan) *s.i.s: in rr: drvn and hdwy over 2f out: styd on bhd plcd horses but nvr anywhere nr ldng duo* **33/1**
6 1 **Fire In Babylon (IRE)** 3-9-3 0........................ AndreaAtzeni 4 52
(Michael Wigham) *in tch: rdn 3f out and nvr nr ldrs: styd on one pce fnl 2f* **20/1**
0-6 **7** hd **Art Thief**[21] 1682 3-9-3 0........................ TravisBlock 1 51
(Sylvester Kirk) *in tch: rdn and one pce fnl 2f* **16/1**
0-0 **8** 5 **Ollywood**[7] 2103 3-9-3 0........................ TedDurcan 6 35
(Tony Carroll) *unruly cnt stalls: in tch tl wknd appr fnl 2f* **28/1**

1m 13.41s (0.41) **Going Correction** +0.075s/f (Good) **8** Ran SP% **123.1**
Speed ratings (Par 99): **100,98,89,89,88 86,86,79**toteswingers: 1&2 £1.20, 1& Canashito £2.30, 1& Choose The Moment £0.50, 2& C £6.80, 2&CTM £1.60. PLACES: £1.02, £1.70, C £2.80, CTM £0.90. CSF £3.53 TOTE £1.50; EX 3.70 TRIFECTA FH,I & C £11.80. Pool: £5,275.18 - 164.15 winning units. FH, I &27 Owner.

FOCUS
An uncompetitive maiden and one run at no more than a fair gallop. The first two pulled a fair way clear in the last furlong and the winner is rated close to his debut form, although the level is fluid.

2312 HILDON H'CAP 1m 5f 61y
8:15 (8:17) (Class 5) (0-75,75) 4-Y-0+ **£2,914** (£867; £433; £216) **Stalls** Low

Form RPR
-253 **1** **High On A Hill (IRE)**[19] 1761 4-9-6 **74**........................ DaneO'Neill 8 84
(Sylvester Kirk) *trckd ldrs: led appr fnl 3f: pushed clr fnl f: comf* **14/1**
1350 **2** 2½ **Gunslinger (FR)**[19] 1761 6-9-4 **72**........................ HayleyTurner 6 77
(Michael Scudamore) *t.k.h: in tch: chsd ldrs fr 3f out: styd on to chse wnr ins fnl f but nvr any ch* **25/1**
2416 **3** 1¾ **Sunset Place**[16] 1839 4-8-13 **67**........................(p) RobertHavlin 3 69
(Jonathan Geake) *s.i.s: hld up towards rr: hdwy and nt clr run whn swtchd lft ins fnl 2f: drvn to chse wnr over 1f out but nvr any ch: one pce into 3rd ins fnl f* **12/1**
3250 **4** 2 **Muzo (USA)**[15] 1847 5-9-7 **75**........................ AndreaAtzeni 11 74
(Chris Dwyer) *sn led: hdd appr fnl 3f: wknd appr fnl f* **25/1**
1012 **5** 2 **Storm Hawk (IRE)**[12] 1956 4-9-0 **68**........................(p) TedDurcan 2 64
(Pat Eddery) *s.i.s: in rr: hdwy over 3f out: rdn over 2f out: nvr gng pce to rch ldrs* **12/1**
00-2 **6** 1 **Marju King (IRE)**[19] 1750 5-8-11 **65**........................ FergusSweeney 10 60
(Stuart Kittow) *in rr: hdwy on outside 5f out: chsd ldrs and rdn 2f out: wknd fnl f* **14/1**
02-4 **7** hd **Raktiman (IRE)**[14] 1914 4-9-0 **68**........................(p) RichardKingscote 5 63
(Tom Dascombe) *chsd ldr to 3f out: wknd ins fnl 2f* **11/1**[3]
0- **8** shd **Rebel Dancer (FR)**[14] 2181 6-9-5 **73**........................(t) JimCrowley 1 69+
(Ian Williams) *in rr: hdwy over 2f out: nvr rchd ldrs and one pce whn hmpd over 1f out* **7/1**[2]
1614 **9** 3¾ **Irish Jugger (USA)**[17] 1817 4-9-1 **69**........................ JamesMillman 13 58
(Rod Millman) *in rr: sme hdwy 3f out but nvr beyond mid-div* **25/1**
505- **10** 6 **Silent Applause**[202] 7252 8-8-11 **65**........................ SteveDrowne 9 45
(Dr Jon Scargill) *in tch tl wknd fr 3f out* **33/1**
11-0 **11** 1½ **Jovial (IRE)**[24] 1608 4-8-8 **65**........................ JohnFahy(3) 4 43
(Denis Coakley) *chsd ldrs tl ins fnl 3f* **14/1**
00-0 **12** 2¼ **Mecox Bay (IRE)**[33] 1443 4-8-8 **65**........................(v[1]) SimonPearce(3) 7 39
(Andrew Balding) *s.i.s: in rr: sme hdwy over 3f out: sn wknd* **25/1**
P **First Point (GER)**[44] 8-9-2 **70**........................ KierenFallon 12 —
(Nicky Henderson) *trckd ldrs tl p.u and dismntd after 5f* **5/4**[1]

2m 50.48s (-1.52) **Going Correction** -0.025s/f (Good) **13** Ran SP% **119.0**
Speed ratings (Par 103): **103,101,100,99,97 97,97,97,94,91 90,88,—**
toteswingers: 1&2 £34.30, 1&3 £31.30, 2&3 £52.50. CSF £330.57 CT £4269.23 TOTE £14.00: £4.60, £6.30, £2.40; EX 248.90 TRIFECTA Not won..
Owner Seahorse Five & Tim Pearson **Bred** Dominic Fagan **Trained** Upper Lambourn, Berks

FOCUS
A fair handicap but one that lost much of its interest when short-priced market leader broke down at the end of the back straight. The gallop was an ordinary one and not many figured. The form is rated around the placed horses and fifth.
First Point(GER) Official explanation: vet said gelding pulled up lame

2313 BETFAIR SUPPORTS ORACLE CANCER TRUST FILLIES' H'CAP 7f (S)
8:45 (8:51) (Class 5) (0-75,75) 3-Y-0+ **£2,914** (£867; £433; £216) **Stalls** Centre

Form RPR
4211 **1** **Saddlers Bend (IRE)**[18] 1789 5-9-8 **72**........................ MatthewDavies(3) 11 81
(George Baker) *chsd ldrs: chal ins fnl 3f: led ins fnl 2f: edgd rt ins fnl f: rdn out* **10/1**
1443 **2** ½ **Caelis**[19] 1766 3-8-4 **62**........................(b) RichardKingscote 14 66
(Ralph Beckett) *hld up in rr: hdwy on ins fr 2f out: swtchd lft ins fnl f: styd on to go 2nd fnl 120yds: fin wl but nt rch wnr* **12/1**
1352 **3** 1¼ **Perfect Ch'I (IRE)**[15] 1866 4-9-9 **70**........................ MartinLane 9 74
(Ian Wood) *led: jnd ins fnl 3f: hdd ins fnl 2f: styd chalng tl outpcd ins fnl f: lost 2nd fnl 120yds* **16/1**
342- **4** ½ **Valencha**[182] 7521 4-9-11 **72**........................ TravisBlock 7 77+
(Hughie Morrison) *in tch: hdwy 2f out: styng on whn hmpd ins fnl f: kpt on again clsng stages* **11/1**
60-1 **5** 1 **Chokurei (IRE)**[47] 1130 3-8-10 **71**........................ JohnFahy(3) 2 67
(Clive Cox) *t.k.h: chsd ldrs: rdn: swtchd lft and effrt to chse ldrs appr fnl f: kpt on same pce* **12/1**
0-24 **6** ½ **Bianca De Medici**[14] 1884 4-9-12 **73**........................ SteveDrowne 6 72
(Hughie Morrison) *chsd ldrs: rdn 2f out: outpcd fnl f* **6/1**[2]
35-2 **7** nk **Russian Rave**[37] 1330 5-9-11 **72**........................ FergusSweeney 3 70+
(Jonathan Portman) *t.k.h in rr: hdwy on outside over 2f out: styd on same pce fnl f* **14/1**
41- **8** 1¼ **Mantatisi**[189] 7448 3-9-0 **72**........................ PatCosgrave 15 63
(James Fanshawe) *hld up in rr: hdwy 2f out: no imp fnl f* **2/1**[1]
1051 **9** 9 **Dualagi**[23] 1630 7-9-3 **64**........................ RobertHavlin 4 34
(Martin Bosley) *chsd ldrs tl wknd qckly over 2f out* **33/1**
514- **10** nk **Poyle Judy**[176] 7572 3-9-2 **74**........................ JimCrowley 12 40
(Ralph Beckett) *t.k.h in rr: sme prog over 2f out: sn wknd* **20/1**
2140 **11** 1¼ **Greenflash**[9] 2018 3-8-11 **74**........................ KieranO'Neill(5) 5 36
(Richard Hannon) *a outpcd* **12/1**
041- **12** 6 **Hippique**[157] 7872 4-9-3 **64**........................(v) HayleyTurner 16 —
(Jeremy Gask) *pressed ldr 3f: wknd over 2f out* **25/1**
303- **13** 4½ **Elegant Muse**[191] 7408 3-8-12 **70**........................ KierenFallon 1 —
(Walter Swinburn) *chsd ldrs: rdn and btn over 2f out* **8/1**[3]

1m 26.16s (0.46) **Going Correction** +0.075s/f (Good)
WFA 3 from 4yo+ 11lb **13** Ran SP% **123.3**
Speed ratings (Par 100): **100,99,98,97,96 95,95,93,83,83 81,75,69**
toteswingers: 1&2 £41.10, 1&3 £11.20, 2&3 £31.20. CSF £125.56 CT £1926.51 TOTE £7.20: £2.30, £5.00, £4.80; EX 174.60 TRIFECTA Not won..
Owner Mrs Christine Cone **Bred** J F Tuthill **Trained** Whitsbury, Hants

FOCUS
No more than a fair fillies' handicap in which a couple of the less-exposed sorts proved a shade disappointing. The gallop was an ordinary one and this was another race on the card in which those held up were at a bit of a disadvantage. The first eight pulled clear but the form looks ordinary rated around those in the frame behind the winner.
Dualagi Official explanation: jockey said mare ran too free
T/Plt: £1,050.80 to a £1 stake. Pool of £77,434.38 - 53.79 winning tickets. T/Qpdt: £89.70 to a £1 stake. Pool of £6,270.31- 51.70 winning tickets. ST

2070 YORK (L-H)
Saturday, May 21

OFFICIAL GOING: Good (good to firm in places; 7.3)
Rail moved out 3m from 1m 6f to entrance of home straight adding 20yds to distances on round course.
Wind: Fresh strong behind Weather: Mixture of sunshine and cloud

2314 SPORTINGBET.COM CLAIMING STKS 1m 4f
2:05 (2:05) (Class 4) 4-Y-0+ **£5,504** (£1,637; £818; £408) **Stalls** Centre

Form RPR
530- **1** **Just Lille (IRE)**[205] 7189 8-8-11 89........................(p) SilvestreDeSousa 1 87
(Ann Duffield) *mde all: rdn over 4f out: drvn over 2f out: kpt on wl* **7/2**[2]
2 2½ **Sunwise (USA)**[196] 6654 5-9-7 94........................(b) JimmyFortune 5 93
(William Haggas) *trckd ldr: chal 4f out: sn drvn: kpt on one pce* **5/1**
0-40 **3** nk **Halla San**[17] 1808 9-8-11 95........................ LeeTopliss(5) 6 88
(Richard Fahey) *in tch: pushed along over 4f out: disp 2nd fr over 2f out: kpt on: eased fnl 50yds* **10/3**[1]
32-2 **4** 10 **Spring Jim**[64] 359 10-9-0 82........................ GeorgeBaker 4 70
(James Fanshawe) *hld up: rdn and hdwy over 3f out: wknd over 1f out: eased ins fnl f* **4/1**[3]
00-0 **5** 6 **Gold Rules**[10] 2002 4-8-9 86........................ DavidSimmonson(7) 3 62
(Michael Easterby) *hld up in tch: rdn over 4f out: sn no imp: wknd fnl 2f* **14/1**
613/ **6** 98 **Scriptwriter (IRE)**[25] 4722 9-8-12 94........................ PaulMulrennan 2 —
(Howard Johnson) *hld up in tch: rdn over 4f out: sn wknd: bhd fnl 3f: eased fnl f* **7/2**[2]

2m 32.44s (-0.76) **Going Correction** +0.125s/f (Good) **6** Ran SP% **110.9**
Speed ratings (Par 105): **107,105,105,98,94 29**
toteswingers: 1&2 £4.40, 1&3 £2.20, 2&3 £3.20. CSF £20.30 TOTE £4.90: £2.60, £2.70; EX 22.50.
Owner Middleham Park Racing XLVI **Bred** Sweetmans Bloodstock **Trained** Constable Burton, N Yorks
■ Stewards' Enquiry : Lee Topliss ten-day ban: failed to ride out for second (Jun 4, 6-14)

FOCUS
A decent race by claiming standards with the third the best guide.

Spring Jim Official explanation: trainer said gelding had a breathing problem

2315 SPORTINGBET.COM CONDITIONS STKS 7f

2:35 (2:35) (Class 3) 3-Y-O+ **£8,418** (£2,505; £1,251; £625) **Stalls** Low

Form RPR

25-3 **1** **Chachamaidee (IRE)**[20] [1718] 4-8-11 105........................[1] EddieAhern 3 108
(Sir Henry Cecil) *dwlt: sn trckd ldng pair: rdn to ld over 1f out: edgd rt 1f out: kpt on* **11/4**[2]

10-2 **2** 1 ½ **Kakatosi**[14] [1889] 4-9-2 103........................ JimmyFortune 4 109
(Andrew Balding) *w ldr: led over 3f out: rdn over 2f out: hdd over 1f out: sltly bmpd 1f out: kpt on* **15/8**[1]

330- **3** nk **Awzaan**[232] [6529] 4-9-2 111........................ RichardHills 5 108
(Mark Johnston) *trckd ldng pair: rdn over 2f out: nt clr run and swtchd lft 1f out: kpt on ins fnl f* **11/4**[2]

040- **4** 2 ½ **Palace Moon**[246] [6147] 6-9-2 109........................(t) GeorgeBaker 1 101
(William Knight) *trckd ldng pair: chal on bit 2f out: sn rdn: wknd ins fnl f* **5/1**[3]

411- **5** 22 **Out Of Nothing**[199] [7308] 8-8-8 80........................ PaulPickard[(3)] 2 —
(Kevin M Prendergast) *led narrowly: rdn whn hdd over 3f out: wknd 2f out* **20/1**

1m 21.85s (-3.45) **Going Correction** -0.30s/f (Firm) course record **5** Ran SP% **109.5**
Speed ratings (Par 107): **107,105,104,102,76**
CSF £8.24 TOTE £3.50: £1.80, £1.70; EX 8.10.

Owner R A H Evans **Bred** Cheval Court Stud **Trained** Newmarket, Suffolk

FOCUS

A good little conditions event which was run at a solid pace and the form looks slightly muddling, with the third and fourth not at their best on reappearances.

NOTEBOOK

Chachamaidee(IRE) built on the level of her comeback over 1m at Newmarket 20 days earlier and, paying a compliment to her conqueror there, I'm A Dreamer, ran out a fairly ready winner. She took a little time to settle, but found plenty when asked for her effort around 2f out and the application of a first-time hood clearly helped her cause. She is not that simple to place off her current sort of mark, but has now won her last two outings here and could just be up to nicking a Group 3 this term if the headgear continues to have the desired effect.

Kakatosi ran a blinder when second on his seasonal debut at Haydock and did so again here, but lacked the class of the winner. He may just be better off being delivered somewhat later in his races and fully deserves to get his head back in front. (op 2-1)

Awzaan failed to score in four outings at three last year, but still showed he retains an engine and was the one to beat at these weights on his comeback. He looked to hit something of a flat spot when it really mattered and ought to come on a good deal. (op 5-2)

Palace Moon looked to be travelling best of all on the outside nearing 2f out, but he couldn't quicken when push came to shove and ultimately got well beaten off. He has become difficult to catch right, but it wouldn't be surprising to see him improve significantly for the outing. (op 11-2)

Out Of Nothing was biting off more than she could chew on her return from a 99-day break and proved a sitting duck after setting the decent early pace.

2316 STOWE FAMILY LAW LLP GRAND CUP (LISTED RACE) 1m 6f

3:10 (3:10) (Class 1) 4-Y-O+

£19,869 (£7,532; £3,769; £1,879; £941; £472) **Stalls** Low

Form RPR

1-41 **1** **Times Up**[20] [1717] 5-9-0 108........................ EddieAhern 3 115
(John Dunlop) *trckd ldrs: led on bit 3f out: rdn and edgd rt over 1f out: kpt on ins fnl f: comf* **5/2**[1]

60-6 **2** 4 **Theology**[24] [1601] 4-9-0 109........................ GeorgeBaker 5 109
(Jeremy Noseda) *hld up: hdwy over 4f out: chal over 2f out: sn rdn: kpt on: no ch w wnr ins fnl f* **7/2**[2]

6010 **3** 3 ¾ **Montaff**[17] [1808] 5-9-0 99........................ SamHitchcott 2 104
(Mick Channon) *in tch: pushed along and hdwy over 4f out: chal 3f out: sn drvn: kpt on one pce* **14/1**

100- **4** ¾ **Prospect Wells (FR)**[196] [7350] 6-9-0 106........................ PaulMulrennan 4 103
(Howard Johnson) *midfield: hdwy over 4f out: rdn and ev ch 3f out: sn outpcd: hung lft 1f out: kpt on towards fin* **12/1**

03-3 **5** 3 ½ **Simenon (IRE)**[21] [1679] 4-9-0 97........................ JimmyFortune 7 98
(Andrew Balding) *trckd ldr: rdn over 3f out: sn one pce: wknd ins fnl f* **5/1**

0-12 **6** 8 **Cracking Lass (IRE)**[8] [2044] 4-8-9 95........................ LeeTopliss 6 82
(Richard Fahey) *hld up: rdn over 5f out: sn no imp* **4/1**[3]

510- **7** 4 ½ **Palomar (USA)**[64] [7350] 9-9-0 90........................ GrahamGibbons 8 81
(Brian Ellison) *s.i.s: hld up: rdn over 4f out: a towards rr* **33/1**

064- **8** 15 **Oasis Knight (IRE)**[15] [2097] 5-9-0 100........................(b) MichaelHills 1 60
(Nicky Henderson) *led: rdn whn hdd 3f out: sn wknd: eased over 1f out* **10/1**

2m 59.03s (-1.17) **Going Correction** +0.125s/f (Good) **8** Ran SP% **113.9**
Speed ratings (Par 111): **108,105,103,103,101 96,94,85**
toteswingers: 1&2 £2.80, 1&3 £6.40, 2&3 £11.00. CSF £11.21 TOTE £3.30: £1.50, £1.60, £3.10; EX 8.40 Trifecta £251.00 Pool: £508.93 - 1.50 winning units..

Owner Mrs I H Stewart-Brown & M J Meacock **Bred** I Stewart-Brown And M Meacock **Trained** Arundel, W Sussex

FOCUS

A competitive Listed event for stayers and there was a decent pace on. The runners once again ignored the far side in the home straight and the form is solid, although limited by the third.

NOTEBOOK

Times Up followed up his Newmarket success 20 days earlier and handed his in-form trainer a third win in the race in the past four seasons. He had failed to win in three previous attempts over this longer trip, but is stronger now and there was a lot to like about the manner of his victory. Despite racing somewhat enthusiastically off the solid early pace, he travelled beautifully into the lead 2f out and saw out the trip without much fuss. This marks him down as now being very much a Pattern performer and surely connections will now look towards the Group 1 Irish St Leger at the Curragh as his big aim in September. The stable won this with Tactic last term, who went on to finish a below-par sixth in that, but won the Curragh Cup over this trip along the way, and that Group 3 event could well be next for this late-maturing 5-y-o. (op 9-4 tchd 11-4 in a place)

Theology, from another in-form stable, was well held by the winner but stepped up as expected on the level of his comeback run in the Group 2 Sagaro Stakes at Ascot last month. He finished a clear second best and will probably come on again for the run. (op 4-1)

Montaff never figured in the Chester Cup last time, but had won at Ripon over 2m on his penultimate outing and returned to that sort of form with a sound enough effort in defeat. (op 16-1)

Prospect Wells(FR) was returning from a 196-day absence, but did score first time up last year. He didn't looks the easiest under pressure, but stayed on stoutly towards the finish and could build on this. Official explanation: jockey said said gelding was unsuited by the good (good to firm in places) ground (op 14-1)

Simenon(IRE), third at Goodwood on his return 21 days earlier, raced handily and wasn't disgraced on ground plenty quick enough. (op 6-1 tchd 9-2)

Cracking Lass(IRE) came under pressure before the home straight and ran below her previous level. Perhaps the run came a bit too soon. (op 9-2)

2317 SPORTINGBET.COM SPRINT (H'CAP) 5f

3:40 (3:41) (Class 2) (0-105,101) 3-Y-O+**£28,494** (£8,478; £4,237; £2,116) **Stalls** Centre

Form RPR

00-3 **1** **Masamah (IRE)**[17] [1809] 5-9-9 100........................ EddieAhern 8 111
(Kevin Ryan) *w ldr: led 2f out: drvn and hld on wl ins fnl f* **8/1**[2]

0-11 **2** ½ **Doctor Parkes**[17] [1809] 5-9-2 93........................ JimmyFortune 5 102
(Eric Alston) *trckd ldrs: drvn and kpt on wl ins fnl f: wnt 2nd towards fin* **11/1**

3 nk **Celerina (IRE)**[50] [1086] 4-8-3 87........................ SAGray[(7)] 2 95
(T Stack, Ire) *w ldr: rdn 1f out: kpt on ins fnl f* **12/1**

5-22 **4** 2 **Waffle (IRE)**[28] [1518] 5-9-9 100........................ SilvestreDeSousa 11 101
(David Barron) *hld up in tch: hdwy over 1f out: rdn and kpt on wl ins fnl f: nt rch ldrs* **15/2**[1]

30-0 **5** ½ **Hazelrigg (IRE)**[9] [2028] 6-8-10 87........................(be) DanielTudhope 15 86
(Tim Easterby) *trckd ldrs towards stands' side: rdn over 1f out: kpt on ins fnl f* **33/1**

04-5 **6** ¾ **Secret Millionaire (IRE)**[9] [2028] 4-8-8 88........................ JamesSullivan[(3)] 18 84
(Patrick Morris) *t.k.h: w ldr towards stands' side: rdn over 1f out: no ex ins fnl f* **10/1**[3]

5-31 **7** nk **Ancient Cross**[9] [2028] 7-9-4 95........................(t) GrahamGibbons 19 90+
(Michael Easterby) *hld up in tch towards stands' side: pushed along and hdwy over 1f out: kpt on ins fnl f: n.d* **10/1**[3]

20-0 **8** nse **Tax Free (IRE)**[42] [1242] 9-9-9 100........................ AdrianNicholls 1 95
(David Nicholls) *chsd ldrs: rdn over 2f out: ev ch over 1f out: wknd ins fnl f* **16/1**

411 **9** hd **Mon Brav**[7] [2116] 4-8-5 85........................ PaulPickard[(3)] 10 79
(Brian Ellison) *in tch: rdn 2f out: sn no imp* **10/1**[3]

-000 **10** ¾ **Johannes (IRE)**[9] [2028] 8-8-12 94........................ LeeTopliss[(5)] 17 86
(Richard Fahey) *hld up: rdn over 2f out: one pce* **15/2**[1]

3400 **11** hd **Barney McGrew (IRE)**[9] [2028] 8-9-7 98........................ GeorgeBaker 4 89+
(Michael Dods) *hld up in tch: rdn over 2f out: one pce* **16/1**

125- **12** hd **Bajan Tryst (USA)**[211] [7073] 5-9-9 100........................ PhillipMakin 3 90
(Kevin Ryan) *w ldr: rdn 2f out: wknd fnl f* **16/1**

35/0 **13** nk **Befortyfour**[9] [2028] 6-9-1 92........................ MichaelHills 12 81
(Richard Guest) *led narrowly: rdn whn hdd 2f out: sn wknd* **40/1**

3203 **14** ¾ **Beat The Bell**[7] [2117] 6-8-13 90........................ LeeNewman 16 77+
(David Barron) *hld up: rdn over 1f out: sn no imp* **20/1**

05-0 **15** 1 ¼ **Kaldoun Kingdom (IRE)**[8] [2075] 6-9-3 101........................ GeorgeChaloner[(7)] 13 83
(Richard Fahey) *hld up in tch: rdn over 1f out: sn no imp* **28/1**

0-44 **16** ½ **Confessional**[17] [1809] 4-9-0 91........................(e) RobertWinston 20 71
(Tim Easterby) *prom towards stands' side: rdn 2f out: wknd fnl f* **14/1**

-000 **17** 1 ¼ **Hotham**[7] [2117] 8-8-7 84........................ PaulQuinn 7 60
(Noel Wilson) *dwlt: hld up: rdn over 2f out: a towards rr* **33/1**

00-4 **18** 8 **Taajub (IRE)**[15] [1848] 4-9-7 98........................ RichardHills 6 45
(William Haggas) *dwlt: hld up: rdn over 2f out: a towards rr* **18/1**

00-0 **19** 2 **Swiss Franc**[9] [2028] 6-9-1 92........................ PaulMulrennan 14 32+
(David Elsworth) *hld up: hmpd over 2f out: sn bhd: eased* **20/1**

56.58 secs (-2.72) **Going Correction** -0.30s/f (Firm) **19** Ran SP% **128.8**
Speed ratings (Par 109): **109,108,107,104,103 102,102,101,101,100 100,99,99,98,96 95,93,80,77**
toteswingers: 1&2 £26.10, 1&3 £11.00, 2&3 £18.50. CSF £88.62 CT £1083.23 TOTE £9.60: £2.60, £2.90, £2.80, £2.00; EX 111.90 Trifecta £1460.70 Pool: £29544.27 - 14.96 winning units..

Owner Dr Marwan Koukash **Bred** Stanley Estate & Stud Co & Mount Coote Stud **Trained** Hambleton, N Yorks

■ Stewards' Enquiry : George Chaloner two-day ban: careless riding (Jun 6-7)

FOCUS

A fiercely competitive sprint handicap and unsurprisingly there was no hanging about. Despite the stands' side proving the place to be at the previous meeting nine days earlier, the main action developed more towards the far side this time and three came clear. The form is rated around the first three.

NOTEBOOK

Masamah(IRE) just came out on top, opening his account for the season at the second time of asking. A sprinter that loves forcing the pace, he travelled sweetly under a positive ride and knuckled down gamely when hard pressed by old rival Doctor Parkes inside the final half furlong. This venue clearly suits as it was this made it 2-3 over C&D and there is every reason to think he can make an impact in a higher grade this year. Trainer Kevin Ryan said afterwards he was not sure where his 5-y-o would head next. (op 12-1)

Doctor Parkes threw down a strong challenge nearing the finish, but was always just being held in this quest for a hat-trick. He was up another 4lb, thus was that amount worse off with the winner on their last-time-out Chester form, and did have the better of the draw that day. This rates another personal-best in defeat, however, and this was probably just that bit too sharp for him. (tchd 12-1)

Celerina(IRE) ◆ was never far away towards the far side and she too turned in her best effort in defeat. This prolific 4-y-o ought to learn for the experience of this big-field race and further prizes look to await her this year. (tchd 14-1)

Waffle(IRE) had his chance and ran right up to par, giving the form a decent look. He hasn't won since his 2-y-o debut, but richly deserves to score again and can do so when reverting to a slightly stiffer test. (op 8-1)

Hazelrigg(IRE) ◆ needed his comeback over C&D at the last meeting and emerged best of the six that reopposed from that race here. He should come on again and looks capable of defying this mark.

Secret Millionaire(IRE) ran a blinder here on his return at the last meeting and was well backed. He had his chance towards the near side and reversed form with his previous conqueror Ancient Cross.

Ancient Cross was up 6lb and didn't get such a charmed passage this time. (op 11-1)

Tax Free(IRE) ◆ was having his first outing in a handicap since finishing fifth off a 7lb higher mark in the 2006 Stewards' Cup. He improved nicely on the level of his seasonal debut last month and is one to keep an eye on with something similar in mind back over a stiffer test.

Mon Brav wasn't disgraced in his quest for a hat-trick in this much hotter company off a 4lb higher mark and may not be weighted out of winning again just yet. His rider later reported his saddle slipped. Official explanation: jockey said saddle slipped (op 12-1)

Johannes(IRE) again attracted strong support, but got a better passage this time and lacked a gear change. (op 8-1)

Barney McGrew(IRE), who finished on the bridle here nine days earlier, had no obvious excuses this time.

Taajub(IRE) was taken off his feet and connections later reported him to have lost his action. Official explanation: jockey said colt klost its action and hung left (op 20-1 tchd 16-1)

Swiss Franc Official explanation: jockey said gelding hung right

2318 YORKSHIRE REGIMENT E B F MEDIAN AUCTION MAIDEN STKS 6f

4:15 (4:15) (Class 3) 2-Y-O **£7,447** (£2,216; £1,107; £553) **Stalls** Centre

Form RPR

2 **1** **Brocklebank (IRE)**[14] 1890 2-9-3 0 .... PhillipMakin 8 89+
(Kevin Ryan) *w ldr: led over 2f out: rdn over 1f out: kpt on wl* **10/3**[2]

02 **2** *1 1/4* **Apostle (IRE)**[9] 2033 2-9-3 0 .... EddieAhern 2 85
(Michael Bell) *led narrowly: hdd over 2f out: sn rdn: kpt on: hld towards fin* **15/8**[1]

3 *7* **Cockney Rocker** 2-9-3 0 .... MichaelHills 9 64+
(Jane Chapple-Hyam) *slowly away: hld up: pushed along and green over 3f out: hdwy over 1f out: wnt 3rd ins fnl f: kpt on but no threat to ldng pair* **12/1**

2233 **4** *2 1/4* **One Kool Dude**[15] 1876 2-8-12 0 .... LeeTopliss(5) 6 58
(Richard Fahey) *trckd ldrs: rdn over 2f out: one pce* **15/2**

5 *2 1/4* **Comical** 2-9-3 0 .... SilvestreDeSousa 11 51+
(Mark Johnston) *s.i.s: hld up: pushed along over 3f out: edgd lft fr over 1f out: kpt on ins fnl f* **6/1**[3]

6 *1* **Inya House** 2-9-3 0 .... GeorgeBaker 3 48
(Nigel Tinkler) *trckd ldrs: rdn 2f out: wknd over 1f out* **40/1**

7 *1/2* **Angel Kiss (IRE)** 2-8-12 0 .... DanielTudhope 7 41
(David O'Meara) *hld up: rdn over 2f out: kpt on ins fnl f: n.d* **25/1**

4 **8** *2* **Tyre Giant Dot Com**[49] 1095 2-9-3 0 .... GrahamGibbons 1 40
(Geoffrey Oldroyd) *slowly away: hld up: rdn over 2f out: no imp* **7/1**

9 *3/4* **Only Orsenfoolsies** 2-9-3 0 .... PaulMulrennan 4 38
(Micky Hammond) *prom: rdn over 2f out: sn wknd* **66/1**

10 *16* **Turn The Page** 2-9-3 0 .... RobertWinston 10 —
(Alan McCabe) *chsd ldrs: rdn 3f out: sn wknd* **25/1**

1m 10.44s (-1.46) **Going Correction** -0.30s/f (Firm) **10** Ran SP% **115.7**
Speed ratings (Par 97): **97,95,86,83,80 78,78,75,74,53**
toteswingers: 1&2 £2.10, 1&3 £8.40, 2&3 £7.80. CSF £9.56 TOTE £4.40: £1.40, £1.30, £4.10; EX 5.90 Trifecta £48.50 Pool of £526.57 - 8.02 winning units..
Owner Mrs Margaret Forsyth **Bred** Vincent Reen **Trained** Hambleton, N Yorks

FOCUS
Probably just an average juvenile maiden, but it was run at a sound pace and the form looks decent with the two market leaders coming nicely clear.

NOTEBOOK
Brocklebank(IRE) finished runner-up on his debut at Haydock a fortnight previously and went one better with a taking display. He proved free through the early parts in share of the lead, but found a turn of foot when asked to win the race and was always holding his main-market rival. Clearly improving, he looks well worth a try in Pattern company. (op 7-2 tchd 3-1)
Apostle(IRE) improved a bundle from his debut when second over C&D nine days earlier and held every chance to go one better, but again just found one too strong. He travels like a good horse and can win a maiden over this trip on a stiffer track. (tchd 2-1)
Cockney Rocker ◆ finished encouragingly from off the pace and fared best of the newcomers. He has speed in his pedigree, but looked to need every yard of this trip. Granted normal improvement he ought to go close next time out. (op 10-1)
One Kool Dude had finished placed on his previous four outings and looked as though this extra furlong would suit pretty much throughout them. He didn't settle that well and hit a flat spot when the tempo got serious, but kept on for pressure. He rates the benchmark, but will probably struggle to win a maiden. (op 6-1)
Comical was always playing catch up after a tardy start and ultimately ran too green to do himself full justice. He has plenty of scope, however, and should leave this form behind when faced with a suitably stiffer test. (op 9-1)
Inya House, speedily bred, showed nice early pace and ought to improve a bundle for the initial outing. (tchd 33-1)

2319 SPORTINGBET AND YORKSHIRE EVENING POST STKS (H'CAP) 7f

4:50 (4:50) (Class 3) (0-90,90) 3-Y-O **£8,418** (£2,505; £1,251; £625) **Stalls** Low

Form RPR

4-21 **1** **Common Touch (IRE)**[10] 2003 3-9-0 **88** .... LeeTopliss(5) 8 101+
(Richard Fahey) *hld up in tch: hdwy to chal over 2f out: rdn to ld 1f out: kpt on strly* **7/2**[1]

5522 **2** *3 1/4* **City Legend**[5] 2147 3-8-4 **76** oh4 .... (bt) DeclanCannon(3) 10 80
(Alan McCabe) *chsd ldrs: rdn over 3f out: led 2f out: sn drvn and edgd lft: hdd 1f out: kpt on: no ch w wnr* **22/1**

0213 **3** *1 1/4* **Iceblast**[10] 2003 3-8-11 **83** .... (b1) JamesSullivan(3) 4 84
(Michael Easterby) *rrd and slowly away: hld up: rdn over 3f out: hdwy over 1f out: kpt on wl ins fnl f: wnt 3rd towards fin* **11/1**

31-2 **4** *3/4* **Majestic Dream (IRE)**[26] 1571 3-9-1 **84** .... (v) GeorgeBaker 13 83
(Walter Swinburn) *trckd ldrs: rdn and ev ch 2f out: kpt on one pce* **8/1**[3]

2-14 **5** *3/4* **Yair Hill (IRE)**[20] 1725 3-8-11 **80** .... EddieAhern 9 77
(John Dunlop) *hld up: hdwy 3f out: chal on bit 2f out: sn rdn: fnd little* **11/1**

0-34 **6** *2* **My Single Malt (IRE)**[8] 2043 3-8-10 **79** .... GrahamGibbons 3 70
(Tom Tate) *trckd ldrs: rdn over 2f out: wknd fnl f* **14/1**

42-3 **7** *3* **Nordic Spruce (USA)**[27] 1546 3-9-3 **86** .... PaulMulrennan 11 69
(Sir Henry Cecil) *hld up in tch on outer: rdn over 2f out: no imp* **8/1**[3]

21-0 **8** *2 1/4* **First Class Favour (IRE)**[16] 1820 3-8-13 **87** .... LanceBetts(5) 2 64
(Tim Easterby) *led: rdn whn hdd 2f out: sn wknd* **40/1**

3-33 **9** *1* **Nawaashi**[14] 1916 3-8-9 **78** .... RichardHills 12 52
(Mark Johnston) *prom: rdn over 2f out: wknd over 1f out* **8/1**[3]

15- **10** *1/2* **Baptist (USA)**[224] 6737 3-9-7 **90** .... JimmyFortune 14 63+
(Andrew Balding) *slowly away: hld up: rdn over 2f out: no imp* **6/1**[2]

-343 **11** *nk* **Boundaries**[16] 1825 3-9-0 **83** .... (v) RobertWinston 5 55
(Tim Easterby) *t.k.h: trckd ldrs: rdn over 3f out: wknd 2f out* **25/1**

110- **12** *1 1/2* **Barista (IRE)**[179] 7544 3-9-1 **84** .... AdrianNicholls 1 52
(Mick Channon) *hld up: a towards rr* **25/1**

00-0 **13** *hd* **Major Conquest (IRE)**[20] 1725 3-8-12 **81** .... MichaelHills 7 49
(J W Hills) *midfield: rdn over 2f out: wknd over 1f out* **16/1**

51 **14** *12* **J R Hartley**[66] 873 3-8-11 **80** .... PhillipMakin 6 —
(Bryan Smart) *prom: rdn and lost pl over 3f out: wknd 2f out: eased* **16/1**

1m 22.12s (-3.18) **Going Correction** -0.30s/f (Firm) **14** Ran SP% **119.4**
Speed ratings (Par 103): **106,102,100,100,99 96,93,90,89,89 88,87,86,73**
toteswingers: 1&2 £20.10, 1&3 £10.60, 2&3 £45.40. CSF £90.55 CT £804.81 TOTE £3.40: £1.80, £6.50, £4.00; EX 94.90 Trifecta £565.10 Part won. Pool of £763.73 - 0.62 winning units..
Owner Nicholas Wrigley & Kevin Hart **Bred** Overbury Stallions Ltd And D Boocock **Trained** Musley Bank, N Yorks

FOCUS
A good 3-y-o handicap, run at a solid pace and they were spread out across the home straight but again ignored the far side. The form looks good for the grade with the third, fourth and fifth close to their marks.

NOTEBOOK
Common Touch(IRE) ◆ made it 2-4 when resuming winning ways over C&D at the Dante meeting nine days previously and he followed up off a 5lb higher mark in the style of a rapidly improving handicapper. He was allowed to find his feet off the pace and made his challenge down the centre. The manner in which he travelled and then put the race to bed was impressive, so it's highly likely he still has more to offer with this being just his fifth outing to-date. The ultra-competitive Britannia Handicap at Royal Ascot over an extra furlong next month could prove up his street, and he would prove popular if heading there next. Rightly so. (tchd 11-4)
City Legend, a runner-up the last twice, quickened to look a definite threat nearing the furlong marker. He was put in his place by the winner where it mattered, but this does rate his best effort to date from 4lb out of the handicap. It wouldn't be surprising to see him out quickly again after this. (op 20-1)
Iceblast was 5lb better off with the winner on their last-time-out C&D form and equipped with first-time blinkers. He came through late on after rearing from the gates and helps to set the level. (op 10-1 tchd 12-1)
Majestic Dream(IRE), 4lb higher, had to race wide early from his draw in 13 and wasn't at all disgraced. He may be ready to tackle 1m again. (op 9-1)
Yair Hill(IRE) travelled as well as anything into contention, but lacked a turn of foot when asked for his effort and the handicapper could have his measure. It could be he is ready to try 1m again, however.
Nordic Spruce(USA) made her way to the stands' rail after turning in, but was soon under the pump and posted a laboured effort. (op 11-1)
Baptist(USA) was something of an unknown quantity on this 3-y-o and handicap debut, having raced just twice at two. Despite carrying top weight he came in for some support back on quicker ground, but wasn't helped by the outside stall and never got involved from out the back. He now has a bit to prove, but is a good-looking colt and it would be rash to write him off just yet. Official explanation: jockey said colt missed the break (op 11-2 tchd 13-2)
Boundaries Official explanation: jockey said colt ran too free

2320 JOHN WRIGHT ELECTRICAL STKS (HANDICAP FOR GENTLEMAN AMATEUR RIDERS) 1m 4f

5:25 (5:25) (Class 4) (0-80,80) 4-Y-O+ **£5,309** (£1,646; £822; £411) **Stalls** Centre

Form RPR

2214 **1** **Ravi River (IRE)**[14] 1909 7-10-10 **69** .... MrSWalker 12 83
(Brian Ellison) *midfield: hdwy over 4f out: led over 2f out: sn drvn: kpt on wl* **9/1**

124- **2** *2 1/4* **Meetings Man (IRE)**[104] 6074 4-10-9 **71** .... MrJHamer(3) 4 81
(Micky Hammond) *midfield: hdwy 5f out: led 4f out: rdn whn hdd over 2f out: kpt on: hld towards fin* **14/1**

2-21 **3** *3* **Sancho Panza**[11] 1994 4-10-4 **66** .... MrRBirkett(3) 9 71
(Julia Feilden) *hld up: gd hdwy on outer over 4f out: chal 3f out: kpt on one pce fnl 2f* **4/1**[2]

24/6 **4** *3 3/4* **John Forbes**[11] 1977 9-10-2 **68** .... MrJohnWilley(7) 3 67
(Brian Ellison) *hld up: rdn over 4f out: hdwy over 2f out: wnt 4th over 1f out: kpt on ins fnl f: nrst fin* **33/1**

3313 **5** *14* **Kames Park (IRE)**[5] 2159 9-10-12 **71** .... MrJMQuinlan 8 48
(Richard Guest) *hld up: rdn and hdwy over 3f out: wknd over 2f out* **11/1**

6340 **6** *1* **Hits Only Jude (IRE)**[2] 2213 8-10-0 **66** oh3 .... (v) MrJHarney(7) 11 41
(Declan Carroll) *chsd ldrs: rdn over 3f out: wknd over 1f out* **25/1**

3551 **7** *2* **Danderek**[19] 1746 5-11-0 **80** .... MrSHuggan(7) 6 52
(Richard Fahey) *trckd ldrs: rdn over 3f out: sn wknd* **11/2**[3]

30-0 **8** *4 1/2* **Kingsdale Orion (IRE)**[14] 1908 7-10-9 **73** .... MrDCottle(5) 1 38
(Brian Ellison) *midfield: rdn over 3f out: sn wknd* **12/1**

-521 **9** *4 1/2* **Jeer (IRE)**[48] 1107 7-11-2 **75** .... (b) MrOGreenall 2 33
(Michael Easterby) *led narrowly: hdd 4f out: wknd qckly* **5/2**[1]

421- **10** *13* **Rubi Dia**[162] 7806 4-10-6 **70** .... BrendanPowell(5) 5 —
(Kevin M Prendergast) *chsd ldrs: rdn over 4f out: sn wknd* **14/1**

1046 **11** *nk* **Trans Sonic**[14] 1909 8-10-7 **73** .... (b) MrSMurray(7) 10 —
(David O'Meara) *prom: lost pl over 7f out: wknd over 4f out* **25/1**

1404 **12** *25* **Record Breaker (IRE)**[20] 1713 7-11-6 **79** .... (b) MrMSeston 7 —
(Mark Johnston) *w ldr: rdn over 4f out: wknd qckly* **11/1**

2m 34.11s (0.91) **Going Correction** +0.125s/f (Good) **12** Ran SP% **122.3**
Speed ratings (Par 105): **101,99,97,95,85 85,83,80,77,69 68,52**
toteswingers: 1&2 £21.90, 1&3 £5.50, 2&3 £11.10. CSF £129.34 CT £593.29 TOTE £11.30: £3.30, £3.80, £1.60; EX 154.60 TRIFECTA Not won..
Owner Koo's Racing Club **Bred** Gainsborough Stud Management Ltd **Trained** Norton, N Yorks

FOCUS
A competitive race of its type and the amateur riders set a searching pace as there was a battle for the lead. The runners spread across the home straight and the centre was the place to be as the principals had it to themselves from 2f out. The runner-up looks the best guide to the level.
Jeer(IRE) Official explanation: trainer's rep had no explanation for the poor form shown
T/Plt: £35.60 to a £1 stake. Pool of £96,470.64 - 1,977.75 winning tickets. T/Qpdt: £7.50 to a £1 stake. Pool of £6,945.20 - 679.10 winning tickets. AS

2321 - (Foreign Racing) - See Raceform Interactive

[1777]CURRAGH (R-H)

Saturday, May 21

OFFICIAL GOING: Good to firm

2322a T P WATERS EUROPEAN BREEDERS FUND MARBLE HILL STKS (LISTED RACE) 5f

2:40 (2:42) 2-Y-O **£26,896** (£7,862; £3,724; £1,241)

RPR

1 **Power**[19] 1777 2-9-1 .... SeamieHeffernan 5 104+
(A P O'Brien, Ire) *led and disp: rdn and narrowly hdd 2f out: kpt on: disp fnl f: led on line* **6/4**[1]

2 *shd* **Tough As Nails (IRE)**[37] 1345 2-9-1 .... GFCarroll 2 104+
(Michael Mulvany, Ire) *prom: impr to take narrow ld 2f out: rdn and strly pressed fr over 1f out: disp ins fnl f: hdd on line* **4/1**[3]

3 *4* **Fire Lily (IRE)**[34] 1426 2-8-12 .... WMLordan 4 86
(David Wachman, Ire) *mid-div: 6th 1/2-way: rdn into 4th 2f out: no imp over 1f out: kpt on same pce fnl f* **7/4**[2]

4 *3* **An Ghalanta (IRE)**[34] 1426 2-8-12 .... KJManning 6 75
(J S Bolger, Ire) *chsd ldrs: 4th 1/2-way: rdn in 5th 2f out: no ex and kpt on one pce fr over 1f out* **12/1**

5 *1* **Gold Lace (IRE)**[48] 1115 2-8-12 .... FMBerry 8 72
(P J Prendergast, Ire) *mid-div: 5th 1/2-way: rdn and dropped to 7th 2f out: kpt on one pce fr over 1f out* **20/1**

6 *shd* **Muckle Bahoochie (IRE)**[8] 2084 2-8-12 .... JMurtagh 1 71
(G M Lyons, Ire) *hld up in 7th: rdn in 6th and no imp 2f out: kpt on one pce* **16/1**

7 *1* **Signifer (IRE)**[5] 2154 2-9-1 .... RichardHughes 7 71
(Mick Channon) *prom: cl 2nd 1/2-way: rdn and no ex 2f out: 3rd and no imp 1 1/2f out: wknd fnl f* **14/1**

8 *dist* **Hexagonal (IRE)**[10] 2010 2-9-1 .... CDHayes 9 —
(Lee Smyth, Ire) *a trailing: t.o* **100/1**
59.39 secs (-3.11) **Going Correction** -0.45s/f (Firm) **8** Ran SP% **122.4**
Speed ratings: **106,105,99,94,93 92,91,—**
CSF £8.88 TOTE £2.10: £1.02, £1.20, £1.20; DF 8.60.
Owner Michael Tabor **Bred** Norelands & Hugo Lascelles **Trained** Ballydoyle, Co Tipperary

FOCUS
This was a terrific contest between two very speedy and high-class colts, neither of whom deserved to lose, particularly the runner-up, considering what happened to him here before. The third looks a solid guide to the level.

NOTEBOOK
Power was dropping back in trip and it just about came off. He has no shortage of early pace as he was positively ridden, and he didn't lack courage either as he really battled on up the hill as he came clear with the runner-up. He has plenty of speed and gets a sixth furlong well so it is a measure of his ability that he was able to drop back to this trip and win a race as good as this one looked. (op 7/4 tchd 5/2)
Tough As Nails(IRE) ◆ was unlucky and hasn't enjoyed any of that at the Curragh this season. He again showed no end of speed and he really sustained it all the way to the line, as measured by the first two pulling as far clear of the opposition as they did. He's tough and speedy and is a smart colt. His trainer is thinking of keeping him in Ireland for the Railway Stakes but a race like the Norfolk Stakes looks made for him. (op 7/2)
Fire Lily(IRE) tracked the pace and was in a good position from which to mount a challenge over a furlong out but the first two just went right away from her inside the last. She's probably decent but was no match for the first two. (op 5/2)
An Ghalanta(IRE) should be well capable of winning a maiden. She showed some early speed, came off the bridle at around halfway and did look beaten but she kept on again late. She should certainly appreciate an extra furlong. (op 10/1)
Gold Lace(IRE) tracked the pace towards the stands' rail and looked reasonably speedy but was left behind in the final furlong or so. (op 20/1 tchd 16/1)
Muckle Bahoochie(IRE) had neither the speed to be competitive early nor could she pick up in the last furlong or so. The margin of her defeat is certainly indicative of this being a strong race.
Hexagonal(IRE) Official explanation: jockey said gekding did not act on today's ground

2323a WEATHERBYS IRELAND GREENLANDS STKS (GROUP 3) 6f
3:10 (3:10) 3-Y-O+ **£35,021** (£10,237; £4,849; £1,616)

RPR
1 **Hitchens (IRE)**[10] 2005 6-9-9 .... FMBerry 9 115
(David Barron) *chsd ldrs: 4th 1/2-way: rdn into 3rd 1 1/2f out: styd on to chal ins fnl f: led fnl 100yds: kpt on wl* **11/4**[2]
2 *1 1/4* **Tiddliwinks**[10] 2005 5-9-9 .... PJSmullen 8 111
(Kevin Ryan) *chsd ldrs: 3rd 1/2-way: impr to chal 2f out: led 1 1/2f out: rdn and chal ins fnl f: hdd fnl 100yds: no ex and kpt on same pce* **10/3**[3]
3 *1 1/2* **Santo Padre (IRE)**[28] 1533 7-9-9 106........ RichardHughes 5 106
(David Marnane, Ire) *dwlt and hmpd leaving stalls: hld up towards rr: rdn into 6th 1 1/2f out: styd on in 4th 1f out: kpt on same pce fnl f* **6/1**
4 *1 1/4* **Sing Softly (USA)**[38] 1319 3-8-11 103........ CO'Donoghue 3 97
(A P O'Brien, Ire) *led: chal 2f out: rdn and hdd 1 1/2f out: no ex ins fnl f: kpt on same pce* **5/2**[1]
5 *2 1/2* **Snaefell (IRE)**[28] 1533 7-9-12 106........(b) JMurtagh 4 97+
(M Halford, Ire) *dwlt and wnt lft leaving stalls: towards rr: rdn in mod 7th and no imp 1f out: kpt on one pce fnl f* **9/1**
6 *shd* **Partner (IRE)**[8] 2078 5-9-9 93........(b) SeamieHeffernan 6 94
(David Marnane, Ire) *chsd ldrs: 5th 1/2-way: rdn 2f out: no imp 1 1/2f out: kpt on one pce* **20/1**
7 *3* **Croisultan (IRE)**[48] 1118 5-9-9 106........ NGMcCullagh 2 84
(Liam McAteer, Ire) *chsd ldr in 2nd: rdn in 3rd 2f out: no ex in 4th 1 1/2f out: kpt on one pce* **12/1**
8 *1* **Tell The Wind (IRE)**[28] 1532 3-8-11 93........ DPMcDonogh 1 80+
(Kevin Prendergast, Ire) *mid-div: 6th 1/2-way: rdn and wknd 2f out* **33/1**
1m 11.44s (-3.56) **Going Correction** -0.45s/f (Firm)
WFA 3 from 4yo+ 9lb **8** Ran SP% **118.0**
Speed ratings: **105,103,101,99,96 96,92,90**
CSF £12.91 TOTE £3.40: £1.30, £1.50, £2.10; DF 14.90.
Owner Laurence O'Kane & Paul Murphy **Bred** Curragh Bloodstock Agency Ltd **Trained** Maunby, N Yorks

FOCUS
Following Sole Power's success in the Temple Stakes, it's ironic that Irish Stakes races seem to be won by English raiders on a regular basis. The third has been rated just off his 5f level and the fourth just off her 7f level.

NOTEBOOK
Hitchens(IRE) turned around the York form with his compatriot and runner-up, doing it convincingly enough. Tracking the pace, Fran Berry had to wait for a gap to open up, but considering that they were running into a bit of a headwind it probably wasn't a bad thing. When he did find some daylight inside the last he picked up well and won going away. He may step up to Group 2 company next. (op 10/3)
Tiddliwinks tracked the pace early on and travelled up well to challenge and lead a furlong out, but so well was he travelling that one might have expected him to find a little bit more than he did. It was a respectable performance. (op 11/4)
Santo Padre(IRE) was unlucky after being slightly hampered at the start and losing valuable lengths. He was eventually brought back into the race but just had that bit more leeway to find than was ideal. He kept on to the line and was nearest at the finish, and it's not hard to have seen him more involved with a clear run. (op 8/1)
Sing Softly(USA) showed early toe and travelled well at the head of the pace, but the likely effect of racing alone into the headwind probably took its toll. She found little enough when headed a furlong or so from the finish. (op 5/2 tchd 9/4)
Snaefell(IRE) jinked a bit coming out of the stalls but didn't lose much momentum. She just wasn't good enough to make his presence felt in the second half of the race having been covered up. (op 10/1)
Partner(IRE) ran better than his finishing position as he tracked the pace towards the stands' rail and had to be pulled quite wide to get a run. He ran on a bit inside the last. (op 20/1 tchd 16/1)
Croisultan(IRE) faded inside the last furlong and a half having chased the early pace. (op 10/1)

2324a ABU DHABI IRISH 2,000 GUINEAS (ENTIRE COLTS & FILLIES) (GROUP 1) 1m
3:45 (3:46) 3-Y-O
£162,500 (£53,232; £25,215; £8,405; £5,603; £2,801)

RPR
1 **Roderic O'Connor (IRE)**[21] 1686 3-9-0 119........ JPO'Brien 3 117
(A P O'Brien, Ire) *mde all: rdn and kpt on wl fnl f* **7/2**[3]
2 *3/4* **Dubawi Gold**[21] 1686 3-9-0 .... RichardHughes 1 117+
(Richard Hannon) *restrained and hld up towards rr: hdwy in 6th 2f out: rdn into 3rd 1f out: styd on fnl f to go 2nd cl home: nt rch wnr* **7/4**[1]
3 *1/2* **Oracle (IRE)**[19] 1778 3-9-0 102........ SeamieHeffernan 8 114
(A P O'Brien, Ire) *settled bhd ldrs: 5th 1/2-way: hdwy into 3rd 2f out: rdn into 2nd 1 1/2f out: no imp on wnr fnl f: lost 2nd cl home* **25/1**
4 *4 1/2* **High Ruler (USA)**[20] 1735 3-9-0 107........ CO'Donoghue 7 104
(A P O'Brien, Ire) *chsd wnr in 2nd and pushed along to go pce: rdn 1/2-way: no ex in 3rd 1 1/2f out: 5th 1f out: kpt on same pce fnl f* **40/1**
5 *hd* **Dunboyne Express (IRE)**[55] 1004 3-9-0 114........ DPMcDonogh 2 103
(Kevin Prendergast, Ire) *chsd ldrs: 4th 1/2-way: rdn 1 1/2f out: no ex over 1f out: kpt on same pce fnl f* **3/1**[2]
6 *3 1/2* **Zabarajad (IRE)**[19] 1778 3-9-0 105........ JMurtagh 6 95
(John M Oxx, Ire) *hld up bhd ldrs: 6th 1/2-way: rdn and no imp 1 1/2f out: kpt on one pce* **4/1**
7 *3/4* **Slim Shadey**[21] 1686 3-9-0 .... LukeMorris 5 94
(J S Moore) *chsd ldrs: 3rd 1/2-way: rdn in 5th 2f out: sn no ex* **16/1**
8 *24* **Foolproof (IRE)**[8] 2078 3-9-0 84........(t) DMGrant 4 38
(John Joseph Murphy, Ire) *a towards rr: rdn and wknd 3f out* **200/1**
1m 37.88s (-8.12) **Going Correction** -0.70s/f (Hard) **8** Ran SP% **116.3**
Speed ratings: **112,111,110,106,106 102,101,77**
CSF £10.18 CT £129.98 TOTE £5.40: £1.90, £1.02, £6.30; DF 14.10.
Owner Mrs John Magnier **Bred** Swettenham Stud **Trained** Ballydoyle, Co Tipperary

FOCUS
A remarkably cool ride by Joseph O'Brien on the winner in a relatively weak renewal of the Irish 2000 Guineas. The runner-up was the only one to make up ground from off the pace and the race has been rated around the winner to his 2-y-o best.

NOTEBOOK
Roderic O'Connor(IRE) went out in front as neither of the horses who one would have thought to be pacemakers couldn't or didn't get there. This led to him being given the run of the race. His rider kicked a furlong and a half out and managed to get the vital couple of lengths that he needed as both the second and third were reeling him in close home. All due respect to the winner for a Classic success and especially to his teenage rider for riding the race he did, but time is likely to tell that this was a weak renewal. The winner is likely to take his chance in the Irish or French Derby. The way his two main rivals were coming back at him, one would expect him to be ridden with some restraint if he takes up one of those options, and it may just be that a stiff mile suits him best. Official explanation: trainer said, regarding the apparent improvement in form shown, that they were very happy with the colt going to Newmarket but that the colt was having its first run of the year and got stage fright in a very fast run race (op 7/2 tchd 3/1)
Dubawi Gold failed to pick up immediately and that cost him. He came home very strongly and his rider said afterwards that he changed his legs a number of times when asked to quicken, as if he was feeling the ground. He's one about whom one wouldn't have much doubt about his ability to stay 1m2f. Official explanation: jockey said colt did not enjoy a clear run in the closing stages (op 2/1 tchd 6/4)
Oracle(IRE) was beaten further in the Tetrarch Stakes than he was beaten here, and that is the primary reason to doubt the form. He was likely to be used in a pacemaking role but he just missed the kick and consequently didn't get there. Seamie Heffernan rode a proper race on him. He was just caught a bit flat-footed when the winner quickened on over a furlong out but was gaining all the way to the line, admittedly not as quickly as the runner-up. He was rated 102 here but it mustn't be forgotten that he was rated 90 before the Tetrarch, and it must be questionable that he has improved enough to be beaten just over a length in what would normally constitute a Classic over 1m. (op 25/1 tchd 28/1)
High Ruler(USA) was in as a pacemaker but he was being hard ridden to get to the front and never got there. He didn't really lose touch either and ended up being beaten just over five lengths. Another stick to beat the form with perhaps. (op 33/1)
Dunboyne Express(IRE) sat on the inside rail, got a bit of cover and a nice lead, but when asked for his effort inside the final 2f the response just wasn't there. (op 11/4)
Zabarajad(IRE) ran about as well as he was entitled to. (op 9/2)
Slim Shadey came off the bridle 3f out and faded inside the distance. (op 20/1)
Foolproof(IRE) was completely out of his depth. Official explanation: jockey said colt did not handle today's ground (op 150/1 tchd 200/1)

2325a TRI EQUESTRIAN STKS (GROUP 3) (F&M) 1m
4:20 (4:21) 4-Y-O+ **£33,620** (£9,827; £4,655; £1,551)

RPR
1 **Emulous**[48] 1118 4-9-3 111........ PJSmullen 10 113+
(D K Weld, Ire) *mid-div: 5th 1/2-way: hdwy in 3rd 2f out: rdn to chal 1f out: led last 150yds: kpt on wl* **11/4**[2]
2 *1 3/4* **Lolly For Dolly (IRE)**[19] 1779 4-9-3 108........(b) WMLordan 9 109
(T Stack, Ire) *chsd ldrs: 3rd 1/2-way: impr to ld 2f out: rdn and chal 1f out: hdd fnl 150yds: no ex and kpt on same pce* **11/10**[1]
3 *3* **Kinky Afro (IRE)**[20] 1718 4-9-0 .... LukeMorris 4 99
(J S Moore) *chsd ldrs early: 6th 1/2-way: rdn in 5th 2f out: 3rd and no imp on ldrs 1f out: kpt on same pce fnl f* **25/1**
4 *1/2* **Headford View (IRE)**[19] 1779 7-9-0 93........(p) FMBerry 6 98
(James Halpin, Ire) *hld up towards rr: rdn in 7th 2f out: no imp in 6th 1f out: kpt on same pce fnl f* **25/1**
5 *hd* **Obama Rule (IRE)**[238] 6379 4-9-3 103........ JMurtagh 2 100
(Ms Joanna Morgan, Ire) *mid-div: 7th 1/2-way: rdn in 6th 2f out: no imp in 5th 1f out: kpt on same pce fnl f* **7/1**[3]
6 *1/2* **Boynagh Joy (IRE)**[164] 7772 6-9-0 100........ SeamieHeffernan 1 96
(James Halpin, Ire) *chsd ldrs: 4th 1/2-way: rdn 2f out: no imp in 3rd 1 1/2f out: 4th 1f out: kpt on one pce fnl f* **16/1**
7 *6* **Good Time Sue (IRE)**[202] 7262 7-9-0 90........(t) GFCarroll 8 82
(Ms M Dowdall Blake, Ire) *towards rr for most: nvr a factor* **25/1**
8 *2* **Cilium (IRE)**[10] 2012 5-9-0 95........ CDHayes 3 78
(Jeffrey Ian Mulhern, Ire) *led early: hdd after 1f: mod 2nd 1/2-way: rdn 3f out: wknd over 2f out* **20/1**
9 *3/4* **Termagant (IRE)**[19] 1781 4-9-0 102........(b[1]) DPMcDonogh 5 76
(Kevin Prendergast, Ire) *t.k.h and led after 1f: sn clr: reduced advantage 3f out: rdn and hdd 2f out: sn no ex and wknd* **8/1**
1m 38.95s (-7.05) **Going Correction** -0.70s/f (Hard) **9** Ran SP% **120.1**
Speed ratings: **107,105,102,101,101 101,95,93,92**
CSF £6.07 TOTE £4.50: £1.70, £1.02, £7.30; DF 7.50.
Owner K Abdulla **Bred** Juddmonte Farms Ltd **Trained** The Curragh, Co Kildare

FOCUS
The third, fourth, ffith and sixth have all been rated to their best.

NOTEBOOK
Emulous put a seasonal bow that she needed behind her as she convincingly turned the tables on the runner-up from last month. Held up and tracking the favourite, she got a nice lead from her until well inside the final furlong and then quickened on inside the last. She's a good filly, improving and seems to be coming to hand a little bit earlier than she did last season. It will be interesting to see whether she can progress enough to be a genuine Group 2 filly over the coming months. (op 9/4)
Lolly For Dolly(IRE) ran another fine race and is a model of consistency this season, but she was outclassed by the winner. Ridden handily, she mounted her challenge over a furlong out and ran all the way to the line but just wasn't good enough to cope with the winner. She's genuinely of this grade or very close to it and it wouldn't be a surprise to see her get a bit of a break. (op 5/4)
Kinky Afro(IRE) ran a very fair race, although she was fairly well beaten. Racing in mid-division, she couldn't make any impression on the leaders when the race developed in earnest but did some useful late work.
Headford View(IRE) ran well and got herself some useful black type. Held up and never really seen with a chance, she was pulled to the outside over 2f out and ran on at the same pace without making an impression. It's an effort that's unlikely to affect her handicap mark too much.

PIMLICO (L-H)

Saturday, May 21

OFFICIAL GOING: Turf: good; dirt: fast

2328a PREAKNESS STKS (GRADE 1) (3YO) (DIRT) 1m 1f 110y(D)

11:16 (12:00) 3-Y-O **£705,128** (£128,205; £70,512; £38,461; £19,230)

RPR

1 **Shackleford (USA)**[14] 1921 3-9-0 0 .... JLCastanon 5 121
(Dale Romans, U.S.A) **126/10**

2 ½ **Animal Kingdom (USA)**[14] 1921 3-9-0 0 .... (b) JRVelazquez 11 121+
(H Graham Motion, U.S.A) **23/10** [1]

3 1¼ **Astrology (USA)**[28] 3-9-0 0 .... MESmith 1 117
(Steven Asmussen, U.S.A) **155/10**

4 2½ **Dialed In (USA)**[14] 1921 3-9-0 0 .... JRLeparoux 10 112+
(Nicholas Zito, U.S.A) **22/5** [2]

5 2 **Dance City (USA)**[35] 3-9-0 0 .... RADominguez 8 108
(Todd Pletcher, U.S.A) **115/10**

6 1¼ **Mucho Macho Man (USA)**[14] 1921 3-9-0 0 .... RMaragh 9 105
(Kathy Ritvo, U.S.A) **26/5** [3]

7 1½ **King Congie (USA)**[35] 3-9-0 0 .... RAlbarado 3 102
(Thomas Albertrani, U.S.A) **219/10**

8 ¾ **Mr. Commons (USA)**[41] 3-9-0 0 .... VEspinoza 14 101
(John Shirreffs, U.S.A) **33/1**

9 1½ **Isn't He Perfect (USA)**[28] 3-9-0 0 .... (b) EPrado 12 97
(Doodnauth Shivmangal, U.S.A) **31/1**

10 1¼ **Concealed Identity (USA)**[14] 3-9-0 0 .... SheldonRussell 13 95
(Edmond D Gaudet, U.S.A) **26/1**

11 nk **Norman Asbjornson (USA)**[42] 1254 3-9-0 0 .... (b) JPimentel 2 94
(Christopher W Grove, U.S.A) **43/1**

12 1¾ **Sway Away (USA)**[35] 3-9-0 0 .... (b) GKGomez 6 90
(Jeff Bonde, U.S.A) **123/10**

13 7 **Midnight Interlude (USA)**[14] 1921 3-9-0 0 .... (b) MGarcia 7 76
(Bob Baffert, U.S.A) **136/10**

14 nk **Flashpoint (USA)**[48] 1123 3-9-0 0 .... CVelasquez 4 75
(Wesley A Ward, U.S.A) **165/10**

1m 56.47s (0.88) **14** Ran SP% **122.9**
PARI-MUTUEL (all including $2 stakes): WIN 27.20; PLACE (1-2) 10.20, 4.20; SHOW (1-2-3) 6.80, 3.60, 8.00; SF 114.80 .
Owner Michael Lauffer & W D Cubbedge **Bred** Michael Lauffer & W D Cubbedge **Trained** USA

NOTEBOOK

Shackleford (USA), fourth behind the runner-up in the Kentucky Derby, was soon in a perfect stalking position and, having taken it up rounding the final bend, stayed on willingly to gain his revenge. He always looked like holding on but there's no doubting he had the run of things, and more will be required once taking on the older horses.

Animal Kingdom (USA) blitzed the Derby field with a fine show of acceleration, but again ridden under restraint, he found the winner had got first run and was unable to reel him in over this shorter trip. There's little doubt he was the best horse and connections will no doubt rue this missed opportunity as he looks to have obvious claims in the Belmont Stakes.

Astrology (USA) was always well placed and kept on for pressure to record a career best.

Dialed In (USA), given far too much to do when a fast-finishing fourth in the Derby, was again ridden right out the back and lacked to pace to be involved on this drop in trip. He looks made for the Belmont over 1m4f.

2321 CURRAGH (R-H)

Sunday, May 22

OFFICIAL GOING: Good

2329a BIG BAD BOB EUROPEAN BREEDERS FUND (C & G) 2YO MAIDEN 6f

1:40 (1:42) 2-Y-O **£10,706** (£2,482; £1,086; £620)

RPR

1 **Reply (IRE)**[29] 1531 2-9-0 .... SeamieHeffernan 4 90+
(A P O'Brien, Ire) *led and disp early: led 1/2-way: rdn clr over 1f out: kpt on strly: easily* **10/3** [3]

2 4 **Slade Power (IRE)** 2-9-0 .... WMLordan 1 78+
(Edward Lynam, Ire) *mid-div: 6th 1/2-way: hdwy into 2nd 2f out: rdn and no imp on wnr over 1f out: kpt on same pce* **14/1**

3 3 **Tenth Star (IRE)** 2-9-0 .... CO'Donoghue 2 69+
(A P O'Brien, Ire) *in rr of mid-div: hdwy into 6th 2f out: rdn into 4th 1f out: kpt on same pce fnl f* **16/1**

4 1¼ **Foot Soldier (IRE)** 2-9-0 .... RyanMoore 5 65+
(A P O'Brien, Ire) *chsd ldrs: 4th 1/2-way: rdn 2f out: no imp in 3rd over 1f out: kpt on same pce* **3/1** [2]

5 4½ **Fastidious** 2-9-0 .... PJSmullen 7 52+
(D K Weld, Ire) *chsd ldrs: 5th 1/2-way: rdn in 7th 2f out: no ex and kpt on one pce* **7/4** [1]

6 hd **Forgiving Light**[9] 2077 2-9-0 .... CDHayes 8 51
(Andrew Oliver, Ire) *chsd ldrs: 3rd 1/2-way: rdn in 5th 2f out: no ex and kpt on one pce* **10/1**

7 1¾ **Dragon Khan (IRE)** 2-9-0 .... FMBerry 10 46
(C Roche, Ire) *hld up towards rr: rdn into 8th 2f out: no imp and kpt on one pce* **25/1**

8 1 **Jjs Pride (IRE)**[7] 2127 2-8-7 .... DarrenEdwardEgan(7) 6 43
(Paul W Flynn, Ire) *led and disp: 2nd 1/2-way: rdn in 3rd 2f out: no ex and wknd over 1f out* **50/1**

9 2 **Aquilonius (IRE)** 2-9-0 .... KJManning 9 37
(J S Bolger, Ire) *a towards rr* **12/1**

10 3 **Speedy Yaki (IRE)** 2-9-0 .... WJSupple 3 28
(Daniel Mark Loughnane, Ire) *dwlt: a towards rr* **66/1**

1m 11.24s (-3.76) **Going Correction** -0.575s/f (Hard) **10** Ran SP% **121.1**
Speed ratings: **102,96,92,91,85 84,82,81,78,74**
CSF £50.39 TOTE £4.60 : £1.50, £3.10, £2.90; DF 84.20.
Owner Mrs John Magnier **Bred** Mrs C Regalado-Gonzalez **Trained** Ballydoyle, Co Tipperary

FOCUS

The majority of the riders described the ground as "good" following rain. This was an impressive winner, and he now goes to Royal Ascot, while the second travelled well and there was definite promise from the third and fourth. It has been rated positively.

NOTEBOOK

Reply (IRE) ◆, third behind the smart Requinto in a four-runner maiden over 5f at Cork on his debut last month, is clearly going the right way judged by his performance here. He showed plenty of speed and was soon disputing the lead before going on 2f out. Trainer Aidan O'Brien said of the winner: "He was travelling very strongly at all stages and looks an Ascot type. It could be the Coventry or maybe the Norfolk as he looks quick enough for 5f." Boylesports introduced the winner into their Coventry market at 12-1. (op 4/1)

Slade Power (IRE) fared best of the newcomers, running a good race after not breaking as smartly from stalls as many of his rivals. He made headway before halfway and was second from under 2f out, chasing the winner without ever threatening to get near him. (op 16/1)

Tenth Star (IRE), a stablemate of the winner, shaped well. Behind early on, he made headway from over 2f out and kept on steadily. (op 14/1)

Foot Soldier (IRE) ◆, another Ballydoyle first-timer, chased the leaders. Fourth at halfway, he was never able to get into serious contention but gave the impression that there will be a good bit better to come. (op 11/4)

Fastidious was backed down from 5-1 in the morning to 7-4 favourite but never looked like justifying that support. Fifth at halfway, he soon lost his place before keeping on inside the final furlong. The rider reported that the colt had run green. Official explanation: jockey said colt ran green (op 15/8 tchd 6/4)

Dragon Khan (IRE) hung right in the closing stages. Official explanation: jockey said colt hung right in the closing stages (op 16/1)

Aquilonius (IRE) ran very green. Official explanation: jockey said colt ran very green (op 10/1)

2331a AIRLIE STUD GALLINULE STKS (GROUP 3) 1m 2f

2:40 (2:44) 3-Y-O **£29,418** (£8,599; £4,073; £1,357)

RPR

1 **Alexander Pope (IRE)**[20] 1778 3-9-1 102 .... CO'Donoghue 8 108+
(A P O'Brien, Ire) *settled bhd ldrs: 5th 1/2-way: rdn in 4th 2f out: styd on to ld under 1f out: kpt on wl* **3/1** [1]

2 1¾ **Moriarty (IRE)**[39] 1320 3-9-1 .... RyanMoore 3 104+
(Richard Hannon) *hld up towards rr: hdwy into 5th 2f out: sn rdn: kpt on wl fnl f to go 2nd cl home* **11/2**

3 hd **Smartcity (USA)**[22] 1704 3-9-1 .... CDHayes 1 104
(Andrew Oliver, Ire) *chsd ldrs: 4th 1/2-way: impr into 2nd 2f out: rdn to ld briefly over 1f out: no ex in 2nd ins fnl f: kpt on same pce: lost 2nd cl home* **25/1**

4 1 **Best Hello**[14] 1927 3-9-1 .... WJSupple 6 102
(P D Deegan, Ire) *chsd ldrs: 3rd 1/2-way: 2nd 4f out: rdn in 3rd 2f out: no ex in 4th 1f out: kpt on same pce* **7/1**

5 3½ **Last Crusade (IRE)**[10] 2035 3-9-1 87 .... SeamieHeffernan 5 95
(A P O'Brien, Ire) *led: rdn and hdd over 1f out: no ex and kpt on same pce* **12/1**

6 1½ **Sapphire Pendant (IRE)**[14] 1928 3-8-12 .... WJLee 4 89
(David Wachman, Ire) *in rr of mid-div: hdwy into 6th 2f out: rdn and no imp 1 1/2f out: kpt on one pce* **8/1**

7 2½ **Swampfire (IRE)**[9] 2082 3-9-1 95 .... (b) NGMcCullagh 2 87
(John M Oxx, Ire) *mid-div: 7th 1/2-way: rdn and no ex in 9th 3f out: kpt on one pce* **20/1**

8 hd **Adilapour (IRE)**[21] 1735 3-9-1 100 .... (p) JMurtagh 10 87
(John M Oxx, Ire) *chsd ldr in 2nd: 3rd 4f out: rdn and wknd over 2f out* **5/1** [3]

9 ½ **Parkers Mill (IRE)**[24] 1643 3-9-1 .... WMLordan 9 86
(T Stack, Ire) *mid-div: 6th 1/2-way: rdn and wknd over 2f out* **9/2** [2]

10 dist **Banksters Bonus (IRE)**[21] 1735 3-9-1 99 .... FMBerry 7 —
(Mrs John Harrington, Ire) *a towards rr: t.o* **9/1**

2m 8.46s (-5.84) **Going Correction** -0.125s/f (Firm) **10** Ran SP% **125.1**
Speed ratings: **111,109,109,108,105 104,102,102,102,** —
CSF £21.29 TOTE £4.30 : £1.70, £2.00, £4.30; DF 23.40.
Owner Derrick Smith **Bred** T Hirschfeld **Trained** Ballydoyle, Co Tipperary

FOCUS

Anything coming out of this race with Classic pretensions will clearly have to improve significantly. The race-fit winner improved for the trip, but the third limits the form.

NOTEBOOK

Alexander Pope (IRE) did it well enough and looks as if he'll have little difficulty stepping up in trip. Held up, he came off the bridle and began his challenge over 2f out, sustaining his effort to get there inside the last. He probably didn't do a huge amount in front and he may need to come with one run but it was an effort that promises a reasonable amount. However, he needs to step forward considerably if he's to be competitive in the French Derby. (op 4/1 tchd 5/2)

Moriarty (IRE) is a reasonable type and improved a bit on past efforts. Held up slightly further back than the winner, he began to stay on from over a furlong out when switched to the outside and kept on to the line. He lacks a bit of a change of gear but will remain competitive in races of this class. He's also likely to get a bit further. (op 4/1)

Smartcity (USA) underlined the good form of his stable. He raced prominently throughout, got a bit of cover towards the inside rail and, while he wasn't able to improve his position inside the final furlong, he kept on to very decent effect. There's a reasonable race to be won with this progressive type.

Best Hello was ridden quite positively and perhaps he might have benefited from an even more positive ride. He lacks a change of pace at this trip and just stayed on at one pace in the final furlong or so. He even gives the impression that he could be a Leger horse later in the year. (op 7/1 tchd 8/1)

Last Crusade (IRE) kept on to reasonable effect when headed. (op 20/1)

Adilapour (IRE) dropped away disappointingly. (op 5/1 tchd 6/1)

Parkers Mill (IRE) also dropped away disappointingly. (op 5/1 tchd 4/1)

Banksters Bonus (IRE) dropped away well before the turn into the straight and ran no race at all. Official explanation: vet said gelding was found to be clinically abnormal post race; jockey said gelding lost its action and was eased (op 9/1 tchd 8/1)

2332a TATTERSALLS GOLD CUP (GROUP 1) 1m 2f 110y

3:10 (3:14) 4-Y-O+ **£112,241** (£34,396; £16,293; £5,431; £1,810)

RPR

1 **So You Think (NZ)**[20] 1781 5-9-1 126 .... RyanMoore 5 127+
(A P O'Brien, Ire) *trckd ldr in 2nd: led under 3f out: pushed along and chal 2f out: asserted over 1f out: kpt on strly: easily* **1/7** [1]

2 4½ **Campanologist (USA)**[22] 1685 6-9-1 .... FrankieDettori 2 117
(Saeed Bin Suroor) *chsd ldrs in 3rd: rdn to chal 2f out: no ex in 2nd over 1f out: kpt on same pce* **14/1** [3]

3 2½ **Famous Name**[14] 1930 6-9-1 117 .... PJSmullen 3 113+
(D K Weld, Ire) *settled 4th: rdn into 3rd 2f out: no imp over 1f out: kpt on same pce* **7/1** [2]

4 8 **Mid Mon Lady (IRE)**[11] 2012 6-8-12 100 .... (b) FMBerry 4 94+
(H Rogers, Ire) *hld up in last: no imp 3f out: mod 4th over 1f out: kpt on one pce* **100/1**

5 10 **Windsor Palace (IRE)**[20] 1781 6-9-1 97 .... JPO'Brien 1 79+
(A P O'Brien, Ire) *led: rdn and hdd under 3f out: wknd over 2f out* **100/1**

2m 14.08s (-5.92) **Going Correction** -0.125s/f (Firm) **5** Ran SP% **108.6**
Speed ratings: **116,112,110,105,97**
CSF £3.27 TOTE £1.10 : £1.02, £2.80; DF 3.70.

Owner Smith/Magnier/Tabor/Dato Tan/Tunku Yahaya **Bred** M J Moran & Piper Farm Ltd **Trained** Ballydoyle, Co Tipperary

FOCUS

So You Think only did what he was entitled to do against this opposition. He's clearly a horse of immense talent, but we're going to have to wait until he takes on other top-class Group 1 horses before we have our excitement fulfilled, as he didn't meet any on this occasion. The runner-up is the best guide to the level of the form.

NOTEBOOK

So You Think(NZ) went to the front 2f out, quickly asserted and did nothing much more than the minimum from there. One would have to be impressed with the manner in which he disposed of inferior rivals, but surely more onerous tests await him. (op 1/6)

Campanologist(USA) ran a very creditable race and connections have every reason to be encouraged that he can win a good race at home this season. Sitting behind the two leaders, he had no answer to the winner's change of pace in the straight, but he kept on well and was always comfortably holding the second favourite in the battle for placings. (op 12/1)

Famous Name fell notably short at this level. Held up off the pace, the winner had too many gears for him, but even so it must have been more than a little bit disappointing that he could make no impression on the runner-up inside the last. He's still likely to farm a good few of those uncompetitive Group 3s that he's been mopping up around Leopardstown for a couple of years. (op 11/2)

Mid Mon Lady(IRE) picked up the handy 8,400euros on offer. (op 100/1 tchd 66/1)

2334a ETIHAD AIRWAYS IRISH 1,000 GUINEAS (GROUP 1) (FILLIES) 1m

4:15 (4:17) 3-Y-O

£162,500 (£53,232; £25,215; £8,405; £5,603; £2,801)

RPR

1 **Misty For Me (IRE)**[21] 1719 3-9-0 113 SeamieHeffernan 15 115
(A P O'Brien, Ire) *prom: 2nd 1/2-way: rdn in 3rd 2f out: cl 4th 1f out: kpt on to chal fnl f: led cl home* **5/1**[3]

2 ¾ **Together (IRE)**[21] 1719 3-9-0 112 RyanMoore 2 113
(A P O'Brien, Ire) *chsd ldrs early: 8th 1/2-way: hdwy into 5th 2f out: rdn to ld over 1f out: strly pressed ins fnl f: hdd cl home* **4/1**[1]

3 1 **Laughing Lashes (USA)**[21] 1719 3-9-0 112 FMBerry 14 111
(Mrs John Harrington, Ire) *mid-div: hdwy in 7th 2f out: rdn into 5th 1f out: kpt on fnl f to go 3rd cl home* **10/1**

4 nk **Claiomh Solais (IRE)**[11] 2015 3-9-0 90 RPWhelan 5 110?
(J S Bolger, Ire) *led: rdn 3f out: hdd over 1f out: kpt on same pce fnl f: lost 3rd cl home* **33/1**

5 nk **Banimpire (IRE)**[11] 2012 3-9-0 108 KJManning 7 109
(J S Bolger, Ire) *prom: 3rd 1/2-way: rdn 2f out: no ex ins fnl f: kpt on same pce* **9/1**

6 ½ **History Note (IRE)**[56] 1006 3-9-0 NGMcCullagh 8 108
(John M Oxx, Ire) *chsd ldrs: 7th 1/2-way: rdn in 6th 2f out: no imp over 1f out: kpt on same pce* **10/1**

7 2½ **Chrysanthemum (IRE)**[238] 6401 3-9-0 104 WMLordan 12 102
(David Wachman, Ire) *hld up towards rr: rdn in 11th 2f out: no imp in 8th 1f out: kpt on one pce* **7/1**

8 ½ **Handassa**[14] 1928 3-9-0 (b[1]) DPMcDonogh 1 101
(Kevin Prendergast, Ire) *in rr of mid-div: rdn and no imp in 10th 2f out: kpt on one pce* **20/1**

9 nk **Rose Bonheur**[11] 2011 3-9-0 97 CDHayes 11 101
(Kevin Prendergast, Ire) *hld up towards rr: rdn into mod 10th 1f out: no imp and kpt on one pce* **33/1**

10 3 **Emiyna (USA)**[20] 1779 3-9-0 106 JMurtagh 9 94
(John M Oxx, Ire) *in rr of mid-div: rdn and no imp over 2f out: kpt on one pce* **9/2**[2]

11 1½ **Majestic Dubawi**[39] 1318 3-9-0 NeilCallan 10 90
(Mick Channon) *chsd ldrs: 6th 1/2-way: rdn in 9th and no ex 2f out: kpt on one pce* **20/1**

12 nk **Ballybacka Lady (IRE)**[14] 1928 3-9-0 102 PJSmullen 4 90
(P A Fahy, Ire) *chsd ldrs: 4th 1/2-way: rdn to chal 2f out: no ex and wknd over 1f out* **25/1**

13 ½ **Seeharn (IRE)**[20] 1779 3-9-0 99 WJSupple 6 88
(Kevin Prendergast, Ire) *a towards rr* **33/1**

14 11 **Wild Wind (GER)**[7] 2137 3-9-0 106 CO'Donoghue 13 63
(A P O'Brien, Ire) *chsd ldrs: 5th 1/2-way: rdn in 8th and no ex 2f out: wknd* **12/1**

15 2 **Look At Me (IRE)**[20] 1779 3-9-0 98 JPO'Brien 3 58
(A P O'Brien, Ire) *in rr of mid-div for most: wknd over 2f out* **16/1**

1m 35.9s (-10.10) **Going Correction** -0.825s/f (Hard) **15** Ran SP% **131.3**
Speed ratings: **117,116,115,114,114 114,111,111,110,107 106,106,105,94,92**
CSF £25.22 TOTE £5.90: £1.80, £1.40, £3.70; DF 27.30.

Owner Michael Tabor **Bred** March Thoroughbreds **Trained** Ballydoyle, Co Tipperary

FOCUS

A Ballydoyle one-two involving two fillies running right up to their best and with little to separate them. The race has been rated up to scratch, with the fifth-nith all rated as improving slightly.

NOTEBOOK

Misty For Me(IRE) put a disappointing effort at Newmarket behind her and came back to the form which saw her win the Moyglare and the Prix Marcel Boussac last season. She was ridden handily by Seamie Heffernan, kept out of trouble towards the outside of the field, gradually upped her effort and sustained her run all the way to the line to beat a stable companion that looked to have first run. She has pace but clearly stays well and connections could prepare her for the Investec Oaks. On the dam's side of her pedigree there's no guarantee that she'll get 1m4f, so it will be interesting to see if she does. Official explanation: trainer said, regarding the apparent improvement in form shown, that filly was having her first run of the year at Newmarket and he was happy with the filly before Newmarket and expected her to run well but had no explanation for her poor performance that day (op 6/1 tchd 4/1)

Together(IRE) has had the misfortune to finish second in the English and Irish 1,000 Guineas, but as both her Newmarket conqueror Blue Bunting and Misty For Me will be stepping up in trip, she now looks the leading 3-y-o miling filly around. She did little enough wrong here. Tracking the leaders, she took a stride or two to pick up when the pace quickened inside the 2f pole but she eventually did and looked to have come to win her race a furlong out. Perhaps she got there a fraction too soon, although it looked a case of her being outstayed more than anything. She's probably a pure miler on a flatter track and deserves to pick up a nice prize. (op 7/2 tchd 9/2)

Laughing Lashes(USA) was held up off the pace and took time to get going inside the final 3f, but she eventually consented to run on inside the final 1 1/2f and came home as well, if not better, than anything. It was a pity for connections that she didn't begin her run earlier, but at least they now know they have their filly back. (op 12/1 tchd 14/1)

Claiomh Solais(IRE) kept up a good gallop and didn't relent until inside the last furlong. Handicaps certainly won't be in her future and one could see her being very competitive under similar tactics in Group races over 7f. She is definitely the fly in the ointment regarding the form of the race. (op 40/1 tchd 50/1)

Banimpire(IRE) was dropping back in trip having seen out 1m2f very convincingly at Naas previously. She tracked her stable companion and came under pressure early enough as they approached the straight. She kept on well under pressure without having the required change of pace and it wouldn't be a surprise to see her go to Epsom as she seems to be thriving on her racing. (op 8/1 tchd 10/1)

History Note(IRE) wasn't good enough but justified the decision to supplement her as she kept going all the way to the line without being able to make much of an impression. She's probably still improving. (op 9/1)

Chrysanthemum(IRE) ran respectably but couldn't make an impression on what was her seasonal debut. (op 10/1)

Handassa could never get into it.

Rose Bonheur was held up to get the trip but had her limitations exposed despite running on a little bit late on.

Emiyna(USA) was held up off the pace but never got close to getting involved. Official explanation: trainer said filly was found to be sore post-race (op 5/1)

Majestic Dubawi dropped away having chased the pace early. (op 33/1)

Ballybacka Lady(IRE) ran like a non-stayer. She was close enough 2f out but weakened considerably inside the last.

Wild Wind(GER) Official explanation: jockey said filly became very tired and was eased

2333 - 2336a (Foreign Racing) - See Raceform Interactive

1931 COLOGNE (R-H)

Sunday, May 22

OFFICIAL GOING: Turf: soft

2337a KARIN BARONIN VON ULLMANN - SCHWARZGOLD-RENNEN (GROUP 3) (3YO FILLIES) (TURF) 1m

3:05 (12:00) 3-Y-O

£32,758 (£10,775; £5,603; £3,448; £2,155; £1,293)

RPR

1 **Djumama (IRE)**[210] 7108 3-9-2 0 AHelfenbein 4 103
(Andreas Lowe, Germany) *broke wl: settled on rail in ldng gp: travelled smoothly into fnl turn: hit traffic problems early in st: qcknd wl whn clr: swept to ld 150yds out: comf* **16/5**[2]

2 nk **Dalarna (GER)**[210] 7108 3-9-2 0 APietsch 5 102
(W Hickst, Germany) *broke fast to ld initially: then restrained to settle bhd ldr: then dropped bk to 4th: qcknd early in st to ld 2f out: r.o wl: hdd 150yds out: r.o wl* **37/10**[3]

3 2½ **Reine Vite (GER)**[203] 3-9-2 0 JiriPalik 6 97
(Uwe Ostmann, Germany) *broke slowly and in rr initially: proged down bk st: qcknd wl early in st: chal ldrs and r.o wl* **215/10**

4 1¾ **Wolkenburg (GER)**[21] 3-9-2 0 THellier 1 93
(P Schiergen, Germany) *broke wl and led on settling: in front ent st: r.o wl: hdd 2f out: styd on* **113/10**

5 ½ **Taleia (GER)**[238] 6407 3-9-2 0 EPedroza 3 91
(A Wohler, Germany) *a.p bhd ldrs: chal ldr early in st: r.o but wknd fnl f* **118/10**

6 1¼ **Aigrette Garzette (IRE)**[210] 7108 3-9-2 0 AStarke 7 89
(P Schiergen, Germany) *racd in midfield: briefly threatened early in st: no ex: fdd* **12/5**[1]

7 1¾ **Salona (GER)**[21] 3-9-2 0 MircoDemuro 9 84
(J-P Carvalho, Germany) *settled in rr: proged arnd fnl turn: threatened briefly early in st: no ex: fdd* **143/10**

8 ¾ **Kellemoi De Pepita**[228] 3-9-2 0 HenkGrewe 8 83
(R Dzubasz, Germany) *settled in midfield: proged ent st: rdn but no ex: fdd* **43/10**

9 3½ **Turia (GER)**[210] 7108 3-9-2 0 GaetanMasure 2 75
(Uwe Ostmann, Germany) *prom fr s: proged early in st: rdn and sn wknd* **242/10**

10 4½ **La Salvita (GER)**[203] 3-9-2 0 ASuborics 10 64
(A Wohler, Germany) *settled in midfield initially then dropped bk to rr: nvr figured* **139/10**

1m 39.2s (0.81) **10** Ran SP% **131.0**
WIN (incl. 10 euro stake): 42. PLACES: 17, 32, 44. SF: 290.

Owner Stall Phillip I **Bred** Colin Kennedy **Trained** Germany

2338a MEHL MULHENS-RENNEN - GERMAN 2,000 GUINEAS (GROUP 2) (3YO COLTS & FILLIES) (TURF) 1m

4:15 (12:00) 3-Y-O **£86,206** (£25,862; £11,206; £6,034; £2,586)

RPR

1 **Excelebration (IRE)**[36] 1405 3-9-2 0 AdamKirby 5 118+
(Marco Botti) *settled in 7th: gd prog arnd fnl turn: patiently rdn early in st: mde move 2f out: qcknd wl in centre of trck to ld 1f out: sn clr: easily* **21/10**[1]

2 7 **Gereon (GER)**[196] 7375 3-9-2 0 GeorgBocskai 10 103+
(C Zschache, Germany) *settled early on bhd eventual wnr: r.o wl in st but short of room: fnd ex gear whn in clr and r.o wl wout threatening wnr* **4/1**[3]

3 ½ **Acadius (GER)**[42] 3-9-2 0 MircoDemuro 7 101
(J-P Carvalho, Germany) *settled in rr: picked up positions arnd fnl turn: rchd ldng gp 1 1/2f out: hrd rdn to go 3rd cl home* **18/5**[2]

4 1½ **Stark Danon (FR)**[42] 3-9-2 0 ASuborics 9 97
(W Hickst, Germany) *settled towards rr: mde move early in st: looked threatening: rdn and r.o wl: lost 3rd ins fnl f* **152/10**

5 4½ **Point Blank (GER)**[15] 3-9-2 0 StefanieHofer 6 87
(Mario Hofer, Germany) *settled in midfield: prog in st: r.o wl but no threat to ldrs* **41/1**

6 3½ **Casual Glimpse**[38] 1341 3-9-2 0 DaneO'Neill 3 79
(Richard Hannon) *a.p in ldng gp: r.o in st but no threat* **159/10**

7 7 **The Paddyman (IRE)**[16] 1850 3-9-2 0 (b[1]) DarryllHolland 4 63
(William Haggas) *broke wl to contest ld: set fast pce: r.o in st: hdd 1f out: no ex* **44/5**

8 ¾ **Rose Danon (GER)**[42] 3-9-2 0 AStarke 2 61
(P Schiergen, Germany) *bkmarker fr s: rn through btn horses in st* **137/10**

9 1¾ **Zantano (GER)**[196] 7375 3-9-2 0 GaetanMasure 11 57
(Uwe Ostmann, Germany) *racd freely bhd ldrs: briefly threatened early in st: sn wknd* **30/1**

10 ¾ **Quinindo (GER)**[35] 1433 3-9-2 0 THellier 8 55
(A Wohler, Germany) *led initially then settled in 2nd: briefly threatened in st: rdn and sn wknd* **36/5**

11 5 **Nice Danon**[35] 1433 3-9-2 0 EPedroza 1 44
(A Wohler, Germany) *racd in midfield: rdn and sn wknd in st* **91/10**

1m 36.2s (-2.19) **11** Ran SP% **130.8**
WIN (incl. 10 euro stake): 31. PLACES: 15, 15, 18. SF: 139.

Owner Giuliano Manfredini **Bred** Owenstown Stud **Trained** Newmarket, Suffolk

NOTEBOOK
Excelebration(IRE) had to do no more than repeat his Greenham second to Frankel to collect this prize, and under a confident ride, he readily asserted to win as he pleased. Clearly very smart, he'd be entitled to take his place in the St James's Palace, but the Jersey Stakes would look very winnable and is perhaps the wiser option.
Casual Glimpse ended well held on ground that would have been softer than ideal.
The Paddyman(IRE) did too much early in the blinkers and had nothing left for the final furlong.

KRANJI (L-H)
Sunday, May 22

OFFICIAL GOING: Turf: good

2339a KRISFLYER INTERNATIONAL SPRINT (GROUP 1) (3YO+) (TURF) 6f
12:50 (12:00) 3-Y-0+

£286,432 (£101,758; £51,507; £25,125; £10,050; £5,025)

RPR

1 **Rocket Man (AUS)**[21] 6-9-0 0 ... FCoetzee 9 125
(Patrick Shaw, Singapore) *broke wl and led: sn hdd and settled on heels of ldr: led 2f out: shkn up and qcknd clr appr fnl f: r.o strly* **1/5**[1]

2 *4 3/4* **Eclair Fastpass (AUS)**[42] 5-9-0 0 ... (b) JVerenzuela 1 110
(D Koh, Singapore) *racd in midfield: 6th and stdd on bnd appr fnl 2f: styd on u.p to go 2nd ins fnl f: no ch w wnr* **38/1**

3 *hd* **Perfect Pins (NZ)**[30] 6-9-0 0 ... (b) JSaimee 3 109
(D Dragon, Singapore) *prom on ins of eventual wnr: outpcd appr 2f out: styd on u.p fnl f* **92/1**

4 *1/2* **Ghozi (AUS)**[21] 6-9-0 0 ... (bt) VladDuric 7 108
(John O'Hara, Singapore) *in rr: last 2f out: effrt and hmpd 1f out: styd on u.p fnl 110yds* **73/1**

5 *nk* **Powerful Ruler (NZ)**[14] 6-9-0 0 ... (b) JoaoMoreira 2 107
(B Dean, Singapore) *midfield: 7th and pushed along 2f out: kpt on wout qckning fnl f* **144/1**

6 *hd* **Sacred Kingdom (AUS)**[21] 1741 8-9-0 0 ... (bt) GlenBoss 6 106
(P F Yiu, Hong Kong) *chsd ldrs: 3rd 2f out: sn rdn and nt qckn fnl 300yds* **23/5**[2]

7 *nk* **Green Birdie (NZ)**[57] 999 8-9-0 0 ... BrettPrebble 10 105
(C Fownes, Hong Kong) *dwlt: settled towards rr: forced four wd fnl bnd: 9th 2f out: no real imp fnl f* **116/10**[3]

8 *nk* **Capablanca (AUS)**[21] 10-9-0 0 ... StevenArnold 5 104
(D Baertschiger, Singapore) *w.w towards rr: mod prog fnl f: n.d* **133/1**

9 *1 3/4* **Better Be The One (AUS)**[21] 5-9-0 0 ... (b) DannyBeasley 4 98
(M Freedman, Singapore) *sn led: hdd 2f out: wknd u.p fnl f* **16/1**

10 *2 3/4* **Happy Dubai (IRE)**[57] 996 4-9-0 0 ... RoystonFfrench 8 90
(A Al Raihe, UAE) *dwlt: sn pushed along to chse ldrs: 4th on outside 2f out: sn rdn and wknd qckly fnl f* **28/1**

69.14 secs (69.14) **10 Ran SP% 124.9**
PARI-MUTUEL (all including 5 sgd stakes): WIN 6.00; PLACE 5.10, 36.00, 92.00; DF 29.00.
Owner Alfredo Leonardo Arnaldo Crabbia **Bred** D R Fleming **Trained** Singapore

NOTEBOOK
Rocket Man(AUS), runner-up in this for each of the past two years, had bolted up over C&D last time and made a very short-price favourite on the back of that. Happy enough to track the early pace, readily asserted once asked and powered right away for an impressive win. A trip to England is now on the cards, although Royal Ascot is likely to come too soon, so the July Cup is likely to be the race.
Sacred Kingdom(AUS), winner of this in 2009, had his chance and just couldn't quicken.
Green Birdie(NZ), last year's winner, could never get into it.

2340a SINGAPORE AIRLINES INTERNATIONAL CUP (GROUP 1) (3YO+) (TURF) 1m 2f
1:40 (12:00) 3-Y-0+

£859,296 (£305,276; £95,163; £95,163; £30,150; £15,075)

RPR

1 **Gitano Hernando** [illegible][21] 1742 5-9-0 0 ... GlynSchofield 4 120
(H J Brown, South Africa) *led setting stdy gallop: hdd after 3f: trckd ldr: chal fnl bnd (over 2f out): led 2f out: r.o wl u.p* **136/10**

2 *1/2* **River Jetez (SAF)**[21] 1742 8-8-10 0 ... BernardFayd'Herbe 9 115
(M F De Kock, South Africa) *chsd ldrs (3rd or 4th most of way): lost pl 3f out: 6th and pushed along 2f out: r.o wl u.p fnl f: a hld by wnr* **66/10**[3]

3 *1* **Waikato (NZ)**[23] 8-9-0 0 ... JoaoMoreira 6 117
(L Laxon, Singapore) *a.p: 2nd and ev ch fnl f: nt qckn u.p fnl 100yds* **212/10**

3 *dht* **Irian (GER)**[21] 1742 5-9-0 0 ... DarrenBeadman 5 117
(J Moore, Hong Kong) *racd in midfield: 8th towards outside 2f out: styd on u.p fnl 150yds: nt pce to chal* **8/1**

5 *1/2* **Chinchon (IRE)**[57] 1001 6-9-0 0 ... GeraldMosse 12 116
(C Laffon-Parias, France) *hld up on outside of main pack in abt 7th: smooth hdwy to go 4th and travelling wl 3f out: rdn 2f out: nt qckn fnl f* **9/1**

6 *nk* **Risky Business (AUS)**[23] 7-9-0 0 ... (tp) GlenBoss 10 115
(S Burridge, Singapore) *w.w towards rr: hdwy on rail fnl bnd: 7th ins fnl 2f: kpt on fnl f wout having pce to chal* **224/10**

7 *1 1/2* **Wigmore Hall (IRE)**[21] 1742 4-9-0 0 ... JamieSpencer 3 112
(Michael Bell) *settled towards rr: 11th 2f out: sme hdwy fnl f: nvr threatened* **148/10**

8 *3/4* **California Memory (USA)**[21] 1742 5-9-0 0 ... MChadwick 13 111
(A S Cruz, Hong Kong) *settled in midfield: rushed up on outside to ld after 3f: hdd 2f out: wknd fnl 150yds* **12/5**[1]

9 *1* **Royal Bench (IRE)**[27] 1576 4-9-0 0 ... ODoleuze 7 109
(Robert Collet, France) *settled in midfield: tk clsr order fr 3f out: 5th and rdn 2f out: nt qckn: fdd ins fnl f* **132/10**

10 *1/2* **Presvis**[27] 1576 7-9-0 0 ... RichardHughes 2 108
(Luca Cumani) *dwlt and settled in last: hdwy on outside 3f out: 10th and wdst of all st (jst over 2f out): no imp* **17/5**[2]

11 *2* **New Rose Wood (AUS)**[23] 6-8-10 0 ... (t) KBSoo 1 100
(D Koh, Singapore) *racd in fnl 3rd: n.d* **53/1**

12 *3/4* **Fat Kid (NZ)**[23] 5-9-0 0 ... IAzhar 8 102
(H K Tan, Singapore) *nvr in contention* **118/10**

2m 3.93s (123.93) **12 Ran SP% 125.1**
PARI-MUTUEL (all including 5 sgd stakes): WIN 73.00; PLACE 17.00, 13.00, 7.00 (Irian), 12.00 (Waikato); DF 167.00.
Owner Ramzan Kadyrov **Bred** Newsells Park Stud Ltd **Trained** South Africa

FOCUS
With just a steady pace it was an advantage to race prominent.

NOTEBOOK
Gitano Hernando, well beaten in the QE II Cup at Sha Tin on his recent debut for the yard, was subject to a complete change of tactics and received a well-judged ride to register a second Group 1 success. It's doubtful whether things will fall so kindly in future, however.
River Jetez(SAF) was never far away and had her chance, but just lacked the pace to win.
Waikato(NZ) held a good position throughout, but lacked the neccessary pace.
Irian(GER) ran really well considering he tried to come from as far back as he did.
Chinchon(IRE) would have gone close to winning had there been more pace on, as having travelled well, he lacked a sufficient finishing kick.
Wigmore Hall(IRE) was completely unsuited by the pace of pace and can have the run safely ignored.
Presvis is a tricky ride and, having been settled in last, he was forced to challenge wide, but never had a hope of closing off such a steady gallop. This wasn't his best form and will now be given a break before returning to Dubai next year.

2240 LONGCHAMP (R-H)
Sunday, May 22

OFFICIAL GOING: Turf: good

2341a PRIX DE L'AVRE (LISTED RACE) (3YO) (TURF) 1m 4f
1:00 (12:00) 3-Y-0 **£23,706** (£9,482; £7,112; £4,741; £2,370)

RPR

1 **Meandre (FR)**[25] 3-9-2 0 ... MaximeGuyon 2 106+
(A Fabre, France) **69/10**

2 *hd* **Genzy (FR)**[28] 1551 3-9-2 0 ... OlivierPeslier 6 105
(J E Pease, France) **13/10**[1]

3 *shd* **Ibicenco (GER)**[30] 3-9-2 0 ... TomQueally 3 105
(J Hirschberger, Germany) **18/1**

4 *3/4* **Beaulieu (IRE)**[46] 3-9-2 0 ... (p) StephanePasquier 7 104
(E Libaud, France) **68/10**

5 *5* **War Is War (IRE)**[34] 1447 3-9-2 0 ... ThomasHuet 1 96
(E J O'Neill, France) **27/1**

6 *2* **Shamar (FR)**[28] 3-9-2 0 ... Christophe-PatriceLemaire 4 92
(A De Royer-Dupre, France) **58/10**[3]

7 *4* **Hurricane Higgins (IRE)**[15] 1895 3-9-2 0 ... JoeFanning 5 86
(Mark Johnston) *settled in 2nd on outer: rdn early in st: no ex: sn fdd* **7/2**[2]

2m 30.3s (-0.10) **7 Ran SP% 114.7**
WIN (incl. 1 euro stake): 7.90. PLACES: 2.30, 1.50. SF: 21.80.
Owner Rothschild Family **Bred** Famille Rothschild **Trained** Chantilly, France

NOTEBOOK
Hurricane Higgins(IRE), who would have won the Lingfield Derby trial had he not hung violently, proved most disappointing and, although clearly talented, he's left with a fair bit to prove now.

2342a MONTJEU COOLMORE PRIX SAINT-ALARY (GROUP 1) (3YO FILLIES) (TURF) 1m 2f
1:30 (12:00) 3-Y-0 **£123,146** (£49,267; £24,633; £12,306; £6,163)

RPR

1 **Wavering (IRE)**[15] 1922 3-9-0 0 ... MickaelBarzalona 6 112+
(A Fabre, France) *settled towards rr: rdn 2f out on wd outside: qcknd wl 1f out: fin strly to ld fnl 50yds* **7/1**

2 *snk* **Epic Love (IRE)**[22] 1709 3-9-0 0 ... StephanePasquier 2 111
(P Bary, France) *settled in midfield: rdn and gd prog 1 1/2f out: qcknd wl to ld briefly ins fnl f: hdd 50yds out: r.o wl* **3/1**[1]

3 *nk* **Nonsuch Way (IRE)**[42] 1264 3-9-0 0 ... SylvainRuis 3 110
(F Vermeulen, France) *sn prom: 3rd into st: rdn and qcknd wl to ld briefly 1 1/2f out: hdd 1f out: r.o wl* **20/1**

4 *3/4* **Glorious Sight (IRE)**[7] 2137 3-9-0 0 ... SebastienMaillot 9 109
(Robert Collet, France) *settled in 4th on rail: rdn 1 1/2f out: r.o wl: no ex fnl 100yds* **11/2**

5 *nse* **Camelia Rose (FR)**[22] 1709 3-9-0 0 ... OlivierPeslier 5 108+
(J-C Rouget, France) *settled towards rr: hrd rdn 1f out: qcknd wl: r.o strly* **12/1**

6 *1/2* **La Pernelle (IRE)**[22] 1709 3-9-0 0 ... Christophe-PatriceLemaire 12 107+
(Y De Nicolay, France) *settled in rr: stl wl bk 1 1/2f out: hrd rdn: fin strly fnl 100yds: clst at fin* **10/1**

7 *shd* **Luna Tune (FR)**[24] 3-9-0 0 ... AnthonyCrastus 1 107
(J-L Pelletan, France) *racd in midfield: rdn 1 1/2f out: styd on wl* **50/1**

8 *1 1/2* **Don't Hurry Me (IRE)**[31] 1513 3-9-0 0 ... IoritzMendizabal 11 104
(J-C Rouget, France) *sn led: rdn and 2 l clr 2f out: hdd and u.p 1 1/2f out: no ex: qckly dropped out* **5/1**[3]

8 *dht* **Dalarua (IRE)**[25] 3-9-0 0 ... ChristopheSoumillon 8 104
(S Wattel, France) *settled towards rr: rdn 1 1/2f out: looked briefly threatening but no ex fnl f* **4/1**[2]

10 *shd* **Triveni (FR)**[55] 3-9-0 0 ... AlexisBadel 7 104
(Mme M Bollack-Badel, France) *racd in midfield: rdn 1 1/2f out: no ex* **33/1**

11 *3* **Pagera (FR)**[31] 1513 3-9-0 0 ... MaximeGuyon 4 98
(Y Fouin, France) *settled in midfield: rdn but no ex 2f out: fdd* **20/1**

12 *3* **Queen Menantie (FR)**[42] 1264 3-9-0 0 ... FranckBlondel 10 92
(J Boisnard, France) *settled in 2nd: stl threatening 1 1/2f out: rdn but no ex: qckly fdd* **25/1**

2m 5.80s (1.80) **Going Correction** +0.075s/f (Good) **12 Ran SP% 124.6**
Speed ratings: **95,94,94,94,94 93,93,92,92,92 89,87**
WIN (incl 1 euro stake): 6.40. Places: 2.10, 1.50, 5.00. DF: 13.40. SF: 31.00..
Owner Godolphin SNC **Bred** Darley Stud Management Co Ltd **Trained** Chantilly, France

NOTEBOOK
Wavering(IRE), third behind potential top-notcher Galikova at Saint-Cloud last time, appreciated coming from off a decent pace and stayed on strongly close home for a first Group 1 success. She's worth her place in the Diane, but a victory there looks doubtful, and it probably won't be until faced with 1m4f that she comes into her own.
Epic Love(IRE) had been progressing nicely and picked up well to challenge, but couldn't quite stay on as strongly as the winner.
Glorious Sight(IRE), runner-up in last weekend's Pouliches, had her chance and again ran well, possibly finding the race coming too soon.

Don't Hurry Me(IRE) was probably made a bit too much use of on this rise in class.

2343a PRIX D'ISPAHAN (GROUP 1) (4YO+) (TURF) 1m 1f 55y
2:45 (12:00) 4-Y-0+ **£123,146** (£49,267; £24,633; £12,306; £6,163)

RPR

1 **Goldikova (IRE)**197 7364 6-8-13 0 OlivierPeslier 6 119+
(F Head, France) *settled in 2nd bhd pcemaker: qcknd to ld 1 1/2f out: chal 1f out: rdn and r.o wl to hold off str chal fnl 50yds* **8/11**1

2 *nk* **Cirrus Des Aigles (FR)**22 1708 5-9-2 0 ChristopheSoumillon 2 121
(Mme C Barande-Barbe, France) *settled in 3rd to shadow eventual wnr: wnt 2nd 1 1/2f out: hrd rdn: r.o strly fnl 100yds: failed narrowly* **14/1**

3 *3/4* **Rajsaman (FR)**21 1740 4-9-2 0 (b) ThierryJarnet 7 120+
(F Head, France) *in rr fr s: last into st: qcknd wl fr 1 1/2f out: r.o strly fnl 100yds: clst at fin* **11/1**

4 *5* **Flash Dance (IRE)**49 1125 5-8-13 0 MickaelBarzalona 5 106
(F Head, France) *set pce for eventual wnr: hdd 1 1/2f out: styd on* **200/1**

5 *1* **Byword**21 1740 5-9-2 0 MaximeGuyon 8 107
(A Fabre, France) *settled in midfield: rdn 2f out: qcknd wl: looked threatening but fnd no ex fr 1f out* **7/2**2

6 *6* **Shamalgan (FR)**21 1740 4-9-2 0 IoritzMendizabal 3 94
(A Savujev, Czech Republic) *racd towards rr: rdn 2f out: no ex: styd on fnl f* **66/1**

7 *4* **Pan River (TUR)**32 6-9-2 0 SelimKaya 4 86
(R Tetik, Turkey) *settled towards rr: rdn early in st: hmpd and dropped out fr 1 1/2f out* **50/1**

8 *1 1/2* **Ransom Note**38 1342 4-9-2 0 MichaelHills 9 83
(B W Hills) *settled in 4th: rdn but no ex fr 2f out: sn wknd* **20/1**

9 *15* **Dick Turpin (IRE)**8 2101 4-9-2 0 JimmyFortune 1 51
(Richard Hannon) *settled in 3rd on rail: rdn 2f out: sn no ex: wknd qckly: eased fnl f* **13/2**3

1m 51.0s (-4.30) **Going Correction** +0.075s/f (Good) **9** Ran SP% **117.2**
Speed ratings: **122,121,121,116,115 110,106,105,92**
WIN (incl 1 euro stake): 1.50 (Goldikova and Flash Dance coupled). Places: 1.10, 1.60, 2.40. DF: 5.90. SF: 8.20..
Owner Wertheimer & Frere **Bred** Wertheimer Et Frere **Trained** France

NOTEBOOK
Goldikova(IRE), although not at her very best for this reappearance, found enough in front to register a 13th Group 1 victory. The outstanding miler of recent times, she was following up last year's win in the race and, with improvement anticipated, heads for a mouth-watering showdown with Canford Cliffs in the Queen Anne at Royal Ascot, a race she also won last year.
Cirrus Des Aigles(FR), third to Planteur in the Ganay, ran every bit as well on this slight drop in trip, just failing to get past the brilliant mare. He seems improved this year and can definitely win at a slightly lower level.
Rajsaman(FR) has definitely been helped by the blinkers and showed his last-time-out Saint-Cloud victory to be no fluke, finishing fast and confirming form with Byword in the process.
Flash Dance(IRE) did well to stick on for fourth having bene in to set up the race for Goldikova.
Byword, runner-up in this last year, was expected to have come on for his recent reappearance behind Rajsaman, but never really posed a threat of winning and was disappointing.
Ransom Note, winner of the Earl Of Sefton, found this big jump in class too much.
Dick Turpin(IRE) was very disappointing. Reappearing only eight days after finding the ground too fast in the Lockinge, he was expected to be helped by the easier conditions, but found little for pressure and stopped quickly. He's left with a fair bit to prove now.

2344a PRIX VICOMTESSE VIGIER (GROUP 2) (4YO+) (TURF) 1m 7f 110y
3:20 (12:00) 4-Y-0+ **£63,879** (£24,655; £11,767; £7,844; £3,922)

RPR

1 **Brigantin (USA)**22 1707 4-8-11 0 Pierre-CharlesBoudot 4 113
(A Fabre, France) *initially 2nd: assumed ld whn Mashoor rn out at grndstand bnd: rdn 2f out: qcknd wl and battled hrd to hold on fnl strides* **7/1**

2 *shd* **Dunaden (FR)**22 1707 5-8-11 0 GregoryBenoist 1 111
(M Delzangles, France) *settled in 4th: rdn early in st: qcknd wl fnl f to chal for ld: r.o strly: failed narrowly* **7/4**1

3 *2* **Marinous (FR)**22 1707 5-9-0 0 ThierryJarnet 3 112
(F Head, France) *settled at rr of field: rdn 2f out: r.o fnl f wout threatening ldrs* **10/1**

4 *hd* **Opinion Poll (IRE)**73 826 5-9-0 0 MickaelBarzalona 6 111
(Mahmood Al Zarooni) *initially towards rr: rdn to cl on ldr down bk st: rdn early in st: briefly threatened ent fnl f: no ex* **10/3**2

5 *3* **Le Larron (IRE)**22 1707 4-8-11 0 ChristopheSoumillon 5 107
(A De Royer-Dupre, France) *settled on rail bhd ldrs: rdn but unable qck 2f out: styd on* **8/1**

R **Mashoor (FR)**22 1707 4-8-11 0 MaximeGuyon 2 —
(A Fabre, France) *sn led: failed to settle and rn out on grndstand bnd* **4/1**3

3m 31.6s (10.10) **Going Correction** +0.075s/f (Good)
WFA 4 from 5yo 1lb **6** Ran SP% **112.1**
Speed ratings: **77,76,75,75,74** —
WIN (incl 1 euro stake): 10.20. Places: 2.70, 1.40. SF: 19.40..
Owner Team Valor **Bred** Team Valor, Mme A Fabre, Denali Stud & Partners **Trained** Chantilly, France

FOCUS
A farcial early gallop means this form is meaningless.

NOTEBOOK
Brigantin(USA) was left in front when his wayward stablemate departed the contest and continued to set a dawdling gallop. He was obviously at an advantage when the dash for home began and held on well, but there's little doubt he was a fluke winner.
Dunaden(FR) had beaten all bar one of these last time, and was favourite to do so again, but his rider asked him too big a question, and the horse couldn't get there in time. He was clearly the best horse and should show it in time, with him remaining a progressive stayer.
Marinous(FR) was going on well late on, but he's far from a certain stayer at this trip, so in some ways the lack of early pace probably helped him.
Opinion Poll(IRE) is a strong stayer who could have been expected to set a decent gallop and draw the finishing kick out of his rivals in such a small field, but bizarrely he was anchored right at the back through the early stages. Although eventully allowed to stride through and sit prominent, he was always going to be found wanting once the sprint began. This was a good opportunity missed.
Le Larron(IRE) doesn't seem to be progressing.
Mashoor(FR) had his mind on other things out in front and ran out on the bend leading to the stables.

MUNICH (L-H)
Sunday, May 22

OFFICIAL GOING: Turf: good

2345a ONEXTWO.COM - BAVARIAN CLASSIC (GROUP 3) (3YO) (TURF) 1m 2f
3:25 (12:00) 3-Y-0
£27,586 (£9,482; £4,741; £2,586; £1,724; £1,293)

RPR

1 **Mawingo (GER)**21 1739 3-9-2 0 FJohansson 7 106
(J Hirschberger, Germany) *settled towards rr in 5th: qcknd wl bef fnl turn: proged smoothly early in st: qcknd to join ldr 1 1/2f out: prevailed cl home* **36/5**

2 *nse* **Arrigo (GER)** 3-9-2 0 ADeVries 3 106
(J Hirschberger, Germany) *sn joint ldr: set gd pce: r.o wl in st: jnd in ld 1 1/2f out: battled to line: btn on line by minimum margin* **8/5**1

3 *3* **Silvaner (GER)**35 1433 3-9-2 0 FilipMinarik 2 100
(P Schiergen, Germany) *racd in 3rd on rail: smooth prog arnd fnl turn: r.o wl: fin strly* **23/5**3

4 *1/2* **Earl Of Tinsdal (GER)**21 1739 3-9-2 0 JBojko 6 99
(A Wohler, Germany) *broke wl to be joint ldr: then settled in 2nd: r.o wl in st: rdn and one pce fnl f* **19/10**2

5 *3/4* **Avanti (GER)**30 3-9-2 0 WPanov 5 97
(H J Groschel, Germany) *bkmarker fr s: rn through btn horses in st* **22/1**

6 *nk* **Impostor (GER)** 3-9-2 0 KKerekes 4 97
(W Figge, Germany) *settled in 6th: briefly threatened in st: rdn but no ex: fdd* **69/10**

7 *1 1/4* **Sandrino (GER)** 3-9-2 0 FlavienPrat 1 94
(J-P Carvalho, Germany) *racd in midfield: r.o wl early in st: rdn but sn fdd: wknd qckly fnl f* **16/1**

2m 7.18s (-1.79) **7** Ran SP% **125.9**
WIN (incl. 10 euro stake): 82. PLACES: 16, 11, 15. SF: 187.
Owner Gestut Schlenderhan **Bred** Gestut Schlenderhan **Trained** Germany

CARLISLE (R-H)
Monday, May 23

OFFICIAL GOING: Good to soft (soft in places 5f & 6f chutes)
Wind: Very strong, half against Weather: Cloudy

2346 CONFERENCES AT CARLISLE MEDIAN AUCTION MAIDEN STKS 5f
2:00 (2:02) (Class 6) 2-Y-0 **£1,619** (£481; £240; £120) **Stalls** Low

Form RPR

1 **Risky Art** 2-8-12 0 GrahamGibbons 8 79+
(Michael Easterby) *mde all: pushed along over 1f out: kpt on strly ins fnl f* **33/1**

56 2 *2* **Jimmy The Lollipop (IRE)**30 1522 2-9-3 0 (b1) PhillipMakin 2 75
(Kevin Ryan) *sn chsng wnr: effrt and rdn 2f out: kpt on fnl f: nt gng pce to chal* **11/2**

3 *1/2* **Wild Sauce** 2-8-12 0 TomEaves 10 68+
(Bryan Smart) *t.k.h: hld up towards rr: rdn and rn green 2f out: edgd rt and kpt on ins fnl f* **9/1**

2 4 *3 1/4* **Flambard House (IRE)**35 1434 2-9-3 0 PaulMulrennan 6 62+
(Howard Johnson) *trckd ldrs: drvn over 2f out: kpt on same pce appr fnl f* **3/1**1

4 5 *1 3/4* **Whisky Bravo**13 1966 2-9-0 0 DeclanCannon(3) 12 55+
(David Brown) *midfield on outside: rdn and hung lft 2f out: edgd rt and kpt on same pce ins fnl f* **7/2**2

34 6 *3/4* **Devlin**10 2042 2-9-3 0 PaulHanagan 3 53
(Richard Fahey) *midfield on ins: drvn along 1/2-way: no imp over 1f out* **6/1**

7 *3/4* **Master Of Ages (IRE)** 2-9-3 0 JoeFanning 9 50+
(Mark Johnston) *in tch on outside: shkn up 2f out: sn outpcd* **5/1**3

63 8 *3* **Made In The Shade**14 1939 2-8-12 0 FrederikTylicki 4 34
(Paul Midgley) *hld up: drvn and effrt 2f out: sn no imp* **20/1**

0 9 *4 1/2* **King Laertis (IRE)**8 2120 2-9-3 0 PJMcDonald 11 23
(Ben Haslam) *sn bhd and drvn along: no ch fr 1/2-way* **100/1**

10 *21* **Ruskins View (IRE)** 2-8-12 0 PatrickMathers 7 —
(Alan Berry) *s.i.s: a wl bhd* **200/1**

11 *3 3/4* **Landaho** 2-8-9 0 JamesSullivan(3) 1 —
(Hugh McWilliams) *bhd: rdn and struggling after 2f: nvr on terms* **200/1**

64.14 secs (3.34) **Going Correction** +0.45s/f (Yiel) **11** Ran SP% **113.2**
Speed ratings (Par 91): **91,87,87,81,79 77,76,71,64,31 25**
toteswingers:1&2:£27.20, 2&3:£8.90, 1&3:£19.70 CSF £196.61 TOTE £30.80: £6.50, £2.30, £3.90; EX 232.00.
Owner Sangster Family **Bred** J M Beever **Trained** Sheriff Hutton, N Yorks

FOCUS
Ground conditions had eased after morning rain, and with a stiff headwind to contend with too, this probably took a bit of getting for 2-y-os. The form is rated positively but could rate higher.

NOTEBOOK
Risky Art had no problems coping with conditions, providing promising first-season sire Dutch Art with another winner. There was no confidence behind her in the betting, but she did it comfortably, showing bright early speed and never really looking in any danger. She knew her job but can be expected to improve and her yard is in good form in general. (op 25-1)
Jimmy The Lollipop(IRE) had gone with a bit of promise in the Brocklesby and bounced back from a disappointing effort with blinkers tried for the first time. There's no obvious indication he's going to prove much better than this, but an ordinary race should come his way at some stage. (op 15-2)
Wild Sauce, a daughter of Exceed And Excel, made a promising start and can be expected to go close in similar event next time with anything like normal improvement, travelling comfortably and keeping on well without being subjected to an unduly hard time. (op 10-1)
Flambard House(IRE) was second had thrown up a couple of winners, but he failed to improve as expected, although the softer conditions do provide an excuse. (op 5-2)
Whisky Bravo failed to build on his debut fourth, though being caught wide throughout was probably no help and he could be worth another chance.
Devlin had made the frame on his two previous starts but the form didn't amount to a great deal and he never threatened to land a serious blow. He's more one for nurseries over further later on (bred to be suited by 6f plus). (op 9-2)

Master Of Ages(IRE), an Exceed And Excel half-brother to three winners up to 1m2f, is in good hands and can be expected to build on this first effort, showing speed early out wide before fading. (tchd 11-2)

2347 LADIES NIGHT ON AUGUST 1ST CLAIMING STKS 7f 200y
2:30 (2:31) (Class 6) 3-Y-0+ **£1,706** (£503; £252) **Stalls** Low

Form RPR
0121 **1** **Fremen (USA)**[7] 2149 11-9-5 **77** .... PaulQuinn 9 77
(David Nicholls) *mde all: rdn 2f out: styd on wl ins fnl f* **7/2**[2]
00-0 **2** ¾ **The Osteopath (IRE)**[10] 2061 8-9-7 **86** .... PatrickDonaghy[(3)] 2 81
(Michael Dods) *hld up in tch: hdwy and edgd rt to chse wnr over 1f out: kpt on u.p* **2/1**[1]
60-2 **3** ¾ **Moody Tunes**[56] 8-9-8 **75** .... AndrewElliott 7 77
(Mrs K Burke) *chsd wnr: rdn over 2f out: sltly outpcd over 1f out: styd on ins fnl f* **7/2**[2]
000- **4** 3¼ **Moheebb (IRE)**[249] 6112 7-9-6 **77** ....(b) PJMcDonald 5 68
(Ruth Carr) *hld up in tch: rdn and hdwy over 1f out: kpt on same pce ins fnl f* **12/1**
6530 **5** 4½ **Mastership (IRE)**[20] 1793 7-9-7 **80** ....(b) PaulHanagan 6 58
(John Quinn) *hld up: effrt on ins 2f out: no imp appr fnl f* **9/2**[3]
0420 **6** 1¾ **Handsome Falcon**[13] 1970 7-9-1 **75** ....(p) LeeTopliss[(5)] 3 53
(Ollie Pears) *t.k.h: cl up tl edgd rt and wknd over 1f out* **16/1**
0 **7** 11 **Bunacurry**[10] 2045 6-8-11 **0** .... GarryWhillans[(7)] 8 26
(Barry Murtagh) *hld up: struggling over 3f out: sn btn* **200/1**
00-0 **8** 14 **Without Prejudice (USA)**[9] 2115 6-9-8 **80** .... GrahamGibbons 4 —
(Michael Easterby) *dwlt: bhd: struggling 1/2-way: nvr on terms* **25/1**
056/ **9** 7 **Hair Of The Dog**[23] 6385 7-9-0 **51** ....(t) SeanLevey[(3)] 1 —
(George Charlton) *in tch on ins tl wknd qckly 3f out* **200/1**

1m 43.45s (3.45) **Going Correction** +0.45s/f (Yiel) **9** Ran SP% **114.4**
Speed ratings (Par 101): **100,99,98,95,90 89,78,64,57**
toteswingers:1&2:£3.90, 2&3:£2.80, 1&3:£2.10 CSF £10.76 TOTE £3.60: £1.10, £1.90, £1.20; EX 12.10.
Owner Middleham Park Racing XXXV C King A Seed **Bred** Flaxman Holdings Ltd **Trained** Sessay, N Yorks

FOCUS
A fair claimer rated slightly negatively around the first two to their recent best.

2348 AMW CONTRACTORS AND MANNING ELLIOTT ARCHITECTS APPRENTICE H'CAP 7f 200y
3:00 (3:00) (Class 6) (0-65,65) 4-Y-0+ **£1,706** (£503; £252) **Stalls** Low

Form RPR
066- **1** **Epernay**[254] 5942 4-9-0 **58** ....(t) MichaelO'Connell 3 69+
(Ian Williams) *prom: drvn over 2f out: rallied to ld appr fnl f: edgd rt: styd on wl* **4/1**[3]
06-2 **2** 2¼ **Silly Gilly (IRE)**[16] 1911 7-8-13 **57** .... LeeTopliss 10 63
(Ron Barr) *hld up in tch: hdwy to ld 2f out: hdd appr fnl f: kpt on same pce ins fnl f* **3/1**[1]
06-0 **3** hd **Mangham (IRE)**[22] 1714 6-9-7 **65** .... DaleSwift 7 70
(George Foster) *t.k.h: hld up in tch: hdwy on ins and ev ch over 1f out: kpt on same pce ins fnl f* **10/1**
-003 **4** 3 **Star Addition**[26] 1615 5-8-8 **52** .... NeilFarley 2 50
(Eric Alston) *prom: rdn and outpcd over 2f out: styd on fnl f: nrst fin* **7/2**[2]
20-0 **5** 6 **Jupiter Fidius**[44] 1244 4-8-13 **62** ....(p) EdmondLinehan[(5)] 8 47
(Kate Walton) *cl up: rdn to ld briefly over 2f out: wknd over 1f out* **8/1**
-600 **6** 9 **Baltimore Jack (IRE)**[16] 1909 7-9-1 **64** .... DavidSimmonson[(5)] 5 28
(G P Kelly) *cl up: effrt and ev ch over 2f out: wknd over 1f out* **33/1**
/500 **7** nse **Velvet Band**[4] 2237 4-8-7 **51** oh1 ....(v) AmyRyan 1 15
(Richard Whitaker) *led to over 2f out: sn rdn and wknd* **100/1**
2-35 **8** 2¾ **It's A Mans World**[5] 793 5-8-7 **51** ....(v) AndrewHeffernan 9 —
(Kevin M Prendergast) *sn pushed along in rr: struggling over 3f out: nvr on terms* **13/2**
2534 **9** 3½ **Classic Descent**[17] 1857 6-9-0 **58** ....(bt) JamesSullivan 6 —
(Ruth Carr) *s.i.s: bhd: rdn over 3f out: sn wknd* **8/1**

1m 43.26s (3.26) **Going Correction** +0.45s/f (Yiel) **9** Ran SP% **115.8**
Speed ratings (Par 101): **101,98,98,95,89 80,80,77,74**
toteswingers:1&2:£3.70, 2&3:£11.00, 1&3:£13.20 CSF £16.48 CT £111.65 TOTE £5.20: £1.50, £3.10, £1.30; EX 22.50.
Owner Mr & Mrs G Middlebrook **Bred** Mr & Mrs G Middlebrook **Trained** Portway, Worcs

FOCUS
Just a modest apprentice event but sound rated through the runner-up.
Epernay Official explanation: trainer's rep said, regarding apparent improvement in form, that the filly had strengthened up over the winter and he felt it was a weak race.

2349 ROBERT ELLIOTT MEMORIAL FILLIES' H'CAP 1m 1f 61y
3:30 (3:30) (Class 5) (0-70,67) 3-Y-0 **£3,238** (£963; £481; £240) **Stalls** Low

Form RPR
00-6 **1** **Tidal Run**[21] 1751 3-8-8 **57** .... MartinHarley[(3)] 1 64
(Mick Channon) *in tch: rdn and outpcd over 3f out: rallied over 1f out: led ins fnl f: r.o wl* **7/1**[3]
4-04 **2** 1¼ **Tarantella Lady**[24] 1653 3-9-7 **67** .... PJMcDonald 4 71
(George Moore) *hld up: outpcd 1/2-way: rallied and swtchd rt over 1f out: styd on to take 2nd nr fin: nt rch wnr* **12/1**
00-0 **3** ½ **Damascus Symphony**[13] 1974 3-8-11 **57** .... AndrewElliott 11 60+
(James Bethell) *led: hrd pressed over 2f out: hdd ins fnl f: kpt on same pce: lost 2nd cl home* **33/1**
35-0 **4** 6 **Inside**[47] 1169 3-8-12 **58** ....(p) PaulHanagan 9 48
(Richard Fahey) *cl up: hdwy to chal over 2f out to ent fnl f: wknd last 100yds* **13/2**[2]
2332 **5** 8 **Paco Belle (IRE)**[60] 951 3-9-4 **67** .... SeanLevey[(3)] 10 39
(Andrew Crook) *trckd ldrs: drvn over 3f out: wknd fr 2f out* **12/1**
3-04 **6** ½ **Monicalew**[11] 2018 3-9-6 **66** .... TomEaves 2 37
(Walter Swinburn) *hld up towards rr: struggling over 3f out: btn fnl 2f* **5/6**[1]
06-0 **7** 15 **Formidable Girl (USA)**[14] 1958 3-8-12 **58** ....(p) PhillipMakin 6 —
(Kevin Ryan) *t.k.h: prom: smooth hdwy on outside over 3f out: sn rdn: wknd 2f out* **9/1**
-366 **8** 2½ **Rainbows Reach**[75] 801 3-8-4 **53** oh6 ....(tp) AndrewHeffernan[(3)] 7 —
(Gay Kelleway) *dwlt: bhd: struggling over 4f out: nvr on terms* **80/1**
0-00 **9** 27 **Allez Leulah (IRE)**[17] 1858 3-8-9 **55** .... JoeFanning 5 —
(Mark Johnston) *hld up towards rr: drvn 1/2-way: wknd over 3f out* **33/1**

2m 2.25s (4.65) **Going Correction** +0.45s/f (Yiel) **9** Ran SP% **112.9**
Speed ratings (Par 96): **97,95,95,90,83 82,69,67,43**
toteswingers:1&2:£9.50, 2&3:£32.50, 1&3:£31.00 CSF £82.33 CT £2552.38 TOTE £10.20: £2.20, £2.10, £5.10; EX 83.10.
Owner M Channon **Bred** Barry Walters Farms **Trained** West Ilsley, Berks
■ Stewards' Enquiry : Sean Levey three-day ban: careless riding (Jun 13,19, one day remedial training)

FOCUS
An ordinary fillies event, and the impression was the leaders pressed for home a bit too far out under the conditions, the complexion of the race changing dramatically in the final 2f. The winner recorded a persoanal best but the form is not the most convincing.
Tidal Run Official explanation: trainer's rep said, regarding apparent improvement in form, that the filly had injured itself on its final run last season and improved from its first run early this month.
Paco Belle(IRE) Official explanation: jockey said filly hung left-handed throughout
Monicalew Official explanation: jockey said filly never travelled

2350 EXPLOSIVE PRODUCTIONS LTD H'CAP (DIV I) 6f 192y
4:00 (4:00) (Class 6) (0-60,60) 3-Y-0 **£1,364** (£403; £201) **Stalls** Low

Form RPR
00-0 **1** **Alluring Star**[7] 2163 3-9-0 **53** .... DavidNolan 3 61
(Michael Easterby) *mde all: jnd over 2f out: rdn and hung rt over 1f out: hld on wl ins fnl f* **9/2**[1]
000 **2** ¾ **Catallout (IRE)**[23] 1693 3-8-12 **56** .... NeilFarley[(5)] 8 62
(Declan Carroll) *hld up: pushed along over 3f out: hdwy 2f out: styd on wl ins fnl f: nrst fin* **6/1**[3]
6-03 **3** 1¼ **Cool In The Shade**[14] 1941 3-9-1 **54** .... BarryMcHugh 2 57
(Paul Midgley) *prom: hdwy and ev ch over 2f out: carried rt appr fnl f: one pce ins fnl f* **9/2**[1]
050 **4** 3¾ **The Nifty Duchess**[17] 1860 3-8-10 **49** .... DavidAllan 7 42
(Tim Easterby) *trckd ldrs: drvn and outpcd 2f out: kpt on fnl f: no imp* **10/1**
00-6 **5** 1¾ **Illawalla**[13] 1971 3-8-4 **46** oh1 .... JamesSullivan[(3)] 5 34
(Hugh McWilliams) *hld up: drvn along 3f out: hdwy appr fnl f: nvr able to chal* **33/1**
0-00 **6** nk **May Burnett (IRE)**[33] 1495 3-8-4 **46** oh1 ....(t) AndrewHeffernan[(3)] 11 33
(Brian Rothwell) *bhd: drvn 1/2-way: styd on fnl f: nvr on terms* **18/1**
30-0 **7** 1 **Spin A Wish**[14] 1945 3-8-8 **50** .... AmyRyan[(3)] 6 35
(Richard Whitaker) *in tch tl rdn and outpcd fr 2f out* **25/1**
65-5 **8** 11 **Robber Stone**[14] 1953 3-8-11 **53** .... MartinHarley[(3)] 4 —
(Mick Channon) *in tch: effrt over 3f out: wknd fr 2f out* **5/1**[2]
060- **9** 1 **Bonne Millie**[300] 4451 3-8-7 **46** .... PaulHanagan 10 —
(Ollie Pears) *trckd ldrs tl rdn and wknd 2f out* **5/1**[2]
000- **10** 9 **Green Pastures (IRE)**[300] 4447 3-9-7 **60** .... PaulMulrennan 9 —
(Howard Johnson) *bhd: struggling 1/2-way: eased whn no ch fnl 2f* **8/1**

1m 31.09s (3.99) **Going Correction** +0.45s/f (Yiel) **10** Ran SP% **116.2**
Speed ratings (Par 97): **95,94,92,88,86 86,84,72,71,60**
toteswingers:1&2:£8.00, 2&3:£7.50, 1&3:£5.40 CSF £31.40 CT £131.14 TOTE £7.40: £2.10, £3.70, £2.30; EX 47.90.
Owner Jeff Hamer & Bernard Bargh **Bred** B Bargh **Trained** Sheriff Hutton, N Yorks

FOCUS
Just a run-of-the-mill 3-y-o handicap in all probability. The third looks the best guide to the level.
Alluring Star Official explanation: trainer said, regarding apparent improvement in form, that the filly had improved in fitness from its previous run.
Catallout(IRE) Official explanation: jockey said filly hung left throughout
Green Pastures(IRE) Official explanation: jockey said gelding never travelled

2351 EXPLOSIVE PRODUCTIONS LTD H'CAP (DIV II) 6f 192y
4:30 (4:30) (Class 6) (0-60,58) 3-Y-0 **£1,364** (£403; £201) **Stalls** Low

Form RPR
5423 **1** **Mini's Destination**[14] 1933 3-9-2 **53** .... PhillipMakin 5 62
(John Holt) *in tch gng wl: hdwy to ld appr fnl f: edgd rt: kpt on wl* **11/1**
60-0 **2** 1¼ **Ryedale Dancer (IRE)**[17] 1880 3-8-13 **50** .... DavidAllan 1 55
(Tim Easterby) *led tl edgd lft and hdd over 1f out: kpt on fnl f: nt gng pce of wnr* **7/2**[2]
-033 **3** 1¼ **Cathcart Castle**[6] 2172 3-9-3 **57** .... MartinHarley[(3)] 7 59
(Mick Channon) *in tch on outside: hdwy to ld briefly over 1f out: edgd rt: one pce ins fnl f* **9/2**
6-04 **4** hd **See The Storm**[34] 1465 3-8-9 **49** .... JamesSullivan[(3)] 8 50
(Patrick Morris) *bhd: rdn 1/2-way: styd on wl ins fnl f: nvr able to chal* **40/1**
3305 **5** 4 **Unwrapit (USA)**[37] 1400 3-9-7 **58** ....(p) TomEaves 2 49
(Bryan Smart) *in tch: drvn over 2f out: wknd over 1f out* **20/1**
5556 **6** 7 **Princess Gail**[14] 1952 3-9-3 **54** .... GrahamGibbons 9 26
(Mark Brisbourne) *hld up: drvn 3f out: sme hdwy over 1f out: nvr on terms* **16/1**
00-0 **7** ½ **Newzflash**[33] 1495 3-8-8 **45** .... BarryMcHugh 10 15
(Ollie Pears) *bhd and sn struggling: nvr on terms* **33/1**
04 **8** hd **Love For Love**[8] 2125 3-9-4 **55** .... DanielTudhope 4 25
(David O'Meara) *trckd ldrs: effrt over 2f out: wknd over 1f out* **3/1**[1]
0-04 **9** 3½ **Decadence**[17] 1880 3-9-1 **52** .... PaulMulrennan 6 12
(Eric Alston) *in tch: rdn 3f out: wkng whn n.m.r over 1f out* **4/1**[3]
06-6 **10** 9 **Rattleyurjewellery**[52] 1078 3-8-5 **45** .... DeclanCannon[(3)] 3 —
(David Brown) *cl up tl rdn and wknd fr 2f out* **20/1**

1m 31.13s (4.03) **Going Correction** +0.45s/f (Yiel) **10** Ran SP% **114.5**
Speed ratings (Par 97): **94,92,91,90,86 78,77,77,73,63**
toteswingers:1&2:£7.40, 2&3:£4.50, 1&3:£3.60 CSF £46.39 CT £206.81 TOTE £14.00: £3.00, £1.10, £1.80; EX 68.10.
Owner J R Holt **Bred** Whatton Manor Stud **Trained** Peckleton, Leics

FOCUS
A similar standard to the first division, with unexposed sorts being pretty thin on the ground. The pace was at least a sound one and the form looks solid enough, rated around the placed horses.

2352 WATCH RACING UK ON SKY 432 H'CAP (DIV I) 5f 193y
5:00 (5:03) (Class 6) (0-65,65) 4-Y-0+ **£1,364** (£403; £201) **Stalls** Low

Form RPR
1022 **1** **Pelmanism**[17] 1861 4-9-6 **64** ....(b) PhillipMakin 5 76+
(Kevin Ryan) *dwlt: hld up: nt clr run over 2f out: hdwy over 1f out: led ins fnl f: sn clr* **15/8**[1]
06-0 **2** 3 **Hansomis (IRE)**[10] 2062 7-8-11 **55** .... PaulMulrennan 10 63+
(Bruce Mactaggart) *hld up in midfield: hdwy over 2f out: cl up and keeping on whn hmpd and snatched up ent fnl f: r.o wl to take 2nd cl home* **16/1**
61-4 **3** shd **Hellbender (IRE)**[22] 1712 5-9-0 **63** .... DaleSwift[(5)] 11 65
(George Foster) *hld up: hdwy on outside over 2f out: led over 1f out: hung rt: rdr dropped reins and hdd ins fnl f: kpt on same pce* **8/1**
0200 **4** 3½ **Colamandis**[45] 1216 4-8-4 **51** oh4 .... JamesSullivan[(3)] 4 42
(Hugh McWilliams) *bhd: drvn 1/2-way: kpt on fnl f: nvr able to chal* **40/1**
-613 **5** hd **Electioneer (USA)**[26] 1612 4-9-6 **64** ....(v[1]) GrahamGibbons 8 54
(Michael Easterby) *trckd ldrs: drvn 1/2-way: nt qckn over 1f out* **11/4**[2]
-066 **6** ¾ **Northern Bolt**[4] 2238 6-9-7 **65** ....(b) PatrickMathers 6 53
(Ian McInnes) *chsd ldng gp: drvn 1/2-way: no imp over 1f out* **9/1**

23-0 **7** ½ **Hot Rod Mamma (IRE)**26 1612 4-8-7 **51**.................. DuranFentiman 1 37
(Dianne Sayer) *prom: hdwy to ld over 2f out: hdd over 1f out: wknd ins fnl f* **20/1**
44-5 **8** 4 **Secret City (IRE)**26 1612 5-8-13 **57**..........................(p) DanielTudhope 2 30
(Robin Bastiman) *led to over 2f out: rdn and wknd over 1f out* **7/1**3
0-0U **9** 4½ **Viking Warrior (IRE)**26 1612 4-9-5 **63**.................. FrederikTylicki 9 22
(Michael Dods) *hld up in tch: drvn 1/2-way: wknd fr 2f out* **28/1**
0-06 **10** 4 **Rio Sands**5 2205 6-8-2 **51** oh1.......................(p) DanielleMcCreery(5) 12 —
(Richard Whitaker) *cl up tl rdn and wknd fr 2f out* **40/1**
000 **11** 2¼ **Boxer Shorts**17 1875 5-8-3 **54** oh6 ow3..................... JosephYoung(7) 3 —
(Michael Mullineaux) *bhd and sn struggling: nvr on terms* **125/1**

1m 16.85s (3.15) **Going Correction** +0.45s/f (Yiel) **11** Ran SP% **114.8**
Speed ratings (Par 101): **97,93,92,88,87 86,86,80,74,69 66**
toteswingers:1&2:£8.50, 2&3:£21.10, 1&3:£4.00 CSF £31.66 CT £203.27 TOTE £2.70: £1.30, £5.70, £1.90; EX 44.20.
Owner Guy Reed **Bred** Guy Reed **Trained** Hambleton, N Yorks

FOCUS
Probably form to view reasonably positively relative to the grade, the principals all being well handicapped.

2353 WATCH RACING UK ON SKY 432 H'CAP (DIV II) 5f 193y
5:30 (5:30) (Class 6) (0-65,64) 4-Y-0+ **£1,364** (£403; £201) **Stalls** Low

Form RPR
2061 **1** **Klynch**17 1861 5-9-3 **63**...(b) JamesSullivan(3) 11 84
(Ruth Carr) *hld up in tch on outside: hdwy to ld over 1f out: drvn out ins fnl f* **10/3**1
200- **2** 2 **Needy McCredie**247 6188 5-8-2 **52** ow2...................... ShaneBKelly(7) 6 66
(James Turner) *t.k.h: hld up: hdwy to chal over 1f out: kpt on same pce ins fnl f* **8/1**
-324 **3** 4½ **Senate Majority**8 2126 4-9-7 **64**....................................... DavidAllan 4 64
(Tim Easterby) *trckd ldrs: effrt and ev ch over 1f out: outpcd fnl f* **9/2**2
0-03 **4** 1¼ **Broctune Papa Gio**20 1803 4-8-7 **50** oh2..................... FrannyNorton 3 46
(Keith Reveley) *trckd ldr: rdn and outpcd 2f out: plugged on fnl f: no imp* **15/2**
5422 **5** nk **Convince (USA)**20 1803 10-8-10 **56**.................. AndrewHeffernan(3) 5 51
(Kevin M Prendergast) *fly-jmpd s: chsd ldng gp: drvn along over 2f out: no imp over 1f out* **8/1**
-636 **6** 2½ **Two Turtle Doves (IRE)**11 2016 5-8-11 **61**.............. JosephYoung(7) 7 48
(Michael Mullineaux) *cl up tl rdn and wknd fr 2f out* **8/1**
-063 **7** 1¾ **Berbice (IRE)**17 1861 6-9-2 **64**....................................... LeeTopliss(5) 8 45
(Linda Perratt) *stdd s: t.k.h in rr: rdn and sme hdwy over 1f out: nvr able to chal* **8/1**
0004 **8** 1½ **Royal Blade (IRE)**17 1856 4-8-7 **50** oh4...................... PatrickMathers 1 27
(Alan Berry) *led tl hdd over 1f out: sn btn* **40/1**
0-00 **9** 1¾ **Cheyenne Red (IRE)**22 1712 5-9-3 **60**......................... FrederikTylicki 2 31
(Michael Dods) *prom tl rdn and wknd fr 2f out* **6/1**3

1m 16.28s (2.58) **Going Correction** +0.45s/f (Yiel) **9** Ran SP% **114.2**
Speed ratings (Par 101): **100,97,91,89,89 85,83,81,79**
toteswingers:1&2:£6.60, 2&3:£7.70, 1&3:£3.30. Tote Super 7: Win: Not won. Place: £137.40 CSF £30.10 CT £120.62 TOTE £4.20: £1.90, £1.80, £1.10; EX 34.50.
Owner Douglas Renton **Bred** J C S Wilson Bloodstock **Trained** Huby, N Yorks

FOCUS
An ordinary sprint to conclude proceedings, though the front two deserve some credit for coming well clear. The winner is rated in line with his best form for the yard and the second posted a slight personal best.
T/Plt: £405.40 to a £1 stake. Pool of £55,044.81 - 99.11 winning tickets. T/Qpdt: £117.10 to a £1 stake. Pool of £5,415.57 - 34.20 winning tickets. RY

2147 LEICESTER (R-H)
Monday, May 23
OFFICIAL GOING: Good to firm (firm in places; 8.8)
Wind: Strong behind Weather: Overcast turning to rain after race 1

2354 LADBROKES.COM H'CAP 7f 9y
2:15 (2:15) (Class 5) (0-70,70) 3-Y-0+ **£2,266** (£674; £337; £168) **Stalls** High

Form RPR
1-02 **1** **Mountrath**21 1756 4-9-7 **64**...(v) RyanMoore 12 75
(Gary Moore) *racd alone on stands' side: w ldrs: rdn and hung rt fr over 1f out: r.o u.p to ld wl ins fnl f* **7/2**2
0-20 **2** nk **Sairaam (IRE)**13 1990 5-8-13 **63**.......................... MatthewLawson(7) 4 73
(Charles Smith) *chsd ldrs: led 1/2-way: rdn over 1f out: hung lft and hdd wl ins fnl f* **16/1**
1320 **3** 6 **Copperwood**16 1917 6-9-11 **68**... LiamKeniry 1 62
(Michael Blanshard) *hld up: hdwy over 2f out: sn rdn: styd on: nt rch ldrs* **20/1**
2205 **4** 1¼ **Mount Hollow**65 915 6-9-5 **62**...(v1) ChrisCatlin 13 53
(Reg Hollinshead) *mid-div: hdwy over 2f out: rdn over 1f out: styd on: nt trble ldrs* **14/1**
-336 **5** 1½ **Cuthbert (IRE)**96 562 4-9-13 **70**.................................(p) TomQueally 11 57
(William Jarvis) *edgd rt s: sn mid-div: hdwy u.p over 2f out: no ex ins fnl f* **12/1**
0300 **6** 4½ **Hip Hip Hooray**13 1990 5-9-3 **60**...................................... IanMongan 7 34
(Luke Dace) *s.s: bhd: styd on ins fnl f: nvr nrr* **20/1**
2211 **7** ½ **George Baker (IRE)**11 2027 4-9-6 **70**........................... DavidKenny(7) 2 43
(George Baker) *hld up: hdwy over 2f out: rdn and wknd over 1f out* **15/8**1
000- **8** ½ **George Thisby**217 6991 5-9-8 **65**.................................. JamesMillman 14 37
(Rod Millman) *hld up: rdn over 2f out: nvr on terms* **25/1**
3000 **9** 2¾ **Ace Of Spies (IRE)**16 1907 6-9-11 **68**...................... KirstyMilczarek 10 32
(Conor Dore) *s.i.s and hmpd s: sn pushed along in rr: nvr on terms* **33/1**
0-00 **10** ½ **Chambers (IRE)**16 1909 5-9-0 **57**.......................... SilvestreDeSousa 6 20
(Eric Alston) *chsd ldrs: rdn 1/2-way: wknd over 1f out* **15/2**3
3-30 **11** 1 **Be Amazing (IRE)**17 1869 3-9-0 **68**.................................. TedDurcan 5 28
(David Lanigan) *chsd ldrs tl rdn and wknd 2f out* **16/1**
0-01 **12** 14 **Dhhamaan (IRE)**16 1911 6-9-1 **58**..(b) SebSanders 9 —
(Ruth Carr) *led to 1/2-way: wknd wl over 1f out: eased fnl f: t.o* **10/1**

1m 22.79s (-3.41) **Going Correction** -0.40s/f (Firm)
WFA 3 from 4yo+ 11lb **12** Ran SP% **120.3**
Speed ratings (Par 103): **103,102,95,94,92 87,86,86,83,82 81,65**
toteswingers:1&2:£18.00, 2&3:£29.00, 1&3:£9.00 CSF £55.71 CT £1010.80 TOTE £4.00: £1.20, £2.40, £6.20; EX 87.90 TRIFECTA Not won..
Owner David Phelan **Bred** A G Antoniades **Trained** Lower Beeding, W Sussex

FOCUS
The ground was officially described as good to firm, firm in places (watered) and times were expected to be quick with a strong tailwind helping the horses up the home straight. Despite a solid winning time, this was a moderate handicap and it was interesting that the winner was the only one to race close to the stands' rail, whilst the rest came down the centre. The first two are rated to the best of their old form.
Hip Hip Hooray Official explanation: jockey said mare was slowly away
George Baker(IRE) Official explanation: jockey said gelding never travelled
Dhhamaan(IRE) Official explanation: jockey said gelding lost its action

2355 LADBROKES.COM MAIDEN STKS 5f 218y
2:45 (2:46) (Class 5) 2-Y-0 **£3,238** (£963; £481; £240) **Stalls** High

Form RPR
4 **1** **St Barths**10 2049 2-9-3 0.. MartinDwyer 8 85+
(Brian Meehan) *trckd ldrs: rdn to ld ins fnl f: r.o* **4/11**1
3 **2** 2 **Verbeeck**25 1628 2-9-3 0... RichardMullen 6 76
(Ed McMahon) *chsd ldr tl led 4f out: rdn and hdd ins fnl f: styd on same pce* **16/1**3
5 **3** 1 **Singalat**11 2023 2-9-3 0... CathyGannon 9 73
(David Evans) *chsd ldrs: rdn over 2f out: styd on* **22/1**
4 hd **Bounty Seeker (USA)** 2-9-3 0.................................. SilvestreDeSousa 2 73
(Mark Johnston) *led 2f: chsd ldrs: shkn up over 1f out: styd on same pce ins fnl f* **9/2**2
5 3¾ **Telwaar** 2-9-3 0.. WilliamBuick 4 62
(Peter Chapple-Hyam) *prom: outpcd over 3f out: styd on ins fnl f* **22/1**
0 **6** ½ **Space Raider (AUS)**10 2049 2-9-3 0.................................. MichaelHills 5 63+
(B W Hills) *dwlt: hdwy over 3f out: wknd over 1f out* **40/1**
6 **7** 12 **Unforgiving (IRE)**24 1657 2-8-12 0................................. SebSanders 3 19
(Alan McCabe) *chsd ldrs: rdn over 3f out: wknd over 2f out* **100/1**
60 **8** hd **Witty Buck**23 1691 2-8-10 0...(v1) RyanTate(7) 1 23
(Alan McCabe) *s.i.s: sn pushed along in rr: bhd fr 1/2-way* **200/1**

1m 10.56s (-2.44) **Going Correction** -0.40s/f (Firm) **8** Ran SP% **110.0**
Speed ratings (Par 93): **100,97,96,95,90 90,74,73**
toteswingers:1&2:£2.20, 2&3:£3.20, 1&3:£2.90 CSF £6.41 TOTE £1.50: £1.10, £2.30, £2.90; EX 6.00 Trifecta £21.40 Pool: £817.83 - 28.24 winning units..
Owner Trelawny II **Bred** Peter Hunt & Mrs Sally Hunt **Trained** Manton, Wilts

FOCUS
A division of this maiden was won by the subsequent dual Group 2 winner King Torus last season and this year's renewal featured a couple of very interesting prospects. On this occasion the runners all came down the centre and the third is the ebst guide to the level at this stage.

NOTEBOOK
St Barths ◆ was unfortunate not to do even better than fourth in a decent Newbury maiden on his debut and proved all the rage to gain compensation. He proved a little edgy before the start and once under way needed a couple of smacks to encourage him to get the better of the runner-up, but he was well on top at the line. Connections think he might be a Royal Ascot horse. (op 2-5 tchd 4-9 in a place)
Verbeeck was far too green when third behind a subsequent winner on his Bath debut last month, but looked different gear this time with that experience under his belt. He made sure the favourite had to fight to get the better of him and should be able to find a maiden sooner rather than later. (op 12-1)
Singalat got outpaced when fifth of seven over 5f on his Salisbury debut and stepped up from that with a solid effort, but considering his pedigree is all stamina, anything he achieves over this sort of trips has to be considered a bonus. (op 28-1 tchd 20-1)
Bounty Seeker(USA), a $285,000 half-brother to three winners in the US and Japan out of a Grade 1 winner in the US, ran a creditable debut having been handy from the off and he should improve as he goes up in trip. (op 11-2 tchd 13-2)
Telwaar, a half-brother to two winners at up to 1m including his stablemate Jaser, was by no means knocked about on this debut and should have learnt plenty from it. (op 16-1)

2356 LADBROKES.COM HICKLING (S) STKS 5f 218y
3:15 (3:15) (Class 6) 3-5-Y-0 **£1,706** (£503; £252) **Stalls** High

Form RPR
0-12 **1** **Cootehill Lass (IRE)**27 1585 3-8-11 **65**..............(p) SilvestreDeSousa 10 72
(Geoffrey Harker) *hld up: hdwy over 2f out: rdn to ld over 1f out: edgd rt: r.o* **6/1**3
3443 **2** 2 **Kingswinford (IRE)**2 2286 5-9-3 **74**.......................... RichardEvans(3) 6 68
(David Evans) *chsd ldrs: rdn and ev ch over 1f out: styd on same pce ins fnl f* **6/4**1
-604 **3** 2½ **Rainy Night**34 1471 5-9-6 **66**...(p) ChrisCatlin 1 60
(Reg Hollinshead) *chsd ldrs: rdn and ev ch over 1f out: no ex ins fnl f* **12/1**
5-U0 **4** 1½ **Dusty Spirit**7 2142 4-8-13 **67**..(t) JakePayne(7) 4 55
(Bill Turner) *dwlt: hdwy over 4f out: rdn over 2f out: no ex ins fnl f* **22/1**
0032 **5** 2¾ **Mark Anthony (IRE)**16 1906 4-9-6 **70**.......................(p) JamieSpencer 8 46
(Kevin Ryan) *led: rdn and hdd over 1f out: wknd ins fnl f* **5/2**2
-066 **6** 1½ **Sophie's Beau (USA)**41 1289 4-8-13 **42**................... LeonnaMayor(7) 9 41
(Michael Chapman) *s.i.s: hld up: rdn and wknd over 1f out* **66/1**
-053 **7** ½ **Brave Battle**33 1482 3-8-11 **65**....................................... AdrianNicholls 7 38
(David Nicholls) *chsd ldrs: rdn over 2f out: hung rt over 1f out: wknd fnl f* **12/1**
630 **8** nse **Sailing North (USA)**21 1753 3-8-11 **60**..................... TomMcLaughlin 2 37
(Ronald Harris) *prom: outpcd 4f out: sme hdwy u.p over 1f out: wknd fnl f* **40/1**
5125 **9** 5 **Polemica (IRE)**7 2165 5-9-6 **63**......................................(bt) JamesDoyle 5 21
(Frank Sheridan) *hld up: rdn over 2f out: wknd over 1f out* **11/1**

1m 10.73s (-2.27) **Going Correction** -0.40s/f (Firm)
WFA 3 from 4yo+ 9lb **9** Ran SP% **114.9**
Speed ratings (Par 101): **99,96,93,91,87 85,84,84,77**
toteswingers:1&2:£2.90, 2&3:£5.40, 1&3:£9.30 CSF £15.13 TOTE £4.90: £1.90, £1.10, £5.00; EX 20.20 Trifecta £122.30 Pool: £877.95 - 5.31 winning units..The winner was bought in for 9,000gns. Kingswinford was claimed by L. S. Keys for £7000.
Owner An Englishman, Irishman & Scotsman **Bred** Speers Bloodstock Ltd **Trained** Thirkleby, N Yorks

FOCUS
A moderate seller, but as in the opening contest the winner utilised the strip closest to the stands' rail. The level is fluid with the winner the best guide.

2357 LADBROKES.COM BELVOIR CASTLE H'CAP 1m 1f 218y
3:45 (3:45) (Class 4) (0-85,85) 3-Y-0 **£3,432** (£1,021) **Stalls** Low

Form RPR
-214 **1** **Ivan Vasilevich (IRE)**4 2230 3-8-13 **77**......................... JamieSpencer 3 78
(Jane Chapple-Hyam) *mde all: shkn up over 3f out: rdn and hung lft fr over 1f out: styd on* **4/9**1

6631 **2** *1 ½* **Bussa**[4] 2226 3-8-11 75 6ex .... CathyGannon 4 73
(David Evans) *dwlt: chsd wnr: rdn and ev ch fr over 2f out tl styd on same pce ins fnl f* **15/8**[2]

2m 8.20s (0.30) **Going Correction** +0.025s/f (Good) **2** Ran SP% **104.0**
Speed ratings (Par 101): **99,97**
TOTE £1.20.
Owner Chris Fahy **Bred** Liam Butler **Trained** Dalham, Suffolk

FOCUS
This contest was reduced to a match following the withdrawal of Albaraka, who would have been sent off a very short-priced favourite. A fascinating game of cat and mouse between Jamie Spencer and Cathy Gannon, with the former keen to make this a proper test aboard the winner. Both are rated close to their recent best.

2358 LADBROKES.COM CHARNWOOD FOREST FILLIES' CONDITIONS STKS 7f 9y
4:15 (4:15) (Class 3) 3-Y-0+ **£7,788** (£2,332; £1,166; £583; £291) **Stalls** High

Form RPR

2111 **1** **Saddlers Bend (IRE)**[2] 2313 5-8-10 72 .... MatthewDavies(3) 5 88
(George Baker) *chsd ldrs: led over 2f out: rdn and hung rt fr over 1f out: all out* **14/1**

5-05 **2** *nk* **Nabah**[22] 1722 3-8-3 90 ow1 .... ChrisCatlin 3 84
(Clive Brittain) *chsd ldr: outpcd wl over 1f out: r.o wl ins fnl f: wnt 2nd nr fin* **16/1**

135- **3** *¾* **Jacqueline Quest (IRE)**[297] 4540 4-8-13 111 .... TomQueally 4 85
(Sir Henry Cecil) *hld up: hdwy 1/2-way: rdn: hung rt and ev ch fr over 1f out: no ex nr fin* **1/4**[1]

2-00 **4** *¾* **Bahati (IRE)**[16] 1884 4-8-13 90 .... RichardKingscote 1 83
(Jonathan Portman) *a.p: rdn over 1f out: r.o* **12/1**[3]

0-50 **5** *¾* **Mortitia**[16] 1902 3-8-6 98 .... AdrianNicholls 2 81
(Brian Meehan) *led over 4f: rdn over 1f out: no ex ins fnl f* **10/1**[2]

1m 23.87s (-2.33) **Going Correction** -0.40s/f (Firm)
WFA 3 from 4yo+ 11lb **5** Ran SP% **109.3**
Speed ratings (Par 104): **97,96,95,94,94**
CSF £155.73 TOTE £7.20: £1.60, £4.80; EX 48.00.
Owner Mrs Christine Cone **Bred** J F Tuthill **Trained** Whitsbury, Hants

FOCUS
A fascinating fillies' conditions event but the pace was modest and the form cannot be taken at face value.

NOTEBOOK
Saddlers Bend(IRE), in-foal to Sakhee's Secret, completed a hat-trick when winning a Newbury handicap off a mark of 72 just two days earlier and had upwards of 18lb to find with her four rivals on these terms. At no stage did she look outclassed here, however, and having made her move at the same time as the favourite, she saw her race out much the best. She is in the form of her life, but is likely to be retired now and is yet another mare for whom impending motherhood seems to have improved her no end. (op 10-1)
Nabah, still a maiden, was taking a big drop in trip after running moderately over 1m2f in her first two starts of the season, so it was perhaps no great surprise that she ran on again to take second after losing her pitch around 2f out. She can surely win a race back over further. (op 20-1)
Jacqueline Quest(IRE) hadn't been seen since a disappointing favourite in a Goodwood Group 3 last July. Even so, she appeared to totally outclass these rivals based on her previous efforts in the 1000 Guineas and Coronation Stakes, and she had upwards of 17lb in hand of them at the weights. Everything seemed to be going well enough for most of the race as she travelled well at the back of the field early and swept though to hold every chance over 1f out, but once there she started to carry her head to one side and was run out of second place near the line. Considering that she had apparently been working well, this was very disappointing, though the vet reported that the filly had finished distressed. Quite where she goes from here is anyone's guess. Official explanation: vet said filly finished distressed (op 2-7)
Bahati(IRE) had shown nothing in her first two starts this season and, although not beaten far, never looked like winning. She remains without a win since her racecourse debut. (op 14-1)
Mortitia lost her chance at the start at Nottingham last time, but didn't run badly in the Fred Darling on her return, so this was disappointing as she faded tamely after making the running to over 2f out.

2359 LADBROKES.COM CLAIMING STKS 1m 1f 218y
4:45 (4:45) (Class 6) 4-Y-0+ **£1,706** (£503; £252) **Stalls** Low

Form RPR

0-24 **1** **Uphold**[18] 1828 4-9-11 85 ....(b) JamieSpencer 1 88+
(Jamie Osborne) *mde all: qcknd over 4f out: rdn clr fr over 1f out: eased nr fin* **9/4**[2]

05-3 **2** *4* **Lang Shining (IRE)**[24] 175 7-9-8 80 .... SophieDoyle(3) 5 77
(Jamie Osborne) *hld up: hdwy over 2f out: styd on to go 2nd wl ins fnl f: no ch w wnr* **5/1**[3]

-065 **3** *nk* **Kheskianto (IRE)**[16] 1905 5-7-9 46 ....(bt) KatiaScallan(7) 2 53
(Michael Chapman) *plld hrd and prom: chsd wnr 4f out: rdn over 1f out: styd on same pce: lost 2nd wl ins fnl f* **50/1**

140 **4** *8* **Ahlawy (IRE)**[17] 1879 8-9-5 78 ....(bt) JamesDoyle 3 54
(Frank Sheridan) *sn pushed along to chse ldrs: rdn over 4f out: wknd over 2f out* **11/2**

6220 **5** *1* **Plush**[27] 1586 8-8-7 60 .... ChrisCatlin 8 40
(Shaun Lycett) *dwlt: hld up: plld hrd: rdn over 3f out: nvr on terms* **11/1**

3352 **6** *6* **Layla's Dancer**[5] 2195 4-9-3 72 .... WilliamBuick 4 38
(Tony Carroll) *chsd wnr 6f: sn rdn: wknd wl over 1f out* **7/4**[1]

6- **7** *12* **Amazingreyce**[199] 7338 6-8-12 0 .... LiamKeniry 6 —
(Owen Brennan) *prom: rdn over 4f out: wknd over 2f out: t.o* **66/1**

2m 6.83s (-1.07) **Going Correction** +0.025s/f (Good) **7** Ran SP% **111.0**
Speed ratings (Par 101): **105,101,101,95,94 89,79**
toteswingers:1&2:£3.20, 2&3:£29.20, 1&3:£13.70 CSF £13.05 TOTE £2.40: £1.10, £2.50; EX 7.80 Trifecta £742.80 Part won. Pool: £1003.80 - 0.82 winning units..Uphold was claimed by Miss Gay Kelleway for £14000.
Owner Dr Marwan Koukash **Bred** Juddmonte Farms Ltd **Trained** Upper Lambourn, Berks
■ Stewards' Enquiry : Jamie Spencer caution: used whip with excessive force.

FOCUS
Very few ever got into this claimer and it resulted in a 1-2 for Jamie Osborne. The third is rated to last year's best but limits the form.

2360 LADBROKES.COM COPLOW MAIDEN STKS 1m 3f 183y
5:15 (5:17) (Class 5) 3-Y-0 **£2,266** (£674; £337; £168) **Stalls** Low

Form RPR

3-2 **1** **No Heretic**[9] 2097 3-9-3 0 .... JamieSpencer 5 88+
(Paul Cole) *mde all: rdn and hung lft fr over 1f out: styd on* **4/9**[1]

0-3 **2** *½* **Starlight Walk**[18] 1840 3-8-12 0 .... MartinDwyer 6 80
(Roger Charlton) *chsd wnr: rdn over 1f out: r.o* **7/2**[2]

03 **3** *4* **Tartan Jura**[37] 1389 3-9-3 0 .... GregFairley 7 78
(Mark Johnston) *chsd ldrs: rdn over 4f out: styd on same pce ins fnl f* **40/1**

2422 **4** *5* **Echos Of Motivator**[14] 1951 3-9-3 69 ....(p) DavidProbert 9 70
(Ronald Harris) *chsd ldrs: rdn over 2f out: wknd ins fnl f* **12/1**[3]

66 **5** *¾* **Ash Cloud (IRE)**[19] 1810 3-8-12 0 .... RichardKingscote 2 64
(Tom Dascombe) *hld up: hdwy over 2f out: wknd ins fnl f* **66/1**

6 *50* **Disco Dancing** 3-8-12 0 .... IanMongan 1 —
(Sir Henry Cecil) *s.i.s: a in rr: bhd fr 1/2-way: t.o* **40/1**

0 **7** *61* **Mir Hy (USA)**[26] 1620 3-9-3 0 .... ChrisCatlin 3 —
(Clive Brittain) *sn pushed along in rr: bhd fr 1/2-way: t.o* **100/1**

2m 33.59s (-0.31) **Going Correction** +0.025s/f (Good) **7** Ran SP% **106.5**
Speed ratings (Par 99): **102,101,99,95,95 61,21**
toteswingers:1&2:£1.10, 2&3:£4.20, 1&3:£4.20 CSF £1.75 TOTE £1.60: £1.10, £1.60; EX 2.50 Trifecta £16.10 Pool: £583.41 - 26.29 winning units..
Owner Mrs Fitri Hay **Bred** Belgrave Bloodstock Ltd **Trained** Whatcombe, Oxon

FOCUS
A maiden lacking strength in depth, but no shortage of drama. The form is a bit muddling and best rated around the fourth and fifth.
Disco Dancing Official explanation: jockey said filly ran green throughout
T/Plt: £189.30 to a £1 stake. Pool of £61,668.72 - 237.80 winning tickets. T/Qpdt: £36.80 to a £1 stake. Pool of £4,409.96 - 88.60 winning tickets. CR

[2112]THIRSK (L-H)
Monday, May 23

OFFICIAL GOING: Good (8.7)
Wind: Strong behind Weather: Cloudy and blustery with sunny periods

2361 BOOK NOW FOR LADIES DAY MAIDEN STKS 7f
6:30 (6:32) (Class 5) 3-Y-0+ **£2,914** (£867; £433; £216) **Stalls** Low

Form RPR

02 **1** **Orbit The Moon (IRE)**[13] 1971 3-8-13 0 ....(t) SeanLevey(3) 4 86
(Michael Dods) *mde all and sn clr: rdn over 2f out: kpt on strly* **15/2**

23- **2** *6* **Self Employed**[282] 5065 4-9-13 0 .... PaulHanagan 6 74
(Garry Woodward) *trckd ldrs: hdwy 3f out: rdn to chse wnr over 2f out: drvn over 1f out and no imp* **9/2**[3]

02 **3** *2 ¾* **Maxamillion Bounty**[23] 1693 3-9-2 0 .... TonyHamilton 5 63
(Michael Dods) *chsd wnr: rdn along over 3f out: drvn over 2f out and sn one pce* **5/1**

04 **4** *hd* **Muffin McLeay (IRE)**[16] 1910 3-9-2 0 .... LeeNewman 3 62
(David Barron) *chsd ldrs: rdn along over 3f out: drvn and kpt on same pce fr over 2f out* **4/1**[2]

5 *3 ½* **Fairy Mist (IRE)**[89] 4-9-13 0 .... PaddyAspell 10 57
(Brian Rothwell) *midfield hdwy 3f out: sn rdn and kpt on fnl 2f: nt rch ldrs* **150/1**

6 *1 ¾* **Langtoon Lass** 3-8-8 0 .... MichaelO'Connell(3) 1 43
(David Nicholls) *chsd ldrs on inner: rdn along 3f out: drvn and plugged on same pce fnl 2f* **16/1**

7 *2 ½* **Storm Blue (IRE)** 3-9-2 0 .... MickyFenton 14 41
(Ollie Pears) *dwlt and swtchd lft s: in rr tl sme hdwy over 2f out: nvr nr ldrs* **33/1**

4- **8** *1 ¼* **Spes Nostra**[289] 4821 3-9-2 0 .... SilvestreDeSousa 7 38
(David Barron) *chsd ldrs: pushed along 1/2-way: rdn 3f out and sn wknd* **11/4**[1]

4 **9** *1* **Wicked Streak (IRE)**[20] 1795 6-9-13 0 .... PJMcDonald 9 39
(Micky Hammond) *a towards rr* **40/1**

5 **10** *½* **Brio**[13] 1984 3-9-2 0 .... TadhgO'Shea 8 34
(Alan McCabe) *in tch: rdn along 3f out: edgd lft over 2f out and sn wknd* **16/1**

0 **11** *7* **Tootie Flutie**[19] 1812 3-8-11 0 .... RussKennemore 13 —
(Richard Whitaker) *dwlt: a in rr* **150/1**

0 **12** *¾* **Eastward Ho**[8] 2125 3-8-13 0 .... BillyCray(3) 12 —
(Jason Ward) *in tch: rdn along 1/2-way: sn wknd* **150/1**

13 *2* **Munaa's Dream** 3-8-11 0 .... AndrewElliott 11 —
(Mrs K Burke) [illegible] **[illegible]**

14 *4* **Jordans Express** 3-8-9 0 .... PNolan(7) 2 —
(Noel Wilson) *v.s.a: a bhd* **100/1**

1m 28.83s (1.63) **Going Correction** +0.325s/f (Good)
WFA 3 from 4yo+ 11lb **14** Ran SP% **118.2**
Speed ratings (Par 103): **103,96,93,92,88 86,83,82,81,80 72,71,69,65**
toteswingers:1&2:£9.10, 2&3:£3.80, 1&3:£5.40 CSF £39.40 TOTE £9.90: £2.20, £1.90, £2.20; EX 39.60.
Owner Andrew Tinkler **Bred** Michael Collins **Trained** Denton, Co Durham

FOCUS
A very strong tail wind in the home straight and after heavy showers the ground was reckoned 'lovely, good ground'. A weak maiden with none of the runners yet to have achieved an official rating and very few seriously involved from halfway. The form is taken at face value with the runner-up setting the level.

2362 BOOK TICKETS @ THIRSKRACECOURSE.NET (S) STKS 6f
7:00 (7:01) (Class 5) 2-Y-0 **£2,914** (£867; £433; £216) **Stalls** High

Form RPR

02 **1** **Arcticality (IRE)**[14] 1939 2-8-7 0 .... PaulHanagan 5 57+
(Richard Fahey) *trckd ldng pair: swtchd lft 1 1/2f out and sn rdn: drvn to chal and edgd rt wl ins fnl f: led fnl 50yds* **11/8**[1]

0 **2** *¾* **Pint Size**[16] 1890 2-8-9 0 .... MichaelO'Connell(3) 10 60
(David Nicholls) *chsd ldr: led wl over 2f out: rdn and hung lft 1 1/2f out: drvn and edgd rt 1f out: hung lft wl ins fnl f: hdd and no ex last 50yds* **7/1**[3]

40 **3** *½* **Mad For Fun (IRE)**[13] 1966 2-8-7 0 .... MickyFenton 8 53
(Paul Midgley) *chsd ldrs: rdn along over 2f out: drvn over 1f out: kpt on wl ins fnl f: tk 3rd nr line* **66/1**

44 **4** *1* **Indian Lizzy**[5] 2194 2-8-7 0 .... SilvestreDeSousa 6 52
(Paul Cole) *chsd ldrs: rdn along and hdwy whn hmpd 1 1/2f out: wandered after: drvn and styng on ins fnl f: hmpd and snatched up ins fnl 100yds: nt rcvr and lost 3rd nr line* **4/1**[2]

653 **5** *hd* **Manderston**[8] 2121 2-8-5 0 .... DarylByrne(7) 7 55
(Mark Johnston) *led: pushed along 1/2-way: hdd wl over 2f out: rdn whn n.m.r and edgd rt 1 1/2f out: drvn and keeping on whn n.m.r ins fnl f: one pce after* **8/1**

4 **6** *1 ½* **Jaci Uzzi (IRE)**[20] 1786 2-8-7 0 .... CathyGannon 2 45
(David Evans) *chsd ldrs: rdn along wl over 2f out: drvn wl over 1f out: kpt on same pce* **12/1**

452 **7** *¾* **Ciara Boo (IRE)**[35] 1435 2-8-7 0 .... AndrewMullen 4 43
(David Evans) *in tch: rdn along wl over 2f out: sn drvn and no hdwy* **7/1**[3]

8 *25* **Mystake (IRE)** 2-8-5 0 .... PNolan(7) 1 —
(David Nicholls) *s.i.s: a outpcd and bhd* **25/1**

9 *dist* **Carrieann's Boy** 2-8-12 0................(v[1]) TomEaves 3 —
(Nigel Tinkler) *v.s.a and rel to r: wl t.o thrght* **80/1**

1m 14.11s (1.41) **Going Correction** -0.15s/f (Firm) **9** Ran SP% **112.5**
Speed ratings (Par 93): **84,83,82,81,80 78,77,44,—**
toteswingers:1&2:£2.80, 2&3:£45.10, 1&3: not won. CSF £11.12 TOTE £2.60: £1.50, £2.70, £21.00; EX 15.40.
Owner Percy Green Racing 3 **Bred** Andrew Farnan **Trained** Musley Bank, N Yorks

FOCUS
A run-of-the-mill juvenile seller and the leaders ducked and dived in the final 2f with a strong wind up their tails. The winner is rated to previous form.

NOTEBOOK
Articality(IRE), runner-up behind a smart subsequent winner in a maiden auction event at Redcar, went one better but she made very hard work of it in the conditions. She edged right in the closing stages slamming the door on the eventual fourth. This looks her grade and connections put their hand in their pocket to retain her at the auction. (op 11-10)
Pint Size, who cost just £800, had beaten just one in maiden company on his debut. He led under the stands' side rail but drifted left away from it and was worn down near the line. As his name suggests he lacks size but is capable of going one better at this level. (op 8-1)
Mad For Fun(IRE), well beaten on her first two starts, finished with quite a rattle hard against the stands' side rail. It remains to be seen if this flatters her. (op 100-1)
Indian Lizzy, who has shown ability in two non-sellers, seemed to get unbalanced and was sticking on when left with nowhere to go in the closing stages. (op 11-2)
Manderston raced upsides on the outer but he wandered and faded in the final furlong.

2363 WEATHERBYS BANK H'CAP 6f
7:30 (7:31) (Class 4) (0-85,83) 3-Y-O **£4,209** (£1,252; £625; £312) **Stalls** High

Form RPR
4250 **1** **Dream Catcher (FR)**[4] 2216 3-8-13 **75**................ JoeFanning 11 79
(David Nicholls) *trckd ldrs on stands' rail: effrt and nt clr run over 1f out: sn swtchd lft and rdn to chal ent fnl f: kpt on to ld last 100yds* **15/2**
331- **2** *hd* **Fieldgunner Kirkup (GER)**[217] 6980 3-9-3 **79**......... GrahamGibbons 6 82
(David Barron) *cl up on inner: effrt to chal over 2f out: sn rdn and ev ch: drvn ins fnl f and edgd lft: kpt on wl towards fin* **10/3**[1]
3-00 **3** *nk* **Captain Kolo (IRE)**[10] 2074 3-8-12 **74**................ KellyHarrison 10 76
(Tim Easterby) *cl up: led 2f out and sn rdn: drvn and edgd rt ent fnl f: hdd and no ex last 100yds* **9/1**
-141 **4** *4 ½* **Another Wise Kid (IRE)**[21] 1745 3-9-1 **77**.............. MickyFenton 4 65+
(Paul Midgley) *in tch: hdwy to chse ldrs 2f out: sn rdn and ch over 1f out: drvn and one pce appr fnl f* **10/1**
-214 **5** *1 ¼* **Oneladyowner**[18] 1825 3-9-2 **78**................ PaulMulrennan 8 62
(David Brown) *prom: cl up 1/2-way: rdn and ev ch over 2f out: sn drvn and wknd over 1f out* **7/2**[2]
21-0 **6** *4 ½* **Black Annis Bower**[8] 2122 3-8-4 **73**.............. DavidSimmonson(7) 3 42+
(Michael Easterby) *prom on outer: rdn along 2f out: grad wknd* **33/1**
312- **7** *½* **Breezolini**[227] 6719 3-8-12 **77**................ AmyRyan(3) 7 45
(Richard Whitaker) *a towards rr* **33/1**
1-03 **8** *¾* **Indieslad**[10] 2043 3-9-2 **78**................ SilvestreDeSousa 1 43+
(Ann Duffield) *wnt lft s: in tch on wd outside: rdn along 1/2-way: drvn wl over 2f out and sn btn* **7/1**[3]
5-20 **9** *1* **Homeboy (IRE)**[39] 1335 3-8-7 **69**................ TadhgO'Shea 2 31
(Marcus Tregoning) *a towards rr* **11/1**
446- **10** *¾* **Lady Royale**[257] 5850 3-9-4 **80**................(p) TomEaves 9 40
(Geoffrey Oldroyd) *a in rr* **40/1**
1111 **11** *nk* **Take Your Partner**[42] 1275 3-9-7 **83**................(b) PhillipMakin 5 42
(Kevin Ryan) *led: rdn along and hdd 2f out: wknd qckly* **15/2**

1m 11.65s (-1.05) **Going Correction** -0.15s/f (Firm) **11** Ran SP% **117.1**
Speed ratings (Par 101): **101,100,100,94,92 86,86,85,83,82 82**
toteswingers:1&2:£4.30, 2&3:£4.20, 1&3:£12.40 CSF £32.09 CT £236.88 TOTE £10.50: £2.60, £2.20, £2.60; EX 40.30.
Owner Dr Marwan Koukash **Bred** Daniel Cherdo **Trained** Sessay, N Yorks

FOCUS
A competitive 3-y-o sprint handicap but a modest first prize. Plenty were almost in a line soon after halfway but in the end the first three came clear.The placed horses are rated improvers on their juvenile form.
Oneladyowner Official explanation: jockey said colt was unsuited by the good ground

2364 WEATHERBYS BLOODSTOCK INSURANCE H'CAP 1m 4f
8:00 (8:04) (Class 4) (0-80,80) 4-Y-0+ **£4,209** (£1,252; £625; £312) **Stalls** Low

Form RPR
232 **1** **War Poet**[16] 1910 4-9-1 **74**................ DanielTudhope 3 86+
(David O'Meara) *hld up in tch: smooth hdwy over 3f out: led wl over 1f out and sn clr: comf* **11/4**[1]
466- **2** *4 ½* **Sirgarfieldsobers (IRE)**[346] 2938 5-9-2 **80**................ NeilFarley(5) 1 82
(Declan Carroll) *t.k.h: chsd ldng pair: hdwy to ld 7f out: clr 5f out: rdn along 3f out: hdd wl over 1f out: sn drvn and kpt on same pce* **9/2**[3]
0-00 **3** *¾* **Green Lightning (IRE)**[16] 1908 4-9-2 **75**................(b) JoeFanning 2 76
(Mark Johnston) *trckd ldrs: hdwy to chse ldr over 3f out: rdn to chal 2f out: sn drvn: put hd in pair and kpt on same pce* **8/1**
24-5 **4** *¾* **Puy D'Arnac (FR)**[54] 1039 8-8-10 **69**................ PJMcDonald 7 69
(George Moore) *hld up in tch: hdwy over 3f out: rdn to chse ldrs wl over 1f out: drvn and one pce ins fnl f* **12/1**
03-0 **5** *2 ½* **Daaweitza**[12] 2006 8-8-13 **77**................ DaleSwift(5) 4 73
(Brian Ellison) *hld up in tch: hdwy over 3f out: rdn over 2f out: drvn wl over 1f out and no imp* **9/1**
25-4 **6** *2 ¼* **Beat The Shower**[16] 1908 5-8-10 **69**................ MickyFenton 6 61
(Peter Niven) *hld up in tch: effrt and sme hdwy 3f out: rdn along 2f out: n.d* **3/1**[2]
26-5 **7** *9* **Pertemps Networks**[54] 1036 7-9-0 **73**................ GrahamGibbons 5 51
(Michael Easterby) *led: hdd over 7f out: rdn along over 4f out: sn wknd* **13/2**

2m 39.7s (3.50) **Going Correction** +0.325s/f (Good) **7** Ran SP% **112.0**
Speed ratings (Par 105): **101,98,97,97,95 93,87**
CSF £14.74 CT £84.73 TOTE £2.60: £1.10, £6.10; EX 17.00.
Owner Mike Kirby & Andrew Crowther **Bred** Darley **Trained** Nawton, N Yorks

FOCUS
A competitive stayers' handicap run at a sound pace produced a clearcut unexposed winner of some potential. The overall form is not strong for the grade.
Beat The Shower Official explanation: jockey said gelding hung left in straight

2365 WELCOMETOHERRIOTCOUNTRY.COM FILLIES' H'CAP 5f
8:30 (8:31) (Class 5) (0-70,70) 3-Y-0+ **£2,914** (£867; £433; £216) **Stalls** High

Form RPR
321- **1** **Beauty Pageant (IRE)**[340] 3125 4-9-5 **63**................ RichardMullen 10 77
(Ed McMahon) *mde all: rdn wl over 1f out: drvn and edgd lft ins fnl f: kpt on wl towards fin* **6/5**[1]
222- **2** *¾* **Crystallus (IRE)**[145] 7997 3-8-13 **65**................ PaulMulrennan 11 73
(Ann Duffield) *trckd ldrs on inner: hdwy wl over 1f out: rdn to chse wnr ins fnl f: sn ev ch tl nt qckn towards fin* **17/2**
24-5 **3** *4 ½* **Crimson Cloud**[23] 1697 3-9-4 **70**................ TonyHamilton 2 62+
(Richard Fahey) *prom: effrt to chal 1/2-way: sn rdn and ev ch tl drvn and wknd ins fnl f* **7/1**[3]
2-04 **4** *½* **Oondiri (IRE)**[28] 1555 4-9-3 **61**................(be) TomEaves 8 54
(Tim Easterby) *s.i.s and in rr: hdwy 2f out: rdn to chse ldrs wl over 1f out: sn no imp* **7/1**[3]
0446 **5** *½* **Gorgeous Goblin (IRE)**[9] 2094 4-8-12 **56** oh1......(tp) GrahamGibbons 6 47
(David C Griffiths) *t.k.h: trckd ldrs: pushed along over 2f out: rdn wl over 1f out and sn one pce* **14/1**
01-1 **6** *2* **Foreign Rhythm (IRE)**[10] 2062 6-9-2 **67**................ ShaneBKelly(7) 7 51+
(Ron Barr) *chsd ldrs on outer: rdn along 2f out: grad wknd* **6/1**[2]
363 **7** *nk* **Poppy's Rocket (IRE)**[13] 1967 3-8-4 **56**................ KellyHarrison 5 36
(Marjorie Fife) *prom: rdn along 1/2-way: sn wknd* **28/1**
0124 **8** *½* **Mini Bon Bon**[77] 788 3-8-5 **57**................ SilvestreDeSousa 1 35
(David O'Meara) *a in rr* **14/1**

58.80 secs (-0.80) **Going Correction** -0.15s/f (Firm)
WFA 3 from 4yo+ 8lb **8** Ran SP% **112.0**
Speed ratings (Par 100): **100,98,91,90,90 86,86,85**
toteswingers:1&2:£4.00, 2&3:£9.50, 1&3:£1.70 CSF £11.63 CT £50.12 TOTE £2.90: £2.10, £1.10, £3.60; EX 12.70.
Owner J C Fretwell **Bred** Mesnil, Mount Coote, New England Stud **Trained** Lichfield, Staffs

FOCUS
A modest 56-67 fillies' sprint handicap but the form could rate a little higher.

2366 BOOK THE CHAMPAGNE & SEAFOOD PACKAGE H'CAP 1m
9:00 (9:00) (Class 5) (0-75,75) 4-Y-0+ **£2,914** (£867; £433; £216) **Stalls** Low

Form RPR
26-3 **1** **Quite Sparky**[16] 1910 4-9-4 **72**................ SilvestreDeSousa 1 87
(David O'Meara) *trckd ldrs: hdwy to chse ldr over 3f out: swtchd rt and rdn over 1f out: chal ent fnl f: drvn to ld last 100yds: sn carried rt: kpt on* **4/1**[1]
0-01 **2** *hd* **Vito Volterra (IRE)**[20] 1800 4-9-3 **74**................ SeanLevey(3) 3 88
(Michael Smith) *led: rdn clr bef 1/2-way: drvn wl over 1f out: jnd and rdr dropped whip ent fnl f: sn hung rt: hdd and no ex last 100yds* **7/1**
3336 **3** *2 ½* **Elijah Pepper (USA)**[13] 1970 6-9-2 **75**................ LMcNiff(5) 4 83
(David Barron) *dwlt: sn in tch: hdwy on inner 4f out: rdn to chse ldrs 2f out: drvn and kpt on same pce ins fnl f* **5/1**[3]
6411 **4** *2 ¾* **Fazza**[16] 1909 4-9-0 **68**................ TonyHamilton 5 70
(Edwin Tuer) *chsd ldrs: effrt 3f out and sn rdn: drvn wl over 1f out and kpt on same pce* **9/2**[2]
00-0 **5** *8* **Come And Go (UAE)**[44] 1244 5-9-3 **71**................ TomEaves 2 55
(Ian McInnes) *hld up in tch: hdwy over 3f out: rdn to chse ldrs over 2f out: drvn over 1f out: sn wknd* **10/1**
500- **6** *hd* **Christmas Light**[219] 6917 4-9-0 **68**................ DanielTudhope 13 51+
(David O'Meara) *towards rr: effrt over 2f out: sme late hdwy* **14/1**
506/ **7** *2 ½* **Miss Beat (IRE)**[681] 3870 5-9-2 **75**................ NeilFarley(5) 12 52
(Declan Carroll) *swtchd lft s and hld up: nvr a factor* **25/1**
8 *1* **Akinndi (IRE)**[79] 6953 4-9-5 **73**................ BarryMcHugh 11 48
(Evan Williams) *a towards rr* **14/1**
-406 **9** *2* **Yahrab (IRE)**[21] 1746 6-9-7 **75**................(b) DavidNolan 8 45
(Declan Carroll) *midfield: rdn along over 3f out: sn wknd* **16/1**
0-05 **10** *4 ½* **Rock 'N' Royal**[21] 1748 4-8-13 **67**................ PJMcDonald 10 27
(Richard Fahey) *in tch: effrt 3f out: sn rdn and wknd over 2f out* **7/1**
05-0 **11** *21* **Red Scintilla**[16] 1909 4-9-0 **68**................ PaulMulrennan 7 —
(Nigel Tinkler) *chsd ldr: rdn along over 3f out: sn drvn and wknd over 2f out* **40/1**

1m 41.94s (1.84) **Going Correction** +0.325s/f (Good) **11** Ran SP% **114.4**
Speed ratings (Par 103): **103,102,100,97,89 89,86,85,83,79 58**
toteswingers:1&2:£3.00, 2&3:£7.10, 1&3:£8.40 CSF £31.02 CT £127.62 TOTE £4.60: £1.60, £2.50, £1.90; EX 38.60.
Owner A Crowther **Bred** Bigwigs Bloodstock **Trained** Nawton, N Yorks
■ Stewards' Enquiry : Sean Levey two-day ban: careless riding (Jun 6-7)

FOCUS
A modest 67-75 handicap run at a strong pace thanks to the front-running runner-up. The placed horses offer the best guide to the form.
T/Plt: £40.00 to a £1 stake. Pool of £65,649.93 - 1,196.34 winning tickets. T/Qpdt: £10.80 to a £1 stake. Pool of £4,909.52 335.27 winning tickets JR

2153 WINDSOR (R-H)
Monday, May 23

OFFICIAL GOING: Good to firm (8.8)
Stands' rail dolled out 12yds at 6f down to 7y at winning post. Top bend dolled out 7yds which added 26yds to races of 1m and over.
Wind: Strong, behind Weather: Overcast becoming fine

2367 E B F PETER PEGG 80TH BIRTHDAY NOVICE STKS 5f 10y
6:10 (6:10) (Class 5) 2-Y-O **£3,302** (£736; £736; £245) **Stalls** Low

Form RPR
6 **1** **Charles The Great (IRE)**[16] 1886 2-9-0 0................ JimmyFortune 4 88
(Andrew Balding) *led after 1f: mde most after: rdn and def advantage over 1f out: styd on wl* **12/1**
21 **2** *1 ½* **Lord Ofthe Shadows (IRE)**[42] 1268 2-9-5 0................ RichardHughes 6 88
(Richard Hannon) *s.i.s: pressed wnr after 1f: rdn and nt qckn wl over 1f out: hld after* **7/2**[2]
1 **2** *dht* **Boomerang Bob (IRE)**[21] 1757 2-9-5 0................ SebSanders 5 88
(J W Hills) *trckd ldrs: rdn and effrt wl over 1f out: kpt on but no imp on wnr ins fnl f* **9/1**[3]
01 **4** *½* **Tioman Legend**[17] 1863 2-9-5 0................ SteveDrowne 3 86
(Roger Charlton) *hld up last: swtchd out wd and effrt 1/2-way: rdn and nt qckn over 1f out: one pce after* **11/10**[1]
51 **5** *6* **Starfly (IRE)**[7] 2153 2-9-0 0................ RyanMoore 1 60
(Jeremy Noseda) *led 1f: unable to hold pl against rail: rdn 2f out: wknd over 1f out* **7/2**[2]
415 **6** *½* **The Dancing Lord**[40] 1316 2-8-13 0................ KierenFox(3) 2 60
(Bill Turner) *w ldr 1f: lost pl qckly and sn struggling in rr* **40/1**

58.69 secs (-1.61) **Going Correction** -0.25s/f (Firm) 2y crse rec **6** Ran SP% **112.2**
Speed ratings (Par 93): **102,99,99,98,89 88**
PL: Boomerang Bob £2.20 Lord Ofthe Shadows £1.20 EX: Charles The Great/BB £53.60 C/L £32.60 CSF: C/B £52.55 C/L £26.42. toteswingers:1&BB:£16.00, BB&L:£9.40, 1&L:£11.80 TOTE £14.90: £5.80.

Owner Kennet Valley Thoroughbreds V **Bred** Michael Woodlock & Seamus Kennedy **Trained** Kingsclere, Hants

FOCUS

The going was good to firm. A useful novice stakes event, involving four last-time-out winners. It was fast and furious and there was a surprise result as it went to the only maiden in the field. The time was 0.31 seconds faster than standard and recent race averages help determine the level.

NOTEBOOK

Charles The Great(IRE) was beaten over 8l at 33-1 in an Ascot maiden on debut, but he was backed at biggish prices and put in a gritty display under a prominent ride to win on this much improved second run. A 33,000gns half-brother to a 1m 2-y-o winner, he should go on to better things and is bred to stay quite a bit further than this in time. (op 20-1)

Lord Ofthe Shadows(IRE) was an easy front-running odds-on winner in an ordinary C&D maiden on his second start. He faced some classy opponents here but put in a solid effort under a positive ride. This son of Kyllachy is from the family of Inchinor and Inchmurrin and should continue to go the right way. Official explanation: jockey said, regarding riding, that he stopped riding shortly before line as he was concerned he would have struck the heels of the winner. (op 3-1 tchd 5-2)

Boomerang Bob(IRE) made a promising start to his career when a comfortable Kempton AW maiden winner. He had a bit to find on a line through the runner-up in that race, but ran creditably and has improved again switched to turf. A £30,000 half-brother to a 7f Listed winner in France, he could continue to progress and should stay an extra furlong or two this season. (op 3-1 tchd 5-2)

Tioman Legend left his debut form well behind when powering clear on fast turf at Lingfield last time. He set the standard and was a solid favourite, but it was slightly disappointing that he couldn't click into gear out wide. (op 6-4 tchd 13-8)

Starfly(IRE) was a much improved trailblazing win in a C&D fillies' event last week, but she couldn't adopt a front-running role here and was left behind by the front four. (op 3-1)

The Dancing Lord has been disappointing in both runs since his easy Folkestone maiden win last month. (tchd 33-1)

2368 SPORTINGBET.COM H'CAP — 1m 67y

6:40 (6:41) (Class 5) (0-75,75) 3-Y-O — **£2,266** (£674; £337; £168) **Stalls** Low

Form — RPR

30-4 **1** **Royal Reverie**[17] 1869 3-9-1 **69** ... AdamKirby 11 — 78+
(Walter Swinburn) *chsd ldrs in 7th: shkn up and prog over 3f out: rdn to chal over 1f out: narrow ld fnl f: hld on wl* **14/1**

24-5 **2** *hd* **Puttingonthestyle (IRE)**[14] 1947 3-9-4 **72** ... RichardHughes 9 — 80+
(Richard Hannon) *trckd ldr: led over 2f out gng strly: rdn and pressed over 1f out: narrowly hdd fnl f: jst hld nr fin* **9/4**[1]

2-26 **3** *3 ½* **Woop Woop (IRE)**[14] 1950 3-8-13 **70** ... JohnFahy(3) 6 — 70
(Stef Higgins) *trckd ldng trio: plld out and effrt 2f out: kpt on same pce fr over 1f out* **16/1**

006- **4** *1* **Swaninstockwell (IRE)**[192] 7417 3-8-2 **61** oh3 ... JemmaMarshall(5) 4 — 59+
(Pat Phelan) *hld up in 8th: effrt on outer 3f out: prog to take 4th 1f out: nt pce to threaten after* **66/1**

0-00 **5** *2 ½* **Evergreen Forest (IRE)**[9] 2103 3-8-12 **66** ... JimmyFortune 13 — 58
(Alastair Lidderdale) *hld up in 9th: effrt 3f out: pushed along and sme prog fnl 2f: nvr nr ldrs* **40/1**

-310 **6** *1 ½* **Cheylesmore (IRE)**[13] 1983 3-9-2 **70** ... (t) WilliamCarson 3 — 58
(Stuart Williams) *taken down early: stdd s: hld up last: stl only 10th 2f out: pushed along and sme prog on outer over 1f out: nvr nr ldrs* **40/1**

05-5 **7** *2 ¼* **Promenadia**[28] 1565 3-9-2 **70** ... SteveDrowne 1 — 53
(Roger Charlton) *led at decent pce to over 2f out: steadily wknd* **8/1**[3]

2144 **8** *hd* **Obsession (IRE)**[10] 2064 3-9-7 **75** ... (v) RyanMoore 8 — 57
(Jeremy Noseda) *trckd ldrs in 6th: jst pushed along fr over 2f out and steadily lost grnd* **5/2**[2]

00-0 **9** *4* **Control Chief**[37] 1392 3-8-9 **63** ... JimCrowley 10 — 36
(Ralph Beckett) *trckd ldng pair to 3f out: sn wknd* **10/1**

56-0 **10** *nk* **Paperetto**[18] 1836 3-8-13 **67** ... StevieDonohoe 12 — 39
(Robert Mills) *a in last pair: struggling 3f out: sn btn* **11/1**

30-0 **11** *¾* **Red Mercury (IRE)**[14] 1947 3-9-0 **68** ... FergusSweeney 7 — 38
(Alan King) *chsd ldrs in 5th: lost pl over 2f out: sn wknd* **16/1**

1m 42.82s (-1.88) **Going Correction** -0.25s/f (Firm) **11** Ran SP% **112.7**
Speed ratings (Par 99): **99,98,95,94,91 90,88,87,83,83 82**
toteswingers:1&2:£3.90, 2&3:£4.70, 1&3:£29.80 CSF £41.57 CT £468.22 TOTE £16.70: £2.50, £1.20, £3.30; EX 50.70 Trifecta £924.80 Pool: £1874.78 - 1.50 winning units..
Owner P W Harris **Bred** Pendley Farm **Trained** Aldbury, Herts

FOCUS

A fair handicap for 3-y-os. It was run at a decent pace and they finished quite strung out. Storm Runner ducked under the stalls and was withdrawn. The race is rated around the third and fourth.

2369 COBRA PREMIUM BEER H'CAP — 6f

7:10 (7:10) (Class 4) (0-80,79) 4-Y-O+ — **£3,561** (£1,059; £529; £264) **Stalls** Low

Form — RPR

505- **1** **Soap Wars**[217] 6987 6-9-7 **79** ... GeorgeBaker 7 — 94
(Hugo Palmer) *mde all: clr and gng strly over 1f out: shkn up fnl f: unchal* **12/1**

4230 **2** *3* **Stevie Gee (IRE)**[9] 2095 7-8-10 **73** ... (b) RyanClark(5) 15 — 78
(Ian Williams) *hld up wl in rr: stdy prog on outer fr 1/2-way: rdn to chse wnr jst over 1f out: kpt on but no imp* **12/1**

1224 **3** *1* **Ivory Silk**[21] 1762 6-9-7 **79** ... AdamKirby 9 — 81
(Jeremy Gask) *sn last: taken to wd outside 1/2-way: rdn and prog over 2f out: kpt on to take 3rd fnl f: no imp* **6/1**[2]

056- **4** *nse* **Macdillon**[217] 6987 5-9-2 **74** ... FergusSweeney 14 — 76
(Stuart Kittow) *wl in tch in midfield: rdn and prog to dispute 2nd briefly over 1f out: one pce after* **18/1**

26-0 **5** *¾* **Quasi Congaree (GER)**[9] 2095 5-9-4 **76** ... (t) RichardHughes 5 — 76
(Ian Wood) *chsd ldrs: rdn to dispute 2nd briefly over 1f out: one pce after* **25/1**

/621 **6** *nk* **Mymumsaysimthebest**[18] 1838 6-9-3 **75** ... RyanMoore 1 — 74+
(Gary Moore) *tried to trck ldrs on inner but sn wl in rr: effrt over 2f out: kpt on but nvr gng pce to threaten* **13/8**[1]

0320 **7** *hd* **Desert Strike**[3] 2250 5-8-8 **73** ... (p) NoraLooby(7) 2 — 71
(Alan McCabe) *taken down early: slihtly awkward s: t.k.h in midfield: nudged along and no imp on ldrs over 1f out* **11/1**[3]

36-0 **8** *hd* **Slugger O'Toole**[16] 1898 6-9-1 **73** ... (t) WilliamCarson 12 — 70
(Stuart Williams) *taken down early: wl in rr: u.p 1/2-way: sme prog on outer wl over 1f out: sn no hdwy* **33/1**

21-0 **9** *1 ½* **Sarah's Art (IRE)**[119] 285 8-9-1 **76** ... (t) JohnFahy(3) 6 — 69
(Stef Higgins) *chsd ldrs: rdn and effrt over 2f out: no prog over 1f out: fdd* **25/1**

1631 **10** *nk* **Silver Wind**[9] 2095 6-9-1 **78** ... (b) KieranO'Neill(5) 3 — 70
(Alan McCabe) *prom early but nt pce to hold pl on inner after 2f: no prog fnl 2f* **6/1**[2]

-540 **11** *2 ¾* **Go Nani Go**[23] 1698 5-9-0 **77** ... HarryBentley(5) 4 — 60
(Ed de Giles) *chsd wnr to over 1f out: wknd qckly* **16/1**

000- **12** *4* **Sunnandaeg**[251] 6048 4-9-1 **73** ... SteveDrowne 10 — 43
(Jeremy Gask) *chsd ldrs 4f: sn wknd* **16/1**

00-0 **13** *2 ½* **Tubby Isaacs**[6] 2179 7-9-1 **73** ... NeilCallan 11 — 35
(Dean Ivory) *dwlt: a in rr: struggling 2f out: sn wknd* **25/1**

1m 10.69s (-2.31) **Going Correction** -0.25s/f (Firm) **13** Ran SP% **121.9**
Speed ratings (Par 105): **105,101,99,99,98 98,97,97,95,95 91,86,82**
CSF £144.60 CT £993.63 TOTE £15.40: £5.20, £3.70, £1.60; EX 143.10 Trifecta £898.40 Part won. Pool of £1214.13 - 0.50 winning units. Pool of £607.06 winning units..
Owner Orr-Ewing, Malins & Barby **Bred** Mrs T Brudenell **Trained** Newmarket, Suffolk

FOCUS

A fair sprint handicap in which there was an impressive all-the-way winner. The placed horses to recent form help to set the standard.

2370 SPORTINGBET.COM STKS (REGISTERED AS THE LEISURE STAKES) (LISTED RACE) — 6f

7:40 (7:40) (Class 1) 3-Y-O+

£17,031 (£6,456; £3,231; £1,611; £807; £405) **Stalls** Low

Form — RPR

4-01 **1** **Bated Breath**[16] 1891 4-9-0 108 ... SteveDrowne 6 — 114+
(Roger Charlton) *trckd ldr over 3f out: led wl over 1f out but jnd: rdn and drew clr ins fnl f: readily* **15/8**[1]

0-05 **2** *1 ¾* **Triple Aspect (IRE)**[12] 2005 5-9-0 107 ... RyanMoore 8 — 108
(William Haggas) *chsd ldrs: rdn over 2f out: prog to chal and w wnr wl over 1f out: outpcd ins fnl f* **7/2**[2]

5-24 **3** *2* **Libranno**[26] 1602 3-8-5 109 ... ChrisCatlin 9 — 100
(Richard Hannon) *led to wl over 1f out: sn outpcd* **5/1**[3]

330/ **4** *1* **Monsieur Chevalier (IRE)**[596] 6522 4-9-0 109 ... RichardHughes 1 — 98+
(Richard Hannon) *stdd s: hld up last: stl there and no ch but gng strly 2f out: rn into trble over 1f out: r.o fnl 150yds: nvr remotely nr ldrs* **14/1**

-152 **5** *½* **Horseradish**[10] 2075 4-9-0 102 ... HayleyTurner 4 — 97
(Michael Bell) *trckd ldrs: rdn 2f out: nt qckn and no imp over 1f out: fdd* **7/2**[2]

-105 **6** *½* **Son Of The Cat (USA)**[9] 2099 5-9-0 91 ... (bt[1]) NeilCallan 10 — 95
(Brian Gubby) *t.k.h: hld up in tch: rdn 2f out: sn outpcd* **100/1**

0203 **7** *hd* **Monsieur Joe (IRE)**[17] 1848 4-9-0 109 ... (v) EddieAhern 5 — 95
(Walter Swinburn) *hld up in 7th: shkn up over 2f out: no real prog* **25/1**

5010 **8** *2 ¼* **Evens And Odds (IRE)**[23] 1687 7-9-0 104 ... AdrianNicholls 7 — 87
(David Nicholls) *chsd ldr over 2f: sn lost pl and u.p: n.d fnl 2f* **16/1**

69.89 secs (-3.11) **Going Correction** -0.25s/f (Firm) course record
WFA 3 from 4yo+ 9lb **8** Ran SP% **113.3**
Speed ratings (Par 111): **110,107,105,103,103 102,102,99**
CSF £8.38 TOTE £3.00: £1.10, £1.80, £2.20; EX 10.40 Trifecta £41.20 Pool: £3755.02 - 67.30 winning units..
Owner K Abdulla **Bred** Juddmonte Farms Ltd **Trained** Beckhampton, Wilts

FOCUS

A hot Listed race, with seven of the runners rated between 102 and 109. The course record time was 0.61 seconds faster than standard with the runner-up rated to recent York form setting the level, although it could rate higher.

NOTEBOOK

Bated Breath was an impressive winner on his first three starts last year. He had suffered a couple of hard-luck stories since then but got back on track in a Haydock conditions event last time and followed up in decent style in this Listed contest. Still very lightly raced, he has scope for further improvement and should develop into a Group-class sprinter. He holds entries in the Group 1 Golden Jubilee and July Cup. (op 2-1 tchd 9-4 and 7-4 in places)

Triple Aspect(IRE) did not get the best of runs when fifth behind Delegator in the Duke of York last time. He was pushed along some way out here but gave it a decent shot in a bid for a repeat success in this race. (tchd 4-1 in places)

Libranno, unpenalised for the first time this year, ran respectably under a forcing ride but could not hang in there. His form has possibly levelled off but he was a dual Group 2 winner in the July and Richmond Stakes last summer. (op 9-2 tchd 11-2 in places)

Monsieur Chevalier(IRE) was sidelined by a pelvic injury last year. He was returning from 596 days off, and ran into some trouble, but shaped with plenty of promise and rates better than the finishing position. This was an eye-catching comeback by a horse who was a smart six-time winner as a juvenile and ended that campaign by finishing on the heels of older sprinters in the Abbaye. He should come on for this run and is entered for the big sprints at Royal Ascot and the July Cup. Official explanation: jockey said colt was denied a clear run (op 12-1)

Horseradish continued his relentless progression when just held off a mark of 100 [illegible] it in a hot York handicap last time. He did not look out of place with his sights raised here but faded out of it in the closing stages. (op 4-1)

Son Of The Cat(USA) was very keen and ultimately well held in first-time blinkers, but he deserves some credit because he had 11lb or more to find with all of his rivals on official figures. Official explanation: jockey said gelding ran too free

Monsieur Joe(IRE) has done all of his winning at 5f and his usual finishing burst was missing on this step back up to 6f. (op 28-1)

2371 COBRA ZERO% MEDIAN AUCTION MAIDEN STKS — 1m 2f 7y

8:10 (8:12) (Class 5) 3-Y-O — **£2,266** (£674; £337; £168) **Stalls** High

Form — RPR

44- **1** **Kinyras (IRE)**[238] 6414 3-9-3 0 ... RyanMoore 12 — 78
(Sir Michael Stoute) *mde all: wound up fr 4f out: veered lft 3f out: drvn clr fr over 1f out: styd on* **5/2**[2]

-3 **2** *2 ¼* **Oneiric**[21] 1767 3-8-12 0 ... JimCrowley 4 — 69
(Ralph Beckett) *prom: cl up bhd ldrs over 2f out: rdn to take 2nd 1f out: styd on but no imp on wnr* **15/2**

4 **3** *3 ½* **Autobahn**[10] 2058 3-9-3 0 ... AhmedAjtebi 7 — 67
(Mahmood Al Zarooni) *prom: effrt whn sltly impeded 3f out: sn chsd wnr: hld and lost 2nd 1f out: fdd* **9/4**[1]

0-0 **4** *1 ½* **Hoofprintinthesnow**[21] 1774 3-9-3 0 ... NeilCallan 10 — 64
(Amanda Perrett) *mostly chsd wnr: bmpd by him 3f out: sn lost 2nd: steadily outpcd after* **16/1**

00 **5** *1* **Take A Spin**[33] 1484 3-8-10 0 ... DuilioDaSilva(7) 9 — 62
(Paul Cole) *hld up in last quartet: taken to outer and pushed along 3f out: kpt on steadily wout threatening* **40/1**

0- **6** *1* **Noble Defender**[224] 6802 3-9-3 0 ... FergusSweeney 8 — 60
(Stuart Kittow) *a abt same pl: shkn up 2f out: sn outpcd: nt disgracd* **66/1**

7 *2 ¾* **What's The Point** 3-9-3 0 ... AdamKirby 6 — 54+
(Walter Swinburn) *settled in 8th: rn green whn pushed along over 3f out: nvr on terms* **20/1**

02- **8** *1 ½* **O Ma Lad (IRE)**[204] 7248 3-9-3 0 ... JamesDoyle 1 — 51
(Sylvester Kirk) *hld up in last pair: no prog 3f out: pushed along over 2f out: reminder and passed wkng rivals ins fnl f* **4/1**[3]

9 *½* **Decana** 3-8-12 0 ... SteveDrowne 3 — 45
(Hughie Morrison) *hld up in last quartet: pushed along 3f out: hanging lft 2f out: no real prog* **20/1**

0- **10** *1 ½* **Star Rebel**[206] 7203 3-9-3 0 ... SebSanders 11 — 47
(George Margarson) *hld up in last pair: shkn up over 4f out: sn struggling* **33/1**

050- **11** *2 3/4* **Rowan Ridge**[214] 7034 3-9-3 73 RichardHughes 2 42
(Jim Boyle) *trckd ldrs in 5th: pushed along over 3f out: steadily lost pl after and eased* **33/1**
12 *5* **Silver Bullitt** 3-9-3 0 JimmyFortune 5 32
(Walter Swinburn) *in tch in 7th: shkn up 3f out: sn wknd* **20/1**

2m 8.42s (-0.28) **Going Correction** -0.25s/f (Firm) **12** Ran SP% **121.1**
Speed ratings (Par 99): **91,89,86,85,84 83,81,80,79,78 76,72**
toteswingers:1&2:£4.20, 2&3:£3.30, 1&3:£2.60 CSF £20.09 TOTE £4.70: £1.10, £4.50, £1.10; EX 23.00 Trifecta £31.70 Pool: £465.97 - 10.87 winning units..
Owner Athos Christodoulou **Bred** A Christodoulou **Trained** Newmarket, Suffolk

FOCUS
An interesting maiden run at a fair pace. They finished quite well strung out and the form looks sound enough, with the third, fourth and fifth close to their marks.

2372 KING COBRA H'CAP — 1m 3f 135y
8:40 (8:40) (Class 6) (0-65,64) 4-Y-O+ **£1,706** (£503; £252) **Stalls High**

Form RPR
4123 **1** **Broughtons Paradis (IRE)**[14] 1956 5-9-5 62 StevieDonohoe 8 68
(Willie Musson) *trckd ldrs: gng best of all 3f out: prog to ld 2f out: drvn and hrd pressed over 1f out: hld on wl* **9/4**[1]
2221 **2** *nk* **Wrecking Crew (IRE)**[14] 1959 7-8-13 56 JamesMillman 3 61
(Rod Millman) *dwlt: hld up in last pair: prog over 3f out: drvn to chal 2f out: pressed wnr over 1f out: kpt on but a hld* **11/4**[2]
010- **3** *1* **Rodrigo De Freitas (IRE)**[209] 7156 4-9-6 63 (v) StephenCraine 5 67
(Jim Boyle) *dwlt: hld up in last pair: drvn 3f out: prog u.p fr 2f out: styd on to take 3rd ins fnl f: nvr gng pce to qckn or chal* **8/1**
030- **4** *1* **Choral Festival**[218] 6959 5-9-2 59 MarcHalford 7 61
(John Bridger) *hld up in tch: trckd ldrs 3f out: cl up and rdn whn nt clr run briefly 1f out: one pce after* **7/1**
0343 **5** *11* **Evident Pride (USA)**[25] 1636 8-9-0 57 ow1 AdamKirby 6 40
(Brett Johnson) *led at str pce: stdd it down dramatically bnd 6f out: booted on again 4f out: hdd & wknd 2f out* **3/1**[3]
00-0 **6** *6* **Rio Prince**[18] 1840 4-8-2 50 oh5 RyanPowell(5) 2 23
(John Bridger) *chsd ldr to wl over 2f out: wknd qckly* **25/1**
0500 **7** *10* **Harrys**[21] 1761 4-8-7 50 oh5 (p) HayleyTurner 10 —
(Michael Squance) *chsd ldng pair: wknd rapidly wl over 2f out: t.o* **33/1**

2m 30.86s (1.36) **Going Correction** -0.25s/f (Firm) **7** Ran SP% **112.8**
Speed ratings (Par 101): **85,84,84,83,76 72,65**
toteswingers:1&2:£1.10, 2&3:£4.40, 1&3:£5.80 CSF £8.44 CT £39.16 TOTE £2.40: £1.60, £2.10; EX 5.90 Trifecta £15.80 Pool: £364.85 - 17.03 winning units..
Owner Broughton Thermal Insulation **Bred** Mount Coote Stud **Trained** Newmarket, Suffolk

FOCUS
An ordinary handicap run at a good pace. The market leaders filled the first two positions and the first four finished a long way clear of the rest. The pace was muddling and the form is weak, with the winner rated close to her turf best.
Evident Pride(USA) Official explanation: jockey said gelding had no more to give
T/Jkpt: Not won. T/Plt: £42.50 to a £1 stake. Pool of £106,802.08 - 1,831.77 winning tickets. T/Qpdt: £6.10 to a £1 stake. Pool of £9,311.06 - 1,124.10 winning tickets. JN

[2208]SAINT-CLOUD (L-H)
Monday, May 23

OFFICIAL GOING: Turf: good to soft

2373a PRIX CORRIDA (GROUP 2) (4YO+ FILLIES & MARES) (TURF) — 1m 2f 110y
2:50 (12:00) 4-Y-O+ **£63,879** (£24,655; £11,767; £7,844; £3,922)

RPR
1 **Sarafina (FR)**[23] 1708 4-9-2 0 Christophe-PatriceLemaire 2 125+
(A De Royer-Dupre, France) *settled in 5th: mde smooth prog on outside 2 1/2f out: qcknd wl 1 1/2f out: led 150yds out: r.o strly: easily* **4/7**[1]
2 *2* **Announce**[21] 1784 4-8-11 0 MaximeGuyon 4 115
(A Fabre, France) *settled 4th: moved into 3rd early in st: rdn 2f out: qcknd wl to ld 1 1/2f out: r.o wl: hdd 150yds out: r.o wl* **6/1**[3]
3 *1 1/2* **One Clever Cat (IRE)**[21] 1784 5-8-9 0 FlavienPrat 6 109
(T Clout, France) *settled at rr tl rdn 2 1/2f out: qcknd wl on outside: r.o wl fnl f: clst at fin* **20/1**
4 *2 1/2* **Contredanse (IRE)**[22] 1718 4-8-9 0 KierenFallon 3 104
(Luca Cumani) *led initially then settled in 2nd: rdn 2 1/2f out: tk ld 2f out: sn hdd: styd on fnl f* **20/1**
5 *1 1/2* **Lily Of The Valley (FR)**[232] 6613 4-9-2 0 IoritzMendizabal 1 108
(J-C Rouget, France) *settled 3rd: rdn 2 1/2f out: briefly short of room: no ex u.p 1 1/2f out: fdd fnl f* **4/1**[2]
6 *2* **Rock My Soul (IRE)**[21] 1784 5-8-9 0 Pierre-CharlesBoudot 5 97
(A Fabre, France) *2nd initially then led down bk st: rdn 2 1/2f out: hdd 2f out: no ex: fdd* **25/1**

2m 10.5s (-9.10) **6** Ran SP% **111.3**
WIN (incl. 1 euro stake): 1.40. PLACES: 1.10, 1.50. SF: 3.00.
Owner H H Aga Khan **Bred** H H Aga Khan **Trained** Chantilly, France

NOTEBOOK
Sarafina(FR) was entitled to have come on for her reappearance in the Ganay, and this took less winning. She quickened up well when asked to the race and won with a fair degree of ease. A return to 1m4f will be in her favour and she could go for the Grand Prix de Saint-Cloud next, although everything will be geared around another crack at the Arc this season.
Announce, beaten only once in her five previous starts, won a Group 3 at Chantilly last time out. She probably ran to a similar level in defeat here and remains open to further improvement.
Contredanse(IRE) won the Italian Oaks last season but has been held in Group company since, and perhaps her best chance of adding another Group race success to her CV will be to travel back to Italy.
Lily Of The Valley(FR), winner of the Prix de l'Opera last season, was making her seasonal reappearance and in the circumstances it would have been some achievement to beat a race-fit Sarafina off levels. She's entitled to come on for the run.

[1750]CHEPSTOW (L-H)
Tuesday, May 24

OFFICIAL GOING: Good (good to firm in places) changing to good to firm (good in places) after race 2 (2.50)
Wind: Moderate across Weather: Sunny spells

2374 SIS LIVE MAIDEN AUCTION STKS — 5f 16y
2:20 (2:21) (Class 5) 2-Y-O **£2,266** (£674; £337; £168) **Stalls High**

Form RPR
4 **1** **Wolfgang (IRE)**[28] 1583 2-8-12 0 RichardHughes 6 79+
(Richard Hannon) *in tch: rdn along after 2f: hdwy 2f out: chsd ldr appr fnl f: edgd lft and str chal ins fnl f: led fnl 100yds: in command clsng stages* **9/2**[2]
2 *nk* **Place In My Heart** 2-8-6 0 MartinDwyer 7 72
(George Baker) *trckd ldrs: led over 3f out: pushed along over 1f out: edgd lft ins fnl f: hdd fnl 100yds: nt pce of wnr but kpt on wl* **9/2**[2]
2200 **3** *4* **Umph (IRE)**[24] 1691 2-8-11 0 (v[1]) CathyGannon 1 63
(David Evans) *slt ld tl over 3f out: chsd ldrs tl outpcd by ldng duo fnl f* **7/1**
4 *1* **Gypsy Rider** 2-8-10 0 DavidProbert 3 58
(Bryn Palling) *s.i.s: in rr and sn pushed along: hdwy over 1f out: styd on ins fnl f: nt rch ldrs* **33/1**
5 *nse* **Emma Jean (IRE)** 2-8-0 0 RyanPowell(5) 5 53
(J S Moore) *s.i.s: in rr: drvn along 3f out: hdwy over 1f out: kpt on wl fnl f: gng on clsng stages* **11/1**
6 *1 1/2* **Split Second (IRE)** 2-8-8 0 SamHitchcott 2 51
(Mick Channon) *s.i.s: sn drvn and in tch 1/2-way: outpcd fr over 1f out* **4/1**[1]
0 **7** *1/2* **Mount McLeod (IRE)**[15] 1946 2-8-8 0 FergusSweeney 11 49
(Jamie Osborne) *chsd ldrs: rdn 2f out: wknd over 1f out* **16/1**
8 *nse* **Fast On (IRE)** 2-8-12 0 RichardMullen 10 53+
(Ed McMahon) *bmpd s: a outpcd* **11/2**[3]
0 **9** *3/4* **Bertorella (IRE)**[8] 2153 2-8-6 0 RichardKingscote 4 44
(Ralph Beckett) *w ldrs to 1/2-way: wknd wl over 1f out* **9/1**
0 **10** *2* **Fanrouge (IRE)**[15] 1957 2-8-6 0 LiamJones 9 37
(Malcolm Saunders) *wnt rt s: sn rcvrd: chsd ldrs 3f* **66/1**
11 *2 1/2* **Molly Jones** 2-8-6 0 ChrisCatlin 8 28
(Derek Haydn Jones) *slowly away: a in rr* **25/1**

59.59 secs (0.29) **Going Correction** -0.175s/f (Firm) **11** Ran SP% **116.7**
Speed ratings (Par 93): **90,89,83,81,81 79,78,78,76,73 69**
Tote Swingers: 1&2 £5.00, 2&3 £4.40 CSF £24.51 TOTE £3.60: £1.50, £1.90, £2.80; EX 19.20.
Owner Andrew Tinkler **Bred** C Marnane **Trained** East Everleigh, Wilts

FOCUS
There was 2.5mm of rain the previous day and the going was good, good to firm in places. An ordinary 2-y-o maiden. The pace was fast and the first two pulled clear. The form is rated conservatively through the third.

NOTEBOOK
Wolfgang(IRE) was a weak 7-2 chance when fourth in an average AW maiden on debut before being a late withdrawal in seller a week later. However, the market vibes were fairly positive this time, and he looked a lot more streetwise, finding a sustained run towards the far side to get off the mark on this improved second run.
Place In My Heart, a Compton Place filly, showed plenty of pace but was just overhauled on this debut. She is out of a 1m2f winner who tends to get speedier types than herself, notably very smart 6f-1m performer Leitrim House. (op 11-2 tchd 4-1)
Umph(IRE) ran poorly last time but he set the standard on his best AW form and was supported in the market. Never far away in a first-time visor, he kept plugging on but couldn't live with the first two. This was a respectable run but this fairly exposed colt could continue to be vulnerable to anything with potential. (op 9-1 tchd 13-2)
Gypsy Rider was retained cheaply as a yearling, but he showed definite signs of ability staying on well from some way back on debut.
Emma Jean(IRE) also finished well after looking inexperienced. She is a half-sister to 2-y-o winners at 6f-7f and should improve for this first run. (op 12-1 tchd 10-1)
Split Second(IRE) has a pedigree that is all about speed and was sent off favourite on this debut, but she ran green and couldn't get involved. (op 5-1)
Fast On(IRE), an £11,000 second foal of a maiden half-sister to three decent winners at up to 8.6f, was prominent in the betting but was always struggling after a slow start on debut. Official explanation: jockey said that the colt suffered interference at the start (op 9-2 tchd 7-1)
Fanrouge(IRE) Official explanation: jockey said that the filly veered badly right on leaving the stalls

2375 GOOD LUCK BACK IN OZ PETER CURL CLASSIFIED STKS — 6f 16y
2:50 (2:50) (Class 6) 3-Y-O **£1,619** (£481; £240; £120) **Stalls High**

Form RPR
64-2 **1** **Shes Rosie**[22] 1753 3-9-0 65 RussKennemore 9 70
(John O'Shea) *pressed ldrs 1f: chsd ldr fr 4f out: chal 2 out: led wl over 1f out: wnt lft sn after: comf* **3/1**[2]
3-20 **2** *2 1/4* **Crucis Abbey (IRE)**[14] 1980 3-9-0 60 (v[1]) LiamJones 8 62
(James Unett) *chsd ldrs: drvn to chse wnr fnl f but no imp* **13/2**
0-52 **3** *2 3/4* **Albany Rose (IRE)**[109] 422 3-9-0 63 SteveDrowne 4 54
(Rae Guest) *in rr but in tch: hdwy over 2f out: styd on to take 3rd fnl f but no imp on ldng duo* **12/1**
4365 **4** *3/4* **Scommettitrice (IRE)**[8] 2163 3-9-0 53 (b) TomMcLaughlin 11 51
(Ronald Harris) *s.i.s: in rr: hdwy over 1f out: styd on wl clsng stages but nvr a threat* **16/1**
0-22 **5** *nk* **Court Applause (IRE)**[18] 1869 3-9-0 64 MartinDwyer 5 50
(William Muir) *in rr: pushed along fr 1/2-way: rdn 2f out: styd on fnl f but nvr gng pce to rch ldrs* **9/4**[1]
60-0 **6** *1* **Putin (IRE)**[12] 2025 3-9-0 60 DaneO'Neill 1 47
(Derek Haydn Jones) *in tch: pushed along 1/2-way: rdn fr 2f out: styd on fnl f: nvr a threat* **12/1**
4053 **7** *2 1/2* **Local Diktator**[7] 2177 3-9-0 59 (p) CathyGannon 6 39
(Ronald Harris) *s.i.s: hung lft: nvr any ch: nt clr run on far rail fnl f* **25/1**
5 **8** *3/4* **Green Warrior**[34] 1494 3-9-0 63 (v[1]) RichardHughes 2 37
(Ann Duffield) *sn led: jnd 2f out: hdd wl over 1f out: sn wknd* **9/2**[3]
000- **9** *19* **Lady Excellentia (IRE)**[202] 7295 3-9-0 50 ChrisCatlin 7 —
(Ronald Harris) *stdd s: sn chsng ldrs: wknd 1/2-way* **66/1**

1m 11.34s (-0.66) **Going Correction** -0.175s/f (Firm) **9** Ran SP% **113.9**
Speed ratings (Par 97): **97,94,90,89,88 87,84,83,57**
Tote Swingers: 1&2 £4.20, 1&3 £4.80, 2&3 £12.10 CSF £22.56 TOTE £3.30: £1.50, £2.00, £3.20; EX 26.20.
Owner S G Martin **Bred** Stewart Martin And Alan Purvis **Trained** Elton, Gloucs

FOCUS
Most of the runners were exposed in this classified event and there was just 7lb between eight of them on BHA ratings. The pace was fast and they raced on the far side. The form is rated around the winner and fourth to their previous course marks.

Local Diktator Official explanation: jockey said, regarding the running and riding, that her instructions were that if the colt started to hang she was to let him go to the rail. She added that the colt began to hang left after two furlongs; she hoped that having reached the rail he would stop hanging but he did not, making it impossible for her to ride him out. She further stated that her progress down the rail was impeded in the final furlong by Green Warrior in front of her and thereafter she was unable to ride the colt to the line.
Green Warrior Official explanation: jockey said that the gelding hung left in the final two furlongs

2376 YOLK RECRUITMENT H'CAP 1m 14y
3:20 (3:20) (Class 5) (0-70,70) 4-Y-0+ **£2,266** (£674; £337; £168) **Stalls** High

Form RPR
0-45 **1** **You've Been Mowed**[12] 2027 5-8-6 **60**............................ RyanClark(5) 7 74
(Richard Price) *mde all: drvn clr over 1f out: unchal* **3/1**[1]
10-5 **2** *5* **Tap Dance Way (IRE)**[21] 1789 4-9-7 **70**............................ LiamKeniry 8 73
(Patrick Chamings) *chsd ldrs: chsd wnr fr 3f out: kpt on wl to hold that position fnl f but no ch w wnr* **10/1**
-601 **3** *nk* **Cape Kimberley**[23] 1730 4-8-5 **61**.................................. DavidKenny(7) 9 63
(Tony Newcombe) *racd alone stands' side and 2nd to 3f out: styd disputing that position to fnl f: nvr any ch w wnr and kpt on same pce* **15/2**
0-01 **4** *2¼* **Bold Cross (IRE)**[4] 2242 8-9-7 **70** 6ex.......................... CathyGannon 10 67
(Edward Bevan) *stdd s: t.k.h and chsd ldrs 1/2-way: rdn 3f out: no ch w ldrs fnl 2f but styd on again clsng stages* **5/1**[3]
51-0 **5** *3½* **One Hit Wonder**[11] 2051 4-9-2 **65**.. NeilCallan 6 54
(Mouse Hamilton-Fairley) *in tch: rdn and effrt over 2f out: no imp: wknd fnl f* **8/1**
50-4 **6** *3* **Tanforan**[54] 1058 9-8-7 **56**.. KellyHarrison 1 38
(Brian Baugh) *chsd ldrs 1/2-way but no ch w wnr: rdn over 2f out: wknd fnl f* **28/1**
6311 **7** *7* **Forward Feline (IRE)**[39] 1373 5-8-11 **63**.................. DeclanCannon(3) 5 29
(Bryn Palling) *slowly away: t.k.h: chsd ldrs 1/2-way: wknd 2f out* **15/2**
60-0 **8** *8* **Swift Chap**[31] 1530 5-9-4 **67**... JimmyFortune 3 14
(Rod Millman) *chsd ldrs tl wknd qckly 2f out* **9/2**[2]
-502 **9** *7* **Come On Safari (IRE)**[12] 2027 4-9-5 **68**....................(b) SteveDrowne 2 —
(Joseph Tuite) *s.i.s: rdn 1/2-way: a bhd* **11/1**

1m 34.15s (-2.05) **Going Correction** -0.175s/f (Firm) **9** Ran SP% **115.4**
Speed ratings (Par 103): **103,98,97,95,91 88,81,73,66**
Tote Swingers: 1&2 £6.70, 1&3 £7.70, 2&3 £12.10 CSF £34.12 CT £206.23 TOTE £4.00: £1.30, £3.60, £2.60; EX 39.40.
Owner Mrs K Oseman **Bred** T E Pocock **Trained** Ullingswick, H'fords

FOCUS
The well-backed favourite hammered her rivals under a forcing ride in this minor handicap. The runner-up is rated to form, backed up by the third to his recent mark.
Come On Safari(IRE) Official explanation: jockey said that the gelding was never travelling

2377 KILSBY AND WILLIAMS H'CAP 2m 49y
3:50 (3:50) (Class 6) (0-60,60) 4-Y-0+ **£1,619** (£481; £240; £120) **Stalls** Low

Form RPR
30-4 **1** **Spinning Waters**[8] 2140 5-8-7 **46** oh1............................ KellyHarrison 2 53
(Dai Burchell) *in tch: drvn to chse ldr 3f out: led 2f out: hdd over 1f out: rallied to ld again fnl 100yds: kpt on wl* **7/1**
430/ **2** *nk* **Orbital Orchid**[563] 6436 6-8-12 **51**.................................. MartinDwyer 14 58+
(Nick Williams) *in rr: hdwy fr 3f out: drvn to ld appr fnl f: no ex and hdd fnl 100yds* **5/1**[2]
20-2 **3** *1½* **Dove Cottage (IRE)**[26] 1631 9-9-1 **54**........................ FergusSweeney 6 59
(Stuart Kittow) *t.k.h: sn led: hdd 1m out: styd trcking ldr tl led again 4f out: hdd 2f out: one pce appr fnl f: styd on again fnl 100yds* **8/1**
0-03 **4** *½* **Court Princess**[19] 1833 8-8-10 **49**................................. DavidProbert 11 53
(Richard Price) *in rr: hdwy u.p over 2f out: styd on fnl f but nvr gng pce to chal* **25/1**
5302 **5** *hd* **Miles Of Sunshine**[8] 2140 6-8-12 **51**............................ SamHitchcott 13 55
(Ron Hodges) *s.i.s: in rr: rdn and hdwy 3f out: chsd ldrs 2f out: one pce fnl f* **9/1**
0543 **6** *13* **Vertueux (FR)**[45] 1080 6-9-3 **56**.. NeilCallan 4 45
(Tony Carroll) *chsd ldrs to 3f out: wknd qckly 2f out* **6/1**[3]
3001 **7** *2¼* **Spiritofthemount (USA)**[1] 2140 6-8-12 **51** 6ex.............(b) ChrisCatlin 9 37
(Peter Hiatt) *chsd ldrs tl racd wd fr 10f out: led 1/2-way: hdd 4f out: wknd ins fnl 3f* **10/1**
/650 **8** *1¼* **Am I Blue**[16] 955 5-8-7 **49**.. SophieDoyle(3) 8 33
(Mrs D Thomas) *chsd ldr to 1/2-way: lost pl 3f out: styd on again cl home* **14/1**
0/0- **9** *1¼* **Troubletimestwo (FR)**[24] 6314 5-8-11 **57**.............. GeorgeDowning(7) 7 40
(Tony Carroll) *sn bhd: mod prog clsng stages* **16/1**
-005 **10** *3½* **Hibba (USA)**[8] 2145 4-8-11 **52**....................................... JimmyFortune 5 31
(Mouse Hamilton-Fairley) *chsd ldrs tl wknd over 3f out* **33/1**
53/5 **11** *31* **Tobago Bay**[18] 560 6-8-13 **52**....................................(b) RichardHughes 10 —
(Gary Moore) *chsd ldrs tl wknd 4f out* **4/1**[1]
12 *13* **Silky Lady (IRE)**[261] 5796 4-8-13 **54**................................. LiamKeniry 3 —
(Jonathan Geake) *sn bhd* **40/1**

3m 35.73s (-3.17) **Going Correction** -0.175s/f (Firm)
WFA 4 from 5yo+ 2lb **12** Ran SP% **115.4**
Speed ratings (Par 101): **100,99,99,98,98 92,91,90,89,88 72,66**
Tote Swingers: 1&2 £7.30, 1&3 £17.30, 2&3 £11.70 CSF £40.00 CT £287.57 TOTE £8.60: £2.60, £2.30, £2.10; EX 45.20.
Owner B M G Group **Bred** R E Crutchley **Trained** Briery Hill, Blaenau Gwent

FOCUS
An ordinary staying handicap with the third, fourth and fifth rated close to their marks. It was run at a fair pace and the first five pulled clear a long way clear.
Tobago Bay Official explanation: jockey said that the gelding lost its action

2378 BREWIN DOLPHIN H'CAP 1m 2f 36y
4:20 (4:21) (Class 5) (0-75,81) 4-Y-0+ **£2,266** (£674; £337; £168) **Stalls** Low

Form RPR
-301 **1** **Beaumont's Party (IRE)**[3] 2282 4-9-13 **81** 6ex.............. DavidProbert 2 96+
(Andrew Balding) *t.k.h early but a gng wl: led on bit ins fnl 3f: in n.d fnl 2f: v easily* **8/13**[1]
1325 **2** *2½* **Yes Chef**[19] 1832 4-9-5 **73**.. JamesMillman 3 78
(Rod Millman) *in tch: hdwy 3f out: disp 2nd fr 2f out: rdn to chse easy wnr fnl f but nvr any ch* **9/1**[3]
043- **3** *3* **Norman The Great**[18] 4226 7-9-2 **70**........................... FergusSweeney 7 69
(Alan King) *chsd ldrs tl rdn and lost pl 4f out: rallied fr 2f out: styd on to take wl hld 3rd fnl 50yds* **16/1**
1134 **4** *¾* **Edgeworth (IRE)**[22] 1772 5-8-11 **72**............................ JoshBaudains(7) 5 70
(David Bridgwater) *stdd to rr s: impr fr 5f out: chsd wnr over 2f out but nvr any ch: one pce into 3rd fnl f and dropped to 4th fnl 50yds* **20/1**
120- **5** *6* **Oriental Girl**[202] 7306 6-9-4 **72**...(p) LiamKeniry 9 58
(Jonathan Geake) *in tch tl rdn and dropped to rr 3f out: no ch after* **25/1**
000- **6** *½* **If I Were A Boy (IRE)**[202] 6957 4-9-5 **73**............................ NeilCallan 6 58
(Dominic Ffrench Davis) *chsd ldr: chal 3f out: wknd 2f out* **40/1**
112- **7** *5* **Hurakan (IRE)**[440] 841 5-9-6 **74**..................................(t) JimmyFortune 8 49
(George Baker) *rrd s and bhd: rdn and sme hdwy over 3f out: sn btn* **9/1**[3]
3250 **8** *15* **Needwood Ridge**[17] 1917 4-8-9 **66**.........................(t) LouisBeuzelin(3) 1 —
(Frank Sheridan) *stdd s: a in rr* **33/1**
012- **9** *17* **Crazy Chris**[341] 3130 6-9-7 **75**.. RichardHughes 4 —
(John Flint) *led tl hdd ins fnl 3f: eased whn no ch ins fnl 2f: virtually p.u clsng stages* **11/2**[2]

2m 7.28s (-3.32) **Going Correction** -0.175s/f (Firm) **9** Ran SP% **117.2**
Speed ratings (Par 103): **106,104,101,101,96 95,91,79,66**
Tote Swingers: 1&2 £2.00, 1&3 £5.70, 2&3 £16.30 CSF £6.73 CT £50.02 TOTE £1.30: £1.20, £1.90, £2.70; EX 7.10.
Owner Thurloe Thoroughbreds XXV **Bred** Mrs Joan Murphy **Trained** Kingsclere, Hants

FOCUS
They went a solid pace in this fair handicap which was won in great style by the hot favourite. The winner is unexposed at the trip and looks value for at least twice the official margin.
Hurakan(IRE) Official explanation: jockey said that the gelding fly leapt on leaving the stalls
Crazy Chris Official explanation: jockey said that the mare hung left handed

2379 LINDLEY CATERING H'CAP 1m 4f 23y
4:50 (4:50) (Class 6) (0-60,58) 3-Y-0 **£1,619** (£481; £240; £120) **Stalls** Low

Form RPR
006- **1** **Kepler's Law**[215] 7036 3-9-6 **57**...................................... JimmyFortune 2 70+
(Sir Mark Prescott Bt) *trckd ldr: drvn along 4f out: led over 2f out: drvn clr fnl f: easily* **5/2**[1]
000- **2** *3¾* **Tanjung Agas (IRE)**[202] 7302 3-9-7 **58**................................ NeilCallan 1 67+
(Roger Varian) *reminders after 3f: tendency to run green and carry hd high: hdwy on ins whn hmpd wl over 2f out: swtchd rt and styd on to chse wnr fnl f but nvr any ch* **5/1**
0651 **3** *nk* **Westhaven (IRE)**[3] 2307 3-9-3 **54** 6ex..........................(b) NickyMackay 7 60
(David Elsworth) *t.k.h: chsd ldrs: drvn to dispute 2nd fr 2f out: no imp on wnr and kpt on same pce ins fnl f* **11/4**[2]
5642 **4** *1½* **Revolutionary**[5] 2239 3-9-4 **58**................................... SophieDoyle(3) 4 62
(Jamie Osborne) *led: edgd lft wl over 2f out and hdd sn after: wknd ins fnl f* **4/1**[3]
2664 **5** *24* **The Absent Mare**[8] 2166 3-8-8 **48**........................(bt) LouisBeuzelin(3) 3 —
(Frank Sheridan) *in rr but in tch tl wknd ins fnl 3f: t.o* **8/1**
43 **6** *76* **Delagoa Bay (IRE)**[57] 1018 3-9-1 **52**........................(b1) RichardHughes 5 —
(Sylvester Kirk) *in rr but in tch tl wknd qckly and eased ins fnl 3f: t.o* **9/1**

2m 37.21s (-1.79) **Going Correction** -0.175s/f (Firm) **6** Ran SP% **113.0**
Speed ratings (Par 97): **98,95,95,94,78 27**
Tote Swingers: 1&2 £2.70, 1&3 £3.30, 2&3 £3.10 CSF £15.46 TOTE £3.30: £1.50, £5.40; EX 18.00.
Owner Rectory Racing **Bred** Chippenham Lodge Stud Ltd **Trained** Newmarket, Suffolk

FOCUS
A low-grade handicap but the winner is an unexposed type who showed much improved form stepped up in trip on handicap debut. The form looks above average for the grade with the fourth rated to recent handicap form.
Kepler's Law Official explanation: trainers representative said, regarding the apparent improvement of form, that the gelding was big and backward and has been gelded
Delagoa Bay(IRE) Official explanation: jockey said that the filly lost its action
T/Plt: £143.30 to a £1 stake. Pool of £60,687.91 - 309.10 winning tickets. T/Qpdt: £39.70 to a £1 stake. Pool of £3,869.19 - 72 winning tickets. ST

2302 LINGFIELD (L-H)
Tuesday, May 24

OFFICIAL GOING: Standard
Wind: fresh, across Weather: bright and breezy

2380 LINGFIELD MARRIOTT HOTEL & COUNTRY CLUB MEDIAN AUCTION MAIDEN STKS 5f (P)
2:30 (2:30) (Class 6) 2-Y-0 **£2,047** (£604; £302) **Stalls** High

Form RPR
44 **1** **Multi Blessing**[15] 1932 2-9-0 0................................ MatthewDavies(3) 4 79
(Alan Jarvis) *mde all: rdn and wnt clr ent fnl 2f: drvn over 1f out: in command and kpt on wl fnl f* **16/1**
6245 **2** *2¾* **Courtland King (IRE)**[8] 2143 2-9-3 0............................... WilliamBuick 7 70
(David Evans) *chsd ldng trio: swtchd ins and effrt wl over 1f out: chsd wnr ins fnl f: kpt on but nvr gng pce to threaten wnr* **5/2**[1]
0224 **3** *1½* **Red Socks (IRE)**[7] 2173 2-8-12 0.....................(b1) AdamBeschizza(5) 1 64
(Gay Kelleway) *chsd wnr: drvn and unable qck ent fnl 2f: one pce and no threat to wnr ent fnl f: lost 2nd ins fnl f* **10/3**[2]
4 *1¼* **Maltease Ah** 2-8-12 0.. DarryllHolland 2 54+
(Richard Fahey) *chsd ldng pair: pushed along and outpcd bnd 2f out: kpt on same pce and no threat to wnr fr over 1f out* **4/1**[3]
5 *½* **Tangtastic (IRE)** 2-8-12 0.. EddieCreighton 5 52
(Edward Creighton) *s.i.s: rn green and sn pushed along and outpcd in last trio: sme hdwy and in tch jst over 2f out: outpcd wl over 1f out: kpt on again ins fnl f* **66/1**
6 *2½* **Calendar King** 2-9-0 0.. MartinHarley(3) 3 48+
(Mick Channon) *dwlt: sn pushed along and outpcd in rr: rdn wl over 1f out: hdwy ins fnl f: gng on fin but nvr gng pce to threaten ldrs* **5/2**[1]
7 *9* **Monessa (IRE)** 2-8-5 0....................................... JenniferFerguson(7) 6 11
(Edward Creighton) *s.i.s: a wl outpcd in rr: lost tch 3f out: t.o* **100/1**

59.82 secs (1.02) **Going Correction** +0.175s/f (Slow) **7** Ran SP% **108.6**
Speed ratings (Par 91): **98,93,91,89,88 84,70**
Tote Swingers: 1&2 £12.00, 1&3 £7.00, 2&3 £1.10 CSF £50.55 TOTE £10.20: £2.00, £3.00; EX 70.00.
Owner Christopher Shankland **Bred** Mickley Stud And R Percival **Trained** Twyford, Bucks

FOCUS
A weak maiden to open proceedings and its likely all of those behind the all-the-way winner will have to have their sights lowered in a bid to get off the mark. The kickback looked worse than normal and experience and was vital. The form is rated through the runner-up.

NOTEBOOK
Multi Blessing hadn't achieved much in either start to date, but he's going the right way and looked much more professional here, breaking well and looking in control from a long way out. He probably doesn't want any further for now and might be best put away for nurseries, as he doesn't look up to winning a novice or conditions event. (op 14-1)
Courtland King(IRE) has had plenty of chances now and, for all he had to be switched entering the straight, he wasn't unlucky. He might do better at 6f on this surface, but will probably need to be dropped into a claimer to get off the mark. (op 3-1)

Red Socks(IRE) hasn't progressed since his second start and connections are running out of options with headgear failing to arrest his slide. (op 11-4 tchd 7-2)
Maltease Ah is related to a 2-y-o 5f winner and her yard do well with their youngsters here, but she looks one of their lesser lights on this evidence for all she was slightly green, tending to hang away to her right on the run to the turn. (op 3-1)
Tangtastic(IRE) hadn't much to recommend her on breeding and never threatened after a slow start, also showing signs of inexperience. (op 80-1)
Calendar King, a half-brother to the 2-y-o 6f winner Jolah out of a mare that won at 6f, was soon on the back foot after a tardy start, looking clueless, but is entitled to do better. (op 7-2)

2381 EDEN BROOK (S) STKS 1m (P)
3:00 (3:00) (Class 6) 3-5-Y-O £1,706 (£503; £252) **Stalls** High

Form RPR
0554 **1** **Charlie Smirke (USA)**[6] 2207 5-9-5 65....(bt) RyanMoore 4 69
(Gary Moore) *pressed ldr tl led ent fnl 2f: drvn over 1f out: clr ins fnl f: rdn out* **5/6**[1]
3240 **2** 3 1/4 **Ilissos (USA)**[36] 1442 3-8-4 66....(t) JohnFahy(3) 5 59
(Jeremy Noseda) *dwlt: hld up in tch in last pair: rdn and effrt 2f out: chsd wnr 1f out: no imp ins fnl f* **8/1**[3]
3300 **3** 1 3/4 **Better Self**[19] 1828 3-8-2 60.... MatthewCosham(5) 3 55
(David Evans) *s.i.s: in tch in rr: rdn and unable qck over 2f out: edgd rt ent fnl f: kpt on to go 3rd wl ins fnl f: no threat to wnr* **11/1**
-210 **4** 3/4 **Broughtons Day**[113] 367 4-9-5 67.... TonyCulhane 1 56
(Willie Musson) *led: hdd ent fnl 2f: rdn and unable qck wl over 1f out: wknd 1f out* **2/1**[2]
3444 **5** 1 **Jackie Love (IRE)**[39] 1369 3-8-2 60.... KirstyMilczarek 2 46
(Olivia Maylam) *chsd ldng pair: rdn and effrt on inner wl over 1f out: wknd fnl f* **33/1**

1m 40.27s (2.07) **Going Correction** +0.175s/f (Slow)
WFA 3 from 4yo+ 12lb 5 Ran SP% **110.3**
Speed ratings (Par 101): **96,92,91,90,89**
CSF £8.32 TOTE £2.10: £1.10, £3.40; EX 6.00.There was no bid for the winner.
Owner R E Anderson **Bred** W S Farish & Kilroy Thoroughbred Partnership **Trained** Lower Beeding, W Sussex

FOCUS
An uncompetitive seller run at just a fair gallop and not form to dwell on. The winner probably only had to run to recent form to score.

2382 NEIL AND LIZ MUNCEY 25TH ANNIVERSARY CLASSIFIED CLAIMING STKS 7f (P)
3:30 (3:30) (Class 6) 3-Y-0+ £1,706 (£503; £252) **Stalls** Low

Form RPR
2111 **1** **I Confess**[6] 2206 6-8-10 70....(b) MatthewCosham(5) 9 73
(David Evans) *chsd ldrs: rdn and chal jst over 1f out: led jst ins fnl f: hld on wl* **10/11**[1]
4501 **2** nk **Loves Theme (IRE)**[7] 2177 3-7-11 64....(b) AmyBaker(3) 5 64
(Alan Bailey) *in tch: rdn and effrt on inner 2f out: ev ch u.p ins fnl f: no ex and hld towards fin* **9/1**
1004 **3** shd **Abriachan**[29] 1557 4-8-10 67.... AdamBeschizza(5) 6 72
(Noel Quinlan) *stdd and short of room sn after s: hld up in last trio: rdn and effrt on outer 2f out: ev ch ins fnl f: kpt on* **13/2**
5500 **4** 2 1/4 **Kipchak (IRE)**[8] 2165 6-8-8 62....(v) HarryBentley(5) 2 64
(Conor Dore) *awkward leaving stalls: chsd ldrs: n.m.r on inner and swtchd rt over 4f out: sn led: hdd and rdn wl over 1f out: rr qckn u.p over 1f out: one pce and hld fnl f* **16/1**
403- **5** 2 1/4 **Kirsty's Boy (IRE)**[24] 1701 4-9-2 68.... MartinHarley(3) 3 64
(J P Broderick, Ire) *led tl over 4f out: chsd ldr after tl rdn to ld again wl over 1f out: hdd jst ins fnl f: wknd fnl 100yds* **6/1**[3]
3240 **6** 1 1/2 **Dichoh**[23] 1730 8-9-3 65....(p) GeorgeBaker 10 58
(Michael Madgwick) *in rr: rdn and effrt wl over 1f out: styd on same pce and no imp fnl f* **7/2**[2]
-565 **7** 3/4 **Stonecrabstomorrow (IRE)**[34] 1497 8-8-9 44 ow3(e) MarkCoumbe(5) 4 53
(Michael Attwater) *rdn along towards rr: sme hdwy on inner over 1f out: sn drvn and no prog: no ch fnl f* **66/1**
4560 **8** 11 **Blade Pirate**[7] 2172 3-7-7 47....(p) BradleyBosley(7) 8 16
(John Ryan) *chsd ldr tl over 4f out: chsd ldrs after tl lost pl and dropped to rr jst over 2f out: lost tch over 1f out* **66/1**

1m 25.61s (0.81) **Going Correction** +0.175s/f (Slow)
WFA 3 from 4yo+ 11lb 8 Ran SP% **121.1**
Speed ratings (Par 101): **102,101,101,98,96 94,93,81**
Tote Swingers: 1&2 £3.70, 1&3 £2.00, 2&3 £6.70 CSF £11.70 TOTE £2.10: £1.10, £2.30, £2.10; EX 9.70.I Confess was claimed by Mr G. A. Harker for £7,000.
Owner J E Abbey **Bred** Gestut Sohrenhof **Trained** Pandy, Monmouths

FOCUS
A weak claimer, with nothing of interest beyond this grade going forward. The pace was fair and the form seems sound with those in the frame behind the winner close to their marks.
Stonecrabstomorrow(IRE) Official explanation: jockey said the gelding hit its head on the stalls and was slowly away

2383 MARSH GREEN H'CAP 7f (P)
4:00 (4:01) (Class 5) (0-75,75) 3-Y-0 £2,388 (£705; £352) **Stalls** Low

Form RPR
4-44 **1** **Firstknight**[26] 1626 3-9-2 72.... AdamKirby 6 80
(Marco Botti) *led for over 1f: chsd ldr after tl rdn to ld jst over 1f out: drvn and kpt on wl fnl f* **11/1**
1522 **2** nk **Ceffyl Gwell**[6] 2200 3-9-5 75.... RyanMoore 5 82
(Richard Hannon) *chsd ldrs: short of room and shuffled bk into midfield over 4f out: hdwy 2f out: rdn to chse wnr 1f out: ev ch ins fnl f: kpt on u.p but a hld* **9/2**[2]
054 **3** 1 1/4 **Dunseverick (IRE)**[14] 1985 3-9-3 73.... TedDurcan 9 77+
(David Lanigan) *hld up in tch in midfield: short of room and hmpd 5f out: rdn and effrt 2f out: hdwy on outer ent fnl f: r.o wl to go 3rd fnl 75yds: nt rch ldrs* **6/1**[3]
52-4 **4** 1 3/4 **Prophet In A Dream**[14] 1983 3-9-0 73.... MartinHarley(3) 7 73
(Mick Channon) *wl in tch in midfield: swtchd rt and effrt u.p over 1f out: nt qckn and styd on same pce fnl f* **12/1**
1-36 **5** 3/4 **Tamareen (IRE)**[17] 1916 3-9-5 75....(t) RichardHills 3 73+
(Ed Dunlop) *broke wl: sn stdd bk towards rr: pushed along and hdwy towards inner wl over 1f out: no threat to ldrs but kpt on steadily fnl f* **6/1**[3]
15 **6** hd **El Djebena (IRE)**[6] 2200 3-9-5 75.... SebSanders 11 73+
(Sir Mark Prescott Bt) *in tch in midfield on outer: hdwy to chse ldrs 3f out: rdn ent fnl 2f: drvn and unable qck over 1f out: btn fnl 150yds: lost 3 pls after* **7/2**[1]
626- **7** nk **Miss Exhibitionist**[211] 7123 3-9-3 73.... GeorgeBaker 12 70+
(James Eustace) *stdd and dropped in bhd after s: hld up in last: hdwy and rdn over 1f out: styd on wl ins fnl f: nvr able to chal* **40/1**
32U0 **8** 1 3/4 **Overwhelm**[38] 1391 3-9-3 73....(p) DarryllHolland 13 66
(Andrew Reid) *chsd ldrs tl led over 5f out: rdn 2f out: hdd jst over 1f out: wknd ins fnl f* **50/1**
22-5 **9** 1/2 **Justbookie Dot Com (IRE)**[56] 1031 3-8-13 72.... KierenFox(3) 1 64
(Louise Best) *stdd s: hld up in tch in last pair: effrt and nt clr run wl over 1f out: styd on ins fnl f: nvr able to chal* **40/1**
310- **10** 3/4 **Jolah**[227] 6734 3-9-4 74.... RussellPrice 14 64
(Clive Brittain) *chsd ldrs: rdn wl over 1f out: btn ent fnl f: wknd qckly fnl f* **33/1**
31-0 **11** 1 **Never Never Land**[40] 1335 3-9-4 74.... WilliamBuick 8 62
(John Gosden) *t.k.h early: hld up wl in tch: rdn and unable qck wl over 2f out: wknd over 1f out* **13/2**
024- **12** nk **Isingy Red (FR)**[147] 7990 3-9-5 75.... StephenCraine 10 62
(Jim Boyle) *stdd after s: hld up in tch in midfield: lost pl and dropped towards rr jst over 2f out: no prog u.p wl over 1f out* **50/1**
1130 **13** 1 1/4 **Aquilifer (IRE)**[41] 1317 3-9-5 75.... ShaneKelly 4 59+
(William Jarvis) *hld up in tch towards rr on inner: rdn and no hdwy over 2f out: no threat to ldrs fnl 2f* **14/1**
00-0 **14** 11 **Rafella (IRE)**[28] 1579 3-8-9 70.... AdamBeschizza(5) 2 —
(Simon Dow) *dwlt: a last trio: rdn and no prog 3f out: wl bhd fr over 1f out: eased wl ins fnl f* **33/1**

1m 25.67s (0.87) **Going Correction** +0.175s/f (Slow) 14 Ran SP% **119.7**
Speed ratings (Par 99): **102,101,100,98,97 97,96,94,94,93 92,91,90,77**
Tote Swingers: 1&2 £10.70, 1&3 £32.10, 2&3 £5.90 CSF £57.05 CT £332.18 TOTE £17.70: £5.00, £2.30, £2.70; EX 98.50.
Owner Andrew Tinkler **Bred** Cheveley Park Stud Ltd **Trained** Newmarket, Suffolk

FOCUS
Easily the most interesting race on the card, but one in which a prominent position was again important given the amount of kickback. The runner-up and fourth give the form some substance.

2384 B W STRAGGLERS H'CAP 7f (P)
4:30 (4:32) (Class 6) (0-55,55) 3-Y-0 £2,047 (£604; £302) **Stalls** Low

Form RPR
0-34 **1** **Lady On Top (IRE)**[7] 2172 3-8-9 48.... FrankieMcDonald 2 54
(Nerys Dutfield) *chsd ldrs: rdn to chse clr ldr ent fnl 2f: clsd fnl 150yds: kpt on wl to ld towards fin* **8/1**
00-0 **2** nk **Golden Compass**[40] 1343 3-8-7 46 oh1.... WilliamCarson 10 51
(Giles Bravery) *led for 1f: chsd ldr after tl rdn to ld 3f out: reminders and wnt clr over 2f out: drvn ins fnl f: worn down and hdd towards fin* **7/1**
000- **3** 2 1/2 **Love Nest**[224] 6827 3-8-11 50.... TedDurcan 5 48+
(John Dunlop) *in tch towards rr: rdn along 4f out: outpcd by ldrs 3f out: hdwy and modest 5th over 1f out: styd on to go 3rd ins fnl f: nvr gng pce to rch ldrs* **10/3**[1]
0- **4** 3/4 **Celestial Flyer (IRE)**[12] 2038 3-8-2 46 oh1.... HarryBentley(5) 11 42
(Tor Sturgis) *towards rr: rdn along 5f out: outpcd and struggling 3f out: hdwy on outer wl over 1f out: styd on wl fnl f* **4/1**[2]
0006 **5** hd **Five Cool Kats (IRE)**[15] 1953 3-8-8 47 ow1....(b[1]) RobbieFitzpatrick 6 43
(Paul Burgoyne) *stdd after s: hld up in rr: outpcd 3f out: hdwy jst over 2f out: kpt on u.p ins fnl f: nvr able to chal* **14/1**
0-05 **6** 3 1/4 **Silca Conegliano (IRE)**[8] 2141 3-8-13 55.... MartinHarley(3) 8 44
(Mick Channon) *hld up towards rr: stl plenty to do and hdwy jst over 2f out: nt clr run over 1f out: swtchd rt 1f out: kpt on but no ch w ldrs fnl f: eased towards fin* **5/1**[3]
6050 **7** 1 3/4 **Add Lib**[7] 2177 3-8-4 46.... JohnFahy(3) 1 28
(Matthew Salaman) *sn rdn along and hdwy to ld after 1f: hdd 3f out: sn rdn and outpcd by ldr: 3rd and wl btn over 1f out: fdd ins fnl f* **20/1**
-600 **8** 1 3/4 **Excellence (IRE)**[22] 1753 3-8-7 46.... JamieMackay 4 24
(Karen George) *stdd after s: hld up towards rr: lost tch w ldrs 3f out: n.d after* **33/1**
3-05 **9** 1/2 **Litotes**[120] 274 3-8-13 52.... AndreaAtzeni 7 28
(Michael Attwater) *in tch in midfield: rdn and outpcd wl over 2f out: wknd and wl btn over 1f out: fdd fnl f* **16/1**
3-60 **10** 5 **Koha (USA)**[7] 2172 3-8-10 49.... JimmyQuinn 14 —
(Dean Ivory) *t.k.h: chsd ldrs: rdn and outpcd wl over 2f out: wl btn 2f out: wknd* **10/1**
-006 **11** 3 **Microlight**[48] 1178 3-9-2 55....(e) RichardThomas 12 —
(John E Long) *hld up in tch in midfield: rdn and nt qckn over 2f out: wknd and wl btn over 1f out* **25/1**
0-60 **12** nk **Fully Armed (IRE)**[15] 1945 3-8-7 46 oh1....(bt[1]) MartinLane 13 —
(Rae Guest) *a towards rr: rdn and struggling 3f out: wl bhd fnl 2f* **18/1**
000- **13** 7 **Bella Nemica**[223] 6849 3-8-7 46 oh1.... EddieCreighton 3 —
(Edward Creighton) *chsd ldrs early: rdn and dropped to rr over 2f out: wl bhd fnl 2f* **40/1**

1m 26.89s (2.09) **Going Correction** +0.175s/f (Slow) 13 Ran SP% **124.2**
Speed ratings (Par 97): **95,94,91,90,90 87,85,83,82,76 73,72,64**
Tote Swingers: 1&2 £7.10, 1&3 £4.70, 2&3 £13.80 CSF £63.12 CT £237.00 TOTE £5.40: £1.90, £3.40, £1.90; EX 57.20.
Owner Simon Dutfield **Bred** Neville O'Byrne And Roderick Ryan **Trained** Axmouth, Devon
■ Stewards' Enquiry : Ted Durcan one-day ban: careless riding (June 7)

FOCUS
A very weak handicap in which those making their handicap debuts looked of most interest, but as things turned out it went to one that looked exposed, so in all probability not a race that will turn out to be strong form even at its own level. The pace was no more than fair, a prominent position once again an advantage. The form is weak but the time was relatively good for the grade.
Golden Compass Official explanation: jockey said that the filly suffered interference in running
Excellence(IRE) Official explanation: jockey said that the filly suffered Interference in running

2385 LINGFIELD PARK COUNTRYSIDE EVENING 4TH JUNE H'CAP (DIV I) 1m (P)
5:00 (5:01) (Class 6) (0-60,60) 4-Y-0+ £1,706 (£503; £252) **Stalls** High

Form RPR
0010 **1** **Hecton Lad (USA)**[4] 2268 4-9-4 57....(b) GeorgeBaker 1 68
(John Best) *led tl over 4f out: chsd ldr after tl led again ent fnl 2f: rdn and asserted ent fnl f: drvn out* **3/1**[1]
30-3 **2** 1 **Byrd In Hand (IRE)**[28] 1582 4-9-0 56.... SeanLevey(3) 8 65
(John Bridger) *chsd ldrs: rdn to press wnr 2f out: unable qck w wnr ent fnl f: plugged on same pce ins fnl f* **3/1**[1]
5460 **3** 2 1/4 **Haulit**[26] 1625 5-8-12 51.... RyanMoore 9 55
(Gary Moore) *in tch towards rr: rdn and effrt over 2f out: pressing for 3rd but no ch w ldrs over 1f out: chsd ldng pair ins fnl f: kpt on but nvr gng pce to chal* **8/1**

-606 **4** *5* **Belle Park**[22] [1755] 4-8-13 **52**.................................. DarryllHolland 7 44
(Karen George) *hld up in tch in rr: rdn and hdwy to chse ldng trio ent fnl 2f: sn outpcd and no threat to ldrs fr over 1f out* **12/1**

4200 **5** *2 ½* **Cavalry Guard (USA)**[48] [1184] 7-8-4 **46**..........................(b) BillyCray(3) 3 33
(Tim McCarthy) *chsd ldrs tl led over 4f out: rdn and hdd ent fnl 2f: 3rd and btn over 1f out: fdd fnl f* **33/1**

0652 **6** *2 ¼* **Spirit Of Love (IRE)**[45] [1233] 4-8-7 **46**............................ AndreaAtzeni 2 27
(Michael Wigham) *in tch: rdn and lost pl over 4f out: nvr looked happy after: lost tch u.p wl over 2f out* **7/2**[2]

0650 **7** *3 ¼* **Tinkerbell Will**[27] [1604] 4-8-10 **49**................................ RichardThomas 5 23
(John E Long) *uns rdr and led to s: sn towards rr: rdn and lost tch wl over 2f out* **100/1**

3003 **8** *nse* **Indian Violet (IRE)**[7] [2171] 5-9-7 **60**............................ JamieGoldstein 6 34
(Ralph Smith) *s.i.s: hdwy to chse ldrs over 6f out: rdn and wknd over 2f out: fdd and wl bhd 1f out* **6/1**[3]

0-00 **9** *8* **Calabaza**[55] [1043] 9-8-2 **46** oh1...............................(p) JemmaMarshall(5) 4 —
(Michael Attwater) *prom early: steadily lost pl and rr 5f out: rdn and lost tch wl over 2f out: wl bhd fnl 2f* **100/1**

1m 39.5s (1.30) **Going Correction** +0.175s/f (Slow) **9** Ran SP% **110.2**
Speed ratings (Par 101): **100,99,96,91,89 87,83,83,75**
Tote Swingers: 1&2 £3.30, 1&3 £7.10, 2&3 £6.80 CSF £11.13 CT £58.20 TOTE £3.90: £1.70, £1.10, £4.10; EX 13.10.
Owner H J Jarvis **Bred** R D Daniels Jr & C B Daniels **Trained** Hucking, Kent
■ Stewards' Enquiry : Andrea Atzeni caution: use of whip

FOCUS
A low-grade handicap in which once again little got into it from behind, the pace once again not strong. The form looks straightforward rated around the placed horses.
Spirit Of Love(IRE) Official explanation: jockey said that the gelding was never travelling; trainer said that the gelding was unsuited by the going, which he considered to be deeper than normal
Indian Violet(IRE) Official explanation: trainer said that the gelding was unsuited by the going, which he considered to be deeper than normal

2386 LINGFIELD PARK COUNTRYSIDE EVENING 4TH JUNE H'CAP (DIV II) 1m (P)

5:30 (5:30) (Class 6) (0-60,60) 4-Y-O+ **£1,706** (£503; £252) **Stalls** High

Form RPR

630- **1** **Mnarani (IRE)**[11] [2089] 4-8-4 **46**..................................(b) MartinHarley(3) 9 59
(Emmet Michael Butterly, Ire) *t.k.h: hld up in tch: chsd clr ldr gng wl over 2f out: racd awkwardly and rdn over 1f out: led 1f out: drvn and r.o strly to draw clr fnl 100yds* **11/8**[1]

5050 **2** *3 ½* **Clearing House**[13] [1995] 6-9-4 **57**.................................. KirstyMilczarek 1 62
(John Ryan) *hld up in last pair: rdn and hdwy jst over 2f out: chsd ldng pair over 1f out: chsd wnr ins fnl f: outpcd and btn fnl 100yds: kpt on for clr 2nd* **6/1**[3]

-005 **3** *3 ¼* **Batchworth Blaise**[23] [1730] 8-8-11 **53**............................(b) KierenFox(3) 6 51
(Eric Wheeler) *stdd s: hld up in last pair: hdwy on outer 5f out: led over 3f out: clr over 2f out: rdn and edging rt over 1f out: hdd 1f out: wknd fnl f* **15/2**

/00- **4** *½* **Toballa**[268] [5560] 6-8-4 **46** oh1...(t) BillyCray(3) 4 42
(Clifford Lines) *s.i.s: racd awkwardly in rr: swtchd to outer and drvn wl over 2f out: hdwy and hanging lft over 1f out: kpt on fnl f: no ch w wnr* **33/1**

6510 **5** *½* **Queenie's Star (IRE)**[61] [957] 4-8-13 **52**............................ AdamKirby 5 47
(Michael Attwater) *chsd ldrs: nt clr run over 2f out: swtchd rt and effrt u.p wl over 1f out: no hdwy and btn 1f out* **11/1**

0-06 **6** *¾* **Shaws Diamond (USA)**[8] [2165] 5-9-5 **58**............................ MartinLane 8 52
(Derek Shaw) *chsd ldr tl over 3f out: u.p and struggling 3f out: wknd ent fnl 2f: no ch after* **7/1**

0415 **7** *2 ¼* **Aggbag**[7] [2171] 7-8-9 **48**.. DarryllHolland 2 36
(Tony Carroll) *in tch in midfield: rdn and lost pl wl over 2f out: no prog and wl btn over 1f out* **9/2**[2]

0460 **8** *2 ¾* **Illuminative (USA)**[13] [862] 5-8-11 **50**..........................(b) TonyCulhane 7 32
(Zoe Davison) *hld up in tch: lost pl and rdn over 2f out: lost tch wl over 1f out* **20/1**

540- **9** *3 ¾* **Cactus King**[177] [7614] 8-9-7 **60**... IanMongan 10 33
(Louise Best) *sn led: hdd over 3f out: rdn and struggling in 3rd ent fnl 2f: wknd wl over 1f out: wl bhd and eased ins fnl f* **[illegible]**

1m 39.7s (1.50) **Going Correction** +0.175s/f (Slow) **9** Ran SP% **118.7**
Speed ratings (Par 101): **99,95,92,91,91 90,88,85,81**
Tote Swingers: 1&2 £1.50, 1&3 £4.00, 2&3 £7.20 CSF £10.11 CT £48.04 TOTE £3.00: £1.70, £1.40, £2.60; EX 12.40.
Owner James Ferry **Bred** Ceka Ireland Ltd **Trained** Letterkenny, Co Donegal

FOCUS
Another low-grade affair, but at least a more strongly-run race than seemed apparent beforehand. The runner-up is rated to his April course form.
Aggbag Official explanation: jockey said that the gelding ran flat
T/Plt: £41.50 to a £1 stake. Pool of £50,687.30 - 891.36 winning tickets. T/Qpdt: £8.90 to a £1 stake. Pool of £4,180.31 - 344.10 winning tickets. SP

2120 RIPON (R-H)

Tuesday, May 24

OFFICIAL GOING: Good (good to firm in places)
Rail at innermost configuration and distances as advertised.
Wind: strong 1/2 behind Weather: fine and sunny but very windy

2387 BRITISH STALLION STUDS SUPPORTING BRITISH RACING E B F MAIDEN STKS 5f

2:10 (2:10) (Class 5) 2-Y-O **£3,561** (£1,059; £529; £264) **Stalls** High

Form RPR

1 **Parc De Launay** 2-9-3 0.. JamieSpencer 2 76+
(Tom Tate) *w ldr: led after 1f: wandered: edgd rt over 1f out: kpt on wl* **13/8**[1]

0 **2** *1 ¼* **Dicky Mint**[13] [2007] 2-9-0 0.. JamesSullivan(3) 1 71
(Michael Easterby) *led 1f: chsd wnr: carried rt and styd on same pce fnl f* **17/2**[3]

3 *1 ¾* **Pen Bal Crag (IRE)** 2-9-3 0.. PaulHanagan 9 64+
(Richard Fahey) *chsd ldrs: drvn and hung rt 2f out: styd on ins fnl f* **3/1**[2]

0 **4** *¾* **Come Hither**[10] [2113] 2-8-12 0.. KierenFallon 3 57
(Michael Easterby) *dwlt: in rr: hdwy 2f out: kpt on wl fnl f* **25/1**

5 *½* **Ave Sofia** 2-8-12 0.. JoeFanning 5 55
(John Holt) *s.s: hdwy on wd outside over 2f out: chsng ldrs over 1f out: kpt on same pce* **66/1**

0 **6** *1 ½* **Beechey's Beauty**[14] [1966] 2-9-3 0................................ PaulMulrennan 6 54
(Ann Duffield) *chsd ldrs: kpt on same pce fnl 2f* **40/1**

7 *nk* **Duke Of Aricabeau (IRE)** 2-9-3 0............................. GrahamGibbons 8 53+
(Michael Easterby) *s.i.s: kpt on fnl 2f: nvr nr ldrs* **12/1**

8 *nk* **Cooldine Cat (IRE)** 2-9-3 0.. BarryMcHugh 11 52+
(John Quinn) *dwlt: mid-div: outpcd and wnt rt over 2f out: kpt on fnl f* **12/1**

9 *3 ¾* **Homeward Strut** 2-9-3 0.. SilvestreDeSousa 10 39
(David O'Meara) *dwlt: mid-div: effrt over 2f out: sn lost pl* **22/1**

10 *nk* **Grippa** 2-9-3 0... PhillipMakin 7 38
(David Brown) *mid-div: outpcd and lost pl over 2f out* **20/1**

364 **11** *5* **Nellie Pickersgill**[10] [2113] 2-8-12 0.................................. DuranFentiman 4 15
(Tim Easterby) *chsd ldrs: lost pl over 2f out* **12/1**

60.03 secs (-0.67) **Going Correction** -0.225s/f (Firm) **11** Ran SP% **113.6**
Speed ratings (Par 93): **96,94,91,90,89 86,86,85,79,79 71**
Tote Swingers: 1&2 £3.70, 1&3 £2.20, 2&3 £4.70 CSF £14.31 TOTE £2.60: £1.40, £1.80, £1.50; EX 17.20 Trifecta £116.10 Pool: £370.48 - 2.36 winning units..
Owner Mrs Fitri Hay **Bred** Equity Bloodstock Partnership **Trained** Tadcaster, N Yorks

FOCUS
The going was officially described as good, with some good to firm patches between the 3f and 1f markers. Probably no more than an ordinary maiden in which the front two dominated throughout, but in all likelihood we saw a useful winner.

NOTEBOOK
Parc De Launay was well backed and won despite hanging right for much of the journey. There had been concerns over the quick ground, so he was perhaps a bit reluctant to fully let himself down, but Jamie Spencer was inclined to put it down to greenness and it's reasonable to expect improvement for having the experience. Rated better than the bare form, the raw speed he displayed suggests he wouldn't be out of place at Royal Ascot and it will be considered, although it's doubtful whether he'll get any give in the ground there. (op 11-8 tchd 7-4)
Dicky Mint, from the in-form Mick Easterby stable, showed plenty of pace from stall one and improved massively on his recent York debut when asked to contest a good-looking novice stakes. He'll have no trouble winning on this evidence. (op 16-1 tchd 15-2)
Pen Bal Crag(IRE) never looked like making a winning debut, but was going on nicely close home and should be capable of winning something similar, possibly over 6f. (op 7-2)
Come Hither, another Mick Easterby runner, was doing his best work late and will be of interest for nurseries later in the season. (op 28-1)
Ave Sofia, a half-sister to a 6f-1m winner, ran better than her 66-1 odds suggested she would, and should improve once upped to 6f.
Duke Of Aricabeau(IRE), the Mick Easterby second string according to the betting, never really got into it following a slow start, but should come on for the experience and is likely to appreciate an additional furlong. (tchd 11-1)

2388 ATTHERACES.COM IS FREE H'CAP 1m 1f 170y

2:40 (2:41) (Class 5) (0-70,70) 4-Y-O+ **£2,331** (£693; £346; £173) **Stalls** Low

Form RPR

5-01 **1** **Easy Terms**[36] [1440] 4-8-13 **65**.. JamesSullivan(3) 4 76
(Edwin Tuer) *sn trcking ldrs: led over 2f out: styd on strly fnl f: eased towards fin* **15/2**[2]

640- **2** *1 ½* **Munaawer (USA)**[220] [6937] 4-8-11 **60**............................ JamieSpencer 14 67
(James Bethell) *hld up in mid-div: hdwy on outer 4f out: chal over 1f out: kpt on same pce* **25/1**

4405 **3** *¾* **Lord Lansing (IRE)**[61] [1012] 4-9-2 **65**............................ AndrewElliott 10 71
(Mrs K Burke) *trckd ldrs: swtchd lft over 1f out: styd on to take 3rd nr fin* **20/1**

05-0 **4** *¾* **Beneath**[21] [1798] 4-8-9 **58** ow1..(b) PhillipMakin 5 62
(Kevin Ryan) *mid-div: hdwy over3f out: chsng ldrs over 1f out: kpt on same pce* **11/1**

-000 **5** *¾* **Sharp Sovereign (USA)**[11] [2059] 5-9-3 **66**........................ LeeNewman 7 69
(David Barron) *trckd ldrs: kpt on same pce over 1f out* **9/1**[3]

-000 **6** *8* **Antoniola (IRE)**[18] [1859] 4-9-3 **66**..........................(be) GrahamGibbons 1 53
(Tim Easterby) *sn trcking ldrs: effrt 3f out: wknd over 1f out* **11/1**

04-2 **7** *1 ¼* **Brockfield**[40] [1324] 5-8-12 **61**.. FrannyNorton 3 52+
(Mel Brittain) *led: hdd over 2f out: wknd over 1f out: stmbld ins fnl f: eased* **9/2**[1]

26-0 **8** *5* **Fama Mac**[45] [1245] 4-8-11 **60**.. BarryMcHugh 6 34
(Neville Bycroft) *mid-div: hdwy on ins 3f out: wknd over 1f out* **33/1**

[illegible] **9** [illegible] **[illegible] (IRE)**[[illegible]] [[illegible]] [illegible]......................... NataliaGemelova(3) 2 29
(David O'Meara) *in rr: nvr a factor* **10/1**

05-0 **10** *2 ½* **More Than Many (USA)**[17] [1909] 5-9-5 **68**...................... PaulHanagan 12 33
(Richard Fahey) *a in rr: nvr a factor* **9/2**[1]

32-0 **11** *27* **Tayacoba (CAN)**[11] [2059] 4-9-7 **70**.................................... TomEaves 13 —
(Martin Todhunter) *s.i.s: a in rr: bhd and eased fnl f: t.o* **40/1**

04-0 **12** *2 ¼* **Hurlingham**[34] [1491] 7-8-11 **60**..................................(b) PaulMulrennan 11 —
(Michael Easterby) *in rr: bhd and eased fnl f: t.o* **16/1**

6-45 **13** *½* **I'm Super Too (IRE)**[18] [1859] 4-9-6 **69**..........................(b[1]) PJMcDonald 9 —
(Alan Swinbank) *chsd ldrs: drvn over 3f out: sn lost pl: bhd and eased fnl f: t.o* **15/2**[2]

66-0 **14** *dist* **Streets Of War (USA)**[45] [1243] 4-9-4 **67**...............(b[1]) SilvestreDeSousa 8 —
(Geoffrey Harker) *s.s: in rr: drvn 4f out: sn bhd: t.o over 1f out: virtually p.u* **20/1**

2m 3.84s (-1.56) **Going Correction** -0.225s/f (Firm) **14** Ran SP% **120.3**
Speed ratings (Par 103): **97,95,95,94,94 87,86,82,80,78 57,55,55,—**
Tote Swingers: 1&2 £25.60, 1&3 £25.20, 2&3 £67.00 CSF £191.09 CT £3578.52 TOTE £8.20: £2.40, £9.00, £7.60; EX 228.20 TRIFECTA Not won..
Owner E Tuer **Bred** T E Pocock **Trained** Great Smeaton, N Yorks

FOCUS
A competitive 0-70 handicap and the form looks pretty straightfoward rated around the first three.
Brockfield Official explanation: jockey said that the colt stumbled in the final furlong
I'm Super Too(IRE) Official explanation: jockey said that that the colt stopped quickly

2389 WEATHERBYS BANK H'CAP 1m 1f 170y

3:10 (3:11) (Class 4) (0-80,80) 3-Y-O **£4,209** (£1,252; £625; £312) **Stalls** Low

Form RPR

432- **1** **Motivado**[200] [7335] 3-9-4 **77**.. StevieDonohoe 5 91+
(Sir Mark Prescott Bt) *gave problems s: dwlt: t.k.h early: hdwy to trck ldrs 7f out: nt clr run fr over 2f out: swtchd lft over 1f out: led last 100yds: v readily* **2/1**[1]

4-1 **2** *2 ¾* **Taqaat (USA)**[14] [1971] 3-9-6 **79**.. TadhgO'Shea 2 85
(Mark Johnston) *trckd ldr: reminders over 3f out: led over 1f out: hung rt: hdd ins fnl f: no ex* **9/2**[3]

04-1 **3** *2 ¼* **Ollon (USA)**[15] [1944] 3-8-9 **68**.. PaulHanagan 7 69
(Richard Fahey) *sn trcking ldrs: drvn over 4f out: kpt on same pce over 1f out* **6/1**

3-15 **4** *1* **Franciscan**[15] [1949] 3-8-11 **70**.. KierenFallon 3 69
(Luca Cumani) *hld up towards rr: drvn over 4f out: kpt on fnl f* **11/4**[2]

0-46 **5** *1 ¼* **Yahafedh Alaih**[40] [1341] 3-8-11 **70**.................................. PhilipRobinson 1 67
(Clive Brittain) *led: qcknd over 4f out: hdd over 1f out: sn wknd* **12/1**

-251 **6** *9* **Muhandis (IRE)**[15] 1934 3-9-7 **80** JimCrowley 6 59
(Ed Dunlop) *t.k.h in rr: effrt 3f out: sn wknd: eased towards fin* **8/1**

2m 4.60s (-0.80) **Going Correction** -0.225s/f (Firm) **6** Ran SP% **111.3**
Speed ratings (Par 101): **94,91,90,89,88 81**
Tote Swingers: 1&2 £2.50, 1&3 £3.10, 2&3 £4.40 CSF £11.11 TOTE £3.90: £2.50, £3.10; EX 12.40.
Owner Syndicate 2009 **Bred** Newsells Park Stud **Trained** Newmarket, Suffolk

FOCUS
A decent-looking handicap rated around the third and fifth.

2390 NICK WILMOT-SMITH MEMORIAL H'CAP 1m
3:40 (3:40) (Class 3) (0-95,95) 4-Y-0+ **£6,623** (£1,982; £991; £495; £246) **Stalls** Low

Form RPR
5122 **1** **Dubai Dynamo**[9] 2123 6-8-11 **85** PJMcDonald 7 97
(Ruth Carr) *s.i.s: hld up in rr: hdwy on inner whn nt clr run over 2f out: qcknd to ld last 100yds: styd on strly: v readily* **11/2**[3]
6-12 **2** *2 1/4* **Lord Aeryn (IRE)**[27] 1603 4-9-0 **88** PaulHanagan 1 95
(Richard Fahey) *trckd ldrs on inner: effrt over 2f out: styd on fnl f: tk 2nd post* **11/4**[1]
1123 **3** *shd* **Snow Bay**[9] 2123 5-9-6 **94** AdrianNicholls 3 101
(David Nicholls) *led: edgd lft over 1f out: hdd and no ex ins fnl f* **7/1**
3-0 **4** *1 1/2* **Bea Remembered**[17] 1884 4-9-5 **93** KierenFallon 9 97
(Brian Meehan) *s.i.s: t.k.h in rr: hdwy on outside over 2f out: kpt on fnl f* **20/1**
2-02 **5** *nk* **Reel Buddy Star**[15] 1942 6-8-12 **86** DanielTudhope 5 89
(George Moore) *sn trcking ldr: chal over 2f out: one pce appr fnl f* **20/1**
0424 **6** *3/4* **Suits Me**[13] 2002 8-9-1 **89** PhillipMakin 4 90
(David Barron) *chsd ldrs: one pce fnl 2f* **5/1**[2]
11-0 **7** *hd* **Saint Pierre (USA)**[38] 1406 4-9-0 **88** J-PGuillambert 6 89
(Luca Cumani) *prom: effrt over 2f out: kpt on fnl f* **12/1**
36-0 **8** *2* **Ginger Jack**[11] 2061 4-9-1 **89** SilvestreDeSousa 2 85
(Geoffrey Harker) *stdd s: hld up in rr: nt clr run on inner over 2f out: kpt on: nvr a factor* **14/1**
-000 **9** *2 3/4* **Prince Of Dance**[38] 1410 5-8-13 **87** GrahamGibbons 8 77
(Tom Tate) *in rr: drvn 4f out: nvr a factor* **9/1**
3030 **10** *20* **Dubai Hills**[38] 1406 5-9-7 **95** TomEaves 10 —
(Bryan Smart) *in rr: drvn over 3f out: sn wknd: eased whn bhd over 1f out: t.o* **22/1**
1042 **11** *hd* **Bowmaker**[17] 1898 4-8-9 **83** JoeFanning 11 —
(Mark Johnston) *mid-div: drvn over 3f out: sn lost pl: bhd and eased over 1f out: t.o* **10/1**

1m 38.1s (-3.30) **Going Correction** -0.225s/f (Firm) **11** Ran SP% **118.5**
Speed ratings (Par 107): **107,104,104,103,102 102,101,99,97,77 76**
Tote Swingers: 1&2 £3.20, 1&3 £4.70, 2&3 £2.90 CSF £20.47 CT £111.22 TOTE £5.50: £2.00, £1.60, £2.80; EX 15.40 Trifecta £47.20 Pool: £823.43 - 12.90 winning units..
Owner The Bottom Liners **Bred** T K & Mrs P A Knox **Trained** Huby, N Yorks

FOCUS
A good, competitive handicap. The form looks solid, with the front three having all been running well of late and the second and fourth the best guides to the level.

NOTEBOOK
Dubai Dynamo has been in good form, finishing second over C&D last time having tried to come from too far back, and although again left with plenty of running to do, he finished strongly and in plenty of time, for his second turf win of the season. He'll now head to Newcastle later in the week and a trip to Royal Ascot may be on the cards as well, with the Buckingham Palace Stakes, in which he was well beaten last year, presumably the aim. (op 5-1)
Lord Aeryn(IRE), who built on his 7f Doncaster win with a good second over this trip at Ascot, was up another 4lb but showed he's still progressing, narrowly doing best of those to have raced prominent. (op 7-2)
Snow Bay, a triple winner earlier this year including over C&D, is a very game horse who ran right up to his best. (tchd 15-2)
Bea Remembered built on her debut for the yard and shaped like a filly who will appreciate 1m2f, finishing well down the outside. (op 25-1 tchd 28-1)
Reel Buddy Star was never far away and had every chance from 2f out, but couldn't stay on as well as others. (tchd 18-1)
Saint Pierre(USA) has yet to show he's progressed much from three to four, but this was at least better than his reappearance effort. (op 9-1)
Ginger Jack would have been closer with a better run. (op 16-1)

2391 WEATHERBYS BLOODSTOCK INSURANCE H'CAP 6f
4:10 (4:10) (Class 5) (0-75,73) 3-Y-0 **£4,209** (£1,252; £625; £312) **Stalls** High

Form RPR
0411 **1** **Barkston Ash**[14] 1980 3-9-2 **68** DuranFentiman 8 78
(Eric Alston) *trckd ldr stands' side: led appr fnl f: pushed out* **9/4**[1]
6-34 **2** *1 1/4* **Nine Before Ten (IRE)**[31] 1521 3-9-7 **73** (t) GregFairley 1 79
(Deborah Sanderson) *led: hdd appr fnl f: no ex* **14/1**
526- **3** *2 3/4* **Guinea Seeker**[228] 6705 3-8-10 **62** DavidAllan 10 59
(Tim Easterby) *mid-div: effrt and hung rt over 2f out: wnt 3rd over 1f out: kpt on same pce* **22/1**
30-6 **4** *3/4* **Maggie Mey (IRE)**[10] 2096 3-9-6 **72** SilvestreDeSousa 3 67
(David O'Meara) *chsd ldrs: rdn and outpcd over 3f out: kpt on fnl f* **4/1**[2]
01-6 **5** *nse* **Lady Del Sol**[36] 1437 3-9-7 **73** PaulMulrennan 6 68+
(Marjorie Fife) *bmpd s: bhd: hdwy on outer over 2f out: kpt on fnl f* **10/1**
04-3 **6** *6* **Proper Charlie**[14] 1984 3-9-6 **72** (v[1]) JamieSpencer 7 47
(William Knight) *wnt rt and bmpd s: sme hdwy on outer 2f out: nvr rchd ldrs: wknd and eased last 100yds* **7/1**
01-4 **7** *1 1/2* **Normandy Maid**[27] 1624 3-9-6 **72** PaulHanagan 2 43
(Richard Fahey) *trckd ldrs: wknd over 1f out* **9/2**[3]
-000 **8** *3/4* **Watts Up Son**[22] 1758 3-9-7 **73** (t) DavidNolan 5 41
(Declan Carroll) *chsd ldrs: lost pl over 2f out* **28/1**
2-11 **9** *8* **Finn's Rainbow**[133] 119 3-9-7 **73** PhillipMakin 9 16
(Kevin Ryan) *in rr: drvn over 2f out: sn bhd* **10/1**
20-0 **10** *1* **Bellemere**[11] 2074 3-9-0 **69** JamesSullivan[(3)] 4 —
(Michael Easterby) *in rr: bhd fnl 3f* **50/1**

1m 11.67s (-1.33) **Going Correction** -0.225s/f (Firm) **10** Ran SP% **116.1**
Speed ratings (Par 99): **99,97,93,92,92 84,82,81,70,69**
Tote Swingers: 1&2 £9.70, 1&3 £9.70, 2&3 £32.60 CSF £35.83 CT £567.66 TOTE £3.60: £1.70, £4.00, £6.80; EX 46.50 Trifecta £358.50 Part won. Pool: £484.57 - 0.70 winning units..
Owner The Selebians **Bred** Jonathan Shack **Trained** Longton, Lancs

FOCUS
Few got into this 3-y-o sprint handicap but the form looks sound enough.

2392 SIS LIVE MAIDEN STKS (DIV I) 1m
4:40 (4:41) (Class 5) 3-Y-0 **£1,596** (£1,596; £365; £182) **Stalls** Low

Form RPR
5-35 **1** **Qenaa**[10] 2103 3-8-12 **80** TadhgO'Shea 2 73
(Mark Johnston) *trckd ldrs: effrt 4f out: led over 1f out: jnd on line* **11/2**
35-5 **1** *dht* **Early Applause**[51] 1108 3-9-3 **75** MichaelHills 1 78
(B W Hills) *led 1f: chsd ldr: styd on fnl f: dead-heated on line* **7/4**[1]
0-20 **3** *5* **Auto Mac**[24] 1693 3-9-3 **73** PaulMulrennan 3 66
(Neville Bycroft) *chsd ldrs: edgd lft appr fnl f: kpt on to take 3rd nr fin* **25/1**
3-3 **4** *hd* **Al Burkaan (IRE)**[11] 2045 3-9-3 **0** JamieSpencer 12 66
(Ed Dunlop) *tk fierce hold: racd wd and led after 1f: hdd over 1f out: wknd towards fin* **5/1**[3]
6 **5** *4* **Le Chat D'Or**[17] 1910 3-9-3 **0** BarryMcHugh 11 56
(Neville Bycroft) *s.i.s and wnt lft s: bhd: hdwy over 3f out: kpt on: nvr nr ldrs* **125/1**
000- **6** *5* **Good Faith**[221] 6894 3-9-3 **37** PJMcDonald 8 45
(George Moore) *sn bhd: kpt on fnl 3f: nvr nr ldrs* **100/1**
33-0 **7** *2 3/4* **Cultural Desert**[51] 1108 3-9-3 **76** JimCrowley 6 39
(Ralph Beckett) *mid-div: drvn over 3f out: sn btn* **9/2**[2]
50 **8** *3/4* **Singzak**[9] 2125 3-9-0 **0** JamesSullivan[(3)] 4 37
(Michael Easterby) *mid-div: drvn over 3f out: nvr a factor* **66/1**
00- **9** *4 1/2* **Hopscotch**[185] 7530 3-8-12 **0** HayleyTurner 10 21
(Michael Bell) *swtchd rt after s: in rr and drvn along: sme hdwy 4f out: lost pl over 2f out* **20/1**
40 **10** *1/2* **Neat Sweep (IRE)**[38] 1399 3-8-12 **0** GrahamGibbons 5 20
(Alan McCabe) *chsd ldrs: wknd over 2f out* **50/1**
0-0 **11** *2 1/4* **Henrys Gift (IRE)**[24] 1693 3-9-0 **0** PatrickDonaghy[(3)] 7 20
(Michael Dods) *hld up in rr: drvn over 3f out: nvr on terms* **50/1**
0- **12** *1/2* **Shirataki (IRE)**[228] 6722 3-9-3 **0** JoeFanning 9 19
(Mark Johnston) *mid-div: drvn over 3f out: sn lost pl* **7/1**

1m 40.22s (-1.18) **Going Correction** -0.225s/f (Firm) **12** Ran SP% **114.9**
Speed ratings (Par 99): **96,96,91,90,86 81,79,78,73,73 71,70**Win: Early Applause £1.50 Qeenaa £1.80. Places: EP £1.80 Q £1.10 Auto Mac £9.70. Ex: EP,Q £5.28 Q,EP £5.70. CSF: EP,Q £5.28 Q,EP £7.20. Trifecta: 4-12-2 £80.60, 12-4-2 £62.70. Tote Swingers: EP&Q £3.10, EP&AM £20.80, Q&AM £7.90, £0.27, £OwnerHamdan Al Maktoum Bred Trifecta £Mrs M Campbell-Andenaes Trained Middleham Moor, N Yorks.
Owner John C Grant **Bred** Lakin Bloodstock, Hillard Bloodstock & Trading Ltd **Trained** Lambourn, Berks

FOCUS
The first division of what looked a fairly modest maiden, with the front two proving inseparable at the line. The form suggests the first two were close to their best.

2393 BET BRITISH WITH TOTEPOOL H'CAP 1m 4f 10y
5:10 (5:10) (Class 5) (0-70,68) 4-Y-0+ **£2,331** (£693; £346; £173) **Stalls** Low

Form RPR
5140 **1** **King's Counsel (IRE)**[10] 2091 5-9-1 **62** (v) DanielTudhope 3 71
(David O'Meara) *mde all: qcknd 4f out: rdn over 2f out: styd on wl: unchal* **7/1**
/0-0 **2** *3* **Fossgate**[27] 1617 10-8-4 **54** oh5 AmyRyan[(3)] 8 58+
(James Bethell) *hld up in mid-div: hdwy and drvn over 3f out: styd on fnl 2f: tk 2nd nr fin* **33/1**
146- **3** *hd* **Mohawk Ridge**[165] 7806 5-9-2 **68** LeeTopliss[(5)] 1 72
(Michael Dods) *trckd ldrs: drvn over 3f out: kpt on same pce fnl f* **14/1**
41-6 **4** *1/2* **Penangdouble O One**[17] 1908 4-9-7 **68** (t) JimCrowley 12 71
(Ralph Beckett) *sn trcking wnr: drvn over 3f out: one pce over 1f out* **9/2**[1]
4242 **5** *2 1/4* **Eijaaz (IRE)**[21] 1792 10-8-13 **60** (p) SilvestreDeSousa 9 60+
(Geoffrey Harker) *s.i.s: hld up in rr: hdwy on ins over 3f out: one pce fnl 2f* **6/1**[3]
6-34 **6** *3/4* **Grey Command (USA)**[18] 1881 6-8-7 **54** oh5 FrannyNorton 4 54+
(Mel Brittain) *chsd ldrs: drvn over 3f out: one pce whn hmpd over 2f out* **20/1**
500 **7** *nse* **Lure of The Night (IRE)**[10] 2114 4-8-13 **60** PaulHanagan 11 58
(Brian Rothwell) *in rr: effrt on outside 4f out: chsng ldrs whn edgd rt over 2f out: one pce* **40/1**
4-45 **8** *1* **Sartingo (IRE)**[17] 1910 4-9-6 **67** PJMcDonald 2 64
(Alan Swinbank) *mid-div: drvn over 3f out: one pce fnl 2f* **8/1**
44/0 **9** *1/2* **Westlin' Winds (IRE)**[11] 2060 5-8-11 **63** DaleSwift[(5)] 5 59
(Brian Ellison) *s.i.s: in last: sme hdwy over 3f out: nvr on terms* **7/1**
4612 **10** *6* **Bring Sweets (IRE)**[62] 645 4-8-4 **54** PaulPickard[(3)] 7 40
(Brian Ellison) *in rr: bhd fnl 2f* **12/1**
5-55 **11** *3/4* **Idealism**[35] 1460 4-9-2 **63** FrederikTylicki 6 48
(Micky Hammond) *t.k.h in mid-div: effrt 4f out: wkng whn bmpd over 2f out* **5/1**[2]
5-60 **12** *2* **Apache Warrior**[17] 1909 4-9-1 **62** TomEaves 10 44
(George Moore) *in rr: bhd fnl 2f* **20/1**

2m 36.11s (-0.59) **Going Correction** -0.225s/f (Firm) **12** Ran SP% **114.5**
Speed ratings (Par 103): **92,90,89,89,88 87,87,86,86,82 82,80**
Tote Swingers: 1&2 £52.80, 1&3 £20.60, 2&3 £49.00 CSF £221.55 CT £3099.47 TOTE £9.60: £3.80, £17.10, £4.80; EX 270.50 Trifecta £556.80 Part won. Pool: £752.50 - 0.62 winning units..
Owner W R B Racing 44 **Bred** Peter And Jackie Grimes **Trained** Nawton, N Yorks

FOCUS
A fine front-running ride by Daniel Tudhope on the winner in this low-grade middle-distance handicap. The form is rated around the third and fourth.

2394 SIS LIVE MAIDEN STKS (DIV II) 1m
5:40 (5:47) (Class 5) 3-Y-0 **£2,460** (£732; £365; £182) **Stalls** Low

Form RPR
5 **1** **Izzy The Ozzy (IRE)**[8] 2151 3-8-12 **0** LeeNewman 9 82
(David Barron) *trckd ldrs: led over 2f out: drew clr appr fnl f: eased nr fin* **9/1**[2]
435 **2** *8* **Carrowbeg (IRE)**[24] 1704 3-9-3 **74** JoeFanning 1 69
(Mark Johnston) *led 1f: chsd ldr: wnt 2nd over 2f out: one pce* **13/8**[1]
06- **3** *3 1/2* **Border Abby**[210] 7152 3-8-12 **0** SilvestreDeSousa 11 56
(Rae Guest) *s.i.s: hdwy to ld after 1f: hdd over 2f out: one pce* **40/1**
6 **4** *6* **Woolamaloo**[21] 1799 3-8-12 **0** DavidAllan 2 42
(Tim Easterby) *s.i.s: sn in tch: outpcd 3f out: sn wknd* **100/1**
-6 **5** *1* **Charles De Mille**[49] 1151 3-9-3 **0** PJMcDonald 7 44
(George Moore) *dwlt: in rr bhd whn hmpd over 3f out: kpt on ins fnl f* **16/1**[3]
0-0 **6** *2 1/2* **Silver Tiger**[52] 1096 3-9-3 **0** GrahamGibbons 10 39
(Chris Wall) *sn trcking ldrs: t.k.h: hung rt and lost pl over 2f out* **28/1**
0-6 **U** **Margot De Medici (FR)**[9] 2125 3-8-12 **0** FrederikTylicki 6 —
(Micky Hammond) *in rr: bhd whn uns rdr over 3f out: fatally injured* **100/1**

1m 40.27s (-1.13) **Going Correction** -0.225s/f (Firm) **7** Ran SP% **61.8**
Speed ratings (Par 99): **96,88,84,78,77 75,—**
Tote Swingers: 1&2 £1.10, 1&3 £8.20, 2&3 £2.30. Tote Super 7: Win: Not won. Place: £28.20 - 12 winning units. CSF £6.37 TOTE £5.80: £2.60, £1.10; EX 6.60 Trifecta £25.30 Pool: £52.78 - 1.54 winning units..
Owner Christopher McHale **Bred** Ennistown Stud **Trained** Maunby, N Yorks

The Form Book, Raceform Ltd, Compton, RG20 6NL

FOCUS
This looked the less competitive of the two divisions. Several of these got worked up down at the stalls, with short-price favourite Tlaad (11/10) refusing to go in, and Thatcherite and Little O J also being withdrawn, the latter having gone down in the stalls. Deduct 55p in the £ under R4. The form looks weaker than the first division but the level is fluid and the time relative to the first leg helps set the level.
T/Jkpt: £1,766.30 to a £1 stake. Pool of £44,456.60 - 17.87 winning tickets. T/Plt: £36.60 to a £1 stake. Pool of £73,164.87 - 1,455.43 winning tickets. T/Qpdt: £6.50 to a £1 stake. Pool of £5,177.11 - 586.45 winning tickets. WG

AYR (L-H)

Wednesday, May 25

OFFICIAL GOING: Good to soft (soft in places; 8.6)
Rails on innermost line and full width of track used.
Wind: Strong,all directions Weather: Cloudy

2395 BRITISH STALLION STUDS SUPPORTING BRITISH RACING E B F MAIDEN STKS — 6f

2:10 (2:11) (Class 4) 2-Y-O **£4,468** (£1,329; £664; £331) **Stalls** High

Form RPR
1 **Bogart** 2-9-3 0 .... PaulMulrennan 6 85+
(Kevin Ryan) *w ldr: led over 1f out: pushed clr fnl f* **10/1**
2 2 ¾ **Holy Roman Warrior (IRE)** 2-9-3 0 .... PaulHanagan 7 76+
(Richard Fahey) *led: rdn and hdd over 1f out: kpt on same pce fnl f* **11/4**[2]
4 3 2 ¾ **Letsgoroundagain (IRE)**[40] 1360 2-9-3 0 .... MichaelHills 1 68
(B W Hills) *prom on outside: pushed along and effrt over 2f out: kpt on same pce over 1f out* **8/11**[1]
3 4 1 **Joshua The First**[12] 2042 2-9-3 0 .... TonyHamilton 4 65+
(Keith Dalgleish) *bhd: rdn over 2f out: hdwy and edgd lft over 1f out: kpt on: nvr able to chal* **25/1**
5 nse **Haafkry** 2-9-0 0 .... JamesSullivan(3) 5 65
(Linda Stubbs) *in tch: drvn and outpcd over 3f out: rallied over 1f out: no imp* **66/1**
0 6 ¾ **Zigazag (IRE)**[13] 2023 2-9-3 0 .... LukeMorris 2 63
(David Evans) *dwlt: bhd: drvn 1/2-way: sme hdwy over 1f out: n.d* **100/1**
0 7 11 **Coach Montana (IRE)**[40] 1360 2-9-3 0 .... KierenFallon 8 30
(Jane Chapple-Hyam) *trckd ldrs: rdn over 2f out: wknd over 1f out* **13/2**[3]
0 8 3 ¾ **Moon Trip**[13] 2033 2-9-3 0 .... JoeFanning 3 18
(Mark Johnston) *cl up: rdn and wknd over 2f out: eased whn no ch fnl f* **16/1**

1m 13.73s (1.33) **Going Correction** 0.0s/f (Good) **8** Ran SP% **119.2**
Speed ratings (Par 95): **99,95,91,90,90 89,74,69**
toteswingers:1&2:£2.40, 1&3:£3.10, 2&3:£1.60 CSF £39.21 TOTE £11.10: £2.20, £1.10, £2.00; EX 41.20 Trifecta £73.60 Pool: £717.43 - 7.21 winning units..
Owner Mrs Angie Bailey **Bred** Toby Barker **Trained** Hambleton, N Yorks

FOCUS
Despite a small amount of rain in the morning, the ground had dried out a little from that advertised and was now Good to Soft, Soft in places, though it was expected to ride softer down the far side. An interesting maiden which has been won by some smart performers in recent years, including the subsequent Middle Park winner Amadeus Wolf in 2005, whilst last year it went to the recent dual Guineas runner-up Dubawi Gold. The front pair raced close to the stands' rail, which may have been an advantage, but even so the feeling is that this year's renewal will have produced a couple of nice sorts. The winner will be one to respect up in grade.

NOTEBOOK
Bogart a £32,000 colt out of a winner over this 6f trip, travelled powerfully up with the pace and quickened up stylishly when asked to assert. From the same yard that produced Amadeus Wolf, he is likely to be given a break now and reappear towards the end of July for a second-half of the season campaign. Clearly highly regarded, his trainer believes he will get 7f-1m. (op 12-1 after early 20-1 in a place)
Holy Roman Warrior(IRE) ran a debut full of promise, sharing the lead until outpaced by the winner from the furlong pole. This £70,000 half-brother to the Group 3-winner Corsica shouldn't take long in going one better. (op 3-1 tchd 10-3)
Letsgoroundagain(IRE) very much caught the eye on his debut when fourth in a hot Newbury maiden which has already produced the winners of six subsequent races, but he failed to step up from that initial effort as much as might have been expected. He was a little marooned towards the outside of the field, but he was still comfortably held by the two newcomers and he has a bit to prove now. (tchd 4-5 and 5-6 in places)
Joshua The First, well held when third of four on his Hamilton debut, was up a furlong here but the way he stayed on suggests that an even stiffer test will suit him better.
Haafkry cost just 1,200gns as a yearling so this debut effort wasn't at all bad, especially as he threatened to finish a long way behind at one stage. He is bred to stay much further than this and looks an interesting prospect for later on. Official explanation: jockey said gelding was denied a clear run shortly before line
Zigazag(IRE) never got into it, but this was still an improvement on his last of seven on his Salisbury debut. (op 66-1)

2396 CHAMBER HEALTH PLAN H'CAP — 6f

2:40 (2:41) (Class 6) (0-60,66) 3-Y-O **£1,706** (£503; £252) **Stalls** High

Form RPR
6-00 1 **Monel**[35] 1494 3-8-12 **51** .... DanielTudhope 11 60+
(Jim Goldie) *hld up: hdwy and weaved through to ld over 1f out: drvn out fnl f* **14/1**
3331 2 1 ¾ **Juarla (IRE)**[9] 2163 3-9-13 **66** 6ex .... LukeMorris 2 69
(Ronald Harris) *cl up: drvn and ev ch over 1f out: kpt on ins fnl f* **8/1**
6055 3 nk **Yours**[42] 1306 3-8-13 **52** .... PaulHanagan 16 54
(Kevin Ryan) *in tch: drvn fr 1/2-way: no imp tl styd on wl fnl f: nrst fin* **7/2**[1]
-005 4 1 ¼ **Tahitian Princess (IRE)**[12] 2047 3-8-9 **48** ow1 .... PaulMulrennan 1 46
(Ann Duffield) *in tch: drvn and outpcd over 2f out: kpt on fnl f: nt pce to chal* **20/1**
4-34 5 ¾ **Dotty Darroch**[42] 1303 3-9-1 **54** .... LeeNewman 5 50
(Robin Bastiman) *cl up: led 1/2-way to over 1f out: sn one pce* **7/1**[3]
50-3 6 hd **Ballinargh Boy**[12] 2047 3-8-10 **54** .... NeilFarley(5) 4 49
(Robert Wylie) *cl up: ev ch 1/2-way to over 1f out: rdn and kpt on same pce* **8/1**
003 7 ¾ **Passing Moment**[40] 1370 3-8-11 **50** .... GrahamGibbons 8 43+
(Brian Baugh) *in tch: rdn over 2f out: n.m.r briefly ent fnl f: no imp* **20/1**
0-54 8 1 **Saxonette**[22] 1802 3-9-5 **58** .... TonyHamilton 13 47
(Linda Perratt) *hld up: rdn over 2f out: sme hdwy over 1f out: nvr able to chal* **15/2**
-630 9 hd **Twennyshortkid**[23] 1749 3-8-11 **50** .... (p) KierenFallon 9 39
(Paul Midgley) *dwlt: hld up: rdn and effrt over 1f out: nvr rchd ldrs* **6/1**[2]
4355 10 shd **These Dreams**[5] 2265 3-8-10 **52** .... RobertLButler(3) 3 40
(Richard Guest) *stdd s: hld up: hdwy on outside to chse ldrs over 1f out: wknd ins fnl f* **15/2**
3500 11 4 **Majestic Ridge (IRE)**[9] 2141 3-9-2 **55** .... (v) AdrianNicholls 14 31
(David Evans) *led to 1/2-way: rdn and wknd over 1f out* **16/1**
50-0 12 1 **Say A Prayer**[23] 1749 3-8-12 **51** .... (b) DuranFentiman 12 23
(Tim Easterby) *hld up: drvn over 2f out: nvr able to chal* **12/1**
-004 13 9 **Sleights Boy (IRE)**[15] 1967 3-8-13 **52** .... PatrickMathers 7 —
(Ian McInnes) *prom tl rdn and wknd over 2f out* **66/1**
0-64 14 17 **Prince Titus (IRE)**[19] 1860 3-9-2 **58** .... JamesSullivan(3) 6 —
(Linda Stubbs) *chsd ldrs to 1/2-way: sn lost pl: eased whn no ch fnl 2f* **20/1**

1m 14.58s (2.18) **Going Correction** 0.0s/f (Good) **14** Ran SP% **130.8**
Speed ratings (Par 97): **93,90,90,88,87 87,86,85,84,84 79,77,65,43**
toteswingers:1&2:£30.90, 1&3:£18.40, 2&3:£4.80 CSF £126.70 CT £507.50 TOTE £18.00: £4.70, £2.30, £2.10; EX 200.10 TRIFECTA Not won..
Owner A L Gregg **Bred** Frank Brady And Brian Scanlon **Trained** Uplawmoor, E Renfrews

FOCUS
It started to rain heavily before this handicap, which may partly explain why the winning time was 0.85 seconds slower than the juveniles in the opener, but this was also a weak contest whilst the 2-y-o race was probably above average. The form looks sound for the level.
Monel Official explanation: trainer said, regarding apparent improvement in form, that the gelding settled better in stalls and was suited by the softer ground.
Twennyshortkid Official explanation: jockey said gelding hung right
Sleights Boy(IRE) Official explanation: jockey said gelding was unsuited by the good to soft (soft in places) ground
Prince Titus(IRE) Official explanation: jockey said gelding lost its action but returned sound

2397 WILLIAM MCCLUSKEY H'CAP — 5f

3:15 (3:15) (Class 3) (0-90,90) 4-Y-0+ **£5,504** (£1,637; £818; £408) **Stalls** High

Form RPR
2-60 1 **Ginger Ted (IRE)**[11] 2116 4-8-12 **81** .... (p) J-PGuillambert 5 91
(Richard Guest) *t.k.h: hld up: hdwy and swtchd lft wl over 1f out: led last 30yds: kpt on wl* **10/1**
4-04 2 nk **The Nifty Fox**[11] 2118 7-8-13 **82** .... (v) GrahamGibbons 4 91
(Tim Easterby) *in tch: hdwy and squeezed through to ld ins fnl f: hdd last 30yds: kpt on* **6/1**[3]
0-06 3 ¾ **Duchess Dora (IRE)**[13] 2028 4-9-2 **85** .... PaulHanagan 3 91
(John Quinn) *t.k.h: trckd ldrs: effrt over 1f out: ev ch ent fnl f: kpt on* **11/4**[1]
0-04 4 1 ½ **Judge 'n Jury**[13] 2028 7-9-7 **90** .... (t) JoeFanning 2 91
(Ronald Harris) *mde most tl hdd ins fnl f: kpt on same pce* **11/2**[2]
101- 5 ¾ **Mayoman (IRE)**[235] 6572 6-8-7 **81** .... NeilFarley(5) 9 79+
(Declan Carroll) *rdr slow to remove blindfold and lost iron briefly sn after s: dwlt: hld up: hdwy and swtchd lft over 1f out: kpt on fnl f: no imp* **9/1**
0230 6 ½ **Dancing Freddy (IRE)**[18] 1907 4-7-11 **71** oh3 .... (p) NathanAlison(5) 1 67
(Richard Guest) *dwlt: sn prom on outside: effrt over 1f out: no ex ins fnl f* **20/1**
63-2 7 hd **Strike Up The Band**[11] 2118 8-9-5 **88** .... AdrianNicholls 10 84
(David Nicholls) *cl up: rdn 2f out: no ex ins fnl f* **7/1**
10-0 8 nse **Captain Royale (IRE)**[37] 1438 6-8-6 **75** .... (p) PatrickMathers 8 73+
(Colin Teague) *in tch: rdn over 2f out: n.m.r briefly appr fnl f: no imp* **25/1**
1401 9 hd **Le Toreador**[11] 2118 6-9-0 **83** .... (p) SilvestreDeSousa 6 78
(Kevin Ryan) *cl up: rdn over 2f out: wknd ins fnl f* **13/2**
10-0 10 3 ½ **Foxy Music**[13] 2028 7-9-3 **86** .... AndrewElliott 7 68
(Eric Alston) *t.k.h: hld up: rdn and edgd rt wl over 1f out: sn btn* **20/1**

59.22 secs (-0.18) **Going Correction** 0.0s/f (Good) **10** Ran SP% **114.6**
Speed ratings (Par 107): **107,106,105,102,101 100,100,100,100,94**
toteswingers:1&2:£7.70, 1&3:£5.70, 2&3:£4.60 CSF £65.55 CT £211.49 TOTE £15.60: £3.00, £2.70, £1.10; EX 79.80 Trifecta £463.20 Part won. Pool: £625.99 - 0.54 winning units.
Owner Maze Rattan Limited **Bred** T Counihan **Trained** Stainforth, S Yorks
■ Stewards' Enquiry : J-P Guillambert one-day ban: careless riding (Jun 8)

FOCUS
A decent sprint handicap, run at a strong pace. The placed horses set the level.

NOTEBOOK
Ginger Ted(IRE) isn't the most consistent, but he likes this ground and, although all his best previous form has been at 6f, the strong pace here would have been in his favour. Held up early, he was searching for a gap from some way out, but one appeared entering the last furlong and he utilised it to hit the front close to the line and win with a bit more in hand than the margin would suggest. The problem is that in his next start following his four previous wins, he has bombed out completely.
The Nifty Fox finished behind Le Toreador and Strike Up The Band at Thirsk last time, but he was closely matched with the pair on these revised terms and turned the form around. He was another to come from off the pace and looked to have done enough when just about hitting the front inside the last, but for the second year in a row in this contest he had the prize snatched from him by a narrow margin. He tries hard, but is now on a losing run of 20. (op 5-1)
Duchess Dora(IRE) signalled a return to form when just behind Judge 'n Jury at York a fortnight earlier and she had every chance a furlong out, but failed to quicken. She is knocking on the door. (op 3-1 tchd 10-3)
Judge 'n Jury came into this on a losing run of 22, but he ran his best race for a while at York and had dropped another 1lb in the meantime. One of three disputing the lead from the start, he fared much the best of the trio but is still finding it hard to get his head back in front. (op 9-2)
Mayoman(IRE) ◆, 4-8 last season, was having his first outing since October but his rider was slow to remove the blindfold after the stalls opened and he gave away ground as a result. Under the circumstances he did extremely well to finish so close and is one to watch with the run under his belt. Official explanation: jockey said he lost an iron leaving stalls (op 12-1)
Dancing Freddy(IRE), the winner's stablemate, was 3lb wrong and was in a much more competitive race than he normally contests. Considering he was stuck on the wide outside of the field from the outside stall throughout, he ran a corker. Official explanation: jockey said gelding became restless in stalls (tchd 25-1)
Strike Up The Band may have done too much too soon in the conditions. (op 5-1)
Captain Royale(IRE) Official explanation: jockey said gelding was denied a clear run
Le Toreador is another who may have done too much too soon in the conditions. (op 8-1)

2398 DUTCH ART H'CAP — 7f 50y

3:50 (3:50) (Class 4) (0-85,84) 4-Y-0+ **£4,079** (£1,214; £606; £303) **Stalls** High

Form RPR
6041 1 **Masked Dance (IRE)**[56] 1035 4-9-3 **80** .... (p) PaulMulrennan 4 93
(Kevin Ryan) *mde all: qcknd clr 2f out: unchal* **10/1**
111- 2 5 **Clumber Place**[207] 7238 5-8-10 **76** .... RobertLButler(3) 1 76
(Richard Guest) *chsd wnr thrght: rdn over 2f out: kpt on fnl f: nt pce of wnr* **12/1**
0-04 3 ½ **Illustrious Prince (IRE)**[25] 1695 4-8-13 **81** .... NeilFarley(5) 7 79
(Declan Carroll) *in tch: effrt over 2f out: kpt on fnl f: no imp* **12/1**
10-0 4 ½ **Bella Noir**[44] 1279 4-8-12 **75** .... AndrewElliott 11 72
(Mrs K Burke) *prom: drvn over 2f out: kpt on same pce fr over 1f out* **16/1**
0302 5 2 ¾ **Academy Blues (USA)**[11] 2115 6-9-7 **84** .... AdrianNicholls 12 73+
(David Nicholls) *slowly away: hld up: hdwy on outside over 2f out: no imp fr over 1f out* **12/1**

-402 **6** *2* **Northern Fling**[11] 2112 7-9-2 **82** GaryBartley(3) 2 66
(Jim Goldie) *hld up: effrt over 2f out: nvr able to chal* **11/2**[2]
0-05 **7** *2 ½* **En Fuego**[16] 1942 4-8-10 **73** SilvestreDeSousa 9 50
(Geoffrey Harker) *prom: drvn over 2f out: wknd wl over 1f out* **16/1**
1-04 **8** *3 ¼* **Cara's Request (AUS)**[11] 2112 6-9-7 **84** AndrewMullen 8 52+
(David Nicholls) *trckd ldrs: effrt over 2f out: wknd over 1f out* **9/1**[3]
00-0 **9** *10* **Aldermoor (USA)**[18] 1898 5-8-7 **70** WilliamCarson 6 —
(Stuart Williams) *missed break: hld up: hdwy on outside over 2f out: wknd over 1f out* **33/1**
321- **10** *14* **Divine Call**[212] 7129 4-9-1 **78** KierenFallon 3 —
(William Haggas) *t.k.h: in tch: outpcd and dropped to rr 1/2-way: eased whn no ch over 1f out* **1/1**[1]

1m 32.29s (-1.11) **Going Correction** -0.02s/f (Good) **10** Ran SP% **122.3**
Speed ratings (Par 105): **105,99,98,98,95 92,89,86,74,58**
toteswingers:1&2:£9.00, 1&3:£17.10, 2&3:£14.80 CSF £128.94 CT £1503.61 TOTE £16.00: £2.30, £2.90, £3.40; EX 95.00 TRIFECTA Not won..
Owner Mrs L D Edwards **Bred** Canice Farrell Jnr **Trained** Hambleton, N Yorks

FOCUS
This had looked quite an interesting handicap, but it turned into an odd race with a couple not performing as expected. Not form to take too literally.
Divine Call Official explanation: trainer had no explanation for the poor form shown

2399 ATLAS COMMUNICATIONS FILLIES' H'CAP 1m
4:25 (4:26) (Class 5) (0-70,67) 4-Y-O+ **£2,331** (£693; £346; £173) **Stalls** Low

Form RPR
360- **1** **Ykikamoocow**[251] 6116 5-9-4 **64** SilvestreDeSousa 7 74
(Geoffrey Harker) *trckd ldrs: hdwy to ld 2f out: sn rdn and edgd lft: styd on strly fnl f* **4/1**[2]
-064 **2** *2 ¼* **Madame Excelerate**[7] 2198 4-9-3 **63** KierenFallon 8 68
(Mark Brisbourne) *taken early to post: in tch on outside: hdwy over 2f out: edgd lft and chsd wnr over 1f out: kpt on fnl f* **6/1**
-421 **3** *2 ¼* **Spavento (IRE)**[12] 2057 5-9-2 **62** AndrewElliott 2 68+
(Eric Alston) *trckd ldrs: nt clr run over 2f out: swtchd rt over 1f out: styd on fnl f: nvr able to chal* **9/2**[3]
-323 **4** *1 ½* **Casino Night**[12] 2046 6-9-2 **67** DaleSwift(5) 5 63
(Barry Murtagh) *cl up: led over 3f out to 2f out: rdn and kpt on same pce* **3/1**[1]
-630 **5** *nk* **Mozayada (USA)**[18] 1909 7-8-11 **57** FrannyNorton 6 53
(Mel Brittain) *trckd ldrs: effrt over 2f out: kpt on same pce over 1f out* **16/1**
0-00 **6** *2* **Eternal Instinct**[12] 2046 4-9-4 **67** GaryBartley(3) 12 58+
(Jim Goldie) *hld up: hdwy on outside over 2f out: kpt on fnl f: no imp* **33/1**
4-06 **7** *2 ¾* **Salerosa (IRE)**[22] 1800 6-9-5 **65** (p) PaulMulrennan 10 50
(Ann Duffield) *midfield: rdn over 2f out: sn no imp* **16/1**
4/2- **8** *4* **Amtaar**[438] 889 4-9-3 **63** PaulHanagan 13 38
(Ian Semple) *hld up: rdn and effrt over 2f out: wknd over 1f out* **13/2**
/560 **9** *2 ¾* **Lilyannabanana**[23] 1755 4-8-7 **53** oh3 LukeMorris 3 22
(David Evans) *hld up on ins: drvn and outpcd 3f out: btn fnl 2f* **50/1**
0-00 **10** *1 ¼* **Child Of Our Time (IRE)**[37] 1440 4-8-13 **59** PatrickMathers 11 25
(Colin Teague) *slowly away and drvn in rr: nvr on terms* **66/1**
22-4 **11** *shd* **Many Welcomes**[83] 747 6-8-13 **59** GrahamGibbons 9 25
(Brian Baugh) *towards rr: struggling over 2f out: sn btn* **14/1**
3060 **12** *8* **Hill Tribe**[18] 1909 4-8-13 **62** (p) RobertLButler(3) 4 —
(Richard Guest) *led to over 3f out: rdn and wknd over 2f out* **20/1**

1m 42.52s (-1.28) **Going Correction** -0.025s/f (Good) **12** Ran SP% **120.4**
Speed ratings (Par 100): **105,102,100,99,98 96,93,89,87,85 85,77**
toteswingers:1&2:£6.10, 1&3:£5.00, 2&3:£6.30 CSF £27.94 CT £116.43 TOTE £4.20: £2.00, £1.10, £1.90; EX 37.50 Trifecta £349.80 Pool: £567.34 - 1.20 winning units..
Owner John J Maguire & PAul Benson **Bred** Mrs Karen Heath **Trained** Thirkleby, N Yorks

FOCUS
An ordinary fillies' handicap and again the principals raced handily. The first two set the level with the sixth to his best from the back.
Many Welcomes Official explanation: jockey said mare ran too free

2400 PLAY POKER AT VICTORCHANDLER.COM H'CAP 1m 7f
4:55 (4:56) (Class 6) (0-60,60) 4-Y-O+ **£1,706** (£503; £252) **Stalls** Low

Form RPR
/0-0 **1** **Blazing Buck**[42] 1310 5-8-9 **48** FrannyNorton 8 57
(Tony Carroll) *in tch: rdn 5f out: hdwy on outside to ld and kicked 3 l clr over 2f out: hrd pressed fnl f: hld on wl* **11/2**[3]
0066 **2** *shd* **Valdan (IRE)**[12] 2060 7-9-3 **56** (t) TonyHamilton 5 65
(Maurice Barnes) *hld up: stdy hdwy gng wl over 4f out: chsd wnr over 2f out: effrt over 1f out: styd on wl fnl f: jst hld* **9/1**
5000 **3** *17* **Jackson (BRZ)**[10] 1458 9-8-12 **54** (b) RobertLButler(3) 9 42
(Richard Guest) *trckd ldrs: effrt over 2f out: outpcd by ldng pair fr wl over 1f out* **25/1**
4-00 **4** *5* **Ballade De La Mer**[32] 1519 5-8-7 **46** oh1 (v[1]) LeeNewman 3 28
(George Foster) *trckd ldrs: drvn over 3f out: wknd fnl 2f* **9/1**
5350 **5** *10* **Duar Mapel (USA)**[52] 1107 5-8-6 **52** GeorgeChaloner(7) 4 22
(Brian Baugh) *hld up: outpcd over 4f out: shortlived effrt over 2f out: nvr on terms* **7/1**
/0-2 **6** *2 ¼* **Oh Landino (GER)**[11] 1519 6-8-7 **46** AndrewMullen 2 14
(Jim Goldie) *led: rdn over 4f out: hdd over 2f out: sn wknd* **7/2**[2]
20-0 **7** *40* **Vittachi**[52] 1107 4-9-1 **55** PaulMulrennan 6 —
(Alistair Whillans) *prom: lost pl 1/2-way: sn struggling: eased whn no ch fnl 3f* **10/1**
-532 **8** *2 ½* **Trojan Gift (USA)**[15] 1973 4-9-6 **60** GrahamGibbons 7 —
(Julie Camacho) *cl up: drvn over 4f out: wknd fr 3f out: t.o* **15/8**[1]

3m 25.23s (4.83) **Going Correction** -0.025s/f (Good)
WFA 4 from 5yo+ 1lb **8** Ran SP% **117.8**
Speed ratings (Par 101): **86,85,76,74,68 67,46,45**
toteswingers:1&2:£9.20, 1&3:£18.30, 2&3:£15.10 CSF £54.93 CT £1146.92 TOTE £8.40: £2.60, £3.10, £3.40; EX 83.90 Trifecta £341.90 Part won. Pool: £462.11 - 0.62 winning units..
Owner Mill House Racing Syndicate **Bred** Charlock Stud **Trained** Cropthorne, Worcs
■ Stewards' Enquiry : Lee Newman two-day ban: careless riding (Jun 8-9)

FOCUS
Staying handicaps don't come much worse than this with recent winning form conspicuous by its absence, but it did produce a thrilling finish. the form could rate higher but not a race to go overboard about.
Vittachi Official explanation: jockey said gelding never travelled
Trojan Gift(USA) Official explanation: jockey said gelding suffered interference in running

2401 DAIKINHEATING.CO.UK APPRENTICE H'CAP 1m 1f 20y
5:25 (5:27) (Class 6) (0-60,60) 4-Y-O+ **£1,706** (£503; £252) **Stalls** Low

Form RPR
3200 **1** **Marino Prince (FR)**[6] 2237 6-8-6 **50** DavidSimmonson(5) 9 59
(Paul Midgley) *hld up: hdwy to ld appr fnl f: styd on strly* **8/1**
0-40 **2** *3* **Tobrata**[18] 1909 5-9-2 **58** EdmondLinehan(3) 13 61
(Mel Brittain) *prom: rdn over 2f out: hdwy to chal over 1f out: kpt on same pce fnl f* **20/1**
24-3 **3** *½* **Prince Rhyddarch**[47] 1216 6-9-1 **54** GarryWhillans 4 55+
(Michael Dods) *missed break: bhd: hdwy on outside over 2f out: kpt on fnl f: nrst fin* **7/4**[1]
540- **4** *2* **Dubai Gem**[266] 5655 5-8-2 **46** JenniferFerguson(5) 2 43
(Olivia Maylam) *prom: rdn over 2f out: led briefly over 1f out: kpt on same pce fnl f* **11/2**[2]
5440 **5** *nk* **Empress Leizu (IRE)**[55] 1068 4-8-8 **52** GeorgeDowning(5) 7 48
(Tony Carroll) *bhd: rdn over 3f out: hdwy on ins over 1f out: nrst fin* **12/1**
-524 **6** *nk* **Hathaway (IRE)**[18] 1905 4-9-1 **54** ShaneBKelly 8 50
(Mark Brisbourne) *midfield: drvn over 2f out: hdwy over 1f out: nvr able to chal* **7/1**[3]
0-06 **7** *1 ¾* **Glenluji**[19] 1857 6-9-7 **60** LMcNiff 1 52
(Jim Goldie) *midfield on ins: rdn over 2f out: edgd rt and no imp over 1f out* **11/1**
2130 **8** *2 ½* **Nevada Desert (IRE)**[21] 1814 11-9-3 **56** LucyKBarry 3 42
(Richard Whitaker) *t.k.h: trckd ldrs: effrt over 2f out: wknd over 1f out* **16/1**
3060 **9** *1 ¾* **Noble Attitude**[5] 2260 5-8-4 **46** oh1 JakePayne(3) 10 28
(Richard Guest) *cl up: rdn and ev ch over 2f out: wknd over 1f out* **40/1**
400- **10** *2* **Street Devil (USA)**[60] 7867 6-9-7 **60** MatthewLawson 5 38
(Pat Murphy) *led to over 1f out: sn rdn and btn* **20/1**
1600 **11** *3 ¼* **Bentley**[9] 2159 7-9-4 **60** GeorgeChaloner(3) 14 31
(Brian Baugh) *prom tl rdn and wknd over 2f out* **20/1**
00/0 **12** *10* **Wing N Prayer (IRE)**[24] 1710 4-8-2 **46** oh1 LauraBarry(5) 6 —
(Alan Berry) *bhd: drvn 3f out: nvr on terms* **100/1**
0-55 **13** *8* **Walleyd (IRE)**[12] 2045 4-9-2 **60** RossSmith(5) 11 —
(Linda Perratt) *hld up: pushed along over 3f out: btn fnl 2f* **25/1**

1m 59.38s (1.88) **Going Correction** -0.025s/f (Good) **13** Ran SP% **118.8**
Speed ratings (Par 101): **94,91,90,89,88 88,87,84,83,81 78,69,62**
toteswingers:1&2:£24.00, 1&3:£4.40, 2&3:£11.80 CSF £151.68 CT £358.86 TOTE £8.00: £2.50, £7.70, £1.10; EX 128.60 TRIFECTA Not won..
Owner A Taylor & N Lomas **Bred** Newsells Park Stud Ltd **Trained** Westow, N Yorks

FOCUS
A moderate apprentice handicap, but notable for a couple of gambles. There was a three-way battle for the early lead, but the trio all finished out the back, suggesting they went off too quick. The winner is a slight improver with the runner-up to his old turf form.
T/Jkpt: Not won. T/Plt: £492.90 to a £1 stake. Pool: £70,268.30. 104.05 winning tickets. T/Qpdt: £500.70 to a £1 stake. Pool: £4,939.34. 7.30 winning tickets. RY

[1966] BEVERLEY (R-H)
Wednesday, May 25

OFFICIAL GOING: Good to firm (8.6)
Bottom bend at widest configuration to provide fresh ground on the inner.
Wind: Light, across Weather: Cloudy and blustery

2402 BEVERLEY-RACECOURSE.CO.UK MAIDEN FILLIES' STKS 7f 100y
6:30 (6:34) (Class 5) 3-Y-O+ **£2,266** (£674; £337; £168) **Stalls** Low

Form RPR
3-2 **1** **Elmaam**[19] 1853 3-8-12 0 RichardHills 7 72+
(William Haggas) *trckd ldrs: smooth hdwy 3f out: led wl over 1f out: rdn ent ins fnl f: kpt on* **1/4**[1]
5 **2** *1 ¼* **Zennor**[15] 1974 4-9-9 0 RichardKingscote 1 73+
(Tom Dascombe) *hld up in rr: swtchd outside and gd hdwy wl over 1f out: rdn to chse wnr ent fnl f: kpt on* **7/1**[2]
60 **3** *3 ¾* **Alkhawarah (USA)**[36] 1459 3-8-12 0 TadhgO'Shea 5 60
(Mark Johnston) *led 1 1/2f: prom on inner: effrt and n.m.r over 2f out: sn rdn to chse wnr: drvn and one pce fr over 1f out* **16/1**[3]
50 **4** *hd* **American Lover (FR)**[24] 1710 4-9-9 0 DavidNolan 2 63
(John Wainwright) *in tch: hdwy 2f out: sn rdn and kpt on same pce appr fnl f* **100/1**
050/ **5** *7* **Can Can Dancer**[955] 6685 6-9-9 48 RobbieFitzpatrick 3 46?
(Charles Smith) *bhd tl sme late hdwy* **100/1**
50 **6** *¾* **Lemon Queen (IRE)**[22] 1795 5-9-9 0 FrederikTylicki 9 44
(John Quinn) *chsd ldrs: cl up 1/2-way: rdn to ld over 2f out: sn drvn and hdd wl over 1f out: wknd qckly over 1f out* **33/1**
7 *23* **Lambrini Belle**[55] 5-9-9 0 TomEaves 8 —
(Lisa Williamson) *t.k.h: led after 1 1/2f: wd bnd after 3f: rdn along 3f out: hdd wl over 2f out and sn wknd* **125/1**

1m 31.99s (-1.81) **Going Correction** -0.325s/f (Firm)
WFA 3 from 4yo+ 11lb **7** Ran SP% **104.1**
Speed ratings (Par 100): **97,95,91,91,83 82,55**
toteswingers: 1&2 £1.02, 1&3 £2.30, 2&3 £3.70 CSF £1.67 TOTE £1.20: £1.10, £1.70; EX 1.90.
Owner Hamdan Al Maktoum **Bred** Shadwell Estate Company **Trained** Newmarket, Suffolk

FOCUS
The watered ground was given as good to firm, with a GoingStick reading of 8.6. The bottom bend was at its widest configuration, providing fresh ground on the inner. A weak race, and the winner is rated 12lb off her best figure.

2403 KEVIN DONKIN MEMORIAL H'CAP 1m 1f 207y
7:00 (7:01) (Class 4) (0-85,85) 4-Y-O+ **£4,079** (£1,214; £606; £303) **Stalls** Low

Form RPR
10-0 **1** **Pass Muster**[39] 1387 4-9-3 **81** RoystonFfrench 8 92
(Geoffrey Harker) *hld up in tch: hdwy wl over 2f out: chsd ldrs and carried rt over 1f out: rdn to ld ent fnl f: styd on strly* **25/1**
-003 **2** *3 ½* **Bollin Dolly**[9] 2150 8-8-10 **74** DavidAllan 2 78
(Tim Easterby) *led: rdn along 3f out: hdd 2f out: drvn and rallied to have ev ch appr fnl f: kpt on same pce* **15/2**
6122 **3** *1 ½* **Sharakti (IRE)**[10] 2124 4-8-10 **74** TadhgO'Shea 1 75
(Alan McCabe) *hld up in rr: swtchd outside and hdwy over 2f out: rdn to chal whn hung rt over 1f out: drvn and kpt on ins fnl f* **7/2**[3]
2-24 **4** *¾* **Saint Thomas (IRE)**[23] 1746 4-8-8 **77** LeeTopliss(5) 4 77
(John Mackie) *trckd ldrs: effrt wl over 2f out: rdn whn n.m.r over 1f out: kpt on same pce ins fnl f* **13/2**
6020 **5** *1* **Doctor Zhivago**[14] 2006 4-9-3 **84** MichaelO'Connell(3) 9 82
(David Nicholls) *trckd ldng pair: hdwy 4f out: cl up on outer 3f out: sn rdn: drvn and hld whn hmpd over 1f out: one pce after* **10/3**[2]
6 *¾* **Satwa Dream (IRE)**[240] 4-9-6 **84** PaulHanagan 3 80
(Ed Dunlop) *hld up in rr: effrt over 2f out: sn rdn and n.d* **14/1**
-330 **7** *nk* **Veiled Applause**[14] 2006 8-9-1 **82** DeclanCannon(3) 6 77
(John Quinn) *hld up in tch on inner: hdwy over 2f out: rdn along wl over 1f out: sn btn* **12/1**

210- **8** ½ **Solicitor**[300] [4504] 4-9-7 **85**................ FrankieDettori 7 79
(Mark Johnston) *trckd ldr: hdwy and cl up 3f out: rdn to ld 2f out: drvn and hdd ent fnl f: sn wknd and eased* **3/1**[1]

2m 2.41s (-4.59) **Going Correction** -0.325s/f (Firm) **8** Ran SP% **113.6**
Speed ratings (Par 105): **105,102,101,100,99 99,98,98**
toteswingers: 1&2 £40.40, 1&3 £13.10, 2&3 £2.60 CSF £195.46 CT £826.20 TOTE £36.80: £7.00, £2.00, £1.70; EX 264.20.

Owner An Englishman, Irishman & Scotsman **Bred** Darley **Trained** Thirkleby, N Yorks

FOCUS
There was a solid gallop and the unexposed winner quickened up well from off the pace. There was a surprise winner but the form looks pretty solid.

2404 HILARY NEEDLER TROPHY CONDITIONS STKS (FILLIES) 5f
7:30 (7:31) (Class 2) 2-Y-O
£13,396 (£4,011; £2,005; £1,004; £500; £251) **Stalls** Low

Form RPR

1 **1** **Dozy (IRE)**[19] [1870] 2-8-12 0................ JamieSpencer 7 98+
(Kevin Ryan) *in tch: hdwy to chse ldrs 2f out: rdn over 1f out: kpt on strly to ld last 100yds* **9/2**[3]

12 **2** 1 ¼ **Vocational (USA)**[12] [2070] 2-8-12 0................ FrankieDettori 8 94
(Mark Johnston) *wnt bdly lft s: sn led: clr after 2f: rdn over 1f out: drvn ent fnl f: hdd and no ex last 100yds* **7/4**[1]

111 **3** ½ **Lily's Angel (IRE)**[21] [1806] 2-8-12 0................ PaulHanagan 5 92
(Richard Fahey) *dwlt and towards rr: hdwy 2f out: sn rdn and styd on wl fnl f: nrst fin* **5/2**[2]

1 **4** nk **Queens Revenge**[48] [1199] 2-8-12 0................ DavidAllan 9 94+
(Tim Easterby) *carried lft s and towards rr: hdwy on wd outside 2f out: rdn to chse ldrs over 1f out: ch ent fnl f: no ex last 100yds* **9/2**[3]

5 7 **Tip Top Gorgeous (IRE)** 2-8-9 0................ SeanLevey 6 62
(David O'Meara) *dwlt and towards rr: pushed along 1/2-way: hdwy over 1f out: kpt on ins fnl f: nrst fin* **100/1**

1161 **6** hd **Van Go Go**[16] [1954] 2-8-12 0................ FrederikTylicki 2 65
(David Nicholls) *prom: rdn along over 2f out: drvn wl over 1f out and grad wknd* **33/1**

1 **7** 1 ¾ **Majestic Rose**[48] [1192] 2-8-12 0................ MartinHarley 4 58
(Mick Channon) *prom: rdn along over 2f out: drvn wl over 1f out and sn wknd* **14/1**

1 **8** ½ **Chevanah (IRE)**[19] [1876] 2-8-12 0................ SilvestreDeSousa 3 57
(Ann Duffield) *chsd ldrs on inner: rdn along over 2f out: sn wknd* **20/1**

9 nse **Rano Pano (USA)** 2-8-9 0................ PaulPickard 1 53
(Brian Ellison) *a towards rr* **100/1**

61.99 secs (-1.51) **Going Correction** -0.325s/f (Firm) **9** Ran SP% **117.6**
Speed ratings (Par 96): **99,97,96,95,84 84,81,80,80**
toteswingers: 1&2 £1.90, 1&3 £4.60, 2&3 £1.40 CSF £12.85 TOTE £5.50: £1.50, £1.50, £1.40; EX 14.30.

Owner D Redvers & J H & S M Wall **Bred** Mountarmstrong Stud **Trained** Hambleton, N Yorks

FOCUS
Despite having lost its Listed status this looked a good renewal of the Hilary Needler, containing five defending unbeaten records, and ironically the form looks well up to Listed grade. A good pace was set by Vocational.

NOTEBOOK
Dozy(IRE) was ridden with a bit of patience behind a fast pace. She hadn't achieved a terrific amount on her debut based on the bare form, but her trainer has a good record in this race and has always regarded her as a Royal Ascot type, so her chance had to be respected. She got a nice tow through the race, stayed on strongly inside the last, and, given her pedigree, looks sure to appreciate another furlong in time. That said, the Queen Mary is likely to be her aim at the Royal meeting, and she'll no doubt appreciate it if the rain continues to stay away. (op 7-1)

Vocational(USA) was the moral winner as she did incredibly well considering she veered left leaving the stalls, hampering Queens Revenge in the process, but still showed enough early speed to get to the front after a furlong, and for most of the race it looked like she would hold them all off. She was eventually overhauled, but she is clearly all speed and will deserve to take her chance in the Queen Mary, although a sharper track will surely suit her style of running better. Official explanation: trainer said filly lost its right-fore shoe (op 9-4)

Lily's Angel(IRE) struggled a little with the early pace but she was putting in her best work at the finish and on this evidence she's crying out for a step up to 6f. (op 2-1 tchd 11-4)

Queens Revenge was drawn worst of all and a difficult task was made even tougher when the favourite, drawn to her inside, veered into her leaving the gates and pushed her even wider out. She stayed on well at the finish and it wouldn't be a surprise to see her given the opportunity to reverse the form at Ascot. (tchd 5-1)

Tip Top Gorgeous(IRE), who was given a patient ride, stayed on past beaten rivals. It was a tough race in which to make her debut and she showed more than enough to suggest she can win a maiden.

Van Go Go was behind Majestic Rose when they both made their debuts in a four-runner Kempton maiden last month, but she has been busy since, winning three times, albeit in minor company, and perhaps her streetwise ability allowed her to reverse that Polytrack form. (tchd 40-1)

Majestic Rose was well placed chasing the leader for much of the race but she dropped out rather tamely once things got serious. (op 11-1 tchd 10-1)

2405 WEATHERBYS BLOODSTOCK INSURANCE CONDITIONS STKS 5f
8:00 (8:00) (Class 4) 3-Y-O **£5,296** (£1,586; £793) **Stalls** Low

Form RPR

2-32 **1** **Move In Time**[13] [2032] 3-8-12 **102**................ TomEaves 1 105
(Bryan Smart) *trckd ldng pair: hdwy 1/2-way: effrt to chal over 1f out: qcknd to ld ent fnl f: pushed clr* **4/7**[1]

30-3 **2** 3 ¼ **The Thrill Is Gone**[13] [2032] 3-8-4 **97**................ MartinHarley(3) 3 88
(Mick Channon) *cl up: led over 2f out: sn rdn: drvn and hdd ent fnl f: one pce* **13/8**[2]

521- **3** 15 **Ice Trooper**[300] [4512] 3-9-1 **78**................ RoystonFfrench 2 42
(Linda Stubbs) *led: rdn along 1/2-way: sn hdd: wknd over 1f out and eased* **16/1**[3]

61.21 secs (-2.29) **Going Correction** -0.325s/f (Firm) **3** Ran SP% **107.6**
Speed ratings (Par 101): **105,99,75**
CSF £1.80 TOTE £1.50; EX 1.30.

Owner A Turton, J Blackburn & R Bond **Bred** Bond Thoroughbred Corporation **Trained** Hambleton, N Yorks

FOCUS
Just the three runners for this conditions race and, with Ice Trooper having plenty to find at the weights with the other two, the betting suggested it was a match between a couple of rivals who ran each other close at York last time. A clear personal best from the winner at face value but the form is rated more cautiously.

2406 PHIL JOSS MEMORIAL H'CAP 1m 100y
8:30 (8:32) (Class 5) (0-70,70) 3-Y-O **£2,266** (£674; £337; £168) **Stalls** Low

Form RPR

1401 **1** **Vetvey (IRE)**[16] [1945] 3-9-2 **65**................ SilvestreDeSousa 10 72
(Mark Johnston) *mde all: clr 1/2-way: rdn 2f out: jnd and drvn over 1f out: kpt on gamely fnl f* **11/4**[1]

2622 **2** hd **Dr Red Eye**[8] [2186] 3-8-13 **65**................ BillyCray(3) 7 72
(David Nicholls) *trckd wnr: hdwy 3f out: rdn to chal wl over 1f out: sn drvn and kpt on: jst hld* **7/2**[3]

6-13 **3** 1 **Lady Gar Gar**[26] [1653] 3-9-6 **69**................(p) PaulHanagan 6 73
(Geoffrey Oldroyd) *trckd ldng pair: hdwy over 2f out: swtchd lft and rdn to chal 1f out: drvn and kpt on ins fnl f* **3/1**[2]

4453 **4** 2 **Ad Vitam (IRE)**[16] [1944] 3-8-9 **61**................(t) MartinHarley(3) 1 61
(David C Griffiths) *chsd ldrs: rdn along over 2f out: drvn wl over 1f out: no imp* **8/1**

0-02 **5** 3 **Alensgrove (IRE)**[23] [1749] 3-8-12 **61**................ MickyFenton 9 54
(Paul Midgley) *towards rr: hdwy over 3f out: rdn wl over 2f out: drvn wl over 1f out: nvr nr ldrs* **13/2**

6-00 **6** 1 ¼ **Wild Hysteria (IRE)**[15] [1967] 3-8-7 **56** oh2................ FrederikTylicki 8 46+
(Tom Tate) *blindfold removed late and dwlt: bhd tl styd on fnl 2f: nvr nr ldrs* **40/1**

05-0 **7** nk **Grazeon Again (IRE)**[28] [1624] 3-8-9 **58**................ TomEaves 3 47
(John Quinn) *in tch: rdn along over 3f out: n.d* **20/1**

6-00 **8** 7 **Kalkan Bay**[11] [2096] 3-9-5 **68**................ PJMcDonald 4 41
(Jedd O'Keeffe) *towards rr: rdn along 3f over out: nvr a factor* **33/1**

3400 **9** 2 ½ **Baharat (IRE)**[11] [2092] 3-9-7 **70**................ RobbieFitzpatrick 2 37
(Richard Guest) *a in rr* **20/1**

00-6 **10** 5 **Last Destination (IRE)**[16] [1944] 3-8-12 **64**................ LouisBeuzelin(3) 5 20
(Nigel Tinkler) *towards rr: sme hdwy 3f out: sn rdn and nvr a factor* **28/1**

1m 45.14s (-2.46) **Going Correction** -0.325s/f (Firm) **10** Ran SP% **116.7**
Speed ratings (Par 99): **99,98,97,95,92 91,91,84,81,76**
toteswingers: 1&2 £3.00, 1&3 £2.90, 2&3 £3.40 CSF £11.66 CT £30.25 TOTE £3.80: £1.60, £1.90, £1.20; EX 12.60.

Owner Brian Yeardley **Bred** Gestut Sohrenhof **Trained** Middleham Moor, N Yorks
■ Stewards' Enquiry : Billy Cray three-day ban: used whip with excessive frequency (Jun 8-10)

FOCUS
This was run at what looked a good gallop, but the first four remained in their positions almost throughout and it was in fact a well-judged front-running ride from Silvestre de Sousa. The winner stepped forward again.

2407 BEVERLEY MIDDLE DISTANCE SERIES H'CAP 1m 4f 16y
9:00 (9:01) (Class 5) (0-70,74) 3-Y-O **£3,561** (£1,059; £529; £264) **Stalls** Low

Form RPR

-064 **1** **Pintrada**[16] [1944] 3-9-3 **65**................ PhilipRobinson 5 71+
(James Bethell) *hld up in rr: hdwy on outer wl over 2f out: rdn to chse ldrs over 1f out: led ent fnl f: sn edgd rt and styd on wl towards fin* **9/2**

-122 **2** 1 **Pretty Diamond (IRE)**[28] [1623] 3-9-7 **69**................ SilvestreDeSousa 1 74
(Mark Johnston) *led: jnd 3f out and sn rdn along: drvn wl over 1f out: hdd ent fnl f: no ex last 100yds* **5/2**[2]

0-35 **3** ½ **Residence And Spa (IRE)**[15] [1972] 3-9-6 **68**................ DavidAllan 2 72
(Tim Easterby) *trckd ldr: hdwy and cl up 3f out: rdn to chal over 2f out: drvn wl over 1f out and ev ch tl no ex last 100yds* **18/1**

0411 **4** 1 **Caravan Rolls On**[9] [2152] 3-9-9 **74** 6ex................ AshleyHamblett(3) 4 76
(Peter Chapple-Hyam) *hld up in tch: hdwy on inner over 2f out: rdn to chse ldrs over 1f out: sn drvn and one pce fnl f* **2/1**[1]

-042 **5** ½ **Lemon Drop Red (USA)**[15] [1972] 3-9-0 **62**................ PaulHanagan 3 64
(Ed Dunlop) *trckd ldng pair: effrt over 2f out: rdn wl over 1f out: drvn and one pce appr fnl f* **3/1**[3]

63-6 **6** 3 ¾ **Royal Bonsai**[30] [1559] 3-8-13 **61**................ TomEaves 7 57
(John Quinn) *hld up: a towards rr* **33/1**

[illegible] **7** [illegible] [illegible] .... SeanLevey(3) 8 46
(David O'Meara) *chsd ldrs: rdn along 3f out: drvn over 2f out and sn wknd* **40/1**

2m 41.21s (1.41) **Going Correction** -0.325s/f (Firm) **7** Ran SP% **115.7**
Speed ratings (Par 99): **82,81,81,80,80 77,75**
toteswingers: 1&2 £2.40, 1&3 £10.30, 2&3 £9.10 CSF £16.61 CT £183.64 TOTE £5.90: £2.80, £1.10; EX 19.40.

Owner Scotyork Partnership I **Bred** Carmel Stud **Trained** Middleham Moor, N Yorks

FOCUS
A modest handicap and a bit of a muddling race. The form is rated around the front-running second.

T/Plt: 8.80 to a £1 stake. Pool: £63,479.69. 5,259.26 winning tickets. T/Qpdt: £5.30 to a £1 stake Pool £4,053.54. 565.11w. tckts JR 2408a (Foreign Racing) - See Raceform Int.

2395 AYR (L-H)
Thursday, May 26

OFFICIAL GOING: Good to soft (soft in places; 8.5)
Rails on innermost line and full width of track used.
Wind: Fresh, half against Weather: Cloudy

2409 BRITISH STALLION STUDS SUPPORTING BRITISH RACING E B F MAIDEN STKS 5f
2:20 (2:20) (Class 4) 2-Y-O **£4,468** (£1,329; £664; £331) **Stalls** Centre

Form RPR

5 **1** **Rent Free**[26] [1691] 2-9-3 0................ J-PGuillambert 1 81+
(Nigel Tinkler) *cl up: rdn to ld appr fnl f: rdn and r.o strly* **11/4**[2]

6 **2** 1 ½ **Red Art (IRE)**[14] [2023] 2-9-3 0................ MichaelHills 4 75+
(B W Hills) *cl up: effrt and ev ch appr fnl f: kpt on ins fnl f* **13/8**[1]

3 3 **Al Jemailiya (IRE)** 2-8-12 0................ PaulMulrennan 2 59+
(Kevin Ryan) *trckd ldrs: shkn up and outpcd over 1f out: kpt on fnl f: nrst fin* **7/2**[3]

553 **4** 1 ¾ **Latte**[8] [2194] 2-9-3 0................ TomEaves 3 58
(Linda Stubbs) *led: rdn over 2f out: hdd appr fnl f: sn no ex* **11/2**

60 **5** *15* **Flying Pickets (IRE)**[40] 1383 2-9-3 0.......................(b[1]) RobertWinston 5 —
(David Brown) *dwlt: sn pushed along in tch: struggling 1/2-way: sn btn: t.o* **11/1**

62.49 secs (3.09) **Going Correction** +0.35s/f (Good) **5** Ran SP% **110.7**
Speed ratings (Par 95): **94,91,86,84,60**
CSF £7.71 TOTE £5.00: £1.90, £1.40; EX 9.80.
Owner Maze Rattan Limited **Bred** L T Roberts **Trained** Langton, N Yorks

FOCUS
Only a fair-looking contest but the form ought to be reliable. The winning time was quicker than the following 3-y-o handicap and the first two both stepped up on their second runs.

NOTEBOOK
Rent Free wasn't beaten far on his debut in a race that has worked out really well, and duly built on that effort with a workmanlike victory. He has plenty of size about him and should only progress the longer the season goes on. This is his trip and he'll probably take his chance in a novice event before the handicaps start. (op 5-2 tchd 3-1)
Red Art(IRE) looks to have come on for his debut effort despite being readily held by Rent Free inside the final furlong. One would imagine he'll find his level in handicaps, but may win a weak maiden before entering that sphere. (op 15-8)
Al Jemailiya(IRE) was twice led out unsold, including at a breeze-up sale, but the fact she represented an in-form stable made her of some interest. She showed pace early but got caught flat-footed as the tempo increased before keeping on. (tchd 3-1)
Latte looks a pacey sort, so he'll no doubt win something at a speed-favouring course as a juvenile. (op 5-1 tchd 6-1)

2410 DOWNLOAD THE BLUE SQUARE APP H'CAP 5f
2:50 (2:50) (Class 5) (0-70,68) 3-Y-O **£2,331** (£693; £346; £173) **Stalls** Centre

Form RPR
-540 **1** **Saxonette**[1] 2396 3-8-11 **58**.. PJMcDonald 8 65
(Linda Perratt) *hld up in tch: qcknd to ld 2f out: edgd lft: sn clr* **11/4**[1]
122 **2** *4* **Rylee Mooch**[94] 632 3-9-3 **67**...................................(e) RobertLButler(3) 1 60
(Richard Guest) *prom: hdwy to chse wnr over 1f out: kpt on fnl f: no imp* **11/4**[1]
0-65 **3** *3* **Novalist**[16] 1967 3-8-6 **53**...(b[1]) LeeNewman 4 35
(Robin Bastiman) *cl up: rdn and outpcd over 2f out: no imp ins fnl f* **10/1**
-050 **4** *2 3/4* **Empress Royal**[6] 2265 3-8-10 **62**.................................(p) LeeTopliss(5) 3 34
(Michael Dods) *led tl hdd 2f out: sn btn: eased whn no ch ins fnl f* **3/1**[2]
42-0 **5** *1 1/4* **Surely This Time (IRE)**[24] 1745 3-9-7 **68**.......................(p) TomEaves 7 35
(Kevin Ryan) *cl up tl rdn and wknd over 2f out* **10/3**[3]

62.99 secs (3.59) **Going Correction** +0.35s/f (Good) **5** Ran SP% **110.5**
Speed ratings (Par 99): **90,83,78,74,72**
CSF £10.62 TOTE £4.30: £1.20, £1.50; EX 9.10.
Owner John Murphy **Bred** Mike Channon Bloodstock Ltd **Trained** East Kilbride, S Lanarks

FOCUS
Despite four non-runners, the horses with the best form remained. The winner apparently improved form the previous day, which points to this being weak.

2411 JOIN BLUESQ.COM FOR £20 OF FREE BETS H'CAP 6f
3:20 (3:20) (Class 4) (0-85,80) 3-Y-O **£3,885** (£1,156; £577; £288) **Stalls** Centre

Form RPR
1215 **1** **Mr Optimistic**[13] 2074 3-9-2 **80**.. LeeTopliss(5) 4 89+
(Richard Fahey) *trckd ldrs: nt clr run over 2f out: swtchd rt and hdwy over 1f out: led ins fnl f: r.o wl* **7/2**[2]
-435 **2** *nk* **Tro Nesa (IRE)**[12] 2096 3-8-13 **72**.................................... FrannyNorton 5 78
(Ann Duffield) *dwlt: hld up: hdwy over 1f out: chsd wnr ins fnl f: kpt on fin* **8/1**
-231 **3** *2* **Thirteen Shivers**[13] 2074 3-9-6 **79**...................................... DavidNolan 1 79
(Michael Easterby) *cl up: rdn to ld over 1f out: hdd ins fnl f: kpt on same pce* **5/1**[3]
3-35 **4** *1 1/2* **Crimson Knot (IRE)**[21] 1825 3-9-1 **79** ow1.................. SladeO'Hara(5) 7 74
(Alan Berry) *hld up in tch: hdwy and ev ch over 1f out to ins fnl f: kpt on same pce* **14/1**
610- **5** *5* **Luv U Too**[259] 5882 3-9-1 **74**... GrahamGibbons 8 53
(Pat Murphy) *cl up tl edgd lft and no ex over 1f out* **11/1**
14-0 **6** *1 1/2* **Rutterkin (USA)**[15] 2008 3-8-5 **71**................................ VictorSantos(7) 2 45
(Alan Berry) *in tch: drvn over 2f out: wknd over 1f out* **66/1**
2404 **7** *6* **Dasho**[6] 2255 3-9-4 **77**... RoystonFfrench 3 32
(Olivia Maylam) *t.k.h: cl up tl rdn and wknd over 1f out* **11/2**
-003 **8** *4 1/2* **Captain Kolo (IRE)**[3] 2363 3-9-1 **74**................................... DavidAllan 6 14
(Tim Easterby) *led tl hdd over 1f out: sn rdn and wknd* **2/1**[1]

1m 15.85s (3.45) **Going Correction** +0.35s/f (Good) **8** Ran SP% **115.2**
Speed ratings (Par 101): **99,98,95,93,87 85,77,71**
toteswingers:1&2:£6.60, 2&3:£5.50, 1&3:£3.40 CSF £31.64 CT £140.46 TOTE £3.60: £1.10, £1.70, £1.30; EX 38.90.
Owner F L F S Ltd **Bred** C J Murfitt **Trained** Musley Bank, N Yorks

FOCUS
The best race on the card, containing some in-form runners. The pace set by the leader looked sound, but it probably paid to be covered up out of the wind. A clear best from the winner who reversed York form with the third.
Dasho Official explanation: jockey said gelding ran too free
Captain Kolo(IRE) Official explanation: jockey said gelding ran flat

2412 PLAY MECCA BINGO ON YOUR IPHONE H'CAP 6f
3:50 (3:52) (Class 6) (0-60,60) 4-Y-O+ **£1,706** (£503; £252) **Stalls** Centre

Form RPR
0523 **1** **Beckermet (IRE)**[19] 1911 9-8-10 **56**.......................... ShaneBKelly(7) 14 71
(Ruth Carr) *in tch: hdwy to ld over 2f out: edgd lft over 1f out: rdn out ins fnl f* **3/1**[1]
0000 **2** *2 1/4* **Caldermud (IRE)**[15] 1995 4-9-5 **58**...........................(t) RoystonFfrench 1 66
(Olivia Maylam) *hld up on outside: hdwy to chse wnr appr fnl f: r.o* **8/1**
-004 **3** *1 3/4* **Eilean Eeve**[32] 1540 5-8-11 **50**..(p) PJMcDonald 7 52
(George Foster) *bhd tl hdwy over 1f out: kpt on ins fnl f: nrst fin* **25/1**
3-06 **4** *3/4* **North Central (USA)**[13] 2048 4-9-3 **59**......................... GaryBartley(3) 4 59
(Jim Goldie) *midfield: effrt and rdn 2f out: kpt on same pce ins fnl f* **8/1**
0- **5** *1 1/4* **Lambrini Lace (IRE)**[78] 7917 6-8-5 **47** oh1 ow1.(b[1]) PatrickDonaghy(3) 3 43
(Lisa Williamson) *cl up tl rdn and no ex ins fnl f* **40/1**
30/0 **6** *1* **Big Slick (IRE)**[48] 1213 6-8-12 **51**................................ RobertWinston 12 44
(Mel Brittain) *bhd: rdn and hdwy over 1f out: nvr able to chal* **10/1**
6-00 **7** *1/2* **Mission Impossible**[22] 1815 6-8-8 **47**.......................... PatrickMathers 8 38
(Colin Teague) *prom: drvn 1/2-way: no ex over 1f out* **40/1**
4-00 **8** *6* **Whatyouwoodwishfor (USA)**[13] 2047 5-8-13 **55**..(b) RobertLButler(3) 6 27
(Richard Guest) *w ldrs tl rdn and wknd over 1f out* **28/1**
600- **9** *1 1/4* **Classlin**[252] 6103 4-8-7 **46** oh1.. AndrewMullen 10 14
(Jim Goldie) *bhd: pushed along over 2f out: nvr on terms* **20/1**
0-50 **10** *2* **Bahamian Jazz (IRE)**[19] 1911 4-8-13 **52**........................(v[1]) LeeNewman 5 14
(Robin Bastiman) *w ldrs tl wknd 2f out: eased whn no ch ins fnl f* **8/1**
20-0 **11** *nk* **Tongalooma**[36] 1493 5-8-10 **52**.. AmyRyan(3) 13 13
(James Moffatt) *hld up: effrt and rdn 2f out: sn no imp* **40/1**
0002 **12** *1 1/4* **Charles Parnell (IRE)**[7] 2238 8-9-0 **60**.......................... LucyKBarry(7) 16 17
(Simon Griffiths) *dwlt: hld up: rdn over 2f out: nvr on terms* **11/2**[2]
-000 **13** *9* **Ya Boy Sir (IRE)**[32] 1544 4-8-8 **52**................................... LeeTopliss(5) 2 —
(Ian Semple) *hld up in tch: drvn over 2f out: wknd over 1f out* **20/1**
00 **14** *2 1/4* **Drive Home (USA)**[23] 1803 4-8-13 **57**............................ NeilFarley(5) 11 —
(Noel Wilson) *prom tl rdn and wknd over 2f out* **7/1**[3]

1m 15.47s (3.07) **Going Correction** +0.35s/f (Good) **14** Ran SP% **119.4**
Speed ratings (Par 101): **101,98,95,94,93 91,91,83,81,78 78,76,64,61**
toteswingers:1&2:£7.40, 2&3:£40.40, 1&3:£17.20 CSF £24.16 CT £510.76 TOTE £4.60: £2.30, £4.90, £8.80; EX 29.10.
Owner Exors of the late David W Chapman **Bred** Fritz Von Ball Moss **Trained** Huby, N Yorks

FOCUS
A weak sprint and not many had shown solid recent form. The winner probably ran his best race since this time last year.
Bahamian Jazz(IRE) Official explanation: jockey said gelding lost its action

2413 WEDDINGS AT WESTERN HOUSE HOTEL H'CAP 1m
4:20 (4:21) (Class 5) (0-75,75) 4-Y-O+ **£2,331** (£693; £346; £173) **Stalls** Low

Form RPR
6-20 **1** **Frontline Girl (IRE)**[5] 2301 5-9-4 **72**.............................. AndrewElliott 10 82
(Mrs K Burke) *prom: hdwy to ld over 2f out: edgd lft over 1f out: kpt on wl ins fnl f* **4/1**[2]
0-45 **2** *1 1/4* **Daring Dream (GER)**[12] 2115 6-8-13 **70**........................ GaryBartley(3) 6 77
(Jim Goldie) *t.k.h: hld up: stdy hdwy over 2f out: rdn over 1f out: styd on to chse wnr towards fin* **9/2**[3]
0-23 **3** *1 1/4* **Moody Tunes**[3] 2347 8-9-4 **75**................................... PatrickDonaghy(3) 2 79
(Mrs K Burke) *cl up: effrt and ev ch over 2f out: one pce fnl f: lost 2nd towards fin* **5/1**
532 **4** *3 3/4* **Dabbers Ridge (IRE)**[13] 2046 9-9-4 **75**................ AndrewHeffernan(3) 4 71
(Ian McInnes) *hld up: hdwy on outside over 2f out: no imp fnl f* **11/1**
0331 **5** *1 1/4* **Gala Casino Star (IRE)**[20] 1859 6-9-1 **74**...................(p) LeeTopliss(5) 5 67
(Richard Fahey) *hld up in tch: rdn and hung lft fr over 2f out: no imp fr over 1f out* **3/1**[1]
0-40 **6** *8* **Seldom (IRE)**[24] 1748 5-8-8 **62** oh2 ow1........................ RobertWinston 7 36
(Mel Brittain) *trckd ldrs: drvn 3f out: wknd over 1f out* **28/1**
00-0 **7** *8* **Street Devil (USA)**[1] 2401 6-8-9 **63** oh1 ow2..........(p) GrahamGibbons 9 19
(Pat Murphy) *led: rdn and hdd over 2f out: sn wknd* **40/1**
3163 **8** *2* **Nolecce**[31] 1573 4-8-7 **61**.. FrannyNorton 1 12
(Richard Guest) *sn prom: rdn over 2f out: wknd wl over 1f out* **4/1**[2]

1m 43.66s (-0.14) **Going Correction** +0.075s/f (Good) **8** Ran SP% **114.1**
Speed ratings (Par 103): **103,101,100,96,95 87,79,77**
toteswingers:1&2:£4.40, 2&3:£5.70, 1&3:£4.90 CSF £22.22 CT £91.46 TOTE £5.60: £1.40, £1.10, £3.90; EX 20.90.
Owner M A Roden **Bred** J Donnelly **Trained** Middleham Moor, North Yorks

FOCUS
The pace didn't look too bad in the early stages, even though the runner-up took a strong hold. Ordinary form, the runner-up the best guide.
Gala Casino Star(IRE) Official explanation: jockey said gelding slipped leaving stalls

2414 BET AT BLUESQ.COM H'CAP 1m 2f
4:50 (4:50) (Class 4) (0-80,80) 4-Y-O+ **£3,885** (£1,156; £577; £288) **Stalls** Low

Form RPR
3-03 **1** **Quanah Parker (IRE)**[7] 2213 5-8-11 **70**........................ RobertWinston 3 78
(Richard Whitaker) *trckd ldr: led and qcknd over 2f out: kpt on u.p ins fnl f: jst hld on* **3/1**[1]
/10- **2** *hd* **Staff Sergeant**[318] 3949 4-9-3 **79**.................................... GaryBartley(3) 8 87
(Jim Goldie) *hld up in tch: effrt over 2f out: chsd wnr over 1f out: r.o wl ins fnl f: jst hld* **7/1**
0-63 **3** *2* **Grams And Ounces**[21] 1829 4-9-3 **76**.................................... JoeFanning 2 80
(Amy Weaver) *trckd ldrs: effrt and rdn over 2f out: kpt on same pce ins fnl f* **7/2**[2]
655- **4** *2 3/4* **Spirit Of A Nation (IRE)**[273] 5436 6-9-4 **80**........................ AmyRyan(3) 6 79
(James Moffatt) *hld up in tch on outside: effrt over 2f out: edgd lft and no imp over 1f out* **25/1**
0-04 **5** *1 1/4* **Lord Raglan (IRE)**[20] 1859 4-9-1 **74**.............................. AndrewElliott 1 70
(Mrs K Burke) *led at ordinary gallop: rdn over 3f out: hdd over 2f out: wknd over 1f out* **7/2**[2]
-451 **6** *hd* **Rosbay (IRE)**[13] 2059 7-9-2 **75**..................................... DuranFentiman 5 71
(Tim Easterby) *hld up in tch: drvn and outpcd 3f out: n.d after* **5/1**[3]
-020 **7** *3/4* **High Resolution**[7] 2217 4-9-2 **80**....................................... LeeTopliss(5) 7 74
(Linda Perratt) *s.i.s: hld up: rdn over 2f out: sn n.d: btn over 1f out* **8/1**

2m 14.25s (2.25) **Going Correction** +0.075s/f (Good) **7** Ran SP% **113.6**
Speed ratings (Par 105): **94,93,92,90,89 88,88**
toteswingers:1&2:£4.60, 2&3:£5.20, 1&3:£2.30 CSF £23.93 CT £75.20 TOTE £3.30: £2.30, £4.40; EX 29.20.
Owner Wham Partnership **Bred** M Fahy **Trained** Scarcroft, W Yorks

FOCUS
This isn't form to take too literally, as the early pace was slow and the fractions only increased as the home straight approached. The form is rated around the second and third.

2415 SEE STACEY SOLOMON HERE ON 17TH JUNE H'CAP 7f 50y
5:20 (5:22) (Class 6) (0-60,60) 4-Y-O+ **£1,619** (£481; £240; £120) **Stalls** High

Form RPR
0-04 **1** **Shunkawakhan (IRE)**[23] 1803 8-8-7 **46** oh1...................(p) JoeFanning 8 54
(Linda Perratt) *trckd ldrs: hdwy to ld over 2f out: edgd lft over 1f out: r.o ins fnl f: jst hld on* **13/2**
6-01 **2** *hd* **Blue Charm**[7] 2233 7-8-12 **54** 6ex................................... GaryBartley(3) 9 63+
(Ian McInnes) *hld up: hdwy whn nt clr run over 2f out and over 1f out: styd on strly ins fnl f: jst hld* **9/2**[2]
0202 **3** *3/4* **On The Cusp (IRE)**[7] 2237 4-8-8 **52**...............................(p) JulieBurke(5) 5 57
(Richard Guest) *led: rdn and hdd over 2f out: rallied: kpt on same pce ins fnl f* **11/4**[1]
00-0 **4** *1 1/4* **Balance On Time (IRE)**[23] 1803 5-8-4 **46** oh1... AndrewHeffernan(3) 10 48
(Linda Perratt) *midfield: effrt over 2f out hrd rdn and edgd lft over 1f out: kpt on same pce ins fnl f* **20/1**
01-0 **5** *shd* **Monsieur Pontaven**[37] 1468 4-9-0 **53**...........................(b) LeeNewman 4 55
(Robin Bastiman) *trckd ldrs: rdn over 2f out: no ex ins fnl f* **6/1**[3]
6-05 **6** *1 1/2* **Spread Boy (IRE)**[23] 1795 4-8-11 **50**...............................(b[1]) PaulQuinn 1 48
(Alan Berry) *hld up: rdn over 2f out: hdwy over 1f out: nvr able to chal* **9/1**
0002 **7** *2 1/4* **Chardonnay Star (IRE)**[13] 2047 4-8-8 **47**.................(v) PatrickMathers 7 39
(Colin Teague) *in tch: drvn and outpcd over 2f out: no imp ins fnl f* **14/1**
00-0 **8** *1/2* **Catcher Of Dreams (IRE)**[48] 1216 5-8-7 **46** oh1(v[1]) RoystonFfrench 12 36
(George Foster) *hld up in midfield: hdwy on outside over 2f out: no ex over 1f out* **12/1**

4-06 **9** *4 1/2* **Russian Brigadier**[19] 1906 4-9-1 **54**.............................. RobertWinston 3 32
(Mel Brittain) *t.k.h: trckd ldrs tl rdn and wknd over 1f out* **22/1**

00/ **10** *nk* **Rue Soleil**[640] 5309 7-8-7 **46** oh1.............................. AndrewElliott 13 23
(John Weymes) *pressed ldr: rdn and ev ch over 2f out: wknd over 1f out* **40/1**

/00- **11** *17* **Fourlanends**[213] 7129 4-8-7 **46** oh1.............................. DuranFentiman 6 —
(Noel Wilson) *plld hrd in rr: rdn over 3f out: sn struggling* **16/1**

000- **12** *1* **Sams Spirit**[180] 7599 5-8-4 **46** oh1.............................. PatrickDonaghy(3) 2 —
(Ian Semple) *bhd: rdn along 1/2-way: sn btn* **16/1**

1m 35.96s (2.56) **Going Correction** +0.075s/f (Good) **12** Ran SP% **120.1**
Speed ratings (Par 101): **88,87,86,85,85 83,81,80,75,75 55,54**
toteswingers:1&2:£3.90, 2&3:£2.90, 1&3:£3.50. Tote Super 7: Win: Not won. Place: Not won. CSF £35.48 CT £101.41 TOTE £8.10: £2.20, £1.30, £2.00; EX 37.60.
Owner Mrs Helen Perratt **Bred** Matthew Duffy **Trained** East Kilbride, S Lanarks
■ Stewards' Enquiry : Andrew Heffernan one-day ban: careless riding (Jun 9)
Duran Fentiman caution: entered wrong stall

FOCUS
Six of these were running from out of the handicap, so this looked a poor contest, although the leaders went off at a good gallop. Straightforward form, but the winner looked unlucky.
T/Plt: £136.90 to £1 stake. Pool of £53,467.54 - 285.08 winning tickets. T/Qpdt: £59.90 to a £1 stake. Pool of £3,727.74 - 46.00 winning tickets. RY

2167 BRIGHTON (L-H)

Thursday, May 26

OFFICIAL GOING: Good to firm (8.4)
Rail dolled out 4m from 4.5f to 2f adding 12yds to distances.
Wind: very strong half against Weather: dry, very windy

2416 MATTHEW CLARK DRINKS MAIDEN AUCTION STKS 5f 59y
2:10 (2:10) (Class 5) 2-Y-O **£2,266** (£674) **Stalls** Low

Form RPR
23 **1** **Bubbly Ballerina**[13] 2070 2-8-10 0.............................. RyanMoore 1 88
(Alan Bailey) *mde all: shkn up and readily drew clr jst over 1f out: v easily* **1/10**[1]

022 **2** *5* **Rooknrasbryripple**[8] 2194 2-8-10 0.............................. SamHitchcott 2 66
(Mick Channon) *chsd wnr: shkn up and unable qck ent fnl 2f: rdn and btn ent fnl f* **7/1**[2]

64.79 secs (2.49) **Going Correction** +0.25s/f (Good) **2** Ran SP% **103.4**
Speed ratings (Par 93): **90,82**
TOTE £1.10.
Owner The Champagne Club **Bred** Whitsbury Manor Stud **Trained** Newmarket, Suffolk

FOCUS
There was a stiff wind blowing against the runners in the home straight. The rails had been dolled out from 4.5f to 2f, adding 12 yards to distances. Just two fillies lined up for this juvenile maiden and the formbook suggested it would be a one-sided affair, as it proved. They went a reasonable pace in the conditions.

NOTEBOOK
Bubbly Ballerina, a decent third in a 5f Listed event at York 13 days earlier, landed the odds without fuss. Quickly away, she led from the start and was always going considerably better than her rival. She needed only to be pushed out to collect and is clearly a fair sort, but how easy she will be to place after this remains to be seen. Plans to target either the Queen Mary or the Windsor Castle Stakes at Royal Ascot seem slightly ambitious, but with black type and a victory already to her credit, she can make a broodmare. (op 1-8)
Rooknrasbryripple, dropped in trip after a last-time-out second at Kempton, was always playing second fiddle. She attempted to match strides with the winner from the outset, but was being nudged along to stay in touch 2f out and was comfortably left behind soon afterwards. She has the ability to take a maiden, but it will need to be weak and such races tend to become harder to find as the season progresses. (op 11-2)

2417 MATTHEW CLARK DRINKS H'CAP 1m 3f 196y
2:40 (2:41) (Class 5) (0-70,69) 4-Y-O+ **£2,266** (£674; £337) **Stalls** High

Form RPR
2211 **1** **Filun**[8] 2202 6-9-0 **62** 6ex.............................. LiamKeniry 3 73
(Anthony Middleton) *stdd s: hld up in 3rd: cruised upsides rivals on bit over 1f out: pushed ahd ins fnl f: sn in command: comf* **15/8**[2]

14-2 **2** *3 1/2* **Celestial Girl**[9] 2170 4-9-7 **69**.............................. SteveDrowne 2 75
(Hughie Morrison) *chsd ldr: rdn and effrt ent fnl 2f: led wl over 1f out: sn drvn: hdd ins fnl f: sn btn and edgd lft* **4/6**[1]

464- **3** *6* **Lauberhorn**[189] 7495 4-9-0 **62**..............................(b) KierenFallon 1 62
(Eve Johnson Houghton) *led: rdn 3f out: hdd wl over 1f out: drvn ent fnl f: wkng whn short of room and hmpd ins fnl f: eased after* **15/2**[3]

2m 38.39s (5.69) **Going Correction** +0.25s/f (Good) **3** Ran SP% **106.5**
Speed ratings (Par 103): **91,88,84**
CSF £3.55 TOTE £2.80; EX 3.40.
Owner R J Matthews **Bred** Azienda Agricola Francesca **Trained** Granborough, Bucks
■ Stewards' Enquiry : Steve Drowne one-day ban: careless riding (Jun 9)

FOCUS
Another small field, but all three runners could have been fancied. They raced in Indian file at just a fair pace until approaching the 2f pole. Perhaps not form to take too literally, but the winner looks better than ever at face value.
Celestial Girl Official explanation: jockey said filly hung left

2418 MAYO WYNNE BAXTER SOLICITORS H'CAP 1m 1f 209y
3:10 (3:11) (Class 6) (0-65,65) 3-Y-O **£1,619** (£481; £240; £120) **Stalls** High

Form RPR
1213 **1** **Jack's Revenge (IRE)**[22] 1819 3-9-3 **61**..............................(tp) TonyCulhane 8 75
(George Baker) *chsd ldng pair: wnt 2nd and travelling wl 3f out: led over 2f out: pushed along and drew clr 2f out: wl clr fnl f: pushed out* **5/2**[1]

6-26 **2** *15* **Silver Show (IRE)**[8] 2196 3-9-7 **65**.............................. SamHitchcott 4 49
(Mick Channon) *wl bhd: rdn 5f out: sme hdwy u.p to go modest 3rd over 2f out: kpt on fnl f to go 2nd fnl 75yds: no ch w wnr* **5/1**[3]

3220 **3** *3 1/4* **Back For Tea (IRE)**[5] 2307 3-8-8 **52**..............................(t) KirstyMilczarek 3 30
(Phil McEntee) *t.k.h: chsd ldr tl led over 3f out: hdd and rdn over 2f out: sn btn: tired and lost modest 2nd fnl 75yds* **20/1**

6442 **4** *4* **Surprise (IRE)**[16] 1969 3-9-0 **58**.............................. SteveDrowne 6 28
(Mark Rimmer) *racd off the pce in last trio: rdn and no hdwy 3f out: 4th and wl btn whn hung lft over 1f out* **4/1**[2]

-055 **5** *6* **Senor Tibor (USA)**[15] 1999 3-8-7 **51** oh3..............................(v) EddieCreighton 7 —
(Edward Creighton) *t.k.h early: hld up in last trio: rdn 1/2-way: lost tch w ldrs wl over 2f out: wl bhd fnl 2f* **100/1**

66-0 **6** *17* **Grecian Goddess (IRE)**[14] 2018 3-9-7 **65**.............................. KierenFallon 2 —
(John Ryan) *led tl over 3f out: sn rdn and struggling: wl bhd fnl 2f: eased ins fnl f: t.o* **13/2**

2m 6.47s (2.87) **Going Correction** +0.25s/f (Good) **6** Ran SP% **84.3**
Speed ratings (Par 97): **98,86,83,80,75 61**
toteswingers:1&2:£1.60, 2&3:£4.30, 1&3:£2.60 CSF £7.96 CT £57.42 TOTE £2.70: £1.10, £2.50; EX 6.40 Trifecta £38.60 Pool: £350.82 - 6.72 winning units..
Owner PJL Racing **Bred** Con Marnane **Trained** Whitsbury, Hants

FOCUS
A modest handicap, with the top weight rated 65, but several seemed to have chances. The eaay winner did not have a great deal to beat but is rated up 9lb.

2419 BRIGHTONANDHOVEJOBS.COM MAIDEN STKS 7f 214y
3:40 (3:41) (Class 5) 3-Y-O+ **£2,266** (£674; £337; £168) **Stalls** Low

Form RPR
54-3 **1** **Bakoura**[41] 1358 3-8-11 70.............................. TadhgO'Shea 7 70
(John Dunlop) *hld up in last pair: hdwy over 3f out: chsd wnr 2f out: pushed along to chal jst over 1f out: hld hd high but pushed ahd ins fnl f: in command fnl 75yds: eased cl home* **2/1**[2]

2 **2** *1* **Burning Stone (USA)**[23] 1795 4-9-9 69.............................. AdamBeschizza(5) 2 75
(Gay Kelleway) *led: rdn over 2f out: hrd drvn over 1f out: hdd ins fnl f: one pce* **7/1**

2-6 **3** *10* **Blue Deer (IRE)**[40] 1408 3-9-2 70.............................. SamHitchcott 6 49
(Mick Channon) *hld up in midfield: hdwy to chse ldr ent fnl 3f tl 2f out: fnd little u.p and sn btn: wknd over 1f out* **15/8**[1]

4 *4* **Miss Excel** 4-9-9 0.............................. EddieCreighton 1 38
(Edward Creighton) *uns rdr and galloped loose to s: sn pushed up to chse ldr: lost 2nd and rdn ent fnl 3f: 4th and wl btn over 1f out* **100/1**

0-0 **5** *7* **Ari Gold (IRE)**[22] 1810 3-9-2 0..............................(v[1]) JimCrowley 4 24
(Tom Dascombe) *blind removed late and s.i.s: t.k.h and sn in tch in midfield: struggling and wandering ent fnl 3f: wl btn fnl 2f* **3/1**[3]

25 **6** *8* **Brent Pelham**[41] 1370 4-10-0 0..............................(t) StevieDonohoe 3 —
(Tobias B P Coles) *sn outpce in last: rdn 5f out: c to centre and lost tch 3f out: t.o* **100/1**

00 **7** *27* **Miming**[37] 1465 3-8-11 0.............................. SteveDrowne 5 —
(Hughie Morrison) *racd freely: w ldrs tl wkng whn sltly hmpd ent fnl 3f: wl bhd fnl 2f: eased ins fnl f: t.o* **33/1**

1m 37.55s (1.55) **Going Correction** +0.25s/f (Good)
WFA 3 from 4yo 12lb **7** Ran SP% **110.5**
Speed ratings (Par 103): **102,101,91,87,80 72,45**
toteswingers:1&2:£1.70, 2&3:£2.20, 1&3:£1.70 CSF £14.85 TOTE £4.30: £2.60, £2.40; EX 11.00.
Owner Hamdan Al Maktoum **Bred** Shadwell Estate Company Limited **Trained** Arundel, W Sussex

FOCUS
Not much obvious depth to this run-of-the-mill maiden. The favourite ran poorly and the form is rated a bit cautiously.
Ari Gold(IRE) Official explanation: jockey said blindfold got caught on visor and gelding was slowly away
Miming Official explanation: jockey said filly ran too free

2420 SPORTING SIGNS H'CAP 7f 214y
4:10 (4:10) (Class 6) (0-60,60) 4-Y-O+ **£1,619** (£481; £240; £120) **Stalls** Low

Form RPR
6533 **1** **Diddums**[6] 2245 5-8-11 **57**.............................. KatiaScallan(7) 1 65
(Alastair Lidderdale) *hld up towards rr: hmpd and swtchd rt over 4f out: rdn and gd hdwy on inner over 1f out: chal ins fnl f: r.o wl to ld towards fin* **15/2**

20-3 **2** *1/2* **Fire King**[6] 2242 5-9-5 **58**..............................(p) NeilCallan 10 65
(Andrew Haynes) *t.k.h: hld up in tch in midfield: hdwy to trck ldrs 2f out: rdn under hands and heels and qcknd to ld jst ins fnl f: hdd and no ex towards fin* **9/4**[1]

54-2 **3** *1 3/4* **Phluke**[9] 2171 10-9-4 **57**.............................. CathyGannon 9 60
(Eve Johnson Houghton) *led tl 6f out: styd prom: ev ch and rdn over 2f out: no ex and btn ins fnl f: one pce fnl 100yds* **7/2**[2]

600P **4** *1 3/4* **Dawson Creek (IRE)**[8] 2202 7-8-4 **46** oh1.............................. SophieDoyle(3) 9 45
(Mark Hoad) *w ldrs: rdn and unable qck 3f out: styd chsng ldrs u.p over 2f out: styd on same pce ins fnl f* **66/1**

0030 **5** *shd* **Regal Rave (USA)**[10] 2144 4-9-7 **60**.............................. DaneO'Neill 6 59
(Mouse Hamilton-Fairley) *bhd in last pair: rdn and no hdwy over 2f out: stl 9th and no imp over 1f out: swtchd rt and hdwy 1f out: r.o strly ins fnl f: nt rch ldrs* **11/1**

0-05 **6** *1 1/2* **Yourgolftravel Com**[10] 2144 6-9-2 **55**..............................(bt) JamesDoyle 5 50
(David Pipe) *t.k.h: hld up in midfield: rdn and effrt over 2f out: drvn and fnd little over 1f out: no threat to ldrs ins fnl f* **14/1**

6065 **7** *1 1/2* **Fedora (IRE)**[28] 1625 5-8-6 **50**..............................(t) AdamBeschizza(5) 4 42
(Olivia Maylam) *chsd ldrs: hdwy to ld over 2f out: rdn 2f out: hdd jst ins fnl f: wknd qckly fnl 150yds* **7/1**[3]

-542 **8** *7* **Giulietta Da Vinci**[28] 1633 4-8-13 **52**..............................(b) JimCrowley 11 28
(Steve Woodman) *t.k.h: hld up in tch towards rr: hdwy 3f out: rdn and no hdwy wl over 1f out: sn wknd* **12/1**

0000 **9** *1 1/4* **Mistress Shy**[24] 1763 4-8-0 **46** oh1..............................(t) JackDuern(7) 7 19
(Robin Dickin) *hld up in last pair: struggling over 3f out: wl bhd fnl 2f* **100/1**

-002 **10** *1/2* **Interakt**[17] 1933 4-9-2 **55**..............................(b) TadhgO'Shea 8 27
(Joseph Tuite) *racd freely: sn chsng ldrs: led 6f out tl over 2f out: wknd qckly wl over 1f out* **8/1**

-560 **11** *12* **Durgan**[22] 1813 5-9-2 **55**..............................(p) SteveDrowne 2 —
(Linda Jewell) *racd in midfield: hmpd and dropped in rr over 4f out: lost tch wl over 2f out: eased ins fnl f: t.o* **25/1**

1m 38.34s (2.34) **Going Correction** +0.25s/f (Good) **11** Ran SP% **117.4**
Speed ratings (Par 101): **98,97,95,94,93 92,90,83,82,82 70**
CSF £24.45 CT £72.31 TOTE £7.50: £2.30, £1.70, £2.10; EX 30.70 Trifecta £160.30 Pool: £335.85 - 1.55 winning units..
Owner C S J Beek **Bred** J B Haggas **Trained** Eastbury, Berks

FOCUS
A very ordinary handicap, with the top weight rated 60, but it seemed wide open on paper. The runner-up looks the best guide to the form.
Interakt Official explanation: jockey said filly ran too free

2421 JUICE 107.2 FM H'CAP 6f 209y
4:40 (4:40) (Class 6) (0-65,64) 3-Y-O **£1,619** (£481; £240; £120) **Stalls** Low

Form RPR
0-61 **1** **Dysios (IRE)**[8] 2197 3-9-8 **64** 6ex.............................. KierenFallon 5 75+
(Luca Cumani) *hld up in tch: rdn and qcknd to ld over 1f out: readily asserted ins fnl f: eased nr fin: comf* **1/4**[1]

0333 2 1 3/4 **Cathcart Castle**[3] 2351 3-9-1 57 SamHitchcott 2 58
(Mick Channon) *taken down early: chsd ldng pair: rdn and effrt over 2f out: drvn and ev ch over 1f out: nt gng pce of wnr and btn ins fnl f* 4/1[2]
5335 3 3 1/2 **Titan Diamond (IRE)**[9] 2177 3-8-9 58 RachealKneller(7) 3 50
(Mark Usher) *racd in last pair: effrt and pushed along on inner ent fnl 2f: chsd ldrs 1f out: no ex and btn fnl 150yds: wknd fnl 100yds* 20/1[3]
6-00 4 nk **Maggie's Treasure (IRE)**[62] 964 3-9-7 63 TadhgO'Shea 1 54
(John Gallagher) *led: rdn over 2f out: drvn and hdd over 1f out: wknd fnl 150yds* 40/1
5-50 5 17 **Robber Stone**[3] 2350 3-8-8 53 MatthewDavies(3) 4 —
(Mick Channon) *taken down early: pressed ldr: rdn over 2f out: wknd u.p wl over 1f out: wl bhd and virtually p.u fnl 75yds* 20/1[3]
1m 25.14s (2.04) **Going Correction** +0.25s/f (Good) 5 Ran SP% **112.0**
Speed ratings (Par 97): **98,96,92,91,72**
CSF £1.57 TOTE £1.60: £1.10, £1.40; EX 1.80.
Owner Leonidas Marinopoulos **Bred** Fin A Co S R L **Trained** Newmarket, Suffolk

FOCUS

A weak affair, with the betting market dominated by a well-backed odds-on favourite. He was 9lb well in and didn't need to improve.
Maggie's Treasure(IRE) Official explanation: jockey said gelding lost a shoe

2422 SUMMER MUSIC NIGHT 21ST JUNE H'CAP 5f 213y
5:10 (5:10) (Class 5) (0-75,75) 4-Y-O+ **£2,266** (£674; £337; £168) **Stalls** Low

Form RPR
4423 1 **Magical Speedfit (IRE)**[9] 2169 6-9-3 74 SimonPearce(3) 3 81
(George Margarson) *sn detached in last: pushed along over 3f out: rdn and clsd over 1f out: wnt 3rd 1f out: hld hd high but kpt on to ld cl home* 2/1[1]
00-3 2 hd **Volito**[19] 1912 5-8-9 63 RussKennemore 1 69
(Anabel K Murphy) *chsd ldr: effrt on inner to chse ldr over 1f out: rdn 1f out: n.m.r on rail but ev ch ins fnl f: led fnl 75yds: hdd cl home* 11/4[2]
1-00 3 shd **Sermons Mount (USA)**[10] 2142 5-8-13 67 DaneO'Neill 5 73
(Mouse Hamilton-Fairley) *chsd ldr: jnd ldr over 2f out: rdn to ld wl over 1f out: edgd lft u.p ins fnl f: hdd fnl 75yds: no ex* 11/2
3352 4 5 **Sherjawy (IRE)**[8] 2193 7-8-10 64 KirstyMilczarek 2 54
(Zoe Davison) *chsd ldng trio: rdn ent fnl 3f: wknd u.p 1f out* 8/1
0-06 5 2 3/4 **Peter Island (FR)**[17] 1937 8-9-7 75 (v) MartinLane 4 56
(John Gallagher) *led: jnd and rdn over 2f out: hdd wl over 1f out: wknd ent fnl f* 3/1[3]
1m 11.12s (0.92) **Going Correction** +0.25s/f (Good) 5 Ran SP% **111.5**
Speed ratings (Par 103): **103,102,102,95,92**
CSF £7.89 TOTE £2.70: £1.02, £2.90; EX 9.30.
Owner John Guest Racing **Bred** John Malone **Trained** Newmarket, Suffolk
■ Stewards' Enquiry : Russ Kennemore three-day ban: used whip down shoulder in the forehand (Jun 9-11)

FOCUS

An interesting finale, for all that the five runners are no great shakes, and none could be categorically discounted. It was sound run and the winner is rated to his best.
T/Plt: £11.50 to a £1 stake. Pool of £37,328.91 - 2,356.90 winning tickets. T/Qpdt: £2.80 to a £1 stake. Pool of £3,342.05 - 857.79 winning tickets. SP

1504 FOLKESTONE (R-H)
Thursday, May 26

OFFICIAL GOING: Good to firm (8.4)
Wind: Strong, half behind Weather: Changeable, heavy shower race 5

2423 LADBROKES.COM MAIDEN STKS 5f
2:30 (2:31) (Class 5) 2-Y-O **£2,388** (£705; £352) **Stalls** High

Form RPR
2 1 **Gentlemans Code (USA)**[21] 2-9-3 0 (bt1) MESmith 2 91+
(Wesley A Ward, U.S.A) *mde all: pushed along to assert fnl f: comf* 1/6[1]
2 1 3/4 **Bear Behind (IRE)** 2-9-3 0 RichardKingscote 3 85+
(Tom Dascombe) *racd against rail: pressed wnr: shkn up over 1f out: readily hld but kpt on wl* 5/1[2]
3 27 **Joe M** 2-9-3 0 TomQueally 4 —
(Simon Dow) *immediately outpcd: sn wl t.o* 40/1[3]
58.78 secs (-1.22) **Going Correction** -0.225s/f (Firm) 3 Ran SP% **104.8**
Speed ratings (Par 93): **100,97,54**
CSF £1.26 TOTE £1.20; EX 1.40.
Owner Wesley A Ward & Ice Wine Stable **Bred** Bridlewood Farm **Trained** North America

FOCUS

A very blustery afternoon with the wind behind the runners in the straight. The ground was as quick as advertised. A low-key and uncompetitive sprint maiden, run at a fair pace for the conditions, and good form from the first two. Much excitement was generated over the appearance of Zenyatta's American Hall of Fame jockey Mike Smith aboard the Wesley Ward-trained favourite, Smith's first ride in Britain.

NOTEBOOK

Gentlemans Code(USA) gave his in-form US stable an easy victory. Odds-on and beaten into second on his debut in a muddy dirt track at Belmont Park (having set the pace and drifting slightly right from halfway), he'd clearly learned plenty from what looked an ordinary race. He has a dirt pedigree and connections were concerned about how he would handle the undulations at the Kent track. Those fears were unfounded, as he looked perfectly well-balanced. Sporting a tongue-tie and headgear, he bounced out of the stalls and made all, drawing clear under minimal pressure, despite drifting left towards the stands' rail, for a visually workmanlike victory, although the suspicion is he much better than the winning margin suggests. He is entitled to take his chance at Royal Ascot, where the stable had two 2-y-o winners two years ago. His jockey felt the colt would be better off staying at 5f for now, so the Norfolk Stakes is on the agenda. (op 1-4 tchd 3-10)
Bear Behind(IRE) clearly knew his job on his debut and was in tandem with the winner until 2f out, where he came under pressure. He ran a little green but looks a genuine sort, who stuck his head down and battled once the penny dropped, but simply came across a winner with the benefit of experience and a touch more class. This was a very decent effort. He looks sure to win races over this trip or slightly further. (op 7-2 tchd 10-3)
Joe M needs more experience. He fell out of the stalls, never got competitive and was beaten a long way. (op 25-1 tchd 20-1)

2424 LADBROKES.COM ON YOUR MOBILE H'CAP 5f
3:00 (3:01) (Class 6) (0-55,55) 3-Y-O+ **£1,706** (£503; £252) **Stalls** High

Form RPR
0060 1 **Gothic Chick**[16] 1980 3-8-2 49 (p) KieranO'Neill(5) 10 53
(Alan McCabe) *racd against rail: trckd ldrs: plld out and effrt to ld jst over 1f out: shkn up and sn wl in command* 4/1[2]
50-0 2 1 1/2 **Ishipink**[10] 2164 4-8-7 46 oh1 HarryBentley(5) 4 47
(Ron Hodges) *led and sn grabbed nr side rail: rdn and hdd jst over 1f out: kpt on but no ch w wnr* 16/1
0465 3 2 1/4 **Radiator Rooney (IRE)**[10] 2161 8-8-12 51 RyanPowell(5) 5 47+
(Patrick Morris) *hld up in rr: effrt 2f out: nt clr run over 1f out: hanging but styd on ins fnl f to take 3rd last stride* 4/1[2]
0255 4 shd **Talamahana**[10] 2142 6-9-6 54 (v) TomQueally 1 47
(Andrew Haynes) *racd towards outer: chsd ldrs: pushed along 1/2-way: rdn and cl enough over 1f out: one pce after* 13/2[3]
544- 4 dht **Luisa Tetrazzini (IRE)**[188] 7505 5-9-2 55 MarkCoumbe(5) 7 48
(Michael Attwater) *s.s: wl off the pce in 8th: prog on outer 2f out: styd on to press for 3rd fin* 7/1
-501 6 3 1/4 **Fathey (IRE)**[20] 1875 5-8-9 50 MatthewLawson(7) 2 31
(Charles Smith) *broke wl: styd wdst of all in centre: outpcd over 3f out: effrt and rdn 2f out: fdd ins fnl f* 3/1[1]
-600 7 1/2 **Place The Duchess**[47] 1247 5-8-12 46 oh1 (vt) RobertHavlin 6 26
(Alastair Lidderdale) *chsd ldr to wl over 1f out: wknd ins fnl f* 20/1
0 8 3/4 **Avonvalley**[101] 537 4-8-13 47 RobbieFitzpatrick 3 24
(Peter Grayson) *awkward s: nvr bttr than midfield: rdn and no prog whn hmpd over 1f out* 22/1
3300 9 10 **Pickled Pumpkin**[10] 2163 3-8-12 54 (b) IanMongan 9 —
(Olivia Maylam) *s.s: outpcd and a wl bhd* 11/1
60.01 secs (0.01) **Going Correction** -0.225s/f (Firm)
WFA 3 from 4yo+ 8lb 9 Ran SP% **114.2**
Speed ratings (Par 101): **90,87,84,83,83 78,77,76,60**
toteswingers:1&2:£23.30, 2&3:£29.30, 1&3:£3.00 CSF £64.09 CT £272.15 TOTE £3.80: £1.30, £3.60, £2.00; EX 79.00.
Owner The Michaelmas Daisy Partnership **Bred** Plantation Stud **Trained** Averham Park, Notts

FOCUS

A dreadfully weak handicap and the pace was even. The first two were well placed against the rail and the winner did not need to run up to her best.
Radiator Rooney(IRE) Official explanation: jockey said gelding was denied a clear run
Luisa Tetrazzini(IRE) Official explanation: jockey said mare was slowly away
Pickled Pumpkin Official explanation: jockey said gelding was reluctant to race

2425 GODFREYS JOHN DEERE TURFCARE CLAIMING STKS 6f
3:30 (3:31) (Class 6) 2-Y-O **£1,706** (£503; £252) **Stalls** High

Form RPR
321 1 **Miss Muga**[11] 2121 2-7-11 0 CharlesBishop(7) 5 61
(Mick Channon) *chsd ldng pair and racd against rail: pushed along 1/2-way: plenty to do whn plld out and rdn over 1f out: clsd to ld last 100yds: styd on wl* 10/11[1]
4310 2 1 1/2 **Mousie**[22] 1806 2-8-3 0 KieranO'Neill(5) 1 61
(Alan McCabe) *pressed ldr: led jst over 2f out and sn kicked 2 l clr: hdd and outpcd last 100yds* 9/4[2]
243 3 5 **She's Cool Too (IRE)**[6] 2267 2-8-1 0 (tp) JakePayne(7) 2 46
(Bill Turner) *led and racd towards nr side rail: hdd jst over 2f out: wknd over 1f out* 12/1
0 4 7 **Thefillyfromsutton**[8] 2187 2-7-10 0 ow1 JemmaMarshall(5) 3 18
(Pat Phelan) *s.s: outpcd and hanging: nvr on terms: bhd fr 1/2-way* 5/1[3]
6 5 2 3/4 **Frankie Valley**[31] 1563 2-8-5 0 LukeMorris 4 13
(J S Moore) *rdn after 2f: sn struggling and bhd* 28/1
1m 12.43s (-0.27) **Going Correction** -0.225s/f (Firm) 5 Ran SP% **111.0**
Speed ratings (Par 91): **92,90,83,74,70**
CSF £3.23 TOTE £3.10: £1.10, £2.10; EX 3.10.Miss Muga was claimed by E. J. Creighton for £7000.
Owner R Bastian **Bred** R Bastian **Trained** West Ilsley, Berks

FOCUS

A fairly solid sprint claimer for the money, run in a decent time for the paucity of runners.

NOTEBOOK

Miss Muga won in good style. Clearly on good terms with herself after breaking her duck at the third attempt at Ripon over this trip, her 7lb claimer was patient, giving her plenty to do to catch the leaders inside the final 2 1/2f. But once he angled her out, she readily went about her work, sticking her head down and winning with the minimum of fuss. She looks as though she needs further and is one to keep on the right side while she remains in this mood. (op 5-6 tchd 8-11)
Mousie had a subsequent winner back in third when winning at Yarmouth last month and, dropped in class after failing to handle the draw in a Class 2 event at Chester last time, she held obvious claims on the book for her 6f debut. She looked to have poached a winning lead 2f from home, but succumbed to an in-form rival. She is bred to get this trip and is worth another try over it. (op 5-2 tchd 11-4)
She's Cool Too(IRE) was wearing cheekpieces for the first time to go with the tongue-tie she wore last time. She showed good early pace and nabbed the rail, but was a spent force approaching the final furlong, her limitations exposed once again. (op 17-2 tchd 8-1)
Thefillyfromsutton missed the break on her Goodwood debut and did so again. She did show a modicum of ability once she got going and will benefit from the experience. (op 11-1 tchd 12-1)
Frankie Valley unshipped her rider going down to the start and was never a factor thereafter. The sun ain't gonna shine any less on this performance. (op 25-1 tchd 22-1)

2426 FREIGHT44.COM H'CAP 6f
4:00 (4:03) (Class 6) (0-65,65) 4-Y-O+ **£1,706** (£503; £252) **Stalls** High

Form RPR
5332 1 **Anjomarba (IRE)**[24] 1770 4-9-0 63 KieranO'Neill(5) 3 73
(Brett Johnson) *trckd ldr and racd one off rail: shkn up over 2f out: led over 1f out: rdn and styd on wl* 10/3[1]
-620 2 1 1/4 **Play The Blues (IRE)**[22] 1814 4-9-2 65 (t) RyanPowell(5) 4 71
(Mark Allen) *dwlt: t.k.h: hld up in last pair: prog on outer 2f out: styd on to take 3rd ins fnl f: nt qckn last 100yds* 16/1
-641 3 3/4 **Kyllachy Storm**[10] 2142 7-9-2 65 6ex HarryBentley(5) 5 69
(Ron Hodges) *chsd ldng trio: rdn and nt qckn 2f out: kpt on to take 3rd ins fnl f* 10/3[1]
0054 4 1 1/4 **Simple Rhythm**[8] 2193 5-8-13 57 (p) AdamKirby 7 57
(John Ryan) *racd against rail: led: rdn and hdd over 1f out: fdd ins fnl f* 9/2[2]
5650 5 nk **Stonecrabstomorrow (IRE)**[2] 2382 8-8-7 51 oh6(v1) RobbieFitzpatrick 2 50
(Michael Attwater) *racd towards outer: chsd ldrs: rdn over 2f out: cl enough but nt qckn over 1f out: fdd ins fnl f* 25/1
00-5 6 3/4 **Yes We Can**[28] 1630 4-9-2 60 PatCosgrave 9 56
(Jeremy Gask) *racd against rail: trckd ldng pair: rdn and nt qckn 2f out: lost pl over 1f out: n.d after* 15/2
00 7 hd **Do More Business (IRE)**[24] 1770 4-8-6 55 JemmaMarshall(5) 6 51
(Pat Phelan) *hld up last: shkn up 2f out and wl off the pce: kpt on ins fnl f* 18/1
1000 8 1 1/4 **Crystallize**[14] 2027 5-9-1 59 TomQueally 8 51
(Andrew Haynes) *towards rr: rdn over 2f out: hanging and no prog over 1f out* 7/1[3]

4320 **9** *10* **Co Dependent (USA)**[31] 1562 5-9-7 **65**...................... FergusSweeney 1 25
(Jamie Osborne) *s.i.s: racd wdst of all: effrt fr rr 1/2-way: wknd qckly wl over 1f out* **14/1**

1m 11.33s (-1.37) **Going Correction** -0.225s/f (Firm) **9** Ran SP% **110.3**
Speed ratings (Par 101): **100,98,97,95,95 94,94,92,79**
toteswingers:1&2:£8.50, 2&3:£8.00, 1&3:£2.60 CSF £54.33 CT £177.47 TOTE £4.40: £1.80, £3.60, £1.60; EX 56.00.
Owner Suresh Sivagnanam **Bred** Tally-Ho Stud **Trained** Ashtead, Surrey
■ Stewards' Enquiry : Kieran O'Neill one-day ban: failed to ride to draw (Jun 9)

FOCUS
An open run-of-the-mill, win-in-their-turn sprint handicap, where the pace was true. Those near the top of the handicap contested the finish. The winner showed her best form since she was a 2yo at face value.

2427 LADBROKESGAMES.COM MEDIAN AUCTION MAIDEN STKS 7f (S)
4:30 (4:31) (Class 6) 3-4-Y-O £1,706 (£503; £252) Stalls High

Form RPR
5-3 **1** **Frozen Over**[27] 1654 3-8-11 0....................................... FergusSweeney 3 76
(Stuart Kittow) *pressed ldr: clr of rest fr 1/2-way: rdn 2f out: led ent fnl f: edgd lft but kpt on wl* **9/2**[3]
0 **2** *3 1/4* **Bravo King (IRE)**[24] 1774 3-8-12 0 ow1................................. PaulDoe 6 67
(Jim Best) *racd against rail: led: clr w wnr fr 1/2-way: rdn 2f out: hdd and no ex ent fnl f* **7/1**
06-5 **3** *2 1/4* **Adone (IRE)**[24] 1774 3-8-8 70.................................(v[1]) LouisBeuzelin(3) 1 60
(Sir Michael Stoute) *chsd ldng pair: pushed along and nt on terms 1/2-way: rdn and no imp over 2f out: plugged on* **11/8**[1]
35-0 **4** *1 1/4* **Winged Valkyrie (IRE)**[20] 1853 3-8-0 74 ow1........ MatthewLawson(7) 2 53
(B W Hills) *chsd ldrs on outer: hanging bef 1/2-way and nt on terms: n.d after: plugged on ins fnl f* **5/2**[2]
5 *shd* **Brenhines** 3-8-2 0 ow1.. LauraPike(5) 7 53
(David Simcock) *s.s: wl bhd in last and rn green: sme prog fr 1/2-way: rchd 4th over 1f out: no ex: nt disgracd* **16/1**
6 *54* **Elusive Lucy (IRE)** 3-8-6 0....................................... FrankieMcDonald 5 —
(Linda Jewell) *sn struggling in last pair: wl t.o sn after 1/2-way* **100/1**
00 **7** *8* **Elby**[16] 1984 4-9-8 0.. PatCosgrave 4 —
(Eve Johnson Houghton) *sltly awkward s: chsd ldng trio: reminders after 3f: sn wknd: wl t.o and eased over 1f out* **100/1**

1m 27.06s (-0.24) **Going Correction** -0.225s/f (Firm)
WFA 3 from 4yo 11lb **7** Ran SP% **109.2**
Speed ratings (Par 101): **92,88,85,84,84 22,13**
toteswingers:1&2:£3.00, 2&3:£2.30, 1&3:£1.80 CSF £31.95 TOTE £7.10: £2.00, £4.10; EX 22.90.
Owner P A & M J Reditt **Bred** Manor Farm Packers Ltd **Trained** Blackborough, Devon

FOCUS
Run amid a heavy shower, the first two were always 1-2 in this weak median auction maiden. The form is rated on the negative side.
Elusive Lucy(IRE) Official explanation: jockey said filly moved poorly

2428 LADBROKESPOKER.COM H'CAP 7f (S)
5:00 (5:00) (Class 4) (0-85,85) 3-Y-O+ £3,548 (£1,047; £524) Stalls High

Form RPR
4006 **1** **Ezdeyaad (USA)**[12] 2105 7-9-12 **85**.................................. JackMitchell 6 91
(Ed Walker) *racd against rail: trckd ldng pair: plld out and effrt 2f out: chsd ldr over 1f out: hrd rdn to chal ins fnl f: styd on to ld last strides* **5/1**[3]
30-0 **2** *hd* **Red Yarn**[19] 1898 4-9-0 **73**...(b) TomQueally 3 78
(Gary Moore) *pressed ldr: reminder over 2f out: led wl over 1f out: edgd rt u.p ins fnl f: hdd last strides* **18/1**
33-6 **3** *1 1/2* **Starclass**[45] 1279 4-9-4 **77**.. AdamKirby 1 78+
(Walter Swinburn) *blindfold stl on as stalls opened and slowly away: hld up in last and swtchd to rail: effrt 2f out: rdn and kpt on to take 3rd ins fnl f: unable to chal* **5/2**[1]
0-43 **4** *1 3/4* **Guilded Warrior**[21] 1832 8-9-11 **84**............................ FergusSweeney 4 81
(Stuart Kittow) *racd towards rail: led: rdn and hdd wl over 1f out: fdd ins fnl f* **5/2**[1]
0-03 **5** *2* **Nezami (IRE)**[19] 1898 6-9-3 **76**....................................... AndreaAtzeni 2 67
(John Akehurst) *chsd ldrs on outer: hanging after 3f: nt qckn over 2f out: wknd over 1f out* **7/2**[2]
0-55 **6** *12* **Desert Auction (IRE)**[61] 1103 4-9-2 **75**.......................... PatCosgrave 5 34
(Dean Ivory) *hld up bhd ldrs: shkn up 1/2-way: wknd 2f out: eased* **11/1**

1m 24.74s (-2.56) **Going Correction** -0.225s/f (Firm) **6** Ran SP% **109.6**
Speed ratings (Par 105): **105,104,103,101,98 85**
toteswingers:1&2:£4.70, 2&3:£4.50, 1&3:£2.40 CSF £72.41 TOTE £7.80: £3.60, £6.40; EX 61.20.
Owner John Nicholls (Trading) Ltd **Bred** Caldara Farm **Trained** Newmarket, Suffolk
■ Stewards' Enquiry : Jack Mitchell three-day ban: used whip with excessive frequency without giving gelding time to respond (Jun 9-11)

FOCUS
Just an ordinary Class 4 handicap for lowly prize money and run at a true pace. Sound form, if a bit limited for the grade.
T/Plt: £117.30 to a £ 1 stake. Pool of £38,506.06 - 239.51 winning tickets. T/Qpdt: £22.80 to a £1 stake. Pool of £2,668.21 - 86.30 winning tickets. JN

2056 NEWCASTLE (L-H)
Thursday, May 26

OFFICIAL GOING: Good to firm (good in places) changing to good after race 2 (6:20)
Rail realignment added 4yds to 2m race and 2yds to 10 & 12f races.
Wind: Virtually nil Weather: Overcast and showers

2429 NEPIC NOVICE STKS 5f
5:50 (5:51) (Class 5) 2-Y-O £2,266 (£674; £337) Stalls Centre

Form RPR
1 **1** **Lexington Spirit (IRE)**[12] 2113 2-9-0 0......................... PaulHanagan 1 76+
(Richard Fahey) *led: pushed along and hdd over 1f out: rdn and led ins fnl f: edgd lft and kpt on* **1/4**[1]
410 **2** *nk* **Princess Banu**[13] 2070 2-8-11 0............................... MartinHarley(3) 2 75
(Mick Channon) *cl up: rdn 2f out and sn edgd lft: led over 1f out: drvn and hdd ins fnl f: kpt on u.p* **3/1**[2]
3 *11* **Island Bird** 2-8-8 0 ow2.. MichaelO'Connell(3) 3 32
(Kate Walton) *chsd ldng pair: rdn along over 2f out: sn outpcd* **33/1**[3]

62.90 secs (1.80) **Going Correction** +0.025s/f (Good) **3** Ran SP% **107.9**
Speed ratings (Par 93): **86,85,67**
CSF £1.34 TOTE £1.30; EX 1.10.
Owner Middleham Park Racing XXXIV **Bred** Kildaragh Stud **Trained** Musley Bank, N Yorks

FOCUS
Only three runners but effectively a match, with less between the first two home than than the betting suggested. A cat-and-mouse affair, with the early pace not strong. Straightforward form at face value, and the winner should rate higher.

NOTEBOOK
Lexington Spirit(IRE) hadn't beaten much at Thirsk in all probability but she'd done it well and looked to have more in hand here than the margin she won by, soon taking a keen hold in front and never really extended or coming under maximum pressure despite edging left as she was pressured continually by the runner-up. She looks to have some scope and will improve again, with a step up to 6f surely on the cards sooner rather than later, though whether she's up to Listed class yet has to be open to doubt. (op 1-3 tchd 4-11)
Princess Banu had her limitations exposed at York last time in Listed grade but this was more like the form that saw her beat two subsequent winners at Newmarket. She was never far away and kept on gamely without threatening to get her head in front. There's not much of her and this might be as good as she is. (op 11-4)
Island Bird, the first foal of a 7f/1m winner, was left behind once the pace increased soon after halfway and what she achieved is questionable.

2430 LOCKTON INSURANCE FOR NEPIC MEMBERS MAIDEN FILLIES' STKS 6f
6:20 (6:20) (Class 4) 2-Y-O £3,497 (£1,040; £520; £259) Stalls Centre

Form RPR
5 **1** **Nimiety**[16] 1981 2-9-0 0.. SilvestreDeSousa 5 73
(Mark Johnston) *cl up: led 1/2-way: pushed clr over 2f out: rdn ent fnl f: kpt on strly* **8/1**
4 **2** *2 1/4* **Naseem Alyasmeen (IRE)**[16] 1981 2-8-11 0............. MartinHarley(3) 9 66
(Mick Channon) *trckd ldrs: hdwy to chse wnr over 2f out and sn rdn: drvn and one pce appr fnl f* **3/1**[1]
3 *hd* **Keyhole Kate** 2-8-11 0.. PaulPickard(3) 2 66
(Tim Walford) *dwlt: sn in tch: hdwy over 2f out: rdn to chse wnr ent fnl f: sn drvn and one pce* **25/1**
0 **4** *2 3/4* **Flurry Of Hands (IRE)**[40] 1414 2-9-0 0......................... TonyHamilton 1 57
(Ann Duffield) *in tch: hdwy over 2f out: sn rdn and no imp appr fnl f* **33/1**
6 **5** *1/2* **Neil's Pride**[17] 1939 2-9-0 0... PaulHanagan 7 56+
(Richard Fahey) *chsd ldrs: rdn along and outpcd over 2f out: kpt on u.p fnl f* **15/2**[3]
5 **6** *6* **Chorister Girl**[12] 2113 2-9-0 0..................................... PaulMulrennan 10 38
(Howard Johnson) *led: pushed along and hdd 1/2-way: rdn over 2f out and sn wknd* **3/1**[1]
7 *nk* **Emley Moor** 2-9-0 0.. KellyHarrison 11 37
(Chris Fairhurst) *s.i.s: in rr tl sme late hdwy* **66/1**
4 **8** *hd* **Phoenix Clubs (IRE)**[17] 1939 2-9-0 0............................ MickyFenton 4 36
(Paul Midgley) *chsd ldrs on outer: rdn along 1/2-way: sn wknd* **7/1**[2]
9 *7* **Angel Of Hope (IRE)** 2-9-0 0.. TomEaves 8 15
(Bryan Smart) *trckd ldrs: pushed along 1/2-way: sn rdn and wknd* **7/1**[2]
10 *7* **Bada Bing** 2-8-11 0.. BillyCray(3) 3 —
(David Nicholls) *s.i.s: a in rr: bhd fr 1/2-way* **11/1**

1m 17.51s (2.91) **Going Correction** +0.025s/f (Good) **10** Ran SP% **114.5**
Speed ratings (Par 92): **81,78,77,74,73 65,65,64,55,46**
toteswingers:1&2:£4.90, 1&3:£67.80, 2&3:£17.60 CSF £31.22 TOTE £9.20: £2.90, £1.80, £4.60; EX 26.00.
Owner Miss K Rausing **Bred** Miss K Rausing **Trained** Middleham Moor, N Yorks

FOCUS
None of those with experience had shown much so probably not a race up to its usual standard, although the winner was clearly the best on the day. The form is rated towards the bottom end of the race averages. The action took place on the stands' side and the early pace was just fair.

NOTEBOOK
Nimiety was well held on her debut at Warwick but it was easy to see why a speed test round a sharp track like that wouldn't have suited her first time out as she still looked green and nothing but a galloper, relishing this stiffer test as her pedigree suggested. She's still got a lot to learn and will be even better suited by 7f-plus. (op 7-1 tchd 17-2)
Naseem Alyasmeen(IRE) who'd finished ahead of the winner at Warwick, had her in her sights from halfway but hasn't made the same improvement in the interim and only the benefit of previous experience enabled her to hold on to second. (op 4-1 tchd 11-4)
Keyhole Kate, the third foal of an Irish maiden who stayed 1m5f, fared best of the newcomers and might have finished second but for a sluggish start and being asked to make her challenge widest of all, while running green all the time. She'll improve quite a bit for this experience. (op 20-1)
Flurry Of Hands(IRE) left her debut form behind without threatening to finish any closer but her pedigree lends hope she may do better yet over further. (op 28-1 tchd 25-1)
Neil's Pride ◆ found, as at Redcar when sixth behind the useful Bannock, the post coming too soon despite this being a stiffer test of stamina. She finished with ruuning still in her and connections may go for a nursery with her after one more run or a seller at 7f (op 7-1 tchd 8-1)
Chorister Girl had finished fifth behind the winner of the opening race on her debut and that possibly accounted for her popularity in the betting, but she was in trouble soon after halfway and is clearly very limited. Official explanation: jockey said filly hung left-handed (op 4-1)
Phoenix Clubs(IRE) had finished ahead of Neil's Pride at Redcar over 5f but didn't seem to see out this stiff 6f and again spoilt her finishing effort by hanging, so is one to have reservations about. (op 6-1)

2431 NEPIC H'CAP 7f
6:55 (6:56) (Class 4) (0-85,91) 4-Y-O+ £3,497 (£1,040; £520; £259) Stalls Centre

Form RPR
26-6 **1** **Xilerator (IRE)**[12] 2112 4-9-6 **84**..................................... AndrewMullen 3 96
(David Nicholls) *led far side gp: rdn along 2f out: sn overall ldr and clr appr fnl f: kpt on wl* **14/1**
1221 **2** *5* **Dubai Dynamo**[2] 2390 6-9-13 **91** 6ex................................. PaulHanagan 4 90+
(Ruth Carr) *hld up in rr stands' side: hdwy 3f out: chsd ldrs 2f out and sn rdn: drvn ent fnl f and kpt on same pce: 1st of 7 in gp* **10/11**[1]
40-0 **3** *shd* **Polish World (USA)**[17] 1942 7-8-11 **75**............................ MickyFenton 9 73+
(Paul Midgley) *swvd rt s: overall ldr stands' side: rdn along 2f out: sn hdd: drvn and one pce appr fnl f: 2nd of 7 in gp* **20/1**
-603 **4** *1 3/4* **Excusez Moi (USA)**[19] 1906 9-8-6 **73**................... JamesSullivan(3) 10 67+
(Ruth Carr) *hmpd and dwlt s: in rr stands' side: hdwy 2f out: rdn over 1f out: styd on wl fnl f: nrst fin: 3rd of 7 in gp* **16/1**
060- **5** *1 3/4* **Last Sovereign**[212] 7146 7-8-13 **77**............................... PaulMulrennan 5 66+
(Ollie Pears) *trckd ldrs stands' side: swtchd lft and hdwy over 2f out: sn cl up tl rdn and wknd appr fnl f: 4th of 7 in gp* **9/1**[3]
4-00 **6** *3 3/4* **Rasselas (IRE)**[122] 279 4-9-1 **82**....................................... BillyCray(3) 1 61
(David Nicholls) *in tch far side: rdn along wl over 2f out: sn wknd: 2nd of 3 in gp* **20/1**
4023 **7** *4 1/2* **Rio Cobolo (IRE)**[17] 1942 5-8-9 **76**......................... MichaelO'Connell(3) 8 43
(David Nicholls) *cl up stands' side: rdn along over 3f out: grad wknd: 5th of 7 in gp* **15/2**[2]
50-5 **8** *2 1/2* **Whispered Times (USA)**[23] 1800 4-8-9 **73**...............(p) FrederikTylicki 6 33
(Tracy Waggott) *trckd ldrs stands' side: pushed along 1/2-way: sn rdn and wknd: 6th of 7 in gp* **16/1**

000- **9** ½ **Horatio Carter**[221] 6962 6-9-2 **80**.............................. SilvestreDeSousa 2 38
(Michael Smith) *chsd wnr far side: rdn along 1/2-way: sn wknd: 3rd of 3 in gp* **12/1**

3230 **10** 4½ **Smalljohn**[47] 1245 5-8-11 **75**..............................(v) TomEaves 7 21
(Bryan Smart) *chsd ldrs stands' side: rdn along 3f out: sn wknd: 7th of 7 in gp* **16/1**

1m 28.27s (0.47) **Going Correction** +0.025s/f (Good) **10** Ran SP% **115.7**
Speed ratings (Par 105): **103,97,97,95,93 88,83,80,80,75**
toteswingers:1&2:£4.40, 1&3:£10.20, 2&3:£6.20 CSF £26.91 CT £273.11 TOTE £20.20: £4.20, £1.10, £4.00; EX 52.50.
Owner J Law **Bred** Denis And Mrs Teresa Bergin **Trained** Sessay, N Yorks

FOCUS
A fairly useful handicap in which the field split with little between the two sides until the winner, who dominated the smaller group on the far side, started to pull clear from 2f out. He rates a 5lb personal best, but it's hard to know what to make of this form.

2432 NEWCASTLE INTERNATIONAL AIRPORT MAIDEN FILLIES' STKS 1m 2f 32y
7:30 (7:33) (Class 5) 3-Y-O+ **£2,331** (£693; £346; £173) **Stalls** Low

Form RPR

4-2 **1** **Caraboss**[41] 1363 3-8-10 0.............................. TomEaves 1 90+
(Sir Michael Stoute) *led 1f: cl up: led again over 4f out: pushed clr 2f out: kpt on strly fnl f* **4/7**[1]

4-0 **2** 6 **Al Mayasah (IRE)**[19] 1894 3-8-10 0.............................. SilvestreDeSousa 4 78+
(David Simcock) *hld up in tch: hdwy 4f out: effrt to chse wnr over 2f out: rdn and hung rt over 1f out: sn drvn and no imp* **3/1**[2]

6-4 **3** 14 **Alemaratiya**[23] 1799 3-8-10 0.............................. MickyFenton 5 50
(David Simcock) *prom: rdn along 4f out: drvn wl over 2f out and sn outpcd* **66/1**

2 **4** ¾ **Brook Star (IRE)**[23] 1799 3-8-10 0.............................. FrederikTylicki 2 49
(Michael Dods) *trckd ldrs: hdwy 4f out: rdn along over 3f out: sn outpcd* **33/1**[3]

-0 **5** 22 **Chickini (IRE)**[13] 2045 6-9-7 0.............................. SeanLevey(3) 3 —
(Simon Waugh) *unruly in preliminaries: t.k.h and led after 1f: rdn along and hdd over 4f out: sn wknd* **100/1**

0 **6** 3¾ **Tobetall**[16] 1974 4-9-7 0.............................. PaulPickard(3) 8 —
(Malcolm Jefferson) *a bhd* **100/1**

2m 13.08s (1.18) **Going Correction** -0.15s/f (Firm)
WFA 3 from 4yo+ 14lb **6** Ran SP% **95.1**
Speed ratings (Par 100): **89,84,73,72,54 51**
toteswingers:1&2:£3.00, 1&3:£3.60, 2&3:£2.10 CSF £1.50 TOTE £1.30: £1.10, £1.30; EX 1.70.
Owner The Queen **Bred** The Queen **Trained** Newmarket, Suffolk

FOCUS
A three-horse affair on form seemingly reduced to a match after Ribblesdale entry Shuhra was withdrawn at the start (refused to enter the stalls), but in the end the favourite won easily. The pace was just fair and the winner is rated up 6lb.

2433 NEPIC PROCESS ENGINEERING GROUP H'CAP 2m 19y
8:05 (8:05) (Class 6) (0-65,65) 4-Y-O+ **£1,683** (£501; £250; £125) **Stalls** Low

Form RPR

4-43 **1** **Maid Of Meft**[13] 2060 4-8-12 **55**.............................. FrederikTylicki 4 69
(Linda Perratt) *hld up in rr: hdwy on outer over 5f out: led wl over 2f out and sn rdn clr: styd on strly* **15/2**

515- **2** 9 **Jeu De Roseau (IRE)**[240] 5497 7-9-4 **59**.............................. PaulHanagan 8 62
(Chris Grant) *hld up in tch: hdwy to trck ldrs 1/2-way: effrt over 3f out: rdn wl over 2f out and ch tl drvn and one pce fr over 1f out* **11/4**[2]

020/ **3** 7 **Orsippus (USA)**[19] 6767 5-9-5 **63**.............................. SeanLevey(3) 5 58
(Michael Smith) *trckd ldr: cl up 6f out: led 4f out: sn rdn and hdd wl over 2f out: sn one pce* **2/1**[1]

0-25 **4** 2¼ **Bandanaman (IRE)**[23] 1794 5-8-13 **61**.............................. GarryWhillans(7) 7 53
(Alan Swinbank) *trckd ldrs on inner: effrt over 4f out: rdn along over 3f out: sn drvn and one pce* **4/1**[3]

05- **5** 2 **Royal And Ancient (IRE)**[27] 7690 4-9-3 **65**.............................. LMcNiff(5) 3 55
(David Thompson) *chsd ldrs on inner: pushed along and lost pl bef 1/2-way: bhd after* **33/1**

2230 **6** 1½ **Light The City (IRE)**[55] 1080 4-8-4 **50**.............................. JamesSullivan(3) 9 38
(Ruth Carr) *trckd ldrs on outer: hdwy and cl up 5f out: rdn along wl over 3f out and sn wknd* **8/1**

0-44 **7** 2¾ **Dechiper (IRE)**[13] 2060 9-8-8 **49** ow1.............................. TonyHamilton 6 34
(Robert Johnson) *led: rdn along over 5f out: hdd over 4f out and sn wknd* **14/1**

3m 36.5s (-2.90) **Going Correction** -0.15s/f (Firm)
WFA 4 from 5yo+ 2lb **7** Ran SP% **112.5**
Speed ratings (Par 101): **101,96,93,91,90 90,88**
toteswingers:1&2:£3.00, 1&3:£4.70, 2&3:£1.30 CSF £27.48 CT £56.36 TOTE £9.00: £3.20, £3.20; EX 24.80.
Owner Ken McGarrity **Bred** Ian Murray Tough **Trained** East Kilbride, S Lanarks

FOCUS
An ordinary staying handicap with little between the runners for much of the way with the gallop not strong, so the fact the winner could pull so far clear down the centre of the track in a short space of time suggests she deserves plenty of credit. She rates a small personal best.

2434 DIGIBET.COM H'CAP 6f
8:35 (8:35) (Class 3) (0-90,90) 4-Y-O+ **£5,504** (£1,637; £818; £408) **Stalls** Centre

Form RPR

343 **1** **Marvellous Value (IRE)**[29] 1618 6-8-8 **77**.............................. FrederikTylicki 1 92
(Michael Dods) *chsd overall ldr far side: hdwy 2f out: rdn to ld appr fnl f: sn clr* **13/2**[3]

5416 **2** 4½ **Cape Vale (IRE)**[26] 1675 6-9-3 **89**.............................. MichaelO'Connell(3) 3 90
(David Nicholls) *overall ldr far side: rdn along 2f out: hdd appr fnl f and kpt on same pce: 2nd of 5 in gp* **6/1**[2]

1001 **3** nk **Dickie Le Davoir**[5] 2299 7-9-2 **88** 6ex..............................(b) RobertLButler(3) 2 88
(Richard Guest) *towards rr far side: hdwy 2f out: sn rdn and kpt on ins fnl f: nrst fin: 3rd of 5 in gp* **7/1**

00-0 **4** 5 **Sonny Red (IRE)**[13] 2075 7-9-7 **90**.............................. AndrewMullen 5 74
(David Nicholls) *towards rr far side: hdwy 2f out: sn rdn and kpt on ins fnl f: nrst fin: 4th of 5 in gp* **25/1**

14-0 **5** 7 **Noodles Blue Boy**[50] 1166 5-9-2 **85**.............................. TonyHamilton 8 46+
(Ollie Pears) *trckd ldr stands' side: hdwy to ld that gp 2f out: sn rdn and kpt on: no ch w far side: 1st of 5 in gp* **9/1**

01-6 **6** nse **Sunrise Safari (IRE)**[20] 1878 8-8-11 **80**..............................(v) PaulHanagan 10 41+
(Richard Fahey) *trckd ldng pair stands' side: hdwy over 2f out: rdn wl over 1f out: drvn and kpt on fnl f: no ch w far side: 2nd of 5 in gp* **8/1**

0-63 **7** shd **Silver Rime (FR)**[13] 2061 6-9-4 **87**.............................. PaulMulrennan 6 48+
(Linda Perratt) *hld up in tch stands' side: swtchd lft and hdwy 2f out: sn rdn and kpt on: 3rd of 5 in gp* **7/1**

-155 **8** 3¼ **Nadeen (IRE)**[20] 1878 4-8-10 **82**.............................. SeanLevey(3) 7 32+
(Michael Smith) *trckd ldrs stands' side: hdwy over 2f out and sn rdn: drvn and btn over 1f out: 4th of 5 in gp* **4/1**[1]

64-0 **9** ½ **Master Rooney (IRE)**[12] 2118 5-9-0 **83**.............................. TomEaves 9 32+
(Bryan Smart) *led stands' side gp: rdn along and hdd 2f out: sn drvn and wknd: 5th of 5 in gp* **12/1**

1-00 **10** 19 **Who's Shirl**[5] 2299 5-9-0 **83**.............................. KellyHarrison 4 —
(Chris Fairhurst) *dwlt: a in rr far side: 5th of 5 in gp* **8/1**

1m 13.7s (-0.90) **Going Correction** +0.025s/f (Good) **10** Ran SP% **116.4**
Speed ratings (Par 107): **107,101,100,93,84 84,84,80,79,54**
toteswingers:1&2:£3.90, 1&3:£5.70, 2&3:£4.20 CSF £45.18 CT £232.63 TOTE £5.50: £1.80, £2.70, £2.20; EX 63.30.
Owner A J Henderson **Bred** John Cullinan **Trained** Denton, Co Durham
■ Stewards' Enquiry : Michael O'Connell one-day ban: failed to ride to draw (Jun 9)

FOCUS
A fairly useful handicap in which the quintet that elected to head for the far rail finished well ahead of the stand-side group. And, as usual, when the field splits into two or more groups, those who seized the initiative the quickest proved hard to peg back. The winner is rated up 8lb on his post-3yo form.

NOTEBOOK
Marvellous Value(IRE) looked ready to run his best race of the season after an encouraging third to King Of Eden over C&D last time but could hardly have had things drop more kindly, cruising in Cape Vale's slipstream on the far side until unleashed inside the last. For all this is likely to prove unreliable form, there was plenty to like about the manner he went about his business and considering how few runs he's had since finishing fifth in the Ayr Silver Cup off a mark of 92, he's going to remain one to be interested in for a while yet. (op 15-2 tchd 8-1)
Cape Vale(IRE) ran well and second place was due reward for the enterprise his rider showed, but the suspicion is that he ended up playing more into the winner's hands than his own after setting off strongly and he's probably a bit better than this makes him look. (op 5-1 tchd 7-1)
Dickie Le Davoir nearly got second as Cape Vale tired and ran well considering he was soon detached in the far-side group, the race not panning out to his strengths as much as bigger-field handicaps do. (op 15-2)
Sonny Red(IRE)'s rider seemed surprisingly indecisive as to which side to head for despite the guarantee of a strong lead from his stablemate drawn nearby and when he'd made his mind up he was well in rear with the race effectively already over. (op 20-1)
Noodles Blue Boy won the race on the stand side but what it's worth is anyone's guess seeing as there was no prize-money for fifth place and it was clear from a long way out the far side were well ahead. (op 12-1)
Sunrise Safari(IRE)'s performance shouldn't be treated too literally in the circumstances. (op 9-1)
Silver Rime(FR) ◆ might be one to keep an eye on given his yard has hit form, 6f is too short for him and he was being asked the impossible being expectede to make ground from last place on the stand rail. (op 13-2)
Nadeen(IRE) is another whose performance shouldn't be treated too literally in the circumstances. Official explanation: trainer had no explanation for the poor form shown (op 9-2)
Who's Shirl Official explanation: vet said mare was sore right-hind

2435 TOTEPOOL H'CAP 1m 4f 93y
9:10 (9:11) (Class 4) (0-85,83) 3-Y-O **£4,079** (£1,214; £606; £303) **Stalls** Low

Form RPR

0-1 **1** **Halifax (IRE)**[89] 699 3-9-4 **80**.............................. SilvestreDeSousa 6 94+
(Mark Johnston) *hld up in rr: tk clsr order on inner 5f out: rdn 3f out: styd on to ld wl over 1f out: drvn out* **4/1**[3]

31-5 **2** 3¼ **Defence Of Duress (IRE)**[15] 2008 3-9-5 **81**.............................. MickyFenton 4 89
(Tom Tate) *trckd ldr: hdwy and cl up 4f out: rdn 3f out: led briefly 2f out: drvn and hdd wl over 1f out: kpt on* **5/2**[2]

562- **3** 3 **Samarkand (IRE)**[173] 7693 3-8-11 **73**.............................. SebSanders 3 76+
(Sir Mark Prescott Bt) *dwlt: sn trcking ldrs: hdwy on outer 5f out: cl up 4f out: rdn over 3f out and ev ch tl drvn 2f out and kpt on same pce* **13/8**[1]

1-62 **4** 5 **Oasis Storm**[27] 1652 3-9-3 **79**.............................. FrederikTylicki 2 74
(Michael Dods) *led: rdn along over 4f out: drvn 3f out: hdd 2f out and grad wknd* **5/1**

52-0 **5** 3½ **Raucous Behaviour (USA)**[15] 2008 3-9-4 **80**.............................. GregFairley 5 70
(Mark Johnston) *chsd ldrs: pushed along 1/2-way: rdn over 4f out: sn wknd* **14/1**

2m 43.53s (-2.07) **Going Correction** -0.15s/f (Firm) **5** Ran SP% **110.0**
Speed ratings (Par 101): **100,97,95,92,90**
CSF £14.24 TOTE £5.30: £1.60, £1.60; EX 12.60.
Owner Sheikh Hamdan Bin Mohammed Al Maktoum **Bred** Rabbah Bloodstock Limited **Trained** Middleham Moor, N Yorks

FOCUS
There was a heavy shower just before the off and the jockeys were reporting the ground was riding slower than earlier than in the evening. The time was still decent and this is potentially good form with the first three all improvers.
T/Plt: £13.80 to a £1 stake. Pool:£43,487.65 - 2,291.88 winning tickets T/Qpdt: £7.30 to a £1 stake. Pool:£5,292.68 - 531.97 winning tickets JR

2227 SANDOWN (R-H)
Thursday, May 26

OFFICIAL GOING: Good (good to firm in places on sprint course) changing to good to soft after race 1 (6:00)
Round course at inner configuration and distances as advertised.
Wind: Brisk across Weather: Overcast, thunderstorms

2436 CARLUCCIO'S PICNIC H'CAP 1m 2f 7y
6:00 (6:01) (Class 5) (0-75,74) 4-Y-O+ **£2,590** (£770; £385; £192) **Stalls** Low

Form RPR

2-04 **1** **Rock The Stars (IRE)**[21] 1829 4-9-2 **69**.............................. RyanMoore 4 82
(J W Hills) *trckd ldrs: drvn and styd on wl fr 3f out to ld appr fnl f: rdn and won gng away fnl 120yds* **7/2**[1]

00-1 **2** 4½ **Chain Of Events**[14] 2021 4-9-7 **74**.............................. EddieAhern 12 78
(Neil King) *chsd ldrs: travelling wl 2f out: slt ld over 1f out: sn hdd: no ch w wnr ins fnl f: all out to hold 2nd clsng stages* **13/2**[3]

53-5 **3** nse **Super Duplex**[33] 1530 4-9-0 **67**.............................. IanMongan 11 71
(Pat Phelan) *chsd ldrs: led over 2f out: hdd over 1f out: one pce into 3rd tl rallied fnl 120yds to press for 2nd clsng staged but nvr any ch w wnr* **8/1**

30-0 **4** 1¼ **Silverglas (IRE)**[24] 1772 5-9-6 **73**.............................. WilliamBuick 8 74
(William Knight) *s.i.s: in rr: drvn and hdwy over 2f out: kpt on fnl f: nt rch ldrs* **12/1**

-424 **5** 2¼ **Potentiale (IRE)**[21] 1834 7-9-7 **74**..............................(p) RichardHills 5 71
(J W Hills) *towards rr but in tch: hdwy fr 2f out: styd on fnl f: nt trble ldrs* **11/1**

020- **6** *3 1/2* **Sagredo (USA)**[198] 6091 7-9-7 74 .... GeorgeBaker 3 64
(Jonjo O'Neill) *bhd tl styd on fnl 2f* **20/1**

3060 **7** *1 1/2* **Turjuman (USA)**[78] 802 6-8-7 60 .... JamieMackay 1 47
(Willie Musson) *slowly away: bhd tl styd on wl fr over 1f out* **12/1**

1304 **8** *4* **Classically (IRE)**[14] 2021 5-9-5 72 .... SteveDrowne 7 51
(Peter Hedger) *s.i.s: sn in tch: chsd ldrs 4f out: wknd over 2f out* **20/1**

-110 **9** *shd* **Boa**[12] 2091 6-8-12 65 .... JamieSpencer 10 44
(Reg Hollinshead) *led 2f: chsd ldr: wknd qckly over 2f out* **15/2**

-236 **10** *3 1/4* **Archie Rice (USA)**[27] 1651 5-9-0 67 .... FrankieDettori 9 39
(Tom Keddy) *w ldr: led after 2f: hdd over 2f out: sn wknd* **10/1**

300- **11** *7* **Bowsers Brave (USA)**[357] 2685 5-9-0 67 .... RichardHughes 2 25
(Marcus Tregoning) *chsd ldrs tl wknd qckly ins fnl 2f* **11/2**[2]

0/U **12** *dist* **Exotic Dream (FR)**[10] 2159 5-9-1 68 .... LukeMorris 6 —
(Ronald Harris) *a bhd: t.o fnl 3f* **66/1**

2m 13.52s (3.02) **Going Correction** +0.30s/f (Good) **12** Ran SP% **117.6**
Speed ratings (Par 103): **99,95,95,94,92 89,88,85,85,82 77,—**
toteswingers:1&2:£6.70, 1&3:£6.40, 2&3:£8.60 CSF £24.73 CT £171.80 TOTE £5.20: £1.90, £1.70, £2.90; EX 24.50 Trifecta £208.00 Pool: £4,636.32 - 16.49 winning units.
Owner David Cohen **Bred** Bernard Cooke **Trained** Upper Lambourn, Berks

FOCUS
Those held up couldn't get involved and unsurprisingly the runners were taken towards the stands' side in the straight. A clear best from the winner with the form taken at face value.
Exotic Dream(FR) Official explanation: vet said mare bled from the nose

2437 PIPER HEIDSIECK CHAMPAGNE NATIONAL STKS (LISTED RACE) 5f 6y
6:30 (6:35) (Class 1) 2-Y-O

£12,205 (£4,626; £2,315; £1,154; £578; £290) **Stalls** Low

Form RPR

315 **1** **Pyman's Theory (IRE)**[13] 2070 2-8-9 0 .... RichardKingscote 4 97
(Tom Dascombe) *sn led: drvn clr over 1f out: hld on wl clsng stages* **12/1**

211 **2** *3/4* **Bannock (IRE)**[10] 2154 2-9-0 0 .... FrankieDettori 2 99
(Mark Johnston) *trckd ldrs: n.m.r on ins over 1f out: drvn and qcknd to go 2nd jst ins fnl f: clsng on wnr nr fin but nvr quite gng to get up* **5/2**[2]

122 **3** *5* **Magic City (IRE)**[10] 2154 2-9-0 0 .... RichardHughes 7 81
(Richard Hannon) *hld up in tch: drvn and edgd rt 2f out: qcknd to dispute 2nd over 1f out but nvr nr wnr: wknd ins fnl f* **10/11**[1]

1 **4** *3* **Sixx**[7] 2221 2-9-0 0 .... KierenFallon 3 71
(Richard Hannon) *outpcd and drvn along after 1f: hdwy over 2f out: disp one pce 3rd whn hung lft over 1f out and no ch after* **14/1**

061 **5** *2* **Powerful Wind (IRE)**[9] 2173 2-9-0 0 .... LukeMorris 1 63
(Ronald Harris) *sn chsng wnr but nvr on terms: rdn over 2f out: wknd 1f out* **66/1**

14 **6** *8* **Foxtrot India (IRE)**[10] 2154 2-9-0 0 .... JimCrowley 6 35
(Peter Winkworth) *chsd ldrs: rdn over 2f out and wknd qckly* **9/1**[3]

62.55 secs (0.95) **Going Correction** +0.225s/f (Good) **6** Ran SP% **106.8**
Speed ratings (Par 101): **101,99,91,87,83 71**
toteswingers:1&2:£4.40, 1&3:£1.10, 2&3:£1.10 CSF £38.08 TOTE £10.40: £4.00, £1.30; EX 36.60.
Owner M Owen & M Williams **Bred** T Whitehead **Trained** Malpas, Cheshire
■ Miss Lahar was withdrawn (25/1, ref to ent stalls).

FOCUS
Not since 2003 has a winner of the National Stakes followed up at Royal Ascot (Russian Valour, Norfolk Stakes), but it's a race often contested by smart types, the most high profile in recent times being Excellent Art, who won in 2006 and added the following year's St James's Palace Stakes. This looked a solid enough edition and Pyman's Theory became the first filly to win the race since Sweepstake in 2007. Decent efforts from the first two to pull clear but the third is not progressing.

NOTEBOOK
Pyman's Theory(IRE) hadn't been able to utilise her speed when sluggishly away from the widest draw in a fillies' Listed event at York last time, but she was much too fast for her rivals on this occasion, perhaps aided by her first try on an easy surface. She had a bit of company for the early lead courtesy of outsider Powerful Wind, but she burnt off that rival before halfway and had the race won when around three lengths clear over a furlong out. It's true to say her cause was helped by the runner-up having to wait for a run after meeting trouble, but it was the winner's superior natural pace that afforded her a better position than Mark Johnston's runner. Pyman's Theory will go to the Queen Mary with a chance. (op 10-1)
Bannock(IRE) might not have had the speed of some of these, but he had looked pretty sharp when winning his last two starts and arguably wouldn't have found himself so poorly placed had Frankie Dettori been more positive. The colt had to wait too long for a run and although he finished strongly once in the clear, the winner already had the race in safe keeping. It's unclear whether he's quite up to winning at Royal Ascot, although he looks the type to go on improving. His connections suggested the Norfolk Stakes could be the plan. (op 11-4 tchd 9-4)
Magic City(IRE) has now been a beaten favourite on all three starts since his impressive debut success, proving unable to reverse recent Windsor placings with Bannock. Like last time, he was again ridden with restraint (unlike for debut win and Ascot defeat), but it was clear almost immediately that he wouldn't settle fully and that gave him little chance of producing a worthwhile challenge on the rain-softened ground. He may never fulfil his potential, but it wouldn't surprise if the Hannon/Hughes combination eventually found the key to him. (op 5-6 tchd 4-5 and evens in places)
Sixx narrowly defeated a better-fancied stablemate without being given a hard ride at Salisbury on his debut a week earlier, but this came a bit soon. Richard Hannon said beforehand the colt is still a bit weak and that's how it looked. Having struggled early, he made a brief bid when switched out wide, but he was rather climbing a bit and couldn't sustain a challenge. There should be better to come. (op 12-1)
Foxtrot India(IRE) has a low, fast-ground action and can be given another chance, although probably not at this level. (op 16-1)

2438 CHARLES HEIDSIECK CHAMPAGNE HENRY II STKS (GROUP 2) 2m 78y
7:05 (7:06) (Class 1) 4-Y-O+

£45,416 (£17,216; £8,616; £4,296; £2,152; £1,080) **Stalls** Centre

Form RPR

2-62 **1** **Blue Bajan (IRE)**[13] 2072 9-9-2 111 .... DanielTudhope 7 111
(David O'Meara) *hld up in tch: trckd ldrs: chal gng wl 2f out: led over 1f out: sn drvn: forged clr fnl 100yds* **4/1**[2]

0103 **2** *2 1/2* **Montaff**[5] 2316 5-9-2 99 .... SamHitchcott 2 108
(Mick Channon) *hld up in rr: hdwy over 2f out: drvn and styd on wl to disp 2nd ins fnl f: chsd wnr clsng stages but nvr any ch* **33/1**

216- **3** *1/2* **Holberg (UAE)**[205] 7291 5-9-2 111 .... FrankieDettori 8 107
(Saeed Bin Suroor) *trckd ldrs: wnt 3rd 6f out: drvn to ld over 2f out: sn rdn and hrd pressed: hdd over 1f out: outpcd by wnr ins fnl f: lost wl hld 2nd clsng stages* **6/4**[1]

31-5 **4** *1 3/4* **Aaim To Prosper (IRE)**[29] 1601 7-9-2 95 .... LouisBeuzelin 1 105
(Brian Meehan) *led tl hdd 10f out: styd chsng ldr to 3f out: sn outpcd: rallied u.p and styd on again to take 4th ins fnl f* **14/1**

330- **5** *2 1/2* **Caucus**[236] 6590 4-9-0 102 .... WilliamBuick 3 102
(John Gosden) *trckd ldrs: outpcd 5f out: drvn and hdwy fr 3f out: pressed ldrs in centre crse 2f out: wknd appr fnl f* **10/1**

03-5 **6** *3/4* **Buxted (IRE)**[13] 2072 5-9-2 107 .... RyanMoore 4 101
(Robert Mills) *chsd ldrs: rdn 3f out: wknd fr 2f out* **15/2**

022/ **7** *32* **Nehaam**[586] 6854 5-9-2 105 .... TadhgO'Shea 6 82
(John Gosden) *t.k.h in rr: in tch 4f out: sn rdn: wknd 3f out* **16/1**

-523 **8** *1/2* **Akmal**[12] 2098 5-9-2 105 .... RichardHills 5 91
(John Dunlop) *sn trcking ldr: led 10f out: hdd over 2f out: wknd sn after* **6/1**[3]

3m 41.33s (2.63) **Going Correction** +0.30s/f (Good)
WFA 4 from 5yo+ 2lb **8** Ran SP% **110.6**
Speed ratings (Par 115): **105,103,103,102,101 101,85,84**
toteswingers:1&2:£18.60, 1&3:£1.80, 2&3:£17.50 CSF £106.23 TOTE £5.30: £2.00, £6.80, £1.20; EX 109.70 Trifecta £692.50 Pool: £4,960.01 - 5.30 winning units.
Owner Dr John Hollowood **Bred** Dr J Hollowood **Trained** Nawton, N Yorks

FOCUS
The last horse to complete the Henry II Stakes/Ascot Gold Cup double was Papineau in 2004, a feat also achieved by Mr Dinos the year before, but this lot looked an ordinary bunch for the level, indeed the runner-up had an official mark of just 99. They raced stands' side in the straight. This looked a weak renewal with the favourite not at his best, and it's doubtful the winner had to run to his best.

NOTEBOOK
Blue Bajan(IRE) had shaped nicely on both runs since joining this yard and returning from a lengthy absence, notably when runner-up in the Yorkshire Cup on his previous start. He travelled strongly, as he so often has in the past, with the easing of the ground in his favour, and despite initially having looked to go to the front too soon, found enough. This was his first success on the Flat since 2007 (triple hurdles winner since) and his first Group-race success, so huge credit must go to his highly promising young trainer David O'Meara. Blue Bajan might be due a short break after three relatively quick runs, but he could still have plenty more to offer in big staying events this season, especially when there is give in the ground. (tchd 9-2)
Montaff improved on last year's fifth place in this race, plugging on dourly for pressure without matching the winner's cruising speed. (op 25-1)
Holberg(UAE) has a good record fresh, but this ground was easier than his ideal. He was having his first start since finishing sixth in last year's Melbourne Cup, when he was said to have been unsuited by conditions on the slow side. (op 11-8)
Aaim To Prosper(IRE), last year's Cesarewitch winner, was prominently ridden and kept plugging away. He needs even more of a test and considering he's not sure to be lowly enough weighted for the Ascot Stakes again (third last year off 88), the Queen Alexandra Stakes may be more suitable.
Caucus, debuting for this yard, looked fit enough for this reappearance but appeared likely to finish well beaten when losing his place turning in but he plugged on to a point. He hadn't been seen for 236 days, though has won when fresh. (tchd 9-1 and 11-1 and 12-1 in places)
Akmal, last year's winner, went to the front a fair way out, although he ultimately dropped away. He might not have appreciated the ground, but better could still have been expected (tchd 13-2)

2439 PIPER HEIDSIECK CHAMPAGNE BRIGADIER GERARD STKS (GROUP 3) 1m 2f 7y
7:40 (7:46) (Class 1) 4-Y-O+

£28,385 (£10,760; £5,385; £2,685; £1,345; £675) **Stalls** Low

Form RPR

151- **1** **Workforce**[235] 6612 4-9-7 128 .... RyanMoore 1 127+
(Sir Michael Stoute) *t.k.h early in chsng pack bhd clr ldr: drvn and hdwy over 3f out: wnt 2nd over 2f out and clsng: rdn to ld fnl 120yds: styd on strly* **1/1**[1]

42-3 **2** *1* **Poet**[40] 1403 6-9-0 114 .... AdamKirby 2 118
(Clive Cox) *led: sn 6 l clr: rdn ins fnl 3f: pressed by wnr ins fnl f: hdd fnl 120yds and no ex clsng stages but stl wl clr of 3rd* **16/1**

433- **3** *11* **Jan Vermeer (IRE)**[316] 4039 4-9-0 115 .... WilliamBuick 8 96
(A P O'Brien, Ire) *hld up in rr of chsng pack bhd clr ldr: rdn and styd on fr over 2f out wl hld 3rd fnl f* **5/1**[2]

303- **4** *1 3/4* **Cavalryman**[221] 6977 5-9-0 115 .... FrankieDettori 5 93
(Saeed Bin Suroor) *in rr of chsng pack bhd clr ldr: drvn and hdwy over 2f out: disp wl hld 3rd fnl f: dropped to 4th fnl 120yds* **10/1**

11-6 **5** *1/2* **Afsare**[33] 1528 4-9-0 113 .... KierenFallon 4 92
(Luca Cumani) *chsd ldrs in pack bhd clr ldr: rdn and no imp over 2f out: one pce fr over 1f out* **12/1**

15-3 **6** *shd* **Elusive Pimpernel (USA)**[42] 1342 4-9-0 115 .... EddieAhern 3 91
(John Dunlop) *in rr of pack chsng clr ldr: hdwy on outside to dispute 2nd over 2f out: styd on same pce* **6/1**[3]

13-2 **7** *3* **Distant Memories (IRE)**[21] 1821 5-9-0 114 .... JamieSpencer 7 85
(Tom Tate) *chsd clr ldr: wknd over 2f out* **16/1**

46-2 **8** *1* **Black Spirit (USA)**[33] 1528 4-9-0 110 .... (t) LukeMorris 9 83
(Clive Cox) *prom in pack chsng ldr: rdn and dropped to rr 4f out: no ch after* **16/1**

2m 9.97s (-0.53) **Going Correction** +0.30s/f (Good) **8** Ran SP% **115.4**
Speed ratings (Par 113): **114,113,104,103,102 102,100,99**
toteswingers:1&2:£6.50, 1&3:£1.90, 2&3:£11.30 CSF £20.18 TOTE £1.80: £1.10, £4.90, £1.80; EX 19.90 Trifecta £120.50 Pool: £8,152.25 - 50.05 winning units.
Owner K Abdulla **Bred** Juddmonte Farms Ltd **Trained** Newmarket, Suffolk

FOCUS
A good renewal. Some may be sceptical of the bare form, but Poet was allowed a lead of at least seven lengths at one stage, and although he set a good pace (time 3.55 seconds quicker than earlier Class 5 handicap), the others pretty much ignored him and this track can favour front-runners. Workforce did extremely well to pick him up. He is rated 3lb off his Arc form, with the level revolving around Poet.

NOTEBOOK
Workforce ◆ deserves immense credit for hauling back Poet considering the other beaten runners, who are all decent types in their own right, finished upwards of 11 lengths behind the runner-up. The winner made up the requisite ground readily, challenging closest to the stands' rail (all raced near side) and, although he faced a renewed challenge from the second, he was always doing enough. This victory is particularly significant considering Sir Michael Stoute's runner became the first to defy a penalty in the race since the same trainer's Notnowcato in 2006 (later added two Group 1s), and that horse had just 3lb extra to contend with. Workforce had a 7lb penalty and in recent times a couple of other Classic winners from this yard failed to defy such a handicap, namely Conduit (St Leger) and North Light (Derby). A fine, big colt who has strengthened up since last year, Workforce can build on this performance and as good as So You Think has looked, it will take a brave punter to oppose the Stoute runner should the pair meet. That said there would be a slight question mark should he return to Ascot considering his below-par effort in last year's King George. (tchd 11-10 in places)
Poet had been threatening a performance like this for a while now. A huge horse who is an out-and-out galloper, he loved the ground and the tactics were spot on. (op 20-1)
Jan Vermeer(IRE), who went off favourite ahead of Workforce when only fourth in last year's Derby, made just an adequate return from 316 days off. His trainer often leaves plenty to work on, however. (op 11-2 tchd 9-2 and 6-1 in a place)
Cavalryman ran okay after a 221-day break but isn't the horse he once was. (op 14-1 tchd 16-1 in a place)

Afsare has to be considered disappointing. His reappearance was expected to have brought him on plenty and the ground should have suited considering he has a knee action, but he didn't pick up. He was a bit fresh early, so perhaps the run was still needed, while he was also re-shod at the start, although he didn't seem to get at all worked up. (op 9-1 tchd 14-1 in a place)
Elusive Pimpernel(USA) shaped nicely on his reappearance but didn't improve for the step up in trip. (op 13-2)

2440 CHARLES HEIDSIECK CHAMPAGNE HERON STKS (LISTED RACE) 1m 14y

8:15 (8:16) (Class 1) 3-Y-O **£17,031** (£6,456; £3,231; £1,611; £807) **Stalls** Low

Form RPR

12-1 **1** **Tazahum (USA)**[32] [1547] 3-8-12 101 RichardHills 2 109
(Sir Michael Stoute) *hld up in rr but in tch: drvn and hdwy on stands' rail fr 2f out: str run fnl f to chse ldr fnl 50yds: led last stride* **5/2**[2]

11-5 **2** *nse* **Fury**[26] [1686] 3-8-12 103 KierenFallon 3 109
(William Haggas) *hld up in rr but in tch: hdwy 2f out: sn drvn: kpt on wl to ld fnl 50yds: hdd last stride* **7/4**[1]

2-01 **3** *1 ½* **Neebras (IRE)**[12] [2110] 3-8-12 113 FrankieDettori 4 105
(Mahmood Al Zarooni) *t.k.h: trckd ldr over 5f out: drvn to ld but jnd appr fnl 2f: asserted 1f out: hdd and outpcd pce fnl 50yds* **7/2**[3]

12-1 **4** *1* **Pausanias**[43] [1318] 3-9-3 106 RichardHughes 5 108
(Richard Hannon) *led: pushed along and hdd appr fnl 2f: styd pressing tl edgd rt over 1f out: styd on same pce fnl f* **7/1**

12-0 **5** *2 ¾* **Loving Spirit**[26] [1686] 3-8-12 98 RobertHavlin 1 97
(James Toller) *chsd ldr tl over 5f out: styd front rnk and drvn to chal fr 2f out tl wknd ins fnl f* **8/1**

1m 47.45s (4.15) **Going Correction** +0.30s/f (Good) **5** Ran SP% **110.8**
Speed ratings (Par 107): **91,90,89,88,85**
CSF £7.36 TOTE £3.60: £1.50, £2.70; EX 8.80.
Owner Hamdan Al Maktoum **Bred** Shadwell Australia Ltd **Trained** Newmarket, Suffolk

FOCUS
A time 3.19 seconds slower than the following Class 3 older-horse handicap shows they didn't go that quick and there was a bunch finish. They all raced stands' side in the straight. Although this is muddling form the five are all relatively unexposed and the form is rated on the positive side.

NOTEBOOK
Tazahum(USA) did well to win having looked held in the final few strides. Following up a C&D handicap success gained off 92 on his reappearance, he changed his legs in the closing stages and still looked a bit green, but he rallied well. Sir Michael Stoute doesn't want to run him in the St James's Palace and isn't sure about a drop to 7f for the Jersey, so he'll probably skip Royal Ascot. The objective is to win a Group race at some stage. (op 10-3)
Fury showed he has taken his well-beaten fifth in the Guineas okay, doing little at all wrong in defeat. Perhaps he could be a Jersey horse. (op 2-1 tchd 9-4 and 12-5 in a place)
Neebras(IRE) beat only two rivals at Newmarket last time and this was tougher, but he ran respectably. He might prefer a faster surface. (op 11-4)
Pausanias, the Free Handicap winner, had no easy task under a 5lb penalty, but this was disappointing. He carried his head to one side in the closing stages and failed to take advantage of an easy lead. The easy ground was expected to suit, seeing as he's a big type, but perhaps it didn't. (op 11-2)
Loving Spirit made a brief bid but couldn't sustain his challenge. (op 11-1)

2441 CARLUCCIO'S ALFRESCO WHITSUN CUP (H'CAP) 1m 14y

8:45 (8:45) (Class 3) (0-95,94) 4-Y-O+
£6,417 (£1,921; £960; £481; £239; £120) **Stalls** Low

Form RPR

25-4 **1** **Dunn'o (IRE)**[33] [1529] 6-9-7 94 PhilipRobinson 12 102
(Clive Cox) *mde all: styd alone far side fr ins fnl 4f: drvn and styd on strly fnl 2f: unchal* **11/2**[2]

0-04 **2** *2 ½* **Leviathan**[13] [2061] 4-9-0 87 SteveDrowne 7 98+
(Tony Newcombe) *in tch: hdwy in main pack on stands' side over 2f out: styd on u.p to ld that gp fnl 120yds but no imp on lone wnr far side* **11/2**[2]

10-3 **3** *1* **Julienas (IRE)**[33] [1529] 4-9-6 93 AdamKirby 6 102+
(Walter Swinburn) *chsd ldrs: led main pack on stands' side but nvr on terms w lone wnr on far side: one pce u.p fnl f and lost 2nd fnl 120yds* **5/2**[1]

1-00 **4** *1 ¾* **Brick Red**[26] [1684] 4-9-5 92 JimmyFortune 14 97+
(Andrew Balding) *chsd ldrs and styd w main gp stands' side: nvr on terms w lone wnr far side and styd on same pce fnl f* **6/1**[3]

1-50 **5** *½* **Nazreef**[12] [2105] 4-9-0 87 (t) TravisBlock 15 91
(Hughie Morrison) *in tch: led main gp whn wnr styd along far side ins fnl 4f but nvr on terms: hdd over 2f out: wknd fnl 120yds* **9/1**

30-5 **6** *1 ½* **First Cat**[21] [1834] 4-8-9 82 ow1 RichardHughes 5 82
(Richard Hannon) *in rr on main gp that styd stands' side: hdwy over 2f out: edgd lft over 1f out: continued to hang ins fnl f: styd on same pce* **16/1**

40-5 **7** *shd* **Dukes Art**[24] [1760] 5-8-10 83 RobertHavlin 3 83
(James Toller) *chsd ldrs in main gp that styd stands' side: nvr on terms w lone wnr far side and wknd fnl f* **12/1**

56-3 **8** *2 ¼* **Moynahan (USA)**[21] [1834] 6-9-0 87 EddieAhern 11 82
(Paul Cole) *in tch: styd w main gp on stands' side and rdn over 3f out: wkng whn pushed lft over 1f out* **12/1**

040- **9** *¾* **Cloudy Start**[224] [6877] 5-9-1 88 FergusSweeney 2 81
(Jamie Osborne) *in rr: styd stands' side w main gp: kpt in fr over 1f out: nvr rchd ldrs* **50/1**

5310 **10** *1* **Zebrano**[11] [2124] 5-8-10 83 (b) JamesDoyle 9 74
(Andrew Haynes) *s.i.s: styd w main gp that styd stands' side: a bhd* **22/1**

0-24 **11** *½* **Masai Moon**[14] [2020] 7-9-0 87 JamesMillman 13 77
(Rod Millman) *chsd ldrs in main gp that c stands' side: wknd over 2f out* **28/1**

1m 44.26s (0.96) **Going Correction** +0.30s/f (Good) **11** Ran SP% **114.7**
Speed ratings (Par 107): **107,104,103,101,101 99,99,97,96,95 95**
toteswingers:1&2:£6.70, 1&3:£1.70, 2&3:£4.90 CSF £34.15 CT £93.65 TOTE £6.80: £2.50, £2.10, £1.50; EX 44.70 Trifecta £77.80 Pool: £804.43 - 7.64 winning units.
Owner Dennis Shaw **Bred** R Hodgins **Trained** Lambourn, Berks

FOCUS
All bar Dunn'o raced towards the stands' side, and the winner was the only runner to stick towards the far rail on the entire card. The winner is rated to his best but this result looks skewed.

NOTEBOOK
Dunn'o(IRE) was only 2lb higher than when winning this in 2009 and 1lb above the mark he ran third off last year. This was the horse's first success since that victory here in 2009 and he's now 4-9 at Sandown. (tchd 5-1 and 6-1 in places)
Leviathan fared best of the main bunch towards the near side. He'll face a hike in the weights despite having been beaten. (op 6-1)
Julienas(IRE) ran well without significantly building on the form of his C&D third on his reappearance. (op 11-4 tchd 9-4)
Brick Red stepped up on his two previous efforts this season on this easier ground. (op 11-2 tchd 5-1)
Nazreef has yet to win on turf. (op 10-1)

First Cat Official explanation: jockey said gelding was denied a clear run
T/Jkpt: £6,845.30 to a £1 stake. Pool:£14,462.01 - 1.50 winning tickets T/Plt: £21.80 to a £1 stake. Pool:£105,375.63 - 3,513.11 winning tickets T/Qpdt: £3.30 to a £1 stake. Pool:£6,206.81 - 1,357.36 winning tickets ST

2442 - 2446a (Foreign Racing) - See Raceform Interactive

2416 BRIGHTON (L-H)

Friday, May 27

OFFICIAL GOING: Good to firm (firm in places; 8.7)
Rail dolled out 4m from 4.5f to 2f adding 12yds to distances.
Wind: light, across Weather: overcast, dry

2447 BRASSERIE ITALIANO BRIGHTON MARINA H'CAP 5f 59y

2:00 (2:00) (Class 5) (0-70,76) 3-Y-O+ **£2,525** (£751; £375; £187) **Stalls** Low

Form RPR

6122 **1** **Wooden King (IRE)**[6] [2304] 6-9-12 70 TomMcLaughlin 5 83
(Malcolm Saunders) *mde all: rdn and asserted over 1f out: clr and styd on wl fnl f: rdn out* **9/4**[1]

0-32 **2** *2 ½* **Volito**[1] [2422] 5-9-5 63 GeorgeBaker 2 67
(Anabel K Murphy) *hmpd s and s.i.s: bhd: rdn and hdwy 2f out: drvn and chsd clr wnr jst ins fnl f: no imp* **3/1**[2]

5502 **3** *2 ¼* **Billy Red**[10] [2167] 7-9-10 68 (b) FergusSweeney 4 64
(J R Jenkins) *chsd wnr: clsd and pressed wnr 1/2-way: rdn and unable qck wl over 1f out: wknd jst ins fnl f* **10/3**[3]

3560 **4** *¾* **Rich And Reckless**[9] [2201] 4-9-1 59 (t) IanMongan 6 53
(Tobias B P Coles) *wnt rt s: sn chsng ldrs: rdn and outpcd 1/2-way: no ch w wnr but kpt on again ins fnl f* **25/1**

2261 **5** *shd* **Rocker**[10] [2167] 7-9-13 76 6ex (v) HarryBentley(5) 1 69
(Gary Moore) *hld up in last pair: effrt on inner ent fnl 2f: rdn and no hdwy over 1f out: wknd ins fnl f* **11/2**

-115 **6** *nk* **Novabridge**[25] [1753] 3-9-0 66 (b) StevieDonohoe 3 55
(Andrew Haynes) *wnt lft s: sn pushed along in midfield: rdn and outpcd jst over 2f out: n.d but plugged on again ins fnl f* **15/2**

61.84 secs (-0.46) **Going Correction** -0.075s/f (Good)
WFA 3 from 4yo+ 8lb **6** Ran SP% **109.8**
Speed ratings (Par 103): **100,96,92,91,91 90**
Tote Swingers: 1&2 £1.90, 1&3 £2.00, 2&3 £2.40 CSF £8.80 TOTE £2.50: £1.40, £1.90; EX 11.60.
Owner Pat Hancock **Bred** Terence E Connelly **Trained** Green Ore, Somerset

FOCUS
This was an uncompetitive sprint handicap.They raced towards the far side, although all bar Rocker avoided the rail. That runner may have been at a disadvantage, although much later on the card a winner did race against the fence in the closing stages. The winner continues on the upgrade.

2448 BRITISH STALLION STUDS SUPPORTING BRITISH RACING E B F MAIDEN STKS 5f 213y

2:30 (2:33) (Class 5) 2-Y-O **£3,173** (£944; £471; £235) **Stalls** Low

Form RPR

20 **1** **Bling King**[10] [2181] 2-9-3 0 FergusSweeney 3 80
(Eve Johnson Houghton) *chsd ldrs: shkn up and effrt to chse ldr wl over 2f out: drvn ent fnl f: r.o wl to ld fnl 100yds: in command and pushed out towards fin* **14/1**

652 **2** *1 ¼* **Night Angel (IRE)**[21] [1870] 2-8-12 0 (b) AndreaAtzeni 5 71
(Rod Millman) *wnt bdly rt s: rcvrd to ld after 1f: rdn over 2f out: drvn 1f out: hdd fnl 100yds: nt pce of wnr after* **10/3**[2]

0 **3** *1 ½* **Yammos (IRE)**[10] [2181] 2-9-0 0 MatthewDavies(3) 4 72
(Mick Channon) *stdd after s: t.k.h: hld up wl in tch in last trio: rdn and effrt wl over 1f out: chsd ldng pair jst over 1f out: kpt on same pce ins fnl f* **33/1**

2 **4** *¾* **Pickled Pelican (IRE)**[17] [1988] 2-9-3 0 DaneO'Neill 6 73
(William Haggas) *hmpd s and s.i.s: plld hrd and sn in tch in last trio: rdn and effrt on outer wl over 1f out: no prog: styd on same pce and no threat to ldrs fnl f* **4/7**[1]

5 *2 ¼* **Dana's Present** 2-9-3 0 TonyCulhane 1 62
(George Baker) *t.k.h: led for 1f: chsd ldr after tl rn green and lost pl downhill wl over 2f out: rallied and pressing for 3rd over 1f out: wknd ins fnl f* **8/1**[3]

6 **6** *1* **Manomine**[13] [2109] 2-9-3 0 PhilipRobinson 7 59
(Clive Brittain) *pushed rt s: sn rcvrd and chsng ldrs: rdn ent fnl 2f: wknd over 1f out* **16/1**

30 **7** *2* **Pius Parker (IRE)**[11] [2148] 2-9-3 0 MartinLane 2 53
(John Gallagher) *wl in tch in last trio: rn green and sltly outpcd downhill 3f out: rallied u.p wl over 1f out: wknd 1f out* **25/1**

1m 11.23s (1.03) **Going Correction** -0.075s/f (Good) **7** Ran SP% **117.2**
Speed ratings (Par 93): **90,88,86,85,82 81,78**
Tote Swingers: 1&2 £4.40, 1&3 £20.70, 2&3 £11.50 CSF £62.33 TOTE £19.30: £4.30, £2.30; EX 51.70 Trifecta £673.30 Part won. Pool: £909.96 - 0.86 winning units..
Owner P Deal & C Brown **Bred** Whitsbury Manor Stud And Mrs M E Slade **Trained** Blewbury, Oxon

FOCUS
A fair maiden for the track which rates surprisingly high on the race averages. They raced up the middle in the straight.

NOTEBOOK
Bling King disappointed last time, failing to build on an encouraging debut, but he was said to have been too buzzed up on that occasion and was this time able to confirm that the initial promise. He won in straightforward enough fashion and has the size to go on improving. His trainer thought a bit of him at one stage and he could yet be quite useful in time. Official explanation: trainer said , regarding apparent improvement in form, that the colt had been more relaxed in the preliminaries. (op 16-1 tchd 20-1)
Night Angel(IRE) was runner-up to subsequent Hilary Needler winner Dozy in first-time blinkers over 5f last time, so she could have been expected to win this, but in fairness she probably bumped into quite a nice type. She was said to have crashed through the rails on the way to the start, and didn't convince she handled the track that well in the race itself, wandering a bit under pressure. The step up in trip shouldn't have been too big an issue as this wasn't a severe stamina test. (tchd 11-4)
Yammos(IRE) stepped up on the form of his debut and might win a weak maiden granted a bit more improvement. (op 40-1)
Pickled Pelican(IRE) didn't confirm the promise of his debut second at Yarmouth, but he was squeezed out at the start and then raced a bit keenly. This was disappointing, but it's too early to give up on him. Dane O'Neill reported the colt suffered interference on leaving the stalls. Official explanation: jockey said colt suffered interference at start (tchd 8-13)

The Form Book, Raceform Ltd, Compton, RG20 6NL

Dana's Present, a 20,000gns April foal and half-brother to six winners, out of a smart type, was sent off at a single-figure price for this debut, so has presumably shown ability. He didn't handle the track and ran green, but showed plenty. There should be better to come. (op 16-1 tchd 18-1)

2449 HARDINGS CATERING SERVICES CLASSIFIED (S) STKS 1m 1f 209y

3:05 (3:05) (Class 6) 3-5-Y-O £1,813 (£539; £269; £134) Stalls High

Form RPR

512 **1** **Song To The Moon (IRE)**[21] 1877 4-9-11 69......(b) MatthewDavies(3) 4 73
(Jim Boyle) *stdd and awkward leaving stalls: hld up in last: c stands' side and qckned to ld 3f out: sn rdn clr: u.p and hung bdly lft fr wl over 1f out: kpt on: eased towards fin* **9/4**[2]

05-5 **2** *2* **Retreat Content (IRE)**[38] 1475 3-8-8 65.................... FergusSweeney 1 62
(Jamie Osborne) *led tl hdd 3f out: sn rdn and outpcd by wnr: plugged on same pce fr over 1f out* **5/1**[3]

0112 **3** *3 ¾* **Integria**[7] 2268 5-10-0 64..(bt) TonyCulhane 3 62
(George Baker) *chsd ldr: rdn and nt pce of wnr wl over 2f out: hung lft and btn over 1f out: wknd fnl f* **8/11**[1]

4600 **4** *9* **Illuminative (USA)**[3] 2386 5-9-8 50.................................(b) IanMongan 2 38
(Zoe Davison) *chsd ldng pair: dropped to last and rdn jst over 3f out: drvn and wknd 2f out: wl bhd and heavily eased wl ins fnl f* **22/1**

2m 6.66s (3.06) **Going Correction** -0.075s/f (Good) **4** Ran SP% **109.7**
WFA 3 from 4yo+ 14lb
Speed ratings (Par 101): **84,82,79,72**
CSF £12.43 TOTE £2.60; EX 10.40.The winner was bought in for 5,400gns. Retreat Content was claimed by Miss L. A. Perratt for £5,000.

Owner M Khan X2 **Bred** Michael Woodlock & Seamus Kennedy **Trained** Epsom, Surrey

FOCUS
An uncompetitive seller in which the main action again unfolded towards the middle of the track. The time was 1.86 seconds quicker than the following Class 6 handicap. A weak race and it's difficult to know what the winner achieved.

2450 RACING EXCELLENCE "HANDS AND HEELS" APPRENTICE SERIES H'CAP 1m 1f 209y

3:40 (3:41) (Class 6) (0-60,60) 4-Y-O+ £1,813 (£539; £269; £134) Stalls High

Form RPR

-00 **1** **Major Eradicator (USA)**[57] 1068 4-8-8 47...............(v1) CharlesBishop 1 54
(Alastair Lidderdale) *mostly chsd ldr: allowed ldr to go clr 6f out: clsd 3f out: ev ch over 2f out: rdn to ld over 1f out: in command and edgd rt ins fnl f: a holding rivals* **7/2**[2]

0020 **2** *¾* **Ede's Dot Com (IRE)**[14] 2051 7-9-7 60.............................. LukeRowe 3 65
(Pat Phelan) *stdd s: hld up in rr: clsd 3f out: chsd ldng pair 2f out: rdn over 1f out: no imp tl kpt on ins fnl f: wnt 2nd cl home* **5/1**[3]

0244 **3** *nk* **Goose Green (IRE)**[10] 2171 7-9-0 53...............................(t) JakePayne 5 57
(Ron Hodges) *chsd ldrs: clsd 3f out: rdn to ld over 2f out: hdd over 1f out: kpt on same pce tl swtchd lft and rallied fnl f towards fin: lost 2nd cl home* **5/2**[1]

5640 **4** *6* **Escardo (GER)**[8] 2233 8-8-2 46 oh1........................... JoshBaudains(5) 4 38
(David Bridgwater) *stdd s: hld up in tch: chsd ldng trio and rdn 2f out: wknd ent fnl f* **11/2**[3]

0-04 **5** *35* **The Chester Giant**[9] 2202 4-8-7 46 oh1............................ NoelGarbutt 2 —
(Patrick Morris) *led at stdy gallop tl hdd 6f out: lost pl and rdn ent fnl 3f: lost tch over 2f out: t.o and virtually p.u ins fnl f* **33/1**

5004 **6** *8* **Kate Skate**[7] 2249 4-9-7 60.. IanBurns 6 —
(Gay Kelleway) *stdd s: plld hrd: hld up in last pair: sddle slipped and dashed up to ld 6f out: sn clr: c bk to field and hdd over 2f out: sn bhd: virtually p.u fnl f: t.o* **8/1**

2m 8.52s (4.92) **Going Correction** -0.075s/f (Good) **6** Ran SP% **108.8**
Speed ratings (Par 101): **77,76,76,71,43 36**
Tote Swingers: 1&2 £2.00, 1&3 £2.80, 2&3 £1.90 CSF £11.83 TOTE £4.10: £2.10, £1.10; EX 14.50.

Owner C S J Beek **Bred** Southern Chase Farm Inc Et Al **Trained** Eastbury, Berks

FOCUS
A moderate contest in which these apprentice riders were not allowed to use their whips. The time was 1.86 seconds slower than the earlier 0-70 seller. They raced towards the far side late on, although not quite against the rail. Weak form, the winner up 3lb on efforts for his previous yard.

Major Eradicator(USA) Official explanation: trainer said, regarding apparent improvement in form, that the gelding benefited from the step up in trip and the first-time visor.

Kate Skate Official explanation: jockey said saddle slipped

2451 PLATINUM LACE BAR & GENTLEMEN'S CLUB, BRIGHTON H'CAP 1m 3f 196y

4:15 (4:16) (Class 6) (0-55,55) 4-Y-O+ £1,813 (£539; £269; £134) Stalls High

Form RPR

3662 **1** **Astroleo**[7] 2272 5-8-0 46 oh1.. CharlesEddery(7) 8 54
(Mark H Tompkins) *in tch: rdn and effrt to chse ldr 4f out: led wl over 2f out: forged ahd jst ins fnl f: pressed again fnl 75yds: fnd ex and asserted towards fin* **6/1**

1602 **2** *¾* **Gems**[11] 2145 4-8-13 52... TomMcLaughlin 7 59
(Peter Hiatt) *led for 1f: chsd ldrs after: rdn to chse ldng pair wl over 3f out: no imp and looked hld 2f out: rallied u.p 1f out: chal fnl 100yds: no ex and hld towards fin* **4/1**[3]

200 **3** *2 ¼* **Iguacu**[17] 1987 7-8-10 49..(p) TonyCulhane 3 52
(George Baker) *s.i.s: hld up in last pair: rdn and effrt to chse ldng trio over 3f out: no imp u.p 2f out: plugged on u.p fnl 100yds to go 3rd cl home* **7/2**[2]

0302 **4** *nk* **Vinces**[29] 1635 7-9-1 54...(p) RobertHavlin 6 57
(Tim McCarthy) *chsd ldrs: led over 4f out: rdn: hdd but clr w wnr wl over 2f out: kpt pressing wnr tl btn fnl 150yds: wknd fnl 75yds* **13/2**

-446 **5** *2* **Galiotto (IRE)**[33] 819 5-9-1 54.. GeorgeBaker 1 54
(Gary Moore) *hld up in last pair: effrt and rdn wl over 3f out: 5th and no prog u.p 2f out: nvr able to chal* **9/4**[1]

0-00 **6** *11* **Corlough Mountain**[108] 450 7-8-2 46 oh1................ NathanAlison(5) 2 28
(Paddy Butler) *hld in tch: rdn and short-lived effrt to chse ldrs 4f out: wknd 3f out: 6th and wl btn fnl 2f* **100/1**

00-0 **7** *2* **Pursestrings**[9] 2204 4-8-8 47 ow1..............................(t) FergusSweeney 5 26
(Laura Mongan) *dwlt: t.k.h: in tch in midfield: rdn and wknd over 4f out: wl bhd fnl 2f* **33/1**

-605 **8** *35* **Final Try**[36] 1508 4-8-7 46 oh1... MartinLane 9 —
(Paddy Butler) *led after 1f tl 7f out: chsd ldr tl led again 5f out: sn hdd and struggling u.p: dropped to rr and lost tch over 3f out: t.o and virtually p.u fnl f* **33/1**

-006 **9** *52* **Double Fortune**[11] 2145 4-9-2 55.......................................(b) IanMongan 4 —
(Jamie Poulton) *hld up in tch: hdwy on outer 9f out: led 7f out tl hdd 5f out: sn dropped out: t.o and virtually p.u fnl 2f* **12/1**

2m 33.84s (1.14) **Going Correction** -0.075s/f (Good) **9** Ran SP% **115.2**
Speed ratings (Par 101): **93,92,91,90,89 82,80,57,22**
Tote Swingers: 1&2 £3.60, 1&3 £5.60, 2&3 £4.40 CSF £29.84 CT £96.87 TOTE £7.10: £2.10, £1.60, £1.20; EX 27.10 Trifecta £82.70 Pool: £793.82 - 7.10 winning units..

Owner Mystic Meg Limited **Bred** Mystic Meg Limited **Trained** Newmarket, Suffolk

FOCUS
Not a bad race for such a lowly level with the front two both officially well in. The form reads fairly sound. They raced middle-to-far side, but not quite on the rail.

2452 PLATINUM LACE GENTLEMEN'S CLUB, BRIGHTON H'CAP 6f 209y

4:50 (4:51) (Class 6) (0-65,65) 4-Y-O+ £2,525 (£751; £375; £187) Stalls Low

Form RPR

5113 **1** **Jonnie Skull (IRE)**[17] 1989 5-8-7 51 oh1..................(vt) KirstyMilczarek 5 63
(Phil McEntee) *t.k.h: chsd ldrs tl led over 5f out: mde rest: rdn clr and hung lft fr 2f out: kpt on wl and in command fnl f: rdn out* **5/1**

/40- **2** *3* **Yanbu (USA)**[255] 6061 6-8-1 52 oh6 ow1.................... CharlesBishop(7) 2 56
(Tobias B P Coles) *t.k.h: hld up in midfield: rdn ent fnl 2f: swtchd rt and hdwy over 1f out: chsd clr wnr fnl 100yds: kpt on but no imp* **25/1**

5331 **3** *¾* **Diddums**[1] 2420 5-8-12 63 6ex.. KatiaScallan(7) 4 59
(Alastair Lidderdale) *stdd s: bhd: stl plenty to do and rdn over 1f out: r.o strly and squeezed between horses fnl 100yds: nvr a threat to wnr* **3/1**[2]

2160 **4** *nk* **Mandhooma**[9] 2201 5-9-5 63... TomMcLaughlin 3 64
(Peter Hiatt) *v.s.a: wl bhd: rdn over 3f out: hdwy u.p to press for placings ins fnl f: kpt on but no threat to wnr* **11/4**[1]

0364 **5** *¾* **Fawley Green**[9] 2206 4-9-2 60.......................................(v) GeorgeBaker 7 59
(William Muir) *in tch: hdwy to dispute 2nd over 2f out: rdn and fnd little over 1f out: hung lft and btn 1f out: lost 3 pls fnl 100yds* **4/1**[3]

3502 **6** *nk* **Dvinsky (USA)**[9] 2205 10-9-7 65.....................................(b) JimmyQuinn 6 63
(Michael Squance) *led tl over 5f out: chsd wnr after: drvn and unable qck 2f out: no prog ent fnl f: lost 2nd fnl 100yds: wknd towards fin* **12/1**

0606 **7** *2 ¾* **Pytheas (USA)**[7] 2242 4-9-6 64.................................(tp) FergusSweeney 1 55
(Michael Attwater) *chsd ldr for over 1f: chsd ldrs after: rdn and nt qckn jst over 2f out: wknd ent fnl f* **25/1**

6004 **8** *3 ¾* **Chinese Democracy (USA)**[22] 1831 4-8-7 56..(v) MatthewCosham(5) 8 37
(Dai Burchell) *stdd s: plld hrd: hld up in midfield: rdn and struggling over 2f out: wknd wl over 1f out* **8/1**

1m 22.37s (-0.73) **Going Correction** -0.075s/f (Good) **8** Ran SP% **114.8**
Speed ratings (Par 101): **101,97,96,96,95 95,92,87**
Tote Swingers: 1&2 £27.20, 1&3 £2.80, 2&3 £12.60 CSF £112.48 CT £433.24 TOTE £4.90: £1.50, £9.20, £1.60; EX 164.40 Trifecta £524.40 Pool: £1,020.56 - 1.44 winning units..

Owner Eventmaker Racehorses **Bred** Canice Farrell Jnr **Trained** Newmarket, Suffolk

FOCUS
They raced middle-to-far side and the winner was the only runner on the card to race tight against the inside rail in the closing stages. It was sound run and the form makes sense.

2453 BRIGHTON FESTIVAL 3RD, 4TH, 5TH AUGUST H'CAP 5f 213y

5:25 (5:25) (Class 5) (0-75,75) 3-Y-O £2,525 (£751; £375; £187) Stalls Low

Form RPR

0-13 **1** **Pick A Little**[15] 2024 3-8-9 68.. HarryBentley(5) 2 72
(Ron Hodges) *led for 1f: chsd ldr after: clsd 2f out: rdn and ev ch ent fnl f: led fnl 100yds: edgd rt but hld on wl towards fin* **11/2**

-122 **2** *nk* **Paradise Place**[25] 1764 3-8-7 61.. MartinLane 1 64
(Robert Cowell) *stdd s: hld up in tch: hdwy over 2f out: rdn to ld ent fnl f: drvn and hdd fnl 100yds: kpt on but a hld* **9/4**[2]

6-32 **3** *2 ¼* **Abadejo**[20] 1900 3-8-12 66.. FergusSweeney 3 62
(J R Jenkins) *hmpd s and s.i.s: plld hrd: hdwy to ld after 1f out: clr 4f out: c to stands' side 3f out: rdn over 1f out: hdd ent fnl f: wknd fnl 100yds* **10/1**

5111 **4** *2 ¼* **Exchange**[15] 2024 3-8-12 66... StevieDonohoe 6 55
(Andrew Haynes) *stdd and dropped in bhd after s: hld up in last: rdn and effrt over 1f out: no imp and btn ins fnl f* **10/3**[3]

-503 **5** *6* **Scarlet Rocks (IRE)**[11] 2158 3-9-2 75................... MatthewCosham(5) 4 44
(David Evans) *stdd s and v awkward leaving stalls: sn chsng ldrs: rdn and lost pl ent fnl 2f: edgd lft and wknd over 1f out* **2/1**[1]

1m 10.58s (0.38) **Going Correction** -0.075s/f (Good) **5** Ran SP% **111.7**
Speed ratings (Par 99): **94,93,90,87,79**
CSF £18.42 TOTE £8.10: £5.60, £1.50; EX 15.90.

Owner K B Hodges **Bred** D R Tucker **Trained** Charlton Mackrell, Somerset

FOCUS
A modest sprint handicap. They raced towards the stands' side, but the rail was not decisive. Weak form but the winner is rated back to his best.

Abadejo Official explanation: jockey said gelding ran too free

T/Plt: £179.30 to £1 stake. Pool of £47,263.19 - 192.38 winning tickets. T/Qpdt: £26.70 to £1 stake. Pool of £3,722.79 - 103.15 winning tickets. SP

2295 HAYDOCK (L-H)

Friday, May 27

OFFICIAL GOING: 5f & 6f (inner home straight) - good to firm (firm in places); 7f & further (outer home straight) - good to firm (good in home straight)
5 and 6f races run on inner home straight, races on round course used outer home straight, adding 20yds to distances on round course.
Wind: Moderate, half-against Weather: Fine

2454 VENDMAN SEQUEL H'CAP (FOR LADY AMATEUR RIDERS) 1m 2f 95y

6:05 (6:06) (Class 5) (0-75,75) 4-Y-O+ £2,498 (£774; £387; £193) Stalls Centre

Form RPR

5402 **1** **Amazing Blue Sky**[8] 2213 5-9-7 61 oh1..................... MissSBrotherton 6 75
(Ruth Carr) *mde all: rdn over 1f out: r.o wl to draw clr fnl 110yds* **11/4**[1]

520 **2** *5* **White Diamond**[21] 1879 4-10-2 73........................... MissRJefferson(3) 9 77
(Malcolm Jefferson) *chsd wnr thrght: rdn over 1f out: no imp ins fnl f and wl outpcd fnl 110yds* **9/1**

-003 **3** *1* **Urban Space**[11] 2156 5-10-4 72.. MissEJJones 8 74
(Conor Dore) *bmpd s: hld up: u.p over 2f out: hung lft and hdwy over 1f out: styd on ins fnl f: nt rch ldrs* **20/1**

65-0 **4** *1 ½* **Amir Pasha (UAE)**[58] 1039 6-9-0 61 oh1..................(p) MissRSmith(7) 4 60
(Micky Hammond) *a.p: rdn over 1f out: kpt on same pce ins fnl f* **50/1**

-043 **5** *1* **Morning Chief (IRE)**[14] 2051 4-9-11 68.............(tp) MissRachelKing(3) 1 65
(Clive Cox) *hld up: rdn over 2f out: hdwy over 1f out: one pce ins fnl f* **17/2**

21-4 **6** 1 **Dream Win**[13] 2115 5-10-2 **75**........ MissHBethell(5) 5 70
(Brian Ellison) *hld up in midfield: pushed along over 2f out: swtchd rt wl over 1f out: kpt on ins fnl f: nvr able to chal* **4/1**[2]

0-22 **7** 2 ¾ **Formulation (IRE)**[45] 1292 4-9-13 **74**........ MissNDumelow(7) 7 64
(Hughie Morrison) *in tch: pushed along over 1f out: faltered whn no real imp ins fnl f: fdd* **10/1**

032- **8** 2 ¼ **Edas**[217] 7054 9-9-7 **66**........ MissHCuthbert(5) 3 52
(Thomas Cuthbert) *hld up: hdwy over 6f out: chsd ldrs 3f out: rdn over 1f out: wknd ins fnl f* **33/1**

-055 **9** 4 ½ **Elmfield Giant (USA)**[21] 1874 4-9-11 **70**........(p) MissTSyddall(5) 2 47
(Richard Fahey) *trckd ldrs: rdn over 2f out: wknd wl over 1f out* **11/1**

0012 **10** 1 ½ **Dazakhee**[14] 2057 4-9-7 **66**........ MissWGibson(5) 11 41
(Paul Midgley) *racd keenly: hld up: hdwy over 4f out: rdn in midfield over 2f out: rdr dropped whip wl over 1f out: sn wknd* **6/1**[3]

10-4 **11** 3 ¾ **Hail Bold Chief (USA)**[38] 1460 4-9-13 **74**........ MissDFowkes(7) 10 41
(Alan Swinbank) *hld up: bhd 5f out: struggling fnl 3f: n.d after* **14/1**

2m 14.04s (-1.96) **Going Correction** -0.10s/f (Good) **11** Ran SP% **115.2**
Speed ratings (Par 103): **103,99,98,97,96 95,93,91,87,86 83**
Tote Swingers: 1&2 £7.90, 1&3 £9.90, 2&3 £37.60 CSF £27.01 CT £412.04 TOTE £3.40: £1.20, £4.40, £7.60; EX 32.50.
Owner Exors of the late David W Chapman **Bred** Hong Kong Breeders Club **Trained** Huby, N Yorks
■ Stewards' Enquiry : Miss H Bethell one-day ban: careless riding (tba)

FOCUS
A competitive handicap perhaps not run at the very strong pace that seemed likely beforehand. The winner was back to something near his best.

2455 BRITISH STALLION STUDS SUPPORTING BRITISH RACING E B F MAIDEN STKS 6f
6:35 (6:36) (Class 5) 2-Y-O **£3,238** (£963; £481; £240) **Stalls** Centre

Form RPR

1 **Mezmaar** 2-9-3 0........ RichardHills 3 88+
(B W Hills) *trckd ldrs: led 2f out: shkn up over 1f out: pushed out and r.o wl fnl f: looks useful* **7/4**[1]

2 1 ¾ **Fort Bastion (IRE)** 2-9-3 0........ RichardHughes 2 80+
(Richard Hannon) *green on way to post and coming out of stalls: hld up: pushed along and hdwy 2f out: chsd wnr 1f out: styd on but no imp ins fnl f* **4/1**[3]

3 **3** 1 ½ **Ballesteros**[20] 1890 2-9-3 0........ ShaneKelly 9 78+
(Brian Meehan) *trckd ldrs: lost pl 2f out: nt clr run over 1f out: sn swtchd rt: styd on ins fnl f wout shaking up front 2* **3/1**[2]

4 3 **Badea** 2-9-3 0........ PaulHanagan 10 69+
(Richard Fahey) *green on way to post: s.s: rn green: hld up: pushed along over 2f out: swtchd rt ins fnl f: styd on wl and gng on at fin: can improve* **9/2**

0 **5** ½ **Lexi's Prince (IRE)**[20] 1890 2-9-3 0........ FrannyNorton 7 65
(Tom Dascombe) *a.p: rdn over 1f out: no ex fnl 110yds* **20/1**

0 **6** 1 ¾ **Stepper Point**[42] 1360 2-9-3 0........ DarryllHolland 11 59+
(William Muir) *plld hrd: hld up: hdwy to go prom over 3f out: rdn over 1f out: fdd ins fnl f* **14/1**

7 nk **Man Of My Word** 2-9-0 0........ BillyCray(3) 5 58
(David Nicholls) *led: pushed along and hdd 2f out: wknd ins fnl f* **33/1**

8 nk **Free Zone** 2-9-3 0........ TomEaves 1 57
(Bryan Smart) *in tch on outer: rdn over 1f out: wknd ins fnl f* **66/1**

3 **9** nk **Priestley's Reward (IRE)**[14] 2056 2-9-3 0........ AndrewElliott 8 57
(Mrs K Burke) *s.s: sn rdn in rr: nvr able to get on terms* **80/1**

10 1 ¾ **Speeding** 2-9-0 0........ PatrickHills(3) 6 51
(J W Hills) *midfield tl rdn and wknd over 1f out* **80/1**

1m 14.42s (0.62) **Going Correction** -0.025s/f (Good) **10** Ran SP% **117.9**
Speed ratings (Par 93): **92,89,87,83,83 80,80,79,79,77**
Tote Swingers: 1&2 £2.20, 1&3 £2.80, 2&3 £3.40 CSF £8.90 TOTE £3.20: £1.10, £1.30, £1.80; EX 11.80.
Owner Hamdan Al Maktoum **Bred** Denford Stud Ltd **Trained** Lambourn, Berks

FOCUS
An ordinary maiden but the first three came clear and are sure to rate higher in time. The pace took 2f or so to pick up and plenty were racing keenly early on. The field raced stands' side.

NOTEBOOK
Mezmaar, a costly son of Teofilo out of the useful 2yo 6f/7f winner Bay Tree, herself a half-sister to the Sprint Cup winner Tante Rose, was a well-backed favourite and made an impressive winning debut. He travelled easily in behind until asked to go and win his race which he did with the minimum of fuss, looking to have plenty in the locker. He looks a useful prospect and it wouldn't be a surprise to see him turn up in the Coventry Stakes next time. (tchd 6-4 and 2-1 and 9-4 in a place)
Fort Bastion(IRE) ◆ looks sure to improve and win a maiden. An expensive colt by Lawman out of a mare who won at around 1m in the States, he looked less the finished article than the winner and took until past halfway to get himself organised. Once the penny dropped, however, he came home strongly and he might leave this form behind next time. (tchd 9-2)
Ballesteros remains on course to win a maiden. His rider had him in a good position early only to then find himself trapped behind a wall of horses going well just as the winner was putting a seal on things, and by the time he got out the race had been lost. His debut second looks solid form. (op 9-4)
Badea, a half-brother to a 2yo 7.5f winner out of a mare who won at around 1m4f, ran a promising first race for all he hung badly a couple of times, probably through inexperience. He looked in a hopeless position at halfway as he dropped back to the rear, but there was some steel to his finishing effort when finally straightened out and 7f will see him in an even better light. (op 10-1 tchd 11-1 in a place)
Lexi's Prince(IRE) doesn't look to be living up to his price tag just yet but this was a big improvement on his debut. (op 25-1)
Stepper Point once again showed a fair amount of speed and is probably capable of better when getting it all together, but he was far too free early on (his rider reported he failed to settle) and wasn't given anything like a hard time. Official explanation: jockey said colt ran too free (op 16-1)
Man Of My Word, a half-brother to the useful 5f/6f winner Even Stevens, showed up well for a long way. (op 50-1)
Free Zone showed up for a long way towards the outside and wasn't punished once it was clear he was beaten.
Speeding Official explanation: jockey said colt ran green

2456 PIPER-HEIDSIECK ACHILLES STKS (LISTED RACE) 5f
7:05 (7:06) (Class 1) 3-Y-O+ **£17,031** (£6,456; £3,231; £1,611; £807) **Stalls** Centre

Form RPR

1-12 **1** **Noble Storm (USA)**[21] 1848 5-9-3 110........ GrahamGibbons 6 111
(Ed McMahon) *mde all: r.o wl fnl f: a in command: comf* **4/5**[1]

0-43 **2** 2 **Santo Padre (IRE)**[6] 2323 7-9-3 106........ RichardHughes 2 104
(David Marnane, Ire) *trckd ldrs: pushed along 2f out: effrt to take 2nd over 1f out: sn hung lft: nt pce of wnr ins fnl f* **5/2**[2]

16-0 **3** ¾ **Arctic Feeling (IRE)**[27] 1687 3-8-13 102........ PaulHanagan 5 102
(Richard Fahey) *hld up: rdn ins fnl f: styd on towards fin: nvr able to chal* **10/1**

5-10 **4** 1 ¾ **Baby Strange**[13] 2099 7-9-3 92........ TomEaves 1 95
(Derek Shaw) *hld up: pushed along over 2f out: rdn over 1f out: kpt on ins fnl f but nvr able to trble ldrs* **33/1**

-560 **5** nk **Mister Manannan (IRE)**[85] 754 4-9-3 102........ KierenFallon 4 94
(David Nicholls) *w wnr: pushed along over 1f out: sn lost 2nd: hung lft ent fnl f: fdd fnl 110yds* **7/1**[3]

59.46 secs (-1.34) **Going Correction** -0.025s/f (Good)
WFA 3 from 4yo+ 8lb **5** Ran SP% **108.7**
Speed ratings (Par 111): **111,107,106,103,103**
CSF £2.90 TOTE £1.90: £1.10, £3.10; EX 3.20.
Owner R L Bedding **Bred** Brereton C Jones **Trained** Lichfield, Staffs

FOCUS
A poor turnout for the money and a straightforward win for the favourite who did not need to match his best with the third and fourth more likely guides to the form. The field came down the centre of the track.

NOTEBOOK
Noble Storm(USA) had been beaten on his all previous sorties into Listed company, so it says much for the quality of the opposition that he was sent off odds-on. Soon getting the better of the other possible front-runner Mister Manannan, he was never seriously challenged thereafter and passed the post easing up. All speed and best at 5f, he's clearly better than ever this year and might well make the step up to Group company before the summer is out. (op 5-6)
Santo Padre(IRE) hadn't found things going his way at the Curragh last time and looked Noble Storm's main danger on form. He ran respectably if not up to his best, seeming inconvenienced by the drop to 5f under quick conditions, soon out of his comfort zone chased along to keep up then carrying his head awkwardly and hanging left. Official explanation: jockey said gelding hung left
Arctic Feeling(IRE) had a good deal to find on the figures and ran as well as he could be expected to for all he never threatened after struggling to go the early pace. He looks ready for a step up to 6f.
Baby Strange was out of his depth but didn't run too badly after not surprisingly finding the early pace too hot.
Mister Manannan(IRE) ◆ still hasn't hit top form this year. He faded and edged left on this first run since early March after chasing the winner to 2f out. That said, it won't have escaped the attentions of his trainer that his handicap mark is easing nicely, and it could be that the valuable Scottish Sprint Cup at Musselburgh next weekend or the Gosforth Park Cup at the Northumberland Plate meeting is in his mind. Official explanation: jockey said gelding hung left (op 13-2)

2457 ZANUSSI MAIDEN STKS 1m
7:40 (7:43) (Class 5) 3-Y-O+ **£2,590** (£770; £385; £192) **Stalls** Low

Form RPR

6 **1** **Voodoo Prince**[41] 1409 3-9-2 0........ KierenFallon 3 90+
(Ed Dunlop) *s.i.s: sn in tch w ldrs: wnt 2nd 2f out: r.o to ld wl ins fnl f: wl in command towards fin* **9/4**[1]

2 2 **Kawssaj** 3-9-2 0........ NeilCallan 10 85+
(Roger Varian) *s.i.s: sn trckd ldrs: led over 2f out: rdn and hdd wl ins fnl f: hld towards fin* **3/1**[2]

66 **3** 3 ½ **Robemaker**[25] 1759 3-9-2 0........ WilliamBuick 11 77+
(John Gosden) *in tch: niggled along and dropped to midfield 4f out: hdwy over 2f out: styd on ins fnl f: eased whn no imp on front 2 fnl 50yds* **4/1**[3]

0 **4** nk **Golden Slipper**[42] 1362 3-8-11 0........ DarryllHolland 9 72
(Chris Wall) *racd keenly: sn led: hdd over 2f out: pushed along and nt qckn over 1f out: styd on same pce fnl f* **20/1**

00 **5** 4 ½ **Ambala**[25] 1774 3-8-11 0........ NickyMackay 6 61
(Chris Wall) *hld up: hdwy into midfield 4f out: chsd ldrs over 1f out: one pce fnl f* **100/1**

6 1 ¾ **Come Here Yew (IRE)** 3-9-2 0........ DavidNolan 7 62
(Declan Carroll) *led early: trckd ldrs: pushed along over 2f out: wknd 1f out* **100/1**

60- **7** shd **Save The Bees**[351] 2882 3-9-2 0........ ShaneKelly 1 62
(Declan Carroll) *trckd ldrs tl pushed along and wknd over 1f out* **33/1**

00 **8** nse **Satwa Sunrise (FR)**[11] 2157 4-9-9 0........ JoeFanning 5 57
(Ed Dunlop) *hld up: pushed along into midfield over 2f out: no imp on ldrs* **25/1**

30- **9** 2 ¾ **Torun City**[270] 5587 3-8-9 0........ GeorgeChaloner(7) 12 56
(Richard Fahey) *hld up: effrt into midfield 3f out: hung lft fr 2f out: unable to trble ldrs* **10/1**

10 4 **Royal Deal** 4-9-7 0........ DavidSimmonson(7) 13 46
(Michael Easterby) *hld up in midfield: u.p and outpcd over 4f out* **100/1**

40 **11** 2 ¾ **Wicked Streak (IRE)**[4] 2361 6-10-0 0........ TomEaves 15 40
(Micky Hammond) *s.i.s: hld up: pushed along 4f out: nvr on terms* **33/1**

00- **12** 1 ¾ **Kalgoolie**[283] 5170 3-8-11 0........ FrannyNorton 4 31
(Rae Guest) *midfield: pushed along 3f out: sn wknd* **66/1**

5 **13** 5 **Chlodan**[28] 1654 4-10-0 0........ GrahamGibbons 14 25
(Ollie Pears) *stdd s: hld up: struggling over 2f out: nvr on terms* **25/1**

14 3 ¾ **Georgeoflancashire** 3-8-13 0........ SimonPearce(3) 16 16
(Bruce Hellier) *prom: u.p and wknd over 2f out: sn hung lft whn btn* **125/1**

1m 43.21s (0.31) **Going Correction** -0.10s/f (Good)
WFA 3 from 4yo+ 12lb **14** Ran SP% **108.5**
Speed ratings (Par 103): **94,92,88,88,83 81,81,81,79,75 72,70,65,61**
Tote Swingers: 1&2 £1.60, 1&3 £2.00, 2&3 £3.10 CSF £6.49 TOTE £2.50: £1.60, £1.50, £1.30; EX 5.00.
Owner Lord Derby **Bred** Stanley Estate And Stud Co **Trained** Newmarket, Suffolk
■ Hitman Hatton was withdrawn (9/1, deduct 10p in the £ under R4).

FOCUS
Plenty of runners but few seriously fancied and those at the head of the market came to the fore at the end of a race run at just a fair pace. Ordinary form, rated around the third.
Georgeoflancashire Official explanation: jockey said gelding got its tongue over the bit

2458 "KIKI" BY KIRSTY DOYLE MAIDEN STKS 1m 3f 200y
8:15 (8:19) (Class 5) 3-Y-O+ **£2,590** (£770; £385; £192) **Stalls** Centre

Form RPR

3-0 **1** **Suhaili**[41] 1407 3-8-11 0........ WilliamBuick 14 87+
(Roger Varian) *midfield: pushed along and nt qckn over 3f out: hdwy 2f out: sn chsd ldrs: styd on to ld wl ins fnl f: on top cl home* **6/4**[1]

0/-2 **2** 1 ¼ **Tappanappa (IRE)**[44] 1311 4-10-0 0........ LiamKeniry 6 85+
(Andrew Balding) *midfield: niggled along 6f out: pushed along over 4f out: sn c bk on bridle: hdwy over 3f out: rdn to ld over 1f out: edgd rt ins fnl f: sn edgd lft and hdd: hld towards fin* **10/3**[2]

24 **3** 1 ½ **Stagecoach Danman (IRE)**[107] 471 3-8-11 0........ JoeFanning 12 82
(Mark Johnston) *a.p: led 3f out: rdn and hdd over 1f out: stl ev ch whn n.m.r wl ins fnl f: kpt on same pce towards fin* **14/1**

03 **4** 7 **Dawn Gale (IRE)**[15] 2026 3-8-6 0........ LukeMorris 15 66
(Hughie Morrison) *in tch: pushed along over 4f out: hung lft and one pce over 1f out* **9/1**

0 **5** *shd* **Al Khawaneej**[8] [2218] 3-8-11 0 .... KierenFallon 2 71
(Ed Dunlop) *hld up: hdwy into midfield after 3f: prog to chse ldrs 2f out: one pce and no imp fr over 1f out* **33/1**

0- **6** *1* **Snow Hill**[241] [6442] 3-8-11 0 .... GrahamGibbons 17 69
(Chris Wall) *midfield: pushed along over 3f out: kpt on fr over 1f out: nvr trbld ldrs* **66/1**

66 **7** *2* **Aeneid**[8] [2219] 6-10-0 0 .... DavidNolan 3 66
(Declan Carroll) *midfield: u.p over 2f out: no imp on ldrs* **25/1**

8 *1/2* **Cape Rising (IRE)** 4-9-9 0 .... DarryllHolland 9 60+
(Alan Swinbank) *hld up in rr: u.p over 3f out: nvr trbld ldrs* **50/1**

23 **9** *nse* **Rio Park (IRE)**[12] [2125] 3-8-11 0 .... TomEaves 10 65
(Bryan Smart) *led for 1f: remained handy: rdn over 3f out: wknd 2f out* **25/1**

4-6 **10** *3 1/4* **Marie Rose**[21] [1845] 3-8-7 0 ow1 .... ShaneKelly 1 56
(Brian Meehan) *prom: chalng 3f out: rdn 2f out: wknd over 1f out* **4/1**[3]

11 *nse* **West Brit (IRE)** 3-8-11 0 .... NeilCallan 11 60+
(Ed Dunlop) *s.i.s: towards rr: rn green: pushed along over 5f out: nt clr run and swtchd rt under 2f out: hung lft over 1f out: nvr on terms* **66/1**

04 **12** *9* **Minkie Moon (IRE)**[9] [2203] 3-8-11 0 .... PaulHanagan 16 46
(Amanda Perrett) *a bhd* **25/1**

0-0 **13** *3* **Neptune Equester**[8] [2219] 8-9-7 0 .... JacobButterfield(7) 7 41
(Brian Ellison) *s.i.s: a in rr div: nvr on terms* **66/1**

00 **14** *1 3/4* **Vibration**[7] [2257] 3-8-11 0 .... TravisBlock 13 38
(Hughie Morrison) *led after 1f: hdd 3f out: wknd 2f out* **66/1**

15 *2 1/4* **Ulla** 3-8-3 0 .... SimonPearce(3) 4 29
(Chris Wall) *towards rr: struggling over 4f out: nvr on terms* **100/1**

2m 32.5s (-1.50) **Going Correction** -0.10s/f (Good)
WFA 3 from 4yo+ 17lb **15** Ran SP% **123.1**
Speed ratings (Par 103): **101,100,99,94,94 93,92,92,92,89 89,83,81,80,79**
Tote Swingers: 1&2 £1.60, 1&3 £4.20, 2&3 £20.70 CSF £5.85 TOTE £2.40: £1.20, £2.30, £3.50; EX 7.80.
Owner B E Nielsen **Bred** Mrs Rebecca Philipps **Trained** Newmarket, Suffolk

FOCUS
An ordinary maiden which went the way the market predicted. A fair pace increased once the runners straightened for home. The front three are all potentially better than the bare form.
Ulla Official explanation: jockey said filly ran very green

2459 THE SCISSOR SISTERS LIVE ON 16TH JULY H'CAP 1m 6f
8:45 (8:47) (Class 5) (0-75,74) 4-Y-0+ **£2,590** (£770; £385; £192) **Stalls** Low

Form RPR

00-4 **1** **Arab League (IRE)**[10] [2183] 6-9-7 **74** .... ShaneKelly 2 81
(Richard Price) *a handy: led over 1f out: styd on ins fnl f: in command towards fin* **20/1**

2110 **2** *1 1/2* **Accumulate**[6] [2285] 8-9-6 **73** .... KierenFallon 4 78
(Bill Moore) *in tch: pushed along over 3f out: effrt 2f out: nt clr run over 1f out: styd on ins fnl f: tk 2nd towards fin: nt rch wnr* **11/2**[3]

3242 **3** *1/2* **Hallstatt (IRE)**[20] [1901] 5-9-0 **67** .... (t) GrahamGibbons 8 71
(John Mackie) *handy: led 2f out: rdn and hdd over 1f out: kpt on same pce fnl 110yds* **8/1**

0-0 **4** *1 1/2* **Rebel Dancer (FR)**[6] [2312] 6-9-6 **73** .... (t) TomEaves 5 75
(Ian Williams) *hld up in midfield: rdn and hdwy to chse ldrs over 1f out: kpt on u.p: one pce towards fin* **3/1**[1]

2222 **5** *2 1/2* **Blackstone Vegas**[15] [2034] 5-8-11 **64** .... RobbieFitzpatrick 1 63
(Derek Shaw) *hld up: rdn and hdwy to chse ldrs over 1f out: one pce ins fnl f* **7/1**

0-60 **6** *1 1/2* **Simonside**[15] [2034] 8-9-4 **71** .... PaulHanagan 7 68
(Brian Ellison) *midfield: hdwy after 6f out: rdn whn chsng ldrs 2f out: wknd ins fnl f* **6/1**

5-63 **7** *1* **Perfect Vision**[10] [2176] 4-8-9 **62** .... LukeMorris 3 57
(Clive Cox) *racd keenly: trckd ldrs: pushed along over 3f out: sn lost pl: rdn 2f out: wl btn over 1f out* **5/1**[2]

05-0 **8** *2* **Think Its All Over (USA)**[48] [1243] 4-9-4 **71** .... DarryllHolland 9 63
(Julie Camacho) *hld up: rdn 2f out: sn swtchd rt: nvr on terms* **25/1**

20-4 **9** *2* **Tobernea (IRE)**[17] [1994] 4-9-5 **72** .... JoeFanning 10 62
(Mark Johnston) *led: hdd 2f out: rdn over 1f out: wknd ins fnl f* **9/1**

110- **10** *3/4* **Maybe I Wont**[230] [6754] 6-9-1 **68** .... LiamKeniry 6 57
(Lucinda Featherstone) *hld up: hdwy into midfield 5f out: rdn and wknd over 1f out* **33/1**

3m 2.52s (1.32) **Going Correction** -0.10s/f (Good) **10** Ran SP% **116.5**
Speed ratings (Par 103): **92,91,90,90,88 87,87,86,84,84**
Tote Swingers: 1&2 £25.90, 1&3 £63.50, 2&3 £5.70 CSF £123.89 CT £970.49 TOTE £36.90: £7.50, £1.60, £2.40; EX 210.00.
Owner Mrs P A Wallis **Bred** D G Iceton **Trained** Ullingswick, H'fords

FOCUS
An open finale run at a fair pace and little between the runners for the most part. Ordinary form, rated around the first three.
T/Jkpt: £2,840.00 to £1 stake. Pool of £10,000.00 - 2.50 winning tickets. T/Plt: £12.10 to £1 stake. Pool of £74,492.74 - 4,464.08 winning tickets. T/Qpdt: £3.60 to £1 stake. Pool of £4,015.11 - 812.70 winning tickets. DO

2429 NEWCASTLE (L-H)
Friday, May 27

OFFICIAL GOING: Good (7.7)
Rail realignment added 2yds to distances on round course.
Wind: Light, across Weather: Cloudy

2460 WARD HADAWAY MEDIAN AUCTION MAIDEN STKS 6f
2:10 (2:10) (Class 6) 2-Y-O **£1,813** (£539; £269; £134) **Stalls** Centre

Form RPR

32 **1** **Grand Gold**[12] [2120] 2-9-0 0 .... MartinHarley(3) 1 76
(Mick Channon) *in tch against far rail: pushed along 2f out: hdwy to ld ins fnl f: hld on wl* **5/2**[1]

6 **2** *nk* **Mizbah**[26] [1721] 2-9-3 0 .... TedDurcan 9 75
(Saeed Bin Suroor) *mde most tl hdd ins fnl f: kpt on u.p towards fin* **11/4**[2]

4 **3** *1 3/4* **Maastricht (IRE)**[12] [2120] 2-9-3 0 .... RoystonFfrench 6 70
(Mark Johnston) *dwlt: sn pushed along and disp ld after 1f: rdn 2f out: kpt on same pce fnl f* **4/1**[3]

4 *nk* **Loyal Master (IRE)** 2-9-3 0 .... FrederikTylicki 11 69+
(George Foster) *hld up on outside: stdy hdwy over 2f out: pushed along and rn green over 1f out: kpt on ins fnl f* **100/1**

5 *1 1/2* **Twin Ivan (IRE)** 2-9-3 0 .... TonyHamilton 2 64
(Howard Johnson) *trckd ldrs: rdn and outpcd over 2f out: styd on ins fnl f* **66/1**

3 **6** *1 1/4* **Rhianna Brianna (IRE)**[13] [2113] 2-8-9 0 .... JamesSullivan(3) 8 56
(Michael Easterby) *t.k.h: in tch: effrt over 2f out: kpt on same pce over 1f out* **7/1**

7 *nk* **Louis Hull** 2-9-3 0 .... LeeNewman 4 60
(George Foster) *dwlt: sn prom: rdn over 2f out: no ex over 1f out* **100/1**

8 *2 1/2* **Night Flash (GER)** 2-9-3 0 .... PaulMulrennan 3 52
(James Given) *s.i.s: bhd: pushed along over 2f out: sn no imp* **25/1**

9 *6* **Well Wishes** 2-8-12 0 .... TomEaves 10 29
(Bryan Smart) *t.k.h: in tch: shkn up over 2f out: wknd wl over 1f out* **20/1**

10 *3/4* **Way Of Love (FR)** 2-9-3 0 .... PJMcDonald 5 32
(Kevin Ryan) *dwlt: hdwy to dispute ld after 1f: rdn over 2f out: wknd wl over 1f out* **11/2**

1m 17.28s (2.68) **Going Correction** 0.0s/f (Good) **10** Ran SP% **115.2**
Speed ratings (Par 91): **82,81,79,78,76 75,74,71,63,62**
Tote Swingers: 1&2 £1.60, 1&3 £3.60, 2&3 £2.10 CSF £9.11 TOTE £4.50: £1.40, £1.50, £1.60; EX 11.50.
Owner Jaber Abdullah **Bred** R J & S A Carter **Trained** West Ilsley, Berks
■ Stewards' Enquiry : Ted Durcan two-day ban: careless riding (Jun 10-11)

FOCUS
Frederik Tylicki reported that the ground was dead and a bit sticky. An ordinary maiden auction for 2-y-os, where the action took place on the far side. The three market leaders filled the first three positions but there was not much separating the first seven home. The winner is rated to his mark.

NOTEBOOK
Grand Gold showed the benefit of his debut run when making a bold bid to justify favouritism in a Ripon maiden last time. He had leading claims and found a sustained run against the far rail to defy a big market drift. He is a half-brother to multiple 1m-1m2f Flat/2m hurdle winner Buddy Holly and is out of a 1m2f German winner, so it is very encouraging that he is showing pace sprinting at this early stage of his career. (op 15-8 tchd 11-4)
Mizbah raced enthusiastically up with the pace but was just worn down in the closing stages by the form pick. This was a much improved second run by a Derby entered son of Dubai Destination, who is bred to be suited by 1m+ in the future.
Maastricht(IRE) was a bit awkward at the start but quickly adopted a prominent role and ran a solid race to finish 3l closer to the winner than he did on debut. This Tiger Hill colt looks a strong galloping type who should appreciate a stiffer test later on. (op 5-1)
Loyal Master(IRE) has already been gelded and doesn't have an eye-catching pedigree, but he ran a big race at 100-1 to nearly snatch third on his first run.
Twin Ivan(IRE) cost just 5,000euros and has already been gelded, but he is related to winners abroad and put in an encouraging staying-on effort on debut, particularly as he is not a precocious type on breeding. (tchd 80-1)
Rhianna Brianna(IRE) confirmed the promise of her 5f Thirsk debut third without really building on it. (op 8-1 tchd 17-2)
Way Of Love(FR), a £20,000 breeze-up buy who is a brother to a 1m4f winner in France, was a springer in the market but dropped away quickly over 2f out on his debut. (op 12-1)

2461 MITIE MEDIAN AUCTION MAIDEN STKS 1m 4f 93y
2:45 (2:45) (Class 6) 3-4-Y-0 **£1,813** (£539; £269; £134) **Stalls** Low

Form RPR

42- **1** **Captain Brown**[224] [6894] 3-8-10 0 .... SebSanders 3 84+
(Sir Mark Prescott Bt) *hld up and bhd: hdwy 3f out: rdn: carried hd high and led over 1f out: drew clr fnl f* **4/11**[1]

3 **2** *7* **Emperor Of Rome (IRE)**[14] [2058] 3-8-10 0 .... FrederikTylicki 10 71
(Michael Dods) *t.k.h: led: clr over 4f out: rdn and hdd over 1f out: kpt on same pce* **5/1**[2]

5-0 **3** *3 1/4* **Bint Nas (IRE)**[21] [1845] 3-8-5 0 .... SamHitchcott 5 61
(Mick Channon) *hld up: hdwy 3f out: plugged on fnl 2f: no imp* **7/1**[3]

54 **4** *13* **Aimee Tricks**[77] [836] 3-8-2 0 .... JamesSullivan(3) 4 40
(Ian Semple) *t.k.h: in tch: rdn over 3f out: wknd over 2f out* **28/1**

0 **5** *13* **Indycisive**[14] [2058] 3-8-7 0 .... PaulPickard(3) 11 24
(Simon West) *chsd ldr tl rdn and wknd over 2f out* **40/1**

5 **6** *17* **Jersey Joe (IRE)**[123] [284] 4-9-8 0 .... DaleSwift(5) 2 —
(Brian Ellison) *bhd: struggling over 5f out: nvr on terms* **33/1**

7 *7* **Ebony Breeze (IRE)** 3-8-10 0 .... TomEaves 9 —
(Ian Semple) *prom: drvn 1/2-way: wknd over 4f out* **18/1**

000 **8** *11* **Poosie Nansie (IRE)**[13] [2114] 4-9-8 31 .... (v1) PaulMulrennan 12 —
(George Foster) *cl up tl rdn and wknd over 4f out* **100/1**

[illegible] **9** [illegible] [illegible][366] [illegible] .... TonyHamilton 1 —
(Chris Grant) *midfield: struggling over 4f out: t.o* **66/1**

2m 41.57s (-4.03) **Going Correction** -0.325s/f (Firm)
WFA 3 from 4yo 17lb **9** Ran SP% **119.1**
Speed ratings (Par 101): **100,95,93,84,75 64,59,52,26**
Tote Swingers: 1&2 £1.02, 1&3 £2.10, 2&3 £2.50 CSF £2.65 TOTE £1.40: £1.02, £1.20, £1.60; EX 3.10.
Owner Mr & Mrs William Rucker **Bred** Mr & Mrs A E Pakenham **Trained** Newmarket, Suffolk

FOCUS
There was little strength in depth in this maiden. The hot favourite delivered in decent style under a confident ride and they finished well strung out behind. The level is rated around the second and third.

2462 TSG ENTERPRISE SOLUTIONS H'CAP 1m 4f 93y
3:20 (3:20) (Class 6) (0-60,58) 4-Y-O+ **£1,813** (£539; £269; £134) **Stalls** Low

Form RPR

0-02 **1** **Fossgate**[3] [2393] 10-8-9 **49** .... AmyRyan(3) 11 64
(James Bethell) *hld up in midfield: hdwy over 4f out: led over 2f out: drvn and hld on wl fnl f* **11/2**[3]

50-0 **2** *3/4* **Spahi (FR)**[38] [1468] 5-8-13 **50** .... DanielTudhope 1 64
(David O'Meara) *t.k.h: hld up: stdy hdwy to chse wnr over 1f out: rdn and clsd ins fnl f: hld last 50yds* **4/1**[2]

30-0 **3** *6* **Golden Future**[13] [2091] 8-9-1 **52** .... PaulMulrennan 3 56
(Peter Niven) *prom: effrt and ev ch over 2f out: sn rdn: outpcd by ldng pair over 1f out* **16/1**

3-40 **4** *6* **Dandarrell**[18] [1956] 4-9-2 **53** .... SebSanders 2 48
(Julie Camacho) *hld up: hdwy on outside and in tch 3f out: rdn and outpcd fr 2f out* **16/1**

60-2 **5** *nse* **Falcun**[30] [1617] 4-8-13 **55** .... LeeTopliss(5) 13 50
(Micky Hammond) *hld up: hdwy over 3f out: rdn and edgd lft over 2f out: sn outpcd* **11/4**[1]

00-0 **6** *1 1/2* **Denison Flyer**[8] [2237] 4-8-12 **49** .... (p) LeeNewman 10 41
(Lawrence Mullaney) *prom: drvn and hung lft over 2f out: wknd wl over 1f out* **50/1**

034 **7** *3* **Valantino Oyster (IRE)**[32] [1556] 4-9-7 **58** .... PJMcDonald 12 45
(Ben Haslam) *bhd: struggling over 4f out: styd on fnl 2f: nvr on terms* **17/2**

201- **8** *3 1/4* **Without Equal**[213] [7149] 5-9-2 **53** .... FrederikTylicki 4 35
(David Thompson) *hld up in midfield: stdy hdwy on ins 4f out: rdn and wknd over 2f out* **25/1**

0 **9** *hd* **Suprise Vendor (IRE)**[9] [1615] 5-9-2 **58** .... DaleSwift(5) 5 40
(Stuart Coltherd) *bhd: struggling over 4f out: nvr on terms* **7/1**

4300 **10** *7* **Eton Fable (IRE)**[13] 2091 6-9-6 **57**............................(p) PatrickMathers 9 28
(Colin Teague) *cl up: rdn over 3f out: sn wknd* **40/1**

-045 **11** *3 ½* **Colonel Sherman (USA)**[18] 1956 6-8-11 **48**..........(t) RussKennemore 6 —
(Philip Kirby) *led to 5f out: rdn and wknd fr 3f out* **17/2**

6-25 **12** *4 ½* **Media Stars**[14] 2057 6-9-0 **51**.. TonyHamilton 8 —
(Robert Johnson) *cl up: led 5f out to over 2f out: sn rdn and wknd* **40/1**

2m 41.34s (-4.26) **Going Correction** -0.325s/f (Firm) **12** Ran SP% **118.1**
Speed ratings (Par 101): **101,100,96,92,92 91,89,87,87,82 80,77**
Tote Swingers: 1&2 £13.10, 1&3 £14.90, 2&3 £11.90 CSF £26.87 CT £336.04 TOTE £6.50: £2.40, £1.40, £6.50; EX 34.80.
Owner Mrs James Bethell **Bred** Mrs P A Clark **Trained** Middleham Moor, N Yorks

FOCUS
An ordinary handicap. It was run at a strong pace and the first two pulled clear. They are both potentially on good marks.

2463 DELOITTE CLASSIFIED STKS 1m 2f 32y
3:55 (3:55) (Class 6) 3-Y-O **£1,813** (£539; £269; £134) **Stalls** Low

Form RPR

0-31 **1** **Flying Phoenix**[105] 516 3-9-0 65...................................... KellyHarrison 2 63
(William Haggas) *set stdy pce: t.k.h: mde all: rdn 2f out: hld on wl fnl f* **7/4**[1]

400- **2** *nk* **Geblah (IRE)**[211] 7198 3-8-11 61..................................... MartinHarley(3) 3 62
(David Simcock) *hld up in tch: hdwy to chse wnr over 1f out: kpt on u.p ins fnl f* **12/1**

331 **3** *1 ¾* **Monster Munchie (JPN)**[48] 1252 3-9-0 65......................... TedDurcan 1 59
(William Knight) *t.k.h: cl up: rdn over 2f out: n.m.r and swtchd rt over 1f out: kpt on same pce fnl f* **9/4**[3]

000- **4** *24* **Invent**[212] 7179 3-9-0 63.. SebSanders 4 —
(Sir Mark Prescott Bt) *trckd ldrs: hdwy 1/2-way: drvn over 3f out: wknd over 2f out: sn lost tch* **2/1**[2]

2m 13.99s (2.09) **Going Correction** -0.325s/f (Firm) **4** Ran SP% **108.2**
Speed ratings (Par 97): **78,77,76,57**
CSF £17.13 TOTE £1.60; EX 14.40.
Owner Winterbeck Manor Stud **Bred** Winterbeck Manor Stud **Trained** Newmarket, Suffolk
■ Stewards' Enquiry : Kelly Harrison caution: careless riding.

FOCUS
A tight classified event. The pace was steady and there was not much separating the first three. The form is not sure to prove reliable.

2464 WATERSTONS H'CAP 6f
4:30 (4:30) (Class 5) (0-70,70) 4-Y-O+ **£2,590** (£770; £385; £192) **Stalls** Centre

Form RPR

0611 **1** **Klynch**[4] 2353 5-9-3 **69** 6ex....................................(b) JamesSullivan(3) 2 86
(Ruth Carr) *sn bhd: swtchd to outside over 3f out: hdwy to ld 1f out: styd on strly* **11/4**[1]

5214 **2** *2 ¾* **We'll Deal Again**[20] 1907 4-9-1 **64**............................(b) PaulMulrennan 11 72
(Michael Easterby) *disp ld: led 2f out to 1f out: kpt on same pce fnl f* **6/1**[3]

006- **3** *1 ¾* **Burnwynd Boy**[239] 6491 6-8-13 **62**..................................... SebSanders 8 65
(Ian Semple) *hld up on outside: hdwy over 2f out: rdn and kpt on same pce fnl f* **15/2**

0412 **4** *hd* **Boy The Bell**[7] 2247 4-8-7 **59**... PaulPickard(3) 12 61
(Brian Ellison) *in tch on outside: rdn and outpcd 2f out: kpt on ins fnl f: nt pce to chal* **7/2**[2]

00-5 **5** *1 ¾* **Newbury Street**[20] 1906 4-8-11 **60**................................ DanielTudhope 3 57
(Patrick Holmes) *trckd ldrs: drvn and edgd lft over 1f out: kpt on same pce* **40/1**

3104 **6** *¾* **Hinton Admiral**[30] 1618 7-9-7 **70**.................................... TonyHamilton 9 64
(Keith Dalgleish) *dwlt: bhd tl rdn and hdwy over 1f out: kpt on: nvr able to chal* **16/1**

0-06 **7** *nk* **Sea Salt**[20] 1907 8-8-12 **66**.. DaleSwift(5) 5 59
(Ron Barr) *prom: drvn fr 1/2-way: rallied: nt qckn fnl f* **20/1**

2504 **8** *1* **Desert Icon (IRE)**[15] 2016 5-9-1 **67**............................. MartinHarley(3) 4 61+
(David Simcock) *hld up towards rr: nt clr run fr 1/2-way to over 1f out: sn rdn and no imp* **8/1**

1-60 **9** *2 ¼* **Accamelia**[8] 2238 5-8-9 **58**.. RoystonFfrench 10 41
(Chris Fairhurst) *towards rr: drvn and outpcd 1/2-way: n.d after* **33/1**

00-6 **10** *3 ¼* **Micky Mac (IRE)**[20] 1899 7-8-9 **58**................................ PatrickMathers 1 31
(Colin Teague) *midfield against far rail: drvn 1/2-way: btn over 1f out* **66/1**

04-2 **11** *1 ¾* **Time Medicean**[37] 1493 5-9-0 **63**................................... MickyFenton 7 30
(Paul Midgley) *slt ld to 2f out: sn rdn and wknd* **7/1**

04-0 **12** *½* **Durham Express (IRE)**[92] 673 4-9-4 **70**....................... SeanLevey(3) 6 35
(Michael Dods) *midfield: drvn and outpcd after 2f: btn fnl 2f* **20/1**

1m 14.11s (-0.49) **Going Correction** 0.0s/f (Good) **12** Ran SP% **120.8**
Speed ratings (Par 103): **103,99,97,96,94 93,93,91,88,84 82,81**
Tote Swingers: 1&2 £4.70, 1&3 £5.80, 2&3 £8.20 CSF £18.69 CT £116.31 TOTE £3.80: £1.10, £2.00, £4.10; EX 24.60.
Owner Douglas Renton **Bred** J C S Wilson Bloodstock **Trained** Huby, N Yorks

FOCUS
An ordinary but fairly competitive sprint handicap. The winner's best form since he was a 3yo. The field raced on the far side.
Time Medicean Official explanation: vet said gelding was struck into

2465 O'BRIENS WASTE MANAGEMENT H'CAP 1m 3y(S)
5:05 (5:05) (Class 6) (0-60,59) 3-Y-O **£1,813** (£539; £269; £134) **Stalls** Centre

Form RPR

2-22 **1** **Whitby Jet (IRE)**[9] 2197 3-9-7 **59**....................................... TedDurcan 10 68
(Edward Vaughan) *hld up in tch: hdwy on outside to ld 2f out: rdn and r.o wl fnl f* **5/2**[1]

-530 **2** *3 ½* **Byron Bear (IRE)**[18] 1945 3-8-12 **50**................................ MickyFenton 9 51
(Paul Midgley) *hld up: hdwy over 2f out: kpt on fnl f to take 2nd nr fin: nt rch wnr* **17/2**

0-20 **3** *nse* **Inca Blue**[11] 2166 3-9-2 **54**... DavidAllan 5 55
(Tim Easterby) *trckd ldrs: effrt and ev ch briefly 2f out: kpt on fnl f: lost 2nd cl home* **4/1**[3]

66-5 **4** *2 ¾* **Purkab**[7] 2264 3-9-4 **59**... GaryBartley(3) 1 54+
(Jim Goldie) *hld up: rdn over 2f out: hdwy over 1f out: nvr able to chal* **3/1**[2]

600- **5** *½* **Phair Winter**[224] 6894 3-8-4 **45**..................................... PaulPickard(3) 4 38
(Alan Brown) *prom: drvn along over 2f out: no ex over 1f out* **50/1**

053- **6** *½* **Syncopated Lady (IRE)**[247] 6294 3-9-1 **53**.................... DanielTudhope 6 45
(David O'Meara) *dwlt: hld up in tch: nt clr run over 2f out: sn rdn: rallied appr fnl f: no imp* **6/1**

-004 **7** *3 ¾* **Commander Veejay**[18] 1945 3-8-4 **45**..............(p) AndrewHeffernan(3) 7 29
(Brian Rothwell) *cl up: drvn 3f out: wknd over 1f out* **20/1**

6104 **8** *9* **Fire Crystal**[7] 2243 3-9-4 **56**.. SamHitchcott 3 19
(Mick Channon) *led: rdn and hdd 2f out: sn wknd* **17/2**

000- **9** *8* **Zoom In**[224] 6891 3-8-8 **49**.. SeanLevey(3) 11 —
(Lee James) *prom: rdn over 3f out: wknd over 2f out* **66/1**

1m 44.31s (0.91) **Going Correction** 0.0s/f (Good) **9** Ran SP% **117.1**
Speed ratings (Par 97): **95,91,91,88,88 87,83,74,66**
Tote Swingers: 1&2 £4.90, 1&3 £3.60, 2&3 £5.40 CSF £24.70 CT £84.19 TOTE £2.50: £1.10, £3.30, £1.60; EX 24.30.
Owner A M Pickering **Bred** Rathasker Stud **Trained** Newmarket, Suffolk

FOCUS
A low-grade handicap, but it was quicker than the following Class 5 race. The favourite scored with quite a bit in hand from off the steady pace, posting a 6lb personal best.

2466 NEWCASTLE INTERNATIONAL AIRPORT FILLIES' H'CAP 1m 3y(S)
5:40 (5:40) (Class 5) (0-75,75) 3-Y-O **£2,590** (£770; £385; £192) **Stalls** Centre

Form RPR

5-13 **1** **Certral**[20] 1904 3-8-4 **61** oh3... PaulPickard(3) 6 67+
(Brian Ellison) *t.k.h early: cl up: led over 2f out: styd on strly fnl f* **15/8**[1]

246- **2** *5* **Fenella Fudge**[163] 7879 3-9-6 **74**.................................. PaulMulrennan 1 69
(James Given) *hld up: rdn over 2f out: hdwy over 1f out: styd on fnl f to take 2nd nr fin: no ch w wnr* **8/1**

00-2 **3** *hd* **Sahafh (USA)**[29] 1626 3-9-5 **73**....................................(p) TedDurcan 9 67
(Saeed Bin Suroor) *slowly away: hld up: rdn and hdwy to chse (clr) wnr 1f out: edgd lft: one pce and lost 2nd nr fin* **7/2**[2]

-030 **4** *¾* **Galloping Queen (IRE)**[15] 2018 3-9-3 **71**..................(v) SamHitchcott 2 63
(Mick Channon) *trckd ldrs: drvn along over 2f out: kpt on same pce fnl f* **12/1**

623- **5** *2 ¼* **Scented**[181] 7603 3-9-4 **72**..(b[1]) TonyHamilton 7 59
(Ian Semple) *taken early to post: dwlt: hld up: rdn and hdwy over 1f out: no imp fnl f* **16/1**

3325 **6** *4* **Paco Belle (IRE)**[4] 2349 3-8-10 **67**................................. SeanLevey(3) 4 45
(Andrew Crook) *trckd ldrs: drvn over 2f out: wknd wl over 1f out* **20/1**

035- **7** *¾* **Bay Of Fires (IRE)**[223] 6920 3-9-7 **75**.......................... DanielTudhope 8 51
(David O'Meara) *led to over 2f out: drvn and wknd over 1f out* **11/2**

01- **8** *1 ¼* **Dan's Martha**[175] 7681 3-9-4 **72**................................... RoystonFfrench 5 45+
(Ben Haslam) *t.k.h: dwlt: sn in tch: rdn over 2f out: wknd wl over 1f out* **5/1**[3]

1m 44.44s (1.04) **Going Correction** 0.0s/f (Good) **8** Ran SP% **118.5**
Speed ratings (Par 96): **94,89,88,88,85 81,81,79**
Tote Swingers: 1&2 £5.00, 1&3 £2.60, 2&3 £5.90 CSF £18.82 CT £50.97 TOTE £2.80: £1.20, £2.70, £1.10; EX 17.90.
Owner L S Keys **Bred** Whatton Manor Stud **Trained** Norton, N Yorks

FOCUS
A big gamble was landed in this fillies' handicap. This is weakish form but the winner is at least going the right way.
Dan's Martha Official explanation: jockey said filly ran too freely
T/Plt: £21.20 to £1 stake. Pool of £54,472.63 - 1,870.16 winning tickets. T/Qpdt: £24.60 to £1 stake. Pool of £2,822.61 - 103.15 winning tickets. RY

2105 NEWMARKET (R-H)
Friday, May 27

OFFICIAL GOING: Good (good to firm in places; 7.4)
Far side track used, stalls on stands side except 5.50 centre.
Wind: Light behind Weather: Overcast

2467 CHEMTEST BRITISH STALLION STUDS E B F MAIDEN FILLIES' STKS 6f
2:20 (2:21) (Class 4) 2-Y-O **£4,533** (£1,348; £674; £336) **Stalls** High

Form RPR

1 **Regal Realm** 2-9-0 0.. JimmyFortune 2 88+
(Jeremy Noseda) *hld up: hdwy over 2f out: r.o wl to ld nr fin* **25/1**

2 *hd* **Gamilati** 2-9-0 0.. MickaelBarzalona 1 87+
(Mahmood Al Zarooni) *chsd ldrs: led over 1f out: rdn ins fnl f: hdd nr fin* **7/2**[1]

3 *¾* **Samitar** 2-9-0 0... JamieSpencer 5 85+
(Mick Channon) *chsd ldrs: led over 3f out: rdn and hdd over 1f out: styd on* **8/1**

0 **4** *4* **Roedean (IRE)**[11] 2153 2-9-0 0... RyanMoore 10 73+
(Richard Hannon) *led: rdn and hdd over 3f out: outpcd over 1f out: styd on ins fnl f* **11/1**

5 *½* **Self Centred** 2-9-0 0.. MichaelHills 4 72+
(B W Hills) *s.s: bhd: rdn over 2f out: hdwy over 1f out: styd on same pce fnl f* **20/1**

6 *nse* **Elbe** 2-9-0 0...(t) TomQueally 7 72+
(Sir Henry Cecil) *hld up: hdwy over 3f out: shkn up and edgd lft over 1f out: no ex ins fnl f* **15/2**

7 *hd* **My Propeller (IRE)** 2-9-0 0... WilliamBuick 8 71+
(Peter Chapple-Hyam) *prom: rdn and edgd lft over 1f out: styd on same pce* **4/1**[2]

8 *2 ½* **Damask (IRE)** 2-9-0 0.. RichardHughes 12 63+
(Richard Hannon) *s.i.s: sn prom: shkn up over 1f out: wknd and eased ins fnl f* **9/2**[3]

5 **9** *½* **Good Clodora (IRE)**[16] 1996 2-9-0 0.............................. MartinDwyer 14 62+
(Brian Meehan) *hld up: rdn over 1f out: nvr on terms* **20/1**

355 **10** *1 ¼* **Summathisnthat**[10] 2173 2-9-0 0...................................... JamesDoyle 11 58
(Des Donovan) *chsd ldrs: rdn over 2f out: wknd over 1f out* **25/1**

11 *3 ¼* **Elusive Flame** 2-9-0 0.. KierenFallon 13 48
(David Elsworth) *sed sl owly: a in rr: wknd over 1f out* **7/1**

12 *3 ¾* **Millibar (IRE)** 2-9-0 0.. LukeMorris 9 37
(Nick Littmoden) *hld up in tch: rdn over 2f out: wknd wl over 1f out* **66/1**

1m 13.43s (1.23) **Going Correction** -0.025s/f (Good) **12** Ran SP% **122.8**
Speed ratings (Par 92): **90,89,88,83,82 82,82,79,78,76 72,67**
Tote Swingers: 1&2 £18.30, 1&3 £14.00, 2&3 £8.10 CSF £109.19 TOTE £19.30: £5.30, £2.10, £3.00; EX 133.70.
Owner Cheveley Park Stud **Bred** Cheveley Park Stud Ltd **Trained** Newmarket, Suffolk

FOCUS
Rain during the hours leading up to racing caused the official going description to be changed to Good, good to firm in places and the track being used was the same as last used for the Craven meeting. A number of major yards were represented in this juvenile fillies' maiden, but only three of the runners had previous racecourse experience. The first three were clear and this was surely decent form, and a race certain to throw up winners.

NOTEBOOK
Regal Realm, the second foal of a 7f AW winner from the family of Cheveley Park winner Regal Rose, was unfancied in the market and was out the back early. However, she picked up well inside the last 2f and found extra for pressure to collar the leader near the line. She had quite a hard race but, if she goes the right way, could prove a decent sort. (op 20-1)

Gamilati ◆, a half-sister to a 6f-7f winner out of a 7f winner (including at Group 3 level), showed plenty of ability on this debut and looked the winner entering the Dip. She kept going for pressure, but was run out of it near the line. Her turn is not far away. (op 4-1 tchd 9-2)
Samitar, a 39,000gns half-sister to three winners including the Group 3 juvenile winner Nijoom Dubai, knew her job on this debut and, after leading 2f out, stuck to her task once headed going into the Dip. She was clear of the rest and should have no difficulty winning races. (op 13-2 tchd 9-1)
Roedean(IRE) cost 50,000gns and is the second foal of a half-sister to a couple of smart types. She had shown ability after a slow start on her debut and was sharper this time, leading early on. However, she lost her place soon after halfway and then was hampered by the sixth horse running down the hill, before staying on nicely once meeting the rising ground. She should be suited by an even longer trip. (op 25-1 tchd 10-1)
Self Centred ◆, a 32,000gns half-sister to three 7f winners from the family of Pushy, was tardy from the stalls on this debut but then was noted staying on nicely in the closing stages. She looks sure to improve on this next time. (op 25-1)
Elbe, a half-sister to winners at 7f-1m2f from the family of All At Sea, was wearing a tongue tie for this debut. She travelled well but after joining the leaders 2f out, tended to wander about running into the Dip and then lost two places on the climb to the line. She can do better with this experience behind her, possibly on a flatter track. (op 8-1 tchd 10-1)
My Propeller(IRE), a 45,000gns half-sister to a 6f AW winner out of a 5f winning half-sister to Twilight Blues, was backed into favouritism and travelled well, if a little keenly, in behind the leaders. However, she ran slightly green and her effort flattened out when asked for more. (op 5-1, tchd 11-2 in a place)
Damask(IRE), a 110,000euros half-sister to Zafisio and Harald Bluetooth out of a juvenile winner, dwelt leaving the stalls and, after racing prominently, showed signs of inexperience in the latter stages. (op 6-1)

2468 LLOYDS TSB COMMERCIAL BRITISH STALLIONS E B F FILLIES' H'CAP 6f

2:55 (2:56) (Class 4) (0-85,84) 3-Y-O **£4,533** (£1,348; £674; £336) **Stalls** High

Form RPR
0-23 **1** **Swiss Dream**[14] 2074 3-9-4 **81** KierenFallon 1 98
(David Elsworth) *mde all: shkn up over 1f out: r.o* **9/1**[3]
21-3 **2** *2 ¾* **Blanche Dubawi (IRE)**[13] 2102 3-9-4 **81** TomQueally 2 89
(Noel Quinlan) *chsd ldrs: rdn over 1f out: hung rt and lft ins fnl f: no ex* **4/1**[2]
1-1 **3** *shd* **Instance**[9] 2199 3-9-5 **82** 6ex RyanMoore 4 89+
(Jeremy Noseda) *sn pushed along in rr: hdwy u.p over 1f out: r.o: nrst fin* **15/8**[1]
41-3 **4** *½* **Shesastar**[25] 1745 3-8-7 **70** JoeFanning 6 76
(David Barron) *mid-div: hdwy over 2f out: sn rdn: styd on* **10/1**
0-50 **5** *½* **Catfish (IRE)**[13] 2102 3-9-3 **80** MartinDwyer 3 84
(Brian Meehan) *chsd ldrs: rdn and edgd lft over 1f out: styd on same pce ins fnl f* **14/1**
42-0 **6** *6* **Golden Tempest (IRE)**[13] 2102 3-9-2 **82** JohnFahy(3) 12 67
(Walter Swinburn) *hld up: rdn over 2f out: nvr on terms* **22/1**
06-0 **7** *nk* **Whoateallthepius (IRE)**[22] 1837 3-8-10 **73** JimCrowley 5 57
(Dean Ivory) *chsd ldrs: rdn over 2f out: wknd over 1f out* **33/1**
3216 **8** *3 ½* **Flashbang**[13] 2102 3-8-8 **78** DuilioDaSilva(7) 9 51
(Paul Cole) *prom unril rdn and wknd over 1f out* **16/1**
0-13 **9** *½* **Azzurra Du Caprio (IRE)**[12] 2122 3-9-7 **84** WilliamBuick 10 55
(Ben Haslam) *hld up: swtchd rt over 1f out: n.d* **14/1**
346- **10** *7* **Turn The Tide**[224] 6900 3-8-7 **77** NatashaEaton(7) 7 26
(Alan Bailey) *s.s: a bhd* **66/1**
211 **11** *½* **Clara Zetkin**[14] 2043 3-9-1 **78** RobertWinston 8 25
(David Brown) *s.i.s: hld up: rdn and wknd over 2f out* **16/1**
2-11 **12** *36* **Freckenham (IRE)**[20] 1916 3-9-1 **78** JamieSpencer 11 —
(Michael Bell) *prom tl wknd and eased 1/2-way: t.o* **9/1**[3]

1m 11.49s (-0.71) **Going Correction** -0.025s/f (Good) **12 Ran SP% 117.8**
Speed ratings (Par 98): **103,99,99,98,97 89,89,84,84,74 74,26**
Tote Swingers: 1&2 £8.00, 1&3 £5.30, 2&3 £3.00 CSF £43.89 CT £98.00 TOTE £10.60: £3.10, £2.10, £1.80; EX 55.10.
Owner Lordship Stud **Bred** Lordship Stud **Trained** Newmarket, Suffolk

FOCUS
A fair fillies' handicap, but quite competitive and the time was just under 2secs faster than the preceding juvenile maiden. Once again those racing up the centre of the track dominated the finish, and those drawn low emerged on top. The winner is rated up 7lb.
Instance Official explanation: jockey said filly suffered interference leaving stalls
Freckenham(IRE) Official explanation: jockey said filly never travelled

2469 PETERS ELWORTHY & MOORE MAIDEN STKS 1m 2f

3:30 (3:31) (Class 5) 3-Y-O **£3,238** (£963; £481; £240) **Stalls** High

Form RPR
2- **1** **Hunter's Light (IRE)**[191] 7478 3-9-3 0 WilliamBuick 6 100+
(Saeed Bin Suroor) *trckd ldrs: racd keenly: led over 3f out: rdn and hung lft over 1f out: r.o wl: easily* **11/2**[2]
5-22 **2** *6* **Maqaraat (IRE)**[21] 1850 3-9-3 99 RichardHills 10 88
(B W Hills) *chsd ldrs: ev ch over 2f out: rdn over 1f out: styd on same pce fnl f* **4/11**[1]
3 *4 ½* **Sandbanks Sizzler (IRE)** 3-9-3 0 JimCrowley 13 79
(Ralph Beckett) *hld up: hdwy over 2f out: rdn over 1f out: styd on same pce* **33/1**
0- **4** *2 ¾* **Quails Hollow (IRE)**[238] 6532 3-9-3 0 LiamJones 11 74+
(William Haggas) *hld up: hdwy over 1f out: r.o: nvr nr to chal* **20/1**
64 **5** *1 ¾* **Planetoid (IRE)**[23] 1810 3-9-3 0 AdamKirby 1 75+
(David Lanigan) *hld up: r.o ins fnl f: nvr nr to chal* **25/1**
6 *nk* **Press Office (USA)** 3-9-3 0 MickaelBarzalona 5 69+
(Mahmood Al Zarooni) *s.s: hld up and bhd: hdwy over 2f out: rdn over 1f out: wknd fnl f* **8/1**[3]
7 *nse* **Suzi's A Class Act** 3-8-12 0 LukeMorris 9 64
(James Eustace) *mid-div: hdwy over 4f out: rdn over 2f out: sn wknd* **66/1**
8 *5* **Green Future (USA)** 3-9-3 0 NeilCallan 3 59
(Amanda Perrett) *chsd ldrs: rdn over 3f out: wknd 2f out* **50/1**
0 **9** *1 ½* **Hursley Hope (IRE)**[15] 2019 3-8-12 0 JimmyFortune 12 51
(David Elsworth) *hld up in tch: rdn and wknd 2f out* **50/1**
00-6 **10** *5* **Kambis**[17] 1974 3-8-10 0 TalibHussain(7) 8 46
(Luca Cumani) *dwlt: plld hrd and sn prom: wknd 3f out* **50/1**
0-0 **11** *2 ½* **Akrias (USA)**[14] 2068 3-9-3 0 J-PGuillambert 2 41
(Luca Cumani) *hld up: wknd over 3f out* **66/1**
12 *13* **Semmsu (IRE)** 3-9-3 0 KierenFallon 4 —
(Luca Cumani) *led over 6f: wknd wl over 1f out: t.o* **16/1**

2m 4.56s (-1.24) **Going Correction** -0.025s/f (Good) **12 Ran SP% 126.1**
Speed ratings (Par 99): **103,98,94,92,91 90,90,86,85,81 79,69**
Tote Swingers: 1&2 £8.10, 1&3 £1.90, 2&3 £11.10 CSF £7.98 TOTE £5.50: £1.70, £1.10, £6.40; EX 12.10.
Owner Godolphin **Bred** Darley **Trained** Newmarket, Suffolk

FOCUS
An interesting maiden whose best recent winner was the prolific Tranquil Tiger. The easy winner showed considerable improvement, while the runner-up, who set a high standard, was 10lb off his best.
Planetoid(IRE) ◆ Official explanation: jockey said colt was unsuited by the good (good to firm places) ground

2470 EDMONDSON HALL SOLICITORS & SPORTS LAWYERS H'CAP 7f

4:05 (4:06) (Class 3) (0-95,94) 4-Y-O+ **£7,447** (£2,216; £1,107; £553) **Stalls** High

Form RPR
33-6 **1** **Folly Bridge**[20] 1889 4-9-6 **93** RichardHughes 6 104
(Roger Charlton) *hld up in tch: rdn over 1f out: r.o to ld nr fin: comf* **20/1**
14-2 **2** *¾* **Red Gulch**[15] 2020 4-8-11 **84** J-PGuillambert 2 93
(Ed Walker) *chsd ldrs: rdn to ld 1f out: hdd nr fin* **12/1**
50-2 **3** *1* **No Hubris (USA)**[32] 1564 4-9-3 **90** JamieSpencer 3 96
(Paul Cole) *led: rdn: edgd rt and hdd 1f out: styd on same pce* **11/1**
3142 **4** *2 ½* **Tevez**[10] 2178 6-8-7 **80** oh1 CathyGannon 7 79+
(Des Donovan) *s.s: hld up: swtchd lft over 2f out: hdwy over 1f out: r.o: nt rch ldrs* **9/1**
651- **5** *nse* **Perfect Silence**[202] 7352 6-8-7 **87** LucyKBarry(7) 11 86+
(Clive Cox) *prom: hung rt over 1f out: styd on same pce ins fnl f* **14/1**
-040 **6** *2 ¾* **Space Station**[25] 1760 5-8-10 **83** (b) TomQueally 4 75
(Simon Dow) *s.i.s: hld up: hdwy u.p 2f out: r.o: nvr nrr* **16/1**
-031 **7** *nk* **Galatian**[13] 2111 4-8-10 **83** JamesMillman 1 74
(Rod Millman) *prom: rdn over 2f out: wknd over 1f out* **14/1**
1-50 **8** *2 ¼* **Gouray Girl (IRE)**[20] 1885 4-9-4 **94** JohnFahy(3) 13 79+
(Walter Swinburn) *s.i.s: hld up: hdwy 1/2-way: rdn over 1f out: wknd fnl f* **12/1**
04-0 **9** *2 ½* **Watch Amigo (IRE)**[25] 1760 5-8-12 **85** KierenFallon 8 63+
(Walter Swinburn) *hld up: hdwy over 2f out: rdn whn hmpd wl over 1f out: n.d after* **5/1**[2]
20-0 **10** *2* **Zero Money (IRE)**[20] 1885 5-9-3 **90** SteveDrowne 9 63+
(Roger Charlton) *prom: rdn whn hmpd wl over 1f out: n.d after* **8/1**[3]
64-0 **11** *½* **Greensward**[15] 2020 5-9-0 **87** MartinDwyer 16 58
(Brian Meehan) *dwlt: outpcd: nvr nrr* **16/1**
0-00 **12** *nk* **Rulesn'regulations**[20] 1885 5-9-7 **94** AdamKirby 10 64
(Matthew Salaman) *hld up: rdn over 2f out: n.d* **25/1**
21-3 **13** *8* **Primaeval**[15] 2020 5-8-13 **86** (v) PatCosgrave 14 35+
(James Fanshawe) *hld up: rdn over 2f out: nvr on terms* **9/2**[1]
0-15 **14** *¾* **Below Zero (IRE)**[78] 830 4-9-5 **92** JoeFanning 5 39
(Mark Johnston) *chsd ldrs: wkng whn hmpd wl over 1f out* **18/1**
1100 **15** *16* **Bravo Echo**[20] 1885 5-9-1 **88** NeilCallan 12 —
(Michael Attwater) *hld up: hdwy 1/2-way: rdn and wknd over 2f out: t.o* **25/1**
100- **16** *12* **Arteus**[163] 7875 5-9-4 **91** (v[1]) TadhgO'Shea 15 —
(George Margarson) *in tch tl rdn and wknd over 2f out: t.o* **66/1**

1m 23.83s (-1.57) **Going Correction** -0.025s/f (Good) **16 Ran SP% 124.0**
Speed ratings (Par 107): **107,106,105,102,102 98,98,96,93,90 90,89,80,79,61 47**
Tote Swingers: 1&2 £28.50, 1&3 £11.60, 2&3 £14.30 CSF £239.35 CT £1675.84 TOTE £19.60: £4.00, £2.60, £1.90, £2.80; EX 322.00.
Owner D J Deer **Bred** The National Stud Never Say Die Club Ltd **Trained** Beckhampton, Wilts

FOCUS
A good handicap, but the field went to race towards the far rail and very few got competitive from off the pace. Low draws were favoured. The winner and second are generally progressive.

NOTEBOOK
Folly Bridge, whose previous win was over 7f on the July Course on fast going, had run well afterwards and as a result was still 6lb above that winning mark. She got a good tow into the race and picked up well under pressure to run down the leaders well inside the last furlong. She is sure to go up again for this, and connections might look for a Listed race for her now to try to earn some valuable black type. (op 16-1)
Red Gulch finished ahead of the favourite Primaeval over C&D last time but was 1lb worse off for half a length. Still progressive, he was always in the leading trio but had to work hard to get past the long-time leader, leaving him vulnerable to the winner's late surge. He deserves to pick up a similar contest before long. (op 9-1)
No Hubris(USA) a useful performer who ran well here on his only previous visit, had been narrowly beaten on his return to action. He set off in front and his rider took the field to the far rail. However, he could not shake off the runner-up and eventually gave best entering the final furlong. (tchd 10-1 and 12-1)
Tevez had been running well on sand of late, but his only two wins on turf were at Leicester on good and easy ground. He also therefore appreciated the rain having fallen and ran well, especially as he went right and was slowly away (something he has done before), and then had to be switched to get a run 2f out. (op 11-1)
Perfect Silence ◆ appreciated the fact that rain had eased the ground and ran well considering she raced up the centre of the track for most of the way, away from the principals. She deserves extra credit and should not be too long in adding to her score. (op 12-1)
Space Station all of whose wins have been over 7f but on turning tracks, did not fare too badly although he never got seriously involved. (op 22-1)
Galatian, raised 7lb for a game C&D win earlier in the month, was up in grade and after tracking the leaders near the rail from the start, had nothing more to offer in the last quarter-mile.
Watch Amigo(IRE) was well backed and tracked the pace, but was already under pressure when getting involved in some scrimmaging with Zero Money running down the hill. (op 7-1)
Zero Money(IRE) was 10lb above his last winning mark and had a bit to find with a couple of these on C&D form. He also tracked the leaders and was struggling when the interference occurred.
Primaeval had performed well on his return over C&D earlier in the month when behind today's runner-up, but was drawn in the group that raced up the centre and, under pressure over 2f out, never got involved. (op 4-1)

2471 NEWMARKET BUSINESS DAY H'CAP 1m 2f

4:40 (4:40) (Class 3) (0-95,94) 3-Y-O **£7,447** (£2,216; £1,107; £553) **Stalls** High

Form RPR
3641 **1** **Malthouse (GER)**[8] 2230 3-9-2 **89** 6ex JoeFanning 7 102
(Mark Johnston) *mde all: rdn and edgd lft over 1f out: r.o wl: eased nr fin* **15/2**
53-1 **2** *2 ½* **Danadana (IRE)**[37] 1492 3-8-9 **82** KierenFallon 8 90+
(Luca Cumani) *hld up: hdwy over 2f out: rdn to chse wnr and hung rt over 1f out: styd on same pce ins fnl f* **5/2**[1]
211- **3** *3 ¾* **Flag Officer**[212] 7165 3-8-13 **86** WilliamBuick 2 87+
(Saeed Bin Suroor) *chsd wnr: rdn over 2f out: edgd lft and no ex fnl f* **8/1**
36-1 **4** *2* **Jehanbux (USA)**[22] 1834 3-9-5 **92** RichardHughes 1 89
(Richard Hannon) *trckd ldrs: rdn over 3f out: styd on same pce appr fnl f* **9/1**
62-1 **5** *½* **Blue Destination**[17] 1991 3-8-10 **83** NeilCallan 6 79
(Philip McBride) *chsd ldrs: rdn over 2f out: styd on same pce appr fnl f* **4/1**[2]

144- **6** *nk* **Shooting Gallery**[209] 7236 3-9-3 **90** MickaelBarzalona 4 85
(Mahmood Al Zarooni) *dwlt: hld up: rdn over 3f out: hung lft over 1f out: nvr trbld ldrs* **8/1**

44-1 **7** *3* **Audacious**[20] 1897 3-9-0 **87** RyanMoore 3 76
(Sir Michael Stoute) *hld up: hdwy 1/2-way: rdn over 2f out: wknd over 1f out* **9/2**[3]

2213 **8** *2 1/4* **Amwell Pinot**[62] 988 3-9-7 **94** (p) CathyGannon 5 78
(Alan Bailey) *hld up: rdn over 2f out: sn wknd* **33/1**

2m 4.83s (-0.97) **Going Correction** -0.025s/f (Good) 8 Ran SP% **113.7**
Speed ratings (Par 103): **102,100,97,95,95 94,92,90**
Tote Swingers: 1&2 £4.70, 1&3 £7.40, 2&3 £4.80 CSF £26.31 CT £154.80 TOTE £8.70: £2.40, £2.00, £1.90; EX 34.70.
Owner Sheikh Hamdan Bin Mohammed Al Maktoum **Bred** Dr Chr Berglar **Trained** Middleham Moor, N Yorks

FOCUS
A high-class handicap in which Mark Johnston was bidding to take the race for the second season running. The time was 0.27secs slower than the earlier maiden and the form is perhaps not as strong as the race promised. The winner progressed again and the second looks likely to improve.

NOTEBOOK
Malthouse(GER) ◆, who improved for the step up to this trip to win at Sandown, had a 6lb penalty to carry but was effectively 2lb well-in compared with his new mark. He made the running and responded well when taken on, drawing away once hitting the rising ground. He will go up again for this, but looks worth keeping on-side in the short term at least. (op 9-1 tchd 7-1)
Danadana(IRE), making his handicap debut, was sent off favourite on the strength of a cosy victory at Newcastle. He was never far away but, despite running on, could not stay with the winner. (op 2-1, tchd 11-4 in places)
Flag Officer, up in trip for his turf debut, was another to race close to the pace and looked to show in front briefly around 2f out. However, once the winner responded he had nothing in reserve and possibly this longer trip found him out. (tchd 9-1)
Jehanbux(USA), 6lb higher for his win at Goodwood, was tucked away on this step up in trip but failed to pick up under pressure and may have preferred it if the rain had stayed away. (op 8-1)
Blue Destination, another making his handicap debut, was close up until losing his place as the pace quickened. He rallied in the closing stages. (tchd 7-2)
Shooting Gallery, who was held up at the back on this return to action, ended up racing nearest the stands' rail, which earlier in the day was not the place to be. (op 10-1)
Audacious got off the mark at Lingfield last time despite not handling the downhill run that well. Held up, he was rather exposed and bit keen on the outside of his field, and failed to pick up. (op 6-1 tchd 7-1)

2472 NGK SPARK PLUGS CLASSIFIED STKS 1m
5:15 (5:15) (Class 5) 3-Y-O **£2,590** (£770; £385; £192) **Stalls** High

Form RPR

31-2 **1** **Jibaal (IRE)**[30] 1624 3-9-0 73 JoeFanning 3 75
(Mark Johnston) *chsd ldr: rdn over 1f out: r.o to ld nr fin* **11/4**[2]

26-3 **2** *shd* **Above All**[21] 1843 3-9-0 75 TadhgO'Shea 4 75
(William Haggas) *led: rdn over 1f out: hdd nr fin* **4/9**[1]

552- **3** *3/4* **Ice Cold Bex**[282] 5204 3-9-0 73 JackMitchell 1 73
(Philip McBride) *chsd ldrs: rdn over 3f out: ev ch fr over 2f out tl unable qck nr fin* **10/1**[3]

6-50 **4** *8* **Battle Of Britain**[30] 1611 3-9-0 67 (t) WilliamCarson 2 55
(Giles Bravery) *chsd ldrs: rdn over 2f out: sn wknd* **25/1**

1m 38.4s (-0.20) **Going Correction** -0.025s/f (Good) 4 Ran SP% **108.9**
Speed ratings (Par 99): **100,99,99,91**
CSF £4.48 TOTE £2.60; EX 4.40.
Owner Hamdan Al Maktoum **Bred** Liam Cashman And M Fahy **Trained** Middleham Moor, N Yorks

FOCUS
Quite a competitive classified stakes despite the small field, with little between the first three on official ratings, and the handicapper had clearly got it right as the trio were involved in a real battle throughout the final 2f. The winner rates a small step up.

2473 TURFTV AMATEUR RIDERS' H'CAP 1m 4f
5:50 (5:50) (Class 5) (0-70,73) 4-Y-O+ **£2,498** (£774; £387; £193) **Stalls** Centre

Form RPR

0306 **1** **Bavarica**[11] 2159 9-11-0 **67** MrRBirkett(3) 5 76
(Julia Feilden) *sn chsng ldr: led over 1f out: rdn clr: eased nr fin* **7/2**[3]

0401 **2** *4 1/2* **Strike Force**[6] 2308 7-11-6 **73** 6ex (t) MissALHutchinson(3) 4 75
(Clifford Lines) *plld hrd and prom: chsd wnr fnl f: no imp* **5/2**[1]

0545 **3** *shd* **Diamond Twister (USA)**[12] 808 5-10-3 **60** (t) MrCEllingham(7) 3 62
(Lisa Williamson) *prom: rdn over 2f out: styd on same pce fnl f* **14/1**

1522 **4** *1/2* **Wily Fox**[18] 1935 4-11-1 **72** ow3 MrDJEustace(7) 7 73
(James Eustace) *led: edgd lft fr over 6f out: rdn and hdd over 1f out: no ex ins fnl f* **11/4**[2]

3106 **5** *3 3/4* **Squad**[25] 1761 5-10-13 **68** (v) MrJCoffill-Brown(5) 2 63
(Simon Dow) *hld up: hdwy over 2f out: sn rdn: nvr trbld ldrs* **5/1**

005- **6** *nk* **Miss Whippy**[169] 7789 4-10-2 **55** oh10 JamesBanks(3) 1 49
(Michael Squance) *chsd ldrs: rdn over 2f out: wknd over 1f out* **18/1**

554/ **7** *22* **Just Observing**[700] 3121 8-9-12 **55** oh5 MissHDukes(7) 6 14
(Neville Bycroft) *rrd and s.v.s: hdwy over 9f out: rdn and wknd over 3f out: t.o* **16/1**

0/6- **8** *10* **Gamedor (FR)**[68] 4794 6-10-4 **61** (b) MrJPearce(7) 8 —
(Daniel O'Brien) *hld up: wknd over 3f out: t.o* **33/1**

2m 34.67s (2.67) **Going Correction** -0.025s/f (Good) 8 Ran SP% **114.9**
Speed ratings (Par 103): **90,87,86,86,84 83,69,62**
Tote Swingers: 1&2 £3.40, 1&3 £8.40, 2&3 £7.40. Tote Super 7: Win: Not won. Place: £140.20 - 10 winning tickets. CSF £12.77 CT £106.27 TOTE £4.30: £1.50, £1.90, £2.60; EX 14.50.
Owner Miss J Feilden **Bred** Juddmonte Farms **Trained** Exning, Suffolk

FOCUS
A modest amateur riders' handicap. The winner is rated back to something like her best.
T/Plt: £61.50 to £1 stake. Pool of £86,501.60 - 1,025.98 winning tickets. T/Qpdt: £16.00 to £1 stake. Pool of £4,573.38 - 210.70 winning tickets. CR

1619 PONTEFRACT (L-H)
Friday, May 27

OFFICIAL GOING: Good to firm (good in places; 7.9)
False rail in place over last 6f, 15ft out from inside running rail.
Wind: Moderate behind Weather: Cloudy and blustery

2474 ST. JOHN AMBULANCE H'CAP 1m 4y
6:25 (6:26) (Class 5) (0-75,75) 4-Y-O+ **£2,590** (£770; £385; £192) **Stalls** Low

Form RPR

02-1 **1** **Mont Ras (IRE)**[7] 2252 4-9-0 **68** 6ex SilvestreDeSousa 3 79+
(David O'Meara) *t.k.h early: trckd ldrs: hdwy and cl up over 2f out: rdn to ld 1/2f out and sn edgd lft: jnd ent fnl f and sn drvn: styd on gamely towards fin* **15/8**[1]

2305 **2** *3/4* **Ours (IRE)**[30] 1621 8-9-1 **74** (p) LeeTopliss(5) 1 83
(John Harris) *dwlt and sn rdn along in rr: hdwy on inner 3f out: swtchd rt and rdn over 1f out: chal ent fnl f and ev ch tl drvn and no ex last 75yds* **12/1**

3406 **3** *6* **Hits Only Jude (IRE)**[6] 2320 8-8-4 **63** (v) NeilFarley(5) 5 58
(Declan Carroll) *towards rr and pushed along early: hdwy on wd outside wl over 1f out: sn rdn and styd on u.p ins fnl f: nrst fin* **9/1**

41-6 **4** *1* **Pirate Coast**[27] 1696 4-9-6 **74** DuranFentiman 6 67
(Tim Easterby) *in tch: hdwy to chse ldrs 3f out: rdn along wl over 1f out: kpt on same pce* **9/1**

0-55 **5** *3 1/2* **Hard Rock City (USA)**[115] 376 11-9-4 **75** (t) PatrickDonaghy(3) 4 60
(Declan Carroll) *cl up: led 3f out: rdn 2f out: hdd 1/2f out and grad wknd* **40/1**

0600 **6** *6* **Raleigh Quay (IRE)**[24] 1793 4-9-1 **69** (p) FrederikTylicki 8 40
(Micky Hammond) *midfield: hdwy over 3f out: sn rdn and n.d* **6/1**[3]

4226 **7** *hd* **Bajan Flash**[26] 1714 4-8-12 **69** MichaelO'Connell(3) 2 40
(David Nicholls) *led: rdn along and hdd 3f out: drvn 2f out and sn wknd* **17/2**

2-04 **8** *2* **So Bazaar (IRE)**[14] 2059 4-8-12 **66** (b[1]) PJMcDonald 9 32
(Alan Swinbank) *a towards rr* **20/1**

-001 **9** *7* **Global**[7] 2260 5-8-8 **62** EddieAhern 10 —
(Brian Ellison) *trckd ldrs on outer: pushed along 4f out: rdn 3f out and sn wknd* **7/2**[2]

1m 44.72s (-1.18) **Going Correction** -0.05s/f (Good) 9 Ran SP% **116.7**
Speed ratings (Par 103): **103,102,96,95,91 85,85,83,76**
toteswingers: 1&2 £6.20, 1&3 £6.50, 2&3 £28.00. CSF £26.96 CT £167.37 TOTE £2.40: £1.10, £2.60, £4.10; EX 33.30.
Owner Colne Valley Racing **Bred** Patrick M Ryan **Trained** Nawton, N Yorks
■ Stewards' Enquiry : Lee Topliss two-day ban: used whip with excessive frequency (Jun 19-20)

FOCUS
A modest handicap run at a sound pace and the first two finished well clear. The winner improved again and can probably do better still.
Global Official explanation: jockey said gelding ran flat

2475 CONSTANT SECURITY SERVING YORKSHIRE RACECOURSES H'CAP 1m 4f 8y
6:55 (6:55) (Class 4) (0-85,85) 4-Y-O+ **£4,533** (£1,348; £674; £336) **Stalls** Low

Form RPR

-012 **1** **Hong Kong Island (IRE)**[28] 1658 4-8-7 **71** FrederikTylicki 4 83
(Micky Hammond) *trckd ldrs: effrt and nt clr run over 1f out: swtchd rt and rdn to ld jst ins fnl f: sn clr: styd on* **5/2**[1]

34-0 **2** *3 1/4* **Perpetually (IRE)**[26] 1717 5-9-7 **85** SilvestreDeSousa 3 92
(Mark Johnston) *led: rdn along over 2f out: drvn and hdd briefly over 1f out: rallied to ld again and n.m.r ent fnl f: sn hdd and kpt on same pce* **4/1**[3]

13-4 **3** *1 3/4* **Leader Of The Land (IRE)**[20] 1892 4-9-5 **83** EddieAhern 7 87
(David Lanigan) *trckd ldr: hdwy and cl up over 4f out: rdn to chal over 2f out: led briefly over 1f out: drvn: edgd lft and hdd ent fnl f: sn wknd* **10/3**[2]

2002 **4** *2 1/2* **The Lock Master (IRE)**[17] 1977 4-8-8 **72** NeilChalmers 6 72
(Michael Appleby) *dwlt and in rr: swtchd wd and hdwy wl over 1f out: sn rdn and no imp fnl f* **22/1**

30-1 **5** *4* **George Adamson (IRE)**[20] 1908 5-9-0 **78** PJMcDonald 5 72
(Alan Swinbank) *trckd ldrs: hdwy over 4f out: cl up 3f out: rdn 2f out and ev ch tl drvn and wknd appr fnl f* **4/1**[3]

016- **6** *13* **Fantino**[242] 6423 5-8-8 **72** DavidProbert 1 45
(John Mackie) *t.k.h: trckd ldrs: hdwy and cl up 4f out: rdn along 3f out: sn wknd* **14/1**

-000 **P** **Speed Dating**[22] 1826 5-8-13 **82** (v[1]) LeeTopliss(5) 2 —
(John Quinn) *dwlt: hld up in rr: in tch whn p.u over 3f out* **9/1**

2m 40.33s (-0.47) **Going Correction** -0.05s/f (Good) 7 Ran SP% **112.7**
Speed ratings (Par 105): **99,96,95,94,91 82,—**
toteswingers: 1&2 £2.50, 1&3 £2.30, 2&3 £2.40. CSF £12.37 TOTE £3.40: £1.20, £1.90; EX 14.70.
Owner Miss Terri Anne Nixon **Bred** The Goldsmith Bloodstock Partnership **Trained** Middleham Moor, N Yorks
■ Stewards' Enquiry : Eddie Ahern one-day ban: used whip in incorrect place (Jun 10)

FOCUS
This was run at a steady pace. The form is rated around the runner-up, who has something of an easy lead.

2476 YOUNGSTERS CONDITIONS STKS 6f
7:30 (7:30) (Class 2) 2-Y-O **£6,231** (£1,866; £933; £467; £233) **Stalls** Low

Form RPR

531 **1** **Misty Conquest (IRE)**[15] 2017 2-8-6 0 RichardKingscote 3 85
(Tom Dascombe) *mde all: rdn and qcknd wl over 1f out: drvn ins fnl f and kpt on gamely* **7/2**[3]

1 **2** *1* **Caspar Netscher**[17] 1966 2-9-0 0 RobertWinston 2 90
(Alan McCabe) *trckd ldng pair: effrt 2f out and sn pushed along: hdwy over 1f out: rdn to chse wnr ent fnl f: sn drvn and no imp towards fin* **11/10**[1]

3 *1/2* **Red Duke (USA)** 2-8-8 0 FrederikTylicki 5 82+
(John Quinn) *hld up in rr: hdwy wl over 1f out: rdn and styd on wl fnl f: nrst fin* **3/1**[2]

1 **4** *6* **Betty Fontaine (IRE)**[7] 2241 2-8-6 0 MartinHarley 4 62
(Mick Channon) *trckd wnr: effrt and cl up 1/2-way: rdn over 2f out and grad wknd* **7/1**

0 **5** *6* **Only Orsenfoolsies**[6] 2318 2-8-11 0 PJMcDonald 1 49
(Micky Hammond) *chsd ldng pair: rdn along 1/2-way: sn outpcd* **50/1**

1m 17.02s (0.12) **Going Correction** -0.05s/f (Good) 5 Ran SP% **109.3**
Speed ratings (Par 99): **97,95,95,87,79**
CSF £7.72 TOTE £3.70: £1.90, £1.50; EX 6.80.
Owner Deva Racing Mujadil Partnership **Bred** Polish Belle Partnership **Trained** Malpas, Cheshire

FOCUS
Three previous winners in this conditions event which has a good history. The winner had the run of things on this pace-favouring track.

NOTEBOOK
Misty Conquest(IRE), from a stable flying high with their juveniles, had progressed on each of her previous three starts. Off the mark when accounting for a field of newcomers at Newmarket, she was given a fine tactical ride from the front. Quickening the pace coming off the home turn, in truth she was always doing enough. She is clearly going the right way. (op 10-3)
Caspar Netscher lost nothing in defeat attempting to concede the up and coming winner 8lb. He went in pursuit once in line for home but hard as he tried he was always being held. There is no reason why he should not take his chance at Royal Ascot now. (op 6-5, tchd 6-4 in places)
Red Duke(USA) ◆ is the one to take out of the race. A nice sort with a mixed pedigree, he cost £140,000 at the breeze-up. Dropped in last, he picked up nicely once in line for home and was closing the first two down at the line under a very sympathetic ride. He looks nailed on to land a maiden and is time could prove very useful. (op 4-1)

The Form Book, Raceform Ltd, Compton, RG20 6NL

Betty Fontaine(IRE), representing last year's winning yard, is not very big and was a cheap purchase. She dropped away in the home straight and connections might be tempted to risk her in a good-money claimer. (op 5-1)

Only Orsenfoolsies, well beaten first time at York, was left for dead once the winner went for home. Even so, he picked up £233 for just turning up. (op 40-1 tchd 33-1)

2477 CONSTANT SECURITY SERVICES H'CAP — 1m 4y
8:05 (8:05) (Class 4) (0-85,80) 3-Y-O — **£4,533** (£1,348; £674; £336) **Stalls** Low

Form — RPR

-321 **1** **Chosen Character (IRE)**[8] 2215 3-9-1 **76** 6ex....(vt) RichardKingscote 6 83+
(Tom Dascombe) *t.k.h: trckd ldrs: hdwy and cl up 1/2-way: rdn to ld wl over 1f out: wandered and drvn ins fnl f: kpt on wl towards fin* **7/4**[1]

-235 **2** 1 ¾ **Tasfeya**[17] 1983 3-9-5 **80** TadhgO'Shea 2 83
(Mark Johnston) *set stdy pce: qcknd 3f out: rdn clr 2f out: hdd and drvn wl over 1f out: rallying whn hung rt ins fnl f: one pce after* **9/2**[3]

1 **3** 1 **Cool Macavity (IRE)**[79] 811 3-8-12 **80** MatthewLawson(7) 4 84+
(B W Hills) *hld up in tch: hdwy 2f out: rdn over 1f out: styng on whn n.m.r and swtchd rt ins fnl f: sn one pce* **11/2**

0-13 **4** hd **Great Shot**[25] 1754 3-9-3 **78** JamesDoyle 3 78
(Sylvester Kirk) *t.k.h: hld up in tch: hdwy 2f out: rdn to chse ldrs over 1f out: drvn and edgd lft ins fnl f: one pce* **7/1**

00-3 **5** 2 ¾ **Dubai Celebration**[13] 2096 3-8-11 **75** PatrickDonaghy(3) 1 69
(Jedd O'Keeffe) *t.k.h: hld up in rr: hdwy 2f out: rdn to chse ldrs over 1f out: sn drvn and no imp* **10/1**

1-05 **6** 6 **Home Office**[8] 2229 3-9-3 **78** SilvestreDeSousa 5 58
(Mark Johnston) *trckd ldrs: effrt 3f out: rdn along over 2f out: sn wknd* **4/1**[2]

1m 46.13s (0.23) **Going Correction** -0.05s/f (Good) **6 Ran SP% 111.5**
Speed ratings (Par 101): **96,94,93,93,90 84**
toteswingers: 1&2 £1.10, 1&3 £3.00, 2&3 £2.90. CSF £9.73 TOTE £2.80: £1.20, £3.20; EX 11.10.
Owner Aykroyd And Sons Ltd **Bred** Moyglare Stud Farm Ltd **Trained** Malpas, Cheshire

FOCUS
Another tactical affair, and muddling form. The winner is rated a bit off his Haydock run.

2478 MSK FILLIES' H'CAP — 1m 2f 6y
8:35 (8:36) (Class 5) (0-70,68) 3-Y-O+ — **£2,590** (£770; £385; £192) **Stalls** Low

Form — RPR

3-02 **1** **Rio's Rosanna (IRE)**[13] 2114 4-10-0 **68** RussKennemore 3 82+
(Richard Whitaker) *hld up in tch: hdwy to trck ldrs on inner 4f out: swtchd rt 2f out: rdn to ld wl over 1f out: sn clr: rdn out* **7/1**[3]

-304 **2** 2 ¼ **Jeu De Vivre (IRE)**[17] 1972 3-8-8 **62** SilvestreDeSousa 9 70+
(Mark Johnston) *trckd ldrs: effrt whn n.m.r and lost pl over 2f out: swtchd lft and rdn over 1f out: drvn to chse wnr ins fnl f: kpt on* **9/2**[2]

24P5 **3** ½ **Beauchamp Xiara**[10] 2176 5-9-11 **65** JamesDoyle 8 70
(Hans Adielsson) *hld up towards rr: swtchd rt and hdwy 3f out: chsd ldrs on outer and rdn wl over 1f out: kpt on* **16/1**

14-5 **4** 2 ¼ **Jaldarshaan (IRE)**[143] 34 4-9-9 **63** PJMcDonald 2 64
(Alan Swinbank) *hld up: hdwy over 3f out: swtchd rt and rdn to chse ldrs wl over 1f out: sn drvn and no imp fnl f* **8/1**

4-56 **5** 6 **Countess Ellen (IRE)**[18] 1958 3-8-13 **67** EddieAhern 6 56
(Gerard Butler) *led: rdn along 3f out: drvn 2f out: sn hdd and grad wknd* **10/1**

30/0 **6** 9 **Burza**[14] 2051 5-9-12 **66** DavidProbert 7 37
(John Mackie) *trckd ldrs: effrt over 3f out: rdn along over 2f out: sn drvn and wknd* **9/1**

1301 **7** 1 ¼ **Sail Home**[17] 1993 4-9-6 **65** AdamBeschizza(5) 1 33
(Julia Feilden) *trckd ldrs: hdwy and cl up 3f out: rdn 2f out: sn drvn and wknd over 1f out* **11/4**[1]

1-04 **8** 34 **Majestic Bright**[25] 1756 4-9-8 **62** J-PGuillambert 10 —
(Luca Cumani) *chsd ldrs: hdwy on outer and cl up 3f out: rdn along 2f out and sn wknd* **7/1**[3]

00-5 **9** 18 **Swish Dish (CAN)**[51] 1167 4-9-6 **60** FrederikTylicki 5 —
(Micky Hammond) *a in rr: bhd fnl 3f* **40/1**

-52L **R** **Wood Fair**[8] 2213 4-8-13 **56** PatrickDonaghy(3) 4 —
(Mrs K Burke) *ref to r* **12/1**

2m 13.21s (-0.49) **Going Correction** -0.05s/f (Good)
WFA 3 from 4yo+ 14lb **10 Ran SP% 116.1**
Speed ratings (Par 100): **99,97,96,95,90 83,82,54,40,—**
toteswingers: 1&2 £5.50, 1&3 £22.00, 2&3 £16.30. CSF £38.36 CT £490.05 TOTE £7.00: £1.40, £1.40, £4.70; EX 31.20.
Owner James Marshall & Mrs Susan Marshall **Bred** Hellwood Stud Farm **Trained** Scarcroft, W Yorks

■ Stewards' Enquiry : Russ Kennemore caution: used whip down shoulder in the forehand.

FOCUS
A modest fillies' handicap run at a sound enough pace, but an unexposed winner of some potentia and she was value for a bit extra. The form seems sound enough.

Sail Home Official explanation: trainer's rep said filly was unsuited by the track

Majestic Bright Official explanation: trainer's rep had no explanation for the poor form shown

2479 SINGLES NIGHT - MONDAY EVENING 6TH JUNE MAIDEN STKS — 6f
9:05 (9:06) (Class 5) 3-Y-O — **£2,590** (£770; £385; £192) **Stalls** Low

Form — RPR

03-2 **1** **Redvers (IRE)**[38] 1459 3-9-3 78 JimCrowley 7 76
(Ralph Beckett) *trckd ldrs on outer: cl up 1/2-way: chal 2f out: rdn to ld jst over 1f out and sn edgd lft: kpt on wl towards fin* **1/1**[1]

03 **2** 1 **Alive And Kicking**[21] 1880 3-9-3 0 PhilipRobinson 4 73
(James Bethell) *led: rdn 2f out: hdd and drvn over 1f out: kpt on u.p ins fnl f* **9/4**[2]

6P-0 **3** 1 ¼ **Muroona (IRE)**[17] 1984 3-8-12 0 TadhgO'Shea 1 64
(Mark Johnston) *trckd ldng pair: effrt on inner and rdn along over 2f out: rdn and sltly outpcd wl over 1f out: kpt on u.p fnl f* **10/1**

5 **4** 7 **Magic Rhythm**[27] 1672 3-8-12 0 AndrewElliott 3 42
(Mrs K Burke) *prom: rdn along over 2f out: sn drvn and one pce* **14/1**

5 1 ½ **Misshollygolightly** 3-8-12 0 RobertWinston 8 37
(Brian Baugh) *towards rr: sme hdwy on outer wl over 1f out: sn rdn and n.d* **25/1**

0 **6** ¾ **Desert Chieftain**[13] 2103 3-9-3 0 J-PGuillambert 5 39
(Luca Cumani) *in rr: outpcd and bhd 1/2-way: styd on fr wl over 1f out: nrst fin* **4/1**[3]

0 **7** nse **Yougoigo**[13] 2094 3-9-3 0 PaulMulrennan 2 39
(Marjorie Fife) *chsd ldrs: rdn along over 2f out: sn wknd* **40/1**

6 **8** 1 ½ **See Vermont**[122] 295 3-9-3 0 LeeNewman 6 34
(Robin Bastiman) *cl up: rdn along 3f out: wknd 2f out* **50/1**

1m 18.08s (1.18) **Going Correction** -0.05s/f (Good) **8 Ran SP% 124.8**
Speed ratings (Par 99): **90,88,87,77,75 74,74,72**
toteswingers: 1&2 £1.10, 1&3 £2.60, 2&3 £5.80. CSF £3.88 TOTE £2.20: £1.10, £1.40, £2.70; EX 4.30.
Owner R A Pegum **Bred** Peter Jones And G G Jones **Trained** Kimpton, Hants

FOCUS
A modest sprint maiden and the first three finished clear. The time was slow and the winner was perhaps not at his best.
T/Plt: £25.70 to £1 stake. Pool of £50,577.60 - 1,432.44 winning tickets. T/Qpdt: £7.60 to £1 stake. Pool of £3,518.51 - 339.70 winning tickets. JR

2480 - 2484a (Foreign Racing) - See Raceform Interactive

2402 BEVERLEY (R-H)
Saturday, May 28

OFFICIAL GOING: Good to firm (good in places; 7.9)
Bottom bend at widest configuration to provide fresh ground on inner.
Wind: Moderate against, gusting. Weather: Cloudy

2485 JULIE-BURKE.CO.UK MEDIAN AUCTION MAIDEN STKS — 5f
2:15 (2:16) (Class 5) 2-Y-O — **£3,238** (£963; £481; £240) **Stalls** Low

Form — RPR

3 **1** **Es Que Love (IRE)**[23] 1827 2-9-3 0 SilvestreDeSousa 12 86+
(Mark Johnston) *qckly away: mde all: clr 1/2-way: rdn over 1f out: styd on strly* **6/5**[1]

04 **2** 3 ¼ **Kool Henry (IRE)**[8] 2261 2-9-3 0 StephenCraine 2 74
(David O'Meara) *trckd ldrs on inner: hdwy to chse wnr 1/2-way: rdn wl over 1f out: kpt on: no ch w wnr* **20/1**

2 **3** 2 **Last Bid**[18] 1966 2-8-12 0 DavidAllan 14 62
(Tim Easterby) *swtchd rt s and towards rr: n.m.r 2f out: hdwy wl over 1f out: swtchd lft and rdn appr fnl f: styd on strly to take 3rd nr line* **7/1**

2 **4** hd **Artists Corner**[14] 2093 2-8-12 0 PaulHanagan 6 61
(Richard Fahey) *in tch: hdwy over 2f out: rdn to chse ldng pair over 1f out: sn drvn and one pce: lost 3rd nr line* **9/2**[3]

5 2 **Selective Spirit** 2-8-12 0 AndrewElliott 11 54
(John Weymes) *in rr: gd hdwy on wd outside 2f out: sn rdn and chsd ldrs whn edgd rt ent fnl f: kpt on same pce* **80/1**

6 1 ¾ **Koalition (IRE)** 2-9-0 0 GaryBartley(3) 9 53+
(Deborah Sanderson) *hmpd s and bhd: swtchd wd and hdwy wl over 1f out: kpt on ins fnl f: nrst fin* **100/1**

4 **7** 1 ½ **Arachis Bow**[8] 2248 2-8-12 0 GrahamGibbons 7 42
(Michael Easterby) *midfield: hdwy 2f out: n.m.r and edgd rt over 1f out: n.d* **25/1**

6 **8** hd **Bop It**[16] 2033 2-9-3 0 TomEaves 3 47
(Bryan Smart) *chsd wnr: rdn along 1/2-way: grad wknd* **4/1**[2]

540 **9** ¾ **Liebesziel**[21] 1886 2-9-0 0 MartinHarley(3) 10 44
(Alan McCabe) *chsd wnr: rdn along 1/2-way: grad wknd* **16/1**

10 nk **Valley Ace** 2-9-3 0 JamesDoyle 13 43
(John Quinn) *a in rr* **100/1**

0 **11** ¾ **Lucky Mark (IRE)**[35] 1515 2-9-3 0 LeeNewman 8 40
(George Foster) *wnt lft s: a in rr* **66/1**

55 **12** ¾ **Kodiac King (IRE)**[35] 1515 2-8-12 0 ChrisDCogan(5) 4 37
(Kevin Ryan) *a towards rr* **25/1**

44 **13** 1 **Red Tyke (IRE)**[14] 2093 2-9-3 0 MickyFenton 5 34
(John Quinn) *nvr nr ldrs* **100/1**

64.30 secs (0.80) **Going Correction** -0.05s/f (Good) **13 Ran SP% 120.2**
Speed ratings (Par 93): **91,85,82,82,79 76,73,73,72,71 70,69,67**
Tote Swingers:1&2:£6.90, 2&3:£11.00, 1&3:£3.20 CSF £34.33 TOTE £2.40: £1.20, £3.90, £2.10; EX 29.60.
Owner Crone Stud Farms Ltd **Bred** Newhall Ltd **Trained** Middleham Moor, N Yorks

FOCUS
This race was won by subsequent Redcar Two-Year-Old Trophy winner Ladies Are Forever last year, and several of these had already shown enough promise to win a contest like this. The winner impressed and looks an Ascot possible.

NOTEBOOK
Es Que Love(IRE) basically threw things away on his Ffos Las debut earlier this month when looking likely to win, but despite that he was the only one punters wanted to know here. Despite a wider than ideal draw, he made a smart exit and was soon able to angle across to the far rail in front. Once there, he never looked likely to be caught and there is a chance he may turn up at Royal Ascot. (op 5-4 tchd 6-4 in a place)
Kool Henry(IRE) ◆ improved from his first start to his second and this was another step up. Always tracking the winner, he couldn't make much impression on him, but never looked like losing second. He should be winning before too long. (op 22-1)
Last Bid caught the eye when runner-up on her debut over C&D earlier this month and ran a similar race here, doing all her best work late having started from the outside stall. A step up to 6f should suit her. (op 8-1 tchd 13-2)
Artists Corner, just beaten in a three-way photo on her Doncaster debut, was always being taken along a stride faster than she cared for and could only plug on into fourth. She is another for whom an extra furlong wouldn't come amiss. (op 7-2)
Selective Spirit ◆, a £10,000 filly out of a multiple winning sprinter, made an eyecatching debut. Slow to break, she sat at the back of the field early but stayed on in pleasing fashion after being switched wide over a furlong from home. She is worth keeping an eye on. (op 66-1)
Koalition(IRE) ◆ looked green in rear early, but also stayed on after being switched left. This 8,500euros half-brother to a winning juvenile over 1m certainly provided something to build on.

2486 IT'S GRAHAM HALLETT'S BIRTHDAY H'CAP — 1m 1f 207y
2:45 (2:46) (Class 5) (0-75,75) 4-Y-O+ — **£3,070** (£906; £453) **Stalls** Low

Form — RPR

-310 **1** **Tribal Myth (IRE)**[15] 2059 4-8-7 **66** JulieBurke(5) 4 76
(Kevin Ryan) *trckd ldr: effrt 2f out: rdn to chal over 1f out: led ins fnl f: sn drvn and kpt on wl* **10/3**[1]

1630 **2** nk **Nolecce**[2] 2413 4-8-4 **61** AndrewHeffernan(3) 3 70
(Richard Guest) *hld up in rr: hdwy on outer over 2f out: rdn and edgd rt over 1f out: drvn to chal ins fnl f and ev ch tl no ex towards fin* **14/1**

-101 **3** 3 **Destiny Of A Diva**[29] 1658 4-9-5 **73** GrahamGibbons 7 76
(Reg Hollinshead) *trckd ldng pair: hdwy to chal 2f out: rdn to ld jst over 1f out: drvn and hdd ins fnl f: kpt on* **10/3**[1]

-003 **4** ¾ **Monkton Vale (IRE)**[15] 2059 4-9-0 **68** (v[1]) PaulHanagan 2 70
(Richard Fahey) *trckd ldrs: hdwy on inner 1/2-way: chsd ldrs over 2f out and sn rdn: drvn and btn over 1f out* **7/2**[2]

241- **5** ¾ **Osgood**[218] 7055 4-9-7 **75** SamHitchcott 1 75
(Mick Channon) *led: rdn along 2f out: drvn and hdd jst over 1f out: sn wknd* **8/1**[3]

0322 **6** 1 3/4 **Zaplamation (IRE)**[15] 2059 6-9-3 71 .... TomEaves 5 68+
(John Quinn) *hld up in rr: hdwy whn n.m.r and stmbld 3f out: nt rcvr* **10/3**[1]
2m 5.63s (-1.37) **Going Correction** -0.05s/f (Good) **6** Ran SP% **109.2**
Speed ratings (Par 103): **103,102,100,99,99 97**
Tote Swingers:1&2:£9.10, 2&3:£7.00, 1&3:£2.60 CSF £42.24 TOTE £4.70: £2.70, £6.40; EX 50.30.
Owner Mr & Mrs K Hughes and Dr J Gozzard **Bred** Norelands Stallions **Trained** Hambleton, N Yorks
■ Stewards' Enquiry : Andrew Heffernan two-day ban: used whip with excessive frequency down shoulder in the forehand (Jun 11-12)
Graham Gibbons caution: careless riding.

FOCUS
A tight little handicap and things got tight for a couple of these on the turn for home. Ordinary form.
Tribal Myth(IRE) Official explanation: trainer said, regarding apparent improvement in form, that the gelding was better suited by the faster ground and the track.

2487 RACING UK ON SKY 432 STKS (H'CAP) 7f 100y
3:15 (3:16) (Class 5) (0-70,70) 4-Y-0+ **£2,914** (£867; £433; £216) **Stalls** Low

Form RPR
01-6 **1** **Burns Night**[26] 1748 5-9-7 **70** .... SilvestreDeSousa 11 78
(Geoffrey Harker) *hld up in rr: pushed along 3f out: hdwy and edgd rt over 2f out: rdn to chse ldrs over 1f out: swtchd rt and drvn ins fnl f: kpt on to ld last 50yds* **2/1**[1]
5-23 **2** 1/2 **Muftarres (IRE)**[22] 1857 6-9-1 **64** .... MickyFenton 5 71
(Paul Midgley) *sltly hmpd s and in rr: gd hdwy over 2f out: swtchd lft and rdn to chal ent fnl f: sn drvn and edgd rt to ld narrowly: hdd and no ex last 50yds* **6/1**[3]
3-10 **3** 1 **Master Leon**[15] 2057 4-8-8 **57** .... (v) TomEaves 4 62
(Bryan Smart) *hld up: hdwy 3f out: rdn to chse ldrs wl over 1f out: styd on to chal ent fnl f and ev ch tl drvn and no ex last 100yds* **20/1**
1351 **4** 1 **Lindoro**[49] 1244 6-8-12 **64** .... AndrewHeffernan(3) 3 66+
(Kevin M Prendergast) *chsd ldr: led 1/2-way: rdn wl over 1f out: drvn and hdd ent fnl f: kpt on same pce* **9/2**[2]
1603 **5** 3/4 **Powerful Pierre**[26] 1748 4-8-12 **64** .... (v) GaryBartley(3) 2 64+
(Ian McInnes) *in tch: hdwy on inner over 2f out: effrt and n.m.r over 1f out: rdn and kpt on ins fnl f: nrst fin* **9/1**
6433 **6** 1 1/4 **Flying Applause**[12] 2161 6-8-8 **57** .... (bt) GrahamGibbons 7 54+
(Roy Bowring) *led: hdd 1/2-way: cl up and rdn over 2f out: sn drvn and grad wknd* **8/1**
335 **7** 6 **Mutamaleq (IRE)**[52] 1190 4-8-9 **63** .... DaleSwift(5) 10 45
(Ian McInnes) *chsd ldrs: rdn along over 2f out: sn drvn and wknd* **14/1**
6-00 **8** 2 1/4 **Emeralds Spirit (IRE)**[8] 2260 4-8-11 **60** .... AndrewElliott 6 36
(John Weymes) *chsd ldrs: rdn along over 2f out: sn drvn and wknd* **16/1**
1000 **9** 3 1/4 **Northern Flyer (GER)**[33] 1558 5-9-0 **63** .... (p) PaulHanagan 8 31
(John Quinn) *hld up in tch: hdwy 3f out: rdn to chse ldrs over 2f out: sn wknd* **8/1**
51-0 **10** 6 **Blue Noodles**[27] 1714 5-8-6 **60** .... AdamBeschizza(5) 9 13
(John Wainwright) *in tch: rdn along 3f out: sn wknd* **20/1**
1m 33.49s (-0.31) **Going Correction** -0.05s/f (Good) **10** Ran SP% **120.1**
Speed ratings (Par 103): **99,98,97,96,95 93,87,84,80,73**
Tote Swingers:1&2:£5.00, 2&3:£18.50, 1&3:£13.60 CSF £14.58 CT £187.51 TOTE £3.20: £1.70, £1.70, £7.10; EX 17.30.
Owner An Englishman, Irishman & Scotsman **Bred** Highclere Stud And Floors Farming **Trained** Thirkleby, N Yorks

FOCUS
A modest handicap in which the leaders went off very fast. It was no accident that the last three at halfway were the first three home. the form makes sense.

2488 BRIAN YEARDLEY CONTINENTAL TWO YEAR OLD TROPHY CONDITIONS STKS (C&G) 5f
3:45 (3:45) (Class 2) 2-Y-0 **£9,346** (£2,799; £1,399; £700; £349) **Stalls** Low

Form RPR
1 **1** **Gabrial (IRE)**[23] 1823 2-9-2 0 .... PaulHanagan 1 89
(Richard Fahey) *trckd ldrs on inner: swtchd lft and effrt over 1f out: rdn to chal ent fnl f: drvn and kpt on wl to ld last 30yds* **6/5**[1]
16 **2** 1/2 **Cravat**[17] 2007 2-8-12 0 .... SilvestreDeSousa 2 83
(Mark Johnston) *led: rdn wl over 1f out: drvn and strly chal ent fnl f: kpt on ganely tl no ex and hdd last 30yds* **12/1**
12 **3** 1/2 **Hamza (IRE)**[17] 2007 2-9-2 0 .... TomEaves 3 85
(Kevin Ryan) *cl up: effrt wl over 1f out: sn rdn and ev ch tl drvn ins fnl f and no ex last 50yds* **11/4**[2]
1 **4** 1/2 **Arnold Lane (IRE)**[12] 2148 2-9-2 0 .... SamHitchcott 4 83
(Mick Channon) *cl up on outer: rdn along and sltly outpcd over 1f out: drvn and rallied to have ev ch ins fnl f: no ex last 75yds* **7/2**[3]
1 **5** nk **Mitchum**[46] 1290 2-9-2 0 .... GrahamGibbons 5 82
(David Barron) *trckd ldrs: effrt and hdwy 2f out: rdn and ch over 1f out: drvn and one pce ins fnl f* **12/1**
64.15 secs (0.65) **Going Correction** -0.05s/f (Good) **5** Ran SP% **109.7**
Speed ratings (Par 99): **92,91,90,89,89**
CSF £15.60 TOTE £2.00: £1.30, £5.00; EX 11.10.
Owner Dr Marwan Koukash **Bred** B Kennedy **Trained** Musley Bank, N Yorks
■ Stewards' Enquiry : Sam Hitchcott two-day ban: used whip with excessive force (Jun 11-12)
Paul Hanagan one-day ban: used whip with excessive frequency (Jun 11)

FOCUS
This year's renewal of the Brian Yeardley looked well up to scratch with all five runners previous winners. They finished in a bit of a heap, but in all likelihood this is decent form. Gabrial has more to offer. The winning time was 0.15 seconds quicker than the opening maiden.

NOTEBOOK
Gabrial(IRE) ◆was immediately nominated for this event after overcoming an ordinary draw to make a winning debut at Chester, a maiden that hadn't really worked out. Nevertheless, he was backed to maintain his unbeaten record, but he had to work very hard and it wasn't until the last 20 yards that he managed to get on top of the pacesetter. This big colt still seems to be learning, however, and the Coventry Stakes (for which he was a top-priced 20-1 straight after this) will be considered, though wherever he runs next it will be over 6f. He's likely to have plenty of improvement left in him. (op 5-4 tchd 11-8)
Cravat finished around 4l behind Hamza at York last time and was just 1lb better off, but he still managed to reverse the form under a positive ride and it looked for much of the race as if he wouldn't be caught. Only nailed very late by the favourite, he looks a tough sort and that should continue to stand him in good stead. (op 11-1 tchd 10-1)
Hamza(IRE), from the stable that took the Hilary Needler here three days earlier, lost little in defeat when runner-up in a decent York novice event last time. It was a similar story here, as he raced up with the pace the whole way and wasn't seen off until very late. (op 3-1 tchd 5-2)
Arnold Lane(IRE), winner of an ordinary maiden on his Leicester debut 12 days earlier, raced widest and saw plenty of daylight. He was close enough entering the last furlong, but just tended to hang left in the closing stages, possibly through greenness. He holds a Railway Stakes entry and there should be more races to be won with him. (op 4-1)
Mitchum bolted up by 8l in a modest Fibresand maiden on his debut, but proved very weak in the market on this very different surface. He wasn't beaten far, although last of the quintet, but may need an easier surface to show his best. (op 17-2)

2489 BRANTINGHAM CONDITIONS STKS 5f
4:20 (4:22) (Class 3) 3-Y-0+
£8,100 (£2,425; £1,212; £607; £302; £152) **Stalls** Low

Form RPR
00-1 **1** **Singeur (IRE)**[14] 2117 4-8-12 97 .... LeeNewman 7 101
(Robin Bastiman) *trckd ldrs: hdwy on outer wl over 1f out: rdn ent fnl f: drvn and kpt on wl to ld and edgd rt nr line* **4/1**[3]
5/00 **2** 1/2 **Befortyfour**[7] 2317 6-8-12 89 .... GrahamGibbons 2 99?
(Richard Guest) *led: rdn along wl over 1f out: drvn ent fnl f: edgd lft and hdd nr fin* **10/1**
5511 **3** 3/4 **Liberty Lady (IRE)**[22] 1864 4-8-7 89 .... JamesDoyle 1 92
(Des Donovan) *trckd ldrs on inner: effrt over 1f out: swtchd lft and rdn 1f out: keeping on whn nt clr run and hmpd wl ins fnl f: one pce after* **15/2**
0-00 **4** hd **Tax Free (IRE)**[7] 2317 9-8-12 98 .... PaulHanagan 5 96
(David Nicholls) *cl up: effrt wl over 1f out: sn rdn: drvn and hld whn n.m.r wl ins fnl f* **5/2**[2]
-030 **5** 3 3/4 **Fitz Flyer (IRE)**[16] 2028 5-8-12 89 .... TomEaves 3 82
(Bryan Smart) *cl up: rdn along wl over 1f out: sn drvn and wknd* **16/1**
00-2 **6** 1/2 **Love Delta (USA)**[7] 2288 4-8-12 98 .... SilvestreDeSousa 4 80
(Mark Johnston) *hld up in rr: effrt 2f out: sn rdn and no hdwy* **2/1**[1]
10-0 **7** 6 **Burning Thread (IRE)**[35] 1518 4-9-4 97 .... DaleSwift(5) 6 70
(Tim Etherington) *chsd ldrs on outer: effrt and cl up 2f out: sn rdn and wknd over 1f out* **33/1**
63.17 secs (-0.33) **Going Correction** -0.05s/f (Good) **7** Ran SP% **111.6**
Speed ratings (Par 107): **100,99,98,97,91 90,81**
Tote Swingers:1&2:£6.20, 2&3:£6.70, 1&3:£2.80 CSF £39.80 TOTE £4.00: £2.10, £5.40; EX 50.80.
Owner Ms M Austerfield **Bred** Patrick Cassidy **Trained** Cowthorpe, N Yorks
■ Stewards' Enquiry : Lee Newman three-day ban: careless riding (Jun 11-13)

FOCUS
A decent conditions sprint but the form of these races is rarely solid. the winner showed slight improvement.

NOTEBOOK
Singeur(IRE) had only 1lb to find with a couple of these at the weights and had suddenly bounced back to winning form on his return from 204 days off at Thirsk a fortnight earlier. He seems to be enjoying himself this year, so much so that he was full of himself beforehand and unshipped his rider going to the start. He did nothing wrong once under way, however, and quickened up nicely from the back of the field to hit the front close to the line. His foot problems seem to be behind him now and he may turn out again at Musselburgh next Saturday, while the Ayr Gold Cup may be a possibility. (op 9-2)
Befortyfour was a smart 3-y-o for Michael Jarvis, but had shown nothing in an abbreviated career including on his debut for this stable last time. However, he ran a blinder under a positive ride here and looked like winning until the prize was snatched from him almost on the line. He still retains plenty of ability judged on this effort, but he wasn't well favoured by the weights so he could have a problem if the handicapper takes this form at face value. (op 8-1)
Liberty Lady(IRE) came in to this chasing a hat-trick after a couple of handicap successes and the form of her latest Lingfield success has worked out extremely well. She ran the first few yards of this race with the blindfold still on, but it didn't seem to affect her and she had every chance to pick up the leader had she been good enough. Official explanation: jockey said filly lowered its head when he tried to remove blindfold causing a delay and being slowly away (op 11-2)
Tax Free(IRE) normally contests better races than this and was well in at the weights. Always up there, he had every chance but couldn't take advantage and has gone two years without a win. (op 11-4 tchd 9-4)
Fitz Flyer(IRE) ran creditably as he had a bit to find on these terms, but is now 0-14 on turf. (op 14-1)
Love Delta(USA) had every chance at the weights having run a blinder to finish runner-up in a hot Goodwood handicap on his reappearance/return to turf seven days earlier, but he was disappointing here and never picked up. Perhaps he bounced. (op 9-4 tchd 5-2)
Burning Thread(IRE) saw plenty of daylight on the outside, but he has now failed to beat a rival in three starts since winning a Sandown Listed event just under a year ago and his penalty meant he was worst in at these weights. (op 28-1)

2490 PRE-ORDER YOUR CHAMPAGNE PICNIC PLATTERS H'CAP 1m 100y
4:55 (4:55) (Class 5) (0-70,67) 4-Y-0+ **£2,914** (£867; £433; £216) **Stalls** Low

Form RPR
0243 **1** **Violent Velocity (IRE)**[8] 2260 8-9-5 **65** .... PaulHanagan 3 75
(John Quinn) *hld up in rr: hdwy 3f out: chsd ldr 2f out: led over 1f out: sn rdn clr: eased towards fin* **2/1**[1]
0-00 **2** 6 **Carlitos Spirit (IRE)**[22] 1857 7-8-12 **61** .... (v) GaryBartley(3) 6 57
(Ian McInnes) *chsd ldr: hdwy to ld 2f out: sn rdn and hdd over 1f out: drvn and one pce fnl f* **7/1**
3033 **3** 3 1/2 **Gordy Bee (USA)**[8] 1978 5-8-6 **55** .... (be) AndrewHeffernan(3) 8 43
(Richard Guest) *led: rdn along 3f out: hdd 2f out and sn one pce* **7/1**
0-16 **4** 2 3/4 **Rowan Lodge (IRE)**[29] 1658 9-9-5 **65** .... (b) TomEaves 5 47
(Ollie Pears) *trckd ldrs: hdwy over 3f out: chsd ldrs 2f out: sn rdn and btn* **11/2**[3]
-562 **5** 1 1/4 **Tilsworth Glenboy**[22] 1867 4-9-7 **67** .... StephenCraine 7 46
(J R Jenkins) *dwlt: hld up towards rr: hdwy on outer wl over 2f out: rdn wl over 1f out: sn wknd* **7/1**
0-56 **6** 9 **Sennockian Storm (USA)**[22] 1859 4-9-3 **63** .... SilvestreDeSousa 1 21
(Mark Johnston) *chsd ldr: pushed along 1/2-way: sn rdn and wknd over 2f out* **3/1**[2]
606- **7** 3 1/4 **No Mean Trick (USA)**[304] 4489 5-9-7 **67** .... MickyFenton 4 18
(Paul Midgley) *in tch on inner: rdn along over 3f out: sn wknd* **20/1**
1m 45.6s (-2.00) **Going Correction** -0.05s/f (Good) **7** Ran SP% **116.0**
Speed ratings (Par 103): **108,102,98,95,94 85,82**
Tote Swingers:1&2:£3.70, 2&3:£6.70, 1&3:£3.70 CSF £17.24 CT £82.73 TOTE £2.80: £2.20, £2.00; EX 18.80.
Owner Mrs S Quinn **Bred** Miss Jill Finegan **Trained** Settrington, N Yorks

FOCUS
An ordinary handicap, but they went a rapid pace thanks to the third horse and that set it up for the winner. He may have been the only one to run his race and this is not form to take too literally.

2491 RACING AGAIN ON 8 JUNE H'CAP 5f
5:30 (5:30) (Class 5) (0-75,77) 4-Y-0+ **£2,914** (£867; £433; £216) **Stalls** Low

Form RPR
3-02 **1** **Verinco**[57] 1073 5-9-2 **75** .... (v) AdamCarter(5) 6 88
(Bryan Smart) *mde all: rdn clr over 1f out: styd on strly* **4/1**[2]
1002 **2** 2 3/4 **Ingleby Star (IRE)**[15] 2048 6-8-12 **69** .... (p) GaryBartley(3) 1 72
(Ian McInnes) *chsd ldrs: hdwy over 2f out: rdn to chse wnr wl over 1f out: sn drvn and no imp fnl f* **8/1**

-031 **3** *hd* **Yurituni**[7] 2303 4-9-6 **77**....................(v) PatrickHills(3) 5 79+
(Eve Johnson Houghton) *dwlt and in rr: swtchd outside and hdwy wl over 1f out: rdn and styd on ins fnl f: nrst fin* **5/1**[3]

164- **4** *2 1/4* **Alis Aquilae (IRE)**[217] 7093 5-9-1 **74**.................... DaleSwift(5) 4 68+
(Tim Etherington) *hld up towards rr: effrt and n.m.r 1/2-way: rdn and nt clr run wl over 1f out: swtchd rt and styd on ent fnl f: nrst fin* **11/4**[1]

0600 **5** *2* **Divertimenti (IRE)**[29] 1656 7-9-6 **74**....................(b) PaulQuinn 10 61
(Roy Bowring) *sn chsng ldrs: rdn along 2f out: sn drvn and one pce* **33/1**

3200 **6** *nk* **Desert Strike**[5] 2369 5-9-2 **73**....................(p) MartinHarley(3) 9 59
(Alan McCabe) *chsd ldng pair: rdn along 2f out: sn drvn and grad wknd* **9/1**

0664 **7** *1/2* **Ryedane (IRE)**[8] 2250 9-8-11 **65**....................(b) GrahamGibbons 11 49
(Tim Easterby) *hld up: a towards rr* **14/1**

-015 **8** *1 1/2* **Silvanus (IRE)**[11] 2182 6-8-11 **65**.................... MickyFenton 8 44
(Paul Midgley) *t.k.h: in tch: hdwy to chse ldrs 2f out: rdn: n.m.r and edgd rt over 1f out: sn wknd* **20/1**

5256 **9** *4* **Northern Dare (IRE)**[7] 2280 7-9-4 **72**....................(b) PaulHanagan 3 36
(Richard Fahey) *a towards rr* **8/1**

6544 **10** *nse* **Fear Nothing**[18] 1968 4-8-8 **62**....................(b) TomEaves 2 26
(Ian McInnes) *cl up: rdn along 1/2-way: sn wknd* **14/1**

62.70 secs (-0.80) **Going Correction** -0.05s/f (Good) **10** Ran SP% **116.6**
Speed ratings (Par 103): **104,99,99,95,92 92,91,88,82,82**
Tote Swingers:1&2:£6.90, 2&3:£5.20, 1&3:£4.20 CSF £36.10 CT £168.33 TOTE £4.70: £1.40, £2.10, £2.10; EX 26.60.
Owner B Smart **Bred** Mrs M Gutkin **Trained** Hambleton, N Yorks

FOCUS
Unusually for a sprint handicap, the early pace was steady and as a result the winner had a charmed life out in front whilst his rivals got in each others' way. They must have quickened up dramatically in the second half of the contest, however, as the winning time was 0.47 seconds quicker than the conditions event. The winner's effort shouldn't be underestimated.
T/Plt: £342.70 to a £1 stake. Pool £58,580.45. 124.76 winning tickets T/Qpdt: £30.00 to a £1 stake. Pool £3,602.88. 88.80 winning tickets JR

2247 CATTERICK (L-H)
Saturday, May 28

OFFICIAL GOING: Good (good to firm in places; 8.2)
Wind: Fresh, half against Weather: Overcast

2492 BET ON THE TOTEPLACEPOT AT TOTESPORT.COM CLASSIFIED CLAIMING STKS — 1m 3f 214y
1:55 (1:55) (Class 6) 4-Y-0+ **£2,047** (£604; £302) **Stalls** Low

Form RPR

3030 **1** **Visions Of Johanna (USA)**[9] 2213 6-8-1 66.................... FrannyNorton 5 56
(Ian Williams) *t.k.h: hld up in tch: hdwy over 2f out: drvn to ld 1f out: styd on wl* **5/4**[1]

0306 **2** *1 1/4* **Viewing**[8] 2251 4-9-4 70.................... JamesSullivan(3) 4 74
(James Given) *sn trcking ldr: led gng wl over 2f out: rdn and hdd 1f out: kpt on same pce ins fnl f* **11/1**

00-5 **3** *4 1/2* **Folk Tune (IRE)**[28] 1156 8-8-8 70.................... DeclanCannon(3) 6 57
(John Quinn) *hld up: hdwy 2f out: rdn and no imp fnl f* **9/2**[3]

0-06 **4** *10* **Dimashq**[31] 1617 9-8-1 43.................... KellyHarrison 3 31
(Paul Midgley) *hld up: drvn over 2f out: sme late hdwy: nvr on terms* **20/1**

54-0 **5** *5* **River Ardeche**[12] 2159 6-8-1 69.................... PatrickDonaghy(3) 2 26
(Ben Haslam) *led: rdn and hdd over 2f out: wknd over 1f out* **5/2**[2]

005- **6** *12* **Binglybonglyboo**[293] 4866 5-8-5 57.................... DuranFentiman 8 8
(Lawrence Mullaney) *prom tl rdn and wknd fr 3f out* **20/1**

000/ **7** *17* **Reel Bluff**[566] 6488 5-8-1 42.................... PaulQuinn 1 —
(Noel Wilson) *t.k.h early: trckd ldrs tl rdn and wknd wl over 2f out* **100/1**

0-00 **8** *7* **Always Dixie (IRE)**[33] 1556 4-7-8 37....................(p) NoelGarbutt(7) 7 —
(Andrew Crook) *in tch: struggling over 3f out: sn btn* **66/1**

2m 38.62s (-0.28) **Going Correction** +0.025s/f (Good) **8** Ran SP% **111.5**
Speed ratings (Par 101): **101,100,97,90,87 70,67,63**
toteswingers:1&2:£6.00, 1&3:£1.10, 2&3:£41.10 CSF £15.15 TOTE £2.40: £1.10, £3.10, £1.20; EX 17.70.Visions of Johanna was claimed by R. C. Guest for £5,000.
Owner Dr Marwan Koukash **Bred** David S Milch **Trained** Portway, Worcs

FOCUS
A muddling claimer and the winner didn't need to match his best.

2493 BET TOTEPOOL AT TOTESPORT.COM MEDIAN AUCTION MAIDEN STKS — 5f
2:30 (2:34) (Class 6) 3-Y-0 **£2,183** (£644; £322) **Stalls** Low

Form RPR

1 **Diamond Blue** 3-8-12 0.................... PaulQuinn 5 68+
(Richard Whitaker) *prom: effrt and chsd ldr over 1f out: styd on to ld towards fin* **6/1**

030 **2** *1 1/4* **Take Root**[16] 2032 3-9-0 60.................... PaulPickard(3) 1 68
(Reg Hollinshead) *led: rdn 2f out: hdd and no ex towards fin* **10/1**

026 **3** *2 1/4* **Mecca's Team**[24] 1813 3-8-12 60.................... FrederikTylicki 6 55
(Michael Dods) *chsd ldr: drvn 1/2-way: kpt on same pce fnl f* **11/4**[1]

2 **4** *1/2* **Triviality (IRE)**[24] 1813 3-9-3 0.................... FrannyNorton 11 58+
(Jamie Osborne) *sn pushed along towards rr on outside: hdwy over 1f out: styd on fnl f: nrst fin* **7/2**[2]

504- **5** *nk* **Wandering Lad**[231] 6740 3-9-3 62.................... PJMcDonald 9 57
(Paul Midgley) *hld up: hdwy over 1f out: edgd lft and kpt on same pce fnl f* **10/1**

-430 **6** *7* **Majestic Millie (IRE)**[33] 1561 3-8-12 46.................... DanielTudhope 3 27
(David O'Meara) *midfield: drvn and outpcd 1/2-way: n.d after* **20/1**

222- **7** *1/2* **Norton Girl**[162] 7910 3-8-9 63.................... MichaelO'Connell(3) 8 25
(Michael Herrington) *midfield: drvn along 1/2-way: btn over 1f out* **9/2**[3]

8 *7* **Donnywardsbird** 3-9-3 0.................... DuranFentiman 10 —
(Eric Alston) *bhd and sn outpcd: no imp whn edgd lft over 1f out* **66/1**

60 **9** *1/2* **Ollianna (IRE)**[12] 2151 3-8-12 0.................... TomMcLaughlin 2 —
(Tom Dascombe) *chsd ldrs to 1/2-way: sn rdn and wknd* **10/1**

500- **10** *7* **Furiosa (IRE)**[234] 6666 3-8-9 47....................(t) MatthewDavies(3) 7 —
(Edward Creighton) *in tch: rdn 1/2-way: sn wknd* **100/1**

0 **11** *3* **Right Credentials**[50] 1217 3-8-12 0.................... RoystonFfrench 4 —
(Bruce Hellier) *walked to post: a outpcd in rr* **125/1**

60.23 secs (0.43) **Going Correction** +0.025s/f (Good) **11** Ran SP% **116.7**
Speed ratings (Par 97): **97,95,91,90,90 78,78,66,66,54 50**
toteswingers:1&2:£20.80, 1&3:£4.20, 2&3:£10.30 CSF £62.58 TOTE £7.10: £2.70, £3.80, £1.60; EX 57.40.
Owner Mrs Jane Newett **Bred** Hellwood Stud Farm **Trained** Scarcroft, W Yorks

FOCUS
An ordinary sprint maiden, the emphasis firmly on speed over this sharp track, very few having the pace to get in a serious blow. The winner is probably a bit better than the bare form.

2494 BET ON LIVE CRICKET AT TOTESPORT.COM H'CAP — 7f
3:00 (3:04) (Class 5) (0-75,75) 4-Y-0+ **£2,388** (£705; £352) **Stalls** Centre

Form RPR

0302 **1** **Not My Choice (IRE)**[7] 2286 6-9-6 **74**....................(t) PJMcDonald 5 84
(David C Griffiths) *mde all: rdn and hrd pressed fnl 2f: hld on wl u.p* **4/1**[1]

00-4 **2** *1* **Timeless Elegance (IRE)**[49] 1239 4-9-0 **68**.................... FrederikTylicki 12 75
(Howard Johnson) *cl up: effrt and ev ch fr 2f out: kpt on same pce wl ins fnl f* **5/1**[3]

3-52 **3** *2 1/4* **Lord Of The Dance (IRE)**[8] 2270 5-9-4 **72**.................... TomMcLaughlin 8 73
(Mark Brisbourne) *hld up in tch: effrt over 2f out: edgd lft and kpt on fnl f* **5/1**[3]

200 **4** *1/2* **Frognal (IRE)**[7] 2280 5-9-3 **74**....................(b) JamesSullivan(3) 3 74
(Ruth Carr) *hld up: stdy hdwy on outside over 2f out: rdn over 1f out: kpt on same pce fnl f* **8/1**

-050 **5** *1 1/4* **Ghost (IRE)**[19] 1942 4-9-4 **75**.................... MichaelO'Connell(3) 4 71
(David Nicholls) *hld up: drvn over 2f out: styd on fnl f: nrst fin* **14/1**

0-05 **6** *1/2* **Jupiter Fidius**[5] 2348 4-8-8 **62**....................(p) KellyHarrison 13 57
(Kate Walton) *bhd: drvn over 3f out: hdwy on outside fr over 1f out: nrst fin* **16/1**

002 **7** *nse* **Prince Of Vasa (IRE)**[19] 1943 4-9-7 **75**.................... DuranFentiman 11 70
(Michael Smith) *trckd ldrs: drvn 3f out: no ex over 1f out* **22/1**

513- **8** *4* **Ginger Grey (IRE)**[185] 7554 4-9-5 **73**.................... DanielTudhope 7 57
(David O'Meara) *hld up: rdn over 2f out: nvr rchd ldrs* **9/2**[2]

0010 **9** *3 1/2* **No Quarter (IRE)**[15] 2057 4-8-7 **61** oh1.................... FrannyNorton 2 36
(Tracy Waggott) *midfield: drvn along 1/2-way: wknd fnl 2f* **11/1**

-000 **10** *6* **Chambers (IRE)**[5] 2354 5-8-4 **61** oh4.................... DeclanCannon(3) 1 19
(Eric Alston) *sn drvn along and prom: struggling over 2f out: sn btn* **16/1**

560- **11** *6* **Nufoudh (IRE)**[244] 6394 7-9-1 **69**.................... PatrickMathers 6 11
(Colin Teague) *midfield: drvn and outpcd 1/2-way: n.d after* **40/1**

1320 **12** *10* **Alpha Tauri (USA)**[14] 2095 5-9-1 **72**....................(t) RobertLButler(3) 9 —
(Richard Guest) *cl up tl rdn and wknd over 2f out* **20/1**

1m 26.74s (-0.26) **Going Correction** +0.025s/f (Good) **12** Ran SP% **120.9**
Speed ratings (Par 103): **102,100,98,97,96 95,95,91,87,80 73,61**
toteswingers:1&2:£2.80, 1&3:£5.80, 2&3:£3.90 CSF £23.66 CT £106.34 TOTE £3.80: £1.10, £3.20, £1.40; EX 33.70.
Owner D Griffiths **Bred** Alan Dargan **Trained** Bawtry, S Yorks
■ Stewards' Enquiry : P J McDonald caution: careless riding.

FOCUS
A fair handicap and another race at this sharp course in which it paid to race handily, the front two in front rank throughout, very few threatening to land a serious blow. The form is rated around the third.
Ghost(IRE) Official explanation: jockey said gelding was denied a clear run

2495 MORE LIVE FOOTBALL BETTING AT TOTESPORT.COM H'CAP — 7f
3:30 (3:31) (Class 3) (0-90,92) 4-Y-0+ **£7,771** (£2,312; £1,155; £577) **Stalls** Centre

Form RPR

4340 **1** **Majuro (IRE)**[14] 2095 7-8-9 **81**....................(t) RobertLButler(3) 15 89
(Richard Guest) *hld up in midfield on outside: hdwy over 1f out: styd on to ld cl home* **16/1**

-502 **2** *nk* **Advanced**[14] 2116 8-9-3 **89**....................(p) AmyRyan(3) 1 96
(Kevin Ryan) *chsd ldrs: rdn to ld over 1f out: kpt on fnl f: hdd cl home* **7/2**[1]

0000 **3** *1* **Collateral Damage (IRE)**[13] 2123 8-8-13 **82**....................(t) KellyHarrison 10 86+
(Tim Easterby) *hld up: hdwy on outside 2f out: kpt on wl fnl f: nrst fin* **28/1**

-000 **4** *2* **Layla's Hero (IRE)**[9] 2217 4-8-12 **84**.................... MichaelO'Connell(3) 8 83
(David Nicholls) *hld up: hdwy 2f out: kpt on same pce wl ins fnl f* **12/1**

-003 **5** *1 3/4* **Sir George (IRE)**[14] 2112 6-8-13 **85**.................... MatthewDavies(3) 2 79
(Ollie Pears) *hld up in midfield on ins: hmpd over 4f out: effrt and hdwy over 2f out: no imp fnl f* **6/1**[3]

-330 **6** *nse* **Malcheek (IRE)**[22] 1854 9-8-13 **82**.................... DuranFentiman 14 76
(Tim Easterby) *mde most to over 1f out: wknd ins fnl f* **14/1**

0-00 **7** *1/2* **Gap Princess (IRE)**[13] 2122 7-9-3 **86**.................... DanielTudhope 4 79+
(Geoffrey Harker) *hld up: rdn over 3f out: styd on fnl f: no imp* **25/1**

4311 **8** *3/4* **Imperial Djay (IRE)**[22] 1854 6-9-7 **90**.................... PJMcDonald 6 81
(Ruth Carr) *hld up: pushed along and shortlived effrt 2f out: btn fnl f* **9/2**[2]

10-6 **9** *1* **Jeannie Galloway (IRE)**[69] 923 4-8-12 **86**.................... LeeTopliss(5) 13 74
(Richard Fahey) *prom: effrt and rdn over 2f out: one pce over 1f out: hld whn n.m.r ins fnl f* **8/1**

0033 **10** *2* **Camerooney**[14] 2105 8-9-1 **87**....................(p) PaulPickard(3) 5 70
(Brian Ellison) *w ldr to 1/2-way: sn drvn: edgd lft and wknd over 1f out* **15/2**

-006 **11** *1 1/4* **Glenridding**[7] 2300 7-8-13 **82**....................(p) FrederikTylicki 12 61
(James Given) *prom: rdn over 3f out: wknd fr 2f out* **33/1**

-000 **12** *1/2* **Al Muheer (IRE)**[21] 1885 6-9-0 **86**....................(p) JamesSullivan(3) 11 64
(Ruth Carr) *s.i.s: bhd: struggling 1/2-way: nvr on terms* **8/1**

1m 25.78s (-1.22) **Going Correction** +0.025s/f (Good) **12** Ran SP% **119.2**
Speed ratings (Par 107): **107,106,105,103,101 101,100,99,98,96 94,94**
toteswingers:1&2:£26.70, 1&3:£62.80, 2&3:£5.80 CSF £70.49 CT £1622.07 TOTE £20.00: £6.90, £1.80, £5.10; EX 92.60.
Owner Willie McKay **Bred** Tally-Ho Stud **Trained** Stainforth, S Yorks

FOCUS
A useful contest. There were a few confirmed front-runners and it was run at a strong pace. The winner rates close to his AW level.

NOTEBOOK
Majuro(IRE) found things happening a bit quick for him over 6f at Doncaster last time but had been going well before that and got back to winning ways returned to further, leading late. His trainer is having a fine year and there's no reason why this one won't give another good account next time. Official explanation: trainer's rep said, regarding apparent improvement in form, that the gelding was suited by the step back in trip to 7f. (tchd 14-1)
Advanced has been sparked back to life by the cheekpieces, backing up his good effort at Thirsk a fortnight ago. He should be thereabouts again next time if the headgear continues to have a positive effect. (op 4-1)
Collateral Damage(IRE) shaped a lot better than previously this term, particularly as 7f round here would be sharp enough for him, keeping on strongly from off the pace. He's now 10lb lower than when gaining the last of his six wins in 2009 and is very much one to bear in mind next time. (tchd 25-1)
Layla's Hero(IRE) had offered little previously this season, so this is clearly very much a step back in the right direction. He's another who's potentially very well treated if building on this. (op 14-1)
Sir George(IRE)'s last two efforts show he's back in decent heart, but he possibly needs to come down a little further in the weights, still 3lb higher than his last winning mark here. (tchd 5-1)
Malcheek(IRE) was better than ever on AW during the winter and continues to leave the impression he has a race in him off his lower turf mark at some point, having to use up plenty of energy to get to the front from a wide stall and paying for it late.

Imperial Djay(IRE) seemed to find a 7lb rise for Thirsk enough to catch him out, not having any obvious excuses on the day. (op 5-1)
Camerooney might have been expected to do better after Newmarket, the cheekpieces possibly not working a second time, though the fact there was plenty of competition for the lead probably didn't help either. (op 7-1 tchd 13-2 in a place)
Al Muheer(IRE) is falling in the weights without giving any indication a return to form is imminent.
Official explanation: trainer said gelding was unsuited by the track (op 10-1 tchd 12-1)

2496 BET ON THE BIG MATCH AT TOTESPORT.COM H'CAP — 1m 7f 177y
4:05 (4:06) (Class 5) (0-70,67) 4-Y-O+ — **£2,266** (£674; £337; £168) **Stalls** Centre

Form — RPR
2-00 **1** **Rosewin (IRE)**[16] 2034 5-9-4 **64**.......... MichaelO'Connell(3) 7 — 78+
(Ollie Pears) *in tch: hdwy to ld over 2f out: sn rdn and edgd lft: kpt on wl to draw clr fnl f* **7/1**
2-10 **2** *8* **Madamlily (IRE)**[49] 1243 5-9-9 **66**.......... FrederikTylicki 8 — 70
(John Quinn) *trckd ldrs: effrt over 2f out: chsd wnr over 1f out: no imp* **3/1**[1]
04-5 **3** *3 1/4* **Dan's Heir**[33] 1556 9-8-6 **52**.......... JamesSullivan(3) 4 — 53
(Wilf Storey) *hld up: rdn 4f out: styd on fnl 2f: nvr able to chal* **8/1**
0204 **4** *1* **Lady Norlela**[38] 1491 5-8-6 **56**.......... ShaneBKelly(7) 1 — 55
(Brian Rothwell) *hld up in tch: rdn 4f out: kpt on same pce fnl 2f* **14/1**
-010 **5** *1 1/2* **Capable Guest (IRE)**[25] 1798 9-9-4 **61**.......... PJMcDonald 9 — 59
(George Moore) *hld up: drvn and outpcd over 4f out: rallied over 1f out: nvr able to chal* **14/1**
435- **6** *shd* **Spiders Star**[342] 3241 8-8-13 **59**.......... PaulPickard(3) 6 — 56
(Simon West) *bhd: drvn and outpcd 1/2-way: plugged on fnl 2f: nvr rchd ldrs* **10/1**
3502 **7** *hd* **Leaving Alone (USA)**[22] 1881 4-8-10 **55**..........(b[1]) PatrickMathers 2 — 52
(Edwin Tuer) *t.k.h: led 4f: chsd ldr: drvn over 3f out: wknd fr 2f out* **10/1**
-661 **8** *4 1/2* **Heart Of Dubai (USA)**[25] 1794 6-8-12 **55**..........(p) KellyHarrison 3 — 47
(Micky Hammond) *t.k.h: cl up: led after 4f: hdd over 2f out: sn btn* **5/1**[3]
2-32 **9** *36* **Motirani**[32] 1596 4-9-8 **67**.......... RoystonFfrench 5 — —
(Lydia Pearce) *trckd ldrs: drvn and lost pl after 6f: lost tch fnl 4f* **9/2**[2]

3m 35.81s (3.81) **Going Correction** +0.025s/f (Good)
WFA 4 from 5yo+ 2lb — **9** Ran SP% **115.0**
Speed ratings (Par 103): **91,87,85,84,84 84,83,81,63**
toteswingers:1&2:£5.20, 1&3:£9.90, 2&3:£6.40 CSF £28.17 CT £172.87 TOTE £10.80: £2.30, £1.50, £2.60; EX 32.30.
Owner Major P H K Steveney **Bred** E A Bourke M R C V S **Trained** Norton, N Yorks

FOCUS
A one-sided handicap, but it was a weak race and the ewide-margin winner is only rated to the best of her previous form.
Heart Of Dubai(USA) Official explanation: jockey said gelding ran too free
Motirani Official explanation: jockey said gelding was unsuited by the track

2497 GET LIVE FOOTBALL STATS AT TOTESPORT.COM H'CAP — 5f 212y
4:40 (4:43) (Class 4) (0-85,83) 4-Y-O+ — **£4,209** (£1,252; £625; £312) **Stalls** Low

Form — RPR
022 **1** **Flowing Cape (IRE)**[8] 2244 6-9-4 **83**.......... PaulPickard(3) 6 — 93
(Reg Hollinshead) *in tch: effrt and hdwy over 1f out: led ins fnl f: kpt on wl* **6/1**[3]
2131 **2** *3/4* **Collect Art (IRE)**[8] 2244 4-8-12 **74**.......... FrederikTylicki 9 — 81+
(Andrew Haynes) *in tch: hdwy on outside and ev ch over 1f out to ins fnl f: kpt on fin* **2/1**[1]
0-03 **3** *shd* **Lost In Paris (IRE)**[14] 2118 5-9-4 **80**.......... DavidAllan 1 — 87
(Tim Easterby) *trckd ldrs: effrt and led over 1f out tl ins fnl f: kpt on* **4/1**[2]
100- **4** *1* **Mango Music**[150] 8005 8-8-9 **76**.......... LeeTopliss(5) 4 — 83+
(Richard Fahey) *s.i.s: hld up: hdwy whn nt clr run over 1f out to ins fnl f: r.o fin* **20/1**
0000 **5** *nk* **Red Cape (FR)**[14] 2095 8-8-10 **75**.......... JamesSullivan(3) 5 — 78
(Ruth Carr) *led: rdn 2f out: hdd over 1f out: kpt on same pce fnl f* **16/1**
-240 **6** *1 1/4* **Fishforcompliments**[14] 2095 7-8-9 **78**.......... LauraBarry(7) 8 — 77
(Richard Fahey) *hld up in midfield: effrt whn nt clr run over 1f out: edgd lft: no imp fnl f* **16/1**
0140 **7** *nk* **Tasmeem (IRE)**[7] 2209 4-9-1 **77**..........(h) FrannyNorton 11 — 75
(David Nicholls) *t.k.h: hld up in midfield: effrt over 1f out: no imp fnl f* **11/1**
2000 **8** *hd* **Solar Spirit (IRE)**[16] 2028 6-8-11 **80**.......... ShaneBKelly(7) 2 — 77
(Tracy Waggott) *trckd ldrs tl rdn and no ex over 1f out* **12/1**
2115 **9** *4* **Best Trip (IRE)**[38] 1476 4-8-12 **77**.......... RobertLButler(3) 7 — 61
(Richard Guest) *cl up tl rdn and wknd over 1f out* **11/1**
4-10 **10** *3 1/4* **Bandstand**[42] 1395 5-9-1 **77**.......... RoystonFfrench 10 — 51
(Bryan Smart) *s.i.s: bhd and outpcd: nvr on terms* **25/1**
-030 **11** *5* **Diamond Johnny G (USA)**[22] 1864 4-8-10 **72** ow1(t) TomMcLaughlin 3 — 30
(Edward Creighton) *slowly away: a outpcd* **22/1**

1m 12.95s (-0.65) **Going Correction** +0.025s/f (Good) — **11** Ran SP% **116.7**
Speed ratings (Par 105): **105,104,103,102,102 100,100,99,94,90 83**
toteswingers:1&2:£3.90, 1&3:£4.30, 2&3:£3.30 CSF £17.63 CT £55.45 TOTE £6.40: £1.80, £1.50, £2.00; EX 13.70.
Owner John L Marriott **Bred** David Maher **Trained** Upper Longdon, Staffs

FOCUS
A fair sprint run in a good time. The form looks pretty solid
Fishforcompliments Official explanation: jockey said gelding was denied a clear run

2498 PLAY POKER AT TSPOKER.COM MEDIAN AUCTION MAIDEN FILLIES' STKS — 5f 212y
5:15 (5:17) (Class 6) 3-4-Y-O — **£2,183** (£644; £322) **Stalls** Low

Form — RPR
1 **Midnight Dynamo** 4-9-7 0.......... DanielTudhope 7 — 62+
(Jim Goldie) *hld up: hdwy on outside over 2f out: led ins fnl f: edgd lft and kpt on: eased cl home* **16/1**
0-34 **2** *1 1/4* **Stilettoesinthemud (IRE)**[8] 2252 3-8-9 59.......... JamesSullivan(3) 2 — 56
(James Given) *trckd ldrs: effrt over 2f out: kpt on ins fnl f: nt pce of wnr* **7/2**[3]
26-4 **3** *3/4* **Tilliemint (IRE)**[39] 1459 3-8-12 70.......... DavidAllan 10 — 54
(Tim Easterby) *led: drvn over 2f out: hdd ins fnl f: kpt on same pce* **7/4**[1]
2- **4** *nk* **Arrivaderci**[199] 7392 3-8-9 0.......... AmyRyan(3) 3 — 53+
(Richard Whitaker) *prom: effrt over 2f out: kpt on same pce ins fnl f* **15/8**[2]
0- **5** *3/4* **Let's Face Facts**[210] 7244 4-9-2 0.......... LMcNiff(5) 4 — 53
(Jim Goldie) *s.i.s: outpcd tl hdwy over 1f out: kpt on wl fnl f: nvr nr ldrs* **33/1**
500 **6** *2* **Ellielusive (IRE)**[18] 1985 4-9-7 49.......... TomMcLaughlin 11 — 46
(Mark Brisbourne) *towards rr: rdn 1/2-way: hdwy over 1f out: nrst fin* **66/1**
-006 **7** *3 1/2* **Bygones For Coins (IRE)**[7] 2281 3-8-12 50.......... FrannyNorton 8 — 33
(Alan Berry) *t.k.h: cl up: ev ch and rdn over 2f out: wknd ent fnl f* **40/1**
605- **8** *6* **Bon Appetit**[183] 7576 3-8-12 58.......... KellyHarrison 12 — 14
(Micky Hammond) *cl up on outside tl rdn and wknd over 1f out* **14/1**
9 *1 3/4* **Miss Emily (IRE)** 3-8-12 0.......... PJMcDonald 9 — —
(George Moore) *sn bhd and drvn along: no ch fr 1/2-way* **16/1**
0060 **10** *5* **Areeg (IRE)**[15] 2047 4-9-0 41.......... VictorSantos(7) 6 — —
(Alan Berry) *s.v.s and wl bhd: nvr on terms* **150/1**

1m 14.91s (1.31) **Going Correction** +0.025s/f (Good)
WFA 3 from 4yo 9lb — **10** Ran SP% **119.3**
Speed ratings (Par 98): **92,90,89,88,87 85,80,72,70,63**
toteswingers:1&2:£7.60, 1&3:£4.40, 2&3:£1.70 CSF £72.61 TOTE £13.10: £3.80, £3.00, £1.20; EX 106.70.
Owner Lorimer Racing **Bred** E W Hyslop **Trained** Uplawmoor, E Renfrews
■ Stewards' Enquiry : James Sullivan two-day ban: careless riding (Jun 11-12)

FOCUS
Clearly a weak maiden but a fair start from the winner. The form is rated around the second.
T/Plt: £25.10 to a £1 stake. Pool:£51,252.53 - 1,487.98 winning tickets T/Qpdt: £16.90 to a £1 stake. Pool:£3,271.51 - 142.90 winning tickets RY

2454 HAYDOCK (L-H)
Saturday, May 28

OFFICIAL GOING: 5f & 6f (inner home straight) - good to firm (firm in places; 8.0); 7f & further (outer home straight) - good to firm (good in home straight; 7.8)
5f and 6f races run on new inner home straight. Other races run on outer home straight and races on round course increased by 27yds.
Wind: Moderate, against Weather: Cloudy

2499 BET AT BLUESQ.COM STKS (H'CAP) — 2m 45y
2:05 (2:05) (Class 3) (0-95,95) 4-Y-O+ — **£8,418** (£2,505; £1,251; £625) **Stalls** Low

Form — RPR
511- **1** **Activate**[254] 6131 4-9-4 **91**.......... JamieSpencer 9 — 101+
(Michael Bell) *hld up: hdwy over 2f out: led under 2f out: styd on for press fnl f: a doing enough towards fin* **9/4**[1]
04 **2** *1/2* **Kayef (GER)**[22] 1847 4-8-3 **83**.......... DavidKenny(7) 6 — 92
(Michael Scudamore) *hld up in rr: rdn and hdwy on outer over 2f out: chsd wnr over 1f out: chalng ins fnl f: clsd towards fin but a looked hld* **12/1**
11- **3** *1 1/2* **Ocean Transit (IRE)**[21] 7307 6-8-6 **77**.......... LukeMorris 11 — 84
(Richard Price) *trckd ldrs: rdn and nt clr run over 2f out: styd on ins fnl f: no imp on front 2 towards fin* **9/1**
0-64 **4** *1 1/4* **Deauville Flyer**[15] 2071 5-9-8 **93**.......... RobertWinston 7 — 100+
(Tim Easterby) *midfield: pushed along 3f out: n.m.r and hmpd twice over 2f out: swtchd rt over 1f out: styd on u.p ins fnl f: unable to rch ldrs* **11/2**[3]
131- **5** *1/2* **Ashbrittle**[218] 7061 4-9-5 **92**.......... JimCrowley 4 — 97
(Ralph Beckett) *trckd ldrs: led 3f out: rdn and hdd under 2f out: no ex fnl 100yds* **5/1**[2]
30-0 **6** *3/4* **Swingkeel (IRE)**[24] 1808 6-9-10 **95**..........(p) TedDurcan 5 — 100+
(John Dunlop) *hld up: pushed along over 3f out: nt clr run over 2f out and over 1f out: sn swtchd rt: kpt on ins fnl f: nvr able to chal* **11/1**
0-00 **7** *2 3/4* **My Arch**[22] 1847 9-9-1 **86**.......... TomQueally 13 — 87
(Ollie Pears) *prom: rdn 3f out: btn 2f out* **14/1**
15-0 **8** *12* **Herostatus**[14] 2107 4-9-4 **91**..........(b) GregFairley 10 — 77
(Mark Johnston) *missed break: hld up in midfield: hdwy to chse ldrs 6f out: rdn 3f out: wknd over 1f out* **25/1**
0-10 **9** *4* **Battleoftrafalgar**[28] 1679 4-8-12 **85**..........(b) NeilCallan 12 — 67
(Michael Attwater) *led: hdd 3f out: sn u.p: wknd over 1f out* **40/1**
13-6 **P** **Colloquial**[27] 1729 10-9-5 **90**..........(v) FergusSweeney 1 — —
(Henry Candy) *trckd ldrs: niggled along and lost pl 1/2-way: t.o whn p.u 6f out* **15/2**

3m 36.86s (0.86) **Going Correction** +0.05s/f (Good)
WFA 4 from 5yo+ 2lb — **10** Ran SP% **113.6**
Speed ratings (Par 107): **99,98,98,97,97 96,95,89,87,—**
toteswingers:1&2:£9.10, 1&3:£7.20, 2&3:£18.10 CSF £30.56 CT £203.57 TOTE £2.80: £1.70, £4.10, £2.40; EX 28.70 Trifecta £165.50 Pool £950.66 - 4.25 winning units..
Owner Highclere Thoroughbred Racing Tudor Min **Bred** Card Bloodstock **Trained** Newmarket, Suffolk

FOCUS
With just 3mm of rain in the morning the going description remained unchanged. A good staying handicap but the field was cut by a third due to withdrawals. It was well run and the first two came from the back. The third helps with the form.

NOTEBOOK
Activate ◆ was a progressive sort last year and came into this unbeaten in two runs at around 1m6f. Racing off 6lb higher than for the second of those successes, he was sent off a well-backed favourite. He was able to make his move down the outside, missed all the scrimmaging halfway up the straight and, although he idled once in front, he never looked like getting beaten. He will head for the Northumberland Plate next, and is sure to be popular for that. (tchd 5-2 in places)
Kayef(GER), an ex-French Flat winner, had won over hurdles in February and ran well enough over 2m on fast ground last time. Held up at the back with the winner, he followed that rival through and gave him a race without ever looking likely to get past. He is another who is going the right way. (tchd 11-1)
Ocean Transit(IRE) is better known as a hurdler (Group 2 placed at Cheltenham in March) but had won twice over 1m2f on the Flat in the autumn. Having her first try at this trip on the Flat and 5lb above her last winning mark, she was involved in the barging around 2f out but stuck to her guns and stayed on nicely for the minor placing. She can pick up a race before her summer break. (op 10-1)
Deauville Flyer ◆ was the unlucky horse in the race, but was held up but had nowhere to go from around 3f out to over a furlong out and was buffeted as a result of My Arch drifting left under pressure. He did well to stay on for fourth and can be rated batter than his final placing. He is best on a flat track and presumably connections will look for compensation back here or at somewhere such as York, although he could take on the winner again at Newcastle. (op 6-1)
Ashbrittle, lightly raced and untried at this trip, having won on his only try at 1m6f was 4lb higher. He wore a visor when last winning but it was left off here, although it did not appear to affect his performance as he just seemed to get tired. (tchd 11-2)
Swingkeel(IRE) whose last win was over hurdles for Nigel Twiston-Davies, had returned to his original trainer since running in the Chester Cup. Still 5lb above his last winning mark, he was trapped on the inside when the scrimmaging occurred before staying on once in the clear. He finished third in the Queen Alexandra at Royal Ascot last season and another crack at that race looks on the cards now. Official explanation: jockey said gelding was denied a clear run (op 12-1)
My Arch, a versatile sort who stays well and is effective at this trip, was up with the pace from the start but the ground was faster than ideal and he wandered under pressure in the straight, exacerbating the trouble on his inside.
Battleoftrafalgar Official explanation: jockey said colt hung left

Colloquial was bidding to win for the second time, having scored back in 2007 but he dropped out quickly around halfway and was eased down as if something was amiss. It was subsequently reported he was distressed. Official explanation: vet said gelding was distressed (op 8-1)

2500 BLUE SQUARE SANDY LANE STKS (LISTED RACE) 6f
2:35 (2:36) (Class 1) 3-Y-O

£17,031 (£6,456; £3,231; £1,611; £807; £405) **Stalls** Centre

Form RPR

-403 **1** **Show Rainbow**[7] 2298 3-8-9 98 .... JamieSpencer 8 96
(Mick Channon) *a.p: rdn to ld over 1f out: r.o for press ins fnl f: all out at fin* **5/2**[1]

21-6 **2** *hd* **March On Beetroot**[14] 2106 3-9-0 85 .... JimCrowley 5 100+
(Robert Cowell) *hld up: rdn and hdwy over 1f out: hung lft whn running on ins fnl f: clsd fin: jst failed* **12/1**

1-64 **3** *nk* **Sweet Cecily (IRE)**[15] 2054 3-8-12 98 .... RyanMoore 6 97
(Richard Hannon) *led narrowly: hdd over 3f out: rdn and nt qckn over 1f out: r.o to chal strly ins fnl f: hld fnl stride* **5/1**[3]

1-50 **4** *½* **Ladies Are Forever**[17] 2005 3-8-12 100 .... TomQueally 4 96
(Geoffrey Oldroyd) *hld up: hdwy over 2f out: rdn to chal fr over 1f out: nt qckn cl home* **5/2**[1]

600- **5** *4* **Oor Jock (IRE)**[215] 7135 3-9-0 95 .... TedDurcan 7 85
(Tracey Collins, Ire) *in tch: rdn over 1f out: one pce fnl f* **25/1**

06-6 **6** *¾* **Murbeh (IRE)**[31] 1602 3-9-0 95 .... TadhgO'Shea 1 83
(Brian Meehan) *w ldrs: led over 3f out: rdn and hdd over 1f out: wknd fnl 100yds* **9/2**[2]

00-5 **7** *9* **Belle Bayardo (IRE)**[34] 1545 3-9-0 89 .... DavidProbert 2 54
(Ronald Harris) *in tch: rdn over 2f out: sn wknd* **80/1**

60-0 **8** *3* **Marine Commando**[31] 1602 3-9-3 99 .... TonyHamilton 3 47
(Richard Fahey) *racd keenly: w ldr tl rdn over 2f out: wknd over 1f out* **14/1**

1m 13.88s (0.08) **Going Correction** 0.0s/f (Good) **8 Ran SP% 111.4**
Speed ratings (Par 107): **97,96,96,95,90 89,77,73**
toteswingers:1&2:£3.70, 1&3:£2.80, 2&3:£10.80 CSF £33.17 TOTE £3.20: £1.20, £3.10, £1.80; EX 29.30 Trifecta £134.50 Pool £1,014.88 - 5.58 winning units..
Owner Jaber Abdullah **Bred** Follow The Flag Partnership **Trained** West Ilsley, Berks

FOCUS
Not the strongest Listed race with the highest-rated runner having a mark of just 100, and sub-par form for the grade. The key to this race was the Nell Gwyn Stakes.

NOTEBOOK
Show Rainbow finished fourth in the Nell Gwyn with today's fourth and third within a length and a half of her and she confirmed that form. She had run well dropped back in trip at this track last time and, ridden with more patience, got the better of a good battle with her old rivals before holding off the strong-finishing runner-up. (op 11-4 tchd 9-4)
March On Beetroot ◆, who won a Polytrack maiden over 7f before running well in a Listed race, was dropped in trip but put up a fine effort, finishing well from the back of the field and only just failing to get there. He looks progressive and might be interesting in something like the Jersey Stakes if sent to Royal Ascot. (op 8-1)
Sweet Cecily(IRE), a dual winner at 6f including at Listed level, finished closer to the winner than she had at Newmarket and put up a brave effort, fighting back after making the running until around halfway. (op 11-2, tchd 6-1 in places)
Ladies Are Forever, the highest rated in the field having won valuable Totepool Two-Year-Old Trophy, probably did not get home in the Nell Gwyn and was out of her depth against older sprinters in the Duke of York. She came to have her chance on the outside of the pack but could not quite sustain her run, but still ran to the pound with the winner compared with Newmarket. (op 11-4, tchd 3-1 in places)
Oor Jock(IRE) had useful juvenile form for Dermot Weld but was having his first run for a new trainer. He moved up to challenge 2f out but faded soon afterwards. (tchd 20-1)
Murbeh(IRE) won his first two starts over 6f but had been held subsequently in better company. He had to prove he was up to this on this seasonal debut but, after leading around halfway, he was beaten off before the final furlong and a drop in class looks likely now. (op 6-1)

2501 E B F NEW APPROACH GROSVENOR CASINOS PINNACLE STKS (LISTED RACE) (F&M) 1m 3f 200y
3:05 (3:06) (Class 1) 4-Y-O+

£17,031 (£6,456; £3,231; £1,611; £807; £405) **Stalls** Centre

Form RPR

112- **1** **Ferdoos**[246] 6320 4-8-12 106 .... NeilCallan 9 118+
(Roger Varian) *trckd ldrs: wnt 2nd over 2f out: rdn over 1f out: chalng whn jinked rt ins fnl f: r.o gamely to ld towards fin* **4/1**[3]

11-1 **2** *nk* **Vita Nova (IRE)**[15] 2066 4-8-12 100 .... TomQueally 1 117+
(Sir Henry Cecil) *led: rdn over 2f out: edgd rt u.p whn pressed ins fnl f: worn down towards fin* **15/8**[1]

430- **3** *4 ½* **Meeznah (USA)**[224] 6928 4-8-12 111 .... TedDurcan 4 110
(David Lanigan) *chsd ldrs: pushed along 3f out: outpcd by front 2 over 1f out: kpt on but no ch ins fnl f* **8/1**

/10- **4** *2 ¾* **Crystal Capella**[167] 7851 6-9-5 115 .... RyanMoore 7 112
(Sir Michael Stoute) *hld up: hdwy on outer over 2f out: chsd ldrs over 1f out: no imp: one pce fnl f* **9/4**[2]

2-33 **5** *1 ¾* **Pink Symphony**[28] 1677 4-8-12 101 .... JamieSpencer 8 103
(Paul Cole) *hld up in rr: rdn over 2f out: mod prog ins fnl f: nvr able to trble ldrs* **20/1**

102- **6** *3 ¼* **Pipette**[374] 2224 4-8-12 100 .... LiamKeniry 2 97
(Andrew Balding) *hld up: rdn over 1f out: no imp* **20/1**

200- **7** *nk* **Shimmering Surf (IRE)**[246] 6320 4-8-12 101 .... LukeMorris 6 97
(Peter Winkworth) *chsd ldr: pushed along over 3f out: lost 2nd over 2f out: wknd wl over 1f out* **33/1**

150- **8** *17* **Never Forget (FR)**[258] 6013 4-8-12 110 .... KirstyMilczarek 3 70
(Luca Cumani) *racd keenly: in tch: wknd u.p 2f out* **25/1**

2m 32.2s (-1.80) **Going Correction** +0.05s/f (Good) **8 Ran SP% 113.0**
Speed ratings (Par 111): **108,107,104,102,101 99,99,88**
toteswingers:1&2:£1.30, 1&3:£6.30, 2&3:£3.90 CSF £11.16 TOTE £5.40: £1.50, £1.40, £1.90; EX 14.00 Trifecta £105.00 Pool £1,406.98 - 9.91 winning units..
Owner Sheikh Ahmed Al Maktoum **Bred** Miss A Shaykhutdinova **Trained** Newmarket, Suffolk

FOCUS
A strong renewal of this fillies' Listed race with all the field rated 100 or above and three of the runners rated 110 or more. It was fought out by two lightly raced but unexposed fillies and the form is above-average for the grade.

NOTEBOOK
Ferdoos ◆ was narrowly beaten in a Listed race on her last start but stepped up to get the better of another progressive filly, the pair clear. She was never far away and closed down on the leader before ducking to the right inside the last furlong, she had done something similar at Ascot as well. Once straightened out she picked up and got the better of her rival near the line. She clearly is not entirely straightforward, but her trainer believes it is more to do with her still being immature, and she is likely to return here for the Lancashire Oaks, with races such as the Park Hill possible targets later in the season. (op 3-1)
Vita Nova(IRE) ◆, unbeaten in three starts coming into this, made the running and had most of her rivals in trouble over 2f out. She looked as though she might hold on when the winner ducked to the right but was ultimately just run out of it. She looks capable of winning at this level at least. (op 11-4)
Meeznah(USA), finished second in the Oaks last season before subsequently disqualified on a technicality. She had subsequently struggled in good races and the drop in grade helped her run better on this return to action. She has yet to win a Listed or Group race but is likely to have easier tasks at this level.
Crystal Capella has a terrific strike-rate but struggled to get involved from off the pace on this return. She should come on a fair bit for the outing. (op 11-4, tchd 3-1 in places)
Pink Symphony was the first under pressure, but at least stayed on in the last quarter-mile. Official explanation: jockey said filly was unsuited by the good to firm ground (op 16-1)
Pipette, who has been off for over a year since chasing home Snow Fairy at Goodwood, had been given a wind operation but appeared too keen early on this return and could not pick up when asked. She is another who should be better for the run. (op 18-1)
Shimmering Surf(IRE) raced close to the lead but was soon in trouble when the pace lifted. She seems to have lost her way a little and might need to drop into a conditions race to restore her confidence.
Never Forget(FR), a Group 2 winner in France for Elie Lellouche, was rather disappointing on this drop in grade and debut for new connections. (op 20-1)

2502 TIMEFORM JURY STKS (REGISTERED AS THE JOHN OF GAUNT STAKES) (GROUP 3) 7f
3:35 (3:37) (Class 1) 4-Y-O+

£28,385 (£10,760; £5,385; £2,685; £1,345; £675) **Stalls** Low

Form RPR

5-22 **1** **The Cheka (IRE)**[19] 1948 5-9-0 108 .... TomQueally 3 113
(Eve Johnson Houghton) *chsd ldr: led 2f out: rdn over 1f out: r.o wl: a looked in control ins fnl f* **6/1**[3]

4-52 **2** *1 ¼* **Regal Parade**[17] 2005 7-9-0 119 .... AdrianNicholls 4 110
(David Nicholls) *trckd ldrs: rdn and nt qckn over 2f out: styd on for press ins fnl f: nt pce of wnr* **7/4**[1]

0400 **3** *shd* **Doncaster Rover (USA)**[44] 1340 5-9-0 102 .... RobertWinston 8 109
(David Brown) *in tch: effrt over 2f out: styd on u.p ins fnl f but a hld* **33/1**

1-50 **4** *1* **Inler (IRE)**[17] 2005 4-9-0 104 .... JamieSpencer 1 109+
(Brian Meehan) *jockey appeared concerned abt mount during r: hld up in midfield: nt clr run and swtchd rt over 1f out: kpt on ins fnl f: unable to get to ldrs* **12/1**

42-1 **5** *1 ¾* **Beacon Lodge (IRE)**[21] 1889 6-9-0 109 .... AdamKirby 7 102
(Clive Cox) *stdd and swtchd lft s: hld up: pushed along 2f out: hdwy u.p whn swtchd and forced rt over 1f out: one pce ins fnl f* **7/2**[2]

56-5 **6** *1 ½* **High Standing (USA)**[42] 1397 6-9-0 109 .... (b[1]) RyanMoore 6 98+
(William Haggas) *hld up: nt clr run fr 2f out tl over 1f out: no imp and one pce ins fnl f* **9/1**

0-00 **7** *¾* **Himalya (IRE)**[21] 1885 5-9-0 108 .... ShaneKelly 5 96
(Jeremy Noseda) *ponied to s: hld up: swtchd rt over 2f out: effrt on outer sn after but no imp on ldrs: wl btn fnl f* **22/1**

0-22 **8** *2 ¼* **Kakatosi**[7] 2315 4-9-0 104 .... LiamKeniry 2 90
(Andrew Balding) *led: hdd 2f out: rdn and wknd over 1f out* **10/1**

00-0 **9** *13* **Shakespearean (IRE)**[86] 759 4-9-0 116 .... (tp) TedDurcan 10 55
(Saeed Bin Suroor) *prom tl rdn and wknd over 1f out* **12/1**

1m 29.37s (-1.53) **Going Correction** +0.05s/f (Good) **9 Ran SP% 114.6**
Speed ratings (Par 113): **110,108,108,107,105 103,102,100,85**
toteswingers:1&2:£3.90, 1&3:£26.90, 2&3:£75.80 CSF £16.75 TOTE £5.50: £1.50, £1.20, £6.60; EX 19.70 Trifecta £495.00 Pool £2,254.41 - 3.37 winning units..
Owner Anthony Pye-Jeary And Mel Smith **Bred** James Robert Mitchell **Trained** Blewbury, Oxon

FOCUS
Battle-hardened older horses have a good record in this Group 3 and the majority of the runners fitted that category. The pace looked good, but the first two were never far from the pace. The form is not strong for the grade.

NOTEBOOK
The Cheka(IRE) was narrowly beaten on his return and then ran into a big improver in his last start, so he deserved this first Group 3 success. He has overcome a few problems in his time and gelding seems to have improved him. He picked up well to go clear inside the last 2f, a move which won him the race, and he is likely to be aimed at the Prix Maurice de Gheest or the Hungerford Stakes in August. (op 7-1)
Regal Parade, runner-up in the Duke of York last time, ran his usual game race despite the ground probably being a little faster than ideal. He will surely add to his score when the going is slightly slower. (op 15-8, tchd 2-1 in places)
Doncaster Rover(USA) was probably the first to come under pressure but stuck on in typically resolute fashion. This was his best effort since returning from Dubai.
Inler(IRE) was held up early and was going well but got locked away on the rail as the field bunched and by the time he was in the clear the principals had gone beyond recall. He has been beaten in all his starts in Group and Listed level but surely will pick up a race before long. Official explanation: trainer's rep said gelding lost a shoe (op 14-1 tchd 16-1)
Beacon Lodge(IRE) was held up but did not get the best of runs as the field closed up halfway up the straight, so can be given another chance. (op 4-1 tchd 9-2)
High Standing(USA), wearing blinkers for the first time, never made much impression. (op 8-1)
Himalya(IRE), who was ponied to the start but failed to get involved from the rear. (op 20-1)
Kakatosi made the running at what looked a good gallop but paid for it in the straight. (op 11-1 tchd 9-1)
Shakespearean(IRE), wearing cheekpieces for the first time, was the disappointment of the race, being one of the first to come off the bridle and he dropped right out. (op 8-1)

2503 PLAY POKER AT GCASINO.COM H'CAP 7f
4:10 (4:11) (Class 3) (0-95,88) 3-Y-O **£8,418** (£2,505; £1,251; £625) **Stalls** Low

Form RPR

1- **1** **Western Aristocrat (USA)**[211] 7203 3-9-7 **88** .... TomQueally 4 102+
(Jeremy Noseda) *hld up: nt clr run on inner 2f out: hdwy over 1f out: r.o ins fnl f to ld post* **7/4**[1]

0-51 **2** *nse* **Rhythm Of Light**[14] 2102 3-9-7 **88** .... RichardKingscote 9 101+
(Tom Dascombe) *s.i.s: hld up: nt clr run over 2f out: hdwy over 1f out: led ins fnl f: hdd post* **5/1**[3]

015- **3** *2 ¾* **Honeymead (IRE)**[217] 7085 3-9-2 **83** .... TonyHamilton 8 88
(Richard Fahey) *chsd ldrs: rdn to ld over 1f out: hdd ins fnl f: one pce towards fin* **14/1**

22-0 **4** *shd* **El Muqbil (IRE)**[43] 1361 3-9-2 **83** .... (t) ShaneKelly 11 88
(Brian Meehan) *hld up: hdwy on outer over 2f out: chsd ldrs over 1f out: styd on same pce fnl 100yds* **12/1**

10-0 **5** *2 ½* **Barista (IRE)**[7] 2319 3-8-7 **81** .... CharlesBishop(7) 12 79
(Mick Channon) *hld up in rr: kpt on ins fnl f: nvr able to chal* **33/1**

23-0 **6** *hd* **Admirable Spirit**[15] 2054 3-9-5 **86** .... JimCrowley 2 84
(Richard Hannon) *in tch: rdn over 2f out: nt qckn over 1f out: one pce ins fnl f* **66/1**

54-3 **7** ½ **Whaileyy (IRE)**[18] 1983 3-9-2 **83** RyanMoore 6 79
(Sir Michael Stoute) *chsd ldr: led over 2f out: rdn and hdd over 1f out: fdd fnl 100yds* **4/1**[2]

0-00 **8** 2¾ **Shafgaan**[23] 1820 3-9-6 **87** NeilCallan 5 76
(Clive Brittain) *midfield: racd on and off the bridle: lost pl 2f out: bhd fnl f* **25/1**

-002 **9** 1½ **Mutajare (IRE)**[14] 2092 3-9-3 **84** TadhgO'Shea 1 69
(Mark Johnston) *midfield: pushed along and outpcd 2f out: eased whn no imp fnl 100yds* **14/1**

1-00 **10** 2 **First Class Favour (IRE)**[7] 2319 3-9-4 **85** TedDurcan 7 64
(Tim Easterby) *led: hdd over 2f out: rdn and wknd over 1f out* **40/1**

-402 **11** nk **Indian Ballad (IRE)**[15] 2043 3-9-5 **86** AdrianNicholls 3 65
(Ed McMahon) *chsd ldrs: u.p over 2f out: wknd 1f out* **16/1**

30-1 **12** ½ **Layla Jamil (IRE)**[22] 1853 3-8-12 **79** JamieSpencer 10 56+
(Mick Channon) *chsd ldrs: ev ch 2f out: u.p to hold pl whn n.m.r and hmpd over 1f out: sn dropped away: eased ins fnl f* **10/1**

1m 30.72s (-0.18) **Going Correction** +0.05s/f (Good) **12** Ran SP% **119.7**
Speed ratings (Par 103): **103,102,99,99,96 96,96,92,91,88 88,87**
toteswingers:1&2:£3.40, 1&3:£14.10, 2&3:£10.20 CSF £10.02 CT £97.17 TOTE £2.60: £1.30, £2.00, £5.00; EX 19.40.
Owner Tom Ludt **Bred** Grapestock Llc **Trained** Newmarket, Suffolk

FOCUS
A good and competitive handicap although the market suggested it was not as tight as the ratings suggested. It was run 1.35secs slower than the preceding Group 3. The form is rated around the fourth and the winner in particular has more to offer.

NOTEBOOK
Western Aristocrat(USA) ◆ was a well-backed winner on his debut last October and, with the yard striking form, was heavily supported again. He was held up at the back and his rider when for a brave run up the rail. Although short of room at one point, things opened up for him and he got through just after the runner-up and managed to win a good battle on the nod. He looks the sort for a race such as the Britannia Stakes and might make a Pattern performer if going on from this. (tchd 13-8 and 15-8 after early 9-4)
Rhythm Of Light ◆ was quite a taking winner of a fillies' handicap at Newbury and the third in that race had run well the previous day. She was held up and, like the winner, did not get the clearest of runs. She got to the front before her main rival though, battled on gamely and the first impression was that she had won. She looks an improver and one to keep on-side. (op 6-1)
Honeymead(IRE) won a valuable nursery last season and this reappearance showed she had retained much of her ability. She was only beaten by two progressive types and should find opportunities to add to her score before long. (op 20-1)
El Muqbil(IRE), in a first-time tongue tie, ran better than on his return to action and has races in him on this evidence. (op 11-1 tchd 14-1)
Barista(IRE) missed the break and was slightly hampered early before staying on in the straight. Easier ground and a drop in the weights might help him. (op 28-1)
Admirable Spirit, dropping in class, tracked the pace throughout but failed to pick up and a return to 6f looks likely. (op 50-1)
Whaileyy(IRE) chased the leader early on but probably did too much too soon and faded in the latter stages. (op 5-1)
Shafgaan Official explanation: jockey said colt was ducking left and right
Mutajare(IRE) Official explanation: jockey said colt was denied a clear run
Layla Jamil(IRE) tracked the pace and had every chance halfway up the straight but stopped quickly and was eased as though something went amiss. (tchd 9-1)

2504 BRITISH STALLION STUDS E B F BLUE SQUARE MAIDEN STKS 5f
4:45 (4:50) (Class 5) 2-Y-O **£3,238** (£963; £481; £240) **Stalls** Centre

Form RPR

1 **Shumoos (USA)** 2-8-12 0 ShaneKelly 12 97+
(Brian Meehan) *green to post: racd keenly: hld up: hdwy over 2f out: sn swtchd lft to trck ldrs: swtchd rt over 1f out: qcknd to ld ins fnl f: shot clr fnl 100yds: impressive* **17/2**

2 **2** 4½ **Frederick Engels**[15] 2042 2-9-3 0 RobertWinston 10 84
(David Brown) *a.p: led over 2f out: rdn and hung lft fr over 1f out: hdd ins fnl f: outpcd and no ch w wnr fnl 100yds* **4/1**[2]

6 **3** 5 **Farang Kondiew**[28] 1691 2-9-3 0 DavidNolan 3 66
(Declan Carroll) *prom: led over 3f out: hdd over 2f out: rdn and stl chalng over 1f out: one pce fnl 100yds* **7/1**[3]

4 ½ **Pink Sapphire (IRE)** 2-8-12 0 RyanMoore 1 59+
(Richard Hannon) *green to post: prom: chalng over 1f out: rdn ins fnl f: one pce fnl 100yds* **10/11**[1]

5 ¾ **Ladykin (IRE)** 2-8-12 0 TonyHamilton 2 57
(Richard Fahey) *green to post and in r: in tch: outpcd over 1f out: kpt on towards fin* **33/1**

6 ¾ **Cape Moss (IRE)** 2-9-3 0 RichardKingscote 6 59
(Tom Dascombe) *missed break: outpcd and bhd: kpt on fnl f: nvr able to get on terms w ldrs* **14/1**

7 1¾ **Alnair (IRE)** 2-8-12 0 NeilFarley(5) 9 53
(Declan Carroll) *towards rr: nvr able to get on terms* **66/1**

0 **8** 3 **Peters Pursuit (IRE)**[23] 1823 2-8-10 0 GeorgeChaloner(7) 4 42
(Richard Fahey) *a outpcd and bhd* **25/1**

00 **9** ¾ **Stans Deelyte**[23] 1823 2-8-12 0 LukeMorris 8 34
(Lisa Williamson) *led: hdd over 3f out: remained handy: rdn and wknd over 1f out* **100/1**

10 6 **Princess Tamina (IRE)** 2-8-12 0 LiamKeniry 11 12
(Patrick Morris) *in tch: rdn and wknd 2f out* **66/1**

61.18 secs (0.38) **Going Correction** 0.0s/f (Good) **10** Ran SP% **112.8**
Speed ratings (Par 93): **98,90,82,82,80 79,76,72,70,61**
toteswingers:1&2:£3.40, 1&3:£5.60, 2&3:£2.00 CSF £37.83 TOTE £9.70: £2.10, £1.40, £1.90; EX 51.90.
Owner Fawzi Abdulla Nass **Bred** Brushwood Stable **Trained** Manton, Wilts

FOCUS
This has proved an ordinary maiden in recent years but there were several interesting newcomers from major yards taking part and it produced a very taking performance from one of them. Shumoos looks a strong Queen Mary Stakes contender on this evidence. The first two were clear and the time was just 0.38secs slower than the following 3-y-o handicap.

NOTEBOOK
Shumoos(USA) ◆, a $375,000 first foal of an unraced half-sister to Ishiguru and Graded winners in the US, was keen early and her rider was at pains to get cover. She could be seen travelling easily behind the leading trio 2f out and, once switched entering the final furlong, she strode clear in impressive fashion. From a yard whose runners usually improve for the outing, she looks a Queen Mary filly and could prove hard to beat if going there. (op 8-1 tchd 10-1)
Frederick Engels, a half-brother to the useful Colonel Mak, missed the break and but he stuck to the task willingly on his debut. He had just won the battle with the third and fourth when the winner swept by. Time might well prove there was no disgrace, and his trainer, who clearly thinks a lot of the colt, is likely to take him to Royal Ascot next, presumably for the Windsor Castle. (op 5-1 tchd 6-1)
Farang Kondiew, an 11,000gns Selkirk colt, looked to run green on his debut and had clearly come on for that. He showed up throughout and might have run into a couple of above average performers. (op 8-1 tchd 9-1)
Pink Sapphire(IRE), a 110,000 euros half-sister to a mile winner who is related to some speedy performers, was a well-backed favourite on this debut. She was never far away and had every chance, but could not pick up under pressure and looks the sort who will benefit from the experience. (op 6-5 tchd 5-6 and 5-4 in places)
Ladykin(IRE), a 13,000euros first foal who is related to winners at middle-distances and over hurdles, was green going to the post and only began to get the hang of things late on. She will be better for the outing and possibly longer trips in time.
Cape Moss(IRE), a 26,000 euros first foal of a 7f winner by a sprinter, was slowly away on this debut but was noted staying on quite well at the finish. He is another who is likely to be much sharper next time. (op 11-1)

2505 G CASINO H'CAP 5f
5:20 (5:21) (Class 4) (0-85,85) 3-Y-O **£5,180** (£1,541; £770; £384) **Stalls** Centre

Form RPR

00-2 **1** **Apace (IRE)**[15] 2074 3-9-2 **80** RyanMoore 5 91+
(Sir Michael Stoute) *shkn up early: in rr: hdwy and swtchd rt over 1f out: led ins fnl f: r.o* **2/1**[1]

6-10 **2** 1½ **Gottcher**[15] 2074 3-8-10 **74** ShaneKelly 4 79
(David Barron) *trckd ldrs: effrt to chal over 1f out: no imp on wnr fnl 75yds* **4/1**[2]

-5 **3** ½ **Cruise Tothelimit (IRE)**[15] 2043 3-8-9 **73** RichardKingscote 9 76
(Patrick Morris) *a.p: led 2f out: sn rdn: hdd ins fnl f: styd on same pce towards fin* **25/1**

-050 **4** 1 **Berberana (IRE)**[15] 2074 3-9-1 **79** TedDurcan 11 78
(Tim Easterby) *hld up: rdn and hdwy whn carried rt over 1f out: styd on ins fnl f: nt rch ldrs* **22/1**

00-1 **5** 1 **On The High Tops (IRE)**[49] 1241 3-9-4 **82** AndrewMullen 6 78
(Tom Tate) *led: hdd 2f out: rdn and chalng over 1f out: no ex fnl 100yds* **15/2**

0-63 **6** ½ **Cadeaux Pearl**[15] 2067 3-9-7 **85** AdrianNicholls 7 79
(David Nicholls) *trckd ldrs: rdn over 2f out: chalng over 1f out: fdd fnl 100yds* **9/1**

3430 **7** nk **Boundaries**[7] 2319 3-9-5 **83** (v) RobertWinston 8 76
(Tim Easterby) *n.m.r and hmpd early: sn trckd ldrs: rdn and sltly hmpd over 1f out: sn lost pl: swtchd lft ent fnl f: no imp on ldrs after* **7/1**[3]

2-30 **8** ¾ **Millyluvstobouggie**[15] 2074 3-8-10 **74** LukeMorris 2 64
(Clive Cox) *midfield: rdn over 1f out: wknd ins fnl f* **16/1**

3021 **9** ¾ **Sugar Beet**[35] 1521 3-8-12 **76** DavidProbert 1 63
(Ronald Harris) *in rr: rdn and sme hdwy over 1f out: no imp on ldrs: wl btn fnl 75yds* **14/1**

44-3 **10** 3¼ **Major Muscari (IRE)**[29] 1650 3-9-2 **80** TomQueally 10 56
(Geoffrey Oldroyd) *midfield: u.p and dropped bhd over 1f out: edgd lft whn n.d ins fnl f* **11/1**

421- **11** 2 **Kinlochrannoch**[249] 6263 3-9-3 **81** NeilCallan 3 49
(Ben Haslam) *hld up: rdn over 1f out: nvr on terms* **16/1**

60.80 secs **Going Correction** 0.0s/f (Good) **11** Ran SP% **122.6**
Speed ratings (Par 101): **101,98,97,96,94 93,93,92,90,85 82**
toteswingers:1&2:£2.40, 1&3:£33.60, 2&3:£41.50 CSF £9.98 CT £163.73 TOTE £2.90: £1.80, £2.00, £5.60; EX 12.50.
Owner Cheveley Park Stud **Bred** Grangecon Stud **Trained** Newmarket, Suffolk

FOCUS
This sprint handicap has often been won by a progressive sort and there were several fitting that description in the line-up this time. The winner confirmed York form with the runner-up.
T/Jkpt: Not won. T/Plt: £43.20 to a £1 stake. Pool:£148,686.20 - 2,506.96 winning tickets T/Qpdt: £16.30 to a £1 stake. Pool:£6,015.58 - 272.50 winning tickets DO

2467 NEWMARKET (R-H)
Saturday, May 28

OFFICIAL GOING: Good (good to firm in places; 7.9)
Far side track used, stalls on far side except 5.45 Centre.
Wind: Strong, across. Weather: overcast, breezy

2506 TURFTV H'CAP 1m
2:20 (2:21) (Class 3) (0-90,89) 3-Y-O **£8,418** (£2,505; £1,251; £625) **Stalls** Low

Form RPR

21- **1** **Maywood**[219] 7036 3-9-4 **86** MickaelBarzalona 11 100+
(Mahmood Al Zarooni) *hld up in tch in last: pushed along 3f out: rdn: c to stands' rail and hdwy 2f out: drvn and pressing ldrs over 1f out: led ins fnl f: styd on wl and gng away at fin* **8/1**

62-1 **2** 1½ **Dubai Queen (USA)**[23] 1836 3-9-1 **83** KierenFallon 10 93+
(Luca Cumani) *t.k.h: hld up wl in tch: hdwy over 2f out: rdn and ev ch ent fnl 2f: led over 1f out: hdd ins fnl f: no ex fnl 100yds* **3/1**[1]

0-11 **3** ¾ **Ektibaas**[18] 1983 3-9-1 **83** RichardHills 6 92
(B W Hills) *led: rdn ent fnl 2f: hdd over 1f out: no ex and styd on same pce ins fnl f* **7/2**[2]

-530 **4** 2 **Cruiser**[7] 2296 3-9-3 **85** RichardHughes 7 89
(William Muir) *stdd s: hld up wl in tch towards rr: rdn and effrt wl over 2f out: drvn and chsd ldrs over 1f out: no ex and btn fnl 100yds* **16/1**

44-1 **5** 4½ **Dimension**[26] 1759 3-9-7 **89** WilliamBuick 4 83+
(James Fanshawe) *t.k.h: chsd ldrs: rdn and effrt jst over 2f out: drvn and btn ent fnl f: wknd ins fnl f* **13/2**[3]

21-1 **6** ½ **Cloud Illusions (USA)**[16] 2018 3-8-13 **81** EddieAhern 2 74
(Heather Main) *hld up wl in tch: chsng ldrs and rdn 2f out: unable qck and struggling ent fnl f: wknd ins fnl f* **14/1**

1-13 **7** ½ **The Tichborne (IRE)**[26] 1773 3-9-6 **88** JackMitchell 12 79
(Roger Teal) *t.k.h: hld up in tch: rdn and effrt wl over 2f out: chsd ldrs 2f out: wknd u.p over 1f out* **25/1**

1-00 **8** 1¾ **Golden Hinde**[27] 1723 3-8-12 **80** JoeFanning 1 67
(Mark Johnston) *pressed ldr tl 1/2-way: rdn wl over 2f out: wknd u.p over 1f out* **40/1**

6-14 **9** 1½ **Biaraafa (IRE)**[14] 2102 3-8-2 **77** IanBurns(7) 9 61
(Michael Bell) *hld up in tch in rr: rdn and no hdwy over 2f out: no ch over 1f out* **12/1**

41 **10** 2 **Quadrant (IRE)**[14] 2103 3-9-0 **82** MartinDwyer 8 61+
(Brian Meehan) *stdd s: t.k.h: hld up in tch: rdn and effrt over 2f out: unable qck whn short of room and hmpd over 1f out: n.d after* **7/1**

2-61 **11** hd **Yojimbo (IRE)**[28] 1682 3-8-11 **79** (v) ChrisCatlin 5 58
(Mick Channon) *hld up towards rr: rdn over 2f out: sn struggling: no ch wl over 1f out* **25/1**

134- **12** *nk* **Catalyze**[231] 6733 3-9-5 **87**....(t) JimmyFortune 3 65
(Andrew Balding) *stdd s: t.k.h: hld up in tch: rdn and struggling over 2f out: bhd wl over 1f out* **11/1**

1m 38.94s (0.34) **Going Correction** -0.05s/f (Good) **12** Ran SP% **122.9**
Speed ratings (Par 103): **96,94,93,91,87 86,86,84,83,81 80,80**
Tote Swingers:1&2:£8.30, 2&3:£2.50, 1&3:£9.60 CSF £32.79 CT £105.44 TOTE £9.30: £3.20, £1.90, £2.10; EX 43.30 Trifecta £123.30 Pool £1,335.16 - 8.01 winning units..
Owner Godolphin **Bred** Wood Hall Stud Limited **Trained** Newmarket, Suffolk

FOCUS
This looked a cracking handicap and it would be slightly surprising if it did not contain a few above-average types for the season, as a lot of these had been winning good races. The bare form doesn't look quite as good as might have been expected.

NOTEBOOK
Maywood ◆, once entered for the Derby, hadn't been seen since landing a Brighton maiden (four subsequent winners in behind) last October and wasn't too quickly into stride here. However, after taking time to get into full stride, his excellent jockey manoeuvred his mount to what was being perceived as the unfavoured side considering the previous day's racing and came home strongly against the rail. One would imagine we'll see him over a bit further in time, so the Tercentenary Stakes (formerly the Hampton Court Stakes) at Royal Ascot could be the right option for him, although connections are sure to have higher-rated horses already for that contest. (op 9-1 tchd 10-1)
Dubai Queen(USA) ◆ made a winning return this season from two horses who went on to win their next start, after catching the eye a couple of times as a juvenile. A half-sister to Dubawi, she went to post keenly and didn't settle too well in the race itself, but she clearly has a lot of ability and was only denied by a rival coming up the rails. One would imagine connections will be desperate to get some black type into her, so although she looks well handicapped, it wouldn't be a surprise to see her in a Listed contest soon. The Sandringham Handicap at Ascot would look ideal for her, but it seems likely that she'll be just short of the handicap mark needed to get in unless she gets a dramatic rise. (op 4-1)
Ektibaas was defending an unbeaten record in 2011, and his last win over Sagramor had been enhanced when that horse won the Silver Bowl the previous weekend. 7lb higher for that Warwick success, he was always thereabouts and stayed on nicely throughout the final stages. There must be a fair chance that, given his miling pedigree, he'll head to the Britannia Stakes in an attempt to follow up his stablemate Ransom Note's victory in it last year. (op 4-1 tchd 9-2)
Cruiser had run well in defeat three times already this season but looked up against it facing some unexposed types, so the fact he finished on the heels of the leaders bodes well for him.
Dimension won with lots in hand from an odds-on favourite at Kempton last time, but still had to prove he was effective on turf considering his best previous performances came on the AW. He travelled well just behind but found his effort flattened out late on, so it doesn't seem as though turf is his favoured surface yet, although he should be allowed another chance on much quicker going. (op 6-1)
Cloud Illusions(USA) was chasing a hat-trick after winning at the end of her 2-y-o campaign and starting her season off with success over C&D earlier this month. She was another to move with purpose before not finding another gear when needed. (op 12-1)
The Tichborne(IRE) wasn't beaten far on his first venture on to turf last time at Windsor, but this course was always going to be something new to him after twisting around turning tracks. He took a while to get going and was staying on at the one pace inside the final furlong. (tchd 20-1)
Quadrant(IRE) built on his promising debut when winning a maiden at Newbury last time (subsequent winner in behind) but gave the impression this was too much too quick, despite being hampered in the latter stages, which isn't a disgrace in company as strong as he faced. He'll no doubt prove to be much better than this performance in time. (op 8-1)

2507 NOVAE BLOODSTOCK INSURANCE FAIRWAY STKS (LISTED RACE) 1m 2f
2:50 (2:52) (Class 1) 3-Y-O

£17,031 (£6,456; £3,231; £1,611; £807; £405) **Stalls** Low

Form RPR
5-14 **1** **Laajooj (IRE)**[22] 1850 3-9-0 98.... MickaelBarzalona 2 108
(Mahmood Al Zarooni) *chsd ldr in far side pair: lft alone far side as ldr hung lft 3f out: on terms w stands' side and sn rdn: rdr dropped whip over 1f out: led ent fnl f: hld hd high but kpt on wl* **11/1**

10-1 **2** *1 ¾* **Buthelezi (USA)**[27] 1723 3-9-0 99.... WilliamBuick 1 105+
(John Gosden) *led far side pair and probably led overall: rdn and hung lft fr 3f out: cut across stands' side quartet and stl in ld wl over 1f out: hdd ent fnl f: styd on same pce after* **7/2**[2]

1-12 **3** *4 ½* **Cai Shen (IRE)**[28] 1689 3-9-0 101.... RichardHughes 4 96
(Richard Hannon) *stdd s: hld up in stands' side quartet: hdwy 3f out: rdn and chsng ldr 2f out: wknd ins fnl f* **4/1**[3]

-452 **4** *nk* **Namibian (IRE)**[10] 2191 3-9-0 103.... JoeFanning 6 97+
(Mark Johnston) *led stands' side quartet: rdn and keeping on same pce whn sltly hmpd wl over 1f out: btn and plugged on same pce fnl f* **13/2**

1142 **5** *nse* **Barbican**[27] 1723 3-9-0 95.... CathyGannon 5 95
(Alan Bailey) *chsd stands' side ldr: rdn and chsng overall ldr wl over 1f out: unable qck and btn ent fnl f* **12/1**

1-1 **6** *32* **Naqshabban (USA)**[34] 1546 3-9-0 98.... KierenFallon 3 31
(Luca Cumani) *stdd after s: in tch in stands' side quartet: rdn 4f out: drvn and btn 2f out: virtually p.u ins fnl f: t.o* **6/4**[1]

2m 3.70s (-2.10) **Going Correction** -0.05s/f (Good) **6** Ran SP% **111.6**
Speed ratings (Par 107): **106,104,101,100,100 75**
Tote Swingers:1&2:£6.50, 2&3:£1.20, 1&3:£10.10 CSF £48.02 TOTE £13.20: £4.50, £1.80; EX 45.90.
Owner Godolphin **Bred** Kildaragh Stud **Trained** Newmarket, Suffolk

FOCUS
This race has produced plenty of good horses in the past, including the likes of Lucarno and Red Rocks, but it seems unlikely that this is reliable form, as the six runners split into two groups miles apart from one another, the runner-up went from one side to another, and the interesting favourite ran badly. The first pair were clear though and showed improved form.

NOTEBOOK
Laajooj(IRE), whose rider dropped his whip over 1f out, probably ran as well as could have been expected in the Dee Stakes last time but easily took this after staying to the far side of the course with only one other runner, who disappeared from his view about 1f out. He's clearly a talented individual and goes well for Barzalona, who is now two from two on him. He is also two from two on straight tracks and holds entries in the Royal Hunt Cup and Coral Eclipse. (op 10-1 tchd 9-1)
Buthelezi(USA) and Barbican finished first and second over C&D at the Guineas meeting and that form was confirmed, although the John Gosden-trained runner appeared to want to test both sides of the track to see which one he fancied. Considering he wasn't beaten far and edged right across the track, he ran a cracker and he has plenty of ability, but whether he'll be inclined to use it every time is anyone's guess. A good race is there for the taking with him but punters will need to factor in that he doesn't look completely straightforward when making their calculations. He's been tried in eyeshields in the past, but that produced his worst performance, so he could be the type to resent headgear if tried in it. Official explanation: jockey said colt hung badly left (op 5-1 tchd 11-2)
Cai Shen(IRE) only lost out to Godolphin's Derby entry Ocean War in an attempt at a four-timer last time and had no chance here on what looked to be the 'wrong' side. However, the way he travelled while under wraps does suggest he has more wins in him. (op 9-2)
Namibian(IRE) got hampered by Buthelezi as he came to the near side. He chased home Masked Marvel in the Cocked Hat Stakes at Goodwood on his previous outing after finishing behind Cai Shen the time before over C&D, so he is a fair marker to the form for those who were on his side of the course. (tchd 7-1)
Barbican kept on really well to the line and looks an honest type. He may well be suited by further. (op 11-1 tchd 16-1)
Naqshabban(USA) was the most interesting runner in this, as he was unbeaten and defeated the Musidora Joviality winner last time, but this was a tame effort and he was under pressure a long way out. Official explanation: trainer had no explanation for the poor form shown (op 5-4)

2508 CORAL.CO.UK SPRINT (H'CAP) 6f
3:25 (3:25) (Class 2) (0-105,95) 3-Y-O

£27,416 (£8,210; £4,105; £2,054; £1,025; £514) **Stalls** Low

Form RPR
125- **1** **Majestic Myles (IRE)**[282] 5245 3-9-5 **93**.... JackMitchell 1 105
(Richard Fahey) *in tch: effrt and rdn to ld narrowly over 1f out: hrd pressed jst ins fnl f: battled on v gamely: all out* **17/2**

201- **2** *nk* **Desert Law (IRE)**[225] 6882 3-9-3 **91**.... JimmyFortune 2 102+
(Andrew Balding) *hld up in tch in midfield: rdn and gd hdwy wl over 1f out: drvn ent fnl f: pressed wnr thrght fnl f: r.o wl u.p but a jst hld* **3/1**[1]

0-31 **3** *2 ¼* **L'Ami Louis (IRE)**[27] 1724 3-8-9 **83**.... DaneO'Neill 8 87
(Henry Candy) *led: rdn 2f out: hdd narrowly over 1f out: stl pressing ldrs 1f out: outpcd and btn fnl 150yds: hld on for 3rd* **7/2**[2]

641- **4** *nk* **What About You (IRE)**[183] 7578 3-8-12 **86**....(t) KierenFallon 11 89
(Richard Fahey) *stdd s: t.k.h: swtchd lft and hdwy wl over 4f out: jnd ldrs over 3f out: ev ch and rdn wl over 1f out: unable qck ent fnl f: plugged on same pce after* **8/1**

6530 **5** *1* **Bathwick Bear (IRE)**[15] 2054 3-9-4 **95**.... RichardEvans(3) 6 95
(David Evans) *w ldrs: ev ch and rdn wl over 1f out: drvn and struggling jst over 1f out: wknd jst ins fnl f* **40/1**

-113 **6** *1* **Apollo D'Negro (IRE)**[16] 2025 3-8-1 **78** ow3.... JohnFahy(3) 3 75
(Clive Cox) *in tch in midfield: rdn and no prog over 2f out: rallied u.p jst over 1f out: styd on steadily fnl f: no threat to ldrs* **10/1**

5-20 **7** *nk* **Avonmore Star**[27] 1725 3-9-6 **94**.... RichardHughes 7 90
(Richard Hannon) *hld up towards rr: effrt and swtchd rt ent fnl 2f: nt clr run and swtchd lft wl over 1f out: kpt on under hands and heels fnl f: no threat to ldrs* **14/1**

30-0 **8** *3 ¼* **Jack Smudge**[23] 1825 3-9-0 **88**.... PaulMulrennan 4 73
(James Given) *chsd ldr: ev ch and rdn ent fnl 2f: drvn and btn over 1f out: wknd 1f out: fdd ins fnl f* **16/1**

-634 **9** *4* **Remotelinx (IRE)**[15] 2067 3-9-0 **88**.... MichaelHills 5 60
(J W Hills) *a towards rr: rdn and effrt over 2f out: stl bhd and drvn over 1f out: n.d* **25/1**

26-0 **10** *¾* **Forty Proof (IRE)**[10] 2199 3-8-8 **82**....(v) MartinDwyer 12 52
(William Knight) *bhd: pushed lft wl over 4f out: struggling and rdn over 3f out: nvr trbld ldrs* **40/1**

0-21 **11** *3 ¾* **Lexi's Hero (IRE)**[23] 1825 3-9-7 **95**.... EddieAhern 10 53
(Kevin Ryan) *hld up towards rr: rdn and struggling wl over 2f out: wl btn fnl 2f* **15/2**[3]

1-02 **12** *10* **El Viento (FR)**[15] 2067 3-9-0 **88**....(b) JimmyQuinn 9 —+
(Richard Fahey) *in tch: rdn and struggling over 2f out: wkng whn pushed lft wl over 1f out: wl bhd and eased ins fnl f* **14/1**

-300 **13** *7* **Breedj (IRE)**[28] 1688 3-9-5 **93**....(t) PhilipRobinson 13 —+
(Clive Brittain) *wnt lft s: sn rcvrd and chsng ldrs: rdn and struggling over 2f out: wkng and towards rr whn bdly hmpd: stmbld and nrly uns rdr wl over 1f out: wl bhd after: eased ins fnl f* **33/1**

1m 11.86s (-0.34) **Going Correction** -0.05s/f (Good) **13** Ran SP% **120.6**
Speed ratings (Par 105): **100,99,96,96,94 93,93,88,83,82 77,64,54**
CSF £33.42 CT £112.44 TOTE £8.30: £3.10, £2.00, £1.80; EX 35.50 Trifecta £341.50 Pool £38,227.90 - 82.82 winning units..
Owner James Gaffney **Bred** Arctic Tack Stud **Trained** Musley Bank, N Yorks

■ Stewards' Enquiry : Richard Hughes one-day ban: careless riding (Jun 11)

FOCUS
It seemed strange that the jockeys decided to come down the middle to near side of the track, considering an earlier race on the card, and ones the previous day, appeared to show that sticking to the far rail would give you an advantage. That said, the two stalls that dominated the race were one and two, and they were berthed against the far-side rail. A good 3yo handicap, rated around the fifth.

NOTEBOOK
Majestic Myles(IRE) ◆ looked the most interesting runner in this on his form at two, which included a 7.5l fifth to Wootton Bassett on his final start. Drawn in stall one, he raced prominently and quickened up well to hold off his persistent challenger. He has resumed in great form again this year and clearly has the will to win. Connections reported afterwards that he'd been off since York, where they'd fancied him to run well against Wootton Bassett, because he had split his pelvis, which makes this victory all the more commendable. (op 12-1)
Desert Law(IRE) ◆ won his maiden over C&D last October and was having his first run since. A son of the very speedy Speed Cop, he took quite a grip in behind runners but did find for pressure and went down narrowly after a good tussle with the winner. The trainer reported that he has high hopes for Desert Law and, with this run now under his belt, he looks destined to win a good handicap at least this year. (op 7-2 tchd 4-1 and 9-2 in places)
L'Ami Louis(IRE) only just managed to hold on last time in a tight finish, but a couple of horses behind him that day have already gone on to win a race, including the runner-up. He didn't appear to have a good starting position here but it didn't matter too much in the end as all the jockeys seemed to follow each other to the middle. Racing a bit keenly in front, he stayed on well and is probably capable of more improvement. (tchd 4-1)
What About You(IRE) ◆ started to show improved form when a tongue-tie was added last year, and finished his season with a win at Wolverhampton - subsequent winners in behind. He raced freely, wide of runners, before keeping on in pleasing style towards the stands' side in the final stages. One would imagine connections will be delighted with his first run of the season and he looks another to follow. (op 7-1)
Bathwick Bear(IRE) has lots of speed at his disposal and only faded in the final furlong. He must be a great horse to own as he rarely runs badly.
Apollo D'Negro(IRE), whose jockey put up 3lb overweight, has been in good heart this season and seemed to run his race. (op 12-1)
Avonmore Star appears to have found his level in handicaps, kept on from rear in the latter stages. (op 12-1)

Lexi's Hero(IRE) has been in good heart this year, winning at Chester on his previous outing. Raised 6lb for that success, this was too bad to be true and should be forgotten. Official explanation: jockey said gelding lost its action (op 13-2)

2509 LA HOGUE FARM SHOP & CAFE H'CAP 1m 2f
4:00 (4:00) (Class 3) (0-95,93) 4-Y-0+ **£8,418** (£2,505; £1,251; £625) **Stalls** Low

Form RPR

55-4 **1** **Huygens**26 1760 4-9-3 **89** .... EddieAhern 2 99
(Denis Coakley) *taken down early: in tch: hdwy to trck ldr over 2f out: shkn up to ld over 1f out: rdn clr ent fnl f: kpt on and a doing enough fnl f: pushed out fnl 100yds* **9/2**2

0-65 **2** *1 3/4* **Shavansky**17 2002 7-9-3 **89** .... JimmyFortune 6 95
(Rod Millman) *stdd after s: hld up in last pair: hdwy to chse ldng pair and hung rt ent fnl 2f: drvn and no imp on ldr over 1f out: kpt on same pce ins fnl f: wnt 2nd fnl 50yds* **7/2**1

-000 **3** *1/2* **Licence To Till (USA)**21 1887 4-9-1 **87** .... JoeFanning 1 92
(Mark Johnston) *led: rdn 3f out: drvn and hdd over 1f out: sn unable qck and outpcd by wnr: plugged on same pce fnl f* **8/1**

0-10 **4** *6* **Bonfire Knight**17 2002 4-9-0 **91** .... HarryBentley(5) 8 84
(John Quinn) *chsd ldrs: rdn and struggling over 2f out: 4th and wl hld over 1f out* **9/2**2

200- **5** *8* **Sour Mash (IRE)**252 6203 4-9-4 **90** .... GeorgeBaker 10 67
(Chris Wall) *chsd ldr tl wl over 2f out: sn rdn: hung rt and btn: 5th and no ch over 1f out* **7/1**

50-6 **6** *3 1/4* **Classic Colori (IRE)**23 1824 4-9-4 **90** .... SebSanders 9 61
(Tom Dascombe) *hld up in tch: hdwy to chse ldrs 5f out: rdn and wknd qckly wl over 2f out: wl bhd over 1f out* **6/1**

31- **7** *14* **Mountain Hiker (IRE)**309 4330 4-9-3 **89** .... DarryllHolland 5 32
(Jeremy Noseda) *taken down early: a in rr and nvr gng wl: rdn and btn 3f out: wl bhd and eased ins fnl f: t.o* **11/2**3

2m 3.35s (-2.45) **Going Correction** -0.05s/f (Good) **7** Ran SP% **111.9**
Speed ratings (Par 107): **107,105,105,100,94 91,80**
Tote Swingers:1&2:£2.80, 2&3:£6.10, 1&3:£12.80 CSF £19.63 CT £118.70 TOTE £6.00: £3.20, £2.10; EX 22.40 Trifecta £116.30 Pool £1,089.98 - 6.92 winning units..
Owner Chris Van Hoorn **Bred** R F And Mrs Knipe **Trained** West Ilsley, Berks

FOCUS
Three came out before the off but it was still a competitive race for the class. It once again appeared to be a positive to finish towards the far-side rail. The form is rated through the third.

NOTEBOOK
Huygens, who went to post early, had only tried this trip once in the past, so was unexposed over it and came into this contest off a fair return at Kempton (1m). He moved really strongly stalking the leaders and bounded clear once in front. There ought to be more to come at this trip. (op 6-1 tchd 13-2)
Shavansky had run two decent races in good handicaps already this season and helps to make this form look reasonably solid. He could do with coming down the weights a bit more to have a really obvious chance of victory. (op 9-2)
Licence To Till(USA) ran a bit better last time after a couple of moderate efforts and followed it up with another fair performance. (tchd 15-2)
Bonfire Knight had his chance but made little impression in the final stages. (tchd 5-1)
Sour Mash(IRE), absent since the middle of September, was having his first start for Chris Wall and had been gelded since his last appearance. He had a stalls handler at the start and didn't do a great deal in the race to suggest he's a winner waiting to happen. (op 6-1)
Classic Colori(IRE) caught the eye on his return at Chester and could easily be fancied on his best form, but he was under pressure a long way out and added another poor effort to his profile. (tchd 13-2)
Mountain Hiker(IRE), another to go down to the start before the others, was by far the least-exposed runner but was having his first start since the end of July last year, a win in maiden company on Newmarket's July course. Dropping 2f in trip, he'd had issues with stalls in the past (he seemed to go in easily this time) and was said to have swished his tail repeatedly while trotted to post. It soon became clear he wasn't going to be winning and he looked a hard ride. Official explanation: jockey said gelding never travelled (op 9-2 tchd 6-1 in places)

2510 BRITISH STALLION STUDS SUPPORTING BRITISH RACING E B F MAIDEN STKS 6f
4:35 (4:36) (Class 4) 2-Y-0 **£4,533** (£1,348; £674; £336) **Stalls** Low

Form RPR

0 **1** **Democretes**27 1721 2-9-3 0 .... RichardHughes 9 77+
(Richard Hannon) *mde all: rdn over 1f out: edgd rt u.p ins fnl f: hld on cl home* **14/1**

2 *nk* **Swiss Spirit** 2-9-3 0 .... KierenFallon 14 77+
(David Elsworth) *in tch: switching rt and effrt whn stmbld wl over 1f out: rallying and nt clr run ent fnl f: sn swtchd sharply rt: str run fnl 150yds: pressing wnr fnl 50yds: nt quite get up* **4/1**2

3 *1/2* **Genius Step (IRE)** 2-9-3 0 .... MickaelBarzalona 13 75+
(Mahmood Al Zarooni) *dwlt and short of room sn after s: hld up in tch towards rr: rdn and hdwy wl over 1f out: r.o wl ins fnl f: wnt 3rd fnl 50yds* **6/1**

4 *1/2* **Sandbetweenourtoes (IRE)** 2-9-3 0 .... EddieCreighton 8 73+
(Brian Meehan) *chsd wnr: rdn wl over 1f out: stl pressing wnr 1f out: no ex and styd on same pce fnl 100yds* **40/1**

3 **5** *shd* **Verse Of Love**9 2221 2-9-3 0 .... CathyGannon 10 73
(David Evans) *w ldrs: rdn ent fnl 2f: drvn and unable qck ent fnl f: styd on same pce fnl 150yds* **25/1**

0 **6** *nse* **Rio Grande**17 2007 2-9-3 0 .... WilliamBuick 1 73+
(Jeremy Noseda) *grad swtchd lft after s: in tch: effrt and chsd ldrs 2f out: rdn and unable qck over 1f out: styd on same pce fnl 150yds* **15/8**1

7 *2 1/2* **Sovereign Debt (IRE)** 2-9-3 0 .... EddieAhern 4 65+
(Michael Bell) *in tch in midfield: rdn and sltly outpcd 2f out: rallied ent fnl f: styd on steadily fnl 150yds: nt pce to threaten ldrs*

0 **8** *nk* **All Nighter (IRE)**15 2049 2-9-3 0 .... MartinDwyer 2 65+
(Brian Meehan) *grad swtchd lft after s: in tch hmpd over 4f out: rdn wl over 1f out: keeping on same pce whn pushed rt jst ins fnl f: no imp after* **5/1**3

9 *1* **Anakindalika** 2-8-12 0 .... RobbieFitzpatrick 11 56
(John Ryan) *in tch in midfield: rdn and lost pl ent fnl 2f: styd on same pce fr over 1f out* **100/1**

10 *1 3/4* **Pacific Islands (IRE)** 2-9-3 0 .... AhmedAjtebi 12 56+
(Mahmood Al Zarooni) *short of room and sltly hmpd sn after s: hld up in tch in rr: rdn and effrt wl over 1f out: no imp and plugged on same pce fnl f* **16/1**

4 **11** *2 1/4* **Casa Bex**14 2109 2-9-3 0 .... JackMitchell 3 54
(Philip McBride) *in tch: rdn wl over 1f out: styng on same pce bdly hmpd jst ins fnl f: nt rcvr and n.d after* **20/1**

12 *2* **Percythepinto (IRE)** 2-9-3 0 .... DaneO'Neill 7 43
(David Elsworth) *wl in tch in rr: rdn and outpcd whn rn green wl over 1f out: no threat to ldrs after* **66/1**

13 *11* **Rocco Breeze (IRE)** 2-9-3 0 .... ChrisCatlin 6 10
(Philip McBride) *sn toiling in rr: lost tch 1/2-way: t.o* **40/1**

U **Thecornishcockney** 2-9-3 0 .... StevieDonohoe 5 —
(John Ryan) *taken down early and ponied to s: v.s.a: veered lft and uns rdr sn after s* **66/1**

1m 14.37s (2.17) **Going Correction** -0.05s/f (Good) **14** Ran SP% **120.5**
Speed ratings (Par 95): **83,82,81,81,81 81,77,77,76,73 70,68,53,—**
Tote Swingers:1&2:£11.60, 2&3:£7.10, 1&3:£10.60 CSF £64.84 TOTE £14.60: £3.50, £2.30, £2.50; EX 69.20 Trifecta £326.10 Pool £3,508.39 - 7.96 winning units..
Owner The High Flyers **Bred** R J Cornelius **Trained** East Everleigh, Wilts
■ Stewards' Enquiry : Kieren Fallon three-day ban: careless riding (Jun 11-13)
Eddie Creighton one-day ban: careless riding (Jun 11)

FOCUS
This race has been won by some decent sorts in the past, including Libranno, who went on to win the July and Richmond Stakes on his next two starts, both of which are Group 2s. Tariq took it in 2006 before developing into a Group performer. Much like other races on the card, it wasn't easy to understand why all of the field came to the stands' side considering some evidence that suggested the far side looked the place to be. There were plenty of promising types in the line-up but the bare form is not worth any better than this.

NOTEBOOK
Democretes, representing last year's winning stable, looked in need of the experience at this course over 5f and duly built on that over this longer trip. It will be interesting to see how he is campaigned now, as he looked in need of this trip despite travelling strongly up front. This effort pays a handsome compliment to the now Godolphin-owned Comissar, who beat him 8l. Connections of Democretes said afterwards that their horse will probably now head to the conditions race that stablemate Casual Glimpse won last year on the July course. (op 10-1)
Swiss Spirit ◆, who is a half-brother to Swiss Diva and Swiss Franc, showed more than enough to suggest he could be above average. He raced a bit greenly and appeared to lose his footing over 1f out and needed to be pulled towards the middle of the course to make his effort. The ground he lost there may have cost him victory but there is little doubt he has the size to keep developing and should win his fair share of races this season. (tchd 9-2 and 5-1 in places)
Genius Step(IRE), a brother to an Italian Group 3 winner, kept on well towards the stands' rail and ought to be sharper next time. (tchd 7-1)
Sandbetweenourtoes(IRE) made an encouraging start to his career, as he got into the right position but didn't seen completely sure what to do when there. He'll be wiser next time and should be tough to beat.
Verse Of Love looks to have some size about him and appeared to at least maintain the level of form he showed on debut at Salisbury. (op 20-1 tchd 33-1 in places)
Rio Grande made his debut in a hot-looking contest at York and was really well backed here on his second outing. It looked for a while as though he was going to be kept to the far side but his jockey steered him across with the others and he failed to make a big impact when the race unfolded. (op 9-4 after early 5-2, 11-4 and 3-1 in places)
Sovereign Debt(IRE), a half-brother to Group 3 winner Puff among others, got a little short of room at one point and outpaced but stayed on in pleasing style. It was a nice debut and he can develop into a fair sort. (op 18-1 tchd 22-1)
All Nighter(IRE) showed plenty of ability at Newbury (form has worked out well) but was another to come stands' side from a low draw, which probably wasn't a positive to his chance. (tchd 4-1)

2511 RACING UK MAIDEN STKS 1m
5:10 (5:11) (Class 5) 3-Y-0 **£3,238** (£963; £481; £240) **Stalls** Low

Form RPR

02 **1** **Rave (IRE)**15 2068 3-9-3 0 .... SebSanders 5 89
(J W Hills) *stdd s: t.k.h: hld up wl in tch: rdn and effrt 2f out: drvn to ld over 1f out: clr ent fnl f: r.o wl: rdn out* **7/4**1

00- **2** *3* **Hayaku (USA)**238 6559 3-8-12 0 .... (t) StevieDonohoe 8 77
(Ralph Beckett) *stdd s: hld up in tch: swtchd lft and effrt wl over 2f out: drvn and outpcd by wnr over 1f out: no threat to wnr but plugged on fnl f to go 2nd fnl 75yds* **8/1**

30 **3** *1 1/2* **El Wasmi**24 1810 3-9-3 0 .... PhilipRobinson 2 79
(Clive Brittain) *w ldr: ev ch and rdn over 2f out: drvn and outpcd by wnr over 1f out: plugged on same pce and wl hld fnl f: lost 2nd fnl 75yds* **8/1**

4- **4** *1* **Guisho (IRE)**211 7203 3-9-3 0 .... MartinDwyer 4 76
(Brian Meehan) *led: rdn 2f out: hdd and edgd lft u.p over 1f out: 4th and wl hld fnl f* **7/2**2

54-5 **5** *3 3/4* **Musnad (USA)**18 1985 3-9-3 80 .... RichardHills 3 68
(B W Hills) *hld up in tch: pushed along and unable qck ent fnl 2f: no imp and wl hld fr over 1f out* **9/2**3

0 **6** *9* **Arkaim**16 2019 3-9-3 0 .... J-PGuillambert 1 47
(Ed Walker) *t.k.h: rdn ent fnl 2f: drvn and wknd qckly wl over 1f out* **20/1**

7 *5* **Dollar Deal** 3-9-3 0 .... MMimmocchi 6 36
(Luca Cumani) *chsd ldrs: rdn 3f out: sn struggling and wknd over 2f out: wl bhd over 1f out* **25/1**

0 **8** *25* **Dresden (IRE)**15 2068 3-9-3 0 .... KierenFallon 7 —
(Luca Cumani) *s.i.s: a in last pair: rn green and btn wl over 3f out: t.o and eased ins fnl f* **12/1**

00- **9** *3 1/4* **Generous Pursuit**214 7152 3-8-12 0 .... ChrisCatlin 9 —
(Phil McEntee) *s.i.s: a bhd: struggling 1/2-way: sn lost tch: t.o* **100/1**

1m 37.96s (-0.64) **Going Correction** -0.05s/f (Good) **9** Ran SP% **116.3**
Speed ratings (Par 99): **101,98,96,95,91 82,77,52,49**
Tote Swingers:1&2:£3.90, 2&3:£7.50, 1&3:£3.30 CSF £16.67 TOTE £2.50: £1.10, £3.20, £2.60; EX 19.10 Trifecta £318.30 Pool £1,492.65 - 3.47 winning units..
Owner Gary And Linnet Woodward **Bred** P E Banahan **Trained** Upper Lambourn, Berks
■ Stewards' Enquiry : Martin Dwyer two-day ban: careless riding (Jun 11-12)

FOCUS
This didn't look a good maiden for the track and it wouldn't be a surprise if quite a few of these don't make the winner's enclosure for a while. The form seems sound.

2512 NEWMARKETRACECOURSES.CO.UK H'CAP 1m 6f
5:45 (5:45) (Class 4) (0-85,85) 4-Y-0+ **£5,180** (£1,541; £770; £384) **Stalls** Centre

Form RPR

/00- **1** **Veiled**21 6201 5-9-2 **80** .... KierenFallon 10 94
(Nicky Henderson) *hld up towards rr: hdwy 5f out: rdn to chse ldrs ent fnl 2f: drvn to ld over 1f out: styd on wl fnl f* **9/2**1

00/0 **2** *1 1/2* **Gifted Leader (USA)**17 2006 6-8-13 **77** .... (v) PaulMulrennan 13 89
(Ian Williams) *hld up in tch: rdn and effrt over 2f out: drvn to press wnr over 1f out: unable qck and styd on same pce ins fnl f* **14/1**

0-43 **3** *6* **Trovare (USA)**14 2107 4-9-7 **85** .... PatDobbs 4 89
(Amanda Perrett) *chsd ldrs: wnt 2nd 10f out: rdn to ld and edgd lft ent fnl 2f: hdd u.p over 1f out: wknd fnl f* **5/1**2

3-11 **4** *1* **Seaside Sizzler**26 1761 4-9-2 **80** .... (bt) StevieDonohoe 8 82
(Ralph Beckett) *chsd ldrs: jostling match w rival 11f out: lost pl and pushed along 7f out: hdwy over 3f out: ev ch whn pushed lft ent fnl 2f: wknd 1f out* **10/1**

2-00 **5** *4 1/2* **Boston Blue**16 2034 4-9-1 **79** .... (v) GeorgeBaker 11 75
(Tim Etherington) *led tl hdd and rdn ent fnl 2f: wknd wl over 1f out* **16/1**

04-4 **6** *1 1/4* **Hayzoom**[17] [2006] 4-9-2 **80** .... JimmyFortune 6 74
(Peter Chapple-Hyam) *stdd s: hld up in rr: rdn and hdwy over 3f out: styd on same pce and no imp fr wl over 1f out* **6/1**[3]

0-60 **7** *4* **Cat O' Nine Tails**[8] [2262] 4-8-12 **76** .... JoeFanning 5 65
(Mark Johnston) *chsd ldr: jostling match w rival 11f out: lost 2nd 10f out: chsd ldrs after tl wknd u.p 2f out* **14/1**

-340 **8** *3/4* **Blue Spartan (IRE)**[15] [2055] 6-8-7 **74** .... LouisBeuzelin(3) 9 62
(Rod Millman) *hld up in midfield: rdn and effrt 3f out: wknd 2f out: edgd rt whn btn ent fnl f* **66/1**

0/5- **9** *18* **Deadly Silence (USA)**[181] [7612] 6-8-12 **76** .... DarryllHolland 1 38
(Dr Jon Scargill) *stdd s: hld up in rr: hdwy on far rail over 4f out: rdn and no hdwy wl over 2f out: wl btn and eased ins fnl f* **20/1**

0-30 **10** *7* **Highland Park (IRE)**[16] [2021] 4-8-2 **66** .... AndreaAtzeni 12 19
(Michael Wigham) *stdd s: hld up in rr: rdn and struggling over 4f out: sn lost tch: t.o* **66/1**

201- **11** *nse* **Saggiatore**[218] [7067] 4-8-13 **77** .... MartinDwyer 2 29
(William Muir) *t.k.h: hld up in midfield: hdwy to chse ldrs 8f out: wknd over 3f out: wl bhd and eased fr over 1f out: t.o* **18/1**

1343 **12** *7* **Parhelion**[22] [1847] 4-9-2 **80** .... DaneO'Neill 3 23
(Derek Haydn Jones) *in tch tl wknd 5f out: eased fr wl over 1f out: t.o* **16/1**

31-1 **13** *2 1/2* **Old Hundred (IRE)**[28] [1676] 4-9-7 **85** ....(v) PatCosgrave 7 24
(James Fanshawe) *in tch tl rdn and no hdwy 4f out: wl btn and eased fr wl over 1f out: t.o* **9/2**[1]

5003 **14** *19* **Denton (NZ)**[39] [1470] 8-9-7 **85** ....(t) SteveDrowne 14 —
(Jeremy Gask) *t.k.h: chsd ldrs for 4f: steadily lost pl: bhd and lost tch over 3f out: virtually p.u fr 2f out: t.o* **25/1**

2m 53.69s (-3.31) **Going Correction** -0.05s/f (Good) course record **14** Ran SP% **118.4**
Speed ratings (Par 105): **107,106,102,102,99 98,96,96,85,81 81,77,76,65**
Tote Swingers:1&2:£15.50, 2&3:£15.30, 1&3:£3.20 CSF £64.81 CT £328.71 TOTE £5.00: £1.40, £6.80, £1.60; EX 72.70 Trifecta £1107.00 Part won. Pool £1,496.01 - 0.59 winning units..
Owner Pump & Plant Services Ltd **Bred** Cheveley Park Stud Ltd **Trained** Upper Lambourn, Berks
■ Stewards' Enquiry : Pat Dobbs two-day ban: careless riding (Jun 11-12)

FOCUS
Plenty of these looked to have a chance on their best form, so this should be sound form for the class. They finished well strung out and the winner recorded her best Flat figure.
Trovare(USA) Official explanation: jockey said gelding hung left
Boston Blue Official explanation: jockey said gelding hung left under pressure
T/Plt: £181.50 to a £1 stake. Pool £139,086.02. 559.22 winning tickets T/Qpdt: £16.40 to a £1 stake. Pool £3,271.51. 308.83 winning tickets SP

2513 - 2519a, 2521 - 2522a (Foreign Racing) - See Raceform Interactive

BADEN-BADEN (L-H)
Saturday, May 28

OFFICIAL GOING: Turf: good

2520a HUBERTUS LIEBRECHT-GEDACHTNISPREIS (SCHERPING-RENNEN) (LISTED RACE) (3YO) (TURF) 6f
4:55 (5:04) 3-Y-O **£10,344** (£4,310; £1,724; £862)

RPR

1 **Exciting Life (IRE)**[34] 3-9-2 0 .... MSrnec 10 95
(Adam Wyrzyk, Poland) **23/5**[3]

2 *nse* **Lips Poison (GER)**[187] [7534] 3-8-8 0 .... AHelfenbein 3 87
(Andreas Lowe, Germany) **31/10**[1]

3 *1/2* **Button Moon (IRE)**[15] [2054] 3-8-13 0 .... MartinLane 5 90
(Ian Wood) **79/10**

4 *2 1/2* **Darnell**[40] 3-9-2 0 ....(b) AStarke 6 85
(P Schiergen, Germany) **77/10**

5 *nk* **Boccalino (GER)**[30] [1646] 3-9-2 0 ....(b) FilipMinarik 4 84
(H-A Pantall, France) **13/1**

6 *4* **Beacon Hill (IRE)**[221] [7002] 3-8-9 0 .... ASuborics 1 64
(J-P Carvalho, Germany) **19/5**[2]

7 *2* **Caesarion (GER)**[48] 3-8-11 0 .... WPanov 9 60
(H J Groschel, Germany) **19/2**

8 *1 3/4* **Birthday Prince (GER)** 3-8-9 0 .... JiriPalik 7 52
(Uwe Ostmann, Germany) **23/5**

9 *1/2* **Malpas Missile (IRE)**[162] [7913] 3-8-8 0 .... RussKennemore 2 50
(Tom Dascombe) *broke wl: sn led: shkn up and qcknd clr 2f out: stl 3 l clr 110yds out: stride sn shortened: hdd fnl 30yds* **44/5**

1m 10.26s (-0.03) **9** Ran SP% **130.5**
WIN (incl. 10 euro stake): 56. PLACES: 20, 17, 27. SF: 248.
Owner Frau Sabina Plavac **Bred** Rathasker Stud **Trained** Poland

NOTEBOOK
Button Moon(IRE) looked set to win when clear inside the final furlong, but was caught after getting tired. She showed enough to suggest she can win at this level in Germany at least, and perhaps 5f will suit even better considering her natural speed.

2180 NOTTINGHAM (L-H)
Sunday, May 29

OFFICIAL GOING: Good to firm (good in places; 8.2)
Outer course used, all rails moved 2m adding 7yds to distances on round course and 14yds to 3.20 race.
Wind: Fresh, half-against. Weather: overcast, breezy

2523 E B F BUDDY REDMOND MAIDEN STKS 5f 13y
1:50 (1:51) (Class 5) 2-Y-O **£3,238** (£963; £481; £240) **Stalls** Centre

Form RPR

42 **1** **Dark Ages (IRE)**[30] [1657] 2-8-12 0 .... AdamKirby 3 70
(Noel Quinlan) *w ldr: led last 100yds: hld on towards fin* **9/4**[2]

05 **2** *hd* **Brimstone Hill (IRE)**[12] [2181] 2-9-3 0 .... MichaelHills 7 74
(B W Hills) *trckd ldrs: swtchd lft 1f out: kpt on: no ex towards fin* **9/2**[3]

020 **3** *3/4* **Beau Mistral (IRE)**[25] [1806] 2-8-12 0 .... SilvestreDeSousa 5 67
(Paul Green) *led: hdd ins fnl f: kpt on same pce* **15/8**[1]

0 **4** *2 1/4* **Lady Nickandy (IRE)**[10] [2214] 2-8-12 0 .... RobertWinston 8 58
(Alan McCabe) *hld up in rr: hdwy and swtchd lft 2f out: kpt on same pce appr fnl f* **40/1**

5 *9* **Finbar** 2-9-3 0 .... PaulMulrennan 6 31
(James Given) *dwlt: hdwy over 2f out: hung lft and wknd over 1f out* **8/1**

04 **6** *1/2* **Abercandy (IRE)**[24] [1827] 2-8-12 0 .... CathyGannon 4 24
(David Evans) *sn trcking ldrs: drvn 3f out: sn outpcd and lost pl* **33/1**

0 **7** *14* **Musical Strike**[20] [1939] 2-9-3 0 .... RobbieFitzpatrick 2 —
(Shaun Harris) *dwlt: sn chsng ldrs: drvn over 2f out: sn lost pl and bhd: fin lame* **100/1**

6 **8** *3/4* **Chater Garden (IRE)**[11] [2194] 2-9-3 0 .... KierenFallon 1 —
(Alan Jarvis) *racd wd: w ldrs: wknd 2f out: sn bhd and eased* **15/2**

61.56 secs (0.56) **Going Correction** +0.125s/f (Good) **8** Ran SP% **113.0**
Speed ratings (Par 93): **100,99,98,94,80 79,57,56**
Tote Swingers: 1&2 £2.10, 1&3 £1.50, 2&3 £3.00 CSF £12.46 TOTE £2.30: £1.20, £2.40, £1.02; EX 14.10 Trifecta £31.00 Pool: £704.59 - 16.81 winning units..
Owner Newtown Anner Stud Farm Ltd **Bred** G W Robinson **Trained** Newmarket, Suffolk

FOCUS
The going was good to firm, good in places. Not a strong maiden but the three market leaders filled the first three places. The third has been rated to her mark.

NOTEBOOK
Dark Ages(IRE) had a strong chance on her fourth behind a pair of subsequent winners at Newmarket on debut and a 5l second behind Pyman's Theory who went on to win the Listed National Stakes at Sandown next time. Well backed in the morning but a drifter on course, she again showed plenty of pace under a prominent ride and battled bravely to repel a late challenger and make it third time lucky. Her progress hasn't been very sharp so far but her trainer thinks she could improve on slower ground. (op 6-4 tchd 11-8)
Brimstone Hill(IRE) improved markedly on his debut form when a 50-1 fifth behind some promising sorts in a 6f maiden here last time. He had a bit to find but produced a good finishing surge back at 5f and was just denied. The dam's side of his pedigree includes 1m-1m4f Flat/jumps winners, and he should continue to get better with time and distance. (op 6-1 tchd 13-2)
Beau Mistral(IRE) had claims on her Ripon second last month and a respectable seventh when lumbered with an outside draw in the Lily Agnes at Chester last time. She raced enthusiastically out in front against the stands' rail and stuck to her task well but couldn't quite fight off her main market rivals. (op 2-1 tchd 9-4)
Lady Nickandy(IRE) was never going the pace on her debut at Haydock, but she stayed on well to finish just off the first three on this much improved second run.
Finbar attracted support at biggish prices but he held his head at an angle when the pace increased and couldn't live with some experienced rivals on debut. He should know a lot more next time. (op 12-1)
Musical Strike was reported to have finished lame. Official explanation: vet said colt finished lame
Chater Garden(IRE) Official explanation: jockey said colt moved poorly

2524 PEPPA PIG RETURNS TWINLAKES - 2ND AUGUST H'CAP 5f 13y
2:20 (2:21) (Class 6) (0-65,65) 3-Y-O **£1,813** (£539; £269; £134) **Stalls** Centre

Form RPR

145 **1** **Royal Bajan (USA)**[19] [1980] 3-9-0 **58** .... PaulMulrennan 12 62
(James Given) *racd stands' side rail: w ldrs: led jst ins fnl f: hld on towards fin* **4/1**[1]

0544 **2** *nk* **Pineapple Pete (IRE)**[12] [2180] 3-9-4 **62** ....(tp) RobertWinston 1 65
(Alan McCabe) *trckd ldrs on outside: hung bdly rt over 1f out: chal ins fnl f: no ex nr fin* **13/2**[3]

306 **3** *2 1/4* **Hootys Agogo**[29] [1672] 3-8-4 **53** .... NeilFarley(5) 5 48
(Declan Carroll) *chsd overall ldr on wd outside: led over 2f out: hdd jst ins fnl f: kpt on same pce* **10/1**

6161 **4** *1 1/4* **Meandmyshadow**[19] [1967] 3-9-7 **65** ....(p) SilvestreDeSousa 7 55
(Alan Brown) *chsd ldrs: outpcd over 2f out: kpt on fnl f* **12/1**

2432 **5** *1/2* **Johnny Hancocks (IRE)**[19] [1967] 3-9-6 **64** .... TomEaves 2 53
(Linda Stubbs) *racd wd: led tl over 2f out: kpt on same pce fnl f* **11/2**[2]

4246 **6** *1/2* **Inde Country**[47] [1294] 3-8-7 **51** oh3 .... CathyGannon 9 38
(Nicky Vaughan) *s.i.s: racd towards stands' side: hdwy and edgd rt over 2f out: kpt on fnl f* **40/1**

4144 **7** *hd* **Ace Master**[13] [2163] 3-9-1 **59** .... JimmyQuinn 10 45
(Roy Bowring) *chsd ldrs: one pce fnl 2f* **17/2**

0-15 **8** *1/2* **Invigilator**[20] [1952] 3-9-0 **58** .... LukeMorris 4 42
(Harry Dunlop) *dwlt: hdwy 2f out: styd on ins fnl f* **10/1**

5-26 **9** *7* **My Love Fajer (IRE)**[33] [1595] 3-9-1 **62** .... AmyBaker(3) 8 21
(George Prodromou) *chsd ldrs: wknd 2f out* **25/1**

0-43 **10** *1/2* **Cara Carmela**[27] [1764] 3-8-7 **51** oh3 .... WilliamCarson 3 8
(Stuart Williams) *chsd ldrs: outpcd and lost pl over 2f out* **10/1**

343- **11** *2 1/2* **Nellie Ellis (IRE)**[239] [6576] 3-9-2 **63** .... MatthewDavies(3) 11 11
(George Baker) *chsd ldrs stands' side: lost pl 2f out* **13/2**[8]

300- **12** *4* **Nettis**[270] [5659] 3-9-1 **59** .... AdamKirby 6 —
(George Prodromou) *in rr: bhd fnl 2f* **22/1**

62.13 secs (1.13) **Going Correction** +0.125s/f (Good) **12** Ran SP% **118.2**
Speed ratings (Par 97): **95,94,90,88,88 87,87,86,75,74 70,63**
Tote Swingers: 1&2 £6.30, 1&3 £10.20, 2&3 £12.70 CSF £28.61 CT £248.55 TOTE £4.20: £1.60, £1.60, £4.30; EX 31.10 Trifecta £403.20 Part won. Pool: £544.93 - 0.79 winning units..
Owner Mrs B E Wilkinson **Bred** West Wind Farm **Trained** Willoughton, Lincs

FOCUS
A modest handicap. The field were spread from the centre to stands' side. The fact the runner-up ran so well suggests the form isn't up to much.

2525 FIREMAN SAM VISITS TWINLAKES - 2ND JULY H'CAP 5f 13y
2:50 (2:50) (Class 3) (0-95,95) 4-Y-O+ **£7,447** (£2,216; £1,107; £553) **Stalls** Centre

Form RPR

-031 **1** **Solemn**[16] [2069] 6-8-10 **84** ....(b) LiamKeniry 7 92
(Milton Bradley) *led against stands' side rail: edgd lft over 1f out: in command whn eased nr fin* **16/1**

131- **2** *nk* **Tagula Night (IRE)**[259] [5995] 5-8-10 **87** ....(vt) JohnFahy(3) 10 93
(Walter Swinburn) *in rr: hung lft and hdwy stands' side over 1f out: styd on fnl 75yds* **14/1**

0004 **3** *1/2* **Rocket Rob (IRE)**[8] [2299] 5-8-9 **83** ow1 .... StevieDonohoe 8 87+
(Willie Musson) *bmpd s: in rr: hdwy and nt clr run over 1f out and jst ins fnl f: swtchd rt to r against stands' side rail: fin wl* **9/1**[3]

-530 **4** *1 1/2* **Whozthecat (IRE)**[15] [2116] 4-8-10 **89** .... NeilFarley(5) 8 88
(Declan Carroll) *w ldrs: kpt on same pce fnl f* **4/1**[2]

-001 **5** *nk* **Humidor (IRE)**[29] [1680] 4-9-2 **93** ....(t) MatthewDavies(3) 11 91
(George Baker) *gave problems and led rdrless to s: hdwy to chse ldrs over 2f out: edgd lft and styd on same pce fnl f* **4/1**[2]

4-56 **6** *1/2* **Secret Millionaire (IRE)**[8] [2317] 4-8-13 **87** .... StephenCraine 5 83
(Patrick Morris) *stdd s: sn trcking ldrs: t.k.h: kpt on same pce over 1f out: nvr rchd ldrs* **3/1**[1]

40-0 **7** *1/2* **Olynard (IRE)**[15] [2099] 5-8-12 **86** .... RoystonFfrench 1 80
(Dr Richard Newland) *wnt rt s: in rr: kpt on over 1f out: nvr a factor* **50/1**

0200 **8** *nk* **Star Rover (IRE)**[16] [2075] 4-9-2 **90** .... CathyGannon 9 83
(David Evans) *chsd ldrs: one pce fnl 2f* **9/1**[3]

0240 **9** *1* **Secret Asset (IRE)**[29] [1687] 6-9-0 **95** .... LewisWalsh(7) 3 84
(Jane Chapple-Hyam) *w ldrs on outside: wknd appr fnl f* **16/1**

3-00 **10** *3/4* **Drawnfromthepast (IRE)**[15] [2099] 6-8-11 **92** .... IanBurns(7) 6 79
(Ed Walker) *trckd ldrs: rdn over 2f out: sn lost pl* **20/1**

0-60 **11** *1 3/4* **Skylla**[17] 2028 4-8-8 **82**.................... FrederikTylicki 4 62
(Richard Fahey) *w ldrs: lost pl 2f out* **10/1**

60.65 secs (-0.35) **Going Correction** +0.125s/f (Good) **11** Ran SP% **119.2**
Speed ratings (Par 107): **107,106,105,103,102 102,101,100,99,97 95**
Tote Swingers: 1&2 £8.20, 1&3 £18.40, 2&3 £12.10 CSF £224.13 CT £2184.62 TOTE £18.20: £4.30, £3.00, £2.70; EX 80.20 Trifecta £219.80 Pool: £787.30 - 2.65 winning units..
Owner E A Hayward **Bred** Cheveley Park Stud Ltd **Trained** Sedbury, Gloucs

FOCUS
A good handicap. The pace was not particularly strong and the winner was always best placed.

NOTEBOOK
Solemn recorded an eighth career win when justifying support over this trip at Newmarket last time. He had a 4lb rise to deal with but put in a tenacious front-running effort and was value for more than the winning margin because he was eased down close home. He could take some stopping in a hat-trick bid. (tchd 14-1)
Tagula Night(IRE) took a while to get going in 2010, but ended the year on a high with wins at Sandown and Goodwood. Soft ground looked a possible key to him last autumn and he has peaked around August in the last two years, but that didn't stop him running a huge race off a career-high mark on this return from 259 days off. He looks set for another productive season and is equally effective at 5f/6f. (op 16-1)
Rocket Rob(IRE) ran his best race since switching yards when a close fourth at Haydock last time. Given another typically patient ride, he weaved his way through some traffic problems before surging home behind the prominently ridden winner. He is well weighted on several close calls last summer and should be able to end a 16-month drought when getting a bit more luck. He was reported to have lost a shoe. Official explanation: jockey said gelding was denied a clear run; vet said gelding lost an off-fore shoe (op 6-1)
Whozthecat(IRE) was well backed and showed plenty of dash with blinkers removed dropped back to what is arguably his best trip. Still relatively lightly raced, he is just 1lb higher than for the second of his two fast turf/AW wins in 2010 and may be most potent when attacking on sharp tracks. (op 11-2)
Humidor(IRE) had a golden spell in the second half of last season and got back in the groove with a tongue-tie applied when winning at Goodwood on his second run back. He gave it a decent shot off 6lb higher but was vulnerable in a bid to improve his strike-rate to 6-14. (tchd 9-2)
Secret Millionaire(IRE) was a big market mover in the morning but couldn't launch a serious attack from just behind the pace. He is a very reliable type who is on a winning mark but has won only one of his last 17 starts. (op 7-2, after 4-1 in places)

2526 WINTER WONDERLAND - TWINLAKES 19TH NOVEMBER ONWARDS H'CAP 1m 6f 15y
3:20 (3:21) (Class 5) (0-70,70) 4-Y-O+ **£2,525** (£751; £375; £187) **Stalls** Low

Form RPR

-400 **1** **No Time For Tears (IRE)**[46] 1310 4-7-12 **52**..........(p) KieranO'Neill(5) 13 59
(Lucinda Featherstone) *s.i.s: swtchd lft after s: hdwy on outer over 4f out: styd on wl fnl f: led fnl strides* **33/1**

0452 **2** *nk* **Dubara Reef (IRE)**[9] 2259 4-9-7 **70**....................(p) SilvestreDeSousa 10 76
(Paul Green) *chsd ldrs: upsides after 3f: hung rt and kpt on to ld nr fin: hdd fnl strides* **11/2**[3]

00-4 **3** *3/4* **Outland (IRE)**[27] 1750 5-8-5 **54**.................................. AdrianMcCarthy 5 59
(J R Jenkins) *trckd ldrs: hdwy on inner to ld over 2f out: hdd and no ex last 50yds* **9/1**

0-04 **4** *1 1/4* **Arashi**[30] 1658 5-8-12 **61**..(p) TomMcLaughlin 8 65
(Lucinda Featherstone) *in tch: hdwy over 3f out: hung lft and chal over 1f out: kpt on same pce* **16/1**

65 **5** *3/4* **Court Wing (IRE)**[19] 1973 5-8-2 **51** oh1........................... LukeMorris 15 54
(Richard Price) *t.k.h in midfield: effrt over 3f out: one pce fnl 2f* **25/1**

4305 **6** *2 1/4* **Camps Bay (USA)**[13] 2159 7-9-4 **67**................................. AdamKirby 9 66
(Conor Dore) *mid-div: reminders 7f out: hdwy over 3f out: kpt on fnl f* **16/1**

0-46 **7** *1 3/4* **Blue Nymph**[16] 1305 5-9-3 **66**.. TomEaves 12 63
(John Quinn) *dwlt: hld up in midfield: hdwy over 4f out: led briefly over 2f out: one pce* **5/1**[2]

0-42 **8** *4* **Kayaan**[11] 2202 4-8-11 **60**... MickyFenton 3 51
(Pam Sly) *dwlt: hld up in rr: hdwy over 2f out: nvr nr ldrs* **20/1**

300- **9** *1/2* **Mighty Mambo**[237] 6623 4-9-4 **67**.................................. TomQueally 1 58
(George Margarson) *led tl over 2f out: wknd over 1f out* **33/1**

000- **10** *1 1/2* **Rannoch Moor**[198] 7419 4-8-5 **54** ow1.......................(v1) MartinDwyer 11 43
(Marcus Tregoning) *chsd ldrs: drvn 6f out: wknd over 2f out* **7/2**[1]

44-3 **11** *4 1/2* **Royal Premier (IRE)**[9] 2272 8-8-2 **51** oh1...................... CathyGannon 6 33
(Tom Keddy) *chsd ldrs: wknd over 2f out* **25/1**

-360 **12** *2* **Quinsman**[44] 1367 5-9-7 **70**.. LiamKeniry 7 50
(J S Moore) *hld up in rr: hdwy 3f out: wknd over 2f out* **14/1**

441- **13** *5* **Maison Brillet (IRE)**[150] 8015 4-9-7 **70**......................(p) SteveDrowne 4 43
(Clive Drew) *hld up in rr: bhd fnl 2f: eased* **33/1**

4401 **14** *9* **Profit's Reality (IRE)**[20] 1956 9-9-0 **66**........................ KierenFox(3) 2 26
(Michael Attwater) *in rr: effrt on outside over 3f out: sn wknd: eased* **18/1**

0001 **15** *10* **Torran Sound**[9] 2272 4-8-8 **57**....................................... KierenFallon 14 3
(James Eustace) *sn chsng ldrs: lost pl over 2f out: eased whn bhd* **15/2**

3m 6.34s (-0.96) **Going Correction** +0.025s/f (Good) **15** Ran SP% **121.0**
Speed ratings (Par 103): **103,102,102,101,101 99,98,96,96,95 92,91,88,83,78**
Tote Swingers: 1&2 £53.00, 1&3 £81.00, 2&3 £8.70 CSF £194.31 CT £1796.63 TOTE £66.10: £16.20, £2.10, £2.30; EX 798.10 TRIFECTA Not won..
Owner Arnie Flower **Bred** P D Savill **Trained** Atlow, Derbyshire
■ Stewards' Enquiry : Kieran O'Neill four-day ban: used whip with excessive frequency (Jun 12-13,19-20)

FOCUS
A minor staying handicap. The pace was fairly steady and a surprise winner prevailed in a tight three-way finish. The race has been rated around the fourth and fifth.
Dubara Reef(IRE) Official explanation: jockey said gelding hung right
Royal Premier(IRE) Official explanation: jockey said gelding had no more to give
Profit's Reality(IRE) Official explanation: trainer said gelding was unsuited by the good (good to firm places) ground
Torran Sound Official explanation: jockey said gelding ran flat

2527 DOH, THE SIMPSONS - WHEELGATE - 27TH JULY H'CAP 1m 75y
3:50 (3:51) (Class 5) (0-75,73) 3-Y-O **£2,525** (£751; £375; £187) **Stalls** Centre

Form RPR

3-15 **1** **Shadow Catcher**[10] 2216 3-9-6 **72**................................ FrederikTylicki 1 77
(Michael Dods) *mid-div: effrt 4f out: styd on to ld over 1f out: hld on towards fin* **4/1**[2]

0-66 **2** *nk* **Ferruccio (IRE)**[16] 2064 3-9-0 **66**.................................(t) PatCosgrave 7 70
(James Fanshawe) *mid-div: pushed along and outpcd over 4f out: hdwy 3f out: styd on to chal ins fnl f: no ex nr fin* **6/1**

3343 **3** *nk* **Urban Kode (IRE)**[104] 540 3-8-10 **62**............................(v) CathyGannon 8 65
(David Evans) *sn chsng ldrs: wd and lost pl bnd over 5f out: hdwy to chse ldrs 3f out: hung both ways: upsides over 1f out: kpt on same pce fnl 50yds* **25/1**

33-1 **4** *4* **My Mate Jake (IRE)**[48] 1277 3-9-5 **71**.......................... PaulMulrennan 9 65
(James Given) *dropped to rr after 1f: in rr: hdwy and nt clr run over 2f out: swtchd rt: kpt on fnl f* **9/1**

311 **5** *3 3/4* **One Pursuit (IRE)**[87] 738 3-8-13 **68**.............................. BillyCray(3) 2 53
(David Nicholls) *trckd ldrs: nt clr run over 1f out: hung lft and wknd jst ins fnl f* **11/2**[3]

610 **6** *1/2* **Absolute Princess**[24] 1837 3-8-12 **71**.......................... LeonnaMayor(7) 4 55
(David Nicholls) *t.k.h: w ldr: led after 2f: hdd over 3f out: wkng whn hmpd 1f out* **28/1**

2503 **7** *1/2* **Sir Randolf (IRE)**[53] 1191 3-8-10 **62**............................(t) JamesDoyle 6 45
(Sylvester Kirk) *s.i.s: kpt on fnl 2f: nvr on terms* **25/1**

3-23 **8** *1* **Matavia Bay (IRE)**[11] 2196 3-8-12 **64**............................ KierenFallon 5 45
(Alan Jarvis) *trckd ldrs: edgd lft and wknd 1f out: b.b.v* **5/2**[1]

1-40 **9** *1 1/2* **Endaxi Mana Mou**[53] 1176 3-8-10 **67**.......................... AdamBeschizza(5) 3 44
(Noel Quinlan) *s.i.s: sme hdwy over 2f out: nvr a factor* **33/1**

0130 **10** *2 1/2* **Bertie Blu Boy**[10] 2216 3-8-11 **63**.............................. SilvestreDeSousa 10 35
(Paul Green) *t.k.h: led 2f: w ldr: led 4f out: hdd over 1f out: sn wknd: eased nr fin* **8/1**

1m 46.19s (0.59) **Going Correction** +0.025s/f (Good) **10** Ran SP% **113.4**
Speed ratings (Par 99): **98,97,97,93,89 89,88,87,86,83**
Tote Swingers: 1&2 £7.40, 1&3 £20.40, 2&3 £24.80 CSF £25.96 CT £535.89 TOTE £6.10: £2.10, £1.80, £3.30; EX 38.40 Trifecta £155.90 Part won. Pool: £210.76 - 0.30 winning units..
Owner A Wynn-Williams, D Graham, D Neale **Bred** Mascalls Stud **Trained** Denton, Co Durham

FOCUS
A fair handicap run at a strong tempo. The first three pulled clear and they all came from off the pace. The bare form is only ordinary.
Urban Kode(IRE) Official explanation: jockey said colt hung left and right
One Pursuit(IRE) Official explanation: jockey said gelding was denied a clear run
Matavia Bay(IRE) Official explanation: vet said gelding bled from the nose
Bertie Blu Boy Official explanation: jockey said gelding hung left early stages

2528 TIMMY - WHEELGATE - BAAAAAA 15TH AUGUST MAIDEN FILLIES' STKS (DIV I) 1m 75y
4:20 (4:22) (Class 5) 3-Y-O **£4,209** (£1,252; £625; £312) **Stalls** Centre

Form RPR

4 **1** **Thistle Bird**[32] 1606 3-9-0 0.. SteveDrowne 11 83+
(Roger Charlton) *t.k.h: trckd ldrs: hung lft and chsd ldr over 1f out: styd on to ld post* **14/1**

2 **2** *shd* **Paoletta (USA)**[13] 2157 3-9-0 0...................................... AhmedAjtebi 1 82+
(Mahmood Al Zarooni) *fly-leaped s: t.k.h: sn trcking ldrs: led and edgd lft over 2f out: hdd post* **2/5**[1]

3 *4* **Totheendoftheearth (IRE)** 3-9-0 0.................................. LiamKeniry 9 73
(Sylvester Kirk) *led early: trckd ldrs: chal 3f out: kpt on same pce appr fnl f* **40/1**

0-4 **4** *hd* **Allumeuse (USA)**[28] 1724 3-9-0 0..................................... DavidProbert 6 72
(Andrew Balding) *sn led: hdd over 2f out: kpt on same pce appr fnl f* **10/1**

5 *1 3/4* **Bashasha (USA)** 3-9-0 0.. RichardHills 2 68+
(Roger Varian) *dwlt: sn trcking ldrs: effrt over 2f out: kpt on same pce: will improve* **6/1**[2]

30- **6** *7* **Loving Thought**[226] 6882 3-9-0 0......................................[1] TomQueally 3 51
(Sir Henry Cecil) *s.i.s: t.k.h: sn trcking ldrs: stdd and dropped bk over 5f out: hdwy over 3f out: hung lft and sn wknd* **8/1**[3]

3- **7** *1* **Reillys Daughter**[339] 3349 3-9-0 0..................................... LukeMorris 10 49
(J S Moore) *chsd ldrs on outer: drvn and lost pl over 5f out: wknd 3f out* **20/1**

00- **8** *1 1/4* **Princesse Fleur**[288] 5066 3-8-7 0................................... DavidKenny(7) 4 46
(Michael Scudamore) *in rr: drvn over 4f out: nvr a factor* **50/1**

0 **9** *1 1/4* **Totally Trusted**[12] 2185 3-8-11 0...................................... BillyCray(3) 7 43
(David Nicholls) *gave probems in stalls: awkward s and rdr lost iron for abt 1f: in rr: rdn 4f out: nvr on terms* **66/1**

1m 45.64s (0.04) **Going Correction** +0.025s/f (Good) **9** Ran SP% **123.2**
Speed ratings (Par 96): **100,99,95,95,93 86,85,84,83**
Tote Swingers: 1&2 £3.60, 1&3 £16.70, 2&3 £9.10 CSF £21.37 TOTE £22.80: £3.80, £1.02, £9.70; EX 37.10 Trifecta £582.30 Part won. Pool: £786.98 - 0.43 winning units..
Owner Lady Rothschild **Bred** The Rt Hon Lord Rothschild **Trained** Beckhampton, Wilts

FOCUS
There didn't seem to be much strength in depth in this fillies' maiden which was run at a stop-start gallop. There was a surprise result as the hot favourite was caught close home but the first two pulled clear and both could be decent. the form has not been rated too positively.

2529 TIMMY - WHEELGATE - BAAAAAA 15TH AUGUST MAIDEN FILLIES' STKS (DIV II) 1m 75y
4:50 (4:51) (Class 5) 3-Y-O **£4,209** (£1,252; £625; £312) **Stalls** Centre

Form RPR

1 **Gracefield (USA)** 3-9-0 0... AhmedAjtebi 4 79+
(Mahmood Al Zarooni) *trckd ldr: t.k.h: drvn and outpcd over 2f out: swtchd rt and rallied over 1f out: styd on to ld cl home* **7/1**[2]

6- **2** *nk* **Focal**[302] 4595 3-9-0 0.. RyanMoore 5 73+
(Sir Michael Stoute) *led: pushed along 3f out: sn jnd: hdd fnl strides* **1/2**[1]

3 *2 1/4* **Deck Walk (USA)** 3-9-0 0.. SteveDrowne 10 68+
(Roger Charlton) *hld up on outer in midfield: hdwy over 4f out: chsng ldrs over 2f out: styd on same pce appr fnl f* **9/1**[3]

50 **4** *1* **Faith And Hope (IRE)**[19] 1974 3-9-0 0..........................(t) PatCosgrave 9 65
(James Fanshawe) *trckd ldrs: chal over 2f out: kpt on same pce fnl f* **25/1**

5 *1 3/4* **Crystal High** 3-9-0 0... AdamKirby 3 61
(Marco Botti) *hld up in mid-div: hdwy on inner to trck ldrs 4f out: edgd rt and fdd appr fnl f* **20/1**

6 *3* **Eraadaat (IRE)** 3-9-0 0... RichardHills 1 54+
(Ed Dunlop) *s.s: towards rr: pushed along over 3f out: kpt on fnl 2f: will improve* **10/1**

40 **7** *1 1/2* **Tortilla (IRE)**[8] 2306 3-8-11 0....................................... MartinHarley(3) 6 50
(Des Donovan) *mid-div: drvn over 3f out: wknd 2f out* **28/1**

8 *2 1/2* **Marina Ballerina** 3-9-0 0... PaulQuinn 8 44
(Roy Bowring) *t.k.h: rn wd and lost pl bnd after 1f: hdwy 4f out: lost pl over 2f out* **50/1**

9 *1/2* **Sistine** 3-9-0 0... PaulMulrennan 7 43
(James Given) *s.i.s: hdwy on outside over 4f out: sn drvn: lost pl 2f out* **14/1**

1m 49.69s (4.09) **Going Correction** +0.025s/f (Good) **9** Ran SP% **118.9**
Speed ratings (Par 96): **80,79,77,76,74 71,70,67,67**
Tote Swingers: 1&2 £2.60, 1&3 £5.60, 2&3 £3.00 CSF £10.88 TOTE £6.50: £2.30, £1.02, £2.40; EX 18.20 Trifecta £57.00 Pool: £741.18 - 9.61 winning units..
Owner Godolphin **Bred** Darley **Trained** Newmarket, Suffolk

FOCUS
The second division of a fillies' maiden. There were a number of runners representing top connections', and there was another upset as the odds-on favourite was just picked off. It was slowly run and there are doubts over the form's worth.

2530 BEN & HOLLY - WHEELGATE - 16TH OCTOBER H'CAP — 1m 2f 50y
5:20 (5:20) (Class 6) (0-65,61) 4-Y-O+ **£1,813** (£539; £269; £134) Stalls Low

Form — RPR

0-60 **1** **Guga (IRE)**[19] 1993 5-8-12 **52**..........(b) SilvestreDeSousa 1 65
(John Mackie) *led: wnt wl clr 5f out: kpt on fnl 2f: unchal* **7/1**

05-3 **2** *3 3/4* **Transfer**[19] 1987 6-8-10 **50**.......... JamesDoyle 11 56+
(Richard Price) *in rr: hdwy u.p over 3f out: wnt 2nd 1f out: no ch of rching wnr* **9/4**[1]

-006 **3** *2 1/2* **Dragon Slayer (IRE)**[23] 1871 9-9-1 **55**.......... PatCosgrave 2 56+
(John Harris) *trckd ldrs: effrt over 3f out: wnt 3rd 1f out: one pce* **16/1**

10-0 **4** *3* **Highland Love**[10] 2213 6-9-3 **57**.......... PaulMulrennan 7 52
(Jedd O'Keeffe) *chsd wnr: wnt 2nd over 3f out: wknd fnl f* **18/1**

4504 **5** *1 1/2* **Straversjoy**[9] 2259 4-9-7 **61**.......... GrahamGibbons 6 53
(Reg Hollinshead) *in tch: effrt over 3f out: one pce fnl 2f* **9/2**[3]

50-0 **6** *3 3/4* **Pattern Mark**[23] 1871 5-8-13 **53**..........(p) TomQueally 10 38
(Ollie Pears) *s.i.s: kpt on fnl 3f: nvr nr ldrs* **4/1**[2]

0564 **7** *3 1/2* **General Tufto**[25] 1814 6-9-0 **61**..........(b) MatthewLawson(7) 4 39
(Charles Smith) *s.i.s: drvn on wd outside over 4f out: wknd over 2f out* **14/1**

0-05 **8** *1/2* **Wiseman's Diamond (USA)**[41] 1440 6-9-2 **56**.......... MickyFenton 5 33
(Paul Midgley) *trckd ldrs: effrt over 3f out: wknd and eased over 1f out* **8/1**

-404 **9** *4 1/2* **Chik's Dream**[30] 1655 4-9-5 **59**.......... AndreaAtzeni 9 27
(Derek Haydn Jones) *hld up in mid-div: lost pl over 3f out: sn bhd* **25/1**

50-0 **10** *9* **Efidium**[34] 1557 13-8-4 **47**.......... PaulPickard(3) 3 —
(Suzzanne France) *dropped to rr after 1f: sme hdwy over 3f out: sn wknd: eased whn bhd ins fnl f* **66/1**

000- **11** *10* **Apurna**[195] 4986 6-8-7 **47** oh2..........(p) CathyGannon 8 —
(John Harris) *sn chsng wnr: drvn 4f out: sn lost pl: bhd whn eased fnl f* **66/1**

2m 10.67s (-1.03) **Going Correction** +0.025s/f (Good) **11** Ran SP% **117.2**
Speed ratings (Par 101): **105,102,100,97,96 93,90,90,86,79 71**
Tote Swingers: 1&2 £3.20, 1&3 £16.60, 2&3 £11.40 CSF £22.77 CT £246.62 TOTE £7.90: £2.80, £1.20, £3.70; EX 24.50 Trifecta £288.00 Pool: £665.66 - 1.71 winning units..
Owner W I Bloomfield **Bred** Azienda Agricola Loreto Luciani **Trained** Church Broughton , Derbys

FOCUS
There was an unchallenged winner in this low-grade handicap. He's rated back to something like his best.
Guga(IRE) Official explanation: trainer said, regarding apparent improvement in form, that the gelding appeared to benefit from the reapplication of blinkers.
T/Jkpt: Not won. T/Plt: £119.50 to a £1 stake. Pool £68,922.56. 420.85 winning tickets T/Qpdt: £33.60 to a £1 stake. Pool £4,123.34. 90.60 winning tickets WG

2531a, 2536 - 2537a - (Foreign Racing) - See Raceform Interactive

[1924]LEOPARDSTOWN (L-H)
Sunday, May 29

OFFICIAL GOING: Good to firm (watered)

2532a IRISH STALLION FARMS EUROPEAN BREEDERS FUND 2YO MAIDEN — 7f
2:55 (2:56) 2-Y-O **£10,112** (£2,344; £1,025; £586)

RPR

1 **Teolane (IRE)**[18] 2009 2-8-12.......... KJManning 6 89+
(J S Bolger, Ire) *sn led and clr of remainder w 2nd: rdn clr 2f out: styd on wl fr over 1f out: easily* **6/4**[2]

2 *5 1/2* **Secretary Of State (IRE)**[17] 2036 2-9-0.......... JPO'Brien(3) 2 80
(A P O'Brien, Ire) *chsd ldrs: mod 3rd for much: no imp u.p and kpt on same pce fr under 2f out* **4/5**[1]

3 *shd* **Precious Dream (USA)** 2-8-12.......... WMLordan 3 [illegible]
(David Wachman, Ire) *dwlt: chsd ldrs: mod 4th for much: no imp u.p and kpt on same pce fr under 2f out* **12/1**[3]

4 *1 1/4* **Jimtown**[17] 2036 2-9-3.......... DPMcDonogh 4 76
(Kevin Prendergast, Ire) *sn trckd ldr: clr of remainder: pushed along appr st: no imp and kpt on same pce fr under 2f out* **14/1**

5 *4 1/2* **French Quebec (IRE)** 2-8-9.......... ShaneFoley(3) 1 60
(K J Condon, Ire) *wl off pce towards rr: mod 5th appr st: sn no imp* **33/1**

6 *24* **Can Do Les (IRE)** 2-9-3.......... PJSmullen 5 —
(D K Weld, Ire) *s.i.s: a towards rr: no imp fr bef st* **22/1**

1m 30.48s (1.78) **Going Correction** +0.25s/f (Good) **6** Ran SP% **117.2**
Speed ratings: **99,92,92,91,86 58**
CSF £3.21 TOTE £1.90: £1.02, £1.10; DF 3.80.
Owner Mrs J S Bolger **Bred** J S Bolger **Trained** Coolcullen, Co Carlow

FOCUS
The winner rates a big improver from her promising debut.

NOTEBOOK
Teolane(IRE) ◆ was sent to the front after about 1f and she was never in much danger after that, stretching out well in the straight for a decisive victory. She is clearly well regarded by her trainer and he might drop her back to 6f for the Albany Stakes at Royal Ascot. (op 9/4)
Secretary Of State(IRE), beaten a head over the trip at Gowran Park on his previous start, was third into the straight and, while he kept on for pressure, he was involved in a scrap for the minors and nothing else as the winner forged clear. (op 4/6 tchd 9/10)
Precious Dream(USA), making her debut, missed the break. She made headway on the outside 2f out and kept on, just losing out on second place but never posing any sort of threat to the winner. (op 10/1)
Jimtown, almost five lengths behind Secretary Of State when fifth on his debut at Gowran Park, led early on and raced in second place for much of the journey, but was unable to raise his game from well over 1f out. (op 12/1)
French Quebec(IRE) trailed the field and, although moving up a place turning for home, she never posed any sort of threat. (op 25/1)

2533a BALLYCORUS STKS (GROUP 3) — 7f
3:25 (3:26) 3-Y-O+ **£32,219** (£9,418; £4,461; £1,487)

RPR

1 **Bewitched (IRE)**[232] 6735 4-9-9 111..........(t) JMurtagh 7 113+
(Charles O'Brien, Ire) *hld up: plld to outer and chal in 5th 1f out: qcknd smartly to ld ins fnl f: eased nr fin* **6/1**[2]

2 *1 1/4* **Zoffany (IRE)**[260] 5975 3-9-3 115.......... CO'Donoghue 4 110
(A P O'Brien, Ire) *chsd ldrs: 5th for much: chal u.p and ev ch on terms 1f out: no imp and kpt on same pce wl ins fnl f* **7/4**[1]

3 *shd* **Glor Na Mara (IRE)**[27] 1778 3-8-12 108..........(p) KJManning 3 105
(J S Bolger, Ire) *trckd ldrs: 4th for much: chal u.p and ev ch on terms fr over 1f out: no ex and kpt on same pce wl ins fnl f* **10/1**

4 *2* **Imperial Rome (IRE)**[14] 2139 3-8-12 106.......... WMLordan 2 99
(David Wachman, Ire) *led: t.k.h: hdd and kpt on same pce fr 1f out* **7/4**[1]

5 *1* **Six Of Hearts**[14] 2128 7-9-12 91..........(b) WJSupple 8 104
(Cecil Ross, Ire) *sn racd in rr: kpt on wout threatening u.p fr under 2f out* **28/1**

6 *3 1/2* **Duff (IRE)**[22] 1889 8-9-9 101.......... FMBerry 5 91
(Edward Lynam, Ire) *dwlt sltly: sn trckd ldr: pushed along to chal 2f out: no ex fr over 1f out* **8/1**[3]

7 *nk* **Finicius (USA)**[31] 1642 7-9-9 102..........(t) JamieSpencer 6 90
(Eoin Griffin, Ire) *towards rr: no imp u.p and kpt on same pce fr under 2f out* **16/1**

8 *nk* **Stunning View (IRE)**[210] 7259 4-9-9 99.......... PJSmullen 1 90
(D K Weld, Ire) *trckd ldrs: 3rd for much: no ex u.p fr over 1f out* **12/1**

1m 30.55s (1.85) **Going Correction** +0.25s/f (Good)
WFA 3 from 4yo+ 11lb **8** Ran SP% **124.2**
Speed ratings: **99,97,97,95,94 90,89,89**
CSF £18.57 TOTE £5.30: £1.90, £1.02, £2.00; DF 16.10.
Owner Mrs John Magnier **Bred** Monsieur J C Coude **Trained** Straffan, Co Kildare

FOCUS
The staying-on winner and fifth have been rated to their 2010 bests.

NOTEBOOK
Bewitched(IRE) ◆ made a taking reappearance under a hold-up ride, quickening well after being switched to the outer, was soon well on top and won comfortably. This was her first win over 7f and it was also the quickest ground she has won on. Cut to 12-1 (from 16-1) by Ladbrokes and to 16-1 (from 20-1) by Paddy Power for the Golden Jubilee Stakes, that event is only a possible target, with races at Deauville and Haydock later in the year in mind.\n\x\x Cut to 12-1 (from 16-1) by Ladbrokes and to 16-1 (from 20-1) by Paddy Power for the Golden Jubilee Stakes, that event is only a possible target, with races at Deauville and Haydock later in the year in mind.\n\x\x made a taking reappearance under a hold-up ride, quickening well after being switched to the outer, was soon well on top and won comfortably. This was her first win over 7f and it was also the quickest ground she has won on. Cut to 12-1 (from 16-1) by Ladbrokes and to 16-1 (from 20-1) by Paddy Power for the Golden Jubilee Stakes, that event is only a possible target, with races at Deauville and Haydock later in the year in mind. (op 5/1)
Zoffany(IRE) had twice won over this course and trip and was making a delayed reappearance after being troubled by a slight colic this month. He came there with every chance 1f out but could raise no extra in the closing stages. His trainer expects him to come on for the run, and the St James's Palace Stakes was mentioned as possibly his next target. had twice won over this course and trip and was making a delayed reappearance after being troubled by a slight colic this month. He came there with every chance 1f out but could raise no extra in the closing stages. His trainer expects him to come on for the run, and the St James's Palace Stakes was mentioned as possibly his next target. had twice won over this course and trip and was making a delayed reappearance after being troubled by a slight colic this month. He came there with every chance 1f out but could raise no extra in the closing stages. His trainer expects him to come on for the run, and the St James's Palace Stakes was mentioned as possibly his next target. (op 13/8 tchd 2/1)
Glor Na Mara(IRE) is something of an enigma and remains a maiden despite being placed a couple of times at Group 1 level last year. He was meeting Zoffany on 5lb better terms for a half length beating by that rival in the Phoenix Stakes and, while he just failed to reverse placings, he performed creditably and a lot better than was the case on his two previous starts this season.
Imperial Rome(IRE), a three-time winner, including at Listed level over this trip at the Curragh early this month, performed creditably in the Poule d'Essai des Poulains. He made the running and only gave best inside the final furlong. (op 11/4)
Six Of Hearts produced his best effort of the season so far, and kept on quite well over the last 2f without posing a serious threat. (op 33/1)

2534a SEAMUS & ROSEMARY MCGRATH MEMORIAL SAVAL BEG STKS (LISTED RACE) — 1m 6f
3:55 (3:55) 4-Y-O+ **£26,616** (£7,780; £3,685; £1,228)

RPR

1 **Fame And Glory**[42] 1427 5-9-8 124.......... JamieSpencer 9 115+
(A P O'Brien, Ire) *chsd ldrs: clsr in 5th fr 4f out: chal in 3rd fr over 1f out: sn led and strly pressed: styd on wl* **30/100**[1]

2 *1/2* **Vivacious Vivienne (IRE)**[7] 2333 5-8-12 97.......... CDHayes 1 104
(Donal Kinsella, Ire) *hld up: clsr in 7th fr 4f out: rdn to chal in 4th over 1f out: 2nd and pressed wnr ins fnl f: kpt on same pce cl home* **50/1**

3 *3/4* **Rite Of Passage**[346] 3102 7-9-8 118.......... PJSmullen 8 113+
(D K Weld, Ire) *chsd ldrs: pushed along in clsr 3rd under 4f out: chal in 2nd over 1f out: dropped to 3rd and kpt on wout matching 1st 2 ins fnl f* **9/2**[2]

4 *nk* **Fictional Account (IRE)**[42] 1427 6-9-1 103.......... FMBerry 5 106
(V C Ward, Ire) *towards rr: clsd fr 4f out: rdn in 5th over 1f out: kpt on wout threatening fnl f* **16/1**

5 *4 1/2* **Nebula Storm (IRE)**[42] 1427 4-9-1 102.......... JMurtagh 3 101
(John M Oxx, Ire) *sn chsd ldr: clsd 4f out: led into st: sn clr: reduced ld and strly pressed over 1f out: sn hdd and no ex* **8/1**[3]

6 *4 1/2* **Admiral Barry (IRE)**[25] 1808 6-9-1 99.......... DPMcDonogh 7 93
(Eoin Griffin, Ire) *sn chsd ldrs: clsr in 4th fr 4f out: no ex fr 2f out* **33/1**

7 *nk* **Dirar (IRE)**[25] 1808 6-9-1 106.......... WMLordan 4 93
(Gordon Elliott, Ire) *sn chsd ldrs: clsr in 6th 4f out: no ex fr 2f out* **20/1**

8 *17* **Universal Truth (IRE)**[225] 6926 6-9-1 83.......... PShanahan 6 69
(D K Weld, Ire) *sn led and clr: hdd bef st: no ex fr 2f out* **66/1**

2m 58.66s (-2.34) **Going Correction** -0.05s/f (Good) **8** Ran SP% **123.3**
Speed ratings: **104,103,103,103,100 97,97,88**
CSF £40.04 TOTE £1.30: £1.10, £5.00, £1.50; DF 30.50.
Owner Mrs Fitri Hay **Bred** Ptarmigan Bloodstock And Miss K Rausing **Trained** Ballydoyle, Co Tipperary

FOCUS
A race seen as something of a dress rehearsal for Ireland's challenge for the Ascot Gold Cup. The second raises questions about the value of the form and it is best rated around the winner and fourth.

NOTEBOOK
Fame And Glory succeeded at his first attempt over 1m6f with a performance which leaves plenty of questions to be answered when he tackles an extra 6f in the Ascot Gold Cup. Yeats won the same Leopardstown event before the second of his four Gold Cup wins in 2007 but how Fame And Glory, two of whose four Group 1 wins were achieved over 1m2f, will deal with 2m4f is another matter. He did enough to prevail here in a race run at a decent enough pace, closing after being held up to hit the front under 2f out and being kept up to his task in the closing stages.
Vivacious Vivienne(IRE) looked up against it but put it up to the winner, coming from the back of the field to go second inside the final furlong. She had every chance and kept on to the line without quite getting there.
Rite Of Passage, having his first run since winning the 2010 Ascot Gold Cup, was said to be in need of the run by his trainer before the race. He was always handy and, after being niggled along leaving the back straight, could find no extra in second over 1f out before staying on again towards the finish. He can be expected to come on well for the run and, with his stamina for 2m4f already proven, it would not be difficult to see him turn the tables on Fame And Glory next time.

Fictional Account(IRE), fourth behind Fame And Glory in the Vintage Crop Stakes at Navan last month, was re-opposing on the same terms and was beaten almost the same distance by the winner on this occasion. She stayed on steadily from behind over the last 2f and was doing her best work towards the finish. (op 20/1)
Nebula Storm(IRE) had run Fame And Glory to half a length when second at Navan and was encountering much quicker ground here. He raced in second place until going to the front on the final bend. Briefly ridden clear, he was headed early in the final furlong and was eased when beaten. The ground was probably a bit lively for him. (op 10/1)

2520 BADEN-BADEN (L-H)
Sunday, May 29

OFFICIAL GOING: Turf: good

2538a OLEANDER-RENNEN (GROUP 3) (4YO+) (TURF) 2m
4:15 (4:21) 4-Y-O+ £27,586 (£9,482; £4,741; £2,586; £1,724)

RPR
1 **Tres Rock Danon (FR)**29 5-9-2 0 ASuborics 2 108
(W Hickst, Germany) *hld up in 3rd on rail: racing freely bhd mod pce: settled down bk st: slow to make prog in st but picked up wl ent fnl f: tk ld 50yds out to win narrowly* **7/10**1
2 *hd* **Earlsalsa (GER)**193 [7492] 7-9-0 0 AHelfenbein 3 106
(C Von Der Recke, Germany) *settled 4th: c through on inner rail ent st: tk ld 2f out: r.o wl u.p fnl f: hdd 50yds out* **98/10**
3 *¾* **Flamingo Fantasy (GER)**385 [1956] 6-8-11 0 THellier 4 102
(S Smrczek, Germany) *bkmarker: wnt wd: ent st: threatened briefly 2f out: tired fnl f but hld on wl for 3rd despite hanging* **54/10**3
4 *3 ½* **Burma Gold (IRE)**29 4-9-2 0 FilipMinarik 6 105
(P Schiergen, Germany) *trckd pce: plld hrd: mde move early in st: no ex* **9/5**2
5 *12* **Cabimas**29 4-8-11 0 EPedroza 1 87
(P Schiergen, Germany) *led at mod pce: stl in front ent st: rdn and sn btn 2f out* **32/5**

3m 27.25s (3.66)
WFA 4 from 5yo+ 2lb 5 Ran SP% **132.9**
WIN (incl. 10 euro stake): 17. PLACES: 12, 16, 14. SF: 134.
Owner Stall D'Angelo **Bred** Haras De Chevotel & Morton Bloodstock **Trained** Germany

1554 SAN SIRO (R-H)
Sunday, May 29

OFFICIAL GOING: Turf: good

2539a OAKS D'ITALIA (GROUP 2) (3YO FILLIES) (TURF) 1m 3f
3:30 (12:00) 3-Y-O £172,413 (£75,862; £41,379; £20,689)

RPR
1 **Danedream (GER)**22 [1920] 3-8-11 0 AStarke 2 112
(P Schiergen, Germany) *settled in 5th on rail: prog 3f out: rdn and r.o to ld 2f out: drew clr u.p appr fnl f* **4/6**1
2 *6 ½* **Good Karma (ITY)**28 [1738] 3-8-11 0 FabioBranca 1 100
(S Botti, Italy) *led: 2 l clr 3f out: hdd 2f out: no ex fnl f: jst hld on for 2nd* **121/10**
3 *hd* **Oeuvre D'Art (IRE)**28 [1738] 3-8-11 0 CristianDemuro 6 100
(B Grizzetti, Italy) *settled towards rr: styd on fnl 2f: jst failed to take 2nd: nvr nr enough to chal wnr* **30/1**
4 *2 ¾* **Senza Rete (IRE)**28 [1738] 3-8-11 0 MKolmarkaj 8 95
(M Gasparini, Italy) *trckd ldr: rdn and nt qckn fr 2f out* **17/2**
5 *2 ¾* **Adamantina**28 [1738] 3-8-11 0 MircoDemuro 5 90
(Vittorio Caruso, Italy) *settled on heels of ldng trio: rdn and nt qckn over 2f out: wknd fnl f* **61/20**2
6 *8* **Giu La Testa (IRE)**175 3-8-11 0 CFiocchi 9 76
(A Giorgi, Italy) *racd in midfield: effrt ins fnl 3f: no imp* **246/10**
7 *¾* **Itasip (IRE)**28 [1738] 3-8-11 0 UmbertoRispoli 7 74
(B Grizzetti, Italy) *a bhd* **30/1**
8 *1 ¼* **A Ma Yen (ITY)**21 3-8-11 0 SUrru 4 72
(Vittorio Caruso, Italy) *settled one fr last: rdn 3f out: no real prog: btn over 2f out* **91/20**3
9 *dist* **Ksenia (ITY)**28 [1738] 3-8-11 0 LManiezzi 3 —
(R Menichetti, Italy) *trckd ldng gp: 6th 3 1/2f out: sn rdn and wknd: t.o* **44/1**

2m 15.2s (-3.40) 9 Ran SP% **133.4**
WIN (incl. 1 euro stake): 1.66. PLACES: 1.20, 2.05, 4.10. DF: 14.10.
Owner Gestut Burg Eberstein **Bred** Gestut Brummerhof **Trained** Germany

NOTEBOOK
Danedream(GER), who was well held in the Marcel Boussac on her second-last start at two, improved for the step up to middle distances when third in the Italian Derby earlier this month. Back racing against her own sex, she drew clear of modest opposition to take this by a lengthy margin.

2540a PREMIO COPPA D'ORO DI MILANO (LISTED RACE) (4YO+) (TURF) 1m 7f
4:10 (12:00) 4-Y-O+ £24,137 (£10,620; £5,793; £2,896)

RPR
1 **Frankenstein (ITY)**22 [1918] 4-9-0 0 DarioVargiu 4 111
(B Grizzetti, Italy) **85/40**2
2 *hd* **Caudillo (GER)**196 8-8-10 0 HenkGrewe 1 106
(Dr A Bolte, Germany) **13/10**1
3 *nk* **Nebukadnezar (GER)**196 4-9-0 0 MSanna 2 111
(P L Giannotti, Italy) **68/10**
4 *snk* **Glorious Grey (IRE)** 4-8-10 0 SSulas 3 106
(Ottavio Di Paolo, Italy) **26/1**
5 *8* **Apprimus (IRE)**15 [2098] 5-8-10 0 UmbertoRispoli 6 96
(Marco Botti) *settled in 4th: wnt 3rd 1/2-way: abt 4 l bhd ldr: pushed along and nt qckn over 2f out: btn and eased fnl f* **79/20**3
6 *5* **Lamool (GER)**21 [1931] 4-9-0 0 AStarke 5 95
(Mario Hofer, Germany) **91/20**

3m 12.4s (-4.00)
WFA 4 from 5yo+ 1lb 6 Ran SP% **130.2**
WIN (incl. 1 euro stake): 3.12. PLACES: 1.53, 1.43. DFD: 6.50.
Owner Freedom Holding **Bred** Azienda Agricola Rosati Colarieti Antonio **Trained** Italy

NOTEBOOK
Apprimus(IRE), who found the ground too fast and dropped out tamely at Newbury last time, again failed to shine and continues to be hard to place.

2541a PREMIO CARLO VITTADINI (EX TURATI) (GROUP 2) (3YO+) (TURF) 1m
4:45 (12:00) 3-Y-O+ £60,344 (£26,551; £14,482; £7,241)

RPR
1 **Worthadd (IRE)**15 [2101] 4-9-7 0 MircoDemuro 5 123+
(Vittorio Caruso, Italy) *sn led: mde all: qcknd clr appr fnl f: easily* **30/100**1
2 *3* **Vanjura (GER)**37 4-9-4 0 APietsch 1 113
(R Dzubasz, Germany) *trckd ldr: sn settled in 4th on rail: rdn and wnt 2nd 1 1/2f out: r.o wl: no ch w wnr* **13/4**2
3 *snk* **Rockhorse (IRE)**21 6-9-5 0 DarioVargiu 3 114+
(B Grizzetti, Italy) *settled in rr: hdwy u.p 2f out: wnt 3rd ins fnl 150yds: r.o wl* **146/10**
4 *2 ½* **Field Of Dream**43 [1397] 4-9-5 0 J-PGuillambert 6 108
(Luca Cumani) *settled in 3rd: pushed along 3 1/2f out: rdn appr 2f out: kpt on at same pce* **37/4**3
5 *snk* **Ransom Hope**14 6-9-5 0 CristianDemuro 2 108
(L Riccardi, Italy) *racd in 5th: rdn and n.m.r 2f out: nt qckn once gap appeared on rail 1 1/2f out* **29/1**
6 *4* **Silver Ocean (USA)**22 3-8-7 0 UmbertoRispoli 4 95
(Riccardo Santini, Italy) *sn trcking ldr: rdn and nt qckn 2f out: wknd fnl f* **104/10**
P **Miles Gloriosus (USA)**14 8-9-5 0 LManiezzi 7 —
(R Menichetti, Italy) *settled towards rr on outside: rdn and no imp 2f out: last whn wnt wrong and p.u appr fnl f* **43/1**

1m 36.8s (-5.30)
WFA 3 from 4yo+ 12lb 7 Ran SP% **131.0**
WIN (incl. 1 euro stake): 1.31. PLACES: 1.03, 1.13. DF: 1.74.
Owner Incolinx **Bred** Compagnia Generale S R L **Trained** Italy

NOTEBOOK
Worthadd(IRE), runner-up to Canford Cliffs in the Lockinge, came home an easy winner on this drop in class. He is likely to reoppse the Hannon runner in the Queen Anne next, with the Prix Jacques Le Marois and Breeders' Cup Mile on his agenda for later in the season.
Field Of Dream, runner-up in a strong Listed event at Leicester on his reappearance, didn't run badly on this step up in class, especially as 7f appears to be his best trip.

2346 CARLISLE (R-H)
Monday, May 30

OFFICIAL GOING: Good to soft (good in home straight; 7.7)
Rail realignment increased distances on round course by about 7yds.
Wind: Fresh, against Weather: Overcast intially, brighter after race 2

2542 BRITISH STALLION STUDS SUPPORTING BRITISH RACING E B F MAIDEN STKS 5f
2:20 (2:21) (Class 5) 2-Y-O £3,367 (£1,002; £500; £250) **Stalls** Low

Form RPR
1 **Worthington (IRE)** 2-8-12 0 PaulHanagan 7 82+
(Richard Fahey) *rn green: sn pushed along towards rr: gd hdwy on inner over 1f out: led fnl 100yds: kpt on wl* **9/2**2
2 *2* **Springinmystep (IRE)** 2-9-3 0 TonyHamilton 10 78+
(Michael Dods) *dwlt: sn in tch on outer: hdwy over 2f out: rdn to ld appr fnl f: hdd fnl 100yds* **15/2**
0 3 *2* **See Clearly**30 [1691] 2-8-12 0 DavidAllan 2 66
(Tim Easterby) *w ldr: rdn over 2f out: no ex fnl 100yds* **9/1**
3 4 *7* **Rougini (IRE)**21 [1946] 2-8-12 0 AndrewElliott 9 41
(Mrs K Burke) *w ldr: rdn to ld 2f out: hdd appr fnl f: sn wknd* **9/2**2
5 *1* **Commanche** 2-9-3 0 TomEaves 5 42
(Bryan Smart) *racd keenly: led narrowly: rdn whn hdd 2f out: wknd ins fnl f* **6/1**3
6 *½* **Dansili Dutch (IRE)** 2-8-12 0 LeeNewman 4 35
(David Barron) *chsd ldrs: wknd over 1f out* **10/1**
00 7 *2* **Come To Mind**10 [2261] 2-9-3 0 PatrickMathers 8 33
(Alan Berry) *slowly away: a outpcd towards rr* **200/1**
0 8 *2 ½* **How Sweet It Is (IRE)**17 [2070] 2-8-12 0 PhillipMakin 1 19
(James Bethell) *prom: rdn over 2f out: wknd over 1f out* **5/2**1
9 *5* **Roy's Legacy** 2-9-0 0 DeclanCannon(3) 3 —
(Shaun Harris) *s.i.s: a outpcd in rr* **66/1**
10 *8* **Johansen** 2-9-0 0 MichaelO'Connell(3) 6 —
(Kate Walton) *midfield: rdn over 2f out: sn wknd* **50/1**

62.64 secs (1.84) **Going Correction** +0.30s/f (Good) 10 Ran SP% **114.0**
Speed ratings (Par 93): **97,93,90,79,77 77,73,69,61,49**
toteswingers: 1&2 £8.30, 1&3 £13.20, 2&3 Not won CSF £37.14 TOTE £5.30: £2.50, £3.70, £2.90; EX 30.30.
Owner David W Armstrong **Bred** Mountarmstrong Stud **Trained** Musley Bank, N Yorks

FOCUS
An ordinary maiden, but they went a fair pace with a three-way battle for the early lead. Newcomers filled the first two places and they probably have a lot more to offer.

NOTEBOOK
Worthington(IRE) ◆, a £45,000 half-sister to four winners over a variety of trips, would have been an unlucky loser here as she met trouble when trying to get closer 2f from home, but eventually found her way through and quickened up well against the inside rail to hit the front half a furlong from home. This scopey filly has a bright future. (op 4-1)
Springinmystep(IRE) ◆, 65,000euros half-brother to three winners including the smart Roker Park, had the disadvantage of starting from the outside stall, but he was produced from off the pace to hold every chance inside the last furlong and just found the winner too strong. He should go one better before long. (tchd 8-1)
See Clearly caught the eye when seventh of 15 on her Thirsk debut and she deserves credit here too for faring best of the trio battling for the early lead. There is a race in her. (op 12-1)
Rougini(IRE), behind a subsequent winner when third of eight on her Windsor debut, was another to help force the pace until weakening inside the last furlong. She is bred to appreciate a bit further. (op 4-1)
Commanche, a £28,000 half-brother to two winners at up to 7f including the smart Instant Recall and in the same ownership as the runner-up, was the other to show good speed before fading and is he likely to come on plenty from this debut. (op 13-2 tchd 7-1 in a place)

How Sweet It Is(IRE), seventh of nine in a York Listed race on her debut, was sent off well backed on this big drop in grade, but after racing close to the pace until past halfway she faded most disappointingly. (op 7-2)

2543 GRAFIX SIGNS H'CAP — 5f 193y
2:55 (2:59) (Class 5) (0-70,70) 4-Y-0+ — £2,266 (£674; £337; £168) Stalls Low

Form — RPR

0-64 **1** — **Feeling Fresh (IRE)**^{24} 1878 6-9-2 **70** .... AdamBeschizza(5) 11 — 84
(Paul Green) *hld up: hdwy on outer over 2f out: r.o strly to ld fnl 100yds* **9/2**^{2}

-250 **2** *2½* **Mandalay King (IRE)**^{23} 1907 6-9-4 **67** .... PJMcDonald 4 — 73
(Marjorie Fife) *hld up: hdwy on outer 2f out: kpt on wl ins fnl f: wnt 2nd fnl 100yds* **22/1**

1020 **3** *1¼* **Apache Ridge (IRE)**^{36} 1539 5-9-7 **70** ....(p) PaulMulrennan 7 — 72
(Keith Dalgleish) *led narrowly: rdn over 2f out: hdd fnl 100yds: no ex* **16/1**

1046 **4** *1¼* **Hinton Admiral**^{3} 2464 7-9-7 **70** .... JoeFanning 14 — 68
(Keith Dalgleish) *w ldr: rdn over 2f out: wknd fnl 100yds* **11/1**

4351 **5** *½* **Toby Tyler**^{29} 1712 5-8-12 **64** ....(v) MichaelO'Connell(3) 5 — 60
(Paul Midgley) *chsd ldrs: rdn over 2f out: kpt on one pce* **15/2**

6-02 **6** *1* **Hansomis (IRE)**^{7} 2352 7-8-7 **56** oh1 .... PaulHanagan 16 — 49
(Bruce Mactaggart) *in tch on outer: rdn over 2f out: one pce* **7/1**^{3}

4356 **7** *hd* **Ubenkor (IRE)**^{27} 1803 6-8-9 **58** ....(p) TonyHamilton 6 — 51
(Michael Herrington) *midfield: rdn 3f out: kpt on ins fnl f: nvr threatened* **20/1**

0006 **8** *1* **Avontuur (FR)**^{14} 2161 9-8-13 **65** ....(b) JamesSullivan(3) 13 — 54
(Ruth Carr) *midfield towards outer: rdn over 2f out: one pce* **25/1**

0221 **9** *½* **Pelmanism**^{7} 2352 4-9-7 **70** 6ex ....(b) PhillipMakin 12 — 58
(Kevin Ryan) *hld up: rdn over 2f out: sn no imp* **5/2**^{1}

04-0 **10** *2½* **Dream Express (IRE)**^{35} 1557 6-8-4 **56** oh8............(p) PaulPickard(3) 15 — 36
(David Thompson) *chsd ldrs: rdn 3f out: wknd over 1f out* **100/1**

00-0 **11** *1* **Blown It (USA)**^{33} 1612 5-8-7 **56** oh1 .... AndrewElliott 2 — 33
(Jim Goldie) *in tch on inner: rdn 3f out: wknd ins fnl f* **12/1**

-155 **12** *4½* **Mottley Crewe**^{34} 1584 4-9-1 **69** .... DaleSwift(5) 10 — 31
(Michael Dods) *sn pushed along in midfield: wknd over 1f out* **12/1**

1550 **13** *1* **Final Salute**^{51} 1244 5-8-9 **58** ....(v) TomEaves 3 — 17
(Bryan Smart) *in tch: rdn over 2f out: wknd over 1f out* **22/1**

4-00 **14** *10* **Durham Express (IRE)**^{3} 2464 4-9-7 **70** ....(p) DavidNolan 1 — —
(Michael Dods) *s.i.s: hld up: a towards rr* **20/1**

1m 14.96s (1.26) **Going Correction** +0.30s/f (Good) — **14** Ran SP% **123.7**
Speed ratings (Par 103): **103,99,98,96,95 94,94,92,92,88 87,81,80,66**
toteswingers: 1&2 £17.40, 1&3 £26.50, 2&3 £19.10 CSF £110.23 CT £1489.54 TOTE £6.20: £2.70, £5.00, £2.30; EX 125.60.
Owner Peter R Ball **Bred** J Mahon **Trained** Lydiate, Merseyside

FOCUS
A competitive handicap and they went a strong pace, which helped the front pair who were held up well off the pace. The runner-up to form sets the level.
Pelmanism Official explanation: trainer's rep had no explanation for the poor form shown
Dream Express(IRE) Official explanation: jockey said gelding hung right-handed final 3f

2544 EDINBURGH WOOLLEN MILL CUMBERLAND PLATE TRIAL (H'CAP) — 1m 3f 107y
3:30 (3:30) (Class 4) (0-80,80) 4-Y-0+ — £6,476 (£1,927; £963; £481) Stalls High

Form — RPR

300- **1** — **Red Fama**^{227} 6895 7-8-7 **66** oh4 .... AndrewElliott 7 — 78
(Neville Bycroft) *hld up in midfield: hdwy over 3f out: chal over 2f out: led 1f out: drvn and kpt on wl ins fnl f* **40/1**

0121 **2** *1½* **Hong Kong Island (IRE)**^{3} 2475 4-8-13 **77** 6ex .... DaleSwift(5) 11 — 87
(Micky Hammond) *in tch: rdn over 2f out: kpt on: wnt 2nd fnl 100yds* **11/4**^{1}

311 **3** *½* **Mcbirney (USA)**^{11} 2213 4-9-3 **79** .... AndrewHeffernan(3) 2 — 88
(Paul D'Arcy) *hld up: smooth hdwy 3f out: led 2f out: drvn whn hdd 1f out: no ex fnl 100yds* **4/1**^{2}

0-20 **4** *5* **Embsay Crag**^{19} 2006 5-9-0 **80** .... ShaneBKelly(7) 8 — 81
(Kate Walton) *s.i.s: sn midfield: rdn over 3f out: kpt on one pce: nvr threatened* **6/1**^{3}

4021 **5** *3½* **Amazing Blue Sky**^{3} 2454 5-8-8 **70** 6ex .... JamesSullivan(3) 4 — 65
(Ruth Carr) *led: rdn whn hdd 2f out: sn wknd* **6/1**^{3}

-555 **6** *2¾* **Jonny Lesters Hair (IRE)**^{15} 2124 6-9-7 **80** .... DavidAllan 10 — 71
(Tim Easterby) *prom: rdn over 2f out: wknd over 1f out* **11/1**

3-01 **7** *7* **Oddsmaker (IRE)**^{37} 1519 10-8-7 **66** oh1 ....(t) PaulHanagan 6 — 46
(Maurice Barnes) *trckd ldng pair: rdn over 3f out: wknd 2f out* **16/1**

-000 **8** *1¼* **Full Speed (GER)**^{15} 2124 6-8-8 **74** .... GarryWhillans(7) 3 — 52
(Alan Swinbank) *hld up: a towards rr* **80/1**

0-45 **9** *3¾* **Fourth Generation (IRE)**^{9} 2282 4-9-3 **76** .... PJMcDonald 5 — 48
(Alan Swinbank) *hld up: a towards rr* **11/1**

0-00 **10** *8* **Kingsdale Orion (IRE)**^{9} 2320 7-8-9 **68** ....(p) TomEaves 1 — 27
(Brian Ellison) *dwlt: hld up: a towards rr* **14/1**

41-0 **11** *19* **Music City (IRE)**^{44} 1390 4-9-5 **78** .... JoeFanning 9 — —
(Mark Johnston) *midfield: rdn over 3f out: sn wknd: t.o* **10/1**

2m 26.46s (3.36) **Going Correction** +0.25s/f (Good) — **11** Ran SP% **117.2**
Speed ratings (Par 105): **97,95,95,91,89 87,82,81,78,72 59**
toteswingers: 1&2 Not won, 1&3 £50.90, 2&3 £4.10 CSF £148.07 CT £564.75 TOTE £65.60: £14.50, £1.50, £1.10; EX 1047.70.
Owner B F Rayner **Bred** N Bycroft **Trained** Brandsby, N Yorks

FOCUS
A fair handicap run at a solid pace, but the result would have left most punters scratching their heads. The winner ran to something like his old form with the placed horses both recording small personal bests.

2545 LLOYD HONDA CARLISLE BELL TRIAL (H'CAP) — 7f 200y
4:05 (4:06) (Class 4) (0-80,80) 4-Y-0+ — £4,533 (£1,348; £674; £336) Stalls Low

Form — RPR

000- **1** — **Toto Skyllachy**^{317} 4154 6-9-3 **76** .... PhillipMakin 5 — 87
(Ollie Pears) *midfield: rdn and hdwy over 2f out: chsd ldr over 1f out: kpt on to ld fnl 50yds* **20/1**

06-1 **2** *½* **Take It To The Max**^{17} 2046 4-9-4 **77** .... PaulHanagan 12 — 87
(Richard Fahey) *hld up in midfield: pushed along wl over 3f out: hdwy over 1f out: kpt on wl ins fnl f: wnt 2nd nr fin* **2/1**^{1}

00-4 **3** *nk* **Moheebb (IRE)**^{7} 2347 7-9-4 **77** ....(b) PJMcDonald 10 — 86
(Ruth Carr) *hld up: rdn and hdwy 2f out: kpt on wl ins fnl f: wnt 3rd line* **12/1**

3450 **4** *nk* **Miami Gator (IRE)**^{62} 1033 4-9-5 **78** ....(v) AndrewElliott 4 — 87+
(Mrs K Burke) *led: rdn over 2f out: hdd fnl 50yds: no ex* **22/1**

3052 **5** *5* **Ours (IRE)**^{3} 2474 8-8-12 **74** ....(p) JamesSullivan(3) 2 — 71
(John Harris) *hld up: rdn over 2f out: kpt on ins fnl f: n.d* **8/1**^{3}

00-5 **6** *½* **Ailsa Craig (IRE)**^{20} 1970 5-9-4 **77** .... TonyHamilton 6 — 73
(Edwin Tuer) *in tch: rdn over 2f out: wknd ins fnl f* **9/1**

4-1 **7** *hd* **Tax Break**^{98} 636 4-9-7 **80** .... LeeNewman 3 — 76
(David Barron) *trckd ldr: rdn over 2f out: wknd ins fnl f* **9/2**^{2}

-044 **8** *1* **Fibs And Flannel**^{9} 2301 4-8-12 **71** .... DavidAllan 11 — 64
(Tim Easterby) *midfield: drvn over 2f out: one pce* **8/1**^{3}

0-00 **9** *1¾* **Marjury Daw (IRE)**^{11} 2217 5-9-5 **78** .... PaulMulrennan 9 — 67
(James Given) *hld up: rdn over 2f out: n.d* **33/1**

-000 **10** *1½* **Legal Legacy**^{23} 1909 5-8-12 **71** .... TomEaves 7 — 57
(Michael Dods) *racd keenly: trckd ldr: rdn over 2f out: wknd fnl f* **25/1**

-060 **11** *½* **Shadowtime**^{20} 1970 6-9-4 **77** .... PatrickMathers 13 — 62
(Colin Teague) *midfield on outer: rdn over 3f out: wknd over 1f out* **66/1**

U-14 **12** *7* **Khandaq (USA)**^{27} 1793 4-9-4 **77** .... JoeFanning 8 — 45
(Keith Dalgleish) *chsd ldrs towards outer: rdn over 2f out: wknd over 1f out* **20/1**

31-5 **13** *8* **Oh So Saucy**^{35} 1569 7-9-2 **75** .... JackMitchell 1 — —
(Chris Wall) *in tch on inner: rdn over 2f out: sn wknd* **12/1**

1m 40.93s (0.93) **Going Correction** +0.25s/f (Good) — **13** Ran SP% **121.3**
Speed ratings (Par 105): **105,104,104,103,98 98,98,97,95,93 93,86,78**
toteswingers: 1&2 £40.00, 1&3 £55.70, 2&3 £13.80 CSF £57.13 CT £553.98 TOTE £28.90: £7.20, £1.10, £5.70; EX 71.80.
Owner Richard Walker **Bred** Mrs G Slater **Trained** Norton, N Yorks

FOCUS
Another good handicap run at a solid gallop and it suited those held up. It produced another decent-priced winner and the form is not easy to assess.

2546 LADIES' NIGHT ON 1ST AUGUST H'CAP (DIV I) — 5f
4:40 (4:40) (Class 6) (0-60,60) 3-Y-0+ — £1,364 (£403; £201) Stalls Low

Form — RPR

00-2 **1** — **Needy McCredie**^{7} 2353 5-9-2 **50** .... PaulHanagan 12 — 61
(James Turner) *in tch: rdn over 2f out: hdwy over 1f out: kpt on wl ins fnl f: led post* **7/4**^{1}

-320 **2** *nse* **Sharp Bullet (IRE)**^{17} 2048 5-9-6 **54** ....(p) TonyHamilton 2 — 65
(Bruce Hellier) *chsd ldr: rdn to ld over 1f out: kpt on: hdd post* **9/1**

-000 **3** *1¼* **Mission Impossible**^{4} 2412 6-8-13 **47** ....(p) PatrickMathers 6 — 54
(Colin Teague) *sn chsd along in midfield: hdwy over 1f out: kpt on wl ins fnl f* **28/1**

3006 **4** *1½* **Tyrannosaurus Rex (IRE)**^{40} 1493 7-8-12 **46** oh1..........(v) TomEaves 8 — 47
(Derek Shaw) *in tch: rdn over 2f out: kpt on one pce* **12/1**

6-60 **5** *2* **Sumay Buoy (IRE)**^{10} 2263 4-8-12 **46** oh1 .... AndrewMullen 11 — 40
(Jean McGregor) *midfield: rdn over 2f out: kpt on ins fnl f: nvr threatened ldrs* **66/1**

5241 **6** *1½* **Dower Glen**^{10} 2263 4-9-9 **57** ....(v) JoeFanning 4 — 46
(Keith Dalgleish) *chsd ldrs: rdn over 2f out: wknd ins fnl f* **7/1**^{3}

0-00 **7** *¾* **Gertmegalush (IRE)**^{20} 1968 4-9-7 **60** .... DaleSwift(5) 7 — 46
(John Harris) *sn outpcd in rr: n.d* **11/2**^{2}

320- **8** *hd* **Speedy Senorita (IRE)**^{270} 5697 6-9-9 **60** .... JamesSullivan(3) 10 — 45
(James Moffatt) *trckd ldr: rdn over 2f out: wknd fnl f* **16/1**

54 **9** *3½* **Your Gifted (IRE)**^{96} 646 4-9-12 **60** .... PaulMulrennan 3 — 32
(Patrick Morris) *led: rdn whn hdd over 1f out: sn wknd* **12/1**

5-04 **10** *1* **Bossy Kitty**^{13} 2182 4-9-9 **57** .... AndrewElliott 9 — 26
(Nigel Tinkler) *slowly away: sn pushed along in rr: a bhd* **7/1**^{3}

06-0 **11** *1* **Elegant Dancer (IRE)**^{136} 169 4-8-7 **46** oh1......... AdamBeschizza(5) 5 — —
(Paul Green) *a outpcd in rr* **16/1**

62.21 secs (1.41) **Going Correction** +0.30s/f (Good)
WFA 3 from 4yo+ 8lb — **11** Ran SP% **118.8**
Speed ratings (Par 101): **100,99,97,95,92 89,88,88,82,81 79**
toteswingers: 1&2 £1.90, 1&3 £18.20, 2&3 £28.40 CSF £18.61 CT £342.44 TOTE £2.60: £1.10, £3.20, £8.40; EX 23.80.
Owner J R Turner **Bred** Mrs C M Brown **Trained** Norton-le-Clay, N Yorks

FOCUS
A moderate sprint handicap and for the first time at the meeting the runners spurned the far rail and came up the centre. The winner is rated to recent C&D form with the second to last year's best.
Bossy Kitty Official explanation: jockey said filly hit gates as stalls opened and was slowly away

2547 LADIES' NIGHT ON 1ST AUGUST H'CAP (DIV II) — 5f
5:15 (5:15) (Class 6) (0-60,60) 3-Y-0+ — £1,364 (£403; £201) Stalls Low

Form — RPR

-504 **1** — **Tournedos (IRE)**^{10} 2247 9-9-5 **53** ....(b) PJMcDonald 11 — 67
(Ruth Carr) *hld up: smooth hdwy 2f out: led over 1f out: rdn clr fnl f* **7/1**^{3}

4061 **2** *2¼* **Shawkantango**^{40} 1503 4-9-7 **60** ....(v) DaleSwift(5) 7 — 66
(Derek Shaw) *midfield: rdn over 2f out: hdwy over 1f out: kpt on to go 2nd ins fnl f: no ch w wnr* **7/2**^{1}

300 **3** *1¾* **Schoolboy Champ**^{9} 2286 4-9-12 **60** ....(v1) PaulHanagan 8 — 60
(Patrick Morris) *midfield: rdn over 2f out: kpt on: wnt 3rd nr fin* **10/1**

0000 **4** *hd* **King Of Swords (IRE)**^{15} 2126 7-9-7 **55** ....(p) AndrewElliott 12 — 54
(Nigel Tinkler) *w ldr on outer: rdn over 2f out: edgd lft over 1f out: kpt on same pce* **9/1**

000- **5** *½* **Media Jury**^{227} 6896 4-9-0 **48** oh1 ow2............................(p) DavidNolan 10 — 45
(John Wainwright) *midfield: rdn over 2f out: kpt on ins fnl f* **66/1**

0544 **6** *¾* **Simple Rhythm**^{4} 2426 5-9-6 **57** ....(p) MichaelO'Connell(3) 6 — 52
(John Ryan) *prom: rdn over 2f out: edgd lft over 1f out: no ex ins fnl f* **4/1**^{2}

1460 **7** *1½* **Bold Bomber**^{70} 933 5-8-7 **46** ....(b) AdamBeschizza(5) 2 — 35
(Paul Green) *w ldr: rdn over 2f out: wknd ins fnl f* **14/1**

0-10 **8** *1¼* **Duke Of Rainford**^{129} 256 4-9-2 **50** .... TonyHamilton 4 — 35
(Michael Herrington) *dwlt: hld up: rdn and hdwy over 1f out: wknd ins fnl f* **8/1**

0046 **9** *1½* **Running Water**^{20} 1967 3-8-1 **46** .... JamesSullivan(3) 9 — 25
(Hugh McWilliams) *midfield on outer: rdn over 2f out: wknd over 1f out* **33/1**

0300 **10** *½* **Tenancy (IRE)**^{15} 2126 7-9-7 **58** ....(b) DeclanCannon(3) 1 — 36
(Shaun Harris) *led: rdn whn hdd over 1f out: sn wknd* **14/1**

-P06 **11** *5* **Blind Stag (IRE)**^{10} 2265 3-8-7 **52** ....(p) PaulPickard(3) 5 — —
(David Thompson) *chsd ldrs tl wknd 2f out* **8/1**

00-0 **12** *2¾* **Cookie Galore**^{20} 1979 4-8-12 **46** oh1 .... TomEaves 3 — —
(John Harris) *in tch: rdn over 2f out: wknd over 1f out* **40/1**

62.70 secs (1.90) **Going Correction** +0.30s/f (Good)
WFA 3 from 4yo+ 8lb — **12** Ran SP% **116.2**
Speed ratings (Par 101): **96,92,89,89,88 87,84,82,80,79 71,67**
toteswingers: 1&2 £2.20, 1&3 £18.80, 2&3 £6.90 CSF £30.68 CT £247.63 TOTE £6.00: £2.30, £1.50, £3.00; EX 25.00.
Owner Exors of the late David W Chapman **Bred** Pat Grogan **Trained** Huby, N Yorks

FOCUS
This time the runners raced centre to far side early, but ended up all over the track. The winning time was 0.49 seconds slower than the first division but the form looks more interesting, rated around the first two.
Simple Rhythm Official explanation: trainer's rep had no explanation for the poor form shown

Tenancy(IRE) Official explanation: jockey said gelding was unsuited by the good to soft (good in home straight) ground
Blind Stag(IRE) Official explanation: jockey said gelding hung right-handed throughout

2548 X-FACTOR FINALISTS HERE 24TH JULY H'CAP 1m 1f 61y
5:50 (5:50) (Class 6) (0-65,64) 4-Y-0+ **£1,619** (£481; £240; £120) **Stalls** Low

Form RPR

06-4 **1** **Sinatramania**[17] 2057 4-8-4 **50** .... PaulPickard(3) 11 63
(Tracy Waggott) *hld up: gd hdwy on outer over 2f out: led 2f out: sn clr: kpt on wl* **18/1**

66-1 **2** *3 ½* **Epernay**[7] 2348 4-9-1 **58** .... (t) PaulHanagan 3 63
(Ian Williams) *hld up in midfield: pushed along wl over 3f out: hdwy over 2f out: wnt 2nd over 1f out: kpt on: no ch w wnr* **4/5**[1]

-350 **3** *1 ¼* **Rub Of The Relic (IRE)**[9] 2308 6-8-10 **56** .... (v) MichaelO'Connell(3) 6 59
(Paul Midgley) *t.k.h: trckd ldrs: rdn to ld wl over 2f out: hdd 2f out: kpt on one pce* **33/1**

4-33 **4** *4 ½* **Prince Rhyddarch**[5] 2401 6-8-11 **54** .... TomEaves 12 47
(Michael Dods) *in tch: rdn over 2f out: one pce* **4/1**[2]

4063 **5** *2 ¼* **Hits Only Jude (IRE)**[3] 2474 8-9-0 **62** .... (b) NeilFarley(5) 2 50
(Declan Carroll) *trckd ldrs: rdn over 2f out: wknd ins fnl f* **8/1**

22-4 **6** *hd* **Strike A Deal (IRE)**[35] 1569 4-9-7 **64** .... JackMitchell 8 51
(Chris Wall) *midfield: rdn and hdwy over 2f out: wknd ins fnl f* **7/1**[3]

400- **7** *3* **Kathlatino**[253] 6225 4-9-3 **60** .... PJMcDonald 4 41
(Micky Hammond) *midfield: rdn over 2f out: wknd over 1f out* **28/1**

2004 **8** *6* **Colamandis**[7] 2352 4-8-4 **50** oh3 .... DeclanCannon(3) 1 —
(Hugh McWilliams) *hld up: n.d* **66/1**

0-65 **9** *13* **Hettie Hubble**[8] 1857 5-8-4 **50** oh4 .... (v) AndrewHeffernan(3) 9 —
(David Thompson) *led: rdn whn hdd wl over 2f out: sn wknd* **80/1**

00-0 **10** *7* **Fifty Moore**[23] 1909 4-9-7 **64** .... AndrewElliott 7 —
(Jedd O'Keeffe) *midfield: rdn over 3f out: sn wknd* **22/1**

0000 **11** *6* **Ninth House (USA)**[10] 2260 9-8-4 **50** oh5 .... (b) JamesSullivan(3) 5 —
(Ruth Carr) *dwlt: hld up: a towards rr* **40/1**

030- **12** *20* **Gypsy Style**[243] 6460 4-9-1 **58** .... (p) PaulMulrennan 10 —
(Kate Walton) *w ldr tl wknd qckly 3f out* **66/1**

1m 59.14s (1.54) **Going Correction** +0.25s/f (Good) **12** Ran SP% **121.8**
Speed ratings (Par 101): **103,99,98,94,92 92,89,84,73,66 61,43**
toteswingers: 1&2 £8.60, 1&3 £57.60, 2&3 £17.60. Tote Super 7: Win: Not won. Place: £31.20 - 36 winning tickets. CSF £32.87 CT £556.24 TOTE £34.40: £4.80, £1.10, £9.60; EX 70.60.
Owner Miss T Waggott **Bred** Kingsmead Breeders **Trained** Spennymoor, Co Durham
■ Stewards' Enquiry : Paul Pickard three-day ban: weighed-in 2lb heavy (Jun 13,19-20)

FOCUS
A moderate handicap with the winner rated a 5lb improver and the runner-up below her recent winning form.
Hits Only Jude(IRE) Official explanation: jockey said gelding failed to handle bend turning for home
T/Jkpt: Not won. T/Plt: £174.10 to a £1 stake. Pool:£53,720.49 - 225.16 winning tickets T/Qpdt: £8.10 to a £1 stake. Pool:£3,211.37 - 292.80 winning tickets AS

2374 CHEPSTOW (L-H)
Monday, May 30

OFFICIAL GOING: Good to soft (soft in places; 6.7) changing to soft after race 2 (3.05)
Wind: Virtually nil Weather: Overcast, showers

2549 BET ON TOTEPLACEPOT AT TOTESPORT.COM H'CAP 5f 16y
2:30 (2:31) (Class 6) (0-60,60) 3-Y-0 **£1,619** (£481; £240; £120) **Stalls** High

Form RPR

4-56 **1** **Steel Rain**[133] 189 3-8-11 **50** .... DarryllHolland 8 62
(Nikki Evans) *wnt lft s: bmpd: trckd ldrs: drvn over 2f out: chal appr fnl f: sn led: styd on u.p fnl 100yds* **20/1**

-234 **2** *½* **Ginzan**[26] 1813 3-9-1 **54** .... JimCrowley 6 64
(Malcolm Saunders) *wnt rt s and bmpd: chsd ldrs: drvn to chal appr fnl f and stl upsides fnl 120yds: no ex clsng stages* **9/2**[2]

3040 **3** *2 ¾* **Quadra Hop (IRE)**[20] 1980 3-9-5 **58** .... (t) DavidProbert 2 58
(Bryn Palling) *racd along in centre crse to 1/2-way and disp ld tl led over 2f out: sn rdn: jnd appr fnl f and sn hdd: outpcd by ldng duo but kpt on for 3rd cl home* **13/2**[3]

542 **4** *¾* **Ladydolly**[14] 2141 3-9-2 **55** .... SteveDrowne 4 52
(Roy Brotherton) *w ldr: slt ld after 1f but jnd tl hdd over 2f out: outpcd fnl f* **7/1**

6-10 **5** *2* **Dreams Of Glory**[28] 1764 3-8-7 **49** .... SimonPearce(3) 11 39
(Ron Hodges) *led 1f: styd chsng ldrs tl wknd fnl f* **11/1**

-056 **6** *1 ¼* **Silca Conegliano (IRE)**[6] 2384 3-8-9 **55** .... CharlesBishop(7) 3 41
(Mick Channon) *chsd ldrs: rdn 1/2-way: wknd over 1f out* **7/1**

00-0 **7** *1 ¾* **Lady Excellentia (IRE)**[6] 2375 3-8-11 **50** .... ChrisCatlin 12 29
(Ronald Harris) *chsd ldrs over 3f* **40/1**

6300 **8** *½* **Sailing North (USA)**[7] 2356 3-9-7 **60** .... CathyGannon 10 38
(Ronald Harris) *s.i.s: outpcd tl mod prog fnl f* **12/1**

0-03 **9** *nk* **Atia**[20] 1980 3-9-6 **59** .... EddieAhern 9 35
(Jonathan Portman) *rdn 1/2-way: a bhd* **4/1**[1]

0-44 **10** *3* **Make My Mark (IRE)**[13] 2168 3-8-10 **49** .... TadhgO'Shea 1 15
(John Gallagher) *racd towards centre crse to 1/2-way: a bhd* **25/1**

-600 **11** *1* **Salesiano**[13] 2172 3-9-3 **56** .... NeilCallan 7 18
(Peter Makin) *bmpd s: a bhd* **10/1**

0000 **12** *8* **Zohan (IRE)**[101] 595 3-8-7 **46** oh1 .... (b) RobbieFitzpatrick 13 —
(Peter Grayson) *s.i.s: a in rr* **100/1**

61.17 secs (1.87) **Going Correction** +0.20s/f (Good) **12** Ran SP% **113.7**
Speed ratings (Par 97): **93,92,87,86,83 81,78,77,77,72 70,58**
toteswingers: 1&2 £22.00, 1&3 £28.80, 2&3 £7.40 CSF £101.12 CT £671.65 TOTE £16.00: £8.30, £1.90, £3.00; EX 161.80.
Owner John Berry (Gwent) **Bred** L T Roberts **Trained** Pandy, Monmouths

FOCUS
After the best part of half an inch of rain throughout the morning the going eased to good to soft, soft in places. They raced mainly stands' side in this weak handicap and it paid to race handily. Not a strong contest form-wise and therefore not rated positively.

2550 BET TOTEPOOL AT TOTESPORT.COM H'CAP 1m 14y
3:05 (3:08) (Class 5) (0-70,69) 3-Y-0 **£2,266** (£674; £337; £168) **Stalls** High

Form RPR

2-20 **1** **Hurricane Lady (IRE)**[20] 1986 3-9-6 **68** .... EddieAhern 13 75
(Walter Swinburn) *in tch: hdwy and bmpd over 2f out: drvn to ld ins fnl f: styd on strly* **8/1**[3]

-236 **2** *1* **Whodathought (IRE)**[49] 1272 3-9-2 **69** .... (b) KieranO'Neill(5) 12 74
(Richard Hannon) *chsd ldrs: led ins fnl 2f: hdd ins fnl f: kpt on but nt pce of wnr* **16/1**

43-4 **3** *nk* **Ice Nelly (IRE)**[12] 2197 3-8-13 **61** .... JimCrowley 9 69+
(Hughie Morrison) *in rr: hdwy 3f out: nt clr run 2f out and again 1f out and sn after: styd on to cl on 2nd nr fin but no imp on wnr* **5/1**[1]

-415 **4** *1* **Coax**[12] 2188 3-9-6 **68** .... GregFairley 15 70
(Mark Johnston) *led tl hdd ins fnl 2f: one pce u.p fnl f* **11/2**[2]

0-53 **5** *3 ¼* **Abergeldie (USA)**[20] 1986 3-9-5 **67** .... DavidProbert 14 62
(Andrew Balding) *trckd ldrs: rdn and ev ch over 1f out: wknd ins fnl f* **11/2**[2]

0U-0 **6** *2* **Red Lite (IRE)**[20] 1986 3-9-3 **65** .... EddieCreighton 16 55
(Brian Meehan) *chsd ldrs: rdn over 2f out: wknd over 1f out* **40/1**

20-5 **7** *¾* **Silken Thoughts**[33] 1624 3-9-4 **66** .... DarryllHolland 10 54
(John Berry) *in rr: drvn and hdwy fr 3f out: nvr gng pce to rch ldrs and one pce fnl 2f* **5/1**[1]

223 **8** *1 ¼* **Kishanda**[69] 937 3-9-2 **64** .... SteveDrowne 5 49
(Hughie Morrison) *in rr: rdn and sme prog fr 3f out: nvr rchd ldrs* **10/1**

0301 **9** *11* **Sienna Blue**[21] 1953 3-9-2 **64** .... WilliamBuick 4 35
(Malcolm Saunders) *chsd ldrs: wknd and edgd lft over 2f out: eased whn no ch ins fnl f* **10/1**

610- **10** *18* **Callie's Angel**[201] 7394 3-8-10 **61** .... LouisBeuzelin(3) 3 —
(Bryn Palling) *chsd ldrs tl wknd qckly 2f out* **20/1**

60-4 **11** *6* **My Elliemay**[37] 1525 3-8-4 **57** .... MatthewCosham(5) 11 —
(David Evans) *hung lft after 1f: a bhd* **50/1**

323- **12** *1 ¾* **Polar Auroras**[227] 6902 3-9-4 **66** .... NeilCallan 1 —
(Tony Carroll) *bhd fr 1/2-way* **14/1**

-050 **13** *6* **Warbond**[73] 887 3-8-12 **60** .... ChrisCatlin 6 —
(Michael Madgwick) *early pce: sn bhd* **100/1**

4242 **P** **Irie Ute**[62] 1022 3-9-1 **63** .... TravisBlock 8 —
(Sylvester Kirk) *reluctant to go bhd stalls: sn t.o: p.u fnl 3f: dismntd fnl f* **25/1**

1m 37.96s (1.76) **Going Correction** +0.20s/f (Good) **14** Ran SP% **119.9**
Speed ratings (Par 99): **99,98,97,96,93 91,90,89,78,60 54,52,46,—**
toteswingers: 1&2 £29.60, 1&3 £7.00, 2&3 £16.40 CSF £122.39 CT £712.75 TOTE £12.40: £2.70, £5.60, £2.50; EX 105.80.
Owner Borgatti & Moir **Bred** Barbara Prendergast **Trained** Aldbury, Herts
■ Stewards' Enquiry : William Buick three-day ban: careless riding (Jun 13,19-20)

FOCUS
A moderate handicap and something of a slow-motion finish on the deteriorating ground. Nevertheless, the form looks sound if limited.
Irie Ute Official explanation: jockey said gelding moved poorly throughout

2551 BET TOTEPOOL ON ALL UK RACING MAIDEN STKS 1m 4f 23y
3:40 (3:41) (Class 5) 3-Y-0 **£2,266** (£674; £337; £168) **Stalls** Low

Form RPR

3302 **1** **The Bells O Peover**[10] 2253 3-9-3 75 .... GregFairley 1 84
(Mark Johnston) *mde all: rdn along fr 2f out: styd on wl whn strly chal fr ins fnl f: all out* **6/1**[2]

0-24 **2** *shd* **Galivant (IRE)**[23] 1894 3-8-12 85 .... DarryllHolland 3 78
(J W Hills) *trckd ldrs: chsd wnr fr 3f out: rdn and styd on u.p to chal fr ins fnl f: nt quite get up clsng stages* **8/1**

64 **3** *7* **Zafarana**[18] 2026 3-8-12 0 .... JimCrowley 10 67
(Ed Dunlop) *mid-div: hdwy fr 4f out: styd on to take 3rd ins fnl f but nver any ch w ldng duo* **12/1**

5 **4** *¾* **Run Rabbit Run**[16] 2097 3-9-3 0 .... NeilCallan 5 71
(Roger Varian) *disp 2nd: rdn 4f out: one pce 3f out: kpt on for mod 3rd over 1f out: wknd into 4th ins fnl f* **3/1**[1]

5 *1 ½* **My Heart's On Fire (IRE)** 3-8-9 0 .... RossAtkinson(3) 13 64+
(Tom Dascombe) *s.i.s: in rr: rdn and styd on fr 3f out: hung bdly lft over 1f out: green and hung rt sn after: styd on clsng stages* **50/1**

30-3 **6** *shd* **Unex Renoir**[16] 2097 3-9-3 82 .... WilliamBuick 6 68
(John Gosden) *disp 2nd rdn 4f out: no imp on wnr u.p over 3f out: wknd over 2f out* **3/1**[1]

26-2 **7** *9* **Kadoodd (IRE)**[30] 1692 3-9-3 79 .... SamHitchcott 2 54
(Mick Channon) *chsd ldrs: rdn along 5f out: no ch w ldrs after: styd on same pce fnl 3f* **7/1**[3]

6 **8** *1* **Springtime Melody (FR)**[16] 2104 3-9-3 0 .... CathyGannon 7 52
(David Bourton) *in rr: mod late prog* **100/1**

0-02 **9** *1* **Sirius Superstar**[29] 1728 3-9-3 80 .... DavidProbert 12 51
(Andrew Balding) *bhd: mod late prog* **7/1**[3]

0 **10** *¾* **Sharp Relief (IRE)**[45] 1363 3-8-12 0 .... TravisBlock 11 45
(Hughie Morrison) *bhd most of way* **40/1**

5 **11** *5* **Band Of Thunder**[29] 1728 3-9-3 0 .... NeilChalmers 9 42
(Andrew Balding) *a in rr* **50/1**

0 **12** *nk* **Sit Tight**[20] 1991 3-9-3 0 .... NickyMackay 14 41
(Chris Wall) *chsd ldrs 1m* **100/1**

00 **13** *25* **Mundesley**[40] 1484 3-9-3 0 .... (t) RussKennemore 8 —
(Tom Dascombe) *a in rr: t.o* **100/1**

14 *19* **Readily Apparent** 3-8-9 0 .... (p) SophieDoyle(3) 4 —
(Brendan Powell) *slowly away: sn rdn and bhd: t.o* **150/1**

2m 42.31s (3.31) **Going Correction** +0.20s/f (Good) **14** Ran SP% **118.1**
Speed ratings (Par 99): **96,95,91,90,89 89,83,83,82,81 78,78,61,49**
toteswingers: 1&2 £19.10, 1&3 £25.60, 2&3 £28.20 CSF £51.74 TOTE £5.80: £2.00, £2.30, £2.90; EX 55.20.
Owner D & G Mercer **Bred** Belgrave Bloodstock Ltd **Trained** Middleham Moor, N Yorks
■ Stewards' Enquiry : Darryll Holland two-day ban: used whip with excessive frequency (Jun 13,19)

FOCUS
Not a bad 3-y-o maiden with the third and fourth rated close to previous maiden form.

2552 E B F / BET ON TODAY'S FOOTBALL AT TOTESPORT.COM FILLIES' H'CAP 1m 4f 23y
4:15 (4:15) (Class 5) (0-75,75) 4-Y-0+ **£3,238** (£963; £481; £240) **Stalls** Low

Form RPR

44-1 **1** **Tweedledrum**[65] 983 4-9-2 **70** .... DavidProbert 8 83
(Andrew Balding) *in tch: lost pl over 5f out: hdwy on outside over 3f out: led ins fnl 2f: drvn clr fnl f: readily* **9/1**

0-46 **2** *3 ½* **Now What**[13] 2176 4-8-10 **64** .... EddieAhern 4 71
(Jonathan Portman) *fly-jmpd s: sn chsng ldrs: led over 3f out: hdd ins fnl 2f: no ch w wnr fnl f but hld on wl for 2nd* **9/1**

0-64 **3** *¾* **Shy**[32] 1631 6-8-3 **57** .... CathyGannon 10 63
(Rod Millman) *chsd ldrs: pushed rt after 2f: chsd ldr 3f out: one pce 2f out: rallied and styd on again fnl f to cl on 2nd nr fin but nvr any ch w wnr* **12/1**

50-5 **4** *1 1/4* **Dancing Storm**[28] [1750] 8-8-6 **60**.................................... TadhgO'Shea 7 64
(Stuart Kittow) *slowly away: towards rr: drvn and styd on fr over 2f out: kpt on clsng stages but nvr a threat* **20/1**

03-0 **5** *2* **On Khee**[17] [2055] 4-9-4 **72**.. SteveDrowne 12 73
(Hughie Morrison) *in tch whn pushed rt after 2f: hdwy 3f out: ev ch 2f out: wknd appr fnl f* **12/1**

2-30 **6** *3/4* **Albeed**[29] [1729] 4-9-1 **74**.. RosieJessop(5) 6 73
(John Dunlop) *in rr: stmbld 7f out: hdwy over 3f out to cl on ldrs whn n.m.r: one pce 2f out: wknd appr fnl f* **12/1**

-430 **7** *3* **Goodlukin Lucy**[13] [2176] 4-9-5 **73**.................................... WilliamBuick 2 68
(Pat Eddery) *in tch: rdn and no imp over 3f out: no ch after* **12/1**

3-44 **8** *3 1/4* **Shades Of Grey**[54] [1174] 4-8-9 **66**..............................(b) JohnFahy(3) 9 55
(Clive Cox) *chsd ldrs: pushed rt after 2f: wknd 4f out* **14/1**

/1-0 **9** *8* **Rock My World (IRE)**[11] [2220] 4-9-7 **75**............................... NeilCallan 1 52
(Roger Varian) *led: edgd rt after 2f: hdd over 3f out: sn btn* **6/1[2]**

3124 **10** *1 1/2* **Where's Susie**[28] [1775] 6-9-6 **74**... ChrisCatlin 11 48
(Michael Madgwick) *in tch whn bmpd after 2f wknd 4f out* **9/1**

25-0 **11** *7* **Issabella Gem (IRE)**[11] [2220] 4-9-7 **75**.............................. AdamKirby 3 38
(Clive Cox) *sn chsng ldr and pushed rt after 2f: wknd qckly appr fnl 3f: eased whn no ch fnl f* **9/2[1]**

-111 **12** *3 1/2* **Laverre (IRE)**[14] [2145] 4-9-5 **73**... JimCrowley 5 30
(Lucy Wadham) *chsd ldrs: rdn over 4f out: sn btn: eased whn no ch fnl f* **13/2[3]**

2m 42.64s (3.64) **Going Correction** +0.20s/f (Good) **12** Ran SP% **118.0**
Speed ratings (Par 100): **95,92,92,91,90 89,87,85,80,79 74,72**
toteswingers: 1&2 Not won, 1&3 £29.00, 2&3 £17.50 CSF £87.19 CT £983.77 TOTE £12.10: £4.10, £3.40, £3.90; EX 75.20.
Owner Kingsclere Racing CLub **Bred** Kingsclere Stud **Trained** Kingsclere, Hants

FOCUS
A modest handicap but the form looks pretty sound with the fourth the best guide.
Issabella Gem(IRE) Official explanation: trainer had no explanation for the poor form shown
Laverre(IRE) Official explanation: jockey said filly was unsuited by the soft ground

2553 MORE LIVE FOOTBALL BETTING AT TOTESPORT.COM FILLIES' H'CAP 6f 16y

4:50 (4:51) (Class 5) (0-70,71) 3-Y-O **£2,266** (£674; £337; £168) **Stalls** High

Form RPR

41-0 **1** **Guided Missile (IRE)**[40] [1483] 3-9-6 **69**........................(v[1]) DavidProbert 9 84+
(Andrew Balding) *chsd ldrs: chal 2f out: led over 1f out: drvn clr ins fnl f: comf* **5/2[1]**

40-0 **2** *4* **Sarangoo**[41] [1472] 3-8-9 **58**.. WilliamBuick 7 60
(Malcolm Saunders) *pressed ldr tl slt ld over 2f out: sn rdn and jnd: hdd over 1f out: sn no ch w wnr: jst hld on for 2nd* **10/1**

0-64 **3** *nse* **Abeer (USA)**[13] [2186] 3-9-0 **63**... TadhgO'Shea 1 64+
(Ed Dunlop) *wnt lft s: stdd in rr but wl in tch: hdwy fr 3f out: chal 2f out: outpcd by wnr fnl f but styd on to press for 2nd clsng stages but jst hld* **5/1[3]**

-061 **4** *4 1/2* **Miss Dutee**[13] [2172] 3-8-9 **63**.. KieranO'Neill(5) 8 51
(Richard Hannon) *chsd ldrs: rdn and outpcd 1/2-way: no ch w ldrs after but styd on for 4th ins fnl f* **10/1**

-200 **5** *1* **Delira (IRE)**[20] [1986] 3-9-0 **63**... EddieAhern 5 47
(Jonathan Portman) *chsd ldrs: rdn 3f out: wknd fr 2f out* **16/1**

4-21 **6** *2 3/4* **Shes Rosie**[6] [2375] 3-9-8 **71** 6ex.................................. RussKennemore 4 47
(John O'Shea) *led tl edgd lft and hdd over 2f out: sn btn* **10/3[2]**

400 **7** *1 1/4* **Serial Sinner (IRE)**[24] [1873] 3-8-11 **67**......................... DuilioDaSilva(7) 3 39
(Paul Cole) *chsd ldrs: rdn over 3f out: sn btn* **5/1[3]**

-150 **8** *11* **Winniepeg**[37] [1521] 3-8-8 **60**..(b[1]) JohnFahy(3) 2 —
(Clive Cox) *sn chsng ldrs: rdn 1/2-way: sn btn* **20/1**

1m 13.19s (1.19) **Going Correction** +0.20s/f (Good) **8** Ran SP% **113.8**
Speed ratings (Par 96): **100,94,94,88,87 83,81,67**
toteswingers: 1&2 £12.70, 1&3 £2.00, 2&3 £18.50 CSF £28.18 CT £116.59 TOTE £3.50: £1.50, £2.50, £2.30; EX 24.90.
Owner J C Smith **Bred** Littleton Stud **Trained** Kingsclere, Hants

FOCUS
A weak fillies' handicap and a ready winner. The placed horses are rated close to their marks.
Shes Rosie Official explanation: jockey said filly was unsuited by the soft ground

2554 GET LIVE FOOTBALL STATS AT TOTESPORT.COM H'CAP (DIV I) 6f 16y

5:25 (5:28) (Class 6) (0-60,60) 4-Y-O+ **£1,295** (£385; £192; £96) **Stalls** High

Form RPR

-032 **1** **Emiratesdotcom**[12] [2201] 5-9-7 **60**....................................... ChrisCatlin 2 69+
(Milton Bradley) *towards rr but in tch: hdwy 2f out: styd on to chal ins fnl f led fnl 120yds: drvn out* **3/1[1]**

0233 **2** *1/2* **Miss Firefly**[13] [2167] 6-9-0 **56**..................................(p) SimonPearce(3) 6 63
(Ron Hodges) *led tl hdd over 3f out: styd pressing ldr and slt ld again 1f out: hdd and nt qckn fnl 120yds: jst hld on for 2nd* **12/1**

05-3 **3** *nk* **Euroquip Boy (IRE)**[23] [1912] 4-9-2 **55**............................. JimCrowley 10 61
(Michael Scudamore) *trckd ldr: led over 3f out: narrowly hdd 1f out: styd chalng tl one pce fnl 120yds* **7/1**

3600 **4** *1 3/4* **Valentino Swing (IRE)**[23] [1912] 8-8-10 **49**...................... NeilChalmers 9 49
(Michael Appleby) *in rr but in tch: hdwy to chse ldrs over 2f out: kpt on fnl f but nvr gng pce of ldng trio* **20/1**

2332 **5** *nse* **Libertino (IRE)**[14] [2161] 4-8-11 **55**....................(p) KieranO'Neill(5) 11 55
(Tony Carroll) *chsd ldrs: rdn over 2f out: outpcd ins fnl f* **6/1[3]**

3041 **6** *2* **Athaakeel (IRE)**[12] [2205] 5-9-0 **53**..........................(b) CathyGannon 12 47
(Ronald Harris) *galloped 4f bef s: in tch: hdwy over 2f out: rdn over 1f out and no imp: wknd fnl f* **8/1**

04-0 **7** *3* **Ridgeway Sapphire**[11] [2238] 4-8-7 **46**..........................(v) DavidProbert 4 30
(Mark Usher) *chsd ldrs: rdn 3f out: wknd fr 2f out* **40/1**

0053 **8** *8* **Little Perisher**[11] [2222] 4-8-12 **51**..................................... DarryllHolland 5 —
(Karen George) *chsd ldrs tl wknd over 2f out* **8/1**

0-06 **9** *4 1/2* **Knightfire (IRE)**[19] [2001] 4-9-5 **58**..................................(t) EddieAhern 3 —
(Walter Swinburn) *chsd ldrs: rdn over 2f out: sn btn* **12/1**

60-3 **10** *14* **Dies Solis**[19] [2001] 4-9-6 **59**... WilliamBuick 7 —
(Jeremy Gask) *in tch and rdn 3f out: no rspnse and wknd over 2f out: eased fnl f* **4/1[2]**

1m 14.09s (2.09) **Going Correction** +0.20s/f (Good) **10** Ran SP% **116.6**
Speed ratings (Par 101): **94,93,92,90,90 87,83,73,67,48**
toteswingers: 1&2 £6.70, 1&3 £3.00, 2&3 £15.20 CSF £40.62 CT £240.61 TOTE £3.70: £1.20, £4.10, £3.20; EX 59.40.
Owner Ms S Howell **Bred** Newsells Park Stud **Trained** Sedbury, Gloucs

FOCUS
An ordinary sprint handicap rated through the runner-up backed up by the winner.
Knightfire(IRE) Official explanation: jockey said gelding ran too freely
Dies Solis Official explanation: jockey said colt was unsuited by the soft ground

2555 GET LIVE FOOTBALL STATS AT TOTESPORT.COM H'CAP (DIV II) 6f 16y

5:55 (5:57) (Class 6) (0-60,60) 4-Y-O+ **£1,295** (£385; £192; £96) **Stalls** High

Form RPR

0-00 **1** **Gracie's Games**[13] [2182] 5-8-10 **52**................................ SophieDoyle(3) 7 64+
(Richard Price) *hmpd s: swtchd rt onto rails and towards rr: hdwy and nt clr run 2f out: drvn through to ld appr fnl f: idled in front: drvn out* **25/1**

0-05 **2** *1 3/4* **Bermondsey Bob (IRE)**[11] [2222] 5-9-6 **59**..................... CathyGannon 6 65+
(John Spearing) *led: rdn over 2f out: hdd appr fnl f: nt pce of wnr but kpt on to hold 2nd clsng stages* **5/2[1]**

0-12 **3** *1 1/4* **Charlietoo**[11] [2233] 5-8-8 **52**................................... MatthewCosham(5) 12 54
(Edward Bevan) *chsd ldrs: drvn to chal over 1f out: styd on same pce ins fnl f* **7/2[2]**

4052 **4** *nse* **Dancing Welcome**[11] [2222] 5-9-2 **55**................................(b) ChrisCatlin 8 57
(Milton Bradley) *in rr: hdwy over 2f out: nvr quite on terms and one pce fnl f* **5/1**

0040 **5** *2 1/2* **Chinese Democracy (USA)**[3] [2452] 4-9-3 **56**............... SamHitchcott 11 50
(Dai Burchell) *chsd ldrs: rdn 1/2-way: wknd fnl f* **12/1**

4130 **6** *1/2* **Itsthursdayalready**[9] [2286] 4-9-7 **60**................................ EddieAhern 10 53
(Mark Brisbourne) *in rr: rdn over 2f out: mod prog fnl f* **17/2**

-050 **7** *7* **Abhainn (IRE)**[23] [1905] 5-8-7 **46** oh1...........................(b[1]) DavidProbert 2 16
(Bryn Palling) *chsd ldrs to 1/2-way: eased whn no clsng stages* **9/2[3]**

1-04 **8** *8* **Crimson Queen**[28] [1766] 4-9-3 **56**.................................... WilliamCarson 4 —
(Roy Brotherton) *bhd fr 1/2-way: eased whn no ch clsng stages* **12/1**

250- **9** *3 1/4* **Aalsmeer**[198] [7446] 4-9-7 **60**... DarryllHolland 1 —
(Karen George) *sn pressing ldr: wknd ins fnl 3f: eased whn no ch clsng stages* **16/1**

1m 14.13s (2.13) **Going Correction** +0.20s/f (Good) **9** Ran SP% **121.3**
Speed ratings (Par 101): **93,90,89,88,85 84,75,64,60**
toteswingers: 1&2 £6.80, 1&3 £8.50, 2&3 £4.50 CSF £91.65 CT £292.13 TOTE £28.00: £5.60, £1.80, £1.90; EX 118.50.
Owner David Prosser & Keith Warrington **Bred** David Prosser & Keith Warrington **Trained** Ullingswick, H'fords

FOCUS
The second division of the ordinary sprint handicap with the winner rated to his best and the runner-up possibly better than the bare form.
Gracie's Games Official explanation: trainer said, regarding apparent improvement in form, that the mare was better suited by the soft ground.
T/Plt: £951.40 to a £1 stake. Pool: £71,775.70. 55.07 winning tickets. T/Qpdt: £36.70 to a £1 stake.. Pool: £4,206.30. 84.70 winning tickets. ST

2288 GOODWOOD (R-H)

Monday, May 30

OFFICIAL GOING: Good to firm (good in places on straight course; 8.1)
First 2f of 1m course dolled out 5yds.
Wind: Moderate, half against Weather: Overcast, drizzle from race 5

2556 CHICHESTER OBSERVER (S) STKS 5f

2:00 (2:01) (Class 4) 2-Y-O **£3,885** (£1,156; £577; £288) **Stalls** High

Form RPR

4156 **1** **The Dancing Lord**[7] [2367] 2-9-0 0..................................... KierenFox(3) 2 70
(Bill Turner) *edgy in stalls and slowest away: rcvrd to ld after 2f: mde rest: drvn and kpt on wl fnl f* **5/2[1]**

546 **2** *1 1/4* **Sea Poet**[21] [1932] 2-8-12 0.. RichardHughes 1 56
(Andrew Haynes) *pressed ldrs: rdn to chse wnr fnl f: styd on but a hld* **6/1[3]**

06 **3** *1 3/4* **River Nova**[13] [2173] 2-8-7 0.. KierenFallon 3 45
(Alan Jarvis) *w ldrs: chsd wnr after 2f: rdn and nt qckn over 1f out: one pce after* **7/1**

4 *3* **Little Ted** 2-8-7 0... HarryBentley(5) 8 39
(David Evans) *pushed along in last and rn green early: taken to outer over 1f out: styd on quite wl fnl f to take 4th nr fin* **11/2[2]**

0 **5** *3 1/4* **Very First Blade**[14] [0100] 2-8-12 0.................................... MartinDwyer 5 27
(Mark Brisbourne) *dwlt: hld up in tch: outpcd fr 2f out: shuffled along and nvr involved after* **33/1**

5 **6** *2 3/4* **I Dream Of Genie**[21] [1932] 2-8-7 0.. LukeMorris 6 12
(Peter Winkworth) *fractious bef ent stalls: led 2f: hanging and nt qckn 2f out: steadily wknd* **5/2[1]**

4 **7** *1 1/2* **I'm Talking (IRE)**[35] [1563] 2-8-7 0.................................. FergusSweeney 4 —
(David Evans) *w ldrs 2f: sn lost pl: struggling in rr 2f out: wknd* **16/1**

0 **8** *3 1/4* **Peering**[14] [2160] 2-8-7 0.. RyanClark(5) 7 —
(Nick Littmoden) *in tch in rr: pushed along and no prog 2f out: sn wknd* **40/1**

61.05 secs (2.65) **Going Correction** +0.125s/f (Good) **8** Ran SP% **110.6**
Speed ratings (Par 95): **83,81,78,73,68 63,61,56**
toteswingers: 1&2 £3.10, 1&3 £4.70, 2&3 £7.80 CSF £16.89 TOTE £2.80: £1.10, £2.50, £2.00; EX 14.00.The winner was bought in for 10,000gns.
Owner Mrs M S Teversham **Bred** Mrs Monica Teversham **Trained** Sigwells, Somerset

FOCUS
They raced towards the stands' side, but the rail was not crucial. A Class 4 seller, but it was just an ordinary race with the time moderate and the runner-up setting the level.

NOTEBOOK
The Dancing Lord overcame an awkward start to win readily enough. He was bought in for £10,000 and should be competitive in nurseries later in the season. (tchd 11-4)
Sea Poet ran better than at Brighton on his previous start, reversing placings with the disappointing I Dream Of Genie, but he simply lacked the speed of the winner. A step up to 6f should help. (op 11-2 tchd 13-2)
River Nova wasn't good enough, but she finished some way clear of the others and might find a lesser race. (op 9-1)
Little Ted, an April foal, made an eyecatching debut relative to the level. He was struggling from some way out, but ran on quite nicely in the closing stages, all the while displaying a significant knee action. There's better to come, especially on easy ground. (op 5-1 tchd 9-2 and 6-1 in a place)
Very First Blade Official explanation: jockey said gelding hung left
I Dream Of Genie failed to build on the form of her debut effort and will have a bit to prove next time. (op 11-4 tchd 9-4 and 3-1 in places)

2557 NEWS VETERANS' H'CAP 6f

2:35 (2:36) (Class 4) (0-80,85) 6-Y-O+ **£2,730** (£2,730; £625; £312) **Stalls** High

Form RPR

-600 **1** **Alfresco**[75] [867] 7-8-11 **70**...(b) KierenFallon 13 81
(John Best) *s.i.s: sn wl in tch: rdn and prog 2f out: chal over 1f out: pressed ldr and drew clr of rest: forced dead-heat post* **10/1**

-066 **1** *dht* **Another Try (IRE)**[28] 1771 6-8-11 **75**.......................... HarryBentley(5) 6 86
(Alan Jarvis) *trckd ldr after 2f: rdn to ld jst over 1f out but sn hrd pressed: r.o to draw clr of rest: jnd post* **8/1**
6216 **3** *5* **Mymumsaysimthebest**[7] 2369 6-9-2 **75**.......................... GeorgeBaker 7 70
(Gary Moore) *w.w in tch: prog over 2f out: rdn to chal over 1f out: sn lft bhd by ldng pair* **3/1**[2]
05-1 **4** *shd* **Soap Wars**[7] 2369 6-9-12 **85** 6ex.......................... RichardHughes 3 80
(Hugo Palmer) *led over 4f out and sn crossed to nr side rail: shkn up and hdd jst over 1f out: fdd and jst pushed along after* **9/4**[1]
2302 **5** *2* **Stevie Gee (IRE)**[7] 2369 7-8-9 **73**..........................(b) RyanClark(5) 2 61
(Ian Williams) *prom: drvn 2f out: wl outpcd fr over 1f out* **7/1**[3]
5064 **6** *shd* **Brandywell Boy (IRE)**[10] 2244 8-8-7 **69**.......................... BillyCray(3) 11 57
(Dominic Ffrench Davis) *nvr bttr than midfield: rdn over 2f out: wl outpcd fr over 1f out* **16/1**
520/ **7** *5* **Billion Dollar Kid**[961] 6650 6-9-4 **77**..........................(t) MartinDwyer 9 49
(Joanna Davis) *led to over 4f out: sltly hmpd over 3f out: wknd 2f out* **33/1**
6603 **8** *shd* **Qadar (IRE)**[24] 1866 9-8-7 **71**..........................(p) NathanAlison(5) 1 43
(Alan McCabe) *restless as stalls opened and slowly away: struggling in last: brief effrt 2f out: sn lft bhd* **20/1**
4256 **9** *½* **Even Bolder**[28] 1752 8-8-10 **72**.......................... KierenFox(3) 4 42
(Eric Wheeler) *v restless jst bef stalls opened and slowly away: effrt on outer fr last pair 1/2-way: wknd 2f out* **28/1**
6310 **10** *2½* **Silver Wind**[7] 2369 6-9-5 **78**.......................... MartinLane 10 40
(Alan McCabe) *a struggling to go the pce in rr: lft wl bhd fnl 2f* **10/1**

1m 12.16s (-0.04) **Going Correction** +0.125s/f (Good) **10** Ran SP% **114.6**
Speed ratings: **105,105,98,98,95 95,88,88,87,84**
WIN: AT £4.00, A £5.40; PL: AT £2.10, A £2.80, M £1.80; EX: AT-A £50.30, A-AT £47.50; CSF: AT-A £40.54, A-AT £41.79; TRICAST: AT-A-M £151.18; A-AT-M £154.13; toteswinger: 1&1 £14.00, 1&3 (AT) £4.80, 1&3 (A) £7.40.
Owner Mrs A M Riney **Bred** Usk Valley Stud **Trained** Hucking, Kent
Owner The Twyford Partnership **Bred** Jarvis Associates **Trained** Twyford, Bucks

FOCUS
A fair sprint handicap in which Alfreco and Another Try could not be separated and they set the level of the form. The field raced towards the stands' side, although once again the rail was not decisive.
Even Bolder Official explanation: jockey said gelding was slowly away

2558 WEST SUSSEX COUNTY TIMES ON HOUSE STKS (LISTED RACE) 1m
3:10 (3:10) (Class 1) 3-Y-O+
£17,031 (£6,456; £3,231; £1,611; £807; £405) **Stalls** Low

Form RPR
10-4 **1** **Set The Trend**[44] 1385 5-9-7 100.......................... JimmyFortune 1 108
(Andrew Balding) *mde all: stretched on fr 3f out: drvn and styd on wl fnl 2f: nvr really chal* **10/1**
6-64 **2** *1¼* **The Rectifier (USA)**[21] 1948 4-9-7 104.......................... MickyFenton 2 105
(Jim Boyle) *chsd wnr to wl over 1f out: kpt on to regain 2nd last 100yds: nvr able to chal* **9/1**
33-0 **3** *nk* **Invincible Soul (IRE)**[37] 1529 4-9-7 97.......................... RichardHughes 4 104?
(Richard Hannon) *trckd ldng pair: rdn to chse wnr wl over 1f out: no imp and lost 2nd last 100yds* **11/1**
11-4 **4** *1* **Tropical Paradise (IRE)**[23] 1893 5-9-2 108.......................... IanMongan 3 97+
(Peter Winkworth) *dwlt: hld up in 5th: rdn 2f out: kpt on fr over 1f out: nvr really threatened* **7/2**[2]
00-3 **5** *1¼* **Fontley**[23] 1884 4-9-2 99.......................... KierenFallon 6 94+
(Eve Johnson Houghton) *hld up last: shkn up 2f out: plugged on but nvr gng pce to threaten* **11/2**[3]
013- **6** *13* **Rainfall (IRE)**[240] 6561 4-9-5 112.......................... TedDurcan 5 78
(Saeed Bin Suroor) *w.w in 4th: rdn and no rspnse 2f out: dropped to last 1f out: eased and t.o* **6/5**[1]

1m 39.52s (-0.38) **Going Correction** +0.125s/f (Good) **6** Ran SP% **110.5**
Speed ratings (Par 111): **106,104,104,103,102 89**
toteswingers: 1&2 £6.60, 1&3 £4.80, 2&3 £9.80 CSF £85.76 TOTE £15.30: £5.60, £6.00; EX 142.90.
Owner Corbett Stud **Bred** Old Suffolk Stud **Trained** Kingsclere, Hants

FOCUS
An ordinary Listed event and the form needs treating with some caution as Set The Trend was allowed a surprisingly soft lead, not facing as much competition up front from The Rectifier as one might have expected, and that pair were one-two for much of the contest. The form is rated around the first three.

NOTEBOOK
Set The Trend had returned with a career best when a close fourth over 1m at this level and he was confirming that promise, though clearly plenty went his way under a good ride from Jimmy Fortune. (op 11-1 tchd 12-1)
The Rectifier(USA) probably would have done too much too soon had he taken on Set The Trend for the lead, so the slightly more patient tactics were understandable, but the colt was going on again the finish having been a bit outpaced in the straight. He's up to winning a similar race if getting his own way. (op 11-1 tchd 12-1)
Invincible Soul(IRE) was better placed than some and ran about as well as he was entitled to on the figures, stepping up a good deal on the form of his reappearance. (tchd 10-1)
Tropical Paradise(IRE) ran some way below her official mark of 108, but she had little chance being held up off the modest pace. A strongly run 7f seems to suit best.
Fontley was another who didn't have the race run to suit. (op 6-1, tchd 13-2 in places)
Rainfall(IRE), last year's Jersey Stakes winner, disappointed on her first start since leaving Mark Johnston. However, her new connections reported she'd bruised a foot only a few days earlier, so she might be worth another chance. who was having her first start since leaving Mark Johnston. However, her new connections reported she'd bruised a foot only a few days earlier, so she might be worth another chance. Official explanation: jockey said filly had no more to give; trainer said filly was subsquently found to be sore on her left fore (op 11-10)

2559 WORTHING HERALD MAIDEN AUCTION STKS 6f
3:45 (3:45) (Class 5) 2-Y-O **£2,914** (£867; £433; £216) **Stalls** High

Form RPR
1 **Sir Glanton (IRE)** 2-9-1 0.......................... PatDobbs 6 84+
(Amanda Perrett) *dwlt: wl in rr: prog over 2f out: sn rdn: sustained effrt fr over 1f out: clsd to ld last stride* **40/1**
5 **2** *shd* **Minal**[28] 1757 2-8-12 0.......................... RichardHughes 4 80
(Richard Hannon) *settled midfield: pushed along 1/2-way: prog and rdn 2f out: clsd on ldrs fnl f: keeping on whn short of room last strides: fin 3rd: plcd 2nd* **9/1**
2 **3** *shd* **Lethal Force (IRE)**[23] 1886 2-8-10 0.......................... LukeMorris 11 78
(Clive Cox) *w ldrs: led 1/2-way: edgd rt u.p over 1f out: edgd lft fnl f: hdd last stride: fin 2nd: disqualified and plcd 3rd* **11/8**[1]
2 **4** *1¼* **Pride And Joy (IRE)**[18] 2017 2-9-0 0.......................... FergusSweeney 9 78
(Jamie Osborne) *prom: effrt 2f out: tried to chal fr over 1f out: kpt on but a hld* **6/1**[3]
5 **5** *2½* **Leenavesta (USA)**[14] 2153 2-8-11 0.......................... JimmyFortune 5 67
(Richard Hannon) *led 1f: w ldrs after: drvn 2f out: wknd ins fnl f* **16/1**
0 **6** *1* **Zammy**[17] 2049 2-8-12 0.......................... MichaelHills 10 65+
(B W Hills) *hld up in rr: pushed along 1/2-way: kpt on steadily fnl 2f: nvr on terms w ldrs but nt disgraced* **50/1**
643 **7** *½* **Marygold**[12] 2187 2-8-4 0.......................... MartinLane 3 55
(John Akehurst) *sn pushed along but pressed ldrs: stl chalng over 1f out: wknd ins fnl f* **16/1**
6 **8** *3¾* **Maroosh**[9] 2291 2-9-1 0.......................... MartinDwyer 14 54
(Brian Meehan) *chsd ldrs: shkn up 1/2-way: outpcd over 2f out: grad wknd* **5/1**[2]
9 *½* **Saffron Park** 2-8-11 0.......................... TedDurcan 8 49
(John Best) *s.s: rn green and detached in last: kpt on steadily fnl 2f: nt wout promise* **33/1**
10 *4* **Gifted Dancer** 2-8-0 0.......................... AmyScott(5) 1 30+
(Henry Candy) *s.s: rn green but rcvrd into midfield by 1/2-way: wknd over 1f out* **25/1**
4 **11** *4* **Tidal's Baby**[18] 2017 2-8-11 0..........................(p) MickyFenton 7 23
(Noel Quinlan) *led after 1f to 1/2-way: wknd rapidly over 2f out* **33/1**
12 *10* **Great Mystery (IRE)** 2-8-11 0.......................... KierenFallon 13 —
(J W Hills) *wl in rr: reminder bef 1/2-way: no prog over 2f out: t.o* **18/1**
13 *1½* **Eagle Of Rome (IRE)** 2-8-10 0.......................... RyanClark(5) 12 —
(Nick Littmoden) *spd 3f: wknd rapidly: t.o* **20/1**
14 *5* **Clone Devil (IRE)** 2-8-4 0.......................... KatiaScallan(7) 2 —
(Alastair Lidderdale) *s.s: a wl in rr: t.o* **20/1**

1m 12.68s (0.48) **Going Correction** +0.125s/f (Good) **14** Ran SP% **123.7**
Speed ratings (Par 93): **101,100,100,99,95 94,93,88,88,82 77,64,62,55**
toteswingers: 1&2 £4.00, 1&3 £46.10, 2&3 £23.00 CSF £357.57 TOTE £58.60: £10.20, £3.30, £1.10; EX 293.20.
Owner Slade, Clouting, Ross, Wells **Bred** Sandra Russell **Trained** Pulborough, W Sussex
■ Stewards' Enquiry : Luke Morris two-day ban: careless riding (Jun 13,19)

FOCUS
The runner-up and fourth-placed finisher had both recorded RPRs of 77 on their respective debuts, and the time was only 0.52 seconds slower than the earlier Class 4 handicap for older horses. The action unfolded up the middle of the track but initial indications are that the form is sound.

NOTEBOOK
Sir Glanton(IRE) did well to make a successful debut considering the next seven finishers all had the benefit of a previous run, and his trainer started the day just 6-141 with 2-y-o newcomers in the last five seasons. A £26,000 half-brother to 6f winner Kielder, he can be expected to come on for this and looks quite useful.
Minal ◆ recorded an RPR of only 49 on his debut over 5f on Polytrack, but he went off joint-favourite on that occasion, so clearly better was expected. This was a significant improvement and he can win a similar race. (op 17-2)
Lethal Force(IRE) edged left under pressure late on, doing Minal few favours, albeit that one did not look an unlucky loser, and the placings were reversed. He confirmed the promise he showed when runner-up over 5f at Ascot on his debut. (tchd 6-4)
Pride And Joy(IRE) ran respectably without seeming to improve much on the form he showed when runner-up at Newmarket on his introduction. He did, though, confirm form with the disappointing Tidal's Baby. (op 13-2 tchd 7-1)
Leenavesta(USA), passed over by Richard Hughes, showed ability, as on her debut at Windsor, and may be one for fillies-only company.
Zammy, who was reportedly too worked up ahead of his debut at Newbury when well beaten, fared better this time and gave the impression there should be more to come.
Maroosh did not confirm the promise he showed over C&D on his debut nine days earlier. (op 8-1)

2560 BOGNOR REGIS OBSERVER H'CAP (DIV I) 1m
4:20 (4:21) (Class 6) (0-65,70) 4-Y-O+ **£1,942** (£578; £288; £144) **Stalls** Low

Form RPR
0-32 **1** **Byrd In Hand (IRE)**[6] 2385 4-8-12 **56**.......................... RichardHughes 6 63
(John Bridger) *trckd ldng trio: pushed along and prog 2f out: shkn up to ld jst ins fnl f: in command after* **9/2**[3]
55-6 **2** *¾* **Catchanova (IRE)**[14] 2144 4-9-4 **62**.......................... JimmyFortune 2 67
(Eve Johnson Houghton) *led: rdn over 1f out: hdd jst ins fnl f: kpt on but readily hld* **5/1**
-021 **3** *shd* **Mountrath**[7] 2354 4-9-12 **70** 6ex.......................... GeorgeBaker 8 75
(Gary Moore) *chsd ldr: rdn 2f out: lost 2nd but cl enough jst over 1f out: fnd little and readily hld* **5/2**[1]
0146 **4** *1¼* **French Art**[18] 2027 6-9-7 **65**..........................(p) KierenFallon 10 67
(Nigel Tinkler) *hld up in 7th: stdy prog fr 3f out to go 4th 2f out: sn rdn and fnd nil: one pce after* **7/2**[2]
-634 **5** *1¾* **Fitz**[19] 1995 5-8-9 **53**.......................... TedDurcan 4 51
(Matthew Salaman) *chsd ldrs in 5th: nt qckn and outpcd 2f out: sltly impeded over 1f out: one pce* **9/1**
0101 **6** *3¾* **Hecton Lad (USA)**[6] 2385 4-9-5 **63** 6ex..........................(b) LukeMorris 3 52
(John Best) *chsd ldng pair: rdn 3f out: reluctant and hanging 2f out and lost pl: no ch after* **11/1**
6060 **7** *3* **Pytheas (USA)**[3] 2452 4-8-13 **60**..........................(t) KierenFox(3) 11 43
(Michael Attwater) *awkward s and slowly away: mostly in last trio: hanging and no prog over 2f out* **20/1**
036- **8** *1* **Annes Rocket (IRE)**[183] 7613 6-9-4 **62**.......................... PatDobbs 5 42
(Jimmy Fox) *stdd s: hld up and mostly in last pair: nvr remotely involved* **20/1**
6030 **9** *39* **Roe Valley (IRE)**[17] 2051 4-9-2 **60**.......................... IanMongan 9 —
(Linda Jewell) *in tch in 6th: wknd over 2f out: virtually p.u fnl f* **50/1**
050- **10** *99* **Hilltop Artistry**[194] 7487 5-8-7 **51** oh4.......................... AdrianMcCarthy 7 —
(J R Jenkins) *bolted over a m to s: in tch 2f: sn t.o: hacked bk* **50/1**

1m 40.96s (1.06) **Going Correction** +0.125s/f (Good) **10** Ran SP% **117.4**
Speed ratings (Par 101): **99,98,98,96,95 91,88,87,48,—**
toteswingers: 1&2 £5.70, 1&3 £2.80, 2&3 £5.30 CSF £26.31 CT £69.37 TOTE £5.50: £2.10, £2.90, £1.10; EX 36.20.
Owner Bird In Hand (Hailey) Racing Partnership **Bred** Bricklow Ltd **Trained** Liphook, Hants

FOCUS
A moderate contest run in a time 0.17 seconds slower than the second division. The winner is rated in line with recent form with the third to his latest mark.
Roe Valley(IRE) Official explanation: jockey said gelding lost its action 3f out
Hilltop Artistry Official explanation: jockey said gelding bolted to post

2561 BOGNOR REGIS OBSERVER H'CAP (DIV II) 1m
4:55 (4:55) (Class 6) (0-65,65) 4-Y-O+ **£1,942** (£578; £288; £144) **Stalls** Low

Form RPR
-521 **1** **Wishformore (IRE)**[12] 2198 4-8-12 **61**..........................(p) RyanPowell(5) 5 67
(J S Moore) *trckd ldng pair: clsd over 2f out: rdn to ld over 1f out: hrd pressed fnl f: clung on* **5/1**[2]
3400 **2** *hd* **Ivory Lace**[101] 589 10-9-2 **65**.......................... HarryBentley(5) 11 71
(Steve Woodman) *trckd ldrs disputing 5th: prog over 2f out: rdn to chal jst over 1f out: kpt on fnl f: jst denied* **11/1**

3-02 **3** ¾ **Fault**[14] 2149 5-9-5 **63**........(t) MickyFenton 10 67
(Stef Higgins) *hld up towards rr: prog on outer fr 3f out: rdn to chal jst over 1f out: nt qckn fnl f* **6/1**[3]
5600 **4** 2½ **Durgan**[4] 2420 5-8-11 **55**........ RichardHughes 3 54
(Linda Jewell) *chsd ldrs disputing 5th: lost pl over 2f out: swtchd lft sn after: kpt on to take 4th ins fnl f: no threat* **10/1**
3313 **5** ½ **Diddums**[3] 2452 5-8-11 **62** 6ex........ KatiaScallan(7) 6 59
(Alastair Lidderdale) *hld up towards rr: swtchd off inner 3f out: pushed along over 2f out: plugged on but nvr on terms* **4/1**[1]
0554 **6** 3 **Graceful Spirit**[10] 2268 4-8-4 **51** oh6........ BillyCray(3) 1 41
(Des Donovan) *led at str pce to over 1f out: wknd qckly* **11/1**
0000 **7** 2¾ **Vezere (USA)**[39] 1508 4-8-7 **51**........ MartinDwyer 2 35
(Simon Dow) *pressed ldr at str pce to 2f out: wknd qckly* **20/1**
/33- **8** 3½ **Push Me (IRE)**[171] 7819 4-9-2 **60**........ IanMongan 8 36
(Jamie Poulton) *chsd ldng trio: wknd tamely fr 2f out* **10/1**
00-0 **9** 12 **Gazboolou**[14] 2165 7-9-6 **64**........ FergusSweeney 9 13
(David Pinder) *awkward s: hld up in last pair and wl off the pce: shuffled along and no prog 3f out: eased fnl f* **14/1**
4666 **10** 2½ **Join Up**[10] 2268 5-8-6 **53**........ KierenFox(3) 7 —
(Mark Brisbourne) *settled towards rr: pushed along over 3f out: sn struggling: wknd u.p over 2f out* **8/1**
0264 **11** 12 **Prince Of Thebes (IRE)**[32] 1637 10-9-0 **58**........ LukeMorris 4 —
(Michael Attwater) *v.s.a: a in last pair: u.p bef 1/2-way: t.o* **9/1**

1m 40.79s (0.89) **Going Correction** +0.125s/f (Good) **11** Ran SP% **118.3**
Speed ratings (Par 101): **100,99,99,96,96 93,90,86,74,72 60**
toteswingers: 1&2 £13.80, 1&3 £5.10, 2&3 £15.40 CSF £59.45 CT £348.16 TOTE £6.50: £2.10, £4.30, £2.30; EX 57.60.
Owner J S Moore **Bred** Tally-Ho Stud **Trained** Upper Lambourn, Berks
■ Stewards' Enquiry : Richard Hughes one-day ban: careless riding (Jun 13)

FOCUS
The time was 0.17 seconds quicker than the first division but just a modest contest with the second rated close to last year's form.
Gazboolou Official explanation: jockey said gelding slipped leaving stalls

2562 WEST SUSSEX GAZETTE H'CAP — 1m 4f
5:30 (5:30) (Class 5) (0-70,70) 4-Y-0+ **£2,914** (£867; £433; £216) **Stalls** High

Form RPR
5-30 **1** **Robby Bobby**[25] 1839 6-8-10 **59**........ FergusSweeney 1 67
(Laura Mongan) *trckd ldrs: prog to chal fr 3f out: led over 1f out: edgd sltly rt ins fnl f: styd on* **6/1**
44-1 **2** 1¾ **Spice Fair**[25] 1839 4-9-7 **70**........ RichardHughes 8 79+
(Mark Usher) *hld up last: enough to do whn asked for effrt 3f out: prog over 2f out and swtchd to inner: wnt 2nd ins fnl f: ambitious effrt against rail and chopped off last 50yds* **11/4**[1]
0325 **3** 1¾ **Trachonitis (IRE)**[20] 1977 7-9-7 **70**........ AdrianMcCarthy 2 72
(J R Jenkins) *hld up in last pair: prog on outer over 4f out: led 3f out: drifted rt 2f out: hdd and nt qckn over 1f out* **8/1**
2212 **4** 3¼ **Miss Bounty**[9] 2308 6-8-7 **61**........(v) NathanAlison(5) 5 58
(Jim Boyle) *t.k.h: hld up in 6th: struggling 4f out: sn outpcd: plugged on to take 4th fnl f* **3/1**[2]
162- **5** 1 **Lombok**[6] 7044 5-9-7 **70**........ GeorgeBaker 7 66
(Gary Moore) *trckd ldr: upsides over 3f out: steadily wknd fr over 2f out* **6/1**
255- **6** 2¼ **Sentosa**[77] 7253 4-9-7 **70**........ LukeMorris 6 62
(Michael Blanshard) *trckd ldrs: rdn to chal 3f out: n.m.r over 2f out: sn wknd* **16/1**
0-06 **7** 7 **Rio Prince**[7] 2372 4-8-7 **56** oh11........(t) MarcHalford 3 37
(John Bridger) *led to 3f out: sn wknd* **66/1**
0266 **8** 28 **Highly Regal (IRE)**[22] 908 6-9-5 **68**........(tp) JimmyFortune 4 —
(Roger Teal) *trckd ldng pair to over 4f out: sn wknd and t.o* **11/2**[3]

2m 42.16s (3.76) **Going Correction** +0.125s/f (Good) **8** Ran SP% **114.1**
Speed ratings (Par 103): **92,90,89,87,86 85,80,62**
toteswingers: 1&2 £4.50, 1&3 £5.90, 2&3 £5.70 CSF £22.79 CT £132.45 TOTE £7.30: £1.90, £1.50, £2.70; EX 23.90.
Owner Mrs L J Mongan **Bred** Highclere Stud **Trained** Epsom, Surrey

FOCUS
An ordinary handicap run at a fair pace and rated around the placed horses.
T/Plt: £333.10 to a £1 stake. Pool: £70,331.58. 154.10 winning tickets. T/Qpdt: £117.50 to a £1 stake. Pool: £3,089.59. 23.10 winning tickets. JN

2354 LEICESTER (R-H)
Monday, May 30

OFFICIAL GOING: Good (good to soft in places; 7.9)
Wind: Light, behind Weather: Raining

2563 ENDERBY MEDIAN AUCTION MAIDEN STKS — 5f 2y
2:05 (2:06) (Class 6) 2-Y-0 **£1,706** (£503; £252) **Stalls** High

Form RPR
2 **1** **Burwaaz**[13] 2181 2-9-3 0........ RichardHills 4 86+
(Ed Dunlop) *chsd ldr tl led 3f out: shkn up over 1f out: r.o wl: eased towards fin* **1/4**[1]
2 **2** 2 **Costa Del Fortune (IRE)**[19] 1996 2-8-12 0........ RyanMoore 6 72
(Richard Hannon) *led: rdn and hdd 3f out: chsd wnr thereafter: edgd rt ins fnl f: styd on same pce* **5/1**[2]
436 **3** 3½ **Reina Sofia**[24] 1846 2-8-12 0........ LiamJones 7 60
(Tony Carroll) *chsd ldrs: rdn 1/2-way: no ex fnl f* **25/1**
3 **4** 3¾ **Fairy Moss (IRE)**[24] 1870 2-8-12 0........ DaneO'Neill 2 46
(Richard Hannon) *s.i.s: sn prom: wknd 1/2-way* **14/1**[3]
5 2 **No More Shoes (IRE)** 2-9-3 0........ LiamKeniry 5 44
(Brendan Powell) *chsd ldrs: rdn 1/2-way: wknd 2f out* **40/1**
6 11 **Sophar** 2-9-3 0........ JamesDoyle 1 —
(Jason Ward) *sn outpcd* **150/1**

62.73 secs (2.73) **Going Correction** +0.125s/f (Good) **6** Ran SP% **110.3**
Speed ratings (Par 91): **83,79,74,68,65 47**
toteswingers: 1&2 £1.10, 1&3 £4.50, 2&3 £4.10 CSF £1.76 TOTE £1.30: £1.10, £1.70; EX 2.40.
Owner Hamdan Al Maktoum **Bred** Shadwell Estate Company Limited **Trained** Newmarket, Suffolk

FOCUS
Watering had taken place before the meeting and after persistent morning rain there were two going changes. 'Good, good to soft in places' was the official description by post time, although there was little wind and the winning rider felt the ground was riding good to soft. The time, over three seconds slower than standard, would appear to back this up. An uncompetitive maiden run at a modest pace early on and few got into it, although the winner looks smart. The third sets the level.

NOTEBOOK
Burwaaz, a strapping colt with a fluid action, who was second on his sole start over 6f at Nottingham, where he ran green, pulling hard in the early stages, was well backed. That form looked solid enough (the seventh home winning subsequently), but connections dropped him back to the minimum here. It clearly suited him, although he still looked babyish. He broke smartly and wasn't helped by the relatively pedestrian early pace, fighting his jockey and cocking his head slightly, but once settling he travelled kindly and was given his head approaching the 2f marker. He quickly put the race to bed, only briefly coming off the bridle. He holds a Two-Year-Old Trophy entry at the backend of the season but, in the short-term, connections must be thinking about Royal Ascot, although perhaps not aiming at the top races such as the Coventry or Norfolk Stakes. (op 4-11 tchd 2-5 in places)
Costa Del Fortune(IRE) was a beaten favourite in a 6f fillies' AW maiden at Kempton on her debut and dropped back in trip here. She broke smartly and was on terms with the winner before his class told. She stuck to the task well though and stayed on well. She won't be long in winning. (op 4-1)
Reina Sofia, the most experienced, having her fourth start, ran well for a long way. She keeps bumping into useful sorts, though but she looks genuine having rallied for pressure, and her turn will come. (op 20-1)
Fairy Moss(IRE), who was switched inside to get more cover approaching the 2f pole. She was somewhat disappointing, given that she had run (albeit a remote) third to subsequent Hilary Needler winner Dozy at Nottingham on her debut. She clearly has ability, though, and can pick up a small race. (op 16-1 tchd 12-1)
No More Shoes(IRE), a half-brother to smart 2-y-o Orizaba, was friendless in the betting ring. Equipped with a noseband, he ran well for a long way and showed enough ability to think he can be competitive in low-grade sprint handicaps.
Sophar, who cost just £1,000, needed this first experience and can only improve.

2564 LEICESTER MERCURY WEEKEND EDITION H'CAP — 5f 218y
2:40 (2:43) (Class 4) (0-80,80) 3-Y-O **£4,079** (£1,214; £606; £303) **Stalls** High

Form RPR
12-0 **1** **Steps (IRE)**[25] 1825 3-9-7 **80**........ AndreaAtzeni 9 90
(Roger Varian) *sn led: rdn over 1f out: r.o wl* **12/1**
5262 **2** 2 **Roman Strait**[18] 2025 3-8-7 **66**........ LiamKeniry 2 70
(Michael Blanshard) *hld up: hdwy over 2f out: rdn to chse wnr over 1f out: r.o* **10/1**
2241 **3** 2¼ **Palais Glide**[13] 2180 3-9-6 **79**........ RyanMoore 6 76
(Richard Hannon) *sn pushed along and prom: outpcd over 1f out: styd on u.p ins fnl f* **11/1**
20-0 **4** ½ **Diamond Vine (IRE)**[17] 2074 3-9-3 **76**........(p) J-PGuillambert 8 71
(Ronald Harris) *chsd wnr tl rdn over 1f out: no ex ins fnl f* **50/1**
11-0 **5** ½ **Rock Ace (IRE)**[16] 2092 3-9-7 **80**........ FrannyNorton 4 74
(Deborah Sanderson) *mid-div: sn pushed along: styd on u.p fr over 1f out: nt trble ldrs* **25/1**
3-13 **5** dht **Materialism**[10] 2264 3-8-4 **70**........ DarylByrne(7) 7 64
(Mark Johnston) *chsd ldrs: rdn over 2f out: no ex fnl f* **9/1**[3]
22-1 **7** 1¼ **Sluggsy Morant**[18] 2025 3-9-3 **76**........ DaneO'Neill 1 66
(Henry Candy) *s.i.s: sn pushed along in rr: rdn over 2f out: nvr on terms* **6/4**[1]
5222 **8** 3¼ **City Legend**[9] 2319 3-9-5 **78**........(bt) PatCosgrave 3 57
(Alan McCabe) *s.i.s: sn drvn along in rr: rdn and hung rt over 2f out: n.d* **5/1**[2]

1m 13.46s (0.46) **Going Correction** +0.125s/f (Good) **8** Ran SP% **97.6**
Speed ratings (Par 101): **101,98,95,94,94 94,92,88**
toteswingers: 1&2 £9.10, 1&3 £3.50, 2&3 £11.00 CSF £85.99 CT £804.11 TOTE £16.40: £3.40, £2.10, £2.30; EX 101.00 Trifecta £199.60 Part won. Pool: £269.73 - 0.10 winning units..
Owner Michael Hill **Bred** Eamon Beston **Trained** Newmarket, Suffolk

FOCUS
A fair sprint handicap run at a consistent pace for the softening conditions, which lost some of its interest when second favourite York Glory was withdrawn after playing up in the stalls. Very few got into it and the form is best rated and limited by the fourth, backed up by the second..

2565 GILMORTON (S) STKS — 1m 1f 218y
3:15 (3:15) (Class 6) 3-5-Y-O **£1,706** (£503; £252) **Stalls** Low

Form RPR
3331 **1** **Bernisdale**[24] 1877 3-8-7 59........ FrannyNorton 5 65
(George Moore) *mde virtually all: rdn clr over 1f out* **5/6**[1]
3060 **2** 16 **Jane's Legacy**[28] 1769 3-8-2 47........ PaulQuinn 2 28
(Reg Hollinshead) *chsd ldrs: rdn over 4f out: wkng whn wnt 2nd over 1f out* **7/1**[3]
344 **3** 7 **Lean Machine**[12] 2195 4-9-12 62........(p) J-PGuillambert 4 25
(Ronald Harris) *chsd wnr: rdn over 2f out: wknd and lost 2nd over 1f out* **9/2**[2]
4 3¼ **Chippy** 3-8-7 0........ AndreaAtzeni 3 13
(John Holt) *s.i.s: hld up: hdwy over 3f out: wknd over 2f out* **9/2**[2]
5 13 **Manager Mick (IRE)** 3-8-7 0........ LiamJones 1 —
(John Norton) *sn outpcd: t.o* **14/1**
00 **6** 3½ **John The Glass**[49] 1277 4-9-0 0........ LucyKBarry(7) 6 —
(Mark Wellings) *s.i.s: hld up: plld hrd: rdn: hung lft and wknd over 3f out* **50/1**

2m 10.42s (2.52) **Going Correction** +0.30s/f (Good)
WFA 3 from 4yo 14lb **6** Ran SP% **112.0**
Speed ratings (Par 101): **101,88,82,80,69 66**
toteswingers: 1&2 £1.40, 1&3 £1.20, 2&3 £6.50 CSF £7.43 TOTE £1.90: £1.60, £1.30; EX 7.10.The winner was sold to Ron Harris for 7,000gns.
Owner Evelyn Duchess Of Sutherland **Bred** Evelyn Duchess Of Sutherland **Trained** Middleham Moor, N Yorks

FOCUS
A weak race, even by selling standards, and very few got into it. The winner is rated to form.

2566 LEICESTER MERCURY FAMILY FUN DAY FILLIES' H'CAP — 7f 9y
3:50 (3:51) (Class 4) (0-80,78) 4-Y-0+
£4,673 (£1,399; £699; £350; £174; £87) **Stalls** High

Form RPR
5-20 **1** **Russian Rave**[9] 2313 5-9-1 **72**........ StephenCraine 8 86
(Jonathan Portman) *s.s: hdwy over 4f out: chsd ldr 1/2-way: rdn and hung rt fr over 1f out: r.o to ld post* **7/1**
414- **2** hd **Bonnie Brae**[315] 4209 4-8-13 **70**........ DaneO'Neill 3 83+
(David Elsworth) *hld up: hdwy over 2f out: led over 1f out: sn rdn: hdd post* **13/2**[3]
0300 **3** 5 **Night Trade (IRE)**[27] 1793 4-9-5 **76**........(p) LiamKeniry 6 76
(Deborah Sanderson) *hld up: hdwy over 2f out: rdn over 1f out: styd on to go 3rd wl ins fnl f: nt trble ldrs* **20/1**
-120 **4** 1½ **Dreamacha**[18] 2016 4-8-13 **70**........ JamesDoyle 10 66
(Stuart Williams) *chsd ldrs: led 1/2-way: rdn: hung rt and hdd over 1f out: wknd ins fnl f* **8/1**

0-40 **5** *¾* **Elusive Sue (USA)**[16] 2095 4-8-6 **70**............................ LauraBarry(7) 12 64
(Richard Fahey) *chsd ldrs: rdn over 2f out: wknd fnl f* **6/1**[2]

2050 **6** *5* **Avonrose**[9] 2300 4-8-10 **74**............................ DavidKenny(7) 4 54
(Derek Shaw) *chsd ldrs: rdn over 2f out: sn wknd* **10/1**

051- **7** *1 ¾* **Piddie's Power**[228] 6879 4-9-4 **75**............................ StevieDonohoe 5 51
(Ed McMahon) *plld hrd and prom: jnd ldrs 1/2-way: rdn over 2f out: wknd over 1f out* **9/2**[1]

2336 **8** *6* **Diapason (IRE)**[28] 1762 5-8-13 **70**............................(t) RyanMoore 1 29
(Tom Dascombe) *s.s: swtchd lft sn after s: rdn over 2f out: a in rr* **9/2**[1]

-300 **9** *4* **Lady Florence**[14] 2149 6-8-5 **69**............................ LeonnaMayor(7) 2 18
(David C Griffiths) *led: hdd over 4f out: wknd over 2f out* **40/1**

1153 **10** *8* **Cat Hunter**[94] 689 4-8-13 **70**............................ J-PGuillambert 9 —
(Ronald Harris) *trckd ldrs: plld hrd: lost pl over 4f out: sn rdn: wknd over 2f out: t.o* **8/1**

1m 26.6s (0.40) **Going Correction** +0.125s/f (Good) **10** Ran SP% **115.0**
Speed ratings (Par 102): **102,101,96,94,93 87,85,78,74,65**
toteswingers: 1&2 £9.80, 1&3 £20.70, 2&3 £21.00 CSF £51.22 CT £867.57 TOTE £8.10: £2.60, £2.60, £7.70; EX 45.90 Trifecta £374.50 Pool: £526.37 - 1.04 winning units..
Owner The Traditionalists **Bred** P A & M J Reditt & Morton Bloodstock **Trained** Compton, Berks

FOCUS
A modest, win-in-their-turn fillies' handicap, run at a decent pace for the conditions. It produced a tight finish, with the front pair drawing clear but no form to take too literally, with the runner-up to her previous mark the best guide.
Dreamacha Official explanation: jockey said filly hung right

2567 DONNA AND STEVE H'CAP — 1m 1f 218y
4:25 (4:26) (Class 5) (0-70,70) 4-Y-O+ **£2,266** (£674; £337; £168) **Stalls** Low

Form RPR

0244 **1** **Zafranagar (IRE)**[17] 2055 6-8-8 **64**............................ GeorgeDowning(7) 3 71+
(Tony Carroll) *stdd s: hld up in tch: plld hrd: led ins fnl f: rdn out* **10/3**[2]

0-11 **2** *1 ¾* **Addikt (IRE)**[28] 1756 6-9-0 **70**............................ DavidKenny(7) 7 74
(Michael Scudamore) *s.i.s: racd keenly and sn chsng ldrs: rdn and ev ch over 1f out: styd on same pce ins fnl f: eased whn hld nr fin* **3/1**[1]

-643 **3** *1 ¼* **Striding Edge (IRE)**[12] 2207 5-9-3 **66**............................ JamesDoyle 2 67
(Hans Adielsson) *chsd ldr: rdn to ld over 1f out: hdd and unable qck ins fnl f* **5/1**

10-2 **4** *1 ¼* **Big Sur**[34] 1582 5-8-10 **59**............................ RobertHavlin 6 58
(Tom Keddy) *chsd ldrs: hung rt over 4f out: led over 3f out: rdn and hdd over 1f out: no ex ins fnl f* **4/1**

2346 **5** *½* **Kyle Of Bute**[9] 2308 5-8-11 **60**............................ J-PGuillambert 4 58
(Brian Baugh) *hld up: hdwy over 2f out: rdn and ev ch over 1f out: no ex ins fnl f* **7/2**[3]

2205 **6** *12* **Plush**[7] 2359 8-8-11 **60**............................ StevieDonohoe 1 34
(Shaun Lycett) *led: racd keenly: rdn and hdd over 3f out: wknd over 2f out* **25/1**

2m 13.4s (5.50) **Going Correction** +0.30s/f (Good) **6** Ran SP% **110.8**
Speed ratings (Par 103): **90,88,87,86,86 76**
toteswingers: 1&2 £1.70, 1&3 £3.30, 2&3 £3.30 CSF £13.32 TOTE £3.60: £2.00, £1.60; EX 9.50.

Owner Paul Downing **Bred** His Highness The Aga Khan's Studs S C **Trained** Cropthorne, Worcs
■ Stewards' Enquiry : James Doyle one-day ban: careless riding (Jun 13)

FOCUS
The rain continued to fall during this ordinary handicap, run at a modest early pace. George Downing has caught the eye in recent weeks and the 7lb claimer produced another patient, polished display. The form looks messy and limited.

2568 KIBWORTH HARCOURT MEDIAN AUCTION MAIDEN STKS — 1m 60y
5:00 (5:00) (Class 5) 3-Y-O **£2,266** (£674; £337; £168) **Stalls** Low

Form RPR

6- **1** **Chilled**[276] 5491 3-9-3 0............................ RyanMoore 11 94+
(Sir Michael Stoute) *hld up: hdwy over 2f out: led over 1f out: pushed out* **11/8**[1]

0-42 **2** *2* **Uppercut**[20] 1984 3-9-3 78............................ DaneO'Neill 2 84
(Stuart Kittow) *led: hdd over 6f out: chsd ldrs: rdn over 1f out: styd on* **7/2**[2]

6 **3** *1 ¼* **Stage Attraction (IRE)**[35] 1565 3-9-3 0............................ LiamKeniry 6 81
(Andrew Balding) *chsd ldrs: rdn over 1f out: edgd rt ins fnl f: styd on* **7/1**

653- **4** *2* **Alshazah**[242] 6498 3-9-3 76............................ JamesMillman 12 77
(Rod Millman) *w ldr tl led over 6f out: rdn and hdd over 1f out: no ex ins fnl f* **50/1**

2- **5** *10* **Methayel (IRE)**[346] 3156 3-8-12 0............................ PhilipRobinson 1 49
(Clive Brittain) *chsd ldrs: rdn over 2f out: wknd over 1f out* **16/1**

325- **6** *1 ¼* **Red Riverman**[244] 6436 3-9-3 81............................ LiamJones 9 51
(William Haggas) *hld up: plld hrd: hdwy over 3f out: wknd 2f out* **11/2**[3]

00 **7** *2 ½* **Duchess Of Magenta (IRE)**[25] 1836 3-8-9 0............................ PatrickHills(3) 3 40
(Eve Johnson Houghton) *sn pushed along in rr: hdwy 1/2-way: rdn and wknd over 2f out* **150/1**

8 *2 ¼* **Brick Dust (IRE)** 3-9-3 0............................ J-PGuillambert 5 40
(Luca Cumani) *s.i.s: hld up: hung rt over 2f out: nvr on terms* **40/1**

4 **9** *3* **Suomi**[34] 1580 3-9-3 0............................ PatCosgrave 4 33
(James Fanshawe) *hld up: shkn up over 3f out: wknd over 2f out* **14/1**

0-3 **10** *6* **Full Footage**[24] 1865 3-8-9 0............................ MatthewDavies(3) 7 —
(Roger Charlton) *prom: chsd ldr over 5f out tl rdn and wknd over 2f out* **12/1**

11 *8* **Full Stretch (USA)** 3-9-3 0............................ RichardHills 8 —
(Pat Eddery) *s.s: outpcd* **33/1**

1m 48.21s (3.11) **Going Correction** +0.30s/f (Good) **11** Ran SP% **120.5**
Speed ratings (Par 99): **96,94,92,90,80 79,77,74,71,65 57**
toteswingers: 1&2 £4.20, 1&3 £4.80, 2&3 £6.50 CSF £6.10 TOTE £2.40: £1.70, £1.70, £2.00; EX 7.00 Trifecta £17.90 Pool: £444.44 - 18.28 winning units..
Owner Cheveley Park Stud **Bred** Cheveley Park Stud Ltd **Trained** Newmarket, Suffolk

FOCUS
A weak maiden for desperate prize-money, run ata steady pace for the conditions. The form makes sense rated around the runner-up and fourth.

2569 TIGERS APPRENTICE H'CAP — 1m 3f 183y
5:35 (5:36) (Class 6) (0-60,57) 4-Y-O+ **£1,706** (£503; £252) **Stalls** Low

Form RPR

0360 **1** **Magnitude**[60] 911 6-8-13 **49**............................(p) LMcNiff 4 54
(Brian Baugh) *hld up: hdwy over 3f out: rdn to ld ins fnl f: r.o* **4/1**[2]

320/ **2** *½* **Ishismart**[535] 7490 7-8-8 **49**............................ NicolaJackson(5) 2 53
(Reg Hollinshead) *chsd ldrs: led over 2f out: rdn and hdd ins fnl f: r.o* **12/1**

26-5 **3** *nse* **Belle Boleyn**[20] 1987 4-9-4 **54**............................ AntiocoMurgia 8 58+
(Chris Wall) *hld up: hdwy and hung rt over 1f out: rdn and r.o ins fnl f: nt quite rch ldrs* **5/2**[1]

-656 **4** *1* **Royal Defence (IRE)**[18] 2021 5-9-2 **57**............................ IanBurns(5) 5 59
(Michael Quinn) *led: rdn and hdd over 2f out: hung rt over 1f out: styd on* **6/1**

0/0- **5** *5* **Almowj**[170] 7840 8-8-9 **45**............................ LucyKBarry 6 39
(George Jones) *s.s: bhd: hdwy over 2f out: rdn over 1f out: wknd fnl f* **100/1**

400- **6** *3 ¼* **Astromoon**[271] 5666 4-9-7 **57**............................ CharlesEddery 1 46
(Mark H Tompkins) *chsd ldrs: rdn over 3f out: wknd over 1f out* **14/1**

00/4 **7** *9* **Lion Road (USA)**[28] 1751 5-9-3 **53**............................ DavidKenny 3 28
(Alan King) *chsd ldrs: rdn over 3f out: wknd 2f out* **9/2**[3]

0-00 **8** *6* **Spacecraft (IRE)**[54] 1190 4-8-4 **45**............................(b[1]) JackDuern(5) 10 —
(Christopher Kellett) *chsd ldrs tl rdn and wknd over 2f out* **33/1**

-502 **9** *2* **Bussell Along (IRE)**[10] 2246 5-8-7 **46**............................ RachealKneller(3) 7 —
(Pam Ford) *s.i.s: hld up: rdn over 3f out: sn lost tch* **7/1**

-000 **10** *25* **Scintillating (IRE)**[35] 1567 4-8-4 **45**............................(p) DavidSimmonson(5) 9 —
(Ray Peacock) *chsd ldrs: rdn 1/2-way: wknd over 3f out: t.o* **50/1**

2m 40.71s (6.81) **Going Correction** +0.30s/f (Good) **10** Ran SP% **113.8**
Speed ratings (Par 101): **89,88,88,87,84 82,76,72,71,54**
toteswingers: 1&2 £6.20, 1&3 £3.10, 2&3 £5.20 CSF £49.04 CT £141.82 TOTE £5.20: £2.50, £2.90, £1.80; EX 54.50 Trifecta £301.30 Part won. Pool: £407.25 - 0.59 winning units..
Owner J H Chrimes And Mr & Mrs G W Hannam **Bred** Cheveley Park Stud Ltd **Trained** Audley, Staffs

FOCUS
A very poor apprentice handicap run at a fair clip for the conditions. The front four drew clear of the remainder, but the form may not prove to be reliable and it is hard to be positive about.
T/Plt: £113.40 to a £1 stake. Pool: £45,077.67. 289.98 winning tickets. T/Qpdt: £24.30 to a £1 stake. Pool: £2,838.11. 86.12 winning tickets. CR

1939 REDCAR (L-H)
Monday, May 30

OFFICIAL GOING: Good to firm (9.0)
Wind: Light across Weather: overcast and showers

2570 BUY YOUR TICKETS ON-LINE @ REDCARRACING.CO.UK MAIDEN AUCTION STKS — 5f
2:25 (2:30) (Class 5) 2-Y-O **£2,388** (£705; £352) **Stalls** High

Form RPR

3 **1** **Kohala (IRE)**[16] 2093 2-8-5 0............................ GrahamGibbons 1 89+
(David Barron) *mde most: qcknd clr wl over 1f out: comf* **11/8**[1]

5 **2** *5* **Tip Top Gorgeous (IRE)**[5] 2404 2-8-5 0............................ SilvestreDeSousa 5 69
(David O'Meara) *in tch: pushed along 1/2-way: rdn and hdwy over 1f out: chsd wnr ins fnl f: no imp* **5/2**[2]

6 **3** *2 ½* **Just Like Heaven (IRE)**[27] 1797 2-8-9 0............................ RobertWinston 4 64
(Tim Easterby) *in tch: hdwy on outer 1/2-way: rdn to chse ldrs 2f out: kpt on same pce ent fnl f* **33/1**

04 **4** *2 ¼* **First Fast Now (IRE)**[28] 1744 2-8-6 0............................ KellyHarrison 6 53
(Nigel Tinkler) *prom: rdn along over 2f out: sn one pce* **14/1**

323 **5** *½* **Blue Shoes (IRE)**[10] 2261 2-8-5 0............................ DuranFentiman 2 50
(Tim Easterby) *chsd ldrs: rdn along 1/2-way: sn wknd* **9/2**[3]

0 **6** *nk* **Musical Valley**[27] 1791 2-8-9 0............................(t) RichardKingscote 7 53+
(Tom Dascombe) *cl up: rdn along over 2f out: sn drvn and wknd wl over 1f out* **11/1**

06 **7** *¾* **Beechey's Beauty**[6] 2387 2-8-11 0............................ SebSanders 9 52
(Ann Duffield) *a towards rr* **20/1**

60 **8** *10* **Metal Dealer (IRE)**[15] 2120 2-8-10 0............................ FrederikTylicki 8 —
(George Foster) *s.i.s: a bhd* **40/1**

58.84 secs (0.24) **Going Correction** -0.10s/f (Good) **8** Ran SP% **114.0**
Speed ratings (Par 93): **94,86,82,78,77 77,75,59**
Tote Swingers: 1&2 £1.50, 1&3 £7.50, 2&3 £12.40 CSF £4.76 TOTE £2.50: £1.40, £1.10, £6.60; EX 5.00.
Owner M Dalby **Bred** Pat Todd **Trained** Maunby, N Yorks

FOCUS
Quite a taking performance in this opening sprint maiden with the runner-up setting a modest standard and limiting things.

NOTEBOOK
Kohala(IRE) ◆, narrowly denied on her Doncaster debut, showed bags of pace and fairly bolted up. On this evidence she'll be competing at a higher level before long, with her looking perfectly entitled to take her chance in something like the Queen Mary. (op 6-4 tchd 5-4)
Tip Top Gorgeous(IRE), making a quick reappearance, stayed on for second and can go one better once faced with a stiffer test. (tchd 9-4)
Just Like Heaven(IRE) improved markedly on his debut effort, showing considerably more speed this time. He's bred to want further and can progress again up to 6f. (op 40-1 tchd 28-1)
First Fast Now(IRE) was well held and looks more a nursery type, with 6f likely to suit. (op 9-1)
Blue Shoes(IRE) doesn't look to be progressing and is left with a bit to prove following this effort. (op 4-1)
Musical Valley again showed pace before weakening. The fact he wears a tongue-tie suggests he struggles with his breathing. (op 16-1)

2571 MARKET CROSS JEWELLERS MAIDEN H'CAP — 1m 6f 19y
3:00 (3:00) (Class 6) (0-65,64) 3-Y-O **£1,706** (£503; £252) **Stalls** Low

Form RPR

6-46 **1** **Mojolika**[14] 2152 3-9-7 **64**............................(e) GrahamGibbons 11 72
(Tim Easterby) *mde all: pushed clr over 4f out: rdn wl over 2f out: drvn over 1f out and kpt on gamely* **7/1**

0-00 **2** *1 ¼* **Hal Of A Lover**[5] 2407 3-8-11 **54**............................ SilvestreDeSousa 13 60
(David O'Meara) *sluggish s and sn swtchd lft to inner: in rr tl hdwy on inner over 4f out: swtchd outside and rdn to chse ldrs over 2f out: drvn and styd on appr fnl f: nrst fin* **20/1**

5-54 **3** *½* **Operateur (IRE)**[24] 1858 3-9-2 **62**............................ PatrickDonaghy(3) 14 67
(Ben Haslam) *in tch: hdwy 4f out: rdn to chse wnr over 2f out: drvn over 1f out: kpt on u.p* **16/1**

00-6 **4** *1 ¾* **Tigerino (IRE)**[20] 1969 3-8-2 **45**............................ KellyHarrison 9 48
(Chris Fairhurst) *bhd: hdwy on inner over 3f out: swtchd wd and rdn over 2f out: sn drvn and edgd lft: kpt on fnl f: nrst fin* **66/1**

0653 **5** *1 ¾* **Bradbury (IRE)**[33] 1623 3-9-3 **60**............................(p) RobertWinston 8 60
(James Bethell) *hld up towards rr: hdwy over 5f out: rdn to chse ldrs 3f out: drvn and one pce fnl 2f* **10/1**

-064 **6** *hd* **Cuban Piece (IRE)**[24] 1872 3-9-3 **60**............................(p) RichardKingscote 1 60
(Tom Dascombe) *in tch on inner: hdwy over 4f out: rdn to chse ldrs 3f out: drvn and plugged on same pce fnl 2f* **6/1**[3]

500 **7** *8* **I'm A Celebrity**[21] 1950 3-8-11 **54**............................(b[1]) JimmyQuinn 2 43
(Marco Botti) *in tch: rdn along over 5f out: n.d* **10/1**

0-20 **8** *2 ¼* **History Girl (IRE)**[33] 1609 3-9-4 **61**.................................. TomQueally 10 47
(Sir Henry Cecil) *chsd ldrs: rdn along over 3f out: drvn over 2f out: wknd* **5/1**[2]

0-05 **9** *8* **Playful Girl (IRE)**[24] 1858 3-8-2 **45**................................. DuranFentiman 6 20
(Tim Easterby) *prom: reminders 1/2-way: rdn along to chse ldng pair 5f out: drvn over 3f out and sn wknd* **25/1**

0033 **10** *23* **Pizzetti (IRE)**[11] 2239 3-9-2 **59**.. SebSanders 5 —
(Sir Mark Prescott Bt) *rn in snatches: prom: trckd wnr after 5f: rdn along over 4f out: drvn wl over 3f out: sn wknd and bhd* **2/1**[1]

06-6 **11** *8* **Smart Violetta (IRE)**[24] 1858 3-8-3 **46** ow1.............(v[1]) AdrianNicholls 12 —
(Ann Duffield) *a towards rr: outpcd and bhd fnl 3f* **28/1**

00-0 **12** *5* **Green Pastures (IRE)**[7] 2350 3-9-3 **60**.......................... FrederikTylicki 4 —
(Howard Johnson) *a in rr: bhd fnl 3f* **40/1**

3m 5.26s (0.56) **Going Correction** -0.10s/f (Good) **12** Ran SP% **116.8**
Speed ratings (Par 97): **94,93,93,92,91 90,86,85,80,67 62,59**
Tote Swingers: 1&2 £16.60, 1&3 £9.70, 2&3 £38.50 CSF £142.36 CT £2151.73 TOTE £9.90: £2.80, £4.70, £5.30; EX 150.40.
Owner A Brannon & Habton Farms **Bred** Miss K Rausing **Trained** Great Habton, N Yorks

FOCUS
An interesting staying handicap for 3-y-os and best rated around the fifth and sixth to their marks.
Pizzetti(IRE) Official explanation: trainer's rep had no explanation for the poor form shown

2572 TRY TOTEQUICKPICK IF YOU'RE FEELING LUCKY H'CAP 1m 2f
3:35 (3:36) (Class 4) (0-85,85) 3-Y-O **£2,590** (£770; £385) **Stalls** Low

Form RPR

0-36 **1** **Well Sharp**[30] 1690 3-9-3 **82**.. FrederikTylicki 1 93
(Michael Dods) *hld up: tk clsr order over 3f: pushed along over 2f out: rdn and hdwy to chal wl over 1f out: led ent fnl f: styd on strly* **11/10**[1]

21-0 **2** *7* **Labore**[11] 2230 3-9-0 **79**... SebSanders 3 78
(Marco Botti) *set gd even pce: pushed along and qcknd 3f out: jnd and rdn over 2f out: drvn and hdd ent fnl f: no ex and sn eased* **4/1**[3]

212- **3** *9* **Next Edition (IRE)**[273] 5597 3-9-1 **85**.............................. LeeTopliss(5) 2 64
(Howard Johnson) *trckd ldr: hdwy and cl up 3f out: rdn to chal over 2f out and ev ch tl drvn and wknd wl over 1f out* **6/4**[2]

2m 5.77s (-1.33) **Going Correction** -0.10s/f (Good) **3** Ran SP% **107.6**
Speed ratings (Par 101): **101,95,88**
CSF £5.05 TOTE £1.70; EX 4.70.
Owner Andrew Tinkler **Bred** Equibreed S R L **Trained** Denton, Co Durham

FOCUS
Just the three runners and, although visually impressive, it would be unwise to get carried away with the performance of the winner as there is a bit of doubt over the form.

2573 TOTEPOOL ZETLAND GOLD CUP (H'CAP) 1m 2f
4:10 (4:11) (Class 2) (0-105,100) 3-Y-O+**£17,809** (£5,299; £2,648; £1,322) **Stalls** Low

Form RPR

-550 **1** **Nanton (USA)**[16] 2107 9-9-8 **98**.................................... DanielTudhope 12 107
(Jim Goldie) *hld up in rr: hdwy over 3f out: chsd ldrs over 2f out: swtchd rt and rdn to chal appr fnl f: styd on strly to ld last 100yds* **25/1**

1-11 **2** *1 ¼* **Prince Of Johanne (IRE)**[24] 1879 5-8-13 **89**...........(p) RobertWinston 3 95
(Tom Tate) *hld up in midfield: hdwy over 4f out: trckd ldrs 3f out: rdn to chal 2f out and ev ch tl drvn and one pce wl ins fnl f* **16/1**

0/10 **3** *shd* **Desert Romance (IRE)**[19] 2002 5-8-13 **89**............. SilvestreDeSousa 9 95+
(David O'Meara) *led: pushed along 3f out: jnd and rdn over 2f out: drvn wl over 1f out and kpt on gamely tl hdd and no ex last 100yds* **25/1**

4264 **4** *¾* **Halicarnassus (IRE)**[9] 2289 7-9-3 **96**.......................... MartinHarley(3) 1 100
(Mick Channon) *trckd ldrs on inner: hdwy over 2f out: effrt and n.m.r wl over 1f out: swtchd lft and rdn whn n.m.r ent fnl f: kpt on same pce towards fin* **16/1**

00-1 **5** *1 ½* **Mirrored**[58] 1097 5-9-1 **91**.. DuranFentiman 5 92
(Tim Easterby) *hld up in rr: hdwy 3f out: rdn over 2f out: styd on strly on inner appr fnl f: nrst fin* **11/1**

10-6 **6** *1* **Pendragon (USA)**[30] 1694 8-8-13 **89**.............................. JimmyQuinn 7 88
(Brian Ellison) *trckd ldrs on inner: hdwy to chse ldr over 4f out: rdn to chal 3f out: drvn over 2f out and ev ch tl wknd over 1f out* **8/1**[3]

-043 **7** *1 ¾* **Breakheart (IRE)**[30] 1684 4-9-0 **90**.............................. FrederikTylicki 6 86
(Michael Dods) *towards rr: pushed along 4f out: rdn over 3f out: sn drvn and sme late hdwy: nvr nr ldrs* **11/4**[1]

-106 **8** *nk* **Ingleby Spirit**[19] [illegible] 4-9-11 [illegible]................................ LeeTopliss(5) 11 87
(Richard Fahey) *midfield: effrt over 3f out and sn rdn along: sme late hdwy* **14/1**

0-00 **9** *3* **Sirvino**[19] 2002 6-9-3 **93**.. GrahamGibbons 2 82
(David Barron) *midfield: effrt and sme hdwy over 3f out: sn rdn and wknd over 2f out* **14/1**

0413 **10** *5* **Arlequin**[19] 2002 4-9-2 **92**... TomQueally 14 71
(James Bethell) *in tch towards outer: hdwy over 3f out: rdn along wl over 2f out: grad wknd* **8/1**[3]

11-6 **11** *3 ¾* **Sarrsar**[15] 2123 4-9-5 **95**.. TonyCulhane 4 67
(Saeed Bin Suroor) *in tch: hdwy over 3f out: rdn to chse ldrs over 2f out: sn edgd lft and wknd* **7/1**[2]

0330 **12** *hd* **Bikini Babe (IRE)**[17] 2044 4-9-3 **93**......................... RoystonFfrench 13 64
(Mark Johnston) *a in rr* **33/1**

2-5 **13** *1 ¼* **Merchant Of Dubai**[17] 2044 6-9-7 **100**........................ GaryBartley(3) 15 69
(Jim Goldie) *cl up on outer: rdn along over 4f out: wknd over 3f out* **10/1**

0-16 **14** *1 ¼* **Jutland**[17] 2044 4-9-6 **96**.. AdrianNicholls 8 62
(Mark Johnston) *prom: rdn along 4f out: wknd over 3f out* **16/1**

020- **15** *3 ½* **Jo'Burg (USA)**[205] 7350 7-9-0 **90**.................................... SebSanders 10 49
(Ollie Pears) *dwlt: a bhd* **25/1**

2m 3.68s (-3.42) **Going Correction** -0.10s/f (Good) **15** Ran SP% **124.3**
Speed ratings (Par 109): **109,108,107,107,106 105,103,103,101,97 94,94,93,92,89**
Tote Swingers: 1&2 £59.00, 1&3 £96.60, 2&3 £29.30 CSF £378.21 CT £9712.73 TOTE £27.60: £7.20, £5.10, £12.60; EX 295.80.
Owner J S Morrison **Bred** Samuel H And Mrs Rogers, Jr **Trained** Uplawmoor, E Renfrews

FOCUS
Often a well contested handicap and this year's running looked particularly competitive. The winner is rated to last year's form with the runner-up improving and the fourth to his latest mark.

NOTEBOOK
Nanton(USA) has been a grand performer over the years and had done enough on his last two starts to suggest his winning days weren't behind him. Down to his lowest turf mark since winning the Mallard Stakes in 2009, he is proven over this shorter trip and picked up strongly from off the pace, always looking the winner once upsides from over 1f out. He's likely to continue to contest the top middle-distance handicaps, but winning one is likely to prove beyond him returned to a mark in the 100s. (op 28-1)
Prince Of Johanne(IRE), in search of a four-timer, was up 4lb for winning narrowly at Ripon last time and almost certainly recorded a career-best in defeat here, just being unable to stay on as strongly as the winner. (tchd 14-1)
Desert Romance(IRE) showed his last-time-out York running to be all wrong, finding plenty out in front under strong pressure and holding on well for a place.
Halicarnassus(IRE) is on a workable mark these days and he ran well considering the trip would have been on the short side, keeping on well close home and looking unfortunate not to finish second. (op 22-1)
Mirrored, back to form with a bang when winning at Doncaster on his reappearance, was up 6lb and ran well, but just couldn't quicken, staying on right the way to the line. (op 12-1)
Breakheart(IRE) proved most disappointing. Soon in rear, he proved laboured under pressure in the straight and, although making some minor late headway, he was never in with a chance. He appeared to run flat, but is left with a bit to prove nonetheless. Official explanation: trainer's rep had no explanation for the poor form shown (op 7-2)
Arlequin was forced to challenge wide and ran below-par. (op 15-2)
Sarrsar didn't improve as expected on the step back up to 1m2f. (tchd 15-2)

2574 WIN A VIP DAY OUT @ REDCARRACING.CO.UK MEDIAN AUCTION MAIDEN STKS 6f
4:45 (4:45) (Class 5) 3-Y-O **£1,942** (£578; £288; £144) **Stalls** High

Form RPR

5- **1** **Namwahjobo (IRE)**[369] 2427 3-9-3 0.......................... DanielTudhope 3 75+
(Jim Goldie) *trckd ldrs: hdwy over 2f out: rdn to chse ldr over 1f out: chal ent fnl f: styd on wl to ld last 100yds* **9/4**[2]

4-42 **2** *1 ¼* **Moral Issue**[24] 1880 3-9-0 72.................................... PatrickDonaghy(3) 2 71
(Jedd O'Keeffe) *led: rdn clr wl over 1f out: drvn ins fnl f: hdd and no ex last 100yds* **1/1**[1]

50 **3** *7* **Crabbies Ginger**[9] 2281 3-9-3 0..................................... FrederikTylicki 6 49
(Lisa Williamson) *cl up: rdn along wl over 2f out: sn one pce* **16/1**

4 *6* **Apreslepetitbois** 3-8-12 0.. TomQueally 1 24
(James Bethell) *chsd ldrs: rdn along 1/2-way: sn outpcd* **5/1**[3]

00-4 **5** *nk* **Dreamweaving (IRE)**[11] 2236 3-8-12 40......................... KellyHarrison 7 23
(Nigel Tinkler) *hld up: effrt and sme hdwy over 2f out: sn rdn and n.d* **25/1**

6 *11* **Styleyf** 3-8-9 0... RobertLButler(3) 5 —
(John Balding) *s.i.s and bhd: hdwy and in tch 1/2-way: sn rdn along and wknd* **16/1**

1m 11.99s (0.19) **Going Correction** -0.10s/f (Good) **6** Ran SP% **113.0**
Speed ratings (Par 99): **94,92,83,75,74 59**
Tote Swingers: 1&2 £1.20, 1&3 £3.30, 2&3 £2.90 CSF £4.94 TOTE £2.30: £1.20, £1.60; EX 4.80.
Owner Ambrose Turnbull **Bred** Rathbarry Stud **Trained** Uplawmoor, E Renfrews

FOCUS
A weak maiden that was there for the taking, especially with the defection of Bertiewhittle. The winner is rated to his latest mark with the second not looking up to his official rating.

2575 TRY TOTEQUICKPICK ON ALL TOTEPOOL BETS H'CAP 1m 6f 19y
5:20 (5:20) (Class 6) (0-65,65) 4-Y-0+ **£1,619** (£481; £240; £120) **Stalls** Low

Form RPR

45/0 **1** **Bajan Parkes**[16] 2091 8-9-7 **65**.. TomQueally 8 72
(John Quinn) *cl up whn carried wd bnd after 2f: sn rcvrd to trck ldr: effrt and cl up 3f out: rdn to ld wl over 1f out: styd on wl towards fin* **6/1**

450- **2** *1 ½* **Finellas Fortune**[227] 6895 6-8-7 **51**............................ RoystonFfrench 3 55
(George Moore) *cl up: lft in ld bnd after 2f: pushed along over 3f out: rdn over 2f out: hdd wl over 1f out: drvn and rallied ent fnl f: no ex last 100yds* **11/1**

0-00 **3** *nk* **Simple Jim (FR)**[40] 1491 7-8-9 **53**........................... SilvestreDeSousa 5 57
(David O'Meara) *sn trcking ldrs: pushed along and outpcd whn n.m.r 3f out: rdn over 2f out: drvn over 1f out: swtchd rt and styd on strly ins fnl f: nrst fin* **6/5**[1]

1-43 **4** *¾* **Leitzu (IRE)**[14] 2145 4-9-3 **64**....................................... MartinHarley(3) 2 67
(Mick Channon) *hld up in rr: hdwy to trck ldrs 4f out: smooth effrt on inner to chal over 2f out: sn rdn and ev ch tl drvn and one pce appr fnl f* **4/1**[2]

-630 **5** *¾* **Escape Artist**[116] 409 4-8-8 **52**...................................... DuranFentiman 1 54
(Tim Easterby) *t.k.h: cl up whn rn wd bnd after 2f: trckd ldrs: effrt and hdwy over 3f out: rdn along over 2f out: sn drvn and one pce fr over 1f out* **9/2**[3]

00- **6** *7* **Ferney Boy**[300] 4683 5-8-10 **54**.. KellyHarrison 7 46
(Chris Fairhurst) *hld up: hdwy and in tch 4f out: rdn to chse ldrs 3f out: sn drvn and no imp* **40/1**

000 **7** *3 ¼* **Molannarch**[27] 1799 5-7-13 **46** oh1........................ NataliaGemelova(3) 4 34
(Keith Reveley) *a in rr: rdn along over 3f out: nvr a factor* **40/1**

640 **F** **Khalashan (FR)**[11] 2219 5-8-7 **51** ow1.........................(p) FrederikTylicki 6 —
(Peter Niven) *trckd ldrs on outer whn carried wd bnd after 2f: in tch: effrt on outer over 3f out: sn rdn and wknd: in rr whn fell over 1f out: fatally injured* **22/1**

3m 7.22s (2.52) **Going Correction** -0.10s/f (Good) **8** Ran SP% **115.5**
Speed ratings (Par 101): **88,87,86,86,86 82,80,—**
Tote Swingers: 1&2 £4.70, 1&3 £2.60, 2&3 £4.10 CSF £66.17 CT £129.10 TOTE £7.30: £1.50, £3.00, £1.10; EX 53.10.
Owner Joseph Heler **Bred** Joseph Heler **Trained** Settrington, N Yorks

FOCUS
It paid to race prominently in a race where the pace wasn't strong and the form looks muddling. Several of the runners were carried wide by Escape Artist at the first bend.
T/Plt: £726.30 to a £1 stake. Pool:£39,055.89 - 39.25 winning tickets T/Qpdt: £59.00 to a £1 stake. Pool:£2,266.57 - 28.40 winning tickets JR

2576 - 2579a (Foreign Racing) - See Raceform Interactive

[2563]LEICESTER (R-H)
Tuesday, May 31

OFFICIAL GOING: Good (good to soft in places; 7.1)
Wind: Light behind Weather: Cloudy with sunny spells

2580 BRITISH STALLION STUDS SUPPORTING BRITISH RACING E B F MAIDEN FILLIES STKS 5f 2y
2:15 (2:15) (Class 4) 2-Y-O **£4,338** (£1,291; £645; £322) **Stalls** High

Form RPR

1 **Nagham (IRE)** 2-9-0 0.. StephenCraine 14 75+
(Kevin Ryan) *a.p: rdn over 2f out: r.o to ld nr fin* **12/1**

4 **2** *shd* **Midas Medusa (FR)**[18] 2063 2-9-0 0.......................... RichardHughes 12 74
(Richard Hannon) *chsd ldr: rdn 1/2-way: ev ch ins fnl f: r.o* **3/1**[1]

02 **3** *nse* **Meloneras**[26] 1827 2-9-0 0.. JamesMillman 16 74
(Rod Millman) *led: rdn over 1f out: hdd nr fin* **5/1**[3]

6 **4** *½* **My Solitaire (IRE)**[47] 1337 2-9-0 0.............................. LukeMorris 1 72
(Clive Cox) *chsd ldrs: rdn and ev ch ins fnl f: r.o* **9/1**

5 *½* **Caledonia Lady** 2-9-0 0.. TadhgO'Shea 11 70
(Pat Murphy) *s.i.s: hld up: plld hrd: hdwy over 2f out: rdn and ev ch ins fnl f: no ex nr fin* **150/1**

5 **6** *shd* **Alabanda (IRE)**[15] 2148 2-9-0 0.................................... TedDurcan 18 70
(Tim Easterby) *chsd ldrs: rdn over 1f out: r.o: n.m.r towards fin* **13/2**

22 **7** ¾ **Toffee Tart**[11] 2241 2-9-0 0 SebSanders 15 67
(J W Hills) *mid-div: pushed along 1/2-way: rdn over 1f out: swtchd rt and r.o ins fnl f: nt rch ldrs* **7/2**[2]
8 1¼ **Royal Red** 2-9-0 0 StevieDonohoe 7 63
(Ralph Beckett) *hld up in tch: rdn over 1f out: styd on same pce* **11/2**
9 1¼ **Dine Out** 2-9-0 0 NeilCallan 13 58
(Mark H Tompkins) *s.i.s: sn pushed along and a in rr* **100/1**
10 3¼ **Street Angel (IRE)** 2-9-0 0 CathyGannon 10 47
(Alan Bailey) *s.s: outpcd* **50/1**

61.62 secs (1.62) **Going Correction** +0.075s/f (Good) **10** Ran SP% **113.9**
Speed ratings (Par 95): **90,89,89,88,88 88,86,84,82,77**
toteswingers:1&2:£7.80, 1&3:£11.50, 2&3:£4.30 CSF £47.03 TOTE £12.60: £2.40, £1.80, £2.10; EX 59.30 Trifecta £325.50 Part won. Pool: £439.94 - 0.10 winning units..
Owner Mubarak Al Naimi **Bred** Yeomanstown Stud **Trained** Hambleton, N Yorks

FOCUS
This was won two years ago by the smart Lady Of The Desert. There were a host of non-runners this time and a bunch finish suggests the form is ordinary, but the race should produce winners. They raced towards the stands' side, although the rail was not decisive.

NOTEBOOK
Nagham(IRE), a 16,000euros February foal, continued her stable's superb run of form with their juveniles. Indeed this was Kevin Ryan's ninth different 2-y-o winner from just 28 individual starters this season, and that record was improved to 10-29 moments later at Redcar. The winner's performance is all the more creditable considering the next three finishers all had the benefit of previous experience. She showed a fine attitude when switched into the clear and should improve. (op 20-1 tchd 8-1)
Midas Medusa(FR) stepped up on the form she showed when last of four on her debut over 6f at Newmarket. She should win a similar race. (tchd 7-2)
Meloneras, runner-up at Ffos Las on her second start, showed good speed against the rail and just missed out after becoming unbalanced under pressure in the final few yards. (tchd 7-2)
My Solitaire(IRE) improved on the form she showed on her first start at Newmarket and was going on at the finish. (op 10-1 tchd 12-1)
Caledonia Lady, a late-April foal, is a half-sister to multiple sprint winner Caledonia Princess. Despite racing keenly, she showed plenty of ability and could win a similar race provided she goes the right way from this. (tchd 125-1)
Toffee Tart had been runner-up on her first two starts, but she was officially reported to have run very green when turned over at 2-13 on her latest outing, and she ran here as though she is still learning. She took an age to respond to pressure, but was going on at the finish and a step up in trip should help. (op 10-3 tchd 4-1)

2581 STATHERN CLAIMING STKS 7f 9y
2:45 (2:45) (Class 6) 3-Y-O **£1,619** (£481; £240; £120) **Stalls** High

Form RPR
2-00 **1** **No Poppy (IRE)**[11] 2255 3-8-13 78 TedDurcan 4 65
(Tim Easterby) *hld up: hdwy over 1f out: r.o to ld wl ins fnl f* **9/2**[2]
-525 **2** 1¼ **Danceyourselfdizzy (IRE)**[13] 2196 3-9-0 63 RichardHughes 5 63
(Richard Hannon) *hld up: hdwy over 2f out: rdn and ev ch ins fnl f: styd on same pce* **5/1**[3]
330 **3** ¾ **Christmas Aria (IRE)**[13] 2200 3-9-4 74 NeilCallan 6 65
(Simon Dow) *chsd ldrs: rdn to ld over 1f out: hdd and no ex wl ins fnl f* **7/1**
22 **4** 5 **New Latin (IRE)**[35] 1578 3-9-4 74 JamesDoyle 1 51
(Frank Sheridan) *trckd ldrs: led 2f out: sn edgd lft and hdd: wknd ins fnl f* **9/1**
46-0 **5** ½ **Turn The Tide**[4] 2468 3-8-5 77 CathyGannon 10 37
(Alan Bailey) *plld hrd: sn led: rdn and hdd 2f out: wknd ins fnl f* **7/4**[1]
0055 **6** ½ **Coracle**[17] 2119 3-8-3 52 LeonnaMayor(7) 3 41
(David Nicholls) *chsd ldrs: rdn over 2f out: wknd ins fnl f* **33/1**
00 **7** nse **What About Now**[15] 2157 3-9-5 0 (p) SebSanders 11 50
(J W Hills) *chsd ldrs: rdn 1/2-way: wknd over 1f out* **33/1**
4151 **8** 2¼ **Sofias Number One (USA)**[41] 1500 3-9-4 67 (p) PaulQuinn 7 43
(Roy Bowring) *s.i.s: hdwy 1/2-way: rdn over 1f out: sn wknd* **12/1**
060- **9** 7 **Deva Le Deva (IRE)**[182] 7643 3-7-12 55 HarryBentley(5) 8 —
(Tom Dascombe) *prom: rdn 1/2-way: wknd over 2f out* **18/1**
00 **10** 7 **Dorothy's Dream (IRE)**[15] 2141 3-8-0 0 RyanPowell(5) 2 —
(John O'Shea) *mid-div: rdn and wknd 3f out* **150/1**
00-0 **11** 18 **Look For Love**[22] 1953 3-8-8 49 LiamKeniry 9 —
(Reg Hollinshead) *trckd ldrs: wknd and eased 1/2-way* **50/1**

1m 27.47s (1.27) **Going Correction** +0.075s/f (Good) **11** Ran SP% **115.2**
Speed ratings (Par 97): **95,93,92,87,86 85,85,83,75,67 46**
toteswingers:1&2:£5.70, 1&3:£6.80, 2&3:£5.30 CSF £26.17 TOTE £3.50: £1.70, £1.80, £3.00; EX 29.50 Trifecta £209.10 Pool: £528.45 - 1.87 winning units..
Owner Mrs P M Easterby **Bred** Michael O'Mahony **Trained** Great Habton, N Yorks

FOCUS
A modest claimer in which the action unfolded towards the middle of the track. The time was 0.95 seconds slower than the following Class 4 handicap and the form is best rated around the placed horses.
Look For Love Official explanation: jockey said gelding moved poorly

2582 ABBEY PARK H'CAP 7f 9y
3:15 (3:15) (Class 4) (0-80,78) 3-Y-O **£4,079** (£1,214; £606; £303) **Stalls** High

Form RPR
10-0 **1** **Azameera (IRE)**[12] 2216 3-9-7 78 AdamKirby 6 90+
(Clive Cox) *s.i.s: racd keenly and sn trcking ldrs: rdn over 1f out: led wl ins fnl f: edgd rt and r.o wl* **10/3**[1]
3-12 **2** 1¾ **Elusivity (IRE)**[18] 2064 3-9-4 75 MartinDwyer 9 82
(Brian Meehan) *led: rdn over 1f out: hdd and unable qck wl ins fnl f* **10/3**[1]
0-46 **3** 2¼ **Arctic Mirage**[34] 1611 3-8-10 67 LukeMorris 5 68
(Michael Blanshard) *hld up: hdwy over 2f out: rdn: hung lft and ev ch over 1f out: no ex ins fnl f* **16/1**
535- **4** 1 **Mr Dream Maker (IRE)**[214] 7201 3-8-8 65 SaleemGolam 3 63+
(Ian Williams) *hld up: rdn over 2f out: r.o ins fnl f: nt rch ldrs* **7/2**[2]
05-4 **5** 4 **Icebuster**[141] 110 3-8-11 68 JamesMillman 8 55
(Rod Millman) *plld hrd: w ldr tl rdn over 2f out: wknd over 1f out* **12/1**
4-35 **6** ½ **Saskia's Dream**[14] 2185 3-9-1 72 KierenFallon 2 58
(Jane Chapple-Hyam) *chsd ldrs: rdn over 2f out: wknd ins fnl f* **8/1**[3]
01-0 **7** 1½ **Adorable Choice (IRE)**[47] 1335 3-8-11 73 HarryBentley(5) 7 55
(Tom Dascombe) *prom: rdn 1/2-way: wknd over 2f out* **20/1**
50-1 **8** nk **Swendab (IRE)**[29] 1753 3-8-4 66 RyanPowell(5) 10 47
(John O'Shea) *racd keenly: prom: rdn over 2f out: wknd fnl f* **12/1**
314- **9** 1½ **Menadati (USA)**[281] 5374 3-9-6 77 TedDurcan 1 54
(David Lanigan) *hld up: rdn over 2f out: wknd over 1f out: eased* **14/1**

1m 26.52s (0.32) **Going Correction** +0.075s/f (Good) **9** Ran SP% **112.2**
Speed ratings (Par 101): **101,99,96,95,90 90,88,88,86**
toteswingers:1&2:£2.30, 1&3:£15.10, 2&3:£7.60 CSF £14.01 CT £150.01 TOTE £3.20: £2.20, £1.10, £4.60; EX 13.10 Trifecta £144.70 Pool: £708.26 - 3.62 winning units..
Owner H E Sheikh Sultan Bin Khalifa Al Nahyan **Bred** P Byrne, Eimear Mulhern & B Grassick **Trained** Lambourn, Berks

FOCUS
A fair handicap and the form looks sound enough. The place to be looked close to the stands'-side rail.
Adorable Choice(IRE) Official explanation: vet said filly lost both front shoes
Menadati(USA) Official explanation: jockey said gelding had no more to give

2583 SWANNINGTON H'CAP (DIV I) 1m 1f 218y
3:45 (3:45) (Class 6) (0-65,66) 3-Y-O **£1,706** (£503; £252) **Stalls** Low

Form RPR
0-45 **1** **Gud Day (IRE)**[21] 1971 3-8-13 57 GregFairley 6 65
(Deborah Sanderson) *hld up: hdwy over 3f out: sn rdn: styd on to ld post* **20/1**
2131 **2** nse **Jack's Revenge (IRE)**[5] 2418 3-9-5 66 5ex (tp) MatthewDavies(3) 9 74
(George Baker) *a.p: led over 2f out: rdn and hung lft over 1f out: hdd post* **5/6**[1]
05-4 **3** 3¼ **Lady Barastar (IRE)**[22] 1958 3-9-6 64 AdamKirby 7 65
(Walter Swinburn) *mid-div: lost pl 1/2-way: sn drvn along: hdwy u.p over 1f out: styd on: nt rch ldrs* **6/1**[3]
0-05 **4** 2¾ **Disturbia (IRE)**[22] 1934 3-8-4 48 HayleyTurner 4 44
(J W Hills) *chsd ldrs: rdn over 2f out: styd on same pce appr fnl f* **50/1**
00-0 **5** nse **Caledonia Prince**[21] 1969 3-8-4 48 oh1 ow2 TadhgO'Shea 1 43
(Pat Murphy) *trckd ldrs: racd keenly: rdn over 3f out: styd on same pce fr over 1f out* **100/1**
6-40 **6** nk **Divine Rule (IRE)**[13] 2196 3-9-5 63 (tp) SteveDrowne 3 58
(Hughie Morrison) *led over 7f: sn rdn: wknd ins fnl f* **15/2**
6000 **7** nk **Tegan (IRE)**[10] 2307 3-8-1 50 KieranO'Neill(5) 11 44
(Richard Hannon) *hld up: pushed along over 6f out: rdn over 4f out: styd on u.p and edgd rt fr over 1f out: nvr nrr* **66/1**
-005 **8** 2½ **Emmeline Pankhurst (IRE)**[10] 2293 3-8-8 52 JimmyQuinn 10 41
(Julia Feilden) *s.i.s: hld up: rdn over 2f out: nvr on terms* **22/1**
040- **9** 6 **Hello Tomorrow (USA)**[266] 5841 3-9-7 65 TedDurcan 8 42
(David Lanigan) *hld up: hdwy over 3f out: rdn and wknd over 2f out* **16/1**
560- **10** 8 **Comrade Bond**[258] 6072 3-9-0 58 NeilCallan 2 19
(Mark H Tompkins) *hld up in tch: racd keenly: rdn over 2f out: wknd over 1f out* **50/1**
0-25 **11** 4 **Iron Green (FR)**[31] 1683 3-9-5 63 KierenFallon 5 16
(Heather Main) *chsd ldr tl rdn over 2f out: wknd over 1f out: eased* **9/2**[2]

2m 9.59s (1.69) **Going Correction** +0.075s/f (Good) **11** Ran SP% **120.2**
Speed ratings (Par 97): **96,95,93,91,91 90,90,88,83,77 74**
toteswingers:1&2:£6.40, 1&3:£14.00, 2&3:£2.40 CSF £37.14 CT £131.05 TOTE £32.60: £8.50, £1.02, £2.00; EX 65.80 Trifecta £251.80 Pool: £850.82 - 2.50 winning units..
Owner R J Budge **Bred** Patrick M Ryan **Trained** Sturton le Steeple, Notts
■ Stewards' Enquiry : Matthew Davies one-day ban: used whip with excessive frequency (Jun 19)

FOCUS
A moderate contest, although the time was 1.72 seconds quicker than the second division. The placed horses are rated to their recent Brighton marks.
Comrade Bond Official explanation: jockey said gelding ran too free
Iron Green(FR) Official explanation: jockey said gelding lost its action

2584 OADBY MAIDEN STKS 5f 218y
4:15 (4:16) (Class 4) 2-Y-O **£3,432** (£1,021; £510; £254) **Stalls** High

Form RPR
6 **1** **Roman Soldier (IRE)**[31] 1678 2-9-3 0 GeorgeBaker 8 92+
(Jeremy Noseda) *mde all: shkn up over 1f out: r.o wl: easily* **6/1**
3 **2** 3½ **Right To Dream (IRE)**[10] 2291 2-9-3 0 MartinDwyer 3 78
(Brian Meehan) *chsd ldrs: rdn over 1f out: styd on same pce fnl f* **2/1**[1]
3 ½ **Mehdi (IRE)** 2-9-3 0 ShaneKelly 7 76+
(Brian Meehan) *s.i.s: hld up: hdwy 2f out: rdn over 1f out: styd on same pce fnl f* **33/1**
4 **4** 1 **Bounty Seeker (USA)**[8] 2355 2-9-3 0 JoeFanning 11 73
(Mark Johnston) *chsd wnr: pushed along over 2f out: no ex fnl f* **7/2**[2]
4 **5** 1 **Universal (IRE)**[14] 2181 2-9-3 0 AhmedAjtebi 10 70+
(Mahmood Al Zarooni) *in rr: hdwy 4f out: outpcd over 2f out: styd on ins fnl f* **9/2**[3]
6 1¼ **Avon Pearl** 2-9-3 0 DaneO'Neill 5 66
(Henry Candy) *mid-div: hdwy over 2f out: shkn up over 1f out: no ex fnl f* **20/1**
7 5 **Maccabees** 2-9-3 0 JamesMillman 9 50
(Rod Millman) *hdwy over 3f out: rdn and wknd over 1f out* **100/1**
6 **8** 2½ **Dovils Date**[26] 1835 2-9-3 0 CathyGannon 1 42
(Rod Millman) *hld up: rdn 1/2-way: sn lost tch* **100/1**
9 2¼ **Flavius Victor (IRE)** 2-9-3 0 RichardHughes 6 35
(Richard Hannon) *hld up: rdn and wknd over 2f out* **16/1**
10 5 **Bu Naaji (IRE)** 2-9-3 0 NeilCallan 2 19
(Roger Varian) *chsd ldrs tl wknd wl over 1f out: eased fnl f* **8/1**

1m 12.88s (-0.12) **Going Correction** +0.075s/f (Good) **10** Ran SP% **114.7**
Speed ratings (Par 95): **103,98,97,96,95 93,86,83,80,73**
toteswingers:1&2:£3.40, 1&3:£16.00, 2&3:£7.60 CSF £17.72 TOTE £6.40: £1.40, £1.10, £9.10; EX 25.20 Trifecta £380.10 Pool: £945.24 - 1.84 winning units..
Owner Mrs Susan Roy **Bred** Fermion Syndicate **Trained** Newmarket, Suffolk

FOCUS
This maiden was won last year by Roayh, who was subsequently third in the Coventry Stakes. They raced towards the stands' side. There's substance to this form with the runner-up and fourth-placed finisher having achieved RPRs in the 70s on their respective debuts.

NOTEBOOK
Roman Soldier(IRE) has clearly improved a good deal on the form he showed over 5f at Goodwood on his debut, and it's interesting to note that he once held an entry in the Group 1 Phoenix Stakes. Evidently he's pretty useful. (op 8-1 tchd 9-2)
Right To Dream(IRE) again showed ability and time might show he bumped into a decent type. (op 5-4)
Mehdi(IRE) ◆, a 50,000gns half-brother to 1m winner Final Approach, who developed into a smart hurdler, is an April foal and made a promising debut. Entered in the Group 2 Railway Stakes, he shaped as though he can improve plenty.
Bounty Seeker(USA) may have run to about the same sort of level as on his debut without necessarily improving significantly. (op 5-1)
Universal(IRE) failed to justify odds of 6-4 at Nottingham on his debut and doesn't look to have gone the right way. He seemed to be hanging right under pressure and did not pick up. (op 5-1)

2585 SIS H'CAP 5f 2y
4:45 (4:45) (Class 5) (0-75,81) 4-Y-O+ **£2,266** (£674; £337; £168) **Stalls** High

Form RPR
5551 **1** **Six Wives**[13] 2193 4-8-5 66 LeonnaMayor(7) 9 76
(David Nicholls) *hld up in tch: swtchd rt over 1f out: led wl ins fnl f: r.o* **16/1**

-021 **2** *1 ½* **Verinco**[3] [2491] 5-9-8 **81** 6ex..(v) AdamCarter(5) 5 86
(Bryan Smart) *led: hdd over 3f out: led again 2f out: rdn and hdd wl ins fnl f* **2/1**[1]

0065 **3** *shd* **Comptonspirit**[21] [1968] 7-8-12 **71**............................ JemmaMarshall(5) 7 76+
(Brian Baugh) *s.i.s: sn pushed along in rr: swtchd lft over 1f out: r.o wl ins fnl f: nrst fin* **12/1**

4512 **4** *nk* **Italian Tom (IRE)**[14] [2179] 4-9-3 **71**.................................. LukeMorris 10 75
(Ronald Harris) *s.i.s: sn pushed along in rr: r.o wl ins fnl f: nt rch ldrs* **8/1**[3]

5-54 **5** *½* **Equuleus Pictor**[43] [1444] 7-9-3 **71**.................................. CathyGannon 8 73
(John Spearing) *prom: rdn 1/2-way: hmpd over 1f out: styd on u.p* **9/2**[2]

5030 **6** *1* **Cape Royal**[17] [2118] 11-9-7 **75**.....................................(bt) PatCosgrave 13 73
(Milton Bradley) *w ldrs: led over 3f out: hdd 2f out: rdn and hung rt fr over 1f out: no ex ins fnl f* **12/1**

0032 **7** *1 ½* **Lesley's Choice**[11] [2263] 5-9-0 **68**..(v) KierenFallon 11 61
(Joanna Davis) *chsd ldrs: rdn over 1f out: no ex ins fnl f* **8/1**[3]

44-0 **8** *1 ½* **Kinigi (IRE)**[14] [2179] 5-9-3 **71**...(b) DavidProbert 12 58
(Ronald Harris) *sn drvn along in rr: nvr on terms* **14/1**

-001 **9** *½* **Make My Dream**[21] [1982] 8-9-4 **72**.................................. TadhgO'Shea 3 58
(John Gallagher) *sn outpcd: nvr nrr* **33/1**

60-3 **10** *1 ¾* **Liberty Ship**[14] [2182] 6-7-12 **57**.....................................(b) KieranO'Neill(5) 6 36
(Mark Buckley) *chsd ldrs: rdn over 1f out: wknd ins fnl f* **12/1**

0-40 **11** *2 ½* **Desperate Dan**[29] [1752] 10-9-3 **71**..(v) NeilCallan 4 41
(Andrew Haynes) *dwlt: outpcd* **40/1**

2-14 **12** *2 ¼* **Bilash**[15] [2142] 4-9-0 **68**.. TonyCulhane 1 30
(Reg Hollinshead) *prom: lost pl 4f out: n.d after* **20/1**

10-6 **13** *2 ¾* **Wreningham**[21] [1982] 6-8-7 **61**.. WilliamCarson 2 13
(Stuart Williams) *chsd ldrs: rdn 1/2-way: wknd wl over 1f out* **50/1**

60.54 secs (0.54) **Going Correction** +0.075s/f (Good) **13** Ran SP% **121.5**
Speed ratings (Par 103): **98,95,95,94,94 92,90,87,86,84 80,76,72**
toteswingers:1&2:£11.60, 1&3:£40.00, 2&3:£10.10 CSF £47.50 CT £426.53 TOTE £22.60: £5.10, £1.10, £5.30; EX 60.20 Trifecta £454.10 Part won. Pool: £613.70 - 0.43 winning units..
Owner Sexy Six Partnership **Bred** Cheveley Park Stud Ltd **Trained** Sessay, N Yorks
■ Stewards' Enquiry : Kieran O'Neill two-day ban: careless riding (Jun 19-20)

FOCUS
A modest sprint handicap but the winner is an imporver and the placed horses are rated close to their marks.
Lesley's Choice Official explanation: jockey said gelding lost its action
Kinigi(IRE) Official explanation: vet said mare lost a front shoe
Bilash Official explanation: jockey said colt lost its action

2586 SWANNINGTON H'CAP (DIV II) 1m 1f 218y
5:15 (5:15) (Class 6) (0-65,65) 3-Y-O **£1,706** (£503; £252) **Stalls** Low

Form RPR

06-3 **1** **May Be Some Time**[18] [2064] 3-9-5 **63**.................................. LiamKeniry 3 73+
(Stuart Kittow) *a.p: led wl over 1f out: rdn clr fnl f: eased fnl 50yds* **11/4**[1]

000- **2** *7* **Toucan Tango (IRE)**[231] [6831] 3-9-5 **63**.............................. NeilCallan 6 54
(Peter Chapple-Hyam) *chsd ldrs: reminders 6f out: rdn over 2f out: wknd over 1f out* **3/1**[2]

40-0 **3** *shd* **Miskin Diamond (IRE)**[22] [1952] 3-8-5 **49**........................ DavidProbert 9 40
(Bryn Palling) *hld up: hdwy u.p over 2f out: hung rt and wknd over 1f out* **20/1**

0113 **4** *nk* **Beach Babe**[22] [1958] 3-9-7 **65**.. NickyMackay 11 55
(Jonathan Portman) *sn chsng ldr: rdn over 2f out: hung rt and wknd over 1f out* **6/1**

00-0 **5** *1 ¼* **Soldiers Point**[15] [2166] 3-8-8 **52**.. KierenFallon 5 40
(Jane Chapple-Hyam) *led: rdn and hdd wl over 1f out: sn wknd* **9/1**

00-0 **6** *2 ¾* **Rasteau (IRE)**[13] [2196] 3-8-3 **47**.. JimmyQuinn 8 29
(Tom Keddy) *hld up: rdn over 3f out: n.d* **33/1**

324- **7** *5* **Educated Son**[209] [7295] 3-9-7 **65**.................................... GeorgeBaker 10 37
(Ben De Haan) *hld up: nvr on terms* **14/1**

000- **8** *10* **Hawridge Knight**[229] [6874] 3-8-6 **50**.................................. CathyGannon 2 —
(Rod Millman) *hld up: hdwy over 3f out: rdn and wknd over 2f out* **9/2**[3]

0-00 **9** *4* **No Refraction (IRE)**[11] [2243] 3-8-2 **46** oh1..................(p) HayleyTurner 1 —
(Mark Usher) *chsd ldrs tl rdn and wknd 3f out* **22/1**

2m 11.31s (3.41) **Going Correction** +0.075s/f (Good) **9** Ran SP% **112.9**
Speed ratings (Par 97): **89,83,83,83,82 79,75,67,64**
toteswingers:1&2:£3.30, 1&3:£8.50, 2&3:£8.80 CSF £10.52 CT £130.38 TOTE £4.70: £2.60, £1.10, £5.90; EX 11.60 Trifecta £150.10 Pool: £700.45 - 3.55 winning units..
Owner Dr G S Plastow **Bred** D R Tucker **Trained** Blackborough, Devon
■ Stewards' Enquiry : Liam Keniry one-day ban: careless riding (Jun 19)

FOCUS
The time was 1.72 seconds slower than the first division and, although the winner was visually impressive, it is hard to know what else ran its race in behind.
Educated Son Official explanation: jockey said gelding had no more to give
T/Plt: £34.20 to a £1 stake. Pool:£78,165.61 - 1,663.95 winning tickets T/Qpdt: £4.80 to a £1 stake. Pool:£5,665.44 - 867.91 winning tickets CR

2570 REDCAR (L-H)
Tuesday, May 31

OFFICIAL GOING: Good to firm (watered; 8.7)
Wind: Light across Weather: Fine and dry

2587 BRITISH STALLION STUDS SUPPORTING BRITISH RACING E B F MEDIAN AUCTION MAIDEN FILLIES' STKS 6f
2:30 (2:33) (Class 5) 2-Y-O **£2,978** (£886; £442; £221) **Stalls** High

Form RPR

1 **Inetrobil (IRE)** 2-9-0 0.. PhillipMakin 4 83+
(Kevin Ryan) *dwlt: sn trcking ldrs: smooth hdwy and cl up wl over 2f out: led on bit over 1f out: sn pushed clr: easily* **5/6**[1]

55 **2** *6* **Yearbook**[17] [2093] 2-9-0 0.. DavidAllan 2 55
(Tim Easterby) *cl up: led 1/2-way: rdn along 2f out: drvn and hdd over 1f out: kpt on u.p fnl f: no ch w wnr* **14/1**

0 **3** *¾* **Angel Kiss (IRE)**[10] [2318] 2-9-0 0.................................. SilvestreDeSousa 3 53
(David O'Meara) *led: hdd 1/2-way and sn pushed along: rdn 2f out and kpt on same pce* **9/4**[2]

4 *1* **Cataract** 2-9-0 0... TomEaves 5 49
(John Weymes) *dwlt and sn outpcd in rr: hdwy wl over 2f out: rdn to chse ldrs wl over 1f out: rn green and one pce ent fnl f* **33/1**

0 **5** *3* **Schmooze (IRE)**[20] [1996] 2-9-0 0.................................. FrederikTylicki 7 40
(Marco Botti) *in tch: pushed along bef 1/2-way: sn rdn and outpcd: sme late hdwy* **9/1**[3]

6 *1 ¼* **Angelic Kitten (IRE)** 2-9-0 0.. PaulMulrennan 1 36
(Howard Johnson) *wnt lft s and in rr: sme hdwy on outer 1/2-way: sn pushed along: rn green and wknd* **20/1**

0 **7** *1 ½* **Lady Gadfly**[31] [1691] 2-9-0 0.. PJMcDonald 6 31
(Micky Hammond) *prom: rdn along bef 1/2-way: sn wknd* **50/1**

1m 13.59s (1.79) **Going Correction** -0.125s/f (Firm) **7** Ran SP% **111.7**
Speed ratings (Par 90): **83,75,74,72,68 67,65**
toteswingers:1&2:£2.60, 1&3:£1.20, 2&3:£2.40 CSF £13.55 TOTE £1.70: £1.30, £3.50; EX 11.10.
Owner Pat Beirne **Bred** P Beirne **Trained** Hambleton, N Yorks

FOCUS
Probably just an ordinary juvenile maiden and. while the winner was impressive, the form behind looks limited.

NOTEBOOK
Inetrobil(IRE) ◆ was always cruising and readily asserted to win impressively. On this evidence she can make her mark at a higher level and it'll be interesting to see where she heads next. (tchd 4-5 and 10-11, after early 11-10 in places)
Yearbook ran her best race yet and should prove suited by 6f. She'll be one for nurseries. (tchd 16-1)
Angel Kiss(IRE) improved on her debut effort, keeping on right the way to the line, and is another for whom an additional furlong should help. (op 11-4)
Cataract, whose dam was a 5f 2-y-o winner, was dismissed in the betting so it was surprising to see her show as much as she did on her debut, keeping on having been outpaced and run green. (op 40-1)
Schmooze(IRE) again found this trip on the short side and looks more a nursery type. (op 15-2 tchd 10-1)
Angelic Kitten(IRE), whose sister was placed at up to 1m2f, showed early signs of greenness and was soon outpaced. Official explanation: trainer's rep said filly was in season (tchd 25-1)

2588 RACING UK SKY 432 (S) STKS 7f
3:00 (3:00) (Class 6) 3-5-Y-O **£1,706** (£503; £252) **Stalls** High

Form RPR

004 **1** **Frognal (IRE)**[3] [2494] 5-9-4 74..(b) JamesSullivan(3) 6 65
(Ruth Carr) *hld up towards rr: smooth hdwy to trck ldrs over 3f out: led over 1f out: rdn and hung rt ins fnl f: drvn out* **11/8**[1]

1-64 **2** *¾* **Chilledtothebone**[41] [1482] 3-8-10 65.................................(v) TomEaves 1 59
(Linda Stubbs) *in tch on wd outside: rdn along and edgd lft 3f out: hdwy to chse ldrs and hung rt over 1f out: drvn and hung lft ins fnl f: kpt on u.p towards fin* **7/1**[3]

0-55 **3** *¾* **Newbury Street**[4] [2464] 4-9-7 60.................................... DanielTudhope 7 61
(Patrick Holmes) *towards rr: hdwy 3f out and sn trcking ldrs: rdn to chse wnr ent fnl f: sn drvn: hung lft and one pce towards fin* **10/1**

-0U0 **4** *1* **Viking Warrior (IRE)**[8] [2352] 4-9-7 63.............................. FrederikTylicki 2 58
(Michael Dods) *cl up: led after 1f: pushed along and hdd 3f out: rdn over 2f out: drvn over 1f out: kpt on same pce* **14/1**

0530 **5** *1 ½* **Brave Battle**[8] [2356] 3-8-10 65......................................(b) AndrewMullen 5 50
(David Nicholls) *cl up: led 3f out: rdn along and hdd over 1f out: sn drvn and wknd ent fnl f* **14/1**

0053 **6** *14* **Anddante (IRE)**[11] [2249] 3-8-10 58..................................(be) DuranFentiman 9 12
(Tim Easterby) *in tch: rdn along over 3f out: sn wknd* **15/2**

4451 **7** *1* **Sinadinou**[11] [2249] 3-9-2 63.. AdrianNicholls 10 16
(David Nicholls) *chsd ldrs: rdn along 3f out: sn drvn and wknd* **9/2**[2]

0666 **8** *6* **Sophie's Beau (USA)**[8] [2356] 4-9-7 42............................ KellyHarrison 11 —
(Michael Chapman) *led 1f: prom tl rdn along 3f out and sn wknd* **100/1**

00-0 **9** *15* **Piste**[12] [2238] 5-9-2 47.. PaulMulrennan 4 —
(Tina Jackson) *plld hrd: chsd ldrs: rdn along over 3f out: sn wknd and bhd fnl 2f* **100/1**

0020 **10** *18* **Uddy Mac**[11] [2249] 4-8-9 52.. TerenceFury(7) 8 —
(Neville Bycroft) *in tch: rdn along bef 1/2-way: sn wknd and bhd fnl 2f* **22/1**

1m 24.51s (0.01) **Going Correction** -0.125s/f (Firm)
WFA 3 from 4yo+ 11lb **10** Ran SP% **113.3**
Speed ratings (Par 101): **94,93,92,91,89 73,72,65,48,27**
toteswingers:1&2:£1.80, 1&3:£3.80, 2&3:£15.20 CSF £10.89 TOTE £1.90: £1.60, £2.30, £2.20; EX 11.50.The winner sold to Richard Guest for 7,000gns.
Owner Reach For The Moon & Mrs R Carr **Bred** Bryan Ryan **Trained** Huby, N Yorks

FOCUS
A modest seller and a straightforward success for the favourite with the placed horses close to their best, but rated on the negative side.
Piste Official explanation: trainer said mare was in season
Uddy Mac Official explanation: trainer's rep said gelding finished distressed

2589 WEATHERBYS BLOODSTOCK INSURANCE H'CAP 1m 1f
3:30 (3:32) (Class 5) (0-70,68) 4-Y-O+ **£1,942** (£578; £288; £144) **Stalls** Low

Form RPR

66-2 **1** **Petsas Pleasure**[11] [2271] 5-8-4 **51**.................................. PaulHanagan 12 62
(Ollie Pears) *stdd and swtchd lft s: hld up and bhd: hdwy on outer 3f out: str run fr wl over 1f out: rdn to ld and hung lft ins fnl f: drvn out* **4/1**[1]

6-00 **2** *2 ¾* **Desert Hunter (IRE)**[42] [1461] 8-8-6 **53**.......................... KellyHarrison 10 58
(Micky Hammond) *led 1f: chsd ldr: hdwy and cl up 3f out: rdn 2f out and ev ch whn n.m.r and swtchd rt ent fnl f: kpt on wl towards fin* **14/1**

5004 **3** *½* **Bajan Pride**[10] [2308] 7-8-7 **57**.. DeclanCannon(3) 4 61
(Paul Midgley) *trckd ldrs: hdwy 4f out: cl up 3f out: rdn to ld briefly over 1f out: drvn and hdd ins fnl f: n.m.r and kpt on same pce* **15/2**[3]

4324 **4** *¾* **Eastern Gift**[22] [1936] 6-9-7 **68**.. RobertWinston 6 70+
(Gay Kelleway) *in tch: hdwy over 2f out: n.m.r wl over 1f out: swtchd rt and rdn ent fnl f: kpt on: nrst fin* **8/1**

4005 **5** *½* **Lady Excel (IRE)**[11] [2260] 5-8-7 **54**.................................. FrederikTylicki 11 55
(Brian Rothwell) *trckd ldrs: hdwy wl over 2f out: rdn wl over 1f out: drvn and hld whn n.m.r ent fnl f* **50/1**

5000 **6** *½* **Mr Emirati (USA)**[24] [1911] 4-8-2 **52**..........................(p) JamesSullivan(3) 5 52
(Bryan Smart) *towards rr: rdn along on inner and bhd 3f out: swtchd rt to wd outside and drvn wl over 1f out: styd on strly fnl f: nrst fin* **33/1**

00-0 **7** *hd* **Song Of Parkes**[36] [1555] 4-9-4 **65**.. DavidAllan 2 65
(Eric Alston) *plld hrd: led after 1f: rdn along over 2f out: drvn and hdd over 1f out: wknd ins fnl f* **14/1**

00-6 **8** *½* **Tropical Duke (IRE)**[34] [1615] 5-8-4 **58**.......................... ShaneBKelly(7) 9 56
(Ron Barr) *hld up towards rr: hdwy over 3f out: rdn over 2f out: sn drvn and one pce appr fnl f* **7/1**[2]

0006 **9** *2* **Antoniola (IRE)**[7] [2388] 4-9-5 **66**..........................(be) GrahamGibbons 13 60
(Tim Easterby) *chsd ldng pair: rdn along 3f out: drvn wl over 1f out and grad wknd* **11/1**

1410 **10** *3 ¼* **Barton Bounty**[34] [1613] 4-8-10 **57**.................................. PhillipMakin 1 44
(Peter Niven) *trckd ldrs on inner: hdwy 4f out: rdn along 3f out: sn drvn and wknd over 2f out* **9/1**

400- **11** *1* **Prime Circle**[257] [6117] 5-8-13 **60**..................................(p) PaulMulrennan 3 45
(Alan Brown) *midfield: hdwy on inner to chse ldrs over 4f out: rdn along over 2f out: sn drvn and wknd* **20/1**

0642 12 2 ¼ **Madame Excelerate**[6] 2399 4-9-0 61 TomEaves 7 41
(Mark Brisbourne) *t.k.h: chsd ldrs on outer: rdn along over 3f out: sn wknd* 4/1[1]

1m 52.77s (-0.23) **Going Correction** -0.125s/f (Firm) 12 Ran SP% **116.7**
Speed ratings (Par 103): **96,93,93,92,92 91,91,90,89,86 85,83**
toteswingers:1&2:£14.40, 1&3:£6.10, 2&3:£21.70 CSF £61.65 CT £413.04 TOTE £3.20: £1.90, £3.70, £2.70; EX 70.70.
Owner P Bottomley **Bred** Psb Holdings Ltd **Trained** Norton, N Yorks

FOCUS
A low-grade handicap with the winner rated to last year's best and backed up by the third to recent form.
Song Of Parkes Official explanation: jockey said filly ran too free
Madame Excelerate Official explanation: jockey said filly ran flat

2590 WEATHERBYS BANK H'CAP 5f
4:00 (4:01) (Class 4) (0-85,85) 4-Y-0+ **£2,590** (£770; £385; £192) **Stalls** High

Form RPR
20-0 **1** **Bedloe's Island (IRE)**[17] 2118 6-8-3 **70** AndrewHeffernan(3) 1 79
(Neville Bycroft) *a.p: effrt and cl up 2f out: rdn over 1f out: kpt on ins fnl f to ld nr fin* 20/1

-001 **2** ¾ **Nomoreblondes**[22] 1940 7-8-1 **68** (v) DeclanCannon(3) 5 74
(Paul Midgley) *cl up: rdn wl over 1f out: led appr fnl f and sn drvn: hdd and no ex nr fin* 10/1

-060 **3** nk **Hamoody (USA)**[17] 2116 7-9-7 **85** AdrianNicholls 2 90
(David Nicholls) *s.i.s and in rr: swtchd lft to outer and gd hdwy 1/2-way: jnd ldrs wl over 1f out: sn rdn and ev ch tl drvn ins fnl f and no ex towards fin* 7/1

0203 **4** ½ **Select Committee**[11] 2250 6-8-5 **76** (b[1]) ShaneBKelly(7) 4 79
(John Quinn) *trckd ldrs: hdwy 2f out: rdn and ev ch whn edgd rt ent fnl f and sn one pce* 9/1

-001 **5** 2 ¼ **Bronze Beau**[11] 2250 4-9-3 **84** (t) JamesSullivan(3) 9 79
(Linda Stubbs) *led: rdn along wl over 1f out: drvn and hdd appr fnl f: grad wknd* 9/2[2]

050- **6** 1 **Ishetoo**[225] 6981 7-8-12 **76** PaulHanagan 7 67
(Ollie Pears) *towards rr: rdn along and outpcd 1/2-way: sme hdwy u.p over 1f out: n.d* 5/1[3]

3-56 **7** nse **Diman Waters (IRE)**[17] 2118 4-9-3 **81** DavidAllan 6 72
(Eric Alston) *chsd ldrs: rdn along 2f out: sn drvn and edgd rt: one pce* 5/2[1]

230- **8** ½ **Milton Of Campsie**[202] 7399 6-8-6 **72** SilvestreDeSousa 3 61
(John Balding) *t.k.h: chsd ldrs: rdn wl over 1f out and sn wknd* 12/1

0-00 **9** 3 ¾ **Pavershooz**[17] 2118 6-9-5 **83** (p) DuranFentiman 8 59
(Noel Wilson) *a in rr* 12/1

58.26 secs (-0.34) **Going Correction** -0.125s/f (Firm) 9 Ran SP% **115.2**
Speed ratings (Par 105): **97,95,95,94,90 89,89,88,82**
toteswingers:1&2:£33.30, 1&3:£20.80, 2&3:£14.00 CSF £203.04 CT £1558.76 TOTE £23.80: £4.60, £2.70, £1.70; EX 184.60.
Owner J G Lumsden & M F Hogan **Bred** Dr Dean Harron **Trained** Brandsby, N Yorks
■ Stewards' Enquiry : Andrew Heffernan caution: used whip with excessive frequency

FOCUS
A wide-open sprint handicap but ordinary for the grade, with the placed horses helping to set the level.
Milton Of Campsie Official explanation: jockey said mare hung right-handed

2591 BUY YOUR TICKETS ON-LINE @ REDCARRACING.CO.UK MEDIAN AUCTION MAIDEN STKS 1m 2f
4:30 (4:32) (Class 5) 3-5-Y-0 **£1,942** (£578; £288; £144) **Stalls** Low

Form RPR
-22 **1** **Lady Chloe**[18] 2058 3-8-8 70 PaulHanagan 3 73+
(Philip Kirby) *mde all: pushed along wl over 2f out: rdn over 1f out: kpt on strly* 5/6[1]

6 **2** 2 ¼ **Diptimat**[11] 2258 3-8-13 0 (b) FrederikTylicki 1 73
(Marco Botti) *trckd ldrs on inner: hdwy 4f out: rdn to chse wnr 2f out: sn drvn and no imp fnl f* 8/1[3]

02-0 **3** 4 ½ **O Ma Lad (IRE)**[8] 2371 3-8-13 0 SilvestreDeSousa 8 64
(Sylvester Kirk) *chsd wnr: pushed along 3f out: rdn over 2f out: sn drvn and kpt on same pce* 7/2[2]

45 **4** 2 **Dark Spirit (IRE)**[42] 1474 3-8-5 0 SeanLevey(3) 11 55
(Tim Pitt) *in tch: hdwy to chse ldrs over 3f out: rdn over 2f out and sn no imp* 22/1

5 8 **Handles For Forks (IRE)** 3-8-8 0 SamHitchcott 10 39
(Mick Channon) *towards rr: hdwy wl over 2f out: sn rdn and plugged on: nvr nr ldrs* 9/1

6 12 **Cherry Tree Hill (IRE)** 3-8-13 0 PJMcDonald 4 20+
(Alan Swinbank) *midfield: hdwy 4f out: in tch and rdn 3f out: sn no imp* 16/1

00/ **7** 1 ½ **Freddie Bolt**[624] 5954 5-9-13 0 TomEaves 9 17
(Frederick Watson) *a in rr* 100/1

00 **8** 4 ½ **Reveal The Light**[11] 2257 4-9-8 0 KellyHarrison 5 —
(Garry Woodward) *dwlt: a in rr* 100/1

64 **9** 3 ¼ **Woolamaloo**[7] 2394 3-8-8 0 DavidAllan 2 —
(Tim Easterby) *dwlt: a in rr* 66/1

0 **10** 14 **Toffee Nose**[28] 1795 4-9-13 0 PhillipMakin 6 —
(Ron Barr) *a in rr* 100/1

00 **11** 10 **Penang Pacific**[24] 1910 3-8-13 0 RobertWinston 7 —
(Alan McCabe) *chsd ldrs on outer: rdn along over 4f out: wknd over 3f out: sn bhd* 16/1

2m 4.44s (-2.66) **Going Correction** -0.125s/f (Firm)
WFA 3 from 4yo+ 14lb 11 Ran SP% **118.5**
Speed ratings (Par 103): **105,103,99,98,91 82,80,77,74,63 55**
toteswingers:1&2:£2.30, 1&3:£2.20, 2&3:£4.50 CSF £8.47 TOTE £1.40: £1.02, £2.30, £1.90; EX 8.20.
Owner The Wiggins Family **Bred** John Ellis **Trained** Castleton, N Yorks

FOCUS
A weak maiden and the level is a bit fluid but the time helps give the form credence.
Penang Pacific Official explanation: jockey said gelding hung left-handed in home straight

2592 WIN A VIP DAY OUT @ REDCARRACING.CO.UK H'CAP 6f
5:00 (5:00) (Class 5) (0-70,70) 3-Y-0 **£1,942** (£578; £288; £144) **Stalls** High

Form RPR
35-3 **1** **Fast Shot**[11] 2265 3-8-11 60 DavidAllan 3 69+
(Tim Easterby) *cl up on wd outside: effrt 2f out: rdn to ld over 1f out: drvn and hung lft ins fnl f: kpt on wl* 5/2[1]

4460 **2** 1 ½ **Fleurie Lover (IRE)**[11] 2264 3-8-3 55 AndrewHeffernan(3) 9 59
(Richard Guest) *in rr: hdwy on outer wl over 1f out: rdn and ev ch ent fnl f: sn edgd lft and no ex towards fin* 22/1

2300 **3** ½ **Mazovian (USA)**[14] 2180 3-8-11 60 KellyHarrison 1 63
(Michael Chapman) *cl up: rdn along 2f out: drvn over 1f out: kpt on same pce fnl f* 12/1

3534 **4** 2 ¾ **Winning Draw (IRE)**[21] 1975 3-8-2 54 (p) DeclanCannon(3) 2 48
(Paul Midgley) *in tch: effrt whn nt clr run wl over 1f out: sn rdn and kpt on ins fnl f: nrest fin* 11/1

3102 **5** 2 **Roodee Queen**[14] 2177 3-9-1 64 PaulHanagan 8 52
(Patrick Morris) *chsd ldrs: rdn along 2f out: drvn and one pce appr fnl f* 8/1

4163 **6** 3 **Misty Morn**[38] 1514 3-8-9 58 PaulMulrennan 7 36
(Alan Brown) *led: rdn along over 2f out: drvn and hdd over 1f out: sn wknd* 16/1

445- **7** shd **Ingleby Exceed (IRE)**[254] 6220 3-9-2 65 SilvestreDeSousa 6 43
(David O'Meara) *sltly hmpd s: sn trcking ldrs: effrt 2f out: sn rdn and wknd* 7/2[2]

0-36 **8** 1 **Consistant**[11] 2252 3-8-13 62 RobertWinston 4 36
(Brian Baugh) *a in rr: rdn along and outpcd fr over 2f out* 7/1

32-1 **9** 1 ¼ **Lady Kildare (IRE)**[22] 1941 3-9-4 70 PatrickDonaghy(3) 5 40
(Jedd O'Keeffe) *wnt lft s: cl up: rdn along over 2f out: sn drvn and wknd* 13/2[3]

1m 11.11s (-0.69) **Going Correction** -0.125s/f (Firm) 9 Ran SP% **114.0**
Speed ratings (Par 99): **99,97,96,92,90 86,85,84,82**
toteswingers:1&2:£16.00, 1&3:£6.90, 2&3:£23.40 CSF £59.47 CT £560.68 TOTE £3.30: £1.60, £9.70, £4.30; EX 70.70.
Owner Habton Farms **Bred** Whitsbury Manor Stud & Pigeon House Stud **Trained** Great Habton, N Yorks

FOCUS
A modest enough 3-y-o sprint handicap with the third and fourth close to recent marks.

2593 FOLLOW REDCARRACING ON FACEBOOK AND TWITTER AMATEUR RIDERS' MAIDEN H'CAP 6f
5:30 (5:34) (Class 6) (0-65,57) 4-Y-0+ **£1,648** (£507; £253) **Stalls** High

Form RPR
-500 **1** **Hambleton**[76] 874 4-10-2 **45** MrsCBartley 3 53
(Bryan Smart) *in tch: hdwy over 2f out: rdn to chal over 1f out: drvn to ld jst ins fnl f: sn edgd rt and styd on* 7/1

5-00 **2** 1 ¾ **Karate Queen**[36] 1557 6-9-11 **45** MissVBarr(5) 9 47
(Ron Barr) *a.p: hdwy to ld over 2f out: rdn wl over 1f out: hdd jst ins fnl f: kpt on same pce* 16/1

40-5 **3** ¾ **Hayek**[32] 1649 4-10-6 **56** (b[1]) MissRRichardson(7) 6 57
(Tim Easterby) *a.p: rdn 2f out: kpt on fnl f* 15/2

3500 **4** hd **King Bertolini (IRE)**[11] 2260 4-10-3 **49** MrCMartin(3) 10 48
(Alan Berry) *midfield: hdwy 2f out: sn rdn and styd on wl fnl f: nrst fin* 40/1

00-0 **5** ½ **Reset To Fit**[28] 1803 4-10-9 **52** MrSWalker 16 50
(Eric Alston) *in tch: hdwy on outer over 2f out: rdn to chal over 1f out: ev ch whn edgd lft ent fnl f and sn one pce* 9/1

0-34 **6** ¾ **Honest Buck**[30] 1710 4-10-3 **53** MissLucyRyan(7) 15 48
(Kate Walton) *in tch: rdn along over 2f out: kpt on appr fnl f: nrst fin* 11/2[3]

0545 **7** 1 **Isle Of Ellis (IRE)**[11] 2249 4-10-6 **49** (v) MissADeniel 8 41
(Ron Barr) *midfield: hdwy 2f out: sn rdn and no imp fnl f* 20/1

0-2 **8** 1 ½ **Dream Dream Dream (IRE)**[22] 1941 4-10-11 **54** MissSBrotherton 17 41
(Kevin M Prendergast) *trckd ldrs: hdwy and cl up 2f out: sn rdn: edgd lft and wknd appr fnl f* 5/1[2]

5006 **9** shd **Ellielusive (IRE)**[3] 2498 4-10-1 **49** MissBeckyBrisbourne(5) 13 36
(Mark Brisbourne) *towards rr: rdn along over 2f out: hdwy whn n.m.r and swtchd rt over 1f out: kpt on ins fnl f: nrst fin* 7/1

-034 **10** 2 ¼ **Broctune Papa Gio**[8] 2353 4-10-0 **48** LucyAlexander(5) 1 28
(Keith Reveley) *in tch: rdn along over 2f out: sn drvn and wknd* 4/1[1]

00-R **11** ¾ **Erfaan (USA)**[15] 2162 4-10-9 **55** MrJHamer(3) 5 32
(Julie Camacho) *a in rr* 33/1

0-00 **12** ¾ **Du Plessis**[28] 1803 4-9-11 **45** (p) MissHBethell(5) 2 20
(Brian Ellison) *a towards rr* 16/1

000/ **13** 2 ¾ **Mrs Medley**[526] 7829 5-9-9 **45** MissINew(7) 7 —
(Garry Woodward) *led: rdn along 1/2-way: sn hdd & wknd* 80/1

00- **14** 1 ¼ **Somewhere Else**[291] 5044 4-9-11 **45** MissWGibson(5) 12 —
(Alan Berry) *a in rr: bhd fr 1/2-way* 100/1

000 **15** 6 **Boxer Shorts**[8] 2352 5-9-13 **45** (p) MissMMullineaux(3) 4 —
(Michael Mullineaux) *a in rr: bhd fr 1/2-way* 66/1

1m 13.13s (1.33) **Going Correction** -0.125s/f (Firm) 15 Ran SP% **124.4**
Speed ratings (Par 101): **86,83,82,82,81 80,79,77,77,74 73,72,68,66,58**
toteswingers:1&2:£33.30, 1&3:£12.30, 2&3:£38.70. Tote Super 7: Win: Not won. Place: £478.80 -1 winning tickets. CSF £111.60 CT £898.18 TOTE £10.00: £3.30, £11.20, £5.00; EX 218.90.
Owner B Smart **Bred** Whitsbury Manor Stud **Trained** Hambleton, N Yorks
■ Stewards' Enquiry : Miss H Bethell two-day ban: used whip when out of contention (Jun 16-17)

FOCUS
This was about as open as handicaps come and the form is very moderate, rated around the runner-up and fourth.
T/Jkpt: £8,373.30 to a £1 stake. Pool:£35,380.38 - 3.00 winning tickets T/Plt: £135.80 to a £1 stake. Pool:£73,063.57 - 392.58 winning tickets T/Qpdt: £38.00 to a £1 stake. Pool:£4,964.71 - 96.50 winning tickets JR

2266 YARMOUTH (L-H)
Tuesday, May 31

OFFICIAL GOING: Good to firm (watered; 7.9)
Rail along back straight and bottom bend dolled out 3m adding 15yds to races on round course.
Wind: light, across Weather: sunny and bright

2594 BRITISH STALLION STUDS SUPPORTING BRITISH RACING E B F NOVICE STKS 6f 3y
5:50 (5:50) (Class 5) 2-Y-0 **£3,561** (£1,059; £529; £264) **Stalls** High

Form RPR
1 **1** **Wise Venture (IRE)**[18] 2049 2-9-5 0 JimCrowley 3 87+
(Alan Jarvis) *hld up wl in tch: rdn and effrt over 1f out: chal ent fnl f: pushed ahd ins fnl f: sn in command: pushed out: readily* 9/4[2]

14 **2** 2 ¼ **Monnoyer**[20] 2007 2-9-5 0 FrankieDettori 7 80+
(Jeremy Noseda) *chsd ldr: pushed to ld and edgd lft over 1f out: hrd pressed and rdn ent fnl f: hdd and nt pce of wnr ins fnl f: wl hld and eased towards fin* 3/1[3]

016 **3** 1 ¾ **Red Hearts (IRE)**[18] 2070 2-8-9 0 AdamBeschizza(5) 2 68
(Julia Feilden) *led: rdn ent fnl 2f: hdd and sltly hmpd over 1f out: edgd lft u.p and one pce fnl f* 10/1

1 4 2 1/2 **Mabroor (USA)**[24] 1890 2-9-5 0 ... RichardHills 1 65
(Mark Johnston) *slipped as stalls opened: sn rcvrd and chsng ldrs: rdn and struggling over 2f out: wknd over 1f out* **11/8**[1]

5 12 **Fen Flyer** 2-9-0 0 ... AndreaAtzeni 6 22
(Chris Dwyer) *wnt lft s and s.i.s: in tch in last trio: rdn after 2f: rn green: hung lft and wknd wl over 1f out* **100/1**

6 1/2 **Selbaar** 2-9-0 0 ... DarryllHolland 5 20
(Chris Dwyer) *sltly hmpd s and s.i.s: in tch in last trio: rdn and struggling 2f out: sn wknd* **100/1**

7 3 **Singspiel Spirit** 2-9-0 0 ... PhilipRobinson 4 11
(Clive Brittain) *s.i.s: a bhd: lost tch ent fnl 2f* **33/1**

1m 12.57s (-1.83) **Going Correction** -0.325s/f (Firm) **7** Ran SP% **111.9**
Speed ratings (Par 93): **99,96,93,90,74 73,69**
toteswingers:1&2:£2.80, 1&3:£3.00, 2&3:£4.40 CSF £8.99 TOTE £2.80: £1.40, £3.50; EX 8.50.
Owner Allen B Pope & Jarvis Associates **Bred** Joe Rogers **Trained** Twyford, Bucks

FOCUS
There was 5mm of overnight rain but a dry and breezy day (fresh sea breeze behind the runners in the straight) and the winning rider stated the ground to be "as the official but with no jar". A race that has thrown up several smart sorts in the last ten years, the pick being Jeremy Noseda's Wilko, who took this in 2004 before going on to land the Breeders Cup Juvenile (dirt) and, although the market leader disappointed the winner looks the sort to hold his own in stronger company. The four with previous experience were all winners and that quartet pulled clear of the newcomers. The gallop was no more than fair but the form looks up to scratch for the grade and is best rated around the placed horses.

NOTEBOOK
Wise Venture(IRE) ◆, whose debut win has been franked by the subsequent wins of the third and fourth, took advantage of the below-par run of the market leader but still showed improved form to post a very useful performance under just a hands-and-heels ride. There was plenty to like about the manner of this win, he will have no problems with 7f, has plenty of physical scope and this very highly regarded sort, who is a possible for the Coventry but who reportedly won't be over-faced this year, appeals strongly as the sort to hold his own at a higher level. (op 5-2 tchd 15-8)
Monnoyer was soon ideally placed in a race run at just an ordinary gallop and duly turned in an improved effort on this first attempt over 6f. While entries in Group 1 and 2 company look a shade optimistic at this stage, there are certainly more races at a lesser level to be won with this strong traveller. (tchd 4-1)
Red Hearts(IRE) had her limitations exposed in Listed company at York on her previous start but was allowed a fairly easy time of it in front and fared better back against the boys. However, there is a fair chance she is flattered by her proximity given the way things unfolded, and she'll have to raise her game to win a similar event. (op 16-1 tchd 9-1)
Mabroor(USA), who raced with the choke out after sitting down as the stalls opened, failed by some way to build on the form shown when beating a subsequent winner on his debut at Haydock. However, he is in very good hands and is almost certainly worth another chance. (op 5-4 tchd 7-4)
Fen Flyer, the first foal of a 1m winner in France, never figured in what looked a stiff task against four previous winners on this racecourse debut. There will be easier opportunities than this one and he should improve. (op 125-1)
Selbaar, the first foal of a half-sister to several winners up to 1m4f, wasn't knocked about but had his limitations exposed on this debut. He should improve for this experience and will be of more interest granted a stiffer test of stamina once qualified for a mark.
Singspiel Spirit, a Derby entry who has several winners in his pedigree and who hails from a yard that has won this race twice in the last ten years, offered little after a slow start. He should do better granted a stiffer test of stamina in lesser company. Official explanation: jockey said colt ran green (op 50-1)

2595 AGRIPLANTSOLUTIONS.CO.UK (S) STKS 6f 3y
6:20 (6:21) (Class 6) 2-Y-O **£1,619** (£481; £240; £120) **Stalls** High

Form RPR
432 1 **Selinda**[11] 2267 2-7-13 0 ... CharlesBishop(7) 4 56
(Mick Channon) *mde all: pushed along and clr over 2f out: wl in command 1f out: eased towards fin: easily* **4/6**[1]

604 2 5 **Masivo Man (IRE)**[11] 2267 2-8-11 0 ... JackMitchell 1 41
(Chris Dwyer) *plld hrd: hld up in tch: chsd wnr 3f out: sn edgd rt and rdn: outpcd 2f out: wl btn 1f out: hld on for 2nd fnl 50yds* **25/1**

654 3 hd **The Coulbeck Kid**[12] 2234 2-8-11 0 ...(b1) JamesDoyle 3 40
(Des Donovan) *hld up in tch: rdn and effrt wl over 2f out: hung lft and outpcd 2f out: no ch w wnr 1f out: plugged on u.p to press for 2nd fnl 50yds* **12/1**[3]

4 8 **Willies Diamond (IRE)** 2-8-6 0 ... AndreaAtzeni 2 —
(Michael Wigham) *t.k.h early: chsd wnr: rdn over 3f out: lost pl and hmpd wl over 2f out: last and wl btn over 1f out* **7/4**[2]

1m 14.7s (0.30) **Going Correction** -0.325s/f (Firm) **4** Ran SP% **107.9**
Speed ratings (Par 91): **85,78,78,67**
CSF £14.16 TOTE £1.40; EX 7.70.The winner was bought in 7,000gns
Owner Dave and Gill Hedley **Bred** G Hedley & Mike Channon Bloodstock Limited **Trained** West Ilsley, Berks

FOCUS
A low-grade and uncompetitive seller in which the gallop was just an ordinary one. The time was slow and the form looks weak.

NOTEBOOK
Selinda, the clear form-choice, had the run of the race and probably didn't have to improve too much to win. She was bought in for 7,000gns but will do well to find another race as weak as this one. (tchd 4-5)
Masivo Man(IRE) wasn't disgraced after racing with the choke out and may do better over 7f in due course but achieved little in terms of form and doesn't appeal as a winner waiting to happen. (op 18-1)
The Coulbeck Kid didn't look the easiest of rides in first-time headgear and he'll have to show a fair bit more before he is worth a bet. (op 11-1)
Willies Diamond(IRE), a half-sister to fair 6f winner Al Mugtareb, attracted support but was the first beaten after taking a good hold on her racecourse debut. She will be one to watch next time. (op 9-4)

2596 LORD NELSON MAIDEN STKS 1m 3y
6:55 (6:57) (Class 5) 3-Y-O+ **£2,266** (£674; £337; £168) **Stalls** High

Form RPR
2- 1 **Albaasil (IRE)**[334] 3602 3-9-0 0 ... RichardHills 6 94+
(Sir Michael Stoute) *t.k.h: hld up in tch: rdn and effrt to chse ldng trio 2f: pressed ldrs ins fnl f: qcknd to ld fnl 100yds: rdn and sn in command: readily* **4/1**

4-3 2 1 1/2 **Burj Hatta (USA)**[14] 2185 3-9-0 0 ... FrankieDettori 4 87
(Saeed Bin Suroor) *led: rdn 2f out: drvn over 1f out: kpt on wl tl hdd and nt pce of wnr fnl 100yds* **3/1**[2]

4 3 3/4 **Polperro (USA)**[36] 1568 3-9-0 0 ... WilliamBuick 7 85
(John Gosden) *taken down early: chsd ldrs: effrt to press ldr 2f out: ev ch and drvn over 1f out: styd on same pce ins fnl f* **7/2**[3]

40-3 4 6 **Whey Sauce (JPN)**[20] 2004 3-8-9 89 ... JackMitchell 10 67
(Peter Chapple-Hyam) *chsd ldr: rdn and unable qck ent fnl 2f: 4th and wknd u.p ent fnl f* **11/4**[1]

0 5 8 **Jumeira Field (USA)**[45] 1409 3-8-11 0 ... LouisBeuzelin(3) 8 53
(Sir Michael Stoute) *chsd ldrs: rdn and nt pce of ldng quartet 2f out: 5th and wknd over 1f out: no ch w ldrs and eased ins fnl f* **12/1**

0 6 2 1/4 **Fluctuation (IRE)**[17] 2103 3-8-11 0 ... GilmarPereira(3) 14 48
(William Haggas) *t.k.h: hld up wl in tch: rdn and struggling over 2f out: wknd 2f out: sn no ch w ldrs: plugged on ins fnl f* **100/1**

40- 7 nse **Makheelah**[224] 7001 3-8-9 0 ... PhilipRobinson 13 43
(Clive Brittain) *in tch in midfield: rdn and outpcd ent fnl 2f: 6th and wl btn over 1f out* **40/1**

55- 8 3/4 **Myboyalfie (USA)**[232] 6815 4-9-12 0 ... JimCrowley 9 49
(J R Jenkins) *stdd s: hld up towards rr: struggling wl over 2f out: plugged on but no threat to ldrs fnl 2f* **33/1**

/00 9 5 **Media Hype**[21] 1985 4-9-12 0 ... J-PGuillambert 3 38
(Luca Cumani) *stdd s: hld up towards rr: rdn and wkng whn rn green and hung lft wl over 2f out: no ch after* **100/1**

6- 10 2 1/4 **Patriotic (IRE)**[221] 7049 3-9-0 0 ... RoystonFfrench 1 29
(Mark Johnston) *chsd ldrs: rdn and losing pl 1/2-way: wl bhd fnl 2f* **22/1**

11 2 **Norcroft Jem** 4-9-7 0 ... TomQueally 5 23
(George Margarson) *s.i.s: a bhd: lost tch 1/2-way* **100/1**

0-0 12 1 1/4 **Handel's Messiah (IRE)**[10] 2306 3-9-0 0 ... MartinLane 2 22
(Michael Bell) *a towards rr: rdn and losing tch whn hung lft wl over 2f out: wl bhd after: t.o* **150/1**

- 13 5 **Height Of Summer (IRE)** 3-8-9 0 ... DarryllHolland 12 —
(Chris Wall) *hld up towards rr: pushed along and struggling whn hmpd and swtchd rt wl over 2f out: wl bhd after: t.o* **66/1**

0- 14 1 3/4 **Centre Stage**[214] 7201 3-9-0 0 ... SebSanders 11 —
(George Margarson) *s.i.s: sn rcvrd and racd in midfield: wknd qckly and unbalanced ent fnl 3f: wl bhd fnl 2f: t.o* **100/1**

1m 36.1s (-4.50) **Going Correction** -0.325s/f (Firm)
WFA 3 from 4yo 12lb **14** Ran SP% **117.4**
Speed ratings (Par 103): **109,107,106,100,92 90,90,89,84,82 80,79,74,72**
toteswingers:1&2:£4.90, 1&3:£5.00, 2&3:£2.40 CSF £15.39 TOTE £3.70: £1.10, £1.40, £2.40; EX 18.70.
Owner Hamdan Al Maktoum **Bred** Castlemartin Stud And Skymarc Farm **Trained** Newmarket, Suffolk

FOCUS
Last year's winner only went on to show fair form but this race has previously been won by several smart performers including Tazeez (2008, subsequent dual Group 3 winner, Grade/Group 1 placed) and Class Is Class (Listed winner/Group 3 placed) who won a division of this in 2009 and this year's winner looks potentially very useful at least. The time was very good for the grade, being 1.18secs faster than the following handicap for older horses, and the front three pulled clear of the below-par favourite. The form looks good and is rated positively.
Myboyalfie(USA) Official explanation: trainer said gelding was unsuited by the good to firm ground

2597 PLT ANTI-MARKETING H'CAP 1m 3y
7:25 (7:25) (Class 4) (0-80,77) 4-Y-O+ **£4,079** (£1,214; £606; £303) **Stalls** High

Form RPR
20-6 1 **Destiny Blue (IRE)**[25] 1874 4-9-4 **74** ... JimCrowley 1 87+
(Jamie Osborne) *hld up in tch in last pair: rdn and effrt 2f out: chsd ldr ent fnl f: rdn to ld ins fnl f: r.o wl: in command and pushed out towards fin* **9/4**[1]

-631 2 1 3/4 **Jewelled**[15] 2144 5-9-2 **72** ... SebSanders 5 78
(Lady Herries) *stdd s: hld up in last pair: hdwy to ld on bit 2f out: rdn over 1f out: hdd ins fnl f: nt pce of wnr fnl 75yds: hld on for 2nd cl home* **9/2**[3]

0444 3 nk **Rough Rock (IRE)**[11] 2270 6-8-7 **68** ... AdamBeschizza(5) 3 73
(Chris Dwyer) *hld up wl in tch: rdn and effrt over 1f out: nt clr run briefly jst over 1f out: r.o u.p and pressing for 2nd cl home: no threat to wnr* **14/1**

2140 4 1 3/4 **Tewin Wood**[19] 2020 4-9-5 **75** ... LiamJones 4 76
(Alan Bailey) *sn bustled along to ld: rdn over 3f out: hdd 2f out: stl chsng ldrs and drvn over 1f out: no ex and btn fnl 150yds* **9/2**

4003 5 3 **Negotiation (IRE)**[19] 2021 5-9-10 **66** ... WilliamBuick 6 60
(Michael Quinn) *in tch: rdn and unable qck 3f out: drvn and wknd over 1f out* **4/1**[2]

2123 6 3/4 **Maze (IRE)**[22] 1937 6-9-7 **77** ... TomQueally 2 70
(Tony Carroll) *travelled wl: chsd ldrs: rdn and fnd little over 1f out: wknd fnl 150yds* **8/1**

162- 7 26 **Darcey**[214] 7209 5-9-3 **73** ... MickyFenton 7 —
(Amy Weaver) *chsd ldr tl lost pl qckly ent fnl 2f: lost tch wl over 1f out: eased ins fnl f: t.o* **12/1**

1m 37.28s (-3.32) **Going Correction** -0.325s/f (Firm) **7** Ran SP% **112.6**
Speed ratings (Par 105): **103,101,100,99,96 95,69**
toteswingers:1&2:£2.60, 1&3:£15.20, 2&3:£24.40 CSF £12.16 TOTE £2.90: £1.30, £2.20; EX 16.90.
Owner Mr & Mrs Ian Bendelow & Mrs F Walwyn **Bred** Barronstown Stud **Trained** Upper Lambourn, Berks

FOCUS
A fair handicap but one run at no more than a moderate early gallop, and the time was 1.18secs slower than the preceding maiden. The placed horses set the standard.

2598 NORFOLKBROADS.COM H'CAP 7f 3y
8:00 (8:00) (Class 6) (0-60,60) 3-Y-O **£1,619** (£481; £240; £120) **Stalls** High

Form RPR
-044 1 **See The Storm**[8] 2351 3-8-10 **49** ... JackMitchell 2 49
(Patrick Morris) *hld up in tch in midfield: rdn and effrt over 2f out: hdwy over 1f out: drvn and ev ch 1f out: led ins fnl f: hld on wl u.p: all out* **7/2**[1]

000- 2 nk **Izzet**[224] 7004 3-9-5 **58** ... TomQueally 4 57
(Mark H Tompkins) *hld up in rr: rdn and effrt over 2f out: hdwy u.p over 1f out: ev ch 1f out: forged to ld w wnr ins fnl f: r.o but a jst hld* **6/1**[2]

-600 3 1 1/2 **Fully Armed (IRE)**[7] 2384 3-8-7 **46** oh1 ...(bt) MartinLane 3 41
(Rae Guest) *t.k.h: chsd ldrs: drvn and ev ch over 1f out: no ex and styd on same pce fnl 100yds* **25/1**

0000 4 shd **Blazing Apostle (IRE)**[14] 2186 3-8-0 **46** oh1 ... DanielHarris(7) 6 43
(Christine Dunnett) *chsd ldr: rdn wl over 3f out: keeping on and stl pressing ldr whn sltly hmpd and swtchd lft jst over 1f out: kpt on ins fnl f* **50/1**

0-4 5 hd **Celestial Flyer (IRE)**[7] 2384 3-8-0 **46** oh1 ... CharlesBishop(7) 1 40
(Tor Sturgis) *led: grad c across to stands' rail: rdn over 2f out: hdd ins fnl f: no ex: kpt on same pce fnl 100yds* **7/2**[1]

0000 6 3/4 **Ajaafa**[14] 2172 3-8-13 **52** ... NeilChalmers 10 44
(Michael Appleby) *hld up towards rr: rdn and effrt ent fnl 2f: hdwy over 1f out: kpt on u.p fnl f: nvr able to rch ldrs* **16/1**

00-0 **7** ½ **Warden Bond**[18] 2064 3-9-0 **58** LauraPike(5) 5 49
(William Stone) *towards rr: pushed along after 2f: swtchd lft 2f out: hdwy u.p jst over 1f out: kpt on steadily ins fnl f: nvr gng pce to threaten ldrs* **12/1**

-550 **8** 2½ **Acclamatory**[21] 1980 3-9-6 **59** (t) JimCrowley 13 43
(Stuart Williams) *hld up in tch towards rr: rdn and effrt towards stands' side ent fnl 2f: no prog over 1f out: one pce and no threat to ldrs fnl f* **8/1**[3]

50-6 **9** 3 **Kaifi (IRE)**[35] 1588 3-8-3 **49** oh1 ow3 AntiocoMurgia(7) 9 25
(Clive Brittain) *in tch in midfield: lost pl and dropped to rr over 2f out: rdn and hung lft 2f out: no threat to ldrs after* **9/1**

3550 **10** 4 **Bodie**[25] 1869 3-9-7 **60** (t) MickyFenton 11 25
(Pam Sly) *chsd ldrs: rdn over 2f out: wkng whn short of room and hmpd over 1f out: wl btn fnl f* **8/1**[3]

0-10 **11** 1¼ **Century Dancer**[22] 1952 3-8-11 **55** RyanPowell(5) 12 17
(Tor Sturgis) *in tch in midfield: rdn and lost pl over 2f out: bhd wl over 1f out* **12/1**

1m 26.64s (0.04) **Going Correction** -0.325s/f (Firm) **11** Ran SP% **118.0**
Speed ratings (Par 97): **86,85,83,83,83 82,82,79,75,71 69**
toteswingers:1&2:£5.50, 1&3:£8.40, 2&3:£59.90 CSF £24.22 CT £375.50 TOTE £3.10: £1.10, £2.10, £9.90; EX 21.70.
Owner Keating Bradley Fold Ltd **Bred** D R Botterill **Trained** Tarporley, Cheshire
■ Stewards' Enquiry : Charles Bishop two-day ban: careless riding (Jun 19-20)

FOCUS
A moderate handicap but one in which two of the least exposed members of the field came to the fore late on. The gallop was just an ordinary one and the form is very limited.

2599 MERRIVALE MODEL VILLAGE H'CAP 1m 3y
8:30 (8:33) (Class 6) (0-60,58) 3-Y-O **£1,619** (£481; £240; £120) **Stalls** High

Form RPR

500- **1** **Dubawi Dancer**[253] 6248 3-8-8 **45** LiamJones 5 58+
(William Haggas) *t.k.h: hld up in tch: hdwy to trck ldrs 3f out: chsd ldr and rdn 2f out: rn green but c clr w ldr ent fnl f: wandered lft and rt u.p: led fnl 75yds: hld on cl home* **8/11**[1]

0-00 **2** shd **Zaheeb**[18] 2068 3-8-10 **52** AdamBeschizza(5) 10 65
(Dave Morris) *chsd ldrs tl led wl over 3f out: drvn and clr w wnr ent fnl f: rdr dropped reins fnl 100yds: sn hdd: kpt on u.p: jst hld cl home* **28/1**

00-5 **3** 8 **Easydoesit (IRE)**[22] 1933 3-8-13 **50** JamesDoyle 2 44
(Des Donovan) *in tch in midfield: rdn and hdwy ent fnl 2f: drvn and outpcd by ldng pair ent fnl f: wnt modest 3rd ins fnl f* **12/1**

2235 **4** 1½ **Trojan Touch (USA)**[12] 2239 3-8-9 **46** (v1) AndreaAtzeni 9 36
(Chris Dwyer) *dwlt: sn pushed along and hdwy to chse ldrs after 1f: led over 6f out: hdd wl over 3f out: chsd ldr tl hld hd high u.p and nt qckn 2f out: 3rd and wknd ent fnl f* **14/1**

0-60 **5** 3 **Art Thief**[10] 2311 3-9-7 **58** TomQueally 11 41
(Sylvester Kirk) *hld up in tch towards rr: rdn and effrt towards stands' side jst over 2f out: drvn: edgd lft and wknd over 1f out: no ch fnl f* **5/1**[2]

0-05 **6** 6 **Russian Ice**[21] 1986 3-9-4 **55** AdrianMcCarthy 4 24
(Dean Ivory) *in tch: pushed along 1/2-way: no prog u.p 2f out: wknd over 1f out: no ch ent fnl f* **16/1**

66-1 **7** 2¼ **Henrys Air**[11] 2243 3-9-5 **56** RobbieFitzpatrick 8 19
(David Bridgwater) *chsd ldrs early: steadily lost pl: in rr and rdn 1/2-way: wknd wl over 1f out: no ch ent fnl f* **14/1**

05-4 **8** nse **Sandtail (IRE)**[22] 1953 3-9-6 **57** SebSanders 7 20
(J W Hills) *led tl over 6f out: chsd ldrs after: rdn and struggling ent fnl 2f: sn btn: fdd and eased ins fnl f* **8/1**[3]

0-05 **9** 2¼ **Rural Pursuits**[35] 1592 3-8-3 **47** (p) DanielHarris(7) 1 —
(Christine Dunnett) *prom: rdn 3f out: wknd ent fnl 2f: wl bhd fnl f* **100/1**

0-00 **10** 5 **Librettela**[14] 2174 3-9-2 **53** JimCrowley 3 —
(Alan Jarvis) *s.i.s: a struggling in last: lost tch over 3f out: t.o fnl f* **40/1**

1m 39.64s (-0.96) **Going Correction** -0.325s/f (Firm) **10** Ran SP% **119.5**
Speed ratings (Par 97): **91,90,82,81,78 72,70,70,67,62**
toteswingers:1&2:£7.10, 1&3:£4.20, 2&3:£39.40 CSF £32.13 CT £169.23 TOTE £1.40: £1.02, £16.00, £7.40; EX 44.00.
Owner F W Golding, E Kirtland & N A Callaghan **Bred** Allan Munnis & Laurance Walwin **Trained** Newmarket, Suffolk

FOCUS
A moderate handicap in which the early gallop was reasonable and in which two unexposed sorts pulled clear in the last furlong. The level looks fluid despite the first two coming clear, with nothing solid in behind.
Dubawi Dancer ◆ Official explanation: trainer's rep said, regarding apparent improvement in form, that the filly had strengthened up over the winter.

2600 TIME AND TIDE MUSEUM H'CAP 1m 2f 21y
9:00 (9:01) (Class 6) (0-55,51) 4-Y-0+ **£1,619** (£481; £240; £120) **Stalls** Low

Form RPR

4-43 **1** **Shouda (IRE)**[53] 1218 5-9-0 **49** TomQueally 5 58+
(Barney Curley) *hld up wl off pce towards rr: clsd on ldrs 4f out: chsd ldrs and rdn 2f out: n.m.r briefly over 1f out: drvn to chse ldng pair ins fnl f: qcknd u.p fnl 75yds to ld last strides* **1/1**[1]

0011 **2** hd **Cane Cat (IRE)**[11] 2268 4-9-2 **51** (t) LiamJones 4 60
(Tony Carroll) *hld up wl off the pce in last pair: hdwy 4f out: chsd ldng pair ent fnl f: drvn to ld and edgd rt fnl 75yds: hdd last strides* **5/1**[3]

0060 **3** ¾ **Art Scholar (IRE)**[21] 1987 4-9-0 **49** NeilChalmers 2 56
(Michael Appleby) *hld up off the pce in midfield: hdwy to chse ldrs 4f out: clsd and led over 2f out: rdn ins fnl f: hdd fnl 75yds: one pce* **12/1**

-004 **4** 5 **Tt's Dream**[21] 1987 4-9-0 **49** (bt) RobertHavlin 1 46
(Alastair Lidderdale) *hld up wl off the pce in rr: stdy hdwy on far rail 4f out: chsd ldrs and hung lft ent fnl 2f: sn rdn and ev ch: wknd qckly ins fnl f* **9/2**[2]

6404 **5** 5 **Escardo (GER)**[4] 2450 8-8-10 **45** (vt) RobbieFitzpatrick 12 32
(David Bridgwater) *hld up off the pce in midfield: clsd on ldrs 4f out: rdn and ev ch 2f out: wknd over 1f out: fdd ins fnl f* **22/1**

00-3 **6** 8 **Chantilly Dancer (IRE)**[21] 1993 5-8-7 **45** LouisBeuzelin(3) 9 16
(Michael Quinn) *prom in main gp: clsd on ldrs 4f out: rdn and struggling over 2f out: sn wknd: wl btn over 1f out* **16/1**

4404 **7** 3¾ **Moment Of Clarity**[12] 2233 9-8-7 **45** (b1) SimonPearce(3) 3 —
(Shaun Harris) *sn led and clr: c bk to field over 3f out: hdd over 2f out: rdn and wknd qckly wl over 1f out* **20/1**

00-0 **8** ¾ **Carlcol Girl**[21] 1993 4-8-10 **45** (v) AdrianMcCarthy 8 —
(Christine Dunnett) *led main gp tl 4f out: wknd u.p 3f out: wl bhd fnl 2f* **100/1**

0-60 **9** 8 **Cragganmore Creek**[70] 939 8-8-5 **45** (v) AdamBeschizza(5) 6 —
(Dave Morris) *s.i.s: a wl bhd: rdn and no rspnse 4f out: wl bhd fnl 3f: t.o* **80/1**

6526 **10** 2¾ **Spirit Of Love (IRE)**[7] 2385 4-8-11 **46** (p) AndreaAtzeni 10 —
(Michael Wigham) *chsd ldr and clr of field tl 4f out: sn struggling: wl bhd fnl 2f: t.o* **9/1**

0560 **11** 76 **Lady Freda**[33] 1633 5-8-3 **45** IanBurns(7) 11 —
(Alan Coogan) *prom in main gp: rdn and losing pl 4f out: lost tch 3f out: wl t.o fnl 2f* **100/1**

2m 7.85s (-2.65) **Going Correction** -0.225s/f (Firm) **11** Ran SP% **120.7**
Speed ratings (Par 101): **101,100,100,96,92 85,82,82,75,73 12**
CSF £6.17 CT £40.28 TOTE £2.10: £1.10, £2.10, £4.00; EX 8.70.
Owner Curley Leisure **Bred** Gestut Schlenderhan **Trained** Newmarket, Suffolk

FOCUS
The back straight and bottom bend were dolled off, adding 15m to the distance of this race. A very moderate handicap run at a decent early gallop to suit those held up, and the first three pulled clear. The form is limited with the placed horses helping to set the level.
Spirit Of Love(IRE) Official explanation: jockey said gelding had no more to give
T/Plt: £43.70 to a £1 stake. Pool:£74,542.61 - 1,243.96 winning tickets T/Qpdt: £13.20 to a £1 stake. Pool:£7,247.95 - 404.04 winning tickets SP

TABY (R-H)
Tuesday, May 31
OFFICIAL GOING: Turf: good

2601a JR FORVALTNING STOCKHOLMS STORA PRIS (GROUP 3) (4YO+) (TURF) 1m 1f 165y
8:08 (12:00) 4-Y-0+ **£67,049** (£23,946; £11,494; £7,662; £4,789)

RPR

1 **Tertullus (FR)**[23] 8-9-2 0 RafaelSchistl 6 101
(Rune Haugen, Norway) *settled in 5th: pushed along and hdwy on outside 2 1/2f out: wnt 2nd ins fnl 2f: led ins fnl f: r.o wl* **115/10**

2 ½ **Sir Lando**[23] 1931 4-9-2 0 EddieAhern 8 100
(Wido Neuroth, Norway) *dwlt s: settled towards rr: hdwy on outside over 2 1/2f out: 9th and swtchd outside ins fnl 2f: swtchd ins and styd on wl fnl f: nrest at fin* **9/5**[1]

3 1 **Erroll (SWE)**[323] 5-9-2 0 (b) Per-AndersGraberg 1 98
(Patrick Wahl, Sweden) *a.p (in first four thrght): pushed along and 2nd st (jst over 2f out): rdn and nt qckn fnl 150yds: jst hld on to 3rd* **131/10**

4 hd **Theatrical Award (NOR)**[14] 6-8-13 0 CarlosLopez 3 95
(Michael Taylor, Norway) *broke wl and keen: restrained in midfield: sn settled: pushed along and prog less than 3f out: c four wd into st: disputing cl 6th 2f out: styd on ins fnl f: nt pce to chal* **61/10**

5 4 **Perks (IRE)**[18] 6-9-2 0 EspenSki 7 89
(Jessica Long, Sweden) *led: shkn up and qcknd ins last 2 1/2f: hdd ins fnl f: wknd* **39/1**

6 2½ **Tertio Bloom (SWE)**[18] 6-9-2 0 ValmirDeAzeredo 14 84
(Fredrik Reuterskiold, Sweden) *plld early and hld up towards rr: 10th and pushed along 2 1/2f out: kpt on at one pce fnl 1 1/2f: nvr able to chal* **169/10**

7 ¾ **Peas And Carrots (DEN)**[18] 8-9-2 0 JacobJohansen 2 83
(Lennart Reuterskiold Jr, Sweden) *w.w in fnl 3rd: prog into 8th 4 1/2f out: pushed along 3f out: hdwy on rail ins last 2f: disp 4th over 1f out: nt qckn: 6th and btn whn clipped heels of perks and nrly fell fnl 75yds* **54/10**[3]

8 3 **Theocritus (USA)**[243] 6-9-2 0 RebeccaColldin 15 77
(Claes Bjorling, Sweden) *last: pushed along 4f out: mod prog passed btn horses fnl f: nvr a factor* **46/1**

9 3 **Walzertraum (USA)**[16] 6-9-2 0 (b) ManuelMartinez 13 70
(Fredrik Reuterskiold, Sweden) *racd in midfield: 7th 3f out: no imp fnl 2f* **66/1**

10 ¾ **Runaway**[31] 9-9-2 0 ManuelSantos 11 68
(Ms K Stenefeldt, Sweden) *prom (2nd or 3rd for much of r): 3l 2nd 3 1/2f out: sn pushed along: nt qckn 2f out: wknd fnl 1 1/2f* **233/10**

D hd **Aces Star (USA)**[243] 4-9-2 0 (b) FJohansson 12 76
(Fredrik Reuterskiold, Sweden) *trckd ldr (in 2nd or 3rd for much of the way): lost pl 3f out: 5th and rallying passing 2f marker: cl 8th whn looked to clip heels of tch of hawk wl ins fnl f and all but fell: then hmpd whn having to jump fallen tch* **165/10**

F **Touch Of Hawk (FR)**[14] 5-9-2 0 Jan-ErikNeuroth 9 —
(Wido Neuroth, Norway) *broke in midfield: hmpd by moe green and shuffled bk after less than a f: racd in rr: 11th and pushed along 2 1/2f out: hdwy on rail fnl bnd: in share of cl 7th passing 2f marker: 5th and styng on at one pce whn fell abt* **176/10**

P **Moe Green (IRE)**[31] 4-9-2 0 ElioneChaves 5 —
(Francisco Castro, Sweden) *midfield whn edgd rt and hmpd tch of hawk after less than 1f: sn outpcd towards rr: rdn 4f out: 12th st: bhd whn p.u ins fnl f* **22/5**[2]

1m 59.4s (0.10) **13** Ran SP% **125.9**
PARI-MUTUEL (all including 1sek stake): WIN 12.49; PLACE 3.64, 1.62, 2.73; DF 39.70.
Owner Stall Nor & Lagulise Racing **Bred** H Volz **Trained** Norway

2194 KEMPTON (A.W) (R-H)
Wednesday, June 1
OFFICIAL GOING: Standard to slow
Wind: Fresh, half against, becoming almost nil last 3 races Weather: Fine

2602 FREE ENTRY FOR BETDAQ MEMBERS MEDIAN AUCTION MAIDEN STKS 5f (P)
6:20 (6:20) (Class 6) 2-Y-O **£1,619** (£481; £240; £120) **Stalls** Low

Form RPR

1 **Mitie Mouse** 2-9-3 0 NeilCallan 2 74
(Mike Murphy) *dwlt: sn cl up: trckd ldr 2f: rdn to chal fnl f: led last 100yds: styd on* **8/1**[3]

2 **2** nk **Excavator**[34] 1628 2-9-3 0 RyanMoore 5 73
(Roger Charlton) *led at mod pce: rdn and pressed over 1f out: hdd and nt qckn last 100yds* **4/7**[1]

5 **3** 1¼ **Lupo D'Oro (IRE)**[13] 2214 2-9-3 0 LukeMorris 1 69
(John Best) *cl up on inner: shkn up over 1f out: kpt on same pce ins fnl f* **7/2**[2]

0 **4** 2 **Percythepinto (IRE)**[4] 2510 2-9-3 0 DaneO'Neill 4 61
(David Elsworth) *racd wd: in tch: pushed along over 2f out: nt qckn over 1f out: grad fdd* **20/1**

5 *nse* **Netley Marsh** 2-9-3 0 .... RichardHughes 6 61+
(Richard Hannon) *v.s.a and lost many l: ct up at bk of field after 2f: pushed along over 1f out: fdd grad ins fnl f: nt disgracd* **12/1**

00 **6** *7* **Raspberry Fizz**[11] 2309 2-8-12 0 .... TomQueally 3 31
(Eve Johnson Houghton) *mostly chsd ldr to 2f out: wknd qckly over 1f out* **40/1**

62.54 secs (2.04) **Going Correction** +0.275s/f (Slow) **6** Ran SP% **111.9**
Speed ratings (Par 91): **94,93,91,88,88 77**
toteswingers: 1&2 £1.40, 1&3 £2.50, 2&3 £1.10 CSF £13.10 TOTE £6.10: £2.50, £1.10; EX 15.60.
Owner Bill Rogerson **Bred** R G Percival **Trained** Westoning, Beds

FOCUS
A final time here of just over three seconds above standard, as well as 1.78 seconds slower than the following Class 5 handicap for older horses, shows Excavator dictated a modest pace and the form is limited and rated slightly negatively.

NOTEBOOK
Mitie Mouse is the first foal of a multiple 5f winner. He raced strongly just off the steady pace, and it was no surprise he showed such a professional attitude under pressure. There might not be significant improvement to come in the short term, but evidently he has plenty of ability and rates a nice sprint prospect. (op 9-1)
Excavator may have run into a useful recruit, but the bare form does not represent significant progression from his debut. (tchd 8-15 and 4-6 in places)
Lupo D'Oro(IRE) had shaped as though worth a try over this trip when tiring over 6f first time up, but he found the front pair too strong after racing a little keenly. There might be more to come when he's able to utilise his speed. (op 4-1 tchd 9-2)
Percythepinto(IRE) seemed to step up a good deal on the form he showed on his debut four days earlier, although the steady pace compressed the beaten margins somewhat. (tchd 25-1)
Netley Marsh was weak in the market for this introduction. He showed ability after losing several lengths when slowly into stride, although the lack of speed in the race probably aided his recovery. Official explanation: jockey said colt was slowly away (op 11-1 tchd 14-1)

2603 BETDAQ.COM EXCHANGE PRICE MULTIPLES H'CAP 5f (P)
6:50 (6:50) (Class 5) (0-70,68) 3-Y-0+ **£2,266** (£674; £337; £168) **Stalls** Low

Form RPR

0-44 **1** **Speightowns Kid (USA)**[12] 2265 3-9-2 **63** .... WilliamBuick 12 78+
(Matthew Salaman) *trckd ldr: pushed firmly into ld over 1f out: rdn and drew rt away after* **11/1**

2313 **2** *4 ½* **Decider (USA)**[23] 1955 8-9-11 **65** .... (b) LukeMorris 6 67
(Ronald Harris) *led: rdn and hdd over 1f out: kpt on but no ch w wnr* **6/1**[2]

2-12 **3** *1 ¼* **Rebecca Romero**[34] 1627 4-9-4 **58** .... (v) RichardHughes 4 55+
(Denis Coakley) *hld up in last trio and sn t.k.h: nvr wl plcd: swtchd lft over 1f out: prog to snatch 3rd fin but no ch* **2/1**[1]

3U24 **4** *nse* **Grudge**[11] 2304 6-9-11 **65** .... (b) HayleyTurner 3 62
(Conor Dore) *chsd ldrs in 5th: pushed along fr 1/2-way on inner: effrt to dispute 3rd fr over 1f out: kpt on same pce* **7/1**[3]

03-5 **5** *1* **Maryolini**[15] 2167 6-8-13 **53** .... JimmyQuinn 5 47
(Tom Keddy) *chsd ldrs in 6th: drvn to dispute 3rd ins fnl f: one pce after* **12/1**

0060 **6** *shd* **Vhujon (IRE)**[21] 2001 6-9-3 **57** .... RobbieFitzpatrick 2 50
(Peter Grayson) *sn drvn in 7th and nvr gng wl: kpt on ins fnl f* **33/1**

-326 **7** *1* **Triple Dream**[17] 2126 6-10-0 **68** .... (tp) LiamKeniry 8 58
(Milton Bradley) *disp 3rd most of way: drvn over 1f out and no imp: wknd ins fnl f* **7/1**[3]

0013 **8** *hd* **Efistorm**[42] 1501 10-9-13 **67** .... KirstyMilczarek 7 56
(Conor Dore) *mostly in last pair and struggling to go the pce: detached in 9th over 1f out: kpt on* **20/1**

5340 **9** *4* **Estonia**[26] 1864 4-9-11 **65** .... AdamKirby 10 40
(Michael Squance) *s.i.s: sn disp 3rd but forced to r wd: stl there over 1f out: wknd qckly ins fnl f* **9/1**

660 **10** *6* **Colourbearer (IRE)**[22] 1984 4-9-2 **56** .... DaneO'Neill 9 —
(Milton Bradley) *s.i.s: a struggling in last trio: wl bhd over 1f out* **15/2**

60.76 secs (0.26) **Going Correction** +0.275s/f (Slow)
WFA 3 from 4yo+ 7lb **10** Ran SP% **118.1**
Speed ratings (Par 103): **108,100,98,98,97 96,95,95,88,79**
toteswingers: 1&2 £9.40, 1&3 £5.40, 2&3 £1.40 CSF £76.57 CT £193.15 TOTE £9.70: £4.60, £1.70, £1.10; EX 63.80.
Owner R P Phillips **Bred** Sandyview Farm **Trained** Upper Lambourn, Berks

FOCUS
The first two finishers filled the front two positions pretty much throughout. The level is fluid witht he runner-up to recent handicap form the best guide.
Estonia Official explanation: jockey said filly had no more to give

2604 LAY BACK AND WIN AT BETDAQ.COM H'CAP 1m 2f (P)
7:20 (7:21) (Class 3) (0-95,92) 4-Y-0+ **£5,310** (£1,580; £789; £394) **Stalls** Low

Form RPR

00-2 **1** **Constant Contact**[27] 1834 4-9-5 **90** .... JimmyFortune 5 102
(Andrew Balding) *trckd ldrs: effrt over 2f out: drvn ahd over 1f out: styd on wl* **9/1**

123- **2** *¾* **Heddwyn (IRE)**[219] 7121 4-9-3 **88** .... MartinDwyer 1 98
(Marcus Tregoning) *wl plcd bhd ldrs: effrt to chal over 1f out: pressed wnr after: jst hld last 150yds* **11/1**

61-1 **3** *¾* **Point North (IRE)**[21] 2000 4-9-2 **87** .... (t) WilliamBuick 14 96+
(Jeremy Noseda) *hld up in last trio fr wdst draw: trapped bhd rivals 3f out: plld out and gd prog fr 2f out: tried to cl on ldng pair fnl f: no ex last 100yds* **5/4**[1]

1110 **4** *1* **Sweet Origin**[31] 1717 4-9-4 **89** .... RyanMoore 6 96+
(Marco Botti) *settled in last trio: plenty to do whn effrt on outer over 2f out: gd prog to chal over 1f out: no ex ins fnl f* **13/2**[2]

3556 **5** *7* **Franco Is My Name**[67] 991 5-9-5 **90** .... (p) DaneO'Neill 4 83
(Peter Hedger) *dwlt: sn trckd ldrs on inner: effrt over 2f out: wl outpcd in 5th ins fnl f* **16/1**

60-0 **6** *nse* **Thin Red Line (IRE)**[27] 1824 5-8-13 **87** .... SeanLevey(3) 9 79
(Michael Dods) *wl in rr: rdn and no prog on inner over 2f out: plugged on past tiring rivals ins fnl f* **16/1**

110- **7** *¾* **Absinthe (IRE)**[242] 6562 5-9-7 **92** .... AdamKirby 8 83
(Walter Swinburn) *settled in midfield: rdn and effrt 2f out: no prog jst over 1f out: wknd* **8/1**[3]

0-00 **8** *¾* **Fremont (IRE)**[39] 1529 4-9-4 **89** .... RichardHughes 13 78
(Richard Hannon) *hld up in last trio fr wd draw: prog on outer 3f out: no hdwy wl over 1f out: wknd* **33/1**

23-0 **9** *¾* **Sing Sweetly**[46] 1388 4-8-11 **82** .... DarryllHolland 10 70
(Gerard Butler) *a towards rr: no prog over 2f out: shkn up and last of main gp over 1f out: nvr a factor* **33/1**

6220 **10** *1 ¼* **Resentful Angel**[32] 1677 6-9-7 **92** .... IanMongan 11 77
(Pat Eddery) *pressed ldr after 2f: led jst over 3f out: drvn and hdd over 1f out: wknd qckly* **22/1**

-030 **11** *3 ¾* **Tinshu (IRE)**[18] 2105 5-9-3 **88** .... AndreaAtzeni 3 66
(Derek Haydn Jones) *pressed ldr 2f: styd prom: drvn to ld briefly over 1f out: sn wknd rapidly* **20/1**

0263 **12** *9* **Kidlat**[8] 1824 6-8-13 **84** .... LiamKeniry 12 44
(Alan Bailey) *prom: drvn and wknd over 3f out on outer: sn bhd* **50/1**

1020 **13** *12* **King Olav (UAE)**[42] 1479 6-9-6 **91** .... NeilCallan 7 27
(Tony Carroll) *sn lost gd position and drvn in midfield: wknd 3f out: t.o* **33/1**

510- **14** *16* **Fastnet Storm (IRE)**[154] 8009 5-9-3 **88** .... GrahamGibbons 2 —
(David Barron) *rousted along to ld: hdd jst over 3f out: wknd rapidly: t.o* **20/1**

2m 8.83s (0.83) **Going Correction** +0.275s/f (Slow) **14** Ran SP% **123.6**
Speed ratings (Par 107): **107,106,105,105,99 99,98,98,97,96 93,86,76,63**
toteswingers: 1&2 £10.70, 1&3 £4.20, 2&3 £3.20 CSF £97.83 CT £211.23 TOTE £8.30: £2.00, £3.40, £2.00; EX 46.30.
Owner Kingsclere Racing CLub **Bred** Kingsclere Stud **Trained** Kingsclere, Hants

FOCUS
A strong handicap, although as is so often the case around the tight, inner course, those held up were at a disadvantage. The pace initially seemed honest but gradually appeared to slow - a view supported by the field bunching up on the final bend and the time being 3.33 seconds above standard. the form is a bit muddling despite the first four being clear.

NOTEBOOK
Constant Contact couldn't take advantage of being allowed to set a modest pace on his recent return from a lengthy absence at Goodwood (first run since being gelded), but the improvement shown here suggests that run was very much needed, for all that he has won when fresh in the past. The more patient tactics this time, as well as the switch to Polytrack, evidently suited and he won well, galloping out strongly after the line. It's true to say he was better placed than some of his rivals under Jimmy Fortune, but this was only the ninth start of his career and there should be more to come.
Heddwyn(IRE), like the winner, was well positioned turning into the straight and posted a pleasing performance on his return from a 219-day absence. This was only his fourth outing and he should improve. (op 8-1)
Point North(IRE) had little hope when last of all turning into the straight, but the manner in which he quickened into a threatening position widest of all, before flattening out near the line, suggests he remains well handicapped (7lb higher than for reappearance win). He also still looked a bit immature, being inclined to edge right and his tongue lolling out in the closing stages. There is more to come, however. (tchd 6-5, 11-8 and 11-10 in a place)
Sweet Origin, back on what looks his favoured surface, did well considering he was only a length up on Point North turning into the straight. (op 10-1 tchd 6-1)
Thin Red Line(IRE), another who raced in an unpromising position, made some late headway. (op 25-1)
Fastnet Storm(IRE) Official explanation: jockey said gelding stopped quickly

2605 BETDAQ MOBILE APPS H'CAP 7f (P)
7:50 (7:50) (Class 6) (0-65,71) 4-Y-0+ **£1,619** (£481; £240; £120) **Stalls** Low

Form RPR

-226 **1** **Grand Piano (IRE)**[31] 1730 4-8-10 **65** .... (v[1]) ThomasBrown(7) 7 73
(Andrew Balding) *dwlt: settled in last trio: plenty to do 3f out: stdy prog over 2f out: shkn up and sustained effrt to ld last 100yds* **8/1**

30-3 **2** *¾* **Foxtrot Alpha (IRE)**[21] 1995 5-9-0 **62** .... LukeMorris 8 68
(Peter Winkworth) *prom: trckd ldr 3f out: clsd to ld 2f out: hdd and one pce fnl 100yds* **9/2**[2]

-005 **3** *½* **Rapid Water**[97] 666 5-9-3 **65** .... DarryllHolland 1 70
(Michael Squance) *prom: chsd ldng pair 3f out: hrd rdn to cl over 1f out: nt qckn ins fnl f* **10/1**

320- **4** *1* **Holiday Snap**[186] 7597 5-9-3 **65** .... (t) JimCrowley 2 67
(Mary Hambro) *led: gng strly 3f out: hdd and fnd nil 2f out: plugged on after* **8/1**

0640 **5** *nk* **Army Of Stars (IRE)**[21] 1995 5-8-9 **62** .... (bt[1]) RyanClark(5) 4 63
(Michael Blake) *chsd ldrs: hrd rdn and effrt 2f out: one pce ins fnl f* **20/1**

0626 **6** *nk* **Pipers Piping (IRE)**[15] 2179 5-8-10 **65** .... LauraSimpson(7) 6 65
(Michael Squance) *trckd ldrs: pushed along over 2f out: cl enough but nt qckn over 1f out: one pce after* **16/1**

5-33 **7** *2 ½* **Eager To Bow (IRE)**[14] 2201 5-9-3 **65** .... GeorgeBaker 11 59
(Patrick Chamings) *in tch towards rr: effrt over 2f out: chsng ldrs u.p over 1f out: fdd* **10/3**[1]

20-1 **8** *1 ¼* **Woolston Ferry (IRE)**[14] 2201 5-8-12 **65** .... JamesRogers(5) 3 55+
(David Pinder) *dwlt: wl off the pce in last pair: sme prog 2f out but nvr on terms: no hdwy after* **8/1**

4320 **9** *10* **Katmai River (IRE)**[14] 2201 4-9-2 **64** .... (v) SteveDrowne 10 27
(Mark Usher) *sn rdn in last trio: a bhd* **7/1**[3]

5530 **10** *15* **Timpanist (USA)**[30] 1766 4-9-1 **63** .... NeilCallan 12 —
(Simon Dow) *chsd ldrs: rdn and wknd 1/2-way: t.o* **40/1**

604- **11** *2 ¾* **Private Olley**[225] 6997 4-9-2 **64** .... TomQueally 14 —
(Harry Dunlop) *chsd ldr to 3f out: wknd rapidly: t.o* **16/1**

1m 28.16s (2.16) **Going Correction** +0.275s/f (Slow) **11** Ran SP% **115.2**
Speed ratings (Par 101): **98,97,96,95,95 94,91,90,79,61 58**
toteswingers: 1&2 £15.60, 1&3 £11.10, 2&3 £23.10 CSF £42.92 CT £373.09 TOTE £8.30: £2.30, £2.00, £4.10; EX 53.00.
Owner D H Back & I A Balding **Bred** B Kennedy **Trained** Kingsclere, Hants
■ Stewards' Enquiry : Ryan Clark two-day ban: used whip with excessive frequency (Jun 19-20)

FOCUS
A bunch finish and ordinary-looking form. The visual impression was that the pace had increased significantly by about halfway (at which point the field were strung out) and that the runners then finished relatively slowly. The third is rated close to his latest C&D form.

2606 BRITISH STALLION STUDS SUPPORTING BRITISH RACING E B F MAIDEN FILLIES' STKS 6f (P)
8:20 (8:24) (Class 5) 2-Y-0 **£3,302** (£982; £491; £245) **Stalls** Low

Form RPR

1 **Hawfinch** 2-9-0 0 .... WilliamBuick 6 84+
(John Gosden) *pushed along in last pair early: stl wl off the pce over 2f out: gd prog on inner over 1f out: sustained effrt to ld last 110yds: sn clr* **25/1**

2 *2 ½* **Rockme Cockney** 2-9-0 0 .... JamesDoyle 1 75
(Jeremy Gask) *prom: chsd ldr over 2f out: clsd to ld ent fnl f: hdd and outpcd last 110yds* **50/1**

4 **3** *1 ¾* **Colorful Notion (IRE)**[11] 2302 2-9-0 0 .... AdamKirby 2 70
(Marco Botti) *trckd ldrs: clsd over 2f out: chal and upsides 1f out: one pce after* **12/1**

36 **4** *½* **Represent (IRE)**[12] 2254 2-8-11 0 .... MartinHarley(3) 3 68
(Mick Channon) *led: rdn over 1f out: hdd and fdd ent fnl f* **7/1**[2]

4 **5** *½* **Tina's Spirit (IRE)**[20] 2023 2-9-0 0 .... DaneO'Neill 4 67
(Richard Hannon) *chsd ldr to over 2f out: nt qckn and sn lost pl: kpt on ins fnl f* **8/1**[3]

6 *6* **More Is To Come (USA)** 2-9-0 0 JimCrowley 12 49
(Ralph Beckett) *racd wd: in tch: outpcd over 2f out: wknd over 1f out* **20/1**
7 *1 ½* **Solfilia** 2-9-0 0 JimmyFortune 8 44
(Hughie Morrison) *chsd ldrs: lost pl bef 1/2-way: wl in rr fnl 2f* **25/1**
8 *12* **Essexvale (IRE)** 2-9-0 0 RichardHughes 7 —
(Richard Hannon) *s.s: mostly last: lost tch 1/2-way: t.o* **12/1**
9 *9* **Sea Of Light (IRE)** 2-9-0 0 (b[1]) SteveDrowne 9 —
(Roger Charlton) *in tch to 1/2-way: sn wknd: t.o* **66/1**
P **Hidden Passion (USA)** 2-9-0 0 MartinDwyer 5 —
(Brian Meehan) *lost action sn after s: eased and p.u* **9/4[1]**
1m 15.86s (2.76) **Going Correction** +0.275s/f (Slow) **10 Ran SP% 85.7**
Speed ratings (Par 90): **92,88,86,85,85 77,75,59,47,—**
toteswingers: 1&2 £67.80, 1&3 £24.20, 2&3 £44.30 CSF £435.99 TOTE £17.50: £4.10, £6.90, £4.30; EX 285.10.
Owner C J Murfitt **Bred** C J Murfitt **Trained** Newmarket, Suffolk

FOCUS
Not as strong a fillies' maiden as had appeared likely but an interesting winner and there was plenty to talk about. Lemon Rock, who was due to go off favourite, was withdrawn after rearing over and unseating Ryan Moore behind the stalls. The filly hit the deck but was soon on her feet and cantered around loose for around a minute or so. It's worth pointing out that she had looked uncomfortable in the paddock, continually swishing her tail and displaying a bizarre stamping action, very much giving the impression something was bothering her.

NOTEBOOK
Hawfinch belied her big odds to make a taking winning debut, and the trainer explained afterwards that the filly is an extremely nervous type, particularly around people. She was understandably given a sympathetic ride by William Buick and looked held when in around fifth place, a good 5l off the lead 2f out, but she quickened nicely, needing just one slap with the whip. A half-sister to a couple of 7f winners, she may now be stepped up in trip, although this run should sharpen her up plenty. She could be quite useful if going the right way.
Rockme Cockney, the first foal of a 1m debut winner at two, showed plenty of ability and is entitled to come on for this.
Colorful Notion(IRE) ran to only a moderate level when sent off at 15-8 for her debut. This seemed a bit better, although she had the benefit of experience over the front pair. (op 10-1)
Represent(IRE) is entered in the Group 2 Railway Stakes, but she faded after showing speed, as she had done when sent off at 6-5 last time. A return to 5f should help. (op 6-1)
Tina's Spirit(IRE) was passed over by Richard Hughes and didn't seem to improve on her Salisbury debut. (tchd 15-2)
Hidden Passion(USA) wasn't in the race for long. Brian Meehan said beforehand the filly goes "very well at home", but she seemed to take a bad step after only a few yards, after which she was not striding out well, and Martin Dwyer, who soon looked down to see if anything was amiss, was quick to try and pull her up. Official explanation: jockey said filly lost its action shortly after leaving stalls and pulled up (op 11-4)

2607 RACING AT SKYSPORTS.COM H'CAP (LONDON MILE QUALIFIER) 1m (P)
8:50 (8:53) (Class 4) (0-85,84) 3-Y-O **£4,079** (£1,214; £606; £303) **Stalls** Low

Form RPR
121- **1** **Humdrum**[222] 7059 3-9-2 **80** RichardHughes 7 93+
(Richard Hannon) *settled in 6th: moved up smartly to ld wl over 1f out: sn clr: eased last 100yds: quite impressive* **9/1**
4-41 **2** *2 ¾* **Sinfonico (IRE)**[14] 2200 3-9-3 **81** RyanMoore 12 85+
(Richard Hannon) *hld up in 8th: rdn on outer over 2f out: prog over 1f out: styd on to take 2nd last 50yds* **5/1[2]**
0-05 **3** *½* **Buxfizz (USA)**[13] 2230 3-8-12 **79** (p) SeanLevey(3) 8 82
(Robert Mills) *led: hdd and brushed aside wl over 1f out: clung on to 2nd tl last 50yds* **16/1**
310- **4** *¾* **Safari Team (IRE)**[255] 6230 3-9-2 **80** JimCrowley 4 81
(Peter Winkworth) *trckd ldr 3f: styd handy: drvn on inner 2f out: plugged on one pce* **20/1**
-400 **5** *nk* **Orientalist**[11] 2296 3-9-5 **83** (p) TomQueally 2 83
(Eve Johnson Houghton) *hld up in 7th: pushed along 3f out: effrt 2f out: kpt on same pce: no threat* **18/1**
11-5 **6** *nk* **Muntasib (USA)**[56] 1175 3-9-6 **84** TadhgO'Shea 3 84
(Marcus Tregoning) *reluctant to enter stalls: hld up in 9th: shkn up over 2f out: no prog and looked less than keen over 1f out: fnlly styd on ins fnl f* **10/1**
51-2 **7** *1* **Prince Of Burma (IRE)**[13] 2215 3-9-2 **80** WilliamBuick 10 77+
(John Gosden) *hld up in last pair: rdn on outer over 2f out and no prog: kpt on ins fnl f: no threat* **2/1[1]**
16 **8** *nse* **Dubaianswer**[35] 1599 3-9-4 **82** AdamKirby 14 79
(Marco Botti) *trckd ldng trio: gng wl 3f out: rdn and nt qckn over 2f out: lost pl fr over 1f out* **14/1**
12-0 **9** *½* **Dunhoy (IRE)**[22] 1983 3-9-0 **78** HayleyTurner 13 74
(Stef Higgins) *stdd s then s.i.s: hld up last: effrt on inner and modest prog 2f out: nvr on terms* **33/1**
34-1 **10** *¾* **Harry Luck (IRE)**[30] 1773 3-9-4 **82** DaneO'Neill 1 76
(Henry Candy) *t.k.h in 5th: pushed along 3f out: no prog 2f out: fdd* **6/1[3]**
13-4 **11** *1* **Marzante (USA)**[30] 1773 3-9-0 **78** (b[1]) SteveDrowne 6 70
(Roger Charlton) *trckd ldr after 3f to 2f out: wknd* **10/1**
1m 41.64s (1.84) **Going Correction** +0.275s/f (Slow) **11 Ran SP% 118.0**
Speed ratings (Par 101): **101,98,97,97,96 96,95,95,94,94 93**
CSF £53.78 CT £720.32 TOTE £9.50: £3.10, £3.10, £9.50; EX 38.10.
Owner The Queen **Bred** The Queen **Trained** East Everleigh, Wilts

FOCUS
Another race run at no more than a fair gallop which has resulted in the form not being rated too positively, despite the winner scoring impressively.
Muntasib(USA) Official explanation: jockey said colt hung left-handed
Dubaianswer Official explanation: jockey said filly had no more to give

2608 KEMPTONLIVE.CO.UK APPRENTICE H'CAP 1m 4f (P)
9:20 (9:21) (Class 6) (0-65,65) 4-Y-O+ **£1,619** (£481; £240; £120) **Stalls** Centre

Form RPR
/351 **1** **Camera Shy (IRE)**[49] 1310 7-9-1 **56** AdamBeschizza 2 60
(Kevin Morgan) *mde all: dictated stdy pce: shkn up and nvr less than 2 l clr fr 2f out: unchal* **4/5[1]**
0-10 **2** *2* **Bubbly Braveheart (IRE)**[42] 1486 4-9-7 **65** LucyKBarry(3) 4 66
(Pat Phelan) *mostly chsd wnr: rdn over 2f out: kpt on same pce: nvr able to chal* **9/2[2]**
0-50 **3** *1* **Boogie Dancer**[27] 954 7-8-6 **47** (t) RyanClark 5 46
(Stuart Howe) *trckd ldrs: rdn over 2f out: wnt 2nd briefly over 1f out: one pce after* **15/2[3]**
0546 **4** *shd* **Paint The Town Red**[13] 2235 6-8-5 **46** oh1 (p) TobyAtkinson 6 45
(Richard Guest) *hld up: last to 5f out: effrt over 2f out: rdn and kpt on: nrly snatched 3rd* **10/1**
40-0 **5** *2 ½* **Trecase**[22] 1987 4-9-0 **55** KieranO'Neill 7 50
(Tony Carroll) *t.k.h: cl up: rdn over 2f out: no prog over 1f out: fdd* **11/1**
050/ **6** *16* **Street Warrior (IRE)**[739] 1014 8-8-13 **57** MatthewCosham(3) 3 26
(James Evans) *s.i.s: t.k.h: in tch tl wknd over 2f out: sn wl bhd* **16/1**
000- **7** *22* **Bonamassa**[219] 7117 4-8-2 **46** oh1 MatthewLawson(3) 1 —
(Michael Attwater) *dropped to last 5f out: sn t.o* **66/1**
2m 42.19s (7.69) **Going Correction** +0.275s/f (Slow) **7 Ran SP% 110.3**
Speed ratings (Par 101): **85,83,83,82,81 70,55**
CSF £4.22 TOTE £1.40: £1.02, £3.70; EX 4.50.
Owner Michael Ogburn **Bred** Haras D'Etreham And Madame Lily Ades **Trained** Newmarket, Suffolk

FOCUS
An uncompetitive apprentices' handicap run at a slow pace (time over 11 seconds above standard) and the first two finishers filled the front two positions pretty much throughout. The form looks unconvincing.
T/Plt: £445.80 to a £1 stake. Pool of £64,679.99 - 105.91 winning units. T/Qpdt: £416.70 to a £1 stake. Pool of £3,998.83 - 7.10 winning units. JN

2523 NOTTINGHAM (L-H)
Wednesday, June 1

OFFICIAL GOING: Good to firm (good in places in straight: 8.2)
Outer course used. Rail moved out 2m adding 7yds to 8 &10f races and 15f to 14f race.
Wind: Light against Weather: Overcast

2609 BET ON TOTEPLACEPOT AT TOTESPORT.COM H'CAP (DIV I) 6f 15y
1:40 (1:41) (Class 5) (0-70,69) 4-Y-O+ **£1,942** (£578; £288; £144) **Stalls** High

Form RPR
-131 **1** **Dashwood**[21] 2001 4-9-7 **69** (t) WilliamCarson 1 81+
(Giles Bravery) *racd alone far side: mde all: rdn out* **13/2[3]**
5300 **2** *1* **Errigal Lad**[16] 2162 6-8-2 **50** oh1 KellyHarrison 4 59+
(Garry Woodward) *racd stands' side: dwlt: hdwy over 1f out: led that gp ins fnl f: r.o* **22/1**
5231 **3** *2* **Beckermet (IRE)**[6] 2412 9-8-7 **62** 6ex ShaneBKelly(7) 8 64
(Ruth Carr) *racd stands' side: chsd ldrs: rdn over 1f out: styd on* **9/4[1]**
2006 **4** *hd* **Primo De Vida (IRE)**[27] 1838 4-8-13 **66** (p) NathanAlison(5) 13 68
(Jim Boyle) *led stands' side: rdn and hung lft fr over 1f out: hdd and no ex that gp ins fnl f* **10/1**
4405 **5** *3 ¼* **Lees Anthem**[17] 2126 4-8-12 **60** PatrickMathers 7 51
(Colin Teague) *racd stands' side: prom: rdn over 2f out: no ex ins fnl f* **33/1**
-052 **6** *2* **Bermondsey Bob (IRE)**[2] 2555 5-8-11 **59** CathyGannon 12 44
(John Spearing) *racd stands' side: chsd ldrs: rdn over 2f out: wknd ins fnl f* **9/2[2]**
0414 **7** *½* **Nubar Boy**[13] 2222 4-9-5 **67** (v) PatCosgrave 3 50
(David Evans) *racd stands' side: prom: rdn over 1f out: wknd ins fnl f* **12/1**
3516 **8** *4 ½* **Absa Lutte (IRE)**[11] 2286 8-9-0 **69** (t) JosephYoung(7) 11 38
(Michael Mullineaux) *racd stands' side: hung lft and outpcd: styd on ins fnl f: nvr nrr* **10/1**
2606 **9** *nk* **Gwilym (GER)**[11] 2304 8-8-12 **60** DaneO'Neill 6 28
(Derek Haydn Jones) *racd stands' side: chsd ldrs: rdn over 2f out: wknd over 1f out* **14/1**
-030 **10** *¾* **Danzoe (IRE)**[98] 646 4-9-4 **69** KierenFox(3) 2 35
(Christine Dunnett) *racd stands' side: sn pushed along in rr: sme hdwy u.p over 2f out: wknd over 1f out* **25/1**
-046 **11** *2 ½* **Whiskey Junction**[105] 554 7-9-3 **65** SebSanders 5 23
(Michael Quinn) *racd stands' side: prom: rdn and wknd over 2f out* **16/1**
-000 **12** *9* **Grand Stitch (USA)**[32] 1698 5-8-13 **66** (v) NeilFarley(5) 10 —
(Declan Carroll) *racd stands' side: rrd s: a in rr* **20/1**
1m 14.25s (-0.65) **Going Correction** -0.025s/f (Good) **12 Ran SP% 116.6**
Speed ratings (Par 103): **103,101,99,98,94 91,91,85,84,83 80,68**
toteswingers:1&2:£18.50, 2&3:£13.10, 1&3:£3.60 CSF £144.67 CT £426.96 TOTE £5.90: £1.80, £5.30, £1.60; EX 108.70 Trifecta £305.20 Part won. Pool of £412.46 - 0.50 winning units..
Owner Macattack, William Lea Screed & Form IT **Bred** Darley **Trained** Cowlinge, Suffolk
■ Stewards' Enquiry : William Carson four-day ban: used whip with excessive frequency (Jun 19-22)

FOCUS
The going was good to firm, good in places in the straight. This looked the stronger of the two divisions of this sprint handicap. Most of the field raced centre to stands' side but it went to a progressive unexposed type who raced solo on the far side in a premeditated manoeuvre. The form is rated through the third to the balance of last year's efforts.

2610 BET ON TOTEPLACEPOT AT TOTESPORT.COM H'CAP (DIV II) 6f 15y
2:10 (2:10) (Class 5) (0-70,69) 4-Y-O+ **£1,942** (£578; £288; £144) **Stalls** High

Form RPR
4336 **1** **Flying Applause**[4] 2487 6-8-9 **57** (bt) RussKennemore 6 72
(Roy Bowring) *edgd lft s: hld up: rdn over 2f out: hdwy over 1f out: led ins fnl f: sn clr: easily* **11/4[1]**
4214 **2** *4* **Steel City Boy (IRE)**[13] 2238 8-8-11 **59** KellyHarrison 8 61
(Garry Woodward) *led: rdn over 1f out: hdd ins fnl f: sn outpcd* **7/1[3]**
0003 **3** *2 ½* **Methaaly (IRE)**[11] 2280 8-8-11 **66** (be) JosephYoung(7) 12 60
(Michael Mullineaux) *chsd ldrs: rdn and hung lft over 1f out: styd on same pce ins fnl f* **7/1[3]**
1625 **4** *shd* **Sleepy Blue Ocean**[85] 794 5-9-7 **69** (p) LukeMorris 5 63
(John Balding) *s.i.s and hmpd s: hld up: hdwy over 1f out: sn rdn: styd on same pce ins fnl f* **11/1**
-020 **5** *1* **Defector (IRE)**[11] 2280 5-9-4 **66** FrankieMcDonald 1 57
(David Bourton) *hung lft thrght: in rr: hdwy 2f out: rdn over 1f out: no ex ins fnl f* **16/1**
13-0 **6** *½* **Bathwick Xaara**[30] 1771 4-9-5 **67** CathyGannon 7 56
(Jonathan Portman) *prom: hung lft over 2f out: sn rdn: wknd ins fnl f* **11/1**
6043 **7** *1* **Rainy Night**[9] 2356 5-9-4 **66** (p) GeorgeBaker 10 52
(Reg Hollinshead) *chsd ldrs: rdn over 1f out: wknd fnl f* **8/1**
00-4 **8** *1 ½* **Kings 'n Dreams**[51] 1267 4-9-7 **69** (b) WilliamCarson 4 50
(Dean Ivory) *sn prom: rdn over 2f out: wknd over 1f out* **6/1[2]**
0200 **9** *hd* **Valmina**[12] 2270 4-8-13 **61** (t) DavidProbert 3 41
(Tony Carroll) *hld up: hdwy 1/2-way: rdn over 1f out: wknd ins fnl f* **14/1**
0-00 **10** *¾* **Hoh Hoh Hoh**[16] 2142 9-8-11 **64** (t) RyanClark(5) 2 42
(Richard Price) *chsd ldrs: rdn over 1f out: wknd ins fnl f* **16/1**
1m 15.3s (0.40) **Going Correction** -0.025s/f (Good) **10 Ran SP% 112.2**
Speed ratings (Par 103): **96,90,87,87,85 85,83,81,81,80**
toteswingers:1&2:£3.90, 2&3:£6.50, 1&3:£5.30 CSF £20.68 CT £119.01 TOTE £3.60: £1.10, £2.50, £2.60; EX 22.50 Trifecta £55.10 Pool: £324.71 - 4.36 winning units..
Owner K Nicholls **Bred** G H Beeby And Viscount Marchwood **Trained** Edwinstowe, Notts

FOCUS
There was an emphatic winner in the second division of this minor sprint handicap. The runner-up is rated to his recent best.
Defector(IRE) Official explanation: jockey said gelding hung left-handed

2611 FREE RACING POST FORM AT TOTESPORT.COM H'CAP 5f 13y
2:40 (2:40) (Class 5) (0-75,75) 3-Y-O **£2,266** (£674; £337; £168) **Stalls** High

Form RPR
21-6 **1** **Manoori (IRE)**[19] 2074 3-9-5 **73** TedDurcan 5 81+
(Chris Wall) *s.i.s: hld up: swtchd lft and hdwy over 1f out: led ins fnl f: sn rdn: jst hld on* **5/6**[1]
-326 **2** *hd* **Alpha Delta Whisky**[16] 2151 3-9-2 **70** TadhgO'Shea 1 77+
(John Gallagher) *hld up: swtchd lft and hdwy over 1f out: r.o wl* **16/1**
463 **3** *shd* **Restless Bay (IRE)**[15] 2180 3-9-7 **75** (v) GeorgeBaker 3 82
(Reg Hollinshead) *s.i.s: hld up: hdwy over 1f out: rdn and r.o wl* **16/1**
5442 **4** *1 ¾* **Pineapple Pete (IRE)**[3] 2524 3-8-8 **62** (tp) RobertWinston 9 63
(Alan McCabe) *hld up: hdwy over 1f out: no ex ins fnl f* **6/1**[2]
00-1 **5** *2 ¾* **Mr Mo Jo**[39] 1514 3-9-0 **68** DuranFentiman 8 59
(Lawrence Mullaney) *w ldrs: led and hung lft over 1f out: hdd and no ex ins fnl f* **10/1**[3]
3-43 **6** *1 ¼* **Circuitous**[16] 2141 3-8-8 **62** SilvestreDeSousa 6 48
(Paul Cole) *s.i.s: sn prom: rdn and hung lft over 1f out: wknd ins fnl f* **12/1**
-633 **7** *nk* **Whitecrest**[11] 2294 3-9-2 **70** SebSanders 4 55
(John Spearing) *led: rdn: edgd lft and hdd over 1f out: wknd ins fnl f* **16/1**
2-05 **8** *3 ¼* **Surely This Time (IRE)**[6] 2410 3-9-0 **68** (b) PhillipMakin 7 42
(Kevin Ryan) *w ldrs: led 1/2-way: sn rdn: hdd over 1f out: wknd ins fnl f* **33/1**
-002 **9** *4 ½* **Style And Panache (IRE)**[16] 2158 3-9-7 **75** PatCosgrave 2 32
(David Evans) *chsd ldrs: rdn 1/2-way: wknd over 1f out* **11/1**

60.95 secs (-0.05) **Going Correction** -0.025s/f (Good) 9 Ran SP% **114.5**
Speed ratings (Par 99): **99,98,98,95,91 89,88,83,76**
toteswingers:1&2:£6.00, 2&3:£14.50, 1&3:£6.20 CSF £16.56 CT £132.36 TOTE £2.00: £1.50, £3.00, £1.90; EX 19.40 Trifecta £122.10 Pool: £518.46 - 3.14 winning units..
Owner Hassan Al Abdulmalik **Bred** T J Monaghan **Trained** Newmarket, Suffolk

FOCUS
A fair handicap, six of the nine runners had finished in the first three on their previous start. The very heavily backed favourite just prevailed in a tight three-way finish and the third, rated to his best, is the guide.
Mr Mo Jo Official explanation: jockey said gelding hung left under pressure

2612 E B F MORE LIVE SPORT BETTING AT TOTESPORT.COM MAIDEN STKS 5f 13y
3:10 (3:10) (Class 5) 2-Y-O **£3,238** (£963; £481; £240) **Stalls** High

Form RPR
2 **1** **Bear Behind (IRE)**[6] 2423 2-9-3 0 RichardKingscote 1 85+
(Tom Dascombe) *led: hdd over 3f out: chsd ldr tl shkn up to ld 1f out: r.o wl* **8/11**[1]
0203 **2** *2 ¾* **Beau Mistral (IRE)**[3] 2523 2-8-12 0 SilvestreDeSousa 2 68
(Paul Green) *w wnr tl led over 3f out: rdn and hdd 1f out: styd on same pce* **17/2**[3]
3 *1 ½* **Justineo** 2-9-3 0 MichaelHills 3 68+
(William Haggas) *dwlt: hdwy to go 3rd 1/2-way: sn rdn: no ex ins fnl f* **2/1**[2]
0 **4** *shd* **Master Of Ages (IRE)**[9] 2346 2-9-3 0 GregFairley 4 67
(Mark Johnston) *chsd ldrs: pushed along 1/2-way: sn outpcd* **12/1**

61.53 secs (0.53) **Going Correction** -0.025s/f (Good) 4 Ran SP% **109.5**
Speed ratings (Par 93): **94,89,87,87**
CSF £7.30 TOTE £1.40; EX 3.50.
Owner Bellman Black Marantelli Owen **Bred** Rory O'Brien **Trained** Malpas, Cheshire

FOCUS
The odds-on favourite was a comfortable winner from a reliable yardstick in this maiden. The form looks straightforward with the runner-up to her latest C&D mark.

NOTEBOOK
Bear Behind(IRE) is by a 6f-7f winner out of a winning miler, but he showed plenty of pace when chasing home useful odds-on US rival Gentlemans Code in a three-runner Folkestone maiden on debut last week. This big, powerful type set a clear standard and travelled smoothly up with the pace before kicking clear without being asked a serious question. He holds entries in the Listed Woodcote Stakes at Epsom and in a valuable conditions race at Musselburgh on Saturday, but his connections may wait and target him at the Windsor Castle at Ascot. (op 4-6 tchd 5-6)
Beau Mistral(IRE) added another solid front-running effort to her five-race profile. She looks a willing type who should continue to go well, but she is consistent rather than progressive and may find better openings in nurseries. (op 15-2 tchd 9-1)
Justineo was slowly away and looked inexperienced but shaped with promise as second favourite behind a useful type on debut. An Oasis Dream first foal of a 1m3f-1m5f (AW Listed) winning half-sister to prolific high-class 5f-7f winner Galeota and useful sprint winner Lady Livius, he should have learned a lot and is bred to stay quite a bit further than this in time. (op 11-4)
Master Of Ages(IRE) looked inexperienced when fading into seventh of 11 in a 5f Carlisle maiden auction on his recent debut and he could never get involved on this second run. Out of a 6.7f-10.5f winning dam who has had three winners at 8.6f-1m2f from three previous foals, he may need more time and distance. (tchd 11-1 and 16-1)

2613 BET ON LIVE TENNIS AT TOTESPORT.COM H'CAP 1m 6f 15y
3:45 (3:45) (Class 5) (0-70,70) 3-Y-O **£2,266** (£674; £337; £168) **Stalls** Low

Form RPR
06-1 **1** **Kepler's Law**[8] 2379 3-9-0 **63** 6ex SebSanders 5 73+
(Sir Mark Prescott Bt) *a.p: led over 2f out: rdn and hung lft ins fnl f: styd on* **8/15**[1]
-516 **2** *½* **Dark Dune (IRE)**[19] 2076 3-9-3 **66** (e) DavidAllan 1 71
(Tim Easterby) *plld hrd and prom: rdn over 2f out: hung lft and rt over 1f out: styd on* **11/1**[3]
0-30 **3** *hd* **C P Joe (IRE)**[16] 2152 3-8-9 **58** ow2 RobertWinston 3 62
(Paul Green) *hld up: hdwy over 3f out: sn rdn: styd on* **22/1**
00-0 **4** *3 ¾* **High Fallutin (IRE)**[47] 1363 3-8-3 **52** CathyGannon 4 51
(Eve Johnson Houghton) *dwlt: hld up: hdwy over 2f out: sn rdn: swtchd rt ins fnl f: nt rch ldrs* **40/1**
060 **5** *hd* **Mina's Boy**[23] 1950 3-8-5 **54** RoystonFfrench 9 53
(Ed Dunlop) *prom: outpcd over 5f out: styd on ins fnl f* **33/1**
6-53 **6** *nk* **Hartforth**[26] 1877 3-8-12 **61** (p) GrahamGibbons 8 59
(James Bethell) *chsd ldrs: rdn over 4f out: sn outpcd: styd on ins fnl f* **33/1**
00-3 **7** *1 ¼* **Peira**[21] 1997 3-9-1 **64** AndreaAtzeni 7 61
(Jane Chapple-Hyam) *chsd ldr tl led over 3f out: rdn and hdd over 2f out: wknd ins fnl f* **12/1**
2144 **8** *12* **Investment World (IRE)**[42] 1502 3-8-13 **62** GregFairley 6 42
(Mark Johnston) *hld up: rdn over 3f out: wknd 2f out* **12/1**
00-2 **9** *53* **Brezza Di Mare (IRE)**[30] 1751 3-9-7 **70** ShaneKelly 2 —
(Brian Meehan) *led: rdn and hdd over 3f out: sn wknd and eased: t.o* **5/1**[2]

3m 7.07s (-0.23) **Going Correction** -0.025s/f (Good) 9 Ran SP% **118.3**
Speed ratings (Par 99): **99,98,98,96,96 96,95,88,58**
CSF £7.60 CT £71.77 TOTE £1.50: £1.10, £3.70, £4.80; EX 8.40 Trifecta £75.60 Pool: £866.04 - 8.47 winning units..
Owner Rectory Racing **Bred** Chippenham Lodge Stud Ltd **Trained** Newmarket, Suffolk

FOCUS
A Sir Mark Prescott-trained hot favourite had to work fairly hard, but showed a lot of staying power to win this handicap, which was run at a fair pace and the first three were clear of the rest. The form is rated through the runner-up but the proximity of the fourth, fifth and sixth raises doubts.
Brezza Di Mare(IRE) Official explanation: trainer's rep had no explanation for the poor form shown

2614 BET ON LIVE CRICKET AT TOTESPORT.COM CONDITIONS STKS 1m 75y
4:15 (4:16) (Class 2) 3-Y-O+ **£9,844** (£2,948; £1,474) **Stalls** Centre

Form RPR
-303 **1** **Balcarce Nov (ARG)**[11] 2284 6-9-1 96 JamieSpencer 5 102
(Tom Tate) *mde all: shkn up over 2f out: sn clr: unchal* **9/4**[2]
34-0 **2** *3 ¾* **Al Zir (USA)**[11] 2290 4-9-1 109 (t) FrankieDettori 3 93
(Saeed Bin Suroor) *dwlt: hld up: outpcd over 3f out: hdwy to chse wnr over 1f out: rdn: hung lft and no imp ins fnl f* **1/2**[1]
54-0 **3** *19* **Vitznau (IRE)**[104] 587 7-9-1 97 RobertWinston 2 66
(Robert Cowell) *chsd wnr: rdn over 2f out: hung lft and wknd over 1f out* **12/1**[3]

1m 45.84s (0.24) **Going Correction** -0.025s/f (Good) 3 Ran SP% **105.1**
Speed ratings (Par 109): **97,93,74**
CSF £3.81 TOTE £3.50; EX 3.40.
Owner Mrs Fitri Hay **Bred** Firmamento **Trained** Tadcaster, N Yorks

FOCUS
The Godolphin hotpot was very disappointing in this small-field conditions race, which went to an unchallenged 96-rated performer. The winner only had to run to previous handicap form to score.

NOTEBOOK
Balcarce Nov(ARG) finished a creditable pacesetting third in a useful 7f Chester handicap last time. He had quite a bit to find on official figures but this tough and consistent performer put in a powerful front-running performance to improve on his second in this race last year. The form looks suspect with the favourite disappointing and the third cutting out quickly, but this 6-y-o is a likeable type who may be able to pick up a minor Listed race this season. (op 5-2 tchd 2-1)
Al Zir(USA) had leading claims on his best form last year, including an Epsom Derby sixth and a fourth in a Group 3 at Newmarket in October. A tame reappearance effort in a 1m2f Listed race at Goodwood added a complication, and this 109-rated performer was toiling some way out after a slow start and could find only a limited response in his attempt to cash in on this good opportunity back at 1m. Official explanation: trainer's rep said colt was unsuited by the good to firm (good in places) ground (op 4-7)
Vitznau(IRE) finished last of 14 off a mark of 99 in a Meydan handicap on debut for this yard in February. He was a big market drifter on return from a break and produced a very short-lived assault on the winner before dropping away and being eased down. (op 15-2 tchd 14-1)

2615 E B F PLAY BLACKJACK AT TOTESPORT.COM FILLIES' H'CAP 1m 75y
4:50 (4:51) (Class 4) (0-85,83) 3-Y-O **£4,533** (£1,348; £674; £336) **Stalls** Centre

Form RPR
10-4 **1** **Submission**[27] 1837 3-9-3 **79** KierenFallon 10 85+
(Luca Cumani) *trckd ldrs: plld hrd: led over 1f out: sn rdn: jst hld on* **11/10**[1]
6224 **2** *shd* **Imaginary World (IRE)**[13] 2229 3-8-10 **72** (be) RobertWinston 1 78
(Alan McCabe) *hld up: hdwy and swtchd rt over 1f out: shkn up ins fnl f: r.o: jst failed* **16/1**
-616 **3** *1 ¼* **Adaria**[19] 2073 3-9-4 **80** PaulMulrennan 5 83
(David C Griffiths) *led: rdn and hdd over 1f out: unable qck nr fin* **20/1**
-131 **4** *1 ¾* **Certral**[5] 2466 3-8-2 **64** 6ex CathyGannon 9 63
(Brian Ellison) *a.p: chsd ldr over 3f out: sn rdn and ev ch: no ex ins fnl f* **3/1**[2]
01 **5** *1 ¾* **Doricemay (IRE)**[14] 2192 3-9-2 **78** PhilipRobinson 2 73
(Clive Cox) *prom: pushed along 1/2-way: sn outpcd: hdwy and swtchd rt over 1f out: styd on* **7/1**[3]
0-05 **6** *6* **Primo Lady**[18] 2102 [illegible] (p) DavidProbert 4 61
(Gay Kelleway) *hld up: rdn and hung lft over 2f out: sn wknd* **25/1**
4-40 **7** *½* **Heatherbird**[26] 1853 3-8-8 **75** HarryBentley(5) 7 55
(William Jarvis) *hld up: plld hrd: hdwy over 3f out: rdn: hung lft and wknd over 2f out* **12/1**
41-0 **8** *2 ½* **Herminella**[18] 2102 3-8-5 **72** JamesRogers(5) 3 46
(William Muir) *hld up: rdn over 3f out: wknd over 2f out* **50/1**
13- **9** *37* **Winnie Dixie (USA)**[271] 5725 3-8-12 **74** JamieSpencer 6 —
(Paul Cole) *chsd ldr tl rdn over 3f out: sn wknd: t.o* **16/1**

1m 45.11s (-0.49) **Going Correction** -0.025s/f (Good) 9 Ran SP% **115.1**
Speed ratings (Par 98): **101,100,99,97,96 90,89,87,50**
toteswingers:1&2:£5.30, 2&3:£11.80, 1&3:£9.10 CSF £21.44 CT £236.48 TOTE £2.10: £1.10, £3.90, £4.70; EX 24.70 Trifecta £547.70 Pool: £977.12 - 1.32 winning units..
Owner Pearl Bloodstock Ltd **Bred** Fittocks Stud Ltd **Trained** Newmarket, Suffolk

FOCUS
A decent fillies' handicap, involving a number of unexposed types. It was run at a decent pace and there was a tight finish but the form appears sound.
Doricemay(IRE) Official explanation: trainer said filly was unsuited by the good to firm (good in places) ground

2616 PLAY ROULETTE AT TOTESPORT.COM "HANDS AND HEELS" APPRENTICE SERIES H'CAP (RACING EXC. INITIATIVE) 1m 2f 50y
5:25 (5:25) (Class 6) (0-65,63) 4-Y-O+ **£1,619** (£481; £240; £120) **Stalls** Low

Form RPR
0063 **1** **Dragon Slayer (IRE)**[3] 2530 9-8-13 **55** LucyKBarry 6 65
(John Harris) *plld hrd: trckd ldr 2f: remained handy: nt clr run 3f out: swtchd rt: led over 1f out: pushed out* **4/1**[2]
3502 **2** *2 ¾* **Aviso (GER)**[12] 2242 7-8-12 **62** KevinLundie(8) 8 66
(David Evans) *led: shkn up over 2f out: edgd lft and hdd over 1f out: styd on same pce ins fnl f: eased nr fin* **11/2**
3060 **3** *½* **Carr Hall (IRE)**[30] 1750 8-8-12 **57** GeorgeDowning(3) 2 60
(Tony Carroll) *hld up: hdwy over 1f out: styd on* **13/2**
4215 **4** *1 ¼* **Ocean Of Peace (FR)**[19] 2051 8-8-8 **58** KirstenSmith(8) 9 59
(Martin Bosley) *a.p: chsd ldr 8f out tl over 3f out: styd on same pce ins fnl f* **5/1**[3]
100- **5** *1 ¾* **Royal Composer (IRE)**[244] 6518 8-8-7 **49** RachealKneller 10 46
(Tim Easterby) *prom: pushed along over 3f out: styd on same pce fr over 1f out* **8/1**
0345 **6** *¾* **Dream Of Fortune (IRE)**[86] 790 7-9-7 **63** (bt) LukeRowe 3 59
(David Evans) *hld up: pushed along over 2f out: styd on ins fnl f: nvr nrr* **11/1**

656/ **7** 3 **Semi Detached (IRE)**[15] 107 8-8-5 47 (t) JakePayne 1 37
(James Unett) *prom: chsd ldr over 3f out: pushed along over 2f out: wknd ins fnl f* **20/1**

2425 **8** 24 **Eijaaz (IRE)**[8] 2393 10-8-10 60 (p) JordanNason(8) 5 —
(Geoffrey Harker) *hld up and a bhd: t.o* **7/2**[1]

2m 12.04s (0.34) **Going Correction** -0.025s/f (Good) **8** Ran SP% **111.8**
Speed ratings (Par 101): **97,94,94,93,92 91,89,69**
toteswingers:1&2:£3.10, 2&3:£2.80, 1&3:£6.40 CSF £24.96 CT £136.07 TOTE £4.00: £1.20, £3.60, £3.90; EX 22.50 Trifecta £132.80 Pool: £865.09 - 4.82 winning units..
Owner Mrs A E Harris **Bred** Arandora Star Syndicate **Trained** Eastwell, Leics

FOCUS
A modest apprentice handicap rated around the placed horses to recent form. It was run at a decent pace and they were quite strung out early on.
T/Plt: £29.60 to a £1 stake. Pool of £49,445.05 - 1,218.16 winning tickets T/Qpdt: £17.40 to a £1 stake. Pool of £2,754.60 - 116.62 winning tickets. CR

2387 RIPON (R-H)
Wednesday, June 1

OFFICIAL GOING: Good (8.5)
Wind: Light half behind Weather: Fine and dry

2617 BRITISH STALLION STUDS SUPPORTING BRITISH RACING E B F MAIDEN STKS 6f
6:40 (6:43) (Class 5) 2-Y-O £3,561 (£1,059; £529; £264) Stalls High

Form RPR

2 **1** **Travis County (IRE)**[19] 2056 2-9-0 0 PaulPickard(3) 11 78+
(Brian Ellison) *mde all: rdn over 1f out: drvn ins fnl f: hld on wl* **8/1**[3]

2 hd **Iffraam (IRE)** 2-9-3 0 FrederikTylicki 6 78+
(Michael Dods) *dwlt: midfield and pushed along 1/2-way: gd hdwy on outer 2f out: rdn to chse ldrs jst over 1f out: drvn and styd on strly ins fnl f: jst failed* **8/1**[3]

2 **3** 3/4 **Right Result (IRE)**[13] 2221 2-9-3 0 PatDobbs 8 75
(Richard Hannon) *cl up: effrt 2f out: rdn and ev ch ent fnl f: sn drvn and no ex last 100yds* **11/10**[1]

3 **4** 2 1/2 **Always Et Toujours**[13] 2234 2-9-3 0 JoeFanning 5 67
(Mark Johnston) *chsd ldrs: rdn along 2f out: sn drvn and kpt on same pce* **33/1**

0 **5** 2 **Giorgio's Dragon (IRE)**[20] 2033 2-9-3 0 TonyHamilton 9 61
(Richard Fahey) *chsd ldrs: rdn along over 2f out: sn one pce* **16/1**

0 **6** 7 **Regal Acclaim (IRE)**[17] 2120 2-9-3 0 TedDurcan 3 39+
(Tim Easterby) *towards rr tl sme late hdwy* **40/1**

7 1 1/4 **Optimum Rose (IRE)** 2-8-12 0 SilvestreDeSousa 12 30+
(David O'Meara) *s.i.s and towards rr: hdwy 1/2-way: sn rdn along and n.d* **25/1**

6 **8** nk **One New Cat (IRE)**[15] 2181 2-9-3 0 TomMcLaughlin 7 34
(Ed Dunlop) *midfield: rdn along wl over 2f out: no hdwy* **20/1**

9 1/2 **Forster Street (IRE)** 2-9-3 0 DavidAllan 13 32
(Tim Easterby) *a towards rr* **66/1**

0 **10** 3/4 **Pontius Pilate (IRE)**[61] 1071 2-9-3 0 (p) TomEaves 4 30
(Bryan Smart) *dwlt: a towards rr* **33/1**

11 2 1/2 **Fifteentwo** 2-9-3 0 AdrianNicholls 1 22
(David Nicholls) *s.i.s and a in rr* **25/1**

0 **12** 1 1/2 **Isolde's Return**[18] 2113 2-8-12 0 PJMcDonald 2 12
(George Moore) *a in rr* **100/1**

13 3 1/2 **Rivington** 2-9-3 0 PaulHanagan 10 —
(Richard Fahey) *trcking ldrs: cl up 1/2-way: sn rdn and wknd qckly: bhd and eased ins fnl f* **3/1**[2]

1m 12.28s (-0.72) **Going Correction** -0.25s/f (Firm) **13** Ran SP% **124.0**
Speed ratings (Par 93): **94,93,92,89,86 77,75,75,74,73 70,68,63**
toteswingers: 1&2 £12.70, 1&3 £2.40, 2&3 £2.70 CSF £67.03 TOTE £10.50: £2.10, £2.40, £1.10; EX 96.20.
Owner D Gilbert, M Lawrence, A Bruce **Bred** Loughbrown Stud **Trained** Norton, N Yorks
■ Stewards' Enquiry : Paul Pickard caution: used whip with excessive frequency.

FOCUS
An interesting juvenile maiden that is likely to produce its share of winners.

NOTEBOOK
Travis County(IRE) put his experience to good use in making the running and just held on. This was a big step up on his initial effort and it will be interesting to see where he goes next, with his future likely to be in handicaps.
Iffraam(IRE) ◆, a son of Iffraaj and entered in next year's Derby, came close to making a winning debut. He showed early signs of inexperience but responded well to pressure, challenging down the centre of the track, and the result might have been different in another stride or two. He should have no trouble going one better. (tchd 10-1)
Right Result(IRE) looked the one to beat having been narrowly denied by a stable companion on his debut at Salisbury, and the step up from 5f looked in his favour. However, having soon been on the pace, he was unable to see it out as well as the front pair. He can win a small maiden. (op 10-11 tchd 5-6)
Always Et Toujours again showed pace but saw it out better than he had done on his Southwell debut. He is bred to stay further and there should be more to come.
Giorgio's Dragon(IRE) showed considerably more than on his debut, travelling nicely before offering up the same pace under pressure. He can come on again and will be suited by 7f. (op 18-1 tchd 22-1)
Rivington, a strong-looking type who was very well backed, proved very disappointing. He showed bright early speed but was quickly in trouble once his rider began to push away, and dropped right out. Clearly thought capable of a good deal better, he deserves a chance to show this running to be wrong. (op 8-1)

2618 EURA AUDIT UK (S) H'CAP 1m 4f 10y
7:10 (7:10) (Class 6) (0-60,60) 4-5-Y-O £1,942 (£578; £288; £144) Stalls Low

Form RPR

0340 **1** **Valantino Oyster (IRE)**[5] 2462 4-9-2 58 (v1) PatrickDonaghy(3) 11 69
(Ben Haslam) *dwlt: hdwy on outer to trck ldrs after 3f: effrt 3f out: rdn to ld 2f out: sn edgd rt and clr ent fnl f* **7/1**

-000 **2** 5 **Drop The Hammer**[7] 1794 5-9-1 54 (v) SilvestreDeSousa 10 57
(David O'Meara) *prom: led over 4f out: rdn along 3f out: hdd 2f out and sn hdd: one pce appr fnl f* **3/1**[2]

-001 **3** 3 1/2 **Major Eradicator (USA)**[5] 2450 4-8-8 47 (v) PaulHanagan 2 44
(Alastair Lidderdale) *midfield: hdwy over 4f out: rdn to chse ldrs 3f out: drvn over 2f out and sn one pce* **9/4**[1]

3004 **4** 2 1/2 **Ay Tay Tate (IRE)**[46] 1386 5-9-2 55 (tp) KellyHarrison 4 48
(David C Griffiths) *hld up in rr: hdwy 4f out: rdn along over 2f out: no imp* **15/2**

00-6 **5** 3 **Fantastic Storm**[12] 2272 4-8-7 46 oh1 (v) LeeNewman 3 35
(Robin Bastiman) *chsd ldrs on inner: rdn along 4f out: sn drvn and grad wknd* **40/1**

2306 **6** 1 **Light The City (IRE)**[6] 2433 4-8-11 50 PJMcDonald 12 37
(Ruth Carr) *prom: effrt and cl up over 4f out: rdn along over 3f out: drvn wl over 2f out and sn wknd* **5/1**[3]

050 **7** 7 **Serenader**[18] 2114 4-9-2 55 (b1) DanielTudhope 5 31
(David O'Meara) *hld up in rr: hdwy 4f out: in tch over 2f out: sn rdn and wknd* **14/1**

-000 **8** 10 **Always Dixie (IRE)**[4] 2492 4-8-7 46 oh1 (b) JoeFanning 9 —
(Andrew Crook) *a towards rr* **50/1**

005- **9** 25 **Chadwell Spring (IRE)**[13] 4591 5-9-3 56 (p) TomEaves 6 —
(Mike Sowersby) *in tch: pushed along over 5f out: wknd 4f out: sn bhd* **66/1**

00/ **10** 31 **Vain Boteli (GER)**[24] 7272 5-9-7 60 (vt1) TonyHamilton 7 —
(Richard Ford) *led: rdn along and hdd over 4 out: sn wknd* **50/1**

2m 35.62s (-1.08) **Going Correction** -0.25s/f (Firm) **10** Ran SP% **113.0**
Speed ratings: **93,89,87,85,83 83,78,71,55,34**
yoteswingers: 1&2 £5.20, 1&3 £4.50, 2&3 £2.70 CSF £23.24 CT £51.85 TOTE £4.30: £1.10, £2.00, £1.10; EX 19.20.There was no bid for the winner.
Owner The Mount Racing Club **Bred** Des Vere Hunt Farm Co And Jack Ronan **Trained** Middleham Moor, N Yorks

FOCUS
A poor selling handicap in which all bar Light The City were sporting some sort of headgear. The runner-up is rated to his best form.

2619 RIPON FARM SERVICES H'CAP 6f
7:40 (7:49) (Class 4) (0-85,85) 3-Y-O £4,209 (£1,252; £625; £312) Stalls High

Form RPR

32-1 **1** **Elusive Prince**[26] 1880 3-9-0 78 LeeNewman 8 88+
(David Barron) *mde virtually all: pushed along 2f out: drvn clr ent fnl f: styd on* **13/8**[1]

1000 **2** 2 1/2 **Sacrosanctus**[19] 2074 3-8-9 76 MichaelO'Connell(3) 4 78
(David Nicholls) *trckd ldrs: effrt 2f out: swtchd rt and rdn over 1f out: kpt on to chse wnr ins fnl f: no imp towards fin* **20/1**

01-1 **3** 2 **Bassett Road (IRE)**[12] 2255 3-9-4 85 RossAtkinson(3) 2 81
(Tom Dascombe) *cl up: rdn and ev ch 2f out: drvn and edgd rt ent fnl f: one pce* **3/1**[2]

2501 **4** 1 **Dream Catcher (FR)**[9] 2363 3-9-2 80 6ex JamieSpencer 7 72
(David Nicholls) *in rr: hdwy on inner 2f out: sn rdn and kpt on u.p ins fnl f: nrst fin* **9/2**[3]

-250 **5** 1 3/4 **Bunce (IRE)**[14] 2199 3-9-4 82 PatDobbs 1 69
(Richard Hannon) *chsd ldrs: rdn along over 2f out: sn drvn and wknd over 1f out* **12/1**

5400 **6** 1 1/4 **Satin Love (USA)**[14] 2200 3-8-8 72 JoeFanning 3 55
(Mark Johnston) *chsd ldrs: rdn along wl over 2f out: sn drvn and wknd* **16/1**

40-0 **7** 2 **Orchid Street (USA)**[27] 1825 3-8-11 75 PaulHanagan 6 51
(Ann Duffield) *s.i.s and in rr: sme hdwy whn n.m.r wl over 1f out: sn btn* **16/1**

1-65 **8** 1/2 **Lady Del Sol**[8] 2391 3-8-9 73 PaulMulrennan 5 48
(Marjorie Fife) *dwlt and towards rr: effrt and sme hdwy on outreer 2f out: sn rdn and btn* **16/1**

1m 11.34s (-1.66) **Going Correction** -0.25s/f (Firm) **8** Ran SP% **111.4**
Speed ratings (Par 101): **101,97,95,93,91 89,87,86**
toteswingers: 1&2 £10.90, 1&3 £1.80, 2&3 £14.30 CSF £35.41 CT £88.17 TOTE £2.80: £1.30, £7.50, £1.10; EX 39.20.
Owner Bridge Extraction Systems Ltd **Bred** Usk Valley Stud **Trained** Maunby, N Yorks

FOCUS
A decent 3yo sprint handicap with the winner building on his previous course success.

2620 DIRECTORS CUP (H'CAP) 6f
8:10 (8:15) (Class 3) (0-95,94) 4-Y-O+ £6,623 (£1,982; £991; £495; £246) Stalls High

Form RPR

4-24 **1** **Addictive Dream (IRE)**[18] 2099 4-9-4 91 JamieSpencer 6 107
(Walter Swinburn) *trckd ldr far side: hdwy to ld that gp 1/2-way: rdn and overall ldr 1 1/2f out: sn clr on far side: drvn out* **4/1**[1]

-520 **2** 2 **Grissom (IRE)**[18] 2095 5-8-5 78 DuranFentiman 11 88
(Tim Easterby) *cl up stands' side: hdwy to ld that gp and overall ldr over 2f out: sn rdn and hdd 1 1/2f out: kpt on: 1st of 8 in gp* **22/1**

0005 **3** 1 1/4 **Red Cape (FR)**[4] 2497 8-8-2 75 KellyHarrison 8 81
(Ruth Carr) *cl up stands' side: effrt 2f out: sn rdn and ev ch tl drvn and one pce ent fnl f: 2nd of 8 in gp* **14/1**

0-20 **4** 1 1/4 **Medici Time**[32] 1675 6-8-8 81 (v) TedDurcan 13 83
(Tim Easterby) *s.i.s and in rr stands' side: hdwy 2f out: rdn over 1f out: kpt on ins fnl f: nrst fin: 3rd of 8 in gp* **20/1**

00-1 **5** 1 1/2 **Saucy Brown (IRE)**[31] 1715 5-8-9 82 AndrewMullen 10 79
(David Nicholls) *chsd ldrs stands' side: hdwy over 2f out: rdn wl over 1f out: kpt on same pce fnl f: 4th of 8 in gp* **16/1**

0-04 **6** nse **Coolminx (IRE)**[55] 1205 4-8-11 84 PaulHanagan 9 81
(Richard Fahey) *chsd ldrs stands' side: rdn along over 2f out: sn drvn and wknd: 5th of 8 in gp* **11/1**

00-0 **7** 1/2 **Kellys Eye (IRE)**[59] 1111 4-9-4 91 PaulMulrennan 1 86
(George Foster) *trckd ldrs far side: hdwy over 2f out: rdn to chse wnr wl over 1f out: sn drvn and no imp: 2nd of 6 in gp* **12/1**

0065 **8** nk **Arganil (USA)**[18] 2116 6-9-0 87 (b) PhillipMakin 12 81
(Kevin Ryan) *towards rr stands' side: effrt and sme hdwy over 2f out: sn rdn and n.d: 6th of 8 in gp* **12/1**

000- **9** 2 **Hogmaneigh (IRE)**[256] 6175 8-9-2 89 JoeFanning 2 77
(Mark Johnston) *hld up in rr far side: hdwy over 2f out: sn rdn and no imp' 3rd of 6 in gp* **22/1**

20-1 **10** 2 1/2 **Pepper Lane**[17] 2122 4-8-10 83 SilvestreDeSousa 16 63
(David O'Meara) *overall ldr stands' side: pushed along and hdd wl over 2f out: sn rdn and wknd: 7th of 8 in gp* **4/1**[1]

10-0 **11** 2 1/4 **Amenable (IRE)**[18] 2116 4-9-2 89 AdrianNicholls 3 61
(David Nicholls) *led far side gp: rdn along 1/2-way: sn hdd and grad wknd: 4th of 6 in gp* **8/1**[3]

0000 **12** shd **Hotham**[11] 2317 8-8-8 81 LeeNewman 4 53
(Noel Wilson) *a towards rr far side: 5th of 6 in gp* **28/1**

0-05 **13** 8 **Noverre To Go (IRE)**[28] 1809 5-9-7 94 (t) RichardKingscote 7 41
(Tom Dascombe) *chsd ldng pair far side: rdn along 1/2-way: sn wknd: 6th of 6 in gp* **6/1**[2]

0101 **14** *5* **Thrust Control (IRE)**[23] [1943] 4-8-7 **85**.......................... LeeTopliss(5) 15 16
(Tracy Waggott) *a in rr stands' side: last of 8 in gp* **25/1**

1m 10.38s (-2.62) **Going Correction** -0.25s/f (Firm) **14** Ran SP% **122.4**
Speed ratings (Par 107): **107,104,102,101,99 98,98,97,95,91 88,88,78,71**
toteswingers: 1&2 £30.00, 1&3 £19.60, 2&3 £64.20 CSF £103.99 CT £1150.06 TOTE £4.30: £1.10, £9.00, £6.90; EX 134.70.

Owner Caveat Emptor Partnership **Bred** Eugene Matthews **Trained** Aldbury, Herts

FOCUS

A competitive sprint handicap. The field split into two groups and the placed horses set the level.

NOTEBOOK

Addictive Dream(IRE) burst clear on the far side to win impressively for the in-form Walter Swinburn. Fourth off the same mark at Newbury the time before, this was a career-best by some way and, having had just the ten runs, it's likely there's more to come. He could feature in some of the top 6f sprints this summer. (old market op 6-1 tchd 9-2 new market op 9-2)

Grissom(IRE), soon prominent on the stands' side, kept on strongly to 'win' the race on his side, but wasn't on terms with Addictive Dream. (new market)

Red Cape(FR) has slipped to a fair mark and now has good back-to-back efforts to his name. He can pick up a handicap at some point. (new market)

Medici Time returned to form following a below-par run at Doncaster, putting in his best work late following a slow start. (old market op 22-1 new market op 22-1)

Saucy Brown(IRE) was well weighted on old form and showed he can compete in handicaps. (new market)

Coolminx(IRE) had her chance and was a touch disappointing. (new market op 12-1)

Kellys Eye(IRE) chased home the winner on the far side and is steadily working his way back to a more workable mark. (old market tchd 14-1 new market)

Pepper Lane, up 9lb for winning with ease over C&D last time, was quickly beaten off and failed to reproduce her best. Official explanation: trainer's rep had no explanation for the poor form shown (old market op 5-1 new market)

Noverre To Go(IRE) was unable to build on his last-time-out Chester fifth. This clearly wasn't his true running. (old market op 13-2 tchd 6-1 new market op 13-2)

2621 SIS PICTURE SERVICES MAIDEN STKS — 1m 1f 170y
8:40 (8:44) (Class 5) 3-Y-0+ **£2,331** (£693; £346; £173) **Stalls** Low

Form RPR

4-2 **1** **Abdicate (IRE)**[19] [2045] 3-8-6 0.......................... PaulHanagan 2 76+
(Richard Fahey) *trckd ldrs: hdwy over 4f out: rdn over 2f out: chal wl over 1f out: drvn ent fnl f: styd on gamely to ld last 50yds* **9/2**[2]

2 **2** *½* **Sir Francis Drake**[17] [2125] 3-8-11 0.......................... AhmedAjtebi 10 80+
(Mahmood Al Zarooni) *trckd ldrs: hdwy on outer over 3f out: rdn to chal 2f out and sn tk slt advantage: jnd over 1f out: drvn and edgd rt ent fnl f: hdd and no ex last 50yds* **6/4**[1]

0 **3** *3* **Daruband**[12] [2257] 3-8-11 0.......................... SilvestreDeSousa 8 74+
(Mahmood Al Zarooni) *trckd ldrs on inner: hdwy over 3f out: rdn over 2f out: chsd ldng pair over 1f out: no imp* **9/1**

5 **4** *7* **Mill Mick**[12] [2257] 4-9-10 0.......................... StephenCraine 6 60
(John Mackie) *hld up in tch: hdwy to chse ldrs 3f out: rdn over 2f out and kpt on same pce* **50/1**

40-5 **5** *2* **Newby Lodge (IRE)**[22] [1991] 3-8-6 0.......................... KellyHarrison 11 50
(William Haggas) *midfield: hdwy on outer over 3f out: rdn to chse ldrs over 2f out: edgd rt and wknd wl over 1f out* **20/1**

6 *½* **Tourtiere** 3-8-11 0.......................... TomEaves 4 54+
(George Moore) *dwlt: bhd tl styd on fnl 2f: n.d* **100/1**

7 *2¾* **Bollin Mandy** 3-8-7 0 ow1.......................... DavidAllan 13 45
(Tim Easterby) *dwlt and bhd: hdwy on outer and in tch 3f out: sn rdn and grad wknd* **80/1**

0-0 **8** *2¾* **Diamond Bob**[12] [2257] 3-8-11 0.......................... TomMcLaughlin 3 43
(Ed Dunlop) *a towards rr* **33/1**

0-0 **9** *½* **Shirataki (IRE)**[8] [2392] 3-8-11 0.......................... JoeFanning 12 42
(Mark Johnston) *trckd ldr: effrt and cl up 4f out: rdn along 3f out: sn drvn and wknd 2f out* **33/1**

10 *1¾* **Charmouth Girl**[60] 5-9-2 0.......................... DeclanCannon(3) 9 33
(John Mackie) *t.k.h: chsd ldrs: pushed along over 4f out: rdn over 3f out and grad wknd* **100/1**

11 *40* **Bonzai Boy (IRE)** 3-8-8 0.......................... MichaelO'Connell(3) 5 —
(George Moore) *dwlt: a towards rr* **80/1**

04 **12** *28* **Plimsoll Line (USA)**[12] [2258] 3-8-11 0.......................... JamieSpencer 15 —
(Michael Bell) *trckd ldrs: hdwy to chse ldng pair over 4f out: rdn along over 3f out and sn wknd: eased* **5/1**[3]

5-00 **P** **Sobea Star (IRE)**[46] [1415] 3-8-7 50 ow1.......................... MickyFenton 16 —
(Pam Sly) *led: rdn along 3f out: drvn over 2f out: jst hdd wl over 1f out whn p.u: fatally injured* **100/1**

2m 3.34s (-2.06) **Going Correction** -0.25s/f (Firm)
WFA 3 from 4yo+ 13lb **13** Ran SP% **102.9**
Speed ratings (Par 103): **98,97,95,89,88 87,85,83,82,81 49,27,—**
toteswingers: 1&2 £1.30, 1&3 £5.40, 2&3 £3.60 CSF £7.86 TOTE £3.90: £1.50, £1.10, £2.70; EX 7.60.

Owner Highclere Thoroughbred Racing Lady Salsa **Bred** Ceka Ireland Ltd **Trained** Musley Bank, N Yorks

FOCUS

An ordinary maiden, but the front three drew clear and the race should produce winners despite the form being rather muddling.

2622 ATTHERACES.COM IS FREE H'CAP — 2m
9:10 (9:10) (Class 5) (0-75,75) 4-Y-0+ **£4,209** (£1,252; £625; £312) **Stalls** Low

Form RPR

1-06 **1** **Jackday (IRE)**[26] [1881] 6-9-3 **68**.......................... (p) DavidAllan 6 73
(Tim Easterby) *hld up in rr: hdwy wl over 2f out: effrt over 1f out: swtchd rt and rdn ins fnl f: styd on to ld nr fin* **12/1**

-612 **2** *hd* **Petella**[19] [2060] 5-8-12 **63**.......................... PJMcDonald 1 68
(George Moore) *hld up towards rr: stdy hdwy over 3f out: trckd ldrs over 2f out: rdn to ld appr fnl f: sn drvn and hdd nr fin* **15/8**[2]

-134 **3** *1¾* **Descaro (USA)**[20] [2034] 5-9-9 **74**.......................... SilvestreDeSousa 8 77
(David O'Meara) *hld up in rr: hdwy 3f out: rdn to chse ldrs and edgd rt wl over 1f out: drvn and kpt on ins fnl f* **13/8**[1]

25-0 **4** *½* **Blazing Desert**[20] [2034] 7-9-7 **72**.......................... TomEaves 2 74
(John Quinn) *trckd ldr: led 4f out: rdn along 3f out: drvn and hdd wl over 1f out: wknd ent fnl f* **15/2**

20-0 **5** *4½* **Hi Dancer**[61] [8] 8-8-11 **62**.......................... PhillipMakin 9 59
(Ben Haslam) *trckd ldng pair: rdn along over 3f out: drvn over 2f out: sn wknd* **7/1**[3]

5050 **6** *1½* **Why So Serious**[20] [2034] 5-8-5 **56** oh6.......................... JoeFanning 3 51?
(Peter Salmon) *led: rdn along 4f out: hdd 3f out: wknd over 2f out* **33/1**

2044 **7** *3½* **Lady Norlela**[4] [2496] 5-8-5 **56**.......................... PaulHanagan 4 47
(Brian Rothwell) *chsd ldng poair: rdn along over 3f out: drvn over 2f out: sn wknd* **18/1**

3m 32.85s (1.05) **Going Correction** -0.25s/f (Firm) **7** Ran SP% **113.0**
Speed ratings (Par 103): **87,86,86,85,83 82,81**
toteswingers: 1&2 £3.60, 1&3 £5.10, 2&3 £1.10 CSF £34.20 CT £57.07 TOTE £15.00: £9.10, £1.20; EX 33.60.

Owner Mrs Jean P Connew **Bred** Mrs H D McCalmont **Trained** Great Habton, N Yorks

FOCUS

The pace was a steady one for this 2m handicap. The third is rated to form but the proximity of the sixth raises doubts.

T/Jkpt: Not won. T/Plt: £12.50 to a £1 stake. Pool of £97,079.19 - 5637.64 winning units. T/Qpdt: £9.70 to a £1 stake. Pool of £5,572.48 - 422.17 winning units. JR

2623 - 2629a (Foreign Racing) - See Raceform Interactive

[2042] HAMILTON (R-H)
Thursday, June 2

OFFICIAL GOING: Good (good to soft in places; 7.8)

Rail realignment reduced distances on round course by 8yds.
Wind: Virtually nil Weather: Overcast

2630 RACING UK ON SKY CHANNEL 432 MAIDEN AUCTION STKS — 6f 5y
2:10 (2:10) (Class 6) 2-Y-0 **£2,590** (£770; £385; £192) **Stalls** High

Form RPR

1 **The Clan Macdonald** 2-8-8 0.......................... LeeNewman 3 79+
(David Barron) *trckd ldrs: hdwy over 1f out: led jst ins fnl f: rdn clr fnl 100yds: comf* **7/1**[3]

5 **2** *3¼* **Nearly A Gift (IRE)**[28] [1823] 2-8-4 0.......................... DuranFentiman 5 65
(Tim Easterby) *in tch: rdn and hdwy over 1f out: kpt on ins fnl f: wnt 2nd nr fin: no ch w wnr* **11/2**[2]

5240 **3** *nk* **Always Ends Well (IRE)**[17] [2148] 2-8-4 0.......................... JoeFanning 2 64
(Mark Johnston) *led narrowly: rdn whn hdd jst ins fnl f: no ex and lost 2nd nr fin* **12/1**

4 *2½* **Darling Lexi (IRE)** 2-8-10 0.......................... PaulHanagan 4 62+
(Richard Fahey) *hld up: pushed along 1/2-way: hdwy over 1f out: edgd lft and no further imp ins fnl f* **11/1**

54 **5** *¾* **Complex**[17] [2160] 2-8-6 0.......................... AdrianNicholls 6 56
(David Evans) *prom: pushed along and lost pl over 2f out: wknd over 1f out* **80/1**

6 *1* **Revitalise** 2-8-9 0.......................... PhillipMakin 8 55+
(Kevin Ryan) *dwlt: sn pushed along in rr: rdn over 2f out: n.d* **20/1**

5 **7** *1½* **Winter Hill**[12] [2309] 2-8-4 0.......................... RichardKingscote 7 46
(Tom Dascombe) *w ldr: rdn over 2f out: wknd over 1f out* **4/6**[1]

1m 12.72s (0.52) **Going Correction** -0.025s/f (Good) **7** Ran SP% **109.9**
Speed ratings (Par 91): **95,90,90,86,85 84,82**
toteswingers:1&2:£3.80, 1&3:£8.20, 2&3:£5.30 CSF £41.02 TOTE £6.70: £5.50, £3.60; EX 52.50.

Owner The Warwickshire Partnership **Bred** Pevens Racing **Trained** Maunby, N Yorks

FOCUS

Probably no more than a fair maiden with the favourite finishing last and the exposed third still in front approaching the last. The field stayed stand side. A decentr start from the winner with the second and third setting the level.

NOTEBOOK

The Clan Macdonald, a filly by Intikhab out of a well-related 7f/7.5f winner, made a promising debut and was never stronger than at the finish after taking some time to warm to her task. She shows a bit of knee action, so it might be the ground here was ideal for her, but she looks a sure improver with 7f not likely to prove a problem. (tchd 15-2)

Nearly A Gift(IRE) had shaped well in a maiden at Chester that's proving muddling form overall, but the step up to 6f promised to suit and it did with her finishing effort suggesting that she'll stay 7f as he pedigree suggests. (op 6-1 tchd 9-2)

Always Ends Well(IRE) looked to have lost her way a little but she bounced back with a solid effort for all she didn't see the sixth furlong out as well as it looked she might, having travelled strongly. She's enough ability to win a small race back at 5f. (op 16-1)

Darling Lexi(IRE)'s pedigree is a tricky-to-interpret mixture of speed and stamina but she looked beaten here more by inexperience than anything else, losing her place at halfway before staying on, albeit without running straight. She'll improve. (op 12-1)

Complex seemed to run his best race yet trying 6f for the first time, but never threatened and would be of more interest down in a claimer. (op 66-1 tchd 100-1)

Revitalise, a gelding by Vital Equine out of the 6f/7.5f winner Tancred Arms, was soon on the back foot after a slow start and will improve for the experience. (op 22-1 tchd 25-1)

Winter Hill was an expensive flop for the second time in succession, readily brushed aside with 2f to run and finishing very tamely. She's quite stoutly bred on her female side so might be better over further, but equally her sire Three Valleys has proved a disappointment to say the least at stud so far. Official explanation: trainer had no explanation for the poor form shown (tchd 8-11 in places)

2631 RACING NEXT WEDNESDAY NIGHT CLAIMING STKS — 6f 5y
2:40 (2:40) (Class 6) 3-5-Y-0 **£2,047** (£604; £302) **Stalls** High

Form RPR

3324 **1** **Carrie's Magic**[20] [2062] 4-8-10 67.......................... (b) LeeNewman 1 68
(David Barron) *chsd ldrs: rdn and hdwy 2f out: led 1f out: kpt on wl* **6/4**[1]

0020 **2** *2* **Prince Of Vasa (IRE)**[5] [2494] 4-9-4 75.......................... PaulMulrennan 6 70
(Michael Smith) *prom: rdn and hung rt over 2f out: sn led: hdd 1f out: kpt on but a hld by wnr fnl 100yds* **11/4**[2]

1630 **3** *3¼* **Dark Lane**[12] [2300] 5-9-5 78.......................... (b[1]) PaulHanagan 4 60
(Richard Fahey) *led after 1f: rdn whn hdd over 2f out: sn hung rt: one pce* **11/4**[2]

4 *1¼* **The Fiery Cross** 4-9-10 0.......................... TomEaves 5 61?
(Ian Semple) *dwlt: hld up in tch: hdwy over 2f out: drvn over 1f out: kpt on same pce* **12/1**[3]

-000 **5** *2½* **Rosbertini**[20] [2057] 5-8-13 50.......................... (p) FrederikTylicki 3 42
(Linda Perratt) *sn outpcd in rr: wl bhd tl kpt on ins fnl f: n.d* **22/1**

-000 **6** *¾* **Country Waltz**[13] [2265] 3-8-1 59.......................... AndrewMullen 8 36
(Linda Perratt) *trckd ldrs: rdn over 2f out: wknd over 1f out* **22/1**

000- **7** *shd* **Reach For The Sky (IRE)**[223] [7051] 4-8-9 47.......................... PatrickMathers 9 35
(Alan Berry) *sn outpcd towards rr: n.d* **100/1**

005- **8** *5* **Old Firm**[187] [7601] 5-9-1 35.......................... DuranFentiman 2 25
(Ian Semple) *led for 1f: remained prom tl wknd 2f out* **66/1**

1m 12.46s (0.26) **Going Correction** -0.025s/f (Good)
WFA 3 from 4yo+ 8lb **8** Ran SP% **112.2**
Speed ratings (Par 101): **97,94,90,88,85 84,83,77**
.Carrie's Magic was claimed by A. C. Whillans for £6000. \n\x\x

Owner J Starbuck **Bred** John Starbuck **Trained** Maunby, N Yorks

FOCUS
A wide variety of abilities on show in an ordinary claimer that largely played out as the betting suggested it would. The field again stayed stands' side. It's doubtful this is form to be positive about.

2632 LANARKSHIRE CHAMBER OF COMMERCE H'CAP — 5f 4y
3:10 (3:10) (Class 6) (0-65,65) 3-Y-0+ £2,047 (£604; £302) Stalls High

Form RPR
4-50 **1** **Doc Hay (USA)**[28] 1838 4-9-13 **64** .... JoeFanning 12 76+
(Keith Dalgleish) *dwlt: sn in tch gng keenly: hdwy over 2f out: led over 1f out: sn edgd rt: hld on wl u.p towards fin* **6/1**[2]
3202 **2** *nk* **Sharp Bullet (IRE)**[3] 2546 5-9-3 **54** .... (p) RichardKingscote 13 65
(Bruce Hellier) *hld up: gd hdwy fr 2f out: rdn to chse wnr jst ins fnl f: kpt on but hld towards fin* **7/2**[1]
310- **3** *½* **Sands Of Dee (USA)**[203] 7405 4-9-12 **63** .... AdrianNicholls 11 72
(David Nicholls) *in tch towards stands' side: reminders bef 1/2-way: hdwy 2f out: chal 1f out: kpt on ins fnl f* **9/1**
00-1 **4** *3 ½* **Blues Jazz**[20] 2047 5-8-11 **55** .... GarryWhillans[(7)] 6 51
(Ian Semple) *in tch: rdn and outpcd over 2f out: kpt on ins fnl f: wnt 4th post: nvr threatened ldrs* **13/2**[3]
0040 **5** *nse* **Royal Blade (IRE)**[10] 2353 4-8-2 **46** .... DanielleMooney[(7)] 4 42
(Alan Berry) *w ldr: rdn to ld over 2f out: hdd over 1f out: no ex ins fnl f* **33/1**
5041 **6** *nk* **Tournedos (IRE)**[3] 2547 9-9-1 **59** 6ex .... (b) ShaneBKelly[(7)] 2 54+
(Ruth Carr) *squeezed s: hld up in rr towards far side: rdn and hdwy over 2f out: no further imp ins fnl f* **7/2**[1]
00-0 **7** *2* **Argentine (IRE)**[62] 1073 7-9-11 **62** .... LeeNewman 8 50
(George Foster) *chsd ldrs: rdn over 2f out: wknd ins fnl f* **20/1**
5140 **8** *½* **Soopacal (IRE)**[64] 1048 6-9-11 **65** .... MichaelO'Connell[(3)] 9 51
(Michael Herrington) *led: rdn whn hdd over 2f out: wknd over 1f out* **18/1**
5-00 **9** *1* **Distant Sun (USA)**[27] 1856 7-9-6 **57** .... PaulHanagan 5 40
(Linda Perratt) *chsd ldrs: rdn over 2f out: wknd ins fnl f* **11/1**
-505 **10** *nk* **Sandwith**[27] 1856 8-9-8 **62** .... (v) GaryBartley[(3)] 1 43
(George Foster) *hld up towards far side: rdn over 2f out: n.d* **12/1**
00-0 **11** *½* **Tabiet**[20] 2062 4-9-2 **53** .... PhillipMakin 10 33
(Linda Perratt) *prom: rdn and outpcd over 2f out: wknd over 1f out* **50/1**
5 **12** *1 ¾* **Lambrini Lace (IRE)**[7] 2412 6-8-9 **46** oh1 .... (b) TomEaves 3 19
(Lisa Williamson) *chsd ldrs towards far side: wknd over 1f out* **33/1**
-605 **13** *4 ½* **Sumay Buoy (IRE)**[3] 2546 4-8-9 **46** oh1 .... AndrewMullen 7 —
(Jean McGregor) *chsd ldrs: rdn over 2f out: sn wknd: eased ins fnl f* **66/1**

60.10 secs (0.10) **Going Correction** -0.025s/f (Good) **13 Ran SP% 117.4**
Speed ratings (Par 101): **98,97,96,91,91 90,87,86,84,84 83,80,73**
toteswingers:1&2: £4.90, 2&3: £6.50, 1&3: £7.00 CSF £25.49 CT £165.87 TOTE £5.70: £2.20, £1.30, £4.20; EX 31.90.
Owner S Laffan **Bred** Colts Neck Stables Llc **Trained** Carluke, South Lanarkshire

FOCUS
An ordinary handicap in which the field split into two groups initially with the first three all staying in the smaller group nearer the stands' rail. Sound, straightforward form.
Sumay Buoy(IRE) Official explanation: jockey said gelding ran flat

2633 GARRY OWEN H'CAP — 6f 5y
3:40 (3:41) (Class 5) (0-75,75) 4-Y-0+ £2,590 (£770; £385; £192) Stalls High

Form RPR
-600 **1** **Jobe (USA)**[19] 2095 5-9-6 **74** .... (p) PhillipMakin 7 86
(Kevin Ryan) *mde all: rdn over 1f out: kpt on strly ins fnl f: comf* **9/1**
1330 **2** *3 ½* **Frequency**[12] 2280 4-9-4 **72** .... (b) JoeFanning 10 73+
(Keith Dalgleish) *slowly away: hld up: hdwy over 1f out: kpt on wl ins fnl f: wnt 2nd nr fin: no ch w wnr* **14/1**
-312 **3** *hd* **Ingleby Arch (USA)**[51] 1289 8-8-11 **70** .... LMcNiff[(5)] 8 70
(David Barron) *trckd ldr: rdn over 2f out: kpt on: lost 2nd towards fin* **13/2**[2]
220- **4** *2 ¼* **Imprimis Tagula (IRE)**[172] 7846 7-9-4 **75** .... (v) AmyBaker[(3)] 4 68
(Alan Bailey) *midfield: rdn over 2f out: hdwy over 1f out: one pce ins fnl f* **11/1**
1-43 **5** *1 ¼* **Hellbender (IRE)**[10] 2352 5-8-9 **63** .... PaulMulrennan 9 52
(George Foster) *hld up: rdn and outpcd over 2f out: kpt on ins fnl f: n.d* **12/1**
1541 **6** *1 ¼* **Memphis Man**[14] 2222 8-8-3 **62** .... MatthewCosham[(5)] 3 47
(David Evans) *hld up: rdn over 2f out: no imp* **25/1**
06-3 **7** *nk* **Burnwynd Boy**[6] 2464 6-8-9 **62** ow1 .... SebSanders 5 47
(Ian Semple) *trckd ldrs: rdn over 2f out: wknd ins fnl f* **15/2**
0630 **8** *1 ½* **Berbice (IRE)**[10] 2353 6-8-10 **64** .... PaulHanagan 6 43
(Linda Perratt) *racd keenly: in tch: rdn over 1f out: wknd ins fnl f* **16/1**
6111 **9** *3 ¼* **Klynch**[6] 2464 5-9-0 **75** 12ex .... (b) ShaneBKelly[(7)] 1 44+
(Ruth Carr) *v.s.a: wl in rr: brief hdwy 1/2-way: nvr able to get competitive* **9/4**[1]
0-00 **10** *3 ¾* **Captain Royale (IRE)**[8] 2397 6-9-7 **75** .... (p) PatrickMathers 11 32
(Colin Teague) *in tch: rdn over 2f out: wknd over 1f out* **16/1**
3-03 **11** *6* **Supreme Spirit (IRE)**[28] 1831 4-9-6 **74** .... (p) AdrianNicholls 2 —
(David Nicholls) *trckd ldr: rdn over 2f out: wknd over 1f out* **7/1**[3]

1m 11.54s (-0.66) **Going Correction** -0.025s/f (Good) **11 Ran SP% 116.7**
Speed ratings (Par 103): **103,98,98,95,93 91,91,89,85,80 72**
toteswingers:1&2: £16.70, 2&3: £15.40, 1&3: £8.80 CSF £126.82 CT £878.28 TOTE £8.60: £2.20, £4.30, £2.90; EX 127.90.
Owner Mrs Angie Bailey **Bred** David Garvin **Trained** Hambleton, N Yorks

FOCUS
Exposed sprinters in a fair handicap in which the field raced as one this time, the winner making all on the stands' side initially before drifting to the centre. He showed his best form since his early 3yo days. It was the pick of the three C&D times.
Jobe(USA) Official explanation: trainer said, regarding the apparent improvement in form shown, gelding was suited by the reapplication of cheekpieces.
Klynch Official explanation: jockey said, regarding running and riding, that as he removed the blindfold gelding turned his head, putting his nose on the framework of the stalls causing him to be slowly away

2634 IRISH E B F CAPTAIN J.C. STEWART FILLIES' H'CAP — 1m 65y
4:10 (4:10) (Class 3) (0-95,90) 3-Y-0+ £7,771 (£2,312; £1,155; £577) Stalls Low

Form RPR
0-63 **1** **Gobama**[22] 2000 4-10-0 **90** .... SebSanders 3 98
(J W Hills) *trckd ldr on inner: short of room 2f out: rdn and chal over 1f out: led narrowly fnl 100yds: kpt on: jst hld on* **5/1**
2416 **2** *shd* **She's A Character**[14] 2217 4-9-4 **80** .... PaulHanagan 2 87
(Richard Fahey) *s.i.s: hld up in tch on inner: swtchd lft 2f out: sn hdwy to chal: pressed wnr strly fnl 100yds: kpt on: jst failed* **4/1**[3]
-060 **3** *2 ¼* **Amethyst Dawn (IRE)**[18] 2123 5-9-9 **85** .... DavidAllan 1 87
(Tim Easterby) *led: rdn over 2f out: hdd fnl 100yds: no ex* **7/2**[2]
140 **4** *¾* **Granny McPhee**[12] 2282 5-9-4 **83** .... AmyBaker[(3)] 7 83
(Alan Bailey) *s.i.s: hld up: briefly short of room over 2f out: rdn 2f out: kpt on: n.d* **8/1**
-500 **5** *3* **Oceanway (USA)**[13] 2256 3-8-9 **82** .... JoeFanning 6 72
(Mark Johnston) *prom: rdn over 2f out: wknd ins fnl f* **7/1**
26-0 **6** *6* **Whispering Spirit (IRE)**[36] 1610 5-8-8 **73** .... AmyRyan[(3)] 5 52
(Ann Duffield) *hld up: rdn over 3f out: wknd 2f out* **16/1**
2-20 **7** *2* **Askaud (IRE)**[15] 2188 3-8-10 **83** .... FrederikTylicki 4 55
(David Nicholls) *trckd ldng pair: rdn 3f out: sn wknd* **3/1**[1]

1m 46.01s (-2.39) **Going Correction** -0.125s/f (Firm)
WFA 3 from 4yo+ 11lb **7 Ran SP% 113.4**
Speed ratings (Par 104): **106,105,103,102,99 93,91**
toteswingers:1&2: £4.50, 2&3: £3.90, 1&3: £3.60 CSF £24.71 CT £77.90 TOTE £5.20: £2.30, £1.80; EX 20.40.
Owner W Y Chen **Bred** Newsells Park Stud **Trained** Upper Lambourn, Berks
■ Stewards' Enquiry : Seb Sanders caution: careless riding

FOCUS
Not a strong race for the grade and a messy one to boot with the eventual third dictating a steady pace, but the best horse won and would have done so more decisively had things panned out more in her favour. The form is rated around the third.

NOTEBOOK
Gobama looked to have been found a good opening back on her favoured turf after her latest third to the very well-handicapped Point North on Polytrack at Kempton, and has to rate value for more than her winning margin. Always a filly that hits a flat spot in her races, the steady pace and being trapped behind the leader at the point she was wouldn't have helped her, even on this stiff track, and she deserves plenty of credit to overcome those obstacles and keep the persistent runner-up at bay. She's on the fringe of Listed class on turf and will probably be given the opportunity in that grade again. (op 9-2)
She's A Character has always struggled off this sort of mark before, but her Doncaster win in April suggested she might be an improved performer this year and she confirmed that seems to be the case over what is her ideal trip. (tchd 9-2)
Amethyst Dawn(IRE) attracted plenty of support beforehand, possibly in the expectation of a return to her normal front-running tactics, but though she was able to dictate she didn't pick up quite as she did on occasions last year and left the impression that she possibly still hasn't fully come to herself. She'll be well handicapped when she does. (op 11-2)
Granny McPhee found being held up off this pace at a trip short of her best against her, but she finished strongly and continues at the top of her game. (op 7-1)
Oceanway(USA) was up there early but was readily brushed aside once the race began in earnest. (op 9-1)
Whispering Spirit(IRE) runs mostly on Polytrack these days and probably isn't up to this grade on that surface, let alone turf. (op 14-1)

2635 TURFTV H'CAP — 1m 3f 16y
4:40 (4:40) (Class 6) (0-65,65) 3-Y-0 £2,047 (£604; £302) Stalls High

Form RPR
-315 **1** **Countrywide Flame**[17] 2152 3-9-2 **65** .... (p) JulieBurke[(5)] 6 80
(Kevin Ryan) *mde all: 4 l clr 1/2-way: rdn over 2f out: kpt on wl ins fnl f* **9/2**[2]
000- **2** *1 ¼* **Fire Fighter (IRE)**[233] 6827 3-9-0 **58** .... SebSanders 1 71
(Sir Mark Prescott Bt) *s.i.s: sn midfield: pushed along wl over 4f out: reminders over 3f out: drvn to chse ldr over 2f out: kpt on u.str.p: hld towards fin* **1/2**[1]
04-0 **3** *7* **Kian's Delight**[29] 1812 3-8-13 **60** .... MichaelO'Connell[(3)] 4 60
(Jedd O'Keeffe) *trckd wnr: drvn over 2f out: kpt on one pce* **50/1**
00-2 **4** *11* **Silver Tigress**[27] 1858 3-8-3 **47** .... PaulHanagan 5 28
(George Moore) *trckd ldrs: rdn over 3f out: wknd fnl 2f* **13/2**[3]
3433 **5** *1 ¼* **Urban Kode (IRE)**[4] 2527 3-8-13 **62** .... (v) MatthewCosham[(5)] 3 40
(David Evans) *midfield: rdn over 3f out: sn no imp* **14/1**
000- **6** *7* **Nay Secret**[223] 7049 3-8-5 **49** .... AndrewMullen 7 —
(Jim Goldie) *midfield: pushed along and lost pl over 5f out: wknd over 2f out* **40/1**
0-00 **7** *6* **Go**[24] 1945 3-8-8 **52** .... FrederikTylicki 2 —
(Micky Hammond) *hld up: rdn over 4f out: sn btn* **66/1**

2m 22.6s (-3.00) **Going Correction** -0.125s/f (Firm) **7 Ran SP% 110.7**
Speed ratings (Par 97): **105,104,99,91,90 85,80**
toteswingers:1&2: £1.80, 2&3: £7.80, 1&3: £11.60 CSF £6.69 TOTE £4.50: £1.20, £1.40; EX 9.50.
Owner Countrywide Racing **Bred** Michael Clarke **Trained** Hambleton, N Yorks
■ Stewards' Enquiry : Seb Sanders caution: used whip with excessive frequency

FOCUS
Little strength in depth to a weak race and more than half the runners never got competitive after the winner set a brisk pace. He improved on his C&D form last month.

2636 DAILY RECORD H'CAP — 1m 5f 9y
5:10 (5:10) (Class 5) (0-70,70) 4-Y-0+ £2,590 (£770; £385; £192) Stalls High

Form RPR
434- **1** **Pokfulham (IRE)**[26] 7229 5-8-5 **54** .... (v) AndrewMullen 6 63+
(Jim Goldie) *trckd ldr: rdn to ld over 1f out: kpt on to go clr ins fnl f: comf* **9/4**[1]
6012 **2** *3 ½* **Houston Dynimo (IRE)**[13] 2251 6-9-7 **70** .... PaulMulrennan 5 74
(Nicky Richards) *led: rdn whn hdd over 1f out: kpt on: no ch w wnr* **7/2**[2]
5000 **3** *2 ¾* **Lure of The Night (IRE)**[9] 2393 4-8-11 **60** .... PaulHanagan 3 60
(Brian Rothwell) *midfield: pushed along over 4f out: drvn over 1f out: kpt on ins fnl f: wnt 3rd towards fin* **9/1**
2-40 **4** *¾* **Birkside**[20] 2059 8-8-11 **60** .... PhillipMakin 2 59
(Linda Perratt) *hld up: hdwy over 2f out: chsd ldng pair over 1f out: sn drvn and no imp: lost 3rd towards fin* **9/2**[3]
-460 **5** *1 ¼* **Terenzium (IRE)**[27] 1881 9-8-4 **53** .... (p) JoeFanning 1 50
(Micky Hammond) *hld up: rdn over 3f out: n.d* **9/1**
3234 **6** *1 ¼* **Casino Night**[8] 2399 6-8-11 **67** .... ShaneBKelly[(7)] 4 62
(Barry Murtagh) *sn midfield: rdn over 2f out: wknd over 1f out* **7/1**
00 **7** *hd* **Suprise Vendor (IRE)**[6] 2462 5-8-9 **58** .... TomEaves 7 53
(Stuart Coltherd) *trckd ldr: rdn 3f out: wknd over 1f out* **9/1**

2m 51.15s (-2.75) **Going Correction** -0.125s/f (Firm) **7 Ran SP% 113.7**
Speed ratings (Par 103): **103,100,99,98,97 97,97**
toteswingers:1&2: £2.70, 2&3: £6.70, 1&3: £6.30 CSF £10.09 TOTE £2.30: £1.02, £3.60; EX 10.70.
Owner Ambrose Turnbull **Bred** Killian Farm **Trained** Uplawmoor, E Renfrews

FOCUS
Something of a lop-sided handicap to end proceedings with only two of the runners officially rated above 60, and a tactical affair to boot, with the eventual second dictating a stop-start gallop. Modest form, rated around the runner-up.
T/Plt: £83.00 to a £1 stake. Pool of £46,848.97 - 411.95 winning tickets. T/Qpdt: £15.90 to a £1 stake. Pool of £3,981.15 - 184.20 winning tickets. AS

2380 LINGFIELD (L-H)

Thursday, June 2

OFFICIAL GOING: Turf course - firm (good to firm in places; 9.3); all-weather - standard

Wind: medium, half against Weather: warm

2637 FREE REPLAYS ON ATTHERACES.COM H'CAP (TURF) 1m 3f 106y

2:20 (2:20) (Class 6) (0-60,63) 3-Y-0 **£1,876** (£554; £277) **Stalls** High

Form RPR

00-0 **1** **Guards Chapel**[28] 1836 3-9-3 **55**.............................. RyanMoore 7 65+
(Luca Cumani) *dwlt: rdn along early: bhd in last pair: rdn and gd hdwy towards inner 3f out: drvn to chse ldrs 2f out: led ent fnl f: edgd rt but r.o wl fnl 150yds* **4/1**[2]

00-4 **2** *1 ¾* **Mokalif**[24] 1934 3-9-4 **56**.............................. HayleyTurner 12 63+
(Michael Bell) *dwlt: rdn along early: bhd in last quartet: rdn 5f out: rdn and effrt u.p 3f out: chsd ldng trio over 1f out: styd on wl to chse wnr ins fnl f: carried sltly rt and no imp fnl 100yds* **10/1**

00-2 **3** *¾* **Drumadoon (IRE)**[12] 2293 3-9-3 **55**.............................. TedDurcan 3 61
(John Dunlop) *hld up in tch: hdwy 4f out: rdn and ev ch over 2f out: led 2f out tl ent fnl f: styd on same pce fnl 150yds* **7/2**[1]

000 **4** *¾* **Formal Dining (USA)**[17] 2157 3-9-6 **58**.............................. NeilCallan 5 63
(Edward Vaughan) *hld up in tch in midfield: hdwy to chse ldrs over 3f out: rdn to ld wl over 2f out: hdd 2f out: unable qck u.p over 1f out: kpt on same pce ins fnl f* **16/1**

5350 **5** *4 ½* **Laffraaj (IRE)**[22] 1997 3-8-12 **55**..............................(v) HarryBentley(5) 6 52
(Pat Eddery) *hld up in midfield: hmpd after 1f: hdwy to chse ldrs 4f out: rdn and fnd little ent fnl 2f: 5th and wl hld over 1f out* **16/1**

-530 **6** *2 ½* **September Draw (USA)**[24] 1951 3-9-7 **59**.............................. RichardHughes 10 52
(Richard Hannon) *hld up in last quartet: rdn and effrt 3f out: hdwy to go modest 6th wl over 1f out: no imp on ldrs and pushed along after: eased wl ins fnl f* **9/1**

0-61 **7** *3 ¾* **Tidal Run**[10] 2349 3-9-8 **63** 6ex.............................. MartinHarley(3) 2 53
(Mick Channon) *led for 1f: chsd ldng trio and travelling wl after: nvr enough room on rail fr over 3f out: shuffled bk and towards rr whn eventually swtchd rt and clr run wl over 1f out: nt rcvr and n.d after* **11/2**[3]

000- **8** *1* **Last Act (IRE)**[175] 7780 3-8-11 **49**.............................. ChrisCatlin 1 34
(Mark Hoad) *t.k.h: chsd ldr tl led after 1f: rdn and hdd wl over 2f out: wknd wl over 1f out* **100/1**

00-6 **9** *1 ¼* **Xenophon**[12] 2305 3-8-10 **48**..............................(p) FrankieMcDonald 14 31
(Brendan Powell) *chsd ldr after 1f tl 3f out: sn struggling u.p: wknd 2f out* **33/1**

5453 **10** *¾* **Dew Reward (IRE)**[12] 2305 3-9-6 **58**..............................(b) CathyGannon 4 40
(Eve Johnson Houghton) *chsd ldrs tl hmpd after 1f: racd in midfield after: dropped towards rr on downhill run 4f out: rdn and no hdwy over 3f out: bhd fnl 2f* **10/1**

00-4 **11** *2* **Ministry**[22] 1997 3-9-7 **59**.............................. LukeMorris 8 37
(John Best) *t.k.h: hld up wl in tch on outer: rdn and struggling ent fnl 3f: wkng and towards rr whn edgd rt over 2f out: wl btn after* **11/1**

00-0 **12** *1 ¾* **Boston Court (IRE)**[14] 2231 3-9-4 **56**.............................. MartinDwyer 9 31
(Brian Meehan) *in tch in midfield: pushed along 8f out: reminders over 5f out: lost pl on downhill run 4f out: towards rr and struggling whn edgd lft and sltly hmpd over 2f out: no ch after* **20/1**

-006 **13** *11* **Dune Island**[22] 1999 3-8-7 **45**.............................. MarcHalford 13 —
(John Bridger) *a bhd: rn wd and lost tch bnd over 3f out* **100/1**

2m 29.5s (-2.00) **Going Correction** -0.25s/f (Firm) **13** Ran SP% **115.6**
Speed ratings (Par 97): **97,95,95,94,91 89,86,86,85,84 83,81,73**
toteswingers:1&2:£10.30, 1&3:£4.60, 2&3:£8.30 CSF £41.13 CT £152.36 TOTE £5.10: £1.90, £3.30, £1.40; EX 39.80 Trifecta £152.00 Pool: £330.80 - 1.61 winning units..
Owner Highclere Thoroughbred Racing (Matilda) **Bred** Mrs J Chandris **Trained** Newmarket, Suffolk

FOCUS

The pace seemed honest enough throughout and four lightly raced, unexposed types finished clear, so the form looks good for the level. The winner in particular looks potentially lot better than his opening mark. The time was 1.33 seconds quicker than the following Class 6 handicap for older horses.

Guards Chapel ◆ Official explanation: trainer's rep said, regarding the apparent improvement in form shown, gelding benefited from today's longer trip and was unluckly in running

Tidal Run Official explanation: jockey said filly was denied a clear run

2638 ATTHERACES.COM EXCLUSIVE HUGH TAYLOR TIPPING H'CAP (TURF) 1m 3f 106y

2:50 (2:50) (Class 6) (0-55,55) 4-Y-0+ **£1,876** (£554; £277) **Stalls** High

Form RPR

4465 **1** **Galiotto (IRE)**[6] 2451 5-9-1 **54**..............................(b) RyanMoore 4 60
(Gary Moore) *trvelled wl: trckd ldrs: lft 3rd bnd over 3f out: rdn and ev ch over 2f out: led wl over 1f out: drvn and forged ahd ent fnl f: edgd rt but in command ins fnl f* **6/4**[1]

4/60 **2** *4 ½* **Drawback (IRE)**[15] 808 8-9-2 **55**..............................(p) StephenCraine 5 53
(Barry Brennan) *hld up in tch in last trio: hdwy and lft 4th bnd over 3f out: rdn over 2f out: drvn and styd on to chse wnr ins fnl f: no imp* **25/1**

2606 **3** *2* **King Kieren (IRE)**[28] 1833 6-9-2 **55**..............................(v[1]) EddieAhern 2 50
(Linda Jewell) *led: rdn and hdd 3f out: unable qck u.p wl over 1f out: one pce and wl hld ins fnl f* **15/2**

2000 **4** *1 ¾* **Lucky Diva**[90] 773 4-8-2 **48**.............................. JakePayne(7) 3 40
(Bill Turner) *chsd ldr: rdn to ld 3f out: hdd wl over 1f out: lost 2nd ins fnl f: wknd fnl 100yds* **22/1**

6004 **5** *1 ¼* **Illuminative (USA)**[6] 2449 5-8-11 **50**..............................(p) SamHitchcott 6 40
(Zoe Davison) *in tch: lft 5th and hmpd bnd over 3f out: rdn: no prog and racd awkwardly 3f out: no threat to ldrs after: plugged on ins fnl f* **25/1**

6030 **6** *16* **Barbirolli**[23] 1987 9-8-3 **47**.............................. LauraPike(5) 8 10
(William Stone) *stdd s: hld up in last pair: lft 6th and hmpd bnd over 3f out: nt rcvr and wl hld after* **13/2**[3]

300/ **7** *3* **Press To Reset**[581] 7139 4-8-5 **47**.............................. KierenFox(3) 7 —
(Bill Turner) *stdd after s: a in last: struggling on downhill run 4f out: losing tch whn hmpd bnd over 3f out* **50/1**

-306 **S** **Aine's Delight (IRE)**[22] 943 5-8-12 **54**.............................. SimonPearce(3) 9 —
(Andy Turnell) *dwlt: sn rcvrd and chsng ldrs: cl 3rd and travelling wl whn slipped up bnd over 3f out* **15/8**[2]

2m 30.83s (-0.67) **Going Correction** -0.25s/f (Firm) **8** Ran SP% **113.9**
Speed ratings (Par 101): **92,88,87,86,85 73,71,—**
toteswingers:1&2:£10.50, 2&3:£32.50, 1&3:£2.40 CSF £44.04 CT £220.29 TOTE £3.00: £1.20, £6.50, £1.10; EX 50.30 Trifecta £443.20 Part won. Pool of £598.99 - 0.61 winning units..
Owner Andrew Bradmore **Bred** Ballintaggart Syndicate **Trained** Lower Beeding, W Sussex

FOCUS

An extremely moderate handicap that was further weakened when Aine's Delight slipped up. The winner is rated back to something like his best.

Illuminative(USA) Official explanation: jockey said gelding suffered interference in running

Barbirolli Official explanation: jockey said gelding lost it's action

2639 LINGFIELD PARK OWNERS CLUB MAIDEN FILLIES' STKS (TURF) 1m 2f

3:20 (3:21) (Class 5) 3-Y-O+ **£2,388** (£705; £352) **Stalls** Low

Form RPR

0 **1** **Street Secret (USA)**[27] 1873 3-8-9 0.............................. NeilCallan 1 73
(Roger Varian) *t.k.h: chsd ldrs: rdn and ev ch ent fnl 2f: led ins fnl f: styd on wl* **8/1**

6- **2** *¾* **Whispered**[220] 7113 3-8-9 0.............................. RyanMoore 8 71
(Sir Michael Stoute) *led: hrd pressed and rdn ent fnl 2f: hdd wl over 1f out: unable qck and sltly outpcd ent fnl f: kpt on fnl 75yds* **3/1**[3]

3 *nse* **Shieldmaiden (USA)** 3-8-9 0.............................. FrankieDettori 9 71
(Mahmood Al Zarooni) *chsd ldr: rdn and ev ch ent fnl 2f: drvn to ld wl over 1f out: changed legs: faltered and hdd ins fnl f: no ex and lost 2nd nr fin* **9/4**[2]

4 *3 ½* **Serenity Star** 3-8-9 0.............................. AhmedAjtebi 2 64
(Mahmood Al Zarooni) *t.k.h: hld up in tch: effrt to chse ldng trio ent fnl 3f: drvn and no imp wl over 1f out: plugged on same pce ins fnl f* **14/1**

2 **5** *1 ½* **Light Blow (USA)**[26] 1915 3-8-9 0.............................. TomQueally 3 61
(Sir Henry Cecil) *hld up in tch: effrt and swtchd rt ent fnl 3f: sn rdn and no hdwy: 5th and wl hld whn hung lft over 1f out* **15/8**[1]

00 **6** *6* **Hint Of Silver (IRE)**[16] 2185 3-8-10 0 ow1.............................. RobertHavlin 6 50?
(Andrew Haynes) *stdd after s: in tch of rr main gp: racd awkwardly downhill 4f out: rdn and wknd qckly 3f out* **200/1**

6 **7** *½* **La Belle Au Bois (IRE)**[31] 1767 5-9-3 0.............................. LeeNewnes(5) 4 48?
(Nick Lampard) *t.k.h: hld up in tch: rdn and wknd wl over 2f out: n.d after* **100/1**

8 *shd* **Veradis** 3-8-9 0.............................. LukeMorris 5 48?
(Clive Cox) *sn bustled along in last trio: in tch tl 3f out: sn outpcd and n.d after* **25/1**

00 **9** *64* **Ellies Girl (IRE)**[22] 1998 3-8-9 0.............................. ChrisCatlin 7 —
(Ronald Harris) *nvr gng wl in last and sn pushed along: lost tch 5f out: t.o fnl 3f* **150/1**

2m 12.43s (1.93) **Going Correction** -0.25s/f (Firm)
WFA 3 from 5yo 13lb **9** Ran SP% **114.3**
Speed ratings (Par 100): **82,81,81,78,77 72,72,72,20**
toteswingers:1&2: £5.20, 2&3: £2.10, 1&3: £4.50 CSF £31.87 TOTE £13.10: £3.40, £1.10, £1.20; EX 40.40 Trifecta £170.00 Pool: £953.91 - 4.15 winning units..
Owner Saif Ali **Bred** Adena Springs **Trained** Newmarket, Suffolk

FOCUS

This looked a potentially decent fillies' maiden - some powerful connections were represented - but the pace was just modest and a couple of likely candidates failed to handle the quick ground. Muddling form, rated around the race averages.

2640 LINGFIELD PARK COUNTRYSIDE EVENING 4TH JUNE MEDIAN AUCTION MAIDEN STKS (DIV I) 6f (P)

3:50 (3:51) (Class 6) 2-Y-O **£1,364** (£403; £201) **Stalls** Low

Form RPR

1 **Redact (IRE)** 2-9-3 0.............................. RichardHughes 1 81+
(Richard Hannon) *s.i.s: sn pushed along and wl outpcd in last trio: hdwy 1/2-way: chsd ldng quartet and in tch 2f out: swtchd wd wl over 1f out: str run 1f out: led fnl 100yds: sn clr: eased nr fin* **11/4**[2]

0222 **2** *3* **Rooknrasbryripple**[7] 2416 2-8-9 0.............................. MartinHarley(3) 6 64
(Mick Channon) *t.k.h: chsd ldrs: rdn and ev ch ent fnl f tl outpcd by wnr fnl 100yds* **5/1**[3]

3 **3** *¾* **Red Alpha (IRE)**[16] 2173 2-9-3 0.............................. RyanMoore 2 67
(Jeremy Noseda) *trckd ldrs: rdn and effrt over 1f out: drvn ent fnl f: ev ch ins fnl f tl outpcd by wnr fnl 100yds* **1/1**[1]

0 **4** *hd* **Illustrious Lad (IRE)**[52] 1268 2-9-3 0.............................. PatCosgrave 9 66
(Jim Boyle) *dwlt: sn rcvrd and pressing ldr: rdn to ld over 1f out: drvn ent fnl f: hdd: outpcd by wnr and lost 2nd fnl 100yds* **66/1**

5 *2 ¼* **Fire Chip** 2-9-3 0.............................. JimCrowley 10 56
(Peter Winkworth) *v.s.a: wl bhd: hdwy on outer into midfield and rn wd bnd 2f out: styd on same pce and no imp after* **14/1**

5 **6** *nse* **Spring Daisy (IRE)**[44] 1451 2-8-12 0.............................. RussKennemore 7 51
(Tom Dascombe) *led tl rdn and hdd over 2f out: wknd ins fnl f* **12/1**

0 **7** *14* **Arbeejay**[31] 1757 2-8-12 0.............................. RichardThomas 5 9
(Paul Burgoyne) *s.i.s: racd in midfield: rdn and struggling over 3f out: lost tch over 2f out* **100/1**

8 *1 ½* **Our Boy Billy** 2-9-3 0.............................. EddieAhern 3 10
(Robert Cowell) *s.i.s: a wl outpcd in last trio* **20/1**

9 *½* **Goldies Band** 2-8-12 0.............................. KirstyMilczarek 8 3
(Phil McEntee) *sn pushed along in midfield: rdn and lost pl qckly over 2f out: wl bhd over 1f out* **100/1**

1m 13.96s (2.06) **Going Correction** +0.20s/f (Slow) **9** Ran SP% **115.9**
Speed ratings (Par 91): **94,90,89,88,84 84,65,63,63**
CSF £16.69 TOTE £4.30: £1.60, £1.10, £1.80; EX 19.10 Trifecta £25.80 Pool: £641.74 - 13.35 winning units..
Owner Kennet Valley Thoroughbreds Iii **Bred** D And Mrs D Veitch **Trained** East Everleigh, Wilts
■ Stewards' Enquiry : Russ Kennemore one-day ban: careless riding (Jun 19)

FOCUS

The visual impression was of an overly strong pace and that view is supported by hand times. The leader made it to the top of the straight around 1.10 seconds quicker than the pacesetter in the second division, yet the final time was only 0.52 seconds faster than the following leg. The runner-up is the key to the form.

NOTEBOOK

Redact(IRE) was detached from the main group early following a sluggish start, but this was still a taking performance. While it's clear the leaders didn't finish particularly quickly, the winner did well to recover into a challenging position and his finishing kick shows he's pretty useful. A half-brother to a 7f winner out of a successful sprinter in Italy, he deserves extra credit considering Richard Hannon's juveniles have not been as forward this year as they were last season. Indeed in 2010 the stable's record with 2-y-o newcomers from March through to May was 15-45 (33.3%), compared to just 6-46 (13%) over the same period in 2011. (op 7-2 tchd 4-1 in places)

Rooknrasbryripple was no match at all for the winner, but she kept on well enough considering she'd been a bit keen chasing the overly strong pace. She has now finished runner-up on her last four starts (including in a match on her previous outing), but she can win a race and looks the type to do okay in nurseries. (op 4-1)

Red Alpha(IRE) didn't build on the form he showed when third over 5f at Kempton on his debut, finding only the one pace. A drop back in trip might help. (op 6-5 tchd 10-11, 5-4 in places)

Illustrious Lad(IRE) paid for racing up with the quick gallop, but this was still a big improvement on the form he showed on his only previous start at Windsor 52 days earlier.

Fire Ship Official explanation: jockey said gelding was slowly away

Spring Daisy(IRE) probably went off a bit too fast. She ran green on her debut, but has clearly learnt plenty and should be suited by a drop in trip. (op 10-1)
Goldies Band Official explanation: jockey said filly ran very green

2641 LINGFIELD PARK COUNTRYSIDE EVENING 4TH JUNE MEDIAN AUCTION MAIDEN STKS (DIV II) 6f (P)
4:20 (4:20) (Class 6) 2-Y-O **£1,364** (£403; £201) **Stalls** Low

Form RPR

1 **Illaunglass (IRE)** 2-8-12 0 RyanMoore 10 77+
(Jeremy Noseda) *flashed tail leaving stalls: sn chsng ldr: shkn up and flashed tail 2f out: rdn to ld over 1f out: in command ins fnl f: rdn out* **8/15**[1]

4 2 2 **Quick Bite (IRE)**[22] 1996 2-8-12 0 LukeMorris 7 71+
(Hugo Palmer) *chsd ldrs: rdn and effrt ent fnl 2f: swtchd rt and drvn ent fnl f: r.o to chse wnr wl ins fnl f: no threat to wnr* **22/1**

4 3 1 ¼ **Maltease Ah**[9] 2380 2-8-12 0 DarryllHolland 6 67
(Richard Fahey) *led: rdn ent fnl 2f: hdd over 1f out: drvn and styd on same pce ins fnl f* **16/1**

0 4 3 ¼ **Dressed In Lace**[12] 2309 2-8-12 0 LiamKeniry 2 57
(Andrew Balding) *chsd ldng pair: rdn and effrt on inner over 1f out: wknd fnl 150yds* **16/1**

6 5 1 ¼ **Calendar King**[9] 2380 2-9-0 0 MartinHarley(3) 9 59
(Mick Channon) *t.k.h: hld up in tch in midfield: rdn and fnd little over 1f out: sn hung lft and btn* **25/1**

6 shd **Responsive** 2-8-12 0 SteveDrowne 5 53+
(Hughie Morrison) *hld up in tch: nt clr run briefly over 2f out: rdn and styd on same pce fr wl over 1f out* **12/1**[3]

7 4 **Gadreel (IRE)** 2-9-3 0 RichardHughes 4 46
(Richard Hannon) *s.i.s: bhd: hdwy on outer over 3f out: no prog and btn wl over 1f out: wl hld and swtchd lft ins fnl f* **16/1**

33 8 1 ½ **Worth**[31] 1765 2-8-12 0 MartinDwyer 8 37
(Brian Meehan) *s.i.s: a in last pair: rdn and wknd wl over 1f out* **4/1**[2]

0 9 ¾ **Fresteem**[28] 1835 2-9-3 0 IanMongan 1 39
(Luke Dace) *taken down early: t.k.h: hld up in tch: rdn wl over 1f out: sn wknd* **100/1**

1m 14.48s (2.58) **Going Correction** +0.20s/f (Slow) **9** Ran SP% **119.8**
Speed ratings (Par 91): **90,87,85,81,79 79,74,72,71**
toteswingers:1&2: £4.60, 2&3: £10.80, 1&3: £4.60 CSF £20.25 TOTE £1.50: £1.10, £4.40, £3.40; EX 21.60 Trifecta £100.00 £1033.82 - 7.65 winning units..
Owner S E Construction (Kent) Ltd **Bred** R O'Callaghan And D Veitch **Trained** Newmarket, Suffolk

FOCUS
The time was 0.52 seconds slower than the first division, although that race was run at a stronger tempo. the winner is the type to rate higher.

NOTEBOOK
Illaunglass(IRE), a 54,000gns half-sister to 1m Listed winner Redolent, has an entry in the Group 1 Moyglare Stud Stakes and Jeremy Noseda said afterwards the filly had worked better than Regal Realm, who made a winning debut at odds of 25-1 at Newmarket the previous week, so that explains a starting price of 8-15 for this one. She fully justified the support, basically proving a notch above this lot, although she did flash her tail on more than occasion including when flicked with the whip. This was a fair performance, with her doing well to get a handy position from stall ten, and she didn't have a hard race. She has the scope to improve and it wouldn't surprise to see her turn up in the Albany Stakes at Royal Ascot, although that will require a lot more and she might not want the ground too quick. (op 8-13 tchd 4-6 in places)
Quick Bite(IRE) stepped up a little on the form of her recent Kempton debut and might find an ordinary maiden. (op 20-1)
Maltease Ah probably improved a bit on the form of her 5f debut here, although she didn't see her race out after leading. (tchd 14-1)
Dressed In Lace left behind the form of a moderate Newbury debut and can be expected to come on again for this.
Responsive, a £50,000 purchase, made a satisfactory introduction. (op 11-1)
Worth was well below the form she showed in a couple of 5f turf maidens, not recovering from a slow start. (op 9-2)

2642 LINGFIELD MARRIOTT HOTEL & COUNTRY CLUB (S) STKS 7f (P)
4:50 (4:50) (Class 6) 3-Y-O+ **£1,706** (£503; £252) **Stalls** Low

Form RPR

2-50 1 **Arrow Storm (USA)**[24] 1949 3-8-11 67 RussKennemore 6 67
(Tom Dascombe) *taken down early: mde all: rdn wl over 1f out: drvn and hrd pressed ins fnl f: hld on cl home: all out* **11/4**[1]

-556 2 nse **Desert Auction (IRE)**[7] 2428 4-9-7 75 (v¹) MartinDwyer 11 71
(Dean Ivory) *chsd wnr thrght: rdn and effrt 2f out: drvn and kpt on to chal 1f out: kpt on: jst hld* **4/1**[2]

0502 3 4 **Clearing House**[9] 2386 6-9-13 57 KirstyMilczarek 7 66
(John Ryan) *wl off the pce towards rr: rdn and effrt whn nt clr run jst over 2f out: wnt modest 4th wl over 1f out: kpt on to go 3rd ins fnl f: nvr trbld ldrs* **6/1**

-003 4 1 ¾ **Custom House (IRE)**[22] 1999 3-8-11 72 RyanMoore 9 51
(Richard Hannon) *hld up in midfield: rdn and struggling enterng fnl 2f: hung lft and no hdwy over 1f out: plugged on to go 4th wl ins fnl f* **5/1**[3]

4550 5 ¾ **Bold Ring**[22] 2001 5-9-2 55 EddieCreighton 4 48
(Edward Creighton) *chsd ldng pair: rdn 4f out: outpcd by ldng pair wl over 1f out: wl btn 1f out: lost 2 pls ins fnl f* **25/1**

4300 6 2 ¾ **Gallantry**[16] 2178 9-9-13 68 JimmyQuinn 8 52
(Michael Squance) *in tch in midfield: drvn and outpcd jst over 2f out: wknd wl over 1f out* **5/1**[3]

1006 7 9 **Guildenstern (IRE)**[15] 2206 9-9-10 50 (t) MartinHarley(3) 10 28
(Alastair Lidderdale) *stdd s: hld up wl off the pce in last trio: rdn and no hdwy ent fnl 2f: sn wl bhd* **25/1**

4-00 8 12 **Bahkov (IRE)**[17] 2155 5-9-2 50 HarryBentley(5) 1 —
(Eric Wheeler) *taken down early: a bhd: lost tch over 2f out: t.o* **20/1**

20-0 9 4 **Moonlight Serenade**[64] 1045 4-9-2 50 SteveDrowne 5 —
(Simon Earle) *a bhd: lost tch over 2f out: t.o* **33/1**

-U04 10 22 **Dusty Spirit**[10] 2356 4-9-0 72 (t) JakePayne(7) 2 —
(Bill Turner) *s.i.s: swtchd to outer after 1f: stdy hdwy to chse ldrs over 4f out tl wknd over 2f out: eased fr wl over 1f out: t.o whn rdr lost irons wl ins fnl f* **20/1**

1m 26.16s (1.36) **Going Correction** +0.20s/f (Slow)
WFA 3 from 4yo+ 10lb **10** Ran SP% **114.4**
Speed ratings (Par 101): **100,99,95,93,92 89,79,65,60,35**
toteswingers:1&2: £3.20, 2&3: £5.60, 1&3: £3.70 CSF £12.16 TOTE £3.40: £2.00, £2.10, £2.30; EX 17.10 Trifecta £85.40 Pool: £1123.88 - 9.73 winning units..The winner was bought in for 5,200gns.
Owner B Keswick **Bred** Fausto Martellozzo **Trained** Malpas, Cheshire

FOCUS
The first two finishers raced one-two pretty much throughout and those held up had little hope. The winner did not need to match his 2yo best.
Clearing House Official explanation: jockey said gelding was denied a clear run
Moonlight Serenade Official explanation: jockey said filly had no more to give
Dusty Spirit Official explanation: jockey said gelding lost a shoe at the start

2643 EDENBROOK FILLIES' H'CAP 7f (P)
5:20 (5:20) (Class 5) (0-75,74) 3-Y-O **£2,388** (£705; £352) **Stalls** Low

Form RPR

2-34 1 **Queen Of Cash (IRE)**[15] 2200 3-9-4 71 JimCrowley 6 80
(Hughie Morrison) *chsd ldr tl led over 2f out: rdn wl over 1f out: in command and styd on wl ins fnl f: rdn out* **15/2**

046- 2 2 ¼ **Pencarrow**[222] 7087 3-9-6 73 FrankieDettori 4 76
(Mahmood Al Zarooni) *in tch: effrt to chse wnr 2f out: styd on same pce u.p ins fnl f* **9/2**[2]

1-23 3 ½ **Romantic Wish**[45] 1446 3-9-4 74 SeanLevey(3) 5 75
(Robert Mills) *dwlt: sn in tch in midfield: rdn and hdwy ent fnl 2f: chsd ldrs over 1f out: styd on same pce u.p ins fnl f* **9/2**[2]

52-2 4 2 ¾ **Psychic's Dream**[36] 1607 3-9-5 72 AdamKirby 11 66+
(Marco Botti) *stdd and swtchd lft after s: hld up in last pair: nt clr run over 2f out: rdn and hdwy wl over 1f out: kpt on to go 4th fnl 100yds: nvr gng to rch ldrs: eased towards fin* **6/1**[3]

3-34 5 2 **Miss Mediator (USA)**[15] 2192 3-9-7 74 PatDobbs 9 63
(Richard Hannon) *chsd ldrs on outer: rdn and unable qck ent fnl 2f: wknd jst over 1f out* **14/1**

350- 6 1 ½ **Fluvial (IRE)**[224] 7035 3-9-5 72 AhmedAjtebi 1 57
(Mahmood Al Zarooni) *chsd ldrs: rdn and effrt wl over 1f out: btn jst ins fnl f: fdd fnl 150yds* **18/1**

43-5 7 1 ½ **Beso (IRE)**[47] 1393 3-9-2 69 RyanMoore 2 50+
(Luca Cumani) *racd in last pair: rdn along over 4f out: drvn and sme hdwy 2f out: no prog and btn ent fnl f* **10/3**[1]

6-26 8 4 ½ **Zafaraan**[17] 2157 3-8-13 66 TomQueally 7 34
(Peter Chapple-Hyam) *in tch: lost pl and wd bnd 2f out: sn wknd wl bhd ins fnl f* **14/1**

524- 9 1 ¾ **Map Of Heaven**[202] 7418 3-9-3 70 LiamJones 8 34
(William Haggas) *hld up in tch: rdn and hung lft wl over 1f out: sn wknd and wl btn* **13/2**

4430 10 ½ **Toms River Tess (IRE)**[15] 2200 3-9-2 69 KirstyMilczarek 3 31
(Zoe Davison) *taken down early and led to s: led tl hdd and rdn over 2f out: wknd qckly over 1f out* **50/1**

1m 26.15s (1.35) **Going Correction** +0.20s/f (Slow) **10** Ran SP% **119.4**
Speed ratings (Par 96): **100,97,96,93,91 89,88,82,80,80**
toteswingers:1&2: £6.80, 2&3: £6.60, 1&3: £8.90 CSF £42.29 CT £173.54 TOTE £10.00: £2.80, £2.00, £1.30; EX 53.40 Trifecta £511.70 Part won. Pool: £691.52 - 0.61 winning units. Pool of £269.69 winning units..
Owner Hugh Scott-Barrett And Partners **Bred** Grangemore Stud **Trained** East Ilsley, Berks

FOCUS
The time was almost identical to the earlier older-horse seller, and like in that race, it paid to be handy. Sound form amongst the principals.
Miss Mediator(USA) Official explanation: jockey said filly hung right
T/Plt: £20.00 to a £1 stake. Pool of £55,057.99 - 2,004.68 winning tickets. T/Qpdt: £10.10 to a £1 stake. Pool of £3,599.21 - 262.58 winning tickets. SP

2436 SANDOWN (R-H)
Thursday, June 2

OFFICIAL GOING: Sprint course - good to firm; round course - good (good to firm in back straight; sprint 8.7, round 8.4)
Back straight and bend at innermost configuration, home straight dolled out 4yds and distances as advertised.
Wind: Light, behind Weather: Sunny, warm

2644 KILLIK & CO WEALTH MANAGEMENT MAIDEN AUCTION STKS 5f 6y
6:00 (6:00) (Class 5) 2-Y-O **£2,266** (£674; £337; £168) **Stalls** Low

Form RPR

1 **I'm Still The Man (IRE)** 2-8-6 0 KierenFox(3) 3 73
(Bill Turner) *trckd ldng trio and racd against rail: gap appeared and rdn to ld over 1f out: sn in command* **25/1**

2 2 1 ½ **Marcus Augustus (IRE)**[21] 2023 2-9-2 0 RichardHughes 9 75
(Richard Hannon) *wnt lft s: pressed ldng pair but wl off the rail: nt qckn over 1f out: styd on to take 2nd nr fin* **4/6**[1]

33 3 ¾ **Red Mischief (IRE)**[12] 2302 2-8-2 0 ow1 JohnFahy(3) 6 61
(Harry Dunlop) *pressed ldr: carried lft and nt qckn over 1f out: chsd wnr but no imp fnl f: lost 2nd nr fin* **5/1**[2]

4 1 ¼ **Imelda Mayhem** 2-8-6 0 LukeMorris 5 57
(J S Moore) *in tch: rdn after 2f: outpcd 2f out: styd on fnl f: nrst fin* **12/1**[3]

6 5 shd **Faraway**[17] 2143 2-8-13 0 ChrisCatlin 4 64
(William Haggas) *settled in 7th: pushed along 1/2-way: sn outpcd: kpt on quite wl fnl f: nrst fin* **20/1**

6 6 2 ¾ **Concordia Notte (IRE)**[12] 2309 2-8-3 0 AndrewHeffernan(3) 1 48
(Paul D'Arcy) *led against rail: edgd lft and hdd over 1f out: rdr sn dropped whip: wkng qckly whn temporarily eased ins fnl f* **5/1**[2]

7 nk **Clarkson (IRE)** 2-8-11 0 FergusSweeney 8 51
(Jamie Osborne) *settled towards rr and off the rail: shkn up and outpcd 2f out: n.d after* **12/1**[3]

8 1 ¾ **High Five Prince (IRE)** 2-8-11 0 LiamKeniry 7 45
(Mark Usher) *s.s: a last: shkn up and no prog 2f out* **66/1**

61.52 secs (-0.08) **Going Correction** -0.125s/f (Firm) **8** Ran SP% **118.8**
Speed ratings (Par 93): **95,92,91,89,89 84,84,81**
toteswingers:1&2:£4.40, 1&3:£8.60, 2&3:£1.90 CSF £43.71 TOTE £36.70: £6.30, £1.10, £1.40; EX 71.10.
Owner Jason Tucker **Bred** Jaykayeen **Trained** Sigwells, Somerset
■ Stewards' Enquiry : John Fahy caution: careless riding; £650 fine - jockey changed his boots after weighing out

FOCUS
The back straight and the bend were at their innermost configuration and the home straight was dolled out four yards. The 5f course was riding quick, and this was ordinary form for the track. The balances of the placed horses sets the level.

NOTEBOOK
I'm Still The Man(IRE), never far away against the rail, was rousted along to lead approaching the furlong pole and held on well to his advantage. Bill Turner's fifth 2yo winner of the season, he is entitled to improve for this but might not be simple to place in the short term. By a sprinter, but with stamina on the dam's side, the colt should stay 6f in time. His target is reportedly a valuable sales race at Ascot in August.

Marcus Augustus(IRE) set the standard on his debut second at Salisbury to stablemate Airborne Again. The outside draw was less than ideal and he compounded matters by swerving to his left when leaving the stalls, but soon raced in touch. He lacked a change of gear when brought under pressure, but moved through into second late on and should go one better in the near future. (tchd 8-11 and 4-5 in places)
Red Mischief(IRE) has finished third on each of her three starts and has probably shown a similar level of form each time. The drop to the minimum trip was no inconvenience to her, but she was not helped by being carried to her left at a crucial stage of the race. (op 4-1)
Imelda Mayhem, a half-sister to several winners out of a Listed juvenile scorer, was the first off the bridle but was keeping on towards the finish and will come on for the experience. (op 14-1)
Faraway was running on late up the rail and improved on what he achieved on his Bath debut. (op 25-1)
Concordia Notte(IRE), who showed a little promise on her debut and was ideally drawn in one, came in for support. After losing her lead and drifting left, she was already dropping back when she stumbled on a crossing inside the last. (op 6-1)
Clarkson(IRE), whose yard won this with Treadwell two years ago, was never a factor from his wide draw but is probably capable of a fair bit better with the experience under his belt. (op 14-1 tchd 16-1)

2645 BET ON LIVE TENNIS AT TOTESPORT.COM H'CAP 5f 6y
6:30 (6:31) (Class 4) (0-85,82) 3-Y-O+ **£4,079** (£1,214; £606; £303) **Stalls** Low

Form RPR
031- **1** **Sharpened Edge**[218] 7180 5-9-8 **76**.............................. FergusSweeney 3 85
(Christopher Mason) *mde all and racd against rail: drvn 2f out: hld on wl nr fin* **12/1**
-005 **2** *nk* **Fantasy Explorer**[20] 2069 8-9-6 **74**.............................. DaneO'Neill 4 82
(John Quinn) *trckd ldng trio: effrt 2f out: rdn to chse wnr fnl f: edgd rt: jst hld* **5/1**[2]
00-3 **3** *hd* **Osiris Way**[20] 2069 9-10-0 **82**.............................. GeorgeBaker 11 89+
(Patrick Chamings) *racd wd: trckd ldrs in 6th: sltly checked over 1f out: r.o fnl f to take 3rd nr fin* **13/2**
0646 **4** *1* **Brandywell Boy (IRE)**[3] 2557 8-9-1 **69**.............................. NeilCallan 1 75+
(Dominic Ffrench Davis) *trckd ldrs in 5th and racd against rail: clsd over 1f out: trying to chal between rivals whn squeezed out last 150yds: nt rcvr* **8/1**
4002 **5** *½* **The Wee Chief (IRE)**[22] 2001 5-8-13 **67**..............................(t) LiamKeniry 2 69
(Jimmy Fox) *dwlt sltly: hld up in 7th: gng bttr than most 2f out: rdn and sme prog jst over 1f out: fnd little and no imp last 150yds* **6/1**[3]
1602 **6** *nk* **Taurus Twins**[13] 2250 5-9-9 **77**..............................(b) RichardHughes 9 78+
(Richard Price) *dwlt sltly: settled in last trio: shkn up 2f out: nt clr run on outer briefly over 1f out: r.o last 150yds: nrst fin* **8/1**
-04 **7** *1* **Poppanan (USA)**[19] 2095 5-9-5 **78**.............................. AdamBeschizza(5) 5 75
(Simon Dow) *scratchy to post: dwlt sltly: settled in last trio: rdn and sme prog over 1f out: keeping on but no ch whn short of room briefly ins fnl f* **9/2**[1]
0306 **8** *2½* **Cape Royal**[2] 2585 11-9-7 **75**..............................(bt) PatCosgrave 10 63+
(Milton Bradley) *racd one off rail: w wnr: rdn 2f out: sing to lose pl whn bdly squeezed out 1f out: eased* **12/1**
2123 **9** *½* **Island Legend (IRE)**[23] 1982 5-8-9 **63**..............................(p) LukeMorris 7 49
(Milton Bradley) *racd wd: pressed ldng pair 3f: edgd lft and wknd over 1f out* **14/1**
2100 **10** *1¼* **Picansort**[96] 698 4-9-1 **69**..............................(v) JimmyQuinn 12 51
(Brett Johnson) *dwlt sltly: hld up and a in last trio: shkn up over 1f out: no ch whn nowhere to go ins fnl f* **25/1**
350- **11** *9* **Imjin River (IRE)**[349] 3174 4-8-11 **70**.............................. AshleyMorgan(5) 6 19
(Mark H Tompkins) *dwlt sltly: struggling after 2f: sn last: t.o* **16/1**

60.29 secs (-1.31) **Going Correction** -0.125s/f (Firm) **11** Ran SP% **116.5**
Speed ratings (Par 105): **105,104,104,102,101 101,99,95,94,92 78**
toteswingers:1&2:£17.90, 1&3:£9.30, 2&3:£4.60 CSF £70.34 CT £438.79 TOTE £15.30: £3.40, £2.90, £2.40; EX 109.00.
Owner Christopher & Annabelle Mason **Bred** Christopher J Mason **Trained** Caewent, Monmouthshire
■ A winner with his first runner for Christopher Mason.
■ Stewards' Enquiry : Dane O'Neill caution: used whip with excessive frequency

FOCUS
A fair handicap where a low draw proved an advantage. Not many got involved with several meeting trouble in running. The winner is rated back to her best.
Island Legend(IRE) Official explanation: jockey said gelding hung left throughout

2646 KATHE KAYE MEMORIAL H'CAP 7f 16y
7:05 (7:05) (Class 4) (0-85,85) 3-Y-O **£4,079** (£1,214; £606; £303) **Stalls** Low

Form RPR
1246 **1** **May's Boy**[17] 2147 3-8-1 **70**..............................(p) HarryBentley(5) 6 79
(Mark Usher) *trckd ldng pair: darted through on inner to ld over 2f out and sn booted more than 2 l clr: styd on strly* **33/1**
33-4 **2** *2½* **Local Singer (IRE)**[15] 2199 3-9-2 **80**.............................. JimCrowley 11 82
(Malcolm Saunders) *hld up in 6th: rdn over 2f out: styd on fr over 1f out to take 2nd last strides* **8/1**
-501 **3** *nk* **Silverware (USA)**[35] 1626 3-8-12 **76**.............................. RichardHughes 3 77
(Richard Hannon) *trckd ldng trio: shkn up 3f out: disp 2nd wl over 1f out but no imp on wnr: kpt on* **4/1**[2]
1-24 **4** *nk* **Majestic Dream (IRE)**[12] 2319 3-9-6 **84**..............................(v) FrankieDettori 7 84
(Walter Swinburn) *trckd ldr to 3f out: sn shkn up: disp 2nd over 1f out but no imp on wnr: one pce last 100yds* **11/4**[1]
61- **5** *1* **Chill (IRE)**[241] 6626 3-8-9 **73**.............................. KierenFallon 2 70+
(Luca Cumani) *settled in 7th: pushed along 3f out and no prog: rdn 2f out: kpt on fnl f: n.d* **11/2**
046- **6** *1¼* **Deny**[220] 7112 3-8-7 **71** ow1.............................. RyanMoore 9 65+
(Sir Michael Stoute) *s.s: hld up in 9th: shkn up wl over 2f out and no prog: kpt on fr over 1f out* **5/1**[3]
5-1 **7** *½* **Great Acclaim**[34] 1654 3-9-0 **78**.............................. PatCosgrave 10 71
(James Fanshawe) *hld up in 8th: swtchd ins and pushed along 2f out: kpt on one pce after: nvr nr to chal* **11/1**
0-00 **8** *3¾* **Serena's Pride**[13] 2255 3-8-8 **75**.............................. MatthewDavies(3) 4 58
(Alan Jarvis) *led to over 2f out: wknd over 1f out* **25/1**
064- **9** *3¾* **Cocohatchee**[238] 6690 3-8-8 **72**.............................. LukeMorris 5 45
(Pat Phelan) *trckd ldrs in 5th: effrt on inner 2f out: trying to chal for a pl whn no room over 1f out: hmpd sn after and eased* **14/1**
-005 **10** *½* **Royal Opera**[31] 1754 3-8-7 **71**.............................. CathyGannon 1 42
(Rod Millman) *hmpd sn after s and stmbld: a in last: no prog over 2f out* **40/1**

1m 28.01s (-1.49) **Going Correction** -0.175s/f (Firm) **10** Ran SP% **114.1**
Speed ratings (Par 101): **101,98,97,97,96 94,94,90,85,85**
toteswingers:1&2:£35.80, 1&3:£22.00, 2&3:£7.40 CSF £268.03 CT £1324.48 TOTE £31.70: £3.50, £2.40, £1.90; EX 307.10.
Owner High Five Racing **Bred** John Richardson **Trained** Upper Lambourn, Berks

FOCUS
Zaahid took this event in 2007 before developing into a smart handicapper. This is ordinary handicap form, with the winner carrying over some of his AW progress and the next three close to form. The pace was not strong and it proved difficult making ground from the back.
Silverware(USA) Official explanation: jockey said colt hung right

2647 BET ON LIVE CRICKET AT TOTESPORT.COM H'CAP 1m 14y
7:35 (7:37) (Class 4) (0-85,85) 4-Y-O+ **£4,079** (£1,214; £606; £303) **Stalls** Low

Form RPR
2550 **1** **Norman Orpen (IRE)**[28] 1826 4-9-7 **85**.............................. KierenFallon 6 93
(Jane Chapple-Hyam) *trckd ldng pair: plld out and rdn jst over 1f out: led last 150yds: drvn out and hld on* **15/2**[1]
0-56 **2** *hd* **First Cat**[7] 2441 4-9-3 **81**.............................. RichardHughes 5 90+
(Richard Hannon) *hld up in last pair: stl there over 2f out: effrt whn nt clr run over 1f out: str run fnl f: jst failed* **12/1**
0536 **3** *½* **First Post (IRE)**[20] 2066 4-8-11 **80**.............................. HarryBentley(5) 7 86
(Derek Haydn Jones) *wl in tch on outer: hung lft fr over 2f out: prog to chal and w ldrs over 1f out: continued to hang lft but styd on: jst hld* **10/1**[3]
6-00 **4** *nse* **Viva Vettori**[19] 2105 7-9-5 **83**.............................. NickyMackay 4 89+
(David Elsworth) *hld up in midfield: effrt and looking for room fr 2f out: rdn and styd on strly ins fnl f: gaining at fin* **15/2**[1]
04-0 **5** *nk* **Directorship**[40] 1529 5-9-7 **85**.............................. GeorgeBaker 14 90
(Patrick Chamings) *forced to r wd early: trckd ldrs: effrt to cl 2f out: rdn to chal and w wnr ins fnl f: nt qckn and lost pls last strides* **8/1**[2]
16-5 **6** *nk* **Fantasy Gladiator**[19] 2111 5-9-2 **80**..............................(p) JimmyQuinn 17 85
(Robert Cowell) *hld up towards rr: stdy prog towards inner fr over 2f out: drvn over 1f out: styd on: nvr quite able to chal* **25/1**
3-40 **7** *½* **Santefisio**[21] 2020 5-9-5 **83**.............................. WilliamBuick 15 86
(Peter Makin) *hld up last and wl off the pce: effrt on outer over 2f out: rdn and styd on fr over 1f out: nrst fin* **14/1**
-130 **8** *hd* **Chilli Green**[22] 2000 4-9-5 **83**.............................. DaneO'Neill 13 86
(John Akehurst) *led: rdn 2f out: hdd and fdd last 150yds* **20/1**
16- **9** *1¼* **Gypsy Carnival**[246] 6467 4-8-12 **76**.............................. JimCrowley 3 76
(Ralph Beckett) *t.k.h: trckd ldrs in 5th: nt qckn 2f out: fdd fnl f* **8/1**[2]
5-00 **10** *shd* **Signor Verdi**[19] 2105 4-9-6 **84**.............................. MartinDwyer 12 84
(Brian Meehan) *hld up in midfield and racd wd: sltly checked over 2f out: nt qckn and lost pl sn after: plugged on* **20/1**
1203 **11** *1¾* **Night Lily (IRE)**[13] 2269 5-8-13 **80**.............................. AndrewHeffernan(3) 16 76
(Paul D'Arcy) *dwlt: hld up in last trio: no room on inner 3f out: n.d after: kpt on fnl f* **8/1**[2]
5216 **12** *nk* **Edgewater (IRE)**[12] 2310 4-9-0 **78**.............................. RyanMoore 1 73
(John Akehurst) *trckd ldrs on inner: nt qckn 2f out: lost pl fr jst over 1f out: fdd* **8/1**[2]
-105 **13** *nse* **Willow Dancer (IRE)**[16] 2178 7-8-13 **77**..............................(p) AdamKirby 11 72
(Walter Swinburn) *pressed ldr to over 1f out: wknd* **14/1**
26-0 **14** *nk* **Kings Bayonet**[36] 1603 4-8-13 **77**.............................. HayleyTurner 8 71
(Alan King) *hld up in midfield: shkn up and no imp on ldrs over 2f out: grad wknd* **25/1**
6-04 **15** *2½* **Master Mylo (IRE)**[19] 2111 4-8-13 **77**.............................. TomQueally 2 66
(Dean Ivory) *hld up in midfield on inner: no prog over 2f out: sn lost pl and btn* **20/1**
0-00 **16** *11* **L'Hirondelle (IRE)**[84] 822 7-8-13 **77**.............................. NeilCallan 10 40
(Michael Attwater) *prom in 4th tl wknd over 2f out: t.o* **66/1**

1m 42.01s (-1.29) **Going Correction** -0.175s/f (Firm) **16** Ran SP% **121.6**
Speed ratings (Par 105): **99,98,98,98,97 97,97,96,95,95 93,93,93,93,90 79**
toteswingers:1&2:£27.00, 1&3:£12.30, 2&3:£14.50 CSF £85.27 CT £918.20 TOTE £8.30: £2.60, £2.50, £2.90, £2.60; EX 92.50.
Owner Gordon Li **Bred** Kevin Walsh **Trained** Dalham, Suffolk

FOCUS
An open handicap which was not strong run considering the size of the field. The winner recorded a 3lb turf best, with the third and fourth the best guides.
First Post(IRE) Official explanation: jockey said gelding hung left

2648 POUR TO PROFIT AND UDS MAIDEN STKS 1m 2f 7y
8:10 (8:13) (Class 5) 3-Y-O **£2,266** (£674; £337; £168) **Stalls** Low

Form RPR
2 **1** **Timeline**[13] 2258 3-9-3 0.............................. AhmedAjtebi 1 98+
(Mahmood Al Zarooni) *t.k.h: trckd ldrs: cruised through to ld over 2f out: rn green whn shkn up but sn drew rt away: eased fnl f: impressive* **11/2**[3]
0 **2** *5* **New Hampshire (USA)**[36] 1606 3-9-3 0.............................. RobertHavlin 6 83
(John Gosden) *wl enough plcd bhd ldrs: shkn up over 2f out: kpt on to take 2nd over 1f out: no ch w wnr* **50/1**
3 *1½* **Highland Castle** 3-9-3 0.............................. DaneO'Neill 8 80
(David Elsworth) *hld up in midfield: drvn 2f out: styd on fr over 1f out to take 3rd nr fin* **66/1**
2 **4** *nk* **Almagest**[14] 2231 3-9-3 0.............................. WilliamBuick 9 79
(John Gosden) *hld up in midfield tl quick prog to trck ldng pair 1/2-way: rdn 3f out: nt qckn 2f out: sn btn* **7/4**[1]
0 **5** *¾* **Midnight Oil**[13] 2258 3-9-3 0.............................. KierenFallon 5 78+
(Luca Cumani) *hld up in rr: swtchd to outer over 3f out: nudged along and stdy prog over 2f out: kpt on nr fin: do bttr* **33/1**
6 *2¾* **Bugler's Dream (USA)** 3-9-3 0.............................. FrankieDettori 17 72
(Mahmood Al Zarooni) *mde most to over 2f out: no ch w wnr: wknd and lost 2nd over 1f out* **14/1**
7 *1* **Astrantia** 3-8-12 0.............................. IanMongan 16 65+
(Sir Henry Cecil) *trckd ldrs on outer: stmbld after 2f: stl in chsng gp but rdn 2f out: fdd* **50/1**
0-6 **8** *3½* **Elrasheed**[50] 1321 3-9-3 0.............................. RichardHills 2 63+
(John Dunlop) *hld up wl in rr: pushed along on inner and nowhere nr ldrs over 2f out: reminder and kpt on fr over 1f out* **16/1**
0 **9** *1* **Shamacam**[36] 1605 3-9-3 0.............................. RyanMoore 10 61
(Sir Michael Stoute) *hld up wl in rr: shkn up over 2f out and nowhere nr ldrs: kpt on fr over 1f out: nrst fin* **8/1**
10 *hd* **Asterism** 3-8-12 0.............................. TomQueally 12 56+
(Sir Henry Cecil) *hld up in last pair: stl there over 2f out: pushed along and kpt on quite encouragingly fnl f* **20/1**
32 **11** *1½* **Danehill Dante (IRE)**[31] 1759 3-9-3 0.............................. RichardHughes 7 58
(Richard Hannon) *trckd ldrs on outer: rdn 3f out: no prog and btn over 2f out in chsng gp: wknd fnl f* **5/2**[2]
12 *hd* **Jiwen (CAN)** 3-8-12 0.............................. TadhgO'Shea 3 52
(Roger Varian) *slowest away: a wl in rr: pushed along and a little late prog* **25/1**
0 **13** *2¼* **Bright Abbey**[14] 2231 3-9-3 0.............................. AdamKirby 14 53
(Walter Swinburn) *hld up wl in rr: pushed along and stl there 3f out: no real prog* **100/1**

5- **14** *1 1/4* **Renoir's Lady**[321] 4103 3-8-12 0 .... HayleyTurner 4 45
(Simon Dow) *prom tl wknd qckly over 2f out* **66/1**
5 **15** *1 1/2* **Dakar (GER)**[43] 1480 3-9-3 0 .... EddieAhern 15 47
(Pat Phelan) *hld up and a wl in rr: no prog in last trio over 2f out* **100/1**
06 **16** *2 1/2* **Speed Dancer**[23] 1991 3-9-3 0 .... LukeMorris 13 42
(James Eustace) *a in rr: struggling 3f out* **150/1**
0 **17** *2 1/4* **Talbot Green**[19] 2097 3-9-3 0 .... MartinDwyer 11 38
(William Muir) *mostly pressed ldr to 3f out: wknd rapidly* **200/1**

2m 9.89s (-0.61) **Going Correction** -0.175s/f (Firm) **17** Ran SP% **125.6**
Speed ratings (Par 99): **95,91,89,89,88 86,85,83,82,82 81,80,79,78,76 74,73**
toteswingers:1&2:£66.20, 1&3:£32.70, 2&3:£207.80 CSF £273.36 TOTE £4.20: £1.70, £37.30, £36.40; EX 507.50.
Owner Godolphin **Bred** Belgrave Bloodstock Ltd **Trained** Newmarket, Suffolk

FOCUS
A fascinating maiden contested by some well-bred runners from the big yards, and plenty of winners should emerge from it in time. The pace was fairly steady. The winner impressed and looks useful.
Astrantia Official explanation: jockey said filly clipped heels

2649 BET ON THE DERBY AT TOTESPORT.COM H'CAP 1m 2f 7y
8:45 (8:45) (Class 4) (0-80,79) 4-Y-O+ **£4,079** (£1,214; £606; £303) **Stalls** Low

Form RPR
/0-6 **1** **Qaraaba**[14] 2232 4-9-1 **73** .... GeorgeBaker 8 81+
(Seamus Durack) *stdd s: hld up wl in rr: prog and looking for room 2f out: hmpd jst over 1f out: str burst ins fnl f to ld last 50yds* **25/1**
1 **2** *3/4* **Mauritino (GER)**[20] 2051 7-9-2 **74** .... JimCrowley 6 80
(Jonjo O'Neill) *hld up towards rr: stdy prog over 2f out: rdn to cl and chal last 100yds: jst outpcd* **3/1**[1]
41- **3** *hd* **Sense Of Pride**[250] 6356 4-9-4 **76** .... WilliamBuick 7 81
(John Gosden) *led 2f: chsd ldr: rdn to ld 2f out: hrd pressed fnl f: clung on tl hdd last 50yds* **6/1**[3]
01 **4** *nse* **Butler (IRE)**[18] 2124 4-9-7 **79** .... KierenFallon 15 84
(Luca Cumani) *hld up wl in rr: effrt on outer over 2f out: styd on wl fr over 1f out: tried to chal fnl f: jst outpcd* **13/2**
130- **5** *nk* **Haljaferia (UAE)**[312] 4405 5-9-5 **77** .... DaneO'Neill 16 81
(David Elsworth) *prom: waiting to chal over 2f out gng strly: chsd ldr over 1f out: rdn and nt qckn: lost pl nr fin* **25/1**
1-04 **6** *3/4* **Significant Move**[20] 2066 4-9-4 **76** .... LiamKeniry 2 79+
(Stuart Kittow) *hld up in midfield on inner: hmpd jst over 2f out: effrt again jst over 1f out: r.o but nt rcvr* **10/3**[2]
40-2 **7** *1/2* **Wiggy Smith**[17] 2150 12-9-2 **79** .... AmyScott[(5)] 12 81
(Henry Candy) *hld up in last pair: gng easily on outer 3f out: rdn 2f out: kpt on fr over 1f out: nvr rchd ldrs* **16/1**
6515 **8** *3/4* **Understory (USA)**[17] 2150 4-9-3 **75** .... NeilCallan 4 75
(Tim McCarthy) *dwlt: rcvrd to chse ldrs: rdn and cl up 2f out tl fdd ins fnl f* **40/1**
20-0 **9** *1/2* **Sohcahtoa (IRE)**[36] 1603 5-9-2 **77** .... SeanLevey[(3)] 14 76
(Robert Mills) *hld up wl in rr: pushed along over 2f out: styd on quite steadily fnl f: nvr nrr* **12/1**
0-12 **10** *3/4* **Allanit (GER)**[85] 802 7-9-2 **74** .... TomQueally 9 72
(Barney Curley) *led after 2f: kicked on over 3f out: hdd 2f out: fdd* **33/1**
05-3 **11** *nse* **Gallant Eagle (IRE)**[16] 2178 4-9-4 **76** .... PatCosgrave 11 74
(Ed de Giles) *pressed ldrs: rdn over 2f out: stl cl enough over 1f out: wknd fnl f* **14/1**
3-53 **12** *1/2* **Super Duplex**[7] 2436 4-8-4 **67** .... JemmaMarshall[(5)] 5 64
(Pat Phelan) *t.k.h: w ldrs tl wknd jst over 1f out* **16/1**
510- **13** *nk* **Broughtons Swinger**[228] 6959 4-8-7 **65** .... JamieMackay 17 61
(Willie Musson) *hld up wl in rr: sltly checked over 2f out: shuffled along and kpt on one pce after: nvr a factor* **50/1**
002 **14** *1* **Inef (IRE)**[14] 2232 4-9-2 **74** .... IanMongan 1 68
(Laura Mongan) *prom: rdn and edgd rt jst over 2f out: struggling over 1f out* **20/1**
2110 **15** *nk* **Beaubrav**[26] 1887 5-9-4 **76** ....(t) AdamKirby 3 70
(Michael Madgwick) *mostly in midfield: rdn 3f out: lost pl and btn 2f out* **22/1**
16 *1/2* **Bold Identity (IRE)**[112] 3746 5-9-6 **78** .... RichardHughes 10 71
(Richard Phillips) *hld up and sn last: rdn over 2f out: no real prog* **40/1**

2m 10.14s (-0.36) **Going Correction** -0.175s/f (Firm) **16** Ran SP% **128.4**
Speed ratings (Par 105): **94,93,93,93,92 92,91,91,90,90 90,89,89,88,88 88**
toteswingers:1&2:£16.00, 1&3:£34.50, 2&3:£6.30 CSF £97.16 CT £546.27 TOTE £38.40: £6.20, £1.30, £1.30, £2.10; EX 269.70.
Owner P A Deal **Bred** Shadwell Estate Company Limited **Trained** Lambourn, Berkshire
■ The first winner as a trainer for former jump jockey Seamus Durack.
■ Stewards' Enquiry : George Baker caution: careless riding

FOCUS
A real bunch finish to this competitive handicap, with the first 13 home separated by not much more than five lengths. The pace wound up in the straight and the time was slightly slower than the earlier 3yo maiden. The winner is rated a bit better than the bare form.
Significant Move Official explanation: jockey said gelding was denied a clear run
T/Jkpt: Not won. T/Plt: £505.70 to a £1 stake. Pool:£92,149.16 - 133.02 winning tickets T/Qpdt: £99.60 to a £1 stake. Pool:£6,393.39 - 47.50 winning tickets JN

2233 SOUTHWELL (L-H)
Thursday, June 2

OFFICIAL GOING: Standard
Wind: Light across Weather: Fine and dry

2650 GOT THE FEELING GET TO LADBROKES MAIDEN STKS 6f (F)
2:30 (2:38) (Class 5) 3-Y-O **£2,388** (£705; £352) **Stalls** Low

Form RPR
32-2 **1** **Formal Demand**[17] 2151 3-9-3 72 .... JamieSpencer 1 79+
(Edward Vaughan) *qckly away and led 2f: chsd clr ldr and wd st to stands' rail: hdwy 2f out: rdn over 1f out: styd on to ld ins fnl f* **13/8**[1]
05 **2** *2 1/4* **Beechcraft Baron (IRE)**[13] 2266 3-9-0 0 .... GilmarPereira[(3)] 2 72+
(William Haggas) *chsd ldrs: rdn along wl over 2f out: styd on ins fnl f: tk 2nd nr line* **14/1**
-500 **3** *shd* **Suddenly Susan (IRE)**[19] 2119 3-8-5 60 ....(b[1]) LeonnaMayor[(7)] 10 66
(David Nicholls) *prom on outer: led after 2f and sn clr: rdn along on inner over 1f out: wknd and hdd ins fnl f: lost 2nd nr line* **8/1**[3]
4 *5* **Stylistickhill (IRE)** 3-8-9 0 .... BillyCray[(3)] 9 50
(David Nicholls) *chsd ldrs: hdwy over 2f out: sn rdn and kpt on same pce* **16/1**
0 **5** *1 1/2* **Ducal**[13] 2266 3-8-12 0 .... RosieJessop[(5)] 13 51+
(Sir Mark Prescott Bt) *dwlt and swtchd lft s: bhd: hdwy 2f out: rdn and kpt on ins fnl f: nt rch ldrs* **12/1**
5 **6** *1/2* **Arabian Heights**[16] 2174 3-9-3 0 .... StevieDonohoe 12 49+
(Sir Mark Prescott Bt) *towards rr tl sme late hdwy* **8/1**[3]
02 **7** *1/2* **Hab Reeh**[23] 1974 3-9-3 0 ....(t) RoystonFfrench 11 47
(Clive Brittain) *reminders s and in rr tl sme late hdwy* **3/1**[2]
8 *2 3/4* **Don't Call Me Tiny (IRE)** 3-8-12 0 .... KellyHarrison 4 34
(Don Cantillon) *bhd tl sme late hdwy* **28/1**
-60 **9** *1 1/2* **Cuckney Bear**[16] 2185 3-9-3 0 .... GrahamGibbons 5 34
(Ed McMahon) *a towards rr* **33/1**
0-0 **10** *7* **Uncle Bryn**[33] 1693 3-9-0 0 .... DeclanCannon[(3)] 7 —
(John Quinn) *chsd ldng pair: wd st: rdn along over 2f out: sn drvn and wknd* **25/1**
11 *shd* **Partly Pickled** 3-9-3 0 .... PaulQuinn 8 —
(David Nicholls) *a towards rr* **20/1**
12 *4* **Minstrel Lad** 3-9-3 0 .... JamesDoyle 6 —
(Des Donovan) *a towards rr* **100/1**
13 *19* **Quebrador (GER)** 3-8-12 0 .... AdamBeschizza[(5)] 3 —
(Gay Kelleway) *dwlt: hdwy and in tch on inner 1/2-way: sn rdn along and wknd* **25/1**

1m 16.54s (0.04) **Going Correction** +0.10s/f (Slow) **13** Ran SP% **125.4**
Speed ratings (Par 99): **103,100,99,93,91 90,89,86,84,74 74,69,44**
CSF £26.79 TOTE £2.60: £1.20, £3.50, £2.20; EX 30.00.
Owner Ali Saeed **Bred** New England Stud, Lord Derby And P Vela **Trained** Newmarket, Suffolk

FOCUS
Just an ordinary maiden, and very few got into it. The level of the form revolves around the runner-up.

2651 E B F LADBROKES.COM MAIDEN FILLIES' STKS 6f (F)
3:00 (3:02) (Class 5) 2-Y-O **£3,238** (£963; £481; £240) **Stalls** Low

Form RPR
6 **1** **Greatest Dancer (IRE)**[22] 1996 2-9-0 0 .... JamieSpencer 5 81+
(Jamie Osborne) *cl up: led wl over 2f out: rdn clr over 1f out: easily* **13/8**[1]
63 **2** *8* **Silvas Romana (IRE)**[12] 2283 2-9-0 0 .... FrannyNorton 4 56
(Mark Brisbourne) *cl up: disp ld over 3f out: rdn wl over 2 out: drvn and one pce fr wl over 1f out* **7/4**[2]
3 *5* **Medam** 2-9-0 0 .... RobbieFitzpatrick 1 41+
(Shaun Harris) *rrd s and v.s.a: bhd: hdwy 1/2-way: rdn over 2f out: kpt on* **9/1**
4 *2 3/4* **Beacon Lady** 2-9-0 0 .... WilliamCarson 3 30
(Bill Turner) *sn rdn along and outpcd: a in rr* **9/2**[3]
5 *2 1/2* **Miss Medici (IRE)** 2-9-0 0 .... JamesDoyle 2 22
(Des Donovan) *slt ld: rdn along over 3f out: hdd wl over 2f out: sn drvn and wknd* **8/1**

1m 18.64s (2.14) **Going Correction** +0.10s/f (Slow) **5** Ran SP% **113.8**
Speed ratings (Par 90): **89,78,71,68,64**
CSF £5.03 TOTE £2.00: £1.10, £1.60; EX 3.90.
Owner David L Dixon **Bred** Ballyhane Stud **Trained** Upper Lambourn, Berks

FOCUS
Two of the five runners gave away whatever chance they had in the early stages, so this isn't strong form. There was an easy winner and the runner-up is the key to the form.

NOTEBOOK
Greatest Dancer(IRE) showed some promise in a fair-looking maiden at Kempton on debut and bolted up here as her only two challengers faded out of contention. (tchd 7-4, 15-8 in a place)
Silvas Romana(IRE) improved on her first run with a better performance at Chester last time, but was made to look one-paced on Fibresand. (op 13-8)
Medam ◆'s dam won a 7f Listed race as a 3-y-o, but she forfeited many lengths with a really slow start on her debut. However, she did make some eye-catching ground up and wasn't given a hard time when it was obvious she wasn't going to get involved. (op 10-1 tchd 8-1)
Beacon Lady, whose dam ran over middle-distances in France, got completely outpaced before making late modest progress. Official explanation: jockey said filly was slow into her stride (op 7-1)
Miss Medici(IRE), a half-sister to a winning Polytrack performer, was able to lay handy for most of the race and showed good speed before greenness saw her start to wander from over 1f out. Official explanation: jockey said filly hung right (op 15-2 tchd 7-1)

2652 LADBROKES MOBILE (S) STKS 1m (F)
3:30 (3:30) (Class 6) 3-Y-O **£1,706** (£503; £252) **Stalls** Low

Form RPR
-225 **1** **Classic Voice (IRE)**[26] 1904 3-8-12 71 .... SilvestreDeSousa 3 69
(Hugo Palmer) *cl up: effrt over 2f out: rdn to ld wl over 1f out: drvn clr ent fnl f: kpt on* **8/11**[1]
3122 **2** *6* **Jay Jays Joy**[14] 2236 3-9-3 65 ....(b) GrahamGibbons 8 60
(David Barron) *cl up on outer: rdn along wl over 2f out and sn outpcd: drvn over 1f out: kpt on to take 2nd nr line* **5/2**[2]
-560 **3** *3/4* **Valley Tiger**[19] 2119 3-8-7 59 .... JamesRogers[(5)] 2 53
(William Muir) *led: rdn along and jnd over 2f out: drvn and hdd wl over 1f out: wknd ent fnl f: lost 2nd nr fin* **12/1**
6604 **4** *2* **Sing Alana Sing**[12] 2307 3-8-7 43 ....(t) WilliamCarson 1 44
(Bill Turner) *chsd ldrs: rdn along bef 1/2-way: sn drvn and outpcd fr wl over 2f out* **50/1**
-660 **5** *8* **Eduardo**[17] 2166 3-8-9 57 .... PatrickDonaghy[(3)] 5 30
(Jedd O'Keeffe) *chsd ldrs: rdn along bef 1/2-way: sn outpcd* **7/1**[3]
4544 **6** *8* **Lindo Erro**[37] 1588 3-8-4 50 .... DeclanCannon[(3)] 6 —
(John Mackie) *dwlt: a in rr* **20/1**
045- **7** *30* **Calormen**[204] 7396 3-8-5 54 .... DavidKenny[(7)] 4 —
(Alan Juckes) *dwlt: a in rr: bhd fnl 3f* **33/1**

1m 44.91s (1.21) **Going Correction** +0.10s/f (Slow) **7** Ran SP% **116.3**
Speed ratings (Par 97): **97,91,90,88,80 72,42**
toteswingers:1&2: £1.80, 2&3: £3.10, 1&3: £2.50 CSF £2.78 TOTE £1.90: £1.20, £2.00; EX 3.20.The winner was sold to R Brotherton for 9,000gns.
Owner H Palmer **Bred** G Flannery Developments **Trained** Newmarket, Suffolk

FOCUS
A few of these hadn't been down to this grade before, but this was a weakish seller. The winner dod not need to mact his Polytrack best.

2653 PLAY ROULETTE AT LADBROKES.COM H'CAP 7f (F)
4:00 (4:03) (Class 5) (0-75,75) 4-Y-O+ **£2,266** (£674; £337; £168) **Stalls** Low

Form RPR
0220 **1** **All Right Now**[16] 2178 4-9-2 **70** .... AndreaAtzeni 5 84
(Derek Haydn Jones) *cl up: led 3f out: rdn over 2f out: drvn clr appr fnl f: styd on* **10/3**[2]
0411 **2** *1 1/4* **Koo And The Gang (IRE)**[23] 1979 4-9-4 **72** .... SilvestreDeSousa 11 83
(Brian Ellison) *cl up on outer: effrt 3f out: rdn and chsd ldng pair 2f out: drvn wl over 1f out: edgd lft and kpt on ins fnl f* **6/4**[1]

60-0 **3** *1 1/2* **Aultcharn (FR)**[15] 2207 4-9-5 **73**.. ShaneKelly 3 81
(Brian Meehan) *trckd ldrs: hdwy 1/2-way: rdn to chse wnr over 2f out: drvn over 1f out: kpt on same pce ins fnl f* **9/1**

6305 **4** *2 1/4* **Mozayada (USA)**[8] 2399 7-9-4 **72**................................ FrannyNorton 10 74
(Mel Brittain) *chsd ldrs: hdwy on inner 3f out: rdn 2f out: drvn over 1f out and no imp ins fnl f* **20/1**

0053 **5** *2* **Elhamri**[15] 2205 7-9-3 **71**.. JamesDoyle 1 69
(Conor Dore) *led: rdn along 1/2-way: hdd 3f out: sn drvn and grad wknd* **25/1**

06-0 **6** *3/4* **Gracie's Gift (IRE)**[17] 2165 9-8-9 **63**......................(v) GrahamGibbons 9 59
(Richard Guest) *hld up: hdwy wl over 2f out: rdn to chse ldrs wl over 1f out: sn drvn: edgd rt and no imp* **10/1**

6000 **7** *nse* **Bentley**[8] 2401 7-9-2 **70**..(p) KellyHarrison 2 66
(Brian Baugh) *towards rr: hdwy over 2f out: sn rdn and n.d* **33/1**

1006 **8** *1* **El Dececy (USA)**[19] 2095 7-9-4 **75**..........................(p) RobertLButler(3) 6 69
(John Balding) *in tch: rdn along wl over 2f out: sn wknd* **20/1**

0000 **9** *1 1/4* **Ace Of Spies (IRE)**[10] 2354 6-9-0 **68**.............................. TonyHamilton 8 59
(Conor Dore) *chsd ldrs: rdn along 3f out: sn wknd* **33/1**

1300 **10** *17* **Double Carpet (IRE)**[48] 1368 8-8-9 **66**.............................. BillyCray(3) 7 18
(Garry Woodward) *in tch: rdn along bef 1/2-way: sn wknd* **20/1**

531 **11** *shd* **El Libertador (USA)**[52] 1276 5-8-7 **61** ow1..............(b) JamieSpencer 13 —
(Jeremy Gask) *in tch: rdn along bef 1/2-way: sn wknd* **13/2**[3]

1m 30.2s (-0.10) **Going Correction** +0.10s/f (Slow) **11** Ran SP% **119.5**
Speed ratings (Par 103): **104,102,100,98,96 95,95,93,92,73 72**
toteswingers:1&2: £1.70, 2&3: £4.00, 1&3: £6.20 CSF £7.90 CT £40.37 TOTE £3.80: £1.10, £1.60, £2.50; EX 10.50.

Owner Justin Hay **Bred** Rolyon Stud **Trained** Efail Isaf, Rhondda C Taff

FOCUS
A good quality handicap run at a solid pace. Plenty of the runners, including the winner, could find only the one pace in the final stages as a result. Both the first two ran a bit better than their meeting here last month.

Ace Of Spies(IRE) Official explanation: jockey said gelding hung left

2654 AT THE RACES SKY 415 H'CAP — 1m 6f (F)
4:30 (4:32) (Class 6) (0-60,60) 4-Y-O+ — **£1,706** (£503; £252) **Stalls** Low

Form — RPR

-031 **1** **Three White Socks (IRE)**[23] 1973 4-8-10 **52**................ PaulPickard(3) 1 75
(Brian Ellison) *rn in snatches early: trckd ldrs tl lost pl after 3f and swtchd to outer: pushed along over 7f out: smooth hdwy and cl up over 4f out: led over 3f out and sn rdn clr: easily* **8/11**[1]

21/ **2** *16* **Im Spartacus**[835] 1638 9-9-2 **60**.. RyanClark(5) 9 67
(Ian Williams) *a.p: effrt 4f out: chsd wnr 3f out: drvn over 2f out and plugged on one pce* **5/1**[3]

-14 **3** *15* **Zed Candy (FR)**[75] 39 8-9-7 **60**................................(p) TonyHamilton 8 40
(Richard Ford) *trckd ldrs: rdn along 1/2-way and sn outpcd: styd on u.p fr over 2f out: tk remote 3rd ins fnl f* **10/3**[2]

00-0 **4** *2* **Orpen Bid (IRE)**[45] 1063 6-8-7 **46** oh1.......................... KellyHarrison 5 23
(Michael Mullineaux) *chsd ldrs: rdn along over 4f out: sn outpcd* **100/1**

6000 **5** *4 1/2* **Hamilton Hill**[13] 2271 4-8-6 **52**................................... CharlesBishop(7) 7 23
(Terry Clement) *chsd ldrs: rdn along 1/2-way: sn outpcd and bhd* **28/1**

005/ **6** *6* **Ritsi**[1025] 4924 8-8-3 **49**.. LukeStrong(7) 2 —
(Marjorie Fife) *hld up: effrt and sme hdwy 1/2-way: rdn along over 4f out: sn outpcd and bhd* **16/1**

-346 **7** *1 1/2* **Grey Command (USA)**[9] 2393 6-9-0 **60**.................. JohnCavanagh(7) 6 —
(Mel Brittain) *led: rdn along 5f out: hdd over 4f out: sn wknd* **12/1**

3m 10.26s (1.96) **Going Correction** +0.10s/f (Slow) **7** Ran SP% **115.7**
Speed ratings (Par 101): **98,88,80,79,76 73,72**
toteswingers:1&2: £1.80, 2&3: £2.50, 1&3: £1.80 CSF £5.11 CT £7.97 TOTE £1.60: £1.10, £2.70; EX 5.70.

Owner Racing Management & Training Ltd **Bred** Hippodromos Y Caballos S A **Trained** Norton, N Yorks

FOCUS
This wasn't a good race and essentially it's guesswork to assess the winner. Hard form to pin down.

2655 AT THE RACES VIRGIN 534 H'CAP — 6f (F)
5:00 (5:01) (Class 6) (0-55,55) 4-Y-O+ — **£1,706** (£503; £252) **Stalls** Low

Form — RPR

3260 **1** **Premier League**[44] 1453 4-9-2 **55**............................(p) RoystonFfrench 3 68
(Julia Feilden) *trckd ldrs: smooth hdwy 2f out: led 1 1/2f out: rdn and hung rt ins fnl f: kpt on* **9/2**[3]

0163 **2** *3 3/4* **St Ignatius**[14] 2233 4-9-1 **54**.. JamesDoyle 9 55
(Michael Appleby) *cl up: led 1/2-way: rdn and hdd 1 1/2f out: sn drvn and kpt on same pce* **7/2**[2]

6066 **3** *2 1/4* **Flow Chart (IRE)**[29] 1815 4-8-7 **46** oh1.................(b) RobbieFitzpatrick 5 40
(Peter Grayson) *chsd ldrs: rdn over 2f out: drvn over 1f out: kpt on u.p ins fnl f* **50/1**

-123 **4** *2* **Charlietoo**[3] 2555 5-8-13 **52**....................................(p) SilvestreDeSousa 6 39
(Edward Bevan) *in rr: pushed along 1/2-way: rdn over 2f out: styd on appr fnl f: nrst fin* **2/1**[1]

0323 **5** *hd* **Kheley (IRE)**[17] 2162 5-8-5 **49**...................................... JamesRogers(5) 7 36
(Mark Brisbourne) *hld up: hdwy to chse ldrs over 2f out: sn rdn and no imp* **11/2**

000- **6** *1 1/2* **Lady Vivien**[324] 3976 5-8-9 **48**.. TonyHamilton 2 30
(George Foster) *led: rdn along and hdd 1/2-way: drvn wl over 1f out and grad wknd* **20/1**

0260 **7** *1 1/2* **Cheveyo (IRE)**[17] 2162 5-8-8 **47**......................................(v) PJMcDonald 8 24
(Lisa Williamson) *chsd ldrs on outer: rdn along over 2f out: drvn wl over 1f out and sn wknd* **25/1**

06-6 **8** *10* **Lujiana**[44] 1464 6-9-0 **53**.. FrannyNorton 1 —
(Mel Brittain) *chsd ldrs on inner: rdn along wl over 2f out: sn wknd* **10/1**

00-0 **9** *4* **Pavement Games**[72] 941 4-8-9 **48**.................................... GrahamGibbons 4 —
(Richard Guest) *hld up: a towards rr* **16/1**

1m 17.58s (1.08) **Going Correction** +0.10s/f (Slow) **9** Ran SP% **114.7**
Speed ratings (Par 101): **96,91,88,85,85 83,81,67,62**
toteswingers:1&2: £3.80, 2&3: £20.50, 1&3: £21.90 CSF £20.02 CT £690.46 TOTE £5.50: £1.60, £2.30, £11.80; EX 27.50.

Owner Mrs Jo Lambert **Bred** Gill Slater **Trained** Exning, Suffolk

FOCUS
A modest contest at best, run in an ordinary time. The winner is rated up a length.

2656 FREE REPLAYS ON ATTHERACES.COM H'CAP — 1m 3f (F)
5:30 (5:30) (Class 5) (0-75,75) 4-Y-O+ — **£2,388** (£705; £352) **Stalls** Low

Form — RPR

0-63 **1** **Hit The Switch**[14] 2237 5-8-5 **59**.............................. SilvestreDeSousa 5 72
(Patrick Morris) *trckd ldr: pushed along over 4f out: hdwy to ld 3f out: swtchd rt and rdn wl over 1f out: drvn ins fnl f and styd on gamely* **8/1**[3]

1-05 **2** *1/2* **Hakuna Matata**[20] 2059 4-8-10 **69**.. DaleSwift(5) 6 81
(Brian Ellison) *trckd ldrs: hdwy 3f out: rdn to chse wnr 2f out: drvn and kpt on ins fnl f tl no ex towards fin* **11/8**[1]

5-03 **3** *6* **Persian Peril**[23] 1977 7-9-1 **69**.. PJMcDonald 3 70
(Alan Swinbank) *trckd ldrs on inner: effrt over 3f oiut and sn pushed along: rdn to chse ldng pair 2f out: swtchd rt and drvn whn edgd rt ent fnl f: one pce* **7/2**[2]

4-25 **4** *nk* **Onyx Of Arabia (IRE)**[14] 2213 4-9-4 **72**...........................(b) ShaneKelly 2 73
(Brian Meehan) *hld up: hdwy 4f out: rdn to chse ldrs over 2f out: drvn and no imp whn sltly hmpd ent fnl f* **7/2**[2]

1043 **5** *10* **Cobo Bay**[14] 2235 6-9-7 **75**...(b) TonyHamilton 4 58
(Conor Dore) *led: rdn along 4f out: hdd 3f out and sn wknd* **12/1**

5023 **6** *20* **Amical Risks (FR)**[13] 2259 7-8-3 **57**................................ KellyHarrison 1 —
(Ollie Pears) *a in rr: rdn along and outpcd over 3f out: sn bhd* **12/1**

-000 **7** *29* **Plenilune (IRE)**[36] 1615 6-8-2 **56** oh11................................ FrannyNorton 7 —
(Mel Brittain) *in tch: rdn along over 4f out: sn wknd and bhd fnl 3f* **80/1**

2m 27.09s (-0.91) **Going Correction** +0.10s/f (Slow) **7** Ran SP% **114.3**
Speed ratings (Par 103): **107,106,102,102,94 80,59**
toteswingers:1&2: £3.40, 2&3: £2.50, 1&3: £3.20. Totesuper 7: Win: Not won. Place £74.60. CSF £19.51 TOTE £5.50: £2.40, £1.10; EX 25.30.

Owner M M Allen **Bred** Mrs M T Dawson **Trained** Tarporley, Cheshire

■ Stewards' Enquiry : P J McDonald one-day ban: careless riding (Jun 19)
Dale Swift one-day ban: used whip with excessive frequency (Jun 19)

FOCUS
This was sound run and probably fair form for the grade, with the first two clear.
T/Plt: £8.70 to a £1 stake. Pool of £55,288.39 - 4,609.07 winning tickets. T/Qpdt: £5.40 to a £1 stake. Pool of £2,962.06 - 398.90 winning tickets. JR

2538 BADEN-BADEN (L-H)
Thursday, June 2

OFFICIAL GOING: Turf: good

2657a UVEX-TROPHY (EX BADENER MEILE (GROUP 3) (3YO+) (TURF) — 1m
6:40 (12:00) 3-Y-O+
£27,586 (£9,482; £4,741; £2,586; £1,724; £1,293)

RPR

1 **Alianthus (GER)**[53] 1263 6-9-6 0.. ADeVries 12 117
(J Hirschberger, Germany) *broke wl to ld: set gd pce: led into st and sn drew clr: eased down ins fnl f: won easily* **39/10**[3]

2 *3/4* **Sehrezad (IRE)**[32] 1740 6-9-6 0.. JiriPalik 9 115
(Andreas Lowe, Germany) *hld up bhd ldng gp: mde early move in st: r.o wl u.p: chsd wnr home wout threatening* **6/4**[1]

3 *1* **Neatico (GER)**[25] 4-9-0 0.. AStarke 2 107
(P Schiergen, Germany) *broke fast: sn prom in ldng gp: r.o wl in st but no imp on first two* **98/10**

4 *2* **Santino (GER)**[25] 4-9-2 0.. JohanVictoire 6 104
(J-P Carvalho, Germany) *amonst ldng gp fr s: looked threatening early in st: r.o wl* **7/2**[2]

5 *3* **Rockatella (IRE)**[46] 1432 4-8-13 0.. KKerekes 10 94
(W Hefter, Germany) *settled towards rr: mde swift prog ent st: qcknd wl on outside: r.o* **183/10**

6 *2* **Magic Eye (IRE)**[53] 1263 6-8-13 0.................................... AHelfenbein 1 90
(Andreas Lowe, Germany) *broked wl: racd in midfield: threatened briefly 1/2-way down st: no ex* **78/10**

7 *1 1/4* **Samardal (FR)**[210] 4-9-2 0.. EPedroza 3 90
(A Wohler, Germany) *bkmarker fr s: passed btn horses in st* **105/10**

8 *1* **Golden Tirol (GER)**[46] 5-9-0 0.. MSrnec 11 86
(Adam Wyrzyk, Poland) *racd in midfield: nvr a factor in st* **42/1**

9 *12* **Le Francois (GER)** 4-9-2 0.. FilipMinarik 5 60
(W Figge, Germany) *broke wl: racd freely: tired sn down bkst: nvr figured in st: t.o* **29/1**

10 *2 1/2* **Forthe Millionkiss (GER)**[196] 7500 7-9-2 0............................ APietsch 4 54
(Uwe Ostmann, Germany) *prom at first: amongst ldng gp: flattered briefly early in st: sn btn: t.o* **19/1**

11 *1/2* **Reine Heureuse (GER)**[41] 4-8-13 0.. DPorcu 7 50
(Uwe Ostmann, Germany) *broke fast to r bhd ldr: pulling freely: looked threateaning early in st: sn fnd no ex: wknd qckly fnl f* **28/1**

1m 37.51s (-1.60) **11** Ran SP% **131.2**
WIN (Incl. 10 euro stake): 49. PLACES: 17, 13, 24. SF: 88.

Owner Baron G Von Ullmann **Bred** Gestut Karlshof **Trained** Germany

Race 2658a - See RI

2241 BATH (L-H)
Friday, June 3

OFFICIAL GOING: Good to firm (firm in places; 9.4)
Wind: mild breeze Weather: sunny

2659 BATH ALES SWAN H'CAP — 1m 5f 22y
6:25 (6:25) (Class 6) (0-60,60) 4-Y-O+ — **£1,813** (£539; £269; £134) **Stalls** High

Form — RPR

2164 **1** **Money Money Money**[18] 2145 5-9-7 **60**........................ JamesMillman 2 70
(Rod Millman) *trckd ldr: wnt upsides over 2f out: sn rdn: edgd lft fr over 1f out: led ins fnl f: styd on wl* **4/1**[3]

3006 **2** *1* **Oak Leaves**[91] 773 4-8-7 **46** oh1.. DavidProbert 6 54
(Nikki Evans) *trckd ldr: led jst over 2f out: rdn and immediately hrd pressed: hdd ins fnl f: no ex* **12/1**

0-23 **3** *1 1/2* **Dove Cottage (IRE)**[10] 2377 9-9-1 **54**......................(p) FergusSweeney 1 61
(Stuart Kittow) *trckd ldr: rdn and hdd jst over 2f out: 3/4 l down and styng on same pce whn short of room on rails ins fnl f* **1/1**[1]

3025 **4** *8* **Miles Of Sunshine**[10] 2377 6-9-1 **54**................................ SteveDrowne 5 48
(Ron Hodges) *hld up: pushed along over 6f out: rdn over 3f out: nvr gng pce to get to ldrs* **7/2**[2]

20-0 **5** *1 ½* **Happy Fleet**[29] 1839 8-9-1 **54**................................ DaneO'Neill 4 46
(Roger Curtis) *hld up: rdn over 3f out: nvr any imp on ldrs* **22/1**

00-4 **6** *8* **Brave Enough (USA)**[25] 1935 4-9-1 **54**.................. FrankieMcDonald 3 34
(Roger Curtis) *trckd ldr: rdn over 3f out: hld 2f out: wknd fnl f* **40/1**

5-04 **7** *½* **Yeomanry**[14] 2272 6-8-7 **46**..(p) MartinLane 7 25
(Ian Williams) *in tch: rn in snatches: pushed along most of way: rdn 6f out: no imp: wknd fnl f* **12/1**

2m 49.08s (-2.92) **Going Correction** -0.275s/f (Firm) **7** Ran SP% **114.4**
Speed ratings (Par 101): **97,96,95,90,89 84,84**
Tote Swingers: 1&2 £5.30, 1&3 £1.20, 2&3 £3.00 CSF £48.51 TOTE £4.70: £2.80, £5.40; EX 55.90.
Owner Mrs Jenny Willment **Bred** Mrs Jenny Willment **Trained** Kentisbeare, Devon

FOCUS
A weak staying handicap but a small personal best from the winner.

2660 BATH ALES GEM FILLIES' H'CAP — 5f 11y

6:55 (6:55) (Class 5) (0-70,70) 3-Y-O **£2,849** (£847; £423; £211) **Stalls** Centre

Form RPR

0-05 **1** **Madame Kintyre**[15] 2223 3-8-11 **60**............................ JamesMillman 7 66
(Rod Millman) *mde all: r.o gamely to assert ins fnl f: rdn out* **8/1**

02-3 **2** *1 ¾* **Volcanic Dust (IRE)**[36] 1630 3-9-7 **70**........................ CathyGannon 2 69
(Milton Bradley) *t.k.h trcking wnr: rdn 2f out: kpt on but a being hld* **13/2**

4-10 **3** *¾* **Best Be Careful (IRE)**[13] 2294 3-9-0 **63**........................ DaneO'Neill 1 59
(Mark Usher) *trckd ldrs: rdn 2f out: kpt on same pce fnl f* **5/1**[3]

00-2 **4** *2 ¾* **Porthgwidden Beach (USA)**[105] 595 3-8-2 **51** oh1...(t) DavidProbert 5 37
(Stuart Williams) *trckd ldrs: rdn over 1f out: nt pce to chal: no ex fnl f* **7/4**[1]

6152 **5** *6* **Vicona (IRE)**[13] 2294 3-9-0 **70**.................................... DuilioDaSilva(7) 4 35
(Paul Cole) *hld up bhd ldrs: rdn 2f out: no imp: fdd fnl f* **2/1**[2]

0-60 **6** *2 ¼* **Aurivorous**[13] 2294 3-8-13 **62**.. SamHitchcott 3 18
(Anabel K Murphy) *hld up: rdn 2f out: no imp: wknd fnl f* **33/1**

61.50 secs (-1.00) **Going Correction** -0.225s/f (Firm) **6** Ran SP% **113.7**
Speed ratings (Par 96): **99,96,95,90,81 77**
Tote Swingers: 1&2 £5.30, 1&3 £5.00, 2&3 £2.20 CSF £57.13 CT £286.61 TOTE £9.50: £4.30, £3.10; EX 34.40.
Owner Rod Millman Racing Club **Bred** Mrs L S Millman **Trained** Kentisbeare, Devon

FOCUS
With the two market leaders underperforming, more so in the case of Vicona, it is debatable whether this form is strong. The winner more than confirmed her latest Salisbury improvement.
Madame Kintyre Official explanation: trainer said, regarding apparent improvement in form, that the filly is big and backward and had been dropped in class.

2661 E B F BATH ALES HOP POLE MAIDEN STKS — 5f 161y

7:30 (7:32) (Class 5) 2-Y-O **£3,173** (£944; £471; £235) **Stalls** Centre

Form RPR

0 **1** **Luv U Forever**[18] 2153 2-8-12 0...................................... CathyGannon 7 74
(Pat Murphy) *mde all: hld on gamely whn chal fnl f: drvn out* **7/1**[3]

6 **2** *nk* **Ivor's Princess**[24] 1981 2-8-12 0................................... JamesMillman 2 73
(Rod Millman) *chsd ldrs: pushed along early: rdn 2f out: chal ent fnl f: kpt on but no ex nring fin* **20/1**

3 **3** *3 ½* **Miss Lahar**[18] 2153 2-8-12 0... SamHitchcott 6 61
(Mick Channon) *racd keenly: trckd ldrs: effrt 2f out: kpt on same pce fnl f* **4/7**[1]

44 **4** *½* **Balm**[18] 2153 2-8-12 0.. DaneO'Neill 1 60
(Richard Hannon) *trckd wnr tl rdn over 2f out: kpt on same pce fnl f* **7/2**[2]

603 **5** *2* **Xinbama (IRE)**[18] 2143 2-9-3 0.. SebSanders 4 58
(J W Hills) *hld up bhd ldrs: effrt 2f out: no ex fnl f* **7/1**[3]

00 **6** *18* **Mount McLeod (IRE)**[10] 2374 2-8-12 0..................... FergusSweeney 3 9
(Jamie Osborne) *rrd and wnt rt leaving stalls: sn rcvrd to trck wnr: effrt over 2f out: wknd over 1f out* **25/1**

1m 10.89s (-0.31) **Going Correction** -0.225s/f (Firm) **6** Ran SP% **119.5**
Speed ratings (Par 93): **93,92,87,87,84 60**
Tote Swingers: 1&2 £20.20, 1&3 £1.70, 2&3 £4.00 CSF £116.92 TOTE £8.00: £4.00, £12.70; EX 63.50.
Owner 21C Telecom.co.uk **Bred** Richard Hunt **Trained** East Garston, Berks

FOCUS
Just an ordinary maiden in which all bar Xinbama were fillies. A race lacking in depth with the third and fourth below previous form and the fifth the best guide.

NOTEBOOK
Luv U Forever had finished behind both Miss Lahar and Balm on her debut at Windsor but has clearly come on a good deal for that experience because this was a huge step forward. She showed excellent early speed to lead her rivals before battling on gamely when Ivor's Princess began to close up the inside. The way she toughed out the closing stages, allied with her pedigree, suggests she'll get 6f no problem, and maybe even seven in time. (op 11-1 tchd 12-1)
Ivor's Princess also stepped up markedly on her debut effort, keeping on well up the inside rail and finishing nicely clear of the rest. There ought to be races in her. (op 25-1 tchd 28-1)
Miss Lahar, who got a little bit worked up beforehand, ruined her chance by racing far too keenly through the early stages and that resulted in a tame finishing effort. She shaped with real promise on her debut so this was disappointing. (op 4-5, tchd 10-11 in places and Evens in a place)
Balm, behind Miss Lahar at Windsor, doesn't look to be progressing and this stiffer test of stamina didn't help. (op 9-2)

2662 BATH ALES SUMMER'S HARE H'CAP — 5f 161y

8:00 (8:01) (Class 4) (0-85,85) 3-Y-O+ **£3,238** (£963; £481; £240) **Stalls** Centre

Form RPR

6413 **1** **Kyllachy Storm**[8] 2426 7-8-6 **66**.................................. MatthewDavies(3) 1 73
(Ron Hodges) *trckd ldrs: pished along over 3f out: rdn over 2f out: str run between horses ent fnl f: led fnl 50yds* **5/1**

0313 **2** *hd* **Yurituni**[6] 2491 4-9-3 **77**..(v) PatrickHills(3) 6 83
(Eve Johnson Houghton) *trckd ldrs: wandered u.p over 1f out: chal ent fnl f: kpt on towards fin* **11/4**[1]

4-05 **3** *½* **Noodles Blue Boy**[8] 2434 5-10-0 **85**.............................. SebSanders 4 89
(Ollie Pears) *trckd ldr: rdn into narrow advantage over 1f out: edgd rt 1f out: no ex whn hdd fnl 50yds* **7/2**[2]

0-51 **4** *¾* **Black Cadillac (IRE)**[18] 2141 3-8-1 **66**.........................(v) DavidProbert 7 66
(Andrew Balding) *hld up bhd ldrs: rdn to chse ldrs 2f out: keeping on whn nt clr run fnl 75yds* **4/1**[3]

2023 **5** *¾* **Ebraam (USA)**[14] 2244 8-9-3 **74**.. LukeMorris 2 73
(Ronald Harris) *hld up last but in tch: hdwy u.p over 1f out: ev ch ent fnl f: no ex fnl 75yds* **9/2**

1156 **6** *2 ¼* **Novabridge**[7] 2447 3-8-1 **66**...(b) CathyGannon 3 56
(Andrew Haynes) *led: rdn and hdd over 1f out: no ex ins fnl f* **12/1**

1m 10.04s (-1.16) **Going Correction** -0.225s/f (Firm)
WFA 3 from 4yo+ 8lb **6** Ran SP% **111.4**
Speed ratings (Par 105): **98,97,97,96,95 92**
Tote Swingers: 1&2 £1.60, 1&3 £4.90, 2&3 £2.80 CSF £18.77 TOTE £4.60: £2.70, £3.50; EX 13.20.
Owner Mrs Angela Hart **Bred** Sir Eric Parker **Trained** Charlton Mackrell, Somerset

FOCUS
A competitive sprint in which the pace was strong from the outset. Ordinary form, and the winner probably only had to run to his recent best.

2663 BATH ALES SALAMANDER H'CAP — 1m 2f 46y

8:35 (8:35) (Class 5) (0-70,70) 4-Y-O+ **£2,525** (£751; £375; £187) **Stalls** Low

Form RPR

2164 **1** **Shamardal Phantom (IRE)**[16] 2204 4-9-5 **68**.................... MartinLane 4 77
(David Simcock) *v awkward leaving stalls: racd in last: stdy prog fr 3f out: shkn up to ld ent fnl f: r.o* **4/1**[3]

1340 **2** *1 ¾* **Very Well Red**[16] 2198 8-9-7 **70**.. WilliamCarson 2 76
(Peter Hiatt) *led: rdn 3f out: hdd ent fnl f: kpt on but no ex* **15/2**

2214 **3** *5* **Duneen Dream (USA)**[14] 2245 6-8-10 **59**........................ DavidProbert 5 54
(Nikki Evans) *trckd ldr: rdn over 3f out: lost 2nd 2f out: kpt on same pce* **3/1**[2]

0-52 **4** *nk* **Tap Dance Way (IRE)**[10] 2376 4-9-7 **70**.............................. DaneO'Neill 6 64
(Patrick Chamings) *trckd ldrs: rdn over 3f out: kpt on same pce fnl 2f* **2/1**[1]

2154 **5** *21* **Ocean Of Peace (FR)**[2] 2616 8-8-9 **58**................................ LukeMorris 1 36
(Martin Bosley) *trckd ldrs: rdn over 3f out: wknd over 1f out: eased fnl f* **4/1**[3]

2m 9.00s (-2.00) **Going Correction** -0.275s/f (Firm) **5** Ran SP% **110.1**
Speed ratings (Par 103): **97,95,91,91,74**
CSF £30.23 TOTE £6.70: £4.30, £5.50; EX 19.50.
Owner Sultan Ali **Bred** Pier House Stud **Trained** Newmarket, Suffolk

FOCUS
This was run at a good pace. The winner recorded a 7lb personal bedst, with the form rated around the second.
Tap Dance Way(IRE) Official explanation: jockey said filly hung left-handed
Ocean Of Peace(FR) Official explanation: jockey said gelding ran flat

2664 BATH ALES BREWERY CLASSIFIED STKS — 1m 2f 46y

9:05 (9:05) (Class 6) 3-Y-O **£1,910** (£564; £282) **Stalls** Low

Form RPR

5-51 **1** **Canaveral**[18] 2146 3-9-0 72.. ShaneKelly 2 78+
(Brian Meehan) *trckd ldrs: rdn to chal ent fnl f: led fnl 75yds: rdn out* **3/1**[2]

40-0 **2** *¾* **Novel Dancer**[20] 2097 3-8-9 69.................................... KieranO'Neill(5) 7 76
(Richard Hannon) *trckd ldr: led 2f out: sn rdn: kpt on but no ex whn hdd fnl 75yds* **12/1**

2203 **3** *¾* **Standout**[14] 2253 3-9-0 73.. DaneO'Neill 6 75
(Richard Hannon) *hld up in tch: hdwy fr 3f out: rdn 2f out: styd on same pce fnl f* **4/1**[3]

5-06 **4** *2* **Misk Khitaam (USA)**[15] 2230 3-9-0 74................................ MartinLane 1 71
(John Dunlop) *in tch: pushed along in last pair 4f out: rdn over 3f out: styd on fnl f* **20/1**

31-4 **5** *5* **Tenby Lady (USA)**[14] 2253 3-9-0 73..................................... SebSanders 5 61
(Sir Mark Prescott Bt) *trckd ldrs: rdn over 2f out: wknd 1f out* **11/8**[1]

3425 **6** *nk* **Black Pond (USA)**[21] 2058 3-9-0 74.....................(v[1]) SilvestreDeSousa 3 60
(Mark Johnston) *sn led: 5 l clr 7f out tl rdn and hdd 2f out: fdd fnl f* **9/1**

-454 **7** *nk* **Persian Herald**[16] 2188 3-9-0 75... LukeMorris 4 59
(William Muir) *s.i.s: in tch but nvr any imp: struggling 4f out: fdd fnl f* **25/1**

2m 8.40s (-2.60) **Going Correction** -0.275s/f (Firm) **7** Ran SP% **113.4**
Speed ratings (Par 97): **99,98,97,96,92 91,91**
Tote Swingers: 1&2 £2.70, 1&3 £2.00, 2&3 £4.60 CSF £36.44 TOTE £4.10: £1.20, £7.50; EX 42.00.
Owner Manton Racing Partnership **Bred** Heather Raw **Trained** Manton, Wilts

FOCUS
Some unexposed 3-y-os on show in a tight classified stakes, an interesting race for the grade. The winner is progressing nicely.
T/Plt: £1,063.10 to a £1 stake. Pool £54,902.62 - 37.70 winning units T/Qpdt: £170.10 to a £1 stake. Pool £4,399.13 - 19.10 winning units TM

2492 CATTERICK (L-H)

Friday, June 3

OFFICIAL GOING: Good to firm (firm in places; 9.2)
Wind: light 1/2 against Weather: fine and sunny

2665 BRITISH STALLION STUDS SUPPORTING BRITISH RACING E B F MAIDEN STKS — 5f

1:50 (1:51) (Class 5) 2-Y-O **£3,238** (£963; £481; £240) **Stalls** Low

Form RPR

1 **Ralphy Boy (IRE)** 2-9-0 0.................................... MichaelO'Connell(3) 8 72+
(David Nicholls) *dwlt: swtchd lft and chsd ldrs after 1f: led over 1f out: styd on to ld again post* **11/4**[2]

525 **2** *nse* **Superplex**[24] 1966 2-9-3 0.. TonyHamilton 6 72
(John Quinn) *w ldr: led over 2f out: hdd over 1f out: narrow ld ins fnl f: hdd last stride* **2/1**[1]

000 **3** *8* **Nameitwhatyoulike**[23] 2007 2-9-0 0......................... JamesSullivan(3) 3 43
(Michael Easterby) *chsd ldrs: lost pl 2f out: tk modest 3rd nr fin* **66/1**

06 **4** *1 ¼* **Dolly Danca**[20] 2113 2-8-12 0.. MickyFenton 5 34
(Paul Midgley) *led tl over 2f out: edgd rt and wknd over 1f out* **9/1**

5 *1 ½* **Look Here's Lady** 2-8-12 0.. FrannyNorton 7 28
(Ed McMahon) *sn outpcd and in rr: kpt on fnl f* **3/1**[3]

6 *15* **Elsie Tanner (IRE)** 2-8-12 0.. PaulQuinn 2 —
(David Nicholls) *s.s: outpcd and bhd: eased last 100yds* **18/1**

59.56 secs (-0.24) **Going Correction** -0.275s/f (Firm) **6** Ran SP% **101.8**
Speed ratings (Par 93): **90,89,77,75,72 48**
Tote Swingers: 1&2 £1.50, 1&3 £28.00, 2&3 £6.00 CSF £7.02 TOTE £2.80: £1.10, £1.80; EX 11.20.
Owner Frank Lowe **Bred** Frank Lowe **Trained** Sessay, N Yorks
■ Minniehaha was withdrawn (8/1, unruly in the stalls). Deduct 10p in the £ under R4.

FOCUS
No depth to this maiden but a decent start from the winner. Straightforward form to rate.

NOTEBOOK
Ralphy Boy(IRE) was able to see off a battle-hardened rival on his debut, impressing with the way he travelled for a long way and just shading a tight finish. This son of Acclamation can only improve with this behind him. (op 4-1)

Superplex probably got back to the form he showed when runner-up at Beverley and should pick up a race at some stage, though it already looks as though he's always going to be vulnerable to anything with potential. (op 7-4 tchd 9-4)
Nameitwhatyoulike had shown nothing previously so this was clearly a step in the right direction. He wasn't unduly knocked about to get third, either, and he's got a bit of potential for low-grade nurseries.
Dolly Danca again showed early speed and is another who will be able to find more realistic opportunities now she's eligible for nurseries. Official explanation: jockey said filly lost its action (op 13-2)
Look Here's Lady, a daughter of Kyllachy out of connections' useful sprinter Look Here's Carol, patently needed the experience, off the bridle throughout but hinting that she was getting the hang of things by the finish. She's in good hands and should be all the sharper next time. (op 4-1)
Elsie Tanner(IRE), a stablemate of the winner, was way too green to do herself justice, slowly away and behind throughout. (op 11-1)

2666 YORKSHIRE-OUTDOORS.CO.UK (S) STKS — 1m 5f 175y

2:25 (2:25) (Class 6) 4-Y-O+ — **£1,706** (£503; £252) **Stalls** Low

Form — RPR

2020 **1** **White Deer (USA)**^{37} [1613] 7-8-12 64 (p) DanielTudhope 2 — 58+
(Geoffrey Harker) *trckd ldrs: smooth hdwy 2f out: shkn up to ld last 100yds: cheekily* **11/4**^{2}

0- **2** *nk* **Summerlea (IRE)**^{196} [7514] 5-8-12 65 AndrewElliott 7 — 58
(Patrick Holmes) *trckd ldrs: drvn 4f out: chal over 1f out: kpt on same pce last 50yds* **9/2**^{3}

0105 **3** *2* **Capable Guest (IRE)**^{6} [2496] 9-9-4 61 PJMcDonald 5 — 61
(George Moore) *trckd ldrs: reminders over 5f out: kpt on same pce fnl 2f: tk 3rd nr fin* **9/4**^{1}

5445 **4** *½* **Silent Lucidity (IRE)**^{122} [373] 7-8-12 52 (p) TonyHamilton 1 — 54
(Peter Niven) *led 2f: chsd ldrs: chal over 3f out: led 2f out: edgd lft: hdd ins fnl f: one pce* **6/1**

6120 **5** *2 ¾* **Bring Sweets (IRE)**^{10} [2393] 4-8-13 54 DaleSwift(5) 3 — 56
(Brian Ellison) *hld up in rr: hdwy over 2f out: n.m.r over 1f out: kpt on one pce* **11/2**

54/0 **6** *1 ½* **Just Observing**^{7} [2473] 8-8-12 50 (p) MickyFenton 4 — 49
(Neville Bycroft) *led after 2f: qcknd 8f out: hdd 2f out: sn n.m.r: wknd and heavily eased last 75yds* **16/1**

0/00 **7** *80* **Wing N Prayer (IRE)**^{9} [2401] 4-8-7 45 FrannyNorton 6 — —
(Alan Berry) *in rr: detached last and drvn after 5f: t.o 3f out: virtually p.u* **125/1**

3m 1.63s (-1.97) **Going Correction** -0.075s/f (Good) **7** Ran SP% **112.0**
Speed ratings (Par 101): **102,101,100,100,98 97,52**
CSF £14.83 TOTE £1.50: £1.50, £2.10; EX 17.20.There was no bid for the winner.
Owner A S Ward **Bred** Fleetwood Bloodstock Et Al **Trained** Thirkleby, N Yorks
■ Stewards' Enquiry : Tony Hamilton caution: careless riding.

FOCUS
A typically modest seller and a steady pace resulted in a bunched finish. Muddling form, rated around the third.

2667 LIONWELD KENNEDY H'CAP — 5f

3:00 (3:00) (Class 5) (0-70,70) 3-Y-O+ — **£2,072** (£616; £308; £153) **Stalls** Low

Form — RPR

1120 **1** **Lucky Art (USA)**^{24} [1968] 5-9-2 **61** JamesSullivan(3) 1 — 78
(Ruth Carr) *mde all: wnt clr appr fnl f: styd on strly* **7/2**^{1}

0105 **2** *3 ½* **Kyzer Chief**^{14} [2247] 6-8-10 **59** ShaneBKelly(7) 2 — 63
(Ron Barr) *dwlt: sn chsng ldrs: wnt 2nd over 2f out: edgd rt and kpt on same pce appr fnl f* **9/1**

03-0 **3** *2 ½* **Bahamian Ballet**^{21} [2048] 9-9-11 **67** GrahamGibbons 4 — 62
(Ed McMahon) *chsd ldrs: outpcd over 2f out: kpt on same pce over 1f out* **6/1**

-040 **4** *1 ½* **Wicked Wilma (IRE)**^{13} [2280] 7-8-13 **60** SladeO'Hara(5) 6 — 50
(Alan Berry) *in rr and sn pushed along: hdwy over 1f out: styd on towards fin* **11/2**

4431 **5** *nk* **Ridley Didley (IRE)**^{14} [2247] 6-9-4 **65** (p) NeilFarley(5) 7 — 54
(Noel Wilson) *chsd wnr: wknd over 1f out* **9/2**^{2}

0055 **6** *2 ½* **Ignatieff (IRE)**^{13} [2304] 4-10-0 **70** DuranFentiman 5 — 50
(Linda Stubbs) *chsd wnr: outpcd over 2f out: hung lft and lost pl over 1f out* **5/1**^{3}

1603 **7** *½* **Spirit Of Coniston**^{14} [2247] 8-9-0 **56** MickyFenton 3 — 34
(Paul Midgley) *in rr: n.m.r over 2f out: hung lft and lost pl* **8/1**

58.00 secs (-1.80) **Going Correction** -0.275s/f (Firm) **7** Ran SP% **107.9**
Speed ratings (Par 103): **103,97,93,91,90 86,85**
CSF £30.71 TOTE £5.00: £3.60, £7.90; EX 30.60.
Owner Exors of the late David W Chapman **Bred** Gaines-Gentry Thoroughbreds **Trained** Huby, N Yorks

FOCUS
This looked a tight little handicap beforehand, but turned out to be anything but. the winner recorded a fast time and rates back to last year's best.
Spirit Of Coniston Official explanation: jockey said gelding hung left-handed

2668 RACINGUK.COM H'CAP — 5f 212y

3:35 (3:36) (Class 4) (0-85,83) 4-Y-O+ — **£4,209** (£1,252; £625; £312) **Stalls** Low

Form — RPR

00-0 **1** **Roker Park (IRE)**^{20} [2116] 6-9-4 **80** DanielTudhope 4 — 92+
(David O'Meara) *chsd ldrs: drvn and outpcd 3f out: hdwy to ld over 1f out: styd on strly* **7/2**^{2}

1-30 **2** *1 ½* **Caranbola**^{24} [1968] 5-8-10 **72** RobertWinston 5 — 77
(Mel Brittain) *w ldr: kpt on same pce fnl f* **11/2**

00-0 **3** *¾* **Bonnie Charlie**^{20} [2116] 5-9-4 **83** MichaelO'Connell(3) 3 — 86
(David Nicholls) *trckd ldrs: effrt on ins over 2f out: kpt on same pce appr fnl f* **15/2**

00-0 **4** *hd* **Viva Ronaldo (IRE)**^{146} [99] 5-8-12 **81** LauraBarry(7) 1 — 85+
(Richard Fahey) *dwlt: hld up: effrt on ins over 2f out: nt clr run over 1f out tl swtchd rt wl ins fnl f: fin strly* **4/1**^{3}

0020 **5** *½* **Legal Eagle (IRE)**^{20} [2118] 6-8-12 **79** (p) AdamBeschizza(5) 2 — 80
(Paul Green) *led: hdd over 1f out: no ex* **11/4**^{1}

6034 **6** *3 ¾* **Excusez Moi (USA)**^{8} [2431] 9-8-11 **73** PJMcDonald 6 — 62+
(Ruth Carr) *s.s: a detached in last* **13/2**

1m 12.84s (-0.76) **Going Correction** -0.075s/f (Good) **6** Ran SP% **109.4**
Speed ratings (Par 105): **102,100,99,98,98 93**
CSF £21.21 TOTE £4.50: £2.30, £6.00; EX 28.00.
Owner T Alderson **Bred** Dr Dean Harron **Trained** Nawton, N Yorks

FOCUS
A small field, but it contained some fairly useful performers and the race was run at a sound pace. The time was ordinary but the form is rated at face value.
Excusez Moi(USA) Official explanation: jockey said gelding missed the break

2669 I DO BRIDAL AND EVENING WEAR MAIDEN STKS — 1m 3f 214y

4:15 (4:16) (Class 5) 3-Y-O+ — **£2,072** (£616; £308; £153) **Stalls** Low

Form — RPR

2-43 **1** **King Of The Celts (IRE)**^{34} [1692] 3-8-11 77 DavidAllan 6 — 65+
(Tim Easterby) *trckd ldr: pushed along to ld 2f out: sn rdn and edgd lft: kpt on* **1/9**^{1}

06-0 **2** *3 ¼* **December**^{45} [1466] 5-9-7 43 (t) DaleSwift(5) 3 — 60
(James Given) *led: drvn over 4f out: hdd 2f out: one pce* **16/1**^{2}

40 **3** *10* **Tasman Tiger**^{14} [2257] 4-9-7 0 KellyHarrison 2 — 39
(Kate Walton) *trckd ldrs: drvn over 4f out: wnt modest 3rd over 3f out: sn wl outpcd* **16/1**^{2}

5-6 **4** *8* **Rosie Raymond**^{20} [2114] 6-9-7 0 RobbieFitzpatrick 4 — 26
(Charles Smith) *racd in last: outpcd and drvn after 3f: nvr on terms* **20/1**^{3}

56 **5** *6* **Jersey Joe (IRE)**^{7} [2461] 4-9-9 0 (v1) PaulPickard(3) 1 — 22
(Brian Ellison) *dwlt and reminders after s: sn chsng ldrs: drvn over 4f out: lost pl over 3f out* **25/1**

2m 36.69s (-2.21) **Going Correction** -0.075s/f (Good)
WFA 3 from 4yo+ 15lb **5** Ran SP% **110.4**
Speed ratings (Par 103): **104,101,95,89,85**
CSF £3.36 TOTE £1.10: £1.10, £3.90; EX 4.10.
Owner Mrs B Oughtred **Bred** Gerrardstown House Stud **Trained** Great Habton, N Yorks

FOCUS
A weak and uncompetitive maiden, but the pace was decent. The winner was 10lb+ off his previous form.

2670 GO RACING IN YORKSHIRE H'CAP — 5f 212y

4:45 (4:46) (Class 6) (0-65,62) 3-Y-O+ — **£2,729** (£806; £403) **Stalls** Low

Form — RPR

-064 **1** **North Central (USA)**^{8} [2412] 4-9-11 **59** (p) DanielTudhope 1 — 70+
(Jim Goldie) *trckd ldr: led over 1f out: styd on wl* **5/1**^{3}

-042 **2** *1 ½* **Baybshambles (IRE)**^{19} [2126] 7-9-10 **58** RobbieFitzpatrick 4 — 63
(Ron Barr) *trckd ldrs: swtchd rt 2f out: wnt 2nd appr fnl f: no imp* **8/1**

4462 **3** *3 ½* **This Ones For Eddy**^{24} [1989] 6-9-2 **50** GrahamGibbons 8 — 44
(John Balding) *mid-div: rdn and outpcd over 3f out: hdwy and swtchd rt 2f out: kpt on to take modest 3rd fnl strides* **3/1**^{2}

0-00 **4** *shd* **Piste**^{3} [2588] 5-8-10 **47** PatrickDonaghy(3) 7 — 40
(Tina Jackson) *dwlt: hdwy and swtchd ins 2f out: tk 3rd ins fnl f: kpt on one pce* **66/1**

4124 **5** *2 ¼* **Boy The Bell**^{7} [2464] 4-9-9 **62** DaleSwift(5) 11 — 56+
(Brian Ellison) *trckd ldrs: effrt whn hmpd 2f out: no ch after* **11/4**^{1}

-000 **6** *½* **Bahamian Kid**^{31} [1803] 6-9-4 **52** (v) TonyHamilton 2 — 36
(George Foster) *drvn to ld: hdd over 1f out: sn wknd* **33/1**

000- **7** *1 ½* **Ursus**^{16} [7148] 6-9-5 **53** (p) PaddyAspell 5 — 33
(Christopher Wilson) *trckd ldrs: hmpd 2f out: sn wknd over 1f out* **20/1**

/0-0 **8** *1 ¼* **Blue Rum (IRE)**^{14} [2247] 4-8-6 **47** LukeStrong(7) 12 — 23
(Alan Kirtley) *chsd ldrs: hmpd 2f out sn wknd* **100/1**

3-00 **9** *½* **Hot Rod Mamma (IRE)**^{11} [2352] 4-9-3 **51** DuranFentiman 9 — 25+
(Dianne Sayer) *in rr: sme hdwy on outer whn hmpd 2f out: nvr a factor* **10/1**

423- **10** *8* **Red Rhythm**^{177} [7757] 4-9-11 **59** PJMcDonald 10 — —
(Micky Hammond) *in rr: wl outpcd and detached over 3f out: sn bhd: b.b.v* **6/1**

1m 13.2s (-0.40) **Going Correction** -0.075s/f (Good) **10** Ran SP% **113.0**
Speed ratings (Par 101): **99,97,92,92,89 88,86,84,84,73**
CSF £41.55 CT £142.26 TOTE £6.80: £2.00, £1.90, £1.40; EX 47.30.
Owner Dogberry Racing **Bred** Tony Holmes & Walter Zent **Trained** Uplawmoor, E Renfrews
■ Stewards' Enquiry : Robbie Fitzpatrick eight-day ban: careless riding (Jun 17-24)

FOCUS
Run-of-the-mill fare, and not form to go overboard about, the principals having the run of the race in a contest where a few of the market leaders lost their chance after some interference 2f out. The first two were clear and the form could rate a bit higher.
This Ones For Eddy ◆ Official explanation: jockey said gelding suffered interference in running
Bahamian Kid Official explanation: jockey said gelding hung left-handed
Red Rhythm Official explanation: vet said gelding bled from the nose

2671 WE RACE AGAIN ON JUNE 29TH H'CAP — 7f

5:15 (5:16) (Class 5) (0-70,70) 3-Y-O+ — **£2,183** (£644; £322) **Stalls** Centre

Form — RPR

2112 **1** **Powerful Presence (IRE)**^{138} [181] 5-9-9 **65** DanielTudhope 4 — 81+
(David O'Meara) *trckd ldrs: wnt 2nd over 2f out: sn led narrowly: styd on wl to forge clr fnl 100yds* **10/3**^{1}

010 **2** *2 ¾* **Dhhamaan (IRE)**^{11} [2354] 6-9-2 **58** (b) PJMcDonald 5 — 67
(Ruth Carr) *mde most: narrowly hdd 2f out: styd on same pce ins fnl f* **14/1**

0-55 **3** *1 ½* **Thinking**^{15} [2233] 4-8-10 **52** DavidAllan 7 — 57
(Tim Easterby) *mid-div: hdwy over 2f out: kpt on to take 3rd last 100yds* **12/1**

3024 **4** *½* **Gemma's Delight (IRE)**^{13} [2280] 4-9-2 **58** (p) LiamJones 9 — 62
(James Unett) *in tch: effrt over 2f out: wnt 3rd over 1f out: one pce* **10/1**

60-0 **5** *6* **Nufoudh (IRE)**^{6} [2494] 7-9-10 **69** PaulPickard(3) 10 — 56
(Colin Teague) *chsd ldrs: wknd over 1f out* **40/1**

3514 **6** *1 ½* **Lindoro**^{6} [2487] 6-9-5 **64** SeanLevey(3) 12 — 47+
(Kevin M Prendergast) *chsd ldrs: wknd over 1f out* **9/2**^{2}

-605 **7** *½* **Cyflymder (IRE)**^{13} [2280] 5-9-8 **69** NeilFarley(5) 8 — 51+
(Declan Carroll) *hld up in rr: sme hdwy over 2f out: kpt on: nvr nr ldrs* **9/2**^{2}

-020 **8** *1 ¼* **Call Of Duty (IRE)**^{21} [2046] 6-9-13 **69** DuranFentiman 11 — 48+
(Dianne Sayer) *dwlt: in rr: sme hdwy over 3f out: kpt on fnl 2f: nvr a factor* **8/1**^{3}

00-0 **9** *7* **Our Boy Barrington (IRE)**^{27} [1909] 4-9-11 **70** (v1) MichaelO'Connell(3) 2 — 30
(David Nicholls) *s.i.s: reminders after 1f: sme hdwy over 2f out: wknd over 1f out* **16/1**

060- **10** *shd* **Island Chief**^{213} [7283] 5-9-4 **67** DavidSimmonson(7) 6 — 26
(Michael Easterby) *s.s: a in rr: nvr on terms* **25/1**

0-60 **11** *13* **Ellies Image**^{48} [1394] 4-9-4 **60** GrahamGibbons 1 — —
(Brian Baugh) *s.i.s: hdwy on ins over 4f out: sn chsng ldrs: lost pl wl over 1f out: sn heavily eased* **17/2**

1m 25.78s (-1.22) **Going Correction** -0.075s/f (Good) **11** Ran SP% **116.7**
Speed ratings (Par 103): **103,99,98,97,90 89,88,87,79,78 64**
CSF £51.92 CT £504.10 TOTE £3.50: £1.10, £4.50, £4.50; EX 32.40.
Owner The Lawton Bamforth Partnership **Bred** Corduff Stud **Trained** Nawton, N Yorks
■ A 438-1 four-timer from four rides for Danny Tudhope.

FOCUS
A handicap in which few got into off the back of a good pace. The winner continues to improve and could do better still.
Ellies Image Official explanation: jockey said filly had no more to give

T/Plt: £39.70 to a £1 stake. Pool:£35,070.89 - 644.04 winning tickets. T/Qpdt: £17.90 to a £1 stake. Pool:£2,209.80 - 91.00 winning tickets. WG

2091 DONCASTER (L-H)

Friday, June 3

OFFICIAL GOING: Good to firm (good in places; 6.8)

Wind: Light half behind Weather: Fine and dry

2672 GUINNESS MAIDEN STKS — 6f
6:05 (6:05) (Class 5) 2-Y-O — £2,525 (£751; £375; £187) Stalls High

Form — RPR

5 **1** **Telwaar**[11] 2355 2-9-3 0 ... NeilCallan 4 — 86+
(Peter Chapple-Hyam) *trckd ldrs: smooth hdwy to ld 2f out: rdn and sn qcknd clr: kpt on strly* **5/1**[3]

2 2 ¾ **Campanology** 2-9-3 0 ... JMurtagh 2 — 78+
(Richard Hannon) *green: edgd lft and outpcd in rr early: hdwy 1/2-way: rdn to chse wnr and edgd rt ent fnl f: kpt on: bttr for r* **15/8**[2]

32 **3** 4 ½ **Tortoni (IRE)**[13] 2283 2-9-3 0 ... JimmyFortune 3 — 64
(Kevin Ryan) *trckd ldrs on outer: hdwy over 2f out: sn rdn and chsd wnr: kpt on same pce* **1/1**[1]

65 **4** 3 ¾ **Topcoat (IRE)**[24] 1988 2-9-3 0 ... RoystonFfrench 5 — 53
(Mark Johnston) *led: rdn along 1/2-way: hdd and drvn 2f out: sn wknd* **14/1**

0 **5** nse **Grippa**[10] 2387 2-9-3 0 ... RobertWinston 1 — 53
(David Brown) *cl up: rdn along wl over 2f out: grad wknd* **28/1**

6 1 **Bitaphon (IRE)** 2-9-3 0 ... IanMongan 7 — 50
(Deborah Sanderson) *cl up: rdn along 1/2-way: grad wknd* **50/1**

0 **7** nk **Spoken Words**[15] 2214 2-8-9 0 ... JamesSullivan(3) 6 — 44
(Hugh McWilliams) *a towards rr* **50/1**

8 10 **Port Star** 2-9-3 0 ... AdamKirby 8 — 19
(John Mackie) *a in rr: outpcd and bhd fr wl over 2f out* **50/1**

1m 11.97s (-1.63) **Going Correction** -0.275s/f (Firm) — 8 Ran SP% **117.4**
Speed ratings (Par 93): **99,95,89,84,84 82,82,69**
Tote Swingers: 1&2:£2.50, 1&3:£1.60, 2&3:£1.10 CSF £15.09 TOTE £5.60: £1.20, £1.90, £1.02; EX 15.70.
Owner Ziad A Galadari **Bred** Galadari Sons Stud Company Limited **Trained** Newmarket, Suffolk

FOCUS
Probably no more than a fair maiden in all probability but the winner was impressive and the second also shaped with plenty of promise. The runners came up the centre of the track and the fourth and fifth help set the level.

NOTEBOOK
Telwaar's debut form looked only ordinary but he'd clearly learnt plenty from that and ran out an easy winner with a performance notable for the good turn of foot he showed to put the race to bed 2f out. He doesn't look in need of any further for now, for all his pedigree suggests he'll stay 7f, and though he lacks the Group entries of the second and third, he won well enough to suggest he wouldn't be out of place in the something like the Coventry Stakes. (tchd 11-2)
Campanology ◆ is a half-bother to the 2000 Guineas runner-up Dubawi Gold and holds an entry in the Group 1 National Stakes. He was too green to do himself justice, but there was plenty to like about his effort from halfway without being given anything like a hard time and he'll leave this form behind next time and win a maiden, either at this trip or 7f. (tchd 13-8)
Tortoni(IRE) had been unsuited by the track at Chester last time, according to his trainer, but once again failed to confirm the promise of his debut or the expectation of his Group 1 entry. He tended to hang left even before the winner went on and then readily left after the winner asserted. He's clearly well thought of, but he's had three quick races and looked here either in need of a break or easier ground. (op 6-5 tchd 5-4)
Topcoat(IRE) looks limited for now, at this sort of trip at least, but this run will qualify him for nurseries and, given that his dam won at 1m4f, he still has potential for improvement at 7f or more.
Grippa was clearly all the better for his recent debut but couldn't go with the leaders once the tempo lifted and probably needs dropping in grade if he's to get off the mark. (op 25-1)
Bitaphon(IRE) hasn't a bad pedigree, being by Acclamation out of a decent sprint winner in Italy, and showed minor promise, up there early and not given a hard time.

2673 EARL OF DONCASTER HOTEL MAIDEN STKS — 7f
6:35 (6:39) (Class 5) 3-Y-O — £2,525 (£751; £375; £187) Stalls High

Form — RPR

22-2 **1** **Johnny Castle**[15] 2216 3-9-3 84 ... NickyMackay 12 — 87
(John Gosden) *prom: hdwy to ld over 2f out: rdn over 1f out: drvn and edgd rt ins fnl f: kpt on* **8/11**[1]

64-3 **2** 1 ¼ **Panoptic**[16] 2192 3-8-12 76 ... IanMongan 14 — 79
(Sir Henry Cecil) *midfield: hdwy 1/2-way: chsd wnr wl over 1f out: rdn and ev ch ent fnl f: sn drvn and kpt on same pce towards fin* **13/2**[3]

3 4 ½ **Raymbek Batyr (IRE)** 3-9-3 0 ... JimmyFortune 11 — 71
(Jeremy Noseda) *midfield: hdwy to trck ldrs 1/2-way: chsd ldng pair 2f out: sn rdn and kpt on same pce* **4/1**[2]

0-4 **4** 7 **Adelina Patti**[15] 2223 3-8-12 0 ... TomEaves 3 — 48
(Walter Swinburn) *t.k.h early: trckd ldrs: effrt wl over 2f out: sn rdn and outpcd: styd on ins fnl f* **16/1**

0 **5** ¾ **Mandatori (IRE)**[49] 1362 3-8-12 0 ... (t) JMurtagh 5 — 46
(Nicky Vaughan) *led: rdn along 3f out: hdd over 2f out: drvn wl over 1f out: sn wknd* **50/1**

6- **6** hd **Dictionary**[293] 5085 3-9-3 0 ... NeilCallan 6 — 50
(William Haggas) *hld up: hdwy on outer 3f out: rdn 2f out: sn no imp* **12/1**

2040 **7** shd **Cold Secret**[37] 1611 3-9-3 67 ... (p) AdamKirby 9 — 50
(David Elsworth) *prom: rdn along 3f out: grad wknd* **28/1**

6-0 **8** 2 ½ **Crabbies Gold (IRE)**[20] 2094 3-9-0 0 ... JamesSullivan(3) 13 — 43
(Lisa Williamson) *a in rr* **100/1**

9 ¾ **Kool Shuffle (GER)** 3-9-3 0 ... MickyFenton 7 — 41
(Tom Tate) *dwlt: a towards rr* **50/1**

10 hd **Toothache** 3-8-12 0 ... KirstyMilczarek 15 — 35
(Garry Woodward) *s.i.s and bhd: swtchd lft and hdwy after 3f: in tch 3f out: sn rdn and wknd 2f out* **100/1**

05 **11** 1 **Anathena**[13] 2281 3-8-12 0 ... TonyCulhane 8 — 33
(Reg Hollinshead) *midfield: hdwy to chse ldrs 1/2-way: rdn along wl over 2f out: sn wknd* **66/1**

12 21 **Powder Keg** 3-9-3 0 ... RoystonFfrench 2 — —
(Mark Johnston) *in tch: rdn along over 3f out: sn wknd* **25/1**

00- **13** 6 **Pope Potter**[202] 7452 3-9-0 0 ... RobertLButler(3) 10 — —
(Richard Guest) *a towards rr: rdn along and bhd fr 1/2-way* **200/1**

1m 24.7s (-1.60) **Going Correction** -0.275s/f (Firm) — 13 Ran SP% **120.0**
Speed ratings (Par 99): **98,96,91,83,82 82,82,79,78,78 77,53,46**
Tote Swingers: 1&2 £2.40, 1&3 £1.80, 2&3 £3.10 CSF £5.74 TOTE £1.40: £1.02, £2.00, £1.70; EX 5.60.
Owner Normandie Stud Ltd **Bred** Normandie Stud Ltd **Trained** Newmarket, Suffolk

FOCUS
A big field but a wide range of abilities on show and it was the form horses who came to the fore with the runners again coming down the centre of the track. The winner sets the standard.
Anathena Official explanation: jockey said filly hung left throughout

2674 CRYER AND STOTT CHEESEMONGER H'CAP — 1m (S)
7:10 (7:11) (Class 4) (0-80,80) 4-Y-O+ — £4,597 (£1,368; £683; £341) Stalls High

Form — RPR

4231 **1** **Sunset Kitty (USA)**[16] 2207 4-9-6 79 ... AdamKirby 8 — 90
(Walter Swinburn) *in tch: hdwy to trck ldrs 1/2-way: effrt 2f out: rdn to ld over 1f out: drvn and edgd rt ins fnl f: styd on* **7/1**[3]

0011 **2** ¾ **Dazeen**[13] 2301 4-8-13 72 ... TonyCulhane 11 — 81
(Paul Midgley) *hld up towards rr: hdwy 3f out: effrt and n.m.r over 2f out: sn swtchd rt and rdn to chal ent fnl f: sn drvn: edgd lft and one pce* **8/1**

0000 **3** 1 ½ **San Cassiano (IRE)**[20] 2105 4-9-4 80 ... (b[1]) JamesSullivan(3) 6 — 87
(Ruth Carr) *a.p: led wl over 2f out: rdn and hdd over 1f out: drvn and edging lft whn n.m.r and swvd lft wl ins fnl f: one pce* **15/2**

5014 **4** ½ **Euston Square**[21] 2046 5-9-4 77 ... TomEaves 9 — 83
(Alistair Whillans) *hld up towards rr: hdwy 3f out: rdn to chal over 1f out: n.m.r and drvn ent fnl f: hld whn hmpd and carried lft last 100yds* **16/1**

3456 **5** 3 **Standpoint**[13] 2301 5-9-4 77 ... NeilCallan 14 — 75
(Reg Hollinshead) *hld up in tch: hdwy to chse ldrs over 3f out: rdn along over 2f out: sn drvn and kpt on same pce* **4/1**[1]

6-13 **6** 3 ¼ **Aquarian Spirit**[24] 1970 4-9-5 78 ... TonyHamilton 10 — 68
(Richard Fahey) *led: rdn along 3f out and sn hdd: drvn 2f out and grad wknd* **5/1**[2]

0-00 **7** ½ **Satwa Laird**[15] 2217 5-9-6 79 ... TomMcLaughlin 5 — 68
(Ed Dunlop) *racd wd: prom: effrt and ev ch over 2f out: sn rdn and wknd over 1f out* **8/1**

0006 **8** 2 ¾ **Aerodynamic (IRE)**[20] 2115 4-8-13 72 ... PaddyAspell 13 — 55
(Clive Mulhall) *a towards rr* **33/1**

5450 **9** hd **Vanilla Rum**[20] 2112 4-8-9 68 ... MickyFenton 2 — 50
(John Mackie) *towards rr: hdwy on wd outside and in tch over 3f out: sn rdn along and wknd wl over 2f out* **25/1**

0-00 **10** 3 ½ **Without Prejudice (USA)**[11] 2347 6-9-7 80 ... GrahamGibbons 3 — 54
(Michael Easterby) *dwlt: sn swtchd rt: a in rr* **66/1**

0-05 **11** ¾ **West End Lad**[57] 1201 8-9-6 79 ... (b) RussKennemore 12 — 52
(Roy Bowring) *cl up on inner: rdn along wl over 2f out: sn wknd* **40/1**

326- **12** 12 **Cabal**[20] 5149 4-9-3 79 ... SeanLevey(3) 1 — 24
(Andrew Crook) *dwlt: a in rr* **40/1**

0-11 **13** 9 **Batgirl**[14] 2270 4-9-0 73 ... PatCosgrave 4 — —
(John Berry) *dwlt and towards rr: hdwy over 3f out: chsd ldrs over 2f out: sn rdn and wknd* **9/1**

1223 **14** 4 ½ **Sharakti (IRE)**[9] 2403 4-9-3 76 ... (p) RobertWinston 7 — —
(Alan McCabe) *cl up: rdn along wl over 2f out: sn wknd* **7/1**[3]

1m 37.18s (-2.12) **Going Correction** -0.275s/f (Firm) — 14 Ran SP% **124.7**
Speed ratings (Par 105): **99,98,96,96,93 90,89,86,86,83 82,70,61,56**
Tote Swingers: 1&2 £14.50, 1&3 £12.60, 2&3 £12.90 CSF £61.98 CT £445.49 TOTE £7.00: £2.80, £2.40, £3.70; EX 38.30.
Owner Cool Cats **Bred** Mckee Stables Inc **Trained** Aldbury, Herts

FOCUS
A fair handicap in which the runners were well bunched for much of the way and it paid not to be too far back. The action took place centre to stands' side and the form looks sound.

2675 STOBART GROUP H'CAP — 1m (R)
7:40 (7:41) (Class 5) (0-75,75) 3-Y-O — £2,525 (£751; £375; £187) Stalls Low

Form — RPR

10-0 **1** **Aciano (IRE)**[15] 2229 3-9-7 75 ... MartinDwyer 8 — 85+
(Brian Meehan) *a.p on outer: cl up 1/2-way: rdn to ld 1 1/2f out: clr ins fnl f* **13/2**[3]

26-1 **2** 2 ¾ **Hernando Torres**[20] 2119 3-8-12 66 ... GrahamGibbons 1 — 69
(Michael Easterby) *trckd ldrs on inner: hdwy and cl up 3f out: effrt 2f out: sn rdn and ev ch tl drvn and one pce ent fnl f* **13/2**[3]

3-14 **3** hd **Konstantin (IRE)**[25] 1949 3-9-1 69 ... HayleyTurner 6 — 72
(Marcus Tregoning) *cl up: rdn to ld over 2f out: hdd 1 1/2f out and sn drvn: one pce ent fnl f* **6/1**[1]

41-0 **4** ½ **Mantatisi**[13] 2313 3-9-4 72 ... PatCosgrave 7 — 73
(James Fanshawe) *trckd ldrs: hdwy 3f out: rdn 2f out: drvn and one pce ent fnl f* **11/4**[1]

05-5 **5** 1 **Arctic Cat (IRE)**[35] 1655 3-8-5 59 ... AndrewElliott 5 — 58+
(Mrs K Burke) *in rr: pushed along 3f out: rdn 2f out: styd on appr fnl f: nrst fin* **20/1**

02-2 **6** 1 ¼ **Nicola's Dream**[14] 2264 3-9-1 69 ... TonyHamilton 4 — 65
(Richard Fahey) *trckd ldrs: pushed along over 3f out: rdn over 2f out: sn drvn and no imp* **8/1**

-430 **7** 1 **Prince Of Passion (CAN)**[14] 2264 3-9-0 68 ... TomEaves 9 — 62
(Michael Dods) *hld up towards rr: effrt and sme hdwy wl over 2f out: sn rdn and n.d* **33/1**

0-11 **8** 15 **Iron Step**[21] 2064 3-9-7 75 ... JMurtagh 2 — 34
(Nicky Vaughan) *sn led: pushed along 4f out: rdn 3f out: sn hrd pressed and hdd over 2f out: wknd qckly and eased* **11/4**[1]

1m 37.82s (-1.88) **Going Correction** -0.275s/f (Firm) — 8 Ran SP% **113.1**
Speed ratings (Par 99): **98,95,95,94,93 92,91,76**
Tote Swingers: 1&2 £7.40, 1&3 £7.80, 2&3 £6.30 CSF £46.80 CT £266.66 TOTE £8.80: £2.60, £3.50, £1.30; EX 62.50.
Owner Mrs Sheila Tucker **Bred** Miss Sarah Thompson **Trained** Manton, Wilts

FOCUS
An ordinary handicap that went the way of one clearly well handicapped at this level. The pace was no more than fair and the runners came up the centre in the straight. The form is rated slightly positively with those in the frame behind the winner all recording personal bests.
Iron Step Official explanation: jockey said gelding hung right

2676 ARICABEAURACING.COM FILLIES' H'CAP — 1m 2f 60y
8:15 (8:15) (Class 3) (0-95,93) 4-Y-O+ — £7,447 (£2,216; £1,107; £553) Stalls Low

Form — RPR

3-04 **1** **Bea Remembered**[10] 2390 4-9-7 93 ... MartinDwyer 7 — 104
(Brian Meehan) *hld up in tch: gd hdwy 3f out: str run to ld 1 1/2f out: sn rdn clr: kpt on strly* **15/2**[3]

21-4 **2** 2 ½ **Opera Gal (IRE)**[44] 1479 4-9-7 93 ... FrannyNorton 3 — 99
(Andrew Balding) *trckd ldng pair: hdwy on inner to ld wl over 2f out: rdn and hdd 1 1/2f out: sn drvn and kpt on same pce* **85/40**[1]

63-2 **3** 1 ¾ **Babycakes (IRE)**[14] 2269 4-9-1 87 ... HayleyTurner 2 — 90
(Michael Bell) *trckd ldrs: hdwy 3f out: rdn 2f out: chsd ldng pair over 1f out: sn drvn and no imp* **9/2**[2]

5215 **4** *1 1/4* **Snow Dancer (IRE)**[29] 1824 7-8-9 **84**........................ JamesSullivan(3) 1 84+
(Hugh McWilliams) *in rr: hdwy 3f out: rdn 2f out: styd on u.p fnl f: nrst fin* **12/1**

20 **5** *shd* **High Figurine (IRE)**[66] 4-8-10 **82**.. LiamJones 6 82
(William Haggas) *chsd ldrs: effrt 3f out: rdn over 2f out: sn drvn and kpt on same pce* **33/1**

16-0 **6** *2 3/4* **Sparkling Smile (IRE)**[27] 1887 4-9-5 **91**.............................. NeilCallan 9 86
(David Lanigan) *hld up: hdwy 3f out: rdn to chse ldrs 2f out: sn drvn and btn over 1f out* **8/1**

-030 **7** *9* **Bahamian Music (IRE)**[13] 2282 4-8-9 **81**....................... TonyHamilton 8 59
(Richard Fahey) *cl up: effrt 3f out and sn rdn: drvn over 2f out and sn wknd* **14/1**

10-0 **8** *7* **Aktia (IRE)**[21] 2066 4-9-0 **86**... KirstyMilczarek 4 50
(Luca Cumani) *hld up in rr: effrt on inner over 3f out: sn rdn and n.d* **8/1**

521- **9** *3/4* **Kristalette (IRE)**[261] 6079 4-9-2 **88**..................................... AdamKirby 5 51
(Walter Swinburn) *led: pushed along over 4f out: rdn 3f out: sn hdd & wknd: bhd and eased fr wl over 1f out* **15/2**[3]

2m 5.65s (-3.75) **Going Correction** -0.275s/f (Firm) **9** Ran SP% **113.2**
Speed ratings (Par 104): **104,102,100,99,99 97,90,84,83**
Tote Swingers: 1&2 £5.10, 1&3 £4.90, 2&3 £3.60 CSF £23.31 CT £80.30 TOTE £11.10: £4.00, £1.02, £2.80; EX 32.00.

Owner Mrs Perle O'Rourke **Bred** Plantation Stud **Trained** Manton, Wilts

FOCUS
A useful handicap run at something of a muddling pace but the winner improved on her best and the third is rated to her best form at the trip. The field stayed far side.

NOTEBOOK
Bea Remembered had run well in a warm Ripon handicap last time and, upped to this trip for the first time, found further improvement ridden closer to the pace than she had been then. Her ability at shorter trips clearly stood her in good stead here as the race was run, but she still won with a lot of authority and is probably a bit better than a handicapper. She looks very well suited by fast ground. (op 7-1)

Opera Gal(IRE) duly made the expected improvement from her reappearance with her yard in excellent form, but simply ran into a better-handicapped rival on the day under the conditions. She'll probably be put back over 1m4f at some point, as she possibly lacks the pace on ground this fast to win a handicap at this trip off her current mark. (op 11-4 tchd 2-1)

Babycakes(IRE) was very briefly short of room but it wasn't an excuse, and she ran as well as might have been expected at a trip that's as far as she wants to go. (op 4-1 tchd 7-2)

Snow Dancer(IRE) ideally needs a stiffer test than this so, considering she wasn't best placed as the race was run and then found trouble, she emerges with a fair amount of credit. (op 14-1)

High Figurine(IRE) seemed to run respectably on her first start since being trained in France while leaving the impression a return to 1m4f (and possibly easier ground) will see her to better effect.

Aktia(IRE) must have been more to her performance than not getting the strong pace that suits ideally. Official explanation: jockey said filly hung left (op 15-2 tchd 13-2)

Kristalette(IRE), who was very progressive last year, was inclined to be too keen on her first run since September and all in all didn't look in the frame of mind to do herself justice. (op 7-1, tchd 8-1 in places)

2677 YORKSHIRE RADIO H'CAP 1m 4f

8:45 (8:46) (Class 5) (0-70,70) 3-Y-O **£2,525** (£751; £375; £187) **Stalls** Low

Form RPR

4561 **1** **L'Hermitage (IRE)**[13] 2305 3-9-7 **70**.............................(p) MartinDwyer 1 79
(Brian Meehan) *hld up in tch: hdwy 3f out: swtchd rt to chse ldrs 2f out: rdn to ld over 1f out: drvn and hdd ins fnl f: rallied wl to ld again last 50yds* **16/1**

-103 **2** *1/2* **Romeo Montague**[13] 2293 3-9-7 **70**......................... TomMcLaughlin 10 78
(Ed Dunlop) *t.k.h: hld up in rr: hdwy 3f out: str run on inner over 2f out: nt clr run and swtchd rt over 1f out: led ins fnl f: sn rdn and edgd lft: hdd and no ex last 50yds* **17/2**

4-50 **3** *hd* **Getabuzz**[48] 1415 3-8-12 **61**.. DavidAllan 9 69
(Tim Easterby) *hld up towards rr: hdwy on outer wl over 2f out: rdn to chal over 1f out and ev ch tl drvn and one pce last 100yds* **10/1**

-212 **4** *3 1/4* **Watered Silk**[15] 2225 3-9-0 **63**.. HayleyTurner 6 66
(Marcus Tregoning) *trckd ldr: cl up 4f out: led wl over 2f out and sn rdn along: drvn and hdd over 1f out: one pce* **13/8**[1]

-413 **5** *2 1/4* **Achalas (IRE)**[15] 2228 3-9-3 **69**... SeanLevey(3) 8 68
(Heather Main) *chsd ldrs: hdwy on outer 3f out: rdn along and ch 2f out tl drvn: n.m.r and wknd ent fnl f* **4/1**[2]

2-10 **6** *2 3/4* **Bouggatti**[21] 2076 3-9-4 **67**... TomEaves 7 62
(William Jarvis) *hld up: effrt on inner and nt clr run 3f out: rdn over 2f out: n.d* **20/1**

-042 **7** *2 1/4* **Tarantella Lady**[11] 2349 3-9-4 **67**...................................... PJMcDonald 5 58
(George Moore) *in tch: rdn along over 3f out: sn wknd* **18/1**

60-6 **8** *3 1/4* **Illustrious Forest**[20] 2119 3-8-8 **57**........................... GrahamGibbons 3 43
(John Mackie) *led: rdn along 4f out: hdd wl over 2f out and sn wknd* **8/1**[3]

40-0 **9** *10* **Tileyf (IRE)**[34] 1683 3-9-5 **68**..(b[1]) AdamKirby 4 38
(Clive Cox) *chsd ldrs: rdn along over 3f out: sn wknd* **33/1**

0-44 **10** *10* **Divinite Green (IRE)**[24] 1991 3-9-7 **70**.......................... JimmyFortune 2 24
(Peter Chapple-Hyam) *trckd ldrs on inner: rdn along over 3f out: sn wknd* **11/1**

2m 31.94s (-2.96) **Going Correction** -0.275s/f (Firm) **10** Ran SP% **116.0**
Speed ratings (Par 99): **98,97,97,95,93 92,90,88,81,75**
Tote Swingers: 1&2 £27.10, 1&3 £22.50, 2&3 £16.60 CSF £144.26 CT £1438.45 TOTE £22.70: £5.30, £4.30, £4.90; EX 141.00.

Owner Paul & Jenny Green **Bred** Paul Green **Trained** Manton, Wilts

FOCUS
An interesting finale and an exciting finish at the end of a race run at decent enough clip from far enough out to ensure a decent test at the trip. The runners again kept to the far rail in the straight and it's probably solid, if ordinary, form for the grade with the fourth to his latest mark.

Divinite Green(IRE) Official explanation: jockey said colt lost its action

T/Plt: £98.20 to a £1 stake. Pool £72,192.11 - 536.51 winning tickets. T/Qpdt: £92.90 to a £1 stake. Pool £4,307.33 - 34.30 winning tickets. JR

1476 EPSOM (L-H)

Friday, June 3

OFFICIAL GOING: Good (overall 8.0; stands' side 8.2; far side 7.8)
Rail dolled out 5yds from 8f to 6f and upto 5yds from 5f to winning post adding approximately 10yds to distances.

2678 PRINCESS ELIZABETH STKS (SPONSORED BY INVESTEC) (GROUP 3) (F&M) 1m 114y

1:40 (1:41) (Class 1) 3-Y-O+

£28,385 (£10,760; £5,385; £2,685; £1,345; £675) **Stalls** Low

Form RPR

202- **1** **Antara (GER)**[222] 7109 5-9-6 116..................................... FrankieDettori 7 108+
(Saeed Bin Suroor) *dwlt: hld up in midfield: hdwy over 2f out: rdn and qcknd to ld over 1f out: kpt on wl and a doing enough ins fnl f* **11/8**[1]

24-6 **2** *3/4* **First City**[34] 1681 5-9-6 101.. WilliamBuick 1 106
(David Simcock) *hld up in last trio: rdn and effrt wl over 2f out: sustained run fr 2f out: chsd wnr fnl 100yds: kpt on wl and clsng on wnr at fin* **16/1**

16- **3** *2 1/2* **Clinical**[300] 4842 3-8-8 91.. SebSanders 8 99+
(Sir Mark Prescott Bt) *chsd ldrs: rdn and effrt wl over 2f out: outpcd by wnr over 1f out: wnt 2nd briefly and edgd lft ins fnl f: kpt on same pce fnl 100yds* **15/2**[3]

21-3 **4** *3 1/2* **Timepiece**[22] 2029 4-9-6 110.. TomQueally 3 97
(Sir Henry Cecil) *lw: w ldr tl led 6f out: rdn and edging lft over 2f out: hdd and nt pce of wnr over 1f out: 4th and btn whn n.m.r and hmpd ins fnl f* **6/4**[2]

5 *1 1/4* **Skyway (IRE)**[26] 1929 4-9-6 87.. KLatham 2 90
(Richard Brabazon, Ire) *swtg: t.k.h: led for 2f: styd w ldr tl rdn over 2f out: sn losing pl: wknd over 1f out* **20/1**

00- **6** *1* **Mountain Rose (GER)**[12] 4-9-6 89.......................... RichardHughes 4 88
(Mario Hofer, Germany) *stdd after s: hld up in rr: rdn and effrt 3f out: no real hdwy: nvr threatened ldrs* **66/1**

-052 **7** *hd* **Nabah**[11] 2358 3-8-8 90... PhilipRobinson 10 85
(Clive Brittain) *swtg: s.i.s: a towards rr: rdn and no hdwy over 3f out: nvr trbld ldrs* **22/1**

1111 **8** *3 3/4* **Saddlers Bend (IRE)**[11] 2358 5-9-6 76........................ MatthewDavies 6 79
(George Baker) *chsd ldrs: rdn over 3f out: drvn and unable qck over 2f out: wknd wl over 1f out* **33/1**

1m 43.72s (-2.38) **Going Correction** -0.075s/f (Good)
WFA 3 from 4yo+ 12lb **8** Ran SP% **113.3**
Speed ratings (Par 113): **107,106,104,101,99 99,98,95**
Tote Swingers: 1&2 £3.60, 1&3 £2.60, 2&3 £5.40 CSF £21.69 TOTE £2.30: £1.10, £2.20, £2.10; EX 14.80 Trifecta £47.10 Pool: £10,020.74 - 157.32 winning units..

Owner Godolphin **Bred** Th Gehrig **Trained** Newmarket, Suffolk

FOCUS
Despite warm weather and a drying wind the official going remained Good before this opening race of the meeting. The rails were dolled out 5yds from the inner for all but a furlong of this mile trip, adding 10yds to race distances, and the riders reported the ground was riding 'perfect' or on the firm side of good. \n\x\x This fillies' Group 3 has been won by some useful types in recent seasons, the best of them being subsequent Group 1 winners Echelon and Eva's Request. This year's contest featured a mixed range of abilities judged on official ratings, with a span of some 40lb between the highest and lowest. Saeed Bin Suroor has a good record in the race, having won three of last seven renewals, and his Antara was a cut above these. She did not need to get close to her best, with the runner-up limiting the form.

NOTEBOOK
Antara(GER), the 2010 winner, was bidding to emulate Echelon by scoring in successive years. Her last win was in this race on her reappearance last year, but she was subsequently placed in three Group 1 races and had the highest official rating. She scored in similar style to last season, coming with a smooth run from off the pace to lead, and then holding off the late challenge of the runner-up under just hands and heels. She looks unlikely to go to Royal Ascot and connections will look for Group 1 races later in the season. (op 5-1 tchd 6-1 in places)

First City, the winner of a mile handicap off 98 and placed in a Group 3 over 7f last August, had to prove she was up to this grade. She put up a fine effort, though, coming from off the pace to close in on the winner near the finish. If she can repeat this there are races to be won at Group 3 or Listed level with her. (tchd 14-1 and 20-1 in places)

Clinical, a winner on her debut over 7f on fast ground, but well beaten in the Group 3 Sweet Solera on her second start in August and not seen since, was interesting on this return despite having a fair amount to find on the ratings. She was well supported and ran creditably, chasing the pace throughout but not being able to go with the principals in the latter stages despite running on. She secured black type though, and her trainer can be expected to find her a suitable opportunity in Listed company at some point, although she might go to Royal Ascot next. (op 10-1 tchd 6-1 and 11-1 in a place)

Timepiece, a smart triple Listed winner and Group placed, was clear second best on the ratings and in the betting. She raced upsides the leader before asserting early in the straight, but had no more to offer when challenged by the winner and dropped away, getting unbalanced in the closing stages. The only previous occasion she finished out of the frame was in last year's Oaks, and it is likely that the course does not suit her. (op 7-4)

Skyway(IRE), a useful Irish mare at up to 1m1f on a sound surface, tried to make the running but was given no peace by the second-favourite and soon dropped away once headed. (op 25-1)

Mountain Rose(GER), a German-trained filly whose best efforts in her home country gave her a lot to find on the form, was never able to get involved from the rear.

Nabah had been narrowly beaten by Saddlers Bend last time in a conditions race on fast. She reversed that form on better terms, but was always out the back. (op 25-1 tchd 28-1)

Saddlers Bend(IRE), an in-foal mare and improved as a result, had posted her best effort yet when giving Nabah 7lb and a neck beating at Leicester. The aim was presumably to try to earn black type before she retired to stud and she gave it her best shot, chasing the leaders before fading in the straight. (op 28-1)

2679 INVESTEC MILE (H'CAP) 1m 114y

2:10 (2:12) (Class 2) (0-105,100) 4-Y-O+

£15,577 (£4,665; £2,332; £1,167; £582; £292) **Stalls** Low

Form RPR

-203 **1** **Dance And Dance (IRE)**[22] 2031 5-9-4 **97**......................... RyanMoore 4 109
(Edward Vaughan) *lw: s.i.s: hld up in tch towards rr: hdwy on inner 3f out: swtchd rt and gd hdwy 2f out: chsd ldr over 1f out: led ent fnl f: clr fnl 150yds: r.o wl* **15/2**[2]

-053 **2** *2 3/4* **Highland Knight (IRE)**[32] 1760 4-8-8 **87**....................(t) DavidProbert 12 93
(Andrew Balding) *chsd ldng pair: rdn to ld and edgd to rail over 2f out: drvn and hdd ent fnl f: nt pce of wnr after: kpt on wl for 2nd* **9/1**

40-4 **3** ½ **Start Right**[127] 332 4-9-5 **98** .... KierenFallon 17 103+
(Luca Cumani) *lw: stdd s and dropped in bhd: pushed along and effrt bhd a wall of horses 3f out: switching rt to outer over 2f out: gd hdwy over 1f out: chsd ldng pair ins fnl f: r.o: nt rch ldrs* **6/1**[1]

00-0 **4** ½ **Vainglory (USA)**[34] 1684 7-8-6 **90** .... LauraPike(5) 15 94+
(David Simcock) *lw: hld up in last pair: pushed along and effrt bhd a wall of horses wl over 2f out: swtchd rt ent fnl 2f: r.o strly fnl f: nt rch ldrs* **33/1**

0600 **5** ¾ **Spirit Of Sharjah (IRE)**[13] 2288 6-9-2 **95** .... JimmyQuinn 9 97
(Julia Feilden) *hld up wl in tch: hdwy to chse ldng pair and nt clr run over 2f out tl 2f out: drvn and kpt on same pce fr over 1f out* **33/1**

0-61 **6** 2½ **Extraterrestrial**[20] 2115 7-9-0 **93** .... PaulHanagan 5 90
(Richard Fahey) *in tch: rdn and effrt to chse ldrs wl over 2f out: unable qck and outpcd wl over 1f out: styd on same pce and no threat to ldrs fnl f* **8/1**[3]

3-62 **7** ½ **Arabian Spirit**[20] 2105 6-8-9 **88** .... PaulMulrennan 2 91+
(Richard Fahey) *lw: chsd ldrs: rdn and effrt whn trapped bhd wkng rival over 2f out: rdn and rallied wl over 1f out: styd on same pce and no imp fnl f* **16/1**

00-0 **8** 1 **Citrus Star (USA)**[33] 1720 4-9-7 **100** .... GeorgeBaker 6 93
(Chris Wall) *in tch: rdn and effrt to chse ldr 2f out tl over 1f out: wknd ent fnl f* **14/1**

0-10 **9** ½ **Wannabe King**[22] 2031 5-9-5 **98** ....(b) TedDurcan 10 90
(David Lanigan) *hld up in tch in midfield: effrt to chse ldrs over 2f out: unable qck u.p ent fnl 2f: wknd over 1f out* **9/1**

014 **10** ¾ **Merchant Of Medici**[13] 2310 4-8-3 **82** .... ChrisCatlin 7 73
(William Muir) *taken down early: hld up in last trio: effrt and switching rt over 2f out: no prog u.p 2f out: n.d after* **25/1**

0406 **11** 1¼ **Space Station**[7] 2470 5-8-4 **83** ....(b) NickyMackay 11 71
(Simon Dow) *hld up in tch towards rr: rdn and effrt wl over 2f out: no imp fr wl over 1f out: nvr threatened ldrs* **33/1**

1251 **12** 7 **Benandonner (USA)**[20] 2105 8-8-11 **90** .... MartinLane 13 62
(Mike Murphy) *chsd ldrs: rdn and struggling over 3f out: wknd qckly ent fnl 2f* **14/1**

-650 **13** 6 **Totally Ours**[22] 2031 4-8-13 **92** .... JimCrowley 14 51
(William Muir) *a bhd: rdn and no hdwy 3f out: nvr on terms* **50/1**

2000 **14** 5 **Tartan Gigha (IRE)**[34] 1684 6-9-1 **94** .... SilvestreDeSousa 3 42
(Mark Johnston) *nvr travelling wl: chsd ldrs and niggled along: rdn and losing pl 3f out: wl bhd fnl f* **8/1**[3]

200- **15** 1¾ **Beauchamp Xerxes**[177] 7776 5-9-6 **99** .... WilliamBuick 16 43
(Gerard Butler) *in tch on outer: rdn and effrt over 2f out: hung lft and sltly hmpd 2f out: sn wknd: eased ins fnl f* **25/1**

2600 **16** 1¼ **Hacienda (IRE)**[15] 2217 4-8-9 **88** .... GregFairley 8 30
(Mark Johnston) *w ldr tl wl over 2f out: sn wknd: wl bhd fnl f* **20/1**

210- **17** 7 **Kajima**[231] 6888 4-9-1 **94** .... RichardHughes 1 —
(Richard Hannon) *led tl over 2f out: sn struggling: wknd rapidly 2f out: wl bhd and eased ins fnl f: t.o* **14/1**

/20- **18** 19 **Sowaylm**[265] 5955 4-8-11 **90** ....(t) FrankieDettori 18 —
(Saeed Bin Suroor) *stdd s: hld up towards rr: rdn and short-lived effrt 3f out: sn wknd: wl bhd and virtually p.u ins fnl f: t.o* **20/1**

1m 43.18s (-2.92) **Going Correction** -0.075s/f (Good) **18** Ran SP% **122.2**
Speed ratings (Par 109): **109,106,106,105,105 102,102,101,101,100 99,93,87,83,81 80,74,57**
Tote Swingers: 1&2 £16.50, 1&3 £4.60, 2&3 £12.40 CSF £64.49 CT £452.62 TOTE £7.10: £2.10, £3.10, £2.00, £9.50; EX 72.90 Trifecta £268.30 Pool: £2,965.93 - 8.10 winning units..
Owner Mohammed Rashid **Bred** Darley **Trained** Newmarket, Suffolk

FOCUS
A competitive, good-quality handicap, although the topweight was racing off 5lb lower than the permitted maximum. The pace was sound and there was a mix of prominent racers and hold-up horses amongst the principals. The time was half a second quicker than the earlier Group 3. The winner is rated up 6lb but had more the run of the race than some.

NOTEBOOK
Dance And Dance(IRE) had run well when third in a similarly competitive event, the Listed Hambleton Handicap, at York last month. Well drawn, he was slow to break in common with recent runs, but made a forward move once into the straight. Going after the leader heading to the final furlong, he was quickly past him and won pulling away. He could run in the Royal Hunt Cup, but jarred himself at Ascot last year and would not want conditions too firm. (op 7-1 tchd 8-1)
Highland Knight(IRE), always close up, kicked for home as the leading pair fell away, and although he was soon cut down by the winner he stuck on well for second. He has been beaten plenty of times off this sort of mark, including on Polytrack latest, but is pretty consistent and unlikely to earn much respite from the handicapper. (op 8-1)
Start Right ◆, off the track since a run in Dubai in January, had stall 17 to overcome. Dropped in at the back by Kieren Fallon, he still had only three behind him at the 3f pole, but soon began to pick up ground once switched out and finished nicely for third. The draw did for him here, but he remains well capable of picking up a nice handicap from his current mark and the Royal Hunt Cup could fit the bill. (op 7-1 tchd 11-2)
Vainglory(USA) was third in this a year ago when 2lb higher. Adopting a change of tactics, he was held up at the back and his rider momentarily appeared to lose an iron on the descent to Tattenham Corner. His path was blocked up the straight, but once switched out for a clear passsage he made rapid progress past rivals and would have been second with a little further to run. He's currently 3lb above his highest winning mark. (tchd 40-1 in a place)
Spirit Of Sharjah(IRE), a winner over 7f here, took a bold route up the rail but, after moving into third, he faded late on. This trip just found him out but an easy mile should not pose him too many problems.
Extraterrestrial was raised 10lb for his easy win at Thirsk but that still left him well handicapped on his best old form and he was 5lb lower than when seventh in this race last year. After jinking leaving the stalls, he had his chance in the straight but was held in the final furlong.
Arabian Spirit was travelling strongly when finding himself trapped behind horses as leader Hacienda dropped back rapidly. He could not recover the lost momentum when in the clear, but is worth another chance back on a more conventional track. His rider confirmed the gelding was denied a clear run. Official explanation: jockey said gelding was denied a clear run
Citrus Star(USA) faded after losing second spot to the winner over a furlong out and may not have stayed the longer trip. (op 16-1)
Wannabe King, behind Dance And Dance at York, performed only respectably here. (tchd 10-1)
Merchant Of Medici made late progress from off the pace and probably remains in form.
Space Station Official explanation: jockey said gelding hung left (tchd 40-1 in a place)
Sowaylm Official explanation: jockey said colt was unsuited by the track

2680 INVESTEC CORONATION CUP (GROUP 1) 1m 4f 10y
2:45 (2:47) (Class 1) 4-Y-O **£141,925** (£53,800; £26,925; £13,425; £6,725) **Stalls** Centre

Form RPR

6-31 **1** **St Nicholas Abbey (IRE)**[28] 1851 4-9-0 122 .... RyanMoore 1 124+
(A P O'Brien, Ire) *t.k.h: chsd ldr: rdn over 3f out: nt pce of ldr and squeezed for room 2f out: swtchd rt wl over 1f out: drvn and rallied ent fnl f: styd on gamely to ld fnl 75yds: gng away at fin* **1/1**[1]

12-1 **2** 1 **Midday**[22] 2029 5-8-11 121 .... TomQueally 3 119
(Sir Henry Cecil) *lw: hld up in tch: qcknd to ld 3f out: edging lft 2f out but sn rdn 2 l clr: drvn ent fnl f: hdd and no ex fnl 75yds* **5/4**[2]

10- **3** 2 **Clowance**[208] 7373 6-8-11 110 .... RichardHughes 4 116
(Roger Charlton) *stdd after s: hld up in last: rdn and hanging lft 3f out: sn outpcd by ldrs: stl hanging lft but styd on to go 3rd 1f out: kpt on same pce after* **40/1**

0-11 **4** 3¼ **Dandino**[34] 1685 4-9-0 113 .... PaulMulrennan 5 114
(James Given) *led at stdy gallop: rdn and qcknd over 3f out: hdd 3f out: unable qck and struggling whn short of room and hmpd 2f out: wknd over 1f out* **10/1**[3]

0-13 **5** 5 **Indian Days**[34] 1685 6-9-0 114 .... PaulHanagan 2 106
(James Given) *t.k.h: chsd ldng pair: rdn whn pce qcknd over 3f out: immediately outpcd: wknd and wl btn over 1f out* **28/1**

2m 37.18s (-1.72) **Going Correction** -0.075s/f (Good) **5** Ran SP% **109.4**
Speed ratings (Par 117): **102,101,100,97,94**
CSF £2.46 TOTE £2.30: £1.80, £1.10; EX 3.30.
Owner D Smith, Mrs J Magnier, M Tabor **Bred** Barton Bloodstock & Villiers Synd **Trained** Ballydoyle, Co Tipperary

FOCUS
This Group 1 over the full Derby distance has been dominated by Aidan O'Brien in recent seasons, as the Coolmore trainer has now been responsible for five of the last seven winners. Fillies generally have a good record in this race, despite the last female winner being In The Groove in 1991, with several having been placed in recent seasons. Two of the five taking part here were females and they filled the places. This lacked pace and Midday was surely not at her best. St Nicholas Abbey rates a small personal best.

NOTEBOOK
St Nicholas Abbey(IRE), the top juvenile of his generation in 2009, only ran once in 2010 when sixth in the 2,000 Guineas. Beaten at odds-on in a Listed race on soft on his reappearance before running away with the Group 3 Ormonde Stakes on fast going, he was up in class here but significantly was the trainer's sole representative. He proved awkward to saddle and was awash with sweat, admittedly on a very warm day, at the start, but he was similarly excitable at Chester. He harried Dandino for the early lead before settling in second, then struggled to handle Tattenham Corner and looked in trouble as the second favourite ranged up on his outside. He was slightly short of room as that rival drifted across to the rail but he responded when switched outside and, despite wandering up the camber, finished strongly to cut down the mare well inside the final furlong. He is clearly back to something near his juvenile form and the big 1m4f races are likely to be on the agenda now. He was quoted at around 7-2 for the King George and 10-1 for the Prix de L'Arc de Triomphe. (tchd 10-11 and 11-10 in places)
Midday, who was touched off by Sariska in the 2009 Oaks, has done nothing but improve since, winning five Group 1s - two Nassau Stakes, a Yorkshire Oaks, a Prix Vermeille and a Breeders' Cup race. She won a Group 2 on her return and had no problem with the ground. Held up early, she swept around the outside, despite being carried wide by the winner, and hit the front fully 3f from home. However, she drifted to the rail and, after looking certain to win, had nothing in reserve when the winner produced his late run. She still looks as good as ever, and the feeling was that she would probably have prevailed if her rider had not committed her so early. There are not many opportunities for her in the near future, unless she takes on colts again, so an attempt to win a third Nassau might be next on the agenda. (op 6-4)
Clowance, a Group-winning mare whose career has been truncated by the need to avoid fast ground, did finish fourth in the Oaks on this track in 2008 and was also narrowly beaten in the Group 1 Irish St Leger. Although the ground was probably faster than ideal, she took her chance in what was due to be her last race, as she is in-foal to Oasis Dream. Held up at the back, she made good progress in the straight, despite not looking happy on the ground, and being slightly hampered as the winner drifted right. She stuck to her task though and was not beaten far, despite also stumbling near the finish. She retires to stud as the winner of nearly £167,000 in just ten starts over five seasons, but is a credit to connections who have done well to enable her to maintain her level of form. (tchd 50-1)
Dandino is a progressive colt who acts on any ground and one who has improved from a mark of 77 13 months previously (including a handicap at this meeting last season off 82) to winning the Jockey Club Stakes last time and a rating of 113. He won the early tussle for the lead and then settled the pace before kicking on turning for home, but was soon challenged by the principals and could not quicken, although he appeared to be responding when rather short of room near the rail as the runner-up drifted down the camber. That cost him momentum, and he had no more to offer. He might not be quite up to this class, but there are more Group races to be won with him, with the Hardwicke or the Princess Of Wales's Stakes possible options. (op 9-1)
Indian Days is a consistent sort at a lower level and was 4lb better off for 4 1/4l with stable-companion Dandino compared with their running in the Jockey Club Stakes. He travelled well enough, but was left behind by the others in the straight. He goes well at Goodwood, and a race such as the Glorious Stakes might be a suitable target before a return to Turkey. (op 33-1 tchd 25-1)

2681 INVESTEC INVESTMENT STKS (H'CAP) 1m 2f 18y
3:25 (3:26) (Class 2) 4-Y-O+
£28,039 (£8,397; £4,198; £2,101; £1,048; £526) **Stalls** Low

Form RPR

5-20 **1** **Resurge (IRE)**[23] 2002 6-9-5 **97** .... FergusSweeney 8 107
(Stuart Kittow) *taken down early: hld up in last trio: swtchd rt and hdwy over 2f out: rdn to chse ldrs over 1f out: led ins fnl f: r.o wl and in comand fnl 50yds* **8/1**

22-2 **2** 1¼ **Right Step**[23] 2002 4-9-5 **97** .... RyanMoore 1 104
(Alan Jarvis) *lw: hld up in tch towards rr: rdn and gd hdwy ent fnl 2f: drvn and ev ch 1f out: styd on same pce fnl 100yds* **9/2**[2]

110- **3** 1½ **Dhaamer (IRE)**[244] 6565 4-8-9 **87** .... RichardHills 5 91+
(John Gosden) *chsd ldrs: rdn and effrt wl over 2f out: kpt edging lft but qcknd to ld ent fnl 2f: rdn and hrd pressed 1f out: hdd ins fnl f: wknd towards fin* **5/1**[3]

3011 **4** 1½ **Beaumont's Party (IRE)**[10] 2378 4-8-11 **89** 6ex........ DavidProbert 7 90
(Andrew Balding) *taken down early: hld up in tch in midfield: rdn and effrt 3f out: cl 4th and keeping on whn nt clr run and hmpd jst over 1f out: one pce and no imp after* **7/2**[1]

-602 **5** ¾ **Tres Coronas (IRE)**[29] 1826 4-8-6 **84** .... ChrisCatlin 3 84
(David Barron) *s.i.s: bhd: stl last over 2f out: hdwy past btn horses jst over 1f out: styd on wl fnl f: nvr trbld ldrs* **16/1**

-430 **6** ¾ **Ramona Chase**[21] 2066 6-8-1 **79** ....(t) AndreaAtzeni 10 77
(Michael Attwater) *in tch towards rr: effrt and rdn 3f out: styd on fnl f: nvr gng pce to threaten ldrs* **20/1**

0003 **7** 1½ **Licence To Till (USA)**[6] 2509 4-8-9 **87** .... GregFairley 6 82
(Mark Johnston) *sn niggled along in midfield: effrt u.p wl over 2f out: no hdwy 2f out: wknd over 1f out* **12/1**

-020 **8** *shd* **Pleasant Day (IRE)**[23] 2002 4-8-11 **89** ....(b) PaulHanagan 4 84
(Richard Fahey) *led: rdn over 3f out: hdd and drvn over 2f out: wknd u.p over 1f out* **14/1**

2000 **9** 3¼ **Sand Skier**[23] 2002 4-8-3 **81** .... SilvestreDeSousa 9 69
(Mark Johnston) *chsd ldr tl over 6f out: rdn 5f out: wknd and n.m.r over 2f out: wl btn fnl f* **25/1**

0-00 **10** *2 ¼* **Oriental Scot**[34] [1694] 4-8-10 **88**.................................... SteveDrowne 11 72
(William Jarvis) *chsd ldrs tl wnt 2nd over 6f out tl over 2f out: wkng whn short of room and hmpd wl over 1f out: wl btn fnl f* **16/1**

06-3 **11** *3 ¾* **Prompter**[61] [1112] 4-9-10 **102**.. JamieSpencer 2 78
(Michael Bell) *in tch in midfield: rdn and unable qck over 2f out: short of room and shuffled bk towards rr 2f out: n.d after* **8/1**

2m 7.07s (-2.63) **Going Correction** -0.075s/f (Good) **11** Ran SP% **114.0**
Speed ratings (Par 109): **107,106,104,103,103 102,101,101,98,96 93**
Tote Swingers: 1&2 £5.80, 1&3 £11.30, 2&3 £4.50 CSF £42.48 CT £199.06 TOTE £8.90: £2.60, £1.70, £2.00; EX 40.50 Trifecta £237.50 Pool: £3,539.35 - 11.02 winning units..
Owner Chris & David Stam **Bred** Sweetmans Bloodstock **Trained** Blackborough, Devon

FOCUS
A well contested handicap, run at a sound pace, and this is solid form which could rate higher at face value.

NOTEBOOK
Resurge(IRE), who produced a sustained run from the rear to sweep to the front inside the last, has a real penchant for Epsom, and took his record to three wins and two seconds from five starts here, including a second in the City and Suburban over this trip at the April meeting. He was 3lb higher now, having been dropped 2lb after an indifferent run at York. There are no immediate plans for him, but he should always be kept in mind at this venue. (tchd 15-2)
Right Step ran another thoroughly solid race, but after coming through to hold every chance he could not contain the winner, who had finished over 9l behind him at York last month but was 5lb better off here. Without a win since taking a maiden on his second racecourse appearance, he has finished runner-up in six handicaps since, including each of his last four starts, but there doesn't appear to be anything much wrong with his attitude. The Listed Wolferton Stakes, a handicap over this trip, looks a suitable Ascot target, but he is currently operating off a career-high mark. (op 5-1)
Dhaamer(IRE) quickened up to lead at the two pole but was soon tackled. Found out by 1m4f in soft ground when last seen back in October, he is capable of landing a handicap in the coming weeks but would not want conditions any quicker than this. (op 9-2)
Beaumont's Party(IRE) was foiled in his hat-trick attempt, improving to chase the leading three but then running into a spot of trouble. He was 8lb higher than when winning easily at Chepstow, but was officially 3lb ahead of the handicapper and although this was a shade disappointing at face value, he is perhaps worth another chance. (tchd 4-1)
Tres Coronas(IRE) was not well away and did not appear to be travelling that sweetly at the back of the field, but ran on strongly when the race was as good as over and could have a bit of improvement in him at 1m4f. He has never run over that trip but did try 1m6f at Musselburgh in April. (op 14-1)
Ramona Chase was another to come from the rear without ever threatening to get involved. He tends to run creditably at his local track and had been third here in the City and Suburban. (op 16-1)
Licence To Till(USA) was never a significant factor on this fairly quick reappearance. (op 14-1 tchd 11-1)
Pleasant Day(IRE), blinkered again, faded after trying to kick clear in the straight. (op 20-1)
Sand Skier was unable to get to the front and has been well held in two tries here this season. (op 28-1 tchd 33-1)
Oriental Scot was poised in second turning in, but did not pick up from there. The track may not have suited this scopey gelding and he could be worth one more chance to fulfil the promise of his reappearance at Doncaster. (op 14-1)
Prompter had been aimed at this race, but was just starting to struggle when he was slightly short of room. He has a bit to prove after this. (op 9-1 tchd 15-2)

2682 INVESTEC OAKS (GROUP 1) (FILLIES) 1m 4f 10y
4:05 (4:05) (Class 1) 3-Y-O

£184,502 (£69,940; £35,002; £17,452; £8,742; £4,387) **Stalls** Centre

Form RPR

2-12 **1** **Dancing Rain (IRE)**[21] [2050] 3-9-0 99.................................... JMurtagh 7 114
(William Haggas) *mde all: set stdy gallop and allowed to go clr 9f out: c bk to field 4f out: rdn and qcknd clr again over 2f out: pressed ins fnl f: kpt finding ex and r.o gamely* **20/1**

2-1 **2** *¾* **Wonder Of Wonders (USA)**[30] [1807] 3-9-0 106........... KierenFallon 12 112
(A P O'Brien, Ire) *lw: chsd wnr thrght: rdn and outpcd by wnr over 2f out: rallied u.p over 1f out: styd on wl to press wnr ins fnl f: no ex and hld fnl 75yds* **3/1**[2]

-131 **3** *4* **Izzi Top**[21] [2050] 3-9-0 100.. WilliamBuick 2 106
(John Gosden) *chsd ldrs: 4th st: rdn and outpcd wl over 2f out: kpt on same pce [illegible] ldng pair over 1f out tl fnl 100yds: wnt 3rd again nr fin* **25/1**

11-1 **4** *shd* **Blue Bunting (USA)**[33] [1719] 3-9-0 114.......................... FrankieDettori 6 107+
(Mahmood Al Zarooni) *lw: t.k.h: hld up in tch: shuffled bk on downhill run and 7th st: swtchd sharply rt and rdn 3f out: styd on fr wl over 1f out: wnt 3rd but no ch w ldng pair fnl 100yds: eased and lost 3rd nr fin* **9/4**[1]

1-01 **5** *2 ¾* **Misty For Me (IRE)**[12] [2334] 3-9-0 113...................... SeamieHeffernan 4 101
(A P O'Brien, Ire) *leggy: chsd ldng pair: 3rd st: drvn and outpcd by ldng pair wl over 2f out: btn and lost 3rd over 1f out: wknd ins fnl f* **5/1**[3]

-511 **6** *½* **Beatrice Aurore (IRE)**[16] [2189] 3-9-0 99........................ TedDurcan 3 101
(John Dunlop) *t.k.h: hld up in midfield: 6th st: rdn and no hdwy over 2f out: pressing for placings but no ch w ldng pair over 1f out: wknd ins fnl f* **20/1**

7 *1 ¾* **Siren's Song (IRE)**[47] [1428] 3-9-0 .... FMBerry 5 98
(Mrs John Harrington, Ire) *hld up in midfield: 9th st: rdn and no real hdwy wl over 2f out: plugged on same pce and no threat to ldrs fnl 2f* **16/1**

0-0 **8** *1 ¼* **Eirnin (IRE)**[23] [2012] 3-9-0 87.. JPO'Brien 10 96
(A P O'Brien, Ire) *stdd s: hld up in rr: 12th st: rdn and sme hdwy towards inner wl over 2f out: no hdwy fr wl over 1f out: nvr trbld ldrs* **100/1**

1-11 **9** *2 ½* **Zain Al Boldan**[27] [1894] 3-9-0 107.................................... SamHitchcott 8 92
(Mick Channon) *stdd s: hld up in last trio: 10th st: rdn and effrt ent fnl 3f: nvr gng pce to get on terms: kpt on one pce and n.d fnl 2f* **10/1**

11-6 **10** *shd* **Havant**[33] [1719] 3-9-0 105.. RyanMoore 9 92+
(Sir Michael Stoute) *lw: hld up in midfield: 8th st: bmpd and came sharply rt 3f out: no prog u.p and wknd 2f out* **7/1**

232 **11** *2 ½* **Blaise Chorus (IRE)**[30] [1807] 3-9-0 100......................... MichaelHills 13 88
(B W Hills) *t.k.h: hld up in midfield: hdwy and 5th st: rdn and outpcd wl over 2f out: wknd wl over 1f out* **66/1**

0-0 **12** *1 ¼* **Why (IRE)**[23] [2012] 3-9-0 96...................................... MickaelBarzalona 11 86
(A P O'Brien, Ire) *tall: stdd s: hld up in last trio: 11th st: rdn and no hdwy 3f out: n.d* **100/1**

34-3 **13** *41* **Fork Handles**[30] [1807] 3-9-0 96.. JamieSpencer 1 —
(Mick Channon) *swtg: stdd s: hld up in last trio: 11th st: sn lost tch: wl bhd fnl 2f: eased: t.o* **40/1**

2m 41.73s (2.83) **Going Correction** -0.075s/f (Good) **13** Ran SP% **119.2**
Speed ratings (Par 110): **87,86,83,83,81 81,80,79,77,77 76,75,48**
Tote Swingers: 1&2 £16.70, 1&3 £33.70, 2&3 £18.20 CSF £76.36 CT £1557.92 TOTE £29.20: £4.40, £2.00, £7.20; EX 147.10 Trifecta £1314.00 Pool: £13,762.45 - 7.75 winning units..
Owner M J & L A Taylor **Bred** Swettenham Stud **Trained** Newmarket, Suffolk
■ Stewards' Enquiry : Frankie Dettori ten-day ban: failed to ride out for third (Jun 17-26)

FOCUS
The third Classic of the season and a race with a longer history than the Derby. The subsequent exploits of recent winners has been varied, but Kazzia, Alexandrova and Sariska all proved to be the best middle-distance fillies of their generation, and Ouija Board and Snow Fairy both went on to international success at the highest level. This year's race looked pretty open but there was a surprise result, particularly notable for the terrific ride given to the winner by Johnny Murtagh, who made all the running and rode his rivals to sleep, as the time - 4.55secs slower than the earlier Coronation Cup - testifies, with the first three being in the first five places throughout. Given the doubts the form is rated to the bottom end of the race averages.

NOTEBOOK
Dancing Rain(IRE) had won a 1m2f Newbury maiden on her return to action and then was just beaten by Izzi Top in the Listed Swettenham Stud Fillies' Trial over the same C&D last time. Stepping up in trip and grade, she went off in front, got an uncontested lead and her rider was able to save something for the closing stages. The filly was not guaranteed to stay, despite her dam being a half-sister to Derby winner Dr Devious, but she saw it out well. There is a possibility she could be supplemented for the Irish Oaks, where she is likely to take on the runner-up again. (tchd 25-1)
Wonder Of Wonders(USA) had bounced back from a below-par reappearance to take a 1m4f maiden prior to winning the Cheshire Oaks, and was guaranteed to stay the trip. She was sensibly ridden close to the pace, as she has shown a slight tendency to hit a flat spot in her races, and had every chance, although her rider reported the filly lost her action briefly halfway up the straight. Although she got close, she could not quite reel in the winner and the stiffer test she will face in the Irish Oaks might play more to her strengths. (op 10-3 tchd 7-2 in places)
Izzi Top disappointed in the Pretty Polly before bouncing back to take a Listed race at Newbury, narrowly defeating today's winner. Out of a half-sister to the stayer top Kayf Tara from the family of an Irish Oaks winner, she always looked likely to stay and was ridden positively. She could not go with the first two, but kept plugging away to finish a slightly fortunate third. She has no immediate engagements and could well be put away with an autumn campaign in mind. (op 33-1)
Blue Bunting(USA) had done nothing but improve before finishing strongly to take the 1,000 Guineas on her reappearance. She was stepping up in trip, but her dam was a stayer and her half-brother has won over 2m2f. This was not to be Frankie Dettori's finest hour though, as the filly lost a good early pitch so that at the top of the hill she was eighth. He was riding her turning into the straight, but then pushed his way out, doing Havant no favours, and could make no impression on the first two. Dettori then dropped his hands after passing Izzi Top in the closing stages and lost third place on the line, which cost him a ten-day ban. He said afterwards that the track and the pace did not suit his filly; she might also go for the Irish Oaks next. (tchd 5-2)
Misty For Me(IRE), a three-time Group 1 winner, taking the Moyglare and Marcel Boussac at two and winning the Irish 1,000 Guineas on her previous start, was closely matched with Blue Bunting through Together, but had finished well behind the former in the 1,000 Guineas at Newmarket. She was in the first five from the start, tucked away on the rail, but could not pick up under pressure in the straight. Connections stated that she was unsuited by the downhill part of the track, but the dam's side of her pedigree suggested she would struggle to get the trip, and that was the impression. She is in the Coronation Stakes, and it will be no surprise if she drops back in trip for that race rather than go to the Curragh. (op 6-1 tchd 8-1 in a place)
Beatrice Aurore(IRE) had won a fillies' handicap at Goodwood on her return to action before stepping back up in trip to win a Listed race at the same track. Going up again in distance and grade, she was expected to stay as her dam got this far, and her close relatives stayed 1m6f. She was always in the leading bunch, but could not produce an extra gear. She is likely to go to the Ribblesdale next, and the stiffer track plus a probable better gallop in a slightly lower grade at Ascot might suit her better. (op 16-1)
Siren's Song(IRE), the winner of a 1m2f Listed race on only her second start but untried on anything faster than easy ground, was stepping up in grade but came home well, despite reportedly getting unbalanced. This probably came too soon in her career, but she will have learnt something and the Ribblesdale is also an option for her. (tchd 20-1 in a place)
Eirnin(IRE), who had been beaten in a handicap and a Group 3 this season, looked a potential pacemaker as, similar to stablemate Why, her form gave her no pretensions to being involved in the race otherwise. However, she was held up at the back and, although she stayed on steadily in the straight, this looked a case of an opportunity missed.
Zain Al Boldan, unbeaten in three starts, including running away with the Lingfield Oaks Trial, did not appear to have strong enough form, but had handled a switchback track and stayed the trip. She was held up here and, although she would have preferred a better pace, her rider offered no excuses. It seems likely she will also go to the Ribblesdale next. (tchd 9-1)
Havant, sixth in the 1,000 Guineas on her return, staying on steadily, was expected to appreciate the longer trip as several of her siblings had won at this distance or further. She was close enough early, but was struggling when hampered by the fourth in the straight and her rider reported that the filly did not like the ground. She might be set for an autumn campaign when conditions are likely to be more in her favour. (op 13-2)
Blaise Chorus(IRE) made the runner-up work to beat her in the Cheshire Oaks and she was in the first five early. However, she dropped away in the straight as if not getting home over the trip. (tchd 80-1)
Why(IRE), well beaten in three starts this time and a with fair amount to find on a couple of her rivals, was always towards the back.
Fork Handles, a well beaten third behind today's runner-up in the Cheshire Oaks and with a lot to find on that form, was held when eased in the last furlong as if something was amiss. (op 66-1 tchd 100-1 in a place)

2683 INVESTEC SURREY STKS (LISTED RACE) 7f
4:50 (4:50) (Class 1) 3-Y-O

£17,031 (£6,456; £3,231; £1,209; £1,209; £405) **Stalls** Low

Form RPR

11-0 **1** **Hooray**[33] [1719] 3-9-3 116.. SebSanders 5 109
(Sir Mark Prescott Bt) *racd keenly: chsd ldr: moved upsides ent st over 3f out: led 2f out: powered over 2 l clr 1f out: sn edgd lft: a doing enough towards fin* **8/11**[1]

0135 **2** *1 ¼* **Lord Of The Stars (USA)**[85] [823] 3-9-0 99 ow1.......... JamieSpencer 1 103
(David Simcock) *led: hdd 2f out: sn rdn: nt qckn w wnr 1f out: styd on towards fin but a looked hld* **14/1**

0-01 **3** *¾* **Chilworth Lad**[33] [1725] 3-8-13 99.. MartinHarley 2 100
(Mick Channon) *lw: trckd ldrs: 3rd ent st over 3f out: effrt on inner to chal over 2f out: nt qckn over 1f out: sn plld off rail: styd on towards fin but nt quite pce of first 2* **7/1**[3]

-035 **4** *1 ½* **Utley (USA)**[20] [2106] 3-8-13 110.. WilliamBuick 3 96
(John Gosden) *lw: broke wl: in tch: pushed along in 4th ent st over 3f out: outpcd after and sn hung lft: kpt on ins fnl f: no real imp* **5/1**[2]

-340 **4** *dht* **Vanguard Dream**[28] [1844] 3-8-13 95.................................... RyanMoore 4 96
(Richard Hannon) *swtg: hld up: 5th ent st over 3f out: rdn over 1f out: kpt on ins fnl f: nt pce to chal* **11/1**

0-46 **6** *6* **Casual Glimpse**[12] [2338] 3-8-13 97.............................. RichardHughes 6 79
(Richard Hannon) *hld up: a looked ill at ease on trck: last ent st and outpcd over 3f out: toiling and hung lft after* **9/1**

1m 21.56s (-1.74) **Going Correction** -0.075s/f (Good) **6** Ran SP% **112.1**
Speed ratings (Par 107): **106,104,103,102,102 95**
Tote Swingers: 1&2 £3.10, 1&3 £2.20, 2&3 £7.40 CSF £12.47 TOTE £1.60: £1.10, £3.40; EX 9.80.
Owner Cheveley Park Stud **Bred** Cheveley Park Stud Ltd **Trained** Newmarket, Suffolk

FOCUS

Not a strong Listed race, and only the first three home ever became involved to a meaningful extent. The pace was decent. Hooray did not need to match her 2yo best.

NOTEBOOK

Hooray was the class act in the line-up, but a 9lb penalty for her Group 1 win in the Cheveley Park Stakes last autumn left her with only 2lb in hand of form rival Utley at these weights. She was back in trip after failing to get home in the 1000 Guineas and her trainer reported that she has pleased him since Newmarket, the filly having taken time to come to hand before the Classic. Unable to grab the immediate lead from stall 5, she raced close up and rather keenly, some way off the rail. She took it up two out and went a couple of lengths clear, but was tying up a little near the end as the runner-up came back at her. The bare form is some way off her best and it may be asking a lot of her to win at the top level again, but she holds entries in both the Coronation Stakes and the Golden Jubilee at the Royal meeting, and that is likely to be her target. She's in the July Cup further down the line. (op 10-11)

Lord Of The Stars(USA), who had been targeted at this race, had made all at Meydan earlier in the year and used the same tactics. The favourite headed him in the straight, but he refused to lie down and was closing on her again near the finish. He is smart and may be worth another try at 1m.

Chilworth Lad was back up in grade after winning a Salisbury handicap, for which he was raised 5lb. Straightening up for home in third place, there was a nice gap for him up the rail and he tried to close on the leading pair, but was always just held. This was a creditable effort. (op 13-2)

Utley(USA) was always in a similar position and never threatened to pick up well enough to trouble the leaders. The track was a feasible excuse, but unsurprisingly he is proving difficult to place this year. His American owner has horses in the States and perhaps this colt will be switched over there. (tchd 10-1)

Vanguard Dream often leads, but hold-up tactics were given a try again and they didn't work, although he was keeping on at the end. He did have the worst chance at the weights. (tchd 10-1)

Casual Glimpse looked uncomfortable throughout and failed to handle the track at all. (op 8-1)

2684 INVESTEC OPPORTUNITY STKS (H'CAP) 7f

5:25 (5:25) (Class 2) (0-100,92) 3-Y-O

£12,462 (£3,732; £1,866; £934; £350; £350) **Stalls** Low

Form RPR

-450 **1** **Norse Blues**[20] 2100 3-8-7 **78** .... JamesDoyle 7 91
(Sylvester Kirk) *prom: 2nd ent st over 3f out: led wl over 1f out: r.o wl and edgd lft whn drew clr ins fnl f* **8/1**[3]

51-3 **2** *5* **Reposer (IRE)**[15] 2215 3-8-9 **80** .... JimmyQuinn 8 80
(John Best) *led after 1f: rdn 2f out: sn hdd: outpcd by wnr and no ch ins fnl f* **8/1**[3]

0-00 **3** *2 3/4* **Sonning Rose (IRE)**[13] 2296 3-9-2 **87** .... ChrisCatlin 9 79
(Mick Channon) *hld up bhd: 11th ent st over 3f out: r.o wl fnl f: fin strly: nt rch front 2* **20/1**

0-00 **4** *shd* **Major Conquest (IRE)**[13] 2319 3-8-7 **78** .... MickaelBarzalona 1 70
(J W Hills) *hld up: 9th ent st over 3f out: rdn and hdwy 2f out: styd on ins fnl f but unable to chal ldrs* **16/1**

25-1 **5** *nse* **Fityaan**[24] 1984 3-8-9 **80** .... RichardHills 10 75+
(B W Hills) *hld up: 7th ent st over 3f out: sn hung lft and nt clr run: hdwy whn swtchd rt over 2f out: kpt on whn chsng ldrs in vain ins fnl f: no ex cl home* **4/1**[1]

44-0 **5** *dht* **Cloud Rock**[34] 1688 3-8-13 **84** .... RyanMoore 11 76+
(Peter Chapple-Hyam) *lw: dwlt: swtchd lft s: hld up: 10th ent st over 3f out: pushed along over 2f out: styd on ins fnl f: gng on at fin* **9/2**[2]

0-40 **7** *nk* **Julius Geezer (IRE)**[28] 1852 3-9-7 **92** .... RichardKingscote 5 83
(Tom Dascombe) *led for 1f: continued to trck ldrs: 4th ent st over 3f out: outpcd by ldrs over 1f out: styd on same pce fnl f* **20/1**

2220 **8** *6* **City Legend**[4] 2564 3-8-2 **78** .... (bt) KieranO'Neill[(5)] 3 53
(Alan McCabe) *midfield: pushed along 4f out: 8th ent st over 3f out: rdn over 2f out: nt clr run over 1f out: wknd fnl f* **9/1**

6221 **9** *5* **Hugely Exciting**[28] 1865 3-8-8 **79** .... (p) LiamKeniry 4 40
(J S Moore) *midfield: 6th ent st over 3f out: pushed along over 2f out: sn wknd* **14/1**

52-0 **10** *3* **Robert The Painter (IRE)**[29] 1825 3-9-0 **85** .... PaulHanagan 2 38+
(Richard Fahey) *trckd ldrs: n.m.r and hmpd after 1f: 5th ent st over 3f out: sn u.p: wknd over 2f out* **4/1**[1]

-120 **11** *6* **Falmouth Bay (USA)**[20] 2096 3-8-10 **81** .... SilvestreDeSousa 6 18
(Mark Johnston) *in tch: prom on outer after 1f: cl 3rd ent st over 3f out: rdn over 2f out: hung lft whn wkng over 1f out* **14/1**

1m 22.2s (-1.10) **Going Correction** -0.075s/f (Good) **11** Ran SP% **119.1**

Speed ratings (Par 105): **103,97,94,94,93 93,93,86,81,77 70**

Tote Swingers: 1&2 £14.40, 1&3 £33.20, 2&3 £32.70 CSF £71.54 CT £1230.74 TOTE £9.70: £2.60, £3.30, £5.80; EX 83.10 Trifecta £1964.60 Pool: £3,185.92 - 1.20 winning units..

Owner J C Smith **Bred** Littleton Stud **Trained** Upper Lambourn, Berks

FOCUS

An ordinary event for the grade, with the topweight racing off 8lb below the ceiling. Few got into the race and it may be wise not to treat the form too positively. A 5lb personal best from the winner, with the second to form.

NOTEBOOK

Norse Blues mastered the runner-up with a furlong and a half left and drew progressively clear to slam the field, despite not looking entirely at ease on the camber. He enjoyed the reversion to positive tactics and was back down in trip after failing to stay 1m2f last time. A mile should pose no problems and he may go for the Britannia Handicap at Royal Ascot. (op 11-1 tchd 12-1 in places)

Reposer(IRE) missed the break when a respectable third at Haydock, but soon got to the front here. Although he was put in his place by the wide-margin winner he boxed on well for a clear second. He just looks held off this mark. (tchd 9-1)

Sonning Rose(IRE) flew home after still being last with a quarter of a mile left, geting the verdict in a five-way photo for third. She was 5lb lower than when well beaten at Haydock last time, when the mile had seemed to stretch her.

Major Conquest(IRE) hinted at better to come when behind Norse Blues at Salisbury last month, but made no show at York. Eased 3lb here, he was never a threat but stayed on from the rear and just missed out on third. (op 20-1 tchd 22-1)

Cloud Rock was awkward leaving the stalls and was behind until running on when it was all too late. (tchd 4-1)

Fityaan, a Warwick maiden winner, went after the leading pair in the straight and looked set to finish third on this handicap debut, only to flag near the finish. It was reported that he had lost his action. Official explanation: jockey said gelding lost its action (tchd 4-1)

Julius Geezer(IRE) chased the pace until his stamina began to ebb away late on this first attempt at 7f. He had been dropped 5lb after a couple of lacklustre efforts in the spring, and promises to stay 6f well enough. (op 18-1)

Robert The Painter(IRE) was reported to have failed to handle the track. Official explanation: jockey said gelding failed to handle the track (tchd 9-2)

Falmouth Bay(USA) raced up with the pace in company with the winner and second, but dropped away in the final couple of furlongs. He has yet to prove himself on turf. (op 12-1)

T/Jkpt: Not won. T/Plt: £46.20 to a £1 stake. Pool:£209,311.39 - 3,301.46 winning tickets. T/Qpdt: £9.60 to a £1 stake. Pool:£10,559.29 - 873.49 winning tickets. SP

[2556] GOODWOOD (R-H)

Friday, June 3

OFFICIAL GOING: Good to firm (good in places on straight course; 8.2)

First 2f of 1m course dolled out 5yds.

Wind: medium, half behind Weather: sunny

2685 GOODWOOD FARM SHOP STKS (H'CAP) (FOR AMATEUR RIDERS) 1m 1f

6:15 (6:16) (Class 5) (0-70,65) 4-Y-O+ **£2,498** (£774; £387; £193) **Stalls** Low

Form RPR

003 **1** **Iguacu**[7] 2451 7-9-12 **49** .... (p) MissSBrotherton 1 58
(George Baker) *dwlt: sn rcvrd and chsng ldrs: led over 2f out: kpt on wl fnl f: all out nr fin* **9/2**[1]

2305 **2** *nk* **Free Tussy (ARG)**[13] 2308 7-10-8 **64** .... (bt) MissHayleyMoore[(5)] 10 72
(Gary Moore) *hld up bhd: rdn and hdwy wl over 2f out: r.o strly fnl f: wnt 2nd last strides: nt quite rch wnr* **13/2**[3]

-003 **3** *hd* **Mr Udagawa**[18] 2144 5-10-3 **59** .... (p) MrRJWilliams[(5)] 6 67
(Bernard Llewellyn) *in tch: rdn to chse ldr wl over 1f out: kpt on ins fnl f: lost 2nd last strides* **12/1**

5320 **4** *2 1/2* **Laconicos (IRE)**[13] 2308 9-10-4 **62** .... (t) MissCScott[(7)] 8 65
(William Stone) *bhd: rdn over 3f out: hdwy 2f out: styd on fnl f: nt rch ldrs* **16/1**

1403 **5** *2 1/4* **Lunar River (FR)**[13] 2308 8-10-8 **59** .... (t) MissEJJones 14 57
(David Pinder) *in rr: effrt ent fnl 3f: edgd rt and styd on same pce fr over 1f out* **9/1**

000- **6** *4* **Megalala (IRE)**[219] 7167 10-10-7 **63** .... MrJackSalmon[(5)] 2 52
(John Bridger) *led: rdn and hdd over 2f out: wknd over 1f out* **5/1**[2]

-043 **7** *3 1/2* **Commerce**[16] 2204 4-10-9 **65** .... MrJCoffill-Brown[(5)] 3 46
(Simon Dow) *chsd ldr tl over 2f out: sn rdn: wknd wl over 1f out: no ch fnl f* **9/2**[1]

0000 **8** *3 1/2* **Novillero**[51] 1308 4-9-4 **46** oh1 .... MrsSarah-JaneFox[(5)] 5 19
(Jimmy Fox) *a towards rr: nvr trbld ldrs* **50/1**

6-05 **9** *1* **King Columbo (IRE)**[28] 1866 6-9-12 **56** .... MissSBirkett[(7)] 4 27
(Julia Feilden) *in tch: rdn and effrt over 3f out: wknd ent fnl 2f* **8/1**

0000 **10** *1/2* **Realt Na Mara (IRE)**[15] 2237 8-10-6 **62** .... MrRPooles[(5)] 11 32
(Hughie Morrison) *chsd ldrs: rdn wl over 3f out: wknd over 2f out* **28/1**

02-5 **11** *1 1/2* **Fifty Cents**[14] 2242 7-10-8 **62** .... MrCMartin[(3)] 13 29
(Milton Harris) *hld up in rr: nvr on terms* **8/1**

-006 **12** *1 3/4* **Corlough Mountain**[7] 2451 7-9-6 **48** oh1 ow2 .... MissMBryant[(5)] 12 11
(Paddy Butler) *a bhd* **80/1**

1m 57.06s (0.76) **Going Correction** -0.25s/f (Firm) **12** Ran SP% **118.8**

Speed ratings (Par 103): **86,85,85,83,81 77,74,71,70,70 68,67**

Tote Swingers: 1&2 £6.10, 1&3 £8.00, 2&3 £11.40 CSF £33.38 CT £337.18 TOTE £6.30: £1.70, £2.00, £3.50; EX 25.70.

Owner Derek & Cheryl Holder **Bred** Cheveley Park Stud Ltd **Trained** Whitsbury, Hants

FOCUS

The going was good to firm (good in places on the straight course). An ordinary amateur riders' handicap rated around the placed horses. Two of market leaders dropped away after getting involved in a duel up with the decent pace.

Fifty Cents Official explanation: jockey said gelding was unsuited by the good to firm ground

2686 RACING UK STKS (H'CAP) 1m 4f

6:45 (6:45) (Class 4) (0-85,85) 4-Y-O+ **£4,533** (£1,348; £674; £336) **Stalls** High

Form RPR

4050 **1** **Porgy**[13] 2285 6-9-1 **79** .... TedDurcan 5 91
(David Simcock) *stdd s: hld up in last: clsd and travelling wl over 3f out: swtchd rt and pushed along to make prog over 2f out: drvn to ld jst over 1f out: drew clr fnl f: comf* **8/1**

0-00 **2** *4 1/2* **Red Courtier**[23] 2006 4-8-11 **75** .... (p) TomQueally 7 80
(Paul Cole) *in tch in midfield: rdn over 4f out: hdwy u.p to chse ldr over 2f out tl wl over 1f out: no ch w wnr but plugged on to go 2nd again ins fnl f* **9/1**

316- **3** *3* **Bramalea**[230] 6929 6-9-7 **85** .... JimCrowley 1 85
(Hughie Morrison) *led at stdy gallop: rdn and clr ent fnl 3f: drvn and hdd jst over 1f out: sn outpcd: wknd fnl f* **7/1**

15-1 **4** *2 3/4* **Huff And Puff**[45] 1450 4-9-2 **80** .... PhilipRobinson 2 76
(Amanda Perrett) *chsd ldng pair: n.m.r on inner 4f out: rdn and btn wl over 2f out: wl btn 2f out: styd on past btn horses fnl f* **11/4**[1]

12-1 **5** *nse* **New Code**[46] 1443 4-9-3 **81** .... GeorgeBaker 4 77
(Gary Moore) *stdd after s: hld up in last pair: hdwy and chsng ldrs over 3f out: rdn and unable qck over 2f out: wknd over 1f out* **11/2**[3]

45-1 **6** *nk* **Rockfella**[43] 1509 5-8-11 **75** .... EddieAhern 6 70
(Denis Coakley) *dwlt: sn rcvrd and in midfield: effrt to chse ldrs and drvn ent fnl 3f: wknd wl over 1f out* **4/1**[2]

0-55 **7** *11* **Cashpoint**[27] 1887 6-9-4 **82** .... JackMitchell 8 59
(Anthony Middleton) *chsd ldr tl 6f out: drvn and unable qck 3f out: wknd u.p wl over 1f out* **15/2**

00- **8** *37* **Baltimore Clipper (USA)**[239] 6698 4-9-2 **80** .... RichardHughes 3 —
(Paul Cole) *chsd ldrs: hdwy to chse ldr 6f out tl over 2f out: sn wknd: virtually p.u fnl f: t.o* **16/1**

2m 33.66s (-4.74) **Going Correction** -0.25s/f (Firm) **8** Ran SP% **113.3**

Speed ratings (Par 105): **105,102,100,98,98 97,90,65**

Tote Swingers: 1&2 £13.70, 1&3 £11.30, 2&3 £14.00 CSF £74.89 CT £527.30 TOTE £11.40: £2.80, £3.60, £2.50; EX 98.50.

Owner Dr Marwan Koukash **Bred** Juddmonte Farms Ltd **Trained** Newmarket, Suffolk

FOCUS

A decent handicap run at a steady pace. The three market leaders were disappointing and the form doesn't look very solid. The winner and third are probably the best guides to the level.

Baltimore Clipper(USA) Official explanation: jockey said gelding lost its action

2687 BRITISH STALLION STUDS SUPPORTING BRITISH RACING EBF MAIDEN STKS 6f

7:20 (7:23) (Class 5) 2-Y-O **£3,238** (£963; £481; £240) **Stalls** High

Form RPR

1 **Chandlery (IRE)** 2-9-3 0 .... PatDobbs 8 83+
(Richard Hannon) *chsd ldr: jnd ldr travelling wl 2f out: pushed ahd over 1f out: hrd pressed ins fnl f: hld on wl fnl 75yds* **11/1**

2 *shd* **Coupe De Ville (IRE)** 2-9-3 0 .... RichardHughes 1 83+
(Richard Hannon) *wnt rt s and s.i.s: sn swtchd lft and nudged along towards rr: rdn and hdwy over 1f out: chal ins fnl f: kpt on under hands and heels: hld towards fin* **4/1**[3]

4 3 1 **Bronze Angel (IRE)**[13] 2291 2-9-3 0 .... TedDurcan 3 80
(Marcus Tregoning) *chsd ldrs in centre: rdn and effrt wl over 1f out: styd on same pce u.p fnl f* **7/2**[2]

4 4 **Shamaal Nibras (USA)** 2-9-3 0 .... JimCrowley 6 68+
(Ed Dunlop) *in tch: effrt to press ldrs over 2f out: btn ent fnl f: wknd fnl 150yds* **10/3**[1]

5 4 ½ **Purple Affair (IRE)** 2-9-3 0 .... TomQueally 7 54
(J S Moore) *chsd ldrs: rdn and struggling over 2f out: wknd qckly 2f out:* **25/1**

6 ½ **Breaking The Bank** 2-9-3 0 .... GeorgeBaker 4 53
(William Muir) *led tl rdn and hdd over 1f out: wknd qckly ent fnl f* **20/1**

7 12 **Laurel Lad (IRE)** 2-9-3 0 .... MichaelHills 2 17
(B W Hills) *s.i.s: rn green and sn pushed along in rr: rdn and wknd qckly ent fnl 2f: wl bhd fnl f* **9/1**

8 29 **Edensor (IRE)** 2-9-3 0 .... EddieAhern 9 —
(John Dunlop) *sltly hmpd s: immediately lost tch: t.o after 2f* **28/1**

1m 11.13s (-1.07) **Going Correction** -0.25s/f (Firm) **8** Ran SP% **95.7**
Speed ratings (Par 93): **97,96,95,90,84 83,67,28**
Tote Swingers: 1&2:£3.80, 1&3:£6.50, 2&3:£1.50 CSF £37.27 TOTE £11.90: £3.80, £1.20, £1.20; EX 24.80.
Owner Mrs J Wood **Bred** Owenstown Stud **Trained** East Everleigh, Wilts
■ Waseem Faris (9/2) was withdrawn (refused to enter stalls). Rule 4 applies, deduct 15p in the £ from all bets.

FOCUS
Eight of the nine runners were newcomers in this maiden for 2-y-os. Two Richard Hannon-trained runners fought out a very tight finish and the runner with experience was a clear third. The form is rated around the averages and the time. Waseem Faris refused to go into the stalls and was withdrawn.

NOTEBOOK
Chandlery(IRE) looked the stable second string but he travelled smoothly for a long way and showed some fighting qualities to hang on from his stablemate on this debut. He is a speedily bred £88,000 buy, who has a powerful physique and looks another good prospect for a top yard with a wealth of 2-y-o talent. (op 10-1)
Coupe De Ville(IRE) was prominent in the betting and gave it a good shot on debut despite showing signs of inexperience. He could improve significantly for the run and is an 82,000gns half-brother to winners at 5f-1m1f, including Fantastico Roberto a 1m1f stakes winner in US. (op 7-2 tchd 9-2)
Bronze Angel(IRE) came home strongly after missing the break when fourth behind a decent type in a C&D maiden last month. Solid in the market, he raced near the pace this time but couldn't quite match the finishing speed of the first two. This was a decent second effort by a £42,000 yearling purchase. His proximity adds some solidity to the form and he should appreciate a stiffer test in time. (op 4-1 tchd 3-1)
Shamaal Nibras(USA), a 45,000gns breeze-up buy who is a half-brother to four winners in North America, was well backed but couldn't sustain his promising mid-race move on this debut. (tchd 3-1 and 7-2)

2688 HALNAKER CLASSIFIED STKS 1m 3f
7:50 (7:54) (Class 5) 3-Y-O **£2,590** (£770; £385; £192) **Stalls** High

Form RPR

14-0 **1** **Aldwick Bay (IRE)**[15] 2230 3-9-0 75 .... RichardHughes 6 82
(Richard Hannon) *hld up wl off the pce in last pair: clsd and in tch 5f out: chsd ldrs and drvn over 1f out: chsd ldr fnl 100yds: r.o wl to ld last strides* **10/1**[3]

5-12 **2** *hd* **Sacred Shield**[22] 2022 3-9-0 71 .... TomQueally 8 82
(Sir Henry Cecil) *t.k.h: chsd clr ldng pair: clsd 5f out: jnd ldr on bit over 1f out: led 1f out: rdn ins fnl f: hdd last strides* **15/8**[1]

3-03 **3** *4* **Magical Flower**[21] 2065 3-8-9 72 .... HarryBentley(5) 1 74
(William Knight) *chsd ldr tl led gng wl over 3f out: rdn over 2f out: hdd 1f out: lost 2nd and wknd fnl 100yds* **16/1**

01-2 **4** *½* **Mountain Range (IRE)**[25] 1947 3-9-0 75 .... EddieAhern 2 74
(John Dunlop) *hld up wl off the pce in midfield: clsd and in tch 5f out: chsd ldrs and swtchd rt ent fnl 2f: unable qck u.p over 1f out: styd on same pce after* **15/8**[1]

354 **5** *hd* **Informed Award**[22] 2019 3-9-0 75 .... RobertHavlin 5 73
(John Gosden) *stdd s: hld up wl off the pce in rr: clsd and in tch 5f out: chsd ldrs and rdn 2f out: no ex and btn jst ins fnl f* **8/1**[2]

524- **6** *12* **Another Laugh**[242] 6634 3-9-0 75 .... JimCrowley 3 52
(Alan King) *hld up wl off the pce in midfield: clsd and in tch 5f out: swtchd lft and rdn ent fnl 3f: wknd 2f out* **8/1**[2]

01-0 **7** *21* **Fly By White (IRE)**[22] 2022 3-9-0 72 .... PatDobbs 4 —
(Richard Hannon) *t.k.h: led and sn clr: rdn and hdd over 3f out: dropped out rapidly wl over 2f out: t.o fnl f* **22/1**

2m 24.88s (-1.62) **Going Correction** -0.25s/f (Firm) **7** Ran SP% **111.1**
Speed ratings (Par 99): **95,94,91,91,91 82,67**
Tote Swingers: 1&2 £5.80, 1&3 £18.80, 2&3 £5.10 CSF £27.58 TOTE £9.20: £3.80, £3.10; EX 28.00.
Owner Mrs Ann Williams **Bred** Ailesbury Bloodstock **Trained** East Everleigh, Wilts

FOCUS
An interesting classified event run at a strong pace and the first three are rated to form. A well-backed Henry Cecil-trained filly looked likely to collect when cruising to the front but was mugged by a fast finisher.

2689 CHICHESTER MAIDEN FILLIES' STKS 1m
8:25 (8:26) (Class 5) 3-Y-O+ **£2,590** (£770; £385; £192) **Stalls** Low

Form RPR

43 **1** **Rougette**[20] 2103 3-8-12 0 .... MichaelHills 9 84+
(B W Hills) *chsd ldrs tl wnt 2nd over 6f out: led 2f out: sn rdn and clr ent fnl f: r.o wl: easily* **8/11**[1]

5 **2** *4 ½* **Brinmore**[16] 2192 3-8-12 0 .... JimCrowley 8 71
(William Knight) *t.k.h: hld up towards rr: hdwy on outer 3f out: rdn to chse clr wnr over 1f out: no imp but kpt on for clr 2nd* **5/1**[3]

0 **3** *4 ½* **Ondeafears (IRE)**[24] 1984 4-9-9 0 .... JimmyQuinn 1 63
(Stuart Howe) *s.i.s: t.k.h: hld up towards rr: hdwy into midfield 5f out: chsd ldng trio and rdn over 2f out: sn outpcd: wl hld but kpt on to go modest 3rd ins fnl f* **66/1**

-0 **4** *1 ¼* **Another Whisper (IRE)**[29] 1836 3-8-12 0 .... RichardHughes 10 57
(Richard Hannon) *led tl rdn and hdd 2f out: sn outpcd by wnr: 3rd and wl hld ent fnl f* **3/1**[2]

5 *2 ½* **County Hotel (IRE)**[39] 4-9-4 0 .... RyanPowell(5) 7 54?
(Barry Brennan) *awkward leaving stalls and s.i.s: hld up in rr: swtchd lft and effrt 3f out: rdn and no prog over 1f out* **100/1**

00 **6** *3* **A B Celebration**[16] 2192 3-8-12 0 .... MarcHalford 3 44?
(John Bridger) *t.k.h: chsd ldr tl over 6f out: wknd over 2f out: wl btn over 1f out* **100/1**

60 **7** *1* **Summerandlightning (IRE)**[71] 952 5-9-9 0 .... LiamKeniry 2 45+
(Mark Usher) *chsd ldrs tl rdn and wknd over 2f out: wl btn and edging rt over 1f out* **66/1**

8 *2 ½* **Adaeze (IRE)** 3-8-12 0 .... StephenCraine 4 36
(Jonathan Portman) *chsd ldrs: rdn and unable qck 3f out: wknd ent fnl 2f: wl bhd over 1f out* **20/1**

9 *4 ½* **Queen Of Epirus** 3-8-5 0 .... DavidKenny(7) 6 25
(George Baker) *s.i.s: sn pushed along towards rr: lost tch over 2f out* **20/1**

3- **10** *2 ¼* **Iztaccihuatl**[433] 1017 3-8-12 0 .... EddieCreighton 5 19
(Michael Scudamore) *in tch in midfield: rdn 5f out: lost pl u.p 3f out: wl bhd fnl 2f* **16/1**

1m 39.47s (-0.43) **Going Correction** -0.25s/f (Firm)
WFA 3 from 4yo+ 11lb **10** Ran SP% **119.9**
Speed ratings (Par 100): **92,87,83,81,79 76,75,72,68,66**
Tote Swingers: 1&2:£2.20, 1&3:£20.60, 2&3:£31.70 CSF £4.85 TOTE £2.00: £1.10, £1.10, £9.00; EX 5.70.
Owner D M James **Bred** D M James **Trained** Lambourn, Berks

FOCUS
There was not much strength in depth in this maiden but the hot favourite did the job in good style and the form is given a chance through the runner-up to his debut form.

2690 BRITISH STALLION STUDS SUPPORTING BRITISH RACING E B F FILLIES' (H'CAP) 6f
8:55 (8:56) (Class 3) (0-95,89) 3-Y-O+ **£7,447** (£2,216; £1,107; £553) **Stalls** High

Form RPR

0-30 **1** **Poppy Seed**[13] 2298 4-9-13 **88** .... RichardHughes 6 97
(Richard Hannon) *mde all: rdn and drew clr w runner-up 1f out: asserted fnl 100yds: eased towards fin* **5/2**[1]

56-0 **2** *1 ¼* **Desert Poppy (IRE)**[34] 1675 4-9-9 **87** .... JohnFahy(3) 3 92
(Walter Swinburn) *chsd ldrs: chsd wnr over 2f out: rdn and ev ch over 1f out: clr w wnr jst ins fnl f: no ex and btn fnl 100yds* **10/3**[2]

313- **3** *1 ¾* **Carrignavar (USA)**[237] 6751 3-9-6 **89** .... JimCrowley 4 86
(Ralph Beckett) *t.k.h: hld up wl in tch: nt clr run ent fnl 2f: sn rdn to chse ldng pair: styd on same pce ent fnl f* **13/2**[3]

5014 **4** *1 ½* **Ray Of Joy**[19] 2122 5-9-6 **81** .... PatDobbs 1 76
(J R Jenkins) *bmpd s: hld up in tch in last pair: rdn and effrt over 1f out: outpcd by ldng pair: styd on same pce after* **10/1**

1111 **5** *4* **Chevise (IRE)**[59] 1145 3-8-8 **82** .... HarryBentley(5) 2 62
(Steve Woodman) *chsd ldrs: rdn and effrt over 2f out: unable qck u.p over 1f out: wknd ent fnl f* **7/1**

00-6 **6** *2* **Idiom (IRE)**[28] 1844 3-8-6 **80** .... LauraPike(5) 5 53
(David Simcock) *dwlt: hld up in tch: rdn and effrt ent fnl 2f: no prog and wknd wl over 1f out* **20/1**

0-12 **7** *1* **Dispol Kylie (IRE)**[21] 2062 5-8-12 **73** .... GregFairley 8 45
(Kate Walton) *racd keenly: chsd ldrs: rdn and unable qck over 2f out: wknd wl over 1f out* **7/1**

/33- **8** *½* **Plume**[357] 2929 4-9-7 **82** .... JackMitchell 7 53
(Roger Teal) *chsd ldr tl over 2f out: sn u.p and struggling: wknd wl over 1f out* **8/1**

1m 10.86s (-1.34) **Going Correction** -0.25s/f (Firm)
WFA 3 from 4yo+ 8lb **8** Ran SP% **114.9**
Speed ratings (Par 104): **98,96,94,92,86 84,82,82**
Tote Swingers: 1&2:£1.40, 1&3:£4.80, 2&3:£6.80 CSF £10.93 CT £47.06 TOTE £4.10: £2.20, £1.10, £2.50; EX 5.70.
Owner Lady Whent **Bred** Raffin Bloodstock **Trained** East Everleigh, Wilts

FOCUS
The pace was not very strong in this decent sprint handicap and the first two were always prominent. The winner is rated to her best backed up by the placed horses.

NOTEBOOK
Poppy Seed found life tough in Listed company on her last three starts but she got within 2l of 102-rated rival on her return two runs back, and travelled smoothly in the lead before knuckling down well to land a gamble off a feasible mark back in this handicap. Still lightly raced, she is best on fast ground and probably has enough speed to be equally effective at 5f. (op 3-1 tchd 100-30)
Desert Poppy(IRE) had a bit to prove from a handicapping perspective off 8lb higher than her third career win at Newbury last August, but she ran a big race on her second run back. She seems best when racing near the pace on fast ground, and would be of strong interest in a similar handicap next time. (op 7-2 tchd 3-1)
Carrignavar(USA), withdrawn from a Haydock Listed race on her intended return, shaped well redirected into a handicap, particularly as she was ridden more patiently than the first two in a steadily run race. A Sandown maiden winner on the second of just three starts last year, this well-regarded type still has plenty of potential as a sprinter. (op 11-2)
Ray Of Joy recorded a sixth career win when landing a gamble over 6f at Kempton last month, but she has been held off slightly lower turf marks in two runs since and is 4lb higher than her sole win on grass. (op 9-1)
Chevise(IRE) had been in unstoppable form in claimers/handicaps on Polytrack since October. She still looked feasibly treated off just 7lb higher than her opening mark, but could find only a short-lived effort in her bid for a six-timer on this switch back on turf. (op 8-1)
T/Plt: £173.30 to a £1 stake. Pool £59,796.00 - 251.85 winning units. T/Qpdt: £7.30 to a £1 stake. Pool £3,927.49 - 394.10 winning units. SP

2260 MUSSELBURGH (R-H)
Friday, June 3

OFFICIAL GOING: Good (good to firm in places; 6.1)
All rail moved in 3m.
Wind: Almost nil Weather: Sunny, hot

2691 ISLE OF SKYE BLENDED SCOTCH WHISKY MAIDEN STKS 1m
2:00 (2:00) (Class 5) 3-Y-O+ **£2,590** (£770; £385; £192) **Stalls** Low

Form RPR

40-2 **1** **Royal Hush**[35] 1648 3-8-12 69 .... PhillipMakin 3 73+
(Kevin Ryan) *mde all: pushed along and qcknd 2f out: edgd lft ins fnl f: styd on strly* **4/1**

- **2** *2* **Tmaam (USA)** 3-9-3 0 .... JoeFanning 8 73+
(Mark Johnston) *dwlt: sn cl up: effrt and drvn over 2f out: styd on ins fnl f: nt rch wnr* **9/4**[1]

36 **3** *1 ½* **To The Spring**[28] 1873 3-8-12 0 .... StevieDonohoe 7 65
(William Haggas) *trckd ldrs: effrt 2f out: kpt on same pce fnl f* **11/4**[3]

000/ **4** *10* **Billy Cadiz**[594] 6847 6-9-7 38 .... JacobButterfield(7) 1 50
(Mark Campion) *t.k.h: trckd ldrs tl pushed along and wknd 2f out* **100/1**

5 *7* **Munaawib** 3-9-3 0 .... TadhgO'Shea 2 31
(Marcus Tregoning) *dwlt: bhd and rdn along after 2f: shortlived effrt whn hung bdly rt over 2f out: sn btn* **5/2**[2]

-400 **6** *2* **Machir Bay**[33] 1710 4-10-0 41 FrederikTylicki 6 26
(Keith Dalgleish) *hld up in tch: struggling over 3f out: sn wknd* **40/1**

1m 40.11s (-1.09) **Going Correction** -0.075s/f (Good)
WFA 3 from 4yo+ 11lb 6 Ran SP% **109.4**
Speed ratings (Par 103): **102,100,98,88,81 79**
Tote Swingers: 1&2 £2.90, 1&3 £3.10, 2&3 £2.50 CSF £12.72 TOTE £5.00: £3.00, £3.00; EX 13.70.
Owner Mr & Mrs R Kelvin Hughes **Bred** C E Stedman **Trained** Hambleton, N Yorks

FOCUS

A beautiful, sunny day in Scotland, and the time of the first race suggested the ground was riding as advertised. The Going Stick was 6.1 after a dry night and there was very little breeze. A weak maiden in both strength and depth, run at a decent pace. It's hard to be confident about the form.

2692 CORNHILL BUILDERS H'CAP (A QUALIFIER FOR THE BETFAIR BONUS SCOTTISH RACING MILE FINAL) 1m

2:35 (2:37) (Class 6) (0-65,71) 4-Y-0+ **£2,590** (£770; £385; £192) **Stalls** Low

Form RPR

-402 **1** **Ra Junior (USA)**[14] 2260 5-9-2 60 FrederikTylicki 4 71
(Paul Midgley) *midfield on ins: effrt and swtchd lft over 2f out: chsng ldrs whn nt clr run over 1f out: rcvrd and led wl ins fnl f: r.o wl* **11/4**[1]

-041 **2** *1 ½* **Shunkawakhan (IRE)**[8] 2415 8-8-7 51 6ex (p) JoeFanning 1 58
(Linda Perratt) *t.k.h: cl up: led after 2f: rdn and edgd lft fr over 1f out: hdd and no ex wl ins fnl f* **14/1**

2431 **3** *2* **Violent Velocity (IRE)**[6] 2490 8-9-10 71 6ex DeclanCannon(3) 8 73
(John Quinn) *midfield: drvn over 3f out: rallied over 2f out: kpt on same pce fnl f* **11/4**[1]

020- **4** *3* **Second Reef**[246] 6495 9-8-5 52 NataliaGemelova(3) 2 47
(Thomas Cuthbert) *prom: drvn over 2f out: outpcd over 1f out: kpt on ins fnl f: no imp* **100/1**

000 **5** *nk* **Drive Home (USA)**[8] 2412 4-8-13 57 AdrianNicholls 3 51
(Noel Wilson) *led 2f: w ldr tl drvn and no ex appr fnl f* **40/1**

00-0 **6** *shd* **Safari Guide**[14] 2252 5-8-5 52 AndrewHeffernan(3) 6 46
(Kevin M Prendergast) *t.k.h: prom: effrt and rdn over 2f out: nt qckn appr fnl f* **20/1**

0320 **7** *1 ½* **Amno Dancer (IRE)**[21] 2057 4-9-0 58 LeeNewman 7 49
(David Barron) *in tch: effrt and hdwy over 2f out: btn ins fnl f* **6/1**[2]

31-0 **8** *nk* **Military Call**[14] 2260 4-8-12 63 GarryWhillans(7) 10 57+
(Alistair Whillans) *hld up: effrt on ins 2f out: no imp fnl f* **16/1**

-056 **9** *2 ¼* **Spread Boy (IRE)**[8] 2415 4-8-6 50 PatrickMathers 11 35
(Alan Berry) *bhd and sn pushed along: drvn and effrt over 3f out: wknd fnl 2f* **28/1**

6-03 **10** *4 ½* **Mangham (IRE)**[11] 2348 6-9-7 65 PhillipMakin 9 39
(George Foster) *hld up on outside: shortlived effrt over 2f out: btn over 1f out* **6/1**[2]

-550 **11** *2 ½* **Walleyd (IRE)**[9] 2401 4-8-11 60 LeeTopliss(5) 12 29
(Linda Perratt) *s.i.s: bhd and pushed along: nvr on terms* **50/1**

46-0 **12** *3 ¼* **Cold Quest (USA)**[41] 1520 7-8-6 55 JulieBurke(5) 5 16
(Linda Perratt) *hld up: shortlived effrt on outside 3f out: btn fnl 2f* **12/1**[3]

1m 40.36s (-0.84) **Going Correction** -0.075s/f (Good) 12 Ran SP% **115.7**
Speed ratings (Par 101): **101,99,97,94,94 94,92,92,90,85 83,79**
CSF £43.41 CT £117.45 TOTE £4.20: £1.10, £3.90, £1.10; EX 33.40.
Owner R Wardlaw **Bred** Darley **Trained** Westow, N Yorks

FOCUS

A modest and wide-open handicap run at a generous clip. Not form to be too positive about.
Mangham(IRE) Official explanation: jockey said gelding ran too free from a wide draw

2693 BRUCE STEVENSON INSURANCE BROKERS (S) STKS 5f

3:10 (3:10) (Class 6) 2-Y-0 **£1,942** (£578; £288; £144) **Stalls** High

Form RPR

1 **Act Your Shoe Size** 2-8-6 0 JoeFanning 5 68+
(Keith Dalgleish) *chsd ldr: pushed along 1/2-way: hdwy to ld wl ins fnl f: r.o* **4/1**[3]

02 **2** *1 ¼* **Pint Size**[11] 2362 2-8-11 0 AdrianNicholls 2 69
(David Nicholls) *led: rdn over 1f out: hdd and no ex wl ins fnl f* **11/4**[2]

3 *9* **Fortune Star (IRE)** 2-8-11 0 FrederikTylicki 6 36
(Linda Perratt) *chsd ldrs: rdn over 1f out: sn btn* **8/1**

0 **4** *3 ¼* **Justine Time (IRE)**[20] 2113 2-8-6 0 LeeNewman 4 19
(David Barron) *sn pushed along to chse ldrs: rdn and edgd rt 1/2-way: wknd wl over 1f out* **11/10**[1]

6 **5** *1* **Mister Tancred**[19] 2121 2-8-11 0 AndrewMullen 1 21
(David Nicholls) *s.i.s: bhd and pushed along: struggling fr 1/2-way* **16/1**

59.28 secs (-1.12) **Going Correction** -0.075s/f (Good) 5 Ran SP% **111.3**
Speed ratings (Par 91): **91,89,74,69,67**
CSF £15.35 TOTE £7.30: £2.50, £2.10; EX 20.90.The winner was bought in for £8,500.
Owner Gordon McDowall **Bred** Gordon McDowall **Trained** Carluke, South Lanarkshire

FOCUS

Few made much appeal upon paddock inspection. It was run at a good clip and the first two finished clear, showing above-average form.

NOTEBOOK

Act Your Shoe Size was fairly easy to back early on, but was nibbled at in the market before the off. Although her pedigree is nothing special, she knew her job and wore down the long-time leader. She did it well in the end, and a further furlong would not go amiss. She was bought back in for £8,500. (op 11-2)

Pint Size will not have many easier opportunities to get off the mark. He made a fist of it from the front and went down fighting. He is capable of winning a race of a similar nature. (op 13-8)

Fortune Star(IRE) needs further. (op 11-1)

Justine Time(IRE) failed to progress from her first run in a fillies' maiden at Thirsk and was beaten a long way. This was a disappointing effort. (op 6-4, tchd 13-8 in a place)

Mister Tancred was again slowly away and never got on terms. (op 22-1 tchd 25-1)

2694 EDGEN MURRAY EUROPE LTD TARTAN TROPHY H'CAP (CONSOLATION RACE FOR THE SCOTTISH SPRINT CUP) 5f

3:45 (3:46) (Class 3) 3-Y-0+ **£7,771** (£2,312; £1,155; £577) **Stalls** High

Form RPR

-033 **1** **Lost In Paris (IRE)**[6] 2497 5-9-8 80 (p) TadhgO'Shea 13 93
(Tim Easterby) *prom: hdwy to ld over 1f out: pushed out fnl f: comf* **4/1**[1]

2066 **2** *2 ¼* **Bosun Breese**[13] 2299 6-8-11 74 LMcNiff(5) 12 79
(David Barron) *mde most to over 1f out: kpt on fnl f: nt pce of wnr* **17/2**[3]

-365 **3** *1 ½* **Red Roar (IRE)**[13] 2286 4-8-7 65 PatrickMathers 14 65
(Alan Berry) *dwlt: bhd and pushed along: hdwy whn checked over 1f out: styd on fnl f: nrst fin* **10/1**

-000 **4** *3 ¾* **Distant Sun (USA)**[1] 2632 7-7-12 59 ow2 AndrewHeffernan(3) 11 45
(Linda Perratt) *bhd and outpcd: hdwy appr fnl f: kpt on: nrst fin* **40/1**

-105 **5** *nk* **Magical Macey (USA)**[20] 2118 4-9-9 81 (b) LeeNewman 4 66
(David Barron) *w ldrs tl rdn and nt qckn appr fnl f* **12/1**

0626 **6** *hd* **Garstang**[38] 1584 8-8-0 61 (b) SimonPearce(3) 3 45
(John Balding) *dwlt: bhd tl hdwy over 1f out: nvr able to chal* **18/1**

4010 **7** *3 ¾* **Le Toreador**[9] 2397 6-9-10 82 (b) PhillipMakin 5 53
(Kevin Ryan) *w ldrs tl wknd appr fnl f* **7/1**[2]

0-60 **8** *nk* **Mullglen**[27] 1907 5-8-8 66 JoeFanning 7 36
(Tim Easterby) *bhd and sn outpcd: hdwy over 1f out: nvr rchd ldrs* **17/2**[3]

-006 **9** *¾* **Mandarin Spirit (IRE)**[14] 2263 11-8-2 63 (b) DeclanCannon(3) 10 30
(Linda Perratt) *w ldrs tl wknd over 1f out* **50/1**

0-36 **10** *2 ¾* **Invincible Lad (IRE)**[37] 1618 7-9-7 79 AndrewMullen 6 36
(David Nicholls) *midfield: drvn 1/2-way: wknd over 1f out* **14/1**

-53 **11** *¾* **Cruise Tothelimit (IRE)**[6] 2505 3-8-8 73 FrederikTylicki 2 27
(Patrick Morris) *midfield on outside: effrt 2f out: wknd over 1f out* **11/1**

0-33 **12** *2* **Arriva La Diva**[21] 2062 5-8-0 63 ow3 JulieBurke(5) 9 10
(Linda Perratt) *w ldrs tl rdn and wknd over 1f out* **16/1**

0-00 **13** *nk* **Tabiet**[1] 2632 4-7-7 56 oh3 DanielleMcCreery(5) 1 —
(Linda Perratt) *midfield on outside: struggling over 2f out: sn btn* **100/1**

2-52 **14** *½* **Jarrow (IRE)**[20] 2095 4-9-6 78 AdrianNicholls 8 —
(David Nicholls) *midfield: drvn along 1/2-way: lost pl whn hmpd over 1f out* **4/1**[1]

59.32 secs (-1.08) **Going Correction** -0.075s/f (Good)
WFA 3 from 4yo+ 7lb 14 Ran SP% **121.9**
Speed ratings (Par 107): **105,101,99,93,92 92,86,85,84,80 78,75,75,74**
Tote Swingers: 1&2 £2.90, 1&3 £7.10, 2&3 £40.90 CSF £38.13 CT £261.61 TOTE £3.90: £1.50, £4.30, £3.30; EX 47.70.
Owner W H Ponsonby **Bred** Yeomanstown Stud **Trained** Great Habton, N Yorks

FOCUS

The consolation race for the Scottish Sprint Cup was hand-timed, but seemingly run at a generous pace and high numbers (stands' side) were to the fore. Very few got into it. The winner posted a 5lb personal best, arguably worth more but few showed their form.

NOTEBOOK

Lost In Paris(IRE) won this race 12 months ago off a mark of 75, but had not scored in 12 subsequent starts, despite running well in defeat. Running off 80 here and with cheekpieces fitted, he had the ideal draw and was given a good tow into the race by the eventual runner-up. Despite hanging right, he won with a bit to spare. (op 7-2)

Bosun Breese ran another game race in defeat, but had no real excuses with ground and draw in his favour. This drop back to 5f suited him and he won't be long in winning again on this evidence. (op 8-1)

Red Roar(IRE) was well backed despite not having the run of the race at Chester last time. She had the rail draw, which was not ideal, and she was very slow into her stride, having to be shoved along to get into contention. She settled quickly, though, and stayed on well. On this evidence, she looks a bit better than her official mark of 65. (op 14-1)

Distant Sun(USA) seemed to be going nowhere and was almost last 2.5f out, but came with a rare old rattle. He didn't show much at Hamilton 24 hours previously, but the run clearly didn't tax him. His is handicapped to win at present. (op 50-1)

Magical Macey(USA) was beaten a fair way, but seems to be running into form. Up with the pace from the start, he travelled well but faded late. He ran to his mark from an unfavourable draw. (op 11-1)

Arriva La Diva showed decent early pace, but found herself squeezed for room when tightened up by Le Toreador at the 2f pole. While she would have had no chance with the winner, her race had not yet been run so it is best to draw a line under this display. (op 14-1)

2695 TRADESMAN'S DERBY H'CAP 1m 4f 100y

4:25 (4:25) (Class 4) (0-80,83) 3-Y-O **£9,714** (£2,890; £1,444; £721) **Stalls** Low

Form RPR

1-03 **1** **Lexington Bay (IRE)**[21] 2076 3-9-2 73 DavidNolan 4 81
(Richard Fahey) *cl up: led 2f out: rdn and edgd rt appr fnl f: hld wl* **13/2**[2]

32-1 **2** *¾* **Motivado**[10] 2389 3-9-12 83 6ex StevieDonohoe 8 90+
(Sir Mark Prescott Bt) *hld up in tch: stdy hdwy 1/2-way: rdn and outpcd over 2f out: rallied to chse wnr 1f out: kpt on u.p but a hld* **1/2**[1]

14-4 **3** *3 ¾* **Sky Falcon (USA)**[27] 1903 3-9-6 77 JoeFanning 1 78
(Mark Johnston) *trckd ldrs: drvn and outpcd over 2f out: rallied appr fnl f: no imp* **25/1**

0311 **4** *1 ¾* **Szabo's Destiny**[28] 1872 3-9-0 71 FrederikTylicki 2 69
(James Given) *led: rdn and hdd 2f out: kpt on same pce fnl f* **8/1**[3]

6-16 **5** *4 ½* **Piave (IRE)**[14] 2253 3-8-13 73 AshleyHamblett(3) 3 64
(Peter Chapple-Hyam) *hld up in tch: drvn and outpcd over 3f out: no imp fnl f* **20/1**

00-3 **6** *2 ¾* **Cosmic Moon**[14] 2256 3-8-11 73 LeeTopliss(5) 6 59
(Richard Fahey) *hld up in tch: effrt on outside 3f out: btn fnl 2f* **12/1**

01- **7** *31* **Quiz Mistress**[202] 7452 3-9-5 76 TadhgO'Shea 5 —
(Gerard Butler) *s.v.s: sn rcvrd to join pack: effrt on outside over 3f out: wknd fr 2f out* **14/1**

2m 41.02s (-0.98) **Going Correction** -0.075s/f (Good) 7 Ran SP% **114.1**
Speed ratings (Par 101): **100,99,97,95,92 91,70**
Tote Swingers: 1&2 £1.80, 1&3 £7.10, 2&3 £3.70 CSF £10.13 CT £77.16 TOTE £5.90: £1.60, £2.20; EX 13.60.
Owner Keith Denham & Tony Denham **Bred** Mrs Vanessa Hutch **Trained** Musley Bank, N Yorks
■ Stewards' Enquiry : Ashley Hamblett caution: used whip down shoulder in the forehand.

FOCUS

Decent money for a competitive handicap and run at only a fair pace, which slackened in the middle stages. The winner confirmed his latest York improvement.
Quiz Mistress Official explanation: jockey said filly was slow away

2696 CRUDEN GROUP H'CAP (A QUALIFIER FOR THE BETFAIR BONUS SCOTTISH RACING STAYERS FINAL) 1m 5f

5:00 (5:00) (Class 6) (0-65,65) 4-Y-0+ **£2,590** (£770; £385; £192) **Stalls** Low

Form RPR

63-3 **1** **Ghufa (IRE)**[49] 1372 7-9-4 65 SimonPearce(3) 2 73
(Lydia Pearce) *in tch: effrt over 2f out: swtchd lft over 1f out: led ins fnl f: rdn out* **15/2**

0-03 **2** *1* **Golden Future**[7] 2462 8-8-5 52 DeclanCannon(3) 8 59
(Peter Niven) *cl up: effrt and drvn over 2f out: hung rt: chal over 1f out to ins fnl f: kpt on fin* **13/2**[3]

5-04 **3** *hd* **Beneath**[10] 2388 4-8-13 57 (b) PhillipMakin 4 63
(Kevin Ryan) *chsd ldr: rdn over 2f out: led over 1f out to ins fnl f: kpt on: hld cl home* **11/2**[2]

-431 **4** *2 ¾* **Maid Of Meft**[8] 2433 4-9-3 61 6ex FrederikTylicki 11 63+
(Linda Perratt) *hld up: rdn 3f out: hdwy over 1f out: nvr able to chal* **9/2**[1]

0662 **5** *3 ¼* **Valdan (IRE)**[9] 2400 7-8-12 56 (t) StevieDonohoe 6 53
(Maurice Barnes) *hld up and bhd: rdn along over 2f out: hdwy over 1f out: nvr able to chal* **8/1**

231- **6** *1* **Los Nadis (GER)**[36] 3496 7-9-4 65 GaryBartley(3) 3 61
(Jim Goldie) *t.k.h: hld up: effrt over 2f out: nvr able to chal* **9/2**[1]

25-5 **7** *½* **Parc Des Princes (USA)**[20] 2091 5-9-2 65 LeeTopliss(5) 9 60
(Nicky Richards) *hld up: rdn 3f out: sme late hdwy: nvr rchd ldrs* **13/2**[3]

56/0 **8** *1 ½* **Hair Of The Dog**[11] 2347 7-8-4 **51**...................(bt[1]) AndrewHeffernan(3) 1 44
(George Charlton) *t.k.h: led to over 1f out: wknd ent fnl f* **66/1**
1635 **9** *4* **French Hollow**[14] 2262 6-8-13 **64**.............................. GarryWhillans(7) 10 51
(Tim Fitzgerald) *t.k.h: hld up: rdn and edgd rt 3f out: sn n.d* **10/1**
000- **10** *21* **Merrion Tiger (IRE)**[332] 3760 6-8-10 **54**.............................. LeeNewman 7 —
(George Foster) *midfield: drvn and outpcd over 5f out: sn btn: t.o* **40/1**

2m 50.44s (-1.56) **Going Correction** -0.075s/f (Good) course record **10** Ran SP% **114.3**
Speed ratings (Par 101): **101,100,100,98,96 95,95,94,92,79**
Tote Swingers: 1&2 £7.00, 1&3 £7.90, 2&3 £10.20 CSF £54.43 CT £289.80 TOTE £7.10: £2.30, £2.70, £2.10; EX 36.70.
Owner S & M Supplies (Aylsham) Ltd **Bred** Shadwell Estate Company Limited **Trained** Newmarket, Suffolk
■ Lydia Pearce's first winner since resuming her training career.
■ Stewards' Enquiry : Phillip Makin caution: used whip down shoulder in the forehand.

FOCUS
A weak handicap run at a pedestrian early pace, which would not have helped many of the runners and it produced a tight finish. A trio kicked clear entering the straight. The winner is rated close to last year's turf best.

2697 RACING UK H'CAP (A QUALIFIER FOR THE BETFAIR BONUS SCOTTISH RACING SPRINT FINAL) 5f
5:35 (5:35) (Class 6) (0-65,65) 3-Y-O **£2,590** (£770; £385; £192) **Stalls** High

Form RPR
5-21 **1** **Rothesay Chancer**[14] 2265 3-9-4 **65**.............................. GaryBartley(3) 4 70
(Jim Goldie) *prom: effrt over 1f out: edgd lft and led last 100yds: kpt on wl* **7/4**[1]
4223 **2** *½* **Tancred Spirit**[39] 1561 3-8-0 **47**..............................(p) DeclanCannon(3) 7 48
(Paul Midgley) *led tl rdn and hdd last 100yds: kpt on towards fin* **11/2**[3]
0060 **3** *nk* **Bygones For Coins (IRE)**[6] 2498 3-8-1 **50**......... DanielleMcCreery(5) 6 50?
(Alan Berry) *fly-jmpd s: bhd: hdwy over 1f out: kpt on ins fnl f: nrst fin* **22/1**
6-00 **4** *1* **Face East (USA)**[14] 2265 3-8-2 **46** oh1.......................... PatrickMathers 8 42?
(Alan Berry) *sn pushed along bhd ldng gp: rdn 1/2-way: imp tl styd on fnl f: nrst fin* **100/1**
23-6 **5** *nk* **Pantella (IRE)**[25] 1941 3-9-7 **65**.............................. PhillipMakin 3 60
(Kevin Ryan) *dwlt: hld up in tch: effrt over 1f out: kpt on same pce fnl f* **6/1**
6650 **6** *7* **Fawara**[14] 2265 3-7-13 **46** oh1.............................. AndrewHeffernan(3) 1 16
(Ruth Carr) *cl up to 1/2-way: rdn and wknd wl over 1f out* **50/1**
5401 **7** *1 ½* **Saxonette**[8] 2410 3-9-1 **64** 6ex.............................. LeeTopliss(5) 2 29
(Linda Perratt) *prom: drvn 1/2-way: wknd fr 2f out* **15/2**
6-52 **8** *9* **Pizzarra**[14] 2265 3-9-0 **58**.............................. FrederikTylicki 5 —
(James Given) *cl up tl rdn and wknd appr fnl f: eased whn no ch last 100yds* **9/4**[2]

60.55 secs (0.15) **Going Correction** -0.075s/f (Good) **8** Ran SP% **115.9**
Speed ratings (Par 97): **95,94,93,92,91 80,78,63**
Tote Swingers: 1&2 £2.90, 1&3 £7.80, 2&3 £10.10 CSF £12.10 CT £156.03 TOTE £2.70: £1.10, £2.40, £6.90; EX 12.20.
Owner Discovery Racing Club 2 **Bred** Mrs S R Kennedy **Trained** Uplawmoor, E Renfrews

FOCUS
A competitive if modest sprint handicap finale, run in the slowest of the three C&D times. The winenr confirmed his C&D latest.
T/Plt: £47.50 to a £1 stake. Pool:£35,070.89 - 644.04 winning tickets. T/Qpdt: £30.20 to a £1 stake. Pool:£2,449.98 - 873.49 winning tickets. RY

2698 - 2704a (Foreign Racing) - See Raceform Interactive

2672 DONCASTER (L-H)
Saturday, June 4

OFFICIAL GOING: Good to firm (7.3)
Wind: Moderate, behind Weather: Fine and dry

2705 WILLIAMHILL.COM H'CAP 1m (S)
2:20 (2:21) (Class 2) (0-105,96) 3-Y-O **£12,952** (£3,854; £1,926; £962) **Stalls** High

Form RPR
1-6 **1** **Chef**[51] 1339 3-9-7 **96**.............................. DavidProbert 7 105+
(Andrew Balding) *trckd ldrs: swtchd lft and hdwy wl over 1f out: rdn to chal ent fnl f: drvn and kpt on to ld last 100yds* **9/4**[1]
0-50 **2** *hd* **Mubtadi**[14] 2296 3-8-6 **81**.............................. MartinLane 3 90+
(David Simcock) *trckd ldrs: hdwy on outer 2f out: rdn to ld briefly ent fnl f: sn drvn: hdd and nt qckn last 100yds* **5/1**[3]
0-61 **3** *3 ¾* **Shamdarley (IRE)**[21] 2092 3-8-3 **78**.............................. HayleyTurner 1 78+
(Michael Dods) *hld up in rr: hdwy 3f out: effrt and n.m.r 2f out: sn rdn: chsd ldng pair ins fnl f: one pce* **5/2**[2]
01-0 **4** *½* **Byrony (IRE)**[38] 1599 3-8-13 **88**.............................. PatDobbs 4 87
(Richard Hannon) *trckd ldng pair: effrt and cl up 2f out: rdn to ld briefly over 1f out: drvn and hdd ent fnl f: sn one pce* **20/1**
0-30 **5** *2 ¼* **Rigolleto (IRE)**[14] 2296 3-9-0 **92**.............................. MartinHarley(3) 6 86
(Mick Channon) *set stdy pce: qcknd wl over 3f out: rdn 2f out: drvn and hdd appr fnl f: wknd* **14/1**
2620 **6** *3 ½* **Fred Willetts (IRE)**[14] 2296 3-9-1 **90**..............................(v) PatCosgrave 8 76
(David Evans) *trckd ldrs on inner: effrt wl over 2f out: rdn wl over 1f out: sn wknd* **9/1**
56-0 **7** *nse* **Waltz Darling (IRE)**[52] 1322 3-9-4 **93**.............................. TonyHamilton 9 79
(Richard Fahey) *dwlt: hld up: a in rr* **33/1**
1410 **8** *hd* **Crown Counsel (IRE)**[14] 2296 3-8-13 **88**.................. RoystonFfrench 2 73
(Mark Johnston) *cl up: rdn along over 2f out: sn wknd* **6/1**

1m 38.4s (-0.90) **Going Correction** -0.10s/f (Good) **8** Ran SP% **114.7**
Speed ratings (Par 105): **100,99,96,95,93 89,89,89**
toteswingers: 1&2 £3.80, 1&3 £2.40, 2&3 £3.90 CSF £14.04 CT £29.38 TOTE £3.20: £1.10, £2.10, £1.50; EX 16.30 Trifecta £115.50 Pool: £965.02 - 6.18 winning units..
Owner Brook Farm Bloodstock **Bred** Bloomsbury Stud **Trained** Kingsclere, Hants

FOCUS
One of the jockeys in the first described it as "beautiful ground, just on the fast side of good. First run in 2008, this event was won in its opening year by subsequent smart performer Redford. This was a decent handicap, but run at only a steady pace until past halfway. The first two did well to pull clear and the winner already looks smart.

NOTEBOOK
Chef was the least exposed runner on view, restricted to two previous outings. Making his handicap debut after finishing sixth in a sales race at Newmarket, just a neck behind subsequent dual 1000 Guineas runner-up Together, he was held up in fifth and had to be switched out for a run. Once in the clear he made steady rather than rapid progress, leading late on and holding off the persistent runner-up. A smart prospect, he is capable of bettering this bare form and has more to offer. (op 5-2)
Mubtadi came with his run from just behind Chef, enjoying an uninterrupted passage. He took a narrow lead and battled on willingly, but just missed out. He had been dropped 2lb since a lacklustre effort at Haydock, where he raced on the wrong side of the track. (op 13-2)
Shamdarley(IRE) still appeared well treated despite a 9lb rise for an easy win on the round mile here. Dropped in at the back from stall one, he did not immediately pick up when asked to improve his position as the pace lifted, but once switched out he came home quite nicely for third. Things did not pan out for him here but he can probably make amends. (op 11-4)
Byrony(IRE), last on her return at Ascot, had every chance at one stage and seems to have trained on. (op 16-1 tchd 14-1)
Rigolleto(IRE) made the running at his own pace and gradually quickened things up, but he could not hold his lead going to the furlong pole and was comfortably beaten in the end. (op 11-1)
Fred Willetts(IRE) finished in front of three of these opponents, including the runner-up, in the Silver Bowl at Haydock last time, but a busy spell appears to have caught up with him. (op 11-1)
Crown Counsel(IRE), whose trainer had won the last two runnings of this, was the first to come under pressure and faded after racing up with the pace. (tchd 9-2)

2706 WILLIAM HILL - HOME OF BETTING H'CAP 7f
2:50 (2:52) (Class 2) (0-105,98) 4-Y-O+ **£12,952** (£3,854; £1,926; £962) **Stalls** High

Form RPR
-600 **1** **Smarty Socks (IRE)**[35] 1694 7-8-11 **88**.............................. DanielTudhope 7 98
(David O'Meara) *dwlt and bhd: stdy hdwy on wd outside 3f out: chsd ldrs wl over 1f out: rdn to chal ins fnl f: kpt on wl to ld nr fin* **9/1**
01-6 **2** *hd* **Webbow (IRE)**[154] 6 9-8-9 **86**.............................. MartinDwyer 9 95
(Mark Campion) *chsd ldrs: gd hdwy over 2f out: led 1 1/2f out: rdn and edgd lft ins fnl f: hdd and no ex towards fin* **25/1**
/0-5 **3** *¾* **Bronze Prince**[23] 2020 4-8-10 **87**.............................. RobertHavlin 1 94
(John Gosden) *hld up: hdwy wl over 2f out: rdn to chse ldrs over 1f out: drvn and kpt on ins fnl f* **7/1**[2]
5022 **4** *¾* **Advanced**[7] 2495 8-8-10 **92**..............................(p) JulieBurke(5) 15 97
(Kevin Ryan) *prom: led wl over 2f out: rdn and hdd 1 1/2f out: drvn and edgd lft ent fnl f: one pce towards fin* **8/1**[3]
-030 **5** *hd* **Space War**[20] 2123 4-9-0 **91**.............................. DavidNolan 11 96
(Michael Easterby) *hld up: hdwy over 2f out: sn rdn and styd on ins fnl f: nrst fin* **20/1**
2243 **6** *1 ½* **Internationaldebut (IRE)**[21] 2116 6-8-11 **88**................ TonyCulhane 14 89
(Paul Midgley) *hld up towards rr: gd hdwy over 2f out: swtchd rt and rdn to chse ldrs over 1f out: edgd lft and kpt on ins fnl f: nrst fin* **9/1**
3110 **7** *shd* **Imperial Djay (IRE)**[7] 2495 6-8-13 **90**.............................. PJMcDonald 13 91
(Ruth Carr) *in tch: hdwy over 2f out: rdn and hung lft over 1f out: drvn and kpt on ins fnl f: nrst fin* **25/1**
-025 **8** *1* **Cheers For Thea (IRE)**[16] 2217 6-8-11 **88**................(bt) DarryllHolland 5 88+
(Tim Easterby) *towards rr: pushed along 1/2-way: rdn and hdwy whn hmpd over 1f out: kpt on ins fnl f: nrst fin* **25/1**
3401 **9** *nse* **Majuro (IRE)**[7] 2495 7-8-8 **85**..............................(t) RobbieFitzpatrick 2 83
(Richard Guest) *in tch: hdwy on wd outside to chse ldrs over 2f out: rdn wl over 1f out: drvn appr fnl f and kpt ons same pce* **16/1**
2121 **10** *¾* **Bawaardi (IRE)**[22] 2061 5-8-13 **90**.............................. TonyHamilton 17 86
(Richard Fahey) *prom: effrt and ch 2f out: sn rdn and wknd ent fnl f* **6/1**[1]
-666 **11** *hd* **Damika (IRE)**[14] 2284 8-9-1 **92**.............................. RussKennemore 19 87
(Richard Whitaker) *in tch: rdn along wl over 2f out: sn drvn and one pce* **14/1**
0450 **12** *1 ½* **Osteopathic Remedy (IRE)**[23] 2031 7-9-1 **95**............ SeanLevey(3) 16 86
(Michael Dods) *chsd ldrs: rdn along over 2f out: hld whn sltly hmpd over 1f out: wknd* **28/1**
4000 **13** *nk* **Barney McGrew (IRE)**[14] 2317 8-9-5 **96**.............................. TomQueally 6 86
(Michael Dods) *t.k.h: chsd ldrs: rdn along over 2f out: wknd over 1f out* **14/1**
0-60 **14** *2* **Noble Citizen (USA)**[28] 1885 6-9-0 **91**..............................(be) MartinLane 3 76
(David Simcock) *hld up towards rr: sme hdwy 1/2-way: pushed along whn sltly hmpd over 1f out: wknd after* **9/1**
00-0 **15** *2 ¼* **Sunraider (IRE)**[28] 1885 4-8-13 **90**.............................. MichaelHills 8 74
(B W Hills) *chsd ldrs: rdn along over 2f out: wkng whn hmpd over 1f out* **28/1**
-440 **16** *hd* **Dhaular Dhar (IRE)**[28] 1885 9-8-6 **88**.............................. HarryBentley(5) 4 66
(Jim Goldie) *a in rr* **16/1**
0040 **17** *¾* **Jack My Boy (IRE)**[34] 1720 4-8-12 **89**..............................(b) PatCosgrave 18 65
(David Evans) *racd wd: prom: rdn along 3f out: sn wknd* **50/1**
-150 **18** *6* **Below Zero (IRE)**[8] 2470 4-8-13 **90**.............................. RoystonFfrench 10 50
(Mark Johnston) *in tch: rdn along wl over 2f out: sn wknd* **66/1**
0000 **19** *2 ¾* **Oasis Dancer**[28] 1885 4-9-7 **98**..............................(b[1]) JimCrowley 12 51
(Ralph Beckett) *led: rdn along and hdd wl over 2f out: sn wknd* **25/1**
00-4 **20** *10* **My Kingdom (IRE)**[29] 1849 5-9-0 **91**.............................. AhmedAjtebi 20 —
(David Nicholls) *a towards rr: bhd and eased fnl 2f* **16/1**

1m 23.96s (-2.34) **Going Correction** -0.10s/f (Good) **20** Ran SP% **130.8**
Speed ratings (Par 109): **109,108,107,107,106 105,105,103,103,102 102,101,100,98,95 95,94,87,84,73**
toteswingers: 1&2 £70.00, 1&3 £62.40, 2&3 £26.50 CSF £231.46 CT £1732.53 TOTE £11.50: £2.80, £6.80, £3.40, £2.70; EX 300.60 Trifecta £1455.40 Part won. Pool: £1,966.80 - 0.10 winning units..
Owner R Fell & K Everitt **Bred** Mick McGinn **Trained** Nawton, N Yorks

FOCUS
A competitive handicap and solid form. The winner is rated back to his best. It initially looked as if they would split into two groups, but that didn't happen. The principals raced down the centre to the far side of the track.

NOTEBOOK
Smarty Socks(IRE) missed the break as he often does and was last at halfway, but he came with a sustained run down the outer to force his nose in front close home. This tough individual was only 3lb higher than when winning here last August, and now has three wins over C&D. He is well suited by fast ground and is equally effective at 1m. His trainer and jockey are in blinding form.
Webbow(IRE) ran a big race on his debut for Mark Campion but could not quite hold on to his advantage. He is an able performer who scored at Dundalk before Christmas, but despite any number of good runs his last win on turf was over a mile here in August 2007. (op 20-1)
Bronze Prince ◆ was far less experienced and less exposed than the rest of the field and he ran a taking race, staying on well for third. There should be a handicap to be won with him before long and he is in the Royal Hunt Cup, although he would struggle to make the cut there. (op 13-2 tchd 11-2)
Advanced has been performing well since the cheekpieces went on and this was another solid effort, but his losing run stretches 22 races now back to September 2009. (op 17-2 tchd 9-1)
Space War ran better ridden with more restraint and the way he was keeping on hinted that a return to 1m will suit. (op 25-1)
Internationaldebut(IRE) raced nearer the stands' side than a lot of the principals and remains in decent heart. It would not be a surprise if headgear was used on him again at some point. (op 10-1)
Imperial Djay(IRE) ran creditably enough but was never a serious factor and the handicapper looks in control for now.
Cheers For Thea(IRE) was running on when it was too late and will be of more interest back at 1m.
Majuro(IRE) could not confirm his Catterick superiority over Advanced.

Bawaardi(IRE) had his chance on this hat-trick bid but a high draw and career-high mark combined to beat him. (op 7-1 tchd 11-2)

2707 VISIT WILLIAMHILL.COM ON YOUR MOBILE! CONDITIONS STKS 1m 2f 60y
3:25 (3:25) (Class 2) 3-Y-O £13,016 (£3,873; £1,935; £966) Stalls Low

Form				RPR
41	1		**Alkimos (IRE)**[26] 1950 3-8-12 93 J-PGuillambert 2 (Luca Cumani) *trckd ldng pair on inner: effrt and nt clr run over 2f out: qcknd to ld over 1f out: rdn and kpt on wl fnl f* **3/1**[2]	105+
32	2	2 1/4	**Maali (IRE)**[18] 2185 3-8-12 0 PhilipRobinson 1 (Clive Brittain) *trckd ldrs: pushed along 3f out: rdn wl over 1f out: kpt on u.p to chse wnr ins fnl f: no imp towards fin* **13/2**	99
0-12	3	1 1/4	**Buthelezi (USA)**[7] 2507 3-8-12 104 RobertHavlin 3 (John Gosden) *led: rdn along and jnd 3f out: drvn 2f out: hdd over 1f out: kpt on same pce* **6/4**[1]	97
10	4	2 1/4	**Midsummer Fair (USA)**[20] 2139 3-8-12 95 AhmedAjtebi 5 (Mahmood Al Zarooni) *trckd ldr: hdwy and cl up 3f out: rdn along 2f out and ev ch tl drvn over 1f out and sn wknd* **5/1**[3]	92
1	P		**Gusting**[22] 2058 3-8-12 0 RoystonFfrench 4 (Mahmood Al Zarooni) *hld up in tch tl p.u wl over 2f out* **15/2**	—

2m 8.87s (-0.53) **Going Correction** -0.10s/f (Good) 5 Ran SP% **106.8**
Speed ratings (Par 105): **98,96,95,93,—**
toteswingers: 1&2 £9.90 CSF £19.67 TOTE £3.80: £2.20, £5.10; EX 21.30.
Owner Leonidas Marinopoulos **Bred** C O'Brien B McGarvey & D Everard **Trained** Newmarket, Suffolk

FOCUS
A valuable and interesting conditions event, but run at just an ordinary gallop and in consequence a little muddling. Their is potentially a fair bit more from the winner.

NOTEBOOK
Alkimos(IRE) was caught in a pocket for a time but when a gap opened in front of him he quickened up smartly to take it, although he edged right once in front. He will be on a stiffish mark after this but that may not matter as he looks well worth his place in Listed company now. The Cumani team won this race a year ago with Afsare, who went on to add the Listed Hampton Court (now Tercentenary) Stakes at Ascot, and it would be no surprise to see this colt take the same route. (op 2-1)
Maali(IRE), an unlucky loser in a Nottingham maiden last time, ran well on this rise in grade but having chased the winner through he gave the impression that his stamina for this longer trip was running out near the finish. A maiden should be his for the taking. (op 15-2 tchd 6-1)
Buthelezi(USA), runner-up in a Listed race last time after hanging aross the track, was 9lb clear on adjusted official figures. Setting the pace and showing no evidence of his quirky side, he was staying on again having been headed and may have a bit of improvement in him at 1m4f. On the face of it though, this was a below-par effort. (op 15-8)
Midsummer Fair(USA) found the French Guineas asking too much of him last time and he was slightly disappointing down in grade, holding every chance but perhaps not seeing out this longer trip. He is the type who may not prove simple to place. (op 11-2 tchd 6-1)
Gusting, a Newcastle maiden winner on his only previous start, unfortunately suffered a serious leg injury with around 3f to run. Official explanation: trainer said gelding was lame (op 7-1)

2708 CLOSE BUILDING SERVICES LTD H'CAP 1m 4f
3:55 (3:55) (Class 4) (0-85,84) 4-Y-O+ £3,885 (£1,156; £577; £288) Stalls Low

Form				RPR
-262	1		**Oriental Cavalier**[14] 2282 5-8-11 **74** (v) JimCrowley 5 (Mark Buckley) *hld up in tch: hdwy 4f out: chsd ldrs 3f out: led 2f out and sn rdn: drvn and edgd rt ins fnl f: kpt on wl* **13/2**	83
2321	2	3/4	**War Poet**[12] 2364 4-9-5 **82** DanielTudhope 6 (David O'Meara) *hld up: smooth hdwy 3f out: rdn to chse wnr over 1f out: swtchd lft and drvn ins fnl f: kpt on* **9/4**[1]	90+
5406	3	2 1/2	**Arizona John (IRE)**[16] 2220 6-9-3 **80** TomQueally 3 (John Mackie) *hld up in tch: smooth hdwy over 3f out: chsd ldng pair 2f out: rdn and n.m.r over 1f out: one pce fnl f* **13/2**	84
-162	4	1 1/4	**Ubi Ace**[24] 2006 5-9-5 **82** PJMcDonald 1 (Tim Walford) *trckd ldrs on inner: hdwy to chse ldr over 4f out: rdn along wl over 2f out: drvn wl over 1f out: sn one pce* **4/1**[2]	84
10-0	5	2 1/2	**Maybe I Wont**[8] 2459 6-8-2 **65** oh1 MartinLane 8 (Lucinda Featherstone) *in tch: hdwy to chse ldrs 3f out: rdn along 2f out: sn drvn and one pce* **14/1**	63
0-05	6	3	**Gold Rules**[14] 2314 4-9-0 **84** (t) DavidSimmonson(7) 2 (Michael Easterby) *chsd ldrs: rdn along 3f out: sn wknd* **33/1**	77
3135	7	1 1/2	**Kames Park (IRE)**[14] 2320 9-8-5 **68** RobbieFitzpatrick 4 (Richard Guest) *dwlt: a in rr* **28/1**	59
326	8	8	**Cloudy Bay (USA)**[29] 1879 4-8-11 **77** (p) SeanLevey(3) 10 (Mrs K Burke) *led: rdn along 4f out: drvn and hdd 2f out: sn wknd* **18/1**	55
11-0	9	30	**Spensley (IRE)**[28] 1887 5-8-13 **76** PatCosgrave 9 (James Fanshawe) *chsd ldrs on outer: rdn along 4f out: sn wknd* **6/1**[3]	—
66-2	10	7	**Sirgarfieldsobers (IRE)**[12] 2364 5-9-3 **80** DavidNolan 7 (Declan Carroll) *chsd ldr: rdn along 1/2-way: sn lost pl and bhd* **12/1**	—

2m 31.1s (-3.80) **Going Correction** -0.10s/f (Good) 10 Ran SP% **117.7**
Speed ratings (Par 105): **108,107,105,105,103 101,100,95,75,70**
toteswingers: 1&2 £5.70, 1&3 £12.30, 2&3 £6.10 CSF £21.69 CT £101.35 TOTE £5.60: £2.00, £1.60, £2.10; EX 23.30 Trifecta £149.10 Pool: £779.81 - 3.87 winning units..
Owner X8 Racing Partnership 2 **Bred** Mrs Claire Massey **Trained** Castle Bytham, Stanford

FOCUS
Just a fair handicap, but it was well run and the form is sound. The winner is rated back to his best.
Sirgarfieldsobers(IRE) Official explanation: jockey said gelding pulled itself up

2709 E B F ONE CALL INSURANCE MAIDEN FILLIES' STKS 6f 110y
4:30 (4:32) (Class 4) 2-Y-O £5,245 (£1,560; £780; £389) Stalls High

Form				RPR
2	1		**Falls Of Lora (IRE)**[17] 2187 2-9-0 0 AhmedAjtebi 1 (Mahmood Al Zarooni) *prom: cl up 1/2-way: led over 2f out: rdn clr over 1f out: kpt on strly* **9/4**[1]	90+
	2	5	**Show Flower** 2-8-11 0 MartinHarley(3) 2 (Mick Channon) *a.p: cl up 1/2-way: rdn to chse wnr 2f out: drvn over 1f out: kpt on same pce* **11/2**[3]	76
3	3	nk	**Vassaria (IRE)**[15] 2254 2-8-11 0 SeanLevey(3) 8 (Michael Dods) *trckd ldrs: hdwy wl over 2f out: rdn wl over 1f out: kpt on same pce fnl f* **4/1**[2]	75
	4	shd	**Elusive Kate (USA)** 2-9-0 0 RobertHavlin 7 (John Gosden) *hld up towards rr: hdwy 2f out: pushed along over 1f out: kpt on fnl f: bttr for r* **11/2**[3]	76+
	5	4	**Piranha (IRE)** 2-9-0 0 JimCrowley 3 (Ed Dunlop) *chsd ldrs: rdn along 2f out: grad wknd* **12/1**	64
	6	2	**Reve Du Jour (IRE)** 2-9-0 0 TomQueally 4 (Alan McCabe) *towards rr: hdwy over 2f out: sn rdn along and n.d* **20/1**	59
	7	3/4	**Correct** 2-9-0 0 HayleyTurner 9 (Michael Bell) *a towards rr* **14/1**	57+
	8	1/2	**Emperors Pearl (IRE)** 2-9-0 0 MichaelHills 5 (B W Hills) *s.i.s and towards rr: sme hdwy on outer 1/2-way: sn rdn and n.d* **14/1**	55
0	9	2 1/4	**She's Flawless (USA)**[15] 2254 2-9-0 0 MartinDwyer 12 (Brian Meehan) *led: rdn along 1/2-way: sn hdd & wknd* **11/1**	49
	10	3	**Wake Up Sioux (IRE)** 2-9-0 0 RobbieFitzpatrick 10 (David C Griffiths) *s.i.s: a in rr: bhd fr 1/2-way* **33/1**	41
0	11	1	**Zain Princess (IRE)**[14] 2309 2-9-0 0 DarryllHolland 11 (Gerard Butler) *a in rr: bhd fr 1/2-way* **33/1**	38

1m 18.88s (-1.02) **Going Correction** -0.10s/f (Good) 11 Ran SP% **121.5**
Speed ratings (Par 92): **101,95,94,94,90 87,87,86,83,80 79**
toteswingers: 1&2 £3.60, 1&3 £2.40, 2&3 £5.30 CSF £14.88 TOTE £2.70: £1.30, £2.60, £1.70; EX 17.30 Trifecta £72.20 Pool: £1,310.89 - 13.43 winning units..
Owner Godolphin **Bred** Darley **Trained** Newmarket, Suffolk

FOCUS
An interesting fillies' maiden run over a testing trip for juveniles this early in the season. The impressive winner looks useful.

NOTEBOOK
Falls Of Lora(IRE), whose debut second to Glee at Goodwood was the best form achieved by any of the four who had previously run, ran out a clear-cut winner. Tacking over from stall one, she struck the front some way out before stretching clear in impressive fashion. There are no big-race entries for her yet, and it remains to be seen what she beat here, but she obviously has an engine and a race like the Albany Stakes at Ascot could come into consideration. She will get further than this later on. (op 11-4 after early 3-1 in places tchd 2-1)
Show Flower made the running and stuck on to secure second after the winner had stamped her authority. A half-sister to Godolphin's smart 7f horse Sirocco Breeze, she holds Group-race entries and is a promising filly, but perhaps the bare 6f would be more suitable for her at the moment than this extended trip. A maiden should soon come her way. (op 9-2)
Vassaria(IRE) did not really build on the form she showed on her debut at Haydock and looks unlikely to be taking up her Moyglare Stud Stakes entry on this evidence. Outpaced by the leaders from the two pole, but sticking on, she may need 7f plus to be seen to best effect. (op 5-1)
Elusive Kate(USA) ◆, the first foal of a 3yo winner in the US, cost $70,000 as a yearling. Picking up nicely from the rear, she was just edged out in a photo for third and promises better to come. (op 7-1 tchd 15-2)
Piranha(IRE) was beaten a fair way in the end but not before showing ability on this debut. There is plenty of stamina on her dam's side. (tchd 11-1)
Reve Du Jour(IRE) faded in the last couple of furlongs and this trip may have stretched her. (op 16-1)
Correct, a half-sister to three winners, one of them an Italian Oaks runner-up, can do better with this debut experience to call on. (op 16-1)

2710 CROWNHOTEL-BAWTRY.COM MAIDEN STKS 5f
5:05 (5:06) (Class 5) 3-Y-O+ £2,914 (£867; £433; £216) Stalls High

Form				RPR
33-4	1		**Eland Ally**[22] 2074 3-9-3 72 TomQueally 6 (Tom Tate) *mde all: shkn up and pushed clr over 1f out: easily* **1/3**[1]	77
0	2	2 3/4	**Crew Cut (IRE)**[21] 2094 3-9-3 0 RobertHavlin 3 (Jeremy Gask) *trckd ldrs: hdwy 2f out: rdn wl over 1f out: kpt on to take 2nd ins fnl f: no ch w wnr* **9/1**[3]	67
45/3	3	3/4	**Bobby's Doll**[51] 1331 4-9-0 55 AdamBeschizza(5) 1 (Terry Clement) *chsd wnr: rdn along 2f out: sn drvn and one pce: lost 2nd ins fnl f* **7/1**[2]	62
4465	4	7	**Gorgeous Goblin (IRE)**[12] 2365 4-9-5 54 (vt) RobbieFitzpatrick 10 (David C Griffiths) *dwlt: hdwy 1/2-way: rdn to chse ldrs 2f out: sn drvn and btn* **10/1**	37
0	5	2 1/2	**Noels Princess**[26] 1941 4-9-5 0 DanielTudhope 9 (David O'Meara) *chsd ldrs: rdn along 2f out: sn wknd* **20/1**	28
56	6	3/4	**Lady Rumba**[19] 2141 3-8-7 0 RyanPowell(5) 2 (John O'Shea) *a towards rr* **12/1**	22
00-	7	3	**First Pressing**[388] 2022 3-8-5 0 HannahNunn(7) 4 (John Berry) *a towards rr* **50/1**	11
60	8	1	**Green Ensign (IRE)**[49] 1399 4-9-7 0 MartinHarley(3) 5 (Alan McCabe) *a in rr* **33/1**	16
	9	2 1/4	**Harmony Wold** 3-9-0 0 ow2 DavidNolan 7 (Declan Carroll) *chsd ldrs: rdn along 1/2-way: sn wknd* **33/1**	—
05-0	10	1 3/4	**Tsarina Louise**[59] 1179 3-8-12 38 JimCrowley 8 (James Given) *a in rr: bhd fr 1/2-way* **33/1**	—

59.18 secs (-1.32) **Going Correction** -0.10s/f (Good)
WFA 3 from 4yo 7lb 10 Ran SP% **129.8**
Speed ratings (Par 103): **106,101,100,89,85 84,79,77,74,71**
toteswingers: 1&2 £2.40, 1&3 £2.20, 2&3 £4.30 CSF £5.15 TOTE £1.40: £1.02, £2.30, £1.90; EX 5.90 Trifecta £32.80 Pool: £1,755.19 - 39.49 winning units..
Owner The Ivy Syndicate **Bred** Peter Webb **Trained** Tadcaster, N Yorks
■ Stewards' Enquiry : Ryan Powell one-day ban: careless riding (Jun 19)

FOCUS
A weak sprint maiden with no depth, but the time was fair. The third is the key to the level.
T/Plt: £18.00 to a £1 stake. Pool: £82,278.82. 3,335.94 winning tickets. T/Qpdt: £7.10 to a £1 stake. Pool: £3,295.51. 341.90 winning tickets. JR

2678 EPSOM (L-H)
Saturday, June 4

OFFICIAL GOING: Good to firm (good in places on derby course; derby course 8.3; sprint course 8.5)
Rails at innermost configuration and distances as advertised.
Wind: modest, across Weather: sunny and warm

2711 INVESTEC HORSES HELP THE HEROES H'CAP 1m 2f 18y
1:40 (1:40) (Class 2) (0-105,98) 3-Y-O
£24,924 (£7,464; £3,732; £1,868; £932; £468) Stalls Low

Form				RPR
41-2	1		**Charles Camoin (IRE)**[16] 2229 3-8-6 **83** ow1 LiamKeniry 7 (Sylvester Kirk) *swtg: stdd after s: t.k.h early: hld up in tch in last trio: dropped to last and rdn over 3f out: hdwy on outer 2f out: 5th ent fnl f: edging lft but r.o wl to ld cl home* **10/1**	95+
4-21	2	shd	**Trojan Nights (USA)**[20] 2125 3-8-7 **84** EddieAhern 6 (William Haggas) *hld up in last trio: hdwy towards inner ent fnl 3f: drvn to chse ldrs 2f out: chal between horses jst ins fnl f: led fnl 100yds: hdd and no ex cl home* **6/1**	96

31-1 **3** *3/4* **Boogie Shoes**[34] [1727] 3-8-12 **89** .... NeilCallan 3 99+
(Roger Varian) *lw: t.k.h: hld up wl in tch: rdn and effrt to chse ldr ent fnl 2f: led over 1f out: rdn and nt qckning whn hung rt 1f out: hdd fnl 100yds: one pce after* **9/4**[1]

-421 **4** *1 1/2* **Tanfeeth**[16] [2231] 3-8-11 **88** .... RichardHills 1 96+
(Ed Dunlop) *lw: hld up in tch in last trio: hdwy over 3f out: rdn and chsng ldrs ent fnl 2f: keeping on same pce and looking hld whn short of room ins fnl f: eased towards fin* **11/2**[3]

6411 **5** *1 1/2* **Malthouse (GER)**[8] [2471] 3-9-7 **98** .... SilvestreDeSousa 4 102
(Mark Johnston) *pressed ldr tl rdn to ld over 2f out: hdd and drvn over 1f out: stl pressing ldrs 1f out: wknd fnl 100yds* **3/1**[2]

-515 **6** *8* **Arabian Star (IRE)**[14] [2287] 3-8-3 **80** ow1 .... ChrisCatlin 2 68
(Mick Channon) *led tl rdn and hdd over 1f out: wknd qckly wl over 1f out: wl btn ent fnl f* **33/1**

0-34 **7** *3/4* **Sergeant Ablett (IRE)**[34] [1723] 3-8-13 **90** .... PaulMulrennan 9 77
(James Given) *chsd ldrs tl dropped bk to midfield 6f out: rdn and struggling over 2f out: wknd and wl btn over 1f out* **8/1**

1164 **8** *2* **Gottany O'S**[14] [2295] 3-8-2 **79** .... CathyGannon 10 62
(Mick Channon) *dwlt: sn rdn along and hdwy to chse ldrs on outer after 1f: rdn and wknd ent fnl 2f: wl btn whn short of room and swtchd lft over 1f out* **20/1**

2m 6.32s (-3.38) **Going Correction** +0.075s/f (Good) **8** Ran SP% **113.3**
Speed ratings (Par 105): **116,115,115,114,112 106,105,104**
toteswingers:1&2:£11.20, 2&3:£3.10, 1&3:£4.70 CSF £67.00 CT £182.61 TOTE £11.40: £2.50, £1.80, £1.30; EX 78.00 Trifecta £132.40 Pool: £2,416.44 - 13.49 winning units..
Owner Chris Wright & The Hon Mrs J M Corbett **Bred** Pat Grogan **Trained** Upper Lambourn, Berks
■ Stewards' Enquiry : Liam Keniry one-day ban: used whip with excessive frequency down shoulder in the forehand (Jun 20)

FOCUS
There was 3mm of water applied to the track following the opening day Oaks card, but the ground had still quickened up a touch, being given as good to firm, good in places on the Derby course, and good to firm on the sprint track. Following this opener the jockeys were in agreement with the official description. The rail was at its innermost configuration and all distances were as advertised. Five of the last ten winners of this 3yo handicap subsequently won in Group company, including two at highest level, namely Lailani and Conduit. Less runners than usual - the last ten runnings all attracted double-figure fields - and the top weight was rated 7lb below the ceiling of 105, although in last year's race it was 12lb. The pace was good and the first five finished wel clear, with the front three in particular looking ahead of their marks, so the form should work out, with the fourth and fifth setting the level.

NOTEBOOK
Charles Camoin(IRE) ◆ was a second winner of the race in the space of three years for Sylvester Kirk. Carrying 1lb overweight, he didn't handle the downhill run into the straight and had dropped back to last just over 2f out, but the decent gallop ensured the leaders came back to him and he produced a sustained challenge out widest. He won his maiden over 1m last year, but had found that trip on the short side when resuming at Sandown and he improved significantly for this longer distance. It's possible he'll get even further and it wouldn't surprise if he was allowed his chance in the King George V handicap at Royal Ascot - Dandino followed up last year's success here in that very race. (op 8-1)
Trojan Nights(USA) ◆ improved for the slight step up in trip and just missed out. He can continue to progress. (op 9-2 tchd 13-2)
Boogie Shoes ◆ impressed many when winning over this trip on his reappearance at Salisbury and, although he couldn't defy a 7lb rise, this was not a bad performance. He travelled with enthusiasm, although that may have been to his detriment as he was committed before the first two finishers, who had raced much further back and he wandered around when getting tired. There's more to come. (op 2-1, tchd 5-2 in places)
Tanfeeth travelled well - if anything, he was a bit keen - but he took an age to respond to pressure and gave the impression he was uncomfortable on the track in the closing stages. He could yet do better. (op 6-1 tchd 5-1 and 13-2 in a place)
Malthouse(GER), who was bidding for a hat-trick, couldn't defy a 9lb rise for his latest win at Newmarket eight days earlier, but he was unable to dominate and chased an overly strong pace. This may have come too soon as well and he can be given another chance. (op 9-2)

2712 INVESTEC WOODCOTE STKS (LISTED RACE) 6f
2:10 (2:11) (Class 1) 2-Y-0

£14,192 (£5,380; £2,692; £1,342; £672; £337) **Stalls** High

Form RPR
31 **1** **Fulbright**[18] [2261] 2-9-0 0 .... SilvestreDeSousa 8 91+
(Mark Johnston) *pressed ldr: rdn over 2f out: led over 1f out: drvn and styd on wl to draw clr ins fnl f: in command fnl 100yds: eased towards fin* **3/1**[2]

51 **2** *1 1/4* **Evervescent (IRE)**[16] [2214] 2-9-0 0 .... NeilCallan 1 87
(J S Moore) *str: chsd ldng pair: swtchd rt and rdn 3f out: outpcd by ldng pair 2f out: rallied ins fnl f: styd on and wnt 2nd fnl 50yds: nt gng pce to threaten wnr* **12/1**

1 **3** *1/2* **On The Dark Side (IRE)**[15] [2248] 2-8-9 0 .... PaulMulrennan 7 81
(Kevin Ryan) *lengthy: led: rdn and drew clr w wnr ent fnl 2f: edgd rt and hdd over 1f out: btn ins fnl f: wknd and lost 2nd fnl 50yds* **8/1**

12 **4** *2* **Caspar Netscher**[8] [2476] 2-9-0 0 .... JMurtagh 6 83
(Alan McCabe) *unf: stdd s: hld up in last pair: struggling and rdn over 2f out: hdwy over 1f out: styd on to go 4th ins fnl f: no imp fnl 100yds:* **11/4**[1]

4102 **5** *hd* **Princess Banu**[9] [2429] 2-8-9 0 .... CathyGannon 2 74
(Mick Channon) *sn in tch in midfield: rdn and outpcd over 2f out: styd on again and swtchd rt ins fnl f: nt gng pce to threaten wnr* **16/1**

3151 **6** *1 1/2* **He's So Cool (IRE)**[22] [2056] 2-9-0 0 .... KierenFox 5 75
(Bill Turner) *racd in midfield: rdn ent fnl 3f: sn drvn and outpcd: kpt on again ins fnl f but no threat to ldrs* **13/2**[3]

1 **7** *1/2* **Norse Gold**[17] [2194] 2-9-0 0 .... KierenFallon 4 73
(David Elsworth) *w'like: scope: t.k.h: hld up in tch: rdn and unable qck over 2f out: sn struggling and outpcd: one pce and no threat to ldrs fr over 1f out* **3/1**[2]

3211 **8** *7* **Miss Muga**[9] [2425] 2-8-9 0 .... EddieCreighton 3 47
(Edward Creighton) *s.i.s: a in rr: rdn and struggling ent fnl 3f: wknd over 2f out* **66/1**

69.44 secs (0.04) **Going Correction** +0.075s/f (Good) **8** Ran SP% **116.2**
Speed ratings (Par 101): **102,100,99,97,96 94,94,84**
toteswingers:1&2:£7.70, 2&3:£7.70, 1&3:£4.00 CSF £38.82 TOTE £4.30: £1.50, £3.30, £2.20; EX 39.70 Trifecta £244.40 Pool: £2,220.20 - 6.72 winning units..
Owner Sheikh Hamdan Bin Mohammed Al Maktoum **Bred** R F And S D Knipe **Trained** Middleham Moor, N Yorks
■ Stewards' Enquiry : Paul Mulrennan two-day ban: careless riding (Jun 19-20)

FOCUS
Not always the strongest of Listed races but last year's contest bucked the trend, with subsequent Guineas runner-up Dubawi Gold finishing second and Norfolk/Gimcrack winner Approve finishing fourth and there's reason for believing that this year's race might work out quite well. Few got into it from off the pace and the placed horses set the level.

NOTEBOOK
Fulbright is bred to be quick and put up a taking display on this step up to 6f. He matched strides with On The Dark Side before asserting approaching the final furlong and drawing clear. Eased close home, he was value for a bit further and now looks a genuine Coventry Stakes candidate. He holds Irish Group 1 entries later in the season, but time will tell whether he proves up to competing at that level. (op 11-4 tchd 7-2 and 4-1 in places)
Evervescent(IRE), winner of what looked an ordinary maiden at Haydock last time, tracked the two leaders and picked off the filly to take second in the last moments. This was a step up and will presumably have given connections enough confidence to chance their arm in the Coventry now. (op 14-1 tchd 9-1)
On The Dark Side(IRE) ◆ had only won a Catterick maiden narrowly on her debut but it looked quite significant that Kevin Ryan, who has a good bunch of 2-y-os this year, relied on the filly here. She showed pace to lead and battled on well when challenged, but she got unbalanced on the track in the closing stages and lost second close home. She clearly has plenty of ability and a return to a more conventional course can see her win again. (tchd 15-2)
Caspar Netscher beat the winner on his debut at Beverley, but that rival has clearly progressed significantly since. Done no favours at the start when squeezed up, he was at the tail of the field turning in, but finished strongly, despite not looking entirely happy on the track. He's capable of better than the bare form of this effort suggests. (tchd 10-3 and 7-2 in a place)
Princess Banu, one of the most experienced in the line-up, was hanging in the closing stages but did keep on reasonably well. She isn't very big, though, and might not have much scope for improvement. (op 12-1 tchd 18-1)
He's So Cool(IRE), who's rider couldn't claim his regular 3lb, didn't handle the bend into the straight and failed to make any headway once in line for home. He's better than this and will be more at home returned to a straight track. (op 8-1 tchd 11-2)
Norse Gold was keen in the early stages and failed to run to the level he showed at Kempton on his debut. While this was disappointing, he has the pedigree to improve over further in time. (op 4-1, tchd 5-1 in places)
Miss Muga, who came here on the back of wins in selling and claiming company, never got into it after a slow start. (tchd 40-1)

2713 INVESTEC DIOMED STKS (GROUP 3) 1m 114y
2:40 (2:40) (Class 1) 3-Y-O+

£28,385 (£10,760; £5,385; £2,685; £1,345; £675) **Stalls** Low

Form RPR
1-23 **1** **Fanunalter**[86] [828] 5-9-4 107 .... AdamKirby 1 111+
(Marco Botti) *lw: t.k.h: hld up in tch in last trio: gng wl but nt clr run over 2f out: swtchd rt and clipped rivals heels wl over 1f out: swtchd sharply lft and hdwy jst ins fnl f: qcknd to ld fnl 75yds: pushed out* **16/1**

1121 **2** *1/2* **St Moritz (IRE)**[23] [2031] 5-9-4 107 .... AdrianNicholls 8 110
(David Nicholls) *swtg: led: rdn ent fnl 3f: drvn and edgd rt over 1f out: kpt on v gamely tl hdd fnl 75yds: no ex cl home* **9/2**[3]

211- **3** *1* **Rio De La Plata (USA)**[209] [7373] 6-9-11 120 .... FrankieDettori 6 115
(Saeed Bin Suroor) *t.k.h: hld up wl in tch: hdwy to press ldr wl over 1f out: rdn and ev ch ent fnl f: styd on same pce u.p ins fnl f: btn fnl 75yds* **7/2**[2]

100- **4** *hd* **Nationalism**[217] [7234] 4-9-4 102 .... WilliamBuick 2 107
(John Gosden) *stdd s: t.k.h: hld up in tch in last trio: rdn and effrt on outer ent fnl 2f: no real hdwy tl r.o strly fnl 100yds: nrly snatched 3rd on post* **16/1**

0600 **5** *1* **Mac Love**[106] [605] 10-9-4 102 .... NeilCallan 4 105
(Stef Higgins) *stdd s: t.k.h: hld up in tch in last pair: looking to switch rt ent fnl 3f: gap opened and hdwy over 2f out: drvn to press ldrs ent fnl f: wknd fnl 75yds* **14/1**

30-3 **6** *nk* **Awzaan**[14] [2315] 4-9-4 110 .... RichardHills 3 104
(Mark Johnston) *chsd ldng pair: nt clr run over 2f out tl gap opened and drvn to press ldrs ent fnl f: no ex and btn fnl 100yds* **17/2**

0-43 **7** *1* **Premio Loco (USA)**[21] [2101] 7-9-4 119 .... GeorgeBaker 7 102
(Chris Wall) *stdd after s: hld up in tch in rr: rdn and effrt on outer jst over 2f out: no prog and btn jst ins fnl f* **15/8**[1]

415- **8** *3 1/4* **Vesuve (IRE)**[232] [6885] 5-9-4 110 .... MickaelBarzalona 5 104
(Saeed Bin Suroor) *chsd ldrs: rdn to press ldr wl over 2f out: unable qck whn rival clipped his heels and lost pl wl over 1f out: wkng whn hmpd and lost pl jst ins fnl f: eased after* **8/1**

1m 45.12s (-0.98) **Going Correction** +0.075s/f (Good) **8** Ran SP% **115.3**
Speed ratings (Par 113): **107,106,105,105,104 104,103,100**
toteswingers:1&2:£9.40, 2&3:£2.50, 1&3:£8.20 CSF £86.91 TOTE £25.80: £4.90, £2.10, £1.10; EX 128.20 Trifecta £362.60 Pool: £8,222.34 - 16.78 winning units..
Owner Scuderia Rencati Srl **Bred** Azienda Agricola Francesca **Trained** Newmarket, Suffolk

FOCUS
The first time the Diomed Stakes has been staged on Derby day, instead of on the Oaks card, since 2007. Several of these were inconvenienced by St Moritz setting a steady pace (time best part of three seconds above standard on quick track), and the form is misleading.

NOTEBOOK
Fanunalter doesn't do much in front, so a troubled trip in the straight was no bad thing, but he still impressed with how well he quickened off the steady pace when finally getting a run, especially as he was one of a few who had been keen. There was also plenty to like about how long he travelled on the bridle and he's extremely smart on his day. This was his first start in about three months following a spell in Dubai and it was his first Group-race success. (tchd 12-1 in places)
St Moritz(IRE) was trying Group company for only the second time in his career, but he could still have been expected to win considering how events unfolded, especially as he had the same chance as Fanunalter judged on official figures. This was still another solid effort, though, and he has yet to finish outside the top two in five starts for this trainer. (op 6-1)
Rio De La Plata(USA) was resurgent last year, his five wins in 2010 including two Italian Group 1s, but he had been off since November and had to concede 7lb all round. Another who was a bit keen, this was a satisfactory return, but his best hope of further success at the top level lies abroad. (tchd 10-3 and 4-1)
Nationalism had been gelded after losing his form towards the backend of last season, although he was officially reported to have lost his action (when blinkered for first time) on his latest start. This was a promising return, as he was keen early, and took a long time to pick up before running on strongly. He will have to prove he can build on this, however.
Mac Love, who had been off for 106 days, didn't have the race run to suit and, having been keen, his run flattened out when he was in the clear. (tchd 12-1 and 16-1)
Awzaan continues to operate below his 2-y-o best. He had to wait for a run towards the inside, but didn't pick up when in the clear. (op 8-1 tchd 9-1)
Premio Loco(USA) was third in the Lockinge on his previous start and had upwards of 6lb in hand on official figures, but the steady pace put him at a major disadvantage. He couldn't make any impression when taken extremely wide in the straight. (op 2-1, tchd 9-4 in places)

Vesuve(IRE), returning from a 232-day absence, had quite a rough race. Official explanation: jockey said horse suffered interference in running (tchd 9-1)

2714 INVESTEC ENTREPRENEURIAL DASH" H'CAP — 5f

3:15 (3:15) (Class 2) 3-Y-0+

£46,732 (£13,995; £6,997; £3,502; £1,747; £877) **Stalls** High

Form				RPR
-622	**1**		**Captain Dunne (IRE)**[20] 2138 6-9-10 **105**.......................(p) DavidAllan 9 (Tim Easterby) *broke fast: sn crossed to chse ldr towards stands' rail: led gng wl ent fnl 2f: rdn over 1f out: hrd pressed wl ins fnl f: hld on gamely cl home: all out* **13/2**[3]	111
-440	**2**	*nk*	**Confessional**[14] 2317 4-8-10 **91**................................(e) PaulMulrennan 13 (Tim Easterby) *in tch: nt clr run ent fnl f: rdn and hdwy fnl 150yds: r.o strly to snatch 2nd on post: nt quite rch wnr* **10/1**	96+
20-0	**3**	*shd*	**La Fortunata**[39] 1584 4-7-13 **80**....................................... AndreaAtzeni 10 (Mike Murphy) *led and crossed to r against stands' rail hdd and rdn ent fnl 2f: swtchd lft and rallied u.p jst over 1f out: ev ch fnl 75yds: lost 2nd on post* **16/1**	85
-600	**4**	*shd*	**Sohraab**[21] 2099 7-7-12 **84**.. KieranO'Neill(5) 1 (Hughie Morrison) *lw: in tch: rdn and effrt wl over 1f out: swtchd lft ent fnl f: r.o wl u.p fnl 150yds: nt quite rch wnr* **25/1**	88+
34-0	**5**	*nse*	**Fathom Five (IRE)**[31] 1809 7-8-10 **91**......................... AdrianNicholls 17 (David Nicholls) *hld up in midfield: effrt on stands' rail 2f out: nt clr run and switching lft 1f out: r.o strly fnl 100yds: nt quite rch wnr* **9/1**	95+
0300	**6**	*nse*	**Indian Trail**[14] 2299 11-8-1 **82**..(v) PaulQuinn 16 (David Nicholls) *bhd: stl in rr and bhd a wall of horses ent fnl f: gap opened and r.o strly fnl 100yds: nt quite rch ldrs* **16/1**	86
0-43	**7**	*hd*	**Jamesway (IRE)**[29] 1852 3-8-0 **88**.................................... JimmyQuinn 5 (Richard Fahey) *taken down early: towards rr: effrt over 1f out: swtchd lft and hdwy 1f out: r.o strly: nt quite rch ldrs* **25/1**	88+
0-31	**8**	*3/4*	**Masamah (IRE)**[14] 2317 5-9-9 **104** 4ex.......................... JamieSpencer 8 (Kevin Ryan) *taken down early: stdd after s: sn bhd: rdn and hdwy in centre over 1f out: chsd ldrs ins fnl f: no imp fnl 50yds* **9/2**[1]	104+
0162	**9**	*hd*	**Falasteen (IRE)**[23] 2028 4-8-11 **92**................................ WilliamBuick 12 (David Nicholls) *bhd: hdwy and switching lft over 1f out: kpt on wl ins fnl f: nt rch ldrs* **6/1**[2]	92+
3210	**10**	*3/4*	**Oldjoesaid**[21] 2117 7-8-2 **83**....................................... SilvestreDeSousa 3 (Kevin Ryan) *in tch towards centre: rdn 1/2-way: hdwy to chse ldng trio ent fnl f: styd on same pce ins fnl f* **16/1**	80+
-004	**11**	*shd*	**Bertoliver**[22] 2069 7-8-2 **83**... LukeMorris 4 (Stuart Williams) *broke fast: chsd ldrs and grad crossing towards stands' side: rdn wl over 1f out: wknd ins fnl f* **20/1**	80
110-	**12**	*1/2*	**Perfect Blossom**[289] 5250 4-8-7 **91**.................................. AmyRyan(3) 6 (Kevin Ryan) *in tch: nt clr run and switching lft ent fnl f: rdn and styd on same pce fnl 150yds: nvr able to chal* **10/1**	86+
2030	**13**	*nse*	**Beat The Bell**[14] 2317 6-8-9 **90**................................... GrahamGibbons 7 (David Barron) *swtg: taken down early: in tch in midfield: rdn and unable qck ent fnl 2f: kpt on again ins fnl f: nvr able to chal* **14/1**	85+
6-03	**14**	*2 1/2*	**Arctic Feeling (IRE)**[8] 2456 3-9-0 **102**.......................... JackMitchell 15 (Richard Fahey) *s.i.s: wl bhd: switching lft and effrt wl over 1f out: kpt on fnl f: nvr trbld ldrs* **12/1**	85
0066	**15**	*nse*	**Masta Plasta (IRE)**[21] 2117 8-9-1 **96**............................ AndrewMullen 2 (David Nicholls) *chsd ldrs: rdn ent fnl 2f: wkng whn bmpd jst ins fnl f* **25/1**	81
3-20	**16**	*7*	**Strike Up The Band**[10] 2397 8-8-3 **84**......................(b1) CathyGannon 11 (David Nicholls) *in tch tl rdn and wknd over 1f out: bhd and eased ins fnl f* **16/1**	55

54.30 secs (-1.40) **Going Correction** -0.05s/f (Good)
WFA 3 from 4yo+ 7lb **16** Ran SP% **128.2**
Speed ratings (Par 109): **109,108,108,108,108 108,107,106,106,105 104,104,103,99,99 88**
toteswingers:1&2:£14.90, 2&3:£37.60, 1&3:£18.50 CSF £70.20 CT £1010.41 TOTE £7.60: £2.20, £2.80, £4.20, £5.10; EX 88.00 Trifecta £1913.30 Pool: £8,741.95 - 3.38 winning units..
Owner Middleham Park Racing XV & Partners **Bred** Ballybrennan Stud Ltd **Trained** Great Habton, N Yorks

FOCUS

There's usually a scramble for the rail in this race and it was no different this year. There was a blanket finish and some hard-luck stories, with several looking better than the bare form.

NOTEBOOK

Captain Dunne(IRE) just held on at the line. With cheekpieces back on he showed good early speed to cross over from stall nine and dispute the lead one off the rail and, once taking over a furlong out, edged over and had the rail to help from then on. Although he was being cut down close home he had enough in hand to hold on, and deserved this after being denied by the narrowest of margins in a Group 3 in France last time. It's easy to see him picking up a Listed/Group 3 race later this season on a speed-favouring track. (tchd 6-1 and 7-1 in a place)
Confessional, who had a high draw, was one of those who didn't get the clearest of runs and, having been beaten only narrowly, could be considered slightly unlucky. He's run three good races in defeat this year and deserves a change of fortune. (op 12-1)
La Fortunata was fast away and grabbed the stands' side rail. She wasn't able to hold that valued position 2f out, giving it up to the winner, but ran on again after being switched. Progressive on turf last summer, she left a poor reappearance effort on the AW well behind here and is clearly not handicapped out of things just yet.
Sohraab ◆, back over 5f, had a tough task on from stall one and was among those who raced furthest away from the favoured stands' rail. He finished really well to take fourth, is on a good mark at the moment and should be capable of winning one of these while the ground remains fast.
Fathom Five(IRE), having his second start for Nicholls, had the best draw and got a nice position early tracking the leader on the rail. He kept on when switched from behind the winner, but didn't quicken sufficiently to make the places. This was still a welcome return to form. (op 15-2)
Indian Trail is a hostage to fortune as he's the type who is held up and needs the gaps to come. From a good draw he was held up on the rail, but it was only well inside the last that a path opened up for him and he finished really well to be nearest at the line. He is now an 11-y-o but he retains plenty of ability and can win again when things fall right. (op 14-1)
Jamesway(IRE) ◆ was drawn low but came over towards the stands' side and didn't get much luck in running. One of only two 3-y-os in the field, he finished really well and shaped like a gelding capable of winning off his current mark. He's one to note for a similar affair. (tchd 28-1 in places)
Masamah(IRE) stumbled crossing the first path and struggled with the camber, but he finished his race off well widest of all up the centre of the track and remains in good form. However, he's already due to go up another 2lb. (op 6-1)
Falasteen(IRE) had a fair draw but he wasn't best away and had to be held up. Switched to challenge wide, things didn't pan out well for him and it'll be tougher in future off a 4lb higher mark. (tchd 13-2 in a place)
Oldjoesaid, drawn low, showed plenty of pace towards the centre but couldn't sustain his challenge inside the last. He ran a better race than his finishing position would suggest. (op 20-1 tchd 22-1)
Bertoliver, last year's winner from stall 15, wasn't so lucky with the draw this time around and used up a lot of energy getting a good early position.
Perfect Blossom has won fresh before so lack of a recent outing wasn't a huge concern. She didn't get an entirely clear run but showed enough to suggest he can be competitive off this mark. (op 11-1 tchd 9-1 and 12-1 in places)
Strike Up The Band Official explanation: jockey said gelding lost its action

2715 INVESTEC DERBY (GROUP 1) — 1m 4f 10y

4:00 (4:00) (Class 1) 3-Y-O

£709,625 (£269,000; £134,625; £67,125; £33,625; £16,875) **Stalls** Centre

Form				RPR
31	**1**		**Pour Moi (IRE)**[28] 1923 3-9-0 113.............................. MickaelBarzalona 7 (A Fabre, France) *w'like: str: stdd after s: hld up bhd: last st: sn swtchd rt and hdwy: 6th and running on whn hung lft over 1f out: swtchd rt: sustained run ins fnl f to ld nr fin: jockey bolt uprt and celebrating last strides* **4/1**[2]	123+
3-1	**2**	*hd*	**Treasure Beach**[30] 1822 3-9-0 107................................. CO'Donoghue 12 (A P O'Brien, Ire) *lw: chsd ldrs: wnt 2nd ent fnl 4f: 6 l 2nd st: drvn and clsd to press ldr 2f out: ev ch wl over 1f out: led ent fnl f: kpt on u.p and forged ahd ins fnl f: hdd cl home* **25/1**	122
21-1	**3**	*3/4*	**Carlton House (USA)**[23] 2030 3-9-0 116......................... RyanMoore 13 (Sir Michael Stoute) *b: hld up towards rr: sltly hmpd and swtchd rt 5f out: 8th st: rdn to chse ldng pair over 2f out: clsd and pressed ldrs ent fnl f: wnt 2nd ins fnl f: no ex and one pce fnl 100yds* **5/2**[1]	121+
2	**4**	*3/4*	**Memphis Tennessee (IRE)**[27] 1927 3-9-0 109.................. JPO'Brien 6 (A P O'Brien, Ire) *str: lw: led: clr after 2f: 6 l clr st: rdn over 2f out: jnd and drvn wl over 1f out: hdd ent fnl f: no ex and lost 2 pls fnl 150yds* **20/1**	119
4-13	**5**	*3/4*	**Native Khan (FR)**[35] 1686 3-9-0 116....................................... JMurtagh 3 (Ed Dunlop) *hld up in midfield: hdwy and 4th st: drvn and clsd on ldrs 2f out: chsng ldrs 1f out: n.m.r and styd on same pce fnl 100yds* **8/1**	118
1-31	**6**	*2*	**Recital (FR)**[27] 1927 3-9-0 115.. PJSmullen 4 (A P O'Brien, Ire) *str: lw: hld up in rr: hdwy on inner and 7th st: clsd and chsng ldrs whn hung lft u.p over 1f out: one pce and no imp ins fnl f* **5/1**[3]	115
3	**7**	*nk*	**Vadamar (FR)**[28] 1923 3-9-0 108................. Christophe-PatriceLemaire 9 (A De Royer-Dupre, France) *medium sized: hld up in midfield: 6th and effrt st: rdn and no prog 2f out: 7th and looked wl hld ent fnl f: swtchd rt and styd on again ins fnl f: nt gng pce to rch ldrs* **14/1**	114
6-51	**8**	*4*	**Masked Marvel**[17] 2191 3-9-0 109.................................... WilliamBuick 5 (John Gosden) *lw: hld up in midfield: 5th and effrt st: sn rdn: unable qck and btn ent fnl 2f: wknd over 1f out* **25/1**	108
20-3	**9**	*19*	**Pisco Sour (USA)**[23] 2030 3-9-0 107............................. JimmyFortune 1 (Hughie Morrison) *chsd ldrs: 3rd st: sn u.p and struggling: wknd 2f out: wl btn over 1f out: eased ins fnl f* **50/1**	78
2-2	**10**	*3*	**Seville (GER)**[23] 2030 3-9-0 117........................... ChristopheSoumillon 2 (A P O'Brien, Ire) *stdd s: hld up towards rr: 9th st: drvn and struggling whn racd awkardly wl over 2f out: sn btn: wl bhd and eased fr over 1f out: t.o* **13/2**	73
5-11	**11**	*7*	**Ocean War**[35] 1689 3-9-0 106... FrankieDettori 10 (Mahmood Al Zarooni) *hld up in midfield: nt clr run and swtchd rnd wkng rival wl over 3f out: 10th st: sn rdn and no hdwy: wl btn fnl 2f: eased fnl f: t.o* **12/1**	62+
60-5	**12**	*3 1/4*	**Castlemorris King**[33] 1769 3-9-0 52.........................(v1) MarkCoumbe 11 (Michael Attwater) *swtg: chsd ldrs: losing pl qckly 5f out: 12th and dropping out st: sn lost tch: t.o fnl 2f: eased ins fnl f* **150/1**	56
1-6	**13**	*55*	**Marhaba Malyoon (IRE)**[28] 1895 3-9-0 78.................. JamieSpencer 8 (David Simcock) *chsd ldr tl ent fnl 4f: sn losing pl and dropping out rapidly: 11th st: sn lost tch: t.o and eased fnl 2f* **100/1**	—

2m 34.54s (-4.36) **Going Correction** +0.075s/f (Good) **13** Ran SP% **120.1**
Speed ratings (Par 113): **117,116,116,115,115 114,113,111,98,96 91,89,53**
toteswingers:1&2:£20.40, 2&3:£18.00, 1&3:£3.10 CSF £110.16 CT £303.63 TOTE £5.30: £1.90, £7.80, £1.40; EX 151.20 Trifecta £708.00 Pool: £43,757.61 - 45.73 winning units..

Owner Mrs John Magnier, M Tabor & D Smith **Bred** Lynch Bages Ltd **Trained** Chantilly, France

■ Stewards' Enquiry : Mickael Barzalona one-day ban: used whip with excessive frequency without giving colt time to respond (Jun 19)

FOCUS

There was no Frankel, the long-term ante-post favourite instead heading to the St James's Palace Stakes, and only one previous Group 1 winner lined up, namely Recital, who took last year's Criterium de Saint-Cloud. Less than three lengths covered the first five finishers, so the bare form looks limited by Derby standards, but there was a strong impression that the winner and third-placed finisher can both rate a good deal higher. The time was 0.76 seconds under standard and 2.31 seconds quicker than the following Class 2 handicap for older horses, but the visual impression was that the pace only gradually increased, aiding both the runner-up and fourth-placed finisher, and consequently both Pour Moi and Carlton House did well to stay on from so far behind. With the proximity of the first five the form is not rated too positively.

NOTEBOOK

Pour Moi(IRE) not only provided Andre Fabre with his first victory in the Derby, but was also a first French-trained winner since Empery in 1976. There was also a first success in the race for 19-year-old Mickael Barzalona, who has a touch of brilliance about him. This was only the jockey's fourth ride at Epsom. The winner got warm beforehand, but he's done that before and it seems to be in his nature. He had been too keen when beaten on his return, but he responded extremely well to hold-up tactics next time, showing exceptional acceleration to come from last to first in the Group 2 Prix Greffulhe and, despite being faced with a much sterner test this time, repeated the trick. He had been taken to Epsom's Breakfast With The Stars event for a workout and he evidently handled the track well. Much has understandably been made of the Carlton House's wide trip into the straight, but Pour Moi followed almost the exact same path. The key difference was that he made his bid a fraction later. When first asked for his effort, the winner couldn't quite match the instant acceleration shown by Sir Michael Stoute's runner but, crucially, he sustained his challenge for longer, despite having hung left halfway up the straight. Incredibly, despite the margin of victory being just a head, Barzalona stood bolt upright in the irons to showboat a couple of yards or so before the line. It's unlikely he mistook the winning post as he also celebrated victory prematurely when taking the UAE Derby aboard Khawlah by an even narrower margin (just a nose on that occasion) in March, and he obviously trusted that his mount's forward momentum meant success was assured, but clearly it wasn't advisable. Andre Fabre said Pour Moi will now be given a break before being trained for the Arc, with the Prix Niel his likely preparation race. The general 5-1 is difficult to argue with, but this colt will surely have to become at least slightly more tactically versatile if he's to maximise his potential. (op 5-1, tchd 6-1 in a place and 11-2 in place)

Treasure Beach, the Chester Vase winner, was ideally placed considering how the race unfolded and just failed. He's another who looks a bit flattered, but evidently he's capable of high-class form. (tchd 28-1 and 33-1 in a place)

Carlton House(USA) ◆ dominated the headlines in the days before, not only because he was bidding to provide the Queen with her first Derby winner, but he was ante-post favourite after his success in the Dante and had suffered a late injury scare. Indeed, his participation was in doubt for much of the week after he knocked a near-fore joint in a routine canter on the Monday. Although allowed his chance, he had small front bandages fitted and didn't impress with his pre-race demeanour, jig-jogging at the start, sweating up, notably on his neck, and then proving reluctant to enter the stalls. He also took a while to load on his previous start. Not much went right for him in the race itself but he ran a blinder considering he endured a desperate trip. He was a bit further back than ideal (albeit the winner was even further behind) having started slowest of all, and met trouble on the downhill run into the straight. First of all he had to switch around the backtracking Castlemorris King, whose participation made no sense considering he was rated just 52, and then he was carried wide on the final part of the bend after Marhaba Malyoon (something presumably amiss) hung right, forcing Ocean War to switch towards the favourite's path. Carlton House was still able to quicken exceptionally to move into a challenging position, taking a good few lengths out of Pour Moi and briefing looking the winner, but it was a tough ask to sustain his challenge having been committed so early after covering extra ground. In the final furlong he got noticeably tired, changing his legs on more than one occasion and he also lost a hind shoe. Even in defeat, this was the performance of a high-class colt and it will be a surprise if he doesn't win at the top level. It's tempting to say 1m2f will be his best trip, but there's a lot of stamina on his female line and he will probably stay better in time. (op 9-4 tchd 2-1 and 3-1 in a place and 7-4 in places)

Memphis Tennessee(IRE) steadily opened up a clear lead without overexerting himself, in much the same fashion to the same trainer's At First Sight when that colt was runner-up to Workforce 12 months ago. Although Joseph O'Brien's mount was pegged back in good time, he had enough left to keep on for a respectable fourth-place finish. This was a step up on the form he showed when runner-up to Recital in the Derrinstown on his reappearance, but while improvement was expected, he's probably flattered. (op 22-1 tchd 25-1 and 33-1 in a place)

Native Khan(FR) was the only representative of the 2000 Guineas form, having finished third. Despite getting warm he ran okay, appearing to just about get the trip, and Johnny Murtagh apparently thinks there's more to come, so the Irish Derby will be considered. (op 9-1)

Recital(FR), who had looked an awkward ride when successful in the Derrinstown, was without the services of Kieren Fallon, who was aboard at Leopardstown, after the owner of Native Khan, who said the rider had agreed to partner Ed Dunlop's runner, took out an injunction. Fallon's absence was a negative, and again the colt hung badly left on to the rail and consequently couldn't showcase his true capabilities. (op 11-2, tchd 6-1 in places)

Vadamar(FR) apparently had excuses when behind Pour Moi last time, but he looked to be exposed as not good enough this time. He still ran respectably. (op 16-1)

Masked Marvel is reportedly considered more of a St Leger horse by connections. (tchd 33-1 in a place)

Pisco Sour(USA) was much too keen. (op 66-1)

Seville(GER) was unbalanced and consequently the Dante runner-up ran no sort of race. (op 11-2, tchd 7-1 in places)

Ocean War did not handle the track. (op 14-1)

2716 INVESTEC SUREFOOTED H'CAP — 1m 4f 10y

4:50 (4:51) (Class 2) (0-100,97) 4-Y-0+

£12,462 (£3,732; £1,866; £934; £466; £234) **Stalls** Centre

Form — RPR

2164 **1** **Fox Hunt (IRE)**[22] 2044 4-9-5 **95**..........................(v[1]) SilvestreDeSousa 3 105
(Mark Johnston) *lw: chsd ldr: rdn and clr w ldr 3f out: led ent fnl f: kpt on wl u.p and a holding on ins fnl f* **15/2**

00-6 **2** *3/4* **Berling (IRE)**[28] 1887 4-8-12 **88**.. EddieAhern 7 97
(John Dunlop) *hld up towards rr: gd hdwy on inner 3f out: chsd ldrs and swtchd rt over 1f out: chsd wnr wl ins fnl f: kpt on* **7/1[3]**

46-4 **3** *3/4* **Zuider Zee (GER)**[28] 1887 4-9-1 **91**................................. WilliamBuick 6 98
(John Gosden) *hld up in midfield: effrt: whn edgd lft and hmpd 3f out: sn swtchd rt and hdwy ent fnl 2f: chsng ldrs and stl edging lft 1f out: styd on wl u.p to snatch 3rd last strides* **8/1**

15-3 **4** *hd* **Life And Soul (IRE)**[34] 1717 4-9-2 **92**................................ NeilCallan 15 99
(Amanda Perrett) *lw: t.k.h: hld up in tch in midfield: hdwy to chse ldrs over 3f out: rdn and chse ldr over 1f out: kpt on but no imp and lost 2 pls wl ins fnl f* **6/1[2]**

4-32 **5** *1* **Aurorian (IRE)**[34] 1729 5-8-11 **87**............................... RichardHughes 10 92
(Richard Hannon) *hld up in midfield: rdn and hdwy over 2f out: chsng ldrs and drvn ent fnl f: no ex and styd on same pce fnl 100yds* **20/1**

4306 **6** *1 1/4* **Ramona Chase**[1] 2681 6-8-3 **79**..................................(t) AndreaAtzeni 14 82
(Michael Attwater) *stdd s: t.k.h: hld up towards rr: hdwy into midfield 6f out: swtchd rt and effrt 3f out: kpt on and chsng ldrs 1f out: no ex and btn whn n.m.r ins fnl f* **40/1**

14-0 **7** *2 3/4* **Coin Of The Realm (IRE)**[34] 1717 6-9-1 **91**..................... RyanMoore 9 90
(Gary Moore) *stdd s: hld up in last quartet: rdn and effrt over 2f out: hdwy and swtchd rt over 1f out: kpt on ins fnl f: nvr threatened ldrs* **6/1[2]**

020/ **8** *4 1/2* **Double Handful (GER)**[83] 6891 5-8-2 **78** oh3............. CathyGannon 11 70
(Venetia Williams) *chsd ldrs: rdn and unable qck ent fnl 3f: outpcd and drvn ent fnl 2f: n.d fr over 1f out* **66/1**

040- **9** *4 1/2* **Blizzard Blues (USA)**[251] 6388 5-9-7 **97**..................(b) JamieSpencer 13 82
(Jamie Osborne) *stdd s: hld up in last quartet: sme hdwy but hanging lft ent fnl 2f: nvr trbld ldrs* **50/1**

00-1 **10** *1 3/4* **Plaisterer**[16] 2220 6-9-3 **93**.. JackMitchell 8 75
(Chris Wall) *led: rdn and clr w wnr 3f out: hdd over 2f: wknd over 1f out: fdd ins fnl f* **14/1**

1-41 **11** *5* **Bourne**[28] 1892 5-8-13 **89**.. KierenFallon 1 63
(Luca Cumani) *in tch: rdn over 3f out: unable qck and switching rt wl over 2f out: no prog and wl hld fnl 2f* **3/1[1]**

-343 **12** *1 3/4* **The Galloping Shoe**[24] 2006 6-8-9 **85**............................ ChrisCatlin 4 56
(Ian Semple) *in tch: rdn and struggling ent fnl 3f: wknd over 2f out* **25/1**

0/0- **13** *nk* **Press The Button (GER)**[420] 1220 8-9-0 **90**................ StephenCraine 2 61
(Jim Boyle) *v slowly: in tch in rr after 1f: rdn and no hdwy 3f out: n.d fnl 2f* **50/1**

20-0 **14** *2 1/4* **Chilly Filly (IRE)**[22] 2071 5-8-13 **89**.............................. PaulMulrennan 5 56
(James Given) *stdd s: a in rr: n.d* **20/1**

0-01 **15** *3* **Yorgunnabelucky (USA)**[21] 2107 5-9-6 **96**.............(p) FrankieDettori 12 58
(Mark Johnston) *chsd ldrs: rdn and struggling over 3f out: wknd over 2f out: wl bhd and eased ins fnl f* **14/1**

2m 36.85s (-2.05) **Going Correction** +0.075s/f (Good) **15** Ran SP% **123.5**
Speed ratings (Par 109): **109,108,108,107,107 106,104,101,98,97 94,92,92,91,89**
toteswingers:1&2:£10.40, 2&3:£10.90, 1&3:£11.30 CSF £56.39 CT £444.05 TOTE £8.70: £2.70, £2.50, £3.20; EX 80.10 Trifecta £851.40 Pool: £4,4422.17 - 3.84 winning units..

Owner Sheikh Hamdan Bin Mohammed Al Maktoum **Bred** Ballylinch Stud **Trained** Middleham Moor, N Yorks

FOCUS

Several of these came into the race looking to have a few pounds in hand of the handicapper and it's a race that is likely to throw up a few winners. The early gallop didn't look strong and it proved tough for those held up to close down the leader. The form looks solid enough with the third and fourth close to their marks.

NOTEBOOK

Fox Hunt(IRE) was prominent throughout and held off the pack to win a shade cosily. Visored for the first time, he raced in second early before taking over approaching the 2f pole and then stayed on strongly to the line against the inside rail. A progressive sort who holds a Hardwicke entry, the more sensible Ascot target would appear to be the Duke of Edinburgh Handicap, but it's worth remembering that he had the run of things here and whether the headgear has such a positive effect second time is debatable. (op 11-1 tchd 12-1)

Berling(IRE) isn't straightforward but he has the raw ability to win off this mark. He didn't get a chance to throw anything away this time as he was sensibly kept next to the rail and his rider only used his whip in the right hand. While he could never get to the winner, keeping him among horses until the last minute does seem the right thing to do. Fifth in the King George V last year, he's entitled to run well in the Duke of Edinburgh Handicap this time around. (op 8-1 tchd 10-1)

Zuider Zee(GER) ◆, fortunate to finish two places in front of Berling at Ascot last time, could have done with a stronger pace as he was staying on stoutly at the finish. He holds an entry in the Northumberland Plate and it'll be interesting to see if his connections decide to go the staying route with him as there's potential for improvement granted a stiffer test of stamina.

Life And Soul(IRE) was another for whom a stronger gallop would have been of help, as he was keen early on. A consistent sort, he ran well at Ascot on a couple of occasions last year and will return there for the Duke of Edinburgh Handicap. (tchd 11-2 and 8-1 in a place)

Aurorian(IRE) had to work to get a clear run in the straight, but kept on quite well once in the open. He gets 2m, so the lack of pace early on was no help but, in any case, the handicapper looks to have his number.

Ramona Chase, making a quick reappearance following his sixth-place finish here the previous day over 1m2f, didn't quite get home. He has a poor strike-rate but does tend to run well at this track. (op 50-1)

Coin Of The Realm(IRE), winner of this race in 2009, was down to a mark 9lb lower than when fourth in this race last year, so had been given a real chance by the handicapper. He was given a lot to do considering how the race unfolded and, while never making up his ground quick enough in the closing stages, was given an easy time once all chance had gone and gave the impression that the ability to win off this mark remains. (op 11-2)

Bourne was being niggled along from some way out and proved disappointing. He'd looked ahead of the handicapper at Haydock last time and deserves another chance back on a more conventional track. (tchd 11-4 and 10-3 in places)

2717 INVESTEC SPECIALIST BANK H'CAP — 6f

5:25 (5:27) (Class 2) (0-100,99) 4-Y-0+

£12,462 (£3,732; £1,866; £934; £466; £234) **Stalls** High

Form — RPR

-031 **1** **Swiss Cross**[18] 2169 4-9-0 **92**...(t) NeilCallan 4 101
(Gerard Butler) *lw: chsd ldr: led gng wl ent fnl 3f: clr and rdn over 1f out: drvn and tiring ins fnl f: a holding on but all out nr fin* **9/2[1]**

0-00 **2** *1/2* **Tajneed (IRE)**[22] 2075 8-9-7 **99**....................................... CathyGannon 7 106
(David Nicholls) *hld up in rr: pushed along 1/2-way: hdwy u.p ent fnl f: r.o strly to snatch 2nd on post* **20/1**

60-0 **3** *nse* **Fireback**[34] 1720 4-8-10 **88**... JimmyFortune 9 95
(Andrew Balding) *chsd ldrs: rdn and outpcd ent fnl 3f: rallied u.p over 1f out: chsd wnr 1f out: kpt on fnl 100yds: lost 2nd on post* **11/2[2]**

3055 **4** *1 1/4* **Lui Rei (ITY)**[14] 2288 5-9-2 **99**...................................... KieranO'Neill[(5)] 16 102
(Robert Cowell) *lw: sn outpcd in rr: stl 14th and switching rt jst over 1f out: str run ins fnl f: wnt 4th last strides: nt rch ldrs* **9/1**

0-10 **5** *hd* **Joseph Henry**[29] 1849 9-9-0 **92**...................................... KierenFallon 13 94
(David Nicholls) *in tch: effrt and hanging bdly lft 2f out: kpt hanging but kpt on to chse ldrs ins fnl f: n.m.r and styd on same pce fnl 100yds* **12/1**

4162 **6** *nk* **Cape Vale (IRE)**[9] 2434 6-8-11 **89**................................... AdrianNicholls 6 90
(David Nicholls) *led: hdd and rdn ent fnl 3f: nt pce of wnr ent fnl 2f: lost 2nd 1f out: wknd ins fnl f* **10/1**

0-03 **7** *3/4* **Secret Witness**[21] 2099 5-9-1 **93**......................................(b) LukeMorris 1 92
(Ronald Harris) *in tch on inner: rdn and outpcd by ldrs 3f out: hrd drvn and rallied over 1f out: styd on same pce ins fnl f* **8/1**

-451 **8** *3/4* **Piazza San Pietro**[26] 1937 5-8-11 **89**.............................. JamesDoyle 12 85
(Andrew Haynes) *racd in midfield: rdn and unable qck ent fnl 3f: hdwy over 1f out: kpt on same pce and no imp ins fnl f* **7/1[3]**

0100 **9** *1/2* **Flipando (IRE)**[14] 2284 10-9-5 **97**............................. GrahamGibbons 10 92
(David Barron) *swtg: in tch: rdn and unable qck 3f out: rallied and hdwy u.p over 1f out: carried lft 1f out: styd on same pce and no imp ins fnl f* **9/1**

-104 **10** *1/2* **Baby Strange**[8] 2456 7-9-0 **92**.. StephenCraine 3 91+
(Derek Shaw) *b: stdd s: hld up towards rr: hdwy towards inner wl over 1f out: nt clr run and bdly hmpd 1f out: nt rcvr: swtchd rt and styd on same pce ins fnl f* **20/1**

0000 **11** *1/2* **Green Park (IRE)**[21] 2117 8-8-3 **86**..............................(b) NeilFarley[(5)] 2 78
(Declan Carroll) *stmbld s and s.i.s: sn rdn along and hdwy to r in midfield: rdn and unable qck 3f out: drvn and wknd over 1f out* **40/1**

0-00 **12** *2 1/2* **Olynard (IRE)**[6] 2525 5-8-8 **86**...................................... FergusSweeney 14 70
(Dr Richard Newland) *a towards rr: rdn and effrt over 2f out: nvr trbld ldrs* **20/1**

-052 **13** *1/2* **Esprit De Midas**[34] 1715 5-8-9 **87**.................................... PaulQuinn 11 69
(David Nicholls) *s.i.s: sn outpcd in rr: hmpd 4f out: nvr trbld ldrs* **25/1**

0-04 **14** *1/2* **Sonny Red (IRE)**[9] 2434 7-8-10 **88**................................ AndrewMullen 8 68
(David Nicholls) *swtg: chsd ldrs: drvn and unable qck 3f out: wknd over 1f out* **28/1**

0-26 **15** *3/4* **Love Delta (USA)**[7] 2489 4-9-6 **98**......................... SilvestreDeSousa 15 76
(Mark Johnston) *racd in midfield on outer: rdn and effrt 3f out: no hdwy and wl btn fnl 2f* **10/1**

68.41 secs (-0.99) **Going Correction** +0.075s/f (Good) **15** Ran SP% **127.1**
Speed ratings (Par 109): **109,108,108,106,106 105,104,103,103,102 101,98,97,97,96**toteswingers:1&2:£20.00, 2&3:£29.30, 1&3:£5.70 CSF £104.43 CT £525.94 TOTE £4.80: £2.10, £6.40, £2.40; EX 130.30 Trifecta £2407.30 Part won. Pool £3,253.22 - 0.61 winning units. Part won. Pool £3,253.22 - 0.61 winning units. .

Owner A D Spence **Bred** Lordship Stud **Trained** Newmarket, Suffolk

■ Stewards' Enquiry : Kieran O'Neill two-day ban: careless riding (Jun 23-24)

FOCUS

This looked quite competitive on paper but in the race itself it was dominated throughout by the winner. The form is rated through the runner-up backed up by the third.

NOTEBOOK

Swiss Cross ◆ never looked like being caught on a day when speed was lasting out well. He's returned to form since being re-fitted with a tongue-tie (form figures wearing it read 3217311), running well from a poor draw at Chester and then winning at Brighton last time. He improved again to take this from the front. He's now living up to his pedigree and he could well have a say in the outcome of the Wokingham, his next target, as he doesn't need to be ridden as prominently as he was here. He stayed further in his youth so should appreciate a strongly run 6f. (op 5-1)

Tajneed(IRE) showed a bit more at York last time and improved again to finish strongly from off the pace and take second. Given his record at Ripon the Great St Wilfrid must again be his main target this season, although he'll no doubt come into consideration for the Wokingham following this effort. (tchd 22-1)

Fireback, all the better for his reappearance at Newmarket, wasn't badly placed in the chasing pack but, although he made some inroads into the winner's advantage close home, he could never quite get there. A stiffer 6f should suit him. (tchd 6-1)
Lui Rei(ITY) ◆, dropped in from his wide draw, finished as well as anything to take fourth. He has back-class, having won the Group 2 Prix Robert Papin at two, and it's not hard to see him winning a handicap off this sort of mark. (op 14-1)
Joseph Henry is a prominent racer but had a double-figure draw to overcome and he ended up racing wide around the bend into the straight. He then hung left in the straight, which didn't help his chances at all. (tchd 11-1)
Cape Vale(IRE) disputed the early lead with the winner but couldn't stay with him from two and a half furlongs. He's the type that needs to dominate to be seen at his best and he didn't appreciate being taken on. (tchd 9-1)
Secret Witness didn't look particularly comfortable on the track. (tchd 10-1 in a place)
Piazza San Pietro struggled to make up ground from off the pace. (tchd 13-2)
Flipando(IRE) also failed to get into it from off the pace. (op 8-1 tchd 10-1)
Baby Strange was denied a clear run and had to be snatched up approaching the final furlong, which prevented him from mounting any meaningful challenge. (op 22-1 tchd 16-1)
Green Park(IRE) is out of form and struggling to take advantage of a declining mark. (tchd 33-1)
T/Jkpt: Not won. T/Plt: £304.50 to a £1 stake. Pool of £294,270.22 - 705.37 winning tickets. T/Qpdt: £60.50 to a £1 stake. Pool of £14,454.16 - 176.70 winning tickets. SP

2637 LINGFIELD (L-H)
Saturday, June 4

OFFICIAL GOING: Turf course - firm (9.4); all-weather - standard
Wind: Light across Weather: Fine

2718 DEBBIE'S BIRTHDAY CELEBRATION/BRITISH STALLION STUDS E B F MAIDEN FILLIES' STKS (TURF) 6f
6:15 (6:16) (Class 5) 2-Y-O **£3,173** (£944; £471; £235) **Stalls** High

Form | | | | RPR
6 **1** **Huma Bird**[16] 2227 2-9-0 0 WilliamBuick 10 80
(Mahmood Al Zarooni) *mde all: rdn and wandered over 1f out: drvn out* **9/4**[2]
22 **2** 1 3/4 **Nayarra (IRE)**[16] 2227 2-9-0 0 (v[1]) SamHitchcott 6 75
(Mick Channon) *chsd wnr: rdn over 2f out: edgd rt over 1f out: styd on same pce* **2/1**[1]
4 **3** 1/2 **Sunrise Dance**[15] 2254 2-8-11 0 MatthewDavies[(3)] 9 74
(Alan Jarvis) *chsd ldrs: rdn over 2f out: styd on same pce fr over 1f out* **7/1**
4 5 **Mention (IRE)** 2-9-0 0 ShaneKelly 5 59+
(Brian Meehan) *prom: rdn over 2f out: sn outpcd* **12/1**
5 nk **Amis Reunis** 2-9-0 0 RichardHughes 2 58+
(Richard Hannon) *sn pushed along in rr: hdwy over 3f out: wknd over 1f out* **7/2**[3]
6 6 **Iced Opal** 2-9-0 0 LiamKeniry 4 40+
(Michael Blanshard) *s.s: outpcd: swtchd lft over 3f out: nvr nrr* **66/1**
5 **7** 3 3/4 **Tangtastic (IRE)**[11] 2380 2-9-0 0 EddieCreighton 3 28
(Edward Creighton) *prom: rdn over 3f out: sn wknd* **66/1**
8 2 **Fire And Sparks** 2-9-0 0 NickyMackay 1 22
(David Simcock) *prom: lost pl 5f out: hdwy over 2f out: wknd over 1f out* **25/1**
9 2 1/2 **Echo Of Dubai (IRE)** 2-9-0 0 ChrisCatlin 8 15
(Clive Brittain) *sn outpcd* **25/1**

1m 10.16s (-1.04) **Going Correction** -0.325s/f (Firm) **9** Ran SP% **117.2**
Speed ratings (Par 90): **93,90,90,83,82 74,69,67,63**
toteswingers: 1&2 £1.70, 1&3 £3.10, 2&3 £2.80 CSF £7.09 TOTE £3.00: £1.10, £2.50, £1.50; EX 8.70.
Owner Godolphin **Bred** Darley **Trained** Newmarket, Suffolk

FOCUS
Fast ground, so business as usual with regards to the stands' rail being favoured. The runner-up is rated to the balance of his two previous starts.

NOTEBOOK
Huma Bird hung all over the course at Sandown on debut but proved a different proposition this time, bouncing out, bagging the rail and setting a good tempo. She kept on well to see off her nearest pursuers in pretty convincing style and the penny has clearly dropped with her. She holds an entry in the sales race at Doncaster this autumn. (op 4-1)
Nayarra(IRE), who had run over the minimum trip in her first two outings, found one too good for the third time, but she saw the trip out well enough having chased the pace and is clearly capable of winning a maiden. (op 6-4 tchd 11-8)
Sunrise Dance stepped up on her Haydock debut and shaped like a filly with more to offer. (op 15-2 tchd 13-2)
Mention(IRE) can be expected to step up on this effort next time. (op 14-1)
Amis Reunis had to be dropped in from her wide draw and couldn't land a blow. She wasn't knocked about and is another likely to fare much better next time. (op 3-1 tchd 4-1)

2719 GODFREYS - A GREAT DEAL MORE THAN MOWERS H'CAP (TURF) 7f
6:45 (6:45) (Class 5) (0-75,75) 4-Y-O+ **£2,914** (£867; £433; £216) **Stalls** High

Form | | | | RPR
0-00 **1** **Kakapuka**[25] 1968 4-9-4 72 RichardHughes 8 81
(Anabel K Murphy) *chsd ldrs: rdn to ld ins fnl f: r.o: eased nr fin* **22/1**
5004 **2** 1/2 **Kipchak (IRE)**[11] 2382 6-7-13 60 (b[1]) SophieSilvester[(7)] 11 68
(Conor Dore) *led: rdn and hdd ins fnl f: styd on same pce* **4/1**[2]
0-13 **3** hd **Rondeau (GR)**[45] 1488 6-9-7 75 GeorgeBaker 6 82+
(Patrick Chamings) *hld up: swtchd lft and hdwy over 1f out: sn rdn: r.o* **3/1**[1]
0-05 **4** 1 **Aleqa**[25] 1990 4-9-3 71 TedDurcan 5 75
(Chris Wall) *sn pushed along in rr: swtchd lft and hdwy over 2f out: rdn over 1f out: styd on same pce ins fnl f* **7/1**
0-00 **5** 2 **Ancient Greece**[19] 2150 4-9-1 72 (t) MatthewDavies[(3)] 9 71
(George Baker) *mid-div: rdn 1/2-way: r.o ins fnl f: nt rch ldrs* **10/1**
005- **6** 1 1/2 **My Learned Friend (IRE)**[270] 5838 7-9-3 74 SimonPearce[(3)] 3 69+
(Andrew Balding) *prom: rdn over 1f out: edgd rt and no ex ins fnl f* **14/1**
6-00 **7** 1/2 **Slugger O'Toole**[12] 2369 6-9-2 70 (t) WilliamCarson 2 64
(Stuart Williams) *swtchd rt after s: outpcd: nt clr run over 1f out: r.o ins fnl f: nvr nrr* **16/1**
3203 **8** 2 **Copperwood**[12] 2354 6-8-13 67 LiamKeniry 4 55
(Michael Blanshard) *mid-div: hdwy over 2f out: rdn over 1f out: btn whn n.m.r ins fnl f: eased* **10/1**
0-01 **9** 3 1/2 **Bidable**[33] 1755 7-9-5 73 RichardKingscote 10 52
(Bryn Palling) *s.i.s: outpcd* **7/1**
201 **10** shd **Deerslayer (USA)**[18] 2168 5-9-6 74 PaulDoe 7 52
(Jim Best) *chsd ldrs: rdn over 2f out: wknd over 1f out* **6/1**[3]
600- **11** 13 **For Life (IRE)**[190] 7573 9-9-2 73 NataliaGemelova[(3)] 1 —
(John E Long) *chsd ldr tl rdn 1/2-way: wknd 2f out* **25/1**

1m 21.45s (-1.85) **Going Correction** -0.325s/f (Firm) **11** Ran SP% **123.2**
Speed ratings (Par 103): **97,96,96,95,92 91,90,88,84,84 69**
CSF £113.33 CT £362.91 TOTE £36.30: £10.70, £1.10, £1.50; EX 88.60.
Owner Mrs E Mills & A Murphy **Bred** Paradime Ltd **Trained** Wilmcote, Warwicks

FOCUS
An ordinary handicap rated through the winner backed up by the runner-up.
Kakapuka ◆ Official explanation: trainer said, regarding apparent improvement in form, that the colt was better suited by the step up in trip from 5f to 7f.
Bidable Official explanation: jockey said masre slipped on leaving stalls

2720 T FROST BAWTRY RACING SADDLERS FILLIES' H'CAP (TURF) 5f
7:15 (7:15) (Class 5) (0-70,70) 3-Y-O+ **£3,070** (£906; £453) **Stalls** High

Form | | | | RPR
1204 **1** **Dreamacha**[5] 2566 4-9-9 70 TobyAtkinson[(5)] 6 91+
(Stuart Williams) *chsd ldrs: gng wl and nt clr run fr over 1f out tl gap appeared and led wl ins fnl f: qcknd clr* **7/2**[2]
0015 **2** 2 1/2 **Miss Polly Plum**[16] 2238 4-8-11 53 (p) AndreaAtzeni 4 63
(Chris Dwyer) *led: rdn over 1f out: edgd lft: hdd and unable qck wl ins fnl f* **8/1**
3 2 1/2 **Queen Grace (IRE)**[35] 1700 4-8-11 53 RichardHughes 1 54+
(Michael J Browne, Ire) *racd alone in centre and up w the ldr: swtchd to stands' side over 3f out: rdn and ev ch ins fnl f: wknd towards fin* **3/1**[1]
3033 **4** 3/4 **Commandingpresence (USA)**[17] 2193 5-8-9 51 oh1 CathyGannon 10 49
(John Bridger) *sn outpcd: hdwy 2f out: rdn over 1f out: nt rch ldrs* **4/1**[3]
60-1 **5** 1 1/2 **Baby Queen (IRE)**[18] 2182 5-9-7 63 J-PGuillambert 5 56
(Brian Baugh) *mid-div: hdwy 1/2-way: rdn over 1f out: wknd ins fnl f* **4/1**[3]
4005 **6** 4 1/2 **Wanchai Whisper**[26] 1938 4-8-13 55 (v) WilliamCarson 9 32
(Michael Wigham) *sn outpcd: sme hdwy over 1f out: nvr on terms* **10/1**
0-00 **7** 10 **Lady Titticaca**[122] 383 3-7-11 51 oh6 HarryBentley[(5)] 2 —
(Ron Hodges) *chsd ldrs: rdn and hung rt 1/2-way: wknd over 1f out* **100/1**
006- **8** 1/2 **Gessabelle**[172] 7869 4-8-2 51 oh6 (t) LeonnaMayor[(7)] 11 —
(Phil McEntee) *sn outpcd* **25/1**
4106 **9** 1/2 **Lois Lane**[58] 1193 3-8-10 59 RichardKingscote 7 —
(Ron Hodges) *mid-div: rdn 1/2-way: wknd wl over 1f out* **33/1**
0-60 **U** **Arowana (IRE)**[122] 380 3-8-7 56 SamHitchcott 8 —
(Zoe Davison) *rrd and uns rdr leaving stalls* **33/1**

57.17 secs (-1.03) **Going Correction** -0.325s/f (Firm)
WFA 3 from 4yo+ 7lb **10** Ran SP% **118.1**
Speed ratings (Par 100): **95,91,87,85,83 76,60,59,58,—**
toteswingers:1&2:£6.70, 2&3:£5.50, 1&3:£2.00 CSF £30.98 CT £94.39 TOTE £5.60: £2.30, £2.70, £1.10; EX 51.00.
Owner Essex Racing Club (Dreamacha) **Bred** Barry Root **Trained** Newmarket, Suffolk

FOCUS
A moderate fillies' handicap best rated through the runner-up to her Yarmouth form.
Baby Queen(IRE) Official explanation: jockey said mare was slowly away

2721 DRY HILL (S) STKS 1m 4f (P)
7:45 (7:45) (Class 6) 3-Y-O+ **£1,706** (£503; £252) **Stalls** Low

Form | | | | RPR
3-31 **1** **Carlton Scroop (FR)**[11] 232 8-10-0 69 PaulDoe 2 72
(Jim Best) *mde all: set stdy pce tl qcknd over 2f out: sn drvn clr: styd on* **7/2**
2432 **2** 3 1/2 **Eagle Nebula**[39] 1577 7-9-11 66 KierenFox[(3)] 4 67
(Brett Johnson) *prom: rdn over 2f out: styd on to go 2nd ins fnl f: no ch w wnr* **11/4**[3]
3056 **3** 1 3/4 **Camps Bay (USA)**[6] 2526 7-10-0 67 (p) LukeMorris 6 64
(Conor Dore) *chsd wnr: rdn over 3f out: styd on same pce fnl 2f: lost 2nd ins fnl f* **5/2**[2]
3435 **4** 10 **Evident Pride (USA)**[12] 2372 8-10-0 71 IanMongan 3 48
(Brett Johnson) *hld up in tch: rdn over 2f out: sn wknd* **2/1**[1]
0555 **5** 3/4 **Senor Tibor (USA)**[9] 2418 3-8-2 45 (v) JenniferFerguson[(7)] 7 43
(Edward Creighton) *s.i.s: hdwy over 7f out: wknd over 3f out* **50/1**

2m 37.96s (4.96) **Going Correction** +0.25s/f (Slow)
WFA 3 from 5yo+ 15lb **5** Ran SP% **112.8**
Speed ratings (Par 101): **93,90,89,82,82**
CSF £13.72 TOTE £3.70: £1.40, £1.90; EX 13.40.There was no bid for the winner.
Owner Carlton Scroope Partnership **Bred** Jonathan Jay **Trained** Lewes, E Sussex

FOCUS
Weak and muddling form, even by selling standards, with the pace moderate.

2722 COUNTRYSIDE ALLIANCE H'CAP 1m 2f (P)
8:15 (8:15) (Class 6) (0-60,60) 3-Y-O **£1,706** (£503; £252) **Stalls** Low

Form | | | | RPR
66-2 **1** **Nutshell**[14] 2307 3-9-3 56 JimmyQuinn 9 65
(Harry Dunlop) *a.p: chsd ldr over 2f out: led over 1f out: rdn out* **7/2**[1]
-362 **2** 1 3/4 **Sukhothai (USA)**[19] 2166 3-9-6 59 JackMitchell 3 64
(James Fanshawe) *hld up: rdn 1/2-way: hdwy over 2f out: styd on u.p to go 2nd ins fnl f: nt rch wnr* **9/2**[2]
6424 **3** 1 1/4 **Revolutionary**[11] 2379 3-9-4 60 SophieDoyle[(3)] 13 63
(Jamie Osborne) *chsd ldrs: rdn 2f out: styd on* **7/1**
0-06 **4** hd **Oliver's Gold**[14] 2293 3-9-0 53 LiamKeniry 14 55
(Amanda Perrett) *hld up in tch: rdn over 1f out: styd on* **10/1**
-053 **5** 6 **Bobby Dazzler (IRE)**[17] 2195 3-9-4 57 PaulDoe 11 47
(Jim Best) *chsd ldr tl rdn over 2f out: styd on same pce appr fnl f* **12/1**
060- **6** nk **Dark And Dangerous (IRE)**[206] 7386 3-9-7 60 LukeMorris 8 50
(Peter Winkworth) *s.i.s: hld up: styd on u.p fnl 2f: nvr trbld ldrs* **11/2**[3]
060- **7** 3 1/2 **Commercial (IRE)**[240] 6694 3-9-7 60 FergusSweeney 12 43
(Jamie Osborne) *led: rdn and hdd over 1f out: wknd ins fnl f* **50/1**
2254 **8** nse **Not So Bright (USA)**[39] 1592 3-9-2 55 (t) CathyGannon 4 37
(Des Donovan) *hld up: rdn over 2f out: n.d* **14/1**
3000 **9** 5 **Sleeping Brave**[17] 2197 3-8-11 53 (v[1]) MatthewDavies[(3)] 1 25
(Jim Boyle) *prom tl rdn and wknd over 2f out* **20/1**
05-0 **10** 2 1/2 **Cuban Quality (USA)**[18] 2186 3-9-7 60 (b[1]) RichardKingscote 10 27
(Tom Dascombe) *hld up: rdn over 3f out: a in rr* **10/1**
060- **11** 4 **Black Iceman**[170] 7888 3-9-5 58 (v[1]) AndreaAtzeni 7 17
(Lydia Pearce) *hld up: rdn over 4f out: a in rr* **40/1**
040- **12** 19 **Chilworth Lass (IRE)**[192] 7552 3-8-13 52 SamHitchcott 5 —
(Mick Channon) *hld up: a in rr: rdn over 3f out: sn lost tch: t.o* **25/1**
5-30 **13** 15 **Dililah**[19] 2157 3-9-2 55 WilliamBuick 2 —
(William Knight) *plld hrd and prom: rdn over 3f out: sn wknd: t.o* **12/1**

2m 9.61s (3.01) **Going Correction** +0.25s/f (Slow) **13** Ran SP% **121.5**
Speed ratings (Par 97): **97,95,94,94,89 89,86,86,82,80 77,62,50**
toteswingers:1&2:£2.20, 2&3:£4.60, 1&3:£4.50 CSF £18.13 CT £107.96 TOTE £3.00: £1.10, £2.00, £2.60; EX 13.00.

The Form Book, Raceform Ltd, Compton, RG20 6NL

Owner The Gauchos **Bred** Stowell Park Stud **Trained** Lambourn, Berks

FOCUS

A weak handicap but the form looks sound rated around the first four.

2723 TANDRIDGE MAIDEN STKS — 1m (P)

8:45 (8:45) (Class 5) 3-Y-O — **£3,070** (£906; £453) **Stalls** High

Form — RPR

6 **1** — **Stand To Reason (IRE)**[14] 2306 3-9-3 0 .... LiamKeniry 12 — 83+
(Mikael Magnusson) *chsd ldrs: rdn over 1f out: hmpd ins fnl f: styd on u.p to ld and edgd lft towards fin* **11/4**[1]

3-5 **2** *nk* **Trumpington Street (IRE)**[57] 1210 3-9-3 0 .... WilliamBuick 2 — 82
(John Gosden) *led: rdn and hung rt ins fnl f: edgd lft and hdd towards fin* **3/1**[2]

0-2 **3** *6* **Daddyow**[39] 1580 3-9-3 0 .... DavidProbert 11 — 68
(Bryn Palling) *hld up in tch: outpcd over 2f out: r.o ins fnl f* **5/1**[3]

4 *½* **Takhreej (IRE)** 3-9-3 0 .... ShaneKelly 1 — 67
(Sir Michael Stoute) *sn chsng ldrs: rdn over 2f out: wknd ins fnl f* **15/2**

6 **4** *dht* **Coupland Lass (IRE)**[25] 1985 3-8-12 0 .... JackMitchell 8 — 62
(Willie Musson) *hld up: hdwy over 1f out: nvr nr to chal* **25/1**

0 **6** *½* **Tanmawy (IRE)**[15] 2258 3-9-3 0 .... RichardHughes 4 — 66+
(Ed Dunlop) *chsd ldrs: rdn over 2f out: wknd ins fnl f* **9/1**

0 **7** *4 ½* **Artisan**[33] 1759 3-9-3 0 .... JamieMackay 3 — 56
(Willie Musson) *s.i.s: a in rr: lost tch fnl 3f* **16/1**

8 *hd* **Ibiza Sunset (IRE)** 3-9-3 0 .... LukeMorris 10 — 55
(Peter Winkworth) *hld up: rdn 1/2-way: wknd over 3f out* **10/1**

9 *hd* **Graceful Act** 3-8-12 0 .... TedDurcan 6 — 50
(James Toller) *prom: lost pl 6f out: n.d after* **16/1**

0 **10** *1 ¼* **Kings Fortune**[14] 2306 3-9-3 0 .... IanMongan 9 — 52
(Michael Bell) *pushed along to chse ldrs: rdn over 2f out: sn wknd: hung lft over 1f out* **66/1**

11 *24* **Oakdown** 3-9-3 0 .... FergusSweeney 5 — —
(Alan King) *s.s: a in rr: bhd fr 1/2-way: t.o* **25/1**

1m 40.37s (2.17) **Going Correction** +0.25s/f (Slow) — **11** Ran SP% **120.1**

Speed ratings (Par 99): **99,98,92,92,92 91,87,87,86,85 61**

toteswingers:1&2:£2.90, 2&3:£4.50, 1&3:£3.10 CSF £11.12 TOTE £4.40: £1.70, £2.00, £1.60; EX 7.50.

Owner B Nielsen & Eastwind Racing & M Trussell **Bred** Coleman Bloodstock Limited **Trained** Upper Lambourn, Berks

■ Stewards' Enquiry : Jamie Mackay 14-day ban (2nd-offence in 24mths): failed to take all reasonable and permissable measures to obtain best possible placing (Jun 18-Jul 1)

FOCUS

Nothing got into this from off the pace and the front two filled those positions throughout. They finished clear though and the form looks reasonable.

Artisan Official explanation: jockey said, regarding running and riding, that his orders were to settle in mid-division, ensure the gelding was relaxed and to wind up from 3f out and finish as close as he could, it was unsuited by the slow early pace.

T/Plt: £11.20 to a £1 stake. Pool:£76,036.03 4,928.65 winning tickets T/Qpdt: £3.10 to a £1 stake. Pool of £4,331.43 - 1,029.60 winning tickets. CR

2691 MUSSELBURGH (R-H)

Saturday, June 4

OFFICIAL GOING: Good to firm (good in places; 6.7)

All rails moved in 3m.

Wind: Fresh, half behind Weather: Overcast

2724 TOTESPORT 0800 221221 SALTIRE SPRINT (H'CAP) — 5f

2:05 (2:06) (Class 2) (0-105,104) 3-Y-O — **£18,693** (£5,598; £2,799; £1,401; £699; £351) **Stalls** High

Form — RPR

3210 **1** — **Barnet Fair**[22] 2074 3-7-11 **80** .... AndrewHeffernan(3) 6 — 86
(Richard Guest) *dwlt: hld up in tch: hdwy to ld 1f out: kpt on strly* **7/2**[2]

0-22 **2** *1 ½* **Bold Bidder**[29] 1852 3-8-7 **87** .... FrannyNorton 2 — 88
(Kevin Ryan) *led tl hdd 1f out: kpt on ins fnl f: nt gng pce of wnr* **4/1**[3]

-354 **3** *hd* **Crimson Knot (IRE)**[9] 2411 3-7-13 **79** oh1 ow1 .... PatrickMathers 4 — 79
(Alan Berry) *trckd ldrs: effrt and drvn over 1f out: kpt on ins fnl f* **12/1**

0-35 **4** *3 ½* **Face The Problem (IRE)**[29] 1852 3-9-3 **97** .... RobertWinston 7 — 85
(B W Hills) *trckd ldrs: drvn 1/2-way: outpcd appr fnl f: sn no imp* **11/4**[1]

0-00 **5** *hd* **Jack Smudge**[7] 2508 3-8-5 **85** .... PaulHanagan 1 — 72
(James Given) *cl up tl rdn and no ex appr fnl f* **17/2**

50-4 **6** *¾* **Mappin Time (IRE)**[29] 1852 3-8-10 **90** .... DuranFentiman 9 — 74
(Tim Easterby) *dwlt: bhd: rdn and swtchd rt over 1f out: nvr able to chal* **7/1**

-102 **7** *3 ¾* **Gottcher**[7] 2505 3-7-11 **80** oh3 ow2 .... JamesSullivan(3) 5 — 51
(David Barron) *hung rt thrght: w ldr: lost pl whn n.m.r 1/2-way: sn btn* **11/2**

58.28 secs (-2.12) **Going Correction** -0.275s/f (Firm) — **7** Ran SP% **115.0**

Speed ratings (Par 105): **105,102,102,96,96 95,89**

toteswingers:1&2:£3.60, 2&3:£4.60, 1&3:£5.40 CSF £18.08 CT £149.26 TOTE £4.10: £2.30, £2.10; EX 22.30 Trifecta £200.70 Pool: £659.07 - 2.43 winning units..

Owner Donald Wheatley **Bred** Mrs J M Russell **Trained** Stainforth, S Yorks

FOCUS

The going had dried out to good to firm, good in places, despite the weather being cooler and more cloudy than the previous day. A good field for this sprint, attracted by decent prize-money, but after a couple of withdrawals the top-weight was rated 8lb below the race ceiling. Not many showed their form, but the winner recorded a length personal best.

NOTEBOOK

Barnet Fair came from the rear to score in decent style. He had progressed with racing on Polytrack over the winter and had run well on his return to turf after starting slowly. He got away much better but was still out the back early here, then travelled well into the race before asserting. He appears still to be on the upgrade and a weight rise may not stop his progress. (tchd 4-1 in a place)

Bold Bidder, who had two of today's rivals behind when runner-up at Chester, was quickly away and eventually got to the rail. She kept on well but the winner proved too strong. She has now finished second on her last three starts but there is nothing wrong with her attitude. (op 7-2)

Crimson Knot(IRE) is a regular over this C&D and gained her only win here. Despite being 2lb wrong, including her rider's 1lb overweight, she performed well again, if unable to find more, having been upsides over 1f out.

Face The Problem(IRE), who finished behind the runner-up at Chester, was sent off a well-backed favourite to reverse the form. He was well drawn but was unable to hold his pitch early and was a little short of room, from which point he never posed a threat. (op 4-1)

Jack Smudge has form over 5f but has been running over 6f of late. He was badly drawn and, in the circumstances, did quite well to get into the firing line around 2f out before fading. (op 8-1)

Mappin Time(IRE) had the best draw on the rail but was unable to hold his place there and was always struggling. (tchd 15-2)

Gottcher broke well but was taken on for the lead early and lost that particular battle, from which point he dropped away tamely. (op 6-1, tchd 7-1 in a place)

2725 TOTEPOOL EDINBURGH CASTLE CONDITIONS STKS — 5f

2:35 (2:37) (Class 2) 2-Y-O — **£12,462** (£3,732; £1,866; £934; £466) **Stalls** High

Form — RPR

22 **1** — **Frederick Engels**[7] 2504 2-8-11 0 .... RobertWinston 1 — 103
(David Brown) *carried sltly rt s: pressed ldr: led over 1f out: rdn and drew clr fnl f: readily* **13/2**[3]

31 **2** *6* **Es Que Love (IRE)**[7] 2485 2-8-11 0 .... JoeFanning 2 — 81
(Mark Johnston) *wnt rt s: led: rdn and hdd over 1f out: sn outpcd* **5/6**[1]

215 **3** *1 ¾* **Alejandro (IRE)**[24] 2007 2-9-0 0 .... PaulHanagan 4 — 78
(Richard Fahey) *chsd ldrs: drvn and outpcd 2f out: no imp ins fnl f* **9/4**[2]

13 **4** *½* **Ponty Acclaim (IRE)**[24] 2007 2-8-6 0 .... DuranFentiman 3 — 68
(Tim Easterby) *trckd ldrs: effrt and rdn 1/2-way: no ex fr over 1f out* **10/1**

033 **5** *1 ½* **Economic Crisis (IRE)**[15] 2248 2-8-6 0 .... PatrickMathers 5 — 63
(Alan Berry) *fly-jmpd s: in tch: rdn and outpcd 1/2-way: n.d after* **66/1**

58.02 secs (-2.38) **Going Correction** -0.275s/f (Firm) — **5** Ran SP% **109.2**

Speed ratings (Par 99): **108,98,95,94,92**

CSF £12.41 TOTE £7.00: £2.60, £1.10; EX 13.60.

Owner Norton Common Farm Racing **Bred** Peter Baldwin **Trained** Averham Park, Notts

FOCUS

All three previous winners of this juvenile conditions race have gone on to make the frame at Group level, and that could be the case again, especially as the winner's time was faster than the two handicaps for older horses. The form is not taken too literally but the winner looks on the upgrade.

NOTEBOOK

Frederick Engels ◆ had run into a couple of potentially high-class performers on his first two starts, but his trainer said after his previous race that he still thought a lot of him and was taking him to Ascot, and this performance justified his faith. He never gave the favourite much rope and, when asked to go on over 1f out, quickly put daylight between himself and the rest. The Windsor Castle, or even the Norfolk Stakes, are his likely targets, and on this evidence he should have a good chance in either. (op 8-1)

Es Que Love(IRE) had absolutely bolted up in a maiden auction at Beverley and was also being talked about as a possible Ascot horse. He went off in front but could never get away from the winner and, when that rival went on, could not respond. (op 8-11, tchd 10-11 in places)

Alejandro(IRE) won his maiden over C&D but had looked unlucky next time at York when hampered. He tracked the pace but was always struggling to stay with the first two, and it looks as though nurseries might be his best option in future. (op 5-2)

Ponty Acclaim(IRE), who finished ahead of today's third last time, was settled early and moved up to chase the leaders soon after halfway, but then paid for her exertions late on. (op 9-1 tchd 11-1)

Economic Crisis(IRE) was outclassed at this level and was always in the rear. (op 40-1)

2726 TOTESPORT.COM EDINBURGH CUP (H'CAP) — 1m 4f 100y

3:10 (3:11) (Class 2) (0-105,103) 3-Y-O — **£49,848** (£14,928; £7,464; £3,736; £1,864; £936) **Stalls** Low

Form — RPR

311 **1** — **Eternal Heart (IRE)**[16] 2228 3-8-5 **87** .... JoeFanning 10 — 95
(Mark Johnston) *mde all: rdn over 2f out: hrd pressed over 1f out: edgd lft ins fnl f: styd on strly* **11/2**[3]

-222 **2** *1* **Mica Mika (IRE)**[14] 2287 3-7-13 **84** .... AndrewHeffernan(3) 5 — 90
(Richard Fahey) *trckd ldrs: effrt and rdn over 2f out: ev ch over 1f out: kpt on ins fnl f* **12/1**

4524 **3** *¾* **Namibian (IRE)**[7] 2507 3-9-7 **103** .... GregFairley 8 — 108
(Mark Johnston) *hld up: hdwy and in tch after 4f: rdn and outpcd over 2f out: rallied over 1f out: styd on ins fnl f* **7/1**

31-1 **4** *1 ¼* **Swift Alhaarth (IRE)**[14] 2287 3-8-1 **83** .... FrannyNorton 2 — 86
(Mark Johnston) *t.k.h: sn trcking wnr: rdn over 2f out: edgd lft: kpt on same pce ins fnl f* **17/2**

24-1 **5** *2 ¼* **Mulaqen**[24] 1998 3-8-3 **85** .... TadhgO'Shea 3 — 84
(Marcus Tregoning) *in tch: rdn and outpcd 3f out: rallied over 1f out: no imp ins fnl f* **8/1**

42-1 **6** *2* **Captain Brown**[8] 2461 3-7-8 **81** .... RosieJessop(5) 7 — 77+
(Sir Mark Prescott Bt) *dwlt: hld up on ins: hdwy over 2f out: edgd lft over 1f out: kpt on ins fnl f: no imp* **3/1**[1]

5111 **7** *2 ½* **Lexi's Boy (IRE)**[35] 1706 3-7-11 **82** oh4 ow2 .... JamesSullivan(3) 6 — 74
(Kevin Ryan) *prom: drvn and outpcd over 3f out: n.d after* **25/1**

1-63 **8** [illegible] **Bridle Belle**[34] [illegible] [illegible] .... PaulHanagan [illegible] — 70
(Richard Fahey) *hld up: rdn and outpcd over 3f out: btn fnl 2f* **9/2**[2]

00-3 **9** *nk* **Colour Vision (FR)**[31] 1811 3-8-4 **86** .... AndrewElliott 1 — 76
(Mark Johnston) *hld up: struggling over 3f out: nvr on terms* **7/1**

2m 38.9s (-3.10) **Going Correction** -0.125s/f (Firm) — **9** Ran SP% **116.7**

Speed ratings (Par 105): **105,104,103,103,101 100,98,98,97**

toteswingers:1&2:£11.00, 2&3:£12.60, 1&3:£7.70 CSF £69.46 CT £470.00 TOTE £5.50: £1.50, £3.70, £2.00; EX 86.00 Trifecta £823.20 Part won. Pool: £1,112.47 - 0.91 winning units..

Owner Mrs Joan Keaney **Bred** Mrs Joan Keaney **Trained** Middleham Moor, N Yorks

■ Stewards' Enquiry : Franny Norton caution: used whip without giving gelding time to respond.

FOCUS

A very valuable handicap for 3-y-os that fell to subsequent dual Listed winner Harris Tweed in 2010. They appeared to go a good gallop but three of the first four were in the first trio virtually throughout. The winner continues to progress.

NOTEBOOK

Eternal Heart(IRE), a half-brother to a couple of smart types, notably Yavana's Pace, was given a positive ride, reminiscent of when winning his maiden over C&D. Under one of the best front-running jockeys around, he made all and stuck on in tenacious style. It seems likely he will go the Royal Ascot for the King George V Handicap, and he is sure to run with credit if he gets over this hard race in time. (op 5-1)

Mica Mika(IRE) has been running consistently well this season and was always close to the winner but, try as he might, could not get past. He has been runner-up in all four starts this season but reversed previous form with the fourth on 7lb better terms. There is nothing wrong with his attitude, and a bit of cut in the ground might enable him to gain that elusive win. (op 14-1 tchd 16-1)

Namibian(IRE) has gone up 18lb this season without winning but ran another decent race giving 16lb and more all round. He just needs to drop a few pounds, but his consistency does not make it easy for the handicapper to relent. (op 10-1)

Swift Alhaarth(IRE) was on a hat-trick but had gone up 7lb from his last success and, despite running his race, was unable to confirm previous form with the runner-up. (op 10-1 tchd 11-1)

Mulaqen, having only his second race on turf, came from off the pace to chase the leaders through the closing stages but could never make sufficient impression. He was clearly best of the hold-up horses though. (op 9-1 tchd 10-1)

Captain Brown, sent off favourite, was held up, as he was on his previous start. However, his apprentice rider appeared to rather overdo the waiting tactics, as the gelding was still last and a fair way behind turning for home. He ran on without ever looking likely to figure and can be forgiven this. (tchd 5-2, 7-2 in a place)

Lexi's Boy(IRE), who has been so progressive on the AW, looked to be feeling the ground back on this fast turf. (op 20-1)

Bridle Belle was also held up at the back of the field and was never able to get competitive. (op 6-1)

Colour Vision(FR) was also held up at the back of the field and was unable to get involved. (op 9-2)

2727 TOTESCOOP6 SCOTTISH SPRINT CUP (H'CAP) 5f
3:40 (3:43) (Class 2) (0-105,98) 3-Y-0+
£24,924 (£7,464; £3,732; £1,868; £932; £468) **Stalls** High

Form				RPR
0-00	**1**		**Burning Thread (IRE)**[7] [2489] 4-9-1 **94** .... DaleSwift(5) 16 (Tim Etherington) *rrd s: sn in tch: effrt and hdwy over 1f out: led ins fnl f: r.o wl* **50/1**	104
0212	**2**	*1*	**Verinco**[4] [2585] 5-8-8 **82** .... (v) TomEaves 7 (Bryan Smart) *cl up: led appr to ins fnl f: kpt on towards fin* **12/1**	88
5-00	**3**	*nk*	**Kaldoun Kingdom (IRE)**[14] [2317] 6-9-3 **98** .... GeorgeChaloner(7) 9 (Richard Fahey) *bhd: hdwy against stands' rail whn n.m.r briefly appr and ent fnl f: r.o wl towards fin* **33/1**	103+
-112	**4**	*½*	**Doctor Parkes**[14] [2317] 5-9-9 **97** .... PaulHanagan 15 (Eric Alston) *midfield: effrt whn n.m.r and blkd over 1f out: kpt on ins fnl f* **11/4**[1]	100+
0-04	**5**	*½*	**Fol Hollow (IRE)**[34] [1715] 6-8-13 **87** .... JoeFanning 17 (David Nicholls) *led tl hdd appr fnl f: kpt on same pce last 100yds* **16/1**	88
20-3	**6**	*3 ¼*	**Racy**[23] [2028] 4-9-3 **91** .... PhillipMakin 5 (Kevin Ryan) *hld up in tch: effrt and hdwy over 1f out: kpt on same pce ins fnl f* **5/1**[2]	81+
0-44	**7**	*shd*	**Favourite Girl (IRE)**[21] [2117] 5-9-3 **91** .... (v) DuranFentiman 11 (Tim Easterby) *prom: rdn and outpcd whn checked over 1f out: kpt on ins fnl f* **12/1**	80
/002	**8**	*hd*	**Befortyfour**[7] [2489] 6-9-4 **95** .... RobertLButler(3) 10 (Richard Guest) *trckd ldrs: rdn over 2f out: no ex appr fnl f* **22/1**	84
0-05	**9**	*1 ½*	**Hazelrigg (IRE)**[14] [2317] 6-8-12 **86** .... (be) FrederikTylicki 14 (Tim Easterby) *hld up: blkd after 1f: effrt over 1f out: nvr able to chal* **10/1**[3]	69+
40-0	**10**	*¾*	**Cheveton**[22] [2075] 7-9-3 **96** .... RyanClark(5) 8 (Richard Price) *hld up: effrt on outside over 2f out: wknd over 1f out* **10/1**[3]	76+
-042	**11**	*½*	**The Nifty Fox**[10] [2397] 7-8-11 **85** .... (v) SebSanders 1 (Tim Easterby) *racd centre: prom: effrt 2f out: edgd lft and wknd appr fnl f* **14/1**	64+
-566	**12**	*3 ¼*	**Secret Millionaire (IRE)**[6] [2525] 4-8-10 **87** .... JamesSullivan(3) 13 (Patrick Morris) *hld up: hdwy 2f out: wknd appr fnl f* **12/1**	54+
0-00	**13**	*½*	**Colonel Mak**[34] [1720] 4-9-5 **98** .... LMcNiff(5) 2 (David Barron) *racd centre: bhd: stuggling 1/2-way: nvr on terms* **16/1**	63+
2-00	**14**	*1*	**Courageous (IRE)**[23] [2028] 5-8-13 **90** .... (v) MichaelO'Connell(3) 6 (David Nicholls) *midfield: drvn 1/2-way: sn struggling* **33/1**	52
-055	**15**	*2 ½*	**Striking Spirit**[28] [1888] 6-9-5 **93** .... (t) RobertWinston 3 (Tim Easterby) *prom centre: edgd lft after 2f: wknd wl over 1f out* **10/1**[3]	46+
-000	**16**	*11*	**Archers Road (IRE)**[21] [2117] 4-9-1 **89** .... LeeNewman 4 (David Barron) *spd centre to 1/2-way: sn rdn and wknd* **33/1**	—+

58.13 secs (-2.27) **Going Correction** -0.275s/f (Firm) **16 Ran SP% 127.2**
Speed ratings (Par 109): **107,105,104,104,103 98,97,97,95,94 93,88,87,85,81 64**
toteswingers:1&2:£107.50, 2&3:£54.00, 1&3:£107.50 CSF £576.66 CT £19009.73 TOTE £114.60: £14.70, £3.10, £8.00, £1.40; EX 1401.80 TRIFECTA Not won..
Owner Tim Etherington **Bred** James Lombard **Trained** Norton, N Yorks

FOCUS
A high-class, competitive sprint handicap that was slower than the earlier juvenile contest and produced a surprise result. Those that were drawn low and raced towards the outside finished well beaten. The form might not be that solid.

NOTEBOOK
Burning Thread(IRE) won a Listed race at Sandown last season but had not beaten a rival in two starts this year, although he had excuses on one occasion. He reared as the stalls opened and struggled to go the pace from his favourable draw, but then picked up from halfway and got to the front inside the last furlong. He is still relatively lightly raced and, if he can build on this, he can pick up more good prizes. He is likely to go for the Wokingham next. Official explanation: trainer said, regarding apparent improvement in form, that the gelding was more relaxed in the stalls and get a better start. (tchd 66-1)
Verinco is a really speedy sort and showed enough pace to get over to the stands' side from his middle-to-high-draw. He made most of the running, only to be caught inside the last. He handles any ground and deserves to gain compensation before long.
Kaldoun Kingdom(IRE) ◆ has not won for 14 months but has only just dropped below his last winning mark. After being out the back, having switched behind runners towards the nearside, he finished best of all next to the rail. Given some ease in the ground, he could soon be back to winning form. (op 28-1)
Doctor Parkes has been in fine form but has gone up 13lb as a result and, having been held up, did not get involved until late on, and then his effort flattened out. (op 4-1)
Fol Hollow(IRE) showed lots of pace but paid for it in the closing stages. (tchd 14-1)
Racy ◆ looks the one to take from the contest, as he was drawn low and ended up racing in the centre. He was unable to build on his unlucky third at York, but looks one to bear in mind as he is relatively lightly raced and open to improvement. (op 4-1)
Favourite Girl(IRE) had run well in her two previous starts but, after showing up for the first half of the race, dropped out under pressure. (op 11-1)
Befortyfour, narrowly beaten in a conditions race the previous weekend, was 6lb higher this time but again performed creditably. (op 16-1)
Hazelrigg(IRE), who looked on the way back last time, didn't have things fall for him here, as he was held up and was faced with a wall of horses for most of the way. (op 9-1)
Cheveton is best with more give in the ground and in the circumstances did well to come from the back of the field, especially as he was forced to race up the middle of the track, but then dropped away again. (op 11-1 tchd 8-1)

2728 STEPHEN HAY AND ASSOCIATES LTD CLASSIFIED STKS 1m 1f
4:15 (4:15) (Class 5) 3-Y-O
£3,238 (£963; £481) **Stalls** Low

Form				RPR
6-52	**1**		**Adlington**[32] [1801] 3-9-0 70 .... PaulHanagan 2 (Richard Fahey) *led 1f: trckd ldrs: plld out and hdwy to ld over 1f out: hung rt ins fnl f: comf* **10/11**[1]	73
221-	**2**	*3*	**Janet's Pearl (IRE)**[264] [6027] 3-9-0 70 .... PhillipMakin 3 (Ann Duffield) *cl up: led over 3f out: hdd over 1f out: carried rt ins fnl f: kpt on same pce last 100yds* **7/2**[3]	66
10-2	**3**	*12*	**Screenprint**[26] [1949] 3-9-0 70 .... (t) JoeFanning 1 (Michael Bell) *plld hrd: led after 1f to over 3f out: rallied: wknd over 1f out* **15/8**[2]	49

1m 53.07s (-0.83) **Going Correction** -0.125s/f (Firm) **3 Ran SP% 109.4**
Speed ratings (Par 99): **98,95,84**
CSF £4.17 TOTE £1.80; EX 3.30.
Owner The Living Legend Racing Partnership **Bred** Highfield Farm Llp **Trained** Musley Bank, N Yorks

FOCUS
Nothing between the trio on official ratings in this classified stakes but it did not prove as tight a race as the figures suggested. It's doubtful if the winner had to improve.

2729 FOUNTAIN COURT APARTMENTS - HOTEL STYLE HOME COMFORT H'CAP 7f 30y
4:45 (4:45) (Class 4) (0-80,80) 3-Y-O
£5,180 (£1,541; £770; £384) **Stalls** Low

Form				RPR
2333	**1**		**Bertiewhittle**[14] [2281] 3-8-13 **72** .... LeeNewman 2 (David Barron) *trckd ldrs: rdn to ld over 1f out: kpt on strly to go clr fnl f* **15/2**	82
4031	**2**	*3 ¾*	**Goal (IRE)**[16] [2236] 3-8-4 **63** .... (t) FrannyNorton 7 (Richard Guest) *set stdy pce: rdn and hdd over 1f out: kpt on same pce* **20/1**	63
24-1	**3**	*¾*	**Lamasaas (USA)**[35] [1693] 3-9-7 **80** .... RobertWinston 5 (B W Hills) *sn trcking ldr: effrt over 2f out: kpt on same pce fnl f* **7/1**	78
0-11	**4**	*1 ¼*	**Lightning Cloud (IRE)**[19] [2147] 3-9-7 **80** .... PhillipMakin 1 (Kevin Ryan) *plld hrd: hld up in tch: effrt over 2f out: kpt on same pce fnl f* **13/8**[1]	75+
2-12	**5**	*2*	**Maverik**[21] [2096] 3-9-5 **78** .... FrederikTylicki 4 (Michael Dods) *t.k.h: in tch: effrt on outside over 2f out: edgd lft: wknd over 1f out* **4/1**[2]	67+
-534	**6**	*3 ½*	**Sabratha (IRE)**[16] [2215] 3-8-6 **65** .... JoeFanning 6 (Linda Perratt) *t.k.h: prom on outside: rdn over 2f out: wknd over 1f out* **10/1**	45+
-330	**7**	*nk*	**Nawaashi**[14] [2319] 3-9-5 **78** .... TadhgO'Shea 3 (Mark Johnston) *hld up: struggling over 3f out: nvr on terms* **5/1**[3]	57

1m 28.01s (-0.99) **Going Correction** -0.125s/f (Firm) **7 Ran SP% 112.9**
Speed ratings (Par 101): **100,95,94,93,91 87,86**
toteswingers:1&2:£13.50, 2&3:£27.10, 1&3:£4.80 CSF £126.49 TOTE £9.80: £3.00, £4.20; EX 79.50.
Owner Norton Common Farm Racing **Bred** E Dafydd **Trained** Maunby, N Yorks

FOCUS
A fair 3-y-o handicap. Several weren't at their best, but the winner stepped up.
Maverik Official explanation: jockey said gelding ran too free

2730 SCOTTISH RACING H'CAP 1m 4f 100y
5:20 (5:20) (Class 6) (0-65,63) 3-Y-O
£2,590 (£770) **Stalls** Low

Form				RPR
3042	**1**		**Jeu De Vivre (IRE)**[8] [2478] 3-9-7 **63** .... JoeFanning 2 (Mark Johnston) *mde all at stdy gallop: qcknd over 2f out: sn clr: easily* **1/7**[1]	71
40-0	**2**	*8*	**A Southside Boy (GER)**[41] [1542] 3-8-4 **46** .... DuranFentiman 1 (Jim Goldie) *t.k.h: trckd wnr: hung bdly lft bnd after 3f: rdn over 2f out: sn btn* **4/1**[2]	41

2m 54.24s (12.24) **Going Correction** -0.125s/f (Firm) **2 Ran SP% 107.5**
Speed ratings (Par 97): **54,48**
TOTE £1.10.
Owner Ms J Bianco **Bred** Rockhart Trading Ltd **Trained** Middleham Moor, N Yorks

FOCUS
This modest handicap was reduced to a match and it proved a non-event, run in a slow time. The winner will be aon a good mark if escaping a rise for this.
T/Plt: £540.80 to a £1 stake. Pool of £67,503.74 - 91.11 winning tickets. T/Qpdt: £213.10 to a £1 stake. Pool of £2,938.49 - 10.20 winning tickets. RY

2460 NEWCASTLE (L-H)
Saturday, June 4

OFFICIAL GOING: Good to firm (good in places on straight course; 8.0)
Rail realignment on round course added 2y to 10f races and 4yd to 2m race.Last 3f of home straight dolled out 3yds.
Wind: light 1/2 behind Weather: overcast

2731 NESTLE CONFECTIONERY CHARITY MAIDEN AUCTION STKS 6f
6:30 (6:30) (Class 5) 2-Y-O
£2,914 (£850, £850, £210) **Stalls** Centre

Form				RPR
	1		**Bellechance** 2-8-3 0 .... DeclanCannon(3) 4 (Nigel Tinkler) *trckd ldrs: styd on to ld 1f out: hld on towards fin* **11/4**[1]	61
5	**2**	*½*	**Haafkry**[10] [2395] 2-8-4 0 .... JamesSullivan(3) 5 (Linda Stubbs) *w ldrs: no ex fnl 50yds* **3/1**[2]	61
0	**2**	*dht*	**Louis Hull**[8] [2460] 2-8-12 0 .... PaulPickard(3) 8 (George Foster) *s.i.s: in rr: drvn to improve 3f out: upsides over 1f out: kpt on same pce last 100yds* **25/1**	69
56	**4**	*shd*	**Fiction Or Fact (IRE)**[16] [2214] 2-8-13 0 .... TonyHamilton 1 (Kevin Ryan) *dwlt: sn chsng ldrs: drvn over 2f out: outpcd over 1f out: styd on fnl f* **4/1**[3]	66
0	**5**	*hd*	**Flosse**[24] [1996] 2-8-2 0 .... KellyHarrison 7 (Ed Walker) *dwlt: sn outpcd and in rr: hdwy: nt clr run and swtchd rt 2f out: sn chsd ldrs: kpt on towards fin* **8/1**	56
5	**6**	*¾*	**Galilee Chapel (IRE)**[26] [1939] 2-8-10 0 .... GaryBartley(3) 3 (Howard Johnson) *led: hdd 1f out: wknd towards fin* **8/1**	63
6	**7**	*3 ¼*	**Arrowroot**[20] [2120] 2-8-8 0 .... LanceBetts(5) 6 (Tim Easterby) *chsd ldrs: rdn over 2f out: wknd over 1f out* **16/1**	54
	8	*1 ¾*	**Bartley** 2-8-13 0 .... TomEaves 2 (Bryan Smart) *outpcd: lost pl and reminders after 2f: bhd tl sme late hdwy* **16/1**	48

1m 14.53s (-0.07) **Going Correction** -0.25s/f (Firm) **8 Ran SP% 109.5**
Speed ratings (Par 93): **90,89,89,89,88 87,83,81**
EX: Belle Chance/Louis Hull £32.10 Belle Chance/Haafkry £6.30 CSF: B/LH £31.09 B/H £5.07. toteswingers:1&LH :£11.10, B&LH:£12.20, 1&H:£2.50 TOTE £3.20: £1.20 TRIFECTA PL: Louis Hull £7.60, Haafkry £1.60.
Owner N Patsalides & M Patel **Bred** Burton Agnes Stud Co Ltd **Trained** Langton, N Yorks

FOCUS
A blanket finish, suggesting the bare form is nothing out of the ordinary, with the five immediately behind the first two all showing minor improvement.

NOTEBOOK
Bellechance showed a willing attitude to justify market support on her debut. A second recent juvenile winner for her yard, this daughter of Acclamation is entitled to build on this. (op 7-2)
Haafkry has shown ability on both starts and may do better still, particularly when given the chance to tackle 7f-plus. (tchd 10-3)
Louis Hull offered more than on his recent debut over C&D and could be the type to improve with racing. (tchd 10-3)
Fiction Or Fact(IRE) is bred for speed but shaped as if a stiffer test would suit, getting outpaced before staying on again late. He's improved a bit with each outing and is the type to do better in nurseries. (op 10-3)

Flosse was a cheap purchase and it could prove money well spent as she clearly has ability. She was left with plenty to do after being short of room 2f out. She's open to further progress. (op 9-1)
Galilee Chapel(IRE) is bred to stay this far but didn't seem to benefit for the step up from 5f at this stage of his career, giving no extra inside the last. (op 7-1 tchd 6-1)
Arrowroot showed enough to suggest he has ability and is probably being brought along with nurseries in mind.
Bartley was too green to do himself justice on this debut but should at least know more next time. (op 12-1 tchd 10-1)

2732 DALKIA GREEN ENERGY CHALLENGE H'CAP 7f
7:00 (7:06) (Class 5) (0-75,78) 4-Y-0+ **£2,914** (£867; £433; £216) **Stalls** Centre

Form				RPR
600-	1		**Pravda Street**230 6963 6-8-13 **72** DaleSwift(5) 4 (Brian Ellison) *hld up: effrt over 2f out: sn chsng ldng pair: styd on ins fnl f: led nr fin* **5/1**3	82
-012	2	½	**Vito Volterra (IRE)**12 2366 4-9-7 **78** SeanLevey(3) 5 (Michael Smith) *led: jnd 2f out: hdd and no ex nr fin* **9/4**2	87
6-10	3	*shd*	**Music Festival (USA)**21 2095 4-8-10 **64** GregFairley 3 (Jim Goldie) *chsd ldr: chal 2f out: kpt on same pce towards fin* **85/40**1	73
6-04	4	8	**Feel The Heat**32 1800 4-9-5 **73** TomEaves 7 (Bryan Smart) *sn trcking ldrs: effrt over 2f out: wknd over 1f out* **7/1**	60
4225	5	½	**Convince (USA)**12 2353 10-7-13 **56** oh1 AndrewHeffernan(3) 9 (Kevin M Prendergast) *fly-jmpd s: hld up: effrt over 3f out: sn rdn and hung lft: nvr trbld ldrs* **14/1**	42
0140	6	3¾	**Tombellini (IRE)**22 2057 4-8-1 **58** BillyCray(3) 1 (David Nicholls) *uns rdr and rn loose gng to s: reluctant to go to s: dwlt: sn chsng ldrs: drvn 4f out: lost pl over 2f out* **14/1**	34
03-0	7	57	**Stonehaugh (IRE)**47 1438 8-8-12 **66** TonyHamilton 8 (Howard Johnson) *w ldrs: wknd 3f out: bhd whn eased ins fnl f: wl t.o* **16/1**	—

1m 26.01s (-1.79) **Going Correction** -0.25s/f (Firm) **7 Ran SP% 111.2**
Speed ratings (Par 103): **105,104,104,95,94 90,25**
toteswingers:1&2:£2.80, 2&3:£1.40, 1&3:£1.90 CSF £15.72 CT £29.02 TOTE £6.60: £4.20, £2.20; EX 20.30.
Owner Ms Z Hatcher **Bred** R A Instone **Trained** Norton, N Yorks

FOCUS
Clearly not a strong handicap overall, but best to take a reasonably positive view of the front three who came well clear of the rest. The winner is rated to his previous best and the form appears sound.
Stonehaugh(IRE) Official explanation: vet said gelding finished distressed

2733 ROWNTREE'S SOUR PASTILLES H'CAP 2m 19y
7:30 (7:31) (Class 6) (0-65,62) 4-Y-0+ **£2,072** (£616; £308; £153) **Stalls** Low

Form				RPR
-440	1		**Dechiper (IRE)**9 2433 9-8-8 **46** TonyHamilton 2 (Robert Johnson) *trckd ldrs: wnt 2nd over 2f out: rdn to ld over 1f out: drvn rt out* **22/1**	53
4/00	2	1	**Westlin' Winds (IRE)**11 2393 5-9-4 **61** DaleSwift(5) 7 (Brian Ellison) *hld up towards rr: hdwy after 4f: effrt over 3f out: styd on to take 3rd jst ins fnl f: kpt on same pce: tk 2nd post* **11/8**1	67
505	3	*shd*	**Pearl Mountain (IRE)**24 1998 4-8-13 **52** MickyFenton 5 (Lydia Pearce) *hld up towards rr: t.k.h: drvn over 4f out: hung lft and wnt 2nd jst ins fnl f: kpt on same pce* **12/1**	58
-034	4	3¾	**Court Princess**11 2377 8-8-12 **50** PaulHanagan 9 (Richard Price) *led after 2f: set modest pce: qcknd gallop 4f out: hdd over 1f out: wknd jst ins fnl f* **5/1**3	51
066-	5	¾	**Harsh But Fair**254 6313 5-8-4 **45** JamesSullivan(3) 6 (Michael Easterby) *hld up in rr: t.k.h: effrt 3f out: kpt on ins fnl f* **9/2**2	45
/06-	6	*hd*	**Word Of Warning**10 4854 7-9-2 **54** PJMcDonald 4 (Martin Todhunter) *hld up in rr: hdwy over 2f out: kpt on ins fnl f* **16/1**	54
0-26	7	5	**Oh Landino (GER)**10 2400 6-8-8 **46** GregFairley 1 (Jim Goldie) *led 2f: chsd ldr: wknd over 1f out* **14/1**	40
300-	8	3¼	**Almutaham (USA)**31 6114 4-8-11 **50** TomEaves 8 (James Moffatt) *trckd ldrs: drvn over 3f out: wknd 2f out* **8/1**	40

3m 39.89s (0.49) **Going Correction** 0.0s/f (Good)
WFA 4 from 5yo+ 1lb **8 Ran SP% 112.7**
Speed ratings (Par 101): **98,97,97,95,95 95,92,90**
toteswingers:1&2:£7.60, 2&3:£5.70, 1&3:£39.90 CSF £51.48 CT £400.73 TOTE £27.80: £5.70, £1.30, £3.90; EX 87.70.
Owner L Armstrong **Bred** Tommy Burns **Trained** Newburn, Tyne & Wear

FOCUS
A modest staying event which was steadily run for the most part and the form looks slightly dubious. The winner is rated to last year's best with the runner-up close to his old Flat form.
Dechiper(IRE) Official explanation: trainer said, regarding apparent improvement in form, that the gelding benefited by being held up.

2734 ROCKCLIFFE HALL H'CAP 1m 2f 32y
8:00 (8:01) (Class 5) (0-75,75) 4-Y-0+ **£2,914** (£867; £433; £216) **Stalls** Low

Form				RPR
0-33	1		**Munsarim (IRE)**29 1859 4-9-7 **75** JoeFanning 9 (Keith Dalgleish) *trckd ldr: led over 2f out: sn rdn: jst hld on* **11/4**1	82
-250	2	*nse*	**Media Stars**8 2462 6-7-13 **56** oh6 JamesSullivan(3) 6 (Robert Johnson) *trckd ldrs: t.k.h: wnt 2nd over 1f out: kpt on: jst hld* **28/1**	63
16-2	3	¾	**Grand Diamond (IRE)**50 1072 7-8-10 **67** GaryBartley(3) 4 (Jim Goldie) *hld up towards rr: hdwy 5f out: styd on to take 4th jst ins fnl f: edgd lft and no ex last 50yds* **11/2**2	72
0050	4	*shd*	**Dean Iarracht (IRE)**15 2251 5-8-3 **60** ow3 PaulPickard(3) 5 (Tracy Waggott) *s.s and reminders sn after s: in rr: hdwy on outer over 2f out: wnt handy 3rd appr fnl f: no ex clsng stages* **14/1**	65+
4516	5	1¾	**Rosbay (IRE)**9 2414 7-9-7 **75** DuranFentiman 7 (Tim Easterby) *led tl over 2f out: wknd over 1f out* **11/2**2	77
0/0-	6	1¼	**Herrera (IRE)**397 1751 6-8-5 **66** LauraBarry(7) 10 (Richard Fahey) *hld up in mid-div: nt clr run over 2f out and over 1f out: styd on fnl 150yds* **9/1**	65+
00-0	7	*nk*	**That'll Do Nicely (IRE)**49 1390 8-9-6 **74** TomEaves 12 (Nicky Richards) *hld up in mid-div: hdwy 5f out: rdn over 3f out: kpt on ins fnl f* **13/2**3	73
600	8	1¾	**Amtired**16 2218 5-8-2 **56** oh1 (b1) PaulHanagan 11 (Brian Ellison) *trckd ldrs: hung lft and lost pl over 1f out* **9/1**	51
21-0	9	3¼	**Rubi Dia**14 2320 4-8-7 **64** AndrewHeffernan(3) 2 (Kevin M Prendergast) *hld up in rr: effrt over 3f out: nvr a factor: wknd over 1f out* **8/1**	53

2m 11.08s (-0.82) **Going Correction** 0.0s/f (Good) **9 Ran SP% 112.0**
Speed ratings (Par 103): **103,102,102,102,100 99,99,98,95**
toteswingers:1&2:£20.50, 2&3:£20.20, 1&3:£3.00 CSF £83.51 CT £393.18 TOTE £3.40: £1.10, £6.90, £1.90; EX 74.30.
Owner Joseph Leckie & Sons Ltd **Bred** Shadwell Estate Company Limited **Trained** Carluke, South Lanarkshire

FOCUS
Another steadily run race and it paid to be up with the pace and the performance of the fourth is worth marking up slightly. The form is not rated too positively otherwise, with the winner to his recent best the safest option.

2735 ALZHEIMER'S SOCIETY MAIDEN STKS 1m 2f 32y
8:30 (8:35) (Class 5) 3-Y-0+ **£2,914** (£867; £433; £216) **Stalls** Low

Form				RPR
23	1		**Miss Aix**41 1549 3-8-7 0 HayleyTurner 3 (Michael Bell) *trckd ldrs: effrt over 3f out: styd on to ld appr fnl f: hld on nr fin* **7/4**1	75
0	2	*hd*	**Covert Desire**18 2185 3-8-12 0 AhmedAjtebi 5 (Mahmood Al Zarooni) *chsd ldrs: styd on to go 2nd last 100yds: struck over hd by rival's whip: jst hld nr fin* **11/2**3	80
2	3	3	**End Or Beginning**21 2104 3-8-12 0 JamieSpencer 10 (Paul Cole) *s.s: jnd ldr after 2f: drvn and hung lft 3f out: kpt on same pce last 100yds* **4/1**2	74
0-20	4	3½	**Lucky Legs (IRE)**51 1339 3-8-8 75 ow1 RobertWinston 4 (B W Hills) *led: qcknd over 3f out: hdd appr fnl f: sn wknd* **28/1**	63
6	5	*nk*	**Maricopa**22 2068 3-8-5 0 (t) AntiocoMurgia(7) 6 (Mahmood Al Zarooni) *trckd ldrs: drvn over 3f out: hung lft and outpcd over 1f out* **11/1**	66
32	6	1½	**Laashak (USA)**28 1897 3-8-12 0 TadhgO'Shea 9 (Sir Michael Stoute) *hld up in midfield: drvn and outpcd 3f out: kpt on ins fnl f* **13/2**	63
46	7	*hd*	**Jonny Delta**22 2045 4-9-8 0 GaryBartley(3) 7 (Jim Goldie) *in rr: outpcd over 3f out: kpt on ins fnl f* **50/1**	63
4	8	*nk*	**Amaze**22 2045 3-8-12 0 PhillipMakin 1 (Brian Ellison) *in rr: drvn over 3f out: kpt on ins fnl f* **28/1**	62
05	9	10	**Indycisive**8 2461 3-8-9 0 PaulPickard(3) 8 (Simon West) *s.i.s: a in rr: bhd fnl 3f* **100/1**	42

2m 11.38s (-0.52) **Going Correction** 0.0s/f (Good)
WFA 3 from 4yo 13lb **9 Ran SP% 112.3**
Speed ratings (Par 103): **102,101,99,96,96 95,95,94,86**
toteswingers:1&2:£2.50, 2&3:£4.80, 1&3:£1.70 CSF £11.14 TOTE £2.50: £1.30, £2.60, £1.30; EX 13.60.
Owner J L C Pearce **Bred** J L C Pearce **Trained** Newmarket, Suffolk

FOCUS
This was an above-average 3-y-o-plus maiden for the time of year. The form is not sure to prove reliable but is best rated around the placed horses.

2736 HAAS-TEK/PPM LTD SERVICES & SALES H'CAP 5f
9:00 (9:02) (Class 5) (0-75,75) 3-Y-O **£2,914** (£867; £433; £216) **Stalls** Centre

Form				RPR
11-0	1		**Cinderkamp**17 2199 3-9-7 **75** JamieSpencer 2 (Edward Vaughan) *stdd s: in rr: hdwy and swtchd lft 2f out: led appr fnl f: hdd ins fnl 150yds: edgd rt and kpt on to ld post* **9/4**1	84
4-53	2	*shd*	**Crimson Cloud**12 2365 3-9-0 **68** PaulHanagan 1 (Richard Fahey) *t.k.h: smooth hdwy over 1f out: sn stmbld: led narrowly last 150yds: hdd post* **5/2**2	76+
6-43	3	3¼	**Tilliemint (IRE)**7 2498 3-8-11 **65** (e1) DuranFentiman 6 (Tim Easterby) *w ldrs: kpt on same pce fnl f* **6/1**	61
460-	4	2¾	**Hygrove Gal**198 7493 3-8-10 **64** TomEaves 3 (Bryan Smart) *w ldrs: wknd fnl f* **12/1**	50
6214	5	1	**Beautiful Day**14 2294 3-8-12 **66** PhillipMakin 4 (Kevin Ryan) *led tl appr fnl f: sn wknd* **10/3**3	48
0-00	6	13	**Bellemere**11 2391 3-8-5 **66** DavidSimmonson(7) 5 (Michael Easterby) *chsd ldrs: outpcd and lost pl over 2f out: sn bhd: eased ins fnl f* **20/1**	—

59.78 secs (-1.32) **Going Correction** -0.25s/f (Firm) **6 Ran SP% 109.2**
Speed ratings (Par 99): **100,99,94,90,88 67**
toteswingers:1&2:£1.40, 2&3:£2.50, 1&3:£2.60 CSF £7.67 TOTE £2.40: £1.10, £2.30; EX 7.40.
Owner Ali Saeed **Bred** Baron F Von Oppenheim **Trained** Newmarket, Suffolk

FOCUS
An uncompetitive event to conclude proceedings, the front two coming clear. The first two could rate higher but there are doubta baout the next three home.
T/Plt: £29.20 to a £1 stake. Pool of £75,620.71 - 1885.17 winning units. T/Qpdt: £9.30 to a £1 stake. Pool of £5,470.37 - 432.90 winning units. WG

2737 - 2743a (Foreign Racing) - See Raceform Interactive

2446 LONGCHAMP (R-H)
Saturday, June 4

OFFICIAL GOING: Turf: good

2744a PRIX DU PALAIS-ROYAL (GROUP 3) (3YO+) (TURF) 7f
2:35 (12:00) 3-Y-0+ **£34,482** (£13,793; £10,344; £6,896; £3,448)

			RPR
1		**Sahpresa (USA)**174 7853 6-9-6 0 GregoryBenoist 8 (Rod Collet, France) *settled at rr of field: mde swift prog on outside 1 1/2f out: qcknd wl to cl on ldrs 100yds out: swept by to ld 25 yds out: easily* **23/5**2	120
2	1½	**Moonlight Cloud**34 1719 3-8-6 0 DavyBonilla 4 (F Head, France) *settled towards rr: rdn 1f out: qcknd wl on outside to ld 100yds out: r.o wl but no answer to eventual wnr cl home* **9/10**1	108
3	1	**Evaporation (FR)**34 4-9-0 0 OlivierPeslier 2 (C Laffon-Parias, France) *settled 3rd: qcknd to ld 1f out: hdd 100yds out: styd on wl* **73/10**	107
4	*shd*	**African Story**15 4-9-3 0 MaximeGuyon 1 (A Fabre, France) *settled 4th: short of room whn making move 1 1/2f out: r.o wl whn in the clr fnl 100yds* **6/1**3	110
5	2	**Pink Gin (FR)**30 1841 4-9-3 0 FranckBlondel 3 (J-M Beguigne, France) *settled 5th: nt qckn 1 1/2f out: styd on fnl f* **20/1**	104
6	3	**As De Trebol (USA)**13 5-9-3 0 BFayosMartin 7 (M Delcher-Sanchez, Spain) *led fr s: set gd pce: led 2f out: hdd 1 1/2f out: no ex* **12/1**	96
7	1½	**Pyrrha**28 1893 5-9-0 0 IoritzMendizabal 6 (Chris Wall) *settled in 2nd: rdn 1 1/2f out: no ex: fdd fnl f* **14/1**	89
8	6	**Personified (GER)**37 1647 4-9-0 0 GaryCarter 5 (Mme J Bidgood, France) *broke slowly and a in rr: no ex in st* **32/1**	73

1m 19.2s (-1.50)
WFA 3 from 4yo+ 10lb **8 Ran SP% 119.0**
WIN (incl. 1 euroi stake): 5.60. PLACES: 1.50, 1.20, 1.60. DF: 4.50. SF: 13.80.
Owner Teruya Yoshida **Bred** Douglas McIntyre **Trained** France

NOTEBOOK
Sahpresa(USA) settled this with an impressive turn of foot and may now head for another crack at the Windsor Forest, in which she finished a disappointing eighth last year.
Moonlight Cloud, who appeared not to get home when favourite for the 1000 Guineas, was dropping back to 7f and appeared to do everthing right, only to be swamped for pace by the older winner well inside the last furlong.
Pyrrha tracked the early pace, but didn't get home.

2745 - 2748a (Foreign Racing) - See Raceform Interactive

2657 BADEN-BADEN (L-H)
Sunday, June 5

OFFICIAL GOING: Turf: good

2749a GROSSER PREIS DER BADISCHEN UNTERNEHMEN (GROUP 2) (4YO+) (TURF) 1m 3f
4:25 (12:00) 4-Y-0+
£34,482 (£13,362; £5,603; £3,448; £2,155; £1,293)

RPR

1 **Night Magic (GER)**28 1931 5-9-3 0 .... KKerekes 4 114
(W Figge, Germany) *broke fast to ld: set gd pce: led into st: r.o wl u.p defying ev chal to hold on narrowly* **8/5**1

2 nk **Russian Tango (GER)**28 4-9-0 0 .... EPedroza 7 110
(A Wohler, Germany) *broke wl: settled in 3rd pursuing ldr: mde move early in st: r.o wl: engaged wnr in battle gng down narrowly cl home* **11/5**2

3 1 1/2 **Durban Thunder (GER)**28 5-9-0 0 .... THellier 3 107
(T Mundry, Germany) *broke wl: racd freely alongside eventual wnr: first to chal in st: kpt on wl: no ex ins fnl f* **11/2**

4 1 1/4 **Val Mondo (GER)**28 1931 4-9-0 0 .... AHelfenbein 9 105
(Uwe Ostmann, Germany) *racd in midfield on outer: rdn early in st: flattered briefly 1 1/2f out: no ex pce to catch ldrs: r.o* **5/1**3

5 2 1/2 **Altair Star (IRE)**42 1554 4-9-0 0 .... FilipMinarik 5 101
(P Schiergen, Germany) *settled in 4th: mde prog to r cl to ldrs down bkst: r.o wl in st wout threatening* **108/10**

6 3/4 **Court Canibal**37 1670 6-9-0 0 .... ASuborics 1 99
(M Delzangles, France) *a the bkmarker: passed btn horses towards fin* **195/10**

7 4 1/2 **Nicea (GER)**21 4-8-10 0 .... AStarke 8 87
(P Schiergen, Germany) *settled in midfield: fnd no ex in st* **116/10**

8 2 1/2 **Wheredreamsare**357 3018 4-9-0 0 .... ADeVries 2 87
(W Figge, Germany) *racd in midfield: styd on in st wout threatening* **124/10**

2m 19.19s (-0.08) **8** Ran SP% **130.5**
WIN (incl. 10 euro stake): 26. PLACES: 12, 13, 15. SF: 69.
Owner Stall Salzburg **Bred** Gestut Etzean **Trained** Germany

2279 CHANTILLY (R-H)
Sunday, June 5

OFFICIAL GOING: Turf: soft

2750a PRIX DE ROYAUMONT (GROUP 3) (3YO FILLIES) (TURF) 1m 4f
1:20 (12:00) 3-Y-0 **£34,482** (£13,793; £10,344; £6,896; £3,448)

RPR

1 **Testosterone (IRE)**21 2135 3-9-0 0 .... StephanePasquier 9 107
(P Bary, France) *chsd ldrs: moved up to ld after 2f: qcknd 2 l clr appr 1 1/2f out: r.o wl fnl f* **7/1**3

2 3 **Chegei Has (FR)**25 3-9-0 0 .... IoritzMendizabal 1 102
(J-P Gallorini, France) *trckd ldr early: settled in 5th after 3f: r.o u.p appr fnl f: wnt 2nd 110yds out: kpt on wl but no ch w wnr* **14/1**

3 2 **Campanillas (IRE)**21 2135 3-9-0 0 .... GeraldMosse 3 99
(C Laffon-Parias, France) *chsng ldng gp: racing 4th or 5th much of the way: 3rd and styng on 2f out: sn rdn: nt qckn fnl f* **14/1**

4 2 1/2 **Avongrove**21 2135 3-9-0 0 .... MickaelBarzalona 5 95
(A Fabre, France) *settled in last pl: hdwy on outside over 2 1/2f out: tk 4th 50yds out: nt pce to chal* **5/2**1

5 1/2 **Gorgeous Sixty (FR)**25 3-9-0 0 .... OlivierPeslier 7 94
(Y Fouin, France) *prom on outside racing keenly: settled after 4f: 2nd and rdn 1 1/2f out: nt qckn: wknd fnl 100yds* **10/1**

6 3/4 **Jehannedarc (IRE)**29 1922 3-9-0 0 .... MaximeGuyon 6 93
(A De Royer-Dupre, France) *v reluctant to enter stalls: broke wl enough: racd in 6th: pushed along over 2f out: sn rdn: no imp fnl f* **8/1**

7 1 1/2 **Ozeta (FR)**21 2135 3-9-0 0 .... AnthonyCrastus 2 90
(E Lellouche, France) *led: hdd after 2f: racd in 3rd: rdn 2 1/2f out: nt qckn: fdd fnl f* **3/1**2

8 snk **Bernieres (IRE)**29 1922 3-9-0 0 .... Christophe-PatriceLemaire 8 90
(Mme Pia Brandt, France) *w.w towards rr: nvr in contention* **12/1**

9 1 **Mourasana**35 3-9-0 0 .... JohanVictoire 10 89
(C Lerner, France) *a bhd: nvr a factor* **16/1**

10 1/2 **Triveni (FR)**14 2342 3-9-0 0 .... AlexisBadel 4 88
(Mme M Bollack-Badel, France) *a bhd: n.d* **20/1**

2m 31.2s (0.20) **Going Correction** +0.275s/f (Good) **10** Ran SP% **117.9**
Speed ratings: **110,108,106,105,104 104,103,103,102,102**
WIN (incl. 1 euro stake): 7.40. PLACES: 2.70, 3.90, 4.60. DF: 44.30. SF: 69.80.
Owner Ecurie La Boetie **Bred** S C E A La Poterie **Trained** Chantilly, France

NOTEBOOK
Testosterone(IRE) won this impressively and will now take a step up in class in the Prix de Malleret.

2751a PRIX DU JOCKEY CLUB (GROUP 1) (3YO COLTS & FILLIES) (TURF) 1m 2f 110y
2:08 (12:00) 3-Y-0 **£738,879** (£295,603; £147,801; £73,836; £36,982)

RPR

1 **Reliable Man**27 3-9-2 0 .... GeraldMosse 10 123
(A De Royer-Dupre, France) *settled towards rr: hdwy fr 2f out: swtchd lft appr 1 1/2f out: styd on u.p and edgd rt: to ld 100yds out: styd on wl* **16/1**

2 3/4 **Bubble Chic (FR)**29 1923 3-9-2 0 .... IoritzMendizabal 2 121
(G Botti, Italy) *trckd ldng gp: disputing 5th over 3f out: qcknd to ld 1 1/2f out: r.o u.p: hdd 100yds out: no ex* **12/1**

3 2 **Baraan (FR)**56 1265 3-9-2 0 .... Christophe-PatriceLemaire 1 120+
(J-C Rouget, France) *dwlt: sn rdn but at least 15 l adrift of next runner: mde gradual hdwy to be on terms w next-to-last runner 3 1/2f out: pushed along and hdwy 2f out: styng on whn n.m.r and swtchd rt ins fnl f: nvr nre* **9/2**1

4 nse **Colombian (IRE)**32 1810 3-9-2 0 .... WilliamBuick 4 117
(John Gosden) *prom early: sn settled in midfield: on rail disputing 7th over 3f out: rdn and styng on 1 1/2f out: 3rd 150yds out: no ex fnl 50yds: lost 3rd cl home* **25/1**

5 nse **Tin Horse (IRE)**21 2139 3-9-2 0 .... ThierryJarnet 12 117
(D Guillemin, France) *settled in midfield: 9th or 10th on outside 3f out: rdn and r.o 1 1/2f out: edgd rt and kpt on same pce fnl f* **6/1**2

6 3 **Prairie Star (FR)**21 2136 3-9-2 0 .... AnthonyCrastus 9 111
(E Lellouche, France) *chsd ldng gp: 4th or 5th much of the way: 3rd and ev ch 2 1/2f out: rdn and nt qckn fnl 1 1/2f* **12/1**

7 1/2 **Glaswegian**21 2139 3-9-2 0 .... StephanePasquier 5 110+
(P Bary, France) *settled towards rr: 14th w 3f to run: rdn over 2f out: styd on fnl f: nt pce to get on terms* **25/1**

8 1/2 **Roderic O'Connor (IRE)**15 2324 3-9-2 0 .... RyanMoore 3 109
(A P O'Brien, Ire) *a prominewnt: cl 4th 2 12f out: effrt to chal 1 1/2f out: wknd fnl 125yds* **9/2**1

9 1/2 **Casamento (IRE)**36 1686 3-9-2 0 .... FrankieDettori 7 108
(Mahmood Al Zarooni) *sn led: rdn 2 1/2f out: hdd appr fnl 1 1/2f: wknd fnl f* **8/1**3

10 1 **Absolutly Yes (FR)**27 1965 3-9-2 0 .... MickaelBarzalona 13 106
(Y-M Porzier, France) *a.p: disp 2nd nring 1 1/2f out: sn rdn and btn: wknd fnl f* **25/1**

11 1/2 **Grand Vent (IRE)**21 2136 3-9-2 0 .... MaximeGuyon 8 105
(A Fabre, France) *w.w in fnl few: hdwy on outside to be in midfield ins last 3f: sn rdn: no imp* **12/1**

12 2 **Nobel Winner (FR)**27 1965 3-9-2 0 .... OlivierPeslier 6 101
(J-M Beguigne, France) *racd in midfield: 8th whn sltly hmpd and hind legs slipped over 3 1/2f out: rdn and nt qckn over 1 1/2f out: sn btn* **40/1**

13 1 1/2 **Veter (FR)**27 3-9-2 0 .... ThierryThulliez 14 98
(N Clement, France) *nvr beyond mid-div: no real impact* **66/1**

14 1/2 **Sandagiyr (FR)**16 2279 3-9-2 0 .... JMurtagh 16 97
(A De Royer-Dupre, France) *chsd ldng gp: 5th 3f out: sn rdn and btn* **14/1**

15 4 **Crackerjack King (IRE)**29 1920 3-9-2 0 .... FabioBranca 11 90
(S Botti, Italy) *racd in fnl 3rd: nvr in contention* **8/1**3

16 6 **Saint Desir**29 1923 3-9-2 0 .... JohanVictoire 15 78
(E Lellouche, France) *nvr a factor* **100/1**

2m 7.70s (-1.10) **Going Correction** +0.275s/f (Good) **16** Ran SP% **125.0**
Speed ratings: **115,114,113,112,112 110,110,110,109,108 108,107,106,105,102 98**
WIN (incl. 1 euro stake): 8.90. PLACES: 2.70, 3.50, 2.20. DF: 59.00. SF: 115.40.
Owner Pride Racing Club **Bred** N P Bloodstock Ltd **Trained** Chantilly, France

FOCUS
A seventh running of this French Classic over its shortened distance and which has produced some big fields, which has counted against high drawn runners who race prominently. The pace was notably strong early but once again there was a lull into the tricky bend at the end of the long downhill run in the back straight, before the dash from the home bend.

NOTEBOOK
Reliable Man maintained his unbeaten record in impressive style. He betrayed his inexperience only when hitting the front and jinking left to lessen the winning distance. Dropped out to counter his high draw, he showed racecraft to weave through the pack to deliver his challenge, and is worth rating a clearer winner and one likely to stay 1m4f if asked. The Grand Prix de Paris is an intended follow-up.
Bubble Chic(FR) finished nicely clear of the rest on his first try at this trip and this Italian challenger did nothing wrong in defeat, doing by far the best of those up with the early pace, strongly suggesting he is on the upgrade this year and deserving of a Group 1 success.
Baraan(FR) was effectively out of the race within 100m, fluffing the start, giving his rivals some ten lengths start and, although attached at the back when the pace eased, he was again on the back foot in the dash home. He lengthened well to get third but sticking to the inside rail did not make any more ground on Reliable Man, who had to switch wider from just in front of him.
Colombian(IRE), another inexperienced runner with just a Chester maiden win in three runs, can be rated better than the bare form and connections feel sure easier ground will bring further improvement. He was up with the pace but got shuffled back into the bend before picking up again in the straight and this is probably as far as he wants to go.
Tin Horse(IRE) got stuck wide from his high draw, in midfield, and was wide in the straight, momentarily threatening a challenge as the winner made his move before stamina became an issue.
Prairie Star(FR), with form against the placed horses, was a shade disappointing.
Glaswegian promised more after a disappointing effort in the French Guineas.
Roderic O'Connor(IRE) increasingly gives the impression he needs to boss a race with his good Dewhurst run and Irish 2000 Guineas win coming in such circumstances. Here he was doing enough early in third and while he edged ahead up the rail early in the straight he was soon a spent force. He got very warm before the race and it might be the race came soon enough after his Classic win.
Casamento(IRE) travelled easily enough in leading at a strong pace but the Racing Post Trophy winner was again disappointing in fading as the race developed in the final 2f. Connections are keeping the faith but stamina does not look a strong suit.
Grand Vent(IRE) could never land a blow from the back and was another to come very wide in the straight before plugging on, suggesting further on easier ground will see him in a better light in time.

2752a PRIX DE SANDRINGHAM (GROUP 2) (3YO FILLIES) (TURF) 1m
2:50 (12:00) 3-Y-0 **£63,879** (£24,655; £11,767; £7,844; £3,922)

RPR

1 **Immortal Verse (IRE)**21 2137 3-8-11 0 .... OlivierPeslier 3 111
(Robert Collet, France) *racd freely towards rr: 6th whn swtchd lft and bmpd Espirita over 1 1/2f out: qcknd fnl f and led on outside 60yds fr home* **8/1**

2 1/2 **Mixed Intention (IRE)**21 2137 3-8-11 0 .... Christophe-PatriceLemaire 5 110
(F Vermeulen, France) *racd in 3rd: qcknd ins fnl f to ld 100yds out: hdd 60yds fr home: no ex* **4/1**2

3 2 1/2 **Peinture Abstraite**25 3-8-11 0 .... GeraldMosse 7 104
(A De Royer-Dupre, France) *settled in 4th or 5th: pushed along 2f out: styd on ins fnl f: nt pce to chal first two* **9/2**3

4 3/4 **Sunday Nectar (IRE)**54 3-8-11 0 .... IoritzMendizabal 2 103
(X Thomas-Demeaulte, France) *led: qcknd 3 l clr over 2f out: strly rdn ins fnl f: hdd 100yds out: fdd* **11/2**

5 1 1/2 **Cerveza**86 841 3-8-11 0 .... MaximeGuyon 1 99
(Mme Pia Brandt, France) *racd in 4th or 5th: last 3f out: kpt on at same pce fr 1 1/2f out* **14/1**

6 3 **Perfect Tribute**[29] 1893 3-8-11 0 .... LukeMorris 4 92
(Clive Cox) *plld hrd on heels of ldr: 2nd 2f out: sn pushed along: nt qckn: fdd* **4/1**[2]

7 3/4 **Espirita (FR)**[21] 2137 3-8-11 0 .... AnthonyCrastus 6 90
(E Lellouche, France) *last: 5th on outside whn bmpd by eventual wnr over 1 1/2f out: sn rdn: no imp fnl f* **3/1**[1]

1m 39.2s (1.20) **Going Correction** +0.275s/f (Good) 7 Ran SP% **116.3**
Speed ratings: **105,104,102,101,99 96,96**
WIN (incl. 1 euro stake): 6.90. PLACES: 3.30, 3.40. SF: 35.40.
Owner R C Strauss **Bred** Kilfrush Stud **Trained** Chantilly, France

NOTEBOOK
Immortal Verse(IRE) quickened up well to win and may now head for the Coronation Stakes.
Perfect Tribute paid for pulling too hard early.

2753a GRAND PRIX DE CHANTILLY (GROUP 2) (4YO+) (TURF) 1m 4f
3:25 (12:00) 4-Y-0+ **£63,879** (£24,655; £11,767; £7,844; £3,922)

RPR

1 **Silver Pond (FR)**[36] 1708 4-8-11 0 .... OlivierPeslier 4 119
(C Laffon-Parias, France) *unruly s bef being loaded: trckd ldr: disp ld 1 1/2f out: hanging appr fnl f: r.o to ld cl home* **8/1**

2 hd **Behkabad (FR)**[211] 7366 4-9-4 0 .... Christophe-PatriceLemaire 1 125
(J-C Rouget, France) *broke wl and racd in 3rd: hdwy on ins to dispute ld 1 1/2f out: r.o but hdd cl home* **6/4**[1]

3 4 **Allied Powers (IRE)**[30] 1851 6-8-11 0 .... IoritzMendizabal 3 112
(Michael Bell) *settled in 5th: rdn and outpcd over 2 1/2f out: styd on wl fnl 150yds: nt pce to chal first two* **12/1**

4 hd **Ley Hunter (USA)**[36] 1708 4-8-11 0 .... MickaelBarzalona 5 112
(A Fabre, France) *last: tk clsr order 3f out: rdn and kpt on fr 1 1/2f out: nvr nrr* **5/1**[2]

5 nk **Ivory Land (FR)**[31] 1842 4-8-11 0 .... GeraldMosse 8 111
(A De Royer-Dupre, France) *racd in 6th: plld wd and rdn to go 3rd fnl 100yds: nt qckn u.p* **5/1**[2]

6 1/2 **Poet**[10] 2439 6-8-11 0 .... AdamKirby 2 110
(Clive Cox) *upset in stalls: sn led: hdd 1 1/2f out: sn strly rdn and nt qckn: wknd and lost 3rd fnl 100yds* **6/1**[3]

7 5 **Celtic Celeb (IRE)**[31] 1842 4-9-2 0 .... ThierryThulliez 6 107
(F Doumen, France) *a bhd: wl btn fnl 1 1/2f* **20/1**

8 8 **Wiener Walzer (GER)**[31] 1842 5-8-11 0 .... MaximeGuyon 7 90
(A Fabre, France) *racd in 4th: tk clsr order 3 1/2f out to go cl 3rd w 3f to run: rdn and fnd nthing ins fnl 2f: wl btn whn eased fnl f* **16/1**

2m 29.6s (-1.40) **Going Correction** +0.275s/f (Good) 8 Ran SP% **117.1**
Speed ratings: **115,114,112,112,111 111,108,102**
WIN (incl. 1 euro stake): 8.80. PLACES: 2.30, 1.50, 2.50. DF: 15.80. SF: 38.20.
Owner Haras Du Quesnay **Bred** Haras Du Quesnay **Trained** Chantilly, France

NOTEBOOK
Silver Pond(FR) battled on well to score despite having played up beforehand. He is likely to go for the Grand Prix de Saint-Cloud next.
Behkabad(FR), last seen finishing fourth in the Arc, just failed to make a winning return but this was still a good effort considering he was conceding weight all round. He may take the winner on again in the Grand Prix de Saint-Cloud or go for the King George.
Allied Powers(IRE) ran creditably in his bid to win this race for the second year in a row.
Poet, fresh from his cracking effort against Workforce, didn't get home this time and perhaps he found this trip too much in the ground or it came too soon after Sandown.

2754a PRIX DU GROS-CHENE (GROUP 2) (3YO+) (TURF) 5f
4:00 (12:00) 3-Y-0+ **£63,879** (£24,655; £11,767; £7,844; £3,922)

RPR

1 **Wizz Kid (IRE)**[59] 1207 3-8-6 0 .... IoritzMendizabal 7 113
(Robert Collet, France) *racd in midfield: swtchd to rail 1/2-way: hdwy and 4th ins fnl 1 1/2f: r.o wl on stands' rail to ld cl home* **25/1**

2 hd **Prohibit**[15] 2297 6-9-2 0 .... (p) JimCrowley 4 118
(Robert Cowell) *trckd ldrs stands' side: r.o wl to ld briefly 50yds out: hdd cl home* **7/1**[2]

3 shd **Inxile (IRE)**[21] [illegible] 6-9-2 0 .... (p) AdrianNicholls 1 118
(David Nicholls) *sn led on stands' rail: drifted rt ins fnl 1 1/2f: hdd 50yds out: no ex* **7/2**[1]

4 1 1/2 **Hamish McGonagall**[15] 2297 6-9-2 0 .... DavidAllan 3 112
(Tim Easterby) *a.p: 2nd and rdn ins fnl 2f: kpt on at same pce fnl f* **11/1**

5 nse **Mar Adentro (FR)**[21] 2138 5-9-2 0 .... (p) JohanVictoire 6 112
(R Chotard, France) *settled towards rr: hdwy 2f out: 5th ins fnl f: nt qckn last 100yds* **11/1**

6 1 1/2 **Total Gallery (IRE)**[61] 5-9-2 0 .... GregoryBenoist 9 107
(M Delzangles, France) *racd towards rr: rdn 1/2-way: styd on fnl f: nt pce to chal* **9/1**

7 3/4 **Marchand D'Or (FR)**[245] 6608 8-9-2 0 .... DavyBonilla 10 104
(M Delzangles, France) *bhd: u.p over 2f out: styd on fnl f: nvr plcd to chal* **8/1**[3]

8 hd **Bluster (FR)**[21] 2138 5-9-2 0 .... WilliamBuick 5 103
(Robert Collet, France) *chsd ldrs in share of 4th: swtchd outside 2f out: sn rdn and no imp: fdd fnl f* **20/1**

9 1 1/2 **Fred Lalloupet**[21] 2138 4-9-2 0 .... OlivierPeslier 2 98
(D Smaga, France) *nvr beyond mid-div* **16/1**

10 nk **Cadeau For Maggi**[38] 1647 6-9-2 0 .... FabriceVeron 13 97
(H-A Pantall, France) *midfield: rdn and no imp fnl 2f* **14/1**

11 hd **Poppet's Treasure**[38] 1647 4-8-13 0 .... StephanePasquier 8 93
(R Pritchard-Gordon, France) *w ldrs: rdn and wknd fnl 2f* **20/1**

12 shd **Split Trois (FR)**[21] 2138 3-8-6 0 .... Christophe-PatriceLemaire 15 90
(Y De Nicolay, France) *in rr: nvr in contention* **7/1**[2]

13 2 1/2 **Piccadilly Filly (IRE)**[21] 2138 4-8-13 0 .... EddieCreighton 11 84
(Edward Creighton) *prom: rdn and wknd fnl 1 1/2f* **12/1**

14 3/4 **Lisselan Diva (IRE)**[36] 1687 5-8-13 0 .... WilliamsSaraiva 12 81
(Mme J Bidgood, France) *trckd ldng gp: rdn and no imp fnl 2f: sn bhd* **20/1**

58.40 secs (58.40)
WFA 3 from 4yo+ 7lb 14 Ran SP% **123.4**
WIN (incl. 1 euro stake): 20.40. PLACES: 5.10, 2.60, 1.80. DF: 100.60. SF: 241.20.
Owner Mme Maeve Mahony **Bred** Ballylinch Stud **Trained** Chantilly, France

NOTEBOOK
Wizz Kid(IRE) put in a sustained effort against the rail and that may have made the difference. There are no plans for him.
Prohibit appeared to have timed his effort just right, but then had the prize snatched from him. He may now go for the King's Stand.
Inxile(IRE) tried to make every yard in his bid for a four-timer and was only just run out of it.
Hamish McGonagall ran his usual honest race but is still to finish nearer than fourth in eight attempts in Group or Listed races.

2423 FOLKESTONE (R-H)
Monday, June 6

OFFICIAL GOING: Good to firm (8.3)
Wind: Virtually nil.

2755 THEPRIVATELINE.COM LADY RIDERS' H'CAP 5f
2:30 (2:30) (Class 6) (0-60,60) 4-Y-0+ **£1,648** (£507; £253) **Stalls** High

Form RPR

0334 1 **Commandingpresence (USA)**[2] 2720 5-9-11 50 .... MissSBrotherton 7 56
(John Bridger) *chsd ldrs: rdn ent fnl 2f: chsd ldr ins fnl f: kpt on to ld nr fin* **11/4**[1]

0-02 2 nk **Imaginary Diva**[28] 1938 5-9-3 49 .... MissKMargarson(7) 3 53
(George Margarson) *chsd ldr tl led 1/2-way: rdn 2f out: pushed along under hands and heels fnl f: hdd nr fin* **9/2**[3]

40 3 2 3/4 **Your Gifted (IRE)**[7] 2546 4-10-7 60 .... MissGAndrews 5 55
(Patrick Morris) *taken down early: t.k.h: hld up wl in tch: hdwy to chse ldr and rdn over 1f out: drvn and btn ins fnl f: wknd towards fin* **13/2**

0432 4 3 1/4 **The Tatling (IRE)**[21] 2164 14-10-1 59 .... MissHDavies(5) 1 42
(Milton Bradley) *bhd: outpcd 1/2-way: rdn ent fnl 2f: wnt modest 4th ent fnl f: nvr gng pce to trble ldrs* **5/1**

0-02 5 3 **Ishipink**[11] 2424 4-9-1 47 .... MissKClark(7) 6 19
(Ron Hodges) *taken down v early and led to s: led tl 1/2-way: wknd wl over 1f out* **7/1**

4653 6 4 1/2 **Radiator Rooney (IRE)**[11] 2424 8-9-9 53 ow2 MissBeckyBrisbourne(5) 2 —
(Patrick Morris) *taken down early: stdd s: hld up in last pair and r out towards centre: rdn: hung rt and btn 2f out* **4/1**[2]

61.42 secs (1.42) **Going Correction** +0.20s/f (Good) 6 Ran SP% **107.3**
Speed ratings (Par 101): **96,95,91,85,81 73**
Tote Swingers:1&2:£2.40, 2&3:£6.50, 1&3:£3.10 CSF £13.78 TOTE £3.00: £1.70, £2.60; EX 13.30.
Owner Mrs Liz Gardner **Bred** Lazy Lane Farms Inc **Trained** Liphook, Hants

FOCUS
This was a moderate amateur riders' handicap and form needs treating with extreme caution. As is so often the case at Folkestone, the rail seemed to provide an advantage. The form is rated negatively.

2756 FREE TRIAL WITH THEPRIVATELINE.COM CLAIMING STKS 6f
3:00 (3:00) (Class 6) 3-Y-0+ **£1,706** (£503; £252) **Stalls** High

Form RPR

1025 1 **Roodee Queen**[6] 2592 3-7-11 64 .... KieranO'Neill(5) 5 58
(Patrick Morris) *chsd ldrs: rdn to ld over 1f out: hld on wl u.p fnl f: ducked lft and uns rdr after fin* **3/1**[1]

3645 2 1 1/4 **Fawley Green**[10] 2452 4-9-2 58 .... (v) DarryllHolland 8 62
(William Muir) *dwlt: rdn along early: in tch: hdwy to chse ldrs 1/2-way: hrd drvn and chsd wnr ins fnl f: one pce after* **7/1**

0300 3 1 1/4 **Diamond Johnny G (USA)**[9] 2497 4-9-0 70 ow1 ...(t) AlanCreighton(3) 3 59
(Edward Creighton) *awkward leaving stalls and s.i.s: swtchd lft after s: bhd: hdwy over 1f out: nt clr run and swtchd rt ent fnl f: no imp fnl 100yds: wnt 3rd last strides* **10/1**

2332 4 hd **Miss Firefly**[7] 2554 6-8-4 56 .... (p) HarryBentley(5) 10 50
(Ron Hodges) *w ldr: led over 2f out: rdn and hung rt whn hdd over 1f out: wknd ins fnl f: lost 3rd last strides* **10/3**[2]

6505 5 2 1/2 **Stonecrabstomorrow (IRE)**[11] 2426 8-8-10 48 ow1(v) MarkCoumbe(5) 7 48
(Michael Attwater) *in tch towards rr: rdn and outpcd 1/2-way: rallied u.p and in tch 2f out: wknd ent fnl f* **66/1**

56-4 6 1 3/4 **Katy's Secret**[26] 2001 4-8-11 58 .... KieronFallon 9 30
(William Jarvis) *hld up in tch: rdn and effrt whn nt clr run over 1f out: drvn and no prog 1f out* **4/1**[3]

0000 7 2 1/4 **Crazy In Love**[28] 1933 3-8-1 46 .... (b) AdrianMcCarthy 6 27
(Olivia Maylam) *led tl over 2f out: wkng whn short of room ent fnl f* **66/1**

00-4 8 shd **Ghost Dancer**[21] 2161 7-9-6 50 .... (p) LiamKeniry 4 40
(Milton Bradley) *t.k.h: hld up in tch: swtchd rt and effrt 2f out: wknd ent fnl f* **25/1**

5026 9 1 1/2 **Dvinsky (USA)**[10] 2452 10-9-0 63 .... (b) JimmyQuinn 1 29
(Michael Squance) *dwlt: early reminders and sn chsng ldrs on outer: wknd u.p over 1f out* **11/2**

-004 10 10 **Public Image**[94] 761 5-8-9 41 .... HayleyTurner 2 —
(Jamie Poulton) *a struggling in rr: lost tch 1/2-way* **80/1**

1m 13.61s (0.91) **Going Correction** +0.20s/f (Good)
WFA 3 from 4yo+ 8lb 10 Ran SP% **113.1**
Speed ratings (Par 101): **101,99,97,97,94 91,88,88,86,73**
CSF £23.26 TOTE £3.30: £1.70, £2.50, £2.90; EX 24.10 Trifecta £407.00 Part won. Pool £550.08 - 0.79 winning units..Diamond Johnny G was the subject of a friendly claim. Roodee Queen was claimed by J. M. Bradley for £5,500.
Owner Chester Racing Club Ltd **Bred** Tom & Evelyn Yates **Trained** Tarporley, Cheshire

FOCUS
A moderate claimer, although the time was 0.5 seconds quicker than the following Class 4 handicap for older horses. They raced stands' side, but this time the rail was not decisive. The winner didn't need to run to her best.
Miss Firefly Official explanation: jockey said mare hung right throughout
Stonecrabstomorrow(IRE) Official explanation: jockey said gelding was unsuited by good to firm ground

2757 HP TECHNOLOGY H'CAP 6f
3:30 (3:31) (Class 4) (0-85,76) 3-Y-0 **£3,238** (£963; £481; £240) **Stalls** High

Form RPR

-131 1 **Pick A Little**[10] 2453 3-8-12 72 .... HarryBentley(5) 5 76
(Ron Hodges) *pressed ldrs: rdn and effrt 2f out: edging rt fr over 1f out: led ent fnl f: kpt on wl* **5/2**[2]

-266 2 2 **Roman Dancer (IRE)**[19] 2199 3-9-7 76 .... DarryllHolland 3 74
(John Gallagher) *hld up in tch: rdn and effrt ent fnl 2f: edging rt and chsd ldng pair ent fnl f: kpt on same pce: wnt 2nd nr fin* **11/4**[3]

2225 3 1/2 **Welsh Inlet (IRE)**[16] 2294 3-8-10 65 .... MarcHalford 4 61
(John Bridger) *led: hung rt fr 2f out: hdd ent fnl f: continued to hang bdly and ended up on far rail: lost 2nd nr fin* **13/2**

4300 4 5 **Toms River Tess (IRE)**[4] 2643 3-9-0 69 .... SamHitchcott 1 49
(Zoe Davison) *in tch: pushed along 1/2-way: drvn and unable qck 2f out: wknd ent fnl f* **10/1**

215 **5** *shd* **Shostakovich (IRE)**[21] 2147 3-9-3 **72**..........................(tp) JamesDoyle 2 52
(Sylvester Kirk) *pressed ldr tl rdn and unable qck ent fnl 2f: wknd ent fnl f* **9/4**[1]

1m 14.11s (1.41) **Going Correction** +0.20s/f (Good) **5** Ran SP% **108.4**
Speed ratings (Par 101): **98,95,94,88,87**
CSF £9.38 TOTE £3.50: £1.70, £1.60; EX 11.00.
Owner K B Hodges **Bred** D R Tucker **Trained** Charlton Mackrell, Somerset

FOCUS
Only five runners and an ordinary handicap for the class. The time was a disappointing 0.5 seconds slower than the earlier Class 6 claimer, although the ground may have been a bit more chewed up for this race. The field drifted away from the stands' rail in the closing stages. A length personal best from the winner.
Welsh Inlet(IRE) Official explanation: jockey said filly hung right throughout

2758 ROD MARTEN'S 80TH BIRTHDAY CELEBRATION H'CAP 2m 93y
4:00 (4:00) (Class 5) (0-75,75) 4-Y-O+ **£2,388** (£705; £352) **Stalls** High

Form RPR
-030 **1** **On Terms (USA)**[37] 1677 5-9-9 **74**.......................... KierenFallon 5 80
(Simon Dow) *sn led: qcknd clr w runner-up 5f out: rdn over 2f out: hdd ent fnl 2f: drvn: kpt on and styd pressing ldr tl led again fnl 100yds: styd on wl* **1/1**[1]
00-3 **2** *½* **Wild Desert (FR)**[30] 1901 6-9-10 **75**.......................... JamieSpencer 1 80
(Charlie Longsdon) *chsd wnr: upsides and qcknd clr w wnr 5f out: looked to be travelling best 3f out: rdn to ld narrowly ent fnl 2f: sn drvn: hdd and no ex fnl 100yds* **7/4**[2]
6 **3** *26* **Anak (IRE)**[46] 597 5-9-7 **72**..........................(b) EddieAhern 3 46
(Jim Best) *chsd ldrs: outpcd 5f out: 3rd and wl btn 3f out* **16/1**
02-5 **4** *6* **Swordsman (GER)**[10] 1282 9-9-1 **66**..........................(vt) ChrisCatlin 4 33
(Chris Gordon) *in tch in last: rdn and outpcd 5f out: lost tch 3f out* **7/1**[3]

3m 44.11s (6.91) **Going Correction** +0.15s/f (Good) **4** Ran SP% **104.7**
Speed ratings (Par 103): **88,87,74,71**
CSF £2.78 TOTE £1.30; EX 2.78.
Owner S Dow **Bred** Juddmonte Farms Inc **Trained** Epsom, Surrey

FOCUS
Only two counted from some way out and this is weak form. It's doubtful if the winner nedded to match his best.

2759 THEPRIVATELINE.COM "ASIAN H'CAP" STKS (H'CAP) 1m 4f
4:30 (4:30) (Class 6) (0-60,59) 4-Y-O+ **£1,706** (£503; £252) **Stalls** High

Form RPR
6022 **1** **Gems**[10] 2451 4-9-4 **56**.......................... ChrisCatlin 7 63
(Peter Hiatt) *mde all: rdn ent fnl 2f: edgd lft but styd on wl fnl f* **3/1**[1]
3024 **2** *1¾* **Vinces**[10] 2451 7-9-2 **54**.......................... HayleyTurner 5 57
(Tim McCarthy) *chsd wnr tl 5f out: rdn and n.m.r over 2f out: kpt on same pce u.p fr over 1f out* **11/2**
0306 **3** *shd* **Barbirolli**[4] 2638 9-8-4 **47**.......................... LauraPike[(5)] 2 50
(William Stone) *t.k.h: hld up in last pair: hdwy and chsng ldrs whn n.m.r jst over 2f out: rdn and disputing 3rd over 1f out: styd on same pce fnl f* **8/1**
30-4 **4** *hd* **Choral Festival**[14] 2372 5-9-7 **59**.......................... MarcHalford 1 62
(John Bridger) *chsd ldrs: rdn to chse wnr wl over 1f out: sn ev ch: no ex and btn ins fnl f: lost 2 pls nr finsh* **9/2**[2]
-244 **5** *4* **Musashi (IRE)**[39] 1636 6-9-7 **59**.......................... IanMongan 3 55
(Laura Mongan) *stdd s: hld up in last pair: gd hdwy to chse wnr 5f out tl wl over 1f out: wknd u.p ent fnl f* **3/1**[1]
3234 **6** *22* **Sunset Boulevard (IRE)**[46] 1508 8-9-0 **52**..........................(b) EddieAhern 4 24
(Jim Best) *hld up in tch in last trio: effrt to chse ldrs on outer over 2f out: wknd over 1f out: wl btn and eased fnl f* **5/1**[3]
6050 **7** *37* **Final Try**[10] 2451 4-8-2 **45**.......................... HarryBentley[(5)] 6 —
(Paddy Butler) *t.k.h: chsd ldrs tl dropped to last and drvn over 3f out: sn lost tch: t.o fnl 2f* **66/1**

2m 42.15s (1.25) **Going Correction** +0.15s/f (Good) **7** Ran SP% **112.8**
Speed ratings (Par 101): **101,99,99,99,96 82,57**
Tote Swingers:1&2:£2.70, 2&3:£6.60, 1&3:£5.40 CSF £19.37 TOTE £4.80: £1.30, £3.90; EX 13.00.
Owner R Robinson **Bred** Bishop Wilton Stud **Trained** Hook Norton, Oxon

FOCUS
A moderate handicap and weak, muddling form.
Gems Official explanation: two-day ban; careless riding (20th-21th June)

2760 THEPRIVATELINE.COM MEDIAN AUCTION MAIDEN STKS 1m 1f 149y
5:00 (5:01) (Class 6) 3-4-Y-O **£1,706** (£503; £252) **Stalls** Centre

Form RPR
05 **1** **Junoob**[32] 1836 3-8-13 0.......................... TadhgO'Shea 7 89+
(John Dunlop) *chsd ldr: rdn to chal over 2f out: led over 1f out: rn green but clr ent fnl f: eased towards fin: comf* **3/1**[3]
6 **2** *3¾* **Satwa Dream (IRE)**[12] 2403 4-9-7 81.......................... HarryBentley[(5)] 2 79
(Ed Dunlop) *chsd ldng pair: rdn and effrt on inner ent fnl 2f: outpcd by wnr over 1f out: wnt 2nd but no threat to wnr jst ins fnl f* **9/4**[2]
5-22 **3** *2¾* **Zakon (IRE)**[27] 1991 3-8-13 75.......................... KierenFallon 6 73
(Denis Coakley) *led: rdn and pressed jst over 2f out: hdd and nt pce of wnr over 1f out: wknd fnl f* **1/1**[1]
4 **4** *7* **Miss Excel**[11] 2419 4-9-7 0.......................... EddieCreighton 5 54
(Edward Creighton) *a chsng ldng trio: pushed along after 2f: rdn and struggling 3f out: wknd over 2f out* **40/1**
5 *5* **Oculist** 3-8-10 0.......................... SophieDoyle[(3)] 4 48+
(Jamie Osborne) *s.i.s: wl off the pce in rr: pushed along over 1f out: styd on past btn horses ins fnl f: n.d* **16/1**
0000 **6** *½* **Officer Lily (USA)**[17] 2271 4-9-0 42.......................... GeorgeanBuckell[(7)] 1 42
(John Best) *s.i.s: a wl off the pce in last trio: n.d* **100/1**
50-0 **7** *1¾* **Rowan Ridge**[14] 2371 3-8-13 69.......................... PatCosgrave 3 43
(Jim Boyle) *racd off the pce in midfield: shortlived effrt over 4f out: wl bhd fnl 3f* **40/1**
8 *1¾* **Dhampas**[226] 3-8-13 0.......................... IanMongan 8 40
(Jim Boyle) *s.i.s: a wl bhd: n.d* **33/1**

2m 4.13s (-0.77) **Going Correction** +0.15s/f (Good) **8** Ran SP% **120.5**
WFA 3 from 4yo 13lb
Speed ratings (Par 101): **109,106,103,98,94 93,92,91**
Tote Swingers:1&2:£2.20, 2&3:£1.40, 1&3:£1.50 CSF £10.72 TOTE £5.20: £1.40, £1.20, £1.10; EX 13.20 Trifecta £22.30 Pool £720.22 - 23.88 winning units..
Owner Hamdan Al Maktoum **Bred** Shadwell Estate Company Limited **Trained** Arundel, W Sussex

FOCUS
Hard to know exactly what to make of the form, but while it may be unwise to take the official marks of the runner-up and third too literally, the time was decent for a race of its type and this is above average form for the track.
T/Plt: £48.00 to a £1 stake. Pool: £70,089.31 - 1,065.58 winning tickets. T/Qpdt: £5.50 to a £1 stake. Pool: £4,041.64 - 540.70 winning tickets. SP

[2474]PONTEFRACT (L-H)
Monday, June 6

OFFICIAL GOING: Good to firm (good in places; 8.0)
Wind: Light, behind. Weather: Fine and dry

2761 JK AND JOEL BREAKFAST SHOW - RADIO AIRE MAIDEN AUCTION FILLIES' STKS 6f
6:30 (6:31) (Class 5) 2-Y-O **£2,388** (£705; £352) **Stalls** Low

Form RPR
0 **1** **Pendle Lady (IRE)**[51] 1414 2-8-4 0.......................... FrannyNorton 3 67
(Mark Brisbourne) *led 1f: cl up tl led again over 2f out: rdn and hung rt wl over 1f out: drvn ent fnl f: kpt on gamely* **40/1**
3 **2** *¾* **Majestic Zafeen**[25] 2017 2-8-3 0.......................... MartinHarley[(3)] 4 67
(Mick Channon) *t.k.h: trckd ldng pair: hdwy to chse wnr over 2f out: rdn to chal wl over 1f out: ev ch tl drvn and one pce ins fnl f* **6/5**[1]
3 *2½* **Sunny Side Up (IRE)** 2-8-6 0.......................... PaulHanagan 5 59+
(Richard Fahey) *trckd ldrs: hdwy over 2f out: rdn whn n.m.r and swtchd lft over 1f out: kpt on same pce* **3/1**[2]
552 **4** *12* **Yearbook**[6] 2587 2-8-4 0.......................... DuranFentiman 2 21
(Tim Easterby) *chsd ldrs: rdn along bef 1/2-way: sn outpcd* **7/1**
5 *¾* **In A Jiffy (IRE)** 2-8-4 0.......................... JoeFanning 6 19
(David Barron) *wnt rt s: t.k.h and led after 1f: pushed along: rn green and hdd over 2f out: rn v wd bnd 2f out: sn bhd* **10/3**[3]

1m 18.04s (1.14) **Going Correction** -0.10s/f (Good) **5** Ran SP% **108.5**
Speed ratings (Par 90): **88,87,83,67,66**
CSF £87.30 TOTE £29.80: £8.10, £1.10; EX 61.10.
Owner Peter Mort **Bred** Rossenarra Bloodstock Limited **Trained** Great Ness, Shropshire
■ Stewards' Enquiry : Franny Norton one-day ban; excessive use of whip (20th June)

FOCUS
After some rain early last week and about 30mm water applied over the past five days the ground was described as beautiful. False rail in place over last 6f 15ft from inside rail.

NOTEBOOK
Pendle Lady(IRE), a neat daughter of Chineur, had finished a well-beaten second-last on her debut at Ripon after a sluggish start. She had sore shins after. She was out first here and after hanging out on the turn for home she showed real grit to repel the favourite. It was no fluke and this speedy type will improve again and should be even better on a flat, right-handed track. (op 50-1)
Majestic Zafeen, third behind a subsequent winner on her debut at Newmarket, moved up on to the heels of the winner once in line for home but could not quite get to grips. She looked to have no excuse. (op Evens tchd 11-8 in a place)
Sunny Side Up(IRE) had to be switched left once in line for home to make her effort on the inside of the first two. She was by no means knocked about and will be suited by a step up to 7f. (op 11-4)
Yearbook, runner-up to an easy debutant winner on her third start at Redcar, never went the pace and may have to drop to claimers or sellers. (op 15-2 tchd 13-2)
In A Jiffy(IRE), attempting to become her trainer's sixth juvenile winner, was very well backed. With nothing on her outside she went right leaving the stalls but was soon upsides the winner. She completely failed to handle the home turn and was allowed to come home in her own time. She had clearly been showing plenty at home and is worth another chance on a straight course. (op 11-2 tchd 3-1)

2762 TONY BETHELL MEMORIAL H'CAP 2m 1f 22y
7:00 (7:00) (Class 4) (0-80,76) 4-Y-O+ **£4,079** (£1,214; £606; £303) **Stalls** Low

Form RPR
0-06 **1** **Wells Lyrical (IRE)**[17] 2262 6-9-10 **76**.......................... TomEaves 4 84
(Bryan Smart) *trckd ldng pair: hdwy to trck ldr 6f out: led 3f out: rdn wl over 1f out: drvn ent fnl f: kpt on wl* **4/1**[1]
06-0 **2** *5* **Hollins**[25] 2034 7-9-9 **75**.......................... FrederikTylicki 1 78
(Micky Hammond) *hld up in tch: hdwy 5f out: trckd ldrs 3f out: rdn to chse wnr over 1f out: drvn and one pce fnl f* **4/1**[1]
-204 **3** *½* **Pittodrie Star (IRE)**[18] 2220 4-9-8 **75**.......................... JimmyFortune 3 77
(Andrew Balding) *hld up in rr: hdwy 6f out: rdn along to chse ldrs over 3f out: drvn and kpt on same pce fr over 1f out* **9/2**[2]
-013 **4** *2½* **Spruzzo**[31] 1881 5-8-8 **60**.......................... KellyHarrison 2 59
(Chris Fairhurst) *trckd ldr: cl up after 8f: led over 6f out: rdn along and hdd 3f out: sn drvn and kpt on same pce* **13/2**
0301 **5** *4½* **Visions Of Johanna (USA)**[9] 2492 6-9-0 **66**.........(t) RobbieFitzpatrick 6 60
(Richard Guest) *hld up: hdwy 5f out: rdn along 3f out: n.d* **16/1**
62-3 **6** *½* **Maoi Chinn Tire (IRE)**[9] 2251 4-9-2 **69**..........................(p) StephenCraine 5 63
(Jennie Candlish) *trckd ldrs: smooth hdwy 6f out: effrt over 3f out: rdn over 2f out and sn btn* **5/1**[3]
1-00 **7** *25* **Dan Buoy (FR)**[48] 1458 8-8-13 **65**..........................(b) GregFairley 8 31
(Richard Guest) *led: rdn along over 7f out: hdd over 6f out: sn drvn and wknd* **8/1**
0003 **8** *5* **Jackson (BRZ)**[12] 2400 9-8-5 **57** oh5..........................(b) PaulHanagan 7 18
(Richard Guest) *trckd ldrs: effrt over 6f out: rdn along 5f out: sn wknd* **20/1**

3m 45.05s (0.45) **Going Correction** -0.10s/f (Good) **8** Ran SP% **109.9**
WFA 4 from 5yo+ 1lb
Speed ratings (Par 105): **94,91,91,90,88 87,76,72**
Tote Swingers:1&2:£1.10, 2&3:£2.10, 1&3:£3.40. CSF £18.39 CT £67.66 TOTE £3.60: £1.10, £2.00, £1.50; EX 16.80.
Owner M Barber **Bred** Brittas House Stud **Trained** Hambleton, N Yorks

FOCUS
A modest stayers' handicap run at a true pace. It was quite competitive and the winner posted his best form since late 2009.

2763 MR WOLF SPRINT H'CAP 6f
7:30 (7:30) (Class 3) (0-90,82) 3-Y-O **£6,670** (£1,984; £991; £495) **Stalls** Low

Form RPR
4-14 **1** **Louis The Pious**[18] 2216 3-8-13 **74**.......................... FrederikTylicki 7 85
(Kevin Ryan) *trckd ldrs on outer: hdwy 2f out: rdn to chal and edgd lft ent fnl f: kpt on to ld last 100yds* **9/1**
1-22 **2** *½* **Jade**[22] 2122 3-8-11 **72**.......................... PaulHanagan 5 81
(Ollie Pears) *cl up: led 2f out: rdn over 1f out: jnd and drvn ent fnl f: hdd and no ex last 100yds* **7/1**
12-0 **3** *5* **Breezolini**[14] 2363 3-9-1 **76**.......................... RobertWinston 3 69
(Richard Whitaker) *hld up in tch: hdwy on inner wl over 1f out: sn rdn and kpt on same pce ins fnl f* **25/1**
-21 **4** *½* **Foxtrot Hotel (IRE)**[16] 2311 3-9-7 **82**.......................... JimCrowley 6 73
(Peter Winkworth) *trckd ldrs: effrt over 2f out: rdn wl over 1f out: kpt on same pce* **15/8**[1]

4-31 **5** *4 ½* **King Ferdinand**[16] 2281 3-9-1 **76**.................................. JimmyFortune 1 53
(Andrew Balding) *cl up on inner: effrt over 2f out and sn rdn: drvn wl over 1f out: wknd appr fnl f* **7/2**[2]

31-2 **6** *nk* **Fieldgunner Kirkup (GER)**[14] 2363 3-9-7 **82**........... GrahamGibbons 4 58
(David Barron) *cl up: effrt over 2f out and ev ch tl drvn and wknd appr fnl f* **9/2**[3]

4100 **7** *16* **Strictly Pink (IRE)**[16] 2298 3-9-4 **79**.................................. LukeMorris 2 —
(Alan Bailey) *led: rdn along 3f out: hdd 2f out: sn drvn and wknd over 1f out: eased* **10/1**

1m 16.5s (-0.40) **Going Correction** -0.10s/f (Good) **7** Ran SP% **110.6**
Speed ratings (Par 103): **98,97,90,90,84 83,62**
Tote Swingers:1&2:£6.20, 2&3:£17.70, 1&3:£22.30 CSF £64.12 TOTE £14.30: £7.80, £3.10; EX 87.10.
Owner F Gillespie **Bred** Ashbrittle Stud **Trained** Hambleton, N Yorks

FOCUS
A highly competitive 3-y-o sprint, but the first two pulled clear in the end. They were the only ones to show their best. The time was nothing special, but was the pick of the three C&D races.

NOTEBOOK
Louis The Pious, too keen when fourth in a stronger event over 7f at Haydock on his first try in handicap company, was tapped for toe soon after the halfway mark. Making his effort on the wide outside he had to dig deep to get the better of the runner-up. He will go up as a result but should be competitive off his new mark. (op 14-1)
Jade, runner-up in an all-aged handicap at Ripon, went on once in line for home. She tended to duck and dive but in the end gave her all. She will be suited by a step up to 7f and deserves to go one better.
Breezolini, who is not that big, stepped up markedly on her return effort at Thirsk. (op 22-1)
Foxtrot Hotel(IRE), making his handicap debut from a mark of 82 after his Newbury maiden success, was quite keen and looked a shade unhappy on the ground in the home straight. The experience will not be lost on him. (op 9-4)
King Ferdinand, who did well to overcome traffic problems when getting off the mark in maiden company at Chester, found an initial mark of 76 too stiff. (op 3-1)
Fieldgunner Kirkup(GER), who had Breezolini well behind when narrowly beaten on his return at Thirsk, had to race from a 3lb higher mark. He looks ready for a step up to seven.
Strictly Pink(IRE), highly tried, dropped right out after setting the pace and may be ready for a mid-summer break. (op 8-1)

2764 RACING UK ON SKY CHANNEL 432 H'CAP — 1m 2f 6y
8:00 (8:00) (Class 4) (0-85,80) 3-Y-O **£4,079** (£1,214; £606; £303) **Stalls** Low

Form RPR

1-2 **1** **Seelo (USA)**[24] 2052 3-9-7 **80**.................................. WilliamBuick 6 96
(John Gosden) *mde all: qcknd clr over 2f out: easily* **9/4**[2]

025- **2** *7* **A Boy Named Suzi**[205] 7444 3-9-4 **77**.................................. LukeMorris 1 79
(James Eustace) *hld up: hdwy on inner over 2f out: rdn wl over 1f out: styd on u.p to take 2nd ins fnl f: no ch w wnr* **22/1**

4-13 **3** *½* **Ollon (USA)**[13] 2389 3-8-9 **68**.................................. PaulHanagan 2 69
(Richard Fahey) *trckd ldng pair: hdwy 3f out: rdn to chse wnr 2f out: sn drvn and one pce: lost 2nd ins fnl f* **11/1**

031- **4** *3 ¾* **Battery Power**[208] 7394 3-8-11 **70**.................................. TomEaves 3 64
(Mark H Tompkins) *chsd wnr: rdn along 3f out: drvn 2f out: sn one pce* **33/1**

5-04 **5** *2 ½* **Watercourse (IRE)**[20] 2185 3-9-3 **76**.................................. AndreaAtzeni 4 65
(Roger Varian) *hld up in tch: hdwy to trck ldrs 1/2-way: effrt over 3f out: rdn over 2f out: sn btn* **13/8**[1]

20-3 **6** *23* **Mutayaser**[19] 2188 3-9-4 **77**.................................. RichardHills 5 20+
(Sir Michael Stoute) *hld up in rr: sme hdwy 3f out: sn rdn and nvr a factor: bhd and eased fnl f* **11/4**[3]

2m 12.4s (-1.30) **Going Correction** -0.10s/f (Good) **6** Ran SP% **111.2**
Speed ratings (Par 101): **101,95,95,92,90 71**
Tote Swingers:1&2:£9.70, 2&3:£25.90, 1&3:£1.50 CSF £41.88 TOTE £3.50: £1.20, £6.70; EX 40.50.
Owner George Strawbridge **Bred** George Strawbridge Jr **Trained** Newmarket, Suffolk

FOCUS
A 3-y-o handicap with some noteworthy winners including Pipedreamer in 2007. The winner was improved but his market rivals disappointed and the second limits the form to an extent .
Watercourse(IRE) Official explanation: trainer said colt was unsuited by good to firm good in places going.
Mutayaser Official explanation: trainer was unable to offer any explanation as to poor run

2765 FATHERS DAY ON JUNE 19TH PACKAGES H'CAP — 6f
8:30 (8:31) (Class 5) (0-70,70) 3-Y-O+ **£2,388** (£705; £352) **Stalls** Low

Form RPR

0203 **1** **Apache Ridge (IRE)**[7] 2543 5-10-0 **70**....................(p) PaulMulrennan 11 81
(Keith Dalgleish) *dwlt: sn prom: effrt to ld 2f out: rdn over 1f out: drvn ins fnl f: hld on wl* **7/1**

2612 **2** *nk* **Close To The Edge (IRE)**[27] 1980 3-9-0 **67**............... MartinHarley[(3)] 9 75
(Alan McCabe) *chsd ldrs: hdwy over 2f out: rdn to chse wnr wl over 1f out: drvn ent fnl f: kpt on* **2/1**[1]

-056 **3** *3 ½* **Stamp Duty (IRE)**[18] 2215 3-9-6 **70**.................................. PaulHanagan 10 67
(Ollie Pears) *in tch on wd outside: pushed along 1/2-way: hdwy 2f out: rdn to chse ldng pair over 1f out: sn drvn and no imp fnl f* **5/1**[2]

-600 **4** *2 ½* **Accamelia**[10] 2464 5-9-0 **56**.................................. JoeFanning 7 47
(Chris Fairhurst) *chsd ldrs: rdn wl over 1f out: drvn and no imp fnl f* **28/1**

6-60 **5** *2 ¾* **Rattleyurjewellery**[14] 2351 3-8-1 **51** oh6.................. FrannyNorton 2 31
(David Brown) *in rr and rdn along 1/2-way: hdwy on inner wl over 1f out: styd on u.p fnl f: nrst fin* **40/1**

-416 **6** *1 ¾* **Watch Chain (IRE)**[17] 2270 4-9-10 **66**.................................. WilliamBuick 1 42
(Mark H Tompkins) *in tch: hdwy to chse ldrs 1/2-way: rdn along 2f out: sn no imp* **11/2**[3]

-060 **7** *¾* **Sea Salt**[10] 2464 8-9-3 **64**.................................. DaleSwift[(5)] 5 38
(Ron Barr) *nvr bttr than midfield* **9/1**

0535 **8** *3 ½* **Elhamri**[4] 2653 7-9-10 **66**.................................. TomEaves 3 29
(Conor Dore) *cl up on inner: rdn along over 2f out: sn wknd* **9/1**

06-0 **9** *2* **No Mean Trick (USA)**[9] 2490 5-9-7 **63**..................(b[1]) MickyFenton 8 19
(Paul Midgley) *led: rdn along and hdd over 2f out: sn drvn and wknd wl over 1f out* **33/1**

0- **10** *28* **Billyruben**[191] 7598 3-8-9 **59**.................................. AdrianNicholls 4 —
(David Nicholls) *a in rr: bhd fr 1/2-way* **11/1**

1m 17.58s (0.68) **Going Correction** -0.10s/f (Good)
WFA 3 from 4yo+ 8lb **10** Ran SP% **115.0**
Speed ratings (Par 103): **91,90,85,82,78 76,75,70,68,30**
Tote Swingers:1&2:£2.20, 2&3:£1.90, 1&3:£3.30 CSF £20.75 CT £77.20 TOTE £8.20: £2.50, £1.50, £1.20; EX 18.20.
Owner A R M Galbraith **Bred** Allevamento Ficomontanino Srl **Trained** Carluke, South Lanarkshire

FOCUS
A modest handicap and the first two pulled clear. The new winner rates back to his best, with a small personal best from the second.

No Mean Trick(USA) Official explanation: jockey said gelding hung right

2766 TOTEPOOL A BETTER WAY TO BET H'CAP — 5f
9:00 (9:00) (Class 5) (0-75,73) 4-Y-O+ **£2,388** (£705; £352) **Stalls** Low

Form RPR

0464 **1** **Hinton Admiral**[7] 2543 7-9-1 **67**.................................. JoeFanning 9 76
(Keith Dalgleish) *s.i.s and in rr: hdwy on outer wl over 1f out: sn rdn and str run ent fnl f: drvn to ld and edgd lft last 40yds* **4/1**[2]

2643 **2** *1* **Jigajig**[17] 2263 4-9-2 **68**..................................(p) PaulHanagan 7 74
(Kevin Ryan) *dwlt: sn trcking ldrs: effrt 2f out: rdn to chal over 1f out: drvn to ld last 100yds: hdd and no ex last 40yds* **5/1**[3]

0150 **3** *½* **Silvanus (IRE)**[9] 2491 6-8-12 **64**.................................. MickyFenton 4 70+
(Paul Midgley) *hld up in rr: hdwy whn nt clr run and swtchd rt jst over 1f out: rdn and styng on whn n.m.r ins fnl f and again last 50yds: nrst fin* **25/1**

0-06 **4** *¾* **Mr Wolf**[17] 2250 10-9-7 **73**..................................(p) FrederikTylicki 8 74
(John Quinn) *led: rdn wl over 1f out: drvn ent fnl f: hdd & wknd last 100yds* **8/1**

-060 **5** *1 ½* **Captain Scooby**[16] 2286 5-9-4 **70**.................................. TonyHamilton 2 66
(Richard Whitaker) *trckd ldrs: swtchd rt and hdwy 2f out: rdn and ev ch wl over 1f out tl drvn and one pce ent fnl f* **5/1**[3]

0653 **6** *nk* **Comptonspirit**[6] 2585 7-9-0 **71**.................................. JemmaMarshall[(5)] 1 66
(Brian Baugh) *chsd ldrs on inner: rdn along wl over 2f out: sn drvn and wknd ent fnl f* **3/1**[1]

0004 **7** *3* **King Of Swords (IRE)**[7] 2547 7-8-0 **55**..................(p) DeclanCannon[(3)] 5 39
(Nigel Tinkler) *chsd ldrs: rdn along 2f out: n.m.r and sn wknd* **6/1**

121- **8** *nk* **Bertie Southstreet**[300] 4938 8-9-5 **71**..................(v) TomEaves 6 54
(Deborah Sanderson) *chsd ldr: rdn along 2f out: sn drvn and wknd* **14/1**

63.97 secs (0.67) **Going Correction** -0.10s/f (Good) **8** Ran SP% **114.2**
Speed ratings (Par 103): **90,88,87,86,84 83,78,78**
Tote Swingers:1&2:£3.00, 2&3:£25.70, 1&3:£10.40. totesuper7: WIN: Not won. PLACE: Not won. CSF £24.23 CT £438.73 TOTE £6.10: £2.60, £1.80, £5.70; EX 25.80.
Owner William Brand & Gordon McDowall **Bred** Gainsborough Stud Management Ltd **Trained** Carluke, South Lanarkshire

FOCUS
A modest sprint handicap featuring Mr Wolf, who had an earlier race named in his honour and who had finished first, second and third in the last three renewals of this contest. it was strong run and the winner showed his best turf form for two years.
Silvanus(IRE) Official explanation: jockey said gelding was denied a clear run
T/Plt: £210.50 to a £1 stake. Pool: £73,080.50 - 253.37 winning tickets. T/Qpdt: £34.00 to a £1 stake. Pool: £5,041.95 - 109.70 winning tickets. JR

2367 WINDSOR (R-H)
Monday, June 6

OFFICIAL GOING: Good to soft (soft in places; 6.5)
Wind: Almost nil Weather: Cloudy

2767 E B F SPORTINGBET.COM MEDIAN AUCTION MAIDEN STKS — 6f
6:15 (6:19) (Class 5) 2-Y-O **£3,238** (£963; £481; £240) **Stalls** Low

Form RPR

1 **Rebellious Guest** 2-9-3 0.................................. TomQueally 5 83+
(George Margarson) *trckd ldrs: rdn and prog 2f out to ld over 1f out: sn wl in command* **9/2**[2]

02 **2** *3* **Red Aggressor (IRE)**[21] 2148 2-9-3 0.......................... PhilipRobinson 10 74
(Clive Brittain) *uns rdr on way to post: trckd ldrs: shkn up 2f out: styd on wl enough to take 2nd ins fnl f: no imp on wnr* **9/2**[2]

3 *2* **Knight Vision** 2-9-3 0.................................. SamHitchcott 13 68+
(David Nicholls) *in tch bhd ldrs: rdn 2f out: styd on to take 3rd nr fin* **20/1**

4 **4** *¾* **Armiger**[21] 2143 2-9-3 0.................................. DarryllHolland 9 66
(William Muir) *free to post: led: tk field to far side: hdd over 1f out: fdd fnl f* **16/1**

5 *nk* **Khazium (IRE)** 2-9-3 0.................................. AdamKirby 2 65+
(Pat Eddery) *slowest away: wl in rr: prog fr 1/2-way: shkn up and kpt on quite wl fnl f* **14/1**

6 *1* **Stellar Express (IRE)** 2-8-5 0.......................... MatthewLawson[(7)] 12 57+
(B W Hills) *towards rr: shkn up over 2f out: kpt on steadily fr over 1f out* **40/1**

7 *nk* **Zuzu Angel (IRE)** 2-8-12 0.................................. ShaneKelly 15 56+
(William Knight) *stdd s: wl in rr: stl there 2f out: stdy prog over 1f out: nrst fin* **25/1**

3 **8** *½* **Cockney Rocker**[16] 2318 2-9-3 0.................................. JamieSpencer 6 59
(Jane Chapple-Hyam) *chsd ldr to 2f out: steadily wknd* **7/2**[1]

0 **9** *1 ½* **Great Mystery (IRE)**[7] 2559 2-9-3 0.................................. SebSanders 3 55
(J W Hills) *pressed ldrs: shkn up over 2f out: wknd over 1f out* **50/1**

10 *¾* **Cashmere Or Caviar (IRE)** 2-8-12 0.......................... MichaelHills 1 48
(B W Hills) *rn green in rr towards outer: effrt 2f out: no prog over 1f out* **10/1**

11 *1* **Merv (IRE)** 2-9-3 0.................................. DaneO'Neill 11 50
(Henry Candy) *dwlt: rn green in rr: modest prog 2f out: sn no hdwy* **5/1**[3]

12 *½* **Wrapped Up** 2-8-12 0.................................. FrankieMcDonald 8 43
(Heather Main) *dwlt: wl in rr: sme prog into midfield 2f out: wknd fnl f* **100/1**

13 *2 ¼* **Music Girl** 2-8-12 0.................................. FergusSweeney 16 36
(Michael Blanshard) *chsd ldrs tl rdn and wknd 2f out* **66/1**

14 *4 ½* **Clean Bowled (IRE)** 2-9-3 0.................................. MartinDwyer 4 28
(Brian Meehan) *rn green and dropped to last after 2f: sn bhd* **12/1**

15 *20* **Don't Tempt Me (IRE)** 2-8-12 0.................................. LiamKeniry 7 —
(Sylvester Kirk) *t.k.h in midfield: wknd 1/2-way: t.o* **50/1**

1m 15.76s (2.76) **Going Correction** +0.40s/f (Good) **15** Ran SP% **122.0**
Speed ratings (Par 93): **97,93,90,89,88 87,87,86,84,83 82,81,78,72,45**
Tote Swingers:1&2:£5.30, 2&3:£21.10, 1&3:£25.50 CSF £23.94 TOTE £6.00: £2.00, £2.80, £6.60; EX 29.70 Trifecta £307.30 Pool £2,866.26 - 6.90 winning units..
Owner John Guest Racing **Bred** Equity Bloodstock Partnership **Trained** Newmarket, Suffolk

FOCUS
After 25mm of rain in the previous 24 hours the going was changed to good to soft, soft in places, and as a result there were plenty of non-runners scattered through the card. The stands' rail was dolled out 12yds at 6f and 7yds at winning post. The top bend was dolled out 7 yards from the normal configuration, adding 26 yards to race distances in the 1m+ contests. An interesting maiden. They went a fair pace in the conditions and raced on the far side. A newcomer stormed clear from a rival who set the standard, and the form looks solid.

NOTEBOOK
Rebellious Guest was prominent in the market and travelled smoothly just off the pace before surging to an emphatic victory on debut. A 54,000gns Cockney Rebel colt, he looks a good prospect and is a half-brother to useful 2-y-o fast-ground sprint winners Di Stefano and Smokey Storm. He is a possible for the Coventry at Royal Ascot. (tchd 4-1 and 5-1 in a place)

Red Aggressor(IRE) showed much improved form when second in a 5f Leicester maiden last time behind a useful rival who ran well in better company next time. He set a decent target for the others to aim at but there was a scare when he unseated his rider on the way to post and then looked reluctant to go into the stalls. However, that didn't stop him running a solid race under a prominent ride, and pulling clear of the third. He may have a bit of temperament but he also has a fair amount of ability and adds some solidity to the form. (op 7-2)

Knight Vision stayed on steadily from just off the pace on a promising debut. He has already been gelded but has plenty of speed in the female line and can build on this. (tchd 22-1)

Armiger showed up well for a long way to confirm the promise of his debut fourth at Bath. (tchd 14-1)

Khazium(IRE) shaped with promise, staying on out wide on debut. A 16,000gns purchase, he is out of an Irish triple 1m2f-1m3f winner off marks in the 50s and should improve with time and distance. (op 25-1, tchd 50-1 in a place)

Stellar Express(IRE) looked the stable second string on jockey bookings, but she stayed on well against the far rail to post an encouraging debut run. Her pedigree is a mix of speed and stamina but she showed some spark here and holds sales-race entries later on. (op 50-1)

Cockney Rocker shaped with promise from well off the pace when 12-1 third in a 6f York maiden on debut. Sent off favourite, he looked more streetwise but couldn't pick up, and may not have been effective in the rain-softened ground.

Merv(IRE) was prominent in the market but looked very inexperienced and didn't show much on his first run. (op 8-1)

2768 AFFORDABLE RACEHORSE SYNDICATION WITH JAMASITR RACING CLAIMING STKS — 1m 2f 7y

6:45 (6:45) (Class 6) 3-Y-0+ — £1,619 (£481; £240; £120) Stalls High

Form / RPR

5121 **1** **Song To The Moon (IRE)**[10] [2449] 4-8-11 70......(b) MatthewDavies(3) 5 — 71
(Jim Boyle) *stdd s: hld up in last pair: prog over 3f out: chsd ldr over 2f out: drvn to ld jst over 1f out: styd on wl* **2/1**[2]

/10- **2** *1 1/4* **Soccerjackpot (USA)**[4] [6357] 7-9-5 88................................ AdamKirby 4 — 74
(Graeme McPherson) *led: set mod pce tl kicked on over 4f out: hdd jst over 1f out: styd on but hld fnl f* **15/2**[3]

4-43 **3** *5* **Experimentalist**[18] [2226] 3-8-10 69.................................. SteveDrowne 3 — 68
(Hughie Morrison) *t.k.h: hld up in last pair: outpcd and pushed along over 4f out: kpt on fr over 2f out to take 3rd ins fnl f* **13/8**[1]

3456 **4** *1/2* **Dream Of Fortune (IRE)**[5] [2616] 7-9-2 63..............(bt) RichardEvans(3) 6 — 63
(David Evans) *cl up: chsd ldr over 3f out to over 2f out: fnd nil and sn wknd* **10/1**

5306 **5** *2* **September Draw (USA)**[4] [2637] 3-7-10 59.................. KieranO'Neill(5) 2 — 54
(Richard Hannon) *t.k.h: chsd ldr to over 3f out: sn lost pl and btn* **15/2**[3]

6 *14* **Triumphus**[467] 7-9-2 0.. FrankieMcDonald 7 — 28
(Paul Fitzsimons) *t.k.h: cl up tl wknd over 3f out: t.o* **20/1**

2m 13.49s (4.79) **Going Correction** +0.275s/f (Good)
WFA 3 from 4yo+ 13lb — **6** Ran SP% **108.8**
Speed ratings (Par 101): **91,90,86,85,84 72**
Tote Swingers:1&2:£2.80, 2&3:£1.70, 1&3:£1.10 CSF £15.76 TOTE £2.60: £1.20, £3.50; EX 13.90 Trifecta £31.30 Pool £7,706.32 - 182.13 winning units..Song To The Moon was the subject of a friendly claim.

Owner M Khan X2 **Bred** Michael Woodlock & Seamus Kennedy **Trained** Epsom, Surrey

FOCUS
They went a stop-start gallop in this claimer and not many got into it. Modest form, best rated around the winner to her recent best.

Experimentalist Official explanation: jockey said gelding injured his shoulder leaving the stalls

2769 MERCERS LAW H'CAP — 1m 2f 7y

7:15 (7:16) (Class 4) (0-80,80) 4-Y-0+ — £3,561 (£1,059; £529; £264) Stalls High

Form / RPR

123- **1** **Ken's Girl**[222] [7182] 7-9-3 76... FergusSweeney 12 — 85
(Stuart Kittow) *taken down early: jockey in stalls bef horse: mde all: rdn 2f out: styd on and a in control* **7/1**[3]

0-12 **2** *1* **Chain Of Events**[11] [2436] 4-9-1 74.................................... EddieAhern 5 — 81
(Neil King) *chsd wnr to over 3f out: drvn to go 2nd again wl over 2f out: styd on: a hld* **9/2**[2]

15-0 **3** *1* **Aspro Mavro (IRE)**[21] [2150] 5-9-4 77................................ AdamKirby 15 — 82
(Jim Best) *chsd ldng trio: rdn 3f out: wnt 3rd 2f out but nt on terms w ldng pair: styd on: unable to chal* **16/1**

1344 **4** *1 3/4* **Edgeworth (IRE)**[13] [2378] 5-8-5 71............................ JoshBaudains(7) 4 — 73+
(David Bridgwater) *blindfold off late and slowly away: rcvrd and sn in 5th: lost pl gng easily 3f out: urged along and wnt 4th over 1f out: nvr able to chal* **20/1**

6/0- **5** *1 3/4* **Duke Of Burgundy (FR)**[9] [1357] 8-8-11 70....................(t) TomQueally 6 — 68
(Jennie Candlish) *towards rr: rdn over 3f out and struggling: kpt on over 2f out to take 5th fnl f: n.d* **28/1**

6-03 **6** *3 3/4* **Rosco Flyer (IRE)**[25] [2021] 5-9-1 74................................(p) DaneO'Neill 1 — 65
(Roger Teal) *chsd ldng pair to over 3f out: steadily wknd u.p fr over 2f out* **8/1**

-061 **7** *2 3/4* **Effigy**[21] [2150] 7-8-11 75.. AmyScott(5) 14 — 60
(Henry Candy) *hld up in last trio: shkn up over 2f out: no great prog: nvr a factor* **12/1**

-120 **8** *1/2* **Uncle Fred**[20] [2178] 6-9-7 80... GeorgeBaker 7 — 64
(Patrick Chamings) *hld up in last trio: jst pushed along over 3f out and no prog: nvr nr ldrs* **9/1**

0-36 **9** *8* **Meglio Ancora**[21] [2156] 4-8-11 70.................................. JamieSpencer 9 — 47
(Jonathan Portman) *hld up in last trio: prog 1/2-way: chsd wnr over 3f out to wl over 2f out: sn wknd and eased* **11/1**

0033 **10** *2 1/2* **Urban Space**[10] [2454] 5-8-12 71...................................... HayleyTurner 3 — 34
(Conor Dore) *sweating: settled in 6th: rdn over 3f out: sn struggling: wknd over 2f out* **7/2**[1]

103- **11** *4 1/2* **Mr Harmoosh (IRE)**[42] [7205] 4-9-1 74............................. JamesDoyle 11 — 28
(Sheena West) *hld up in 7th: rdn over 3f out: struggling over 2f out: wknd and bhd* **7/1**[3]

2m 12.43s (3.73) **Going Correction** +0.275s/f (Good) — **11** Ran SP% **116.6**
Speed ratings (Par 105): **96,95,94,93,91 88,86,86,79,77 74**
Tote Swingers:1&2:£4.60, 2&3:£14.50, 1&3:£31.80 CSF £38.19 CT £491.18 TOTE £11.20: £4.30, £1.10, £5.80; EX 48.60 Trifecta £1825.20 Part won. Pool £2,466.58 - 0.45 winning units..

Owner Midd Shire Racing **Bred** D R Tucker **Trained** Blackborough, Devon

FOCUS
There was an all-the-way winner in this fair handicap, and the runner-up was always prominent too. The field all went to the far side in the straight. The form is rated around the front pair.

Urban Space Official explanation: trainer was unable to offer any explanation as to poor show

2770 CHEVRON MALTA HOLIDAYS H'CAP — 5f 10y

7:45 (7:45) (Class 4) (0-85,83) 3-Y-0 — £4,079 (£1,214; £606; £303) Stalls Low

Form / RPR

0020 **1** **Style And Panache (IRE)**[5] [2611] 3-8-13 75.................. PatCosgrave 1 — 78
(David Evans) *mostly chsd clr ldr: rdn 2f out: clsd to ld ins fnl f: drvn out* **7/1**[3]

5035 **2** *1/2* **Scarlet Rocks (IRE)**[10] [2453] 3-8-13 75......................... CathyGannon 3 — 76
(David Evans) *disp 2nd bhd clr ldr and sn clr of rest: rdn 2f out: clsd w wnr to chal fnl f: nt qckn last 100yds* **17/2**

-636 **3** *nk* **Cadeaux Pearl**[9] [2505] 3-9-4 83.......................................(b[1]) BillyCray(3) 2 — 83
(David Nicholls) *blasted off in front and sn clr: c bk to rivals over 1f out: hdd and no ex ins fnl f* **10/3**[2]

0-31 **4** *1 1/4* **Perfect Pastime**[16] [2294] 3-9-2 78....................................... TedDurcan 5 — 79+
(Walter Swinburn) *stdd s: hld up in last pair and sn wl bhd: rdn 1/2-way: sed to make grnd 1f out: clsng whn nowhere to go last 100yds* **5/2**[1]

L-03 **5** *1/2* **Regal Approval**[17] [2255] 3-9-2 78.................................... HayleyTurner 4 — 72
(Hughie Morrison) *taken down early: settled in 4th but sn wl outpcd: rdn 1/2-way: nvr on terms: kpt on* **5/2**[1]

5012 **6** *3/4* **Loves Theme (IRE)**[13] [2382] 3-7-13 64.........................(b) AmyBaker(3) 7 — 55
(Alan Bailey) *hld up in last and sn outpcd: rdn 1/2-way: nvr on terms: kpt on* **14/1**

62.71 secs (2.41) **Going Correction** +0.40s/f (Good) — **6** Ran SP% **109.9**
Speed ratings (Par 101): **96,95,94,92,91 90**
Tote Swingers:1&2:£8.70, 2&3:£10.80, 1&3:£4.00 CSF £57.81 TOTE £9.90: £5.20, £4.50; EX 23.60.

Owner Roger Ambrose,Sean Ambrose & Bill Reilly **Bred** Rathasker Stud **Trained** Pandy, Monmouths

FOCUS
David Evans trained the first two in this sprint handicap. There was a bunch finish and the fourth was unlucky. The first two were closely matched on last month's C&D form.

2771 SPORTINGBET.COM H'CAP — 1m 67y

8:15 (8:15) (Class 5) (0-75,74) 4-Y-0+ — £2,266 (£674; £337; £168) Stalls Low

Form / RPR

00-5 **1** **Prince Of Sorrento**[19] [2207] 4-8-8 61................................ TedDurcan 3 — 77+
(John Akehurst) *awkward s: rcvrd to chse ldng pair: led over 2f out and sn rdn wl clr: eased last 75yds* **5/1**[3]

1-05 **2** *4 1/2* **One Hit Wonder**[13] [2376] 4-8-10 63................................... LiamKeniry 10 — 66
(Mouse Hamilton-Fairley) *hld up last: pushed along bef 1/2-way: detached 3f out: drvn and styd on wl fr over 1f out: tk 2nd last strides* **9/1**

314- **3** *1/2* **Indian Valley (USA)**[229] [7019] 4-9-2 74.......................... HarryBentley(5) 4 — 76
(Hugo Palmer) *hld up disputing 5th: rdn wl over 2f out: kpt on to chal for 2nd 1f out: wnr wl clr* **9/4**[1]

00-6 **4** *1/2* **If I Were A Boy (IRE)**[13] [2378] 4-9-2 69............................(p) JamesDoyle 1 — 70
(Dominic Ffrench Davis) *led to over 2f out: no ch w wnr after: lost pls ins fnl f* **11/1**

246- **5** *nk* **Royal Etiquette (IRE)**[158] [8021] 4-8-12 65............................ DaneO'Neill 11 — 65
(Lawney Hill) *dwlt: hld up in 7th: rdn 3f out: effrt u.p to chal for a pl 1f out: one pce* **16/1**

1246 **6** *3/4* **Al Aqabah (IRE)**[19] [2207] 6-9-2 72............................ AdamBeschizza(3) 5 — 70
(Brian Gubby) *settled disputing 5th: drvn 3f out: tried to cl on plcd horses over 1f out: one pce* **9/1**

5043 **7** *5* **Salient**[31] [1868] 7-9-0 67..(v) KirstyMilczarek 2 — 54
(Michael Attwater) *chsd ldng trio: rdn 3f out: no prog 2f out: wknd over 1f out* **7/1**

0-35 **8** *14* **Mingun Bell (USA)**[16] [2301] 4-9-5 72................................ TomQueally 7 — 27
(Ed de Giles) *chsd ldr to 3f out: wknd qckly: t.o and eased fnl f* **9/2**[2]

1m 46.22s (1.52) **Going Correction** +0.275s/f (Good) — **8** Ran SP% **112.3**
Speed ratings (Par 103): **103,98,98,97,97 96,91,77**
Tote Swingers:1&2:£9.80, 2&3:£5.90, 1&3:£4.50 CSF £46.80 CT £127.92 TOTE £6.10: £2.20, £2.40, £1.40; EX 51.90 Trifecta £223.60 Pool £625.60 - 2.07 winning units..

Owner Mrs Pam Akhurst **Bred** Mrs P Akhurst **Trained** Epsom, Surrey

FOCUS
A number of runners had something to prove in this handicap. The pace was decent and there was a runaway winner, who rates back to his early best.

2772 READ PAUL HANAGAN'S BLOG AT ATTHERACES.COM CLASSIFIED STKS — 6f

8:45 (8:45) (Class 5) 3-Y-0 — £2,266 (£674; £337; £168) Stalls Low

Form / RPR

20-2 **1** **Muffraaj**[16] [2281] 3-9-0 74.. MartinDwyer 1 — 81
(David Simcock) *mde all: rdn and styd on wl whn pressed fnl f* **2/1**[1]

316- **2** *3/4* **Expose**[212] [7347] 3-9-0 73... RichardHughes 4 — 79+
(William Haggas) *stdd s: tk fierce hold: hld up in 4th: clsd on ldrs gng strly 2f out: plld out to press wnr fnl f: sn rdn and nt qckn* **2/1**[1]

1-4 **3** *1 3/4* **Echo Ridge (IRE)**[25] [2025] 3-9-0 75............................ StevieDonohoe 2 — 73
(Ralph Beckett) *chsd wnr to 1f out: kpt on same pce* **7/2**[2]

2420 **4** *7* **Reginald Claude**[109] [578] 3-9-0 71................................ DaneO'Neill 5 — 51
(Mark Usher) *hld up last: rdn over 2f out: wknd over 1f out* **14/1**

2-05 **5** *3/4* **Khaleeji**[21] [2158] 3-9-0 74.. SebSanders 3 — 48
(J W Hills) *chsd ldng pair to wl over 1f out: wknd* **13/2**[3]

1m 15.51s (2.51) **Going Correction** +0.40s/f (Good) — **5** Ran SP% **108.9**
Speed ratings (Par 99): **99,98,95,86,85**
CSF £6.04 TOTE £3.00: £1.10, £2.00; EX 5.80.

Owner Dr Ali Ridha **Bred** Tibthorpe Stud **Trained** Newmarket, Suffolk

FOCUS
An interesting classified event, involving some unexposed types.The two market leaders fought out a tight finish. The winner is rated up a length on his Chester form.

T/Jkpt: Not won. T/Plt: £604.00 to a £1 stake. Pool: £107,751.92 - 130.21 winning tickets.
T/Qpdt: £71.70 to a £1 stake. Pool: £7,620.85 - 78.60 winning tickets. JN

2773 - 2775a (Foreign Racing) - See Raceform Interactive

2009 NAAS (L-H)

Monday, June 6

OFFICIAL GOING: Good to firm

2776a ALFRED NOBEL ROCHESTOWN (C & G) STKS (LISTED RACE) — 6f

4:10 (4:10) 2-Y-0 — £33,620 (£9,827; £4,655; £1,551)

RPR

1 **Lilbourne Lad (IRE)**[23] [2109] 2-9-0 .... RichardHughes 3 — 105+
(Richard Hannon) *mde all: asserted over 1f out: pushed out and stretched clr fnl f: impressive* **9/4**[2]

2 *6* **Snowflake Dancer (IRE)**[22] 2127 2-9-0 .... KJManning 5 87
(J S Bolger, Ire) *trckd ldr in 2nd: rdn 2f out: no ch w wnr fr over 1f out: kpt on one pce* **8/1**

3 *½* **French Emperor (IRE)**[29] 1924 2-9-0 .... CO'Donoghue 6 86
(Edward Lynam, Ire) *trckd ldrs mainly 3rd: rdn 2f out: no imp on easy wnr fr over 1f out: kpt on one pce* **11/2**

4 *½* **Raphael Santi (IRE)**[36] 1731 2-9-0 ....(p) JPO'Brien 2 84
(A P O'Brien, Ire) *trckd ldrs mainly 4th: rdn 2f out: sn swtchd rt and bmpd rival: no imp and sltly hmpd ins fnl f* **4/1**[3]

5 *½* **Requinto (IRE)**[44] 1531 2-9-0 .... WMLordan 4 83
(David Wachman, Ire) *t.k.h and settled bk in rr: pushed along under 2f out: bmpd over 1f out: no imp and repeatedly bmpd rival ins fnl f* **6/4**[1]

1m 11.24s (-1.96) **5** Ran SP% **117.3**
CSF £20.03 TOTE £2.50: £1.60, £3.80; DF 19.20.
Owner Andrew Russell **Bred** Swordlestown Little **Trained** East Everleigh, Wilts
■ Stewards' Enquiry : J P O'Brien caution: careless riding

FOCUS
Lilbourne Lad impressed and this was the best Listed performance by a 2-y-o before the end of June for a number of years. He looks an obvious contender for the Coventry Stakes but more will be needed there.

NOTEBOOK
Lilbourne Lad(IRE) ◆ made the home runners look distinctly ordinary with a blistering display. Sent to the front by Richard Hughes, he travelled powerfully from the outset and it was soon apparent that the others were labouring. He barely had to be shaken up to pull readily clear and this fine-looking colt now has Royal Ascot on his agenda. Connections did not mention specific targets after the race, but he has an entry in the Railway Stakes and a couple of sales contests. It is just possible that the visual impression slightly flatters him, as the favourite disappointed, but it can still be deemed a high-class performance on his third start. (op 9/4 tchd 5/2)
Snowflake Dancer(IRE) produced a career-best effort on his third start and continues to go the right way. He has a good attitude, like his father, but was blown away by the winner. (op 9/1)
French Emperor(IRE) is another progressive type who shaped a shade keenly but showed plenty of raw pace. It was apparent at halfway that he was struggling to make an impact, but he kept on resolutely and is clearly a pretty useful colt. (op 10/1)
Raphael Santi(IRE) had plenty on his plate after winning a Gowran maiden over further. He ran to debut form with the fifth but never really got into the race. (op 7/2)
Requinto(IRE) was held up here, perhaps to get the trip or in recognition of the likely pacesetting of the winner. The writing was on the wall a long way out and he made no impression when in the clear. (op 6/4 tchd 7/4)

2777a COOLMORE STUD EUROPEAN BREEDERS FUND FILLIES SPRINT STKS (LISTED RACE) 6f
4:40 (4:42) 2-Y-O **£37,823** (£11,056; £5,237; £1,745)

RPR

1 **Teolane (IRE)**[8] 2532 2-9-0 .... KJManning 1 101+
(J S Bolger, Ire) *mde all: rdn and styd on wl fr over 1f out* **11/10**[1]

2 *2 ½* **Princess Sinead (IRE)**[26] 2009 2-9-0 .... FMBerry 2 94
(Mrs John Harrington, Ire) *trckd ldrs: 3rd 1/2-way: 2nd 2f out: sn rdn and no imp on wnr fr over 1f out: kpt on same pce* **3/1**[2]

3 *2* **Naseem Sea (IRE)**[26] 2010 2-9-0 .... WJSupple 5 88
(P D Deegan, Ire) *slowly away: sn in tch: wnt 3rd under 2f out: sn rdn and no imp fr over 1f out: kpt on one pce fnl f* **6/1**[3]

4 *7* **Basantee**[18] 2234 2-9-0 .... RichardKingscote 3 67
(Tom Dascombe) *chsd ldrs: 6th 2f out: mod 5th and no imp over 1f out: kpt on one pce* **16/1**

5 *2* **Feathers And Bows (USA)**[16] 2321 2-9-0 .... WMLordan 4 61
(David Wachman, Ire) *trckd ldr in 2nd: pushed along in 3rd 2f out: sn no ex* **12/1**

6 *1 ¼* **Guru Girl**[31] 1846 2-9-0 .... AndrewElliott 6 57
(Mrs K Burke) *prom early: rdn in 5th 2f out: sn no ex* **20/1**

7 *½* **Crimson Sunrise (IRE)**[9] 2513 2-9-0 .... PJSmullen 8 55+
(D K Weld, Ire) *settled in rr: rdn and no threat fr 2f out* **12/1**

8 *½* **Gold Lace (IRE)**[16] 2322 2-9-0 .... CDHayes 9 54
(P J Prendergast, Ire) *chsd ldrs: drvn along fr 1/2-way: no ex fr 2f out* **25/1**

9 *8* **Homecoming Queen (IRE)**[9] 2513 2-9-0 ....(p) SeamieHeffernan 7 30
(A P O'Brien, Ire) *chsd ldrs: nvr a factor: rdn 2f out and sn no ex: eased whn btn fnl f* **12/1**

1m 11.56s (-1.64) **9** Ran SP% **124.5**
CSF £4.89 TOTE £1.70: £1.02, £2.10, £2.80; DF 5.20.
Owner Mrs J S Bolger **Bred** J S Bolger **Trained** Coolcullen, Co Carlow

NOTEBOOK
Teolane(IRE) won this in a manner highly remininiscent of Cuis Ghaire from the same yard in 2008. Soon in front, she grabbed the rail and, although clearly in need of further than this trip, she has plenty of speed and ultimately won readily. A daughter of the brilliant Teofilo, she certainly has the size to progress further and her trainer reckons she might get 1m4f next year. Whether or not she goes to the Albany - like Cuis Ghaire - is up for debate, and it must be a shade worrying that a trip to Royal Ascot would represent her third run in little over a month. She looks an ideal type for the Moyglare and that is on her agenda. (op 4/5)
Princess Sinead(IRE) lost little in defeat. She had a grand position to track the winner but never really looked like making any impression on her. She settled better and is clearly a smart type, though she would be more of a 6f horse than the winner. (op 5/1)
Naseem Sea(IRE) continues to progress. She travelled well off the pace and trounced everything else, making no impact on the first two. She gained black type here and is thriving with racing. (op 7/1)
Basantee fared pretty well, considering this was a massive step up in class. She ran a respectable race. (op 14/1)
Feathers And Bows(USA) faced a huge task here but showed enough ability to suggest she should win a maiden. (op 20/1)
Homecoming Queen(IRE) shaping as though she struggled with the track. (op 12/1 tchd 14/1)

2778 - 2779a (Foreign Racing) - See Raceform Interactive

[2587]REDCAR (L-H)
Tuesday, June 7

OFFICIAL GOING: Good to firm (8.7)
Wind: Light across Weather: Cloudy with sunny periods

2780 FOLLOW REDCARRACING ON FACEBOOK AND TWITTER MEDIAN AUCTION MAIDEN STKS 6f
2:00 (2:01) (Class 5) 2-Y-O **£1,942** (£578; £288; £144) **Stalls** High

Form RPR

0 1 **Roger Sez (IRE)**[24] 2113 2-8-12 0 .... DavidAllan 3 72+
(Tim Easterby) *wnt lft s: trckd ldrs: hdwy on outer to chal 2f out: sn led: rdn over 1f out: kpt on wl* **25/1**

05 2 *2* **Lexi's Prince (IRE)**[11] 2455 2-9-3 0.....................(v[1]) RichardKingscote 1 71
(Tom Dascombe) *sn led: pushed along 1/2-way: rdn and edgd lft 2f out: sn hdd: drvn over 1f out: kpt on same pce* **3/1**[2]

2243 3 *4* **Red Socks (IRE)**[14] 2380 2-9-0 0 .... AdamBeschizza(3) 4 58
(Gay Kelleway) *trckd ldrs: effrt whn n.m.r 2f out: sn rdn and kpt on same pce* **5/1**[3]

45 4 *¾* **Whisky Bravo**[15] 2346 2-9-3 0 .... PhillipMakin 8 55
(David Brown) *in tch: rdn along 1/2-way: hdwy to chse ldrs 2f out: sn drvn and one pce* **2/1**[1]

4 5 *2 ¾* **Cataract**[7] 2587 2-8-12 0 .... TomEaves 2 42
(John Weymes) *chsd ldr: rdn along wl over 2f out: drvn and wknd wl over 1f out* **16/1**

2 6 *2 ¼* **Ingleby Angel (IRE)**[19] 2234 2-9-3 0 .... DanielTudhope 6 39
(David O'Meara) *s.i.s: effrt on wd outside and rdn along 1/2-way: nvr a factor* **3/1**[2]

00 7 *3 ½* **King Laertis (IRE)**[15] 2346 2-9-3 0 .... PJMcDonald 5 28
(Ben Haslam) *prom: rdn along 1/2-way: sn wknd* **150/1**

05 8 *2 ½* **Only Orsenfoolsies**[11] 2476 2-9-3 0 .... FrederikTylicki 7 20
(Micky Hammond) *chsd ldrs: rdn along bef 1/2-way: sn outpcd and bhd* **20/1**

1m 10.81s (-0.99) **Going Correction** -0.15s/f (Firm) **8** Ran SP% **115.2**
Speed ratings (Par 93): **100,97,92,91,87 84,79,76**
Tote Swingers: 1&2 £11.80, 1&3 £10.90, 2&3 £2.10 CSF £98.51 TOTE £39.00: £9.20, £2.20, £1.70; EX 171.90 TRIFECTA Not won..
Owner R Sidebottom **Bred** B Kennedy **Trained** Great Habton, N Yorks

FOCUS
Apart from a sharp shower on Sunday evening, it had been dry and breezy since the last meeting and a total of 32mm of water had been applied to the track since Thursday. The jockeys confirmed the ground was on the quick side. A modest maiden and, as is often the case at this course, the field raced in the centre. The gallop was ordinary and the first two pulled clear.

NOTEBOOK
Roger Sez(IRE) ◆, too green to do herself justice on her debut, was much more professional this time and, after travelling strongly, showed a decent attitude and much-improved form to win with ears pricked over this longer trip. She'll have no problems with 7f and, as this form can't be rated too highly, she will be one to watch out for when the nursery season begins. (op 33-1 tchd 40-1)
Lexi's Prince(IRE) looked to have decent claims judged on his previous run but, while he matched that improved Haydock form, he didn't look straightforward in the first-time visor and isn't one to be taking too short a price about. (op 7-2 tchd 11-4)
Red Socks(IRE) wasn't disgraced with the headgear left off returned to turf upped to 6f for the first time, but he doesn't look to be progressing and is likely to remain vulnerable in this type of event. (op 11-2 tchd 9-2)
Whisky Bravo attracted support but again failed to confirm debut promise back on a sound surface and over 6f for the first time and is likely to remain vulnerable in this grade. (op 5-2 tchd 11-4)
Cataract travelled strongly for a long way, but was quickly left behind once the tempo increased and failed to build on her debut run over this course and distance. She may do better in time. (tchd 14-1)
Ingleby Angel(IRE), a leggy, unfurnished type, was below his debut form on Fibresand last month on this first turf run. (op 5-2 tchd 10-3)

2781 WIN A VIP DAY OUT @ REDCARRACING.CO.UK MAIDEN FILLIES' STKS 7f
2:30 (2:31) (Class 5) 3-Y-0+ **£2,047** (£604; £302) **Stalls** High

Form RPR

0- 1 **Willbeme**[235] 6892 3-9-0 0 .... AndrewElliott 5 60
(Neville Bycroft) *cl up: led 3f out: rdn wl over 1f out: hdd briefly ins fnl f: rallied to ld again nr fin* **22/1**

504 2 *hd* **American Lover (FR)**[13] 2402 4-9-10 62 .... DavidNolan 3 63
(John Wainwright) *trckd ldng pair: hdwy to chse wnr 1/2-way: rdn to chal 2f out: drvn over 1f out: led briefly ins fnl f: edgd lft and hdd nr fin* **9/2**[3]

4-0 3 *4 ½* **Crabbies Bay**[22] 2151 3-9-0 0 .... TomEaves 6 47
(Lisa Williamson) *chsd ldrs: rdn along over 2f out: sn drvn and one pce* **33/1**

0-5 4 *nk* **Let's Face Facts**[10] 2498 4-9-10 0 .... DanielTudhope 10 50+
(Jim Goldie) *in rr: hdwy wl over 2f out: rdn wl over 1f out: nt rch ldrs* **4/1**[2]

-025 5 *5* **Alensgrove (IRE)**[10] 2400 3-9-0 61 .... MickyFenton 4 33
(Paul Midgley) *s.i.s and bhd: swtchd rt towards stands' rail wl over 2f out: styd on u.p fnl 2f: nvr nr ldrs* **13/8**[1]

00- 6 *3 ¼* **Karens Legacy (IRE)**[258] 6293 3-8-11 0 .... GaryBartley(3) 1 28
(Ian McInnes) *in rr: hdwy 1/2-way: rdn along wl over 2f out: plugged on: nvr a factor* **28/1**

0-0 7 *2 ¼* **Stella Marris**[43] 1559 4-9-10 0 .... PaddyAspell 8 22
(Christopher Wilson) *a in midfield* **66/1**

000- 8 *8* **Hot Toddie**[215] 7309 3-9-0 38 .... PaulMulrennan 9 —
(James Given) *midfield: rdn along over 3f out: sn wknd* **28/1**

-650 9 *1 ¾* **Hettie Hubble**[6] 2548 5-9-7 46 ....(v) PaulPickard(3) 12 —
(David Thompson) *chsd ldrs: rdn along 1/2-way: sn wknd* **25/1**

10 *shd* **Atyaab**[249] 6547 4-9-10 65 .... PJMcDonald 7 —
(Alan Swinbank) *led: rdn along 1/2-way: sn hdd & wknd 2f out* **9/2**[3]

00 11 *½* **Right Credentials**[10] 2493 3-9-0 0 .... JoeFanning 2 —
(Bruce Hellier) *a in rr* **100/1**

300- 12 *11* **Annalika**[265] 6092 3-9-0 37 .... PatrickMathers 11 —
(Colin Teague) *dwlt: a bhd* **100/1**

1m 25.12s (0.62) **Going Correction** -0.15s/f (Firm)
WFA 3 from 4yo+ 10lb **12** Ran SP% **116.0**
Speed ratings (Par 100): **90,89,84,84,78 74,72,63,61,61 60,47**
Tote Swingers: 1&2 £19.70, 1&3 £45.00, 2&3 £21.80 CSF £110.66 TOTE £48.40: £7.00, £2.20, £6.00; EX 141.50 TRIFECTA Not won..
Owner P D Burrow **Bred** Mrs J M Russell **Trained** Brandsby, N Yorks

FOCUS
A low-grade fillies' maiden in which three of the market leaders disappointed to varying degrees. The gallop was reasonable and the first two pulled clear. Weak form, rated around the runner-up.
Alensgrove(IRE) Official explanation: jockey said filly was never travelling

2782 VOLTIGEUR RESTAURANT #10.95 TWO COURSE SPECIAL H'CAP 7f
3:00 (3:01) (Class 5) (0-70,70) 3-Y-O **£1,942** (£578; £288; £144) **Stalls** High

Form RPR

0-64 1 **Maggie Mey (IRE)**[14] 2391 3-9-7 70 .... DanielTudhope 5 77
(David O'Meara) *cl up: led 2 1/2f out: rdn edgd lft and hdd ent fnl f: sn drvn and rallied to ld again last 50yds* **10/3**[1]

2020 2 *½* **Finefrenzyrolling (IRE)**[28] 1986 3-8-10 62........(b[1]) PatrickDonaghy(3) 1 68
(Mrs K Burke) *trckd ldrs: smooth hdwy over 2f out: rdn to ld ent fnl f: sn drvn and edgd lft: hdd and no ex last 50yds* **12/1**

33-4 3 *4* **Hoppy's Flyer (FR)**[60] 1220 3-9-7 70 .... MickyFenton 3 65
(Paul Midgley) *s.i.s and bhd: stdy hdwy 1/2-way: rdn 2f out: kpt on ins fnl f: nrst fin* **18/1**

4602 **4** 1½ **Fleurie Lover (IRE)**[7] 2592 3-8-3 **55**.................... AndrewHeffernan(3) 12 46
(Richard Guest) *towards rr: hdwy 3f out: rdn along 2f out: styd on appr fnl f: nrst fin* **7/1**
533- **5** 2¼ **Sovereign Street**[235] 6892 3-9-3 **66**............................ PaulMulrennan 10 51
(Ann Duffield) *trckd ldrs: smooth hdwy 3f out: rdn and ev ch over 2f out: sn drvn and wknd over 1f out* **13/2**[3]
3630 **6** nk **Poppy's Rocket (IRE)**[15] 2365 3-8-6 **55**........................ KellyHarrison 9 39
(Marjorie Fife) *towards rr: hdwy wl over 2f out: sn rdn and kpt on fnl f: nrst fin* **25/1**
6300 **7** 1½ **Twennyshortkid**[13] 2396 3-7-13 **51** oh2.................. DeclanCannon(3) 13 31
(Paul Midgley) *hmpd s and rr tl styd on fnl 2f: n.d* **14/1**
000- **8** nk **Ice Girl**[259] 6264 3-8-2 **54**..(e[1]) JamesSullivan(3) 15 33
(Michael Easterby) *wnt lft and hmpd s: in rr tl sme late hdwy* **18/1**
4010 **9** ½ **Spirit Of Grace**[19] 2215 3-9-5 **68**....................................... JoeFanning 7 46
(Alan McCabe) *led: rdn along 1/2-way: hdd 2 1/2f out: sn drvn and wknd* **15/2**
0-02 **10** 2 **Ryedale Dancer (IRE)**[15] 2351 3-8-3 **52**..................... DuranFentiman 8 25
(Tim Easterby) *prom: rdn along wl over 2f out: sn wknd* **7/2**[2]
140- **11** 1½ **Whats For Pudding (IRE)**[256] 6325 3-7-13 **53**.............. NeilFarley(5) 11 22
(Declan Carroll) *chsd ldrs: rdn along over 2f out: sn wknd* **33/1**
0-00 **12** ¾ **Spin A Wish**[15] 2350 3-8-2 **51** oh4.. PaulQuinn 2 18
(Richard Whitaker) *midfield: rdn along 1/2-way: sn wknd* **40/1**
06-0 **13** 2¾ **Cannon Bolt (IRE)**[34] 1812 3-8-5 **54** oh3 ow3............... LeeNewman 14 13
(Robin Bastiman) *hmpd s: a in rr* **50/1**

1m 23.46s (-1.04) **Going Correction** -0.15s/f (Firm) **13** Ran SP% **119.0**
Speed ratings (Par 99): **99,98,93,92,89 89,87,87,86,84 82,81,78**
Tote Swingers: 1&2 £12.10, 1&3 £13.40, 2&3 £29.40 CSF £42.36 CT £491.13 TOTE £3.70: £1.40, £5.30, £5.50; EX 54.50 Trifecta £161.10 Pool: £479.05 - 2.20 winning units..
Owner The Ten Commandments **Bred** Roger O'Callaghan **Trained** Nawton, N Yorks
■ Stewards' Enquiry : Daniel Tudhope one-day ban: used wip down the shoulder in the forehand position (Jun 21)

FOCUS
A couple of unexposed sorts in a modest handicap. The gallop was reasonable, but this was another race in which the prominent racers held the edge. Improved form from the first two.
Sovereign Street Official explanation: jockey said filly ran too free

2783 JOHN SMITH'S REDCAR STRAIGHT-MILE CHAMPIONSHIP H'CAP (QUALIFIER) 1m
3:35 (3:36) (Class 3) (0-95,90) 3-Y-O+
£3,738 (£1,119; £559; £280; £139; £70) **Stalls** High

Form RPR
2-11 **1** **Boom And Bust (IRE)**[17] 2310 4-9-6 **86**......................... HayleyTurner 7 99+
(Marcus Tregoning) *trckd ldrs: hdwy and cl up 3f out: rdn to ld wl over 1f out: clr ins fnl f* **4/1**[1]
4221 **2** 2¼ **Just Bond (IRE)**[28] 1970 9-9-5 **85**................................. PaulMulrennan 2 91
(Geoffrey Oldroyd) *hld up and bhd: swtchd rt to stands' rail over 2f out: gd hdwy wl over 1f out: rdn and styd on strly ins fnl f* **14/1**
-025 **3** 1 **Reel Buddy Star**[14] 2390 6-9-5 **85**................................ DanielTudhope 3 89
(George Moore) *cl up: rdn and ev ch 2f out tl drvn and one pce ent fnl f* **7/1**[3]
0003 **4** 1½ **San Cassiano (IRE)**[4] 2674 4-9-0 **80**...........................(b) PJMcDonald 10 80
(Ruth Carr) *led: rdn along 3f out: drvn and hdd wl over 1f out: sn edgd lft and one pce* **9/2**[2]
-000 **5** 1 **Kiwi Bay**[23] 2123 6-9-10 **90**... TomEaves 4 88
(Michael Dods) *cl up: rdn along wl over 2f out: drvn wl over 1f out: grad wknd* **8/1**
0000 **6** ½ **Al Muheer (IRE)**[10] 2495 6-9-0 **83**.........................(p) JamesSullivan(3) 11 80
(Ruth Carr) *hld up towards rr: hdwy and n.m.r 3f out: rdn 2f out: kpt on same pce* **25/1**
0003 **7** 1½ **Collateral Damage (IRE)**[10] 2495 8-9-3 **83**......................(t) DavidAllan 6 76
(Tim Easterby) *hld up towards rr: hdwy wl over 2f out: rdn wl over 1f out: sn no imp* **9/2**[2]
6-00 **8** 1 **Ginger Jack**[14] 2390 4-9-7 **87**....................................... DuranFentiman 12 78
(Geoffrey Harker) *hld up towards rr: n.d* **14/1**
3130 **9** nk **Mujaadel (USA)**[25] 2061 6-8-13 **82**.....................(p) MichaelO'Connell(3) 8 72
(David Nicholls) *rrd s and s.i.s: sn in midfield: rdn along over 2f out and sn wknd* **25/1**
-040 **10** 5 **Cara's Request (AUS)**[13] 2398 6-9-3 **83**...................... AdrianNicholls 1 62
(David Nicholls) *t.k.h: prom to 1/2-way: sn lost pl and bhd* **20/1**
-006 **11** 2½ **Rasselas (IRE)**[12] 2431 4-8-11 **80**....................................... BillyCray(3) 5 53
(David Nicholls) *chsd ldrs: rdn along 3f out: sn wknd* **18/1**
4026 **12** 6 **Northern Fling**[13] 2398 7-9-2 **82**.. KierenFallon 9 41
(Jim Goldie) *in tch: rdn along over 3f out: sn wknd and bhd whn eased wl over 1f out* **14/1**

1m 35.37s (-2.63) **Going Correction** -0.15s/f (Firm) **12** Ran SP% **117.7**
Speed ratings (Par 107): **107,104,103,102,101 100,99,98,97,92 90,84**
Tote Swingers: 1&2 £4.30, 1&3 £6.80, 2&3 £12.90 CSF £58.75 CT £383.90 TOTE £3.20: £1.20, £3.80, £2.80; EX 47.30 Trifecta £188.80 Pool: £699.11 - 2.74 winning units..
Owner Jas Singh **Bred** Duncan A McGregor **Trained** Lambourn, Berks

FOCUS
There was a heavy shower on the run up to this race, but the riders reported it hadn't got into the ground. Mainly exposed handicappers, but a useful contest in which the gallop was reasonable. The winner should cope with a higher grade and is rated a little better than the bare form.

NOTEBOOK
Boom And Bust(IRE) ◆ is a progressive sort who showed he didn't have to make the running when beating a competitive-looking field to register another career-best, despite edging off a true line late on. He is thriving and, on this evidence, this strong-traveller may be capable of further improvement. (op 9-2 tchd 11-2)
Just Bond(IRE), fresh from an improved turf run, ran at least as well from this 4lb higher mark to chase home a progressive sort. He deserves plenty of credit given he came from a long way back and, although vulnerable to a younger rival, should win again on turf when things pan out. (op 10-1)
Reel Buddy Star doesn't have much in hand from his current mark, but he had the run of the race and posted another solid effort. He looks a good guide to the worth of this form and should continue to give a good account. (op 10-1 tchd 13-2)
San Cassiano(IRE), who was well-backed throughout the day, has slipped to a fair mark and, although he may not be entirely straightforward, again showed enough in blinkers to suggest he's capable of picking up a handicap for his in-form yard. (op 5-1 tchd 4-1)
Kiwi Bay, who took this race last year, was ridden much more prominently than is usually the case but was far from disgraced after racing a shade keen early on. He may be seen to best effect coming from off a stronger gallop and wouldn't be one to write off just yet. (op 7-1 tchd 13-2)
Al Muheer(IRE) ◆, who has slipped a fair way in the weights, ran his best race for some time on only this third run for the yard. Consistency hasn't been his strong suit, but he's the type to win a race or two for these connections. (op 20-1)
Collateral Damage(IRE), sixth in this race last year, failed to build in the anticipated manner on his latest Catterick run back over this more suitable trip, but wasn't disgraced after attempting to come from off the pace. He is 11lb lower than at this stage last year and is worth another chance. (tchd 5-1 in a place)

2784 RACING UK CHANNEL 432 MAIDEN CLAIMING STKS 6f
4:10 (4:10) (Class 6) 2-Y-O **£1,706** (£503; £252) **Stalls** High

Form RPR
022 **1** **Pint Size**[4] 2693 2-8-7 0.. AdrianNicholls 3 69+
(David Nicholls) *qckly away and mde all: clr fr wl over 1f out: easily* **6/4**[1]
5534 **2** 8 **Latte**[12] 2409 2-8-11 0.. KierenFallon 4 50
(Linda Stubbs) *trckd ldrs: hdwy over 2f out: rdn to chse wnr fr wl over 1f out: sn no imp* **7/4**[2]
605 **3** 5 **Flying Pickets (IRE)**[12] 2409 2-8-2 0.......................... DeclanCannon(3) 1 25
(David Brown) *trckd ldrs: hdwy to chse wnr wl over 2f out and sn rdn: drvn and one pce fr wl over 1f out* **9/1**
403 **4** 4 **Mad For Fun (IRE)**[15] 2362 2-7-13 0.......................... JamesSullivan(3) 7 10
(Paul Midgley) *towards rr: sme hdwy 2f out: sn rdn and n.d* **6/1**[3]
60 **5** 1¾ **Unforgiving (IRE)**[15] 2355 2-8-0 0................................. AndrewMullen 2 —
(Alan McCabe) *in tch on outer: rdn along to chse ldrs 1/2-way: drvn and outpcd fnl 2f* **16/1**
6 **6** ¾ **Sophar**[8] 2563 2-8-8 0.. BillyCray(3) 5 11
(Jason Ward) *a in rr* **66/1**
7 7 **Prebends Bridge** 2-8-2 0.. AndrewHeffernan(3) 6 —
(Howard Johnson) *chsd wnr: rdn along 1/2-way: sn wknd* **20/1**

1m 11.14s (-0.66) **Going Correction** -0.15s/f (Firm) **7** Ran SP% **112.8**
Speed ratings (Par 91): **98,87,80,75,73 72,62**
Tote Swingers: 1&2 £1.40, 1&3 £2.30, 2&3 £3.40 CSF £4.22 TOTE £2.20: £1.20, £1.80; EX 3.30.The winner was claimed by Mr Kristian Strangeway for £6,000.
Owner D Nicholls & M Love **Bred** Bambi Bloodstock **Trained** Sessay, N Yorks

FOCUS
A modest and uncompetitive claimer and run in the rain. The gallop was a fair. The winner is rated to his pre-race mark, but could be worth up to 10lb higher.

NOTEBOOK
Pint Size had no problems with the return to 6f and, although uneasy in the market, ran up to his best to win an uncompetitive event with plenty in hand. He has bags of foot and, although subsequently claimed, can add to his tally in this grade. (op Evens)
Latte, who unlike the winner, has plenty of size and scope, but was firmly put in his place over this longer trip in this lesser grade after attracting support. He will be worth a try over 7f in due course and should be able to pick up a race. (op 5-2 tchd 11-4)
Flying Pickets(IRE), with the blinkers left off this time, was nibbled at in the market but again had his limitations exposed and she is of little immediate interest. (op 20-1)
Mad For Fun(IRE) finished much further behind the winner than at Thirsk last time and is likely to remain vulnerable to the better sorts in this grade or in maidens. (op 7-1 tchd 8-1)

2785 LADIES' DAY ON SATURDAY 18TH JUNE MEDIAN AUCTION MAIDEN STKS 1m
4:45 (4:48) (Class 6) 3-5-Y-O **£1,706** (£503; £252) **Stalls** High

Form RPR
03-2 **1** **Set Me Free (IRE)**[21] 2174 3-9-2 76.................................. KierenFallon 4 67+
(Luca Cumani) *trckd ldng pair: hdwy to ld wl over 3f out: clr 2f out: easily* **1/8**[1]
30 **2** 6 **Bella Montagna**[21] 2185 3-8-11 0... TomEaves 7 48
(John Quinn) *towards rr: pushed along 1/2-way: hdwy over 2f out: swtchd lft over 1f out: kpt on to take 2nd ins fnl f: no ch w wnr* **14/1**[3]
-000 **3** 3¾ **Into Mac**[24] 2114 5-9-6 40.. TerenceFury(7) 6 47?
(Neville Bycroft) *cl up: led after 1 1/2f: pushed along and hdd over 3f out: rdn and hung bdly rt wl over 1f out: one pce and lost 2nd ins fnl f* **50/1**
4 2¼ **Born To Shine (USA)** 3-9-2 0.. PJMcDonald 5 39
(Alan Swinbank) *s.i.s and in rr: hdwy 3f out: sn rdn and n.d* **9/1**[2]
00-0 **5** 11 **Pope Potter**[4] 2673 3-8-13 0..(p) RobertLButler(3) 2 14
(Richard Guest) *led 1 1/2f: cl up to 1/2-way: sn wknd and bhd fnl 2f* **66/1**
00- **6** 20 **Cono (IRE)**[321] 4241 3-9-2 0.. PatrickMathers 1 —
(Colin Teague) *a in rr: outpcd and wl bhd fr over 2f out* **100/1**

1m 39.41s (1.41) **Going Correction** -0.15s/f (Firm)
WFA 3 from 5yo 11lb **6** Ran SP% **110.0**
Speed ratings (Par 101): **86,80,76,74,63 43**
Tote Swingers: 1&2 £1.10, 1&3 £3.70, 2&3 £6.10 CSF £2.88 TOTE £1.10: £1.02, £2.50; EX 2.70.
Owner Leonidas Marinopoulos **Bred** Skymarc Farm **Trained** Newmarket, Suffolk
■ Stewards' Enquiry : Terence Fury caution: used whip without giving gelding time to respond

FOCUS
Maiden races rarely come as uncompetitive as this one and the proximity of the 40-rated third confirms the form behind the winner is very moderate. The winner did not need to match his reappearance form. The gallop was an ordinary one and the time was slow.

2786 YORKSHIRE RACING SUMMER FESTIVAL 16TH - 24TH JULY H'CAP 1m 2f
5:15 (5:18) (Class 6) (0-55,55) 3-Y-O **£1,706** (£503; £252) **Stalls** Low

Form RPR
5-25 **1** **Pinotage**[29] 1944 3-9-0 **53**... RobertWinston 1 59
(Richard Whitaker) *hld up towards rr: stdy hdwy 4f out: chsd ldrs over 2f out: rdn to ld jst over 1f out: flashed tail and hung lft ins fnl f: kpt on strly* **7/1**
-354 **2** 2½ **Goodmanyourself**[19] 2239 3-8-7 **46**................................ MickyFenton 5 48
(Paul Midgley) *trckd ldrs: hdwy over 3f out: led 3f out: rdn 2f out: drvn and hdd jst over 1f out: hld whn n.m.r ins fnl f* **4/1**[1]
0040 **3** 1¾ **Commander Veejay**[11] 2465 3-8-4 **46** oh1......(p) AndrewHeffernan(3) 14 43
(Brian Rothwell) *hld up in rr: hdwy 3f out: nt clr run and swtchd outside wl over 1f out: sn rdn and styd on wl fnl f: tk 3rd on line* **20/1**
00-3 **4** nse **Ninth Parallel (USA)**[37] 1710 3-9-1 **54**.......................(p) FrannyNorton 11 51
(Ann Duffield) *hld up in tch: hdwy over 3f out: rdn to chse ldr 2f out: sn drvn and ev ch tl one pce appr fnl f* **13/2**
-050 **5** 2½ **Playful Girl (IRE)**[8] 2571 3-8-7 **46** oh1............................ DuranFentiman 2 38
(Tim Easterby) *chsd ldrs: rdn along over 3f out: drvn over 2f out: sn one pce* **16/1**
000- **6** ¾ **Final Liberation (FR)**[203] 7470 3-9-2 **55**............................ SebSanders 9 45
(Sir Mark Prescott Bt) *chsd ldrs: rdn along 3f out: drvn over 2f out: sn one pce* **9/2**[2]
6-43 **7** 3½ **Alemaratiya**[12] 2432 3-9-0 **53**.. MartinLane 12 36
(David Simcock) *hld up towards rr: hdwy over 3f out: in tch and rdn over 2f out: sn drvn and n.d* **9/1**
040 **8** 4 **Love For Love**[15] 2351 3-9-0 **53**..................................... DanielTudhope 13 28
(David O'Meara) *cl up: led over 4f out: rdn along and hdd 3f out: sn wknd* **5/1**[3]

00-0 **9** *2 1/4* **Be My Spy**[31] 1910 3-8-7 **46** oh1 (p) GregFairley 15 17
(Peter Salmon) *midfield: pushed along and lost pl bef 1/2-way: sn in rr* **100/1**

0-00 **10** *1/2* **Newzflash**[15] 2351 3-8-7 **46** oh1 (p) TomEaves 4 16
(Ollie Pears) *led: pushed along and hdd over 4f out: rdn over 3f out: sn drvn and grad wknd* **28/1**

000 **11** *1* **Hey Up There (IRE)**[18] 2249 3-8-4 **46** oh1 JamesSullivan(3) 3 14
(Ruth Carr) *in tch on inner: hdwy to chse ldrs 4f out: rdn along 3f out: n.m.r and lost pl wl over 2f out: sn bhd* **66/1**

-000 **12** *34* **Go**[5] 2635 3-8-13 **52** (v[1]) FrederikTylicki 10 —
(Micky Hammond) *prom on outer: rdn along over 4f out: sn wknd and bhd fnl 2f* **28/1**

2m 9.75s (2.65) **Going Correction** -0.15s/f (Firm) **12** Ran SP% **110.7**
Speed ratings (Par 97): **83,81,79,79,77 76,74,70,69,68 67,40**
Tote Swingers: 1&2 £4.90, 1&3 £22.10, 2&3 £14.60 CSF £29.69 CT £459.70 TOTE £8.60: £2.40, £2.10, £4.70; EX 33.80 Trifecta £378.50 Part won. Pool: £511.61 - 0.61 winning units..
Owner Nice Day Out Partnership **Bred** Hellwood Stud Farm **Trained** Scarcroft, W Yorks
■ May Burnett (40/1, ref to ent stalls) and Wild Hysteria (14/1, unruly in stalls) were withdrawn. Deduct 5p in the £ under R4.
■ Stewards' Enquiry : Robert Winston one-day ban: careless riding (Jun 21)

FOCUS
A moderate handicap run in driving rain. Weak form rated through the second. The gallop was just a modest one.
T/Plt: £157.10 to a £1 stake. Pool: £63,069.00 - 292.98 winning tickets. T/Qpdt: £7.60 to a £1 stake. Pool: £5,445.00 - 526.68 winning tickets. JR

2221 SALISBURY (R-H)
Tuesday, June 7

OFFICIAL GOING: Good to firm

2787 GEORGE SMITH HORSEBOXES MAIDEN AUCTION STKS (DIV I) 6f
2:15 (2:17) (Class 5) 2-Y-O **£2,590** (£770; £385; £192) **Stalls** Low

Form RPR

3 **1** **Blackdown Fair**[17] 2309 2-8-4 0 AndreaAtzeni 4 80+
(Rod Millman) *mde all: pushed clr 2f out and in n.d after: easily* **7/2[2]**

2 *4 1/2* **Rafaella** 2-8-7 0 LukeMorris 6 70
(Harry Dunlop) *chsd ldrs: wnt 2nd 1f out but nvr any ch w wnr: edgd lft and kpt on cl home* **16/1**

3 *1 3/4* **Miss Conduct** 2-8-4 0 NickyMackay 3 61
(John Spearing) *chsd ldrs: wnt 2nd 2f out but nvr nr wnr: lost 2nd 1f out and styd on same pce* **25/1**

4 *2 1/4* **My Sharona** 2-7-13 0 KieranO'Neill(5) 13 55
(Sylvester Kirk) *s.i.s: green: drvn and hdwy 3f out: styd on wl fnl f: nt rch ldrs* **25/1**

4 **5** *hd* **Gypsy Rider**[14] 2374 2-8-9 0 CathyGannon 12 59
(Bryn Palling) *chsd ldrs and wnt 2nd 3f out to 2f out: one pce fnl f* **14/1**

6 *1 1/2* **Viscount Vert (IRE)** 2-9-2 0 DavidProbert 2 62
(Andrew Balding) *rdn along fr stalls: hdwy 2f out: styd on fnl f but nvr a threat* **11/4[1]**

0 **7** *hd* **Plym**[17] 2309 2-8-11 0 PatDobbs 5 56
(Richard Hannon) *s.i.s: in rr: hdwy fr 2f out: kpt on fnl f but nvr a threat* **8/1**

8 *3/4* **Mr Knightley (IRE)** 2-9-2 0 DaneO'Neill 14 59
(Richard Hannon) *in rr: drvn along over 2f out: hdwy over 1f out: kpt on cl home* **13/2[3]**

9 *1 1/4* **Meanwhile (IRE)** 2-7-13 0 HarryBentley(5) 15 43
(William Knight) *s.i.s: in rr: drvn and green over 2f out: kpt on along stages* **22/1**

0 **10** *1* **Native Hedgerow (IRE)**[25] 2049 2-8-9 0 JohnFahy(3) 11 48
(Peter Hedger) *in rr: drvn and hdwy fr 3f out: nvr rchd ldrs and kpt on same pce appr fnl f* **33/1**

11 *1/2* **Hi There (IRE)** 2-8-12 0 EddieAhern 8 46
(J W Hills) *sn in tch and chsng ldrs: wknd fr 2f out* **14/1**

0 **12** *2 1/2* **Calusa Bay (IRE)**[22] 2153 2-7-13 0 JemmaMarshall(5) 16 31
(Pat Phelan) *in rr: no ch whn hung rt 2f out* **100/1**

13 *2 1/2* **One More Roman (IRE)** 2-8-9 0 JamieSpencer 7 28
(J S Moore) *chsd wnr to 3f out: wknd sn after* **8/1**

0 **14** *2 1/4* **Sea Of Light (IRE)**[6] 2606 2-8-4 0 ChrisCatlin 9 17
(Roger Charlton) *spd over 3f* **50/1**

15 *29* **Kathryn Perry (IRE)** 2-8-7 0 RobbieFitzpatrick 10 —+
(Andrew Haynes) *slowly away and veered bdly rt to far rails sn after: a t.o* **33/1**

1m 15.44s (0.64) **Going Correction** -0.10s/f (Good) **15** Ran SP% **124.5**
Speed ratings (Par 93): **91,85,82,79,79 77,77,76,74,73 72,69,65,62,24**
Tote Swingers: 1&2 £20.10, 1&3 £20.80, 2&3 £23.00 CSF £56.11 TOTE £3.00: £1.30, £5.60, £9.70; EX 76.80.
Owner Roy Brooke **Bred** Brookridge Timber Ltd **Trained** Kentisbeare, Devon

FOCUS
This was a non-bonus auction maiden, so not obviously strong form, and a low draw seemed helpful (first three drawn in single figures), with the main action unfolding towards the far rail. The time was 0.25 seconds quicker than the second division.

NOTEBOOK
Blackdown Fair had plenty in her favour, racing against the fence for much of the way until edging slightly left in the closing stages, and she had the benefit of experience over the next three finishers. Plus she was getting weight from most of her rivals. However, she's an extremely quick filly and evidently has a fair amount of ability. Her dam didn't progress in the long-term after a winning debut, but this one was improving on an encouraging introduction and her natural speed can see her hold her own in better company, provided she continues to go the right way. (op 3-1 tchd 4-1)
Rafaella, an 8,000gns first foal of a quite useful 1m winner (Listed placed at 1m2f), fared best of the newcomers. She was favourably drawn but can still be expected to improve. (op 25-1)
Miss Conduct is a half-sister to multiple 6f-7f winner Mister Elegant and 7f scorer Zeffirelli, out of a successful mare. She was another who was helped by a low draw, but she's a late April foal so there should be better to come. (op 20-1)
My Sharona, a 6,000gns April foal, fared best of those from off the pace and a double-figure stall. She was keeping on nicely enough at the finish and can improve. (op 28-1 tchd 22-1)
Gypsy Rider raced a bit further away from the far rail than a few of these and didn't step up significantly on his Chepstow debut. (op 12-1)

Viscount Vert(IRE), a 21,000euros purchase, was sent off favourite so has presumably shown plenty at home. He was not away well enough to make use of his low draw, but he kept on to post a respectable introduction. Official explanation: jockey said colt was slowly away (op 7-2 tchd 4-1)

2788 GEORGE SMITH HORSEBOXES MAIDEN AUCTION STKS (DIV II) 6f
2:45 (2:47) (Class 5) 2-Y-O **£2,590** (£770; £385; £192) **Stalls** Low

Form RPR

5 **1** **Netley Marsh**[6] 2602 2-8-12 0 DaneO'Neill 14 73
(Richard Hannon) *mid-div: swtchd lft and hdwy whn rdn jst over 2f out: r.o wl ins fnl f: led fnl 75yds* **5/1[2]**

004 **2** *1/2* **Bajan Hero**[17] 2283 2-8-12 0 CathyGannon 8 71
(David Evans) *stmbld leaving stalls: sn pushed into ld: rdn over 2f out: edgd lft and no ex whn hdd fnl 75yds* **10/1**

3 *1/2* **Royal Reyah** 2-8-9 0 FergusSweeney 2 67+
(Stuart Kittow) *sn nudged along towards rr: swtchd lft 3f out: hdwy 2f out: r.o ins fnl f: nrst fin* **11/2[3]**

5 **4** *3/4* **Emma Jean (IRE)**[14] 2374 2-7-11 0 HarryBentley(7) 9 59
(J S Moore) *chsd ldrs: rdn to chse ldr 2f out tl ins fnl f: edgd lft: kpt on same pce* **4/1[1]**

5 *1 3/4* **Sovereign Waters** 2-8-4 0 LukeMorris 11 55+
(Eve Johnson Houghton) *s.i.s: towards rr: hdwy whn nt clr run briefly 2f out: swtchd lft: kpt on ins fnl f: nrst fin* **16/1**

025 **6** *nk* **Fromthestables Com (IRE)**[20] 2194 2-8-12 0 EddieAhern 15 61
(J W Hills) *in tch: rdn over 2f out: swtchd rt over 1f out: kpt on same pce* **12/1**

7 *1 1/2* **Flying Kitty** 2-8-6 0 ow2 MarcHalford 1 51
(John Bridger) *towards rr: c centre and stdy hdwy fr over 2f out: kpt on same pce fnl f* **80/1**

8 *3/4* **The Name Is Don (IRE)** 2-8-9 0 DavidProbert 4 52
(Mark Gillard) *mid-div: rdn and sme hdwy over 2f out: fdd fnl 120yds* **33/1**

9 *1* **The New Black (IRE)** 2-8-2 0 KieranO'Neill(5) 10 46
(Richard Hannon) *sn pushed along in midfield: sme prog 2f out: fdd fnl 120yds* **8/1**

6 **10** *nse* **Single Girl (IRE)**[20] 2187 2-8-7 0 NickyMackay 6 46
(Jonathan Portman) *chsd ldr: rdn over 2f out: wknd over 1f out* **12/1**

11 *1/2* **Island Melody (IRE)** 2-8-9 0 LiamKeniry 13 47
(J S Moore) *s.i.s: racd green: detached in last: styd on past btn horses fnl f: nvr a factor* **14/1**

12 *4 1/2* **Doc Hill** 2-8-9 0 ChrisCatlin 5 33
(Michael Blanshard) *chsd ldrs: rdn over 3f out: wknd 2f out* **28/1**

0 **13** *6* **Joli Colourful (IRE)**[64] 1136 2-8-2 0 DavidKenny(7) 7 15
(Tony Newcombe) *bmpd leaving stalls: trckd ldrs racing keenly: effrt 3f out: wknd 2f out* **20/1**

14 *nk* **Stag Hill (IRE)** 2-8-9 0 JamesDoyle 3 14
(Sylvester Kirk) *mid-div tl wknd 2f out* **12/1**

1m 15.69s (0.89) **Going Correction** -0.10s/f (Good) **14** Ran SP% **120.3**
Speed ratings (Par 93): **90,89,88,87,85 84,82,81,80,80 79,73,65,65**
Tote Swingers: 1&2 £12.60, 1&3 £7.80, 2&3 £7.10 CSF £52.38 TOTE £6.20: £1.90, £3.50, £2.40; EX 60.00.
Owner The Major Shear **Bred** Bishop Wilton Stud **Trained** East Everleigh, Wilts

FOCUS
The second division of this non-bonus auction maiden, and the time was 0.25 seconds slower than the first leg, so modest-looking form.

NOTEBOOK
Netley Marsh ◆ ruined his chance with a slow start on his debut on Polytrack six days earlier, but he showed some ability on that occasion and had learnt just enough. He wasn't best away once again but produced a sustained challenge, and he turned out to be the only winner from six races run on the straight track on this card who came from some way off the pace. His dam won over 2m, so it's reasonable to assume he can continue to progress with time and distance. (tchd 9-2)
Bajan Hero raced in much the same fashion to the winner of the first division, showing good speed against the far rail, only he didn't see his race out quite as well. He's improving, though. (op 17-2)
Royal Reyah ◆, an April foal, is from a family Stuart Kittow knows well and he should soon be winning. A half-brother to two successful sprinters for this yard, his dam was a 6f winner for the stable. He stayed on from a long way back and was really going on at the finish to fare best of the newcomers. (op 13-2)
Emma Jean(IRE)'s Chepstow debut, when she was fifth, looks pretty limited form. The fourth-placed finisher from that race could only manage fifth in the first division of this maiden. (op 9-2)
Sovereign Waters ran to only a moderate level, but there's good reason to expect quite a bit more in due course. A May foal who's a half-sister to Oaks runner-up Something Exciting, she was doing her best work at the finish. Much like the winner, she really should do better with time and distance.
Flying Kitty cost only £400, but she's related to a few winners at around this trip and showed ability, despite ending up out widest having started against the rail. She's a May foal, so should be able to do better. (op 100-1 tchd 66-1)
Stag Hill(IRE) Official explanation: jockey said colt hung right-handed

2789 DOUGLAND CLAIMING STKS 6f 212y
3:20 (3:20) (Class 5) 3-Y-O+ **£2,428** (£722; £361; £180) **Stalls** Low

Form RPR

1120 **1** **April Fool**[17] 2300 7-9-4 81 (b) RichardEvans(3) 10 81
(David Evans) *mde all: rdr dropped reins 2f out: pushed along and styd on wl whn chal ins fnl 2f: readily* **2/1[1]**

525 **2** *2 1/2* **Stefanki (IRE)**[20] 2206 4-9-9 82 (p) MatthewDavies(3) 4 79
(George Baker) *s.i.s: in rr: hdwy on outside 3f out: styd on to chse wnr over 1f out: drvn to chal sn after but continually hung lft and nt keen: wl hld fnl 100yds* **7/2[2]**

0-10 **3** *1 1/4* **Spanish Bounty**[24] 2099 6-9-12 87 EddieAhern 3 79+
(Jonathan Portman) *awkward stalls: in tch: hdwy 3f out: chsd wnr 2f out: one pce into 3rd and hld whn hmpd fnl 150yds* **5/1[3]**

5252 **4** *1 1/4* **Danceyourselfdizzy (IRE)**[7] 2581 3-8-4 63 KieranO'Neill(5) 1 61
(Richard Hannon) *chsd ldrs: rdn over 2f out: wknd appr fnl f* **5/1[3]**

6-14 **5** *1 3/4* **Red Zeus (IRE)**[39] 1659 3-8-7 63 (p) LiamKeniry 2 54
(J S Moore) *in rr: hdwy and hung rt 2f out: styd on fnl f: nvr any ch* **20/1**

0-46 **6** *1/2* **The Name Is Frank**[22] 2142 6-9-5 60 (t) FergusSweeney 7 59
(Mark Gillard) *chsd ldr to 2f out: sn btn* **33/1**

04-0 **7** *2 1/2* **Hobson**[36] 1755 6-8-11 69 AmyScott(5) 5 49
(Eve Johnson Houghton) *a outpcd* **12/1**

5562 **8** *5* **Desert Auction (IRE)**[5] 2642 4-9-5 72 (v) MartinDwyer 8 39
(Dean Ivory) *chsd ldrs tl wknd 2f out* **10/1**

006 9 11 **Sunrise Lyric (IRE)**[22] 2155 4-8-13 54 ChrisCatlin 6 —
(Paul Cole) *s.i.s: a in rr* **40/1**

1m 27.79s (-0.81) **Going Correction** -0.10s/f (Good)
WFA 3 from 4yo+ 10lb **9** Ran SP% **115.8**
Speed ratings (Par 103): **100,97,95,94,92 91,88,83,70**
Tote Swingers: 1&2 £1.90, 1&3 £1.40, 2&3 £3.60 CSF £8.79 TOTE £3.20: £1.10, £1.10, £3.50; EX 12.50.The winner was claimed by Ron Harris for £10,000.
Owner Mrs E Evans **Bred** Miss B Swire **Trained** Pandy, Monmouths

FOCUS
A decent enough claimer but it's doubtful if the first three were at their best.
Spanish Bounty Official explanation: jockey said gelding reared leaving the stalls

2790 CASTLEPOINT SHOPPING PARK A3060 BOURNEMOUTH MAIDEN STKS 6f 212y
3:55 (3:56) (Class 5) 3-Y-O+ **£2,914** (£867; £433; £216) **Stalls** Low

Form RPR

5-2 1 **Emilio Largo**[29] 1934 3-9-3 0 TomQueally 9 87+
(Sir Henry Cecil) *t.k.h: trckd ldrs: shkn up: swtchd lft and chal between horses whn n.m.r 1f out: qcknd to ld fnl 100yds: comf* **7/2**[2]

05- 2 1 **Sea Soldier (IRE)**[223] 7178 3-9-3 0 JimmyFortune 17 81
(Andrew Balding) *sn trcking ldr: led wl over 2f out: sn drvn: jnd over 1f out: strly chal ins fnl f: hdd and outpcd fnl 100yds* **6/1**[3]

22 3 ¾ **Moone's My Name**[24] 2103 3-8-12 0 JimCrowley 15 74
(Ralph Beckett) *front rnk: pressed ldrs fr 2f out and chal appr fnl f: outpcd by ldng duo fnl 100yds* **4/5**[1]

0- 4 4 **Thunda**[297] 5078 3-8-12 0 CathyGannon 8 63
(Eve Johnson Houghton) *t.k.h: chsd ldrs: rdn along 2f out: styng on same pce whn rdr dropped whip ins fnl f* **40/1**

0 5 2½ **Joyful Sound (IRE)**[32] 1865 3-9-3 0 RobertHavlin 12 61
(Andrew Haynes) *t.k.h: in tch: swtchd lft to outside and hdwy fr 2f out: styd on same pce ins fnl f* **50/1**

0-0 6 ½ **Heezararity**[24] 2103 3-9-3 0 AdamKirby 6 60
(Stuart Kittow) *chsd ldrs: rdn over 2f out: wknd over 1f out* **9/1**

7 nk **Budley** 3-8-10 0 JakePayne(7) 7 59
(Bill Turner) *slowly away: in rr: swtchd lft to outside and hdwy over 2f out: styd on fr over 1f out: could nt rch ldrs* **66/1**

8 1¼ **Noverton** 3-8-12 0 DaneO'Neill 3 51
(James Eustace) *mid-div: pushed along and one pce 1/2-way: kpt on fnl f but nvr a threat* **40/1**

5-0 9 1¼ **Dusty Bluebells (IRE)**[41] 1607 3-8-12 0 LukeMorris 5 47
(J S Moore) *chsd ldrs: rdn 3f out: wknd ins fnl 2f* **33/1**

0 10 2¼ **Bop Till Dawn (IRE)**[42] 1580 3-8-12 0 EddieAhern 18 41
(Harry Dunlop) *drvn to ld after 1f: hdd wl over 2f out: sn hanging rt: eased whn no ch fnl f* **100/1**

11 2 **Concrete Jungle (IRE)** 3-9-3 0 StevieDonohoe 13 41
(Andrew Haynes) *s.i.s: a towards rr* **100/1**

00 12 ½ **Hertford Street**[28] 1985 3-9-3 0 FergusSweeney 10 40
(Peter Makin) *chsd ldrs: swtchd lft and rdn over 2f out: sn wknd* **100/1**

13 1½ **Phlorian**[12] 2443 5-9-8 0 (tp) KieranO'Neill(5) 4 35
(Ian Patrick Browne, Ire) *in rr: sme hdwy into mid-div over 3f out: sn wknd* **80/1**

06 14 nk **Desert Chieftain**[11] 2479 3-9-3 0 J-PGuillambert 14 35
(Luca Cumani) *nvr in contention* **25/1**

00 15 ½ **Hector The Brave (IRE)**[41] 1606 4-9-13 0 SamHitchcott 16 33
(John E Long) *chsd ldrs tl wknd over 2f out* **150/1**

16 nse **Lady Bayside** 3-8-12 0 TomMcLaughlin 2 28
(Malcolm Saunders) *s.i.s: a in rr* **80/1**

17 15 **Dark Pegasus** 3-9-3 0 ChrisCatlin 11 —
(Karen George) *a in rr* **100/1**

18 1¼ **Tuscan Blue** 3-9-3 0 PatDobbs 1 —
(Richard Hannon) *a in rr* **20/1**

1m 27.8s (-0.80) **Going Correction** -0.10s/f (Good)
WFA 3 from 4yo+ 10lb **18** Ran SP% **129.0**
Speed ratings (Par 103): **100,98,98,93,90 90,89,88,86,84 81,81,79,79,78 78,61,60**
CSF £24.38 TOTE £3.80: £1.50, £2.00, £1.10; EX 23.30.
Owner Malcolm C Denmark **Bred** Mrs M Chaworth-Musters **Trained** Newmarket, Suffolk

FOCUS
A fair 3-y-o maiden for the time of the year and the time was almost identical to the earlier claimer, which was an above-average race for the grade won by the 81-rated April Fool. Once again the race unfolded towards the far rail. The form seems sound enough with the first three clear.

2791 BRITISH STALLION STUDS SUPPORTING BRITISH RACING E B F MARGADALE FILLIES' H'CAP 1m 1f 198y
4:30 (4:31) (Class 4) (0-85,84) 3-Y-O+ **£5,180** (£1,541; £770; £384) **Stalls** Low

Form RPR

0-60 1 **Golden Aria (IRE)**[19] 2232 4-9-2 72 PatDobbs 7 81
(Richard Hannon) *hld up last: rdn 3f out: centre fr 2f out: wnt 3rd ent fnl f: styd on strly to ld on line* **14/1**

510- 2 nse **Isolate**[220] 7235 3-8-9 78 EddieAhern 2 86
(Hughie Morrison) *in tch: jnd ldr travelling wl jst over 2f out: sn rdn: tk narrow advantage jst ins fnl f: hdd line* **11/2**[3]

3 ¾ **Love Over Gold (FR)**[208] 4-9-10 80 JimCrowley 5 87
(Ralph Beckett) *chsd ldr: rdn to ld jst over 2f out: hdd jst ins fnl f: no ex* **22/1**

51-3 4 4 **Istishaara (USA)**[26] 2022 3-8-8 77 TadhgO'Shea 4 75
(John Dunlop) *sn pushed along in last trio: rdn and hdwy over 3f out: chal briefly jst over 2f out: one pce after* **7/4**[1]

5-30 5 2 **Goldtrek (USA)**[19] 2220 4-9-6 76 JimmyFortune 3 71
(Roger Charlton) *led: rdn and hdd jst over 2f out: fdd fnl f* **9/2**[2]

2115 6 nk **Saint Helena (IRE)**[31] 1894 3-9-1 84 ChrisCatlin 1 77
(Harry Dunlop) *trckd ldrs: rdn over 3f out: wknd ent fnl f* **14/1**

15-4 7 7 **Beyeh (IRE)**[21] 2184 3-7-13 73 KieranO'Neill(5) 6 52
(Clive Brittain) *trckd ldrs: rdn over 3f out: wknd 2f out* **7/1**

4-61 8 1¾ **Miss Chicane**[19] 2232 3-8-5 74 LukeMorris 8 50
(Walter Swinburn) *s.i.s: rdn 3f out: a in last pair: wknd 2f out* **9/2**[2]

2m 7.71s (-2.19) **Going Correction** -0.10s/f (Good)
WFA 3 from 4yo 13lb **8** Ran SP% **118.3**
Speed ratings (Par 102): **104,103,103,100,98 98,92,91**
Tote Swingers: 1&2 £15.40, 1&3 £10.70, 2&3 £11.40 CSF £91.40 CT £1708.14 TOTE £28.10: £3.60, £2.30, £3.50; EX 145.70.
Owner Thurloe Thoroughbreds XX **Bred** Mrs Mary Coonan **Trained** East Everleigh, Wilts

FOCUS
A fair fillies' handicap run at a strong pace. The time was good and there;s a chance this form is better than rated.

2792 DOUGLAND H'CAP 6f 212y
5:00 (5:01) (Class 6) (0-65,65) 3-Y-O **£1,942** (£578; £216; £216) **Stalls** Low

Form RPR

-016 1 **Cadmium Loch**[18] 2243 3-9-0 58 RussKennemore 6 66
(Reg Hollinshead) *trckd ldr: rdn to ld appr fnl 2f: styd on wl u.p fnl f: all out* **20/1**

0-33 2 nk **El Maachi**[20] 2197 3-9-6 64 RobbieFitzpatrick 10 71
(Jim Best) *led: hdd appr fnl 2f: rallied to press wnr ins fnl f: no ex cl home* **14/1**

4231 3 hd **Mini's Destination**[15] 2351 3-9-0 58 NickyMackay 2 64+
(John Holt) *chsd ldrs: rdn 2f out: styd on wl thrght fnl f and clsng nr fin: nt quite get up* **10/1**

00-0 3 dht **Camberley Two**[37] 1724 3-8-6 50 ChrisCatlin 3 56
(Roger Charlton) *chsd ldrs: rdn over 2f out: styd on u.p fnl f: gng on cl home: nt quite get up* **6/1**[2]

066- 5 ¾ **Mrs Greeley**[227] 7094 3-9-7 65 TomQueally 11 69+
(Eve Johnson Houghton) *s.i.s: in rr: swtchd lft to outside and hdwy fr 2f out: str run fnl f: gng on cl home* **5/1**[1]

5-40 6 2¼ **Hawk Moth (IRE)**[29] 1949 3-9-4 62 CathyGannon 1 60+
(John Spearing) *s.i.s: in rr: and t.k.h: rdn over 2f out: n.m.r and hdwy over 1f out: kpt on fnl f: nt rch ldrs* **14/1**

6-00 7 1 **Paperetto**[15] 2368 3-9-7 65 EddieAhern 14 61
(Robert Mills) *sn in tch: drvn and styd on to chse ldrs ins fnl 2f: one pce fnl f* **10/1**

3353 8 nk **Titan Diamond (IRE)**[12] 2421 3-8-4 55 RachealKneller(7) 13 50
(Mark Usher) *chsd ldrs: rdn over 2f out: wknd 1f out* **16/1**

0614 9 2 **Miss Dutee**[8] 2553 3-9-0 63 KieranO'Neill(5) 15 52
(Richard Hannon) *in rr: hdwy over 2f out: in tch w ldrs over 1f out: sn shkn up and one pce* **16/1**

3332 10 1¾ **Cathcart Castle**[12] 2421 3-8-10 57 MartinHarley(3) 17 42
(Mick Channon) *chsd ldrs: rdn over 2f out: wknd appr fnl f* **15/2**

3615 11 1¼ **Spirit Of Oakdale (IRE)**[20] 2197 3-9-4 62 (p) AdamKirby 8 43
(Walter Swinburn) *chsd ldrs: rdn over 2f out: wknd wl over 1f out* **9/1**

106- 12 3¾ **Rather Cool**[222] 7197 3-8-11 55 StevieDonohoe 16 26
(Andrew Haynes) *in rr: hdwy over 2f out: keeping on whn nt clr run over 1f out: no ch after* **40/1**

00-6 13 2¼ **Piccolete**[37] 1724 3-8-10 54 DaneO'Neill 4 19
(Richard Hannon) *chsd ldrs over 4f* **7/1**[3]

0530 14 hd **Local Diktator**[14] 2375 3-9-2 60 LukeMorris 5 25
(Ronald Harris) *s.i.s: t.k.h: rdn 3f out: no prog and stl rr whn hung lft wl over 1f out* **33/1**

-341 15 1¾ **Lady On Top (IRE)**[14] 2384 3-8-9 53 FrankieMcDonald 18 13
(Nerys Dutfield) *in rr: rdn and hdwy on outside over 2f out: nvr on terms: sn wknd* **16/1**

-060 16 1 **One Cool Chick**[17] 2294 3-8-6 50 MarcHalford 7 —
(John Bridger) *t.k.h: chsd ldrs over 4f* **50/1**

1m 28.49s (-0.11) **Going Correction** -0.10s/f (Good) **16** Ran SP% **126.5**
Speed ratings (Par 97): **96,95,95,95,94 92,90,90,88,86 84,80,77,77,75 74**
Place: Mini's Destination £3.00 Camberley Two £2.90. Tricast: CL,EM,MD £1,550.73 CL,EM,CT £955.83. Tote Swingers: 1&2 £43.10, 1&MD £14.60, 1&CT £21.30, 2&MD £9.10, 2&CT£15.00. CSF £279.86 TOTE £36.20: £5.70, £3.00; EX 449.50.
Owner M Johnson **Bred** R Hollinshead And M Johnson **Trained** Upper Longdon, Staffs

FOCUS
A modest handicap in which it paid to race prominently and near the rail. The form has been given a bit of a chance.
Local Diktator Official explanation: jockey said colt hung left-handed

2793 CASTLEPOINT SHOPPING PARK A3060 BOURNEMOUTH H'CAP 1m 4f
5:30 (5:31) (Class 5) (0-75,74) 4-Y-O+ **£2,428** (£722; £361; £180) **Stalls** Low

Form RPR

12-1 1 **Danvilla**[21] 2176 4-9-3 70 WilliamCarson 4 80
(Paul Webber) *s.i.s: towards rr: drvn along over 5f out: last whn swtchd to centre over 3f out: hdwy over 2f out: styd on strly to ld ins fnl f: drifted rt: drvn out* **13/2**

26-4 2 1¾ **Rowan Tiger**[63] 1156 5-9-7 74 PatCosgrave 12 81
(Jim Boyle) *trckd ldr: led over 3f out: rdn over 2f out: hdd ins fnl f: styd on but no ex* **16/1**

2111 3 1¼ **Filun**[12] 2417 6-9-4 71 LiamKeniry 1 76
(Anthony Middleton) *hld up bhd: smooth hdwy fr over 2f out: rdn to dispute 2nd briefly over 1f out: styd on same pce* **9/1**

-303 4 ½ **Eshtyaaq**[19] 2224 4-9-2 69 CathyGannon 11 73
(David Evans) *in tch: swtchd lft and hdwy over 3f out: sn rdn: chsd ldr over 2f out tl jst over 1f out: styd on same pce* **7/2**[2]

0-10 5 4 **Gloucester**[22] 2156 8-8-11 71 DavidKenny(7) 9 69
(Michael Scudamore) *slowly away: towards rr: hdwy 4f out: rdn 3f out: one pce fnl 2f* **25/1**

03-2 6 nse **Eastern Magic**[25] 2055 4-9-0 67 ChrisCatlin 5 65
(Reg Hollinshead) *mid-div: rdn 3f out: styd on same pce fnl 2f* **9/1**

14-0 7 1¼ **True To Form (IRE)**[36] 1772 4-9-6 73 (p) TonyCulhane 3 69
(George Baker) *mid-div tl pushed along and lost pl over 3f out: sme late prog fnl f: n.d* **11/1**

-060 8 ½ **Rio Prince**[8] 2562 4-7-11 55 oh10 (t) HarryBentley(5) 2 50
(John Bridger) *trckd ldrs: rdn over 3f out: wknd over 1f out* **100/1**

-514 9 1 **Mons Calpe (IRE)**[22] 2156 5-9-1 73 (p) KieranO'Neill(5) 8 66
(Paul Cole) *led tl rdn over 3f out: kpt chsng ldrs tl wknd ent fnl f* **6/1**[3]

300/ 10 5 **Petito (IRE)**[397] 5546 8-7-13 55 oh5 SimonPearce(3) 7 40
(Mark Gillard) *s.i.s: steadily rcvrd to trck ldrs after 2f: rdn over 3f out: wknd 2f out* **66/1**

30/0 11 19 **Phonic (IRE)**[25] 2051 4-9-2 69 JimmyFortune 6 24
(John Dunlop) *mid-div tl wknd over 2f out: eased whn btn* **11/4**[1]

2m 35.73s (-2.27) **Going Correction** -0.10s/f (Good) **11** Ran SP% **117.1**
Speed ratings (Par 103): **103,101,101,100,98 97,97,96,96,92 80**
Tote Swingers: 1&2 £7.40, 1&3 £7.40, 2&3 £13.50 CSF £102.98 CT £940.40 TOTE £6.70: £1.80, £3.80, £2.20; EX 77.40.
Owner Shully Liebermann **Bred** Minster Stud **Trained** Mollington, Oxon

FOCUS
A fair handicap run at a good pace, and straightforward form.

Phonic(IRE) Official explanation: jockey said gelding would not let himself down on the ground

2794 AXMINSTER CARPETS RACING EXCELLENCE APPRENTICE H'CAP (WHIPS SHALL BE CARRIED BUT NOT USED) 6f

6:00 (6:07) (Class 5) (0-75,75) 4-Y-0+ **£2,428** (£722; £361; £180) **Stalls** Low

Form RPR

1312 **1** **Collect Art (IRE)**[10] 2497 4-9-10 **75** LucyKBarry 6 84
(Andrew Haynes) *wnt sltly rt s: mde all: fnd plenty whn briefly chal fnl 130yds: pushed out: readily* **11/8**[1]

-304 **2** *1* **Getcarter**[22] 2155 5-9-6 **71** MatthewLawson 3 77
(Richard Hannon) *in tch: pushed along 3f out: hdwy over 1f out: kpt on to go 2nd towards fin* **13/2**

0-33 **3** *½* **Witchry**[22] 2142 9-8-12 **63** CharlesBishop 1 67
(Tony Newcombe) *chsd wnr: pushed along 3f out: kpt on to hold ch briefly fnl 130yds: no ex* **9/2**[2]

0430 **4** *nse* **Rainy Night**[6] 2610 5-8-7 **63** (p) JackDuern(5) 8 67
(Reg Hollinshead) *chsd ldrs: pushed along 3f out: disp 2nd over 1f out: kpt on but no ex* **20/1**

5124 **5** *½* **Italian Tom (IRE)**[7] 2585 4-9-3 **71** LeonnaMayor(3) 2 73
(Ronald Harris) *in tch: pushed along to dispute 2nd over 1f out: kpt on to hold ch briefly fnl 130yds: no ex nring fin* **5/1**[3]

000 **6** *3 ¾* **Do More Business (IRE)**[12] 2426 4-8-2 **56** oh4 JakePayne(3) 5 46
(Pat Phelan) *in tch: pushed along 3f out: nvr gng pce to chal: fdd fnl f* **40/1**

5416 **7** *1 ¾* **Memphis Man**[5] 2633 8-8-4 **62** KevinLundie(7) 4 47
(David Evans) *taken slowly to s: s.i.s: bhd: nvr gng pce to get on terms* **14/1**

012- **8** *3 ¼* **Hidden Destiny**[188] 7655 4-8-11 **67** GeorgeDowning(5) 7 41
(Peter Makin) *trckd wnr: pushed along and edgd rt 3f out: wknd over 1f out* **10/1**

1m 14.34s (-0.46) **Going Correction** -0.10s/f (Good) **8** Ran SP% **113.2**
Speed ratings (Par 103): **99,97,97,96,96 91,88,84**
Tote Swingers: 1&2 £2.30, 1&3 £2.00, 2&3 £6.00. Totesuper 7: Win: Not won. Place: £147.60. CSF £10.63 CT £31.52 TOTE £2.30: £1.30, £1.30, £1.70; EX 13.10.
Owner Athos Racing **Bred** Pier House Stud **Trained** Limpley Stoke, Bath

FOCUS
For the first time on the straight track on this card, the runners initially shunned the far rail, but they tended to drift towards the fence in the closing stages. This looked a weakish handicap, rated around the third.
T/Jkpt: Part won. £7,323.10 to a £1 stake. Pool: £10,314 - 0.50 winning tickets. T/Plt: £263.20 to a £1 stake. Pool: £81,622.00 - 226.30 winning tickets. T/Qpdt: £31.40 to a £1 stake. Pool: £5,995.00 - 141.10 winning tickets. TM

2795 - 2796a (Foreign Racing) - See Raceform Interactive

2485 BEVERLEY (R-H)

Wednesday, June 8

OFFICIAL GOING: Good to firm (8.4)
Wind: Light, half behind Weather: Cloudy with sunny periods

2797 TIDMARSH TWINS BIRTHDAY CLAIMING STKS 5f

2:00 (2:00) (Class 6) 2-Y-0 **£1,619** (£481; £240; £120) **Stalls** Low

Form RPR

1 **Beaumaris (IRE)** 2-9-0 0 TomEaves 3 63+
(Ann Duffield) *in tch: pushed along 1/2-way: hdwy wl over 1f out: rdn to chal ent fnl f: sn led and kpt on wl* **7/1**[3]

6053 **2** *3* **Flying Pickets (IRE)**[1] 2784 2-8-2 0 DeclanCannon(3) 1 43
(David Brown) *cl up: rdn along 1/2-way: drvn and ch over 1f out: kpt on same pce ins fnl f* **13/2**[2]

3102 **3** *1 ½* **Mousie**[13] 2425 2-8-6 0 SilvestreDeSousa 5 39
(Alan McCabe) *led: rdn along 1 1/2f out: drvn ent fnl f: sn hdd & wknd* **2/5**[1]

3 **4** *6* **Island Bird**[13] 2429 2-7-9 0 NeilFarley(5) 6 11
(Kate Walton) *cl up: rdn along on outer 1/2-way: drvn over 1f out: wknd ent fnl f* **14/1**

6 **5** *53* **Elsie Tanner (IRE)**[5] 2665 2-8-0 0 PaulQuinn 4 —
(David Nicholls) *rrd and swvd violently lft s: virtually ref to r* **16/1**

64.92 secs (1.42) **Going Correction** -0.05s/f (Good) **5** Ran SP% **109.8**
Speed ratings (Par 91): **86,81,78,69,—**
toteswingers: 1&2 £11.40 CSF £46.22 TOTE £5.90: £1.20, £3.10; EX 24.40.
Owner Derek Iceton **Bred** D G Iceton **Trained** Constable Burton, N Yorks

FOCUS
A weak claimer even before the favourite ran well below form and one of the other runners virtually took no part. This is tricky form to pin down, but the winner made a pleasing start.

NOTEBOOK
Beaumaris(IRE) is bred to need further than this, being by Sir Percy out of mare by Fantastic Light, but she's clearly more precocious than her pedigree would suggest and won with something in hand after taking time to find her stride. It's hard to think she won't improve as she steps up in trip and might be one for nurseries if she's not exposed too much before they begin. (op 11-2)
Flying Pickets(IRE) had been well held in a similar event at Redcar the preceding day so his proximity back in trip suggests the form is probably only very modest, not least as he looked as if this trip on a stiff track is a bare minimum. (op 7-1 tchd 8-1)
Mousie looked to have solid form claims at her best but her profile, even for one with not many runs to her name, is patchy and she faded tamely once headed after being able to dictate on the rail. (op 1-2)
Island Bird's proximity in a steadily-run novice on her debut flatters her on this evidence for all it looked here as if easier ground wouldn't come amiss. (op 16-1)
Elsie Tanner(IRE) still hasn't got the hang of racing, losing all chance with an extremely slow start. Official explanation: jockey said filly was reluctant to race (op 14-1 tchd 18-1)

2798 BOND TYRES H'CAP 5f

2:30 (2:34) (Class 6) (0-65,65) 3-Y-0+ **£1,942** (£578; £288; £144) **Stalls** Low

Form RPR

-336 **1** **Choc'A'Moca (IRE)**[19] 2247 4-9-4 **55** (v) MickyFenton 4 70
(Paul Midgley) *mde all: rdn clr over 1f out: drvn and edgd rt ins fnl f: kpt on wl* **15/2**

6640 **2** *1 ¼* **Ryedane (IRE)**[11] 2491 9-9-8 **64** (b) LanceBetts(5) 10 74
(Tim Easterby) *in tch: hdwy to trck ldrs 1/2-way: rdn to chse wnr over 1f out: drvn ins fnl f and no imp towards fin* **13/2**[3]

0416 **3** *3 ½* **Tournedos (IRE)**[6] 2632 9-9-5 **59** 6ex (b) JamesSullivan(3) 13 57+
(Ruth Carr) *midfield: hdwy 2f out: n.m.r and swtchd to outer over 1f out: sn rdn and styd on ins fnl f: nrst fin* **6/1**[2]

00-5 **4** *nk* **Media Jury**[9] 2547 4-8-9 **46** oh1 (p) TonyHamilton 2 43
(John Wainwright) *prom: rdn along 2f out: drvn over 1f out: kpt on same pce* **16/1**

000- **5** *hd* **Port Ronan (USA)**[284] 5535 5-8-9 **49** oh1 ow3 GaryBartley(3) 8 45
(John Wainwright) *cl up: rdn along 2f out: drvn over 1f out: grad wknd* **25/1**

00-0 **6** *1* **Sea Crest**[62] 1204 5-8-12 **49** AndrewHeffernan 3 41
(Mel Brittain) *in tch: hdwy 2f out: sn rdn and kpt on same pce appr fnl f* **15/2**

410 **7** *½* **Rio's Girl**[24] 2126 4-9-2 **58** (p) ChrisDCogan(5) 11 49
(Kevin Ryan) *chsd ldrs on outer: hdwy over 2f out: rdn wl over 1f out: sn one pce* **13/2**[3]

-060 **8** *1* **Rio Sands**[16] 2352 6-8-8 **48** AmyRyan(3) 12 35
(Richard Whitaker) *s.i.s and swtchd rt s: bhd: hdwy 2f out: rdn along over 1f out: nvr nr ldrs* **16/1**

5440 **9** *3* **Fear Nothing**[11] 2491 4-9-10 **61** TomEaves 7 37
(Ian McInnes) *a towards rr* **16/1**

00-6 **10** *2 ¾* **Hitches Dubai (BRZ)**[30] 1940 6-9-8 **59** SilvestreDeSousa 14 25
(Geoffrey Harker) *a towards rr* **14/1**

-040 **11** *1* **Bossy Kitty**[9] 2546 4-9-6 **57** J-PGuillambert 1 20
(Nigel Tinkler) *chsd ldrs on inner: rdn along bef 1/2-way: sn wknd* **8/1**

60-0 **12** *3 ½* **Bonne Millie**[16] 2350 3-7-13 **46** oh1 DeclanCannon(3) 5 —
(Ollie Pears) *chsd ldrs: rdn along bef 1/2-way and sn wknd* **33/1**

1614 **13** *¾* **Meandmyshadow**[10] 2524 3-9-0 **65** (p) ShaneBKelly(7) 6 12
(Alan Brown) *rdn along 1/2-way: a bhd* **11/2**[1]

63.08 secs (-0.42) **Going Correction** -0.05s/f (Good)
WFA 3 from 4yo+ 7lb **13** Ran SP% **122.1**
Speed ratings (Par 101): **101,99,93,92,92 91,90,88,83,79 77,72,71**
toteswingers: 1&2 £5.40, 1&3 £9.20, 2&3 £5.40 CSF £56.93 CT £329.61 TOTE £6.70: £2.20, £2.40, £2.50; EX 62.80.
Owner John Milburn - Andrew Stephenson **Bred** Yeomanstown Stud **Trained** Westow, N Yorks

FOCUS
There was a heavy shower before and during this race, which was little more than a fair sprint handicap in which bang-in-form runners were few and far between. The field stayed far side and few got into it from behind. The time was relatively good and the form has been given a slight chance.
Meandmyshadow Official explanation: jockey said filly was never travelling

2799 MARSHAL TYRES H'CAP 7f 100y

3:00 (3:01) (Class 5) (0-70,65) 4-Y-0+ **£2,590** (£770; £385; £192) **Stalls** Low

Form RPR

-553 **1** **Thinking**[5] 2671 4-8-8 **52** DuranFentiman 8 62
(Tim Easterby) *cl up: led 2f out: rdn over 1f out: drvn ins fnl f: jst hld on* **6/1**[3]

6035 **2** *nse* **Powerful Pierre**[11] 2487 4-9-1 **64** (v) DaleSwift(5) 7 74
(Ian McInnes) *in tch on inner: hdwy wl over 2f out: effrt and nt clr run wl over 1f out: sn swtchd lft and rdn: drvn and styd on to chal ins fnl f: ev ch tl no ex nr line* **12/1**

1604 **3** *3 ½* **Mandhooma**[12] 2452 5-9-4 **62** WilliamCarson 3 63
(Peter Hiatt) *trckd ldrs: hdwy over 3f out: rdn to chse wnr wl over 1f out: drvn ent fnl f: kpt on same pce* **11/1**

1401 **4** *1 ¼* **Positivity**[20] 2237 5-9-1 **59** (p) TomEaves 4 57
(Bryan Smart) *chsd ldrs: effrt over 2f out and sn rdn: drvn over 1f out: wknd ent fnl f* **15/2**

R-50 **5** *nse* **Just The Tonic**[44] 1558 4-9-5 **63** TonyHamilton 5 61
(Marjorie Fife) *hld up in rr: hdwy wl over 2f out: rdn wl over 1f out: kpt on u.p fnl f: nrst fin* **33/1**

2-40 **6** *1* **Many Welcomes**[14] 2399 6-8-13 **57** J-PGuillambert 2 52
(Brian Baugh) *dwlt: in rr: hdwy over 2f out: sn rdn and kpt on appr fnl f: nt rch ldrs* **9/1**

-232 **7** *2 ¾* **Muftarres (IRE)**[11] 2487 6-9-7 **65** MickyFenton 6 54
(Paul Midgley) *dwlt and in rr: effrt and sme hdwy over 2f out: sn rdn and n.d* **3/1**[1]

-002 **8** *1 ¾* **Carlitos Spirit (IRE)**[11] 2490 7-8-13 **60** (v) GaryBartley(3) 1 44
(Ian McInnes) *led: rdn along 3f out: hdd 2f out: sn drvn and grad wknd* **4/1**[2]

2030 **9** *¾* **Wotatomboy**[20] 2233 5-8-2 **46** (b) PaulQuinn 11 28
(Richard Whitaker) *chsd ldng pair: rdn along over 2f out: drvn wl over 1f out: wknd appr fnl f* **20/1**

00-0 **10** *4 ½* **Prime Circle**[8] 2589 5-9-2 **60** (v[1]) SilvestreDeSousa 10 31
(Alan Brown) *in tch: rdn along over 3f out: sn wknd* **16/1**

00-0 **11** *12* **Luv U Noo**[58] 1273 4-8-8 **55** DeclanCannon(3) 9 —
(Brian Baugh) *t.k.h: hld up: a in rr* **10/1**

1m 31.97s (-1.83) **Going Correction** -0.20s/f (Firm) **11** Ran SP% **119.8**
Speed ratings (Par 103): **102,101,97,96,96 95,92,90,89,84 70**
toteswingers: 1&2 £5.00, 1&3 £7.10, 2&3 £13.90 CSF £77.32 CT £796.25 TOTE £7.80: £2.20, £3.20, £3.40; EX 68.60.
Owner Habton Farms **Bred** L T Roberts **Trained** Great Habton, N Yorks
■ Stewards' Enquiry : Dale Swift two-day ban: used whip in incorrect place (Jun 22-23)

FOCUS
An ordinary handicap run at a decent pace but as often happens here, those in rear on the turn found it tough getting competitive. The form is sound enough amongst the principals.
Muftarres(IRE) Official explanation: jockey said gelding ran flat

2800 ADMIRAL TYRES H'CAP 1m 1f 207y

3:30 (3:31) (Class 5) (0-70,70) 4-Y-0+ **£2,590** (£770; £385; £192) **Stalls** Low

Form RPR

6-40 **1** **Judicious**[39] 1692 4-9-2 **65** SilvestreDeSousa 8 76+
(Geoffrey Harker) *prom: trckd ldr 1/2-way: effrt 2f out: rdn over 1f out: led jst ins fnl f: kpt on* **11/8**[1]

40-2 **2** *2 ¾* **Munaawer (USA)**[15] 2388 4-8-11 **63** AmyRyan(3) 2 68
(James Bethell) *hld up: hdwy on outer 3f out: rdn to chse ldng pair over 1f out: kpt on ins fnl f* **10/3**[2]

0055 **3** *1* **Lady Excel (IRE)**[8] 2589 5-8-5 **54** AndrewHeffernan 7 57
(Brian Rothwell) *led: rdn along 2f out: drvn over 1f out: hdd jst ins fnl f: kpt on same pce* **18/1**

6006 **4** *6* **Baltimore Jack (IRE)**[16] 2348 7-8-9 **61** JamesSullivan(3) 4 52
(G P Kelly) *prom: trckd ldng pair fr 1/2-way: rdn along 2f out: drvn over 1f out and sn btn* **25/1**

00-5 **5** *nse* **Royal Composer (IRE)**[7] 2616 8-8-2 **51** oh2 DuranFentiman 6 42
(Tim Easterby) *trckd ldrs: hdwy 3f out: rdn over 2f out: drvn wl over 1f out and sn one pce* **16/1**

3226 **6** *½* **Zaplamation (IRE)**[11] 2486 6-9-4 **70** DeclanCannon(3) 3 60
(John Quinn) *t.k.h: hld up towards rr: sme hdwy 3f out: sn rdn along and nvr a factor* **7/2**[3]

-164 **7** *hd* **Rowan Lodge (IRE)**[11] 2490 9-9-1 **64** (b) TomEaves 1 54
(Ollie Pears) *hld up: hdwy 3f out: rdn to chse ldrs over 2f out: sn drvn and wknd* **14/1**

4100 **8** *5* **Barton Bounty**[8] 2589 4-8-1 **57**.....(b) ShaneBKelly(7) 5 37
(Peter Niven) *dwlt: sn outpcd and a bhd* **16/1**
2m 4.03s (-2.97) **Going Correction** -0.20s/f (Firm) **8** Ran SP% **114.9**
Speed ratings (Par 103): **103,100,100,95,95 94,94,90**
toteswingers: 1&2 £2.70, 1&3 £8.80, 2&3 £12.50 CSF £6.06 CT £53.64 TOTE £2.60: £1.40, £1.70, £5.40; EX 10.20.

Owner The Unique Partnership **Bred** Cheveley Park Stud Ltd **Trained** Thirkleby, N Yorks

FOCUS
A fair handicap contested largely by exposed runners and no surprise perhaps that it went to the only one that wasn't, and who was heavily backed too. The pace was steady, as it looked it might be beforehand. The form is rated around the third.

Barton Bounty Official explanation: jockey said gelding became upset in the stalls and was slow away

2801 ROTALLA TYRES H'CAP 1m 4f 16y
4:00 (4:00) (Class 6) (0-55,52) 3-Y-O **£2,590** (£770; £385; £192) **Stalls** Low

Form RPR
-002 **1** **Hal Of A Lover**[9] 2571 3-9-4 **52**..... SilvestreDeSousa 3 62
(David O'Meara) *hld up in rr: hdwy on outer wl over 2f out: rdn to chal over 1f out: led appr fnl f: drvn out* **11/8**[1]

-046 **2** *1 3/4* **Market Maker (IRE)**[20] 2239 3-9-3 **51**..... TomEaves 4 58
(Tim Easterby) *trckd ldrs: hdwy over 3f out: rdn to chal 2f out: drvn and ev ch 1f out: kpt on same pce* **9/2**[3]

0-30 **3** *9* **Mayan Flight (IRE)**[20] 2239 3-9-4 **52**..... TonyHamilton 5 45
(Richard Whitaker) *cl up: effrt to chal 3f out: rdn and slt ld 2f out: sn drvn and hdd appr fnl f: one pce* **4/1**[2]

-054 **4** *2* **Disturbia (IRE)**[8] 2583 3-9-0 **48**..... J-PGuillambert 1 37
(J W Hills) *trckd ldrs: effrt and hdwy over 3f out: rdn along over 2f out: sn drvn and wknd* **4/1**[2]

660 **5** *11* **Rainbows Reach**[16] 2349 3-8-9 **46**.....(b) DeclanCannon(3) 6 18
(Gay Kelleway) *t.k.h: chsd ldng pair: rdn along wl over 2f out: sn wknd* **33/1**

0602 **6** *1 1/2* **Jane's Legacy**[9] 2565 3-8-13 **47**.....(p) PaulQuinn 2 16
(Reg Hollinshead) *led: rdn along 4f out: drvn over 2f out: sn hdd & wknd* **16/1**

2m 40.15s (0.35) **Going Correction** -0.20s/f (Firm) **6** Ran SP% **109.1**
Speed ratings (Par 97): **90,88,82,81,74 73**
toteswingers: 1&2 £2.90, 1&3 £1.50, 2&3 £2.10 CSF £7.41 TOTE £1.70: £1.10, £4.00; EX 7.50.

Owner Glenn Briers & The Dreamers **Bred** Genesis Green Stud Ltd **Trained** Nawton, N Yorks

FOCUS
A low-grade handicap run at a muddling pace. The first pair were clear and their form is sound.

Jane's Legacy Official explanation: trainer's rep said filly finished distressed

2802 JINYU TYRES MAIDEN STKS 7f 100y
4:30 (4:35) (Class 5) 3-Y-O+ **£2,396** (£712; £356; £177) **Stalls** Low

Form RPR
36-3 **1** **Power Punch (IRE)**[29] 1971 3-9-0 75..... WilliamCarson 2 81
(B W Hills) *mde all: pushed clr 2f out: rdn over 1f out: drvn and hung lft ins fnl f: kpt on wl towards fin* **11/4**[2]

2325 **2** *2 1/4* **Striking The Wind (USA)**[49] 1496 3-9-0 74..... SilvestreDeSousa 13 75
(Mark Johnston) *prom: chsd wnr over 4f out: rdn 2f out: swtchd rt and drvn ins fnl f: sn one pce* **9/4**[1]

325 **3** *6* **Dark Isle**[25] 2094 3-9-0 80..... TomEaves 5 60
(J W Hills) *prom: rdn to chse ldng pair over 2f out: drvn wl over 1f out: sn one pce* **9/2**[3]

4 *3* **Circle Of Angels** 3-8-9 0..... GregFairley 1 52+
(Mark Johnston) *dwlt: rapid prog on inner to chse ldrs after 1f: pushed along and sltly outpcd 3f out: rdn and styng on whn hmpd over 1f out: swtchd lft and styd on ins fnl f* **12/1**

5 **5** *hd* **Fairy Mist (IRE)**[16] 2361 4-9-10 0..... PaddyAspell 12 56
(Brian Rothwell) *in tch: effrt to chse ldrs 3f out: rdn over 2f out: hld whn hmpd over 1f out* **50/1**

36- **6** *2 1/4* **Free Art**[22] 2209 3-9-0 76.....(p) DuranFentiman 7 46+
(Geoffrey Harker) *hld up in rr: effrt 3f out: sn rdn and sme late hdwy* **15/2**

7 *nk* **Prices Lane** 4-8-12 0..... DavidSimmonson(7) 3 45
(Michael Easterby) *dwlt and towards rr: sme hdwy into midfield whn hmpd over 2f out: swtchd lft and rdn wl over 1f out: sn no imp* **100/1**

50 **8** *1/2* **Brio**[16] 2361 3-8-9 0..... NeilFarley(5) 14 44
(Alan McCabe) *in tch: hdwy on outer to chse ldrs 3f out: rdn and hung rt 2f out: sn drvn and wknd* **33/1**

0 **9** *3/4* **Royal Deal**[12] 2457 4-9-10 0..... DavidNolan 6 47
(Michael Easterby) *a towards rr* **66/1**

0 **10** *1 1/2* **Miss Emily (IRE)**[11] 2498 3-8-9 0..... PaulQuinn 4 34
(George Moore) *a towards rr* **100/1**

11 *nk* **Merito** 3-8-11 0..... AmyRyan(3) 15 38+
(Kevin Ryan) *stdd s and hld up in rr: swtchd lft to outer and sme hdwy over 2f out: sn rdn and wknd* **12/1**

0 **12** *3 1/4* **Hard Rok (IRE)**[32] 1910 3-9-0 0..... TonyHamilton 8 30
(Richard Whitaker) *a in rr* **100/1**

0- **13** *1 3/4* **Valentine's Gift**[234] 6964 3-9-0 0..... AndrewHeffernan 10 26
(Neville Bycroft) *a towards rr* **33/1**

5 **14** *13* **Misshollygolightly**[12] 2479 3-8-11 0 ow2..... J-PGuillambert 9 —
(Brian Baugh) *chsd ldrs: rdn along 1/2-way: sn wknd* **40/1**

1m 31.74s (-2.06) **Going Correction** -0.20s/f (Firm)
WFA 3 from 4yo 10lb **14** Ran SP% **117.5**
Speed ratings (Par 103): **103,100,93,90,89 87,87,86,85,83 83,79,77,62**
toteswingers: 1&2 £2.30, 1&3 £3.50, 2&3 £2.70 CSF £8.71 TOTE £5.00: £2.20, £1.10, £1.20; EX 11.20.

Owner J Hanson **Bred** Barouche Stud Ireland Ltd **Trained** Lambourn, Berks

FOCUS
An ordinary maiden that was run at a fair gallop and in which little behind early got into it. The winner improved with the second close to his best.

Circle Of Angels Official explanation: jockey said filly suffered interference in running

Free Art Official explanation: jockey said colt was denied a clear run

Misshollygolightly Official explanation: jockey said filly hung left throughout

T/Plt: £146.90 to a £1 stake. Pool: £48,051.22. 238.69 winning tickets. T/Qpdt: £9.80 to a £1 stake. Pool: £4,558.21. 341.50 winning tickets. JR

2630 HAMILTON (R-H)
Wednesday, June 8

OFFICIAL GOING: Good changing to good to soft (good in places) after race 1 (6.00)
Wind: Almost nil Weather: Overcast, showers

2803 JOIN HAMILTON PARK ON FACEBOOK AMATEUR RIDERS' H'CAP 6f 5y
6:00 (6:03) (Class 6) (0-60,63) 4-Y-O+ **£1,977** (£608; £304) **Stalls** Centre

Form RPR
0-53 **1** **Hayek**[8] 2593 4-10-3 **56**.....(b) MissRRichardson(7) 15 67
(Tim Easterby) *bhd centre: plenty to do 1/2-way: gd hdwy over 1f out: led ins fnl f: comf* **12/1**

5001 **2** *1 1/4* **Hambleton**[8] 2593 4-10-5 **51** 6ex..... MissSBrotherton 10 58
(Bryan Smart) *prom centre: led over 1f out to ins fnl f: kpt on same pce* **11/2**[2]

6366 **3** *1 3/4* **Two Turtle Doves (IRE)**[16] 2353 5-10-11 **60**..... MissMMullineaux(3) 12 61
(Michael Mullineaux) *hld up stands' side: rdn 1/2-way: hdwy over 1f out: kpt on fin* **9/1**[3]

00-3 **4** *nk* **Ivestar (IRE)**[128] 362 6-10-9 **60**.....(vt) MissCharlotteHolmes(5) 14 60
(Ben Haslam) *bhd centre tl hdwy over 1f out: kpt on fnl f: nvr able to chal* **12/1**

0641 **5** *1 3/4* **North Central (USA)**[5] 2670 4-11-3 **63** 6ex.....(p) MrsCBartley 8 58
(Jim Goldie) *prom: pushed along over 2f out: sn outpcd: rallied over 1f out: no imp fnl f* **4/1**[1]

0043 **6** *1 3/4* **Eilean Eeve**[13] 2412 5-10-3 **49**.....(p) MrSWalker 9 38
(George Foster) *in tch centre: drvn 1/2-way: no ex appr fnl f* **9/1**[3]

-000 **7** *1* **Hot Rod Mamma (IRE)**[5] 2670 4-9-13 **50**..... MissECSayer(5) 11 36
(Dianne Sayer) *spd stands' side tl rdn and no ex appr fnl f* **12/1**

8 *1/2* **Zeruth (IRE)**[336] 3799 5-9-13 **50**..... MissPhillipaTutty(5) 4 34
(Ann Duffield) *t.k.h: in tch centre tl rdn and wknd appr fnl f* **12/1**

0002 **9** *1/2* **Almaty Express**[23] 2162 9-10-2 **55**.....(b) MrEKingsley(7) 16 38
(John Weymes) *bhd stands' side: edgd rt and hdwy over 1f out: nvr able to chal* **16/1**

2416 **10** *2 3/4* **Dower Glen**[9] 2546 4-10-11 **57**.....(v) MrSDobson 3 31
(Keith Dalgleish) *chsd overall ldr towards far side: rdn 1/2-way: wknd 2f out* **11/1**

505- **11** *3/4* **Cross Of Lorraine (IRE)**[224] 7170 8-10-6 **59**...(b) MissCharlieJones(7) 6 31
(Chris Grant) *overall ldr towards far side: hdd over 1f out: sn btn* **16/1**

5004 **12** *1/2* **King Bertolini (IRE)**[8] 2593 4-9-12 **49**..... MissWGibson(5) 1 19
(Alan Berry) *s.i.s: wl bhd centre tl sme late hdwy: nvr on terms* **33/1**

0000 **13** *6* **Ya Boy Sir (IRE)**[13] 2412 4-9-10 **49**..... MrSFeeney(7) 7 —
(Ian Semple) *wl bhd centre: pushed along 1/2-way: nvr on terms* **50/1**

4-50 **14** *8* **Secret City (IRE)**[16] 2352 5-10-4 **55**.....(b) MrSBushby(5) 13 —
(Robin Bastiman) *cl up towards stands' side to 1/2-way: sn rdn and wknd: eased whn no ch fnl f* **12/1**

1m 15.39s (3.19) **Going Correction** +0.375s/f (Good) **14** Ran SP% **118.8**
Speed ratings (Par 101): **93,91,89,88,86 83,82,81,81,77 76,75,67,57**
toteswingers: 1&2 £7.50, 1&3 £16.20, 2&3 £9.30 CSF £75.60 CT £635.12 TOTE £16.50: £5.20, £2.00, £3.50; EX 82.80.

Owner Habton Farms **Bred** Cranford Stud **Trained** Great Habton, N Yorks

FOCUS
The going was given as good (GoingStick 8.4), although there was a heavy shower in the hour before the start of racing. All races over 6f plus were run over approximately 8yds shorter than the official measurements owing to movements of rails. A competitive amateur riders' event run at a decent gallop and it was set up for a closer. The form is moderate and not a race to be positive about.

North Central(USA) Official explanation: jockey said gelding was unsuited by the good to soft, good in places ground

Almaty Express Official explanation: jockey said gelding was unsuited by the good to soft, good in places ground

2804 SODEXO STOP HUNGER CHARITY H'CAP (QUALIFIER FOR THE BETFAIR BONUS SCOTTISH RACING STAYERS FINAL) 1m 3f 16y
6:30 (6:30) (Class 6) (0-65,65) 4-Y-O+ **£2,729** (£806; £403) **Stalls** Low

Form RPR
-334 **1** **Prince Rhyddarch**[9] 2548 6-8-7 **54**..... SeanLevey(3) 11 63
(Michael Dods) *hld up in tch: effrt over 2f out: edgd rt and led appr fnl f: kpt on wl* **4/1**[2]

0005 **2** *nk* **Sharp Sovereign (USA)**[15] 2388 5-9-2 **65**..... LMcNiff(5) 3 73
(David Barron) *led: rdn and hrd pressed fr over 3f out: hdd appr fnl f: rallied: hld towards fin* **3/1**[1]

0-04 **3** *3 1/2* **Highland Love**[10] 2530 6-8-13 **57**..... PaulMulrennan 7 59
(Jedd O'Keeffe) *chsd ldr: rdn and ev ch over 3f out: outpcd by ldng pair appr fnl f* **16/1**

4-00 **4** *2* **Hurlingham**[15] 2388 7-8-13 **57**.....(b) DavidAllan 10 56
(Michael Easterby) *hld up in tch: smooth hdwy over 3f out: cl up and rdn over 2f out: edgd rt and no ex over 1f out* **18/1**

0504 **5** *3/4* **Dean Iarracht (IRE)**[4] 2734 5-8-10 **57**..... PaulPickard(3) 4 54
(Tracy Waggott) *dwlt: bhd: rdn and hdwy on outside over 2f out: no imp fnl f* **7/1**[3]

0-00 **6** *5* **Fifty Moore**[9] 2548 4-9-3 **64**.....(b[1]) MichaelO'Connell(3) 5 52
(Jedd O'Keeffe) *trckd ldrs: drvn and outpcd over 2f out: btn over 1f out* **40/1**

3401 **7** *1* **Valantino Oyster (IRE)**[7] 2618 4-9-2 **63** 6ex.....(v) PatrickDonaghy(3) 12 49
(Ben Haslam) *bhd: drvn and outpcd 4f out: n.d after* **7/1**[3]

001/ **8** *8* **Key Decision (IRE)**[30] 1963 7-8-9 **56**.....(tp) MartinHarley(3) 6 28
(Shaun Harley, Ire) *hld up bhd ldng gp: effrt and drvn over 3f out: wknd fnl 2f* **3/1**[1]

0006 **9** *37* **Mr Emirati (USA)**[8] 2589 4-8-8 **52**.....(p) RoystonFfrench 9 —
(Bryan Smart) *trckd ldrs tl hung rt and wknd fr 4f out: t.o* **16/1**

2m 26.99s (1.39) **Going Correction** +0.075s/f (Good) **9** Ran SP% **114.5**
Speed ratings (Par 101): **97,96,94,92,92 88,87,82,55**
toteswingers: 1&2 £2.00, 1&3 £7.10, 2&3 £7.60 CSF £16.26 CT £170.19 TOTE £4.00: £1.80, £1.50, £3.30; EX 17.40.

Owner Mr & Mrs Charles Villiers **Bred** Ian Murray Tough **Trained** Denton, Co Durham

■ Stewards' Enquiry : Sean Levey caution: careless riding

FOCUS
The going was changed to good to soft, good in places before this event, and Paul Mulrennan, aboard the third, agreed, reporting it to be on the slow side of good. A gamble on Key Decision went astray and the race was fought out by two previous course winners, who are rated to last September's course form.

2805 HAMILTON-PARK.CO.UK H'CAP (A QUALIFIER FOR THE BETFAIR BONUS SCOTTISH RACING SPRINT FINAL) 5f 4y
7:00 (7:00) (Class 6) (0-65,54) 3-Y-O **£2,729** (£806; £403) **Stalls** Centre

Form RPR
-345 **1** **Dotty Darroch**[14] 2396 3-9-0 **52**.......................... JulieBurke(5) 7 56
(Robin Bastiman) *cl up: edgd rt and led over 1f out: pushed out fnl f: comf* **13/8**[1]
4306 **2** 1 ½ **Majestic Millie (IRE)**[11] 2493 3-8-10 **46**.......................... SeanLevey(3) 6 45
(David O'Meara) *led tl rdn and hdd over 1f out: rallied: kpt on same pce ins fnl f* **11/2**
0460 **3** 1 ½ **Running Water**[9] 2547 3-8-13 **46**..........................(t) PhillipMakin 5 40
(Hugh McWilliams) *hld up in tch: effrt and hdwy over 1f out: kpt on same pce ins fnl f* **16/1**
3000 **4** 2 **Alfraamsey**[29] 1980 3-9-4 **54**.......................... MartinHarley(3) 3 40
(Mick Channon) *hld up in tch: rdn over 2f out: no imp tl styd on fnl f: nvr able to chal* **9/1**
0603 **5** 3 ¾ **Bygones For Coins (IRE)**[5] 2697 3-8-12 **50**....... DanielleMcCreery(5) 4 23
(Alan Berry) *t.k.h: cl up tl rdn and wknd over 1f out* **3/1**[2]
0-05 **6** 1 **Vintage Grape (IRE)**[33] 1860 3-9-3 **50**.......................... DavidAllan 1 19
(Eric Alston) *t.k.h: cl up: rdn over 2f out: wknd over 1f out* **9/2**[3]
62.29 secs (2.29) **Going Correction** +0.375s/f (Good) **6** Ran SP% **112.5**
Speed ratings (Par 97): **96,93,91,88,82 80**
toteswingers: 1&2 £1.60, 1&3 £4.50, 2&3 £10.00 CSF £11.12 TOTE £2.00: £1.10, £1.50; EX 9.50.
Owner The McMaster Springford Partnership **Bred** Ptarmigan Bloodstock Ltd **Trained** Cowthorpe, N Yorks

FOCUS
A poor sprint handicap considering the weight band for the race, as the top-weight, the only previous winner in the field, was rated 11lb below the ceiling. It was run during a heavy hail shower. The form looks weak despite the first two running close to form.

2806 PRESTIGE SCOTLAND H'CAP 6f 5y
7:30 (7:30) (Class 4) (0-80,80) 4-Y-O+ **£4,533** (£1,348; £674; £336) **Stalls** Centre

Form RPR
5202 **1** **Grissom (IRE)**[7] 2620 5-9-5 **78**.......................... DavidAllan 12 88
(Tim Easterby) *midfield: hdwy and narrow ld over 1f out: kpt on gamely u.p fnl f: all out* **11/4**[1]
0-04 **2** shd **Ursula (IRE)**[25] 2116 5-9-0 **76**.......................... MartinHarley(3) 9 86
(Mrs K Burke) *towards rr and drvn after 2f: rallied over 2f out: disp ld over 1f out: kpt on wl fnl f: jst hld* **7/1**
0332 **3** nk **Karaka Jack**[18] 2299 4-9-1 **77**.......................... MichaelO'Connell(3) 2 86+
(David Nicholls) *prom: ev ch and hung lft wl over 1f out: kpt on u.p fnl f: hld nr fin* **11/2**[3]
5040 **4** 4 ½ **Desert Icon (IRE)**[12] 2464 5-8-7 **66**.......................... MartinLane 1 61
(David Simcock) *bhd and outpcd: hdwy over 1f out: nvr able to chal* **22/1**
3123 **5** nk **Ingleby Arch (USA)**[6] 2633 8-8-6 **70**.......................... LMcNiff(5) 11 64
(David Barron) *chsd ldrs: drvn 1/2-way: wknd appr fnl f* **12/1**
6001 **6** ¾ **Jobe (USA)**[6] 2633 5-9-7 **80** 6ex..........................(p) PhillipMakin 7 71
(Kevin Ryan) *led tl rdn and hdd over 1f out: sn wknd* **4/1**[2]
0-50 **7** 4 **Whispered Times (USA)**[13] 2431 4-8-8 **70**..............(p) PaulPickard(3) 4 48
(Tracy Waggott) *w ldr: rdn 1/2-way: checked over 1f out: sn wknd* **50/1**
64-0 **8** shd **Kerrys Requiem (IRE)**[24] 2122 5-9-4 **80**.......................... SeanLevey(3) 8 58
(Tim Pitt) *bhd and sn outpcd: nvr rchd ldrs* **28/1**
3302 **9** 3 **Frequency**[6] 2633 4-8-13 **72**..........................(b) PaulMulrennan 5 49
(Keith Dalgleish) *trckd ldrs: smooth hdwy over 2f out: rdn whn hmpd over 1f out: nt rcvr* **6/1**
0-60 **10** 1 ¼ **Great Charm (IRE)**[18] 2299 6-9-4 **77**.......................... RoystonFfrench 6 42
(Eric Alston) *midfield: outpcd after 2f: struggling fr over 2f out* **10/1**
1m 13.69s (1.49) **Going Correction** +0.375s/f (Good) **10** Ran SP% **115.4**
Speed ratings (Par 105): **105,104,104,98,98 97,91,91,87,85**
toteswingers: 1&2 £3.50, 1&3 £3.20, 2&3 £7.80 CSF £21.73 CT £101.47 TOTE £2.80: £1.10, £2.10, £2.00; EX 23.60.
Owner Jim & Helen Bowers **Bred** Michael McGlynn **Trained** Great Habton, N Yorks
■ Stewards' Enquiry : L McNiff two-day ban: careless riding (Jun 22-23)
Michael O'Connell three-day ban: two for careless riding (Jun 22-23); one for excessive use of whip down the shoulder in the forehand position (Jun 24)

FOCUS
They went a good clip up front and the first two came from off the pace. The form is fair for the grade with the placed horses setting the level.

2807 RACING UK (S) STKS 1m 1f 36y
8:00 (8:02) (Class 6) 4-Y-O+ **£1,942** (£578; £288; £144) **Stalls** Low

Form RPR
-233 **1** **Moody Tunes**[13] 2413 8-9-0 75.......................... SeanLevey(3) 7 81
(Mrs K Burke) *mde all: rdn and hrd pressed fnl 2f: kpt on gamely fnl f* **6/4**[1]
/11- **2** 3 **Belle Noverre (IRE)**[66] 1117 7-8-9 77.......................... MartinHarley(3) 6 69
(Shaun Harley, Ire) *hld up in tch: stdy hdwy to press wnr over 3f out: drvn and ev ch 2f out: hung rt and no ex ins fnl f* **9/4**[3]
1211 **3** 2 ¼ **Fremen (USA)**[16] 2347 11-9-3 77.......................... AdrianNicholls 3 69
(David Nicholls) *trckd ldrs: drvn 3f out: one pce fnl f* **2/1**[2]
-000 **4** 5 **Child Of Our Time (IRE)**[14] 2399 4-8-0 55............ DanielleMooney(7) 4 48
(Colin Teague) *s.i.s: bhd: hdwy and edgd rt over 3f out: no imp fnl 2f* **66/1**
500- **5** 46 **Psalm Twentythree**[243] 6716 5-8-12 0.......................... PaulMulrennan 2 —
(Ian Semple) *trckd ldrs: hdwy to press wnr after 3f: rdn and wknd over 3f out: t.o* **66/1**
000- **6** 44 **Matilda May**[209] 7406 4-8-7 20.......................... PatrickMathers 8 —
(Colin Teague) *in tch: rdn after 3f: wknd fr 4f out: t.o* **100/1**
2m 1.15s (1.45) **Going Correction** +0.075s/f (Good) **6** Ran SP% **108.1**
Speed ratings (Par 101): **96,93,91,86,46 6**
toteswingers: 1&2 £1.02, 1&3 £1.10, 2&3 £1.20 CSF £4.80 TOTE £2.20: £1.70, £1.10; EX 3.80.The winner was bought in for 4,800gns.
Owner Aricabeau Racing Limited **Bred** Llety Stud **Trained** Middleham Moor, North Yorks
■ Stewards' Enquiry : Adrian Nicholls one-day ban: careless riding (Jun 22)

FOCUS
A three-horse contest on paper and in the race itself. The first three are above average for the grade with the winner the best guide.

2808 TURFTV CLASSIFIED STKS 1m 1f 36y
8:30 (8:31) (Class 5) 3-4-Y-O **£2,729** (£806; £403) **Stalls** Low

Form RPR
52 **1** **Zennor**[14] 2402 4-9-7 70.......................... RichardKingscote 6 86+
(Tom Dascombe) *hld up: smooth hdwy over 3f out: led over 1f out: rdn and r.o strly* **3/1**[1]
0-41 **2** ½ **King Kurt (IRE)**[19] 2251 3-8-9 69.......................... PhillipMakin 4 83
(Kevin Ryan) *led 2f: cl up: led 3f out to over 1f out: rallied: hld towards fin* **10/3**[2]
203- **3** 10 **U A E Storm (USA)**[287] 5413 3-8-9 69.......................... MartinLane 7 61
(David Simcock) *dwlt: bhd: drvn 1/2-way: rallied over 3f out: chsd ldrs and hung rt 2f out: sn outpcd* **9/1**[3]
3-21 **4** 2 ¾ **Abidhabidubai**[22] 2186 3-8-9 70.......................... FrederikTylicki 5 35+
(John Quinn) *sddle slipped sn after s: cl up: shkn up 3f out: wknd wl over 1f out: fin 5th: plcd 4th* **3/1**[1]
51-0 **5** 3 **Cape Of Dance (IRE)**[53] 1392 3-8-9 70.......................... JoeFanning 1 28
(Mark Johnston) *trckd ldrs: checked after 3f: rdn and wknd over 2f out: eased whn no ch: fin sixth: plcd 5th* **9/1**[3]
0304 **6** 13 **Galloping Queen (IRE)**[12] 2466 3-8-6 70................(v) MartinHarley(3) 8 —
(Mick Channon) *led after 2f to 3f out: wknd 2f out: fin seventh: plcd sixth* **12/1**
23-5 **7** ½ **Scented**[12] 2466 3-8-9 70..........................(b) PaulMulrennan 3 —
(Ian Semple) *t.k.h: trckd ldrs tl rdn and wknd over 2f out: fin eighth: plcd seventh* **33/1**
00-6 **D** 9 **Christmas Light**[16] 2366 4-9-4 68.......................... SeanLevey(3) 2 43
(David O'Meara) *prom: effrt and rdn over 2f out: edgd rt and wknd over 1f out: fin 4th: disqualified and plcd last: rdr failed to weigh in* **10/1**
1m 59.61s (-0.09) **Going Correction** +0.075s/f (Good)
WFA 3 from 4yo 12lb **8** Ran SP% **112.8**
Speed ratings (Par 103): **103,102,93,83,80 69,68,85**
toteswingers: 1&2 £2.10, 1&3 £7.00, 2&3 £4.70 CSF £12.81 TOTE £4.90: £2.30, £2.00, £3.90; EX 13.10.
Owner Miss Amy Murphy **Bred** D P Martin **Trained** Malpas, Cheshire
■ Stewards' Enquiry : Sean Levey three-day ban: failed to weigh in (Jun 22-24)
Phillip Makin caution: careless riding

FOCUS
A competitive race on paper, with just 2lb separating the entire field on official ratings, but there was a fair pace on and the first two came nicely clear. The form looks a bit fluid but is rated positively with the first two clear.
Abidhabidubai Official explanation: jockey said saddle slipped
Scented Official explanation: jockey said filly ran too free

2809 BOOK NOW FOR CASH FOR KIDS NIGHT H'CAP (QUALIFIER FOR BETFAIR BONUS SCOTTISH RACING MILE FINAL) 1m 65y
9:00 (9:00) (Class 6) (0-60,58) 3-Y-O+ **£2,590** (£770; £385; £192) **Stalls** Low

Form RPR
2023 **1** **On The Cusp (IRE)**[13] 2415 4-9-5 **52**..........................(p) MartinHarley(3) 2 62
(Richard Guest) *cl up: led after 2f: mde rest: rdn and clr 2f out: styd on strly* **4/1**[1]
5550 **2** 3 ¼ **Carnival Dream**[36] 1803 6-9-1 **45**..........................(p) PhillipMakin 10 48
(Hugh McWilliams) *hld up: effrt on outside over 2f out: chsd clr wnr ins fnl f: no imp* **20/1**
4006 **3** 1 ¾ **Machir Bay**[5] 2691 4-9-1 **45**..........................(p) PaulMulrennan 7 44
(Keith Dalgleish) *hld up in tch: drvn and outpcd over 3f out: rallied to chse clr wnr appr fnl f: no ex* **11/1**
2102 **4** 2 ¼ **Mr Chocolate Drop (IRE)**[32] 1905 7-9-11 **58**..............(t) SeanLevey(3) 4 51
(Mandy Rowland) *hld up in tch: effrt over 2f out: disp 2nd appr fnl f: sn one pce* **6/1**[3]
-012 **5** 5 **Blue Charm**[13] 2415 7-9-9 **56**.......................... GaryBartley(3) 14 38
(Ian McInnes) *hld up: pushed along over 2f out: sme hdwy over 1f out: nvr able to chal* **4/1**[1]
-535 **6** ½ **One Of Twins**[23] 2166 3-8-3 **47**..........................(b[1]) JamesSullivan(3) 3 28
(Michael Easterby) *trckd ldrs: drvn over 2f out: wandered and wknd appr fnl f* **9/2**[2]
0-04 **7** 4 ½ **Balance On Time (IRE)**[13] 2415 5-9-1 **45**.................. FrederikTylicki 12 15
(Linda Perratt) *towards rr on ins: drvn along over 3f out: wknd fnl 2f* **10/1**
2246 **8** 4 ½ **Meydan Style (USA)**[29] 1979 5-9-3 **47**.......................... JoeFanning 6 —
(Bruce Hellier) *prom: drvn and outpcd over 3f out: n.d after* **14/1**
0-00 **9** nk **Charity Fair**[49] 1497 4-8-12 **45**.......................... PaulPickard(3) 13 —
(Ron Barr) *bhd: struggling 1/2-way: nvr on terms* **28/1**
000- **10** 3 ¾ **Peter Tchaikovsky**[288] 4156 5-9-11 **55**.......................... PatrickMathers 5 —
(Ian McInnes) *trckd ldrs tl rdn and wknd over 2f out* **33/1**
05-0 **11** ½ **Old Firm**[6] 2631 5-8-12 **45**..........................(b[1]) PatrickDonaghy(3) 15 —
(Ian Semple) *bhd: outpcd and hung rt over 3f out: nvr on terms* **50/1**
0000 **12** 45 **Ninth House (USA)**[9] 2548 9-9-1 **45**..........................(b) PJMcDonald 9 —
(Ruth Carr) *s.v.s: t.o thrght* **16/1**
1m 50.52s (2.12) **Going Correction** +0.075s/f (Good)
WFA 3 from 4yo+ 11lb **12** Ran SP% **115.6**
Speed ratings (Par 101): **92,88,87,84,79 79,74,70,69,66 65,20**
toteswingers: 1&2 £17.50, 1&3 £13.00, 2&3 £25.30 CSF £87.39 CT £825.49 TOTE £5.30: £1.70, £8.00, £5.50; EX 63.20.
Owner Rakebackmypoker.com **Bred** J Stan Cosgrove **Trained** Stainforth, S Yorks

FOCUS
Very few got into this.
Ninth House(USA) Official explanation: jockey said horse reared as stalls opened
T/Plt: £49.50 to a £1 stake. Pool: £65,684.69. 967.93 winning tickets. T/Qpdt: £7.90 to a £1 stake. Pool: £5,948.42. 554.20 winning tickets. RY

2499 HAYDOCK (L-H)
Wednesday, June 8

OFFICIAL GOING: Good changing to good to soft after race 1 (2.20)
Wind: Light to moderate, half-against Weather: Cloudy, unsettled

2810 PHS WASHROOM SERVICES H'CAP 1m 2f 95y
2:20 (2:20) (Class 4) (0-85,85) 4-Y-O+ **£4,209** (£1,252; £625; £312) **Stalls** Centre

Form RPR
6-23 **1** **Udabaa (IRE)**[32] 1887 4-9-5 **83**..........................(p) RichardHills 6 97
(Marcus Tregoning) *mde all: rdn over 2f out: styd on dourly to draw clr ins fnl f* **5/4**[1]

6134 **2** *6* **Prince Apollo**[24] 2124 6-8-12 **76**....(t) PaulHanagan 5 79
(Gerard Butler) *racd keenly in tch: rdn and wanted to lugg lft jst over 1f out: sn chsd wnr but no imp* **9/1**

126- **3** *1 1/4* **Boss's Destination**[345] 3519 4-8-10 **74**.... PJMcDonald 3 75
(Alan Swinbank) *chsd ldrs: rdn and nt qckn over 3f out: styd on towards fin: nt pce to chal* **9/1**

-111 **4** *1/2* **Frontline Phantom (IRE)**[33] 1874 4-8-3 **74**.... MatthewLawson(7) 8 74
(Mrs K Burke) *chsd wnr: rdn over 2f out: lost 2nd 1f out and one pce: no ex fnl 75yds* **4/1**[2]

0312 **5** *1/2* **Pelham Crescent (IRE)**[23] 2156 8-9-1 **79**.... DavidProbert 1 78
(Bryn Palling) *s.i.s: racd keenly: hld up: niggled along over 3f out: no imp tl styd on towards fin* **16/1**

2030 **6** *12* **Dahaam**[20] 2220 4-8-13 **77**.... JamieSpencer 4 53
(David Simcock) *hld up: u.p over 2f out: nvr a threat* **6/1**[3]

10-0 **7** *21* **Mistoffelees**[53] 1390 5-8-12 **76**.... KierenFallon 2 29
(Luca Cumani) *hld up: toiling over 3f out: nvr on terms* **14/1**

2m 16.49s (0.49) **Going Correction** +0.175s/f (Good) **7** Ran SP% **111.3**
Speed ratings (Par 105): **105,100,99,98,98 88,72**
toteswingers: 1&2 £5.30, 1&3 £9.10, 2&3 £4.50 CSF £12.73 CT £67.68 TOTE £2.20: £1.50, £4.10; EX 13.40.
Owner Hamdan Al Maktoum **Bred** Philip Brady **Trained** Lambourn, Berks

FOCUS
Sprints on inner home straight. Races on round course on outer home straight, adding 27yds to distances on round course. This looked a decent handicap, which was run at a solid pace. However, surprisingly, hardly any of the runners got involved with a winning chance. Probably not strong form for the grade, but a 5lb personal best from the winner.
Mistoffelees Official explanation: jockey said something was amiss with gelding

2811 PHS COMPLIANCE BRITISH STALLION STUDS E B F MAIDEN FILLIES STKS 6f
2:50 (2:51) (Class 5) 2-Y-O **£3,238** (£963; £481; £240) **Stalls** Centre

Form RPR

1 **Viola D'Amour (IRE)** 2-9-0 0.... RichardKingscote 7 81+
(Tom Dascombe) *chsd ldrs: rdn over 1f out: styd on to ld wl ins fnl f: a doing enough towards fin* **20/1**

P **2** *nk* **Hidden Passion (USA)**[7] 2606 2-9-0 0.... ShaneKelly 1 80
(Brian Meehan) *trckd ldrs: led wl over 1f out: rdn ins fnl f: sn hdd: styd on for press but a looked hld after* **13/2**[3]

0 **3** *1 1/2* **Lady Gibraltar**[18] 2309 2-9-0 0.... KierenFallon 4 75
(Alan Jarvis) *a.p: rdn to chal fr 2f out: one pce towards fin* **15/2**

4 *1/2* **Proud Pearl (USA)** 2-9-0 0.... MartinDwyer 11 74+
(Brian Meehan) *in rr: pushed along over 2f out: prog over 1f out: styd on ins fnl f but nt pce to chal* **17/2**

2 **5** *nk* **Dare To Dream**[19] 2254 2-9-0 0.... PatDobbs 2 73
(Richard Hannon) *led: rdn and hdd wl over 1f out: kpt on same pce ins fnl f* **4/1**[1]

6 *3/4* **Savanna Days (IRE)** 2-9-0 0.... JamieSpencer 3 71
(Mick Channon) *dwlt: prom: rdn to chal fr 2f out: no ex fnl 100yds* **12/1**

7 *2 1/4* **Eraada** 2-9-0 0.... RichardHills 9 64
(Mark Johnston) *dwlt: in rr: rdn over 1f out: nvr able to get to ldrs* **16/1**

8 *3/4* **Mahkama (USA)** 2-9-0 0.... FrankieDettori 10 62
(Saeed Bin Suroor) *hld up: hdwy over 2f out: chalng 1f out: wknd fnl 110yds: eased whn btn towards fin* **4/1**[1]

9 *3* **Minne Wa Wa** 2-9-0 0.... PaulHanagan 6 53
(David Brown) *prom: effrt 2f out: wknd over 1f out* **33/1**

3 **10** *6* **Al Jemailiya (IRE)**[13] 2409 2-9-0 0.... PhillipMakin 5 35
(Kevin Ryan) *s.i.s: hld up: pushed along over 2f out: nvr on terms* **11/2**[2]

11 *3* **Weood (IRE)** 2-9-0 0.... TomQueally 8 26
(Clive Brittain) *dwlt: hld up: toiling over 1f out: fin wl bhd* **40/1**

1m 16.33s (2.53) **Going Correction** +0.225s/f (Good) **11** Ran SP% **114.7**
Speed ratings (Par 93): **90,89,87,86,86 85,82,81,77,69 65**
toteswingers: 1&2 £37.50, 1&3 £19.60, 2&3 £18.60 CSF £139.28 TOTE £25.30: £5.50, £2.90, £3.20; EX 169.90.
Owner Laurence A Bellman **Bred** Denis Brosnan And Patsy Byrne **Trained** Malpas, Cheshire

FOCUS
Most of these hadn't run before, but the fifth does give the form a solid look judged on her initial outing. One would imagine that plenty of horses capable of winning as juveniles will emerge from this.

NOTEBOOK
Viola D'Amour(IRE), from the first crop of Teofilo, out of 1m scorer who has produced four winners, wasn't seriously fancied in the betting but came home really strongly to post a pleasing debut. The trainer, who said the victory was far from a surprise, felt the rain that fell helped his filly, as she needs further than 6f ideally. (op 25-1)
Hidden Passion(USA)'s connections did not know exactly what happened to her on her first run. Martin Dwyer reportedly felt her take a bad step and pulled her up, but she was fine the following morning and since, and had worked well for some time. This was more like it and she put up a bold show before being worn down in the final stages. (op 11-2)
Lady Gibraltar improved on her first racecourse start at Newbury, and is progressing in the right direction. Official explanation: jockey said filly hung left and right (op 7-1 tchd 11-2)
Proud Pearl(USA) ◆, a $250,000 sister to 5f-1m2f winner in America, is entered in the Moyglare Stud Stakes and caught the eye with the way she finished under a mainly hands-and-heels ride in the final furlong. (op 8-1 tchd 9-1)
Dare To Dream finished runner-up to a useful-looking type over C&D on debut trained by Tom Dascombe, and appeared to run to a similar level here, despite needing to be hard ridden from over 1f out. (tchd 10-3)
Savanna Days(IRE), a 150,000gns first foal of German 1m3f Listed winner/German Oaks runner-up, is entered in the Moyglare Stud and made a satisfactory start to her career after coming down the far-side rail in the latter stages. (tchd 14-1)
Eraada, a half-sister to Dubai World Cup winner Almutawakel, 1,000 Guineas runner-up Muwakleh and the useful middle-distance performer Elmustanser among plenty of winners, was a bit slow to start and never got into a position where she could make a winning run. That said, she kept on well and will no doubt be much better than this performance.
Mahkama(USA), a $270,000 half-sister to US 1m 2-y-o Grade 3 winner Summer Raven, travelled into contention going well but didn't get home. On breeding, she may not have handled the easy ground, as she looked really tired in the final half a furlong. Official explanation: jockey said filly tired quickly in the closing stages (op 7-2)
Al Jemailiya(IRE) showed promise in a small-field 5f contest at Ayr last month but never made any impression here. (op 14-1)

2812 PHS WATERLOGIC H'CAP 1m 3f 200y
3:20 (3:20) (Class 3) (0-95,92) 4-Y-O+ **£7,123** (£2,119; £1,059; £529) **Stalls** Centre

Form RPR

34-0 **1** **Classic Vintage (USA)**[18] 2289 5-9-7 **92**.... TomQueally 8 98
(Amanda Perrett) *led after 2f: hdd 2f out: sn rdn but continued to press ldr: styd on to regain ld nr fin* **11/1**

0-13 **2** *nk* **Granston (IRE)**[33] 1879 10-9-3 **88**.... GrahamGibbons 9 94
(James Bethell) *cl up: upsides 3f out: led 2f out: rdn over 1f out and continually pressed: edgd lft ins fnl f: hdd nr fin* **25/1**

0236 **3** *3/4* **Tominator**[25] 2107 4-9-5 **90**.... TonyCulhane 7 95
(Reg Hollinshead) *hld up: hdwy over 2f out: rdn whn chsng ldrs over 1f out: styd on towards fin* **16/1**

0501 **4** *2 1/4* **Porgy**[5] 2686 6-9-0 **85** 6ex.... JamieSpencer 2 86
(David Simcock) *s.i.s: hld up: rdn over 1f out: kpt on ins fnl f: nvr able to chal* **7/2**[2]

-000 **5** *1 1/4* **Mister Angry (IRE)**[18] 2289 4-9-0 **85**.... JoeFanning 6 84
(Mark Johnston) *prom: rdn 2f out: one pce ins fnl f* **25/1**

1-20 **6** *3/4* **Dansili Dancer**[32] 1887 9-9-4 **92**.... JohnFahy(3) 1 90
(Clive Cox) *led early: racd in tch: rdn 2f out: no imp fnl f* **9/2**[3]

31-2 **7** *1 3/4* **Kitty Wells**[20] 2220 4-9-0 **85**.... KierenFallon 5 80
(Luca Cumani) *in tch: pushed along over 3f out: bhd over 1f out* **15/8**[1]

60-1 **8** *1 3/4* **Dance Tempo**[23] 2156 4-9-1 **86**.... JimmyFortune 4 78
(Hughie Morrison) *sn led: hdd after 2f: trckd ldrs after: pushed along 3f out: wknd over 1f out* **6/1**

2m 38.1s (4.10) **Going Correction** +0.175s/f (Good) **8** Ran SP% **111.4**
Speed ratings (Par 107): **93,92,92,90,89 89,88,87**
toteswingers: 1&2 £24.10, 1&3 £26.90, 2&3 £5.90 CSF £221.74 CT £4213.45 TOTE £12.80: £2.60, £4.70, £3.20; EX 177.90.
Owner R & P Scott A & J Powell Gallagher Stud **Bred** Gallagher's Stud **Trained** Pulborough, W Sussex

FOCUS
The early pace didn't look frenetic and it again paid to race handily with the first pair always 1-2. This doesn't look reliable form.

NOTEBOOK
Classic Vintage(USA) didn't run very well last time after attracting some market support and had gone some time without success, mainly due to his consistency giving the handicapper little leeway, but he fought on really well after racing prominently to get the better of a tight finish. Whether he can repeat this form next time considering his overall profile is debatable. (op 12-1)
Granston(IRE) has started this season in great heart and kept on bravely for pressure after appearing to assume command inside the final furlong. It's fair to say this 10-y-o ran up to his best. (op 20-1)
Tominator, back down in trip, kept on fairly well but he looks handicapped up to the hilt on his winning turf form.
Porgy, raised 6lb for his Goodwood success, sat in behind runners and failed to quicken when Jamie Spencer got really serious with him inside the final furlong. His winning form has come on better ground. (op 5-1)
Mister Angry(IRE) hasn't really run that well since winning last August, including in blinkers on his previous outing, which were swiftly dispensed with here. This was only a bit better and at least he wasn't beaten a really long way. (tchd 33-1)
Dansili Dancer has gone well here in the past, including when taking the 2007 Old Newton Cup over this C&D, so this was a shade disappointing, although the easy ground is a plausible excuse. Official explanation: trainer said gelding was unsuited by the good to soft ground (tchd 4-1)
Kitty Wells shaped promisingly on her return to action over C&D last month but didn't repeat that sort of effort. The ground may have been the problem, as she'd only raced on better ground in the past but her rider did report afterwards that she wasn't suited by the slow early pace. Official explanation: jockey said filly was unsuited by the slow early pace (op 13-8 tchd 6-4)
Dance Tempo, up 9lb after winning on his handicap debut, ran poorly and is another who may not have handled conditions. (tchd 13-2)

2813 PHS DATASHRED MAIDEN STKS 1m 3f 200y
3:50 (3:51) (Class 5) 3-Y-O+ **£2,266** (£674; £337; £168) **Stalls** Centre

Form RPR

2 **1** **Wild Coco (GER)**[27] 2019 3-8-8 0.... TomQueally 8 102+
(Sir Henry Cecil) *midfield: hdwy 5f out: led over 3f out: effrtlessly wnt clr ins fnl f: v easily* **4/5**[1]

0-2 **2** *8* **Thubiaan (USA)**[34] 1840 3-8-13 0.... RichardHills 6 95+
(William Haggas) *handy: led 4f out: hdd over 3f out: continued to chse wnr: rdn over 2f out: one pce over 1f out: eased whn no ch fnl 110yds* **4/1**[3]

00 **3** *9* **Crimson Knight**[25] 2097 3-8-13 0.... MartinDwyer 9 77
(Brian Meehan) *midfield: hdwy 3f out: rdn over 2f out to chse ldrs: kpt on to take 3rd towards fin: n.d to ldrs* **25/1**

2 **4** *3/4* **Keys (IRE)**[28] 1998 4-10-0 0.... PaulHanagan 4 76
(Roger Charlton) *led for 3f: remained handy: effrt over 3f out: one pce fr over 1f out: no ch after* **5/2**[2]

25 **5** *5* **Body Language (IRE)**[25] 2114 3-8-8 0.... FrannyNorton 11 63
(Ann Duffield) *hld up: struggling over 3f out: kpt on modly fr 2f out: nvr a threat* **33/1**

6 *6* **Ithoughtitwasover (IRE)** 3-8-13 0.... JoeFanning 2 58
(Mark Johnston) *midfield: hdwy and effrt to chse ldrs 3f out: rn green u.p: no imp fnl 2f: wl btn fnl f* **28/1**

0 **7** *4* **Sacred Sound (IRE)**[53] 1407 3-8-13 0.... SamHitchcott 1 52
(Mick Channon) *trckd ldrs: rdn 3f out: wknd over 2f out* **40/1**

4-0 **8** *2 3/4* **Navigation Track**[53] 1407 3-8-13 0.... JamieSpencer 12 47
(David Simcock) *hld up: sme hdwy over 4f out: no imp on ldrs: wl btn over 1f out* **50/1**

60 **9** *1 1/2* **Springtime Melody (FR)**[9] 2551 3-8-13 0.... FrankieMcDonald 10 45
(David Bourton) *in rr: u.p over 2f out: edgd lft over 1f out: nvr a threat* **100/1**

06/ **10** *6* **Alltheclews**[1013] 5477 6-9-7 0.... NoelGarbutt(7) 5 35
(Lucinda Featherstone) *prom: led after 3f: hdd 4f out: wknd 3f out* **100/1**

11 *nk* **Union Zak**[894] 7-10-0 0.... GrahamGibbons 7 35
(Rod Millman) *s.s: hdwy to go prom after 3f: wknd over 3f out* **66/1**

12 *41* **Patricias Pride**[24] 4-10-0 0.... AndrewElliott 3 —
(Lucinda Featherstone) *hld up: struggling 4f out: nvr on terms: t.o* **100/1**

2m 31.93s (-2.07) **Going Correction** +0.175s/f (Good)
WFA 3 from 4yo+ 15lb **12** Ran SP% **123.2**
Speed ratings (Par 103): **113,107,101,101,97 93,91,89,88,84 84,56**
toteswingers: 1&2 £1.10, 1&3 £12.90, 2&3 £23.20 CSF £4.49 TOTE £1.60: £1.20, £1.60, £4.10; EX 6.10.
Owner Gestut Rottgen **Bred** Gestut Rottgen **Trained** Newmarket, Suffolk

FOCUS
Not a race with much depth but the winner was extremely impressive and looks sure to go on to much better things. The winning time was really good in comparison to the handicap over the same trip, where the winner ran off 92, and the field was well strung out. The level of the form is set around the third.

Springtime Melody(FR) Official explanation: jockey said gelding stumbled on the bend into the home straight

2814 PHS TREADSMART H'CAP 1m
4:20 (4:20) (Class 4) (0-85,85) 4-Y-0+ **£4,209** (£1,252; £625; £312) **Stalls** Low

Form RPR
-503 **1** **Magic Cat**[18] 2300 5-9-4 **82** AndrewElliott 7 91
(Mrs K Burke) *hld up: u.p over 2f out: swtchd rt and hdwy over 1f out: styd on ins fnl f to ld nr fin* **10/1**

5-42 **2** *hd* **Dolphin Rock**[18] 2301 4-9-4 **82** TomQueally 10 91
(David Barron) *in tch: pushed along over 3f out: rdn over 2f out: styd on to ld ins fnl f: hdd nr fin* **9/2**[2]

60-0 **3** *½* **Venutius**[20] 2217 4-9-7 **85** GrahamGibbons 8 92
(Ed McMahon) *prom: rdn and outpcd 3f out: rallied ins fnl f: styd on towards fin* **17/2**

0000 **4** *1¼* **Prince Of Dance**[15] 2390 5-9-5 **83** RobertWinston 11 88
(Tom Tate) *racd keenly: in tch: wnt prom over 5f out: rdn over 2f out: chalng over 1f out: led briefly ins fnl f: one pce towards fin* **15/2**

-352 **5** *½* **One Scoop Or Two**[18] 2282 5-8-13 **77** RussKennemore 2 80
(Reg Hollinshead) *led: rdn 2f out: hdd ins fnl f: no ex towards fin* **9/2**[2]

0035 **6** *13* **Sir George (IRE)**[11] 2495 6-9-5 **83** PaulHanagan 4 56
(Ollie Pears) *trckd ldrs: u.p 3f out: wknd over 1f out* **7/1**[3]

0000 **7** *2¾* **Greyfriarschorista**[24] 2123 4-9-2 **80** (p) JoeFanning 9 47
(Mark Johnston) *prom: rdn 3f out: wknd ins fnl f* **16/1**

0112 **8** *1½* **Dazeen**[5] 2674 4-8-8 **72** TonyCulhane 5 36
(Paul Midgley) *hld up in midfield: u.p over 2f out: no imp: wl btn fnl f* **4/1**[1]

0-20 **9** *hd* **Oneofapear (IRE)**[24] 2124 5-9-7 **85** PJMcDonald 6 48
(Alan Swinbank) *hld up: pushed along over 4f out: toiling over 2f out* **12/1**

6/6- **10** *16* **July Days (IRE)**[248] 6599 5-9-0 **78** KellyHarrison 3 —
(Brian Baugh) *a bhd: toiling over 1f out* **50/1**

1m 44.93s (2.03) **Going Correction** +0.175s/f (Good) **10** Ran SP% **115.8**
Speed ratings (Par 105): **96,95,95,94,93 80,77,76,76,60**
toteswingers: 1&2 £8.80, 1&3 £20.30, 2&3 £7.50 CSF £54.24 CT £404.23 TOTE £12.30: £3.50, £1.70, £3.10; EX 62.80.
Owner Ray Bailey **Bred** R Bailey **Trained** Middleham Moor, North Yorks

FOCUS
A really good handicap with enough in-form horses at this level to suggest this is good form for the grade. it was sound run.
Dazeen Official explanation: trainer said gelding was unsuited by the good to soft ground

2815 PHS DIRECT H'CAP 1m
4:50 (4:51) (Class 5) (0-70,69) 4-Y-0+ **£2,266** (£674; £337; £168) **Stalls** Low

Form RPR
4316 **1** **Bold Marc (IRE)**[26] 2046 9-9-5 **67** AndrewElliott 1 78
(Mrs K Burke) *mde all: shkn up over 1f out: styd on wl: looked in command fnl 100yds* **4/1**[3]

5340 **2** *2* **Classic Descent**[16] 2348 6-8-9 **57** (bt) RobertWinston 3 63
(Ruth Carr) *dwlt: hld up: hdwy 2f out: rdn to take 2nd over 1f out: no real imp on wnr ins fnl f* **14/1**

0034 **3** *½* **Star Addition**[16] 2348 5-8-3 **51** PaulHanagan 5 56
(Eric Alston) *a.p: rdn and nt qckn over 1f out: kpt on u.p but a hld* **7/2**[2]

0-34 **4** *2* **Intiqaal (IRE)**[19] 2266 4-9-6 **68** (t) RichardHills 8 68
(Ed Dunlop) *racd keenly in midfield: pushed along and nt clr run over 2f out: rdn over 1f out: edgd lft ins fnl f: one pce* **10/3**[1]

3- **5** *1¾* **Red Dagger (IRE)**[41] 7006 5-8-5 **53** AndrewMullen 6 49
(Richard Price) *trckd ldrs: effrt to take 2nd over 3f out: lost 2nd over 1f out: carried hd to one side u.p: wknd fnl 100yds* **16/1**

0-46 **6** *2½* **Tanforan**[15] 2376 9-8-5 **53** KellyHarrison 10 43
(Brian Baugh) *racd keenly: hld up: hdwy over 3f out: rdn over 2f out: no imp: wl btn ins fnl f* **10/1**

0120 **7** *4½* **Dazakhee**[12] 2454 4-9-4 **66** TonyCulhane 2 46
(Paul Midgley) *dwlt: sn trckd ldrs: pushed along over 3f out: wknd over 2f out* **6/1**

00-0 **8** *1¾* **Cawdor (IRE)**[60] 1239 5-9-0 **69** KristinStubbs(7) 4 45
(Linda Stubbs) *racd keenly in midfield: dropped to rr after 2f: effrt over 2f out: no imp: wknd 1f out* **25/1**

335 **9** *3¾* **Redhotdoc**[20] 2219 7-9-5 **67** (p) JoeFanning 7 34
(Bill Moore) *in rr: u.p over 4f out: nvr on terms* **8/1**

1m 46.0s (3.10) **Going Correction** +0.175s/f (Good) **9** Ran SP% **116.2**
Speed ratings (Par 103): **91,89,88,86,84 82,77,76,72**
toteswingers: 1&2 £11.20, 1&3 £3.60, 2&3 £8.40 CSF £58.28 CT £216.16 TOTE £4.60: £1.10, £3.30, £3.20; EX 67.90.
Owner Aricabeau Racing Limited **Bred** Eamon D Delany **Trained** Middleham Moor, North Yorks

FOCUS
A modest handicap run at slow-early fractions, which meant quite a few didn't settle until the tempo lifted in the home straight. The winner had an easy lead and is rated to his best form since September 2009.
T/Jkpt: Not won. T/Plt: £1,198.30 to a £1 stake. Pool: £77,643.74. 47.30 winning tickets. T/Qpdt: £98.20 to a £1 stake. Pool: £5,361.64. 40.40 winning tickets. DO

2602 KEMPTON (A.W) (R-H)
Wednesday, June 8

OFFICIAL GOING: Standard
Wind: Across, fresh becoming moderate Weather: Fine

2816 BETDAQ.COM EVERY WEDNESDAY AT KEMPTON PARK APPRENTICE H'CAP 1m (P)
6:15 (6:15) (Class 5) (0-70,70) 4-Y-0+ **£2,266** (£674; £337; £168) **Stalls** Low

Form RPR
5-62 **1** **Catchanova (IRE)**[9] 2560 4-8-13 **62** AmyScott(3) 4 71
(Eve Johnson Houghton) *w.w bhd clr ldng quintet: clsd over 2f out: led wl over 1f out: rdn and kpt on wl* **5/1**[1]

2300 **2** *1½* **Jungle Bay**[29] 1977 4-9-5 **70** LewisWalsh(5) 1 76
(Jane Chapple-Hyam) *pressed ldng pair at str pce: rdn to chal 2f out: chsd wnr sn after: kpt on but a hld* **8/1**

1016 **3** *nk* **Hecton Lad (USA)**[9] 2560 4-8-9 **62** (b) GeorgeanBuckell(7) 14 67+
(John Best) *prom on outer: urged along over 2f out: kpt on after but a hld fnl f* **8/1**

00-5 **4** *¾* **Cool Hand Jake**[62] 1198 5-9-7 **70** JamesRogers(3) 6 73
(Peter Makin) *hld up in last pair and wl off the pce: prog over 2f out: swtchd ins and styd on fr over 1f out: tk 4th nr fin* **8/1**

2-50 **5** *hd* **Inpursuitoffreedom**[27] 2021 4-9-9 **69** AshleyMorgan 10 72
(Philip McBride) *settled off the pce in midfield: prog over 2f out: chsd ldrs over 1f out: kpt on one pce after* **16/1**

3006 **6** *2½* **Gallantry**[6] 2642 9-9-5 **68** MatthewCosham(3) 8 65
(Michael Squance) *settled off the pce in midfield: lost pl and rdn over 2f out: kpt on again fr over 1f out* **20/1**

3244 **7** *1½* **Eastern Gift**[8] 2589 6-9-8 **68** AdamBeschizza 11 61
(Gay Kelleway) *hld up in towards rr: rdn over 2f out on outer: plugged on but nvr a threat* **6/1**[2]

0053 **8** *¾* **Rapid Water**[7] 2605 5-9-5 **65** (p) RyanClark 12 57
(Michael Squance) *pressed ldr at str pce: led over 2f out to wl over 1f out: wknd* **12/1**

0060 **9** *½* **Guildenstern (IRE)**[6] 2642 9-8-0 **51** oh1 KatiaScallan(5) 5 42
(Alastair Lidderdale) *racd wd in midfield: rdn and no prog over 2f out: one pce after* **25/1**

5134 **10** *2* **Sasheen**[19] 2242 4-9-7 **67** (p) HarryBentley 13 53
(Jeremy Gask) *chsd ldng trio tl wknd fr 2f out* **7/1**[3]

2000 **11** *hd* **Having A Ball**[55] 1333 7-8-11 **60** MatthewLawson(3) 2 46
(Jonathan Portman) *dwlt: a in last quartet: rdn and no prog over 2f out* **16/1**

0-00 **12** *5* **Rock With You**[33] 1866 4-8-13 **62** LucyKBarry(3) 3 36
(Pat Phelan) *s.s: a bhd: detached in last 3f out* **20/1**

40-0 **13** *1¼* **Cactus King**[15] 2386 8-8-7 **56** NathanAlison(3) 9 27
(Louise Best) *settled in last quartet: hmpd on inner over 4f out: no prog over 2f out* **50/1**

1225 **14** *1½* **San Antonio**[106] 640 11-9-3 **70** (b) ChristyMews(7) 7 38
(Pam Sly) *led at str pce to over 2f out: wknd rapidly and eased* **16/1**

1m 41.12s (1.32) **Going Correction** +0.20s/f (Slow) **14** Ran SP% **117.5**
Speed ratings (Par 103): **101,99,99,98,98 95,94,93,93,91 90,85,84,83**
toteswingers: 1&2 £7.00, 1&3 £9.10, 2&3 £10.40 CSF £40.60 CT £325.54 TOTE £6.20: £2.20, £3.10, £2.30; EX 59.20.
Owner Andrew Wyer Darrell Blake Hugh Arthur **Bred** G J King **Trained** Blewbury, Oxon

FOCUS
This was just a modest apprentices' handicap, but they went a fair pace. Straightforward form.
Cool Hand Jake Official explanation: jockey said geling missed the break

2817 BETDAQ.COM EXCHANGE PRICE MULTIPLES MAIDEN STKS 6f (P)
6:45 (6:46) (Class 5) 2-Y-O **£2,266** (£674; £337; £168) **Stalls** Low

Form RPR
06 **1** **Main Focus (USA)**[26] 2049 2-9-3 0 WilliamBuick 3 82+
(John Gosden) *mde all: clr whn hung lft and reminders over 1f out: pushed out fnl f: comf* **10/11**[1]

2 *3* **Pearl Mix (IRE)** 2-9-3 0 JimCrowley 10 74+
(Ralph Beckett) *s.s: rn green in rr: shkn up on outer 2f out: r.o wl to take 2nd last 100yds: promising debut* **6/1**[2]

3 **3** *2½* **Finalist**[20] 2227 2-8-12 0 PhilipRobinson 9 61
(Dean Ivory) *racd wd: prom: chsd wnr over 2f out: no imp: fdd and lost 2nd last 100yds: jst hld on for 3rd* **25/1**

4 *nk* **Flying Trader (USA)** 2-9-3 0 KierenFallon 5 65+
(Jane Chapple-Hyam) *s.i.s: sn in midfield: outpcd and shkn up 2f out: kpt on again fnl f: nrly snatched 3rd* **15/2**[3]

5 *1¼* **House Limit (IRE)** 2-9-3 0 ChrisCatlin 1 61
(Harry Dunlop) *chsd wnr 2f: styd prom tl fdd over 1f out* **33/1**

6 *¾* **Littlecote Lady** 2-8-12 0 LiamKeniry 7 54
(Mark Usher) *restless stalls: s.s: rn green in rr: no prog tl kpt on ins fnl f* **66/1**

6 **7** *1¼* **Finley Connolly (IRE)**[27] 2017 2-9-3 0 MartinDwyer 2 55
(Brian Meehan) *chsd wnr after 2f to over 2f out: steadily wknd* **9/1**

8 *1¼* **Pond Life (IRE)** 2-9-3 0 HayleyTurner 6 51
(Amy Weaver) *chsd ldng quartet: outpcd fr 2f out: no imp 1f out: fdd after* **25/1**

9 *1¼* **Freddy Q (IRE)** 2-9-3 0 RyanMoore 11 47+
(Richard Hannon) *s.s: rn green and bucking early: detached in last tl effrt on inner 2f out: sn no prog* **8/1**

10 *½* **Nifty Shiftin** 2-9-3 0 DaneO'Neill 8 46
(David Elsworth) *s.s: rn green but sn in midfield: shkn up over 2f out: wknd over 1f out* **16/1**

1m 15.2s (2.10) **Going Correction** +0.20s/f (Slow) **10** Ran SP% **117.6**
Speed ratings (Par 93): **94,90,86,86,84 83,81,80,78,77**
toteswingers: 1&2 £2.30, 1&3 £9.30, 2&3 £30.70 CSF £6.38 TOTE £2.00: £1.10, £2.20, £5.60; EX 8.20.
Owner K Abdulla **Bred** Juddmonte Farms Inc **Trained** Newmarket, Suffolk

FOCUS
A fair maiden.

NOTEBOOK
Main Focus(USA) set a fair standard judged on his second-time out fifth-place finish in a hot maiden at Newbury (winner, third and fourth all successful since), and he was too quick for this lot. Plenty keen enough to post, he looked a headstrong type in the race itself, racing powerfully in the lead, and although he found enough, he didn't finish as fast as the eyecatching Pearl Mix, who probably would have won had he not run green. Main Focus is a half-brother to a Polytrack winner, so it's no surprise the surface suited, although his chances of progressing well in the long term depend on him learning to settle. (op 5-4 tchd 11-8 in places)
Pearl Mix(IRE) ◆, a 120,000euros first foal of a 7f winner (on 2-y-o debut in France), raced off the pace after a slow start and showed further signs of inexperience when first asked for his effort, having had a wide trip into the straight, but he was really going on at the finish. He should have learnt plenty. (op 8-1 tchd 11-1 in a place)
Finalist had a three-wide trip but still stepped up on the form he showed on his debut over 5f on turf.
Flying Trader(USA), a 55,000gns purchase, didn't break well enough to get a worthwhile position but he finished reasonably okay and this was a respectable introduction. (op 7-1 tchd 13-2)
House Limit(IRE), a £16,000 April foal, looked reasonably well educated for much of the way but didn't see his race out.
Littlecote Lady shaped as though she'll be better for the experience.
Freddy Q(IRE) looked badly in need of the experience. He also covered a lot of ground on the first of the bend, before being taken towards the inside rail, and an awful lot better is expected next time. (op 6-1)

2818 LAY BACK AND WIN AT BETDAQ.COM H'CAP 6f (P)
7:15 (7:17) (Class 5) (0-75,75) 3-Y-O **£2,266** (£674; £337; £168) **Stalls** Low

Form RPR
3-1 **1** **Mosaicist (IRE)**[19] 2266 3-9-6 **74** KierenFallon 2 89+
(James Fanshawe) *t.k.h: prom: trckd ldr 1/2-way: led wl over 1f out: pushed clr: comf* **3/1**[2]

-441 **2** *2¼* **Speightowns Kid (USA)**[7] 2603 3-9-1 **69** 6ex WilliamBuick 5 74+
(Matthew Salaman) *chsd ldrs: shkn up over 2f out: outpcd and drvn over 1f out: styd on to take 2nd last 150yds: no ch w wnr* **11/10**[1]

21-1 **3** *1¾* **Magic Cross**[49] 1482 3-8-9 **66** AdamBeschizza(3) 4 65
(Philip McBride) *settled in rr: pushed along and prog on inner 2f out: shkn up and styd on to take 3rd last 75yds* **16/1**

-442 **4** *1* **Climaxfortackle (IRE)**[23] 2163 3-8-9 **63** .... JimCrowley 9 59+
(Derek Shaw) *dwlt: mostly last: shkn up over 2f out: styd on fr over 1f out to take 4th last strides* **16/1**

2U00 **5** *1 ¼* **Overwhelm**[15] 2383 3-9-3 **71** .... (p) SebSanders 1 63
(Andrew Reid) *led to wl over 1f out: wknd qckly fnl f* **22/1**

-103 **6** *½* **Green Apple**[21] 2199 3-9-5 **73** .... FergusSweeney 3 63
(Peter Makin) *chsd ldr to 1/2-way: wknd over 1f out* **14/1**

15-0 **7** *nk* **Silver Alliance**[21] 2199 3-9-6 **74** .... AdamKirby 6 63
(Walter Swinburn) *trckd ldrs: shkn up and hanging over 2f out: lost pl and outpcd: n.d after* **13/2**[3]

16-0 **8** *nse* **Rowan Spirit (IRE)**[22] 2180 3-9-6 **74** .... TomMcLaughlin 11 63
(Mark Brisbourne) *nvr beyond midfield: rdn over 2f out: sn outpcd and btn* **50/1**

60-0 **9** *½* **Jeeran**[64] 1152 3-9-1 **69** .... (t) PhilipRobinson 7 56
(Clive Brittain) *racd wd in rr: rdn and no prog over 2f out: no ch after* **66/1**

3-60 **10** *1 ¼* **Pippa's Gift**[22] 2180 3-9-2 **70** .... MartinDwyer 12 53
(William Muir) *racd wd: prom: wknd 2f out: eased fnl f* **33/1**

-436 **11** *1* **Circuitous**[7] 2611 3-8-8 **62** .... ChrisCatlin 8 42
(Paul Cole) *wnt lft s: a towards rr: rdn and no prog over 2f out* **20/1**

1m 14.33s (1.23) **Going Correction** +0.20s/f (Slow) **11** Ran SP% **119.9**
Speed ratings (Par 99): **99,96,93,92,90 90,89,89,88,87 85**
toteswingers: 1&2 £1.20, 1&3 £4.10, 2&3 £5.90 CSF £6.40 CT £44.56 TOTE £3.60: £1.60, £1.10, £2.80; EX 7.40.
Owner Shooting Star Racing **Bred** Newberry Stud Company **Trained** Newmarket, Suffolk

FOCUS
A strong race for the grade with the first three finishers all having won last-time out, and the front two in particular looking well handicapped. The form is rated around the third.

2819 BETDAQ MOBILE APPS H'CAP — 1m 4f (P)
7:45 (7:45) (Class 4) (0-85,85) 3-Y-O **£4,079** (£1,214; £606; £303) **Stalls** Centre

Form RPR

62-3 **1** **Samarkand (IRE)**[13] 2435 3-8-8 **72** .... SebSanders 9 88+
(Sir Mark Prescott Bt) *racd wd in midfield: prog on outer 4f out to chse ldr over 2f out: urged along to cl and led wl over 1f out: forged clr* **9/1**

0-1 **2** *5* **Area Fifty One**[133] 300 3-8-7 **76** .... JamesRogers(5) 8 84
(William Muir) *led narrowly at decent pce and clr of rest: def advantage 4f out: drvn and hdd wl over 1f out: kpt on but no match for wnr* **33/1**

3-34 **3** *1 ¼* **El Mansour (USA)**[26] 2052 3-9-0 **78** .... AdamKirby 12 84
(Clive Cox) *sn chsd clr ldng pair: chsd ldr 4f out to over 2f out: nt qckn u.p: kpt on wl fnl f* **13/2**[2]

1 **4** *5* **Western Prize**[144] 176 3-8-13 **77** .... JimCrowley 14 75+
(Ralph Beckett) *hld up wl in rr: gng wl over 3f out: prog over 2f out but ldrs already gone: drvn over 1f out: styd on to take 4th fnl f* **7/1**[3]

1 **5** *1 ¾* **Antarctic (IRE)**[19] 2257 3-9-4 **82** .... WilliamBuick 11 77+
(John Gosden) *dwlt: rousted along to chse ldng trio: drvn and outpcd over 2f out: wl btn after* **7/2**[1]

1136 **6** *1* **Tijori (IRE)**[30] 1947 3-8-9 **73** .... RyanMoore 2 67
(Richard Hannon) *hld up in last trio: rdn over 3f out: plugged on fnl 2f: n.d* **16/1**

2-53 **7** *hd* **Malanos (IRE)**[19] 2257 3-8-13 **77** .... DaneO'Neill 4 70
(David Elsworth) *chsd ldrs: rdn 3f out: sn outpcd and btn* **14/1**

055 **8** *10* **Montegonian (USA)**[37] 1759 3-8-11 **75** .... MartinDwyer 13 52
(Marcus Tregoning) *sn wl plcd bhd clr ldrs: rdn 3f out: sn wknd and bhd* **9/1**

1220 **9** *1 ½* **Gower Rules (IRE)**[18] 2293 3-7-11 **66** oh3 .... KieranO'Neill(5) 1 41
(John Bridger) *pressed ldr and clr of rest: lost 2nd 4f out: wknd over 2f out: sn bhd* **33/1**

1 **10** *2 ¾* **Action Front (USA)**[34] 1840 3-9-7 **85** .... PatDobbs 5 55
(Amanda Perrett) *hld up towards rr: gng wl enough 4f out: rdn over 2f out: wknd and sn bhd* **9/1**

4313 **11** *2 ¼* **Diplomasi**[23] 2152 3-8-5 **69** .... ChrisCatlin 7 36
(Clive Brittain) *s.i.s: t.k.h and hld up in rr: rdn and no prog 3f out: sn bhd* **28/1**

2215 **12** *9* **Blue Cossack (IRE)**[84] 866 3-8-2 **66** oh3 .... DavidProbert 6 18
(Mark Usher) *a in rr: rdn and struggling 3f out: sn bhd* **40/1**

21 **13** *38* **Baltic Light (USA)**[22] 2175 3-9-2 **80** .... IanMongan 3 —
(Sir Henry Cecil) *s.i.s: last whn snatched up after 2f: brief effrt over 4f out: drvn and wknd over 3f out: t.o* **7/1**[3]

2m 35.15s (0.65) **Going Correction** +0.20s/f (Slow) **13** Ran SP% **114.9**
Speed ratings (Par 101): **105,101,100,97,96 95,95,88,87,86 84,78,53**
toteswingers: 1&2 £19.80, 1&3 £5.50, 2&3 £45.70 CSF £278.58 CT £2047.02 TOTE £9.60: £3.40, £5.40, £2.70; EX 178.20.
Owner Moyglare Stud Farm **Bred** Moyglare Stud Farm Ltd **Trained** Newmarket, Suffolk

FOCUS
Plenty of unexposed types, including five last-time-out winners, so this looked a good race for the class, but not many got into it. The pace had appeared plenty strong enough, with Area Fifty One and Gower Rules getting involved in a speed duel down the back straight, but the former kept on surprisingly well. The form is set around the third.
Baltic Light(USA) Official explanation: jockey said filly anticipated the start and hit her head on the gate

2820 HEART FM SUPPORTS KEMPTON LIVE H'CAP — 1m 3f (P)
8:15 (8:15) (Class 6) (0-55,55) 4-Y-O+ **£1,619** (£481; £240; £120) **Stalls** Low

Form RPR

400/ **1** **Lunar Promise (IRE)**[894] 7786 9-8-13 **55** .... RyanClark(5) 4 71+
(Ian Williams) *t.k.h: hld up in tch: smooth prog over 2f out: led over 1f out: sn clr: easily* **10/3**[2]

-400 **2** *6* **Herecomethegirls**[30] 1959 5-8-11 **53** ow1 .... (b) KylieManser(5) 8 55
(Olivia Maylam) *racd wd: hld up in tch: prog over 3f out: led over 2f out gng strly: hdd over 1f out: no ch w wnr after: wknd last 150yds: jst hld on for 2nd* **28/1**

0450 **3** *nk* **Colonel Sherman (USA)**[12] 2462 6-8-11 **55** .... (t) DavidKenny(7) 2 57+
(Philip Kirby) *plld hrd early: hld up and sn in rr: rdn and prog over 2f out: styd on fr over 1f out: nrly snatched 2nd* **9/2**[3]

03/0 **4** *nse* **Appointment**[21] 2198 6-8-13 **50** .... JamieGoldstein 12 52
(Ralph Smith) *wl away fr wd draw: led: rdn and hdd over 2f out: sn outpcd: kpt on fnl f* **66/1**

50-5 **5** *4* **Motarjm (USA)**[36] 1310 7-8-13 **50** .... (t) ChrisCatlin 3 44
(Lydia Pearce) *hld up in last quartet: rdn and prog over 2f out: kpt on same pce to take 5th ins fnl f* **10/1**

-343 **6** *3 ¾* **Prince Blue**[71] 1025 4-9-1 **52** .... SamHitchcott 6 40
(John E Long) *trckd ldrs: wl there and rdn over 2f out: sn fdd* **9/1**

000- **7** *2 ¼* **Lunar Limelight**[256] 6375 6-9-4 **55** .... FergusSweeney 7 39
(Peter Makin) *hld up in last pair: rdn and prog over 2f out: nvr rchd ldrs: wknd over 1f out* **20/1**

205 **8** *nk* **Battle Axe (FR)**[110] 588 6-8-12 **49** ow1 .... IanMongan 13 32
(Laura Mongan) *awkward s: hld up in last quartet: rdn and modest prog over 2f out: nvr a real factor* **20/1**

6-53 **9** *11* **Belle Boleyn**[9] 2569 4-9-3 **54** .... GeorgeBaker 11 17
(Chris Wall) *prog to join ldr after 3f tl wknd over 3f out: sn bhd* **9/4**[1]

-040 **10** *2 ¼* **Burnbrake**[112] 553 6-9-3 **54** .... (b) JamesMillman 5 13
(Les Hall) *hld up and sn last: pushed along and virtually t.o over 2f out: nvr in the hunt* **16/1**

600- **11** *3 ¼* **Cils Blancs (IRE)**[113] 6460 5-8-13 **50** .... (p) PatCosgrave 9 —
(Jane Chapple-Hyam) *trckd ldrs: wnt 2nd over 3f out to wl over 2f out: wknd qckly* **25/1**

0 **12** *3 ¼* **Silky Lady (IRE)**[15] 2377 4-8-12 **49** .... LiamKeniry 1 —
(Jonathan Geake) *t.k.h: hld up in midfield on inner: wknd wl over 2f out: sn bhd* **33/1**

6505 **13** *3 ¾* **Ocean Rosie (IRE)**[19] 2271 4-8-11 **48** .... LiamJones 14 —
(Tony Carroll) *pressed ldr 3f: wknd wl over 3f out: sn bhd* **33/1**

2m 23.76s (1.86) **Going Correction** +0.20s/f (Slow) **13** Ran SP% **121.2**
Speed ratings (Par 101): **101,96,96,96,93 90,89,88,80,79 76,74,71**
toteswingers: 1&2 £31.20, 1&3 £3.20, 2&3 £72.80 CSF £101.40 CT £436.36 TOTE £3.70: £1.20, £6.20, £1.80; EX 189.70.
Owner Richard Edwards **Bred** Deer Forest Stud Ltd **Trained** Portway, Worcs

FOCUS
An extremely moderate, uncompetitive event, but a well-handicapped winner. He's rated back to his late 2008 form.

2821 REWARDS4RACING.COM FILLIES' H'CAP — 7f (P)
8:45 (8:45) (Class 5) (0-70,70) 3-Y-O **£2,266** (£674; £337; £168) **Stalls** Low

Form RPR

0-15 **1** **Chokurei (IRE)**[18] 2313 3-9-7 **70** .... AdamKirby 5 86
(Clive Cox) *trckd ldrs: rdn and prog over 2f out: led over 1f out: sn clr: readily* **9/1**

5-20 **2** *3 ¾* **Empress Charlotte**[29] 1986 3-8-13 **62** .... HayleyTurner 8 68
(Michael Bell) *hld up in last pair: stdy prog over 2f out: styd on wl fnl f to take 2nd last strides* **12/1**

0-55 **3** *nk* **Mawjoodah**[27] 2018 3-9-5 **68** .... PhilipRobinson 4 73
(Clive Brittain) *led: gng strly over 2f out: hdd and no ex over 1f out: lost 2nd last strides* **8/1**

-142 **4** *shd* **Ellie In The Pink (IRE)**[29] 1986 3-8-10 **64** .... HarryBentley(5) 10 69
(Alan Jarvis) *trckd ldrs: rdn and effrt over 2f out: kpt on fr over 1f out to press for pl nr fin* **7/1**[3]

4432 **5** *½* **Caelis**[18] 2313 3-9-2 **65** .... (b) JimCrowley 7 71+
(Ralph Beckett) *unable to secure gd position and sn in last quartet: drvn over 2f out: styd on after: nrst fin* **4/1**[2]

26-0 **6** *1* **Blue Maisey**[29] 1986 3-9-3 **66** .... FergusSweeney 3 67
(Peter Makin) *prom on inner: chsd ldr wl over 2f out to wl over 1f out: fdd fnl f* **20/1**

06-0 **7** *½* **Coin Box**[22] 2174 3-9-6 **69** .... AhmedAjtebi 14 68
(Mahmood Al Zarooni) *forced to r wd in midfield: effrt over 2f out: kpt on same pce u.p: nvr able to chal* **14/1**

4445 **8** *3 ¾* **Jackie Love (IRE)**[15] 2381 3-8-0 **56** .... JenniferFerguson(7) 9 45
(Olivia Maylam) *racd wd in rr: effrt over 2f out: nvr on terms w ldrs* **66/1**

00-6 **9** *¾* **Moonlight Mystery**[42] 1606 3-8-13 **62** .... JackMitchell 1 49
(Chris Wall) *nvr gng that wl on inner: effrt u.p to chse ldrs 2f out: sn wknd* **10/3**[1]

-020 **10** *2 ¼* **Looksmart**[29] 1986 3-9-0 **63** .... RyanMoore 2 44
(Richard Hannon) *nvr beyond midfield: rdn 3f out: no prog and btn over 2f out* **10/1**

5-52 **11** *5* **Tinaheely (IRE)**[39] 1682 3-9-7 **70** .... StephenCraine 11 38
(Jonathan Portman) *chsd ldr to wl over 2f out: wknd qckly* **12/1**

1-60 **12** *2 ½* **Opera Dancer**[25] 2102 3-9-7 **70** .... LiamKeniry 13 31
(Sylvester Kirk) *hld up wl in rr: shkn up and no prog over 2f out: no ch after: eased* **20/1**

6600 **13** *16* **Encore View**[23] 2163 3-8-7 **56** .... (t) ChrisCatlin 6 —
(Nick Littmoden) *lost midfield pl rapidly 4f out and sn last: t.o* **50/1**

1m 27.49s (1.49) **Going Correction** +0.20s/f (Slow) **13** Ran SP% **120.8**
Speed ratings (Par 96): **99,94,94,94,93 92,91,87,86,84 78,75,57**
toteswingers: 1&2 £11.70, 1&3 £16.30, 2&3 £18.00 CSF £109.26 CT £912.14 TOTE £12.30: £3.60, £4.30, £3.40; EX 156.50.
Owner H E Sheikh Sultan Bin Khalifa Al Nahyan **Bred** Sheikh Sultan Bin Khalifa Al Nayhan **Trained** Lambourn, Berks

FOCUS
A modest fillies' handicap, but reasonably competitive. The pace was fair and the time was a respectable 0.92 seconds slower than the following Class 4 handicap for older horses. A clear personal best from the winner.

2822 PROBIZ H'CAP — 7f (P)
9:15 (9:15) (Class 4) (0-80,80) 4-Y-O+ **£4,079** (£1,214; £606; £303) **Stalls** Low

Form RPR

21-0 **1** **Divine Call**[14] 2398 4-9-5 **78** .... RyanMoore 2 89+
(William Haggas) *led 1f: styd prom: effrt again to ld over 1f out: drvn out and styd on wl* **7/4**[1]

3-63 **2** *½* **Starclass**[13] 2428 4-9-4 **77** .... AdamKirby 5 87+
(Walter Swinburn) *hld up in last pair: gd prog on outer jst over 2f out: chsd wnr ins fnl f: styd on but no imp nr fin* **12/1**

0-66 **3** *2* **Sakhee's Pearl**[42] 1610 5-9-4 **77** .... (b) DaneO'Neill 3 81
(Jo Crowley) *trckd ldrs on inner: effrt 2f out: chsd wnr briefly 1f out: outpcd* **16/1**

0-22 **4** *½* **Mashatu**[29] 1990 4-8-13 **72** .... PatCosgrave 7 75+
(James Fanshawe) *hld up in rr: pushed along over 2f out: stdy prog over 1f out: nvr gng pce to threaten but styd on* **10/3**[2]

5-54 **5** *½* **Spa's Dancer (IRE)**[22] 2178 4-9-5 **78** .... (p) SebSanders 4 87+
(J W Hills) *hld up in midfield: repeatedly failed to get clr run fr 2f out tl fnl f: r.o after: nrst fin* **11/2**[3]

45-0 **6** *3* **Mazamorra (USA)**[19] 2269 4-9-2 **80** .... TobyAtkinson(5) 6 73+
(Marco Botti) *hld up in midfield: nt clr run 2f out: sn wl outpcd and no ch* **33/1**

0030 **7** *nk* **Hereford Boy**[22] 2178 7-8-11 **70** .... (p) ChrisCatlin 9 63
(Dean Ivory) *hld up in midfield: prog over 2f out: tried to chal wl over 1f out: wknd qckly fnl f* **50/1**

05-6 **8** *1 ¾* **Mishrif (USA)**[22] 2178 5-9-0 **73** .... (v) PatDobbs 12 61
(J R Jenkins) *trckd ldrs: lost pl wl over 1f out: no ch whn short of room ent fnl f* **16/1**

3523 **9** *½* **Perfect Ch'l (IRE)**[18] 2313 4-8-11 **70** .... LiamKeniry 14 57
(Ian Wood) *led after 1f tl over 1f out: wknd* **25/1**

10-5 **10** *nk* **Baby Dottie**[37] 1771 4-8-11 **70** .... IanMongan 10 56
(Pat Phelan) *prom: rdn to chal 2f out: wknd qckly over 1f out* **16/1**

40-0 **11** *2 1/4* **Rio Tinto**[44] [1569] 4-8-10 **69**.. WilliamCarson 13 49
(Giles Bravery) *racd wd in tch: v wd bnd 3f out whn on terms: sn wknd* **66/1**

531- **12** *nse* **Scottish Glen**[207] [7439] 5-8-11 **70**.. JimCrowley 8 50
(Patrick Chamings) *hld up in last: nudged along and no prog over 2f out* **9/1**

1m 26.57s (0.57) **Going Correction** +0.20s/f (Slow) **12** Ran SP% **120.4**
Speed ratings (Par 105): **104,103,101,100,100 96,96,94,93,93 90,90**
toteswingers: 1&2 £10.50, 1&3 £9.40, 2&3 £19.40 CSF £25.04 CT £243.32 TOTE £2.70: £1.90, £2.80, £4.30; EX 18.60.
Owner Cheveley Park Stud **Bred** Cheveley Park Stud Ltd **Trained** Newmarket, Suffolk

FOCUS
A fair handicap run at a good pace, and the time was 0.92 seconds quicker than the earlier Class 5 for 3-y-os. The winner built on his Southwell form.
Spa's Dancer(IRE) Official explanation: jockey said gelding was denied a clear run
T/Plt: £585.50 to a £1 stake. Pool: £68,176.56. 84.99 winning tickets. T/Qpdt: £205.60 to a £1 stake. Pool: £6,670.20. 24.00 winning tickets. JN

2594 YARMOUTH (L-H)
Wednesday, June 8

OFFICIAL GOING: Good to firm (8.0)
Wind: Modest, half against Weather: Cloudy, brighter spells

2823 NORFOLK NELSON MUSEUM MAIDEN AUCTION STKS 5f 43y
2:10 (2:15) (Class 5) 2-Y-O **£2,266** (£674; £337; £168) **Stalls** High

Form RPR

04 **1** **Lady Nickandy (IRE)**[10] [2523] 2-8-0 0.......................... KieranO'Neill(5) 1 59
(Alan McCabe) *w ldr: pushed along 1/2-way: rdn to ld over 1f out: drvn and hrd pressed ins fnl f: kpt on and a jst holding rival: drvn out* **2/7**[1]

2 *1/2* **Mystery Cool (IRE)**[28] [2009] 2-8-5 0................................. CathyGannon 3 57
(David Peter Nagle, Ire) *taken down early: s.i.s: chsd ldng pair: effrt and swtchd lft over 1f out: drvn and ev ch ins fnl f: kpt on but a jst hld* **4/1**[2]

6042 **3** *3 1/4* **Masivo Man (IRE)**[8] [2595] 2-8-10 0.................................. AndreaAtzeni 4 50
(Chris Dwyer) *broke fast: led tl rdn and hdd over 1f out: drvn and unable qck ent fnl f: wknd fnl 150yds* **16/1**[3]

4 **4** *14* **Willies Diamond (IRE)**[8] [2595] 2-8-5 0.................................. AWhelan 2 —
(Michael Wigham) *sn pushed along and struggling to go pce: dropped to last over 3f out: rdn 1/2-way: lost tch wl over 1f out* **25/1**

64.88 secs (2.18) **Going Correction** -0.075s/f (Good) 4 Ran SP% **107.5**
Speed ratings (Par 93): **79,78,73,50**
CSF £1.72 TOTE £1.30.
Owner K N Lane **Bred** Martin Francis **Trained** Averham Park, Notts

FOCUS
A weak juvenile maiden in which the two main form picks had it to themselves inside the final furlong. Selling-class form with the winner rated to her pre-race mark. The runners were faced with a fair headwind. Back straight and bottom bend dolled out 3m adding 15m to races on Round course.

NOTEBOOK
Lady Nickandy(IRE) proved all the rage and shed her maiden tag at the third time of asking, but had to work much harder than her prohibitive odds suggested she would. The drop to this trip had seen her improve on her second outing at Nottingham last time, but she tended to race lazily here and didn't seem totally at ease on the track. Returning to 6f ought to prove more suitable as she matures, but if she gets into the Listed Windsor Castle Stakes over this trip at Royal Ascot next week, she is an intended runner to give her owners a day out. (op 8-15 tchd 4-7 in a place)
Mystery Cool(IRE) proved very easy to back down in trip. She didn't help her cause with a slow start, but still threw down a strong challenge when switched mid-track from the furlong pole. Ultimately this sharper test just found her out, but she has now found his sort of level. (op 5-2)
Masivo Man(IRE), runner-up in a seller here eight days earlier, set out from the front on this drop back to the minimum and was left behind by the first pair before the last furlong. (tchd 14-1 and 18-1)
Willies Diamond(IRE) was outpaced from the gates over this sharper test and, eased off when well beaten passing the 2f pole, something presumably went amiss. (op 16-1)

2824 GREAT YARMOUTH GREYHOUND HOMEFINDERS H'CAP 1m 2f 21y
2:40 (2:40) (Class 6) (0-65,65) 4-Y-O+ **£1,619** (£481; £240; £120) **Stalls** Low

Form RPR

0603 **1** **Art Scholar (IRE)**[8] [2600] 4-8-5 **49**.................................... NeilChalmers 3 67+
(Michael Appleby) *hld up in last pair: smooth hdwy to trck ldr ent fnl 2f: led on bit over 1f out: readily c clr fnl f: easily* **3/1**[2]

00-3 **2** *4* **Golden Waters**[20] [2232] 4-9-7 **65**...................................... CathyGannon 4 72
(Eve Johnson Houghton) *led at stdy gallop: pushed along and flashed tail 4f out: flashed tail again u.p and hdd over 1f out: no ch w wnr ins fnl f* **2/1**[1]

00-0 **3** *3 3/4* **Sanctum**[29] [1987] 5-8-2 **46**..(b[1]) AdrianMcCarthy 2 46
(Dr Jon Scargill) *dwlt: sn pushed along and rcvrd to chse ldng pair: rdn and effrt over 3f out: drvn and outpcd 2f out: 3rd and wl btn ins fnl f* **11/1**

0-05 **4** *2* **Spiritual Art**[21] [2204] 5-9-5 **63**.. RobertHavlin 1 59
(Luke Dace) *hld up in last pair: effrt on outer ent fnl 2f: rdn and unable qck 2f out: 4th and wl btn 1f out* **4/1**[3]

26-2 **5** *6* **Locum**[44] [1573] 6-8-8 **59**... CharlesEddery(7) 7 43
(Mark H Tompkins) *dwlt: in tch: rdn and fnd little over 2f out: wknd wl over 1f out* **4/1**[3]

-600 **6** *11* **Libre**[96] [773] 11-8-2 **46** oh1...(p) JimmyQuinn 8 —
(Violet M Jordan) *stdd s: t.k.h: hld up in tch in last trio: rdn and fnd nil over 3f out: wknd and hung lft 2f out: eased ins fnl f* **25/1**

0-00 **7** *21* **Carlcol Girl**[8] [2600] 4-8-2 **46** oh1...................................(b[1]) AndreaAtzeni 5 —
(Christine Dunnett) *racd keenly: chsd ldr: effrt and ev ch ent fnl 4f: wknd rapidly over 2f out: t.o and virtually p.u ins fnl f* **66/1**

2m 9.58s (-0.92) **Going Correction** -0.075s/f (Good) 7 Ran SP% **112.0**
Speed ratings (Par 101): **100,96,93,92,87 78,61**
toteswingers: 1&2 £1.60, 1&3 £6.20, 2&3 £4.20 CSF £9.02 CT £53.60 TOTE £3.20: £1.80, £1.60; EX 10.00 Trifecta £63.60 Pool: £302.52 - 3.52 winning units..
Owner D J Lewin **Bred** John Ramsbottom **Trained** Danethorpe, Notts
■ Michael Appleby's first winner from his new base near Newark.

FOCUS
An ordinary handicap, run at an average pace. Pretty limited form and the runner-up rates the benchmark.

2825 NORFOLK AND SUFFOLK ANIMAL TRUST APPRENTICE (S) STKS 1m 1f
3:10 (3:10) (Class 6) 3-Y-O **£1,619** (£481; £240; £120) **Stalls** Low

Form RPR

36-4 **1** **Unex Goya (IRE)**[109] [610] 3-8-12 68.........................(tp) MatthewDavies 3 52
(George Baker) *chsd ldng trio: pushed along over 3f out: drvn and clsd to chse ldr over 1f out: hrd drvn and edgd rt ins fnl f: led fnl 75yds: drvn out* **4/7**[1]

1600 **2** *nk* **Onlyfoalsandhorses (IRE)**[21] [2196] 3-8-10 53..........(p) RyanPowell(3) 5 52
(J S Moore) *chsd ldr tl over 5f out: rdn to chse wnr again over 2f out: led and hung rt 2f out: drvn ent fnl f: hdd fnl 75yds: no ex* **12/1**

00- **3** *1/2* **Dolly Colman (IRE)**[243] [6711] 3-8-2 0............................ DavidKenny(5) 7 45
(Andrew Haynes) *t.k.h: hld up off the pce in last quartet: rdn and effrt ent fnl 3f: chsd ldng pair over 1f out: swtchd rt ins fnl f: styng on and clsng at fin* **25/1**

0 **4** *6* **Circus Master**[22] [2174] 3-8-12 0..(bt[1]) KierenFox 1 37
(James Eustace) *s.i.s: racd wl off the pce in last quartet: rdn and hung lft ent fnl 4f: modest hdwy but racing awkwardly u.p fr 2f out: nvr on terms* **16/1**

2200 **5** *7* **Hackett (IRE)**[26] [2064] 3-8-5 60..(v[1]) IanBurns(7) 6 21
(Michael Quinn) *led: hdd and rdn 2f out: wknd over 1f out: fdd fnl f* **7/1**[3]

5600 **6** *6* **Blade Pirate**[15] [2382] 3-8-5 45.....................................[1] BradleyBosley(7) 8 —
(John Ryan) *stdd s: plld hrd and sn chsng ldrs: jnd ldr over 5f out tl over 2f out: wknd qckly wl over 1f out* **66/1**

00-0 **7** *16* **Generous Pursuit**[11] [2511] 3-8-4 0.............................. TobyAtkinson(3) 2 —
(Phil McEntee) *stdd s: hld up off the pce in last trio: rdn and short-lived effrt 3f out: wl bhd and eased ins fnl f: t.o* **66/1**

8 *75* **Double Dice** 3-8-7 0... AshleyHamblett 4 —
(George Margarson) *hld up off the pce in last quartet: struggling in last 4f out: sn lost tch: wl t.o and virtually p.u fnl 2f* **9/2**[2]

1m 58.26s (2.46) **Going Correction** -0.075s/f (Good) 8 Ran SP% **114.7**
Speed ratings (Par 97): **86,85,85,79,73 68,54,—**
toteswingers: 1&2 £2.40, 1&3 £5.80, 2&3 £26.20 CSF £9.06 TOTE £1.40: £1.02, £2.60, £6.10; EX 9.70 Trifecta £90.80 Pool: £391.69 - 3.19 winning units..The winner was sold to Michael Smith for 3,600gns.
Owner M Khan X2 **Bred** Iona Equine **Trained** Whitsbury, Hants

FOCUS
The front three were clear in this weak seller. The winner did not need to match even his AW form.
Double Dice Official explanation: jockey said filly lost its action on the bend and was never travelling thereafter

2826 DIGIBET.COM H'CAP 6f 3y
3:40 (3:40) (Class 3) (0-90,90) 3-Y-O+ **£6,670** (£1,984; £991; £495) **Stalls** High

Form RPR

3121 **1** **Collect Art (IRE)**[1] [2794] 4-8-13 **75**................................ StevieDonohoe 6 85
(Andrew Haynes) *w ldrs: shkn up to ld over 1f out: rdn and asserted ent fnl f: in command fnl 100yds: r.o wl* **9/4**[2]

10-0 **2** *1 1/2* **Kanaf (IRE)**[39] [1680] 4-9-13 **89**.. TadhgO'Shea 7 94
(Ed Dunlop) *taken down early: dwlt: in tch in last pair: hdwy over 1f out: rdn to chse wnr 1f out: kpt on but no real imp after* **11/2**[3]

4231 **3** *1/2* **Magical Speedfit (IRE)**[13] [2422] 6-8-10 **75**................ SimonPearce(3) 1 79
(George Margarson) *hld up in last pair: effrt on outer over 1f out: pressing for 2nd fnl 100yds: kpt on same pce after and no threat to wnr* **10/1**

10-0 **4** *1 1/4* **Oil Strike**[25] [2099] 4-9-13 **89**.. LukeMorris 2 89
(Peter Winkworth) *in tch: rdn ent fnl 2f: effrt between horses and edgd lft ent fnl f: styd on same pce fnl 150yds* **2/1**[1]

4-40 **5** *1 3/4* **We Have A Dream**[39] [1675] 6-9-5 **81**.............................(b) AndreaAtzeni 5 75
(William Muir) *led: hdd and rdn over 1f out: unable qck ent fnl f: wknd ins fnl f* **9/1**

-000 **6** *hd* **Judd Street**[25] [2099] 9-10-0 **90**...................................... CathyGannon 3 83
(Eve Johnson Houghton) *in tch towards rr: rdn and effrt wl over 1f out: no imp u.p fnl f* **10/1**

1222 **7** *1/2* **Rylee Mooch**[18] [2410] 3-8-1 **71** oh4.................................(e) JimmyQuinn 4 61
(Richard Guest) *racd keenly: w ldr: rdn and unable qck over 1f out: wknd fnl f* **20/1**

1m 12.84s (-1.56) **Going Correction** -0.075s/f (Good)
WFA 3 from 4yo+ 8lb 7 Ran SP% **112.4**
Speed ratings (Par 107): **107,105,104,102,100 100,99**
toteswingers: 1&2 £3.60, 1&3 £3.00, 2&3 £6.00 CSF £14.50 TOTE £3.60: £2.30, £4.50; EX 15.70.
Owner Athos Racing **Bred** Pier House Stud **Trained** Limpley Stoke, Bath

FOCUS
The feature handicap wasn't a strong race for the class and it had an open look about it. There was a decent pace on and the main action developed down the middle of the track. The winner improved on the form of his win the day before and the next two were close to their best.

NOTEBOOK
Collect Art(IRE) readily followed up his win at Salisbury the previous day with a career-best effort and landed his sixth success of 2011. He escaped a penalty and is a dual course winner, but has had a very busy time of it already this term so there had to be a slight worry about how he would shape up here. One wouldn't have known at any stage of the race he had raced just 24 hours earlier, however, and he could have been called the winner passing the furlong marker. He's a credit to connections and, well entered up, it wouldn't be surprising to see him out again in the next week while in such form. (op 2-1 tchd 3-1)
Kanaf(IRE) ◆ didn't look happy at any stage on the undulations, but still kept on to be closest at the finish and his turn could well be nearing again. (op 13-2)
Magical Speedfit(IRE) just got up to resume winning ways at his beloved Brighton 13 days earlier and was just 1lb higher. He posted a sound effort without seriously threatening and helps to set the level. (op 17-2)
Oil Strike was another that didn't appear happy on the track, in his case in the second half of the race. He's on a good mark, though, and can be placed to effect again before too long. (op 5-2 tchd 15-8)
We Have A Dream, who attracted some support, showed up better again with blinkers re-applied but ultimately paid for his early exertions. (op 10-1 tchd 7-1)
Judd Street went without his usual headgear and looks to need further respite from the handicapper. (op 9-1 tchd 11-1)
Rylee Mooch found this too hot from 4lb out of the handicap. (tchd 16-1)

2827 YARMOUTH STADIUM H'CAP 6f 3y
4:10 (4:16) (Class 6) (0-65,65) 3-Y-O **£1,619** (£481; £240; £120) **Stalls** High

Form RPR

415 **1** **Bahia Emerald (IRE)**[22] [2180] 3-9-4 **62**............................ DarryllHolland 2 76
(Jeremy Noseda) *towards rr and nudged along: hdwy ent fnl 2f: chal over 1f out: led 1f out: r.o wl and drew clr ins fnl f: easily* **9/4**[1]

-523 **2** *4 ½* **Albany Rose (IRE)**[15] 2375 3-9-1 **59**.................................. TedDurcan 1 59
(Rae Guest) *chsd ldrs: rdn to chal 2f out: led over 1f out: hdd 1f out: outpcd and no ch w wnr fnl 150yds: kpt on for clr 2nd* **6/1**

1566 **3** *2 ¼* **Novabridge**[5] 2662 3-9-7 **65**..(b) JimmyQuinn 7 58
(Andrew Haynes) *hld up in tch: hdwy to chse ldrs wl over 1f out: rdn and wanting to hang lft over 1f out: hung lft and outpcd 1f out: no ch w wnr after* **11/2**[3]

0-60 **4** *hd* **Alspritza**[23] 2141 3-8-2 **46** oh1.. NickyMackay 5 38
(Chris Wall) *led: rdn and rn green wl over 1f out: hdd over 1f out: wandered lft and rt u.p and outpcd fnl f* **20/1**

1222 **5** *6* **Paradise Place**[12] 2453 3-9-6 **64**................................(p) AndreaAtzeni 10 37
(Robert Cowell) *chsd ldr tl jst over 1f out: sn rdn and unable qck: wknd over 1f out: wl btn fnl f* **3/1**[2]

0006 **6** *1* **Ajaafa**[8] 2598 3-8-8 **52**.. NeilChalmers 6 22
(Michael Appleby) *in tch towards rr: rdn and struggling over 2f out: no threat to ldrs fnl 2f* **25/1**

6-00 **7** *1 ½* **Eyes On**[30] 1958 3-9-0 **58**...(b[1]) CathyGannon 8 23
(Philip McBride) *t.k.h early: in tch: rdn and nt qckn ent fnl 2f: wknd u.p wl over 1f out* **11/1**

655- **8** *18* **Cat Island**[243] 6722 3-8-8 **59**...................................... CharlesEddery(7) 4 —
(Mark H Tompkins) *in tch: rdn 3f out: wknd qckly jst over 2f out: t.o and eased ins fnl f* **11/1**

050- **9** *13* **Sirens**[259] 6286 3-8-8 **52**.. KirstyMilczarek 9 —
(Phil McEntee) *a struggling in last: lost tch over 3f out: t.o fnl 2f* **40/1**

1m 13.34s (-1.06) **Going Correction** -0.075s/f (Good) **9** Ran SP% **113.2**
Speed ratings (Par 97): **104,98,95,94,86 85,83,59,42**
toteswingers: 1&2 £4.10, 1&3 £3.10, 2&3 £5.60 CSF £15.37 CT £65.05 TOTE £3.50: £1.10, £3.50, £2.80; EX 16.00 Trifecta £81.60 Pool: £1,106.08 - 10.03 winning units..
Owner Cheveley Park Stud **Bred** Corduff Stud **Trained** Newmarket, Suffolk

FOCUS
A low-grade 3-y-o sprint handicap. The form looks fair for the class, rated around the second. The winenr can rate higher.

2828 SIS LIVE MAIDEN H'CAP 1m 3y
4:40 (4:43) (Class 6) (0-65,57) 4-Y-0+ **£1,619** (£481; £240; £120) **Stalls** High

Form RPR

000/ **1** **Dannios**[487] 4734 5-8-7 **50**...(t) HayleyBurton(7) 2 57
(Ed Walker) *s.i.s: sn rcvrd and in tch: j. path 6f out: pushed along to chse ldrs over 1f out: ev ch ins fnl f: kpt on wl under hands and heels to ld nr fin* **33/1**

0650 **2** *hd* **Fedora (IRE)**[13] 2420 5-8-13 **49**.......................................(t) CathyGannon 6 56
(Olivia Maylam) *t.k.h: hld up wl in tch: nt clr run 3f out: rdn and hdwy 2f out: drvn to chal ent fnl f: led jst ins fnl f: sn hrd pressed: hdd and no ex nr fin* **6/1**

220- **3** *2* **Master Of Song**[225] 7156 4-9-2 **52**..................................(p) JimmyQuinn 5 54
(Roy Bowring) *t.k.h: hld up wl in tch towards rr: hdwy towards far side ent fnl 2f: rdn to chse ldrs over 1f out: kpt on same pce ins fnl f* **4/1**[2]

5546 **4** *1* **Graceful Spirit**[9] 2561 4-8-9 **45**.. LukeMorris 9 45
(Des Donovan) *in tch: hdwy jst over 2f out: rdn to ld wl over 1f out: drvn and hdd jst ins fnl f: hung lft and outpcd fnl 150yds* **4/1**[2]

50/5 **5** *4* **Can Can Dancer**[14] 2402 6-8-12 **48**.......................... RobbieFitzpatrick 4 39
(Charles Smith) *t.k.h: hld up in tch: rdn and effrt to chse ldrs wl over 1f out: wknd 1f out* **25/1**

400- **6** *½* **Raise All In (IRE)**[377] 2454 5-8-6 **45**...................... NataliaGemelova(3) 7 34
(Ian McInnes) *chsd ldr tl led and rdn jst over 2f out: hdd wl over 1f out: wknd ent fnl f* **40/1**

0333 **7** *5* **Gordy Bee (USA)**[11] 2490 5-9-1 **54**.........................(be) RobertLButler(3) 1 32
(Richard Guest) *led tl hdd and rdn jst over 2f out: racd awkwardly u.p and wknd wl over 1f out* **5/1**[3]

60-5 **8** *1 ¾* **Hotfoot**[19] 2268 4-9-7 **57**.. TedDurcan 8 31
(John Berry) *awkward leaving stalls: hld up wl in tch in rr: effrt towards stands' side over 2f out: rdn and fnd little ent fnl 2f: sn wknd: no ch over 1f out* **7/2**[1]

50-0 **9** *6* **Hilltop Artistry**[9] 2560 5-8-11 **47**.. NickyMackay 3 —
(J R Jenkins) *taken down early: chsd ldrs: rdn and struggling over 2f out: wknd qckly 2f out: wl bhd fnl f* **16/1**

5260 **10** *1 ¾* **Spirit Of Love (IRE)**[8] 2600 4-8-10 **46**........................(p) AndreaAtzeni 10 —
(Michael Wigham) *stdd s: hld up in tch: rdn and fnd little over 2f out: btn 2f out: sn wl bhd* **12/1**

1m 41.0s (0.40) **Going Correction** -0.075s/f (Good) **10** Ran SP% **116.0**
Speed ratings (Par 101): **95,94,92,91,87 87,82,80,74,72**
toteswingers: 1&2 £47.30, 1&3 £38.20, 2&3 £4.70 CSF £216.60 CT £983.72 TOTE £59.50: £10.90, £1.70, £2.00; EX 296.70 TRIFECTA Not won..
Owner Mrs T Walker **Bred** Roseland Thoroughbreds Ltd **Trained** Newmarket, Suffolk
■ Hayley Burton's first ride, and first winner.

FOCUS
A desperately weak maiden handicap. The winner had shown nothing since his first 2yo starts for Luca Cumani, and the second continues below his winter AW form.

2829 NORFOLKTOURISTATTRACTIONS.CO.UK H'CAP 7f 3y
5:10 (5:12) (Class 6) (0-60,60) 3-Y-0+ **£1,619** (£481; £240; £120) **Stalls** High

Form RPR

-000 **1** **Rileys Crane**[19] 2268 4-9-0 **46** oh1..................................(v[1]) SaleemGolam 1 58
(Christine Dunnett) *chsd ldrs: pushed along 1/2-way: rdn to chse ldr ent fnl 2f: led over 1f out: drvn and kpt on to forge ahd ins fnl f* **100/1**

3006 **2** *1 ¼* **Hip Hip Hooray**[16] 2354 5-9-12 **58**... RobertHavlin 3 67
(Luke Dace) *hld up in tch towards rr: hdwy wl over 2f out: rdn to chse ldng pair wl over 1f out: ev ch u.p and clr w wnr ins fnl f: no ex and btn fnl 75yds* **8/1**

0-00 **3** *5* **Captainrisk (IRE)**[21] 2201 5-9-7 **60**..............................(v) DanielHarris(7) 4 56
(Christine Dunnett) *chsd ldr tl led 1/2-way: rdn ent fnl 2f: hdd over 1f out: nt pce of ldng pair and btn jst ins fnl f: hld on for 3rd fnl 100yds* **22/1**

046 **4** *¾* **Kate Skate**[12] 2450 4-9-5 **58**.. NatashaEaton(7) 7 51
(Gay Kelleway) *in tch: hdwy and rdn over 2f out: chsd ldrs over 1f out: outpcd u.p and btn jst ins fnl f: plugged on same pce and wl hld after* **33/1**

1131 **5** *nk* **Jonnie Skull (IRE)**[12] 2452 5-9-11 **57**.....................(vt) KirstyMilczarek 6 50
(Phil McEntee) *led tl hdd 1/2-way: rdn over 2f out: wknd u.p ent fnl f: wl hld and edgd lft ins fnl f* **4/1**[1]

6060 **6** *2* **Yakama (IRE)**[99] 722 6-9-1 **50**.......................................(v) KierenFox(3) 9 37
(Christine Dunnett) *stdd s: hld up in rr: hdwy ent fnl 2f: chsng ldrs and rdn over 1f out: drvn and btn 1f out: wknd fnl f* **33/1**

030- **7** *1 ¼* **Wodian (IRE)**[175] 7879 3-9-2 **58**... TedDurcan 5 38
(David Lanigan) *bhd: swtchd lft and effrt 2f out: rdn and no hdwy over 1f out: wknd ent fnl f* **9/2**[2]

0050 **8** *hd* **Avec Moi**[19] 2268 4-9-0 **46** oh1.. CathyGannon 12 29
(Christine Dunnett) *in tch in midfield: rdn: lost pl and struggling 1/2-way: rallied u.p ent fnl f: kpt on but no threat to ldrs* **50/1**

2202 **9** *½* **Sweet Possession (USA)**[21] 2198 5-9-8 **57**...........(p) SimonPearce(3) 8 39
(Pat Eddery) *in tch: pushed along and effrt whn unbalanced over 2f out: rdn and no hdwy whn unbalanced again 2f out: sn wl btn* **7/1**[3]

00-3 **10** *1 ¾* **Excellent Aim**[19] 2270 4-9-13 **59**.................................... DarryllHolland 11 36
(George Margarson) *hld up in tch towards rr: swtchd rt and effrt ent fnl 2f: sn rdn and fnd little: drvn and btn over 1f out* **4/1**[1]

5016 **11** *1 ¼* **Fathey (IRE)**[13] 2424 5-9-4 **50**................................... RobbieFitzpatrick 2 24
(Charles Smith) *chsd ldrs: rdn over 2f out: wknd u.p 2f out* **18/1**

6426 **12** *6* **Crocodile Bay (IRE)**[44] 1570 8-9-3 **52**..................(b) RobertLButler(3) 14 10
(Richard Guest) *in tch towards stands' side: shkn up and fnd nil 2f out: sn btn and fdd tamely over 1f out* **12/1**

0-03 **13** *5* **Koraleva Tectona (IRE)**[125] 397 6-9-6 **59**............ CharlesEddery(7) 13 —
(Mark H Tompkins) *taken down early: in tch: lost pl and dropped to rr 1/2-way: wl bhd fnl 2f* **16/1**

6003 **14** *5* **Fully Armed (IRE)**[8] 2598 3-8-4 **46** oh1....................(bt) NickyMackay 15 —
(Rae Guest) *racd alone towards stands' side: in tch: rdn ent fnl 3f: sn struggling: wl bhd and eased ins fnl f* **12/1**

1m 26.57s (-0.03) **Going Correction** -0.075s/f (Good)
WFA 3 from 4yo+ 10lb **14** Ran SP% **121.5**
Speed ratings (Par 101): **97,95,89,89,88 86,84,84,84,82 80,73,68,62**
toteswingers: 1&2 £67.50, 1&3 £116.90, 2&3 £29.00 CSF £775.86 CT £9746.54 TOTE £76.40: £19.20, £4.30, £8.30; EX 603.40 TRIFECTA Not won..
Owner M Riley & S Crane **Bred** David & Julie Andrews **Trained** Hingham, Norfolk

FOCUS
A weak and wide-open handicap. The first pair came nicely clear and it's hard to know how literally to take this form.
Rileys Crane Official explanation: trainer said, regarding the running and riding, gelding appeared to benefit from racing over 7f for the first time and application of a visor
Excellent Aim Official explanation: jockey said gelding hung right
Fathey(IRE) Official explanation: trainer said gelding made a noise
T/Plt: £50.80 to a £1 stake. Pool: £55,473.81. 796.82 winning tickets. T/Qpdt: £21.20 to a £1 stake. Pool: £4,004.34. 139.35 winning tickets. SP

2810 HAYDOCK (L-H)
Thursday, June 9

OFFICIAL GOING: Good to soft (5f, 6f 7.3; 1m & plus 7.0)
Wind: light 1/2 against Weather: fine

2830 BETDAQ THE BETTING EXCHANGE APPRENTICE TRAINING SERIES H'CAP (RACING EXCELLENCE INITIATIVE) 1m 3f 200y
6:20 (6:20) (Class 5) (0-70,70) 4-Y-0+ **£2,266** (£674; £337; £168) **Stalls** Centre

Form RPR

5-32 **1** **Transfer**[11] 2530 6-8-5 **51** oh1.. RyanClark 9 68+
(Richard Price) *hld up in rr: hdwy 6f out: led on bit over 2f out: pushed clr 1f out: eased fnl 50yds* **10/3**[1]

5-04 **2** *3 ¾* **Amir Pasha (UAE)**[13] 2454 6-8-13 **59**................................(p) DaleSwift 2 66
(Micky Hammond) *mid-div: hdwy over 3f out: wnt 2nd over 1f out: no ch w wnr* **5/1**[2]

0-40 **3** *1 ¼* **Brasingaman Eric**[43] 1615 4-8-7 **53**.. NeilFarley 6 58
(George Moore) *in rr-div: hdwy over 3f out: wnt 3rd over 1f out: one pce* **9/1**

0036 **4** *6* **Donna Elvira**[26] 2091 4-9-0 **60**..(p) JulieBurke 10 55
(Edwin Tuer) *chsd ldrs: wknd over 1f out* **5/1**[2]

2-40 **5** *1 ½* **Raktiman (IRE)**[19] 2312 4-9-0 **67**..............................(p) BenWilliams(7) 4 60
(Tom Dascombe) *s.s: hdwy over 4f out: swtchd violently lft over 2f out: one pce* **6/1**[3]

-212 **6** *4* **Bright Sparky (GER)**[61] 631 8-8-2 **53** ow2....(vt) DavidSimmonson(5) 7 40
(Michael Easterby) *hld up in rr: hdwy over 4f out: wknd 2f out* **16/1**

-434 **7** *¾* **Leitzu (IRE)**[10] 2575 4-8-13 **64**................................... CharlesBishop(5) 3 49
(Mick Channon) *chsd ldrs: wknd 2f out* **15/2**

-023 **8** *2* **Alubari**[23] 2170 4-9-0 **60**.. TobyAtkinson 11 61
(David Simcock) *trckd ldr: t.k.h: led over 7f out: hdd over 2f out: sn wknd* **8/1**

62-0 **9** *15* **Saloon (USA)**[24] 2159 7-9-3 **70**................................. LauraSimpson(7) 5 28
(Jane Chapple-Hyam) *hld up in rr: lost pl 4f out: sn bhd: t.o* **25/1**

00/0 **10** *2 ¼* **Lord Wheathill**[30] 1987 4-8-0 **51** oh6.......................... NatashaEaton(5) 1 —
(Lisa Williamson) *led: hdd over 7f out: lost pl over 2f out: sn bhd: t.o* **100/1**

2m 34.85s (0.85) **Going Correction** -0.05s/f (Good) **10** Ran SP% **114.3**
Speed ratings (Par 103): **95,92,91,87,86 84,83,82,72,70**
toteswingers:1&2:£5.80, 1&3:£8.40, 2&3:£9.30 CSF £19.23 CT £135.29 TOTE £3.60: £1.10, £1.90, £8.00; EX 14.80.
Owner G Ivall & R J Price **Bred** Kingsclere Stud **Trained** Ullingswick, H'fords
■ Stewards' Enquiry : David Simmonson one-day ban: careless riding (Jun 23)

FOCUS
Sprints on inner home straight. Races on round course on outer home straight adding 35yds to distances on round course. An ordinary apprentice handicap but one run at a strong pace, suiting those ridden with some patience. The field came stands' side in the straight. They were well strung out behind the easy winner, who was value for 6l.

2831 WATCH RACES LIVE AT RACINGUK.COM MAIDEN STKS 6f
6:50 (6:50) (Class 5) 2-Y-0 **£2,266** (£674; £337; £168) **Stalls** Centre

Form RPR

5 **1** **Barolo Top (IRE)**[28] 2033 2-9-0 0.................................. RichardKingscote 5 80+
(Tom Dascombe) *wnt rt s: trckd ldrs: wnt 2nd and edgd rt over 1f out: led last 100yds: styd on wl towards fin* **1/1**[1]

2 *1 ¼* **Wolf Spirit (IRE)** 2-9-0 0.. PhillipMakin 6 77+
(Kevin Ryan) *dwlt: hld up: hdwy to trck ldrs over 3f out: edgd rt and led over 1f out: hdd and no ex last 100yds* **6/4**[2]

00 **3** *4 ½* **Art Dzeko**[28] 2033 2-9-0 0... DavidAllan 4 63
(Tim Easterby) *led: hung rt and hdd over 1f out: one pce* **18/1**

4 *3 ¾* **Elkhart (IRE)** 2-9-0 0.. SilvestreDeSousa 1 52
(Mark Johnston) *chsd ldrs: drvn over 2f out: edgd rt and outpcd over 1f out: sn wknd* **7/1**[3]

5 *15* **Elammato (IRE)** 2-9-0 0.. TomEaves 3 —
(Lisa Williamson) *chsd ldrs: lost pl 3f out: sn bhd* **100/1**

6 *3 ½* **Brasingaman Espee** 2-9-0 0... PJMcDonald 2 —
(George Moore) *chsd ldrs: edgd rt and wknd over 2f out: sn bhd* **33/1**

1m 16.54s (2.74) **Going Correction** +0.225s/f (Good) **6** Ran SP% **111.7**
Speed ratings (Par 93): **88,86,80,75,55 50**
toteswingers:1&2:£1.02, 1&3:£3.20, 2&3:£3.10 CSF £2.69 TOTE £3.30: £1.60, £1.60; EX 2.80.
Owner Jones, Seed, Woodgate **Bred** P G Lyons **Trained** Malpas, Cheshire

FOCUS
Little strength in depth to this maiden but a couple of the newcomers shaped with promise and the runner-up looks a useful prospect. The form has been rated positively.

NOTEBOOK
Barolo Top(IRE) set the standard such as it was and the benefit of previous experience as well possibly as greater stamina enabled him to get the better of the runner-up, looking held 2f out but readily on top by the line for a slightly flattering success given he only came clear late. He's clearly held in some regard as his trainer reported afterwards that he might have left him a gallop short and was expecting a more comfortable win, but both his starts suggest strongly he'll need 7f before long taking on better horses, so the Coventry Stakes next week for which he's engaged looks one step too far too soon. (op 11-8)
Wolf Spirit(IRE) ◆ is a surefire winner of a similar event. A colt by Amadeus Wolf, who his trainer had in his care, out of an Irish 7f winner, he had presumably breezed very well for his purchase price to have increased dramatically this year and for a long way here looked comfortably the best horse in the race, still on the bridle 2f out but edging left thereafter and beaten more by lack of condition in the ground than by lack of ability. He'll be a different proposition under faster conditions. (op 5-4 tchd 13-8)
Art Dzeko hadn't shown much so far but he's some size about him and has probably been running himself. He showed up more prominently here with his yard in better form, sticking on gamely after making the running and leaving the impression he's more a 7f nursery prospect for later in the year. He has a round-pounding action, so might always be best on soft ground. (op 20-1 tchd 16-1)
Elkhart(IRE), by Refuse To Bend out of a 7f winner, was changing his legs early then ran very green with over 2f to run, losing his position. He'll step up quite a bit on this next time in all probability. (tchd 8-1)

2832 TOM JONES LIVE ON 18TH JUNE H'CAP — 5f
7:20 (7:23) (Class 4) (0-80,79) 3-Y-0+ **£4,209** (£1,252; £625; £312) **Stalls** Centre

Form — RPR
6026 **1** **Taurus Twins**[7] 2645 5-9-7 **77**.....(b) DaleSwift(5) 11 — 88
(Richard Price) *mde all stands' side: kpt on wl fnl f* **4/1**[1]
-601 **2** *3/4* **Angelo Poliziano**[25] 2126 5-9-10 **75**.....(p) SilvestreDeSousa 6 — 83
(Ann Duffield) *chsd ldrs towards centre: edgd lft over 1f out: no ex last 50yds* **15/2**[3]
0022 **3** *1 1/4* **Ingleby Star (IRE)**[12] 2491 6-9-1 **69**.....(p) GaryBartley(3) 7 — 73
(Ian McInnes) *chsd wnr: edgd lft and kpt on same pce fnl f* **10/1**
00-0 **4** *1* **Tyfos**[54] 1395 6-10-0 **79**..... J-PGuillambert 8 — 79
(Brian Baugh) *chsd ldrs: kpt on same pce appr fnl f* **12/1**
46-0 **5** *2 1/2* **Lady Royale**[17] 2363 3-9-3 **78**.....(p) SeanLevey(3) 2 — 69+
(Geoffrey Oldroyd) *hld up in rr: hdwy over 2f out: kpt on same pce fnl f* **20/1**
0450 **6** *1 1/2* **Atlantic Beach**[20] 2244 6-9-5 **70**.....(p) RichardKingscote 10 — 56
(Milton Bradley) *mid-div: effrt over 2f out: nvr nr ldrs* **20/1**
0-06 **7** *1 1/2* **Mey Blossom**[25] 2122 6-9-13 **78**..... TonyHamilton 9 — 58
(Richard Whitaker) *dwlt: hdwy over 2f out: chsng ldrs over 1f out: sn wknd* **17/2**
650- **8** *hd* **Ryan Style (IRE)**[265] 6140 5-9-13 **78**..... TomEaves 13 — 57
(Lisa Williamson) *dwlt: hdwy to chse ldrs over 3f out: wknd over 1f out* **16/1**
3260 **9** *2* **Triple Dream**[8] 2603 6-9-3 **68**.....(tp) LiamKeniry 4 — 40
(Milton Bradley) *racd far side: chsd ldr that side: led that gp 1f out: no ch w stands' side* **16/1**
3653 **10** *1/2* **Red Roar (IRE)**[6] 2694 4-9-0 **65**..... FrannyNorton 5 — 35
(Alan Berry) *reluctant to go to s: dwlt: lost pl over 3f out: sn bhd* **4/1**[1]
4-06 **11** *3 1/2* **Rutterkin (USA)**[14] 2411 3-8-3 **68**..... VictorSantos(7) 1 — 26
(Alan Berry) *chsd two others far side: bhd fnl 2f* **50/1**
-143 **12** *5* **Ballarina**[39] 1716 5-8-11 **62**..... DavidAllan 3 — —
(Eric Alston) *led two others far side: hdd 1f out: heavily eased* **6/1**[2]

61.43 secs (0.63) **Going Correction** +0.225s/f (Good)
WFA 3 from 4yo+ 7lb **12** Ran SP% **116.6**
Speed ratings (Par 105): **105,103,101,100,96 93,91,91,87,87 81,73**
toteswingers:1&2:£9.10, 1&3:£9.30, 2&3:£14.90 CSF £32.27 CT £285.86 TOTE £4.60: £2.50, £1.70, £3.50; EX 44.20.
Owner G E Amey **Bred** G E Amey **Trained** Ullingswick, H'fords

FOCUS
A fair handicap in which the field split into two groups, the trio on the far side always behind the group on the stand side in which the rather-isolated winner made all hard against the rail. It proved very difficult to get into the race from off the pace. The form is rated around the second and third.
Ballarina Official explanation: jockey said mare lost its action

2833 REWARDS4RACING.COM H'CAP — 1m
7:50 (7:50) (Class 3) (0-95,89) 3-Y-0 **£7,123** (£2,119; £1,059; £529) **Stalls** Low

Form — RPR
-1 **1** **Nahrain**[24] 2157 3-9-5 **87**..... WilliamBuick 5 — 104+
(Roger Varian) *hld up: smooth hdwy over 3f out: led on bit 2f out: pushed clr 1f out: v easily* **8/15**[1]
-166 **2** *5* **Belle Royale (IRE)**[22] 2189 3-9-7 **89**..... FrannyNorton 6 — 87
(Mark Brisbourne) *trckd ldrs on outer: t.k.h: rdn and outpcd over 2f out: styd on stands' side to chse wnr appr fnl f* **20/1**
-550 **3** *1 3/4* **Weapon Of Choice (IRE)**[19] 2296 3-9-0 **82**..... TomEaves 1 — 76
(David Simcock) *sn led: hdd 2f out: kpt on one pce* **10/1**[3]
2352 **4** *1* **Tasfeya**[13] 2477 3-8-13 **81**..... TadhgO'Shea 7 — 73
(Mark Johnston) *led early: chsd ldrs: one pce fnl 2f* **7/1**[2]
-014 **5** *6* **Ventura Sands (IRE)**[26] 2092 3-8-3 **71**..... PaulHanagan 3 — 49
(Richard Fahey) *trckd ldrs: drvn over 3f out: wknd 2f out* **14/1**
414- **6** *nk* **Top Care (USA)**[204] 7481 3-8-11 **79**..... SilvestreDeSousa 4 — 56
(Mark Johnston) *n.m.r and lost pl sn after s: in rr: drvn over 3f out: wknd 2f out* **7/1**[2]

1m 43.7s (0.80) **Going Correction** -0.05s/f (Good) **6** Ran SP% **110.8**
Speed ratings (Par 103): **94,89,87,86,80 79**
toteswingers:1&2:£1.90, 1&3:£2.40, 2&3:£8.70 CSF £13.00 CT £51.79 TOTE £1.20: £1.02, £9.70; EX 10.30.
Owner Sheikh Ahmed Al Maktoum **Bred** Darley **Trained** Newmarket, Suffolk
■ Stewards' Enquiry : Tadhg O'Shea one-day ban: careless riding (Jun 23)

FOCUS
A handicap in all but name as the unexposed once-raced maiden winner routed her exposed rivals as easily as the betting suggested she would. She was probably the only one to run her race. The pace was fair and the field came centre to stands' side in the straight.

NOTEBOOK
Nahrain, who held an entry in the Coronation Stakes until recently, won in the style befitting one considered good enough for an entry in that race but able to run here off a mark of 87 here even allowing for the shortcomings of some of the rivals behind her. Her mark wasn't obviously lenient given that the form of the race she won at Windsor hadn't exactly been advertised since, but she would still have won this quite readily with another 14lb on her back. She's no shortage of speed, and looks up to winning at Listed level with the Valiant Stakes at Ascot next month one possible target. (op 4-7)
Belle Royale(IRE) plugged on well for second on ground to her liking but never at any point looked in the same race as the winner. She'd been beaten some way in a Listed race trying 1m2f last time, but left the impression here she'd be worth another try at it in handicap company for all she's always going to be vulnerable to something less exposed. (op 16-1)
Weapon Of Choice(IRE) showed signs of a return to form, possibly helped by an easier surface than of late. (op 12-1)
Tasfeya looked quirky under pressure between horses and might be something of a soft touch.
Ventura Sands(IRE) was almost certainly out of his depth in this grade.
Top Care(USA) looked very rusty on his first start since last autumn (gelded in the meantime). (op 8-1)

2834 SCISSOR SISTERS LIVE ON 16TH JULY H'CAP — 7f
8:20 (8:20) (Class 4) (0-85,85) 3-Y-0 **£4,209** (£1,252; £625; £312) **Stalls** Low

Form — RPR
0-00 **1** **Regimental (IRE)**[37] 1801 3-8-2 **66**..... PaulHanagan 1 — 80
(Ann Duffield) *mid-div: hdwy towards centre over 2f out: sn w ldrs: carried lft and led ins fnl f: hung bdly rt and hld on towards fin* **6/1**
-122 **2** *1/2* **Elusivity (IRE)**[9] 2582 3-8-11 **75**..... MartinDwyer 3 — 88
(Brian Meehan) *trckd ldrs: led 2f out: edgd lft over 1f out: hdd ins fnl f: hdd ins fnl f: hld whn carried rt and bmpd nr line* **7/2**[1]
5-00 **3** *5* **Icy Blue**[43] 1624 3-8-2 **66** oh1..... FrannyNorton 5 — 65
(Richard Whitaker) *mid-div: hdwy over 3f out: kpt on one pce over 1f out* **14/1**
021 **4** *2 1/2* **Orbit The Moon (IRE)**[17] 2361 3-9-4 **85**.....(t) SeanLevey(3) 2 — 77
(Michael Dods) *hld up towards rr: drvn and hdwy towards centre over 2f out: chsng ldng pair over 1f out: one pce* **9/2**[3]
3-60 **5** *hd* **Whipphound**[21] 2215 3-8-11 **75**..... GrahamGibbons 4 — 67
(Mark Brisbourne) *hld up: t.k.h: effrt over 2f out: edgd lft and one pce* **22/1**
0-05 **6** *4 1/2* **Barista (IRE)**[12] 2503 3-8-9 **80**..... CharlesBishop(7) 8 — 60
(Mick Channon) *hld up in rr: hdwy stands' side over 2f out: edgd lft over 1f out: sn wknd* **4/1**[2]
-000 **7** *3/4* **First Class Favour (IRE)**[12] 2503 3-8-11 **80**..... LanceBetts(5) 6 — 58
(Tim Easterby) *led: hdd 2f out: sn wknd* **16/1**
046- **8** *15* **Colorado Gold**[238] 6870 3-9-7 **85**..... PhillipMakin 9 — 22
(Ed de Giles) *trckd ldrs: drvn 3f out: sn wknd: bhd whn eased clsng stages: t.o* **12/1**
-056 **9** *3 1/4* **Home Office**[13] 2477 3-8-12 **76**..... SilvestreDeSousa 7 — —
(Mark Johnston) *trckd ldr: drvn 3f out: sn lost pl: bhd whn eased clsng stages: t.o* **15/2**

1m 30.37s (-0.53) **Going Correction** -0.05s/f (Good) **9** Ran SP% **111.0**
Speed ratings (Par 101): **101,100,94,91,91 86,85,68,64**
toteswingers:1&2:£4.70, 1&3:£23.60, 2&3:£11.20 CSF £25.70 CT £270.03 TOTE £8.70: £1.90, £2.10, £5.90; EX 39.70.
Owner I Farrington & R Chapman **Bred** Deer Forest Stud **Trained** Constable Burton, N Yorks

FOCUS
Not too many in-form runners in what was a fair handicap and it may not be wise to read too much into the fact the first two pulled well clear at the end of a well-run race. The runners again came stands' side in the straight. The time was slow and the form is not rated too positively.

2835 RACING UK IN YOUR PUB 0870 351 8834 H'CAP — 1m 2f 95y
8:50 (8:50) (Class 5) (0-70,70) 3-Y-0 **£2,266** (£674; £337; £168) **Stalls** Centre

Form — RPR
2-01 **1** **Good Boy Jackson**[33] 1904 3-9-6 **69**..... PhillipMakin 4 — 89+
(Kevin Ryan) *mde all: rdn wl clr over 1f out: heavily eased fnl 50yds* **10/3**[2]
5-34 **2** *11* **Number Theory**[33] 1904 3-9-7 **70**..... NickyMackay 8 — 67
(John Holt) *in rr: hdwy over 4f out: wnt 3rd over 3f out: chsd wnr over 1f out: no imp* **12/1**
5-00 **3** *4* **Oldmeldrum (IRE)**[38] 1749 3-8-11 **60**..... GregFairley 3 — 49
(Peter Salmon) *s.i.s: t.k.h in rr: drvn over 6f out: hdwy over 3f out: kpt on to take modest 3rd post* **40/1**
4534 **4** *shd* **Ad Vitam (IRE)**[15] 2406 3-8-5 **61**.....(p) LeonnaMayor(7) 7 — 50
(David C Griffiths) *in rr: hdwy over 4f out: sn outpcd kpt on fnl 2f: tk modest 3rd ins fnl f: one pce* **25/1**
-133 **5** *6* **Lady Gar Gar**[15] 2406 3-9-7 **70**.....(p) PaulHanagan 1 — 47
(Geoffrey Oldroyd) *mid-div: effrt and 4th over 2f out: wknd fnl f* **9/2**[3]
[illegible] **6** [illegible] [illegible] [illegible] [illegible] **70**..... AhmedAjtebi 5 — 46
(Mahmood Al Zarooni) *in rr: stmbld 6f out: drvn and sme hdwy over 3f out: wknd over 1f out* **6/1**
6-31 **7** *9* **May Be Some Time**[9] 2586 3-9-6 **69** 6ex..... LiamKeniry 11 — 27
(Stuart Kittow) *trckd ldrs: chsd wnr 6f out: drvn 3f out: wknd over 1f out: eased clsng stages* **9/4**[1]
4320 **8** *15* **Barnum (USA)**[40] 1683 3-9-6 **69**..... SilvestreDeSousa 9 — —
(Mark Johnston) *trckd ldrs: drvn and hmpd over 4f out: wknd 3f out: sn bhd: t.o* **10/1**
3241 **9** *50* **Bountiful Guest**[82] 916 3-9-5 **68**..... GrahamGibbons 2 — —
(Brian Baugh) *t.k.h: sn trcking ldrs: wknd over 3f out: bhd whn heavily eased fnl f: wl t.o: eventually completed* **16/1**

2m 15.97s (-0.03) **Going Correction** -0.05s/f (Good) **9** Ran SP% **115.3**
Speed ratings (Par 99): **98,89,86,85,81 80,73,61,21**
toteswingers:1&2:£10.90, 1&3:£23.50, 2&3:£84.80 CSF £42.62 CT £1346.66 TOTE £4.80: £2.10, £3.90, £15.50; EX 48.40.
Owner The C H F Partnership **Bred** The C H F Partnership **Trained** Hambleton, N Yorks

FOCUS
No more than an ordinary 3yo handicap but it still provided an impressive winner well ahead of his mark. The pace was fair, increasing early in the straight as the runners came stands' side. The winner impressed and was value for 12l, but none of the others ran to their best.
Bountiful Guest Official explanation: jockey said gelding got very tired
T/Plt: £59.10 to a £1 stake. Pool:£66,681.51 - 823.58 winning tickets T/Qpdt: £24.70 to a £1 stake. Pool:£4,607.39 - 137.50 winning tickets WG

2308 NEWBURY (L-H)
Thursday, June 9

OFFICIAL GOING: Good to firm (good in places; 6.4)
Wind: Virtually nil Weather: Sunny spells

2836 DOWNLOAD THE BLUE SQUARE APP MAIDEN FILLIES' STKS (DIV I) — 1m 2f 6y
1:30 (1:30) (Class 5) 3-Y-0 **£3,756** (£1,117; £558; £278) **Stalls** Low

Form — RPR
0 **1** **Gosbeck**[28] 2026 3-9-0 0..... DaneO'Neill 5 — 85+
(Henry Candy) *trckd ldrs: pushed along fr 4f out: styng on whn nt clr run and swtchd rt 1f out: rdn and styd on wl to ld fnl 30yds: kpt on strly* **12/1**

3 **2** *1* **Floral Beauty**[34] [1845] 3-9-0 0 RyanMoore 6 83+
(Sir Michael Stoute) *led: jnd 5f out: narrowly hdd over 4f out: led again over 3f out: rdn along 2f out: styd on wl tl hdd and outpcd fnl 30yds* **4/11**[1]

4- **3** *3 1/4* **Misty Isles**[241] [6804] 3-9-0 0 KierenFallon 10 77
(Heather Main) *t.k.h: chsd ldrs: rdn over 2f out: hung lft u.p over 1f out: chsd ldng duo ins fnl f but no imp* **20/1**

0 **4** *1 3/4* **Tarkeeba (IRE)**[55] [1363] 3-9-0 0 RichardHills 8 74+
(Roger Varian) *chsd ldr: chal 5f out tl slt ld over 4f out: hdd over 3f out: one pce fr 2f out and btn whn sltly hmpd 1f out* **8/1**[2]

5- **5** *1 1/2* **New River (IRE)**[306] [4844] 3-9-0 0 RichardHughes 1 70+
(Richard Hannon) *in tch: outpcd and pushed along 3f out: styd on wl fnl f but nvr a threat* **12/1**

6 *1 3/4* **Fairy Pose** 3-9-0 0 EddieAhern 7 67
(Amanda Perrett) *chsd ldrs: pushed along fr 4f out: wknd fr 2f out* **33/1**

7 *3/4* **Cardrona** 3-9-0 0 WilliamBuick 9 65+
(John Gosden) *s.i.s: in rr: pushed along over 3f out: hung lft and green fr over 2f out: kpt on ins fnl f but nvr a threat* **20/1**

8 *6* **Emsiyah (USA)** 3-9-0 0 FrankieDettori 3 53
(Saeed Bin Suroor) *in tch: pushed along 3f out: rdn and wknd 2f out* **10/1**[3]

9 *3/4* **Heart Of Dixie (IRE)** 3-9-0 0 JimmyFortune 4 52
(Paul Cole) *in rr: rdn and sme prog 3f out but nvr beyond mid-div and sn wknd* **50/1**

0 **10** *2* **Satwa Ballerina**[19] [2306] 3-9-0 0 JimCrowley 11 48
(Ed Dunlop) *stdd and swtchd lft s: bhd most of way* **100/1**

2m 10.01s (1.21) **Going Correction** -0.025s/f (Good) **10** Ran SP% **124.3**
Speed ratings (Par 96): **94,93,90,89,88 86,86,81,80,79**
toteswingers:1&2:£3.30, 1&3:£26.50, 2&3:£4.90 CSF £17.46 TOTE £16.00: £3.20, £1.02, £4.40; EX 30.70.
Owner Major M G Wyatt **Bred** Dunchurch Lodge Stud Co **Trained** Kingston Warren, Oxon

FOCUS
After a heavy shower before racing, the ground was said to be on the good side of good to firm according to clerk of the course. He also reported that the bottom bend was out, meaning there was an extra 30 metres added to all distances on the round course. A couple of interesting newcomers took on some who had already shown fair form. The winner improved and can rate higher, with the tentative level set around the second and fifth.

2837 NEWVOICEMEDIA MAIDEN STKS (C&G) 6f 110y
2:00 (2:04) (Class 4) 2-Y-O **£3,432** (£1,021; £510; £254) **Stalls** Centre

Form RPR

1 **Eastern Sun (IRE)** 2-9-0 0 WilliamBuick 12 88+
(John Gosden) *trckd ldr: led ins fnl 3f: shkn up and qcknd over 1f out: edgd lft and c clr fnl 120yds: easily* **6/1**[3]

2 *2 1/4* **Moustache (IRE)** 2-9-0 0 RichardHughes 5 80+
(Richard Hannon) *led tl hdd ins fnl 3f: styd chsng wnr but pushed along and one pce fnl f: sn no ch and hung rt nr fin but kpt on wl for clr 2nd* **5/4**[1]

3 *1 1/4* **Spiritual Star (IRE)** 2-9-0 0 JimmyFortune 10 76+
(Andrew Balding) *in tch: pushed along and hdwy 2f out: drvn to chse ldng duo appr fnl f: one pce whn pushed rt nr fin* **15/2**

4 *3 3/4* **Tidal Way (IRE)** 2-9-0 0 KierenFallon 6 66
(Mick Channon) *chsd ldrs: rdn and outpcd 2f out: styd on again ins fnl f* **16/1**

5 *1* **Acer Diamonds (IRE)** 2-8-11 0 AdamBeschizza(3) 4 63
(Julia Feilden) *wnt lft s: chsd ldrs: rdn over 2f out: wknd over 1f out* **13/2**

6 *1/2* **Graphic (IRE)** 2-9-0 0 RyanMoore 1 62+
(Richard Hannon) *sn chsng ldrs: rdn over 2f out: wknd sn after* **11/2**[2]

7 *1 1/2* **Doctor Banner** 2-8-11 0 MartinHarley(3) 9 58
(Mick Channon) *chsd ldrs: rdn and wknd 2f out* **33/1**

8 *2* **Valley Of Stars (IRE)** 2-9-0 0 EddieCreighton 11 52
(Edward Creighton) *s.i.s: rdn over 2f out: a outpcd* **100/1**

9 *1 1/2* **Nassau Storm** 2-9-0 0 (t) JimCrowley 14 48+
(William Knight) *s.i.s: in rr: pushed along over 2f out: kpt on clsng stages* **33/1**

10 *14* **Nic Nok** 2-9-0 0 FergusSweeney 7 10
(Harry Dunlop) *in rr but in tch: rdn: hung lft and btn over 2f out* **66/1**

1m 21.13s (1.83) **Going Correction** +0.05s/f (Good) **10** Ran SP% **113.5**
Speed ratings (Par 95): **91,88,87,82,81 81,79,77,75,59**
toteswingers:1&2:£3.10, 1&3:£6.40, 2&3:£3.50 CSF £13.29 TOTE £7.20: £1.80, £1.20, £2.30; EX 17.60.
Owner Prince AA Faisal & Rachel Hood **Bred** Saad Bin Mishrif **Trained** Newmarket, Suffolk

FOCUS
This maiden has produced some decent performers, most notably Group 1-winning juvenile Arcano. The race only contained newcomers.

NOTEBOOK
Eastern Sun(IRE) ◆, a half-brother to plenty of winners, including Group 2 winner Allied Powers, didn't appear to have the physical scope of some of his rivals but he looks built to excel this year. Always travelling well, he lengthened nicely once in full command and came home a fairly impressive winner. The trainer hinted that his horse may head for the 7f Superlative Stakes at Newmarket next month, won last year by King Torus. (op 13-2 tchd 15-2)
Moustache(IRE) ◆, a half-brother to Lightning Cloud, who has won twice this year for Kevin Ryan, has size about him and seemed to know his job considering the way he jumped out and led. However, once passed he displayed signs of greenness and edged left and right close to the end. He should be more battle hardened next time. (op 11-8 tchd 6-4, 6-5 and 13-8 in places)
Spiritual Star(IRE), the first foal of a dam who won as a 2-y-o, and is half-sister to juvenile winners, was another who wasn't as imposing as some but he knew his job and kept on well, despite being hampered by the runner-up. (op 8-1 tchd 7-1)
Tidal Way(IRE), related to Silver Suitor and winning chaser Indian Groom, made a fair start to his career after becoming one paced when the tempo really lifted. (op 11-1)
Acer Diamonds(IRE), a half-brother to the smart Bay Willow, has a bit of size about him and shaped okay after meeting with some market support. He'll no doubt be better for the run. (op 17-2)
Graphic(IRE), weak in the market, is a nice looker and will surely be better than this effort suggests. He looked a little green under pressure, so should have learnt something. (op 9-2 tchd 7-2)
Doctor Banner was a little keen to post and during the race. Inexperience got the better of him in the end, but this run wasn't without some promise.
Nassau Storm, a half-brother to very useful handicapper Swift Gift, wore a tongue-tie for his debut and made some fair late headway after getting behind. (op 25-1 tchd 22-1)

2838 PERTEMPS H'CAP 1m (S)
2:30 (2:33) (Class 5) (0-75,75) 3-Y-O **£2,266** (£674; £337; £168) **Stalls** Centre

Form RPR

303 **1** **El Wasmi**[12] [2511] 3-9-7 **75** (b[1]) PhilipRobinson 8 86
(Clive Brittain) *s.i.s: sn chsng ldrs: wnt 2nd over 2f out: drvn to chal ins fnl f: led fnl 100yds: drvn out* **16/1**

663 **2** *1/2* **Robemaker**[13] [2457] 3-9-5 **73** WilliamBuick 3 82
(John Gosden) *led 1f: trckd ldr tl led again over 2f out: drvn over 1f out: jnd ins fnl f: hdd and no ex fnl 100yds* **6/1**[2]

40-3 **3** *2* **Levitate**[21] [2229] 3-9-6 **74** RyanMoore 14 79+
(Sir Michael Stoute) *in rr: swtchd rt and hdwy on stands' rail fr 2f out: str run fnl f: fin wl to take 3rd fnl 120yds: clsng on ldng duo nr fin* **9/4**[1]

0163 **4** *1 1/4* **Zamina (IRE)**[24] [2146] 3-8-13 **67** JamesDoyle 6 69
(Sylvester Kirk) *in rr: hdwy over 2f out: styd on to take 4th ins fnl f but nt pce of ldng trio* **12/1**

3143 **5** *1* **Beautiful Lando (FR)**[34] [1869] 3-8-2 **59** ow1 JohnFahy(3) 2 59
(Heather Main) *chsd ldrs: rdn over 2f out: styd on same pce u.p fr over 1f out* **20/1**

506- **6** *shd* **Hot Spice**[240] [6827] 3-8-10 **64** EddieAhern 1 63
(John Dunlop) *led after 1f: hdd over 2f out and sn rdn: wknd fnl f* **14/1**

-611 **7** *2* **Dysios (IRE)**[14] [2421] 3-9-5 **73** KierenFallon 16 68+
(Luca Cumani) *hld up in rr: rdn and sme hdwy over 2f out: no imp on ldrs and styd on same pce* **6/1**[2]

55-0 **8** *3/4* **Arctic Maiden**[31] [1958] 3-8-6 **60** MartinDwyer 11 53
(Willie Musson) *in rr: drvn and hdwy fr 2f out: no imp on ldrs ins fnl f* **40/1**

300- **9** *nk* **Honourable Knight (IRE)**[286] [5490] 3-9-2 **70** DaneO'Neill 7 62
(Mark Usher) *in tch: rdn over 2f out: sn btn* **33/1**

24-0 **10** *3/4* **Isingy Red (FR)**[16] [2383] 3-9-5 **73** StephenCraine 5 64
(Jim Boyle) *chsd ldrs tl wknd 1f out* **40/1**

3106 **11** *2* **Cheylesmore (IRE)**[17] [2368] 3-8-13 **67** (t) JimCrowley 9 53
(Stuart Williams) *in rr: hdwy over 2f out: nvr gng pce to rch ldrs and wknd ins fnl f* **33/1**

30-1 **12** *shd* **Fettuccine (IRE)**[139] [253] 3-9-4 **72** FergusSweeney 15 58
(John Gallagher) *in rr: rdn and sme hdwy over 2f out: nvr beyond mid-div and wknd fnl f* **50/1**

020 **13** *1 3/4* **Red Copper**[56] [1328] 3-8-1 **60** HarryBentley(5) 13 42
(Michael Bell) *in tch: rdn 3f out: wknd fr 2f out* **33/1**

0-41 **14** *1* **Royal Reverie**[17] [2368] 3-9-7 **75** AdamKirby 12 55
(Walter Swinburn) *chsd ldrs over 5f* **7/1**[3]

2362 **15** *3 1/2* **Whodathought (IRE)**[10] [2550] 3-9-1 **69** (b) RichardHughes 4 41
(Richard Hannon) *hld up in mid-div: brief effrt over 2f out: sn btn* **10/1**

1m 40.22s (0.52) **Going Correction** +0.05s/f (Good) **15** Ran SP% **121.6**
Speed ratings (Par 99): **99,98,96,95,94 94,92,91,91,90 88,88,86,85,82**
toteswingers:1&2:£17.60, 1&3:£9.40, 2&3:£5.20 CSF £103.24 CT £312.01 TOTE £24.10: £5.50, £2.70, £1.30; EX 84.30.
Owner Saeed Manana **Bred** Glebe Stud And Partners **Trained** Newmarket, Suffolk
■ Stewards' Enquiry : Philip Robinson three-day ban: used whip with excessive frequency and without giving gelding time to respond (Jun 23-25)

FOCUS
Plenty of these looked capable of better than they'd shown, but even so this was probably only an ordinary 3yo handicap for the track, rated around the fourth to sixth. The early gallop didn't look strong and the field came down the middle as a bunch.

2839 LORD WEINSTOCK MEMORIAL STKS (REGISTERED AS THE BALLYMACOLL STUD STAKES) (LISTED RACE) 1m 2f 6y
3:05 (3:06) (Class 1) 3-Y-O
£17,031 (£6,456; £3,231; £1,611; £807; £405) **Stalls** Low

Form RPR

01-3 **1** **Rumh (GER)**[27] [2050] 3-8-12 93 FrankieDettori 1 103
(Saeed Bin Suroor) *mde all: rdn clr appr fnl f: edgd rt: clsng stages: unchal* **5/2**[1]

13 **2** *6* **Imperial Pippin (USA)**[22] [2189] 3-8-12 93 WilliamBuick 3 91
(John Gosden) *chsd ldrs: rdn over 2f out: styd on to chse wnr over 1f out but nvr any ch: pushed out and jst hld on for 2nd clsng stages* **9/2**[2]

52 **3** *hd* **Moment Of Time**[31] [1950] 3-8-12 0 JimmyFortune 8 91
(Andrew Balding) *disp 2nd: rdn over 2f out and outpcd into 3rd over 1f out: rallied ins fnl f and styd on again to press for 2nd cl home but nvr any ch w wnr* **7/1**

1110 **4** *nse* **Palm Pilot (IRE)**[33] [1894] 3-8-12 79 (p) RyanMoore 4 91
(Ed Dunlop) *dropped in rr 7f out and wl bhd 4f out: rdn over 2f out: hdwy over 1f out: edging lft but styd on fnl 120yds to press for 2nd cl home but nvr any ch w wnr* **40/1**

544- **5** *3* **Fanny May**[256] [6407] 3-8-12 92 EddieAhern 2 85
(Denis Coakley) *disp 2nd: rdn over 2f out: wknd over 1f out* **20/1**

3-54 **6** *3 1/4* **Poplin**[22] [2189] 3-8-12 91 KierenFallon 6 78
(Luca Cumani) *in tch: hdwy to chse ldrs: rdn over 2f out: wknd wl over 1f out* **6/1**[3]

16- **7** *2 1/4* **Matula (IRE)**[222] [7235] 3-8-12 88 JimCrowley 9 74
(Ralph Beckett) *in rr: rdn and sme hdwy over 2f out but nvr in contention and wknd sn after* **10/1**

1 **8** *2 3/4* **Gracefield (USA)**[11] [2529] 3-8-12 0 AhmedAjtebi 7 68
(Mahmood Al Zarooni) *t.k.h: in tch: rdn and wknd over 2f out* **14/1**

21 **9** *4 1/2* **Albaraka**[117] [529] 3-8-12 85 SebSanders 5 59
(Sir Mark Prescott Bt) *in rr: rdn and mod improvement wl over 2f out but nvr any threat: sn wknd* **9/2**[2]

2m 6.35s (-2.45) **Going Correction** -0.025s/f (Good) **9** Ran SP% **114.7**
Speed ratings (Par 107): **108,103,103,103,100 98,96,94,90**
toteswingers:1&2:£2.90, 1&3:£4.00, 2&3:£5.70 CSF £13.50 TOTE £3.10: £1.30, £1.40, £2.60; EX 8.70.
Owner Godolphin **Bred** Stiftung Gestut Fahrhof **Trained** Newmarket, Suffolk

FOCUS
A couple of these still held Group 2 Ribblesdale entries at Royal Ascot, and the winner had bumped into the first and third in the Epsom Oaks already this season, so for a Listed contest the field looked strong. The winner has improved with each run and this was the clear pick of the four C&D times.

NOTEBOOK
Rumh(GER) ◆, who had little chance on her seasonal return here (same trip) when bumping into subsequent Oaks winner and third Dancing Rain and Izzi Top, was taken to the front by Frankie Dettori, dominated while there and kept going to record a comfortable success. Although it will come quite quickly, she is now likely to take her chance at Royal Ascot next week, especially as her stablemate Khawlah is far from certain to take up her engagement in the Ribblesdale. (tchd 2-1, 11-4 in places and 3-1 in places)
Imperial Pippin(USA) wasn't disgraced behind Oaks sixth Beatrice Aurore at Goodwood last time in a Listed contest, which was only her second run, and shaped like a horse who will get further here after coming home at the one pace throughout the final stages. (op 7-2)
Moment Of Time bumped into a decent sort last time after a sound first run, and again progressed with a positive run. This looks her right distance and surely connections will be looking for a win soon, now she has some valuable black type. (op 11-2)

Palm Pilot(IRE) ran poorly in the Lingfield Oaks Trial last time but had excuses, both the trip and going. Connections reached for cheekpieces for the first time, but she looked a hard ride and wasn't going anywhere quickly over 3f out. It seemed sure she was going to finish last at one point, but she ran on, albeit looking a shade reluctant, and almost claimed third. She obviously has ability, as the hat-trick on the AW proves, but needs to brighten her outlook to racing before becoming a viable win selection. (op 50-1)

Fanny May is a well-travelled filly after running in France and Germany as a 2-y-o in Listed contests. She was soon up with the leaders on her seasonal reappearance and ran her race without being good enough. (op 25-1)

Poplin, a place behind Imperial Pippin last time, pulled a bit in behind and was disappointing. (op 13-2 tchd 15-2)

Matula(IRE) wasn't beaten far by Blue Bunting on her second start last season in the Montrose Stakes, but hadn't been out since that effort. A filly with a bit of size, she'll need to come on a bit for this to be of interest next time. (op 14-1)

Gracefield(USA) was making a fairly quick reappearance after winning a maiden at Nottingham 11 days previously from an odds-on shot. One got the impression that she wasn't good enough and pulled too hard. (tchd 12-1)

Albaraka, whose sister won a Listed race for these connections, hadn't been out on a racecourse since easily winning a Wolverhampton maiden in mid-February but attracted plenty of market interest. Not the quickest away, she never looked like landing the money and was well beaten. (op 11-2 tchd 6-1)

2840 DOWNLOAD THE BLUE SQUARE APP MAIDEN FILLIES' STKS (DIV II) 1m 2f 6y

3:40 (3:40) (Class 5) 3-Y-O **£3,756** (£1,117; £558; £278) **Stalls** Low

Form RPR

3- **1** **Polygon (USA)**[265] 6155 3-9-0 0 .... MartinDwyer 8 88+
(John Gosden) *hld up in rr: hdwy on ins to ld appr fnl f: pushed clr fnl 120yds: easily* **17/2**[3]

34 **2** *2* **Stella Point (IRE)**[27] 2050 3-9-0 0 .... RichardHughes 1 83+
(Mick Channon) *trckd ldrs: travelling wl 2f out: drvn and qcknd to chse wnr fnl f but no ch but styd on one pce* **1/1**[1]

3 *1* **Inner Secret (USA)** 3-9-0 0 .... FrankieDettori 3 80+
(Mahmood Al Zarooni) *in tch: hdwy on outside over 2f out: drvn and styd on to chal over 1f out: nt pce of ldng duo ins fnl f* **20/1**

3-32 **4** *1 ½* **Rainbow Springs**[34] 1845 3-9-0 100 .... WilliamBuick 5 77
(John Gosden) *t.k.h: trckd ldrs: hd to one side over 2f out: drvn and styd on to chal over 1f out: no ex ins fnl f* **7/2**[2]

6-2 **5** *2* **Hairstyle**[28] 2026 3-9-0 0 .... RyanMoore 4 73
(Sir Michael Stoute) *chsd ldrs: rdn 2f out: wknd and hung lft fnl f* **7/2**[2]

6 *¾* **Rusoom** 3-9-0 0 .... RichardHills 7 72
(Marcus Tregoning) *chsd ldr: led over 2f out tl hdd appr fnl f: wknd sn after* **33/1**

7 *1 ½* **Convention** 3-9-0 0 .... JimCrowley 10 69+
(Ed Dunlop) *s.i.s: in rr: shkn up over 2f out: mod prog clsng stages* **80/1**

06 **8** *¾* **Compassion**[27] 2065 3-9-0 0 .... AdamKirby 9 67
(Michael Bell) *s.i.s: in rr: rdn 3f out: mod prog clsng stages* **100/1**

3-0 **9** *shd* **Reillys Daughter**[11] 2528 3-9-0 0 .... FergusSweeney 2 67?
(J S Moore) *in rr: rdn over 3f out: mod prog clsng stages* **100/1**

00 **10** *6* **Hursley Hope (IRE)**[13] 2469 3-9-0 0 .... DaneO'Neill 6 55
(David Elsworth) *led tl hdd over 2f out: sn btn* **100/1**

2m 10.28s (1.48) **Going Correction** -0.025s/f (Good) **10** Ran SP% **116.9**
Speed ratings (Par 96): **93,91,90,89,87 87,86,85,85,80**
toteswingers:1&2:£2.80, 1&3:£9.00, 2&3:£4.80 CSF £17.40 TOTE £11.90: £1.50, £1.30, £2.70; EX 26.00.
Owner Lady Rothschild **Bred** Carwell Equities Ltd **Trained** Newmarket, Suffolk

FOCUS
The second division of the maiden looked the stronger, considering one of the market leaders had a third place in a 2-y-o Group 1 in her profile already. It was run in a similar time. It produced what looks to be a good prospect in Polygon, with the form rated through the fourth.

2841 BE WISER INSURANCE H'CAP 7f (S)

4:15 (4:15) (Class 5) (0-75,75) 3-Y-O **£1,470** (£1,470; £337; £168) **Stalls** Centre

Form RPR

-346 **1** **Rajan Bear**[23] 2180 3-8-12 66 .... DaneO'Neill 6 73
(Michael Blanshard) *s.i.s: in rr: gd hdwy over 1f out: drvn to ld ins fnl f: ct and forced to dead-heat last stride* **16/1**

36-4 **1** *dht* **Muzdahi (USA)**[27] 2068 3-9-7 75 .... RichardHills 2 86+
(John Dunlop) *in rr: nt clr run 2f out: swtchd rt appr fnl f: str run on rails and n.m.r fnl 120yds: got up to force dead-heat last stride* **7/2**[1]

34-6 **3** *1 ¼* **Orthodox Lad**[21] 2216 3-9-2 70 .... AdamKirby 15 74
(John Best) *s.i.s: in rr: rdn 3f out: hdwy and nt clr run over 1f out: styd on wl fnl f: tk 3rd cl home but nt pce of ldng duo* **7/1**[2]

10-0 **4** *½* **Kingarrick**[21] 2229 3-9-6 74 .... SebSanders 10 77
(Eve Johnson Houghton) *chsd ldrs: rdn to chal 1f out: kpt on same pce ins fnl f* **12/1**

00-3 **5** *1 ¼* **Oetzi**[26] 2119 3-8-3 62 .... HarryBentley(5) 11 61
(Alan Jarvis) *chsd ldr: led over 2f out: sn rdn: kpt narrow ld tl ins fnl f: wknd fnl 120yds* **15/2**[3]

24-0 **6** *1 ¾* **Silenzio**[34] 1843 3-9-5 73 .... RyanMoore 7 68
(Richard Hannon) *chsd ldrs: rdn over 2f out and ev ch 1f out: wknd ins fnl f* **8/1**

2-44 **7** *1 ¾* **Prophet In A Dream**[16] 2383 3-9-1 72 .... MartinHarley(3) 9 62+
(Mick Channon) *in tch: travelling ok ins fnl 2f: rdn over 1f out and sn one pce* **8/1**

1-00 **8** *nk* **Never Never Land**[16] 2383 3-9-4 72 ....(b[1]) WilliamBuick 4 61
(John Gosden) *chsd ldrs: rdn 2f out: ev ch 1f out: wknd qckly fnl f* **10/1**

20-0 **9** *1 ½* **Hard Bargain (IRE)**[38] 1774 3-9-2 70 .... EddieAhern 3 55
(Denis Coakley) *in rr: drvn and hdwy fr 2f out: tried to cl on ldrs appr fnl f but no imp: sn wknd* **25/1**

24-0 **10** *1 ½* **Sylas Ings**[31] 1947 3-9-2 70 .... IanMongan 5 51
(Pat Phelan) *in rr: nt clr run fr 2f out: swtchd sharply lft over 1f out: hung lft sn after: sme prog clsng stages* **40/1**

2-54 **11** *½* **Amhran (IRE)**[19] 2306 3-9-6 74 .... MartinDwyer 8 54
(Brian Meehan) *chsd ldrs: chal u.p fr 2f out to 1f out: wknd ins fnl f* **9/1**

4000 **12** *4* **Serial Sinner (IRE)**[10] 2553 3-8-6 67 .... DuilioDaSilva(7) 13 36
(Paul Cole) *in tch: rdn and effrt 2f out: no imp and wknd fnl f* **40/1**

3205 **13** *8* **Rojo Boy**[27] 2068 3-9-4 72 ....(b) KierenFallon 14 19
(David Elsworth) *led tl hdd over 2f out: sn wknd* **9/1**

1m 27.16s (1.46) **Going Correction** +0.05s/f (Good) **13** Ran SP% **120.1**
Speed ratings (Par 99): **93,93,91,91,89 87,85,85,83,81 81,76,67**
WIN: Muzdahi £2.10 Bajan Bear £9.10 PL: M £1.60, BB £4.90, OL £2.70 EX: M/BB £58.90 BB/M £44.20 CSF: M/BB £32.11 BB/M £35.56 TC: M/BB/OL £194.86. BB/M/OL £228.17. toteswingers: M&BB £15.00, BB&OL £20.90, M&OL £6.90.
Owner Hamdan Al Maktoum **Bred** Shadwell Farm LLC **Trained** Arundel, W Sussex

FOCUS
Quite a few of these seemed unexposed and open to improvement, but the race was a bit messy and a couple looked unlucky. The judge was unable to split the front two, but Muzdahi was unlucky not to win outright. Pretty ordinary form for the track.

2842 INSURE WISER H'CAP 1m 4f 5y

4:50 (4:50) (Class 5) (0-75,75) 3-Y-O **£2,266** (£674; £337; £168) **Stalls** Low

Form RPR

-411 **1** **Anton Dolin (IRE)**[19] 2293 3-9-4 72 .... EddieAhern 3 87+
(John Dunlop) *trckd ldrs: led over 2f out: shkn up fnl f: kpt on strly and a in command* **3/1**[2]

00-1 **2** *¾* **Four Nations (USA)**[40] 1683 3-9-4 72 .... JimCrowley 11 83+
(Amanda Perrett) *in rr: hdwy over 3f out: drvn to go 2nd over 1f out: styd on wl u.p clsng stages but a readily hld* **11/4**[1]

21-4 **3** *3 ¾* **Slight Advantage (IRE)**[31] 1951 3-9-2 73 .... JohnFahy(3) 10 78
(Clive Cox) *broke wl: stdd towards rr: swtchd rt to outside 3f out: rdn and styd on to take 3rd ins fnl f but no imp on ldng duo* **12/1**

0-36 **4** *1 ¼* **Waterborne**[29] 1997 3-8-9 63 ....(t) RichardHughes 12 66
(Roger Charlton) *stdd in rr: swtchd rt to outside ins fnl 3f: sn rdn: hanging lft u.p fr 2f out: clsd u.p over 1f out but stl hanging and nt resolute: btn fnl f* **20/1**

3111 **5** *nse* **Dubai Glory**[21] 2225 3-9-7 75 .... JamesDoyle 7 78+
(Sheena West) *chsd ldrs: led over 6f out: hdd over 2f out: wknd and lost 3rd fnl f* **8/1**[3]

1-50 **6** *1 ¾* **Mattoral**[27] 2076 3-9-7 75 .... SebSanders 4 75
(Peter Makin) *drvn fr stalls and chsd ldrs after 2f: hrd drvn over 2f out: no prog and sn btn* **11/1**

000- **7** *10* **Lejaam**[234] 6978 3-9-0 68 .... RichardHills 9 52
(John Dunlop) *in rr: sme hdwy into mid-div fr 3f out: no further prog and sn wknd* **16/1**

-404 **8** *4* **Ugo (USA)**[24] 2152 3-9-2 70 .... KierenFallon 1 48
(Heather Main) *chsd ldrs: rdn and n.m.r 3f out: wknd over 2f out* **22/1**

62-4 **9** *5* **Levantera (IRE)**[31] 1947 3-9-4 72 .... PhilipRobinson 2 42
(Clive Cox) *led tl hdd over 6f out: wknd qckly over 2f out* **9/1**

60-6 **10** *13* **Royal Reason**[64] 1189 3-8-8 65 .... MartinHarley(3) 8 14
(Mick Channon) *in rr: sme hdwy on ins whn n.m.r 3f out: sn wknd* **50/1**

-021 **11** *20* **Captain Bellamy (USA)**[21] 2239 3-8-7 61 .... WilliamBuick 5 —
(Hughie Morrison) *chsd ldrs: rdn 4f out: wknd 3f out: eased whn no ch fnl f* **8/1**[3]

2m 35.31s (-0.19) **Going Correction** -0.025s/f (Good) **11** Ran SP% **116.9**
Speed ratings (Par 99): **99,98,96,95,95 93,87,84,81,72 59**
toteswingers:1&2:£3.20, 1&3:£8.30, 2&3:£10.00 CSF £11.28 CT £85.50 TOTE £3.40: £1.10, £1.60, £4.60; EX 11.10.
Owner Windflower Overseas Holdings Inc **Bred** Windflower Overseas Holdings Inc **Trained** Arundel, W Sussex

FOCUS
Much like the previous race on the card, most of these had the potential to be a good bit better than they'd already shown, but the winner is the one to concentrate on. he is value for extra, and this is good form for the grade, rated fairly positively.
Levantera(IRE) Official explanation: trainer said filly would prefer softer ground
Captain Bellamy(USA) Official explanation: trainer said gelding would prefer softer ground

2843 BE WISER INSURANCE GENTLEMAN AMATEUR RIDERS' H'CAP 1m 2f 6y

5:20 (5:23) (Class 5) (0-70,70) 4-Y-0+ **£2,186** (£677; £338; £169) **Stalls** Low

Form RPR

-040 **1** **Mustajed**[19] 2308 10-10-3 57 ....(b) MrPMillman(5) 5 66
(Rod Millman) *in rr but in tch: hdwy on ins over 2f out: styng on whn nt clr run and swtchd rt to chal between horses fnl 120yds: pushed out to ld last strides* **8/1**

00-6 **2** *nk* **Megalala (IRE)**[6] 2685 10-10-9 63 .... MrJackSalmon(5) 1 71
(John Bridger) *fly-jmpd s: led: clr over 3f out: rdn along over 2f out: kpt narrow advantage whn chal thrght fnl f: hdd last strides* **11/2**[3]

6345 **3** *1* **Fitz**[10] 2560 5-10-1 53 .... JamesBanks(3) 8 59
(Matthew Salaman) *chsd ldrs: rdn: edgd lft and styd on to chal fnl f: no ex and one pce fnl 100yds* **6/1**

00-0 **4** *3* **Northern Spy (USA)**[19] 2308 7-10-8 62 .... MrJCoffill-Brown(5) 2 62
(Simon Dow) *chsd ldrs: pushed along fr 2f out: one pce fnl f* **10/1**

4603 **5** *½* **Lady Lam**[22] 2202 5-10-4 58 ....(t) BrendanPowell(5) 6 57
(Sylvester Kirk) *in rr: pushed along over 2f out: styd on fnl f but nvr gng pce to rch ldrs* **13/2**

-050 **6** *4 ½* **King Columbo (IRE)**[6] 2685 6-10-4 56 ....(p) MrRBirkett(3) 4 46
(Julia Feilden) *chsd ldr tl over 2f out: sn btn* **5/1**[2]

2-50 **7** *2* **Fifty Cents**[6] 2685 7-10-10 62 .... MrCMartin(3) 3 48
(Milton Harris) *s.i.s: rdn along 4f out: a bhd* **16/1**

112 **8** *2 ¼* **Addikt (IRE)**[10] 2567 6-11-7 70 .... MrSWalker 7 52
(Michael Scudamore) *stdd s: in rr: hdwy on outside 3f out: sn rdn: hung lft over 2f out: sn wknd* **5/2**[1]

2m 11.16s (2.36) **Going Correction** -0.025s/f (Good) **8** Ran SP% **112.9**
Speed ratings (Par 103): **89,88,87,85,85 81,79,78**
toteswingers:1&2:£7.20, 1&3:£8.00, 2&3:£6.40 CSF £49.92 CT £282.29 TOTE £9.00: £2.50, £1.20, £2.40; EX 45.80.
Owner Rod Millman Racing Club **Bred** Shadwell Estate Company Limited **Trained** Kentisbeare, Devon
■ Stewards' Enquiry : Mr P Millman trainer said, regarding the apparent improvement in form shown, gelding had too much to do from a wide draw last time.

FOCUS
A modest handicap, but most held some sort of chance. The pace was decent and the form is sound and limited.
King Columbo(IRE) Official explanation: jockey said gelding hung right-handed
T/Jkpt: Not won. T/Plt: £10.80 to a £1 stake. Pool:£65,930.51 - 4,421.05 winning tickets T/Qpdt: £9.50 to a £1 stake. Pool:£5,044.37 - 390.90 winning tickets ST

2609 NOTTINGHAM (L-H)

Thursday, June 9

OFFICIAL GOING: Good to firm (good in places; watered; 7.4)
Wind: Light against Weather: Cloudy with sunny spells

2844 BRITISH STALLION STUDS SUPPORTING BRITISH RACING EBF MAIDEN STKS 6f 15y

1:50 (1:50) (Class 5) 2-Y-O **£3,238** (£963; £481; £240) **Stalls** High

Form RPR

1 **Sans Loi (IRE)** 2-9-3 0 .... RobertWinston 9 86+
(Alan McCabe) *chsd ldrs: led wl over 1f out: sn pushed clr: easily* **5/2**[1]

2 5 **West Leake Hare (IRE)** 2-9-3 0 .... MichaelHills 4 68+
(B W Hills) *s.i.s: racd keenly and sn prom: shkn up over 2f out: styd on same pce fr over 1f out: wnt 2nd wl ins fnl f* **7/1**[3]

56 3 1 **Darnathean**[30] 1988 2-9-3 0 .... (b) TonyCulhane 3 67+
(Paul D'Arcy) *chsd ldrs: rdn over 2f out: styd on same pce appr fnl f* **28/1**

4 3/4 **Daunt (IRE)** 2-9-3 0 .... JamieSpencer 6 63
(Richard Hannon) *led: hdd over 4f out: chsd ldr: rdn over 1f out: wknd fnl f* **3/1**[2]

5 1 **Storm Belt (USA)** 2-9-3 0 .... TomQueally 10 60+
(Mahmood Al Zarooni) *chsd ldr tl led over 4f out: rdn and hdd wl over 1f out: edgd lft and wknd fnl f* **3/1**[2]

6 2 1/4 **Not Bad For A Boy (IRE)** 2-9-3 0 .... PatDobbs 7 53
(Richard Hannon) *s.i.s: sn in tch: rdn and wknd over 1f out* **10/1**

0 7 3 3/4 **Hawaiian Freeze**[20] 2248 2-8-12 0 .... AndrewMullen 1 37
(Richard Ford) *chsd ldrs: pushed along and lost pl over 4f out: wknd wl over 1f out* **66/1**

8 3/4 **Berlusca (IRE)** 2-9-3 0 .... PaulHanagan 5 40
(William Jarvis) *s.i.s: hld up: hung lft fr over 2f out: sn wknd* **7/1**[3]

1m 17.13s (2.23) **Going Correction** +0.15s/f (Good) **8** Ran SP% **117.6**
Speed ratings (Par 93): **91,84,83,82,80 77,72,71**
toteswingers:1&2:£4.80, 1&3:£8.70, 2&3:£16.30 CSF £21.53 TOTE £2.70: £1.30, £2.10, £4.40; EX 27.30.
Owner Mrs Z Wentworth **Bred** Joan Murphy & Lawman Syndicate **Trained** Averham Park, Notts

FOCUS
All races on outer course and inner rail out 2m adding 13yds to distances on Round course. This was the first of two sprint races where runners came down the centre of the track. The winner impressed and can do better.

NOTEBOOK
Sans Loi(IRE), who has been given an entry in next week's Coventry, was very popular in the market and seemed to know his job. Stalking the early leaders, he was still travelling powerfully running into the final 2f and quickly began to draw clear once asked for his effort. He was a touch green once racing in isolation, edging to his left briefly, so it's probable there's improvement to come, but his trainer was inclined to think Ascot may come too soon. (op 10-3)
West Leake Hare(IRE), half-brother to winners over further, is by a speedy sire and he showed more than enough to suggest he'll be winning races, overcoming a tardy start and keenness to take second.
Darnathean had worn a visor and blinkers on his first two starts, and retained the latter aid here. Not ridden as positively as he had been previously, it enabled him to see his race out and he should be capable of getting an extra furlong in time (op 20-1)
Daunt(IRE), a half-brother to the very useful 6f performer Acclamazing, was soon on the speed but quickly got left trailing by the winner and was run out of the places. He should improve. (op 5-2)
Storm Belt(USA), from a yard whose juveniles have been needing a run, showed ability before tiring and should improve. (op 7-2)
Not Bad For A Boy(IRE), the Hannon second string, was readily outpaced when the tempo quickened and should leave this running behind next time, with 7f likely to suit later in the season. (op 17-2)
Berlusca(IRE), whose dam is from a fine French middle distance family, was hanging and clearly failed to run to expectations. (op 15-2 tchd 13-2)

2845 WARREN BOARD - GRAPHIC BOARD H'CAP 6f 15y
2:20 (2:22) (Class 6) (0-65,65) 3-Y-0+ £1,780 (£529; £264; £132) Stalls High

Form RPR

3361 1 **Flying Applause**[8] 2610 6-9-10 62 6ex .... (bt) JimmyQuinn 8 75
(Roy Bowring) *s.i.s: sn mid-div: rdn 1/2-way: hdwy over 1f out: r.o u.p to ld wl ins fnl f* **3/1**[1]

0526 2 1 **Bermondsey Bob (IRE)**[8] 2609 5-9-4 59 .... KierenFox(3) 10 69
(John Spearing) *led: rdn over 1f out: hdd and unable qck wl ins fnl f* **11/1**

00 3 2 3/4 **Gertmegalush (IRE)**[10] 2546 4-9-5 60 .... RobertLButler(3) 6 61
(John Harris) *s.i.s: bhd: hdwy over 1f out: r.o: nt rch ldrs* **16/1**

0-14 4 3/4 **Arch Walker (IRE)**[34] 1861 4-9-8 63 .... MichaelO'Connell(3) 12 62
(Jedd O'Keeffe) *prom: pushed along 1/2-way: rdn over 1f out: styd on same pce fnl f* **14/1**

0401 5 2 1/4 **First Blade**[24] 2164 5-9-13 65 .... (b) PaulQuinn 16 56
(Roy Bowring) *hld up: hdwy over 1f out: wknd ins fnl f* **20/1**

010 6 2 1/2 **Delaware Dancer (IRE)**[193] 7613 4-9-11 63 .... RobertHavlin 17 46
(Jeremy Gask) *s.i.s: hld up: hdwy 1/2-way: rdn over 1f out: wknd fnl f* **9/2**[2]

4-65 7 nk **Griffin Point (IRE)**[24] 2155 4-9-1 53 .... PaulHanagan 11 35
(William Muir) *chsd ldrs: rdn over 2f out: wknd fnl f* **20/1**

4424 8 6 **Pineapple Pete (IRE)**[8] 2611 3-9-2 62 .... (tp) RobertWinston 13 25
(Alan McCabe) *s.i.s: hld up: shkn up over 2f out: hdwy over 1f out: wknd fnl f* **11/1**

0-25 9 3/4 **Oh So Spicy**[20] 2270 4-9-7 59 .... TedDurcan 9 20+
(Chris Wall) *chsd ldrs: pushed along 1/2-way: edgd lft over 1f out: sn wknd and eased* **12/1**

0-05 10 1 3/4 **Reset To Fit**[9] 2593 4-9-0 52 .... DavidAllan 7 —
(Eric Alston) *prom: rdn 1/2-way: wknd over 2f out* **16/1**

0224 11 nk **Exceedingly Good (IRE)**[34] 1875 5-8-10 55 .... LucyKBarry(7) 15 —
(Roy Bowring) *hld up: a in rr: wknd over 2f out* **15/2**[3]

5003 12 4 **Suddenly Susan (IRE)**[7] 2650 3-8-7 60 .... (b) LeonnaMayor(7) 3 —
(David Nicholls) *chsd ldr to 1/2-way: hung lft and wknd 2f out* **10/1**

401/ 13 25 **Half A Crown (IRE)**[594] 6989 6-9-5 57 .... PhillipMakin 4 —
(Noel Quinlan) *s.i.s: sn prom: rdn and wknd wl over 2f out: t.o* **10/1**

U244 14 5 **Grudge**[8] 2603 6-9-13 65 .... (b) TomEaves 5 —
(Conor Dore) *s.i.s: sn prom: wknd over 3f out: t.o* **33/1**

1m 15.61s (0.71) **Going Correction** +0.15s/f (Good)
WFA 3 from 4yo+ 8lb **14** Ran SP% **128.4**
Speed ratings (Par 101): **101,99,96,95,92 88,88,80,79,76 76,71,37,31**
toteswingers:1&2:£9.60, 1&3:£21.00, 2&3:£51.20 CSF £38.87 CT £485.44 TOTE £2.40: £1.10, £6.10, £6.50; EX 52.70.
Owner K Nicholls **Bred** G H Beeby And Viscount Marchwood **Trained** Edwinstowe, Notts
■ Stewards' Enquiry : Kieren Fox two-day ban: used whip with excessive frequency and without giving gelding time to respond (Jun 23-24)

FOCUS
The front pair drew a little way clear on in what was a modest sprint handicap. The winner is rated back to his 2009 C&D form.

2846 HANNAH JAYNE PHILLIPS 21ST BIRTHDAY CELEBRATION H'CAP 1m 6f 15y
2:50 (2:50) (Class 5) (0-75,74) 4-Y-0+ £2,266 (£674; £337; £168) Stalls Low

Form RPR

3502 1 **Gunslinger (FR)**[19] 2312 6-9-7 74 .... JoeFanning 3 82
(Michael Scudamore) *chsd ldr 1f: remained handy: led over 2f out: rdn over 1f out: all out* **9/2**[2]

2423 2 nse **Hallstatt (IRE)**[13] 2459 5-9-1 68 .... (t) GrahamGibbons 6 76
(John Mackie) *chsd ldr after 1f tl led over 8f out: hdd over 5f out: led again 4f out: hdd over 2f out: rallied and ev ch fnl f: jst failed* **9/2**[2]

05-5 3 8 **Hawridge King**[21] 2224 9-9-5 72 .... JamesMillman 1 69
(Stuart Kittow) *prom: rdn over 3f out: styd on to go 3rd over 1f out: no ex fnl f* **2/1**[1]

1110 4 4 1/2 **Laverre (IRE)**[10] 2552 4-9-6 73 .... PaulHanagan 4 64
(Lucy Wadham) *prom: rdn over 3f out: ev ch over 2f out: wknd over 1f out* **5/1**[3]

5362 5 1 3/4 **Frameit (IRE)**[97] 769 4-8-8 61 .... PaulMulrennan 8 49
(James Given) *hld up: rdn over 2f out: n.d* **16/1**

2536 6 2 1/4 **Leyte Gulf (USA)**[31] 1956 8-8-9 62 .... LiamKeniry 7 47
(Chris Bealby) *dwlt: hld up: rdn and hung lft over 2f out: n.d* **20/1**

5-54 7 3 **Bin End**[44] 1577 5-9-5 72 .... FrankieMcDonald 5 53
(Barry Brennan) *hld up: hdwy 4f out: rdn: edgd lft and wknd over 1f out* **16/1**

-044 8 9 **Arashi**[11] 2526 5-8-9 62 ow1 .... (v) TomMcLaughlin 2 30
(Lucinda Featherstone) *led over 5f: remained w ldr tl led again over 5f out: hdd 4f out: sn rdn: wknd over 2f out* **13/2**

3m 8.14s (0.84) **Going Correction** +0.15s/f (Good) **8** Ran SP% **116.2**
Speed ratings (Par 103): **103,102,98,95,94 93,91,86**
toteswingers:1&2:£3.70, 1&3:£3.00, 2&3:£3.00 CSF £25.50 CT £52.60 TOTE £3.20: £1.10, £1.40, £1.80; EX 27.10.
Owner S M Smith & Keith Hunter **Bred** Dayton Investments Ltd **Trained** Bromsash, Herefordshire
■ Stewards' Enquiry : Paul Mulrennan two-day ban: careless riding (Jun 23-24)

FOCUS
There was little pace on in this modest staying handicap, yet the front two managed to draw clear.

2847 PIPER HEIDSIECK CHAMPAGNE H'CAP 1m 75y
3:25 (3:25) (Class 3) (0-95,93) 3-Y-0 £6,670 (£1,984; £991; £495) Stalls Centre

Form RPR

1112 1 **Kuala Limper (IRE)**[75] 988 3-9-0 86 .... PaulHanagan 1 94
(David Elsworth) *mde all: rdn over 1f out: styd on wl* **10/1**

5-51 2 2 1/4 **Early Applause**[16] 2392 3-8-7 79 .... MichaelHills 2 82
(B W Hills) *chsd wnr: ev ch over 2f out: sn rdn: styd on same pce ins fnl f* **11/2**

1-04 3 1 1/4 **Byrony (IRE)**[5] 2705 3-9-2 88 .... PatDobbs 6 88
(Richard Hannon) *chsd ldrs: rdn over 2f out: no ex ins fnl f* **16/1**

2-04 4 nk **El Muqbil (IRE)**[12] 2503 3-8-11 83 .... (t) TadhgO'Shea 5 82
(Brian Meehan) *hld up: hdwy over 2f out: rdn over 1f out: styd on same pce fnl f* **4/1**[2]

122- 5 4 1/2 **Seattle Drive (IRE)**[239] 6845 3-9-7 93 .... TedDurcan 8 82
(David Elsworth) *s.i.s: hld up: hdwy over 3f out: rdn over 2f out: wknd ins fnl f* **7/1**

1-21 6 1 **Jibaal (IRE)**[13] 2472 3-8-4 76 .... JoeFanning 3 63
(Mark Johnston) *chsd ldrs: rdn over 2f out: wknd over 1f out* **5/1**[3]

32-2 7 20 **Ajeeb (USA)**[19] 2306 3-8-7 79 ow2 .... JamieSpencer 7 20
(David Simcock) *hld up: pushed along 1/2-way: wknd over 2f out: t.o* **11/4**[1]

-323 8 18 **Azrael**[26] 2110 3-9-7 93 .... RobertWinston 4 —
(Alan McCabe) *plld hrd and prom: rdn over 3f out: wknd over 2f out: t.o* **9/1**

1m 46.48s (0.88) **Going Correction** +0.15s/f (Good) **8** Ran SP% **116.2**
Speed ratings (Par 103): **101,98,97,97,92 91,71,53**
toteswingers:1&2:£11.70, 1&3:£14.70, 2&3:£13.40 CSF £64.71 CT £887.45 TOTE £9.90: £2.40, £2.00, £3.20; EX 73.90.
Owner John Dwyer **Bred** Oghill House Stud & Jimmy Hyland **Trained** Newmarket, Suffolk

FOCUS
A decent handicap, but few got into it. The time compared well with that of the following maiden and the winner produced a clear personal best back on turf.

NOTEBOOK
Kuala Limper(IRE) was given a good front-running ride. Most progressive at up to 1m on the AW at Kempton earlier this year, he slowed things down in front before the home bend, and then caught out many when kicking again. Although things went his way, his trainer expects he has more to offer in good handicaps. (op 9-1)
Early Applause, who dead-heated in a minor Ripon maiden last month, was never far away and appeared to run up to his best. (op 15-2)
Byrony(IRE), reappearing just five days after finishing fourth at Doncaster, ran to a similar level and is still a few pounds too high in the handicap. (op 14-1)
El Muqbil(IRE) was the only one to make any headway from off the pace and his performance can be upgraded, meaning he's probably worth one more chance to build on his 2-y-o promise. (op 9-2)
Seattle Drive(IRE) was keen and didn't get home having made a brief forward move. He should come on for this and remains capable of better, presuming he relaxes more in future. (op 6-1)
Jibaal(IRE) found this tougher than the minor Newmarket handicap he won last time. (op 4-1)
Ajeeb(USA) found little for pressure and was virtually tailed off on this handicap debut. Something was presumably amiss. (op 3-1)
Azrael Official explanation: jockey said colt failed to handle the bend

2848 WARREN BOARD - CARTON BOARD MAIDEN STKS 1m 75y
4:00 (4:12) (Class 5) 3-Y-0+ £2,266 (£674; £337; £168) Stalls Centre

Form RPR

0 1 **Silver Bullitt**[17] 2371 3-9-0 0 .... TedDurcan 8 81
(Walter Swinburn) *mde all: hung lft over 4f out: rdn over 1f out: styd on* **25/1**

43/ 2 1/2 **Vimiero (USA)**[607] 6663 4-9-11 0 .... JamieSpencer 9 83
(Walter Swinburn) *a.p: chsd wnr 2f out: sn rdn: r.o* **7/4**[1]

6 3 5 **Hawridge Song**[30] 1984 3-9-0 0 .... JamesMillman 7 68
(Rod Millman) *prom: rdn and swtchd rt over 2f out: styd on to go 3rd ins fnl f: nt trble ldrs* **28/1**

46 4 1 1/4 **Dervisher (IRE)**[23] 2185 3-9-0 0 .... (b[1]) TomQueally 15 65
(Sir Henry Cecil) *chsd wnr tl rdn over 2f out: sn hung lft: no ex fnl f* **5/1**[3]

46- 5 2 1/2 **Ela Gonda Mou**[275] 5842 4-9-6 0 .... RobertWinston 17 57+
(Peter Charalambous) *mid-div: rdn over 2f out: styd on: nt trble ldrs* **25/1**

5 dht **Wordiness** 3-9-0 0 .... FrankieMcDonald 13 59+
(Barry Brennan) *hld up: r.o ins fnl f: nrst fin* **66/1**

0 7 1 1/2 **Carpentras**[23] 2174 3-8-9 0 .... RobertHavlin 12 51
(Dr Jon Scargill) *hld up: rdn over 2f out: styd on ins fnl f: nvr nrr* **40/1**

0 8 3 1/4 **Semmsu (IRE)**[13] 2469 3-9-0 0 .... J-PGuillambert 14 48+
(Luca Cumani) *plld hrd and prom: rdn over 2f out: wknd over 1f out* **14/1**

0-6 9 nk **Burst Of Stardust**[21] 2223 3-8-6 0 .... KierenFox(3) 1 43
(Bryn Palling) *chsd ldrs: rdn over 2f out: wknd over 1f out* **25/1**

10 nk **Fascinating (IRE)** 3-8-7 0 .... AntiocoMurgia(7) 2 47
(Mahmood Al Zarooni) *s.i.s: in rr and rdn over 3f out: n.d* **11/2**

06 11 1 3/4 **Arkaim**[12] 2511 3-9-0 0 .... LiamKeniry 5 43
(Ed Walker) *s.i.s: hld up: a in rr* **33/1**

0 12 1 1/4 **Gambatte**[30] 1984 4-9-6 0 .... LiamJones 10 38
(Tony Carroll) *plld hrd and prom: rdn over 3f out: wknd over 2f out* **66/1**

13 *hd* **Anatolian** 3-9-0 0 .... PaulHanagan 11 40
(Mahmood Al Zarooni) *s.i.s: hld up: rdn over 3f out: nvr on terms* **4/1**[2]

14 *4* **Deraasa (USA)** 3-8-9 0 .... TadhgO'Shea 3 26
(Saeed Bin Suroor) *s.i.s: a in rr* **15/2**

15 *73* **Astroverdi** 3-8-7 0 .... CharlesEddery(7) 4 —
(Mark H Tompkins) *s.s: outpcd: t.o fr 1/2-way* **66/1**

1m 48.56s (2.96) **Going Correction** +0.15s/f (Good)
WFA 3 from 4yo 11lb **15** Ran SP% **131.7**
Speed ratings (Par 103): **91,90,85,84,81 81,80,77,76,76 74,73,73,69,—**
toteswingers:1&2:£18.20, 1&3:£96.70, 2&3:£23.40 CSF £70.84 TOTE £45.70: £8.60, £1.50, £7.10; EX 163.20.
Owner Antoniades Family **Bred** Overbury Stallions Ltd **Trained** Aldbury, Herts
■ Shopping Oasis (14/1) was withdrawn after breaking out of the stalls. R4 applies, deduct 5p in the £.

FOCUS
Bit of a turn up in this interesting maiden, which saw a 1-2 for Walter Swinburn. They were clear but this was ordinary maiden form.
Arkaim Official explanation: jockey said gelding hung right

2849 TRY TIMEFORM.BETFAIR.COM RACING APP FILLIES' H'CAP (DIV I) 1m 2f 50y
4:35 (4:37) (Class 5) (0-75,75) 3-Y-O **£4,209** (£1,252; £625; £312) **Stalls** Low

Form RPR

3116 **1** **Apache Glory (USA)**[28] 2022 3-9-2 **70** .... PatDobbs 1 85
(Richard Hannon) *chsd ldrs: led over 1f out: shkn up and r.o wl* **15/2**

00-3 **2** *2 ½* **Mystic Edge**[24] 2166 3-8-4 **58** .... JoeFanning 4 68
(Michael Bell) *s.i.s: sn pushed along and prom: rdn and ev ch over 1f out: styd on same pce ins fnl f* **9/2**[2]

52-5 **3** *2 ½* **Lucy Limelites**[34] 1862 3-9-5 **73** ....(b[1]) TomQueally 6 78
(Roger Charlton) *led: rdn and hdd over 1f out: no ex ins fnl f* **6/1**

442- **4** *10* **Alareen (USA)**[217] 7312 3-8-12 **66** .... TedDurcan 7 51
(Saeed Bin Suroor) *sn chsng ldr: rdn and ev ch over 2f out: wknd over 1f out* **7/2**[1]

01-0 **5** *¾* **Pink Diva (IRE)**[27] 2076 3-9-7 **75** .... JamieSpencer 10 59
(Tom Tate) *hld up: rdn over 2f out: nvr on terms* **13/2**

40-4 **6** *4 ½* **Norse Wing**[38] 1774 3-8-9 **63** .... RichardThomas 2 38
(Ralph Beckett) *prom: rdn over 3f out: wknd over 2f out* **14/1**

03-0 **7** *1 ¾* **Fennica (USA)**[46] 1549 3-9-2 **70** .... RobertHavlin 8 41
(John Gosden) *sn prom: shkn up 1/2-way: rdn and wknd over 2f out* **5/1**[3]

1 **8** *½* **Merton Lady**[29] 1999 3-8-11 **68** .... KierenFox(3) 9 38
(John Flint) *s.i.s: hld up and a in rr: swtchd rt over 4f out: wknd 3f out* **6/1**

2m 12.96s (1.26) **Going Correction** +0.15s/f (Good) **8** Ran SP% **117.4**
Speed ratings (Par 96): **100,98,96,88,87 83,82,82**
toteswingers:1&2:£7.90, 1&3:£7.30, 2&3:£6.60 CSF £42.25 CT £219.18 TOTE £5.90: £1.80, £1.90, £2.60; EX 42.40.
Owner Malih Lahej Al Basti **Bred** Malih Al Basti **Trained** East Everleigh, Wilts

FOCUS
The front three drew clear in what was a pretty ordinary handicap. It was the pick of the C&D times and looks much stronger form than division II. The third sets the standard.
Merton Lady Official explanation: jockey said filly hung right

2850 TRY TIMEFORM.BETFAIR.COM RACING APP FILLIES' H'CAP (DIV II) 1m 2f 50y
5:10 (5:10) (Class 5) (0-75,74) 3-Y-O **£4,209** (£1,252; £625; £312) **Stalls** Low

Form RPR

5455 **1** **Entrance**[106] 649 3-8-4 **57** .... JimmyQuinn 7 61
(Julia Feilden) *a.p: rdn to ld over 1f out: hung lft ins fnl f: styd on u.p* **40/1**

5-56 **2** *¾* **Celani**[51] 1456 3-8-13 **66** .... GrahamGibbons 1 68
(Tim Walford) *led: rdn and hdd over 1f out: styd on* **20/1**

-600 **3** *½* **Corvette**[22] 2196 3-8-7 **60** .... JoeFanning 3 61
(J R Jenkins) *chsd ldrs: rdn over 2f out: nt clr run ins fnl f: styd on* **33/1**

56-0 **4** *2 ¾* **Spade**[28] 2018 3-9-0 **67** .... JamieSpencer 9 63
(David Elsworth) *s.i.s: hld up: hdwy over 2f out: rdn ins fnl f: no ex* **8/1**

2213 **5** *2 ½* **Little Jazz**[23] 2186 3-9-1 **68** .... LiamJones 4 59
(Paul D'Arcy) *hld up: pushed along over 3f out: swtchd rt over 2f out: sn rdn and hung lft: no imp fnl f* **7/1**[3]

46-2 **6** *6* **Fenella Fudge**[13] 2466 3-9-7 **74** .... PaulMulrennan 2 53
(James Given) *chsd ldr: rdn and ev ch over 2f out: wknd over 1f out* **17/2**

0-01 **7** *16* **Miss Topsy Turvy (IRE)**[28] 2022 3-8-11 **64** .... TedDurcan 5 11+
(John Dunlop) *unruly in stalls: s.s: bhd: rdn over 3f out: sn wknd* **11/10**[1]

-311 **8** *¾* **Flying Phoenix**[13] 2463 3-9-0 **67** .... KellyHarrison 6 12
(William Haggas) *trckd ldrs: racd keenly: rdn and wknd wl over 2f out* **9/2**[2]

40-6 **9** *7* **Fortunateencounter (FR)**[77] 952 3-9-3 **70** .... RobertHavlin 10 —
(John Gosden) *s.i.s: hld up: rdn over 3f out: sn hung lft and lost tch: t.o* **9/1**

2m 14.09s (2.39) **Going Correction** +0.15s/f (Good) **9** Ran SP% **120.1**
Speed ratings (Par 96): **96,95,95,92,90 86,73,72,67**
toteswingers:1&2:£19.00, 1&3:£23.70, 2&3:£20.60 CSF £654.19 CT £23479.96 TOTE £44.60: £9.90, £5.50, £10.50; EX 359.40.
Owner Hoofbeats Racing Club **Bred** Cheveley Park Stud Ltd **Trained** Exning, Suffolk

FOCUS
Certainly the less competitive of the two divisions, and much the weaker one too looking at the result. The favourite disappointed and the time was relatively slow.
Miss Topsy Turvy(IRE) Official explanation: jockey said filly hit her head coming out of the stalls
Flying Phoenix Official explanation: trainer's rep had no explanation for the poor form shown

2851 BOOK NOW FOR LADIES' NIGHT 2ND JULY H'CAP 1m 2f 50y
5:40 (5:40) (Class 6) (0-60,60) 4-Y-O+ **£1,619** (£481; £240; £120) **Stalls** Low

Form RPR

0112 **1** **Cane Cat (IRE)**[9] 2600 4-8-12 **51** .... LiamJones 3 59
(Tony Carroll) *hld up: hdwy to ld over 2f out: sn rdn: styd on* **9/2**[2]

5535 **2** *1 ½* **Naledi**[16] 1253 7-8-4 **46** oh1 .... SophieDoyle(3) 9 51
(Richard Price) *chsd ldrs: rdn over 2f out: styd on* **20/1**

0343 **3** *3 ½* **Star Addition**[1] 2815 5-8-12 **51** .... RobertWinston 5 49
(Eric Alston) *hld up: hdwy over 2f out: rdn over 1f out: no ex ins fnl f* **5/1**[3]

0653 **4** *6* **Kheskianto (IRE)**[17] 2359 5-8-2 **48** ....(bt) KatiaScallan(7) 6 34
(Michael Chapman) *mid-div: hdwy 3f out: wknd fnl f* **20/1**

0631 **5** *½* **Dragon Slayer (IRE)**[8] 2616 9-8-9 **55** .... LucyKBarry(7) 4 40
(John Harris) *s.i.s: hld up: hdwy u.p over 1f out: nvr trbld ldrs* **11/4**[1]

-000 **6** *¾* **Quaestor (IRE)**[21] 2233 4-8-9 **48** ow1 ....(p) JamieSpencer 1 32
(Andrew Crook) *stdd s: hld up: rdn over 1f out: nvr nrr* **25/1**

6620 **7** *9* **Professor John (IRE)**[19] 2308 4-9-7 **60** .... TomQueally 2 26
(Ian Wood) *chsd ldrs: hmpd 6f out: rdn over 2f out: wknd over 1f out* **9/1**

-601 **8** *10* **Guga (IRE)**[11] 2530 5-9-5 **58** 6ex ....(b) GrahamGibbons 10 —
(John Mackie) *led and sn clr: rdn over 3f out: hdd over 2f out: wknd over 1f out* **11/4**[1]

30/3 **P** **Moonlight Fantasy (IRE)**[20] 2271 8-8-12 **51** .... TomMcLaughlin 8 —
(Lucinda Featherstone) *chsd ldrs tl hung lft and wknd over 4f out: eased and sn t.o: p.u and dismntd fnl f* **12/1**

2m 13.96s (2.26) **Going Correction** +0.15s/f (Good) **9** Ran SP% **119.2**
Speed ratings (Par 101): **96,94,92,87,86 86,79,71,—**
toteswingers:1&2:£10.80, 1&3:£5.80, 2&3:£9.10. Totesuper 7: Win: Not won. Place: Not won CSF £92.48 CT £473.43 TOTE £4.90: £1.40, £6.20, £2.40; EX 89.10.
Owner John W Egan **Bred** Mrs G P Booth And J Porteous **Trained** Cropthorne, Worcs
■ Stewards' Enquiry : Sophie Doyle three-day ban: used whip with excessive frequency (Jun 23-25)

FOCUS
A lowly handicap, but the form is sound. The winner confirmed her Yarmouth latest.
Moonlight Fantasy(IRE) Official explanation: jockey said gelding lost its action
T/Plt: £282.70 to a £1 stake. Pool:£49,173.56 - 126.94 winning tickets T/Qpdt: £78.10 to a £1 stake. Pool:£3,578.71 - 33.90 winning tickets CR

2823 YARMOUTH (L-H)
Thursday, June 9

OFFICIAL GOING: Good to firm (watered; 8.0)
Wind: medium, half against Weather: overcast

2852 AVENUE PUB BEATTY ROAD MAIDEN STKS 6f 3y
2:10 (2:11) (Class 5) 3-Y-O+ **£2,266** (£674; £337; £168) **Stalls** High

Form RPR

0-52 **1** **Chaussini**[23] 2168 4-9-3 73 .... RoystonFfrench 1 78
(James Toller) *mde all: readily drew clr ent fnl 2f: in n.d after: v easily* **5/1**[3]

25-6 **2** *10* **Red Riverman**[10] 2568 3-9-0 81 .... ShaneKelly 2 49
(William Haggas) *chsd ldrs: rdn to chse wnr ent fnl 2f: sn wl outpcd and no ch w wnr after* **6/4**[1]

3 *2 ¾* **My Own Way Home** 3-8-9 0 .... CathyGannon 5 35
(Des Donovan) *chsd ldrs: pushed along and rn green 4f out: rdn and struggling over 2f out: no ch over 1f out: wnt modest 3rd 1f out* **33/1**

0 **4** *nk* **Don't Call Me Tiny (IRE)**[7] 2650 3-8-9 0 .... HayleyTurner 4 34
(Don Cantillon) *t.k.h early: chsd wnr tl ent fnl 2f: sn rdn and wl btn* **20/1**

5 *1* **Roy The Boy (USA)** 3-8-7 0 .... LewisWalsh(7) 8 36
(Jane Chapple-Hyam) *stdd after s: rn green and a in last pair after: wl btn 1/2-way: sme modest late hdwy* **13/8**[2]

6 **6** *4 ½* **Fire In Babylon (IRE)**[19] 2311 3-9-0 0 .... AndreaAtzeni 9 22
(Michael Wigham) *stdd after s: a bhd: struggling and switching lft 4f out: lost tch 1/2-way* **16/1**

1m 11.34s (-3.06) **Going Correction** -0.30s/f (Firm)
WFA 3 from 4yo+ 8lb **6** Ran SP% **108.3**
Speed ratings (Par 103): **108,94,91,90,89 83**
toteswingers:1&2:£1.80, 1&3:£8.20, 2&3:£6.30 CSF £12.06 TOTE £2.30: £1.10, £1.70; EX 9.70 Trifecta £61.80 Pool: £341.87 - 4.09 winning units..
Owner M E Wates **Bred** Langton Stud **Trained** Newmarket, Suffolk

FOCUS
Back straight and bottom bend dolled out 3m adding 15m to races on Round course. A weak maiden and ultimately a one-horse race. The time was modest and the favourite disappointed, so it's doubtful if the winner had to improve.

2853 VIKINGFSG.CO.UK CLASSIFIED STKS 1m 3y
2:40 (2:40) (Class 6) 3-Y-O **£1,619** (£481; £240; £120) **Stalls** High

Form RPR

-504 **1** **Battle Of Britain**[13] 2472 3-9-0 65 ....(t) WilliamCarson 8 83
(Giles Bravery) *wnt rt s: mde all and racd against stands' rail: rdn 2f out: wl clr ent fnl f: pushed out: easily* **10/1**[3]

00-0 **2** *11* **Ride The Wind**[45] 1565 3-9-0 63 .... GeorgeBaker 7 53+
(Chris Wall) *racd in centre: stdd after s: hld up in last pair: rdn and effrt ent fnl 2f: chsd clr wnr 1f out: no imp 1st of 6 in gp* **10/1**[3]

-221 **3** *1 ¼* **Whitby Jet (IRE)**[13] 2465 3-9-0 65 .... ShaneKelly 3 50+
(Edward Vaughan) *racd in centre: in tch: rdn and effrt to ld gp and chse wnr 2f out: no ch w wnr over 1f out: plugged on same pce: 2nd of 6 in gp* **1/1**[1]

-262 **4** *¾* **Silver Show (IRE)**[14] 2418 3-9-0 64 .... SamHitchcott 4 48+
(Mick Channon) *racd in centre: chsd ldrs: rdn over 3f out: styd on same pce u.p fnl 2f: no ch w wnr over 1f out: 3rd of 6 in gp* **16/1**

-005 **5** *¾* **Talkative Guest (IRE)**[23] 2172 3-8-11 60 .... AshleyHamblett(3) 9 46
(George Margarson) *bmpd s: chsd wnr on stands' rail: rdn and struggling jst over 2f out: no ch w wnr over 1f out: 2nd of 2 in gp* **20/1**

5-02 **6** *1 ¼* **Mister Ben Vereen**[20] 2243 3-9-0 63 .... CathyGannon 6 43+
(Eve Johnson Houghton) *racd in centre: t.k.h: prom: rdn ent fnl 2f: no ch w wnr and edging lft over 1f out: wknd fnl f: 4th of 6 in gp* **5/1**[2]

0-50 **7** *2 ¾* **I Hate To Lose (USA)**[22] 2192 3-9-0 65 .... HayleyTurner 1 44+
(Philip McBride) *racd in centre: stdd after s: hld up in rr: rdn and effrt ent fnl 2f: no ch w wnr over 1f out: wknd fnl f: 5th of 6 in gp* **5/1**[2]

2540 **8** *11* **Not So Bright (USA)**[5] 2722 3-9-0 55 ....(t) AndreaAtzeni 5 —
(Des Donovan) *racd in centre: led that gp and chsd wnr overall tl 2f out: sn wknd: wl bhd and eased ins fnl f* **33/1**

1m 36.67s (-3.93) **Going Correction** -0.30s/f (Firm) **8** Ran SP% **115.1**
Speed ratings (Par 97): **107,96,94,94,93 92,89,78**
toteswingers:1&2:£10.40, 1&3:£3.10, 2&3:£3.40 CSF £103.74 TOTE £16.30: £2.20, £2.90, £1.20; EX 170.10 Trifecta £316.10 Part won. Pool: £427.18 - 0.30 winning units..
Owner Christopher Wright & Minster Stud **Bred** Petra Bloodstock Agency Ltd **Trained** Cowlinge, Suffolk

FOCUS
A modest event and for form purposes a meaningless contest, as two of the eight runners raced away from the others up the stands' rail, including the wide-margin winner. The winner is rated around the best view of his 2yo form, but this is unconvincing.

2854 GREAT YARMOUTH SEALIFE CENTRE (S) STKS 7f 3y
3:15 (3:16) (Class 6) 2-Y-O **£1,619** (£481; £240; £120) **Stalls** High

Form RPR

05 **1** **Schmooze (IRE)**[9] 2587 2-8-6 0 ....(b[1]) AndreaAtzeni 5 61
(Marco Botti) *in tch: hdwy to chse ldr over 2f out: pushed ahd ent fnl f: drvn clr ins fnl f: in command and idling fnl 75yds: eased towards fin* **11/2**[3]

2 *5* **Artic Dancer (IRE)**[39] 1731 2-8-6 0 .... WilliamCarson 7 48
(David Peter Nagle, Ire) *led: rdn ent fnl 2f: hdd ent fnl f: no ch w wnr but battled on to hold 2nd fnl 150yds* **8/1**

5462 **3** nse **Sea Poet**[10] 2556 2-8-11 0 MartinLane 4 53
(Andrew Haynes) *stdd after s: hld up bhd: pushed along and hdwy 3f out: chsd ldng pair and swtchd lft wl over 1f out: battling for 2nd and kpt on fnl 150yds but no ch w wnr* **5/2**[1]

6535 **4** 8 **Manderston**[17] 2362 2-8-4 0 DarylByrne(7) 2 32+
(Mark Johnston) *chsd ldrs: rdn over 2f out: wknd u.p wl over 1f out: 4th and wl btn fnl f* **11/4**[2]

5 4 1/2 **Bridgets Call** 2-8-6 0 CathyGannon 6 15+
(Des Donovan) *in tch in last trio: pushed along 4f out: struggling and swtchd lft jst over 2f out: sn wknd and wl bhd* **13/2**

6 2 **Godber (IRE)** 2-8-11 0 SamHitchcott 1 15+
(Mick Channon) *sn pushed along in last trio: rdn after 2f: wknd jst over 2f out: sn wl bhd* **6/1**

5 **7** 46 **Tumbleowtashoes**[20] 2267 2-8-11 0 KirstyMilczarek 3 —
(John Ryan) *awkward leaving stalls: sn rcvrd and chsd ldr tl over 2f out: sn dropped out: t.o over 1f out* **80/1**

1m 26.1s (-0.50) **Going Correction** -0.30s/f (Firm) 7 Ran SP% **110.6**
Speed ratings (Par 91): **90,84,84,75,69 67,15**
toteswingers:1&2:£5.80, 1&3:£2.90, 2&3:£3.80 CSF £44.25 TOTE £9.10: £3.30, £5.90; EX 37.20.The winner was sold to Linda Perratt for 9,800gns
Owner Christopher McHale **Bred** Chris McHale And Oghill House Stud **Trained** Newmarket, Suffolk

FOCUS
The first 7f race of the season for juveniles in this country, but no more than an ordinary seller. The stands' side appeared to hold a significant edge.

NOTEBOOK
Schmooze(IRE) looked the winner from some way out and, once in front, she quickly bolted clear. She had looked short of pace in a couple of 6f maidens, but the extra furlong, drop in class and first-time blinkers combined to turn her into the emphatic winner of a bad race. (op 5-1 tchd 13-2)
Artic Dancer(IRE)'s rider attempted the same tactics as had proved so successful on Battle Of Britain in the previous contest, trying to make all the running against the stands' rail. She did her best, but the winner was running all over her from over a furlong out. She had only beaten a total of one rival in two Irish maidens but, although this was an improvement, she was probably flattered by racing against the rail. (op 15-2 tchd 13-2)
Sea Poet had the best form on offer after finishing runner-up in a Goodwood seller last time, but this was his first run beyond 5f and he was ridden with that in mind. He did stay on over the last 2f, but was never in the same parish as the winner and couldn't even get past the pace-setter. (op 2-1 tchd 11-4)
Manderston, already twice held at this level, appeared to find 6f beyond him last time and dropped right away after coming under pressure over 2f from home. (op 5-2 tchd 2-1)

2855 SEAL SANCTUARY WINTERTON FILLIES' H'CAP 7f 3y
3:50 (3:51) (Class 4) (0-85,83) 3-Y-O+ **£4,079** (£1,214; £606; £303) **Stalls** High

Form RPR

0-60 **1** **Roodle**[43] 1603 4-9-9 **78** (b[1]) CathyGannon 5 87
(Eve Johnson Houghton) *stdd and awkward leaving stalls: t.k.h: hld up in rr: rdn and hdwy to chse ldng pair 2f out: nt clr run ent fnl f: drvn and qcknd through on stands' rail to ld fnl 75yds: sn in command* **13/2**

-202 **2** 2 1/2 **Sairaam (IRE)**[17] 2354 5-8-13 **68** RobbieFitzpatrick 4 70
(Charles Smith) *led: rdn 2f out: drvn and edging lft ent fnl f: hdd fnl 75yds: sn btn* **11/4**[2]

53-5 **3** 3 3/4 **Ming Meng (IRE)**[67] 1109 4-9-6 **75** HayleyTurner 6 67
(Michael Bell) *chsd ldrs: swtchd lft and chsd ldr over 2f out: drvn and unable qck ent fnl f: wknd fnl 100yds: fin lame* **11/8**[1]

0-0 **4** 3 1/4 **Amoya (GER)**[31] 1950 4-9-8 **77** (t) StevieDonohoe 2 60
(Philip McBride) *chsd ldr tl over 2f out: sn struggling u.p: wknd over 1f out* **20/1**

534- **5** 6 **Eshoog (IRE)**[328] 4095 3-8-11 **76** ChrisCatlin 1 43
(Clive Brittain) *in tch in last pair: rdn and struggling ent fnl 2f: wknd wl over 1f out* **7/2**[3]

1m 24.15s (-2.45) **Going Correction** -0.30s/f (Firm)
WFA 3 from 4yo+ 10lb 5 Ran SP% **109.1**
Speed ratings (Par 102): **102,99,94,91,84**
CSF £23.79 TOTE £5.60: £2.80, £4.10; EX 28.20.
Owner Mrs R F Johnson Houghton **Bred** Mrs H Johnson Houghton & Mrs R F Johnson Hought **Trained** Blewbury, Oxon

FOCUS
Not a very competitive fillies' handicap and again the stands' rail was the place to be. Modest form, the winner rated back to something like her best.
Roodle Official explanation: trainer's rep said, regarding the apparent improvement in form shown, filly benefited from the application of blinkers.
Ming Meng(IRE) Official explanation: vet said filly finished lame

2856 MERRIVALE MODEL VILLAGE GREAT YARMOUTH H'CAP 2m
4:25 (4:25) (Class 6) (0-60,60) 4-Y-O+ **£1,619** (£481; £240; £120) **Stalls** High

Form RPR

3313 **1** **Annelko**[20] 2246 4-9-0 **54** MartinLane 5 64
(Andrew Haynes) *mde all: pushed along and clr ent fnl 2f: styd on wl and in command fr over 1f out* **10/3**[2]

3-40 **2** 4 **Dr Finley (IRE)**[31] 1956 4-9-3 **60** SimonPearce(3) 1 65
(Lydia Pearce) *in tch: effrt to chse ldng pair and drvn ent fnl 2f: no imp on wnr over 1f out: wnt 2nd ins fnl f: kpt on* **7/1**

05-6 **3** 3 1/4 **Miss Whippy**[13] 2473 4-8-6 **46** KirstyMilczarek 4 47
(Michael Squance) *chsd wnr: pushed along 4f out: flashed tail after: drvn and no imp wl over 1f out: lost 2nd and wknd ins fnl f* **25/1**

-326 **4** 1 1/4 **Night Orbit**[28] 2034 7-9-6 **59** RoystonFfrench 2 59
(Julia Feilden) *pushed along at times in last trio: rdn and effrt 3f out: drvn and no prog fr wl over 1f out: wnt 4th wl ins fnl f* **9/2**[3]

00-6 **5** 1 3/4 **Astromoon**[10] 2569 4-8-12 **57** AshleyMorgan(5) 7 55
(Mark H Tompkins) *t.k.h: hld up in last trio: rdn and effrt on outer 3f out: no prog u.p wl over 1f out: wl btn after* **25/1**

64-3 **6** 1 1/4 **Lauberhorn**[14] 2417 4-9-5 **59** CathyGannon 6 55
(Eve Johnson Houghton) *in tch in midfield: rdn and effrt 3f out: no prog u.p 2f out: sn wknd* **17/2**

-344 **7** 6 **Marcus Antonius**[35] 1839 4-9-4 **58** (p) PatCosgrave 8 47
(Jim Boyle) *chsd ldrs: rdn ent 4f out: rdn and nt qckn wl over 2f out: wknd wl over 1f out* **2/1**[1]

6564 **8** 3 1/4 **Royal Defence (IRE)**[10] 2569 5-8-11 **57** IanBurns(7) 3 42
(Michael Quinn) *hld up in rr: rdn and effrt whn stmbld over 2f out: no hdwy and wl btn fnl 2f* **14/1**

3m 32.23s (-0.17) **Going Correction** -0.10s/f (Good)
WFA 4 from 5yo+ 1lb 8 Ran SP% **112.0**
Speed ratings (Par 101): **96,94,92,91,90 90,87,85**
toteswingers:1&2:£5.20, 1&3:£16.90, 2&3:£20.40 CSF £25.60 CT £487.07 TOTE £4.60: £1.30, £1.10, £8.70; EX 29.30 TRIFECTA Not won..
Owner David Prosser **Bred** Paul Wyatt Ranby Hall **Trained** Limpley Stoke, Bath

FOCUS
A moderate staying handicap, but at least the winner made sure it was a fair test. He rates a clear personal best, but the opposition was dubious.
Marcus Antonius Official explanation: vet said gelding was lame on its off fore leg

2857 DIGIBET.COM H'CAP 1m 6f 17y
5:00 (5:00) (Class 5) (0-70,67) 3-Y-O **£2,266** (£674; £337; £168) **Stalls** High

Form RPR

0-42 **1** **Mokalif**[7] 2637 3-8-10 **56** HayleyTurner 8 62+
(Michael Bell) *chsd ldr tl carried wd and lost pl bnd after 2f: racd in midfield after: rdn over 3f out: swtchd rt and drvn to chse ldr 2f out: chal ins fnl f: kpt on to ld towards fin* **5/4**[1]

0002 **2** nk **May Contain Nuts**[24] 2152 3-9-2 **62** GeorgeBaker 1 68
(Brendan Powell) *in tch in midfield: rdn and effrt over 3f out: chsd ldr 3f out: drvn to ld over 1f out: hrd pressed and kpt on gamely ins fnl f: hdd and no ex towards fin* **11/2**[3]

0-61 **3** 2 1/4 **Ivanov (IRE)**[50] 1502 3-8-5 **51** JamieMackay 4 54
(Willie Musson) *hld up in last pair: pushed along and effrt on inner 3f out: chsng ldrs and swtchd rt ent fnl f: kpt on: unable to chal* **8/1**

65-4 **4** 2 1/2 **Memory Lane**[19] 2293 3-9-7 **67** StevieDonohoe 6 66
(Sir Mark Prescott Bt) *chsd ldrs tl lft in ld bnd after 2f: hdd 12f out: chsd ldr after tl 3f out: kpt plugging on u.p and styd chsng ldrs: struggling and btn whn pushed rt ent fnl f* **7/2**[2]

2354 **5** 3/4 **Trojan Touch (USA)**[9] 2599 3-8-2 **48** oh2 (p) AndreaAtzeni 5 46
(Chris Dwyer) *dwlt: sn rdn along and rcvrd to ld sn after s: hung bdly rt and hdd bnd after 2f: rcvrd to ld again 12f out: drvn and hdd over 1f out: wknd ins fnl f* **16/1**

0-04 **6** 3 **High Fallutin (IRE)**[8] 2613 3-8-7 **53** CathyGannon 7 47
(Eve Johnson Houghton) *in tch in midfield: rdn and effrt whn hung lft 3f out: stl in tch but unable qck after: wknd and hung lft 1f out* **12/1**

006- **7** 14 **Colzium**[210] 7400 3-8-4 **50** ow1 ChrisCatlin 3 25
(Mark H Tompkins) *plld hrd early: chsd ldrs tl stdd bk to r in last pair after 1f: rdn and effrt over 3f out: wknd ent fnl 2f: sn bhd* **20/1**

3m 6.35s (-1.25) **Going Correction** -0.10s/f (Good) 7 Ran SP% **111.5**
Speed ratings (Par 99): **99,98,97,96,95 93,85**
toteswingers:1&2:£2.30, 1&3:£2.70, 2&3:£3.60 CSF £8.06 CT £36.19 TOTE £2.60: £1.10, £1.50; EX 7.70 Trifecta £31.80 Pool: £597.05 - 13.88 winning units.
Owner Ahmed Ali **Bred** R E Crutchley **Trained** Newmarket, Suffolk

FOCUS
An ordinary 3-y-o staying handicap and the pace was modest, but it was quite a dramatic contest. Muddling form, rated around the runner-up.

2858 INJURED JOCKEYS FUND H'CAP 1m 3f 101y
5:30 (5:30) (Class 6) (0-65,63) 3-Y-O **£1,619** (£481; £240; £120) **Stalls** Low

Form RPR

00-0 **1** **Cotton Grass**[27] 2068 3-8-11 **58** AshleyMorgan(5) 6 64+
(Mark H Tompkins) *in tch in midfield: rdn and hdwy on outer 3f out: chsd ldr ent fnl f: styd on wl to ld on post* **11/2**[2]

4424 **2** nse **Surprise (IRE)**[14] 2418 3-9-1 **57** MarcHalford 3 63
(Mark Rimmer) *dwlt: in tch in midfield: hdwy on inner over 3f out: sqeezed through on rail to press ldr 2f out: rdn to ld over 1f out: kpt on fnl f: hdd on post* **11/1**

00-0 **3** 4 **Tommy Tiger**[26] 2119 3-8-11 **53** ChrisCatlin 5 52+
(Stuart Williams) *led for 2f: chsd ldrs after: nt clr run over 2f out: swtchd rt and rdn 2f out: styd on same pce fnl f* **12/1**

00-2 **4** 3/4 **Toucan Tango (IRE)**[9] 2586 3-9-7 **63** DarryllHolland 11 61
(Peter Chapple-Hyam) *chsd ldrs tl led after 2f: rdn over 3f out: drvn and hdd over 1f out: wknd ins fnl f* **4/1**[1]

6-36 **5** 5 **Thymesthree (IRE)**[117] 529 3-9-6 **62** GeorgeBaker 2 51
(Chris Wall) *in tch towards rr: effrt and hung lft over 2f out: sme hdwy past btn horses over 1f out: nvr trbld ldrs* **9/1**

0-53 **6** 2 1/2 **Easydoesit (IRE)**[9] 2599 3-8-8 **50** CathyGannon 12 35
(Des Donovan) *bhd: pushed along and reminder 8f out: rdn and effrt 3f out: nt clr run 2f out: styd on past btn horses fnl f: nvr trbld ldrs* **10/1**

00-4 **7** 3/4 **Invent**[13] 2463 3-9-5 **61** StevieDonohoe 7 45
(Sir Mark Prescott Bt) *s.i.s: hld up in tch in rr: hdwy on outer over 4f out: rdn to chse ldrs 3f out: wknd qckly over 1f out* **8/1**

2500 **8** 2 **Ippi N Tombi (IRE)**[19] 2307 3-8-3 **45** KirstyMilczarek 8 26
(Phil McEntee) *chsd ldrs: rdn over 3f out: wknd u.p wl over 1f out* **33/1**

-055 **9** 3 1/2 **Generous Genella**[50] 1502 3-8-3 **45** (t) AndreaAtzeni 9 20
(Julia Feilden) *chsd ldrs: wnt 2nd 8f out tl 2f out: sn wknd u.p* **22/1**

-615 **10** 2 1/4 **Runaway Tiger (IRE)**[36] 1819 3-9-6 **62** (b) PatCosgrave 1 33
(Paul D'Arcy) *s.i.s: a towards rr: rdn and no real hdwy 3f out: n.d* **8/1**

5-03 **11** 2 1/4 **Bint Nas (IRE)**[13] 2461 3-9-7 **63** SamHitchcott 10 30
(Mick Channon) *t.k.h: chsd ldrs: rdn and unable qck 3f out: wknd wl over 1f out: wl btn and eased fnl 75yds* **7/1**[3]

000 **12** 75 **Donnaconna (CAN)**[27] 2045 3-8-3 **45** HayleyTurner 4 —
(Mark Johnston) *chsd ldrs: dropped to midfield and u.p 6f out: drvn and dropped out over 3f out: wl t.o and eased fr over 1f out* **16/1**

2m 28.19s (-0.51) **Going Correction** -0.10s/f (Good) 12 Ran SP% **118.4**
Speed ratings (Par 97): **97,96,94,93,89 88,87,86,83,81 80,25**
toteswingers:1&2:£14.10, 1&3:£16.30, 2&3:£14.60 CSF £64.77 CT £703.34 TOTE £7.60: £3.20, £4.00, £4.60; EX 85.40 TRIFECTA Not won..
Owner Kingsville Promotions Ltd **Bred** Mystic Meg Limited **Trained** Newmarket, Suffolk

FOCUS
A moderate handicap and only one of these had tasted success before. The first four pulled well clear of the others.
Cotton Grass Official explanation: trainer said, regarding the apparent improvement in form shown, filly has needed time to mature and would appear to have been suited by running over this longer trip
T/Plt: £89.30 to a £1 stake. Pool:£50,604.80 - 413.53 winning tickets T/Qpdt: £32.70 to a £1 stake. Pool:£3,963.78 - 89.60 winning tickets SP

2859 - 2860a (Foreign Racing) - See Raceform Interactive

^{2531}LEOPARDSTOWN (L-H)

Thursday, June 9

OFFICIAL GOING: Good changing to good to yielding after race 3 (6:55)

2861a BALLYOGAN STKS (GROUP 3) (F&M) — 6f

6:55 (6:56) 3-Y-0+ **£32,219** (£9,418; £4,461; £1,487)

RPR

1 **Radharcnafarraige (IRE)**^{32} [1928] 3-9-1 97 .... KJManning 11 103
(J S Bolger, Ire) *chsd ldrs: 6th on outer 1/2-way: hdwy to chal over 1f out: led early fnl f and kpt on wl: hld on* **14/1**

2 *hd* **Peahen**^{27} [2087] 3-8-12 95 .... JMurtagh 7 99
(G M Lyons, Ire) *slowly away and in rr: sme hdwy on outer early st: drvn along in 9th over 1f out: styd on wl ins fnl f: jst failed* **14/1**

3 *nk* **Knock Stars (IRE)**^{27} [2078] 3-8-12 95 .... PBBeggy 12 98
(Patrick Martin, Ire) *settled towards rr: hdwy fr 2f out: 6th 1f out: kpt on wl u.p wout rching wnr* **14/1**

4 *1 3/4* **Beyond Desire**^{33} [1902] 4-9-6 .... NeilCallan 9 94
(Roger Varian) *trckd ldrs racing keenly: 3rd 2f out: chal over 1f out: no imp u.p ins fnl f* **9/2**^{3}

5 *hd* **Capercaillie (USA)**^{19} [2298] 4-9-6 .... LukeMorris 3 94
(Clive Cox) *trckd ldrs on inner: 7th 1/2-way: pushed along fr early st: rdn and kpt on ins fnl f* **12/1**

6 *1* **Invincible Ash (IRE)**^{75} [996] 6-9-6 111 ....(tp) GFCarroll 1 91
(M Halford, Ire) *trckd ldrs on inner: 3rd 1/2-way: drvn along early st: no ex ins fnl f* **4/1**^{2}

7 *1 1/4* **Tweedy (IRE)**^{19} [2298] 4-9-6 96 .... WMLordan 4 87
(Edward Lynam, Ire) *trckd ldr in 2nd: chal and led briefly over 1f out: no ex ins fnl f* **16/1**

8 *3 1/2* **Sing Softly (USA)**^{19} [2323] 3-8-12 103 .... CO'Donoghue 6 73
(A P O'Brien, Ire) *chsd ldrs: 8th 1/2-way: no ex fr over 1f out* **7/4**^{1}

9 *1* **Dawn Eclipse (IRE)**^{39} [1732] 6-9-6 93 .... BACurtis 10 72
(T G McCourt, Ire) *trckd ldrs on outer: 5th 1/2-way: rdn and no ex fr over 1f out* **20/1**

10 *1 3/4* **Timeless Call (IRE)**^{47} [1532] 3-8-12 93 .... NGMcCullagh 2 65
(Reginald Roberts, Ire) *led: strly pressed 2f out: hdd wl over 1f out: wknd* **7/1**

11 *2 1/2* **Sun Queen (USA)**^{8} [2624] 3-8-12 83 .... SeamieHeffernan 8 57
(A P O'Brien, Ire) *a bhd* **50/1**

1m 13.59s (-0.51) **Going Correction** +0.075s/f (Good)
WFA 3 from 4yo+ 8lb **11** Ran SP% **127.3**
Speed ratings: **106,105,105,103,102 101,99,95,93,91 88**
CSF £210.08 TOTE £18.90: £4.10, £3.40, £5.90; DF 114.70.
Owner Ms Grainne Seoige **Bred** J S Bolger **Trained** Coolcullen, Co Carlow

FOCUS
A prolonged shower before this contest resulted in the rain starting to get into the ground and the official description was changed from good to good to yielding after the race. It has been rated around the third, fourth and fifth.

NOTEBOOK
Radharcnafarraige(IRE) had won twice last season, once at Group 3 level over this trip, and had performed creditably in the Albany Stakes and the Cherry Hinton, finishing fourth in both races. Tried over 1m and over 7f on her two previous attempts this year, she appreciated the drop back in trip and after hitting the front entering the final furlong was all out to hold on in a three-way photo. (op 16/1)
Peahen, another dropping in distance, lost ground at the start and did well to get as close as she did. She still had eight rivals in front of her approaching the final furlong and finished well. Official explanation: jockey said filly missed the break
Knock Stars(IRE) won three nurseries last year and had run well, including second at Listed level over 5f, this season. She produced another good effort here, coming from the back of the field and running on well from over 1f out.
Beyond Desire, runner-up in this event a year ago and having her second outing of the season, didn't help her cause by racing keenly just behind the leaders. (op 9/2 tchd 5/1)
Capercaillie(USA) had finished just in front of Beyond Desire in a similar event over the same trip at Nottingham last month, before running fourth in another Listed event at Haydock. She kept on in the closing stages having come under pressure early in the straight. The rain probably didn't help her chance. (op 12/1 tchd 14/1)
Invincible Ash(IRE) had produced a career-best effort when a close fourth in the Group 2 Al Quoz Sprint (5f) at Meydan in March. A seven-time winner, including at Listed level, she came under pressure under 2f out and could make little impression over the final furlong on ground which was turning against her. Official explanation: jockey said mare did not act on today's easing conditions (op 3/1)
Sing Softly(USA), the Nell Gwyn Stakes runner-up and twice a winner on soft ground this year, had finished fourth in the Group 3 Greenlands Stakes last month on her first attempt against older horses other than in a maiden. Back against her own sex here, she proved disappointing and was beaten early in the straight. Official explanation: jockey said filly was unable to go the early pace and may benefit from stepping back up in trip (op 9/4)

2862 - 2865a (Foreign Racing) - See Raceform Interactive

^{1447}MAISONS-LAFFITTE (R-H)

Thursday, June 9

OFFICIAL GOING: Turf: good to soft

2866a PRIX LA FLECHE (LISTED RACE) (2YO) (TURF) — 5f

4:10 (12:00) 2-Y-0 **£23,706** (£9,482; £7,112; £4,741; £2,370)

RPR

1 **Dijarvo**^{27} [2053] 2-8-10 0 .... DavidProbert 4 97
(Tony Carroll) *broke smartly: racd 2nd: rdn 2f out: qcknd to ld 1 1/2f out: r.o wl fnl f* **93/10**

2 *3/4* **Ponte Vespucci (FR)**^{14} [2446] 2-8-10 0 ...... Christophe-PatriceLemaire 3 94
(Y De Nicolay, France) **23/10**^{1}

3 *1 1/2* **Robert Le Diable (FR)**^{19} 2-9-0 0 .... OlivierPeslier 2 93
(D Prod'Homme, France) **58/10**^{3}

4 *shd* **Louve Rouge (FR)**^{21} 2-8-10 0 .... JohanVictoire 1 89
(C Boutin, France) **8/1**

5 *3* **Uccellina (FR)**^{31} 2-8-10 0 .... Pierre-CharlesBoudot 7 72
(A Fabre, France) **5/2**^{2}

5 *1 1/2* **Sotka**^{19} 2-8-10 0 .... IoritzMendizabal 5 72
(Mme G Rarick, France) **11/1**

7 *2 1/2* **Susukino (FR)**^{21} 2-8-10 0 ....(p) GregoryBenoist 8 63
(S Kobayashi, France) **30/1**

8 *4* **Wakidoun (FR)** 2-9-0 0 .... MaximeGuyon 6 53
(D Allard, France) **17/2**

59.20 secs (59.20) **8** Ran SP% **116.5**
WIN (incl. 1 euro stake): 10.30. PLACES: 2.40, 1.50, 1.80. DF: 15.80. SF: 31.90.
Owner The Dijarvo Partnership **Bred** B Minty **Trained** Cropthorne, Worcs

NOTEBOOK
Dijarvo, whose connections decided to skip Royal Ascot as they didn't believe they could reverse form with Best Terms in the Queen Mary, gained a valuable Listed success with her here.

2867a PRIX D'ANDRESY (CLAIMER) (4YO+) (TURF) — 7f

6:10 (12:00) 4-Y-0+ **£6,465** (£2,586; £1,939; £1,293; £646)

RPR

1 **Jordaura**^{19} [2301] 5-9-2 0 .... DavidProbert 9 82
(Tony Carroll) *racd towards rr: gd prog through field 2f out: hrd rdn to chal ins fnl f: got up on line to win by minimum margin* **13/1**

2 *nse* **Freminius (GER)**^{256} [6408] 7-9-2 0 .... DominiqueBoeuf 11 82
(W Baltromei, Germany) **9/5**^{1}

3 *3* **Tigron (USA)**^{14} 10-8-8 0 ....(b) JulienMagniez$^{(8)}$ 4 74
(Mme C Barande-Barbe, France) **68/10**^{2}

4 *nk* **Glasshoughton**^{604} [6764] 8-9-2 0 .... JohanVictoire 6 73
(T Potters, Germany) **14/1**

5 *snk* **Vianello (IRE)**^{120} [481] 4-8-11 0 ....(b) MaximeGuyon 3 68
(Mario Hofer, Germany) **11/1**

6 *snk* **Selena (FR)**^{239} 4-8-8 0 .... Pierre-CharlesBoudot 8 64
(M Boutin, France) **26/1**

7 *3/4* **Easterland (IRE)**^{94} 5-8-13 0 .... YoannRousset$^{(3)}$ 7 70
(F Chappet, France) **12/1**

8 *nk* **Allez Bailey (FR)**^{21} 5-9-2 0 .... GeraldMosse 1 70
(P Lacroix, France) **89/10**^{3}

9 *1/2* **Poker Face (SWI)**^{42} 4-8-11 0 .... SebastienMaillot 17 63
(U Suter, France) **26/1**

10 *3/4* **Nachos (FR)**^{63} 7-8-6 0 ....(b) StevanBourgois$^{(5)}$ 2 61
(R Chotard, France) **57/1**

0 **Satchmo Bay (FR)**^{330} 10-9-2 0 ....(p) MarcNobili 12 —
(C Boutin, France) **35/1**

0 **Prorisks (FR)**^{21} 5-8-13 0 ....(p) BenjaminBoutin$^{(7)}$ 10 —
(C Boutin, France) **32/1**

0 **Solarea (FR)**^{24} 4-8-8 0 .... FlavienPrat 5 —
(T Clout, France) **13/1**

0 **Elpais (ITY)**^{24} 4-9-2 0 .... StephanePasquier 14 —
(G Botti, Italy) **11/1**

1m 28.8s (88.80) **14** Ran SP% **118.9**
WIN (incl. 1 euro stake): 14.70. PLACES: 3.70, 1.50, 2.20. DF: 20.90. SF: 62.80.
Owner Carl Hodgson **Bred** Pendley Farm **Trained** Cropthorne, Worcs

NOTEBOOK
Jordaura, brought over with Dijarvo, who won a Listed race for the stable earlier on the card, narrowly completed a double for her trainer and rider with their first runners in France.

^{2549}CHEPSTOW (L-H)

Friday, June 10

OFFICIAL GOING: Good to firm (8.2)

Wind: Virtually nil Weather: Overcast, rain race 6

2868 BRITISH STALLION STUDS SUPPORTING BRITISH RACING E B F NOVICE STKS — 6f 16y

6:25 (6:25) (Class 4) 2-Y-0 **£4,468** (£1,329; £664; £331) **Stalls** High

Form RPR

1 **1** **Factory Time (IRE)**^{52} [1451] 2-9-2 0 .... ChrisCatlin 6 87+
(Mick Channon) *on trcking ldrs: led 2f out: drvn along over 1f out: clrd on strly and in command fnl 120yds* **6/4**^{1}

201 **2** *2* **Bling King**^{14} [2448] 2-9-5 0 .... DaneO'Neill 4 83
(Eve Johnson Houghton) *trckd ldrs: chsd wnr wl over 2f out: rdn over 1f out: kpt on but no imp and one pce ins fnl f* **7/1**

1 **3** *2* **Percy Jackson**^{25} [2143] 2-9-5 0 .... NeilCallan 2 77
(Denis Coakley) *chsd ldrs: rdn 3f out: hung lft whn in 3rd over 2f out: no imp fr over 1f out* **9/4**^{2}

416 **4** *3 1/2* **Ortea**^{25} [2154] 2-9-5 0 .... CathyGannon 5 67
(David Evans) *slt ld 3f: wknd into 4th over 2f out* **12/1**

5 *10* **Peak Storm** 2-9-0 0 .... JimCrowley 1 34
(John Gallagher) *wnt lft s: a wl bhd* **66/1**

14 **6** *11* **Sixx**^{15} [2437] 2-9-5 0 .... PatDobbs 3 —
(Richard Hannon) *w ldr 3f: wknd rapidly wl over 2f out* **11/2**^{3}

1m 10.66s (-1.34) **Going Correction** -0.30s/f (Firm) **6** Ran SP% **107.8**
Speed ratings (Par 95): **96,93,90,86,72 58**
Tote Swingers:1&2:£1.90, 2&3:£2.60, 1&3:£1.30 CSF £11.49 TOTE £2.30: £1.60, £1.50; EX 6.90.
Owner Jaber Abdullah **Bred** Tally-Ho Stud **Trained** West Ilsley, Berks

FOCUS
There were a couple of light showers before racing and riders in the first were complimentary about the going, the winning jockey calling it "good, fast flat ground with no jar". A decent novice stakes contested by five previous winners and run in a respectable time. The winner should have more to offer and the standard looks solid rated around the second and third.

NOTEBOOK
Factory Time(IRE) travelled up well and found plenty to shake off the runner-up. He was receiving 3lb from his principal rivals, his debut success at Bath in April having come in a Class 5 maiden auction, but nonetheless looks a useful prospect. He has something more to prove if he is to justify his Group-race entries, however, and raced on the quickest ground here. He should stay further. (op 5-4)
Bling King's yard won this in 2002 with Tout Seul, who went on to land the Dewhurst. This colt was on his toes in the paddock, but it did not prevent him from running a sound race and he was a clear second best. He has done all his racing so far on fast ground. (op 13-2 tchd 15-2)
Percy Jackson was caught wide of his opponents and lacked the pace of the first two but was keeping on inside the last. He will stay further and a less undulating track may suit. (op 3-1)
Ortea, who looked on good terms with himself in the preliminaries, showed pace to dispute the lead but faded under pressure on this first try at 6f. He is able and looks the type for nurseries a little later on. (op 11-1)
Peak Storm, a half-brother to four winners, looked green beforehand. Facing a very stiff task in this company, he went badly left leaving the stalls and was never a factor but he should improve. (op 50-1)

Sixx represented a yard which had won three of the last five runnings of this event, the best of those winners being useful filly Penny's Gift. His fourth in a Listed race last time was perhaps the best form on offer, but he weakened rather quickly after sharing the lead. Whether a stumble after two furlongs had anything to do with this disappointing effort is unclear. He was reported by Pat Dobbs to have run too free, and the stewards ordered the colt to be routine tested. Official explanation: jockey said colt ran too free (op 5-1 tchd 6-1)

2869 ONSHORE MARINE MEDICAL SERVICES BRISTOL MAIDEN H'CAP 6f 16y

6:55 (6:55) (Class 5) (0-70,68) 3-Y-0+ **£2,525** (£751; £375; £187) **Stalls** High

Form RPR

400- **1** **Questionnaire (IRE)**[209] 7447 3-8-9 **57** .... JamesDoyle 8 71
(Nicky Vaughan) *pressed ldrs on stands' side tl led after 2f: drvn clr ins fnl 2f: readily* **25/1**

-643 **2** 3 ½ **Abeer (USA)**[11] 2553 3-9-1 **63** ....(p) JimCrowley 1 66+
(Ed Dunlop) *racd towards centre of crse: drvn and outpcd 1/2-way: hdwy 2f out: rdn to chse wnr 1f out but nvr any ch: jst hld on for 2nd* **6/1**[2]

P-03 **3** nk **Muroona (IRE)**[14] 2479 3-9-0 **62** .... RoystonFfrench 9 64+
(Mark Johnston) *in tch: hmpd and outpcd over 2f out: hdwy over 1f out: styd on u.p to go 3rd fnl 120yds: clsng on 2nd nr fin but no ch w wnr* **12/1**

-63 **4** 1 ½ **Blue Deer (IRE)**[15] 2419 3-9-6 **68** .... SamHitchcott 7 65
(Mick Channon) *chsd ldrs: rdn 2f out: styd on same pce appr fnl f* **13/2**[3]

0-02 **5** 1 ¼ **Sarangoo**[11] 2553 3-8-10 **58** .... NeilCallan 12 51
(Malcolm Saunders) *s.i.s: sn chsng ldrs: wnt 2nd 1/2-way but no imp on wnr: lost 2nd 1f out: wknd fnl 120yds* **13/2**[3]

2-03 **6** 3 ½ **Choose The Moment**[20] 2311 3-9-1 **63** .... DaneO'Neill 6 45
(Eve Johnson Houghton) *chsd ldrs: rdn over 2f out: wknd appr fnl f* **10/1**

6600 **7** 1 ¾ **Colourbearer (IRE)**[9] 2603 4-9-2 **56** .... RichardKingscote 11 34
(Milton Bradley) *s.i.s: sn in tch: rdn 1/2-way: wknd ins fnl 2f* **20/1**

30-4 **8** 1 ¼ **Meia Noite**[23] 2201 4-9-6 **60** .... GeorgeBaker 10 34+
(Chris Wall) *in rr: hdwy and n.m.r over 3f out: nvr in contention after* **4/1**[1]

22-5 **9** ¾ **Suzhou**[23] 2201 4-9-6 **60** ....(v) CathyGannon 2 32
(Denis Coakley) *s.i.s: racd in centre crse: a outpcd* **13/2**[3]

-025 **10** 1 **Ishipink**[4] 2755 4-8-6 **49** oh2........................ MatthewDavies(3) 3 18
(Ron Hodges) *led 2f: racd in centre crse: wknd 2f out* **25/1**

-423 **11** nk **Cristaliyev**[36] 1830 3-8-11 **62** ....(v[1]) KierenFox(3) 4 28
(Jim Boyle) *chsd ldrs in centre crse 4f* **17/2**

-000 **12** 2 ¼ **Excellent Vision**[25] 2142 4-9-1 **55** ....(p) LiamKeniry 5 15
(Milton Bradley) *s.i.s: in tch over 3f* **40/1**

1m 10.22s (-1.78) **Going Correction** -0.30s/f (Firm)
WFA 3 from 4yo 8lb **12** Ran SP% **116.5**
Speed ratings (Par 103): **99,94,93,91,90 85,83,81,80,79 78,75**
Tote Swingers:1&2:£38.70, 2&3:£15.00, 1&3:£43.00 CSF £160.36 CT £1938.21 TOTE £19.30: £7.20, £2.70, £3.70; EX 320.30.
Owner Gordon Kendrick **Bred** Pheroze Sorabjee **Trained** Helshaw Grange, Shropshire

FOCUS
Obviously a moderate race but it went to a progressive sort 12 months ago in Joe Packet. The winner raced on the favoured stands' rail but the form is taken at face value, with the second and third close to their marks.
Meia Noite Official explanation: vet said filly was coughing
Cristaliyev Official explanation: jockey said colt was never travelling

2870 HAMPTON BY HILTON NEWPORT EAST H'CAP 7f 16y

7:30 (7:30) (Class 5) (0-70,70) 4-Y-0+ **£2,525** (£751; £375; £187) **Stalls** High

Form RPR

-050 **1** **Polar Annie**[29] 2027 6-8-13 **62** .... CathyGannon 12 73
(Malcolm Saunders) *s.i.s: in rr: hdwy over 2f out: rdn and str run appr fnl f to ld fnl 150yds: r.o strly* **10/1**

-023 **2** 1 ½ **Fault**[11] 2561 5-9-0 **63** ....(t) NeilCallan 13 70
(Stef Higgins) *hld up in tch: hdwy 2f out: slt ld 1f out: hdd and outpcd fnl 150yds but styd on wl for clr 2nd* **9/2**[2]

-451 **3** 2 ¾ **You've Been Mowed**[17] 2376 5-9-2 **70** .... RyanClark(5) 11 70
(Richard Price) *led: rdn 2f out: hdd 1f out: sn one pce in 3rd: wknd fnl 75yds* **5/2**[1]

0-00 **4** 1 ¼ **Lutine Charlie (IRE)**[29] 2027 4-9-0 **66** .... KierenFox(3) 14 62
(Ronald Harris) *chsd ldr: chal fr 3f out to 1f out: sn wknd* **16/1**

4-00 **5** ½ **Hobson**[3] 2789 6-9-3 **69** ....(b) SimonPearce(3) 8 64
(Eve Johnson Houghton) *chsd ldrs: chal fr 2f out to 1f out: sn wknd* **16/1**

0321 **6** hd **Emiratesdotcom**[11] 2554 5-9-3 **66** 6ex........................ LiamKeniry 5 60
(Milton Bradley) *in rr but in tch: hdwy to chse ldrs ins fnl 2f: wknd fnl f* **8/1**

310 **7** 3 ¼ **El Libertador (USA)**[8] 2653 5-8-11 **60** ....(b) ChrisCatlin 1 46
(Jeremy Gask) *in rr tl styd on fnl f: nvr a threat* **22/1**

2534 **8** 1 ¾ **Hand Painted**[36] 1838 5-9-3 **66** .... TravisBlock 4 47
(Peter Makin) *chsd ldrs tl wknd over 1f out* **14/1**

41-0 **9** 5 **Hippique**[20] 2313 4-8-13 **62** .... JamesDoyle 10 29
(Jeremy Gask) *chsd ldrs tl wknd over 2f out* **33/1**

6202 **10** 1 ¼ **Play The Blues (IRE)**[15] 2426 4-8-13 **67** .... RyanPowell(5) 7 31
(Mark Allen) *rn wout declared tongue strap: chsd ldrs 4f* **10/1**

6013 **11** ¾ **Cape Kimberley**[17] 2376 4-8-5 **61** .... DavidKenny(7) 2 23
(Tony Newcombe) *s.i.s: sme prog into mid-div 1/2-way: sn wknd* **7/1**[3]

-406 **12** 4 **Exceedingly Bold**[51] 1488 4-9-5 **68** ....(t) DaneO'Neill 9 19
(Jo Crowley) *s.i.s: a in rr* **14/1**

1m 21.37s (-1.83) **Going Correction** -0.30s/f (Firm) **12** Ran SP% **120.9**
Speed ratings (Par 103): **98,96,93,91,91 90,87,85,79,78 77,72**
Tote Swingers:1&2:£16.10, 2&3:£3.50, 1&3:£11.70 CSF £55.70 CT £145.67 TOTE £13.30: £3.70, £1.40, £1.40; EX 35.30.
Owner Lockstone Business Services Ltd **Bred** Cobhall Court Stud **Trained** Green Ore, Somerset

FOCUS
An open and competitive handicap for the grade, but those racing nearest the stands' rail dominated with the first four home coming out of the top four boxes. The form should therefore be treated with a degree of caution. The winner was closely matched with the favourite on last July's C&D win, and showed her best form since.
Play The Blues(IRE) Official explanation: jockey said fillies tongue strap came loose going into stalls

2871 LINDLEY CATERING MAIDEN FILLIES' STKS 1m 4f 23y

8:05 (8:07) (Class 5) 3-Y-0+ **£2,525** (£751; £375; £187) **Stalls** Low

Form RPR

4-5 **1** **Schism**[28] 2065 3-8-12 0........................ DaneO'Neill 11 75
(Henry Candy) *s.i.s: sn rcvrd to trck ldr: drvn to chal over 2f out: rdn to ld fnl 140yds: sn in command: readily* **3/1**[2]

-32 **2** 1 ½ **Oneiric**[18] 2371 3-8-12 0........................ JimCrowley 8 72
(Ralph Beckett) *led: drvn whn jnd over 2f out: hdd and outpcd fnl 140yds* **7/4**[1]

66 **3** 2 ¼ **Golden City (IRE)**[22] 2218 3-8-12 0........................ ChrisCatlin 9 68
(Chris Wall) *trckd ldrs in 3rd: pushed along under hand driving fnl 3f: nvr gng pce of ldng duo but kpt on wl fnl f* **8/1**

0 **4** 2 ½ **Ace Serve**[29] 2026 3-8-12 0........................ NeilCallan 6 64
(Roger Varian) *chsd ldrs in 4th: rdn and one pce fnl 3f* **9/2**[3]

02 **5** 2 ¼ **Host The Band**[22] 2235 7-9-6 0........................ DavidKenny(7) 12 60
(Tony Newcombe) *in tch: pushed along and hdwy 4f out: nvr rchd ldrs and outpcd fnl 2f* **12/1**

6 nk **Cluain Dara (IRE)** 3-8-12 0........................ RoystonFfrench 7 60+
(Mark Johnston) *rn green: n.m.r after s: faltered and bhd: drvn and hdwy 3f out: styd on fnl f but nvr in contention* **9/1**

00-0 **7** ½ **Princesse Fleur**[12] 2528 3-8-12 0........................ JamieGoldstein 5 59?
(Michael Scudamore) *chsd ldrs: rdn 4f out: wknd ins fnl 3f* **50/1**

60 **8** 7 **La Belle Au Bois (IRE)**[8] 2639 5-9-8 0........................ LeeNewnes(5) 4 48
(Nick Lampard) *bhd most of way* **50/1**

9 1 ½ **Hope Point** 3-8-12 0........................ LiamKeniry 10 46
(Mark Usher) *slowly away: a bhd* **33/1**

5 **10** 37 **Sally Anne**[23] 2195 3-8-12 0........................ JimmyQuinn 1 —
(John Holt) *slowly away: a wl bhd: t.o* **66/1**

2m 38.63s (-0.37) **Going Correction** 0.0s/f (Good)
WFA 3 from 5yo+ 15lb **10** Ran SP% **116.7**
Speed ratings (Par 100): **101,100,98,96,95 95,94,90,89,64**
Tote Swingers:1&2:£2.80, 2&3:£3.80, 1&3:£3.20 CSF £8.51 TOTE £4.10: £1.40, £1.30, £1.90; EX 9.80.
Owner Major M G Wyatt **Bred** Ashbrittle Stud **Trained** Kingston Warren, Oxon

FOCUS
A modest fillies' maiden, run at a fairly steady pace. The principals were always prominent and the form has been rated around the runner-up.
Cluain Dara(IRE) Official explanation: jockey said filly was slowly away

2872 OFFICE IMAGE H'CAP 1m 2f 36y

8:40 (8:40) (Class 5) (0-75,74) 4-Y-0+ **£2,525** (£751; £375; £187) **Stalls** Low

Form RPR

3252 **1** **Yes Chef**[17] 2378 4-9-7 **74** .... JamesMillman 2 81
(Rod Millman) *mde all and set modest pce tl qcknd over 3f out: shkn up over 1f out and styd on strly: unchal* **5/4**[1]

12-0 **2** 2 **Hurakan (IRE)**[17] 2378 5-9-5 **72** ....(t) TonyCulhane 8 76
(George Baker) *chsd ldrs off mod pce: drvn and hdwy over 2f out to chse wnr wl over 1f out: kpt on but a wl hld* **9/1**[3]

-014 **3** 1 ¾ **Bold Cross (IRE)**[17] 2376 8-9-1 **68** .... CathyGannon 4 68+
(Edward Bevan) *s.i.s: t.k.h and stdd in rr off mod pce: drvn whn pce qcknd over 3f out: styd on fr over 1f out to take 3rd ins fnl f but nt rch 2nd and no ch w wnr* **9/1**[3]

20-6 **4** 1 **Sagredo (USA)**[15] 2436 7-9-6 **73** .... GeorgeBaker 9 71
(Jonjo O'Neill) *in rr but in tch off mod pce: rdn whn pce qcknd over 3f out: styd on fnl 2f but nvr any threat* **3/1**[2]

5-56 **5** 1 ¾ **Mister Fantastic**[16] 1828 5-8-2 **55** oh8........................ KellyHarrison 5 49
(Dai Burchell) *racd in 2nd as wnr set mod pce: rdn whn gallop increased over 3f out but nvr quite on terms: lost 2nd wl over 1f out: wknd fnl f* **25/1**

20-5 **6** nse **Oriental Girl**[17] 2378 6-9-3 **70** ....(p) LiamKeniry 7 64
(Jonathan Geake) *in rr but in tch off modest pce tl gallop increased over 3f out and sme prog: one pce fnl 2f* **9/1**[3]

06-6 **7** nk **Ashkalara**[35] 1868 4-8-10 **63** .... JimmyQuinn 6 56
(Stuart Howe) *stdd s: t.k.h in rr off mod pce: rdn and effrt whn gallop increased over 3f out: one pce fnl 2f* **14/1**

55-6 **8** 1 ¾ **Sentosa**[11] 2562 4-9-3 **70** .... DaneO'Neill 3 60
(Michael Blanshard) *chsd ldrs off mod pce: rdn whn gallop increased over 3f out: wknd over 1f out* **20/1**

2m 9.72s (-0.88) **Going Correction** 0.0s/f (Good) **8** Ran SP% **114.7**
Speed ratings (Par 103): **103,101,100,99,97 97,97,96**
Tote Swingers:1&2:£3.20, 2&3:£4.40, 1&3:£2.40 CSF £13.86 CT £72.40 TOTE £2.00: £1.20, £2.60, £2.50; EX 13.30.
Owner Coombeshead Racing **Bred** Percys (north Harrow) Ltd **Trained** Kentisbeare, Devon

FOCUS
An ordinary handicap run at a steady pace. The winner got an easy lead and recorded a small personal best.

2873 FESTIVAL RACING H'CAP 2m 49y

9:10 (9:10) (Class 6) (0-65,65) 4-Y-0+ **£1,813** (£539; £269; £134) **Stalls** Low

Form RPR

0-41 **1** **Spinning Waters**[17] 2377 5-8-9 **50** .... KellyHarrison 5 57
(Dai Burchell) *trckd ldrs: led 3f out: rdn 2f out: narrowly hdd ins fnl f: rallied gamely to ld again last stride* **5/1**[2]

31-5 **2** shd **Salontyre (GER)**[35] 1847 5-9-10 **65** ....(p) DavidProbert 4 72
(Bernard Llewellyn) *chsd ldrs: drvn to chal over 1f out: led ins fnl f: kpt on u.p: ct last stride* **10/3**[1]

30/2 **3** nk **Orbital Orchid**[17] 2377 6-8-13 **54** .... DaneO'Neill 2 60
(Nick Williams) *mid-div: dropped to rr 6f out: rdn and hdwy over 2f out: styd on strly u.p thrght fnl f: nt quite rch ldng duo* **5/1**[2]

0254 **4** 1 **Miles Of Sunshine**[7] 2659 6-8-9 **53** .... MatthewDavies(3) 6 58
(Ron Hodges) *s.i.s: in rr: hdwy and swtchd rt to outside over 2f out: styd on wl thrght fnl f but nt rch ldrs* **16/1**

445- **5** 2 ½ **The Composer**[10] 6416 9-8-5 **46** oh1........................ JimmyQuinn 12 48
(Michael Blanshard) *in rr: rdn and hdwy over 2f out: styd on same pce ins fnl f and no imp on ldrs* **13/2**[3]

-462 **6** 2 **Now What**[11] 2552 4-9-8 **64** .... JimCrowley 8 64
(Jonathan Portman) *in tch: chsd ldrs 10f out: drvn to chal over 1f: no ex and wknd ins fnl f* **8/1**

55 **7** 1 ¾ **Court Wing (IRE)**[12] 2526 5-8-9 **50** .... CathyGannon 10 48
(Richard Price) *in rr: rdn and hdwy on outside over 2f out: no imp over 1f out: wknd fnl f* **9/1**

-253 **8** 2 ¼ **Stormy Morning**[34] 1914 5-9-10 **65** ....(p) LiamKeniry 1 60
(J S Moore) *chsd ldr tl led 11f out: hdd 3f out: wknd over 1f out* **12/1**

0-01 **9** 9 **Blazing Buck**[16] 2400 5-8-12 **53** .... FrannyNorton 3 37
(Tony Carroll) *chsd ldrs: rdn 3f out: btn over 2f out* **10/1**

0-00 **10** 15 **Nobbys Girl**[31] 1973 6-8-5 **46** oh1........................ ChrisCatlin 7 12
(Ronald Harris) *led 5f: wknd 3f out* **66/1**

3m 39.18s (0.28) **Going Correction** 0.0s/f (Good)
WFA 4 from 5yo+ 1lb **10** Ran SP% **115.0**
Speed ratings (Par 101): **99,98,98,98,97 96,95,94,89,82**
Tote Swingers:1&2:£5.30, 2&3:£3.50, 1&3:£6.00 CSF £21.69 CT £87.28 TOTE £5.40: £1.70, £1.10, £2.30; EX 12.60.
Owner B M G Group **Bred** R E Crutchley **Trained** Briery Hill, Blaenau Gwent

FOCUS
Run in the rain, this was a very moderate staying handicap but probably a decent race for the grade. The pace was only steady before picking up in the straight, and there was something of a bunch finish. The winner, third and fourth met over C&D latest and showed similar form.

Miles Of Sunshine Official explanation: jockey said gelding hung left handed throughout
The Composer Official explanation: jockey said gelding stumbled in the back straight
T/Plt: £20.60 to a £1 stake. Pool:£55,004.77 - 1,946.52 winning tickets T/Qpdt: £3.60 to a £1 stake. Pool:£5,712.45 - 1,160.79 winning tickets ST

2685 GOODWOOD (R-H)

Friday, June 10

OFFICIAL GOING: Good to firm (good in places; 8.4)
Wind: Mild breeze against Weather: sunny with some cloud

2874 TOYO TIRES MAIDEN H'CAP — 1m 6f

6:15 (6:16) (Class 5) (0-75,74) 3-Y-O — **£2,590** (£770; £385; £192) **Stalls** High

Form — RPR

-332 **1** **Cunning Act**[22] 2226 3-9-4 **71** .... StephenCraine 2 — 83
(Jonathan Portman) *hld up towards rr: hdwy fr 4f out: rdn to chal over 1f out: kpt on u.str.p to ld fnl stride* **14/1**

243 **2** *shd* **Stagecoach Danman (IRE)**[14] 2458 3-9-7 **74** .... JoeFanning 9 — 85
(Mark Johnston) *led after 1f: rdn 2f out: kpt on gamely fnl f: hdd fnl stride* **3/1**[1]

-353 **3** *2 ½* **Bow River Arch (USA)**[35] 1872 3-9-4 **71** ....(p) RyanMoore 4 — 79
(Jeremy Noseda) *mid-div: hdwy over 2f out: sn rdn: styd on to chse ldng pair ent fnl f: no ex nring fin* **9/2**[2]

0425 **4** *4* **Lemon Drop Red (USA)**[16] 2407 3-8-9 **62** .... RichardHughes 11 — 64
(Ed Dunlop) *in tch: pushed along briefly over 3f out: nt clr run whn swtchd rt 2f out: sn rdn: styd on same pce fnl f* **12/1**

0-03 **5** *1 ¾* **Fleeting Tiger**[22] 2225 3-8-2 **55** oh1 .... NickyMackay 10 — 55
(John Dunlop) *trckd ldrs: rdn 2f out: hung rt over 1f out: one pce fnl f* **7/1**[3]

-060 **6** *1* **Sum Satisfaction**[22] 2225 3-8-6 **59** .... HayleyTurner 5 — 57
(Dominic Ffrench Davis) *t.k.h: hld up towards rr: rapid hdwy to trck ldrs over 6f out: rdn over 3f out: fdd fnl f* **33/1**

0-34 **7** *2 ¾* **Deceptive**[22] 2225 3-8-9 **62** .... SteveDrowne 1 — 56
(Roger Charlton) *mid-div tl dropped to rr over 5f out: rdn whn swtchd lft over 2f out: little imp* **9/1**

460 **8** *3 ¾* **Star Alliance (IRE)**[22] 2218 3-8-12 **65** .... MartinLane 7 — 54
(John Dunlop) *a towards rr* **16/1**

6-23 **9** *nk* **Madrasa (IRE)**[22] 2218 3-9-5 **72** .... JamieSpencer 8 — 61
(Ed McMahon) *led for 1f: trckd ldr: rdn 3f out: short of room wl over 1f out: sn wknd* **7/1**[3]

043- **10** *5* **Dictate**[192] 7644 3-9-5 **72** .... DarryllHolland 6 — 54
(Mark H Tompkins) *dwlt: rdn over 3f out: a in rr* **25/1**

0-25 **11** *4* **Circus Star (USA)**[28] 2076 3-9-4 **71** .... MartinDwyer 3 — 47
(Brian Meehan) *trckd ldrs tl lost pl after being squeezed up 6f out: in tch: rdn over 3f out: wknd over 2f out* **8/1**

3m 6.64s (3.04) **Going Correction** +0.125s/f (Good) — **11** Ran SP% **116.3**
Speed ratings (Par 99): **96,95,94,92,91 90,89,86,86,83 81**
Tote Swingers:1&2:£7.30, 2&3:£3.30, 1&3:£12.70 CSF £55.22 CT £226.23 TOTE £10.20: £3.00, £1.70, £1.10; EX 31.90.
Owner M J Vandenberghe **Bred** The Hon Mrs R Pease **Trained** Compton, Berks
■ Stewards' Enquiry : Stephen Craine one-day ban; excessive use of whip (24th June)

FOCUS
Top bend dolled out 3yds; lower bend dolled out 4yds. A dry night but, although 3mm of rain fell in the morning, one leading rider described the ground as perfect. Several unexposed sorts in a fair handicap and one in which only a couple had previously run over this trip. An ordinary gallop increased passing the three furlong pole and the first three finished a few lengths clear. The form is rated fairly positively.

2875 FRANKIE'S 24TH ANNIVERSARY MAIDEN STKS — 1m

6:45 (6:46) (Class 5) 3-Y-O — **£2,590** (£770; £385; £192) **Stalls** Low

Form — RPR

\- **1** **Galiando** 3-9-3 0 .... JimmyFortune 6 — 85+
(Jeremy Noseda) *hld up in tch: pushed along whn swtchd to centre over 3f out: rdn and stdy hdwy over 2f out: wnt 3rd 1f out: str run fnl 100yds to ld nring fin* **8/1**[3]

23 **2** *½* **Cala Santanyi**[35] 1853 3-8-12 0 .... RyanMoore 8 — 78
(Gerard Butler) *broke wl: sn stdd bhd ldr: led over 1f out: sn rdn whn strly pressed: kpt on: hdd fnl 30yds* **11/10**[1]

4-52 **3** *nk* **Puttingonthestyle (IRE)**[18] 2368 3-9-3 77 ....(v[1]) RichardHughes 1 — 82
(Richard Hannon) *trckd ldr: rdn for str chal fr over 1f out: ev ch fnl f: kpt on* **2/1**[2]

30- **4** *5* **Sally Friday (IRE)**[253] 6511 3-8-12 0 .... LukeMorris 7 — 65
(Peter Winkworth) *s.i.s: in last pair but in tch: rdn wl over 2f out: wnt 4th ins fnl f: nvr gng pce to threaten* **12/1**

4-36 **5** *2 ½* **Proper Charlie**[17] 2391 3-8-12 70 .... HarryBentley(5) 5 — 64
(William Knight) *trckd ldrs: rdn 2f out: wknd ins fnl f* **20/1**

0 **6** *2 ½* **Pagan Warrior (IRE)**[58] 1315 3-9-3 0 ....(t) AdamKirby 4 — 58
(Clive Cox) *sn drvn to ld: rdn over 2f out: hdd over 1f out: wknd* **12/1**

0050 **7** *8* **Emmeline Pankhurst (IRE)**[10] 2583 3-8-12 52 .... DarryllHolland 2 — 34
(Julia Feilden) *in tch: rdn over 2f out: wknd over 1f out* **40/1**

0- **8** *12* **Amor Patrice**[224] 7203 3-9-3 0 .... RobertHavlin 3 — 10
(Les Hall) *hld up in last pair but in tch: rdn 3f out: wknd 2f out* **100/1**

1m 40.96s (1.06) **Going Correction** +0.125s/f (Good) — **8** Ran SP% **115.6**
Speed ratings (Par 99): **99,98,98,93,90 88,80,68**
Tote Swingers:1&2:£3.10, 2&3:£1.02, 1&3:£3.30 CSF £17.37 TOTE £10.50: £2.80, £1.10, £1.10; EX 19.00.
Owner Bluehills Racing Limited **Bred** Hesmonds Stud Ltd **Trained** Newmarket, Suffolk

FOCUS
Group 1-placed Indian Creek won this in 2001 and this has also gone to smart performers Three Graces (2003) and Dansili Dancer (2005) but, although this bare form is no more than fair, it'll be a bit of a surprise if the winner doesn't step up a fair way on this in due course. Not the most competitive of races and just an ordinary gallop in which the first three (including both market leaders) pulled clear in the closing stages. The form looks sound enough.

2876 GOLF AT GOODWOOD STKS (H'CAP) — 7f

7:20 (7:25) (Class 4) (0-85,84) 4-Y-O+ — **£4,533** (£1,348; £674; £336) **Stalls** Low

Form — RPR

00-0 **1** **Truism**[20] 2310 5-9-3 **80** .... RyanMoore 12 — 95
(Amanda Perrett) *hld up towards rr: pushed along and stdy prog fr 2f out: str run whn rdn ent fnl f: led fnl 120yds: won gng away* **4/1**[2]

42-4 **2** *3* **Valencha**[20] 2313 4-8-9 **72** .... RichardHughes 4 — 79
(Hughie Morrison) *hld up towards rr: pushed along and hdwy over 3f out: swtchd lft whn nt clr run 2f out: sn rdn: styd on to have ev ch v briefly fnl 120yds: nt pce of wnr* **3/1**[1]

0-05 **3** *¾* **Huzzah (IRE)**[20] 2310 6-9-0 **77** .... MichaelHills 3 — 82
(B W Hills) *led: rdn 2f out: kpt on gamely but no ex whn hdd fnl 120yds* **6/1**[3]

0355 **4** *¾* **Seek The Fair Land**[20] 2300 5-9-2 **79** ....(b) PatCosgrave 7 — 82
(Jim Boyle) *mid-div: hdwy over 3f out: rdn over 2f out: chsd ldr over 1f out tl hung rt ent fnl f: kpt on same pce* **15/2**

-250 **5** *1 ¼* **Shifting Star (IRE)**[35] 1854 6-9-7 **84** .... AdamKirby 2 — 83
(Walter Swinburn) *in tch: rdn to chse ldrs over 2f out: styng on at same pce whn short of room jst ins fnl f* **9/1**

-060 **6** *2* **Mujood**[36] 1834 8-9-2 **84** .... AmyScott(5) 9 — 78
(Eve Johnson Houghton) *v reluctant to go down and led fnl 3f to stalls where virtually ref to go bhd: sn pushed along in rr: rdn over 3f out: hdwy over 1f out: no further imp fnl f* **16/1**

-035 **7** *8* **Nezami (IRE)**[15] 2428 6-8-11 **74** .... MartinLane 6 — 46
(John Akehurst) *mid-div tl outpcd over 3f out: wknd over 1f out* **12/1**

0420 **8** *2 ¼* **Bowmaker**[17] 2390 4-9-6 **83** .... JoeFanning 1 — 49
(Mark Johnston) *trckd ldr tl rdn 3f out: wknd over 1f out* **9/1**

0-0 **9** *4* **Bashir Biyoum Zain (IRE)**[35] 1854 4-9-5 **82** .... HayleyTurner 11 — 38
(Amy Weaver) *sn pushed along to chse ldrs: rdn over 3f out: wknd 2f out* **9/1**

62-0 **10** *1* **Darcey**[10] 2597 5-8-7 **73** .... JohnFahy(3) 10 — 26
(Amy Weaver) *sn pushed along to chse ldr: rdn over 3f out: wkng whn sltly hmpd over 2f out* **33/1**

1m 26.75s (-0.15) **Going Correction** +0.125s/f (Good) — **10** Ran SP% **117.6**
Speed ratings (Par 105): **105,101,100,99,98 96,87,84,79,78**
Tote Swingers:1&2:£2.30, 2&3:£2.70, 1&3:£5.90 CSF £16.57 CT £73.20 TOTE £5.00: £2.10, £1.60, £2.20; EX 11.80.
Owner George Materna & John McInerney **Bred** Juddmonte Farms Ltd **Trained** Pulborough, W Sussex
■ Stewards' Enquiry : Richard Hughes one-day ban; careless riding (24th June)

FOCUS
Mainly exposed performers in a reasonable handicap. The gallop seemed an ordinary one but the first two came from off the pace. The winner is rated back to his best with the second to form.
Truism Official explanation: trainer said regarding apparent improvement in form gelding wasb suited by the track

2877 CRIMBOURNE STUD STKS (H'CAP) — 1m 1f 192y

7:55 (7:55) (Class 3) (0-90,88) 3-Y-O — **£7,447** (£2,216; £1,107; £553) **Stalls** Low

Form — RPR

1-31 **1** **Club Oceanic**[23] 2188 3-9-7 **88** ....(p) FrankieDettori 4 — 98+
(Jeremy Noseda) *hld up in last pair: hdwy 3f out: rdn through gap to chal over 1f out: led fnl 130yds: drvn out* **5/4**[1]

2-31 **2** *nk* **Zain Shamardal (IRE)**[28] 2068 3-9-4 **85** .... MartinDwyer 8 — 94
(Brian Meehan) *hld up in tch: hdwy into narrow ld wl over 2f out: sn rdn: hdd fnl 130yds: kpt on but no ex* **11/4**[2]

10-5 **3** *2 ½* **Profondo Rosso (IRE)**[34] 1903 3-8-13 **80** ....(v[1]) RyanMoore 7 — 84
(Sir Michael Stoute) *trckd ldrs: rdn and ev ch wl over 2f out tl ent fnl f: kpt on same pce* **10/1**

31-0 **4** *½* **Rutland Boy**[30] 2008 3-8-10 **77** .... JamieSpencer 6 — 80+
(Ed Dunlop) *hld up last: rdn 3f out: no imp tl edgd rt and styd on ent fnl f: wnt 4th nr fin* **16/1**

-133 **5** *½* **Little Black Book (IRE)**[22] 2230 3-8-10 **77** .... DarryllHolland 2 — 79
(Gerard Butler) *hld up in tch: trck ldrs wl over 2f out: sn rdn: nvr quite upsides ldrs: kpt on same pce* **11/2**[3]

3-41 **6** *1 ½* **Tiger Webb**[23] 2203 3-8-12 **86** .... CharlesEddery(7) 1 — 85
(Sir Henry Cecil) *prom: rdn to chal 3f out tl over 1f out: fdd ins fnl f* **8/1**

215- **7** *2* **One Lucky Lady**[205] 7481 3-8-8 **75** .... MichaelHills 5 — 70
(B W Hills) *led: rdn 3f out: sn hdd: wknd fnl f* **33/1**

31-6 **8** *2* **Mr Perceptive (IRE)**[31] 1983 3-8-10 **77** .... RichardHughes 3 — 68
(Richard Hannon) *trckd ldrs: rdn 2f out: wknd over 1f out: sltly hmpd jst ins fnl f* **25/1**

2m 9.31s (1.31) **Going Correction** +0.125s/f (Good) — **8** Ran SP% **119.4**
Speed ratings (Par 103): **99,98,96,96,95 94,93,91**
Tote Swingers:1&2:£1.20, 2&3:£6.70, 1&3:£5.10 CSF £5.06 CT £23.55 TOTE £2.30: £1.10, £1.80, £2.60; EX 4.20.
Owner Sir Robert Ogden **Bred** Card Bloodstock **Trained** Newmarket, Suffolk

FOCUS
A useful handicap in which all of the eight were winners. The gallop was a steady one to halfway but the first two, who pulled clear late on, are progressive sorts and this race should throw up winners. The winner rates up 5lb.

NOTEBOOK
Club Oceanic ◆, with the cheekpieces on again, appreciated the step up in trip and showed a good attitude to defy this 6lb rise in the weights. He'd have been even better suited by a better gallop at this trip and this progressive sort, who was having only his fifth start, left the impression that there's even more to come. He will reportedly be targeted for a race at the Glorious meeting here. (op 11-8 tchd 6-4)
Zain Shamardal(IRE) ◆, whose Newmarket victory threw up several subsequent winners, showed he was even better over this longer trip - in a race that didn't place the full emphasis on stamina at least. He pulled clear of the remainder in the last 100yds and won't always bump into such a progressive rival. He looks sure to win another race. (op 5-2)
Profondo Rosso(IRE), with the visor on for the first time, had the run of the race and was anything but disgraced against a couple of progressive rivals to post his best effort in handicaps. A stronger overall gallop may have suited better and he may be even better with more give underfoot. (tchd 11-1)
Rutland Boy ◆, who wasn't disgraced on his reappearance in a useful handicap at York, caught the eye in a race that wasn't really run to suit. As with several of these, he'd have been much better suited by a stronger pace and he is well worth another chance over this trip granted a better gallop. (tchd 20-1)
Little Black Book(IRE) has been running creditably in turf handicaps over this trip but, while unable to build on that form in this muddling event, he was far from disgraced and should continue to give a good account. (op 7-1)
Tiger Webb, who won an uncompetitive maiden in good style on his previous start, was well placed in a race in which the pace was found out in this stronger company after being raised a fairly harsh-looking 8lb for that win. He'll have to improve to defy this mark. (tchd 9-1)
Mr Perceptive(IRE)'s rider reported he was unsuited by the good to firm ground and the undulating nature of the course. Official explanation: jockey said gelding was unsuited by ground and undulating track

2878 HILDON STKS (H'CAP) — 6f

8:30 (8:31) (Class 4) (0-85,84) 3-Y-O — **£4,533** (£1,348; £674; £336) **Stalls** High

Form — RPR

01-2 **1** **St Augustine (IRE)**[21] 2255 3-9-3 **80** .... LukeMorris 2 — 89+
(John Best) *trckd ldrs: led over 2f out: rdn clr fnl f: eased nr fin* **7/2**[1]

4-30 **2** *½* **Whaileyy (IRE)**[13] 2503 3-9-4 **81** ....(v[1]) RyanMoore 4 — 86
(Sir Michael Stoute) *trckd ldrs: upsides wnr over 2f out: sn rdn: kpt on but nt pce of wnr ent fnl f* **7/2**[1]

1136 **3** *1* **Apollo D'Negro (IRE)**[13] 2508 3-8-9 **75**........................(p) JohnFahy(3) 3 77
(Clive Cox) *hld up wl in tch: trckd ldrs over 2f out: sn rdn: kpt on same pce fnl f* **9/2**[2]

3-06 **4** *nk* **Admirable Spirit**[13] 2503 3-9-7 **84**................................ RichardHughes 7 85
(Richard Hannon) *cl up: rdn 2f out: kpt on but nt pce to chal* **7/1**[3]

1115 **5** *1* **Chevise (IRE)**[7] 2690 3-9-0 **82**...................................... HarryBentley(5) 1 80
(Steve Woodman) *cl up: rdn 2f out: kpt on same pce fnl f* **14/1**

-145 **6** *4 ½* **Yair Hill (IRE)**[20] 2319 3-9-1 **78**..............................(b¹) EddieAhern 6 61
(John Dunlop) *s.i.s: hdwy to trck ldrs over 4f out: effrt 2f out: wknd fnl f* **7/2**[1]

1400 **7** *5* **Greenflash**[20] 2313 3-8-9 **72**.. JamieSpencer 5 39
(Richard Hannon) *led tl over 2f out: sn wknd* **14/1**

2253 **8** *2 ¼* **Welsh Inlet (IRE)**[4] 2757 3-8-2 **65**...................................... JoeFanning 8 25
(John Bridger) *hung rt thrght: w ldr tl over 2f out: no ch whn hung bdly rt to centre over 1f out* **14/1**

1m 12.4s (0.20) **Going Correction** +0.125s/f (Good) **8 Ran SP% 117.3**
Speed ratings (Par 101): **103,102,101,100,99 93,86,83**
Tote Swingers:1&2:£4.60, 2&3:£3.30, 1&3:£5.00 CSF £16.26 CT £56.08 TOTE £4.60: £1.80, £1.30, £2.10; EX 12.40.
Owner B Malt, S Malcolm & A Longman **Bred** Paget Bloodstock **Trained** Hucking, Kent

FOCUS
Not too many in-form types but a reasonable handicap that went to the least exposed runner. The gallop was a decent one and this form should prove reliable, with the second and third rated to their marks.
Welsh Inlet(IRE) Official explanation: jockey said filly hung right

2879 TANQUERAY H'CAP 6f
9:00 (9:00) (Class 5) (0-70,75) 4-Y-0+ **£2,590** (£770; £385; £192) **Stalls** High

Form RPR

-322 **1** **Volito**[14] 2447 5-9-0 **63**.. RichardHughes 2 73+
(Anabel K Murphy) *hld up: hdwy whn nt clr run and swtchd to stands' side rail 2f out: swtchd rt to chal ins fnl f sn led: comf* **3/1**[2]

03-4 **2** *¾* **C'Mon You Irons (IRE)**[39] 1770 6-8-13 **62**.....................(b) IanMongan 1 68
(Mark Hoad) *led: rdn 2f out: kpt on but no ex whn hdd fnl 130yds* **10/1**

1311 **3** *3 ¾* **Dashwood**[9] 2609 4-9-12 **75** 6ex...........................(t) WilliamCarson 8 69
(Giles Bravery) *chsd ldrs: rdn over 2f out: kpt being leaned on by chalr: nt pce to get on terms* **11/8**[1]

-540 **4** *1 ¾* **Seamus Shindig**[27] 2095 9-9-2 **70**.................................... AmyScott(5) 3 58
(Henry Candy) *hld up: hdwy to chse ldrs 3f out: sn rdn and hung lft: kpt on same pce fnl f* **4/1**[3]

6400 **5** *3 ½* **Starwatch**[24] 2179 4-8-7 **61**.. HarryBentley(5) 4 38
(John Bridger) *chsd ldrs tl rdn over 2f out: wknd over 1f out* **8/1**

5446 **6** *½* **Simple Rhythm**[11] 2547 5-8-6 **55**.....................................(p) MartinLane 5 30
(John Ryan) *trckd ldr: rdn over 2f out: wknd over 1f out* **20/1**

1m 12.72s (0.52) **Going Correction** +0.125s/f (Good) **6 Ran SP% 112.1**
Speed ratings (Par 103): **101,100,95,92,88 87**
Tote Swingers:1&2:£5.70, 2&3:£1.50, 1&3:£1.70 CSF £30.59 CT £56.49 TOTE £2.90: £1.10, £2.50; EX 17.10.
Owner Mrs Anabel K Murphy **Bred** A J And Mrs L Brazier **Trained** Wilmcote, Warwicks

FOCUS
Not a strong handicaps, even for the grade, but a decent gallop and the first two pulled clear late on. They raced on the rail which may or may not have been significant. The form is rated around the runner-up.
T/Plt: £8.30 to a £1 stake. Pool:£67,214.97 - 5,870.26 winning tickets T/Qpdt: £4.30 to a £1 stake. Pool:£4,157.33 - 711.24 winning tickets TM

2644 SANDOWN (R-H)
Friday, June 10

OFFICIAL GOING: Sprint course - good to soft (good in places); round course - good (good to soft in places) (7.3) changing to good to soft after race 4 (4.00)
Wind: Virtually nil. Weather: bright spells and showers

2880 IRISH STALLION FARMS E B F MAIDEN STKS 5f 6y
2:20 (2:20) (Class 5) 2-Y-0 **£3,885** (£1,156; £577; £288) **Stalls** Low

Form RPR

32 **1** **Verbeeck**[18] 2355 2-9-3 0... JamieSpencer 5 78
(Ed McMahon) *broke wl: chsd ldr: sltly outpcd 2f out: rdn and effrt over 1f out: led ins fnl f: kpt on wl* **15/8**[1]

0 **2** *¾* **Orders From Rome (IRE)**[20] 2291 2-9-3 0...................... TomQueally 1 76+
(Eve Johnson Houghton) *hld up in tch: nt clr run wl over 1f out: switching lft fr over 1f out: in the clr and r.o wl ins fnl f: chsd wnr fnl 75yds: r.o wl* **9/1**

52 **3** *1 ¾* **Dream Whisperer**[38] 1785 2-8-12 0..................................... NeilCallan 2 64
(Dominic Ffrench Davis) *pushed along early: led after 1f: rdn and forged clr wl over 1f out: sn drvn: hdd ins fnl f: wknd and edgd rt fnl 75yds* **12/1**

4 *1 ¼* **El Diamante (FR)** 2-8-12 0.. RichardHughes 7 64+
(Richard Hannon) *s.i.s: wl bhd in last trio: nudged along and clsd 1/2-way: nt clr run and switching rt 1f out: kpt on to go 4th nr fin: nvr threatened ldrs* **5/1**[3]

4 **5** *nk* **Backtrade (IRE)**[41] 1678 2-9-3 0...................................... DavidProbert 4 67
(Andrew Balding) *pushed along early to chse ldrs: rdn 1/2-way: nt qckn u.p and styd on same pce fr over 1f out: 4th and hld whn squeezed for room and eased wl ins fnl f* **85/40**[2]

6 *hd* **Whinging Willie (IRE)** 2-9-3 0.. RyanMoore 3 65+
(Gary Moore) *s.i.s: sn rdn and wl outpcd in last: hdwy 1f out: r.o v strly ins fnl f: nvr trbld ldrs* **20/1**

0 **7** *1 ¼* **Millibar (IRE)**[14] 2467 2-8-12 0... LukeMorris 9 53
(Nick Littmoden) *t.k.h: hld up in midfield: rdn and effrt ent fnl 2f: chsng ldrs and carried lft jst ins fnl f: wknd fnl 150yds* **50/1**

0 **8** *3* **Mister Musicmaster**[28] 2049 2-9-3 0.............................. JamesMillman 8 47
(Rod Millman) *chsd ldrs on outer: rdn and unable qck ent fnl 2f: wknd over 1f out* **33/1**

9 *1 ¾* **Lulla** 2-8-12 0.. PatDobbs 10 36
(Marcus Tregoning) *s.i.s and flashed tail leaving stalls: bhd in last trio: pushed along and clsd 1/2-way: no hdwy over 1f out: wknd fnl f* **25/1**

10 *½* **Princess Alessia** 2-8-12 0.. RobertHavlin 6 34
(Terry Clement) *chsd ldrs: rdn 1/2-way: wknd u.p over 1f out: wl btn and eased fnl 50yds* **25/1**

64.19 secs (2.59) **Going Correction** +0.35s/f (Good) **10 Ran SP% 118.5**
Speed ratings (Par 93): **93,91,89,87,86 86,84,79,76,75**
Tote Swingers:1&2:£6.70, 2&3:£10.80, 1&3:£3.70 CSF £18.48 TOTE £3.40: £1.30, £3.10, £2.50; EX 24.40.
Owner J C Fretwell **Bred** Peter Winkworth **Trained** Lichfield, Staffs

FOCUS
Home bend at mid-configuration. Home straight dolled out 5yds and distances on round course increased by about 5yds. This maiden has generally been the source of useful handicappers at best, but did see the initial success of subsequent Group 2 winner and useful sire Acclamation back in 2001. It was a bit of a messy race and there were several eyecatchers amongst the beaten horses. The winner improved but the second had to wait for a run.

NOTEBOOK
Verbeeck had been placed behind some decent sorts in two previous starts, and was ridden positively on this drop back to 5f. He had to be driven to assert and may have been fortunate that the second did not get out sooner, but he could be the sort for one of the sales races later on, contests his owner often targets. (op 5-2)
Orders From Rome(IRE) ◆, a 30,000gns colt related to some smart performers in the USA, had shown promise on his debut and looked unlucky here. He tracked the leaders up the rail, but Backtrade rather got in his way when he needed to get out and, although finishing well, the winner had got first run. He should not be long in making amends. (tchd 10-1 in a place)
Dream Whisperer built on her debut when runner-up up on her second outing. She helped force the pace and tried to get away from the winner inside the last 2f, but was worn down in the closing stages. Her turn should come, possibly against her own sex. (op 10-1)
El Diamante(FR), a 200,000euros half-sister to winners at various trips in France, missed the break on this debut but was noted staying on nicely late on under considerate handling. She should have learnt a lot and is likely to be a different proposition next time. (tchd 9-2)
Backtrade(IRE), a 37,000euros half-brother to, among others, dual 6f winner Shaard, out of a useful triple 6f winner at two, had finished fourth in a Goodwood maiden which could not have worked out better, with the other five beaten horses all going on to score next time. However, he was struggling from the halfway point and then seemed to run green and wander before getting hampered next to the rail late on, something his rider later confirmed. Possibly the rain-softened ground did not suit and he can be given another chance. Official explanation: jockey said colt suffered interference in running (op 9-4 tchd 11-4)
Whinging Willie(IRE) ◆, a 44,000gns tenth foal and brother to a smart 6f juvenile winner, fell out of the stalls on this debut and was detached until past halfway. However, once he worked out what was required he picked up strongly and was in fourth a few strides after the line. He looks one to note. (op 16-1)

2881 J T C DOBELL H'CAP 5f 6y
2:50 (2:50) (Class 5) (0-75,74) 3-Y-0 **£2,590** (£770; £385; £192) **Stalls** Low

Form RPR

3262 **1** **Alpha Delta Whisky**[9] 2611 3-9-3 **70**................................ TomQueally 2 81
(John Gallagher) *dwlt: sn pushed along and rcvrd to ld after 1f: mde rest: rdn and wnt 2 l clr over 1f out: edgd lft u.p ins fnl f: styd on wl and a holding rivals* **3/1**[2]

1360 **2** *2* **Grandmas Dream**[48] 1521 3-9-7 **74**..................................(b¹) PaulDoe 4 77
(Jim Best) *trckd ldrs on far rail: rdn and effrt 2f out: drvn over 1f out: chsd wnr ins fnl f: kpt on but a hld* **22/1**

4412 **3** *1 ½* **Speightowns Kid (USA)**[2] 2818 3-9-2 **69** 6ex................. WilliamBuick 5 67
(Matthew Salaman) *chsd ldrs: rdn and effrt 2f out: drvn and chsd wnr over 1f out tl ins fnl f: no ex and one pce after* **6/4**[1]

-213 **4** *2 ½* **Indian Shuffle (IRE)**[25] 2155 3-9-2 **69**............................... EddieAhern 3 58
(Jonathan Portman) *led for 1f: chsd wnr after: drvn and unable qck 2f out: wknd ins fnl f* **10/1**

-300 **5** *1 ½* **Millyluvstobouggie**[13] 2505 3-9-4 **71**................................. AdamKirby 7 55
(Clive Cox) *hld up wl in tch: effrt and drvn 2f out: no hdwy and btn whn edgd rt ent fnl f: wknd ins fnl f* **4/1**[3]

4-10 **6** *hd* **Oh So Kool**[28] 2074 3-9-1 **73**...(t) RyanClark(5) 6 56
(Stuart Williams) *dwlt: hld up wl in tch in rr: pushed along and effrt 2f out: edgd rt u.p and no hdwy ent fnl f: wknd ins fnl f* **16/1**

6-00 **7** *4 ½* **Whoateallthepius (IRE)**[14] 2468 3-9-3 **70**................... RichardHughes 8 37
(Dean Ivory) *taken down early: racd towards centre: in tch in last trio: rdn and btn 2f out: eased whn wl bhd fnl f* **11/1**

63.43 secs (1.83) **Going Correction** +0.35s/f (Good) **7 Ran SP% 112.7**
Speed ratings (Par 99): **99,95,93,89,87 86,79**
Tote Swingers:1&2:£5.60, 2&3:£5.50, 1&3:£1.40 CSF £58.21 CT £132.30 TOTE £4.30: £2.40, £4.20; EX 20.00.
Owner Adweb Ltd **Bred** Kentford Farm Stud Ltd **Trained** Chastleton, Oxon

FOCUS
A fair but quite competitive sprint handicap run 0.76secs faster than the earlier juvenile maiden. The first two raced nearest the far rail and the form is rated around the runner-up.

2882 BRITISH STALLION STUDS SUPPORTING BRITISH RACING E B F MAIDEN STKS 7f 16y
3:25 (3:25) (Class 5) 2-Y-0 **£3,885** (£1,156; £577; £288) **Stalls** Low

Form RPR

1 **John Lightbody** 2-9-3 0.. JoeFanning 7 82+
(Mark Johnston) *chsd ldr: jnd ldr ent fnl 3f: rdn to ld 2f out: in command and styd on wl fnl f: rdn out* **3/1**[1]

54 **2** *1 ¾* **Iceni Girl**[23] 2187 2-8-12 0.. WilliamBuick 8 73
(John Gosden) *chsd ldrs: rdn ent fnl 2f: chsd wnr over 1f out: kpt on wl but no imp on wnr fnl f* **9/2**[3]

3 *½* **Polydamos** 2-9-3 0.. LukeMorris 11 76+
(Harry Dunlop) *sn outpcd in last quartet: rdn along 5f out: hdwy and edging rt 3f out: swtchd arnd wkng rival over 1f out: edgd bk to far rail and chsd ldrs ins fnl f: r.o wl to go 3rd nr fin* **25/1**

3 **4** *½* **Rock Canyon (IRE)**[31] 1988 2-9-0 0................................ SeanLevey(3) 6 75
(Robert Mills) *hld up in midfield: swtchd lft and effrt over 2f out: disputing 2nd and drvn over 1f out: styd on same pce fnl f: no ex towards fin* **7/1**

5 *4* **Goldoni (IRE)** 2-9-3 0... DavidProbert 3 65
(Andrew Balding) *in tch in midfield: rdn and effrt ent fnl 2f: no hdwy and btn over 1f out: plugged on same pce fnl f* **14/1**

6 *1 ¾* **Poetic Lord** 2-9-3 0.. RichardHughes 1 61
(Richard Hannon) *dwlt: sn in tch in midfield: rdn and effrt ent fnl 2f: no hdwy and btn over 1f out: wknd ent fnl f* **6/1**

0 **7** *5* **Special Boy (IRE)**[34] 1890 2-9-3 0.................................. FrankieDettori 2 48
(Saeed Bin Suroor) *led tl hdd and rdn 2f out: wknd over 1f out: fdd fnl f* **7/2**[2]

8 *¾* **Red Czar (IRE)** 2-9-3 0.. TomQueally 5 46
(Alan McCabe) *sn wl outpcd in last pair: sme hdwy but hanging rt 3f out: no hdwy: wl btn and stl hanging over 1f out* **9/1**

9 *4 ½* **Midnight Bahia (IRE)** 2-8-12 0.. JimmyQuinn 9 30
(Dean Ivory) *s.i.s: wl bhd in last quartet: clsd and jst abt in tch 3f out: wknd 2f out* **50/1**

10 *22* **Captain Cardington (IRE)** 2-9-3 0.................................. SamHitchcott 4 —
(Mick Channon) *bmpd s: sn outpcd in last: t.o after 2f* **20/1**

1m 32.54s (3.04) **Going Correction** +0.45s/f (Yiel) **10 Ran SP% 119.4**
Speed ratings (Par 93): **100,98,97,96,92 90,84,83,78,53**
Tote Swingers:1&2:£4.10, 2&3:£22.20, 1&3:£20.50 CSF £16.77 TOTE £3.90: £1.90, £1.80, £7.70; EX 11.70.
Owner Netherfield House Stud **Bred** Netherfield House Stud **Trained** Middleham Moor, N Yorks

FOCUS

Usually quite an informative maiden in which the best recent winner was probably Magistretti, who went on to win the Dante Stakes, while several others were up to Listed level. Very few of these had previous experience and it fell to a well-backed newcomer. The form fits with the race averages.

NOTEBOOK

John Lightbody, a 55,000gns colt closely related to Freemantle, has a Derby entry. He clearly knew his job on this debut and was always close to the pace before taking over around 2f out. He then stayed on well to justify favouritism and can be expected to go on to better things. (op 4-1 tchd 9-2)

Iceni Girl had shown promise in maidens at 5f and 6f despite running green and, up in trip, she put up a good show against the colts. This trip seemed to suit, despite the fact she is related to several sprinters. (op 4-1)

Polydamos, a 20,000gns son of the high-class mare Spotlight, was under the pump soon after halfway on this debut, but responded to pressure and finished best of all. Better can be expected with this under his belt. (op 33-1)

Rock Canyon(IRE), a brother to a 1m6f winner, had stayed on towards to the finish on his debut over 6f on fast ground, was expected to appreciate the step up in trip and had his chance before fading late on. (op 8-1 tchd 13-2)

Goldoni(IRE), a 16,000gns half-brother to Gunner Lindley, ran with promise and looks as if he will get a bit further. (op 12-1)

Poetic Lord, a 38,000gns half-brother to Millenium Force out of a 1m2f winner, missed the break slightly on this debut but showed ability. (op 5-1)

Special Boy(IRE), another Derby entry, was too keen in front on this second start and paid for it once the winner went by. (op 4-1 tchd 9-2, 5-1 in a place)

Red Czar(IRE)'s rider reported that the colt hung right throughout. Official explanation: jockey said colt hung badly right (tchd 7-1)

2883 MOUSETRAP CHALLENGE CUP FILLIES' H'CAP 1m 14y

4:00 (4:01) (Class 4) (0-85,83) 3-Y-O **£4,533** (£1,348; £674; £336) **Stalls** Low

Form RPR

1-3 **1** **Watneya**[23] 2200 3-8-12 **74** .... RyanMoore 9 85+
(William Haggas) *stdd s: hld up in tch in midfield: rdn and effrt wl over 1f out: drvn to ld 1f out: r.o strly: rdn out* **3/1**[1]

0-20 **2** *2 1/4* **Barathea Dancer (IRE)**[34] 1894 3-8-11 **76** .... SeanLevey(3) 6 81
(Roger Teal) *chsd ldrs: wnt 2nd 4f out tl rdn to ld over 2f out: hdd 1f out: nt pce of wnr but kpt on to hold 2nd fnl f* **14/1**

26-0 **3** *1/2* **Miss Exhibitionist**[17] 2383 3-8-10 **72** .... WilliamBuick 1 76
(James Eustace) *hld up towards rr: rdn and hdwy over 2f out: drvn and chsd ldrs over 1f out: kpt on to go 3rd ins fnl f* **16/1**

512 **4** *1 3/4* **Sure Route**[27] 2102 3-9-7 **83** .... RichardHughes 3 83
(Richard Hannon) *t.k.h: hld up in tch: rdn and effrt to chse ldrs 2f out: unable qck over 1f out: kpt on same pce fnl f* **4/1**[2]

01- **5** *1/2* **Spanish Pride (IRE)**[350] 3399 3-8-5 **67** .... MartinDwyer 10 66+
(John Dunlop) *stdd and dropped in bhd after s: hld up in last: pushed along and sme hdwy over 1f out: kpt on ins fnl f: nvr threatened ldrs* **15/2**[3]

0-26 **6** *nse* **Lunar Phase (IRE)**[29] 2026 3-9-2 **78** .... LukeMorris 5 77
(Clive Cox) *t.k.h: hld up in tch: rdn and unable qck ent fnl 3f: outpcd and edgd rt u.p wl over 1f out: rallied and styd on again ins fnl f: nvr gng pce to threaten ldrs* **12/1**

-351 **7** *3* **Qenaa**[17] 2392 3-8-12 **74** .... JoeFanning 2 66
(Mark Johnston) *chsd ldr tl 4f out: rdn to chse ldr again ent fnl 2f tl over 1f out: wknd fnl f* **12/1**

1-5 **8** *4* **Manaaber (USA)**[21] 2256 3-8-12 **74** .... RichardHills 7 57
(B W Hills) *restless in stalls: hld up in last trio: rdn and shortlived effrt 2f out: no prog and wl hld over 1f out: n.d* **3/1**[1]

-460 **9** *9* **Cheque Book**[27] 2102 3-8-13 **75** .... MichaelHills 8 37
(B W Hills) *restless in stalls: led tl over 2f out: sn rdn: wknd over 1f out: fdd fnl f* **28/1**

0-23 **10** *7* **Sahafh (USA)**[14] 2466 3-8-11 **73** ....(p) FrankieDettori 4 19
(Saeed Bin Suroor) *restless in stalls: hld up in last trio: rdn and no hdwy over 2f out: wl bhd over 1f out* **14/1**

1m 46.18s (2.88) **Going Correction** +0.45s/f (Yiel) **10** Ran SP% **119.8**
Speed ratings (Par 98): **103,100,100,98,98 97,94,90,81,74**
Tote Swingers:1&2:£14.40, 2&3:£41.00, 1&3:£15.50 CSF £49.12 CT £603.41 TOTE £3.80: £1.10, £5.70, £4.40; EX 60.50.

Owner Sheikh Ahmed Al Maktoum **Bred** J Breslin **Trained** Newmarket, Suffolk

FOCUS

A competitive-looking fillies' handicap in which they came to the stands' side in the straight. The form is rated on the positive side with the runner-up setting the standard.

Manaaber(USA) Official explanation: jockey said filly became upset in stalls and cut her head

2884 VAL AND RAY GOLDEN H'CAP 1m 2f 7y

4:35 (4:35) (Class 3) (0-90,90) 4-Y-O+

£7,165 (£2,145; £1,072; £537; £267; £134) **Stalls** Low

Form RPR

3-30 **1** **The Only Key**[22] 2220 5-8-12 **81** .... LukeMorris 1 90
(Jane Chapple-Hyam) *chsd ldrs: rdn wl over 2f out: ev ch ent fnl f: drvn ahd ins fnl f: kpt on wl: all out* **20/1**

1-62 **2** *nk* **All Action (USA)**[39] 1760 4-9-2 **85** .... TomQueally 2 93
(Sir Henry Cecil) *dwlt: sn pushed along and rcvrd to chse ldrs: wnt 2nd 4f out: ev ch and rdn 2f out: drvn ahd over 1f out: hdd ins fnl f: no ex towards fin* **5/2**[1]

0-43 **3** *3/4* **Ela Gorrie Mou**[21] 2269 5-8-4 **73** .... JimmyQuinn 11 80+
(Peter Charalambous) *taken down early: pushed along early: in tch in midfield and t.k.h 8f out: rdn and nt clr run over 2f out: hdwy jst over 1f out: nt clr run and swtchd sharply lft ins fnl f: r.o wl to go 3rd towards fin* **25/1**

000- **4** *1 1/2* **Markazzi**[297] 5188 4-9-2 **85** .... RichardHills 4 89
(Sir Michael Stoute) *dwlt: hld up in last trio: rdn and hdwy wl over 2f out: chsd ldrs and drvn over 1f out: wknd ins fnl f* **9/1**

0-22 **5** *3/4* **Incendo**[28] 2066 5-8-13 **82** ....(t) PatCosgrave 14 84
(James Fanshawe) *hld up in last trio: nt clr run ent fnl 2f: rdn and hdwy ent fnl f: no imp and plugged on same pce fnl 100yds* **14/1**

0-05 **6** *nk* **Greylami (IRE)**[20] 2289 6-9-4 **90** .... SeanLevey(3) 15 92+
(Robert Mills) *stdd after s: hld up in tch in rr: bhd and nt clr run over 2f out: switching rt and hdwy ent fnl f: kpt on wl: nt rch ldrs* **16/1**

-041 **7** *1/2* **Rock The Stars (IRE)**[15] 2436 4-8-7 **76** .... WilliamBuick 12 77+
(J W Hills) *in tch in midfield: shuffled bk towards rr over 4f out: rdn over 2f out: hdwy ent fnl f: styd on: nt pce to rch ldrs* **8/1**

-652 **8** *nk* **Shavansky**[13] 2509 7-9-7 **90** .... JamesMillman 3 90
(Rod Millman) *s.i.s: hld up in last: hdwy in centre 3f out: chsd ldrs and rdn wl over 1f out: wknd ins fnl f* **7/1**[3]

6-30 **9** *3 1/2* **Moynahan (USA)**[15] 2441 6-9-3 **86** .... FrankieDettori 5 79
(Paul Cole) *in tch in midfield: drvn and effrt jst over 2f out: no prog and btn ent fnl f: wknd fnl f* **20/1**

-350 **10** *1 1/4* **Ellemujie**[28] 2066 6-8-12 **81** .... ShaneKelly 6 72
(Dean Ivory) *hld up in tch in midfield: rdn and effrt towards centre 2f out: no real hdwy: one pce and wl hld fnl f* **33/1**

1330 **11** *nse* **Layline (IRE)**[76] 991 4-9-3 **86** .... JamieSpencer 8 77+
(Gay Kelleway) *taken down early: led and styd wd: rdn over 2f out: hdd over 1f out: styng on same pce and struggling whn pushed lft and bdly hmpd ins fnl f: no ch and eased after* **20/1**

1-23 **12** *1 3/4* **Shallow Bay**[28] 2066 4-9-3 **86** .... EddieAhern 13 73+
(Walter Swinburn) *hld up in tch in midfield: nt clr run and shuffled bk towards rr 3f out: swtchd lft and hdwy on stands' rail over 1f out: chsng ldrs and styng on whn bdly hmpd ins fnl f: no ch after and eased fnl 100yds* **13/2**[2]

2012 **13** *3 3/4* **Avon River**[20] 2310 4-9-4 **87** ....(b) RichardHughes 9 67
(Richard Hannon) *t.k.h: chsd ldrs: rdn and unable qck over 2f out: wkng whn short of room ent fnl f* **16/1**

654- **14** *nk* **Silver Point (FR)**[373] 2640 8-9-6 **89** .... DavidProbert 7 68
(Bryn Palling) *chsd ldr tl 4f out: wknd u.p wl over 1f out: bhd fnl f* **50/1**

4-02 **15** *1* **Perpetually (IRE)**[14] 2475 5-9-2 **85** .... JimmyFortune 10 62
(Mark Johnston) *chsd ldrs and racd wd: rdn and unable qck over 2f out: wknd over 1f out* **16/1**

2m 13.19s (2.69) **Going Correction** +0.45s/f (Yiel) **15** Ran SP% **122.9**
Speed ratings (Par 107): **107,106,106,104,104 104,103,103,100,99 99,98,95,95,94**
Tote Swingers:1&2:£16.10, 2&3:£20.60, 1&3:£59.60 CSF £65.73 CT £1330.93 TOTE £29.70: £7.90, £1.50, £10.30; EX 170.00.

Owner B Liversage **Bred** Newsells Park Stud **Trained** Dalham, Suffolk

■ Stewards' Enquiry : Jimmy Quinn two-day ban: careless riding (24th-25th June)

FOCUS

A good and very competitive-looking handicap on paper, but the field got rather compressed against the stands' rail in the straight and there were several hard-luck stories. The time wasn't great and the winner is basically rated to his British best.

NOTEBOOK

The Only Key, a dual winner at around this trip in Germany, had finished a close third on her reappearance before not appearing to stay over further next time. She tracked the leaders on the inside early and followed the runner-up until making her effort, then responded gamely to pressure to get on top well inside the last. Her trainer reported they had been waiting for cut in the ground for her, she should not go up much for this, and her attitude will be an advantage in future. Official explanation: trainer said regarding apparent improvement in form that mare was suited by being prominently ridden and appreciated the good ground

All Action(USA) had run well on Polytrack last time and the ease in the ground was no negative, as he had won his maiden on heavy. He showed up throughout and fought off several challenges in the straight, but the late effort of the winner proved too much. His turn cannot be far away. (op 9-4)

Ela Gorrie Mou was unlucky as he was faced with a wall of horses when looking for a run early in the straight, and then had to switch as the runner-up drifted, doing the weakening front-runner Layline no favours as he did so; a manoeuvre that cost his rider a two-day ban. All ground comes alike and, although he handled this stiff finish, his wins have all been on flat tracks. (op 33-1)

Markazzi lost his form completely last season, but it was significant that his powerful connections had persevered and he had also been gelded. He ran quite well on this return, having been held up early, and looks capable of winning races of this sort of mark. (op 7-1)

Incendo was another who had nowhere to go in the straight before staying on, and he is likely to benefit for a return to 1m4f in any case.

Greylami(IRE)'s best form on turf has been on fast ground, but he did handle soft in the distant past. He stayed on steadily from the rear and, now back to his last winning mark, this was more like it from him.

Rock The Stars(IRE), a recent C&D winner, was another who stayed on late. (op 11-1)

Shavansky moved up from the back to join the leaders halfway up the straight, but probably got there too soon and faded. He needs things to fall just right. (op 10-1)

Shallow Bay was another who was unlucky as he had nowhere to go up the stands' rail for most of the straight and was impeded more than once. He can be forgiven this. (op 8-1)

2885 DECK INTENIONO FOUNDENO H'OAP 1m 2f 7y

5:05 (5:06) (Class 5) (0-75,73) 3-Y-O **£2,590** (£770; £385; £192) **Stalls** Low

Form RPR

0-31 **1** **Grumeti**[21] 2253 3-9-7 **73** .... JamieSpencer 13 86+
(Michael Bell) *hld up in midfield: hdwy to chse ldrs jst over 2f out: rdn and ev ch over 1f out: drvn to ld ent fnl f: hld on wl u.p fnl 100yds* **11/10**[1]

06-4 **2** *hd* **Swaninstockwell (IRE)**[18] 2368 3-8-1 **58** .... JemmaMarshall(5) 9 66
(Pat Phelan) *chsd ldr: ev ch and rdn wl over 1f out: pressed wnr thrght fnl f: kpt on wl but a jst hld* **20/1**

14-0 **3** *2 1/2* **Spyder**[20] 2295 3-9-7 **73** .... AndreaAtzeni 11 76
(Jane Chapple-Hyam) *led: rdn over 2f out: hrd pressed and drvn wl over 1f out: hdd ent fnl f: no ex and btn fnl 100yds* **14/1**

32-0 **4** *1* **Pandorica**[32] 1949 3-9-0 **69** .... JohnFahy(3) 12 70
(Clive Cox) *chsd ldrs: rdn and unable qck over 2f out: outpcd 2f out: rallied u.p and edging rt over 1f out: kpt on steadily fnl f* **18/1**

2260 **5** *1/2* **Uncle Dermot (IRE)**[28] 2064 3-9-0 **66** .... TomQueally 2 66+
(Brendan Powell) *dwlt: t.k.h: hld up towards rr: gd hdwy in centre 3f out: drvn and ev ch over 1f out: wknd ins fnl f* **20/1**

3-00 **6** *2* **Cultural Desert**[17] 2392 3-9-6 **72** .... WilliamBuick 7 68+
(Ralph Beckett) *t.k.h early: stdd bk to rr 8f out: hdwy over 3f out: chsd ldrs and drvn 2f out: no imp and edgd lft over 1f out* **22/1**

30-0 **7** *2 1/2* **Sugar Hiccup (IRE)**[32] 1950 3-9-0 **66** .... LukeMorris 10 57
(Clive Cox) *in tch in midfield: rdn and effrt over 2f out: sme hdwy u.p 2f out: no hdwy and btn ent fnl f* **40/1**

45-0 **8** *1* **Face Value**[51] 1481 3-9-5 **71** .... ShaneKelly 3 60
(Brian Meehan) *hld up towards rr: rdn and unable qck wl over 2f out: sn outpcd and no threat to ldrs wl over 1f out: modest hdwy ins fnl f* **25/1**

563- **9** *1* **Secret Edge**[226] 7179 3-9-4 **70** .... FergusSweeney 6 57
(Alan King) *dwlt: sn rcvrd and in midfield: rdn and dropped to rr ent fnl 3f: n.d after: sme modest hdwy past btn horses fnl f* **10/1**[3]

430 **10** *2* **Prime Mover**[39] 1759 3-9-6 **72** .... FrankieDettori 1 55
(Ed Dunlop) *dwlt: in tch towards rr: pushed along and hdwy over 3f out: wknd ent fnl 2f: wl bhd fnl f* **9/2**[2]

51- **11** *1/2* **Amerthyst**[194] 7609 3-9-5 **71** .... IanMongan 8 53
(Jo Crowley) *chsd ldrs: rdn and struggling ent fnl 3f: wknd over 2f out: wl bhd over 1f out* **16/1**

0-30 **12** *13* **Peira**[9] 2613 3-8-12 **64** .... MichaelHills 5 20
(Jane Chapple-Hyam) *in tch: rdn and struggling over 3f out: wl bhd fnl 2f* **18/1**

630- **13** *5* **Conjuror's Bluff**[226] [7178] 3-9-7 **73**................................ RichardHughes 4 19
(Richard Hannon) *chsd ldrs: rdn and unable qck over 2f out: wknd ent fnl 2f: wl bhd and eased ins fnl f* **20/1**

2m 14.95s (4.45) **Going Correction** +0.45s/f (Yiel) **13** Ran SP% **122.9**
Speed ratings (Par 99): **100,99,97,97,96 95,93,92,91,89 89,79,75**
Tote Swingers:1&2:£10.10, 2&3:£53.10, 1&3:£5.30 CSF £34.37 CT £232.29 TOTE £2.00: £1.20, £5.30, £4.00; EX 39.60.
Owner Thurloe Thoroughbred XXVIII **Bred** Catridge Farm Stud Ltd **Trained** Newmarket, Suffolk

FOCUS
An ordinary but tight-knit 3-y-o handicap, although the betting suggested only two mattered, and run a respectable 1.76secs slower than the preceding race for older horses over the same trip. A prominent position looked an advantage and the level is set around the third and fourth.
T/Plt: £138.20 to a £1 stake. Pool:£79,198.02 - 418.27 winning tickets T/Qpdt: £15.00 to a £1 stake. Pool:£4,656.58 - 228.70 winning tickets SP

2314 YORK (L-H)
Friday, June 10

OFFICIAL GOING: Good (good to firm in places; 7.2)
Wind: Virtually nil Weather: Cloudy, odd shower before racing

2886 ACTURIS E B F MAIDEN STKS 5f
2:10 (2:11) (Class 3) 2-Y-O **£6,476** (£1,927; £963; £481) **Stalls** Centre

Form RPR

1 **Church Music (IRE)** 2-9-3 0.. GrahamGibbons 2 88+
(Kevin Ryan) *w ldr: led on bit over 2f out: pushed clr over 1f out: eased fnl 100yds: readily* **15/8**[1]

23 **2** *1 ¾* **Right Result (IRE)**[9] [2617] 2-9-3 0.................................... KierenFallon 6 76
(Richard Hannon) *w ldr: rdn to ld wl over 2f out: sn hdd: kpt on: no ch w wnr* **9/4**[2]

3 **3** *2 ¼* **Pen Bal Crag (IRE)**[17] [2387] 2-9-3 0................................ PaulHanagan 7 68
(Richard Fahey) *chsd ldrs: rdn over 2f out: kpt on: wnt 3rd fnl 100yds* **11/2**[3]

0 **4** *nk* **Busy Bimbo (IRE)**[27] [2113] 2-8-12 0.............................. PatrickMathers 8 62
(Alan Berry) *sn in tch: rdn over 2f out: kpt on ins fnl f* **50/1**

5 *1* **La Taniere** 2-9-0 0.. JamesSullivan(3) 1 63+
(Michael Easterby) *outpcd towards rr tl kpt on fr over 1f out: nrst fin* **80/1**

40 **6** *½* **Phoenix Clubs (IRE)**[15] [2430] 2-8-12 0............................ PJMcDonald 10 60+
(Paul Midgley) *bdly hmpd s: in rr tl kpt on fr over 1f out: nrst fin* **100/1**

03 **7** *1 ¼* **See Clearly**[11] [2542] 2-8-12 0... DavidAllan 9 52
(Tim Easterby) *wnt rt s: in tch: rdn and hdwy to go 3rd over 1f out: wknd ins fnl f* **10/1**

8 *shd* **Blue Ridges (IRE)** 2-8-12 0.................................. SilvestreDeSousa 11 52+
(Geoffrey Harker) *hld up: rdn and outpcd over 2f out: kpt on fnl f: n.d* **20/1**

042 **9** *3 ½* **Red Shadow**[27] [2113] 2-8-12 0.. PaulMulrennan 5 39
(Alan Brown) *led narrowly: rdn whn hdd wl over 2f out: wknd over 1f out* **20/1**

2403 **10** *1 ¼* **Always Ends Well (IRE)**[8] [2630] 2-8-5 0.......................... DarylByrne(7) 3 35
(Mark Johnston) *w ldr: rdn and lost pl over 2f out: wknd over 1f out* **16/1**

0 **11** *2* **Man Of My Word**[14] [2455] 2-9-0 0............................ MichaelO'Connell(3) 4 32
(David Nicholls) *s.i.s: a outpcd towards rr* **14/1**

60.07 secs (0.77) **Going Correction** +0.075s/f (Good) **11** Ran SP% **116.3**
Speed ratings (Par 97): **96,93,89,89,87 86,84,84,78,76 73**
Tote Swingers:1&2:£1.70, 2&3:£1.40, 1&3:£2.80 CSF £5.73 TOTE £2.90: £1.20, £1.50, £2.10; EX 7.90 Trifecta £35.50 Pool £814.06 - 16.93 winning units..
Owner J C Fretwell **Bred** Mrs Ellen Lyons **Trained** Hambleton, N Yorks

FOCUS
Races on original inside line and distances as advertised. Not a bad juvenile maiden and an impressive winner who was value for two extra lengths. The second and third help with the level.

NOTEBOOK
Church Music(IRE) ◆ delivered in the style of a very useful colt, travelling strongly and stretching clear inside the final 1 1/2f to win with any amount in hand, eased down. A half-brother to four winners, his stable has a wealth of talent in the juvenile division this year, and this son of Amadeus Wolf will be well worth his place in pattern company, with the Gimcrack a likely target. (op 2-1 tchd 11-4)
Right Result(IRE) recorded RPRs of 81 and 76 in his first two starts and looked to hold sound claims on paper, but he was left for dead by the winner in the final furlong. There's no reason to suppose he has taken a step back, which puts the winner's performance in perspective. (op 5-2 tchd 11-4 in a place)
Pen Bal Crag(IRE) hung left under pressure but kept on well enough. He looks more of a nursery type in due course. (op 6-1 tchd 5-1)
Busy Bimbo(IRE) is a half-sister to those prolific mares Look Busy and The City Kid. This was a big step up on her debut effort at Thirsk and races will be won with her. (op 40-1)
La Taniere hails from a stable that rarely has first-time-out winners so this was a creditable effort, especially as he was green throughout. (op 66-1)
Phoenix Clubs(IRE) was slowly away and got badly bumped at the start. Running on at the finish, a return to 6f will suit her once she gets to race in nurseries. Official explanation: jockey said filly was hampered at start
See Clearly weakened in the closing stages having raced prominently, and she's another for whom handicaps will offer better opportunities. (op 9-1 tchd 8-1)

2887 WILLIAM BIRCH & SONS LTD STKS (H'CAP) 1m 208y
2:40 (2:42) (Class 4) (0-80,79) 4-Y-0+ **£5,245** (£1,560; £780; £389) **Stalls** Low

Form RPR

0005 **1** **Barren Brook**[27] [2112] 4-9-4 **76**.................................... PaulMulrennan 3 91
(Michael Easterby) *t.k.h early: sn midfield: hdwy 3f out: rdn to ld over 1f out: kpt on wl ins fnl f* **11/2**[1]

0055 **2** *3 ¼* **Negotiation (IRE)**[10] [2597] 5-8-8 **66**.............................. FrannyNorton 15 73
(Michael Quinn) *s.i.s: hld up: sn swtchd to inner: rdn and hdwy over 2f out: kpt on wl: wnt 2nd fnl 75yds* **33/1**

1014 **3** *½* **Count Bertoni (IRE)**[44] [1621] 4-9-7 **79**......................... DanielTudhope 16 85
(David O'Meara) *in tch: rdn and hdwy over 3f out: ev ch 2f out: kpt on* **16/1**

3525 **4** *1* **One Scoop Or Two**[2] [2814] 5-9-5 **77**............................ GrahamGibbons 13 81
(Reg Hollinshead) *trckd ldrs: rdn over 3f out: kpt on* **13/2**[2]

3315 **5** *nk* **Gala Casino Star (IRE)**[15] [2413] 6-9-1 **73**....................... PaulHanagan 9 76
(Richard Fahey) *midfield: rdn over 3f out: hdwy over 1f out: kpt on fnl f* **8/1**[3]

0525 **6** *nse* **Ours (IRE)**[11] [2545] 8-9-3 **78**...........................(p) RobertLButler(3) 14 81
(John Harris) *s.i.s: sn outpcd in rr: hdwy 2f out: kpt on wl ins fnl f: n.d* **28/1**

4213 **7** *4* **Spavento (IRE)**[16] [2399] 5-7-13 **62**............................ NathanAlison(5) 8 56
(Eric Alston) *hld up: hdwy over 2f out: chsd ldrs over 1f out: no ex fnl f* **11/1**

0-43 **8** *½* **Moheebb (IRE)**[11] [2545] 7-9-3 **75**.................................(b) PJMcDonald 1 68
(Ruth Carr) *midfield on inner: rdn over 3f out: one pce* **8/1**[3]

0/06 **9** *hd* **Burza**[14] [2478] 5-8-5 **63**... AdrianNicholls 10 56
(John Mackie) *hld up: rdn over 3f out: kpt on fnl f: n.d* **40/1**

0010 **10** *½* **Global**[14] [2474] 5-8-6 **67**... PaulPickard(3) 5 59
(Brian Ellison) *prom: rdn to ld over 2f out: hdd over 1f out: sn wknd* **16/1**

6-23 **11** *hd* **Grand Diamond (IRE)**[6] [2734] 7-8-9 **67**.....................(p) AndrewMullen 12 58
(Jim Goldie) *hld up in midfield: rdn over 3f out: no imp* **16/1**

4313 **12** *5* **Violent Velocity (IRE)**[7] [2692] 8-8-7 **72**........................ ShaneBKelly(7) 6 52
(John Quinn) *in tch: rdn over 3f out: wknd over 1f out* **12/1**

1-64 **13** *2 ¼* **Pirate Coast**[14] [2474] 4-9-0 **72**...................................... DuranFentiman 2 47
(Tim Easterby) *led for 1f: trckd ldrs: rdn over 3f out: wknd over 1f out* **14/1**

0310 **14** *2 ½* **Mountain Cat (IRE)**[27] [2115] 7-9-5 **77**............................ RobertWinston 4 47
(Mrs K Burke) *trckd ldrs: rdn over 2f out: sn wknd* **20/1**

-540 **15** *1* **Desert Vision**[27] [2112] 7-8-10 **71**..............................(vt) JamesSullivan(3) 17 39
(Michael Easterby) *midfield on outer: rdn over 3f out: sn wknd* **33/1**

2230 **16** *2 ¼* **Sharakti (IRE)**[7] [2674] 4-8-13 **76**................................ KieranO'Neill(5) 7 39
(Alan McCabe) *hld up in midfield: rdn over 3f out: wknd over 2f out* **25/1**

4-20 **17** *7* **Brockfield**[17] [2388] 5-8-3 **61**..................................... SilvestreDeSousa 11 —
(Mel Brittain) *midfield: brought stands' side over 3f out: sn rdn: edgd lft and wknd over 1f out* **16/1**

0213 **18** *16* **Mountrath**[11] [2560] 4-8-12 **70**.....................................(v) KierenFallon 18 —
(Gary Moore) *led after 1f: rdn whn hdd over 3f out: sn wknd: eased fnl f* **9/1**

1m 50.41s (-1.59) **Going Correction** -0.05s/f (Good) **18** Ran SP% **127.5**
Speed ratings (Par 105): **105,102,101,100,100 100,96,96,96,95 95,91,89,87,86 84,77,63**
Tote Swingers:1&2:£127.40, 2&3:£102.00, 1&3:£61.00 CSF £204.76 CT £2860.29 TOTE £8.80: £2.70, £11.50, £4.60, £1.90; EX 351.60 TRIFECTA Not won..
Owner D Scott, Mrs E Wright & J Clark **Bred** David Allan **Trained** Sheriff Hutton, N Yorks

FOCUS
A fair handicap. Sound form set around the second and third.
Brockfield Official explanation: jockey said horse hung right
Mountrath Official explanation: trainer said gelding was made to much use of in the early stages from a early stage

2888 BOND TYRES STKS (H'CAP) 2m 88y
3:15 (3:15) (Class 3) (0-90,88) 4-Y-O+ **£11,333** (£3,372; £1,685; £841) **Stalls** Low

Form RPR

2-31 **1** **Bollin Judith**[28] [2060] 5-8-11 **75**.......................................(t) DavidAllan 14 86
(Tim Easterby) *t.k.h early: hld up: hdwy 3f out: chsd ldr over 1f out: styd on gamely to ld towards fin* **12/1**

10-1 **2** *nk* **Hawk Mountain (UAE)**[21] [2262] 6-9-8 **86**........................ FrederikTylicki 7 96
(John Quinn) *hld up in midfield on outside: rdn and outpcd over 4f out: rallied on outside 2f out: kpt on wl fnl f: jst hld* **6/1**[1]

31-0 **3** *hd* **Mountain Hiker (IRE)**[13] [2509] 4-9-7 **86**....................(p) PaulHanagan 6 96
(Jeremy Noseda) *led: rdn clr whn hung lft over 2f out: kpt on fnl f: hdd and no ex towards fin* **9/1**[3]

0-63 **4** *2 ¼* **Dazinski**[23] [2190] 5-9-6 **84**... PaulMulrennan 10 91
(Mark H Tompkins) *prom: drvn along 4f out: rallied: kpt on u.p ins fnl f* **14/1**

1343 **5** *3 ¼* **Descaro (USA)**[9] [2622] 5-8-10 **74**...............................(p) DanielTudhope 4 77
(David O'Meara) *hld up in tch: drvn along fr over 3f out: kpt on same pce fr 2f out* **14/1**

-600 **6** *¾* **Cat O' Nine Tails**[13] [2512] 4-8-9 **74**.......................... SilvestreDeSousa 13 77
(Mark Johnston) *bhd: rdn over 4f out: hdwy on outside 2f out: edgd lft and styd on: nvr able to chal* **12/1**

-200 **7** *¾* **Montparnasse (IRE)**[28] [2071] 4-9-6 **85**............................. PhillipMakin 2 87
(Kevin Ryan) *prom: chsd ldr 3f out to over 1f out: edgd lft and sn no ex* **20/1**

0/02 **8** *nse* **Gifted Leader (USA)**[13] [2512] 6-9-4 **82**........................(v) PJMcDonald 9 84
(Ian Williams) *hld up: drvn and hdwy over 2f out: kpt on fnl f: nvr able to chal* **8/1**[2]

4-03 **9** *3* **Gordonsville**[21] [2262] 8-9-3 **84**................................. JamesSullivan(3) 11 82
(Jim Goldie) *hld up towards rr: rdn along over 3f out: no imp fnl 2f* **16/1**

11-3 **10** *1 ½* **Ocean Transit (IRE)**[13] [2499] 6-8-11 **78**...................... AdamBeschizza(3) 1 74
(Richard Price) *midfield on ins: drvn and outpcd 3f out: btn fnl 2f* **8/1**[2]

1-51 **11** *3 ¼* **Dark Ranger**[29] [2034] 5-8-4 **71** ow1.............................. MartinHarley(3) 17 63
(Tim Pitt) *swtchd lft sn after s: hld up on ins: rdn over 3f out: wknd fr 2f out* **9/1**[3]

11-0 **12** *27* **Kazbow (IRE)**[27] [2107] 5-9-10 **88**...................................... KierenFallon 8 48
(Luca Cumani) *cl up: chsd ldr over 6f out to 3f out: wknd 2f out: t.o* **20/1**

1102 **13** *shd* **Accumulate**[14] [2459] 8-8-11 **75**.................................. J-PGuillambert 3 35
(Bill Moore) *in tch: drvn over 4f out: wknd over 3f out: eased whn no ch fnl 2f* **11/1**

20-3 **14** *4* **Beat The Rush**[48] [1517] 4-9-6 **85**...................................... TomEaves 15 40
(Julie Camacho) *t.k.h: swtchd lft after 1f: hld up: struggling over 3f out: sn btn: t.o* **20/1**

4522 **15** *18* **Dubara Reef (IRE)**[12] [2526] 4-8-0 **70**........................(p) KieranO'Neill(5) 12 —
(Paul Green) *sn chsng ldr: drvn and lost 2nd over 6f out: wknd over 4f out: t.o* **16/1**

3-61 **16** *22* **Grande Caiman (IRE)**[93] [813] 7-8-8 **75** ow2..... MichaelO'Connell(3) 16 —
(Geoffrey Harker) *swtchd lft sn after s: hld up: struggling over 3f out: sn btn: eased whn no ch* **50/1**

3m 31.91s (-2.59) **Going Correction** -0.05s/f (Good) **16** Ran SP% **121.6**
WFA 4 from 5yo+ 1lb
Speed ratings (Par 107): **104,103,103,102,101 100,100,100,98,97 96,82,82,80,71 60**
Tote Swingers:1&2:£5.90, 2&3:£13.60, 1&3:£35.00 CSF £77.79 CT £696.14 TOTE £11.70: £2.20, £2.20, £3.00, £3.70; EX 51.90 Trifecta £314.70 Pool £1,063.18 - 2.50 winning units..
Owner Sir Neil Westbrook **Bred** Sir Neil & Exors Of Late Lady Westbrook **Trained** Great Habton, N Yorks
■ Stewards' Enquiry : Frederik Tylicki two-day ban; excessive use of whip (24th-25th June)

FOCUS
A good staying handicap. The winner improved again with the next two bigger improvers. Fairly sound form overall.

NOTEBOOK
Bollin Judith faced no easy task having gone up 7lb for her latest win at Newcastle, but she's progressive and had conditions to suit, and she finished strongly to edge things close home.
Hawk Mountain(UAE), a winner at Musselburgh on his reappearance, ran a career best in defeat, keeping on really well for pressure. He's a possible for the Northumberland Plate in a fortnight's time. (op 13-2)
Mountain Hiker(IRE), the least exposed horse in the field, wore cheekpieces and a noseband and, while perhaps not entirely straightforward (hung left under pressure in the closing stages), he was given a fine ride, stretching the field early on before slowing things down, then kicking again from the turn in. He clearly stays well and is open to further improvement, but on this occasion he was just run down close home. (op 8-1)
Dazinski, never too far off the gallop, ran up to his recent best. (op 12-1 tchd 11-1)
Descaro(USA) again ran his race, this time in first-time cheekpieces.

Cat O' Nine Tails stayed on from off the pace to be nearest at the finish. She's probably more effective when ridden more positively. (op 18-1)
Montparnasse(IRE) looked threatening at the top of the straight, but his effort flattened out under pressure. The handicapper still seems to have his measure.
Accumulate Official explanation: jockey said gelding was never travelling
Beat The Rush Official explanation: jockey said gelding failed to stay
Dubara Reef(IRE) Official explanation: jockey said gelding ran flat
Grande Caiman(IRE) Official explanation: jockey said gelding was unsuited by ground

2889 SKF ROUS (S) STKS — 6f

3:50 (3:50) (Class 4) 2-Y-O — £6,476 (£1,927; £963; £481) Stalls Centre

Form					RPR
0003	1		**Nameitwhatyoulike**[7] [2665] 2-8-11 0 (Michael Easterby) *led: rdn whn hdd over 1f out: rallied to ld again fnl 75yds: kpt on* **14/1**	(b[1]) PaulMulrennan 2	69
5302	2	¾	**Aquasulis (IRE)**[32] [1954] 2-8-6 0 (David Evans) *w ldr: rdn over 2f out: led over 1f out: hdd fnl 75yds: no ex* **16/1**	SilvestreDeSousa 1	62
515	3	¾	**Snowed In (IRE)**[27] [2109] 2-8-11 0 (J S Moore) *hld up: rdn and hdwy over 1f out: wnt 3rd ins fnl f: kpt on wl: nrst fin* **13/2**	StevieDonohoe 12	65+
021	4	3 ¼	**Arcticality (IRE)**[18] [2362] 2-8-6 0 (Richard Fahey) *chsd ldrs: rdn 3f out: kpt on one pce* **9/2**[3]	PaulHanagan 14	50
2222	5	½	**Rooknrasbryripple**[8] [2640] 2-8-4 0 ow1 (Mick Channon) *in tch on outer: hdwy over 2f out: ev ch over 1f out: sn edgd lft: wknd ins fnl f* **7/2**[2]	MartinHarley(3) 13	49
2003	6	3	**Umph (IRE)**[17] [2374] 2-8-11 0 (David Evans) *chsd ldrs: rdn over 2f out: wknd fnl f* **12/1**	(v) PhillipMakin 7	44
0	7	½	**Valley Ace**[13] [2485] 2-8-11 0 (John Quinn) *in tch: rdn and lost pl over 3f out: bhd tl kpt on ins fnl f: n.d* **18/1**	TomEaves 10	43
66	8	½	**Sonko (IRE)**[21] [2261] 2-8-3 0 (Tim Pitt) *trckd ldrs: rdn over 2f out: wknd over 1f out* **50/1**	JamesSullivan(3) 3	36
24	9	1 ¾	**Artists Corner**[13] [2485] 2-8-6 0 (Richard Fahey) *chsd ldrs: rdn over 2f out: wknd over 1f out* **5/2**[1]	AndrewHeffernan 4	31
5400	10	¾	**Liebesziel**[13] [2485] 2-8-11 0 (Alan McCabe) *hld up: rdn 1/2-way: hdwy 2f out: wknd fnl f* **14/1**	(p) RobertWinston 5	34
40	11	19	**Si Sealy (IRE)**[50] [1505] 2-8-11 0 (David Evans) *chsd ldrs: lost pl over 3f out: sn bhd* **40/1**	GrahamGibbons 9	—

1m 12.9s (1.00) **Going Correction** +0.075s/f (Good) **11** Ran SP% **118.9**
Speed ratings (Par 95): **96,95,94,89,89 85,84,83,81,80 55**
Tote Swingers:1&2:£54.00, 2&3:£21.60, 1&3:£19.90 CSF £220.33 TOTE £19.80: £3.20, £4.30, £2.50; EX 130.40 TRIFECTA Not won..There was no bid for the winner.
Owner S Bowett **Bred** A E Smith And Co **Trained** Sheriff Hutton, N Yorks

FOCUS

A valuable juvenile seller and a better than average field for the grade. The first two improved and this is sound form.

NOTEBOOK

Nameitwhatyoulike had been available at 40-1 earlier in the day, but was steadily backed. He was hard to fancy on his previous form, but was stepping up a furlong in distance and had blinkers on for the first time. Given a positive ride, he rallied well after being headed. (op 33-1)
Aquasulis(IRE), prominent throughout, hit the front inside the final 2f but just couldn't hold off the rallying winner close home. The step up to 6f suited him.
Snowed In(IRE), detached in last through the early part of the race, stayed on strongly from 2f out and was never nearer than at the line. A stiffer track should help him. (op 8-1)
Arcticality(IRE), winner of a lower-grade seller at Thirsk last time, ran a sound enough race, seeing the trip out well. (op 11-4)
Rooknrasbryripple, having had five previous starts, was one of the more experienced runners in the field. She failed to see it out that well. (op 4-1)
Artists Corner took a step back from her debut effort on her second start and this was another disappointing performance. Official explanation: jockey said filly had no more to give (op 3-1)

2890 CHARLES CLINKARD FINE FOOTWEAR ANNIVERSARY STKS (H'CAP) — 5f

4:25 (4:26) (Class 3) (0-95,95) 3-Y-O+ — £7,447 (£2,216; £1,107; £553) Stalls Centre

Form					RPR
-204	1		**Medici Time**[9] [2620] 6-9-0 81 (Tim Easterby) *hld up: gd hdwy nr side over 1f out: led ins fnl f: kpt on strly* **25/1**	(v) TomEaves 14	94
1055	2	1	**Magical Macey (USA)**[7] [2694] 4-9-0 81 (David Barron) *cl up: effrt and disp ld over 1f out to ins fnl f: kpt on: nt pce of wnr* **16/1**	(b) LeeNewman 11	90
-310	3	shd	**Ancient Cross**[20] [2317] 7-10-0 95 (Michael Easterby) *hld up in midfield: smooth hdwy to ld briefly ins fnl f: rdn and kpt on same pce towards fin* **8/1**	(t) GrahamGibbons 15	104
4-33	4	nse	**Captain Carey**[41] [1680] 5-9-11 92 (Malcolm Saunders) *hld up: n.m.r and pushed along after 2f: no imp tl styd on wl fnl f: nrst fin* **7/1**[2]	TomMcLaughlin 3	100
0603	5	shd	**Hamoody (USA)**[10] [2590] 7-9-4 85 (David Nicholls) *midfield: drvn along 1/2-way: kpt on strly fnl f: nvr able to chal* **25/1**	AndrewMullen 9	93
0-01	6	¾	**Bedloe's Island (IRE)**[10] [2590] 6-8-9 76 6ex (Neville Bycroft) *trckd ldrs: drvn along over 2f out: kpt on same pce fnl f* **25/1**	FrannyNorton 4	81
5-00	7	½	**Tombi (USA)**[28] [2075] 7-9-7 88 (Geoffrey Harker) *towards rr and sn pushed along: no imp tl styd on fnl f: nrst fin* **9/1**	(p) SilvestreDeSousa 10	92
-063	8	¾	**Duchess Dora (IRE)**[16] [2397] 4-9-2 86 (John Quinn) *trckd ldrs on outside of gp tl rdn and no ex fr over 1f out* **13/2**[1]	DeclanCannon(3) 2	87
0043	9	nk	**Rocket Rob (IRE)**[12] [2525] 5-9-1 82 (Willie Musson) *bhd and outpcd: gd hdwy fnl f: nrst fin* **7/1**[2]	StevieDonohoe 6	82
0000	10	¾	**Haajes**[20] [2299] 7-9-0 81 (Paul Midgley) *midfield: drvn along 1/2-way: kpt on fnl f: nrst fin* **20/1**	MickyFenton 13	78
0020	11	nse	**Befortyfour**[6] [2727] 6-10-0 95 (Richard Guest) *bhd and sn pushed along: sme late hdwy: nvr able to chal* **33/1**	RobbieFitzpatrick 8	92
2510	12	shd	**Discanti (IRE)**[27] [2116] 6-9-7 88 (Tim Easterby) *midfield: drvn and outpcd 1/2-way: no imp fr over 1f out* **33/1**	(t) DuranFentiman 12	85
1550	13	nse	**Nadeen (IRE)**[15] [2434] 4-9-0 81 (Michael Smith) *bhd on outside: rdn along 1/2-way: effrt wl over 1f out: nvr rchd ldrs* **9/1**	KierenFallon 5	77
6363	14	1	**Cadeaux Pearl**[4] [2770] 3-8-9 83 (David Nicholls) *gd spd towards nr side of gp: led over 1f out: edgd lft and hdd ins fnl f: sn btn* **22/1**	(b) AdrianNicholls 16	73
2151	15	shd	**Mr Optimistic**[15] [2411] 3-8-11 85 (Richard Fahey) *in tch on outside of gp: outpcd after 2f: btn over 1f out* **7/1**[2]	PaulHanagan 1	74
01-5	16	7	**Mayoman (IRE)**[16] [2397] 6-9-0 81 (Declan Carroll) *led: rdn and hdd over 1f out: wknd qckly* **15/2**[3]	(v) DavidNolan 7	48

58.75 secs (-0.55) **Going Correction** +0.075s/f (Good)
WFA 3 from 4yo+ 7lb **16** Ran SP% **126.1**
Speed ratings (Par 107): **107,105,105,105,105 103,103,101,101,100 100,99,99,98,98 86**
Tote Swingers:1&2:£64.00, 2&3:£25.70, 1&3:£33.60 CSF £367.42 CT £2093.63 TOTE £29.60: £4.90, £4.40, £2.80, £1.60; EX 520.50 Trifecta £984.30 Part won. Pool £1,330.24 - 0.30 winning units..
Owner Mrs C A Hodgetts **Bred** Mrs Fiona Denniff **Trained** Great Habton, N Yorks

FOCUS

A competitive sprint handicap, but a fourth success on the card for the Easterby clan. Straightforward form.

NOTEBOOK

Medici Time finished fourth in a race won by Wokingham fancy Addictive Dream at Ripon last time, and that form had already been given a boost when his stablemate and runner-up in the race Grissom won at Hamilton two days earlier. He came with his usual late run to win a shade comfortably, but he's likely to be upped to a career-high mark on the back of this, so following up will not be easy.
Magical Macey(USA) showed good pace throughout and performed with credit off what looks a stiff mark.
Ancient Cross ◆ travelled well into contention, but perhaps he could have done with being covered up as he didn't find a great deal once let down. He can defy this sort of mark. (op 17-2 tchd 15-2)
Captain Carey is running consistently well, but there's little margin for error off his current mark. (tchd 8-1)
Hamoody(USA) didn't shape too badly considering he didn't have the clearest of runs. (op 33-1)
Bedloe's Island(IRE) ran right up to his best under his penalty, which meant he was effectively 3lb badly in at the weights.
Tombi(USA) ◆, backed from 25-1 in the morning, was running on nicely at the finish and hinted heavily at a return to form. His stable has been in amongst the winners recently, he's well handicapped now, and a return to 6f could well pay dividends. (op 8-1)
Duchess Dora(IRE) didn't quite run up the form she showed at Ayr last time. (op 8-1)
Rocket Rob(IRE) was 5lb well in at the weights following his unlucky-in-running third at Nottingham last time and looked to hold obvious claims, even allowing for this track not being ideal for his style of running. He drifted in the betting beforehand, though, fell out of the stalls and was struggling behind for most of the race before staying on through beaten horses late on. Official explanation: jockey said gelding was outpaced in the early stages (op 11-2 tchd 5-1)
Mayoman(IRE) Official explanation: jockey said gelding had no more to give

2891 BETFAIR CLASSIFIED STKS — 1m 2f 88y

4:55 (4:56) (Class 5) 3-Y-O — £5,245 (£1,560; £780; £389) Stalls Low

Form					RPR
5-10	1		**Dragonera**[22] [2232] 3-9-0 75 (Ed Dunlop) *hld up in tch: hdwy over 3f out: rdn to chal over 2f out: kpt on: led post* **15/2**	PaulMulrennan 5	84
1-04	2	hd	**El Torbellino (IRE)**[30] [2008] 3-9-0 75 (David O'Meara) *w ldr: rdn to ld narrowly over 2f out: kpt on: hdd post* **7/2**[2]	DanielTudhope 6	83
6-32	3	1	**Above All**[14] [2472] 3-9-0 75 (William Haggas) *racd keenly: led narrowly: rdn whn hdd over 2f out: remained w ev ch tl no ex nr fin* **7/2**[2]	TadhgO'Shea 2	81
2342	4	3 ¾	**Dressing Room (USA)**[25] [2146] 3-9-0 74 (Mark Johnston) *trckd ldrs: rdn over 3f out: one pce* **5/1**[3]	(v) SilvestreDeSousa 3	74
21-4	5	8	**Corsicanrun (IRE)**[65] [1168] 3-9-0 74 (Richard Fahey) *hld up in tch: pushed along 5f out: rdn over 3f out: sn no imp: wknd over 1f out* **2/1**[1]	PaulHanagan 1	58
36-2	6	21	**Matilda's Waltz**[44] [1620] 3-9-0 74 (Ralph Beckett) *hld up: a in rr* **16/1**	StevieDonohoe 4	16

2m 11.82s (-0.68) **Going Correction** -0.05s/f (Good) **6** Ran SP% **112.1**
Speed ratings (Par 99): **100,99,99,96,89 72**
Tote Swingers:1&2:£5.70, 2&3:£1.50, 1&3:£3.00 CSF £33.34 TOTE £9.90: £3.60, £1.70; EX 40.00.
Owner J Weatherby, Champneys **Bred** Preston Lodge Stud **Trained** Newmarket, Suffolk
■ Stewards' Enquiry : Tadhg O'Shea one-day ban: excessive use of whip (24th June)
Daniel Tudhope caution: used whip down shoulder

FOCUS

A very tight 3-y-o affair and a close finish. Fair form with the front three looking a bit ahead of their marks.
Matilda's Waltz Official explanation: jockey said filly was never travelling

2892 FUTURE CLEANING SERVICES APPRENTICE STKS (H'CAP) — 1m 4f

5:30 (5:34) (Class 4) (0-80,80) 4-Y-O+ — £5,245 (£1,560; £780; £389) Stalls Centre

Form					RPR
3-14	1		**Odin's Raven (IRE)**[23] [117] 6-8-13 69 (Brian Ellison) *hld up: gd hdwy 3f out: rdn to ld over 1f out: kpt on wl fnl f* **25/1**	PaulPickard 13	79
2111	2	1 ¼	**Tenhoo**[21] [2259] 5-8-11 72 (Eric Alston) *hld up in midfield: hdwy over 3f out: chsd ldrs 2f out: kpt on wl ins fnl f: wnt 2nd towards fin* **9/2**[2]	NathanAlison(5) 6	80+
34-1	3	½	**Pokfulham (IRE)**[8] [2636] 5-8-2 61 6ex (Jim Goldie) *t.k.h early: prom: rdn to ld over 2f out: edgd lft and hdd over 1f out: kpt on: lost 2nd towards fin* **7/2**[1]	(v) KieranO'Neill(3) 14	69
13-0	4	2 ¼	**Kathleen Frances**[30] [2006] 4-9-5 78 (Mark H Tompkins) *midfield: smooth hdwy over 3f out: rdn to chal 2f out: no ex fnl f* **5/1**[3]	AshleyMorgan(3) 4	82
0000	5	1 ¾	**Full Speed (GER)**[11] [2544] 6-8-13 74 (Alan Swinbank) *midfield: hdwy over 3f out: rdn and ev ch whn hmpd over 1f out: one pce after* **40/1**	GarryWhillans(5) 2	75
05-0	6	4 ½	**Pevensey (IRE)**[22] [2220] 9-9-1 76 (David Barron) *v.s.a: sn rcvrd into midfield: rdn over 3f out: kpt on one pce* **10/1**	LMcNiff(5) 9	70
-003	7	hd	**Green Lightning (IRE)**[18] [2364] 4-8-13 74 (Mark Johnston) *hld up: bhd tl kpt on fr over 1f out: n.d* **18/1**	(b) DarylByrne(5) 16	68
3300	8	½	**Veiled Applause**[16] [2403] 8-9-5 80 (John Quinn) *midfield: rdn over 3f out: one pce* **33/1**	ShaneBKelly(5) 7	73
-005	9	3 ¼	**Boston Blue**[13] [2512] 4-9-4 77 (Tim Etherington) *hld up towards outer: rdn over 3f out: n.d* **10/1**	(v) DaleSwift(3) 12	65
/2-2	10	¾	**Indochina**[91] [836] 4-8-13 72 (David Simcock) *hld up: rdn over 3f out: n.d* **12/1**	AdamBeschizza(3) 1	58
0034	11	shd	**Monkton Vale (IRE)**[13] [2486] 4-8-4 67 (Richard Fahey) *trckd ldrs: rdn over 3f out: wknd over 1f out* **16/1**	(b) LauraBarry(7) 5	53
16-6	12	2 ½	**Fantino**[14] [2475] 5-9-0 70 (John Mackie) *trckd ldrs: rdn to chal over 3f out: wknd over 2f out* **28/1**	DeclanCannon 11	52

0-03 **13** *hd* **King Zeal (IRE)**[22] 2220 7-9-3 **78**.................... JamesRogers(5) 10 60
(Barry Leavy) *led: rdn whn hdd over 2f out: wknd over 1f out* **10/1**

060- **14** *8* **Bavarian Nordic (USA)**[305] 4891 6-8-13 **69**.................... AmyRyan 8 38
(Richard Whitaker) *midfield on outer: rdn over 3f out: wknd over 2f out* **33/1**

00-0 **15** *13* **Dzesmin (POL)**[34] 1908 9-8-13 **69**.................... JamesSullivan 3 17
(David O'Meara) *trckd ldrs: wknd over 2f out* **33/1**

200/ **16** *½* **Hada Men (USA)**[633] 5961 6-8-12 **71**.................... JulieBurke(3) 15 19
(Tina Jackson) *dwlt: hld up: a towards rr* **33/1**

2m 32.5s (-0.70) **Going Correction** -0.05s/f (Good) **16** Ran SP% **124.7**
Speed ratings (Par 105): **100,99,98,97,96 93,93,92,90,90 89,88,88,82,74 73**
Tote Swingers:1&2:£19.10, 2&3:£5.70, 1&3:£21.10. Totesuper 7: Win: Not won. Place: £1,374.10 CSF £130.81 CT £512.41 TOTE £20.30: £3.50, £1.60, £1.70, £1.30; EX 186.20 Trifecta £218.20 Pool £1,064.66 - 3.61 winning units..
Owner Racing Management & Training Ltd **Bred** Newberry Stud Company **Trained** Norton, N Yorks
■ Stewards' Enquiry : Garry Whillans two-day ban: careless riding (25th-26th June)
Declan Cannon five-day ban: careless riding (24th-28th June)

FOCUS
A modest handicap, confined to apprentice riders. It was well run and the form is rated to face value around the fourth.
T/Jkpt: Not won. T/Plt: £2,032.40 to a £1 stake. Pool:£108,722.35 - 39.05 winning tickets T/Qpdt: £189.50 to a £1 stake. Pool:£6,827.00 - 26.65 winning tickets AS

2893 - 2899a (Foreign Racing) - See Raceform Interactive

2659 BATH (L-H)
Saturday, June 11

OFFICIAL GOING: Good (7.6)
Wind: Moderate across Weather: Sunny spells

2900 TOTEPLACEPOT WIN WITHOUT BACKING A WINNER H'CAP 1m 2f 46y
2:20 (2:20) (Class 6) (0-55,58) 4-Y-0+ **£2,183** (£644; £322) **Stalls** Low

Form RPR

6031 **1** **Art Scholar (IRE)**[3] 2824 4-9-2 **55** 6ex.................... NeilChalmers 12 73
(Michael Appleby) *hld up in rr: stl bhd and plenty to do ins fnl 3f: hdwy and nt clr run over 2f out: hdwy sn after to chse ldr over 1f out: rdn to ld fnl 120yds: readily* **11/10**[1]

3543 **2** *3¾* **Corrib (IRE)**[57] 1374 8-8-9 **48** ow2....................(p) StevieDonohoe 10 58
(Bryn Palling) *s.i.s: t.k.h and led after 1f: sn clr: rdn over 2f out: hdd and no ex fnl 120yds but wl clr of 3rd* **9/1**[3]

1530 **3** *5* **Chief Exec**[36] 1868 9-8-13 **52**.................... RobertHavlin 13 52
(Jeremy Gask) *s.i.s: in rr: hdwy over 2f out: styd on to take 3rd fnl f but nvr any ch w ldng duo* **12/1**

2443 **4** *3½* **Goose Green (IRE)**[15] 2450 7-8-10 **52**....................(t) MatthewDavies(3) 3 45
(Ron Hodges) *prom: rdn 3f out but nvr nr clr ldr: wknd over 1f out* **4/1**[2]

0004 **5** *hd* **Lucky Diva**[9] 2638 4-8-0 **46** oh1.................... JakePayne(7) 1 39
(Bill Turner) *led 1f: chsd clr ldr tl wknd over 1f out* **25/1**

0403 **6** *1¼* **Christmas Coming**[40] 1805 4-8-13 **55**....................(t) MichaelGeran(3) 7 45
(Tony Carroll) *prom early: stdd in mid-div: hdwy 3f out: styd on towards outside fr 2f out but no imp on ldrs* **20/1**

0534 **7** *1½* **Market Puzzle (IRE)**[22] 2271 4-8-3 **47**.................... KieranO'Neill(5) 4 34
(Mark Brisbourne) *chsd ldrs: rdn 3f out: wknd ins fnl 2f* **11/1**

5105 **8** *½* **Queenie's Star (IRE)**[18] 2386 4-8-9 **51**.................... KierenFox(3) 9 37
(Michael Attwater) *in rr: rdn and sme hdwy on outside over 2f out: styd on same pce and nvr rchd ldrs* **22/1**

0045 **9** *1¼* **Love In The Park**[80] 943 6-8-11 **53**.................... AdamBeschizza(3) 5 37
(Roy Brotherton) *a in rr* **9/1**[3]

-000 **10** *6* **Spacecraft (IRE)**[12] 2569 4-8-8 **47** oh1 ow1....................(b) SaleemGolam 6 19
(Christopher Kellett) *sn chsng ldrs in 3rd: rdn 3f out: sn btn* **100/1**

0650 **11** *4½* **Dauntsey Park (IRE)**[61] 1273 4-8-13 **52**.................... JamesDoyle 8 15
(Tor Sturgis) *prom early: dropped to rr 1/2-way: sme prog on outside over 2f out: nvr rchd ldrs and sn btn* **33/1**

2m 9.59s (-1.41) **Going Correction** -0.10s/f (Good) **11** Ran SP% **120.5**
Speed ratings (Par 101): **101,98,94,91,91 90,88,88,87,82 79**
toteswingers:1&2:£4.50, 1&3:£4.60, 2&3:£17.40 CSF £11.53 CT £86.18 TOTE £2.20: £1.10, £2.60, £3.20; EX 16.40 Trifecta £41.10 Pool £146.70 - 2.46 winning units..
Owner D J Lewin **Bred** John Ramsbottom **Trained** Danethorpe, Notts

FOCUS
A weak contest run at no pace early until the runner-up went on. The runner-up built on his recent form.

2901 TOTEEXACTA BETTER VALUE FORECAST MAIDEN AUCTION STKS 5f 11y
2:50 (2:54) (Class 6) 2-Y-0 **£2,072** (£616; £308; £153) **Stalls** Centre

Form RPR

00 **1** **Fanrouge (IRE)**[18] 2374 2-8-7 0 ow1.................... SaleemGolam 4 67
(Malcolm Saunders) *chsd ldrs: drvn to ld over 1f out: strly chal ins fnl f: styd on gamely clsng stages* **33/1**

06 **2** *½* **Musical Valley**[12] 2570 2-8-6 0....................(t) RossAtkinson(3) 8 67
(Tom Dascombe) *awkward s: towards rr: hdwy over 2f out: wnt 2nd 1f out: styd on to chal ins fnl f: no ex clsng stages* **33/1**

4 **3** *shd* **Imelda Mayhem**[9] 2644 2-8-1 0.................... RyanPowell(5) 1 64
(J S Moore) *in tch: hdwy 2f out: squeezed through on inner ins fnl f and ev ch fnl 100yds: no ex cl home* **4/1**[3]

0 **4** *1¼* **Nude (IRE)**[21] 2309 2-7-13 0.................... KieranO'Neill(5) 5 58
(Sylvester Kirk) *chsd ldrs: rdn 2f out: styng on fnl f but nvr gng pce to press ldrs* **4/1**[3]

6320 **5** *3¾* **Triggerlo**[42] 1691 2-8-8 0.................... MatthewDavies(3) 6 51
(Mick Channon) *slt ld: rdn 2f out: hdd appr fnl f: sn btn* **3/1**[2]

6 *1* **Misred Melissa (IRE)** 2-8-4 0 ow1.................... AdamBeschizza(3) 2 43
(John Gallagher) *slowly away: in rr: stl last over 1f out: styd on wl fnl f: gng on clsng stages* **20/1**

00 **7** *½* **Bertorella (IRE)**[18] 2374 2-8-8 0 ow2.................... StevieDonohoe 9 43
(Ralph Beckett) *uns rdr then led 3f to post: in tch: rdn and hdwy over 2f out: styd on same pce over 1f out* **16/1**

8 *¾* **Best In Show** 2-8-10 0.................... PatrickHills(3) 7 45
(J W Hills) *s.i.s: in rr: rdn and sme hdwy on outside over 2f out: nvr rchd ldrs and styd on same pce* **5/2**[1]

9 *hd* **Ernest Speak (IRE)** 2-8-10 0.................... KierenFox(3) 3 44
(Bill Turner) *s.i.s: a outpcd* **12/1**

05 **10** *2½* **Purple Angel**[22] 2241 2-8-4 0.................... NeilChalmers 10 26
(Jonathan Portman) *pressed ldr: stl upsides over 1f out: sn wknd* **40/1**

63.97 secs (1.47) **Going Correction** +0.15s/f (Good) **10** Ran SP% **120.2**
Speed ratings (Par 91): **94,93,93,91,85 83,82,81,81,77**
toteswingers:1&2:£42.10, 1&3:£42.10, 2&3:£24.40 CSF £825.66 TOTE £42.40: £7.00, £5.70, £1.70; EX 1048.50 TRIFECTA Not won..
Owner Chris Scott **Bred** Silk Fan Syndicate **Trained** Green Ore, Somerset

FOCUS
A weak-maiden beforehand proved little better in practice, with two big outsiders occupying first and second spot and the two market leaders underperforming. The early pace did at least seem good, however. The third and seventh offer perspective on the form.

NOTEBOOK
Fanrouge(IRE) had beaten only one home in each of her two previous outings and carried 1lb overweight this time, so the omens weren't good. This stiffest track yet encountered inspired her to raise her game, however, as perhaps befitting a filly whose immediately family have needed at 6f and further to show their best, and she proved most tenacious to get the better of a three-way battle up the run-in. The form looks nothing special, but she could hold her own in modest fillies' handicaps following this. (tchd 40-1)
Musical Valley was ridden more patiently than on either previous start and briefly looked as if he might emerge on top in the scramble for the line, but ultimately found the winner too determined. Another to have appreciated this tougher course, there is a low-grade handicap to be won with him, too. (op 22-1 tchd 20-1)
Imelda Mayhem is out of a juvenile 5f winner and can number another among her half-siblings, but she already looked in need of something a touch stiffer on her staying-on Sandown debut last time and couldn't quite muster sufficient late pace to gain the day here either, even in a well-run contest at the trip. (op 3-1)
Nude(IRE), as on her debut at Newbury over 6f, was starting to feel the pinch around halfway and she still has work to do to before emulating the juvenile sprint winners on her dam's side. (op 13-2)
Triggerlo, who lost favouritism shortly before the off, didn't fully revive for the return to a stiff 5f and is starting to look exposed and disappointing. (op 7-2 tchd 11-4)
Best In Show, who ousted Triggerlo as favourite, looked beforehand as if this might be needed and ran accordingly, albeit he was just starting to get the hang of things very late on. (op 7-2 tchd 4-1)

2902 TOTESWINGER MORE WAYS TO WIN E B F NOVICE STKS 5f 11y
3:25 (3:26) (Class 4) 2-Y-0 **£4,468** (£1,329; £664; £331) **Stalls** Centre

Form RPR

14 **1** **Betty Fontaine (IRE)**[15] 2476 2-8-8 0.................... MatthewDavies(3) 6 76
(Mick Channon) *bmpd s: in rr but in tch: swtchd rt 2f out: rdn and str run to ld ins fnl f: hung lft last 120yds: styd on wl* **7/2**[3]

6 **2** *1½* **Cape Moss (IRE)**[14] 2504 2-8-11 0.................... RossAtkinson(3) 7 74
(Tom Dascombe) *pushed rt s: hdwy on outer and hung rt over 1f out: styng on to dispute 2nd ins fnl f whn crossed and swtchd rt: hung lft u.p sn after: kpt on to take 2nd cl home but no imp on wnr* **5/2**[2]

1561 **3** *nk* **The Dancing Lord**[12] 2556 2-8-13 0.................... KierenFox(3) 4 75
(Bill Turner) *wnt rt s: pressed ldr tl led ins fnl 3f: hdd ins fnl f: one pce: lost 2nd cl home* **9/2**

0163 **4** *3½* **Red Hearts (IRE)**[11] 2594 2-8-11 0.................... AdamBeschizza(3) 2 60
(Julia Feilden) *chsd ldrs: drvn to chal 2f out: wknd ins fnl f* **9/4**[1]

0310 **5** *4½* **Steady The Buffs**[26] 2154 2-8-4 0.................... DavidKenny(7) 1 41
(Hugo Palmer) *led tl hdd ins fnl 3f: wknd wl over 1f out* **14/1**

5 **6** *½* **No More Shoes (IRE)**[12] 2563 2-9-0 0.................... StevieDonohoe 3 42
(Brendan Powell) *chsd ldrs: rdn 3f out: wknd wl over 1f out* **12/1**

63.49 secs (0.99) **Going Correction** +0.15s/f (Good) **6** Ran SP% **114.1**
Speed ratings (Par 95): **98,95,95,89,82 81**
toteswingers:1&2:£2.00, 1&3:£5.70, 2&3:£3.50 CSF £13.00 TOTE £5.40: £2.30, £3.10; EX 21.70.
Owner Billy Parish **Bred** Tony And Mary McKiernan **Trained** West Ilsley, Berks
■ Stewards' Enquiry : Kieren Fox caution: used whip without giving horse time to respond

FOCUS
A bruised foot deprived likely market leader Arnold Lane of the chance to run, but the Channon yard still collected the spoils with its other representative. Modest form, rated through the third.

NOTEBOOK
Betty Fontaine(IRE) was a debut maiden winner over 150yds further on her previous course visit. This wasn't entirely plain sailing as she received a bump leaving the stalls and had to switch round the outside of the runner-up 2f out to deliver her challenge. The response once in the clear was whole-hearted and sustained, and she was anything but coming to the end of her tether late on despite veering left. Out of a filly that stayed 7f as a juvenile, a step back up in trip should pose no problems. (op 10-3)
Cape Moss(IRE) broke on better terms than on his Haydock debut, despite being bumped early by another runner. Delivering his challenge after the winner had already made hers, he was never going to reel her in even if he'd been able to chart a straighter course in the later stages. He will need winding up earlier if he is going to score at this trip, though as one with greater prowess over 6f-1m trips in his immediate family a step up in trip may be preferable in any event. (op 3-1 tchd 7-2)
The Dancing Lord, the perpetrator of the early interference suffered by the first two home, had nothing left to fight back with once headed a furlong out. A winner already at Goodwood and Folkestone, he is best kept to sharper 5f tracks than this one. (op 11-2)
Red Hearts(IRE) was a scorer over Brighton's speedy 5f in April, but most recently held over 6f at Yarmouth despite being gifted an easy lead. Today's effort dropped back to the minimum trip was disappointing even so, with little offered when asked after halfway. (tchd 5-2)

2903 TRY TOTEQUICKPICK IF YOU'RE FEELING LUCKY H'CAP 5f 161y
4:00 (4:00) (Class 4) (0-80,79) 3-Y-0+ **£3,238** (£963; £481; £240) **Stalls** Centre

Form RPR

66-0 **1** **Barons Spy (IRE)**[35] 1888 10-10-0 **79**.................... JamesDoyle 7 87
(Richard Price) *bmpd s: in tch: chsd ldrs and rdn 3f out: hdwy 2f out: chal fr 2f out tl led ins fnl f: hld on wl* **10/1**

550- **2** *nk* **Titus Gent**[164] 8004 6-9-2 **67**.................... TravisBlock 5 74
(Jeremy Gask) *wnt rt s: chsd ldrs: chal 2f out: slt ld u.p 1f out: hdd ins fnl f: kpt on wl but a hld clsng stages* **16/1**

-333 **3** *¾* **Witchry**[4] 2794 9-8-5 **63**.................... DavidKenny(7) 4 68
(Tony Newcombe) *in rr: hdwy towards outside 2f out: styd on to take 3rd fnl 120yds: nt rch ldng duo* **7/2**[1]

0010 **4** *3* **Make My Dream**[11] 2585 8-9-6 **71**.................... RobertHavlin 3 66
(John Gallagher) *chsd ldrs: ev ch 2f out: wknd ins fnl f* **16/1**

5023 **5** *1¾* **Billy Red**[15] 2447 7-9-4 **69**....................(b) StevieDonohoe 11 58
(J R Jenkins) *broke wl: sn led: rdn 2f out: hdd 1f out: wknd and edgd lft ins fnl f* **11/1**

1-00 **6** *1½* **Sarah's Art (IRE)**[19] 2369 8-9-5 **73**....................(t) MichaelGeran(3) 6 57
(Stef Higgins) *hmpd s: in rr: hdwy over 1f out: styd on fnl f: nvr a threat* **6/1**

6464 **7** *nk* **Brandywell Boy (IRE)**[9] 2645 8-9-2 **70**.................... BillyCray(3) 2 53
(Dominic Ffrench Davis) *chsd ldrs on ins: wkng whn n.m.r on rails ins fnl f* **4/1**[2]

2550 **8** *3* **Secret Queen**[30] 2027 4-8-12 **66**.................... KierenFox(3) 8 39
(Martin Hill) *hmpd s: in rr: swtchd rt to outside over 2f out: nvr gng pce to rch ldrs* **14/1**

123- **9** *11* **Superior Edge**[240] 6879 4-9-6 **76**.................... KieranO'Neill(5) 1 13
(Christopher Mason) *chsd ldrs tl wknd 2f out* **11/2**[3]

0064 **10** *1 3/4* **Primo De Vida (IRE)**[10] 2609 4-8-10 **64**...........(b[1]) MatthewDavies(3) 10 —
(Jim Boyle) *hmpd s: in rr: swtchd rt to outside over 2f out and brief effrt: nvr in contention and sn wknd* **7/1**

1m 11.22s (0.02) **Going Correction** +0.15s/f (Good) **10** Ran SP% **120.2**
Speed ratings (Par 105): **105,104,103,99,97 95,94,90,76,73**
toteswingers:1&2:£1.90, 1&3:£3.10, 2&3:£1.80 CSF £161.71 CT £679.10 TOTE £13.10: £3.60, £5.70, £1.10; EX 112.70 Trifecta £121.10 Part won. Pool £163.74 - 0.10 winning units..
Owner Barry Veasey **Bred** Tally-Ho Stud **Trained** Ullingswick, H'fords

FOCUS
Ordinary form for the grade, but sound.

2904 TRY TOTEQUICKPICK ON ALL TOTEPOOL BETS H'CAP 1m 3f 144y
4:35 (4:36) (Class 5) (0-70,66) 3-Y-O **£2,914** (£867; £433; £216) **Stalls** Low

Form RPR
-610 **1** **Tidal Run**[9] 2637 3-9-0 **62**.......................... MatthewDavies(3) 8 70
(Mick Channon) *hld up in rr: hdwy 3f out: drvn to dispute 2nd fr ins fnl 2f: chsd ldr fnl 120yds: styd on wl to ld last stride* **6/1**[3]

0-25 **2** *shd* **Dr Darcey**[23] 2225 3-8-11 **61**..........................(b[1]) KieranO'Neill(5) 7 69
(Richard Hannon) *led: rdn over 2f out: kpt on wl u.p fnl f: hdd last stride* **5/2**[2]

55-0 **3** *1* **Undulant Way**[33] 1947 3-9-7 **66**.......................... JamesDoyle 4 72
(Amanda Perrett) *chsd ldrs: drvn to dispute 2nd fr ins fnl 2f: no imp u.p: one pce fnl 120yds* **7/4**[1]

436 **4** *4* **Delagoa Bay (IRE)**[18] 2379 3-7-13 **47** oh1.................. SophieDoyle(3) 3 46
(Sylvester Kirk) *in tch: hdwy on outside 2f out: nvr gng pce to chal and one pce fr over 1f out* **25/1**

0-45 **5** *6* **Golestan Palace (IRE)**[21] 2307 3-8-12 **57**.................. RobertHavlin 5 46
(Ed Walker) *chsd ldr 7f out tl ins fnl 2f: sn wknd* **14/1**

0-04 **6** *4* **Like A Boy**[28] 2104 3-9-0 **59**.......................... TravisBlock 2 41
(Peter Makin) *t.k.h: chsd ldrs: rdn 4f out: wknd over 2f out* **7/1**

2150 **7** *4 1/2* **Blue Cossack (IRE)**[3] 2819 3-8-13 **63**.................. LeeNewnes(5) 1 38
(Mark Usher) *slowly away: in rr: hdwy 5f out: in tch 4f out: wknd over 2f out* **11/1**

0-03 **8** *1 1/2* **Miskin Diamond (IRE)**[11] 2586 3-8-4 **49** ow2.............. NeilChalmers 6 21
(Bryn Palling) *rdn over 3f out: a towards rr* **12/1**

2m 29.69s (-0.91) **Going Correction** -0.10s/f (Good) **8** Ran SP% **118.3**
Speed ratings (Par 99): **99,98,98,95,91 88,85,84**
toteswingers:1&2:£1.90, 1&3:£3.10, 2&3:£1.80 CSF £22.23 CT £37.77 TOTE £7.00: £2.50, £1.70, £1.02; EX 18.60 Trifecta £56.10 Pool £214.90 - 2.83 winning units..
Owner M Channon **Bred** Barry Walters Farms **Trained** West Ilsley, Berks

FOCUS
Not that strong a race for the grade, with only half the field within 10lb of the ratings ceiling. It produced a thrilling finish, however, and the form seems sound.

2905 TOTEPOOL A BETTER WAY TO BET H'CAP 1m 3f 144y
5:10 (5:12) (Class 6) (0-60,61) 4-Y-O+ **£2,072** (£616; £308; £153) **Stalls** Low

Form RPR
/050 **1** **Dancing Primo**[22] 2258 5-8-3 **45**.......................... KieranO'Neill(5) 9 54+
(Mark Brisbourne) *in tch: hdwy 4f out: led ins fnl 3f: rdn: idled and wandered 1f out: rdn and fnd ex whn got to far rail fnl 120yds* **12/1**

00- **2** *1* **Waldsee (GER)**[171] 7967 6-8-13 **50**.......................... JamesDoyle 7 55
(Joanna Davis) *in rr: hdwy 6f out: awkward and lost pl bnd ins fnl 5f: hdwy again 3f out: styd on to cl on idling wnr jst ins fnl f: kpt on but a hld clsng stages* **25/1**

/50- **3** *1 3/4* **Jocheski (IRE)**[9] 3084 7-9-0 **54**.......................... BillyCray(3) 8 56
(Tony Newcombe) *chsd ldrs: wnt 2nd ins fnl 3f: no imp on wnr: one pce and lost 2nd fnl f* **8/1**

5020 **4** *9* **Bussell Along (IRE)**[12] 2569 5-8-1 **45**.................. RachealKneller(7) 1 32
(Pam Ford) *s.i.s: in rr: hdwy 3f out and in tch over 2f out: wknd wl over 1f out* **16/1**

2143 **5** *1* **Duneen Dream (USA)**[8] 2663 6-9-4 **58**.................. KierenFox(3) 11 43+
(Nikki Evans) *led tl hdd ins fnl 3f: wknd 2f out* **9/2**[2]

0044 **6** *2 1/2* **Tt's Dream**[11] 2600 4-8-10 **47**..........................(b) RobertHavlin 3 28
(Alastair Lidderdale) *s.i.s: in rr: hdwy 3f out: nvr rchd ldrs and wknd 2f out* **5/1**[3]

0110 **7** *6* **Fastinthestraight (IRE)**[109] 645 4-9-2 **56**...........(p) MatthewDavies(3) 2 27
(Jim Doyle) *s.i.s: in rr: sme hdwy 3f out: sn wknd* **7/1**

0-00 **8** *2* **Le Corvee (IRE)**[10] 998 9-8-8 **52**.......................... GeorgeDowning(7) 5 19
(Tony Carroll) *s.i.s: sme prog 3f out: sn wknd* **8/1**

0401 **9** *45* **Zagarock**[22] 2246 4-9-0 **51**.......................... NeilChalmers 6 —+
(Bryn Palling) *chsd ldr tl wknd qckly 3f out: eased whn btn fnl 2f* **2/1**[1]

2m 29.49s (-1.11) **Going Correction** -0.10s/f (Good) **9** Ran SP% **120.3**
Speed ratings (Par 101): **99,98,97,91,90 88,84,83,53**
toteswingers:1&2:£44.00, 1&3:£5.10, 2&3:£16.70 CSF £271.84 CT £2542.50 TOTE £18.90: £4.70, £9.90, £1.40; EX 718.30 TRIFECTA Not won..
Owner L R Owen **Bred** L R Owen **Trained** Great Ness, Shropshire

FOCUS
A decent clip from the outset in this weak handicap. The winner was showing her first form.
Dancing Primo Official explanation: trainer said regarding apparent improvement in form he had no explanation as to mares improvement
T/Plt: £1,123.90 to a £1 stake. Pool:£56,735.47 - 36.85 winning tickets T/Qpdt: £186.70 to a £1 stake. Pool:£3,684.34 - 14.60 winning tickets ST

2280 CHESTER (L-H)
Saturday, June 11

OFFICIAL GOING: Good to firm (8.1)
Wind: light 1/2 against Weather: overcast, changeable, heavy showers

2906 CORBETTS BEST DRESSED FILLIES' H'CAP 1m 4f 66y
2:15 (2:15) (Class 4) (0-85,82) 4-Y-O+ **£5,828** (£1,734; £866; £432) **Stalls** Low

Form RPR
1-42 **1** **Never Can Tell (IRE)**[39] 1788 4-9-3 **78**.......................... JoeFanning 1 86
(Jamie Osborne) *dwlt: drvn to ld after 1f: drvn clr over 1f out: styd on strly* **11/2**

4-11 **2** *3 1/4* **Tweedledrum**[12] 2552 4-9-3 **78**.......................... FrannyNorton 8 81+
(Andrew Balding) *swtchd lft after s: hld up in rr: pushed along 6f out: hung lft over 1f out: styd on to take 2nd last 75yds* **3/1**[1]

-021 **3** *1/2* **Rio's Rosanna (IRE)**[15] 2478 4-9-1 **76**.................. TonyHamilton 4 78+
(Richard Whitaker) *hld up in mid-div: effrt over 2f out: n.m.r on inner appr fnl f: kpt on to take 3rd last 100yds* **7/2**[2]

0032 **4** *1 1/2* **Bollin Dolly**[17] 2403 8-9-0 **75**.......................... PJMcDonald 5 75
(Tim Easterby) *trckd ldrs: wnt 2nd over 1f out: kpt on one pce* **7/1**

3-53 **5** *7* **Countess Comet (IRE)**[32] 1992 4-9-3 **78**............(p) RichardKingscote 2 66
(Ralph Beckett) *led 1f: chsd ldrs: wkng whn n.m.r appr fnl f* **5/1**

26-0 **6** *9* **Cabal**[8] 2674 4-8-11 **75**.......................... SeanLevey(3) 6 49
(Andrew Crook) *hld up towards rr: pushed along 3f out: nvr on terms* **50/1**

1404 **7** *18* **Granny McPhee**[9] 2634 5-9-7 **82**.......................... LiamJones 3 27
(Alan Bailey) *s.i.s: hld up in rr: hdwy over 5f of out: chsng ldrs over 2f out: wknd over 1f out: eased clsng stages* **9/2**[3]

0/0 **8** *18* **Qeethaara (USA)**[21] 2282 7-8-12 **73**.......................... DuranFentiman 7 —
(Mark Brisbourne) *mid-div: hdwy to chse ldrs over 3f out: wknd 2f out: bhd whn eased clsng stages* **33/1**

2m 36.25s (-2.25) **Going Correction** -0.025s/f (Good) **8** Ran SP% **114.9**
Speed ratings (Par 102): **106,103,103,102,97 91,79,67**
Tote Swingers: 1&2 £3.80, 1&3 £6.10, 2&3 £2.60 CSF £22.50 CT £65.69 TOTE £6.70: £1.90, £1.60, £1.80; EX 26.20.
Owner Dr Marwan Koukash **Bred** Shaanara Syndicate **Trained** Upper Lambourn, Berks
■ Stewards' Enquiry : Franny Norton caution: careless riding

FOCUS
No false rail. Rail realignment added 10yds to 5f races and 22yds to all others. Probably only a fair handicap, which was effectively stolen from the front, so messy form which is rated on the negative side. Winning jockey Joe Fanning reported afterwards it was 'good, fast ground'.

2907 CORBETTSPORTS.COM FREE BET MAIDEN STKS 5f 16y
2:45 (2:49) (Class 4) 2-Y-O **£5,018** (£1,493; £746; £372) **Stalls** Low

Form RPR
1 **Big Note (IRE)** 2-9-3 0.......................... FrannyNorton 10 83+
(Andrew Balding) *dwlt: swtchd lft after s: hdwy on ins whn nt clr run 2f out: chsd ldr over 1f out: r.o to ld last 100yds: readily* **14/1**

042 **2** *2 3/4* **Kool Henry (IRE)**[14] 2485 2-9-0 0.......................... SeanLevey(3) 5 71
(David O'Meara) *chsd ldr: styd on to take 2nd towards fin* **9/2**[2]

2452 **3** *hd* **Courtland King (IRE)**[18] 2380 2-9-3 0.................. AdrianNicholls 1 70
(David Evans) *led: hdd ins fnl f: kpt on same pce* **6/1**[3]

33 **4** *1 1/2* **Shere Khan**[26] 2148 2-9-3 0.......................... TonyHamilton 4 65
(Richard Hannon) *in rr-div: hdwy to chse ldrs over 2f out: kpt on same pce appr fnl f* **3/1**[1]

25 **5** *2* **Blodwen Abbey**[22] 2254 2-8-12 0.......................... LiamJones 7 53
(James Unett) *chsd ldrs: outpcd 2f out: styd on fnl f* **8/1**

52 **6** *2* **Nearly A Gift (IRE)**[9] 2630 2-8-12 0.................. DuranFentiman 8 46
(Tim Easterby) *s.i.s: hdwy 3f out: nvr trbld ldrs* **9/1**

0335 **7** *3/4* **Economic Crisis (IRE)**[7] 2725 2-8-12 0.................. PatrickMathers 2 43
(Alan Berry) *chsd ldrs: wknd over 1f out* **14/1**

56 **8** *2 1/4* **Spring Daisy (IRE)**[9] 2640 2-8-12 0.................. RichardKingscote 3 35
(Tom Dascombe) *chsd ldrs: lost pl over 2f out* **16/1**

9 *1 3/4* **Prince Gabriel (IRE)** 2-9-3 0.......................... JoeFanning 6 33
(David Nicholls) *dwlt: in rr: nvr a factor* **13/2**

61.15 secs (0.15) **Going Correction** -0.025s/f (Good) **9** Ran SP% **111.1**
Speed ratings (Par 95): **97,92,92,89,86 83,82,78,75**
toteswingers:1&2:£17.80, 1&3:£8.10, 2&3:£1.80 CSF £69.71 TOTE £18.70: £4.20, £1.50, £1.90; EX 71.60.
Owner N Botica **Bred** Willow Tree Stud Farm **Trained** Kingsclere, Hants

FOCUS
This didn't look a really strong race but there is no doubt the winner looks one with a future. The third sets the level.

NOTEBOOK
Big Note(IRE) ◆, by a sprinter out of a French Listed winner, sat towards the rear early before proving easily the best of these when asked to quicken, even after half-jumping or slipping on a path in the home straight. He has a couple of sales race entries later in the year and may head to Newmarket's July meeting next. (op 16-1)
Kool Henry(IRE) caught the eye on his last outing at Beverley but got a little stirred up at the start, so the fact he ran on nicely bodes well for his future. (tchd 7-2)
Courtland King(IRE) got to the front and had every chance, but couldn't hang on. (op 5-1)
Shere Khan made progress from his debut at Leicester last time and seemed fancied for this, but he didn't have the change of gear to get to the front, and probably needs further. (op 4-1)
Blodwen Abbey was down in trip again after showing speed at Haydock before faltering. Ridden with a bit of restraint here, she wasn't able to quicken after coming a bit wide off the final bend and jumping the same path the winner has a problem with. (op 16-1)
Prince Gabriel(IRE), a half-brother to a winning 2-y-o sprinter, got upset in the stalls and didn't make any impression after starting slowly. (op 7-1 tchd 8-1)

2908 RAYMOND CORBETT MEMORIAL H'CAP 7f 122y
3:20 (3:21) (Class 2) (0-105,90) 3-Y-O **£12,952** (£3,854; £1,926; £962) **Stalls** Low

Form RPR
6206 **1** **Fred Willetts (IRE)**[7] 2705 3-9-0 **88**..................(v) MatthewCosham(5) 2 94
(David Evans) *mde all: hld on wl* **5/1**[2]

1304 **2** *1/2* **Kingscroft (IRE)**[37] 1820 3-8-13 **82**.......................... JoeFanning 3 87
(Mark Johnston) *chsd wnr: chal over 1f out: styd on same pce last 75yds* **6/1**[3]

-305 **3** *5* **Rigolleto (IRE)**[7] 2705 3-9-7 **90**.......................... ChrisCatlin 4 82
(Mick Channon) *chsd ldrs: one pce over 1f out* **6/1**[3]

1000 **4** *3 3/4* **Strictly Pink (IRE)**[5] 2763 3-8-10 **79**.......................... LiamJones 1 62
(Alan Bailey) *rrd s: in rr: effrt over 3f out: swtchd rt 1f out: tk n.d 4th nr fin* **8/1**

13 **5** *1* **Cool Macavity (IRE)**[15] 2477 3-8-11 **80**.................. FrannyNorton 6 60
(B W Hills) *s.i.s: swtchd lft after 1f: sn chsng ldrs: effrt over 2f out: floundered and wknd over 1f out* **2/1**[1]

-056 **6** *3/4* **Barista (IRE)**[2] 2834 3-8-4 **80**.......................... CharlesBishop(7) 5 59
(Mick Channon) *swtchd lft after s: in rr: pushed along and n.m.r on inner over 2f out: wknd over 1f out* **10/1**

-400 **7** *1 3/4* **Julius Geezer (IRE)**[8] 2684 3-9-7 **90**.................. RichardKingscote 7 64
(Tom Dascombe) *trckd ldrs on outer: t.k.h: drvn over 2f out: lost pl over 1f out* **6/1**[3]

1m 32.5s (-1.30) **Going Correction** -0.025s/f (Good) **7** Ran SP% **113.1**
Speed ratings (Par 105): **105,104,99,95,94 94,92**
Tote Swingers: 1&2 £2.60, 1&3 £2.00, 2&3 £2.90 CSF £33.61 TOTE £5.60: £2.50, £3.80; EX 23.10.
Owner 24 - 7 Recruitment/ Allan Jones **Bred** Liam Queally **Trained** Pandy, Monmouths

FOCUS
It was an advantage to be up the pace in this contest, as the first two home were first and second throughout, finishing clear. The winner is rated in line with his previous best.

NOTEBOOK
Fred Willetts(IRE) finished a place behind Rigolleto when they met at Haydock a week previously, but comfortably reversed that form after making all the running. Any rise in the handicap will make things really hard for him next time judged on previous efforts off official marks in the 90s. (op 9-2)
Kingscroft(IRE) was behind Fred Willetts when they met here in May, and wasn't able to get his revenge despite looking the more likely winner about 1f out. (op 9-2)
Rigolleto(IRE) was defending a one-from-one record at the course (his only victory), but didn't have the speed when needed to close down the two that shot clear. (op 7-1)
Strictly Pink(IRE) never made any impression in this after starting slowly.

Cool Macavity(IRE) was the least exposed of this bunch and was having only his third racecourse start, and second on turf. Not the quickest into stride, he raced keenly surrounded by horses and had nothing more to give late on. He can be given another chance because he still looked a bit green at times. The jockey reported afterwards that his mount lost his action in the home straight. (op 11-4)
Barista(IRE) had been a little disappointing this year and this wasn't any better. (op 9-1 tchd 12-1)
Julius Geezer(IRE) won the Lily Agnes last season and had been mainly consistent since without getting his head in front, but ruined his chance in this by pulling very hard while pace was modest. (op 7-1)

2909 BET AT CORBETTSPORTS.COM H'CAP — 1m 2f 75y
3:55 (3:56) (Class 2) (0-105,101) 4-Y-O+ **£12,708** (£6,796; £3,398; £1,699; £846) **Stalls** High

Form				RPR
-160	1		**Jutland**[12] 2573 4-9-4 **95** JoeFanning 2 (Mark Johnston) *trckd ldrs: effrt over 2f out: led last 150yds: hld on wl towards fin* **8/1**	102
-100	2	*nk*	**Lost In The Moment (IRE)**[93] 824 4-9-9 **100** (p) ChrisCatlin 10 (Saeed Bin Suroor) *hld up towards rr: effrt over 2f out: styd on to chse wnr ins fnl f: no ex towards fin* **14/1**	107+
1-42	3	*1 ¼*	**Opera Gal (IRE)**[8] 2676 4-9-3 **94** FrannyNorton 8 (Andrew Balding) *led: qcknd over 2f out: hdd and no ex ins fnl f* **3/1**[1]	98
6-56	4	*1 ¾*	**Fantasy Gladiator**[9] 2647 5-8-3 **80** (p) AndrewElliott 1 (Robert Cowell) *trckd ldrs: t.k.h: effrt over 2f out: kpt on one pce appr fnl f* **22/1**	81
4400	5	*shd*	**Dhaular Dhar (IRE)**[7] 2706 9-8-6 **86** PaulPickard(3) 12 (Jim Goldie) *t.k.h in rr: hdwy on ins 2f out: styd on fnl f* **25/1**	86+
-064	6	*nk*	**Tartan Gunna**[21] 2282 5-8-5 **82** (b) LiamJones 3 (Mark Johnston) *s.s: detached in rr: hdwy over 3f out: kpt on fnl 2f: nrst fin* **9/1**	82
0-15	7	*shd*	**Mirrored**[12] 2573 5-9-0 **91** DuranFentiman 4 (Tim Easterby) *dwlt: t.k.h in rr: effrt on outside over 3f out: styd on fnl f* **8/1**	91+
440-	8	*3*	**Gritstone**[248] 6677 4-7-13 **83** LauraBarry(7) 6 (Richard Fahey) *t.k.h in mid-div: nt clr run and lost pl 2f out: styd on steadily fnl f: will improve* **20/1**	77+
20-1	9	*1 ¾*	**Sam Sharp (USA)**[23] 2217 5-8-12 **89** RichardKingscote 5 (Ian Williams) *trckd ldrs: effrt over 2f out: wknd over 1f out* **13/2**[3]	79
10-0	10	*nk*	**Absinthe (IRE)**[10] 2604 5-8-7 **87** JohnFahy(3) 9 (Walter Swinburn) *s.i.s: mid-div: effrt over 2f out: wknd over 1f out* **11/2**[2]	76+
-104	11	*6*	**Bonfire Knight**[14] 2509 4-8-13 **90** (v1) TonyHamilton 7 (John Quinn) *trckd ldrs: effrt over 2f out: sn lost pl* **14/1**	67
-010	12	*15*	**Light From Mars**[30] 2031 6-9-10 **101** AdrianNicholls 11 (David Nicholls) *trckd ldr: t.k.h: drvn over 2f out: lost pl over 1f out: eased whn bhd* **14/1**	48

2m 10.87s (-0.33) **Going Correction** -0.025s/f (Good) **12 Ran SP% 118.9**
Speed ratings (Par 109): **100,99,98,97,97 97,96,94,93,92 88,76**
Tote Swingers: 1&2 £19.30, 1&3 £5.50, 2&3 £8.10 CSF £111.44 CT £415.68 TOTE £9.50: £3.20, £3.00, £1.40; EX 157.90.
Owner Sheikh Hamdan Bin Mohammed Al Maktoum **Bred** Darley **Trained** Middleham Moor, N Yorks

FOCUS
A really strong-looking handicap, but the form won't be that reliable because the early pace was far from quick, meaning plenty of these took strong holds and not many got involved. Improved form from the first two.

NOTEBOOK
Jutland, a winner over C&D on his first start of the year, didn't run very well last time but obviously likes his trips to this course as, after being well placed near the leader, he forced his way to the front and did enough to hang on. Official explanation: trainer said regarding apparent improvement in form gelding was suited by track (op 9-1)
Lost In The Moment(IRE), who ran three times at Meydan on the AW earlier in the year, raced keenly towards the rear early but came with a strong finish to make Jutland work for success. (tchd 10-1)
Opera Gal(IRE), a previous C&D winner, is a consistent performer and once again posted a sound effort, although she did have the luxury of dictating from the front. She is said to need a bit of ease in the ground. (op 7-2)
Fantasy Gladiator ◆ had never tried this trip before but there is no doubt he can win over it considering this performance. It surely can't be long before he wins in turf for the first time. (op 20-1)
Dhaular Dhar(IRE) likes it here and was lower in the weights than his last visit, but he wasn't well placed off a slow pace and couldn't get to the leaders. (tchd 28-1)
Tartan Gunna usually runs well but doesn't win that often, but this was an odd run. He started slowly and often didn't look to be enjoying things as much as he should have, but he got back involved and kept on for pressure. The over-riding impression was that he doesn't look one to trust for now. (op 8-1)
Mirrored finished a long way in front of Jutland in the Zetland Gold Cup recently and seemed sure to be a major player as he loomed up on the outside. However, his effort soon levelled out and he couldn't compete. (tchd 9-1)
Gritstone ◆ caught the eye staying on from the rear after his 248-day absence and will no doubt be better for the run. (op 25-1 tchd 28-1)
Sam Sharp(USA), up 7lb for winning at 1m at Haydock last time, found only the one pace when the tempo lifted. (op 5-1)
Absinthe(IRE), dropped 5lb since his last start on turf, didn't make much impression. (op 13-2 tchd 5-1)
Light From Mars wasn't beaten far in a solid-looking Listed race on his previous run, but this trip wasn't certain to suit. He didn't appear to get home but his jockey reported afterwards that his mount didn't handle the track. (op 12-1)

2910 KATHLEEN CORBETT MEMORIAL CLASSIFIED CLAIMING STKS — 7f 2y
4:30 (4:31) (Class 4) 3-Y-O+ **£5,180** (£1,541; £770; £384) **Stalls** Low

Form				RPR
4432	1		**Kingswinford (IRE)**[19] 2356 5-8-13 70 PaulPickard(3) 5 (Brian Ellison) *trckd ldrs: drvn over 2f out: chal over 1f out: edgd rt fnl 75yds: styd on to ld nr fin* **4/1**[3]	77
5014	2	*nk*	**Dream Catcher (FR)**[10] 2619 3-8-11 79 FrannyNorton 6 (David Nicholls) *swtchd rt s: led: jnd over 1f out: hdd and no ex nr fin* **3/1**[1]	77
14-3	3	*¾*	**Bilko Pak (IRE)**[160] 10 3-8-5 78 AdrianNicholls 2 (Ann Duffield) *hmpd s: hld up in mid-div: effrt 3f out: styd on fnl f: no ex fnl 50yds* **8/1**	69
3042	4	*shd*	**Getcarter**[4] 2794 5-9-3 71 (p) RichardKingscote 1 (Richard Hannon) *hmpd s: sn chsng ldrs: effrt over 2f out: swtchd rt and then lft ins fnl f: styd on towards fin* **7/2**[2]	75
05-6	5	*5*	**Saharia (IRE)**[148] 168 4-9-5 77 (p) TonyHamilton 4 (Ollie Pears) *n.m.r and dropped bk sn after s: hdwy over 2f out: nvr nr ldrs* **14/1**	63
5-24	6	*¾*	**Opus Maximus (IRE)**[66] 1164 6-9-2 80 (p) JoeFanning 10 (Jennie Candlish) *in rr: sme hdwy over 2f out: nvr on terms* **11/2**	58
-523	7	*11*	**Lord Of The Dance (IRE)**[14] 2494 5-9-5 72 LiamJones 8 (Mark Brisbourne) *bmpd s: mid-div: drvn 3f out: sn lost pl and bhd* **8/1**	32
0/0-	8	*1*	**Danzig Fox**[326] 3122 6-8-10 40 JosephYoung(7) 7 (Michael Mullineaux) *bmpd s: chsd ldrs: lost pl over 2f out* **33/1**	27
4654	9	*1*	**Gorgeous Goblin (IRE)**[7] 2710 4-9-1 52 (vt) ChrisCatlin 3 (David C Griffiths) *in rr: bhd fnl 2f* **25/1**	22

1m 26.38s (-0.12) **Going Correction** -0.025s/f (Good)
WFA 3 from 4yo+ 10lb **9 Ran SP% 118.3**
Speed ratings (Par 105): **99,98,97,97,91 91,78,77,76**
Tote Swingers: 1&2 £3.80, 1&3 £6.90, 2&3 £6.00 CSF £16.90 TOTE £4.50: £1.80, £1.60, £2.90; EX 18.00.The winner was subject to a friendly claim. Dream Catcher was claimed by A D W Pinder for £19,000.
Owner L S Keys **Bred** J Costello **Trained** Norton, N Yorks

FOCUS
Plenty of varying abilities on show in this claimer, but a good, honest performer took the contest. He's rated to this year's form. Again, not many got involved.
Dream Catcher(FR) Official explanation: two-day ban: careless riding (25th-26th June)

2911 CHESTER ROCKS 2 & 3 JULY H'CAP — 5f 16y
5:05 (5:05) (Class 3) (0-95,95) 3-Y-O **£8,418** (£2,505; £1,251; £625) **Stalls** Low

Form				RPR
1110	1		**Lord Avon**[30] 2032 3-9-3 **91** JoeFanning 1 (Bill Turner) *mde all: drvn 2 l clr 1f out: hld on towards fin* **9/2**[3]	96
6-66	2	*1*	**Murbeh (IRE)**[14] 2500 3-9-7 **95** LiamJones 4 (Brian Meehan) *hld up towards rr: effrt over 2f out: plld wd over 1f out: fin wl* **7/2**[2]	96+
-006	3	*hd*	**Ballista (IRE)**[36] 1852 3-9-0 **88** RichardKingscote 7 (Tom Dascombe) *chsd wnr: kpt on same pce fnl f* **15/2**	88
0504	4	*2 ½*	**Berberana (IRE)**[14] 2505 3-8-4 **78** AndrewElliott 2 (Tim Easterby) *hood removed v late: dwlt: sn chsng ldrs: one pce over 1f out* **8/1**	69+
4111	5	*6*	**Barkston Ash**[18] 2391 3-8-2 **76** oh1 DuranFentiman 3 (Eric Alston) *mid-div: drvn over 2f out: outpcd and lost pl over 1f out* **9/4**[1]	46
4300	6	*1*	**Boundaries**[14] 2505 3-8-8 **82** (v) FrannyNorton 8 (Tim Easterby) *mid-div: drvn over 2f out: sn wl outpcd* **11/2**	48
21-0	7	*7*	**Kinlochrannoch**[14] 2505 3-8-6 **80** ChrisCatlin 6 (Ben Haslam) *sn outpcd and detached in last: wl bhd fnl 2f* **20/1**	21

60.19 secs (-0.81) **Going Correction** -0.025s/f (Good) **7 Ran SP% 114.2**
Speed ratings (Par 103): **105,103,103,99,89 87,76**
Tote Swingers: 1&2 £3.50, 1&3 £5.00, 2&3 £4.90 CSF £20.51 CT £114.26 TOTE £4.50: £2.20, £2.60; EX 22.60.
Owner Mrs M S Teversham **Bred** Mrs Monica Teversham **Trained** Sigwells, Somerset

FOCUS
By this point on the card, it had become completely obvious that making or being close to the pace was a big advantage over 1m or less. Most of these didn't run their races.

NOTEBOOK
Lord Avon, who has progressed well from a win in a seller during March, was bounced out from the lowest draw and was virtually untroubled to make all. Much like the first winner on the card, it would be surprising if things fell in place like they did here too many times. (op 4-1)
Murbeh(IRE) hadn't been beaten a long way in a couple of Listed contests this year (both 6f) and this was his first try over 5f. Once again he kept on well but wasn't good enough to win. (op 4-1)
Ballista(IRE), dropped 5lb since a fair effort over C&D, chased the leader throughout but was never going to catch him. (op 7-1)
Berberana(IRE) finished well in front of Kinlochrannoch last time, and there was never any danger that form was going to be reversed. The Tim Easterby runner held every chance but became one paced late on. (op 13-2)
Barkston Ash, now 20lb higher than the first of his previous three wins, was chasing a four-timer, but this big sort didn't appear to handle the track, so is easily afforded another chance. (op 5-2)
Boundaries has run well here in the past so it was a surprise to see him have trouble handling the bend. (op 8-1)

2912 F VODKA FILLIES' H'CAP — 1m 2f 75y
5:40 (5:42) (Class 5) (0-70,70) 4-Y-O+ **£4,047** (£1,204; £601; £300) **Stalls** High

Form				RPR
2-32	1		**Kenyan Cat**[24] 2204 4-9-5 **68** AdrianNicholls 8 (Ed McMahon) *hld up in midfield: smooth hdwy over 2f out: edgd lft and led appr fnl f: styd on wl* **11/4**[1]	79+
5045	2	*2 ½*	**Straversjoy**[13] 2530 4-8-6 **58** PaulPickard(3) 12 (Reg Hollinshead) *hld up in rr: wd bnd 7f out: stdy hdwy on outer over 3f out: chsd wnr 1f out: no imp* **16/1**	64
32-0	3	*3 ¼*	**Magic Millie (IRE)**[18] 2388 4-8-7 **59** SeanLevey(3) 3 (David O'Meara) *sn chsng ldrs: styd on same pce over 1f out* **13/2**[3]	58
2130	4	*½*	**Spavento (IRE)**[1] 2887 5-8-13 **62** DuranFentiman 4 (Eric Alston) *in tch: drvn 5f out: styd on one pce over 1f out* **15/2**	60
4P53	5	*shd*	**Beauchamp Xiara**[15] 2478 5-9-1 **64** JoeFanning 11 (Hans Adielsson) *t.k.h in rr: hdwy over 3f out: kpt on fnl f* **10/1**	62
3402	6	*1 ¼*	**Very Well Red**[8] 2663 8-9-7 **70** ChrisCatlin 6 (Peter Hiatt) *led 1f: chsd ldrs: led 2f out: wnt lft and hdd over 1f out: wknd towards fin* **7/1**	65
224-	7	*½*	**Zenarinda**[253] 6535 4-8-13 **67** AshleyMorgan(5) 10 (Mark H Tompkins) *s.i.s: hdwy 4f out: n.m.r over 1 1/2f out: kpt on one pce* **10/1**	61
0-42	8	*shd*	**Sacco D'Oro**[25] 771 5-7-11 **51** oh4 NeilFarley(5) 1 (Michael Mullineaux) *s.i.s: mid-div: kpt on fnl f: nvr a factor* **25/1**	45
000-	9	*6*	**Grethel (IRE)**[10] 6051 7-7-11 **51** oh6 DanielleMcCreery(5) 5 (Alan Berry) *in rr: wd bnd 7f out: hdwy over 4f out: lost pl and carried wd bnd wl over 1f out: sn bhd* **40/1**	33
6420	10	*1 ¾*	**Madame Excelerate**[11] 2589 4-9-0 **63** LiamJones 9 (Mark Brisbourne) *led after 1f: wd bnd 7f out: hdd 2f out: sn hmpd and lost pl: eased* **14/1**	42+
0110	11	*5*	**Princess Lexi (IRE)**[23] 2232 4-9-1 **64** FrannyNorton 2 (Ian Williams) *s.i.s: sn trcking ldrs: wkng whn hmpd over 1f out: eased ins fnl f* **5/1**[2]	33+
5246	12	*7*	**Hathaway (IRE)**[17] 2401 4-8-4 **53** AndrewElliott 7 (Mark Brisbourne) *chsd ldrs on outer: drvn 6f out: hung bdly rt and lost pl bnd wl over 1f out: eased and sn bhd* **18/1**	—

2m 11.98s (0.78) **Going Correction** -0.025s/f (Good) **12 Ran SP% 123.2**
Speed ratings (Par 100): **95,93,90,90,89 88,88,88,83,82 78,72**
Tote Swingers: 1&2 £13.50, 1&3 £4.20, 2&3 £18.30 CSF £53.94 CT £275.38 TOTE £4.30: £1.50, £5.50, £2.60; EX 68.90.
Owner David Botterill & John Guest **Bred** D R Botterill **Trained** Lichfield, Staffs
■ Stewards' Enquiry : Franny Norton two-day ban: careless riding (25th-26th June)

FOCUS
This was a messy race in which quite a few were produced to have a chance. The winner posted a clear personal best.
T/Plt: £114.40 to a £1 stake. Pool:£69,560.58 - 443.54 winning tickets T/Qpdt: £34.40 to a £1 stake. Pool:£3,278.94 - 70.40 winning tickets WG

The Form Book, Raceform Ltd, Compton, RG20 6NL

2580 LEICESTER (R-H)

Saturday, June 11

OFFICIAL GOING: Good (good to firm in places; watered; 7.2)

Wind: Light behind Weather: Cloudy with sunny spells

2913 CREAM GORSE H'CAP 5f 2y

6:30 (6:30) (Class 5) (0-70,72) 3-Y-O+ £2,914 (£867; £433; £216) Stalls High

Form RPR

0-26 **1** **Musical Bridge**[36] 1856 5-9-9 **65**........................(b) TomEaves 1 73
(Lisa Williamson) *w ldr tl led 1/2-way: rdn and edgd rt fr over 1f out: r.o* **9/2**[3]

5511 **2** *3/4* **Six Wives**[11] 2585 4-9-9 **72**........................ LeonnaMayor(7) 5 78
(David Nicholls) *trckd ldrs: rdn over 1f out: ev ch ins fnl f: unable qck towards fin* **6/4**[1]

2306 **3** *1/2* **Dancing Freddy (IRE)**[17] 2397 4-9-8 **67**..............(p) RobertLButler(3) 2 71
(Richard Guest) *chsd ldrs: rdn over 1f out: styd on same pce ins fnl f* **11/2**

5150 **4** *shd* **Bateleur**[26] 2142 7-9-2 **61**........................ MartinHarley(3) 3 65
(Mick Channon) *hld up: hdwy on outer over 1f out: sn rdn: styd on same pce ins fnl f* **11/1**

3132 **5** *1 1/4* **Decider (USA)**[10] 2603 8-9-0 **56**........................(b) LukeMorris 4 55
(Ronald Harris) *led to 1/2-way: rdn over 1f out: no ex ins fnl f* **11/4**[2]

59.32 secs (-0.68) **Going Correction** -0.25s/f (Firm) **5** Ran SP% **108.6**
Speed ratings (Par 103): **95,93,93,92,90**
CSF £11.42 TOTE £4.20: £1.10, £1.10; EX 7.90.
Owner John Conway **Bred** John Starbuck **Trained** Saighton, Cheshire

FOCUS
A workaday handicap in which little more than a couple of lengths covered all five runners at the line. The form is taken at face value.

2914 INSPIRATIONAL HEALTH CARE MAIDEN FILLIES' STKS 5f 218y

7:00 (7:00) (Class 5) 2-Y-O £2,914 (£867; £433; £216) Stalls High

Form RPR

1 **Russelliana** 2-9-0 0........................ DavidProbert 3 85+
(Sir Michael Stoute) *a.p: edgd lft fr over 1f out: styd on to ld wl ins fnl f* **7/2**[3]

2 *1 1/4* **Tickled Pink (IRE)** 2-9-0 0........................ TomQueally 5 81+
(Sir Henry Cecil) *s.i.s: hdwy over 2f out: led over 1f out: hdd and unable qck wl ins fnl f* **5/1**

3 *1 1/2* **Pearl Diva (IRE)** 2-9-0 0........................ NeilCallan 6 77+
(Peter Chapple-Hyam) *chsd ldrs: rdn over 2f out: ev ch wl over 1f out: styd on same pce ins fnl f* **11/4**[1]

0 **4** *4 1/2* **Damask (IRE)**[15] 2467 2-9-0 0........................ DarryllHolland 11 63
(Richard Hannon) *chsd ldrs: rdn over 2f out: styd on same pce fr over 1f out: hung rt wl ins fnl f* **4/1**

5 *1* **Besito (IRE)** 2-9-0 0........................ TomEaves 2 60
(William Jarvis) *chsd ldrs: led 2f out: sn hdd: wknd ins fnl f* **12/1**

2 **6** *8* **Lemon Rock**[29] 2063 2-9-0 0........................ AdamKirby 1 35
(Noel Quinlan) *led 4f: sn rdn and wknd* **10/3**[2]

5 **7** *4 1/2* **Ave Sofia**[18] 2387 2-9-0 0........................ NickyMackay 9 22
(John Holt) *mid-div: rdn: hung rt and wknd over 2f out* **33/1**

0 **8** *11* **Street Angel (IRE)**[11] 2580 2-8-7 0........................ NatashaEaton(7) 7 —
(Alan Bailey) *s.i.s: a in rr: bhd fr 1/2-way: t.o* **100/1**

9 *1 1/2* **Song Of Joy (IRE)** 2-9-0 0........................ KellyHarrison 10 —
(Paul D'Arcy) *sn pushed along in rr: bhd fr 1/2-way: t.o* **80/1**

1m 11.7s (-1.30) **Going Correction** -0.25s/f (Firm) **9** Ran SP% **121.5**
Speed ratings (Par 90): **98,96,94,88,87 76,70,55,53**
toteswingers:1&2:£3.50, 1&3:£3.70, 2&3:£5.10 CSF £22.60 TOTE £7.30: £1.60, £3.00, £2.00; EX 50.60.
Owner Sir Evelyn De Rothschild **Bred** Southcourt Stud **Trained** Newmarket, Suffolk

FOCUS
An interesting maiden with the front three clear. The race is rated towards the top end of the averages.

NOTEBOOK
Russelliana was heavily backed and the daughter of Medicean didn't disappoint on debut, seeing this out in really pleasing style to beat another potentially smart filly. Despite her inexperience, she travelled smoothly and was the last to come off the bridle. She edged left once coming under pressure but it was probably greenness more than anything and it didn't stop her staying on really nicely to make a winning debut. She looks to have a bright future and she has the potential to stay 1m-plus on breeding. (op 7-1 after early 10-1 in places)
Tickled Pink(IRE), Group 1 entered, is clearly held in high regard and she shaped really nicely in second, coming down the middle of the track. She looked to have put her rivals in trouble when quickening up to lead just over a furlong out and although beaten, shaped with real promise. She will be short odds to go one better next time. (op 7-2)
Pearl Diva(IRE) also shaped like a certain future winner in third and she pulled nicely clear of the remainder. (op 3-1 tchd 2-1)
Damask(IRE) seemed to improve a little on her moderate Newmarket debut. She was readily left behind in the closing stages and hung under pressure, however. (tchd 9-2)
Lemon Rock shaped with a deal of promise on debut but fared nowhere near as well here, dropping away tamely from halfway. (op 3-1)

2915 F.P. BIRTHDAY H'CAP 1m 1f 218y

7:30 (7:31) (Class 5) (0-75,75) 4-Y-O+ £2,914 (£867; £433; £216) Stalls Low

Form RPR

1013 **1** **Destiny Of A Diva**[14] 2486 4-9-5 **73**........................ AdamKirby 6 87
(Reg Hollinshead) *hld up: hdwy and swtchd lft 3f out: led 2f out: sn rdn and hung lft: r.o: eased nr fin* **7/2**[2]

4-25 **2** *2 1/2* **Shabak Hom (IRE)**[29] 2046 4-9-5 **73**........................ MartinLane 5 81
(David Simcock) *hld up: hdwy over 3f out: rdn and hung rt over 2f out: chsd wnr over 1f out: no imp* **3/1**[1]

U2-0 **3** *8* **Emeebee**[36] 1867 5-8-13 **67**........................ TonyCulhane 8 59
(Willie Musson) *s.i.s and wnt lft s: bhd: t.o 1/2-way: stl last over 2f out: styd on u.p fnl f: nrst fin* **9/2**[3]

0-00 **4** *1 1/2* **Swift Chap**[18] 2376 5-8-10 **64**........................(v[1]) DarryllHolland 4 53
(Rod Millman) *prom: rdn and hmpd 3f out: sn outpcd: styd on ins fnl f* **10/1**

41-5 **5** *3* **Osgood**[14] 2486 4-9-0 **75**........................ CharlesBishop(7) 1 58
(Mick Channon) *led: hdd over 2f out: sn rdn: wknd over 1f out* **11/2**

4160 **6** *1/2* **Silent Oasis**[23] 2232 5-9-2 **70**........................ FergusSweeney 2 52
(Brendan Powell) *chsd ldrs: rdn over 2f out: wknd over 1f out* **14/1**

5150 **7** *3/4* **Understory (USA)**[9] 2649 4-9-6 **74**........................ NeilCallan 3 55
(Tim McCarthy) *chsd ldr tl led over 2f out: sn rdn and hdd: wknd fnl f:* **8/1**

/000 **8** *14* **Focail Eile**[36] 1867 6-8-11 **65**........................ TomQueally 7 18
(Noel Quinlan) *hld up: rdn whn hmpd 3f out: sn wknd: t.o* **14/1**

2m 5.50s (-2.40) **Going Correction** -0.15s/f (Firm) **8** Ran SP% **114.3**
Speed ratings (Par 103): **103,101,94,93,91 90,90,78**
toteswingers:1&2:£1.30, 1&3:£3.40, 2&3:£3.70 CSF £14.44 CT £46.81 TOTE £2.50: £1.10, £1.80, £2.40; EX 9.90.
Owner M A Massarella **Bred** M Massarella **Trained** Upper Longdon, Staffs
■ Stewards' Enquiry : Adam Kirby two-day ban: careless riding (27th-28th June)

FOCUS
Osgood ensured they went a decent gallop and that suited the hold-up horses. The first two finished clear and were the only ones to show their form.

2916 INSPIRATIONAL HEALTH CARE SPRINT H'CAP 5f 218y

8:00 (8:27) (Class 4) (0-80,79) 3-Y-O £5,180 (£1,541; £770; £384) Stalls High

Form RPR

-505 **1** **Catfish (IRE)**[15] 2468 3-9-7 **79**........................ ShaneKelly 1 87
(Brian Meehan) *mde all: crossed over to stands' side rail over 4f out: rdn over 1f out: jst hld on* **3/1**[1]

3003 **2** *hd* **Mazovian (USA)**[11] 2592 3-8-2 **60**........................ SilvestreDeSousa 6 67
(Michael Chapman) *chsd ldrs: rdn over 2f out: swtchd rt over 1f out: chsd wnr ins fnl f: r.o: jst failed* **12/1**

0002 **3** *2 1/4* **Sacrosanctus**[10] 2619 3-9-3 **78**........................ MichaelO'Connell(3) 4 78
(David Nicholls) *chsd wnr: rdn over 1f out: styd on same pce ins fnl f* **8/1**[3]

633 **4** *1 1/4* **Restless Bay (IRE)**[10] 2611 3-9-6 **78**........................(v) AdamKirby 2 74+
(Reg Hollinshead) *s.i.s: hld up: hdwy and hmpd over 1f out: no ex ins fnl f* **8/1**[3]

5-31 **5** *3 1/4* **Frozen Over**[16] 2427 3-9-3 **75**........................ FergusSweeney 9 60
(Stuart Kittow) *s.i.s: hld up: hdwy over 2f out: rdn over 1f out: wknd wl ins fnl f* **11/1**

613- **6** *3 3/4* **Picabo (IRE)**[229] 7116 3-9-1 **73**........................ TomQueally 8 46
(Lucy Wadham) *s.i.s: hld up: swtchd rt 1/2-way: hdwy over 2f out: rdn over 1f out: wknd fnl f* **3/1**[1]

3-40 **7** *5* **Gay Gallivanter**[30] 2018 3-8-9 **67**........................ MartinLane 7 24
(Michael Quinn) *mid-div: sn drvn along: bhd fr 1/2-way* **33/1**

0-04 **8** *2 1/4* **Diamond Vine (IRE)**[12] 2564 3-9-3 **75**........................(p) LukeMorris 5 25
(Ronald Harris) *chsd ldrs: rdn 1/2-way: wknd over 1f out: eased* **20/1**

41-0 **9** *7* **Indian Emperor (IRE)**[23] 2215 3-9-4 **76**........................ NeilCallan 3 —
(Roger Varian) *chsd ldrs: rdn 1/2-way: wknd 2f out* **10/3**[2]

1m 11.28s (-1.72) **Going Correction** -0.25s/f (Firm) **9** Ran SP% **119.0**
Speed ratings (Par 101): **101,100,97,96,91 86,80,77,67**
toteswingers:1&2:£7.80, 1&3:£2.90, 2&3:£14.90 CSF £41.37 CT £268.78 TOTE £3.70: £1.60, £3.50, £3.10; EX 42.40.
Owner Raymond Tooth **Bred** Castellane Partnership **Trained** Manton, Wilts
■ Stewards' Enquiry : Silvestre De Sousa one-day ban: careless riding (25th June)

FOCUS
Racing was delayed after a handler was injured loading a horse for the previous race. Ordinary form for the grade, and the principals were always prominent. The stands' rail may have been favoured.

2917 JUNE JORDAN 70TH BIRTHDAY CELEBRATION H'CAP 7f 9y

8:30 (8:59) (Class 4) (0-80,79) 3-Y-O+ £5,180 (£1,541; £770; £384) Stalls High

Form RPR

0041 **1** **Frognal (IRE)**[11] 2588 5-9-3 **73**........................(b) RobertLButler(3) 8 82
(Richard Guest) *got loose on the way to post: s.i.s: hld up: nt clr run wl over 1f out: hdwy and hung rt sn after: rdn to ld wl ins fnl f: r.o* **14/1**

60-5 **2** *2* **Last Sovereign**[16] 2431 7-9-9 **76**........................ TomQueally 4 80
(Ollie Pears) *chsd ldrs: led over 2f out: rdn and hdd wl ins fnl f* **4/1**[1]

-040 **3** *1 1/2* **Master Mylo (IRE)**[9] 2647 4-9-8 **75**........................ ShaneKelly 7 75
(Dean Ivory) *hld up: hdwy over 2f out: rdn and hung rt over 1f out: styd on same pce ins fnl f* **10/1**

22-1 **4** *hd* **Choral**[73] 1047 3-9-0 **77**........................ DarryllHolland 3 72
(Richard Hannon) *hld up: hdwy over 2f out: rdn over 1f out: styd on same pce ins fnl f* **4/1**[1]

-000 **5** *4* **Slugger O'Toole**[7] 2719 6-9-1 **68**........................(t) DavidProbert 9 56
(Stuart Williams) *chsd ldrs: lost pl over 2f out: n.d after* **9/1**[3]

20-4 **6** *7* **Imprimis Tagula (IRE)**[9] 2633 7-9-8 **75**..............(v) SilvestreDeSousa 2 44
(Alan Bailey) *hld up in tch: rdn over 1f out: wknd fnl f* **4/1**[1]

4060 **7** *3 1/2* **Yahrab (IRE)**[19] 2366 6-9-5 **72**........................(b) DavidNolan 5 32
(Declan Carroll) *led over 4f: sn rdn and wknd* **11/1**

00-0 **8** *1 3/4* **Arabian Pearl (IRE)**[21] 2286 5-9-5 **72**........................ NeilCallan 6 27
(Peter Chapple-Hyam) *hld up: hdwy 1/2-way: rdn over 2f out: wknd wl over 1f out* **9/2**[2]

1m 24.3s (-1.90) **Going Correction** -0.25s/f (Firm)
WFA 3 from 4yo+ 10lb **8** Ran SP% **113.4**
Speed ratings (Par 105): **100,97,96,95,91 83,79,77**
toteswingers:1&2:£4.40, 1&3:£22.10, 2&3:£5.70 CSF £67.98 CT £596.72 TOTE £14.60: £3.60, £1.80, £2.40; EX 64.30.
Owner Rakebackmypoker.com **Bred** Bryan Ryan **Trained** Stainforth, S Yorks

FOCUS
Weak form for the grade, but the pace was good and the winner is rated to last year's best.

2918 ASFORDBY H'CAP 5f 2y

9:00 (9:24) (Class 6) (0-60,60) 3-Y-O £2,072 (£616; £308; £153) Stalls High

Form RPR

-455 **1** **Chester Deelyte (IRE)**[40] 1764 3-8-7 **46** oh1..............(v[1]) TomEaves 11 54
(Lisa Williamson) *a.p: rdn to ld 1f out: r.o: hung rt nr fin* **25/1**

50 **2** *1 1/2* **Green Warrior**[18] 2375 3-9-7 **60**........................(p) TomQueally 1 63+
(Ann Duffield) *hld up: hdwy 1/2-way: rdn and hung lft ins fnl f: r.o* **13/2**

3063 **3** *1 1/2* **Hootys Agogo**[13] 2524 3-8-8 **52**........................ NeilFarley(5) 10 49
(Declan Carroll) *chsd ldr tl led over 3f out: rdn over 1f out: hung rt and hdd 1f out: styd on same pce ins fnl f* **10/3**[2]

0040 **4** *2 1/4* **Sleights Boy (IRE)**[17] 2396 3-8-13 **52**..............(b) PatrickMathers 8 41
(Ian McInnes) *prom: drvn along 1/2-way: styd on same pce fnl f* **33/1**

206 **5** *4* **Reachtothestars (USA)**[25] 2177 3-9-7 **60**........................ AdamKirby 6 35
(Noel Quinlan) *hld up: hrd rdn over 1f out: n.d* **10/1**

6440 **6** *3 1/4* **Hereselle (IRE)**[81] 936 3-9-4 **57**........................ SilvestreDeSousa 9 20
(Michael Chapman) *chsd ldrs: rdn 1/2-way: wknd over 1f out* **22/1**

0403 **7** *1* **Quadra Hop (IRE)**[12] 2549 3-9-4 **57**........................(t) DavidProbert 2 16
(Bryn Palling) *chsd ldrs: rdn 1/2-way: wknd fnl f* **9/2**[3]

-550 **8** *1 1/2* **Bobbyow**[100] 745 3-9-2 **55**........................(p) MartinLane 3 —
(Bryn Palling) *chsd ldrs: rdn over 3f out: wknd wl over 1f out* **10/1**

0601 **9** *hd* **Gothic Chick**[16] 2424 3-8-13 **55**........................(p) MartinHarley(3) 5 —
(Alan McCabe) *mid-div: rdn and wknd wl over 1f out* **3/1**[1]

0-00 **10** *3 3/4* **Lady Excellentia (IRE)**[12] 2549 3-8-8 **47**........................ LukeMorris 4 —
(Ronald Harris) *s.s: a in rr* **20/1**

-350 **11** *18* **Una Vita Pius (IRE)**[113] 595 3-8-10 **49**........................ JamieMackay 7 —
(Patrick Gilligan) *led: hdd over 3f out: wknd 1/2-way: t.o* **20/1**

59.94 secs (-0.06) **Going Correction** -0.25s/f (Firm) **11** Ran SP% **118.4**
Speed ratings (Par 97): **90,87,85,81,75 70,68,66,65,59 30**
toteswingers:1&2:£31.30, 1&3:£12.90, 2&3:£7.20 CSF £169.75 CT £710.06 TOTE £26.30: £6.60, £2.70, £1.10; EX 193.50.
Owner Hindford Oak Racing **Bred** Yeomanstown Stud **Trained** Saighton, Cheshire
FOCUS
A weak 3-y-o handicap. The winner is rated back to her 2yo best.
T/Plt: £91.80 to a £1 stake. Pool:£67,678.03 - 537.70 winning tickets T/Qpdt: £34.10 to a £1 stake. Pool:£5,234.78 - 113.58 winning tickets CR

[2718]LINGFIELD (L-H)

Saturday, June 11

OFFICIAL GOING: Turf course - good to firm (good in places) changing to good to firm after race 1 (6:10); all-weather - standard
Wind: Strong, behind - Race 1. Light, behind , races 2-3. Light against remainder. Weather: Fine but cloudy

2919 PARTY PACKAGES AT LINGFIELD PARK MEDIAN AUCTION MAIDEN FILLIES' STKS (TURF) 5f

6:10 (6:10) (Class 6) 2-Y-O **£2,388** (£705; £352) **Stalls** High

Form RPR

1 **Quite A Thing** 2-9-0 0.. SebSanders 4 86+
(Sir Mark Prescott Bt) *mde virtually all: grabbed rail 2f out: shkn up and sn drew rt away: eased last 75yds: impressive debut* **3/1**[2]

6 **2** *8* **Split Second (IRE)**[18] 2374 2-9-0 0.................. PatCosgrave 5 61+
(Mick Channon) *prom: chsd wnr 2f out: sn brushed aside* **3/1**[2]

3 *2 1/4* **Van Der Art** 2-8-9 0.. HarryBentley(5) 1 50+
(Alan Jarvis) *green in preliminaries: dwlt: rn green and sn wl bhd in last: shkn up 1/2-way: styd on over 1f out: wnt 3rd ins fnl f: gng on at fin* **5/2**[1]

06 **4** *5* **Imperial Weapon (IRE)**[39] 1791 2-9-0 0.................. WilliamCarson 2 30
(John Spearing) *dwlt: chsd ldrs and in tch: rdn and wknd qckly 2f out* **50/1**

063 **5** *nk* **Ida Inkley (IRE)**[22] 2241 2-9-0 0.................. StephenCraine 6 29+
(Jonathan Portman) *racd against rail: w wnr to 1/2-way: wknd qckly 2f out* **5/1**[3]

4 **6** *1/2* **J Cunningham**[36] 1870 2-9-0 0.................. DaneO'Neill 3 27
(Mark Usher) *dwlt: outpcd in 5th: nvr on terms and no ch fnl 2f* **11/1**

7 *4 1/2* **Liquid Sunshine** 2-9-0 0.................. LiamKeniry 7 11
(Sylvester Kirk) *s.s: wl outpcd in 6th: a bhd* **12/1**

57.07 secs (-1.13) **Going Correction** -0.15s/f (Firm) 2y crse rec **7** Ran SP% **113.2**
Speed ratings (Par 88): **103,90,86,78,78 77,70**
toteswingers:1&2:£1.30, 1&3:£2.30, 2&3:£2.60 CSF £12.19 TOTE £3.30: £2.40, £2.00; EX 7.80.
Owner Lady Fairhaven & The Hon C & H Broughton **Bred** Whitsbury Manor Stud & Pigeon House Stud **Trained** Newmarket, Suffolk
FOCUS
A modest juvenile maiden, but a very impressive debut winner who set a juvenile course record that had previously stood for 12 years. The fourth and sixth offer perspective.
NOTEBOOK
Quite A Thing ◆ looks to have a bright future. First-time-out winners are not the norm from this stable and, despite taking the preliminaries like an old handicapper, the market didn't obviously scream she was fancied to make a winning start. She was still solid, however, and after breaking professionally it was clear from halfway she would take the beating. While this form may not amount to that much, she stretched clear without breaking sweat and broke the juvenile course record. It will take a smart one to lower her colours if heading for a novice race next and she appears as a pattern class sprinter in the making. (op 11-4 tchd 5-2 and 4-1 in a place)
Split Second(IRE) was a beaten favourite on her debut last month. She lacked the natural speed to get seriously involved and looks ready for a stiffer test. (op 11-4, tchd 7-2 in a place)
Van Der Art ◆ attracted support and turned in an eyecatching debut effort. She fell out of the gates and was last at halfway, but once the penny dropped she stayed on encouragingly under hands-and-heels riding. She ought to prove more streetwise next time and a stiffer test should also suit. (op 10-3)
Imperial Weapon(IRE) ran a touch more encouragingly on his third appearance. (op 40-1)
Ida Inkley(IRE), having her fourth outing, had the plum draw and once again set out to make all. She was hassled by the winner, though, and wilted from 2f out. (tchd 6-1)

2920 HAPPY 50TH BIRTHDAY ALBERT MACKEY H'CAP (TURF) 6f

6:40 (6:42) (Class 6) (0-60,63) 3-Y-O+ **£1,706** (£503; £252) **Stalls** High

Form RPR

0152 **1** **Miss Polly Plum**[7] 2720 4-9-5 **53**..................(p) AndreaAtzeni 2 67
(Chris Dwyer) *mde all: gd spd fr outside draw and crossed to rail over 4f out: clr 2f out: rdn fnl f: unchal* **14/1**

0012 **2** *1 1/4* **Running Mate (IRE)**[58] 1336 4-9-5 **53**..................(t) IanMongan 18 63
(Jo Crowley) *hld up bhd ldrs against rail: rdn 2f out: styd on to take 2nd fnl f: unable to chal* **9/2**[1]

3341 **3** *nk* **Commandingpresence (USA)**[5] 2755 5-9-3 **56** 6ex HarryBentley(5) 12 65
(John Bridger) *chsd ldrs: rdn 2f out: outpcd by wnr: styd on to take 3rd ins fnl f* **8/1**[3]

6452 **4** *2 3/4* **Fawley Green**[5] 2756 4-9-5 **58**..................(v) JamesRogers(5) 16 58
(William Muir) *racd against rail: prom: chsd wnr 1/2-way: no imp 2f out: wknd ins fnl f* **5/1**[2]

0500 **5** *2 1/2* **Fantasy Fighter (IRE)**[35] 1912 6-9-0 **48**.................. JimmyQuinn 7 40+
(John Quinn) *racd wd towards rr: effrt 2f out: styd on fr over 1f out: nvr a threat* **16/1**

1500 **6** *shd* **Loyal Royal (IRE)**[25] 2179 8-9-10 **58**..................(bt) LiamKeniry 13 50+
(Milton Bradley) *dwlt: hld up in last trio: swtchd lft to outer wl over 1f out: styd on after: nrst fin* **25/1**

44-0 **7** *1 1/2* **Doctor Hilary**[26] 2155 9-9-11 **59**..................(b) DaneO'Neill 10 46
(Mark Hoad) *racd wd in midfield: effrt 2f out: sn outpcd: no ch after: kpt on* **12/1**

-000 **8** *3/4* **Green Earth (IRE)**[77] 985 4-9-6 **59**.................. JemmaMarshall(5) 15 44
(Pat Phelan) *hld up wl in rr against rail: swtchd lft and out wd over 1f out: kpt on: nvr a threat* **12/1**

1-50 **9** *1* **Swansea Jack**[22] 2270 4-9-4 **57**..................(t) RyanClark(5) 14 38
(Stuart Williams) *dwlt: hld up wl in rr and against rail: asked for effrt over 2f out: hanging and nt qckn* **9/2**[1]

0606 **10** *1 1/4* **Vhujon (IRE)**[10] 2603 6-9-7 **55**.................. RobbieFitzpatrick 17 32
(Peter Grayson) *sn rdn in midfield: nvr able to make any prog* **20/1**

-150 **11** *1 1/4* **Replicator**[107] 664 6-9-2 **53**..................(e) AshleyHamblett(3) 6 26
(Patrick Gilligan) *racd wd in midfield: outpcd over 2f out: no ch after* **33/1**

0-56 **12** *1/2* **Yes We Can**[16] 2426 4-9-6 **57**.................. SimonPearce(3) 11 29
(Jeremy Gask) *dwlt: a towards rr and off the pce: no prog fnl 2f* **20/1**

-600 **13** *nk* **Canadian Danehill (IRE)**[27] 2126 9-9-5 **53**..................(p) PatCosgrave 5 24
(Robert Cowell) *got across fr wd draw and prom over 3f: sn wknd* **66/1**

2002 **14** *7* **Tymismoni (IRE)**[25] 2172 3-9-0 **56**.................. SebSanders 3 —
(Brett Johnson) *racd alone far side: a wl off the pce* **16/1**

000- **15** *10* **Thalia Grace**[203] 7519 4-9-7 **55**.................. JamesMillman 4 —
(Les Hall) *racd on wd outside: nvr on terms: t.o* **33/1**

0000 **16** *6* **Crystallize**[16] 2426 5-9-10 **58**..................(b[1]) RichardHughes 8 —
(Andrew Haynes) *chsd wnr to 1/2-way: sn wknd rapidly: eased over 1f out: t.o* **20/1**

400- **17** *34* **Eye For The Girls**[235] 7007 5-9-5 **53**.................. WilliamCarson 9 —
(Les Hall) *a wl in rr: wl t.o* **33/1**

1m 10.1s (-1.10) **Going Correction** -0.15s/f (Firm)
WFA 3 from 4yo+ 8lb **17** Ran SP% **126.4**
Speed ratings (Par 101): **101,99,98,95,91 91,89,88,87,85 84,83,83,73,60 52,7**
toteswingers:1&2:£5.10, 1&3:£10.50, 2&3:£9.00 CSF £70.34 CT £580.79 TOTE £11.60: £2.80, £1.70, £1.70, £1.90; EX 63.60.
Owner Mrs J Hughes & Miss C Hughes **Bred** Brookfield Stud & Partners **Trained** Burrough Green, Cambs
FOCUS
A moderate sprint handicap and once again racing near to the stands' side rail proved vital. A length personal best from the winner.

2921 RONNIE SCOTT'S NIGHT HERE 18TH JUNE H'CAP (TURF) 7f

7:10 (7:12) (Class 6) (0-55,55) 3-Y-O+ **£2,183** (£644; £322) **Stalls** High

Form RPR

4003 **1** **Kenswick**[26] 2149 4-9-6 **52**..................(v) DaneO'Neill 9 60
(Pat Eddery) *stdd s: dropped in and hld up in last trio: swtchd lft and prog over 1f out but stl plenty to do: str run fnl f to ld last 75yds: won gng away* **11/1**

2554 **2** *1 1/2* **Talamahana**[16] 2424 6-9-7 **53**..................(v) EddieAhern 6 57
(Andrew Haynes) *settled midfield towards outer: prog over 2f out: rdn and clsd to ld last 100yds: sn hdd and outpcd* **40/1**

0-40 **3** *1* **Ghost Dancer**[5] 2756 7-9-4 **50**..................(p) TomMcLaughlin 15 51
(Milton Bradley) *slowest away: hld up in last pair: prog towards outer fr 2f out: kpt on fr over 1f out: outpcd but tk 3rd nr fin* **9/1**

0020 **4** *nk* **Interakt**[16] 2420 4-9-4 **55**..................(b) HarryBentley(5) 14 55
(Joseph Tuite) *dwlt: sn pressed ldng pair: rdn to ld 2f out but nt against rail: hdd and outpcd last 100yds* **10/1**

6004 **5** *shd* **Durgan**[12] 2561 5-9-7 **53**..................(v[1]) RichardHughes 16 53
(Linda Jewell) *racd against rail: led: rdn 1/2-way: hdd 2f out: sn btn but kpt on fnl f* **9/2**[2]

0000 **6** *1 3/4* **Vezere (USA)**[12] 2561 4-9-1 **47**..................(b[1]) SebSanders 7 42
(Simon Dow) *dwlt: wl in rr: pushed along and struggling 1/2-way: styd on fr over 1f out: nrst fin* **22/1**

6502 **7** *2* **Fedora (IRE)**[3] 2828 5-8-12 **49**..................(p) KylieManser(5) 3 39+
(Olivia Maylam) *stdd s: hld up towards rr but racd wd: prog 3f out: tried to cl on ldrs over 1f out: sn wknd* **7/1**[3]

0034 **8** *nk* **Set To Go**[33] 1933 4-9-1 **47**.................. GeorgeBaker 8 36
(Tor Sturgis) *prom on outer: rdn 3f out: steadily wknd u.p fr 2f out* **11/1**

524 **9** *3 1/4* **Dancing Welcome**[12] 2555 5-9-8 **54**..................(b) LiamKeniry 1 41+
(Milton Bradley) *towards rr on outer: rdn over 2f out: effrt but no real threat whn hmpd over 1f out* **12/1**

5-33 **10** *hd* **Euroquip Boy (IRE)**[12] 2554 4-9-2 **55**.................. DavidKenny(7) 13 35
(Michael Scudamore) *dwlt: tk fierce hold: w ldr: upsides 2f out: sn hrd rdn and wknd* **7/2**[1]

5420 **11** *nk* **Giulietta Da Vinci**[16] 2420 4-9-6 **52**..................(v[1]) HayleyTurner 4 31
(Steve Woodman) *wl in rr: rdn in last trio over 2f out and no prog: modest late hdwy* **25/1**

-650 **12** *1/2* **Griffin Point (IRE)**[2] 2845 4-9-2 **53**.................. JamesRogers(5) 5 31
(William Muir) *prom on outer: rdn 3f out: wknd and hung rt 2f out* **16/1**

0655 **13** *5* **Rightcar**[26] 2164 4-9-1 **47**..................(b) RobbieFitzpatrick 12 11
(Peter Grayson) *nvr beyond midfield: wknd over 2f out* **50/1**

000 **14** *2 1/2* **Elby**[16] 2427 4-9-0 **46**.................. AndreaAtzeni 10 4
(Eve Johnson Houghton) *chsd ldrs 4f: sn wknd* **33/1**

-635 **15** *1/2* **Flying Cherry (IRE)**[58] 1331 4-9-4 **50**.................. IanMongan 18 6
(Jo Crowley) *racd against rail in midfield: rdn 1/2-way: sn struggling: wknd 2f out: eased* **16/1**

4-00 **16** *11* **Millden**[26] 2142 4-9-8 **54**..................(tp) PatCosgrave 17 —
(Milton Bradley) *racd against rail: trckd ldrs: rdn 3f out: sn wknd and eased: t.o* **22/1**

1m 23.22s (-0.08) **Going Correction** -0.15s/f (Firm) **16** Ran SP% **128.0**
Speed ratings (Par 101): **94,92,91,90,90 88,86,86,82,82 81,81,75,72,72 59**
toteswingers:1&2:£53.70, 1&3:£19.90, 2&3:£154.00 CSF £421.39 CT £4263.46 TOTE £13.90: £3.10, £8.40, £2.80, £2.40; EX 456.30.
Owner P J J Eddery **Bred** Burton Agnes Stud Co Ltd **Trained** Nether Winchendon, Bucks
FOCUS
This weak handicap, run at a solid pace, was again expected to revolve around those drawn nearest to the stands' rail. The winner emerged mid-track, however. The winner rates a small personal best.

2922 ATR ROYAL ASCOT MICROSITE NOW LIVE H'CAP 1m (P)

7:40 (7:40) (Class 6) (0-60,63) 4-Y-O+ **£1,706** (£503; £252) **Stalls** High

Form RPR

0042 **1** **Kipchak (IRE)**[7] 2719 6-9-9 **62**..................(b) HayleyTurner 1 71
(Conor Dore) *mde all: clr after 3f: c bk to rivals 2f out: hrd rdn over 1f out: hld on gamely* **4/1**[1]

2553 **2** *1* **Kai Mook**[24] 2198 4-8-13 **59**..................(bt[1]) HarryPoulton(7) 6 66
(Roger Ingram) *hld up in 7th: prog fr 3f out gng wl: in tch in 5th whn n.m.r briefly wl over 1f out: rdn and styd on to take 2nd last 75yds: unable to chal* **7/1**

0600 **3** *1 1/4* **Pytheas (USA)**[12] 2560 4-8-13 **57**.................. MarkCoumbe(5) 8 61
(Michael Attwater) *racd wd: trckd ldrs in 5th: rdn and prog to dispute 2nd 2f out: nt qckn over 1f out: kpt on same pce* **20/1**

5023 **4** *3/4* **Clearing House**[9] 2642 6-9-10 **63**.................. KirstyMilczarek 2 65
(John Ryan) *trckd ldng trio: effrt on inner to dispute 2nd 2f out: drvn over 1f out: no imp on wnr ins fnl f: wknd last 100yds* **5/1**[2]

313/ **5** *1 3/4* **Surwaki (USA)**[852] 471 9-9-1 **54**..................(p) PatCosgrave 3 52
(Robert Cowell) *chsd wnr: rdn and lost 2nd 2f out: fdd* **9/1**

60-6 **6** *hd* **Poor Prince**[31] 1995 4-9-7 **60**.................. LiamKeniry 7 58
(Chris Gordon) *chsd ldrs in 6th: rdn 3f out and no prog: plugged on u.p over 1f out* **15/2**

0600 **7** *shd* **Guildenstern (IRE)**[3] 2816 9-8-3 **49**.................. KatiaScallan(7) 10 46
(Alastair Lidderdale) *allowed to s slowly: hld up in 10th: long way off the pce over 2f out: nudged along and styd on steadily after: hopeless task* **16/1**

The Form Book, Raceform Ltd, Compton, RG20 6NL

450- **8** *9* **Michael's Nook**[248] 6672 4-9-2 **55**........................ IanMongan 5 32
(Stuart Kittow) *chsd ldng pair: rdn over 3f out: sn lost pl and btn* **11/2**[3]

5644 **9** *½* **Lopinot (IRE)**[84] 906 8-9-6 **59**........................(v) GeorgeBaker 11 35
(Martin Bosley) *allowed to s slowly: hld up in last trio: nvr remotely nr ldrs: pushed along and no real prog over 2f out* **8/1**

040- **10** *9* **Fair Breeze**[243] 6814 4-9-2 **55**........................ RichardHughes 12 10
(Richard Phillips) *allowed to s slowly: hld up in last: taken wd then hung rt bnd 4f out: t.o after* **16/1**

0000 **11** *8* **Dingaan (IRE)**[31] 1995 8-9-5 **58**........................ RobbieFitzpatrick 9 —
(Peter Grayson) *allowed to s slowly: hld up in rr: wknd 3f out: t.o* **40/1**

1m 38.68s (0.48) **Going Correction** +0.10s/f (Slow) **11** Ran SP% **116.4**
Speed ratings (Par 101): **101,100,98,98,96 96,95,86,86,77 69**
toteswingers:1&2:£1.10, 1&3:Not won, 2&3:Not won CSF £31.51 CT £508.85 TOTE £3.40: £1.90, £1.90, £8.60; EX 12.00.
Owner Liam Breslin **Bred** Miss Mary Davidson & Mrs Steffi Von Schilcher **Trained** Cowbit, Lincs

FOCUS
A moderate handicap and straightforward form. All three AW races on the card were won from the front. The winner ran to his winter best.

2923 VISIT ATTHERACES.COM/ASCOT H'CAP 1m 2f (P)
8:10 (8:10) (Class 5) (0-70,66) 4-Y-0+ **£3,070** (£906; £453) **Stalls** Low

Form RPR

360 **1** **Archie Rice (USA)**[16] 2436 5-9-7 **66**........................ GeorgeBaker 9 73
(Tom Keddy) *sn led: untrbld in front despite mod pce: increased tempo over 2f out: hrd rdn fnl f: jst lasted* **15/2**

0-32 **2** *nk* **On The Feather**[25] 2176 5-9-5 **64**........................ JamesMillman 3 70
(Rod Millman) *hld up in tch: effrt on outer 2f out: drvn and r.o to take 2nd last 100yds: clsd on wnr fin* **9/2**[2]

6433 **3** *1 ¼* **Striding Edge (IRE)**[12] 2567 5-9-6 **65**........................ JamesDoyle 1 69
(Hans Adielsson) *sn hld up towards rr: rdn 2f out: prog over 1f out: styd on to take 3rd wl ins fnl f* **11/2**[3]

150- **4** *1* **Recalcitrant**[223] 7255 8-9-6 **65**........................ EddieAhern 7 67
(Simon Dow) *prom: chsd wnr after 3f: drvn 2f out: nt qckn over 1f out: fdd last 100yds* **20/1**

-130 **5** *1* **Mister Frosty (IRE)**[85] 645 5-9-0 **59**........................ KirstyMilczarek 5 59
(George Prodromou) *t.k.h: hld up in last trio: rdn over 2f out: no prog tl styd on fnl f* **12/1**

-321 **6** *½* **Byrd In Hand (IRE)**[12] 2560 4-9-0 **59**........................ RichardHughes 8 59
(John Bridger) *trckd wnr 3f: styd handy: rdn 2f out: disp 2nd but nt qckn over 1f out: wknd fnl f* **6/4**[1]

2250 **7** *¾* **The Blue Dog (IRE)**[32] 1992 4-9-5 **64**........................(v[1]) WilliamCarson 2 61
(Michael Wigham) *hld up in rr: prog on inner 3f out: sn rdn and nt qckn: n.d over 1f out* **10/1**

110- **8** *2 ¾* **Count Ceprano (IRE)**[301] 5071 7-9-3 **65**........................ SimonPearce(3) 4 57
(Lydia Pearce) *racd wd in tch: rdn over 2f out: wknd over 1f out* **16/1**

566- **9** *3 ½* **Bell's Ocean (USA)**[255] 6452 4-9-1 **60**........................ RobbieFitzpatrick 6 45
(John Ryan) *hld up in last trio: rdn over 2f out: no prog and sn btn* **28/1**

2m 9.40s (2.80) **Going Correction** +0.10s/f (Slow) **9** Ran SP% **116.2**
Speed ratings (Par 103): **92,91,90,89,89 88,88,85,83**
toteswingers:1&2:£6.40, 1&3:£6.70, 2&3:£3.70 CSF £41.47 CT £202.58 TOTE £9.40: £2.30, £1.50, £2.00; EX 46.40.
Owner Andrew Duffield **Bred** Baltusrol Thoughbreds Llc Et Al **Trained** Newmarket, Suffolk

FOCUS
A modest handicap in which the winner scored under a fine front-running ride. The winner is rated to his winter form.

2924 WIN A HOLIDAY ON LADIES NIGHT MEDIAN AUCTION MAIDEN STKS 7f (P)
8:40 (8:42) (Class 6) 3-4-Y-0 **£2,388** (£705; £352) **Stalls** Low

Form RPR

4 **1** **Gladys' Gal**[45] 1607 3-8-8 0........................ AndreaAtzeni 5 91
(Roger Varian) *mde all: shkn up 2f out: styd on stoutly fnl f* **13/2**[3]

2 **2** *2* **Outsmart**[22] 2266 3-8-13 0........................ AhmedAjtebi 2 90
(Mahmood Al Zarooni) *chsd ldng pair: rdn over 2f out: wnt 2nd 1f out: hd quite high and no imp last 100yds* **7/4**[1]

023- **3** *1 ½* **Midnight Feast**[303] 3785 3-8-13 84 IanMongan 6 86
(Peter Winkworth) *chsd wnr: rdn over 2f out: nt qckn and lost 2nd 1f out: one pce* **15/2**

56 **4** *6* **Arabian Heights**[9] 2650 3-8-13 0........................ SebSanders 11 70+
(Sir Mark Prescott Bt) *s.s: hld up wl in rr: pushed along 3f out: pushed along more firmly in 8th over 1f out: styd on encouragingly to take 4th post* **22/1**

00- **5** *nk* **Proud Chieftain**[223] 7248 3-8-13 0........................ JamesDoyle 3 69
(Clifford Lines) *towards rr: shkn up over 2f out and wl outpcd: styd on fr over 1f out: nrst fin* **50/1**

0 **6** *½* **Brick Dust (IRE)**[12] 2568 3-8-13 0........................ KirstyMilczarek 7 68
(Luca Cumani) *trckd ldrs: pushed along and outpcd in 4th over 2f out: no imp after: lost pl last strides* **28/1**

05 **7** *½* **Ducal**[9] 2650 3-8-8 0........................ RosieJessop(5) 10 66
(Sir Mark Prescott Bt) *s.s: hld up in rr: rchd 6th over 2f out but wl outpcd: shkn up over 1f out: plugged on* **50/1**

02-3 **8** *3* **Top Diktat**[25] 2174 3-8-13 75........................ RichardHughes 9 58
(Sir Michael Stoute) *racd wd: hld up: shkn up and outpcd in 5th over 2f out: no ch after: wknd fnl f* **15/8**[2]

- **9** *4 ½* **Steely** 3-8-13 0........................ PaulDoe 4 46
(Jim Best) *prom 3f: sn lost pl: wl in rr over 2f out* **100/1**

10 *9* **Insidious** 3-8-13 0........................ DaneO'Neill 8 22
(William Jarvis) *dwlt: sn last and wl bhd: t.o* **50/1**

0-0 **11** *18* **Go On The Badger**[25] 2174 3-8-8 0........................ HayleyTurner 1 —
(James Toller) *chsd ldrs: rdn 1/2-way: sn wknd rapidly: t.o* **100/1**

U **Kantata** 3-8-8 0........................ EddieAhern 13 —
(James Toller) *uns rdr bef gng in stalls: rrd as stalls opened and c out wout rdr* **100/1**

1m 24.85s (0.05) **Going Correction** +0.10s/f (Slow) **12** Ran SP% **112.9**
WFA 3 from 4yo 10lb
Speed ratings (Par 101): **103,100,99,92,91 91,90,87,82,71 51,—**
toteswingers:1&2:£3.40, 1&3:£6.80, 2&3:£2.80 CSF £13.96 TOTE £8.70: £2.50, £1.30, £2.60; EX 8.30.
Owner Fishlake Commercial Motors Ltd **Bred** Mike Gosse **Trained** Newmarket, Suffolk

FOCUS
This wasn't a bad maiden, but there was drama from the stalls as the two outside stalls failed to jump out, including 4/1 shot Escape To Glory who was deemed a non-runner. The form still looks fair with the principals coming clear. All three AW races were won from the front. The winner was a big improver.
T/Plt: £63.90 to a £1 stake. Pool:£69,151.35 - 788.86 winning tickets T/Qpdt: £18.80 to a £1 stake. Pool:£5,395.04 - 211.76 winning tickets JN

2880 SANDOWN (R-H)
Saturday, June 11

OFFICIAL GOING: Sprint course - soft; round course - good to soft (soft in places)
Wind: virtually nil Weather: sunny, light cloud

2925 BET ON TOTEPLACEPOT AT TOTESPORT.COM H'CAP 1m 1f
1:55 (1:55) (Class 3) (0-90,88) 3-Y-0
£9,346 (£2,799; £1,399; £700; £349; £175) **Stalls** Low

Form RPR

0-16 **1** **Barney Rebel (IRE)**[41] 1723 3-9-0 **81**........................ MichaelHills 12 90
(B W Hills) *hld up in last quartet: hdwy 3f out: rdn to chal wl over 1f out: led narrowly ent fnl f: edgd rt ins fnl f: forged to ld fnl 75yds* **20/1**

21-1 **2** *¾* **Tullius (IRE)**[23] 2229 3-9-2 **83**........................ IanMongan 9 91+
(Peter Winkworth) *chsd ldrs: rdn to ld jst over 2f out: drvn and narrowly hdd ent fnl f: battled on gamely and stl ev ch whn squeezed for room and btn fnl 75yds* **8/1**

4-30 **3** *1 ¼* **Star Surprise**[21] 2296 3-9-7 **88**........................ EddieAhern 4 93
(Michael Bell) *chsd ldrs: rdn and chsd ldr 2f out tl wl over 1f out: drvn and unable qck over 1f out: styd on again fnl 100yds* **8/1**

61 **4** *2 ½* **Mashaaref**[25] 2185 3-9-2 **83**........................ RichardHills 7 83+
(Roger Varian) *hld up in midfield: rdn and effrt whn swtchd rt and hmpd rivals wl over 2f out: hdwy to chse ldng trio wl over 1f out: plugged on but no real imp fr over 1f out* **4/1**[2]

61 **5** *4 ½* **Voodoo Prince**[15] 2457 3-9-4 **85**........................ FrankieDettori 3 75+
(Ed Dunlop) *towards rr early: hdwy into midfield after 2f out: rdn and effrt whn bmpd and hmpd wl over 2f out: hdwy ent fnl 2f: 5th and wl hld over 1f out* **7/2**[1]

-630 **6** *7* **Planet Waves (IRE)**[38] 1811 3-8-13 **80**........................ PhilipRobinson 5 54
(Clive Brittain) *dwlt: sn pushed along and qckly rcvrd to ld: rdn and hdd jst over 2f out: wknd over 1f out* **25/1**

4-10 **7** *7* **Harry Luck (IRE)**[10] 2607 3-9-0 **81**........................ DaneO'Neill 6 40
(Henry Candy) *sn pushed along in last trio: rdn and no hdwy 3f out: 7th and wl btn over 1f out: eased fnl f* **12/1**

41 **8** *shd* **England Rules (IRE)**[40] 1774 3-8-12 **79**........................(t) WilliamBuick 2 38+
(Jeremy Noseda) *hld up in tch: rdn wl over 3f out: bdly hmpd and lost pl wl over 2f out: nt rcvr and no ch after* **11/2**[3]

21-0 **9** *2 ¾* **Twice Bitten**[42] 1690 3-8-10 **77**........................ LiamKeniry 11 30
(James Toller) *stdd after s: t.k.h: hld up in last trio: rdn and effrt ent 3f out: no real prog: wl btn 2f out: eased ins fnl f* **20/1**

0-06 **10** *2* **Kalahaag (IRE)**[24] 2188 3-8-11 **78**........................ RichardHughes 1 26
(Richard Hannon) *a in rr: rdn and no rspnse wl over 3f out: wl bhd and eased fnl f* **16/1**

-111 **11** *9* **Memorabilia**[131] 365 3-8-7 **74**........................ SilvestreDeSousa 8 —
(Mark Johnston) *chsd ldr: rdn wl over 3f out: struggling and lost pl 3f out: sn bhd: t.o and eased fnl f* **11/1**

1m 57.4s (1.70) **Going Correction** +0.275s/f (Good) **11** Ran SP% **115.1**
Speed ratings (Par 103): **103,102,101,99,95 88,82,82,80,78 70**
toteswingers:1&2:£18.80, 1&3:£26.30, 2&3:£8.30 CSF £164.34 CT £1421.88 TOTE £25.00: £6.40, £2.40, £2.60; EX 235.40.
Owner Rebel Racing **Bred** Marston Stud And Fleming Thoroughbreds **Trained** Lambourn, Berks
■ Stewards' Enquiry : Michael Hills two-day ban: careless riding (25th-26th June)

FOCUS
Home bend at mid-configuration; home straight dolled out 5yds and distances on round course increased by about 5yds. This was a decent handicap run at a far pace, but quite a rough one, and following a stewards' inquiry the result was allowed to stand. Despite the soft ground, the jockeys decided to stay towards the far side in the home straight.

NOTEBOOK
Barney Rebel(IRE) was well held off 1lb higher on his handicap debut over a furlong further at Newmarket last month, but appeared to settle much better this time. Brought with a steady run down the outside over 2f from home, he did edge to his right once in front in the latter stages, but looked the winner on merit. He still has a bit of scope. (tchd 22-1)
Tullius(IRE) was put up 6lb after beating a subsequent winner over a furlong shorter here on his reappearance last month, but showed here that this sort of mark isn't beyond him. Never far away, he was in front over 2f out and though headed a furlong later, he battled on really well and wasn't done many favours by the winner close home. He remains in top form. (tchd 15-2)
Star Surprise, up a furlong in trip, was always up there and had every chance. He has gained both of his victories at this track so obviously likes it here. (op 12-1)
Mashaaref, making his handicap debut after his game Nottingham success, was in midfield when taken inside to avoid the weakening Memorabilia over 3f out, but in doing so he knocked Voodoo Prince into England Rules and none of the trio were done many favours by the incident. He remains unexposed, but may need quicker ground. (op 7-2)
Voodoo Prince came into this a complete unknown quantity after his convincing Haydock maiden success, but he was already being niggled when hampered over 3f out. He also may not have appreciated the rain. (op 11-4)
England Rules(IRE) had a tongue tie on for this handicap debut following his battling Windsor maiden success. He suffered worst in the melee over 3f out, but he too didn't appear to be travelling that well at the time. (op 13-2)

2926 TOTESCOOP6 H'CAP 7f 16y
2:25 (2:28) (Class 3) (0-90,84) 3-Y-0
£9,346 (£2,799; £1,399; £700; £349; £175) **Stalls** Low

Form RPR

-412 **1** **Sinfonico (IRE)**[10] 2607 3-9-7 **84**........................ RichardHughes 4 94
(Richard Hannon) *in tch: hmpd over 5f out: hdwy to trck ldng pair ent fnl 2f: rdn to chal over 1f out: led ins fnl f: r.o wl* **12/1**

2-1 **2** *1* **Anoint**[32] 1985 3-9-5 **82**........................ FrankieDettori 2 89
(William Haggas) *chsd ldrs: effrt to chse ldr ent fnl 2f: rdn and ev ch over 1f out: led ins fnl f: sn hdd and styd on same pce fnl 75yds* **3/1**[1]

10 **3** *hd* **Deity**[37] 1837 3-9-5 **82**........................ WilliamBuick 13 89
(Jeremy Noseda) *chsd ldr tl led over 5f out: rdn wl over 1f out: sn hrd pressed: hdd and n.m.r briefly ins fnl f: styd on same pce fnl 100yds* **11/1**

3-42 **4** *1 ¼* **Local Singer (IRE)**[9] 2646 3-9-3 **80**........................ TomMcLaughlin 12 86+
(Malcolm Saunders) *t.k.h: hld up in midfield: nt clr run and shuffled bk over 2f out: swtchd lft and hdwy over 1f out: r.o wl and switching rt ins fnl f: nt rch ldrs* **11/1**

32-1 **5** *1* **Wiqaaya (IRE)**[75] 1015 3-9-7 **84**........................ RichardHills 5 85
(Ed Dunlop) *stdd after s: hld up in last trio: effrt towards centre over 2f out: rdn 2f out: styd on steadily ins fnl f: nvr gng pce to rch ldrs* **14/1**

64-6 **6** *2* **Buckland (IRE)**36 1843 3-9-2 **79** ShaneKelly 8 74+
(Brian Meehan) *towards rr whn pushed rt and hmpd after 1f: rdn over 2f out: nt clr run and swtchd rt over 1f out: no threat to ldrs but styd on wl ins fnl f* **10/1**

-116 **7** *1* **Flynn's Boy**58 1335 3-8-13 **76** MartinLane 3 69
(Rae Guest) *bmpd s: in tch: rdn and effrt ent fnl 2f: styng on same pce and no imp whn edgd lft u.p over 1f out: wl hld whn n.m.r ins fnl f* **22/1**

41- **8** *4* **Premium Coffee**338 3811 3-9-4 **81** LukeMorris 11 63
(Mick Channon) *towards rr whn hmpd after 1f: rdn wl over 3f out: no hdwy and no ch w ldrs wl over 1f out: plugged on past btn horses ins fnl f: n.d* **25/1**

2461 **9** *nk* **May's Boy**9 2646 3-8-8 **76** (p) HarryBentley(5) 7 57
(Mark Usher) *in tch: nt clr run and swtchd rt ent fnl 2f: unable qck u.p wl over 1f out: wknd and pushed lft over 1f out* **9/1**3

320- **10** *1 3/4* **Tipsy Girl**252 6563 3-9-1 **78** EddieAhern 6 54
(Denis Coakley) *hld up in tch: hmpd over 5f out: hmpd and snatched up over 2f out: swtchd rt and rdn over 1f out: no prog* **20/1**

-000 **11** *8* **Shafgaan**14 2503 3-9-6 **83** (t) PhilipRobinson 15 38
(Clive Brittain) *dwlt: sn rdn along and rcvrd to chse ldrs on outer: rdn and struggling over 2f out: wknd wl over 1f out* **16/1**

111 **12** *hd* **Sound Amigo (IRE)**23 2216 3-8-11 **74** TomQueally 10 28
(Ollie Pears) *t.k.h: hld up in tch: edgd rt after 1f: rdn and effrt over 2f out: wknd wl over 1f out: bhd and eased ins fnl f* **7/2**2

15-0 **13** *1 3/4* **My Delirium**28 2102 3-9-5 **82** JimCrowley 1 31
(Ralph Beckett) *led tl over 5f out: chsd ldr after tl ent fnl 2f: sn struggling u.p: wkng whn short of room and hmpd ent fnl f* **33/1**

2-50 **14** *4* **Justbookie Dot Com (IRE)**18 2383 3-8-6 **69** SilvestreDeSousa 9 —
(Louise Best) *t.k.h: hld up in tch: hmpd and lost pl after 1f: hmpd again over 5f out: bhd after: rdn and btn 3f out: wl bhd and eased ins fnl f* **40/1**

1m 32.3s (2.80) **Going Correction** +0.275s/f (Good) **14** Ran SP% **121.6**
Speed ratings (Par 103): **95,93,93,92,91 88,87,83,82,80 71,71,69,64**
toteswingers:1&2:£9.10, 1&3:£30.10, 2&3:£6.60 CSF £45.30 CT £436.53 TOTE £15.50: £4.60, £1.60, £4.80; EX 60.40 Trifecta £495.10 Part won. Pool £495.10 - 0.50 winning units..
Owner White Beech Farm **Bred** P Doyle Bloodstock & J K Thoroughbred **Trained** East Everleigh, Wilts

FOCUS
Another decent and competitive handicap, but unlike in the opener the jockeys decided to come up the stands' rail and there was inevitably trouble. The winner got back on track with a small personal best.

NOTEBOOK
Sinfonico(IRE) had shown much better form on Polytrack coming into this, but he stays further and his trainer believed that the stiff uphill finish here would suit him. That is how it looked, as he was always travelling nicely behind the leaders and quickened up well when asked to go and win his race. (op 10-1 tchd 14-1)
Anoint was making his handicap debut after making hard work of landing the odds in a Warwick maiden on his return, but he was never far off the pace, had every chance, and never stopped trying. This was only his third start so he is entitled to still have a bit more improvement in him. (op 10-3 tchd 11-4)
Deity came into this still unexposed, but had questions to answer following a poor effort on her handicap debut at Goodwood last month. This was much better and she put that last effort behind her, but she did very much have the run of the race out in front. (op 10-1)
Local Singer(IRE) ◆ was beaten over two lengths by May's Boy over C&D nine days earlier and enjoyed a 6lb pull. He turned the form around and would have finished even closer had he not become short of room over 2f from home. He is one to note. (op 12-1)
Wiqaaya(IRE), making her handicap debut, was 1-14 when winning a terrible Wolverhampton maiden in March, but she can also be rated a bit closer here as she had to be taken out into the centre of the track in order to make her run from the back of the field, which wasn't ideal. (op 12-1)
Buckland(IRE) hasn't really built on early promise, but he didn't run badly here considering he was badly hampered after 2f. (op 14-1)
Flynn's Boy, a dual winner on the AW earlier this year, can also be rated a bit better than his final position as he was hampered by the runner-up exiting the stalls. (op 16-1)
Tipsy Girl ◆ was returning from 252 days off, though she did make a successful racecourse debut last term. Backed at fancy prices, she was still full of running when completely running out of room soon after turning in. She is worth bearing in mind. (op 40-1)

2927 TOTESPORT 0800 221 221 H'CAP 7f 16y
2:55 (2:59) (Class 2) (0-100,99) 3-Y-O+

£21,808 (£6,531; £3,265; £1,634; £815; £409) **Stalls** Low

Form RPR

1-41 **1** **Law Of The Range**35 1884 4-9-2 **88** SilvestreDeSousa 7 100
(Marco Botti) *chsd ldr tl led over 5f out: styd far side st: rdn ent fnl f: clr ins fnl f: styd on wl: rdn out* **13/2**3

-331 **2** *1 1/2* **Our Jonathan**21 2284 4-9-13 **99** WilliamBuick 15 107+
(Kevin Ryan) *stdd s and dropped in bhd: hld up in rr: c centre to stands' side st: hdwy ent fnl 2f: chsd ldrs ent fnl f: hung rt ins fnl f: chsd wnr and no imp fnl 100yds* **4/1**1

115- **3** *1 1/4* **The Confessor**299 5143 4-9-1 **87** DaneO'Neill 1 91+
(Henry Candy) *led: switching lft to r wd after 1f: hdd over 5f out: chsd wnr after and c centre to stands' side: rdn 2f out: hung rt fr over 1f out: styd on same pce fnl f: lost 2nd fnl 100yds* **7/1**

51-5 **4** *1/2* **Perfect Silence**15 2470 6-9-1 **87** LukeMorris 8 90
(Clive Cox) *chsd ldrs: styd far side st: rdn over 2f out: drvn and no imp over 1f out: styd on same pce fnl f* **11/2**2

60-5 **5** *3/4* **Mr Rainbow**27 2123 5-9-3 **89** PhilipRobinson 11 90+
(Alan Swinbank) *in tch: c centre to stands' side st: nt clr run against stands' rail ent fnl f: rdn and chsng ldrs over 1f out: hung rt and styd on same pce fnl f* **14/1**

/4-0 **6** *2 1/2* **Namecheck (GER)**42 1684 4-9-11 **97** FrankieDettori 9 91+
(Mahmood Al Zarooni) *towards rr: c centre to stands' side: hdwy in centre and rdn over 2f out: chsng ldrs and drvn 2f out: hung rt and wknd fnl f* **12/1**

4-03 **7** *3 1/4* **Vitznau (IRE)**10 2614 7-9-7 **93** (p) JimCrowley 4 78
(Robert Cowell) *stdd s: hld up in rr: c centre to stands' side st: rdn 2f out: styd on past btn horses fnl f: nvr trbld ldrs* **50/1**

20-0 **8** *1/2* **Mass Rally (IRE)**30 2031 4-9-9 **95** TomEaves 3 79
(Michael Dods) *hld up towards rr: c centre to stands' side st: rdn and effrt ent fnl 2f: no imp and btn ent fnl f* **18/1**

0-02 **9** *2 1/2* **Mon Cadeaux**21 2284 4-9-9 **95** DavidProbert 5 72
(Andrew Balding) *t.k.h: chsd ldrs: c centre to stands' side st: rdn ent fnl 2f: wknd jst over 1f out* **13/2**3

100- **10** *shd* **Mirza**210 7443 4-9-1 **87** RichardHughes 10 64
(Rae Guest) *in tch: c centre to stands' side st: rdn and unable qck ent fnl 2f: wknd ent fnl f* **20/1**

1-00 **11** *1 1/4* **Suited And Booted (IRE)**49 1529 4-9-7 **93** TomQueally 6 67
(Richard Hannon) *chsd ldrs: c centre to stands' side st: rdn and effrt ent fnl 2f: styng on same pce and carried rt 1f out: wknd fnl f* **20/1**

3-00 **12** *16* **Irish Heartbeat (IRE)**29 2075 6-9-9 **95** (b1) DavidNolan 2 —
(Richard Fahey) *t.k.h: chsd ldrs: c centre to stands' side st: rdn and wknd rapidly wl over 1f out: wl bhd and eased ins fnl f: t.o* **15/2**

005- **13** *10* **Mahadee (IRE)**268 6123 6-9-7 **93** (b) PatCosgrave 12 —
(Ed de Giles) *s.i.s: bhd: c centre to stands' side st: rdn and no hdwy ent fnl 2f: wl bhd and eased ins fnl f: t.o* **40/1**

1m 32.02s (2.52) **Going Correction** +0.275s/f (Good) **13** Ran SP% **119.9**
Speed ratings (Par 109): **96,94,92,92,91 88,84,84,81,81 79,61,50**
toteswingers:1&2:£4.00, 1&3:£9.30, 2&3:£7.00 CSF £31.36 CT £198.76 TOTE £7.40: £2.00, £2.30, £2.50; EX 25.40 Trifecta £299.70 Pool £1,223.43 - 3.02 winning units..
Owner Christopher McHale **Bred** Brookside Breeders Club **Trained** Newmarket, Suffolk
■ Stewards' Enquiry : Silvestre De Sousa one-day ban: careless riding (25th June)

FOCUS
They went down the inside rail in the opener and down the stands' rail in the second, but in this there was a bit of both and the riders of the first and fourth horses both deserve plenty of plaudits for having the bottle to stay on the inside, while their rivals took the more traditional soft-ground route. It does make the form rather suspect, however. The winner and fourth were probably favoured.

NOTEBOOK
Law Of The Range, put up 6lb for last month's game Ascot success, had never tackled a trip this short before, but the easing of the ground would have made this more of a test of stamina. However, the credit for this victory must go down to her replacement jockey, who stuck determinedly to the inside rail after turning in and it was soon obvious that she wasn't going to be caught. She looks the type that can continue to thrive. (op 11-2)
Our Jonathan was put up 4lb after making his first attempt at this trip a winning one at Chester last month. This stiffer track, and the easy ground, would have made this an even greater stamina test, but as it turned out he saw the trip out well having been among the group that came up the stands' side in the straight. It's debatable how much closer he might have finished had he stayed on the inside, but either way there is no doubt that he stays this trip really well. (op 9-2)
The Confessor ◆, winner of three of his four starts last season, was returning from 299 days off, but he made a successful reappearance last term and the softening ground wasn't a problem. Kept wide right from the start, he ran on again after hitting a flat spot around 2f out and this bodes well for the future.
Perfect Silence ran well on her return from a lengthy layoff at Newmarket last month, though the softening of the ground was in her favour. This was another good effort from her, though she was undoubtedly helped by being the only other one to stay towards the inside rail along with the winner. (op 7-1 tchd 15-2 and 9-1 in a place)
Mr Rainbow ◆ was entitled to come on from last month's encouraging Ripon return following a lengthy absence and was noted doing all his best work late, though his rider reported that he had hung badly right. He is one to keep an eye on in the coming weeks. (op 16-1)
Namecheck(GER) has been very lightly raced since the autumn of his 2-y-o career and ran poorly following another long absence at Newmarket in April. However, he was just about in front of the stands' side group passing the 2f pole here before fading, so obviously retains some ability. (op 16-1)
Mirza reportedly lost a front shoe. (op 16-1)

2928 TOTESPORT.COM SCURRY STKS (LISTED RACE) 5f 6y
3:30 (3:30) (Class 1) 3-Y-O

£17,031 (£6,456; £3,231; £1,611; £807; £405) **Stalls** Low

Form RPR

5-34 **1** **Margot Did (IRE)**30 2032 3-8-8 105 HayleyTurner 1 112
(Michael Bell) *pressed ldr tl led 2f out: sn rdn and qcknd clr: in n.d fnl f: r.o wl: easily* **4/1**2

4-33 **2** *5* **Dinkum Diamond (IRE)**29 2054 3-9-2 106 DaneO'Neill 5 105+
(Henry Candy) *dwlt: hld up in last trio: rdn and effrt whn nt clr run wl over 1f out tl 1f out: hdwy to press for placings ins fnl f: no ch w wnr but kpt on to go 2nd wl ins fnl f* **9/2**3

-321 **3** *3/4* **Move In Time**17 2405 3-8-13 102 TomEaves 2 96
(Bryan Smart) *t.k.h: chsd ldrs: rdn and nt qng pce of wnr wl over 1f out: drvn and chsd clr wnr over 1f out: no imp: lost 2nd wl ins fnl f* **5/1**

2-11 **4** *1 1/4* **Night Carnation**30 2032 3-8-8 109 DavidProbert 9 87
(Andrew Balding) *hld up in tch in midfield: rdn and effrt 2f out: ev ch of 2nd but no ch w wnr ent fnl f: wknd fnl 75yds* **5/2**1

-030 **5** *3 3/4* **Arctic Feeling (IRE)**7 2714 3-9-2 102 DavidNolan 8 81
(Richard Fahey) *sn pushed along in last trio: rdn and outpcd 2f out: wl btn but plugging on whn nt clr run and swtchd lft ins fnl f* **33/1**

4103 **6** *1* **Button Moon (IRE)**14 2520 3-8-8 96 (p) MartinLane 4 70
(Ian Wood) *led: hdd and rdn 2f out: sn outpcd by wnr: wknd and wl btn whn hung rt ent fnl f* **11/1**

20-6 **7** *nk* **Pabusar**29 2054 3-8-13 104 JimCrowley 3 74
(Ralph Beckett) *chsd ldrs: rdn and unable qck 2f out: wknd and btn over 1f out: fdd fnl f* **16/1**

0-32 **8** *19* **The Thrill Is Gone**17 2405 3-8-8 96 RichardHughes 7 —
(Mick Channon) *chsd ldrs: rdn and struggling ent fnl 2f: sn wknd: wl btn over 1f out: virtually p.u fnl f: t.o* **25/1**

1-21 **9** *1 1/4* **Ahtoug**36 1852 3-8-13 96 FrankieDettori 10 —
(Mahmood Al Zarooni) *taken down early: wnt lft s: a outpcd in rr: lost tch wl over 1f out: virtually p.u ins fnl f: t.o* **7/1**

61.84 secs (0.24) **Going Correction** +0.325s/f (Good) **9** Ran SP% **116.9**
Speed ratings (Par 107): **111,103,101,99,93 92,91,61,59**
toteswingers:1&2:£3.90, 1&3:£5.10, 2&3:£3.80 CSF £22.72 TOTE £6.10: £1.60, £1.80, £2.30; EX 26.40 Trifecta £130.10 Pool £1,684.17 - 9.57 winning units..
Owner T Redman And P Philipps **Bred** N Hartery **Trained** Newmarket, Suffolk

FOCUS
This has gone to some nice young sprinters in recent years with the 2007 winner Hoh Mike and the 2009 winner Triple Aspect both going on to win at Group level. This year it proved to be a one-horse race, but Margot Did had the best draw against the rail, and the ground and time lend doubts to the strength of the form.

NOTEBOOK
Margot Did(IRE) is a classy filly on her day having been placed in three Group contests as a juvenile, but not for the first time she didn't enjoy the best of luck when behind Night Carnation and Move In Time at York last month. However, she enjoyed a clear run this time around and having seen off fellow pacesetter Button Moon at halfway, fairly bolted up. She can still make the grade as a sprinter and may be aimed at the Nunthorpe and the Abbaye later in the season, while she may take in the King George Stakes at Goodwood along the way. (op 9-2)
Dinkum Diamond(IRE), winner of a Listed race over C&D at two and a close third behind his elders in the Abernant on his return, was given a patient ride and still appeared to be going well when having to wait for a gap between the weakening Button Moon and Pabusar over a furlong from home, but even had he got through when he wanted to he wouldn't have troubled the winner. (tchd 5-1)
Move In Time achieved little in landing the odds in a three-runner Beverley conditions event last time, but was closely matched with Night Carnation on previous York running. Always in vain pursuit of the winner, this looks about as good as he is. (op 6-1 tchd 7-1 in a place)
Night Carnation was bidding for a hat-trick and had three of today's rivals behind her when narrowly winning at York last month. Admittedly she wasn't well drawn in stall nine here and although she made a promising move inside the last 2f, it soon flattened out. (op 9-4 tchd 11-4 in places)

Arctic Feeling(IRE) scored at this level at a juvenile, but his penalty made things tricky on these terms and he never got into the race at any stage.

Ahtoug may have been worst in at the weights and started from the worst draw, but it was still disappointing to see him beaten after 2f. His rider reported that he was unsuited by the soft ground. (op 8-1)

2929 BET TOTEPOOL AT TOTESPORT.COM H'CAP — 5f 6y
4:05 (4:06) (Class 4) (0-80,83) 4-Y-0+ — **£6,152** (£1,830; £914; £456) **Stalls** Low

Form — RPR

56-4 **1** **Macdillon**[19] 2369 5-9-1 **74** .... LiamKeniry 4 — 85
(Stuart Kittow) *travelled strly: trckd ldrs: effrt and swtchd lft over 1f out: rdn to chal 1f out: drvn ahd fnl 100yds: styd on wl and drew clr towards fin* **7/2**[2]

0261 **2** *1 1/4* **Taurus Twins**[2] 2832 5-9-5 **83** 6ex..........(b) HarryBentley(5) 13 — 89
(Richard Price) *racd keenly: pressed ldrs: wnt 2nd 3f out: rdn to ld wl over 1f out: hdd fnl 100yds: no ex and wknd towards fin* **13/2**

0025 **3** *1 3/4* **The Wee Chief (IRE)**[9] 2645 5-8-8 **67**..........(tp) EddieAhern 3 — 67
(Jimmy Fox) *hld up in tch: effrt and swtchd lft over 1f out: chsd ldng pair ins fnl f: kpt on but nt gng pce to threaten wnr* **8/1**

31-1 **4** *2 1/2* **Sharpened Edge**[9] 2645 5-9-7 **80**.......... DavidProbert 2 — 71
(Christopher Mason) *broke v fast and led: rdn ent fnl 2f: hdd and drvn wl over 1f out: wknd ins fnl f* **9/4**[1]

00-0 **5** *1 1/4* **The Strig**[54] 1444 4-8-6 **65**..........(t) WilliamCarson 1 — 51
(Stuart Williams) *racd in last pair: rdn and effrt on far rail 2f out: no real imp: swtchd lft and kpt on ins fnl f: nvr trbld ldrs* **16/1**

2615 **6** *1* **Rocker**[15] 2447 7-9-1 **74**..........(be) GeorgeBaker 10 — 57
(Gary Moore) *in tch: rdn and nt qckn ent fnl 2f: drvn and btn over 1f out: no ch w wnr but plugged on wl ins fnl f* **25/1**

1221 **7** *1* **Wooden King (IRE)**[15] 2447 6-9-3 **76**.......... TomMcLaughlin 5 — 55
(Malcolm Saunders) *chsd ldr for 2f: rdn and struggling ent fnl 2f: wknd u.p over 1f out* **6/1**[3]

1000 **8** *4* **Picansort**[9] 2645 4-8-8 **67**.......... JimmyQuinn 7 — 32
(Brett Johnson) *dwlt: a in last pair: rdn and no hdwy ent fnl 2f: edging rt and wl hld ent fnl f* **25/1**

24-0 **9** *11* **Love You Louis**[158] 29 5-9-1 **74**.......... RichardHughes 11 — —
(J R Jenkins) *in tch in midfield: rdn and effrt ent fnl 2f: btn ent fnl f: eased and dropped to last fnl 150yds* **14/1**

62.56 secs (0.96) **Going Correction** +0.325s/f (Good) — **9** Ran SP% **112.0**
Speed ratings (Par 105): **105,103,100,96,94 92,91,84,67**
toteswingers:1&2:£4.10, 1&3:£5.60, 2&3:£8.50 CSF £24.56 CT £143.17 TOTE £4.70: £1.30, £2.40, £2.80; EX 27.10.
Owner Boswell,Pillans,Harris,Urquhart & Kittow **Bred** Hopkins, Kittow & Mrs Perry **Trained** Blackborough, Devon

FOCUS
This wasn't as competitive a sprint handicap as it might have been with five non-runners, and that became six when Boogie Waltzer was withdrawn after bursting her stall. The pace was sound, however, with a three-way battle for the early lead. The rail again proved best. The winner is rated back to last year's form.

2930 BET TOTEPOOL ON 0800 221 221 MAIDEN STKS — 1m 2f 7y
4:40 (4:40) (Class 5) 3-Y-O — **£3,885** (£1,156; £577; £288) **Stalls** Low

Form — RPR

0 **1** **Arch Fire (USA)**[58] 1338 3-9-3 0..........(v1) RichardHughes 6 — 94
(Sir Michael Stoute) *in tch: rdn to chse ldng pair over 2f out: wnt 2nd over 1f out: styd on and drvn to ld ins fnl f: forged clr fnl 75yds* **8/1**

43 **2** *2 1/2* **Polperro (USA)**[11] 2596 3-9-3 0.......... WilliamBuick 2 — 89+
(John Gosden) *chsd ldr tl rdn to ld and edgd lft wl over 2f out: clr 2f out: wandering u.p over 1f out: hdd ins fnl f: sn btn* **9/4**[1]

-2 **3** *3 3/4* **Tmaam (USA)**[8] 2691 3-9-3 0.......... SilvestreDeSousa 13 — 82+
(Mark Johnston) *chsd ldrs but sn rdn along: rdn 5f out: 5th and wl outpcd over 2f out: styd on again u.p fr over 1f out: wnt 3rd wl ins fnl f: nvr gng pce to threaten ldrs* **13/2**[3]

0-3 **4** *1* **Monopolize**[23] 2231 3-9-3 0.......... IanMongan 4 — 80
(Sir Henry Cecil) *chsd ldrs: swtchd lft 2f out: sn rdn to chse ldr: no imp and lost 2nd over 1f out: styd on same pce fnl f* **4/1**[2]

5 *4 1/2* **Qahriman** 3-9-3 0.......... J-PGuillambert 3 — 71+
(Luca Cumani) *s.i.s: pushed along and rn green wl off the pce in rr: hdwy over 2f out: styd on past btn horses to go modest 5th over 1f out: kpt on fnl f: nvr trbld ldrs* **50/1**

6 **6** *4 1/2* **Momaris**[22] 2257 3-9-3 0.......... AndreaAtzeni 8 — 62
(Roger Varian) *sn pushed along and wl off the pce towards rr: plugged on past btn horses fnl 2f: wnt modest 6th over 1f out: nvr trbld ldrs* **9/1**

7 *2 1/4* **Aiken** 3-9-3 0.......... DaneO'Neill 1 — 57+
(John Gosden) *v.s.a: wl bhd in last trio: rdn over 3f out: plugged on past btn horses fr over 1f out: nvr on terms* **16/1**

0 **8** *3 3/4* **Green Future (USA)**[15] 2469 3-9-3 0.......... PatCosgrave 14 — 50
(Amanda Perrett) *hld up off the pce in midfield: sltly hmpd after 2f: rdn and effrt 3f out: 7th and no imp over 2f out: wl btn fnl 2f* **40/1**

05 **9** *10* **Al Khawaneej**[15] 2458 3-9-3 0.......... TomMcLaughlin 5 — 30+
(Ed Dunlop) *sn pushed along and wl off the pce in rr: rdn and lost tch wl over 3f out: t.o and eased fnl f* **28/1**

4-4 **10** *3* **Unex Picasso**[28] 2114 3-9-3 0..........(b1) RichardHills 7 — 24
(William Haggas) *led: hdd and hmpd wl over 2f out: sn rdn and btn: wknd and wl btn over 1f out: eased fnl f: t.o* **12/1**

2-4 **11** *1 3/4* **Hermes**[116] 546 3-9-3 0..........(v1) JimCrowley 12 — 20
(Ralph Beckett) *hld up in midfield: rdn and effrt 3f out: 6th and no prog whn veered bdly lft 2f out: wl btn after: eased ins fnl f: t.o* **18/1**

0 **12** *shd* **What's The Point**[19] 2371 3-9-3 0.......... EddieAhern 10 — 20+
(Walter Swinburn) *racd in midfield: rdn and struggling over 3f out: wkng and wl btn whn hmpd and pushed lft 2f out: no ch and eased after: t.o* **25/1**

13 *10* **Ownwan (USA)** 3-8-12 0.......... FrankieDettori 15 — —
(Saeed Bin Suroor) *s.i.s: a bhd lost tch wl over 3f out: t.o and eased fnl 2f* **9/1**

0-6 **14** *22* **Noble Defender**[19] 2371 3-9-3 0.......... LiamKeniry 11 — —
(Stuart Kittow) *in tch in midfield: rdn and losing pl 4f out: wknd over 3f out: wl t.o and eased fnl f* **50/1**

2m 13.48s (2.98) **Going Correction** +0.275s/f (Good) — **14** Ran SP% **128.3**
Speed ratings (Par 99): **99,97,94,93,89 86,84,81,73,70 69,69,61,43**
toteswingers:1&2:£4.70, 1&3:£7.70, 2&3:£4.20 CSF £27.03 TOTE £10.40: £3.20, £1.50, £2.40; EX 33.70.
Owner K Abdulla **Bred** Juddmonte Farms Inc **Trained** Newmarket, Suffolk

FOCUS
A big field, but few could be seriously considered and some of these are going to need even more time. Not many got involved or showed their form. The second set a good standard and the winner was much improved.

2931 BET TOTEPOOL ON ALL UK RACING H'CAP — 1m 6f
5:15 (5:15) (Class 4) (0-85,85) 4-Y-0+ — **£6,152** (£1,830; £914; £456) **Stalls** Low

Form — RPR

/020 **1** **Gifted Leader (USA)**[1] 2888 6-8-13 **82**..........(v) RyanClark(5) 4 — 92
(Ian Williams) *in tch in midfield: lost pl and pushed along over 4f out: swtchd lft and hdwy u.p 2f out: edging rt but chsng ldrs ent fnl f: led ins fnl f: styd on wl: rdn out* **11/2**[1]

10-0 **2** *2* **Regal Park (IRE)**[21] 2285 4-9-7 **85**.......... WilliamBuick 3 — 92
(Marco Botti) *stdd s: hld up in rr: hdwy 6f out: rdn 4f out: hdwy on outer 3f out: hung rt and upsides ldr 2f out: rdn to ld narrowly over 1f out: hdd and no ex ins fnl f* **6/1**[2]

4-02 **3** *1/2* **Crocus Rose**[53] 1470 5-9-4 **82**.......... JimmyQuinn 6 — 88
(Harry Dunlop) *hld up towards rr: hdwy on inner 1/2-way: chsng ldrs whn nt clr run and swtchd lft over 1f out: drvn and hanging rt 1f out: kpt hanging and kpt on same pce ins fnl f* **12/1**

-002 **4** *nk* **Red Courtier**[8] 2686 4-8-11 **75**..........(p) JimCrowley 8 — 83+
(Paul Cole) *hld up in midfield: rdn and effrt whn short of room and bdly hmpd 2f out: rallying u.p and edging rt over 1f out: swtchd lft ins fnl f: styd on wl fnl 100yds: nt rch ldrs* **12/1**

6/20 **5** *1 3/4* **Advisor (FR)**[36] 1847 5-9-2 **80**.......... HayleyTurner 10 — 83
(Michael Bell) *led: rdn wl over 2f out: jnd and drvn 2f out: hdd over 1f out: kpt on u.p and stl ev ch tl wknd ins fnl f* **8/1**

0-41 **6** *3/4* **Arab League (IRE)**[15] 2459 6-9-1 **79**.......... ShaneKelly 1 — 81
(Richard Price) *chsd ldrs: swtchd lft and tried to chal between horses over 2f out: short of room 2f out: sn rdn and unable qck: one pce and btn fnl f* **14/1**

04-0 **7** *3/4* **Bow To No One (IRE)**[36] 1847 5-9-0 **78**.......... KirstyMilczarek 2 — 80+
(Alan Jarvis) *in tch in midfield: rdn and effrt on inner whn hmpd and swtchd rt ent fnl 2f: rallied u.p on rail ent fnl f: keeping on same pce and hld whn nt clr run wl ins fnl f* **16/1**

3/5- **8** *6* **Kazzene (USA)**[49] 4-9-5 **83**..........(tp) AndreaAtzeni 15 — 76
(David Pipe) *hld up in last trio: rdn wl over 4f out: swtchd lft and hdwy u.p 2f out: styd on wl: nvr trbld ldrs* **22/1**

-600 **9** *3 1/2* **Dynamic Drive (IRE)**[23] 2224 4-9-2 **80**.......... EddieAhern 12 — 68
(Walter Swinburn) *in tch in midfield on outer: effrt and in tch whn short of room and hmpd 2f out: rdn: edgd rt and no hdwy over 1f out* **14/1**

04-4 **10** *2 1/2* **Magicalmysterytour (IRE)**[63] 1238 8-9-6 **84**.......... SilvestreDeSousa 13 — 69
(Willie Musson) *hld up in last trio: rdn and effrt over 2f out: nt clr run ent fnl 2f: nt rcvr and n.d after: eased ins fnl f* **12/1**

60-0 **11** *5* **Kid Charlemagne (IRE)**[21] 2289 8-9-5 **83**..........(t) IanMongan 7 — 68
(Warren Greatrex) *t.k.h: rdn and effrt to chse ldr briefly over 2f out: drvn and struggling 2f out: wknd over 1f out: eased ins fnl f* **20/1**

5-14 **12** *7* **Huff And Puff**[8] 2686 4-9-1 **79**.......... PhilipRobinson 9 — 47
(Amanda Perrett) *in tch: pushed along and effrt 4f out: rdn and hdwy to chse ldrs ent fnl 3f: wknd and edgd rt 2f out: sn bhd* **6/1**[2]

2531 **13** *7* **High On A Hill (IRE)**[21] 2312 4-9-3 **81**.......... RichardHughes 5 — 39
(Sylvester Kirk) *chsd ldr tl over 2f out: struggling whn short of 2f out: sn wknd: eased ins fnl f: t.o* **15/2**[3]

32-2 **14** *1 3/4* **Right Stuff (FR)**[13] 1105 8-9-7 **85**.......... GeorgeBaker 14 — 40
(Gary Moore) *hld up towards rr: hdwy into midfield 1/2-way: rdn and struggling 3f out: sn wknd: lost tch and eased fr 2f out: t.o* **14/1**

3m 9.28s (4.78) **Going Correction** +0.275s/f (Good) — **14** Ran SP% **124.9**
Speed ratings (Par 105): **97,95,95,95,94 93,93,90,88,86 83,79,75,74**
toteswingers:1&2:£9.70, 1&3:£13.60, 2&3:£17.10 CSF £38.85 CT £394.75 TOTE £6.00: £2.50, £3.00, £3.30; EX 49.90.
Owner Gifted Leader Partners **Bred** Juddmonte Farms Inc **Trained** Portway, Worcs

FOCUS
They didn't seem to go a great gallop in this staying handicap, but even so the front two came from well off the pace. Things got a bit messy but the form is taken at face value.
T/Jkpt: Not won. T/Plt: £209.10 to a £1 stake. Pool:£142,119.69 - 496.06 winning tickets T/Qpdt: £23.00 to a £1 stake. Pool:£8,961.40 - 287.54 winning tickets SP

2886 YORK (L-H)
Saturday, June 11

OFFICIAL GOING: Good (good to firm in places; 7.2; home straight: far side 7.2; centre 6.9; stands' side 6.8)
Wind: fresh against Weather: mixture of cloud and sunshine

2932 QUEEN MOTHER'S CUP (LADY AMATEUR RIDERS' H'CAP) — 1m 4f
2:10 (2:10) (Class 3) (0-95,89) 3-Y-0+ — **£9,369** (£2,905; £1,452; £726) **Stalls** Centre

Form — RPR

-530 **1** **Crackentorp**[29] 2071 6-10-8 **83**.......... MissJCoward 9 — 91
(Tim Easterby) *hld up in midfield: hdwy over 3f out: chsd ldr over 1f out: kpt on wl: led post* **8/1**[2]

0-46 **2** *hd* **Inspirina (IRE)**[21] 2282 7-10-4 **79**.......... MissPernillaHermansson 12 — 87
(Richard Ford) *led: rdn over 3f out: kpt on: hdd post* **20/1**

24-2 **3** *2 1/2* **Meetings Man (IRE)**[21] 2320 4-9-7 **74**.......... MissRSmith(6) 19 — 78
(Micky Hammond) *in tch on outer: hdwy over 2f out: wnt 3rd over 1f out: kpt on* **11/1**

-364 **4** *1 1/4* **Bowdler's Magic**[21] 2285 4-10-12 **87**.......... MsKWalsh 14 — 89
(Mark Johnston) *dwlt: hld up: hdwy over 3f out: short of room 2f out: wnt 4th 1f out: kpt on* **15/2**[1]

10-2 **5** *2 1/4* **Staff Sergeant**[16] 2414 4-10-7 **82**.......... MrsCBartley 11 — 80
(Jim Goldie) *midfield: rdn over 3f out: drvn over 1f out: kpt on ins fnl f: n.d* **9/1**[3]

021- **6** *nk* **Trip The Light**[164] 8003 6-10-5 **83**..........(v) MissTSyddall(3) 6 — 81
(Richard Fahey) *prom: rdn over 3f out: one pce* **11/1**

2-06 **7** *2* **Ejteyaaz**[27] 2124 4-10-3 **78**.......... MissADeniel 20 — 73
(Richard Fahey) *hld up: hdwy on outer over 3f out: outpcd over 2f out: kpt on fnl f* **25/1**

2123 **8** *3/4* **Sir Boss (IRE)**[21] 2285 6-10-12 **87**.......... MissMMullineaux 13 — 81
(Michael Mullineaux) *trckd ldr: rdn over 3f out: stl ev ch 2f out: wknd over 1f out* **9/1**[3]

3-35 **9** *nk* **Antigua Sunrise (IRE)**[31] 2006 5-10-3 **81**.......... MissPhillipaTutty(3) 4 — 74
(Richard Fahey) *midfield: rdn and hdwy over 3f out: one pce* **15/2**[1]

-056 **10** *nse* **Gold Rules**[7] 2708 4-10-4 **82**..........(t) MissJoannaMason(3) 8 — 75
(Michael Easterby) *trckd ldrs: rdn and lost pl over 3f out: kpt on ins fnl f* **14/1**

3061 **11** 3 1/4 **Bavarica**[15] 2473 9-9-5 **72** MissSBirkett(6) 7 60
(Julia Feilden) *midfield on outer: rdn over 3f out: wknd over 1f out* **22/1**

30-5 **12** 1 1/2 **Haljaferia (UAE)**[9] 2649 5-10-2 **77** MissLAllan 2 62
(David Elsworth) *midfield on inner: rdn over 3f out: wknd over 1f out* **8/1**[2]

145- **13** 15 **Baralaka**[12] 6654 4-10-9 **87** LucyAlexander(3) 5 48
(Rose Dobbin) *hld up: rdn over 3f out: sn wknd* **33/1**

000- **14** 1/2 **Epic (IRE)**[231] 7084 4-10-10 **85** (b) MissLHorner 17 46
(Mark Johnston) *hld up: a towards rr* **25/1**

050- **15** 14 **Umverti**[78] 6984 6-9-8 **72** MissJFoster(3) 18 10
(Joanne Foster) *prom: lost pl over 5f out: wknd over 3f out: t.o* **50/1**

-204 **F** **Embsay Crag**[12] 2544 5-10-4 **79** MissSBrotherton 3 —
(Kate Walton) *midfield whn fell after 1f* **9/1**[3]

2m 34.04s (0.84) **Going Correction** +0.05s/f (Good)
WFA 3 from 4yo+ 15lb **16** Ran SP% **120.8**
Speed ratings (Par 107): **99,98,97,96,94 94,93,92,92,92 90,89,79,79,69** —
toteswingers:1&2:£26.50, 1&3:£16.50, 2&3:£50.60 CSF £167.24 CT £1773.43 TOTE £8.40: £2.10, £4.60, £2.70, £2.30; EX 179.20 Trifecta £903.10 Part won. Pool £1,220.54 - 0.60 winning units..
Owner C H Stevens **Bred** C A Cyzer **Trained** Great Habton, N Yorks

FOCUS
Races on original inside line and distances as advertised. Traditionally a highly competitive handicap and this year's running was no different, although plenty of interest was lost when lowly-weighted 3-y-o Defence Of Duress, who was forecast to go off favourite, came out. The winner had slipped to a good mark and rates a few pounds off last year's best, with the runner-up the best guide to the form.

NOTEBOOK
Crackentorp, 9lb lower than when third last term, picked up well, having raced in midfield, and his extra stamina was a huge help in the closing stages. It would be no surprise to see him contest the Northumberland Plate again now, as he did last season, albeit without success. (op 7-1)
Inspirina(IRE) was stepping back up to 1m4f and returned to his best under a well-judged ride, fending off all bar the winner. He'll be bumped up a few pounds for this, though, which may stop him winning.
Meetings Man(IRE) ran well when third over C&D off 3lb lower last month, and he confirmed his wellbeing with another solid effort. He may want 1m6f now. (op 12-1)
Bowdler's Magic stays well, therefore it was far from ideal he was held up following a sluggish start. Predictably, he got going all too late. (op 13-2)
Staff Sergeant again ran well and has more to offer. (op 15-2)
Trip The Light, making his reappearance, was a bit keen early and then outpaced at the business end. (op 12-1)
Ejteyaaz made some ground from the rear and will soon become of interest. (op 28-1 tchd 33-1)
Sir Boss(IRE) had his chance and wasn't good enough. (op 12-1)
Antigua Sunrise(IRE) never got close enough and was a touch disappointing (op 8-1)
Haljaferia(UAE) failed to build on a promising reappearance, not looking at his best. (op 15-2)
Embsay Crag clipped heels after 1f and Serena Brotherton had no chance of staying aboard. (op 11-1 tchd 12-1)

2933 LADBROKES.COM STKS (H'CAP) 1m 208y
2:40 (2:42) (Class 2) (0-105,105) 3-Y-O+ **£17,485** (£5,202; £2,600; £1,298) **Stalls** Low

Form RPR

654- **1** **Confront**[285] 5590 6-9-11 **102** RyanMoore 16 111
(Sir Michael Stoute) *a.p: chsd ldr 3f out: rdn to ld wl over 1f out: edgd rt: styd on u.p* **8/1**[3]

1-60 **2** 1/2 **Sarrsar**[12] 2573 4-9-2 **93** (v1) NeilCallan 3 101
(Saeed Bin Suroor) *a.p: rdn over 2f out: chsd wnr over 1f out: edgd rt: r.o* **14/1**

-141 **3** 1/2 **Kay Gee Be (IRE)**[27] 2123 7-9-0 **91** PaulHanagan 7 98
(Richard Fahey) *prom: outpcd over 2f out: rallied over 1f out: r.o* **9/2**[1]

0-04 **4** 1 **Vainglory (USA)**[8] 2679 7-8-8 **90** LauraPike(5) 4 95+
(David Simcock) *hld up: hdwy over 1f out: r.o: nt rch ldrs* **9/1**

-042 **5** 1 1/4 **Leviathan**[16] 2441 4-8-12 **89** FergusSweeney 8 91+
(Tony Newcombe) *hld up: hdwy over 3f out: rdn over 1f out: styd on same pce ins fnl f* **6/1**[2]

0044 **6** 1 3/4 **Charlie Cool**[23] 2217 8-8-11 **88** (b) RobertWinston 9 86
(Ruth Carr) *mid-div: hdwy over 3f out: rdn over 1f out: no ex ins fnl f* **8/1**[3]

-050 **7** shd **Itlaaq**[31] 2002 5-8-12 **89** PaulMulrennan 11 87
(Michael Easterby) *led 1f: chsd ldrs: rdn over 2f out: no ex fnl f* **20/1**

0-00 **8** 3/4 **Harrison George (IRE)**[30] 2031 6-9-7 **105** GeorgeChaloner(7) 2 101+
(Richard Fahey) *hld up: racd keenly: rdn over 2f out: r.o ins fnl f: nrst fin* **20/1**

0250 **9** 3 1/2 **Cheers For Thea (IRE)**[7] 2706 6-8-10 **87** (bt) DavidAllan 15 76
(Tim Easterby) *s.i.s: hld up: rdn over 3f out: styd on ins fnl f: nvr nrr* **16/1**

3031 **10** shd **Balcarce Nov (ARG)**[10] 2614 6-9-5 **96** JamieSpencer 13 84
(Tom Tate) *led 8f out: rdn and hdd wl over 1f out: wknd ins fnl f* **10/1**

0430 **11** 2 **Tiger Reigns**[42] 1684 5-9-8 **99** PhillipMakin 6 83
(Michael Dods) *hld up: rdn over 2f out: a in rr* **25/1**

0000 **12** 1/2 **Tartan Gigha (IRE)**[8] 2679 6-9-1 **92** RoystonFfrench 12 75
(Mark Johnston) *prom: rdn over 3f out: edgd lft and wknd over 1f out* **33/1**

360- **13** 6 **Classic Punch (IRE)**[220] 7297 8-9-10 **101** AdamKirby 17 71
(David Elsworth) *hld up in tch: rdn over 2f out: sn wknd* **33/1**

-022 **14** 6 **Tartan Trip**[23] 2217 4-8-10 **87** oh3 (v) JimmyFortune 1 44
(Andrew Balding) *hld up: rdn over 2f out: wknd over 1f out* **6/1**[2]

4500 **15** 1 1/4 **Osteopathic Remedy (IRE)**[7] 2706 7-9-3 **94** FrederikTylicki 10 48
(Michael Dods) *plld hrd and prom: rdn and wknd over 2f out* **28/1**

1m 50.3s (-1.70) **Going Correction** +0.05s/f (Good) **15** Ran SP% **123.3**
Speed ratings (Par 109): **109,108,108,107,106 104,104,103,100,100 98,98,93,87,86**
toteswingers:1&2:£17.20, 1&3:£6.20, 2&3:£9.80 CSF £105.72 CT £585.84 TOTE £10.50: £3.70, £4.90, £1.80; EX 138.50 Trifecta £406.30 Pool £1,768.25 - 3.22 winning units..
Owner K Abdulla **Bred** Juddmonte Farms Ltd **Trained** Newmarket, Suffolk

FOCUS
A good-quality 0-105 handicap run at an ordinary pace. The winner took advantage of a much reduced mark and showed his best form since winning a Group 3 in late 2009.

NOTEBOOK
Confront, who was a bit below his best last season, returned to something like his best to triumph. Given a fine ride by Ryan Moore, who always had him perfectly positioned, he didn't initially do much in front, but found extra when the runner-up got to his quarters and was good value for the win. He'll be forced back into pattern-company now.
Sarrsar, a touch disappointing on two previous starts this year, had every chance to get past the winner and returned to his 3-y-o best, the first-time visor no doubt contributing heavily.
Kay Gee Be(IRE) has improved since joining this yard, winning two of his last three, but he never looked like plundering this prize, just lacking a change of pace. (op 5-1)
Vainglory(USA) got going too late having been held up. (tchd 10-1)
Leviathan was another keeping on late. (tchd 13-2)
Itlaaq will be of interest again once the handicapper relents. (op 16-1)
Harrison George(IRE) will be of interest again once the handicapper relents. (tchd 16-1)

Tartan Trip was well fancied despite racing from 3lb wrong', but he couldn't reproduce his best. (op 8-1 tchd 17-2)

2934 BOND TYRES TROPHY STKS (H'CAP) 6f
3:15 (3:16) (Class 2) (0-105,105) 3-Y-O **£51,808** (£11,560; £11,560; £3,848) **Stalls** Centre

Form RPR

-210 **1** **Lexi's Hero (IRE)**[14] 2508 3-8-11 **95** JamieSpencer 18 103
(Kevin Ryan) *mde all against stands' rail: rdn 2f out: drvn and hld on wl ins fnl f* **20/1**

4-52 **2** 1 **Cocktail Charlie**[41] 1711 3-8-8 **92** DavidAllan 16 97
(Tim Easterby) *trckd ldrs: rdn over 2f out: edgd lft over 1f out: kpt on ins fnl f: nt rch wnr* **20/1**

1112 **2** dht **Acclamazing (IRE)**[36] 1844 3-9-0 **98** (t) AdamKirby 2 103+
(Marco Botti) *hld up: hdwy in centre over 2f out: drvn and kpt on ins fnl f: edgd rt wl ins fnl f: unable to rch wnr* **8/1**[3]

-231 **4** nk **Swiss Dream**[15] 2468 3-8-5 **89** NickyMackay 15 93
(David Elsworth) *prom: rdn over 2f out: kpt on ins fnl f* **11/1**

25-1 **5** shd **Majestic Myles (IRE)**[14] 2508 3-9-2 **100** PaulHanagan 3 104+
(Richard Fahey) *trckd ldrs: rdn over 2f out: kpt on ins fnl f: n.m.r and bmpd towards fin* **9/1**

13-0 **6** 1 1/4 **New Planet (IRE)**[21] 2297 3-9-7 **105** PhillipMakin 20 105
(John Quinn) *hld up stands' side: rdn and hdwy over 1f out: kpt on ins fnl f* **33/1**

1-60 **7** nk **Majestic Dubawi**[20] 2334 3-8-13 **100** MartinHarley(3) 7 99
(Mick Channon) *chsd ldrs: rdn over 2f out: kpt on one pce* **28/1**

1-11 **8** nk **Seal Rock**[29] 2067 3-8-12 **96** FergusSweeney 4 99+
(Henry Candy) *trckd ldrs: rdn over 2f out: keeping on whn short of room wl ins fnl f* **7/1**[2]

-430 **9** 1 1/4 **Jamesway (IRE)**[7] 2714 3-8-4 **88** PaulQuinn 11 82+
(Richard Fahey) *hld up in rr: rdn over 2f out: kpt on ins fnl f: nvr threatened* **16/1**

00-4 **10** hd **Forjatt (IRE)**[42] 1688 3-9-2 **100** NeilCallan 8 102+
(Roger Varian) *in tch: rdn over 2f out: keeping on whn hmpd 1f out: no ch after* **8/1**[3]

33-2 **11** 1/2 **Dozy Joe**[24] 2199 3-8-6 **90** oh1 GrahamGibbons 13 82
(Ian Wood) *hld up: rdn and outpcd over 2f out: kpt on fnl f: n.d* **25/1**

2-11 **12** nk **Elusive Prince**[10] 2619 3-8-2 **86** KellyHarrison 1 77
(David Barron) *prom towards centre: rdn over 2f out: wknd ins fnl f* **14/1**

50-6 **13** 1 1/2 **Waking Warrior**[30] 2032 3-8-1 **90** JulieBurke(5) 12 76
(Kevin Ryan) *hld up: rdn over 2f out: edgd lft fr over 1f out: n.d* **40/1**

41-4 **14** nse **What About You (IRE)**[14] 2508 3-7-13 **86** (t) DeclanCannon(3) 19 72
(Richard Fahey) *chsd ldr against stands' rail: rdn and outpcd 2f out: wknd fnl f* **14/1**

0-25 **15** hd **Madany (IRE)**[45] 1602 3-8-9 **93** TadhgO'Shea 10 78
(B W Hills) *hld up: rdn 2f out: no imp* **18/1**

0-46 **16** hd **Mappin Time (IRE)**[7] 2724 3-8-4 **88** (b) RoystonFfrench 17 72
(Tim Easterby) *prom stands' side: rdn over 2f out: wknd over 1f out* **50/1**

5305 **17** 1/2 **Bathwick Bear (IRE)**[14] 2508 3-8-9 **93** CathyGannon 9 76
(David Evans) *midfield: pushed along 1/2-way: lost pl over 1f out: eased nr fin* **40/1**

4-32 **18** 8 **Cape To Rio (IRE)**[29] 2054 3-9-1 **99** RyanMoore 5 56
(Richard Hannon) *hld up: rdn over 2f out: a towards rr* **16/1**

01-2 **19** 8 **Desert Law (IRE)**[14] 2508 3-8-13 **97** JimmyFortune 6 29+
(Andrew Balding) *prom: lost pl qckly over 2f out: sn wknd: eased* **13/2**[1]

0-00 **20** 1 **Marine Commando**[14] 2500 3-8-10 **94** FrederikTylicki 14 22
(Richard Fahey) *s.i.s: a bhd* **50/1**

1m 11.44s (-0.46) **Going Correction** +0.05s/f (Good) **20** Ran SP% **125.3**
Speed ratings (Par 105): **105,103,103,103,103 101,101,100,99,98 98,97,95,95,95 95,94,83,73,71**PL: AC £1.90, CC £3.90 EX: LH/AC £161.90 LH/CC £325.80 CSF: LH/AC £79.82 LH/CC £177.43 TC: LH/AC/CC £1,663.23. LH/CC/AC £1,759.74. toteswingers: LH&AC £31.70, LH&CC £94.40, AC&CC £47.30 TOTE £26.40: £4.90 TRIFECTA Trifecta: LH/AC/C27 Owner.

FOCUS
As usual this valuable 3-y-o sprint handicap was wide-open. The winner got the rail and confirmed the good impression of his Chester win, but there was something of a bunch finish and the principals may not be as far ahead of their marks as they might have been.

NOTEBOOK
Lexi's Hero(IRE) came out on top, receiving a fine ride from Jamie Spencer who was quick the bag the stands' rail. A winner at Chester's May meeting, he failed to give his running when held up off this 6lb higher mark last time, but the return to more positive tactics suited him well and he found plenty for pressure for a well deserved win. He's expected to step up to Listed level now. (op 25-1)
Cocktail Charlie looked likely to benefit from the return to 6f and he travelled smoothly into contention. He couldn't quicken instantly, though, and despite staying on right the way to the line, he never quite looked like getting on top. This was a career-best. (op 15-2 tchd 6-1)
Acclamazing(IRE) interfered with several by edging right. A most progressive sprinter who didn't get the best of runs over 7f at Ascot last time, he challenged down the centre, but couldn't get there in time. He's likely to prove just as effective back at 7f. (op 15-2 tchd 6-1)
Swiss Dream was soon prominent and ran every bit as well in a more competitive race off 8lb higher. (op 9-1)
Majestic Myles(IRE), who had a few of these behind when making a winning return off 7lb lower at Newmarket, had every chance form over 1f out, being slightly squeezed up close home when held. (op 10-1)
New Planet(IRE), last of 12 against his elders in the Temple Stakes last month, had clearly come on from that and the step up to 6f was clearly a help, keeping on nicely close home. He isn't the easiest to place, however. (op 40-1 tchd 25-1)
Majestic Dubawi, 11th in the Irish 1,000 Guineas, ran a good race from a mark of 100, but is another tricky to place. (op 40-1)
Seal Rock, up 4lb from last time, was staying on in the battle for the places when badly squeezed up by Acclamazing. This was only his fourth start, and he remains capable of better, with a slower surface possibly being in his favour. (op 15-2)
Jamesway(IRE) caught the eye finishing fast in last weekend's Epsom Dash, but he again got going late back against his own age return to 6f. (op 14-1)
Forjatt(IRE) was trying to stay on when hampered just over 1f out. He'd have been a good bit closer and can be rated better than the bare form. (op 9-1)
Elusive Prince found this more competitive than the Ripon handicap he dominated last time. (op 12-1)
What About You(IRE) looked a bit awkward under pressure initially and only ran on in the last 100 yards. (op 12-1)

Desert Law(IRE) had run such a good race on his reappearance at Newmarket and possibly 'bounced' here. (tchd 7-1)

2935 GIVE GENEROUSLY TO MACMILLAN STKS (H'CAP) 1m 2f 88y
3:50 (3:51) (Class 2) (0-100,92) 3-Y-O **£12,952** (£3,854; £1,926; £962) **Stalls** Low

Form RPR
21- **1** **Sea Moon**[228] 7152 3-9-7 **92**.......... RyanMoore 5 111+
(Sir Michael Stoute) *hld up: pushed along over 4f out: hdwy over 3f out: rdn to chse ldr over 1f out: styd on u.p to ld wl ins fnl f* **4/6**[1]
11-3 **2** *1 3/4* **Flag Officer**[15] 2471 3-9-1 **86**.......... NeilCallan 2 101
(Saeed Bin Suroor) *chsd ldrs: led 3f out: rdn and hung rt fr over 1f out: hdd wl ins fnl f* **7/1**[3]
6-00 **3** *8* **Waltz Darling (IRE)**[7] 2705 3-9-4 **89**.......... FrederikTylicki 9 88
(Richard Fahey) *hld up: rdn over 2f out: r.o ins fnl f: wnt 3rd nr fin: nt trble ldrs* **40/1**
2-44 **4** *1/2* **Mariachi Man**[21] 2296 3-9-5 **90**.......... DavidAllan 8 88
(Tim Easterby) *chsd ldr tl led over 3f out: sn rdn and hdd: wknd ins fnl f: lost 3rd nr fin* **13/2**[2]
2133 **5** *4* **Iceblast**[21] 2319 3-8-12 **83**.......... GrahamGibbons 6 73
(Michael Easterby) *hld up: hdwy u.p over 1f out: sn wknd* **10/1**
-336 **6** *1 1/2* **Angelic Upstart (IRE)**[58] 1344 3-8-10 **81** ow3.......... JimmyFortune 1 68
(Andrew Balding) *prom: rdn over 2f out: wknd fnl f* **20/1**
6163 **7** *3* **Adaria**[10] 2615 3-8-9 **80**.......... PaulMulrennan 7 61
(David C Griffiths) *led: hdd over 3f out: sn rdn: wknd over 1f out* **14/1**
-521 **8** *6* **Adlington**[7] 2728 3-8-2 **73** oh1.......... PaulHanagan 3 42
(Richard Fahey) *prom: rdn over 3f out: wknd wl over 1f out* **12/1**

2m 8.88s (-3.62) **Going Correction** +0.05s/f (Good) **8** Ran SP% **116.5**
Speed ratings (Par 105): **116,114,108,107,104 103,101,96**
toteswingers:1&2:£2.30, 1&3:£8.40, 2&3:£18.70 CSF £6.17 CT £100.07 TOTE £1.60: £1.10, £2.00, £4.40; EX 4.30 Trifecta £87.20 Pool £2,317.96 - 20.12 winning units..
Owner K Abdulla **Bred** Juddmonte Farms Ltd **Trained** Newmarket, Suffolk
■ This event was formerly known as the Daniel Prenn Royal Yorkshire Handicap.

FOCUS
The front pair drew some 8l clear in a handicap that lacked strength in depth. Sea Moon is clearly a lot better than his opening mark and the second looks much improved too.

NOTEBOOK
Sea Moon, the one time Derby Hope who wasn't forward enough to be prepped for Epsom, was making his handicap debut from a mark of 92. Sent off at 4-6, he wasn't the best away and then took a bit of a grip. His prospects didn't look good at one stage, with the runner-up taking a couple of lengths out of him, but Moore always seemed confident he would get there, and the son of Beat Hollow saw it out dourly to ultimately score with a bit in hand. Very much expected to come on for this, he's expected to want all of 1m4f and should leave this form behind in time. Still in the Irish Derby, he isn't up to that level yet, but it would be no surprise to see him take his chance in a St Leger trial next, being related to Brian Boru, who won the Doncaster classic. (op 4-5 tchd evens in a place)
Flag Officer took a marked step forward on his reappearance third, going on over 3f out and really making the winner dig in. He remains capable of better, but can expect to go up a bit in the weights. (op 15-2)
Waltz Darling(IRE) had offered little this year, trying 1m for the first time latest, and although he appeared to keep on well for third, he was probably just keeping on past tired horses. (op 28-1)
Mariachi Man had run well in the Silver Bowl at Haydock, but his stamina gave way on this first try at 1m2f. (op 7-1)
Iceblast looked a doubtful stayer up 3f in trip, and he was duly well held. (tchd 12-1)

2936 REG GRIFFIN APPRECIATION EBF MAIDEN STKS 6f
4:25 (4:27) (Class 3) 2-Y-O **£7,447** (£2,216; £1,107; £553) **Stalls** Centre

Form RPR
2 **1** **Swiss Spirit**[14] 2510 2-9-3 0.......... RyanMoore 10 86
(David Elsworth) *racd keenly: trckd ldr: led wl over 2f out: jnd and pressed over 1f out: drvn and kpt on to assert fnl 100yds* **4/6**[1]
2 *1* **Discression** 2-9-3 0.......... PhillipMakin 6 84+
(Kevin Ryan) *slowly away: sn in tch: hdwy to chse wnr over 2f out: upsides ent fnl f: no ex fnl 100yds* **6/1**[2]
3 *3* **Bedlam** 2-8-12 0.......... DavidAllan 1 69+
(Tim Easterby) *dwlt and wnt lft s: sn pushed along towards rr: hdwy 2f out: wnt 3rd 1f out: [illegible] no threat ldng pair* **[illegible]/1**
4 *2 1/4* **Ventura Spirit** 2-9-3 0.......... PaulHanagan 4 69+
(Richard Fahey) *chsd ldrs: rdn and lost pl over 2f out: kpt on again ins fnl f* **10/1**
5 *1 1/2* **All Or Nothin (IRE)** 2-9-3 0.......... JimmyFortune 5 63
(John Quinn) *hld up: hdwy over 2f out: rdn to chse ldng pair over 1f out: wknd ins fnl f* **10/1**
02 **6** *1 1/2* **Dicky Mint**[18] 2387 2-9-3 0..........(t) GrahamGibbons 2 58
(Michael Easterby) *trckd ldrs: rdn over 2f out: edgd rt over 1f out: wknd ins fnl f* **9/1**[3]
7 *1/2* **Sinai (IRE)** 2-8-9 0.......... MichaelO'Connell(3) 7 52
(Geoffrey Harker) *dwlt: sn in tch: pushed along over 2f out: no imp* **66/1**
35 **8** *4* **Verse Of Love**[14] 2510 2-9-3 0.......... CathyGannon 8 45
(David Evans) *w ldr: rdn over 2f out: sn lost pl: wknd over 1f out* **25/1**
0 **9** *nk* **Hamis Al Bin (IRE)**[21] 2291 2-9-3 0.......... RoystonFfrench 3 44
(Mark Johnston) *led narrowly: hdd over 2f out: sn hung lft: wknd over 1f out* **25/1**
10 *43* **Dutch Heritage** 2-9-3 0.......... FrederikTylicki 9 —
(Richard Fahey) *s.i.s: sn pushed along in rr: t.o 1/2-way* **33/1**

1m 12.52s (0.62) **Going Correction** +0.05s/f (Good) **10** Ran SP% **119.3**
Speed ratings (Par 97): **97,95,91,88,86 84,84,78,78,20**
toteswingers:1&2:£1.80, 1&3:£5.90, 2&3:£11.80 CSF £4.68 TOTE £1.60: £1.10, £2.50, £4.20; EX 5.80.
Owner Lordship Stud **Bred** Lordship Stud **Trained** Newmarket, Suffolk

FOCUS
The front two drew 3l clear in what was a decent-looking maiden. The winner is rated roughly to his debut form

NOTEBOOK
Swiss Spirit made hard enough work of it, racing a lot keener than ideal and in the end his experience giving him the edge over the runner-up. Clearly very pacey, as many in the family are, he should prove just as effective over 5f for the time being and remains capable of better. (op 10-11tchd evens in a place)
Discression ◆ comes from a yard that can do little wrong with its juvenile at present, and he travelled strongly on this racecourse debut. However, he was unable to get away from the favourite, and ultimately the lack of a previous outing may have made the difference. He should come on and can go one better. (op 7-1 tchd 8-1)
Bedlam ◆, a daughter of Auction House, was green early, but finished to good effect and looks a ready-made winner of a fillies' maiden, with 7f likely to suit in time. (op 16-1 tchd 22-1)
Ventura Spirit looked the part and made a satisfactory debut. He should come on appreciably. (op 9-1 tchd 8-1)
All Or Nothin(IRE) showed a bit of ability and should come on. (op 8-1 tchd 11-1)

Dicky Mint failed to improve for the fitting of a tongue-tie and may be more of a nursery type. (op 7-1)

2937 YORK COMMITTEE CLASSIFIED STKS 7f
5:00 (5:01) (Class 4) 3-4-Y-O **£6,476** (£1,927; £963; £481) **Stalls** Low

Form RPR
5-53 **1** **My Son Max**[26] 2147 3-8-11 80.......... RyanMoore 6 83
(Richard Hannon) *hld up in tch: pushed along over 2f out: hdwy over 1f out: drvn and kpt on ins fnl f: led post* **4/1**[2]
44-3 **2** *hd* **Suffolk Punch (IRE)**[28] 2111 4-9-7 79..........(v) JimmyFortune 5 86
(Andrew Balding) *trckd ldr: rdn to ld over 1f out: drvn and kpt on ins fnl f: edgd lft towards fin: hdd post* **9/2**[3]
3331 **3** *1/2* **Bertiewhittle**[7] 2729 3-8-11 79.......... GrahamGibbons 3 81
(David Barron) *hld up in tch: rdn and hdwy 2f out: ev ch ent fnl f: kpt on* **15/8**[1]
6-31 **4** *shd* **Quite Sparky**[19] 2366 4-9-7 78.......... DanielTudhope 2 85+
(David O'Meara) *trckd ldr: rdn 2f out: kpt on ins fnl f: n.m.r towards fin* **5/1**
0-10 **5** *3/4* **Layla Jamil (IRE)**[14] 2503 3-8-11 79.......... JamieSpencer 1 78
(Mick Channon) *led: rdn whn hdd over 1f out: no ex ins fnl f* **6/1**
555- **6** *1 1/2* **Wisecraic**[290] 5421 4-9-7 78.......... PaulHanagan 4 78
(J S Moore) *s.i.s: hld up: pushed along over 3f out: sn no imp* **16/1**

1m 24.46s (-0.84) **Going Correction** +0.05s/f (Good)
WFA 3 from 4yo 10lb **6** Ran SP% **109.8**
Speed ratings (Par 105): **106,105,105,105,104 102**
toteswingers:1&2:£3.20, 1&3:£2.20, 2&3:£2.40 CSF £20.89 TOTE £5.10: £2.50, £2.40; EX 23.10.
Owner Dougie McKay **Bred** Mrs Fiona Denniff **Trained** East Everleigh, Wilts

FOCUS
Just 2lb separated these on BHA ratings, but it was no surprise to see one of the 3-y-os, who were receiving 10lb, come out on top. The winner is rated in line with recent efforts.

2938 CHARLES HENRY MEMORIAL STKS (H'CAP) 6f
5:30 (5:33) (Class 4) (0-80,81) 3-Y-O+ **£7,123** (£2,119; £1,059; £529) **Stalls** Centre

Form RPR
21-0 **1** **Entitled**[35] 1884 4-9-7 **79**.......... RyanMoore 17 92
(Sir Michael Stoute) *s.i.s: hld up: pushed along and hdwy over 1f out: rdn and r.o strly ins fnl f: led nr fin* **9/2**[2]
1211 **2** *1/2* **Collect Art (IRE)**[3] 2826 4-9-2 **81** 6ex.......... LucyKBarry(7) 14 92
(Andrew Haynes) *led: rdn over 1f out: kpt on: hdd towards fin* **4/1**[1]
1-66 **3** *2* **Dancing Maite**[56] 1395 6-8-11 **72**.......... DeclanCannon(3) 1 77
(Roy Bowring) *chsd ldrs: rdn over 2f out: kpt on ins fnl f* **14/1**
-010 **4** *nk* **River Falcon**[28] 2116 11-9-6 **78**.......... DanielTudhope 2 82
(Jim Goldie) *hld up in rr: rdn over 2f out: hdwy in centre over 1f out: kpt on strly ins fnl f* **20/1**
2034 **5** *hd* **Select Committee**[11] 2590 6-8-10 **75**..........(b) ShaneBKelly(7) 10 78
(John Quinn) *trckd ldrs: rdn over 1f out: kpt on ins fnl f* **40/1**
40-2 **6** *3/4* **Jack Luey**[21] 2280 4-9-4 **76**.......... PaulHanagan 5 77
(Lawrence Mullaney) *chsd ldrs: rdn over 2f out: kpt on ins fnl f* **7/1**[3]
0130 **7** *shd* **Efistorm**[10] 2603 10-9-5 **77**.......... PaulMulrennan 6 78
(Conor Dore) *midfield: rdn over 2f out: kpt on ins fnl f* **40/1**
-302 **8** *nse* **Caranbola**[8] 2668 5-9-0 **72**.......... RobertWinston 20 72
(Mel Brittain) *chsd ldrs: rdn over 2f out: kpt on same pce* **18/1**
-305 **9** *3/4* **Summer Dancer (IRE)**[33] 1942 7-9-4 **79**.......... MichaelO'Connell(3) 15 77+
(Paul Midgley) *midfield: rdn and outpcd over 1f out: kpt on fnl f: n.d* **25/1**
50-6 **10** *1/2* **Ishetoo**[11] 2590 7-9-2 **74**.......... JimmyFortune 19 70
(Ollie Pears) *hld up: rdn over 2f out: kpt on: nvr threatened* **16/1**
4-30 **11** *1* **Lujeanie**[135] 316 5-9-8 **80**..........(p) RoystonFfrench 16 73
(Dean Ivory) *midfield: rdn over 2f out: one pce* **50/1**
1511 **12** *nk* **Steelcut**[21] 2280 7-9-4 **76**..........(p) CathyGannon 18 68
(David Evans) *midfield: rdn over 2f out: no imp* **16/1**
-060 **13** *1/2* **Bahamian Lad**[103] 708 6-9-2 **74**.......... PaulQuinn 11 65
(Reg Hollinshead) *wnt bdly lft s: sn chsd ldrs: rdn over 2f out: wknd over 1f out* **40/1**
2006 **14** *1 1/4* **Desert Strike**[14] 2491 5-8-7 **72**..........(tp) NoraLooby(7) 8 59
(Alan McCabe) *s.i.s: hld up: rdn over 2f out: nvr threatened* **50/1**
[illegible] **15** *hd* **[illegible] (IRE)**[21] [illegible] [illegible].......... PJMcDonald 4 [illegible]
(Ruth Carr) *hld up: pushed along bef 1/2-way: a towards rr* **14/1**
51-0 **16** *3/4* **Piddie's Power**[12] 2566 4-9-3 **75**.......... GrahamGibbons 12 59
(Ed McMahon) *prom: rdn over 2f out: wknd over 1f out* **14/1**
-641 **17** *1 1/2* **Feeling Fresh (IRE)**[12] 2543 6-9-4 **76**.......... JamieSpencer 9 55+
(Paul Green) *s.i.s and swtchd rt s: hld up in rr: rdn over 2f out: n.d* **11/1**
4565 **18** *3/4* **Green Manalishi**[22] 2250 10-9-5 **77**..........(tp) PhillipMakin 7 53
(Kevin Ryan) *midfield: rdn over 2f out: wknd over 1f out* **40/1**
0-55 **19** *1 1/4* **Bond Fastrac**[28] 2095 4-9-1 **73**..........(p) FrederikTylicki 13 45
(Geoffrey Oldroyd) *chsd ldrs: rdn over 2f out: wknd over 1f out* **12/1**
441- **20** *2 1/2* **Hatta Stream (IRE)**[184] 7782 5-9-2 **74**.......... MickyFenton 3 38
(Lydia Pearce) *hld up: rdn over 2f out: wknd over 1f out* **33/1**

1m 11.48s (-0.42) **Going Correction** +0.05s/f (Good) **20** Ran SP% **129.0**
Speed ratings (Par 105): **104,103,100,100,100 99,98,98,97,97 95,95,94,93,92 91,89,88,87,83**
Tote Swingers: 1&2 £3.50, 1&3 £14.50, 2&3 £11.90. Totesuper 7: Win: Not won. Place: £116.60 CSF £21.24 CT £251.62 TOTE £5.20: £2.10, £1.80, £3.30, £5.00; EX 22.80.
Owner Cheveley Park Stud **Bred** Cheveley Park Stud Ltd **Trained** Newmarket, Suffolk

FOCUS
A good sprint handicap. The winning time compared favourably with that recorded by Lexi's Hero in the 3-y-o handicap earlier on the card. the winner recorded a clear personal best and the second improved again.
T/Plt: £78.70 to a £1 stake. Pool:£208,093.16 - 1,930.13 winning tickets T/Qpdt: £15.50 to a £1 stake. Pool:£7,333.71- 349.49 winning tickets AS

2939 - 2949a, 2951a (Foreign Racing) - See Raceform Interactive

2579 BELMONT PARK (L-H)
Saturday, June 11

OFFICIAL GOING: Turf: 9.43 good; 10.39 yielding; dirt: 7.34 - 8.59 muddy; 11.35 sloppy

2950a BELMONT STKS (GRADE 1) (3YO) (DIRT) 1m 4f (D)
11:35 (11:39) 3-Y-O **£384,615** (£128,205; £70,512; £38,461; £19,230)

RPR
1 **Ruler On Ice (USA)**[35] 3-9-0 0..........(b[1]) JValdiviaJr 3 122
(Kelly Breen, U.S.A) *smartly away and chsd ldr: led over 1f out: r.o gamely u.p* **248/10**

2 ¾ **Stay Thirsty (USA)**35 [1921] 3-9-0 0 ... JJCastellano 2 121
(Todd Pletcher, U.S.A) *a.p in 3rd: rdn 3 1/2f out: outpcd 2 1/2f out: rallied on rail to press wnr 1f out: styd on wout being able to qckn* **162/10**

3 1½ **Brilliant Speed (USA)**35 [1921] 3-9-0 0 ... JRosario 5 119+
(Thomas Albertrani, U.S.A) *racd towards rr early: prog on outside after 2f and racd in midfield: 6th and running on 3f out: 3rd and ev ch over 1 1/2f out: nt qckn ins fnl f* **109/10**

4 5¼ **Nehro (USA)**35 [1921] 3-9-0 0 ... CNakatani 6 111
(Steven Asmussen, U.S.A) *chsd ldng gp: swtchd ins to rail after 1f and sn settled in 5th and then 6th on bk st: rdn to hold position fr 3 1/2f out: 6th st: styd on fnl f to take 4th on line* **49/10**2

5 nk **Shackleford (USA)**21 [2328] 3-9-0 0 ... JLCastanon 12 110+
(Dale Romans, U.S.A) *led: hdd over 1f out: fdd fnl f: lost 4th on line* **63/10**

6 1½ **Animal Kingdom (USA)**21 [2328] 3-9-0 0 ... (b) JRVelazquez 9 108+
(H Graham Motion, U.S.A) *bmpd by Mucho Macho Man sn after s: stmbld: rdr lost iron and lft last: 15l adrift of ldr at 1/2-way: rapid hdwy on outside 4f out: 5th 2f out: rdn and no ex appr fnl f: wknd* **13/5**1

7 15 **Mucho Macho Man (USA)**21 [2328] 3-9-0 0 ... RADominguez 10 86
(Kathy Ritvo, U.S.A) *bmpd Animal Kingdom sn after s: chsd ldng gp tl rdn and wknd fnl 1 1/2f* **41/5**

8 3½ **Santiva (USA)**35 [1921] 3-9-0 0 ... SXBridgmohan 4 80
(Eddie Kenneally, U.S.A) *racd in 4th: pushed along and nt qckn 3f out: wknd fr 2f out: eased fnl f* **133/10**

9 nse **Monzon (USA)**28 3-9-0 0 ... JLezcano 7 80
(Ignacio Correas IV, U.S.A) *towards rr: riden and no imp fr 3f out: nvr a factor* **28/1**

10 1½ **Master Of Hounds (USA)**35 [1921] 3-9-0 0 ... GKGomez 1 78
(A P O'Brien, Ire) *settled towards rr: tk clsr order and racd in 7th appr 4f fr home: no imp on ldrs 2 1/2f out: wknd* **6/1**3

11 1 **Prime Cut (USA)**28 3-9-0 0 ... EPrado 8 76
(Neil J Howard, U.S.A) *n.d* **211/10**

12 1 **Isn't He Perfect (USA)**21 [2328] 3-9-0 0 ... (b) RMaragh 11 75
(Doodnauth Shivmangal, U.S.A) *a bhd: nvr in contention* **31/1**

2m 30.88s (1.92) **12 Ran SP% 119.8**
PARI-MUTUEL (all including $2 stakes): WIN 51.50; PLACE (1-2) 26.00, 19.40; SHOW (1-2-3) 13.60, 10.80, 7.90; SF 928.00.
Owner George & Lori Hall **Bred** Liberation Farm & Brandywine Farm **Trained** USA

FOCUS
A sloppy track that favoured speed led to a shock result. The bulk of this year's Triple Crown contenders will be easily forgotten.

NOTEBOOK
Ruler On Ice(USA) left his previous form behind, helped by a number of factors, but is flattered. A maiden winner on sloppy, he was the only runner with form on such a surface, plus he was well placed considering how the track was playing, and he also had blinkers fitted for the first time.
Stay Thirsty(USA) is a half-brother to Belmont Stakes runner-up Andromeda's Hero, so this test suited and he ran well having held a good position.
Brilliant Speed(USA) was better than his seventh-place finish in the Kentucky Derby indicated as he had a wide trip, and he's better than he showed here too. He was the only runner to produce a sustained challenge from off the pace, despite being four-wide into the straight. This was a missed opportunity as he's bred to stay well.
Nehro(USA) came out of the race with a small chip in his right front ankle and will have surgery.
Shackleford(USA), the Preakness winner, did not stay, despite the track riding to suit his style.
Animal Kingdom(USA), the Kentucky Derby winner and Preakness runner-up, lost his chance when squeezed out soon after the start, nearly unseating his rider. Detached for the most part, he made a sweeping move starting out of the backstretch and passed six rivals, but the racetrack gave him no hope of sustaining his effort. There was talk of him switching back to turf for the Arlington Million, but he may now stick to dirt for the Haskell at Monmouth on July 30 and/or the Travers at Saratoga on August 27. The long-term plan is the 2012 Dubai World Cup, but he may struggle outside of this division.
Master Of Hounds(USA), like when a staying-on fifth in the Kentucky Derby, started slowly and this time he made no progress. The sloppy surface did not suit a colt with a turf pedigree.

2705 DONCASTER (L-H)

Sunday, June 12

OFFICIAL GOING: Straight course - good changing to good to soft after race 2 (2.50) round course - good to firm (good in places) changing to good after race 1 (2.15) and good to soft (soft in places) after race 4 (4.00)
fresh 1/2 against raining, very breezy

2952 CROWNHOTEL-BAWTRY.COM APPRENTICE H'CAP — 1m 6f 132y
2:15 (2:15) (Class 5) (0-70,70) 4-Y-0+ **£2,525** (£751; £375; £187) **Stalls** Low

Form / RPR

4/64 1 **John Forbes**22 [2320] 9-8-13 **66** ... JacobButterfield(7) 9 74
(Brian Ellison) *hld up in rr: gd hdwy 3f out: led jst ins fnl f: styd on: eased cl home* **14/1**

-132 2 1¼ **Shifting Gold (IRE)**39 [1817] 5-9-2 **62** ... (b) AmyRyan 12 67
(Kevin Ryan) *s.i.s: in rr: drvn and plld wd over 4f out: gd hdwy over 2f out: fin wl to take 2nd fnl strides* **10/1**

-213 3 nk **Sancho Panza**22 [2320] 4-9-3 **66** ... AdamBeschizza(3) 2 71
(Julia Feilden) *trckd ldrs: styd on to go 2nd ins fnl f: no ex* **9/2**1

660 4 ½ **Aeneid**16 [2458] 6-9-6 **69** ... NeilFarley(3) 16 73
(Declan Carroll) *s.i.s: hld up in rr: hdwy to join ldrs 5f out: led over 3f out: hdd over 2f out: led appr fnl f: sn hdd: kpt on same pce fnl f* **18/1**

3015 5 3 **Visions Of Johanna (USA)**6 [2762] 6-9-3 **66** ... (p) RyanClark(3) 7 66
(Richard Guest) *mid-div: hdwy to ld over 2f out: hdd appr fnl f: wknd clsng stages* **12/1**

46-3 6 1¼ **Mohawk Ridge**19 [2393] 5-9-9 **69** ... SeanLevey 10 68
(Michael Dods) *trckd ldrs: t.k.h: one pce appr fnl f* **10/1**

5/01 7 5 **Bajan Parkes**13 [2575] 8-9-10 **70** ... DeclanCannon 11 62
(John Quinn) *in rr: effrt over 4f out: chsng ldrs over 2f out: wknd over 1f out* **16/1**

3-26 8 1¼ **Eastern Magic**5 [2793] 4-9-0 **67** ... JackDuern(7) 15 58
(Reg Hollinshead) *in rr: hdwy 8f out: sn chsng ldrs: wknd 2f out* **14/1**

-054 9 hd **Aegean Destiny**29 [2091] 4-8-10 **59** ... JulieBurke(3) 3 49
(John Mackie) *hld up in rr: chsng ldrs over 2f out: sn wknd* **9/1**3

265- 10 2½ **Tillietudlem (FR)**218 [6983] 5-8-12 **63** ... LMcNiff(5) 13 50
(Jim Goldie) *in rr: hdwy on outside over 7f out: drvn over 4f out: wknd 2f out* **11/2**2

5-00 11 9 **Think Its All Over (USA)**16 [2459] 4-9-4 **67** ... DaleSwift(3) 1 42
(Julie Camacho) *led tl hdd over 2f out: wknd over 2f out* **16/1**

0003 12 10 **Lure of The Night (IRE)**10 [2636] 4-8-6 **59** ... DavidSimmonson(7) 8 21
(Brian Rothwell) *trckd ldrs: lost pl over 2f out* **28/1**

3-03 13 8 **Cornish Beau (IRE)**30 [2055] 4-9-6 **69** ... AshleyMorgan(3) 4 21
(Mark H Tompkins) *chsd ldrs: lost pl 3f out* **10/1**

2126 14 9 **Bright Sparky (GER)**3 [2830] 8-8-5 **51** ... (bt) PatrickDonaghy 5 —
(Michael Easterby) *chsd ldrs: lost pl 3f out* **20/1**

4454 15 ¾ **Silent Lucidity (IRE)**9 [2666] 7-7-13 **52** ... (p) LauraBarry(7) 14 —
(Peter Niven) *chsd ldrs: lost pl over 3f out* **20/1**

3m 11.31s (3.91) **Going Correction** +0.275s/f (Good) **15 Ran SP% 121.9**
Speed ratings (Par 103): **100,99,99,98,97 96,93,93,93,91 87,81,77,72,72**
Tote Swingers: 1&2 £12.80, 1&3 £8.10, 2&3 £5.00 CSF £144.27 CT £744.49 TOTE £18.80: £4.90, £2.70, £1.90; EX 112.70 Trifecta £379.30 Part won. Pool £512.58 - 0.70 winning units..
Owner Brian Ellison **Bred** Northmore Stud **Trained** Norton, N Yorks

FOCUS
A good test at the distance for this apprentice handicap. Ordinary form, the winner back to his old Flat best.

2953 E B F POLYPIPE MEDIAN AUCTION MAIDEN STKS — 6f
2:50 (2:51) (Class 5) 2-Y-O **£3,302** (£982; £491; £245) **Stalls** High

Form / RPR

0 1 **Sovereign Debt (IRE)**15 [2510] 2-9-3 0 ... JamieSpencer 4 82
(Michael Bell) *mid-div: hdwy to chse ldrs over 2f out: edgd rt and led appr fnl f: styd on wl* **7/2**2

62 2 2 **Mizbah**16 [2460] 2-9-3 0 ... TomQueally 13 76
(Saeed Bin Suroor) *w ldrs: led 3f out: hdd appr fnl f: no ex* **11/2**3

5 3 2½ **Finbar**14 [2523] 2-9-3 0 ... PaulMulrennan 3 69
(James Given) *w ldrs: n.m.r over 1f out: kpt on same pce* **50/1**

4 nk **Balti's Sister (IRE)** 2-8-12 0 ... GrahamGibbons 17 63
(Michael Easterby) *hld up in rr stands' side: hdwy over 2f out: kpt on same pce fnl f* **100/1**

30 5 1¾ **Come On Blue Chip (IRE)**31 [2033] 2-9-3 0 ... TonyCulhane 9 62
(Paul D'Arcy) *mid-div: effrt over 2f out: styd on fnl f* **11/1**

6 nk **Chapter Seven** 2-9-3 0 ... PaulHanagan 2 61+
(Richard Fahey) *dwlt: sn chsng ldrs on outside: hung lft over 1f out: sn wknd* **14/1**

7 shd **Talwar (IRE)** 2-9-3 0 ... WilliamBuick 6 61+
(Jeremy Noseda) *mid-div: hdwy over 2f out: sn chsng ldrs: wknd over 1f out* **7/1**

8 1 **Laffan (IRE)** 2-9-3 0 ... StephenCraine 16 58+
(Kevin Ryan) *dwlt: hdwy to chse ldrs 3f out: wknd fnl f* **20/1**

02 9 3¾ **Louis Hull**8 [2731] 2-9-3 0 ... RoystonFfrench 15 47
(George Foster) *chsd ldrs: wknd over 1f out* **33/1**

300 10 ½ **Pius Parker (IRE)**16 [2448] 2-9-3 0 ... RobertHavlin 10 45
(John Gallagher) *led tl 3f out: wknd over 1f out* **100/1**

05 11 4½ **Samasana (IRE)**37 [1870] 2-8-12 0 ... MartinLane 7 27
(Ian Wood) *in rr: sme hdwy over 2f out: sn wknd* **100/1**

4 12 1½ **Sandbetweenourtoes (IRE)**15 [2510] 2-9-3 0 ... ShaneKelly 8 27
(Brian Meehan) *chsd ldrs: outpcd over 2f out: lost pl over 1f out* **13/8**1

13 1¾ **Miserere Mei (IRE)** 2-8-9 0 ... SeanLevey(3) 5 17
(Alan McCabe) *s.i.s: a towards rr* **66/1**

05 14 ½ **Grippa**9 [2672] 2-9-3 0 ... RobertWinston 12 21
(David Brown) *chsd ldrs: wknd over 2f out* **100/1**

0 15 14 **Turn The Page**22 [2318] 2-9-3 0 ... DanielTudhope 14 —
(Alan McCabe) *hld up in rr: lost pl over 2f out: sn bhd* **100/1**

16 2½ **Festival Spirit** 2-9-3 0 ... SilvestreDeSousa 1 —
(Mark Johnston) *chsd ldrs on outer: hung lft and lost pl over 2f out* **25/1**

17 26 **Ohceecee** 2-9-0 0 ... BillyCray(3) 11 —
(Jason Ward) *s.s: a detached in last: t.o 3f out* **100/1**

1m 14.22s (0.62) **Going Correction** +0.075s/f (Good) **17 Ran SP% 124.1**
Speed ratings (Par 93): **98,95,92,91,89 88,88,87,82,81 75,73,71,70,52 48,14**
Tote Swingers: 1&2 £5.10, 1&3 £29.60, 2&3 £27.40 CSF £22.18 TOTE £4.80: £2.10, £1.90, £7.20; EX 27.90 Trifecta £380.40 Pool £545.01 - 1.06 winning units..
Owner Lawrie Inman **Bred** Yeomanstown Stud **Trained** Newmarket, Suffolk
■ Stewards' Enquiry : Jamie Spencer caution: careless riding

FOCUS
Quite an interesting juvenile maiden. The time and race averages help with the ratings.

NOTEBOOK
Sovereign Debt(IRE) shaped as though his debut experience at Newmarket would do him good (behind Sandbetweenourtoes) and he duly took a marked step forward, justifying good market support in the process. Drawn low, he didn't pick up immediately, but really motored from over 1f out and looks the type to progress again, being a half-brother to smart 6f-7f performer Duff. (op 11-2)
Mizbah was soon up there and saw it out well, but the winner was that bit too good. He has improved with each run and can win a small maiden, with 7f likely to suit. (tchd 5-1)
Finbar improved markedly on his debut effort, possibly appreciating the slower conditions. He should benefit from 7f and can win races.
Balti's Sister(IRE), from a yard that is going well with its juveniles this season, was dismissed in the betting, but made some good late headway and should improve.
Come On Blue Chip(IRE) looks more of a nursery type. (op 14-1 tchd 10-1)
Chapter Seven was expected to need this experience and he should improve markedly as he matures.
Talwar(IRE), Group 1-entered, could make no impact, but certainly deserves another chance on better ground. (op 13-2)
Sandbetweenourtoes(IRE) proved most disappointing, never travelling and failing to confirm debut form with the winner. This clearly wasn't his best form, and he can be given another chance, although may be one for nurseries now. Official explanation: jockey said colt was never travelling (op 6-4 tchd 15-8 and 2-1 in a place)
Turn The Page Official explanation: jockey said colt lost his action
Festival Spirit Official explanation: jockey said colt hung left

2954 JOSH WALKER HAPPY 18TH BIRTHDAY H'CAP — 6f
3:25 (3:27) (Class 3) (0-95,95) 3-Y-0+ **£7,447** (£2,216; £1,107; £553) **Stalls** High

Form / RPR

2-06 1 **Dungannon**22 [2288] 4-9-7 **90** ... JimmyFortune 13 103+
(Andrew Balding) *mid-div: hdwy over 2f out: led jst ins fnl f: edgd rt: kpt on wl* **15/2**3

110 2 1 **Mon Brav**22 [2317] 4-8-13 **85** ... SeanLevey(3) 15 95+
(Brian Ellison) *hld up towards rr: hdwy 2f out: struck on hd by winning rdr's whip ins fnl f: crowded: styd on wl to take 2nd last 50yds* **9/1**

-200 3 ½ **Medicean Man**30 [2075] 5-9-10 **93** ... WilliamBuick 10 101
(Jeremy Gask) *mid-div: sn drvn along: hdwy 2f out: styd on wl ins fnl f: tk 3rd nr fin* **6/1**2

2000 4 1½ **Star Rover (IRE)**14 [2525] 4-9-5 **88** ... (v1) SilvestreDeSousa 9 91
(David Evans) *mde most: hdd jst ins fnl f: no ex* **20/1**

5304 5 nk **Whozthecat (IRE)**14 [2525] 4-9-1 **89** ... NeilFarley(5) 16 91
(Declan Carroll) *w ldr: kpt on same pce last 150yds* **20/1**

-404 6 nse **Lutine Bell**22 [2288] 4-9-9 **92** ... (b) MartinLane 12 94
(Mike Murphy) *s.i.s: hdwy 2f out: n.m.r: kpt on same pce ins fnl f* **11/1**

31-2 **7** *hd* **Tagula Night (IRE)**[14] 2525 5-9-5 **91**............................(vt) JohnFahy(3) 6 92
(Walter Swinburn) *mid-div: effrt over 2f out: chsng ldrs over 1f out: kpt on same pce fnl f* **16/1**

1124 **8** *1* **Norville (IRE)**[22] 2284 4-9-12 **95**..................................(b) CathyGannon 3 93
(David Evans) *chsd ldrs: kpt on same pce appr fnl f* **16/1**

0305 **9** *3/4* **Fitz Flyer (IRE)**[15] 2489 5-9-4 **87**.. TomEaves 5 83
(Bryan Smart) *w ldrs: wknd fnl 100yds* **33/1**

-115 **10** *1 3/4* **King Of Eden (IRE)**[30] 2061 5-9-5 **88**.................................. DavidAllan 8 78
(Eric Alston) *in rr: hdwy over 2f out: chsng ldrs over 1f out: wknd last 100yds* **14/1**

1040 **11** *3/4* **Baby Strange**[8] 2717 7-9-7 **90**.. StephenCraine 19 78+
(Derek Shaw) *towards rr: hdwy whn nt clr run over 2f out: nvr on terms* **12/1**

0013 **12** *2 1/2* **Dickie Le Davoir**[17] 2434 7-9-0 **86**..........................(b) RobertLButler(3) 11 66
(Richard Guest) *sn bhd: nvr on terms* **18/1**

1010 **13** *1 1/4* **Thrust Control (IRE)**[11] 2620 4-9-0 **83**.......................... PaulMulrennan 14 59
(Tracy Waggott) *chsd ldrs: wknd 2f out* **66/1**

/3-6 **14** *2* **Dorback**[29] 2099 4-9-7 **90**.. JamieSpencer 18 59
(Henry Candy) *hld up in rr: nvr on terms* **11/2[1]**

-000 **15** *1 1/2* **Corporal Maddox**[22] 2288 4-9-11 **94**................................ TomQueally 2 59
(Jamie Osborne) *s.s: hdwy over 4f out: wknd over 1f out* **33/1**

000- **16** *2* **Able Master (IRE)**[246] 6752 5-9-9 **92**................................ RobertHavlin 4 50
(Jeremy Gask) *in rr: bhd fnl 2f* **25/1**

1m 12.96s (-0.64) **Going Correction** +0.075s/f (Good) **16** Ran SP% **111.9**
Speed ratings (Par 107): **107,105,105,103,102 102,102,100,99,97 96,93,91,88,86 84**
Tote Swingers: 1&2 £11.40, 1&3 £6.80, 2&3 £8.30 CSF £57.79 CT £374.32 TOTE £6.90: £2.10, £2.50, £1.90, £5.70; EX 54.40 Trifecta £656.60 Part won. Pool £887.38 - 0.80 winning units..
Owner I G Burbidge **Bred** J A E Hobby **Trained** Kingsclere, Hants
■ Marvellous Value was withdrawn (unruly in stalls, 10/1). Deduct 5p in the £ under R4.
■ Stewards' Enquiry : Sean Levey two-day ban: excessive use of whip (26th-27th June)
Jimmy Fortune caution: careless riding

FOCUS
A competitive sprint handicap, and fair form. The winner may do better again.

NOTEBOOK
Dungannon returned to winning form, moving nicely into a challenging position and finding plenty for pressure. This is his trip and it's likely there's more to come, although he'll be forced back into top sprint handicaps now. (op 8-1 tchd 7-1)
Mon Brav failed in his bid for a hat-trick in a valuable sprint at York, but came right back to his best in taking second. He was hit with the winning rider's whip, but it didn't affect the result. (op 14-1 tchd 8-1)
Medicean Man is on a decent mark and he came home well for third. (op 13-2 tchd 7-1 and 11-2)
Star Rover(IRE) gave his all in the first-time visor. (op 25-1)
Whozthecat(IRE) was soon prominent and had his chance. (tchd 22-1)
Lutine Bell came to challenge but couldn't quicken on. (op 10-1)
King Of Eden(IRE)'s progression seems to have flattened out.
Dorback never got into it and was disappointing. Official explanation: jockey said gelding lost his action (op 9-2 tchd 6-1)

2955 TOTEPOOL FLEXI BETTING H'CAP — 1m (R)
4:00 (4:02) (Class 4) (0-85,85) 4-Y-0+ **£4,597** (£1,368; £683; £341) **Stalls** Low

Form RPR

6313 **1** **Veroon (IRE)**[78] 995 5-8-13 **77**..................................(p) PaulMulrennan 3 85
(James Given) *trckd ldrs: effrt and swtchd rt over 2f out: edgd rt fnl f: styd on to ld last stride* **7/1**

0014 **2** *nse* **Hail Promenader (IRE)**[33] 1970 5-9-0 **78**...................... RobertWinston 1 86
(B W Hills) *trckd ldrs: wnt 2nd over 3f out: led over 1f out: hdd post* **11/2[3]**

2100 **3** *1 1/2* **Cono Zur (FR)**[22] 2301 4-8-12 **76**.. PaulHanagan 6 81
(Ruth Carr) *led: hdd over 1f out: kpt on same pce ins fnl f* **6/1**

4010 **4** *2 1/4* **Majuro (IRE)**[8] 2706 7-9-7 **85**...................................(t) RobbieFitzpatrick 7 84
(Richard Guest) *in rr: hdwy and swtchd lft over 2f out: kpt on same pce: nvr nr to chal* **7/2[1]**

40-0 **5** *2 1/2* **Cloudy Start**[17] 2441 5-9-7 **85**...................................(p) FergusSweeney 9 79
(Jamie Osborne) *chsd ldrs: drvn 3f out: wknd over 1f out* **15/2**

-000 **6** *nk* **Signor Verdi**[10] 2647 4-9-4 **82**..(b1) ShaneKelly 5 75
(Brian Meehan) *s.i.s: reminders 3f out: kpt on fnl f: nvr a factor* **5/1[2]**

00-0 **7** *6* **Gumnq (IRE)**[80] 2124 4-8-7 **71**.. GrahamGibbons 8 50
(James Bethell) *dwlt: t.k.h in rr: sme hdwy 3f out: sn lost pl* **25/1**

8 *1* **Born To Be Achamp (BRZ)**[393] 5-9-7 **85**............ SilvestreDeSousa 11 62
(Geoffrey Harker) *t.k.h: w ldrs: lost pl over 4f out: sn bhd* **11/1**

0650 **9** *1/2* **Ajdaad (USA)**[31] 2021 4-8-6 **70**...................................(p) AndrewMullen 4 46
(Alan McCabe) *chsd ldrs: drvn over 2f out: sn wknd* **12/1**

1m 40.73s (1.03) **Going Correction** +0.275s/f (Good) **9** Ran SP% **112.7**
Speed ratings (Par 105): **105,104,103,101,98 98,92,91,90**
Tote Swingers: 1&2 £4.10, 1&3 £6.20, 2&3 £4.30 CSF £43.93 CT £245.33 TOTE £8.60: £2.40, £1.90, £1.40; EX 23.30 Trifecta £138.90 Pool £963.39 - 5.13 winning units.
Owner Danethorpe Racing Partnership **Bred** C M Farrell **Trained** Willoughton, Lincs
■ Stewards' Enquiry : Robert Winston one-day ban: excessive use of whip (26th June)

FOCUS
An ordinary handicap in which several could be given a chance. A career best from the winner, who was previously slightly better on Polytrack.

2956 TOTEPOOL QUICK PICK MAIDEN STKS — 1m 4f
4:30 (4:32) (Class 5) 3-Y-0+ **£2,525** (£751; £375; £187) **Stalls** Low

Form RPR

4-3 **1** **High Jinx (IRE)**[23] 2258 3-8-12 0.. PatCosgrave 1 97+
(James Fanshawe) *trckd ldrs: smooth hdwy to trck ldr over 3f out: hung rt and led over 1f out: drvn clr* **4/1[3]**

43 **2** *5* **Lidar (FR)**[24] 2219 6-9-13 0... JimmyFortune 4 86
(Alan King) *led: hdd over 1f out: styd on same pce* **18/1**

0-36 **3** *3/4* **Unex Renoir**[13] 2551 3-8-12 82.. RobertHavlin 2 85
(John Gosden) *trckd ldrs: drvn and outpcd over 3f out: styd on to take 3rd 2f out: one pce* **9/1**

0 **4** *hd* **Korabushka**[62] 1271 3-8-7 0.. PaulHanagan 7 80
(Jeremy Noseda) *s.i.s: sn chsng ldrs: outpcd over 3f out: styd on to take 4th 2f out: one pce* **25/1**

5 *1 3/4* **Light Well (IRE)** 3-8-12 0... WilliamBuick 16 82+
(John Gosden) *in rr: hdwy over 2f out: kpt on: should improve* **10/1**

2-40 **6** *6* **Wayward Glance**[22] 2295 3-8-12 83.................................. JamieSpencer 9 72
(Michael Bell) *hld up in rr: effrt 4f of out: sn chsng ldrs: wknd over 1f out* **7/2[2]**

0-0 **7** *23* **Star Rebel**[20] 2371 3-8-12 0... TomEaves 8 35
(George Margarson) *swvd lft s: in tch: lost pl over 3f out* **100/1**

54-3 **8** *2 1/2* **Muqtarrib (IRE)**[31] 2019 3-8-12 84..................................... RichardHills 13 31
(Brian Meehan) *trckd ldr: drvn 3f out: wknd over 1f out* **11/4[1]**

0- **9** *1 1/4* **Sulliman**[241] 6876 4-9-13 0.. DanielTudhope 5 29
(George Margarson) *in rr: drvn over 3f out: nvr on terms* **100/1**

0-6 **10** *3/4* **Snow Hill**[16] 2458 3-8-12 0.. JackMitchell 3 28
(Chris Wall) *in rr: sme hdwy over 3f out: sn wknd* **25/1**

04- **11** *1 1/2* **Gale Green**[367] 2890 4-9-8 0.. FergusSweeney 15 21
(Henry Candy) *in rr: bhd fnl 3f* **33/1**

44 **12** *5* **Sciampin**[24] 2218 3-8-5 0.. AntiocoMurgia(7) 11 18
(Marco Botti) *trckd ldr: t.k.h: wknd over 2f out* **66/1**

0-5 **13** *6* **Pyjoma**[59] 1332 4-9-8 0.. TonyCulhane 14 —
(Julia Feilden) *s.i.s: t.k.h in rr: bhd fnl 3f: eased* **100/1**

0 **14** *7* **Searing Heat (USA)**[29] 2097 3-8-12 0.............................. TomQueally 6 —
(Sir Henry Cecil) *t.k.h: trckd ldrs: drvn and lost pl 5f out: hung lft over 3f out: sn bhd: eased* **9/1**

2m 35.64s (0.74) **Going Correction** +0.275s/f (Good)
WFA 3 from 4yo+ 15lb **14** Ran SP% **118.3**
Speed ratings (Par 103): **108,104,104,104,102 98,83,81,81,80 79,76,72,67**
Tote Swingers: 1&2 £11.30, 1&3 £9.20, 2&3 £13.30 CSF £68.78 TOTE £4.60: £1.90, £3.90, £3.50; EX 76.50 Trifecta £509.30 Pool £839.69 - 1.22 winning units.
Owner Mr & Mrs W J Williams **Bred** Haras De La Perelle **Trained** Newmarket, Suffolk

FOCUS
The strongest stayers came to the fore in this 1m4f maiden. Few showed their form, with the first six a long way clear, but the winner looks potentially a smart stayer.

2957 YORKSHIRE RACING FESTIVAL 16TH-24TH JULY CLASSIFIED STKS — 1m 2f 60y
5:05 (5:06) (Class 5) 3-Y-0 **£4,209** (£1,252; £625; £312) **Stalls** Low

Form RPR

03-3 **1** **Set To Music (IRE)**[64] 1251 3-9-0 70.............................. JamieSpencer 5 85
(Michael Bell) *trckd ldrs: led on wd outside over 2f out: kpt on fnl f: jst hld on* **11/4[1]**

5340 **2** *shd* **Calaf**[24] 2215 3-9-0 70.. TonyHamilton 2 84
(Richard Fahey) *tk fierce hold: trckd ldrs: wnt 2nd over 1f out: styd on ins fnl f: jst hld* **14/1**

3-45 **3** *8* **Glyn Ceiriog**[34] 1950 3-9-0 70.. TonyCulhane 4 68
(George Baker) *hld up in mid-div: effrt over 3f out: outpcd over 2f out: kpt on to take modest 3rd 1f out* **13/2**

6222 **4** *3 1/2* **Dr Red Eye**[18] 2406 3-8-11 69.. BillyCray(3) 10 61
(David Nicholls) *sn led: hdd over 2f out: edgd rt and wknd over 1f out* **10/1**

2-50 **5** *3 3/4* **Layla's King**[24] 2228 3-9-0 69.. PaulHanagan 3 54
(Richard Fahey) *led early: chsd ldrs: wknd 2f out* **13/2**

1032 **6** *3 1/2* **Romeo Montague**[9] 2677 3-9-4 74..........................(p) TomMcLaughlin 1 51
(Ed Dunlop) *dwlt: in rr: hdwy 3f out: wkng whn hmpd over 1f out* **3/1[2]**

46-6 **7** *6* **Deny**[10] 2646 3-9-0 70... JimmyFortune 6 35
(Sir Michael Stoute) *hld up: effrt over 3f out: outpcd over 2f out: sn btn: eased ins fnl f* **4/1[3]**

2m 13.03s (3.63) **Going Correction** +0.275s/f (Good) **7** Ran SP% **114.1**
Speed ratings (Par 99): **96,95,89,86,83 80,76**
Tote Swingers: 1&2 £6.90, 1&3 £3.90, 2&3 £11.30. Totesuper 7: Win: Not won. Place: £550.20 CSF £39.79 TOTE £3.70: £1.90, £6.60; EX 40.70 Trifecta £329.10 Pool £1,289.83 - 2.90 winning units.
Owner The Queen **Bred** His Highness The Aga Khan's Studs S C **Trained** Newmarket, Suffolk
■ Stewards' Enquiry : Billy Cray caution: carless riding

FOCUS
A trappy conditions race run in the worst of the ground. The first pair were clear, and only they showed their form.
Romeo Montague Official explanation: trainer said gelding was unsuited by ground
T/Jkpt: Not won. T/Plt: £665.00 to a £1 stake. Pool:£127,725.00 - 140.20 winning tickets T/Qpdt: £110.90 to a £1 stake. Pool:£9,624.00 - 64.20 winning tickets WG

2707 SALISBURY (R-H)
Sunday, June 12

OFFICIAL GOING: Good to soft (soft in places) changing to soft after race 1 (2.00)
Wind: strong across Weather: persistent rain

2958 ALBERT SAMUEL "CITY BOWL" H'CAP — 1m 4f
2:00 (2:00) (Class 4) (0-85,85) 4-Y-0+ **£4,533** (£1,348; £674; £336) **Stalls** High

Form RPR

241 **1** **Uphold**[20] 2359 4-9-7 **85**..(e1) NeilCallan 9 93
(Gay Kelleway) *mde all: led gp to stands-side rails over 4f out: rdn 3f out: hung rt 2f out: drifted lft ent fnl f: styd on dourly: drvn out* **11/1**

-015 **2** *1* **Warlu Way**[24] 2220 4-9-3 **81**... TedDurcan 2 87
(John Dunlop) *mid-div: rdn 3f out: no imp tl styd on fr over 1f out: wnt 2nd towards fin* **3/1[2]**

200- **3** *1 1/4* **Mildoura (FR)**[226] 7206 6-9-7 **85**.. IanMongan 3 89+
(Laura Mongan) *mid-div: rdn 3f out: chsd ldrs 2f out: styng on to mount chal whn short of room against rails: kpt on but hld after* **16/1**

4245 **4** *1/2* **Potentiale (IRE)**[17] 2436 7-8-9 **73** ow1............................(p) EddieAhern 1 77
(J W Hills) *trckd ldrs: rdn 3f out: chsd wnr fr over 1f out tl no ex fnl 75yds* **20/1**

0-26 **5** *1* **Nibani (IRE)**[38] 1826 4-9-4 **82**... RyanMoore 8 84
(Sir Michael Stoute) *mid-div tl outpcd over 3f out: hdwy over 1f out: styd on fnl f* **9/4[1]**

00-0 **6** *nk* **Baltimore Clipper (USA)**[9] 2686 4-8-12 **76**...................... ChrisCatlin 5 78
(Paul Cole) *trckd ldrs tl lost pl over 4f out: sn rdn: styd on fnl 2f* **50/1**

4-12 **7** *nk* **Spice Fair**[13] 2562 4-8-8 **72**.. HayleyTurner 4 73
(Mark Usher) *hld up towards rr: hdwy to join wnr 5f out: rdn over 3f out: styd on same pce fnl f* **9/1**

-254 **8** *nk* **Onyx Of Arabia (IRE)**[10] 2656 4-8-7 **71**..................(b) EddieCreighton 7 72
(Brian Meehan) *awkward leaving stalls: hld up towards rr: pushed along 6f out: rdn over 3f out: styd on fnl 2f* **17/2**

1-14 **9** *12* **Milnagavie**[24] 2224 4-9-4 **82**... RichardHughes 10 63
(Richard Hannon) *trckd wnr: rdn 3f out: wknd fnl f* **5/1[3]**

2m 41.61s (3.61) **Going Correction** +0.325s/f (Good) **9** Ran SP% **113.9**
Speed ratings (Par 105): **100,99,98,98,97 97,97,96,88**
Tote Swingers: 1&2 £8.10, 1&3 £21.80, 2&3 £11.10 CSF £43.50 CT £533.90 TOTE £15.40: £4.00, £1.70, £4.70; EX 63.90.
Owner Whispering Winds **Bred** Juddmonte Farms Ltd **Trained** Exning, Suffolk

FOCUS
Rail 18ft off permanent far side rail between 6.5f and winning post. The first going forecast was good to firm at the overnight stage, but plenty of rain fell on the track, leading to a plethora of non-runners during the afternoon and going changes. Before this first race, it was good to soft with soft in places in the home straight, and good on the loop but afterwards (the loop wasn't used) the going changed to soft all round. They didn't go too quickly early on and the finish was a bit of a mess. The winner got a fairly easy lead and this is shaky form.

2959 PICADOR CHEVROLET H'CAP 5f
2:30 (2:30) (Class 4) (0-85,90) 3-Y-0+ £4,533 (£1,348; £674; £336) Stalls Centre

Form RPR
6004 1 **Sohraab**[8] 2714 7-9-13 **84**........................ RyanMoore 10 95
(Hughie Morrison) *in tch: pushed along fr 3f out: hdwy and swtchd rt over 1f out: r.o strly to ld fnl 140yds: drew clr: comf* **9/4**[1]
0311 2 2 ¾ **Solemn**[14] 2525 6-10-5 **90**........................(b) LiamKeniry 2 91
(Milton Bradley) *prom: rdn and ev ch fr wl over 1f out: kpt on but nt pce of wnr ins fnl f* **13/2**[3]
26-3 3 1 ¾ **Sutton Veny (IRE)**[22] 2299 5-9-13 **84**........................ TedDurcan 9 79
(Jeremy Gask) *prom: rdn and ev ch 2f out: kpt on same pce fnl f* **11/2**[2]
0-33 4 nse **Osiris Way**[10] 2645 9-10-0 **85**........................ GeorgeBaker 8 80
(Patrick Chamings) *led: rdn and hrd pressed fr wl over 1f out: hdd ins fnl f: no ex fnl 75yds* **11/2**[2]
5110 5 ½ **Steelcut**[1] 2938 7-9-0 **76**........................(p) MatthewCosham(5) 1 69
(David Evans) *pushed along in last pair: rdn over 2f out: kpt on but nvr gng pce to get on terms* **9/1**
220- 6 1 ¾ **Avrilo**[339] 3818 5-8-13 **70**........................ JimCrowley 11 57+
(Malcolm Saunders) *trckd ldrs: nt clr run briefly whn rdn over 1f out: no ex fnl 75yds* **25/1**
4131 7 ½ **Kyllachy Storm**[9] 2662 7-8-11 **68**........................ HayleyTurner 12 53
(Ron Hodges) *s.i.s: bhd but in tch: nvr gng pce to get involved* **14/1**
0201 8 9 **Style And Panache (IRE)**[6] 2770 3-9-3 **81** 6ex........ RichardHughes 3 33
(David Evans) *chsd ldrs: rdn over 2f out: wknd ins fnl f* **8/1**
-260 9 3 ¾ **Matterofact (IRE)**[22] 2304 8-9-1 **75**........................ MartinHarley(3) 5 14
(Malcolm Saunders) *w ldrs tl over 3f out: sn rdn: wknd fnl f* **16/1**

61.88 secs (0.88) **Going Correction** +0.325s/f (Good)
WFA 3 from 4yo+ 7lb 9 Ran SP% **112.4**
Speed ratings (Par 105): **105,100,97,97,96 94,93,78,72**
Tote Swingers: 1&2 £4.20, 1&3 £4.20, 2&3 £5.50 CSF £16.30 CT £70.31 TOTE £3.10: £1.40, £2.60, £1.10; EX 18.40.
Owner Pangfield Racing **Bred** T J Billington **Trained** East Ilsley, Berks

FOCUS
The impression was that some of the jockeys were keen to preserve as much energy as they could, but that meant a few took a keen hold early. This was not a strong race for the grade. The winner is rated back to last summer's form.

2960 WATERAID MILDREN CONSTRUCTION MAIDEN FILLIES' STKS 1m
3:05 (3:05) (Class 5) 3-Y-0 £2,914 (£867; £433; £216) Stalls Low

Form RPR
06- 1 **Making Eyes (IRE)**[225] 7231 3-9-0 0........................ IanMongan 3 92
(Hugo Palmer) *mid-div: smooth hdwy fr 3f out: led wl over 1f out: clr fnl f: r.o strly* **20/1**
302- 2 6 **Electra Star**[227] 7198 3-9-0 79........................ RichardHughes 1 78+
(William Haggas) *hld up towards rr: hdwy 3f out: ev ch briefly wl over 1f out: sn rdn and edgd lft: no ch w wnr fnl f* **11/4**[1]
3 3 1 ¾ **Totheendoftheearth (IRE)**[14] 2528 3-9-0 0........................ LiamKeniry 14 74
(Sylvester Kirk) *led: rdn whn hdd wl over 1f out: kpt on same pce* **11/1**
0-2 4 nk **Ssafa**[68] 1146 3-9-0 0........................ EddieAhern 7 73+
(J W Hills) *mid-div: rdn over 2f out: hdwy over 1f out: styd on wout threatening* **20/1**
4 5 1 ¼ **Sedaine**[37] 1873 3-9-0 0........................ JimCrowley 9 71
(Ralph Beckett) *prom: rdn over 2f out: kpt on same pce fr over 1f out* **8/1**
26- 6 2 **Complexion**[233] 7057 3-9-0 0........................ RyanMoore 2 66
(Sir Michael Stoute) *hld up towards rr: sme prog u.p over 2f out: no further imp fr over 1f out* **7/2**[2]
7 1 ½ **Lupa Montana (USA)** 3-9-0 0........................ StevieDonohoe 6 63+
(Ralph Beckett) *s.i.s: towards rr: sme stdy prog fr 2f out: nvr trbld ldrs* **40/1**
8 shd **Eastern Breeze (IRE)** 3-9-0 0........................ TedDurcan 8 62+
(Saeed Bin Suroor) *s.i.s: towards rr: hdwy fr 4f out to chse ldrs 3f out: sn rdn: wknd ent fnl f* **10/1**
35 9 3 ¾ **Misrepresent (USA)**[37] 1873 3-9-0 0........................ NickyMackay 13 54
(John Gosden) *wnt rt leaving stalls: sn chsng ldrs: rdn over 2f out: wknd ent fnl f* **15/2**[3]
- 10 8 **Amazing Win (IRE)** 3-9-0 0........................ ChrisCatlin 11 35
(Mick Channon) *trckd ldrs: rdn over 2f out: wknd over 1f out* **33/1**
11 2 ¼ **Little Cottonsocks** 3-9-0 0........................(t) LukeMorris 10 30
(Clive Cox) *chsd ldrs: rdn over 3f out: wknd over 2f out* **40/1**
5 12 1 ¼ **Bashasha (USA)**[14] 2528 3-9-0 0........................ TadhgO'Shea 4 27
(Roger Varian) *trckd ldrs tl rdn 3f out: sn wknd* **8/1**
0 13 4 **Funny Enough**[31] 2026 3-9-0 0........................ DaneO'Neill 5 18
(George Baker) *chsd ldrs: rdn over 2f out: sn wknd* **16/1**

1m 44.82s (1.32) **Going Correction** +0.325s/f (Good) 13 Ran SP% **123.5**
Speed ratings (Par 96): **106,100,98,97,96 94,93,93,89,81 79,77,73**
Tote Swingers: 1&2 £18.40, 1&3 £38.70, 2&3 £8.50 CSF £73.69 TOTE £32.40: £8.60, £1.40, £6.00; EX 147.10.
Owner Starter For Ten Partnership **Bred** F Dunne **Trained** Newmarket, Suffolk

FOCUS
Visibility wasn't good for the last part of this race and, in the main, it appeared to be a last filly standing contest, because lots seemed to be produced to have every chance before faltering. The runner-up set a fair standard and the winner was much improved, but this may not be as good as it looks.

Electra Star Official explanation: jockey said filly hung left

2961 BRIDGET SWIRE'S PALACE AFFAIR & SAKHEE'S SECRET CATHEDRAL STKS (LISTED RACE) 6f
3:40 (3:40) (Class 1) 3-Y-0+ £17,031 (£6,456; £3,231; £1,611) Stalls Low

Form RPR
1-41 1 **Elnawin**[37] 1848 5-9-4 105........................ RichardHughes 6 113
(Richard Hannon) *prom: led over 3f out: pushed clr fr over 1f out: easily* **9/2**[3]
6-56 2 8 **High Standing (USA)**[15] 2502 6-9-4 107........................(b) RyanMoore 2 87
(William Haggas) *trckd ldrs: rdn to chse wnr over 2f out: no ch fr over 1f out: all out to hold on for 2nd* **15/8**[1]
/00- 3 ½ **Border Patrol**[364] 3017 5-9-4 112........................ EddieAhern 3 86
(Roger Charlton) *squeezed out s: racd in cl 4th: rdn 2f out: nvr threatened: wnt 3rd ent fnl f: styd on same pce* **15/8**[1]
21-0 4 11 **Russian Spirit**[22] 2298 5-9-3 98........................ NeilCallan 5 50
(Roger Varian) *racd keenly: led tl over 3f out: sn rdn: wknd ent fnl f* **4/1**[2]

1m 15.28s (0.48) **Going Correction** +0.325s/f (Good) 4 Ran SP% **107.7**
Speed ratings (Par 111): **109,98,97,83**
CSF £12.99 TOTE £4.00; EX 7.60.
Owner Noodles Racing **Bred** D R Tucker **Trained** East Everleigh, Wilts

FOCUS
This is not form to take seriously because of conditions but the winner was extremely impressive. It's hard to know what he achieved with the others below par, and he's rated in line with his previous best.

NOTEBOOK
Elnawin, runner-up in this last year, got away quickly and had all of his rivals in trouble over 2f, which is where he edged across and bagged the stands' rail. Richard Hughes did need to get serious for a few strides to make him lengthen, but that effort probably wasn't needed as everything behind him ran poorly. This performance does at least show that he handles soft-looking conditions and is in great heart this year. Hopefully the handicapper won't over-react to the result. (op 4-1)

High Standing(USA), down in trip, had winning form in soft ground but was made to look pedestrian as the winner shot clear. The fitting of blinkers hasn't done a lot for him. (tchd 7-4)

Border Patrol was having his first run for almost a year and was sluggish leaving the stalls before being squeezed up. In truth, this was a disappointing return for a horse that is known to handle easy ground, but he's entitled to improve for the run and will be better judged after that. (op 5-2)

Russian Spirit was another to have gone well in soft ground in the past to run disappointingly, although she did have quite a bit to find with these on official figures. (op 7-2)

2962 BRIDGET SWIRE MEMORIAL MAIDEN STKS 6f
4:15 (4:16) (Class 2) 2-Y-0 £8,742 (£2,601; £1,300; £649) Stalls Low

Form RPR
1 **Harbour Watch (IRE)** 2-9-3 0........................ RichardHughes 7 83+
(Richard Hannon) *trckd ldrs: travelling wl whn swtchd rt over 1f out: led jst ins fnl f: pushed clr: readily* **11/4**[2]
6 2 3 ¾ **Avon Pearl**[12] 2584 2-9-3 0........................ DaneO'Neill 3 70
(Henry Candy) *trckd ldrs: rdn for str chal fr 2f out: led v briefly jst ins fnl f: nt pce of wnr* **2/1**[1]
03 3 ½ **Yammos (IRE)**[16] 2448 2-9-3 0........................ ChrisCatlin 9 69
(Mick Channon) *trckd ldrs: led 2f out: sn rdn: hdd jst ins fnl f: no ex* **4/1**[3]
4 2 ¾ **King's Ciel** 2-9-3 0........................ MatthewDavies 4 60
(George Baker) *prom: chsng ldrs whn swtchd lft 2f out: kpt on same pce fnl f* **33/1**
5 nk **Opera Buff** 2-9-3 0........................ LiamKeniry 8 59
(Sylvester Kirk) *s.i.s: in rr but in tch: rdn 2f out: styd on same pce fnl f* **9/1**
0 6 ½ **Eagle Of Rome (IRE)**[13] 2559 2-9-3 0........................ LukeMorris 1 58
(Nick Littmoden) *led tl rdn 2f out: chsd ldrs: fdd fnl 100yds:* **33/1**
0 7 2 ¾ **Solfilia**[11] 2606 2-8-12 0........................ HayleyTurner 2 45
(Hughie Morrison) *hld up in tch: rdn 3f out: no imp* **11/1**
8 2 **Poker Hospital** 2-8-12 0........................ TedDurcan 5 39
(George Baker) *hld up but in tch: hated kickbk and swtchd rt over 3f out: rdn over 2f out: nvr any imp* **8/1**

1m 18.56s (3.76) **Going Correction** +0.65s/f (Yiel) 8 Ran SP% **115.3**
Speed ratings (Par 99): **100,95,94,90,90 89,85,83**
Tote Swingers: 1&2 £2.20, 1&3 £3.10, 2&3 £2.70 CSF £8.76 TOTE £3.80: £1.60, £2.30, £1.10; EX 10.00.
Owner H Robin Heffer **Bred** T Molan **Trained** East Everleigh, Wilts

FOCUS
Quite what this form will amount to in the coming weeks, unless the ground stays soft, is debateable, but the winner did it well.

NOTEBOOK
Harbour Watch(IRE) ◆ proved far too good for a pair of horses with fair efforts already under their belts. A 58,000gns purchase, he has seemingly always been well regarded so one would imagine we'll see him pitched in against some decent sorts next time. He may head to the July meeting at Newmarket next amd looks to have a bright future. (op 3-1)

Avon Pearl had run well at a big price on his only previous outing, so gives the race some substance, as he should be good enough to win as a juvenile considering what he has shown so far. (op 13-8)

Yammos(IRE) was the most experienced in the field, which undoubtedly helped him in these conditions. One would imagine connections have their eyes on handicaps with him. (op 7-2 tchd 3-1)

King's Ciel looks to have a bit of size about him and he came home nicely when it was all too late. (op 28-1)

Opera Buff also looks to have substance and ought to come on for this. His half-sister won over 1m2f-1m3f, so he could be a longer-term project rather than one to pick up lots of races at two. (op 10-1 tchd 11-1)

Eagle Of Rome(IRE) showed quite a bit of toe but steadily faded out of contention. (op 50-1)

Poker Hospital attracted market interest but she didn't look to be happy early and then got thrown a bit wide of her rivals as the jockey tried to avoid Solfilia, who started to edge across her. She didn't get involved thereafter. (op 14-1)

2963 CHARLIE GENGE MEMORIAL FILLIES' H'CAP 6f 212y
4:45 (4:45) (Class 5) (0-75,75) 3-Y-0+ £2,590 (£770; £385; £192) Stalls Centre

Form RPR
14-2 1 **Bonnie Brae**[13] 2566 4-10-0 **75**........................ RyanMoore 3 90
(David Elsworth) *trckd ldrs: rdn to ld led jst over 1f out: r.o wl to draw clr: comf* **13/8**[1]
203- 2 5 **Duquesa (IRE)**[230] 7118 3-8-2 **64**........................ MatthewCosham(5) 9 62
(David Evans) *led: rdn 2f out: hdd jst over 1f out: sn hld by wnr: kpt on same pce* **11/4**[2]
3010 3 2 **Sienna Blue**[13] 2550 3-8-7 **64**........................ LukeMorris 2 56
(Malcolm Saunders) *trckd ldrs: rdn over 2f out: kpt on same pce* **7/1**
04-0 4 1 ¼ **Dualite (IRE)**[25] 2192 3-8-10 **67**........................ TedDurcan 10 56
(John Dunlop) *trckd ldrs: rdn to chal 2f out: hld by wnr ent fnl f: fdd fnl 100yds* **13/2**
054- 5 4 ½ **Aristeia**[248] 6688 3-8-10 **67** ow1........................ RichardHughes 8 50
(Richard Hannon) *hld up in cl 5th: effrt fr 2f out: wknd fnl f* **4/1**[3]

1m 33.94s (5.34) **Going Correction** +0.65s/f (Yiel)
WFA 3 from 4yo 10lb 5 Ran SP% **110.6**
Speed ratings (Par 100): **95,89,87,85,80**
CSF £6.37 TOTE £2.10: £1.10, £2.60; EX 4.60.
Owner Mrs T A Foreman **Bred** Rosyground Stud **Trained** Newmarket, Suffolk

FOCUS
Plenty of connections seemingly didn't want their horses running in the soft ground, so six of the intended 11 runners were withdrawn. This meant the remaining five could all ran in a bunch towards the stands' side. Only the winner showed her form.

2964 LIZZIESHATHIRE.CO.UK RACING EXCELLENCE "HANDS AND HEELS" APPRENTICE SERIES H'CAP 1m
5:20 (5:21) (Class 6) (0-65,64) 3-Y-O **£1,942** (£578; £288; £144) **Stalls** Low

Form RPR

2313 **1** **Mini's Destination**[5] 2792 3-9-1 **58**................................ LucyKBarry 12 69
(John Holt) *trckd ldrs: shkn up to ld wl over 1f out: sn in command: comf* **5/1**[3]

06-3 **2** *2 ¾* **Border Abby**[19] 2394 3-8-5 **51**.................................. NoelGarbutt(3) 13 56
(Rae Guest) *wnt lft s: towards rr: hdwy over 4f out: chsd wnr over 1f out: kpt on but a being readily hld* **25/1**

3-43 **3** *4 ½* **Ice Nelly (IRE)**[13] 2550 3-9-2 **62**............................ JacobMoore(3) 14 57+
(Hughie Morrison) *bmpd leaving stalls: bhd: pushed along and stdy prog fr 4f out: styd on to go 3rd ent fnl f but no ch w ldrs* **9/4**[2]

0312 **4** *5* **Goal (IRE)**[8] 2729 3-9-6 **63**..(t) JakePayne 10 46
(Richard Guest) *led: clr 3f out: hdd wl over 1f out: sn hld: fdd ins fnl f* **10/1**

00-3 **5** *1* **Quite A Catch (IRE)**[69] 1137 3-9-3 **60**........................ JustinNewman 7 41
(Jonathan Portman) *trckd ldrs: pushed along and styd on same pce fnl 2f* **33/1**

1134 **6** *hd* **Beach Babe**[12] 2586 3-9-7 **64**.. LukeRowe 9 44+
(Jonathan Portman) *hld up towards rr: pushed along and stdy prog fr over 3f out but nvr troubling ldrs* **20/1**

4335 **7** *9* **Urban Kode (IRE)**[10] 2635 3-8-12 **63**......................(v) KevinLundie(8) 8 23
(David Evans) *chsd ldrs: rdn 3f out: wknd ent fnl f* **18/1**

030 **8** *4* **Valdaw**[32] 1997 3-9-3 **60**...(b[1]) CharlesBishop 4 10
(Joseph Tuite) *mid-div: hdwy 3f out to chse ldrs: wknd over 1f out* **33/1**

-640 **9** *1* **Blaze On By**[100] 760 3-8-4 **47**....................................... GeorgeDowning 11 —
(John Bridger) *sn pushed along in midfield: wknd over 2f out* **50/1**

5000 **10** *½* **Miss Boops (IRE)**[32] 1999 3-9-0 **62**......................... GerardGalligan(5) 6 —
(Zoe Davison) *mid-div: pushed along over 4f out: wknd over 2f out* **50/1**

0-50 **11** *1 ¾* **Bumbling Bertie**[27] 2166 3-8-1 **47**......................(v) SophieSilvester(3) 1 —
(Andrew Balding) *a towards rr* **16/1**

00-1 **12** *16* **Dubawi Dancer**[12] 2599 3-8-9 **52**.. IanBurns 5 —+
(William Haggas) *t.k.h early: restrained bhd ldrs after 1f: rdn 3f out: wknd qckly* **7/4**[1]

500- **13** *13* **Coedmor Boy**[206] 7496 3-8-5 **48**... LukeStrong 2 —
(John Flint) *chsd ldrs tl wknd over 2f out* **40/1**

1m 49.12s (5.62) **Going Correction** +0.65s/f (Yiel) **13** Ran SP% **124.9**
Speed ratings (Par 97): **97,94,89,84,83 83,74,70,69,69 67,51,38**
Tote Swingers: 1&2 £12.70, 1&3 £3.70, 2&3 £15.30. Totesuper 7: Win: Not won. Place: £55.20. CSF £131.53 CT £334.13 TOTE £5.60: £1.80, £4.80, £1.60.
Owner J R Holt **Bred** Whatton Manor Stud **Trained** Peckleton, Leics

FOCUS
With the ground by now churned up a bit, and the jockeys not allowed to carry whips, a good rider and judgement of pace was definitely required. Few showed their form and this is not a race to be positive about.
T/Plt: £43.00 to a £1 stake. Pool:£90,560.00 - 1,535.18 winning tickets T/Qpdt: £9.20 to a £1 stake. Pool:£6,192.00 - 497.04 winning tickets TM

2077 CORK (R-H)
Sunday, June 12

OFFICIAL GOING: Sprint course - good (good to yielding in places); round course - good (good to firm in places)

2967a GALTEE MIDSUMMER SPRINT STKS (LISTED RACE) 5f
3:35 (3:38) 3-Y-O+ **£25,215** (£7,370; £3,491; £1,163)

RPR

1 **Inxile (IRE)**[7] 2754 6-9-12 ....(p) AdrianNicholls 8 111
(David Nicholls) *sn led and mde virtually all: rdn over 1f out: kpt on wl u.p fnl f* **1/1**[1]

2 *¾* **Liberty Lady (IRE)**[15] 2489 4-9-4 .... JamesDoyle 5 100
(Des Donovan) *chsd ldrs: 4th 1/2-way: swtchd rt 2f out: wnt 2nd early fnl f: kpt on wl u.p but nt match wnr* **16/1**

3 *2* **Oor Jock (IRE)**[15] 2500 3-9-0 95.. PShanahan 6 93
(Tracey Collins, Ire) *prom: 3rd 1/2-way: drvn along and dropped to 5th 1f out: kpt on same pce fnl f wout threatening principals* **33/1**

4 *2* **Calm Bay (IRE)**[2] 2894 5-9-7 92.....................................(bt) PJSmullen 2 89
(H Rogers, Ire) *prom: 2nd 1/2-way: drvn along fr 2f out: no ex fr early fnl f* **16/1**

5 *hd* **Glor Na Mara (IRE)**[6] 2774 3-9-0 105............................(tp) KJManning 4 85
(J S Bolger, Ire) *chsd ldrs: 6th and rdn 2f out: no imp fr over 1f out: kpt on one pce* **7/1**[3]

6 *½* **Lechevalier Choisi (IRE)**[11] 2624 3-9-0 89......................... CDHayes 3 83
(James Bernard McCabe, Ire) *towards rr: drvn along 1/2-way: nvr a factor: kpt on one pce fnl f* **14/1**

7 *½* **Tiddliwinks**[22] 2323 5-9-7 .... PhillipMakin 1 96+
(Kevin Ryan) *chsd ldrs: 5th 1/2-way: rdn and no imp in 4th early fnl f whn rdr lost iron and nrly uns: nt rcvr* **9/4**[2]

8 *1* **Blue Dahlia (IRE)**[16] 2480 4-9-4 96...................................... WMLordan 7 78
(T Stack, Ire) *chsd ldrs: 6th 1 1/2f out: sn no ex* **12/1**

58.64 secs (-0.56)
WFA 3 from 4yo+ 7lb **8** Ran SP% **122.3**
CSF £22.60 TOTE £2.10: £1.10, £2.30, £6.90; DF 28.10.
Owner D Nicholls & Mrs J Love **Bred** Denis And Mrs Teresa Bergin **Trained** Sessay, N Yorks
■ Stewards' Enquiry : Phillip Makin one-day ban: careless riding (Jun 28)

FOCUS
The standard is set around the third and fourth.

NOTEBOOK
Inxile(IRE) returned to Ireland to record his third win here this season, two of them at this track, and there never really seemed to be much doubt. From his stands' side draw, he managed to get to the front early on, but the speed he showed when really asked to go about his business 2f out killed his rivals and he was always just holding the late effort of the runner-up. He's admirably consistent, seems to thrive on his racing and also has no objections to travelling. This was a good performance giving weight away all round and the time was impressive on ground a bit slower than good. (op 5/4 tchd 9/10)
Liberty Lady(IRE) came home well. She may have been slightly flattered by her proximity to the winner, but it was a good run and it's hard to see handicaps in her future after this. (op 14/1)
Oor Jock(IRE) could well be on the progressive side also. He showed plenty of early speed, couldn't match the winner when he opened up but he kept on well and did best of those who laid up with the winner early on. There could be a nice conditions race to be won with him. (op 33/1 tchd 25/1)
Calm Bay(IRE) has been running well of late and did so again here, showing plenty of early pace himself before he was found to be a bit one paced inside the last. He's a horse in good form but may well find himself going up a couple of pounds more after this. (op 16/1 tchd 20/1)
Glor Na Mara(IRE) kept on close home but didn't have the toe to be competitive. (op 9/1)
Tiddliwinks was off the bridle early on, tried to challenge over a furlong out but was struggling to get on terms when the rider lost an iron and was close to being unseated inside the last. He would have finished closer but not close enough. Official explanation: jockey said gelding became unbalanced and as a result he lost an iron (op 7/4)

2968a KERRY GROUP NOBLESSE STKS (GROUP 3) (F&M) 1m 4f
4:10 (4:10) 3-Y-O+ **£46,228** (£13,512; £6,400; £2,133)

RPR

1 **Banimpire (IRE)**[21] 2334 3-8-12 109.................................... KJManning 2 107+
(J S Bolger, Ire) *trckd ldrs in 4th: wnt 2nd and chal 2f out: sn led and edgd rt fr over 1f out: styd on wl fnl f* **7/4**[1]

2 *3* **Sense Of Purpose (IRE)**[26] 2212 4-9-9 95.......................... PJSmullen 6 98
(D K Weld, Ire) *led: strly pressed 2f out: sn hdd and no imp fnl f: kpt on same pce* **14/1**

3 *1 ¾* **Amazing Beauty (IRE)**[32] 2004 3-8-9 89....................... CO'Donoghue 9 96
(A P O'Brien, Ire) *trckd ldrs in 3rd: rdn 2f out: no imp and kpt on one pce fr over 1f out* **12/1**

4 *½* **Polly's Mark (IRE)**[29] 2098 5-9-9 .... AdamKirby 3 94
(Clive Cox) *trckd ldr in 2nd: drvn along early st and dropped to 4th: sltly checked 2f out: no imp fr over 1f out: kpt on one pce* **2/1**[2]

5 *1* **Gemstone (IRE)**[35] 1928 3-8-9 100.................................... WMLordan 4 94
(A P O'Brien, Ire) *chsd ldrs in 6th: pushed along early st: kpt on one pce wout threatening* **20/1**

6 *hd* **Why (IRE)**[9] 2682 3-8-9 95... DavidMcCabe 7 93
(A P O'Brien, Ire) *slowly away: sn in tch in rr: sme hdwy 2f out: no imp fr 1f out: kpt on one pce* **25/1**

7 *1* **Mesariya (IRE)**[32] 2012 3-8-9 .... JMurtagh 1 92
(John M Oxx, Ire) *settled in 5th: rdn over 2f out: sn no imp* **9/2**[3]

8 *1* **High Vintage (IRE)**[9] 2700 6-9-9 75..................................... FMBerry 5 89?
(Edmond Kent, Ire) *towards rr: 7th 1/2-way: sme hdwy on inner into 5th 2f out: no imp whn sltly hmpd ins fnl f* **50/1**

9 *shd* **Eirnin (IRE)**[9] 2682 3-8-9 93.. WJLee 8 90
(A P O'Brien, Ire) *a towards rr: no imp fr 2f out: kpt on one pce* **16/1**

2m 37.81s (-10.09)
WFA 3 from 4yo+ 15lb **9** Ran SP% **118.7**
CSF £28.01 TOTE £2.80: £1.02, £2.70, £2.70; DF 31.30.
Owner Mrs J S Bolger **Bred** Kilcarn Stud **Trained** Coolcullen, Co Carlow

FOCUS
The form fits to the top end of the race averages, rated around the second.

NOTEBOOK
Banimpire(IRE) ◆ travelled like a dream throughout, quickened to the front over a furlong out and galloped to the line. Her attitude matches her ability and she seems to be thriving on her busy schedule. She looks even better over this trip and we may not have to wait long to see if she's a filly of genuine Group 1 class. If continuing her current rate of progression there's no reason why she shouldn't be. (op 2/1 tchd 9/4)
Sense Of Purpose(IRE) is a decent filly. Again, Pat Smullen rode a terrific race from the front and tried to draw the sting from her opponents by kicking on 2f out. The winner outclassed her but she ran an honest race and deserves to pick up a Listed race. (op 12/1)
Amazing Beauty(IRE) looked more at home with more patient tactics here than when trying to make all in the Musidora Stakes last time. A bit more was kept in reserve for the business end, but she wasn't good enough having challenged briefly. She probably saw out the trip and is a filly good enough to possibly win in Listed company. (op 14/1)
Polly's Mark(IRE) was a bit disappointing. She travelled well on the heels of the leaders but she was coming off the bridle before the straight and never really looked like getting on terms from there. (op 2/1 tchd 9/4)
Gemstone(IRE) was trying this trip for the first time and didn't run badly. It's inconclusive as to whether she stayed but she is turning into a bit of a disappointing filly. (op 14/1)
Mesariya(IRE) got a bit of a bump in the straight but didn't look like getting on terms and is better than this effort would suggest. (op 4/1)

2965 - 2966a, 2969 - 2976a (Foreign Racing) - See Raceform Interactive

2750 CHANTILLY (R-H)
Sunday, June 12

OFFICIAL GOING: Turf: good to soft

2977a PRIX DE DIANE - LONGINES (GROUP 1) (3YO FILLIES) (TURF) 1m 2f 110y
2:30 (12:00) 3-Y-O **£418,698** (£167,508; £83,754; £41,840; £20,956)

RPR

1 **Golden Lilac (IRE)**[28] 2137 3-9-0 0................................ MaximeGuyon 1 116
(A Fabre, France) *t.k.h early but sn settled in 4th: shkn up 2f out: qcknd to ld ins fnl f: hld on wl fnl 50yds* **2/1**[2]

2 *1* **Galikova (FR)**[36] 1922 3-9-0 0... OlivierPeslier 7 114+
(F Head, France) *racd in 5th on outside of eventual wnr: shkn up and nt qckn over 2f out: 5th and strly rdn 1 1/2f out: styd on strly fnl 110yds: nt quite rch wnr* **11/8**[1]

3 *nk* **Glorious Sight (IRE)**[21] 2342 3-9-0 0............................. GeraldMosse 5 113
(Robert Collet, France) *a.p in ldng gp chsng clr ldr: 3rd and travelling wl 3f out: led ins fnl 1 1/2f: hdd ins fnl f: no ex last 100yds* **20/1**

4 *2* **Haya Landa (FR)**[24] 3-9-0 0...................................... JohannBensimon 4 110
(Mme L Audon, France) *hdd gp chsng clr ldr: rdn and one pce fr 1 1/2f out: jst hld on to 4th* **50/1**

5 *nse* **Andromeda Galaxy (FR)**[34] 3-9-0 0.................. ChristopheSoumillon 2 109
(E Lellouche, France) *settled towards rr: tk clsr order fr 4 1/2f out: 6th appr 3f out: kpt on one pce fr 2f out: nt pce to chal ldrs* **14/1**

6 *¾* **Wavering (IRE)**[21] 2342 3-9-0 0................................. MickaelBarzalona 3 108
(A Fabre, France) *racd towards rr: 8th 3f out: strly rdn 1 1/2f out: kpt on fnl f wout having pce to trble ldrs* **9/1**[3]

7 *snk* **Shareta (IRE)**[34] 3-9-0 0............................. Christophe-PatriceLemaire 6 108
(A De Royer-Dupre, France) *hld up: 7th 3f out: rdn and no imp last 1 1/2f* **9/1**[3]

8 *hd* **Epic Love (IRE)**[21] 2342 3-9-0 0............................... StephanePasquier 8 107
(P Bary, France) *in rr: last 3f out: nvr in contention* **12/1**

9 *10* **Polemique (IRE)**[36] 1922 3-9-0 0 AurelienLemaitre 9 88
(F Head, France) *sn in clr ld: hdd ins fnl 1 1/2f: wknd qckly and eased* **100/1**

2m 7.90s (-0.90) **Going Correction** +0.175s/f (Good) **9** Ran SP% **117.5**
Speed ratings: **110,109,109,107,107 107,106,106,99**
WIN (incl. 1 euro stake): 3.60. PLACES: 1.40, 1.10, 3.20. DF: 2.40. SF: 5.80.
Owner Gestut Ammerland **Bred** Gestut Ammerland **Trained** Chantilly, France

FOCUS
The Prix de Diane invariably attracts a small field compared with most major European Classics, but the race has nevertheless been every bit as strong as the British and French Oaks in recent seasons. This year was no exception, with the nine-runner field containing two fillies who were vying to be crowned the finest of their age group in Europe. They finished in a bit of abunch which limits Golden Lilac's rating. She's rated just off her Pouliches figure.

NOTEBOOK
Golden Lilac(IRE) came to Chantilly having won her four previous starts, most recently when enhancing an already glowing reputation by storming to victory in the Poule d'Essai des Pouliches. That, however, was not enough for her to be favourite as punters perhaps heeded the words of trainer Andre Fabre, who had doubts about the daughter of Galileo's stamina. Those doubts proved unfounded at face value, but the pace set by Galikova's pacemaker Polemique, while respectable, was not overly demanding and nor was it immediately followed by the other eight runners. Indeed, Polemique continued to hold the lead until 300 metres from home, while the other eight were relatively close together at the finish, suggestive of a race that turned into more of a sprint than a test of stamina. Nevertheless, Golden Lilac emerges with plenty of credit for the way she immediately put her stamp on the race before fending off the sustained challenge of eventual third Glorious Sight. Some bookmakers reacted by quoting her as short as 10-1 for the Prix de l'Arc de Triomphe, but just her participation must be doubtful given Fabre's trip worries. That said, her Boreal half-sister won over 1m4f and Galileo imparts plenty of stamina, so there must be a chance the Arc distance will be within her range. There must also be a chance, though, that connections will choose to use her speed over 1m and 1m2f. If she is to be tried over further, the 1m3f Breeders' Cup Filly & Mare Turf could be the ideal option.
Galikova(FR), Goldikova's half-sister, was hot favourite after her extremely impressive success in a Saint-Cloud trial. Another daughter of Galileo, she seemed to be beaten for speed, pure and simple. Perfectly positioned turning for home, she failed to find the same instant response as Golden Lilac and appeared sure to be well beaten until making ground hand over fist inside the final furlong. She is certain to do better over 1m4f and would be favourite to reverse form with the winner over the longer trip, although it's worth noting that this is the second time she has flopped on the Group 1 stage after performing below par in last season's Prix Marcel Boussac. She'll be given a break now before being brought back for the Prix Vermeille in September.
Glorious Sight(IRE), racing for the eighth time this season, once again showed herself to be a model of consistency and arguably produced the best effort of her career. A three-length second to Golden Lilac in the Pouliches, she was beaten by only a smidgeon over a length this time. A harsh observer could claim that she was suited by racing close to the steady pace, but that should not hide the fact that she is a most admirable filly who thoroughly deserves a first Group win.
Haya Landa(FR) had a huge amount on her plate having won no more than a small Longchamp conditions race, but she also came to this Classic having run only three times and with plenty of potential to improve. She duly did but, like Glorious Sight, enjoyed the run of the race.
Andromeda Galaxy(FR) is held in high regard and ran a respectable race to take fifth on just her third outing. Her future is bright.
Wavering(IRE) enjoyed her moment in the sun when landing a substandard Prix Saint-Alary, a contest that retains Group 1 status but should not.
Shareta(IRE), too good for Andromeda Galaxy last time, was unable to quicken and needs a greater test of stamina.

2978a PRIX PAUL DE MOUSSAC (GROUP 3) (3YO COLTS & GELDINGS) (TURF) 1m
3:10 (12:00) 3-Y-O **£34,482** (£13,793; £10,344; £6,896; £3,448)

RPR
1 **Mutual Trust**[25] 3-8-10 0 MaximeGuyon 11 114
(A Fabre, France) *trckd ldng pair: 4th 3f out: shkn up and qcknd appr fnl f: led 60yds out: r.o wl* **2/1**[1]
2 *3/4* **Ch'Tio Bilote (FR)**[34] 1965 3-8-10 0 IoritzMendizabal 8 112
(J-P Gallorini, France) *racd in 4th: hdwy and rn wd fnl bnd: 3rd 3f out: wnt 2nd and pressing ldr u.p appr fnl f: led narrowly 100yds out: hdd w 60yds to run: no ex* **16/1**
3 *1* **Blue Soave (FR)**[24] 2240 3-8-10 0 ThierryThulliez 4 110
(F Chappet, France) *chsd pcemaker: led ins fnl 2 1/2f: hdd 100yds out: no more to give* **33/1**
4 *1 1/2* **Slow Pace (USA)**[55] 1447 3-8-10 0 OlivierPeslier 7 106
(F Head, France) *settled towards rr: 7th on outside 3f out: outpcd and u.p 1 1/2f out: styd on ins fnl f: nvr threatened* **13/2**
5 *1/2* **Barocci (JPN)**[28] 2139 3-8-10 0 (p) ChristopheSoumillon 6 105
(E Lellouche, France) *racd in midfield: 6th 3f out: rdn over 1 1/2f out: kpt on wout qckning* **6/1**[3]
6 *nk* **Venomous**[28] 2139 3-8-10 0 FlavienPrat 10 104
(T Clout, France) *hld up: 10th 3f out: swtchd outside 2f out: styd on fnl f: nt pce to chal* **11/4**[2]
7 *1/2* **Modern History (IRE)**[28] 2139 3-8-10 0 MickaelBarzalona 1 103
(A Fabre, France) *w.w: 8th 3f out: hdwy to go 4th appr fnl f: sn rdn and nt qckn: fdd fnl 50yds* **10/1**
8 *2 1/2* **Maiguri (IRE)**[28] 2139 3-8-10 0 JohanVictoire 2 98
(C Baillet, France) *hld up: last 3f out: no imp fnl 2f* **16/1**
9 *shd* **Woodstock City (FR)**[17] 3-8-10 0 BernardFayd'Herbe 3 97
(R Chotard, France) *chsd ldrs: 5th 3f out: widden and wknd fr 1 1/2f out* **16/1**
10 *20* **Invincible Viking (IRE)**[23] 3-8-10 0 (b) DominiqueBoeuf 9 —
(Y Barberot, France) *led: 3 l clr 3f out: hdd ins fnl 2 1/2f: eased fnl f* **66/1**

1m 36.59s (-1.41) **Going Correction** +0.175s/f (Good) **10** Ran SP% **118.8**
Speed ratings: **114,113,112,110,110 109,109,106,106,86**
WIN (incl. 1 euro stake): 3.20. PLACES: 2.10, 3.70, 6.70. DF: 25.30. SF: 38.50.
Owner K Abdulla **Bred** Juddmonte Farms **Trained** Chantilly, France

NOTEBOOK
Mutual Trust, whose trainer was winning this race for the eighth time, swooped on the outside of a couple of longshots for a comfortable 3/4l victory in a race run at an unusually good clip by French standards. A step up to Group 1 company is now on the cards, with the Prix Jean Prat a possible target.

2979a PRIX DU LYS (GROUP 3) (3YO COLTS & GELDINGS) (TURF) 1m 4f
3:45 (12:00) 3-Y-O **£34,482** (£13,793; £10,344; £6,896; £3,448)

RPR
1 **Kreem**[24] 3-8-11 0 MaximeGuyon 4 107
(A Fabre, France) *racd in 6th: hdwy appr fnl 3f: 5th and styng on u.p 1 1/2f out: r.o wl fnl 110yds to get up on line* **7/1**[3]
2 *shd* **Ibicenco (GER)**[21] 2341 3-8-11 0 ADeVries 7 106
(J Hirschberger, Germany) *racd in 5th: disputing 3rd 3f out: led narrowly appr fnl f: kpt on wl u.p: ct post* **10/1**
3 *1 1/2* **Beaulieu (IRE)**[21] 2341 3-8-11 0 (p) Christophe-PatriceLemaire 6 104
(E Libaud, France) *racd in 3rd: 8 l off ldr: hdwy gng wl 2 1/2f out: led appr fnl 1 1/2f: hdd narrowly nring fnl f: no ex fnl 100yds* **14/1**
4 *3/4* **Sano Di Pietro**[32] 3-8-11 0 ChristopheSoumillon 2 103
(A De Royer-Dupre, France) *settled in last: at least 15 l bhd pcemaker 4f out: rdn fr 2f out: styd on to go 4th 110yds out: nt pce to chal* **8/11**[1]
5 *shd* **Genzy (FR)**[21] 2341 3-8-11 0 OlivierPeslier 1 103
(J E Pease, France) *hld up next to last: 5th 3f out: n.m.r 2f out: nt qckn u.p appr fnl f* **6/1**[2]
6 *3/4* **Touz Price (FR)**[49] 1551 3-8-11 0 FranckBlondel 5 101
(J-M Lefebvre, France) *chsd clr ldr: led 2f out: hdd appr fnl f: wknd fnl 110yds* **9/1**
7 *15* **Arlington (GER)**[15] 3-8-11 0 MCadeddu 3 77
(J Hirschberger, Germany) *led: qcknd 8 l clr 4f out: hdd 2f out: eased last f* **25/1**

2m 28.71s (-2.29) **Going Correction** +0.175s/f (Good) **7** Ran SP% **114.3**
Speed ratings: **114,113,112,112,112 111,101**
WIN (incl. 1 euro stake): 7.30. PLACES: 3.70, 5.40. SF: 64.60.
Owner Muteb Bin Abdullah **Bred** F. Bianco **Trained** Chantilly, France

NOTEBOOK
Kreem, much improved since being stepped up in trip, came with a late run to get up right on the line. According to his breeder Frederic Blanco he's likely to go for the Group 1 Grand Prix de Paris next.

2980a PRIX DU CHEMIN DE FER DU NORD (GROUP 3) (4YO+) (TURF) 1m
4:20 (12:00) 4-Y-O+ **£34,482** (£13,793; £10,344; £6,896; £3,448)

RPR
1 **Byword**[21] 2343 5-8-11 0 MaximeGuyon 8 114+
(A Fabre, France) *a cl up in share of 3rd or 4th: qcknd to ld fnl f: eased cl home* **8/11**[1]
2 *3/4* **Vagabond Shoes (IRE)**[38] 1841 4-8-11 0 OlivierPeslier 6 113
(Y Durepaire, Spain) *pressed ldr: led ins fnl 2f: hdd 1f out: kpt on wl* **25/1**
3 *3/4* **Beacon Lodge (IRE)**[15] 2502 6-8-11 0 GeraldMosse 7 111
(Clive Cox) *w.w towards rr: 7th 3f out: swtchd outside 2f out: r.o to go 3rd ins fnl f: hmpd by runner-up cl home but mde no difference to position* **5/1**[2]
4 *1 1/2* **Unnefer (FR)**[38] 1841 6-8-11 0 StephanePasquier 4 108
(P Bary, France) *racd in midfield: in middle of 3 horses sharing 4th 3f out: 6th and styng on whn short of room and swtchd outside 1f out: kpt on fnl 100yds* **7/1**[3]
5 *nse* **Blue Panis (FR)**[168] 4-8-11 0 Christophe-PatriceLemaire 1 107
(F Chappet, France) *chsd ldrs on rail: 3rd 3f out and ev ch 2f out: nt qckn u.p fnl f* **10/1**
6 *1* **Sir Oscar (GER)**[38] 1841 4-8-11 0 ADeVries 5 105
(T Potters, Germany) *w.w in last pl: sme hdwy fnl f: nvr in contention* **14/1**
7 *1 1/2* **Trajano (USA)**[24] 6-8-11 0 GregoryBenoist 2 102?
(M Delzangles, France) *racd in midfield: rdn and no imp fnl 2f* **25/1**
8 *1* **Konig Bernard (FR)**[38] 1841 5-8-11 0 DominiqueBoeuf 3 99
(W Baltromei, Germany) *led: hdd ins fnl 2f: fdd fnl f* **16/1**

1m 36.76s (-1.24) **Going Correction** +0.175s/f (Good) **8** Ran SP% **116.4**
Speed ratings: **113,112,111,110,109 108,107,106**
WIN (incl. 1 euro stake): 1.90. PLACES: 1.30, 3.40, 1.70. DF: 25.40. SF: 31.30.
Owner K Abdulla **Bred** Juddmonte Farms Ltd **Trained** Chantilly, France

NOTEBOOK
Byword disappointed behind Goldikova last time but, down in grade here, outclassed his opponents to score a comfortable success. Although the winning margin was only 3/4l, he was value for much more, having been eased down by his jockey.
Beacon Lodge(IRE) won this race in 2009 but this was a stronger renewal and he wasn't disgraced in third.

HOPPEGARTEN (R-H)
Sunday, June 12

OFFICIAL GOING: Turf: good

2981a DIANA-TRIAL (GROUP 2) (3YO FILLIES) (TURF) 1m 2f
3:55 (12:00) 3-Y-O
£34,482 (£13,362; £5,603; £3,448; £2,155; £1,293)

RPR
1 **Selkis (GER)**[259] 6407 3-9-2 0 VSchulepov 8 97
(J Hirschberger, Germany) *settled in midfield: gd prog through field on fnl turn: u.p early in st: slow to qckn but grad picked up 1 1/2f out and mde gd prog in centre of trck: r.o strly fnl f to get up on line for narrow win* **172/10**
2 *nse* **Julie's Love**[25] 3-9-2 0 AlexisBadel 6 97
(Manfred Hofer, Germany) *racd 5th: mde swift prog arnd fnl turn: short of room early in st: qcknd wl whn clr to join ldrs 1f out: tk ld 100yds out: ct on line* **41/5**
3 *1* **Night Of Dubai (IRE)**[259] 6407 3-9-2 0 THellier 1 95
(Mario Hofer, Germany) *broke wl: rushed to ld: set decent pce: led into st: r.o wl: hdd 100yds out: styd on wl* **104/10**
4 *shd* **Paragua (GER)** 3-9-2 0 EPedroza 3 95
(A Wohler, Germany) *racd in 4th: gd prog arnd fnl turn: qcknd to chal for ld: r.o wl but no ex ins fnl 100yds* **13/5**[2]
5 *1/2* **Leopardin (GER)** 3-9-2 0 WPanov 5 94
(H J Groschel, Germany) *broke slowly: settled towards rr: mde gd prog down bkst: looked threatening ent st and ev ch 1 1/2f out: no ex: styd on* **29/1**
6 *1* **Directa Princess (GER)** 3-9-2 0 AHelfenbein 10 92
(Andreas Lowe, Germany) *broke poorly: had to work through field to join ldng gp: r.o wl in st wout threatening ldrs* **91/10**
7 *shd* **Dalarna (GER)**[21] 2337 3-9-2 0 APietsch 11 92
(W Hickst, Germany) *broke wl: settled bhd ldrs: then dropped bk into midfield on bkst: styd on in st but unable qck w ldrs* **21/10**[1]
8 *1 1/2* **Alkhana (IRE)** 3-9-2 0 FilipMinarik 4 89
(P Schiergen, Germany) *settled midfield: u.p early in st: styd on but nvr a force* **31/1**
9 *1 1/4* **Jardina (GER)**[259] 6407 3-9-2 0 AStarke 7 86
(P Schiergen, Germany) *broke smartly to ld early: then settled bhd ldr: briefly threatened early in st but qckly fdd and dropped away* **74/10**[3]

10 *hd* **Kellemoi De Pepita**[21] 2337 3-9-2 0.. JBojko 2 86
(R Dzubasz, Germany) *broke slowly: racd as bkmarker: rdn early in st on wd outside but fnd no ex* **9/1**

11 *1* **Serafina (GER)**[294] 3-9-2 0.. DarryllHolland 9 84
(W Hickst, Germany) *racd midfield: proged to join ldrs down bkst: threatened briefly early in st: sn btn* **172/10**

2m 5.00s (-1.70) **11** Ran SP% **128.9**
WIN (incl. 10 euro stake): 182. PLACES: 59, 27, 31. SF: 1,452..
Owner Gestut Schlenderhan **Bred** Gestut Schlenderhan **Trained** Germany

2539 SAN SIRO (R-H)
Sunday, June 12

OFFICIAL GOING: Turf: heavy

2982a GRAN PREMIO DI MILANO (GROUP 1) (3YO+) (TURF) 1m 4f
4:10 (4:43) 3-Y-0+ **£116,379** (£51,206; £27,931; £13,965)

RPR

1 **Voila Ici (IRE)**[28] 2134 6-9-7 0.. MircoDemuro 2 114
(Vittorio Caruso, Italy) *trckd ldr thrght: led 2 1/2f out: strly pressed by Jakkalberry tl 1 1/2f out: r.o gamely to hold off runner-up* **43/10**[3]

2 *nk* **Scalo**[35] 1931 4-9-7 0.. FrankieDettori 4 114
(A Wohler, Germany) *settled in midfield towards outside: 8th after 4f: rdn and prog 3f out: swtchd ins 1 1/2f out: styd on wl and wnt 2nd ins fnl f: no ex cl home* **13/20**[1]

3 *shd* **Saratoga Black (IRE)**[217] 7373 4-9-7 0........................ CristianDemuro 5 113
(B Grizzetti, Italy) *a.p: 3rd on outside 3f out: pressed ldr sn after: outpcd 1 1/2f out: styd on again fnl f: clsng fin* **246/10**

4 *2 1/2* **Jakkalberry (IRE)**[36] 1918 5-9-7 0.. FabioBranca 9 109
(E Botti, Italy) *settled in midfield: prog 4f out to press ldrs 3f out: cl 2nd and ev ch 2f out: rdn and nt qckn fnl 1 1/2f* **23/10**[2]

5 *1/2* **Branderburgo (IRE)**[28] 2134 4-9-7 0.. GBietolini 6 109
(L Riccardi, Italy) *missed break: rushed up to ld after 100yds: hdd 2 1/2f out: no ex and fdd last 150yds* **58/1**

6 *10* **Frankenstein (ITY)**[14] 2540 4-9-7 0.. GArena 7 93
(B Grizzetti, Italy) *racd in 4th: rdn and wknd fnl 2f* **30/1**

7 *1* **Toi Et Moi (IRE)**[41] 1784 4-9-4 0.. UmbertoRispoli 3 88
(P Bary, France) *settled towards rr: effrt 2 1/2f out: no imp and nvr in contention* **61/10**

8 *hd* **Silver Arrow (ITY)**[63] 6-9-7 0.. LManiezzi 8 91
(R Menichetti, Italy) *chsd ldng gp: rdn and wknd fr 2 1/2f out* **51/1**

9 *2* **Cima De Pluie**[28] 2134 4-9-7 0.. DarioVargiu 1 87
(B Grizzetti, Italy) *racd in fnl three: rdn and nt qckn 3f out: nvr a threat* **192/10**

2m 34.4s (2.90) **9** Ran SP% **139.6**
WIN (incl. 1 euro stake): 5.34. PLACES: 1.52, 1.11, 2.52; DF 13.30.
Owner Incolinx **Bred** Soc Finanza Locale Consulting Srl **Trained** Italy

NOTEBOOK
Voila Ici(IRE) dug deep for a gutsy victory.

2542 CARLISLE (R-H)
Monday, June 13

OFFICIAL GOING: Good to soft (good in places with soft in places in 5f/6f chute; 7.5)
Old stable bend moved out further 2yds, 4yds from inside line and distances increased by 12yds.
Wind: Fresh, half against Weather: Cloudy

2983 BOOK YOUR CONFERENCE AT CARLISLE RACECOURSE MAIDEN AUCTION STKS 5f 193y
1:45 (1:47) (Class 5) 2-Y-0 **£2,388** (£705; £352) **Stalls** Low

Form RPR

0 **1** **Bartley**[9] 2731 2-8-13 0.. TomEaves 8 78
(Bryan Smart) *towards rr: pushed along 1/2-way: hdwy far side gp over 2f out: edgd rt and led ins fnl f: r.o* **40/1**

42 **2** *1 1/2* **Auntie Joy**[28] 2160 2-8-1 0.. JamesSullivan(3) 4 64
(Michael Easterby) *chsd ldrs: effrt and led far side over 1f out to ins fnl f: kpt on same pce towards fin* **9/2**[1]

0 **3** *2 1/4* **Fast On (IRE)**[20] 2374 2-8-13 0.. RichardMullen 6 66+
(Ed McMahon) *midfield: effrt and c stands' side over 2f out: led that gp over 1f out: kpt on: nt pce of first two far side* **9/2**[1]

4 *1 1/2* **Medieval Bishop (IRE)** 2-8-11 0.. TonyHamilton 9 60
(Howard Johnson) *s.i.s: bhd: hdwy in centre over 2f out: hung lft over 1f out: kpt on fin* **50/1**

6 **5** *3 1/4* **Koalition (IRE)**[16] 2485 2-8-11 0.. GregFairley 7 50
(Deborah Sanderson) *cl up: effrt and ev ch far side gp over 2f out: rdn and no ex over 1f out* **16/1**

6 *nk* **Jay Kay** 2-8-11 0.. AndrewElliott 11 49
(Robert Wylie) *dwlt: sn pushed along towards rr: effrt and chsd stands' side ldrs 2f out: kpt on same pce fnl f* **22/1**

7 *1/2* **Sir Elmo (IRE)** 2-8-11 0.. SilvestreDeSousa 5 48
(Declan Carroll) *dwlt: bhd: hdwy far side over 2f out: kpt on fnl f: no imp* **25/1**

0 **8** *nk* **Mick Slates (IRE)**[68] 1165 2-8-6 0.. NeilFarley(5) 17 47
(Declan Carroll) *s.i.s: sn wl bhd: hdwy in centre 2f out: nrst fin* **100/1**

64 **9** *1* **Mebsuta (IRE)**[41] 1791 2-8-8 0.. PaulHanagan 16 41
(Kevin Ryan) *in tch on outside: effrt stands' side gp over 2f out: no imp over 1f out* **6/1**[2]

10 *3/4* **Flirty Gerty (IRE)** 2-8-11 0.. RichardKingscote 13 41
(Tom Dascombe) *prom: hdwy and led stands' side gp over 2f out to over 1f out: sn btn* **14/1**

6 **11** *1/2* **Revitalise**[11] 2630 2-8-11 0.. PhillipMakin 15 40
(Kevin Ryan) *in tch on outside: rdn stands' side over 2f out: wknd over 1f out* **11/1**

63 **12** *1* **Just Like Heaven (IRE)**[14] 2570 2-8-9 0.. DavidAllan 3 35
(Tim Easterby) *sn drvn along towards rr: outpcd far side over 2f out: n.d after* **9/1**[3]

13 *9* **Hopes Rebellion** 2-8-10 0 ow1.. RobertWinston 10 9
(Declan Carroll) *in tch: effrt and ch far side over 2f out: wknd over 1f out* **66/1**

14 *1 1/4* **Red Alex** 2-8-13 0.. PaulMulrennan 14 8
(James Given) *dwlt: bhd and drvn on outside: c stands' side over 2f out: nvr on terms* **33/1**

0 **15** *3/4* **Roy's Legacy**[14] 2542 2-8-6 0.. DeclanCannon(3) 2 2
(Shaun Harris) *led: styd far side ent st: hdd over 1f out: sn btn* **200/1**

16 *9* **Reemeya (USA)** 2-8-8 0.. JoeFanning 12 —
(Mark Johnston) *chsd ldrs on outside: rdn in stands' side gp over 2f out: wknd wl over 1f out* **14/1**

3 **17** *14* **Keyhole Kate**[18] 2430 2-8-6 0.. DuranFentiman 1 —
(Tim Walford) *dwlt: sn in tch: rdn far side gp over 2f out: sn wknd* **6/1**[2]

1m 16.27s (2.57) **Going Correction** +0.35s/f (Good) **17** Ran SP% **121.0**
Speed ratings (Par 93): **96,94,91,89,84 84,83,83,81,80 80,78,66,65,64 52,33**
toteswingers: 1&2 £29.80, 1&3 £27.10, 2&3 £5.60. CSF £203.95 TOTE £38.50: £9.40, £1.70, £2.30; EX 389.90 TRIFECTA Not won..
Owner Mrs V R Smart **Bred** B Smart **Trained** Hambleton, N Yorks

FOCUS
An ordinary maiden and a difference of opinion with the larger group of ten staying far side, whilst seven made a move towards the stands' rail on the crown of the bend. A messy race to assess, and it has been rated around the race averages and the runner-up.

NOTEBOOK
Bartley had run green when last of eight on his Newcastle debut, hence his massive odds here, but he had obviously learnt from that and improved plenty. Given a bit to do in the far-side group, he quickened up very nicely to hit the front half a furlong from home and there should be more improvement in him, with a step up to 7f not expected to be a problem.
Auntie Joy had run really well in her first two starts and looked as though she would relish this extra furlong. She was in front against the inside rail over a furlong from home, but couldn't withstand the winner's finishing effort. She could be interesting with the nurseries about three weeks away. (op 5-1 tchd 11-2)
Fast On(IRE), outpaced over 5f on his Chepstow debut, was drawn low but ended up in the stands'-side group, so he did well to emerge best of those that came that side and should be up to winning an ordinary maiden. (op 4-1 tchd 7-2)
Medieval Bishop(IRE) ◆, out of a half-sister to nine winners, started out in the far-side group but hung over towards the nearside over a furlong out. Nonetheless, he stayed on the fare best of the newcomers and has a future.
Koalition(IRE) was ridden more positively than when sixth of 13 on his Beverley debut at odds of 100-1, but didn't get home over this extra furlong. Perhaps he needs quicker ground. (op 22-1 tchd 14-1)
Jay Kay, a half-brother to two winners at up to 1m4f, was noted doing some good late work and can be expected to improve over time and distance. (op 25-1)

2984 ULTIMATE LADIES' NIGHT ON 1ST AUGUST CLAIMING STKS 1m 1f 61y
2:15 (2:15) (Class 6) 3-Y-0+ **£1,706** (£503; £252) **Stalls** Low

Form RPR

2331 **1** **Moody Tunes**[5] 2807 8-9-13 75.. AndrewElliott 5 74
(Mrs K Burke) *chsd ldrs: rdn and hdwy to chal over 1f out: edgd rt: kpt on gamely fnl f: led nr fin* **8/11**[1]

2-02 **2** *hd* **Baby Driver**[24] 2249 3-8-12 59.. PaulMulrennan 3 69
(Howard Johnson) *led at decent gallop: rdn: edgd lft and jnd over 1f out: kpt on wl fnl f: hdd nr fin* **22/1**

0-02 **3** *1/2* **The Osteopath (IRE)**[21] 2347 8-9-12 83.. PhillipMakin 6 71
(Michael Dods) *hld up: effrt whn nt clr run over 2f out: gd hdwy over 1f out: kpt on fnl f: jst hld* **13/8**[2]

0043 **4** *15* **Bajan Pride**[11] 2589 7-9-3 56.. MickyFenton 4 29
(Paul Midgley) *hld up in tch: rdn over 3f out: outpcd 2f out: btn fnl f* **14/1**[3]

06-0 **5** *2 1/2* **Peppercorn Rent (IRE)**[73] 1074 3-8-2 50 ow1.....(e) AndrewHeffernan 2 19
(Tracy Waggott) *pressed ldr: drvn 4f out: wknd fnl 2f* **66/1**

00 **6** *1/2* **Bunacurry**[21] 2347 6-8-10 0.. GarryWhillans(7) 1 23
(Barry Murtagh) *hld up in tch: rdn along over 3f out: wknd fr 2f out* **125/1**

1m 59.15s (1.55) **Going Correction** +0.125s/f (Good)
WFA 3 from 6yo+ 12lb **6** Ran SP% **109.3**
Speed ratings (Par 101): **98,97,97,84,81 81**
toteswingers: 1&2 £2.50, 1&3 £1.10, 2&3 £2.20. CSF £16.57 TOTE £2.00: £1.10, £3.60; EX 10.00.The winner was claimed by Paul Murphy for £15,000. Baby Driver was claimed by Tom Dascombe for £12,000.
Owner Aricabeau Racing Limited **Bred** Llety Stud **Trained** Middleham Moor, North Yorks
■ Stewards' Enquiry : Paul Mulrennan one-day ban: used whip in incorrect place (Jun 27)

FOCUS
Only two mattered in this moderate claimer according to the market, but it wasn't that straightforward. The form looks suspect with the front pair both showing awkward head-carriages inside the last 2f. Tricky form to assess, as it depends on how much the runner-up improved.

2985 BELL & PLATE DAY NEXT WEDNESDAY H'CAP 7f 200y
2:45 (2:45) (Class 5) (0-70,70) 4-Y-0+ **£2,266** (£674; £337; £168) **Stalls** Low

Form RPR

4114 **1** **Fazza**[21] 2366 4-9-5 **68**.. TonyHamilton 10 79
(Edwin Tuer) *trckd ldr: led over 2f out: drvn and kpt on wl fnl f* **7/2**[1]

0000 **2** *1 1/2* **Bentley**[11] 2653 7-8-5 **54**..(p) SilvestreDeSousa 4 62
(Brian Baugh) *t.k.h: in tch: effrt and chsd wnr over 1f out: kpt on same pce wl ins fnl f* **18/1**

-002 **3** *2* **Desert Hunter (IRE)**[13] 2589 8-8-4 **53**.. KellyHarrison 2 56
(Micky Hammond) *led to over 2f out: sn rdn: kpt on same pce fnl f* **10/1**

4021 **4** *nse* **Ra Junior (USA)**[10] 2692 5-9-4 **67**.. FrederikTylicki 9 70+
(Paul Midgley) *bhd: drvn over 3f out: hdwy on outside over 1f out: kpt on fnl f: nvr able to chal* **7/2**[1]

4-54 **5** *1 1/2* **Jaldarshaan (IRE)**[17] 2478 4-8-13 **62**.. RobertWinston 3 62
(Alan Swinbank) *dwlt: sn in tch: effrt over 2f out: edgd rt and one pce over 1f out* **13/2**[3]

0-66 **6** *nk* **Twisted**[26] 1613 5-8-8 **60**..(b) JamesSullivan(3) 1 59
(Michael Easterby) *trckd ldrs: drvn and outpcd over 2f out: rallied over 1f out: kpt on fnl f* **17/2**

3000 **7** *2 1/2* **Lady Florence**[14] 2566 6-8-11 **67**.. JacobButterfield(7) 12 60
(David C Griffiths) *prom on outside: rdn 3f out: wknd fnl f* **40/1**

-103 **8** *1 1/2* **Master Leon**[16] 2487 4-8-8 **57**..(v) TomEaves 5 47
(Bryan Smart) *midfield: effrt and rdn over 2f out: edgd rt over 1f out: btn fnl f* **14/1**

005- **9** *1 1/4* **Solis**[57] 2523 5-8-12 **61**.. PJMcDonald 13 48
(Micky Hammond) *hld up: drvn over 3f out: nvr able to chal* **16/1**

-020 **10** *1 1/4* **Swiftly Done (IRE)**[43] 1714 4-9-0 **68**..(b) NeilFarley(5) 14 52
(Declan Carroll) *hld up: pushed along over 3f out: nvr rchd ldrs* **6/1**[2]

0-50 **11** *2* **Kalahari Desert (IRE)**[24] 2249 4-8-2 **51** oh4.. PaulQuinn 8 31
(Richard Whitaker) *t.k.h: hld up: rdn 3f out: nvr able to chal* **80/1**

-006 **12** *hd* **Aussie Blue (IRE)**[47] 1621 7-9-0 **63**.. FrannyNorton 6 47
(Richard Whitaker) *midfield: drvn along over 2f out: wknd over 1f out* **14/1**

000- **13** 20 **Big Whitfield**[354] 3369 5-8-3 **52** AndrewHeffernan 11 —
(Tracy Waggott) *midfield on outside: struggling over 3f out: sn btn: t.o* **28/1**

1m 41.91s (1.91) **Going Correction** +0.125s/f (Good) **13** Ran SP% **123.3**
Speed ratings (Par 103): **95,93,91,91,89 89,87,85,84,83 81,80,60**
toteswingers: 1&2 £13.90, 1&3 £8.10, 2&3 £26.80. CSF £76.24 CT £616.29 TOTE £2.60: £1.10, £8.20, £4.40; EX 88.60 Trifecta £256.40 Part won. Pool: £346.52 - 0.10 winning units..
Owner E Tuer **Bred** D R Tucker **Trained** Great Smeaton, N Yorks
FOCUS
An ordinary handicap but the form looks sound. Only the fourth got involved from the rear.

2986 PIPER HEIDSIECK FILLIES' H'CAP 6f 192y
3:15 (3:16) (Class 4) (0-80,77) 3-Y-O £4,079 (£1,214; £606; £303) Stalls Low

Form RPR
0-01 **1** **Alluring Star**[21] 2350 3-7-13 **58** oh1 JamesSullivan(3) 6 67+
(Michael Easterby) *mde all: rdn 2f out: styd on strly fnl f* **7/1**
5-51 **2** 1 3/4 **Fairlie Dinkum**[24] 2264 3-9-3 **73** TomEaves 12 76
(Bryan Smart) *hld up in tch: effrt over 1f out: styd on to take 2nd nr fin: nt rch wnr* **15/2**
1-30 **3** 1/2 **Camache Queen (IRE)**[30] 2102 3-9-6 **76** JoeFanning 1 78
(Denis Coakley) *trckd ldrs: effrt and chsd wnr over 1f out: kpt on fnl f: lost 2nd nr fin* **6/1**[2]
-001 **4** 1 **No Poppy (IRE)**[13] 2581 3-9-2 **77** LanceBetts(5) 7 76
(Tim Easterby) *hld up: effrt on outside over 1f out: kpt on fnl f: nvr able to chal* **13/2**[3]
35-0 **5** 2 3/4 **Bay Of Fires (IRE)**[17] 2466 3-9-3 **73** SilvestreDeSousa 8 65
(David O'Meara) *t.k.h: cl up: hung lft after 2f: effrt over 1f out: kpt on same pce fnl f* **10/1**
0002 **6** 1/2 **Catallout (IRE)**[21] 2350 3-7-11 **58** NeilFarley(5) 13 49
(Declan Carroll) *hld up: hdwy on outside and prom over 2f out: wknd ins fnl f* **16/1**
4-25 **7** 6 **Spinatrix**[35] 1941 3-8-4 **60** DuranFentiman 2 34
(Michael Dods) *hld up: rdn over 3f out: nvr able to chal* **20/1**
-222 **8** 1 **Jade**[7] 2763 3-9-2 **72** PaulMulrennan 5 44
(Ollie Pears) *hld up: effrt and pushed along over 2f out: wknd over 1f out* **11/4**[1]
556- **9** 3/4 **Ballinargh Girl (IRE)**[288] 5547 3-9-3 **73** AndrewElliott 11 43
(Robert Wylie) *plld hrd: cl up tl rdn and wknd over 1f out* **28/1**
052 **10** 3 3/4 **Daisyclipper**[30] 2094 3-8-13 **69** PaulHanagan 4 28
(Ann Duffield) *in tch: drvn and outpcd over 3f out: n.d after* **9/1**
1-00 **11** 20 **Adorable Choice (IRE)**[13] 2582 3-9-3 **73** (t) RichardKingscote 3 —
(Tom Dascombe) *sn bhd and pushed along: nvr on terms* **25/1**

1m 28.05s (0.95) **Going Correction** +0.125s/f (Good) **11** Ran SP% **115.6**
Speed ratings (Par 98): **99,97,96,95,92 91,84,83,82,78 55**
toteswingers: 1&2 £11.10, 1&3 £6.60, 2&3 £11.90. CSF £56.01 CT £342.49 TOTE £10.00: £3.80, £2.80, £2.90; EX 73.70 TRIFECTA Not won..
Owner Jeff Hamer & Bernard Bargh **Bred** B Bargh **Trained** Sheriff Hutton, N Yorks
FOCUS
A fair fillies' handicap, but not many got into it. The winner is progressing nicely.
Bay Of Fires(IRE) Official explanation: jockey said filly hung left-handed on bend
Jade Official explanation: jockey said filly ran flat

2987 STOBART GROUP & HOSPICE AT HOME H'CAP 5f
3:45 (3:46) (Class 5) (0-70,70) 3-Y-O+ £2,266 (£674; £337; £168) Stalls Low

Form RPR
-501 **1** **Doc Hay (USA)**[11] 2632 4-9-11 **69** JoeFanning 2 83+
(Keith Dalgleish) *hld up: stdy hdwy whn nt clr run over 2f out to ent fnl f: swtchd lft and qcknd to ld last 100yds: kpt on wl* **7/2**[2]
-600 **2** 1/2 **Mullglen**[10] 2694 5-9-6 **64** (p) DavidAllan 6 73
(Tim Easterby) *hld up: rdn 1/2-way: hdwy on outside to ld 1f out: rdr sn dropped whip: hdd last 100yds: kpt on* **6/1**
2022 **3** 2 **Sharp Bullet (IRE)**[11] 2632 5-9-0 **58** (p) PaulHanagan 3 60
(Bruce Hellier) *cl up: rdn and ev ch 1f out: kpt on same pce fnl f* **9/2**[3]
21-1 **4** 1 **Beauty Pageant (IRE)**[21] 2365 4-9-11 **69** RichardMullen 8 67
(Ed McMahon) *led to over 2f out: sn rdn and edgd lft: kpt on same pce ins fnl f* **6/4**[1]
4163 **5** hd **Tournedos (IRE)**[5] 2798 9-9-2 **60** (b) PJMcDonald 4 58
(Ruth Carr) *prom: effrt over 1f out: kpt on same pce fnl f* **12/1**
0404 **6** 1 1/2 **Wicked Wilma (IRE)**[10] 2667 7-9-0 **58** PatrickMathers 1 50
(Alan Berry) *midfield on ins: drvn after 2f: rallied 2f out: kpt on same pce fnl f* **16/1**
150- **7** 3 3/4 **Avertuoso**[229] 7169 7-9-5 **70** (v) JustinNewman(7) 10 49
(Bryan Smart) *dwlt: sn cl up: led over 2f out to 1f out: sn btn* **33/1**
-200 **8** 1 1/4 **Lake Chini (IRE)**[38] 1856 9-9-7 **65** (b) GrahamGibbons 9 39
(Michael Easterby) *cl up tl rdn and wknd appr fnl f* **22/1**
0-00 **9** hd **Argentine (IRE)**[11] 2632 7-9-1 **59** PaulMulrennan 11 33
(George Foster) *hld up: rdn along 1/2-way: nvr on terms* **25/1**
050- **10** 1 1/4 **Cayman Fox**[229] 7169 6-9-12 **70** TomEaves 7 39
(Linda Perratt) *t.k.h: in tch: effrt over 2f out: wknd over 1f out* **40/1**

62.13 secs (1.33) **Going Correction** +0.35s/f (Good) **10** Ran SP% **121.8**
Speed ratings (Par 103): **103,102,99,97,97 94,88,86,86,84**
toteswingers: 1&2 £5.30, 1&3 £3.50, 2&3 £6.80. CSF £25.01 CT £99.17 TOTE £5.50: £1.40, £2.90, £2.50; EX 39.80 Trifecta £224.40 Pool: £515.61 - 1.70 winning units..
Owner S Laffan **Bred** Colts Neck Stables Llc **Trained** Carluke, South Lanarkshire
FOCUS
An ordinary sprint handicap in which the leaders may have gone off too quick, as the first two home came from well off the pace. Fair form for the grade, with the winner a bit better than the bare figures.

2988 WEST MOOR STUD H'CAP 1m 1f 61y
4:15 (4:15) (Class 5) (0-70,71) 4-Y-O+ £2,266 (£674; £337; £168) Stalls Low

Form RPR
0044 **1** **Ay Tay Tate (IRE)**[12] 2618 5-8-5 **53** FrannyNorton 5 69
(David C Griffiths) *cl up: led after 2f: mde rest: drvn clr fr over 1f out* **20/1**
3503 **2** 8 **Rub Of The Relic (IRE)**[14] 2548 6-8-7 **55** (v) MickyFenton 11 53
(Paul Midgley) *trckd ldrs: effrt and rdn over 3f out: styd on fnl f: tk 2nd cl home: no ch w wnr* **14/1**
-401 **3** shd **Judicious**[5] 2800 4-9-9 **71** 6ex SilvestreDeSousa 4 69
(Geoffrey Harker) *led 2f: cl up: rdn and effrt over 2f out: one pce fr over 1f out: lost 2nd cl home* **11/10**[1]
-030 **4** 1 1/2 **Mangham (IRE)**[10] 2692 6-9-3 **65** PaulMulrennan 8 60
(George Foster) *hld up in tch: effrt over 3f out: rdn and no imp fr 2f out* **20/1**
6-41 **5** shd **Sinatramania**[14] 2548 4-8-11 **59** AndrewHeffernan 1 54
(Tracy Waggott) *t.k.h: in tch on ins: rdn over 2f out: no imp fr over 1f out* **5/2**[2]
-404 **6** 2 1/2 **Dandarrell**[17] 2462 4-8-1 **52** (p) JamesSullivan(3) 6 41
(Julie Camacho) *hld up on ins: effrt over 3f out: nvr able to chal* **9/1**[3]
-040 **7** 1/2 **So Bazaar (IRE)**[17] 2474 4-9-2 **64** RobertWinston 10 52
(Alan Swinbank) *hld up towards rr: effrt over 2f out: hung rt over 1f out: sn btn* **20/1**
-550 **8** 12 **Idealism**[20] 2393 4-8-12 **60** FrederikTylicki 2 22
(Micky Hammond) *t.k.h: prom tl rdn and wknd over 2f out* **20/1**
00-0 **9** 1/2 **Kathlatino**[14] 2548 4-8-9 **57** PJMcDonald 9 18
(Micky Hammond) *bhd: struggling 4f out: nvr on terms* **50/1**

1m 57.99s (0.39) **Going Correction** +0.125s/f (Good) **9** Ran SP% **113.9**
Speed ratings (Par 103): **103,95,95,94,94 92,91,81,80**
toteswingers: 1&2 £11.80, 1&3 £6.50, 2&3 £4.00. CSF £235.48 CT £569.33 TOTE £22.30: £4.50, £3.00, £1.02; EX 99.70 Trifecta £272.60 Part won. Pool: £368.46 - 0.62 winning units..
Owner Andrew Langan **Bred** Kelly's Vintage Partnership **Trained** Bawtry, S Yorks
FOCUS
An ordinary handicap and ultimately a one-horse race. A surprise return to his best from the winner, but nothing else ran their race.

2989 WATCH RACING UK ON SKY 432 H'CAP (DIV I) 5f 193y
4:45 (4:45) (Class 6) (0-60,61) 3-Y-O+ £1,364 (£403; £201) Stalls Low

Form RPR
3361 **1** **Choc'A'Moca (IRE)**[5] 2798 4-10-2 **61** 6ex (v) MickyFenton 2 72
(Paul Midgley) *led to over 2f out: regained ld over 1f out: kpt on strly fnl f* **9/2**[2]
0-21 **2** 2 **Needy McCredie**[14] 2546 5-9-11 **56** PaulHanagan 11 61
(James Turner) *dwlt: sn in tch on outside: effrt and edgd lft over 2f out: edgd rt and chsd wnr over 1f out: kpt on* **15/8**[1]
0004 **3** nk **Distant Sun (USA)**[10] 2694 7-9-10 **55** FrederikTylicki 10 59
(Linda Perratt) *hld up: effrt on outside 2f out: edgd rt and kpt on fnl f: nt gng pce to chal* **14/1**
01 **4** 2 1/2 **Gracie's Games**[14] 2555 5-9-9 **57** SophieDoyle(3) 6 53
(Richard Price) *t.k.h: hld up: rdn and effrt over 2f out: edgd rt over 1f out: kpt on same pce fnl f* **7/1**
0300 **5** 1 1/2 **Wotatomboy**[5] 2799 5-9-1 **46** (v) PaulQuinn 13 37
(Richard Whitaker) *cl up: led over 2f out to over 1f out: wknd ins fnl f* **12/1**
6004 **6** 1/2 **Accamelia**[7] 2765 5-9-11 **56** JoeFanning 7 45
(Chris Fairhurst) *in tch: rdn over 2f out: edgd rt over 1f out: wknd ins fnl f* **11/2**[3]
4-00 **7** 1 1/2 **Dream Express (IRE)**[14] 2543 6-9-3 **48** PJMcDonald 4 32
(David Thompson) *midfield: drvn along 1/2-way: sn no imp* **28/1**
-000 **8** 9 **Hold On Tiger (IRE)**[73] 1077 4-8-8 **46** ShirleyTeasdale(7) 8 —
(Nicky Richards) *prom tl rdn and wknd over 2f out* **10/1**
40-0 **9** nk **Whipperoo (IRE)**[61] 1303 3-8-3 **45** JamesSullivan(3) 1 —
(Patrick Morris) *in tch on ins: struggling 1/2-way: sn btn* **40/1**
00/0 **10** 3 **Rue Soleil**[18] 2415 7-9-0 **45** AndrewElliott 3 —
(John Weymes) *sn towards rr: struggling 1/2-way: nvr on terms* **50/1**

1m 15.61s (1.91) **Going Correction** +0.35s/f (Good)
WFA 3 from 4yo+ 8lb **10** Ran SP% **112.1**
Speed ratings (Par 101): **101,98,97,94,92 91,89,77,77,73**
toteswingers: 1&2 £3.30, 1&3 £7.90, 2&3 £6.40. CSF £12.55 CT £107.53 TOTE £4.40: £1.10, £1.50, £3.20; EX 14.70 Trifecta £94.70 Pool: £632.47 - 4.94 winning units..
Owner John Milburn - Andrew Stephenson **Bred** Yeomanstown Stud **Trained** Westow, N Yorks
FOCUS
This looked the stronger of the two divisions with three last-time-out winners amongst the field. Those horses that had stuck to the inside rail seemed to run well throughout the meeting, even if they didn't win, so it was a surprise that the winner was left alone there whilst his rivals all raced a bit wider. It was the pick of the C&D times and the form looks sound.

2990 WATCH RACING UK ON SKY 432 H'CAP (DIV II) 5f 193y
5:15 (5:15) (Class 6) (0-60,58) 3-Y-O+ £1,364 (£403; £201) Stalls Low

Form RPR
355- **1** **Bid For Gold**[231] 7125 7-9-6 **55** PatrickDonaghy(3) 13 63
(Jedd O'Keeffe) *hld up in midfield: hdwy to ld wl over 1f out: hung rt: kpt on wl fnl f* **11/1**
0054 **2** nk **Tahitian Princess (IRE)**[19] 2396 3-8-7 **47** (p) FrannyNorton 8 52
(Ann Duffield) *hld up in tch: effrt on outside over 1f out: chsd wnr ins fnl f: kpt on fin* **9/2**[2]
003 **3** 1 3/4 **Schoolboy Champ**[14] 2547 4-9-12 **58** (v) PaulHanagan 9 59
(Patrick Morris) *prom: effrt and ev ch over 1f out: kpt on same pce fnl f* **13/2**[3]
-446 **4** 2 1/4 **Avoncreek**[28] 2162 7-9-0 **46** KellyHarrison 6 40
(Brian Baugh) *in tch: effrt and ev ch wl over 1f out: sn rdn and one pce* **10/1**
-026 **5** 1 **Hansomis (IRE)**[14] 2543 7-9-10 **56** PaulMulrennan 2 47
(Bruce Mactaggart) *hld up towards rr: rdn over 2f out: hdwy over 1f out: kpt on ins fnl f: nrst fin* **7/2**[1]
-200 **6** 1/2 **Forzarzi (IRE)**[47] 1621 7-9-2 **48** (p) PhillipMakin 3 37
(Hugh McWilliams) *in tch: effrt over 2f out: no ex over 1f out* **12/1**
5-00 **7** 1 3/4 **Real Diamond**[25] 2238 5-9-6 **52** SilvestreDeSousa 1 36
(Ollie Pears) *led: styd alone far side and hdd over 2f out: wknd over 1f out* **9/2**[2]
0-00 **8** 4 1/2 **Catcher Of Dreams (IRE)**[18] 2415 5-8-10 **45** (vt) JamesSullivan(3) 7 14
(George Foster) *sn towards rr: drvn and outpcd 1/2-way: sn struggling* **18/1**
-004 **9** 1/2 **Piste**[10] 2670 5-8-13 **45** AndrewHeffernan 10 —
(Tina Jackson) *s.i.s: bhd and sn outpcd: nvr on terms* **16/1**
2466 **10** 3 **Inde Country**[15] 2524 3-8-5 **48** SophieDoyle(3) 4 —
(Nicky Vaughan) *hld up in midfield: drvn and outpcd 1/2-way: n.d after* **16/1**
300- **11** 1/2 **Future Gem**[251] 6643 5-8-13 **45** (p) PJMcDonald 5 —
(David Thompson) *cl up: led centre over 2f out to wl over 1f out: sn struggling* **33/1**

1m 15.69s (1.99) **Going Correction** +0.35s/f (Good)
WFA 3 from 4yo+ 8lb **11** Ran SP% **117.0**
Speed ratings (Par 101): **100,99,97,94,92 92,89,83,83,79 78**
toteswingers: 1&2 £10.70, 1&3 £5.20, 2&3 £6.30. CSF £59.66 CT £289.24 TOTE £14.70: £3.60, £2.30, £2.20; EX 61.20 TRIFECTA Not won..
Owner Jedd O'Keeffe **Bred** B Minty **Trained** Middleham Moor, N Yorks
■ Stewards' Enquiry : Patrick Donaghy three-day ban: careless riding (Jun 27-29)
FOCUS
Unlike in the first division, those taking part in this had basically forgotten how to win. The winning time was 8/100ths of a second slower than the first leg. The winner is rated to last year's form.
T/Plt: £88.70 to a £1 stake. Pool:£60,181.37 - 495.02 winning tickets. T/Qpdt: £44.60 to a £1 stake. Pool:£4,917.67 - 81.52 winning tickets. RY

[1980]WARWICK (L-H)

Monday, June 13

OFFICIAL GOING: Good (good to soft in places; 7.2)

Wind: Fresh across Weather: Cloudy with sunny spells

2991 CRABBIE'S "SPIFFING" ALCOHOLIC GINGER BEER AMATEUR RIDERS' H'CAP — 1m 4f 134y

6:10 (6:10) (Class 6) (0-60,60) 4-Y-0+ **£1,977** (£608; £304) **Stalls** Low

Form					RPR
6	**1**		**Amana (USA)**[24] 2259 7-10-8 59 (Mark Brisbourne) *chsd ldrs: lost pl over 4f out: nt clr run over 3f out: hdwy over 2f out: rdn to ld over 1f out: hung rt ins fnl f: styd on wl* **14/1**	MissBeckyBrisbourne(5) 8	69
6035	**2**	*3*	**Lady Lam**[4] 2843 5-10-7 58 (t) (Sylvester Kirk) *hld up: hdwy over 2f out: chsd wnr over 1f out: styd on* **15/2**[3]	MissCBoxall(5) 4	64
2212	**3**	*1 1/4*	**Wrecking Crew (IRE)**[21] 2372 7-10-7 58 (Rod Millman) *s.s: hld up: hdwy and nt clr run over 1f out: r.o: nt rch ldrs* **9/2**[1]	MrsDBamonte(5) 1	62+
506-	**4**	*1*	**Bon Spiel**[15] 5888 7-10-9 60 (tp) (Chris Gordon) *hld up: hdwy over 4f out: rdn over 1f out: hung rt and styd on same pce ins fnl f* **16/1**	BrendanPowell(5) 2	62
6621	**5**	*nk*	**Astroleo**[17] 2451 5-9-12 51 (Mark H Tompkins) *led: rdn and hdd over 1f out: edgd rt: no ex fnl f* **10/1**	MissNMcCaffrey(7) 11	53
056-	**6**	*3/4*	**Harare**[314] 4676 10-10-2 55 (v) (Karen Tutty) *plld hrd: hld up: hdwy over 1f out: rdn and hung lft ins fnl f: nvr trbld ldrs* **28/1**	MissGTutty(7) 7	56
4651	**7**	*3/4*	**Galiotto (IRE)**[11] 2638 5-10-8 59 (b) (Gary Moore) *hdwy to chse ldr over 9f out to over 6f out: remained handy: rdn over 1f out: no ex* **8/1**	MissHayleyMoore(5) 9	58
-643	**8**	*1 1/4*	**Shy**[14] 2552 6-10-7 58 (Rod Millman) *chsd ldrs: rdn over 2f out: wknd over 1f out* **9/2**[1]	MrPMillman(5) 13	56
0603	**9**	*1*	**Carr Hall (IRE)**[12] 2616 8-10-3 56 (Tony Carroll) *hld up: hdwy 8f out: rdn and edgd rt over 1f out: sn wknd* **16/1**	MrCCarroll(7) 12	52
5-00	**10**	*1/2*	**Jinto**[32] 2021 4-10-8 57 (David Elsworth) *hld up: rdn over 2f out: nvr on terms* **7/1**[2]	MissLAllan(3) 3	52
010-	**11**	*6*	**Hurricane Thomas (IRE)**[221] 7323 7-10-8 59 (Karen Tutty) *chsd ldrs: rdn over 2f out: wknd over 1f out* **22/1**	MissPhillipaTutty(5) 6	45
5453	**12**	*1/2*	**Diamond Twister (USA)**[17] 2473 5-10-5 58 (t) (Lisa Williamson) *s.i.s: hld up: racd keenly: hdwy 8f out: chsd ldr over 6f out: rdn over 2f out: wknd over 1f out* **16/1**	MrCEllingham(7) 10	44
000-	**13**	*15*	**Business Bay (USA)**[289] 5522 4-9-13 52 (Patrick Clinton) *hld up: a in rr: bhd fnl 3f: t.o* **50/1**	MissABlakemore(7) 5	—

2m 48.52s (3.92) **Going Correction** +0.125s/f (Good) **13 Ran SP% 114.9**

Speed ratings (Par 101): **92,90,89,88,88 88,87,86,86,85 82,81,72**

toteswingers: 1&2 £24.70, 1&3 £32.50, 2&3 £10.60. CSF £108.89 CT £553.40 TOTE £23.30: £6.60, £3.60, £1.90; EX 187.40.

Owner Mark Brisbourne **Bred** Shadwell Farm LLC **Trained** Great Ness, Shropshire

FOCUS

The official going changed to good, good to soft in places from good to firm after 23mm of rain fell in the preceding 36 hours. However, there was a stiff, warm, drying breeze throughout the afternoon. A weak amateurs' handicap run at only a steady pace and the time was ten seconds outside the standard. The form looks open to question, with the winner rated back to her Irish best. The pacesetters made for the faster strip of ground up the stands' rail coming off the bend, although they eventually fanned out across the track.

2992 CRABBIE'S "TICKETY BOO" ALCOHOLIC GINGER BEER MEDIAN AUCTION MAIDEN STKS — 5f

6:40 (6:41) (Class 5) 2-Y-0 **£2,590** (£770; £385; £192) **Stalls** Low

Form					RPR
	1		**Pressure Drop (IRE)** 2-8-9 0 (Pat Murphy) *dwlt: outpcd: hdwy u.p over 1f out: sn edgd lft: jinked rt ins fnl f: r.o to ld towards fin* **20/1**	MarkLawson(3) 8	68+
06	**2**	*1 1/4*	**Stepper Point**[17] 2455 2-9-3 0 (William Muir) *led: rdn and hdd towards fin* **9/4**[1]	DaneO'Neill 1	69
	3	*3/4*	**Lana (IRE)** 2-8-12 0 (Michael Bell) *a.p: chsd ldr over 3f out: shkn up over 1f out: styd on* **7/2**[2]	JamieSpencer 4	61+
6522	**4**	*nk*	**Night Angel (IRE)**[17] 2448 2-8-12 0 (b) (Rod Millman) *chsd ldr to over 3f out: rdn over 1f out: styd on* **9/4**[1]	JamesMillman 3	60
0	**5**	*1 1/4*	**Alnair (IRE)**[16] 2504 2-9-3 0 (Declan Carroll) *prom: rdn: hung rt and outpcd 1/2-way: styd on ins fnl f* **5/1**[3]	DavidNolan 5	60
0	**6**	*2 3/4*	**Lucifers Shadow (IRE)**[27] 2181 2-9-3 0 (Sylvester Kirk) *sn pushed along and prom: outpcd 1/2-way: n.d after* **16/1**	JamesDoyle 9	50
	7	*2 1/2*	**Especially Red (IRE)** 2-8-8 0 ow1 (Lisa Williamson) *sn prom: outpcd fr over 3f out* **33/1**	DaleSwift(5) 2	37

60.52 secs (0.92) **Going Correction** +0.125s/f (Good) **7 Ran SP% 114.0**

Speed ratings (Par 93): **97,95,93,93,91 86,82**

toteswingers: 1&2 £11.30, 1&3 £18.00, 2&3 £3.70. CSF £64.75 TOTE £25.50: £8.60, £1.10; EX 99.90.

Owner Sterling Racing I **Bred** Kilnamoragh Stud **Trained** East Garston, Berks

FOCUS

A modest sprint maiden run at a fair pace and they fanned out off the bend, with the winner racing up the centre of the track. While the form may not amount to much, the unfancied debutant winner looks above average.

NOTEBOOK

Pressure Drop(IRE), a strongly-made filly, hails from a yard not noted for juvenile maiden winners but she clearly knew her job, despite not looking fully wound-up. Though she was green in the early stages and broke slowly, she travelled sweetly and powered home, clearly enjoying the near-perfect ground. He rider had a job pulling her up. She will have learned plenty and could be worth following. (op 16-1)

Stepper Point had shaped well on his second run, a 6f affair at Haydock, but was back to the minimum here. He showed plenty of early pace and made for the far rail in the straight, but didn't quite get home, being niggled at from 2f out. He is clearly going the right way. (op 10-3)

Lana(IRE) missed her intended debut at Leicester when the ground had eased, so the conditions here may not have suited. She showed plenty of early dash but wasn't given an overly taxing introduction by her rider. Given the stable's juveniles usually benefit for their first run, and given that she would have learned plenty, she can be expected to do much better next time. (op 3-1 tchd 5-2)

Night Angel(IRE) had bumped into a couple of decent type on her last two runs but had few excuses here, particularly with a decent draw. In fairness, this was easier ground than she has encountered previously and she stayed on promisingly, suggesting a return to 6f may suit. (op 13-8)

Alnair(IRE) improved on his debut, but not greatly. He looks a modest sprinter at best. (op 11-1)

2993 BRAKES TRUST MEMBERS H'CAP — 6f

7:10 (7:12) (Class 6) (0-65,65) 3-Y-0 **£2,388** (£705; £352) **Stalls** Low

Form					RPR
55-3	**1**		**Ma Quillet**[25] 2223 3-9-7 65 (Henry Candy) *chsd ldr: rdn over 1f out: r.o to ld nr fin* **11/4**[1]	DaneO'Neill 6	72
-430	**2**	*1/2*	**Look Twice**[28] 2163 3-8-12 56 (Alex Hales) *led: rdn over 1f out: hdd nr fin* **20/1**	ChrisCatlin 7	61
340	**3**	*3/4*	**Full Shilling (IRE)**[66] 1220 3-8-8 52 (John Spearing) *dwlt: hld up: hdwy and edgd lft 1f out: r.o wl u.p: nt rch ldrs* **13/2**[3]	LiamJones 1	55
0030	**4**	*2 3/4*	**Passing Moment**[19] 2396 3-8-6 50 (Brian Baugh) *prom: rdn 1/2-way: sn outpcd: rallied over 1f out: styd on* **9/1**	SaleemGolam 9	44
00-0	**5**	*2 1/2*	**Nettis**[15] 2524 3-8-13 57 (t) (George Prodromou) *s.i.s: sn pushed along in rr: rdn over 2f out: nt trble ldrs* **25/1**	KirstyMilczarek 12	43
600-	**6**	*nk*	**Love Club**[322] 4432 3-8-3 50 (Brian Baugh) *chsd ldrs: rdn over 2f out: wknd fnl f* **28/1**	BillyCray(3) 16	35
635-	**7**	*3/4*	**Babich Bay (IRE)**[275] 5936 3-9-4 65 (Pat Murphy) *mid-div: drvn along 1/2-way: hmpd 1f out: n.d* **15/2**	MarkLawson(3) 4	48
23-0	**8**	*1*	**Polar Auroras**[14] 2550 3-9-4 62 (Tony Carroll) *sn pushed along in rr: nvr on terms* **17/2**	SebSanders 15	42
3654	**9**	*nk*	**Scommettitrice (IRE)**[20] 2375 3-8-1 52 ow1 (b) (Ronald Harris) *hld up: rdn over 2f out: n.d* **15/2**	MatthewLawson(7) 14	31
3000	**10**	*nk*	**Pickled Pumpkin**[18] 2424 3-8-8 52 (Olivia Maylam) *s.i.s: rdn over 2f out: n.d* **40/1**	MarcHalford 17	30
3003	**11**	*6*	**Stravsambition**[28] 2163 3-9-1 59 (Reg Hollinshead) *chsd ldrs: rdn over 2f out: wknd over 1f out* **6/1**[2]	JamieSpencer 2	18

1m 13.13s (1.33) **Going Correction** +0.125s/f (Good) **11 Ran SP% 112.8**

Speed ratings (Par 97): **96,95,94,90,87 86,85,84,84,83 75**

toteswingers: 1&2 £12.30, 1&3 £14.00, 2&3 £31.20. CSF £64.18 CT £325.05 TOTE £2.20: £1.10, £7.30, £3.50; EX 30.40.

Owner Geoff Buck **Bred** Geoff Buck **Trained** Kingston Warren, Oxon

■ Stewards' Enquiry : Chris Catlin caution: used whip with excessive frequency

Dane O'Neill one-day ban: used whip with excessive frequency (Jun 27)

FOCUS

A weak sprint handicap, run at a decent pace and the times of the preceding sprint and this 6f affair suggested that the going was nearer to good ground than the official verdict of good, good to soft in places. Very few got into it and the place to be was up with the pace. The winner was less exposed than most.

2994 VOUTE SALES WARWICKSHIRE OAKS STKS (LISTED RACE) (FILLIES) — 1m 2f 188y

7:40 (7:41) (Class 1) 4-Y-0+

£17,031 (£6,456; £3,231; £1,611; £807; £405) **Stalls** Low

Form					RPR
1-34	**1**		**Timepiece**[10] 2678 4-9-1 110 (Sir Henry Cecil) *trckd ldrs: led over 1f out: rdn out* **11/8**[1]	TomQueally 1	106+
4-24	**2**	*1/2*	**Sea Of Heartbreak (IRE)**[23] 2290 4-8-12 103 (Roger Charlton) *chsd ldrs: hmpd 2f out: sn rdn: chsd wnr fnl f: edgd lft: r.o* **6/1**[3]	KirstyMilczarek 2	102
001-	**3**	*1*	**Ceilidh House**[219] 7349 4-9-1 100 (t) (Ralph Beckett) *hld up: rdn over 2f out: r.o wl ins fnl f: nt rch ldrs* **16/1**	JimCrowley 10	103+
12-5	**4**	*nk*	**Mirror Lake**[43] 1718 4-8-12 108 (Amanda Perrett) *trckd ldrs: nt clr run 2f out: rdn over 1f out: r.o* **4/1**[2]	PatDobbs 11	100
1-41	**5**	*nk*	**Piano**[34] 1992 4-8-12 90 (John Gosden) *hld up: hdwy over 1f out: sn rdn and edgd lft: r.o* **7/1**	SebSanders 7	99+
0-00	**6**	*1 1/4*	**Crystal Gal (IRE)**[32] 2031 4-8-12 96 (Lucy Wadham) *prom: stdd and lost pl over 8f out: hdwy over 1f out: styd on same pce ins fnl f* **16/1**	DaneO'Neill 3	97
225	**7**	*2*	**Pink Symphony**[16] 2501 4-8-12 101 (Paul Cole) *chsd ldrs: rdn and edgd lft 2f out: wknd ins fnl f* **16/1**	JamieSpencer 4	91
0-06	**8**	*1 1/2*	**Gallic Star (IRE)**[44] 1677 4-8-12 100 (Mick Channon) *hld up: plld hrd: hdwy over 8f out: rdn over 3f out: wknd over 1f out* **33/1**	ChrisCatlin 9	89
02-6	**9**	*8*	**Pipette**[16] 2501 4-8-12 100 (Andrew Balding) *s.i.s: hld up: rdn over 2f out: wknd over 1f out* **14/1**	RichardMullen 5	74
56-5	**10**	*1/2*	**Conciliatory**[44] 1681 4-8-12 84 (Rae Guest) *led: rdn over 2f out: hdd & wknd over 1f out* **100/1**	LiamJones 6	73

2m 20.21s (-0.89) **Going Correction** +0.125s/f (Good) **10 Ran SP% 117.1**

Speed ratings (Par 108): **108,107,106,106,106 105,103,102,96,96**

toteswingers: 1&2 £3.10, 1&3 £6.20, 2&3 £53.00. CSF £9.97 TOTE £2.50: £1.40, £2.40, £4.30; EX 11.10.

Owner K Abdulla **Bred** Juddmonte Farms Ltd **Trained** Newmarket, Suffolk

■ The first winner for Sir Henry Cecil since the announcement of his knighthood.

FOCUS

A cracking renewal of this Listed fillies' event but the bare form is only ordinary for the grade. The time was under five seconds slower than standard, thanks largely to the modest early pace. The winner did not need to be at her best.

NOTEBOOK

Timepiece had somewhat disappointed in a Group 3 on Oaks day at Epsom, a track that doesn't appear to suit her. She had shown much better form on hear seasonal return prior to that behind stablemate Midday at York and had plenty of support here, justifiably so, given she'd already won three times at this level. Upped in trip after having plenty of use made of her last time, she jumped out well and settled early, always looking the likely winner from some way out. She had the far rail to run against and coped with the step up in trip well, but whether she can cope with this trip when upped in class again is open to question. This will have helped her confidence, nevertheless. (op 6-4 tchd 5-4 and 13-8 in places)

Sea Of Heartbreak(IRE) is nothing but consistent and appears at the top of her game this season. Always up with the pace, she stuck to her guns as she tried to close on the classy winner and gave her plenty to think about. She is not going to be easy to place this season, but deserves to win a nice prize. (tchd 15-2)

Ceilidh House was held up at the back of the field and was last turning in, but she made up plenty of ground and was never nearer than at the finish. She would have preferred more pace to aim at and needs a truly run affair to show her best. She does tend to run best when fresh and it remains to be seen if she will reproduce her best next time, but she gives the impression there is a good race to be won with her this season. (op 14-1 tchd 12-1)

Mirror Lake ran a game race. She hasn't had a lot of experience and she clearly benefited from her seasonal debut when fifth over an inadequate 1m1f at Newmarket on her reappearance last month. She still looks on an upward curve and this looks her trip. (op 5-1)

Piano was taking a step up in class and seemed to handle it well, though her run just flattened out in closing stages. She was quite free in the early stages, but is worth another crack at this level. (op 8-1 tchd 9-1)

2995 CRABBIE'S "STEADY ON" ALCOHOLIC GINGER BEER H'CAP — 7f 26y
8:10 (8:11) (Class 4) (0-85,85) 4-Y-0+ — **£4,079** (£1,214; £606; £303) Stalls Low

Form — RPR

22-0 **1** **Duster**[47] 1603 4-9-5 **83** .... DaneO'Neill 4 — 94
(Hughie Morrison) *a.p: chsd ldr 4f out: led over 1f out: rdn out* — **9/1**

31-3 **2** *1* **Amazing Star (IRE)**[44] 1696 6-8-7 **76** .... NeilFarley(5) 9 — 84+
(Declan Carroll) *hld up: hdwy over 1f out: sn rdn: r.o* — **8/1**

-545 **3** *1 1/2* **Spa's Dancer (IRE)**[5] 2822 4-9-0 **78** .... (p) SebSanders 6 — 82
(J W Hills) *mid-div: lost pl 4f out: hdwy u.p over 1f out: r.o* — **3/1**[1]

20/0 **4** *1 1/4* **Billion Dollar Kid**[14] 2557 6-8-10 **74** .... (t) JamesDoyle 2 — 75
(Joanna Davis) *chsd ldrs: rdn over 1f out: edgd rt and styd on same pce ins fnl f* — **25/1**

1412 **5** *3/4* **Unlimited**[42] 1804 9-8-4 **68** .... LiamJones 14 — 67
(Tony Carroll) *prom: racd keenly: rdn over 1f out: styd on same pce ins fnl f* — **16/1**

0060 **6** *1* **Glenridding**[16] 2495 7-8-10 **79** .... (p) DaleSwift(5) 3 — 75
(James Given) *chsd ldr 3f: remained handy: rdn over 1f out: no ex ins fnl f* — **10/1**

6-00 **7** *nk* **Kings Bayonet**[11] 2647 4-8-10 **74** .... TomQueally 5 — 69
(Alan King) *s.i.s: hdwy u.p over 1f out: no ex ins fnl f* — **11/1**

-400 **8** *nk* **Santefisio**[11] 2647 5-9-4 **82** .... PatDobbs 8 — 77
(Peter Makin) *hld up: rdn over 1f out: n.d* — **11/2**[2]

0-03 **9** *1/2* **Aultcharn (FR)**[11] 2653 4-8-9 **73** .... ShaneKelly 10 — 66
(Brian Meehan) *led: rdn and hdd over 1f out: wknd and eased ins fnl f* — **11/1**

-240 **10** *1 1/4* **Masai Moon**[18] 2441 7-9-7 **85** .... JamesMillman 12 — 75
(Rod Millman) *chsd ldrs: rdn over 2f out: wknd fnl f* — **13/2**[3]

-064 **11** *2* **Ghostwing**[27] 2169 4-9-4 **82** .... (v) ChrisCatlin 7 — 66
(John Gallagher) *hld up: a in rr: rdn and wknd over 1f out* — **14/1**

1m 24.59s (-0.01) **Going Correction** +0.125s/f (Good) — **11** Ran SP% **117.0**
Speed ratings (Par 105): **105,103,102,100,99 98,98,98,97,96 93**
toteswingers: 1&2 £15.50, 1&3 £5.30, 2&3 £3.80. CSF £78.69 CT £275.19 TOTE £11.30: £3.30, £2.40, £1.70; EX 91.20.
Owner M T Bevan **Bred** Paddock Space **Trained** East Ilsley, Berks

FOCUS
A decent handicap for modest prize-money and run at a sporadic pace, initially quick, then steady during the middle part. It helped those who were to the fore. A length personal best from the winner.

2996 ELIZA DOOLITTLE AFTER RACING ON AUGUST 23RD H'CAP — 1m 2f 188y
8:40 (8:46) (Class 6) (0-65,64) 4-Y-0+ — **£2,047** (£604; £302) Stalls Low

Form — RPR

003- **1** **Command Marshal (FR)**[338] 3896 8-9-1 **58** .... TomQueally 5 — 66
(Ed de Giles) *mde all: rdn and hung lft ins fnl f: styd on wl* — **12/1**

0635 **2** *2 1/4* **Hits Only Jude (IRE)**[14] 2548 8-8-12 **60** .... (v) NeilFarley(5) 2 — 64
(Declan Carroll) *a.p: rdn to chse wnr over 1f out: styd on same pce ins fnl f* — **4/1**[3]

0600 **3** *2* **Beetuna (IRE)**[74] 1058 6-9-6 **63** .... FrankieMcDonald 6 — 63
(David Bourton) *chsd wnr: rdn over 1f out: rdr dropped whip sn after: styd on same pce* — **11/1**

45-6 **4** *shd* **Supa Seeker (USA)**[28] 2150 5-9-7 **64** .... SebSanders 8 — 64
(Tony Carroll) *a.p: rdn and hung lft fr over 1f out: styd on same pce* — **7/2**[2]

4635 **5** *2* **Waahej**[47] 1608 5-9-6 **63** .... ChrisCatlin 10 — 59
(Peter Hiatt) *hld up: hdwy over 4f out: rdn over 2f out: no ex fnl f* — **3/1**[1]

143 **6** *hd* **Madame Boot (FR)**[47] 1604 4-9-2 **59** .... PatDobbs 7 — 55
(Peter Makin) *hld up: rdn over 1f out: nvr trbld ldrs* — **9/2**

444- **7** *3 1/4* **Only You Maggie (IRE)**[290] 5474 4-9-2 **64** .... MarkCoumbe(5) 1 — 54
(Gary Harrison) *hld up: rdn over 2f out: a in rr* — **20/1**

0030 **8** *3 1/4* **Warrior Nation (FR)**[28] 2140 5-8-0 **46** ow1 .... LouisBeuzelin(3) 4 — 29
(Adrian Chamberlain) *s.i.s: racd keenly and sn prom: rdn: hung lft and wknd over 1f out* — **16/1**

2m 24.31s (3.21) **Going Correction** +0.125s/f (Good) — **8** Ran SP% **112.1**
Speed ratings (Par 101): **93,91,89,89,88 88,85,83**
toteswingers: 1&2 £3.90, 1&3 £12.80, 2&3 £6.00. CSF £57.08 CT £545.83 TOTE £12.20: £1.50, £1.90, £3.70; EX 57.60.
Owner E B De Giles **Bred** Werner Wolf **Trained** Ledbury, Herefordshire
■ The first training success for Ed De Giles.

FOCUS
A modest handicap, run at a crawl, which turned into a 3f sprint. Not many got involved and the form has been rated negatively.
T/Plt: £289.50 to a £1 stake. Pool:£56,947.89 - 143.55 winning tickets. T/Qpdt: £45.00 to a £1 stake. Pool:£5,575.91 - 91.66 winning tickets. CR

2767 WINDSOR (R-H)
Monday, June 13

OFFICIAL GOING: Good (good to soft in places; 7.1)
Stands' rail dolled out 15yds at 6f and 7yds at winning post. Top bend dolled out 7yds from normal configuration adding 27yds to races of 1m and over.
Wind: Fresh, behind Weather: Fine

2997 IRISH STALLION FARMS EBF MAIDEN STKS — 5f 10y
6:00 (6:02) (Class 5) 2-Y-0 — **£3,238** (£963; £481; £240) Stalls Low

Form — RPR

62 **1** **Red Art (IRE)**[18] 2409 2-9-3 0 .... MichaelHills 3 — 85+
(B W Hills) *trckd ldng pair: led 2f out: pushed along and drew clr over 1f out* — **11/4**[1]

5 **2** *4 1/2* **Amis Reunis**[9] 2718 2-8-12 0 .... RichardHughes 11 — 64+
(Richard Hannon) *restless stalls: prom but sn pushed along: effrt 2f out: rdn to take 2nd jst ins fnl f: no ch w wnr* — **11/4**[1]

3 *3/4* **Billyrayvalentine (CAN)** 2-9-3 0 .... TonyCulhane 10 — 66+
(George Baker) *chsd ldrs in 6th: shkn up 2f out: rdn and kpt on to take 3rd nr fin* — **9/2**[2]

4 *hd* **Absent Amy (IRE)** 2-8-12 0 .... JamieMackay 8 — 60+
(Willie Musson) *s.i.s: rn green in rr: prog on outer over 1f out: styd on and nrly snatched 3rd* — **100/1**

0 **5** *hd* **Clarkson (IRE)**[11] 2644 2-9-3 0 .... FergusSweeney 5 — 65
(Jamie Osborne) *in tch in 8th: prog 2f out: rdn and kpt on same pce fnl f* — **16/1**

330 **6** *1 1/2* **Lord Ali McJones**[28] 2143 2-9-3 0 .... RussKennemore 9 — 59
(Tom Dascombe) *led to 2f out: lost 2nd jst ins fnl f: wknd* — **14/1**

7 *shd* **Emerald Smile (IRE)** 2-8-12 0 .... CathyGannon 1 — 54
(J S Moore) *taken down early and ponied to s: chsd ldr to jst over 2f out: rn green and wkng whn short of room briefly over 1f out* — **40/1**

8 *3/4* **Son Du Silence (IRE)** 2-9-3 0 .... AdamKirby 2 — 56
(J S Moore) *s.i.s: rcvrd and sn in tch in 7th: no prog over 1f out: fdd* — **28/1**

46 **9** *2 1/4* **Karuga**[38] 1846 2-8-12 0 .... JimmyFortune 12 — 43
(Richard Hannon) *racd on outer in rr: no prog 2f out: fdd over 1f out* — **9/1**

10 *1 3/4* **Fugitive Motel (IRE)** 2-9-3 0 .... RyanMoore 6 — 42
(Richard Hannon) *outpcd and sn wl bhd: nvr a factor: kpt on fnl f* — **7/1**[3]

3 **11** *1 1/2* **Joe M**[18] 2423 2-9-3 0 .... NeilCallan 4 — 36
(Simon Dow) *spd to 1/2-way: sn wknd* — **66/1**

12 *4 1/2* **Laura's Bairn** 2-9-3 0 .... EddieAhern 7 — 20
(J R Jenkins) *green preliminaries: v s.i.s: rn v green and virtually t.o in last 1/2-way: kpt on* — **33/1**

60.42 secs (0.12) **Going Correction** +0.05s/f (Good) — **12** Ran SP% **117.9**
Speed ratings (Par 93): **101,93,92,92,91 89,89,88,84,81 79,71**
toteswingers: 1&2 £1.80, 1&3 £4.80, 2&3 £4.30. CSF £9.36 TOTE £3.90: £1.20, £1.60, £1.30; EX 11.90 Trifecta £37.00 Pool: £4,726.55 - 94.35 winning units..
Owner Des Anderson & R J Arculli **Bred** H Q Spooner **Trained** Lambourn, Berks

FOCUS
They raced stands' side. Probably not a strong maiden.

NOTEBOOK
Red Art(IRE) was much the best, improving on the form he showed on his first two starts. The ease in the ground suited and he should be contesting some reasonable nurseries in due course. (op 10-3 tchd 7-2)
Amis Reunis was the choice of Richard Hughes over two other Richard Hannon runners and improved on a moderate debut. She got set upset in the stalls, but calmed down soon enough. In the race itself she rather ran in snatches early and was off the bridle before halfway, so she can be expected to progress again, but she looks nothing out of the ordinary. (op 5-2 tchd 3-1)
Billyrayvalentine(CAN) took the eye on pedigree, being a £105,000 half-brother to Careless Jewel, a Grade 1 scorer over 1m2f on dirt in the US, but there had to be a doubt about how he'd cope with easy turf. Solid in the market but by no means heavily backed, he ran okay and might have been slightly closer with more room in the closing stages. He can probably do better on a sounder surface. (op 5-1)
Absent Amy(IRE) cost only 2,500gns but she's a half-sister to three winners and showed ability, doing her best work at the finish having been pushed along early. She can improve and should stay further. (tchd 80-1)
Clarkson(IRE) didn't improve significantly on his Sandown debut and looks more of a nursery type. (op 14-1)
Karuga Official explanation: jockey said, regarding running and riding, his instructions were to do his best in the race, adding filly started from an unfavourable draw and raced flat out from the start. He added the filly appears genuine but moderate.

2998 SPORTINGBET.COM (S) STKS — 6f
6:30 (6:31) (Class 5) 2-Y-0 — **£2,266** (£674; £337; £168) Stalls Low

Form — RPR

3022 **1** **Aquasulis (IRE)**[3] 2889 2-8-6 0 .... CathyGannon 7 — 60
(David Evans) *led: rdn over 2f out: hdd ins fnl f: hung lft but rallied to ld last strides* — **3/1**[1]

54 **2** *hd* **Emma Jean (IRE)**[6] 2788 2-8-1 0 .... RyanPowell(5) 10 — 59
(J S Moore) *hld up at rr of main gp: plld out wd and prog over 2f out: clsd to ld ins fnl f: hung lft after: hdd last strides* — **4/1**[2]

50 **3** *10* **Aljosan**[44] 1691 2-8-6 0 .... MartinLane 9 — 29
(David Evans) *pressed wnr to jst over 2f out: wl outpcd fr over 1f out* — **33/1**

455 **4** *1 1/4* **First Rebellion**[46] 1632 2-8-11 0 .... NeilCallan 11 — 31
(Tony Carroll) *trckd ldng trio: rdn over 2f out: lft wl bhd fr over 1f out* — **16/1**

2110 **5** *2 1/2* **Miss Muga**[9] 2712 2-8-11 0 .... EddieCreighton 5 — 23
(Edward Creighton) *sn pushed along in rr and unable to go the pce: modest prog u.p 2f out: no threat* — **14/1**

4623 **6** *1* **Sea Poet**[4] 2854 2-8-11 0 .... JimmyFortune 3 — 20
(Andrew Haynes) *chsd ldrs: prog against rail to chal over 2f out: wknd wl over 1f out* — **8/1**

4321 **7** *2 1/4* **Selinda**[13] 2595 2-8-11 0 .... RyanMoore 12 — 13
(Mick Channon) *chsd ldrs: cl enough over 2f out: wknd wl over 1f out* — **15/2**[3]

060 **8** *1* **Jettie**[28] 2153 2-8-6 0 .... RoystonFfrench 1 — 5
(David Evans) *s.i.s: rdn in rr over 4f out: nvr on terms* — **100/1**

9 *shd* **Masters Club** 2-8-11 0 .... JackMitchell 2 — 10
(John Ryan) *s.s: outpcd and wl bhd in last pair: nvr a factor* — **25/1**

444 **10** *shd* **Indian Lizzy**[21] 2362 2-8-6 0 .... HayleyTurner 4 — 5
(Paul Cole) *trckd ldrs: gng strly 1/2-way: wknd rapidly 2f out* — **9/1**

04 **11** *9* **Thefillyfromsutton**[18] 2425 2-8-1 0 .... JemmaMarshall(5) 8 — —
(Pat Phelan) *pressed ldng pair to 1/2-way: wknd v rapidly: t.o* — **66/1**

12 *45* **June Thirteen (IRE)** 2-8-11 0 .... RichardHughes 6 — —
(Richard Hannon) *s.s: rn v green and sn t.o: hung to far rail and allowed to coast home fr 1/2-way* — **4/1**[2]

1m 13.87s (0.87) **Going Correction** +0.05s/f (Good) — **12** Ran SP% **119.7**
Speed ratings (Par 93): **96,95,82,80,77 76,73,71,71,71 59,—**
toteswingers: 1&2 £3.80, 1&3 £20.10, 2&3 £44.10. CSF £14.53 TOTE £3.20: £1.80, £1.40, £10.70; EX 20.60 Trifecta £512.10 Pool: £4,498.91 - 6.50 winning units..The winner was bought in for £9,200. Emma Jean was the subject of a friendly claim.
Owner Bathwick Gold Partnership **Bred** Rathasker Stud **Trained** Pandy, Monmouths

FOCUS
The field raced stands' side for much of the straight, but the front two ended up far side in the closing stages. They finished well clear.

NOTEBOOK
Aquasulis(IRE) finished second in a stronger seller at York three days earlier and she went one better in gutsy fashion, her first win at the sixth attempt. She went left under pressure late on, but did well to sustain her challenge considering she had helped set a good pace and the runner-up came from further behind. Her connections bought her back at the auction for £9,000. (op 11-4 tchd 7-2)
Emma Jean(IRE), dropped in class, couldn't match the winner for early speed but she picked up well when taken widest with her challenge and was only just worried out of it, perhaps being a bit intimidated by the more battle-hardened winner, who carried her a bit left. She was a long way clear of the others and can win a similar race. (op 11-2 tchd 6-1)
Aljosan showed early speed but was beaten a long way. (op 25-1)
Selinda made all for a wide-margin success at this level (6f, good to firm) at Yarmouth two weeks earlier, but she couldn't dominate this time and Ryan Moore was looking down from over a furlong out, presumably feeling as though something was amiss. Official explanation: jockey said filly moved poorly (op 6-1)

June Thirteen(IRE), named after the date on which he was making his debut, represented a trainer with a fine record in the race (won last three runnings), but he was weak in the market and showed nothing. He lost several lengths at the start and was eased off. Official explanation: jockey said bit pulled through colts mouth (tchd 9-2)

2999 THANK YOU AND GOOD LUCK GEMMA CHARRINGTON H'CAP — 1m 67y

7:00 (7:00) (Class 5) (0-75,75) 4-Y-0+ **£2,266** (£674; £337; £168) **Stalls** Low

Form — RPR

61-1 **1** **Rustic Deacon**[160] 30 4-9-4 **72** ... RichardHughes 14 — 82+
(Willie Musson) *sn trckd ldr: led 2f out gng easily: shkn up whn pressed jst over 1f out: rdn out last 100yds: a holding on* **7/2**[2]

-000 **2** *nk* **Marjury Daw (IRE)**[14] 2545 5-9-7 **75** ... JimmyFortune 13 — 82
(James Given) *trckd ldrs in 6th: prog on outer 2f out: hrd rdn to chal fnl f: styd on* **12/1**

0346 **3** *hd* **Miss Bootylishes**[26] 2198 6-8-10 **67** ... JohnFahy(3) 9 — 74
(Paul Burgoyne) *trckd ldng trio: rdn to go 2nd wl over 1f out: tried to chal u.p after: a hld* **16/1**

0-51 **4** *3/4* **Prince Of Sorrento**[7] 2771 4-8-13 **67** 6ex ... TedDurcan 6 — 72+
(John Akehurst) *sn restrained bhd ldng pair: tried to chal against rail 2f out but tight for room: tried again fnl f: styd on but all too late* **2/1**[1]

10-5 **5** *1 1/4* **Rosedale**[24] 2269 4-9-2 **70** ... RoystonFfrench 8 — 72+
(James Toller) *s.s and rousted along early in last pair: effrt on outer 3f out: drvn and sme prog fr 2f out: nvr able to rch ldrs* **8/1**[3]

5-60 **6** *1 1/4* **Mishrif (USA)**[5] 2822 5-9-5 **73** ... IanMongan 1 — 73
(J R Jenkins) *hld up in 8th: rdn over 2f out: no real prog* **9/1**

3-00 **7** *2* **Skyfire**[97] 799 4-9-7 **75** ... PatCosgrave 4 — 70
(Ed de Giles) *hld up in last: stl in last pair over 2f out: pushed along over 1f out: rdn and styd on fnl f: nvr nr ldrs* **33/1**

14-0 **8** *1 1/4* **Flag Of Glory**[86] 908 4-9-4 **72** ... GeorgeBaker 7 — 64
(Chris Wall) *led to 2f out: steadily wknd* **12/1**

-000 **9** *1 1/2* **L'Hirondelle (IRE)**[11] 2647 7-9-5 **73** ... NeilCallan 2 — 62
(Michael Attwater) *trckd ldrs in 5th: rdn over 2f out and no prog: fdd over 1f out* **25/1**

240- **10** *4* **Sweet Secret**[222] 7305 4-8-12 **66** ... HayleyTurner 3 — 45
(Jeremy Gask) *t.k.h: hld up in midfield: rdn over 2f out: sn lost pl and btn* **10/1**

0100 **11** *6* **Big Bay (USA)**[23] 2301 5-9-2 **70** ... AndreaAtzeni 5 — 36
(Jane Chapple-Hyam) *pushed along in rr bef 1/2-way: sn struggling* **33/1**

1m 46.27s (1.57) **Going Correction** +0.275s/f (Good) **11** Ran SP% **116.8**
Speed ratings (Par 103): **103,102,102,101,100 99,97,96,94,90 84**
toteswingers: 1&2 £11.70, 1&3 £17.30, 2&3 £44.40. CSF £43.84 CT £457.54 TOTE £5.40: £2.30, £3.70, £4.10; EX 48.10 Trifecta £1470.90 Pool: £2,782.92 - 1.40 winning units..
Owner Mrs Rita Brown **Bred** P V Jackson **Trained** Newmarket, Suffolk

FOCUS
They raced stands' side. This looked a decent race for the grade, and the winner was value for a bit extra, but not many got involved.
Rosedale ◆ Official explanation: jockey said filly missed the break

3000 SPORTINGBET.COM H'CAP — 6f

7:30 (7:31) (Class 4) (0-85,85) 4-Y-0+ **£3,885** (£867; £867; £288) **Stalls** Low

Form — RPR

-405 **1** **We Have A Dream**[5] 2826 6-9-3 **81** ... MartinDwyer 1 — 90
(William Muir) *racd against rail: w ldr: rdn over 2f out: edgd lft fnl f: r.o to ld last strides* **16/1**

-015 **2** *hd* **Victorian Bounty**[24] 2244 6-9-3 **81** ... NeilCallan 15 — 89
(Stef Higgins) *mde most in narrow ld: hdd ins fnl f: styd on u.p: jst hld* **16/1**

2031 **2** *dht* **Apache Ridge (IRE)**[7] 2765 5-8-7 **74** 6ex ... (p) MartinHarley(3) 13 — 82
(Keith Dalgleish) *racd on outer: trckd ldrs: rdn to chal fnl f: narrow ld ins fnl f: hdd last strides* **8/1**[3]

601 **4** *3/4* **Ginger Ted (IRE)**[19] 2397 4-9-7 **85** ... (p) J-PGuillambert 7 — 91+
(Richard Guest) *towards rr: hmpd and snatched up wl over 3f out: effrt u.p over 2f out: styd on: nrst fin* **8/1**[3]

1236 **5** *nk* **Maze (IRE)**[13] 2597 6-8-10 **77** ... MichaelO'Connell(3) 5 — 82
(Tony Carroll) *taken down early: pressed ldrs: poised to chal gng strly over 2f out: rdn and nrly upsides over 1f out: nt qckn fnl f* **16/1**

1326 **6** *3/4* **New Leyf (IRE)**[31] 2061 5-9-4 **82** ... RyanMoore 6 — 84
(Jeremy Gask) *towards rr: effrt over 2f out: rdn in midfield over 1f out: kpt on but nt pce to threaten* **11/4**[1]

0-40 **7** *shd* **Kings 'n Dreams**[12] 2610 4-8-3 **67** ... (b) WilliamCarson 11 — 69
(Dean Ivory) *wl in tch in midfield: rdn and nt qckn 2f out: kpt on again fnl f* **25/1**

4-50 **8** *nk* **Cardinal**[110] 651 6-8-12 **76** ... HayleyTurner 3 — 77
(Robert Cowell) *stdd s: hld up wl in rr: hanging lft and reminders wl over 1f out: kpt on fnl f: nvr on terms* **20/1**

3100 **9** *hd* **Silver Wind**[14] 2557 6-8-13 **77** ... (v) AdamKirby 2 — 77
(Alan McCabe) *trckd ldrs against rail: pushed along 1/2-way: nt qckn 2f out: one pce after* **20/1**

-000 **10** *1 1/4* **Olynard (IRE)**[9] 2717 5-9-5 **83** ... (v[1]) RichardHughes 12 — 79
(Dr Richard Newland) *hld up wl in rr: pushed along on wd outside 2f out: no imp on ldrs 1f out: fdd* **14/1**

4-45 **11** *5* **Aye Aye Digby (IRE)**[27] 2169 6-9-4 **82** ... EddieAhern 10 — 62
(Patrick Chamings) *w ldrs over 3f: sn lost pl and btn* **10/1**

-100 **12** *1/2* **Diriculous**[74] 1067 7-9-2 **80** ... JimmyFortune 14 — 59
(Robert Mills) *s.s: a wl in rr: rdn and no prog over 2f out* **25/1**

040 **P** **Poppanan (USA)**[11] 2645 5-8-10 **77** ... AdamBeschizza(3) 9 — —
(Simon Dow) *prom: broke down after 2f and p.u: fatally injured* **13/2**[2]

20-0 **P** **Slip Sliding Away (IRE)**[23] 2288 4-9-0 **81** ... JohnFahy(3) 8 — —
(Peter Hedger) *dwlt: last whn lost action and p.u after 2f: lame bhd* **14/1**

1m 12.48s (-0.52) **Going Correction** +0.05s/f (Good) **14** Ran SP% **119.5**
Speed ratings (Par 105): **105,104,104,103,103 102,102,101,101,99 93,92,—,—**toteswingers: 1&VB £55.70, 1&AR £11.90, VB&AR £13.90. PLACES: £7.40, VB £6.50, AR £2.70. CSF: We Have A Dream & VB £117.52, WHAD & AR £65.20. EXACTA: WHAD & VB £118.50, WHAD & AR £80.00. TRICAST: WHAD, VB & AR £1,127.02, WHAD, VB & AR £1,070.85. CT £0.0027 TOTE £Owner: £The Dreaming Squires, £Bred, £Whitsbury Manor Stud, £TrainedLambourn, Berks.

FOCUS
It paid to be handy and this looks like ordinary form for the class. Not many got involved. The winner is rated to last year's latter form. They raced towards the stands' side for much of the straight, but were well spread out at the line.
Ginger Ted(IRE) ◆ Official explanation: jockey said gelding was denied a clear run
Slip Sliding Away(IRE) Official explanation: jockey said gelding was lame

3001 VESTRA WEALTH MANAGEMENT MAIDEN STKS — 1m 2f 7y

8:00 (8:02) (Class 5) 3-Y-0+ **£2,266** (£674; £337; £168) **Stalls** Centre

Form — RPR

3 **1** **Highland Castle**[11] 2648 3-9-0 0 ... AdamKirby 8 — 83+
(David Elsworth) *trckd ldrs in 5th: rdn to ld jst over 2f out: drvn and kpt on wl fnl f* **4/1**[2]

2 *nk* **Gatewood** 3-9-0 0 ... NickyMackay 7 — 82+
(John Gosden) *trckd ldrs in 6th: outpcd fr 3f out: rdn and renewed effrt 2f out: styd on wl to take 2nd ins fnl f: clsd on wnr: jst hld* **7/1**

04 **3** *2* **Golden Slipper**[17] 2457 3-8-9 0 ... NeilCallan 2 — 73
(Chris Wall) *trckd ldng trio: moved up on inner to chal over 2f out: upsides wl over 1f out: nt qckn fnl f* **25/1**

0 **4** *nse* **Suzi's A Class Act**[17] 2469 3-8-9 0 ... JackMitchell 15 — 73
(James Eustace) *led: rdn and hdd jst over 2f out: sn sltly outpcd: kpt on again fnl f* **40/1**

22 **5** *3 1/2* **Sir Francis Drake**[12] 2621 3-9-0 0 ... AhmedAjtebi 5 — 71
(Mahmood Al Zarooni) *trckd ldng pair: rdn to chal and upsides jst over 2f out: nt qckn: wknd fnl f* **2/1**[1]

3 **6** *2 1/2* **Kleitomachos (IRE)**[42] 1774 3-9-0 0 ... RichardHughes 13 — 66+
(Stuart Kittow) *settled in midfield: outpcd in abt 8th fr 3f out: pushed along and styd on quite takingly fnl 2f* **9/1**

7 *nse* **Proof (IRE)** 3-8-7 0 ... AntiocoMurgia(7) 4 — 66+
(Mahmood Al Zarooni) *dwlt: hld up in rr: sme prog on outer 4f out: sn outpcd: plugged on again fnl 2f* **25/1**

4- **8** *2* **Red Eyes**[304] 5033 3-9-0 0 ... MartinDwyer 9 — 62
(Brian Meehan) *pressed ldr to 3f out: wknd over 2f out* **11/2**[3]

9 *2 1/2* **Roubiliac (USA)** 4-9-13 0 ... JimmyFortune 14 — 57
(Paul Webber) *settled in midfield: shkn up 4f out: sn wl outpcd and btn* **12/1**

5 **10** *6* **Oculist**[7] 2760 3-9-0 0 ... FergusSweeney 3 — 45
(Jamie Osborne) *s.i.s: a in rr: rdn and bhd fr over 2f out* **66/1**

0 **11** *1 1/2* **Decana**[21] 2371 3-8-9 0 ... TravisBlock 10 — 37
(Hughie Morrison) *in tch in midfield: wkng whn bmpd on outer over 2f out* **66/1**

12 *nse* **So Wise (USA)** 3-9-0 0 ... (v[1]) RyanMoore 12 — 42
(Sir Michael Stoute) *t.k.h in midfield: outpcd 3f out: sn wknd* **14/1**

13 *5* **Farmers Hill** 3-9-0 0 ... WilliamCarson 6 — 32
(Mark Hoad) *dwlt: hld up in last: shkn up over 4f out: no prog: bhd after* **100/1**

-0 **14** *10* **Height Of Summer (IRE)**[13] 2596 3-8-9 0 ... TedDurcan 16 — —
(Chris Wall) *a in rr: lost tch fr 4f out: t.o* **100/1**

15 *40* **Imperial Unity (USA)** 3-9-0 0 ... IanMongan 1 — —
(Sir Henry Cecil) *hld up towards rr: pushed along over 4f out: wknd over 3f out: virtually p.u* **16/1**

2m 9.77s (1.07) **Going Correction** +0.275s/f (Good)
WFA 3 from 4yo 13lb **15** Ran SP% **126.6**
Speed ratings (Par 103): **106,105,104,104,101 99,99,97,95,90 89,89,85,77,45**
toteswingers: 1&2 £5.80, 1&3 £33.00, 2&3 £14.30. CSF £32.67 TOTE £6.40: £2.30, £3.50, £8.40; EX 38.50 TRIFECTA Not won..
Owner J Wotherspoon & W Harrison-Allan **Bred** John Wotherspoon **Trained** Newmarket, Suffolk

FOCUS
A fair maiden, although it proved difficult to come from well off the pace. The time was good, being 1.54 seconds quicker than the following Class 5 handicap won by the impressive Sim Sala Bim. The form is sound enough but only ordinary for the track.
Imperial Unity(USA) Official explanation: vet said colt had a breathing problem

3002 VESTRA WEALTH PRIVATE CLIENT H'CAP — 1m 2f 7y

8:30 (8:32) (Class 5) (0-70,70) 3-Y-0 **£2,266** (£674; £337; £168) **Stalls** Centre

Form — RPR

06-2 **1** **Sim Sala Bim**[105] 713 3-9-4 **67** ... WilliamCarson 8 — 80+
(Stuart Williams) *s.s: rousted along to catch up in rr: urged along and gd prog over 4f out to press ldrs over 3f out: led over 2f out: clr and in command over 1f out: won w plenty in hand* **15/8**

040- **2** *2 1/4* **Frederick William**[107] 7003 3-9-4 **67** ... FergusSweeney 9 — 72
(Peter Makin) *hld up towards rr: gng bttr than most but plenty to do whn ldrs drew clr 4f out: prog on outer 3f out: styd on to take 2nd ins fnl f: no ch w wnr* **20/1**

-600 **3** *1/2* **Atlas Shrugged (IRE)**[24] 2253 3-9-2 **65** ... (b) AdamKirby 14 — 69
(Clive Cox) *chsd ldrs: off the bridle by 1/2-way: responded to press and stl cl enough over 2f out: kpt on same pce* **14/1**

2230 **4** *2 3/4* **Kishanda**[14] 2550 3-8-13 **62** ... NickyMackay 15 — 61
(Hughie Morrison) *pressed ldr to over 2f out: fdd over 1f out* **14/1**

0-36 **5** *1 1/4* **Sixty Roses (IRE)**[35] 1951 3-9-2 **65** ... EddieAhern 7 — 61
(John Dunlop) *hld up in last pair: lost tch whn ldrs drew clr 4f out: shkn up 3f out: styd on steadily after: nrst fin* **9/2**[1]

6-53 **6** *1 1/4* **Adone (IRE)**[18] 2427 3-9-4 **67** ... (v) RyanMoore 13 — 61
(Sir Michael Stoute) *mde most to over 2f out: steadily wknd over 1f out* **11/2**[2]

-006 **7** *1 1/2* **Ringstead Bay (FR)**[25] 2226 3-8-12 **61** ... StevieDonohoe 12 — 52
(Ralph Beckett) *chsd ldrs: u.p fr 1/2-way: lft bhd 4f out: no hdwy after* **33/1**

3-14 **8** *1 3/4* **My Mate Jake (IRE)**[15] 2527 3-9-7 **70** ... JimmyFortune 6 — 57
(James Given) *pressed ldrs: rdn 4f out: steadily wknd fr over 2f out* **7/1**[3]

0-06 **9** *2 1/4* **Joe Strummer (IRE)**[42] 1774 3-9-2 **65** ... HayleyTurner 10 — 48+
(Michael Bell) *lost midfield pl 7f out: rdn in rr 4f out: no ch after: modest late prog* **8/1**

4-30 **10** *1 1/2* **Sky Diamond (IRE)**[142] 260 3-8-8 **62** ... JamesO'Reilly(5) 5 — 42
(James Given) *hld up in rr: lft bhd fr over 4f out: shkn up 3f out and threatened a little prog: fdd fnl 2f* **16/1**

U-06 **11** *1 1/4* **Red Lite (IRE)**[14] 2550 3-9-0 **63** ... EddieCreighton 1 — 40
(Brian Meehan) *t.k.h: hld up last: lft bhd fr 4f out: no ch after* **25/1**

1-45 **12** *13* **Night Witch (IRE)**[132] 379 3-9-2 **68** ... AlanCreighton(3) 2 — 19
(Edward Creighton) *chsd ldrs: drvn over 4f out: wknd u.p after* **66/1**

040- **13** *9* **Piccarello**[281] 5784 3-9-1 **69** ... AshleyMorgan(5) 4 — —
(Mark H Tompkins) *towards rr whn hmpd 7f out: lost tch 4f out: pushed along and wknd after: eased* **20/1**

2106 **14** *6* **Tagansky**[35] 1949 3-9-2 **65** ... NeilCallan 11 — —
(Simon Dow) *w ldng pair to over 3f out: wknd rapidly: eased and t.o* **16/1**

2m 11.31s (2.61) **Going Correction** +0.275s/f (Good) **14** Ran SP% **111.8**
Speed ratings (Par 99): **100,98,97,95,94 93,92,91,89,88 87,76,69,64**
toteswingers: 1&2 £50.40, 1&3 £25.50, 2&3 £44.10. CSF £140.16 CT £1757.55 TOTE £6.80: £2.20, £6.40, £5.40; EX 129.60 TRIFECTA Not won..
Owner A Atkins **Bred** Old Mill Stud **Trained** Newmarket, Suffolk

FOCUS
A modest contest, rated around the third, but a progressive winner who was value for further. The impression was they went a good pace (winner, runner-up and fifth all well behind early) and perhaps the gallop was overly strong as the time was somewhat surprisingly 1.54 seconds slower than the earlier maiden won by Highland Castle.

3003 VESTRAWEALTH.COM H'CAP — 1m 3f 135y
9:00 (9:00) (Class 5) (0-70,68) 4-Y-O+ — **£2,266** (£674; £337; £168) **Stalls** Centre

Form / RPR

0-44 **1** **Choral Festival**[7] 2759 5-8-7 **59** HarryBentley(5) 1 — 68
(John Bridger) *hld up in midfield: stdy prog over 3f out: chsd ldr over 1f out: rdn to ld ins fnl f: kpt on* **6/1**[3]

0-26 **2** ½ **Marju King (IRE)**[23] 2312 5-9-3 **64** (b[1]) FergusSweeney 9 — 72
(Stuart Kittow) *prom: trckd ldr 4f: led over 2f out: drvn over 1f out: hdd and nt qckn ins fnl f* **13/2**

1231 **3** 3¼ **Broughtons Paradis (IRE)**[21] 2372 5-9-4 **65** StevieDonohoe 3 — 67
(Willie Musson) *hld up in last trio: prog on outer fr over 2f out: styd on to take 3rd ins fnl f: nvr able to chal* **7/2**[1]

0600 **4** 2¼ **It's Dubai Dolly**[23] 2308 5-8-9 **56** (b[1]) MartinDwyer 7 — 55
(Alastair Lidderdale) *led and clr: stdd pce over 6f out: kicked on again over 4f out: hdd over 2f out: reminders and steadily outpcd* **16/1**

0024 **5** 1¼ **The Lock Master (IRE)**[17] 2475 4-9-7 **68** NeilChalmers 11 — 65
(Michael Appleby) *trckd ldrs early: lost pl completely 7f out: last over 4f out: stl there over 2f out: rdn and kpt on fnl 2f* **8/1**

1065 **6** 1¾ **Squad**[17] 2473 5-9-5 **66** (v) NeilCallan 4 — 60
(Simon Dow) *hld up towards rr: rdn and no prog over 3f out: modest late hdwy* **16/1**

1/46 **7** ½ **Shesha Bear**[31] 2055 6-8-11 **58** (b) RichardHughes 6 — 51
(Jonathan Portman) *prom: rdn over 3f out: nt qckn over 2f out: steadily fdd* **5/1**[2]

10-3 **8** 1½ **Rodrigo De Freitas (IRE)**[21] 2372 4-9-2 **63** (v) JimmyFortune 5 — 53
(Jim Boyle) *dwlt: in tch: nt qckn over 3f out: fdd fnl 2f* **8/1**

-301 **9** 3¾ **Robby Bobby**[14] 2562 6-9-1 **62** IanMongan 2 — 46
(Laura Mongan) *hld up in last trio: shkn up and no prog over 3f out: btn after* **17/2**

0-05 **10** 4 **Trecase**[12] 2608 4-8-5 **52** CathyGannon 8 — 29
(Tony Carroll) *chsd ldr to 4f out: losing pl whn short of room sn after: wknd* **33/1**

05P- **11** 7 **Spring Stock**[245] 6816 4-8-13 **60** WilliamCarson 10 — 25
(Brendan Powell) *dwlt: towards rr: brought wd and effrt 3f out: sn wknd qckly* **28/1**

2m 33.95s (4.45) **Going Correction** +0.275s/f (Good) **11 Ran SP% 117.4**
Speed ratings (Par 103): **96,95,93,92,91 90,89,88,86,83 78**
toteswingers: 1&2 £8.40, 1&3 £5.20, 2&3 £6.60. CSF £44.74 CT £158.61 TOTE £7.00: £2.40, £2.30, £1.60; EX 46.20 Trifecta £196.80 Pool: £611.80 - 2.30 winning units..
Owner Mrs Liz Gardner **Bred** Cheveley Park Stud Ltd **Trained** Liphook, Hants
■ Stewards' Enquiry : Stevie Donohoe caution: careless riding

FOCUS
They went a muddling pace and this is modest form.
T/Jkpt: Not won. T/Plt: £611.70 to a £1 stake. Pool:£103,075.83 - 123.00 winning tickets. T/Qpdt: £354.40 to a £1 stake. Pool:£6,825.69 - 14.25 winning tickets. JN

3004 - 3006a (Foreign Racing) - See Raceform Interactive

2337 COLOGNE (R-H)
Monday, June 13

OFFICIAL GOING: Turf: good

3007a OPPENHEIM-UNION-RENNEN (GROUP 2) (3YO) (TURF) — 1m 3f
4:20 (12:00) 3-Y-O
£51,724 (£18,103; £8,620; £4,310; £2,155; £1,293)

RPR

1 **Arrigo (GER)**[22] 2345 3-9-2 0 ADeVries 6 — 105
(J Hirschberger, Germany) *broke wl: racd keenly early on: checked at first turn: dropped towards rr to settle: in rr ent st: patiently rdn: mde move 1 1/2f out: qcknd wl ins fnl f to ld 50yds out* **2/1**[2]

2 nk **Ametrin (IRE)**[29] 3-9-2 0 FilipMinarik 1 — 104
(J Hirschberger, Germany) *sent to ld: nt handle first turn and swung wd but maintained ld: set gd pce: r.o wl in st to hold off all chals tl hdd fnl 50yds* **173/10**

3 1¾ **Gereon (GER)**[22] 2338 3-9-2 0 GeorgBocskai 5 — 101
(C Zschache, Germany) *racd on rail bhd ldrs: short of room in st: fin strly whn in clr to take 3rd but too late to chal for ld: unlucky* **7/5**[1]

4 nse **Saltas (GER)**[43] 1739 3-9-2 0 AStarke 4 — 101
(P Schiergen, Germany) *racd freely bhd ldr: mde early move in st to chal ldr: r.o wl but no answer to first two home in fnl f: ct for 3rd on line* **9/2**[3]

5 ½ **Theo Danon (GER)**[29] 3-9-2 0 ASuborics 7 — 100
(P Schiergen, Germany) *settled towards rr: mde move over 1 1/2f out in middle of trck: r.o but no threat to ldrs* **13/2**

6 1¾ **Sindaco (GER)**[29] 3-9-2 0 THellier 2 — 97
(W Hickst, Germany) *settled at rr of field: r.o in st but failed to threaten* **125/10**

7 hd **Ordensritter (GER)**[64] 3-9-2 0 HenkGrewe 8 — 97
(H Steinmetz, Germany) *settled at rr and nvr proved a factor in r* **41/1**

8 1¾ **Sundream (GER)**[29] 3-9-2 0 EPedroza 3 — 93
(A Wohler, Germany) *broke wl: a.p: chal early in st but wknd 2f out* **9/1**

2m 17.87s (-2.93) **8 Ran SP% 131.8**
WIN (incl. 10 euro stake): 30. PLACES: 13, 23, 13. SF: 308.
Owner Gestut Schlenderhan **Bred** Gestut Schlenderhan **Trained** Germany

2796 LONGCHAMP (R-H)
Monday, June 13

OFFICIAL GOING: Turf: good to soft

3008a LA COUPE (GROUP 3) (4YO+) (TURF) — 1m 2f
2:55 (12:00) 4-Y-O+ **£34,482** (£13,793; £10,344; £6,896; £3,448)

RPR

1 **Cirrus Des Aigles (FR)**[22] 2343 5-9-4 0 FranckBlondel 1 — 122
(Mme C Barande-Barbe, France) *led at mod pce on settling: qcknd 2f out: r.o wl whn chal ins fnl f: a in command* **11/10**[1]

2 ¾ **Announce**[21] 2373 4-8-13 0 MaximeGuyon 6 — 115
(A Fabre, France) *settled 4th on outside: rdn and qcknd wl 1f out: chal ldr ins fnl f: ev ch: no ex fnl 50yds: a hld* **3/1**[2]

3 2½ **Stacelita (FR)**[183] 7854 5-8-8 0 Christophe-PatriceLemaire 7 — 105
(J-C Rouget, France) *settled 5th: rdn 2f out: nt qckn: styd on wl fnl f: no threat to ldrs* **3/1**[2]

4 1 **One Clever Cat (IRE)**[21] 2373 5-8-8 0 FlavienPrat 3 — 103
(T Clout, France) *settled 4th on rail: rdn 2f out: nt qckn: styd on fnl f* **20/1**

5 1½ **Grand Tard (FR)**[19] 2408 5-8-11 0 FabienLefebvre 4 — 103
(Y-M Porzier, France) *settled in cl 2nd: rdn 2f out: no ex: r.o one pce fnl 1 1/2f* **11/1**[3]

6 3 **Zillione Beauty (FR)**[30] 5-8-8 0 (p) Pierre-CharlesBoudot 5 — 94
(Mme P Butel, France) *a in rr: rdn 2f out but no ex: nvr a factor* **12/1**

2m 7.66s (3.66) **6 Ran SP% 118.4**
WIN (incl. 1 euro stake): 2.10. PLACES: 1.20, 1.70. SF: 5.00.
Owner Jean-Claude-Alain Dupouy **Bred** Y Lelimouzin And B Deschamps **Trained** France

1883 ASCOT (R-H)
Tuesday, June 14

OFFICIAL GOING: Good (good to soft in places on round course; stands' side 9.2, centre 9.6, far side 9.0, rnd 8.1)
Rail on round course out 3m from inside line from 9f to home straight adding 6yds to Old Mile and 12yds to 5.00 race.
Weather: fine

3009 QUEEN ANNE STKS (BRITISH CHAMPIONS' SERIES) (GROUP 1) — 1m (S)
2:30 (2:30) (Class 1) 4-Y-O+
£141,925 (£53,800; £26,925; £13,425; £6,725; £3,375) **Stalls** Centre

Form / RPR

11-1 **1** **Canford Cliffs (IRE)**[31] 2101 4-9-0 127 RichardHughes 6 — 130+
(Richard Hannon) *stdd after s: t.k.h early: hld up in last trio: hdwy to trck ldrs ent fnl 2f: rdn to chal ent fnl f: led fnl 100yds: r.o wl* **11/8**[2]

11-1 **2** 1 **Goldikova (IRE)**[23] 2343 6-8-13 125 ow2 OlivierPeslier 1 — 126
(F Head, France) *trckd ldrs: hdwy to press ldr gng wl over 2f out: rdn to ld over 1f out: hrd pressed ent fnl f: drvn and battled on gamely tl hdd and no ex fnl 100yds: eased nr fin* **5/4**[1]

11-2 **3** 1¾ **Cityscape**[52] 1527 5-9-0 119 RyanMoore 3 — 123
(Roger Charlton) *hld up in tch in rr: rdn and effrt to chse ldrs wl over 1f out: drvn and pressed ldng pair 1f out: no ex and outpcd fnl 100yds* **14/1**

11-3 **4** 2¼ **Rio De La Plata (USA)**[10] 2713 6-9-0 120 FrankieDettori 7 — 118
(Saeed Bin Suroor) *stdd s: t.k.h early: hld up in last trio: smooth hdwy to ld over 2f out: rdn and hdd over 1f out: drvn ent fnl f: wknd fnl 150yds* **25/1**

0-10 **5** 6 **Ransom Note**[23] 2343 4-9-0 114 MichaelHills 5 — 104
(B W Hills) *chsd ldrs: niggled along after 2f: rdn and struggling ent fnl 2f: wknd over 1f out* **50/1**

0-44 **6** 5 **Cape Blanco (IRE)**[45] 1708 4-9-0 122 JamieSpencer 4 — 93
(A P O'Brien, Ire) *led tl drvn and hdd ent fnl 3f: sn dropped out u.p: wl bhd over 1f out* **8/1**[3]

2-04 **7** 6 **Flash Dance (IRE)**[23] 2343 5-8-11 104 MickaelBarzalona 2 — 76
(F Head, France) *chsd ldr tl led ent fnl 3f: hdd and dropped out qckly u.p over 2f out: wl bhd over 1f out* **100/1**

1m 38.38s (-2.22) **Going Correction** +0.10s/f (Good) course record **7 Ran SP% 111.1**
Speed ratings (Par 117): **115,114,112,110,104 99,93**
Tote Swingers: 1&2 £1.10, 1&3 £3.00, 2&3 £2.60 CSF £3.18 TOTE £2.10: £1.30, £1.10; EX 2.80.
Owner The Heffer Syndicate, M Tabor & D Smith **Bred** S And S Hubbard Rodwell **Trained** East Everleigh, Wilts
■ Stewards' Enquiry : Olivier Peslier £650: changed his boots after weighing out

FOCUS
Little doubt the ground was drying all the time on a hot, sunny day. GoingStick readings suggested the middle of the track was riding quickest - 9.6 - compared to 9.2 on the stands' side and 9.0 on the far side. The round course was 8.1. \n\x\x Arguably the most eagerly anticipated race of the week to kick things off, certainly the biggest clash, and, whilst in many respects it was a shame for it to be the first contest of the meeting, talk about starting with a bang. Apart from the 'big' two, last season's Irish Derby and Irish Champion Stakes winner Cape Blanco, dropping in trip, and three-time Group 1 winner Rio De La Plata, made it one of the stronger editions of the race in recent memory. The pace was always likely to be a good one. Canford Cliffs confirmed himself the leading older miler, matching his Sussex Stakes figure. The form is sound.

NOTEBOOK
Canford Cliffs(IRE) drew alongside Goldikova as the race for home really began and proved the stronger, finding plenty for pressure and asserting in the final 100 yards. Bidding to achieve a unique feat of winning on the opening day of the meeting for a third consecutive season, having taken the Coventry at two, and the St James's Palace Stakes last year, he was a ready winner of the Lockinge on last month's reappearance, and had pleased his trainer with a recent Kempton workout. Applying simple logic that he is a better horse than former stablemate Paco Boy, who almost toppled the mare in this a year ago, it was easy to see why he was initially made favourite to beat her, and in doing so he confirmed himself the best older miler in the world. Whether he'll get a chance to prove himself the best overall in a meeting with Frankel remains to be seen, but it'll be the Sussex Stakes again next, before a probable crack at the QEII back here in September. (tchd 6-5 and 6-4 in places)

Goldikova(IRE), a 13-time Group 1 winner (including this race last year) and the outstanding miler of recent times, did what was required when making a winning reappearance in the Prix d'Ispahan and good late support saw her spearhead the market at the off. Unlike a year ago, she had the presence of a pacemaker, but it probably did more to aid the winner than her, and despite travelling through the race with her usual exuberance, she was unable to fend off her younger rival. Crucially, however, Olivier Peslier was putting up 2lb overweight, which is frankly unforgiveable in a race of such importance, and in theory that would have entitled her to dead-heat with the winner. With that in mind, there's every reason to believe she's run to around her best. She'll now be given a short break and return to Deauville in August for the Prix Jacques Le Marois, with the ultimate aim being a fourth successive Breeders' Cup Mile. \n\x\x This was a huge effort by \bCityscape\p, a career-best by some way in fact. Although the ground was drying, there was enough moisture left in it not to inconvenience the son of Selkirk, who ideally likes it soft, and he briefly looked like joining in with the front pair over 1f out. Ultimately, though, he just lacked that extra touch of class to race on. This was only the 5-y-o's 11th start, and he can be expected to go where the ground dictates, with the Jacques Le Marois looking the obvious target. (op 6-4 tchd 13-8 in places)

Cityscape put up a career-best by some way. Although the ground was drying, there was enough moisture left in it not to inconvenience the son of Selkirk, who ideally likes it soft, and he briefly looked like joining in with the front pair over 1f out. Ultimately, though, he just lacked that extra touch of class to race on. This was only the 5-y-o's 11th start, and he can be expected to go where the ground dictates, with the Jacques Le Marois looking the obvious target. (op 12-1 tchd 16-1 in places)

Rio De La Plata(USA) was brought back to his best last season, winning five times, including twice at the top level in Italy. A satisfactory third on his reappearance in the Diomed at Epsom just ten days earlier (gave weight, got tired late on), the carpet-like surface would have been in his favour, and he made a most impressive mid-race move, but it turned out he'd fired his round too soon, and his run ultimately petered out. He's a likely candidate for end-of-season Group 1 honours abroad once more. (op 20-1)

Ransom Note made a successful debut in Group company by winning the Earl Of Sefton on his reappearance, but he failed to match that level down the field behind Goldikova in the Prix d'Ispahan and, although faring better, was one of the first under pressure and simply doesn't look up to this level. (op 66-1 tchd 80-1 in a place)

Cape Blanco(IRE) was viewed by many as a potential dark horse on this first try at 1m (three-time winner over 7f at two). He had a bit to prove after coming up short in both the Dubai World Cup and Prix Ganay this year, though, and despite taking them along at a good clip early, he was already under pressure and beaten when edging over towards the rail, and ultimately dropped right out. (tchd 9-1 and 10-1 in places)

Flash Dance(IRE) was in here to cut out the running for Goldikova, but she had to go plenty quick enough to get past early leader Cape Blanco.

3010 KING'S STAND STKS (BRITISH CHAMPIONS' SERIES & GLOBAL SPRINT CHALLENGE) (GROUP 1) 5f

3:05 (3:09) (Class 1) 3-Y-O+

£170,310 (£64,560; £32,310; £16,110; £8,070; £4,050) **Stalls** Centre

Form RPR

0432 **1** **Prohibit**[9] [2754] 6-9-4 113 ....(p) JimCrowley 14 121
(Robert Cowell) *hld up: hdwy over 2f out: r.o and edgd rt ins fnl f: gd run to ld towards fin* **7/1**

1-0 **2** ½ **Star Witness (AUS)**[94] 4-9-4 116 ....(t) StevenArnold 18 119
(Danny O'Brien, Australia) *hld up: hdwy over 2f out: hung rt fr over 1f out: r.o ins fnl f: gng on at fin* **6/1**[2]

3 ½ **Sweet Sanette (SAF)**[66] 6-9-1 106 ....(t) JamieSpencer 10 114
(A T Millard, Hong Kong) *unruly gng to post and walked down to s: displayed gd spd to press ldr: led jst over 2f out: hdd and no ex towards fin* **16/1**

10-0 **4** nk **Overdose**[24] [2297] 6-9-4 0 .... ASuborics 15 116
(Jozef Roszival, Hungary) *displayed gd spd and prom: rdn over 1f out: stl chalng ins fnl f: hld and styd on same pce fnl strides* **12/1**

-012 **5** 2 ¼ **War Artist (AUS)**[80] [996] 8-9-4 115 .... OlivierPeslier 7 108+
(Markus Klug, Germany) *towards rr: swtchd rt and hdwy over 2f out: swtchd rt again over 1f out and sn carried wd: r.o ins fnl f: gng on at fin* **12/1**

36-2 **6** shd **Kingsgate Native (IRE)**[24] [2297] 6-9-4 115 .... RyanMoore 8 107
(Sir Michael Stoute) *midfield: effrt and hdwy over 1f out: styd on to chse ldrs ins fnl f: nt pce to chal* **11/2**[1]

2120 **7** hd **Iver Bridge Lad**[45] [1687] 4-9-4 106 ....(b) MichaelO'Connell 13 107
(John Ryan) *towards rr: rdn over 1f out: prog ins fnl f: r.o towards fin: unable to rch ldrs* **25/1**

-031 **8** ½ **Sole Power**[24] [2297] 4-9-4 117 .... WMLordan 2 105
(Edward Lynam, Ire) *s.i.s: hld up: sn in midfield: trckd ldrs over 2f out: rdn over 1f out: styd on same pce ins fnl f* **13/2**[3]

-055 **9** 1 **Mar Adentro (FR)**[9] [2754] 5-9-4 106 ....(tp) JohanVictoire 4 101
(R Chotard, France) *towards rr: hdwy 2f out: rdn and swtchd rt over 1f out: no imp on ldrs: one pce fnl 50yds* **33/1**

11-0 **10** shd **Astrophysical Jet**[45] [1687] 4-9-1 110 .... GrahamGibbons 12 98
(Ed McMahon) *midfield: pushed along over 2f out: one pce and no imp ins fnl f* **12/1**

30/4 **11** ½ **Monsieur Chevalier (IRE)**[22] [2370] 4-9-4 109 .... RichardHughes 16 99+
(Richard Hannon) *bhd: rdn and swtchd rt over 1f out: kpt on ins fnl f: nvr gng pce to get competitive* **12/1**

/54- **12** shd **Bridgetown (USA)**[38] 4-9-4 108 .... JRVelazquez 11 99
(Todd Pletcher, U.S.A) *chsd ldrs: rdn and outpcd over 1f out: n.d after* **11/1**

13 ¾ **Holiday For Kitten (USA)**[52] [9040] 3-8-9 108 ....(bt) MESmith 17 91
(Wesley A Ward, U.S.A) *bhd: outpcd 2f out: nvr able to trble ldrs* **25/1**

0-05 **14** nk **Group Therapy**[24] [2297] 6-9-4 108 .... ShaneKelly 19 95
(David Barron) *towards rr: pushed along whn n.m.r under 2f out: nvr able to trble ldrs* **20/1**

050- **15** ½ **Arctic (IRE)**[225] [7278] 4-9-4 109 .... PShanahan 6 93
(Tracey Collins, Ire) *bhd: hdwy into midfield towards centre of trck over 2f out: no imp over 1f out: outpcd fnl f* **50/1**

0-10 **16** nse **Stone Of Folca**[24] [2297] 3-8-12 104 .... LukeMorris 9 91
(John Best) *midfield: u.p over 1f out: outpcd and n.d after* **66/1**

0-06 **17** 1 ¼ **Rose Blossom**[24] [2297] 4-9-1 106 ....(b1) PaulHanagan 5 86
(Richard Fahey) *displayed gd spd to ld: hdd jst over 2f out: wknd over 1f out* **40/1**

110- **18** nk **Swiss Diva**[254] [6608] 5-9-1 110 .... IoritzMendizabal 1 84
(David Elsworth) *chsd ldrs tl rdn and wknd over 1f out* **20/1**

1-10 **19** 5 **Tangerine Trees**[24] [2297] 6-9-4 107 ....(v) TomEaves 3 69
(Bryan Smart) *chsd ldrs: u.p 2f out: wknd over 1f out* **25/1**

59.50 secs (-1.70) **Going Correction** +0.10s/f (Good)
WFA 3 from 4yo+ 7lb **19** Ran SP% **130.4**
Speed ratings (Par 117): **112,111,110,109,106 106,105,105,103,103 102,102,101,100,99 99,97,97,89**
Tote Swingers: 1&2 £12.90, 1&3 £35.60, 2&3 £17.20 CSF £45.24 CT £696.95 TOTE £10.40: £3.30, £2.30, £9.20; EX 93.50 Trifecta £3385.70 Pool: £14,107.12 - 3.08 winning units..
Owner Dasmal, Rix, Barr, Morley, Mrs Penney **Bred** Juddmonte Farms Ltd **Trained** Six Mile Bottom, Cambs

■ Robert Cowell's first Group 1 winner, and Jim Crowley's first domestic Group 1 and first Royal Ascot winner.

FOCUS

This was as international a race as one could possibly get, with the 19 runners representing eight different countries. The field threatened to split into two early with a group of seven racing closer to the stands' rail, including the eventual winner, second and fourth, while the larger group of 12 started off more towards the centre, but the two groups had emerged before halfway. Unsurprisingly they went a scorching pace. However this wasn't a strong renewal and the time compared unfavourably with the Windsor Castle Stakes. The third holds down the form a little.

NOTEBOOK

Prohibit certainly isn't work-shy with this being his ninth start of the campaign, but his trainer had stated that he thrives on his racing and that was certainly borne out here. He also likes to come late off a strong pace and he was always going to get that in this race, a fact that punters must have latched on to as he was well backed before the off. Despite getting a little outpaced in the middle part of the contest, he took off approaching the last furlong and forged to the front around 30 yards from the line. A real 5f specialist, he may head for the Nunthorpe next. (op 12-1)

Star Witness(AUS) is a dual Group 1-winning sprinter in Australia though firmly put in his place on the three occasions he took on the great Black Caviar. Connections had been worried about the rain that had fallen leading up to the meeting, but the winning time suggests that the ground was certainly not soft. Held up in the nearside group, he finished strongly inside the last furlong but couldn't quite match the winner. He may turn out again in the Golden Jubilee on Saturday or wait for the July Cup. (tchd 7-1 and 8-1 in a place)

Sweet Sanette(SAF), who was getting 16lb from Sacred Kingdom when beating him a neck at Sha Tin last time, was very much on her toes beforehand and eventually had to be led to the start. She showed blinding speed before taking over in front at halfway and looked as though she would take plenty of catching, but she folded well inside the last furlong and was mugged in the last 30 yards. (op 14-1 tchd 20-1)

Overdose had carried all before him around Europe until losing his unbeaten record in a German Group 2 last August, while his performance in the Temple Stakes when behind five of today's rivals appeared to show his limitations, but despite getting warm beforehand he ran a blinder here, showing plenty of speed towards the nearside of the track and keeping on all the way to the line. (op 11-1)

War Artist(AUS), last seen narrowly beaten by J J The Jet Plane in the Al Quoz Sprint at Meydan in March, was making his debut for his new German yard. Held up in the far-side group, he ran on well towards the far side of the field, away from the main action, and fared best of those starting from single-figure draws. He should be able to win another Group sprint on the continent. (op 14-1 tchd 10-1)

Kingsgate Native(IRE), who was taken to post very early, was beaten less than a length by Sole Power in the Temple Stakes on his reappearance and turned that form around, but although he stayed on from the middle of the field he couldn't make much impression on the principals. This was his third appearance in this race and his record in it now reads 066. (op 7-1)

Iver Bridge Lad was struggling to go the early pace, but made up plenty of late ground. He has been successful in Listed company and may be able to find a lesser Group sprint in due course.

Sole Power showed that his 100-1 success in last season's Nunthorpe was no fluke when beating seven of today's rivals in the Temple Stakes at Haydock last month, but his trainer was worried about the rain that had fallen. A mid-race move came to little and he would probably have preferred rattling fast ground. (op 7-1)

Monsieur Chevalier(IRE) was a very smart 2-y-o, but missed the whole of last year with a pelvic injury. He made a fine comeback when fourth in a Windsor Listed event last month, but he seemed to find everything happening too quickly for him early here, though he did make up some late ground and seems to have retained plenty of ability. (op 14-1)

Bridgetown(USA) did show up for some of the way before weakening having become restless in the stalls. (op 12-1 tchd 10-1)

Holiday For Kitten(USA) was always struggling.

Rose Blossom went off far too quick in the first-time blinkers and paid the penalty.

3011 ST JAMES'S PALACE STKS (BRITISH CHAMPIONS' SERIES) (GROUP 1) (ENTIRE COLTS) 1m (R)

3:45 (3:47) (Class 1) 3-Y-O

£141,925 (£53,800; £26,925; £13,425; £6,725; £3,375) **Stalls** Low

Form RPR

1-11 **1** **Frankel**[45] [1686] 3-9-0 130 .... TomQueally 5 122+
(Sir Henry Cecil) *hld up in 4th: shkn up and chsd clr ldr 5f out: clsd on ldr and led ent fnl 3f: 6 l clr 2f out: sn rdn: coming bk to field qckly fnl 100yds: a holding on but all out nr fin: rdn out* **30/100**[1]

13-2 **2** ¾ **Zoffany (IRE)**[16] [2533] 3-9-0 115 .... RyanMoore 8 120
(A P O'Brien, Ire) *stdd and dropped in after s: hld up in rr: stl last over 2f out: hdwy u.p wl over 1f out: swtchd lft jst ins fnl f: r.o wl to chse wnr fnl 100yds: clsng after but nvr quite getting to wnr* **20/1**

1-21 **3** 1 ½ **Excelebration (IRE)**[23] [2338] 3-9-0 116 .... AdamKirby 1 117+
(Marco Botti) *awkward s: t.k.h early: hld up in midfield: hmpd over 4f out: rdn and effrt to chse clr wnr 2f out: hung rt u.p but styd on and clsng steadily on wnr ins fnl f: lost 2nd fnl 100yds* **10/1**[2]

-013 **4** hd **Neebras (IRE)**[19] [2440] 3-9-0 110 .... FrankieDettori 4 116
(Mahmood Al Zarooni) *taken direct to s: stdd s: hld up in last pair: rdn: hdwy and switching lft ent fnl 2f: pressing for placings 1f out: kpt on wl u.p fnl f but nvr a threat to wnr* **50/1**

115- **5** 3 ¼ **Dream Ahead (USA)**[241] [6924] 3-9-0 126 .... WilliamBuick 3 110
(David Simcock) *hld up in last trio: c wd and effrt wl over 2f out: pressing for placings but stl 5 l fr wnr whn edgd lft ent fnl f: hung rt and no prog jst ins fnl f: eased towards fin* **14/1**

1122 **6** 8 **Dubawi Gold**[24] [2324] 3-9-0 117 .... RichardHughes 7 90+
(Richard Hannon) *chsd ldrs: swtchd rt and wnt 3rd over 4f out: rdn and chsd clr wnr briefly ent fnl 2f: sn struggling and edging rt u.p: wknd over 1f out* **12/1**[3]

11-5 **7** nse **Wootton Bassett**[30] [2139] 3-9-0 120 .... PaulHanagan 9 90
(Richard Fahey) *hld up off the pce in midfield: rdn and struggling in 6th wl over 2f out: wknd 2f out* **12/1**[3]

8 13 **Grand Prix Boss (JPN)**[37] 3-9-0 114 .... MircoDemuro 6 60
(Yoshito Yahagi, Japan) *chsd clr ldr tl 5f out: modest 4th and struggling wl over 2f out: wknd ent fnl 2f: wl bhd and eased fnl f* **16/1**

4-20 **9** 15 **Rerouted (USA)**[45] [1686] 3-9-0 110 .... MichaelHills 2 26
(B W Hills) *led and sn wl clr: hdd ent fnl 3f: lost 2nd ent fnl 2f: lost pl rapidly and eased fr over 1f out: t.o* **66/1**

1m 39.24s (-1.46) **Going Correction** +0.20s/f (Good) **9** Ran SP% **122.2**
Speed ratings (Par 113): **115,114,112,112,109 101,101,88,73**
Tote Swingers: 1&2 £3.70, 1&3 £2.00, 2&3 £19.20 CSF £12.67 CT £37.26 TOTE £1.20: £1.02, £4.70, £2.40; EX 10.80 Trifecta £70.60 Pool: £45,611.01 - 477.52 winning units..
Owner K Abdulla **Bred** Juddmonte Farms Ltd **Trained** Newmarket, Suffolk

■ Stewards' Enquiry : Richard Hughes three-day ban: careless riding (Jun 28-30)

FOCUS

A fascinating renewal of the St James's Palace featuring the winners of 29 races between them and four of the nine runners were previous Group/Grade 1 winners, but all the attention was directed towards one horse. Frankel duly won, but was not as impressive as at Newmarket and the bare form was 10lb off his Guineas figure. The second and fourth are rated up 5lb, with the third close to his German mark.

NOTEBOOK

Frankel has become a real superstar in remaining unbeaten in six previous starts and his breathtaking success in the 2,000 Guineas was still very much fresh in the memory. He was bidding to match the exploits of Rock Of Gibraltar (2002) and Henrythenavigator (2008) by following up his Newmarket success in this and he seemed to have no chinks in his armour with regard to trip, track or ground. However, although he won, the feeling is that we didn't see the best of him here and he just about got away with it. Tom Queally was obviously concerned not to get caught in a pocket in the main pack and sent his mount in pursuit of the pacemaker a long way out. Having collared him over 3f from home, he was soon in a clear lead, but it can be a long way home at Ascot and the colt appeared to get tired inside the last furlong and didn't have a lot to spare at the line, though connections were more of the opinion that he just idled. He is obviously better than this and a mouth-watering clash with Canford Cliffs in the Sussex Stakes could be on, while a step up to 1m2f for the Juddmonte International remains a possibility. (op 1-3 tchd 2-7 and 4-11 in places)

Zoffany(IRE), bidding to give his trainer his seventh success in this race since 2000, was a high-class 2-y-o, culminating in a success in the Group 1 Phoenix Stakes, and he made a creditable return from a bout of colic when runner-up in a Leopardstown Group 3, but his trainer had voiced concerns over his stamina on this first attempt at 1m. Soon settled in last place, he ran on well inside the last 2f and was closing down the favourite at the line. He may be a bit flattered by how close he got, but he obviously saw the trip out well and may take the winner on again in the Sussex. (tchd 33-1 in places and 16-1 in places)

Excelebration(IRE) was the only one to get anywhere near Frankel in the Greenham on his return, albeit beaten 4l, and the form of his subsequent annihilation of ten rivals on soft ground in the German 2,000 Guineas was hard to quantify. Making his debut at Group 1 level, he didn't get the ideal break when stumbling at the start and didn't enjoy the smoothest of passages either, but he ran on well over the last 2f and should be up to winning another Group race or two. (op 8-1)

Neebras(IRE) had his limitations exposed in a Sandown Listed event last time and had 20lb to find with Frankel on official ratings, so the fact that he finished where he did may have been down to him running on past a couple of disappointments and his rider seemed genuinely thrilled that he managed to grab fourth.

Dream Ahead(USA) was last seen finishing 7l behind Frankel in the Dewhurst on his first attempt at 7f, having previously been unbeaten in three starts including a brilliant 9l success in the Middle Park. He relishes soft ground and lack of rain was the reason for him not making his reappearance until now, but although conditions had come more in his favour here it also put more of an emphasis on stamina, which was already a question mark against him. Ridden to get the trip, he made an effort on the wide outside after turning in, but then started to hang about and was making no impression inside the last furlong. He was entitled to need it, but it may be that he is a sprinter. (op 12-1)

Dubawi Gold has done connections proud his year, finishing runner-up in the English and Irish 2,000 Guineas' and he probably should have won the Curragh version last time, but he had 6l to find with Frankel on Newmarket running. Ridden more prominently this time, he made an effort rounding the home bend but it came to little and he soon dropped away. He has been on the go since March, so could probably do with a break. (op 16-1 tchd 22-1 in a place)

Wootton Bassett developed into a high-class 2-y-o culminating with a soft-ground success in the Group 1 Prix Jean-Luc Lagardere, but lost his unbeaten record in the French 2,000 Guineas on his return when not drawn to advantage. The ground shouldn't have been a problem to him here, but he put in a laboured effort, coming off the bridle at halfway and finding nothing. He has plenty to prove now.

Grand Prix Boss(JPN) was very impressive when winning a very valuable Grade 1 in Tokyo last month, though his trainer had given the impression he would have been happy with a first-four finish here. He led the main group until gradually losing his place at halfway and he was well beaten before reaching the 2f pole.

Rerouted(USA) was in as a pacemaker for Frankel, but his jockey must have thought he was taking part in the King's Stand and quickly blazed off into a massive advantage before being swamped by the winner a good 3f from home. (op 100-1)

3012 COVENTRY STKS (GROUP 2) — 6f

4:25 (4:27) (Class 1) 2-Y-O

£48,254 (£18,292; £9,154; £4,564; £2,286; £1,147) **Stalls** Centre

Form				RPR
1	**1**		**Power**[24] 2322 2-9-1 0 ... RyanMoore 19 (A P O'Brien, Ire) *hld up: pushed along and hdwy over 2f out: rdn over 1f out: r.o to ld and edgd rt fnl 110yds: on top at fin* **4/1**[1]	110
61	**2**	*nk*	**Roman Soldier (IRE)**[14] 2584 2-9-1 0 ... GeorgeBaker 23 (Jeremy Noseda) *a.p: led 2f out: rdn over 1f out: hdd fnl 110yds and carried rt: hld fnl strides* **10/1**	109
41	**3**	*1 ¼*	**St Barths**[22] 2355 2-9-1 0 ... MartinDwyer 22 (Brian Meehan) *hld up: hdwy whn nt clr run over 2f out: r.o and edgd rt ins fnl f: nt get to ldrs* **14/1**	105
22	**4**	*hd*	**Lethal Force (IRE)**[15] 2559 2-9-1 0 ... AdamKirby 8 (Clive Cox) *in tch on far-side: outpcd whn gps merged over 3f out: rdn and hdwy over 1f out: styd on and edgd lft ins fnl f: nt pce to get to ldrs* **50/1**	105+
11	**5**	*½*	**Gatepost (IRE)**[34] 2007 2-9-1 0 ... JamieSpencer 4 (Mick Channon) *hld up in rr: swtchd lft to join main gp over 3f out: edgd rt and hdwy over 1f out: r.o ins fnl f: run flattened out towards fin* **7/1**[3]	105+
011	**6**	*3*	**B Fifty Two (IRE)**[31] 2109 2-9-1 0 ... SebSanders 21 (J W Hills) *hld up in midfield: rdn and hdwy over 1f out: styd on tl one pce fnl 100yds* **25/1**	94
21	**7**	*nk*	**North Star Boy (IRE)**[38] 1886 2-9-1 0 ... JimmyFortune 20 (Richard Hannon) *hld up: rdn and hdwy over 1f out: styd on ins fnl f: nt rch ldrs* **25/1**	93
11	**8**	*¾*	**Jack Who's He (IRE)**[62] 1316 2-9-1 0 ... CathyGannon 12 (David Evans) *unruly at s: midfield: hdwy over 3f out: rdn to chal over 2f out: nt qckn over 1f out: n.m.r and snatched up jst ins fnl f: kpt on but no imp after* **50/1**	92
022	**9**	*shd*	**Red Aggressor (IRE)**[8] 2767 2-9-1 0 ... PhilipRobinson 2 (Clive Brittain) *led far-side gp tl gps merged over 3f out: overall ld briefly over 2f out: wknd fnl 100yds* **100/1**	91+
1	**10**	*nk*	**Mezmaar**[18] 2455 2-9-1 0 ... RichardHills 1 (B W Hills) *racd keenly prom on far side: gps merged over 3f out: one pce over 1f out: eased whn btn fnl 100yds* **13/2**[2]	92+
1	**11**	*½*	**Chandlery (IRE)**[11] 2687 2-9-1 0 ... PatDobbs 7 (Richard Hannon) *hld up in rr on far side gp: gps merged over 3f out: rdn over 1f out: kpt on ins fnl f: nt trble ldrs* **50/1**	88+
1	**12**	*¾*	**Rebellious Guest**[8] 2767 2-9-1 0 ... TomQueally 13 (George Margarson) *prom: rdn to chal 2f out: wknd fnl 100yds* **20/1**	86
2	**13**	*2*	**Campanology**[11] 2672 2-9-1 0 ... JMurtagh 5 (Richard Hannon) *hld up in far side gp: gps merged over 3f out: rdn and hdwy over 1f out: one pce ins fnl f* **40/1**	80+
31	**14**	*1*	**Trumpet Major (IRE)**[24] 2291 2-9-1 0 ... RichardHughes 18 (Richard Hannon) *hld up: hmpd 2f out: kpt on into midfield over 1f out: no imp on ldrs* **12/1**	77+
51	**15**	*½*	**Barolo Top (IRE)**[5] 2831 2-9-1 0 ... RichardKingscote 10 (Tom Dascombe) *trckd ldrs on far-side tl outpcd whn gps merged over 3f out: n.d after* **66/1**	76
311	**16**	*1 ¼*	**Fulbright**[10] 2712 2-9-1 0 ... SilvestreDeSousa 17 (Mark Johnston) *midfield: effrt to chse ldrs over 2f out: wknd ins fnl f* **14/1**	72
512	**17**	*½*	**Evervescent (IRE)**[10] 2712 2-9-1 0 ... NeilCallan 3 (J S Moore) *racd on far-side in midfield: gps merged over 3f out: rdn over 2f out: nvr a threat* **66/1**	70
24	**18**	*½*	**Pride And Joy (IRE)**[15] 2559 2-9-1 0 ... FergusSweeney 16 (Jamie Osborne) *midfield: effrt over 2f out: hmpd 2f out: sn lost pl: n.d after* **100/1**	69
15	**19**	*1 ½*	**Mitchum**[17] 2488 2-9-1 0 ... GrahamGibbons 11 (David Barron) *swtchd lft s: in tch: pushed along over 3f out: wknd wl over 1f out* **66/1**	64
11	**20**	*2 ½*	**Gabrial (IRE)**[17] 2488 2-9-1 0 ... PaulHanagan 15 (Richard Fahey) *trckd ldrs tl rdn and wknd over 2f out* **20/1**	57
21	**21**	*5*	**Brocklebank (IRE)**[24] 2318 2-9-1 0 ... PhillipMakin 9 (Kevin Ryan) *prom on far side: gps merged over 3f out: pushed along and wknd over 2f out* **14/1**	42
31	**22**	*8*	**Commissar**[44] 1721 2-9-1 0 ... FrankieDettori 6 (Mahmood Al Zarooni) *in tch on far side: gps merged over 3f out: u.p over 2f out: wknd over 1f out* **8/1**	18
	23	*1 ¾*	**Italo (USA)**[19] 2446 2-9-1 0 ... (bt) JASanchez 14 (Wesley A Ward, U.S.A) *led: hdd over 2f out: sn wknd* **16/1**	13

1m 13.55s (-0.85) **Going Correction** +0.10s/f (Good) 2y crse rec **23** Ran SP% **131.6**

Speed ratings (Par 105): **109,108,106,106,106 102,101,100,100,100 99,98,95,94,93 92,91,90,88,85 78,68,65**

Tote Swingers: 1&2 £7.70, 1&3 £31.70, 2&3 £32.40 CSF £40.03 CT £402.48 TOTE £3.70: £1.60, £5.20, £8.20; EX 47.80 Trifecta £576.10 Pool: £13,542.28 - 17.39 winning units..

Owner M Tabor, D Smith & Mrs John Magnier **Bred** Norelands & Hugo Lascelles **Trained** Ballydoyle, Co Tipperary

■ Stewards' Enquiry : J A Sanchez four-day ban: used whip when out of contention and when gelding was showing no response (Jun 28- Jul 1)

FOCUS

This was the largest field the race has attracted in some time and it featured no end of fascinating contenders, with no less than 17 of them having scored last time, but it did not look a strong renewal. Predictably, the field split into two early, albeit they did end up merging back into one, and those who raced more towards the stands' side were favoured. Power maintained his progress to edge out the second and third, who are also on the up. There was a lengthy stewards' enquiry before the result was confirmed.

NOTEBOOK

Power, O'Brien's only runner, had been successful despite the drop to 5f in a Listed race at the Curragh last time. Ryan Moore was happy enough to chase the leaders in the stands' side pack, and the gaps opened perfectly for him as horses began to stake their claim. Having tracked the runner-up through, this rather imposing looking juvenile gradually wore him down, albeit with the help of some interference which he caused - Ryan Moore putting that down to the fact he was feeling his legs as he'd been lame all week, making the effort all the more commendable. It wasn't deemed enough to have affected the result, however, and there's little doubt he was the best horse. Described as a "strong, tough sort" by his trainer, he's expected to get further and both the National Stakes and Dewhurst will come under strong consideration for him later in the campaign. A general 12-1 shot for next year's 2,000 Guineas, he didn't stamp his authority on the race like the stable's subsequent Newmarket victor Henrythenavigator did in 2007, but it's still early days and we're likely to learn more about him still in the Phoenix Stakes, his next intended target. (tchd 9-2 and 5-1 in places)

Roman Soldier(IRE) proved popular in the run up to the race and adopted a prominent position stands' side. He picked up well to come to the front and briefly looked to be holding the winner when challenged, but received a couple of bumps off his more physically imposing rival, and was forced to settle for second. Clearly smart, he ought to have no trouble with 7f. (op 12-1 tchd 9-1)

St Barths, another who shed his maiden second time at Leicester, would have appreciated the slightly easier surface and stepped up markedly in terms of form to take third, covering more ground than most in the final 2f. A more positive ride may suit and he could be one for the July Stakes at Newmarket next month. (op 16-1)

Lethal Force(IRE) was one of the few maidens in the race. He brought course form into the race, having finished runner-up over 5f on debut, and did really well considering he was berthed in stall eight, whereas the front three came from 19 or higher. He should have no trouble winning a maiden. (op 66-1)

Gatepost(IRE)'s jockey will no doubt come in for some criticism for his ride. Although one could see what he was doing in switching more towards the stands' side from stall four, by the time he'd explored most of the track the principals had got first run and he couldn't make up the ground. He can probably be rated better than the bare form. (tchd 13-2)

B Fifty Two(IRE) acquitted himself well on this rise in grade. Already a dual winner, he edged out a useful-looking sort at Newmarket last time and this effort seemed to confirm he's up to contesting Group races.

North Star Boy(IRE) had beaten the fourth Lethal Force in a 5f course maiden last month, but didn't improve enough for the longer trip to confirm form. He was going on close home, and can make his mark at a lesser level. (op 20-1)

Jack Who's He(IRE), twice a winner over 5f earlier in the season, ran well up in grade on this first try at 6f and would have finished closer still but for interference. He could be up to winning a Listed race (entered in Redcar Two-Year-Old Trophy), and also has sales race entries. (tchd 80-1 in place)

Red Aggressor(IRE) again showed plenty of speed and kept on well.

Mezmaar, a son of Teofilo whose dam is a half-sister to high-class sprinter Tante Rose, saw plenty of daylight from stall one, which as it turned out was a bad draw, raced keenly and didn't get home. While disappointing, it would be unwise to assume this is as good as he is. Richard Hills later reported the colt raced too freely. Official explanation: jockey said colt ran too free (op 7-1 tchd 8-1 in a place 15-2 in places)

Chandlery(IRE) kept on without threatening and will find easier opportunities. (op 66-1)

Rebellious Guest ran well until over 1f out and wasn't given a hard time once beaten. He is highly regarded and could have more to offer, with this race perhaps coming too soon after his debut win. (tchd 25-1 in a place)

Trumpet Major(IRE) looked the best of Richard Hannon's, but never made a show. (tchd 14-1)

Fulbright, the Woodcote winner, found this altogether tougher. (op 16-1)

Gabrial(IRE) briefly made a forward move, but couldn't go through with his challenge. (op 18-1 tchd 16-1)

Brocklebank(IRE) appeared to run flat.

Commissar was snapped up by Godolphin after his impressive victory in a 5f maiden at Newmarket last month, and looked a potential improver for the extra furlong. He failed to give his running, though, fading quite tamely. (op 11-1 tchd 12-1 in places)

Italo(USA), as expected, cut out the early running before fading. (tchd 20-1)

3013 ASCOT STKS (H'CAP) — 2m 4f

5:00 (5:01) (Class 2) (0-95,95) 4-Y-O+

£31,155 (£9,330; £4,665; £2,335; £1,165; £585) **Stalls** Low

Form				RPR
00-1	**1**		**Veiled**[17] 2512 5-9-3 **88** ... EddieAhern 10 (Nicky Henderson) *hld up in tch and a travelling wl: chsd ldr and clr of field ent fnl 3f: rdn over 2f out: drvn to ld over 1f out: styd on wl and in command fnl 150yds* **11/2**[3]	98+
01-2	**2**	*2 ¾*	**Ermyn Lodge**[39] 1847 5-9-2 **87** ... (v) IanMongan 18 (Pat Phelan) *chsd ldrs tl wnt 2nd 14f out: jnd ldr 8f out tl led 5f out: clr w wnr chsng 3f out: rdn over 2f out: hdd over 1f out: no ex and btn ins fnl f* **16/1**	93
-100	**3**	*shd*	**Phoenix Flight (IRE)**[30] 1105 6-9-1 **86** ... OlivierPeslier 14 (James Evans) *t.k.h: hld up towards rr: hdwy into 7th and gng wl over 3f out: rdn and effrt to chse ldng pair 2f out: edgd rt fr over 1f out: styd on fnl f: nrly snatched 2nd* **50/1**	92
4-51	**4**	*hd*	**Zigato**[39] 1847 4-9-4 **92** ... WilliamBuick 9 (John Gosden) *hld up in rr: last and stuck bhd and wall of horses over 3f out: c wd and hdwy wl over 2f out: stl only 11th over 1f out: r.o strly ins fnl f: nt rch ldrs* **7/2**[1]	98+

11 **5** *3/4* **La Estrella (USA)**[26] 2235 8-9-1 **86** .... DaneO'Neill 15 91
(Don Cantillon) *stdd s: hld up towards rr: rdn and effrt whn barging match w rivals over 3f out: hdwy wl over 2f out: kpt on fr over 1f out: nt rch ldrs* **20/1**

220/ **6** *3 3/4* **Rattan (USA)**[40] 5522 6-9-1 **86** .... RichardHughes 12 87
(W P Mullins, Ire) *hld up towards rr: hmpd and swtchd lft over 3f out: gd hdwy 3f out: styng on whn swtchd lft ent fnl 2f: edgd rt and no imp jst over 1f out* **16/1**

10-0 **7** *1 3/4* **Palomar (USA)**[24] 2316 9-9-4 **89** .... PaulHanagan 2 89
(Brian Ellison) *stdd s: hld up in rr: effrt whn nt clr run over 3f out: c wd and hdwy 3f out: edgd rt and kpt on same pce fr over 1f out: nvr trbld ldrs* **20/1**

2 **8** *nk* **Sunwise (USA)**[24] 2314 5-9-7 **92** ....(b) JimmyFortune 19 91
(William Haggas) *in tch in midfield: effrt and rdn ent fnl 4f: hrd drvn and no imp over 2f out: plugged on same pce after* **25/1**

/12- **9** *19* **Junior**[89] 4467 8-9-10 **95** ....(b) RyanMoore 7 75
(David Pipe) *led but niggled along: jnd 8f out: drvn and hdd 5f out: wknd u.p wl over 2f out: eased fr over 1f out* **4/1**[2]

31-5 **10** *11* **Ashbrittle**[17] 2499 4-9-4 **92** .... JimCrowley 1 61
(Ralph Beckett) *hld up in midfield: rdn and swtchd rt over 3f out: nt clr run and immediately swtchd lft and barging match w rivals: no real hdwy and btn ent fnl 2f: eased fr over 1f out: t.o* **10/1**

-210 **11** *1 1/2* **Becausewecan (USA)**[34] 2006 5-9-5 **90** .... JoeFanning 3 58
(Mark Johnston) *chsd ldrs: rdn and unable qck over 3f out: wknd 3f out: wl btn and eased fr over 1f out: t.o* **40/1**

250- **12** *10* **Australia Day (IRE)**[220] 5307 8-9-8 **93** .... JMurtagh 5 51
(Paul Webber) *racd keenly: chsd ldr tl 14f out: chsd ldng pair after: rdn and struggling ent fnl 3f: wknd wl over 2f out: virtually p.u fnl f: t.o* **18/1**

060- **13** *33* **Private Story (USA)**[30] 6889 4-9-3 **91** ....(t) FergusSweeney 17 —
(Tim Vaughan) *hld up in midfield: rdn and losing pl whn barging match w rivals over 3f out: no ch wl over 2f out: eased fr wl over 1f out: wl t.o* **66/1**

-010 **14** *1/2* **Yorgunnabelucky (USA)**[10] 2716 5-9-10 **95** ......(p) SilvestreDeSousa 13 —
(Mark Johnston) *t.k.h: hld up in midfield: lost pl and struggling 4f out: lost tch u.p wl over 2f out: eased fr wl over 1f out: wl t.o* **50/1**

3-00 **15** *2 1/4* **Plymouth Rock (IRE)**[41] 1808 5-9-10 **95** ....(v) FrankieDettori 8 —
(Jeremy Noseda) *hld up in rr: rdn and effrt over 3f out: nt clr run briefly and no prog ent fnl 3f: wl bhd and eased fnl 2f: wl t.o* **8/1**

40-0 **16** *39* **Blizzard Blues (USA)**[10] 2716 5-9-9 **94** ....(b) TomQueally 11 —
(Jamie Osborne) *awkward leaving stalls and v.s.a: rcvrd and clsd on to bk of field after 2f: veered lft 10f out: rdn and no rspnse 4f out: virtually p.u fnl 2f: wl t.o* **66/1**

2/0- **17** *13* **Tyrrells Wood (IRE)**[364] 3050 6-9-5 **90** .... JamieSpencer 16 —
(Ian Williams) *chsd ldrs: struggling and losing pl u.p 5f out: towards rr whn hmpd 3f out: wl bhd and virtually p.u fr over 2f out: wl t.o* **14/1**

60-4 **18** *54* **Desert Sea (IRE)**[73] 1105 8-9-7 **92** .... NeilCallan 4 —
(David Arbuthnot) *hld up in midfield: rdn and unable qck over 3f out: no prog 3f out and wl btn after: virtually p.u fnl 2f: wl t.o* **22/1**

/00- **P** **Unleashed (IRE)**[65] 3050 6-9-5 **90** .... GeorgeBaker 20 —
(Charlie Mann) *stdd s: hld up in rr: lost action and p.u 9f out: dismntd* **100/1**

4m 24.82s (0.02) **Going Correction** +0.20s/f (Good)
WFA 4 from 5yo+ 3lb **19** Ran SP% **129.6**
Speed ratings (Par 109): **107,105,105,105,105 103,103,103,95,91 90,86,73,73,72 56,51,29,—**
Tote Swingers: 1&2 £22.70, 1&3 £72.70, 2&3 £131.80 CSF £86.18 CT £4061.44 TOTE £6.90: £1.70, £3.10, £11.20, £1.50; EX 106.10 Trifecta £8044.10 Part won. Pool: £10,870.53 - 0.61 winning units..
Owner Pump & Plant Services Ltd **Bred** Cheveley Park Stud Ltd **Trained** Upper Lambourn, Berks

FOCUS
A typical running of this race, featuring a blend of hardened Flat stayers and dual-purpose horses reverting from hurdles/fences. The draw has been of little consequence in recent times since the safety limit was reduced. The early pace was a fast one, with last year's winner Junior wanting to ensure it was proper test, although it did slow briefly before Ermyn Lodge helped crank it up again on the far side. The third and fourth set the standard but the form of this race often doesn't work out.

NOTEBOOK
Veiled and the runner-up were the only ones to cope with the strong pace by the time they reached the home bend, and it was Nicky Henderson's mare who emerged victorious, going on over 1f out under replacement jockey Eddie Ahern and finding more than enough to hold on. A much-improved hurdler last jumps season, when winning at up to 2m5f, she had scored off 8lb lower on her recent return to the Flat, and had no trouble with the marathon distance. Presumably, she'll be aimed towards the Cesarewitch later in the season. (op 6-1 tchd 13-2)
Ermyn Lodge committed such a long way out, so did remarkably well to hang on for second. Now 3lb higher than when runner-up over 2m at the course on his reappearance, he may have been a tad fortunate to reverse form with Zigato, but is clearly a thoroughly tough and progressive stayer.
Phoenix Flight(IRE) had won over hurdles last month and transferred his good form back to the level. He was noted travelling well quite a way out, and finished well without ever looking likely to reach the winner. The marathon trip clearly suited. (op 40-1 tchd 66-1 in places)
Zigato should have given the winner more to do, finding himself given a ridiculous amount of ground to make up and getting going all too late having been forced to come wide rounding the final bend. Impressive winner of a 2m course handicap last time, readily beating Ermyn Lodge, he finished strongly and, considering this was only his eighth start, there's probably more to come. (tchd 4-1 in places and 9-2 in places)
La Estrella(USA), who has notched up six straight victories on the Southwell Fibresand (mainly in claimers), kept on well considering he had to try and barge his way out of trouble, and probably should have finished closer. He isn't the easiest to keep sound, but can win more races at a lower level. (op 33-1)
Rattan(USA) met trouble at a crucial stage and got going all too late.
Palomar(USA) tried to come from a similarly long way back having also been denied a clear run.
Sunwise(USA) was reported to have hung right-handed, but still drew a long way clear of the remainder. Official explanation: jockey said gelding hung right throughout; vet said gelding lost its right fore shoe
Junior has improved over jumps since last season's 5l win in this and was last seen storming to a 24l victory in the Kim Muir. Although 10lb higher this time round, he was beaten too far for it to be put down to that, and instead it's probable he was made to go too hard early and was then taken on by Ermyn Lodge a long way out, which wasn't the case last year when he pretty much dominated his own tempo. It's hoped he'll bounce back. (op 9-2)
Ashbrittle looked in need of the run on his reappearance at Haydock, and the step up to this marathon trip promised to suit, but he was forced to try and switch when short of room and then got into a barging match. He could make no headway afterwards and it would be no surprise to see connections reach for the visor next time (successful only previous try in them). (tchd 12-1 in places)
Australia Day(IRE) had stamina to prove and raced far too freely. Official explanation: jockey said gelding was unsuited by the trip (op 16-1 tchd 20-1 and 25-1 in a place)
Plymouth Rock(IRE), although briefly denied a clear run, is now running out of excuses. (op 11-1 tchd 12-1)
Blizzard Blues(USA) Official explanation: vet said gelding finished distressed

Tyrrells Wood(IRE) has now flopped in this two years in a row. (op 16-1)

3014 WINDSOR CASTLE STKS (LISTED RACE) 5f
5:35 (5:40) (Class 1) 2-Y-O

£28,385 (£10,760; £5,385; £2,685; £1,345; £675) **Stalls** Centre

Form RPR

221 **1** **Frederick Engels**[10] 2725 2-9-3 0 .... JMurtagh 22 106
(David Brown) *midfield: hdwy 2f out: r.o to ld ins fnl f: in command towards fin* **9/4**[1]

221 **2** *2 1/4* **Stonefield Flyer**[42] 1797 2-9-3 0 .... PaulMulrennan 13 97
(Keith Dalgleish) *prom: swtchd rt over 2f out: chalng fr over 1f out: styd on same pce and wl hld by wnr towards fin* **16/1**

124 **3** *hd* **Caspar Netscher**[10] 2712 2-9-3 0 .... RobertWinston 20 96
(Alan McCabe) *midfield: hdwy whn carried rt over 2f out: tried to chal ins fnl f: styd on same pce fnl 75yds* **25/1**

21 **4** *1/2* **Gentlemans Code (USA)**[19] 2423 2-9-3 0 ....(bt) MESmith 10 94
(Wesley A Ward, U.S.A) *displayed gd spd to ld far-side gp: gps merged 3f out: pressed over 1f out: hdd ins fnl f: kpt on same pce towards fin* **13/2**[2]

21 **5** *3 3/4* **Bear Behind (IRE)**[13] 2612 2-9-3 0 .... RichardKingscote 5 81
(Tom Dascombe) *chsd ldrs on far side: gps merged 3f out: effrt over 2f out: outpcd by front 4 ins fnl f* **16/1**

123 **6** *3/4* **Hamza (IRE)**[17] 2488 2-9-3 0 .... PhillipMakin 18 78
(Kevin Ryan) *in tch: n.m.r over 2f out: rdn over 1f out: one pce ins fnl f* **16/1**

23 **7** *1/2* **Bayleyf (IRE)**[38] 1886 2-9-3 0 .... LukeMorris 19 76
(John Best) *midfield: pushed along over 3f out: styd on ins fnl f: unable to rch ldrs* **25/1**

2 **8** *nk* **Springinmystep (IRE)**[15] 2542 2-9-3 0 .... TomQueally 15 77+
(Michael Dods) *bmpd s: towards rr: rdn over 1f out: prog ins fnl f: r.o: gng on at fin* **40/1**

312 **9** *1 1/2* **Es Que Love (IRE)**[10] 2725 2-9-3 0 .... SilvestreDeSousa 27 70
(Mark Johnston) *racd nr side rail: led main gp but nt overall: rdn and stl ev ch 2f out: fdd fnl 100yds* **22/1**

1 **10** *1* **The Penny Horse (IRE)**[69] 1185 2-9-3 0 .... JamesDoyle 6 66
(J S Moore) *chsd ldrs on far side: gps merged 3f out: rdn 2f out: one pce fnl f* **66/1**

1 **11** *shd* **Worthington (IRE)**[15] 2542 2-8-12 0 .... PaulHanagan 17 61
(Richard Fahey) *bhd: kpt on u.p fnl f: nvr nrr* **9/1**[3]

11 **12** *1/2* **Lexington Spirit (IRE)**[19] 2429 2-8-12 0 .... TomEaves 23 59
(Richard Fahey) *midfield: pushed along over 2f out: wknd over 1f out* **33/1**

43 **13** *3/4* **Caledonian Spring (IRE)**[28] 2181 2-9-3 0 .... EddieAhern 14 61
(Paul D'Arcy) *in tch: rdn over 1f out: sn wknd* **25/1**

33 **14** *nse* **Ballesteros**[18] 2455 2-9-3 0 .... ShaneKelly 7 61
(Brian Meehan) *hld up: racd on far side: gps merged 3f out: hdwy into midfield 2f out: sn u.p: no imp* **28/1**

61 **15** *1/2* **Huma Bird**[10] 2718 2-8-12 0 .... WilliamBuick 25 54
(Mahmood Al Zarooni) *chsd ldrs: rdn 2f out: wknd over 1f out* **16/1**

41 **16** *1 1/2* **Wolfgang (IRE)**[21] 2374 2-9-3 0 .... RyanMoore 21 54
(Richard Hannon) *bhd: tried to keep on fnl f: nvr able to get competitive* **33/1**

1223 **17** *1 3/4* **Magic City (IRE)**[19] 2437 2-9-3 0 .... RichardHughes 9 48
(Richard Hannon) *bhd on far-side: gps merged 3f out: u.p and moved into midfield over 2f out: no imp on ldrs* **10/1**

142 **18** *2 3/4* **Monnoyer**[14] 2594 2-9-3 0 ....(v[1]) FrankieDettori 8 38+
(Jeremy Noseda) *hld up on far side: gps merged 3f out: effrt in midfield over 2f out: wknd and eased over 1f out* **16/1**

1 **19** *1 1/4* **I'm Still The Man (IRE)**[12] 2644 2-9-3 0 .... KierenFox 16 33
(Bill Turner) *towards rr: u.p over 2f out: nvr on terms* **50/1**

34 **20** *shd* **Crowning Star (IRE)**[29] 2148 2-9-3 0 .... MickaelBarzalona 12 36
(J S Moore) *in rr: swtchd lft after 1f: nt clr run over 1f out: nvr a threat* **33/1**

51 **21** *3/4* **Rent Free**[19] 2409 2-9-3 0 .... J-PGuillambert 3 30
(Nigel Tinkler) *in tch on far side: pushed along whn gps merged 3f out: wknd over 1f out* **80/1**

423 **22** *1* **Copper Falls**[43] 1757 2-8-12 0 .... FergusSweeney 11 22
(Brendan Powell) *missed break: swtchd lft after 1f: a bhd* **100/1**

53 **23** *3/4* **Lupo D'Oro (IRE)**[13] 2602 2-9-3 0 .... GeorgeBaker 2 27
(John Best) *in tch on far side: gps merged 3f out: wknd over 1f out: eased whn btn ins fnl f* **80/1**

1 **24** *2 1/4* **Mitie Mouse**[13] 2602 2-9-3 0 .... NeilCallan 1 16
(Mike Murphy) *racd on far side: midfield: gps merged over 3f out: effrt over 2f out: no imp: wknd over 1f out* **33/1**

59.91 secs (-1.29) **Going Correction** +0.10s/f (Good) **24** Ran SP% **133.3**
Speed ratings (Par 101): **108,104,104,103,97 96,95,94,92,90 90,89,88,88,87 85,82,78,76,76 74,73,72,68**
Tote Swingers: 1&2 £7.40, 1&3 £13.60, 2&3 £255.10 CSF £35.40 CT £806.63 TOTE £3.60: £1.80, £4.90, £11.80; EX 47.80 Trifecta £4201.90 Pool: £7,069.13 - 1.24 winning units..
Owner Qatar Bloodstock Ltd **Bred** Peter Baldwin **Trained** Averham Park, Notts
■ David Brown's first Royal Ascot winner.

FOCUS
Even with the two non-runners and one withdrawal, a massive field lined up for the Windsor Castle with 17 of the 24 remaining runners previous winners. The field started off in two groups with the larger bunch of 15 coming stands' side while nine started off down the middle, but the centre group made a dramatic diagonal move to their left so that the two groups had merged before halfway. Again those drawn high held sway. The time was excellent and Frederick Engels rates the best winner of this in the past decade. Pretty solid form.

NOTEBOOK
Frederick Engels had chased home the current Queen Mary favourite Shumoos on his second start before recording a very fast time when thrashing Es Que Love by 6l at Musselburgh. He was off the bridle in the middle of the nearside group at halfway, but then showed a nice turn of foot to sweep through between horses and lead inside the last furlong. He should stay 6f without any problem and will now be aimed at the July Stakes. (op 5-2 tchd 11-4 in places)
Stonefield Flyer ◆ bolted up by 6l in a Newcastle median auction maiden on his third start and ran a cracker in this much stiffer company, racing close to the pace throughout and keeping on well for second. His young trainer has made a very impressive start to his career and this colt should win a nice race.
Caspar Netscher didn't seem to handle Epsom when a beaten favourite in the Woodcote and ran much better here. Having moved into a challenging position over a furlong from home, he ran on well, and a return to 6f should help him.
Gentlemans Code(USA), representing the yard that took this race two years ago, comfortably beat Bear Behind in a three-runner event at Folkestone last time and deserves credit for this performance as he led the centre-group early and used up a bit of energy in order to move across to his left and take the overall lead over a furlong from home. He couldn't see it out, but still finished nicely clear of the rest. (op 7-1)

Bear Behind(IRE) started off in the centre group and had every chance before fading inside the last furlong. (op 20-1)
Hamza(IRE) had twice run well in defeat since making a winning debut at Musselburgh and he plugged on to record another creditable effort, though he lacks the scope of a few of these.
Bayleyf(IRE), whose stable took this with a 100-1 shot in 2008, had shown ability in a couple of maidens but he probably improved on that here, staying on from well back to finish a highly creditable seventh. (op 40-1)
Springinmystep(IRE) ◆ had an awful lot of ground to make up over a furlong from home, but finished with quite a rattle and comprehensively reversed form with his Beverley conqueror Worthington. There is surely much better to come from him. (op 50-1 tchd 66-1 in a place)
Magic City(IRE) had raced more often any of his rivals and had been beaten at odds-on three times since his extremely impressive debut victory. He never looked happy here, and this was a bigger disappointment even allowing for him starting off in the centre-field group. (op 9-1 tchd 11-1 in a place)
Copper Falls Official explanation: jockey said filly was slowly away
T/Jkpt: £3,046.20 to a £1 stake. Pool of £182,343.93 - 42.50 winning units. T/Plt: £40.20 to a £1 stake. Pool of £500,493.52 - 9,069.29 winning units. T/Qpdt: £11.50 to a £1 stake. Pool of £21,667.19 - 127.31 winning units. SP

2447 BRIGHTON (L-H)

Tuesday, June 14

OFFICIAL GOING: Good (7.4)
Rail dolled out 6yds from 4.5f to 2f adding 12yds to all distances.
Wind: Light, against Weather: Sunny

3015 3663 FIRST FOR FOOD SERVICE H'CAP — 5f 59y

6:00 (6:00) (Class 6) (0-60,59) 3-Y-O+ **£1,619** (£481; £240; £120) **Stalls** Low

Form / RPR

5055 **1** **Stonecrabstomorrow (IRE)**[8] 2756 8-8-10 **48**.......(v) MarkCoumbe(5) 3 — 59
(Michael Attwater) *jst in tch in last pair: drvn 2f out: prog over 1f out: sustained effrt to ld last 150yds* **18/1**

4324 **2** *1* **The Tatling (IRE)**[8] 2755 14-9-12 **59**.................. LiamKeniry 6 — 67
(Milton Bradley) *settled in 5th: prog gng strly 2f out: c to chal fnl f: shkn up and nt qckn last 100yds* **11/2**[3]

4110 **3** *2 ¾* **Spic 'n Span**[42] 1787 6-9-8 **55**..................(b) KirstyMilczarek 1 — 53
(Ronald Harris) *wnt to post early after showing reluctance to do so: led at str pce and sn clr: wknd and hdd last 150yds* **13/2**

-060 **4** *nse* **Knightfire (IRE)**[15] 2554 4-9-5 **55**..................(tp) JohnFahy(3) 5 — 53
(Walter Swinburn) *jst in tch in last pair: rdn 2f out: no prog tl styd on ins fnl f* **10/1**

4006 **5** *1 ¾* **Lithaam (IRE)**[28] 861 7-8-7 **45**..................(tp) RyanClark(5) 2 — 37
(Milton Bradley) *chsd ldrs: effrt 2f out: nt qckn over 1f out: fdd* **25/1**

1210 **6** *nk* **Straboe (USA)**[39] 1856 5-9-9 **56**..................(v) WilliamCarson 7 — 47
(Stuart Williams) *chsd ldr: rdn and nt qckn 2f out: sn lost 2nd: fdd jst over 1f out* **11/8**[1]

-022 **7** *2 ¾* **Imaginary Diva**[8] 2755 5-9-2 **49**.................. ChrisCatlin 4 — 30
(George Margarson) *chsd ldng pair: wnt 2nd briefly wl over 1f out: sn wknd* **9/4**[2]

62.56 secs (0.26) **Going Correction** +0.10s/f (Good) **7** Ran SP% **119.8**
Speed ratings (Par 101): **101,99,95,94,92 91,87**
Tote Swingers: 1&2 £13.80, 1&3 £14.80, 2&3 £3.60 CSF £117.80 TOTE £20.00: £8.10, £2.20; EX 101.30.
Owner Miss Nicola Carroll **Bred** P Dillon **Trained** Epsom, Surrey

FOCUS
The front two in the betting both ran below form and the pace was overly strong, so extremely moderate form. The surprise winner ran to his winter AW best. They tended to race up the middle in the straight.

3016 BRITISH STALLION STUDS SUPPORTING BRITISH RACING E B F MAIDEN STKS — 5f 213y

6:30 (6:30) (Class 5) 2-Y-O **£3,238** (£963; £481; £240) **Stalls** Low

Form / RPR

46 **1** **My Lucky Liz (IRE)**[29] 2153 2-8-12 0.................. MartinLane 5 — 70
(David Simcock) *hld up last: shkn up and prog 2f out: led jst over 1f out: sn in command: pushed out firmly* **9/4**[1]

5 **2** *1 ¾* **Sheila's Buddy**[33] 2017 2-9-3 0.................. LiamKeniry 4 — 70
(J S Moore) *mde most: drvn and hdd jst over 1f out: kpt on same pce* **18/1**

3 *½* **Tones (IRE)** 2-8-12 0.................. KieranO'Neill(5) 1 — 68
(Richard Hannon) *hld up in 4th: effrt and wl on terms 2f out: outpcd 1f out: fdd nr fin* **9/4**[1]

04 **4** *1 ¾* **Master Of Ages (IRE)**[13] 2612 2-8-10 0.................. DarylByrne(7) 6 — 63
(Mark Johnston) *rrd s: rcvrd to press ldr after 1f: upsides over 3f out to wl over 1f out: nt qckn and sn btn* **5/2**[2]

65 **5** *hd* **Faraway**[12] 2644 2-9-3 0.................. LiamJones 3 — 62
(William Haggas) *t.k.h: trckd ldr 1f: pushed along 1/2-way: nt qckn 2f out: fdd* **11/2**[3]

1m 11.06s (0.86) **Going Correction** +0.10s/f (Good) **5** Ran SP% **110.8**
Speed ratings (Par 93): **98,95,95,92,92**
CSF £33.79 TOTE £2.80: £1.10, £5.60; EX 23.40.
Owner Ahmed Jaber **Bred** Rabbah Bloodstock Limited **Trained** Newmarket, Suffolk

FOCUS
A modest maiden with the winner rated to her debut form. The action unfolded up the middle of the track.

NOTEBOOK
My Lucky Liz(IRE) was a bit disappointing at Windsor last time, but she had previously shaped well when not beaten far at Ascot and she was confirming that initial promise. Stepped up in trip, she benefited from a patient ride and was too good for this lot. Ordinary nurseries may provide her with the best chance of further juvenile success. (op 2-1 tchd 15-8)
Sheila's Buddy stepped up on his debut effort, keeping on well having been positively ridden. He needs further. (op 16-1)
Tones(IRE), a £25,000 purchase of a multiple 6f-1m winner in Italy, made a respectable start. He's open to improvement and should win. (op 10-3)
Master Of Ages(IRE) was well placed by his 7lb claimer, but he didn't handle the track starting from the downhill run into the straight. (op 10-3 tchd 9-4)
Faraway raced keenly and found nothing for pressure. Perhaps he's another who didn't take to the track. (op 4-1 tchd 7-1)

3017 RENDEZ-VOUS CASINO AT BRIGHTON MARINA H'CAP — 7f 214y

7:00 (7:00) (Class 6) (0-65,64) 4-Y-O+ **£2,266** (£674; £337; £168) **Stalls** Low

Form / RPR

0440 **1** **Inquisitress**[111] 652 7-8-7 **50**.................. CathyGannon 4 — 57
(John Bridger) *covered up bhd ldrs: effrt 2f out: rdn and wnt between rivals to ld jst ins fnl f: idled but hld on* **12/1**

44-3 **2** *½* **Rich Boy**[158] 78 4-8-13 **56**..................(p) JackMitchell 8 — 62
(Laura Mongan) *pressed ldr: led 2f out: hdd jst ins fnl f: kpt on but a hld* **13/2**[3]

0305 **3** *1 ¼* **Regal Rave (USA)**[19] 2420 4-9-1 **58**.................. LiamKeniry 3 — 61+
(Mouse Hamilton-Fairley) *hld up in last pair: stl there 2f out: effrt and rdn over 1f out: kpt on to take 3rd last stride: no ch to chal* **11/2**[2]

-000 **4** *shd* **Fly By Nelly**[28] 2171 5-8-5 **48**.................. WilliamCarson 5 — 51
(Mark Hoad) *led: rdn and hdd 2f out: nt qckn but kpt pressing tl no ex fnl f* **20/1**

5211 **5** *½* **Wishformore (IRE)**[15] 2561 4-9-2 **64**..................(p) RyanPowell(5) 7 — 66+
(J S Moore) *t.k.h: sn hld up in 5th: lost pl over 2f out: rdn wl over 1f out: plugged on fnl f* **7/4**[1]

-056 **6** *1 ½* **Yourgolftravel Com**[19] 2420 6-8-9 **52**..................(bt) ChrisCatlin 9 — 50
(David Pipe) *hld up in 6th: smooth prog to press ldrs wl over 2f out: rdn and fnd nil wl over 1f out: sn btn* **8/1**

00P4 **7** *½* **Dawson Creek (IRE)**[19] 2420 7-7-13 **45**.................. SophieDoyle(3) 10 — 42
(Mark Hoad) *sn trckd ldng pair: wl on terms 3f out: wknd fr 2f out* **13/2**[3]

5650 **8** *1 ¾* **Spinning Ridge (IRE)**[34] 1995 6-9-1 **58**..................(b) KirstyMilczarek 2 — 51
(Ronald Harris) *reluctant to go to post: rel to r and lost several l: in tch in last pair: rdn over 2f out: wknd over 1f out* **8/1**

1m 36.81s (0.81) **Going Correction** +0.10s/f (Good) **8** Ran SP% **113.1**
Speed ratings (Par 101): **99,98,97,97,96 95,94,92**
Tote Swingers: 1&2 £7.60, 1&3 £9.20, 2&3 £5.80 CSF £84.93 CT £484.90 TOTE £14.90: £4.80, £1.70, £1.20; EX 79.70.
Owner C Marshall T Wallace J J Bridger **Bred** A Saccomando **Trained** Liphook, Hants

FOCUS
This is very moderate form, with the winner probably the best guide. They raced far side in the straight.
Spinning Ridge(IRE) Official explanation: jockey said gelding was slowly away

3018 BRIGHTON SHEET METAL CENTENARY H'CAP — 1m 1f 209y

7:30 (7:30) (Class 6) (0-65,65) 3-Y-O **£1,619** (£481; £240; £120) **Stalls** High

Form / RPR

054- **1** **Lady Gabrielle (IRE)**[202] 7558 3-9-2 **60**.................. NickyMackay 1 — 68+
(David Elsworth) *prom: rdn over 3f out: prog to ld 2f out: drvn and kpt on wl after* **9/1**

4-60 **2** *2 ½* **Around The Clock (USA)**[32] 2068 3-9-5 **63**.................. DarryllHolland 2 — 66
(Amanda Perrett) *led at fair pce: hrd rdn over 2f out: sn hdd and nt qckn: wandering but kpt on fnl f* **3/1**[2]

0-00 **3** *½* **Viking Rose (IRE)**[34] 1997 3-9-1 **59**.................. JackMitchell 4 — 61
(James Eustace) *prom: rdn to chal 3f out: stl upsides 2f out: nt qckn over 1f out: one pce after* **12/1**

0506 **4** *½* **Harry Lime**[55] 1487 3-8-13 **57**.................. CathyGannon 6 — 58
(William Jarvis) *hld up in 6th: rdn over 4f out: effrt u.p wl over 2f out: kpt on same pce after* **20/1**

60-6 **5** *1* **Dark And Dangerous (IRE)**[10] 2722 3-9-1 **59**..............(v[1]) IanMongan 9 — 58
(Peter Winkworth) *dwlt: hld up in last pair: rdn over 3f out: cl enough and n.m.r 2f out: nt qckn after* **11/2**

3303 **6** *1 ¾* **Roman Flame**[50] 1572 3-9-2 **60**..................(v) SebSanders 8 — 56
(Michael Quinn) *hld up bhd ldrs: prog on outer 4f out: rdn to chal wl over 2f out: wknd over 1f out* **14/1**

4451 **7** *4 ½* **Highlife Dancer**[59] 1413 3-9-7 **65**.................. ChrisCatlin 3 — 52
(Mick Channon) *hld up in last pair: pushed along and nt on terms w rest fr 4f out: no prog fnl 2f* **5/1**[3]

0-00 **8** *14* **Shirataki (IRE)**[13] 2621 3-8-6 **50**.................. JoeFanning 7 — —
(Mark Johnston) *sn pressed ldr: rdn whn bmpd by rival 3f out: wknd qckly sn after: virtually p.u fnl f* **11/4**[1]

2m 3.47s (-0.13) **Going Correction** +0.10s/f (Good) **8** Ran SP% **112.8**
Speed ratings (Par 97): **104,102,101,101,100 99,95,84**
Tote Swingers: 1&2 £9.60, 1&3 £16.70, 2&3 £12.60 CSF £35.25 CT £326.54 TOTE £13.30: £3.20, £2.30, £3.00; EX 51.90.
Owner The Lady Gabrielle Partnership **Bred** Mount Coote Partnership **Trained** Newmarket, Suffolk

FOCUS
A few lightly raced types from decent stables lined up, but they still looked an ordinary bunch. The form is rated around the third and fourth. They were spread out across the track in the closing stages.

3019 DIGIBET.COM H'CAP — 6f 209y

8:00 (8:01) (Class 6) (0-65,64) 4-Y-O+ **£1,619** (£481; £240; £120) **Stalls** Low

Form / RPR

6043 **1** **Mandhooma**[6] 2799 5-9-5 **62**.................. ChrisCatlin 7 — 73
(Peter Hiatt) *hld up in last pair: brought to nr side rail and prog 2f out: drvn and r.o to ld last 100yds* **11/2**[3]

0-32 **2** *hd* **Foxtrot Alpha (IRE)**[13] 2605 5-9-6 **63**.................. LukeMorris 8 — 73
(Peter Winkworth) *pressed ldr: upsides 2f out: pressed new ldr after: upsides again inss fnl f: jst outpcd nr fin* **7/2**[2]

0204 **3** *¾* **Interakt**[3] 2921 4-8-7 **55**.................. HarryBentley(5) 3 — 63
(Joseph Tuite) *t.k.h: cl up bhd ldrs: effrt to ld 2f out: drvn and hdd last 100yds: nt qckn* **6/1**

40-2 **4** *2 ¾* **Yanbu (USA)**[18] 2452 6-8-9 **52**.................. StevieDonohoe 6 — 53+
(Tobias B P Coles) *t.k.h: hld up in last pair: nt qckn 2f out: plugged on fnl f: no ch* **12/1**

1632 **5** *½* **St Ignatius**[12] 2655 4-8-11 **54**..................(p) JamesDoyle 5 — 53
(Michael Appleby) *led: c towards nr side in st: hdd 2f out: fdd over 1f out* **8/1**

0232 **6** *2* **Fault**[4] 2870 5-9-7 **64**..................(t) SebSanders 2 — 58
(Stef Higgins) *sn restrained into 5th: prog over 2f out to chal wl over 1f out: hanging lft and fnd nil: sn wknd* **6/4**[1]

3200 **7** *8* **Co Dependent (USA)**[19] 2426 5-9-2 **62**..................(p) SophieDoyle(3) 1 — 34
(Jamie Osborne) *t.k.h: hld up bhd ldng pair: styd alone far side in st: bhd fnl 2f* **25/1**

1m 23.53s (0.43) **Going Correction** +0.10s/f (Good) **7** Ran SP% **114.5**
Speed ratings (Par 101): **101,100,99,96,96 93,84**
Tote Swingers: 1&2 £4.90, 1&3 £6.00, 2&3 £3.30 CSF £25.07 CT £119.01 TOTE £4.80: £2.60, £1.70; EX 29.50.
Owner P W Hiatt **Bred** Shadwell Estate Company Limited **Trained** Hook Norton, Oxon

FOCUS
For the first time on this card the majority of the field raced stands' side in the closing stages and the one-two-three were closest to the rail in the order in which they finished. However, the following race seemed to prove there was no bias. It didn't look strong run and the form is rated around the runner-up.

3020 BRASSERIE ITALIAN MARINA SQUARE BRIGHTON H'CAP 5f 213y
8:30 (8:30) (Class 5) (0-70,69) 3-Y-O+ **£2,266** (£674; £337; £168) **Stalls** Low

Form RPR
40-2 **1** **Elsie's Orphan**[49] 1581 4-9-9 **64**.. LiamKeniry 8 76
(Patrick Chamings) *dwlt: hld up in rr but wl in tch: outpcd 2f out and rdn: gd prog over 1f out: led ins fnl f: sn clr* **3/1**[1]
4-00 **2** *2 ½* **Kinigi (IRE)**[14] 2585 5-9-9 **69**..(b) RyanClark(5) 1 73
(Ronald Harris) *led 1f: prom after: styd in centre st and wl on terms: rdn 2f out: led again briefly jst ins fnl f but sddle slipped: sn outpcd* **8/1**
1504 **3** *½* **Bateleur**[3] 2913 7-9-3 **61**.. MartinHarley(3) 9 63
(Mick Channon) *trckd ldrs: c to nr side rail in st: chal 2f out: upsides 1f out: sn outpcd* **10/1**
0504 **4** *1* **Highland Harvest**[28] 2167 7-9-9 **64**.. IanMongan 7 63
(Jamie Poulton) *led after 1f: c towards nr side in st: hdd & wknd jst ins fnl f* **13/2**
0510 **5** *2* **Dualagi**[24] 2313 7-9-9 **64**.. GeorgeBaker 4 56
(Martin Bosley) *hld up in rr but in tch: outpcd 2f out: rdn and one pce after* **11/1**
-000 **6** *¾* **Zowington**[24] 2304 9-9-9 **64**..(v) WilliamCarson 2 54
(Stuart Williams) *dwlt: hld up in rr but in tch: outpcd and rdn 2f out: no prog after* **11/1**
2260 **7** *1 ¾* **Rio Royale (IRE)**[40] 1838 5-9-8 **63**.. PatDobbs 5 47
(Amanda Perrett) *in tch: outpcd and rdn 2f out: nvr on terms after* **7/2**[2]
-003 **8** *2 ¼* **Sermons Mount (USA)**[19] 2422 5-9-12 **67**.. ChrisCatlin 3 44
(Mouse Hamilton-Fairley) *hld up in tch: outpcd and rdn 2f out: btn after* **9/2**[3]

1m 10.33s (0.13) **Going Correction** +0.10s/f (Good) **8** Ran SP% **115.6**
Speed ratings (Par 103): **103,99,99,97,95 94,91,88**
Tote Swingers: 1&2 £3.70, 1&3 £5.00, 2&3 £17.80 CSF £27.82 CT £214.86 TOTE £2.50: £1.10, £3.80, £3.90; EX 26.80.
Owner Mrs J E L Wright **Bred** Wheelers Land Stud **Trained** Baughurst, Hants

FOCUS
A race full of exposed types, the one exception being Elsie's Orphan. The form seems sound. The majority of these came towards the stands' side in the closing stages, but the winner was well away from the rail and the runner-up was the only runner who raced up the middle all the way up the straight.
Kinigi(IRE) Official explanation: jockey said saddle slipped
T/Plt: £963.20 to a £1 stake. Pool of £59,759.00 - 45.29 winning units. T/Qpdt: £67.60 to a £1 stake. Pool of £9,201.00 - 100.66 winning units. JN

2361 THIRSK (L-H)
Tuesday, June 14

OFFICIAL GOING: Good (8.4)
Wind: light 1/2 behind Weather: fine and sunny

3021 TURFTV (S) STKS 6f
1:45 (1:47) (Class 6) 2-Y-O **£2,590** (£770; £385; £192) **Stalls** High

Form RPR
2225 **1** **Rooknrasbryripple**[4] 2889 2-8-9 0.. SamHitchcott 7 64
(Mick Channon) *trckd ldrs: led on stands' side rail 3f out: kpt on strly: readily* **3/1**[2]
060 **2** *2 ½* **Beechey's Beauty**[15] 2570 2-9-0 0..(p) DavidNolan 9 62
(Ann Duffield) *in tch: hdwy on ins over 2f out: styd on to take 2nd nr fin* **25/1**
61 **3** *½* **First Bid**[25] 2267 2-9-7 0.. RichardMullen 1 67
(Kevin Ryan) *wnt lft s: chsd ldrs: drvn 3f out: chsd wnr over 1f out: kpt on same pce* **4/6**[1]
4 *2 ½* **Blue Belle Lady** 2-8-9 0.. TonyHamilton 3 48
(Richard Fahey) *dwlt: in rr: hdwy on outer whn nt clr run and swtchd rt 2f out: kpt on fnl f* **12/1**
04 **5** *1 ½* **Justine Time (IRE)**[11] 2693 2-8-9 0..(p) LeeNewman 5 43
(David Barron) *led over 2f: edgd lft and wknd over 1f out* **20/1**
0036 **6** *nk* **Umph (IRE)**[4] 2889 2-9-0 0..(v) AndrewMullen 4 47
(David Evans) *w ldr: led over 3f out: sn hdd: wknd fnl f* **22/1**
7 *6* **Low Pastures** 2-8-11 0.. JamesSullivan(3) 8 29
(Michael Easterby) *s.i.s: hung lft and a bhd* **33/1**
0 **8** *1 ¾* **Ruskins View (IRE)**[22] 2346 2-8-9 0.. PatrickMathers 11 19
(Alan Berry) *sn outpcd: sme hdwy over 2f out: hung lft: wknd over 1f out: fin lame* **100/1**
9 *7* **Come On Dave (IRE)** 2-9-0 0.. AdrianNicholls 6 —
(David Nicholls) *dwlt: t.k.h in mid-div: hung bdly lft over 2f out: sn wknd* **11/1**[3]
0 **10** *1 ½* **Johansen**[15] 2542 2-9-0 0.. PJMcDonald 2 —
(Kate Walton) *chsd ldrs on outer: wknd over 1f out* **100/1**
11 *1* **Tiny Tittle (IRE)** 2-8-9 0.. DuranFentiman 10 —
(Deborah Sanderson) *dwlt: a in rr* **100/1**

1m 14.51s (1.81) **Going Correction** +0.05s/f (Good) **11** Ran SP% **119.9**
Speed ratings (Par 91): **89,85,85,81,79 79,71,68,59,57 56**
Tote Swingers: 1&2 £8.10, 1&3 £1.50, 2&3 £6.70 CSF £78.22 TOTE £2.80: £1.30, £4.90, £1.10; EX 73.80.There was no bid for the winner.
Owner Wessex Downs Racing **Bred** Downfield Cottage Stud & D F Powell **Trained** West Ilsley, Berks

FOCUS
An ordinary seller.
NOTEBOOK
Rooknrasbryripple, who'd been runner-up four times in maidens, didn't have to improve to get off the mark at the seventh time of asking. It'll be a bit of a surprise if she proves much better than she's shown to date but she'll continue to hold her own kept to this level. (op 7-2)
Beechey's Beauty improved for a combination of a drop in grade and first-time cheekpieces. The longer trip was also a help given the way he stayed on. It's possible he could have more to give. (op 28-1)
First Bid wasn't best drawn and went left leaving his stall, but he might still have been expected to do better, never really going that well despite having shown plenty of speed over shorter previously. (tchd 4-5 and 8-11 in places)
Blue Belle Lady's presence in a seller on debut suggests she can't have been showing a great deal at home but this daughter of Orientor certainly offered enough to suggest she has a race in her at this level at least. Clearly green (missed break), she also met trouble just under 2f out but was staying on well at the finish. She should be all the sharper next time. (op 14-1)
Justine Time(IRE) fared only a little better for the fitting of cheekpieces and looks just poor at this stage. (op 22-1 tchd 25-1)
Umph(IRE) seems to be going backwards judged on his last two efforts down at this level.
Low Pastures Official explanation: jockey said gelding was slowly away
Ruskins View(IRE) Official explanation: jockey said filly finished lame
Come On Dave(IRE) very much needed the experience but did hint at ability towards the outside and should be up to making more of an impact in this grade next time. (op 12-1)

3022 BRITISH STALLION STUDS SUPPORTING BRITISH RACING E B F NOVICE STKS 5f
2:15 (2:16) (Class 4) 2-Y-O **£4,533** (£1,348; £674; £336) **Stalls** High

Form RPR
134 **1** **Ponty Acclaim (IRE)**[10] 2725 2-8-11 0.. DavidAllan 3 86+
(Tim Easterby) *trckd ldrs: t.k.h: swtchd rt over 1f out: str run on ins to ld last 100yds: readily* **10/3**[3]
1 **2** *2* **Nagham (IRE)**[14] 2580 2-9-0 0.. StephenCraine 4 82
(Kevin Ryan) *led: hung lft thrght: hdd and no ex ins fnl f* **8/1**
21 **3** *2 ¼* **Amadeus Denton (IRE)**[31] 2093 2-9-2 0.. FrederikTylicki 2 76
(Michael Dods) *w ldr on outer: kpt on same pce fnl f* **3/1**[2]
2 **4** *1 ¾* **Slenningford**[25] 2248 2-8-9 0.. PJMcDonald 5 63
(Ollie Pears) *chsd ldrs: outpcd over 1f out: kpt on ins fnl f* **12/1**
1 **5** *3 ¼* **Risky Art**[22] 2346 2-8-8 0.. JamesSullivan(3) 7 53
(Michael Easterby) *dwlt: hdwy on ins to chse ldrs 3f out: swtchd lft 2f out: wknd over 1f out* **11/8**[1]
65 **6** *2* **Neil's Pride**[19] 2430 2-8-9 0.. TonyHamilton 6 44
(Richard Fahey) *in rr: outpcd 3f out: nvr on terms* **50/1**
0 **7** *10* **Red Samantha (IRE)**[56] 1455 2-8-9 0.. PatrickMathers 1 8
(Alan Berry) *swvd lft s: in rr: bhd fnl 2f* **200/1**

59.56 secs (-0.04) **Going Correction** +0.05s/f (Good) **7** Ran SP% **111.4**
Speed ratings (Par 95): **102,98,95,92,87 84,68**
Tote Swingers: 1&2 £4.10, 1&3 £1.70, 2&3 £3.10 CSF £27.87 TOTE £3.70: £1.80, £6.60; EX 31.20.
Owner Rapcalone **Bred** T Darcy & Vincent McCarthy **Trained** Great Habton, N Yorks

FOCUS
A fairly useful conditions event.
NOTEBOOK
Ponty Acclaim(IRE), who had run into a few really useful sorts since her debut success at Ripon, found this level more to her liking and was readily on top by the finish. She's got a low weight in the Super Sprint at Newbury and it wouldn't be a surprise to see her go well at reasonbale odds. (op 4-1 tchd 9-2)
Nagham(IRE) was clearly all the sharper for Leicester, leading from the off this time, and emerges with credit conceding the winner 3lb. She's had just two starts so there may be more to come. (op 7-1)
Amadeus Denton(IRE), the only male horse in the race, had made a bit of a meal of justifying short odds at Doncaster last time and had no apparent excuses on this occasion, finding no extra inside the last. (op 4-1 tchd 11-4)
Slenningford's Catterick form had been boosted by On The Dark Side finishing placed in the Woodcote, but she probably ran to just a similar level, though once again offering enough to suggest she has a small race in her before long.
Risky Art had been impressive at Carlisle so this was disappointing. She'd made all there but missed a beat at the start here and never looked comfortable, clearly not herself for whatever reason. She deserves another chance. Official explanation: jockey said filly ran flat (op 5-4 tchd 11-10)
Neil's Pride has ability and is one to keep in mind for nurseries after this third run. Further is sure to suit judged on her breeding (dam won at up to 1m6f). (op 40-1)

3023 PORRITT'S STRIPE H'CAP 1m 4f
2:50 (2:50) (Class 4) (0-80,80) 4-Y-O+ **£4,209** (£1,252; £625; £312) **Stalls** Low

Form RPR
-011 **1** **Easy Terms**[21] 2388 4-8-10 **72**.. JamesSullivan(3) 5 91+
(Edwin Tuer) *trckd ldrs: hmpd over 2f out: led over 1f out: readily* **7/2**[1]
-120 **2** *3 ¼* **Lady Chaparral**[26] 2220 4-9-0 **73**.. TonyHamilton 13 85
(George Moore) *swtchd lft after s: t.k.h: sn trcking ldr: led 3f out: hdd over 1f out: styd on same pce* **13/2**[2]
6-20 **3** *7* **Sirgarfieldsobers (IRE)**[10] 2708 5-9-2 **80**.. NeilFarley(5) 2 81
(Declan Carroll) *trckd ldrs: t.k.h: hung lft over 2f out: kpt on one pce* **9/1**
-244 **4** *1 ¾* **Saint Thomas (IRE)**[20] 2403 4-9-2 **75**.. StephenCraine 11 73+
(John Mackie) *chsd ldrs: outpcd over 2f out: kpt on fnl f* **12/1**
3101 **5** *shd* **Tribal Myth (IRE)**[17] 2486 4-8-8 **72**.. JulieBurke(5) 4 70
(Kevin Ryan) *trckd ldrs: one pce fnl 2f* **9/1**
0215 **6** *½* **Amazing Blue Sky**[15] 2544 5-8-11 **70**.. PJMcDonald 1 67
(Ruth Carr) *led: hdd 3f out: edgd rt: wknd over 1f out* **8/1**
42-0 **7** *¾* **Danceintothelight**[76] 1039 4-8-5 **64**.. KellyHarrison 9 60
(Micky Hammond) *in rr: kpt on fnl 2f: nt clr run and swtchd rt ins fnl f: nvr nr ldrs* **16/1**
104- **8** *1 ½* **Royal Trooper (IRE)**[227] 7226 5-9-5 **78**.. FrederikTylicki 10 71
(James Given) *hld up in mid-div: drvn over 4f out: nvr a factor* **15/2**[3]
43-5 **9** *½* **Shernando**[38] 1901 4-9-7 **80**.. RoystonFfrench 12 73
(Mark Johnston) *s.i.s: in rr: drvn over 5f out: bhd 3f out: nvr on terms* **9/1**
6-50 **10** *1* **Pertemps Networks**[22] 2364 7-8-12 **71**.. DavidAllan 7 62
(Michael Easterby) *in rr: drvn over 4f out: kpt on fnl 2f: nvr a factor* **18/1**
1350 **11** *2* **Kames Park (IRE)**[10] 2708 9-8-6 **65**.. RobbieFitzpatrick 3 53
(Richard Guest) *s.i.s: in rr: hung lft over 1f out: nvr on terms* **22/1**
200/ **12** *2 ¼* **Shaloo Diamond**[612] 6681 6-9-1 **74**.. RussKennemore 8 58
(Richard Whitaker) *stmbld s: t.k.h in midfield: wknd 3f out* **16/1**
2-00 **13** *3 ¼* **Tayacoba (CAN)**[21] 2388 4-8-3 **65**.. PatrickDonaghy(3) 6 44
(Martin Todhunter) *mid-div: drvn over 3f out: sn bhd* **66/1**

2m 35.38s (-0.82) **Going Correction** +0.05s/f (Good) **13** Ran SP% **119.0**
Speed ratings (Par 105): **104,101,97,96,95 95,95,94,93,93 91,90,88**
Tote Swingers: 1&2 £5.20, 1&3 £6.90, 2&3 £10.90 CSF £24.61 CT £192.32 TOTE £4.40: £2.30, £3.10, £3.50; EX 28.30.
Owner E Tuer **Bred** T E Pocock **Trained** Great Smeaton, N Yorks

FOCUS
A fair contest which was well run. The performances of the first two need viewing in a positive light as the pair of them finished well clear of the rest, and post earn personal bests.
Danceintothelight Official explanation: jockey said gelding was denied a clear run

3024 FAIRFAX ARMS, GILLING H'CAP (DIV I) 7f
3:25 (3:26) (Class 5) (0-70,70) 3-Y-O+ **£2,590** (£770; £385; £192) **Stalls** Low

Form RPR
0U04 **1** **Viking Warrior (IRE)**[14] 2588 4-9-0 **56**.. FrederikTylicki 5 64
(Michael Dods) *led 1f: chsd ldr: led and hung lft over 1f out: jst hld on* **9/1**
0100 **2** *½* **No Quarter (IRE)**[17] 2494 4-9-4 **60**.. FrannyNorton 8 67+
(Tracy Waggott) *mid-div: wnt modest 4th over 2f out: swtchd rt jst ins fnl f: fin wl* **18/1**

-405 **3** *1 1/4* **Elusive Sue (USA)**[15] 2566 4-9-6 **69**.................... LauraBarry(7) 1 72
(Richard Fahey) *chsd ldrs: kpt on same pce fnl f* **4/1**[2]
102 **4** *1 1/2* **Dhhamaan (IRE)**[11] 2671 6-9-2 **58**....................(b) PJMcDonald 3 57
(Ruth Carr) *chsd ldrs: led after 1f: hdd and swtchd rt over 1f out: fdd ins fnl f* **10/3**[1]
-555 **5** *1 3/4* **Hard Rock City (USA)**[18] 2474 11-9-9 **70**....................(t) NeilFarley(5) 11 65+
(Declan Carroll) *t.k.h in rr: hdwy on outside over 2f out: edgd lft: nvr nr to chal* **10/1**
0/06 **6** *3* **Big Slick (IRE)**[19] 2412 6-8-9 **51** oh2.................... DavidAllan 4 37
(Mel Brittain) *rr-div: swtchd rt over 2f out: kpt on: nvr nr ldrs* **16/1**
-135 **7** *2 1/2* **Materialism**[15] 2564 3-9-4 **70**.................... RoystonFfrench 6 46
(Mark Johnston) *s.i.s: sn drvn along in rr: last over 3f out: sme hdwy and swtchd rt over 1f out: kpt on: nvr on terms* **11/2**[3]
00 **8** *2 3/4* **Strong Knight**[43] 1746 4-9-9 **65**.................... DuranFentiman 7 37
(Tim Walford) *towards rr: nvr a factor* **18/1**
6-06 **9** *12* **Gracie's Gift (IRE)**[12] 2653 9-9-4 **63**....................(v) RobertLButler(3) 2 —
(Richard Guest) *trckd ldrs: wknd over 2f out* **22/1**
0-26 **10** *1 3/4* **Downtown Boy (IRE)**[36] 1945 3-7-13 **51** oh1.................... AndrewMullen 10 —
(Tom Tate) *chsd ldrs on outer: lost pl bnd over 4f out: sn bhd* **7/1**
-060 **11** *6* **Little Pete (IRE)**[29] 2165 6-9-8 **64**....................(p) PatrickMathers 9 —
(Ian McInnes) *sn prom: lost pl over 4f out: bhd whn eased over 1f out* **50/1**
30-0 **12** *33* **Gypsy Style**[15] 2548 4-8-9 **51**....................(b[1]) TonyHamilton 12 —
(Kate Walton) *racd v wd: chsd ldrs: lost pl bnd over 4f out: bhd whn heavily eased 2f out: t.o* **40/1**

1m 28.23s (1.03) **Going Correction** +0.05s/f (Good)
WFA 3 from 4yo+ 10lb **12** Ran SP% **115.2**
Speed ratings (Par 103): **96,95,94,92,90 86,84,80,67,65 58,20**
Tote Swingers: 1&2 £25.10, 1&3 £9.00, 2&3 £15.70 CSF £151.99 CT £760.51 TOTE £16.30: £4.40, £8.80, £1.30; EX 191.60.
Owner Transpennine Partnership **Bred** Darley **Trained** Denton, Co Durham

FOCUS
Run-of-the-mill fare and, as is often the case over this C&D, a handy position was vital. Not that many ever threatened to land a serious blow. The winner showed much his best form this year.

3025 FAIRFAX ARMS, GILLING H'CAP (DIV II) 7f
4:05 (4:05) (Class 5) (0-70,70) 3-Y-O+ **£2,590** (£770; £385; £192) **Stalls** Low

Form RPR
2210 **1** **Pelmanism**[15] 2543 4-9-9 **70**....................(b) BrianToomey(5) 3 78
(Kevin Ryan) *hld up in mid-div: effrt and swtchd rt over 2f out: chsng ldrs over 1f out: hung rt: kpt on to ld nr fin* **7/1**[3]
5146 **2** *1/2* **Lindoro**[11] 2671 6-9-7 **63**.................... AndrewHeffernan 10 70
(Kevin M Prendergast) *led 1f: chsd clr ldr: led over 1f out: hdd and no ex nr fin* **8/1**
2313 **3** *nk* **Beckermet (IRE)**[13] 2609 9-9-0 **63**.................... ShaneBKelly(7) 4 69
(Ruth Carr) *mid-div: hmpd and lost pl bnd over 4f out: hdwy on outside 2f out: kpt on ins fnl f* **4/1**[2]
3515 **4** *nk* **Toby Tyler**[15] 2543 5-9-8 **64**....................(v) MickyFenton 7 69+
(Paul Midgley) *hood removed v late: s.i.s: in rr: hmpd and swtchd lft over 2f out: gd hdwy on ins over 1f out: styd on wl fnl f* **11/1**
4260 **5** *nk* **Crocodile Bay (IRE)**[6] 2829 8-8-10 **52**....................(b) RobbieFitzpatrick 6 57
(Richard Guest) *mid-div: hmpd over 2f out: gd hdwy over 1f out: styd on same pce fnl 100yds* **33/1**
100- **6** *3 1/4* **Angaric (IRE)**[210] 7468 8-8-11 **60**.................... JustinNewman(7) 11 56
(Bryan Smart) *swtchd lft s: in rr: kpt on fnl 2f: nvr nr to chal* **22/1**
0-06 **7** *1* **Sea Crest**[6] 2798 5-8-9 **51** oh2.................... DavidAllan 1 44
(Mel Brittain) *led after 1f: clr over 3f out: hdd over 1f out: wknd fnl 75yds* **16/1**
6-22 **8** *1 3/4* **Silly Gilly (IRE)**[22] 2348 7-8-10 **57**.................... DaleSwift(5) 5 45
(Ron Barr) *mid-div: lost pl bnd over 4f out: no threat after* **2/1**[1]
0-05 **9** *1 1/4* **Come And Go (UAE)**[22] 2366 5-9-12 **68**.................... PJMcDonald 2 53
(Ian McInnes) *in tch: effrt over 2f out: wknd over 1f out* **14/1**
5000 **10** *1/2* **Velvet Band**[22] 2348 4-8-9 **51** oh6....................(b[1]) FrannyNorton 9 35
(Richard Whitaker) *chsd ldrs: lost pl over 1f out* **33/1**
3-20 **11** *8* **Diablo Dancer**[31] 2094 3-9-2 **68**.................... DanielTudhope 8 26
(Tim Walford) *t.k.h: lost pl bnd over 4f out: bhd fnl 2f* **15/2**

1m 28.07s (0.87) **Going Correction** +0.05s/f (Good)
WFA 3 from 4yo+ 10lb **11** Ran SP% **119.8**
Speed ratings (Par 103): **97,96,96,95,95 91,90,88,87,86 77**
Tote Swingers: 1&2 £11.90, 1&3 £6.30, 2&3 £7.10 CSF £61.88 CT £261.35 TOTE £9.30: £3.10, £2.70, £1.60; EX 39.70.
Owner Guy Reed **Bred** Guy Reed **Trained** Hambleton, N Yorks
■ Brian Toomey's first winner on the Flat.
■ Stewards' Enquiry : Brian Toomey two-day ban: careless riding (Jun 28-29)

FOCUS
A modest contest. They went off hard up front and the field ended up in a bit of a heap as the leaders came back late on. It was slightly faster than division I and the form seems sound enough.
Silly Gilly(IRE) Official explanation: jockey said mare never travelled
Diablo Dancer Official explanation: jockey said filly suffered interference in running

3026 BRITISH STALLION STUDS SUPPORTING BRITISH RACING E B F FILLIES' H'CAP 1m
4:40 (4:40) (Class 3) (0-90,89) 3-Y-O+ **£6,799** (£2,023; £1,011; £505) **Stalls** Low

Form RPR
0603 **1** **Amethyst Dawn (IRE)**[12] 2634 5-9-9 **84**.................... DavidAllan 2 91
(Tim Easterby) *dwlt: sn trcking ldrs: hdwy on ins to ld over 5f out: rdn over 1f out: edgd rt: kpt on wl* **9/4**[1]
4162 **2** *1 1/2* **She's A Character**[12] 2634 4-9-7 **82**.................... TonyHamilton 5 86
(Richard Fahey) *swtchd lft after s: hdwy to chse ldrs over 5f out: kpt on to take 2nd ins fnl f: no imp* **10/3**[2]
6500 **3** *2* **Totally Ours**[11] 2679 4-9-9 **89**.................... JamesRogers(5) 3 88
(William Muir) *trckd ldrs: effrt over 3f out: sn outpcd: edgd rt over 1f out: styd on ins fnl f: tk 3rd nr line* **9/2**
11-2 **4** *3/4* **Clumber Place**[20] 2398 5-8-12 **76**.................... RobertLButler(3) 8 74
(Richard Guest) *w ldrs on outer: t.k.h: chsd wnr over 1f out: fdd last 100yds* **9/2**
1-05 **5** *4 1/2* **Snow Magic (IRE)**[35] 1992 4-8-12 **73**....................[1] PatCosgrave 6 60
(James Fanshawe) *hld up towards rr: effrt over 3f out: swtchd rt over 1f out: nvr trbld ldrs: eased clsng stages* **4/1**[3]
11-5 **6** *18* **Out Of Nothing**[24] 2315 8-9-3 **78**.................... AndrewHeffernan 7 24
(Kevin M Prendergast) *led tl over 5f out: lost pl over 2f out: sn bhd: t.o* **16/1**

1m 41.48s (1.38) **Going Correction** +0.05s/f (Good)
WFA 3 from 4yo+ 11lb **6** Ran SP% **116.1**
Speed ratings (Par 104): **95,93,91,90,86 68**
Tote Swingers: 1&2 £2.10, 1&3 £2.20, 2&3 £3.30 CSF £10.52 CT £30.52 TOTE £2.50: £1.10, £3.10; EX 9.20.
Owner D A West **Bred** W Kane **Trained** Great Habton, N Yorks

FOCUS
A fair fillies' event in which the winner dictated. She turned round Hamilton form with the runner-up and is rated close to her best.

NOTEBOOK
Amethyst Dawn(IRE) had a 3lb swing in the weights with She's A Character for Hamilton and that was enough to see her turn the tables. Tim Easterby's likeable mare should continue to hold her own and has a particularly good record when the ground is on the soft side. (op 5-2 tchd 11-4)
She's A Character will probably go up a little more in the weights without winning, which won't make life any easier, but she's clearly in a good vein of form at present. (op 3-1 tchd 11-4)
Totally Ours had run in a couple of really competitive handicaps prior to this and found this more to her liking. She left the impression a return to 1m2f will suit ideally as she got outpaced before keeping on well at the death. (op 8-1)
Clumber Place is best at 7f, and that was underlined by the fact she faded a bit late on here. She remains at the top of her game. (op 4-1 tchd 5-1)
Snow Magic(IRE) did well on Polytrack at the end of last season but hasn't been able to carry that over to turf this time round, a first-time hood not making any difference. (op 9-2 tchd 11-2)
Out Of Nothing had a more realistic chance back in this company but dropped away tamely. (tchd 14-1)

3027 STONEACRE FORD H'CAP 5f
5:15 (5:17) (Class 6) (0-65,65) 3-Y-O+ **£2,729** (£806; £403) **Stalls** High

Form RPR
03 **1** **Your Gifted (IRE)**[8] 2755 4-9-2 **58**.................... MatthewCosham(5) 18 75
(Patrick Morris) *dwlt: gd hdwy on ins to ld over 3f out: clr over 1f out: edgd lft: unchal* **12/1**
4055 **2** *4 1/2* **Lees Anthem**[13] 2609 4-9-2 **58**.................... DaleSwift(5) 1 59
(Colin Teague) *hdwy to chse ldrs on outside over 2f out: edgd rt: kpt on to take 2nd nr fin* **12/1**
0003 **3** *1/2* **Mission Impossible**[15] 2546 6-8-11 **48**....................(p) PatrickMathers 2 47+
(Colin Teague) *in rr: gd hdwy over 2f out: wnt 2nd over 1f out: kpt on same pce* **20/1**
100 **4** *1* **Rio's Girl**[6] 2798 4-9-4 **58**....................(p) AmyRyan(3) 16 53
(Kevin Ryan) *chsd ldrs: carried rt jst ins fnl f: kpt on same pce* **13/2**[2]
2142 **5** *nk* **We'll Deal Again**[18] 2464 4-9-13 **64**.................... DavidNolan 8 58
(Michael Easterby) *mid-div: effrt 2f out: kpt on same pce* **3/1**[1]
3550 **6** *1* **These Dreams**[20] 2396 3-8-6 **50**.................... AndrewMullen 9 38
(Richard Guest) *in rr: kpt on fnl 2f: nrst fin* **11/1**
3313 **7** *1/2* **Sparking**[29] 2164 4-9-7 **58**.................... LeeNewman 6 47
(David Barron) *mid-div: styd on fnl 2f: nvr nr to chal* **15/2**
3064 **8** *3/4* **Dispol Grand (IRE)**[44] 1716 5-9-3 **54**.................... MickyFenton 3 40
(Paul Midgley) *mid-div: hdwy whn hmpd over 1f out: kpt on: nvr nr ldrs* **16/1**
0-00 **9** *1 1/4* **Blue Rum (IRE)**[11] 2670 4-8-6 **46** oh1.................... PaulPickard(3) 4 28
(Alan Kirtley) *in rr: sme hdwy over 1f out: nvr a factor* **50/1**
0-60 **10** *nk* **Micky Mac (IRE)**[18] 2464 7-9-5 **56**.................... FrederikTylicki 15 37
(Colin Teague) *prom: wknd over 1f out* **33/1**
6266 **11** *1* **Garstang**[11] 2694 8-9-8 **59**....................(b) DavidAllan 12 36
(John Balding) *mid-div: effrt over 2f out: n.m.r: nvr nr ldrs* **7/1**[3]
2600 **12** *1/2* **Cheveyo (IRE)**[12] 2655 5-8-9 **46**....................(v) AndrewHeffernan 10 21
(Lisa Williamson) *sn in rr* **40/1**
20-0 **13** *3/4* **Speedy Senorita (IRE)**[15] 2546 6-9-5 **59**.................... JamesSullivan(3) 11 32
(James Moffatt) *led tl over 3f out: wknd 2f out* **20/1**
0000 **14** *3 1/2* **Grand Stitch (USA)**[13] 2609 5-9-9 **65**....................(v) NeilFarley(5) 13 25
(Declan Carroll) *mid-div: in rr fnl 2f* **20/1**
4315 **15** *2* **Ridley Didley (IRE)**[11] 2667 6-9-9 **65**....................(p) BrianToomey(5) 7 18
(Noel Wilson) *chsd ldrs: wknd qckly over 1f out* **20/1**
000 **16** *1 3/4* **Gala Spirit (IRE)**[34] 2001 4-9-7 **58**.................... AWhelan 5 —
(Michael Wigham) *s.s and sn swtchd rt: a in rr* **25/1**
60-0 **17** *1* **Midget**[44] 1716 4-9-4 **55**.................... TonyHamilton 17 —
(Declan Carroll) *sn bhd* **33/1**

59.22 secs (-0.38) **Going Correction** +0.05s/f (Good)
WFA 3 from 4yo+ 7lb **17** Ran SP% **125.4**
Speed ratings (Par 101): **105,97,97,95,94 93,92,91,89,88 87,86,85,79,76 73,72**
Tote Swingers: 1&2 £31.80, 1&3 £30.80, 2&3 £39.90 CSF £131.56 CT £2974.93 TOTE £10.00: £1.80, £4.30, £5.80, £1.20; EX 173.70.
Owner L Walsh **Bred** Rathasker Stud **Trained** Tarporley, Cheshire
■ Stewards' Enquiry : Dale Swift five-day ban: careless riding (Jun 28 - Jul 2)
Amy Ryan one-day ban: careless riding (Jun 28)

FOCUS
This looked very open beforehand. The runners stayed in one group and the performances of the second and third, who both came from low stalls, are probably worth marking up slightly. The winner had the avnatage of the rail and is rated back to her best, with the second 10lb off.
Ridley Didley(IRE) Official explanation: jockey said gelding had no more to give

3028 STATION WHIN H'CAP 6f
5:50 (5:51) (Class 4) (0-85,85) 3-Y-O+ **£4,209** (£1,252; £625; £312) **Stalls** High

Form RPR
014 **1** **Ginger Ted (IRE)**[1] 3000 4-9-11 **85**....................(p) RobertLButler(3) 12 96+
(Richard Guest) *hld up in rr: effrt and nt clr run over 2f out: styd on wl to ld lat 50yds: hld on towards fin* **6/1**[3]
0053 **2** *hd* **Red Cape (FR)**[13] 2620 8-9-0 **74**.................... JamesSullivan(3) 8 84
(Ruth Carr) *w ldr: led 3f out: hdd ins fnl f: no ex nr fin* **9/2**[1]
1400 **3** *1 1/2* **Tasmeem (IRE)**[17] 2497 4-9-4 **75**....................(v[1]) FrannyNorton 14 80
(David Nicholls) *chsd ldrs: chal over 1f out: kpt on same pce last 100yds* **10/1**
3306 **4** *1* **Malcheek (IRE)**[17] 2495 9-9-9 **80**.................... DavidAllan 10 82+
(Tim Easterby) *in rr: hdwy over 2f out: chsng ldrs appr fnl f: kpt on same pce* **7/1**
45-0 **5** *1* **Walvis Bay (IRE)**[39] 1878 4-9-10 **81**.................... MickyFenton 15 80
(Tom Tate) *led 3f: one pce whn hung lft ins fnl f* **11/2**[2]
-520 **6** *1 1/2* **Jarrow (IRE)**[11] 2694 4-9-6 **77**.................... AdrianNicholls 3 71+
(David Nicholls) *sn chsng ldrs on outside: kpt on same pce appr fnl f* **8/1**
3006 **7** *3/4* **Indian Trail**[10] 2714 11-9-11 **82**....................(v) PaulQuinn 11 74
(David Nicholls) *towards rr: hdwy over 1f out: kpt on: nvr nr ldrs* **14/1**
0000 **8** *nk* **Hotham**[13] 2620 8-9-7 **78**.................... DanielTudhope 7 69
(Noel Wilson) *hld up in mid-div: effrt 2f out: sn outpcd: kpt on towards fin* **25/1**
5650 **9** *1/2* **Green Manalishi**[3] 2938 10-9-3 **77**....................(p) AmyRyan(3) 13 66
(Kevin Ryan) *chsd ldrs: wknd over 1f out* **20/1**
-043 **10** *1 1/2* **Illustrious Prince (IRE)**[20] 2398 4-9-4 **80**.................... NeilFarley(5) 9 64
(Declan Carroll) *in rr: sme hdwy over 2f out: sn wknd* **9/1**
2502 **11** *2* **Mandalay King (IRE)**[15] 2543 6-8-10 **67**.................... PJMcDonald 4 45
(Marjorie Fife) *rrd s: mid-div: outpcd and lost pl over 3f out: sme hdwy whn nt clr run over 2f out: sn wknd* **16/1**

4-00 **12** *1* **Baldemar**[44] 1720 6-9-11 82 .... FrederikTylicki 1 57
(Richard Fahey) *chsd ldrs: wkng whn struck over face by rival rdr's ship over 1f out* **14/1**

00-0 **13** *8* **Haadeeth**[24] 2299 4-9-6 77 .... TonyHamilton 5 26
(Richard Fahey) *w ldrs: hung lft and lost pl over 1f out: sn bhd: eased* **25/1**

1m 12.15s (-0.55) **Going Correction** +0.05s/f (Good) **13** Ran SP% **122.2**
Speed ratings (Par 105): **105,104,102,101,100 98,97,96,96,94 91,90,79**
Tote Swingers: 1&2 £8.20, 1&3 £8.60, 2&3 £9.40. Totesuper7: WIN: Not won. PLACE: Not won. CSF £33.03 CT £279.37 TOTE £5.70: £2.60, £2.50, £4.50; EX 33.10.
Owner Maze Rattan Limited **Bred** T Counihan **Trained** Stainforth, S Yorks

FOCUS
A fairly useful sprint. They stayed in one group towards the stands' rail and the pace was a good one.The winner did it smoothly and the form is rated around the runner-up.
Haadeeth Official explanation: jockey said gelding hung left-handed
T/Plt: £112.50 to a £1 stake. Pool of £54,525.86 - 353.61 winning units. T/Qpdt: £31.10 to a £1 stake. Pool of £3,957.42 - 94.12 winning units. WG

3009 ASCOT (R-H)
Wednesday, June 15

OFFICIAL GOING: Good (stands' side 9.4, centre 10.0, far side 9.5, round 8.4)

Rail on round course out 3m from inside line from 9f to home straight adding \n\x\x 9yd to 1m2f race.
Wind: Moderate, half against Weather: Showers late afternoon

3029 JERSEY STKS (GROUP 3) 7f
2:30 (2:30) (Class 1) 3-Y-0

£39,739 (£15,064; £7,539; £3,759; £1,883; £945) **Stalls** Centre

Form RPR

32-6 **1** **Strong Suit (USA)**[60] 1405 3-9-6 113 .... RichardHughes 5 119
(Richard Hannon) *trckd ldr gng wl: shkn up to ld over 1f out: sn rdn: edgd sltly lft jst ins fnl f: kpt on and a in full control* **11/1**

12-1 **2** *½* **Codemaster**[32] 2106 3-9-1 110 .... DaneO'Neill 8 112
(Henry Candy) *in tch: rdn 2f out: styd on ins fnl f: clsd towards fin but nt quite pce of wnr and nvr gng to get there* **7/4**[1]

1-1 **3** *nk* **Western Aristocrat (USA)**[18] 2503 3-9-1 95 .... JMurtagh 9 111+
(Jeremy Noseda) *hld up: rdn and nt qckn over 2f out: hdwy over 1f out: r.o ins fnl f: gng on at fin* **9/2**[3]

00-3 **4** *¾* **Oracle (IRE)**[25] 2324 3-9-1 116 .... RyanMoore 3 109
(A P O'Brien, Ire) *in tch: effrt to chse ldrs over 1f out: ch ins fnl f: one pce fnl 50yds* **7/1**

-210 **5** *½* **Splash Point (USA)**[81] 998 3-9-4 104 .... FrankieDettori 2 111
(Mahmood Al Zarooni) *hld up: rdn and hdwy over 1f out: chsng ldrs and in cl contention ins fnl f: one pce fnl 50yds* **16/1**

-120 **6** *1* **Sikeeb (IRE)**[25] 2296 3-9-1 97 .... (t) PhilipRobinson 1 105
(Clive Brittain) *chsd ldrs: rdn 2f out: sn outpcd: kpt on ins fnl f: nt pce to chal* **40/1**

5-15 **7** *½* **Majestic Myles (IRE)**[4] 2934 3-9-1 100 .... PaulHanagan 7 104
(Richard Fahey) *racd keenly: chsd ldrs: rdn and nt qckn over 1f out: one pce ins fnl f* **20/1**

0-22 **8** *3½* **Havane Smoker**[31] 2139 3-9-1 111 .... ChristopheSoumillon 10 95
(J-C Rouget, France) *stdd s: racd keenly: hld up in last pl: rdn over 1f out: failed to pick-up: eased whn n.d fnl 75yds* **3/1**[2]

0354 **9** *¾* **Utley (USA)**[12] 2683 3-9-1 108 .... (b[1]) WilliamBuick 6 92
(John Gosden) *racd keenly: led: shkn up over 2f out: rdn and hdd over 1f out: sn wknd* **33/1**

1m 26.09s (-1.11) **Going Correction** +0.025s/f (Good) **9** Ran SP% **116.4**
Speed ratings (Par 109): **111,110,110,109,108 107,106,102,102**
toteswingers: 1&2 £4.90, 1&3 £7.80, 2&3 £2.60 CSF £30.46 CT £104.32 TOTE £11.80: £2.60, £1.50, £2.00; EX 31.10 Trifecta £232.60 Pool: £14,983.86 - 47.65 winning units..
Owner Mrs J Wood **Bred** Mcdowell Farm, Gainsborough Farm Et Al **Trained** East Everleigh, Wilts

FOCUS
Since the turn of the millennium four winners of this race subsequently won in Group 1 company, namely Observatory, Mozart, Proclamation and Aqlaam. The action unfolded up the middle of the track and the pace was good, courtesy of the free-running Utley, who raced in a clear lead. A field of nine represented the lowest turnout for well over 20 years, but this was an up-to-scratch Jersey and the penalised Strong Suit is a bit above the usual winner, up a length on last year's Coventry victory. The level of the form is set around the fifth and sixth.

NOTEBOOK
Strong Suit(USA) produced a very smart performance considering he was shouldering a 5lb penalty and had to concede weight all round. He was given a positive ride, leading the chasing pack, and it was clear from some way out he was going well. It was just a question of what he would find on this first start after a notable setback and return from two months off, but despite wandering a bit, he did enough. He was reported to have lost his action when well behind Frankel in the Greenham on his reappearance and it turned out he was suffering from a breathing problem, so he was operated on. His connections originally doubted he'd make Ascot, but Richard Hannon revealed afterwards the colt had worked "brilliantly" with Canford Cliffs on the Thursday prior to this meeting. Strong Suit was finally confirming the promise of his high-class juvenile form and was gaining a second straight Royal Ascot success, adding to last year's win in the Coventry. It's not out of the question he could bid to emulate stablemate Canford Cliffs by going for a third in next year's Queen Anne - he certainly deserves another shot in Group 1 company with improvement expected form this performance. In the shorter term he could go for the Prix Jean Prat over 1m at Chantilly, a race his stable won last year with Dick Turpin, and he should get the extra furlong. (op 10-1 tchd 12-1)
Codemaster won a Listed race at Newmarket on his reappearance that had provided two Jersey winners in recent years, Jeremy and Tariq, as well as a runner-up in Fokine. Henry Candy's runner upheld that tradition with a good, keeping-on second, but he was always held. (op 15-8 tchd 2-1 in places)
Western Aristocrat(USA) ◆ was up in class after a couple of wins in minor company (last time he defeated Rhythm Of Light, who later won the Sandringham on this card) and ran a race full of promise. A bit enthusiastic early, it was understandable he was ridden with cover and Johnny Murtagh chose to follow the favourite, but that left the colt with too much to do, especially as he was outpaced when belatedly asked for an effort. He was really going on at the finish and considering he still has plenty of scope for physical development, he could be high class at around 1m. (tchd 5-1)
Oracle(IRE)'s third in the Irish Guineas has yet to work out, but he ran with credit. He briefly looked a threat challenging towards the far side of the group, but his bid flattened out late on. (op 6-1)
Splash Point(USA), the UAE 2,000 Guineas winner, was closest to the far rail and shaped quite well. A return to further ought to suit. (op 20-1 tchd 25-1 in places)
Sikeeb(IRE) returned to form in a first-time tongue-tie on this drop in trip, but was still well held. (op 50-1)
Majestic Myles(IRE) was turned out only four days after being beaten in a good handicap at York and was keen.
Havane Smoker was runner-up in the French 2,000 Guineas last time, but the combined record of runners to come out that race now stands at 0-10. Excitable beforehand and requiring two handlers, he raced keenly under exaggerated hold-up tactics and never featured. (op 7-2 tchd 4-1 in places)
Utley(USA) was warm down his neck and didn't settle in front in first-time blinkers. (op 40-1)

3030 WINDSOR FOREST STKS (GROUP 2) (F&M) 1m (S)
3:05 (3:09) (Class 1) 4-Y-0+

£56,770 (£21,520; £10,770; £5,370; £2,690; £1,350) **Stalls** Centre

Form RPR

1122 **1** **Lolly For Dolly (IRE)**[25] 2325 4-8-12 108 .... (b) WMLordan 5 115
(T Stack, Ire) *swtchd to r in centre gp for 3f: towards rr: rdn 3f out: hdwy wl over 1f out: nt clr run and swtchd lft jst over 1f out: drvn to ld ins fnl f: styd on wl and gng away fin: drvn out* **11/1**

5-31 **2** *1½* **Chachamaidee (IRE)**[25] 2315 4-8-12 105 .... TomQueally 3 111
(Sir Henry Cecil) *racd in centre gp for 3f: in tch: hdwy to trck ldrs and travelling wl ent fnl 2f: pushed to ld over 1f out: edgd lft u.p and hdd ins fnl f: one pce after* **16/1**

4-62 **3** *1* **First City**[12] 2678 5-8-12 105 .... JamieSpencer 7 109
(David Simcock) *stdd s: swtchd to r in centre gp for 3f: hld up in rr: hdwy 2f out: nt clr run over 1f out tl ent fnl f: drvn and chsd ldng pair ins fnl f: kpt on* **25/1**

21-2 **4** *2¾* **Sajjhaa**[34] 2029 4-8-12 111 .... FrankieDettori 4 103
(Saeed Bin Suroor) *mounted on crse and taken down early: racd in centre gp: overall ldr and grad led gp across to merge w stands' side trio 5f out: rdn jst over 2f out: drvn and hdd over 1f out: wknd ins fnl f* **10/3**[1]

53-1 **5** *½* **I'm A Dreamer (IRE)**[45] 1718 4-8-12 110 .... WilliamBuick 12 102
(David Simcock) *racd in centre gp for 3f: hld up towards rr: rdn and effrt over 2f out: drvn and unable qck over 1f out: edgd lft and outpcd fnl f* **7/2**[2]

4-40 **6** *1¼* **Field Day (IRE)**[34] 2029 4-8-12 107 .... (t) RyanMoore 6 99
(Brian Meehan) *racd in centre gp for 3f: in tch: rdn and effrt 2f out: hanging rt and unable qck over 1f out: continued to hang rt and wknd fnl f* **14/1**

4-44 **7** *3* **Music Show (IRE)**[34] 2029 4-8-12 112 .... RichardHughes 8 92+
(Mick Channon) *swtchd lft s and racd in centre gp for 3f: rdn and effrt over 2f out: keeping on but stl plenty to do whn nt clr run over 1f out: lost any ch: pushed along and no imp fnl f* **8/1**

10-1 **8** *½* **Seta**[46] 1681 4-8-12 110 .... KierenFallon 1 91
(Luca Cumani) *racd in centre gp for 3f: chsd ldrs: rdn 3f out: ev ch u.p ent fnl 2f: drvn and btn jst over 1f out: wknd fnl f* **7/1**[3]

0-35 **9** *¾* **Fontley**[16] 2558 4-8-12 99 .... DarryllHolland 2 89
(Eve Johnson Houghton) *racd in centre gp for 3f: a towards rr: rdn and struggling 3f out: wl btn over 1f out: no ch but styng u.p whn nt clr run and swtchd lft fnl 100yds* **50/1**

11-5 **10** *¾* **Dever Dream**[39] 1893 4-8-12 105 .... EddieAhern 10 87
(William Haggas) *immediately swtchd to r on stands' rail: in tch: rdn and unable qck jst over 2f out: wknd u.p over 1f out: wl btn fnl f* **14/1**

20-2 **11** *½* **Anna Salai (USA)**[46] 1681 4-8-12 109 .... MickaelBarzalona 13 86
(Mahmood Al Zarooni) *immediately crossed to racd against stands' rail: in tch in midfield: rdn and struggling ent fnl 2f: wknd wl over 1f out* **12/1**

15/0 **12** *2¾* **Shamandar (FR)**[39] 1885 4-8-12 100 .... MichaelHills 9 80
(William Haggas) *immediately swtchd to r against stands' rail: chsd overall ldr tl jst over 2f out: sn struggling u.p: wknd wl over 1f out* **33/1**

35-3 **R** **Jacqueline Quest (IRE)**[23] 2358 4-8-12 111 .... JMurtagh 11 —
(Sir Henry Cecil) *ref to r: tk no part* **20/1**

1m 38.72s (-1.88) **Going Correction** +0.025s/f (Good) **13** Ran SP% **117.7**
Speed ratings (Par 115): **110,108,107,104,104 103,100,99,98,98 97,94,—**
toteswingers: 1&2 £26.40, 1&3 £35.90, 2&3 £61.40 CSF £164.75 CT £4241.39 TOTE £14.20: £3.00, £4.30, £9.10; EX 200.70 Trifecta £13018.30 Part won. Pool: £17,592.38 - 0.80 winning units..
Owner David Keoghan **Bred** J Jamgotchian **Trained** Golden, Co Tipperary
■ The first Royal Ascot winner for both Tommy Stack and Wayne Lordan.
■ Stewards' Enquiry : W M Lordan 4-day ban: used whip in incorrect place (Jun 29 - Jul 2)

FOCUS
This race has been won by some of the top fillies and mares in its relatively short history, but the last three winners all reached their peak at Group 2 level and never won in the highest grade. This looked a pretty competitive renewal with only 7lb covering the majority of the field on official ratings, and it produced a surprise result. The time comes out as the same as the Royal Hunt Cup and this form is a bit below the average for this race. The winner is rated in line with the best view of her Irish form. A number of others didn't show their best.

NOTEBOOK
Lolly For Dolly(IRE), a progressive filly at Group 3 level this season and since blinkers have been fitted, had shown her best form on soft ground and she was up in grade here. Held up at the back early, she was being ridden along fully 3f out and went as long as 150-1 in running on the exchanges, but then picked up as others faded and finished strongly next to the rail to lead inside the last furlong. She was never going better than at the finish and might get further. She will go to Tipperary next, but the target will be the Matron Stakes. (op 14-1 tchd 10-1)
Chachamaidee(IRE) showed a return to form when dropped in trip and grade at York with a hood fitted for the first time. Back up to 1m, she coped well with being re-saddled on the way to the start and she travelled well in behind the leaders. She looked the most likely winner when taking over from the favourite over a furlong out, but was run down by the Irish filly. She is likely to go to the Oak Tree Stakes, back at 7f, at Glorious Goodwood. (op 14-1)
First City, who had run well when second in a Group 3 on her previous outing, was held up at the back before cruising up to the leaders 2f out. She was briefly short of room, but got out and looked a big danger entering the last furlong, only for her effort to peter out. She stays the trip, but has yet to score at Group or Listed level and, as she carries her head awkwardly, might be worth a try in some form of headgear. (op 28-1)
Sajjhaa was a worthy favourite as she had the beating of I'm A Dreamer and Music Show on recent form. Dropping back in trip having finished runner-up to Midday at York, she made the running but could not hold off the challengers in the last 2f. She has gone well fresh in the past and not necessarily improved next time, so she might be given more of a break before her next run. (op 3-1 tchd 7-2)
I'm A Dreamer(IRE), an impressive winner of a 1m1f Group 3 on her reappearance with today's runner-up and Field Day behind, had finished behind Sajjhaa in a Listed race last autumn and was worse off at the weights today. That said, she was still rather disappointing, fading tamely after looking to have every chance. (tchd 10-3 and 9-2 in a place and 4-1 in places)
Field Day(IRE), who beat Chachamaidee when the winner of a Listed race over the round mile here last season, was given every chance as she was tucked away just behind the pace throughout. She has to prove she can win at Group level. (op 20-1)
Music Show(IRE) was the only Group 1 winner taking part this time and she avoided a penalty for that success. She was making headway when she ran into a bottleneck over a furlong out, and by the time she was in the clear the race was over. She can be given another chance. (tchd 9-1)
Seta is a three-time Listed winner, but has been held so far in Group company. She was ridden close to the pace, but faded under pressure and it looks as if Group company is beyond her. (op 11-2)

Fontley, a decent handicapper who ran well over C&D on her reappearance, was always struggling in this better grade. (op 100-1)

Dever Dream, a multiple winner at 6f-7f in 2010, was up in both trip and grade here. She appeared to have her chance, but did not seem to get home. (tchd 16-1)

Anna Salai(USA), runner-up in the Irish 1,000 Guineas in 2010, was having her first run for over ten months when runner-up to Seta at Goodwood, but failed to improve on that performance here. (op 16-1)

Shamandar(FR) missed all last season, but put up a promising effort in the Victoria Cup on her return to action. She raced up with the pace near the stands' side before fading. (tchd 28-1 and 50-1)

Jacqueline Quest(IRE), disqualified after winning the 2010 1,000 Guineas, had run well below her best on her reappearance and refused to race at all this time.

3031 PRINCE OF WALES'S STKS (BRITISH CHAMPIONS' SERIES) (GROUP 1) 1m 2f

3:45 (3:47) (Class 1) 4-Y-O+

£227,080 (£86,080; £43,080; £21,480; £10,760; £5,400) **Stalls** Low

Form RPR

16-1 **1** **Rewilding**[81] 1001 4-9-0 121 .... FrankieDettori 6 130
(Mahmood Al Zarooni) *hld up in last pl: rdn and hdwy over 2f out: chsd ldr ent fnl 2f: r.o for press ins fnl f: led cl home* **17/2**[3]

3-11 **2** *nk* **So You Think (NZ)**[24] 2332 5-9-0 126 .... RyanMoore 4 129
(A P O'Brien, Ire) *racd keenly: disp ld for 2f: chsd ldrs: wnt 2nd over 3f out: kicked into ld wl over 2f out and sn edgd rt: jst over 2 l clr ent fnl 2f: hrd rdn over 1f out: all out ins fnl f: worn down cl home* **4/11**[1]

00-2 **3** *6* **Sri Putra**[39] 1896 5-9-0 113 .... NeilCallan 1 117
(Roger Varian) *hld up: rdn 2f out: chsd ldrs for press over 1f out but no imp: kpt on to take 3rd cl home: no ch w front pair* **66/1**

5-11 **4** *½* **Planteur (IRE)**[46] 1708 4-9-0 122 .... ChristopheSoumillon 3 116
(E Lellouche, France) *hld up in tch: effrt over 2f out: unable to chal ldr: one pce over 1f out: no ch w front pair ins fnl f: lost 3rd cl home* **11/2**[2]

-106 **5** *10* **Twice Over**[32] 2101 6-9-0 125 .... TomQueally 7 96
(Sir Henry Cecil) *hld up in tch: effrt over 2f out: unable to chal ldr: wknd over 1f out* **14/1**

33-3 **6** *43* **Jan Vermeer (IRE)**[20] 2439 4-9-0 115 .... JPO'Brien 5 —
(A P O'Brien, Ire) *s.i.s: hdwy to ld after 2f: abt 7 l clr 1/2-way: rdn and hdd wl over 2f out: sn wknd and eased: t.o* **28/1**

5-00 **7** *95* **Debussy (IRE)**[81] 1000 5-9-0 120 .... AhmedAjtebi 2 —
(Mahmood Al Zarooni) *disp ld for 2f: racd keenly chsd ldr tl over 3f out: wkng whn bdly hmpd sn after: sn completely t.o* **66/1**

2m 4.24s (-2.76) **Going Correction** +0.125s/f (Good) **7 Ran SP% 112.3**
Speed ratings (Par 117): **116,115,110,110,102 68,—**
toteswingers: 1&2 £1.40, 1&3 £19.80, 2&3 £8.30 CSF £11.78 TOTE £10.80: £3.50, £1.10; EX 18.30.

Owner Godolphin **Bred** Watership Down Stud **Trained** Newmarket, Suffolk
■ Mahmood Al Zarooni's first Royal Ascot winner.

■ Stewards' Enquiry : Frankie Dettori 9-day ban: used whip with excessive frequency (Jun 29 - Jul7)

FOCUS

All eyes were on a colt who had well and truly caught the imagination on a global scale, the New Zealand-bred, ex-Australian-trained and now Irish-based So You Think. However, the six-time Group 1 winner surprisingly came up short, just losing out in a memorable finish. The first two posted top-class efforts to pull clear, although the fourth and fifth weren't at their best. Rewilding produced a clear personal best and So You Think is rated to his Australian mark. The pace was strong when Jan Vermeer went to the front after 2f.

NOTEBOOK

Rewilding followed up his Sheema Classic success to make it back-to-back Group 1 wins and he's evidently a really high-class colt. There was a doubt about how he'd cope with the drop back from 1m4f, but he just got away with it under an inspired Frankie Dettori. The jockey did, however, pick up a ban for using his whip with excessive frequency. The key to the winner is to keep him fresh as there's not a great deal of him and he hasn't always taken his racing well, hence this being his first start since the aforementioned Dubai success, so it's possible this will leave its mark in the relative short term. However, his connections want to run him in the King George back here on July 23, and if he does recover in time then he should go well, with the extra distance sure to help him. (op 12-1)

So You Think(NZ) may not be the superstar we were led to believe as he was fully expected to have the beating of Rewilding over 1m2f, but there's reason to think he may yet prove himself genuinely top class. Aidan O'Brien blamed himself for the defeat, believing his runner was "not fit enough" following two wins against overmatched rivals at the Curragh since switching hemispheres. The trainer felt he hadn't done enough with the horse since that latest victory, and while such excuses often need taking with a pinch of salt, in this case O'Brien's view makes sense. So You Think is a big, gross horse and it's notable that when trained in Australia he raced much more regularly than is the norm for European middle-distance runners. Indeed last year he was out six times between August 28 and November 2, and his Cox Plate victory (the second of his career) came only three days before his third in the Melbourne Cup. He certainly behaved like a horse who was much too fresh and the race did not go to plan. Sweating a bit under his saddle, he was too enthusiastic through the early stages, not helped by stable companion and apparent intended pacemaker Jan Vermeer missing the break. A further hindrance to So You Think was the persistent presence of Debussy, who sat about as close to the runner-up as possible for as long as possible, not being allowed to stride on and consequently racing keenly. He certainly didn't aid Ryan Moore's attempts to settle his mount. The runner-up quickened early in the straight, but it soon became apparent he wasn't going away from his field in the manner many had anticipated, and despite keeping on gamely, he was eventually overhauled in agonising fashion. All things considered he's worth another chance and provided he takes the race okay it makes sense to turn him out quickly for the Eclipse. (op 2-5 tchd 4-9 and 1-2 in places)

Sri Putra is a hard horse to win with these days but he's capable of really smart form, like when third in a sub-par Eclipse last season. This was a much better race and he ran as well as could have been expected.

Planteur(IRE) was bidding to become the fourth French-trained winner of the race in five years and the form of his Prix Ganay win has worked out well (runner-up Sarafina and third-placed Cirrus Des Aigles have since won in Group company), but he disappointed. He moved into contention going okay, but proved one-paced under pressure in the straight. His round action suggests he may have found the ground quicker than ideal. (op 9-2)

Twice Over was fourth in this in 2009 and runner-up last year, but he doesn't look as good now. A heavy defeat in the Lockinge hinted as much and he's now 3-16 in Group 1s.

Jan Vermeer(IRE) acted as the pacemaker, being rushed up to lead after missing the break. (op 40-1)

Debussy(IRE) Official explanation: jockey said he eased horse closing stages having clipped the rail turning in

3032 ROYAL HUNT CUP (HERITAGE H'CAP) 1m (S)

4:25 (4:25) (Class 2) 3-Y-O+

£62,310 (£18,660; £9,330; £4,670; £2,330; £1,170) **Stalls** Centre

Form RPR

0-33 **1** **Julienas (IRE)**[20] 2441 4-8-8 93 .... EddieAhern 24 105
(Walter Swinburn) *racd stands' side: hld up wl in tch: rdn and effrt to ld 2f out: drvn and edgd lft ins fnl f: kpt on wl* **12/1**[3]

2031 **2** *½* **Dance And Dance (IRE)**[12] 2679 5-9-3 102 5ex .... RyanMoore 30 113+
(Edward Vaughan) *racd stands' side: hld up in rr: effrt and bhd a wall of horses wl over 1f out: swtchd lft and hdwy to chse ldrs 1f out: pressing wnr whn gap clsd and swtchd rt ins fnl f: r.o wl: 2nd of 22 in gp* **7/1**[1]

-400 **3** *2* **Invisible Man**[97] 828 5-9-6 105 .... (b) FrankieDettori 25 111
(Saeed Bin Suroor) *racd stands' side: stdd s: hld up in rr: stl plenty to do and bhd a wall of horses 2f out: hdwy over 1f out: chsng ldrs whn sltly hmpd ins fnl f: styd on wl: 3rd of 22 in gp* **20/1**

0-66 **4** *nse* **Pendragon (USA)**[16] 2573 8-8-4 89 .... JimmyQuinn 14 95+
(Brian Ellison) *racd stands' side: hld up in tch in midfield: nt clr run and switching rt wl over 1f out: kpt on wl u.p fnl f: 4th of 22 in gp* **33/1**

5-14 **5** *4* **Eton Forever (IRE)**[49] 1600 4-9-4 103 .... NeilCallan 15 100+
(Roger Varian) *racd stands' side: chsd ldrs: swtchd rt and effrt to chse wnr over 1f out drvn and pressing ldr 1f out: wknd fnl 150yds: 5th of 22 in gp* **14/1**

0-43 **6** *¾* **Start Right**[12] 2679 4-8-13 98 .... KierenFallon 12 93+
(Luca Cumani) *racd stands' side: in tch in midfield: pushed along over 3f out: drvn and chsd ldrs wl over 1f out: unable qck and no imp ent fnl f: wknd ins fnl f: 6th of 22 in gp* **8/1**[2]

3010 **7** *nk* **Kyllachy Star**[25] 2284 5-8-12 97 .... PhillipMakin 31 91
(Richard Fahey) *racd stands' side: hld up in tch in midfield: rdn and effrt jst over 2f out: unable qck u.p over 1f out: wknd 1f out: 7th of 22 in gp* **40/1**

3250 **8** *hd* **Fareer**[34] 2031 5-9-10 109 .... (b[1]) RichardHills 16 103+
(Ed Dunlop) *racd stands' side: hld up towards rr: swtchd rt and effrt jst over 2f out: drvn to chse ldrs over 1f out: no prog 1f out: wknd ins fnl f: 8th of 22 in gp* **25/1**

6-06 **9** *1* **Chapter And Verse (IRE)**[46] 1684 5-7-11 87 .... KieranO'Neill(5) 21 79
(Mike Murphy) *racd stands' side: stdd s and t.k.h early: hld up in tch in midfield: rdn and effrt over 2f out: nt clr run and switching rt over 1f out: plugged on same pce fnl f: 9th of 22 in gp* **20/1**

0-P0 **10** *½* **Capital Attraction (USA)**[34] 2031 4-8-10 95 .... (b[1]) TomQueally 22 85
(Sir Henry Cecil) *racd stands' side: in tch: hdwy to chse ldrs over 3f out: rdn and pressing ldrs whn hung rt wl over 1f out: wknd jst over 1f out: 10th of 22 in gp* **50/1**

0/-0 **11** *¾* **Stunning View (IRE)**[17] 2533 4-9-0 99 .... (p) PJSmullen 18 88
(D K Weld, Ire) *taken down early: racd stands' side: hld up towards rr: rdn and effrt whn short of room wl over 1f out: swtchd rt and plugged on fr over 1f out: nvr able to chal: 11th of 22 in gp* **28/1**

0224 **12** *½* **Pintura**[34] 2031 4-8-10 95 .... JamieSpencer 9 82+
(David Simcock) *racd stands' side: hld up in rr: rdn and hdwy wl over 1f out: kpt on fnl f: nvr trbld ldrs: 12th of 22 in gp* **20/1**

0-02 **13** *1* **Sooraah**[39] 1884 4-8-4 92 .... JohnFahy(3) 8 77
(William Haggas) *racd far side: hld up in rr: hdwy over 2f out: rdn to ld far side 2f out: kpt on and fin wl clr of gp but no ch w overall ldrs: 1st of 4 in gp* **25/1**

1-13 **14** *1* **Point North (IRE)**[14] 2604 4-8-3 88 ow1 .... (t) MickaelBarzalona 13 71+
(Jeremy Noseda) *racd stands' side: hld up towards rr: rdn and effrt over 2f out: drvn and no prog over 1f out: wknd 1f out: 13th of 22 in gp* **8/1**[2]

0-53 **15** *1 ¼* **Bronze Prince**[11] 2706 4-8-2 87 .... NickyMackay 28 67
(John Gosden) *racd stands' side: chsd ldr tl led 1/2-way: rdn wl over 2f out: hdd 2f out: wknd u.p over 1f out: 14th of 22 in gp* **12/1**[3]

1-00 **16** *1 ¾* **Gunner Lindley (IRE)**[53] 1529 4-8-7 92 .... MichaelHills 17 68
(B W Hills) *racd stands' side: hld up towards rr: swtchd rt and effrt towards centre over 2f out: no imp and wl hld over 1f out: 15th of 22 in gp* **40/1**

1413 **17** *¾* **Kay Gee Be (IRE)**[4] 2933 7-8-6 91 .... PaulHanagan 33 65
(Richard Fahey) *racd stands' side: led tl 1/2-way: lost pl qckly u.p jst over 2f out: wl bhd fnl f: 16th of 22 in gp* **16/1**

6000 **18** *1* **Hacienda (IRE)**[12] 2679 4-8-3 88 .... SilvestreDeSousa 26 60
(Mark Johnston) *chsd ldrs stands' side: wnt 2nd 1/2-way tl jst over 2f out: sn struggling u.p: wknd over 1f out: 17th of 22 in gp* **50/1**

0-42 **19** *3 ¼* **Proponent (IRE)**[46] 1684 7-8-8 98 .... HarryBentley(5) 19 62
(Roger Charlton) *t.k.h: chsd ldrs stands' side: rdn and ev ch ent fnl 2f: struggling whn pushed rt wl over 1f out: sn wknd: wl btn and eased ins fnl f: 18th of 22 in gp* **20/1**

0430 **20** *1 ½* **Breakheart (IRE)**[16] 2573 4-8-5 90 .... FrannyNorton 23 51
(Michael Dods) *racd stands' side: hld up in midfield: swtchd rt and effrt over 2f out: no real hdwy: wknd wl over 1f out: 19th of 22 in gp* **28/1**

60-2 **21** *¾* **Mont Agel**[34] 2031 4-8-12 97 .... JMurtagh 3 56
(Michael Bell) *racd far side: hld up in last pair of gp: rdn and btn over 2f out: no ch w ldrs fnl 2f: 2nd of 4 in gp* **14/1**

00-2 **22** *1 ¾* **Albaqaa**[49] 1614 6-8-13 98 .... (t) DarryllHolland 27 53
(P J O'Gorman) *racd stands' side: stdd s: hld up in tch: rdn and struggling over 2f out: wl bhd over 1f out: wl btn fnl f: 20th of 22 in gp* **100/1**

600- **23** *3* **Mr David (USA)**[249] 6735 4-8-13 98 .... HayleyTurner 11 46
(Jamie Osborne) *racd in centre pair: rdn wl over 2f out: no prog and no ch fr wl over 1f out: 1st of 2 in gp* **66/1**

2640 **24** *1 ¼* **Brae Hill (IRE)**[25] 2284 5-8-7 97 .... LeeTopliss(5) 7 43
(Richard Fahey) *led centre pair and in tch overall: rdn and struggling wl over 2f out: sn wknd: wl bhd fnl f: 2nd of 2 in gp* **33/1**

-004 **25** *1 ¼* **Brick Red**[20] 2441 4-8-7 92 .... WilliamBuick 4 35
(Andrew Balding) *racd far side: chsd ldr of gp: rdn to ld gp over 2f out tl 2f out: no ch w ldrs and wl btn fnl 2f: eased ins fnl f: 3rd of 4 in gp* **22/1**

-122 **26** *9* **Lord Aeryn (IRE)**[22] 2390 4-8-3 88 .... (p) ChrisCatlin 6 10+
(Richard Fahey) *taken down early: grad swtchd lft and jnd stands' side gp after 2f: chsd ldrs tl rdn and wknd over 2f out: t.o and eased ins fnl f: 21 of 22 in gp* **33/1**

3- **27** *1 ¼* **Super Say (IRE)**[25] 2326 5-8-10 98 .... BACurtis(3) 10 17+
(Andrew Oliver, Ire) *taken down early: grad swtchd lft to join stands' side gp after 2f: chsd ldrs tl rdn and wknd over 2f out: t.o and eased ins fnl f: 22nd of 22 in gp* **20/1**

3-03 **28** *57* **Invincible Soul (IRE)**[16] 2558 4-8-12 **97**..................(p) RichardHughes 2 —
(Richard Hannon) *racd far side: led gp tl over 2f out: sn wl bhd and virtually p.u fr over 1f out: wl t.o: 4th of 4 in gp* **18/1**

1m 38.53s (-2.07) **Going Correction** +0.025s/f (Good) **28** Ran SP% **137.4**
Speed ratings (Par 109): **111,110,108,108,104 103,103,103,102,101 100,100,99,98,97 95,94,93,90,88 88,86,83,82,80 71,70,**
toteswingers: 1&2 £15.80, 1&3 £41.50, 2&3 £20.30 CSF £76.40 CT £1741.62 TOTE £14.70: £3.70, £2.00, £4.30, £9.20; EX 128.30 Trifecta £2358.20 Pool: £13,518.47 - 4.24 winning units..
Owner P W Harris **Bred** Pendley Farm **Trained** Aldbury, Herts
■ Walter Swinburn's first Royal Ascot success as a trainer.
■ Stewards' Enquiry : Eddie Ahern two-day ban: careless riding (Jun 29-30); two-day ban: used whip with excessive frequency (Jul 1,3)

FOCUS
Arguably the hottest mile handicap of the season and recent winners have been a mixture of the battle-hardened handicapper, such as Mine, and the unexposed, for instance Forgotten Voice and it was an unexposed type that prevailed. Leading ante-post fancy Green Destiny was rerouted to the Wolferton Handicap Stakes. In recent seasons it has been an advantage to race on one flank or the other, and this time the clear advantage lay with those racing close to the stands' rail. the winner is generally progressive and the second produced another personal best.

NOTEBOOK
Julienas(IRE) is a steadily progressive handicapper, but all his previous form had been on turning tracks. He was produced to lead over a furlong out and, despite doing the runner-up no favours, put his stamina for 1m2f to good use to hold on. He survived a stewards' enquiry, but it cost his rider a two-day ban. His dam was a Group winning juvenile and he might be up to winning at Pattern level if going on again from this. (op 14-1 tchd 16-1 in a place)
Dance And Dance(IRE) ◆ finished jarred up in the Buckingham Palace here last year, but had been running well since recovering and had won a good handicap at Epsom last time. He was switched to get a run nearest the rail and the winner left a gap briefly, but then closed the door causing his rider to switch. He was reducing the gap all the way to the line, but could not quite get there and surely deserves to pick up a similar contest before long. (op 10-1 tchd 13-2)
Invisible Man won this race last year in first-time blinkers, but had not won since and was 10lb higher. He ran another good race without threatening the first two, but his opportunities are limited off this rating. (op 25-1)
Pendragon(USA) improved when upped to 1m2f last season, including winning here, but was 4lb above his last winning mark. He performed well and had his chance. (op 40-1)
Eton Forever(IRE) won the Doncaster Spring Mile in authoritative fashion from Dance And Dance at the beginning of the turf season, but was 11lb higher. He travelled well and looked the most likely winner 2f out, but when asked for more he drifted towards the stands' rail and had no more to offer. He probably needs a little more cut in the ground.
Start Right looked unlucky when third to Dance And Dance at Epsom and was 5lb better off, but 10lb above his last winning mark. He tracked the pace, if rather wider on the course than ideal, and couldn't produce extra in the closing stages. (tchd 15-2 and 10-1 in a place)
Kyllachy Star, whose best form has been around Chester, did finish third in the Irish Lincolnshire on soft ground. He again ran with credit and is the sort who could make his mark in one of the big autumn handicaps when the ground is more in his favour. (tchd 50-1 in a place)
Fareer, a progressive handicapper who was well beaten in this last season off 107, was 2lb higher but had placed in Group company in Dubai when fitted with a visor over the winter. Wearing first-time blinkers, he did well considering he ended up more towards the centre of the track than most.
Chapter And Verse(IRE) had shown his best form on Polytrack and had a bit to do with a couple of these on his latest Newmarket form. He was noted staying on late without posing a threat, but gives the impression there is a good race in him, possible over further. (op 25-1 tchd 40-1 in a place)
Capital Attraction(USA) has not had much racing, but had been well beaten in two starts this season and his best form was on Polytrack. However, dropped 5lb and in blinkers on for the first time, he did much better and would have finished closer had he not been hampered by the fifth, although admittedly he was just beginning to struggle at the time.
Stunning View(IRE) was another who was lightly raced, but had shown decent form in Ireland on soft ground. Wearing first-time cheekpieces, he was another staying on at the end. (op 33-1 tchd 25-1)
Pintura should have finished closer judged on his run behind today's second last time, when he looked unlucky.
Sooraah did by far the best of those who raced far side.
Point North(IRE) was lightly raced and was well supported although his best form was on Polytrack or soft turf. He moved up to have a chance over 2f out, but dropped away in the closing stages. (op 9-1 tchd 10-1 in a place)
Bronze Prince was also very lightly raced and his only win came on Polytrack. However, he raced prominently on this step up in trip and failed to get home. (tchd 14-1 in places)
Invincible Soul(IRE) Official explanation: jockey said colt stopped quickly

3033 QUEEN MARY STKS (GROUP 2) (FILLIES) 5f

5:00 (5:00) (Class 1) 2-Y-O

£42,577 (£16,140; £8,077; £4,027; £2,017; £1,012) **Stalls** Centre

Form RPR

11 **1** **Best Terms**[33] 2053 2-8-12 0.. RichardHughes 7 102
(Richard Hannon) *chsd ldrs: effrt and swtchd rt wl over 1f out: led ins fnl f and pressed: kpt finding for press: hld on wl at fin* **12/1**

1 **2** *shd* **Shumoos (USA)**[18] 2504 2-8-12 0.................................... MartinDwyer 3 102
(Brian Meehan) *in tch: pushed along over 2f out: clsd over 1f out: chalng ins fnl f: r.o u.p whn pressing wnr: hld at fin* **6/5**[1]

5 **3** *hd* **Caledonia Lady**[15] 2580 2-8-12 0.................................. DarryllHolland 4 101
(Pat Murphy) *hld up in rr: hdwy over 2f out: swtchd lft over 1f out: r.o ins fnl f: edgd rt and clsd on front 2 towards fin* **100/1**

3 **4** *1 ½* **Fire Lily (IRE)**[25] 2322 2-8-12 0.. RyanMoore 11 96
(David Wachman, Ire) *midfield: pushed along and outpcd over 2f out: u.p and r.o ins fnl f: gng on at fin: nt rch ldrs* **8/1**[3]

31 **5** *¾* **Kohala (IRE)**[16] 2570 2-8-12 0.................................. GrahamGibbons 2 93
(David Barron) *hld up: hdwy 3f out: rdn to chse ldrs over 1f out: kpt on same pce fnl 100yds* **40/1**

6 *shd* **Ruby's Day**[26] 2-8-12 0.. FrankieDettori 10 92+
(E J O'Neill, France) *midfield: rdn over 1f out: styd on ins fnl f: nt rch ldrs: one pce cl home* **20/1**

7 *1* **Gypsy Robin (USA)**[54] 2-8-12 0....................................(bt) JASanchez 9 89
(Wesley A Ward, U.S.A) *chsd ldr: drew level over 2f out: def ld over 1f out: rdn and hdd ins fnl f: no ex fnl 50yds* **13/2**[2]

122 **8** *½* **Vocational (USA)**[21] 2404 2-8-12 0.......................... SilvestreDeSousa 6 87
(Mark Johnston) *hld up: hdwy whn rdn and swtchd rt 2f out: chsd ldrs over 1f out: one pce fnl 110yds* **12/1**

13 **9** *1 ½* **On The Dark Side (IRE)**[11] 2712 2-8-12 0.................. JamieSpencer 14 82
(Kevin Ryan) *led: jnd over 2f out: rdn and hdd over 1f out: fdd fnl 75yds* **25/1**

10 *2 ½* **Somasach (USA)**[14] 2623 2-8-12 0.................................. KJManning 13 73
(J S Bolger, Ire) *towards rr: pushed along and hdwy into midfield over 2f out: no imp u.p over 1f out: outpcd after* **12/1**

1 **11** *1 ¼* **Charlotte Rosina**[27] 2227 2-8-12 0...................................... JohnFahy 12 68
(Roger Teal) *chsd ldrs: rdn 2f out: wknd ent fnl f* **33/1**

11 **12** *½* **Dozy (IRE)**[21] 2404 2-8-12 0.. PhillipMakin 8 66
(Kevin Ryan) *hld up: rdn 2f out: no imp: nvr on terms w ldrs* **9/1**

1 **13** *2 ½* **Ebony Clarets**[57] 1455 2-8-12 0.................................... PaulHanagan 5 57
(Richard Fahey) *sn pushed along in rr div: wl bhd fnl 2f* **50/1**

231 **14** *4 ½* **Bubbly Ballerina**[20] 2416 2-8-12 0.......................... MickaelBarzalona 1 41
(Alan Bailey) *chsd ldrs: rdn 2f out: sn wknd* **33/1**

60.22 secs (-0.98) **Going Correction** +0.025s/f (Good) **14** Ran SP% **122.9**
Speed ratings (Par 102): **103,102,102,100,98 98,97,96,93,89 87,87,83,75**
toteswingers: 1&2 £5.10, 1&3 £75.80, 2&3 £33.60 CSF £25.81 CT £1528.32 TOTE £11.20: £2.90, £1.20, £19.00; EX 31.60 Trifecta £1701.10 Pool: £16,436.50 - 7.15 winning units..
Owner R Barnett **Bred** W And R Barnett Ltd **Trained** East Everleigh, Wilts

FOCUS
This Group 2 often falls to a precocious type for whom this has proved to be a career peak, but there have also been plenty that have gone on to better things, such as multiple Classic and Group 1 winner Attraction and last year's winner Maqaasid, who subsequently finished third in the Cheveley Park and 1,000 Guineas. A typically strong field of early types produced a desperate finish with the well-backed favourite being touched off. The field finished compressed and this has the look of a lesser renewal, with the third and fifth key to the form. Best Terms progressed and Shumoos built slightly on her debut effort.

NOTEBOOK
Best Terms had beaten subsequent winners in both her starts over 5f on fast ground and won this in gallant fashion. She raced upsides the runner-up for most of the way, but once in front refused to give way and just prevailed; her rider has made a habit of narrow successes in juvenile races here in the last couple of years. She is not very big and is a May foal, so deserves credit for being able to win this. She is likely to be aimed at the Lowther and the Cheveley Park now and, along with the runner-up is quoted at 20-1 for next year's 1000 Guineas. (op 10-1)
Shumoos(USA) dominated the market after her impressive Haydock debut success was emphatically boosted - her nearest pursuer there ran out a decisive winner of the Windsor Castle Stakes the previous day. She tracked the leaders and was upsides the winner from around halfway but, despite her persistent efforts, could not quite get past. She is likely to take her chance in the Cherry Hinton next as connections feel she needs 6f, and it will be interesting to see if she is able to go on from this hard race. (op 5-4 tchd 11-8 in a places)
Caledonia Lady ◆ nearly caused a major surprise. A half-sister to multiple sprint-winner Caledonia Princess, she had been too keen on her debut but her rider was able to settle her out the back and she really picked up in the second half of the race. She had to switch around the weakening leaders, but might have won with a clear passage. A maiden should be a formality on this evidence.
Fire Lily(IRE) ◆ won a fillies' maiden on easy ground, but then finished third to the subsequent Coventry Stakes winner in a Listed race at the Curragh on fast. She was unable to go the early gallop, but picked up in the second half of the race and finished strongly, suggesting she will be more of a threat to the winner in races such as the Lowther later on. (tchd 7-1 and 9-1 in a place)
Kohala(IRE) had taken a 5f maiden at Redcar in good style and did pretty well on this step up in grade, especially as she raced more towards the far side than most. (op 33-1)
Ruby's Day was narrowly beaten on her debut at Chantilly before getting home in a conditions race on the same track. She was held up behind the principals, but could not go with those rivals when they went for home, although she did keep on in the closing stages. (tchd 18-1)
Gypsy Robin(USA) had made all to win a 4.5f fillies' maiden on her US debut on synthetics, but she was unable to get an uncontested lead here and her efforts to reach the front left her vulnerable in the closing stages. (tchd 8-1)
Vocational(USA) had won on her debut at Warwick before finishing second in a York Listed race, then second to Dozy in Hilary Needler, form which suggested she was a good yardstick. She missed the break before getting involved from halfway, but raced towards the far side and her effort petered out in the last furlong. (op 16-1 tchd 11-1)
On The Dark Side(IRE) finished a good third in the Woodcote after making the running and adopted the same tactics over this shorter trip. She did a lot of early running though and paid for it in the closing stages. (tchd 28-1)
Somasach(USA) was outpaced from an early stage. (op 14-1 tchd 11-1)
Dozy(IRE) was slowly into her stride and failed to get involved. Official explanation: vet said filly was found to be lame (op 11-1)
Ebony Clarets probably needs further now. (tchd 66-1)

3034 SANDRINGHAM H'CAP (LISTED RACE) (FILLIES) 1m (S)

5:35 (5:35) (Class 1) (0-110,103) 3-Y-O

£28,385 (£10,760; £5,385; £2,685; £1,345; £675) **Stalls** Centre

Form RPR

512 **1** **Rhythm Of Light**[18] [illegible] 3-8-12 **91**........................ RichardKingscote 1 100
(Tom Dascombe) *stdd and swtchd lft s: t.k.h: hld up in rr: swtchd rt and hdwy over 2f out: rdn to chal and edgd lft 1f out: led ins fnl f: r.o wl* **8/1**[3]

2-12 **2** *1 ¼* **Dubai Queen (USA)**[18] 2506 3-8-7 **89** oh1..................... KierenFallon 10 99
(Luca Cumani) *in tch towards rr: pushed along and hdwy 3f out: rdn to ld 2f out: hrd pressed and drvn 1f out: sn hdd and no ex fnl 150yds* **9/2**[1]

6-13 **3** *2* **Winter's Night (IRE)**[25] 2296 3-9-0 **96**........................... LukeMorris 6 101
(Clive Cox) *t.k.h: hld up in tch: swtchd rt and hdwy to press ldrs over 2f out: ev ch and drvn over 1f out: outpcd by ldng pair fnl f: kpt on same pce* **11/2**[2]

1-00 **4** *2 ¾* **Cape Dollar (IRE)**[45] 1719 3-9-7 **103**................................ RyanMoore 9 106+
(Sir Michael Stoute) *t.k.h: hld up in tch in midfield: hdwy whn bdly hmpd and lost pl over 2f out: swtchd lft and rallied over 1f out: kpt on but no threat to ldrs fnl f* **11/1**

21-1 **5** *1 ½* **Humdrum**[14] 2607 3-8-8 **90**.. RichardHughes 11 85
(Richard Hannon) *hld up in tch in midfield: rdn and effrt over 2f out: hung rt and no imp ent fnl f* **9/2**[1]

460- **6** *1 ¾* **Blessed Biata (USA)**[235] 7098 3-8-11 **93**........................... JMurtagh 13 84
(William Haggas) *stdd s: hld up in rr: rdn wl over 2f out: swtchd lft and sme hdwy u.p over 1f out: one pce and no imp fnl f: nvr trbld ldrs* **11/2**[2]

-003 **7** *nse* **Sonning Rose (IRE)**[12] 2684 3-8-7 **89** oh2......................... ChrisCatlin 2 80
(Mick Channon) *hld up in tch in midfield: rdn and effrt over 2f out: unable qck and btn whn hung rt over 1f out* **25/1**

431 **8** *hd* **Rougette**[12] 2689 3-8-7 **89** oh2.. MichaelHills 8 80
(B W Hills) *hld up in tch: rdn and unable qck over 2f out: hung rt and no threat to ldrs over 1f out* **14/1**

123- **9** *1 ¼* **Sweetie Time**[235] 7098 3-8-10 **92**....................................... HayleyTurner 4 80
(Michael Bell) *chsd ldrs: rdn and edgd rt over 2f out: wknd u.p wl over 1f out* **25/1**

-015 **10** *¾* **Emma's Gift (IRE)**[33] 2073 3-8-10 **92**......................... AdamBeschizza 14 78
(Julia Feilden) *stdd s: hld up in rr: rdn and effrt 3f out: swtchd lft and no prog over press 2f out: wl hld over 1f out* **25/1**

10-6 **11** *2 ¼* **Secret Love (IRE)**[33] 2050 3-8-7 **89** oh2.......................... PaulHanagan 7 70
(Mikael Magnusson) *w ldr tl led over 4f out: rdn and hdd 2f out: wknd over 1f out* **8/1**[3]

55-1 **12** *18* **Traffic Sister (USA)**[40] 1873 3-8-8 **90**........................... JamieSpencer 5 29
(J S Moore) *racd freely: led tl over 4f out: lost pl qckly over 2f out: wl bhd fnl 2f: t.o and eased ins fnl f* **20/1**

5-13 **13** *½* **Wrekin Sunset**[33] 2073 3-8-8 **90**.................................... AndrewElliott 3 28+
(Mrs K Burke) *plld hrd: chsd ldrs: rdn and losing pl whn bmpd and hmpd over 2f out: sn wl bhd: t.o and eased ins fnl f* **33/1**

-505 **14** *2 ½* **Mortitia**[23] 2358 3-8-13 **95**.......... PhillipMakin 12 28
(Brian Meehan) *broke wl: sn stdd towards rr: t.k.h: rdn and no rspnse over 2f out: sn wl bhd: t.o and eased ins fnl f* **66/1**

1m 39.93s (-0.67) **Going Correction** +0.025s/f (Good) **14** Ran SP% **125.1**
Speed ratings (Par 104): **104,102,100,98,96 94,94,94,93,92 90,72,71,69**
toteswingers: 1&2 £7.10, 1&3 £10.60, 2&3 £3.10 CSF £42.14 CT £230.13 TOTE £11.70: £3.40, £2.00, £2.40; EX 59.20 Trifecta £248.70 Pool: £11,384.18 - 33.86 winning units..
Owner Lowe Silver Deal **Bred** Hermes Services Ltd **Trained** Malpas, Cheshire
■ The first winner at the royal meeting for both Tom Dascombe and Richard Kingscote.

FOCUS
The top-weight Cape Dollar was rated 7lb below the race ceiling of 110 and was the only runner with a three-figure official mark. The race was not up to its usual standard, but this was still a strong fillies' handicap and the form is solid. The winner is rated up 5lb. The pace seemed good and they raced up the middle of the track before tending to edge towards the far side, although not onto the rail. It's understandable the time was a good deal slower than both the Windsor Forest and Hunt Cup.

NOTEBOOK
Rhythm Of Light's nose defeat on her latest start over 7f at Haydock received a boost when the winner that day, Western Aristocrat, finished a highly promising third in the Jersey. She was 6lb higher, but the step up in trip really suited and she won well. There should be more to come.
Dubai Queen(USA) was beaten fair and square, but she was 6lb higher than when runner-up last time and this represented further improvement. She's superbly bred - half-sister to Dubawi - and this was important black type. (op 4-1 tchd 5-1 and 11-2 in a place)
Winter's Night(IRE) had won on both her previous visits to Ascot and she again showed her liking for the course with a decent performance.
Cape Dollar(IRE) lost her chance when hampered just as she was beginning to make a move around 2f out. She may well have produced a career-best granted a clear run and is one to keep on-side. (op 12-1 tchd 10-1)
Humdrum was up 10lb for winning at Kempton on her reappearance and faced with better company. Official explanation: jockey said filly hung right (op 5-1)
Blessed Biata(USA) was a popular choice having shown plenty of ability over 6f-7f in a light juvenile campaign and she didn't look badly treated, but she took far too long to pick up, only making modest late progress. This was her first start for 235 days and the run appeared needed. (op 8-1)
Secret Love(IRE) Official explanation: jockey said filly hung right
T/Jkpt: Not won. T/Plt: £393.10 to a £1 stake. Pool: £492,309.06. 914.03 winning tickets. T/Qpdt: £12.20 to a £1 stake. Pool: £29,970.64. 1,814.19 winning tickets. SP

2803 HAMILTON (R-H)

Wednesday, June 15

OFFICIAL GOING: Good (8.2)
Rail realignment reduced distance son round course by 8yds.
Wind: Light, half behind Weather: Overcast

3035 BRITISH STALLION STUDS SUPPORTING BRITISH RACING E B F MAIDEN STKS — 6f 5y
2:20 (2:20) (Class 5) 2-Y-O **£3,238** (£963; £481; £240) **Stalls** High

Form — RPR

50 **1** **Indepub**[31] 2120 2-9-0 0.......... AmyRyan(3) 6 74+
(Kevin Ryan) *cl up: led gng wl over 2f out: rdn out fnl f* **33/1**

34 **2** *1* **Joshua The First**[21] 2395 2-9-3 0.......... PaulMulrennan 3 71+
(Keith Dalgleish) *prom: drvn and outpcd over 2f out: kpt on to chse wnr ins fnl f: r.o* **2/1**[1]

52 **3** *nk* **Haafkry**[11] 2731 2-9-0 0.......... JamesSullivan(3) 7 70
(Linda Stubbs) *cl up: rdn and ev ch over 2f out: kpt on same pce ins fnl f* **9/2**[2]

4 *4* **Dubious Escapade (IRE)** 2-8-9 0.......... RoystonFfrench 4 50
(Ann Duffield) *dwlt: chsd ldng gp: effrt and hdwy whn short of room briefly over 1f out: no imp fnl f* **10/1**

654 **5** *1 ¾* **Topcoat (IRE)**[12] 2672 2-9-3 0.......... JoeFanning 2 53
(Mark Johnston) *led to over 2f out: rdn and no ex over 1f out* **14/1**

6 *3 ½* **Nayef Flyer** 2-9-0 0.......... TonyHamilton 5 39
(Richard Fahey) *dwlt: sn pushed along bhd main gp: no imp fnl 2f* **5/1**[3]

052 **7** *nse* **Lexi's Prince (IRE)**[8] 2780 2-9-3 0..........(v) StevieDonohoe 1 42
(Tom Dascombe) *cl up tl edgd both ways and wknd over 1f out* **9/2**[2]

8 *12* **Angel Warrior (IRE)** 2-9-0 0.......... PJMcDonald 8 —
(Ben Haslam) *slowly away: bhd and outpcd: nvr on terms* **20/1**

1m 12.04s (-0.16) **Going Correction** -0.15s/f (Firm) **8** Ran SP% **109.8**
Speed ratings (Par 93): **95,93,93,87,85 80,80,64**
toteswingers: 1&2 £27.80, 1&3 £27.40, 2&3 £1.30 CSF £91.68 TOTE £44.10: £11.40, £1.10, £1.30; EX 127.70.
Owner D W Barker **Bred** Mrs Deborah O'Brien **Trained** Hambleton, N Yorks

FOCUS
This ordinary juvenile maiden was run at just an average pace and it saw many chances 2f out. The winner improved but it looked no fluke, with the third helping with the level.

NOTEBOOK
Indepub had not shone on his two previous outings, but his bang in-form yard has a decent record in this event and he stepped up markedly to make it third time lucky. He is evidently going the right way and ought to make his mark when the nurseries kick off. Official explanation: trainer's rep said, regarding apparent improvement in form, that the colt started better. (tchd 25-1)
Joshua The First, whose in-form stable saddled a 2-y-o to finish second at Royal Ascot the previous day, was well supported. He had looked as though a seventh furlong might be ideal on his previous outing, however, and he really found the first half of this contest happening too quickly. He can win when faced with a suitably stiffer test. (op 5-2 tchd 11-4 in a place)
Haafkry wanted to hang early on, but straightened up as the race developed and ran another sound race in defeat, helping to set the standard. (tchd 4-1)
Dubious Escapade(IRE), backed at long odds, advertised her inexperience but was doing some fair work late on and ought to improve a deal. Another furlong should prove to her liking in due course. (op 16-1)
Topcoat(IRE), although from a top stable, dropped away after racing up with the pace and has now been unplaced in four career starts. (op 16-1 tchd 12-1)
Nayef Flyer, whose decent yard is operating below-par at present, is the first foal of a useful and well bred sprinter. She lacked the pace to land a telling blow and, while entitled to improve, doesn't have much scope. (op 6-1 tchd 13-2)
Lexi's Prince(IRE) was the form choice here, but he looked wayward in a first-time visor on his previous outing eight days earlier and did so again here. It's a case of back to the drawing board for his connections. (op 9-4)

3036 SAM COLLINGWOOD-CAMERON H'CAP — 6f 5y
2:55 (2:55) (Class 5) (0-75,75) 3-Y-O+ **£3,238** (£963; £481; £240) **Stalls** High

Form — RPR

5154 **1** **Toby Tyler**[1] 3025 5-9-3 **64**..........(v) FrederikTylicki 1 72
(Paul Midgley) *in tch on outside: rdn 1/2-way: hdwy to ld ins fnl f: kpt on wl* **4/1**[1]

3003 **2** *1* **Night Trade (IRE)**[16] 2566 4-9-9 **75**..........(p) NeilFarley(5) 3 80
(Deborah Sanderson) *prom: effrt over 2f out: edgd lft and chsd wnr ins fnl f: r.o* **9/1**

4641 **3** *½* **Hinton Admiral**[9] 2766 7-9-12 **73** 6ex.......... JoeFanning 2 76
(Keith Dalgleish) *prom: smooth hdwy over 2f out: rdn over 1f out: kpt on same pce ins fnl f* **4/1**[1]

0-46 **4** *½* **Imprimis Tagula (IRE)**[4] 2917 7-9-7 **75**..........(v) MissAlexOwen(7) 5 77
(Alan Bailey) *led tl hdd ins fnl f: kpt on same pce* **14/1**

1 **5** *2 ¾* **Midnight Dynamo**[18] 2498 4-9-7 **68**.......... DanielTudhope 7 61+
(Jim Goldie) *dwlt: bhd and outpcd: hdwy over 2f out: rdn and one pce appr fnl f* **16/1**

-060 **6** *1 ½* **Salerosa (IRE)**[21] 2399 6-9-1 **62**..........(p) PaulMulrennan 9 50
(Ann Duffield) *chsd main gp: rdn and effrt 2f out: kpt on fnl f: nvr able to chal* **18/1**

0202 **7** *½* **Prince Of Vasa (IRE)**[13] 2631 4-9-6 **70**.......... SeanLevey(3) 10 56
(Michael Smith) *chsd ldrs tl rdn and wknd appr fnl f* **15/2**[3]

0563 **8** *nse* **Stamp Duty (IRE)**[9] 2765 3-8-12 **70**.......... MichaelO'Connell(3) 4 56
(Ollie Pears) *in tch: drvn and outpcd over 2f out: n.d after* **7/1**[2]

0043 **9** *1 ½* **Distant Sun (USA)**[2] 2989 7-8-9 **56** oh1.......... AndrewHeffernan 11 37
(Linda Perratt) *hld up: hdwy nr side over 2f out: no imp over 1f out* **11/1**

-000 **10** *3 ½* **Cheyenne Red (IRE)**[23] 2353 5-8-10 **57**.......... PJMcDonald 6 27
(Michael Dods) *hld up: pushed along over 2f out: sn btn* **16/1**

-034 **11** *6* **Devil You Know (IRE)**[30] 2165 5-9-6 **67**..........(t) DavidNolan 8 18
(Michael Easterby) *prom: drvn over 2f out: wknd over 1f out* **14/1**

1m 10.83s (-1.37) **Going Correction** -0.15s/f (Firm)
WFA 3 from 4yo+ 8lb **11** Ran SP% **113.0**
Speed ratings (Par 103): **103,101,101,100,96 94,94,93,91,87 79**
toteswingers: 1&2 £6.80, 1&3 £8.10, 2&3 £11.60 CSF £38.47 CT £137.13 TOTE £5.70: £1.90, £4.60, £2.30; EX 53.40.
Owner Anthony D Copley **Bred** Whitsbury Manor Stud **Trained** Westow, N Yorks

FOCUS
A moderate sprint handicap. The runners wanted to race more mid-track and the form is straightforward enough, the winner rated to last year's best.
Prince Of Vasa(IRE) Official explanation: jockey said gelding hung right
Stamp Duty(IRE) Official explanation: jockey said saddle slipped
Cheyenne Red(IRE) Official explanation: jockey said gelding lost a near-fore shoe

3037 CASH FOR KIDS NIGHT MEDIAN AUCTION MAIDEN STKS — 1m 1f 36y
3:35 (3:35) (Class 6) 3-5-Y-O **£2,047** (£604; £302) **Stalls** Low

Form — RPR

4 **1** **Circle Of Angels**[7] 2802 3-8-9 0.......... JoeFanning 7 75+
(Mark Johnston) *in tch: hdwy on outside to ld over 2f out: kpt on strly to go clr fnl f: eased nr fin* **5/2**[2]

023 **2** *3 ¼* **Maxamillion Bounty**[23] 2361 3-8-11 70.......... SeanLevey(3) 6 70
(Michael Dods) *t.k.h: led to over 2f out: edgd rt and rallied over 1f out: kpt on same pce fnl f* **7/2**[3]

424- **3** *½* **Lion Court (IRE)**[233] 7119 3-9-0 73.......... StevieDonohoe 2 69
(Sir Mark Prescott Bt) *prom: drvn and outpcd over 3f out: rallied wl over 1f out: kpt on fnl f: nvr able to chal* **6/4**[1]

24 **4** *7* **Brook Star (IRE)**[20] 2432 3-8-9 0.......... FrederikTylicki 4 49
(Michael Dods) *hld up: pushed along and outpcd 4f out: rallied and swtchd lft over 1f out: kpt on: nvr able to chal* **28/1**

30-0 **5** *3 ½* **Torun City**[19] 2457 3-9-0 70.......... TonyHamilton 1 46
(Richard Fahey) *cl up tl drvn and wknd fr 2f out* **8/1**

6 **6** *3 ¼* **Tourtiere**[14] 2621 3-9-0 0.......... PJMcDonald 5 39
(George Moore) *trckd ldrs: rdn along over 3f out: edgd rt and wknd 2f out* **14/1**

0 **7** *6* **Ebony Breeze (IRE)**[19] 2461 3-9-0 0.......... PaulMulrennan 3 25
(Ian Semple) *hld up towards rr: struggling over 3f out: btn fnl 2f* **100/1**

1m 56.39s (-3.31) **Going Correction** -0.15s/f (Firm) **7** Ran SP% **113.0**
Speed ratings (Par 101): **104,101,100,94,91 88,83**
toteswingers: 1&2 £1.40, 1&3 £2.60, 2&3 £1.10 CSF £11.43 TOTE £3.40: £2.00, £1.40; EX 12.00.
Owner R S Brookhouse **Bred** R S Brookhouse **Trained** Middleham Moor, N Yorks

FOCUS
A moderate maiden, run at a fair pace. The winner looks sure to do better than the bare form.

3038 HAMILTONPARK.CO.UK H'CAP — 1m 65y
4:10 (4:12) (Class 4) (0-80,77) 3-Y-O+ **£4,533** (£1,348; £674; £336) **Stalls** Low

Form — RPR

-201 **1** **Unknown Rebel (IRE)**[36] 1972 3-8-6 **69**.......... AmyRyan(3) 5 73
(Kevin Ryan) *mde all at ordinary gallop: rdn and qckn over 2f out: hld on wl fnl f* **9/4**[1]

2-26 **2** *shd* **Nicola's Dream**[12] 2675 3-8-9 **69**.......... FrederikTylicki 2 73
(Richard Fahey) *trckd ldrs: rdn over 2f out: styd on wl fnl f: jst hld* **5/1**[3]

3115 **3** *nk* **One Pursuit (IRE)**[17] 2527 3-8-4 **67**.......... BillyCray(3) 3 70+
(David Nicholls) *in tch: checked after 2f: lost pl and outpcd over 3f out: hung lft and hdwy over 1f out: kpt on strly fnl f: jst hld* **7/1**

-060 **4** *1 ¾* **Glenluji**[21] 2401 6-8-6 **58** oh1.......... PaulPickard(3) 6 60+
(Jim Goldie) *s.i.s: t.k.h: hld up: hdwy and prom over 3f out: rdn and one pce fnl f* **14/1**

4352 **5** *1* **Carrowbeg (IRE)**[22] 2394 3-8-12 **72**.......... JoeFanning 9 69
(Mark Johnston) *cl up: rdn over 2f out: edgd lft: no ex appr fnl f* **7/1**

00-0 **6** *¾* **Horatio Carter**[20] 2431 6-10-0 **77**.......... PaulMulrennan 1 75
(Michael Smith) *hld up: stdy hdwy on ins wl over 1f out: shkn up and no imp fnl f* **22/1**

-000 **7** *1* **Without Prejudice (USA)**[12] 2674 6-9-11 **74**.......... DavidNolan 4 70
(Michael Easterby) *hld up: drvn and hdwy over 2f out: no imp over 1f out* **33/1**

0336 **8** *2 ½* **Law To Himself (IRE)**[27] 2213 4-9-6 **69**.......... PJMcDonald 8 59
(Alan Swinbank) *trckd ldrs tl rdn and wknd over 1f out* **4/1**[2]

6-06 **9** *7* **Whispering Spirit (IRE)**[13] 2634 5-9-5 **68**..........(v) RoystonFfrench 7 42
(Ann Duffield) *prom: rdn over 2f out: wknd wl over 1f out* **16/1**

1m 47.13s (-1.27) **Going Correction** -0.25s/f (Firm)
WFA 3 from 4yo+ 11lb **9** Ran SP% **112.3**
Speed ratings (Par 105): **96,95,95,93,92 92,91,88,81**
toteswingers: 1&2 £4.30, 1&3 £2.90, 2&3 £4.30 CSF £12.96 CT £65.39 TOTE £2.30: £1.10, £2.00, £3.90; EX 13.00.
Owner D Reilly & Mrs C Reilly **Bred** Kilfrush Stud **Trained** Hambleton, N Yorks
■ Stewards' Enquiry : Billy Cray caution: careless riding; caution: used whip with excessive frequency.

FOCUS
This was competitive enough for the grade. It was run at something of an uneven pace, though. The winner got an easy lead but keeps progressing.

3039 RACING UK ON VIRGIN MEDIA 536 H'CAP — 1m 65y
4:45 (4:46) (Class 6) (0-60,60) 3-Y-O — £1,942 (£578; £288; £144) Stalls Low

Form — RPR

60-0 **1** **Save The Bees**[19] 2457 3-9-0 **58** .... NeilFarley(5) 8 — 68+
(Declan Carroll) *in tch: hdwy to chal over 2f out: led over 1f out: hld on wl fnl f* **14/1**

00-5 **2** ¾ **Phair Winter**[19] 2465 3-8-4 **46** oh1 .... PaulPickard(3) 12 — 54+
(Alan Brown) *bhd: rdn and hdwy on outside 3f out: chsd wnr ins fnl f: r.o* **40/1**

600- **3** *nk* **Sangar**[242] 6919 3-8-12 **54** .... MichaelO'Connell(3) 14 — 61
(Ollie Pears) *midfield: outpcd 4f out: rallied over 2f out: chsd ldrs ins fnl f: r.o* **16/1**

5-04 **4** *5* **Inside**[23] 2349 3-9-3 **56** ....(p) DavidNolan 6 — 51
(Richard Fahey) *in tch: drvn and effrt over 2f out: outpcd over 1f out* **8/1**[3]

00-0 **5** *1 ¼* **Little Book**[63] 1312 3-9-6 **59** .... StevieDonohoe 7 — 51
(Edward Vaughan) *hld up: rdn over 3f out: hdwy over 1f out: nvr able to chal* **10/1**

6605 **6** *1* **Eduardo**[13] 2652 3-8-8 **50** ....(t) PatrickDonaghy(3) 5 — 40
(Jedd O'Keeffe) *midfield: drvn over 3f out: hdwy 2f out: sn no imp* **11/1**

5-06 **7** *1* **Smart Step**[36] 1972 3-9-4 **57** .... JoeFanning 2 — 45
(Mark Johnston) *chsd clr ldr: rdn over 3f out: wknd over 1f out* **13/2**[2]

-043 **8** ½ **Deep Applause**[26] 2252 3-9-7 **60** .... FrederikTylicki 9 — 46
(Michael Dods) *hld up and bhd: rdn over 3f out: hdwy over 1f out: nvr able to chal* **4/1**[1]

0-36 **9** *2 ¼* **Ballinargh Boy**[21] 2396 3-8-13 **52** .... GregFairley 11 — 33
(Robert Wylie) *t.k.h early: trckd ldrs: rdn over 3f out: wknd over 1f out* **8/1**[3]

3000 **10** ¾ **Twennyshortkid**[8] 2782 3-8-7 **49** .... DeclanCannon(3) 1 — 28
(Paul Midgley) *prom: led over 2f out to over 1f out: sn wknd* **12/1**

25-4 **11** *hd* **Geronimo Chief (IRE)**[64] 1293 3-9-6 **59** .... AndrewHeffernan 10 — 38
(Ben Haslam) *hld up: hdwy on outside 3f out: wknd over 1f out* **14/1**

6-00 **12** *hd* **Crabbies Gold (IRE)**[12] 2673 3-9-2 **60** .... DaleSwift(5) 13 — 39
(Lisa Williamson) *bhd: drvn along over 3f out: nvr on terms* **50/1**

0504 **13** *7* **The Nifty Duchess**[23] 2350 3-8-9 **48** .... KellyHarrison 3 — 10
(Tim Easterby) *midfield: drvn and outpcd over 3f out: btn fnl 2f* **22/1**

6-00 **14** *3 ¾* **Formidable Girl (USA)**[23] 2349 3-8-11 **55** ....(b1) JulieBurke(5) 4 — 9
(Kevin Ryan) *led at str gallop and sn clr: hdd over 2f out: sn wknd* **12/1**

1m 46.87s (-1.53) **Going Correction** -0.25s/f (Firm) — **14** Ran SP% **116.3**
Speed ratings (Par 97): **97,96,95,90,89 88,87,87,84,84 84,83,76,73**
toteswingers: 1&2 £126.90, 1&3 £42.30, 2&3 £92.20 CSF £483.43 CT £8937.10 TOTE £17.20: £4.60, £13.70, £8.10; EX 406.50.
Owner Steve Ryan **Bred** S P Ryan **Trained** Sledmere, E Yorks

FOCUS
A weak handicap, but it was run at a strong pace. The winner improved and the first three were clear.
Save The Bees Official explanation: trainer's rep said, regarding apparent improvement in form, that it was only the gelding's second run for the yard, which has been out of form, but have been running much better recently.
Deep Applause Official explanation: jockey said gelding missed the break

3040 BOOK NOW FOR LADIES NIGHT CLASSIFIED CLAIMING STKS — 5f 4y
5:20 (5:20) (Class 6) 3-Y-O+ — £1,942 (£578; £288; £144) Stalls High

Form — RPR

10-3 **1** **Sands Of Dee (USA)**[13] 2632 4-9-4 66 .... BillyCray(3) 2 — 78+
(David Nicholls) *trckd ldrs: effrt 2f out: led ins fnl f: rdn out* **3/1**[2]

3063 **2** ¾ **Dancing Freddy (IRE)**[4] 2913 4-9-0 67 ....(p) MartinHarley(3) 1 — 71
(Richard Guest) *cl up: led over 1f out: sn rdn: hdd ins fnl f: kpt on* **9/4**[1]

0060 **3** *3 ¼* **Boundless Spirit**[29] 2180 3-8-8 67 ow1 ....(t) MichaelO'Connell(3) 3 — 57
(David Nicholls) *in tch: pushed along 1/2-way: effrt on outside over 1f out: one pce ins fnl f* **11/2**

2560 **4** ¾ **Northern Dare (IRE)**[18] 2491 7-8-11 69 ....(b) AndrewHeffernan 6 — 51
(Richard Fahey) *missed break: outpcd and bhd: hdwy fnl f: nvr able to chal* **9/2**[3]

0060 **5** *2 ¼* **Mandarin Spirit (IRE)**[12] 2694 11-8-6 60 ....(b) JulieBurke(5) 4 — 43
(Linda Perratt) *led to over 1f out: sn wknd* **25/1**

5-24 **6** *nk* **Patch Patch**[37] 1940 4-9-1 67 ....(p) FrederikTylicki 5 — 45
(Michael Dods) *dwlt: hld up in tch: rdn and hung rt 2f out: sn wknd* **9/2**[3]

59.51 secs (-0.49) **Going Correction** -0.15s/f (Firm)
WFA 3 from 4yo+ 7lb — **6** Ran SP% **111.4**
Speed ratings (Par 101): **97,95,90,89,85 85**
toteswingers: 1&2 £1.80, 1&3 £3.50, 2&3 £2.60 CSF £10.01 TOTE £3.70: £1.90, £1.50; EX 10.00.
Owner Paul J Dixon & Brian Morton **Bred** Mike Abraham **Trained** Sessay, N Yorks

FOCUS
This classified claimer saw a shambles of a start as three horses independently messed up as the gates opened. The leaders went off at a decent pace. The winner weas officially worst in but the form is taken at face value.
Northern Dare(IRE) Official explanation: jockey said gelding missed the break
Patch Patch Official explanation: jockey said gelding missed the break

3041 TURFTV IN YOUR BETTING SHOP APPRENTICE H'CAP (ROUND 2 HAMILTON PARK APPRENTICE SERIES) — 1m 4f 17y
5:50 (5:50) (Class 6) (0-60,60) 4-Y-O+ — £2,047 (£604; £302) Stalls High

Form — RPR

01-0 **1** **Without Equal**[19] 2462 5-8-13 **52** .... ShaneBKelly 4 — 61
(David Thompson) *bhd: rdn over 4f out: hdwy over 2f out: led ins fnl f: styd on wl* **16/1**

1-00 **2** *1 ¼* **Rubi Dia**[11] 2734 4-9-2 **60** .... DavidSimmonson(5) 7 — 67
(Kevin M Prendergast) *hld up: hdwy over 3f out: effrt and edgd rt over 2f out: chsd wnr ins fnl f: r.o* **11/1**

044/ **3** *1 ½* **Wood Fairy**[555] 7665 5-8-11 **55** .... LauraBarry(5) 10 — 60+
(Richard Fahey) *t.k.h: led: rdn over 2f out: hdd ins fnl f: kpt on same pce* **4/1**[2]

4605 **4** ¾ **Terenzium (IRE)**[13] 2636 9-8-8 **50** ....(p) GeorgeChaloner(3) 1 — 53
(Micky Hammond) *hld up: pushed along over 4f out: hdwy on outside over 2f out: kpt on same pce ins fnl f* **8/1**

3341 **5** *4* **Prince Rhyddarch**[7] 2804 6-9-6 **59** 6ex .... GarryWhillans 5 — 56
(Michael Dods) *trckd ldrs: rdn and edgd rt over 2f out: sn no ex* **6/4**[1]

56-0 **6** *2 ¾* **Deferto Delphi**[36] 1979 4-8-11 **55** .... JustinNewman(5) 8 — 48
(Barry Murtagh) *hld up: hdwy to chse ldr 1/2-way: rdn over 2f out: wknd over 1f out* **33/1**

6625 **7** *7* **Valdan (IRE)**[12] 2696 7-9-3 **59** ....(t) EdmondLinehan(3) 9 — 40
(Maurice Barnes) *trckd ldrs tl rdn and wknd over 2f out* **9/2**[3]

-045 **8** *12* **The Chester Giant**[19] 2450 4-8-4 **46** oh1 ....(v1) JakePayne(3) 6 — —
(Patrick Morris) *prom: outpcd and hung bdly rt over 3f out: sn btn* **40/1**

0/0- **9** ½ **Petrosian**[10] 469 7-8-4 **46** oh1 ....(v1) SophieSilvester(3) 3 — —
(Lisa Williamson) *missed break: sn wl bhd: nvr on terms* **66/1**

0-00 **10** *32* **Flyjack (USA)**[16] 173 4-8-3 **47** oh1 ow1 ....(v1) JosephYoung(5) 2 — —
(Lisa Williamson) *prom tl rdn and wknd over 3f out* **40/1**

2m 37.09s (-1.51) **Going Correction** -0.25s/f (Firm) — **10** Ran SP% **112.8**
Speed ratings (Par 101): **95,94,93,92,90 88,83,75,75,53**
toteswingers: 1&2 £12.20, 1&3 £9.10, 2&3 £7.70 CSF £167.06 CT £842.20 TOTE £13.30: £1.90, £3.10, £2.20; EX 87.30.
Owner K Fitzsimons **Bred** The Brookfield Stud **Trained** Bolam, Co Durham
■ Stewards' Enquiry : David Simmonson two-day ban: careless riding (Jun 29-30)

FOCUS
An ordinary middle-distance handicap, confined to apprentice riders. There was a fair pace on. The winner is rated up 5lb.
T/Plt: £402.90 to a £1 stake. Pool: £44,448.64. 80.53 winning units. T/Qpdt: £57.50 to a £1 stake. Pool: £2,921.88. 37.60 winning units. RY

2816 KEMPTON (A.W) (R-H)
Wednesday, June 15

OFFICIAL GOING: Standard
Wind: Moderate, half behind Weather: Cloudy

3042 FREE ENTRY FOR BETDAQ MEMBERS APPRENTICE H'CAP — 1m 2f (P)
6:10 (6:11) (Class 4) (0-60,80) 4-Y-O+ — £4,079 (£1,214; £606; £303) Stalls Low

Form — RPR

21/1 **1** **Troopingthecolour**[67] 1250 5-9-7 **80** .... MatthewLawson(3) 12 — 92
(Steve Gollings) *trckd ldr as field spread out: led 1/2-way: hung bdly lft bnd 2f out and ended against nr side rail: styd on wl* **15/2**

6302 **2** *2 ½* **Nolecce**[18] 2486 4-8-7 **66** .... MatthewCosham(3) 10 — 73
(Richard Guest) *taken down early: trckd ldng trio: prog to go 2nd 3f out: rdn and kpt on fnl 2f: no imp on wnr* **5/1**[1]

00-0 **3** *2 ¼* **Bowsers Brave (USA)**[20] 2436 5-9-0 **75** ....(t) KatiaScallan(5) 7 — 78
(Marcus Tregoning) *restless stalls: dwlt: hld up in last quintet and wl bhd: prog on inner fr 3f out: pushed along to take 3rd fnl f: nvr able to chal* **11/1**

3-00 **4** *2* **Sing Sweetly**[14] 2604 4-9-8 **78** .... TobyAtkinson 9 — 77+
(Gerard Butler) *hld up: pushed along in remote 12th 1/2-way: prog on inner 2f out: styd on to take 4th last 75yds* **8/1**

3040 **5** *2 ¼* **Classically (IRE)**[20] 2436 5-9-5 **75** .... KieranO'Neill 2 — 69
(Peter Hedger) *taken down early: chsd ldrs in 6th but nt on terms: tried to cl 3f out: nt clr run over 2f out: sme prog over 1f out: wknd fnl f* **12/1**

0-04 **6** *1 ½* **Silverglas (IRE)**[20] 2436 5-8-11 **72** .... LukeRowe(5) 3 — 63
(William Knight) *taken down early: chsd ldrs in 5th: rdn over 2f out: disp 3rd over 1f out: wknd* **13/2**[3]

0435 **7** *nk* **Morning Chief (IRE)**[19] 2454 4-8-9 **68** ....(bt) LucyKBarry(3) 5 — 58
(Clive Cox) *led at str pce: hanging lft and hdd 1/2-way: sn rdn: lost pl 3f out: wknd over 1f out* **6/1**[2]

4405 **8** *2* **Hawaana (IRE)**[41] 1829 6-9-8 **78** .... RyanPowell 11 — 64
(Gay Kelleway) *hld up in last quintet and wl bhd: tried to make prog 3f out: rdn and no hdwy over 1f out* **14/1**

6206 **9** *3 ¾* **Pertuis (IRE)**[41] 1829 5-9-1 **76** .... DavidCoyle(5) 6 — 55
(Harry Dunlop) *hld up in last quintet and wl bhd: clsd on ldrs 3f out but wd: wknd wl over 1f out* **10/1**

2423 **10** *3 ¼* **Florio Vincitore (IRE)**[67] 1232 4-8-4 **65** .... JenniferFerguson(5) 13 — 37
(Edward Creighton) *wl off the pce in 8th: rn wd bnd 3f out: sn bhd* **10/1**

0200 **11** *8* **Buddy Holly**[33] 2051 6-8-8 **64** ....(b1) AshleyMorgan 14 — 20
(Robert Eddery) *pressed ldng pair tl wknd rapidly wl over 2f out: t.o* **20/1**

364- **12** *22* **Present Story**[256] 6557 4-8-1 **62** .... NoelGarbutt(5) 4 — —
(Gary Harrison) *chsd ldrs in 7th: rdn after 3f: wknd 4f out: t.o* **50/1**

213- **13** *16* **Drizzi (IRE)**[427] 1303 10-8-2 **63** .... LeonnaMayor(5) 1 — —
(Phil McEntee) *a bhd: t.o fr 1/2-way* **40/1**

2m 8.15s (0.15) **Going Correction** +0.20s/f (Slow) — **13** Ran SP% **117.2**
Speed ratings (Par 105): **107,105,103,101,99 98,98,96,93,91 84,67,54**
toteswingers: 1&2 £5.80, 1&3 £19.30, 2&3 £20.30 CSF £43.13 CT £416.30 TOTE £7.90: £2.00, £2.30, £4.50; EX 35.60.
Owner Northern Bloodstock Racing **Bred** Meon Valley Stud **Trained** Scamblesby, Lincs

FOCUS
They went fast early in this apprentice handicap, but it did slow. It was still the fastest of the three C&D times. The winner rates a 6lb personal best.
Present Story Official explanation: jockey said filly never travelled

3043 BETDAQ.COM EXCHANGE PRICE MULTIPLES MAIDEN FILLIES' STKS — 1m 2f (P)
6:40 (6:41) (Class 5) 3-Y-O+ — £2,266 (£674; £337; £168) Stalls Low

Form — RPR

1 **Val O'Hara (IRE)** 3-8-12 0 .... JimCrowley 4 — 81+
(Peter Winkworth) *slowest away: hld up in last trio: gd prog on wd outside fr 2f out: sustained effrt against nr side to ld last 100yds* **25/1**

2 *1* **Neumark (GER)** 3-8-12 0 .... TomQueally 2 — 79+
(Sir Henry Cecil) *trckd ldng trio: wnt 3rd 3f out: lft in ld wl over 1f out: hanging lft and rn green after: hdd and outpcd last 100yds* **8/1**

3- **3** *1 ¾* **Shuhra (IRE)**[259] 6468 3-8-12 0 .... EddieAhern 8 — 75
(William Haggas) *prom: trckd ldr 1/2-way: led 3f out: hung bdly lft bnd 2f out and looked reluctant: sn hdd: nt qckn after* **7/2**[1]

4-6 **4** *4 ½* **Sleek Gold**[41] 1836 3-8-12 0 .... MartinDwyer 10 — 66
(Brian Meehan) *trckd ldrs: pushed along in 4th over 2f out: no imp over 1f out: fdd* **4/1**[2]

3 **5** ½ **Shieldmaiden (USA)**[13] 2639 3-8-12 0 .... AhmedAjtebi 14 — 65
(Mahmood Al Zarooni) *trckd ldr to 1/2-way: styd prom: chalng whn carried v wd bnd 2f out: fdd over 1f out* **4/1**[2]

6 *4* **Oasis Memory (IRE)** 3-8-12 0 .... WilliamBuick 6 — 57
(John Gosden) *a abt same pl: pushed along and no imp over 2f out: fdd fnl f* **11/2**[3]

7 ¾ **Cordillera** 3-8-12 0 .... J-PGuillambert 7 — 56
(Luca Cumani) *settled in rr: pushed along 2f out: no real prog* **25/1**

8 *1* **Etheldreda (IRE)** 3-8-9 0 .... JohnFahy(3) 9 — 54
(Clive Cox) *rdn towards rr after 3f: nvr gng wl after: styd in tch to 2f out: wknd* **16/1**

9 *3 ¼* **All My Heart** 3-8-12 0 .... SebSanders 3 — 47+
(Sir Mark Prescott Bt) *rdn after 3f: a in rr: no prog whn trapped bhd wkng rival over 2f out* **12/1**

10 2 3/4 **Chatterer (IRE)** 3-8-12 0 PatDobbs 11 42
(Marcus Tregoning) *dwlt: a in rr: rdn and no prog 3f out: hanging and green over 1f out* **25/1**

11 3 **Princesse Gaelle** 3-8-7 0 TobyAtkinson(5) 1 36
(Marco Botti) *dwlt: hmpd on inner after 100yds: a in rr: no ch fnl 2f* **20/1**

40- 12 29 **Transeggselence**253 6655 4-9-11 0 LiamKeniry 13 —
(Gary Harrison) *led to 3f out: wknd rapidly: t.o* **66/1**

2m 9.66s (1.66) **Going Correction** +0.20s/f (Slow)
WFA 3 from 4yo 13lb 12 Ran SP% **120.1**
Speed ratings (Par 100): **101,100,98,95,94 91,91,90,87,85 83,59**
toteswingers: 1&2 £51.50, 1&3 £102.40, 2&3 £9.70 CSF £205.27 TOTE £29.40: £6.00, £2.50, £1.20; EX 472.40.
Owner M Stewkesbury **Bred** Mervyn Stewkesbury **Trained** Chiddingfold, Surrey
■ Stewards' Enquiry : Seb Sanders two-day ban: careless riding (Jun 29-30)

FOCUS
The betting suggested this was an open fillies' maiden. There was a distinct lack of early pace and the bare form is probably only ordinary, with little to go on. The first two should both improve.

3044 LAY BACK AND WIN AT BETDAQ.COM H'CAP 1m 2f (P)
7:10 (7:12) (Class 4) (0-85,86) 3-Y-O **£4,079** (£1,214; £606; £303) **Stalls** Low

Form RPR

2141 1 **Ivan Vasilevich (IRE)**23 2357 3-9-2 **77** MartinDwyer 9 90+
(Jane Chapple-Hyam) *won battle for ld: mde all: kicked clr 2f out: styd on wl: unchal* **12/1**

0-1 2 2 1/2 **Spifer (IRE)**32 2104 3-9-3 **78** KierenFallon 2 84+
(Luca Cumani) *hld up last: stl there wl over 1f out: taken to outer and gd prog after: r.o to take 2nd last 100yds: no ch w wnr: do bttr* **6/1**2

1-21 3 1/2 **Seelo (USA)**9 2764 3-9-11 **86** 6ex WilliamBuick 5 91
(John Gosden) *chsd wnr 2f: settled in abt 4th after: pushed along and prog to chse wnr again 2f out: no imp fnl f: lost 2nd last 100yds* **4/11**1

5-20 4 4 1/2 **Shewalksinbeauty (IRE)**27 2229 3-9-2 **77** PatDobbs 7 73
(Richard Hannon) *chsd wnr after 2f to 2f out: wknd fnl f* **25/1**

-430 5 1/2 **Ibsaar**45 1727 3-9-2 **77** (p) LiamJones 4 72
(William Haggas) *hld up in tch: rdn wl over 2f out: hd high and nt look keen after: sn btn* **25/1**

4 6 1 1/2 **Deorai (IRE)**45 1727 3-9-7 **82** DaneO'Neill 3 74
(Jo Crowley) *hld up in rr: rdn on outer over 2f out: no prog and wl outpcd after* **16/1**

4-05 7 2 1/2 **Goodness**25 2306 3-8-10 **74** LouisBeuzelin(3) 6 61
(Sir Michael Stoute) *in tch: rdn and struggling in rr over 3f out: n.d fnl 2f* **20/1**

10-4 8 3 3/4 **Safari Team (IRE)**14 2607 3-9-5 **80** JimCrowley 10 60
(Peter Winkworth) *hld up tl chsd ldrs on outer after 4f: rdn wl over 2f out: wknd over 1f out* **16/1**

3-22 9 10 **My Vindication (USA)**49 1609 3-8-10 **76** KieranO'Neill(5) 1 36
(Richard Hannon) *plld hrd: prom tl wknd rapidly over 2f out* **11/1**3

2m 8.78s (0.78) **Going Correction** +0.20s/f (Slow) 9 Ran SP% **127.8**
Speed ratings (Par 101): **104,102,101,98,97 96,94,91,83**
toteswingers: 1&2 £3.70, 1&3 £2.60, 2&3 £2.00 CSF £88.22 CT £95.75 TOTE £14.70: £2.10, £1.60, £1.10; EX 47.00.
Owner Chris Fahy **Bred** Liam Butler **Trained** Dalham, Suffolk

FOCUS
A fair handicap. The winner had an easy ttime in front which was the place to be on this card, and the favourite was 8lb off his Pontefract win.

3045 BETDAQ MOBILE APPS H'CAP 7f (P)
7:40 (7:41) (Class 4) (0-85,85) 3-Y-O+ **£4,079** (£1,214; £606; £303) **Stalls** Low

Form RPR

5140 1 **Thunderball**40 1854 5-9-4 **82** (b) LeonnaMayor(7) 4 92
(David Nicholls) *mde all: sn clr: at least 7 l clr 2f out: c to end of tether fnl f: hld on* **15/2**

1-62 2 1 1/4 **Kingsdine (IRE)**32 2111 4-9-12 **83** TomMcLaughlin 7 90
(Malcolm Saunders) *trckd ldng trio: gng easily 3f out: prog to go 2nd 2f out but wnr wl clr: grad clsd fnl f: too much to do* **6/1**2

1210 3 3/4 **Almahaza (IRE)**35 2000 7-9-10 **81** NeilChalmers 8 86
(Adrian Chamberlain) *settled in midfield: rdn and prog over 2f out: wnt 3rd over 1f out: clsd fnl f: nvr able to chal* **25/1**

140 4 1/2 **Merchant Of Medici**12 2679 4-9-10 **81** MartinDwyer 13 85+
(William Muir) *dwlt: hld up in last pair: stl there over 2f out: prog on inner after: styd on wl to take 4th nr fin: too much to do* **3/1**1

-315 5 1 1/2 **Tiradito (USA)**35 2000 4-9-12 **83** (p) AdamKirby 10 83
(Marco Botti) *settled in midfield: hrd rdn on outer over 2f out: styd on: nvr rchd ldrs* **10/1**

1236 6 1 **Jake The Snake (IRE)**32 2111 10-9-7 **85** LucyKBarry(7) 3 82
(Tony Carroll) *wl plcd in chsng gp: effrt over 2f out: no imp on wnr and one pce over 1f out* **16/1**

16-0 7 1 1/2 **Moretta Blanche**40 1854 4-9-12 **83** JimCrowley 5 76
(Ralph Beckett) *stdd s: hld up in last pair: sme prog over 2f out: rdn and plugged on: n.d* **16/1**

5230 8 nse **Perfect Ch'l (IRE)**7 2822 4-8-13 **70** JamesDoyle 12 63
(Ian Wood) *in tch in midfield: rdn and no prog over 2f out: n.d after* **25/1**

64-5 9 2 1/4 **Micky P**29 2179 4-8-9 **66** (t) WilliamCarson 6 53
(Stuart Williams) *chsd ldrs: u.p sn after 3f out and sn lost pl: no hdwy fnl 2f* **18/1**

3311 10 2 3/4 **Cavitie**30 2165 5-8-9 **66** (p) DarryllHolland 2 45
(Andrew Reid) *chsd ldng pair to over 2f out: sn wknd qckly* **11/1**

555- 11 3/4 **Hurricane Spirit (IRE)**350 3565 7-9-11 **82** DaneO'Neill 9 59
(Terry Clement) *awkward s: a in rr: rdn and no prog over 2f out* **28/1**

210- 12 10 **Zip Lock (IRE)**237 7033 5-9-7 **78** KierenFallon 1 28
(David Elsworth) *chsd clr wnr to 2f out: wknd rapidly: t.o* **7/1**3

41- 13 2 1/2 **Irons On Fire (USA)**249 6742 3-8-10 **77** TonyCulhane 11 16
(George Baker) *racd wd towards rr: dropped away fr 3f out: t.o and eased* **10/1**

1m 26.58s (0.58) **Going Correction** +0.20s/f (Slow)
WFA 3 from 4yo+ 10lb 13 Ran SP% **118.2**
Speed ratings (Par 105): **104,102,101,101,99 98,96,96,93,90 89,78,75**
toteswingers: 1&2 £10.30, 1&3 £24.80, 2&3 £26.40 CSF £50.27 CT £1080.95 TOTE £8.50: £3.10, £2.60, £10.00; EX 44.50.
Owner Paul J Dixon & Brian Morton **Bred** Mrs Yvette Dixon **Trained** Sessay, N Yorks

FOCUS
A decent handicap run at a good pace. Another all the way winner, who was allowed to establish a clear lead. The form has not been rated too literally.

Perfect Ch'l(IRE) Official explanation: jockey said filly lost its action close home

3046 BRITISH STALLION STUDS SUPPORTING BRITISH RACING E B F MAIDEN FILLIES' STKS 7f (P)
8:10 (8:11) (Class 5) 2-Y-O **£3,238** (£963; £481; £240) **Stalls** Low

Form RPR

4 1 **Elusive Kate (USA)**11 2709 2-9-0 0 WilliamBuick 4 81+
(John Gosden) *chsd ldng pair: shkn up 3f out: wnt 2nd over 2f out: urged along and clsd to ld over 1f out: hrd pressed last 150yds: rdn and hld on wl* **5/4**1

2 hd **Kinetica** 2-9-0 0 SebSanders 5 80+
(Sir Mark Prescott Bt) *hld up in last pair: pushed along 3f out: prog 2f out: rdn to chal ins fnl f: jst hld last 100yds* **2/1**2

04 3 2 1/2 **Roedean (IRE)**19 2467 2-9-0 0 PatDobbs 2 74
(Richard Hannon) *fractious bef ent stalls: chsd ldng trio: shkn up 3f out: clsd to chal over 1f out: nt qckn* **4/1**3

4 1 **Arsaadi (IRE)** 2-9-0 0 TomMcLaughlin 7 71+
(Ed Dunlop) *slowly away and rn green in last: shkn up 3f out: prog to chse ldrs over 1f out: one pce fnl f: bttr for experience* **14/1**

5 3 1/2 **Tweet Lady** 2-9-0 0 JamesMillman 1 62
(Rod Millman) *chsd ldr to over 2f out: wknd over 1f out* **25/1**

4 6 13 **Sister Guru**69 1192 2-9-0 0 DaneO'Neill 6 28
(Peter Hedger) *racd freely: led and sn clr: wknd rapidly and hdd over 1f out: sn bhd* **22/1**

1m 28.88s (2.88) **Going Correction** +0.20s/f (Slow) 6 Ran SP% **112.6**
Speed ratings (Par 90): **91,90,87,86,82 67**
toteswingers: 1&2 £1.20, 1&3 £1.10, 2&3 £1.60 CSF £4.01 TOTE £2.60: £1.10, £2.30; EX 4.10.
Owner Magnolia Racing LLC & Ms Rachel Hood **Bred** Clovelly Farms **Trained** Newmarket, Suffolk

FOCUS
An ordinary maiden in which the sixth set a good tempo. The winner didn't ned to improve on her debut effort.

NOTEBOOK
Elusive Kate(USA) narrowly prevailed. A promising fourth at Doncaster on debut, she looks destined for nurseries and should stay 1m later in the season. (op 5-6 tchd 11-8)
Kinetica, a half-sister to 1m2f winner Four Nations, came strong in the final 2f, and briefly looked set to go past the winner. She should improve and can go one better. (op 3-1)
Roedean(IRE), who played up a bit beforehand, didn't have more use made of her, proving one-paced under pressure. She's another set for nurseries. (op 9-2)
Arsaadi(IRE), whose dam won up to 1m6f, was very green before staying on and ran as though there'll be significant improvement to come. (op 20-1)
Tweet Lady holds a Super Sprint entry and showed enough to suggest she'll win a small maiden, possibly over 6f. (op 40-1)

3047 SKYSPORTS.COM RACING H'CAP 2m (P)
8:40 (8:41) (Class 6) (0-65,65) 4-Y-O+ **£1,619** (£481; £240; £120) **Stalls** Low

Form RPR

1641 1 **Money Money Money**12 2659 5-9-9 **64** JamesMillman 5 73
(Rod Millman) *hld up in last quartet: stl there 4f out: prog 3f out: rdn to chse ldr over 1f out: looked hld tl styd on to ld last stride* **15/2**3

6204 2 shd **Kavaloti (IRE)**44 1761 7-9-10 **65** (b) GeorgeBaker 9 74+
(Gary Moore) *hld up in 7th: smooth prog to go 3rd over 3f out: led over 2f out: sed idling and looking arnd: hrd rdn over 1f out: looked like holding on tl gave up and hdd last stride* **6/1**2

-160 3 4 1/2 **Kadouchski (FR)**31 1839 7-8-12 **53** ClareLindop 2 57
(John Berry) *prom: lost pl on inner over 4f out: prog again over 3f out: chal and w ldr over 2f out: one pce over 1f out* **16/1**

/05- 4 1 **Summer Affair (IRE)**516 198 6-8-11 **52** ow1 JimCrowley 12 54
(Ben Case) *hld up in last quartet: prog 5f out: chsd ldrs and cl enough 3f out: nt qckn 2f out: one pce after* **33/1**

6P31 5 hd **Maydream**70 1181 4-8-8 **50** FrankieMcDonald 14 52
(Jimmy Fox) *dropped in fr wd draw and hld up last: prog over 3f out: nt on terms over 2f out: plugged on* **14/1**

4322 6 5 **Eagle Nebula**11 2721 7-9-5 **65** MarkCoumbe(5) 4 61
(Brett Johnson) *settled midfield: lost pl over 5f out: in last trio over 3f out: sme prog over 2f out: no imp on ldrs over 1f out* **10/1**

/5-4 7 1 **Sommersturm (GER)**70 1181 7-8-11 **52** TomQueally 1 47
(Barney Curley) *led: jnd after 5f: hdd over 2f out: wknd grad* **11/1**

-530 8 12 **L'Homme De Nuit (GER)**41 1839 7-9-1 **63** MartinLeonard(7) 7 44
(Jim Best) *racd wd: hld up wl in rr: effrt over 3f out: sn no prog and wknd* **40/1**

40-2 9 3 **Black Tor Figarro (IRE)**59 33 6-9-0 **55** DaneO'Neill 10 32
(Lawney Hill) *prom: jnd ldr after 5f: upsides wl over 2f out: sn wknd qckly* **7/4**1

3436 10 9 **Prince Blue**7 2820 4-8-10 **52** SamHitchcott 13 18
(John E Long) *trckd ldr 5f: prom after: rdn and wknd qckly over 3f out* **28/1**

-453 11 36 **Carbon Print (USA)**19 769 6-8-8 **52** (tp) JohnFahy(3) 11 —
(James Evans) *towards rr: str reminders 7f out: drvn up to go prom briefly over 4f out: sn wknd: t.o* **33/1**

0563 12 29 **Camps Bay (USA)**11 2721 7-9-10 **65** (p) HayleyTurner 6 —
(Conor Dore) *prom: wknd 5f out: sn t.o and eased* **16/1**

6063 13 10 **King Kieren (IRE)**13 2638 6-8-12 **53** (p) KierenFallon 3 —
(Linda Jewell) *prom tl wknd over 5f out: eased and t.o* **16/1**

3m 33.31s (3.21) **Going Correction** +0.20s/f (Slow)
WFA 4 from 5yo+ 1lb 13 Ran SP% **115.9**
Speed ratings (Par 101): **99,98,96,96,96 93,93,87,85,81 63,48,43**
toteswingers: 1&2 £9.40, 1&3 £19.90, 2&3 £16.80 CSF £48.72 CT £702.53 TOTE £9.60: £2.40, £1.60, £4.90; EX 45.90.
Owner Mrs Jenny Willment **Bred** Mrs Jenny Willment **Trained** Kentisbeare, Devon

FOCUS
A moderate staying handicap. The form is probably sound.
Eagle Nebula Official explanation: jockey said gelding ran flat

3048 RACING@SKYSPORTS.COM H'CAP 6f (P)
9:10 (9:11) (Class 4) (0-85,84) 3-Y-O **£4,079** (£1,214; £606; £303) **Stalls** Low

Form RPR

2101 1 **Barnet Fair**11 2724 3-9-7 **84** KierenFallon 1 92+
(Richard Guest) *dwlt: settled in last pair: urged along and prog 2f out: drvn and fnl f to ld last 100yds: readily* **5/2**1

-600 2 3/4 **Pippa's Gift**7 2818 3-8-7 **70** MartinDwyer 3 73
(William Muir) *led: rdn and hdd over 2f out: rallied over 1f out: chal and upsides ins fnl f: sn outpcd* **25/1**

-441 3 3/4 **Firstknight**22 2383 3-8-13 **76** AdamKirby 4 77
(Marco Botti) *chsd ldrs: effrt over 2f out: hrd rdn to cl 1f out: kpt on same pce after* **11/4**2

-140 **4** *nse* **Sand Owl**[32] 2102 3-9-2 **79** .... DarryllHolland 2 79
(Peter Chapple-Hyam) *trckd ldng pair: prog to ld over 2f out: drvn over 1f out: hdd and one pce last 100yds* **4/1**[3]

-314 **5** *2 ½* **Perfect Pastime**[9] 2770 3-9-1 **78** .... TedDurcan 5 70
(Walter Swinburn) *mostly in last pair: hanging u.p 1/2-way and sn detached: kpt on again fr over 1f out* **10/1**

3-21 **6** *¾* **Redvers (IRE)**[19] 2479 3-8-13 **76** .... JimCrowley 8 66
(Ralph Beckett) *racd wd: chsd ldrs: rdn over 2f out and nt qckn: fdd over 1f out* **11/2**

2160 **7** *4* **Flashbang**[19] 2468 3-8-13 **76** .... TomQueally 7 53
(Paul Cole) *dwlt: sn pressed ldr: lost pl wl over 2f out: steadily wknd* **10/1**

-006 **8** *1* **Penny's Pearl (IRE)**[30] 2158 3-9-4 **81** .... CathyGannon 6 55
(David Evans) *chsd ldrs: rdn 1/2-way: struggling in rr over 2f out* **25/1**

1m 14.22s (1.12) **Going Correction** +0.20s/f (Slow) **8** Ran SP% **116.5**
Speed ratings (Par 101): **100,99,98,97,94 93,88,86**
toteswingers: 1&2 £7.70, 1&3 £2.80, 2&3 £8.00 CSF £64.11 CT £181.32 TOTE £4.00: £1.60, £7.30, £2.00; EX 60.00.
Owner Donald Wheatley **Bred** Mrs J M Russell **Trained** Stainforth, S Yorks

FOCUS
A fair sprint handicap. The winner was probably a bit better than the bare form on a card where prominent runners did best.
T/Plt: £79.20 to a £1 stake. Pool: £66,700.51. 614.33 winning tickets. T/Qpdt: £10.00 to a £1 stake. Pool: £4,430.41. 325.33 winning tickets. JN

2617 RIPON (R-H)

Wednesday, June 15

OFFICIAL GOING: Good to soft (8.3)
Wind: Light, half behind Weather: Rain for about 90 minutes before racing, overcast becoming fine

3049 SUNDOWN SKY APPRENTICE CLASSIFIED (S) STKS 6f
6:50 (6:57) (Class 6) 3-4-Y-O £1,942 (£578; £288; £144) Stalls High

Form RPR

1245 **1** **Boy The Bell**[12] 2670 4-9-13 61 .... KevinLundie 7 59
(Brian Ellison) *chsd ldrs: led 2f out: edgd rt: drvn out* **7/4**[1]

0405 **2** *1 ½* **Royal Blade (IRE)**[13] 2632 4-9-8 45 .... DanielleMooney 2 49
(Alan Berry) *led tl 2f out: kpt on same pce fnl f* **18/1**

604- **3** *hd* **Be A Good Lady**[216] 7404 3-9-0 47 .... TerenceFury 8 46
(Neville Bycroft) *s.s: bhd: hdwy over 2f out: styd on fnl f* **20/1**

0-30 **4** *½* **Chillie Peppar**[57] 1472 3-9-0 55 .... RichardOliver 4 45
(George Prodromou) *dwlt: sn outpcd and in rr: hdwy over 1f out: styd on towards fin* **14/1**

6540 **5** *3* **Gorgeous Goblin (IRE)**[4] 2910 4-9-8 52 ....(t[1]) JasonHart 3 37
(David C Griffiths) *sn chsng ldrs: wknd fnl f* **11/1**

0-45 **6** *shd* **Dreamweaving (IRE)**[16] 2574 3-9-0 40 .... EvaMoscrop 6 35
(Nigel Tinkler) *mid-div: outpcd over 2f out: nvr a factor* **80/1**

3106 **7** *4 ½* **Dolly Parton (IRE)**[26] 2264 3-9-5 66 ....(p) ShirleyTeasdale 5 25
(David Nicholls) *chsd ldrs: wknd over 1f out* **9/2**[3]

-501 **8** *hd* **Arrow Storm (USA)**[13] 2642 3-9-5 70 .... BenWilliams 1 25
(Tom Dascombe) *awkward to load: w ldr: wknd over 2f out* **2/1**[2]

1m 14.63s (1.63) **Going Correction** -0.05s/f (Good)
WFA 3 from 4yo 8lb **8** Ran SP% **114.1**
Speed ratings (Par 101): **87,85,84,84,80 79,73,73**
toteswingers: 1&2 £6.40, 1&3 £11.90, 2&3 £18.80 CSF £34.46 TOTE £3.30: £1.10, £5.30, £3.10; EX 37.10.There was no bid for the winner.
Owner L S Keys **Bred** D J P Turner **Trained** Norton, N Yorks
■ Stewards' Enquiry : Richard Oliver caution: used whip with excessive frequency.

FOCUS
A weak apprentice seller which took place on rain-softened ground, the time nearly four seconds over RP standard. It's doubtful the winner had to match his recent form.
Arrow Storm(USA) Official explanation: trainer's rep had no explanation for the poor form shown

3050 RIPON RACES.CO.UK MEDIAN AUCTION MAIDEN STKS 5f
7:20 (7:20) (Class 5) 2-Y-O £2,331 (£693; £346; £173) Stalls High

Form RPR

23 **1** **Last Bid**[18] 2485 2-8-12 0 .... DavidAllan 8 74+
(Tim Easterby) *trckd ldrs: led appr fnl f: r.o wl* **11/8**[1]

5252 **2** *2* **Superplex**[12] 2665 2-9-3 0 .... PJMcDonald 9 72
(John Quinn) *chsd ldrs: upsides 1f out: kpt on same pce* **10/3**[2]

43 **3** *nse* **Maltease Ah**[13] 2641 2-8-12 0 .... TonyHamilton 5 67
(Richard Fahey) *led: hdd appr fnl f: kpt on same pce* **8/1**

6 **4** *6* **Inya House**[25] 2318 2-9-3 0 .... TomEaves 3 50
(Nigel Tinkler) *chsd ldrs: rdn 2f out: sn outpcd* **7/1**[3]

5 *hd* **Baltic Bomber (IRE)** 2-9-3 0 .... JackMitchell 2 49
(John Quinn) *mid-div: outpcd and lost pl 3f out: kpt on fnl f* **25/1**

40 **6** *nk* **Arachis Bow**[18] 2485 2-8-9 0 .... JamesSullivan(3) 1 43
(Michael Easterby) *swvd rt s: mid-div: effrt over 2f out: sn outpcd* **33/1**

7 *4 ½* **Johnson's Cat (IRE)** 2-9-0 0 .... RobertLButler(3) 7 35+
(Richard Guest) *dwlt: in rr: sme hdwy over 2f out: sn wknd* **25/1**

8 *4 ½* **Simpson Millar** 2-9-3 0 .... DuranFentiman 6 16
(Noel Wilson) *dwlt: mid-div: wknd 2f out* **20/1**

9 *3 ¾* **Wish Again (IRE)** 2-9-3 0 .... AdrianNicholls 4 —
(David Nicholls) *s.s: swtchd lft sn after s: a outpcd in last* **9/1**

60.66 secs (-0.04) **Going Correction** -0.05s/f (Good) **9** Ran SP% **114.2**
Speed ratings (Par 93): **98,94,94,85,84 84,77,69,63**
toteswingers: 1&2 £1.70, 1&3 £3.60, 2&3 £3.60 CSF £5.39 TOTE £2.30: £1.30, £1.10, £2.50; EX 6.40.
Owner C H Stevens **Bred** Bearstone Stud **Trained** Great Habton, N Yorks

FOCUS
An ordinary maiden, experience coming to the fore, the front three pulling clear. Straightforward form.

NOTEBOOK
Last Bid hadn't helped her cause with slow starts previously but was away more on terms this time and found a bit of improvement, not that hard pressed to quicken clear inside the last. From a yard enjoying a good run, she's an obvious type for sprint nurseries. (op 2-1 tchd 9-4 in places)
Superplex gave his running again, showing his customary speed, but he's clearly vulnerable in these events. He'll look more exposed than many in nurseries, too. (op 5-2)
Maltease Ah at least matched the form she showed on Polytrack at Lingfield last time and, in excellent hands, could be the type to do better still, particularly with nurseries looming. (op 7-1)
Inya House had shown speed on his debut at York but seemed at sea on this undulating track. He remains capable of better. (op 8-1)
Baltic Bomber(IRE), a son of Baltic King, clearly needed the experience, missing the break and soon off the bridle, but showed promise as he got the hang of things late on and could be the sort to do quite a bit better next time. (tchd 22-1)
Arachis Bow has hinted at ability on all three starts and this half-sister to the useful Bow Bridge appeals as one who'll do better in nurseries. She shouldn't get too high a mark. (op 50-1)
Wish Again(IRE), a gelded son of Moss Vale, was green but didn't shape with promise all the same. (op 8-1)

3051 YOU'RE BETTER OFF WITH BETFAIR H'CAP 1m 1f 170y
7:50 (7:50) (Class 4) (0-85,85) 4-Y-O+ £4,209 (£1,252; £625; £312) Stalls Low

Form RPR

0-03 **1** **City Of The Kings (IRE)**[31] 2124 6-9-7 **85** ....(p) DanielTudhope 3 93
(Geoffrey Harker) *hld up in rr: effrt over 3f out: rdn over 2f out: styd on wl to ld fnl strides* **5/4**[1]

0-56 **2** *shd* **Ailsa Craig (IRE)**[16] 2545 5-8-11 **75** .... TonyHamilton 6 83
(Edwin Tuer) *trckd ldr: led over 1f out: hdd towards fin* **11/4**[2]

1000 **3** *3* **Hidden Glory**[81] 991 4-9-1 **79** .... PaulMulrennan 2 81
(James Given) *trckd ldrs: drvn over 4f out: one pce appr fnl f* **12/1**

5165 **4** *3* **Rosbay (IRE)**[11] 2734 7-8-9 **73** .... DuranFentiman 7 69
(Tim Easterby) *dwlt: t.k.h in rr: drvn over 4f out: sn wl outpcd: kpt on fnl 2f: tk 4th last 50yds* **9/1**

260 **5** *3* **Cloudy Bay (USA)**[11] 2708 4-8-6 **73** ....(p) SeanLevey(3) 5 63
(Mrs K Burke) *led: qcknd clr over 6f out: drvn over 3f out: hdd over 1f out: sn wknd* **6/1**[3]

0-40 **6** *7* **Hail Bold Chief (USA)**[19] 2454 4-8-9 **73** .... PJMcDonald 1 48
(Alan Swinbank) *trckd ldrs: drvn over 4f out: wknd over 3f out* **10/1**

2m 5.32s (-0.08) **Going Correction** +0.125s/f (Good) **6** Ran SP% **112.2**
Speed ratings (Par 105): **105,104,102,100,97 92**
toteswingers: 1&2 £1.10, 1&3 £10.40, 2&3 £3.90 CSF £4.83 TOTE £2.30: £1.10, £3.40; EX 5.50.
Owner John J Maguire **Bred** Tom McDonald **Trained** Thirkleby, N Yorks

FOCUS
Cloudy Bay set a sound pace and the field was quite well strung out at the top of the straight. Ordinary form.

3052 NORMAN WELLS MEMORIAL CHALLENGE TROPHY H'CAP 6f
8:20 (8:20) (Class 3) (0-95,93) 3-Y-O £6,623 (£1,982; £991; £495; £246) Stalls High

Form RPR

2313 **1** **Thirteen Shivers**[20] 2411 3-8-4 **79** .... JamesSullivan(3) 10 88
(Michael Easterby) *mid-div: hdwy on outer to ld 2f out: hld on towards fin* **5/1**[3]

4020 **2** *¾* **Indian Ballad (IRE)**[18] 2503 3-8-13 **85** .... AdrianNicholls 3 91
(Ed McMahon) *wnt lft s: in rr: hdwy 2f out: chsng ldrs 1f out: no ex clsng stages* **8/1**

1414 **3** *shd* **Another Wise Kid (IRE)**[23] 2363 3-8-2 **77** .... DeclanCannon(3) 7 83
(Paul Midgley) *chsd ldrs: chal over 1f out: kpt on same pce last 50yds* **10/1**

-020 **4** *nk* **El Viento (FR)**[18] 2508 3-9-1 **87** ....(b) TonyHamilton 6 92
(Richard Fahey) *hmpd s: in rr: hdwy over 2f out: chsng ldrs 1f out: kpt on same pce last 100yds* **20/1**

0250 **5** *¾* **Another Citizen (IRE)**[26] 2256 3-8-2 **74** .... DuranFentiman 5 77
(Tim Easterby) *hmpd s: in rr: hdwy on outer over 2f out: chsng ldrs 1f out: kpt on same pce* **16/1**

2-03 **6** *nk* **Breezolini**[9] 2763 3-8-1 **76** .... AmyRyan(3) 11 78
(Richard Whitaker) *in rr: hdwy and swtchd rt over 1f: kpt on: eased nr fin* **12/1**

0-1 **7** *3 ¼* **Amazing Amoray (IRE)**[30] 2151 3-8-10 **82** .... LeeNewman 12 73
(David Barron) *led tl over 3f out: wknd over 1f out* **11/4**[1]

-030 **8** *6* **Indiesład**[23] 2363 3-8-5 **77** .... RoystonFfrench 9 49
(Ann Duffield) *chsd ldrs: sn drvn along: lost pl 2f out* **14/1**

5-1 **9** *4* **Dickie's Lad (IRE)**[39] 1900 3-9-4 **90** ....(t) TomEaves 10 49
(Kevin Ryan) *w ldr: led over 3f out: hdd 2f out: sn wknd* **9/2**[2]

-005 **10** *½* **Jack Smudge**[11] 2724 3-8-10 **82** .... PaulMulrennan 2 40
(James Given) *chsd ldrs: lost pl over 1f out* **12/1**

1m 12.16s (-0.84) **Going Correction** -0.05s/f (Good) **10** Ran SP% **114.4**
Speed ratings (Par 103): **103,102,101,101,100 100,95,87,82,81**
toteswingers: 1&2 £5.20, 1&3 £14.70, 2&3 £10.60 CSF £43.78 CT £391.39 TOTE £4.50: £1.70, £1.90, £2.90; EX 31.10.
Owner Keith Wreglesworth & Andre Fordham **Bred** Cheveley Park Stud Ltd **Trained** Sheriff Hutton, N Yorks

FOCUS
A competitive 3yo sprint which was set up for those coming from behind by the two market leaders taking each other on up front. The form is rated on the positive side.

NOTEBOOK
Thirteen Shivers's York form has proved to be really strong, a number of winners emeging from the race, and he put a slight blip at Ayr behind him, leaving the impression he was only doing what was required late on, so there's a fair he'll do better again next time.
Indian Ballad(IRE) didn't get home over 7f at Haydock last time and wasted no time showing he's still in good heart back at sprint trips. He's a reliable sort who should continue to give a good account. (op 10-1)
Another Wise Kid(IRE) is another enjoying a good season, back on the up here after a slightly below-par effort at Thirsk last time. (tchd 12-1)
El Viento(FR) had found it tough in a strong handicap at Newmarket the time before but bounced back in this slightly easier grade without having any excuses. (op 18-1)
Another Citizen(IRE) put a couple of poor runs behind him, the drop back to sprinting clearly no hindrance, though merely keeping on late having been taken off his feet early.
Breezolini is back in form and would have finished closer had she not got caught in behind a weakening rival for much of the penultimate 1f, keeping on well at the finish. A strongly-run 6f suits her down to the ground. (op 16-1)
Amazing Amoray(IRE) appealed as the type to do better in handicaps but was taken on up front by Dickie's Lad. It is probably best to give both the benefit of the doubt for the time being. Official explanation: trainer had no explanation for the poor form shown (tchd 5-2 and 3-1)
Dickie's Lad(IRE) got a bit worked up in the preliminaries and could perhaps do with settling down a bit if he is to progress. Official explanation: trainer's rep had no explanation for the poor form shown (op 4-1 tchd 5-1 in places)

3053 SIS LIVE MAIDEN STKS 6f
8:50 (8:52) (Class 5) 3-Y-O £2,331 (£693; £346; £173) Stalls High

Form RPR

32- **1** **Long Awaited (IRE)**[232] 7150 3-9-3 0 .... JackMitchell 5 88+
(Roger Varian) *trckd ldr: led over 3f out: wnt easily clr fnl f: eased fnl 50yds* **8/11**[1]

4- **2** *3 ¾* **Easy Over (IRE)**[320] 4543 3-9-3 0 .... AdrianNicholls 8 74+
(Ed McMahon) *dwlt: sn drvn to chse ldrs: sn t.k.h: n.m.r over 4f out: drvn and hdwy 3f out: chsd wnr over 1f out: no ch w wnr* **15/8**[2]

0 **3** *6* **Powder Keg**[12] 2673 3-9-3 0 .... JoeFanning 1 55
(Mark Johnston) *chsd ldrs: drvn 3f out: one pce fnl 2f* **16/1**[3]

60 **4** *2* **See Vermont**[19] 2479 3-8-12 0 .... LMcNiff(5) 7 48
(Robin Bastiman) *s.i.s: in rr: kpt on fnl 2f: nvr nrr* **80/1**

00- **5** *3 ¼* **Indigo Sands (IRE)**[225] 7279 3-9-3 0........................ PatrickMathers 3 38
(Alan Berry) *chsd ldrs: wknd over 1f out* **100/1**

5- **6** *4* **Russian Winter**[228] 7240 3-8-12 0................................ DaleSwift(5) 9 25
(Tim Etherington) *chsd ldrs: lost pl over 2f out* **16/1**[3]

66 **7** *nse* **Fire In Babylon (IRE)**[6] 2852 3-9-3 0........................ AndreaAtzeni 2 25
(Michael Wigham) *sn outpcd and in rr* **40/1**

6 **8** *nk* **Langtoon Lass**[23] 2361 3-8-12 0................................ AndrewMullen 6 19
(David Nicholls) *swtchd lft after s: led hdd over 3f out: wknd over 2f out* **25/1**

1m 12.83s (-0.17) **Going Correction** -0.05s/f (Good) **8** Ran SP% **113.0**
Speed ratings (Par 99): **99,94,86,83,79 73,73,73**
toteswingers: 1&2 £1.02, 1&3 £1.50, 2&3 £3.80 CSF £2.13 TOTE £1.50: £1.02, £1.10, £2.80; EX 2.30.
Owner Saif Ali & Saeed H Altayer **Bred** Mrs C Regalado-Gonzalez **Trained** Newmarket, Suffolk

FOCUS
No depth to this maiden whatsoever but the form pair came clear in a fair time. These figures could underrate them.
Fire In Babylon(IRE) Official explanation: jockey said colt never travelled

3054 ATTHERACES.COM ROYAL ASCOT MEGASITE H'CAP 1m 4f 10y
9:20 (9:20) (Class 5) (0-75,74) 4-Y-O+ **£4,209** (£1,252; £625; £312) **Stalls** Low

Form RPR

-021 **1** **Fossgate**[19] 2462 10-8-1 **57** ow2.. AmyRyan(3) 1 68+
(James Bethell) *hld up: hdwy on inner over 3f out: led over 2f out: over 2 l clr 1f out: jst lasted* **5/1**[3]

0-54 **2** *nse* **The Caped Crusader (IRE)**[27] 2213 4-9-4 **74**..... MichaelO'Connell(3) 5 84+
(Ollie Pears) *s.i.s: sn trcking ldrs: nt clr run on inner over 2f out: swtchd outside: tk 3rd appr fnl f: edgd lft: fin wl: jst failed* **4/1**[1]

0052 **3** *nk* **Sharp Sovereign (USA)**[7] 2804 5-8-7 **65**........................... LMcNiff(5) 2 73
(David Barron) *led 1f: chsd ldrs: drvn over 4f out: rallied fnl f: styd on towards fin* **9/2**[2]

3240 **4** *9* **Hail Tiberius**[27] 2213 4-9-2 **69**........................ DuranFentiman 10 63
(Tim Walford) *s.i.s: drvn and hdwy 4f out: sn chsng ldrs: wknd over 1f out* **11/1**

1401 **5** *5* **King's Counsel (IRE)**[22] 2393 5-9-1 **68**....................(v) DanielTudhope 4 54
(David O'Meara) *trckd ldrs: wnt 2nd over 6f out: led 3f out: sn hdd: wknd over 1f out* **9/2**[2]

4053 **6** *1 ¾* **Lord Lansing (IRE)**[22] 2388 4-8-10 **66**.................... PatrickDonaghy(3) 7 49
(Mrs K Burke) *t.k.h in midfield: trckd ldrs 5f out: chal 3f out: wknd over 1f out* **11/2**

3511 **7** *13* **Camera Shy (IRE)**[14] 2608 7-8-8 **61**................................ AndreaAtzeni 8 23
(Kevin Morgan) *hld up in rr: effrt over 3f out: lost pl over 1f out: eased* **9/1**

3062 **8** *13* **Viewing**[18] 2492 4-9-6 **73**.. PaulMulrennan 3 14
(James Given) *led after 1f: t.k.h: hdd 3f out: sn lost pl and bhd: eased* **16/1**

2m 38.52s (1.82) **Going Correction** +0.125s/f (Good) **8** Ran SP% **112.6**
Speed ratings (Par 103): **98,97,97,91,88 87,78,69**
toteswingers: 1&2 £3.60, 1&3 £5.50, 2&3 £3.10 CSF £24.49 CT £94.79 TOTE £4.60: £1.50, £1.30, £1.40; EX 23.10.
Owner Mrs James Bethell **Bred** Mrs P A Clark **Trained** Middleham Moor, N Yorks
■ Stewards' Enquiry : L McNiff three-day ban: used whip with excessive frequency (Jun 29-Jul 1)

FOCUS
Form to view positively, the front three pulling well clear off what was a sound gallop. The first two look a bit better than the bare form.
Viewing Official explanation: jockey said filly ran too free
T/Plt: £21.40 to a £1 stake. Pool: £67,295.16. 2,285.77 winning tickets. T/Qpdt: £9.40 to a £1 stake. Pool: £5,731.29. 447.74 winning tickets. WG

3055 - 3063a (Foreign Racing) - See Raceform Interactive

3029 ASCOT (R-H)
Thursday, June 16

OFFICIAL GOING: Good to soft (soft in places)
Rail on round course out 3m from inside line from 9f to home straight adding 12yds to races of 12f and over and 9yds to 10f race.
Wind: Light against Weather: Main dry with light showers after wet morning

3064 NORFOLK STKS (GROUP 2) 5f
2:30 (2:31) (Class 1) 2-Y-O
£42,577 (£16,140; £8,077; £4,027; £2,017; £1,012) **Stalls** Centre

Form RPR

1 **1** **Bapak Chinta (USA)**[34] 2042 2-9-1 0........................... PhillipMakin 2 106+
(Kevin Ryan) *racd in centre: pressed ldr tl led 1/2-way: mde rest: r.o wl u.p fnl f: asserted fnl 100yds: rdn out* **6/1**[3]

12 **2** *1* **Boomerang Bob (IRE)**[24] 2367 2-9-1 0........................ SebSanders 13 102
(J W Hills) *racd in centre: hld up in tch towards rr: hdwy 1/2-way: drvn and ev ch ent fnl f: no ex and btn fnl 100yds: kpt on: 2nd of 10 in gp* **20/1**

1 **3** *1 ¼* **Crown Dependency (IRE)**[42] 1835 2-9-1 0............... RichardHughes 5 98+
(Richard Hannon) *racd in centre: pushed along for 1f: hld up in tch after: nt clr run 3f out: rdn: hdwy and edging rt wl over 1f out: chsd ldrs 1f out: styd on same pce and no imp fnl 150yds: 3rd of 10 in gp* **8/1**

21 **4** *½* **Burwaaz**[17] 2563 2-9-1 0.. RichardHills 17 96+
(Ed Dunlop) *racd stands' side and against rail: midfield overall: rdn and effrt over 2f out: led gp and chsng overall ldrs 2f out: drvn and kpt on same pce fnl f: 1st of 5 in gp* **12/1**

2130 **5** *3 ¾* **Signifer (IRE)**[26] 2322 2-9-1 0..................................... JamieSpencer 21 83
(Mick Channon) *racd stands' side: stdd s: hld up wl bhd: rdn and hdwy 2f out: sn edging rt and midfield overall over 1f out: styd on same pce and no imp fnl f: nvr trbld ldrs: 2nd of 5 in gp* **40/1**

2112 **6** *nk* **Bannock (IRE)**[21] 2437 2-9-1 0.............................. SilvestreDeSousa 7 82
(Mark Johnston) *racd in centre: in tch but sn niggled along: n.m.r and jostling match w rival over 3f out: rdn and unable qck 2f out: styd on same pce and no threat to ldrs fnl f: 4th of 10 in gp* **9/2**[2]

314 **7** *¾* **Forevertheoptimist (IRE)**[34] 2056 2-9-1 0.............. KierenFallon 10 79
(Linda Stubbs) *racd in centre: s.i.s: and sn pushed along and struggling to go pce in rr: hdwy and edging rt over 1f out: no imp fnl f: nvr trbld ldrs: 5th of 10 in gp* **33/1**

1 **8** *½* **Silverheels (IRE)**[73] 1136 2-9-1 0.................................. RyanMoore 20 77
(Paul Cole) *racd stands' side: dwlt: sn pushed along and outpcd in rr: sme hdwy but edging rt 1/2-way: plugged on fnl f but n.d: 3rd of 5 in gp* **4/1**[1]

3151 **9** *½* **Pyman's Theory (IRE)**[21] 2437 2-8-12 0............... RichardKingscote 3 72
(Tom Dascombe) *racd in centre: chsd overall ldr tl led after 1f: hdd 1/2-way: drvn and unable qck 2f out: btn jst over 1f out: wknd fnl f: 6th of 10 in gp* **9/1**

61 **10** *½* **Charles The Great (IRE)**[24] 2367 2-9-1 0.................... JimmyFortune 12 73+
(Andrew Balding) *racd in centre: chsd ldrs: rdn and unable qck jst over 2f out: wknd u.p over 1f out: 7th of 10 in gp* **16/1**

11 *¾* **Everyday Dave (CAN)**[45] 2-9-1 0.................................(bt) JASanchez 16 71
(Wesley A Ward, U.S.A) *racd stands' side: broke fast and overall ldr for 1f: chsd ldrs after: rdn ent fnl 2f: wknd qckly over 1f out: 4th of 5 in gp* **8/1**

223 **12** *1 ¼* **Tell Dad**[33] 2109 2-9-1 0.. PatDobbs 11 66
(Richard Hannon) *racd in centre: in tch: edgd rt and jostling match w rival over 3f out: towards rr after: rdn and no hdwy ent fnl 2f: wknd wl over 1f out: 8th of 10 in gp* **25/1**

1 **13** *2* **Sans Loi (IRE)**[7] 2844 2-9-1 0....................................... RobertWinston 9 59
(Alan McCabe) *racd in centre: s.i.s: sn rcvrd and in tch: rdn and unable qckn 2f out: btn and wknd over 1f out: fdd fnl f: 9th of 10 in gp* **14/1**

162 **14** *¾* **Cravat**[19] 2488 2-9-1 0.. JoeFanning 1 56
(Mark Johnston) *racd in centre: sn pushed along: in tch towards rr: rdn and struggling 1/2-way: wknd wl over 1f out: sn bhd: 10th of 10 in gp* **66/1**

22 **15** *2 ¼* **Marcus Augustus (IRE)**[14] 2644 2-9-1 0......................... TomQueally 15 48
(Richard Hannon) *racd stands' side: chsd gp ldr but midfield overall tl 1/2-way: sn rdn and wknd 2f out: wl bhd fnl f: 5th of 5 in gp* **50/1**

63.03 secs (1.83) **Going Correction** +0.625s/f (Yiel) **15** Ran SP% **122.4**
Speed ratings (Par 105): **104,102,100,99,93 93,91,91,90,89 88,86,83,81,78**
toteswingers:1&2:£67.80, 1&3:£8.10, 2&3:£45.80 CSF £130.51 CT £999.57 TOTE £7.30: £2.60, £6.40, £2.80; EX 460.00 Trifecta £2645.00 Pool: £7,184.54 - 2.01 winning units..
Owner T A Rahman **Bred** E T Buckley, S Varney & A O'Donnell **Trained** Hambleton, N Yorks
■ Phillip Makin's first Royal Ascot winner.
■ Stewards' Enquiry : Seb Sanders one-day ban: used whip with excessive frequency (Jul 1)

FOCUS
The going was changed to good to soft, soft in places following 11mm of rain after 7am, and a perceived draw bias on the straight course was reversed, as those who raced down the middle had the upper hand. Some very smart 2-y-os have won this contest down the years. Names such as seven-time juvenile winner Superpower, the Lester Piggott-ridden filly Niche, subsequent Irish 2000 Guineas winner Turtle Island and Jack Berry's flying Mind Games have graced the winners' roster before the turn the millennium. However, recent winners haven't always gone on as expected. The classy pair Dutch Art and Winker Watson, who is now back in training, promised so much but failed to deliver a win at three and beyond, while last year's winner Approve got packed off to stud before having a chance to prove himself. That said, the horse in tenth in the 2010 running was Dubawi Gold (then trained by Michael Dods), who was runner-up in the English and Irish Guineas this year. This year's renewal didn't look to contain an obvious 'exciting' type, and there were six non-runners, but virtually all of those who remained had won at least once. Straightforward form, rated to the race average.

NOTEBOOK
Bapak Chinta(USA) ◆'s first win could not have worked out much better. It was only a four-runner race at Hamilton, but the runner-up Frederick Engels, who was due to run in this until taken out in the morning, went on to finish runner-up to the Queen Mary second next time, before winning a conditions stakes and the Windsor Castle Stakes. Said to have never come off the bridle at home and in need of an older horse to lead him, the winner showed lots of speed and a pleasing attitude under pressure to run all the way to the line, holding off a persistent challenger. Kevin Ryan's juveniles have been in exceptional form this season, but this colt must be the best seen out so far from that stable and, long-term, a race like the Nunthorpe should be on his agenda. Quicker ground is expected to suit him better. (op 15-2 tchd 8-1)
Boomerang Bob(IRE) finished behind Charles The Great last time (conceding 5lb), but easily reversed that form and made the winner work hard inside the final furlong. His stable has been in good form this season and one would imagine he will have no trouble getting a bit further on pedigree. He has an entry in the Railway Stakes later this month, although that may come a bit quick, but connections nominated the Prix Robert Papin as his likely next target. (op 25-1 tchd 28-1)
Crown Dependency(IRE) ◆, the first string on jockey bookings for the in-form Hannon stable, needed a few reminders to get into the firing line before keeping on at the one pace - the trainer said afterwards that his horse got a hefty bump, that may have cost him the race interestingly. There is certainly no disgrace in finishing third in a Group 2, but the drop in trip didn't appear to suit. He will possibly be given a break and head to Goodwood for either the Molecomb or Richmond, and connections rate him very highly. (op 7-1)
Burwaaz ◆ raced away from the action nearer the stands' rail, and should definitely be marked up for his effort as he was nicely clear of the next home that side. A horse with plenty of size, he will develop into an above-average performer and connections will surely want to be take on the winner again on a level playing field. (op 14-1)
Signifer(IRE) got upsides the fourth with about a furlong to go but couldn't go with that rival as he extended clear. (tchd 50-1)
Bannock(IRE), who in some ways it wasn't a huge surprise to see reverse National Stakes form with Pyman's Theory, as he'd got stuck in a pocket for a while at Sandown before staying on strongly. He needed to be ridden along here for a few strides before keeping on, while Tom Dascombe's filly showed really good speed in the centre before tiring late on. (op 13-2)
Silverheels(IRE) was sent off favourite possibly as a result of his sire's other progeny being well suited by soft ground. However, he had excuses as he missed the break and raced on the unfavoured stands' side. He might need a step up in trip. (op 5-1 tchd 11-2 and 6-1 in places)
Charles The Great(IRE)'s rider reported that the colt lost his right hind shoe. Official explanation: jockey said colt lost its right-hind shoe
Everyday Dave(CAN), an unbeaten American challenger, faded steadily after leading the stands'-side group, probably finding the ground too testing, and Wesley Ward's horses haven't quite hit the heights this week after Gentlemans Code's good performance on the first day. (op 11-2)

3065 RIBBLESDALE STKS (GROUP 2) (FILLIES) 1m 4f
3:05 (3:05) (Class 1) 3-Y-O
£56,770 (£21,520; £10,770; £5,370; £2,690; £1,350) **Stalls** Low

Form RPR

1151 **1** **Banimpire (IRE)**[4] 2968 3-8-12 **109**.................................... KJManning 2 111
(J S Bolger, Ire) *midfield: hdwy gng wl over 3f out: effrt to chse ldr over 2f out: styd on to ld 110yds out: sn wnt a nk up: all out at fin* **3/1**[1]

4-12 **2** *shd* **Field Of Miracles (IRE)**[40] 1894 3-8-12 **95**............ RichardHughes 11 110
(John Gosden) *prom: led after 2f: kicked ent st: 2 l clr 2f out: hdd 110yds out and sn a nk down: rallied fnl strides* **16/1**

1221 **3** *7* **Dorcas Lane**[46] 1722 3-8-12 **100**.................................... PaulHanagan 6 100
(Lucy Wadham) *towards rr: hdwy 3f out: wnt 3rd 2f out: sn hung rt: styd on fnl f: no imp on front pair but clr of remainder* **10/1**

2-60 **4** *6* **Look At Me (IRE)**[25] 2334 3-8-12 **95**................................... RyanMoore 4 91+
(A P O'Brien, Ire) *racd keenly: hld up: hdwy on inner over 3f out: plld off rail to chse ldrs over 2f out: carried rt and n.m.r briefly ent fnl 2f: one pce and no imp after* **12/1**

-110 **5** *4* **Zain Al Boldan**[13] 2682 3-8-12 **105**.................................. KierenFallon 12 85
(Mick Channon) *s.i.s: bhd and a niggled along: styd on fr 2f out: wnt mod 5th ins fnl f: nvr a danger* **8/1**[3]

1-31 **6** *6* **Rumh (GER)**[7] 2839 3-8-12 **93**.. FrankieDettori 5 76
(Saeed Bin Suroor) *hld up in midfield: hdwy over 4f out: chsd ldr over 3f out tl over 2f out: wknd jst ins fnl 2f* **7/2**[2]

-212 **7** *18* **Highest**[29] 2189 3-8-12 95 WilliamBuick 10 49
(John Gosden) *prom: niggled along over 7f out: rdn and wknd over 3f out* **9/1**

0-64 **8** *5* **Musharakaat (IRE)**[43] 1807 3-8-12 95 RichardHills 8 42
(Ed Dunlop) *prom: pushed along over 2f out: sn wknd* **33/1**

3-14 **9** *9* **Arizona Jewel**[36] 2004 3-8-12 89 TomQueally 7 28
(Sir Henry Cecil) *hld up in midfield on outer: rdn 4f out: wknd over 3f out* **14/1**

10 *1 3/4* **Make My Heart Sing (IRE)**[34] 2083 3-8-12 90 PJSmullen 1 26
(A P O'Brien, Ire) *in tch: niggled along over 5f out: wknd 4f out: sn bhd: t.o* **14/1**

41 **11** *1 1/2* **Creme Anglaise**[41] 1845 3-8-12 86 HayleyTurner 9 23
(Michael Bell) *in tch: pushed along over 4f out: wknd over 3f out: t.o* **14/1**

-402 **12** *6* **Sunday Bess (JPN)**[28] 2219 3-8-12 83 (v[1]) RichardKingscote 3 14
(Tom Dascombe) *led for 2f: trckd ldr tl over 4f out: rdn and wknd 4f out: t.o* **40/1**

2m 37.06s (4.56) **Going Correction** +0.625s/f (Yiel) **12** Ran SP% **116.4**
Speed ratings (Par 108): **109,108,104,100,97 93,81,78,72,71 70,66**
toteswingers:1&2:£10.80, 1&3:£7.90, 2&3:£26.00 CSF £51.88 CT £430.76 TOTE £3.80: £1.70, £4.70, £3.80; EX 54.30 Trifecta £608.40 Pool: £7,958.75 - 9.67 winning units..
Owner Mrs J S Bolger **Bred** Kilcarn Stud **Trained** Coolcullen, Co Carlow

■ Stewards' Enquiry : K J Manning two-day ban: used whip with excessive frequency in incorrect place (Jun 30-Jul 1)

FOCUS

As the previous day, the rail on the round course was positioned 3m out from the inside, adding approximately 12yards to the race distance. This race is often won by an improver, but only Punctilious in recent years has gone on to Group 1 success in Europe, and for four of the last five winners it has proved to be a highlight and final success of their careers. This year's line-up did not look strong with only three having official ratings of 100 or above, and with the rain-softened ground having its effect, the field finished strung out. The first pair finished clear and the form fits with the race averages.

NOTEBOOK

Banimpire(IRE) has been a progressive performer since upped in trip, and her only defeat in her previous five starts was when a close fifth dropped back to 1m in the Irish 1000 Guineas. She had shown before she handled soft ground and, after being hampered early when held up, followed the favourite through and went in pursuit of the leader when that one kicked over 2f out. She managed to get her head in front entering the last half-furlong but then had to dig deep to hold on as the runner-up rallied. She is a really tough sort as this was her fifth win of the season from seven starts, the latest being just four days previously. She will now have the Irish Oaks as her target. Her rider picked up a two-day ban for his use of the whip. (op 4-1)

Field Of Miracles(IRE) ◆ improved from her 1m4f Polytrack success to finish second in the Lingfield Oaks Trial but that left her with a lot to find with Zain Al Boldan. However, she was ridden positively and, after going on in Swinley Bottom, kicked clear off the home turn. She was caught by the winner inside the last furlong but battled back gamely and was only just held. She is clearly on the upgrade and should be winning a Group race before long. (op 20-1)

Dorcas Lane had progressed from her winning debut to take the Pretty Polly Stakes at Newmarket, but was up in trip and drifted in the betting after connections expressed concerns about the soft ground. She ran well though, making ground from the back on the home turn and staying on stoutly without troubling the principals. She was well clear of the rest and probably goes for the Lancashire Oaks next, with the Yorkshire Oaks a possibility later on. (op 8-1 tchd 12-1)

Look At Me(IRE), a 7f winner on soft before finishing runner-up in a Group 3 last season, had finished well beaten both starts in Group company this year and was taking a big step up in trip. Although her breeding didn't suggest stamina, she acted on the ground and kept on steadily, although well beaten. (tchd 11-1)

Zain Al Boldan who completed a hat-trick when winning the Lingfield Oaks Trial from today's runner-up but was well beaten in the Oaks, missed the break and was soon being pushed along at the back. She just stayed on past beaten rivals in the straight and looks the sort for a race like the Park Hill later on. (tchd 9-1)

Rumh(GER) was sent off favourite, having finished third behind the Oaks third and winner in a 1m2f Newbury Listed race and had then made all to win similar event over same C&D next time. Over this longer distance she was held up before moving onto the heels of the leaders nearing the home turn, but she failed to pick up and gave the impression a combination of the trip and the soft ground beat her. The rider confirmed his filly did not handle the ground. Official explanation: jockey said filly was unsuited by the good to soft (soft in places) ground (tchd 3-1, 4-1 in places)

Highest raced prominently but failed to get home in the conditions. (tchd 10-1 in a place)

Musharakaat(IRE), another prominent racer, also failed to get home in the conditions.

Creme Anglaise another prominent racer, was struggling before the home turn. (op 12-1)

Sunday Bess(JPN), the early leader, was beaten before the straight, although the jockey reported the filly was unsuited by the ground. Official explanation: jockey said filly was unsuited by the good to soft (soft in places) ground (op 33-1)

3066 GOLD CUP (BRITISH CHAMPIONS' SERIES) (GROUP 1) 2m 4f

3:45 (3:47) (Class 1) 4-Y-0+

£154,698 (£58,642; £29,348; £14,633; £7,330; £3,678) **Stalls** Low

Form RPR

5-11 **1** **Fame And Glory**[18] 2534 5-9-2 122 JamieSpencer 3 121+
(A P O'Brien, Ire) *travelled wl: hld up in tch: rdn and effrt over 2f out: led and hung rt to rail over 1f out: sn drvn clr: kpt on wl and in command fnl f: rdn out* **11/8**[1]

2234 **2** *3* **Opinion Poll (IRE)**[25] 2344 5-9-2 112 MickaelBarzalona 1 118
(Mahmood Al Zarooni) *hld up in last quartet: effrt and swtchd sharply lft over 2f out: hdwy u.p 2f out: chsd wnr 1f out: kpt on wl but no imp fnl 150yds* **16/1**

6-41 **3** *4 1/2* **Brigantin (USA)**[25] 2344 4-9-0 113 Pierre-CharlesBoudot 13 114+
(A Fabre, France) *hld up in tch in midfield: rdn and sltly outpcd wl over 2f out: 7th and hdwy u.p over 1f out: swtchd rt jst ins fnl f: styd on to go 3rd nr fin: no threat to wnr* **16/1**

03-3 **4** *1/2* **Manighar (FR)**[34] 2072 5-9-2 114 KierenFallon 8 113
(Luca Cumani) *in tch: hdwy to press ldr and rdn over 3f out: drvn and ev ch ent fnl 2f: nt gng pce of wnr over 1f out and btn whn edgd lft 1f out: plugged on same pce fnl f* **14/1**

-316 **5** *1/2* **Askar Tau (FR)**[34] 2072 6-9-2 106 (v) GeorgeBaker 6 113
(Marcus Tregoning) *hld up in tch in midfield: hdwy to chse ldng trio 3f out: drvn and pressing ldrs 2f out: nt pce of wnr over 1f out and btn 1f out: plugged on same pce fnl f* **66/1**

10-1 **6** *2 1/4* **Duncan**[34] 2072 6-9-2 119 WilliamBuick 12 110
(John Gosden) *t.k.h: chsd ldrs: wnt 2nd 6f out tl led over 4f out: hrd pressed and rdn over 2f out: hdd and nt pce of wnr over 1f out: btn and lost 2nd 1f out: wknd ins fnl f* **8/1**[2]

-413 **7** *shd* **Kasbah Bliss (FR)**[47] 1707 9-9-2 111 ThierryThulliez 4 110+
(F Doumen, France) *hld up in tch in midfield: shuffled bk towards rr over 3f out: swtchd lft and hdwy jst over 2f out: plugged on fnl 2f but no threat to wnr* **16/1**

1-54 **8** *1 3/4* **Aaim To Prosper (IRE)**[21] 2438 7-9-2 100 RyanMoore 15 108
(Brian Meehan) *chsd ldr tl 10f out: styd chsng ldrs: pressing ldr and rdn 4f out: drvn and unable qck jst over 3f out: sn struggling: one pce and no threat fnl 2f* **22/1**

332- **9** *6* **Motrice**[243] 6929 4-8-11 108 SebSanders 14 99
(Sir Mark Prescott Bt) *stdd and swtchd rt after s: t.k.h: hld up towards rr: hdwy 6f out: 6th and rdn wl over 2f out: wknd and btn 2f out* **22/1**

-621 **10** *1/2* **Blue Bajan (IRE)**[21] 2438 9-9-2 111 DanielTudhope 10 102
(David O'Meara) *hld up in midfield: shuffled bk towards rr 5f out: rdn and modest hdwy over 2f out: no imp and wl hld whn hung rt over 1f out* **11/1**

2-14 **11** *26* **The Betchworth Kid**[50] 1601 6-9-2 103 HayleyTurner 5 76
(Alan King) *stdd s: hld up in rr: rdn and short-lived effrt 3f out: wknd and wl btn over 2f out: eased ins fnl f: t.o* **40/1**

1-34 **12** *2 1/4* **Fictional Account (IRE)**[18] 2534 6-8-13 103 FMBerry 7 71
(V C Ward, Ire) *stdd s: hld up in last quartet: hdwy 6f out: rdn: edgd rt and struggling ent fnl 3f: wknd and wl bhd 2f out: t.o* **20/1**

16-3 **13** *73* **Holberg (UAE)**[21] 2438 5-9-2 111 FrankieDettori 2 —
(Saeed Bin Suroor) *chsd ldrs: rdn and struggling 4f out: wknd ent fnl 3f: wl bhd and virtually p.u fnl 2f: wl t.o* **10/1**[3]

133/ **P** **Geordieland (FR)**[643] 5824 10-9-2 109 RichardHughes 9 —
(Jamie Osborne) *stdd s: plld hrd and hld up in last quartet: swtchd to outer and hdwy 14f out: led 10f out and sn clr: hdd over 6f out: immediately dropped out and eased: p.u 5f out* **25/1**

41-2 **P** **Tastahil (IRE)**[43] 1808 7-9-2 115 RichardHills 11 —
(B W Hills) *led tl 10f out: chsd ldr tl led again over 6f out: rdn and hdd over 4f out: immediately dropped out: t.o and eased fr over 2f out: p.u ins fnl f* **16/1**

4m 37.51s (12.71) **Going Correction** +0.625s/f (Yiel)
WFA 4 from 5yo+ 2lb **15** Ran SP% **122.1**
Speed ratings (Par 117): **99,97,96,95,95 94,94,93,91,91 80,80,50,—,—**
toteswingers:1&2:£6.50, 1&3:£9.00, 2&3:£56.90 CSF £22.97 CT £272.62 TOTE £2.40: £1.20, £4.70, £4.60; EX 32.60 Trifecta £387.70 Pool: £16,422.10 - 31.33 winning units..
Owner D Smith/Mrs J Magnier/M Tabor/Mrs F Hay **Bred** Ptarmigan Bloodstock And Miss K Rausing **Trained** Ballydoyle, Co Tipperary

■ Stewards' Enquiry : Jamie Spencer one-day ban: careless riding (Jun 30); three-day ban: used whip down shoulder in the forehand (Jul 1,3,4)

FOCUS

It's fair to say last year's race didn't work out well. The winner Rite Of Passage wasn't seen again until fairly recently, and despite shaping with promise at Leopardstown, training issues prevented him from defending his crown. Runner-up Age Of Aquarius sadly managed only one more race, the third Purple Moon hasn't been out since the Goodwood Cup, and fifth-placed Ask was retired to stud. Only Gallic raider Kasbah Bliss and outsider Tastahil came back for another go. \n\x\x The 2011 running had plenty of queries hanging over it as the favourite hadn't been shaping like a definite stayer, while plenty of the others either didn't look good enough or also had questions to answer regarding stamina, but as it turned out the race got a high-class winner. The early pace wasn't fast by any means and the time was relatively slow. Fame And Glory is still rated 6lb off last season's best with the next pair close to form.

NOTEBOOK

Fame And Glory was the clear pick of these on raw ability. In his 3-y-o campaign he regularly duelled with Sea The Stars, putting up some solid efforts in defeat, and also won the Irish Derby, while a fifth in last season's Arc confirmed him to be still capable of mixing it with the best. He hadn't impressed in two victories in Listed company this year, including when stepped up to 1m6f on his previous outing, so when the rain came during the morning, bookies were seemingly keen to get him - Stan James pushed him out to 3-1 at one point. However, he was heavily backed, with a couple of five-figure bets reportedly struck with William Hill at 5-2, and the Ballydoyle runner landed a major punt, being sent off at just 11-8. Settled just in behind, he stalked the ordinary pace before coming home strongly once getting into the clear, again proving that a class horse can get home over extended distances. Yeats dominated this event over a period of four years and, if campaigned in the same manner, Fame And Glory will be hard to beat. Bookmakers were offering 66-1 afterwards that he emulates his stablemate with four successes and that's by no means a bad price if one was prepared to wait for a potential payout. He is due to have a break now prior to being prepared for another assault on the Arc. (op 15-8 tchd 2-1 in places and 9-4 in places)

Opinion Poll(IRE) ◆, whose owners Godolphin had a surprisingly moderate recent record in this contest, ran a blinder on ground that came right for him. Had he been closer to the winner when he made his final move, there seems little doubt Fame And Glory would have been made to work harder, and it certainly was impressive the way he changed gear to get involved. (op 14-1)

Brigantin(USA) had got the better of Opinion Poll last time in the Prix Vicomtesse Vigier but got caught seriously flat-footed before keeping on. He certainly shouldn't be beating the runner-up any time soon over staying trips, but he is only four and can come back again next year a stronger horse. The Melbourne Cup is his long-term target. (tchd 20-1 in places)

Manighar(FR), who was suited by the ease in the ground, swept into the home straight looking a live danger, but he had been keen and just kept on at the one pace. He was slightly hampered as the winner came past (Jamie Spencer was banned), but it made little difference to his final position. The Melbourne Cup is said to be on his agenda again - he was seventh last year. (op 12-1 tchd 16-1 in places)

Askar Tau(FR) needs producing late, and while it's easy to argue that he got in a battle earlier than he would have liked, there wasn't much George Baker could do about that. He wouldn't have wanted the rain. (op 40-1)

Duncan came into this well fancied after winning the Yorkshire Cup, his first run after being gelded, but there was a doubt over the trip with him - connections had toyed with running him the Hardwicke Stakes later in the week. Racing a bit freely early, he took a time to settle but was in an ideal position on turning in. However, he steadily lost his place the further he went down the home straight, and he didn't stay 2m4f under these circumstances. Dropped down to 1m6f-2m again, and if settling, he could be hard to beat.

Kasbah Bliss(FR) deliberately missed the Prix Vicomtesse Vigier this year, as they felt it had taken the edge of him when he ran modestly in this race last year, but that didn't help him to have a winning chance this time. (op 14-1)

Aaim To Prosper(IRE), last season's Cesarewitch winner, had no stamina issues as he'd finished third in last year's Ascot Stakes over this distance, and he ran as well as could have been expected. (op 33-1)

Motrice made good progress through handicaps last year before finding the step up to Group company on her last three outings a bit too much. Absent since finishing second to Tastahil (getting 13lb) in the Jockey Club Cup last October, she had her chance off the final bend but weakened quickly under pressure. (tchd 25-1)

Blue Bajan(IRE), supplemented for this race for £25,000, was well below the form he showed when winning the Henry II at Sandown last time. (op 10-1 tchd 9-1)

Holberg(UAE) seemed to have a leading chance if reproducing his best over a trip he'd not attempted before, but the 2009 winner of the Queen's Vase was not helped by the rain-softened ground. Official explanation: jockey said horse was unsuited by the good to soft (soft in places) ground (op 9-1 tchd 12-1)

Geordieland(FR) was having his first outing since running in the 2009 Doncaster Cup. He was rushed into the lead at one point after taking a fierce hold, but dropped out very quickly. The trainer reported afterwards that his horse returned okay and lives to fight another day. (op 20-1)

3067 BRITANNIA STKS (HERITAGE H'CAP) (C&G) 1m (S)

4:25 (4:27) (Class 2) (0-105,101) 3-Y-O

£62,310 (£18,660; £9,330; £4,670; £2,330; £1,170) **Stalls** Centre

Form — RPR

2-21 **1** **Sagramor**[26] 2296 3-8-13 **93** NickyMackay 23 102+
(Hughie Morrison) *racd in stands' side gp: in tch: effrt 3f out: r.o ins fnl f: led fnl 75yds: in command cl home* **8/1**[2]

-123 **2** *½* **Cai Shen (IRE)**[19] 2507 3-9-7 **101** RyanMoore 15 109+
(Richard Hannon) *racd on far-side: hld up: hdwy over 2f out: r.o ins fnl f: clsng towards fin: nvr gng to get there* **20/1**

-130 **3** *hd* **The Tichborne (IRE)**[19] 2506 3-8-7 **87** JackMitchell 18 94
(Roger Teal) *racd on far-side: led: swtchd to r stands' side 6f out and stl overall ldr: rdn over 2f out: hdd fnl 75yds: kpt on but hld fnl strides* **100/1**

26-1 **4** *nse* **Belgian Bill**[61] 1384 3-9-3 **97** (t) TonyCulhane 30 104+
(George Baker) *racd in stands' side gp: midfield: hdwy over 3f out: nt clr run 3f out: swtchd lft over 2f out: r.o u.p ins fnl f: gng on at fin* **10/1**[3]

4-14 **5** *1* **Trade Storm**[33] 2106 3-9-4 **98** DarryllHolland 22 103
(John Gallagher) *racd in stands' side gp: midfield: hdwy 3f out: rdn to chal over 1f out: nt qckn towards fin* **50/1**

5304 **6** *nk* **Cruiser**[19] 2506 3-8-5 **85** MartinDwyer 25 89
(William Muir) *racd in stands' side gp: in tch: rdn over 2f out: styd on towards fin: nt quite gng pce of ldrs* **25/1**

00-1 **7** *½* **Bahceli (IRE)**[47] 1690 3-8-12 **92** NeilCallan 13 95+
(Richard Hannon) *racd far-side: hld up: swtchd to r stands' side over 6f out: hdwy 2f out: rdn and nt clr run over 1f out: styng on whn swtchd rt ins fnl f: nt get to ldrs* **33/1**

21-1 **8** *½* **Chain Lightning**[53] 1550 3-8-11 **91** RichardHughes 11 93+
(Richard Hannon) *racd in far-side gp: hld up: swtchd to r stands' side 6f out: hdwy over 3f out: chsd ldrs 2f out: kpt on same pce towards fin* **6/1**[1]

4-05 **9** *nk* **Madawi**[42] 1822 3-8-13 **93** PhilipRobinson 29 94
(Clive Brittain) *racd in stands' side gp: midfield: rdn 2f out: kpt on u.p ins fnl f: no real imp on ldrs* **16/1**

4122 **10** *hd* **Tropical Beat**[29] 2188 3-8-6 **86** (b[1]) WilliamBuick 31 87+
(John Gosden) *racd in stands' side gp: hld up: hdwy whn nt clr run and swtchd rt over 1f out: r.o ins fnl f: gng on at fin* **10/1**[3]

1532 **11** *¾* **Tinkertown (IRE)**[33] 2110 3-9-5 **99** JamieSpencer 14 98
(Paul Cole) *s.s: racd far-side: in rr: hdwy 2f out: chsd ldrs ins fnl f: one pce fnl 75yds* **33/1**

-145 **12** *shd* **Ashva (USA)**[35] 2030 3-8-5 **85** FrannyNorton 1 84+
(Michael Dods) *racd on far-side: prom: rdn to chal wl over 1f out: fdd fnl 75yds* **40/1**

-502 **13** *2* **Mubtadi**[12] 2705 3-8-6 **86** MartinLane 17 80+
(David Simcock) *racd on far-side: hld up: nt clr run over 2f out: hdwy over 1f out: styd on ins fnl f: nt gng pce to rch ldrs* **33/1**

3404 **14** *¾* **Vanguard Dream**[13] 2683 3-9-1 **95** PatDobbs 27 88
(Richard Hannon) *racd in stands'side gp: hld up: rdn 2f out: sme hdwy into midfield ins fnl f: unable to trble ldrs* **33/1**

-345 **15** *hd* **Bridgefield (USA)**[105] 753 3-9-6 **100** FrankieDettori 16 92+
(Mahmood Al Zarooni) *racd on far-side: swtchd to stands' side gp after 1f: hld up: hdwy 2f out: rdn to chse ldrs over 1f out: no ex fnl 100yds* **33/1**

001- **16** *1 ¾* **Capaill Liath (IRE)**[263] 6386 3-8-2 **87** (p) HarryBentley[(5)] 5 75
(Michael Bell) *racd in far-side gp: bhd: nt clr run over 2f out: sn swtchd rt: styd on ins fnl f: nt pce to trble ldrs* **25/1**

1-16 **17** *hd* **Polar Kite (IRE)**[26] 2296 3-8-7 **87** PaulHanagan 2 75
(Richard Fahey) *racd in far-side gp: hld up: hdwy 3f out: chsd ldrs over 2f out: no ex fnl 100yds* **20/1**

-211 **18** *½* **Common Touch (IRE)**[26] 2319 3-8-12 **97** LeeTopliss[(5)] 7 83
(Richard Fahey) *racd in far-side gp and in tch: rdn and nt qckn over 2f out: no imp fnl f* **16/1**

-013 **19** *hd* **Chilworth Lad**[13] 2683 3-9-2 **99** MartinHarley[(3)] 12 85
(Mick Channon) *racd in stands' side gp: in tch: effrt 2f out: wknd ins fnl f* **50/1**

4100 **20** *1 ¾* **Crown Counsel (IRE)**[12] 2705 3-8-6 **86** SilvestreDeSousa 19 68
(Mark Johnston) *racd in stands' side gp: prom: pushed along 1/2-way: wknd over 1f out* **66/1**

34-0 **21** *shd* **Catalyze**[19] 2506 3-8-5 **85** (t) DavidProbert 33 67
(Andrew Balding) *racd in stands' side gp: hld up: rdn into midfield over 2f out: bhd fnl f* **33/1**

1-23 **22** *2* **Captain Bertie (IRE)**[42] 1820 3-8-10 **90** MichaelHills 9 67
(B W Hills) *racd in far-side gp: in tch tl pushed along and wknd 3f out* **14/1**

0- **23** *11* **Honey Of A Kitten (USA)**[61] 1418 3-9-1 **95** PJSmullen 6 47
(D K Weld, Ire) *racd on far-side: trckd ldrs tl rdn and wknd 2f out* **20/1**

15-0 **24** *1 ¾* **Baptist (USA)**[26] 2319 3-8-10 **90** JimmyFortune 32 38
(Andrew Balding) *racd in stands' side gp: in tch tl wknd over 3f out* **22/1**

-113 **25** *1 ¼* **Ektibaas**[19] 2506 3-8-7 **87** RichardHills 10 32
(B W Hills) *racd in far-side gp: prom tl rdn and wknd over 2f out* **16/1**

1121 **26** *¾* **Kuala Limper (IRE)**[7] 2847 3-8-11 **91** 5ex TomQueally 24 34
(David Elsworth) *racd in stands' side gp: prom: pushed along and wknd over 2f out* **16/1**

3053 **27** *1 ¼* **Rigolleto (IRE)**[5] 2908 3-8-10 **90** SamHitchcott 3 30
(Mick Channon) *racd in far-side gp: prom: led gp at 1/2-way tl gps merged 3f out: wknd ent fnl 2f* **100/1**

4501 **28** *10* **Norse Blues**[13] 2684 3-8-10 **90** JamesDoyle 8 —
(Sylvester Kirk) *prom: led far-side gp 6f out to 1/2-way: rdn and wknd 2f out* **33/1**

5-31 **29** *34* **Dream Achieved**[50] 1606 3-8-12 **92** RobertWinston 26 —
(B W Hills) *racd in stands' side gp: prom tl wknd qckly over 3f out: t.o fnl f* **14/1**

1m 44.55s (3.95) **Going Correction** +0.625s/f (Yiel) **29** Ran SP% **137.2**
Speed ratings (Par 105): **105,104,104,104,103 102,102,101,101,101 100,100,98,97,97 95,95,95,95,93 93,91,80,78,77 76,75,**
toteswingers:1&2:£27.40, 1&3:Not won, 2&3:Not won CSF £164.79 CT £14178.21 TOTE £7.20: £2.40, £7.30, £29.50, £3.10; EX 223.80 TRIFECTA Not won..
Owner Melksham Craic **Bred** Melksham Craic **Trained** East Ilsley, Berks
■ Stewards' Enquiry : Nicky Mackay four-day ban: used whip with excessive frequency (Jun 30,Jul 1,3,4)
Jack Mitchell seven-day ban: used whip with excessive frequency (Jun 30-Jul 6)

FOCUS
A typically competitive renewal of a race that usually falls to an improving type. As with the previous day's Royal Hunt Cup, in recent years it has paid to race on either flank but, after the previous two days' events the stands' rail seemed the place to be and, despite the rain, that proved to be the case again. There was a certain amount of indecision in the early stages amongst the jockeys, as some switched from the group racing up the centre to the nearside, but in the end the whole field converged towards the stands' rail. The form looks sound amongst the principals with the third the key to the form.

NOTEBOOK
Sagramor won a valuable Haydock handicap over this trip on his previous start and the form had been working out reasonably well. He handled the ground well enough and, produced over 2f out, kept plugging away under pressure. He is clearly tough and genuine and presumably will be aimed at the big all-aged handicaps now. (op 9-1 tchd 10-1 in a place)
Cai Shen(IRE) completed a hat-trick when winning a conditions race at Newbury on his reappearance but had been held in Listed company on both starts since. Down in trip and grade, he handled the ground on his first try on it, and came from out of the pack racing towards the centre to chase home the winner. This was a brave effort but he will not find things easy if he goes up from his current rating. (op 28-1)
The Tichborne(IRE), a dual winner on Polytrack whose form this year had not worked out, was untried on soft but ran a terrific race. He came across from the centre and was soon helping set the pace and, once over towards the rail, showed in a clear advantage. He battled on gamely and was only worn down inside the final furlong, although his rider's efforts with the whip cost him a seven-day ban.
Belgian Bill ◆, a winner at up to 1m on fast and placed on easy ground, had gained both wins on a flat track. Up 5lb for his last success, he came through up the rail to challenge the leader but could not pick up enough to go through the gap. He will be interesting for similar races at York and Doncaster later on. (tchd 17-2)
Trade Storm, a winner at up to 7f on fast ground but held in Listed and Group company, was another untried on softer than good. He ran his race and only just missed a place in the frame.
Cruiser won his maiden over 6f on soft ground and, although he had a bit to find with a couple of these on more recent form, ran creditably with the conditions to suit.
Bahceli(IRE) ◆, the winner of a decent 1m Newmarket handicap on his seasonal reappearance, had appeared best on fast ground but was noted staying on despite not getting the clearest of runs. He might be more potent back on a sounder surface and the Newmarket July meeting might offer him a suitable opportunity.
Chain Lightning won his maiden over this trip at Salisbury on soft ground from four subsequent winners, and took a Sandown handicap on his return. Racing off 6lb higher, he was heavily backed leading up to the race but, after coming to have his chance 2f from home, his effort petered out. (op 8-1)
Madawi is still a maiden but has run well in sales races and in Group 3s and, proven with cut, stayed on steadily. (tchd 40-1 in a place)
Tropical Beat ◆ was the unlucky horse in the race. He stays further than this but had not encountered cut in the ground previously and had blinkers on for the first time. He was held up out the back was short of room at a crucial stage before making significant late headway. With a clear run he could well have been involved in the finish. Official explanation: jockey said colt was denied a clear run
Tinkertown(IRE) gained his wins on Polytrack and fast ground and finished placed in Group 3 Dee Stakes. He had been well beaten on his only previous try on soft but handled this ground well enough and finished as if needing a return to further. (op 50-1)
Ashva(USA) won his maiden on Fibresand at this trip but, after being well beaten in the Dante, was down in trip and grade. He ran creditably from the lowest draw of all, the only one from a single figure box to finish in the first dozen, only to pay for his efforts late on. (op 33-1)
Dream Achieved showed up early but dropped right away and was eased as if something was amiss.

3068 TERCENTENARY STKS (GROUP 3) (FORMERLY THE HAMPTON COURT STAKES) 1m 2f

5:00 (5:03) (Class 1) 3-Y-O

£39,739 (£15,064; £7,539; £3,759; £1,883; £945) **Stalls** Low

Form — RPR

0-30 **1** **Pisco Sour (USA)**[12] 2715 3-9-0 107 JimmyFortune 11 113
(Hughie Morrison) *hld up in tch: swtchd lft and effrt over 2f out: rdn and qcknd to ld wl over 1f out: drvn and r.o wl fnl f* **20/1**

411 **2** *1 ¾* **Alkimos (IRE)**[12] 2707 3-9-0 103 KierenFallon 5 110
(Luca Cumani) *s.i.s: hld up towards rr: hdwy on outer jst over 3f out: pressed ldrs and hung rt jst ins fnl 2f: chsd wnr over 1f out: r.o wl u.p but a hld fnl f* **13/2**[3]

0-13 **3** *2* **Slumber**[42] 1822 3-9-0 101 MichaelHills 3 109+
(B W Hills) *bustled along leaving stalls: hld up in tch: nt clr run ent fnl 2f and switching lft after: eventually in the clr ent fnl f: r.o wl to go 3rd wl ins fnl f: unable to chal ldrs* **10/1**

1-40 **4** *¾* **Specific Gravity (FR)**[53] 1548 3-9-0 95 IanMongan 15 104
(Sir Henry Cecil) *t.k.h: hld up in tch: swtchd lft and effrt ent fnl 2f: chsd ldrs and drvn over 1f out: kpt on same pce fnl f* **50/1**

2-11 **5** *¾* **Tazahum (USA)**[21] 2440 3-9-0 107 RichardHills 14 103+
(Sir Michael Stoute) *t.k.h: chsd ldrs on outer: rdn and pressing ldrs ent fnl 2f: unable qck w ldng pair and sltly hmpd wl over 1f out: kpt on same pce after* **5/1**[2]

-141 **6** *hd* **Laajooj (IRE)**[19] 2507 3-9-0 108 MickaelBarzalona 16 102
(Mahmood Al Zarooni) *stdd and swtchd rt after s: hld up in last pair: effrt on outer whn bmpd over 2f out: gd hdwy u.p over 1f out: edgd rt and styd on same pce ins fnl f* **10/1**

7 *nk* **Marksmanship (IRE)**[74] 1120 3-9-0 0 RyanMoore 10 102+
(A P O'Brien, Ire) *t.k.h: hld up towards rr: effrt: swtchd lft and bmpd rival over 2f out: n.m.r and no hdwy 2f out: hdwy over 1f out: edgd rt but styd on wl u.p fnl f: unable to chal* **10/3**[1]

2-1 **8** *3 ½* **Hunter's Light (IRE)**[20] 2469 3-9-0 101 FrankieDettori 12 95
(Saeed Bin Suroor) *t.k.h: chsd ldrs tl wnt 2nd wl over 3f out: rdn to ld jst over 2f out: hdd over 1f out: sn struggling and btn ent fnl f: wknd fnl 150yds* **7/1**

2205 **9** *2 ¼* **Ahlaain (USA)**[63] 1341 3-9-0 100 WilliamBuick 9 90
(David Simcock) *stdd and swtchd rt s: hld up in last pair: effrt but stl plenty to do whn nt clr run 2f out: sn swtchd lft: styd on u.p fnl f: nvr trbld ldrs* **66/1**

-134 **10** *2* **Auld Burns**[29] 2191 3-9-0 104 JamieSpencer 4 86
(Richard Hannon) *hld up in last trio: rdn and struggling wl over 2f out: edging rt u.p over 1f out: styd on past btn horses but no ch fnl f* **18/1**

1-32 **11** *½* **Moriarty (IRE)**[25] 2331 3-9-0 105 (v[1]) RichardHughes 7 85
(Richard Hannon) *wnt direct to s: led for over 1f: chsd ldr tl wl over 3f out: n.m.r and swtchd lft over 2f out: sn rdn: wknd over 1f out* **16/1**

322 **12** *¾* **Maali (IRE)**[12] 2707 3-9-0 95 PhilipRobinson 8 84
(Clive Brittain) *chsd ldrs: rdn and unable qck whn sltly hmpd wl over 2f out: struggling whn short of room ent fnl 2f: wkng whn pushed lft over 1f out: n.d after* **40/1**

51 **13** ½ **Midsummer Sun**[28] 2218 3-9-0 88 .... TomQueally 6 83
(Sir Henry Cecil) *hld up in midfield: swtchd lft and unable qck whn rdn over 2f out: edging rt u.p and no hdwy over 1f out* **14/1**

2-05 **14** 5 **Loving Spirit**[21] 2440 3-9-0 98 .... RobertHavlin 1 73
(James Toller) *t.k.h: hld up towards rr: rdn and effrt whn swtchd rt over 2f out: no prog and wl hld whn swtchd lft over 1f out* **33/1**

1-26 **15** 14 **Happy Today (USA)**[47] 1686 3-9-0 102 .... MartinDwyer 13 45
(Brian Meehan) *chsd ldr tl led over 8f out: drvn and hdd ent fnl 2f: wknd qckly u.p over 1f out: wl btn and eased ins fnl f* **16/1**

5-40 **16** 5 **Slim Shadey**[26] 2324 3-9-0 101 .... LukeMorris 2 35
(J S Moore) *a towards rr: rdn and struggling over 3f out: wl bhd fnl 2f: t.o* **33/1**

2m 11.84s (4.84) **Going Correction** +0.625s/f (Yiel) **16** Ran SP% **124.0**
Speed ratings (Par 109): **105,103,102,101,100 100,100,97,95,94 93,93,92,88,77 73**
toteswingers:1&2:£29.60, 1&3:£46.10, 2&3:£21.80 CSF £141.68 CT £1413.10 TOTE £28.60: £6.70, £2.10, £4.40; EX 210.60 Trifecta £7150.00 Part won. Pool: £9,662.26 - 0.04 winning units..

Owner Michael Kerr-Dineen **Bred** Hascombe Stud **Trained** East Ilsley, Berks

■ Stewards' Enquiry : Michael Hills two-day ban: careless riding (Jun 30-Jul 1)

FOCUS

A change of name for this Group 3 contest, in recognition of the 300th anniversary of the Royal meeting. A competitive contest with only 7lb covering the majority of the field on official ratings beforehand, and it produced a somewhat surprise result.

NOTEBOOK

Pisco Sour(USA) had gained his wins on soft ground and on Fibresand, and had finished third in the Dante at this trip before being much too keen in the Derby. Helped by a drop in trip and grade and with the going to suit, he came from off the pace to lead inside the last 2f and ran on strongly to the line. He proved himself a decent performer on soft ground and connections will consider the St Leger later on, although his ability to get further than today's trip has yet to be proven. Official explanation: trainer said regarding apparent improvement in form that on it's previous run the colt ran too fresh. (op 16-1)

Alkimos(IRE) has been progressive this season, improving from his debut to score twice on a sound surface. He handled the soft ground well enough and, after racing wide, went in pursuit of the winner in the last 2f but could make no impression in the last furlong. (op 5-1 tchd 9-2)

Slumber ◆, the winner of a Derby trial at Epsom before finishing third in the Chester Vase, had shown his form on a sound surface. He tracked the leaders but then got caught on the heels of weakening rivals early in the straight before staying on quite well. He should have finished closer and will appreciate a return to 1m4f. (op 12-1)

Specific Gravity(FR) beat seven winners when taking his maiden on soft ground but had been held in two runs on a sound surface in Listed and Group company since. He ran better on this easier surface, as he followed the runner-up through, but his effort flattened out in the final furlong. (op 40-1)

Tazahum(USA)'s only defeat in four previous starts was by Dubawi Gold. He had form on easy ground but was stepping up in trip and grade and, after looking sure to play a part turning for home, failed to pick up under pressure, giving the impression he did not stay. (op 9-2 tchd 11-2 in places)

Laajooj(IRE), a dual winner on a sound surface, including his previous start in a 1m2f Listed race, was held up well behind but was running on from some way back despite carrying his head awkwardly. He can be given another chance back on a sound surface. (op 11-1 tchd 12-1)

Marksmanship(IRE) had beaten five subsequent winners when taking his maiden over this trip on soft ground at the Curragh, but was up in grade and gave the impression that his inexperience cost him. He was held up but looked to be going nowhere under pressure early in the straight, before finding his feet and finishing quite well. He can be given another chance. (op 9-2 tchd 5-1 in places)

Hunter's Light(IRE) built on his promising juvenile debut to take a 1m2f Newmarket maiden on his return last month, but was up in grade and raced keenly close to the pace. He faded once in line for home and is another who should do better, especially back on faster ground. (op 8-1)

Auld Burns was reported as being unsuited by the going. Official explanation: jockey said gelding was unsuited by the good to soft (soft in places) ground (op 25-1 tchd 33-1)

Moriarty(IRE) was also reported as being unsuited by the going. Official explanation: jockey said colt was unsuited by the good to soft (soft in places) ground (op 14-1)

Happy Today(USA) was reported by the vet as being lame on his off hind. Official explanation: vet said colt finished lame off-hind (op 33-1)

3069 KING GEORGE V STKS (H'CAP) 1m 4f

5:35 (5:36) (Class 2) (0-105,99) 3-Y-O

£31,155 (£9,330; £4,665; £2,335; £1,165; £585) Stalls Low

Form RPR

-411 **1** **Brown Panther**[26] 2295 3-8-13 91 .... RichardKingscote 12 112+
(Tom Dascombe) *midfield: hdwy 4f out: led over 3f out: rdn clr fnl f and in command: eased cl home* **4/1**[1]

21-1 **2** 6 **Census (IRE)**[34] 2052 3-9-2 94 .... RichardHughes 10 105+
(Richard Hannon) *midfield: hdwy over 2f out: styd on ins fnl f: tk 2nd fnl 75yds: no ch w wnr* **6/1**[2]

-361 **3** 1 **Well Sharp**[17] 2572 3-8-12 90 .... PhillipMakin 20 98
(Michael Dods) *midfield: hdwy 4f out: chsd wnr 3f out: rdn and ev ch over 2f out: no imp and outpcd by wnr over 1f out: no ex and lost 2nd fnl 75yds* **40/1**

-621 **4** 2 **Communicator**[34] 2076 3-8-10 88 .... JamieSpencer 11 93
(Michael Bell) *hld up: hdwy over 2f out: sn swtchd rt and chsd ldrs: styd on ins fnl f: unable to chal* **16/1**

3-12 **5** 6 **Danadana (IRE)**[20] 2471 3-8-8 86 .... KierenFallon 14 81
(Luca Cumani) *midfield: hmpd on bnd and forced wd over 3f out: hdwy to chse ldrs over 2f out: edgd rt ent fnl 2f: no imp: wl btn ins fnl f* **12/1**

2-11 **6** 1¾ **Sud Pacifique (IRE)**[36] 2008 3-9-0 92 .... RyanMoore 13 84
(Jeremy Noseda) *hld up: hdwy over 2f out: u.p in 6th over 1f out: no imp* **7/1**[3]

4210 **7** ¾ **Greyfriars Drummer**[26] 2295 3-8-10 88 .... JoeFanning 16 79
(Mark Johnston) *in rr-div: rdn and hdwy on outer 2f out: edgd rt over 1f out: nvr able to trble ldrs* **66/1**

4115 **8** 4½ **Malthouse (GER)**[12] 2711 3-9-6 98 .... MickaelBarzalona 2 82
(Mark Johnston) *midfield: pushed along 3f out: swtchd lft whn outpcd over 2f out: nvr on terms w ldrs* **20/1**

1-21 **9** ¾ **Charles Camoin (IRE)**[12] 2711 3-8-12 90 .... LiamKeniry 18 73
(Sylvester Kirk) *hld up in rr: rdn over 2f out: no imp* **20/1**

6-14 **10** ½ **Jehanbux (USA)**[20] 2471 3-9-0 92 .... FrankieDettori 8 74
(Richard Hannon) *prom: rdn over 2f out: sn wknd* **50/1**

3-53 **11** nk **Picture Editor**[29] 2191 3-9-7 99 .... TomQueally 9 81
(Sir Henry Cecil) *midfield: hmpd and forced wd on bnd over 3f out: snatched up whn nt clr run under 3f out: no imp fr 2f out: wknd over 1f out* **22/1**

2222 **12** 13 **Mica Mika (IRE)**[12] 2726 3-8-7 85 .... FrannyNorton 5 46
(Richard Fahey) *led: hdd over 3f out: rdn over 2f out: sn wknd* **25/1**

1115 **13** 3¼ **Art History (IRE)**[46] 1723 3-8-10 88 .... SilvestreDeSousa 22 44
(Mark Johnston) *bhd: struggling 3f out: nvr on terms* **33/1**

14 6 **Apache (IRE)**[18] 2537 3-9-4 99 .... JPO'Brien(3) 1 45
(A P O'Brien, Ire) *racd keenly: sn trckd ldrs: niggled along whn n.m.r and stmbld on bnd over 3f out: carried hd to one side and wknd over 2f out* **4/1**[1]

02-1 **15** 27 **Purification (IRE)**[59] 1445 3-8-10 88 .... WilliamBuick 7 —
(John Gosden) *in tch: pushed along and wknd over 2f out* **8/1**

3-14 **16** nk **Discoteca**[47] 1689 3-9-0 92 .... JimmyFortune 4 —
(Andrew Balding) *midfield: u.p 2f out: sn bhd* **40/1**

3021 **17** 2¼ **The Bells O Peover**[17] 2551 3-8-12 90 .... RichardHills 6 —
(Mark Johnston) *w ldr tl over 3f out: sn pushed along: wknd over 2f out* **40/1**

-312 **18** 9 **Reflect (IRE)**[26] 2295 3-8-11 89 .... PatDobbs 3 —
(Richard Hannon) *midfield: pushed along over 5f out: sn lost pl: bhd fnl 4f: t.o* **25/1**

2m 36.93s (4.43) **Going Correction** +0.625s/f (Yiel) **18** Ran SP% **126.7**
Speed ratings (Par 105): **110,106,105,104,100 98,98,95,94,94 94,85,83,79,61 61,59,53**
toteswingers:1&2:£3.90, 1&3:£44.40, 2&3:£60.30 CSF £23.88 CT £878.16 TOTE £5.90: £1.60, £1.70, £8.10, £4.60; EX 24.00 Trifecta £3201.40 Pool: £8,783.74 - 2.03 winning units..

Owner Owen Promotions Limited **Bred** Owen Promotions Ltd **Trained** Malpas, Cheshire

■ Stewards' Enquiry : Richard Kingscote two-day ban: careless riding (Jun 30,Jul 1)

FOCUS

Mainly unexposed potential improvers lined up and the time was slightly quicker than the Ribblesdale. The form can be viewed quite positively despite the fact that a few met some trouble in running and some of those held up did appear to be at a disadvantage. Brown Panther impressed and looks every inch a Group horse. The runner-up improved too.

NOTEBOOK

Brown Panther ◆'s performance suggested there was little doubt that he was up to Group company. The winner of his only race at two and seemingly always well regarded, he presumably needed the run when beaten on his return at Kempton, but had won his next two starts on turf, rising from a mark of 73 to the 91. His jockey made a bold forward move off the final bend, looking to get there plenty soon enough, but Brown Panther found plenty to post an impressive success. It's not difficult to see him to develop into a St Leger candidate if remaining progressive, as he looks to have plenty of stamina. (op 9-2 tchd 5-1 in places)

Census(IRE) ◆ didn't appear to get stopped in his run when the rush for the line started but flew home once hitting top gear. The further he went, the better he looked, so a step up in trip again won't go amiss. (op 7-1)

Well Sharp ◆, who still holds an Irish Derby entry, matched strides with the winner for a while on turning but weakened in the final stages. He looks to have plenty of pace and is worth considering over a shorter distance.

Communicator ◆ took quite a grip in rear and made his move wide of the field entering the home straight before heading towards the inside rail. There was plenty to like about the performance, despite never looking likely to win, and he can be given another chance over a similar trip. (op 14-1 tchd 20-1)

Danadana(IRE) looked sure to be involved in the finish when he got into a challenging position, even after being knocked wide in some scrimmaging about 3f out, but he gave the impression that he didn't get home in this company. (op 14-1 tchd 16-1 in places)

Sud Pacifique(IRE) kept on from the rear but had little of chance of getting involved in the final outcome from his starting position. (op 15-2 tchd 8-1)

Charles Camoin(IRE) ◆ was never in the hunt but did make some good late progress, and is worth keeping in mind for a lesser event. (op 22-1 tchd 25-1)

Picture Editor, whose 3-y-o campaign hadn't started well, albeit he was a pacemaker on his seasonal return, was in the process of running well when hampered at least once. He would have been closer with a clear passage. (op 25-1)

Apache(IRE), who has four Group 1 entries, raced keenly early and didn't really settle until the field headed back for home. He wasn't completely done with when appearing to be hampered by the winner about 3f out, but it's difficult to believe he had a great deal left in the tank after his earlier exertions. Jospeh O'Brien reported afterwards that his mount suffered interference. Official explanation: jockey said colt suffered interference in running (op 7-2 tchd 9-2 in places)

Purification(IRE), a handicap debutant, looked to have leading form claims (he finished in front of Communicator on his previous run over 1m2f at Windsor), but failed to live up to expectations. He had an entry in the King Edward VII, so must be though capable of a lot better, and did give the impression at stages that he was still a bit inexperienced. (op 11-2)

T/Jkpt: Not won. T/Plt: £209.20 to a £1 stake. Pool:£542,101.94 - 1,891.18 winning tickets
T/Qpdt: £41.50 to a £1 stake. Pool:£29,257.48 - 521.61 winning tickets SP

2797 BEVERLEY (R-H)

Thursday, June 16

OFFICIAL GOING: Good to firm (good in places; 8.4)

Wind: almost nil Weather: fine, shower after race 5

3070 BEVERLEY-RACECOURSE.CO.UK MAIDEN AUCTION STKS 7f 100y

6:40 (6:41) (Class 6) 2-Y-O £1,706 (£503; £252) Stalls Low

Form RPR

4 **1** **Loyal Master (IRE)**[20] 2460 2-9-3 0 .... LeeNewman 1 75+
(George Foster) *sn trcking ldrs: drvn 3f out: qcknd to ld over 1f out: hung rt: drvn clr* **5/2**[2]

04 **2** 5 **Flurry Of Hands (IRE)**[21] 2430 2-8-12 0 .... AndrewHeffernan 3 58
(Ann Duffield) *led: hdd over 1f out: kpt on same pce* **14/1**

223 **3** 1½ **Queen Of The Hop**[59] 1435 2-8-12 0 .... GrahamGibbons 2 54
(J S Moore) *in rr: drvn and outpcd 3f out: kpt on to take 3rd last 50yds* **14/1**

05 **4** 1¼ **Flosse**[12] 2731 2-8-12 0 .... J-PGuillambert 4 53
(Ed Walker) *trckd ldrs: t.k.h: chal over 2f out: sltly hmpd and swtchd lft appr fnl f: wknd last 150yds* **10/3**[3]

564 **5** 1¼ **Fiction Or Fact (IRE)**[12] 2731 2-9-3 0 .... PaulMulrennan 6 54
(Kevin Ryan) *trckd ldrs: t.k.h: effrt over 2f out: sn rdn and no imp* **6/4**[1]

6 3¼ **Karma Chameleon** 2-9-3 0 .... PaddyAspell 7 46
(Richard Guest) *wnt lft s: in rr: hdwy on outer to chse ldrs over 3f out: edgd rt and wknd over 2f out* **10/1**

1m 32.89s (-0.91) **Going Correction** -0.375s/f (Firm) **6** Ran SP% **114.1**
Speed ratings (Par 91): **90,84,82,81,79 76**
toteswingers:1&2:£10.90, 1&3:£3.20, 2&3:£3.30 CSF £34.44 TOTE £4.10: £2.00, £6.20; EX 31.20.

Owner Ron Hull **Bred** Castleton Lyons & Kilboy Estate **Trained** Haddington, East Lothian

FOCUS

There had been 2mm of overnight rain but, after a warm and muggy day, the going was changed before racing to good to firm, good in places. The ground was described as perfect. A modest and uncompetitive maiden in which an ordinary gallop resulted in a time nearly three seconds outside the Racing Post Standard. The winner impressed but the form is no more than fair.

NOTEBOOK

Loyal Master(IRE) ◆ duly confirmed debut promise over a trip that looked sure to suit and turned in an improved effort to win with plenty in hand despite edging right late on. He's a scopey individual who would have been even better suited by a stronger gallop and he'll be interesting in nurseries. (op 11-4 tchd 7-2)

Flurry Of Hands(IRE) is a steadily progressive sort and, although she had the run of the race, turned in her best effort on her first run over this trip. She'll remain vulnerable to the better sorts in this grade but will be of more interest in run-of-the-mill nursery company.

Queen Of The Hop, with the cheekpieces left off on this first run for nearly two months, was easy in the market but wasn't disgraced on this first start beyond 5f. She didn't fail through lack of stamina but she lacks in physical scope and is likely to continue to find things hard going in this grade. (op 10-1)

Flosse had the run of the race but, although looking dangerous early in the straight, didn't get home in the anticipated manner after racing with the choke out over this longer trip. She should stay 7f but will have to settle better than she did here. (op 3-1 tchd 11-4)

Fiction Or Fact(IRE) couldn't confirm previous placings with Flosse over a trip that was expected to suit and was the disappointment. The yard's juveniles have been in good form and, although this one is starting to look exposed, he's probably worth another chance. Official explanation: trainer's rep had no explanation for the poor form shown (op 15-8 tchd 11-8)

3071 HULL DAILY MAIL H'CAP — 7f 100y
7:10 (7:12) (Class 4) (0-80,80) 4-Y-0+ — **£4,079** (£1,214; £606; £303) **Stalls** Low

Form — RPR

5460 **1** **Striker Torres (IRE)**[28] 2213 5-8-9 **68** ... PaulMulrennan 1 — 78
(Geoffrey Oldroyd) *stdd s: hld up in rr: effrt over 2f out: swtchd lft over 1f out: r.o to ld jst ins fnl f: drvn out* **8/1**

1-66 **2** *1 ¾* **Sunrise Safari (IRE)**[21] 2434 8-9-6 **79** ... (v) TonyHamilton 8 — 85
(Richard Fahey) *hld up in rr: effrt over 2f out: hung rt over 1f out: styd on to take 2nd nr fin* **16/1**

0352 **3** *nk* **Powerful Pierre**[8] 2799 4-8-2 **64** ... (v) DeclanCannon(3) 9 — 69
(Ian McInnes) *chsd ldrs: led appr fnl f: sn hdd: kpt on same pce* **11/2**

621 **4** *1 ½* **Catchanova (IRE)**[8] 2816 4-8-3 **62** ... DuranFentiman 5 — 63
(Eve Johnson Houghton) *mid-div: hung lft bnd 4f out: hdwy over 2f out: kpt on one pce appr fnl f* **5/1**[3]

3363 **5** *1 ½* **Elijah Pepper (USA)**[24] 2366 6-9-2 **75** ... GrahamGibbons 2 — 72+
(David Barron) *mid-div: drvn over 2f out: one pce appr fnl f* **4/1**[2]

-010 **6** *1 ¾* **My Gacho (IRE)**[26] 2300 9-9-4 **77** ... (v) AdrianNicholls 4 — 70
(David Nicholls) *t.k.h: led after 1f: hdd appr fnl f: wknd fnl 75yds* **11/1**

3050 **7** *1 ¼* **Summer Dancer (IRE)**[5] 2938 7-9-6 **79** ... MickyFenton 6 — 69
(Paul Midgley) *hld up in rr: effrt over 2f out: kpt on fnl f: nvr a factor* **7/2**[1]

3021 **8** *3 ¾* **Not My Choice (IRE)**[19] 2494 6-9-7 **80** ... (t) DavidNolan 7 — 61
(David C Griffiths) *swtchd rt after s: led 1f: chsd ldrs: wknd appr fnl f* **8/1**

0600 **9** *19* **Yahrab (IRE)**[5] 2917 6-8-13 **72** ... (b) KellyHarrison 3 — —
(Declan Carroll) *trckd ldrs: lost pl over 2f out: sn bhd: t.o* **18/1**

1m 30.17s (-3.63) **Going Correction** -0.375s/f (Firm) — **9** Ran SP% **116.0**
Speed ratings (Par 105): **105,103,102,100,99 97,95,91,69**
toteswingers:1&2:£30.40, 1&3:£4.00, 2&3:£18.10 CSF £125.55 CT £770.31 TOTE £12.20: £3.60, £7.30, £2.00; EX 147.10.
Owner R C Bond **Bred** T Stack & Lynchbages Ltd **Trained** Brawby, N Yorks

FOCUS
Mainly exposed sorts in a fair handicap. The gallop was a good one and the hold-up horses came to the fore late on. The winner is rated back to his old turf form.

3072 LUCKY IN LOVE NIGHT H'CAP — 2m 35y
7:40 (7:40) (Class 5) (0-70,69) 4-Y-0+ — **£2,266** (£674; £337; £168) **Stalls** Low

Form — RPR

35-6 **1** **Spiders Star**[19] 2496 8-8-8 **59** ow1 ... MichaelO'Connell(3) 7 — 72
(Simon West) *s.s: hld up in rr: gd hdwy and swtchd outside over 1f out: wnt 4 l 2nd appr fnl f: styd on strly to ld fnl strides* **8/1**

15-2 **2** *nk* **Jeu De Roseau (IRE)**[21] 2433 7-8-11 **59** ... TonyHamilton 9 — 71+
(Chris Grant) *trckd ldrs: led over 2f out: pushed clr appr fnl f: hdd nr fin* **5/1**[2]

600- **3** *10* **Strikemaster (IRE)**[233] 7157 5-7-13 **52** ... (t) DanielleMcCreery(5) 6 — 52
(Lee James) *s.s: in rr: hdwy on outside over 2f out: styd on to take modest 3rd fnl 75yds* **40/1**

21/2 **4** *3 ½* **Im Spartacus**[14] 2654 9-9-1 **63** ... PaulMulrennan 10 — 59
(Ian Williams) *trckd ldrs: led 3f out: sn hdd: wknd ins fnl f* **9/2**[1]

0134 **5** *1 ¾* **Spruzzo**[10] 2762 5-8-12 **60** ... KellyHarrison 13 — 54
(Chris Fairhurst) *chsd ldrs: drvn 4f out: one pce fnl 2f* **7/1**[3]

1205 **6** *1 ¼* **Bring Sweets (IRE)**[13] 2666 4-8-3 **54** ... PaulPickard(3) 12 — 46
(Brian Ellison) *hld up in rr: hdwy 9f out: chal 3f out: wknd appr fnl f* **10/1**

6305 **7** *¾* **Escape Artist**[17] 2575 4-8-3 **51** ... (e) DuranFentiman 11 — 43
(Tim Easterby) *s.i.s: in rr-div: t.k.h: hdwy 7f out: one pce fnl 3f* **9/2**[1]

0-40 **8** *6* **Tobernea (IRE)**[20] 2459 4-9-7 **69** ... TomEaves 1 — 53
(Mark Johnston) *chsd ldrs: wknd over 1f out* **7/1**[3]

6/0- **9** *4 ½* **Oniz Tiptoes (IRE)**[15] 166 10-8-2 **50** oh5 ... (p) AndrewHeffernan 2 — 29
(John Wainwright) *chsd ldrs: drvn along after 4f: lost pl over 2f out* **20/1**

4/06 **10** *9* **Just Observing**[13] 2666 8-7-13 **50** oh4 ... (p) DeclanCannon(3) 3 — 18
(Neville Bycroft) *led: hdd 3f out: sn lost pl and bhd* **22/1**

00-0 **11** *22* **Rannoch Moor**[18] 2526 4-8-3 **51** ... (b[1]) AdrianNicholls 5 — —
(Marcus Tregoning) *mid-div: sn drvn along: bhd whn hmpd and swvd bdly lft over 2f out: sn eased: t.o* **7/1**[3]

3m 33.64s (-6.16) **Going Correction** -0.375s/f (Firm) — **11** Ran SP% **122.3**
Speed ratings (Par 103): **100,99,94,93,92 91,91,88,85,81 70**
toteswingers:1&2:£13.90, 1&3:£59.00, 2&3:£23.90 CSF £48.66 CT £1544.52 TOTE £11.50: £4.40, £1.50, £6.00; EX 59.40.
Owner Miss Kate Milligan **Bred** Acrum Lodge Stud **Trained** Middleham Moor, N Yorks

FOCUS
A modest staying handicap. The gallop was a fair one but the first two deserve plenty of credit for pulling so far clear in the closing stages. It's hard to know how much credit they deserve though.

3073 MIKE AND ANNE GUEST CONDITIONS STKS — 5f
8:10 (8:14) (Class 4) 3-Y-0+ — **£5,828** (£1,734; £866; £432) **Stalls** Low

Form — RPR

-004 **1** **Tax Free (IRE)**[19] 2489 9-9-0 96 ... AdrianNicholls 2 — 99
(David Nicholls) *trckd ldrs: effrt 2f out: led over 1f out: hld on towards fin* **4/1**[3]

0-11 **2** *nk* **Singeur (IRE)**[19] 2489 4-9-4 97 ... LeeNewman 1 — 102
(Robin Bastiman) *chsd ldng pair on ins: effrt over 2f out: swtchd outside over 1f out: styd on ins fnl f: jst hld* **2/1**[2]

2122 **3** *2 ¾* **Verinco**[12] 2727 5-9-0 83 ... (v) TomEaves 3 — 88
(Bryan Smart) *led: jnd 2f out: hdd over 1f out: wknd fnl 50yds* **9/2**

600- **4** *6* **Tropical Treat**[263] 6390 4-9-3 101 ... JimCrowley 4 — 70
(Ralph Beckett) *t.k.h: trckd ldrs: effrt over 2f out: nvr a threat: wknd appr fnl f: eased clsng stages* **13/8**[1]

61.46 secs (-2.04) **Going Correction** -0.175s/f (Firm) — **4** Ran SP% **109.6**
Speed ratings (Par 105): **109,108,104,94**
CSF £12.24 TOTE £4.20; EX 8.20.
Owner Ian Hewitson **Bred** Denis And Mrs Teresa Bergin **Trained** Sessay, N Yorks

FOCUS
A poor turnout for the money on offer, and ordinary conditions form. The market leader disappointed but the finish was fought out by a couple of very useful sorts. The gallop wasn't overly strong.

3074 MATCH YOUR PADLOCK AND KEY H'CAP — 1m 1f 207y
8:40 (8:41) (Class 6) (0-60,61) 4-Y-0+ — **£1,780** (£529; £264; £132) **Stalls** Low

Form — RPR

00/1 **1** **Lunar Promise (IRE)**[8] 2820 9-9-5 **61** 6ex ... DaleSwift(5) 1 — 76
(Ian Williams) *trckd ldrs: wnt 2nd 3f out: styd on to ld last 150yds* **9/4**[1]

0441 **2** *2 ½* **Ay Tay Tate (IRE)**[3] 2988 5-9-8 **59** 6ex ... GrahamGibbons 10 — 69
(David C Griffiths) *led: hdd and no ex jst ins fnl f* **9/4**[1]

5640 **3** *7* **General Tufto**[18] 2530 6-9-2 **58** ... (b) JulieBurke(5) 2 — 54
(Charles Smith) *midfield: reminders after 1f: wnt 3rd 2f out: one pce* **14/1**

-450 **4** *nk* **Lucayan Dancer**[50] 1615 11-9-0 **51** ... AdrianNicholls 9 — 46
(David Nicholls) *hld up towards rr: effrt on outside over 2f out: kpt on fnl f* **11/1**[3]

065- **5** *4* **Obara D'Avril (FR)**[333] 4173 9-8-5 **45** ... PaulPickard(3) 4 — 32
(Simon West) *led rdrless to post: s.v.s: in rr: kpt on fnl 2f: nvr a factor* **40/1**

-043 **6** *3 ¾* **Highland Love**[8] 2804 6-9-4 **55** ... PaulMulrennan 7 — 35
(Jedd O'Keeffe) *trckd ldrs: effrt over 2f out: wknd over 1f out* **7/2**[2]

0553 **7** *3 ¼* **Lady Excel (IRE)**[8] 2800 5-9-0 **51** ... AndrewHeffernan 6 — 24
(Brian Rothwell) *trckd ldrs: t.k.h: wnt 3rd over 2f out: wknd over 1f out* **11/1**[3]

560 **8** *10* **Jack's Rocket**[121] 546 4-8-8 **45** ... (e) PatrickMathers 5 — —
(Richard Guest) *stdd s: t.k.h in rr: drvn over 3f out: sn lost pl and bhd* **40/1**

6-00 **9** *1 ¾* **Fama Mac**[23] 2388 4-9-6 **57** ... AndrewElliott 11 — —
(Neville Bycroft) *sn trcking ldrs: t.k.h: lost pl over 2f out* **25/1**

2m 2.66s (-4.34) **Going Correction** -0.375s/f (Firm) — **9** Ran SP% **115.8**
Speed ratings (Par 101): **102,100,94,94,90 87,85,77,75**
toteswingers:1&2:£2.40, 1&3:£7.60, 2&3:£5.10 CSF £7.12 CT £52.78 TOTE £3.20: £1.60, £1.70, £4.00; EX 9.10.
Owner Richard Edwards **Bred** Deer Forest Stud Ltd **Trained** Portway, Worcs

FOCUS
A reasonable event for the 0-60 grade in which two progressive previous winners pulled clear in the last furlong and half. An ordinary gallop increased in the last 3f. The winner was well in on his olf doem and this win could be rated higher.
Highland Love Official explanation: jockey said gelding was unable to dominate

3075 VISIT THE TOAD TO WIN PRIZES MAIDEN STKS — 5f
9:10 (9:13) (Class 5) 3-4-Y-0 — **£2,266** (£674; £337; £168) **Stalls** Low

Form — RPR

04- **1** **Farlow (IRE)**[288] 5657 3-9-3 0 ... JimCrowley 5 — 72+
(Ralph Beckett) *chsd ldrs: drvn over 2f out: led ins fnl f: jst hld on* **10/3**[1]

2-4 **2** *hd* **Arrivaderci**[19] 2498 3-8-9 0 ... AmyRyan(3) 6 — 66
(Richard Whitaker) *mid-div: hdwy over 1f out: styd on wl ins fnl f: jst hld* **9/2**[3]

3-65 **3** *nk* **Pantella (IRE)**[13] 2697 3-8-12 63 ... (p) PaulMulrennan 13 — 65
(Kevin Ryan) *w ldr: led over 1f out: hung lft and hdd ins fnl f: no ex* **11/2**

-200 **4** *2* **Homeboy (IRE)**[24] 2363 3-8-12 66 ... JulieBurke(5) 7 — 63
(Marcus Tregoning) *mid-div: hdwy 2f out: chsng ldrs 1f out: kpt on same pce* **7/2**[2]

55 **5** *3 ¾* **Fairy Mist (IRE)**[8] 2802 4-9-9 0 ... PaddyAspell 8 — 51+
(Brian Rothwell) *in rr: sme hdwy 2f out: nvr nr ldrs* **14/1**

000- **6** *1 ¼* **Kwik Time**[241] 6980 3-9-3 30 ... LeeNewman 14 — 45
(Robin Bastiman) *in rr: edgd lft over 1f out: kpt on* **66/1**

7 *1* **Missile Attack (IRE)** 3-9-3 0 ... TomEaves 1 — 41
(Ian Semple) *chsd ldrs: wknd fnl f* **9/1**

-260 **8** *1 ¼* **My Love Fajer (IRE)**[18] 2524 3-9-3 59 ... (p) GrahamGibbons 2 — 37
(Alan McCabe) *led tl over 1f out: sn wknd* **10/1**

00 **9** *2 ½* **Yougoigo**[20] 2479 3-9-3 0 ... PaulQuinn 4 — 28
(Marjorie Fife) *mid-div: effrt over 2f out: no imp* **50/1**

625- **10** *1 ¾* **Ruler's Honour (IRE)**[209] 7505 4-9-2 55 ... JacobButterfield(7) 10 — 23
(Tim Etherington) *gave problems gng to s: a towards rr* **16/1**

-0 **11** *hd* **Ivory Trilogy (IRE)**[33] 2094 3-8-12 0 ... DaleSwift(5) 15 — 21
(Tim Etherington) *unruly befhand: swvd lft and almost uns rdr s: bhd: edgd rt and sme hdwy over 1f out: nvr on terms* **33/1**

04-5 **12** *2 ¼* **Wandering Lad**[19] 2493 3-9-3 62 ... MickyFenton 12 — 13
(Paul Midgley) *chsd ldrs: wknd over 1f out* **10/1**

13 *1 ¼* **Lovely Lynn (IRE)** 3-8-12 0 ... AndrewElliott 11 — —
(Declan Carroll) *mid-div: wknd 2f out* **33/1**

0 **14** *1* **Harmony Wold**[12] 2710 3-8-12 0 ... KellyHarrison 16 — —
(Declan Carroll) *s.i.s: in rr* **66/1**

6 **15** *1 ¾* **Styleyf**[17] 2574 3-8-9 0 ... RobertLButler(3) 9 — —
(John Balding) *s.i.s: a in rr* **66/1**

63.17 secs (-0.33) **Going Correction** -0.125s/f (Firm)
WFA 3 from 4yo 6lb — **15** Ran SP% **131.9**
Speed ratings (Par 103): **97,96,96,93,87 85,83,81,77,74 73,70,68,66,63**
toteswingers:1&2:£6.60, 1&3:£5.30, 2&3:£4.00 CSF £19.80 TOTE £5.10: £2.30, £2.60, £2.20; EX 17.70.
Owner Lawrence, Deal & Carolyn Thornton **Bred** Patrick J Monahan **Trained** Kimpton, Hants

FOCUS
No more than a modest maiden and one run in driving rain. The gallop was sound and the first four pulled clear. The form is best judged around the first two.
T/Plt: £392.20 to a £1 stake. Pool:£38,900.70 - 72.40 winning tickets T/Qpdt: £26.40 to a £1 stake. Pool:£3,441.60 - 96.20 winning tickets WG

2913 LEICESTER (R-H)
Thursday, June 16

OFFICIAL GOING: Good to firm (good in places; 8.7)
Wind: Light behind Weather: Showers

3076 OADBY MAIDEN STKS — 7f 9y
6:50 (6:52) (Class 4) 2-Y-0 — **£3,561** (£1,059; £529; £264) **Stalls** High

Form — RPR

1 **Leqqaa (USA)** 2-9-3 0 ... AdamKirby 1 — 84+
(Mark Johnston) *chsd ldrs: rdn over 2f out: led over 1f out: r.o wl* **3/1**[1]

06 **2** *6* **Space Raider (AUS)**[24] 2355 2-8-10 0 ... MatthewLawson(7) 3 — 69
(B W Hills) *chsd ldr tl led 4f out: rdn and hdd over 1f out: wknd ins fnl f* **8/1**

3 1¾ **Repeater** 2-9-3 0 .... SebSanders 6 66+
(Sir Mark Prescott Bt) *got loose on the way to post: s.i.s: hdwy 5f out: rdn and ev ch over 1f out: wknd ins fnl f* **3/1**[1]

4 hd **Juno The Muffinman (IRE)** 2-9-3 0 .... RussKennemore 5 64+
(Tom Dascombe) *trckd ldrs: rdn over 2f out: sn outpcd: styd on ins fnl f* **7/2**[2]

06 5 3½ **Zigzag (IRE)**[22] 2395 2-9-3 0 .... CathyGannon 7 55
(David Evans) *sn led: hdd 4f out: rdn over 2f out: edgd rt and wknd over 1f out* **7/1**[3]

6 9 **Bathwick Street** 2-9-0 0 .... RichardEvans(3) 4 33
(David Evans) *uns rdr on the way to post: s.i.s: sn pushed along and prom: rdn 1/2-way: sn wknd* **16/1**

7 6 **Dutchman's Field** 2-9-3 0 .... TomMcLaughlin 2 18
(Ed Dunlop) *s.s: outpcd* **9/1**

1m 25.7s (-0.50) **Going Correction** -0.125s/f (Firm) **7 Ran SP% 111.7**
Speed ratings (Par 95): **97,90,88,87,83 73,66**
toteswingers:1&2:£4.10, 1&3:£3.80, 2&3:£4.60 CSF £25.85 TOTE £3.40: £2.40, £3.30; EX 34.30.

Owner Hamdan Al Maktoum **Bred** London Thoroughbred Services Ltd **Trained** Middleham Moor, N Yorks

FOCUS
There was an open market for this maiden, but a well-bred newcomer gradually got the hang of things and surged clear for his powerful connections. There is more to come from him. The time was almost three seconds slower than RP standard.

NOTEBOOK
Leqqaa(USA) was sent off a joint favourite in his chosen target from a stack of entries in the next few days and produced a powerful burst to kick clear on debut. The form is hard to weigh up but this was a good start by a $310,000 Derby entered half-brother to highly progressive Zaham, who landed the 2007 1m2f Listed Hampton Court Stakes for the same owner/trainer combination. (op 11-4 tchd 9-4)

Space Raider(AUS) finished a remote second but showed a decent attitude to keep battling under a prominent ride. He is quietly progressing and seems to be working his way towards nurseries over a bit further. (tchd 9-1)

Repeater, a Montjeu colt who is out of a 1m2f winning half-sister to French Oaks-placed pair Time Ahead and Time Away, got loose and was very coltish before the start and then missed the break, but he showed ability to get into contention before fading in the closing stages on debut. (op 10-3 tchd 7-2)

Juno The Muffinman(IRE), a 55,000euos half-brother to three middle-distance Flat/hurdle winners, got tapped for speed before staying on late on debut. (op 9-2 tchd 5-1)

Zigzag(IRE) was a market springer but the step up in trip failed to inpsire improvement and he was left behind when things got serious. (op 16-1)

Dutchman's Field was always trailing after a very slow start on debut. (op 5-1)

3077 TOWN HALL (S) STKS 1m 1f 218y

7:20 (7:20) (Class 6) 3-Y-O £1,619 (£481; £240; £120) Stalls Low

Form RPR

-451 1 **Gud Day (IRE)**[16] 2583 3-9-8 64 .... SebSanders 4 72
(Deborah Sanderson) *w ldr tl led 8f out: rdn and hung lft 2f out: sn clr: eased nr fin* **11/10**[1]

005 2 3¾ **Take A Spin**[24] 2371 3-9-3 66 .... ChrisCatlin 5 59
(Paul Cole) *sn pushed along in rr: hdwy to chse wnr over 2f out: sn rdn: styd on same pce appr fnl f* **5/2**[2]

0-00 3 1¼ **Boston Court (IRE)**[14] 2637 3-9-3 54 .... (b[1]) ShaneKelly 7 56
(Brian Meehan) *a.p: rdn over 4f out: chsd wnr over 3f out to over 2f out: styd on same pce appr fnl f* **10/1**

1222 4 5 **Jay Jays Joy**[14] 2652 3-9-8 65 .... (b) CathyGannon 3 51
(David Barron) *prom: rdn over 3f out: wknd over 1f out* **9/2**[3]

00 5 13 **Eastward Ho**[24] 2361 3-9-3 0 .... PatCosgrave 2 20
(Jason Ward) *led 2f: chsd wnr tl rdn over 3f out: wknd wl over 1f out* **100/1**

-000 6 5 **Dancing Cavalier (IRE)**[31] 2166 3-9-3 45 .... AdamKirby 6 10
(Reg Hollinshead) *s.s: hld up: hdwy 1/2-way: rdn over 2f out: sn wknd* **00/1**

2m 8.38s (0.48) **Going Correction** +0.05s/f (Good) **6 Ran SP% 107.4**
Speed ratings (Par 97): **100,97,96,92,81 77**
toteswingers:1&2:£1.10, 1&3:£4.70, 2&3:£2.00 CSF £3.61 TOTE £2.10: £1.20, £1.30; EX 4.60.The winner was sold to Ron Harris for 12,000gns

Owner R J Budge **Bred** Patrick M Ryan **Trained** Sturton le Steeple, Notts

FOCUS
A 64-rated favourite did the job in professional style under a forcing ride in this seller. He improved on his recent C&D win but the level of the form is a bit shaky.

3078 SIS LIVE H'CAP 5f 2y

7:50 (7:50) (Class 4) (0-80,78) 3-Y-O+ £4,079 (£1,214; £606; £303) Stalls High

Form RPR

2041 1 **Dreamacha**[12] 2720 4-9-7 78 .... RyanClark(5) 4 93+
(Stuart Williams) *trckd ldrs: a gng wl: led 1f out: r.o wl* **9/4**[2]

0612 2 2¼ **Shawkantango**[17] 2547 4-8-8 60 .... (v) RobbieFitzpatrick 2 64
(Derek Shaw) *mid-div: edgd rt over 3f out: hdwy u.p over 1f out: r.o to go 2nd wl ins fnl f: nt trble wnr* **11/1**

0060 3 ¾ **Desert Strike**[5] 2938 5-9-6 72 .... (p) ShaneKelly 5 73
(Alan McCabe) *w ldr tl led over 3f out: rdn over 1f out: sn hdd: styd on same pce: lost 2nd wl ins fnl f* **14/1**

0662 4 nk **Bosun Breese**[13] 2694 6-9-3 74 .... LMcNiff(5) 7 74
(David Barron) *chsd ldrs: rdn and ev ch 1f out: styd on same pce* **2/1**[1]

6334 5 2¼ **Restless Bay (IRE)**[5] 2916 3-9-6 78 .... (v) ChrisCatlin 6 68
(Reg Hollinshead) *sn outpcd: hdwy and nt clr run over 1f out: nvr able to chal* **7/1**[3]

3132 6 3¾ **Yurituni**[13] 2662 4-9-9 78 .... (v) PatrickHills(3) 1 57
(Eve Johnson Houghton) *s.i.s: outpcd: eased ins fnl f* **8/1**

3060 7 4½ **Cape Royal**[14] 2645 11-9-7 73 .... (bt) PatCosgrave 3 35
(Milton Bradley) *sn led: hdd over 3f out: rdn 1/2-way: wknd and eased fnl f* **14/1**

59.57 secs (-0.43) **Going Correction** -0.125s/f (Firm)
WFA 3 from 4yo+ 6lb **7 Ran SP% 109.4**
Speed ratings (Par 105): **98,94,93,92,89 83,75**
toteswingers:1&2:£7.00, 1&3:£11.90, 2&3:£45.80 CSF £24.01 TOTE £2.60: £2.40, £5.20; EX 13.50.

Owner Essex Racing Club (Dreamacha) **Bred** Barry Root **Trained** Newmarket, Suffolk

FOCUS
A fair sprint handicap won in very smooth style by a highly progressive performer who was making it five wins from her last ten starts. The level of the form is a bit fluid.

Yurituni Official explanation: trainer's rep said filly was unsuited by the good to firm (good in places) ground

3079 WALTHAM-ON-THE-WOLDS FILLIES' H'CAP 5f 218y

8:20 (8:20) (Class 5) (0-75,75) 3-Y-O+ £2,590 (£770; £385; £192) Stalls High

Form RPR

2-24 1 **Psychic's Dream**[14] 2643 3-9-2 70 .... AndreaAtzeni 2 82+
(Marco Botti) *hld up: swtchd lft and hdwy 2f out: led over 1f out: shkn up and r.o wl* **3/1**[1]

0-3 2 2¾ **Basle**[26] 2303 4-9-12 73 .... ChrisCatlin 8 78
(Gay Kelleway) *chsd ldrs: rdn and ev ch over 1f out: edgd rt and styd on same pce ins fnl f* **9/1**

2124 3 hd **Mata Hari Blue**[64] 1307 5-8-8 62 .... LucyKBarry(7) 6 66
(John Holt) *hld up: rdn over 2f out: hdwy over 1f out: styd on same pce ins fnl f* **7/2**[2]

4424 4 1½ **Climaxfortackle (IRE)**[8] 2818 3-8-9 63 .... RobbieFitzpatrick 9 61
(Derek Shaw) *s.s: in rr and rdn over 2f out: hdwy over 1f out: eased whn hld towards fin* **14/1**

0-02 5 1¾ **Red Yarn**[21] 2428 4-9-10 74 .... (b) SeanLevey(3) 7 68
(Gary Moore) *sn led: rdn over 2f out: sn hung rt: hdd over 1f out: no ex fnl f* **11/2**[3]

21-0 6 2½ **Celtic Sixpence (IRE)**[30] 2180 3-9-7 75 .... AdamKirby 5 59
(Noel Quinlan) *prom: rdn and swtchd rt over 2f out: hung rt over 1f out: wknd fnl f* **8/1**

-130 7 3¼ **Dream Number (IRE)**[51] 1581 4-9-0 66 .... JamesRogers(5) 4 42
(William Muir) *w ldr: rdn and ev ch whn carried rt 2f out: wknd fnl f* **9/1**

3-06 8 shd **Bathwick Xaara**[15] 2610 4-9-4 65 .... CathyGannon 3 40
(Jonathan Portman) *chsd ldrs: rdn and hmpd over 2f out: wknd fnl f* **6/1**

1m 12.18s (-0.82) **Going Correction** -0.125s/f (Firm)
WFA 3 from 4yo+ 7lb **8 Ran SP% 114.7**
Speed ratings (Par 100): **100,96,96,94,91 88,84,83**
toteswingers:1&2:£15.30, 1&3:£2.40, 2&3:£10.80 CSF £30.55 CT £98.58 TOTE £4.00: £1.10, £2.10, £2.10; EX 36.70.

Owner R G & T E Levin **Bred** R G Levin **Trained** Newmarket, Suffolk

■ Stewards' Enquiry : Sean Levey two-day ban: careless riding (Jun 30-Jul 1)
Adam Kirby two-day ban: careless riding (Jul 1,3)

FOCUS
This looked a competitive fillies' handicap but the unexposed, well backed favourite ran out an emphatic winner. She recorded a clear personal best, the form rated round the third and fourth.

Celtic Sixpence(IRE) Official explanation: jockey said filly hung right-handed from halfway

3080 LEICESTER RACECOURSE CONFERENCE CENTRE MAIDEN STKS 1m 3f 183y

8:50 (8:52) (Class 5) 3-Y-O+ £2,266 (£674; £337; £168) Stalls Low

Form RPR

05 1 **Midnight Oil**[14] 2648 3-8-10 0 .... KierenFallon 11 89+
(Luca Cumani) *led after 1f: clr 2f out: easily* **11/8**[1]

00 2 3½ **Shamacam**[14] 2648 3-8-7 0 .... LouisBeuzelin(3) 6 73
(Sir Michael Stoute) *chsd ldrs: rdn over 2f out: styd on to go 2nd wl ins fnl f: no ch w wnr* **8/1**

0 3 ½ **Rishikesh**[28] 2218 3-8-10 0 .... ShaneKelly 3 72
(Michael Bell) *dwlt: hdwy 10f out: chsd wnr 4f out: rdn over 2f out: sn outpcd: lost 2nd wl ins fnl f* **7/1**

0-25 4 ½ **High Samana**[42] 1840 3-8-10 78 .... StevieDonohoe 5 71
(Ralph Beckett) *chsd ldrs: rdn over 2f out: styd on same pce* **5/1**[3]

00 5 4 **Talbot Green**[14] 2648 3-8-5 0 .... (t) JamesRogers(5) 8 65?
(William Muir) *prom: rdn over 3f out: disp 2nd over 2f out: wknd fnl f* **100/1**

62 6 4½ **Diptimat**[16] 2591 3-8-10 0 .... (b) AndreaAtzeni 1 58
(Marco Botti) *hld up: hdwy 1/2-way: rdn over 3f out: wknd wl over 1f out* **7/2**[2]

0-0 7 2¼ **Strength And Stay (IRE)**[61] 1407 3-8-10 0 .... CathyGannon 4 54
(Eve Johnson Houghton) *hld up: bhd 1/2-way: nvr nr* **40/1**

5 8 1½ **Gilt (USA)**[33] 2104 3-8-5 0 .... ChrisCatlin 2 47
(Ed Dunlop) *hld up: shkn up over 2f out: nvr on terms* **28/1**

4 9 20 **Chippy**[17] 2565 3-8-10 0 .... NickyMackay 7 20
(John Holt) *led 1f: chsd wnr tl rdn 4f out: wknd wl over 2f out: t.o* **100/1**

0 10 ¾ **Oakdown**[12] 2723 3-8-7 0 .... SimonPearce(3) 10 19
(Alan King) *hld up: bhd fr 1/2-way: t.o* **66/1**

0 11 nk **Milton Hill**[28] 2231 4-9-7 0 .... BillyCray(3) 9 18
(Dominic Ffrench Davis) *hld up: bhd fr 1/2-way: t.o* **125/1**

2m 35.3s (1.40) **Going Correction** +0.05s/f (Good)
WFA 3 from 4yo 14lb **11 Ran SP% 114.8**
Speed ratings (Par 103): **97,94,94,94,91 88,86,85,72,72 71**
toteswingers:1&2:£5.10, 1&3:£7.70, 2&3:£9.40 CSF £12.93 TOTE £2.30: £1.40, £1.90, £2.40; EX 11.00.

Owner Castle Down Racing **Bred** Meon Valley Stud **Trained** Newmarket, Suffolk

FOCUS
The well backed favourite hammered his rivals under a forcing ride in this fair maiden, and the third shaped a bit better than the finishing position suggests. The winner impressed and the form is rated fairly positively.

3081 NELSON RESTAURANT H'CAP 1m 60y

9:20 (9:22) (Class 4) (0-85,83) 3-Y-O+ £4,079 (£1,214; £606; £303) Stalls Low

Form RPR

4-00 1 **Watch Amigo (IRE)**[20] 2470 5-10-0 83 .... KierenFallon 2 92
(Walter Swinburn) *plld hrd and prom: led over 5f out: rdn over 1f out: styd on gamely* **2/1**[1]

-004 2 nk **Viva Vettori**[14] 2647 7-10-0 83 .... NickyMackay 8 91
(David Elsworth) *stdd s: hld up: hdwy over 2f out: rdn and ev ch fr over 1f out: edgd rt: styd on* **2/1**[1]

1-02 3 6 **Labore**[17] 2572 3-8-11 76 .... AndreaAtzeni 4 68
(Marco Botti) *led 3f: chsd ldrs: rdn over 1f out: wknd ins fnl f* **5/1**[2]

-050 4 2 **West End Lad**[13] 2674 8-9-8 77 .... (b) RussKennemore 6 67
(Roy Bowring) *chsd ldrs: rdn over 3f out: sn outpcd: styd on ins fnl f* **33/1**

2516 5 3 **Muhandis (IRE)**[23] 2389 3-8-11 76 .... (b[1]) TomMcLaughlin 1 57
(Ed Dunlop) *dwlt: hdwy 1/2-way: rdn over 1f out: wknd ins fnl f* **11/1**

-060 6 6 **Kavachi (IRE)**[26] 2310 8-9-2 74 .... RossAtkinson(3) 3 43
(Gary Moore) *s.i.s: hld up: rdn over 3f out: wknd over 2f out* **25/1**

1200 7 1¼ **Falmouth Bay (USA)**[13] 2684 3-8-6 78 .... DarylByrne(7) 5 42
(Mark Johnston) *w ldr 4f: rdn and wknd over 1f out* **14/1**

20- **8** 1 3/4 **Flameoftheforest (IRE)**[202] 7586 4-9-13 **82** PatCosgrave 7 44
(Ed de Giles) *unruly in stalls: s.i.s: sn prom: rdn over 3f out: wknd over 2f out* **9/1**[3]

1m 44.44s (-0.66) **Going Correction** +0.05s/f (Good)
WFA 3 from 4yo+ 10lb **8 Ran SP% 115.1**
Speed ratings (Par 105): **105,104,98,96,93 87,86,84**
toteswingers:1&2:£1.10, 1&3:£4.30, 2&3:£4.40 CSF £5.75 CT £16.24 TOTE £2.60: £1.02, £1.70, £2.60; EX 8.20.
Owner Ian Harris & Tim Halpin **Bred** Thurso Limited **Trained** Aldbury, Herts

FOCUS
The two market leaders pulled a long way clear in this decent handicap which was run at a fairly steady pace. The form is rated around the second.
T/Plt: £9.50 to a £1 stake. Pool:£48,260.22 - 3,703.91 winning tickets T/Qpdt: £4.10 to a £1 stake. Pool:£4,276.96 - 760.00 winning tickets CR

3049 RIPON (R-H)
Thursday, June 16

OFFICIAL GOING: Good to soft (good in places; 8.2)
Wind: Wind light half behind Weather: Sunny

3082 E B F "ARABIAN GLEAM" MAIDEN STKS 6f
2:10 (2:11) (Class 5) 2-Y-O **£3,561** (£1,059; £529; £264) **Stalls** High

Form RPR
4 **1** **Overpowered**[35] 2033 2-9-3 0 TomEaves 1 80
(Paul Cole) *wnt rt s: sn in tch on outer: hdwy over 2f out: rdn to ld jst ins fnl f: kpt on wl* **4/1**[3]
2334 **2** 2 1/2 **One Kool Dude**[26] 2318 2-9-3 0 FrederikTylicki 3 72
(Richard Fahey) *prom: rdn over 2f out: led appr fnl f: sn hdd: kpt on: no ch w wnr* **9/1**
3 **3** 1/2 **Knight Vision**[10] 2767 2-9-3 0 AdrianNicholls 8 71
(David Nicholls) *w ldr: rdn over 2f out: kpt on one pce* **7/2**[2]
4 3/4 **Kenny Powers** 2-9-3 0 (t) RussKennemore 6 69+
(Tom Dascombe) *dwlt: hld up: racd keenly: hdwy over 1f out: kpt on wl ins fnl f: nrst fin* **4/1**[3]
6 **5** 2 3/4 **Bitaphon (IRE)**[13] 2672 2-9-3 0 DavidNolan 5 60
(Deborah Sanderson) *chsd ldrs: rdn over 2f out: one pce* **66/1**
6 1 **Lady Caprice** 2-8-12 0 MickyFenton 7 52
(Ann Duffield) *led narrowly: rdn whn hdd over 1f out: wknd ins fnl f* **25/1**
7 3 **New Decade** 2-9-3 0 RoystonFfrench 4 48
(Mark Johnston) *hld up: pushed along 1/2-way: n.d* **10/1**
8 nk **Premier Choice** 2-9-3 0 DavidAllan 11 47
(Tim Easterby) *dwlt: hld up: pushed along 1/2-way: rn green and no imp* **5/2**[1]
000 **9** 1 1/4 **Come To Mind**[17] 2542 2-9-3 0 PatrickMathers 10 43
(Alan Berry) *chsd ldrs towards inner tl wknd over 1f out* **125/1**
5 **10** nk **In A Jiffy (IRE)**[10] 2761 2-8-12 0 LeeNewman 9 37
(David Barron) *chsd ldrs: pushed along and losing pl whn bmpd 2f out: sn wknd* **20/1**

1m 13.21s (0.21) **Going Correction** -0.175s/f (Firm) **10 Ran SP% 120.8**
Speed ratings (Par 93): **91,87,87,86,82 81,77,76,74,74**
toteswingers:1&2:£2.30, 1&3:£3.70, 2&3:£4.40 CSF £39.79 TOTE £5.20: £1.80, £2.00, £1.80; EX 23.80.
Owner Mrs Jill Haines & Jared Sullivan **Bred** Tafiya Syndicate **Trained** Whatcombe, Oxon
■ Stewards' Enquiry : Russ Kennemore two-day ban: careless riding (Jun 30-Jul 1)

FOCUS
Jockeys returning after the first agreed that the ground was on the slow side. An ordinary looking maiden and solid if limited form.

NOTEBOOK
Overpowered, who finished fourth in a stronger heat at York on his debut, didn't have to step up a great deal to take this. However, having been drawn in stall one, he deserves some credit for winning despite racing wide throughout (tchd 9-2)
One Kool Dude, the most experienced runner in the line-up, showed up well the whole way and ran his race. He is beginning to look exposed. (op 7-1)
Knight Vision had the rail to help throughout and posted a respectable effort. He looks one for nurseries in due course. (op 10-3)
Kenny Powers ◆, a half-brother to Italian Group 1 winner Hearts On Fire, cost 50,000gns. Tongue-tied on his debut, he was quite keen early but shaped with a deal of promise. He can build on this and should be capable of winning something similar in the coming weeks. (op 7-2 tchd 9-2)
Bitaphon(IRE) is another whose hopes of success will be better in handicaps.
Premier Choice, who is related to lots of winners, was sent off a well-backed favourite on his debut. Held up out the back, he ran green under pressure and clearly much better was expected. He can be given another chance with this experience under his belt. (op 11-2)

3083 SIS LIVE CLAIMING STKS 6f
2:45 (2:45) (Class 5) 3-Y-O+ **£2,331** (£693; £346; £173) **Stalls** High

Form RPR
0-50 **1** **Zomerlust**[34] 2061 9-9-8 85 (v) TomEaves 3 89
(John Quinn) *mde all: rdn over 1f out: drvn and hld on wl ins fnl f* **5/2**[1]
1300 **2** 1 1/2 **Efistorm**[5] 2938 10-8-10 77 PJMcDonald 4 72
(Conor Dore) *trckd ldr: rdn over 2f out: pressed wnr ent fnl f: kpt on: hld towards fin* **11/4**[2]
-120 **3** 1/2 **Dispol Kylie (IRE)**[13] 2690 5-8-7 73 MichaelO'Connell(3) 5 70
(Kate Walton) *hld up: rdn and hdwy over 1f out: wnt 3rd 1f out: kpt on* **9/2**
1545 **4** 2 1/4 **Bonnie Prince Blue**[29] 2205 8-8-5 70 (b) JulieBurke(5) 8 63
(Ian McInnes) *hld up: pushed along 1/2-way: rdn and hdwy over 1f out: edgd rt jst ins fnl f: one pce* **10/1**
-040 **5** hd **Sonny Red (IRE)**[12] 2717 7-9-7 85 AdrianNicholls 6 74
(David Nicholls) *trckd ldr: rdn over 2f out: drvn over 1f out: wknd ins fnl f* **3/1**[3]
60-0 **6** 6 **Deva Le Deva (IRE)**[16] 2581 3-7-7 53 (p) DanielleMcCreery(5) 7 36
(Tom Dascombe) *hld up in tch: rdn over 2f out: wknd over 1f out* **33/1**

1m 12.26s (-0.74) **Going Correction** -0.175s/f (Firm)
WFA 3 from 4yo+ 7lb **6 Ran SP% 110.5**
Speed ratings (Par 103): **97,95,94,91,91 83**
toteswingers:1&2:£1.40, 1&3:£1.20, 2&3:£2.40 CSF £9.35 TOTE £3.60: £2.10, £1.70; EX 10.80.
Owner Dawson And Quinn **Bred** The Lavington Stud **Trained** Settrington, N Yorks

FOCUS
A fair claimer but the form has been rated fairly negatively.

3084 BET ON ROYAL ASCOT AT TOTESPORT.COM H'CAP 1m 4f 10y
3:20 (3:21) (Class 4) (0-85,81) 3-Y-O **£4,209** (£1,252; £625; £312) **Stalls** Low

Form RPR
03-2 **1** **Lady Amakhala**[28] 2218 3-8-12 **72** PJMcDonald 1 81
(George Moore) *trckd ldng pair: pushed along and outpcd over 3f out: hdwy 2f out: led appr fnl f: kpt on wl* **18/1**
1-52 **2** 3 **Defence Of Duress (IRE)**[21] 2435 3-9-7 **81** MickyFenton 2 85
(Tom Tate) *led narrowly: rdn over 3f out: drvn whn hdd appr fnl f: no ch w wnr* **9/4**[2]
4-43 **3** 1/2 **Sky Falcon (USA)**[13] 2695 3-9-3 **77** RoystonFfrench 5 80
(Mark Johnston) *stdd s: hld up: rdn and hdwy over 2f out: chal wl over 1f out: one pce fnl f* **14/1**
-031 **4** 3 **Lexington Bay (IRE)**[13] 2695 3-9-7 **81** DavidNolan 3 79
(Richard Fahey) *midfield: hdwy over 3f out: rdn and ev ch 2f out: no ex ins fnl f* **5/1**[3]
5162 **5** 11 **Dark Dune (IRE)**[15] 2613 3-8-9 **69** (e) DavidAllan 4 50
(Tim Easterby) *trckd ldng pair: rdn over 4f out: wknd over 2f out* **11/1**
00-6 **6** 7 **Good Faith**[23] 2392 3-7-13 **62** oh12 JamesSullivan(3) 7 31
(George Moore) *hld up: pushed along over 5f out: a towards rr* **66/1**
2-31 **7** 3 3/4 **Samarkand (IRE)**[8] 2819 3-9-4 **78** 6ex StevieDonohoe 6 41
(Sir Mark Prescott Bt) *prom: rdn and pressed ldr over 4f out: wknd over 1f out: eased* **5/4**[1]

2m 36.46s (-0.24) **Going Correction** 0.0s/f (Good) **7 Ran SP% 113.6**
Speed ratings (Par 101): **100,98,97,95,88 83,81**
toteswingers:1&2:£9.40, 1&3:£31.80, 2&3:£13.30 CSF £57.97 TOTE £12.40: £5.70, £1.30; EX 71.80.
Owner Mrs D N B Pearson **Bred** Mrs D N B Pearson **Trained** Middleham Moor, N Yorks
■ Stewards' Enquiry : David Nolan caution: used whip down shoulder in the forehand.

FOCUS
This was a well-run race. The two market leaders were both disappointing but the time was reasonable and the winner is credited with a 10lb personal best.
Samarkand(IRE) Official explanation: trainer's rep said gelding was unsuited by the good to soft (good in places) ground

3085 LADIES DAY H'CAP 1m 1f
4:00 (4:01) (Class 3) (0-90,88) 4-Y-O+ **£6,623** (£1,982; £991; £495; £246) **Stalls** Low

Form RPR
0200 **1** **Pleasant Day (IRE)**[13] 2681 4-9-7 **88** (b) FrederikTylicki 1 98
(Richard Fahey) *hld up in tch: chsd ldrs over 2f out: drvn and kpt on wl ins fnl f: led towards fin* **8/1**
-422 **2** nk **Dolphin Rock**[8] 2814 4-9-1 **82** LeeNewman 2 91
(David Barron) *led for 1f: trckd ldr: rdn to ld again 2f out: edgd rt over 1f out: kpt on: hdd towards fin* **5/2**[1]
0446 **3** 1 **Charlie Cool**[5] 2933 8-9-7 **88** (b) PJMcDonald 5 95
(Ruth Carr) *trckd ldrs: hdwy to chal 2f out: sn rdn: kpt on: hld towards fin* **5/2**[1]
5556 **4** 4 **Jonny Lesters Hair (IRE)**[17] 2544 6-8-10 **77** DavidAllan 6 75
(Tim Easterby) *led after 1f: rdn whn hdd 2f out: sltly short of room over 1f out: wknd ins fnl f* **10/3**[2]
3300 **5** 3/4 **Layline (IRE)**[6] 2884 4-9-5 **86** TomEaves 3 83
(Gay Kelleway) *racd keenly: hld up on inner: rdn over 1f out: no imp* **12/1**
0646 **6** 4 1/2 **Tartan Gunna**[5] 2909 5-9-1 **82** (b) RoystonFfrench 4 69
(Mark Johnston) *dwlt: hld up in tch: pushed along over 2f out: sn no imp: wknd ins fnl f* **7/1**[3]

1m 53.04s (-1.66) **Going Correction** 0.0s/f (Good) **6 Ran SP% 111.5**
Speed ratings (Par 107): **107,106,105,102,101 97**
toteswingers:1&2:£2.60, 1&3:£3.20, 2&3:£1.30 CSF £27.88 TOTE £8.70: £3.90, £1.10; EX 32.10.
Owner J C Parsons & J J Gilmartin **Bred** Patrick J Gleeson **Trained** Musley Bank, N Yorks
■ Stewards' Enquiry : Lee Newman one-day ban: careless riding (Jun 30)

FOCUS
A pretty competitive little handicap, which was well run. The winner was up 3lb on his good effort here in May.

NOTEBOOK
Pleasant Day(IRE) got a nice run through the race on the rail and picked up well when switched between horses inside the last. He had too much use made of him at Epsom and goes well here - his previous good effort this term came here in May - and he's clearly versatile when it comes to ground. (op 13-2)
Dolphin Rock, 3lb well in at the weights following his good effort at Haydock eight days earlier, was well placed chasing the pace throughout but had to settle for the runner-up spot for the seventh time in his last 14 starts. (tchd 3-1)
Charlie Cool, racing off the same mark as when successful in this race last year, had every chance a furlong out but was just run out of it. (op 3-1 tchd 10-3)
Jonny Lesters Hair(IRE), 3lb lower than when last successful, was left alone in front but couldn't take advantage. (op 4-1 tchd 3-1)
Layline(IRE) struggled to get into it from off the pace. (op 11-1 tchd 10-1)
Tartan Gunna didn't look happy on the track. (op 11-2)

3086 BEAUMONT ROBINSON LADIES' DERBY H'CAP (LADY AMATEUR RIDERS) 1m 4f 10y
4:35 (4:37) (Class 6) (0-65,62) 4-Y-O+ **£2,248** (£697; £348; £174) **Stalls** Low

Form RPR
-064 **1** **Dimashq**[19] 2492 9-9-0 **45** MissWGibson(5) 5 53
(Paul Midgley) *hld up: hdwy over 3f out: chal over 1f out: kpt on ins fnl f: led towards fin* **14/1**
0221 **2** nk **Gems**[10] 2759 4-10-8 **62** 6ex MissEJJones 7 69
(Peter Hiatt) *prom: led after 3f: rdn over 2f out: strly pressed appr fnl f: kpt on: hdd towards fin* **6/1**[3]
0-30 **3** shd **Talk Of Saafend (IRE)**[15] 1959 6-9-8 **53** MissECSayer(5) 1 60
(Dianne Sayer) *trckd ldrs on inner: rdn over 2f out: hdwy to chal appr fnl f: kpt on: jst hld* **16/1**
-032 **4** 3 **Golden Future**[13] 2696 8-9-10 **55** MissJoannaMason(5) 6 57
(Peter Niven) *in tch: rdn over 2f out: hdwy to chal over 1f out: no ex ins fnl f* **3/1**[1]
403 **5** 2 1/4 **Tasman Tiger**[13] 2669 4-9-10 **50** MissSBrotherton 2 49
(Kate Walton) *midfield: hdwy over 3f out: rdn and ev ch 2f out: wknd ins fnl f* **11/1**
0-60 **6** 4 1/2 **Tropical Duke (IRE)**[16] 2589 5-9-11 **56** MissVBarr(5) 14 47
(Ron Barr) *hld up: hdwy on inner over 3f out: swtchd lft over 2f out: sn rdn: no further imp appr fnl f* **10/1**
4-30 **7** 1/2 **Royal Premier (IRE)**[18] 2526 8-9-3 **48** MissPhillipaTutty(5) 11 39
(Tom Keddy) *slowly away: hld up: pushed along over 2f out: kpt on ins fnl f: n.d* **20/1**

606- **8** *shd* **Wind Shuffle (GER)**50 2086 8-10-7 **61**............................ MissADeniel 3 51
(Richard Fahey) *led for 3f: trckd ldr: rdn over 3f out: wknd over 1f out* **8/1**

1000 **9** *1* **Barton Bounty**8 2800 4-10-0 **54**.................................. MissJCoward 13 43
(Peter Niven) *hld up: rdn over 3f out: n.d* **25/1**

0-05 **10** *½* **Hi Dancer**15 2622 8-10-1 **60**.......................... MissCharlotteHolmes(5) 4 48
(Ben Haslam) *midfield on outer: rdn over 3f out: wknd over 1f out* **5/1**2

1260 **11** *11* **Bright Sparky (GER)**4 2952 8-9-6 **51**..................(bt) LucyAlexander(5) 9 21
(Michael Easterby) *hld up: a towards rr* **16/1**

-420 **12** *12* **Sacco D'Oro**5 2912 5-9-4 **47**.............................. MissMMullineaux(3) 10 —
(Michael Mullineaux) *trckd ldrs: lost pl 5f out: wknd over 3f out* **20/1**

6-02 **13** *hd* **December**13 2669 5-10-3 **57**..(t) MrsCBartley 8 8
(James Given) *sn prom: lost pl over 4f out: wknd over 3f out* **16/1**

2m 38.71s (2.01) **Going Correction** 0.0s/f (Good) **13** Ran SP% **122.2**
Speed ratings (Par 101): **93,92,92,90,89 86,85,85,85,84 77,69,69**
toteswingers:1&2:£23.40, 1&3:£41.00, 2&3:£24.10 CSF £95.33 CT £1388.92 TOTE £21.30: £5.70, £2.50, £4.70; EX 184.90.
Owner A Bell **Bred** Darley **Trained** Westow, N Yorks

FOCUS
An ordinary handicap. The winner showed similar form to his win in this in 2009.
Dimashq Official explanation: trainer had no explanation for the apparent improvement in form
Royal Premier(IRE) Official explanation: jockey said gelding was slowly away when she missed handle to remove blindfold.

3087 BUY YOUR TICKETS ON-LINE @ RIPON-RACES.CO.UK H'CAP 5f
5:10 (5:11) (Class 5) (0-75,75) 3-Y-0+ **£2,331** (£520; £520; £173) **Stalls** High

Form RPR

1201 **1** **Lucky Art (USA)**13 2667 5-9-6 **70**.............................. JamesSullivan(3) 9 86+
(Ruth Carr) *mde all: clr 1/2-way: rdn out fnl f: easily* **3/1**1

0422 **2** *3 ¾* **Baybshambles (IRE)**13 2670 7-8-8 **58**.......................... PaulPickard(3) 3 59
(Ron Barr) *midfield: rdn over 2f out: hdwy over 1f out: kpt on ins fnl f: no threat to wnr* **3/1**1

-000 **2** *dht* **Captain Royale (IRE)**14 2633 6-9-7 **73**.........................(p) DaleSwift(5) 4 74
(Colin Teague) *chsd wnr: rdn over 2f out: kpt on: no ch w wnr* **16/1**

4046 **4** *1 ¼* **Wicked Wilma (IRE)**3 2987 7-8-11 **58**.......................... StevieDonohoe 1 55
(Alan Berry) *chsd wnr: rdn over 2f out: no ex ins fnl f* **9/1**

6012 **5** *¾* **Angelo Poliziano**7 2832 5-10-0 **75**...............................(p) DavidNolan 7 69+
(Ann Duffield) *dwlt: hld up: rdn and hdwy over 1f out: one pce fnl f* **7/2**2

0605 **6** *nk* **Captain Scooby**10 2766 5-9-6 **70**.............................. SeanLevey(3) 10 63
(Richard Whitaker) *midfield: rdn over 2f out: one pce* **11/2**3

-015 **7** *1 ¼* **Highland Warrior**27 2263 12-9-12 **73**............................ MickyFenton 2 61
(Paul Midgley) *hld up: rdn and hdwy on outer 2f out: sn chsd clr ldr: wknd ins fnl f* **20/1**

-006 **8** *5* **Bellemere**12 2736 3-8-3 **63**.................................... DavidSimmonson(7) 8 33
(Michael Easterby) *midfield: rdn over 2f out: wknd over 1f out* **28/1**

1050 **9** *nk* **Sloop Johnb**78 1048 5-9-6 **67**....................................(e1) PJMcDonald 6 36
(Conor Dore) *sn pushed along in rr: a bhd* **18/1**

58.63 secs (-2.07) **Going Correction** -0.175s/f (Firm)
WFA 3 from 5yo+ 6lb **9** Ran SP% **117.0**
Speed ratings (Par 103): **109,103,103,101,99 99,97,89,88**
PL: CR £5.00, BS £2.10 EX: LA/CR £26.60, LA/BS £6.60 CSF: LA/CR £26.57 LA/BS £6.12 T/C: LA/CR/BS £79.05, LA/BS/CR £61.50. toteswingers: LA&CR £6.80, LA&BS £2.20, CR&BS £9.90. TOTE £4.30: £1.80.
Owner Exors of the late David W Chapman **Bred** Gaines-Gentry Thoroughbreds **Trained** Huby, N Yorks

FOCUS
Only one horse counted here, the winner making all from a good draw in a decent time. He looks as good as ever.

3088 RACING AGAIN ON MONDAY 4TH JULY H'CAP 1m
5:45 (5:45) (Class 6) (0-65,65) 4-Y-0+ **£2,331** (£693; £346; £173) **Stalls** Low

Form RPR

3402 **1** **Classic Descent**8 2815 6-8-10 **57**.........................(bt) JamesSullivan(3) 5 66
(Ruth Carr) *dwlt: hld up: hdwy over 2f out: sn chsd ldrs: pressed ldr 1f out: kpt on: led post* **13/2**3

066 **2** *hd* **Jupiter Fidius**19 2494 4-8-0 **60** (p) ShaneBKelly(7) 13 68
(Kate Walton) *trckd ldrs: rdn over 2f out: led narrowly 1f out: kpt on: hdd post* **9/1**

-050 **3** *1 ½* **Wiseman's Diamond (USA)**18 2530 6-8-3 **54**(b1) DavidSimmonson(7) 15 59
(Paul Midgley) *w ldr on outer: rdn to ld 3f out: hdd 1f out: kpt on* **14/1**

1300 **4** *3 ¼* **Nevada Desert (IRE)**22 2401 11-8-8 **55**.......................... SeanLevey(3) 2 53
(Richard Whitaker) *midfield: rdn over 2f out: kpt on fnl f: wnt 4th post: nvr threatened ldrs* **14/1**

0602 **5** *hd* **Master Of Dance (IRE)**65 1295 4-9-7 **65**.......................(p) GregFairley 4 62
(Peter Salmon) *led: rdn whn hdd 3f out: remained w ev ch tl over 1f out: no ex fnl f* **11/1**

0-00 **6** *¾* **Prime Circle**8 2799 5-9-0 **58**..................................... FrederikTylicki 16 53
(Alan Brown) *dwlt: hld up: rdn and hdwy on outer over 2f out: one pce fnl f* **25/1**

-566 **7** *nk* **Sennockian Storm (USA)**19 2490 4-9-1 **59**........... RoystonFfrench 12 54
(Mark Johnston) *prom: rdn over 3f out: one pce: wknd ins fnl f* **20/1**

-553 **8** *½* **Newbury Street**16 2588 4-9-0 **58**.............................. AndrewElliott 14 52
(Patrick Holmes) *midfield on outer: rdn and hdwy to chse ldrs over 1f out: wknd ins fnl f* **12/1**

1464 **9** *3* **French Art**17 2560 6-9-1 **64**....................................(p) TobyAtkinson(5) 11 51
(Nigel Tinkler) *hld up: rdn over 3f out: no imp* **4/1**1

506 **10** *2 ¾* **Lemon Queen (IRE)**22 2402 5-8-11 **55**............................ PJMcDonald 3 35
(John Quinn) *in tch on inner: rdn over 2f out: wknd over 1f out* **18/1**

-600 **11** *1 ¼* **Apache Warrior**23 2393 4-9-0 **58**................................. TomEaves 7 35
(George Moore) *midfield: lost pl over 3f out: wknd over 2f out* **12/1**

2-26 **12** *nse* **Lakeman (IRE)**154 148 5-9-0 **65**............................ JacobButterfield(7) 8 42
(Brian Ellison) *midfield: rdn and lost pl over 3f out: wknd over 2f out* **8/1**

5-53 **13** *7* **Cross The Boss (IRE)**34 2057 4-9-0 **58**...........................(t) DavidAllan 9 19
(Ben Haslam) *dwlt: hld up: pushed along over 3f out: a towards rr* **11/2**2

1m 40.89s (-0.51) **Going Correction** 0.0s/f (Good) **13** Ran SP% **120.8**
Speed ratings (Par 101): **102,101,100,97,96 96,95,95,92,89 88,88,81**
toteswingers:1&2:£7.80, 1&3:£31.00, 2&3:£37.90. Totesuper7: Win: Not won. Place: Not won. CSF £64.72 CT £834.17 TOTE £6.40: £1.70, £3.50, £4.70; EX 90.30.
Owner Exors of the late David W Chapman **Bred** Mrs M L Parry **Trained** Huby, N Yorks

FOCUS
A moderate affair. The first two are rated close to last year's form.
Cross The Boss(IRE) Official explanation: trainer said, regarding running, that the gelding had a breathing problem
T/Plt: £110.70 to a £1 stake. Pool:£54,796.06 - 361.08 winning tickets T/Qpdt: £37.50 to a £1 stake. Pool:£3,451.41 - 67.96 winning tickets AS

2991 WARWICK (L-H)
Thursday, June 16

OFFICIAL GOING: Good (good to firm in places; 7.1)
Wind: quite strong breeze behind Weather: sunny periods with showers, heavy at times.

3089 WARWICK MUSIC NIGHT AUGUST 23RD CLAIMING STKS 1m 22y
1:50 (1:50) (Class 5) 3-Y-0+ **£2,590** (£770; £385; £192) **Stalls** Low

Form RPR

-640 **1** **High Five Society**28 2213 7-9-9 70..............................(b) JimmyQuinn 2 66
(Roy Bowring) *s.i.s: in rr: hdwy to trck ldrs 5f out: rdn to ld jst over 1f out: r.o* **3/1**2

3350 **2** *2 ¾* **Urban Kode (IRE)**4 2964 3-8-10 63.........................(v) CathyGannon 1 55
(David Evans) *chsd ldrs: outpcd over 2f out: styd on ins fnl f: wnt 2nd nr fin* **7/2**3

2524 **3** *nk* **Danceyourselfdizzy (IRE)**9 2789 3-8-6 65................ KieranO'Neill(5) 4 55
(Richard Hannon) *trckd ldrs: rdn over 2f out: styd on same pce* **5/2**1

-406 **4** *¾* **Divine Rule (IRE)**16 2583 3-9-1 60..............................(vt1) DaneO'Neill 3 58
(Hughie Morrison) *led for over 3f: prom: led over 2f out: sn rdn: hdd jst over 1f out: no ex whn lost 2 pls towards fin* **3/1**2

3443 **5** *6* **Lean Machine**17 2565 4-9-7 60..............................(p) WilliamCarson 8 42
(Ronald Harris) *hld up: rdn over 2f out: nvr any imp* **22/1**

-655 **6** *½* **Vogarth**37 1979 7-8-12 42..(b) KatiaScallan(7) 6 39
(Michael Chapman) *t.k.h: trckd ldrs: rdn over 2f out: wknd fnl f* **80/1**

00-0 **7** *hd* **Algurayn (IRE)**51 1591 3-8-6 55..................................(b1) AmyBaker(3) 5 36
(George Prodromou) *dwlt: rdn 3f out: a in rr* **50/1**

005- **8** *17* **Fajer Al Kuwait**245 6869 3-8-5 54 ow3.................. RichardOliver(7) 7 —
(George Prodromou) *prom: led over 5f out: rdn and hdd over 2f out: sn wknd* **40/1**

1m 41.52s (0.52) **Going Correction** +0.075s/f (Good)
WFA 3 from 4yo+ 10lb **8** Ran SP% **110.8**
Speed ratings (Par 103): **100,97,96,96,90 89,89,72**
toteswingers:1&2:£2.60, 1&3:£2.30, 2&3:£2.50 CSF £12.81 TOTE £4.20: £1.80, £2.10, £1.10; EX 14.70.
Owner S R Bowring **Bred** A C M Spalding **Trained** Edwinstowe, Notts
■ Stewards' Enquiry : Richard Oliver caution: used whip when out of contention.

FOCUS
The ground had dried out since Monday's meeting and was officially described as good, good to firm last 2f. There was a sharp shower before the opener and the winning time was 4.92 seconds outside standard, but the early pace was modest and this was a poor race. The field stayed centre-to-far side on reaching the home straight. The form has been rated negatively through the fourth.

3090 RACING UK ON CHANNEL 432 MAIDEN FILLIES' STKS (DIV I) 6f
2:20 (2:21) (Class 5) 3-Y-0+ **£2,266** (£674; £337; £168) **Stalls** Low

Form RPR

3-3 **1** **Bless You**50 1607 3-9-0 0.. DaneO'Neill 11 84+
(Henry Candy) *trckd ldr: led jst over 2f out: sn rdn: edgd sltly lft: r.o wl fnl f: eased nr fin* **10/3**2

0-2 **2** *2 ½* **Vizean (IRE)**37 1985 3-9-0 0.................................... RichardMullen 3 75
(Ed McMahon) *wnt to s early: led: rdn and hdd over 2f out: sn wandered u.p: kpt on but a being hld by wnr: jst hld on for 2nd* **4/1**

-345 **3** *nse* **Miss Mediator (USA)**14 2643 3-8-9 74..................... KieranO'Neill(5) 6 75
(Richard Hannon) *chsd ldrs: rdn over 2f out: nt quite gng pce to chal: styd on: jst failed to snatch 2nd* **7/2**3

5/33 **4** *8* **Bobby's Doll**12 2710 4-9-4 55................................. AdamBeschizza(3) 10 51
(Terry Clement) *chsd ldrs: rdn over 2f out: sn one pce* **25/1**

06 **5** *1* **Amber Heights**30 2174 3-9-0 0.................................... FergusSweeney 9 46
(David Pinder) *in tch: rdn over 2f out: sn one pce* **22/1**

24 **6** *¾* **Cheherazad (IRE)**41 1853 3-9-0 0................................... TedDurcan 13 44
(Paul Cole) *wnt rt s: sn in tch: rdn wl over 2f out: sn one pce* **9/4**1

05 **7** *½* **Mistress Quick**26 2311 3-9-0 0...................................... AdamKirby 14 42
(Ben De Haan) *nvr bttr than mid-div* **50/1**

5- **8** *3* **Queen's Choice (IRE)**265 6323 3-9-0 0........................ StephenCraine 4 32
(Anabel K Murphy) *nvr bttr than mid-div* **80/1**

06-0 **9** *6* **Gessabelle**12 2720 4-9-0 36...(t) LeonnaMayor(7) 2 15
(Phil McEntee) *mid-div: rdn wl over 2f out: wknd over 1f out* **100/1**

53 **10** *1 ¾* **Waterbury Girl**40 1900 3-9-0 0.................................... CathyGannon 12 —
(Bryn Palling) *hung rt ent fnl f: a towards rr* **50/1**

\- **11** *2* **Bowmans Well (IRE)** 6-9-7 0.. NeilChalmers 5 —
(Peter Purdy) *s.i.s: sn outpcd: a in rr* **100/1**

12 *1* **Present Laughter** 3-8-11 0...................................... MatthewDavies(3) 7 —
(Ron Hodges) *s.i.s: a towards rr* **80/1**

3-0 **13** *3 ½* **Iztacchiuatl**13 2689 3-8-7 0.. DavidKenny(7) 1 —
(Michael Scudamore) *dismntd and ld to s: s.i.s: a towards rr* **40/1**

0060 **14** *2* **Ellielusive (IRE)**16 2593 4-9-7 52............................... TomMcLaughlin 8 —
(Mark Brisbourne) *s.i.s: a towards rr* **80/1**

1m 11.4s (-0.40) **Going Correction** +0.075s/f (Good) course record
WFA 3 from 4yo+ 7lb **14** Ran SP% **116.3**
Speed ratings (Par 100): **105,101,101,90,89 88,87,83,75,73 70,69,64,62**
toteswingers:1&2:£3.80, 1&3:£3.50, 2&3:£3.60 CSF £15.47 TOTE £5.60: £1.40, £1.80, £1.90; EX 20.00.
Owner T A F Frost **Bred** Roan Rocket Partners **Trained** Kingston Warren, Oxon

FOCUS
A weak older-fillies' maiden in which only four counted in the market and three of them pulled right away. They produced decent form but there was little depth.

3091 RACING UK ON CHANNEL 432 MAIDEN FILLIES' STKS (DIV II) 6f
2:55 (2:56) (Class 5) 3-Y-0+ **£2,266** (£674; £337; £168) **Stalls** Low

Form RPR

00 **1** **Pinch Of Posh (IRE)**50 1607 3-9-0 0................................ TedDurcan 2 66
(Paul Cole) *trckd ldrs: rdn over 2f out: led fnl 140yds: r.o wl: rdn out* **5/1**2

2 *1 ¾* **Sannibel** 3-9-0 0.. ShaneKelly 9 60
(Kevin Morgan) *wnt lft leaving stalls: led: rdn whn hdd 2f out: rallied to hold ev ch ins fnl f: no ex fnl 100yds* **33/1**

05 **3** *nk* **Mandatori (IRE)**13 2673 3-9-0 0...................................(t) CathyGannon 1 59+
(Nicky Vaughan) *t.k.h towards rr of midfield: rdn 2f out: sn swtchd rt: styd on wl fnl f* **10/1**

0 **4** *1 ½* **Adaeze (IRE)**13 2689 3-9-0 0...................................... StephenCraine 12 54
(Jonathan Portman) *trckd ldrs: rdn to ld 2f out: hdd fnl 140yds: hld in 4th whn stmbld nr fin* **40/1**

0-62 **5** *½* **Catalinas Diamond (IRE)**28 2223 3-9-0 74.................. DaneO'Neill 10 53
(Pat Murphy) *mid-div: rdn to chse ldrs 2f out: styd on same pce fnl f* **9/4**1

6 1 1/4 **Nafa (IRE)** 3-9-0 0 RichardMullen 4 49
(Michael Mullineaux) *mid-div: rdn over 2f out: styd on wout threatening fnl f* **25/1**

00 7 hd **Zagalinis Speech**[40] 1900 3-9-0 0 AdrianMcCarthy 13 48
(J R Jenkins) *chsd ldrs: rdn over 3f out: fading whn carried rt over 1f out* **100/1**

00 8 nse **Gambatte**[7] 2848 4-9-7 0 LiamJones 5 50
(Tony Carroll) *mid-div tl outpcd over 2f out: styd on again ins fnl f: nvr trbld ldrs* **80/1**

9 4 1/2 **Festival Dance** 3-8-11 0 MatthewDavies(3) 8 33
(Ron Hodges) *swvd bdly rt leaving stalls: a towards rr* **25/1**

2/3- 10 1/2 **Tomodachi (IRE)**[276] 6039 4-9-7 0 AdamKirby 3 34
(Marco Botti) *chsd ldrs: rdn wl over 2f out: nt gng pce to get on terms: wknd fnl f* **9/4**[1]

50 11 1 3/4 **Misshollygolightly**[8] 2802 3-9-0 0 SaleemGolam 6 26
(Brian Baugh) *mid-div: rdn over 2f out: wknd over 1f out* **80/1**

12 1 1/4 **Quest For Silver** 3-9-0 0 JamesMillman 7 22
(Jeremy Gask) *s.i.s: a towards rr* **9/1**[3]

1m 12.97s (1.17) **Going Correction** +0.075s/f (Good)
WFA 3 from 4yo+ 7lb 12 Ran SP% **113.8**
Speed ratings (Par 100): **95,92,92,90,89 87,87,87,81,80 78,76**
toteswingers:1&2:£9.40, 1&3:£31.80, 2&3:£13.30 CSF £156.71 TOTE £6.20: £2.90, £9.50, £2.90; EX 160.40.
Owner Mrs Melba Bryce **Bred** Swordlestown Stud **Trained** Whatcombe, Oxon

FOCUS
The winning time was a massive 1.57 seconds slower than the first division, which suggests this form is really weak. The race is rated on the negative side.
Catalinas Diamond(IRE) Official explanation: jockey said filly hit the gates; trainer said filly returned with cut nose
Festival Dance Official explanation: jockey said filly veered right leaving stalls

3092 BRITISH STALLION STUDS SUPPORTING BRITISH RACING E B F MAIDEN FILLIES' STKS 5f
3:35 (3:36) (Class 5) 2-Y-O **£3,626** (£1,079; £539; £269) **Stalls** Low

Form RPR

1 **Dam Beautiful** 2-9-0 0 StephenCraine 14 81+
(Kevin Ryan) *travelled wl: trckd ldr: led wl over 1f out: shkn up to assert fnl 120yds: r.o wl: readily* **12/1**

2 2 **Impassive** 2-9-0 0 RichardMullen 10 74
(Ed McMahon) *chsd ldr: rdn to chal wl over 1f out: kpt on but nt pce of wnr fnl 120yds* **10/3**[1]

55 3 2 1/4 **Leenavesta (USA)**[17] 2559 2-8-9 0 KieranO'Neill(5) 6 66
(Richard Hannon) *wnt rt leaving stalls: chsd ldrs: rdn over 2f out: kpt on but nt pce to chal* **15/2**

0 4 nk **Royal Red**[16] 2580 2-9-0 0 JimCrowley 5 65
(Ralph Beckett) *hld up: hdwy 2f out: sn rdn: kpt on same pce fnl f* **7/2**[2]

6 5 1 1/4 **Reve Du Jour (IRE)**[12] 2709 2-9-0 0 ShaneKelly 9 60
(Alan McCabe) *in tch: rdn over 2f out: hung lft: kpt on same pce* **25/1**

00 6 nk **Millibar (IRE)**[6] 2880 2-9-0 0 TomMcLaughlin 13 59+
(Nick Littmoden) *s.i.s: towards rr: styd on fr over 1f out: nvr threatened ldrs* **50/1**

7 3/4 **Anginola (IRE)** 2-9-0 0 EddieCreighton 11 56
(Joseph Tuite) *s.i.s: bhd: sn pushed along: styd on fnl f: nvr trbld ldrs* **100/1**

523 8 1 **Dream Whisperer**[6] 2880 2-8-11 0 BillyCray(3) 7 53
(Dominic Ffrench Davis) *in tch: rdn over 2f out: wknd fnl f* **8/1**

9 2 3/4 **Get The Trip** 2-9-0 0 KirstyMilczarek 3 43
(James Toller) *s.i.s: a towards rr* **33/1**

10 1 **Orrell Post** 2-9-0 0 TonyHamilton 1 39
(Richard Fahey) *chsd ldrs: rdn over 2f out: wknd over 1f out* **14/1**

023 11 3/4 **Meloneras**[16] 2580 2-9-0 0 (b1) JamesMillman 4 37
(Rod Millman) *led: rdn over 2f out: hdd wl over 1f out: sn wknd* **13/2**[3]

12 4 **White Spirit (IRE)** 2-9-0 0 AdamKirby 8 22
(Marco Botti) *mid-div: rdn over 2f out: sn wknd* **17/2**

59.92 secs (0.32) **Going Correction** +0.075s/f (Good) 12 Ran SP% **116.1**
Speed ratings (Par 90): **100,96,93,92,90 90,89,87,83,81 80,73**
toteswingers:1&2:£8.80, 1&3:£11.80, 2&3:£6.30 CSF £49.74 TOTE £12.00: £3.90, £1.50, £3.00; EX 70.30.
Owner Mrs Lisa Dartnell **Bred** Lady Lonsdale **Trained** Hambleton, N Yorks

FOCUS
An ordinary maiden, but the first two home were both newcomers so can probably go on to better things.

NOTEBOOK
Dam Beautiful, a 20,000gns half-sister to Bosun Breeze, defied the market negatives, and the fact that she was always trapped out wide from the outside stall makes this performance even better. From a stable in cracking form with its juveniles, she produced a smart turn of foot to pull away from the runner-up and she is a filly with a future. (op 8-1)
Impassive, in contrast to the winner, was popular in the market. Another ridden close to the pace, she disputed the lead over a furlong out but couldn't match the winner's turn of foot. A £9,000 filly out of a half-sister to Forte Dei Marmi and Savarain, she holds a Super Sprint entry and there are certainly races to be won with her. (op 9-2)
Leenavesta(USA) showed ability in finishing fifth in her first two starts and again ran well having always been up there throughout. She could be an early nursery type. (op 7-1)
Royal Red finished around 3l behind Meloneras on her Leicester debut and turned that form around. She also fared best of those held up, so seems likely to progress again from this. (op 5-1)
Reve Du Jour(IRE) didn't seem to see out the extra 1.5f on her Doncaster debut, but the way she stayed on out wide here suggests she needs to go back up in trip. (op 33-1)
Millibar(IRE), 3l behind Dream Whisperer at Sandown last time, was again done few favours by the draw and although now unplaced in all three starts, is better than her form figures suggest.
Meloneras was only narrowly beaten in her previous two starts, but may have done too much too soon in the first-time blinkers here. Her rider reported that she had hung right handed. Official explanation: jockey said filly hung right-handed (op 9-2)

3093 NIDEK UK 5TH ANNIVERSARY H'CAP 7f 26y
4:10 (4:12) (Class 5) (0-70,70) 3-Y-O+ **£2,729** (£806; £403) **Stalls** Low

Form RPR

6-42 1 **Tamasou (IRE)**[31] 2165 6-9-13 70 RichardMullen 13 78
(Ed McMahon) *in tch: pushed along and hdwy fr 2f out: styd on wl to ld fnl 75yds: rdn out* **6/1**[2]

1240 2 1/2 **The Big Haerth (IRE)**[29] 2207 5-9-9 69 RichardEvans(3) 11 76
(David Evans) *sn pushed into ld: rdn 2f out: styd on gamely: hdd fnl 75yds* **25/1**

6050 3 1 1/2 **Cyflymder (IRE)**[13] 2671 5-9-5 67 NeilFarley(5) 10 70
(Declan Carroll) *chsd ldrs: rdn wl over 2f out: nt pce to chal: styd on* **12/1**

2446 4 nk **Midnight Trader (IRE)**[41] 1869 3-9-0 66 (t) AdamKirby 9 65+
(Paul D'Arcy) *mid-div: outpcd over 2f out: wd ent st: styd on wl fnl f: snatched 4th nring fin* **9/2**[1]

0-04 5 hd **Glass Mountain (IRE)**[33] 2094 3-9-3 69 PatCosgrave 8 68+
(James Fanshawe) *in tch: pushed along 3f out: rdn over 2f out: styd on same pce fnl f* **6/1**[2]

1306 6 1 **Itsthursdayalready**[17] 2555 4-9-0 57 ShaneKelly 6 56
(Mark Brisbourne) *trckd ldrs: rdn over 2f out: one pce fnl f* **22/1**

2000 7 1/2 **Valmina**[15] 2610 4-8-9 59 (t) GeorgeDowning(7) 2 57
(Tony Carroll) *hld up towards rr: pushed along and hdwy fr 2f out: styd on same pce fnl f* **20/1**

0-10 8 1/2 **Woolston Ferry (IRE)**[15] 2605 5-9-3 65 JamesRogers(5) 3 61
(David Pinder) *towards rr of midfield: rdn over 2f out: styd on same pce: nvr threatened ldrs* **25/1**

0243 9 3 1/2 **Khajaaly (IRE)**[31] 2165 4-9-11 68 JimmyQuinn 7 55
(Julia Feilden) *s.i.s: sn taking t.k.h towards rr of midfield: rdn over 2f out: wknd ins fnl f* **12/1**

63-5 10 1 1/2 **Too Many Questions (IRE)**[157] 110 3-9-4 70 CathyGannon 1 50
(David Evans) *a towards rr* **15/2**

-600 11 6 **Ellies Image**[13] 2671 4-9-1 58 SaleemGolam 4 25
(Brian Baugh) *a towards rr* **50/1**

40-1 12 5 **Saturn Way (GR)**[36] 1995 5-9-10 67 TedDurcan 12 20
(Patrick Chamings) *chsd ldr: rdn wl over 2f out: wknd over 1f out* **7/1**[3]

1m 25.32s (0.72) **Going Correction** +0.075s/f (Good)
WFA 3 from 4yo+ 9lb 12 Ran SP% **105.2**
Speed ratings (Par 103): **98,97,95,95,95 94,93,92,88,87 80,74**
toteswingers:1&2:£20.00, 1&3:£10.60, 2&3:£32.50 CSF £125.13 CT £887.26 TOTE £3.70: £1.20, £8.40, £4.40; EX 108.30.
Owner Brooklands Racing **Bred** Garry Gleeson **Trained** Lichfield, Staffs
■ Holiday Snap (9/1) was withdrawn after losing s shoe. Deduct 10p in the £ under R4.
■ Stewards' Enquiry : Adam Kirby one-day ban: used whip with excessive frequency (Jun 30)

FOCUS
An ordinary handicap dominated by the two top weights. The form is rated around the runner-up.
Glass Mountain(IRE) Official explanation: jockey said gelding lost a right-hind shoe
Saturn Way(GR) Official explanation: trainer's rep said gelding bled from the nose

3094 HOUSE OF FRASER LEAMINGTON H'CAP 1m 2f 188y
4:45 (4:46) (Class 6) (0-55,53) 4-Y-O+ **£2,047** (£604; £302) **Stalls** Low

Form RPR

-321 1 **Transfer**[7] 2830 6-8-11 51 RyanClark(5) 1 74+
(Richard Price) *travelled wl in mid-div: smooth hdwy over 2f out: led over 1f out: pushed clr: easily* **4/9**[1]

5432 2 5 **Corrib (IRE)**[5] 2900 8-8-11 46 (p) CathyGannon 3 57
(Bryn Palling) *hld up bhd: hdwy 5f out to trck ldrs 3f out: rdn and ev ch 2f out tl jst ins fnl f: no ch w wnr* **7/2**[2]

0/40 3 9 **Lion Road (USA)**[17] 2569 5-9-2 51 FergusSweeney 12 46
(Alan King) *chsd ldrs: rdn and ev ch 2f out tl over 1f out: hung rt fnl f: jst hld on for 3rd* **12/1**

3601 4 hd **Magnitude**[17] 2569 6-8-12 52 (p) LMcNiff(5) 7 46
(Brian Baugh) *hld up towards rr: rdn and hdwy fr over 2f out: wnt 4th wl over 1f out: nvr threatened ldrs* **8/1**[3]

0300 5 4 1/2 **Warrior Nation (FR)**[3] 2996 5-8-10 45 NeilChalmers 6 31
(Adrian Chamberlain) *led: rdn and hdd whn hung lft over 1f out: sn wknd* **14/1**

6006 6 1 1/2 **Libre**[8] 2824 11-8-11 46 ow1 TomMcLaughlin 5 30
(Violet M Jordan) *hld up towards rr: rdn and sme imp over 2f out: fdd fnl f* **50/1**

565- 7 5 **Robbmaa (FR)**[23] 4530 6-8-3 45 (p) JakePayne(7) 10 20
(Tony Carroll) *chsd ldrs tl 4f out: nt a danger after* **33/1**

0/0- 8 29 **Scarlet Ridge**[509] 274 4-8-10 45 JimmyQuinn 11 —
(Dean Ivory) *mid-div: lost pl and struggling over 4f out: wl bhd fnl 2f* **50/1**

000- 9 18 **Chill Out Charley**[291] 5557 4-8-10 45 WilliamCarson 8 —
(Ronald Harris) *t.k.h early: trckd ldr: hung rt fr over 4f out: wkng whn hanging bdly rt 3f out: sn wl bhd* **33/1**

2m 21.72s (0.62) **Going Correction** +0.075s/f (Good) 9 Ran SP% **126.7**
Speed ratings (Par 101): **100,96,89,89,86 85,81,60,47**
toteswingers:1&2:£1.30, 1&3:£3.40, 2&3:£5.40 CSF £2.71 CT £10.04 TOTE £1.30: £1.02, £1.90, £2.40; EX 3.00.
Owner G Ivall & R J Price **Bred** Kingsclere Stud **Trained** Ullingswick, H'fords
■ Ishismart (10/1) was withdrawn on vet's advice. Deduct 5p in the £ under R4.

FOCUS
An extremely weak and uncompetitive handicap which looked a penalty kick for the red-hot favourite, and so it proved. He's rated back to his post-3yo best. More than half the field were wrong at the weights by 5lb or more.
Chill Out Charley Official explanation: jockey said gelding hung right

3095 WHITES OF COVENTRY LTD METAL PROCESSORS H'CAP 1m 6f 213y
5:20 (5:20) (Class 5) (0-75,75) 4-Y-O+ **£2,590** (£770; £385; £192) **Stalls** Low

Form RPR

040/ 1 **Riptide**[43] 4178 5-8-8 62 (v1) JamieGoldstein 7 71+
(Michael Scudamore) *s.i.s: towards rr: midfield 1/2-way: rdn and hdwy 2f out: styd on for str run ins fnl f: led nr fin* **20/1**

0-32 2 nk **Wild Desert (FR)**[10] 2758 6-9-7 75 CathyGannon 5 83
(Charlie Longsdon) *trckd ldr: rdn to ld over 2f out: clr ent fnl f: ct fnl strides* **4/1**[1]

130- 3 5 **Broughtons Point**[237] 7061 5-9-0 68 JamieMackay 2 70
(Willie Musson) *mid-div: rdn and hdwy fr over 2f out: styd on to chse ldr over 1f out tl no ex fnl f* **7/1**[2]

1-64 4 2 1/2 **Penangdouble O One**[23] 2393 4-8-11 68 (t) JohnFahy(3) 12 67
(Ralph Beckett) *mid-div: rdn to chse ldrs 6f out: one pce fnl f* **4/1**[1]

01-0 5 3/4 **Saggiatore**[19] 2512 4-9-7 75 DaneO'Neill 13 73
(William Muir) *in tch tl lost pl over 4f out: rdn and hdwy fr 2f out: swtchd lft and styd on ent fnl f* **11/1**

43-3 6 1/2 **Norman The Great**[23] 2378 7-9-0 68 FergusSweeney 10 65
(Alan King) *hld up towards rr: rdn whn c wd into st: sn swtchd lft: styd on fnl f: nvr trbld ldrs* **8/1**[3]

0125 7 1 1/4 **Storm Hawk (IRE)**[26] 2312 4-8-13 67 (p) ChrisCatlin 6 62
(Pat Eddery) *trckd ldrs: rdn over 2f out: fdd ins fnl f* **11/1**

550 8 1/2 **Court Wing (IRE)**[6] 2873 5-7-11 56 oh6 KieranO'Neill(5) 9 51
(Richard Price) *led tl rdn over 2f out: wknd ent fnl f* **12/1**

0320 9 9 **Epsom Salts**[62] 1367 6-9-2 70 TedDurcan 3 53
(Pat Phelan) *rdn over 3f out: a towards rr* **12/1**

65-2 10 1 3/4 **My Mate Max**[27] 1914 6-9-6 74 StephenCraine 14 55
(Reg Hollinshead) *slowly away: sn trcking ldrs: rdn over 4f out: wknd over 2f out* **9/1**

1100 **11** *8* **Beaubrav**[14] 2649 5-9-3 **71**...(t) AdamKirby 11 41
(Michael Madgwick) *rdn 4f out: a towards rr* **12/1**
2421 **12** *3 1/4* **Calculating (IRE)**[43] 1817 7-8-8 **62**... JimmyQuinn 4 28
(Mark Usher) *rdn over 3f out: a towards rr* **11/1**
3m 18.94s (-0.06) **Going Correction** +0.075s/f (Good) **12** Ran SP% **126.4**
Speed ratings (Par 103): **103,102,100,98,98 98,97,97,92,91 87,85**
toteswingers:1&2:£19.40, 1&3:£59.20, 2&3:£13.70 CSF £104.97 CT £648.19 TOTE £16.90: £4.00, £3.00, £2.40; EX 108.10.
Owner Middletons **Bred** D Robb **Trained** Bromsash, Herefordshire
■ Stewards' Enquiry : Dane O'Neill one-day ban: careless riding (Jun 30)

FOCUS
An ordinary staying handicap, run at a fair pace thanks to a disputed lead. Typically for Warwick few got involved. The form is rated around the runner-up.
Beaubrav Official explanation: trainer said gelding had a breathing problem; vet said gelding lost left-front shoe

3096 JOIN TODAY AT REWARDS4RACING.COM APPRENTICE RIDERS' H'CAP 1m 22y
5:55 (5:56) (Class 6) (0-60,58) 4-Y-0+ **£2,047** (£604; £302) **Stalls** Low

Form RPR
03/0 **1** **Invincible Hero (IRE)**[77] 1065 4-9-2 **58**...(t) NeilFarley(3) 5 66
(Declan Carroll) *slowly away and squeezed up s: sn taking t.k.h and trcking ldrs: rdn to ld over 2f out: drifted rt fnl f: a doing enough to hold on* **7/1**
4150 **2** *1 1/4* **Aggbag**[23] 2386 7-8-5 **47**... AdamBeschizza(3) 1 52
(Tony Carroll) *chsd ldrs tl lost pl over 3f out: rdn and prog 2f out: chsd wnr ins fnl f: hung rt: kpt on but a being hld* **5/2**[1]
4440 **3** *nse* **Kielty's Folly**[66] 1273 7-8-10 **54**... LMcNiff(5) 9 59
(Brian Baugh) *trckd ldrs: rdn to chse wnr ent fnl f: kpt on but no ex* **8/1**
005- **4** *1* **My Jeanie (IRE)**[275] 6061 7-8-3 **45**... KieranO'Neill(3) 10 48
(Jimmy Fox) *hld up in last: hdwy fr 2f out: rdn over 1f out: styd on* **11/1**
2406 **5** *2* **Dichoh**[23] 2382 8-9-3 **56**...(v) KierenFox 4 54
(Michael Madgwick) *mid-div: pushed along over 3f out: rdn over 2f out: styd on wout threatening ldrs* **6/1**[3]
2240 **6** *13* **Exceedingly Good (IRE)**[7] 2845 5-8-11 **55**... LeonnaMayor(5) 3 24
(Roy Bowring) *wnt to s early: led: rdn and hdd over 2f out: wknd fnl f* **9/2**[2]
-500 **7** *1* **Valkov**[63] 1333 4-8-8 **54**... GeorgeDowning(7) 11 20
(Tony Carroll) *a towards rr* **10/1**
0060 **8** *2* **Sweet Mirasol (IRE)**[31] 2162 4-8-3 **47**...(t) NathanAlison(5) 6 —
(Mandy Rowland) *a towards rr* **11/1**
060- **9** *33* **Red Flash (IRE)**[260] 6454 4-8-13 **52**... MatthewDavies 2 —
(Gary Harrison) *prom for over 3f: sn pushed along: wl bhd fnl 2f* **18/1**
1m 42.26s (1.26) **Going Correction** +0.075s/f (Good) **9** Ran SP% **115.7**
Speed ratings (Par 101): **96,94,94,93,91 78,77,75,42**
toteswingers:1&2:£4.90, 1&3:£6.70, 2&3:£3.90 CSF £24.90 CT £145.67 TOTE £5.90: £1.30, £2.70, £3.10; EX 20.40.
Owner Mrs Sarah Bryan **Bred** Fortbarrington Stud **Trained** Sledmere, E Yorks

FOCUS
A moderate apprentice handicap, and obviously limited form, rated around the second and fourth.
T/Plt: £159.30 to a £1 stake. Pool:£32,845.82 - 150.45 winning tickets T/Qpdt: £184.10 to a £1 stake. Pool:£2,239.31 - 9.00 winning tickets TM

3097 - 3103a (Foreign Racing) - See Raceform Interactive

3064 ASCOT (R-H)
Friday, June 17

OFFICIAL GOING: Good to soft (soft in places) changing to soft after race 5 (5.00)
Course at normal configuration and distances as advertised.
Wind: moderate Weather: cloudy turning wet

3104 ALBANY STKS (GROUP 3) (FILLIES) 6f
2:30 (2:30) (Class 1) 2-Y-0
£34,062 (£12,912; £6,462; £3,222; £1,614; £810) **Stalls** Centre

Form RPR
3 **1** **Samitar**[21] 2467 2-8-12 0... JamieSpencer 14 105+
(Mick Channon) *hld up: hdwy over 2f out: swtchd lft arnd ldrs over 1f out: r.o to ld fnl 110yds: edgd rt whn in full control towards fin* **16/1**
1 **2** *3/4* **Inetrobil (IRE)**[17] 2587 2-8-12 0... PhillipMakin 16 103+
(Kevin Ryan) *athletic: lw: a.p: led wl over 1f out: sn rdn: hdd fnl 110yds: styd on for press but hld cl home* **17/2**
1 **3** *1 3/4* **Illaunglass (IRE)**[15] 2641 2-8-12 0... RyanMoore 6 98
(Jeremy Noseda) *str: midfield: hdwy to chse ldrs over 1f out: styd on but unable to mount serious chal to front pair: no further imp fnl 75yds* **10/1**
1 **4** *1/2* **Switcher (IRE)**[28] 2254 2-8-12 0... RichardKingscote 9 96
(Tom Dascombe) *str: midfield: rdn over 2f out: hdwy to chse ldrs over 1f out: styd on ins fnl f: nt pce to chal* **6/1**[2]
1113 **5** *1 1/4* **Lily's Angel (IRE)**[23] 2404 2-8-12 0... RichardHughes 1 92
(Richard Fahey) *hld up: rdn over 2f out: hdwy and wnt through gap between horses wl over 1f out: styd on to chse ldrs ins fnl f: one pce fnl 100yds* **10/1**
01 **6** *1 3/4* **Luv U Forever**[14] 2661 2-8-12 0... DarryllHolland 12 87
(Pat Murphy) *w'like: led: hdd wl over 1f out: sn rdn: stl ch ins fnl f: fdd fnl 100yds* **33/1**
1 **7** *2* **Sajwah (IRE)**[38] 1981 2-8-12 0... RichardHills 13 81
(B W Hills) *tall: athletic: lw: racd keenly: chsd ldrs: rdn over 2f out: sn outpcd: no imp after* **8/1**[3]
314 **8** *2 3/4* **Sweet Chilli (IRE)**[35] 2070 2-8-12 0... GrahamGibbons 2 73
(David Barron) *hld up: rdn 2f out: sme hdwy over 1f out: one pce and no imp ins fnl f* **12/1**
1 **9** *2 1/2* **Judas Jo (FR)**[45] 1791 2-8-12 0... NeilCallan 8 65
(Gay Kelleway) *w'like: tall: hld up: pushed along whn n.m.r jst over 2f out: swtchd lft wl over 1f out: no imp on ldrs: wl btn fnl f* **40/1**
220 **10** *1 3/4* **Toffee Tart**[17] 2580 2-8-12 0... SebSanders 4 60
(J W Hills) *midfield: impr to trck ldrs over 4f out: rdn over 2f out: wknd over 1f out* **66/1**
0 **11** *3/4* **Anakindalika**[20] 2510 2-8-12 0... KirstyMilczarek 3 58
(John Ryan) *athletic: lw: prom: rdn 2f out: wknd wl over 1f out* **100/1**
11 **12** *3/4* **Teolane (IRE)**[11] 2777 2-8-12 0... KJManning 7 56
(J S Bolger, Ire) *w'like: scope: awkward leaving stalls: racd keenly: hld up: rdn 2f out: failed to pick-up: toiling fr over 1f out* **5/4**[1]
52 **13** *1/2* **Tip Top Gorgeous (IRE)**[18] 2570 2-8-12 0... SilvestreDeSousa 15 54
(David O'Meara) *unf: midfield: pushed along over 2f out: sn lost pl: bhd and n.d over 1f out* **80/1**
1m 15.93s (1.53) **Going Correction** +0.375s/f (Good) **13** Ran SP% **121.2**
Speed ratings (Par 100): **104,103,100,100,98 96,93,89,86,84 83,82,81**
toteswingers:1&2:£17.50, 2&3:£9.70, 1&3:£13.70 CSF £145.37 CT £1511.03 TOTE £16.70: £4.50, £3.10, £3.60; EX 163.50 Trifecta £1040.00 Pool: £9251.38 - 6.58 winning units..
Owner Nick & Olga Dhandsa & John & Zoe Webster **Bred** Norman Court Stud **Trained** West Ilsley, Berks

FOCUS
Ground conditions were very different to when declarations had been made on Wednesday morning, and there were quite a number of absentees through the card. Jamie Spencer, the winning jockey in the opener, thought the ground was riding good to soft, but several of the other riders reported conditions to be slow or soft. The time was reasonable given the conditions, only around 2.5sec outside the Racing Post standard. \n\x\x This was the tenth running of this event and it looked a decent edition, although it lost some of its international interest when American-trained Judy The Beauty was ruled out because of the ground. The field raced in one bunch down the centre, and although the first two were drawn high there did not appear to be any meaningful advantage. Not many were able to get involved and the favourite's poor run takes some of the gloss off the form, but the winner impressed and is rated at the top end of the race averages. The fifth helps put the form into perspective.

NOTEBOOK
Samitar became the fourth maiden to take this, the previous one having been her half-sister Nijoom Dubai, also trained by Mick Channon, in 2007. Channon had been on target with Silca's Gift too four years earlier. A close third at Newmarket on her debut, the winner produced a taking display, making smooth headway to close on the two leaders and seeing it out well after claiming the runner-up. A smart prospect who should progress, she will get further than this in time. Races like the Cherry Hinton and Princess Margaret Stakes would be obvious targets, but her trainer is inclined to put her away until the autumn. She has been given quotes of 25-1 for next season's 1,000 Guineas. (tchd 18-1 and 20-1 in places)
Inetrobil(IRE), bought into by Highclere Thoroughbreds after her easy Redcar debut win, represented the powerful team of juveniles in the Kevin Ryan yard, successful in Thursday's Norfolk Stakes with Bapak Chinta. She travelled well before taking it up but took time to fully subdue the pacesetter, and when she had she was left vulnerable to the winner's challenge. Connections offered no excuses but considered she could have done with getting a lead for a bit longer. The Cherry Hinton could come under consideration. (op 8-1 tchd 10-1)
Illaunglass(IRE)'s yard had twice won this with once-raced fillies and this Lingfield maiden winner ran very well on her turf bow. She had flashed her tail first time but did nothing wrong here, running on gamely for third after racing on the opposite side of the group from the first two. She could take on the runner-up again at Newmarket in the Cherry Hinton. (op 8-1 tchd 15-2)
Switcher(IRE), like the second and third, was stepping up considerably in grade after winning her sole previous start. From a stable enjoying a fine meeting, she lacked the pace to get in a challenge to the leaders but stuck on for fourth. (op 9-1)
Lily's Angel(IRE) incurred her first defeat in four starts when third in the Hilary Needler at Beverley, and the two fillies who finished in front of her there, Dozy and Vocational, were both unplaced in the Queen Mary Stakes this week. Richard Fahey's runner, on whom Richard Hughes replaced the injured Paul Hanagan, made progress from the rear nearest to the far side without threatening the principals, and is worth another try at this trip. (tchd 9-1)
Luv U Forever showed good pace and did not lie down when headed by the runner-up, only fading inside the last. Her small stable's Caledonia Lady, regarded as the quicker filly of the pair, had been a close third in the Queen Mary. (op 40-1)
Sajwah(IRE), successful at Warwick first time, was unable to pick up after tracking the pace and may not have acted on the ground. (tchd 9-1)
Sweet Chilli(IRE)'s limitations had been exposed when she was fourth in a York Listed race and the extra furlong here did not bring about sufficient improvement. (op 14-1)
Teolane(IRE) appeared to have strong credentials, already successful in Listed company at Naas in a race won by her stable's Cuis Ghaire (it was Group 3 then) on her way to taking this prize in 2008. She was a solid favourite but she ran no sort of race, leaving the stalls very awkwardly then failing to pick up from the rear, not acting on the ground. A fairly busy spell may have taken its toll too. Official explanation: jockey said filly never travelled in the good to soft (soft in places) ground (op 11-8 tchd 6-4 in places and 13-8 in places)

3105 KING EDWARD VII STKS (GROUP 2) (C&G) 1m 4f
3:05 (3:05) (Class 1) 3-Y-0
£86,750 (£32,884; £16,457; £8,205; £4,110; £2,062) **Stalls** Low

Form RPR
2-12 **1** **Nathaniel (IRE)**[43] 1822 3-8-12 106... WilliamBuick 5 120+
(John Gosden) *swtg: on toes: chsd ldrs and a travelling wl: hdwy to press ldr 4f out: going strly ent fnl 3f: sn drew clr: rdn and in command 2f out: edgd lft ins fnl f: r.o strly: comf* **11/4**[1]
51 **2** *5* **Fiorente (IRE)**[34] 2097 3-8-12 92... RyanMoore 10 111+
(Sir Michael Stoute) *lw: swtchd lft s and racd wd tl crossed over and in rr 9f out: rdn 4f out: hdwy u.p over 2f out: modest 6th over 1f out: styd on wl to chse clr wnr ins fnl f: kpt on: no ch w wnr* **9/1**
61 **3** *2* **Alexander Pope (IRE)**[26] 2331 3-8-12 109... CO'Donoghue 6 108
(A P O'Brien, Ire) *w'like: edgy: t.k.h early: hld up in last trio: rdn and hdwy 3f out: wnt modest 3rd 2f out: no imp on wnr and styd on same pce u.p after* **12/1**
2-1 **4** *1 3/4* **Mijhaar**[28] 2258 3-8-12 94... NeilCallan 11 105+
(Roger Varian) *lw: t.k.h: swtchd lft s and racd wd tl crossed over and in rr 9f out: hdwy 4f out: edging rt over 3f out: rdn to chse clr wnr and edgd rt 2f out: no imp: no ex and lost 2 pls ins fnl f* **10/3**[2]
1-03 **5** *4 1/2* **Fulgur**[34] 2100 3-8-12 87... KierenFallon 2 98+
(Luca Cumani) *t.k.h: hld up in midfield: effrt whn short of room and sltly hmpd over 3f out: hdwy wl over 2f out: 5th and no imp whn edgd rt and n.m.r wl over 1f out: wl btn after* **14/1**
1-13 **6** *6* **Genius Beast (USA)**[33] 2136 3-8-12 110... AhmedAjtebi 8 88
(Mahmood Al Zarooni) *in tch in midfield: rdn and effrt to chse ldng pair over 3f out: drvn and chsd clr wnr over 2f out tl 2f out: sn wknd* **11/1**
1-11 **7** *29* **Glen's Diamond**[42] 1850 3-8-12 105... JimmyFortune 3 42
(Richard Fahey) *dwlt: niggled along thrght and nvr travelling: in tch in midfield: rdn and struggling 4f out: lost tch over 2f out: t.o and eased fnl f* **6/1**[3]
1220 **8** *1 3/4* **Hurricane Higgins (IRE)**[26] 2341 3-8-12 103...(b[1]) JoeFanning 4 39
(Mark Johnston) *led for 2f: chsd ldr after tl 4f out: wkng whn short of room and jostled over 3f out: wl bhd over 2f out: t.o and eased ins fnl f* **20/1**
-231 **9** *2* **Glencadam Gold (IRE)**[34] 2108 3-8-12 95... IanMongan 1 36
(Sir Henry Cecil) *lw: t.k.h early: chsd ldrs: rdn and struggling over 3f out: wknd wl over 2f out: sn wl bhd: t.o and eased fnl f* **25/1**
14 **10** *nk* **World Domination (USA)**[36] 2030 3-8-12 101... TomQueally 7 36
(Sir Henry Cecil) *lw: plld hrd: chsd ldrs tl led after 2f: hdd and rdn ent fnl 3f: wknd rapidly over 2f out: t.o and eased ins fnl f* **8/1**
2m 34.48s (1.98) **Going Correction** +0.425s/f (Yiel) **10** Ran SP% **116.4**
Speed ratings (Par 111): **110,106,105,104,101 97,77,76,75,75**
toteswingers:1&2:£6.80, 2&3:£14.40, 1&3:£5.70 CSF £28.27 CT £257.26 TOTE £3.90: £1.60, £3.60, £2.20; EX 36.40 Trifecta £290.60 Pool: £12631.60 - 32.15 winning units..

Owner Lady Rothschild **Bred** Kincorth Investments Inc **Trained** Newmarket, Suffolk

FOCUS

There are usually one or two Derby also-rans in the line-up for this race, but this year the field was made up entirely of horses who had skipped Epsom. The softening ground put an even greater emphasis on stamina and, as is often the case, it looks a race that will have a huge bearing on the St Leger. The winning time was 2.45sec quicker than that recorded by Brown Panther (now a 14-1 shot for the Leger) in the King George V Handicap the previous day. The form is rated positively, with Nathaniel an above-average winner, improving in line with Treasure Beach in the Derby.

NOTEBOOK

Nathaniel(IRE) ◆'s trainer sent out subsequent Leger winner Arctic Cosmos to finish second in this race last year, and this colt looks an ideal candidate for the Doncaster Classic on the back of this impressive success. A strong galloper, he came here boasting obvious form claims, having run the subsequent Derby runner-up Treasure Beach close at Chester last time. The softer ground was always going to suit him and, while he got edgy and warm in the preliminaries, his trainer was unconcerned (apparently it's a trait of the family) and it clearly didn't have any negative affect on the way he ran. He did benefit from racing on the inside, in contrast to the runner-up and fourth, who raced wide early and lost ground, but there was plenty to like about the way he stretched clear in the straight, and he shouldn't have any trouble with the longer trip at Doncaster, for which he's a best price 7-2. The Voltigeur or the Geoffrey Freer will be next, although he wouldn't want fast ground. (op 9-4 tchd 2-1 and 3-1 in places)

Fiorente(IRE) ◆ came here rather than going for the handicap the previous day, where he could have run off 92, and he ran a very promising race in second. Slowly away, he was soon pushed along to lead Mijhaar under the trees on the far side in the early stages - a tactic that can often work on soft ground - but when they both crossed over to rejoin the main bunch it was clear the decision had backfired, as they were forced to tuck in at the rear of the field. Still at the back of the field turning in, Fiorente kept on really strongly to take second. There's no question that this lightly raced colt has plenty of improvement in him, and he could well develop into a Leger candidate himself (12-1 generally) - his connections' Conduit was second in this race in 2009 before going one better in the Leger - but his trainer gave a hint that he might have bigger prizes in mind for him. In any case, whatever he does this year he'll make a better 4-y-o. (op 14-1 tchd 16-1 in a place)

Alexander Pope(IRE), winner of a 1m2f Group 3 in Ireland last time out, looks to be steadily improving and, despite racing keenly early, stayed on well enough to take third. He got the trip alright, but might be at his best over 1m2f. (tchd 10-1)

Mijhaar ◆ bounded clear of two subsequent winners at Haydock last time and, while this was a big step up in class, he is clearly well regarded, was sure to be suited by the testing ground and on pedigree the step up in distance looked likely to suit. He was unsurprisingly well backed, but the tactic of following Fiorente over to the far side early didn't work out (raced freely as well) and, while he travelled strongly into contention, that loss of ground early on and attempt to go in pursuit of the winner from the top of the straight finally told, and he was run out of the places late on. He is better than the bare form suggests and is quiet capable of winning Group races. Perhaps the Princess Of Wales's Stakes could come into consideration, although he has a soft-ground action and would want a bit of dig. (op 7-2 tchd 3-1 and 4-1 in places)

Fulgur looked to have a bit to do on this step up in grade, but he ran a fine race given he was quite keen early, improving for the longer trip. (op 12-1)

Genius Beast(USA), who twice finished behind Nathaniel at two, won the Classic Trial at Sandown on his reappearance and ran a solid race in a French Group 2 last time. He ran like a non-stayer here, but whether that was down to the trip alone, or the ground was against him remains to be seen. (op 12-1)

Glen's Diamond was never going that well and the ground was probably just too soft for him. (op 8-1 tchd 10-1 in places)

Hurricane Higgins(IRE) ran a shocker in France last month but he was fitted with blinkers for the first time here and his connections were hopeful he would handle the ground. He again ran poorly, though, and has a few questions to answer now. (op 22-1)

Glencadam Gold(IRE) presumably didn't handle these very different ground conditions. (op 28-1 tchd 33-1)

World Domination(USA) was weak in the betting and, having made the running to the turn in, dropped right out. The ground was probably all against him too. (tchd 9-1)

3106 CORONATION STKS (BRITISH CHAMPIONS' SERIES) (GROUP 1) (FILLIES) 1m (R)

3:45 (3:48) (Class 1) 3-Y-O

£141,925 (£53,800; £26,925; £13,425; £6,725; £3,375) **Stalls** Low

Form | | | | RPR

2-01 **1** **Immortal Verse (IRE)**[12] 2752 3-9-0 109........................ GeraldMosse 11 115
(Robert Collet, France) *stdd s: hld up in last pl: swtchd lft to outside and mde hdwy 2f out: str run to ld over 1f out: stretched out wl and in command thrght fnl f* **8/1**

2-44 **2** *2 1/4* **Nova Hawk**[33] 2137 3-9-0 107................................(t) StephanePasquier 10 110+
(Rod Collet, France) *hld up: hdwy whn nt clr run over 1f out: sn swtchd rt: r.o to take 2nd fnl 110yds: nt pce to trble wnr* **9/2**[2]

-152 **3** *1/2* **Barefoot Lady (IRE)**[37] 2004 3-9-0 104........................... KierenFallon 6 109
(Richard Fahey) *prom: pushed along 3f out: effrt to chal wl over 1f out: nt qckn ent fnl f: styd on u.p but hld after* **16/1**

3-02 **4** *1/2* **I Love Me**[34] 2106 3-9-0 101.. DavidProbert 5 108
(Andrew Balding) *on toes: in tch: rdn 2f out: effrt whn n.m.r jst over 1f out: nt qckn: kpt on u.p ins fnl f but jst lacked pce of ldrs* **14/1**

-522 **5** *shd* **Together (IRE)**[26] 2334 3-9-0 112...................................... RyanMoore 13 108
(A P O'Brien, Ire) *swtg: hld up: pushed along and hdwy over 2f out: swtchd rt and tried to chal over 1f out: kpt on same pce fnl 100yds* **7/2**[1]

3-21 **6** *3/4* **Joviality**[37] 2004 3-9-0 105.. WilliamBuick 3 106
(John Gosden) *prom: pushed along over 2f out: rdn to ld wl over 1f out: sn hdd: nt pce of wnr ins fnl f: no ex fnl 100yds* **10/1**

16-0 **7** *1 3/4* **Memory (IRE)**[47] 1719 3-9-0 111.................................... RichardHughes 9 102+
(Richard Hannon) *racd keenly: hld up: effrt wl over 1f out: sn nt clr run and carried rt: kpt on under hands and heels whn n.d ins fnl f* **10/1**

36-1 **8** *6* **Theyskens' Theory (USA)**[35] 2073 3-9-0 108................. MartinDwyer 8 88
(Brian Meehan) *lw: prom: chsd ldr over 5f out: rdn and chalng wl over 1f out: wknd ent fnl f* **6/1**[3]

-54 **9** *2 3/4* **Claiomh Solais (IRE)**[26] 2334 3-9-0 109........................... KJManning 2 82
(J S Bolger, Ire) *str: led: shkn up to increase pce over 3f out: rdn and hdd wl over 1f out: wknd appr fnl f* **9/1**

2004 **10** *7* **Elshabakiya (IRE)**[27] 2298 3-9-0 94............................. PhilipRobinson 4 66
(Clive Brittain) *racd keenly in midfield: pushed along and outpcd over 2f out: bhd over 1f out* **80/1**

1- **11** *5* **More Than Real (USA)**[224] 7340 3-9-0 113..................... OlivierPeslier 1 54
(Todd Pletcher, U.S.A) *wl made: lw: midfield: pushed along over 2f out: sn wknd: wl bhd over 1f out* **12/1**

16-3 **12** *4 1/2* **Clinical**[14] 2678 3-9-0 100.. SebSanders 12 44
(Sir Mark Prescott Bt) *midfield: pushed along 3f out: n.m.r whn outpcd ent fnl 2f: eased whn wl btn over 1f out* **25/1**

1m 42.75s (2.05) **Going Correction** +0.525s/f (Yiel) **12** Ran SP% **119.3**

Speed ratings (Par 110): **110,107,107,106,106 105,104,98,95,88 83,78**

toteswingers:1&2:£8.30, 2&3:£16.80, 1&3:£31.50 CSF £44.14 CT £574.37 TOTE £8.80: £2.60, £1.90, £6.00; EX 36.60 Trifecta £724.40 Pool: £23544.03 - 24.05 winning units..

Owner R C Strauss **Bred** Kilfrush Stud **Trained** Chantilly, France

■ A 1-2 for French father and son Robert and Rodolphe Collet.

FOCUS

This was an open renewal of the Coronation Stakes but not a strong one, lacking as it did any previous Group 1 winners. It didn't happen in 2008 or in 2010 either if the disqualified Jacqueline Quest is discounted, but in the majority of seasons at least one Guineas winner turns up here. This year Blue Bunting, Golden Lilac and Misty For Me, successful at Newmarket, Longchamp and the Curragh respectively, were absent having already stepped up beyond a mile. The form of the three Classics was still represented, by the second, fourth and fifth at Newmarket, the second and fourth from the Curragh and the fourth home at Longchamp, as well as the 11th home in the latter race who ran out an impressive winner here. The pace was strong and the first two home were the last pair turning into the straight. The winner and second are French trained, strengthening the already strong hand of 3yo fillies in France this year, which also numbers the Prix de Diane 1-2, Golden Lilac and Galikova. The ground complicates things and there are one or two doubts over how reliable this is. The form is on a par with the English and Irish Guineas.

NOTEBOOK

Immortal Verse(IRE) was last of all turning in, but then unleashed a striking turn of foot down the outside to win very comfortably. She had been withdrawn from the Newmarket Classic after playing up in the stalls, when an unconsidered 66-1 chance, and ran on into midfield in an unsatisfactory French Guineas, a race in which her pacemaker Glorious Sight finished second. A win in the Group 2 Prix de Sandringham at Chantilly proved her well-being as well as underlining her effectiveness in soft ground, and she is clearly a high-class filly with more to offer at the top level. The Prix Rothschild at Deauville is likely to be her next target, where Goldikova could well be in opposition. A fast pace is important to her, as is getting her to relax. She has yet to run on a sound surface. (tchd 15-2)

Nova Hawk brought solid form here after finishing fourth in both the English and French Guineas, and is well at home in soft conditions. One place ahead of the winner turning for home, she endured a slightly troublesome passage when picking up ground but it did not affect the result. She has plenty of speed and could drop back to 7f. (op 13-2 tchd 7-1)

Barefoot Lady(IRE)'s connections were worried about the ground, but she got through it well and stayed on bravely for third after racing not far from the pace. The 1,000 Guineas fifth was dropping back in trip after her narrow second to Joviality in the Musidora, and has the option of going back up to 1m2f now. (tchd 20-1 in places)

I Love Me, runner-up to Jersey Stakes second Codemaster in a 7f Listed race latest, had her stamina to prove after fading in the Newmarket Guineas but she belied those concerns with a brave effort in fourth. This was also the first time she has raced around a bend. (op 16-1 tchd 10-1)

Together(IRE) represented the stable successful in this 12 months ago with Lillie Langtry and was sent off favourite. Runner-up in two Guineas, she ran on near the inside to get involved in the battle for the places but the mile looks the outer limit of her stamina and this ground was not ideal. This classy filly is without a win in her last nine starts now, five of them at the top level. (tchd 9-2 in places)

Joviality was John Gosden's only runner after 1,000 Guineas third Maqaasid was taken out. Down in trip after her slender victory over Barefoot Lady in a steadily run Musidora at York, she was more battle-hardened here and led briefly before giving best inside the last. She has more to offer. (op 8-1)

Memory(IRE) all but refused to race in the 1,000 Guineas and missed the French version after coming into season. Last year's Albany Stakes winner had plenty to prove, having disappointed in the Moyglare Stud Stakes on her final start at two, but she went some way to restoring her reputation here. There were no problems at the stalls following her extensive course of schooling and she ran a pleasing race, not given a hard time after running into a spot of trouble when trying to pick up the leaders from the back. The Falmouth Stakes at Newmarket next month looks the ideal target. (op 8-1)

Theyskens' Theory(USA) easily accounted for inferior opposition in a Newmarket Listed race on her return but this was the acid test for a filly who beat Blue Bunting by five lengths in her maiden. She turned for home in second spot but the effort of chasing a fast pace told. She has won in soft ground but is perhaps more at home on a sound surface. Apparently she returned with a slightly high heart rate, but she scoped fine. (op 11-2)

Claiomh Solais(IRE) represented connections of 2008 winner Lush Lashes and finished a neck in front of stablemate Banimpire, Thursday's Ribblesdale winner, in the Irish Guineas. A late-maturing filly who didn't appear at two but was running for the sixth time this season, she set a brisk gallop in the conditions and tried to kick away in the straight, but was swallowed up before the final furlong. Her trainer will be keen to secure some black type for her. (tchd 12-1 in places)

More Than Real(USA), an American challenger, had not been seen since taking the Breeders' Cup Juvenile Fillies' Turf at Churchill Downs last November, and faced a very stiff task attempting to win this first time out. The easy ground was alien to her too and she dropped away in the straight. (op 14-1)

3107 WOLFERTON H'CAP (LISTED RACE) 1m 2f

4:25 (4:25) (Class 1) (0-110,110) 4-Y-O+

£28,385 (£10,760; £5,385; £2,685; £1,345; £675) **Stalls** Low

Form | | | | RPR

-523 **1** **Beachfire**[27] 2289 4-8-9 **98**...(b) WilliamBuick 15 111+
(John Gosden) *lw: stdd s: hld up in last: stl plenty to do and rdn over 2f out: str run and switching rt over 1f out: led ins fnl f: r.o strly and sn clr* **12/1**[3]

1002 **2** *2 1/4* **Lost In The Moment (IRE)**[6] 2909 4-8-11 **100**...(p) MickaelBarzalona 11 108
(Saeed Bin Suroor) *chsd ldrs: rdn and qcknd to ld over 2f out: hrd pressed and drvn ent fnl f: hdd and nt pce of wnr ins fnl f: kpt on* **8/1**[2]

6 **3** *1* **Waydownsouth (IRE)**[14] 2701 4-8-10 **99**.............................. DMGrant 10 105
(Patrick J Flynn, Ire) *t.k.h: hld up wl in tch: rdn and effrt 3f out: hdwy u.p over 1f out: pressed ldr ent fnl f: no ex and outpcd fnl 150yds* **20/1**

2-22 **4** *4 1/2* **Right Step**[14] 2681 4-8-11 **100**.. JimCrowley 12 97
(Alan Jarvis) *lw: stdd and dropped in bhd after s: hld up in rr: effrt and switching lft over 2f out: no imp tl styd on u.p ent fnl f: wnt 4th ins fnl f: no threat to ldrs* **16/1**

-041 **5** *1 3/4* **Bea Remembered**[14] 2676 4-8-11 **100**............................. MartinDwyer 4 94
(Brian Meehan) *t.k.h: hld up in tch: rdn and effrt to chse ldrs jst over 2f out: drvn and unable qck over 1f out: btn 1f out: wknd ins fnl f* **16/1**

-060 **6** *1 3/4* **Gallic Star (IRE)**[4] 2994 4-8-11 **100**.............................. HughBowman 13 90
(Mick Channon) *lw: hld up towards rr: rdn and effrt on outer over 2f out: no real prog and no ch w ldrs 1f out: plugged on fnl f* **40/1**

11-1 **7** *nk* **Green Destiny (IRE)**[48] 1684 4-8-10 **99**........................... MichaelHills 2 88+
(William Haggas) *lw: in tch tl hmpd and dropped to rr after 1f: in last pair and bhd a wall of horses 4f out: nt clr run over 3f out: rdn and sme hdwy towards inner ent fnl 2f: no prog and wl hld over 1f out: wknd ins fnl furlon* **6/4**[1]

41-0 **8** *nse* **Riggins (IRE)**[141] 326 7-9-5 **108**....................................... NeilCallan 8 97
(Ed Walker) *t.k.h: in midfield early: grad stdd bk towards rr: switching rt and effrt u.p 2f out: no hdwy and btn 1f out: wknd ins fnl f* **40/1**

23-0 **9** *3* **Balducci**[36] 2031 4-8-13 **102**.. JimmyFortune 16 85
(Andrew Balding) *t.k.h: chsd ldr: rdn and unable qck wl over 2f out: swtchd rt and struggling 2f out: losing pl and btn whn pushed rt and hmpd over 1f out: n.d after* **25/1**

530- **10** *3/4* **Circumvent**[258] 6562 4-9-4 **107**.. TomQueally 6 89
(Paul Cole) *led: hdd and drvn over 2f out: edgd lft u.p 2f out: wknd over 1f out: wl btn and eased ins fnl f* **20/1**

-132 **11** *8* **Shamali**[41] 1883 6-9-3 **106**........................ RyanMoore 5 72
(William Haggas) *lw: restless in stalls: hld up in midfield: rdn and effrt 2f out: chsd ldrs and drvn over 1f out: keeping on same pce and looked btn whn hmpd 1f out: no ch after and eased ins fnl f* **8/1**[2]

-201 **12** *2* **Resurge (IRE)**[14] 2681 6-9-0 **103**........................ FergusSweeney 1 65
(Stuart Kittow) *in tch short of room hmpd over 9f out: sn rcvrd and chsd ldrs 8f out: rdn and unable qck over 2f out: struggling whn sltly hmpd and swtchd rt wl over 1f out: sn wknd: eased ins fnl f* **16/1**

0-54 **13** *3 ¼* **World Heritage**[41] 1883 5-8-11 **100**........................ DarryllHolland 3 55
(Robert Eddery) *t.k.h: chsd ldrs tl wknd u.p over 2f out: wl bhd and eased ins fnl f* **33/1**

0-10 **14** *20* **Spanish Duke (IRE)**[27] 2290 4-9-0 **103**........................ EddieAhern 7 18
(John Dunlop) *t.k.h: hld up in midfield: shuffled bk towards rr whn nt clr run and hmpd over 3f out: rdn and short--lived effrt over 2f out: wl bhd and eased 1f out: t.o* **8/1**[2]

2m 10.48s (3.48) **Going Correction** +0.625s/f (Yiel) **14** Ran SP% **119.9**
Speed ratings (Par 111): **111,109,108,104,103 102,101,101,99,98 92,90,88,72**
toteswingers:1&2:£11.30, 2&3:£36.20, 1&3:£28.80 CSF £95.49 CT £1911.07 TOTE £13.50: £3.80, £1.90, £6.70; EX 110.60 Trifecta £8167.00 Pool: £11036.60 - 1.00 winning unit.
Owner H R H Princess Haya Of Jordan **Bred** Bridgewater Equine Ltd **Trained** Newmarket, Suffolk
■ Stewards' Enquiry : William Buick two-day ban: careless riding (Jul 1,3)

FOCUS
A similar betting heat to last year, in that the market was headed by a well-backed, short-priced favourite, who was unexposed, well drawn and had pretensions to being a Group horse. However, in contrast to last year, the supposed handicap good thing did not deliver. Probably sound form enough among the principals with a smart performance from the winner.

NOTEBOOK
Beachfire is a bit of a quirky customer but is talented and at his best running on late through beaten horses. The pace was a good one, which he needs, and Buick timed things well, coming from last on the turn in to first inside the final furlong. He gave a couple of rivals a bump along the way as he hung under pressure, but he won on merit. The return of the blinkers was a big plus and, as a son of Indian Haven, who won the Irish 2,000 Guineas in soft ground, it was no great surprise to see him improve for getting to race on this sort of surface. (op 14-1)
Lost In The Moment(IRE) ◆ ran a blinder at Chester last time when finishing fast from off the pace to take second in a tactical affair, and he might have won this if given a more patient ride. He did best of those that raced close to the pace, kicking for home off the turn, and was there to be shot at in the closing stages, appearing to idle in front. While the winner went flying by on his inner, he readily held off Waydownsouth for second place, and he can win a good race (the John Smith's Cup, perhaps) when delivered with his challenge later.
Waydownsouth(IRE) had no ground worries and showed his wellbeing a fortnight earlier with a career-best effort in a Listed race at the Curragh. He's clearly an improving sort, and this was another fine effort. (op 16-1 tchd 25-1 in places)
Right Step has a poor strike-rate but he likes to run on late off a good pace and he got that here. He never looked like winning, though, and the handicapper is likely to remain in charge. (tchd 18-1)
Bea Remembered, who was a bit keen early, might prefer better ground, but this was still a solid effort. (op 14-1)
Gallic Star(IRE) hadn't shown a great deal in three previous runs this season, but she was third in the Ribblesdale last year and the return to this track brought about some improvement. (op 50-1 tchd 33-1)
Green Destiny(IRE) missed the Hunt Cup for this. The ground had come right for him and he appeared to have plenty in his favour, with his trainer confident the longer trip would cause him no problems. Held up out the back alongside the winner, he got a bit messed around early on and, having stuck to the inside from the turn in, didn't really pick up for pressure. Things got a little tight as Riggins edged towards the rail in front of him, but he was going nowhere at the time and this was clearly a very disappointing performance. His Newmarket win tells us he's better than this. Official explanation: jockey said gelding suffered interference shortly after start (op 13-8 tchd 15-8 in places)
Riggins(IRE) has gone well fresh in the past so his absence since January wasn't necessarily a concern, but he's on a stiff mark and his cause wasn't helped by racing keenly. (op 33-1)
Balducci was prominent for a long way and looked to have too much use made of them in a race which favoured closers. (op 20-1)
Circumvent, who looked fit for this reappearance, like Balducci, was prominent for a long way and looked to have too much use made of them in a race which favoured closers. (op 22-1)
Shamali was keeping on when hampered by the winner a furlong out. He weakened quickly afterwards and is better than the bare form suggests. Official explanation: jockey said gelding had no more to give (op 10-1 tchd 11-1)
Spanish Duke(IRE) pulled too hard in the early stages and gave himself no chance of seeing out the race. Official explanation: jockey said gelding ran flat (tchd 7-1)

3108 QUEEN'S VASE (GROUP 3) 2m
5:00 (5:00) (Class 1) 3-Y-O

£34,062 (£12,912; £6,462; £3,222; £1,614; £810) **Stalls** Low

Form RPR

5243 **1** **Namibian (IRE)**[13] 2726 3-9-1 103........................ SilvestreDeSousa 8 106
(Mark Johnston) *midfield: hdwy over 3f out: led jst over 2f out: sn hung rt: hdd narrowly jst ins fnl f: gamely regained slender ld fnl 110yds whn drifting lft: styd on and a doing enough cl home* **7/2**[1]

21 **2** *nk* **Solar Sky**[29] 2219 3-9-1 89........................ TomQueally 9 105
(Sir Henry Cecil) *lw: in tch: effrt and swtchd lft over 2f out: wnt 2nd over 1f out: led narrowly jst ins fnl f: hdd fnl 110yds: continued to chal whn carried lft: styd on but jst hld cl home* **9/2**[2]

3111 **3** *7* **Eternal Heart (IRE)**[13] 2726 3-9-1 91........................ JoeFanning 11 97
(Mark Johnston) *lw: led: increased pce 3f out: hdd jst over 2f out: kpt on u.p after: no ch w front pair ins fnl f* **6/1**[3]

23 **4** *1* **Regent Street (IRE)**[40] 1927 3-9-1 106........................(p) RyanMoore 2 96
(A P O'Brien, Ire) *prom: rdn to chal jst over 2f out: nt qckn over 1f out: styd on same pce ins fnl f: no ch w front pair ins fnl f* **9/2**[2]

0-11 **5** *¾* **Halifax (IRE)**[22] 2435 3-9-1 87........................ RichardHughes 12 95
(Mark Johnston) *racd on outer: a.p: effrt to chal jst over 2f out: nt qckn: kpt on same pce ins fnl f whn n.d to front pair* **7/1**

-222 **6** *3* **Hawaafez**[34] 2108 3-8-12 86........................ RichardHills 10 88
(Marcus Tregoning) *hld up: rdn over 2f out: moved into mod 6th 1f out: nvr a threat* **20/1**

23 **7** *3 ½* **End Or Beginning**[13] 2735 3-9-1 0........................ JamieSpencer 3 87?
(Paul Cole) *hld up: pushed along 3f out: kpt on u.p fr 2f out but nvr able to get nr ldrs: wl btn ins fnl f* **20/1**

5324 **8** *12* **Borug (USA)**[41] 1895 3-9-1 93........................(p) MickaelBarzalona 5 73
(Saeed Bin Suroor) *racd keenly: hld up: u.p 3f out: no imp 2f out: wl bhd over 1f out* **25/1**

2-12 **9** *6* **Ittirad (USA)**[35] 2076 3-9-1 87........................ NeilCallan 6 66
(Roger Varian) *lw: ref to settle: in tch: pushed along 3f out: wknd wl over 1f out* **9/1**

5611 **10** *25* **L'Hermitage (IRE)**[14] 2677 3-9-1 75........................(p) MartinDwyer 7 36
(Brian Meehan) *hld up in rr: u.p over 3f out: bhd fnl 2f: t.o* **50/1**

-033 **11** *56* **Qushchi**[27] 2295 3-8-12 86........................ JimCrowley 1 —
(William Jarvis) *racd keenly: prom: pushed along and wknd over 3f out: bhd fnl 2f: t.o* **20/1**

3m 40.97s (11.97) **Going Correction** +0.725s/f (Yiel) **11** Ran SP% **115.5**
Speed ratings (Par 109): **99,98,95,94,94 92,91,85,82,69 41**
toteswingers:1&2:£3.60, 2&3:£5.60, 1&3:£5.90 CSF £16.98 CT £90.92 TOTE £4.50: £2.00, £2.30, £1.80; EX 20.40 Trifecta £159.90 Pool: £14174.56 - 65.56 winning units..
Owner Sheikh Hamdan Bin Mohammed Al Maktoum **Bred** Hascombe And Valiant Studs **Trained** Middleham Moor, N Yorks
■ Silvestre de Sousa's first Royal Ascot winner.
■ Stewards' Enquiry : Silvestre De Sousa three-day ban: careless riding (Jul 1,3,4)

FOCUS
Subsequent Gold Cup runner-up Patkai was perhaps the best recent winner of this Group 3, while Mastery was third here in 2009 before landing the St Leger. This looked an up-to-scratch field. The pace was fairly steady but it still proved a true test of stamina for these 3-y-os, none of whom had tackled this far before. The first two came well clear as they contested the finish. The form makes a fair bit of sense among the first six, with the winner rated to his Musselburgh latest and the second up a stone on his maiden form. Mark Johnston has a superb record in this event.

NOTEBOOK
Namibian(IRE) gave Mark Johnston his sixth win in the last 11 years. The colt burst to the front in the straight, drifting to the rail as he did so, then edged to his left as he withstood a strong challege from the runner-up. Silvestre De Sousa had his whip in his right hand, the incorrect one, as his mount drifted over, and the pair had to survive a Stewards' enquiry. The son of Cape Cross had run well in defeat in Listed company and off 103 in a Musselburgh handicap earlier this season, but the rise in trip saw him to fine effect here in this better grade. A game performer likely to have further improvement in him, he could go for the St Leger, but would have work to do if he was to beat Nathaniel, for one. (op 9-2 tchd 5-1 in places)
Solar Sky ◆'s trainer first won this event back in 1972, and nearly made it nine victories in all. The chestnut made heavy weather of landing the odds in a maiden at Haydock but much better was expected of him over this extra half-mile. He just allowed Namibian to take first run, but then produced a sweeping burst which took him narrowly to the front, only to be edged out late on. He was being carried to his left by the rallying winner near the finish. He was one of the most inexperienced members of the field and there is more to come from this half-brother to Oaks winner Love Divine. That filly produced St Leger winner Sixties Icon, and that race could come into consideration for this colt. (tchd 4-1 and 5-1 in places)
Eternal Heart(IRE), the winner's stablemate, had notched a hat-trick of victories, two from the front, and he adopted those tactics here, but after trying to wind it up before the straight he was cut down by the first two. He stuck on well enough for third, but the rain perhaps just took the edge off his stamina. He had Namibian behind when winning a valuable handicap at Musselburgh, but was 16lb worse off here. (tchd 7-1 in places)
Regent Street(IRE) acted as pacemaker for Recital in the Ballysax Stakes and Derrinstown Stud Derby Trial this spring, acquitting himself well both times. Equipped with first-time cheekpieces in place of blinkers, he was never too far from the lead but lacked a change of gear as his stamina for this longer trip was put to the test. (op 10-3 tchd 5-1)
Halifax(IRE) ◆, the third of the Johnston trio and representing the same owner as the winner, ran with plenty of credit without quite convincing he truly saw out this longer trip. He can win more races back over a little shorter. (tchd 8-1 in places)
Hawaafez seemed sure to be suited by this greater test of stamina and she was staying on well when it was all over, but in truth she was never in the race. (op 22-1)
End Or Beginning, a lightly raced maiden, was worth a try at this trip, being a half-brother to Jockey Club Cup winner Royal And Regal. He did run on from the back but was not seen with a realistic chance. (op 25-1 tchd 16-1)
Borug(USA) was well held and has yet to prove he acts on soft ground. (op 33-1)
Ittirad(USA) was much too keen and didn't see it out. He could be worth another try over this sort of trip but he does need to settle. (op 8-1)

3109 BUCKINGHAM PALACE STKS (H'CAP) 7f
5:35 (5:37) (Class 2) (0-105,105) 3-Y-O+

£31,155 (£9,330; £4,665; £2,335; £1,165; £585) **Stalls** Centre

Form RPR

-302 **1** **Manassas (IRE)**[41] 1885 6-9-0 **95**........................ MartinDwyer 29 104
(Brian Meehan) *racd stands' side: chsd ldrs: rdn to chse ldr over 2f out: drvn ahd jst over 1f out: kpt on gamely fnl 100yds* **12/1**

1-10 **2** *1* **Excellent Guest**[41] 1885 4-8-9 **90**........................ TomQueally 28 96
(George Margarson) *racd stands' side: hld up in tch: hdwy jst over 2f out: rdn and chsd ldrs over 1f out: drvn and chsd wnr ins fnl f: kpt on but no imp fnl 75yds: 2nd of 10 in gp* **16/1**

0550 **3** *nk* **Striking Spirit**[13] 2727 6-8-10 **91**........................ SebSanders 2 96+
(Tim Easterby) *racd far side tl grad crossed to centre after 2f: in tch: rdn and effrt over 2f out: drvn to chse ldrs over 1f out: kpt on same pce fnl 100yds: 1st of 15 in gp* **50/1**

0-14 **4** *nk* **Decent Fella (IRE)**[27] 2300 5-8-9 **90**........................(v) LiamKeniry 23 95
(Andrew Balding) *racd stands' side: hld up in tch: rdn to chse ldrs 2f out: drvn over 1f out: styd on u.p fnl 100yds: 3rd of 10 in gp* **16/1**

2634 **5** *hd* **Docofthebay (IRE)**[35] 2075 7-9-0 **95**........................(b) IanMongan 32 99
(David Nicholls) *racd stands' side: hld up towards rr: switching rt and hdwy over 2f out: drvn to chse ldrs over 1f out: kpt on u.p fnl 100yds: nvr quite pce to chal ldrs: 4th of 10 in gp* **8/1**[3]

-000 **6** *nk* **Courageous (IRE)**[13] 2727 5-8-7 **88**........................ KierenFallon 31 91
(David Nicholls) *racd stands' side: overall ldr: rdn over 2f out: drvn and hdd jst over 1f out: kpt on same pce fnl 150yds: 5th of 10 in gp* **20/1**

6001 **7** *½* **Smarty Socks (IRE)**[13] 2706 7-8-12 **93**........................ DanielTudhope 25 95
(David O'Meara) *racd stands' side: wnt rt s and s.i.s: in rr: swtchd rt 1/2-way and pushed along: hdwy u.p over 1f out: kpt on wl ins fnl f: nt rch ldrs: 6th of 10 in gp* **20/1**

3312 **8** *5* **Our Jonathan**[6] 2927 4-9-4 **99**........................ FrannyNorton 9 87
(Kevin Ryan) *racd in centre: hld up in midfield: effrt whn bmpd over 2f out: hdwy u.p and chsd ldrs wl over 1f out: sn drvn and unable qck: btn 1f out: eased wl ins fnl f: 2nd of 15 in gp* **5/1**[1]

2000 **9** *¾* **Freeforaday (USA)**[62] 1406 4-8-12 **93**........................ HayleyTurner 22 79
(John Best) *racd stands' side: towards rr: rdn and struggling 3f out: no threat to ldrs but kpt on again ins fnl f: 7th Of 10 in gp* **50/1**

1002 **10** *1 ½* **Across The Rhine (USA)**[40] 1930 5-9-4 **104**........................ HarryBentley(5) 30 86
(Tracey Collins, Ire) *racd stands' side: s.i.s: sn rcvrd and chsd ldr after 1f tl over 2f out: struggling u.p 2f out: wknd over 1f out: wl btn fnl f: 8th of 10 in gp* **25/1**

6-56 **11** *nk* **Moonreach (IRE)**[55] 1533 4-8-8 **94**........................ SHJames(5) 5 76
(James J Hartnett, Ire) *racd in centre: t.k.h: in tch: effrt u.p wl over 2f out: drvn and unable qck ent fnl 2f: wknd over 1f out: 3rd of 15 in gp* **50/1**

-1 **12** *2* **Free For All (IRE)**[41] 1898 4-8-9 **90**........................ JamesDoyle 6 66
(Sylvester Kirk) *racd in centre: chsd gp ldr and prom overall: led gp over 2f out and sn rdn: wknd u.p over 1f out: fdd fnl f: 4th of 15 in gp* **14/1**

5444 **13** *1* **Atlantic Sport (USA)**[98] 6-9-7 **102**........................ HughBowman 10 75
(Mick Channon) *racd in centre: in tch: rdn and effrt to chse ldrs over 2f out: wknd u.p jst over 1f out: fdd ins fnl f: eased towards fin: 5th of 15 in gp* **40/1**

31-0 **14** *2 ¼* **Kalk Bay (IRE)**[76] 1092 4-8-11 **92**................................ JimmyFortune 12 59
(William Haggas) *racd in centre: stdd s: hld up towards rr: effrt: swtchd lft and bmpd rival over 2f out: hdwy u.p 2f out: wknd over 1f out: eased whn no ch ins fnl f: 6th of 15 in gp* **6/1**[2]

1500 **15** *1 ½* **Below Zero (IRE)**[13] 2706 4-8-7 **88**.......................... SilvestreDeSousa 3 51
(Mark Johnston) *racd on far side tl grad crossed to chse ldrs in centre after 2f: rdn over 2f out: wknd u.p over 1f out: 7th of 15 in gp* **50/1**

-600 **16** *¾* **Noble Citizen (USA)**[13] 2706 6-8-8 **89**.............(be) MickaelBarzalona 26 50
(David Simcock) *racd stands' side: hld up towards rr: rdn along over 3f out: sme hdwy u.p over 2f out: wknd wl over 1f out: eased whn no ch ins fnl f: 9th of 10 in gp* **14/1**

0224 **17** *4* **Advanced**[13] 2706 8-8-8 **92**.................................(b) AmyRyan(3) 16 43
(Kevin Ryan) *racd in centre: led gp and prom overall: rdn and struggling over 2f out: wknd wl over 1f out: wl btn fnl f: 8th of 15 in gp* **20/1**

-040 **18** *½* **Castles In The Air**[41] 1885 6-9-5 **100**........................ RichardHughes 14 49
(Richard Fahey) *racd in centre: stdd s and hld up in rr: rdn and effrt over 2f out: wandering lft and rt wl over 1f out: no imp and wl btn 1f out: eased ins fnl f: 9th of 15 in gp* **18/1**

0403 **19** *4 ½* **Kinky Afro (IRE)**[27] 2325 4-9-3 **98**.................................... LukeMorris 18 35
(J S Moore) *racd in centre: s.i.s: a towards rr: rdn and edging rt over 3f out: no ch fnl 2f: 10th of 15 in gp* **25/1**

1000 **20** *4 ½* **Flipando (IRE)**[13] 2717 10-9-1 **96**............................ GrahamGibbons 17 21
(David Barron) *racd in centre: hld up towards rr: rdn and effrt over 2f out: no prog and sn struggling: no ch wl over 1f out: eased ins fnl f: 11th of 15 in gp* **50/1**

3305 **21** *19* **Lowther**[27] 2284 6-9-4 **102**.......................................(be) MartinHarley(3) 15 —
(Alan Bailey) *racd in centre: in tch: rdn and struggling 1/2-way: lost tch jst over 2f out: eased fr over 1f out: t.o: 12th of 15 in gp* **33/1**

-410 **22** *4 ½* **Rakaan (IRE)**[119] 606 4-9-6 **101**..................................... RyanMoore 13 —
(Jamie Osborne) *racd in centre: stdd s: hld up in rr: swtchd rt and rdn 3f out: no hdwy 2f out: eased fr over 1f out: t.o: 13th of 15 in gp* **12/1**

40-0 **23** *13* **King Of Dixie (USA)**[51] 1600 7-9-10 **105**........................ JimCrowley 24 —
(William Knight) *racd stands' side: in tch in midfield: rdn wl over 3f out: lost pl 3f out and sn bhd: eased fr over 1f out: t.o: 10th of 10 in gp* **33/1**

0-40 **24** *6* **Axiom**[55] 1529 7-9-3 **98**.. NeilCallan 21 —
(Ed Walker) *racd in centre: in tch but sn niggled along: drvn and struggling whn edgd rt over 2f out: wl btn and eased fr over 1f out: t.o: 14th of 15 in gp* **10/1**

00-0 **25** *6* **Beauchamp Xerxes**[14] 2679 5-9-3 **98**......................(p) DarryllHolland 11 —
(Gerard Butler) *racd in centre: chsd ldrs but sn pushed along: rdn and struggling 1/2-way: wl bhd and eased fnl 2f: t.o: 15th of 15 in gp* **40/1**

1m 29.71s (2.51) **Going Correction** +0.475s/f (Yiel)
WFA 3 from 4yo+ 9lb **25 Ran SP% 139.4**
Speed ratings (Par 109): **109,107,107,107,106 106,106,100,99,97 97,95,93,91,89 88,84,83,78,73 51,46,31,24,17**
toteswingers:1&2:£31.00, 2&3:£576.00, 1&3:not won. Tote Super 7: Win: Not won Place: Not won. CSF £179.82 CT £9100.06 TOTE £15.30: £3.60, £5.00, £16.50, £4.40; EX 169.10 TRIFECTA Not won..
Owner Mrs R Philipps **Bred** Mrs Rebecca Philipps **Trained** Manton, Wilts

FOCUS
The GoingStick had suggested that the ground on the stands' side was five ticks slower than in the middle and on the far side, and a bigger group did form up the centre of the track, but it was out of the ten-strong stands' side group that the first two emerged, together with six of the next eight home. The winner is rated to his old best and the third is rated back to the form of his Wokingham second last year.

NOTEBOOK
Manassas(IRE), 2lb higher than when runner-up over this C&D in the Victoria Cup last time out, is a tough, reliable performer in these big handicaps, and he finally had his day. He was placed a couple of times last August on good to soft and, while he might not want the ground any worse than this, he handled this surface perfectly well, and obviously had the benefit of racing on the right part of the track. The Bunbury Cup would look the ideal target for him now.
Excellent Guest, a winner over this C&D last autumn on easy ground, had quite a bit of use made of him in the Victoria Cup and appreciated being covered up and ridden with more patience. He's clearly still improving.
Striking Spirit ◆ ran a screamer from stall two and is the one to take from the race. He tracked the leaders on the outer of the far-side group before being sent on inside the final 2f, quickly put distance between himself and rest of his group and stayed on really well to take third, 6l clear of his nearest centre group pursuer. He never raced beyond 6f in 27 starts for previous trainers but, on his second start for Tim Easterby, showed that the distance is far from beyond him, while also confirming his love for this track. This opens up new options for him, and he is clearly capable of winning a similar race off this sort of mark.
Decent Fella(IRE), relatively lightly raced for a 5-y-o, seems to be at his best at this trip and, from a good draw, travelled well into contention before staying on for a place. He remains open to further improvement.
Docofthebay(IRE) looked to have conditions in his favour and, as it turned out, was also drawn on the right side. He ran a solid race.
Courageous(IRE) looked interesting on his best form from last year, which included a narrow defeat in the Ayr Bronze Cup, but he'd shown nothing in three previous starts this term, albeit over 5f. Making the running from his good stands' side draw, he didn't quite see it out, but this was a return to something like his best and he'll be interesting back over 6f.
Smarty Socks(IRE), 5lb higher for his Doncaster win, stayed on from off the pace up the stands' side, but he could never quite land a blow. He might be ideally suited by quicker ground.
Our Jonathan ◆ got a bump from Kalk Bay approaching the 2f marker and, although he stayed on, his jockey let him coast home from more or less a furlong out when his chance of making the places had gone and he was secure in his position. Second home from the centre group, he's probably still on a mark he can win off when things fall kinder. (op 6-1)
Freeforaday(USA) had the advantage of racing in the stands' side group. (tchd 66-1 in a place)
Across The Rhine(USA) had the advantage of racing in the stands' side group. (tchd 20-1)
Moonreach(IRE), drawn low, was third-best from the centre group. This was a fair effort from this son of Chineur, but a strongly run 6f might see him at his very best. (tchd 80-1 in a place)
Free For All(IRE) raced quite freely towards the head of affairs in the centre group, and he paid for that later on. On the plus side, though, he did keep pretty straight under pressure this time. (op 12-1 tchd 16-1 in a place)
Atlantic Sport(USA) hasn't won for a long time and looks held off his current mark. (op 50-1)
Kalk Bay(IRE) came to have his chance out of the centre group but his effort quickly flattened out. He was expected to appreciate these ground conditions but was ultimately disappointing. (op 7-1)
Below Zero(IRE) showed a bit more than of late, leading Striking Spirit briefly towards the far side before edging back towards the larger centre group and holding a prominent position for much of the race. Official explanation: jockey said gelding had no more to give
Noble Citizen(USA) likes it here but he's a fast-ground merchant and this soft surface was no good to him. (op 16-1)
Rakaan(IRE) Official explanation: jockey said gelding had no more to give
Axiom should have been at home on the ground so his performance was very disappointing. (op 14-1 tchd 16-1 in a place)
T/Jkpt: Not won. T/Plt: £2,568.10 to a £1 stake. Pool of £534,672.56 - 151.98 winning tickets. T/Qpdt: £263.80 to a £1 stake. Pool of £36,062.46 - 101.16 winning tickets. DO

2409 AYR (L-H)
Friday, June 17

OFFICIAL GOING: Good to soft (good in places) changing to good to soft (soft in places) after race 4 (7.45)
Wind: Fresh, half behind Weather: Overcast, showers

3110 L&M SURVEY SERVICES APPRENTICE H'CAP 1m
6:10 (6:11) (Class 6) (0-55,54) 4-Y-0+ **£1,942** (£578; £288; £144) **Stalls** Low

Form RPR
3-56 **1** **Botham (USA)**[28] 2260 7-9-1 **53**.............................. GeorgeDowning(3) 8 62
(Jim Goldie) *prom: effrt over 2f out: chsd ldr over 1f out: styd on wl to ld nr fin* **3/1**[2]

40-4 **2** *nk* **Dubai Gem**[23] 2401 5-8-5 **45**.................................. JenniferFerguson(5) 6 53
(Olivia Maylam) *t.k.h: trckd ldrs: led gng wl 2f out: sn rdn: edgd lft 1f out: kpt on: hdd nr fin* **7/2**[3]

0-00 **3** *3* **Coolella (IRE)**[28] 2260 4-8-11 **49**.............................. JustinNewman(3) 9 50
(John Weymes) *cl up: rdn and ev ch over 3f out to 2f out: kpt on same pce ins fnl f* **16/1**

0063 **4** *¾* **Machir Bay**[9] 2809 4-8-10 **45**....................................(p) GeorgeChaloner 1 44
(Keith Dalgleish) *set stdy pce: hdd over 3f out: outpcd over 2f out: rallied ins fnl f: no imp* **11/4**[1]

6000 **5** *1* **Amtired**[13] 2734 5-8-13 **53**.....................................(b) JacobButterfield(5) 7 50
(Brian Ellison) *cl up: hdwy on ins to ld over 3f out: hdd 2f out: sn outpcd* **5/1**

063- **6** *6* **Richo**[226] 7299 5-9-0 **54**... JackDuern(5) 4 37
(Shaun Harris) *missed break: hld up in tch: effrt over 3f out: wknd 2f out* **11/1**

0005 **7** *4* **Rosbertini**[15] 2631 5-8-10 **50**.. RossSmith(5) 3 24
(Linda Perratt) *rrd s: hld up: hdwy on outside over 2f out: wknd wl over 1f out* **18/1**

6-00 **8** *13* **Cold Quest (USA)**[14] 2692 7-8-11 **53**......................... DanielMorgan(7) 5 —
(Linda Perratt) *hld up: outpcd over 2f out: sn btn* **16/1**

1m 47.44s (3.64) **Going Correction** +0.30s/f (Good) **8 Ran SP% 115.9**
Speed ratings (Par 101): **93,92,89,88,87 81,77,64**
toteswingers:1&2:£3.10, 2&3:£18.00, 1&3:£12.60 CSF £14.22 CT £142.17 TOTE £3.10: £1.40, £1.50, £4.10; EX 10.70.
Owner Caledonia Racing **Bred** France Weiner & Neal Hayias **Trained** Uplawmoor, E Renfrews

FOCUS
Persistent rain had softened the going to good to soft with good places. The full width of the track was in use. They went just a steady pace mindful of the conditions and, still closely bunched, they fanned out entering the straight. Weak form, rated around the winner and third.

3111 LIZ AND MARTIN BRAWLEY RUBY WEDDING MAIDEN STKS 7f 50y
6:40 (6:41) (Class 5) 3-Y-0+ **£2,719** (£809; £404; £202) **Stalls** High

Form RPR
4-0 **1** **Spes Nostra**[25] 2361 3-9-3 0.. LeeNewman 7 75
(David Barron) *led to 3f out: cl up: effrt 2f out: led wl ins fnl f: styd on wl* **13/2**[3]

-422 **2** *½* **Moral Issue**[18] 2574 3-9-0 70..................................... PatrickDonaghy(3) 6 73
(Jedd O'Keeffe) *pressed wnr: led 3f out: sn drvn: hdd wl ins fnl f: no ex cl home* **2/1**[2]

04- **3** *7* **Sole Danser (IRE)**[320] 4614 3-9-3 0.............................. RobertWinston 8 55
(B W Hills) *dwlt: hld up: stdy hdwy on outside to chse clr ldrs over 1f out: sn rdn and no imp* **6/4**[1]

4 **4** *½* **Apreslepetitbois**[18] 2574 3-8-12 0.................................. AndrewElliott 3 49
(James Bethell) *t.k.h: trckd ldrs: rdn over 2f out: wknd over 1f out* **25/1**

6-0 **5** *3 ¼* **Patriotic (IRE)**[17] 2596 3-9-3 0.................................. RoystonFfrench 2 45
(Mark Johnston) *sn niggled in tch: drvn and outpcd over 3f out: n.d after* **8/1**

4 **6** *3* **The Fiery Cross**[15] 2631 4-9-12 0.................................... PJMcDonald 4 40
(Ian Semple) *prom: drvn and outpcd over 2f out: sn btn* **11/1**

/ **7** *21* **Toote Forest (USA)** 5 0 7 0.................................... AndrewHeffernan 1 —
(Lisa Williamson) *s.i.s: t.k.h in rr: struggling 1/2-way: sn lost tch* **33/1**

1m 35.29s (1.89) **Going Correction** +0.30s/f (Good)
WFA 3 from 4yo+ 9lb **7 Ran SP% 112.9**
Speed ratings (Par 103): **101,100,92,91,88 84,60**
CSF £19.44 TOTE £7.50: £1.60, £2.10; EX 25.90.
Owner J Cringan & D Pryde **Bred** James A Cringan **Trained** Maunby, N Yorks

FOCUS
The first two battled throughout at a good pace and burnt off the rest. Modest form, with the favourite disappointing.

3112 GLENFIDDICH H'CAP 1m
7:15 (7:15) (Class 5) (0-75,74) 4-Y-0+ **£2,590** (£770; £385; £192) **Stalls** Low

Form RPR
-452 **1** **Daring Dream (GER)**[22] 2413 6-9-0 **70**.......................... GaryBartley(3) 5 83
(Jim Goldie) *cl up on outside: smooth hdwy to ld over 2f out: rdn and edgd lft over 1f out: sn clr* **11/8**[1]

1-46 **2** *5* **Dream Win**[21] 2454 5-9-2 **74**.. DaleSwift(5) 3 76
(Brian Ellison) *pressed ldr: effrt and ev ch over 2f out: nt gng pce of wnr fr over 1f out* **3/1**[2]

0-04 **3** *2* **Bella Noir**[23] 2398 4-9-6 **73**.. AndrewElliott 2 70
(Mrs K Burke) *set modest pce: rdn and hdd over 2f out: sn outpcd* **3/1**[2]

1-00 **4** *shd* **Military Call**[14] 2692 4-8-7 **60**.. PJMcDonald 4 57
(Alistair Whillans) *trckd ldrs: rdn over 2f out: swtchd rt over 1f out: nvr able to chal* **10/1**

5-40 **5** *3 ½* **Key Breeze**[35] 2046 4-8-5 **63**...(t) JulieBurke(5) 1 52
(Kevin Ryan) *dwlt: t.k.h: hld up in tch: rdn over 2f out: sn outpcd* **8/1**[3]

1m 45.37s (1.57) **Going Correction** +0.30s/f (Good) **5 Ran SP% 112.3**
Speed ratings (Par 103): **104,99,97,96,93**
CSF £5.94 TOTE £2.40: £1.40, £1.80; EX 5.60.
Owner George Barclay & Graeme McGinlay **Bred** Gestut Auenquelle **Trained** Uplawmoor, E Renfrews

FOCUS
Not that strong a contest and they went just a steady pace. The winner didn't need to improve much.

3113 CLYDE COAST CONTRACTS H'CAP 7f 50y
7:45 (7:46) (Class 4) (0-85,82) 4-Y-0+ **£5,180** (£1,541; £770; £384) **Stalls** High

Form RPR
00-1 **1** **Pravda Street**[13] 2732 6-8-10 **76**...................................... DaleSwift(5) 5 89+
(Brian Ellison) *early ldr: chsd ldr: led over 2f out: pushed clr fr over 1f out: readily* **5/2**[1]

1-24 **2** 4 ½ **Clumber Place**[3] 3026 5-9-1 **76**.................................... RobertWinston 2 77
(Richard Guest) *t.k.h early: sn led: c to centre st: hdd over 2f out: kpt on same pce fr over 1f out* **3/1**[2]

-046 **3** 1 ¼ **Coolminx (IRE)**[16] 2620 4-9-7 **82**.................................. FrederikTylicki 6 80
(Richard Fahey) *t.k.h: prom: outpcd over 2f out: rallied fnl f: no imp* **9/2**

-103 **4** 2 ¼ **Music Festival (USA)**[13] 2732 4-8-5 **66**........................ AndrewMullen 3 58
(Jim Goldie) *prom: rdn over 2f out: sme hdwy appr fnl f: no imp* **7/2**[3]

-140 **5** 3 **Khandaq (USA)**[18] 2545 4-9-0 **75**.............................. AndrewHeffernan 4 59
(Keith Dalgleish) *trckd ldrs: rdn over 2f out: hung lft and wknd over 1f out* **9/1**

133- **6** 15 **Social Rhythm**[238] 7055 7-8-6 **67**.................................... PJMcDonald 7 12
(Alistair Whillans) *hld up: struggling over 2f out: sn lost tch* **9/1**

1m 34.62s (1.22) **Going Correction** +0.30s/f (Good) **6** Ran SP% **114.0**
Speed ratings (Par 105): **105,99,98,95,92 75**
toteswingers:1&2:£2.90, 2&3:£2.30, 1&3:£4.10 CSF £10.54 TOTE £3.60: £2.50, £1.30; EX 9.60.
Owner Ms Z Hatcher **Bred** R A Instone **Trained** Norton, N Yorks

FOCUS
The three horses most suited by easier ground filled the first three places, though none were a match for the winner who romped away. The form is rated around the runner-up.

3114 AKELA CONSTRUCTION H'CAP 6f
8:20 (8:21) (Class 4) (0-80,79) 3-Y-O **£4,857** (£1,445; £722; £360) **Stalls** Centre

Form RPR

5-1 **1** **Namwahjobo (IRE)**[18] 2574 3-9-2 **74**................................ LeeNewman 5 88
(Jim Goldie) *rrd s: sn prom: rdn to ld over 1f out: drew clr ins fnl f* **7/2**[2]

4352 **2** 4 ½ **Tro Nesa (IRE)**[22] 2411 3-8-12 **75**.................................... DaleSwift(5) 4 75
(Ann Duffield) *trckd ldrs: drvn and outpcd over 2f out: rallied over 2f out: wnt 2nd wl ins fnl f: no ch w wnr* **13/8**[1]

0004 **3** 1 ¾ **Strictly Pink (IRE)**[6] 2908 3-9-4 **79**................................ AmyBaker(3) 7 73
(Alan Bailey) *in tch: hdwy and ev ch over 1f out: sn rdn: lost 2nd and no ex wl ins fnl f* **8/1**

1-40 **4** 2 **Normandy Maid**[24] 2391 3-8-13 **71**................................ FrederikTylicki 3 59
(Richard Fahey) *hld up in tch: drvn and outpcd over 2f out: sme hdwy over 1f out* **13/2**[3]

603 **5** 9 **Alkhawarah (USA)**[23] 2402 3-8-4 **62**.......................... RoystonFfrench 1 21
(Mark Johnston) *prom: pushed along after 2f: rallied: wknd wl over 1f out* **7/1**

-110 **6** 6 **Finn's Rainbow**[24] 2391 3-8-7 **70**.................................... JulieBurke(5) 6 —
(Kevin Ryan) *disp ld to over 2f out: sn rdn: wknd wl over 1f out* **10/1**

16- **P** **Sweet Cheeks (IRE)**[335] 4150 3-8-9 **67**.......................... PJMcDonald 2 —
(Linda Perratt) *led tl rdn and hdd over 1f out: wknd qckly ins fnl f: p.u and dismntd nr fin* **14/1**

1m 16.04s (3.64) **Going Correction** +0.45s/f (Yiel) **7** Ran SP% **113.0**
Speed ratings (Par 101): **101,95,92,90,78 70,—**
toteswingers:1&2:£3.70, 2&3:£1.50, 1&3:£5.00 CSF £9.37 TOTE £4.70: £1.60, £1.20; EX 7.40.
Owner Ambrose Turnbull **Bred** Rathbarry Stud **Trained** Uplawmoor, E Renfrews

FOCUS
The going had changed to good to soft with soft places by the fifth race. This was not that competitive and they finished strung out, but take nothing away from an impressive winner who rates a 10lb personal best.

3115 WEDDINGS AT WESTERN HOUSE HOTEL H'CAP 1m 5f 13y
8:50 (8:50) (Class 5) (0-75,75) 4-Y-O+ **£2,784** (£828; £414; £206) **Stalls** Low

Form RPR

-606 **1** **Simonside**[21] 2459 8-8-10 **69**.. DaleSwift(5) 4 78
(Brian Ellison) *trckd ldrs: led over 2f out: edgd lft ins fnl f: hld on wl* **7/1**

4-13 **2** nk **Pokfulham (IRE)**[7] 2892 5-8-9 **63**..............................(v) AndrewMullen 1 71
(Jim Goldie) *t.k.h early: in tch: effrt and swtchd lft 2f out: kpt on ins fnl f: a hld* **11/8**[1]

4-54 **3** 4 ½ **Puy D'Arnac (FR)**[20] 2364 8-9-0 **68**.............................. RobertWinston 8 69
(George Moore) *hld up: smooth hdwy to trck ldrs over 2f out: sn rdn: one pce over 1f out* **6/1**[3]

540- **4** ½ **Forrest Flyer (IRE)**[264] 6397 7-9-0 **68**.............................. LeeNewman 3 68
(Jim Goldie) *trckd ldrs: rdn and ev ch over 3f out to over 2f out: one pce over 1f out* **12/1**

-434 **5** 1 ¾ **The Oil Magnate**[79] 1036 6-9-7 **75**.............................. FrederikTylicki 6 73
(Michael Dods) *hld up: stdy hdwy whn nt clr run over 2f out: sn rdn: fnd little over 1f out* **10/1**

-360 **6** 8 **Chookie Hamilton**[28] 2262 7-9-7 **75**................................ PJMcDonald 5 60
(Keith Dalgleish) *cl up: led over 3f out to over 2f out: wknd over 1f out* **9/1**

6006 **7** 63 **Cat O' Nine Tails**[7] 2888 4-9-6 **74**................................ RoystonFfrench 2 —
(Mark Johnston) *led: rdn and hdd over 3f out: lost tch over 2f out: eased* **4/1**[2]

3m 2.25s (8.25) **Going Correction** +0.45s/f (Yiel) **7** Ran SP% **115.7**
Speed ratings (Par 103): **92,91,89,88,87 82,43**
toteswingers:1&2:£6.40, 2&3:£6.10, 1&3:£10.50 CSF £17.55 CT £62.62 TOTE £9.80: £7.00, £1.20; EX 23.10.
Owner Racing Management & Training Ltd **Bred** Keith Richardson **Trained** Norton, N Yorks

FOCUS
The winner went for home from 2f out and held off the ever-gaining challenge of the favourite and they pulled clear of the rest. Ordinary form with the winner rated back to his best.

3116 GUESTS OF PRINCESS ROYAL EVENTS CENTRE H'CAP 1m 2f
9:20 (9:21) (Class 6) (0-65,65) 3-Y-O **£2,047** (£604; £302) **Stalls** Low

Form RPR

5-52 **1** **Retreat Content (IRE)**[21] 2449 3-8-12 **61**........................ DaleSwift(5) 5 65
(Linda Perratt) *trckd ldr to over 4f out: cl up: rdn to ld over 1f out: edgd lft: hld on gamely ins fnl f* **8/1**

0-03 **2** ½ **Damascus Symphony**[25] 2349 3-9-0 **58**........................ AndrewElliott 1 61
(James Bethell) *led: rdn over 3f out: hdd over 1f out: rallied: hld towards fin* **4/1**[3]

0-00 **3** shd **Henrys Gift (IRE)**[24] 2392 3-8-13 **57**.......................... FrederikTylicki 9 60
(Michael Dods) *hld up: drvn and outpcd 3f out: rallied over 1f out: styd on wl ins fnl f* **14/1**

6-54 **4** 2 ¼ **Purkab**[21] 2465 3-8-10 **57**.. GaryBartley(3) 4 55
(Jim Goldie) *hld up in tch: drvn and outpcd over 2f out: rallied over 1f out: kpt on same pce ins fnl f* **3/1**[2]

0403 **5** ½ **Commander Veejay**[10] 2786 3-8-2 **46** oh1............(p) AndrewHeffernan 3 43
(Brian Rothwell) *hld up: rdn over 3f out: sme hdwy wl over 1f out: no imp ins fnl f* **9/1**

0421 **6** hd **Jeu De Vivre (IRE)**[13] 2730 3-9-7 **65**.......................... RoystonFfrench 7 62
(Mark Johnston) *in tch: drvn and outpcd over 3f out: rallied over 1f out: kpt on: nrst fin* **5/2**[1]

544 **7** 4 ½ **Aimee Tricks**[21] 2461 3-8-5 **52** ow3.......................... PatrickDonaghy(3) 6 40
(Ian Semple) *cl up: chal over 3f out: rdn and wknd appr fnl f* **12/1**

650 **8** 2 ¾ **Abernethy (IRE)**[35] 2058 3-8-6 **50**.................................... PJMcDonald 2 32
(Linda Perratt) *trckd ldrs: smooth hdwy over 2f out: rdn and wknd appr fnl f* **14/1**

2m 19.71s (7.71) **Going Correction** +0.45s/f (Yiel) **8** Ran SP% **115.7**
Speed ratings (Par 97): **87,86,86,84,84 84,80,78**
toteswingers:1&2:£6.30, 2&3:£9.50, 1&3:£36.60 CSF £40.48 CT £445.34 TOTE £12.60: £3.30, £2.20, £4.60; EX 57.70.
Owner Jackton Racing Club **Bred** Darley **Trained** East Kilbride, S Lanarks

FOCUS
Moderate fare run at an ordinary early pace, with the first two racing prominently throughout. The winner is rated back close to his early form.
T/Plt: £18.90 to a £1 stake. Pool of £33,800.33 - 1,300.75 winning tickets. T/Qpdt: £3.90 to a £1 stake. Pool of £3,027.00 - 563.18 winning tickets. RY

2874 GOODWOOD (R-H)
Friday, June 17

OFFICIAL GOING: Soft
First 2f of 1m course dolled out 5yds, Top bend out 3yds and lower bend out 4yds.
Wind: quite strong against Weather: persistent rain sometimes heavy

3117 TANQUERAY MAIDEN AUCTION FILLIES' STKS 6f
6:20 (6:21) (Class 4) 2-Y-O **£3,885** (£1,156; £577; £288) **Stalls** High

Form RPR

64 **1** **My Solitaire (IRE)**[17] 2580 2-8-13 0.................................... AdamKirby 5 71
(Clive Cox) *trckd ldrs: rdn over 2f out: chal ent fnl f: led fnl 100yds: rdn out* **11/8**[1]

5 **2** ½ **Alice's Dancer (IRE)**[27] 2302 2-8-13 0.......................... RichardMullen 7 69+
(William Muir) *awkward away: sn prom: rdn to ld jst over 2f out: hdd ins fnl f: kpt on but no ex* **16/1**

6 **3** 4 **Stellar Express (IRE)**[11] 2767 2-8-8 0.......................... WilliamCarson 1 52
(B W Hills) *s.i.s: in last pair: pushed along 3f out: rdn and styd on fr over 1f out* **9/2**[3]

0 **4** 1 ¾ **Zuzu Angel (IRE)**[11] 2767 2-8-12 0.................................... ShaneKelly 2 51+
(William Knight) *hld up bhd ldrs: pushed along 3f out: styd on fr over 1f out* **13/2**

0 **5** shd **Kathryn Perry (IRE)**[10] 2787 2-8-5 0.......................... LouisBeuzelin(3) 6 46
(Andrew Haynes) *led tl rdn jst over 2f out: wknd fnl f* **50/1**

6 3 ¼ **Guava** 2-8-13 0.. EddieAhern 4 42
(Richard Hannon) *chsd ldrs: rdn 4f out: wknd 2f out* **3/1**[2]

04 **7** 6 **Nude (IRE)**[6] 2901 2-8-7 0.. ChrisCatlin 3 18
(Sylvester Kirk) *in tch: rdn over 3f out: wknd over 2f out* **9/1**

1m 17.22s (5.02) **Going Correction** +0.50s/f (Yiel) **7** Ran SP% **116.5**
Speed ratings (Par 92): **86,85,80,77,77 73,65**
toteswingers:1&2:£6.30, 2&3:£6.50, 1&3:£1.90 CSF £27.05 TOTE £2.60: £1.10, £5.90; EX 31.30.
Owner T Y Bissett **Bred** Highfort Stud **Trained** Lambourn, Berks
■ Stewards' Enquiry : Adam Kirby two-day ban: used whip with excessive frequency (Jul 4-5)

FOCUS
After 9mm of rain during the day the going was changed to soft. The favourite had to work hard to get past an outsider in this fillies' maiden in which none of the other fancied runners got involved. The third and fourth set the level.

NOTEBOOK
My Solitaire(IRE) set the standard on her close fourth from an unfavourable draw at Leicester last month when she finished just ahead of subsequent Queen Mary third Caledonia Lady. She had to show plenty of determination but this daughter of top-class French five-time 5f-1m soft-ground winner Clodovil handled the conditions and eventually got on top in the closing stages. The form looks a bit suspect but this half-sister to very useful 6f winner Kaldoun Kingdom and useful 1m-1m1f French winner Mary Boleyn, has some staying power and should be open to further progress. (op 13-8 tchd 7-4)
Alice's Dancer(IRE) had a negative debut experience at Lingfield, where she reared over backwards and galloped loose to the start before finishing tailed off, but this sister to a couple of 2-y-o winners deserves plenty of credit for a big run under a prominent ride against the stands' rail on this second start.
Stellar Express(IRE) did some encouraging late work in a Windsor maiden on debut and it was a similar story here from a filly who should get better with time and distance. (op 11-2 tchd 4-1)
Zuzu Angel(IRE) was never involved but stayed on when it was all over, running near her debut form when she finished just behind Stellar Express. (op 11-2)
Kathryn Perry(IRE) was always tailed off on her debut, but she outran her 50-1 price for a long way here before getting tired. Official explanation: jockey said filly hung right-handed (op 40-1)
Guava, a £30,000 Kyllachy first foal of a dual 1m-1m2f winner at two, was prominent in the betting and showed some early speed but she looked inexperienced when the leaders cranked it up and couldn't find a response. (op 7-2)

3118 WAVE FM STKS (H'CAP) 1m 1f 192y
6:50 (6:53) (Class 5) (0-75,75) 3-Y-O **£2,590** (£770; £385; £192) **Stalls** Low

Form RPR

2-04 **1** **Pandorica**[7] 2885 3-9-1 **69**.. AdamKirby 1 76
(Clive Cox) *chsd ldrs: rdn over 3f out: led over 1f out: styd on wl: drvn out* **8/1**

4540 **2** ¾ **Persian Herald**[14] 2664 3-9-3 **71**.................................... RichardMullen 5 75
(William Muir) *s.i.s: towards rr: hdwy fr 3f out: sn rdn: swtchd rt and styd on ins fnl f: a being hld* **12/1**

00-0 **3** ½ **Korngold**[35] 2064 3-8-8 **62**.. EddieAhern 11 65
(John Dunlop) *slowly away: towards rr: rdn and hdwy over 2f out: swtchd rt ins fnl f: styd on* **8/1**

06-1 **4** 2 ½ **Robin Hoods Bay**[30] 2196 3-9-7 **75**................................ GeorgeBaker 8 73+
(Edward Vaughan) *hld up towards rr: hdwy over 3f out: rdn to chse ldrs over 2f out: styd on ins fnl f* **3/1**[1]

6-42 **5** shd **Swaninstockwell (IRE)**[7] 2885 3-7-13 **58**.............. JemmaMarshall(5) 9 56
(Pat Phelan) *t.k.h: led: rdn: drifted lft and hdd over 1f out: no ex ins fnl f* **5/1**[2]

000- **6** 9 **Mujarah (IRE)**[238] 7057 3-8-6 **60**.................................... ChrisCatlin 6 40
(John Dunlop) *sme late prog: mainly towards rr* **20/1**

4-60 **7** 14 **Marie Rose**[21] 2458 3-8-12 **69**.................................... LouisBeuzelin(3) 4 21
(Brian Meehan) *a towards rr* **11/1**

22-0 **8** ¾ **Songsmith**[52] 1580 3-9-7 **75**.. WilliamCarson 3 25
(Lucy Wadham) *t.k.h: trckd ldrs: rdn 4f out: sn wknd* **8/1**

1312 **9** 3 ¼ **Jack's Revenge (IRE)**[17] 2583 3-9-6 **74**..................(tp) TonyCulhane 14 18
(George Baker) *chsd ldrs: rdn 4f out: sn wknd* **5/1**[2]

44-3 **10** 20 **Kyllachy Spirit**[37] 1998 3-9-5 **73**.................................... ShaneKelly 10 —
(William Knight) *chsd ldrs: rdn over 3f out: sn wknd* **16/1**

3545 **11** *11* **Informed Award**[14] 2688 3-9-5 **73** .... WilliamBuick 13 —
(John Gosden) *racd wd but in tch: rdn and effrt 3f out: sn hung rt and wknd: eased* **13/2**[3]
2m 15.8s (7.80) **Going Correction** +0.70s/f (Yiel) **11** Ran SP% **131.7**
Speed ratings (Par 99): **96,95,95,93,92 85,74,73,71,55 46**
toteswingers:1&2:£31.00, 2&3:£34.30, 1&3:£20.90 CSF £112.09 CT £822.99 TOTE £10.70: £2.80, £4.60, £3.40; EX 120.50.
Owner C V Cruden **Bred** Ambersham Stud **Trained** Lambourn, Berks

FOCUS
There was a lively market for this competitive handicap. The pace was steady but it was a war of attrition in the closing stages and the first five pulled clear. Ordinary form.
Jack's Revenge(IRE) Official explanation: jockey said colt had no more to give
Informed Award Official explanation: jockey said colt had no more to give

3119 GOODWOOD HOTEL MAIDEN FILLIES' STKS 1m 1f
7:25 (7:26) (Class 5) 3-Y-0+ **£2,590** (£770; £385; £192) **Stalls** Low

Form RPR
-324 **1** **Rainbow Springs**[8] 2840 3-9-0 100 .... WilliamBuick 1 83+
(John Gosden) *mde all: drew readily clr over 1f out: heavily eased towards fin* **2/7**[1]
0 **2** *7* **Queen Of Epirus**[14] 2689 3-9-0 0 .... TonyCulhane 7 57
(George Baker) *trckd ldrs: rdn 3f out: sn chsd wnr but nvr any ch fr over 1f out: kpt on same pce* **28/1**
3 *3/4* **Minaret (IRE)** 3-9-0 0 .... ChrisCatlin 5 55
(Mahmood Al Zarooni) *s.i.s: hdwy to trck ldr after 2f: rdn over 3f out: sn hld: kpt on same pce* **7/2**[2]
5 **4** *2 3/4* **County Hotel (IRE)**[14] 2689 4-9-11 0 .... FrankieMcDonald 4 50
(Barry Brennan) *s.i.s: hdwy into 4th after 3f: rdn over 3f out: one pce fnl 2f* **33/1**
00 **5** *8* **Rachael's Ruby**[37] 1998 4-9-8 0 .... JohnFahy(3) 2 33
(Roger Teal) *trckd ldr: effrt 3f out: wknd 2f out* **25/1**
0-0 **6** *22* **Unbeatable**[32] 2157 3-9-0 0 .... ShaneKelly 6 —
(William Knight) *chsd ldrs for 3f: sn in rr and struggling: t.o fnl 3f* **16/1**[3]
2m 4.66s (8.36) **Going Correction** +0.70s/f (Yiel)
WFA 3 from 4yo 11lb **6** Ran SP% **116.1**
Speed ratings (Par 100): **90,83,83,80,73 54**
toteswingers:1&2:£3.40, 2&3:£4.10, 1&3:£1.10 CSF £15.68 TOTE £1.40: £1.10, £9.00; EX 10.80.
Owner George Strawbridge **Bred** George Strawbridge **Trained** Newmarket, Suffolk

FOCUS
The Group 1-placed hot favourite had no trouble capitalizing on a golden opportunity in a maiden that had very little strength in depth. She was value for extra but probably ran more in line with this year's form than last.

3120 CAPITAL FM STKS (H'CAP) 1m 6f
7:55 (7:58) (Class 3) (0-95,94) 4-Y-0+
£7,165 (£2,145; £1,072; £537; £267; £134) **Stalls** High

Form RPR
0-04 **1** **Chiberta King**[34] 2107 5-9-4 **91** .... LiamKeniry 5 106+
(Andrew Balding) *trckd ldr: led after 3f: drew wl clr over 1f out: heavily eased ins fnl f* **17/2**
02-2 **2** *3 1/4* **Plato (JPN)**[27] 2285 4-8-13 **86** .... IanMongan 13 90
(Sir Henry Cecil) *hld up: pushed along and hdwy over 4f out: rdn in 4th over 3f out: styd on to go 2nd ins fnl f: nvr any ch w heavily eased wnr* **5/2**[2]
30-5 **3** *1 1/2* **Western Pearl**[34] 2098 4-9-6 **93** .... ShaneKelly 2 95
(William Knight) *led after 1f: hdd after 3f: chsd wnr: rdn over 2f out: wl hld by wnr fr over 1f out: no ex whn lost 2nd ins fnl f* **8/1**[3]
6-43 **4** *7* **Zuider Zee (GER)**[13] 2716 4-9-5 **92** .... WilliamBuick 10 85
(John Gosden) *little s.i.s: hdwy to trck ldrs after 2f: rdn over 3f out: wknd jst over 1f out* **15/8**[1]
0000 **5** *11* **Sand Skier**[14] 2681 4-8-3 **76** .... JoeFanning 1 53
(Mark Johnston) *led for 1f: trckd ldrs: rdn over 3f out: sn one pce: wknd over 1f out* **8/1**[3]
2-10 **6** *25* **Warne's Way (IRE)**[36] 2034 8-8-2 **75** oh2 .... (b) LukeMorris 3 17
(Brendan Powell) *in tch tl dropped in rr over 6f out: sn struggling: no ch fr 4f out: virtually p.u* **9/1**
3310 **7** *4 1/2* **Admirable Duque (IRE)**[32] 2156 5-8-0 **76** ow1 .... (p) SophieDoyle(3) 8 12
(Dominic Ffrench Davis) *s.i.s: in last pair: rdn over 3f out: nvr any imp: wknd over 1f out: virtually p.u* **25/1**
20/5 **8** *36* **Harry Tricker**[48] 1679 7-9-1 **88** .... (p) GeorgeBaker 9 —
(Gary Moore) *hld up: rdn 3f out: wknd 2f out: virtually p.u* **8/1**[3]
3m 13.39s (9.79) **Going Correction** +0.70s/f (Yiel) **8** Ran SP% **121.1**
Speed ratings (Par 107): **100,98,97,93,87 72,70,49**
toteswingers:1&2:£6.40, 2&3:£5.80, 1&3:£9.50 CSF £32.00 CT £184.87 TOTE £11.50: £2.70, £1.70, £1.80; EX 40.50.
Owner The Pink Hat Racing Partnership **Bred** Watership Down Stud **Trained** Kingsclere, Hants
■ Stewards' Enquiry : Sophie Doyle two-day ban: failing to ride out for 6th (Jul 1,3)

FOCUS
A good staying handicap. They were tightly grouped for a long way but well strung out at the end. The winner is rated value for 8l and back to his best, but the form is not totally convincing.

NOTEBOOK
Chiberta King got back to form in cheekpieces when a front-running fourth in bid for a repeat success in 1m6f Newmarket handicap last month. The defection of several confirmed front-runners was a bonus to his cause and he fought of all potential dangers before romping clear with headgear discarded to record a fourth win. He could face a sharp rise in mark after this but is still relatively lightly raced for his age and was a comfortable winner off 3lb higher on fast ground at Newmarket last spring. (op 11-1)
Plato(JPN) was a maiden winner on slow ground, and pushed a well backed Mark Johnston-trained springer all the way in a Chester handicap last month, but he couldn't pose a serious threat off 2lb higher here. (op 11-4)
Western Pearl ran respectably under a prominent ride back in a handicap, but she is still paying the price in handicapping terms for her third in a 1m6f Listed Newmarket event last September and may need to drop back down the weights.
Zuider Zee(GER) shaped like a return to this trip would suit when eye-catcher at Ascot and Epsom recently, but his promising effort flattened out and the soft ground may have dulled his powers. A progressive triple 1m2f-1m4f winner in 2010, he could be worth another chance back on quick ground next time. (op 7-4 tchd 2-1)
Sand Skier attracted support in his bid to revive on his first run off a mark in the 70s, but he was left behind when the pace quickened in the straight. (op 12-1)

Harry Tricker Official explanation: jockey said gelding had no more to give

3121 HARDWARE ASSOCIATES FILLIES' STKS (H'CAP) 7f
8:30 (8:30) (Class 4) (0-85,85) 3-Y-0+ **£4,533** (£1,348; £674; £336) **Stalls** Low

Form RPR
2-42 **1** **Valencha**[7] 2876 4-9-1 **72** .... RichardHughes 2 81+
(Hughie Morrison) *trckd ldr: rdn over 2f out: led over 1f out: sn edgd rt whn pressed: kpt on wl: on top at fin* **6/5**[1]
-201 **2** *1/2* **Russian Rave**[18] 2566 5-9-7 **78** .... SebSanders 7 86
(Jonathan Portman) *s.i.s: trckd front 3: rdn 2f out: chal jst over 1f out: sn edgd lft: kpt on: hld nr fin* **4/1**[3]
1300 **3** *2 1/2* **Chilli Green**[15] 2647 4-9-11 **82** .... DaneO'Neill 5 83
(John Akehurst) *led: rdn and hdd over 1f out: kpt on same pce: regained 3rd nr fin* **5/2**[2]
221- **4** *1* **Zing Wing**[270] 6247 3-8-11 **77** .... JimmyFortune 4 72
(Paul Cole) *trckd ldng pair: rdn 2f out: chal over 1f out: 3/4 l 3rd and styng on at same pce whn squeezed out ins fnl f: lost 3rd sn after* **9/2**
1m 31.32s (4.42) **Going Correction** +0.70s/f (Yiel)
WFA 3 from 4yo+ 9lb **4** Ran SP% **112.2**
Speed ratings (Par 102): **102,101,98,97**
CSF £6.50 TOTE £2.10; EX 9.30.
Owner Pangfield Partners **Bred** T J Billington **Trained** East Ilsley, Berks

FOCUS
It was very gloomy before this fillies' handicap which was weakened by four withdrawals. The pace was reasonable and the winner is generally progressive.

3122 GOODWOOD FARM SHOP STKS (H'CAP) 6f
9:00 (9:00) (Class 5) (0-75,75) 3-Y-0 **£2,729** (£806; £403) **Stalls** High

Form RPR
6-20 **1** **Da Ponte**[31] 2180 3-9-5 **73** .... ShaneKelly 4 79
(Walter Swinburn) *chsd ldrs: rdn 2f out: led over 1f out: edgd rt: r.o: drvn out* **13/2**[3]
54-5 **2** *1/2* **Aristeia**[5] 2963 3-8-12 **66** .... RichardHughes 1 70+
(Richard Hannon) *hld up bhd: pushed along and hdwy over 1f out: r.o wl through horses ins fnl f: nrest finsh whn wnt 2nd cl home* **8/1**
64-0 **3** *nk* **Cocohatchee**[15] 2646 3-9-4 **72** .... IanMongan 13 75
(Pat Phelan) *chsd ldrs: rdn 2f out: kpt on ins fnl f: no ex whn lost 2nd nr fin* **8/1**
4151 **4** *nse* **Bahia Emerald (IRE)**[9] 2827 3-9-0 **68** 6ex .... DarryllHolland 2 71
(Jeremy Noseda) *mid-div: hdwy over 2f out: sn rdn: ev ch wl over 1f out: wandered ent fnl f: no ex whn lost disp 2nd nr fin* **2/1**[1]
-463 **5** *2* **Arctic Mirage**[17] 2582 3-8-13 **67** .... (b[1]) LukeMorris 6 63
(Michael Blanshard) *s.i.s: towards rr: drvn and hdwy over 2f out: kpt on same pce ins fnl f* **10/1**
-130 **6** *2* **Golden Taurus (IRE)**[30] 2200 3-9-6 **74** .... SebSanders 8 64
(J W Hills) *hld up: pushed along over 3f out: hdwy and effrt over 2f out: fdd ins fnl f* **11/1**
0-30 **7** *1 1/4* **Obiter Dicta**[34] 2102 3-9-2 **70** .... DaneO'Neill 7 56
(Henry Candy) *s.i.s: towards rr: rdn over 2f out: styd on wout troubling ldrs* **5/1**[2]
155 **8** *2 3/4* **Shostakovich (IRE)**[11] 2757 3-9-4 **72** .... (p) JamesDoyle 5 49
(Sylvester Kirk) *prom: rdn and ev ch 2f out: fdd ins fnl f* **16/1**
4204 **9** *1/2* **Reginald Claude**[11] 2772 3-9-3 **71** .... LiamKeniry 9 47
(Mark Usher) *mid-div: rdn 2f out: kpt on same pce* **28/1**
-336 **10** *4 1/2* **His Grace (IRE)**[59] 1449 3-8-13 **67** .... FrankieMcDonald 3 28
(Andrew Haynes) *mid-div: rdn over 2f out: wknd over 1f out* **20/1**
36 **11** *3/4* **Hoover**[30] 2200 3-9-5 **73** .... StephenCraine 12 32
(Jim Boyle) *led: rdn and hdd over 1f out: sn wknd* **11/1**
1m 15.23s (3.03) **Going Correction** +0.50s/f (Yiel) **11** Ran SP% **125.4**
Speed ratings (Par 99): **99,98,97,97,95 92,90,87,86,80 79**
toteswingers:1&2:£5.30, 2&3:£9.50, 1&3:£5.90 CSF £61.82 CT £442.93 TOTE £8.20: £2.10, £3.70, £3.40; EX 100.80.
Owner Mrs Bettine Evans **Bred** R P Williams **Trained** Aldbury, Herts

FOCUS
A fair sprint handicap. It was run at a strong pace and they raced up the centre of the track. The form is rated around the third.
T/Plt: £664.40 to a £1 stake. Pool of £52,102.01 - 57.24 winning units. T/Qpdt: £29.20 to a £1 stake. Pool of £4,832.50 - 122.33 winning units. TM

2724 MUSSELBURGH (R-H)
Friday, June 17

OFFICIAL GOING: Good (6.4)
Bottom bend moved out 3m adding 24m to races on round course.
Wind: light, half behind Weather: Cloudy

3123 BALFOUR BEATTY ENGINEERING SERVICES (BBES) EBF MAIDEN STKS 7f 30y
1:50 (1:50) (Class 5) 2-Y-0 **£3,238** (£963; £481; £240) **Stalls** High

Form RPR
1 **Sound Advice** 2-9-3 0 .... PaulMulrennan 6 82+
(Keith Dalgleish) *stmbld and s.i.s: hld up in rr: hung lft to r alone stands' side st: gd hdwy over 1f out: led jst ins fnl f: kpt on* **15/2**
56 **2** *1 3/4* **Alabanda (IRE)**[17] 2580 2-8-12 0 .... DavidAllan 1 73
(Tim Easterby) *in tch: hdwy over 2f out: rdn to ld narrowly over 1f out: hdd jst ins fnl f: kpt on: no ch w wnr towards fin* **4/1**[3]
3 *hd* **Marching On (IRE)** 2-9-3 0 .... PJMcDonald 4 78
(Kevin Ryan) *led after 1f: wnt wd on bnd 4f out: rdn whn hdd narrowly over 1f out: kpt on: no ch w wnr towards fin* **7/1**
4 **4** *hd* **Badea**[21] 2455 2-9-3 0 .... TonyHamilton 2 77+
(Richard Fahey) *dwlt: hld up in tch: pushed along 3f out: rdn and hdwy over 1f out: kpt on fnl 100yds* **5/4**[1]
43 **5** *3 3/4* **Maastricht (IRE)**[21] 2460 2-9-3 0 .... RoystonFfrench 3 68
(Mark Johnston) *trckd ldr: rdn over 2f out: sn one pce: no ex ins fnl f* **7/2**[2]
0 **6** *12* **Lady Of Edge**[55] 1515 2-8-12 0 .... FrederikTylicki 5 33
(Keith Dalgleish) *led for 1f: trckd ldr: rdn 3f out: wknd over 1f out* **50/1**
1m 29.55s (0.55) **Going Correction** -0.05s/f (Good) **6** Ran SP% **112.9**
Speed ratings (Par 93): **94,92,91,91,87 73**
toteswingers:1&2:£6.50, 2&3:£3.30, 1&3:£9.50 CSF £37.21 TOTE £9.20: £2.70, £2.10; EX 36.10.
Owner G L S Partnership **Bred** G L S Partnership **Trained** Carluke, South Lanarkshire

FOCUS
An overcast afternoon and the official going was changed to good after 1.5mm of overnight rain. An interesting maiden which will throw up winners and run at a fair pace for the conditions. However, it was a messy affair, with the eventual winner racing alone up the stands' rail. He showed plenty of ability, and the form is pitched around the far-side runners.

NOTEBOOK
Sound Advice, well supported for his debut, did virtually everything wrong, despite winning. He stumbled out of the stalls, was very slow into his stride and was still detached from his rivals by three lengths turning into the straight, where he hung left towards the stands' rail. He has abundant speed in his pedigree and patent ability, but he looks a tricky ride. His rider had a job pulling him up and, just as his quirky sire had done in a Windsor maiden, he crashed through a running rail after the winning post, giving Paul Mulrennan a nasty fall and a broken leg. His stable remains in superb form and this was the third winner from ten juvenile runners so far this season. (op 12-1)
Alabanda(IRE), having her third start, was upped in trip and only just failed, having taken up the running inside the 2f marker before tiring late. She shows a very willing attitude and looks progressive. (op 9-2)
Marching On(IRE), hailing from stable that has done well with its juveniles this season, came wide into bend showing a little greenness, but he stayed on really well. He has a decent pedigree and on the evidence of this thoroughly pleasing performance, he will win races sooner rather than later. (op 15-2)
Badea was green on his debut but stayed on really well when fourth in a decent Haydock maiden, so it was no surprise that there was good money for him. He still seemed a little inexperienced, but certainly improved for the step up in trip and was doing his best work late on, suggesting a mile would suit. The stable had been in the doldrums over the past few weeks (54 runners without a winner until Pleasant Day struck at Ripon yesterday), so this was a decent performance in the circumstances. He won't be long in winning. (op 11-8 tchd Evens)
Maastricht(IRE), having his third start, reared in the stalls but he settled well once they got going. Upped in trip here, he didn't seem to get the distance and was eased once beaten. (op 11-4)
Lady Of Edge showed plenty of pace early on, but faded. This was her second start, but a watching brief is advised until she shows ability. (op 33-1)

3124 HBJ CLAIM SOLUTIONS H'CAP (QUALIFIER FOR THE BETFAIR BONUS SCOTTISH RACING MILE FINAL) 1m
2:20 (2:26) (Class 5) (0-70,72) 3-Y-O **£4,209** (£1,252; £625; £312) **Stalls** High

Form RPR
-001 **1** **Regimental (IRE)**[8] 2834 3-9-4 **72** 6ex DaleSwift(5) 1 80+
(Ann Duffield) *trckd ldng pair: pushed along over 2f out and sn hdwy: swtchd lft appr fnl f: led fnl 100yds: hld on rdn out* **5/2**[1]
4154 **2** *hd* **Coax**[18] 2550 3-9-5 **68** RoystonFfrench 4 75
(Mark Johnston) *led: rdn over 2f out: hdd fnl 100yds: kpt on but a jst hld* **7/2**[2]
0-20 **3** *1 1/2* **Pivot Bridge**[39] 1949 3-9-2 **65** RobertWinston 6 69
(B W Hills) *trckd ldr: rdn over 2f out: chal over 1f out: one pce ins fnl f* **7/2**[2]
60 **4** *5* **Imperator Augustus (IRE)**[28] 2256 3-9-7 **70** AndrewElliott 5 63
(Patrick Holmes) *midfield: rdn and hdwy on outer over 2f out: chsd ldrs over 1f out: hung rt ins fnl f: sn wknd* **22/1**
-203 **5** *1 3/4* **Inca Blue**[21] 2465 3-8-4 **53** DuranFentiman 2 41
(Tim Easterby) *t.k.h: in midfield: rdn over 3f out: sn no imp* **5/1**[3]
5346 **6** *shd* **Sabratha (IRE)**[13] 2729 3-9-0 **63** FrederikTylicki 3 51
(Linda Perratt) *dwlt: hld up in last pair: rdn over 2f out: kpt on ins fnl f: n.d* **17/2**
5-00 **7** *3/4* **Grazeon Again (IRE)**[23] 2406 3-8-6 **55** ow1 (v[1]) PJMcDonald 8 42
(John Quinn) *racd keenly: trckd ldng pair: rdn over 2f out: wknd over 1f out* **16/1**
3-50 **8** *4* **Scented**[9] 2808 3-9-7 **70** (b) TonyHamilton 7 47
(Ian Semple) *slowly away: hld up in last pair: rdn over 2f out: a towards rr* **33/1**

1m 40.81s (-0.39) **Going Correction** -0.05s/f (Good) **8** Ran SP% **113.4**
Speed ratings (Par 99): **99,98,97,92,90 90,89,85**
toteswingers:1&2:£3.30, 2&3:£2.90, 1&3:£3.80 CSF £11.14 CT £29.47 TOTE £3.80: £1.50, £1.80, £1.30; EX 11.60.
Owner I Farrington & R Chapman **Bred** Deer Forest Stud **Trained** Constable Burton, N Yorks

FOCUS
There was a delay while the running rail was mended, which left the runners at the start longer than they would have anticipated. A well-contested handicap, run at a sensible pace and a well-backed winner, who built on his latest Haydock run.

3125 POMMERY CHAMPAGNE MAIDEN AUCTION STKS 5f
2:55 (2:55) (Class 5) 2-Y-O **£1,942** (£578; £288; £144) **Stalls** Low

Form RPR
1 **Lupin Pooter** 2-8-10 **0** LeeNewman 2 64+
(David Barron) *chsd ldng pair: rdn and hdwy to ld narrowly over 1f out: strly pressed ins fnl f: hld on wl* **6/4**[1]
044 **2** *nk* **First Fast Now (IRE)**[18] 2570 2-8-9 **0** AndrewMullen 4 62
(Nigel Tinkler) *w ldr: rdn over 2f out: edgd rt ins fnl f: kpt on: hld nr fin* **7/1**
0 **3** *1 3/4* **Angel Of Hope (IRE)**[22] 2430 2-8-10 **0** RoystonFfrench 1 57
(Bryan Smart) *wnt rt s: sn pushed along in tch: hdwy to chse ldng pair ent fnl f: kpt on* **9/2**[3]
3 **4** *6* **Fortune Star (IRE)**[14] 2693 2-8-11 **0** FrederikTylicki 5 36
(Linda Perratt) *trckd ldng pair: rdn over 2f out: sn one pce: no ex fnl f* **8/1**
33 **5** *2* **Nannerl (IRE)**[65] 1301 2-8-2 **0** JulieBurke(5) 3 25
(Kevin Ryan) *led narrowly: hdd over 1f out: wknd ins fnl f* **3/1**[2]
6 *2 1/4* **Tuibama (IRE)** 2-8-13 **0** PJMcDonald 6 23
(Ben Haslam) *chsd ldng pair: rdn over 2f out: wknd over 1f out* **12/1**

60.61 secs (0.21) **Going Correction** -0.30s/f (Firm) **6** Ran SP% **114.5**
Speed ratings (Par 93): **86,85,82,73,69 66**
toteswingers:1&2:£2.70, 2&3:£3.90, 1&3:£1.50 CSF £13.12 TOTE £2.50: £1.70, £3.40; EX 12.30.
Owner Harrowgate Bloodstock Ltd **Bred** John Starbuck **Trained** Maunby, N Yorks

FOCUS
This weak sprint was run at a decent pace and didn't take a lot of winning. Selling form in all but name.

NOTEBOOK
Lupin Pooter, for whom there was good money in the offices and on course, clearly knew his job, was always in a prominent position and won despite his inexperience, wandering right in the closing stages. He only cost 800gns so already looks a bargain. (op 13-8 tchd 5-4 and 2-1 in a place, and 7-4 in places)
First Fast Now(IRE) showed plenty of dash but, when it came to a fight, she showed an awkward head carriage and didn't really go through with her effort. She has ability and may pick up a small race. (op 11-2)
Angel Of Hope(IRE) was beaten a long way on her 6f debut in a Newcastle maiden and that experience, combined with a drop in trip, appeared to help her. She stuck to the task well and may be better over extra distance. (op 13-2)
Fortune Star(IRE) looked one-paced over this minimum trip. He needs further. (op 17-2)
Nannerl(IRE), returning from a two-month break, helped set the early pace but tired before the 1f marker. She has shown better form than this and, in the context of this weak race, she was a bit disappointing. (tchd 7-2)
Tuibama(IRE), a 7,000gns half-brother to seven winners including useful sprinters Grand Lad and Galloway Boy (both successful during their 2-y-o season), showed very little and was always behind. He needs more experience and looked as if he will improve for the run. (op 14-1)

3126 M & F FUNERAL SERVICES H'CAP (QUALIFIER FOR THE BETFAIR BONUS SCOTTISH RACING SPRINT FINAL) 5f
3:35 (3:36) (Class 5) (0-70,70) 3-Y-O **£4,209** (£1,252; £625; £312) **Stalls** Low

Form RPR
1210 **1** **Irish Boy (IRE)**[28] 2265 3-8-13 **59** DuranFentiman 2 69
(Noel Wilson) *pressed ldr: rdn over 2f out: hung rt ins fnl f: kpt on: mde contact w 2nd whn ldng towards fin* **6/1**[3]
-211 **2** *nk* **Rothesay Chancer**[14] 2697 3-9-7 **70** GaryBartley(3) 3 79
(Jim Goldie) *trckd ldng pair: hdwy to ld over 1f out: sn drvn: edgd lft ins fnl f: mde contact w wnr and hdd towards fin* **5/2**[2]
5-31 **3** *1 1/4* **Fast Shot**[17] 2592 3-9-5 **65** DavidAllan 6 69+
(Tim Easterby) *trckd ldng pair: rdn 2f out: kpt on ins fnl f* **11/10**[1]
0-40 **4** *2* **Bailadeira**[42] 1853 3-8-9 **60** DaleSwift(5) 4 57
(Tim Etherington) *trckd ldng pair: rdn over 2f out: sltly short of room ent fnl f: one pce after* **20/1**
0302 **5** *5* **Take Root**[20] 2493 3-9-7 **70** PaulPickard(3) 1 49
(Reg Hollinshead) *led: rdn over 2f out: hdd over 1f out: wknd ins fnl f* **7/1**
4010 **6** *4 1/2* **Saxonette**[14] 2697 3-9-5 **65** PJMcDonald 5 28
(Linda Perratt) *sn outpcd in rr: a bhd* **20/1**

58.97 secs (-1.43) **Going Correction** -0.30s/f (Firm) **6** Ran SP% **112.5**
Speed ratings (Par 99): **99,98,96,93,85 78**
toteswingers:1&2:£2.80, 2&3:£1.10, 1&3:£1.30 CSF £21.43 TOTE £5.80: £2.70, £1.30; EX 18.00.
Owner Annwell Inn Syndicate **Bred** Seamus McMullan **Trained** Sandhutton, N Yorks

FOCUS
A reasonably competitive sprint handicap despite the paucity of runners and run in a quicker time than the previous 5f sprint. They came up the stands' rail and there was a tight finish in more ways than one. The form is rated on the positive side and should hold up.

3127 HBJ CLAIM SOLUTIONS H'CAP 1m 6f
4:10 (4:10) (Class 4) (0-85,79) 4-Y-0+ **£7,771** (£2,312; £1,155; £577) **Stalls** High

Form RPR
2120 **1** **Red Kestrel (USA)**[49] 1651 6-9-2 **76** JulieBurke(5) 1 86
(Kevin Ryan) *mde all: pushed along over 2f out: rdn and kpt on ins fnl f: wl in command towards fin* **7/1**
-141 **2** *1* **Odin's Raven (IRE)**[7] 2892 6-8-11 **69** PaulPickard(3) 3 77
(Brian Ellison) *dwlt: hld up: gd hdwy on inner 3f out: sn chsd wnr: kpt on: hld towards fin* **9/4**[2]
-406 **3** *1 1/4* **Dazzling Light (UAE)**[27] 2285 6-9-4 **76** GaryBartley(3) 6 82
(Jim Goldie) *hld up: hdwy 3f out: sltly short of room over 2f out and again over 1f out: in clr appr fnl f: kpt on: nt rch ldng pair* **2/1**[1]
5-46 **4** *2 3/4* **Beat The Shower**[25] 2364 5-8-11 **66** PJMcDonald 5 68
(Peter Niven) *midfield: hdwy on outer over 2f out: sn rdn: kpt on one pce* **9/1**
31-6 **5** *2 3/4* **Los Nadis (GER)**[14] 2696 7-8-9 **64** AndrewMullen 8 62
(Jim Goldie) *trckd ldrs: rdn over 2f out: no imp over 1f out* **16/1**
-061 **6** *3 1/2* **Jackday (IRE)**[16] 2622 6-9-2 **71** (p) DavidAllan 2 64
(Tim Easterby) *midfield: rdn over 2f out: wknd over 1f out* **11/2**[3]
4040 **7** *1 3/4* **Record Breaker (IRE)**[27] 2320 7-9-9 **78** (b) RoystonFfrench 4 69
(Mark Johnston) *trckd ldrs: rdn over 2f out: wknd ins fnl f* **18/1**
050- **8** *91* **Wicked Daze (IRE)**[233] 7173 8-9-10 **79** FrederikTylicki 7 —
(Linda Perratt) *w ldr: rdn and lost pl over 3f out: wknd over 2f out: t.o* **20/1**

3m 2.54s (-2.76) **Going Correction** -0.05s/f (Good) **8** Ran SP% **117.9**
Speed ratings (Par 105): **105,104,103,102,100 98,97,45**
toteswingers:1&2:£4.70, 2&3:£1.40, 1&3:£2.60 CSF £23.98 CT £44.13 TOTE £6.40: £1.40, £1.70, £1.40; EX 21.90.
Owner Hambleton Racing Ltd XII **Bred** Darley **Trained** Hambleton, N Yorks

FOCUS
A steady, but even tempo for this staying handicap, which very few got into. The winner produced his best form since his early 4yo days to beat the 6lb well-in runner-up.

3128 TURFTV IN BETTING SHOPS FOR ROYAL ASCOT H'CAP 7f 30y
4:45 (4:45) (Class 6) (0-65,64) 4-Y-0+ **£1,942** (£578; £288; £144) **Stalls** High

Form RPR
0005 **1** **Drive Home (USA)**[14] 2692 4-8-8 **51** (p) DuranFentiman 4 59
(Noel Wilson) *sn led: rdn over 2f out: led over 1f out: kpt on* **8/1**
6300 **2** *1/2* **Berbice (IRE)**[15] 2633 6-9-5 **62** FrederikTylicki 2 69
(Linda Perratt) *dwlt: sn in tch: smooth hdwy to trck ldr over 1f out: rdn to chal jst ins fnl f: one pce: hld towards fin* **5/1**
0412 **3** *2 3/4* **Shunkawakhan (IRE)**[14] 2692 8-8-12 **55** (p) PJMcDonald 1 55
(Linda Perratt) *trckd ldr: rdn over 2f out: ev ch over 1f out: one pce fnl f* **7/2**[2]
0-14 **4** *1/2* **Blues Jazz**[15] 2632 5-8-12 **55** TonyHamilton 6 53+
(Ian Semple) *midfield: pushed along over 3f out: rdn over 2f out: kpt on ins fnl f: nvr threatened ldrs* **9/2**[3]
-435 **5** *3/4* **Hellbender (IRE)**[15] 2633 5-9-0 **62** DaleSwift(5) 7 58+
(George Foster) *hld up: stl on bridle over 2f out: rdn over 1f out: kpt on: n.d* **5/2**[1]
0436 **6** *nk* **Eilean Eeve**[9] 2803 5-8-6 **49** (p) LeeNewman 9 44
(George Foster) *sn led: rdn over 2f out: hdd over 1f out: wknd ins fnl f* **12/1**
-040 **7** *1 1/4* **Balance On Time (IRE)**[9] 2809 5-8-2 **45** AndrewHeffernan 3 37
(Linda Perratt) *s.i.s: sn in midfield: rdn over 2f out: no imp* **22/1**
060- **8** *3 1/4* **Shamo Hill Theatre**[268] 6296 4-8-2 **45** AndrewMullen 8 28
(Colin Teague) *trckd ldr: rdn over 2f out: sn lost pl: wknd ins fnl f* **40/1**
20-4 **9** *4 1/2* **Second Reef**[14] 2692 9-8-5 **51** NataliaGemelova(3) 5 22
(Thomas Cuthbert) *hld up: rdn over 2f out: a towards rr* **16/1**

1m 29.11s (0.11) **Going Correction** -0.05s/f (Good) **9** Ran SP% **117.1**
Speed ratings (Par 101): **97,96,93,92,91 91,90,86,81**
toteswingers:1&2:£5.80, 2&3:£2.80, 1&3:£6.10 CSF £48.40 CT £167.68 TOTE £7.50: £1.90, £1.90, £2.30; EX 58.80.
Owner Noel Wilson Steven Downes Gary Kennedy **Bred** Moyglare Stud **Trained** Sandhutton, N Yorks

FOCUS
An ordinary, win-in-their-turn handicap, run at an average pace and in a time just half a second quicker than the earlier 2-y-o race. Weak form, rated around the second and third.

3129 NICOLA MARTIN LADY RIDERS' H'CAP (QUALIFIER FOR THE BETFAIR BONUS SCOTTISH RACING STAYERS FINAL) 1m 4f 100y
5:20 (5:20) (Class 5) (0-70,76) 4-Y-0+ £4,059 (£1,259; £629; £314) Stalls High

Form				RPR
-354	1		**Patavium (IRE)**[28] 2251 8-10-6 **69** MissSBrotherton 5 (Edwin Tuer) *trckd ldrs: led over 3f out: sn rdn: kpt on* **7/2**[1]	77
521	2	1	**Zennor**[9] 2808 4-10-6 **76** 6ex MissALMurphy(7) 3 (Tom Dascombe) *dwlt: hld up: sltly short of room over 2f out: stl plenty to do 2f out: sn hdwy: styd on strly ins fnl f: wnt 2nd nr fin* **7/2**[1]	85+
0324	3	¾	**Golden Future**[1] 3086 8-9-1 **55** MissJoannaMason(5) 8 (Peter Niven) *in tch: hdwy to chse wnr over 2f out: ev ch over 1f out: one pce ins fnl f: lost 2nd nr fin* **4/1**[2]	59
-043	4	2 ¼	**Beneath**[14] 2696 4-9-4 **60** (b) MissLSutcliffe(7) 2 (Kevin Ryan) *racd keenly: in tch: hdwy over 2f out: ev ch over 1f out: no ex ins fnl f* **15/2**[3]	61
0641	5	hd	**Dimashq**[1] 3086 9-8-11 **51** 6ex MissWGibson(5) 12 (Paul Midgley) *hld up in rr: hdwy over 3f out: chsd ldrs 2f out: one pce appr fnl f* **12/1**	52+
5032	6	11	**Rub Of The Relic (IRE)**[4] 2988 6-8-13 **55** (v) MissHDukes(7) 10 (Paul Midgley) *hld up: hdwy on outer over 3f out: wknd over 2f out* **9/1**	39
32-0	7	¾	**Edas**[21] 2454 9-9-12 **66** MissHCuthbert(5) 1 (Thomas Cuthbert) *trckd ldrs: rdn over 3f out: wknd over 1f out* **22/1**	48
46/	8	½	**Sergeant Pink (IRE)**[126] 7084 5-9-6 **62** MissRobynGray(7) 4 (Dianne Sayer) *rrd s: hld up: dropped in rr over 5f out: nvr a factor* **22/1**	44
-010	9	2 ¼	**Oddsmaker (IRE)**[18] 2544 10-9-11 **65** (t) LucyAlexander(5) 11 (Maurice Barnes) *prom: led over 7f out: rdn whn hdd over 3f out: wknd over 2f out* **12/1**	43
-404	10	3 ½	**Birkside**[15] 2636 8-9-9 **58** MrsCBartley 9 (Linda Perratt) *midfield: rdn over 3f out: wknd 2f out* **18/1**	31
30-6	11	2 ¾	**Cool Baranca (GER)**[15] 1440 5-9-7 **61** MissECSayer(5) 13 (Dianne Sayer) *dwlt: hld up: hdwy into midfield over 5f out: wknd over 3f out* **14/1**	30
30-0	12	3 ½	**Red Skipper (IRE)**[16] 1099 6-9-0 **54** MissKBannon(5) 6 (Noel Wilson) *led: hdd over 7f out: wknd over 2f out* **33/1**	17

2m 41.72s (-0.28) **Going Correction** -0.05s/f (Good) **12** Ran SP% **125.2**
Speed ratings (Par 103): **98,97,96,95,95 87,87,87,85,83 81,79**
toteswingers:1&2:£3.90, 2&3:£2.20, 1&3:£15.20 CSF £16.05 CT £53.69 TOTE £5.30: £2.30, £1.80, £1.90; EX 17.40.
Owner J A Nixon **Bred** M Channon **Trained** Great Smeaton, N Yorks
■ Serena Brotherton's 100th career victory.

FOCUS
A well-contested lady riders' handicap, run at a generous pace. A small personal best from the winner at face value.
T/Plt: £89.50 to a £1 stake. Pool of £38,340.46 - 312.40 winning tickets. T/Qpdt: £14.90 to a £1 stake. Pool of £3,356.24 - 166.01 winning tickets. AS

2506 NEWMARKET (R-H)
Friday, June 17

OFFICIAL GOING: Good to firm (good in places) changing to good after race 2 (6.30)
First meeting of year on July Course. Stalls on near side of stands' side track except for 6.30 & 8.40, centre.
Wind: Light across Weather: Raining

3130 NEWMARKET NIGHTS APPRENTICE H'CAP 1m
6:00 (6:01) (Class 5) (0-70,70) 4-Y-0+ £2,590 (£770; £385; £192) Stalls High

Form				RPR
001-	1		**Two Certainties**[189] 7810 4-9-0 **60** RyanClark 10 (Stuart Williams) *hld up: hdwy u.p over 1f out: led wl ins fnl f: styd on* **14/1**	70+
4443	2	¾	**Rough Rock (IRE)**[17] 2597 6-9-7 **67** KieranO'Neill 16 (Chris Dwyer) *hld up: hdwy over 2f out: rdn to ld 1f out: hdd wl ins fnl f* **8/1**[3]	73
-420	3	nk	**Exopuntia**[152] 181 5-8-10 **56** AdamBeschizza 13 (Julia Feilden) *chsd ldrs: rdn and ev ch 1f out: styd on* **12/1**	61
3040	4	½	**Red Somerset (USA)**[37] 2000 8-9-1 **64** MatthewLawson(3) 15 (Mike Murphy) *hld up: hdwy over 2f out: rdn ins fnl f: styd on* **9/1**	68
5022	5	hd	**Aviso (GER)**[16] 2616 7-9-0 **63** MatthewCosham(3) 5 (David Evans) *chsd ldr tl led over 2f out: rdn and hdd 1f out: styd on* **6/1**[1]	67
6500	6	shd	**Ajdaad (USA)**[5] 2955 4-9-5 **70** RyanTate(5) 6 (Alan McCabe) *s.i.s: hld up: hdwy over 1f out: r.o: nt rch ldrs* **25/1**	73
0-3	7	shd	**Colinca's Lad (IRE)**[28] 2268 9-8-10 **56** TobyAtkinson 4 (Peter Charalambous) *mid-div: hdwy over 2f out: rdn and edgd lft fr over 1f out: styd on* **8/1**[3]	59
-505	8	1 ¾	**Inpursuitoffreedom**[9] 2816 4-9-9 **69** AshleyMorgan 2 (Philip McBride) *hld up: hdwy u.p and hung lft fr over 1f out: styd on* **15/2**[2]	68
55-5	9	½	**Mudhish (IRE)**[38] 1978 6-9-1 **64** (b) AntiocoMurgia(3) 7 (Clive Brittain) *prom: rdn and ev ch over 1f out: no ex ins fnl f* **33/1**	62
0554	10	5	**Ilie Nastase (FR)**[71] 1198 7-8-13 **64** (b) SophieSilvester(5) 8 (Conor Dore) *mid-div: rdn over 2f out: sn wknd* **16/1**	51
0000	11	1 ¼	**Focail Eile**[6] 2915 6-9-0 **65** (b[1]) IanBurns(5) 11 (Noel Quinlan) *sn led: racd keenly: hdd over 2f out: wknd ins fnl f* **28/1**	49
040-	12	7	**Fidler Bay**[335] 4133 5-9-4 **67** AmyScott(3) 1 (Henry Candy) *s.i.s: outpcd* **16/1**	35
0-24	13	5	**Big Sur**[18] 2567 5-8-8 **57** (b[1]) LucyKBarry(3) 3 (Tom Keddy) *s.i.s: hdwy over 6f out: rdn and wknd over 2f out* **6/1**[1]	13
0066	14	½	**Gallantry**[9] 2816 9-9-6 **66** RyanPowell 9 (Michael Squance) *prom: rdn over 3f out: wknd over 2f out* **33/1**	21
2440	15	7	**Eastern Gift**[9] 2816 6-9-2 **67** NatashaEaton(5) 12 (Gay Kelleway) *prom tl rdn and wknd 2f out* **14/1**	—
6266	16	2 ¼	**Pipers Piping (IRE)**[16] 2605 5-8-10 **63** (p) LauraSimpson(7) 14 (Michael Squance) *chsd ldrs 6f* **22/1**	—

1m 42.75s (2.75) **Going Correction** +0.15s/f (Good) **16** Ran SP% **122.9**
Speed ratings (Par 103): **92,91,90,90,90 90,90,88,87,82 81,74,69,69,62 59**
toteswingers:1&2:£12.50, 2&3:£36.30, 1&3:£66.70 CSF £115.42 CT £1402.41 TOTE £12.60: £2.30, £2.40, £4.30, £3.00; EX 94.20.
Owner A Simpson, M Kerr-Dineen & D Shekells **Bred** Old Mill Stud Ltd And Oomswell Ltd **Trained** Newmarket, Suffolk

FOCUS
The time was six seconds beyond standard but that was not surprising, bearing in mind the grade of the race. There was an acceptable pace on. The winner was unexposed and looks sure to do better.

3131 RACING UK CLASSIFIED STKS 1m 4f
6:30 (6:33) (Class 5) 3-Y-O £2,590 (£770; £385; £192) Stalls Centre

Form				RPR
0641	1		**Pintrada**[23] 2407 3-9-0 **69** TedDurcan 3 (James Bethell) *s.i.s: hld up: hdwy over 4f out: led 2f out: rdn over 1f out: styd on wl: eased nr fin* **7/2**[2]	81
31-4	2	3 ¼	**Battery Power**[11] 2764 3-8-9 **70** AshleyMorgan(5) 8 (Mark H Tompkins) *chsd ldrs: ev ch 2f out: sn rdn: styd on same pce ins fnl f* **10/1**	75
-412	3	6	**King Kurt (IRE)**[9] 2808 3-9-0 **69** PhillipMakin 2 (Kevin Ryan) *chsd ldrs: rdn and hung lft over 1f out: wknd ins fnl f* **5/4**[1]	65
6-25	4	6	**See The Smile (USA)**[77] 1076 3-9-0 **70** AndreaAtzeni 11 (Gay Kelleway) *led: rdn and hdd 2f out: wknd over 1f out: edgd lft ins fnl f* **28/1**	56
63-1	5	½	**Medaille D'Or**[146] 260 3-9-0 **70** JackMitchell 10 (Roger Varian) *hld up: hdwy over 3f out: rdn over 2f out: wknd over 1f out* **11/2**[3]	55
5320	6	4 ½	**Enriching (USA)**[28] 2253 3-9-0 **70** (t) NickyMackay 4 (David Elsworth) *hld up: hdwy 4f out: rdn over 2f out: sn wknd* **20/1**	48
-330	7	2 ½	**Warrant**[37] 1997 3-9-0 **61** JimmyQuinn 1 (Jane Chapple-Hyam) *hld up: rdn over 2f out: wkng whn hung lft over 1f out* **28/1**	44
0-00	8	3 ¼	**Diamond Bob**[16] 2621 3-9-0 **69** TomMcLaughlin 9 (Ed Dunlop) *s.i.s: hld up: rdn and wknd over 2f out* **14/1**	39
4006	9	29	**Satin Love (USA)**[16] 2619 3-9-0 **69** J-PGuillambert 7 (Mark Johnston) *unruly in stalls: sn chsng ldr: rdn over 3f out: wknd over 2f out: t.o* **16/1**	—

2m 34.99s (2.09) **Going Correction** +0.15s/f (Good) **9** Ran SP% **115.3**
Speed ratings (Par 99): **99,96,92,88,88 85,83,81,62**
toteswingers:1&2:£5.70, 2&3:£3.30, 1&3:£2.00 CSF £36.76 TOTE £5.20: £1.90, £2.60, £1.10; EX 45.20.
Owner Scotyork Partnership I **Bred** Carmel Stud **Trained** Middleham Moor, N Yorks

FOCUS
A modest race. The winner progressed nicely and is rated up 10lb. The second improved too but the rest were a stone or more off.

3132 RUSSIAN STANDARD VODKA MAIDEN STKS 6f
7:05 (7:08) (Class 5) 2-Y-O £3,238 (£963; £481; £240) Stalls High

Form				RPR
	1		**Hadaj** 2-9-3 **0** PhilipRobinson 4 (Clive Brittain) *a.p: led over 1f out: sn rdn and hung lft: r.o* **6/1**[3]	83
5	2	2 ¾	**Radiomarelli (USA)**[27] 2291 2-9-3 **0** PatCosgrave 11 (Ralph Beckett) *chsd ldrs: led wl over 1f out: sn hdd: styd on same pce ins fnl f* **6/1**[3]	75
	3	½	**Sehnsucht (IRE)** 2-9-3 **0** PhillipMakin 2 (Alan McCabe) *hld up: rdn over 2f out: hdwy over 1f out: r.o wl towards fin: nt rch ldrs* **5/1**[2]	73+
	4	1	**Thirsty Bear** 2-9-3 **0** J-PGuillambert 7 (Rebecca Curtis) *chsd ldrs: rdn over 1f out: no ex ins fnl f* **20/1**	70
	5	4	**Enjoying (IRE)** 2-8-12 **0** KieranO'Neill(5) 13 (Richard Hannon) *sn pushed along in rr: swtchd rt and r.o ins fnl f: nvr nrr* **20/1**	58+
36	6	hd	**Chillie Billie**[57] 1505 2-9-3 **0** CathyGannon 16 (Phil McEntee) *led: rdn and hdd wl over 1f out: wknd ins fnl f* **12/1**	58
	7	3 ¾	**Elite** 2-8-12 **0** JimmyQuinn 3 (Sir Michael Stoute) *hld up in tch: racd keenly: rdn and hung lft fr over 1f out: sn wknd* **9/2**[1]	41
	8	¾	**Tudor Empire (IRE)** 2-9-3 **0** RobertHavlin 9 (John Gosden) *sn pushed along in rr: nvr nrr* **12/1**	44
0	9	nse	**Rocco Breeze (IRE)**[20] 2510 2-9-3 **0** JackMitchell 8 (Philip McBride) *s.i.s and hmpd s: nvr on terms* **50/1**	44
	10	¾	**My Guardian Angel** 2-8-12 **0** AshleyMorgan(5) 1 (Mark H Tompkins) *sn pushed along and a in rr* **33/1**	42
	11	3	**Shamardeliah (IRE)** 2-8-12 **0** TomMcLaughlin 10 (Ed Dunlop) *prom tl wknd over 1f out* **16/1**	28
0	12	4	**Nifty Shiftin**[9] 2817 2-9-3 **0** TedDurcan 14 (David Elsworth) *prom tl rdn and wknd over 1f out* **25/1**	21
0	12	dht	**Masters Club**[4] 2998 2-8-12 **0** RyanPowell(5) 6 (John Ryan) *mid-div: rdn over 2f out: sn wknd* **100/1**	21
5	14	8	**Fen Flyer**[17] 2594 2-9-3 **0** AndreaAtzeni 15 (Chris Dwyer) *chsd ldrs tl rdn and wknd over 1f out* **66/1**	—
	15	1 ¼	**Bewilder** 2-9-3 **0** NickyMackay 5 (John Gosden) *dwlt: outpcd* **7/1**	—

1m 14.45s (1.95) **Going Correction** +0.15s/f (Good) **15** Ran SP% **117.9**
Speed ratings (Par 93): **93,89,88,87,82 81,76,75,75,74 70,65,65,54,53**
toteswingers:1&2:£9.30, 2&3:£7.60, 1&3:£11.30 CSF £37.75 TOTE £7.50: £3.50, £2.90, £2.60; EX 48.50.
Owner Saeed Manana **Bred** Rabbah Bloodstock Limited **Trained** Newmarket, Suffolk

FOCUS
Over half of these were having their first race, so the time and race averages help with the level. It was a decent start from the winner.

NOTEBOOK
Hadaj put up a good debut display, albeit winning in a time that was considerably beyond standard. He was somewhat green in the preliminaries but showed a willing attitude in the race, knuckling down to finish the job. The way he ran on through the closing stages was most encouraging and a further furlong won't be beyond him. But before that he will return to compete over course and distance in the Group 2 July Stakes. He will have to improve to make his mark in that company, however. (op 13-2 tchd 4-1)
Radiomarelli(USA) was among the half dozen to have seen previous racecourse action and he put the experience to good use. He moved smoothly into contention but was unable to see off the late charge of the winner. He should break his maiden in the not-too-distant future. (op 7-1)
Sehnsucht(IRE) was very well backed to make a winning start to his career but his chance wasn't helped by slightly missing the break. That said, he showed plenty of promise, rattling home through the closing strides. Compensation won't be far off with the experience of this sure to benefit him next time. (op 11-1)
Thirsty Bear, who cost 13,000gns as a yearling, showed enough on this debut to suggest a maiden will be within his grasp. He was one of several who are bound to improve as the season unfolds. (op 16-1)
Enjoying(IRE), a February foal who cost 88,000 euros, is bred to be competitive over this trip and beyond. He should improve next time. (op 25-1)

Elite is half-sister to five winners, including Group 1 performer Olden Times, and is likely to add to her family's reputation. She was a little green, edging left in behind the front-runners and progression can be expected. (op 4-1)
Bewilder, the first foal out of an unraced sister to the top-class Dubai Millennium, was very green. A good-actioned colt, judged by the way he went to post, he was slowly away and never got involved. He is bound to know a lot more next time. (op 6-1)

3133 INVESCO PERPETUAL H'CAP — 1m
7:35 (7:38) (Class 5) (0-75,75) 3-Y-O — **£5,180** (£1,541; £770; £384) **Stalls** High

Form — RPR

2-00 **1** — **Dunhoy (IRE)**[16] [2607] 3-9-6 **74** .... JimmyQuinn 7 — 87+
(Stef Higgins) *hld up: swtchd rt and hdwy over 1f out: r.o u.p to ld wl ins fnl f* **25/1**

5-45 **2** *3/4* **Icebuster**[17] [2582] 3-8-12 **66** .... JamesMillman 12 — 74
(Rod Millman) *hld up: hdwy over 2f out: rdn and ev ch ins fnl f: r.o* **25/1**

-460 **3** *2 1/2* **Focail Maith**[35] [2064] 3-8-13 **70** .... (b) AdamBeschizza(3) 15 — 72
(Noel Quinlan) *hld up in tch: hmpd 7f out: led 1f out: rdn and hdd wl ins fnl f* **33/1**

030- **4** *1* **Etarre (IRE)**[261] [6469] 3-8-8 **67** .... KieranO'Neill(5) 2 — 67+
(Gerard Butler) *led: racd keenly: rdn and hdd 1f out: styd on same pce* **7/1**[3]

3-20 **5** *nk* **Cinta**[47] [1722] 3-9-5 **73** .... AndreaAtzeni 13 — 72
(Marco Botti) *chsd ldrs: rdn over 1f out: styd on same pce ins fnl f* **8/1**

000- **6** *3 1/4* **Wom**[231] [7202] 3-8-6 **60** .... LiamJones 4 — 52+
(William Haggas) *s.i.s: hld up: hdwy u.p and hung lft fr over 1f out: nt trble ldrs* **17/2**

0543 **7** *5* **Dunseverick (IRE)**[24] [2383] 3-9-6 **74** .... TedDurcan 14 — 54
(David Lanigan) *hld up: swtchd rt and hdwy over 2f out: rdn over 1f out: wknd ins fnl f* **9/2**[2]

00-2 **8** *4* **Storm Runner (IRE)**[49] [1655] 3-8-11 **68** .... AshleyHamblett(3) 11 — 39
(George Margarson) *hld up: rdn over 2f out: swtchd lft over 1f out: n.d* **25/1**

52-3 **9** *1 1/2* **Ice Cold Bex**[21] [2472] 3-9-5 **73** .... JackMitchell 6 — 41
(Philip McBride) *hld up: effrt and nt clr run over 1f out: sn hung lft: n.d* **10/1**

150 **10** *1/2* **Loch Fleet (IRE)**[54] [1550] 3-9-7 **75** .... KirstyMilczarek 8 — 42
(Andrew Balding) *chsd ldrs tl rdn and wknd over 2f out* **12/1**

30-0 **11** *5* **Conjuror's Bluff**[7] [2885] 3-9-5 **73** .... CathyGannon 1 — 28+
(Richard Hannon) *hld up: hdwy u.p over 2f out: hung lft and wknd over 1f out* **33/1**

020 **12** *12* **Hab Reeh**[15] [2650] 3-9-5 **73** .... (bt[1]) AhmedAjtebi 10 — —
(Clive Brittain) *chsd ldr: rdn over 2f out: wknd and eased over 1f out: t.o* **40/1**

2251 **13** *2* **Classic Voice (IRE)**[15] [2652] 3-9-3 **71** .... PatCosgrave 9 — —
(Roy Brotherton) *chsd ldrs tl rdn and wknd over 2f out: t.o* **14/1**

030- **14** *8* **Point Du Jour (FR)**[177] [7974] 3-9-4 **72** .... (t) PhillipMakin 5 — —+
(Ian Wood) *trckd ldrs: racd keenly: wknd over 2f out: t.o* **40/1**

6632 **15** *6* **Robemaker**[8] [2838] 3-9-5 **73** .... NickyMackay 3 — —+
(John Gosden) *hld up: hdwy over 4f out: rdn and wknd 2f out: t.o* **11/4**[1]

1m 40.44s (0.44) **Going Correction** +0.15s/f (Good) **15** Ran SP% **124.7**
Speed ratings (Par 99): **103,102,99,98,98 95,90,86,84,84 79,67,65,57,51**
toteswingers:1&2:£240.80, 2&3:£142.90, 1&3:£256.10 CSF £534.82 CT £19025.96 TOTE £46.00: £10.80, £8.00, £13.30; EX 791.70.
Owner David Gilbert **Bred** Rossenarra Bloodstock Limited **Trained** Lambourn, Berks

FOCUS
There were several unexposed types having their first run in handicap company, but it went to the relatively experienced Dunhoy, who won in dramatic fashion. The time was relatively quick and the form is rated on the positive side.

3134 BET365 H'CAP — 7f
8:10 (8:10) (Class 3) (0-95,94) 3-Y-O+ — **£7,447** (£2,216; £1,107; £553) **Stalls** High

Form — RPR

3042 **1** — **Kingscroft (IRE)**[6] [2908] 3-8-7 **82** .... LiamJones 10 — 88
(Mark Johnston) *mde all: rdn over 1f out: styd on gamely* **11/1**

1 [illegible] **2** *shd* **Red Gulch**[21] [2470] 4-9-8 **88** .... J-PGuillambert 11 — 97
(Ed Wall[illegible]) [illegible] **8/1**

-003 **3** *nk* **Marajaa (IRE)**[27] [2310] 9-9-3 **83** .... [illegible] — [illegible]
(Willie Musson) *hld up: hdwy over 1f out: r.o* **13/2**[2]

4030 **4** *1* **Captain Ramius (IRE)**[42] [1849] 5-9-7 **87** .... CathyGannon 9 — 92
(Kevin Ryan) *hood removed late and s.i.s: sn chsng ldrs: rdn over 1f out: styd on* **25/1**

-500 **5** *shd* **Gouray Girl (IRE)**[21] [2470] 4-9-12 **92** .... DavidProbert 13 — 97
(Walter Swinburn) *hld up: hdwy over 1f out: sn rdn: r.o* **9/1**

-562 **6** *nk* **First Cat**[15] [2647] 4-8-11 **82** .... KieranO'Neill(5) 2 — 86+
(Richard Hannon) *hld up: rdn and hung lft fr over 1f out: r.o ins fnl f: nt rch ldrs* **9/1**

0411 **7** *3/4* **Masked Dance (IRE)**[23] [2398] 4-9-8 **88** .... (p) PhillipMakin 4 — 90
(Kevin Ryan) *chsd ldr: rdn over 1f out: styd on same pce* **10/1**

0-00 **8** *3/4* **Big Noise**[27] [2310] 7-9-2 **82** .... TedDurcan 8 — 82
(Dr Jon Scargill) *chsd ldrs: rdn over 1f out: eased whn hld nr fin* **16/1**

6-21 **9** *nse* **Tariq Too**[27] [2300] 4-9-0 **80** .... MartinLane 7 — 80+
(David Simcock) *hld up: hdwy over 1f out: styd on same pce ins fnl f* **11/2**[1]

1100 **10** *nk* **Imperial Djay (IRE)**[13] [2706] 6-9-9 **89** .... RobertHavlin 3 — 88+
(Ruth Carr) *hld up: nt clr run fr over 1f out: nvr able to chal* **16/1**

6005 **11** *1/2* **Spirit Of Sharjah (IRE)**[14] [2679] 6-10-0 **94** .... JimmyQuinn 6 — 94
(Julia Feilden) *hld up in tch: rdn over 1f out: styng on same pce whn nt clr run towards fin* **12/1**

0-00 **12** *2* **Kellys Eye (IRE)**[16] [2620] 4-9-9 **89** .... NickyMackay 12 — 82
(George Foster) *hld up: plld hrd: rdn and hung lft ins fnl f: n.d* **16/1**

13- **13** *4 1/2* **Zacynthus (IRE)**[338] [4036] 3-9-2 **91** .... AhmedAjtebi 14 — 69
(Mahmood Al Zarooni) *hld up: plld hrd: hung lft and wknd over 1f out* **7/1**[3]

1m 26.79s (1.09) **Going Correction** +0.225s/f (Good)
WFA 3 from 4yo+ 9lb **13** Ran SP% **118.9**
Speed ratings (Par 107): **102,101,101,100,100 99,99,98,98,97 97,94,89**
toteswingers:1&2:£11.20, 2&3:£6.60, 1&3:£21.00 CSF £95.88 CT £648.01 TOTE £9.60: £2.30, £2.90, £2.80; EX 86.20.
Owner Dr Marwan Koukash **Bred** J Beckett **Trained** Middleham Moor, N Yorks

FOCUS
This looked a tight race on paper and a length and half covered the first six home. The winner had an easy lead and the second is progressing.

NOTEBOOK
Kingscroft(IRE) was given a fine front-running ride. The time was over three and half seconds outside standard but was in line with conditions which were deteriorating as the rain continued. Due to go up 3lb for running well at Chester the previous weekend, the bottom weight underlined his current wellbeing and he's sure to get another rise in the ratings for this. (op 10-1)
Red Gulch may also be in line for a further hike, only his increases keep coming for finishing second. He has been a victim of his own consistency this season and has now finished second on each of his three starts this season. But this was a genuine effort and it has to be hoped that his consistency is rewarded at some point in the near future. (op 15-2)
Marajaa(IRE) is almost two years without a win and edging down the weights to what appears a playable mark. He came from quite far back with a concerted challenge, finishing the race with real purpose. But it is hard to ignore that he has been on such a long losing run. (op 8-1)
Captain Ramius(IRE) was slowly away after his hood was removed. He lost by only a length and a quarter and the ground conceded at the start certainly didn't help his cause. (tchd 22-1)
Gouray Girl(IRE) has been easing down the weights and can't be discounted next time. (op 12-1)
First Cat, dropped in trip after a narrow reverse over 1m at Sandown a fortnight ago, he ran a race that was hard to assess. Perhaps not the most straightforward of rides, he edged left in behind Marajaa but then ran on late. He couldn't be totally discounted but a total of one win from 22 starts means he is hard to plead a strong case for. (op 8-1)

3135 BET365 MAIDEN STKS — 1m 2f
8:40 (8:43) (Class 5) 3-Y-O — **£3,238** (£963; £481; £240) **Stalls** Centre

Form — RPR

02 **1** — **New Hampshire (USA)**[15] [2648] 3-9-3 0 .... RobertHavlin 5 — 84+
(John Gosden) *alwys prom: rdn to ld 1f out: edgd lft: r.o* **9/4**[1]

5- **2** *1 3/4* **Raahin (IRE)**[248] [6827] 3-9-3 0 .... RichardHills 1 — 81+
(Sir Michael Stoute) *chsd ldrs: led over 1f out: sn rdn: hdd and hung lft: hit on nose by rivals whip ins fnl f: r.o* **9/2**[3]

5-5 **3** *hd* **New River (IRE)**[8] [2836] 3-8-12 0 .... RyanMoore 4 — 76+
(Richard Hannon) *hld up: hdwy over 1f out: r.o* **4/1**[2]

4 *5* **Sohar** 3-8-12 0 .... KirstyMilczarek 7 — 66
(James Toller) *plld hrd: trckd ldr: led over 2f out: rdn and hdd over 1f out: wknd ins fnl f* **50/1**

65 **5** *1 3/4* **Maricopa**[13] [2735] 3-8-10 0 .... (t) AntiocoMurgia(7) 10 — 67
(Mahmood Al Zarooni) *chsd ldrs: ev ch over 2f out: sn rdn: wknd ins fnl f* **16/1**

6 *4* **Portrait Painter (USA)** 3-9-3 0 .... PhillipMakin 2 — 59
(Rebecca Curtis) *led: rdn and hdd over 2f out: wknd over 1f out* **7/1**

7 *2 1/4* **Najraan** 3-8-12 0 .... PhilipRobinson 3 — 50
(Clive Brittain) *hld up: rdn over 2f out: wknd wl over 1f out* **20/1**

8 *12* **Zee Zee Dan (IRE)** 3-9-3 0 .... AWhelan 8 — 31
(Noel Quinlan) *hld up: rdn over 3f out: wknd 2f out* **50/1**

2m 9.07s (3.57) **Going Correction** +0.225s/f (Good) **8** Ran SP% **96.0**
Speed ratings (Par 99): **94,92,92,88,87 83,82,72**
toteswingers:1&2:£2.10, 2&3:£1.40, 1&3:£1.90 CSF £8.28 TOTE £2.20: £1.10, £1.80, £1.50; EX 9.40.
Owner H R H Princess Haya Of Jordan **Bred** Everest Stables Inc **Trained** Newmarket, Suffolk

FOCUS
It is hard to evaluate the form with nothing in the race having previously had more than two starts, but the time was over six seconds beyond standard. It was run at a sensible pace and the form gave another boost to Timeline's Sandown race.

3136 BET365.COM H'CAP — 5f
9:10 (9:10) (Class 5) (0-75,73) 3-Y-O — **£2,590** (£770; £385; £192) **Stalls** High

Form — RPR

16-2 **1** — **Expose**[11] [2772] 3-9-7 **73** .... RyanMoore 5 — 94+
(William Haggas) *trckd ldrs: led ins fnl f: shkn up and r.o wl* **8/11**[1]

2220 **2** *3* **Rylee Mooch**[9] [2826] 3-9-1 **67** .... (e) JamieSpencer 9 — 74
(Richard Guest) *chsd ldrs: rdn to ld and hung rt fr over 1f out: hdd and unable qck ins fnl f* **8/1**

-051 **3** *2 1/4* **Madame Kintyre**[14] [2660] 3-8-13 **65** .... JamesMillman 4 — 64
(Rod Millman) *led: rdn and hdd over 1f out: no ex ins fnl f* **13/2**[2]

2115 **4** *nk* **Rambo Will**[58] [1483] 3-9-0 **66** .... DavidProbert 8 — 64
(J R Jenkins) *chsd ldrs: rdn and hung rt fr over 1f out: styd on same pce* **12/1**

0-00 **5** *1 1/4* **Jeeran**[9] [2818] 3-9-3 **69** .... (bt[1]) PhilipRobinson 7 — 62
(Clive Brittain) *sn pushed along and prom: rdn 1/2-way: wknd ins fnl f* **25/1**

1525 **6** *2* **Vicona (IRE)**[14] [2660] 3-8-9 **68** .... DuilioDaSilva(7) 1 — 54
(Paul Cole) *s.i.s: sme hdwy u.p over 1f out: wknd ins fnl f* **22/1**

1-13 **7** *nk* **Magic Cross**[9] [2818] 3-8-11 **66** .... AdamBeschizza(3) 6 — 51+
(Philip McBride) *s.s: bhd: hdwy u.p over 1f out: wknd ins fnl f* **7/1**[3]

[illegible] **8** [illegible] **Dangerous Illusion (IRE)**[52] [1595] 3-8-2 **54** oh8 .... FrannyNorton 2 — 37
(Michael Quinn) *chsd ldrs: [illegible] wknd ins fnl f* **40/1**

0-05 **9** *20* **Instructress**[88] [929] 3-8-5 **57** .... (p) AndreaAtzeni 3 — —
(Robert Cowell) *chsd ldrs: rdn 1/2-way: wknd wl over 1f out: t.o* **25/1**

60.33 secs (1.23) **Going Correction** +0.225s/f (Good) **9** Ran SP% **117.0**
Speed ratings (Par 99): **99,94,90,90,88 84,84,83,51**
toteswingers:1&2:£2.00, 2&3:£2.40, 1&3:£2.20 CSF £6.90 TOTE £1.80: £1.10, £1.70, £1.80; EX 7.40.
Owner The Royal Ascot Racing Club **Bred** John And Susan Davis **Trained** Newmarket, Suffolk

FOCUS
A one-sided handicap with the winner 4lb well in and unexposed. The form is not the strongest but he is potentially smart.
T/Plt: £1,044.50 to a £1 stake. Pool of £67,898.30 - 47.45 winning tickets. T/Qpdt: £218.20 to a £1 stake. Pool:£4,776.83 - 16.20 winning tickets. CR

2780 REDCAR (L-H)
Friday, June 17

OFFICIAL GOING: Good to firm (good in places; 8.3)
Wind: fresh 1/2 behind Weather: overcast, very breezy

3137 BUY YOUR TICKETS ON-LINE @ REDCARRACING.CO.UK (S) STKS — 7f
2:10 (2:12) (Class 6) 2-Y-O — **£1,619** (£481; £240; £120) **Stalls** High

Form — RPR

0532 **1** — **Flying Pickets (IRE)**[9] [2797] 2-8-8 0 .... JamesSullivan(3) 2 — 53
(David C Griffiths) *trckd ldrs: wnt 2nd over 3f out: led over 1f out: drvn clr* **7/4**[2]

4034 **2** *2 1/2* **Mad For Fun (IRE)**[10] [2784] 2-8-7 0 ow1 .... MickyFenton 3 — 43
(Paul Midgley) *led: hdd over 1f out: kpt on same pce* **4/1**[3]

66 **3** *3 3/4* **Sophar**[10] [2784] 2-8-11 0 .... StevieDonohoe 1 — 37
(Jason Ward) *trckd ldr: drvn and hung lft 3f out: one pce* **16/1**

00 **4** *6* **Valley Ace**[7] [2889] 2-8-11 0 .... (v[1]) TomEaves 4 — 21
(John Quinn) *dwlt: sn drvn along: lost pl after 2f: sn rdn: nt run on* **1/1**[1]

1m 26.33s (1.83) **Going Correction** -0.125s/f (Firm) **4** Ran SP% **112.2**
Speed ratings (Par 91): **84,81,76,70**
CSF £8.90 TOTE £2.60; EX 6.20.There was no bid for the winner.
Owner Norton Common Farm Racing **Bred** Richard Frayne **Trained** Bawtry, S Yorks

FOCUS
A modest card and all seven races were below tariff. After a dry night the going was good to firm, good in places ahead of the opening contest. This was one of the worst 2yo races run in recent years. It was the first time all of these had tried 7f.

NOTEBOOK
Flying Pickets(IRE), the most exposed of the quartet, saw it out best and stayed on well to get his head in front at the sixth time of asking. This looks an improved effort on the face of it, so maybe this trip proved the key. The form is very weak though. (op 2-1 tchd 9-4)
Mad For Fun(IRE) was 4l behind Flying Pickets over 6f last week and couldn't turn the form around over this longer trip, but she set a decent gallop and deserves credit for seeing the other two off fairly convincingly. (op 2-1)
Sophar has shown very little in two previous starts and doesn't appear to have improved much for the longer trip. (op 10-1)
Valley Ace, heavily backed, was niggled along early and never got into contention. The first-time blinkers look to have had a negative effect on him. (op 7-4)

3138 REDCAR RACECOURSE FOR YOUR WEDDING VENUE MAIDEN STKS — 1m 2f
2:45 (2:49) (Class 5) 3-Y-0+ — **£1,942** (£578; £288; £144) **Stalls** Low

Form				RPR
32	1		**Emperor Of Rome (IRE)**[21] 2461 3-8-11 0 .... SeanLevey(3) 9 (Michael Dods) *mde all: rdn over 2f out: kpt on: unchal* **6/5**[1]	75
30	2	4	**Harvey's Hope**[34] 2114 5-9-12 0 .... PaddyAspell 1 (Keith Reveley) *s.s: sn trcking ldrs: wnt 2nd over 1f out: styd on same pce* **20/1**	67
44	3	1½	**Chapter Five**[51] 1616 4-9-0 0 .... GarryWhillans(7) 8 (Keith Reveley) *s.i.s: in rr: drvn 4f out: styd on to take 3rd ins fnl f: gng on at fin* **12/1**	59+
	4	3	**John Louis** 3-9-0 0 .... AdrianNicholls 14 (Philip McBride) *trckd ldrs: one pce fnl 3f* **9/4**[2]	58
05	5	3¾	**Joyful Sound (IRE)**[10] 2790 3-9-0 0 .... StevieDonohoe 10 (Andrew Haynes) *mid-div: kpt on one pce fnl 3f* **10/1**	51
65	6	4½	**Le Chat D'Or**[24] 2392 3-9-0 0 .... DavidNolan 13 (Neville Bycroft) *trckd ldrs: t.k.h: wknd over 1f out* **10/1**	42
-040	7	½	**Decadence**[25] 2351 3-8-7 52 ow1 .... MichaelO'Connell(3) 7 (Eric Alston) *in rr: kpt on fnl 2f: nvr nr ldrs* **14/1**	37
	8	1½	**Sugar Apple** 3-8-6 0 .... JamesSullivan(3) 12 (James Given) *trckd ldrs: outpcd 4f out: kpt on fnl 2f* **8/1**[3]	33
00	9	5	**Miss Emily (IRE)**[9] 2802 3-8-6 0 .... DeclanCannon(3) 11 (George Moore) *mid-div: nvr a factor* **50/1**	23
0-	10	15	**Regythelion**[245] 6896 5-9-7 0 .... NeilFarley(5) 6 (Frederick Watson) *mid-div: lost pl over 3f out: sn bhd and eased: t.o* **66/1**	—
00-0	11	17	**Annalika**[10] 2781 3-8-6 37 .... BillyCray(3) 4 (Colin Teague) *t.k.h in rr: bhd fnl 3f: eased* **66/1**	—
	12	2¾	**Chalkie** 3-9-0 0 .... (p) MickyFenton 3 (Marjorie Fife) *s.s: bhd: t.k.h: t.o 4f out* **50/1**	—
	13	2¼	**Regy From Sedgy** 4-9-12 0 .... GregFairley 2 (Frederick Watson) *s.s: bhd: t.o 4f out* **66/1**	—

2m 6.82s (-0.28) **Going Correction** +0.025s/f (Good)
WFA 3 from 4yo+ 12lb — **13** Ran SP% **133.0**

Owner J M & Mrs E E Ranson **Bred** G J King **Trained** Denton, Co Durham
FOCUS
A weak maiden and the winner probably didn't need to improve.

3139 WIN A VIP DAY OUT @ REDCARRACING.CO.UK H'CAP — 1m 2f
3:20 (3:20) (Class 5) (0-70,69) 4-Y-0+ — **£1,942** (£578; £288; £144) **Stalls** Low

Form				RPR
2502	1		**Media Stars**[13] 2734 6-8-5 **56** .... JamesSullivan(3) 6 (Robert Johnson) *trckd ldrs: hdwy over 2f out: led over 1f out: rdn out* **5/1**[3]	64
6-21	2	1¼	**Petsas Pleasure**[17] 2589 5-8-9 **57** .... TomEaves 5 (Ollie Pears) *stdd s: hld up in last: hdwy over 3f out: drvn over 1f out: styd on to take 2nd last 50yds* **9/4**[1]	62
122	3	1¾	**Timocracy**[28] 2245 6-9-7 **69** .... StevieDonohoe 1 (Andrew Haynes) *set str pce: hdd over 1f out: kpt on same pce: wknd towards fin* **5/2**[2]	71
5502	4	2½	**Carnival Dream**[9] 2809 6-7-13 **50** oh5 .... (p) DeclanCannon(3) 3 (Hugh McWilliams) *trckd ldrs: drvn over 2f out: one pce* **11/1**	47
001	5	1	**Marino Prince (FR)**[23] 2401 6-8-8 **56** .... MickyFenton 7 (Paul Midgley) *hld up in rr: drvn 4f out: sn wl outpcd: kpt on ins fnl f* **7/1**	51
153-	6	12	**Smirfy's Silver**[324] 4481 7-9-5 **67** .... GregFairley 2 (Deborah Sanderson) *t.k.h: sn w ldr: wknd over 2f out: eased over 1f out* **5/1**[3]	38

2m 6.57s (-0.53) **Going Correction** +0.025s/f (Good) — **6** Ran SP% **113.5**
Speed ratings (Par 103): **103,102,100,98,97 88**
toteswingers:1&2:£3.50, 2&3:£2.60, 1&3:£3.80 CSF £17.00 TOTE £4.30: £2.60, £1.60; EX 18.30.
Owner Robert C Whitelock **Bred** Newsells Park Stud **Trained** Newburn, Tyne & Wear
FOCUS
A modest handicap in which Timocracy and Smirfy's Silver took each other on for the early lead and set too strong a gallop. That set things up for the closers. Straightforward form.

3140 ANDERSON BARROWCLIFF H'CAP — 6f
4:00 (4:00) (Class 3) (0-95,90) 3-Y-0+ — **£3,885** (£1,156; £577; £288) **Stalls** High

Form				RPR
3050	1		**Fitz Flyer (IRE)**[5] 2954 5-9-3 **87** .... (v1) TomEaves 2 (Bryan Smart) *mde all: rdn over 1f out: hld on towards fin* **3/1**[2]	96
053	2	½	**Noodles Blue Boy**[14] 2662 5-8-11 **84** .... MichaelO'Connell(3) 5 (Ollie Pears) *chsd wnr: drvn over 1f out: styd on ins fnl f: a jst hld* **11/4**[1]	91
4400	3	½	**Five Star Junior (USA)**[47] 1720 5-9-3 **90** .... JamesSullivan(3) 1 (Linda Stubbs) *dwlt: sn trcking ldrs: edgd lft fnl f: kpt on same pce last 100yds* **7/2**[3]	96
4510	4	¾	**Piazza San Pietro**[13] 2717 5-9-5 **89** .... StevieDonohoe 3 (Andrew Haynes) *hld up towards rr: effrt over 2f out: kpt on same pce ins fnl f* **11/4**[1]	92
0130	5	7	**Dickie Le Davoir**[5] 2954 7-8-13 **86** .... (b) RobertLButler(3) 4 (Richard Guest) *hld up in rr: effrt over 2f out: lost pl over 1f out: eased* **13/2**	67

69.89 secs (-1.91) **Going Correction** -0.125s/f (Firm) — **5** Ran SP% **113.9**
Speed ratings (Par 107): **107,106,105,104,95**
CSF £12.00 TOTE £4.10: £3.10, £1.40; EX 16.10.
Owner Ron Hull **Bred** Colin Kennedy **Trained** Hambleton, N Yorks
FOCUS
A competitive little sprint but not form to be positive about and the time was modest.

NOTEBOOK
Fitz Flyer(IRE) led his rivals a merry dance from the front and he found plenty in the closing stages to score in decisive fashion. This was quite a turnaround in fortunes for a horse who had failed to win in 15 previous efforts on turf, and his finishing efforts have often been weak, but he proved a different proposition in the headgear and displayed bundles of natural speed. The big question now is whether the visor will continue to work, because if it does he can win again. (op 4-1)
Noodles Blue Boy was always tracking the winner but he could never get to grips with that rival at the business end and he is better suited by being able to dominate over the minimum trip. (op 3-1 tchd 7-2)
Five Star Junior(USA) travelled well and looked a major threat approaching the final furlong but he found less than anticipated when coming under pressure. (op 4-1)
Piazza San Pietro had every chance but was only one paced in the final furlong and this class of opposition is a little too hot for him. (op 9-4)
Dickie Le Davoir was soon detached and never figured. (op 9-2 tchd 7-1)

3141 RACING UK ON SKY 432 CLASSIFIED CLAIMING STKS — 1m 2f
4:35 (4:35) (Class 6) 3-Y-0+ — **£1,706** (£503; £252) **Stalls** Low

Form				RPR
4250	1		**Eijaaz (IRE)**[16] 2616 10-8-13 58 .... (p) MichaelO'Connell(3) 6 (Geoffrey Harker) *hld up in rr: smooth hdwy over 3f out: chal on bit over 1f out: shkn up and led jst ins fnl f: sn rdn: hld on towards fin* **3/1**[2]	63
054	2	nk	**Just Five (IRE)**[32] 2149 5-9-11 70 .... SeanLevey(3) 7 (John Weymes) *hld up: effrt over 3f out: rdn and outpcd over 2f out: styd on wl ins fnl f: jst hld* **7/1**[3]	74
021	3	2¾	**Humor Me Rene (USA)**[30] 2195 4-9-6 72 .... MatthewDavies(3) 1 (George Baker) *trckd ldrs: drvn over 2f out: led over 1f out: hdd jst ins fnl f: wknd towards fin* **4/7**[1]	64
3256	4	4½	**Paco Belle (IRE)**[21] 2466 3-8-3 64 .... DeclanCannon(3) 3 (Andrew Crook) *w ldr: led over 3f out: rdn over 2f out: hdd over 1f out: sn wknd* **10/1**	50
/000	5	6	**Wing N Prayer (IRE)**[14] 2666 4-9-2 34 .... (t) StevieDonohoe 2 (Alan Berry) *hld up: hdwy to chse ldrs 4f out: n.m.r over 2f out: wknd over 1f out* **66/1**	36
5/4-	6	2½	**Oskari**[33] 858 6-8-13 51 .... (t) JamesSullivan(3) 5 (Mike Sowersby) *led: hdd over 3f out: lost pl over 2f out* **33/1**	31
30-0	7	8	**Bold Indian (IRE)**[15] 1164 7-9-2 52 .... TomEaves 4 (Mike Sowersby) *trckd ldrs on outer: t.k.h: lost pl over 2f out: sn bhd* **33/1**	15

2m 9.17s (2.07) **Going Correction** +0.025s/f (Good)
WFA 3 from 4yo+ 12lb — **7** Ran SP% **117.6**
Speed ratings (Par 101): **92,91,89,85,81 79,72**
toteswingers:1&2:£2.10, 2&3:£2.10, 1&3:£1.60 CSF £24.20 TOTE £3.20: £1.40, £1.50; EX 22.10.
Owner A S Ward **Bred** Shadwell Estate Company Limited **Trained** Thirkleby, N Yorks
FOCUS
Weak stuff, run much slower than the earlier C&D races. Muddling form, rated around the winner.

3142 FOLLOW REDCARRACING ON FACEBOOK & TWITTER H'CAP — 1m
5:10 (5:10) (Class 5) (0-70,67) 3-Y-0+ — **£1,942** (£578; £288; £144) **Stalls** High

Form				RPR
0340	1		**Broctune Papa Gio**[17] 2593 4-8-6 **48** oh1 .... DeclanCannon(3) 1 (Keith Reveley) *chsd ldrs: drvn over 3f out: styd on to ld last 75yds: hld on* **20/1**	56
045-	2	¾	**Lujano**[195] 7705 6-9-1 **54** .... TomEaves 8 (Ollie Pears) *t.k.h: mde most: hdd and no ex last 75yds* **16/1**	60
0441	3	¾	**See The Storm**[17] 2598 3-7-12 **52** .... NeilFarley(5) 2 (Patrick Morris) *hld up towards rr: effrt 3f out: chal over 1f out: styd on same pce ins fnl f* **13/2**[3]	54
5302	4	hd	**Byron Bear (IRE)**[21] 2465 3-8-1 **50** .... PaulQuinn 3 (Paul Midgley) *hld up in rr: hdwy 3f out: swtchd rt jst ins fnl f: kpt on towards fin* **10/1**	52
05-4	5	2¾	**Dialogue**[53] 1558 5-9-11 **67** .... MichaelO'Connell(3) 7 (Geoffrey Harker) *trckd ldrs: effrt 3f out: wknd appr fnl f* **1/2**[1]	64
0040	6	½	**Colamandis**[18] 2548 4-8-6 **48** oh3 .... (p) JamesSullivan(3) 4 (Hugh McWilliams) *mid-div: drvn and hdwy 3f out: one pce over 1f out* **33/1**	44
0-32	7	2¼	**Fire King**[22] 2420 5-9-7 **60** .... (p) StevieDonohoe 5 (Andrew Haynes) *s.i.s: effrt on outside over 3f out: wknd appr fnl f: eased nr fin* **6/1**[2]	51
1-05	8	nse	**Monsieur Pontaven**[22] 2415 4-8-13 **52** .... (b) MickyFenton 6 (Robin Bastiman) *hld up in rr: effrt over 2f out: nvr nr ldrs* **22/1**	43
000-	9	10	**Royal Premium**[392] 2278 5-8-6 **48** .... (b) BillyCray(3) 9 (Bruce Hellier) *w ldr: t.k.h: wknd over 1f out: eased whn bhd* **33/1**	16

1m 36.08s (-1.92) **Going Correction** -0.125s/f (Firm)
WFA 3 from 4yo+ 10lb — **9** Ran SP% **124.3**
Speed ratings (Par 103): **104,103,102,102,99 99,96,96,86**
toteswingers:1&2:£10.70, 2&3:£8.30, 1&3:£10.80 CSF £297.68 CT £2330.49 TOTE £26.60: £3.30, £3.30, £2.50; EX 140.00.
Owner Broctune Partners I **Bred** Lesley Winn And Reveley Farms **Trained** Lingdale, Redcar & Cleveland
FOCUS
An open event although there was a disappointing favourite. Fairly weak but straightforward form.

3143 COME RACING TOMORROW ON LADIES' DAY MAIDEN H'CAP — 5f
5:45 (5:45) (Class 5) (0-70,61) 3-Y-0+ — **£1,942** (£578; £288; £144) **Stalls** High

Form				RPR
0263	1		**Mecca's Team**[20] 2493 3-9-4 **60** .... SeanLevey(3) 6 (Michael Dods) *mde virtually all: styd on u.p ins fnl f: all out* **7/2**[2]	63
60-0	2	hd	**Brian Sprout**[28] 2252 3-8-13 **55** .... DeclanCannon(3) 1 (John Weymes) *chsd ldrs: rdn and outpcd 3f out: hdwy on wd outside over 1f out: styd on fnl 100yds: jst hld* **20/1**	57
0633	3	hd	**Hootys Agogo**[6] 2918 3-8-8 **52** .... NeilFarley(5) 3 (Declan Carroll) *w wnr: kpt on ins fnl f: no ex nr fin* **5/2**[1]	54
4603	4	3¾	**Running Water**[9] 2805 3-8-3 **45** .... (bt1) JamesSullivan(3) 4 (Hugh McWilliams) *s.i.s: sme hdwy 2f out: sn rdn: kpt on towards fin* **11/1**	33
2232	5	hd	**Tancred Spirit**[14] 2697 3-8-9 **48** .... MickyFenton 2 (Paul Midgley) *chsd ldrs: wknd jst ins fnl f* **7/2**[2]	35
6035	6	1½	**Bygones For Coins (IRE)**[9] 2805 3-8-6 **50** .... DanielleMcCreery(5) 7 (Alan Berry) *hld up towards rr: rdn 2f out: edgd lft: nvr nr ldrs* **14/1**	32
-056	7	2¾	**Vintage Grape (IRE)**[9] 2805 3-8-8 **50** .... (p) MichaelO'Connell(3) 5 (Eric Alston) *mid-div: rdn over 2f out: nvr a factor* **20/1**	22
0-54	8	1¾	**Media Jury**[9] 2798 4-9-0 **47** ow2 .... (p) DavidNolan 8 (John Wainwright) *chsd ldrs: hung lft and wknd over 1f out* **9/1**	15

60-4 **9** *3 ¾* **Hygrove Gal**[13] 2736 3-9-8 **61**.. TomEaves 9 13
(Bryan Smart) *s.i.s: outpcd and a bhd* **13/2**[3]

57.61 secs (-0.99) **Going Correction** -0.125s/f (Firm)
WFA 3 from 4yo 6lb **9** Ran SP% **120.9**
Speed ratings (Par 103): **102,101,101,95,95 92,88,85,79**
toteswingers:1&2:£16.50, 2&3:£12.30, 1&3:£2.70 CSF £72.84 CT £206.12 TOTE £6.20: £1.30, £5.70, £1.10; EX 79.40.
Owner David T J Metcalfe & D W Barker **Bred** Redmyre Bloodstock Ltd **Trained** Denton, Co Durham

FOCUS
More weak form, this time a field of maidens. A small personal best from the winner.
T/Plt: £276.00 to a £1 stake. Pool of £35,585.34 - 94.09 winning tickets. T/Qpdt: £50.10 to a £1 stake. Pool of £2,129.44 - 31.45 winning tickets. WG

3144 - 3151a (Foreign Racing) - See Raceform Interactive

[3104] ASCOT (R-H)

Saturday, June 18

OFFICIAL GOING: Soft (stands' side 8.3, centre 8.8, far side 8.8, round 7.1)
Course at normal configuration and distances as advertised.
Wind: fresh, against Weather: bright spells and showers

3152 CHESHAM STKS (LISTED RACE) 7f
2:30 (2:37) (Class 1) 2-Y-O

£28,385 (£10,760; £5,385; £2,685; £1,345; £675) **Stalls** Centre

Form RPR

1 **Maybe (IRE)**[38] 2009 2-8-12 0.. RyanMoore 5 98+
(A P O'Brien, Ire) *in tch and a travelling wl: led 2f out: clr w runner-up over 1f out: rdn hands and heels and asserted 1f out: styd on wl: impressive* **5/2**[1]

2 **2** *2 ¼* **Fort Bastion (IRE)**[22] 2455 2-9-3 0.............................. RichardHughes 12 97
(Richard Hannon) *hld up in tch: pushed along and effrt over 2f out: rdn to press wnr and drew clr of field wl over 1f out: nt pce of wnr ent fnl f: kpt on for clr 2nd but no threat to wnr after* **9/2**[2]

5 **3** *3* **Self Centred**[22] 2467 2-8-12 0.. MichaelHills 4 85
(B W Hills) *t.k.h: hld up in tch: hdwy to chse ldrs over 2f out: rdn ent fnl 2f: outpcd by ldng pair and btn over 1f out: kpt on same pce fnl f* **18/1**

332 **4** *½* **Esentepe (IRE)**[28] 2309 2-8-12 0.................................. JimmyFortune 11 84
(Richard Hannon) *t.k.h: chsd ldrs: rdn and effrt over 2f out: outpcd by ldng pair over 1f out and btn whn hung rt ent fnl f: kpt on same pce* **22/1**

5 *1 ½* **Swing Alone (IRE)** 2-9-3 0.. AdamKirby 7 85+
(Gay Kelleway) *stdd s: hld up towards rr: rdn and effrt over 2f out: hdwy u.p over 1f out: no threat to ldrs but kpt on steadily ins fnl f* **40/1**

51 **6** *nse* **Telwaar**[15] 2672 2-9-3 0.. NeilCallan 13 85
(Peter Chapple-Hyam) *t.k.h: hung rt thrght: hld up towards rr: effrt over 2f out: sn outpcd and no threat to ldrs: hung rt and kpt on same pce fr over 1f out* **13/2**

2012 **7** *4* **Bling King**[8] 2868 2-9-3 0.. FergusSweeney 3 75
(Eve Johnson Houghton) *in tch in midfield: effrt jst over 2f out: rdn and btn wl over 1f out: sn wknd* **16/1**

21 **8** *nk* **Falls Of Lora (IRE)**[14] 2709 2-8-12 0.................................. AhmedAjtebi 6 69
(Mahmood Al Zarooni) *restless in stalls: hld up towards rr: hdwy over 2f out: sn rdn and hung rt: wknd over 1f out* **8/1**[3]

3 **9** *½* **Polydamos**[8] 2882 2-9-3 0.. LukeMorris 16 73
(Harry Dunlop) *uns rdr on way to s: in tch: lost pl and pushed along wl over 3f out: rdn and hung rt over 2f out: sn struggling and n.d wl over 1f out* **12/1**

5 **9** *dht* **Goldoni (IRE)**[8] 2882 2-9-3 0.. DavidProbert 8 73
(Andrew Balding) *pressed ldr tl led briefly over 2f out: sn hdd and rdn: wknd wl over 1f out* **25/1**

53 **11** *shd* **Singalat**[26] 2355 2-9-3 0.. TomQueally 1 73
(James Given) *wnt rt s: sn rcvrd to chse ldrs: rdn and wknd over 2f out* **25/1**

0 **12** *1 ½* **Island Melody (IRE)**[11] 2788 2-9-3 0.................................. LiamKeniry 2 69
(J S Moore) *stdd and dropped in bhd after s: hld up in rr: rdn and btn ent fnl 2f* **100/1**

033 **13** *2 ¼* **Yammos (IRE)**[6] 2962 2-9-3 0.. SamHitchcott 10 63
(Mick Channon) *a towards rr: rdn and struggling 3f out: sn bhd* **40/1**

10 **14** *1 ¼* **Majestic Rose**[24] 2404 2-8-12 0.. HughBowman 14 55
(Mick Channon) *t.k.h: hld up towards rr: hdwy wl over 2f out: sn rdn and wknd 2f out* **33/1**

66 **15** *1* **Manomine**[22] 2448 2-9-3 0.. PhilipRobinson 9 58
(Clive Brittain) *in tch early: lost pl and struggling 1/2-way: bhd fnl 2f* **100/1**

44 **16** *7* **Bounty Seeker (USA)**[18] 2584 2-9-3 0.......................... SilvestreDeSousa 15 40
(Mark Johnston) *led tl over 2f out: sn drvn and wknd 2f out: wl bhd and eased ins fnl f* **16/1**

1m 32.46s (5.26) **Going Correction** +0.70s/f (Yiel) **16** Ran SP% **120.9**
Speed ratings (Par 101): **102,99,96,95,93 93,89,88,88,88 88,86,83,82,81 73**
toteswingers:1&2:£3.00, 2&3:£19.30, 1&3:£9.80 CSF £11.50 CT £175.64 TOTE £3.10: £1.30, £2.00, £6.10; EX 12.20 Trifecta £271.10 Pool: £12,735.03 - 34.75 winning units..
Owner M Tabor, D Smith & Mrs John Magnier **Bred** Epona Bloodstock Ltd **Trained** Ballydoyle, Co Tipperary

FOCUS
There had been 7mm of rain overnight, plus a couple of heavy showers from lunchtime along with a drying wind. Jockeys in the first were unanimous that the ground was soft and the words 'holding' and 'sticky' were also mentioned. The first-race winning time was over five seconds outside the standard. Restricted to the progeny of stallions who won over at least 1m2f, this race caters for the later-maturing juveniles. The majority of recent Chesham scorers have been unable to build on their victories, but this year's winner could well buck the trend. The runners raced in one group down the centre and finished quite well strung out. There didn't appear any discernible draw advantage. Last-time-out winners have dominated this race in the past decade, but there were only three in this line-up, among them the impressive winner. The form has been rated in line with the race averages, with the fourth and seventh among those offering perspective, but the winner can rate higher.

NOTEBOOK
Maybe(IRE) ◆ came here as the only unbeaten runner. Her Naas debut win, over 6f on fast ground, had been boosted by the runner-up and fourth home Teolane, although the latter filly blew out in the Albany Stakes on Friday. An easy-to-back favourite, with the ground a concern to her trainer, she sweated up in the paddock. There were few worries in the race as she travelled smoothly up with the pace and found more than enough when let down, shrugging off the challenge of the runner-up to win comfortably. Only the third filly to take the Chesham in the last 20 years, and Aidan O'Brien's second winner in the race, following Bach 12 years ago, she looks a very nice prospect and a good deal more should be heard of her. She will get a mile in time but is likely to be kept to this trip for now and take in the Moyglare Stud Stakes at the Curragh in August. That would represent a considerable rise in grade and she will need to step up considerably on this bare form, but she may well be up the task. She is as short as 9-2 for next year's 1,000 Guineas, a price that does not appeal at this stage for all her potential. (op 9-4 tchd 11-4, 3-1 in places and 2-1 in places)
Fort Bastion(IRE)'s trainer has had this race in mind for the colt since his debut second at Haydock behind Coventry also-ran Mezmaar, and the Hannon yard won this in both 2008 and 2009. The colt came under pressure before the winner and proved no match in the end, but was clear of the remainder. He lost little in defeat to a very useful filly and the Group 3 Superlative Stakes at the Newmarket July festival could be his next run. (tchd 5-1 and 11-2 in places)
Self Centred ◆ had been two places behind Albany Stakes winner Samitar when they were making their debuts on the Rowley Mile last month. She stayed on nicely for third over this extra furlong and looks a filly with a future. Newmarket's Sweet Solera Stakes could be next for her, while the Prestige Stakes at Goodwood also makes some appeal, her connections having won that race with Geminiani in 2002. (op 20-1)
Esentepe(IRE), the third filly in the first four and the runner-up's stablemate, had every chance at one stage but lacked a change of pace. She has progressed with each run and she stayed the seventh furlong well enough. (op 20-1 tchd 25-1)
Swing Alone(IRE), sold for £15,000 earlier this year, came under pressure at halfway but kept on in pleasing fashion for fifth, albeit beaten a good way by the winner. This was a promising effort from a debutant. (op 50-1)
Telwaar, who became upset by the antics of Polydamos down at the start, probably stayed the trip but might not mind a drop back to 6f. The Doncaster winner was fifth to Coventry third St Barths first time out and turned around form in that race with both Singalat and Bounty Seeker. (op 9-1)
Bling King, not for the first time, became keyed up in the paddock. This was his first run on ground with give and he performed respectably. (op 25-1)
Falls Of Lora(IRE), an impressive Doncaster winner, was a little restless in the stalls and didn't fire in the race. The ground could have been against her and it may be worth forgiving her this. (op 11-2)
Polydamos got loose for a while down at the start and was never really a factor, dead-heating for ninth with \bGoldoni\p whom he had beaten on his debut. (op 16-1 tchd 11-1 and 20-1 in places)
Bounty Seeker(USA), who looked more developed than most on paddock inspection, weakened after making the running. He failed to confirm the decent impression he had made in Leicester maidens won by St Barths and Roman Soldier, both of whom were placed in the Coventry on Tuesday. (op 20-1 tchd 25-1 in places)

3153 HARDWICKE STKS (GROUP 2) 1m 4f
3:05 (3:07) (Class 1) 4-Y-O+

£61,964 (£23,489; £11,755; £5,861; £2,936; £1,473) **Stalls** Low

Form RPR

/1-1 **1** **Await The Dawn (USA)**[44] 1821 4-9-0 120........................ RyanMoore 9 124+
(A P O'Brien, Ire) *midfield: wnt down centre of trck fr over 6f out to fnl bnd: hdwy over 2f out: sn wnt 2nd: powered into ld over 1f out: r.o wl thrght fnl f: pushed out whn in command towards fin* **4/6**[1]

11-3 **2** *3* **Harris Tweed**[43] 1851 4-9-0 112.................................... RichardHughes 2 118
(William Haggas) *led: wnt down centre of trck fr over 6f out to fnl bnd: rdn 2f out: hdd over 1f out: kpt on u.p ins fnl f but a hld* **12/1**

4461 **3** *2 ½* **Drunken Sailor (IRE)**[35] 2098 6-9-0 115......................(b) KierenFallon 7 114
(Luca Cumani) *hld up: wnt down centre of trck fr over 6f out to fnl bnd: prog and styd on over 1f out: wnt 3rd fnl 110yds: no imp on front 2* **9/1**[3]

1-45 **4** *nk* **Laaheb**[49] 1685 5-9-0 115.. RichardHills 6 114
(Roger Varian) *trckd ldrs: wnt down centre of trck fr over 6f out to fnl bnd: effrt to chse ldr briefly over 2f out but unable to mount serious chal: kpt on same pce ins fnl f* **16/1**

0-42 **5** *2 ¼* **Campanologist (USA)**[27] 2332 6-9-0 116.......................... TedDurcan 4 110
(Saeed Bin Suroor) *hld up in midfield: wnt down centre of trck fr over 6f out to fnl bnd: hdwy over 4f out: rdn and chsd ldrs over 2f out: hung rt ent fnl 2f: one pce and no imp fr over 1f out* **14/1**

2123 **6** *10* **Calvados Blues (FR)**[84] 1001 5-9-0 116.............................. JMurtagh 8 94
(Mahmood Al Zarooni) *racd keenly: hld up: wnt down centre of trck fr over 6f out to fnl bnd: effrt over 2f out and edgd lft: failed to pick-up and carried hd awkwardly: sn wl btn* **14/1**

2-21 **7** *1 ¼* **Kings Gambit (SAF)**[56] 1528 7-9-0 111.......................... JamieSpencer 10 92
(Tom Tate) *trckd ldrs: wnt 2nd over 6f out and racd down centre of trck tl fnl bnd: lost 2nd over 2f out: u.p whn carried rt ent fnl 2f: sn wknd and wl btn* **33/1**

-326 **8** *41* **Poet**[13] 2753 6-9-0 115..(p) AdamKirby 3 26
(Clive Cox) *chsd ldr tl elected to r against ins rail over 6f out whn most wnt down centre of trck: rdn and wknd over 4f out: eased whn wl btn over 2f out: t.o* **8/1**[2]

1/31 **9** *45* **Passion For Gold (USA)**[28] 2292 4-9-0 113........... MickaelBarzalona 1 —
(Saeed Bin Suroor) *hld up: elected to r against ins rail whn most wnt down centre of trck over 6f out: u.p and wl bhd fnl 5f: eased over 2f out: t.o* **11/1**

2m 38.4s (5.90) **Going Correction** +0.875s/f (Soft) **9** Ran SP% **119.3**
Speed ratings (Par 115): **115,113,111,111,109 102,102,74,44**
toteswingers:1&2:£3.00, 2&3:£12.50, 1&3:£2.70 CSF £10.87 CT £46.58 TOTE £1.60: £1.10, £3.10, £1.90; EX 12.30 Trifecta £92.30 Pool: £14,535.82 - 116.48 winning units..
Owner M Tabor & Mrs John Magnier **Bred** Juddmonte Farms Inc **Trained** Ballydoyle, Co Tipperary

FOCUS
The form looks sound among the front four, the only ones to show their form on the ground. Await The Dawn is rated to his Chester form but is up to Group 1 level and theres little between him and St Nicholas Abbey.

NOTEBOOK
Await The Dawn(USA) came into the race rated 4lb clear of his nearest rival and had more scope for improvement than anything else in the field. However, having been so impressive on his reappearance, the question mark hanging over him here was how well he'd cope with the greater test of stamina compared to the one he faced at Chester. A longer trip coupled with softer ground and several rivals who like to force the issue promised to expose any stamina frailties, but in the event he coped admirably, running on strongly from the turn in to win by a clear-cut margin. These conditions were far from ideal and the fact he was still able to win fairly easily underlines his ability and class. He'll appreciate getting back on a decent surface and is clearly well capable of competing in top company between 1m2f and 1m4f, and given his pedigree it's understandable why connections feel he could make up into a Breeders' Cup Classic contender later in the season. There are several Group 1 options open to him on turf before he tries the dirt, but he's bred to go on the surface, and the venue this year, Churchill Downs, is where his sire Giant's Causeway was so narrowly denied by Tiznow in the Classic of 2000. (op 4-7 tchd 4-5 in places)

Harris Tweed took them along out in front. Edging away from the inside rail in search of better ground when possible, he stayed on strongly up the straight, holding off all bar the impressive winner. He probably won't have to take him on again, which will be a relief to connections, and the Princess Of Wales's Stakes might be suitable short-term target for him, although the Melbourne Cup was also mentioned as a possible long-term aim. (op 14-1 tchd 16-1 in places)

Drunken Sailor(IRE) had ground conditions in his favour and he also had the race run to suit, as he likes to come from behind off a good gallop. A dual winner in Listed company, he ran about as well as could be expected in this class. (op 12-1)

Laaheb, whose trainer expected him to appreciate the give in the ground, won a Group 3 here last autumn. He ran a sound race, just being run out of third close home, and is another who could well go for the Princess Of Wales's Stakes, as he has a good record on the July course. (tchd 20-1 in a place)

Campanologist(USA), second in a weaker renewal of this race two years ago, might not want the ground this soft. (op 16-1)

Calvados Blues(FR) failed to run to anywhere near the form he showed out in Dubai in the spring. He's another who might need quicker ground to be seen at his best.

Kings Gambit(SAF) was in second place turning in but soon dropped right out. He ran like a blatant non-stayer. (tchd 40-1 in a place)

Poet had an excuse in France last time but his previous effort behind Workforce at Sandown appeared to give him place claims at least in this company, especially as the ground appeared to be just as he would like it. Wearing cheekpieces for the first time, he took a lead off Harris Tweed and stayed on the inside when the Haggas runner edged out wide in search of better ground. He was under pressure and going nowhere with 6f to go, though, and might be the type who needs to have his own way in front. Adam Kirby reported that his mount ran flat. Official explanation: jockey said horse ran flat (op 10-1)

Passion For Gold(USA) was struggling from a fairly early stage. He had Group 1-winning form in testing ground as a juvenile, so conditions shouldn't have been a problem for him. He has been very lightly raced and clearly had issues, so perhaps all was not well. (op 12-1)

3154 GOLDEN JUBILEE STKS (BRITISH CHAMPIONS' SERIES & GLOBAL SPRINT CHALLENGE) (GROUP 1) 6f

3:45 (3:45) (Class 1) 3-Y-O+

£227,080 (£86,080; £43,080; £21,480; £10,760; £5,400) **Stalls** Centre

Form RPR

0-02 **1** **Society Rock (IRE)**[42] 1891 4-9-4 112 PatCosgrave 3 119
(James Fanshawe) *racd far side: hld up in tch: barging match w rival after 1f: rdn and effrt 2f out: drvn and hdwy between horses jst ins fnl f: styd on wl to ld fnl 75yds* **25/1**

0/40 **2** *½* **Monsieur Chevalier (IRE)**[4] 3010 4-9-4 109 KierenFallon 7 117
(Richard Hannon) *racd far side: in tch in midfield: rdn and lost pl 1/2-way: rallied u.p and swtchd lft over 1f out: styd on wl ins fnl f: wnt 2nd towards fin: 2nd of 11 in gp* **25/1**

1-02 **3** *1 ¼* **Star Witness (AUS)**[4] 3010 4-9-4 116 (t) StevenArnold 11 113
(Danny O'Brien, Australia) *swtchd to r far side after 1f: hld up in tch: pushed along to ld overall over 1f out: rdn fnl f: hdd fnl 75yds: no ex and wknd towards fin: 3rd of 11 in gp* **4/1**[2]

3-51 **4** *hd* **Elzaam (AUS)**[36] 2054 3-8-11 114 RichardHills 10 111+
(Roger Varian) *swtchd to r far side after 1f: pushed along and outpcd in rr 4f out: rdn over 2f out: hdwy u.p jst over 1f out: kpt on wl fnl f: styng on wl fin: 4th of 11 in gp* **12/1**

-011 **5** *nk* **Bated Breath**[26] 2370 4-9-4 113 RichardHughes 4 112
(Roger Charlton) *t.k.h: racd far side: hld up wl in tch: barging match w rival after 1f: rdn and chsd ldrs 2f out: drvn and sltly outpcd over 1f out: kpt on again u.p ins fnl f: 5th of 11 in gp* **8/1**[3]

00-1 **6** *¾* **Amico Fritz (GER)**[54] 1575 5-9-4 112 MaximeGuyon 13 109+
(H-A Pantall, France) *racd stands' side: chsd gp ldr tl led overall 2f out: sn drvn: hdd over 1f out: kpt on same pce fnl 150yds: 1st of 5 in gp* **14/1**

1-01 **7** *¾* **Hooray**[15] 2683 3-8-8 116 SebSanders 2 102
(Sir Mark Prescott Bt) *racd far side: led gp and chsd ldrs overall: rdn ent fnl 2f: drvn over 1f out: styd on same pce fnl f: 6th of 11 in gp* **11/1**

2-10 **8** *nk* **Genki (IRE)**[38] 2005 7-9-4 111 (v) JamieSpencer 1 108
(Roger Charlton) *racd far side: in tch: rdn and effrt to press ldrs over 1f out: drvn and btn ins fnl f: wknd fnl 100yds: 7th of 11 in gp* **20/1**

6310 **9** *¾* **Jimmy Styles**[65] 1340 7-9-4 107 (p) AdamKirby 8 104
(Clive Cox) *racd far side: stdd after s: hld up in rr: effrt and rdn 2f out: hdwy u.p over 1f out: kpt on same pce and no imp fnl f: 8th of 11 in gp* **66/1**

6-26 **10** *1 ¼* **Kingsgate Native (IRE)**[4] 3010 6-9-4 115 (p) RyanMoore 5 100
(Sir Michael Stoute) *racd far side: chsd gp ldr: rdn ent fnl 2f: drvn and unable qck over 1f out: wknd jst ins fnl f: 9th of 11 in gp* **14/1**

5441 **11** *1* **Hitchens (IRE)**[28] 2323 6-9-4 109 FMBerry 16 96+
(David Barron) *racd stands' side: chsd ldng stands' side pair but no bttr than midfield overall: rdn and effrt 2f out: kpt on same pce and no threat to far side fr over 1f out: 2nd of 5 in gp* **33/1**

23-6 **12** *½* **Dalghar (FR)**[38] 2005 5-9-4 113 JimmyFortune 15 95+
(Andrew Balding) *racd stands' side: a in rr: rdn over 2f out: kpt on fnl f but nvr trbld ldrs: 3rd of 5 in gp* **8/1**[3]

0-63 **13** *nse* **Royal Rock**[42] 1891 7-9-4 103 GeorgeBaker 6 98
(Chris Wall) *racd far side: hld up in rr: rdn and effrt 2f out: no imp ent fnl f: btn and eased fnl 100yds: 10 of 11 in gp* **40/1**

11-1 **14** *2 ½* **Bewitched (IRE)**[20] 2533 4-9-1 111 (t) JMurtagh 12 84
(Charles O'Brien, Ire) *swtchd to r far side after 1f: hld up towards rr: rdn and fnd little 2f out: edgd rt u.p and wl btn over 1f out: 11 of 11 in gp* **3/1**[1]

210- **15** *hd* **Definightly**[216] 7459 5-9-4 114 (b) OlivierPeslier 17 86+
(Roger Charlton) *racd stands' side: overall ldr tl 2f out: sn rdn: wknd qckly jst over 1f out: 4th of 5 in gp* **12/1**

40-4 **16** *31* **Palace Moon**[28] 2315 6-9-4 106 (t) JimCrowley 14 —+
(William Knight) *swtchd to r stands' side after s: v.s.a: a struggling in rr: lost tch over 2f out: virtually p.u fnl f: t.o: 5 of 5 in gp* **66/1**

1m 17.22s (2.82) **Going Correction** +0.70s/f (Yiel)
WFA 3 from 4yo+ 7lb **16** Ran **SP%** **125.1**
Speed ratings (Par 117): **109,108,106,106,106 105,104,103,102,100 99,98,98,95,95 53**
toteswingers:1&2:£128.20, 2&3:£30.90, 1&3:£25.30 CSF £537.85 CT £3143.54 TOTE £36.80: £8.30, £5.90, £2.10; EX 720.20 Trifecta £16472.00 Part won. Pool: £22,259.58 - 0.40 winning units..

Owner Simon Gibson **Bred** San Gabriel Investments **Trained** Newmarket, Suffolk
■ Pat Cosgrave's first Royal Ascot winner.

FOCUS
This looked a sub-par edition of the race, which was renamed and elevated to Group 1 status in 2002. Duke of York Stakes winner Delegator was taken out because of the ground, and intended Australian runner Hinchinbrook was ruled out through injury. This has been a real international event in recent seasons, but this year 13 of the runners were British-trained, with one challenger apiece from Australia, France and Ireland. Only three runners had won at the top level and there was not much between the principal contenders either on BHA or Racing Post Ratings. The time was slower then the Wokingham. Society Rock is rated up a length on last year's form in this race, with a bigger personal best from the second, while the third was a length off his King's Stand Mark. The field quickly split into two groups, with the highest-drawn five going down the stands' rail and the other 11 racing on the far side. The larger group came out well on top, with the first five home and nine of the first ten taking that option.

NOTEBOOK
Society Rock(IRE) put in a career-best when runner-up to Starspangledbanner in this a year ago and although he had not matched that since, he had been restricted to just three runs in the interim and there were signs of better to come at Haydock last time when he was runner-up to Bated Breath. The ground was an unknown, as he had never encountered going faster than good, but he obviously handled it well and burst through between horses to lead inside the last. The lightly raced 4yo has the July Cup at Newmarket as his intended target, where he would probably be taken on by a number of those he beat here. He was seventh in last year's July Cup, a race the Fanshawe yard won in 2004 with Frizzante.
Monsieur Chevalier(IRE) made a brave bid to enhance the statistic that four of the last eight Golden Jubilee winners had run in the King's Stand Stakes earlier in the week. Taken off his legs on Tuesday, he was much more at home over this 6f and, after losing his pitch, he stayed on well late on, running past the third home at the same time as the winner, who just had his measure. Along with the fourth, he raced on the near side of his bunch. He is likely to run in the July Cup, too. (tchd 22-1)
Star Witness(AUS), runner-up to Prohibit in the King's Stand, was expected to improve for this extra furlong, having won two Group 1s at home in Australia. He looked in command when bursting to the front, only to tie up late on with the soft ground just finding him out in the last 50 yards. He will remain in Britain and looks sure to run a bold race in the July Cup.\n (op 6-1 tchd 13-2 in places)
Elzaam(AUS) ◆, another who may be July Cup-bound, was one of just two 3yos in this field. He looked in trouble at the rear of the far-side bunch with 2f left, but ran on steadily once finding himself edging more towards the centre of the track. He is very likely to appreciate the return to a sound surface and must be on the shortlist at Newmarket. (tchd 11-1)
Bated Breath held a verdict over both the winner and runner-up from earlier in the season and he did best of his trainer's three runners, only giving best inside the last. This was his first try in a Group race, let alone at this level, and he comes out with plenty of credit. (op 9-1 tchd 10-1)
Amico Fritz(GER), who did best of the five who took the stands-side route, was only beaten around three lengths and loses little in defeat given the circumstances. Fifth in this last year, he had his ground this time but the draw beat him. (op 16-1)
Hooray, back down in trip, showed plenty of pace to lead her elders but could not hold off the challengers inside the last. She is worth a crack at the July Cup. (op 10-1)
Genki(IRE)'s Stewards' Cup win in 2009 came in soft ground but most of his best form has been in fast conditions. He ran well for a long way but was beaten when he was eased in the last few strides. It was reported that he was unsuited by the loose ground. Official explanation: trainer said gelding was unsuited by the loose ground
Jimmy Styles had a bit to find with most of these and the rain cannot have helped him. (tchd 80-1 in a place)
Kingsgate Native(IRE), the 2008 winner, finished down the field a year ago and has now been beaten in his last 11 starts at Group 1 level, including this week's King's Stand Stakes. He wore cheekpieces for the first time. (op 16-1)
Dalghar(FR) was never seen with a chance among the near-side group. He had been coltish in the paddock.
Bewitched(IRE)'s rider could have gone down the stands' side from stall 12 but sensibly made the right call. It did not make much difference as it turned out, as the filly, who beat St James's Palace Stakes runner-up Zoffany over 7f first time out, never picked up and was most disappointing. Her trainer could initially offer no explanation and the stewards ordered her to be routine tested. The following morning, however, she was found to be lame behind. Official explanation: trainer had no explanation for the poor form shown (op 10-3 tchd 7-2 and 4-1 in a place)
Definightly had his ground and was well backed, but after showing fine pace down the unfavoured stands' side he faded badly. (op 10-1)

3155 WOKINGHAM STKS (HERITAGE H'CAP) 6f

4:25 (4:30) (Class 2) (0-110,109) 3-Y-O+

£62,310 (£18,660; £9,330; £4,670; £2,330; £1,170) **Stalls** Centre

Form RPR

30-2 **1** **Deacon Blues**[42] 1888 4-8-13 **98** JMurtagh 11 112
(James Fanshawe) *racd on far-side: hld up in midfield: hdwy wl over 1f out: sn led: r.o ins fnl f: a doing enough whn pressed cl home: 1st of 16 in gp* **15/2**[2]

-224 **2** *nk* **Waffle (IRE)**[28] 2317 5-9-1 **100** FMBerry 16 113
(David Barron) *racd far-side: hld up: hdwy 2f out: wnt 2nd 1f out: r.o to chal ins fnl f: looked hld cl home: 2nd of 16 in gp* **12/1**

01-1 **3** *2 ¾* **Pastoral Player**[48] 1720 4-9-4 **103** RichardHughes 15 108
(Hughie Morrison) *dwlt: racd on far side: hld up in rr: hdwy and swtchd rt 2f out: r.o ins fnl f: nt pce of front two: 3rd of 16 in gp* **12/1**

1401 **4** *1 ¾* **Anne Of Kiev (IRE)**[28] 2298 6-9-3 **102** (t) LukeMorris 3 101
(Jeremy Gask) *racd on far side: midfield: hdwy to chse ldrs over 1f out: styd on ins fnl f: nt quite pce to get to ldrs: 4th of 16 in gp* **25/1**

0P0- **5** *¾* **Gramercy (IRE)**[252] 6752 4-8-13 **98** JamieSpencer 1 95
(Michael Bell) *racd on far side: hld up: hdwy and swtchd rt 2f out: chsd ldrs over 1f out: styd on: 5th of 16 in gp* **20/1**

0160 **6** *1 ¼* **Fathsta (IRE)**[28] 2288 6-8-13 **98** JimmyFortune 5 91
(David Simcock) *racd on far side: trckd ldrs: rdn over 1f out: styd on same pce ins fnl f: 6th of 16 in gp* **14/1**

21-1 **7** *nk* **Hoof It**[36] 2075 4-9-6 **105** KierenFallon 13 97
(Michael Easterby) *racd on far side: trckd ldrs: led gp briefly over 1f out: kpt on same pce ins fnl f: 7th of 16 in gp* **9/2**[1]

14-2 **8** *hd* **Mac's Power (IRE)**[35] 2099 5-9-1 **100** (t) PatCosgrave 22 91+
(James Fanshawe) *racd stands' side: hld up in rr: hdwy over 2f out: led gp over 1f out: styd on but no ch w far-side ldrs: 1st of 9 in gp* **10/1**[3]

0554 **9** *2* **Lui Rei (ITY)**[14] 2717 5-9-0 **99** (p) JimCrowley 25 84
(Robert Cowell) *racd stands' side: hld up in midfield: swtchd rt and hdwy over 1f out: styd on ins fnl f: nt pce of ldrs: 2nd of 9 in gp* **20/1**

-000 **10** *½* **Colonel Mak**[14] 2727 4-8-13 **98** LeeNewman 24 81
(David Barron) *racd stands' side: midfield: rdn over 1f out: kpt on same pce ins fnl f: 3rd of 9 in gp* **33/1**

0100 **11** *hd* **Evens And Odds (IRE)**[26] 2370 7-9-5 **104** GeorgeBaker 28 86
(David Nicholls) *racd stands' side: prom: rdn over 1f out: one pce fnl f: 4th of 9 in gp* **50/1**

0-00 **12** *nse* **Cheveton**[14] 2727 7-8-11 **96** SilvestreDeSousa 12 78
(Richard Price) *racd far side: midfield: effrt over 1f out: kpt on same pce fnl f: 8th of 16 in gp* **18/1**

34-1 **13** *nk* **Imperial Guest**[42] 1888 5-8-13 **98**................................ PhilipRobinson 9 79
(George Margarson) *racd far side: trckd ldrs: rdn over 1f out: wknd ins fnl f: 9th of 16 in gp* **16/1**

-013 **14** *½* **Nasri**[42] 1885 5-8-9 **97**.. MichaelO'Connell(3) 29 77
(David Nicholls) *led stands' side gp tl rdn and hdd over 1f out: wknd ins fnl f: 5th of 9 in gp* **12/1**

-562 **15** *1* **High Standing (USA)**[6] 2961 6-9-10 **109**........................ RyanMoore 21 85
(William Haggas) *racd far side: hld up in rr: effrt over 1f out: kpt on ins fnl f: nt pce to chal: 10th of 16 in gp* **25/1**

0000 **16** *½* **Barney McGrew (IRE)**[14] 2706 8-8-11 **96**...................... LiamKeniry 27 71
(Michael Dods) *racd stands' side: hld up in midfield: effrt to chse ldrs over 1f out: outpcd fnl f: 6th of 9 in gp* **50/1**

0-00 **17** *½* **Swilly Ferry (USA)**[36] 2075 4-8-13 **98**.............................. MichaelHills 8 71
(B W Hills) *racd far side: trckd ldrs: rdn over 1f out: fdd ins fnl f: 11th of 16 in gp* **40/1**

0311 **18** *2* **Swiss Cross**[14] 2717 4-8-12 **97** 5ex.....................................(t) NeilCallan 4 64
(Gerard Butler) *racd far side: overall ldr tl over 1f out: sn wknd: 12th of 16 in gp* **20/1**

0000 **19** *1¾* **Golden Desert (IRE)**[42] 1885 7-8-11 **96**......................... TomQueally 20 57
(Robert Mills) *racd far side: hld up: outpcd over 1f out: 13th of 16 in gp* **66/1**

0600 **20** *hd* **Prime Defender**[38] 2005 7-9-3 **102**.................................. OlivierPeslier 17 63
(B W Hills) *racd far side: midfield: pushed along over 2f out: wknd over 1f out: 14th of 16 in gp* **33/1**

0-00 **21** *½* **Blue Jack**[37] 2028 6-9-3 **102**.................................(v) RichardKingscote 26 61
(Tom Dascombe) *racd stands' side: trckd ldrs: rdn to chal 2f out: wknd over 1f out: 7th of 9 in gp* **33/1**

-260 **22** *4* **Love Delta (USA)**[14] 2717 4-8-13 **98**................................ JoeFanning 30 44
(Mark Johnston) *racd stands' side: prom tl rdn and wknd over 1f out: 8th of 9 in gp* **66/1**

22-4 **23** *3¾* **Victoire De Lyphar (IRE)**[42] 1891 4-9-4 **103**............. AdrianNicholls 14 37
(David Nicholls) *racd far side: in tch: rdn 1/2-way: wknd over 1f out: 15th of 16 in gp* **14/1**

0-00 **24** *1½* **Mister Hughie (IRE)**[36] 2075 4-9-4 **103**....................(p) SamHitchcott 19 32
(Tim Easterby) *racd far side tl swtchd to stands' side gp after 1f: struggling over 2f out: a bhd: 9th of 9 in gp* **40/1**

-001 **25** *11* **Burning Thread (IRE)**[14] 2727 4-8-12 **102** 5ex.............. DaleSwift(5) 10 —
(Tim Etherington) *racd far side: w ldr and t.k.h: rdn over 2f out: wknd over 1f out: 16th of 16 in gp* **50/1**

1m 16.9s (2.50) **Going Correction** +0.70s/f (Yiel) **25** Ran SP% **131.1**
Speed ratings (Par 109): **111,110,106,104,103 101,101,101,98,97 97,97,97,96,95 94,93,91,88,88 87,82,77,75,60**
toteswingers:1&2:£13.30, 2&3:£22.00, 1&3:£9.30 CSF £80.08 CT £1103.85 TOTE £7.90: £2.10, £2.60, £3.00, £6.40; EX 76.80 Trifecta £1817.60 Pool: £135,025.09 - 54.97 winning units..

Owner Jan & Peter Hopper & Michelle Morris **Bred** Mr & Mrs K W Grundy, Mr & Mrs P Hopper **Trained** Newmarket, Suffolk

FOCUS
Ultra-competitive stuff as usual. The field split into two groups, with the larger bunch, which also contained the majority of the market leaders, racing towards the far side, while nine horses formed a smaller stands' side group. The first seven raced on the far side. The time was quicker than the Golden Jubilee and the form looks up to scratch. The winner looks progressive.

NOTEBOOK
Deacon Blues ran well in defeat over this C&D on his reappearance, having been gelded over the winter, and had the look of an ideal type for this cavalry charge, as he travels strongly off a good gallop and gets the trip well. Covered up behind the pace, he was switched out and asked to quicken approaching the final furlong and soon got a gap on his pursuers. While chased down by Waffle well inside the last, he was never in any danger of being passed, and in reality he won this easily. He can have his challenge delayed longer in future, and he could well follow up in the Stewards' Cup. (op 8-1 tchd 9-1 in a place)

Waffle(IRE) has plenty of talent but he's only ever won one race, a maiden on his debut, and despite quickening up smartly to chase down the winner, it would have been a surprise had he gone past. He tends to do enough to get close but is reluctant to lead, and while the way this type of race is run suits him really well, it'll require a very cute ride for him to win one. (op 14-1)

Pastoral Player, a winner at Newmarket on his reappearance, was taken to the far-side rail to be delivered with his challenge and kept on well to take third. He reportedly lost a shoe during the race. Whether he wants the ground this soft is open to question and there's probably more to come from him back on proper summer ground. He could step out of handicap company, possibly in the Nunthorpe down at 5f. (op 11-1 tchd 14-1 in a place)

Anne Of Kiev(IRE), winner of a fillies' Listed race last time out, has a style of running suited to this sort of race. She ran a fine race in defeat but, while she proved that she can act with cut in the ground, a quicker surface is probably still ideal.

Gramercy(IRE) performed with a deal of credit considering he was making his seasonal reappearance. He likes this track and gets 7f so no doubt he'll be back here for the heritage handicaps later in the season. (op 22-1 tchd 28-1 in a place)

Fathsta(IRE) is a consistent sort but his current mark does leave him vulnerable to younger improvers. (op 16-1 tchd 20-1 in a place)

Hoof It showed up well on the far side but he didn't see his race out. An easier 6f or a drop back to the minimum looks like it'll suit him better. (op 11-2)

Mac's Power(IRE) was first home from the group that raced on the stands' side, so it seems his trainer would have won the race no matter which side had been favoured. Always travelling strongly, he quickened away from his rivals when asked, and he was simply unlucky to be on the wrong side. There will be other days for him.

Lui Rei(ITY), second home on the stands' side, has hinted on more than one occasion now that he has a race in him. Quicker ground will help. (op 16-1)

Colonel Mak hasn't been quite at his best this season, and he was 2lb wrong at the weights here, but he likes to get his toe in and so conditions had been right for him. Racing towards the outer of the stands' side group, he posted a respectable effort. (op 25-1)

Evens And Odds(IRE) got a nice lead from his stablemate Nasri on the stands' side but couldn't pick up for pressure. Goodwood is more his track and, given his record in the Stewards' Cup (runner-up and winner last two years), he'll deserve more respect for that big sprint. Official explanation: jockey said gelding hung right under pressure

Cheveton, who is at his best over 5f or an easier 6f, didn't get the trip well enough here. (op 25-1)

Imperial Guest, who beat Deacon Blues here on his reappearance, didn't settle particularly well, which hampered his finishing effort.

High Standing(USA), who was replated at the start, won this race two years ago, but he faced a stiff task this time around off top-weight.

Swiss Cross was found out by the easier ground. (op 33-1)

Victoire De Lyphar(IRE), who drifted in the betting beforehand, was beaten and eased down a long way out. Even allowing for the ground, this was not his true running. Adrian Nicholls reported that he was never travelling. Official explanation: jockey said gelding never travelled (op 10-1)

3156 DUKE OF EDINBURGH STKS (H'CAP) 1m 4f

5:00 (5:01) (Class 2) (0-105,102) 3-Y-O+

£31,155 (£9,330; £4,665; £2,335; £1,165; £585) **Stalls** Low

Form RPR

1641 **1** **Fox Hunt (IRE)**[14] 2716 4-9-8 **99**..........................(v) SilvestreDeSousa 21 112
(Mark Johnston) *chsd ldrs: rdn over 2f out: drvn to ld jst over 1f out: edgd rt but r.o strly ins fnl f: wl in command fin* **12/1**

01-2 **2** *2¼* **Blissful Moment (USA)**[42] 1887 4-9-5 **96**...................... KierenFallon 10 105
(Sir Michael Stoute) *chsd ldr: rdn and ev ch over 2f out: drvn ahd over 1f out: sn hdd: nt pce of wnr fnl f but kpt on for 2nd* **11/1**

2-62 **3** *1* **Averroes (IRE)**[36] 2071 4-9-3 **94**.. AdamKirby 8 101
(Clive Cox) *hld up wl in tch in midfield: rdn and effrt jst over 2f out: hdwy u.p to chse ldrs ent fnl f: styd on wl to go 3rd fnl 100yds: no threat to wnr* **11/1**

6-31 **4** *¾* **Rock A Doodle Doo (IRE)**[42] 1887 4-9-6 **97**................ OlivierPeslier 15 105+
(William Jarvis) *hld up wl in tch in midfield: shuffled bk to rr over 3f out: nt clr run ent fnl 2f: switching rt and hdwy over 1f out: edgd rt but str run fnl f: wnt 4th towards fin: unable to chal* **8/1**[3]

2644 **5** *¾* **Halicarnassus (IRE)**[19] 2573 7-9-7 **98**.......................... HughBowman 2 103
(Mick Channon) *led: rdn over 2f out: drvn and hrd pressed 2f out: hdd over 1f out: no ex and styd on same pce ins fnl f* **40/1**

4/ **6** *1¼* **Ile De Re (FR)**[26] 5-9-2 **93**.. JimCrowley 19 96
(F Head, France) *hld up wl in tch towards rr: rdn and effrt over 2f out: kpt on u.p fnl f: nvr gng pce to threaten ldrs* **20/1**

6-30 **7** *hd* **Prompter**[15] 2681 4-9-10 **101**... RichardHughes 9 104
(Michael Bell) *chsd ldrs early: grad stdd to r in last trio after 2f: in tch in tightly packed field: rdn and effrt on inner over 2f out: chsd ldrs and drvn over 1f out: no ex and btn jst ins fnl f* **22/1**

4-00 **8** *4½* **Coin Of The Realm (IRE)**[14] 2716 6-9-0 **91**.................... TomQueally 6 86
(Gary Moore) *stdd after s: hld up in rr in tightly packed field: rdn and effrt on outer over 2f out: no imp tl kpt on fnl 150yds: nvr gng pce to threaten ldrs* **28/1**

11-0 **9** *shd* **Awsaal**[36] 2071 4-9-5 **96**.. EddieAhern 18 91
(John Dunlop) *hld up wl in tch in midfield: rdn and effrt to chse ldrs ent fnl 2f: drvn and unable qck over 1f out: one pce and btn whn hmpd jst ins fnl f* **20/1**

12-2 **10** *6* **Sharaayeen**[48] 1717 4-9-7 **98**.. RichardHills 3 84
(B W Hills) *hld up wl in tch: effrt towards inner and rdn to chse ldrs ent fnl 2f: drvn and wknd over 1f out* **8/1**[3]

50-0 **11** *1¾* **Very Good Day (FR)**[49] 1679 4-9-4 **95**.......................(v[1]) SamHitchcott 5 78
(Mick Channon) *hld up in rr in tightly packed field: rdn and effrt on inner over 2f out: no imp and wl hld over 1f out* **33/1**

16-0 **12** *4½* **Taqleed (IRE)**[38] 2002 4-9-3 **94**.................................. JimmyFortune 22 70
(John Gosden) *in tch in midfield: rdn and effrt over 2f out: no real prog and btn over 1f out: eased ins fnl f* **7/1**[2]

12-1 **13** *3½* **Modun (IRE)**[63] 1402 4-9-8 **99**.. RyanMoore 13 69
(Sir Michael Stoute) *t.k.h early: hld up wl in tch: rdn 3f out: unable qck and struggling whn short of room jst over 2f out: no hdwy wl hld over 1f out: eased ins fnl f* **10/3**[1]

1601 **14** *12* **Jutland**[7] 2909 4-9-9 **100**... JoeFanning 11 51
(Mark Johnston) *chsd ldr tl over 2f out: sn wknd u.p: eased ins fnl f: t.o* **40/1**

5-34 **15** *25* **Life And Soul (IRE)**[14] 2716 4-9-2 **93**................................ JMurtagh 14 —
(Amanda Perrett) *t.k.h: chsd ldrs tl wknd qckly ent fnl 2f: wl bhd and eased fr over 1f out: t.o* **11/1**

23-2 **16** *2¾* **Heddwyn (IRE)**[17] 2604 4-9-2 **93**.................................... GeorgeBaker 1 —
(Marcus Tregoning) *t.k.h: chsd ldrs tl wknd rapidly ent fnl 2f: wl bhd and eased fr over 1f out* **14/1**

2m 40.03s (7.53) **Going Correction** +0.875s/f (Soft) **16** Ran SP% **122.3**
Speed ratings (Par 109): **109,107,106,106,105 105,104,101,101,97 96,93,91,83,66 64**
toteswingers:1&2:£31.40, 2&3:£108.90, 1&3:£35.90 CSF £126.38 CT £1506.71 TOTE £18.70: £3.70, £1.70, £4.10, £1.40; EX 227.80 Trifecta £5420.50 Pool: £10,426.06 - 1.42 winning units..

Owner Sheikh Hamdan Bin Mohammed Al Maktoum **Bred** Ballylinch Stud **Trained** Middleham Moor, N Yorks

■ Stewards' Enquiry : Richard Hughes two-day ban: careless riding (Jul [illegible])

FOCUS
A fair renewal of what is always a competitive handicap, but not many showed their form on the ground and it may have been an advantage to race positively. The form is rated around the second and third. The time compared favourably with that for the Hardwicke Stakes earlier in the day. The field kept away from the inside rail down the far side and in Swinley Bottom, until tacking back over before the home turn.

NOTEBOOK
Fox Hunt(IRE) ◆ was drawn right on the outside but overcame that to win in striking fashion, never far from the pace and keeping on strongly once in front. He went up only 4lb when winning at Epsom on Derby day and the visor has elicited more improvement from this progressive 4yo, who appears to act on most types of ground. There is more to come from this gelding, who should get further, and might be an interesting type for the Ebor. Mark Johnston has now won this race twice in three years, following his 1-2 in 2009. (op 14-1)

Blissful Moment(USA), the longer priced of the Stoute pair, was always towards the fore and stuck on well for second. Another on the upgrade, he went up 5lb after finishing second over C&D to Rock A Doodle Do last month and he could have further improvement in him, as this was only his seventh outing. (op 8-1)

Averroes(IRE) is commendably consistent and he made the frame again from a career-high mark, staying on well for pressure. He deserves to win a race but the handicapper is unlikely to drop him, unfortunately. (op 12-1 tchd 14-1)

Rock A Doodle Doo(IRE) ◆, the eyecatcher, travelled well towards the rear only to be hampered when he was beginning to pick up ground. He ran on strongly once in the clear, and, while it is unlikely he would have got to the winner, he would probably have finished in front of the runner-up, whom he had beaten on 3lb better terms here last time. He should be kept on the right side. (op 9-1)

Halicarnassus(IRE) ran well for a long way and only missed out on the placings late on. He clearly acts well in soft ground and there is life in him yet, although this globe-trotter has won just once in Britain since 2007. (op 33-1)

Ile De Re(FR), a French runner who gets further and is proven in soft ground, made headway from the rear without troubling the leaders.

Prompter had disappointed on his first two starts of the year but the topweight ran better here. He could still do with being eased in the weights. (tchd 25-1 in places)

Awsaal, dropped 3lb since his return from injury, was fading when he was hampered inside the last. He remains relatively unexposed. (op 25-1)

Sharaayeen, touched off by subsequent Listed winner Times Up at Newmarket, didn't seem to get home here, which is a surprise as he was a good runner-up over 1m4f in soft ground last October. (op 7-1 tchd 9-1 and 10-1 in places)

Taqleed(IRE) looked interesting upped to this trip, but he was drawn out wide and was never a factor. He may not be one to give up on yet. (op 8-1)
Modun(IRE) was disappointing, coming under pressure on the home turn and weakening to finish well back. The least experienced in this field, he went up 15lb for his easy win at Newbury, which won't have helped, but more of a problem was the soft ground. Sir Michael Stoute has won this twice in the past decade and had the runner-up here, but has had three beaten favourites in that period too now. (op 7-2 tchd 3-1 in places)
Life And Soul(IRE) is usually consistent, but failed to settle and ended up walking over the line. (op 12-1)
Heddwyn(IRE) took a keen tug and didn't stay. (op 12-1)

3157 QUEEN ALEXANDRA STKS (CONDITIONS RACE) 2m 5f 159y

5:35 (5:36) (Class 2) 4-Y-0+

£31,155 (£9,330; £4,665; £2,335; £1,165; £585) **Stalls** Low

Form RPR
0-06 **1** **Swingkeel (IRE)**[21] 2499 6-9-2 95 (p) TedDurcan 15 104
(John Dunlop) *hld up in last pl: hdwy 5f out: rdn to chal 2f out: led over 1f out: sn edgd lft: styd on gamely ins fnl f and a looked in command* **11/2**[2]
/20- **2** 3 ½ **Elyaadi**[42] 5776 7-8-11 95 FMBerry 13 96
(John Queally, Ire) *racd keenly: hld up: hdwy 5f out: trckd ldrs over 3f out: rdn to ld 2f out: hdd over 1f out: kpt on u.p ins fnl f but a looked hld* **4/1**[1]
610- **3** 2 ½ **Ajaan**[245] 6926 7-9-5 101 (b) TomQueally 11 102
(Sir Henry Cecil) *midfield: hdwy over 5f out: rdn whn chsng ldrs over 2f out: wnt 3rd jst over 1f out: hung rt u.p ins fnl f: kpt on but no imp on front 2* **10/1**
001- **4** 2 **Dayia (IRE)**[217] 7457 7-9-2 100 OlivierPeslier 4 97
(Lydia Pearce) *chsd ldrs: chalng over 3f out: led over 2f out: sn hdd: rdn over 1f out: one pce ins fnl f* **13/2**[3]
06- **5** 9 **L Frank Baum (IRE)**[261] 6506 4-9-0 87 NeilCallan 12 89
(Gay Kelleway) *midfield: hdwy over 7f out: sn handy: led over 4f out: rdn and hdd over 2f out: wknd over 1f out* **33/1**
340/ **6** 2 ¾ **Font**[38] 6169 8-9-2 80 (t) RichardKingscote 16 87
(Lawney Hill) *midfield: hdwy 5f out: chsd ldrs over 4f out: sn chalng on outer: pushed along 3f out: one pce fr over 2f out* **25/1**
341/ **7** 11 **Degas Art (IRE)**[13] 5657 8-9-2 105 (p) RyanMoore 6 82
(Lucinda Russell) *in tch: wnt prom 5f out: chalng over 3f out: sn rdn: wknd over 1f out: eased whn btn ins fnl f* **14/1**
5/0- **8** 15 **Deutschland (USA)**[42] 5225 8-9-2 96 RichardHughes 17 63
(W P Mullins, Ire) *hld up: hdwy into midfield 5f out: pushed along 4f out: rdn whn chsd ldrs over 2f out: sn no imp: eased whn wl btn over 1f out* **11/2**[2]
4-65 **9** 8 **Gaselee (USA)**[45] 1817 5-8-11 72 DavidProbert 20 51
(Rae Guest) *chsd ldr to 6f out: rdn and wknd 4f out* **50/1**
042 **10** 3 ¼ **Kayef (GER)**[21] 2499 4-9-0 85 PatCosgrave 7 53
(Michael Scudamore) *hld up: rdn and struggling over 6f out: plugged on u.p but no imp fnl 3f* **16/1**
1616 **11** 6 **Momkinzain (USA)**[30] 2224 4-9-0 80 HughBowman 2 48
(Mick Channon) *midfield: hdwy to chse ldrs over 5f out: pushed along over 2f out: sn wknd and eased* **33/1**
000/ **12** 60 **Ladies Best**[16] 7720 7-9-2 80 (t) JimCrowley 10 —
(James Given) *hld up: rdn 8f out: pushed along and hdwy into midfield over 5f out: wknd over 4f out: t.o* **40/1**
-311 **13** ½ **Not Til Monday (IRE)**[32] 2183 5-9-2 74 (b) KierenFallon 14 —
(J R Jenkins) *led: hdd over 4f out: sn rdn and wknd: t.o* **12/1**
60-5 **14** 21 **Chink Of Light**[43] 1851 4-9-0 94 (v) JimmyFortune 1 —
(Andrew Balding) *in tch tl wknd over 4f out: t.o* **16/1**
5-00 **15** 46 **Herostatus**[21] 2499 4-9-0 85 (v[1]) SilvestreDeSousa 5 —
(Mark Johnston) *chsd ldrs: pushed along over 7f out: wknd over 6f out: bhd fnl 5f: t.o* **22/1**
-403 **16** 38 **Halla San**[28] 2314 9-9-2 94 JamieSpencer 9 —
(Richard Fahey) *midfield: hdwy to chse ldrs over 7f out: wknd over 5f out: t.o* **22/1**
635- **17** 54 **Grand Art (IRE)**[170] 8013 7-9-2 73 JamesDoyle 3 —
(Tim Vaughan) *midfield: rdn and lost pl 8f out: bhd fnl 7f: eased whn wl btn over 4f out: t.o: walked over line* **66/1**

5m 2.73s (13.33) **Going Correction** +0.875s/f (Soft)
WFA 4 from 5yo+ 2lb **17** Ran SP% **123.6**
Speed ratings (Par 109): **110,108,107,107,103 102,98,93,90,89 87,65,65,57,40 26,7**
toteswingers:1&2:£2.00, 2&3:£10.40, 1&3:£12.80 CSF £25.34 CT £223.23 TOTE £6.80: £2.60, £1.90, £3.80; EX 21.90 Trifecta £213.40 Pool: £11,501.64 - 39.86 winning units..
Owner Mrs M E Slade **Bred** R J Cornelius **Trained** Arundel, W Sussex

FOCUS
Quite a test in the conditions, but the form makes surprising sense at face value. The winner is rated back to his old best.

NOTEBOOK
Swingkeel(IRE) proved best equipped to deal with this extreme test. He's been a little frustrating in the past but there was no doubting his stamina for this task, having finished third in the race last year on quicker ground and since won a 3m hurdle race, and this softer surface helped him more than others. Ridden patiently, he didn't always travel like the winner, but he had the stamina reserves when it counted and he never looked like shirking things once he hit the front. (op 13-2)
Elyaadi was second in the Ascot Stakes last year, running on late from an impossible position, and so this longer trip was less of a concern for her than many of her rivals. She'd run a solid race over hurdles last month so came here in good form, and she put up a fine effort in defeat, providing her sire Singspiel with a one-two in the race. (op 9-2 tchd 5-1 and 11-2 in a place)
Ajaan, last seen finishing tailed off in the Cesarewitch, had to give weight all round but performed with great credit on his return, probably matching his performance when fifth in a stronger renewal of this race, behind Honolulu, back in 2008. (op 8-1 tchd 11-1)
Dayia(IRE) relishes testing conditions, as she showed when taking a French Listed race on her final start last year. Fourth in the Ascot Stakes last year, two places behind Elyaadi, she travelled strongly through the race but, when it came to where it mattered, didn't see it out as well as the first three. (op 6-1 tchd 7-1)
L Frank Baum(IRE), a lightly raced gelding with soft ground form in Italy, is bred to stay all day, and he put up a good effort on his first outing since September. He's currently rated 87 and he should be capable of winning a handicap off that sort of mark.
Font, a winner over hurdles at Fontwell on his debut for this yard last month, was last seen on the Flat in October 2007. He faced a stiff task at the weights and in the circumstances ran a big race, which augurs well for a summer jumping campaign. (op 33-1)
Degas Art(IRE), another who won over hurdles on his debut for a new stable last time out, last ran on the Flat in September 2006. He was a Listed-class middle-distance performer back then and, while he stays 2m4f over hurdles, this race distance back on the level proved beyond him. Beaten off from the turn in, Ryan Moore reported that the gelding had no more to give. Official explanation: jockey said gelding had no more to give (op 11-1)
Deutschland(USA) was sent off 6-1 for this race last year and finished well beaten. The softer ground gave hope for a better showing this time round but, having been given a patient ride and crept into contention, he found little off the home turn and was eased down. He ran like a non-stayer. (tchd 5-1)
Ladies Best (op 50-1)
Chink Of Light Official explanation: jockey said gelding finished very tired
T/Jkpt: Not won. T/Plt: £262.70 to a £1 stake. Pool of £508016.54 - 1,411.50 winning units. T/Qpdt: £103.70 to a £1 stake. Pool of £19,331.47 -137.88 winning units. DO

[3110] AYR (L-H)

Saturday, June 18

OFFICIAL GOING: Soft (good to soft in places changing to soft after race 4 (4.05)
Home bend out 2m adding 6yds to races between 7f -10f and 12yds to races of over 11f.
Wind: Breezy, half behind Weather: Cloudy, dull

3158 SCOTTISH NEWS OF THE WORLD E B F "MAJOR CADEAUX" LAND O'BURNS FILLIES' STKS (LISTED RACE) 5f

2:20 (2:20) (Class 1) 3-Y-0+

£22,708 (£8,608; £4,308; £2,148; £1,076; £540) **Stalls** Centre

Form RPR
-341 **1** **Margot Did (IRE)**[7] 2928 3-9-1 112 HayleyTurner 3 106
(Michael Bell) *w ldr: rdn to ld over 1f out: kpt on wl ins fnl f* **10/11**[1]
3 **2** nk **Celerina (IRE)**[28] 2317 4-9-3 91 WMLordan 5 103
(T Stack, Ire) *prom: drvn along 2f out: styd on wl ins fnl f but a hld* **8/1**[3]
-504 **3** ¾ **Ladies Are Forever**[21] 2500 3-9-1 97 FrederikTylicki 1 102
(Geoffrey Oldroyd) *trckd ldrs: effrt and drvn 2f out: kpt on same pce wl ins fnl f* **8/1**[3]
3-02 **4** 1 **Katla (IRE)**[56] 1533 3-9-1 101 WJLee 9 98
(J F Grogan, Ire) *in tch: hdwy to chse ldrs appr fnl f: edgd lft: kpt on same pce* **9/2**[2]
-440 **5** ¾ **Favourite Girl (IRE)**[14] 2727 5-9-3 90 (v) DavidAllan 7 94
(Tim Easterby) *led to over 1f out: sn drvn and one pce* **11/1**
-222 **6** 5 **Bold Bidder**[14] 2724 3-8-11 87 PhillipMakin 8 74
(Kevin Ryan) *t.k.h: trckd ldrs tl rdn and wknd over 1f out* **25/1**
21- **7** 9 **Googlette (IRE)**[250] 6796 3-8-11 89 GrahamGibbons 11 41
(Edward Vaughan) *hld up bhd ldrs: rdn 2f out: sn struggling* **16/1**

61.27 secs (1.87) **Going Correction** +0.45s/f (Yiel)
WFA 3 from 4yo+ 6lb **7** Ran SP% **110.8**
Speed ratings (Par 108): **108,107,106,104,103 95,81**
toteswingers:1&2:£1.60, 2&3:£5.70, 1&3:£3.10 CSF £8.32 TOTE £1.70: £1.20, £3.80; EX 8.70 Trifecta £28.80 Pool: £614.60 - 15.77 winning units..
Owner T Redman And P Philipps **Bred** N Hartery **Trained** Newmarket, Suffolk

FOCUS
Four non-runners took some competitive gloss off this Listed event but the favourite was still made to work harder than her chance on official ratings suggested. The runners kept to the centre, the pace only fair with the field well bunched. Ordinary fillies' Listed form and Margot Did didn't need to match her Sandown run.

NOTEBOOK
Margot Did(IRE) might have been a touch flattered by the margin of her Listed win at Sandown last week but a tactical switch to being ridden more prominently and leaving less to chance has certainly been rewarded the last twice and she always had things just under control here despite being pressed late. She's an obvious contender for the King George at Goodwood, but the better 5f sprints later in the year will probably elude her unless she improves further. (op 4-5)
Celerina(IRE)'s progression shows no sign of stopping and she turned in another excellent effort, not least given that she left the impression a stronger gallop would have been more in her favour as she finished strongly after being caught flat-footed. Her recent form is at 5f, but she might also be worth another try at 6f as she's previously shown she stays at least that far. (tchd 15-2)
Ladies Are Forever boasted the third highest official rating and probably ran somewhere near form, never far away and keeping on without ever really threatening to finish any closer. (op 9-1)
Katla(IRE) hadn't run for nearly two months, but more than that left the impression 5f is on the sharp side, moving smoothly while the pace had still to pick up but then outspeeded when it did. (op 6-1)
Favourite Girl(IRE) hadn't run in a race of this nature since 2009 and her run confirmed she's no more than a useful handicapper nowadays, one who ran as well as her chance at the weights beforehand suggested. (op 12-1 tchd 10-1)
Bold Bidder was biting off more than she could chew, even allowing for her being ridden more patiently than usual up in grade, but she was well and truly put in her place once the race developed in earnest. (tchd 28-1)
Googlette(IRE) looked promising last year but things presumably haven't gone smoothly and she was never a factor after an awkward start on her first run since October and first at 5f, carrying her head awkwardly as she was left behind. (op 14-1)

3159 SCOTTISH SUN H'CAP 1m

2:50 (2:52) (Class 2) (0-100,89) 3-Y-0

£15,577 (£4,665; £2,332; £1,167; £582; £292) **Stalls** Low

Form RPR
-444 **1** **Mariachi Man**[7] 2935 3-9-7 **89** DavidAllan 4 102
(Tim Easterby) *cl up: led over 3f out: rdn and styd on strly fr 2f out* **10/3**[2]
021 **2** 3 ½ **Rave (IRE)**[21] 2511 3-9-0 **85** PatrickHills[(3)] 5 90
(J W Hills) *dwlt: hld up: stdy hdwy over 2f out: rdn to chse wnr over 1f out: kpt on ins fnl f: no imp* **7/1**
-161 **3** 2 ¾ **Barney Rebel (IRE)**[7] 2925 3-9-5 **87** RobertWinston 6 86
(B W Hills) *t.k.h: trckd ldrs: effrt over 2f out: edgd lft and no ex over 1f out* **9/2**[3]
-613 **4** ¾ **Shamdarley (IRE)**[14] 2705 3-8-10 **78** FrederikTylicki 3 75
(Michael Dods) *t.k.h: trckd ldrs: effrt whn n.m.r briefly over 2f out: rdn and one pce over 1f out* **7/1**
2-12 **5** 3 ¼ **Calypso Magic (IRE)**[56] 1516 3-9-7 **89** PhillipMakin 7 78
(Howard Johnson) *hld up: struggling over 3f out: sn btn* **6/1**
0020 **6** 5 **Mutajare (IRE)**[21] 2503 3-9-2 **84** WMLordan 9 62
(Mark Johnston) *dwlt: hld up: drvn and outpcd over 2f out: n.d after* **20/1**
15-3 **7** 12 **Honeymead (IRE)**[21] 2503 3-9-1 **83** GrahamGibbons 1 33
(Richard Fahey) *trckd ldrs: effrt and rdn over 2f out: wknd wl over 1f out* **3/1**[1]
106- **8** 3 ¼ **Hawdyerwheesht**[234] 7165 3-9-0 **82** RoystonFfrench 2 25
(Mark Johnston) *led to over 3f out: rdn and wknd over 2f out* **40/1**

1m 46.04s (2.24) **Going Correction** +0.45s/f (Yiel) **8** Ran SP% **112.7**
Speed ratings (Par 105): **106,102,99,99,95 90,78,75**
toteswingers:1&2:£3.50, 2&3:£9.60, 1&3:£3.00 CSF £25.98 CT £103.76 TOTE £4.10: £1.50, £2.50, £1.70; EX 27.40 Trifecta £354.60 Pool: £757.31 - 1.58 winning units..
Owner Jeremy Gompertz **Bred** Jeremy Gompertz **Trained** Great Habton, N Yorks

FOCUS
A useful 3yo handicap, won by the useful Firebet in 2009. There wasn't anything quite so progressive this time round but the winner is clearly very useful in these conditions and improved again, and the second also has more to offer. The pace was reasonable and the runners stayed in the centre.

NOTEBOOK

Mariachi Man hails from a yard in cracking form and with the ground turning in his favour, made the most of the drop back in trip after trying to match strides with Sea Moon at York last week over 1m2f, always travelling strongly and drawing clear readily. He's pretty about him and he might have a good handicap in him if the going remains on the soft side. (op 3-1)

Rave(IRE) ◆ was a bit slow to break but wasn't beaten because of that, simply running into a better handicapped horse under the conditions after looking briefly looking threatening. That said, he didn't seem to handle the soft ground as well as the winner once really asked to pick up, but this was still another good effort and he can progress further back on faster ground. (tchd 13-2)

Barney Rebel(IRE) seemed to run his race and, proven under the conditions and not beaten by the drop back to 1m, seems to act as a good marker for the value of the form.

Shamdarley(IRE) had run well in a stronger race than this at Doncaster last time but didn't seen to pick up as well here as he had then and probably ideally wants faster conditions than this. (tchd 6-1)

Calypso Magic(IRE) seemed to be going nowhere on the home turn but stayed on past beaten rivals and almost certainly found the drop back to 1m against him. (op 13-2 tchd 7-1)

Mutajare(IRE)'s profile this year has been patchy to say the least and he never figured. (op 25-1)

Honeymead(IRE) is a winner on soft ground before so can't have conditions as an excuse. She wasn't beaten by the extra distance either, and her performance is probably worth striking a line through given that the form of her previous race could hardly have worked out better. (op 7-2)

Hawdyerwheesht ran as though badly in need of his first run since October.

3160 SCOTTISH SUN MISS SCOTLAND H'CAP 5f

3:25 (3:25) (Class 3) (0-95,94) 3-Y-O+ **£9,714** (£2,890; £1,444; £721) **Stalls** Centre

Form				RPR
00-6	**1**		**Quest For Success (IRE)**[76] 1111 6-9-9 **94** .... JamesSullivan(3) 8 (Richard Fahey) *in tch: hdwy to ld ent fnl f: styd on wl: jst hld on* **7/2**[1]	101
2100	**2**	*shd*	**Oldjoesaid**[14] 2714 7-9-0 **82** .... PhillipMakin 9 (Kevin Ryan) *hld up last: rdn and hdwy over 1f out: kpt on strly ins fnl f: jst failed* **4/1**[2]	89
-05	**3**	*3/4*	**Go Go Green (IRE)**[48] 1715 5-8-7 **75** oh1 .... HayleyTurner 7 (Jim Goldie) *t.k.h: trckd ldrs: effrt over 1f out: kpt on ins fnl f* **16/1**	79
0300	**4**	*1/2*	**Beat The Bell**[14] 2714 6-9-8 **90** .... GrahamGibbons 3 (David Barron) *hld up in tch: drvn fr 2f out: kpt on wl ins fnl f: nrst fin* **7/1**	93
0420	**5**	*1 1/2*	**The Nifty Fox**[14] 2727 7-9-3 **85** ....(v) DavidAllan 1 (Tim Easterby) *cl up: led 2f out to ent fnl f: kpt on same pce* **4/1**[2]	82
00-4	**6**	*nse*	**Mango Music**[21] 2497 8-8-8 **76** .... FrederikTylicki 5 (Richard Fahey) *led to 2f out: one pce whn nt clr run briefly over 1f out* **5/1**[3]	73
200-	**7**	*1/2*	**Johnstown Lad (IRE)**[8] 2894 7-8-7 **75** ....(t) WMLordan 4 (Daniel Mark Loughnane, Ire) *prom: effrt and rdn 2f out: kpt on same pce ins fnl f* **25/1**	70
4-05	**8**	*1 1/4*	**Fathom Five (IRE)**[14] 2714 7-9-9 **91** .... AndrewMullen 6 (David Nicholls) *t.k.h: cl up tl rdn and wknd appr fnl f* **5/1**[3]	82

62.20 secs (2.80) **Going Correction** +0.45s/f (Yiel) **8** Ran SP% **117.8**

Speed ratings (Par 107): **101,100,99,98,96 96,95,93**

toteswingers:1&2:£4.40, 2&3:£11.10, 1&3:£10.40 CSF £18.32 CT £178.60 TOTE £5.20: £1.50, £1.90, £2.60; EX 29.00 Trifecta £653.40 Part won. Pool: £883.08 - 0.54 winning units..

Owner S & G Clayton **Bred** Desmond Monaghan **Trained** Musley Bank, N Yorks

FOCUS

A fairly useful sprint handicap in which the field, who kept to the centre again, were well bunched throughout. The form seems sound enough with the winner close to his best.

NOTEBOOK

Quest For Success(IRE) might have appeared to be the second string initially on jockey bookings but the betting public weren't fooled given he had finished third to Tangerine Trees in a Newmarket Listed race just five runs ago, hadn't appeared to have lost his form in the meantime and yet remarkably was racing off a 4lb lower mark here. Always doing enough once hitting the front, he was value for more than his winning margin and has another handicap in him when the ground is on the soft side. (op 11-2)

Oldjoesaid was another who'd quickly been given respite by the handicapper despite being poorly drawn on his last two starts and he almost took advantage, for all the winner always just held the edge, putting in a spirited late burst from the rear. (op 5-1)

Go Go Green(IRE) didn't have much racing last year and hadn't shown much this season since joining this yard but this was a step in the right direction and he is starting to look well handicapped if he can build on this.

Beat The Bell didn't have quite the clear run through from the rear that the eventual second did but can't be counted as unlucky. (op 8-1 tchd 9-1)

The Nifty Fox was well ridden as the race developed, getting first run, so it was slightly disappointing if not unexpected given his modest win record that he didn't see it out as well as looked likely. (op 7-2)

Mango Music left the impression she still hasn't come to herself, but the manner in which she rallied after getting tapped for toe suggests she might be ripe next time. (op 11-2 tchd 6-1)

Johnstown Lad(IRE) is another that ran as if needing this run to put him straight.

Fathom Five(IRE) had shaped well at Epsom last time but he was well drawn there at a track he'd won at twice before and he ran disappointingly, dropping out of things rather tamely. (op 7-2 tchd 3-1)

3161 REAL RADIO EUROPEAN BREEDERS' FUND MAIDEN STKS 6f

4:05 (4:08) (Class 5) 2-Y-O **£3,885** (£1,156; £577; £288) **Stalls** Centre

Form				RPR
5	**1**		**Ladykin (IRE)**[21] 2504 2-8-12 0 .... FrederikTylicki 5 (Richard Fahey) *mde virtually all: rdn and edgd rt over 1f out: edgd lft and hld on gamely ins fnl f* **20/1**	76+
43	**2**	*1/2*	**Letsgoroundagain (IRE)**[24] 2395 2-9-3 0 .... RobertWinston 3 (B W Hills) *hld up in tch: smooth hdwy and ev ch over 1f out to ins fnl f: kpt on: hld nr fin* **8/1**	80
32	**3**	*1 3/4*	**Tight Lipped (IRE)**[30] 2214 2-9-3 0 .... RichardMullen 4 (David Brown) *cl up: rdn and edgd lft over 2f out: kpt on same pce ins fnl f* **13/2**[3]	74
2	**4**	*1/2*	**Holy Roman Warrior (IRE)**[24] 2395 2-9-3 0 .... PhillipMakin 1 (Richard Fahey) *prom: effrt over 2f out: edgd lft: kpt on same pce ins fnl f* **9/4**[1]	73
40	**5**	*5*	**Tyre Giant Dot Com**[28] 2318 2-8-12 0 .... DanielleMcCreery(5) 7 (Geoffrey Oldroyd) *t.k.h: w wnr tl wknd over 1f out* **33/1**	58
	6	*nse*	**Thirkleby (IRE)** 2-9-3 0 .... GrahamGibbons 9 (David Barron) *in tch: drvn and outpcd over 2f out: btn over 1f out* **6/1**[2]	58

1m 16.41s (4.01) **Going Correction** +0.45s/f (Yiel) **6** Ran SP% **77.2**

Speed ratings (Par 93): **99,98,96,95,88 88**

toteswingers:1&2:£4.00, 2&3:£3.10, 1&3:£15.20 CSF £70.44 TOTE £21.70: £7.30, £2.80; EX 45.50.

Owner Mrs H Steel **Bred** Jennifer & Evelyn Cullen **Trained** Musley Bank, N Yorks

FOCUS

Probably no more than a fair maiden and nothing in the field remotely of the quality of Wootton Bassett or Easy Ticket, who finished first and second last year, for all their respective stables provided half the runners. The field fanned out, with the advantage being with those that stayed in the centre. The form makes sense.

NOTEBOOK

Ladykin(IRE) had shaped well behind Royal Ascot duo Shumoos and Frederick Engels on her debut at Haydock over what was an inadequate 5f, and despite winning this gamely she still left the impression the trip isn't really far enough for her, even under these conditions. She was apt to roll around off a straight line too, still looking green, so there's good reason to expect better again next time. (op 25-1)

Letsgoroundagain(IRE) had finished behind Holy Roman Warrior over this C&D last time but he reversed placings with ease on this occasion while looking more the horse he promised to be at Newbury on his debut, impressing with the manner with which he travelled. He might be the sort for a decent nursery back on faster ground. (op 7-1 tchd 9-1)

Tight Lipped(IRE) had been gelded since his last run at Haydock and he ran as though he might just have needed this after looking sure to finish closer for much of the way, though he didn't keep to the centre as did the pair that beat him. (tchd 7-1)

Holy Roman Warrior(IRE) was disappointing. He'd handled this sort of ground on his debut and his action is one normally associated with a soft-ground performer but he was labouring some way out and was possibly disadvantaged by racing nearer the far rail than the others. (tchd 13-8)

Tyre Giant Dot Com showed plenty of pace for a long way and might end up being best for now at 5f.

Thirkleby(IRE), a half-brother by Haafhd to a useful 2yo 7f winner, was very green initially but was noted making late progress and should improve. (tchd 8-1)

3162 ARNOLD CLARK H'CAP 6f

4:40 (4:41) (Class 4) (0-80,80) 3-Y-O+ **£5,828** (£1,734; £866; £432) **Stalls** Centre

Form				RPR
1110	**1**		**Klynch**[16] 2633 5-9-7 **76** ....(b) JamesSullivan(3) 6 (Ruth Carr) *mde all: qcknd clr over 1f out: readily* **6/1**	91
0104	**2**	*4 1/2*	**River Falcon**[7] 2938 11-9-11 **77** .... DanielTudhope 2 (Jim Goldie) *chsd ldrs: drvn along over 2f out: kpt on same pce fr over 1f out* **4/1**[2]	77
0-15	**3**	*nk*	**Saucy Brown (IRE)**[17] 2620 5-10-0 **80** .... AndrewMullen 7 (David Nicholls) *t.k.h: cl up tl rdn and one pce over 1f out* **9/1**	79
3020	**4**	*2 3/4*	**Frequency**[10] 2806 4-9-5 **71** ....(b) HayleyTurner 10 (Keith Dalgleish) *hld up in tch: smooth hdwy over 2f out: rdn over 1f out: fnd little* **13/2**	61
-006	**5**	*2*	**Eternal Instinct**[24] 2399 4-8-9 **64** .... GaryBartley(3) 4 (Jim Goldie) *in tch: drvn over 2f out: btn over 1f out* **9/1**	47
042	**6**	*4 1/2*	**Ursula (IRE)**[10] 2806 5-9-13 **79** .... RobertWinston 5 (Mrs K Burke) *hld up in tch: drvn over 2f out: btn over 1f out* **11/4**[1]	48
-464	**7**	*nk*	**Imprimis Tagula (IRE)**[3] 3036 7-9-5 **74** ....(v) AmyBaker(3) 9 (Alan Bailey) *trckd ldrs: rdn over 2f out: wknd wl over 1f out* **5/1**[3]	42

1m 15.51s (3.11) **Going Correction** +0.45s/f (Yiel)

WFA 3 from 4yo+ 7lb **7** Ran SP% **111.0**

Speed ratings (Par 105): **105,99,98,94,92 86,85**

toteswingers:1&2:£4.50, 2&3:£6.20, 1&3:£6.90 CSF £28.19 CT £204.71 TOTE £6.60: £2.60, £2.10; EX 36.90.

Owner Douglas Renton **Bred** J C S Wilson Bloodstock **Trained** Huby, N Yorks

FOCUS

The official going was changed to soft before this race. No more than a fair handicap and a messy one too, the winner allowed to dictate a steady pace. He's rated back to his best old soft-ground form. The field stayed centre to stand side.

3163 FAVOURITE H'CAP 1m 5f 13y

5:15 (5:15) (Class 3) (0-95,90) 4-Y-O+ **£9,714** (£2,890; £1,444; £721) **Stalls** Low

Form				RPR
161-	**1**		**Bondage (IRE)**[17] 2628 4-9-0 **83** .... WMLordan 7 (Gordon Elliott, Ire) *hld up: smooth hdwy over 3f out: led over 1f out: drvn and styd on wl* **9/4**[1]	93+
5-10	**2**	*1 1/2*	**High Office**[35] 2107 5-9-7 **90** .... FrederikTylicki 2 (Richard Fahey) *hld up in tch: smooth hdwy over 3f out: led briefly wl over 1f out: rallied: kpt on ins fnl f* **5/1**[3]	96
0-21	**3**	*6*	**Line Of Duty (IRE)**[38] 2006 4-9-7 **90** .... RobertWinston 4 (Alan Swinbank) *led to 1/2-way: led over 3f out to wl over 1f out: kpt on same pce* **5/1**[3]	87
3430	**4**	*7*	**The Galloping Shoe**[14] 2716 6-9-1 **84** ....(v1) PhillipMakin 3 (Ian Semple) *s.i.s: hld up: hdwy over 2f out: no imp over 1f out* **12/1**	80
-030	**5**	*1/2*	**Gordonsville**[8] 2888 8-8-13 **82** .... DanielTudhope 1 (Jim Goldie) *trckd ldrs tl rdn and wknd over 2f out* **6/1**	77
3644	**6**	*2*	**Bowdler's Magic**[7] 2932 4-9-4 **87** .... RoystonFfrench 6 (Mark Johnston) *prom: drvn over 3f out: wknd fr 2f out* **9/2**[2]	79
316-	**7**	*3 1/4*	**Graceful Descent (FR)**[234] 7173 6-8-8 **80** ow1 .... GaryBartley(3) 5 (Jim Goldie) *cl up: led 1/2-way to over 3f out: wknd over 2f out* **10/1**	67

3m 2.24s (8.24) **Going Correction** +0.60s/f (Yiel) **7** Ran SP% **113.4**

Speed ratings (Par 107): **98,97,93,92,92 91,89**

toteswingers:1&2:£3.10, 2&3:£2.50, 1&3:£2.70 CSF £13.47 TOTE £2.40: £2.10, £4.90; EX 14.40.

Owner Bodhran Makers Syndicate **Bred** Mesnil Investments Ltd & Carrigbeg Stud **Trained** Trim, Co Meath

FOCUS

Quite a useful handicap, albeit one run at a just a fair pace for a long way, and once again the runners shunned either rail. The winner continues his rapid progress for this yard.

NOTEBOOK

Bondage(IRE) ◆, representing the yard that won this race 12 months ago with subsequent Ebor winner Dirar, justified favouritism in winning almost as readily ultimately as his stable companion had, though not after a brief scare, drawing clear late after travelling strongly throughout. He's a good cruising speed for a budding stayer and likely has plenty more improvement in him now some of his quirks are being ironed out. The Cesarewitch would almost certainly be on his list of late-season targets. (op 5-2 tchd 2-1)

High Office was very unfortunate to come up against such a well-treated winner. He was travelling equally as strongly early in the straight, but despite pulling clear of the rest always looked as if he was going to come off second best. He's in the Northumberland Plate next week, and would have to be of interest there if allowed to take his chance as the trip will surely be within reach and he'll be well in compared to future handicaps taking into account the rise he'll receive in his mark for this. (op 9-2)

Line Of Duty(IRE) found this a much tougher assignment than the bigger-field handicap he won at York last time and though he ran respectably, he was well held from a long way out. (op 9-2)

The Galloping Shoe hasn't been with his current yard long and put a modest Epsom run behind him with a respectable effort trying his longest trip yet in a first-time visor, albeit never looking likely to finish any closer.

Gordonsville isn't quite firing at the minute yet is slow in getting any respite from the handicapper, which looks to be what he needs.

Graceful Descent(FR) didn't run as badly as her position suggests after lack of a previous run this season found her out badly late on. (op 9-1)

3164 BARRHEAD TRAVEL H'CAP 1m 2f
5:50 (5:51) (Class 4) (0-85,83) 4-Y-0+ **£6,476** (£1,927; £963; £481) **Stalls** Low

Form RPR
0300 **1** **Bahamian Music (IRE)**[15] 2676 4-9-2 **78** FrederikTylicki 8 87
(Richard Fahey) *hld up in tch: smooth hdwy over 2f out: led over 1f out: drvn out ins fnl f* **11/1**
0205 **2** *1* **Doctor Zhivago**[24] 2403 4-9-7 **83** AndrewMullen 6 89
(David Nicholls) *sn w ldr: led after 4f: rdn over 2f out: hdd over 1f out: edgd lft and kpt on ins fnl f* **11/1**
-201 **3** *hd* **Frontline Girl (IRE)**[23] 2413 5-8-13 **75** RobertWinston 10 81
(Mrs K Burke) *hld up: stdy hdwy over 2f out: rdn and edgd lft over 1f out: kpt on same pce ins fnl f* **5/2**[1]
6025 **4** *6* **Tres Coronas (IRE)**[15] 2681 4-9-7 **83** GrahamGibbons 1 77
(David Barron) *s.i.s: hld up in tch: effrt over 2f out: wknd over 1f out* **7/2**[2]
55-4 **5** *1* **Spirit Of A Nation (IRE)**[23] 2414 6-8-13 **78** AmyRyan(3) 3 70
(James Moffatt) *hld up: drvn along over 2f out: nvr able to chal* **20/1**
0-25 **6** *nse* **Staff Sergeant**[7] 2932 4-9-6 **82** DanielTudhope 2 74
(Jim Goldie) *prom tl rdn and wknd fr 2f out* **5/2**[1]
62 **7** *14* **Satwa Dream (IRE)**[12] 2760 4-9-3 **79** TomMcLaughlin 4 43
(Ed Dunlop) *hld up in tch: rdn over 2f out: sn wknd: eased whn no ch* **10/1**[3]
060- **8** *1 ¼* **Stags Leap (IRE)**[237] 6224 4-8-8 **77** GarryWhillans(7) 7 38
(Alistair Whillans) *led 4f: cl up: ev ch and rdn over 3f out: wknd over 2f out* **25/1**
2630 **9** *33* **Kidlat**[17] 2604 6-9-7 **83** RoystonFfrench 9 —
(Alan Bailey) *trckd ldrs tl wknd qckly 4f out: sn lost tch* **28/1**

2m 16.62s (4.62) **Going Correction** +0.60s/f (Yiel) **9** Ran SP% **117.2**
Speed ratings (Par 105): **105,104,104,99,98 98,87,86,59**
toteswingers:1&2:£11.00, 2&3:£5.70, 1&3:£4.90 CSF £121.11 CT £400.99 TOTE £10.50: £2.60, £2.50, £1.50; EX 122.60.
Owner R A Fahey **Bred** Genesis Green Stud Ltd **Trained** Musley Bank, N Yorks

FOCUS
An ordinary handicap to end the card and the runners were finding things hard work by now. Again the action took place in the centre. Ordinary form with the first three basically to their marks.
T/Plt: £1,282.70 to a £1 stake. Pool of £69,303.00 - 39.44 winning tickets. T/Qpdt: £275.90 to a £1 stake. Pool of £3,766.72 10.10 winning tickets. RY

2830 HAYDOCK (L-H)
Saturday, June 18

OFFICIAL GOING: Straight course - good to firm changing to good to firm (firm in places) after race 1 (6.15); round course - good (8.7)
Sprints on inner home straight, races on round course on outer home straight adding 33yds to distances on round course.
Wind: moderate 1/2 against Weather: fine

3165 ANGEL MAIDEN STKS 5f
6:15 (6:16) (Class 5) 2-Y-0 **£2,914** (£867; £433; £216) **Stalls** Centre

Form RPR
1 **West Leake Diman (IRE)** 2-9-3 0 RobertHavlin 6 79+
(B W Hills) *dwlt: hld up: smooth hdwy to trck ldrs over 2f out: led ins fnl f: edgd lft: eased towards fin* **7/2**[2]
4 **2** *1 ½* **Excelette (IRE)**[43] 1876 2-8-12 0 TomEaves 8 69
(Bryan Smart) *w ldr: led over 1f out: hdd ins fnl f: no ex* **3/1**[1]
3 *1 ¼* **The Rising (IRE)** 2-9-3 0 MartinLane 3 69+
(Ed McMahon) *wnt lft s: chsd ldrs: drvn over 2f out: sn outpcd: styd on fnl f* **4/1**[3]
60 **4** *hd* **Gin Twist**[40] 1946 2-8-12 0 StephenCraine 4 63
(Tom Dascombe) *led tl hdd over 1f out: kpt on same pce* **11/1**
62 **5** *¾* **Split Second (IRE)**[7] 2919 2-8-9 0 MartinHarley(3) 2 61
(Mick Channon) *sltly hmpd s: w ldrs: drvn over 2f out: one pce over 1f out* **3/1**[1]
6 *8* **Punta Lara Lady (IRE)** 2-8-12 0 GregFairley 5 32
(Paul Green) *chsd ldrs: drvn over 2f out: sn lost pl* **33/1**
7 *¾* **M J Woodward** 2-9-0 0 PatrickDonaghy(3) 7 34
(Paul Green) *s.i.s: in rr: hung lft 2f out: sn wknd and bhd* **40/1**
36 **8** *9* **Rhianna Brianna (IRE)**[22] 2460 2-8-9 0 SeanLevey(3) 1 —
(Michael Easterby) *chsd ldrs on outside: drvn and hung lft over 2f out: sn wknd: eased whn bhd clsng stages* **10/1**

61.72 secs (0.92) **Going Correction** 0.0s/f (Good) **8** Ran SP% **115.0**
Speed ratings (Par 93): **94,91,89,89,88 75,74,59**
toteswingers: 1&2 £3.00, 1&3 £4.30, 2&3 £4.80. CSF £14.56 TOTE £4.40: £1.70, £1.70, £1.70; EX 16.90.
Owner Henry Barton **Bred** Mr & Mrs G Middlebrook **Trained** Lambourn, Berks

FOCUS
Probably just an ordinary maiden but a nice start from the winner. The runner-up improved.

NOTEBOOK
West Leake Diman(IRE) saw off some more experienced rivals to make a winning debut. He clearly knew his job as he travelled very smoothly throughout, was the last to come off the bridle and found enough for pressure to assert in the final furlong. There are mixed messages from his pedigree as to what sort of trips will prove his optimum in the future, but he is obviously not short of natural speed and he's impressed connections enough to warrant entries in a couple of the valuable sales races later in the season. (op 10-3)
Excelette(IRE) had shaped with promise at Ripon on debut and she showed the benefit of that outing with a more polished effort here. She looks well up to winning in similar company. (op 10-3 tchd 7-2)
The Rising(IRE), who wasn't best away from the stalls, put up an eyecatching effort. He took time to hit top stride but the penny really dropped in the final furlong and he took off down the near side. Although it's often unwise to get carried away with fast finishers, this colt looks sure to benefit from this experience, in which case he'll soon be winning. (op 11-2)
Gin Twist looked a bit one-paced and doesn't appear to be progressing. (op 12-1 tchd 9-1)
Split Second(IRE) was under pressure well over 2f out and couldn't find any extra. This was a step backwards after her good run at Lingfield second time up. (op 4-1)

3166 REWARDSRACING.COM H'CAP 5f
6:45 (6:50) (Class 5) (0-75,75) 3-Y-0+ **£2,914** (£867; £433; £216) **Stalls** Centre

Form RPR
3243 **1** **Senate Majority**[26] 2353 4-9-0 **63** (b) DavidNolan 9 74+
(Tim Easterby) *w ldrs: led over 3f out: wnt clr appr fnl f: drvn out* **8/1**[3]
5160 **2** *1 ¼* **Absa Lutte (IRE)**[17] 2609 8-9-5 **68** TomEaves 13 74
(Michael Mullineaux) *dwlt: hld up in rr: hdwy stands' side over 2f out: chsd wnr 1f out: kpt on wl* **25/1**
6254 **3** *2* **Sleepy Blue Ocean**[17] 2610 5-9-4 **67** (p) MartinLane 17 66
(John Balding) *in rr stands' side: hdwy 2f out: kpt on to take 3rd post* **14/1**
0223 **4** *nk* **Sharp Bullet (IRE)**[5] 2987 5-8-9 **58** (p) TadhgO'Shea 4 56
(Bruce Hellier) *t.k.h: sn trcking ldrs: kpt on same pce fnl 2f* **8/1**[3]
0033 **5** *nk* **Schoolboy Champ**[5] 2990 4-8-4 **58** MatthewCosham(5) 6 55
(Patrick Morris) *mid-div: hdwy 2f out: kpt on: nt rch ldrs* **8/1**[3]
6530 **6** *hd* **Red Roar (IRE)**[9] 2832 4-9-1 **64** PatrickMathers 16 60
(Alan Berry) *reluctant and led rdrless to post: s.i.s: sn drvn along: kpt on fnl 2f: nvr a threat* **14/1**
-532 **7** *1* **Crimson Cloud**[14] 2736 3-8-12 **72** LeeTopliss(5) 2 62
(Richard Fahey) *chsd ldrs on outer: kpt on same pce fnl 2f* **11/2**[2]
05- **8** *½* **Atlantic Cycle (IRE)**[246] 6906 4-9-8 **74** (t) PatrickDonaghy(3) 7 65+
(Mrs K Burke) *hld up in rr: kpt on fnl 2f: nvr nr ldrs* **16/1**
4-20 **9** *½* **Time Medicean**[22] 2464 5-9-0 **63** TonyCulhane 3 52
(Paul Midgley) *mid-div: effrt over 2f out: wknd over 1f out* **12/1**
530 **10** *hd* **Cruise Tothelimit (IRE)**[15] 2694 3-8-13 **73** NeilFarley(5) 1 59
(Patrick Morris) *chsd ldrs on outer: wknd over 1f out* **10/1**
00-6 **11** *hd* **Timber Treasure (USA)**[107] 748 7-8-8 **57** (b) GregFairley 11 44
(Paul Green) *in rr: nt clr run and swtchd rt over 1f out: nvr on terms* **33/1**
-013 **12** *6* **Tillys Tale**[34] 2126 4-9-5 **75** DavidSimmonson(7) 14 41
(Paul Midgley) *led over 1f: w ldrs: wknd 2f out: eased whn bhd clsng stages* **10/1**
6035 **13** *4 ½* **Chosen One (IRE)**[42] 1907 6-9-3 **66** PJMcDonald 12 15
(Ruth Carr) *w ldrs: wknd 2f out: eased whn bhd clsng stages* **9/2**[1]

60.55 secs (-0.25) **Going Correction** 0.0s/f (Good)
WFA 3 from 4yo+ 6lb **13** Ran SP% **118.8**
Speed ratings (Par 103): **103,101,97,97,96 96,94,94,93,93 92,83,75**
toteswingers: 1&2 £38.70, 1&3 £25.80, 2&3 £33.10. CSF £190.33 CT £2825.50 TOTE £7.90: £1.90, £7.20, £4.90; EX 225.40.
Owner The Senators **Bred** Wheelers Land Stud **Trained** Great Habton, N Yorks

FOCUS
This looked quite an open handicap on paper, but it was pretty much over as a contest entering the final furlong.
Timber Treasure(USA) Official explanation: jockey said gelding was denied a clear run
Chosen One(IRE) Official explanation: trainer had no explanation for the poor form shown

3167 ABACUS SECURITIES MAIDEN STKS 1m
7:15 (7:16) (Class 5) 3-Y-0+ **£2,914** (£867; £433; £216) **Stalls** Low

Form RPR
-222 **1** **Maqaraat (IRE)**[22] 2469 3-9-2 99 TadhgO'Shea 12 87+
(B W Hills) *trckd ldrs: smooth hdwy to ld 2f out: sn pushed clr: v easily* **1/4**[1]
4- **2** *7* **Secret Era**[231] 7244 4-9-2 0 JamesRogers(5) 4 65
(William Muir) *s.s: detached in last: hdwy and swtchd outside over 2f out: styd on wl to take 2nd last 75yds* **10/1**[3]
54 **3** *2 ¼* **Magic Rhythm**[22] 2479 3-8-11 0 AndrewElliott 11 58
(Mrs K Burke) *w ldrs: led over 2f out: sn hdd: one pce fnl f* **12/1**
4 *1* **Knowe Head (NZ)** 4-9-11 0 PatrickMathers 8 62
(James Unett) *s.i.s: t.k.h in rr: hdwy over 3f out: kpt on same pce fnl f* **33/1**
0 **5** *1 ¼* **Dollar Deal**[21] 2511 3-9-2 0 KirstyMilczarek 6 58
(Luca Cumani) *chsd ldrs: kpt on one pce fnl 3f* **12/1**
00 **6** *1 ¾* **Royal Deal**[10] 2802 4-9-12 0 DavidNolan 2 56
(Michael Easterby) *sn bhd: sme hdwy over 2f out: nvr on terms* **33/1**
4- **7** *nk* **Palagonia**[194] 7723 3-8-9 0 DarylByrne(7) 5 53+
(Mark Johnston) *led: hdd over 2f out: sn wknd* **5/1**[2]
0 **8** *4 ½* **Bollin Mandy**[17] 2621 3-8-11 0 PJMcDonald 7 38
(Tim Easterby) *chsd ldrs: drvn over 3f out: wknd over 2f out* **25/1**
0 **9** *4* **Prices Lane**[10] 2802 4-9-0 0 DavidSimmonson(7) 1 31
(Michael Easterby) *mid-div: drvn over 3f out: lost pl over 2f out* **50/1**
5 **10** *1 ¾* **Kindlelight Soleil (FR)**[42] 1897 4-9-5 0 RichardOld(7) 13 32
(Nick Littmoden) *swtchd lft after s: a in rr* **66/1**
0 **11** *3* **Ossie Ardiles (IRE)**[31] 2206 3-8-9 0 JustinNewman(7) 10 23
(Michael Appleby) *chsd ldrs: drvn over 3f out: wknd over 2f out* **66/1**

1m 44.55s (1.65) **Going Correction** +0.10s/f (Good)
WFA 3 from 4yo 10lb **11** Ran SP% **135.8**
Speed ratings (Par 103): **95,88,85,84,83 81,81,76,72,71 68**
toteswingers: 1&2 £1.60, 1&3 £2.80, 2&3 £12.40. CSF £5.58 TOTE £1.40: £1.02, £2.20, £2.60; EX 4.70.
Owner Hamdan Al Maktoum **Bred** James F Hanly **Trained** Lambourn, Berks

FOCUS
Absolutely no depth to this maiden.

3168 BLACKBELT SMARTPHONE DEFENCE H'CAP 1m
7:45 (7:45) (Class 4) (0-85,87) 3-Y-0 **£5,180** (£1,541; £770; £384) **Stalls** Low

Form RPR
2-12 **1** **Las Verglas Star (IRE)**[71] 1214 3-8-8 **79** LauraBarry(7) 3 93
(Richard Fahey) *chsd ldrs: wnt 2nd 3f out: led jst over 2f out: drvn clr ent fnl f: styd on wl* **7/1**
61-5 **2** *3 ½* **Chill (IRE)**[16] 2646 3-8-9 **73** KirstyMilczarek 5 79+
(Luca Cumani) *sn chsng ldrs: drvn and outpcd 4f out: swtchd outside and chsd clr wnr over 1f out: kpt on* **3/1**[2]
22-1 **3** *6* **Little Rocky**[36] 2045 3-9-9 **87** MartinLane 8 79
(David Simcock) *stdd s: sn detached in last: hrd drvn over 5f out: hdwy over 3f out: edgd lft 1f out: one pce* **2/1**[1]
-151 **4** *2 ½* **Shadow Catcher**[20] 2527 3-8-11 **75** TomEaves 7 61
(Michael Dods) *mid-div: hdwy to chse clr ldr 4f out: one pce whn hmpd 1f out* **7/1**
41-0 **5** *2* **Malpas Missile (IRE)**[21] 2520 3-9-0 **78** RussKennemore 6 60
(Tom Dascombe) *hld up in rr: effrt over 3f out: wknd 1f out* **16/1**
06-1 **6** *3 ½* **The Mellor Fella**[35] 2096 3-9-1 **84** LeeTopliss(5) 4 58
(Richard Fahey) *chsd ldrs: effrt over 3f out: wknd over 1f out* **4/1**[3]
0560 **7** *17* **Home Office**[9] 2834 3-8-8 **72** (b[1]) PJMcDonald 2 —
(Mark Johnston) *led: wnt wl clr after 2f: wknd and hdd jst over 2f out: t.o* **25/1**

1m 43.47s (0.57) **Going Correction** +0.10s/f (Good) **7** Ran SP% **113.1**
Speed ratings (Par 101): **101,97,91,89,87 83,66**
toteswingers: 1&2 £4.70, 1&3 £5.00, 2&3 £2.10. CSF £27.60 CT £57.06 TOTE £5.30: £2.50, £3.30; EX 26.00.
Owner CBWS Partnership **Bred** Brendan Holland And P Connell **Trained** Musley Bank, N Yorks

FOCUS
Some improving 3yos on show in what looked an informative event on paper. However, it was run at a furious gallop as Home Office was lit up by the first-time blinkers and they came home at quite long intervals.

3169 SCISSOR SISTERS HERE ON 16TH JULY H'CAP — 1m
8:15 (8:15) (Class 4) (0-85,86) 4-Y-O+ **£5,180** (£1,541; £770; £384) **Stalls** Low

Form RPR
2-11 **1** **Mont Ras (IRE)**[22] 2474 4-8-10 **74**........................ TomEaves 5 92+
(David O'Meara) *chsd ldr: led over 2f out: drvn clr appr fnl f: eased towards fin* **4/1**[2]
1120 **2** *6* **Dazeen**[10] 2814 4-8-11 **75**........................ TonyCulhane 2 81+
(Paul Midgley) *s.s: hld up in rr: hdwy on ins 3f out: nt clr run over 2f out: swtchd rt over 1f out: styd on to chse wnr fnl 100yds: no imp* **8/1**
1-32 **3** *1 ¼* **Amazing Star (IRE)**[5] 2995 6-8-7 **76**........................ NeilFarley(5) 4 76
(Declan Carroll) *hld up in midfield: effrt over 2f out: chsd wnr over 1f out: kpt on same pce* **7/2**[1]
0030 **4** *4 ½* **Collateral Damage (IRE)**[11] 2783 8-8-13 **82**...............(t) LanceBetts(5) 7 72
(Tim Easterby) *s.s: hdwy u.p over 2f out: sn chsng ldrs: wknd 1f out* **8/1**
0006 **5** *1 ½* **Al Muheer (IRE)**[11] 2783 6-9-2 **80**........................(p) PJMcDonald 1 66
(Ruth Carr) *chsd ldrs: wknd fnl f* **7/1**
5031 **6** *1 ¾* **Magic Cat**[10] 2814 5-9-8 **86**........................ AndrewElliott 8 68
(Mrs K Burke) *mid-div: hdwy on outside over 3f out: wknd over 1f out* **9/2**[3]
6410 **7** *shd* **Feeling Fresh (IRE)**[7] 2938 6-8-9 **76**........................ PatrickDonaghy(3) 6 58
(Paul Green) *t.k.h in rr: hdwy 3f out: sn chsng ldrs: wknd over 1f out* **16/1**
0-00 **8** *1 ½* **Invincible Force (IRE)**[28] 2299 7-9-4 **82**........................ GregFairley 10 61
(Paul Green) *trckd ldrs: drvn over 3f out: wknd over 1f out* **33/1**
14-5 **9** *9* **Christmas Carnival**[71] 1223 4-9-5 **83**........................(b) DavidNolan 11 41
(Michael Easterby) *led: hdd over 2f out: wknd over 1f out: eased whn bhd clsng stages* **15/2**

1m 43.3s (0.40) **Going Correction** +0.10s/f (Good) **9** Ran SP% **115.7**
Speed ratings (Par 105): **102,96,94,90,88 87,86,85,76**
toteswingers: 1&2 £7.80, 1&3 £2.00, 2&3 £6.70. CSF £36.00 CT £122.42 TOTE £5.30: £1.20, £3.60, £2.20; EX 39.70.
Owner Colne Valley Racing **Bred** Patrick M Ryan **Trained** Nawton, N Yorks

FOCUS
Not a bad race for the grade.
Magic Cat Official explanation: trainer said gelding was unsuited by the good ground

3170 ANDY FARRELL 30TH BIRTHDAY H'CAP — 1m 2f 95y
8:45 (8:45) (Class 5) (0-75,74) 4-Y-O+ **£2,914** (£867; £433; £216) **Stalls** Centre

Form RPR
3155 **1** **Gala Casino Star (IRE)**[8] 2887 6-9-1 **73**........................ LeeTopliss(5) 5 81
(Richard Fahey) *trckd ldrs: effrt over 3f out: led narrowly over 1f out: struck over hd by runner-up rdr's whip: kpt on: all out* **5/2**[1]
1216 **2** *nk* **Fashionable Gal (IRE)**[20] 1388 4-9-2 **74**........................ RosieJessop(5) 9 81
(Neil King) *w ldr: t.k.h: led 7f out: narrowly hdd over 1f out: no ex clsng stages* **13/2**
/0-5 **3** *½* **Duke Of Burgundy (FR)**[12] 2769 8-9-1 **68**...............(t) StephenCraine 8 74
(Jennie Candlish) *trckd ldrs: drvn over 3f out: chal over 1f out: kpt on same pce fnl 150yds* **10/1**
24-0 **4** *½* **Zenarinda**[7] 2912 4-8-13 **66**........................ MartinLane 2 71
(Mark H Tompkins) *hld up towards rr: effrt on outside over 3f out: chsng ldrs whn edgd lft jst ins fnl f: no ex* **7/2**[2]
0143 **5** *3 ¼* **Bold Cross (IRE)**[8] 2872 8-9-1 **68**........................ TomEaves 1 67
(Edward Bevan) *stdd s: t.k.h in rr: hdwy over 3f out: sn chsng ldrs: wkng whn hmpd ins fnl f* **5/1**[3]
-045 **6** *1 ½* **Lord Raglan (IRE)**[23] 2414 4-9-4 **71**........................ AndrewElliott 4 67
(Mrs K Burke) *led tl 7f out: drvn over 3f out: wknd over 1f out* **5/1**[3]
2/3- **7** *6* **Alhaque (USA)**[30] 179 5-9-3 **70**........................ TonyCulhane 6 54
(Paul Midgley) *trckd ldrs: drvn over 3f out: sn lost pl* **14/1**

2m 16.09s (0.09) **Going Correction** +0.10s/f (Good) **7** Ran SP% **113.2**
Speed ratings (Par 103): **103,102,102,101,99 98,93**
toteswingers: 1&2 £5.10, 1&3 £5.70, 2&3 £6.50. CSF £18.79 CT £135.92 TOTE £4.20: £2.30, £2.00; EX 18.40.
Owner The Friar Tuck Racing Club **Bred** Glashare House Stud **Trained** Musley Bank, N Yorks

FOCUS
Exposed performers in this ordinary affair and there was only a length or so covering the first four home at the line, so not form to get excited about.
T/Plt: £136.80 to a £1 stake. Pool of £67,745.43 - 361.44 winning units. T/Qpdt: 12.90 to a £1 stake. Pool of £5,108.77 - 292.57 winning units. WG

2919 LINGFIELD (L-H)
Saturday, June 18

OFFICIAL GOING: Turf course - soft; all-weather - standard
Normally a high draw is essential on the straight course, bur recent rain turned the ground to soft, bringing those drawn towards the middle of the track into it.
Wind: Strong, half behind Weather: Fine but cloudy

3171 PREMIER PENSIONS GROUP MAIDEN AUCTION STKS (TURF) — 7f
6:00 (6:01) (Class 6) 2-Y-O **£1,706** (£503; £252) **Stalls** High

Form RPR
5 **1** **Fire Ship**[16] 2640 2-8-9 0........................ LukeMorris 2 71
(Peter Winkworth) *chsd ldrs in 6th: rdn 1/2-way: prog u.p over 2f out: clsng to chal whn hmpd jst over 1f out: styd on to ld ins fnl f* **5/1**[3]
60 **2** *1* **Dovils Date**[18] 2584 2-8-11 0........................ JamesMillman 3 69+
(Rod Millman) *mostly in 7th and racd against rail: pushed along after 3f: struggling tl styd on wl fr 2f out: tk 2nd nr fin* **33/1**
5 **3** *½* **Khazium (IRE)**[12] 2767 2-9-0 0........................ DaneO'Neill 1 71
(Pat Eddery) *t.k.h: pressed ldng pair: led wl over 1f out: hanging lft after and veered lft jst over 1f out: hdd and nt qckn ins fnl f: lost 2nd nr fin* **13/8**[1]
333 **4** *4* **Red Mischief (IRE)**[16] 2644 2-8-4 0........................ NickyMackay 5 51
(Harry Dunlop) *w ldr to over 2f out: nt qckn u.p: fdd over 1f out* **11/2**
5 **5** *nk* **Purple Affair (IRE)**[15] 2687 2-8-11 0........................ LiamKeniry 6 57
(J S Moore) *trckd ldng trio: rdn and no rspnse 2f out: grad fdd* **4/1**[2]
0 **6** *5* **Ernest Speak (IRE)**[7] 2901 2-8-10 0........................ KierenFox(3) 4 47
(Bill Turner) *chsd ldrs: hrd rdn and dropped to rr 3f out: struggling after* **33/1**
2 **7** *2 ½* **Mystery Cool (IRE)**[10] 2823 2-8-5 0........................ WilliamCarson 9 33
(Stuart Williams) *racd against rail: led to wl over 1f out: hanging and wknd* **9/1**
8 *3 ¾* **Siouxperhero (IRE)** 2-8-13 0........................ FergusSweeney 7 31
(William Muir) *rn green: a in last pair: struggling bef 1/2-way* **20/1**
9 *7* **Cool Fantasy (IRE)** 2-8-10 0........................ CathyGannon 8 11
(Paul D'Arcy) *a in last pair: hanging after 3f and ended in centre of crse over 2f out: t.o* **20/1**

1m 27.72s (4.42) **Going Correction** +0.475s/f (Yiel) **9** Ran SP% **115.6**
Speed ratings (Par 91): **93,91,91,86,86 80,77,73,65**
toteswingers: 1&2 £3.00, 1&3 £4.50, 2&3 £7.90. CSF £156.84 TOTE £8.40: £2.50, £3.10, £1.10; EX 44.40.
Owner IGP Partnership & Partner **Bred** Yorton Farm **Trained** Chiddingfold, Surrey

FOCUS
A routine maiden, though different from normal as a low stall is normally a disadvantage, but not on this ground. The runners raced mainly in the stands' side half of the course. The race is rated at the bottom end of the race averages.

NOTEBOOK
Fire Ship had shown ability when not getting the run of the race on his debut, on sand, and the extra furlong played to his strengths. He knuckled down well, despite being leaned on, and showed he has what it takes to hold his own in modest nurseries. (op 6-1)
Dovils Date, suited by the step up in trip, ran by far his best race to date. He is now qualified for handicaps and should have no problem staying 1m. (op 25-1)
Khazium(IRE) has demonstrated in his first two races that he is capable of winning. A small maiden is within reach and faster ground would help him see out 7f better. Official explanation: jockey said colt hung left (op 10-3)
Red Mischief(IRE) did not improve for the step up to 7f, although the easy ground helped to stretch her stamina. She is good enough to win a little maiden, but nurseries will be attractive before long (op 3-1)
Purple Affair(IRE) improved a bit from his debut but needs to find more to win a maiden. (op 11-2)
Ernest Speak(IRE) already looks as if he needs a handicap mark. (op 40-1)
Mystery Cool(IRE) Official explanation: trainer said filly lost right-hind shoe
Cool Fantasy(IRE) Official explanation: jockey said gelding hung left

3172 PREMIER PENSIONS MANAGEMENT H'CAP (TURF) — 7f 140y
6:30 (6:31) (Class 5) (0-75,75) 3-Y-O+ **£3,070** (£906; £453) **Stalls** Centre

Form RPR
1050 **1** **Willow Dancer (IRE)**[16] 2647 7-10-0 **75**........................(p) AdamKirby 2 84
(Walter Swinburn) *racd alone against far rail: a on terms w main gp: rdn over 2f out: upsides main gp ldr 1f out: ld nr fin* **7/2**[1]
4062 **2** *½* **Lastkingofscotland (IRE)**[31] 2206 5-9-11 **72**...........(b) GeorgeBaker 10 79
(Conor Dore) *racd against rail: led main gp: gng bttr than rest over 2f out: rdn and styd on fr over 1f out: nt on terms w far side wnr nr fin* **10/1**
-123 **3** *1 ¾* **Sammy Alexander**[53] 1593 3-9-0 **71**........................ NickyMackay 3 72
(David Simcock) *hld up in rr: prog on outer 1/2-way: rdn over 2f out: styd on to take 2nd in gp nr fin* **8/1**
1434 **4** *¾* **But Beautiful (IRE)**[36] 2051 4-9-8 **69**........................ DaneO'Neill 8 70
(Robert Mills) *chsd ldr: rdn over 2f out: hld over 1f out: lost 2nd in gp nr fin* **4/1**[2]
0100 **5** *3 ¾* **Cativo Cavallino**[31] 2207 8-9-1 **65**........................ NataliaGemelova(3) 9 56
(John E Long) *s.i.s: hld up in rr: prog on outer 1/2-way: rdn over 2f out: wknd over 1f out* **25/1**
2200 **6** *1 ¼* **Sunshine Always (IRE)**[31] 2207 5-9-5 **71**.............. JemmaMarshall(5) 1 59
(Michael Attwater) *t.k.h: trckd ldrs: gng wl enough 3f out: wknd 2f out* **10/1**
3532 **7** *7* **Ongoodform (IRE)**[37] 2016 4-10-0 **75**........................(p) LukeMorris 12 46
(Paul D'Arcy) *racd against rail: chsd ldng pair: rdn 3f out: wknd qckly 2f out* **5/1**[3]
51-2 **8** *18* **Amazon Twilight**[156] 140 3-9-1 **72**........................ LiamKeniry 11 —
(Brett Johnson) *t.k.h: hld up in rr against rail: wknd rapidly over 2f out: t.o and eased* **8/1**
1435 **9** *7* **Beautiful Lando (FR)**[9] 2838 3-8-2 **59** ow1...........(v) FrankieMcDonald 5 —
(Heather Main) *hld up in rr: wknd over 2f out: t.o and eased* **14/1**
55-5 **10** *4 ½* **Paphos**[38] 2001 4-8-10 **62**........................(v) RyanClark(5) 4 —
(Stuart Williams) *prom 4f: sn wknd qckly: t.o and eased* **12/1**

1m 33.52s (0.00) **Going Correction** +0.475s/f (Yiel)
WFA 3 from 4yo+ 10lb **10** Ran SP% **117.5**
Speed ratings (Par 103): **102,101,99,99,95 94,87,69,62,57**
toteswingers: 1&2 £5.00, 1&3 £8.30, 2&3 £15.90. CSF £39.51 CT £270.89 TOTE £5.40: £1.10, £4.10, £3.00; EX 21.70.
Owner The Weeping Willows **Bred** Exors Of The Late R E Sangster **Trained** Aldbury, Herts

FOCUS
With the ground soft, it was always likely that someone would attempt the far side route, particularly in view of the first-race result.
Amazon Twilight Official explanation: trainer said filly lost its action

3173 PREMIER BENEFIT SOLUTIONS MAIDEN STKS (TURF) — 6f
7:00 (7:02) (Class 5) 3-Y-O+ **£3,070** (£906; £453) **Stalls** High

Form RPR
23 **1** **Firebeam**[59] 1496 3-9-0 0........................ DaneO'Neill 1 95
(William Haggas) *prom: trckd ldr over 3f out: led 2f out: shkn up and drew clr over 1f out: comf* **4/7**[1]
3 **2** *6* **Escape To Glory (USA)**[28] 2306 3-9-0 0........................ GeorgeBaker 10 76
(Mikael Magnusson) *led against rail: rdn and hdd 2f out: clr of rest but no match for wnr* **9/4**[2]
604 **3** *4 ½* **Abacist (IRE)**[91] 905 3-9-1 0 ow1........................ AdamKirby 9 62
(Ralph Beckett) *prom: pushed along 1/2-way: chsd ldng pair 2f out: sn lft bhd* **16/1**
0 **4** *4 ½* **Dark Pegasus**[11] 2790 3-8-11 0........................ KierenFox(3) 3 47
(Karen George) *towards rr in centre: reminder over 4f out: sme prog fr 1/2-way: plugged on fnl f: no threat* **80/1**
54 **5** *2* **Bambika**[81] 1020 3-8-9 0........................ FergusSweeney 5 36
(Jo Crowley) *chsd ldrs in 5th but nt on terms: rdn 1/2-way: no prog* **12/1**[3]
04 **6** *1 ¼* **Don't Call Me Tiny (IRE)**[9] 2852 3-8-9 0........................ CathyGannon 8 32
(Don Cantillon) *sn pushed along in midfield and nt on terms: no real prog fr 1/2-way* **25/1**
0 **7** *1* **Aaranyow (IRE)**[54] 1565 3-9-0 0........................ PaulDoe 11 33
(Bryn Palling) *chsd ldr to over 3f out: steadily wknd over 2f out* **25/1**
0 **8** *hd* **Beggers Belief**[48] 1724 3-9-0 0........................ EddieCreighton 6 33
(Eric Wheeler) *outpcd and bhd in last trio: nvr on terms* **100/1**
9 *1 ¼* **Pastoral Jet** 3-8-7 0........................ LukeRowe(7) 2 29
(Richard Rowe) *dwlt: sn t.o in last pair: sme modest late prog* **80/1**
060 **10** *6* **Bird Dog**[45] 1813 5-9-7 43........................ LukeMorris 4 —
(Phil McEntee) *chsd ldrs 2f: sn wknd and bhd* **100/1**

11 *40* **Pressbuttonb** 4-9-7 0 .... WilliamCarson 7 —
(Giles Bravery) restless in stalls: dwlt: sn wl t.o **33/1**

1m 13.03s (1.83) **Going Correction** +0.475s/f (Yiel)
WFA 3 from 4yo+ 7lb **11** Ran SP% **123.1**
Speed ratings (Par 103): **106,98,92,86,83 81,80,80,78,70 17**
toteswingers: 1&2 £1.10, 1&3 £4.60, 2&3 £4.40. CSF £2.04 TOTE £1.50: £1.02, £1.10, £3.10; EX 2.30.
Owner Highclere Thoroughbred Racing-Blue Peter **Bred** Dukes Stud & Overbury Stallions Ltd **Trained** Newmarket, Suffolk

FOCUS
An ordinary maiden, with the exception of the winner, who looked much better than his rivals. They finished well spaced out, with nobody attempting to repeat the winning far-side tactics in the previous race.
Abacist(IRE) Official explanation: jockey said gelding hung left first half of race
Don't Call Me Tiny(IRE) Official explanation: jockey said filly jumped right
Bird Dog Official explanation: jockey said gelding had no more to give

3174 PREMIER WEALTH PLANNING H'CAP (TURF) 5f
7:30 (7:30) (Class 5) (0-75,74) 3-Y-0+ **£3,070** (£906; £453) **Stalls** High

Form RPR

3343 **1** **Ajjaadd (USA)**[28] 2304 5-9-9 **71** .... J-PGuillambert 4 79+
(Ted Powell) hld up in last: plld out and prog to press ldr jst over 1f out: shkn up and narrow ld ins fnl f: rdr in tangle w reins nr fin: a holding on **15/8**[1]

3602 **2** *shd* **Grandmas Dream**[8] 2881 3-9-6 **74** .... (b) PaulDoe 5 79
(Jim Best) racd against rail: mde most: fought off two rivals over 1f out: narrowly hdd ins fnl f: kpt on wl: jst hld **2/1**[2]

16-6 **3** *10* **Dubai Affair**[51] 1630 3-8-13 **67** .... LukeMorris 3 36
(Ronald Harris) w ldr to 2f out: wknd over 1f out **8/1**

26 **4** *3* **Boragh Jamal (IRE)**[87] 946 4-9-3 **65** .... (b) ShaneKelly 1 25
(Brian Meehan) trckd ldng pair: effrt to chal and w ldr wl over 1f out: sn wknd rapidly **5/2**[3]

60.11 secs (1.91) **Going Correction** +0.475s/f (Yiel)
WFA 3 from 4yo+ 6lb **4** Ran SP% **107.8**
Speed ratings (Par 103): **103,102,86,82**
toteswinger: 1&2 £9.00. CSF £5.88 TOTE £3.90; EX 4.30.
Owner Katy & Lol Pratt **Bred** Darley **Trained** Reigate, Surrey
■ Stewards' Enquiry : Paul Doe three-day ban: used whip with excessive frequency without giving filly time to respond (Jul 3-5)

FOCUS
Uncompetitive on paper, but this small field produced a cracking finish.
Boragh Jamal(IRE) Official explanation: vet said filly lost both front shoes

3175 PREMIER PENSIONS ADMINISTRATION (S) STKS 1m 4f (P)
8:00 (8:00) (Class 6) 3-Y-0 **£1,706** (£503; £252) **Stalls** Low

Form RPR

4530 **1** **Dew Reward (IRE)**[16] 2637 3-8-12 57 .... CathyGannon 7 59
(Eve Johnson Houghton) trckd ldrs: prog to ld over 7f out: mde rest: kicked on over 2f out: hrd pressed and edgd rt fnl f: hld on wl **11/4**[1]

-200 **2** *½* **History Girl (IRE)**[19] 2571 3-8-7 59 .... TomQueally 3 53
(Sir Henry Cecil) hld up in last pair: rdn 5f out: prog on wd outside u.p over 3f out: chsd wnr 2f out: clsd to chal fnl f: nt go by **3/1**[2]

0-40 **3** *3 ½* **Breton Star**[33] 2152 3-8-12 55 .... NickyMackay 2 53+
(David Simcock) trckd ldrs: lost pl 4f out: pushed along whn nt clr run 3f out to over 2f out: prog over 1f out: styd on to take 3rd last 150yds: no imp after **11/4**[1]

0-60 **4** *7* **Xenophon**[16] 2637 3-8-12 45 .... (tp) FrankieMcDonald 4 41
(Brendan Powell) in tch: reminders over 6f out: prog to join wnr over 5f out tl over 2f out: wknd over 1f out **25/1**

0 **5** *1* **Blowing A Hoolie (IRE)**[84] 983 3-8-7 0 .... DavidProbert 1 35
(Gay Kelleway) in tch: drvn over 3f out: wknd 2f out **9/1**

5000 **6** *1* **Ippi N Tombi (IRE)**[9] 2858 3-8-7 40 .... (t) WilliamCarson 8 33
(Phil McEntee) fast away: led to over 7f out: rdn 4f out: wknd 2f out **25/1**

04 **7** *1 ¼* **Circus Master**[10] 2825 3-8-12 0 .... (bt) LukeMorris 6 36
(James Eustace) trckd ldr 4f: styd prom: rdn over 4f out: wknd over 2f out **8/1**[3]

6002 **8** *1 ½* **Onlyfoalsandhorses (IRE)**[10] 2825 3-8-7 53 .... RyanPowell(5) 5 34
(J S Moore) mostly in last: rdn 3f out: no prog: wknd 2f out **8/1**[3]

2m 35.12s (2.12) **Going Correction** +0.125s/f (Slow) **8** Ran SP% **116.8**
Speed ratings (Par 97): **97,96,94,89,89 88,87,86**
toteswingers: 1&2 £1.10, 1&3 £2.50, 1&3 £2.30. CSF £11.59 TOTE £4.20: £2.00, £1.10, £1.70; EX 11.30.The winner was bought by Jason Tucker for 3,000gns.
Owner Mrs R F Johnson Houghton **Bred** Tim Hyde Jnr **Trained** Blewbury, Oxon

FOCUS
A low-grade race even by selling standards, run at an ordinary gallop.

3176 PREMIER PENSIONS ACTUARIAL H'CAP 1m 2f (P)
8:30 (8:30) (Class 6) (0-60,60) 4-Y-0+ **£1,706** (£503; £252) **Stalls** Low

Form RPR

2346 **1** **Sunset Boulevard (IRE)**[12] 2759 8-9-2 **55** .... (b) PaulDoe 11 63
(Jim Best) hld up in rr: stdy prog on outer wl over 3f out: led 2f out: clr over 1f out: drvn and hld on **12/1**

306S **2** *½* **Aine's Delight (IRE)**[16] 2638 5-8-12 **54** .... SimonPearce(3) 9 61
(Andy Turnell) hld up towards rr: prog over 2f out: rdn and r.o to take 2nd ins fnl f: clsng on wnr fin **5/1**[2]

5320 **3** *1 ½* **Abigails Angel**[66] 1308 4-9-5 **58** .... AdamKirby 4 62
(Brett Johnson) trckd ldrs: rdn in 4th 2f out: styd on fr over 1f out: nvr able to chal **8/1**

1100 **4** *1* **Fastinthestraight (IRE)**[7] 2905 4-9-2 **55** .... (p) DaneO'Neill 12 57+
(Jim Boyle) hld up towards rr: nt clr run 3f out and plenty to do after: rdn and r.o strly fr over 1f out: gaining fast at fin **9/2**[1]

1545 **5** *nk* **Ocean Of Peace (FR)**[15] 2663 8-9-5 **58** .... LukeMorris 6 60+
(Martin Bosley) chsd ldrs: rdn over 4f out: n.m.r whn u.p over 2f out: kpt on for driving fr over 1f out **13/2**

1050 **6** *¾* **Queenie's Star (IRE)**[7] 2900 4-8-9 **51** .... KierenFox(3) 8 51
(Michael Attwater) prom: rdn to chse ldr over 3f out: upsides 2f out: wknd jst over 1f out **25/1**

4435 **7** *3 ¾* **Lean Machine**[2] 3089 4-9-7 **60** .... (p) CathyGannon 2 52
(Ronald Harris) led to 2f out: wknd qckly over 1f out **12/1**

-310 **8** *1* **Ermyntrude**[108] 727 4-9-0 **58** .... JemmaMarshall(5) 5 48
(Pat Phelan) hld up in last pair: stl there over 2f out: pushed along over 1f out: sme late prog: nvr nr ldrs **10/1**

0/3P **9** *¾* **Moonlight Fantasy (IRE)**[9] 2851 8-8-12 **51** .... JamieGoldstein 7 40
(Lucinda Featherstone) hld up in midfield: n.m.r over 2f out: no real prog over 1f out **25/1**

3204 **10** *2* **Laconicos (IRE)**[15] 2685 9-8-13 **57** .... (t) LauraPike(5) 14 42
(William Stone) sn prom: u.p wl over 4f out: sn lost pl: wl btn over 2f out **11/2**[3]

4035 **11** *3* **Lunar River (FR)**[15] 2685 8-8-13 **59** .... (t) DavidKenny(7) 1 38
(David Pinder) dwlt: sn in midfield on inner: rdn 3f out: no prog whn tight for room over 2f out: wknd **10/1**

-000 **12** *1 ¼* **Heading To First**[70] 1233 4-8-9 **51** .... (p) RobertLButler(3) 3 27
(Paddy Butler) chsd ldr to over 3f out: sn wknd **20/1**

0300 **13** *2 ½* **Roe Valley (IRE)**[19] 2560 4-9-7 **60** .... FergusSweeney 13 31
(Linda Jewell) stdd s: hld up in last: taken wd over 3f out: shkn up 2f out: wknd **50/1**

/602 **14** *14* **Drawback (IRE)**[16] 2638 8-9-0 **53** .... (p) FrankieMcDonald 10 —
(Barry Brennan) nvr bttr than midfield: wknd 3f out: t.o **16/1**

2m 7.66s (1.06) **Going Correction** +0.125s/f (Slow) **14** Ran SP% **128.5**
Speed ratings (Par 101): **100,99,98,97,97 96,93,92,92,90 88,87,85,74**
toteswingers: 1&2 £25.50, 1&3 £26.30, 2&3 £15.20. CSF £73.04 CT £533.59 TOTE £14.20: £3.60, £3.00, £4.10; EX 81.60.
Owner Cavendish Star Racing **Bred** A J Martin **Trained** Lewes, E Sussex

FOCUS
A moderate but competitive race, run at a fair pace which gave everyone a chance.
T/Plt: £65.80 to a £1 stake. Pool of £67,019.92 - 742.72 winning units. T/Qpdt: £12.60 to a £1 stake. Pool of £6,258.62 - 365.30 winning units. JN

3130 NEWMARKET (R-H)
Saturday, June 18

OFFICIAL GOING: Good to soft (good in places; 7.4)
Stalls on near side of stands' side track except for 5.25, centre.
Wind: Light across Weather: Cloudy with sunny spells

3177 TURNERS TRANSPORT MAIDEN STKS (DIV I) 1m
1:35 (1:35) (Class 5) 3-Y-0 **£2,914** (£867; £433; £216) **Stalls** Low

Form RPR

2-0 **1** **Kirthill (IRE)**[63] 1408 3-9-3 0 .... J-PGuillambert 4 79+
(Luca Cumani) chsd ldrs: led over 1f out: r.o wl: readily **15/8**[1]

5 **2** *2 ¼* **Roy The Boy (USA)**[9] 2852 3-9-3 0 .... ShaneKelly 7 74
(Jane Chapple-Hyam) chsd ldr tl led over 3f out: rdn and hdd over 1f out: styd on same pce ins fnl f **11/1**

3 *¾* **Carinya (IRE)** 3-8-12 0 .... StevieDonohoe 3 67
(Amy Weaver) a.p: rdn and hung rt over 1f out: styd on **66/1**

4 *3* **Earl Of Carrick (USA)** 3-9-3 0 .... WilliamBuick 2 65+
(Mahmood Al Zarooni) s.s: hld up: hdwy and hung lft over 1f out: nt rch ldrs **10/3**[2]

5 *1 ¼* **Raasekha** 3-8-12 0 .... TadhgO'Shea 1 57+
(B W Hills) dwlt: hld up: rdn over 3f out: hdwy over 1f out: nt trble ldrs **4/1**[3]

6 *3 ¾* **Tamara Bay** 3-8-9 0 ....[1] GilmarPereira(3) 10 49+
(William Haggas) hld up: hdwy over 1f out: wknd ins fnl f **40/1**

0- **7** *1* **Switchback**[277] 6053 3-9-0 0 .... LouisBeuzelin(3) 9 51+
(Sir Michael Stoute) dwlt: hld up: rdn and hung rt over 1f out: n.d **7/1**

06 **8** *1* **Fluctuation (IRE)**[18] 2596 3-9-3 0 .... LiamJones 5 49
(William Haggas) led over 4f: rdn over 1f out: wknd fnl f **25/1**

0 **9** *7* **Astroverdi**[9] 2848 3-9-3 0 .... NickyMackay 8 33
(Mark H Tompkins) chsd ldrs: rdn over 3f out: wknd over 2f out **100/1**

00- **10** *4* **Unex Monet**[309] 5047 3-9-3 0 .... ChrisCatlin 11 24
(Michael Bell) hld up: wknd over 2f out **66/1**

11 *18* **Mafroodh** 3-9-3 0 .... IanMongan 6 —
(John Dunlop) mid-div: wknd over 2f out: t.o **14/1**

1m 39.76s (-0.24) **Going Correction** +0.025s/f (Good) **11** Ran SP% **115.6**
Speed ratings (Par 99): **102,99,99,96,94 91,90,89,82,78 60**
toteswingers: 1&2 £6.00, 1&3 £14.80, 2&3 £37.30. CSF £23.52 TOTE £2.80: £1.20, £2.20, £10.30; EX 16.60.
Owner Leonidas Marinopoulos **Bred** Giacinto Guglielmi **Trained** Newmarket, Suffolk

FOCUS
The second day of the first meeting on the July course this year and 7.5mm of rain had eased the ground to good to soft, good in places. The riders reported after this race that it was riding much as the official description indicated. An ordinary 3yo maiden in which the best recent winner was the subsequently useful handicapper Harald Bluetooth. The pace was fairly steady and the field raced centre to stands' side, ending up nearer the stands' rail. Ordinary form at best for the track, without strength in depth, although it was a bit faster than division II.

3178 CASINO AT BET365.COM H'CAP 7f
2:05 (2:06) (Class 4) (0-85,85) 3-Y-0 **£5,180** (£1,541; £770; £384) **Stalls** Low

Form RPR

2-21 **1** **Johnny Castle**[15] 2673 3-9-6 **84** .... WilliamBuick 12 102
(John Gosden) hld up: hdwy over 2f out: led and hung rt ins fnl f: r.o wl: comf **9/4**[1]

31-0 **2** *1 ¼* **Sirius Prospect (USA)**[73] 1175 3-9-1 **79** .... ShaneKelly 6 93
(Dean Ivory) led: rdn over 1f out: hdd ins fnl f: sn outpcd **8/1**

03-2 **3** *1 ¼* **Cape Classic (IRE)**[55] 1540 3-8-9 **73** .... LiamJones 2 83
(William Haggas) hld up: hdwy over 2f out: rdn over 1f out: styd on same pce ins fnl f **11/2**[2]

-064 **4** *2 ¼* **Admirable Spirit**[8] 2878 3-9-4 **82** .... PatDobbs 8 86
(Richard Hannon) chsd ldrs: rdn over 2f out: no ex fnl f **13/2**

331 **5** *¾* **Poyle Punch**[32] 2174 3-9-0 **78** .... StevieDonohoe 3 80
(Ralph Beckett) chsd ldrs: rdn over 2f out: no ex fnl f **20/1**

-125 **6** *nk* **Maverik**[14] 2729 3-9-0 **78** .... DarrylHolland 4 79
(Michael Dods) hld up in tch: plld hrd: rdn over 1f out: styd on same pce **10/1**

4-13 **7** *½* **Lamasaas (USA)**[14] 2729 3-9-2 **80** .... TadhgO'Shea 7 80
(B W Hills) trckd ldrs: rdn over 1f out: sn btn **14/1**

1-13 **8** *hd* **Bassett Road (IRE)**[17] 2619 3-9-7 **85** .... RussKennemore 11 84
(Tom Dascombe) plld hrd and prom: rdn over 1f out: hung rt and wknd ins fnl f **6/1**[3]

-220 **9** *2* **Islesman**[30] 2229 3-9-1 **79** .... DaneO'Neill 1 73
(Heather Main) hld up: rdn and hung rt over 1f out: nvr on terms **22/1**

-106 **10** *1 ¼* **Oh So Kool**[8] 2881 3-8-6 **70** .... WilliamCarson 9 61
(Stuart Williams) plld hrd and prom: rdn over 1f out: wknd fnl f **40/1**

5-40 **10** *dht* **Conducting**[48] 1725 3-9-2 **80** .... MartinDwyer 5 71
(Brian Meehan) chsd ldrs: rdn over 1f out: sn wknd **20/1**

1m 25.49s (-0.21) **Going Correction** +0.025s/f (Good) **11** Ran SP% **117.0**
Speed ratings (Par 101): **102,100,99,96,95 95,94,94,92,90 90**
toteswingers: 1&2 £7.50, 1&3 £1.60, 2&3 £13.70. CSF £19.30 CT £91.28 TOTE £2.90: £1.40, £2.10, £2.00; EX 28.70 Trifecta £445.60 Part won. Pool: £602.26 - 0.72 winning units..
Owner Normandie Stud Ltd **Bred** Normandie Stud Ltd **Trained** Newmarket, Suffolk

FOCUS
A competitive 3-y-o handicap that trainer Richard Hannon was bidding to win for the third successive year. The winner's penultimate Haydock form has worked out well.

3179 BET365 H'CAP — 6f
2:35 (2:35) (Class 4) (0-85,83) 3-Y-O+ — **£5,180** (£1,541; £770; £384) **Stalls** Low

Form				RPR
2243	**1**		**Ivory Silk**[26] 2369 6-9-10 **79** ....(b) ClareLindop 4 (Jeremy Gask) *a.p: led wl over 1f out: r.o wl* **8/1**	91
3554	**2**	*1 ½*	**Seek The Fair Land**[8] 2876 5-9-6 **78** ....(b) MatthewDavies(3) 7 (Jim Boyle) *hmpd s: hld up: hdwy over 2f out: rdn to chse wnr fnl f: r.o* **9/2**[1]	85
000-	**3**	*3 ½*	**Our Piccadilly (IRE)**[251] 6772 6-8-11 **69** .... LouisBeuzelin(3) 8 (Stuart Kittow) *prom: nt clr run over 1f out: styd on same pce fnl f* **20/1**	65
-450	**4**	*hd*	**Mac Gille Eoin**[42] 1888 7-10-0 **83** .... IanMongan 11 (John Gallagher) *led: hdd over 4f out: rdn over 1f out: no ex ins fnl f* **12/1**	78
2505	**5**	*hd*	**Bunce (IRE)**[17] 2619 3-9-4 **80** .... PatDobbs 2 (Richard Hannon) *hld up: rdn over 2f out: hung lft and styd on ins fnl f: nvr nrr* **7/1**[3]	73+
4432	**6**	*1 ¾*	**Rough Rock (IRE)**[1] 3130 6-8-9 **67** .... AdamBeschizza(3) 3 (Chris Dwyer) *s.i.s: hld up: rdn over 1f out: nt trble ldrs* **7/1**[3]	56
-500	**7**	*1 ¼*	**Cardinal**[5] 3000 6-9-7 **76** .... ShaneKelly 6 (Robert Cowell) *hld up: hdwy over 1f out: no ex ins fnl f* **7/1**[3]	61
6005	**8**	*4*	**Divertimenti (IRE)**[21] 2491 7-9-2 **71** ....(b) RussKennemore 9 (Roy Bowring) *chsd ldrs: rdn over 2f out: hung rt over 1f out: sn wknd* **28/1**	43
600-	**9**	*¾*	**Spitfire**[206] 7554 6-9-11 **80** .... TonyCulhane 1 (J R Jenkins) *hld up: rdn over 2f out: wknd over 1f out* **15/2**	50
3025	**10**	*2 ¼*	**Stevie Gee (IRE)**[19] 2557 7-8-13 **73** ....(v) RyanClark(5) 12 (Ian Williams) *hld up: rdn over 2f out: wknd over 1f out* **6/1**[2]	36
50-0	**11**	*2 ¼*	**Imjin River (IRE)**[16] 2645 4-8-6 **66** .... AshleyMorgan(5) 10 (Mark H Tompkins) *prom: rdn and ev ch over 1f out: wknd ins fnl f* **40/1**	21
0-05	**12**	*½*	**The Strig**[7] 2929 4-8-9 **64** oh2 ....(v[1]) WilliamCarson 5 (Stuart Williams) *chsd ldr tl led over 4f out: hdd & wknd wl over 1f out* **16/1**	18

1m 11.78s (-0.72) **Going Correction** +0.025s/f (Good)
WFA 3 from 4yo+ 7lb — **12** Ran SP% **117.1**
Speed ratings (Par 105): **105,103,98,98,97 95,93,88,87,84 81,80**
toteswingers: 1&2 £12.90, 1&3 not won, 2&3 £19.70. CSF £42.36 CT £703.36 TOTE £8.70: £2.50, £2.40, £6.00; EX 52.00 TRIFECTA Not won..
Owner Resurrection Partners **Bred** K T Ivory **Trained** Sutton Veny, Wilts

FOCUS
A decent sprint handicap that has fallen to the likes of subsequent Stewards' Cup winner Zidane and useful sire Kodiac in the past. This year's line-up had no such potential stars but did result in a 'first'. The winner is rated back to his old AW best.

3180 BET365.COM E B F FILLIES' H'CAP — 1m
3:10 (3:10) (Class 4) (0-85,84) 3-Y-O+ — **£5,180** (£1,541; £770; £384) **Stalls** Low

Form				RPR
3-21	**1**		**Elmaam**[24] 2402 3-8-10 **76** .... TadhgO'Shea 2 (William Haggas) *led: rdn and hdd over 1f out: rallied to ld post* **11/4**[1]	85+
4-21	**2**	*shd*	**Bonnie Brae**[6] 2963 4-9-11 **81** 6ex .... WilliamBuick 3 (David Elsworth) *chsd ldr tl led over 1f out: sn rdn: hdd post* **7/2**[3]	92
2311	**3**	*3*	**Sunset Kitty (USA)**[15] 2674 4-10-0 **84** .... ShaneKelly 6 (Walter Swinburn) *chsd ldrs: rdn over 1f out: styd on same pce ins fnl f* **10/3**[2]	88
601-	**4**	*½*	**Tameen**[262] 6469 3-8-9 **75** .... DaneO'Neill 5 (John Dunlop) *hld up: r.o ins fnl f: nrst fin* **5/1**	76
5-1	**5**	*1 ¾*	**Countermarch**[98] 850 3-8-5 **76** .... KieranO'Neill(5) 7 (Richard Hannon) *dwlt: hld up: hdwy over 3f out: rdn and hung rt over 1f out: sn wknd* **11/2**	73
-553	**6**	*½*	**Merrjanah**[29] 2266 3-7-13 **65** oh1 .... JimmyQuinn 8 (Clive Brittain) *prom: lost pl over 3f out: sn rdn: wknd over 1f out* **12/1**	61

1m 41.71s (1.71) **Going Correction** +0.025s/f (Good)
WFA 3 from 4yo 10lb — **6** Ran SP% **111.7**
Speed ratings (Par 102): **92,91,88,88,86 86**
toteswingers: 1&2 £1.70, 1&3 £1.80, 2&3 £3.40. CSF £12.47 CT £31.06 TOTE £4.00: £2.20, £1.50; EX 9.40 Trifecta £10.80 Pool: £411.67 - 27.98 winning units..
Owner Hamdan Al Maktoum **Bred** Shadwell Estate Company **Trained** Newmarket, Suffolk

FOCUS
Subsequent Group 3 winner I'm A Dreamer took this fillies' handicap in 2010 and there were several progressive and unexposed types with prospects of emulating her here. The pace was steady though, the time being nearly two seconds slower than the opening maiden, and the positions didn't change much throughout. The winner is unexposed and the second confirmed her recent improvement.

3181 GET MOBILE AT BET365 H'CAP — 5f
3:40 (3:41) (Class 3) (0-95,94) 3-Y-O
£8,100 (£2,425; £1,212; £607; £302; £152) **Stalls** Low

Form				RPR
2-01	**1**		**Steps (IRE)**[19] 2564 3-9-0 **87** .... JackMitchell 6 (Roger Varian) *chsd ldrs: rdn over 1f out: r.o to ld towards fin* **13/2**	96+
0063	**2**	*¾*	**Ballista (IRE)**[7] 2911 3-9-1 **88** .... RussKennemore 2 (Tom Dascombe) *chsd ldr: rdn over 1f out: led ins fnl f: edgd rt: hdd towards fin* **10/1**	94
3-24	**3**	*1*	**Coeus**[43] 1844 3-9-1 **88** .... StevieDonohoe 5 (Sir Mark Prescott Bt) *a.p: rdn over 1f out: r.o to go 3rd nr fin* **4/1**[2]	90
1211	**4**	*nk*	**Quality Art (USA)**[33] 2158 3-9-3 **90** .... PatDobbs 1 (Gary Moore) *led: edgd lft 1/2-way: rdn over 1f out: hdd and unable qck ins fnl f* **11/2**	91
0-21	**5**	*1 ½*	**Muffraaj**[12] 2772 3-8-6 **79** .... MartinDwyer 4 (David Simcock) *hld up in tch: pushed along 1/2-way: nt clr run over 1f out: styd on ins fnl f* **5/1**[3]	75
0-21	**6**	*1 ¼*	**Apace (IRE)**[21] 2505 3-9-0 **87** .... WilliamBuick 3 (Sir Michael Stoute) *sn pushed along in rr: swtchd lft 2f out: nvr trbld ldrs* **9/4**[1]	78+
-354	**7**	*2 ¼*	**Face The Problem (IRE)**[14] 2724 3-9-0 **94** .... MatthewLawson(7) 8 (B W Hills) *chsd ldrs: rdn over 1f out: wknd fnl f* **14/1**	77
340-	**8**	*1 ¼*	**Excello**[309] 5036 3-9-6 **93** .... IanMongan 7 (Malcolm Saunders) *hld up: racd keenly: rdn over 1f out: wknd fnl f* **33/1**	72

58.82 secs (-0.28) **Going Correction** +0.025s/f (Good) — **8** Ran SP% **114.9**
Speed ratings (Par 103): **103,101,100,99,97 95,91,89**
toteswingers: 1&2 £25.40, 1&3 £9.00, 2&3 £9.90. CSF £68.45 CT £295.75 TOTE £8.60: £2.50, £3.10, £1.80; EX 117.00 Trifecta £720.80 Pool: £1,392.96 - 1.43 winning units..
Owner Michael Hill **Bred** Eamon Beston **Trained** Newmarket, Suffolk

FOCUS
This sprint has fallen to the likes of Moorhouse Lad and Green Manalishi in the last decade and there were several progressive types involved here. The winner continues on the up but the second had not been at his best this year and may limit the form.

NOTEBOOK
Steps(IRE) ◆ is a consistent performer on good ground and Polytrack, but the fact that he was by Verglas suggested that he would probably handle conditions and he did in determined fashion. Always close up after a fast start, he delivered his challenge entering the last furlong and kept on strongly to defy a 7lb rise in the weights. He looks one to keep on-side. (op 9-2)
Ballista(IRE) had won his maiden on soft ground and appreciated the return to it here. He was always in the leading trio and went on around 2f out, but could not hold the winner's effort on his outside. His stable is in good form at present, and he might be able to gain compensation before long. (tchd 12-1)
Coeus was dropping to this trip for the first time since his debut. He handled the easier ground and, having chased the pace throughout, was staying on nicely up the hill. (op 9-2 tchd 5-1)
Quality Art(USA) had only ever raced on a sound surface and Polytrack and, after making the running, could not sustain his effort in the closing stages on this softer surface. (op 5-1 tchd 9-2)
Muffraaj had shown all his form on good and softer ground and chased the leaders up the rail. However, dropping in trip, he could make no impression in the last 2f. (op 6-1 tchd 13-2)
Apace(IRE) was well fancied to build on her taking success at Haydock, but she was outpaced early and then short of room and did not pick up much when switched. It is probable she did not handle the soft ground as she had been well beaten on two previous tries on it. (op 3-1)
Face The Problem(IRE) had shown all his form on fast ground and was not helped by having to race on the outside of the pack. (op 12-1)
Excello, who was Listed placed last season, was making her reappearance and handicap debut, but was too keen early and never figured. (op 28-1)

3182 NEWBUILD FRAMES MAIDEN STKS — 7f
4:15 (4:17) (Class 5) 2-Y-O — **£3,238** (£963; £481; £240) **Stalls** Low

Form				RPR
2	**1**		**Coupe De Ville (IRE)**[15] 2687 2-9-3 0 .... PatDobbs 12 (Richard Hannon) *trckd ldrs: plld hrd: rdn to ld ins fnl f: r.o wl* **11/4**[1]	88+
3	**2**	*2 ½*	**Mehdi (IRE)**[18] 2584 2-9-3 0 .... ShaneKelly 6 (Brian Meehan) *led 6f out: rdn over 1f out: hdd and unable qck ins fnl f* **3/1**[2]	81
	3	*½*	**Right Regal (IRE)** 2-9-3 0 .... AndreaAtzeni 13 (Marco Botti) *a.p: rdn and ev ch over 1f out: styd on same pce ins fnl f* **18/1**	80+
	4	*3*	**Rayvin Black** 2-8-12 0 .... AshleyMorgan(5) 4 (Mark H Tompkins) *chsd ldrs: rdn over 1f out: no ex fnl f* **22/1**	72+
	5	*3 ¼*	**Protect** 2-8-9 0 .... LouisBeuzelin(3) 14 (Sir Michael Stoute) *prom: rdn over 2f out: edgd rt and wknd over 1f out* **16/1**	59
	6	*1*	**Stateos (IRE)** 2-9-3 0 .... IanMongan 15 (Sir Henry Cecil) *dwlt: hld up: rdn over 2f out: hdwy over 1f out: wknd ins fnl f* **14/1**	61
	7	*1*	**Hazaz (IRE)** 2-9-3 0 .... J-PGuillambert 9 (Clive Brittain) *led 1f: chsd ldr: rdn over 1f out: wknd fnl f* **50/1**	59
	8	*2*	**The Blue Banana (IRE)** 2-9-3 0 .... MartinDwyer 10 (Brian Meehan) *in rr and pushed along: styd on ins fnl f: nvr nrr* **25/1**	54+
45	**9**	*nk*	**Universal (IRE)**[18] 2584 2-9-3 0 .... ChrisCatlin 7 (Mahmood Al Zarooni) *prom: rdn over 2f out: wknd over 1f out* **10/1**[3]	53
	10	*1*	**Pugnacious (IRE)** 2-8-10 0 .... AntiocoMurgia(7) 8 (Mahmood Al Zarooni) *mid-div: rdn over 2f out: n.d* **25/1**	51+
	11	*nk*	**Amoure Medici** 2-9-0 0 .... AdamBeschizza(3) 2 (Noel Quinlan) *s.i.s: hld up: plld hrd: hdwy and hung lft fr over 2f out: sn wknd* **25/1**	50
	12	*1 ½*	**Angel Cake (IRE)** 2-8-12 0 .... DarryllHolland 1 (Amy Weaver) *s.i.s: rn green and a in rr* **66/1**	41
	13	*1 ¾*	**Ex Oriente (IRE)** 2-9-3 0 .... WilliamBuick 5 (John Gosden) *mid-div: hdwy over 3f out: wknd over 1f out* **11/4**[1]	42
	14	*6*	**Mormoran** 2-8-12 0 .... JimmyQuinn 11 (Chris Dwyer) *hood removed late and s.i.s: sn mid-div: rdn and wknd over 2f out* **100/1**	22
	15	*hd*	**Alshahir Zain (IRE)** 2-9-3 0 .... JackMitchell 3 (Clive Brittain) *hld up: a in rr: wknd over 2f out* **25/1**	26

1m 26.9s (1.20) **Going Correction** +0.025s/f (Good) — **15** Ran SP% **129.4**
Speed ratings (Par 93): **94,91,90,87,83 82,81,78,78,77 77,75,73,66,66**
toteswingers: 1&2 £1.40, 1&3 £16.70, 2&3 £27.70. CSF £10.88 TOTE £3.60: £1.90, £2.00, £6.40; EX 9.90.
Owner Coupe de Ville Partnership **Bred** Flor Ryan **Trained** East Everleigh, Wilts

FOCUS
A big field for this maiden and only three had previous experience, and two of those filled the first two places. The time was 1.41secs slower than the earlier 3-y-o handicap and the first three were clear of the fourth, who in turn was clear of the rest. The winner impressed and there is more to come.

NOTEBOOK
Coupe De Ville(IRE) ◆, an 82,000gns half-brother to winners at 5f-1m1f, was touched off on his debut over 6f on fast ground. He handled this softer surface without any problem and won in good style, suggesting he can go on to better things. (op 3-1 tchd 5-2)
Mehdi(IRE), a 50,000gns half-brother to 1m winner Final Approach, had made a promising debut behind the subsequent Coventry Stakes runner-up at Leicester. He made the running and kept battling away, but the winner proved too good. He should win a maiden before long though. (op 6-1)
Right Regal(IRE) ◆, a 30,000gns first foal of a dual winner in the US, travelled really well into the race and looked as if he might win over a furlong out, but had to give best to his more experienced rivals. This was a promising debut and he looks sure to go on to win a race. (op 25-1)
Rayvin Black, a half-brother to winners at 7f-1m3f out of a dual 7f winner, showed up throughout and only faded in the final furlong. This was a decent effort as he was clear of the remainder. (tchd 20-1)
Protect, a half-sister to a 1m juvenile winner, was weak in the market and, after chasing the leaders, faded at the business end. She should do better over further in time. (op 17-2)
Stateos(IRE), a 48,000gns first foal of a half-sister to six winners at 1m-1m4f, was out the back and did not get the hang of things until late on. He can be expected to do better in due course. (tchd 12-1)

3183 TURNERS TRANSPORT MAIDEN STKS (DIV II) — 1m
4:50 (4:51) (Class 5) 3-Y-O — **£2,914** (£867; £433; £216) **Stalls** Low

Form				RPR
55-	**1**		**Maraheb**[252] 6748 3-9-3 0 .... IanMongan 8 (John Dunlop) *led 7f out: rdn and flashed tail 1f out: r.o wl* **3/1**[2]	85+
320	**2**	*6*	**Danehill Dante (IRE)**[16] 2648 3-9-3 **79** .... PatDobbs 9 (Richard Hannon) *a.p: rdn to chse wnr over 1f out: styd on same pce ins fnl f* **5/2**[1]	71

3 ¾ **Gobooll** 3-9-3 0 WilliamBuick 3 69+
(William Haggas) *in rr and pushed along: nt clr run over 1f out: siwtched lft: r.o ins fnl f: nt trble ldrs* 6/1

4 ½ **Tadabeer** 3-9-3 0 LiamJones 5 68
(William Haggas) *s.i.s: hld up: hdwy over 1f out: no ex ins fnl f* 14/1

0- 5 ¾ **Our Play (IRE)**[224] 7345 3-9-3 0 DarrylHolland 10 66
(B W Hills) *chsd ldrs: rdn over 2f out: no ex fnl f* 16/1

50 6 2 **Dakar (GER)**[16] 2648 3-9-3 0 ShaneKelly 7 62
(Pat Phelan) *led 1f: chsd wnr: rdn over 2f out: wknd over 1f out* 100/1

30-2 7 nk **Our Gal**[43] 1873 3-8-12 77 ChrisCatlin 4 56
(Noel Quinlan) *prom: rdn over 2f out: wknd over 1f out* 4/1[3]

0 8 1 **Llewellyn**[52] 1606 3-9-3 0 JackMitchell 1 59
(James Fanshawe) *s.i.s: hld up: hdwy over 2f out: rdn and wknd over 1f out* 8/1

0- 9 9 **Cantor**[230] 7248 3-9-3 0 J-PGuillambert 6 38
(Giles Bravery) *hld up: rdn over 3f out: wknd 2f out* 50/1

00 10 4½ **Kings Fortune**[14] 2723 3-9-3 0 MartinDwyer 2 28
(Michael Bell) *hld up: a in rr: rdn and wknd 2f out* 33/1

1m 40.0s **Going Correction** +0.025s/f (Good) 10 Ran SP% **117.4**
Speed ratings (Par 99): **101,95,94,93,93 91,90,89,80,76**
toteswingers: 1&2 £2.60, 1&3 £4.10, 2&3 £5.10. CSF £10.95 TOTE £3.90: £1.20, £1.50, £2.50; EX 12.20.

Owner Hamdan Al Maktoum **Bred** Shadwell Estate Company Limited **Trained** Arundel, W Sussex

FOCUS

The second division of the 3-y-o maiden was run just under a quarter of a second slower than the first, but resulted in a runaway winner. There is a bit of doubt over what he beat.

3184 ROTARY CLUB OF NEWMARKET H'CAP 1m 5f

5:25 (5:27) (Class 5) (0-75,75) 4-Y-O+ **£3,238** (£963; £481; £240) **Stalls** Centre

Form RPR

1- 1 **Roberto Pegasus (USA)**[299] 5376 5-9-6 74 IanMongan 8 83+
(Pat Phelan) *a.p: led over 1f out: rdn out* 7/1[3]

0-43 2 ¾ **Outland (IRE)**[20] 2526 5-8-2 56 oh3 AdrianMcCarthy 14 64
(J R Jenkins) *hld up: hdwy over 2f out: rdn to chse wnr ins fnl f: styd on* 6/1[2]

0-54 3 ½ **Dancing Storm**[19] 2552 8-8-3 60 LouisBeuzelin(3) 11 67
(Stuart Kittow) *hld up: hdwy over 3f out: rdn and edgd lft over 1f out: styd on* 6/1[2]

0600 4 1 **Turjuman (USA)**[23] 2436 6-7-13 58 KieranO'Neill(5) 7 64
(Willie Musson) *hld up: hdwy and swtchd lft over 1f out: rdn and hung rt ins fnl f: r.o* 4/1[1]

/30- 5 1¼ **Penang Princess**[395] 2228 5-9-7 75 LiamJones 15 79
(Chris Gordon) *sn led: rdn over 2f out: hdd over 1f out: no ex ins fnl f* 14/1

6-25 6 1¼ **Locum**[10] 2824 6-8-3 57 JimmyQuinn 4 59
(Mark H Tompkins) *hld up: hdwy over 4f out: sn rdn: nt clr run and swtchd lft over 1f out: r.o u.p* 16/1

16-0 7 1 **Morar**[150] 209 5-9-6 74 JackMitchell 6 74
(Laura Mongan) *prom: rdn and ev ch 2f out: no ex fnl f* 28/1

5640 8 7 **Royal Defence (IRE)**[9] 2856 5-7-13 56 oh1 SimonPearce(3) 5 46
(Michael Quinn) *chsd ldrs: rdn over 2f out: wkng whn hung lft over 1f out* 25/1

3-03 9 1¾ **Kerchak (USA)**[40] 1935 4-9-4 72 MartinDwyer 9 59
(William Jarvis) *chsd ldrs: rdn over 2f out: wknd over 1f out* 8/1

-142 10 15 **Treacle Tart**[128] 484 6-9-1 69 WilliamBuick 2 34
(Peter Charalambous) *chsd ldr: rdn over 2f out: sn wknd: eased over 1f out* 8/1

00- 11 6 **Whitcombe Spirit**[89] 6693 6-7-11 56 oh8 (b) RyanPowell(5) 12 12
(Jamie Poulton) *s.i.s: hld up: hung lft and wknd 3f out* 50/1

-300 12 ½ **Highland Park (IRE)**[21] 2512 4-8-6 60 AndreaAtzeni 10 15
(Michael Wigham) *chsd ldrs: rdn over 4f out: wknd over 2f out: eased* 20/1

2540 P **Onyx Of Arabia (IRE)**[6] 2958 4-9-3 71 (b) ShaneKelly 13 —
(Brian Meehan) *hld up: a in rr: p.u wl over 1f out: lame* 8/1

2m 45.93s (1.93) **Going Correction** +0.025s/f (Good) 13 Ran SP% **121.0**
Speed ratings (Par 103): **95,94,94,93,92 92,91,87,86,76 73,72,—**
toteswingers: 1&2 £3.30, 1&3 £9.40, 2&3 £7.20. CSF £47.27 CT £273.37 TOTE £4.70: £2.80, £2.40, £2.90; EX 23.30.

Owner J Daniels **Bred** Gigginstown House Stud **Trained** Epsom, Surrey

FOCUS

An ordinary handicap but a good-sized field. The second and third set a sound standard.

T/Plt: £36.70 to a £1 stake. Pool of £82,536.17 - 1,638.14 winning units. T/Qpdt: £15.80 to a £1 stake. Pool of £4,080.26 - 191.10 winning units. CR

3137 REDCAR (L-H)

Saturday, June 18

OFFICIAL GOING: Good (good to firm in places) changing to good after race 2 (2.15) changing to good to soft after race 3 (2.45) changing to soft after race 5 (3.55)

Wind: Light against Weather: steady rain

3185 KATE FEARNLEY & CHIC HATS FASHION SHOW H'CAP (DIV I) 1m 6f 19y

1:45 (1:50) (Class 6) (0-60,59) 4-Y-O+ **£1,295** (£385; £192; £96) **Stalls** Low

Form RPR

0-06 1 **Denison Flyer**[22] 2462 4-8-5 46 (b[1]) DeclanCannon(3) 9 53
(Lawrence Mullaney) *trckd ldr: rdn and hung lft over 3f out: led over 2f out: kpt on drvn out* 9/1

06-6 2 ¾ **Word Of Warning**[14] 2733 7-8-10 53 LeeTopliss(5) 2 59
(Martin Todhunter) *midfield: hdwy over 2f out: rdn over 1f out: styd on fnl f: wnt 2nd fnl 100yds: nt rch wnr* 15/2

6610 3 1¼ **Heart Of Dubai (USA)**[17] 2496 6-9-3 55 (p) KellyHarrison 11 59
(Micky Hammond) *hld up on inner: hdwy over 2f out: rdn over 1f out: styd on ins fnl f: wnt 3rd towards fin* 4/1[2]

6250 4 hd **Valdan (IRE)**[3] 3041 7-9-7 59 TonyHamilton 5 63
(Maurice Barnes) *trckd ldrs: smooth hdwy over 2f out: rdn to chal over 1f out: sn one pce: lost 3rd nr fin* 11/2[3]

0006 5 2¾ **Quaestor (IRE)**[9] 2851 4-8-4 45 (p) PaulPickard(3) 1 45
(Andrew Crook) *stdd s: hld up: rdn over 2f out: hdwy over 1f out: styd on ins fnl f: nvr threatened ldrs* 20/1

0000 6 nk **Molannarch**[19] 2575 5-8-7 45 DuranFentiman 3 45
(Keith Reveley) *led: rdn whn hdd over 2f out: wknd ins fnl f* 33/1

0320 7 3½ **They All Laughed**[36] 2060 8-8-5 50 ow2 (p) LucyKBarry(7) 8 45
(Marjorie Fife) *hld up towards outer: rdn over 3f out: sn no imp* 7/1

050- 8 1¾ **Turf Trivia**[17] 4481 4-8-13 51 PJMcDonald 6 43
(George Moore) *trckd ldr: rdn and lost pl over 4f out: wknd over 1f out* 12/1

5464 9 2¼ **Paint The Town Red**[17] 2608 6-8-7 45 (p) MickyFenton 7 34
(Richard Guest) *midfield: rdn over 2f out: sn wknd* 10/1

66-5 10 1¾ **Harsh But Fair**[14] 2733 5-8-7 45 TomEaves 10 32
(Michael Easterby) *dwlt: sn midfield: pushed along over 3f out: wknd over 2f out* 7/2[1]

3m 6.42s (1.72) **Going Correction** +0.15s/f (Good) 10 Ran SP% **116.4**
Speed ratings (Par 101): **101,100,99,99,98 98,96,95,93,92**
toteswingers:1&2:£6.60, 2&3:£8.30, 1&3:£7.60 CSF £74.59 CT £315.44 TOTE £13.70: £4.20, £1.70, £1.60; EX 94.10.

Owner L Mullaney, W Bavill & D Bavill **Bred** Ms R A Myatt **Trained** Great Habton, N Yorks

FOCUS

After some steady rain the going eased from the previous day's meeting to good, good to firm in places. Division 1 of an ordinary 46-60 staying handicap for which Molannarch ensured this was a good test before tiring when headed 3f out.

3186 BRITISH STALLION STUDS E B F MARKET CROSS JEWELLERS MAIDEN STKS 7f

2:15 (2:18) (Class 5) 2-Y-O **£2,978** (£886; £442; £221) **Stalls** High

Form RPR

3 1 **Red Duke (USA)**[22] 2476 2-9-3 0 TomEaves 5 83+
(John Quinn) *in tch: smooth hdwy over 2f out: chsd ldr over 1f out: led fnl 100yds: kpt on* 1/2[1]

2 1 **Rock Supreme (IRE)** 2-9-0 0 SeanLevey(3) 8 81+
(Michael Dods) *led: rdn and edgd lft over 1f out: hdd fnl 100yds: kpt on* 15/2[3]

5 3 1¼ **Comical**[28] 2318 2-9-3 0 PJMcDonald 1 77
(Mark Johnston) *wnt lft s: sn prom: rdn over 2f out: kpt on ins fnl f* 13/2[2]

4 8 **Fine Kingdom** 2-9-3 0 TonyHamilton 3 57
(Michael Dods) *hld up: rdn and hdwy over 1f out: styd on fnl f: nvr threatened ldrs* 25/1

5 5 **Keep Swinging (IRE)** 2-9-3 0 MickyFenton 4 45
(Tom Tate) *tk v t.k.h early: in tch: rdn and lost pl over 2f out: wknd over 1f out* 8/1

6 4 **Dubai Destiny** 2-9-3 0 DavidNolan 7 35
(Tim Easterby) *prom: rdn and outpcd over 3f out: wknd over 1f out* 20/1

30 7 1 **Priestley's Reward (IRE)**[22] 2455 2-9-0 0 MichaelGeran(3) 6 32
(Mrs K Burke) *dwlt: sn in tch on outer: rdn over 2f out: sn wknd* 33/1

8 11 **Lady Advocate (IRE)** 2-8-12 0 DuranFentiman 2 —
(Tim Easterby) *trckd ldrs: rdn and lost pl over 3f out: sn wknd* 25/1

1m 26.6s (2.10) **Going Correction** +0.275s/f (Good) 8 Ran SP% **118.3**
Speed ratings (Par 93): **99,97,96,87,81 77,75,63**
toteswingers:1&2:£1.70, 2&3:£20.10, 1&3:£1.10 CSF £4.84 TOTE £1.60: £1.10, £2.10, £2.00; EX 8.00.

Owner Maxilead Limited **Bred** B P Walden Jr & H Sexton **Trained** Settrington, N Yorks

FOCUS

The ground changed to good all round after further rain. An interesting maiden with the front three finishing clear of the remainder and looking ones to keep an eye on in the future. the winner is rated to the form of his solid debut.

NOTEBOOK

Red Duke(USA) ◆, for whom this looked a good opportunity to build on his debut promise when chasing home Misty Conquest and Caspar Netscher, with the latter franking the form when third in the Windsor Castle at Royal Ascot earlier this week. He had to be only nudged out to stamp his authority after travelling well most of the way but looks a useful prospect and it will be no surprise to see further improvement when stepped up again in trip as his pedigree would suggest. (op 4-6, tchd 5-6 in places)

Rock Supreme(IRE) is a brother to the smart middle-distance stayer Yellowstone and half-brother to the useful Londoner. This was a very pleasing debut and he will not be long in getting off the mark judged on this performance. (op 13-2)

Comical shaped with promise on his debut and again, this big strapping son of Dubai Destination confirmed that promise. He will be seen to even better effect when upped in distance as he could never quite find the pace to lay down a serious challenge in the latter stages.

Fine Kingdom ran respectably and was a little unlucky to bump into some useful prospects.

Keep Swinging(IRE), a 250,000euros yearling and related to the smart Royaaty, will come on for the experience as he took a very strong hold in the early stages before tiring entering the final furlong.

3187 KATE FEARNLEY & CHIC HATS FASHION SHOW H'CAP (DIV II) 1m 6f 19y

2:45 (2:48) (Class 6) (0-60,55) 4-Y-O+ **£1,295** (£385; £192; £96) **Stalls** Low

Form RPR

60-6 1 **Zefooha (FR)**[150] 89 7-9-7 55 (p) DuranFentiman 3 62
(Tim Walford) *in tch: rdn and outpcd over 4f out: hdwy u.p 2f out: led ins fnl f: styd on* 7/1

0-25 2 1¾ **Falcun**[22] 2462 4-9-6 54 TomEaves 8 58
(Micky Hammond) *midfield: rdn and outpcd over 4f out: hdwy over 2f out: styd on ins fnl f: wnt 2nd post* 3/1[2]

606- 3 shd **Haka Dancer (USA)**[24] 6076 8-8-8 45 (p) PaulPickard(3) 5 49
(Philip Kirby) *midfield: rdn over 5f out: hdwy over 3f out: chsd ldr over 1f out: kpt on one pce: lost 2nd post* 10/1

0-6 4 2¼ **Ferney Boy**[19] 2575 5-8-13 50 SeanLevey(3) 2 51
(Chris Fairhurst) *led: clr 5f out tl over 1f out: hdd ins fnl f: wknd* 8/1

/400 5 12 **Cause For Applause (IRE)**[65] 675 5-8-11 45 TonyHamilton 6 29
(Ray Craggs) *hld up: rdn over 4f out: sn no imp* 25/1

46-0 6 ½ **Perez (IRE)**[23] 1556 9-8-6 45 (tp) JulieBurke(5) 1 28
(Wilf Storey) *hld up: reminders 10f out: nvr threatened* 16/1

7 3 **Doberdan (USA)**[351] 2308 6-8-6 45 (p) ChrisDCogan(5) 7 24
(Patrick Holmes) *trckd ldr: rdn and lost pl over 4f out: wknd over 2f out* 33/1

50-2 8 2½ **Finellas Fortune**[19] 2575 6-9-5 53 PJMcDonald 9 29
(George Moore) *trckd ldr: rdn over 4f out: wknd over 2f out* 11/4[1]

065 R **Silvers Spirit**[46] 1799 5-8-11 45 AndrewHeffernan 10 —
(Keith Reveley) *ref to r* 5/1[3]

3m 7.93s (3.23) **Going Correction** +0.275s/f (Good) 9 Ran SP% **113.7**
Speed ratings (Par 101): **101,100,99,98,91 91,89,88,—**
toteswingers:1&2:£3.00, 2&3:£4.60, 1&3:£11.60 CSF £27.84 CT £209.83 TOTE £8.40: £2.50, £1.10, £3.20; EX 34.20.

Owner Shaun Conway **Bred** Darley Stud Management Co Ltd **Trained** Sheriff Hutton, N Yorks

FOCUS
A fair pace for the second division of the 46-60 handicap in a time just over a second slower but there had been further ease in conditions. Some interest was lost when Silvers Spirit, who was being thoroughly unco-operative, refused to come out of the stalls. The form of the race has to be treated with caution as it contained a large number of out-of-sorts performers or exposed types.

3188 BET ON ROYAL ASCOT AT TOTESPORT.COM H'CAP 7f
3:20 (3:22) (Class 3) (0-90,89) 4-Y-0+ £3,885 (£1,156; £577; £288) Stalls High

Form RPR
4112 **1** **Koo And The Gang (IRE)**[16] 2653 4-8-2 **73** ow1......... PaulPickard(3) 2 83
(Brian Ellison) *dwlt: sn trckd ldr: rdn over 2f out: led over 1f out: kpt on ins fnl f* **5/2**[2]
0-03 **2** *1* **Polish World (USA)**[23] 2431 7-8-3 **74**...................... DeclanCannon(3) 1 81
(Paul Midgley) *led: rdn whn hdd over 1f out: kpt on: hld towards fin* **11/4**[3]
0600 **3** *2* **Shadowtime**[19] 2545 6-8-1 **74**...................... JulieBurke(5) 3 76
(Colin Teague) *trckd ldrs in 3rd: rdn over 2f out: kpt on one pce* **12/1**
0-60 **4** *1 1/4* **Ishetoo**[7] 2938 7-8-4 **72**...................... AndrewHeffernan 5 70
(Ollie Pears) *hld up in tch: rdn over 2f out: kpt on one pce: nvr threatened* **13/2**
0-55 **5** *2 3/4* **Mr Rainbow**[7] 2927 5-9-7 **89**...................... PJMcDonald 6 80
(Alan Swinbank) *hld up in tch: rdn over 2f out: sn no imp* **9/4**[1]
1m 30.01s (5.51) **Going Correction** +0.875s/f (Soft) **5** Ran SP% **107.0**
Speed ratings (Par 107): **103,101,99,98,95**
CSF £9.11 TOTE £3.40: £1.90, £1.50; EX 7.00.
Owner Koo's Racing Club **Bred** Vincent Howley **Trained** Norton, N Yorks

FOCUS
A confirmed front-runner in the field ensured a decent pace for this tricky little handicap.

NOTEBOOK
Koo And The Gang(IRE) missed the break slightly but kept finding after coming under pressure to get the upper hand inside the final furlong. He has been in fine fettle on the Fibresand but this was a good effort off an 11lb higher mark when last seen on turf. (op 11-4)
Polish World(USA) took up his customary role at the head of affairs but could not quite last out. A sound effort but he was given a soft lead and looks to be still in the grip of the handicapper. (op 3-1 tchd 5-2)
Shadowtime became unsettled in the stalls and had something to prove on recent form but ran well enough without threatening to lay down a serious challenge. He shaped as though he could be returning to form and might be worth keeping on-side when returning to Beverley. (op 14-1 tchd 11-1)
Ishetoo, who has not won for over two years but is relatively well-treated, still has to convince he sees out this trip. (op 7-1)
Mr Rainbow failed to pick up when asked for his effort and his run petered out entering the final furlong. He had shown he retains all his ability on his two previous efforts this season, notably in a stronger race at Sandown last time, so this was disappointing with the yard not firing. (op 7-4 tchd 5-2)

3189 H JARVIS 133RD ANNIVERSARY H'CAP 5f
3:55 (3:56) (Class 4) (0-85,78) 3-Y-0 £2,590 (£770; £385; £192) Stalls High

Form RPR
4143 **1** **Another Wise Kid (IRE)**[3] 3052 3-9-6 **77**...................... MickyFenton 4 84+
(Paul Midgley) *hld up: hdwy over 2f out: rdn to ld appr fnl f: kpt on wl* **6/4**[1]
6-05 **2** *2 3/4* **Lady Royale**[9] 2832 3-9-2 **76**......................(b) DeclanCannon(3) 6 73
(Geoffrey Oldroyd) *dwlt: hld up in tch: rdn over 2f out: hdwy over 1f out: edgd lft ent fnl f: wnt 2nd fnl 100yds: kpt on: no ch w wnr* **6/1**[3]
1 **3** *1 3/4* **Diamond Blue**[21] 2493 3-8-13 **70**...................... PaulQuinn 3 61
(Richard Whitaker) *chsd ldrs: rdn and hdwy over 2f out: led narrowly over 1f out: sn hdd: no ex and lost 2nd fnl 100yds* **11/4**[2]
4325 **4** *2 1/4* **Johnny Hancocks (IRE)**[20] 2524 3-7-12 **62**.............. KristinStubbs(7) 2 45
(Linda Stubbs) *led after 1f: rdn whn hdd over 1f out: wknd ins fnl f* **7/1**
0-15 **5** *3* **Mr Mo Jo**[17] 2611 3-8-11 **68**...................... DuranFentiman 5 40
(Lawrence Mullaney) *led for 1f: w ldr: rdn over 2f out: wknd over 1f out* **9/1**
21-3 **6** *3/4* **Ice Trooper**[24] 2405 3-9-7 **78**...................... TonyHamilton 1 47
(Linda Stubbs) *trckd ldrs: rdn over 2f out: wknd over 1f out* **12/1**
61.32 secs (2.72) **Going Correction** +0.55s/f (Yiel) **6** Ran SP% **111.1**
Speed ratings (Par [illegible]): **[illegible] 83**
toteswingers:1&2:£2.10, 2&3:£4.10, 1&3:£1.30 CSF £10.77 TOTE [illegible]
Owner Michael Ng **Bred** Paul Kavanagh **Trained** Westow, N Yorks

FOCUS
The ground was now described as good to soft. A strong gallop for this competitive sprint with half of the six liking to bowl along, which probably set it up for the two who struggled to go the early pace.

3190 LADIES' AND GENTS EVENING - 27TH AUGUST CLAIMING STKS 7f
4:30 (4:32) (Class 5) 3-Y-0+ £1,942 (£578; £288; £144) Stalls High

Form RPR
0-00 **1** **Spying**[47] 1747 4-9-8 73......................(e1) TonyHamilton 3 76
(Ann Duffield) *trckd ldr: drvn and lost pl over 3f out: rallied over 1f out: styd on ins fnl f: led post* **3/1**[2]
0-00 **2** *nk* **Cawdor (IRE)**[10] 2815 5-8-8 67...................... KristinStubbs(7) 2 68
(Linda Stubbs) *in tch: rdn and hdwy over 2f out: led over 1f out: kpt on: hdd post* **14/1**
3025 **3** *5* **Academy Blues (USA)**[24] 2398 6-9-5 84...................... PaulQuinn 5 59
(David Nicholls) *in tch: rdn and hdwy to chal over 2f out: stl ev ch over 1f out: wknd ins fnl f* **4/5**[1]
0600 **4** *5* **Sea Salt**[12] 2765 8-8-13 62...................... PaddyAspell 1 40
(Ron Barr) *led: rdn whn hdd over 1f out: sn wknd* **9/1**[3]
-500 **5** *3 3/4* **Whispered Times (USA)**[10] 2806 4-9-0 67..............(p) PaulPickard(3) 4 34
(Tracy Waggott) *hld up in tch: rdn and hdwy to ld narrowly over 2f out: hdd over 1f out: sn wknd* **12/1**
464 **6** *10* **Kate Skate**[10] 2829 4-8-0 55...................... NatashaEaton(7) 6 —
(Gay Kelleway) *t.k.h: trckd ldr: rdn and edgd lft over 2f out: sn wknd* **12/1**
1m 31.27s (6.77) **Going Correction** +0.875s/f (Soft) **6** Ran SP% **112.6**
Speed ratings (Par 103): **96,95,89,84,79 68**
toteswingers:1&2:£5.70, 2&3:£3.30, 1&3:£1.10 CSF £39.86 TOTE £3.80: £1.40, £6.90; EX 39.80.
Owner Evelyn Duchess Of Sutherland **Bred** Evelyn Duchess Of Sutherland **Trained** Constable Burton, N Yorks

FOCUS
As the rain continued to fall the ground had turned officially to soft.

3191 CAPTURE LE COEUR PHOTOGRAPHY MEDIAN AUCTION MAIDEN STKS 6f
5:05 (5:07) (Class 5) 3-5-Y-0 £1,942 (£578; £288; £144) Stalls High

Form RPR
-230 **1** **Mother Jones**[43] 1880 3-8-12 74...................... TonyHamilton 2 76
(Bryan Smart) *mde all: shkn up over 1f out: rdn clr fnl f: comf* **10/11**[1]
-033 **2** *7* **Cool In The Shade**[26] 2350 3-8-12 54......................(p) DuranFentiman 10 54
(Paul Midgley) *chsd ldr: rdn over 2f out: ev ch over 1f out: no ex and no ch w wnr ins fnl f* **5/1**[3]
53- **3** *4 1/2* **Avon Supreme**[196] 7686 3-8-9 0...................... PaulPickard(3) 8 39
(Gay Kelleway) *in tch: rdn and outpcd 1/2-way: kpt on to go 3rd ins fnl f: no ch ldng pair* **9/2**[2]
00 **4** *1 1/2* **Toffee Nose**[18] 2591 4-9-3 0...................... ShaneBKelly(7) 6 41
(Ron Barr) *chsd ldrs: rdn and outpcd over 3f out: no imp* **16/1**
06- **5** *1 1/4* **Tinzo (IRE)**[231] 7223 3-9-3 0...................... PaulQuinn 1 35
(Alan Berry) *chsd ldng pair: rdn and outpcd 1/2-way: lost 3rd ins fnl f: wknd* **50/1**
6 *hd* **Classical Chloe** 3-8-9 0...................... DeclanCannon(3) 4 30
(Richard Guest) *wnt lft s and s.i.s: rn green and outpcd in rr: edgd lft into centre after 2f: hdwy to chal for 3rd ent fnl f: eased fnl 100yds* **10/1**
0020 **7** *shd* **Chardonnay Star (IRE)**[23] 2415 4-9-5 47.............(v) AndrewHeffernan 7 31
(Colin Teague) *sn outpcd towards rr: n.d* **12/1**
0040 **8** *3/4* **King Bertolini (IRE)**[10] 2803 4-9-7 47......................(b1) MichaelGeran(3) 9 34
(Alan Berry) *a outpcd in rr* **20/1**
1m 16.98s (5.18) **Going Correction** +0.875s/f (Soft)
WFA 3 from 4yo+ 7lb **8** Ran SP% **116.6**
Speed ratings (Par 103): **100,90,84,82,81 80,80,79**
toteswingers:1&2:£2.00, 2&3:£2.30, 1&3:£2.30 CSF £5.99 TOTE £1.90: £1.10, £1.40, £1.10; EX 5.30.
Owner Ron Hull **Bred** New Hall Stud **Trained** Hambleton, N Yorks

FOCUS
Only three on paper could be seriously considered for this ordinary maiden and it resulted in a deserved success for the well-supported favourite.

3192 WIN A VIP DAY OUT @ REDCARRACING.CO.UK H'CAP 5f
5:40 (5:43) (Class 6) (0-60,62) 3-Y-0 £1,706 (£503; £252) Stalls High

Form RPR
-653 **1** **Novalist**[23] 2410 3-8-8 **50**......................(b) BillyCray(3) 4 56
(Robin Bastiman) *mde all: pressed by 2nd fr s: drvn over 1f out: hld on towards fin: all out* **12/1**
4330 **2** *nk* **Ever Roses**[29] 2249 3-8-12 **51**......................(b1) MickyFenton 8 56
(Paul Midgley) *pressed wnr fr s: drvn over 1f out: kpt on ins fnl f: jst hld* **12/1**
5506 **3** *1/2* **These Dreams**[4] 3027 3-8-11 **50**...................... DuranFentiman 1 53
(Richard Guest) *trckd ldng pair: rdn and hdwy to chal over 1f out: kpt on ins fnl f: hld towards fin* **4/1**[2]
4551 **4** *3* **Chester Deelyte (IRE)**[7] 2918 3-8-6 **52**....................(v) ShaneBKelly(7) 6 44
(Lisa Williamson) *dwlt: hld up: pushed along 1/2-way: hdwy to chse ldrs 2f out: hung lft over 1f out: one pce ins fnl f* **5/1**[3]
502 **5** *3/4* **Green Warrior**[7] 2918 3-9-9 **62**......................(p) TonyHamilton 7 52
(Ann Duffield) *in tch: rdn 1/2-way: one pce* **7/2**[1]
6506 **6** *1 1/2* **Fawara**[15] 2697 3-8-7 **46** oh1...................... AndrewHeffernan 11 30
(Ruth Carr) *sn outpcd towards rr: nvr threatened* **33/1**
05-0 **7** *hd* **Bon Appetit**[21] 2498 3-9-3 **56**...................... KellyHarrison 5 40
(Micky Hammond) *sn outpcd towards rr: nvr threatened* **20/1**
0356 **8** *1/2* **Bygones For Coins (IRE)**[1] 3143 3-8-11 **50**...................... PaulQuinn 2 32
(Alan Berry) *chsd ldrs: rdn and lost pl over 2f out: wknd over 1f out* **11/1**
P060 **9** *13* **Blind Stag (IRE)**[19] 2547 3-8-10 **52**...................... PaulPickard(3) 10 —
(David Thompson) *hld up: bhd 1/2-way* **14/1**
61.40 secs (2.80) **Going Correction** +0.50s/f (Yiel) **9** Ran SP% **97.0**
Speed ratings (Par 97): **97,96,95,90,89 87,87,86,65**
toteswingers:1&2:£6.40, 2&3:£7.70, 1&3:£8.90 CSF £98.37 CT £366.06 TOTE £13.70: £3.30, £2.30, £1.10; EX 54.90.
Owner Ms M Austerfield **Bred** Whitsbury Manor Stud **Trained** Cowthorpe, N Yorks

FOCUS
A modest sprint handicap.
T/Plt: £177.50 to a £1 stake. Pool of £42,514.10 - 174.80 winning tickets. T/Qpdt: £77.20 to a £1 stake. Pool of £2,441.70 - 23.40 winning tickets. AS

3193 - 3199a (Foreign Racing) - See Raceform Interactive

2761 PONTEFRACT (L-H)
Sunday, June 19

OFFICIAL GOING: Good (good to firm in places; 7.6)
False rail in place over last 6f, 15ft off inside rail.
Wind: Moderate 1/2 behind Weather: Overcast

3200 E B F TOTEPLACEPOT MAIDEN FILLIES' STKS (DIV I) 6f
2:10 (2:12) (Class 5) 2-Y-0 £3,238 (£963; £481; £240) Stalls Low

Form RPR
526 **1** **Nearly A Gift (IRE)**[8] 2907 2-9-0 0...................... DavidAllan 9 80+
(Tim Easterby) *mde all: pushed clr over 2f out: eased nr fin* **3/1**[1]
2 *7* **Goal Hanger** 2-9-0 0...................... RichardKingscote 5 59
(Tom Dascombe) *chsd ldrs: effrt over 2f out: hung rt and wnt 2nd over 1f out: no ch w wnr* **5/1**[3]
3 *2 1/4* **Quiet Appeal (IRE)** 2-9-0 0...................... SilvestreDeSousa 11 52
(Mark Johnston) *chsd ldrs: drvn over 2f out: kpt on to take mod 3rd 1f out* **11/2**
04 **4** *3* **Busy Bimbo (IRE)**[9] 2886 2-9-0 0...................... PatrickMathers 1 43
(Alan Berry) *chsd ldrs: drvn over 2f out: one pce* **7/2**[2]
5 *nse* **Chandigarh (IRE)** 2-9-0 0...................... FrankieMcDonald 10 43
(Paul Fitzsimons) *chsd ldrs: wnt 2nd over 2f out: wknd 1f out* **33/1**
6 *1 1/2* **More Bottle (IRE)** 2-9-0 0...................... MickyFenton 2 39+
(Tom Tate) *s.i.s: in rr: outpcd over 2f out: edgd rt over 1f out: nvr nr ldrs* **12/1**
0 **7** *1* **Wake Up Sioux (IRE)**[15] 2709 2-9-0 0...................... NickyMackay 6 36
(David C Griffiths) *trckd ldrs: wknd over 1f out* **40/1**
0 **8** *16* **Miserere Mei (IRE)**[7] 2953 2-8-11 0...................... MartinHarley(3) 7 —
(Alan McCabe) *gave problems gng to s: fly j. and rdr lost iron and almost uns s: s.s: bhd fnl 3f: t.o* **40/1**
00 **9** *9* **Isolde's Return**[18] 2617 2-9-0 0...................... PJMcDonald 4 —
(George Moore) *in rr: bhd fnl 3f: t.o over 1f out: virtually p.u* **100/1**
1m 18.7s (1.80) **Going Correction** +0.175s/f (Good) **9** Ran SP% **95.8**
Speed ratings (Par 90): **95,85,82,78,78 76,75,53,41**
toteswingers: 1&2 £2.20, 1&3 £2.70, 2&3 £4.30. CSF £11.86 TOTE £2.90: £1.20, £1.60, £2.10; EX 10.20 Trifecta £22.40 Pool: £113.96 - 3.76 winning units..
Owner Habton Farms **Bred** Carrigbeg Stud & David Powell **Trained** Great Habton, N Yorks

FOCUS
False rail in place over last 6f, 15ft off inside rail. Following 10mm of rain during the morning, the going was changed to good, good to firm in places, and jockeys returning after the first race reported it to have plenty of juice in it. As is often the case, experience proved the key in this fillies' maiden.

NOTEBOOK

Nearly A Gift(IRE), representing an in-form stable, bounced out of the gates, soon got over to the rail to lead and had her rivals in trouble on the turn in. She stretched clear to win by a wide margin, clearly suited by the return to a stiff track, and looks the type who could well have more to offer once switched to nurseries. (op 7-2)

Goal Hanger, a sister to a 5f 2yo winner and a half-sister to six other winners, was smartly away and chased the leader early on, but she lost her position on the turn before running on again in the straight, while all the time showing signs of greenness. She'll have learnt plenty from this and should go closer next time. (op 7-2 tchd 11-2 in places)

Quiet Appeal(IRE), drawn worst of all, looked very much in need of this experience-wise. She had to be given reminders around halfway but did respond and was keeping on nicely at the finish. She'll be all the better for this debut effort and won't mind stepping up to 7f in time. (op 5-1 tchd 6-1)

Busy Bimbo(IRE) was well drawn but under pressure before the turn in and could only plug on one-paced. This was a step back following her fair effort at York last time. (op 11-2)

Chandigarh(IRE) showed up well for a long way before tiring, and is entitled to come on for this debut run. (op 50-1)

More Bottle(IRE), who struggled to go the pace early, was staying on at the end. She's out of a mare who won over 1m1f and a longer trip will suit her in time. (op 14-1)

3201 E B F TOTEPLACEPOT MAIDEN FILLIES' STKS (DIV II) 6f

2:40 (2:41) (Class 5) 2-Y-O **£3,238** (£963; £481; £240) **Stalls** Low

Form RPR

0 **1** **My Propeller (IRE)**[23] 2467 2-9-0 0 .... JamieSpencer 1 96+
(Peter Chapple-Hyam) *mde all: wnt clr over 2f out: canter* **11/10**[1]

2 *17* **Delia Mary** 2-9-0 0 .... AndrewElliott 5 45
(Jedd O'Keeffe) *chsd ldrs on outer: drvn and outpcd over 2f out: styd on to take 2nd ins fnl f* **66/1**

3 *1 1/2* **Rosie's Lady (IRE)** 2-9-0 0 .... DanielTudhope 6 41
(David O'Meara) *s.i.s: outpcd over 3f out: hdwy over 1f out: swvd rt jst ins fnl f: kpt on* **14/1**

4 *1 1/4* **Margo Channing** 2-9-0 0 .... PJMcDonald 9 37
(Micky Hammond) *chsd ldrs: outpcd and hung rt over 3f out: sn bhd: styd on fnl f* **50/1**

6 **5** *2 3/4* **Dansili Dutch (IRE)**[20] 2542 2-9-0 0 .... GrahamGibbons 10 29
(David Barron) *s.i.s: hld up in rr: sme hdwy over 2f out: nvr a factor* **25/1**

32 **6** *nk* **Majestic Zafeen**[13] 2761 2-9-0 0 .... SamHitchcott 4 28
(Mick Channon) *chsd ldrs: drvn over 2f out: wknd ins fnl f* **7/1**

7 *1 1/4* **Jumeirah Palm Star** 2-9-0 0 .... JimmyFortune 2 24
(Richard Hannon) *sn chsng ldrs: wnt 2nd over 1f out: wknd ins fnl f* **5/1**[2]

2 **8** *2 1/2* **Rockme Cockney**[18] 2606 2-9-0 0 .... JamesDoyle 8 16
(Jeremy Gask) *chsd wnr: wknd over 1f out* **6/1**[3]

9 *nk* **Maliha (IRE)** 2-9-0 0 .... PhillipMakin 7 15+
(Kevin Ryan) *s.s: a bhd* **7/1**

10 *22* **Nadia's Place** 2-9-0 0 .... TomEaves 3 —
(Nigel Tinkler) *s.s: a bhd: t.o 2f out* **66/1**

1m 17.34s (0.44) **Going Correction** +0.175s/f (Good) **10** Ran SP% **119.0**
Speed ratings (Par 90): **104,81,79,77,74 73,71,68,68,38**
toteswingers: 1&2 £14.90, 1&3 £5.00, 2&3 £52.10. CSF £119.14 TOTE £2.00: £1.10, £6.00, £3.20; EX 99.60 Trifecta £306.80 Part won. Pool: £414.61 - 0.10 winning units..
Owner Joseph Barton **Bred** D J & Mrs Brown **Trained** Newmarket, Suffolk

FOCUS

The quicker of the two divisions by 1.36sec, and a seriously impressive performance from the winner.

NOTEBOOK

My Propeller(IRE) ◆ finished seventh in a Newmarket maiden on her debut which has turned out to be a hot contest, with the third going on to win the Albany and the fifth finishing third in the Chesham. Clearly well regarded - she was well backed and sent off second-favourite at Newmarket, and again well supported here - she pinged out of the gates and was soon taking her field along at a really good pace, but without being out of her comfort zone. Once into the straight she continued to draw further clear, with her rider virtually motionless. Eased down close home, she eventually won by 17 lengths, but that flatters the opposition, as she could surely have won by even further had Spencer wanted. \n\x\x Not the biggest, she looks a 2yo through and through and has plenty of speed - Spencer was of the opinion that she wouldn't want to be going any further than 6f. She's fully entitled to go for some big prizes on the back of this, and the Cherry Hinton looks a perfectly reasonable short-term target. (op 15-8 tchd 2-1)

Delia Mary got outpaced on the turn in before running on again past beaten rivals. A half-sister to multiple 5f winner Nickel Silver, she'll come on for this.

Rosie's Lady(IRE) couldn't go the early pace, but that helped in a way as she had something left in the locker for the finish, while those that had tried to chase the strong gallop set by the winner fell in a heap in the straight. (op 16-1)

Margo Channing, another to stay on from a long way back, looked very green. (op 66-1)

Dansili Dutch(IRE), although one of only four in the race with previous experience, failed to get involved.

Rockme Cockney paid for trying to keep tabs with the impressive winner through the early stages. (op 7-2)

3202 TOTEEXACTA FILLIES' H'CAP 1m 4y

3:10 (3:10) (Class 5) (0-70,70) 3-Y-O+ **£2,590** (£770; £385; £192) **Stalls** Low

Form RPR

1100 **1** **Princess Lexi (IRE)**[8] 2912 4-9-8 **64** .... FrannyNorton 7 75
(Ian Williams) *s.i.s: hdwy on ins over 2f out: led ins fnl f: drvn out* **13/2**[3]

-220 **2** *1* **Silly Gilly (IRE)**[5] 3025 7-9-1 **57** .... DanielTudhope 6 65
(Ron Barr) *trckd ldrs: swtchd to outside over 2f out: led over 1f out: hdd and no ex ins fnl f* **4/1**[1]

-215 **3** *1 3/4* **Abidhabidubai**[11] 2808 3-9-4 **70** .... TomEaves 10 72
(John Quinn) *in rr: hdwy over 2f out: kpt on same pce to take 3rd appr fnl f* **4/1**[1]

40-0 **4** *11* **Whats For Pudding (IRE)**[12] 2782 3-7-8 **51** .... NeilFarley(5) 1 28
(Declan Carroll) *led: hdd over 1f out: sn wknd* **20/1**

-263 **5** *4* **Woop Woop (IRE)**[27] 2368 3-9-3 **69** .... TomQueally 11 37
(Stef Higgins) *sn chsng ldrs: wknd over 1f out* **11/2**[2]

0-44 **6** *1 3/4* **Adelina Patti**[16] 2673 3-8-10 **62** .... KierenFallon 3 26
(Walter Swinburn) *t.k.h: trckd ldrs: upsides 4f out: lost pl over 2f out* **4/1**[1]

-066 **7** *10* **Shaws Diamond (USA)**[26] 2386 5-8-13 **55** .... JimCrowley 5 —
(Derek Shaw) *chsd ldrs: drvn 5f out: lost pl over 2f out: sn bhd* **17/2**

-030 **8** *10* **Koraleva Tectona (IRE)**[11] 2829 6-9-2 **58** .... PaulHanagan 2 —
(Mark H Tompkins) *s.i.s: t.k.h in midfield: lost pl 3f out: sn bhd* **20/1**

200 **9** *63* **Sizzle (FR)**[30] 2258 3-8-8 **60** ....(t) RichardKingscote 8 —
(Tom Dascombe) *mid-div: lost pl and heavily eased over 3f out: sn t.o: eventually completed: lame* **12/1**

1m 46.94s (1.04) **Going Correction** +0.175s/f (Good)
WFA 3 from 4yo+ 10lb **9** Ran SP% **116.5**
Speed ratings (Par 100): **101,100,98,87,83 81,71,61,—**
toteswingers: 1&2 £7.40, 1&3 £4.90, 2&3 £2.70. CSF £32.99 CT £115.98 TOTE £9.20: £2.80, £2.20, £2.20; EX 35.50 Trifecta £228.80 Part won. Pool: £309.19 - 0.10 winning units..
Owner Dr Marwan Koukash **Bred** Epona Bloodstock Ltd And P A Byrne **Trained** Portway, Worcs

FOCUS

There was a disputed lead here and that set things up for a closer.

3203 TOTESPORT 0800 221 221 H'CAP 1m 2f 6y

3:40 (3:40) (Class 3) (0-90,89) 3-Y-O+

£7,165 (£2,145; £1,072; £537; £267; £134) **Stalls** Low

Form RPR

4246 **1** **Suits Me**[26] 2390 8-9-11 **87** .... MickyFenton 11 96
(David Barron) *swtchd lft after s: led: drvn over 1f out: hld on wl* **16/1**

0003 **2** *1* **Our Joe Mac (IRE)**[31] 2217 4-9-13 **89** ....(p) PaulHanagan 4 98+
(Richard Fahey) *hmpd s: hld up in mid-div: hdwy and nt clr run fr over 1f out tl ins fnl f: fin wl to take 2nd clsng stages* **15/2**[3]

14-0 **3** *1/2* **Diescentric (USA)**[39] 2002 4-9-9 **85** .... TomQueally 5 91
(Sir Henry Cecil) *wnt lft s: trckd ldrs: t.k.h: swtchd rt and styd on same pce ins fnl f* **11/1**

10-3 **4** *3/4* **Dhaamer (IRE)**[16] 2681 4-9-12 **88** .... RichardHills 6 93+
(John Gosden) *hld up in rr: hdwy on outside over 2f out: kpt on same pce ins fnl f* **9/4**[1]

0030 **5** *nk* **Licence To Till (USA)**[16] 2681 4-9-10 **86** .... RoystonFfrench 1 90+
(Mark Johnston) *s.s: t.k.h in rr: hdwy and plld wd over 2f out: kpt on fnl f: nt rch ldrs* **12/1**

10-0 **6** *1* **Fastnet Storm (IRE)**[18] 2604 5-9-10 **86** .... GrahamGibbons 8 88
(David Barron) *chsd ldrs: one pce appr fnl f* **28/1**

1104 **7** *nk* **Sweet Origin**[18] 2604 4-9-9 **85** .... AdamKirby 2 88+
(Marco Botti) *hld up in mid-div: hdwy and nt clr run over 1f out: hmpd ins fnl f: hit over hd by rival rdr's whip: nt rcvr* **17/2**

20-0 **8** *1 1/2* **Jo'Burg (USA)**[20] 2573 7-9-11 **87** .... PhillipMakin 12 85
(Ollie Pears) *dwlt: hld up in rr: hdwy on wd outside over 1f out: nvr nr ldrs* **22/1**

-230 **9** *9* **Shallow Bay**[9] 2884 4-9-10 **86** .... KierenFallon 7 66
(Walter Swinburn) *chsd ldrs: chal over 5f out: wknd and n.m.r fnl f: eased clsng stages* **4/1**[2]

0-01 **10** *1 1/2* **Pass Muster**[25] 2403 4-9-13 **89** .... SilvestreDeSousa 13 66
(Geoffrey Harker) *chsd ldrs: wknd appr fnl f: eased clsng stages* **8/1**

5-00 **11** *6* **Snoqualmie Star**[37] 2066 4-9-9 **85** ....(b) JimCrowley 10 50
(David Elsworth) *mid-div: hdwy 7f out: sn chsng ldrs: wknd appr fnl f: eased* **22/1**

20-0 **12** *dist* **Sowaylm**[16] 2679 4-9-12 **88** ....(t) TedDurcan 3 —
(Saeed Bin Suroor) *s.i.s: in rr: sme hdwy on outside over 3f out: sn rdn and lost pl: bhd whn virtually p.u over 2f out: wl t.o* **40/1**

2m 13.63s (-0.07) **Going Correction** +0.175s/f (Good) **12** Ran SP% **120.7**
Speed ratings (Par 107): **107,106,105,105,104 104,103,102,95,94 89,—**
toteswingers: 1&2 £11.80, 1&3 £25.00, 2&3 £13.00. CSF £127.88 CT £1398.90 TOTE £14.80: £5.10, £2.70, £6.20; EX 99.20 TRIFECTA Not won..
Owner D E Cook **Bred** R S A Urquhart **Trained** Maunby, N Yorks

FOCUS

This looked pretty competitive but it was dominated from the front by the winner.

NOTEBOOK

Suits Me was left alone on the lead and proceeded to make just about every yard. There were one or two hard-luck stories in behind, but the winner was on a mark he was fully entitled to go close off, and he has always been a tough horse to pass when allowed the run of things.

Our Joe Mac(IRE) ◆, who showed more in the cheekpieces at Haydock last time, likes to get his toe in so the morning rain was in his favour. Held up in midfield, he was faced with a wall of horses in front of him entering the straight and by the time the gap finally arrived it was all too late. He looked unlucky, is clearly back in form and is handicapped to win, so is one to keep in mind for a similar race. (op 17-2)

Diescentric(USA) was never too far off the pace but he was a little keen and that counted against him in the closing stages. Apparently nothing came to light following his poor performance at York, but at least this was a return to form. (op 14-1)

Dhaamer(IRE), held up back in the pack, was given plenty to do considering the way the race was run. Brought with his challenge out wide in the straight, he hung left into the whip under pressure and couldn't muster the pace to challenge. (tchd 5-2)

Licence To Till(USA), who has won over this C&D in the past, made up late ground from the back but was never quite getting there. (tchd 14-1)

Fastnet Storm(IRE), winner of this race two years ago when trained by Tom Tate, got a nice lead through the race from his stablemate Suits Me, but in an ideal world he'd have been making the running himself. (tchd 25-1)

Sweet Origin ◆ was another who got little luck as he tried to find a way through from the back of the field in the straight. Hampered and denied a clear run, he shaped better than his finishing position suggests and should remain of interest as he's well handicapped on turf compared to his AW mark. (op 10-1 tchd 8-1)

Shallow Bay was never too far off the pace and so was ultimately disappointing. (op 9-2)

3204 TOTEPOOL PONTEFRACT CASTLE STKS (LISTED RACE) 1m 4f 8y

4:10 (4:11) (Class 1) 4-Y-O+

£17,031 (£6,456; £3,231; £1,611; £807; £405) **Stalls** Low

Form RPR

3-20 **1** **Distant Memories (IRE)**[24] 2439 5-9-1 113 .... JamieSpencer 5 107
(Tom Tate) *trckd ldrs: wnt 2nd 6f out: shkn up to ld 2f out: wandered: jst hld on* **5/2**[1]

000- **2** *nse* **Ted Spread**[239] 7096 4-9-1 98 .... KierenFallon 3 107
(Mark H Tompkins) *hld up in rr: effrt 4f out: swtchd rt and chsng ldrs on outside over 1f out: styd on ins fnl f: jst failed* **9/1**

110- **3** *3/4* **Vulcanite (IRE)**[238] 7110 4-9-1 103 .... JimCrowley 6 106+
(Ralph Beckett) *t.k.h: trckd ldrs: hung lft over 1f out: crowded and wnt lft ins fnl f: kpt on same pce clsng stages* **10/3**[2]

-201 **4** *6* **Red Cadeaux**[37] 2044 5-9-4 106 .... TomMcLaughlin 2 107+
(Ed Dunlop) *hld up in rr: effrt over 3f out: chsng ldrs on ins over 1f out: 3rd and keeping on same pce whn bdly hmpd ins fnl f: nt rcvr* **4/1**[3]

16-3 **5** *1 1/2* **Bramalea**[16] 2686 6-8-10 83 .... NickyMackay 7 89
(Hughie Morrison) *led: hung rt and hdd 2f out: 4th and wkng whn lft short of room ins fnl f: sn wknd* **22/1**

5-00 **6** *nse* **La De Two (IRE)**[101] 826 5-9-1 108 ....(t) TedDurcan 4 94
(Saeed Bin Suroor) *dwlt: hld up: jnd ldrs over 5f out: sn drvn: hung lft and wknd over 1f out* **9/2**

-230 **7** *31* **Free Agent**[37] 2072 5-9-1 104 .... JimmyFortune 8 44
(Richard Hannon) *trckd ldrs: drvn over 3f out: wd bnd and lost pl over 2f out: sn bhd: virtually p.u: t.o* **9/1**

2m 38.66s (-2.14) **Going Correction** +0.175s/f (Good) **7** Ran SP% **114.2**
Speed ratings (Par 111): **114,113,113,109,108 108,87**
toteswingers: 1&2 £3.70, 1&3 £3.00, 2&3 £7.20. CSF £25.52 TOTE £3.00: £1.40, £6.20; EX 33.70 Trifecta £457.90 Pool: £618.90 - 1.00 winning units..
Owner Mrs Fitri Hay **Bred** Kildaragh Stud **Trained** Tadcaster, N Yorks

FOCUS

A tight finish to this Listed race.

NOTEBOOK

Distant Memories(IRE) just held off the late challenge of Ted Spread to win by the narrowest of margins. This was a drop in class for him as he's been taking on some top-notchers in Group company of late, but he had his stamina to prove over this trip and it was no walk in the park. Made to work hard for his victory, he would have been beaten in another stride, and it's probably fair to say that this trip is a little beyond his optimum, but that he might be more effective over it on an easier track. (op 10-3)

Ted Spread gives the impression of being a stayer in the making and was doing all his best work in the closing stages. He'd have got up in another stride, and this was a really promising effort with the rest of the season in mind. (op 10-1)

Vulcanite(IRE) ◆ travelled best of all but, when let down, lack of race-fitness seemed to find him out and he didn't find as much as he'd promised. A winner of five races last year, he looks to have trained on well and should be well capable of winning something similar before stepping into Group company. (op 7-2 tchd 3-1 and 4-1 in places)

Red Cadeaux got a nice run up the rail in the straight but was badly hampered by Vulcanite when that one hung into him a furlong out. His race was over at that point and, while he looked to be playing for a place only, he would clearly have finished a lot closer with a clear passage. (op 7-2 tchd 9-2)

Bramalea had plenty to find in this company and didn't run badly in the circumstances, although she was allowed the run of things out in front for much of the way. Nicky Mackay reported that the mare hung right. (op 25-1)

La De Two(IRE) has won when fresh before so a three-month absence wasn't a concern, but he was being pushed along some way out here and hung left in the straight, and clearly wasn't at his best.

Free Agent was beaten off before the turn in and this was too bad to be true. (tchd 17-2)

3205 TOTESPORT.COM PONTEFRACT CUP (H'CAP) 2m 1f 216y

4:40 (4:42) (Class 4) (0-85,85) 4-Y-O+ **£4,533** (£1,348; £674; £336) **Stalls** Low

Form RPR

-000 **1** **My Arch**[22] 2499 9-9-10 **85**.. TomQueally 4 93
(Ollie Pears) *hld up in midfield: effrt on ins over 3f out: nt clr run and swtchd rt over 1f out: str run to ld nr fin* **8/1**

-634 **2** *nk* **Dazinski**[9] 2888 5-9-10 **85**.. KierenFallon 9 93
(Mark H Tompkins) *hld up in rr: hdwy over 5f out: led and edgd lft 2f out: 4 l clr 1f out: jst ct* **7/1**[3]

-061 **3** *7* **Wells Lyrical (IRE)**[13] 2762 6-9-7 **82**.................................. TomEaves 10 82
(Bryan Smart) *t.k.h: sn trcking ldr: led briefly over 2f out: kpt on same pce* **10/3**[1]

2225 **4** *3 1/2* **Blackstone Vegas**[23] 2459 5-8-0 **66** oh3.......................... NeilFarley(5) 3 62
(Derek Shaw) *in rr: hdwy on outside over 5f out: chal over 2f out: one pce over 1f out* **15/2**

2-05 **5** *3* **Comedy Act**[29] 2285 4-9-9 **85**.................................. SilvestreDeSousa 1 78
(Mark Johnston) *trckd ldrs: drvn over 3f out: hung lft 1f out: one pce* **8/1**

2512 **6** *2 1/2* **Rosewood Lad**[83] 1016 4-8-10 **72** ow1................................ NeilCallan 6 63
(J S Moore) *trckd ldrs: drvn 4f out: one pce whn hmpd over 1f out: eased clsng stages* **16/1**

6-02 **7** *2* **Hollins**[13] 2762 7-8-10 **76**.. JamesRogers(5) 8 64
(Micky Hammond) *in rr: dropped bk last over 4f out: kpt on appr fnl f* **8/1**

00-3 **8** *9* **Baddam**[23] 1788 9-9-0 **75**..(v) PaulHanagan 7 56
(Ian Williams) *led: hdd over 2f out: wkng whn hmpd wl over 1f out: eased whn bhd* **22/1**

3264 **9** *8* **Night Orbit**[10] 2856 7-8-6 **67** oh8 ow1.......................... RoystonFfrench 11 39
(Julia Feilden) *sn chsng ldrs: drvn 6f out: lost pl over 3f out: eased whn bhd* **40/1**

2-51 **10** *12* **Cosimo de Medici**[32] 2190 4-9-4 **80**...............................(t) JimmyFortune 5 57
(Hughie Morrison) *in rr: hdwy 6f out: sn chsng ldrs: lost pl over 2f out: eased whn bhd* **7/2**[2]

4m 3.10s (6.90) **Going Correction** +0.175s/f (Good)
WFA 4 from 5yo+ 1lb **10** Ran SP% **115.6**
Speed ratings (Par 105): **91,90,87,86,84 83,82,78,75,69**
toteswingers: 1&2 £9.20, 1&3 £6.50, 2&3 £4.80. CSF £62.36 CT £224.21 TOTE £10.40: £2.90, £2.80, £1.60; EX 78.70 Trifecta £197.00 Pool: [illegible] - [illegible] winning units.
Owner J D Spensley & Mrs M A Spensley **Bred** J And A Spensley **Trained** Norton, N Yorks

FOCUS
There was a true pace to this marathon handicap, thanks to front-runner Baddam.

3206 TRY TOTEQUICKPICK ON ALL TOTEPOOL BETS MAIDEN STKS 1m 4f 8y

5:10 (5:12) (Class 5) 3-Y-O **£2,590** (£770; £385; £192) **Stalls** Low

Form RPR

2432 **1** **Stagecoach Danman (IRE)**[9] 2874 3-9-3 78.......... SilvestreDeSousa 6 89+
(Mark Johnston) *w ldr: led after 1f: styd on strly to forge clr appr fnl f: heavily eased clsng stages* **13/8**[1]

5-23 **2** *6* **Star Commander**[40] 1991 3-9-3 73.................................... KierenFallon 9 79
(Mark H Tompkins) *led 1f: w ldr: kpt on same pce fnl 2f* **8/1**

62-2 **3** *5* **She's Got The Luck (IRE)**[30] 2257 3-8-12 71............... PaulHanagan 8 66
(Richard Fahey) *mid-div: hdwy 4f out: kpt on to take 3rd last 100yds* **6/1**[3]

03 **4** *1 1/4* **Daruband**[18] 2621 3-9-3 0.. RoystonFfrench 5 69
(Mahmood Al Zarooni) *trckd ldrs: rdn over 2f out: one pce* **14/1**

54 **5** *1/2* **Run Rabbit Run**[20] 2551 3-9-3 0.. NeilCallan 4 69
(Roger Varian) *dwlt: sn trcking ldrs: one pce fnl 2f* **7/2**[2]

6-20 **6** *21* **Kadoodd (IRE)**[20] 2551 3-9-3 79.................................... SamHitchcott 3 35
(Mick Channon) *hld up in rr: drvn over 4f out: wl outpcd over 2f out: heavily eased towards fin* **14/1**

2 **7** *7* **Favorite Girl (GER)**[32] 2203 3-8-12 0................................ TomQueally 2 19
(Sir Henry Cecil) *dwlt: in rr-div: hdwy 6f out: lost pl over 2f out: eased whn bhd* **6/1**[3]

8 *1/2* **Essex Boy** 3-9-0 0...(e1) RobertLButler(3) 7 23
(Richard Guest) *s.i.s: mid-div: lost pl 8f out: bhd fnl 3f* **50/1**

9 *5* **Morning Air (IRE)** 3-8-12 0.. PhillipMakin 1 —
(Ann Duffield) *hld up in rr: hdwy 6f out: rdn and lost pl over 2f out: eased over 1f out* **50/1**

0-00 **10** *53* **Be My Spy**[12] 2786 3-8-12 30...(v1) GregFairley 10 —
(Peter Salmon) *chsd ldrs: rdn and lost pl over 4f out: sn bhd: t.o 2f out: virtually p.u* **100/1**

2m 41.33s (0.53) **Going Correction** +0.175s/f (Good) **10** Ran SP% **118.2**
Speed ratings (Par 99): **105,101,97,96,96 82,77,77,74,38**
toteswingers: 1&2 £4.10, 1&3 £2.30, 2&3 £9.00. CSF £16.08 TOTE £2.50: £1.30, £2.70, £1.70; EX 22.30 Trifecta £84.60 Pool: £436.72 - 3.82 winning units..
Owner Mrs Jacqueline Conroy **Bred** Newberry Stud Company **Trained** Middleham Moor, N Yorks

FOCUS
No more than a fair maiden.

3207 TRY TOTEQUICKPICK IF YOU'RE FEELING LUCKY H'CAP 6f

5:40 (5:41) (Class 5) (0-75,74) 3-Y-O **£2,590** (£770; £385; £192) **Stalls** Low

Form RPR

6122 **1** **Close To The Edge (IRE)**[13] 2765 3-9-0 **70**................ MartinHarley(3) 8 79
(Alan McCabe) *rrd leaving stalls and s.s: hdwy on outside over 3f out: chsng ldrs over 2f out: led 1f out: styd on* **5/1**[2]

340- **2** *1 1/2* **I Got You Babe (IRE)**[225] 7347 3-8-7 **60**........................ KierenFallon 12 64
(Richard Guest) *w ldrs on outer: led over 1f out: sn hdd: kpt on same pce* **7/1**[3]

2622 **3** *3/4* **Roman Strait**[20] 2564 3-9-1 **68**.. FrannyNorton 4 70
(Michael Blanshard) *in rr: hdwy over 1f out: styd on wl to take 3rd last 50yds* **5/1**[2]

0202 **4** *1* **Finefrenzyrolling (IRE)**[12] 2782 3-8-9 **65**...........(b) PatrickDonaghy(3) 5 63
(Mrs K Burke) *mid-div: effrt over 2f out: chsng ldrs over 1f out: kpt on same pce* **7/1**[3]

-641 **5** *3* **Maggie Mey (IRE)**[12] 2782 3-9-7 **74**..........................(p) DanielTudhope 6 63
(David O'Meara) *led tl over 2f out: wknd fnl 50yds* **10/3**[1]

-342 **6** *nse* **Stilettoesinthemud (IRE)**[22] 2498 3-8-6 **62**........... JamesSullivan(3) 11 51
(James Given) *w ldrs: led 2f out: hdd over 1f out: edgd lft: sn wknd* **22/1**

6024 **7** *1 1/4* **Fleurie Lover (IRE)**[12] 2782 3-8-3 **56**........................ AndrewHeffernan 1 41
(Richard Guest) *in rr: kpt on fnl 2f: nvr nr ldrs* **16/1**

5344 **8** *1 1/2* **Winning Draw (IRE)**[19] 2592 3-7-13 **55** oh2........(p) DeclanCannon(3) 10 35
(Paul Midgley) *w ldr: led over 2f out: sn hdd: wkng whn hung bdly rt ins fnl f* **28/1**

545- **9** *7* **Myjestic Melody (IRE)**[304] 5239 3-8-3 **56**..................... DuranFentiman 7 —
(Noel Wilson) *s.i.s: sn mid-div: lost pl over 2f out: sn bhd* **40/1**

04-1 **10** *3 1/4* **Paper Dreams (IRE)**[40] 1975 3-8-9 **62**............................(p) PhillipMakin 2 —
(Kevin Ryan) *chsd ldrs: lost pl over 2f out: eased whn bhd* **12/1**

-121 **11** *2* **Cootehill Lass (IRE)**[27] 2356 3-9-3 **70**...................(p) SilvestreDeSousa 9 —
(Geoffrey Harker) *in rr: bhd whn eased ins fnl f* **8/1**

1m 17.78s (0.88) **Going Correction** +0.175s/f (Good) **11** Ran SP% **116.3**
Speed ratings (Par 99): **101,99,98,96,92 92,90,88,79,75 72**
toteswingers: 1&2 £7.70, 1&3 £2.90, 2&3 £10.30. totesuper7: WIN: Not won. PLACE: £236.70 - 7 winning units. CSF £38.61 CT £188.43 TOTE £6.10: £2.00, £2.80, £1.50; EX 58.30 Trifecta £299.50 Pool: £501.96 - 1.24 winning units..
Owner Charles Wentworth **Bred** Martin Francis **Trained** Averham Park, Notts

FOCUS
A pretty open handicap.
T/Jkpt: Not won. T/Plt: £242.80 to a £1 stake. Pool of £104,357.39 - 313.75 winning units. T/Qpdt: £72.40 to a £1 stake. Pool of £5,512.75 - 56.30 winning units. WG

WOODBINE (R-H)

Saturday, June 18

OFFICIAL GOING: Turf: firm; polytrack: fast

3208a ALLOWANCE RACE (CONDITIONS) (3YO+ FILLIES & MARES) (TURF) 1m 110y

7:27 (7:27) 3-Y-0+

£28,653 (£9,551; £5,253; £2,865; £1,432; £256)

RPR

1 **Lemon Twirl (USA)**[272] 6235 7-8-6 0.................................. LContreras 4 95
(John Mattine, Canada) **33/4**[3]

2 *nse* **No Explaining (IRE)**[28] 4-8-12 0.................................. ERosaDaSilva 6 101
(Roger L Attfield, Canada) **7/10**[1]

3 *2 1/2* **Honimiere (IRE)**[51] 5-8-6 0.. PHusbands 1 90
(Roger L Attfield, Canada) **43/20**[2]

4 *nk* **World Cup (USA)** 4-8-8 0.. ERamsammy 5 91
(Michael P De Paulo, Canada) **117/10**

5 *[illegible]* **[illegible]**[28] 4-8-6 0.. DJMoran 2 75
(Gerard Butler) *trckd ldrs: rdn 2f out: unable qck: [illegible]* **[illegible]**

6 *hd* **Silent Wisper (CAN)**[258] 4-8-1 0.................................. RLatchman 3 70
(Michael Keogh, Canada) **37/1**

1m 39.74s (99.74) **6** Ran SP% **121.1**
PARI-MUTUEL (all including $2 stakes): WIN 18.50; PLACE (1-2) 5.00, 2.60; SHOW (1-2-3) 2.50, 2.10, 2.20; SF 35.30.
Owner George Robertson **Bred** Malec Thoroughbreds, Inc **Trained** Canada

1263 DUSSELDORF (R-H)

Sunday, June 19

OFFICIAL GOING: Turf: soft

3209a DUSSELDORFER REITER UND RENNVEREINS (GERMAN 1,000 GUINEAS) (GROUP 2) (3YO FILLIES) (TURF) 1m

4:10 (12:00) 3-Y-0

£60,344 (£24,137; £12,068; £6,034; £3,017; £2,155)

RPR

1 **Lips Poison (GER)**[22] 2520 3-9-2 0.................................. DavyBonilla 1 104
(Andreas Lowe, Germany) *broke fast then settled bhd ldr: first to chal on inner early in st: qcknd wl: grabbed ld 1f out: r.o* **92/10**

2 *1 1/4* **Wolkenburg (GER)**[28] 2337 3-9-2 0.................................. AStarke 9 101
(P Schiergen, Germany) *sn prom in 3rd: sn chal in st: led 1 1/2f out: hdd 1f out: r.o wl* **58/10**[3]

3 *nk* **Temida (IRE)**[238] 7108 3-9-2 0.................................. MartinDwyer 2 100
(M G Mintchev, Germany) *amongst bkmarkers: slow to prog in st: shkn up and fin strly fnl f* **37/1**

4 *1/2* **Aigrette Garzette (IRE)**[28] 2337 3-9-2 0.................................. FilipMinarik 7 99
(P Schiergen, Germany) *amongst ldrs: one pce early in st: shkn up 1 1/2f out and r.o wl* **87/10**

5 *hd* **Djumama (IRE)**[28] 2337 3-9-2 0.................................. AHelfenbein 5 99
(Andreas Lowe, Germany) *racd midfield: mde smooth prog bef st: rdn but no ex: r.o clsng stages* **7/10**[1]

6 *2 1/2* **Taleia (GER)**[28] 2337 3-9-2 0.................................. EPedroza 6 93
(A Wohler, Germany) *led fr s: hdd ent st: rdn but no ex* **126/10**

7 shd **Salona (GER)**[28] 2337 3-9-2 0 .... JohanVictoire 4 93
(J-P Carvalho, Germany) *settled in 6th: threatened briefly ent st: sn wknd* **243/10**

8 4 1/2 **Reine Vite (GER)**[28] 2337 3-9-2 0 .... GaetanMasure 8 82
(Uwe Ostmann, Germany) *settled towards rr: mde prog down bkst: rdn but no ex in st: fdd* **117/10**

9 8 **Quesada (IRE)**[49] 3-9-2 0 .... APietsch 3 64
(W Hickst, Germany) *prom early: then settled midfield: flattered briefly early in st: rdn but qckly wknd* **41/10**[2]

1m 41.03s (-0.13) **9** Ran SP% **135.1**
WIN (incl. 10 euro stake): 102. PLACES: 27, 23, 39. SF: 1,638.
Owner Stall Lintec **Bred** Stall Parthenaue **Trained** Germany

Race 3210 - 3211a - See RI

[2982]SAN SIRO (R-H)
Sunday, June 19

OFFICIAL GOING: Turf: soft

3212a PREMIO PRIMI PASSI (GROUP 3) (2YO) (TURF) 6f
4:50 (12:00) 2-Y-0 **£34,482** (£15,172; £8,275; £4,137)

RPR

1 **Vedelago (IRE)**[17] 2-8-11 0 .... MEsposito 2 109
(L Polito, Italy) *broke wl: settled in 5th: tk share of 3rd 1/2-way: shkn up 1 1/2f out: qcknd to ld fnl f: gng away fnl 100yds* **6/4**[2]

2 2 **Salure**[12] 2-8-11 0 .... DarioVargiu 5 103
(B Grizzetti, Italy) *sn led: hdd fnl f: kpt on wout qckning* **29/4**

3 1 3/4 **Strategic Game (IRE)**[45] 2-8-11 0 .... FabioBranca 3 98
(S Botti, Italy) *sn trcking ldr: rdn and kpt on wout qckning fr 1 1/2f out* **21/20**[1]

4 1 3/4 **Art Of Dreams (FR)** 2-8-11 0 .... CristianDemuro 7 93
(L Riccardi, Italy) *towards rr early: in share of 3rd 1/2-way: rdn and nt qckn fr 1 1/2f out* **61/10**

5 1/2 **Vanity Woman** 2-8-8 0 .... MircoDemuro 9 88
(Vittorio Caruso, Italy) *chsd ldrs on wd outside early: dropped bk to be 6th after 1 1/2f: mod hdwy u.p fnl f* **107/20**[3]

6 1/2 **Peccato Di Gola**[17] 2-8-11 0 .... CColombi 1 90
(B Grizzetti, Italy) *led early but in rr after 1f: last and rdn 1/2-way: sme hdwy fnl 1 1/2f: nvr nr to chal* **29/4**

7 3 **Light Lustre (IRE)**[17] 2-8-8 0 .... PAragoni 4 78
(A Peraino, Italy) *broke wl: sn outpcd: 7th 1/2-way: rdn and nt qckn fr 2f out: fdd* **239/10**

8 5 **Rivertime (ITY)**[17] 2-8-11 0 .... LManiezzi 8 66
(R Menichetti, Italy) *prom on outside to 1/2-way: sn rdn and wknd fnl 1 1/2f* **146/10**

1m 10.7s (-1.10) **8** Ran SP% **153.3**
WIN (incl. 1 euro stake): 2.49. PLACES: 1.27, 1.87, 1.15. DF: 38.42.
Owner G T A **Bred** G T A Srl **Trained** Italy

3213a LXXVIII ROYAL MARES (LISTED RACE) (3YO+ FILLIES & MARES) 1m
5:25 (12:00) 3-Y-0+ **£30,172** (£13,275; £7,241; £3,620)

RPR

1 **Rockatella (IRE)**[17] 2657 4-9-4 0 .... MEsposito 8 105
(W Hefter, Germany) **81/10**

2 3/4 **Malagenia (IRE)**[14] 3-8-5 0 .... CristianDemuro 2 98
(L Riccardi, Italy) **164/10**

3 hd **Monblue**[28] 2336 4-9-4 0 .... DarioVargiu 9 103
(B Grizzetti, Italy) **604/100**

4 1/2 **Waldjagd**[31] 4-9-1 0 .... UmbertoRispoli 1 99
(A Wohler, Germany) **58/10**

5 3/4 **Sakheart**[253] 6763 5-9-4 0 .... FabioBranca 3 100
(V Luka Jr, Czech Republic) **21/10**[2]

6 3/4 **Gobama**[17] 2634 4-9-1 0 .... SebSanders 5 95
(J W Hills) *racd in 5th: strly rdn ins fnl 2f: no imp on ldrs* **41/10**[3]

7 hd **Quiza Quiza Quiza**[35] 2134 5-9-6 0 .... MircoDemuro 6 100
(L Riccardi, Italy) **5/3**[1]

8 1/2 **Cronsa (GER)**[28] 2336 4-9-1 0 .... CColombi 7 94
(S Botti, Italy) **36/1**

9 5 **Mountain Rose (GER)**[16] 2678 4-9-1 0 .... GBietolini 4 82
(Mario Hofer, Germany) **26/1**

1m 36.3s (-5.80)
WFA 3 from 4yo+ 10lb **9** Ran SP% **141.4**
WIN (incl. 1 euro stake): 9.09. PLACES: 2.94, 3.98, 2.91. DF: 99.32.
Owner Stall H20 **Bred** Ennistown Stud **Trained** Germany

[2868]CHEPSTOW (L-H)
Monday, June 20

OFFICIAL GOING: Soft
Wind: Quite strong, across Weather: Rain

3214 DUNRAVEN WINDOWS MAIDEN STKS 1m 4f 23y
6:30 (6:31) (Class 5) 3-Y-0+ **£2,266** (£674; £337; £168) **Stalls** Low

Form RPR

-242 1 **Galivant (IRE)**[21] 2551 3-8-7 84 .... MartinDwyer 5 79+
(J W Hills) *trckd ldr: led over 3f out: eased clr: unextended* **1/9**[1]

3-64 2 12 **Captain Sharpe**[13] 1137 3-8-12 65 ....(p) TomMcLaughlin 4 55
(Bernard Llewellyn) *trckd ldrs: dropped to last pair but in tch over 6f out: rdn and hdwy fr 4f out: chal for 2nd over 2f out: kpt on but nvr any ch w wnr* **33/1**

6 3 2 3/4 **Cluain Dara (IRE)**[10] 2871 3-8-7 0 .... RoystonFfrench 3 46
(Mark Johnston) *trckd ldr: rdn to chse wnr 3f out tl ent fnl f: no ex* **7/1**[2]

50 4 6 **Band Of Thunder**[21] 2551 3-8-12 0 .... DavidProbert 2 41
(Andrew Balding) *s.i.s: in last pair: wnt 4th over 6f out: rdn over 4f out: wknd over 2f out* **25/1**[3]

-030 5 20 **Miskin Diamond (IRE)**[9] 2904 3-8-7 46 .... NeilChalmers 6 —
(Bryn Palling) *led tl rdn over 3f out: sn wknd: t.o* **66/1**

6 21 **Ballina Blue** 3-8-12 0 .... TadhgO'Shea 1 —
(John Gallagher) *slowly away: in last pair: nudged along 7f out: rdn 5f out: no imp: wknd 3f out: t.o* **50/1**

2m 47.51s (8.51) **Going Correction** +0.70s/f (Yiel) **6** Ran SP% **112.7**
Speed ratings (Par 103): **99,91,89,85,71 57**
toteswingers: 1&2 £1.90, 1&3 £1.10, 2&3 £4.10. CSF £10.66 TOTE £1.10: £1.02, £6.50; EX 6.30.
Owner Wauchope, Cottam, Mason, Baxter, Caroe **Bred** Barronstown Stud **Trained** Upper Lambourn, Berks

FOCUS
An extremely uncompetitive maiden and the winner cruised home. It's doubtful she had to improve.

3215 EASYODDS.COM H'CAP 1m 2f 36y
7:00 (7:00) (Class 5) (0-75,73) 4-Y-0+ **£2,266** (£674; £337; £168) **Stalls** Low

Form RPR

1-55 1 **Osgood**[9] 2915 4-9-7 73 .... SamHitchcott 3 83
(Mick Channon) *mde all: styd on gamely fnl f: rdn out* **4/1**[3]

-322 2 3/4 **On The Feather**[9] 2923 5-9-0 66 .... JamesMillman 2 75
(Rod Millman) *trckd ldrs: rdn to chse wnr over 1f out: styd on towards fin but a being hld* **5/2**[1]

4513 3 5 **You've Been Mowed**[10] 2870 5-8-13 70 .... DaleSwift(5) 4 69
(Richard Price) *hld up bhd ldrs: hdwy 3f out: rdn 2f out: styd on same pce* **5/2**[1]

1-25 4 1/2 **Spring Secret**[97] 858 5-9-6 72 .... DavidProbert 5 70
(Bryn Palling) *trckd wnr: rdn over 2f out* **3/1**[2]

305/ 5 1/2 **Mega Watt (IRE)**[128] 4207 6-9-0 66 .... KellyHarrison 1 63
(Dai Burchell) *trckd ldrs: rdn over 2f out: kpt on same pce* **20/1**

2100 6 18 **Dubai Miracle (USA)**[58] 1530 4-9-7 73 ....(t) KirstyMilczarek 6 34
(Laura Young) *sn pushed along chsng ldrs: rdn over 4f out: sn btn* **16/1**

2m 16.74s (6.14) **Going Correction** +0.70s/f (Yiel) **6** Ran SP% **112.8**
Speed ratings (Par 103): **103,102,98,98,97 83**
toteswingers: 1&2 £1.80, 1&3 £3.20, 2&3 £1.70. CSF £14.55 TOTE £2.50: £2.10, £1.80; EX 19.00.
Owner Billy Parish **Bred** Eurostrait Ltd **Trained** West Ilsley, Berks

FOCUS
A modest handicap in which Osgood benefited from being allowed an uncontested lead. He's rated in line with the best view of his previous form.

3216 CWMTILLERY GLASS CENTRE GWENT H'CAP 5f 16y
7:30 (7:31) (Class 6) (0-60,64) 3-Y-0+ **£1,619** (£481; £240; £120) **Stalls** High

Form RPR

4-00 1 **Royal Box**[140] 363 4-8-13 49 ....(p) KellyHarrison 1 58
(Dai Burchell) *sn pushed along chsng ldrs: lost pl u.p 3f out: hdwy ent fnl f: drifted rt: r.o strly to ld towards fin* **12/1**

1325 2 1 **Decider (USA)**[9] 2913 8-9-5 55 ....(b) KirstyMilczarek 4 60
(Ronald Harris) *led: rdn and drifted lft fr over 2f out: kpt on but no ex whn ct towards fin* **8/1**[3]

0065 3 3/4 **Lithaam (IRE)**[6] 3015 7-8-10 46 oh1 ....(tp) RussKennemore 10 48
(Milton Bradley) *chsd ldrs: rdn to chse ldr fr 2f out: kpt on same pce fnl f* **25/1**

2342 4 1/2 **Ginzan**[21] 2549 3-9-2 58 .... TomMcLaughlin 6 57
(Malcolm Saunders) *chsd ldrs: rdn to chse ldr fr 2f out: kpt on same pce: no ex nring fin* **11/4**[2]

50-0 5 nk **Aalsmeer**[21] 2555 4-9-7 57 .... MartinDwyer 7 56
(Karen George) *prom tl rdn over 2f out: kpt on same pce* **20/1**

6000 6 nk **Colourbearer (IRE)**[10] 2869 4-9-3 53 ....(t) RoystonFfrench 11 51
(Milton Bradley) *mid-div: rdn over 2f out: styd on fnl f: nvr trbld ldrs* **14/1**

031 7 3/4 **Your Gifted (IRE)**[6] 3027 4-9-9 64 6ex .... MatthewCosham(5) 8 60
(Patrick Morris) *chsd ldrs: rdn to chse ldr 2f out: wknd ins fnl f* **9/4**[1]

-000 8 2 **Hoh Hoh Hoh**[19] 2610 9-9-5 60 ....(t) DaleSwift(5) 9 48
(Richard Price) *outpcd towards rr: sme late prog: nvr a factor* **8/1**[3]

1060 9 2 **Lois Lane**[16] 2720 3-8-10 55 .... MatthewDavies(3) 2 34
(Ron Hodges) *nvr bttr than mid-div* **50/1**

04-0 10 hd **Private Olley**[19] 2605 4-9-2 57 .... LeeNewnes(5) 3 38
(Harry Dunlop) *a outpcd in rr* **25/1**

5500 11 4 **Bobbyow**[9] 2918 3-8-11 53 ....(b[1]) DavidProbert 12 17
(Bryn Palling) *mid-div: rdn over 2f out: wknd over 1f out* **14/1**

0-00 12 1 1/4 **Madam Isshe**[32] 2222 4-9-6 56 .... SamHitchcott 5 18
(Malcolm Saunders) *mid-div: drvn along 1/2-way: sn wknd* **16/1**

63.99 secs (4.69) **Going Correction** +0.75s/f (Yiel)
WFA 3 from 4yo+ 6lb **12** Ran SP% **121.0**
Speed ratings (Par 101): **92,90,89,88,87 87,86,83,79,79 73,71**
toteswingers: 1&2 £13.60, 1&3 £72.40, 2&3 £13.50. CSF £102.28 CT £2420.46 TOTE £12.80: £3.30, £1.90, £13.20; EX 134.70.
Owner T R Pearson **Bred** The Queen **Trained** Briery Hill, Blaenau Gwent

FOCUS
The first race of the evening on the straight course and the field were spread out across the track, but there was no obvious bias. This is moderate form, with the ground a factor. Probably not a race to take too literally.

3217 WYVERN ICES H'CAP 6f 16y
8:00 (8:00) (Class 5) (0-70,69) 3-Y-0+ **£2,266** (£674; £337; £168) **Stalls** High

Form RPR

014 1 **Gracie's Games**[7] 2989 5-8-11 57 .... SophieDoyle(3) 6 65
(Richard Price) *trckd ldr: rdn 2f out: edgd lft ent fnl f: sn chalng ldr: kpt on wl to ld line* **4/1**[2]

3216 2 shd **Emiratesdotcom**[10] 2870 5-9-6 63 .... AdamKirby 2 71
(Milton Bradley) *s.i.s: in last: drvn and hdwy 2f out: led ent fnl f: kpt on but no ex whn hdd line* **2/1**[1]

0300 3 1 **Hereford Boy**[12] 2822 7-9-8 68 ....(b) PatrickHills(3) 7 73
(Dean Ivory) *hld up bhd ldrs: rdn over 1f out: styd on ins fnl f* **14/1**

3324 4 3/4 **Miss Firefly**[14] 2756 6-8-11 57 ....(p) MatthewDavies(3) 5 59
(Ron Hodges) *led: rdn 2f out: hdd ent fnl f: no ex* **7/1**[3]

-002 5 2 3/4 **Kinigi (IRE)**[6] 3020 5-9-7 69 ....(b) DaleSwift(5) 1 63
(Ronald Harris) *chsd ldrs: rdn 3f out: ev ch ent fnl f: fdd fnl 100yds* **4/1**[2]

-060 6 hd **Bathwick Xaara**[4] 3079 4-9-8 65 .... StephenCraine 4 58
(Jonathan Portman) *trckd ldr: rdn over 2f out: fdd fnl 100yds* **7/1**[3]

1-00 7 14 **Spinning Spirit (IRE)**[50] 1730 4-9-6 63 ....(p) TomMcLaughlin 8 11
(Milton Bradley) *trckd ldr: rdn over 2f out: wknd over 1f out* **12/1**

1m 15.96s (3.96) **Going Correction** +0.75s/f (Yiel) **7** Ran SP% **112.7**
Speed ratings (Par 103): **103,102,101,100,96 96,77**
toteswingers: 1&2 £1.20, 1&3 £17.00, 2&3 £7.20. CSF £12.06 CT £97.46 TOTE £2.70: £1.10, £3.30; EX 15.40.
Owner David Prosser & Keith Warrington **Bred** David Prosser & Keith Warrington **Trained** Ullingswick, H'fords

■ Stewards' Enquiry : Adam Kirby caution: used whip with excessive frequency.
Sophie Doyle caution: used whip with excessive freaquency.

The Form Book, Raceform Ltd, Compton, RG20 6NL

FOCUS
A modest sprint handicap where they raced towards the stands' side. The form is rated around the front pair.

3218 KELLANDS MAIDEN STKS — 1m 14y
8:30 (8:31) (Class 5) 3-Y-O+ **£2,266** (£674; £337; £168) **Stalls** High

Form — RPR
63 **1** **Stage Attraction (IRE)**[21] 2568 3-9-2 0 .... DavidProbert 10 90+
(Andrew Balding) *trckd ldrs: led over 1f out: sn rdn: edgd lft: r.o wl fnl 120yds: readily* **4/1**[3]
36- **2** *2* **Aerial Acclaim (IRE)**[276] 6149 3-9-2 0 .... AdamKirby 5 85+
(Clive Cox) *sn trcking ldrs: rdn to chal over 1f out: kpt on but no ex fnl 75yds* **6/4**[2]
4-32 **3** *5* **Burj Hatta (USA)**[20] 2596 3-9-2 82 .... TedDurcan 1 74
(Saeed Bin Suroor) *trckd ldrs: carried lft after 1f: led over 2f out: sn rdn: hdd over 1f out: no ex fnl f* **5/4**[1]
0 **4** *3 ¾* **Lady Bayside**[13] 2790 3-8-12 0 ow1 .... TomMcLaughlin 8 61
(Malcolm Saunders) *mid-div: rdn 3f out: styd on to go 4th fnl f but nvr a threat* **50/1**
5 *nk* **Madam Tessa (IRE)** 3-8-11 0 .... NeilChalmers 6 59+
(Bryn Palling) *hld up towards rr: rdn over 2f out: styd on fr over 1f out: nvr threatened ldrs* **66/1**
2-5 **6** *1 ¼* **Methayel (IRE)**[21] 2568 3-8-11 0 .... PhilipRobinson 9 56
(Clive Brittain) *trckd ldrs: ev ch 2f out: sn rdn: wknd over 1f out* **12/1**
0 **7** *6* **Charmouth Girl**[19] 2621 5-9-7 0 .... StephenCraine 4 45
(John Mackie) *cl up whn squeezed out after 1f: in tch: rdn 3f out: wknd over 1f out* **66/1**
06- **8** *4 ½* **Cherrego (USA)**[220] 7427 3-8-11 0 .... (t) MartinDwyer 11 32
(Bryn Palling) *led tl rdn over 2f out: sn wknd* **66/1**
9 *1 ¾* **Tawseef (IRE)** 3-9-2 0 .... AndrewHeffernan 3 33
(Roy Brotherton) *chsng ldrs whn hmpd after 1f: rdn 3f out: wknd over 1f out* **66/1**
10 *6* **Greyemkay** 3-8-11 0 .... DaleSwift[(5)] 2 19
(Richard Price) *s.i.s: racd v green: a bhd* **50/1**

1m 41.15s (4.95) **Going Correction** +0.75s/f (Yiel)
WFA 3 from 5yo 10lb **10** Ran SP% **122.0**
Speed ratings (Par 103): **105,103,98,94,93 92,86,82,80,74**
toteswingers: 1&2 £1.30, 1&3 £1.30, 2&3 £1.10. CSF £10.97 TOTE £3.90: £1.10, £1.40, £1.10; EX 11.60.
Owner Miss A V Hill **Bred** Dermot Cantillon And Forenaghts Stud **Trained** Kingsclere, Hants
FOCUS
They raced up the middle of the track. A reasonable maiden, although there was a bit of trouble early on when Cherrego went left and a few runners became short of room. The front pair improved.
Methayel(IRE) Official explanation: jockey said filly ran too free and ran green

3219 LINDLEY CATERING CLASSIFIED STKS — 1m 14y
9:00 (9:00) (Class 5) 3-Y-O **£2,266** (£674; £337; £168) **Stalls** High

Form — RPR
30-4 **1** **Uptown Guy (USA)**[54] 1611 3-9-0 70 .... (b[1]) TedDurcan 4 72
(William Haggas) *trckd ldrs: rdn wl over 1f out: r.o wl fnl 120yds: led fnl strides* **11/4**[2]
-520 **2** *nk* **Tinaheely (IRE)**[12] 2821 3-9-0 70 .... StephenCraine 3 71
(Jonathan Portman) *led: rdn over 1f out: kpt on gamely: hdd fnl strides* **8/1**
15 **3** *1 ¼* **Foxley (IRE)**[32] 2232 3-9-0 67 .... MartinDwyer 1 68
(Brian Meehan) *racd keenly w ldr: rdn and ev ch fr over 1f out tl no ex fnl 75yds* **10/3**[3]
4-31 **4** *½* **Bakoura**[25] 2419 3-9-0 70 .... TadhgO'Shea 2 67
(John Dunlop) *trckd ldrs: pushed along over 2f out: sn rdn: kpt on but nt pce to chal* **4/5**[1]

1m 45.71s (9.51) **Going Correction** +0.75s/f (Yiel) **4** Ran SP% **116.4**
Speed ratings (Par 99): **82,81,80,79**
CSF £20.54 TOTE £2.70; EX 13.70.
Owner [illegible] **Bred** Tom Clark & Nancy Clark **Trained** Newmarket, Suffolk
FOCUS
A race run in gloomy conditions. The pace was steady even allowing for the ground (time over four seconds slower than earlier maiden), and a relative dash to the line ensued. They raced up the middle of the track for much of the way although Uptown Guy hung left on to the stands' side rail late on. The time was very slow and the first three are rated basically to form.
T/Plt: £95.50 to a £1 stake. Pool: £50,173.17. 383.52 winning tickets. T/Qpdt: £34.60 to a £1 stake. Pool: £3,894.21. 83.10 winning tickets. TM

3042 KEMPTON (A.W) (R-H)
Monday, June 20

OFFICIAL GOING: Standard
Wind: Fairly light, half behind Weather: Dry, cloudy, brighter spells

3220 PETER ANDRE 06.07.11 H'CAP — 1m 2f (P)
2:15 (2:17) (Class 6) (0-60,60) 3-Y-O **£1,619** (£481; £240; £120) **Stalls** Low

Form — RPR
6513 **1** **Westhaven (IRE)**[27] 2379 3-9-2 55 .... (b) NickyMackay 10 71
(David Elsworth) *rdn along early: chsd ldr after 1f: led over 2f out: sn clr and in n.d fr over 1f out: rdn out* **7/2**[2]
-043 **2** *7* **Arctic Reach**[31] 2243 3-8-8 47 .... (p) FrankieMcDonald 3 49+
(Brendan Powell) *hld up towards rr: travelling wl but nt clr run over 3f out: rdn and hdwy to modest 3rd over 1f out: kpt on u.p to chse wnr ins fnl f: no ch* **20/1**
0004 **3** *nk* **Formal Dining (USA)**[18] 2637 3-9-6 59 .... NeilCallan 8 60+
(Edward Vaughan) *short of room sn after s: hld up in last quartet: hdwy 1/2-way: nt clr run jst over 3f out: rdn and hdwy 3f out: chsd clr wnr over 1f out: no imp: lost 2nd ins fnl f* **3/1**[1]
-400 **4** *3 ½* **Lady Morganna (IRE)**[77] 1134 3-9-5 58 .... CathyGannon 5 52
(Olivia Maylam) *t.k.h: hld up in last quartet: rdn and hdwy into midfield 3f out: plugged on u.p fnl f: no ch w wnr* **33/1**
5030 **5** *hd* **Sir Randolf (IRE)**[22] 2527 3-9-6 59 .... (t) JamesDoyle 1 53
(Sylvester Kirk) *hld up in rr: rdn and hdwy into midfield 3f out: kpt on u.p fr over 1f out: no ch w wnr* **25/1**
0-60 **6** *7* **Royal Reason**[11] 2842 3-9-7 60 .... HughBowman 4 40
(Mick Channon) *led for 1f: chsd ldrs after: rdn and chsd ldng pair over 3f out: outpcd and no ch w wnr 2f out: ev ch of 2nd tl wknd fnl f* **16/1**
0-05 **7** *10* **Soldiers Point**[20] 2586 3-8-11 50 .... (p) PatCosgrave 7 10
(Jane Chapple-Hyam) *rdn along leaving stalls: led after 1f: drvn and hdd over 2f out: outpcd by wnr and btn wl over 1f out: lost 2nd over 1f out: wknd and eased ins fnl f* **16/1**
00-0 **8** *½* **Dixie Land Band**[33] 2192 3-8-8 47 .... RichardThomas 9 6
(Paul Burgoyne) *hld up in last quartet: rdn and struggling over 3f out: wl bhd fnl 2f* **100/1**
0-00 **9** *1 ¾* **Control Chief**[28] 2368 3-9-5 58 .... (t) JimCrowley 6 13
(Ralph Beckett) *chsd ldrs: reminders 1/2-way: rdn and wknd over 3f out: wl bhd fnl 2f* **11/2**
500- **10** *nse* **Trend (IRE)**[242] 7036 3-9-7 60 .... (v[1]) JamieSpencer 2 15
(Michael Bell) *t.k.h: hld up in midfield: nt clr run over 3f out: hdwy to chse ldng trio over 2f out: drvn and fnd nil whn rn wd bnd 2f out: sn gave up and wl btn over 1f out* **5/1**[3]
000 **11** *8* **What About Now**[20] 2581 3-9-4 57 .... (p) MichaelHills 12 —
(J W Hills) *chsd ldrs on outer: rdn and struggling 4f out: wknd and wl bhd fnl 2f: t.o* **25/1**
60-0 **12** *½* **Drummer Boy**[33] 2196 3-9-2 55 .... LukeMorris 11 —
(Peter Winkworth) *chsd ldrs: rdn and struggling over 3f out: wl bhd fnl 2f: t.o* **10/1**

2m 10.28s (2.28) **Going Correction** +0.225s/f (Slow) **12** Ran SP% **116.5**
Speed ratings (Par 97): **99,93,93,90,90 84,76,76,74,74 68,67**
toteswingers: 1&2 £5.70, 1&3 £3.20, 2&3 £11.40. CSF £77.48 CT £234.88 TOTE £3.50: £1.20, £5.40, £1.20; EX 32.00 Trifecta £511.30 Part won. Pool: £691.06 - 0.88 winning units..
Owner J C Smith **Bred** Littleton Stud **Trained** Newmarket, Suffolk
FOCUS
A very poor handicap with 11 of the 12 runners being maidens coming into it, a situation that remained after the contest. They finished well spread out. There's little doubt the winner showed big improvement.

3221 BRITISH BIG BAND 22.06.11 MAIDEN STKS — 5f (P)
2:45 (2:45) (Class 5) 2-Y-O **£2,266** (£674; £337; £168) **Stalls** Low

Form — RPR
5 **1** **Piranha (IRE)**[16] 2709 2-8-12 0 .... RichardHughes 2 81+
(Ed Dunlop) *t.k.h: chsd ldr tl rdn to ld 1f out: sn rdn clr and in total command fnl 150yds: eased towards fin* **13/8**[2]
42 **2** *3 ½* **Banksy**[34] 2173 2-9-3 0 .... NickyMackay 7 73
(John Gosden) *sn led: rdn over 1f out: hdd 1f out: sn outpcd and no ch w wnr fnl 150yds* **5/4**[1]
05 **3** *4 ½* **Clarkson (IRE)**[7] 2997 2-9-3 0 .... FergusSweeney 4 57
(Jamie Osborne) *a chsng ldng pair: effrt and clsd over 2f out: rdn and unable qck over 1f out: styd on same pce and wl hld fnl f* **7/1**[3]
0 **4** *2 ¼* **Flying Kitty**[13] 2788 2-8-9 0 .... SeanLevey[(3)] 5 44
(John Bridger) *a chsng ldng trio but nvr on terms: rdn and plugged on same pce fr wl over 1f out* **20/1**
5 *2* **Mr Hendrix** 2-8-12 0 .... MarkCoumbe[(5)] 3 42
(Brett Johnson) *v.s.a: a wl outpcd in last pair: nvr on terms* **40/1**
6 *5* **Papal Power (IRE)** 2-9-3 0 .... MichaelHills 1 24
(J W Hills) *v.s.a: a wl outpcd in rr: t.o fr 1/2-way* **12/1**

61.70 secs (1.20) **Going Correction** +0.225s/f (Slow) **6** Ran SP% **109.9**
Speed ratings (Par 93): **99,93,86,82,79 71**
toteswingers: 1&2 £1.30, 1&3 £1.60, 2&3 £1.50. CSF £3.80 TOTE £1.60: £1.20, £1.30; EX 4.60.
Owner St Albans Bloodstock LLP **Bred** Epona Bloodstock Ltd **Trained** Newmarket, Suffolk
FOCUS
A weakish maiden and a match according to the market, which is how it turned out. The time was decent and the form is straightforward.
NOTEBOOK
Piranha(IRE) was dropping 1.5f from her Doncaster debut, but it made no difference and she picked off the runner-up over 1f from home with the minimum of fuss. The form is modest, but she is going the right way and a return to further won't bother her. (op 11-8 tchd 5-4)
Banksy, runner-up over C&D last time, tried to make every yard but was made to look slow by the filly from the furlong pole. He looks modest and a drop in grade or nurseries may be his best chance of winning a race. (tchd 11-8)
Clarkson(IRE) showed a bit more on his second start at Windsor seven days earlier and was close enough turning in, but could then make little impression on the front pair. Nurseries may also be his best option. (op [illegible])
Flying Kitty looks very much a modest long-term handicap prospect. (op [illegible])

3222 REWARDS4RACING.COM H'CAP — 5f (P)
3:15 (3:17) (Class 4) (0-85,85) 3-Y-O+ **£4,079** (£1,214; £606; £303) **Stalls** Low

Form — RPR
2163 **1** **Mymumsaysimthebest**[21] 2557 6-9-2 75 .... GeorgeBaker 5 89
(Gary Moore) *chsd ldrs: effrt and rdn to chal over 1f out: led and edgd rt jst over 1f out: clr and in command ins fnl f: comf* **11/2**
1150 **2** *2* **Best Trip (IRE)**[23] 2497 4-9-7 80 .... FrannyNorton 1 90+
(Richard Guest) *taken down early: led tl 3f out: chsd ldr after: gng for gap between horses over 1f out: squeezed and lost pl jst over 1f out: rallied to chse wnr ins fnl f: kpt on but no threat to wnr* **9/4**[1]
10-0 **3** *¾* **Brynfa Boy**[38] 2069 5-9-3 76 .... TonyCulhane 2 80+
(Paul D'Arcy) *taken down early: broke wl: sn stdd and racd off the pce in midfield: pushed along 1/2-way: hdwy u.p over 1f out: styd on wl fnl f: nt rch ldrs* **12/1**
0-00 **4** *½* **Kingsgate Choice (IRE)**[37] 2099 4-9-12 85 .... (b[1]) LukeMorris 4 87
(John Best) *sn rdn along and outpcd in rr: swtchd lft and hdwy over 1f out: styd on strly fnl f: nt rch ldrs* **3/1**[2]
34-5 **5** *2 ½* **Eshoog (IRE)**[11] 2855 3-8-9 74 .... PhilipRobinson 3 65
(Clive Brittain) *sn rdn along and outpcd in rr: hdwy over 1f out: swtchd lft and styd on ins fnl f: nvr trbld ldrs* **20/1**
1230 **6** *nk* **Island Legend (IRE)**[18] 2645 5-9-9 82 .... (p) DaneO'Neill 8 74
(Milton Bradley) *pressed ldr tl led 3f out: rdn over 1f out: hdd jst over 1f out: lost 2nd ins fnl f: fdd fnl 100yds* **16/1**
2660 **7** *nk* **Garstang**[6] 3027 8-9-2 75 .... (b) NeilCallan 6 66
(John Balding) *racd in midfield: hdwy over 2f out: rdn and unable qck over 1f out: styd on same pce and no imp after* **25/1**
-06 **8** *¾* **Night Affair**[31] 2244 5-9-1 74 .... CathyGannon 10 62
(David Arbuthnot) *taken down early: dwlt: sn rdn along: chsd ldrs on outer over 3f out: wknd wl over 1f out* **25/1**
4321 **9** *1 ¾* **Kylladdie**[34] 2179 4-9-7 80 .... (b) JamieSpencer 9 62
(Steve Gollings) *sn rdn along and outpcd in rr: nvr on terms* **7/2**[3]
3200 **10** *13* **Alpha Tauri (USA)**[23] 2494 5-9-4 77 .... (t) JamesDoyle 7 —
(Richard Guest) *taken down early: chsd ldrs tl 1/2-way: wknd qckly 2f out: virtually p.u fnl f: t.o* **40/1**

60.85 secs (0.35) **Going Correction** +0.225s/f (Slow)
WFA 3 from 4yo+ 6lb **10** Ran SP% **121.8**
Speed ratings (Par 105): **106,102,101,100,96 96,95,94,91,71**
toteswingers: 1&2 £3.90, 1&3 £10.70, 2&3 £8.00. CSF £18.39 CT £148.98 TOTE £8.10: £2.00, £1.70, £3.10; EX 23.30 Trifecta £200.10 Pool: £914.08 - 3.38 winning units..

Owner Mrs M J George **Bred** Bearstone Stud **Trained** Lower Beeding, W Sussex
FOCUS
A competitive sprint handicap and, with a few established front-runners in opposition, a truly run race was a near certainty. The winner is rated back to his May Goodwood form.
Kylladdie Official explanation: jockey said gelding suffered interference at start

3223 IRISH NIGHT AT KEMPTON 03.08.11 H'CAP 7f (P)
3:45 (3:46) (Class 6) (0-60,60) 3-Y-O **£1,619** (£481; £240; £120) **Stalls** Low

Form RPR
-056 **1** **Russian Ice**[20] 2599 3-9-0 **53**.....(b[1]) AdrianMcCarthy 2 63
(Dean Ivory) *chsd ldrs: rdn and effrt on inner to ld 1f out: r.o strly and drew clr fnl 100yds: rdn out* **16/1**
5603 **2** 3 ¾ **Valley Tiger**[18] 2652 3-9-1 **59**..... JamesRogers(5) 7 59
(William Muir) *dwlt: sn in tch in midfield: rdn and effrt on inner jst over 2f out: styd on wl u.p fnl f: chsd wnr wl ins fnl f: nvr able to chal* **5/1**[1]
6620 **3** nk **Lady Mango (IRE)**[41] 1980 3-9-3 **56**..... LukeMorris 1 55
(Ronald Harris) *in tch in midfield: rdn and effrt over 2f out: drvn and chsng ldrs ent fnl f: swtchd lft fnl 150yds: kpt on wl to go 3rd nr fin: no threat to wnr* **16/1**
0-30 **4** nk **Loose Quality (USA)**[34] 2180 3-9-6 **59**..... DaneO'Neill 3 57
(Chris Gordon) *led: rdn wl over 1f out: hdd and squeezed for room 1f out: chse clr wnr again ins fnl f: no imp and lost 2 pls wl ins fnl f* **10/1**
0-24 **5** 1 **Porthgwidden Beach (USA)**[17] 2660 3-8-11 **50**.....(t) NeilCallan 10 46
(Stuart Williams) *t.k.h: hld up wl in tch: swtchd lft and effrt to chal over 1f out: ev ch and edgd rt 1f out: nt pce of wnr and no drvn jst ins fnl f: lost 2nd and wknd fnl 110yds* **6/1**[2]
56-0 **6** 5 **Polish Sunset**[31] 2266 3-9-2 **55**..... CathyGannon 6 37
(Amy Weaver) *in tch in midfield: rdn and unable qck over 2f out: styd on same pce and no imp fr over 1f out* **16/1**
04-6 **7** 1 **Wong Again**[63] 1436 3-9-7 **60**..... MichaelHills 5 39
(J W Hills) *chsd ldrs on outer: rdn and pressing ldr 2f out: btn ent fnl f: fdd fnl f* **8/1**
30-0 **8** nk **Wodian (IRE)**[12] 2829 3-9-3 **56**..... RichardMullen 12 35
(David Lanigan) *stdd and dropped in bhd after s: hld up in last trio: rdn and racd awkwardly over 2f out: plugged on same pce fr over 1f out: nvr trbld ldrs* **12/1**
3530 **9** ½ **Titan Diamond (IRE)**[13] 2792 3-8-10 **56**..... RachealKneller(7) 9 33
(Mark Usher) *in tch in midfield: pushed along and outpcd over 2f out: plugged on same pce and no threat to ldrs fr over 1f out* **14/1**
3320 **10** 2 ¾ **Cathcart Castle**[13] 2792 3-9-4 **57**..... HughBowman 11 27
(Mick Channon) *taken down early: stdd s: hld up in rr: effrt and rdn over 2f out: stl plenty to do whn nt clr run 2f out: no ch after* **7/1**[3]
0020 **11** ½ **Tymismoni (IRE)**[9] 2920 3-9-0 **56**.....(v) KierenFox(3) 13 24
(Brett Johnson) *stdd and dropped in bhd after s: hld up in rr: rdn and no real hdwy over 2f out: nvr trbld ldrs* **12/1**
0-00 **12** 4 **Warden Bond**[20] 2598 3-8-11 **55**..... LauraPike(5) 8 13
(William Stone) *in tch towards rr: rdn and struggling wl over 2f out: sn wknd* **20/1**
-100 **13** 5 **Century Dancer**[20] 2598 3-8-9 **53**.....(b[1]) RyanPowell(5) 14 —
(Tor Sturgis) *stdd and dropped in bhd after s: hld up in rr: rdn and short-lived effrt on outer over 2f out: wl btn fnl 2f* **40/1**
0604 **14** 7 **Shaunas Spirit (IRE)**[41] 1980 3-8-10 **49**..... FergusSweeney 4 —
(Dean Ivory) *racd freely: chsd ldr tl jst over 2f out: wknd qckly wl over 1f out: wl bhd fnl f: eased ins fnl f* **10/1**

1m 27.86s (1.86) **Going Correction** +0.225s/f (Slow) **14** Ran SP% **119.6**
Speed ratings (Par 97): **98,93,93,93,91 86,85,84,84,80 80,75,70,62**
toteswingers: 1&2 £36.40, 1&3 £50.40, 2&3 £27.40. CSF £93.49 CT £1363.76 TOTE £34.60: £11.50, £1.50, £5.80; EX 255.00 Trifecta £268.50 Part won. Pool: £362.04 - 0.33 winning units..
Owner Roger Beadle & Ben Bennett **Bred** Kingwood Bloodstock & Mrs M Gutkin **Trained** Radlett, Herts
■ Adrian McCarthy's first winner for well over a year.
FOCUS
A poor handicap with only two of these having hit the target before. The winner is rated back to her 2yo best.

3224 KEMPTON LIVE MAIDEN FILLIES' STKS 1m 4f (P)
4:15 (4:18) (Class 5) 3-Y-O+ **£2,266** (£674; £337; £168) **Stalls** Low

Form RPR
02 **1** **Crassula**[38] 2065 3-8-12 0..... PatDobbs 10 77+
(Terry Clement) *trckd ldrs: rdn and effrt to chal 2f out: led over 1f out: r.o wl and readily drew clr fnl 150yds: comf* **15/8**[1]
23 **2** 3 ½ **Lady Elsie**[68] 1311 3-8-12 0..... LiamJones 3 71
(William Haggas) *led: rdn over 2f out: hdd over 1f out: outpcd by wnr fnl f: kpt on for clr 2nd* **6/1**
0-3 **3** 1 **Moment Juste**[67] 1332 3-8-12 0..... NickyMackay 11 69
(John Gosden) *dwlt: pushed along early: in tch: rdn and effrt over 2f out: unable qck and plugged on same pce fr over 1f out: no ch w wnr fnl f: wnt 3rd towards fin* **7/2**[3]
5 **4** nk **Handles For Forks (IRE)**[20] 2591 3-8-13 0 ow1..... HughBowman 14 70
(Mick Channon) *chsd ldrs: rdn and effrt towards inner to chse ldng pair jst over 2f out: one pce and no threat to wnr ins fnl f: lost 3rd towards fin* **33/1**
0 **5** ¾ **Astrantia**[18] 2648 3-8-12 0..... TomQueally 7 68
(Sir Henry Cecil) *hld up in tch: rdn and unable qck over 2f out: chsd ldrs and plugged on same pce fr over 1f out* **10/3**[2]
0 **6** 3 ½ **All My Heart**[5] 3043 3-8-12 0..... StevieDonohoe 12 62+
(Sir Mark Prescott Bt) *hld up in rr: pushed along and outpcd 3f out: rdn over 2f out: rallied and swtchd rt 1f out: styd on wl ins fnl f: no threat to ldrs* **33/1**
7 1 **Rose Of Sarratt (IRE)** 3-8-12 0..... MartinLane 9 61+
(Rae Guest) *s.i.s: hld up towards rr: rdn and struggling over 3f out: rallied and styd on fr over 1f out: no threat to ldrs* **25/1**
4 **8** ½ **Serenity Star**[18] 2639 3-8-12 0..... AhmedAjtebi 13 60
(Mahmood Al Zarooni) *hld up towards rr: stdy hdwy 7f out: rdn and effrt on outer over 2f out: one pce and btn wl over 1f out: wknd fnl f* **16/1**
0 **9** 5 **Heart Of Dixie (IRE)**[11] 2836 3-8-12 0.....(t) JimCrowley 5 52
(Paul Cole) *t.k.h early: hld up in tch towards rr: hdwy 4f out: rdn and unable qck over 2f out: wknd u.p over 1f out* **40/1**
00 **10** 13 **Satwa Ballerina**[11] 2836 3-8-12 0..... RichardHughes 4 31
(Ed Dunlop) *chsd ldr tl over 2f out: drvn and wknd qckly wl over 1f out: eased whn no ch ins fnl f* **66/1**
11 1 ¼ **Famagusta**[100] 4-9-7 0.....(v) LauraPike(5) 2 29
(Peter Charalambous) *t.k.h: chsd ldrs: rdn over 2f out: wknd qckly u.p over 1f out: eased whn no ch ins fnl f* **100/1**
12 99 **Polly Adler** 4-9-12 0..... DaneO'Neill 8 —
(Stuart Howe) *v.s.a and swishing tail in detached last: clsd and tagged on to bk of field 7f out: rdn and lost tch 5f out: sn t.o* **100/1**
0 **13** 10 **Readily Apparent**[21] 2551 3-8-12 0..... FergusSweeney 1 —
(Brendan Powell) *in tch: rdn and lost pl rapidly 4f out: t.o 2f out: eased to a trot ins fnl f* **100/1**

2m 37.08s (2.58) **Going Correction** +0.225s/f (Slow)
WFA 3 from 4yo 14lb **13** Ran SP% **116.9**
Speed ratings (Par 100): **100,97,97,96,96 93,93,92,89,80 80,14,7**
toteswingers: 1&2 £3.10, 1&3 £3.10, 2&3 £4.90. CSF £12.78 TOTE £3.40: £1.10, £1.70, £1.80; EX 13.90 Trifecta £50.20 Pool: £557.30 - 8.21 winning units..
Owner J R May **Bred** Millsec Limited **Trained** Newmarket, Suffolk
FOCUS
An ordinary middle-distance fillies' maiden and the early pace was nothing special. The winner didn't need to match her latest form.

3225 HAPPY RETIREMENT ROBERT WATSON H'CAP 1m 4f (P)
4:45 (4:47) (Class 5) (0-70,70) 4-Y-O+ **£2,266** (£674; £337; £168) **Stalls** Low

Form RPR
2000 **1** **Buddy Holly**[5] 3042 6-9-1 **64**..... DarryllHolland 4 73
(Robert Eddery) *t.k.h: chsd ldr tl led 6f out: rdn and qcknd clr ent fnl 2f: in drvn and in n.d over 1f out: pushed out ins fnl f: comf* **16/1**
0016 **2** 3 ½ **Lytham (IRE)**[31] 2271 10-8-8 **57**..... LukeMorris 5 60
(Tony Carroll) *stdd s: t.k.h: hld up in tch: rdn 3f out: 4th and no ch w wnr over 1f out: plugged on ins fnl f to go 2nd last strides* **9/1**
5032 **3** hd **Beat Route**[75] 1174 4-9-2 **70**..... JemmaMarshall(5) 2 72
(Michael Attwater) *hld up in tch: effrt on inner and rdn over 2f out: chsd wnr 2f out: sn outpcd and btn: kpt on same pce fnl f and lost 2nd last strides* **5/1**[3]
1-00 **4** 2 **Jovial (IRE)**[30] 2312 4-9-1 **64**..... ShaneKelly 8 63
(Denis Coakley) *chsd ldr tl rdn and nt pce of wnr 2f out: edging rt 2f out: one pce and wl hld after* **10/3**[1]
4503 **5** 1 ¼ **Colonel Sherman (USA)**[12] 2820 6-8-6 **55**.....(t) AndrewHeffernan 1 52
(Philip Kirby) *sn led: hdd 6f out: rdn and struggling over 3f out: outpcd and wl hld fnl 2f* **7/2**[2]
41-0 **6** 3 ¾ **Maison Brillet (IRE)**[22] 2526 4-9-4 **67**.....(p) FrannyNorton 6 58
(Clive Drew) *hld up in tch in rr: effrt and rdn over 2f out: sn outpcd and no threat to ldrs fnl 2f* **15/2**
4530 **7** 42 **Diamond Twister (USA)**[7] 2991 5-8-6 **58**.....(t) KierenFox(3) 7 —
(Lisa Williamson) *in tch: rdn over 5f out: lost tch wl over 2f out: virtually p.u fnl f: t.o* **16/1**
3010 **8** nk **Robby Bobby**[7] 3003 6-8-13 **62**..... IanMongan 3 —
(Laura Mongan) *bhd: hdwy on outer to chse ldrs 6f out: rdn and fnd nil wl over 2f out: wknd jst over 2f out: virtually p.u fnl f: t.o* **11/2**

2m 35.64s (1.14) **Going Correction** +0.225s/f (Slow) **8** Ran SP% **110.9**
Speed ratings (Par 103): **105,102,102,101,100 97,69,69**
toteswingers: 1&2 £20.40, 1&3 £10.40, 2&3 £9.20. CSF £140.27 CT £800.41 TOTE £23.50: £6.10, £3.20, £1.80; EX 150.40 TRIFECTA Not won..
Owner EDS Roofing Supplies Ltd **Bred** R J & S A Carter **Trained** Newmarket, Suffolk
■ Robert Eddery's first winner as a trainer.
FOCUS
An ordinary handicap and though the early pace was solid, it had slowed by halfway. Even so the winning time 1.44 seconds quicker than the fillies' maiden. Sound enough form.
Buddy Holly Official explanation: trainer had no explanation for the apparent improvement in form.
Robby Bobby Official explanation: jockey said gelding ran flat

3226 OLLY MURS 12.08.11 H'CAP (DIV I) 1m (P)
5:15 (5:17) (Class 6) (0-55,55) 3-Y-O **£1,619** (£481; £240; £120) **Stalls** Low

Form RPR
-050 **1** **Litotes**[27] 2384 3-8-8 **50**.....(p) MarkCoumbe(5) 13 57
(Michael Attwater) *racd keenly: chsd ldrs tl led over 5f out: mde rest: rdn and wnt clr 2f out: being ct but a holding on toward fin* **50/1**
-064 **2** ½ **Oliver's Gold**[16] 2722 3-9-1 **52**..... PatDobbs 8 58
(Amanda Perrett) *hld up towards rr: gd hdwy on inner over 2f out: chsd clr wnr 1f out: kpt on u.p: nvr quite getting to wnr* **11/4**[1]
1040 **3** 3 ¼ **Fire Crystal**[24] 2465 3-9-0 **54**..... MartinHarley(3) 10 53
(Mick Channon) *led tl hdd 5f out: chsd ldr after: drvn and unable qck ent fnl 2f: plugged on same pce fnl and wl hld fnl f* **9/1**
5566 **4** hd **Princess Gail**[28] 2351 3-9-2 **53**..... ShaneKelly 1 51
(Mark Brisbourne) *awkward leaving stalls: sn in tch in midfield: rdn and effrt to chse ldrs 2f out: no imp over 1f out: styd on same pce fnl f* **12/1**
0065 **5** 3 **Five Cool Kats (IRE)**[27] 2384 3-8-9 **46**..... JamieSpencer 3 37
(Paul Burgoyne) *t.k.h: in tch: effrt to chse ldrs over 2f out: hrd drvn and wknd jst over 1f out* **8/1**[3]
00-0 **6** ¾ **Hawridge Knight**[20] 2586 3-8-12 **49**.....(v[1]) DarryllHolland 12 38
(Rod Millman) *s.i.s: rcvrd to chse ldrs after 2f: drvn and unable qck over 2f out: wknd u.p over 1f out* **9/1**
4535 **7** 1 ¼ **Magical Star**[61] 1482 3-8-9 **46** oh1..... AWhelan 4 33
(Michael Wigham) *bhd: rdn and effrt over 2f out: styd on steadily fnl f: n.d* **16/1**
6540 **8** ¾ **Scommettitrice (IRE)**[7] 2993 3-9-0 **51**.....(p) JimCrowley 7 36
(Ronald Harris) *t.k.h: chsd ldrs: rdn and struggling over 2f out: wknd wl over 1f out* **10/1**
0-10 **9** 3 ¾ **Appyjack**[137] 406 3-9-3 **54**.....(t) LukeMorris 6 30
(Tony Carroll) *sn pushed and dropped to rr over 6f out: lost tch u.p 3f out: wl bhd fnl f* **7/1**[2]
060- **10** nk **All In A Paddy**[255] 6712 3-9-4 **55**..... FrannyNorton 5 31
(Ed McMahon) *in tch: rdn and struggling wl over 2f out: sn wknd: wl bhd and eased ins fnl f* **7/1**[2]
00-0 **11** 4 **Jody Bear**[33] 2192 3-9-1 **52**..... JackMitchell 2 18
(Jonathan Portman) *dwlt: sn rcvrd and in tch in midfield: drvn and nt qckn over 2f out: wl btn and eased over 1f out* **25/1**
00-0 **12** shd **Kalgoolie**[24] 2457 3-9-4 **55**..... MartinLane 9 21
(Rae Guest) *in tch on outer: lost pl over 3f out: towards rr whn rdn and hung rt wl over 2f out: wl btn fnl 2f: eased ins fnl f* **16/1**
000 **13** hd **Duchess Of Magenta (IRE)**[21] 2568 3-9-1 **52**.....(p) CathyGannon 11 18
(Eve Johnson Houghton) *a towards rr: rdn 4f out: struggling u.p wl over 2f out: bhd fnl 2f* **16/1**

1m 43.1s (3.30) **Going Correction** +0.225s/f (Slow) **13** Ran SP% **123.0**
Speed ratings (Par 97): **92,91,88,88,85 84,83,82,78,78 74,74,73**
toteswingers: 1&2 £38.40, 1&3 £78.40, 2&3 £5.60. CSF £190.51 CT £1435.30 TOTE £67.60: £17.60, £1.60, £3.50; EX 257.30 TRIFECTA Not won..
Owner Canisbay Bloodstock **Bred** Canisbay Bloodstock Ltd **Trained** Epsom, Surrey
FOCUS
A very moderate handicap and a result that would have left most punters reeling. Not form to dwell on, the weakness of the race demonstrated by the runner-up starting favourite.

Litotes Official explanation: trainer said regarding apparent improvement in form that the filly benefited from the application of cheekpieces.
Jody Bear Official explanation: trainer said filly did not face the kickback

3227 OLLY MURS 12.08.11 H'CAP (DIV II) 1m (P)
5:45 (5:45) (Class 6) (0-55,55) 3-Y-O **£1,619** (£481; £240; £120) **Stalls** Low

Form RPR

00-5 **1** **Hi Note**[84] 1018 3-8-9 **49**........ MartinHarley(3) 8 55
(Mick Channon) *sn pushed along and wl off pce in last trio: hdwy and rdn 3f out: chsd ldr jst over 1f out: kpt on dourly to ld wl ins fnl f* **16/1**

00-3 **2** ½ **Love Nest**[27] 2384 3-8-13 **50**........ ShaneKelly 3 55
(John Dunlop) *chsd ldr tl over 4f out: 3rd and rdn over 3f out: ev ch over 1f out: led 1f out: kpt on u.p tl hdd and no ex wl ins fnl f* **11/4**[1]

-000 **3** 1½ **Scarborough Lily**[30] 2307 3-9-0 **51**........(b[1]) NeilCallan 2 52
(Edward Vaughan) *chsd ldrs tl wnt 2nd over 4f out: clsd on ldr and hung rt jst over 2f out: led over 1f out tl 1f out: wknd fnl 100yds* **6/1**[3]

4450 **4** 4½ **Jackie Love (IRE)**[12] 2821 3-8-12 **52**........ AdamBeschizza(3) 9 43
(Olivia Maylam) *dwlt: bhd: hdwy and modest 7th over 2f out: plugged on to go 4th wl ins fnl f: nvr trbld ldrs* **20/1**

6-32 **5** *nk* **Border Abby**[8] 2964 3-9-0 **51**........ MartinLane 1 41
(Rae Guest) *dwlt: sn bustled along and racd off the pce in midfield: clsd on ldr and hung lft 2f out: no imp fr jst over 1f out* **7/2**[2]

0460 **6** 3¾ **Ereka (IRE)**[34] 2177 3-9-2 **53**........ StevieDonohoe 5 35
(Murty McGrath) *dwlt: sn niggled along and racd off the pce in midfield: rdn over 3f out: clsd on ldrs 2f out: no imp and btn 1f out* **25/1**

0060 **7** 9 **Microlight**[27] 2384 3-8-12 **52**........(b) NataliaGemelova(3) 4 13
(John E Long) *led and sn clr: rdn over 2f out: hung rt 2f out: sn hdd over 1f out: sn fdd* **40/1**

0-45 **8** 11 **Celestial Flyer (IRE)**[20] 2598 3-8-9 **46** oh1........ FergusSweeney 10 —
(Tor Sturgis) *stdd after s: a wl bhd: rdn and no real hdwy over 2f out: eased fnl f* **11/1**

4-03 **9** 15 **Crabbies Bay**[13] 2781 3-9-3 **54**........ GeorgeBaker 12 —
(Lisa Williamson) *racd off the pce in midfield: struggling 3f out: wl bhd and eased fr wl over 1f out: t.o* **12/1**

00-0 **10** 2 **Hopscotch**[27] 2392 3-9-4 **55**........ JamieSpencer 11 —
(Michael Bell) *a outpcd in rr: lost tch 3f out: eased fr wl over 1f out: t.o* **8/1**

5-40 **11** ½ **Sandtail (IRE)**[20] 2599 3-9-3 **54**........ MichaelHills 6 —
(J W Hills) *racd off the pce in midfield: rdn and struggling 1/2-way: lost tch over 3f out: eased fr wl over 1f out: t.o* **12/1**

60-0 **12** 8 **Black Iceman**[16] 2722 3-9-2 **53**........(v) MickyFenton 7 —
(Lydia Pearce) *chsd ldrs: rdn and struggling over 4f out: wl bhd and virtually p.u fr wl over 1f out: wl t.o* **33/1**

1m 43.12s (3.32) **Going Correction** +0.225s/f (Slow) **12** Ran SP% **117.9**
Speed ratings (Par 97): **92,91,90,85,85 81,72,61,46,44 43,35**
toteswingers: 1&2 £9.80, 1&3 £17.20, 2&3 £5.50. CSF £57.28 CT £309.84 TOTE £25.10: £4.70, £1.70, £3.30; EX 82.50 Trifecta £290.60 Part won. Pool: £392.75 - 0.40 winning units..
Owner Jon and Julia Aisbitt **Bred** J A And Mrs Duffy **Trained** West Ilsley, Berks

FOCUS
Only one of these had tasted success before. The early tempo was furious but the pace collapsed so much in the second-half of the contest that the winning time was marginally slower than the first division. Weak form although the first three were clear.
Hi Note Official explanation: trainer's rep said, regarding apparent improvement in form, that the filly benefited from a poor race.
Ereka(IRE) Official explanation: jockey said filly lost its action
Crabbies Bay Official explanation: jockey said filly had no more to give
Black Iceman Official explanation: jockey said gelding had no more to give
T/Plt: £48.60 to a £1 stake. Pool: £60,847.45. 913.25 winning tickets. T/Qpdt: £51.20 to a £1 stake. Pool £3,751.36. 54.14 winning tickets. SP

2997 WINDSOR (R H)
Monday, June 20

OFFICIAL GOING: Good to soft changing to good to soft (soft in places) after race 1 (6.40) changing to soft after race 3 (7.40)
Wind: Almost nil Weather: Steady rain first 3 races

3228 PERTEMPS FILLIES' H'CAP 1m 2f 7y
6:40 (6:42) (Class 5) (0-70,70) 3-Y-0+ **£2,266** (£674; £337; £168) **Stalls** High

Form RPR

1634 **1** **Zamina (IRE)**[11] 2838 3-8-13 **67**........ JamesDoyle 7 74
(Sylvester Kirk) *trckd ldrs: prog to ld against far rail wl over 1f out: hrd pressed fnl f: hld on wl* **17/2**

54-1 **2** *nk* **Lady Gabrielle (IRE)**[6] 3018 3-8-7 **66** 6ex........ HarryBentley(5) 4 72+
(David Elsworth) *trckd ldrs: shkn up over 2f out: nt qckn wl over 1f out: styd on to take 2nd ins fnl f: clsng at fin* **9/2**[2]

3-05 **3** ½ **On Khee**[21] 2552 4-10-0 **70**........ RichardHughes 3 75
(Hughie Morrison) *t.k.h: hld up in last trio: swtchd wd and prog wl over 1f out: wnt 2nd briefly ins fnl f: kpt on but nt qckn last 100yds* **4/1**[1]

03-2 **4** 1¼ **Duquesa (IRE)**[8] 2963 3-8-10 **64**........ CathyGannon 9 67
(David Evans) *wl in rr: rdn in last trio over 4f out: fnlly sed to make prog 2f out: styd on wl fnl f to take 4th last strides* **9/1**

3564 **5** *nse* **Peachez**[30] 2305 3-7-11 **56** ow1........(p) AmyScott(5) 10 59
(Alastair Lidderdale) *hld up in last trio: effrt 4f out: rdn and prog 3f out: kpt on fr over 1f out: nvr able to chal* **40/1**

4340 **6** *shd* **Leitzu (IRE)**[11] 2830 4-9-7 **63**........ HughBowman 12 66
(Mick Channon) *led 1f: stdd: chsd ldr 6f out: led over 2f out to wl over 1f out: wknd ins fnl f* **28/1**

1121 **7** ½ **Cane Cat (IRE)**[11] 2851 4-9-0 **56**........(t) LiamJones 5 58
(Tony Carroll) *hld up in rr: stdy prog fr 3f out: rdn to press ldrs over 1f out: wknd ins fnl f* **12/1**

405- **8** *shd* **Susan Stroman**[219] 7448 3-8-7 **61**........ NickyMackay 11 62
(Ed Dunlop) *hld up in midfield: prog 4f out: nt qckn 3f out: tried to cl again over 1f out: one pce* **6/1**[3]

5-43 **9** 4 **Lady Barastar (IRE)**[20] 2583 3-8-10 **64**........(p) KierenFallon 1 57
(Walter Swinburn) *pressed ldrs: rdn to chal over 2f out: wknd over 1f out: eased* **8/1**

-420 **10** 4½ **Elfine (IRE)**[32] 2232 3-9-2 **70**........ DaneO'Neill 6 54
(Harry Dunlop) *led after 1f to over 2f out: wknd wl over 1f out* **16/1**

6106 **11** 6 **Absolute Princess**[22] 2527 3-8-11 **68**........ BillyCray(3) 13 40
(David Nicholls) *a in last trio: u.p over 4f out: sn struggling* **40/1**

P535 **12** ½ **Beauchamp Xiara**[9] 2912 5-9-8 **64**........ JimmyFortune 8 35
(Hans Adielsson) *in tch: rdn on outer 3f out: wknd 2f out* **16/1**

333- **13** ½ **Phase Shift**[185] 7907 3-8-13 **67**........ LukeMorris 2 37
(William Muir) *chsd ldrs: rdn and lost pl 3f out: sn wknd* **25/1**

2m 11.95s (3.25) **Going Correction** +0.325s/f (Good)
WFA 3 from 4yo+ 12lb **13** Ran SP% **115.7**
Speed ratings (Par 100): **100,99,99,98,98 98,97,97,94,90 86,85,85**
toteswingers: 1&2 £18.00, 1&3 £6.90, 2&3 £3.90. CSF £43.45 CT £176.83 TOTE £11.10: £4.20, £2.10, £1.70; EX 76.40 Trifecta £944.40 Pool: £2,680.23 - 2.10 winning units..
Owner N Pickett & S Kirk **Bred** Churchtown Bloodstock **Trained** Upper Lambourn, Berks

FOCUS
The stands rail was dolled out 15yds at the 6f marker and 7yds at the winning post. The top bend was dolled out 7yds from its normal configuration adding 27yds to distances of 1m and above. Mainly dry on Sunday and Monday but, as forecast, the rain arrived on the run up to the first race. The riders reported the ground was "soft" and "definitely on the slow side" and the official going was changed to good to soft, soft in places after the opener. A modest fillies' handicap in which the gallop was an ordinary one and, as usual when the ground is on the easy side, the field headed for the far rail early in the straight. There was a bunch finish and the winner is rated up 3lb. The fifth limits the form.

3229 COOLMORE ALFRED NOBLE MAIDEN AUCTION STKS 6f
7:10 (7:11) (Class 5) 2-Y-O **£2,266** (£674; £337; £168) **Stalls** Low

Form RPR

0 **1** **Son Du Silence (IRE)**[7] 2997 2-8-9 0........ LiamKeniry 12 75
(J S Moore) *mde virtually all: drew clr 2f out against far rail: rdn over 1f out: styd on wl* **10/1**

2 1¾ **Halling Dancer** 2-8-10 0 ow1........ DarryllHolland 4 71+
(John Akehurst) *trckd ldrs: veered lft over 2f out: prog to chse wnr over 1f out: hanging lft but styd on: no imp* **25/1**

3 1¾ **Buster Brown (IRE)** 2-9-2 0........ JimmyFortune 14 72
(James Given) *in tch: in midfield: effrt over 2f out: shkn up and kpt on fr over 1f out: tk 3rd nr fin* **8/1**

4 **4** *nk* **Dixie's Dream (IRE)**[44] 1913 2-8-11 0........ RichardHughes 6 66
(Richard Hannon) *in tch: prog 2f out: rdn to dispute 3rd over 1f out: styd on same pce* **9/4**[1]

5 1 **Courtland Avenue (IRE)** 2-8-9 0........ KierenFallon 16 62
(Jonathan Portman) *dwlt: sn prom: pushed along to dispute 2nd briefly over 1f out: hld after: eased last 50yds* **16/1**

6 2½ **Glad Eye Gladys** 2-8-3 0........ BillyCray(3) 3 51
(David Nicholls) *s.s: m green in last pair and pushed along: taken to wd outside and prog 1/2-way: tried to cl on ldrs over 1f out: no ex* **25/1**

7 2 **The Wicked Lord** 2-8-9 0........ MartinLane 10 48
(Stuart Kittow) *towards rr: rdn 2f out and no prog: modest hdwy fnl f* **33/1**

04 **8** 1¾ **Percythepinto (IRE)**[19] 2602 2-8-11 0........ DaneO'Neill 9 44
(David Elsworth) *hld up in rr: pushed along in last trio 2f out: styd on ins fnl f* **6/1**[3]

9 *nse* **King Of Wing (IRE)** 2-8-11 0........ PatDobbs 8 44
(Richard Hannon) *dwlt: trckd ldrs: no imp 2f out: grad wknd* **11/2**[2]

10 1¼ **Four Richer** 2-8-13 0........ FergusSweeney 13 42
(Jamie Osborne) *in tch: dropped to rr over 2f out: pushed along and no real prog after* **20/1**

11 ¾ **King's Future** 2-8-11 0........ IanMongan 1 38
(John Akehurst) *pressed ldrs to 2f out: wknd* **40/1**

12 ½ **Kelpie Blitz (IRE)** 2-8-11 0........ MickyFenton 2 37
(Seamus Durack) *s.i.s: sn wl in tch: wknd wl over 1f out* **28/1**

0 **13** ½ **Laura's Bairn**[7] 2997 2-8-8 0........ KierenFox(3) 15 35
(J R Jenkins) *w wnr to 1/2-way: wknd rapidly and lost 2nd over 1f out* **50/1**

14 8 **Bengaline** 2-8-13 0........ PaulQuinn 7 13
(David Nicholls) *a in last trio: struggling fr 1/2-way: t.o* **20/1**

4 **15** 2¾ **Denton Dancer**[45] 1863 2-9-2 0........ LukeMorris 11 8
(James Eustace) *prom 1f: sn lost pl rapidly: t.o* **14/1**

1m 16.0s (3.00) **Going Correction** +0.325s/f (Good) **15** Ran SP% **121.2**
Speed ratings (Par 93): **93,90,88,87,86 83,80,78,78,76 75,74,74,63,59**
toteswingers: 1&2 £49.10, 1&3 £32.00, 2&3 £54.00. CSF £242.88 TOTE £15.10: £4.20, £6.30, £2.00; EX 325.30 Trifecta £1286.50 Part won. Pool: £1,738.60 - 0.40 winning units..
Owner Dennis Deegan & Partners Ltd B J Duggan, C Holt And D Thorpe **Trained** Upper Lambourn, Berks

FOCUS
This race has thrown up a few smart types in the past, but this race lacked much in the way of strength and the bare form of this uncompetitive event doesn't look anything out of the ordinary. The gallop was a fair one in the conditions and the field raced centre to far side.

NOTEBOOK
Son Du Silence(IRE) stepped up a good deal on the form shown over 5f here a week ago over this longer trip in softer ground. Although this didn't look a strong maiden, he could do no more than win with something in hand after travelling strongly and he may be capable of better in this sort of ground. (op 14-1)
Halling Dancer, from a yard not associated with debut juvenile winners, showed ability under a hands and heels ride despite his apparent greenness with his rider posting 1lb overweight. Everything about his pedigree suggests further will suit and he should be able to pick up a small event granted a suitable test in due course. (op 22-1)
Buster Brown(IRE) ◆ has plenty of middle-distance blood in his pedigree and, although his Derby entry looks optimistic, he shaped with promise over an inadequate trip on this racecourse debut. He wasn't knocked about, will be well suited by 7f and beyond, is open to improvement and appeals as the sort to win races. (tchd 13-2 and 17-2)
Dixie's Dream(IRE), from a yard that has won this race three times since 2002, attracted support and wasn't totally disgraced in terms of form, but he never really looked happy at any stage on this rain-soaked ground. He'll be suited by the return to a sound surface but will be of more interest in ordinary nurseries. (op 5-2 tchd 2-1)
Courtland Avenue(IRE), the first foal of a modest sprinter, showed ability at a low level after a tardy start on this debut. He's entitled to improve for this, but is likely to remain vulnerable in this type of event. (tchd 14-1)
Glad Eye Gladys, out of an unraced half-sister to several winners up to 1m2f, shaped on this debut run as though the step up to 7f would suit.
King Of Wing(IRE), an 8,000 euro first foal of a half-sister to a couple of winners up to 1m, attracted support, but had his limitations exposed in these testing conditions on this racecourse debut. He should improve for this experience. (op 5-1 tchd 6-1)

3230 LADBROKES H'CAP 6f
7:40 (7:41) (Class 6) (0-65,65) 3-Y-O **£1,619** (£481; £240; £120) **Stalls** Low

Form RPR

00-3 **1** **Pearl Blue (IRE)**[55] 1591 3-9-0 **58**........ JackMitchell 3 81
(Chris Wall) *gd spd fr wd draw and pressed ldr: led 1/2-way: drew clr over 2f out: shkn up over 1f out: unchal* **10/1**

0-02 **2** 5 **Golden Compass**[27] 2384 3-8-6 **50**........ SaleemGolam 7 57
(Giles Bravery) *prom: chal 1/2-way: chsd wnr after: sn wl outpcd: hld on for 2nd* **14/1**

3403 **3** ½ **Full Shilling (IRE)**[7] 2993 3-8-8 **52** LiamJones 12 57
(John Spearing) *v restless in stalls: settled in rr: rdn 1/2-way: hanging but prog on outer 2f out: styd on wl to take 3rd ins fnl f: nrly snatched 2nd* **8/1**

-331 **4** 1¾ **Liberal Lady**[138] 380 3-9-3 **61** RichardHughes 15 61
(Hughie Morrison) *chsd ldrs against far rail: outpcd over 2f out: kpt on to chse ldng pair over 1f out: no imp: lost 3rd ins fnl f* **9/2**[2]

2005 **5** 2¼ **Delira (IRE)**[21] 2553 3-9-3 **61** JimmyFortune 6 54
(Jonathan Portman) *chsd ldrs: outpcd fr over 2f out: one pce and n.d after* **33/1**

400 **6** 6 **Tortilla (IRE)**[22] 2529 3-9-3 **64** MartinHarley[(3)] 14 37
(Des Donovan) *in tch: hmpd and swtchd lft wl over 2f out: outpcd sn after: wknd over 1f out* **22/1**

0-06 **7** 1 **Putin (IRE)**[27] 2375 3-8-13 **57** DaneO'Neill 2 27
(Derek Haydn Jones) *chsd ldrs on wd outside: rdn and effrt 2f out: wknd over 1f out* **16/1**

0-60 **8** 2¼ **Sensational Love (IRE)**[30] 2294 3-9-7 **65** RobertHavlin 1 28
(Robert Mills) *restless stalls: hld up in rr: rdn and modest prog over 2f out: wknd sn after* **16/1**

-000 **9** 1 **Paperetto**[13] 2792 3-9-2 **63** (b[1]) SeanLevey[(3)] 10 23
(Robert Mills) *led to 1/2-way: sn lost pl: continued to weaken u.p* **7/1**

052 **10** 4 **Beechcraft Baron (IRE)**[18] 2650 3-9-7 **65** KierenFallon 4 —
(William Haggas) *s.i.s: sn chsd ldrs: wknd fr 2f out* **10/3**[1]

0032 **11** 2¼ **Mazovian (USA)**[9] 2916 3-9-6 **64** NeilCallan 5 —
(Michael Chapman) *in tch: rdn whn short of room wl over 2f out: sn wknd: no ch whn hmpd over 1f out: eased* **6/1**[3]

1500 **12** 1 **Winniepeg**[21] 2553 3-9-0 **58** (v[1]) LukeMorris 9 —
(Clive Cox) *rdn and struggling in rr bef 1/2-way: sn no ch* **50/1**

3-65 **13** 4½ **Kokojo (IRE)**[110] 729 3-9-3 **61** FergusSweeney 13 —
(Brendan Powell) *hld up in last: nvr remotely involved: eased over 1f out* **25/1**

1m 14.64s (1.64) **Going Correction** +0.325s/f (Good) **13** Ran SP% **119.8**
Speed ratings (Par 97): **102,95,94,92,89 81,80,77,75,70 67,66,60**
toteswingers: 1&2 £9.80, 1&3 £17.30, 2&3 £13.60. CSF £136.80 CT £1217.16 TOTE £15.70: £4.00, £5.50, £3.30; EX 121.00 Trifecta £1442.20 Part won. Pool: £1,442.20 - 0.30 winning units..
Owner Archangels 2 **Bred** L Queally **Trained** Newmarket, Suffolk
■ Stewards' Enquiry : Sean Levey two-day ban: careless riding (Jul 4-5)

FOCUS
A moderate handicap featuring several unexposed sorts. The gallop was a reasonable one but once again very few figured. This was over a second quicker than the previous race over this trip and the field again raced on the far side. It's hard to know how literally to take the form.

3231 JOHN SUNLEY MEMORIAL H'CAP 1m 67y
8:10 (8:11) (Class 4) (0-85,84) 3-Y-O **£4,079** (£1,214; £606; £151; £151) **Stalls** Low

Form RPR

-422 **1** **Whistle On By**[49] 1774 3-9-0 **77** MichaelHills 8 85
(B W Hills) *sn settled to trck ldng pair: wnt 2nd over 4f out: grabbed far rail over 2f out: led wl over 1f out: rdn and styd on wl* **10/1**

-516 **2** 1¼ **Ree's Rascal (IRE)**[32] 2229 3-9-0 **77** PatCosgrave 6 82
(Jim Boyle) *hld up in last pair: stdy prog over 2f out: rdn over 1f out: wnt 2nd and edgd lft jst ins fnl f: no imp on wnr nr fin* **9/2**[2]

0-53 **3** 1½ **Profondo Rosso (IRE)**[10] 2877 3-9-3 **80** (v) KierenFallon 2 82
(Sir Michael Stoute) *won battle for ld after 2f and stdd pce sn after: hrd pressed over 2f out: hanging and nt qckn whn hdd wl over 1f out: cl up but hld whn hmpd jst ins fnl f* **5/2**[1]

4005 **4** 5 **Orientalist**[19] 2607 3-9-4 **81** SebSanders 3 72
(Eve Johnson Houghton) *cl up: shkn up and outpcd fr 2f out: pushed along and no ch after* **10/1**

0566 **4** dht **Barista (IRE)**[9] 2908 3-9-0 **77** HughBowman 7 68
(Mick Channon) *hld up in last pair: shkn up and effrt 3f out: plugged on fnl f: nvr a threat* **11/1**

1651 **6** 7 **Malice Or Mischief (IRE)**[49] 1754 3-9-3 **80** NeilCallan 5 54
(Tony Carroll) *s.s: sn in tch: rdn 3f out: wknd 2f out* **14/1**

5-15 **7** ¾ **Laughing Jack**[44] 1895 3-9-7 **84** JimmyFortune 4 57
(Ed Dunlop) *narrow ld 2f: trckd ldr to over 4f out: rdn and wknd wl over 2f out* **11/2**[3]

-053 **8** 1¼ **Buxfizz (USA)**[19] 2607 3-8-13 **79** (p) SeanLevey[(3)] 1 49
(Robert Mills) *urged along s and reminder: chsd ldrs: u.str.p 1/2-way: wknd over 2f out* **9/2**[2]

1m 47.08s (2.38) **Going Correction** +0.325s/f (Good) **8** Ran SP% **113.5**
Speed ratings (Par 101): **101,99,98,93,93 86,85,84**
toteswingers: 1&2 £5.30, 1&3 £5.10, 2&3 £3.00. CSF £53.59 CT £148.83 TOTE £6.70: £1.20, £1.10, £1.20; EX 55.30 Trifecta £422.90 Part won. Pool: £571.59 - 0.94 winning units..
Owner James Netherthorpe & Richard Morecombe **Bred** Mrs C A Russell **Trained** Lambourn, Berks
■ Stewards' Enquiry : Pat Cosgrave three-day ban: careless riding (Jul 4-6)

FOCUS
The ground was changed to "soft" before this race. A useful handicap in which a decent gallop steadied before halfway before picking up again over a quarter of a mile from home. The field again raced far side and the first three pulled clear. The winner is rated up 8lb.
Buxfizz(USA) Official explanation: vet said gelding had been struck into

3232 FEE GROUP PLC MAIDEN STKS 1m 67y
8:40 (8:40) (Class 5) 3-Y-O **£2,266** (£674; £337; £168) **Stalls** Low

Form RPR

63- **1** **Shooting Line (IRE)**[250] 6844 3-9-3 0 KierenFallon 7 88+
(Walter Swinburn) *hld up: effrt whn n.m.r briefly 3f out: prog against rail over 2f out: rdn to ld jst over 1f out: sn clr* **11/2**

-523 **2** 4 **Puttingonthestyle (IRE)**[10] 2875 3-9-3 77 RichardHughes 5 80
(Richard Hannon) *led 100yds: trckd ldr: led wl over 2f out: sn pressed: edgd lft u.p over 1f out: sn hdd and nt qckn* **15/8**[1]

0 **3** 1¾ **West Brit (IRE)**[24] 2458 3-9-3 0 JimCrowley 3 75
(Ed Dunlop) *chsd ldrs: shkn up 3f out: in tch in 4th whn lft 3rd over 1f out: one pce* **28/1**

00 **4** 17 **Artisan**[16] 2723 3-9-3 0 StevieDonohoe 2 36+
(Willie Musson) *led after 100yds: clr after 2f: styd centre st: wknd and hdd wl over 2f out: no ch whn hmpd over 1f out* **33/1**

- **5** 26 **Rockerfellow** 3-9-3 0 SebSanders 4 —+
(J W Hills) *a wl in rr: wl bhd whn bdly hmpd over 1f out* **25/1**

00- **6** 15 **Misefi**[249] 6866 3-8-12 0 LiamKeniry 9 —
(Martin Bosley) *a in last pair: wl bhd whn bdly hmpd over 1f out* **66/1**

-4 **7** 17 **Ever The Optimist (IRE)**[166] 52 3-9-3 0 NeilCallan 10 —
(Stef Higgins) *t.k.h: chsd ldrs: wknd rapidly over 2f out: t.o* **8/1**

02- **U** **Numeral (IRE)**[394] 2319 3-9-3 0 JimmyFortune 8 62
(Richard Hannon) *hld up towards rr: pushed along and nt on terms over 2f out: keeping on in 5th but no ch whn bdly hmpd and uns rdr over 1f out* **4/1**[3]

6- **F** **Mrs Dee Bee (IRE)**[252] 6803 3-8-12 0 MichaelHills 1 73
(B W Hills) *prom: clsd to chal over 2f out: squeezed out over 1f out then hmpd and fell* **7/2**[2]

1m 47.16s (2.46) **Going Correction** +0.325s/f (Good) **9** Ran SP% **115.2**
Speed ratings (Par 99): **100,96,94,77,51 36,19,—,—**
toteswingers: 1&2 £2.90, 1&3 £17.50, 2&3 £10.70. CSF £15.76 TOTE £5.20: £2.20, £1.10, £9.40; EX 10.40 Trifecta £473.30 Part won. Pool: £639.69 - 0.62 winning units..
Owner P W Harris **Bred** Pendley Farm **Trained** Aldbury, Herts
■ Stewards' Enquiry : Richard Hughes seven-day ban: careless riding (Jul 5-9,11-12)

FOCUS
Not the most competitive of maidens but an eventful race in which two of the fancied runners came to grief with about a furlong and a half to run. The gallop was reasonable and the time suggests the ground was not that bad. The form is rated around the runner-up.

3233 STARLIGHT AND ST JOHN H'CAP 1m 3f 135y
9:10 (9:10) (Class 5) (0-75,75) 3-Y-O **£2,266** (£674; £337; £168) **Stalls** High

Form RPR

4135 **1** **Achalas (IRE)**[17] 2677 3-9-0 **68** KierenFallon 1 78
(Heather Main) *trckd ldng pair: led 3f out: sn jnd: rdn and forged clr fr over 1f out* **7/1**

16-3 **2** 2¼ **Devoted (IRE)**[62] 1456 3-9-5 **73** JimCrowley 7 78
(Ralph Beckett) *hld up in midfield: rdn and prog over 3f out: jnd wnr over 2f out against rail: nt qckn over 1f out: outpcd after* **11/4**[1]

2033 **3** ½ **Standout**[17] 2664 3-9-5 **73** (b[1]) RichardHughes 9 77
(Richard Hannon) *hld up last: prog over 2f out: shkn up and styd on to take 3rd fnl f: nvr nr to chal* **5/1**[2]

-433 **4** 2 **Experimentalist**[14] 2768 3-9-1 **69** JimmyFortune 4 70
(Hughie Morrison) *hld up in midfield: rdn and prog over 3f out: chsd ldng pair wl over 1f out: one pce after* **10/1**

1115 **5** 4½ **Dubai Glory**[11] 2842 3-9-7 **75** JamesDoyle 6 68
(Sheena West) *hld up in last trio: shkn up over 2f out: sme prog wl over 1f out: nvr nr ldrs* **5/1**[2]

2-40 **6** 3½ **Levantera (IRE)**[11] 2842 3-8-12 **69** JohnFahy[(3)] 3 56
(Clive Cox) *led to 1/2-way: led again over 4f out to 3f out: wknd 2f out* **7/1**

4-03 **7** 4½ **Spyder**[10] 2885 3-9-6 **74** (p) AndreaAtzeni 5 54
(Jane Chapple-Hyam) *t.k.h: pressed ldng pair: rdn and wknd over 2f out: eased* **6/1**[3]

000 **8** 2¾ **Vibration**[24] 2458 3-8-2 **56** oh3 NickyMackay 2 31
(Hughie Morrison) *w ldr: led 1/2-way to over 4f out: wknd over 2f out: eased* **33/1**

6150 **9** 2 **Runaway Tiger (IRE)**[11] 2858 3-8-3 **60** (b) KierenFox[(3)] 8 31
(Paul D'Arcy) *stdd s: hld up in last trio: wknd over 2f out* **28/1**

2m 36.43s (6.93) **Going Correction** +0.325s/f (Good) **9** Ran SP% **114.8**
Speed ratings (Par 99): **89,87,87,85,82 80,77,75,74**
toteswingers: 1&2 £6.30, 1&3 £3.10, 2&3 £2.60. CSF £26.41 CT £105.62 TOTE £5.80: £1.50, £2.60, £3.50; EX 38.30 Trifecta £416.60 Pool: £979.63 - 1.74 winning units..
Owner Mr & Mrs D R Guest **Bred** Stonethorn Stud Farms Ltd **Trained** Kingston Lisle, Oxon

FOCUS
No more than a fair handicap and one in which the gallop was just an ordinary one. As in the previous races, the field headed for the far side in the straight. The form makes enough sense at face value.
T/Jkpt: Not won. T/Plt: £339.10 to a £1 stake. Pool: £115,886.93. 249.44 winning tickets. T/Qpdt: £22.30 to a £1 stake. Pool: £8,173.96. 270.82 winning tickets. JN

2159 WOLVERHAMPTON (A.W) (L-H)
Monday, June 20

OFFICIAL GOING: Standard
Wind: Fresh, behind Weather: Fine

3234 32 FOR BETTING H'CAP (DIV I) 7f 32y(P)
2:00 (2:00) (Class 6) (0-60,60) 3-Y-O+ **£1,364** (£403; £201) **Stalls** High

Form RPR

2460 **1** **Meydan Style (USA)**[12] 2809 5-8-12 **46** JoeFanning 4 56
(Bruce Hellier) *a.p: chsd ldr 4f out: led wl over 1f out: rdn out* **16/1**

001- **2** 2¼ **Tell Halaf**[172] 8024 4-9-12 **60** AdamKirby 2 64
(Noel Quinlan) *hld up: hdwy 2f out: chsd wnr fnl f: sn hrd rdn: no imp* **6/4**[1]

3066 **3** 3½ **Itsthursdayalready**[4] 3093 4-9-12 **60** GrahamGibbons 3 54
(Mark Brisbourne) *a.p: rdn over 1f out: styd on same pce* **13/2**[3]

0244 **4** 2¾ **Gemma's Delight (IRE)**[17] 2671 4-9-9 **57** (p) HayleyTurner 10 44
(James Unett) *w ldr tl led over 5f out: rdn and hdd wl over 1f out: wknd ins fnl f* **13/2**[3]

-403 **5** nk **Ghost Dancer**[9] 2921 7-9-1 **49** (p) RichardKingscote 11 35
(Milton Bradley) *s.i.s: hld up: hdwy over 1f out: sn rdn: no imp fnl f* **7/1**

2020 **6** 3¾ **Sweet Possession (USA)**[12] 2829 5-9-6 **57** (p) JamesSullivan[(3)] 7 33
(Pat Eddery) *hld up: hdwy u.p over 2f out: wknd over 1f out* **5/1**[2]

4600 **7** 6 **Bold Bomber**[21] 2547 5-8-12 **46** oh1 PhillipMakin 5 —
(Paul Green) *chsd ldrs: rdn over 2f out: wknd over 1f out* **22/1**

051/ **8** 2¾ **Diamond Fire (IRE)**[24] 2483 7-8-12 **46** oh1 (bt) LiamKeniry 8 —
(Adrian McGuinness, Ire) *hld up: hdwy over 2f out: rdn and wknd over 1f out* **25/1**

0-60 **9** 6 **Macie (IRE)**[91] 934 4-8-13 **47** PaulHanagan 9 —
(Derek Shaw) *hld up: a in rr: rdn and wknd wl over 1f out* **33/1**

350 **P** **Mutamaleq (IRE)**[10] 2487 4-9-9 **60** (p) GaryBartley[(3)] 1 —
(Ian McInnes) *led: hdd over 4f out: rdn and wknd over 2f out: p.u ins fnl f: lame* **12/1**

1m 29.99s (0.39) **Going Correction** +0.10s/f (Slow) **10** Ran SP% **120.5**
Speed ratings (Par 101): **101,98,94,91,90 86,79,76,69,—**
toteswingers: 1&2 £9.10, 1&3 £13.10, 2&3 £3.70. CSF £41.09 CT £186.36 TOTE £21.20: £3.50, £1.10, £2.60; EX 77.00.
Owner The Style Council **Bred** William F Murphy & Annabel Murphy **Trained** Garstang, Lancs
■ Bruce Hellier's first winner since coming out of retirement.

FOCUS
A low-grade opener and a surprise winner, who improved in line with his C&D March form. The time was a bit quicker than division II.

3235 32 ONLINE CASINO H'CAP 1m 141y(P)
2:30 (2:31) (Class 6) (0-65,65) 3-Y-0+ **£1,706** (£503; £252) **Stalls** Low

Form RPR

3124 **1** **Goal (IRE)**[8] 2964 3-9-1 **63**.............................. SebSanders 10 72
(Richard Guest) *a.p: chsd ldr 1/2-way: rdn to ld wl over 1f out: styd on u.p* **11/2**[2]

3465 **2** *3/4* **Kyle Of Bute**[21] 2567 5-9-8 **59**.............................. J-PGuillambert 3 67
(Brian Baugh) *hld up: hdwy over 2f out: chsd wnr over 1f out: sn rdn and ev ch: unable qck wl ins fnl f* **5/1**[1]

3020 **3** *1 1/2* **Serious Drinking (USA)**[49] 1756 5-9-12 **63**....................(t) AdamKirby 6 68
(Walter Swinburn) *hld up: hdwy u.p over 1f out: r.o: wnt 3rd nr fin: nt rch ldrs* **7/1**[3]

4230 **4** *1/2* **Florio Vincitore (IRE)**[5] 3042 4-9-7 **65**............(v[1]) JenniferFerguson(7) 7 68
(Edward Creighton) *dwlt: hld up: hdwy over 1f out: r.o: nrst fin* **10/1**

0000 **5** *hd* **Justcallmehandsome**[35] 2165 9-9-0 **58**....................(v) LucyKBarry(7) 9 61
(Dominic Ffrench Davis) *hld up: hdwy over 1f out: edgd lft ins fnl f: styd on same pce* **14/1**

0421 **6** *3* **Kipchak (IRE)**[9] 2922 6-10-0 **65**..............................(b) HayleyTurner 12 61
(Conor Dore) *led: clr 6f out: rdn and hdd wl over 1f out: wknd ins fnl f* **7/1**[3]

-040 **7** *3 1/4* **Sumbe (USA)**[37] 2111 5-10-0 **65**.............................. AndreaAtzeni 2 54
(Michael Wigham) *prom: rdn over 3f out: wknd fnl f* **5/1**[1]

3300 **8** *1 1/4* **I'Lldoit**[32] 2237 4-8-12 **56**.............................. DavidKenny(7) 8 42
(Michael Scudamore) *s.s: outpcd: nvr nrr* **40/1**

6000 **9** *3/4* **Guildenstern (IRE)**[9] 2922 9-8-5 **49**.............................. KatiaScallan(7) 11 33
(Alastair Lidderdale) *hld up: nvr on terms* **33/1**

00-0 **10** *1/2* **Peter Tchaikovsky**[12] 2809 5-9-4 **55**.............................. PatrickMathers 13 38
(Ian McInnes) *s.s: hmpd over 3f out: a in rr* **66/1**

4140 **11** *1* **Pilgrim Dancer (IRE)**[126] 544 4-9-8 **59**....................(v) StephenCraine 4 40
(Patrick Morris) *hld up in tch: rdn over 2f out: wknd over 1f out* **16/1**

1435 **12** *1/2* **Duneen Dream (USA)**[9] 2905 6-9-7 **58**.............................. RobertWinston 5 37
(Nikki Evans) *chsd ldr to 1/2-way: wknd over 1f out* **7/1**[3]

-145 **13** *2 1/2* **Red Zeus (IRE)**[13] 2789 3-9-0 **62**..............................(p) LiamKeniry 1 35
(J S Moore) *chsd ldrs: rdn 1/2-way: wknd over 3f out* **12/1**

1m 51.43s (0.93) **Going Correction** +0.10s/f (Slow) **13** Ran SP% **122.4**
WFA 3 from 4yo+ 11lb
Speed ratings (Par 101): **99,98,97,96,96 93,90,89,89,88 87,87,85**
toteswingers: 1&2 £7.30, 1&3 £5.10, 2&3 £4.40. CSF £33.71 CT £207.22 TOTE £5.00: £2.10, £1.80, £3.00; EX 47.40.
Owner Willie McKay **Bred** A M F Persse **Trained** Stainforth, S Yorks

FOCUS
No hanging about in this low-grade handicap. The second and third set a sound standard.
Duneen Dream(USA) Official explanation: jockey said gelding hung right-handed

3236 32 FOR SLOTS MEDIAN AUCTION MAIDEN STKS 1m 141y(P)
3:00 (3:00) (Class 6) 3-Y-O **£1,706** (£503; £252) **Stalls** Low

Form RPR

1 **Rawaki (IRE)** 3-9-3 0.............................. LiamKeniry 5 84
(Andrew Balding) *chsd ldrs: pushed along over 3f out: rdn to ld wl ins fnl f: r.o* **16/1**

0-4 **2** *3/4* **Starbound (IRE)**[34] 2174 3-8-12 0.............................. PaulHanagan 6 77
(William Haggas) *led 7f out: rdn and hung rt over 1f out: edgd lft and hdd wl ins fnl f* **11/2**[3]

3-52 **3** *1 1/2* **Trumpington Street (IRE)**[16] 2723 3-9-3 79.................. RobertHavlin 3 79
(John Gosden) *hmpd s: sn led: hdd 7f out: remained handy: chsd ldr over 2f out: rdn and nt clr run over 1f out: ev ch ins fnl f: styd on same pce* **4/7**[1]

20 **4** *3 1/2* **Inklet**[35] 2157 3-8-12 0.............................. AdamKirby 8 66
(Marco Botti) *hdwy over 6f out: rdn over 2f out: no ex fnl f* **3/1**[2]

0 **5** *7* **Budley**[13] 2790 3-9-3 0.............................. JoeFanning 2 55
(Bill Turner) *s.i.s and hmpd s: hld: sme hdwy over 1f out: nvr on terms* **14/1**

0 **6** *5* **Tigerbill**[35] 2151 3-9-3 0.............................. GrahamGibbons 7 43
(Nicky Vaughan) *chsd ldr over 6f out tl rdn over 2f out: wknd over 1f out* **50/1**

0 **7** *15* **Voodoo Queen**[41] 1984 3-8-12 0..............................[1] AndreaAtzeni 4 —
(Marco Botti) *s.s: a in rr: rdn and wknd over 2f out* **20/1**

26 **8** *3* **Silk Lingerie**[89] 945 3-8-12 0.............................. JimmyQuinn 1 —
(Mandy Rowland) *edgd rt s: hld up: a in rr: rdn and wknd over 2f out* **40/1**

1m 51.29s (0.79) **Going Correction** +0.10s/f (Slow) **8** Ran SP% **125.7**
Speed ratings (Par 97): **100,99,98,94,88 84,70,68**
toteswingers: 1&2 £11.00, 1&3 £5.20, 2&3 £1.70. CSF £107.74 TOTE £24.10: £8.40, £1.40, £1.02; EX 83.10.
Owner Kingsclere Racing CLub **Bred** Kingsclere Stud **Trained** Kingsclere, Hants

FOCUS
A modest maiden and the pace slackened right off down the back stretch. The beaten favoutite probably ran close to form and the winner made a nice start.
Silk Lingerie Official explanation: jockey said filly hung right leaving stalls

3237 BRITISH STALLION STUDS SUPPORTING BRITISH RACING E B F MAIDEN STKS 5f 216y(P)
3:30 (3:38) (Class 5) 2-Y-O **£3,238** (£963; £481; £240) **Stalls** Low

Form RPR

4 **1** **Shamaal Nibras (USA)**[17] 2687 2-9-3 0.............................. PaulHanagan 11 84+
(Ed Dunlop) *a.p: rdn over 2f out: led 1f out: styd on wl* **4/7**[1]

0 **2** *4* **Flavius Victor (IRE)**[20] 2584 2-9-3 0.............................. HayleyTurner 8 72
(Richard Hannon) *chsd ldrs: rdn over 2f out: styd on same pce fnl f* **14/1**

2032 **3** *1* **Beau Mistral (IRE)**[19] 2612 2-8-12 0.............................. PhillipMakin 12 64
(Paul Green) *sn led: rdn and hdd 1f out: no ex* **15/2**[2]

4 *3 1/4* **Gooseberry Fool** 2-8-12 0.............................. SebSanders 9 54
(Sir Mark Prescott Bt) *prom: chsd ldr 4f out: rdn over 1f out: sn wknd* **8/1**[3]

5 **5** *6* **Look Here's Lady**[17] 2665 2-8-12 0.............................. GrahamGibbons 5 36
(Ed McMahon) *prom: rdn over 2f out: wknd over 1f out* **25/1**

50 **6** *3/4* **Tangtastic (IRE)**[16] 2718 2-8-12 0.............................. EddieCreighton 3 34
(Edward Creighton) *mid-div: sn drvn along: nvr on terms* **100/1**

7 *2* **Monty Fay (IRE)** 2-9-3 0.............................. AdamKirby 1 33
(Derek Haydn Jones) *sn outpcd* **40/1**

0 **8** *5* **Laurel Lad (IRE)**[17] 2687 2-9-3 0.............................. RobertWinston 6 21
(B W Hills) *s.i.s: hdwy into mid-div whn carried wd by loose horse over 3f out: n.d after* **20/1**

5 **9** *3/4* **La Taniere**[10] 2886 2-8-10 0.............................. DavidSimmonson(7) 2 16
(Michael Easterby) *s.i.s: sn outpcd* **12/1**

0 **10** *nk* **Low Pastures**[6] 3021 2-9-0 0.............................. JamesSullivan(3) 4 15
(Michael Easterby) *s.i.s: sn outpcd* **80/1**

0 **U** **Berlusca (IRE)**[11] 2844 2-9-3 0.............................. JoeFanning 10 —
(William Jarvis) *sddle slipped and uns rdr sn after s* **22/1**

1m 15.84s (0.84) **Going Correction** +0.10s/f (Slow) **11** Ran SP% **118.5**
Speed ratings (Par 93): **98,92,91,87,79 78,75,68,67,67** —
toteswingers: 1&2 £4.70, 1&3 £2.30, 2&3 £8.20. CSF £9.21 TOTE £1.70: £1.10, £2.40, £1.70; EX 12.70.
Owner Tariq S Al Tayer **Bred** Andrew Cowen & Gary Tolchin **Trained** Newmarket, Suffolk

FOCUS
Drama before and during this juvenile maiden which had plenty of deadwood. 100/1 shot Dream Walker was withdrawn after rider Gary Bartley was unseated and injured. The third is a reasonable guide to the form.

NOTEBOOK
Shamaal Nibras(USA), a 45,000gns yearling purchase, had shown his inexperience when only fourth when sent off favourite first time at Goodwood. He still has something to learn but overcame his outside draw to score in most decisive fashion in the end. He will be suited by a step up to seven and will improve again. (op 10-11)
Flavius Victor(IRE) a leggy type, cost 55,000euros. Very green on his debut, he shaped a lot better here. He will improve again and looks sure to go one better. (op 12-1 tchd 16-1)
Beau Mistral(IRE), placed three times from five starts on turf, had the worst of the draw. She took them along but is looking fully exposed now. (op 11-2)
Gooseberry Fool, out of a mare that has already produced seven winners including the French 2,000 Guineas winner Aussie Rules, isn't very big but showed ability and was certainly not knocked about on her debut. (op 11-2 tchd 5-1)
Look Here's Lady, another who's not very big, improved on her debut effort at Catterick and looks potential nursery material after one more outing. (op 20-1)
Tangtastic(IRE) Official explanation: jockey said filly was hampered by loose horse
Laurel Lad(IRE) Official explanation: jockey said colt was hampered by loose horse
La Taniere Official explanation: jockey said gelding was slowly away and resented the kickback

3238 32 FOR BLACKJACK CLAIMING STKS 5f 216y(P)
4:00 (4:06) (Class 5) 3-Y-O **£2,266** (£674; £337; £168) **Stalls** Low

Form RPR

1550 **1** **Shostakovich (IRE)**[3] 3122 3-9-1 77..............................(p) LiamKeniry 4 73
(Sylvester Kirk) *chsd ldr: rdn over 2f out: led ins fnl f: drvn out* **10/3**[2]

4-33 **2** *nk* **Bilko Pak (IRE)**[9] 2910 3-8-11 76.............................. PhillipMakin 6 69+
(Ann Duffield) *s.i.s: hld up: hdwy over 2f out: rdn and j. what looked like a tyre mark ins fnl f: r.o u.p* **4/6**[1]

-230 **3** *nk* **Lady Platinum Club**[61] 1494 3-8-6 62..............................(p) PaulHanagan 1 62
(Geoffrey Oldroyd) *sn led: rdn and hdd ins fnl f: r.o* **8/1**[3]

2240 **4** *4* **Kassaab**[49] 1776 3-8-2 61..............................(b) RaulDaSilva(7) 5 52
(Jeremy Gask) *chsd ldrs: rdn and ev ch over 2f out: no ex fnl f* **25/1**

-500 **5** *nk* **Justbookie Dot Com (IRE)**[9] 2926 3-9-1 66.................. SebSanders 2 57
(Louise Best) *prom: rdn over 2f out: styd on same pce appr fnl f* **14/1**

4644 **6** *4* **Fifth In Line (IRE)**[34] 2177 3-8-4 60.............................. JimmyQuinn 3 33
(David Flood) *prom: rdn over 2f out: wknd over 1f out* **28/1**

1m 15.88s (0.88) **Going Correction** +0.10s/f (Slow) **6** Ran SP% **108.1**
Speed ratings (Par 99): **98,97,97,91,91 86**
toteswingers: 1&2 £1.60, 1&3 £2.00, 2&3 £2.00. CSF £5.46 TOTE £4.50: £1.80, £1.50; EX 6.20.Bilko Pak was subject to a friendly claim.
Owner F J Stephens **Bred** Marchwood Aggregates **Trained** Upper Lambourn, Berks
■ Stewards' Enquiry : Liam Keniry one-day ban: used whip in incorrect place (Jul 4)

FOCUS
The first three are rated to their pre-race marks at face value, but the time was slow.

3239 32 FOR POKER H'CAP 5f 20y(P)
4:30 (4:30) (Class 5) (0-75,73) 3-Y-O **£2,266** (£674; £337; £168) **Stalls** Low

Form RPR

1451 **1** **Royal Bajan (USA)**[22] 2524 3-8-11 **63**.............................. PaulHanagan 7 73+
(James Given) *chsd ldrs: rdn over 1f out: r.o to ld wl ins fnl f* **2/1**[1]

2-32 **2** *1* **Volcanic Dust (IRE)**[17] 2660 3-9-4 **70**.............................. RichardKingscote 2 76
(Milton Bradley) *w ldr tl led 4f out: rdn over 1f out: hdd and unable qck wl ins fnl f* **13/2**

300 **3** *2* **Cruise Tothelimit (IRE)**[2] 3166 3-9-4 **73**.............................. JamesSullivan(3) 4 72
(Patrick Morris) *w ldr: rdn and ev ch over 1f out: styd on same pce ins fnl f* **5/1**[0]

1 **4** *1* **Twice Red**[97] 855 3-9-6 **72**.............................. RobertWinston 1 67
(Derek Shaw) *s.i.s: outpcd: r.o ins fnl f: nrst fin* **2/1**[1]

3025 **5** *1/2* **Take Root**[3] 3126 3-9-4 **70**.............................. StephenCraine 5 63
(Reg Hollinshead) *prom: rdn over 1f out: no ex ins fnl f* **14/1**

U005 **6** *3* **Overwhelm**[12] 2818 3-9-3 **69**..............................(b[1]) J-PGuillambert 3 52
(Andrew Reid) *led 1f: chsd ldrs: rdn over 1f out: wknd ins fnl f* **6/1**[3]

62.78 secs (0.48) **Going Correction** +0.10s/f (Slow) **6** Ran SP% **117.6**
Speed ratings (Par 99): **100,98,95,93,92 88**
toteswingers: 1&2 £2.00, 1&3 £2.50, 2&3 £5.00. CSF £16.94 TOTE £2.30: £1.50, £4.40; EX 10.00.
Owner Danethorpe Racing Partnership **Bred** West Wind Farm **Trained** Willoughton, Lincs

FOCUS
A tight 3-y-o sprint handicap. Weakish form but the winner is progressing now.

3240 32 FOR BINGO AMATEUR RIDERS' (S) STKS 1m 4f 50y(P)
5:00 (5:00) (Class 6) 4-Y-O+ **£1,648** (£507; £253) **Stalls** Low

Form RPR

0155 **1** **Visions Of Johanna (USA)**[8] 2952 6-11-3 64.....(p) MissSBrotherton 11 69+
(Richard Guest) *hld up: hdwy over 6f out: chsd ldr over 3f out: led over 1f out: sn clr: styd on* **9/4**[2]

0401 **2** *2 1/4* **Mustajed**[11] 2843 10-10-12 64..............................(b) MrPMillman(5) 5 66
(Rod Millman) *s.s: hld up: hdwy over 2f out: r.o: wnt 2nd post: nt rch wnr* **8/1**[3]

4564 **3** *shd* **Dream Of Fortune (IRE)**[14] 2768 7-10-12 60..............(bt) MrsEEvans 2 60
(David Evans) *hld up: hdwy over 2f out: chsd wnr fnl f: styd on: lost 2nd post* **14/1**

3505 **4** *4* **Duar Mapel (USA)**[18] 2400 5-10-9 50..............................(v) MrCMartin(3) 10 54
(Brian Baugh) *chsd ldrs: rdn over 3f out: styd on same pce fnl 2f* **28/1**

56-6 **5** *hd* **Harare**[7] 2991 10-10-5 55..............................(v) MissGTutty(7) 8 54
(Karen Tutty) *hld up: hmpd 10f out: r.o ins fnl f: nrst fin* **14/1**

241- **6** *1/2* **Country Road (IRE)**[217] 7463 5-10-9 78..............(be) MrMJJSmith(3) 9 53+
(Tony Carroll) *hld up in tch: plld hrd: led over 5f out: rdn and hdd over 1f out: wknd fnl f* **13/8**[1]

200/ **7** *8* **Just Mossie**[399] 1496 6-10-5 50..............................(p) RyanWhile(7) 6 40
(Bill Turner) *led after 1f: hdd 7f out: sn rdn: wknd over 3f out* **50/1**

4036 **8** *11* **Christmas Coming**[9] 2900 4-10-9 52..............................(t) MissLAllan(3) 3 22
(Tony Carroll) *hld up: hmpd over 8f out: wknd over 3f out* **33/1**

0/0- **9** *13* **Vitruvian Man**[35] 6343 5-10-9 80....................(tp) MissHannahWatson(3) 7 —
(Sophie Leech) *chsd ldrs 7f: t.o* **8/1**[3]

015 **10** *25* **Golan Heights (IRE)**[8] 2975 5-10-7 53..................(b) ThomasGarner(5) 4 —
(Adrian McGuinness, Ire) *led 1f: chsd ldrs: led again 7f out: hdd over 5f out: wknd over 3f out: t.o* **33/1**

2m 45.33s (4.23) **Going Correction** +0.10s/f (Slow) **10** Ran SP% **115.7**
Speed ratings (Par 101): **89,87,87,84,84 84,78,71,62,46**
toteswingers: 1&2 £3.80, 1&3 £7.80, 2&3 £8.70. CSF £19.76 TOTE £3.30: £1.70, £2.10, £2.60; EX 17.10.There was no bid for the winner.
Owner David Kilpatrick **Bred** David S Milch **Trained** Stainforth, S Yorks
■ Stewards' Enquiry : Mrs E Evans ten-day ban: failed to ride out for 2nd (Jul 7,8,23,24,26,29-Aug 1)

FOCUS
An amateur riders' selling race run at a strong pace, with just two being in serious contention in the final 4f. The winner is rated to his winter C&D form.

3241 32 FOR BETTING H'CAP (DIV II) 7f 32y(P)
5:30 (5:30) (Class 6) (0-60,60) 3-Y-0+ **£1,364** (£403; £201) **Stalls** High

Form RPR
4623 **1** **This Ones For Eddy**[17] 2670 6-9-8 **56**........................ GrahamGibbons 9 64
(John Balding) *hld up: hdwy u.p over 2f out: rdn to ld ins fnl f: r.o* **7/2**[1]

6405 **2** *½* **Army Of Stars (IRE)**[19] 2605 5-9-12 **60**.........................(bt) PaulHanagan 3 67
(Michael Blake) *chsd ldrs: rdn over 2f out: led briefly ins fnl f: styd on same pce* **9/2**[2]

0340 **3** *¾* **Set To Go**[9] 2921 4-8-9 **46**...(b) RossAtkinson(3) 7 51
(Tor Sturgis) *led 6f out: rdn over 2f out: hdd and edgd lft ins fnl f: styd on same pce* **9/1**

0200 **4** *¾* **Lily Wood**[35] 2161 5-9-3 **51**.. HayleyTurner 2 54
(James Unett) *chsd ldrs: rdn over 1f out: hmpd ins fnl f: styd on same pce* **17/2**

5310 **5** *2 ½* **Bold Diva**[47] 1814 6-9-6 **57**..................................(v) MichaelO'Connell(3) 10 53
(Tony Carroll) *hld up: hdwy over 2f out: rdn and hung lft over 1f out: styd on same pce* **6/1**[3]

1254 **6** *2 ¼* **Piccolo Express**[91] 933 5-9-10 **58**............................ J-PGuillambert 8 48
(Brian Baugh) *hld up: pushed along 1/2-way: hdwy over 1f out: no ex ins fnl f* **7/2**[1]

6-00 **7** *¾* **Best Known Secret (IRE)**[115] 690 5-8-9 **46** oh1...... SimonPearce(3) 4 34
(Chris Bealby) *mid-div: drvn along over 4f out: wknd fnl f* **20/1**

-000 **8** *8* **Millden**[9] 2921 4-9-1 **49**..(bt) RichardKingscote 1 15
(Milton Bradley) *led 1f: chsd ldrs: rdn over 2f out: sn wknd* **33/1**

-000 **9** *4 ½* **Bishopbriggs (USA)**[40] 1995 6-9-12 **60**.......................... AdamKirby 5 14
(K F Clutterbuck) *prom: rdn 1/2-way: wknd over 2f out* **10/1**

0-00 **10** *2 ½* **Chateau Zara**[94] 893 4-8-9 **46** oh1............................ JamesSullivan(3) 6 —
(Derek Shaw) *hld up: hdwy 5f out: rdn and wknd over 2f out* **18/1**

1m 30.27s (0.67) **Going Correction** +0.10s/f (Slow) **10** Ran SP% **119.5**
Speed ratings (Par 101): **100,99,98,97,94 92,91,82,77,74**
toteswingers: 1&2 £3.30, 1&3 £7.90, 2&3 £9.70. CSF £19.66 CT £135.76 TOTE £4.50: £1.50, £2.20, £2.20; EX 20.80.
Owner Billy Herring **Bred** Broughton Bloodstock **Trained** Scrooby, Notts

FOCUS
A modest handicap, run at a strong pace but a bit slower than division I. The winner's best run since late 2009.
Bishopbriggs(USA) Official explanation: jockey said gelding hung right and had no more to give
Chateau Zara Official explanation: jockey said filly hung right-handed
T/Plt: £17.30 to a £1 stake. Pool: £58,492.69. 2,457.58 winning tickets. T/Qpdt: £2.90 to a £1 stake. Pool: £5,340.50. 1,350.76 winning tickets. CR

3070 BEVERLEY (R-H)
Tuesday, June 21

OFFICIAL GOING: Good (8.2)
Wind: Light half against Weather: Showers

3242 RACING AGAIN ON FRIDAY 1 JULY MAIDEN AUCTION STKS 7f 100y
2:15 (2:15) (Class 6) 2-Y-0 **£1,619** (£481; £240; £120) **Stalls** Low

Form RPR
1 **Broxbourne (IRE)** 2-8-6 0.. SilvestreDeSousa 5 68+
(Mark Johnston) *trckd ldr: hdwy and cl up 3f out: chal 2f out: rdn over 1f out: slt advantage ent fnl f: sn edgd rt: kpt on wl towards fin* **3/1**[3]

52 **2** *½* **Sheila's Buddy**[7] 3016 2-8-9 0.. LiamKeniry 6 70
(J S Moore) *led: jnd 3f out: rdn 2f out: drvn and hdd ent fnl f: no ex towards fin* **2/1**[2]

6 **3** *6* **Godber (IRE)**[12] 2854 2-8-11 0.................................. SamHitchcott 1 58
(Mick Channon) *trckd ldrs: effrt and green 2f out: sn rdn: kpt on same pce appr fnl f* **40/1**

4 *¾* **Pearl Catcher (IRE)** 2-8-9 0.. DavidAllan 3 54
(Tim Easterby) *s.i.s: green and pushed along in rr: hdwy 3f out: swtchd lft and rdn to chse ldng pair over 2f out: wknd over 1f out* **14/1**

422 **5** *5* **Auntie Joy**[8] 2983 2-8-1 0.. JamesSullivan(3) 4 37
(Michael Easterby) *trckd ldrs: hdwy on outer 3f out: effrt over 2f out: sn rdn: hung rt and wknd wl over 1f out* **6/4**[1]

1m 34.4s (0.60) **Going Correction** -0.15s/f (Firm) **5** Ran SP% **107.4**
Speed ratings (Par 91): **90,89,82,81,76**
CSF £8.92 TOTE £2.90: £2.00, £1.80; EX 9.60.
Owner Racegoers Club Owners Group **Bred** Mount Coote Stud And M Johnston **Trained** Middleham Moor, N Yorks

FOCUS
A modest maiden auction and not a test of stamina at the trip with the pace only steady until a sprint for home began. The winner seems sure to build on this.

NOTEBOOK
Broxbourne(IRE), who's a close relative of the useful 1m winner Colorado Rapid, made a promising debut for all she didn't beat much, looking green as she took some time to get organised but always having things under control and value for more than the winning margin. Her dam won at 1m4f and she seems sure to improve granted a stiffer test of stamina. (op 5-2 tchd 2-1)
Sheila's Buddy set the standard and probably ran as well here as he had at Brighton last time, keeping on strongly in the manner of one whose stamina hadn't been tested enough. He may have a bit more to offer once nurseries begin. (op 9-4 tchd 5-2)
Godber(IRE)'s proximity doesn't do much for the form considering he was well held in a seller on his debut, but he's been gelded since and looked much more at home over this longer trip, for all he that he looked far from straightforward under pressure, probably explaining why he's been cut already. (op 33-1)
Pearl Catcher(IRE), a cheaply-bought son of Catcher In The Rye, briefly made a threatening move early in the straight but was always on the back foot trying to catch rivals who'd got first run on him. He's entitled to do better. (op 12-1)
Auntie Joy had looked last time as though this sort of trip might suit but she was too keen under restraint and didn't get home. Official explanation: trainer had no explanation for the poor form shown (op 13-8 tchd 7-4)

3243 ST JOHN AMBULANCE CLAIMING STKS 1m 4f 16y
2:45 (2:45) (Class 6) 3-Y-0+ **£1,619** (£481; £240; £120) **Stalls** Low

Form RPR
5014 **1** **Porgy**[13] 2812 6-9-13 87.. PhillipMakin 3 86+
(David Simcock) *hld up in midfield: smooth hdwy 3f out: trckd ldrs on bridle 2f out: led over 1f out: sn pushed clr* **2/1**[2]

0201 **2** *5* **White Deer (USA)**[18] 2666 7-9-5 64........................(p) SilvestreDeSousa 6 68
(Geoffrey Harker) *hld up in rr: hdwy over 3f out: chsd ldrs whn n.m.r and swtchd ins wl over 1f out: drvn and kpt on to take 2nd ins fnl f: no ch w wnr* **12/1**

6-15 **3** *1* **Hel's Angel (IRE)**[32] 2251 5-8-12 73.................................. DaleSwift(5) 8 64
(Ann Duffield) *trckd ldr: led 1/2-way: rdn along wl over 2f out: drvn and hdd over 1f out: kpt on same pce* **9/2**[3]

0-00 **4** *3 ½* **Palomar (USA)**[7] 3013 9-9-9 89.. StephenCraine 2 65
(Brian Ellison) *trckd ldrs: effrt 3f out: rdn over 2f out: drvn wl over 1f out and sn one pce* **11/8**[1]

00-0 **5** *1* **Jenny Soba**[44] 1107 8-8-10 47..(p) SeanLevey(3) 1 53
(Lucinda Featherstone) *in tch: effrt and rdn along 3f out: sn no imp* **66/1**

5-00 **6** *1 ¾* **Miss Wendy**[87] 796 4-8-9 53.. AshleyMorgan(5) 10 51
(Mark H Tompkins) *led to 1/2-way: cl up: rdn along over 2f out: sn edgd lft and wknd* **50/1**

3500 **7** *3 ¼* **Kames Park (IRE)**[7] 3023 9-9-1 65.................................. RobertLButler(3) 5 50
(Richard Guest) *hld up in rr: effrt and sme hdwy on outer over 2f out: sn rdn and nvr a factor* **12/1**

00-3 **8** *48* **Kathindi (IRE)**[42] 1976 4-8-10 52.................................. LeonnaMayor(7) 7 —
(Michael Chapman) *chsd ldrs: pushed along bef 1/2-way: sn lost pl and bhd fnl 3f* **100/1**

2m 35.7s (-4.10) **Going Correction** -0.15s/f (Firm) course record
WFA 3 from 4yo+ 14lb **8** Ran SP% **113.4**
Speed ratings (Par 101): **107,103,103,100,100 98,96,64**
.Porgy was subject to a friendly claim.\n\x\x
Owner Dr Marwan Koukash **Bred** Juddmonte Farms Ltd **Trained** Newmarket, Suffolk

FOCUS
An uncompetitive claimer but at least it was run at a good pace with the field well strung out from an early stage. The time was good and although the favourite disappointed, the form is rated slightly positively.

3244 SIEMENS CHEMICAL PROCESS H'CAP 1m 1f 207y
3:15 (3:17) (Class 4) (0-80,79) 4-Y-0+ **£4,209** (£1,252; £625; £312) **Stalls** Low

Form RPR
63-0 **1** **Eltheeb**[68] 1324 4-9-0 **69**.. PJMcDonald 7 78
(George Moore) *hld up in rr: hdwy over 2f out: trckd ldrs whn nt clr run over 1f out: swtchd lft and rdn ent fnl f: qcknd to ld last 100yds: kpt on strly* **7/1**

4012 **2** *1 ½* **Strike Force**[25] 2473 7-9-2 **71**..(t) TomEaves 1 77
(Clifford Lines) *hld up in tch: hdwy 3f out: rdn to chse ldrs 2f out: drvn and n.m.r over 1f out: sn swtchd lft: kpt on to take 2nd nr fin* **4/1**[2]

542 **3** *hd* **Just Five (IRE)**[4] 3141 5-8-12 **70**.. SeanLevey(3) 4 76
(John Weymes) *trckd ldrs: hdwy over 2f out: rdn to chal and edgd rt over 1f out: drvn and slt ld jst ins fnl f: hdd & wknd last 100yds* **13/2**

1015 **4** *4* **Tribal Myth (IRE)**[7] 3023 4-8-12 **72**.................................. JulieBurke(5) 2 70
(Kevin Ryan) *trckd ldng pair: hdwy 3f out: led 2f out: sn rdn and edgd rt over 1f out: drvn and hdd jst ins fnl f: sn wknd* **15/8**[1]

601 **5** *2 ¾* **Archie Rice (USA)**[10] 2923 5-9-0 **69**.......................... SilvestreDeSousa 5 61
(Tom Keddy) *cl up: rdn along over 2f out: drvn whn nt clr run and hmpd over 1f out: sn wknd* **8/1**

46-5 **6** *2* **Ela Gonda Mou**[12] 2848 4-9-0 **69**.................................. RobertWinston 6 57
(Peter Charalambous) *chsd ldrs: wd and lost pl bnd over 4f out: in rr after* **14/1**

551 **7** *1* **Osgood**[1] 3215 4-9-10 **79** 6ex.. SamHitchcott 3 65
(Mick Channon) *led: rdn along over 2f out: sn hdd: drvn and rallied appr fnl f: sn wknd* **11/2**[3]

2m 5.57s (-1.43) **Going Correction** -0.15s/f (Firm) **7** Ran SP% **113.8**
Speed ratings (Par 105): **99,97,97,94,92 90,89**
toteswingers:1&2:£6.00, 2&3:£2.20, 1&3:£8.40 CSF £34.50 TOTE £10.70: £4.80, £1.40; EX 41.30.
Owner Geoff & Sandra Turnbull **Bred** Bricklow Ltd **Trained** Middleham Moor, N Yorks

FOCUS
A fair handicap but not obviously strong form with the pace taking a while to pick up and the runners bunching in the straight and a couple getting in each other's way. The winner is rated back to his 3yo best.

3245 CHRIS COOLE CHAMPAGNE H'CAP 7f 100y
3:45 (3:48) (Class 5) (0-70,70) 3-Y-0+ **£2,266** (£674; £337; £168) **Stalls** Low

Form RPR
4014 **1** **Positivity**[13] 2799 5-9-1 **57**..(p) TomEaves 9 64
(Bryan Smart) *trckd ldrs: hdwy over 2f out: rdn over 1f out: drvn ent fnl f: led last 100yds: hld on gamely* **8/1**

5531 **2** *hd* **Thinking**[13] 2799 4-9-1 **57**.. DuranFentiman 3 64+
(Tim Easterby) *hld up: hdwy over 2f out: rdn over 1f out: styng on whn n.m.r jst ins fnl f: drvn and kpt on wl towards fin: jst failed* **7/2**[1]

-505 **3** *nk* **Just The Tonic**[13] 2799 4-9-5 **61**.. LeeNewman 11 67
(Marjorie Fife) *prom: hdwy and cl up over 2f out: led wl over 1f out and sn rdn: drvn ent fnl f: hdd and no ex last 100yds* **12/1**

2-40 **4** *shd* **Nicholas Pocock (IRE)**[166] 61 5-9-4 **60**.......................... StephenCraine 4 66
(Brian Ellison) *chsd ldrs: hdwy over 2f out: rdn and ch over 1f out: drvn ent fnl f: kpt on* **6/1**

3523 **5** *1 ¼* **Powerful Pierre**[5] 3071 4-9-7 **68**..................................(v) DaleSwift(5) 10 71
(Ian McInnes) *hld up in tch: hdwy over 2f out: nt clr run and swtchd lft over 1f out: drvn and kpt on ins fnl f: nrst fin* **9/2**[3]

0-30 **6** *shd* **Eeny Mac (IRE)**[33] 2233 4-8-2 **51** oh6.......................... TerenceFury(7) 2 53
(Neville Bycroft) *hld up towards rr: hdwy on outer over 3f out: rdn to chse ldrs 2f out: kpt on ins fnl f: nrst fin* **20/1**

604- **7** *¾* **Xpres Maite**[278] 6116 8-9-4 **60**..(b) PaulQuinn 5 61
(Roy Bowring) *t.k.h: hdwy to dispute ld after 2f: rdn along over 2f out: drvn over 1f out: kpt on same pce u.p fnl f* **8/1**

6534 **8** *10* **Kheskianto (IRE)**[12] 2851 5-8-2 **51** oh5......................(bt) KatiaScallan(7) 1 27
(Michael Chapman) *hld up in rr: effrt and sme hdwy on inner over 2f out: sn rdn and n.d* **22/1**

3-30 **9** 1/2 **Azimuth (USA)**[45] 1892 4-10-0 **70**..............................(p) PhillipMakin 7 44
(Ann Duffield) *led: rdn along over 2f out: drvn and hdd wl over 1f out: sn wknd* **4/1**[2]
30-5 **10** 9 **Boy Blue**[129] 528 6-9-13 **69**.............................. PatCosgrave 8 21
(Peter Salmon) *dwlt: a in rr* **22/1**

1m 33.07s (-0.73) **Going Correction** -0.15s/f (Firm) **10** Ran SP% **118.1**
Speed ratings (Par 103): **98,97,97,97,95 95,94,83,82,72**
toteswingers:1&2:£4.10, 2&3:£10.80, 1&3:£13.00 CSF £35.60 CT £343.66 TOTE £7.40: £2.00, £1.10, £4.40; EX 21.60.
Owner Mrs F Denniff **Bred** Mrs Fiona Denniff **Trained** Hambleton, N Yorks

FOCUS
An ordinary handicap in which the first three places were filled by horses who'd met each other in a similar race here a fortnight earlier. The gallop was something of a muddling one and the field were well bunched for much of the straight. The winner is rated back to his old turf form.

3246 RACING UK ON SKY 432 MEDIAN AUCTION MAIDEN STKS 1m 100y
4:15 (4:16) (Class 5) 3-Y-O **£2,388** (£705; £352) **Stalls** Low

Form RPR
006 **1** **The Guru Of Gloom (IRE)**[38] 2103 3-9-3 72.......... SilvestreDeSousa 2 66
(William Muir) *trckd ldrs on inner: hdwy over 2f out: led wl over 1f out and sn rdn: drvn ins fnl f: kpt on* **6/4**[1]
2 1/2 **Iulus** 3-9-3 0.............................. TomEaves 4 65
(John Quinn) *hld up towards rr: effrt on inner over 2f out: swtchd lft over 1f out: rdn ent fnl f: kpt on wl towards fin* **16/1**
3 shd **Flaming Nora** 3-8-12 0.............................. PatCosgrave 5 60
(James Fanshawe) *sltly hmpd s and in rr: hdwy 2f out: rdn over 1f out: fin wl* **7/1**[3]
4 **4** 2 1/4 **Stylistickhill (IRE)**[19] 2650 3-8-9 0.............................. BillyCray(3) 3 54
(David Nicholls) *t.k.h: chsd ldrs: rdn along wl over 1f out: kpt on same pce* **14/1**
0-52 **5** hd **Phair Winter**[6] 3039 3-8-9 40.............................. PaulPickard(3) 6 54
(Alan Brown) *trckd ldrs: effrt on outer over 2f out: rdn wl over 1f out: kpt on same pce ins fnl f* **20/1**
0 **6** 3/4 **Kool Shuffle (GER)**[18] 2673 3-9-3 0.............................. MickyFenton 1 57
(Tom Tate) *disp ld on inner: rdn along over 2f out: drvn wl over 1f out: grad wknd* **28/1**
-203 **7** 1/2 **Auto Mac**[28] 2392 3-9-3 70.............................. AndrewElliott 7 56
(Neville Bycroft) *slt ld: rdn along over 2f out: drvn and hdd wl over 1f out: grad wknd* **9/1**
5- **8** 5 **Five Hearts**[234] 7231 3-8-7 0.............................. AshleyMorgan(5) 8 40
(Mark H Tompkins) *t.k.h: hld up towards rr hdwy on outer 3f out: rdn along wl over 1f out: sn wknd* **2/1**[2]

1m 46.37s (-1.23) **Going Correction** -0.15s/f (Firm) **8** Ran SP% **116.6**
Speed ratings (Par 99): **100,99,99,97,96 96,95,90**
toteswingers:1&2:£5.00, 2&3:£16.80, 1&3:£3.30 CSF £28.39 TOTE £2.60: £1.10, £2.90, £2.30; EX 26.00.
Owner R Haim **Bred** Oak Lodge Bloodstock **Trained** Lambourn, Berks

FOCUS
A modest maiden run at a muddling gallop, the greater experience of the winner just gaining the day. It's dfoubtful if he had to be at his best, with his main rival disappointing.

3247 STARS OF THE FUTURE APPRENTICE H'CAP (DIV I) 5f
4:45 (4:46) (Class 6) (0-55,55) 3-Y-O+ **£1,295** (£385; £192; £96) **Stalls** Low

Form RPR
3-55 **1** **Maryolini**[20] 2603 6-9-5 **54**.............................. CharlesBishop 12 65
(Tom Keddy) *trckd ldrs: effrt over 1f out: rdn ent fnl f: sn led and kpt on wl* **6/1**[1]
00-5 **2** 1 3/4 **Port Ronan (USA)**[13] 2798 5-8-11 **46** oh1.............................. GeorgeChaloner 7 51
(John Wainwright) *dwlt and towards rr: hdwy over 2f out: rdn wl over 1f out: styd on wl ins fnl f* **7/1**[3]
3005 **3** hd **Wotatomboy**[8] 2989 5-8-6 **46** oh1.............................. NoelGarbutt(5) 5 50
(Richard Whitaker) *cl up: led 2f out: rdn over 1f out: drvn and hdd ins fnl f: kpt on same pce* **15/2**
0010 **4** [illegible] [illegible] **40** [illegible].............................. LauraBarry(5) 4 49
(Karen Tutty) *dwlt: sn trcking ldrs: hdwy 2f out: [illegible] fnl f* **20/1**
0640 **5** shd **Dispol Grand (IRE)**[7] 3027 5-9-0 **54**..............(v1) DavidSimmonson(5) 11 57
(Paul Midgley) *prom: rdn along 2f out: drvn and n.m.r over 1f out: kpt on u.p towards fin* **13/2**[2]
-100 **6** nk **Duke Of Rainford**[22] 2547 4-8-11 **49**.............................. JustinNewman(3) 9 51
(Michael Herrington) *in tch: effrt 2f out: sn rdn and kpt on ins fnl f* **14/1**
0040 **7** shd **King Of Swords (IRE)**[15] 2766 7-8-10 **52**..............(p) EvaMoscrop(7) 8 53+
(Nigel Tinkler) *hld up: effrt and nt clr run wl over 1f out: swtchd lft and n.m.r 1f out: swtchd wd ins fnl f: styd on wl: nrst fin* **9/1**
0600 **8** 3/4 **Rio Sands**[13] 2798 6-8-11 **46**.............................. NatashaEaton 2 45+
(Richard Whitaker) *in tch on inner: effrt 2f out: rdn and nt clr run over 1f out: rdn and no imp ins fnl f* **8/1**
0404 **9** 1 3/4 **Sleights Boy (IRE)**[10] 2918 3-8-6 **50**..............(b) IanBurns(3) 3 40
(Ian McInnes) *chsd ldrs: rdn along over 2f out: sn wknd* **12/1**
6306 **10** 5 **Poppy's Rocket (IRE)**[14] 2782 3-8-9 **53**.............................. LewisWalsh(3) 6 25
(Marjorie Fife) *towards rr: outpcd fr 1/2-way* **7/1**[3]
4406 **11** 1 1/4 **Hereselle (IRE)**[10] 2918 3-8-11 **55**.............................. KatiaScallan(3) 1 23
(Michael Chapman) *led: rdn along 1/2-way: hdd 2f out and sn wknd* **25/1**
25-0 **12** 10 **Ruler's Honour (IRE)**[5] 3075 4-9-1 **55**..........(be1) JacobButterfield(5) 10 —
(Tim Etherington) *v.s.a: a wl bhd* **11/1**

63.63 secs (0.13) **Going Correction** +0.025s/f (Good)
WFA 3 from 4yo+ 6lb **12** Ran SP% **116.8**
Speed ratings (Par 101): **99,96,95,95,95 94,94,93,90,82 80,64**
toteswingers:1&2:£7.20, 2&3:£11.90, 1&3:£9.50 CSF £46.31 CT £326.42 TOTE £5.50: £1.50, £1.20, £3.60; EX 56.50.
Owner Keith Warth **Bred** Mrs Mary Rowlands **Trained** Newmarket, Suffolk

FOCUS
Wide-open betting in the first division of an extremely modest handicap contested by exposed sprinters, most of whom are on the downgrade, and not form to dwell on. The winner is rated back to last year's best.
Sleights Boy(IRE) Official explanation: jockey said gelding was denied a clear run
Ruler's Honour(IRE) Official explanation: jockey said gelding did not face the first time eyeshield/blinkers.

3248 STARS OF THE FUTURE APPRENTICE H'CAP (DIV II) 5f
5:15 (5:17) (Class 6) (0-55,55) 3-Y-O+ **£1,295** (£385; £192; £96) **Stalls** Low

Form RPR
3055 **1** **Unwrapit (USA)**[29] 2351 3-8-11 **55**..............(p) JustinNewman(3) 4 64
(Bryan Smart) *in rr and rdn along on inner 1/2-way: hdwy wl over 1f out: nt clr run and swtchd lft ent fnl f: str run to ld last 75yds* **9/1**
4052 **2** 2 **Royal Blade (IRE)**[6] 3049 4-8-4 **46** oh1.............................. DanielleMooney(7) 7 50
(Alan Berry) *prom: led 2f out: rdn ent fnl f: hdd and no ex last 75yds* **6/1**[2]
0400 **3** 1 3/4 **Bossy Kitty**[13] 2798 4-9-5 **54**.............................. EdmondLinehan 1 52
(Nigel Tinkler) *trckd ldrs: hdwy 2f out: rdn and ch over 1f out: kpt on same pce ins fnl f* **8/1**
2406 **4** 3/4 **Exceedingly Good (IRE)**[5] 3096 5-9-5 **54**.............................. LeonnaMayor 6 49+
(Roy Bowring) *in tch: pushed along and lost pl 1/2-way: swtchd outside and styd on wl appr fnl f: nrst fin* **6/1**[2]
0000 **5** nk **Crazy In Love**[15] 2756 3-8-0 **46** oh1..............(b) JenniferFerguson(5) 2 38
(Olivia Maylam) *led: rdn along and hdd 2f out: drvn over 1f out: grad wknd* **20/1**
-000 **6** 1 **Blue Rum (IRE)**[7] 3027 4-8-6 **46** oh1.............................. LukeStrong(5) 8 36
(Alan Kirtley) *towards rr: hdwy on inner over 1f out: rdn and kpt on ins fnl f: nrst fin* **25/1**
0033 **7** nk **Mission Impossible**[7] 3027 6-8-10 **48**..............(p) JosephYoung(3) 3 37
(Colin Teague) *prom: rdn along over 2f out: grad wknd fr over 1f out* **4/1**[1]
-500 **8** hd **Kalahari Desert (IRE)**[8] 2985 4-8-12 **47**..............(p) NatashaEaton 12 36
(Richard Whitaker) *in tch on outer: edgd rt after 1 1/2f: rdn along 2f out: wknd over 1f out* **25/1**
00-0 **9** 3 3/4 **Ice Girl**[14] 2782 3-8-5 **51**..............(e) LauraBarry(5) 5 24
(Michael Easterby) *chsd ldrs: rdn along over 2f out: sn wknd* **12/1**
-330 **10** shd **Pinball (IRE)**[156] 185 5-9-2 **51**..............(b) GeorgeChaloner 9 26
(Lisa Williamson) *s.i.s and in rr: hdwy and in tch 2f out: sn rdn and wknd over 1f out* **14/1**
3302 **11** 3 3/4 **Ever Roses**[3] 3192 3-8-5 **51**..............(b) DavidSimmonson(5) 11 10
(Paul Midgley) *in tch on outer: edgd rt after 1 1/2f: rdn over 2f out and sn wknd* **7/1**[3]
-000 **12** 8 **Real Diamond**[8] 2990 5-9-3 **52**..............(p) CharlesBishop 10 —+
(Ollie Pears) *chsd ldrs whn hmpd and squeezed out after 1 1/2f: bhd after* **17/2**

63.75 secs (0.25) **Going Correction** +0.025s/f (Good)
WFA 3 from 4yo+ 6lb **12** Ran SP% **119.5**
Speed ratings (Par 101): **99,95,93,91,91 89,89,88,82,82 76,63**
toteswingers:1&2:£12.80, 2&3:£11.60, 1&3:£13.70 CSF £61.09 CT £460.02 TOTE £11.10: £3.40, £3.20, £4.90; EX 77.50.
Owner Crossfields Racing **Bred** Coffeepot Stable **Trained** Hambleton, N Yorks
■ Justin Newman's first winner as an apprentice, following several as an amateur.
■ Stewards' Enquiry : Luke Strong two-day ban: used whip with excessive force (Jul 6-7)

FOCUS
Not much solid recent form on show rather like the first division and not a race likely to throw up many future winners. It was slightly slower than the first division and the winner is rated back to her maiden form.
T/Plt: £125.10 to a £1 stake. Pool of £58,420.82 - 340.71 winning tickets T/Qpdt: £25.80 to a £1 stake. Pool of £5,251.77 - 150.44 winning tickets. JR

3015 BRIGHTON (L-H)
Tuesday, June 21

OFFICIAL GOING: Good to soft
Wind: Fresh, against Weather: Cloudy

3249 BET ON TOTEPLACEPOT AT TOTESPORT.VOM MAIDEN AUCTION STKS 5f 213y
2:30 (2:30) (Class 5) 2-Y-O **£2,266** (£674; £337; £168) **Stalls** Low

Form RPR
6430 **1** **Marygold**[22] 2559 2-8-5 .... HayleyTurner 3 72
(John Akehurst) *mde all: led field to stands' rail and hmpd clst rival 3f out: [illegible]* **13/8**[1]
3 **2** 2 3/4 **Miss Conduct**[14] 2787 2-8-5 .... [illegible] 1 [illegible]
(John Spearing) *trckd ldrs in 3rd: wnt 2nd 3f out: ch over 1f out: hrd rdn: nt qckn* **11/4**[2]
0 **3** 7 **The New Black (IRE)**[14] 2788 2-8-8 .... PatDobbs 6 46
(Richard Hannon) *fair 4th most of way: rdn 3f out: wnt modest 3rd ins fnl f* **7/2**[3]
3205 **4** 1 **Triggerlo**[10] 2901 2-8-10 .... MartinHarley(3) 5 54
(Mick Channon) *pressed wnr tl bdly hmpd on stands' rail 3f out: outpcd fnl 2f* **7/1**
5 nk **Our Cool Cat (IRE)** 2-8-11 .... RichardMullen 2 45
(Gary Moore) *dwlt: pushed along in 5th: no hdwy fnl 3f* **10/1**
0 **6** 3/4 **Monessa (IRE)**[28] 2380 2-8-6 .... EddieCreighton 1 38
(Edward Creighton) *rring in stalls and s.s: a in last: rdn and n.d fnl 3f* **100/1**

1m 12.23s (2.03) **Going Correction** +0.20s/f (Good) **6** Ran SP% **109.6**
Speed ratings (Par 93): **94,90,81,79,79 78**
toteswingers:1&2:£1.60, 2&3:£2.10, 1&3:£1.60 CSF £5.98 TOTE £2.10: £1.60, £2.00; EX 6.30.
Owner The No Water Partnership **Bred** Green Pastures Farm **Trained** Epsom, Surrey
■ Stewards' Enquiry : Hayley Turner three-day ban: careless riding (July 5-7)

FOCUS
Course at inner configuration and distances as advertised. A modest and uncompetitive maiden auction in which the runners took the conventional soft-ground route by coming over to the stands' rail. The winner is rated to form and at the top end of the race averages.

NOTEBOOK
Marygold had shown enough ability in her first four starts to suggest she could win a race like this. Quickly away, her rider must have had a complete brainstorm as she wasn't sufficiently clear of Triggerlo when grabbing the nearside rail 3f out, which could have resulted in a very nasty accident, so Hayley Turner can possibly count herself lucky to have got away with just a three-day ban for careless riding. Having got to the rail, she was never getting to be caught and was able to saunter clear for an easy success, but the form looks modest. (op 7-4 tchd 6-4)
Miss Conduct, an encouraging third of 15 on her Salisbury debut, had every chance to pick up the winner had she been good enough, but she wasn't. She missed an engagement at Windsor the previous evening because of the going, so may need better ground. (op 9-4 tchd 3-1)
The New Black(IRE) showed a glimmer of ability when ninth of 14 on her Salisbury debut and attracted market support here, but she never managed to land a blow. (op 6-1 tchd 3-1)
Triggerlo was obviously done no favours when badly hampered by the winner 3f out, but how he would have fared without it is hard to say as he had been particularly disappointing the last twice after showing early ability. Official explanation: jockey said gelding suffered interference in running (op 5-1)
Our Cool Cat(IRE), retained for £5,500 as a 2-y-o and out of a half-sister to a couple of winning juveniles, was taken off his feet from the start. (tchd 9-1 and 12-1)

Monessa(IRE) Official explanation: jockey said filly reared when stalls opened

3250 FREE RACING POST FORM AT TOTESPORT.COM H'CAP 6f 209y
3:00 (3:00) (Class 5) (0-75,72) 3-Y-O+ **£2,266** (£674; £337; £168) **Stalls** Low

Form RPR
-322 1 **Foxtrot Alpha (IRE)**[7] 3019 5-8-9 **63** .... JamesRogers(5) 6 74
(Peter Winkworth) *mde all: led field to stands' rail 3f out: rdn out* **7/4**[1]
4002 2 3 ¾ **Ivory Lace**[22] 2561 10-8-13 **67** .... HarryBentley(5) 3 68
(Steve Woodman) *hld up in 5th: hdwy 2f out: hung lft over 1f out: nt qckn* **11/2**[3]
4125 3 3 ¾ **Unlimited**[8] 2995 9-9-5 **68** .... LiamJones 5 59
(Tony Carroll) *stdd s: hld up in rr: hrd rdn and sme hdwy over 1f out: no imp* **9/1**
0622 4 ¾ **Lastkingofscotland (IRE)**[3] 3172 5-9-9 **72** ....(b) HayleyTurner 2 61
(Conor Dore) *sn prom: chsd wnr after 2f: wknd over 1f out* **5/2**[2]
153- 5 2 ¼ **Seamster**[447] 1070 4-9-6 **69** .... CathyGannon 7 52
(Richard Ford) *chsd wnr 2f: wknd wl over 1f out* **20/1**
0005 6 6 **Slugger O'Toole**[10] 2917 6-9-5 **68** ....(e[1]) SaleemGolam 4 34
(Stuart Williams) *in tch in 4th: drvn along over 2f out: sn wknd* **13/2**

1m 23.91s (0.81) **Going Correction** +0.20s/f (Good) **6** Ran SP% **108.4**
Speed ratings (Par 103): **103,98,94,93,91 84**
toteswingers:1&2:£2.20, 2&3:£5.90, 1&3:£3.30 CSF £10.88 TOTE £2.40: £1.40, £5.10; EX 10.30.
Owner P Winkworth **Bred** Irish National Stud **Trained** Chiddingfold, Surrey

FOCUS
An ordinary handicap and, as in the opener, the race went to the horse who managed to bag the stands' rail in front 3f out. The form could be worth more at face value.

3251 BET TOTEPOOL AT TOTESPORT.COM H'CAP 1m 1f 209y
3:30 (3:31) (Class 6) (0-65,65) 3-Y-O+ **£1,619** (£481; £240; £120) **Stalls** High

Form RPR
0-32 1 **Golden Waters**[13] 2824 4-10-0 **65** .... CathyGannon 5 74
(Eve Johnson Houghton) *chsd ldng pair: led over 3f out: pushed out and in control ins fnl f* **15/8**[1]
0530 2 2 ½ **Out Of The Storm**[34] 2197 3-8-5 **57** .... SimonPearce(3) 4 61
(Simon Dow) *led tl over 3f out: nt qckn appr fnl f* **16/1**
-260 3 1 ¼ **Zafaraan**[19] 2643 3-9-2 **65** .... JackMitchell 1 66
(Peter Chapple-Hyam) *cl up: jnd ldrs 3f out: one pce appr fnl f* **5/2**[2]
6003 4 7 **Beetuna (IRE)**[8] 2996 6-9-12 **63** .... FrankieMcDonald 3 50
(David Bourton) *in tch: wnt prom over 5f out: rdn and btn over 2f out* **8/1**[3]
0500 5 2 ½ **Emmeline Pankhurst (IRE)**[11] 2875 3-8-2 **51** .... JimmyQuinn 6 33
(Julia Feilden) *dwlt: towards rr: styd alone on ins rail and sme hdwy 3f out: wknd wl over 1f out* **8/1**[3]
2566 6 nse **Kathleen Kennet**[42] 1987 11-8-11 **48** oh2 ow1 .... SebSanders 7 30
(Jonathan Geake) *chsd ldr tl over 3f out: wknd over 2f out* **8/1**[3]
555 7 5 **Ocean Countess (IRE)**[43] 1936 5-9-8 **59** .... LiamJones 2 31
(Tony Carroll) *s.s: bhd: mod effrt 2f out: sn wknd* **9/1**

2m 6.64s (3.04) **Going Correction** +0.30s/f (Good)
WFA 3 from 4yo+ 12lb **7** Ran SP% **112.6**
Speed ratings (Par 101): **99,97,96,90,88 88,84**
toteswingers:1&2:£7.90, 2&3:£10.40, 1&3:£2.10 CSF £31.34 TOTE £2.50: £1.30, £6.70; EX 32.90.
Owner R Crutchley **Bred** R E Crutchley **Trained** Blewbury, Oxon

FOCUS
A modest handicap in which all bar Emmeline Pankhurst came over to the stands' rail. The form makes a fair bit of sense.

3252 MORE WIMBLEDON BETTING AT TOTESPORT.COM H'CAP 1m 3f 196y
4:00 (4:01) (Class 6) (0-65,64) 4-Y-O+ **£1,619** (£481; £240; £120) **Stalls** High

Form RPR
0-62 1 **Megalala (IRE)**[12] 2843 10-9-7 **64** .... NeilChalmers 3 71
(John Bridger) *mde all: jnd by runner-up 3f out: hld on gamely and edgd ahd again fnl 150yds* **7/4**[2]
0414 2 1 ¼ **Penang Cinta**[32] 2246 8-9-4 **61** .... CathyGannon 4 66
(David Evans) *trckd ldr: drvn level over 2f out: worn down by game wnr fnl 150yds* **1/1**[1]
0-03 3 11 **Sanctum**[13] 2824 5-8-2 **45** ....(b) AdrianMcCarthy 5 37
(Dr Jon Scargill) *s.i.s and rdn s: sn cl up: wknd over 3f out* **5/1**[3]
2050 4 47 **Battle Axe (FR)**[13] 2820 6-7-13 **45** .... SimonPearce(3) 2 —
(Laura Mongan) *s.s: a in last: rdn over 6f out: sn t.o* **16/1**

2m 36.46s (3.76) **Going Correction** +0.30s/f (Good) **4** Ran SP% **108.9**
Speed ratings (Par 101): **99,98,90,59**
CSF £3.92 TOTE £2.30; EX 2.90.
Owner Tommy Ware **Bred** Joseph Gallagher **Trained** Liphook, Hants

FOCUS
This looked a two-horse race on paper, and that's how it turned out. The first three all came stands' side. The winner is rated to her best when ridden by a non-claimer.

3253 BET ON LIVE TENNIS AT TOTESPORT.COM H'CAP 7f 214y
4:30 (4:30) (Class 6) (0-55,56) 3-Y-O+ **£1,619** (£481; £240; £120) **Stalls** Low

Form RPR
0-03 1 **Camberley Two**[14] 2792 3-8-11 **53** .... RichardKingscote 2 70+
(Roger Charlton) *hld up in midfield: hdwy to ld wl over 1f out: sn clr: comf* **11/10**[1]
5505 2 4 **Bold Ring**[19] 2642 5-9-4 **53** .... AlanCreighton(3) 10 60
(Edward Creighton) *chsd ldrs: effrt and n.m.r over 2f out: drvn to chse wnr 1f out: a wl hld* **33/1**
6500 3 2 **Tinkerbell Will**[28] 2385 4-9-0 **46** oh1 .... RichardThomas 13 48
(John E Long) *sn pushed along: mid-div: hdwy u.p over 1f out: styd on same pce* **50/1**
0006 4 shd **Vezere (USA)**[10] 2921 4-9-0 **46** oh1 ....(b) SebSanders 7 48+
(Simon Dow) *hld up towards rr: nt clr run over 2f out: drvn along and gd hdwy fr over 1f out: fin wl* **8/1**
5400 5 1 ½ **Not So Bright (USA)**[12] 2853 3-8-10 **52** ....(bt) JamesDoyle 4 48
(Des Donovan) *hld up towards rr: rdn and hdwy 2f out: no imp* **10/1**
4401 6 5 **Inquisitress**[7] 3017 7-9-10 **56** 6ex .... CathyGannon 3 43
(John Bridger) *prom: led briefly 2f out: wknd 1f out* **13/2**[2]
3065 7 3 ¾ **September Draw (USA)**[15] 2768 3-8-11 **53** .... PatDobbs 1 29
(Richard Hannon) *towards rr: drvn along 3f out: nt rch ldrs* **7/1**[3]
4200 8 3 **Giulietta Da Vinci**[10] 2921 4-9-5 **51** .... GeorgeBaker 8 22
(Steve Woodman) *prom: led 3f out tl 2f out: hrd rdn and wknd over 1f out* **16/1**
0005 9 3 ¾ **The Wonga Coup (IRE)**[35] 2170 4-9-4 **50** .... IanMongan 12 13
(Pat Phelan) *cl up: jnd ldrs 3f out: wknd 2f out* **20/1**
40-0 10 1 ½ **Prince Valentine**[35] 2171 10-9-0 **46** oh1 ....(p) RichardMullen 6 —
(Gary Moore) *hld up in rr: rdn 4f out: nvr trbld ldrs* **25/1**
3-46 11 4 ½ **Minortransgression (USA)**[145] 320 4-9-7 **53** ....(p) KirstyMilczarek 9 —
(H Edward Haynes) *led tl 3f out: sing to lose pl whn n.m.r over 2f out* **25/1**
5050 12 11 **Ocean Rosie (IRE)**[13] 2820 4-9-0 **46** oh1 .... LiamJones 14 —
(Tony Carroll) *prom 4f* **25/1**
000- 13 16 **Michelle (IRE)**[322] 4681 5-9-0 **46** oh1 .... NickyMackay 11 —
(Paddy Butler) *prom 2f: sn lost pl: wl bhd and eased fnl 3f* **80/1**

1m 38.05s (2.05) **Going Correction** +0.30s/f (Good)
WFA 3 from 4yo+ 10lb **13** Ran SP% **122.0**
Speed ratings (Par 101): **101,97,95,94,93 88,84,81,77,76 71,60,44**
toteswingers:1&2:£12.30, 2&3:£44.90, 1&3:£23.20 CSF £58.53 CT £1334.06 TOTE £2.30: £1.40, £8.10, £12.20; EX 60.40 TRIFECTA Not won..
Owner H R H Sultan Ahmad Shah **Bred** Barry Walters Farms **Trained** Beckhampton, Wilts
■ Stewards' Enquiry : Richard Thomas two-day ban: careless riding (Jul 5-6)

FOCUS
The biggest field of the day, but a weak handicap with over half the field maidens coming into it. The whole field came stands' side. The winner is rated value for a bit more than the bare form.
Michelle(IRE) Official explanation: jockey said mare ran too free early

3254 TRY TOTEQUICKPICK ON ALL TOTEPOOL BETS H'CAP 5f 213y
5:00 (5:01) (Class 6) (0-60,59) 3-Y-O+ **£1,619** (£481; £240; £120) **Stalls** Low

Form RPR
0416 1 **Athaakeel (IRE)**[22] 2554 5-9-5 **52** ....(b) CathyGannon 6 63
(Ronald Harris) *in tch: styd alone far side st: led 2f out: rdn clr 1f out: comf* **11/4**[1]
0006 2 3 ½ **Do More Business (IRE)**[14] 2794 4-9-5 **52** .... IanMongan 2 52
(Pat Phelan) *in tch: rdn to chal for 2nd over 1f out: wl hld by wnr on far side* **3/1**[2]
0020 3 1 ¼ **Jemimaville (IRE)**[121] 619 4-8-13 **46** ....(v) TravisBlock 1 42
(Giles Bravery) *hld up in rr: hdwy to ld briefly over 2f out: wl hld by wnr on far side ins fnl f* **9/2**[3]
030- 4 2 ½ **Manasha**[322] 4675 3-8-10 **50** .... MartinLane 5 38
(John Dunlop) *in tch tl outpcd and btn 2f out* **9/2**[3]
4360 5 nse **Fairy Tales**[40] 2025 3-9-1 **55** .... RichardKingscote 4 43
(John Bridger) *led tl over 2f out: wknd wl over 1f out* **8/1**
0000 6 nse **Young Simon**[42] 1989 4-9-8 **55** .... GeorgeBaker 7 43
(George Margarson) *chsd ldr tl over 2f out: wknd wl over 1f out* **15/2**

1m 12.85s (2.65) **Going Correction** +0.30s/f (Good)
WFA 3 from 4yo+ 7lb **6** Ran SP% **110.9**
Speed ratings (Par 101): **94,89,87,84,84 84**
toteswingers:1&2:£2.40, 2&3:£2.70, 1&3:£2.20 CSF £10.97 TOTE £2.20: £1.10, £2.80; EX 12.60.
Owner Drag Star On Swan **Bred** Shadwell Estate Company Limited **Trained** Earlswood, Monmouths

FOCUS
A moderate handicap, but notable for a decent piece of judgement by the winning rider. With the winner racing solo the form is dubious.

3255 TRY TOTEQUICKPICK IF YOU'RE FEELING LUCKY H'CAP 5f 59y
5:30 (5:30) (Class 6) (0-65,64) 3-Y-O+ **£1,619** (£481; £240; £120) **Stalls** Low

Form RPR
0551 1 **Stonecrabstomorrow (IRE)**[7] 3015 8-8-9 **55** 6ex..(v) MarkCoumbe(5) 6 63
(Michael Attwater) *patiently rdn in last: styd far side st: hrd rdn and hdwy 1f out: r.o to ld fnl 75yds* **9/2**[2]
0460 2 1 ¼ **Whiskey Junction**[20] 2609 7-9-8 **63** .... SebSanders 2 67
(Michael Quinn) *w ldr: styd far side st: nt qckn ins fnl f* **11/2**
2530 3 nk **Welsh Inlet (IRE)**[11] 2878 3-9-2 **63** .... NeilChalmers 5 64
(John Bridger) *sn led: c alone to stands' rail st: remained overall ldr tl hdd and no ex fnl 75yds* **6/1**
5262 4 1 ½ **Bermondsey Bob (IRE)**[12] 2845 5-9-6 **61** .... CathyGannon 4 59
(John Spearing) *cl up: styd far side st: no ex ins fnl f* **11/10**[1]
5044 5 3 ¾ **Highland Harvest**[7] 3020 7-9-9 **64** .... IanMongan 1 49
(Jamie Poulton) *chsd ldrs: styd far side st: wknd ins fnl f* **5/1**[3]

63.69 secs (1.39) **Going Correction** +0.30s/f (Good)
WFA 3 from 4yo+ 6lb **5** Ran SP% **112.1**
Speed ratings (Par 101): **100,98,97,95,89**
Tote Super 7: Win: Not won. Place: Not won. CSF £27.72 TOTE £5.40: £2.70, £5.00; EX 27.20.
Owner Miss Nicola Carroll **Bred** P Dillon **Trained** Epsom, Surrey

FOCUS
A moderate sprint handicap and this time only Welsh Inlet was brought to race stands' side. The way things panned out suggests the leaders may have gone off too quick. The winner's best form since early last year.
Welsh Inlet(IRE) Official explanation: jockey said saddle slipped
T/Plt: £30.60 to a £1 stake. Pool of £67,571.22 - 1,609.29 winning tickets. T/Qpdt: £7.80 to a £1 stake. Pool of £4,270.31 - 404.01 winning tickets. LM

2836 NEWBURY (L-H)
Tuesday, June 21

OFFICIAL GOING: Good (good to soft in places; 6.7)
Wind: strong, half against Weather: bright and breezy

3256 PUMP TECHNOLOGY APPRENTICE H'CAP 1m 3f 5y
6:10 (6:10) (Class 5) (0-70,70) 4-Y-O+ **£2,590** (£770; £385; £192) **Stalls** Low

Form RPR
10-0 1 **Broughtons Swinger**[19] 2649 4-9-4 **64** .... AdamBeschizza 5 71+
(Willie Musson) *chsd ldrs: rdn and effrt over 2f out: led over 1f out: forged ahd fnl 50yds: drvn out* **4/1**[1]
3444 2 ½ **Edgeworth (IRE)**[15] 2769 5-9-3 **70** .... JoshBaudains(7) 3 76
(David Bridgwater) *stdd s: hld up in last quartet: gd hdwy to chse ldrs and swtchd rt over 2f out: chsd wnr 1f out: ev ch ins fnl f: no ex and btn fnl 50yds* **6/1**[2]
-102 3 nk **Bubbly Braveheart (IRE)**[20] 2608 4-9-2 **65** .... LucyKBarry(3) 11 70
(Pat Phelan) *chsd ldrs: rdn to ld over 2f out: hdd over 1f out: kpt on u.p but unable qck fnl 150yds* **10/1**
0501 4 1 **Dancing Primo**[10] 2905 5-8-5 **51** .... RyanClark 4 55
(Mark Brisbourne) *hld up in tch in midfield: rdn and effrt wl over 1f out: unable qck and no imp over 1f out: kpt on ins fnl f: nvr quite gng pce to chal* **6/1**[2]
4333 5 ½ **Striding Edge (IRE)**[10] 2923 5-9-2 **65** .... MatthewLawson(3) 2 68
(Hans Adielsson) *stdd after s: hld up in last quartet: hdwy on outer 3f out: chsd ldrs and drvn over 1f out: no ex and btn ins fnl f* **13/2**[3]
4300 6 3 ¼ **Goodlukin Lucy**[22] 2552 4-9-10 **70** .... HarryBentley 9 67
(Pat Eddery) *hld up in tch: hdwy to chse ldrs and rdn over 2f out: no imp over 1f out: plugged on same pce ins fnl f* **7/1**

031 **7** *2* **Iguacu**[18] 2685 7-8-3 **52**............(p) DavidKenny(3) 8 45
(George Baker) *hld up in last quartet: rdn and effrt over 2f out: drvn and no hdwy 2f out: plugged on ins fnl f: nvr gng pce to chal* **9/1**

3135 **8** *½* **Diddums**[22] 2561 5-8-12 **61**............ RosieJessop(3) 10 53
(Alastair Lidderdale) *in tch: effrt to chse ldrs and rdn ent fnl 3f: wknd over 1f out* **12/1**

0600 **9** *4 ½* **Rio Prince**[14] 2793 4-8-0 **51** oh5............(t) JakePayne(5) 6 35
(John Bridger) *led: rdn and hdd over 2f out: wkng and wl hld whn hung rt over 1f out* **40/1**

-503 **10** *11* **Boogie Dancer**[20] 2608 7-8-5 **51** oh5............ RyanPowell 1 16
(Stuart Howe) *stdd s: hld up in rr: rdn and effrt on inner over 3f out: no hdwy: wl bhd over 1f out* **33/1**

0013 **11** *20* **Major Eradicator (USA)**[20] 2618 4-8-2 **51** oh2............(p) AmyScott(3) 7 —
(Alastair Lidderdale) *in tch: dropped in rr and u.p wl over 3f out: lost tch wl over 2f out: t.o* **12/1**

2m 23.0s (1.80) **Going Correction** +0.075s/f (Good) **11** Ran SP% **114.3**
Speed ratings (Par 103): **96,95,95,94,94 91,90,90,86,78 64**
toteswingers:1&2:£5.80, 2&3:£11.90, 1&3:£11.20 CSF £26.37 CT £222.13 TOTE £4.80: £1.10, £3.80, £2.80; EX 26.60.
Owner Broughton Thermal Insulation **Bred** Michael E Broughton **Trained** Newmarket, Suffolk

FOCUS
The rails were moved in from the 1m pole to the 5f pole so the round course was approximately 11 yards longer than standard. Only 2.1mm of rain fell in the 24 hours before racing and the professionals who rode in the arabian race at 5.40 reported the ground to be "good" and "just on the easy side". A modest handicap in which the ordinary gallop combined with a fresh wind (half-against) resulted in a time approximately six seconds above Racing Post standard. It's doubtful the winner had to improve.
Rio Prince Official explanation: jockey said gelding hung right

3257 PUMP TECHNOLOGY & FRIENDS REMEMBER RICHARD DINES MAIDEN AUCTION FILLIES' STKS 6f 8y

6:40 (6:48) (Class 4) 2-Y-O **£3,885** (£1,156; £577; £288) **Stalls** Centre

Form RPR

4 **1** **Mention (IRE)**[17] 2718 2-8-10 0............ ShaneKelly 14 81+
(Brian Meehan) *w ldr: rdn over 1f out: lft in narrow ld jst ins fnl f: kpt on wl and forged ahd fnl 50yds: rdn out* **8/1**[3]

03 **2** *¾* **Lady Gibraltar**[13] 2811 2-8-1 0............ HarryBentley(5) 10 75
(Alan Jarvis) *led: rdn and veered bdly lft ent fnl f: swvd bk rt and hdd jst ins fnl f: hung lft u.p and btn fnl 75yds* **2/1**[1]

3 *nk* **Lady Jameela** 2-8-5 0............ MartinHarley(3) 12 76+
(Mick Channon) *trckd ldrs: pushed along to chal ent fnl f: kpt on same pce and hld fnl 100yds: improve* **10/1**

4 *¾* **Kune Kune** 2-8-6 0............ MartinDwyer 2 75+
(Marco Botti) *chsd ldrs: rdn and pressing ldrs whn bdly hmpd and snatched up ent fnl f: trying to rally whn hmpd again ins fnl f: styd on same pce towards fin* **16/1**

4 **5** *½* **My Sharona**[14] 2787 2-8-4 0............ DavidProbert 13 68
(Sylvester Kirk) *t.k.h: hld up wl in tch: rdn and unable qck over 1f out: rallied u.p and kpt on fnl 150yds* **12/1**

6 *2* **Baltic Flyer (IRE)** 2-8-8 0............ AndreaAtzeni 4 66+
(Robert Eddery) *hld up wl in tch: rdn and unable qck whn hmpd ent fnl f: kpt on same pce under hands and heels riding fnl f* **8/1**[3]

7 *nse* **Jungle** 2-8-8 0............ MichaelHills 15 66+
(B W Hills) *hld up in tch towards rr: rdn and unable qck wl over 1f out: rallied and styd on steadily ins fnl f: unable to chal* **10/1**

2 **8** *2 ½* **Rafaella**[14] 2787 2-8-6 0............ LukeMorris 7 57
(Harry Dunlop) *hld up wl in tch: rdn and unable qck wl over 1f out: drvn and no imp ent fnl f: kpt on same pce and no threat to ldrs ins fnl f* **6/1**[2]

5 **9** *½* **Ermyn Flyer**[73] 1235 2-7-13 0............ JemmaMarshall(5) 16 53
(Pat Phelan) *dwlt: sn in tch: rdn and unable qck 2f out: wknd over 1f out* **100/1**

0 **10** *nse* **Love Grows Wild (USA)**[31] 2309 2-8-8 0............ HayleyTurner 11 57
(Michael Bell) *stdd s: hld up wl in tch: rdn and unable qck 2f out: sn outpcd and no threat to ldrs over 1f out: styd on same pce ins fnl f* **12/1**

0 **11** *3 ¼* **Cashmere Or Caviar (IRE)**[15] 2767 2-8-8 0............ RichardHills 5 47
(B W Hills) *hld up wl in tch towards rr: rdn and unable qck 2f out: sn wknd* **22/1**

12 *2* **Clodhopper (IRE)** 2-8-1 0............ SophieDoyle(3) 8 37
(Jamie Osborne) *hld up in midfield: rdn 2f out: sn wknd* **40/1**

13 *1 ¾* **What's Up (IRE)** 2-8-8 0............ FergusSweeney 6 36
(Jim Boyle) *in tch in rr: rdn and struggling over 2f out: wknd 2f out: sn bhd* **33/1**

14 *18* **Ellie Arter** 2-8-4 0............ FrankieMcDonald 1 —
(Richard Hannon) *bhd and sn pushed along: lost tch 1/2-way: t.o fnl 2f* **66/1**

1m 16.92s (3.92) **Going Correction** +0.40s/f (Good) **14** Ran SP% **121.5**
Speed ratings (Par 92): **89,88,87,86,85 83,83,79,79,79 74,72,69,45**
toteswingers:1&2:£6.00, 2&3:£5.70, 1&3:£26.30 CSF £23.66 TOTE £13.10: £4.10, £1.10, £4.10; EX 35.30.
Owner Raymond Tooth **Bred** Mrs Noelle Walsh **Trained** Manton, Wilts
■ Stewards' Enquiry : Harry Bentley one-day ban: careless riding (Jul 5)

FOCUS
Pyrrha (subsequently smart performer) in 2008 was the clear pick of the four previous winners of this race but, although ths bare form looks no better than fair, and is not the most solid given the way the race was run, this event should throw up winners. The modest gallop suited those up with the pace and the field raced in the centre.

NOTEBOOK
Mention(IRE), like several from this yard, improved a fair bit on her debut run and showed a good attitude after attracting market support to beat an errant rival. She had the run of the race but should have no problems with 7f and this highly regarded sort, who hold entries in several sales races, is almost certainly capable of further improvement. (op 12-1)
Lady Gibraltar didn't help her cause by wandering at Haydock and, after travelling strongly, she looked to throw away a winning opportunity by hanging markedly both ways in the closing stages. She's a fair sort - and more than capable of winning a similar race - but on this evidence doesn't look one to be placing maximum faith in. (op 11-4)
Lady Jameela ◆, who cost £14,000 and who is out of a sister to to very useful dual juvenile winner (up to 1m) Sundari, attracted support and created a favourable impression against a couple of more experienced rivals on this racecourse debut. She'll have no problems with 7f and is sure to win a race. (op 9-1 tchd 12-1)
Kune Kune, who has several Fibresand winners in her pedigree shaped a bit better than the bare form on this racecourse debut after being hampered twice by the wayward runner-up in the closing stages. She'll be even better suited by 7f and is entitled to come on for the run. (op 12-1)
My Sharona duly stepped up on her debut effort and may be a bit better than the bare facts imply given she fared the best of those to come from just off the pace. She'll be well suited by 7f and will be of interest granted a stiffer test in nursery company. (op 18-1)
Baltic Flyer(IRE), who has several winners up to 1m in her pedigree, ran well for a long way before tiring and should come on for the run. (op 15-2)
Jungle ◆ has several winners in her pedigree and a bit to recommend her on looks, caught the eye without being unduly knocked about after losing ground at the start. She should improve a fair bit for this experience and is sure to win a race. (op 14-1 tchd 9-1)
Rafaella pulled far too hard in this muddling event and failed by some way to confirm debut placings with My Sharona. (op 5-1)

3258 PUMPMATIC PUMP STATIONS BY PUMP TECHNOLOGY MAIDEN FILLIES' STKS 7f (S)

7:15 (7:17) (Class 4) 2-Y-O **£3,885** (£1,156; £577; £288) **Stalls** Centre

Form RPR

1 **Questing** 2-9-0 0............ WilliamBuick 7 89+
(John Gosden) *trckd ldrs: wnt 2nd 4f out: pushed ahd over 1f out: sn qcknd: readily c clr 1f out and in n.d fnl f: v easily* **5/1**[2]

2 *3 ½* **Way Too Hot** 2-9-0 0............ AdamKirby 1 77+
(Clive Cox) *in tch: hdwy to chse ldrs over 2f out: rdn to chse wnr over 1f out: sn outpcd by wnr and btn 1f out: no threat to wnr but kpt on for clr 2nd* **9/4**[1]

3 *2 ¼* **Ballyea (IRE)** 2-9-0 0............ RichardHughes 9 74+
(Richard Hannon) *hld up in last pair: clsng and looking for room whn swtchd sharply lft 2f out: pushed lft and hdwy to dispute 3rd over 1f out: kpt on but no ch w wnr fnl f* **13/2**[3]

4 *nk* **Musically** 2-9-0 0............ HughBowman 10 71+
(Mick Channon) *hld up in tch: edging lft over 2f out: swtchd lft and rdn to chse ldng pair over 1f out: battling for 3rd but no ch w wnr fnl f* **16/1**

5 *7* **Rain Dance** 2-9-0 0............ JimmyFortune 6 53+
(Richard Hannon) *hld up in midfield: short of room over 2f out: pushed lft 2f out: sn rdn and outpcd: 6th and wl btn 1f out* **12/1**

6 *¾* **Madame St Clair (IRE)** 2-9-0 0............ MartinDwyer 5 54+
(Brian Meehan) *s.i.s: hld up in last pair: clsd whn sltly hmpd 2f out: sn pushed along and outpcd: wl btn ent fnl f* **5/1**[2]

7 *2 ½* **Cool Light** 2-8-11 0............ MatthewDavies(3) 8 45
(Alan Jarvis) *chsd ldr for 3f: rdn and unable qck in midfield over 2f out: wknd wl over 1f out* **25/1**

0 **8** *½* **Strictly Mine**[31] 2309 2-9-0 0............ KierenFallon 2 44
(Jonathan Portman) *led and grad led field to stands' rail: rdn and hdd over 1f out: sn btn: 5th and wl btn 1f out: eased wl ins fnl f* **20/1**

9 *10* **Waterloo Girl** 2-9-0 0............ LiamKeniry 3 19
(Michael Blanshard) *in tch: short of room and dropped to rr over 2f out: rdn and no hdwy whn rdr dropped whip wl over 1f out: sn wl bhd* **66/1**

5 **10** *1 ¼* **Sovereign Waters**[14] 2788 2-9-0 0............ TomQueally 4 16
(Eve Johnson Houghton) *awkward leaving stalls and s.i.s: rdn and struggling over 2f out: wknd wl over 1f out: sn wl bhd* **5/1**[2]

1m 28.68s (2.98) **Going Correction** +0.40s/f (Good) **10** Ran SP% **117.8**
Speed ratings (Par 92): **98,94,91,91,83 82,79,78,67,65**
toteswingers:1&2:£4.30, 2&3:£5.20, 1&3:£3.00 CSF £16.50 TOTE £6.70: £1.70, £1.90, £2.90; EX 20.40.
Owner H R H Princess Haya Of Jordan **Bred** Darley **Trained** Newmarket, Suffolk

FOCUS
Not much form to go on but this race is regularly won by a decent performer, the picks being Nasheej (rated 111 at best) in 2005, Muthabara (rated 107 at best) in 2007 and Cape Dollar (rated 103) last year and the winner of this year's renewal looks another potentially smart prospect. The gallop was an ordinary one and time was only ordinary. The field congregated towards the stands rail this time.

NOTEBOOK
Questing ◆, who has several winners up to middle distances in her pedigree, had the run of the race but created a very favourable impression when showing a fine turn of foot to beat the well-backed market leader easing down on this racecourse debut. She's a leggy type at present but impressed her rider and is open to plenty of improvement. She appeals as the sort to hold her own in stronger company. (op 7-2)
Way Too Hot ◆, the first foal of an unraced half-sister to a very useful 6f/7f juvenile winner, was well supported throughout the day and, although out-speeded late on, shaped with a fair bit of promise on this racecourse debut. She's a bigger type than the winner - very much the type to improve again - and looks nailed on to win a similar event at the very least. (op 5-2 tchd 10-3)
Ballyea(IRE) ◆, a 75,000gns half-sister to smart turf and Tapeta winner Rakaan, shaped a fair bit better than the bare facts suggest after having to wait for some time to get a run against two rivals who got first run. She wasn't knocked about which clearly [illegible] and she's up to winning her maiden at least. (tchd 6-1 and 7-1)
Musically, a half-sister to a couple of winners up to 1m, has stamina on both sides of her pedigree and she showed a useful level of form on this racecourse debut. She'll have no problems with 1m, is sure to come on for this run and is sure to win races. (op 14-1 tchd 12-1)
Rain Dance, who has several winners over a variety of distances in her pedigree, showed ability without being knocked about on this racecourse debut. She'll have no problems with 1m and is sure to improve. (op 9-1)
Madame St Clair(IRE), the first foal of an unraced half-sister to a couple of winners around 1m1f; attracted plenty of support but failed to land a blow after a tardy start on this debut run. It's a fair bet she'll improve and leave this bare form a fair way behind in due course. (op 14-1)
Cool Light, a half-sister to a 1m all-weather winner out of a 1m4f scorer, wasn't disgraced on this debut. She should improve for this experience and there will be plenty of easier opportunities than this one. (op 40-1)
Strictly Mine Official explanation: jockey said filly hung right

3259 JUNG PUMPEN & PUMP TECHNOLOGY H'CAP 1m 7y(R)

7:45 (7:48) (Class 5) (0-70,70) 3-Y-O **£2,590** (£770; £385; £192) **Stalls** Low

Form RPR

-202 **1** **Snow Trooper**[34] 2196 3-9-0 **63**............ AdamKirby 9 75
(Dean Ivory) *racd off the pce in midfield on outer: clsd and in tch 5f out: rdn: edgd lft but chsd ldr over 1f out: drvn to ld fnl 150yds: drew clr fnl 75yds: rdn out* **9/1**

0050 **2** *2 ¼* **Royal Opera**[19] 2646 3-9-5 **68**............(v[1]) JamesMillman 1 75
(Rod Millman) *led: rdn jst over 2f out: drvn ent fnl f: hdd fnl 150yds: no ex and btn fnl 75yds* **11/1**

33-3 **3** *1 ¾* **Destiny Of Dreams**[77] 1146 3-9-5 **68**............ FergusSweeney 5 71
(Jo Crowley) *chsd clr ldng trio: clsd and in tch 5f out: rdn to chse ldr over 2f out tl over 1f out: plugged on same pce and no imp fnl f* **14/1**

6-04 **4** *4* **Spade**[12] 2850 3-9-3 **66**............(b[1]) JimCrowley 4 60
(David Elsworth) *stdd s: hld up wl bhd: hdwy and in tch 5f out: weaved through field and hdwy to go modest 4th jst over 1f out: no imp fnl f* **11/2**[2]

5-04 **5** *3* **Winged Valkyrie (IRE)**[26] 2427 3-9-7 **70**............ MichaelHills 3 57
(B W Hills) *chsd ldr and clr of field tl 5f out: lost 2nd and rdn over 2f out: hld hd high u.p and wknd over 1f out* **25/1**

001- **6** *1 ¼* **Folly Drove**[257] 6694 3-9-3 **66**............ JamesDoyle 12 52+
(Jonathan Portman) *racd off the pce in midfield: clsd and in tch 5f out: n.m.r over 3f out: rdn and unable qck jst over 2f out: one pce and no threat to ldrs whn nt clr run and eased ins fnl f* **12/1**

0-00 **7** *shd* **Hard Bargain (IRE)**[12] 2841 3-9-4 **67**.............................. KierenFallon 8 51
(Denis Coakley) *racd wl off the pce towards rr: clsd and in tch 5f out: rdn and no prog jst over 2f out: plugging on same pce and wl hld whn edgd lft over 1f out* **8/1**[3]

1-00 **8** *shd* **Herminella**[20] 2615 3-9-4 **67**.............................. DavidProbert 10 51
(William Muir) *racd off the pce in midfield: clsd and in tch 5f out: rdn and fnd little ent fnl 2f: drvn and wknd over 1f out* **17/2**

0-54 **9** 2 ¼ **High On The Hog (IRE)**[36] 2146 3-9-2 **65**.................... JimmyFortune 2 45+
(John Dunlop) *s.i.s: wl off the pce towards rr tl clsd and in tch 5f out: effrt and swtchd lft jst over 2f out: sn nt clr run and lost any ch: no ch and eased ins fnl f* **7/2**[1]

056- **10** 2 ¾ **Jahanara (IRE)**[257] 6697 3-9-5 **68**.............................. RichardHughes 7 40+
(Richard Hannon) *racd freely: chsd ldrs and clr of field for 3f: rdn: unable qck and edgd lft wl over 1f out: wknd over 1f out* **11/1**

00-0 **11** 2 ½ **Honourable Knight (IRE)**[12] 2838 3-9-5 **68**.................. MartinDwyer 6 36+
(Mark Usher) *racd off the pce in midfield: clsd and in tch 5f out: rdn and effrt on inner jst over 2f out: no hdwy and struggling whn nt clr run and hmpd over 1f out: no ch and eased ins fnl f* **11/1**

3104 **12** 5 **Silly Billy (IRE)**[40] 2024 3-9-7 **70**.............................. LiamKeniry 11 25
(Sylvester Kirk) *hld up wl off the pce towards rr: clsd and in tch 5f out: rdn and no hdwy 2f out: wknd over 1f out: wl bhd and eased ins fnl f* **20/1**

1m 39.47s (0.77) **Going Correction** +0.075s/f (Good) **12** Ran SP% **117.2**
Speed ratings (Par 99): **99,96,95,91,88 86,86,86,84,81 79,74**
toteswingers:1&2:£38.60, 2&3:£43.20, 1&3:£17.20 CSF £102.97 CT £1397.96 TOTE £13.60: £4.20, £4.10, £5.40; EX 170.20.
Owner K B Taylor **Bred** Ashridge Farm Stud **Trained** Radlett, Herts

FOCUS
A modest handicap but, although the gallop was reasonable (best comparative time of the evening), not many figured and the first three finished clear. A 5lb personal best from the winner.
High On The Hog(IRE) Official explanation: jockey said colt was denied a clear run

3260 ENJOY JUNIOR RUGBY WITH TADLEY TIGERS FILLIES' H'CAP 1m 2f 6y
8:20 (8:21) (Class 4) (0-85,82) 3-Y-O **£4,079** (£1,214; £606; £303) **Stalls** Low

Form RPR

42-0 **1** **Miss Diagnosis (IRE)**[39] 2050 3-9-4 **79**.............................. JimCrowley 9 92+
(Ralph Beckett) *stdd and dropped in bhd after s: hld up in last quartet: smooth hdwy on outer to join ldrs gng wl 2f out: rdn to ld jst over 1f out: kpt on wl and in command towards fin: rdn out* **10/1**

1-61 **2** 1 ¼ **Masaraat (FR)**[35] 2184 3-9-4 **79**.............................. RichardHills 1 90+
(John Dunlop) *in tch in midfield: switching rt off rail over 3f out: nt clr run and swtchd rt again 2f out: styd on u.p to chse wnr ins fnl f: one pce and hld fnl 75yds* **15/2**[3]

31-1 **3** ¾ **Fine Threads**[43] 1947 3-9-2 **77**.............................. MichaelHills 11 86
(B W Hills) *chsd ldrs: effrt u.p over 2f out: drvn ahd wl over 1f out: hdd jst over 1f out: no ex and styd on same pce fnl 100yds* **9/2**[2]

-122 **4** 1 ¼ **Sacred Shield**[18] 2688 3-9-0 **75**.............................. TomQueally 3 82
(Sir Henry Cecil) *hld up in last quartet: hdwy and travelling wl whn nt clr run over 2f out: rdn and hdwy 2f out: ev ch and drvn jst over 1f out: no ex and btn fnl 100yds: wknd towards fin* **11/4**[1]

-060 **5** 2 **Kalahaag (IRE)**[10] 2925 3-9-0 **75**..............................(b[1]) PatDobbs 7 78?
(Richard Hannon) *chsd ldr: rdn over 2f out: pressing ldrs and drvn over 1f out: wknd fnl 150yds* **33/1**

-266 **6** 2 **Lunar Phase (IRE)**[11] 2883 3-9-2 **77**.............................. AdamKirby 8 76
(Clive Cox) *in tch towards rr: u.p and struggling to qckn wl over 3f out: outpcd 2f out: no threat to ldrs and plugged on same pce ins fnl f* **10/1**

4-21 **7** 5 **Abdicate (IRE)**[20] 2621 3-9-1 **76**.............................. TonyHamilton 2 65
(Richard Fahey) *chsd ldng pair: rdn and effrt over 2f out: drvn and unable qck wl over 1f out: wknd ent fnl f* **14/1**

3-50 **8** ¾ **Beso (IRE)**[19] 2643 3-8-8 **69**.............................. KierenFallon 5 56
(Luca Cumani) *taken down early: a towards rr: pushed along and no hdwy wl over 2f out: wknd ent fnl 2f* **14/1**

10-0 **9** 3 ½ **Sister Red (IRE)**[51] 1725 3-9-5 **80**.............................. RichardHughes 10 60
(Richard Hannon) *led: rdn over 2f out: hdd wl over 1f out: sn btn: fdd ent fnl f: eased wl ins fnl f* **16/1**

10-2 **10** ½ **Isolate**[14] 2791 3-9-7 **82**.............................. JimmyFortune 4 61
(Hughie Morrison) *t.k.h: hld up in tch: lost pl and rdn ent fnl 2f: sn wknd: wl btn and eased wl ins fnl f* **9/2**[2]

2m 7.27s (-1.53) **Going Correction** +0.075s/f (Good) **10** Ran SP% **115.1**
Speed ratings (Par 98): **109,108,107,106,104 103,99,98,95,95**
toteswingers:1&2:£6.80, 2&3:£7.20, 1&3:£8.70 CSF £81.75 CT £387.28 TOTE £12.90: £4.30, £3.60, £1.40; EX 97.20.
Owner J H Richmond-Watson **Bred** M Morrissey **Trained** Kimpton, Hants

FOCUS
A useful-looking and competitive handicap featuring several lightly raced sorts from leading stables and a race in which the winner of three of the last four renewals has gone on to show smart form. The gallop was no more than fair and this race should throw up winners. A clear personal best from Miss Diagnosis.
Isolate Official explanation: jockey said filly ran too freely

3261 SHREDDING FOR BEDDING H'CAP 5f 34y
8:50 (8:50) (Class 5) (0-70,70) 3-Y-O+ **£2,590** (£770; £385; £192) **Stalls** Centre

Form RPR

3-56 **1** **Bouncy Bouncy (IRE)**[35] 2182 4-8-11 **55**..............................(t) HayleyTurner 9 66
(Michael Bell) *chsd ldrs: wnt 2nd 2f out: rdn and effrt over 1f out: led fnl 75yds: r.o wl and sn in command* **11/2**[3]

45 **2** 1 ½ **Equuleus Pictor**[21] 2585 7-9-12 **70**..............................(p) CathyGannon 6 76
(John Spearing) *led: rdn 2f out: drvn over 1f out: hdd fnl 75yds: sn btn* **7/2**[1]

4-00 **3** ½ **Doctor Hilary**[10] 2920 9-8-9 **56**..............................(v) KierenFox[(3)] 2 60
(Mark Hoad) *in tch in last pair: rdn and effrt ent fnl 2f: hdwy and nt clr run whn swtchd lft ins fnl f: r.o wl fnl 100yds* **6/1**

-123 **4** ¾ **Rebecca Romero**[20] 2603 4-8-13 **57**..............................(v) RichardHughes 1 58
(Denis Coakley) *hld up in tch towards rr: hdwy 2f out: rdn to chse ldrs 1f out: styd on same pce fnl 100yds* **4/1**[2]

20-0 **5** 1 ½ **Towy Boy (IRE)**[47] 1838 6-9-2 **60**..............................(bt) JamesDoyle 8 56
(Ian Wood) *chsd ldrs: rdn and effrt wl over 1f out: unable qck u.p ent fnl f: styd on same pce fnl 150yds* **11/1**

64 **6** 1 ½ **Boragh Jamal (IRE)**[3] 3174 4-9-7 **65**..............................(b) MartinDwyer 3 55+
(Brian Meehan) *s.i.s: hld up in last: hdwy and nt clr run over 1f out: swtchd lft 1f out: kpt on: nvr able to chal* **17/2**

2601 **7** 1 ¼ **Premier League**[19] 2655 4-9-2 **60**..............................(p) RoystonFfrench 11 46
(Julia Feilden) *dwlt: sn in tch in midfield: rdn ent fnl 2f: wknd u.p jst ins fnl f* **8/1**

0-00 **8** 2 ½ **Comadoir (IRE)**[132] 470 5-9-7 **65**..............................(t) FergusSweeney 10 42
(Jo Crowley) *chsd ldr tl 2f out: wknd qckly jst over 1f out: wl bhd ins fnl f* **8/1**

62.98 secs (1.58) **Going Correction** +0.40s/f (Good)
WFA 3 from 4yo+ 6lb **8** Ran SP% **113.0**
Speed ratings (Par 103): **103,100,99,98,96 93,91,87**
toteswingers:1&2:£2.00, 2&3:£4.90, 1&3:£9.20 CSF £24.44 CT £118.90 TOTE £4.10: £1.10, £1.30, £2.90; EX 27.30.
Owner Mrs A Scotney Mrs D Asplin A Symonds **Bred** Ms Adelaide Foley & Roger O'Callaghan **Trained** Newmarket, Suffolk

FOCUS
A modest sprint run at a good gallop in which the field came to the stands side. The form is rated at face value around the runner-up.
T/Jkpt: £362,765.00 to a £1 stake. Pool of £1,277,341.75 - 2.50 winning tickets. T/Plt: £104.10 to a £1 stake. Pool of £136,486.84 - 956.39 winning tickets. T/Qpdt: £32.90 to a £1 stake. Pool of £7,160.58 - 160.85 winning tickets. SP

3262 - 3265a (Foreign Racing) - See Raceform Interactive

2900 BATH (L-H)
Wednesday, June 22

OFFICIAL GOING: Good (good to firm in places; 8.6)
GOOD (Good to firm in places; 8.6)
Wind: Fresh against Weather: Dry and breezy

3266 DIGIBET.COM H'CAP 1m 5y
6:10 (6:12) (Class 5) (0-70,70) 4-Y-O+ **£2,266** (£674; £337; £168) **Stalls** Low

Form RPR

0430 **1** **Salient**[16] 2771 7-9-4 **67**.............................. J-PGuillambert 7 76
(Michael Attwater) *led: rdn and hdd 2f out: kpt on gamely to ld again jst ins fnl f: kpt on wl* **5/1**

040- **2** ½ **Daneside (IRE)**[299] 5479 4-8-2 **51** oh3.............................. DavidProbert 2 59
(Gary Harrison) *chsd ldng pair: rdn and effrt over 2f out: swtchd rt over 1f out: pressed ldrs and edgd lft 1f out: pressed wnr and kpt on u.p fnl 100yds* **25/1**

-004 **3** 1 ¼ **Lutine Charlie (IRE)**[12] 2870 4-9-1 **64**.............................. KirstyMilczarek 9 69
(Ronald Harris) *chsd wnr: rdn and led narrowly 2f out: drvn over 1f out: hdd jst ins fnl f: no ex and btn fnl 75yds* **7/2**[3]

-052 **4** *shd* **One Hit Wonder**[16] 2771 4-9-0 **63**.............................. ChrisCatlin 3 68
(Mouse Hamilton-Fairley) *in tch in midfield: rdn 3f out: drvn and outpcd 2f out: rallied and kpt on u.p ins fnl f* **9/4**[1]

44-0 **5** 1 ½ **Only You Maggie (IRE)**[9] 2996 4-8-10 **64**.............................. MarkCoumbe[(5)] 6 65
(Gary Harrison) *in tch in midfield: rdn and effrt on outer over 2f out: kpt on same pce and no imp fnl f* **14/1**

0000 **6** ½ **Having A Ball**[14] 2816 7-8-2 **51** oh2..............................(v) FrankieMcDonald 5 51
(Jonathan Portman) *s.i.s: t.k.h: hld up in last pair: hdwy to chse ldng trio 3f out: rdn and nt qckn wl over 1f out: one pce and btn fnl f* **16/1**

1123 **7** 2 ½ **Integria**[26] 2449 5-9-2 **68**..............................(bt) MatthewDavies[(3)] 4 63
(George Baker) *s.i.s: hld up in rr: slipped and rdr lost iron over 4f out: rdr unbalanced trying to rcvr 4f out: rdn and effrt on outer 2f out: hung lft and no prog 1f out* **11/4**[2]

1m 42.14s (1.34) **Going Correction** 0.0s/f (Good) **7** Ran SP% **112.7**
Speed ratings (Par 103): **93,92,91,91,89 89,86**
toteswingers: 1&2 £6.80, 1&3 £3.60, 2&3 £12.00. CSF £102.09 CT £488.51 TOTE £3.10: £1.10, £23.70; EX 85.50.
Owner Canisbay Bloodstock **Bred** Hesmonds Stud Ltd **Trained** Epsom, Surrey

FOCUS
The first three finishers raced in first, third and second respectively for much of the way, and this is not strong form.
Integria Official explanation: jockey said the gelding slipped on the bend

3267 BRISTOL PORT COMPANY MAIDEN STKS 1m 3f 144y
6:40 (6:50) (Class 5) 3-Y-O+ **£2,266** (£674; £337; £168) **Stalls** Low

Form RPR

6 **1** **Ithoughtitwasover (IRE)**[14] 2813 3-8-13 0.............................. J-PGuillambert 4 87+
(Mark Johnston) *sn niggled along in rr of main gp: awkward and nt handle bnd over 4f out: rdn and hdwy 3f out: led ent fnl f: rn green but forged ahd fnl 150yds: wl in command at fin* **16/1**

30-4 **2** 2 ¼ **Parvana (IRE)**[47] 1845 3-8-8 76.............................. TedDurcan 9 77
(William Haggas) *chsd ldrs: rdn to press ldr 2f out: hung lft 1f out: kpt on same pce ins fnl f: wnt 2nd towards fin* **5/2**[1]

-033 **3** *nk* **Magical Flower**[19] 2688 3-8-3 71.............................. HarryBentley[(5)] 8 76
(William Knight) *led: rdn over 2f out: drvn and hdd 1f out: no ex fnl 150yds: lost 2nd towards fin* **9/1**[3]

3- **4** 1 ½ **Star In Flight**[221] 7451 4-9-13 0.............................. ShaneKelly 3 78
(Brian Meehan) *t.k.h: chsd ldr for 2f: hld up wl in tch after: rdn and unable qck over 1f out: rallied u.p ent fnl f: plugged on same pce fnl f* **33/1**

0-02 **5** 5 **Novel Dancer**[19] 2664 3-8-13 73.............................. PatDobbs 2 70
(Richard Hannon) *chsd ldr after 2f tl rdn and nt qckn jst over 2f out: wknd u.p wl over 1f out* **13/2**[2]

00 **6** 8 **Green Future (USA)**[11] 2930 3-8-13 0.............................. NeilCallan 12 56
(Amanda Perrett) *in tch: slipped on bnd over 4f out: rdn and unable qck wl over 2f out: drvn and wknd 2f out* **25/1**

0 **7** 3 ¾ **Fascinating (IRE)**[13] 2848 3-8-13 0.............................. AhmedAjtebi 11 50
(Mahmood Al Zarooni) *s.i.s: sn pushed along in last pair: rdn and toiling over 2f out: n.d* **20/1**

44 **8** 1 ¾ **Hygrove Welshlady (IRE)**[36] 2175 3-8-8 0.............................. ChrisCatlin 7 42
(J W Hills) *t.k.h: hld up wl in tch: rdn and wknd qckly over 2f out: wl bhd over 1f out* **66/1**

9 26 **Vitobello** 4-9-13 0.............................. NeilChalmers 5 —
(Bryn Palling) *s.i.s: a bhd: lost tch 4f out: t.o and eased ins fnl f* **100/1**

2m 29.65s (-0.95) **Going Correction** 0.0s/f (Good)
WFA 3 from 4yo 14lb **9** Ran SP% **71.8**
Speed ratings (Par 103): **103,101,101,100,96 91,89,87,70**
toteswingers: 1&2 £3.70, 1&3 £5.10, 2&3 £1.80. CSF £20.88 TOTE £14.00: £3.50, £1.10, £1.40; EX 23.50.
Owner Crone Stud Farms Ltd **Bred** Stonethorn Stud Farms Ltd **Trained** Middleham Moor, N Yorks

FOCUS
The official ratings of the runner-up (76) and third (71) suggest this was no more than a fair maiden, although the time was 1.83 seconds faster than the following Class 6 handicap.

Green Future(USA) Official explanation: jockey said the gelding slipped on the bend

3268 BATH CHRONICLE H'CAP 1m 3f 144y

7:10 (7:16) (Class 6) (0-60,60) 3-Y-O **£1,706** (£503; £252) **Stalls** Low

Form RPR

00-2 **1** **Tanjung Agas (IRE)**[29] 2379 3-9-7 **60**....................(p) NeilCallan 11 67+
(Roger Varian) *chsd ldrs: pushed along over 8f out: chsd ldr 6f out: slipped bnd over 4f out: drvn to ld wl over 2f out: wandering lft and rt u.p after: drvn and pricking ears ins fnl f: all out nr fin* **4/1**[2]

000- **2** *nk* **Sea The Flames (IRE)**[273] 6294 3-8-13 **52**.................... TadhgO'Shea 1 58+
(Marcus Tregoning) *dwlt: wl off the pce in rr: stl plenty to do whn nt clr run 3f out: sn swtchd rt: gd hdwy but hld hd high after: chsd ldrs and stl racing awkwardly 1f out: hung lft tl surged ahd to press wnr nr fin* **40/1**

0606 **3** *1/2* **Sum Satisfaction**[12] 2874 3-9-4 **57**.................... JamesDoyle 4 63
(Dominic Ffrench Davis) *in tch: rdn and effrt to chse wnr over 2f out: drvn and pressing wnr 2f out: unable qck ins fnl f* **16/1**

4243 **4** *3 3/4* **Revolutionary**[18] 2722 3-9-1 **57**.................... SophieDoyle(3) 3 56
(Jamie Osborne) *chsd ldrs: rdn to chse ldng pair 4f out: one pce and no imp fnl 2f* **9/1**

0-23 **5** *1/2* **Drumadoon (IRE)**[20] 2637 3-9-4 **57**.................... TedDurcan 10 55
(John Dunlop) *wl off the pce towards rr: rdn over 4f out: hdwy over 4f out: styng on steadily u.p after but nvr gng pce to rch ldrs* **7/2**[1]

0230 **6** *2* **Fleeting Storm**[86] 1018 3-9-6 **59**....................(b1) NickyMackay 8 54
(Hughie Morrison) *racd off the pce in midfield: rdn and no imp over 3f out: no threat to ldrs but plugged on fnl 2f* **25/1**

3505 **7** *2 1/2* **Laffraaj (IRE)**[20] 2637 3-8-8 **52**....................(b1) HarryBentley(5) 6 43
(Pat Eddery) *sn pushed along and wl off the pce in last quartet: sme hdwy on inner 3f out: kpt on but nvr any ch of rching ldrs* **12/1**

0 **8** *1 3/4* **Dhampas**[16] 2760 3-8-7 **46**.................... SamHitchcott 14 34
(Jim Boyle) *racd wl of the pce towards rr: rdn and effrt over 3f out: kpt on steadily but nvr any ch* **33/1**

040 **9** *4 1/2* **Minkie Moon (IRE)**[26] 2458 3-9-5 **58**.................... PatDobbs 13 38
(Amanda Perrett) *midfield tl stern reminders and dropped towards rr after 1f: sme modest hdwy u.p fnl 2f: n.d* **16/1**

3050 **10** *3 1/4* **Mountain Myst**[32] 2307 3-9-3 **56**....................(b1) RichardMullen 12 31
(William Muir) *wl off the pce towards rr: rdn and effrt over 3f out: n.d* **33/1**

006 **11** *1 3/4* **Hint Of Silver (IRE)**[20] 2639 3-8-13 **52**.................... StevieDonohoe 17 24
(Andrew Haynes) *s.i.s: wl off the pce in detached last: sme hdwy and tagged on to bkmarkers 3f out: passed btn horses fr over 2f out: n.d* **50/1**

0544 **12** *3 1/4* **Disturbia (IRE)**[14] 2801 3-8-7 **46**.................... MartinLane 5 12
(J W Hills) *led tl wl over 2f out: sn fdd and wl bhd fr wl over 1f out* **25/1**

0-55 **13** *1/2* **Newby Lodge (IRE)**[21] 2621 3-9-2 **55**.................... ShaneKelly 9 20
(William Haggas) *s.i.s: hmpd sn after s and in rr early: hdwy into midfield 7f out: 5th and drvn 3f out: sn wknd* **8/1**

30-0 **14** *3* **Fastada (IRE)**[42] 1997 3-9-2 **58**.................... MatthewDavies(3) 7 18
(Jonathan Portman) *chsd ldrs: losing pl and pushed along 6f out: wl bhd fnl 3f* **33/1**

500- **15** *2* **Special Endeavour (IRE)**[216] 7497 3-9-5 **58**.................... DavidProbert 16 15
(William Muir) *chsd ldrs tl 6f out: rdn and dropped out qckly over 4f out: wl bhd fnl 3f* **28/1**

0-03 **16** *20* **Tommy Tiger**[13] 2858 3-9-0 **53**.................... ChrisCatlin 15 —
(Stuart Williams) *t.k.h: chsd ldr tl 6f out: rdn and dropped out qckly over 3f out: t.o and eased ins fnl f* **7/1**[3]

600 **17** *3 1/4* **Springtime Melody (FR)**[14] 2813 3-9-2 **55**.................... FrankieMcDonald 2 —
(David Bourton) *racd in midfield: rdn and struggling over 4f out: t.o and eased ins fnl f* **28/1**

2m 31.48s (0.88) **Going Correction** 0.0s/f (Good) **17** Ran SP% **123.1**
Speed ratings (Par 97): **97,96,96,93,93 92,90,89,86,84 83,80,80,78,77 63,61**
toteswingers: 1&2 £55.80, 1&3 £13.90, 2&3 £107.90. CSF £171.47 CT £2360.07 TOTE £4.90: £1.30, £12.80, £1.80, £2.00; EX 249.10.
Owner H R H Sultan Ahmad Shah **Bred** T Molan **Trained** Newmarket, Suffolk

FOCUS
The first two were reluctant to run on for pressure, yet finished one-two, and the time was 1.83 seconds slower than the earlier maiden. Consequently it's hard to view this form particularly highly.
Newby Lodge(IRE) Official explanation: jockey said that the filly was hampered leaving the stalls

3269 PREMIER FOOD COURTS H'CAP 5f 11y

7:40 (7:42) (Class 4) (0-85,78) 3-Y-O **£3,238** (£963; £481; £240) **Stalls** Centre

Form RPR

1311 **1** **Pick A Little**[16] 2757 3-9-1 **77**.................... HarryBentley(5) 5 84
(Ron Hodges) *outpcd in last trio: clsd and chsng ldrs 2f out: swtchd rt and rdn to chse ldr over 1f out: pushed ahd ins fnl f: r.o wl: pushed out* **9/2**[3]

3345 **2** *1* **Restless Bay (IRE)**[6] 3078 3-9-7 **78**....................(v) ChrisCatlin 6 81
(Reg Hollinshead) *outpcd in last trio: pushed along and effrt over 2f out: hdwy over 1f out: styd on to chse wnr fnl 75yds: no imp* **8/1**

-216 **3** *hd* **Shes Rosie**[23] 2553 3-8-10 **67**.................... RussKennemore 4 69
(John O'Shea) *chsd ldng pair: rdn to chse ldr wl over 1f out tl over 1f out: styd on same pce u.p fnl f* **15/2**

2621 **4** *3* **Alpha Delta Whisky**[12] 2881 3-9-5 **76**.................... NeilCallan 3 67
(John Gallagher) *w ldr and clr: led 1/2-way: rdn over 1f out: drvn and hdd ins fnl f: wknd fnl 75yds* **9/4**[2]

2-10 **5** *shd* **Sluggsy Morant**[23] 2564 3-9-0 **76**.................... AmyScott(5) 1 67
(Henry Candy) *sn outpcd in last: rdn over 3f out: u.p 1/2-way: hdwy 1f out and swtchd lft ins fnl f: nvr gng pce to chal* **2/1**[1]

0210 **6** *13* **Sugar Beet**[25] 2505 3-9-5 **76**.................... DavidProbert 2 20
(Ronald Harris) *led and clr w rival: hdd 1/2-way: wknd u.p over 1f out: wl bhd and eased ins fnl f* **11/1**

62.76 secs (0.26) **Going Correction** +0.10s/f (Good) **6** Ran SP% **113.5**
Speed ratings (Par 101): **101,99,99,94,94 73**
toteswingers: 1&2 £1.90, 1&3 £6.10, 2&3 £5.60. CSF £38.50 TOTE £7.50: £5.40, £1.20; EX 45.10.
Owner K B Hodges **Bred** D R Tucker **Trained** Charlton Mackrell, Somerset

FOCUS
The pace was overly strong, with Alpha Delta Whisky and Sugar Beet (reported by David Probert to have run too free) taking each other on, and this was set up for those ridden with patience.
Sugar Beet Official explanation: jockey said that the filly ran too freely

3270 BRITISH STALLION STUDS E B F MAIDEN FILLIES' STKS 5f 161y

8:10 (8:11) (Class 5) 2-Y-O **£3,173** (£944; £471; £235) **Stalls** Centre

Form RPR

6 **1** **Responsive**[20] 2641 2-9-0 **0**.................... NickyMackay 5 81+
(Hughie Morrison) *chsd ldrs tl led over 3f out: mde rest: rdn clr wl over 1f out: in command and r.o wl fnl f: rdn out* **7/2**[2]

42 **2** *2 1/4* **Midas Medusa (FR)**[22] 2580 2-9-0 **0**.................... PatDobbs 2 74
(Richard Hannon) *chsd ldr tl shied at kink in rail and lost pl over 4f out: chsd ldrs after: swtchd rt and effrt to chse wnr wl over 1f out: drvn and no imp fr over 1f out* **2/1**[1]

62 **3** *nk* **Ivor's Princess**[19] 2661 2-9-0 **0**.................... JamesMillman 7 73+
(Rod Millman) *outpcd towards rr: pushed along over 3f out: stl in rr whn pushed rt and hmpd 2f out: hung lft over 1f out: nt clr run and swtchd rt 1f out: str run fnl 150yds: nvr able to chal* **5/1**[3]

0 **4** *2 1/2* **Molly Jones**[29] 2374 2-9-0 **0**.................... ChrisCatlin 1 65
(Derek Haydn Jones) *in tch in midfield: pushed along over 3f out: swtchd rt and hdwy on outer to dispute 3rd 1f out: styd on same pce after* **40/1**

5 *1 1/4* **Pindrop** 2-9-0 **0**.................... ShaneKelly 12 61+
(Walter Swinburn) *v.s.a: bhd in last trio: hdwy and swtchd sharply rt 2f out: kpt on ins fnl f: nvr able to chal* **11/1**

6 *hd* **Ocean Myth** 2-9-0 **0**.................... TedDurcan 6 60
(William Haggas) *s.i.s: bhd in last trio: rdn over 3f out: hdwy on inner 2f out: disputing modest 3rd 1f out: no prog and lost 3 pls fnl 150yds* **9/1**

7 *1/2* **Picura** 2-9-0 **0**.................... DavidProbert 3 58
(William Muir) *in tch: rdn and outpcd 3f out: rallied u.p over 1f out: styd on same pce fnl f* **28/1**

8 *1 1/2* **Affectionate** 2-9-0 **0**.................... AhmedAjtebi 9 53+
(Mahmood Al Zarooni) *veered lft and v.s.a: rn green in last: hdwy u.p on inner over 1f out: kpt on same pce ins fnl f: nvr trbld ldrs* **13/2**

00 **9** *3* **Hawaiian Freeze**[13] 2844 2-9-0 **0**.................... J-PGuillambert 10 43
(Richard Ford) *chsd ldrs: rdn ent fnl 2f: wknd over 1f out* **100/1**

6 **10** *nse* **Misred Melissa (IRE)**[11] 2901 2-9-0 **0**.................... NeilCallan 4 43
(John Gallagher) *led tl over 3f out: rdn and struggling 2f out: lost modest 3rd 1f out and fdd fnl f* **20/1**

11 *2 3/4* **Empressive** 2-9-0 **0**.................... RichardMullen 8 34
(William Muir) *in tch in midfield: rdn and struggling 3f out: rn green and dropped to rr wl over 1f out: bhd and edgd lft 1f out* **20/1**

1m 13.59s (2.39) **Going Correction** +0.10s/f (Good) **11** Ran SP% **120.3**
Speed ratings (Par 90): **88,85,84,81,79 79,78,76,72,72 68**
toteswingers: 1&2 £3.30, 1&3 £5.40, 2&3 £2.50. CSF £10.53 TOTE £3.00: £1.10, £1.10, £2.60; EX 19.10.
Owner Thurloe Thoroughbreds XXIX **Bred** Mrs S Field **Trained** East Ilsley, Berks

FOCUS
Some respected connections were represented and this looked a reasonable fillies' maiden, rated around the second and third.

NOTEBOOK
Responsive stepped up plenty on the form she showed behind the talented Illaunglass (subsequently third in the Albany) over 6f on Polytrack first time up. She looks useful and her connections think there's more to come, even back at 5f. (op 4-1 tchd 9-2)
Midas Medusa(FR) was in the clear for long enough if good enough but didn't see her race out. She again showed enough to suggest she can win a similar race, however. (op 5-2)
Ivor's Princess lacked the early speed to get a good position and was denied a clear run in the closing stages. She would have finished closer with a better trip and can win a maiden, probably back over 6f. (tchd 9-2 and 11-2)
Molly Jones stepped up hugely on her debut performance and showed enough to suggest she can go close in a nursery. (tchd 50-1)
Pindrop ◆ made an eyecatching debut, racing out the back after a slow start and not enjoying a clear run before finishing well. She cost 28,000gns and is a half-sister to nine winners, notably Leporello, who was high class at around 1m2f, latterly for this stable. There should be a lot more to come. (op 9-1)
Ocean Myth ran as though she'll come on for the outing. (op 12-1)
Affectionate looked awkward. She was very slowly away and then raced keenly when latching onto the back of the pack. (op 6-1 tchd 11-2)

3271 LINDLEYS GROUP CLASSIFIED STKS 5f 161y

8:40 (8:40) (Class 5) 3-Y-O **£2,266** (£674; £337; £168) **Stalls** Centre

Form RPR

2134 **1** **Indian Shuffle (IRE)**[12] 2881 3-9-0 **68**.................... NeilCallan 5 73
(Jonathan Portman) *mde all: rdn wl over 1f out: r.o wl and in command fnl 100yds: rdn out* **11/2**

31-6 **2** *1 3/4* **Yasmeena (USA)**[32] 2294 3-9-0 **70**.................... TadhgO'Shea 1 67+
(B W Hills) *taken down early: stdd s and hld up in last: t.k.h 4f out: [illegible] hdwy to chse ldrs over 3f out: rdn 2f out: chsd wnr over 1f out: drvn and one pce ins fnl f* **[illegible]**

0-10 **3** *1 1/4* **Swendab (IRE)**[22] 2582 3-8-9 **66**.................... RyanPowell(5) 3 63
(John O'Shea) *in tch: rdn and effrt 2f out: drvn and wnt 3rd 1f out: no imp and one pce fnl 150yds* **8/1**

6002 **4** *1 3/4* **Pippa's Gift**[7] 3048 3-9-0 **67**.................... RichardMullen 4 57
(William Muir) *in tch: swtchd rt and effrt 2f out: sn drvn and unable qck: wknd ins fnl f* **9/2**[3]

-514 **5** *5* **Black Cadillac (IRE)**[19] 2662 3-9-0 **64**....................(v) DavidProbert 6 41
(Andrew Balding) *w wnr tl wl over 1f out: sn drvn and lost 2nd: wknd ent fnl f* **11/4**[2]

1m 12.46s (1.26) **Going Correction** +0.10s/f (Good) **5** Ran SP% **109.4**
Speed ratings (Par 99): **95,92,91,88,82**
toteswinger: 1&2 £5.60. CSF £14.77 TOTE £5.60: £1.50, £3.00; EX 22.90.
Owner Out To Grass Partnership **Bred** Anglia Bloodstock And Tsarina Stud **Trained** Compton, Berks

FOCUS
A modest classified event run in a time 0.71 seconds slower than the following Class 6 handicap.

3272 EVENT MOBILE BARS H'CAP 5f 161y

9:10 (9:10) (Class 6) (0-60,59) 3-Y-O **£1,706** (£503; £252) **Stalls** Centre

Form RPR

5232 **1** **Albany Rose (IRE)**[14] 2827 3-9-7 **59**.................... TedDurcan 10 76+
(Rae Guest) *chsd ldr: rdn and effrt to ld over 1f out: clr and in command 1f out: r.o strly: rdn out* **9/2**[2]

-025 **2** *3 1/4* **Sarangoo**[12] 2869 3-9-6 **58**.................... TomMcLaughlin 12 64
(Malcolm Saunders) *dwlt: sn rcvrd and in tch in midfield: swtchd rt and hdwy over 1f out: chsd clr wnr fnl 100yds: no imp* **8/1**

-105 **3** *1 3/4* **Dreams Of Glory**[23] 2549 3-8-4 **47**.................... HarryBentley(5) 6 48
(Ron Hodges) *led tl over 3f out: styd w ldr tl drvn ahd again wl over 1f out: sn hdd and outpcd by wnr: wl hld ins fnl f: lost 2nd fnl 100yds* **10/1**

4302 **4** *5* **Look Twice**[9] 2993 3-9-4 **56**.................... ChrisCatlin 7 40
(Alex Hales) *towards rr: rdn over 3f out: hdwy u.p over 1f out: kpt on but no ch w ldrs fnl f* **6/1**

5-40 **5** *1/2* **Regal Bullet (IRE)**[32] 2294 3-9-2 **57**.................... MatthewDavies(3) 13 39
(Dean Ivory) *chsd ldrs on outer: rdn and effrt to press ldrs 2f out: edgd lft u.p and wknd over 1f out* **11/2**[3]

0566 **6** *3 1/2* **Silca Conegliano (IRE)**[23] 2549 3-9-0 **52**.................... SamHitchcott 3 23
(Mick Channon) *towards rr: rdn over 3f out: passed btn horses on inner jst over 1f out: nvr trbld ldrs* **12/1**

-000 **7** 1 1/2 **Lady Excellentia (IRE)**[11] 2918 3-8-7 **45**.................. FrankieMcDonald 1 11
(Ronald Harris) *v s.i.s: bhd: styd on passed btn horses fnl f: n.d* **50/1**

4360 **8** 3/4 **Circuitous**[14] 2818 3-9-6 **58**...(tp) NeilCallan 8 21
(Paul Cole) *chsd ldrs: rdn wl over 2f out: wknd u.p over 1f out: wl btn fnl f* **12/1**

0-02 **9** 1 1/4 **Brian Sprout**[5] 3143 3-9-0 **55**....................................... DeclanCannon(3) 5 14
(John Weymes) *w ldr tl led over 3f out: drvn and hdd wl over 1f out: sn wknd: fdd ins fnl f* **4/1**[1]

566 **10** 1/2 **Lady Rumba**[18] 2710 3-8-4 **47**....................................... RyanPowell(5) 14 —
(John O'Shea) *in tch on outer: rdn over 2f out: sn struggling: wknd u.p wl over 1f out* **33/1**

3000 **11** 1 1/4 **Sailing North (USA)**[23] 2549 3-9-5 **57**.......................(p) KirstyMilczarek 2 —
(Ronald Harris) *in tch on inner: struggling u.p jst over 2f out: wknd over 1f out* **33/1**

4030 **12** *nse* **Quadra Hop (IRE)**[11] 2918 3-9-3 **55**............................(t) DavidProbert 11 —
(Bryn Palling) *t.k.h: chsd ldrs tl 2f out: drvn and wknd over 1f out: fdd 1f out* **14/1**

000 **13** *24* **Dorothy's Dream (IRE)**[22] 2581 3-8-8 **46** ow1.......... RussKennemore 4 —
(John O'Shea) *dwlt: a in rr: rdn and struggling 3f out: t.o and eased ins fnl f* **50/1**

1m 11.75s (0.55) **Going Correction** +0.10s/f (Good) **13** Ran SP% **119.9**
Speed ratings (Par 97): **100,95,93,86,86 81,79,78,76,76 74,74,42**
toteswingers: 1&2 £5.10, 1&3 £7.10, 2&3 £12.20. CSF £39.66 CT £345.71 TOTE £6.20: £1.90, £3.10, £6.10; EX 43.70.
Owner E P Duggan **Bred** Blue Bloodstock Ltd **Trained** Newmarket, Suffolk

FOCUS
The time was the quickest of three races over the trip, 0.71 seconds faster than the earlier 0-70 classified event for 3-y-os.
T/Plt: £244.30 to a £1 stake. Pool of £69,894.17 - 208.81 winning tickets. T/Qpdt: £25.30 to a £1 stake. Pool of £7,017.95 - 205.10 winning tickets. SP

2983 CARLISLE (R-H)
Wednesday, June 22

OFFICIAL GOING: Good (good to soft down the hill; soft in 6f chute) changing to good to soft (good in places) after race 3 (3.05) changing to soft after race 6 (4.40)
Wind: Light, half behind Weather: Cloudy

3273 EDMUNDSON ELECTRICAL MAIDEN AUCTION STKS 5f
2:00 (2:06) (Class 5) 2-Y-O **£2,266** (£674; £337; £168) **Stalls** Low

Form RPR

33 **1** **Pen Bal Crag (IRE)**[12] 2886 2-9-2 0.............................. PaulHanagan 11 78
(Richard Fahey) *cl up: rdn over 2f out: led ins fnl f: edgd lft and styd on strly* **7/2**[1]

2 1/2 **Half A Billion (IRE)** 2-9-2 0... FrederikTylicki 12 76+
(Michael Dods) *trckd ldrs on outside: led 2f out to ins fnl f: kpt on fin* **25/1**

030 **3** 3/4 **See Clearly**[12] 2886 2-8-4 0... DuranFentiman 1 62
(Tim Easterby) *trckd ldrs: effrt and rdn over 2f out: kpt on u.p ins fnl f: hld nr fin* **9/2**[2]

4 1 **Byronic Hero** 2-8-6 0.. PatrickDonaghy(3) 8 63+
(Jedd O'Keeffe) *green in preliminaries and walked to s: missed break and bhd: hdwy on outside 1/2-way: rdn and rn green over 1f out: styd on wl fnl f: bttr for r* **7/1**

56 **5** *hd* **Galilee Chapel (IRE)**[18] 2731 2-8-11 0......................... TonyHamilton 4 64
(Howard Johnson) *led: hdd 2f out: sn rdn: rallied: kpt on same pce ins fnl f* **10/1**

6 **6** 2 1/2 **Lady Caprice**[6] 3082 2-8-6 0...................................... AndrewHeffernan 5 50
(Ann Duffield) *trckd ldrs: effrt and drvn over 2f out: edgd lft and one pce over 1f out* **5/1**[3]

7 1 **Dazzlin Bluebell (IRE)** 2-8-6 0 ow2................................ DavidAllan 10 47+
(Tim Easterby) *rrd over and fell bef s: bhd and sn pushed along: hdwy on outside over 1f out: kpt on: nrst fin* **16/1**

8 1 **Elusive Bonus (IRE)** 2-8-4 0...................................... SilvestreDeSousa 3 41
(David O'Meara) *bhd: pushed along and swtchd rt 2f out: no imp fnl f* **20/1**

0 **9** 2 1/4 **Cooldine Cat (IRE)**[29] 2387 2-8-13 0.............................. TomEaves 9 42
(John Quinn) *midfield: rdn and outpcd 1/2-way: n.d after* **8/1**

45 **10** 2 **Cataract**[15] 2780 2-8-6 0... AndrewMullen 6 28
(John Weymes) *dwlt: t.k.h towards rr: outpcd over 2f out: sn btn* **40/1**

0 **11** 7 **Flirty Gerty (IRE)**[9] 2983 2-8-8 0................................. RichardKingscote 2 4
(Tom Dascombe) *midfield: rdn 1/2-way: wknd over 1f out* **12/1**

12 4 1/2 **Never In (IRE)** 2-8-4 0.. PatrickMathers 7 —
(Alan Berry) *missed break: bhd and pushed along: no ch fr 1/2-way* **100/1**

61.96 secs (1.16) **Going Correction** +0.075s/f (Good) **12** Ran SP% **115.4**
Speed ratings (Par 93): **93,92,91,89,89 85,83,81,78,75 63,56**
toteswingers:1&2:£10.70, 2&3:£9.40, 1&3:£2.80 CSF £98.64 TOTE £3.60: £1.50, £6.10, £1.90; EX 48.70 Trifecta £356.00 Part won. Pool of £481.09 - 0.94 - winning units..
Owner Havelock Racing / R J Partnership **Bred** Hascombe And Valiant Studs **Trained** Musley Bank, N Yorks

■ Stewards' Enquiry : Duran Fentiman caution: used whip with excessive frequency

FOCUS
Rail realignment added 12yds to distances on Round course. The ground was just on the slow side of good at this stage and they raced in one group towards the far side rail. An ordinary maiden auction race but decent efforts from the front pair.

NOTEBOOK
Pen Bal Crag(IRE), third behind a highly-rated newcomer on his second start at York, had to battle hard. He gained the upper hand near the line and a step up to 6f in nursery company now beckons. (op 10-3)
Half A Billion(IRE), an unconsidered newcomer, certainly knew his job. He travelled very strongly but had to give best near the line. Like the winner he had to give weight away and looks a ready-made maiden race winner. (op 20-1)
See Clearly, four places behind the winner at York, had run well here on her previous outing. She stuck to her guns without ever threatening to do enough and should be able to find a race. (op 5-1 tchd 4-1)
Byronic Hero, a cheap buy, came in for support. He had to be led riderless to post and stood still when the stalls opened. He made ground at halfway and stuck on well all the way to the line. He looked the best horse on the day and can gain compensation. (tchd 5-1)
Galilee Chapel(IRE), back over 5f, was keen to post. He took them along but did not quite see it out. A less-demanding track will suit him. (op 8-1 tchd 15-2)
Lady Caprice, who made her debut over 6f, showed a bit more and there may be even better to come. (op 8-1)
Dazzlin Bluebell(IRE) reared over backwards and unseated her rider at the start. After a tardy break she took the eye staying on steadily down the wide outside. She has quite a stout pedigree and will be suited by a much stiffer test. (tchd 18-1)

3274 BRITISH STALLION STUDS E B F EDINBURGH WOOLLEN MILL MAIDEN STKS 5f 193y
2:30 (2:34) (Class 4) 2-Y-O **£4,533** (£1,348; £674; £336) **Stalls** Low

Form RPR

60 **1** **Bop It**[25] 2485 2-9-3 0.. TomEaves 3 76+
(Bryan Smart) *t.k.h early: trckd ldrs: rdn to ld appr fnl f: styd on strly* **7/1**[3]

342 **2** 1/2 **Joshua The First**[7] 3035 2-9-3 0.............................. SilvestreDeSousa 6 74
(Keith Dalgleish) *cl up: led over 2f out: wandered fr over 1f out: hdd appr fnl f: kpt on towards fin* **7/2**[2]

3 2 1/4 **Yeomanoftheguard** 2-9-3 0... PaulHanagan 7 67+
(Richard Fahey) *dwlt: bhd and sn pushed along: hdwy 2f out: kpt on ins fnl f: nt rch first two* **20/1**

4 *nk* **Be Calm** 2-8-9 0.. JamesSullivan(3) 11 61+
(Michael Easterby) *hld up in midfield on outside: rdn and flashed tail fr 1/2-way: hung rt and kpt on ins fnl f: nrst fin* **100/1**

5 2 **Electrickery** 2-8-12 0... PhillipMakin 2 55+
(Mark Johnston) *midfield: effrt and swtchd lft 2f out: edgd lft: kpt on ins fnl f: nvr able to chal* **15/2**

26 **6** 4 1/2 **Ingleby Angel (IRE)**[15] 2780 2-9-3 0.......................... DanielTudhope 10 46
(David O'Meara) *trckd ldrs: rdn and ev ch over 2f out: wknd over 1f out* **28/1**

3 **7** 3/4 **Bedlam**[11] 2936 2-8-12 0... DavidAllan 5 39
(Tim Easterby) *sn drvn along towards rr: sme hdwy over 1f out: nvr on terms* **1/1**[1]

8 1 1/4 **Knight Express** 2-9-3 0.. TonyHamilton 8 40+
(Richard Fahey) *towards rr: sn pushed along: no imp fr 1/2-way* **22/1**

5 **9** 1/2 **Twin Ivan (IRE)**[26] 2460 2-9-3 0.................................... FrederikTylicki 4 38
(Howard Johnson) *cl up tl rdn and wknd fr 2f out* **25/1**

10 2 1/4 **On The Hoof** 2-9-3 0... GrahamGibbons 1 31
(Michael Easterby) *s.i.s: sn pushed along in rr: nvr on terms* **20/1**

0 **11** 2 1/2 **Dylan's Dream (IRE)**[34] 2214 2-8-12 0......................... DuranFentiman 12 18
(Tim Easterby) *led to over 2f out: edgd lft and sn wknd* **66/1**

60 **12** 1 3/4 **Arrowroot**[18] 2731 2-8-12 0... LanceBetts(5) 9 18
(Tim Easterby) *prom: drvn along 1/2-way: sn lost pl* **100/1**

1m 15.44s (1.74) **Going Correction** +0.075s/f (Good) **12** Ran SP% **121.1**
Speed ratings (Par 95): **91,90,87,86,84 78,77,75,74,71 68,66**
toteswingers:1&2:£2.30, 2&3:£7.60, 1&3:£13.70 CSF £29.75 TOTE £8.30: £2.10, £1.10, £5.20; EX 30.60 Trifecta £569.90 Part won. Pool of £770.17 - 0.89 winning units..
Owner A Turton, J Blackburn & R Bond **Bred** Bond Thoroughbred Corporation **Trained** Hambleton, N Yorks

FOCUS
An ordinary maiden with little depth. The winner is an improver, the second quietly progressive.

NOTEBOOK
Bop It, closely related to Hoof It, had been a shade too keen for his own good on his first two starts. His trainer was confident of a much better showing and he did not lack market support. Given a good tow into the race, he showed a willing attitude to wear down the runner-up. Now he is on the right path there should be even better to come. (op 11-1 tchd 6-1)
Joshua The First, beaten by a rank outsider on his third start at Hamilton, did nothing wrong and sets the standard. He will surely find an opening. (tchd 10-3)
Yeomanoftheguard, slowly away on his debut, made up a deal of ground in the second half of the contest. He will be suited by a step up to 7f and looks a sure fire future winner. (op 18-1 tchd 16-1)
Be Calm, on her toes beforehand on her first taste of racecourse action, raced on the wide outside. She hung right but kept on all the way to the line and she should come on for the outing.
Electrickery, drawn one off the inside rail, was switched wide. She kept on in her own time and will know a lot more next time. (op 12-1 tchd 7-1)
Bedlam, a promising third first time at York, never fired. She is well worth another chance. Official explanation: jockey said filly was never travelling (op 10-11 tchd 5-4)

3275 LLOYD LTD CARLISLE BELL CONSOLATION RACE (H'CAP) 7f 200y
3:05 (3:07) (Class 4) (0-80,78) 3-Y-O+ **£5,180** (£1,541; £770; £384) **Stalls** Low

Form RPR

-314 **1** **Quite Sparky**[11] 2937 4-9-4 **78**................................(v[1]) SilvestreDeSousa 8 90+
(David O'Meara) *t.k.h: hld up: hdwy on outside over 2f out: led ins fnl f: kpt on strly* **13/2**[2]

5254 **2** 2 **One Scoop Or Two**[12] 2887 5-9-3 **77**.....................(p) GrahamGibbons 10 84
(Reg Hollinshead) *led: rdn and hung lft wl over 1f out: hdd ins fnl f: kpt on u.p* **8/1**[3]

-430 **3** *hd* **Moheebb (IRE)**[12] 2887 7-9-3 **77**.....................................(b) PJMcDonald 7 83
(Ruth Carr) *hld up: effrt 2f out: kpt on wl ins fnl f: nrst fin* **13/2**[2]

0-50 **4** 1 1/2 **One Way Or Another (AUS)**[39] 2095 8-9-3 **77**.............. ClareLindop 14 80
(Jeremy Gask) *plld hrd in midfield on outside: hdwy and ev ch over 1f out: kpt on same pce ins fnl f* **10/1**

010- **5** *nk* **Scrapper Smith (IRE)**[248] 6960 5-8-11 **78**.............. GarryWhillans(7) 16 80+
(Alistair Whillans) *missed break: bhd: hdwy on ins wl over 1f out: kpt on ins fnl f: nvr able to chal* **33/1**

0030 **6** *hd* **Champagne Style (USA)**[32] 2301 4-9-3 **77**..............(p) PaulHanagan 17 79
(Richard Guest) *hld up: hdwy on outside over 1f out: checked ins fnl f: r.o* **16/1**

5256 **7** 1 **Ours (IRE)**[12] 2887 8-9-0 **77**...(p) RobertLButler(3) 4 77
(John Harris) *bhd tl hdwy over 1f out: kpt on ins fnl f: nrst fin* **16/1**

0000 **8** 1/2 **Solar Spirit (IRE)**[25] 2497 6-9-4 **78**........................... FrannyNorton 1 76
(Tracy Waggott) *hld up on ins: effrt 2f out: no imp ins fnl f* **40/1**

0002 **9** 3 1/2 **Marjury Daw (IRE)**[9] 2999 5-9-1 **75**.............................. MickyFenton 13 65
(James Given) *trckd ldrs: drvn along 3f out: wknd over 1f out* **16/1**

331 **10** 1 **Munsarim (IRE)**[18] 2734 4-9-3 **77**................................... TomEaves 15 65
(Keith Dalgleish) *midfield: rdn and outpcd over 3f out: rallied 2f out: sn no imp* **12/1**

2406 **11** 1 1/2 **Fishforcompliments**[25] 2497 7-8-10 **77**..................... LauraBarry(7) 6 62
(Richard Fahey) *hld up: shkn up over 2f out: nvr able to chal* **11/1**

-562 **12** 3 1/4 **Ailsa Craig (IRE)**[7] 3051 5-9-1 **75**.................................. TonyHamilton 3 52
(Edwin Tuer) *cl up: rdn 3f out: wknd over 1f out* **4/1**[1]

0504 **13** *nk* **West End Lad**[6] 3081 8-9-3 **77**.......................................(b) PhillipMakin 12 53
(Roy Bowring) *prom: drvn along over 3f out: wknd fr 2f out* **50/1**

-246 **14** 1 1/4 **Opus Maximus (IRE)**[11] 2910 6-9-4 **78**...................(p) StephenCraine 5 52
(Jennie Candlish) *trckd ldrs tl rdn and wknd fr 2f out* **66/1**

324 **15** 2 1/2 **Dabbers Ridge (IRE)**[27] 2413 9-9-1 **75**....................... DanielTudhope 11 43
(Ian McInnes) *hld up: rdn on outside over 2f out: btn over 1f out* **20/1**

0500 **16** *5* **Keys Of Cyprus**[32] 2301 9-9-3 **77**.............................. AdrianNicholls 9 33
(David Nicholls) *t.k.h: in tch tl rdn and wknd qckly 2f out* **25/1**

1m 41.08s (1.08) **Going Correction** +0.25s/f (Good) **16** Ran SP% **118.0**
Speed ratings (Par 105): **104,102,101,100,100 99,98,98,94,93 92,89,88,87,85 80**
toteswingers:1&2:£7.20, 2&3:£7.70, 1&3:£6.70 CSF £51.83 CT £355.50 TOTE £7.60: £1.70, £2.00, £1.90, £3.40; EX 66.50 Trifecta £85.80 Pool: £666.10 - 5.74 winning units..
Owner A Crowther **Bred** Bigwigs Bloodstock **Trained** Nawton, N Yorks

FOCUS
The rain had arrived ahead of this consolation race for the Carlisle Bell. There was a weight range of just 3lb and the gallop was unrelenting. The time was similar to the Bell itself and the form is pretty solid.
Ailsa Craig(IRE) Official explanation: trainer said that the mare finished distressed

3276 LLOYD MOTOR GROUP CARLISLE BELL (H'CAP) 7f 200y
3:35 (3:35) (Class 4) (0-80,83) 3-Y-0+ **£15,542** (£4,624; £2,311; £1,154) **Stalls** Low

Form RPR
4504 **1** **Miami Gator (IRE)**[23] 2545 4-9-0 **78**..............................(v) AndrewElliott 6 89
(Mrs K Burke) *mde virtually all: hrd pressed fr 2f out: hld on gamely ins fnl f* **12/1**
0122 **2** *1 ¾* **Vito Volterra (IRE)**[18] 2732 4-9-2 **80**.............................. TonyHamilton 10 87
(Michael Smith) *cl up: rdn and chal over 2f out to ins fnl f: kpt on: hld towards fin* **20/1**
6-12 **3** *1 ½* **Take It To The Max**[23] 2545 4-9-1 **79**.............................. PaulHanagan 2 83
(Richard Fahey) *t.k.h early: trckd ldrs: rdn over 2f out: styd on ins fnl f* **4/1**[1]
3131 **4** *hd* **Veroon (IRE)**[10] 2955 5-9-5 **83** 6ex..............................(p) MickyFenton 3 86
(James Given) *hld up: rdn over 2f out: styd on ins fnl f: nvr able to chal* **22/1**
0143 **5** *¾* **Count Bertoni (IRE)**[12] 2887 4-9-1 **79**.................... SilvestreDeSousa 7 80+
(David O'Meara) *hld up in midfield: rdn and hung rt over 2f out: edgd lft and styd on ins fnl f: nrst fin* **14/1**
0200 **6** *nk* **High Resolution**[27] 2414 4-8-11 **78**.................... JamesSullivan(3) 12 79
(Linda Perratt) *hld up: hdwy 2f out: kpt on fnl f: nvr able to chal* **50/1**
5-41 **7** *1 ¾* **Kensei (IRE)**[39] 2112 4-9-2 **80**.............................. DanielTudhope 5 77
(David O'Meara) *hld up in midfield: rdn over 2f out: no imp ins fnl f* **13/2**[3]
0-61 **8** *1 ½* **Destiny Blue (IRE)**[22] 2597 4-9-1 **79**.............................. PJMcDonald 8 72
(Jamie Osborne) *trckd ldrs: rdn and outpcd over 2f out: rallied appr fnl f: no imp* **11/1**
5453 **9** *¾* **Spa's Dancer (IRE)**[9] 2995 4-9-0 **78**..............................(p) DarryllHolland 9 69
(J W Hills) *trckd ldrs: effrt and ev ch over 2f out: no ex over 1f out* **16/1**
0260 **10** *1 ½* **Northern Fling**[15] 2783 7-9-2 **80**.............................. FrederikTylicki 14 68
(Jim Goldie) *bhd: struggling 1/2-way: sme hdwy over 1f out: nvr able to chal* **33/1**
0-52 **11** *hd* **Sunnyside Tom (IRE)**[32] 2300 7-8-11 **80**.................... LeeTopliss(5) 13 68
(Richard Fahey) *in tch on outside: effrt over 2f out: wknd over 1f out* **12/1**
30-0 **12** *1 ¼* **Union Island (IRE)**[34] 2220 5-9-0 **78**.............................. StephenCraine 4 63
(Brian Ellison) *hld up on ins: rdn and effrt over 2f out: btn over 1f out* **20/1**
0-11 **13** *nk* **Pravda Street**[5] 3113 6-9-4 **82** 6ex.............................. TomEaves 17 66
(Brian Ellison) *midfield on outside: rdn over 2f out: wknd over 1f out* **9/2**[2]
00-1 **14** *7* **Toto Skyllachy**[23] 2545 6-9-1 **79**.............................. PhillipMakin 15 47
(Ollie Pears) *hld up: struggling over 2f out: nvr on terms* **12/1**
0411 **15** *6* **Frognal (IRE)**[11] 2917 5-8-12 **79**..............................(b) RobertLButler(3) 16 33
(Richard Guest) *hld up on outside: rdn and hung rt over 2f out: btn over 1f out* **25/1**
511- **16** *5* **Flipping**[231] 7305 4-9-1 **79**.............................. LiamKeniry 11 22
(Stuart Kittow) *trckd ldrs tl rdn and wknd over 2f out* **20/1**

1m 41.0s (1.00) **Going Correction** +0.25s/f (Good) **16** Ran SP% **122.9**
Speed ratings (Par 105): **105,103,101,101,100 100,98,97,96,95 94,93,93,86,80 75**
totesSwingers:1&2:£42.30, 2&3:£20.10, 1&3:£11.80 CSF £236.77 CT £1186.03 TOTE £13.20: £2.90, £4.90, £1.20, £3.90; EX 362.00 TRIFECTA Not won..
Owner Aricabeau Racing Limited **Bred** Newlands House Stud **Trained** Middleham Moor, North Yorks

FOCUS
A fiercely competitive renewal of a historic race, this year a 78-83 handicap. Again a strong pace, yet the first two home were one-two throughout and it appeared very hard to make ground from off the pace. The first two both raced towards the centre in the home straight. A 1lb personal best from the winner.
Spa's Dancer(IRE) Official explanation: jockey said that the gelding hung left handed
Northern Fling Official explanation: jockey said that the gelding was never travelling
Pravda Street Official explanation: jockey said that the gelding ran flat
Toto Skyllachy Official explanation: the trainer was unable to offer any explanation for the poor performance shown

3277 TOTESPORT.COM CUMBERLAND PLATE (H'CAP) 1m 3f 107y
4:10 (4:10) (Class 4) (0-80,80) 3-Y-0+ **£15,542** (£4,624; £2,311; £1,154) **Stalls** High

Form RPR
0111 **1** **Easy Terms**[8] 3023 4-8-13 **78** 6ex.............................. JamesSullivan(3) 6 90
(Edwin Tuer) *hld up in midfield: smooth hdwy to ld over 2f out: rdn over 1f out: hld on wl ins fnl f* **9/2**[1]
3-04 **2** *1 ¾* **Kathleen Frances**[12] 2892 4-8-11 **78**.................... AshleyMorgan(5) 12 86
(Mark H Tompkins) *hld up: smooth hdwy over 3f out: effrt and pressed wnr 2f out: kpt on ins fnl f: hld and eased cl home* **9/2**[1]
2141 **3** *¾* **Ravi River (IRE)**[32] 2320 7-9-1 **77**.............................. StephenCraine 4 84
(Brian Ellison) *hld up: hdwy over 2f out: kpt on ins fnl f: nt rch first two* **12/1**
-112 **4** *6* **Tweedledrum**[11] 2906 4-9-3 **79**.............................. LiamKeniry 11 76
(Andrew Balding) *hld up: sn niggled along: rdn over 3f out: styd on over 1f out: nrst fin* **6/1**[2]
-550 **5** *1* **Cashpoint**[19] 2686 6-9-4 **80**.............................. RichardKingscote 13 75
(Anthony Middleton) *cl up: effrt and ev ch over 2f out: wknd ins fnl f* **16/1**
0410 **6** *3* **Rock The Stars (IRE)**[12] 2884 4-9-0 **76**.............................. DarryllHolland 5 66
(J W Hills) *prom: drvn 4f out: edgd rt and wknd wl over 1f out* **8/1**[3]
61/ **7** *2 ½* **Praxiteles (IRE)**[22] 6821 7-9-4 **80**..............................(t) FrannyNorton 3 65
(Rebecca Curtis) *hld up ins midfield: drvn and outpcd wl over 2f out: n.d after* **12/1**
-060 **8** *3 ¼* **Ejteyaaz**[11] 2932 4-9-1 **77**.............................. PaulHanagan 10 57
(Richard Fahey) *in tch: rdn over 3f out: wknd over 2f out* **11/1**
6-42 **9** *2 ¼* **Rowan Tiger**[15] 2793 5-9-1 **77**.............................. SilvestreDeSousa 9 53
(Jim Boyle) *led at decent gallop: hdd over 2f out: sn wknd* **12/1**
0560 **10** *1 ¼* **Gold Rules**[11] 2932 4-9-4 **80**.............................. GrahamGibbons 7 54
(Michael Easterby) *hld up: pushed along over 3f out: nvr on terms* **25/1**
-350 **11** *1 ¾* **Antigua Sunrise (IRE)**[11] 2932 5-8-13 **80**.................... LeeTopliss(5) 14 51
(Richard Fahey) *in tch: rdn over 3f out: sn btn* **10/1**
3000 **12** *1* **Veiled Applause**[12] 2892 8-8-8 **77**.............................. ShaneBKelly(7) 15 46
(John Quinn) *hld up: pushed along over 4f out: effrt over 3f out: sn btn* **40/1**
0003 **13** *18* **Hidden Glory**[7] 3051 4-9-3 **79**.............................. MickyFenton 17 18
(James Given) *hld up: drvn along over 3f out: sn wknd* **20/1**
50-0 **14** *43* **Wicked Daze (IRE)**[5] 3127 8-9-3 **79**.............................. PhillipMakin 2 —
(Linda Perratt) *cl up tl wknd fr over 3f out: eased whn no ch fnl 2f* **80/1**

2m 27.44s (4.34) **Going Correction** +0.525s/f (Yiel) **14** Ran SP% **120.4**
Speed ratings (Par 105): **105,103,103,98,98 95,94,91,90,89 87,87,74,42**
toteswingers:1&2:£5.30, 2&3:£14.90, 1&3:£8.50 CSF £22.35 CT £232.85 TOTE £6.30: £2.20, £2.20, £4.70; EX 20.00 Trifecta £142.50 Pool: £346.67 - 1.80 winning units..
Owner E Tuer **Bred** T E Pocock **Trained** Great Smeaton, N Yorks
■ Stewards' Enquiry : Franny Norton one-day ban: careless riding

FOCUS
The rain continued to fall. A highly competitive and truly run renewal of the Cumberland Plate, this year a 76-80 handicap. Good form for the grade, with a progressive winner.

3278 BRITISH STALLION STUDS SUPPORTING BRITISH RACING E B F FILLIES' H'CAP 6f 192y
4:40 (4:41) (Class 4) (0-85,84) 3-Y-0+ **£6,476** (£1,927; £963; £481) **Stalls** Low

Form RPR
4053 **1** **Elusive Sue (USA)**[8] 3024 4-8-13 **69**.............................. PaulHanagan 5 78
(Richard Fahey) *hld up in tch: hdwy over 2f out: led ins fnl f: kpt on strly* **13/2**
0014 **2** *½* **No Poppy (IRE)**[9] 2986 3-8-12 **77**.............................. DavidAllan 2 82
(Tim Easterby) *t.k.h early: in tch: hdwy to ld over 1f out: hdd ins fnl f: r.o* **4/1**[3]
-512 **3** *8* **Fairlie Dinkum**[9] 2986 3-8-8 **73**.............................. TomEaves 3 56
(Bryan Smart) *trckd ldrs gng wl: led over 2f out to 1f out: sn btn* **5/2**[1]
0-60 **4** *2* **Jeannie Galloway (IRE)**[25] 2495 4-9-9 **84**.................... LeeTopliss(5) 6 65
(Richard Fahey) *trckd ldrs: drvn over 2f out: wknd over 1f out* **15/2**
-246 **5** *6* **Bianca De Medici**[32] 2313 4-9-2 **72**.............................. DarryllHolland 4 37
(Hughie Morrison) *led to over 2f out: sn rdn and wknd* **10/3**[2]
3300 **6** *4* **Nawaashi**[18] 2729 3-8-11 **76**.............................. PhillipMakin 7 27
(Mark Johnston) *trckd ldrs: drvn and outpcd wl over 2f out: sn btn* **8/1**
053- **7** *2* **Bint Mazyouna**[284] 5961 3-8-0 **65**.............................. SilvestreDeSousa 1 14
(Richard Guest) *hld up: effrt over 3f out: wknd fnl 2f* **20/1**

1m 29.12s (2.02) **Going Correction** +0.525s/f (Yiel)
WFA 3 from 4yo 9lb **7** Ran SP% **112.6**
Speed ratings (Par 102): **109,108,99,97,90 85,83**
toteswingers:1&2:£3.30, 2&3:£2.70, 1&3:£3.00 CSF £31.43 TOTE £6.30: £3.50, £4.00; EX 25.70.
Owner P D Smith Holdings Ltd **Bred** Mike G Rutherford **Trained** Musley Bank, N Yorks

FOCUS
After the rain the ground was described as 'soft on top'. This 65-84 fillies' handicap was run in heavy rain and all seven runners came towards the stands' rail. The pace seemed over-generous and significantly the first two home were ridden with a degree of restraint. The winner is rated back to her best, which came over C&D last August.
Bianca De Medici Official explanation: trainer said that the filly hung left on the bend

3279 BET ON LIVE TENNIS AT TOTESPORT.COM H'CAP 5f
5:15 (5:16) (Class 4) (0-85,85) 3-Y-0+ **£3,238** (£963; £481; £240) **Stalls** Low

Form RPR
0100 **1** **Le Toreador**[19] 2694 6-9-11 **82**..............................(tp) PhillipMakin 4 91
(Kevin Ryan) *cl up: drvn to ld over 1f out: hld on gamely u.p ins fnl f* **20/1**
-016 **2** *shd* **Bedloe's Island (IRE)**[12] 2890 6-9-3 **74**.................... FrannyNorton 10 83
(Neville Bycroft) *towards rr: drvn over 2f out: gd hdwy fnl f: kpt on wl: jst hld* **10/1**[3]
000- **3** *nk* **Valery Borzov (IRE)**[270] 6363 7-9-11 **82**....................(v) PaulHanagan 5 89
(Richard Fahey) *towards rr: drvn and effrt over 1f out: edgd rt and styd on ins fnl f* **15/2**[2]
0-42 **4** *1* **Timeless Elegance (IRE)**[25] 2494 4-9-1 **72**................ FrederikTylicki 1 76
(Howard Johnson) *trckd ldrs: effrt over 2f out: kpt on same pce ins fnl f* **11/1**
[illegible] **5** *shd* **Captain Scooby**[6] 3087 5-8-11 **68**.............................. TonyHamilton 3 71+
(Richard Whitaker) *hld up: [illegible] outside over 2f out: kpt on u.p ins fnl f: nrst fin* **10/1**
5011 **6** *hd* **Doc Hay (USA)**[9] 2987 4-9-4 **75** 6ex.............................. PJMcDonald 7 78+
(Keith Dalgleish) *missed break: bhd: stdy hdwy whn no room and swtchd lft over 1f out: nt clr run and swtchd repeatedly ins fnl f: kpt on fin* **9/4**[1]
4-00 **7** *shd* **Master Rooney (IRE)**[27] 2434 5-9-9 **80**.............................. TomEaves 9 82
(Bryan Smart) *trckd ldrs: effrt and ev ch over 1f out: kpt on same pce ins fnl f* **12/1**
0-00 **8** *¾* **Foxy Music**[28] 2397 7-10-0 **85**.............................. GrahamGibbons 6 85
(Eric Alston) *led tl hdd over 1f out: kpt on same pce ins fnl f* **33/1**
4003 **9** *2 ¾* **Tasmeem (IRE)**[8] 3028 4-9-4 **75**..............................(v) AdrianNicholls 2 68
(David Nicholls) *trckd ldrs: drvn over 2f out: edgd rt and wknd over 1f out* **14/1**
5500 **10** *3* **Nadeen (IRE)**[12] 2890 4-9-3 **79**.............................. LeeTopliss(5) 8 61
(Michael Smith) *towards rr: drvn along 1/2-way: no imp fr over 1f out* **15/2**[2]
0000 **11** *shd* **Green Park (IRE)**[18] 2717 8-9-7 **83**..............................(b) NeilFarley(5) 11 62
(Declan Carroll) *in tch: drvn along over 3f out: edgd rt and wknd 2f out* **14/1**
6402 **12** *2 ¼* **Ryedane (IRE)**[14] 2798 9-8-9 **66**..............................(b) DavidAllan 12 37
(Tim Easterby) *bhd and sn struggling: no ch fr 1/2-way* **10/1**[3]

62.80 secs (2.00) **Going Correction** +0.525s/f (Yiel) **12** Ran SP% **118.6**
Speed ratings (Par 105): **105,104,104,102,102 102,102,100,96,91 91,87**
toteswingers:1&2:£36.10, 2&3:£12.10, 1&3:£25.00 CSF £207.45 CT £1679.16 TOTE £30.60: £7.90, £3.00, £2.70; EX 257.70 Trifecta £489.50 Part won. Pool of £661.56 - 0.60 winning units..
Owner Guy Reed **Bred** G Reed **Trained** Hambleton, N Yorks
■ Stewards' Enquiry : P J McDonald two-day ban: careless riding (July 6-7)

FOCUS
The rain continued to fall and the going was changed to soft ahead of this 66-85 sprint handicap. The winner's best turf run since late 2009.
Bedloe's Island(IRE) Official explanation: jockey said the gelding hung right handed
Doc Hay(USA) Official explanation: gelding was denied a clear run
Nadeen(IRE) Official explanation: jockey gelding had no more to give
T/Jkpt: Not won. T/Plt: £132.70 to a £1 stake. Pool of £77,831.64 - 427.90 winning tickets. T/Qpdt: £25.60 to a £1 stake. Pool of £5,819.41 - 167.75 winning tickets. RY

3220 KEMPTON (A.W) (R-H)

Wednesday, June 22

OFFICIAL GOING: Standard

Wind: Moderate, half behind Weather: Fine

3280 BETDAQ.COM EVERY WEDNESDAY AT KEMPTON APPRENTICE H'CAP — 1m (P)

6:20 (6:20) (Class 6) (0-60,60) 4-Y-O+ **£1,619** (£481; £240; £120) **Stalls** Low

Form — RPR

4403 **1** **Kielty's Folly**[6] 3096 7-8-12 **54** JamesRogers(3) 8 — 62
(Brian Baugh) *trckd ldr: led 2f out: sn shkn up: hrd pressed ins fnl f: hld on wl* **4/1**[1]

235 **2** *nk* **Lilli Palmer (IRE)**[35] 2198 4-9-1 **54** RyanClark 6 — 61
(Mike Murphy) *dwlt: hld up in last pair: prog on inner over 2f out: wnt 2nd jst ins fnl f and sn chalng: nt qckn nr fin* **11/2**[2]

1502 **3** *1* **Aggbag**[6] 3096 7-8-8 **47** AdamBeschizza 4 — 52
(Tony Carroll) *chsd ldng trio: rdn over 2f out: tried to chal fr over 1f out: kpt on* **4/1**[1]

-P23 **4** *1 1/4* **Signora Frasi (IRE)**[64] 1448 6-9-4 **60** DavidKenny(3) 5 — 62
(Tony Newcombe) *hld up in midfield: effrt 2f out: rdn and stdy on fr over 1f out: tk 4th nr fin: nvr able to chal* **17/2**

4020 **5** *nk* **Goodbye Cash (IRE)**[117] 689 7-8-13 **55** MatthewLawson(3) 9 — 56
(Ralph Smith) *sn led: rdn and hdd 2f out: lost 2nd jst ins fnl f: fdd* **11/1**

-306 **6** *4 1/2* **Lady Rossetti**[125] 575 4-8-3 **47** KatiaScallan(5) 1 — 38
(Marcus Tregoning) *chsd ldrs on inner: rdn 2f out: wknd over 1f out* **10/1**

0031 **7** *1/2* **Kenswick**[11] 2921 4-8-11 **50** (v) TobyAtkinson 3 — 40
(Pat Eddery) *in tch: pushed along 1/2-way: sltly short of room over 2f out: sn lost pl and btn* **6/1**[3]

6500 **8** *1 1/2* **Dauntsey Park (IRE)**[11] 2900 4-8-9 **48** (b[1]) RyanPowell 2 — 34
(Tor Sturgis) *t.k.h: trckd ldng pair tl wknd over 1f out* **20/1**

6440 **9** *3/4* **Lopinot (IRE)**[11] 2922 8-8-12 **58** (v) KirstenSmith(7) 7 — 43
(Martin Bosley) *hld up in last pair: effrt whn squeezed out over 2f out: pushed along after: no ch whn nt clr run 1f out* **22/1**

0125 **10** *2 1/4* **Blue Charm**[14] 2809 7-9-3 **56** JamesO'Reilly 10 — 36
(Ian McInnes) *racd wd: in tch: lost pl over 2f out: sn bhd* **14/1**

1m 41.83s (2.03) **Going Correction** +0.15s/f (Slow) **10 Ran SP% 113.4**
Speed ratings (Par 101): **95,94,93,92,92 87,87,85,84,82**
toteswingers: 1&2 £4.20, 1&3 £3.50, 2&3 £6.30. CSF £24.80 CT £92.05 TOTE £5.40: £3.70, £2.60, £1.90; EX 25.40.
Owner Saddle Up Racing **Bred** Stanneylands Livery **Trained** Audley, Staffs

FOCUS
The going was standard and there was a strong tailwind in the straight. An apprentice handicap. The pace was fairly steady and the first five pulled clear.

3281 BETDAQ.COM EXCHANGE PRICE MULTIPLES H'CAP — 2m (P)

6:50 (6:54) (Class 6) (0-65,65) 4-Y-O+ **£1,619** (£481; £240; £120) **Stalls** Low

Form — RPR

2042 **1** **Kavaloti (IRE)**[7] 3047 7-9-7 **65** (b) GeorgeBaker 2 — 74+
(Gary Moore) *hld up in midfield: smooth prog to chal 2f out: led over 1f out and sn pressed: urged along and fnd enough to assert fnl f* **11/10**[1]

1603 **2** *1 1/2* **Kadouchski (FR)**[7] 3047 7-8-2 **53** HannahNunn(7) 3 — 60
(John Berry) *hld up in midfield: smooth prog fr 3f out to chal over 1f out: shkn up ent fnl f: nt qckn* **10/1**[3]

-402 **3** *2 3/4* **Dr Finley (IRE)**[13] 2856 4-8-13 **60** SimonPearce(3) 4 — 64
(Lydia Pearce) *trckd ldng pair: wnt 2nd 3f out: rdn to ld on suffernce 2f out: hdd and easily outpcd over 1f out* **8/1**[2]

3625 **4** *3 1/2* **Frameit (IRE)**[13] 2846 4-9-2 **60** (v) JimCrowley 9 — 60
(James Given) *hld up in last pair: prog over 4f out: gng strly 3f out: darted up inner to chal wl over 1f out: sn rdn and fnd nil: wknd* **8/1**[2]

654- **5** *2 1/4* **Poppy Gregg**[401] 2169 6-7-13 **46** oh1 (v) AmyBaker(3) 1 — 43
(Dr Jeremy Naylor) *hld up in last: sme prog fr 4f out: nt on terms w ldrs over 2f out: plugged on* **16/1**

3/04 **6** *4* **Appointment**[14] 2820 6-8-5 **49** JamieGoldstein 8 — 41
(Ralph Smith) *led: jnd 1/2-way: drvn and hdd 2f out: wknd* **25/1**

0344 **7** *6* **Court Princess**[18] 2733 8-8-5 **49** HayleyTurner 5 — 34
(Richard Price) *reminder in midfield after 5f: dropped to rr and struggling sn after 1/2-way: plugged on into 6th 2f out: no hdwy after: wknd fnl f* **12/1**

0-60 **8** *20* **Cossack Prince**[24] 1635 6-8-11 **55** (p) IanMongan 12 — 16
(Laura Mongan) *pressed ldr after 5f: upsides 8f out tl wknd rapidly 3f out: t.o* **16/1**

-010 **9** *nk* **Blazing Buck**[12] 2873 5-8-8 **52** LukeMorris 6 — 13
(Tony Carroll) *nvr gng wl: wl in rr fr 6f out: t.o* **10/1**[3]

50/6 **10** *44* **Street Warrior (IRE)**[21] 2608 8-8-8 **52** FergusSweeney 11 — —
(James Evans) *in tch: rdn 6f out: wknd v rapidly: sn wl t.o* **40/1**

00-0 **11** *17* **Bonamassa**[21] 2608 4-7-9 **46** oh1 (v[1]) KatiaScallan(7) 10 — —
(Michael Attwater) *trckd ldr 5f: wknd over 4f out: wl bhd whn rdr dropped whip 3f out: wl t.o* **80/1**

3m 32.58s (2.48) **Going Correction** +0.15s/f (Slow) **11 Ran SP% 115.0**
Speed ratings (Par 101): **99,98,96,95,94 92,89,79,78,56 48**
toteswingers: 1&2 £2.10, 1&3 £2.30, 2&3 £8.20. CSF £12.29 CT £61.73 TOTE £2.10: £1.10, £2.90, £1.90; EX 11.30.
Owner Graham Gillespie **Bred** Mme Henri Devin **Trained** Lower Beeding, W Sussex

FOCUS
A minor staying handicap in which the smooth travelling favourite scored with something in hand.

3282 LAY BACK AND WIN AT BETDAQ.COM MAIDEN STKS — 7f (P)

7:20 (7:22) (Class 5) 2-Y-O **£2,266** (£674; £337; £168) **Stalls** Low

Form — RPR

2 **1** **Pearl Mix (IRE)**[14] 2817 2-9-3 0 JimCrowley 9 — 94+
(Ralph Beckett) *mde all: pushed along over 2f out: gng clr whn shkn up and edgd lft over 1f out: in n.d after* **5/6**[1]

42 **2** *7* **Quick Bite (IRE)**[20] 2641 2-8-12 0 LukeMorris 2 — 71
(Hugo Palmer) *chsd ldng pair: wnt 2nd over 2f out: rdn and no imp on wnr over 1f out: kpt on* **7/1**[2]

3 *4 1/2* **Devdas (IRE)** 2-9-3 0 AdamKirby 11 — 64
(Clive Cox) *hld up in rr: prog over 2f out but ldrs already gone: hanging and rn green but styd on to take 3rd jst ins fnl f* **20/1**

5 **4** *7* **Storm Belt (USA)**[13] 2844 2-9-3 0 WilliamBuick 12 — 46
(Mahmood Al Zarooni) *chsd wnr to over 2f out: wknd over 1f out: jst clung on for 4th* **11/1**

0 **5** *1/2* **Clean Bowled (IRE)**[16] 2767 2-9-3 0 MartinDwyer 3 — 45
(Brian Meehan) *chsd ldrs: easily outpcd fr over 2f out: no ch after* **33/1**

00 **6** *2* **Coach Montana (IRE)**[28] 2395 2-9-3 0 (b[1]) KierenFallon 10 — 40
(Jane Chapple-Hyam) *t.k.h: trckd ldrs: outpcd in 4th over 2f out: steadily fdd* **7/1**[2]

7 *1/2* **Spirit Of The Law (IRE)** 2-9-3 0 GeorgeBaker 8 — 38
(Ed Dunlop) *in tch in midfield: wl outpcd fr over 2f out: no ch after* **28/1**

8 *4* **Position** 2-9-3 0 SebSanders 5 — 28
(Sir Mark Prescott Bt) *s.i.s: rn v green and sn last: nvr a factor: modest late prog* **10/1**[3]

9 *1 3/4* **Carolingian (IRE)** 2-9-3 0 HayleyTurner 7 — 23
(William Knight) *sn rdn in rr: rn green thrght: wl bhd fnl 3f* **66/1**

10 *7* **My Scat Daddy (USA)** 2-9-3 0 IanMongan 1 — 5
(Brett Johnson) *in tch in midfield tl wknd wl over 2f out: t.o* **20/1**

0 **11** *2* **Midnight Bahia (IRE)**[12] 2882 2-8-12 0 PatCosgrave 4 — —
(Dean Ivory) *s.i.s: in tch in midfield: wknd wl over 2f out: t.o* **66/1**

0 **12** *8* **Leading Star**[34] 2227 2-8-12 0 RobertHavlin 6 — —
(Michael Madgwick) *a towards rr: rn green and wknd qckly 3f out: t.o* **100/1**

1m 27.24s (1.24) **Going Correction** +0.15s/f (Slow) **12 Ran SP% 116.9**
Speed ratings (Par 93): **98,90,84,76,76 74,73,68,66,58 56,47**
toteswingers: 1&2 £1.20, 1&3 £5.00, 2&3 £18.90. CSF £6.06 TOTE £2.00: £1.40, £2.00, £6.30; EX 6.90.
Owner Pearl Bloodstock Ltd **Bred** Jean Etienne Dubois **Trained** Kimpton, Hants

FOCUS
There was not much strength in depth in this maiden but the favourite was impressive under a prominent ride.

NOTEBOOK
Pearl Mix(IRE) showed plenty of promise when staying on well for second after looking inexperienced in a 6f maiden here on debut. He had strong form claims and blew his rivals away with an emphatic win under a front-running ride. A 120,000euros colt, he has a few classy 7f-1m2f winners on his dam's side. (op 10-11 tchd evens in places)
Quick Bite(IRE) finished in the frame in a pair of 6f AW maidens here and at Lingfield, the latest when second to the subsequent Group 3 Albany Stakes third Illaunglass. She had fair claims and ran respectably to finish a clear second but was no match for the winner. (tchd 13-2)
Devdas(IRE) showed promise, staying on strongly from a long way back on debut. A first foal of an Irish 6f winner who is from the family of champion 2-y-o/Derby hero New Approach, he should have learned quite a bit and should improve next time. (tchd 25-1)
Storm Belt(USA), out of an unraced half-sister to top-class US dirt performer Congaree, showed speed before tiring when 3-1 for his 6f Nottingham debut. He attracted a bit of support for this second run but again faded after racing near the pace. (op 14-1)
Coach Montana(IRE), beaten 14l-plus in two previous runs, was a market springer in the morning, but he was keen and found a limited response upped in trip with blinkers tried back from a gelding operation. (tchd 13-2)
Position, a Medicean colt out of a 1m2f winner, was slowly away and ran very green in a never competitive debut run. (op 17-2)

3283 BETDAQ MOBILE APPS FILLIES' H'CAP — 6f (P)

7:50 (7:57) (Class 4) (0-80,80) 3-Y-O+ **£4,079** (£1,214; £606; £303) **Stalls** Low

Form — RPR

1- **1** **Hallelujah**[246] 7002 3-9-1 **74** PatCosgrave 9 — 83+
(James Fanshawe) *hld up in last pair: stl last wl over 1f out: gd prog on outer sn after: clsd to ld last 75yds: r.o wl* **5/1**[3]

3005 **2** *1/2* **Millyluvstobougie**[12] 2881 3-8-10 **69** LukeMorris 2 — 76
(Clive Cox) *trckd ldng pair: rdn to ld over 1f out: kpt on u.p fnl f: hdd and outpcd last 75yds* **10/1**

2-06 **3** *hd* **Golden Tempest (IRE)**[26] 2468 3-9-7 **80** DaneO'Neill 3 — 86
(Walter Swinburn) *hld up in midfield: nt clrest of runs 2f out and over 1f out: wnt in pursuit of ldr fnl f but outpcd by wnr last 75yds* **4/1**[2]

1155 **4** *2 1/4* **Chevise (IRE)**[12] 2878 3-9-7 **80** JimCrowley 5 — 79
(Steve Woodman) *trckd ldr: shkn up to chal 2f out: nt qckn over 1f out: fdd last 100yds* **6/1**

160 **5** *3/4* **Dubaianswer**[21] 2607 3-9-6 **79** AdamKirby 8 — 76+
(Marco Botti) *hld up in 7th: gng wl enough over 2f out: pushed along and nt clr run over 1f out: r.o fnl f: nvr nr ldrs* **7/1**

5500 **6** *1/2* **Secret Queen**[11] 2903 4-8-9 **64** KierenFox(3) 7 — 61
(Martin Hill) *settled in last pair: effrt on inner 2f out: no prog jst over 1f out* **25/1**

22-3 **7** *1 1/2* **Les Verguettes (IRE)**[169] 36 3-8-12 **71** SebSanders 1 — 61
(Stef Higgins) *led to over 1f out: sn wknd* **20/1**

31- **8** *6* **Little Curtsey**[230] 7311 3-9-2 **75** KierenFallon 4 — 46
(Hughie Morrison) *uns rdr: broke though rails and rn loose bef s: chsd ldrs: shkn up and cl enough 2f out: wknd jst over 1f out: eased* **7/2**[1]

-110 **9** *1 3/4* **Freckenham (IRE)**[26] 2468 3-9-5 **78** HayleyTurner 6 — 44
(Michael Bell) *chsd ldrs tl wknd qckly wl over 1f out* **13/2**

1m 13.15s (0.05) **Going Correction** +0.15s/f (Slow)
WFA 3 from 4yo 7lb **9 Ran SP% 116.7**
Speed ratings (Par 102): **105,104,104,101,100 99,97,89,87**
toteswingers: 1&2 £7.20, 1&3 £6.50, 2&3 £9.20. CSF £54.32 CT £221.85 TOTE £7.20: £2.60, £3.70, £1.50; EX 79.10.
Owner Chippenham Lodge Stud **Bred** Chippenham Lodge Stud Ltd **Trained** Newmarket, Suffolk

FOCUS
A competitive fillies' handicap won in good style by an unbeaten filly who was returning from a lengthy absence.
Little Curtsey Official explanation: vet said filly had bled from the nose

3284 BRITISH STALLION STUDS E B F NOVICE STKS — 6f (P)

8:20 (8:21) (Class 5) 2-Y-O **£3,238** (£963; £481; £240) **Stalls** Low

Form — RPR

14 **1** **Mabroor (USA)**[22] 2594 2-9-5 0 RichardHills 4 — 88+
(Mark Johnston) *mde all: set ordinary pce tl past 1/2-way: shkn up over 1f out: styd on: unchal* **13/8**[1]

10 **2** *1 3/4* **Norse Gold**[18] 2712 2-9-2 0 DaneO'Neill 3 — 80
(David Elsworth) *t.k.h: trckd wnr after 2f: shkn up and nt qckn 2f out: kpt on but no real imp fnl f* **15/8**[2]

41 **3** *1 1/2* **Mr Majeika (IRE)**[48] 1827 2-9-5 0 JamieSpencer 2 — 79
(Richard Hannon) *hld up in last: rdn and outpcd over 2f out: no imp tl styd on to take 3rd ins fnl f* **4/1**[3]

10 **4** *2 3/4* **I'm Still The Man (IRE)**[8] 3014 2-8-13 0 KierenFox(3) 1 — 67
(Bill Turner) *chsd wnr 2f: styd cl up: shkn up and nt qckn over 2f out: disp 2nd over 1f out: wknd fnl f* **13/2**

1m 15.3s (2.20) **Going Correction** +0.15s/f (Slow) **4 Ran SP% 106.2**
Speed ratings (Par 93): **91,88,86,83**
CSF £4.79 TOTE £4.50; EX 2.80.
Owner Hamdan Al Maktoum **Bred** Falcon Wood Partners **Trained** Middleham Moor, N Yorks

FOCUS
The four runners were quite closely matched on form in this decent novice event but the strong favourite ran his rivals into gradual submission.

NOTEBOOK

Mabroor(USA) cost $300,000 as a yearling and made an impressive debut when beating a decent subsequent winner in a 6f Haydock maiden last month. Things didn't go very well after an awkward start when favourite at Yarmouth last time, but he attracted plenty of support and put in a strong front-running performance to get back on track in style. A half-brother to two US winners, he still has plenty of potential and looks a useful prospect who should stay 1m in time. (op 7-4 tchd 2-1)

Norse Gold scored in great style at 9-1 in a C&D maiden auction on debut, but he didn't seem to cope very well with the undulations in a Listed race at Epsom last time and was a bit too keen in this tactical race. (op 2-1 tchd 13-8)

Mr Majeika(IRE) improved significantly on his debut form when pouncing late in a 5f Ffos Las maiden last time. He was the chosen one of four stable entries, but raced a bit awkwardly early on before staying on when it was all over.He was reported to have finished lame. (op 3-1)

I'm Still The Man(IRE), a 25-1 winner of a Sandown maiden auction on debut, found the opposition too hot to handle in the Windsor Castle at Royal Ascot and couldn't sustain a promising move early in the straight in this decent event on this third run in 20 days. (op 15-2 tchd 8-1)

3285 LEONARD CURTIS H'CAP (LONDON MILE QUALIFIER) 1m (P)

8:50 (8:51) (Class 4) (0-85,85) 3-Y-O+ **£4,079** (£1,214; £606; £303) **Stalls** Low

Form / RPR

-006 **1** **Shamir**[51] 1760 4-10-0 **85**........ IanMongan 3 — 96
(Jo Crowley) *hld up towards rr: prog over 2f out: rdn to cl on ldr over 1f out: styd on wl to ld last 100yds* **16/1**

0-50 **2** ¾ **Dukes Art**[27] 2441 5-9-10 **81**........ RobertHavlin 5 — 90
(James Toller) *settled in midfield in 7th: prog on outer over 2f out: led wl over 1f out gng strly: styd on: hdd and no ex last 100yds* **13/2**[2]

2310 **3** ¾ **Loyalty**[81] 1097 4-9-8 **79**........(v) DaneO'Neill 1 — 86
(Derek Shaw) *late into paddock: hld up in rr: shkn up over 2f out: sing to run on whn nt clr run over 1f out: gd prog fnl f: tk 3rd last strides* **20/1**

400 **4** ½ **Pegasus Again (USA)**[42] 2000 6-9-7 **78**........ JamieSpencer 10 — 84
(Robert Mills) *hld up in rr: prog on outer over 2f out: chsd ldng pair and cl enough u.p 1f out: kpt on same pce: lost 3rd last strides* **10/1**

1424 **5** 1 ¼ **Tevez**[26] 2470 6-9-8 **82**........ MartinHarley(3) 8 — 85
(Des Donovan) *hld up wl in rr: prog on inner jst over 2f out: tried to cl on ldrs 1f out: fdd* **8/1**[3]

0-01 **6** ¾ **Aciano (IRE)**[19] 2675 3-9-1 **82**........ MartinDwyer 7 — 82
(Brian Meehan) *chsd ldrs: rdn over 3f out: struggling to hold pl over 2f out: kpt on fr over 1f out: n.d* **2/1**[1]

-632 **7** 2 **Starclass**[14] 2822 4-9-9 **80**........ AdamKirby 14 — 77
(Walter Swinburn) *mounted on crse: restrained after s: hld up in last trio: rdn over 2f out: prog jst over 1f out: n.d* **10/1**

0000 **8** 4 ½ **L'Hirondelle (IRE)**[9] 2999 7-9-9 **80**........ PaulDoe 2 — 67
(Michael Attwater) *mounted on crse: reluctant to enter stalls: prom early: sn settled bhd ldrs: nt qckn 2f out: fdd fnl f* **25/1**

0526 **9** 4 ½ **Den's Gift (IRE)**[46] 1898 7-9-8 **82**........(b) JohnFahy(3) 12 — 58
(Clive Cox) *led after 2f at str pce: hdd & wknd wl over 1f out* **25/1**

2130 **10** 1 ½ **Mountrath**[12] 2887 4-8-13 **70**........(v) PatCosgrave 6 — 43
(Gary Moore) *led 2f: styd cl up: rdn over 3f out: wknd fr 2f out* **22/1**

-002 **11** 9 **Aspectus (IRE)**[35] 2207 8-9-6 **77**........(p) FergusSweeney 9 — 29
(Jamie Osborne) *prom: chsd ldr 5f out to over 3f out: wknd rapidly 2f out: t.o and eased* **20/1**

2200 **12** 2 ½ **Buaiteoir (FR)**[53] 1684 5-9-10 **84**........(e) KierenFox(3) 4 — 30
(Paul D'Arcy) *dwlt: mostly last: detached fr rest over 2f out: t.o* **12/1**

0000 **13** 1 ½ **Greyfriarschorista**[14] 2814 4-9-6 **77**........ KierenFallon 11 — 20
(Mark Johnston) *in tch: prog on outer to chse ldr over 3f out to 2f out: wknd qckly and eased: t.o* **14/1**

1m 39.77s (-0.03) **Going Correction** +0.15s/f (Slow)
WFA 3 from 4yo+ 10lb **13** Ran SP% **117.8**
Speed ratings (Par 105): **106,105,104,104,102 102,100,95,91,89 80,78,76**
toteswingers: 1&2 £20.50, 1&3 £78.10, 2&3 £26.20. CSF £105.46 CT £1367.95 TOTE £23.20: £6.00, £1.10, £7.00; EX 126.20.
Owner Kilstone Limited **Bred** Plantation Stud **Trained** Whitcombe, Dorset

FOCUS

A good handicap. It was run at a decent tempo and the first five all came from off the pace.

Buaiteoir(FR) Official explanation: vet said gelding finished lame

3286 RACING AT SKYSPORTS.COM H'CAP 1m 4f (P)

9:20 (9:20) (Class 4) (0-85,85) 4-Y-O+ **£4,079** (£1,214; £606; £303) **Stalls** Low

Form / RPR

0030 **1** **Denton (NZ)**[25] 2512 8-9-5 **83**........(t) LukeMorris 1 — 91
(Jeremy Gask) *in tch: first one u.p over 3f out: struggling over 2f out: styd on fr over 1f out: clsd fnl f: led post* **8/1**

1-20 **2** shd **Loden**[34] 2224 4-8-10 **74**........ KierenFallon 7 — 82
(Luca Cumani) *t.k.h: hld up: trckd ldng pair over 7f out: drvn over 2f out: clsd to ld 1f out: hdd post* **6/4**[1]

10-0 **3** 2 ½ **Solicitor**[28] 2403 4-9-3 **81**........ AdamKirby 3 — 85
(Mark Johnston) *led after 1f tl after 4f: chsd ldr: clsd 2f out: drvn to ld over 1f out: hdd and one pce 1f out* **11/2**

6-5 **4** hd **Alsadaa (USA)**[35] 2190 8-9-7 **85**........ IanMongan 4 — 89
(Laura Mongan) *hld up tl led after 4f: drew clr 4f out: rdn 2f out: hdd over 1f out: one pce* **4/1**[2]

501/ **5** nk **Spate River**[324] 6462 6-9-4 **82**........ GeorgeBaker 2 — 85
(Jonjo O'Neill) *led 1f: dropped bk through field and last after 5f: cl enough and reminder 2f out: kpt on steadily wout chalng* **20/1**

1342 **6** 23 **Prince Apollo**[14] 2810 6-8-11 **75**........(t) JamieSpencer 5 — 57
(Gerard Butler) *t.k.h: hld up in tch: shkn up 2f out: wknd rapidly and eased: t.o* **9/2**[3]

2m 35.0s (0.50) **Going Correction** +0.15s/f (Slow) **6** Ran SP% **109.4**
Speed ratings (Par 105): **104,103,102,102,101 86**
toteswingers: 1&2 £1.10, 1&3 £8.60, 2&3 £2.90. CSF £19.55 TOTE £10.70: £4.80, £1.10; EX 20.40.
Owner G Carstairs **Bred** Windsor Park Stud Ltd **Trained** Sutton Veny, Wilts

FOCUS

The favourite was just mugged close home in this decent middle-distance handicap which was run at a steady early pace.

Denton(NZ) Official explanation: trainer's representative stated that after its last race the gelding had scoped badly

T/Plt: £125.00 to a £1 stake. Pool of £54,906.00 - 320.57 winning tickets. T/Qpdt: £55.20 to a £1 stake. Pool of £4,017.42 - 53.80 winning tickets. JN

2958 SALISBURY (R-H)

Wednesday, June 22

OFFICIAL GOING: Good to soft (soft in places) changing to soft after race 1 (2.10)

Wind: strong breeze against Weather: overcast with few sunny periods and showers

3287 BRITISH STALLION STUDS E B F ASHBRITTLE STUD MAIDEN FILLIES' STKS 5f

2:10 (2:10) (Class 4) 2-Y-O **£4,241** (£1,262; £630; £315) **Stalls** Low

Form / RPR

4 **1** **Pink Sapphire (IRE)**[25] 2504 2-9-0 0........ RichardHughes 6 — 81+
(Richard Hannon) *in tch: hdwy 3f out: led jst ins fnl f: r.o wl: readily* **4/11**[1]

04 **2** 2 ¾ **Dressed In Lace**[20] 2641 2-9-0 0........ MartinDwyer 2 — 68
(Andrew Balding) *led: rdn 2f out: hdd jst ins fnl f: kpt on: nt gng pce of wnr* **10/1**[3]

3 ¾ **School Fees** 2-9-0 0........ DaneO'Neill 8 — 65+
(Henry Candy) *s.i.s: towards rr: hdwy over 2f out: sn rdn: styd on ins fnl f* **4/1**[2]

4 1 ¾ **Kyleakin Lass** 2-9-0 0........ MartinLane 4 — 59
(Ian Wood) *sn chsng ldrs: rdn and n.m.r on far rails fr over 2f out: keeping on whn swtchd lft ins fnl f: no ex* **40/1**

54 **5** 2 ¼ **Sweet Ovation**[34] 2227 2-9-0 0........ DavidProbert 7 — 51
(Mark Usher) *in tch: rdn over 2f out: kpt on same pce* **33/1**

6 ½ **Royal Award** 2-9-0 0........ NeilCallan 3 — 49
(Ian Wood) *prom: rdn over 2f out: wknd ent fnl f* **33/1**

7 ½ **Shannon Spree** 2-9-0 0........ PatDobbs 1 — 47
(Richard Hannon) *towards rr: sn pushed along: nvr a factor* **16/1**

8 1 ¼ **Make Up** 2-9-0 0........ RichardMullen 9 — 43
(Richard Hannon) *s.i.s: sn pushed along in rr: nvr a factor* **20/1**

9 7 **End Of May (IRE)** 2-9-0 0........ JamieSpencer 5 — 18
(Rebecca Curtis) *trckd ldrs: rdn wl over 2f out: sn wknd* **20/1**

63.05 secs (2.05) **Going Correction** +0.225s/f (Good) **9** Ran SP% **126.1**
Speed ratings (Par 92): **92,87,86,83,80 79,78,76,65**
toteswingers:1&2:£3.10, 2&3:£5.20, 1&3:£1.02 CSF £5.75 TOTE £1.50: £1.02, £2.30, £1.50; EX 7.00.
Owner M Tabor, D Smith & Mrs J Magnier **Bred** Ms E Flynn **Trained** East Everleigh, Wilts

FOCUS

Rail erected up to 16ft off permanent stands' side rail on straight course between 7.5f and 2.5f. This wasn't the most competitive of maidens outside of the favourite, but there were a couple of eye-catching performances in behind. Ther's more to come from the winner, and the standard is rated around the race averages.

NOTEBOOK

Pink Sapphire(IRE) was only fourth when odds-on for her Haydock debut last month, but considering the first two home that day were Shumoos and Frederick Engels she obviously faced a very stiff task. Entered for the Group 1 Moyglare Stud Stakes and amongst the five-day entries for a Listed race at Newmarket on Saturday, she found the necessary turn of foot to take the gap between the leaders a furlong out and won with plenty in hand. She can go on to better things. (op 4-9 after 1-2 and 4-7 in a place)

Dressed In Lace had improved from her first start to her second and was dropping in trip here. She showed the benefit of her experience by making the running to the furlong pole and could be of some interest with the nurseries just around the corner. (tchd 8-1)

School Fees ◆, first foal of a 1m1f winner, took some time to realise what was required and also saw plenty of daylight on the wide outside. She was doing some pleasing late work, however, and is likely to have learnt plenty from this. (tchd 9-2)

Kyleakin Lass, a 14,000gns half-sister to a winning juvenile sprinter, fared best of the two Ian Wood-trained newcomers and was staying on well against the inside rail at the line. She should find an opportunity.

Sweet Ovation showed limited ability in her first two starts and probably ran to a similar level of form here. She will also qualify for nurseries when they start.

Royal Award showed good speed to press the leader for half a mile and can be expected to last longer next time.

3288 BEGBIES TRAYNOR GROUP MAIDEN STKS 6f

2:45 (2:45) (Class 5) 2-Y-O **£2,914** (£867; £433; £216) **Stalls** Low

Form / RPR

1 **Red Seventy** 2-9-3 0........ PatDobbs 8 — 81+
(Richard Hannon) *mid-div: hdwy 3f out: pushed along over 1f out: chal ins fnl f: kpt on wl: led fnl strides* **14/1**

53 **2** shd **Minal**[23] 2559 2-9-3 0........ RichardHughes 11 — 79
(Richard Hannon) *prom: rdn 2f out: led jst ins fnl f: kpt on: hdd fnl strides* **5/6**[1]

3 ¾ **Diamondhead (IRE)** 2-9-3 0........ MartinDwyer 1 — 79+
(Brian Meehan) *trckd ldrs: nt clr run fr over 1f out: pushed along whn clr run jst ins fnl f: r.o* **7/1**[3]

4 1 ¼ **Tidy Affair (IRE)** 2-9-3 0........ KierenFallon 13 — 74+
(Richard Hannon) *wnt sltly lft leaving stalls: sn trcking ldrs: chal 2f out: sn rdn: ch 1f out: no ex fnl 100yds* **16/1**

5 1 ¼ **Invincible Dream (IRE)** 2-9-3 0........ NeilCallan 4 — 70+
(Robert Mills) *trckd ldrs: nt clr run fr over 2f out tl swtchd rt ent fnl f: sn hmpd again: no ch after* **12/1**

0 **6** 1 ½ **The Name Is Don (IRE)**[15] 2788 2-9-3 0........ FergusSweeney 10 — 65
(Mark Gillard) *led: ducked sltly lft after 1f: rdn 2f out: tended to hang lft: hdd jst ins fnl f: no ex* **40/1**

7 nk **Dickens Rules (IRE)** 2-9-3 0........ JamesDoyle 9 — 64
(Sylvester Kirk) *untidy leaving stalls: towards rr: rdn over 3f out: sme late prog: nvr a threat* **33/1**

8 nk **Red Senor (IRE)** 2-9-3 0........ MichaelHills 2 — 63
(B W Hills) *mid-div: hdwy over 2f out: sn rdn: wknd ins fnl f* **4/1**[2]

0 **9** 1 ¼ **Doctor Banner**[13] 2837 2-9-3 0........ HughBowman 6 — 59
(Mick Channon) *trckd ldrs: rdn and ev ch on far rails 2f out: wknd ins fnl f* **12/1**

10 1 **Ice Loch** 2-9-3 0........ DaneO'Neill 3 — 56
(Michael Blanshard) *rdn over 3f out: a towards rr* **50/1**

00 **11** 11 **Arbeejay**[20] 2640 2-8-12 0........ RichardThomas 12 — 18
(Paul Burgoyne) *mid-div tl hung lft and wknd 2f out* **100/1**

1m 18.42s (3.62) **Going Correction** +0.55s/f (Yiel) **11** Ran SP% **123.3**
Speed ratings (Par 93): **97,96,95,94,92 90,90,89,88,86 72**
toteswingers:1&2:£8.00, 2&3:£2.20, 1&3:£26.90 CSF £27.19 TOTE £23.00: £4.80, £1.10, £1.70; EX 38.40.
Owner Terry Neill **Bred** Sir Eric Parker **Trained** East Everleigh, Wilts

FOCUS
The ground was changed to Soft before this race. A fair maiden and a something of a Richard Hannon benefit with his three runners finishing 1-2-4, though not in the order most would have anticipated. Straightforward form.

NOTEBOOK
Red Seventy ◆, a half-brother to four winners over a variety of trips, travelled well behind the leaders and produced a nice turn of foot to catch his stable-companion right on the line. The market didn't suggest that this was expected, so it was a very encouraging start. (op 12-1 tchd 16-1)
Minal didn't enjoy a smooth passage when narrowly beaten at Goodwood last time and provided the benchmark for the others to aim at. Despite his high draw, he was able to get across and establish a handy position nearer the inside, but he was having to be niggled along from some way out and although in front over a furlong from home, he could never put the race to bed and was collared by his stablemate right on the line. He doesn't have the scope of the winner, but should still win races and nurseries are coming at just the right time for him. (op 11-10 after 11-8 in places tchd 4-5)
Diamondhead(IRE) ◆, a 50,000euros colt out of a half-sister to three winners at up to 1m1f, still seemed to be going well when not enjoying much room over a furlong out, though it would be hard to say it cost him the race. He did attract some market support beforehand and would have to be taken very seriously next time. (op 8-1 tchd 11-2)
Tidy Affair(IRE) ◆ ran a cracker on this debut considering he was drawn on the wide outside. Always thereabouts, he never stopped trying and this 38,000gns half-brother to three winners, including the multiple winning sprinter Night Prospector, should find a race before long. (op 12-1)
Invincible Dream(IRE) ◆, retained for £30,000 as a 2-y-o, was another not to enjoy a great deal of room a furlong out, but he still wasn't beaten far and there was plenty of encouragement in this debut effort. (op 10-1)
The Name Is Don(IRE)'s performance wasn't without promise on his C&D debut earlier this month, but despite that experience he was still inclined to run green at the head of affairs early and may need a bit more time. (op 33-1)
Red Senor(IRE) travelled well off the pace and made a brief effort 2f out, but it came to little. A 130,000euros half-brother to three winners including the Group 3 winner Killybegs, he is surely capable of better. (op 9-2 tchd 6-1)

3289 SMITH & WILLIAMSON MAIDEN FILLIES' STKS — 6f 212y
3:15 (3:16) (Class 5) 3-Y-O — £2,914 (£867; £433; £216) Stalls Low

Form					RPR
2	1		**Mundana (IRE)**35 2192 3-9-0 0 ... KierenFallon 9 (Luca Cumani) *racd keenly: trckd ldrs: pushed along fr 2f out: led fnl 140yds: kpt on wl: pushed out* **1/3**1		74+
0	2	3/4	**Noverton**15 2790 3-9-0 0 ... DaneO'Neill 3 (James Eustace) *trckd ldr: led 2f out: sn rdn: hdd fnl 140yds: no ex* **16/1**		71
33	3	2	**Totheendoftheearth (IRE)**10 2960 3-9-0 0 ... RichardHughes 7 (Sylvester Kirk) *mid-div tl squeezed up and lost pl 5f out: swtchd lft and rdn 2f out: styd on ins fnl f but no ch w ldng pair* **4/1**2		66
-0	4	2 1/2	**Amazing Win (IRE)**10 2960 3-9-0 0 ... HughBowman 6 (Mick Channon) *hld up towards rr: rdn and stdy hdwy fr 2f out: styd on ins fnl f: nvr trbld ldrs* **20/1**		59
05-	5	3/4	**Rosairlie (IRE)**253 6831 3-9-0 0 ... LukeMorris 8 (Harry Dunlop) *squeezed up s: towards rr: rdn over 2f out: styd on ins fnl f: nvr a threat* **14/1**3		57
-050	6	3/4	**Lady Bridget**37 2152 3-9-0 62 ... FergusSweeney 2 (Mark Gillard) *trckd ldrs: rdn over 2f out: fdd ins fnl f* **40/1**		55
0-0	7	3/4	**Swing Door (IRE)**39 2103 3-9-0 0 ... MichaelHills 1 (B W Hills) *led tl rdn 2f out: kpt on tl fdd fnl 140yds* **14/1**3		53?
006	8	3 3/4	**A B Celebration**19 2689 3-9-0 51 ... DavidProbert 5 (John Bridger) *mid-div: rdn 3f out: wknd ent fnl f* **66/1**		43?
00-	9	15	**Zartina (IRE)**230 7311 3-9-0 0 ... JamesDoyle 11 (Sylvester Kirk) *a towards rr: wknd 2f out* **33/1**		—

1m 30.94s (2.34) **Going Correction** +0.55s/f (Yiel) **9** Ran SP% **125.9**
Speed ratings (Par 96): **108,107,104,102,101 100,99,95,78**
toteswingers:1&2:£6.00, 2&3:£7.30, 1&3:£1.02 CSF £9.59 TOTE £1.40: £1.02, £4.90, £1.40; EX 13.80.
Owner Sheikh Mohammed Obaid Al Maktoum **Bred** Scuderia Archi Romani **Trained** Newmarket, Suffolk

FOCUS
A modest fillies' maiden in which few could be fancied and another race featuring a short-priced favourite. The form makes a fair bit of sense around the winner and third.

3290 MOLSON COORS NOEL CANNON MEMORIAL TROPHY (H'CAP) — 1m
3:50 (3:50) (Class 2) (0-100,100) 3-Y-0+
£9,969 (£2,985; £1,492; £747; £372; £187) Stalls Low

Form			Horse	RPR
0425	1		**Leviathan**11 2933 4-9-3 89 ... KierenFallon 5 (Tony Newcombe) *hld up: followed stands' side gp after 2f: hdwy in centre fr 4f out: rdn 2f out: kpt on wl: edgd rt led fnl stride* **5/2**1	97+
-044	2	shd	**Vainglory (USA)**11 2933 7-8-13 90 ... LauraPike(5) 2 (David Simcock) *chsd ldrs: racd far side: rdn to ld 2f out: kpt on: hdd fnl stride* **5/1**2	98
6520	3	1 1/4	**Shavansky**12 2884 7-9-3 89 ... JamesMillman 6 (Rod Millman) *s.i.s: bhd: racd stand-side after 2f: swtchd to centre and hdwy fr 3f out: sn rdn: drifted rt but styd on ins fnl f* **8/1**	94+
505	4	1 1/4	**Nazreef**27 2441 4-8-13 85 ... (t) TravisBlock 1 (Hughie Morrison) *overall ldr on farside after 2f: rdn and edgd lft whn hdd 2f out: kpt on tl no ex towards fin* **6/1**3	87
-053	5	8	**Huzzah (IRE)**12 2876 6-8-9 81 oh4 ... MichaelHills 7 (B W Hills) *s.i.s: bhd: c stand-side after 2f out: swtchd to centre and stdy hdwy fr over 2f out: nvr trbld ldrs* **12/1**	65
-564	6	1	**Fantasy Gladiator**11 2909 5-8-9 81 oh2 ... (p) JamieSpencer 8 (Robert Cowell) *overall ldr tl swtchd to stand-side after 2f: prom: rdn over 2f out: wknd over 1f out* **16/1**	63
4-00	7	2	**Linnens Star (IRE)**41 2020 4-8-12 84 ... JimCrowley 12 (Ralph Beckett) *hld up towards rr: racd stands' side after 2f: hdwy over 3f out: sn rdn: wknd over 1f out* **14/1**	61
-000	8	5	**Suited And Booted (IRE)**11 2927 4-9-5 91 ... PatDobbs 9 (Richard Hannon) *trckd ldr: racd stands' side after 2f: rdn 3f out: wknd 2f out* **33/1**	56
1-00	9	1 1/2	**South Cape**34 2217 8-8-9 86 ... HarryBentley(5) 10 (Gary Moore) *mid-div: racd stands' side after 2f: rdn 3f out: wknd 2f out* **25/1**	48
52-2	10	1	**Hot Spark**56 1610 4-8-12 84 ... (t) DaneO'Neill 3 (John Akehurst) *chsd ldr on far side: rdn over 3f out: wknd 2f out: eased* **11/1**	58
1000	11	nk	**Bravo Echo**26 2470 5-8-13 85 ... LukeMorris 11 (Michael Attwater) *mid-div: swtchd to stands' side after 2f: rdn 3f out: wknd 2f out* **33/1**	44
666-	12	19	**Ordnance Row**284 5948 8-9-13 99 ... NeilCallan 13 (Roger Varian) *chsd ldrs: racd stands' side after 2f: rdn over 3f out* **16/1**	14
-030	13	4	**Invincible Soul (IRE)**7 3032 4-10-0 100 ... RichardHughes 4 (Richard Hannon) *mid-div: racd stands' side after 2f: wknd over 2f out* **14/1**	—

1m 45.95s (2.45) **Going Correction** +0.55s/f (Yiel) **13** Ran SP% **121.5**
Speed ratings (Par 109): **109,108,107,106,98 97,95,90,88,87 87,68,64**
toteswingers:1&2:£2.10, 2&3:£7.90, 1&3:£3.60 CSF £13.85 CT £88.68 TOTE £2.90: £1.10, £1.90, £3.10; EX 16.00.
Owner Paul Moulton **Bred** Laundry Cottage Stud Farm **Trained** Yarnscombe, Devon

FOCUS
A decent and competitive handicap, but somewhat of a messy race with a group of ten exploring the stands' side of the track for the first time on the card, while three stayed far side. As the trio on the far side included the eventual second and fourth, it may be best to mark up the performances of the winner and third. The winner basically ran to form.

NOTEBOOK
Leviathan hadn't won a race since October 2009, but had been running very well in defeat recently and was sent off a well-backed favourite. He had a bit to do in the nearside group at halfway and his rider, probably conscious that the far-side group were getting away, sent him to the front of his side well over 2f from home. He still had a decent amount of ground to make up, but he showed real determination to get up on the line. (op 3-1)
Vainglory(USA), 4lb lower than when fifth in this last year, needs his run timing to perfection so may have found things not panning out in his favour as he was in front of the far-side group a long way from home. Neither he nor his rider did anything wrong, but it seemed inevitable that something would come out of the pack to snatch the prize from him in the last stride. (op 6-1 tchd 9-2)
Shavansky, without a win in over a year, was down to 1m for the first time since September and that may have counted against him. Held up in the nearside group, he stayed on strongly over the last 2f, despite edging away to his right, but was never quite getting there. (op 12-1)
Nazreef ran very well in the far side group and although now 0-8 on turf and 5-5 on the all-weather, there seems no reason at all why he can't win races on the grass. (tchd 7-1)
Huzzah(IRE) was once rated 99, but he hasn't won in over three years and was 4lb wrong here. He was never going to win this, but his performance can be marked up as he gave away plenty of ground with a tardy start which was always going to be fatal at this level. Official explanation: jockey said that the gelding missed the break (op 10-1)
Fantasy Gladiator, a four-time winner on the all-weather and 2lb wrong, led the nearside group until over 2f from home. He is now 0-12 on turf, though he has finished runner-up three times and can win a race on this surface.

3291 ASHBRITTLE STUD BIBURY CUP (H'CAP) — 1m 4f
4:20 (4:21) (Class 3) (0-95,90) 3-Y-O — £7,771 (£2,312; £1,155; £577) Stalls High

Form			Horse	RPR
3-20	1		**Whiplash Willie**32 2295 3-8-10 79 ... (v1) DavidProbert 5 (Andrew Balding) *mid-div: lost pl over 5f out: hdwy over 4f out: rdn over 2f out: led 1f out: styd on strly to draw comf clr* **16/1**	94
44-1	2	7	**Kinyras (IRE)**30 2371 3-8-13 82 ... (v1) RichardHughes 4 (Sir Michael Stoute) *mid-div: hdwy 5f out: rdn to ld 2f out: hdd 1f out: no ex: jst hld on for 2nd* **8/1**	86
0-61	3	shd	**Ardlui (IRE)**39 2114 3-9-2 85 ... FergusSweeney 6 (Henry Candy) *trckd ldrs tl squeezed up after 2f: mid-div: hdwy 4f out to chse ldrs: rdn 3f out: styd on same pce fnl 2f: jst failed to snatch 2nd* **5/2**1	89
1-43	4	1	**Slight Advantage (IRE)**13 2842 3-8-5 74 ... LukeMorris 11 (Clive Cox) *chsd ldrs: rdn 3f out: swtchd lft and rt and wandered u.p fr 2f out: styd on same pce* **10/1**	76
-530	5	1 1/4	**Malanos (IRE)**14 2819 3-8-0 74 ... HarryBentley(5) 2 (David Elsworth) *led: rdn and hdd 2f out: wknd ins fnl f* **8/1**	74
6-12	6	hd	**Fadhaa (IRE)**49 1811 3-9-0 83 ... RichardHills 8 (B W Hills) *racd keenly: trcking ldrs whn short of room and dropped towards rr after 1f: hdwy to trck ldr after 2f: rdn to chal 3f out: wknd ent fnl f* **9/2**2	83+
0-30	7	4 1/2	**Colour Vision (FR)**18 2726 3-9-1 84 ... KierenFallon 3 (Mark Johnston) *trckd ldr: pushed along to chal 4f out: rdn 3f out: wknd jst over 1f out* **16/1**	76
14-0	8	11	**Bloodsweatandtears**42 2008 3-8-12 81 ... (v1) JimCrowley 7 (William Knight) *hld up towards rr: rdn and hdwy over 3f out: wknd 2f out* **25/1**	56
1-	9	2 1/4	**Mahab El Shamaal**261 6618 3-8-6 75 ... MartinLane 9 (David Simcock) *s.i.s: sn pushed along towards rr: rdn on outer over 4f out: wknd 2f out* **6/1**3	46
1-04	10	3/4	**Rutland Boy**12 2877 3-8-9 78 ow1 ... JamieSpencer 1 (Ed Dunlop) *rdn over 3f out: a in rr: eased whn btn* **12/1**	48
15-	11	38	**Pivotman**250 6884 3-9-7 90 ... NeilCallan 10 (Amanda Perrett) *mid-div: rdn over 3f out: wknd 2f out: eased* **12/1**	—

2m 38.72s (0.72) **Going Correction** +0.15s/f (Good) **11** Ran SP% **123.3**
Speed ratings (Par 103): **103,98,98,97,96 96,93,86,84,84 58**
toteswingers:1&2:£11.00, 2&3:£5.20, 1&3:£10.10 CSF £144.92 CT £438.95 TOTE £17.00: £5.00, £3.30, £1.40; EX 167.50.
Owner J C & S R Hitchins **Bred** J C & S R Hitchins **Trained** Kingsclere, Hants

FOCUS
A good handicap full of unexposed and progressive middle-distance performers, but perhaps not up to the race's usual standard. They didn't seem to go much of a pace early, but this trip still proved a decent test of stamina for these 3-y-os in the conditions. The winner was much improved for the visor.

NOTEBOOK
Whiplash Willie didn't improve for the step up to this trip at Haydock last time, but was tried in a first-time visor here and the difference was dramatic. Brought to challenge over a furlong out, once in front he fairly bolted clear and it may be that the easier ground had as much to do with this effort as the headgear. It will be interesting to see if he can reproduce this.
Kinyras(IRE), racing on softer ground and visored for the first time over an extra 2f, proved awkward beforehand but was in front against the inside rail over 2f out and it looked as though he would take some catching. However, the winner swept past him a furlong out and, as he got tired, he only just held on for second. (op 17-2 tchd 9-1 in a place)
Ardlui(IRE), making his handicap debut after slamming a subsequent winner by 7l in a Thirsk maiden over this trip last month, was off the bridle some way out and took plenty of time to respond, but the way he kept on late suggests he is a real stayer and he may be worth a try over even further. (op 2-1 tchd 3-1)
Slight Advantage(IRE) likes this ground and had her chance, but she was inclined to hang about under pressure passing the 2f pole. (op 12-1)
Malanos(IRE), still a maiden, didn't shine on his handicap debut over this trip at Kempton last time and didn't quite see it out after making much of the running here. (op 11-1)
Fadhaa(IRE)'s narrow defeat by Brown Panther at Chester last month looks very smart form now, but he wasn't ridden to best advantage here as he made a sudden move around the outside to take a handy position rounding the loop and that was always likely to tell against him later on. He isn't one to give up on yet. Official explanation: jockey said that the colt ran too free; vet said the colt was listless (op 11-2)
Colour Vision(FR) was weighted to reverse last month's Chester form with Fadhaa and had every chance, but he had run his race coming to the last furlong. (op 12-1)

Mahab El Shamaal was a complete unknown having won a 1m2f Pontefract maiden last October, his only start to date, but he ran in snatches after breaking slowly and never threatened (op 12-1)

3292 NEW FOREST FARM MACHINERY/JOHN DEERE FILLIES' H'CAP 6f
4:55 (4:56) (Class 5) (0-70,69) 3-Y-O **£2,428** (£722; £361; £180) **Stalls** Low

Form RPR

51 **1** **Dead Cool**[34] 2223 3-9-6 **68** .... KierenFallon 7 72+
(Hughie Morrison) *s.i.s: in tch: pushed along whn short of room and lost pl under 3f out: hdwy 2f out: led ins fnl f: drvn out* **3/1**[2]

66-5 **2** *3/4* **Mrs Greeley**[15] 2792 3-9-5 **67** .... CathyGannon 5 69+
(Eve Johnson Houghton) *s.i.s: tk str hold in last pair: rdn over 2f out: stdy prog over 1f out: r.o ins fnl f: wnt 2nd nr fin* **5/2**[1]

-000 **3** *nk* **Whoateallthepius (IRE)**[12] 2881 3-9-5 **67** ....(p) ShaneKelly 8 68
(Dean Ivory) *led: rdn 2f out: hdd ins fnl f: kpt on but no ex whn lost 2nd nr fin* **12/1**

0600 **4** *shd* **One Cool Chick**[15] 2792 3-8-3 **51** oh4 ow1 .... RichardThomas 2 52
(John Bridger) *s.i.s: in last pair: hdwy over 2f out: rdn over 1f out: styd on wout pce to chal* **40/1**

32-3 **5** *3 1/2* **Royal Liaison**[47] 1860 3-9-7 **69** .... JamieSpencer 1 59
(Michael Bell) *in tch: rdn to chse ldrs over 2f out: styng on same pce whn briefly short of room ins fnl f* **4/1**

0-60 **6** *1 1/2* **All Honesty**[35] 2192 3-8-11 **64** .... HarryBentley[(5)] 6 49
(William Knight) *chsd ldrs tl hung lft and wknd over 1f out* **16/1**

0-14 **7** *3 1/4* **Here To Eternity (USA)**[43] 1986 3-9-7 **69** .... JackMitchell 4 43
(Peter Chapple-Hyam) *trckd ldr: rdn 2f out: wknd ent fnl f* **10/3**[3]

3004 **8** *2 1/4* **Toms River Tess (IRE)**[16] 2757 3-9-1 **63** .... SamHitchcott 9 30
(Zoe Davison) *chsd ldrs tl wknd 2f out* **28/1**

1m 18.39s (3.59) **Going Correction** +0.55s/f (Yiel) 8 Ran SP% **116.1**
Speed ratings (Par 96): **98,97,96,96,91 89,85,82**
toteswingers:1&2:£2.70, 2&3:£7.30, 1&3:£7.00 CSF £11.16 CT £76.91 TOTE £4.10: £1.10, £1.10, £3.20; EX 11.20.
Owner C E Trading & Crichel Farms Limited **Bred** Crichel Farms Ltd **Trained** East Ilsley, Berks

FOCUS
A weakish and muddling fillies' handicap with the proximity of the 46-rated fourth doing little for the form.
Mrs Greeley Official explanation: jockey said that the filly suffered interference on leaving the stalls

3293 MOBILE TEA DANCE AFTER RACING H'CAP (FOR GENTLEMAN AMATEUR RIDERS) 6f 212y
5:30 (5:30) (Class 6) (0-65,64) 4-Y-O+ **£1,873** (£581; £290; £145) **Stalls** Low

Form RPR

0-04 **1** **Northern Spy (USA)**[13] 2843 7-10-12 **60** .... MrJCoffill-Brown[(5)] 9 68
(Simon Dow) *mid-div tl dropped in rr whn pushed along 4f out: hdwy 2f out: kpt on ins fnl f: led fnl strides* **6/1**[2]

3453 **2** *hd* **Fitz**[13] 2843 5-10-4 **52** .... ThomasGarner[(5)] 6 59
(Matthew Salaman) *mid-div: rdn and hdwy 2f out: led jst over 1f out: hung rt u.p: ct fnl strides* **7/2**[1]

0000 **3** *1 1/4* **Advertise**[37] 2149 5-10-10 **58** .... MrARawlinson[(5)] 12 62
(Joseph Tuite) *hld up towards rr: hdwy on rails over 3f out: rdn to chse ldrs over 2f out: styd on ins fnl f* **11/1**

10-4 **4** *1* **Silvee**[169] 34 4-10-5 **51** .... MrRBirkett[(3)] 13 52
(John Bridger) *hld up towards rr: swtchd lft and hdwy over 2f out: sn rdn: styd on same pce* **9/1**

-466 **5** *1* **The Name Is Frank**[15] 2789 6-11-0 **62** ....(t) BrendanPowell[(5)] 3 61+
(Mark Gillard) *led for 2f: chsd ldr: rdn over 3f out: ev ch jst over 1f out: no ex* **9/1**

-000 **6** *1/2* **Bahkov (IRE)**[20] 2642 5-10-2 **48** ....(b[1]) MrCMartin[(3)] 4 45
(Eric Wheeler) *chsd ldrs: rdn over 3f out: edgd rt over 1f out: kpt on same pce* **25/1**

04P- **7** *1* **Into The Wind**[293] 5689 4-11-0 **60** .... MrPMillman[(3)] 5 55
(Rod Millman) *mid-div: pushed along 3f out: chsd ldrs over 1f out: fdd ins fnl f* **16/1**

0000 **8** *5* **Realt Na Mara (IRE)**[19] 2685 8-10-9 **57** ....(b) MrRPooles[(5)] 7 38+
(Hughie Morrison) *s.i.s: bhd: sn swtchd rt and hdwy: led after 2f: rdn and hdd jst over 1f out: wknd* **12/1**

0060 **9** *4 1/2* **[illegible] (IRE)**[15] 2789 4-10-7 **50** ....(p) MrDHDunsdon 14 19
(Paul Cole) *chsd ldrs early: bhd fnl 3f* [illegible]

0033 **10** *10* **Mr Udagawa**[19] 2685 5-10-13 **61** ....(b[1]) MrRJWilliams[(5)] 11 —
(Bernard Llewellyn) *chsd ldrs: rdn over 3f out: wknd 2f out* **7/2**[1]

36-0 **11** *4* **Annes Rocket (IRE)**[23] 2560 6-11-4 **61** .... MrTomDavid 2 —
(Jimmy Fox) *v awkwardly away: bhd: hdwy to chse ldng pair over 4f out: wknd over 2f out* **13/2**[3]

0U00 **12** *7* **Cinderella**[49] 1815 4-9-12 **48** ow3 ....(p) MrWFeatherstone[(7)] 1 —
(Lucinda Featherstone) *prom for over 2f: wknd over 3f out* **66/1**

1m 34.66s (6.06) **Going Correction** +0.55s/f (Yiel) 12 Ran SP% **123.7**
Speed ratings (Par 101): **87,86,85,84,83 82,81,75,70,59 54,46**
toteswingers:1&2:£4.60, 2&3:£8.80, 1&3:£11.80. Tote Super 7: Win: Not won. Pool: Not won. CSF £28.03 CT £235.41 TOTE £9.60: £3.00, £1.30, £5.30; EX 35.70.
Owner John Marsden **Bred** Gainsborough Farm Llc **Trained** Epsom, Surrey

FOCUS
A messy amateur riders' event in which the leaders went off much too quick. Not form to be confident about.
T/Plt: £7.10 to a £1 stake. Pool of £48,655.64 - 4,973.34 winning tickets. T/Qpdt: £5.80 to a £1 stake. Pool of £3,198.90 - 403.50 winning tickets. TM

3294 - 3299a (Foreign Racing) - See Raceform Interactive

3035 HAMILTON (R-H)
Thursday, June 23

OFFICIAL GOING: Soft (good to soft in places; 7.2)
Wind: Breezy, across Weather: Cloudy, dry

3300 HAMILTON PARK LADY AMATEUR RIDERS' H'CAP 1m 5f 9y
6:00 (6:01) (Class 6) (0-65,65) 4-Y-O+ **£1,977** (£608; £304) **Stalls** High

Form RPR

6054 **1** **Terenzium (IRE)**[8] 3041 9-9-2 **50** ....(p) MissRSmith[(7)] 3 58
(Micky Hammond) *hld up: stdy hdwy 1/2-way: led and hrd pressed 2f out: edgd lft and styd on wl fnl f* **5/1**[3]

05/6 **2** *1/2* **Ritsi**[21] 2654 8-8-11 **45** .... MissNHayes[(7)] 1 52
(Marjorie Fife) *hld up: hdwy over 2f out: chsd wnr ins fnl f: kpt on: hld towards fin* **16/1**

-303 **3** *2* **Talk Of Saafend (IRE)**[7] 3086 6-9-7 **53** .... MissECSayer[(5)] 2 57
(Dianne Sayer) *prom: effrt and ev ch fr 2f out to ins fnl f: kpt on same pce last 100yds* **5/1**[3]

6/0 **4** *2* **Sergeant Pink (IRE)**[6] 3129 5-10-0 **62** .... MissNSayer[(7)] 9 63
(Dianne Sayer) *dwlt: hld up: pushed along over 3f out: styd on fnl 2f: nrst fin* **12/1**

5054 **5** *1 1/2* **Duar Mapel (USA)**[3] 3240 5-9-4 **50** ....(v) MissHCuthbert[(5)] 6 49
(Brian Baugh) *prom: rdn and outpcd over 3f out: rallied over 1f out: no imp fnl f* **14/1**

1-01 **6** *1 3/4* **Without Equal**[8] 3041 5-9-11 **52** .... MissLHorner 12 48
(David Thompson) *s.i.s: hld up: stdy hdwy 1/2-way: effrt on outside over 2f out: no imp over 1f out* **7/2**[2]

0/0- **7** *3 1/4* **Samizdat (FR)**[28] 5202 8-8-11 **45** .... MissRobynGray[(7)] 10 36
(Dianne Sayer) *led to over 3f out: sn outpcd: hung lft and sme hdwy over 1f out: no imp* **33/1**

150/ **8** *1 1/4* **Rustic Gold**[498] 6132 7-10-0 **58** .... MissPernillaHermansson[(3)] 11 47
(Richard Ford) *cl up: led 3f out to over 2f out: sn btn* **40/1**

61 **9** *hd* **Amana (USA)**[10] 2991 7-10-5 **65** 6ex .... MissBeckyBrisbourne[(5)] 4 54+
(Mark Brisbourne) *t.k.h: hld up towards rr: n.m.r and lost pl 1/2-way: gd hdwy on outside to ld over 2f out: hung rt and sn hdd: wknd* **9/4**[1]

2m 59.38s (5.48) **Going Correction** +0.30s/f (Good) 9 Ran SP% **111.9**
Speed ratings (Par 101): **95,94,93,92,91 90,88,87,87**
toteswingers:1&2:£17.60, 1&3:£4.40, 2&3:£25.40 CSF £76.82 CT £414.74 TOTE £4.10: £1.10, £6.20, £2.10; EX 162.60.
Owner O'Sunburn Partnership **Bred** Azienda Agricola Patrizia **Trained** Middleham Moor, N Yorks
■ Stewards' Enquiry : Miss Becky Brisbourne two-day ban: used whip with excessive frequency, whilst mare was showing no response (tbn)

FOCUS
Rails realignment reduced distances on Round course by 8yds. A modest amateur event which was run at an even gallop. The winner showed similar form to his previous two wins, over the same C&D off this mark.
Without Equal Official explanation: jockey said mare was unsuited by the soft, good to soft in places ground
Amana(USA) Official explanation: trainer's rep had no explanation for the poor form shown

3301 TAGGARTS JAGUAR/LAND ROVER H'CAP (QUALIFIER FOR THE BETFAIR BONUS SCOTTISH RACING STAYERS FINAL) 1m 3f 16y
6:30 (6:31) (Class 6) (0-65,65) 3-Y-O+ **£2,729** (£806; £403) **Stalls** High

Form RPR

4216 **1** **Jeu De Vivre (IRE)**[6] 3116 3-9-1 **65** .... WilliamBuick 2 74
(Mark Johnston) *mde all at stdy pce: qcknd 3f out: kpt on strly fnl f* **7/2**[2]

0-24 **2** *1 1/2* **Silver Tigress**[21] 2635 3-7-12 **48** oh1 .... PatrickMathers 4 53
(George Moore) *hld up in tch: hdwy to chse wnr over 2f out: kpt on ins fnl f* **14/1**

-611 **3** *3* **Miss Blink**[34] 2271 4-9-12 **63** .... LeeNewman 6 63
(Robin Bastiman) *trckd wnr: rdn and effrt 3f out: edgd rt and kpt on same pce fr 2f out* **7/2**[2]

-042 **4** *1 1/4* **Amir Pasha (UAE)**[14] 2830 6-9-5 **61** ....(p) LeeTopliss[(5)] 3 59
(Micky Hammond) *trckd ldrs: rdn along over 2f out: kpt on same pce* **3/1**[1]

0646 **5** *1* **Cuban Piece (IRE)**[24] 2571 3-8-5 **58** ....(p) RossAtkinson[(3)] 5 54
(Tom Dascombe) *in tch: outpcd and edgd rt over 2f out: n.d after* **15/2**

0-0 **6** *1* **Bavarian Nordic (USA)**[13] 2892 6-9-9 **65** .... BrianToomey[(5)] 1 59
(Richard Whitaker) *hld up in tch: n.m.r briefly over 3f out: outpcd over 2f out: n.d after* **9/2**[3]

00-6 **7** *15* **Nay Secret**[21] 2635 3-7-10 **49** oh1 ow1 .... NataliaGemelova[(3)] 8 16
(Jim Goldie) *trckd ldrs tl rdn and wknd over 2f out: eased whn btn fnl f* **50/1**

2m 32.99s (7.39) **Going Correction** +0.30s/f (Good)
WFA 3 from 4yo+ 13lb 7 Ran SP% **108.0**
Speed ratings (Par 101): **85,83,81,80,80 79,68**
toteswingers:1&2:£4.00, 1&3:£2.00, 2&3:£3.90 CSF £43.05 CT £158.48 TOTE £4.30: £2.20, £9.10; EX 33.90.
Owner Ms J Bianco **Bred** Rockhart Trading Ltd **Trained** Middleham Moor, N Yorks
■ Stewards' Enquiry : William Buick two-day ban: careless riding (Jul 7, 11)

FOCUS
Not a strong handicap by any means, although a pair of relatively unexposed 3yos did at least come to the fore and showed minor improvement. The winner dictated what was no more than a fair gallop for much of the way.

3302 DECATHLON MAIDEN AUCTION STKS 6f 5y
7:00 (7:01) (Class 6) 2-Y-O **£1,942** (£578; £288; £144) **Stalls** High

Form RPR

1 **La Salida** 2-8-4 0 .... LeeNewman 8 68+
(David Barron) *rn green in tch: effrt and edgd rt over 1f out: styd on wl fnl f: led nr fin* **6/1**

523 **2** *nk* **Haafkry**[8] 3035 2-8-6 0 .... JamesSullivan[(3)] 2 72
(Linda Stubbs) *cl up: rdn to ld over 1f out: kpt on fnl f: hdd cl home* **2/1**[1]

0 **3** *4 1/2* **New Decade**[7] 3082 2-8-13 0 .... WilliamBuick 7 63
(Mark Johnston) *led: rdn 1/2-way: edgd rt and hdd over 1f out: outpcd fnl f* **3/1**[2]

4 *1 3/4* **Ptolemaic** 2-8-13 0 .... TomEaves 1 60+
(Bryan Smart) *dwlt and wnt bdly rt s: sn wl bhd and green: styd on wl fr 2f out: bttr for r* **9/2**[3]

5 *nk* **Bit A Craic** 2-8-4 0 .... KirstyMilczarek 3 47+
(John Ryan) *s.i.s: bhd and outpcd: hdwy over 1f out: nvr rchd ldrs* **16/1**

60 **6** *1* **Revitalise**[10] 2983 2-8-9 0 .... PhillipMakin 5 49
(Kevin Ryan) *cl up: rdn and ev ch over 2f out: wknd over 1f out* **10/1**

34 **7** *3/4* **Fortune Star (IRE)**[6] 3125 2-8-9 0 .... PJMcDonald 6 47
(Linda Perratt) *prom: rdn over 2f out: wknd wl over 1f out* **25/1**

50 **8** *8* **Maria Anna (IRE)**[40] 2113 2-8-6 0 .... PatrickMathers 4 20
(Ann Duffield) *prom: sn rdn along: wknd fr over 2f out* **50/1**

1m 15.51s (3.31) **Going Correction** +0.30s/f (Good) 8 Ran SP% **111.6**
Speed ratings (Par 91): **89,88,82,80,79 78,77,66**
toteswingers:1&2:£2.90, 1&3:£3.50, 2&3:£1.20 CSF £17.50 TOTE £4.70: £1.10, £1.10, £2.50; EX 23.50.
Owner J G Brown **Bred** Charlock Farm Stud **Trained** Maunby, N Yorks
■ Stewards' Enquiry : Lee Newman caution: used whip down the shoulder in the forehand position

FOCUS
Not a strong maiden with the front two pulling clear, though a few shaped with a bit of promise for the future.

NOTEBOOK
La Salida, a daughter of Proclamation, was a very cheap purchase and looks a bargain after making a winning start to her career, green early but picking up well late on to nail the runner-up close home. She'll stay at least 7f and there should be more to come for a yard enjoying a good run with its juveniles. (op 17-2)
Haafkry is proving consistent but he'll always be a little vulnerable in these events and was collared near the finish having looked in control over 1f out. (op 13-8)
New Decade was duly sharper with last week's debut behind him, prominent from the off this time. A well-bred sort in excellent hands, he appeals as the type to keep on improving. (tchd 5-2)

Ptolemaic, a son of Excellent Art, did well to finish as close as he did given how much ground he sacrificed at the start (veered badly right). He could be the type to do quite a bit better next time. (op 5-1 tchd 11-2)

Bit A Craic was also too green to do herself justice and can be expected to achieve a fair bit more next time, more than hinting at ability by the finish. (op 20-1)

Revitalise went well up with the pace for a long way on his third start and is one to keep in mind for nurseries as the handicapper can hardly go overboard with him. (tchd 11-1)

Fortune Star(IRE) also has something to work with for low-grade nurseries, travelling comfortably to halfway.

3303 HAMILTON-PARK.CO.UK FILLIES' H'CAP 1m 1f 36y

7:30 (7:30) (Class 5) (0-70,67) 3-Y-O+ **£2,590** (£770; £385; £192) **Stalls** Low

Form RPR

2346 **1** **Casino Night**[21] 2636 6-9-5 **65** ShaneBKelly(7) 3 76
(Barry Murtagh) *cl up: led over 3f out: rdn and edgd lft over 2f out: hung lft ins fnl f: styd on wl* **85/40**[1]

665 **2** *5* **Ash Cloud (IRE)**[31] 2360 3-8-10 **60** (p) RussKennemore 2 59
(Tom Dascombe) *chsd ldr: effrt and chsd wnr over 2f out: edgd rt: styd on fnl f: no ex last 100yds* **7/2**[2]

1-06 **3** *1 3/4* **Cape Of Dance (IRE)**[15] 2808 3-9-1 **65** WilliamBuick 4 60
(Mark Johnston) *hld up: struggling over 4f out: hdwy over 1f out: kpt on: no ch w first two* **13/2**

0-54 **4** *5* **Let's Face Facts**[16] 2781 4-9-7 **60** DanielTudhope 1 45
(Jim Goldie) *t.k.h: hld up in tch: lost pl over 4f out: sme late hdwy: n.d* **8/1**

0-50 **5** *3/4* **Swish Dish (CAN)**[27] 2478 4-9-0 **53** (p) PJMcDonald 8 37
(Micky Hammond) *prom tl rdn: edgd rt and wknd over 2f out* **40/1**

66-0 **6** *1 1/4* **Bell's Ocean (USA)**[12] 2923 4-9-2 **55** KirstyMilczarek 5 36
(John Ryan) *cl up tl rdn and wknd over 2f out* **16/1**

-500 **7** *13* **Scented**[6] 3124 3-9-3 **67** TomEaves 6 18
(Ian Semple) *led and clr after 3f: hdd over 3f out: sn wknd* **25/1**

42-4 **8** *1 1/4* **Alareen (USA)**[14] 2849 3-9-2 **66** (t) PhillipMakin 7 14
(Saeed Bin Suroor) *s.i.s: hld up: hdwy and in tch over 3f out: wknd over 2f out* **4/1**[3]

2m 2.49s (2.79) **Going Correction** +0.30s/f (Good)
WFA 3 from 4yo+ 11lb **8** Ran SP% **110.8**
Speed ratings (Par 100): **99,94,93,88,87 86,74,73**
toteswingers:1&2:£2.30, 1&3:£4.50, 2&3:£5.60 CSF £8.92 CT £37.13 TOTE £2.30: £1.10, £2.90, £3.30; EX 10.40.
Owner Barry Robson **Bred** Kingsmead Breeders **Trained** Low Braithwaite, Cumbria
■ Stewards' Enquiry : Shane B Kelly one-day ban: used whip in incorrect place (Jul 7)

FOCUS
Probably not a handicap that took a great deal of winning with only Casino Night showing her form.

3304 PATERSONS OF GREENOAKHILL OPEN MAIDEN STKS 1m 1f 36y

8:00 (8:00) (Class 5) 3-4-Y-O **£2,590** (£770; £385; £192) **Stalls** Low

Form RPR

044 **1** **Muffin McLeay (IRE)**[31] 2361 3-9-0 70 LeeNewman 5 83
(David Barron) *t.k.h: in tch: gd hdwy to ld 2f out: sn clr: easily* **11/2**[3]

3252 **2** *7* **Striking The Wind (USA)**[15] 2802 3-9-0 75 WilliamBuick 4 68
(Mark Johnston) *led to over 2f out: sn drvn along: plugged on fnl f: no ch w wnr* **2/5**[1]

3 *1 3/4* **Shalloon (IRE)** 3-9-0 0 PhillipMakin 7 64
(Mark Johnston) *trckd ldr: led briefly over 2f out: sn rdn: kpt on same pce over 1f out* **4/1**[2]

4 *8* **Goninodaethat** 3-9-0 0 DanielTudhope 3 46
(Jim Goldie) *t.k.h: hld up: rdn and outpcd 3f out: n.d after* **33/1**

00 **5** *7* **Hard Rok (IRE)**[15] 2802 3-8-11 0 JamesSullivan(3) 1 31
(Richard Whitaker) *hld up: outpcd over 3f out: btn fnl 2f* **66/1**

00 **6** *12* **Ebony Breeze (IRE)**[8] 3037 3-9-0 0 (b[1]) TomEaves 2 —
(Ian Semple) *trckd ldrs tl rdn and wknd over 3f out* **66/1**

2m 3.21s (3.51) **Going Correction** +0.30s/f (Good) **6** Ran SP% **112.7**
Speed ratings (Par 103): **96,89,88,81,74 64**
toteswingers:1&2:£1.10, 1&3:£1.60, 2&3:£1.10 CSF £8.37 TOTE £7.50: £2.40, £1.10; EX 8.80.
Owner Harrowgate Bloodstock Ltd **Bred** Mrs Josephine Hughes **Trained** Maunby, N Yorks

FOCUS
No depth to this maiden. There is a bit of doubt over how much the winner improved and the form is rated conservatively.

3305 WANTED AND WESTLIFE LIVE IN JULY SPRINT H'CAP (QUALIFIER FOR THE BETFAIR SCOTTISH RACING FINAL) 5f 4y

8:30 (8:30) (Class 5) (0-75,75) 3-Y-O+ **£4,209** (£1,252; £625; £312) **Stalls** High

Form RPR

0116 **1** **Doc Hay (USA)**[1] 3279 4-10-2 **75** 6ex PJMcDonald 5 89+
(Keith Dalgleish) *dwlt: hld up: hdwy on outside over 1f out: edgd lft and qcknd to ld ins fnl f: sn clr: readily* **5/4**[1]

3241 **2** *3* **Carrie's Magic**[21] 2631 4-9-1 **67** (b) GarryWhillans(7) 9 70
(Alistair Whillans) *hld up bhd ldng gp: rdn over 2f out: hdwy over 1f out: kpt on to take 2nd nr fin: no ch w wnr* **8/1**

0310 **3** *1/2* **Your Gifted (IRE)**[3] 3216 4-9-0 **64** 6ex LeeTopliss(5) 7 65
(Patrick Morris) *t.k.h early: led: qcknd clr 2f out: hdd ins fnl f: one pce: lost 2nd cl home* **15/2**[3]

0565 **4** *1 1/2* **Captain Scooby**[1] 3279 5-9-9 **68** TonyHamilton 1 64
(Richard Whitaker) *prom: drvn over 2f out: one pce over 1f out* **8/1**

331- **5** *1 3/4* **Tadalavil**[339] 4192 6-9-9 **68** PhillipMakin 8 58
(Linda Perratt) *chsd ldr: rdn over 2f out: no ex over 1f out* **10/1**

05-0 **6** *2 3/4* **Cross Of Lorraine (IRE)**[15] 2803 8-8-12 **57** (b) TomEaves 3 37
(Chris Grant) *fly-jmpd s: bhd on outside: struggling over 2f out: nvr on terms* **20/1**

0150 **7** *2 3/4* **Highland Warrior**[7] 3087 12-10-0 **73** MickyFenton 4 43
(Paul Midgley) *trckd ldrs tl rdn and wknd over 1f out* **25/1**

0011 **8** *1/2* **Sharp Shoes**[41] 2048 4-9-1 **67** (p) LauraBarry(7) 2 35
(Ann Duffield) *missed break: sn in tch on outside: hung rt and wknd 2f out* **11/2**[2]

61.12 secs (1.12) **Going Correction** +0.30s/f (Good) **8** Ran SP% **111.5**
Speed ratings (Par 103): **103,98,97,95,92 87,83,82**
toteswingers:1&2:£3.90, 1&3:£4.00, 2&3:£9.40 CSF £11.24 CT £51.27 TOTE £1.90: £1.10, £5.10, £3.40; EX 12.70.
Owner S Laffan **Bred** Colts Neck Stables Llc **Trained** Carluke, South Lanarkshire

FOCUS
A one-sided sprint, the winner clearly a long way ahead of his mark. The form is rated around the runner-up. The speedy Your Gifted took the field along but few ever threatened to land a serious blow.

3306 HAMILTON PARK SUPPORTS CASH FOR KIDS H'CAP (QUALIFIER FOR THE BETFAIR SCOTTISH RACING MILE FINAL) 1m 65y

9:00 (9:01) (Class 6) (0-65,62) 3-Y-O+ **£2,729** (£806; £403) **Stalls** Low

Form RPR

-561 **1** **Botham (USA)**[6] 3110 7-9-5 **53** DanielTudhope 2 69
(Jim Goldie) *hld up: hdwy on ins 3f out: led over 1f out: drew clr fnl f* **9/2**[2]

0002 **2** *5* **Bentley**[10] 2985 7-9-6 **54** KellyHarrison 8 59
(Brian Baugh) *chsd ldr: led 2f out to over 1f out: kpt on fnl f: no ch w wnr* **10/1**

0562 **3** *shd* **Jupiter Fidius**[7] 3088 4-9-5 **60** (p) ShaneBKelly(7) 11 64
(Kate Walton) *hld up: drvn and outpcd 4f out: gd hdwy on outside over 1f out: edgd rt and kpt on fnl f: nrst fin* **4/1**[1]

4200 **4** *2 1/4* **Madame Excelerate**[12] 2912 4-10-0 **62** PhillipMakin 4 61
(Mark Brisbourne) *in tch: drvn over 2f out: kpt on same pce over 1f out* **9/1**[3]

231 **5** *nk* **On The Cusp (IRE)**[15] 2809 4-9-8 **59** (p) MartinHarley(3) 6 57
(Richard Guest) *led tl hdd over 2f out: one pce fr over 1f out* **4/1**[1]

203- **6** *5* **Broughtons Silk**[236] 7229 6-8-12 **46** PJMcDonald 5 33
(Alistair Whillans) *hld up: swtchd rt and sme hdwy 2f out: no imp appr fnl f* **25/1**

230 **7** *nk* **Rio Park (IRE)**[27] 2458 3-9-4 **62** TomEaves 9 48
(Bryan Smart) *t.k.h: trckd ldrs: rdn over 2f out: wknd over 1f out* **4/1**[1]

0434 **8** *1 1/2* **Bajan Pride**[10] 2984 7-9-8 **56** MickyFenton 1 39
(Paul Midgley) *prom: drvn 3f out: wknd fr 2f out* **20/1**

3004 **9** *2 1/4* **Nevada Desert (IRE)**[7] 3088 11-9-7 **55** TonyHamilton 10 33
(Richard Whitaker) *midfield on outside: effrt over 2f out: wknd wl over 1f out* **12/1**

355- **10** *6* **Weetentherty**[263] 5438 4-8-8 **45** JamesSullivan(3) 3 —
(Linda Perratt) *hld up: rdn and shortlived effrt on outside over 2f out: sn btn* **80/1**

1m 50.41s (2.01) **Going Correction** +0.30s/f (Good)
WFA 3 from 4yo+ 10lb **10** Ran SP% **114.8**
Speed ratings (Par 101): **101,96,95,93,93 88,88,86,84,78**
toteswingers:1&2:£12.90, 1&3:£5.10, 2&3:£7.50 CSF £46.81 CT £198.51 TOTE £2.40: £1.02, £4.80, £3.00; EX 24.80.
Owner Caledonia Racing **Bred** France Weiner & Neal Hayias **Trained** Uplawmoor, E Renfrews

FOCUS
Another one-sided handicap to finish off the card. It was the best round course time and fair form for the grade.
T/Plt: £25.70 to a £1 stake. Pool:£55,288.94 - 1,569.81 winning tickets T/Qpdt: £2.70 to a £1 stake. Pool:£4,793.85 - 1,283.70 winning tickets RY

3076 LEICESTER (R-H)

Thursday, June 23

OFFICIAL GOING: Good to firm (good in places; watered; 8.2)
Wind: Light behind Weather: Overcast

3307 RAINBOWS CHILDREN AND YOUNG PEOPLE'S HOSPICE LADIES' H'CAP (LADY AMATEUR RIDERS) 5f 2y

6:40 (6:41) (Class 6) (0-65,65) 3-Y-O+ **£1,648** (£507; £253) **Stalls** High

Form RPR

6405 **1** **Dispol Grand (IRE)**[2] 3247 5-9-7 **54** (v) MissWGibson(3) 4 62
(Paul Midgley) *sn pushed along in rr: hdwy over 1f out: r.o to ld wl ins fnl f* **8/1**

3663 **2** *nk* **Two Turtle Doves (IRE)**[15] 2803 5-9-12 **59** MissMMullineaux(3) 5 66
(Michael Mullineaux) *mid-div: hdwy 1/2-way: rdn over 1f out: r.o* **9/1**

2201 **3** *1/2* **Clear Ice (IRE)**[35] 2238 4-10-7 **65** (b) MissSBrotherton 9 70
(Richard Guest) *sn chsng ldrs: rdn over 1f out: r.o* **9/4**[1]

0220 **4** *1/2* **Imaginary Diva**[9] 3015 5-9-1 **52** MissKMargarson(7) 2 55
(George Margarson) *chsd ldrs: led 2f out: rdn and hdd wl ins fnl f* **14/1**

4222 **5** *1 3/4* **Baybshambles (IRE)**[7] 3087 7-9-9 **58** MissVBarr(5) 3 55
(Ron Barr) *sn prom: rdn over 1f out: styd on same pce ins fnl f* **10/3**[2]

1243 **6** *3/4* **Mata Hari Blue**[7] 3079 5-9-11 **62** MissJessicaHolt(7) 1 56
(John Holt) *chsd ldrs: rdn over 1f out: no ex ins fnl f* **13/2**[3]

2600 **7** *1 1/4* **My Love Fajer (IRE)**[7] 3075 3-9-9 **59** MissZoeLilly 8 47
(Alan McCabe) *hld up: rdn 1/2-way: nvr on terms* **40/1**

0-60 **8** *1* **Wreningham**[23] 2585 6-9-8 **59** MissSBirkett(7) 7 45
(Stuart Williams) *led 3f: wknd ins fnl f* **33/1**

4602 **9** *1* **Whiskey Junction**[2] 3255 7-9-12 **63** MissBAndrews(7) 10 46
(Michael Quinn) *prom: rdn 1/2-way: sn lost pl* **9/1**

0250 **10** *1 3/4* **Ishipink**[13] 2869 4-8-9 **46** MissKClark(7) 11 22
(Ron Hodges) *chsd ldrs: rdn 1/2-way: wknd over 1f out* **33/1**

60.55 secs (0.55) **Going Correction** -0.05s/f (Good)
WFA 3 from 4yo+ 6lb **10** Ran SP% **113.3**
Speed ratings (Par 101): **93,92,91,90,88 86,84,83,81,78**
toteswingers:1&2:£4.00, 1&3:£2.00, 2&3:£3.90 CSF £73.98 CT £214.50 TOTE £21.90: £8.30, £4.50, £1.10; EX 90.40.
Owner T W Midgley **Bred** Martyn J McEnery **Trained** Westow, N Yorks
■ Stewards' Enquiry : Miss K Clark one-day ban: used whip when out of contention (tbn)

FOCUS
A modest sprint handicap for lady riders, run on ground with a GoingStick reading of 8.2. Most of the runners stayed 'in lane' from the stalls. Straightforward form, best judged around the second.

3308 JAYNE FERGUSON MEMORIAL MAIDEN AUCTION STKS 5f 218y

7:10 (7:11) (Class 5) 2-Y-O **£2,266** (£674; £337; £168) **Stalls** High

Form RPR

2 **1** **West Leake Hare (IRE)**[14] 2844 2-8-13 0 RobertWinston 2 75+
(B W Hills) *trckd ldr: racd keenly: led over 2f out: rdn over 1f out: r.o* **10/11**[1]

2 *2 1/2* **Alice Rose (IRE)** 2-8-6 0 MartinLane 5 59
(Rae Guest) *chsd ldrs: outpcd over 2f out: rallied over 1f out: r.o* **40/1**

0 **3** *nk* **Hi There (IRE)**[16] 2787 2-8-11 0 SebSanders 10 63+
(J W Hills) *hld up: hdwy over 1f out: r.o: nrst fin* **16/1**

4 *1* **Ashpan Sam** 2-8-9 0 LiamJones 1 58+
(John Spearing) *prom: rdn over 2f out: styd on same pce fnl f* **66/1**

0 **5** *1 1/4* **Gadreel (IRE)**[21] 2641 2-8-9 0 HayleyTurner 3 54
(Richard Hannon) *led over 3f: sn rdn: no ex fnl f* **16/1**

6 *2 1/4* **Orwellian** 2-8-13 0 MartinDwyer 6 51+
(Brian Meehan) *s.i.s: sn prom: rdn over 2f out: sn outpcd* **12/1**

2433 **7** ½ **Red Socks (IRE)**[16] 2780 2-9-2 0 DavidProbert 4 53
(Gay Kelleway) *chsd ldrs: rdn over 2f out: wknd over 1f out* **11/1**

8 ½ **Levi Draper** 2-8-9 0 PatCosgrave 8 44
(James Fanshawe) *s.i.s: hld up: rdn over 2f out: nvr on terms* **4/1**[2]

5 **9** 2¾ **House Limit (IRE)**[15] 2817 2-8-11 0 ChrisCatlin 9 38
(Harry Dunlop) *hld up in tch: rdn over 2f out: wknd over 1f out* **8/1**[3]

0 **10** 5 **High Five Prince (IRE)**[21] 2644 2-8-11 0 LiamKeniry 7 23
(Mark Usher) *hld up: a in rr: rdn and wknd over 2f out* **40/1**

1m 13.36s (0.36) **Going Correction** -0.05s/f (Good) **10** Ran SP% **117.7**
Speed ratings (Par 93): **95,91,91,89,88 85,84,83,80,73**
toteswingers:1&2:£12.50, 1&3:£3.60, 2&3:£73.20 CSF £55.32 TOTE £1.50: £1.02, £12.00, £6.70; EX 55.30.
Owner Henry Barton **Bred** Churchtown House Stud **Trained** Lambourn, Berks

FOCUS
Just a run-of-the-mill juvenile maiden, but it featured a clutch of nicely-bred newcomers.

NOTEBOOK
West Leake Hare(IRE), beaten 5l when second on his Nottingham debut, comfortably went one better. A fraction keen in the early stages, he was always close to the pace and took the lead approaching 2f out. Once in front, he quickly asserted and should win again. (op 11-10 tchd 6-5)
Alice Rose(IRE), the only filly in the line-up, posted an encouraging debut effort. In front early on, she seemed a little outpaced in mid-race, but came home well and ought to appreciate an extra furlong in due course.
Hi There(IRE), well beaten at Salisbury on his debut, ran better here. Towards the rear in the early stages, he made decent late progress and appears to be going the right way. (op 14-1)
Ashpan Sam, whose dam won over 1m4f, was another to run on nicely towards the finish. He should handle another furlong without a problem.
Gadreel(IRE), seventh of nine in just a fair contest at Lingfield first time out, showed good early speed before fading in the closing stages. He will struggle to win a maiden on the form his two starts to date.
Orwellian, an already gelded newcomer from the family of Fantastic Light, was always in the first half-dozen. Not disgraced, he is likely to come on for this, as most of his stable's youngsters improve for a run. (op 11-1)

3309 A & N MEDIA I.T. SOLUTIONS (S) STKS 7f 9y
7:40 (7:41) (Class 6) 3-Y-O **£1,706** (£503; £252) **Stalls** High

Form RPR

0-00 **1** **Orchid Street (USA)**[22] 2619 3-8-9 72 PatCosgrave 4 63
(Ann Duffield) *hld up in tch: led over 1f out: drvn out* **9/4**[2]

-642 **2** 3¼ **Chilledtothebone**[23] 2588 3-9-0 62 (v) KierenFallon 6 59
(Linda Stubbs) *dwlt: pushed along in rr: hdwy u.p 2f out: chsd wnr fnl f: edgd rt: styd on same pce* **15/8**[1]

00-2 **3** *nk* **Izzet**[23] 2598 3-9-0 60 TomQueally 10 58
(Mark H Tompkins) *sn pushed along in rr: hdwy 1/2-way: rdn over 1f out: styd on same pce* **5/1**[3]

3523 **4** 4 **So Is She (IRE)**[35] 2236 3-9-0 64 (b) LiamJones 8 47
(Alan Bailey) *chsd ldrs: rdn over 2f out: wknd ins fnl f* **15/2**

5300 **5** 7 **Local Diktator**[16] 2792 3-9-5 57 TomMcLaughlin 2 33
(Ronald Harris) *prom: led over 2f out: rdn and hdd over 1f out: wknd fnl f* **50/1**

-304 **6** 1½ **Chillie Peppar**[8] 3049 3-9-0 55 MartinDwyer 1 24
(George Prodromou) *led over 4f: wknd over 1f out* **20/1**

0030 **7** 1 **Fully Armed (IRE)**[15] 2829 3-8-9 44 (bt) MartinLane 3 17
(Rae Guest) *chsd ldrs: rdn 1/2-way: wknd over 1f out* **50/1**

060 **8** 4½ **The Blind Side (IRE)**[38] 2149 3-9-0 32 (p) NeilChalmers 7 10
(Michael Appleby) *chsd ldrs: rdn over 4f out: wknd over 2f out* **150/1**

4213 **9** ½ **Eternal Youth (IRE)**[58] 1585 3-9-5 66 (b) LukeMorris 5 13
(Ronald Harris) *s.s: a bhd* **17/2**

1m 26.12s (-0.08) **Going Correction** -0.05s/f (Good) **9** Ran SP% **113.9**
Speed ratings (Par 97): **98,94,93,89,81 79,78,73,72**
toteswingers:1&2:£1.20, 1&3:£2.40, 2&3:£2.80 CSF £6.59 TOTE £3.50: £2.50, £1.10, £3.20; EX 9.20.The winner was bought in for 6,500gns
Owner David & Carole McMahon **Bred** H Allen Poindexter **Trained** Constable Burton, N Yorks

FOCUS
A modest seller, with a wide range of official ratings. The time was reasonable and the first three all showed their best form this year.

3310 NEXT BEST THING FILLIES' H'CAP 7f 9y
8:10 (8:10) (Class 4) (0-85,84) 3-Y-O **£4,079** (£1,214; £606; £303) **Stalls** High

Form RPR

-151 **1** **Chokurei (IRE)**[15] 2821 3-9-0 77 AdamKirby 4 85
(Clive Cox) *mde virtually all: rdn and hung rt fr over 2f out: r.o* **7/2**[1]

2-15 **2** 1¾ **Wiqaaya (IRE)**[12] 2926 3-9-7 84 RichardHills 3 87
(Ed Dunlop) *a.p: rdn over 1f out: chsd wnr ins fnl f: no imp* **7/2**[1]

2-14 **3** ¾ **Choral**[12] 2917 3-9-0 77 JimmyFortune 1 78
(Richard Hannon) *chsd ldrs: rdn and ev ch over 1f out: styd on same pce ins fnl f* **10/1**

242 **4** 2½ **Imaginary World (IRE)**[22] 2615 3-8-11 74 (be) RobertWinston 9 68
(Alan McCabe) *s.i.s: hld up: hdwy 2f out: shkn up over 1f out: nt run on* **5/1**[3]

1-43 **5** ¾ **Echo Ridge (IRE)**[17] 2772 3-8-11 74 StevieDonohoe 2 66
(Ralph Beckett) *chsd wnr: rdn over 2f out: styd on same pce appr fnl f* **5/1**[3]

1- **6** ½ **Pandorea**[255] 6803 3-9-1 78 DaneO'Neill 7 69
(Henry Candy) *hld up in tch: rdn over 2f out: styd on same pce fr over 1f out* **4/1**[2]

1- **7** 21 **Tedsmore Dame**[346] 3964 3-9-3 80 LiamJones 8 14
(James Unett) *s.i.s: hld up: plld hrd: rdn over 2f out: sn wknd* **25/1**

1m 26.1s (-0.10) **Going Correction** -0.05s/f (Good) **7** Ran SP% **110.7**
Speed ratings (Par 98): **98,96,95,92,91 90,66**
toteswingers:1&2:£2.60, 1&3:£6.60, 2&3:£5.00 CSF £14.84 CT £102.91 TOTE £6.50: £2.60, £1.10; EX 12.80.
Owner H E Sheikh Sultan Bin Khalifa Al Nahyan **Bred** Sheikh Sultan Bin Khalifa Al Nayhan **Trained** Lambourn, Berks

FOCUS
Three overnight withdrawals slightly weakened this competitive fillies' handicap. They went no pace for the first half-mile and the time was only 5lb faster than the seller. The winner confirmed her latest improvement.

3311 ROTARY CLUB OF LEICESTER H'CAP 1m 3f 183y
8:40 (8:41) (Class 6) (0-65,65) 4-Y-O+ **£1,706** (£503; £252) **Stalls** Low

Form RPR

-420 **1** **Kayaan**[25] 2526 4-9-1 59 AdamKirby 13 70
(Pam Sly) *s.i.s: hld up: hdwy over 3f out: led over 2f out: sn rdn and edgd lft: styd on u.p* **17/2**

0440 **2** ½ **Arashi**[14] 2846 5-9-1 59 (v) DaneO'Neill 2 69
(Lucinda Featherstone) *hld up: hdwy over 2f out: rdn and ev ch ins fnl f: nt run on* **6/1**[2]

5352 **3** 4½ **Naledi**[14] 2851 7-7-13 48 HarryBentley(5) 7 51
(Richard Price) *hld up: plld hrd: hdwy over 2f out: rdn over 1f out: styd on same pce fnl f* **8/1**[3]

00-0 **4** 3½ **Mighty Mambo**[25] 2526 4-9-6 64 SebSanders 5 61
(George Margarson) *chsd ldrs: led over 3f out: hdd over 2f out: wknd ins fnl f* **16/1**

600/ **5** 2 **Dream Catcher (SWE)**[25] 5983 8-9-2 60 GeorgeBaker 10 54
(Jonjo O'Neill) *hld up in tch: rdn over 2f out: wknd over 1f out* **10/1**

0/U0 **6** ¾ **Exotic Dream (FR)**[28] 2436 5-9-5 63 LukeMorris 9 55
(Ronald Harris) *hld up: rdn over 2f out: nvr on terms* **66/1**

364 **7** 1¾ **Olimamu (IRE)**[75] 1252 4-8-10 57 SimonPearce(3) 3 47
(Lydia Pearce) *chsd ldrs: rdn over 3f out: wknd over 1f out* **33/1**

2212 **8** ½ **Gems**[7] 3086 4-9-1 59 ChrisCatlin 6 48
(Peter Hiatt) *led: hdd over 3f out: wknd over 1f out* **7/2**[1]

0-02 **9** 1 **Astrodiva**[92] 569 5-8-5 49 NickyMackay 4 36
(Mark H Tompkins) *chsd ldrs: rdn over 3f out: wknd over 1f out* **9/1**

0/0- **10** 3 **Nesnaas (USA)**[14] 3348 10-8-4 48 LiamJones 12 30
(Mark Rimell) *chsd ldr tl rdn over 4f out: wknd 2f out* **100/1**

3022 **11** 2¼ **Nolecce**[6] 3042 4-9-7 65 (p) KierenFallon 1 43
(Richard Guest) *hld up: rdn and wknd over 2f out* **7/2**[1]

005- **12** 2¾ **All Guns Firing (IRE)**[219] 7475 5-8-5 54 JamesRogers(5) 11 28
(Barry Leavy) *s.i.s: hld up: rdn and wknd over 2f out* **25/1**

600 **13** 19 **Summerandlightning (IRE)**[20] 2689 5-8-6 50 DavidProbert 8 —
(Mark Usher) *hld up: last and rdn over 5f out: sn lost tch: t.o* **33/1**

2m 32.32s (-1.58) **Going Correction** -0.05s/f (Good) **13** Ran SP% **117.6**
Speed ratings (Par 101): **103,102,99,97,96 95,94,94,93,91 89,88,75**
toteswingers:1&2:£9.50, 1&3:£15.50, 2&3:£10.00 CSF £55.82 CT £429.14 TOTE £15.80: £6.80, £1.90, £3.00; EX 70.30.
Owner David L Bayliss **Bred** Shadwell Estate Company Limited **Trained** Thorney, Cambs

FOCUS
A weak handicap, with the top weight rated 65, but few could be completely discounted. The pace was decent. A 3;n personal best from the winner.

3312 SANDICLIFFE "SERVICE DRIVEN BY YOU" H'CAP 1m 60y
9:10 (9:10) (Class 5) (0-75,75) 3-Y-O **£2,266** (£674; £337; £168) **Stalls** Low

Form RPR

-201 **1** **Hurricane Lady (IRE)**[24] 2550 3-9-4 72 KierenFallon 2 81+
(Walter Swinburn) *mde all: rdn over 1f out: styd on gamely* **7/4**[1]

-662 **2** ½ **Ferruccio (IRE)**[25] 2527 3-9-0 68 (t) PatCosgrave 1 75
(James Fanshawe) *chsd ldrs: n.m.r over 1f out: r.o* **7/2**[2]

0-04 **3** *hd* **Kalendar Girl (IRE)**[44] 1984 3-8-7 61 StevieDonohoe 4 67+
(Willie Musson) *hld up: nt clr run and swtchd lft over 1f out: sn rdn: r.o wl towards fin* **6/1**

1-60 **4** 1 **Mr Perceptive (IRE)**[13] 2877 3-9-7 75 JimmyFortune 3 79
(Richard Hannon) *a.p: chsd wnr over 5f out: rdn over 1f out: no ex ins fnl f* **11/1**

4464 **5** 4 **Midnight Trader (IRE)**[7] 3093 3-8-12 66 (t) AdamKirby 6 61
(Paul D'Arcy) *hld up: hdwy over 2f out: rdn over 1f out: wknd ins fnl f* **11/2**[3]

0-04 **6** 1¼ **Kingarrick**[14] 2841 3-9-6 74 SebSanders 5 66
(Eve Johnson Houghton) *prom: rdn over 2f out: wknd fnl f* **8/1**

4-56 **7** 9 **Shelovestobouggie**[58] 1580 3-9-2 70 TomQueally 8 41
(Sir Henry Cecil) *hld up: rdn over 2f out: sn hung rt and wknd* **11/1**

1m 45.26s (0.16) **Going Correction** -0.05s/f (Good) **7** Ran SP% **116.0**
Speed ratings (Par 99): **97,96,96,95,91 90,81**
toteswingers:1&2:£1.20, 1&3:£4.80, 2&3:£4.60 CSF £8.25 CT £29.45 TOTE £1.70: £1.10, £7.10; EX 8.20.
Owner Borgatti & Moir **Bred** Barbara Prendergast **Trained** Aldbury, Herts

FOCUS
A competitive finale, in which the winner was given a superb ride. She is a bit more progressive than her rivals, with the fourth setting the standard.
T/Plt: £54.30 to a £1 stake. Pool:£76,825.61 - 1,031.33 winning tickets T/Qpdt: £20.20 to a £1 stake. Pool:£6,166.40 - 225.60 winning tickets CR

2731 NEWCASTLE (L-H)
Thursday, June 23

OFFICIAL GOING: Good to soft changing to soft (good to soft in places) after race 5 (4:30)
Wind: almost nil Weather: overcast, showers, turning to heavy rain

3313 TRADERSBETTINGEXCHANGE.CO.UK NOVICE STKS 6f
2:10 (2:12) (Class 5) 2-Y-O **£2,266** (£674; £337; £168) **Stalls** Centre

Form RPR

1 **1** **Parc De Launay**[30] 2387 2-9-5 0 JamieSpencer 2 84+
(Tom Tate) *trckd ldrs: effrt over 2f out: hmpd jst ins fnl f: styd on wl: led nr fin* **6/4**[1]

1 **2** *nk* **Piece By Piece**[39] 2120 2-9-5 0 DavidAllan 1 83+
(Tim Easterby) *w ldrs: chal over 1f out: crowded: no ex nr fin* **13/2**[3]

4 **3** *hd* **Kenny Powers**[7] 3082 2-9-0 0 (t) RichardKingscote 7 78+
(Tom Dascombe) *led: qckng over 2f out: edgd lft 1f out: hung rt: no ex and hdd towards fin* **2/1**[2]

1 **4** 2 **Act Your Shoe Size**[20] 2693 2-8-9 0 PJMcDonald 3 67
(Keith Dalgleish) *w ldrs: hung lft and outpcd over 2f out: kpt on same pce* **9/1**

01 **5** 3½ **Bartley**[10] 2983 2-9-2 0 TomEaves 5 63
(Bryan Smart) *in rr: sn drvn along: nvr nr ldrs: fin lame* **8/1**

6 *nk* **Bang Tidy (IRE)** 2-8-11 0 PaulPickard(3) 6 60
(Brian Ellison) *dwlt: t.k.h: sn tracxking ldrs: wknd over 2f out* **25/1**

1m 15.04s (0.44) **Going Correction** -0.125s/f (Firm) **6** Ran SP% **111.6**
Speed ratings (Par 93): **92,91,91,88,84 83**
toteswingers:1&2:£2.60, 1&3:£1.30, 2&3:£2.30 CSF £11.68 TOTE £2.70: £1.10, £2.20; EX 10.00.
Owner Mrs Fitri Hay **Bred** Equity Bloodstock Partnership **Trained** Tadcaster, N Yorks
■ Stewards' Enquiry : David Allan two-day ban: used whip with excessive frequency (Jul 7, 11)
Richard Kingscote one-day ban: careless riding (Jul 7)

FOCUS
Course at normal inner configuration. This was an interesting novice event to kick off proceedings, with four previous winners in attendance, and it proved a keen betting heat. With the stalls in the centre they unsurprisingly raced mid-track, going an average pace, and it produced a very tight three-way finish.

NOTEBOOK

Parc De Launay made it two wins from as many starts with a game success and he rates value for a little better than the bare margin. He showed plenty of dash when overcoming greenness on his debut at Ripon a month earlier, but despite being bred to get further, it wasn't surprising to see him waited with over this extra furlong on a stiffer track. He travelled nicely into contention, but still ran green when asked for his effort and took time to pick up. However, he wasn't helped when the third drifted right late on and he deserves credit for getting there where it mattered. The experience should see him go forward again and he rates a very useful prospect. (tchd 13-8 and 7-4 in a place)

Piece By Piece got up late when nosing out a subsequent winner on his debut over this trip at Ripon last month, but had clearly learnt plenty from that experience as he was smartly away this time. He mad a bold bid more towards the far rail and was only just caught near the line. This was a competitive event of its type, and he can be found something similar in which to go one better again. (op 7-1 tchd 15-2)

Kenny Powers ◆ needed his debut outing at Ripon last week, but wasn't unfancied that day and the money poured in for him here. He was much better away and also made a bold show, but his inexperience caught him out when under maximum pressure. Not beaten at all far, he won't be long in winning. (op 11-4 tchd 15-8 and 3-1 in a place)

Act Your Shoe Size was claimed by new connections after winning a 5f seller on her debut 20 days earlier. She found this too hot, but ran her race and may be better off back over the minimum in the short term. (op 11-2)

Bartley was arguably the form pick after winning at the second attempt at Carlisle ten days earlier. He was easy to back, however, and never threatened after getting markedly outpaced from the gates. Considering the leaders didn't go that quick, he could well need a stiffer test now (dam 7f 2-y-o winner). Official explanation: vet said colt was lame on its left hind (op 7-1)

Bang Tidy(IRE) showed ability, but was outclassed and needed the run. (op 50-1)

3314 COOPERS MARQUEES MEDIAN AUCTION MAIDEN STKS 6f

2:45 (2:50) (Class 5) 2-Y-O **£2,331** (£693; £346; £173) **Stalls** Centre

Form	Pos	Dist	Horse / details	Odds	RPR
	1		**Citizen's Charter (USA)** 2-9-3 0 ... AhmedAjtebi 12 (Mahmood Al Zarooni) *mid-div: gd hdwy over 1f out: styd on strly to ld last 75yds: readily*	**16/1**	76+
24	2	1 ¼	**Flambard House (IRE)**[31] 2346 2-9-3 0 ... TonyHamilton 13 (Howard Johnson) *led tl 2f out: styd on same pce last 100yds*	**16/1**	72
	3	*nk*	**Electric Qatar** 2-9-3 0 ... RichardKingscote 10 (Tom Dascombe) *wnt lft s: w ldr: led 2f out: hung bdly lft: wknd and hdd wl ins fnl f*	**5/4**[1]	71+
5	4	1 ¼	**Commanche**[24] 2542 2-9-3 0 ... TomEaves 16 (Bryan Smart) *trckd ldrs: kpt on wl fnl f*	**9/1**	68
24	5	1	**Slenningford**[9] 3022 2-8-12 0 ... PJMcDonald 9 (Ollie Pears) *trckd ldrs: effrt 2f out: kpt on same pce*	**11/2**[2]	60
	6	½	**Bomber Jet** 2-9-3 0 ... PhillipMakin 11 (Nigel Tinkler) *s.s: styd on fnl 2f: nvr rchd ldrs*	**100/1**	63
00	7	2 ¾	**Peters Pursuit (IRE)**[26] 2504 2-9-3 0 ... FrederikTylicki 14 (Richard Fahey) *in rr: kpt on fnl 2f: nvr a factor*	**28/1**	59+
64	8	1	**Inya House**[8] 3050 2-9-3 0 ... GrahamGibbons 15 (Nigel Tinkler) *mid-div: kpt on fnl f: nvr nr ldrs*	**50/1**	52
	9	*nk*	**Sonsie Lass** 2-8-12 0 ... SilvestreDeSousa 4 (Mark Johnston) *chsd ldrs: upsides over 2f out: wknd over 1f out*	**25/1**	46
	10	1 ¼	**Captivity** 2-9-3 0 ... JamieSpencer 2 (Mahmood Al Zarooni) *trckd ldrs: chal over 2f out: wknd over 1f out: eased*	**6/1**[3]	51+
0	11	8	**Emley Moor**[28] 2430 2-8-12 0 ... KellyHarrison 7 (Chris Fairhurst) *s.i.s: a bhd*	**100/1**	18
	12	2 ¾	**Roll Of Thunder** 2-9-3 0 ... PaulHanagan 6 (John Quinn) *a in rr*	**18/1**	15
00	13	*shd*	**Roy's Legacy**[10] 2983 2-8-12 0 ... DanielleMcCreery(5) 5 (Shaun Harris) *mid-div: lost pl over 2f out: sn bhd*	**150/1**	15
	14	1 ½	**Koolgreycat (IRE)** 2-8-12 0 ... AdrianNicholls 3 (Noel Wilson) *mid-div: hdwy over 2f out: wknd over 1f out*	**50/1**	5
04	15	2 ¾	**Come Hither**[30] 2387 2-8-9 0 ... JamesSullivan(3) 8 (Michael Easterby) *s.i.s: a bhd*	**16/1**	—
	16	13	**Lucky Last** 2-8-12 0 ... DavidAllan 1 (Tim Easterby) *in rr: reminders after 2f: sn wl bhd*	**50/1**	—

1m 15.32s (0.72) **Going Correction** -0.125s/f (Firm) **16** Ran SP% **122.8**

Speed ratings (Par 93): **90,88,87,86,84 84,80,79,78,77 66,62,62,60,57 39**

toteswingers:1&2:£26.10, 1&3:£7.70, 2&3:£7.80 CSF £242.23 TOTE £20.70: £5.00, £4.20, £1.30; EX 192.20 TRIFECTA Not won..

Owner Godolphin **Bred** Brereton C Jones **Trained** Newmarket, Suffolk

■ Stewards' Enquiry : Jamie Spencer caution: entered the wrong stall

FOCUS

This didn't look a bad juvenile maiden, which was run at a fair pace, and stamina appeared to be crucial inside the final furlong on the dead surface.

NOTEBOOK

Citizen's Charter(USA) has a decent US pedigree and considering his powerful owners it was surprising he proved so easy to back ahead of this racecourse debut. However, last week's Royal Ascot hero Rewilding aside, his trainer didn't look in the best form beforehand and this does rate a fairly welcome success for the yard. Things didn't look good for the winner as he came under pressure passing the four-furlong marker, but the penny dropped from 2f out and he ultimately won going away. The trip was a minimum for him and he should only improve for the experience, so it will be interesting to see where he turns up next.

Flambard House(IRE), having his third outing, showed his best form to date on this step up a furlong and clearly stays well. He looks the type for nurseries, but could nick a small maiden before making that transition.

Electric Qatar ◆, who holds two Group 1 entries, proved all the rage to make a winning debut for his bang in-form connections. He raced professionally and went clear when asked to win the race. However, he drifted left to the far rail as his stamina ebbed away and he was done with half a furlong out. This will disappoint some, but he is speedily bred and will very likely win if reverting to a sharper test on his next outing. (op 10-11 tchd 11-8)

Commanche, fifth on his debut, was drawn nearest the stands' rail and ran a fair race yet looked to find things a bit too testing. (op 16-1)

Slenningford probably ran close enough to her previous level, but was another that just found this surface too much up in trip. She helps to set the standard. (op 6-1 tchd 5-1)

Bomber Jet, an already gelded son of Avonbridge, posted an encouraging effort on his debut and could improve a deal next time.

Captivity was the better fancied of the Godolphin runners according to the market and showed early speed. He dropped away from 2f out and wants a sharper test at this stage. (op 10-1 tchd 12-1)

Come Hither Official explanation: jockey said filly was never travelling

3315 TRADERSBETTINGEXCHANGE.CO.UK SEATON DELAVAL H'CAP 1m 3y(S)

3:20 (3:23) (Class 2) (0-105,97) 4-Y-O+

£9,844 (£2,948; £1,474; £737; £368; £184) **Stalls** Centre

Form	Pos	Dist	Horse / details	Odds	RPR
1222	1		**Vito Volterra (IRE)**[1] 3276 4-8-4 80 ... AdrianNicholls 7 (Michael Smith) *led centre gp: sn overall ldr: edgd lft fnl f: hld on gamely*	**13/2**[2]	88
0004	2	*nk*	**Prince Of Dance**[15] 2814 5-8-7 83 ... GrahamGibbons 2 (Tom Tate) *trckd ldrs: wnt 2nd 4f out: chal fnl f: no ex nr fin*	**7/1**[3]	90
-620	3	¾	**Arabian Spirit**[20] 2679 6-8-12 88 ... TonyHamilton 3 (Richard Fahey) *hld up: hdwy over 2f out: chsng ldng pair over 2f out: kpt on same pce last 75yds*	**10/1**	94
-616	4	3 ¼	**Extraterrestrial**[20] 2679 7-9-3 93 ... PaulHanagan 4 (Richard Fahey) *trckd ldrs: effrt over 2f out: one pce over 1f out*	**15/2**	91
4300	5	1	**Tiger Reigns**[12] 2933 5-9-7 97 ... FrederikTylicki 1 (Michael Dods) *trckd ldrs on outer: effrt over 2f out: kpt on one pce*	**16/1**	93
4463	6	*shd*	**Charlie Cool**[7] 3085 8-8-8 87 ...(b) JamesSullivan(3) 6 (Ruth Carr) *hld up in rr: effrt over 2f out: kpt on fnl f*	**6/1**[1]	83
0304	7	¾	**Collateral Damage (IRE)**[5] 3169 8-8-6 82 ...(t) DavidAllan 9 (Tim Easterby) *hld up stands' side: effrt over 2f out: kpt on fnl f*	**11/1**	76+
1000	8	3 ¾	**Imperial Djay (IRE)**[6] 3134 6-8-13 89 ... PJMcDonald 8 (Ruth Carr) *s.i.s: effrt over 2f out: sn wknd*	**16/1**	74
-630	9	1 ¾	**Silver Rime (FR)**[28] 2434 6-8-11 87 ... PhillipMakin 12 (Linda Perratt) *trckd ldrs stands' side: led that gp over 2f out: no threat*	**11/1**	68+
1040	10	7	**Bonfire Knight**[12] 2909 4-8-5 88 ... ShaneBKelly(7) 5 (John Quinn) *chsd ldrs: drvn over 3f out: wknd 2f out*	**16/1**	53
0005	11	14	**Kiwi Bay**[16] 2783 6-8-13 89 ... TomEaves 11 (Michael Dods) *hld up stands' side: lost pl over 3f out: sn bhd*	**11/1**	22
330	12	1 ¼	**Camerooney**[26] 2495 8-8-11 87 ... JamieSpencer 10 (Brian Ellison) *led stands' side gp: hdd over 2f out: sn wknd: eased whn bhd*	**11/1**	17
0000	13	15	**Tartan Gigha (IRE)**[12] 2933 6-8-12 88 ...(b[1]) SilvestreDeSousa 13 (Mark Johnston) *chsd ldrs stands' side: drvn over 4f out: sn lost pl and bhd: eased: t.o*	**12/1**	—

1m 40.58s (-2.82) **Going Correction** -0.125s/f (Firm) **13** Ran SP% **119.6**

Speed ratings (Par 109): **109,108,107,104,103 103,102,99,97,90 76,75,60**

toteswingers:1&2:£6.40, 1&3:£12.40, 2&3:£9.50 CSF £51.63 CT £458.93 TOTE £8.00: £3.10, £3.30, £3.50; EX 59.30 Trifecta £580.10 Part won. Pool: £783.95 - 0.75 winning units..

Owner Ace Racing **Bred** O McElroy **Trained** Kirkheaton, Northumberland

■ Stewards' Enquiry : Graham Gibbons one-day ban: careless riding (Jul 7)

FOCUS

A good handicap. The front pair were always 1-2 in the centre group and the winner confirmed his recent progress.

NOTEBOOK

Vito Volterra(IRE) arrived here having finished second on his three outings since winning on his return to turf over 7f here in May, including on similar ground in the Carlisle Bell the previous day. There was a worry beforehand about him being taken on in front, but the other known pacemaker Camerooney raced on the near rail, and he got his own way down the centre. He looked vulnerable 2f out, but kept finding for pressure and was always just doing enough inside the last furlong. He's evidently thriving and this rates a career-best. (op 9-1)

Prince Of Dance posted his best effort for a while last time and was on a decent mark. He emerged as the biggest danger to the winner and held every chance, but found that rival too resolute. He likes some cut, but this surface was perhaps just a bit too demanding over the trip and his turn looks to be nearing again.

Arabian Spirit showed his true colours and was doing all of his best work towards the finish. He likes this sort of ground and deserves to find another opening. (op 11-1)

Extraterrestrial was the first string from his yard according to jockey bookings, but was unable to confirm last-time-out form with his stablemate in third. He needs all to fall right. (op 7-1 tchd 8-1)

Tiger Reigns proved a bit free early, but kept on to register his most encouraging effort for some time and is now back down to his last winning mark. (tchd 14-1)

Charlie Cool didn't look too happy on this ground and is capable of better, but has become hard to catch right. (op 13-2)

3316 LA TAXIS H'CAP 2m 19y

3:55 (3:55) (Class 4) (0-80,73) 4-Y-O+ **£3,238** (£963; £481; £240) **Stalls** Low

Form	Pos	Dist	Horse / details	Odds	RPR
/641	1		**John Forbes**[11] 2952 9-9-0 66 ... TomEaves 7 (Brian Ellison) *hld up in rr: hdwy 6f out: styd on to ld jst ins fnl f: drvn out*	**9/4**[1]	78
-001	2	1 ¼	**Rosewin (IRE)**[26] 2496 5-9-4 73 ... JamesSullivan(3) 5 (Ollie Pears) *hld up in rr: hdwy 7f out: wnt 3rd over 3f out: led appr fnl f: sn hdd: styd on same pce*	**13/2**	84
6015	3	4 ½	**King In Waiting (IRE)**[29] 1881 8-8-7 59 ...(p) SilvestreDeSousa 6 (David O'Meara) *led: drvn over 3f out: hdd appr fnl f: one pce*	**12/1**	64
6122	4	2 ¾	**Petella**[22] 2622 5-8-13 65 ... PJMcDonald 4 (George Moore) *hld up in midfield: outpcd and reminders over 5f out: hdwy over 2f out: kpt on*	**6/1**[3]	67
0122	5	2 ¼	**Houston Dynimo (IRE)**[21] 2636 6-9-6 72 ... PaulHanagan 8 (Nicky Richards) *trckd ldr: wknd fnl f*	**11/1**	71
-102	6	1 ¾	**Madamlily (IRE)**[26] 2496 5-9-1 67 ... TonyHamilton 2 (John Quinn) *hld up in midfield: outpcd over 3f out: kpt on fnl 2f*	**12/1**	64
4314	7	1	**Maid Of Meft**[20] 2696 4-8-12 64 ... FrederikTylicki 10 (Linda Perratt) *hld up in rr: hdwy 8f out: one pce fnl 3f*	**15/2**	60
1322	8	1 ½	**Shifting Gold (IRE)**[11] 2952 5-8-7 62 ...(b) AmyRyan(3) 1 (Kevin Ryan) *dwlt: hdwy 8f out: lost pl over 6f out: sn bhd: kpt on fnl 2f*	**5/1**[2]	56
4401	9	21	**Dechiper (IRE)**[19] 2733 9-7-13 54 oh5 ... DeclanCannon(3) 3 (Robert Johnson) *trckd ldrs: lost pl over 2f out: bhd whn eased last 100yds*	**40/1**	23
	10	48	**Prideus (IRE)**[29] 7-8-10 62 ...(tp) PhillipMakin 9 (Brian Storey) *chsd ldrs: rdn over 4f out: sn lost pl and bhd: t.o 2f out: eased*	**100/1**	—

3m 35.22s (-4.18) **Going Correction** -0.125s/f (Firm) **10** Ran SP% **114.0**

Speed ratings (Par 105): **105,104,102,100,99 98,98,97,87,63**

toteswingers:1&2:£3.80, 1&3:£6.90, 2&3:£11.00 CSF £16.53 CT £141.74 TOTE £3.50: £1.10, £2.10, £2.70; EX 17.10 Trifecta £141.90 Pool: £684.97 - 3.57 winning units..

Owner Brian Ellison **Bred** Northmore Stud **Trained** Norton, N Yorks

FOCUS
This modest staying handicap was run at a decent early pace. Things slowed up a bit nearing the final turn and the first two home made their way more towards the middle of the track in the home straight. Sound enough form with the winner confirming his Doncaster latest and rated to his old turf best.

3317 IGNITION FESTIVAL H'CAP — 1m 2f 32y
4:30 (4:30) (Class 6) (0-55,59) 4-Y-O+ — **£1,050** (£1,050; £240; £120) **Stalls** Low

Form — RPR

0-06 **1** — **Pattern Mark**^{25} [2530] 5-8-13 **51** .... PaulHanagan 5 — 64
(Ollie Pears) *mid-div: hdwy to chse ldrs over 2f out: led last 100yds: jnd post* **12/1**

0-56 **1** *dht* **Dane Cottage**^{39} [115] 4-8-8 **46** .... RichardKingscote 4 — 59
(Brian Ellison) *trckd ldrs: wnt 2nd 100yds out: styd on to draw level last stride* **7/1**^{3}

4412 **3** *2¼* **Ay Tay Tate (IRE)**^{7} [3074] 5-9-7 **59** 6ex .... FrannyNorton 13 — 67
(David C Griffiths) *w ldr: led over 2f out: hdd ins fnl f: no ex* **3/1**^{1}

0-02 **4** *2¾* **Spahi (FR)**^{27} [2462] 5-9-2 **54** .... DanielTudhope 2 — 57
(David O'Meara) *trckd ldrs: chal 2f out: edgd rt: one pce ins fnl f* **3/1**^{1}

0236 **5** *¾* **Amical Risks (FR)**^{21} [2656] 7-8-12 **55** .... JulieBurke(5) 1 — 56
(Ollie Pears) *s.s: hdwy over 2f out: chsng ldrs over 1f out: kpt on same pce* **20/1**

0004 **6** *2* **Child Of Our Time (IRE)**^{15} [2807] 4-9-0 **52** .... DavidAllan 8 — 49
(Colin Teague) *mid-div: hdwy over 2f out: nvr rchd ldrs* **40/1**

6-66 **7** *2¼* **Maxi Moo (IRE)**^{41} [2057] 4-8-10 **48** .... SilvestreDeSousa 7 — 41
(Geoffrey Harker) *mid-div: drvn 6f out: hrd rdn and sme hdwy over 3f out: one pce fnl 2f* **9/2**^{2}

5024 **8** *1¼* **Carnival Dream**^{6} [3139] 6-8-5 **46** oh1 ....(p) DeclanCannon(3) 6 — 36
(Hugh McWilliams) *trckd ldrs: t.k.h: effrt 3f out: one pce* **25/1**

4046 **9** *hd* **Dandarrell**^{10} [2988] 4-9-0 **52** ....(b¹) GrahamGibbons 3 — 42
(Julie Camacho) *trckd ldrs: t.k.h: wknd 2f out* **22/1**

0600 **10** *1¼* **Pictures (IRE)**^{92} [943] 4-8-8 **46** oh1 .... AndrewMullen 10 — 33
(Ron Barr) *mid-div: effrt 3f out: wknd over 1f out* **50/1**

63-6 **11** *2¾* **Richo**^{6} [3110] 5-8-11 **54** ....(b) DanielleMcCreery(5) 16 — 36
(Shaun Harris) *s.v.s: bhd: nt clr run and swtchd rt 2f out: nvr a factor* **66/1**

030- **12** *2* **Catawollow**^{12} [5819] 4-8-11 **49** ....(e) JamieSpencer 15 — 27
(Richard Guest) *in rr: sme hdwy over 2f out: nvr nr ldrs: eased towards fin* **20/1**

-006 **13** *2¼* **Prime Circle**^{7} [3088] 5-9-0 **55** ....(p) PaulPickard(3) 11 — 28
(Alan Brown) *in rr: sme hdwy on ins whn hmpd 1f out: nvr on terms* **40/1**

0000 **14** *3* **Barton Bounty**^{7} [3086] 4-8-12 **50** .... FrederikTylicki 12 — 17
(Peter Niven) *hld up in rr: nvr a factor* **40/1**

6/00 **15** *7* **Hair Of The Dog**^{20} [2696] 7-8-7 **48** ....(bt) PatrickDonaghy(3) 9 — —
(George Charlton) *t.k.h: led: hdd over 2f out: sn wknd: eased* **50/1**

000/ **16** *1¼* **Amongst Amigos (IRE)**^{1122} [2494] 10-8-8 **46** oh1..(b) DuranFentiman 14 — —
(Ian McInnes) *in rr: bhd fnl 3f* **28/1**

0-05 **P** — **Weetfromthechaff**^{35} [1615] 6-8-11 **49** ....(t) TonyHamilton 17 — —
(Maurice Barnes) *trckd ldrs: drvn 4f out: sn wknd: t.o 2f out: heavily eased: p.u and dismntd nr fin* **25/1**

2m 12.53s (0.63) **Going Correction** -0.05s/f (Good) — **17** Ran SP% **126.1**
Speed ratings (Par 101): **95,95,93,91,90 88,87,86,85,84 82,81,79,76,71 70**,—WIN: Pattern Mark £3.20, Dane Cottage £4.20 PL: PM £1.10, DC £4.00 A £1.10, S £1.30 EX: PM/DC £48.10 DC/PM £54.20 CSF: PM/DC £41.42 DC/PM £38.28. T/C: PM/DC/ATT £163.82 , DC/PM/ATT£157.18 toteswingers: PM&DC £20.50, DC&ATT £11.10, PM&ATT £8.00 TOTE £027: £Owner, £David Scott and Co (Pattern Makers) Ltd, £Bred, £D ScottTrained Norton, N Yorks.
Owner Koo's Racing Club **Bred** Winterbeck Manor Stud **Trained** Norton, N Yorks
■ Stewards' Enquiry : Paul Hanagan trainer had no explanation for the apparent improvement in form shown

FOCUS
The rain arrived prior to this moderate handicap. It was run at a solid pace and once again the main action developed down the middle of the home straight, resulting in a dead-heat. The form is rated on the positive side.
Child Of Our Time(IRE) Official explanation: trainer said filly lost a front shoe
Weetfromthechaff Official explanation: jockey said gelding lost its action

3318 CFK FUN DAY 31ST JULY H'CAP — 7f
5:05 (5:05) (Class 5) (0-75,74) 3-Y-O — **£2,266** (£674; £337; £168) **Stalls** Centre

Form — RPR

04-0 **1** — **Ted's Brother (IRE)**^{38} [2163] 3-8-4 **57** .... PaulHanagan 6 — 66+
(Richard Guest) *trckd ldrs: t.k.h: effrt 2f out: styd on to ld ins fnl f: drvn out* **7/1**^{2}

-003 **2** *2* **Icy Blue**^{14} [2834] 3-8-12 **65** .... FrannyNorton 10 — 69
(Richard Whitaker) *hld up: swtchd centre over 5f out: chsng ldrs 3f out: wnt 2nd last 100yds: no imp* **15/2**^{3}

26-3 **3** *2* **Guinea Seeker**^{30} [2391] 3-8-7 **60** .... DavidAllan 5 — 59
(Tim Easterby) *w ldr: led over 2f out: hdd ins fnl f: kpt on same pce* **6/1**^{1}

4300 **4** *½* **Prince Of Passion (CAN)**^{20} [2675] 3-8-12 **65** ....(b¹) FrederikTylicki 3 — 63
(Michael Dods) *led: hdd over 1f out: no ex last 100yds* **28/1**

3042 **5** *½* **Philharmonic Hall**^{34} [2252] 3-8-11 **64** ....(v) TonyHamilton 2 — 60
(Richard Fahey) *trckd ldrs: upsides over 1f out: kpt on same pce* **12/1**

0-35 **6** *¾* **Dubai Celebration**^{27} [2477] 3-9-4 **74** .... PatrickDonaghy(3) 9 — 68
(Jedd O'Keeffe) *hld up in mid-div: effrt over 2f out: kpt on one pce over 1f out* **16/1**

5-02 **7** *1* **White Fusion**^{40} [2119] 3-8-1 **57** .... DeclanCannon(3) 11 — 49
(Howard Johnson) *mid-div: drvn 3f out: sn chsng ldrs: one pce over 1f out* **7/1**^{2}

-310 **8** *1* **Tapis Libre**^{43} [2008] 3-9-1 **68** .... GrahamGibbons 7 — 57
(Michael Easterby) *mid-div: sn drvn along: outpcd over 2f out: no threat after* **15/2**^{3}

6-41 **9** *4* **Unex Goya (IRE)**^{15} [2825] 3-8-9 **65** ....(t) PaulPickard(3) 4 — 44
(Michael Smith) *dwlt and wnt rt s: hdwy on outside to chse ldrs 4f out: wknd over 1f out* **16/1**

5-05 **10** *3¾* **Bay Of Fires (IRE)**^{10} [2986] 3-9-6 **73** .... SilvestreDeSousa 12 — 42
(David O'Meara) *in rr stands' side: drvn over 2f out: hung lft and wknd over 1f out* **6/1**^{1}

0430 **11** *9* **Deep Applause**^{8} [3039] 3-8-7 **60** .... DuranFentiman 1 — —
(Michael Dods) *mid-div: reminders over 3f out: lost pl over 2f out: eased whn bhd ins fnl f* **14/1**

1114 **12** *18* **Exchange**^{27} [2453] 3-8-13 **66** .... JamieSpencer 8 — —
(Andrew Haynes) *in rr: bhd fnl 2f: eased ins fnl f: t.o* **9/1**

1m 28.47s (0.67) **Going Correction** -0.05s/f (Good) — **12** Ran SP% **116.7**
Speed ratings (Par 99): **99,96,94,93,93 92,91,90,85,81 71,50**
toteswingers:1&2:£14.00, 1&3:£8.70, 2&3:£12.80 CSF £57.75 CT £341.36 TOTE £8.40: £2.50, £4.20, £2.80; EX 70.10 Trifecta £426.70 Part won. Pool: £576.69 - 0.82 winning units..
Owner Maze Rattan Limited **Bred** T Counihan **Trained** Stainforth, S Yorks

FOCUS
An ordinary 3-y-o handicap and another race that looked wide open. Yet again the place to be was down the middle of the track. The winner is rated back to his early maiden form.
Exchange Official explanation: jockey said gelding was unsuited by the soft, good to soft in places ground

3319 SENDRIG CONSTRUCTION H'CAP — 1m 2f 32y
5:40 (5:40) (Class 5) (0-75,74) 4-Y-O+ — **£3,238** (£963; £481; £240) **Stalls** Low

Form — RPR

-031 **1** — **Quanah Parker (IRE)**^{28} [2414] 5-9-7 **74** .... GrahamGibbons 6 — 83
(Richard Whitaker) *mid-div: drvn over 3f out: sn chsng ldrs: styd on wl to ld last 50yds despite taking a bump* **9/2**^{2}

1-61 **2** *¾* **Burns Night**^{26} [2487] 5-9-6 **73** ....(p) SilvestreDeSousa 7 — 80
(Geoffrey Harker) *swtchd lft s: effrt over 3f out: led 2f out: edgd rt: hdd and no ex wl ins fnl f* **9/1**

-415 **3** *1½* **Sinatramania**^{10} [2988] 4-8-3 **59** .... PaulPickard(3) 10 — 63
(Tracy Waggott) *hld up in last: hdwy on ins over 2f out: chal over 1f out: styd on same pce last 150yds* **8/1**^{3}

1654 **4** *3½* **Rosbay (IRE)**^{8} [3051] 7-9-6 **73** ....(p) DuranFentiman 1 — 70
(Tim Easterby) *dwlt: t.k.h: sn trcking ldrs: lost pl over 4f out: hdwy on ins 3f out: kpt on one pce fnl 1f* **8/1**^{3}

-052 **5** *1½* **Hakuna Matata**^{21} [2656] 4-9-5 **72** ....(b¹) RichardKingscote 2 — 66
(Brian Ellison) *s.i.s: drvn along to ld over 8f out: hdd 2f out: wknd fnl f* **5/2**^{1}

6 *2¾* **Morning Time (IRE)**^{18} [2106] 5-9-7 **74** .... JamieSpencer 5 — 63
(Lucinda Russell) *in rr: shkn up over 5f out: hrd rdn and sme hdwy over 2f out: hung lft over 1f out: nvr a factor* **20/1**

0550 **7** *4* **Elmfield Giant (USA)**^{27} [2454] 4-9-0 **67** .... PaulHanagan 9 — 48
(Richard Fahey) *led 1f: chsd ldrs: wknd over 1f out* **14/1**

5045 **8** *½* **Dean Iarracht (IRE)**^{15} [2804] 5-8-5 **58** ....(p) FrannyNorton 8 — 38
(Tracy Waggott) *in rr: drvn over 3f out: nvr a factor* **14/1**

/0-6 **9** *nk* **Herrera (IRE)**^{19} [2734] 6-8-6 **66** .... GeorgeChaloner(7) 11 — 45
(Richard Fahey) *trckd ldrs on outside: t.k.h: wkrid 2f out* **20/1**

2-03 **10** *2¾* **Magic Millie (IRE)**^{12} [2912] 4-8-2 **58** .... DeclanCannon(3) 4 — 31
(David O'Meara) *dwlt: drvn to ld after 1f: sn hdd: drvn over 3f out: wknd 2f out* **9/1**

5021 **11** *22* **Media Stars**^{6} [3139] 6-8-9 **62** 6ex .... FrederikTylicki 3 — —
(Robert Johnson) *t.k.h in midfield: wknd over 2f out: eased whn bhd: t.o* **18/1**

2m 12.59s (0.69) **Going Correction** -0.05s/f (Good) — **11** Ran SP% **117.1**
Speed ratings (Par 103): **95,94,93,90,89 87,83,83,83,80 63**
toteswingers:1&2:£7.20, 1&3:£7.80, 2&3:£23.10 CSF £44.62 CT £310.45 TOTE £7.40: £2.70, £4.70, £3.80; EX 49.20 Trifecta £525.20 Part won. Pool: £709.82 - 0.95 winning units..
Owner Wham Partnership **Bred** M Fahy **Trained** Scarcroft, W Yorks

FOCUS
A moderate handicap, run at a fair pace but on the worst ground on the card. Ordinary form for the grade, rated around the first two.
Magic Millie(IRE) Official explanation: trainer had no explanation for the poor form shown
Media Stars Official explanation: trainer's rep said gelding was unsuited by the soft, good to soft in places ground
T/Jkpt: Not won. T/Plt: £48.10 to a £1 stake. Pool:£79,464.85 - 1,204.18 winning tickets T/Qpdt: £22.70 to a £1 stake. Pool:£5,555.07 - 180.60 winning tickets WG

3089 WARWICK (L-H)
Thursday, June 23

OFFICIAL GOING: Good to firm (good in places; 7.4)
Wind: fresh, behind Weather: dry, breezy

3320 WEATHERBYS BANK MAIDEN STKS (DIV I) — 7f 26y
2:20 (2:20) (Class 5) 3-Y-O+ — **£2,266** (£674; £337; £168) **Stalls** Low

Form — RPR

05-2 **1** — **Sea Soldier (IRE)**^{16} [2790] 3-9-3 78 .... JimmyFortune 6 — 78
(Andrew Balding) *chsd ldr tl led after 1f: mde rest: rdn 2f out: drvn and kpt on wl fnl f* **11/4**^{2}

2 **2** *¾* **Kawssaj**^{27} [2457] 3-9-3 0 .... NeilCallan 1 — 76
(Roger Varian) *chsd ldng pair: wnt 2nd wl over 1f out: rdn to chal jst over 1f out: drvn and a hld fnl f* **4/9**^{1}

40- **3** *3½* **Minety Lass**^{317} [4921] 3-8-12 0 .... NeilChalmers 7 — 62
(Adrian Chamberlain) *led for 1f: chsd ldr after tl wl over 1f out: edgd lft and styd on same pce u.p fr over 1f out* **100/1**

6-03 **4** *1¾* **Logans Legend (IRE)**^{38} [2151] 3-9-3 70 .... MichaelHills 8 — 62
(B W Hills) *chsd ldng trio: rdn and unable qck 2f out: 4th and wl hld 1f out* **6/1**^{3}

60 **5** *nk* **Isdaal**^{33} [2306] 4-9-7 0 .... JackMitchell 5 — 59
(Kevin Morgan) *racd off the pce in last trio: rdn and hdwy 2f out: kpt on fr over 1f out: nvr trbld ldrs* **50/1**

5 **6** *2* **Wordiness**^{14} [2848] 3-9-3 0 .... FrankieMcDonald 2 — 56
(Barry Brennan) *s.i.s: wl off the pce in last pair: rdn over 2f out: kpt on fr over 1f out: nvr trbld ldrs* **25/1**

7 *1* **The Buska (IRE)** 3-8-12 0 .... NeilFarley(5) 4 — 53
(Declan Carroll) *s.i.s: sn pushed along and rcvrd to r in midfield: rdn over 2f out: wknd qckly u.p over 1f out* **40/1**

0 **8** *6* **Phlorian**^{16} [2790] 5-9-12 0 ....(tp) HayleyTurner 10 — 40
(Ian Patrick Browne, Ire) *t.k.h: hld up in tch: rdn and struggling 3f out: sn wknd: wl bhd fnl 2f* **66/1**

0- **9** *10* **Poppet's Joy**^{260} [6675] 3-8-12 0 .... ChrisCatlin 9 — —
(Reg Hollinshead) *sn struggling in last: lost tch 3f out* **50/1**

1m 25.01s (0.41) **Going Correction** +0.125s/f (Good)
WFA 3 from 4yo+ 9lb — **9** Ran SP% **122.9**
Speed ratings (Par 103): **102,101,97,95,94 92,91,84,73**
toteswingers:1&2:£1.10, 1&3:£11.60, 2&3:£11.00 CSF £4.60 TOTE £2.90: £1.10, £1.02, £20.40; EX 5.20.
Owner Mrs M E Wates **Bred** M E Wates **Trained** Kingsclere, Hants

FOCUS
Rail from 1m start to 2f moved out 3yds. Not much strength in depth for a maiden that was run at a steady pace, and the form is muddling. They came wide off the bend, up the stands' side and the market principals drew clear after a protracted battle. The favourite disappointed and the form is rated around the winner.

Wordiness Official explanation: jockey said colt reared on leaving stalls

3321 WARWICK MUSIC NIGHT AUGUST 23RD H'CAP 5f
2:55 (2:55) (Class 5) (0-70,68) 3-Y-O £2,729 (£806; £403) Stalls Low

Form RPR

2321 **1** **Albany Rose (IRE)**[1] 3272 3-9-4 **65** 6ex.............................. TedDurcan 8 78+
(Rae Guest) *in tch: pushed along and hdwy to ld over 1f out: rdn clr ent fnl f: in command and rdn out fnl 100yds* **15/8**[1]

6330 **2** *3* **Whitecrest**[22] 2611 3-9-7 **68**.. CathyGannon 2 70
(John Spearing) *chsd ldrs: drvn and pressed ldrs 2f out: unable qck and outpcd by wnr jst over 1f out: wnt 2nd ins fnl f: kpt on but no ch w wnr* **8/1**

3254 **3** *2 ½* **Johnny Hancocks (IRE)**[5] 3189 3-9-1 **62**........................ KierenFallon 4 55
(Linda Stubbs) *led: rdn and hrd pressed 2f out: hdd over 1f out: sn outpcd by wnr and btn 1f out: plugged on same pce fnl f* **6/1**[3]

5663 **4** *1 ¼* **Novabridge**[15] 2827 3-9-3 **64**.. NeilCallan 1 53
(Andrew Haynes) *in tch: pushed along over 3f out: drvn and unable qck wl over 1f out: sn outpcd and no ch w wnr 1f out: plugged on same pce fnl f* **8/1**

6333 **5** *hd* **Hootys Agogo**[6] 3143 3-7-13 **51**.. NeilFarley(5) 7 39
(Declan Carroll) *pressed ldr: rdn and ev ch whn stmbld wl over 1f out: nt qckn u.p over 1f out and btn ent fnl f: wknd ins fnl f* **5/2**[2]

4-02 **6** *7* **Ezzles (USA)**[70] 1334 3-9-4 **65**..................................(tp) RobertWinston 3 28
(Alan McCabe) *taken down early: in tch: rdn and unable qck 2f out: wknd and wl btn whn edgd lft 1f out* **16/1**

00-6 **7** *1* **Love Club**[10] 2993 3-8-3 **50**... PaulQuinn 5 —
(Brian Baugh) *fly-jmpd as stalls opened and slowly away: reminder sn after s: a in rr: wknd wl over 1f out* **25/1**

59.65 secs (0.05) **Going Correction** +0.05s/f (Good) **7** Ran SP% **109.6**
Speed ratings (Par 99): **101,96,92,90,89 78,77**
toteswingers:1&2:£4.00, 1&3:£2.80, 2&3:£8.20 CSF £15.97 CT £67.31 TOTE £2.00: £1.10, £7.40; EX 18.00.
Owner E P Duggan **Bred** Blue Bloodstock Ltd **Trained** Newmarket, Suffolk

FOCUS
A weak sprint handicap run at a fair pace. The form does not look that solid, rated around the second.

3322 WEATHERBYS BLOODSTOCK INSURANCE H'CAP 6f
3:30 (3:34) (Class 4) (0-80,79) 3-Y-O+ £4,079 (£1,214; £606; £303) Stalls Low

Form RPR

-000 **1** **Serena's Pride**[21] 2646 3-8-10 **73**.................................. HarryBentley(5) 8 80
(Alan Jarvis) *chsd ldrs: rdn to chal ent fnl f: led fnl 100yds: pushed along hands and heels and r.o wl after* **7/1**[3]

0250 **2** *hd* **Stevie Gee (IRE)**[5] 3179 7-9-3 **73**.................................... RyanClark(5) 9 81
(Ian Williams) *in tch in midfield: swtchd rt and effrt on stands' rail 2f out: drvn and ev ch ins fnl f: r.o but a jst hld* **10/1**

0-04 **3** *2* **Tyfos**[14] 2832 6-9-13 **78**... J-PGuillambert 12 80
(Brian Baugh) *led: rdn and edgd lft ent fnl f: hdd fnl 100yds: wknd towards fin* **11/2**[2]

1000 **4** *¾* **Silver Wind**[10] 3000 6-9-12 **77**..(b) RobertWinston 7 76
(Alan McCabe) *in tch: drvn wl over 1f out: chsd ldng trio 1f out: styd on same pce u.p after* **9/1**

20-4 **5** *1 ¾* **Holiday Snap**[22] 2605 5-8-12 **63**......................................(t) TravisBlock 15 57
(Mary Hambro) *in tch: sltly outpcd and lost pl whn n.m.r on stands' rail 2f out: drvn over 1f out: styd on u.p ins fnl f: no threat to ldrs* **10/1**

0253 **6** *nk* **The Wee Chief (IRE)**[12] 2929 5-9-1 **66**........................(tp) KierenFallon 5 59
(Jimmy Fox) *hld up towards rr: hdwy into midfield 1/2-way: rdn and kpt on same pce fnl f* **11/2**[2]

2142 **7** *¾* **Steel City Boy (IRE)**[22] 2610 8-8-9 **60** oh1...................... MartinLane 14 50
(Garry Woodward) *chsd ldr: rdn over 2f out: lost 2nd over 1f out: wknd u.p jst over 1f out* **12/1**

13-6 **8** *1 ¼* **Picabo (IRE)**[12] 2916 3-9-1 **73**.. JimCrowley 3 57+
(Lucy Wadham) *hld up in midfield: rdn and effrt in centre 2f out: drvn and no prog over 1f out: no threat to ldrs fnl f* **7/2**[1]

5400 **9** *1 ¼* **Go Nani Go**[31] 2369 5-9-10 **75**... PatCosgrave 6 57
(Ed de Giles) *stdd s: hld up in rr: rdn and effrt over 1f out: no imp: nvr trbld ldrs* **20/1**

4304 **10** *hd* **Rainy Night**[16] 2794 5-8-5 **63**...(p) JackDuern(7) 1 45+
(Reg Hollinshead) *chsd ldrs: rdn ent fnl 2f: wknd over 1f out* **18/1**

0315 **11** *2 ¾* **Mary's Pet**[86] 1024 4-8-10 **64**... SimonPearce(3) 13 37
(John Akehurst) *a towards rr: rdn and no hdwy over 1f out: wl btn fnl f* **28/1**

41-0 **12** *nk* **Hatta Stream (IRE)**[12] 2938 5-9-7 **72**............................. RobertHavlin 10 44
(Lydia Pearce) *dwlt: a bhd: rdn and no hdwy wl over 1f out: wl btn fnl f* **14/1**

1m 11.3s (-0.50) **Going Correction** +0.05s/f (Good) course record
WFA 3 from 4yo+ 7lb **12** Ran SP% **121.5**
Speed ratings (Par 105): **105,104,102,101,98 98,97,95,94,93 90,89**
toteswingers:1&2:£11.90, 1&3:£10.30, 2&3:£12.20 CSF £77.24 CT £421.22 TOTE £12.40: £3.20, £4.60, £4.40; EX 87.50.
Owner Baydoun & Harake Partnership **Bred** Mrs Ann Jarvis **Trained** Twyford, Bucks

FOCUS
An open sprint handicap with not many coming here in form, and it lost much of its appeal with the withdrawal of the 9/2 market leader Flying Applause who unshipped his 5lb claimer on the way to the start (deduct 15p in the 3 under R4). Run at a decent pace, they came wide off the final bend to the stands' side rail. There were plenty in with a chance at the 1f pole. The winner showed her best form since last summer.
Serena's Pride Official explanation: trainer's rep said, regarding the apparent improvement in form shown, filly has been dropped in the weights, appeared suited by racing over a shorter trip and from being ridden sympathetically.
The Wee Chief(IRE) Official explanation: trainer's rep said gelding had a breathing problem
Hatta Stream(IRE) Official explanation: trainer said gelding had knocked a joint

3323 COLLIERS INTERNATIONAL RATING SERVICES ETERNAL STKS (LISTED RACE) (FILLIES) 7f 26y
4:05 (4:07) (Class 1) 3-Y-O

£17,031 (£6,456; £3,231; £1,611; £807; £405) Stalls Low

Form RPR

0-32 **1** **Khor Sheed**[47] 1902 3-9-3 100.. KierenFallon 2 107+
(Luca Cumani) *t.k.h: hld up in midfield: shkn up and chal ent fnl f: led and reminder ins fnl f: sn clr: eased towards fin* **15/8**[1]

23-0 **2** *2 ¼* **Sweetie Time**[8] 3034 3-8-12 92.. HayleyTurner 3 93
(Michael Bell) *chsd ldr tl over 3f out: drvn wl over 1f out: kpt on same pce ins fnl f: snatched 2nd on post* **12/1**

1-63 **3** *shd* **Masaya**[40] 2106 3-8-12 97.. ChrisCatlin 6 93
(Clive Brittain) *led: rdn jst over 2f out: hdd ins fnl f: unable qck and no ch w wnr after: lost 2nd on post* **3/1**[2]

13-3 **4** *1 ¾* **Carrignavar (USA)**[20] 2690 3-8-12 88................................ JimCrowley 5 88
(Ralph Beckett) *stdd s: t.k.h: hld up in midfield: rdn and effrt 2f out: drvn jst over 1f out: edgd lft and styd on same pce ins fnl f* **9/1**

1-36 **5** *1 ½* **Eucharist (IRE)**[47] 1893 3-8-12 100.................................... JimmyFortune 4 84
(Richard Hannon) *stdd s: hld up in last pair: rdn and effrt 2f out: styng on same pce whn pushed lft 1f out: no imp and no ch w wnr whn swtchd rt ins fnl f* **9/2**[3]

-200 **6** *nse* **Glas Burn**[47] 1902 3-8-12 93... StephenCraine 7 84
(Jonathan Portman) *chsd ldrs: wnt 2nd over 3f out tl over 1f out: wknd u.p 1f out* **50/1**

13-2 **7** *7* **Sadafiya**[83] 1079 3-8-12 85.. RichardHills 1 65
(Ed Dunlop) *stdd s: hld up in last: rdn and effrt ent fnl 2f: no hdwy u.p over 1f out: bhd and eased wl ins fnl f* **15/2**

1m 23.8s (-0.80) **Going Correction** +0.125s/f (Good) **7** Ran SP% **109.4**
Speed ratings (Par 104): **109,106,106,104,102 102,94**
toteswingers:1&2:£4.70, 1&3:£2.00, 2&3:£6.50 CSF £23.15 TOTE £2.20: £1.30, £6.80; EX 19.10.
Owner Sheikh Mohammed Obaid Al Maktoum **Bred** Card Bloodstock **Trained** Newmarket, Suffolk
■ Stewards' Enquiry : Jim Crowley caution: careless riding

FOCUS
A decent renewal of this 7f Listed fillies' race but the pace was only modest, the time just slightly quicker than the earlier maiden, and it turned into something of a sprint. They came stands' side off the bend. The form is rated at face value and the winner is value for an extra length.

NOTEBOOK
Khor Sheed, from the same stable that won this last year, produced a very taking display, giving her rivals 5lb for a short-head victory in a 6f Listed event at Newmarket last September. She had subsequent winner Poppy Seed behind her when a close second in another 6f Listed race at Nottingham last time, and looked tuned to the minute. She settled better than most off the sluggish early pace and only had to be shaken up to win under a confident ride. She drew clear with the minimum of fuss after Kieren Fallon gave her just one reminder, and was eased in the last few strides. This step up to 7f appeared to suit and now that she has found her confidence, she should acquit herself well when making the jump into Group company. She looks capable of getting a mile. (op 6-4 tchd 2-1 in a place)
Sweetie Time ran a fine race in defeat. Dropping back in trip after a pleasing return in the 1m Listed Sandringham Handicap at Royal Ascot last week, she stuck to her guns and battled. She would appreciate more cut in the ground and is worth another chance at this trip. (tchd 14-1)
Masaya dictated the pace, such as it was, and ran to a similar level of form that she showed when third to the useful Codemaster at Newmarket in a 7f Listed event last month. She didn't have the pace to stay with the winner and the ground may have been plenty quick enough for her. (tchd 11-4)
Carrignavar(USA) pulled hard early on and would certainly have done better if the pace had been sufficient. This was her first try at 7f and she is worth another crack at it. (op 11-1)
Eucharist(IRE) was a progressive handicapper last season and while she started the season well with a good third in a Group 3 at Newbury, she flopped last month at Lingfield and didn't really fire again here. There were no obvious excuses and the jury is out on her at present. (op 13-2)
Glas Burn had plenty on her plate and was beaten a long way.
Sadafiya didn't get the trip. (op 17-2 tchd 7-1)

3324 WEATHERBYS BANK MAIDEN STKS (DIV II) 7f 26y
4:40 (4:41) (Class 5) 3-Y-O+ £2,266 (£674; £337; £168) Stalls Low

Form RPR

5 **1** **Above Standard (IRE)**[70] 1338 3-9-3 0.................................. MichaelHills 3 81+
(B W Hills) *chsd ldr: rdn to ld wl over 1f out: clr and in command whn rn green and drvn ins fnl f: pushed out towards fin: comf* **8/11**[1]

06 **2** *2* **Brick Dust (IRE)**[12] 2924 3-9-3 0.. KierenFallon 7 73+
(Luca Cumani) *in tch in midfield: pushed along and effrt in centre over 2f out: edgd rt over 1f out: chsd ldng pair 1f out: pushed along and kpt on to go 2nd towards fin: no threat to wnr* **10/1**

0-4 **3** *½* **Thunda**[16] 2790 3-8-12 0.. CathyGannon 1 66
(Eve Johnson Houghton) *led: rdn jst over 2f out: hdd and unable qck wl over 1f out: kpt on same pce u.p fnl f: lost 2nd towards fin* **17/2**[3]

4-20 **4** *2 ¼* **Perfect Mission**[35] 2215 3-9-3 77..................................... JimmyFortune 8 65
(Andrew Balding) *chsd ldrs: rdn and unable qck jst over 2f out: drvn and styd on same pce ent fnl f* **9/4**[2]

5 *1 ½* **Ffajir (IRE)** 3-8-12 0.. ChrisCatlin 9 56+
(Clive Brittain) *outpcd in last quartet: clsd over 3f out: rdn 2f out: styd on steadily past btn horse fnl f: nvr trbld ldrs* **20/1**

0 **6** *2 ¾* **Concrete Jungle (IRE)**[16] 2790 3-9-3 0............................. MartinLane 4 54?
(Andrew Haynes) *sn rdn along in midfield: struggling and outpcd over 2f out: styd on same pce u.p and no threat to ldrs fnl 2f* **66/1**

50 **7** *nk* **Kindlelight Soleil (FR)**[5] 3167 4-9-12 0................(b[1]) TomMcLaughlin 2 56?
(Nick Littmoden) *s.i.s: rdn along and outpcd in rr: hdwy and tagged on to bk of field 1/2-way: struggling u.p jst over 2f out: wknd wl over 1f out* **66/1**

00 **8** *9* **Harmony Wold**[7] 3075 3-8-7 0... NeilFarley(5) 10 24
(Declan Carroll) *chsd ldrs: rdn and struggling over 2f out: wknd qckly wl over 1f out: wl bhd fnl f* **100/1**

\- **9** *16* **Seawood**[13] 5-9-12 0.. PaulQuinn 6 —
(Roy Bowring) *v.s.a: wl outpcd in last: clsd and jst in tch 1/2-way: rdn and lost tch 3f out: t.o* **80/1**

1m 25.31s (0.71) **Going Correction** +0.125s/f (Good)
WFA 3 from 4yo+ 9lb **9** Ran SP% **118.3**
Speed ratings (Par 103): **100,97,97,94,92 89,89,79,60**
toteswingers:1&2:£3.50, 1&3:£2.00, 2&3:£5.80 CSF £9.93 TOTE £2.10: £1.10, £2.80, £1.40; EX 10.80.
Owner J Hanson,Cavendish InvLtd,Sir A Ferguson **Bred** Sandro Garavelli **Trained** Lambourn, Berks

FOCUS
The second division of the 7f maiden was run in a slightly slower time than the opening first division. The pace was sensible. A typically muddling Warwick race and the bare form is only modest.

3325 ELIZA DOOLITTLE AFTER RACING ON AUGUST 23RD H'CAP 1m 2f 188y
5:15 (5:16) (Class 5) (0-70,73) 3-Y-O £2,590 (£770; £385; £192) Stalls Low

Form RPR

4040 **1** **Ugo (USA)**[14] 2842 3-9-5 **68**.. KierenFallon 3 74
(Heather Main) *hld up in midfield: rdn and effrt jst over 2f out: drvn and ev ch jst ins fnl f: led fnl 75yds: jst hld on* **5/1**[2]

-115 **2** *shd* **Amistress**[42] 2022 3-9-2 **65**... CathyGannon 7 73+
(Eve Johnson Houghton) *hld up in tch towards rr: rdn and effrt over 2f out: chsng ldrs on stands' rail and nt clr run jst over 1f out: switching lft arnd 3 rivals 1f out: eventually clr run fnl 100yds: r.o wl u.p: jst failed* **10/3**[1]

5-55 **3** 1/2 **Arctic Cat (IRE)**[20] 2675 3-8-8 **57**.............................. RobertWinston 6 62
(Mrs K Burke) *hld up in tch: chsd ldrs and gng wl 3f out: drvn to chal over 1f out: led 1f out: edgd rt u.p and hdd fnl 100yds: kpt on same pce after* **11/2**[3]

-133 **4** 1 1/2 **Moonlight Rhapsody (IRE)**[55] 1659 3-9-5 **68**.................. MichaelHills 4 71
(B W Hills) *chsd ldrs: rdn to ld jst over 2f out: drvn and hdd 1f out: stl pressing but one pce and looking hld whn hit by rivals whip ins fnl f: hmpd and snatched up fnl 100yds: nt rcvr and one pce after* **7/1**

04-0 **5** 3/4 **Astromagick**[41] 2065 3-8-8 **62**.................................. AshleyMorgan(5) 1 63
(Mark H Tompkins) *dwlt and bustled along in midfield tl 8f out: rdn and effrt over 2f out: chsd ldrs and drvn over 1f out: styd on same pce fnl f* **14/1**

2135 **6** 3 1/2 **Little Jazz**[14] 2850 3-8-10 **66**.............................. ChristopherGraham(7) 8 61
(Paul D'Arcy) *stdd s: hld up in last pair: nudged along and short-lived effrt over 1f out: no prog and btn 1f out* **8/1**

-165 **7** 3 **Piave (IRE)**[20] 2695 3-9-7 **70**...(b1) JackMitchell 2 59
(Peter Chapple-Hyam) *pushed into ld sn after s: hdd over 8f out: chsd ldr after tl rdn to ld wl over 2f out: hdd jst over 2f out: wknd u.p and hung rt 1f out* **11/2**[3]

5344 **8** 4 1/2 **Ad Vitam (IRE)**[14] 2835 3-8-3 **59**............................(p) LeonnaMayor(7) 10 40
(David C Griffiths) *stdd s: hld up in last pair: rdn and short-lived effrt in centre 2f out: wl btn over 1f out* **20/1**

5-00 **9** 2 1/4 **Face Value**[13] 2885 3-9-5 **68**...(b1) ShaneKelly 11 45
(Brian Meehan) *dashed up to ld over 8f out: hdd and rdn wl over 2f out: dropped out qckly 2f out: wl bhd ent fnl f* **11/1**

2m 20.19s (-0.91) **Going Correction** -0.10s/f (Good) **9** Ran SP% **113.9**
Speed ratings (Par 99): **99,98,98,97,96 94,92,88,87**
toteswingers:1&2:£1.80, 1&3:£4.20, 2&3:£3.20 CSF £21.70 CT £93.90 TOTE £5.50: £2.60, £1.10, £3.00; EX 25.60.
Owner Norman Brunskill **Bred** Liberation Farm, J Stuart & P Bance **Trained** Kingston Lisle, Oxon
■ Stewards' Enquiry : Robert Winston one-day ban: careless riding (Jul 7)

FOCUS
A modest handicap, run at a muddling, stop-start pace. They came towards the stands' rail and there were a couple of hard-luck stories, including the second. The form is rated around the winner.

3326 WARWICK APPRENTICE H'CAP 1m 22y
5:45 (5:45) (Class 5) (0-70,68) 4-Y-0+ **£2,388** (£705; £352) **Stalls** Low

Form RPR

0/00 **1** **Qeethaara (USA)**[12] 2906 7-9-8 **66**.............................. RyanClark 5 73+
(Mark Brisbourne) *hld up in midfield: hdwy to trck ldrs and gng wl over 1f out: rdn and qcknd to ld ins fnl f: in command and pushed out towards fin* **9/1**

650- **2** 1 **Genes Of A Dancer (AUS)**[296] 5631 5-8-7 **54**............. LucyKBarry(3) 1 59
(Adrian Chamberlain) *led: rdn 2f out: drvn ent fnl f: hdd and nt pce of wnr ins fnl f: kpt on* **11/2**

1435 **3** 1 **Bold Cross (IRE)**[5] 3170 8-9-10 **68**.......................... MatthewCosham 4 71+
(Edward Bevan) *hld up in last pair: rdn over 1f out: hdwy ent fnl f: styd on same pce u.p fnl 100yds* **15/8**[1]

1230 **4** shd **Integria**[1] 3266 5-9-7 **68**...(bt) DavidKenny(3) 2 70
(George Baker) *in tch: rdn and effrt wl over 1f out: edgd lft u.p jst ins fnl f: kpt on same pce after* **5/1**[3]

0-00 **5** 3 3/4 **Gazboolou**[24] 2561 7-9-1 **62**.. JamesRogers(3) 9 56
(David Pinder) *chsd ldr tl over 6f out: styd chsng ldrs: rdn wl over 2f out: unable qck ent fnl f: wknd ins fnl f* **12/1**

0000 **6** 3 1/2 **Lady Florence**[10] 2985 6-9-2 **67**.................................. ClaireMurray(7) 7 53
(David C Griffiths) *dwlt: racd in centre: hdwy to chse ldr over 6f out: c stands' rail st and pushed along wl over 1f out: rdn and edgd lft ent fnl f: sn wknd* **16/1**

00/4 **7** 1 1/2 **Billy Cadiz**[20] 2691 6-8-5 **49** oh4.................................. HarryBentley 3 31
(Mark Campion) *in tch in midfield: rdn and effrt in centre jst over 2f out: wknd jst over 1f out* **20/1**

4640 **8** shd **French Art**[7] 3088 6-9-6 **64**...(p) TobyAtkinson 6 46
(Nigel Tinkler) *hld up in last pair: rdn and effrt 2f out: no imp over 1f out: wknd fnl f* **9/2**[2]

1m 41.76s (0.76) **Going Correction** +0.10s/f (Good) **8** Ran SP% **113.4**
Speed ratings (Par 103): **101,100,99,98,95 91,90,90**
Tote Super 7: Win: £13,595.40. Place: £115.50. toteswingers:1&2:£13.40, 1&3:£7.30, 2&3:£6.70 CSF £56.43 CT £133.65 TOTE £12.40: £2.20, £2.20, £1.60; EX 85.90.
Owner Mark Brisbourne **Bred** Shadwell Farm LLC **Trained** Great Ness, Shropshire

FOCUS
A modest apprentices' handicap, run at pedestrian pace, and as they had done throughout the afternoon, they came across to the stands' side. The winner's first form for this yarrd.
Bold Cross(IRE) Official explanation: jockey said gelding missed the break
Billy Cadiz Official explanation: trainer said gelding made a noise
T/Plt: £71.40 to a £1 stake. Pool:£53,125.49 - 542.90 winning tickets T/Qpdt: £23.10 to a £1 stake. Pool:£3,861.02 - 123.60 winning tickets SP

3327 - 3333a & 3335a (Foreign Racing) - See Raceform Interactive

DORTMUND (R-H)
Thursday, June 23

OFFICIAL GOING: Turf: good

3334a GROSSER PREIS DER WIRTSCHAFT - 125 JAHRE DORTMUNDER RENNVEREIN (GROUP 3) (3YO+) (TURF) 1m 2f
4:45 (12:00) 3-Y-0+

£27,586 (£9,482; £4,741; £2,586; £1,724; £1,293)

RPR

1 **Elle Shadow (IRE)**[215] 7532 4-9-2 0.. AStarke 6 112
(P Schiergen, Germany) *hld up in 5th: travelled smoothly on outside: mde gd prog through fnl turn: qcknd to chal and tk ld over 1 1/2f out: sn drew clr: easily* **19/10**[1]

2 3 1/2 **Illo (GER)**[46] 5-9-5 0.. ADeVries 7 108
(J Hirschberger, Germany) *settled in 4th: proged to join ldrs down bkst: sn chal in st: r.o wl but no answer to wnr* **2/1**[2]

3 1 1/2 **Ovambo Queen (GER)**[39] 4-9-2 0................................... HenkGrewe 2 102
(Dr A Bolte, Germany) *settled in 3rd: kpt on wl in st: styd on for 3rd ins fnl f* **71/10**[3]

4 2 **Acadius (GER)**[32] 2338 3-8-5 0................................... AnthonyCrastus 2 99
(J-P Carvalho, Germany) *broke fast and sent to ld: set gd pce: hdd over 1 1/2f out: kpt on wl u.p in st: lost 3rd ins fnl f* **2/1**[2]

5 3 **Zaungast (IRE)**[46] 7-9-3 0.. APietsch 5 93
(W Hickst, Germany) *hld up in rr: proged arnd fnl turn: kpt on wl in st but no threat to ldrs* **78/10**

6 15 **Derwisch (IRE)**[46] 1931 5-9-1 0.. AHelfenbein 8 61
(Andreas Lowe, Germany) *a.p: racd bhd ldr: rdn and sn btn in st: wknd* **14/1**

2m 2.65s (122.65)
WFA 3 from 4yo+ 12lb **6** Ran SP% **131.5**
WIN (incl. 10 euro stake): 29. PLACES: 16, 15. SF: 62.
Owner Gestut Wittekindshof **Bred** Gestut Wittekindshof **Trained** Germany

2906 CHESTER (L-H)
Friday, June 24

OFFICIAL GOING: Good to soft (soft in places) changing to soft after race 5 (8.50)
Wind: light 1/2 behind Weather: overcast, persitant rain

3336 TETLEY'S BITTER MAIDEN FILLIES' STKS 7f 2y
6:40 (6:41) (Class 4) 2-Y-O **£4,047** (£1,204; £601; £300) **Stalls** Low

Form RPR

2 **1** **Kinetica**[9] 3046 2-9-0 0.. SebSanders 4 79
(Sir Mark Prescott Bt) *chsd ldr: chal over 2f out: led over 1f out: drvn out* **4/6**[1]

30 **2** 2 1/4 **Al Jemailiya (IRE)**[16] 2811 2-9-0 0........................... SilvestreDeSousa 3 73
(Kevin Ryan) *chsd ldng pair: styd on to take 2nd last 75yds: no imp* **9/1**[3]

2 **3** 1 1/4 **Goal Hanger**[5] 3200 2-9-0 0..................................... RichardKingscote 1 70
(Tom Dascombe) *led: hdd over 1f out: edgd rt and kpt on same pce* **4/1**[2]

4 hd **Royal Majestic** 2-8-11 0.. MatthewDavies(3) 6 70
(Mick Channon) *hld up in rr: drvn and outpcd over 2f out: kpt on fnl f* **33/1**

5 1 **Gabrial's Princess (IRE)** 2-9-0 0.................................. TonyHamilton 2 67
(Bryan Smart) *dwlt: hdwy to trck ldrs 4f out: effrt over 2f out: kpt on same pce fnl f* **10/1**

632 **6** 5 **Silvas Romana (IRE)**[22] 2651 2-9-0 0........................... FrannyNorton 7 55
(Mark Brisbourne) *hld up towards rr: effrt over 2f out: wknd over 1f out* **18/1**

6 **7** 15 **Punta Lara Lady (IRE)**[6] 3165 2-9-0 0.............................. GregFairley 5 17
(Paul Green) *dwlt: sn outpcd and drvn along in rr: hdwy to chse ldrs 4f out: hung rt lost pl over 2f out: sn bhd* **100/1**

1m 30.38s (3.88) **Going Correction** +0.40s/f (Good) **7** Ran SP% **108.3**
Speed ratings (Par 92): **93,90,89,88,87 81,64**
Tote Swingers: 1&2 £1.20, 1&3 £2.10, 2&3 £2.70 CSF £6.64 TOTE £1.60: £1.10, £3.50; EX 6.90.

Owner Miss K Rausing **Bred** Miss K Rausing **Trained** Newmarket, Suffolk

FOCUS
Rail out 6yds from 6f pole to 1.5f with a drop in at that point. Races of 7f and 7.5f increased in distance by 20yds and other races by 22yds. The going was good to soft, soft in places and steady rain was falling. The heavily backed odds-on favourite scored in good style in this fillies' maiden. The race averages limit the form.

NOTEBOOK
Kinetica finished well but was just denied by her main market rival in a 7f Kempton fillies' maiden on debut last week. She set a clear standard and travelled well near the pace before surging to a comfortable win. A half-sister to 1m2f 3-y-o winner Four Nations, out of a 1m-1m6f (German Listed) winner, she has a powerful physique and looks a potentially useful prospect. (op 10-11 tchd 8-13 and evens in places)
Al Jemailiya(IRE) showed some promise when a keeping on third of five at 7-2 in a 5f Ayr maiden on debut. She was laboured over 6f at Hamilton next time, but stayed on well for second on this step up to 7f to confirm her initial promise. (tchd 8-1 and 10-1)
Goal Hanger showed ability when second behind a wide-margin winner in a 6f Pontefract maiden on Sunday. Turned out quickly, this sister to a 5f maiden winner and a stack of other 5f-1m2f winners, ran respectably under a prominent ride before fading late on. This was another pleasing effort from this Exceed And Excel filly, particularly as most of her family have shown their best form on fast ground. (op 7-2)
Royal Majestic was a big market drifter, but made promising late headway after running green for a long way. A £10,000 half-sister to two minor 6f/7f Polytrack winners, she should improve for this debut run. (op 18-1)
Gabrial's Princess(IRE), a 45,000euros Royal Applause first foal of a fairly useful 1m-1m2f AW/turf winner, was niggled along some way out but stuck to her task quite well on debut and should know more next time. (op 7-1 tchd 13-2)
Punta Lara Lady(IRE) Official explanation: jockey said filly hung right-handed throughout

3337 IRVING SOLICITORS H'CAP 7f 122y
7:15 (7:15) (Class 5) (0-70,70) 3-Y-O **£4,047** (£1,204; £601; £300) **Stalls** High

Form RPR

4-00 **1** **Isingy Red (FR)**[15] 2838 3-9-4 **70**.............................. MatthewDavies(3) 3 74
(Jim Boyle) *mid-div: hdwy over 2f out: swtchd outside over 1f out: styd on to ld last 50yds* **16/1**

3-24 **2** 1/2 **Duquesa (IRE)**[4] 3228 3-9-1 **64**...................................(v1) CathyGannon 13 67+
(David Evans) *swtchd lft s: in rr: gd hdwy on outer over 2f out: styd on wl fnl f: jst hld* **7/1**[3]

3-43 **3** nk **Hoppy's Flyer (FR)**[17] 2782 3-9-2 **68**...................... MichaelO'Connell(3) 4 70
(Paul Midgley) *chsd ldr: led over 2f out: hdd and no ex wl ins fnl f* **8/1**

0000 **4** hd **Watts Up Son**[31] 2391 3-9-2 **70**......................................(t) NeilFarley(5) 1 72
(Declan Carroll) *led: hdd over 2f out: ev ch ins fnl f: no ex* **20/1**

1542 **5** 1 1/2 **Coax**[7] 3124 3-9-5 **68**.. SilvestreDeSousa 7 66
(Mark Johnston) *chsd ldrs: swtchd lft over 1f out: upsides ins fnl f: fdd towards fin* **2/1**[1]

0145 **6** 2 **Ventura Sands (IRE)**[15] 2833 3-9-2 **70**.......................... LeeTopliss(5) 8 63
(Richard Fahey) *mid-div: effrt over 2f out: kpt on: nvr trbld ldrs* **16/1**

0161 **7** 1 1/2 **Cadmium Loch**[17] 2792 3-8-6 **62**...................................... JackDuern(7) 12 51
(Reg Hollinshead) *trckd ldrs: effrt over 2f out: one pce over 1f out* **16/1**

006- **8** 1 1/4 **Spartan King (IRE)**[273] 6333 3-9-1 **64**................................ GregFairley 2 50+
(Ian Williams) *t.k.h in rr: sme hdwy and swtchd outside over 2f out: nvr a factor* **11/2**[2]

-202 **9** shd **Crucis Abbey (IRE)**[31] 2375 3-8-11 **60**..........................(v) AndrewElliott 6 46
(James Unett) *t.k.h in rr: nt clr run over 2f out: kpt on: nvr nr ldrs* **14/1**

6-00 **10** nse **Rowan Spirit (IRE)**[16] 2818 3-9-6 **69**.............................. SebSanders 14 55
(Mark Brisbourne) *swtchd lft s: in rr: sme hdwy on outer over 2f out: nvr nr ldrs* **33/1**

3-50 **11** shd **Wolf Slayer**[48] 1916 3-9-4 **67**...................................... RichardKingscote 9 52
(Tom Dascombe) *chsd ldrs: effrt over 2f out: wkng whn hmpd over 1f out* **33/1**

-440 **12** 1/2 **Prophet In A Dream**[15] 2841 3-9-7 **70**........................ FrannyNorton 10 57
(Mick Channon) *chsd ldrs: wknd fnl f* **17/2**

-000 **13** 3 3/4 **Kalkan Bay**[30] 2406 3-9-1 **64**............ TonyHamilton 5 39
(Jedd O'Keeffe) *in rr: sn drvn along: nvr on terms* **50/1**

-35 **14** 4 1/2 **Ivy And Gold**[72] 1302 3-8-0 **54**............ DanielleMcCreery(5) 11 17
(Alan Berry) *chsd ldrs on outer: lost pl over 3f out: sn bhd* **100/1**

1m 37.25s (3.45) **Going Correction** +0.40s/f (Good) 14 Ran SP% **120.8**
Speed ratings (Par 99): **98,97,97,97,95 93,92,90,90,90 90,90,86,81**
Tote Swingers: 1&2 £12.90, 1&3 £23.10, 2&3 £7.50 CSF £119.72 CT £1010.74 TOTE £28.90: £7.00, £2.00, £2.90; EX 223.70.
Owner The Idle B's **Bred** J-Pascal Liberge & J-Charles Haimet **Trained** Epsom, Surrey

FOCUS
There was a tight finish to this modest handicap, which was run at a reasonable pace. The winner is rated back to his 2yo AW form.
Spartan King(IRE) Official explanation: jockey said gelding ran too free

3338 E B F SIXTIES ICON FILLIES' H'CAP — 1m 2f 75y
7:45 (7:47) (Class 3) (0-90,87) 3-Y-O+ **£9,714** (£2,890; £1,444; £721) **Stalls** High

Form — RPR

5005 **1** **Oceanway (USA)**[22] 2634 3-8-8 **79**............ SilvestreDeSousa 7 99+
(Mark Johnston) *led 1f: chsd ldr: drvn to ld over 2f out: styd on strly: eased towards fin* **16/1**

2-11 **2** 2 **Captivator**[69] 1388 4-9-9 **82**............ PatCosgrave 1 97
(James Fanshawe) *s.i.s: hdwy to trck ldrs over 2f out: n.m.r over 1f out: kpt on same pce* **10/3**[2]

3-23 **3** 3 1/4 **Babycakes (IRE)**[21] 2676 4-9-9 **87**............ LeeTopliss(5) 6 96
(Michael Bell) *trckd ldrs: t.k.h: chal over 2f out: kpt on one pce appr fnl f* **11/2**[3]

-433 **4** 3 1/4 **Ela Gorrie Mou**[14] 2884 5-8-13 **75**............ MichaelO'Connell(3) 5 77
(Peter Charalambous) *led after 1f: hdd over 2f out: hung lft and one pce* **7/1**

2013 **5** 3 **Frontline Girl (IRE)**[6] 3164 5-9-2 **75**............ AndrewElliott 2 71
(Mrs K Burke) *w ldrs: drvn over 5f out: outpcd over 2f out: sn wknd* **9/4**[1]

1001 **6** 3 3/4 **Princess Lexi (IRE)**[5] 3202 4-8-11 **70** 6ex............ FrannyNorton 3 59
(Ian Williams) *in rr: drvn along 8f out: nvr a factor* **12/1**

0131 **7** 3 1/2 **Destiny Of A Diva**[13] 2915 4-9-7 **80**............ CathyGannon 4 62
(Reg Hollinshead) *s.s: hld up in rr: effrt over 3f out: sn outpcd: wknd 2f out: hood removed late* **6/1**

2m 13.91s (2.71) **Going Correction** +0.40s/f (Good)
WFA 3 from 4yo+ 12lb 7 Ran SP% **109.6**
Speed ratings (Par 104): **105,103,100,98,95 92,90**
Tote Swingers: 1&2 £4.20, 1&3 £9.40, 2&3 £2.40 CSF £62.95 TOTE £19.00: £6.30, £1.70; EX 49.90.
Owner Sheikh Hamdan Bin Mohammed Al Maktoum **Bred** Darley **Trained** Middleham Moor, N Yorks

FOCUS
Three last-time-out winners lined up in this decent fillies' handicap, but there was a surprise result as the winner burst back to form after a quiet spell. It looked no fluke.

NOTEBOOK
Oceanway(USA) had been a bit disappointing in four runs since a 7f Kempton maiden win last November, but she bounced back with a gritty display stepped up to 1m2f and switched to testing ground for the first time. Out of a 1m2f winner, she should have more to offer in similar conditions and could continue her resurgence. (op 12-1)
Captivator got off the mark with a hood applied in a Wolverhampton maiden before winning a 1m2f Doncaster handicap in very smooth style in April. A hat-trick looked on the cards when she cruised into contention off a 7lb higher mark on the switch to slow ground, but she couldn't maintain a serious challenge to the gutsy winner after getting a split. However, this was a creditable clear-second by this smooth travelling half-sister to smart soft-ground winners Azarole and Pistachio, and she should be able to win more races. (op 3-1 tchd 7-2)
Babycakes(IRE) was a bit keen and couldn't sustain her run. This was a third consecutive placed effort since returning from a break, but she looks exposed after 12 starts and could continue to be vulnerable unless she can emulate her smart half-sister Rosaleen, who continued to improve with age. (op 6-1)
Ela Gorrie Mou didn't get much luck when a close third in a stronger Sandown handicap last time, but she got an easy lead in this race and it was a disappointing that she was a spent force some way out.
Frontline Girl(IRE) arrived here after a win and third on slow ground at Ayr. She was well backed but went in snatches in a very laboured run and may not have handled the track. Official explanation: jockey said mare ran flat (op 11-4 tchd 3-1)
Destiny Of A Diva made it three wins from seven starts when scoring with plenty in hand in a 1m2f Leicester handicap last time, but she put a huge dent in her chance by starting very slowly and was never involved off a 7lb higher mark. Official explanation: jockey said filly was slowly away as blinds were too tight and stuck when she tried to remove them (tchd 11-2 and 13-2)

3339 C.V.A.M. H'CAP — 7f 2y
8:15 (8:15) (Class 4) (0-85,82) 4-Y-O+ **£4,857** (£1,445; £722; £360) **Stalls** Low

Form — RPR

0-04 **1** **Viva Ronaldo (IRE)**[21] 2668 5-9-6 **81**............ TonyHamilton 2 93
(Richard Fahey) *hld up in midfield: led over 1f out: r.o strly* **4/1**[3]

4-32 **2** 3 **Suffolk Punch (IRE)**[13] 2937 4-9-4 **79**............(v) FrannyNorton 6 83
(Andrew Balding) *hmpd s: in rr: hdwy over 2f out: styd on to take 2nd last 75yds: no imp* **11/4**[1]

-560 **3** 2 **Diman Waters (IRE)**[24] 2590 4-9-5 **80**............ PatCosgrave 1 79
(Eric Alston) *trckd ldrs: t.k.h: edgd rt and kpt on same pce ins fnl f* **8/1**

0004 **4** 1/2 **Layla's Hero (IRE)**[27] 2495 4-9-7 **82**............ CathyGannon 4 79
(David Nicholls) *s.s: in rr: hdwy over 2f out: kpt on: nvr rchd ldrs* **7/2**[2]

-000 **5** 1 1/4 **Invincible Force (IRE)**[6] 3169 7-9-7 **82**............(b) GregFairley 7 76
(Paul Green) *swtchd lft after s: led: hdd over 1f out: wknd ins fnl f* **16/1**

0230 **6** 2 1/2 **Rio Cobolo (IRE)**[29] 2431 5-8-12 **76**............ MichaelO'Connell(3) 3 63
(David Nicholls) *chsd ldr: drvn over 3f out: wknd fnl f* **8/1**

0000 **7** 7 **Hotham**[10] 3028 8-9-3 **78**............ SebSanders 9 46
(Noel Wilson) *hld up in rr: nvr a factor: wknd over 1f out* **22/1**

0600 **8** 10 **Bahamian Lad**[13] 2938 6-8-12 **73**............(p) PaulQuinn 10 14
(Reg Hollinshead) *mid-div on outer: drvn over 4f out: lost pl 2f out: bhd whn eased ins fnl f* **20/1**

4200 **9** 6 **Bowmaker**[14] 2876 4-9-7 **82**............ SilvestreDeSousa 5 —
(Mark Johnston) *chsd ldrs: lost pl 3f out: bhd whn eased ins fnl f* **9/1**

1m 29.09s (2.59) **Going Correction** +0.50s/f (Yiel) 9 Ran SP% **116.1**
Speed ratings (Par 105): **105,101,99,98,97 94,86,75,68**
Tote Swingers: 1&2 £2.50, 1&3 £10.80, 2&3 £4.00 CSF £15.52 CT £84.23 TOTE £4.10: £1.80, £1.10, £2.50; EX 9.90.
Owner Aykroyd And Sons Ltd **Bred** Thomas Foy **Trained** Musley Bank, N Yorks

FOCUS
There was an emphatic winner in this decent handicap which was run at a fair pace. The winner's best run since he was a 3yo.

3340 HOLLYOAKS H'CAP — 1m 2f 75y
8:50 (8:50) (Class 5) (0-75,74) 3-Y-O **£4,047** (£1,204; £601; £300) **Stalls** High

Form — RPR

12- **1** **Tahaamah**[249] 6979 3-9-7 **74**............ FrannyNorton 2 91+
(Saeed Bin Suroor) *hld up: effrt and nt clr run over 2f out: swtchd ins over 1f out: styd on wl to ld ins fnl f: readily* **9/4**[1]

3402 **2** 1 **Calaf**[12] 2957 3-9-3 **70**............ TonyHamilton 6 84
(Richard Fahey) *t.k.h: trckd ldrs: led over 1f out: hdd and no ex ins fnl f* **7/2**[2]

6-21 **3** 4 1/2 **Sim Sala Bim**[11] 3002 3-9-6 **73** 6ex............ WilliamCarson 5 78+
(Stuart Williams) *hld up in rr: bdly hmpd on ins bnd 4f out: styd on to take modest 3rd 1f out* **7/2**[2]

2-45 **4** 6 **Cadore (IRE)**[42] 2052 3-9-7 **74**............ RobertHavlin 3 67
(Peter Chapple-Hyam) *led 2f: led 6f out tl over 1f out: sn wknd* **8/1**[3]

05-3 **5** 1 1/2 **Another For Joe**[45] 1985 3-9-7 **74**............ RichardKingscote 7 64
(Ian Williams) *dwlt: in rr: sme hdwy over 2f out: nvr nr ldrs* **9/1**

3200 **6** 3 1/4 **Barnum (USA)**[15] 2835 3-8-12 **65**............(b[1]) SilvestreDeSousa 1 49
(Mark Johnston) *chsd ldrs: drvn over 3f out: lost pl over 2f out* **33/1**

-140 **7** 1 3/4 **My Mate Jake (IRE)**[11] 3002 3-8-12 **70**............(b[1]) LeeTopliss(5) 8 50
(James Given) *drvn early: sn t.k.h and trckd ldrs: led after 2f: hdd 6f out: wknd over 1f out* **16/1**

6312 **8** 5 **Bussa**[32] 2357 3-9-5 **72**............ CathyGannon 4 42
(David Evans) *stmbld s: in rr: hdwy on outside over 4f out: hung rt and lost pl over 1f out: bhd whn eased towards fin* **10/1**

2m 17.36s (6.16) **Going Correction** +0.60s/f (Yiel) 8 Ran SP% **114.2**
Speed ratings (Par 99): **99,98,94,89,88 86,84,80**
Tote Swingers: 1&2 £1.80, 1&3 £4.10, 2&3 £4.90 CSF £10.15 CT £25.78 TOTE £3.30: £1.50, £1.30, £2.40; EX 9.10.
Owner Godolphin **Bred** Darley **Trained** Newmarket, Suffolk

FOCUS
An interesting handicap for 3-y-os, run in a slower time then the fillies' race. They finished quite well strung out and the unexposed winner looks one to follow.
Bussa Official explanation: jockey said gelding hung right throughout and lost its action in home straight

3341 TRAFFORD CENTRE BEST DRESSED COMPETITION H'CAP — 7f 122y
9:20 (9:20) (Class 5) (0-70,69) 4-Y-O+ **£4,047** (£1,204; £601; £300) **Stalls** Low

Form — RPR

2444 **1** **Gemma's Delight (IRE)**[4] 3234 4-8-9 **57**............(p) LiamJones 17 65
(James Unett) *s.i.s and swtchd lft sn after s: gd hdwy on inner and nt clr run over 1f out: squeezed through ins fnl f: led towards fin* **7/1**

4450 **2** 1 **Lockantanks**[66] 1467 4-9-6 **68**............ CathyGannon 8 74
(Michael Appleby) *trckd ldrs: led over 1f out: hdd and no ex fnl 50yds* **8/1**

-406 **3** 1 **Many Welcomes**[16] 2799 6-8-7 **55**............ AndrewElliott 2 58
(Brian Baugh) *in rr: hdwy over 2f out: styd on to take 3rd towards fin* **9/2**[1]

0-60 **4** 3/4 **Timber Treasure (USA)**[6] 3166 7-8-9 **57**............(b) SilvestreDeSousa 14 58
(Paul Green) *hld up in mid-div: hdwy on ins over 1f out: n.m.r ins fnl f: kpt on same pce* **20/1**

0503 **5** hd **Cyflymder (IRE)**[8] 3093 5-9-0 **67**............ NeilFarley(5) 6 68+
(Declan Carroll) *chsd ldrs: nt clr run over 2f out: hmpd and lost pl over 1f out: kpt on wl fnl f* **9/2**[1]

6415 **5** dht **North Central (USA)**[16] 2803 4-9-3 **65**............(p) DanielTudhope 3 66
(Jim Goldie) *trckd ldrs: effrt and nt clr run over 2f out: swtchd rt over 1f out: hung lft and one pce ins fnl f* **5/1**[2]

0-00 **7** 3 3/4 **Song Of Parkes**[24] 2589 4-9-0 **62**............ PatCosgrave 7 58+
(Eric Alston) *led: hdd over 1f out: wkng whn hmpd ins fnl f: eased* **9/1**

2402 **8** 9 **The Big Haerth (IRE)**[8] 3093 5-9-4 **69**............ RichardEvans(3) 15 38+
(David Evans) *chsd ldrs: lost pl over 1f out: eased ins fnl f* **13/2**[3]

1-00 **9** 2 1/2 **Hippique**[14] 2870 4-8-10 **58**............(v) RobertHavlin 1 21
(Jeremy Gask) *mid-div: hdwy on outside over 2f out: sn wknd: bhd whn eased ins fnl f* **18/1**

/0-0 **10** 1 **Danzig Fox**[13] 2910 6-8-2 **50** oh5............ PaulQuinn 9 10
(Michael Mullineaux) *in rr: sn drvn along: nvr on terms* **66/1**

4400 **11** 6 **Takajan (IRE)**[99] 880 4-8-10 **58**............ FrannyNorton 13 —
(Mark Brisbourne) *swtchd lft after s: in rr: bhd fnl 2f* **16/1**

1m 39.92s (6.12) **Going Correction** +0.70s/f (Yiel) 11 Ran SP% **117.4**
Speed ratings (Par 103): **97,96,95,94,94 94,90,81,78,77 71**
CSF £61.89 CT £286.62 TOTE £9.80: £3.20, £1.80, £1.80; EX 140.70.
Owner Miss Ciara Doyle **Bred** John Doyle **Trained** Tedsmore Hall, Shropshire
■ Stewards' Enquiry : Daniel Tudhope two-day ban: careless riding (Jul 11-12)

FOCUS
There were plenty of defectors but this was still a competitive handicap. The pace was decent and the winner came from a long way back. She posted a small personal best.
T/Plt: £132.10 to a £1 stake. Pool:£60,813.11 - 335.94 winning tickets T/Qpdt: £21.50 to a £1 stake. Pool:£4,231.34 - 145.10 winning tickets WG

2952 DONCASTER (L-H)
Friday, June 24

OFFICIAL GOING: Good to firm (6.5)
Wind: Light half againsr Weather: Fine and dry

3342 CWU LEGAL SERVICES E B F MAIDEN FILLIES' STKS — 6f
2:20 (2:22) (Class 5) 2-Y-O **£3,173** (£944; £471; £235) **Stalls** High

Form — RPR

43 **1** **Colorful Notion (IRE)**[23] 2606 2-9-0 0............ AdamKirby 2 78
(Marco Botti) *trckd ldrs: hdwy 1/2-way: rdn to chse ldr over 1f out: kpt on ins fnl f to ld last 100yds* **5/1**[3]

2 1 1/2 **Lesotho (IRE)** 2-9-0 0............ SilvestreDeSousa 1 74+
(Noel Quinlan) *led 2f: cl up on outer: led again 2f out and sn pushed clr: rdn ent fnl f and flashed tail: hdd and no ex last 100yds* **16/1**

3 2 **Oddysey (IRE)** 2-9-0 0............ TomEaves 7 68
(Michael Dods) *chsd ldrs: hdwy over 2f out: rdn wl over 1f out: kpt on same pce* **33/1**

4 1 3/4 **Al Mahmeyah** 2-9-0 0............ DaneO'Neill 5 62+
(Richard Hannon) *s.i.s and bhd: hdwy 1/2-way: rdn wl over 1f out: kpt on fnl f: nrst fin* **3/1**[2]

5 1 1/4 **Tahnee Mara (IRE)** 2-9-0 0............ PhillipMakin 3 59
(Kevin Ryan) *prom: led after 2f: rdn along and hdd 2f out: sn wknd* **10/1**

6 14 **Roman Seal (IRE)** 2-9-0 0............ RichardKingscote 8 17
(Tom Dascombe) *a in rr* **8/1**

4 **7** *2 1/4* **Balti's Sister (IRE)**[12] 2953 2-9-0 0 .... GrahamGibbons 6 10
(Michael Easterby) *cl up: effrt over 2f out: sn rdn and wknd wl over 1f out* **5/2**[1]

0 **8** *20* **Correct**[20] 2709 2-9-0 0 .... JamieSpencer 4 —+
(Michael Bell) *hld up in rr: pushed along 1/2-way: sn outpcd and bhd whn eased over 1f out* **13/2**

1m 14.0s (0.40) **Going Correction** +0.05s/f (Good) **8** Ran SP% **112.6**
Speed ratings (Par 90): **99,97,94,92,90 71,68,42**
Tote Swingers: 1&2 £5.60, 1&3 £12.60, 2&3 £13.80 CSF £75.81 TOTE £5.90: £1.80, £3.90, £5.60; EX 63.90 TRIFECTA Not won..
Owner H E Sheikh Sultan Bin Khalifa Al Nahyan **Bred** Sheikh Sultan Bin Khalifa Al Nayhan **Trained** Newmarket, Suffolk

FOCUS
A few interesting types lined up and hand times compared well to the other two 6f races on the card (both for older horses), being 1.31 seconds faster than the following maiden and only 0.03 seconds off the Class 5 handicap. The race averages help with the form.

NOTEBOOK
Colorful Notion(IRE) ◆ stepped up a good deal on her first two efforts. She took a while to respond to pressure, and though well on top at the line, shaped as though she'll get another furlong. There should be more to come as she continues to learn what's required and she looks useful, although she might not want to be out again too soon after recording such a fast time. (op 3-1)
Lesotho(IRE) ◆ appeared unfancied in the market, but she's a half-sister to a number of decent sorts, the pick of them being Group 1-winning sprinter Pipalong, and she shaped well. She looked the likeliest winner for much of the way, showing good speed having started alertly and being the last to come under pressure, but she got tired late on (pace horses struggled on the straight track). It will be a surprise if she doesn't win a similar race before going up in class. (op 14-1)
Oddysey(IRE), a 12,000euros half-sister to a 1m juvenile winner in Germany, kept on gradually and should be sharper next time. (tchd 28-1)
Al Mahmeyah ◆, a May foal, cost 46,000gns and the dam's four earlier offspring all won more than once. A slow start compromised her chance and she took a while to respond to her rider's urgings, but she kept on steadily. There should be plenty of improvement to come. (op 4-1)
Tahnee Mara(IRE), a £23,000 purchase, made some appeal on breeding, being a half-sister to Totally Ours, a 7f-1m Polytrack winner (also Listed placed over 1m2f on turf), out of a dual 5f scorer half-sister to the Dewhurst winner Tout Seul. However, she didn't see her race out after showing early speed. (op 6-1)
Roman Seal(IRE), a 65,000euros half-sister to 6f soft-ground winner Desert Icon, out of a 5f soft-ground winner, was outpaced for most of the way and made no progress. She might need an easier surface. (op 16-1)
Balti's Sister(IRE) was strong in the market as she looked to build on an encouraging C&D debut, but she dropped out after showing speed. Official explanation: trainer's rep said filly was unsuited by the good to firm ground (op 7-2 tchd 9-4)
Correct Official explanation: jockey said filly hung right throughout

3343 MG LAW EDUCATION AND SOCIAL CARE LAW MAIDEN STKS 6f
2:50 (2:51) (Class 5) 3-Y-0+ **£2,525** (£751; £375; £187) **Stalls** High

Form RPR
1 **Little Jimmy Odsox (IRE)** 3-9-3 0 .... DavidAllan 1 67+
(Tim Easterby) *dwlt and in rr: hdwy on outer wl over 2f out: rdn wl over 1f out: styd on strly appr fnl f: led fnl 75yds* **16/1**

3 **2** *1/2* **My Own Way Home**[15] 2852 3-8-12 0 .... DavidProbert 10 60
(Des Donovan) *hld up towards rr: hdwy wl over 2f out: rdn to chse ldrs wl over 1f out: kpt on u.p ent fnl f: sn ev ch tl no ex towards fin* **20/1**

6-6 **3** *nk* **Dictionary**[21] 2673 3-9-3 0 .... JamieSpencer 8 64
(William Haggas) *led: qcknd clr over 2f out: rdn over 1f out: drvn and wknd ins fnl f: hdd and no ex fnl 75yds* **6/1**[3]

54 **4** *4* **West Side (IRE)**[39] 2151 3-9-3 0 .... (t) DarryllHolland 6 51
(Jeremy Noseda) *trckd ldrs: rdn along and outpcd 1/2-way: styd on u.p fr over 1f out* **1/2**[1]

5-2 **5** *1/2* **Trojan Rocket (IRE)**[76] 1236 3-9-3 0 .... SilvestreDeSousa 4 50
(George Prodromou) *t.k.h: hld up: hdwy 1/2-way: rdn to chse ldr 2f out: drvn and wknd over 1f out* **4/1**[2]

06 **6** *2* **Noola Princess**[20] 2710 4-9-5 0 .... DanielTudhope 3 40
(David O'Meara) *hld up and bhd tl sme late hdwy* **66/1**

5-6 **7** *3/4* **Russian Winter**[9] 3053 3-8-12 0 .... DaleSwift[(5)] 7 41
(Tim Etherington) *chsd ldrs: effrt 3f out: sn rdn along and wknd wl over 1f out* **33/1**

00- **8** *nk* **Deslaya (IRE)**[239] 7185 3-8-12 0 .... JackMitchell 9 35
(Chris Wall) *prom: rdn along wl over 2f out: sn wknd* **18/1**

0 **9** *13* **Lovely Lynn (IRE)**[8] 3075 3-8-7 0 .... NeilFarley[(5)] 2 —
(Declan Carroll) *midfield: rdn along and lost pl bef 1/2-way: sn in rr* **66/1**

1m 15.31s (1.71) **Going Correction** +0.05s/f (Good)
WFA 3 from 4yo 7lb **9** Ran SP% **122.8**
Speed ratings (Par 103): **90,89,88,83,82 80,79,78,61**
Tote Swingers: 1&2 £10.30, 1&3 £4.80, 2&3 £8.60 CSF £276.06 TOTE £14.30: £3.30, £3.70, £2.00; EX 175.20 Trifecta £489.00 Part won. Pool: £660.86 - 0.40 winning units..
Owner Reality Partnerships III **Bred** Dr D Crone & P Lafarge & P Johnston **Trained** Great Habton, N Yorks

FOCUS
Despite the pace appearing strong, the time was poor, being well over a second slower than the earlier 2-y-o maiden and the later Class 5 handicap for 3-y-os, suggesting they went too quick. However, while the level of form looks weak, a few of these can do a lot better, in particular those who were prominent. The form is rated slightly negatively.

3344 MARCH FOR THE ALTERNATIVE H'CAP 1m 6f 132y
3:25 (3:25) (Class 4) (0-85,85) 4-Y-0+ **£4,533** (£1,348; £674; £336) **Stalls** Low

Form RPR
1-00 **1** **Kazbow (IRE)**[14] 2888 5-9-6 **84** .... J-PGuillambert 1 94
(Luca Cumani) *mde all: qcknd over 3f out: rdn along 2f out: drvn and kpt on gamely fnl f* **7/1**[2]

1-10 **2** *3/4* **Old Hundred (IRE)**[27] 2512 4-9-7 **85** .... (v) PatCosgrave 7 93
(James Fanshawe) *hld up towards rr: hdwy 4f out: effrt to chse wnr 2f out: drvn ent fnl f: kpt on* **9/2**[1]

6-10 **3** *nk* **Bollin Greta**[35] 2262 6-8-11 **75** .... (t) DavidAllan 11 83
(Tim Easterby) *hld up in rr: gd hdwy over 3f out: str run to join ldrs 2f out: sn rdn and ev ch tl drvn and kpt on same pce ins fnl f* **14/1**

00-1 **4** *4 1/2* **Red Fama**[25] 2544 7-8-10 **74** .... AndrewElliott 6 76+
(Neville Bycroft) *hld up in rr: hdwy on outer 3f out: rdn along 2f out: styd on appr fnl f: nrst fin* **14/1**

-000 **5** *1 1/4* **Overrule (USA)**[42] 2059 7-7-7 **76** .... DaleSwift[(5)] 10 76
(Brian Ellison) *hld up in rr: hdwy over 3f out: swtchd rt and rdn over 2f out: kpt on same pce* **16/1**

4063 **6** *4 1/2* **Arizona John (IRE)**[20] 2708 6-9-2 **80** .... StephenCraine 2 74
(John Mackie) *trckd ldrs on inner: smooth prog 4f out: trckd wnr over 3f out: rdn over 2f out: grad wknd* **9/1**

2000 **7** *2* **Montparnasse (IRE)**[14] 2888 4-9-6 **84** .... PhillipMakin 8 75
(Kevin Ryan) *hld up towards rr: stdy hdwy on wd outside over 3f out: rdn to chse ldrs over 2f out: drvn wl over 1f out and sn wknd* **15/2**[3]

4-23 **8** *1 3/4* **Meetings Man (IRE)**[13] 2932 4-8-11 **75** .... TomEaves 3 64
(Micky Hammond) *trckd ldrs on inner: effrt over 4f out: rdn along over 3f out: sn wknd* **7/1**[2]

00-4 **9** *hd* **Rajeh (IRE)**[39] 1729 8-9-7 **85** .... CathyGannon 9 73
(John Spearing) *prom: rdn along 4f out: sn wknd* **12/1**

3430 **10** *3 3/4* **Parhelion**[27] 2512 4-9-1 **79** .... DaneO'Neill 5 62
(Derek Haydn Jones) *in tch: rdn along 4f out: sn wknd* **16/1**

-020 **11** *3 1/2* **Perpetually (IRE)**[14] 2884 5-9-7 **85** .... SilvestreDeSousa 4 64
(Mark Johnston) *trckd ldrs: rdn along wl over 3f out: sn wknd* **7/1**[2]

0-12 **12** *nk* **Rare Ruby (IRE)**[38] 2183 7-8-13 **77** .... JamieSpencer 12 55
(Jennie Candlish) *in tch on outer: hdwy to chse ldrs over 4f out: rdn along over 3f out and sn wknd* **10/1**

3m 8.76s (1.36) **Going Correction** +0.225s/f (Good) **12** Ran SP% **119.3**
Speed ratings (Par 105): **105,104,104,102,101 98,97,96,96,94 93,92**
Tote Swingers: 1&2 £9.10, 1&3 £24.80, 2&3 £15.30 CSF £38.76 CT £438.15 TOTE £9.00: £2.70, £2.20, £4.50; EX 38.80 Trifecta £59.80 Pool: £575.63 - 7.12 winning units..
Owner Bruce Corman **Bred** Airlie Stud **Trained** Newmarket, Suffolk

FOCUS
A fair staying handicap in which Kazbow took advantage of a relatively soft lead. He's rated back to his old form, while the second progressed again.
Kazbow(IRE) Official explanation: trainer's rep said, regarding apparent improvement in form, that the gelding was suited by a drop in trip and the faster ground.

3345 SIMPSON MILLAR LEGAL SERVICES NOVICE STKS 7f
4:00 (4:00) (Class 5) 2-Y-0 **£2,525** (£751; £375; £187) **Stalls** High

Form RPR
410 **1** **Wolfgang (IRE)**[10] 3014 2-9-2 0 .... DaneO'Neill 5 79+
(Richard Hannon) *hld up in rr: str run over 2f out: rdn to ld over 1f out: comf* **5/2**[2]

514 **2** *1 1/4* **Basantee**[18] 2777 2-9-0 0 .... RichardKingscote 2 71
(Tom Dascombe) *led to over 4f out: cl up: rdn 2f out and ev ch tl drvn and one pce fnl f* **15/8**[1]

1 **3** *1 1/4* **Beaumaris (IRE)**[16] 2797 2-8-11 0 .... AndrewHeffernan 4 65
(Ann Duffield) *cl up: effrt over 2f out: sn rdn along and sltly outpcd: swtchd lft and drvn ent fnl f: kpt on towards fin* **7/1**

5342 **4** *hd* **Latte**[17] 2784 2-9-0 0 .... DarryllHolland 3 67
(Linda Stubbs) *trckd ldrs: pushed along 1/2-way: rdn wl over 2f out: drvn and kpt on same pce appr fnl f* **14/1**

1516 **5** *1/2* **He's So Cool (IRE)**[20] 2712 2-9-3 0 .... JakePayne[(7)] 1 76
(Bill Turner) *t.k.h: cl up: led over 4f out: rdn along wl over 2f out: hdd over 1f out: wknd fnl f* **11/4**[3]

1m 30.03s (3.73) **Going Correction** +0.05s/f (Good) **5** Ran SP% **109.2**
Speed ratings (Par 93): **80,78,77,76,76**
CSF £7.47 TOTE £3.70: £1.40, £1.10; EX 6.80.
Owner Andrew Tinkler **Bred** C Marnane **Trained** East Everleigh, Wilts
■ Stewards' Enquiry : Jake Payne caution: used whip with excessive frequency.

FOCUS
A pretty ordinary novice event and certainly not form to get carried away with. The fourth is the key to the race.

NOTEBOOK
Wolfgang(IRE)'s Chepstow maiden win has not worked out and he was then beaten a long way in the Windsor Castle. However, the fact he was sent to Royal Ascot suggests his connections think a bit of him and this was his first start beyond 5f. The step up in trip really suited, although this was a soft race and he may find things tougher next time. (op 11-4 tchd 9-4)
Basantee was thought good enough to contest a Naas Listed race last time having won a Southwell maiden by a wide margin, though she was well beaten. Dropped in class and upped in trip, this was better but she was no match for the winner. (op 3-1)
Beaumaris(IRE) found this quite a bit tougher than the 5f Beverley claimer she won on her debut. (tchd 6-1)
Latte is exposed as short of this class but seemed to improve for the longer trip. (op 16-1)
He's So Cool(IRE) hadn't been shaping as though he wanted a step up to 7f and was well beaten after being keen, having raced without cover. He had also got a bit warm. (op 7-4)

3346 TRADE UNION CONGRESS H'CAP 7f
4:35 (4:36) (Class 4) (0-80,80) 3-Y-0 **£3,886** (£1,156; £577; £288) **Stalls** High

Form RPR
3461 **1** **Bajan Bear**[15] 2841 3-8-12 **70** .... DaneO'Neill 2 79+
(Michael Blanshard) *dwlt and in rr: hdwy over 2f out: trckd ldrs whn nt clr run wl over 1f out: swtchd lft and rdn ent fnl f: styd on strly to ld last 50yds* **10/1**

1222 **2** *3/4* **Elusivity (IRE)**[15] 2834 3-9-7 **79** .... JamieSpencer 8 86+
(Brian Meehan) *hld up in rr: gd hdwy wl over 2f out: nt clr run and swtchd lft to chal 2f out: sn led and hung rt over 1f out: drvn ins fnl f: hdd and no ex last 50yds* **5/2**[1]

4-63 **3** *1 1/2* **Orthodox Lad**[15] 2841 3-8-13 **71** .... (b[1]) LukeMorris 4 74
(John Best) *trckd ldrs: hdwy over 2f out: rdn and n.m.r wl over 1f out: kpt on ins fnl f* **7/1**[3]

5-11 **4** *1 3/4* **Namwahjobo (IRE)**[7] 3114 3-9-8 **80** 6ex .... DanielTudhope 1 78
(Jim Goldie) *hld up in tch: hdwy 3f out: rdn to chse ldrs wl over 1f out: drvn and no imp fnl f* **11/4**[2]

2505 **5** *hd* **Another Citizen (IRE)**[9] 3052 3-9-2 **74** .... DuranFentiman 5 72
(Tim Easterby) *a.p: effrt 1/2-way: rdn to ld briefly 2f out: sn hdd and drvn: grad wknd* **14/1**

0000 **6** *8* **First Class Favour (IRE)**[15] 2834 3-9-0 **77** .... LanceBetts[(5)] 7 53
(Tim Easterby) *led: rdn along 3f out: drvn and hdd 2f out: grad wknd* **25/1**

5-10 **7** *3 3/4* **Great Acclaim**[22] 2646 3-9-6 **78** .... PatCosgrave 6 44
(James Fanshawe) *plld hrd: chsd ldrs: hdwy and ev ch over 2f out: sn rdn and wknd wl over 1f out* **9/1**

1-05 **8** *2* **Rock Ace (IRE)**[25] 2564 3-9-3 **78** .... PatrickDonaghy[(3)] 3 39
(Deborah Sanderson) *chsd ldrs on outer: hanging lft thrght: rdn along 1/2-way and sn wknd* **20/1**

1256 **9** *2* **Maverik**[6] 3178 3-9-6 **78** .... DarryllHolland 9 33
(Michael Dods) *plld hrd: chsd ldrs: cl up 1/2-way: rdn and ev ch 2f out: sn wknd* **8/1**

1m 27.87s (1.57) **Going Correction** +0.05s/f (Good) **9** Ran SP% **113.2**
Speed ratings (Par 101): **93,92,90,88,88 79,74,72,70**
Tote Swingers: 1&2 £5.80, 1&3 £9.30, 2&3 £3.00 CSF £34.57 CT £189.84 TOTE £12.20: £3.00, £1.20, £3.20; EX 47.50 Trifecta £234.20 Pool: £629.94 - 1.99 winning units..
Owner C McKenna **Bred** Mr And Mrs C McKenna **Trained** Upper Lambourn, Berks
■ Stewards' Enquiry : Dane O'Neill caution: used whip down the shoulder in the forehand.

FOCUS
The pace was good and the first two finishers filled the last two positions for much of the way. They both shaped a bit better than the bare form.
Rock Ace(IRE) Official explanation: trainer said filly returned lame right-hind

Maverik Official explanation: jockey said gelding ran too free

3347 COMMUNICATION WORKERS UNION HUMANITARIAN AID H'CAP — 6f

5:05 (5:06) (Class 5) (0-70,70) 3-Y-O — **£2,525** (£751; £375; £187) **Stalls** High

Form				RPR
1-34	1		**Shesastar**[28] 2468 3-9-7 **70** ... JamieSpencer 3 (David Barron) *in rr and rdn along 1/2-way: swtchd rt and hdwy wl over 1f out: styd on u.p to ld ent fnl f: sn hung lft and drvn out* **7/4**[1]	81
6223	2	1 1/2	**Roman Strait**[5] 3207 3-9-5 **68** ... LukeMorris 2 (Michael Blanshard) *chsd ldrs: rdn along over 2f out: swtchd lft and drvn over 1f out: ev ch tl one pce ins fnl f* **7/2**[2]	74
-313	3	hd	**Fast Shot**[7] 3126 3-9-2 **65** ... DuranFentiman 4 (Tim Easterby) *led: rdn along wl over 2f out: drvn over 1f out: hdd ent fnl f: one pce* **11/2**[3]	70
-650	4	1 1/2	**Lady Del Sol**[23] 2619 3-9-7 **70** ... DanielTudhope 1 (Marjorie Fife) *trckd ldrs on outer: hdwy and cl up 1/2-way: rdn and ev ch 2f out: sn drvn and one pce fnl f* **18/1**	70
-000	5	1 1/2	**Never Never Land**[15] 2841 3-9-6 **69** ...(b) RobertHavlin 7 (John Gosden) *hld up: hdwy 2f out: sn rdn and no imp appr fnl f* **8/1**	64
0240	6	nse	**Fleurie Lover (IRE)**[5] 3207 3-8-4 **56** ...(e[1]) JamesSullivan[(3)] 9 (Richard Guest) *dwlt and towards rr: hdwy to chse ldrs over 2f out: sn rdn and one pce appr fnl f* **20/1**	51
33-5	7	6	**Sovereign Street**[17] 2782 3-9-3 **66** ... AndrewHeffernan 6 (Ann Duffield) *t.k.h: chsd ldrs: rdn along over 2f out: grad wknd* **12/1**	42
1060	8	3/4	**Cheylesmore (IRE)**[15] 2838 3-9-2 **65** ...(t) WilliamCarson 8 (Stuart Williams) *dwlt: a in rr* **16/1**	39
4-00	9	nk	**Brave Dream**[52] 1802 3-8-13 **67** ... JulieBurke[(5)] 10 (Kevin Ryan) *chsd ldrs: rdn along wl over 2f out: sn wknd* **20/1**	40
-060	10	28	**Rutterkin (USA)**[15] 2832 3-8-9 **65** ... VictorSantos[(7)] 5 (Alan Berry) *cl up: rdn along 1/2-way: sn wknd and bhd* **50/1**	—

1m 13.97s (0.37) **Going Correction** +0.05s/f (Good) — **10** Ran SP% **115.4**
Speed ratings (Par 99): **99,97,96,94,92 92,84,83,83,45**
Tote Swingers: 1&2 £2.50, 2&3 £2.90 CSF £7.26 CT £27.12 TOTE £2.20: £1.10, £1.80, £2.20; EX 7.80 Trifecta £18.20 Pool: £710.44 - 28.79 winning units..
Owner Star Alliance 4 - Lancs 2 Lincs **Bred** The Welcome Alliance **Trained** Maunby, N Yorks
■ Stewards' Enquiry : Luke Morris caution: used whip down shoulder in the forehand

FOCUS
An ordinary handicap and another race on the straight track that went to a hold-up horse. The form is rated through the second and third.

3348 GMB - BRITAIN'S GENERAL UNION H'CAP — 7f

5:40 (5:40) (Class 4) (0-80,77) 4-Y-O+ — **£3,561** (£1,059; £529; £264) **Stalls** High

Form				RPR
0000	1		**Legal Legacy**[25] 2545 5-8-12 **68** ... DarryllHolland 1 (Michael Dods) *hld up towards rr: hdwy over 2f out: rdn over 1f out: drvn to ld jst ins fnl f: kpt on wl* **4/1**[1]	77
3133	2	1/2	**Beckermet (IRE)**[10] 3025 9-8-4 **63** ... JamesSullivan[(3)] 7 (Ruth Carr) *trckd ldrs on inner: hdwy 2f out: swtchd lft and rdn over 1f out: ev ch entyering fnl f: sn drvn and no ex towards fin* **7/1**	71
13-0	3	1 1/4	**Ginger Grey (IRE)**[27] 2494 4-9-3 **73** ...(b) DanielTudhope 2 (David O'Meara) *trckd ldrs on outer: hdwy 2f out: sn rdn and ev ch ent fnl f: sn drvn and one pce* **5/1**[2]	78
-001	4	1	**Kakapuka**[20] 2719 4-9-7 **77** ... JamieSpencer 4 (Anabel K Murphy) *stdd s and hld up in rr: swtchd lft and rapid hdwy wl over 1f out: rdn to chal and ev ch ent fnl f: sn drvn and one pce* **4/1**[1]	79+
0431	5	2	**Jordaura**[15] 2867 5-9-6 **76** ... DavidProbert 9 (Tony Carroll) *trckd ldrs: effrt over 2f out: sn rdn and one pce* **11/2**[3]	75+
2054	6	hd	**Mount Hollow**[32] 2354 6-8-4 **60** ...(v) LukeMorris 6 (Reg Hollinshead) *trckd ldng pair on inner: hdwy 2f out: rdn to ld 1 1/2f out: drvn and hdd ins fnl f: wknd qckly* **12/1**	56
0060	7	2 3/4	**El Dececy (USA)**[22] 2653 7-8-13 **69** ow1 ...(p) AdamKirby 8 (John Balding) *led: rdn along over 2f out: drvn and hdd 1 1/2f out: sn wknd* **10/1**	58
2201	7	dht	**All Right Now**[22] 2653 4-9-5 **75** ... DaneO'Neill 3 (Derek Haydn Jones) *prom: cl up 1/2-way: rdn and ev ch over 2f out: sn drvn and wknd* **17/2**	64
-400	9	4 1/2	**Kings 'n Dreams**[11] 3000 4-8-11 **67** ...(b) WilliamCarson 5 (Dean Ivory) *chsd ldrs: rdn along 2f out: sn wknd* **18/1**	43

1m 27.76s (1.46) **Going Correction** +0.05s/f (Good) — **9** Ran SP% **117.1**
Speed ratings (Par 105): **93,92,91,89,87 87,84,84,79**
Tote Swingers: 1&2 £6.00, 2&3 £5.30 CSF £32.76 CT £144.42 TOTE £3.80: £1.10, £2.20, £2.40; EX 36.60 Trifecta £267.80 Pool: £749.12 - 2.07 winning units..
Owner D Vic Roper **Bred** D Dowling **Trained** Denton, Co Durham

FOCUS
The pace was decent - time fractionally quicker than earlier Class 4 handicap for 3-y-os - and once again on the straight track the pace horses failed to see their race out. The form looks sound.
El Dececy(USA) Official explanation: jockey said gelding had no more to give
T/Plt: £238.70 to a £1 stake. Pool:£72,506.50 - 221.66 winning tickets T/Qpdt: £7.60 to a £1 stake. Pool:£6,151.72 - 598.51 winning tickets JR

2755 FOLKESTONE (R-H)

Friday, June 24

OFFICIAL GOING: Good (good to firm in places; 7.3)
Wind: light, across Weather: dry, bright spells

3349 O'CONNELL'S DRYWALL CONTRACTORS MEDIAN AUCTION MAIDEN STKS — 7f (S)

2:30 (2:32) (Class 6) 2-Y-O — **£1,910** (£564; £282) **Stalls** High

Form				RPR
622	1		**Mizbah**[12] 2953 2-9-3 0 ... TedDurcan 1 (Saeed Bin Suroor) *chsd ldng pair: wnt 2nd ent fnl 3f: rdn to ld over 1f out: a doing enough fnl f: rdn out* **4/9**[1]	75+
4	2	1/2	**Tidal Way (IRE)**[15] 2837 2-9-3 0 ... SamHitchcott 2 (Mick Channon) *hld up in tch: pushed along and hmpd jst over 3f out: rdn over 2f out: clsd on ldrs and swtchd rt over 1f out: edgd lft u.p 1f out: chsd wnr fnl 75yds: kpt on* **6/1**[3]	74
30	3	2	**Cockney Rocker**[18] 2767 2-9-3 0 ... MichaelHills 3 (Jane Chapple-Hyam) *led: jnd 2f out: rdn and hdd over 1f out: styd on same pce ins fnl f* **11/2**[2]	69
0	4	3/4	**Mr Knightley (IRE)**[17] 2787 2-9-3 0 ... RichardMullen 5 (Richard Hannon) *chsd ldr tl short of room and hmpd ent fnl 3f: rallied and chsng ldrs whn nt clr run ent fnl f: swtchd rt and kpt on same pce ins fnl f* **20/1**	67
0	5	6	**Valley Of Stars (IRE)**[15] 2837 2-9-3 0 ... EddieCreighton 6 (Edward Creighton) *in tch: pushed along 5f out: hmpd and wnt rt ent fnl 3f: sn rdn and struggling: wknd 2f out* **100/1**	52
	6	3	**Artistic Thread (IRE)** 2-9-3 0 ... StevieDonohoe 8 (Sir Mark Prescott Bt) *s.i.s: sn bustled along in last pair: rdn 4f out: lost tch over 2f out* **28/1**	50+
	7	14	**Welease Bwian (IRE)** 2-9-3 0 ... SaleemGolam 7 (Stuart Williams) *s.i.s: t.k.h: hld up in last pair: in tch whn sltly hmpd ent fnl 3f: wknd qckly over 2f out: wl bhd and eased fnl 100yds* **80/1**	10

1m 29.24s (1.94) **Going Correction** +0.025s/f (Good) — **7** Ran SP% **109.4**
Speed ratings (Par 91): **89,88,86,85,78 75,59**
Tote Swingers: 1&2 £1.10, 1&3 £1.10, 2&3 £2.20 CSF £3.02 TOTE £1.50: £1.20, £2.60; EX 2.80.

Owner Godolphin **Bred** Darley **Trained** Newmarket, Suffolk

FOCUS
Quite blustery conditions and this looked quite hard work for these 2-y-os. Not easy form to assess but the winner certainly didn't need to improve.

NOTEBOOK
Mizbah brought the best form to the table and he was well-backed to make it fourth-time lucky. Stepping up in trip was always going to suit this Derby entry and, having travelled well in behind the pace, he found plenty for pressure to get the job done in reasonable, if not outstanding, style. He'll do better still when stepped up in trip again, but as things stand this form is only ordinary. (op 4-7 tchd 8-13 in places)
Tidal Way(IRE), having just his second start, came under pressure some 3f out, but he was doing his best work in the final furlong and closed right in on Mizbah close home. He looks to be going the right way and a maiden success looks a formality. (tchd 5-1 and 13-2)
Cockney Rocker didn't see his race out as well as the front two and hasn't really built on a promising debut. He is qualified for a mark now. Official explanation: jockey said colt hung (op 5-1 tchd 6-1)
Mr Knightley(IRE) got squeezed out at halfway and was closing in on the leaders again entering the final furlong where he didn't get a clear run. He can be rated a bit better than the bare result and this was a big improvement on his debut run. (op 14-1)

3350 SHEPWAY BUILDING CONTRACTORS CLAIMING STKS — 6f

3:05 (3:05) (Class 6) 3-Y-O+ — **£1,910** (£564; £282) **Stalls** High

Form				RPR
-450	1		**Aye Aye Digby (IRE)**[11] 3000 6-9-8 82 ... GeorgeBaker 4 (Patrick Chamings) *chsd ldr: sltly hmpd after 1f: led 2f out: shkn up jst over 1f out: pushed along and readily asserted ins fnl f: comf* **6/4**[1]	83
3002	2	1 1/2	**Efistorm**[8] 3083 10-9-0 75 ... HayleyTurner 6 (Conor Dore) *trckd ldrs: rdn and effrt between horses ent fnl f: chsd wnr fnl 150yds: readily brushed aside and kpt on same pce fnl 100yds* **7/4**[2]	70
4066	3	2 1/4	**Boldinor**[36] 2222 8-8-12 59 ... MartinLane 2 (Martin Bosley) *chsd ldrs: rdn to press wnr 2f out: drvn and unable qck ent fnl f: wknd fnl 100yds* **16/1**	61
3003	4	1 1/2	**Diamond Johnny G (USA)**[18] 2756 4-9-5 67 ...(t) AlanCreighton[(3)] 3 (Edward Creighton) *taken down early: stdd s: t.k.h: hld up wl in tch: swtchd rt and effrt over 1f out: drvn and unable qck 1f out: wknd fnl 150yds* **20/1**	66
-064	5	7	**Veuveveuvevoom**[73] 1280 3-7-11 36 ...(p) SimonPearce[(3)] 1 (Gerry Enright) *led and crossed to r on stands' rail: rdn and hdd 2f out: wknd qckly over 1f out* **150/1**	27
3303	6	5	**Christmas Aria (IRE)**[24] 2581 3-8-9 73 ...(p) AdamBeschizza[(3)] 5 (Simon Dow) *s.i.s: nvr gng wl and sn pushed along in last: rdn over 3f out: lost tch over 2f out* **4/1**[3]	23

1m 12.37s (-0.33) **Going Correction** +0.025s/f (Good)
WFA 3 from 4yo+ 7lb — **6** Ran SP% **107.7**
Speed ratings (Par 101): **103,101,98,96,86 80**
Tote Swingers: 1&2 £1.40, 1&3 £4.00, 2&3 £4.90 CSF £3.97 TOTE £2.70: £1.80, £1.60; EX 5.10.

Owner Trolley Action **Bred** G J King **Trained** Baughurst, Hants

FOCUS
An ordinary contest. The first pair dominated but weren't at their best.

3351 BSS MAIDSTONE FOLKESTONE HAMMER STKS (H'CAP) — 6f

3:40 (3:40) (Class 4) (0-85,85) 3-Y-O+ — **£4,533** (£1,348; £674; £336) **Stalls** High

Form				RPR
4051	1		**We Have A Dream**[11] 3000 6-10-0 **85** 6ex ... GeorgeBaker 3 (William Muir) *mde all and crossed to r on stands' rail: rdn and asserted over 1f out: in command and pushed out ins fnl f: eased nr fin: comf* **2/1**[1]	94+
0144	2	1 1/4	**Ray Of Joy**[21] 2690 5-9-9 **80** ... FergusSweeney 6 (J R Jenkins) *chsd ldrs: swtchd rt and rdn over 1f out: chsd wnr ins fnl f: kpt on u.p but no threat to wnr* **7/2**[2]	85
-100	3	1 1/4	**Curtains**[48] 1902 4-9-11 **85** ... SimonPearce[(3)] 5 (Simon Dow) *stdd s: hld up in last pair: rdn and effrt on outer wl over 1f out: wnt 3rd fnl 100yds: kpt on but no threat to wnr* **7/1**	86
2010	4	2	**Deerslayer (USA)**[20] 2719 5-9-3 **74** ...(b[1]) PaulDoe 2 (Jim Best) *w ldr: rdn wl over 1f out: unable qck and drvn over 1f out: edgd lft and btn 1f out: wknd ins fnl f* **6/1**[3]	69
60-0	5	3/4	**Goodwood Treasure**[43] 2025 3-8-3 **67** ... ChrisCatlin 8 (John Dunlop) *in tch in last pair: rdn 1/2-way: drvn and no hdwy over 1f out: styd on same pce and no threat to ldrs fnl f* **12/1**	57
-000	6	nse	**Earlsmedic**[41] 2116 6-8-10 **72** ...(v) RyanClark[(5)] 1 (Stuart Williams) *racd in midfield on outer: rdn and effrt 2f out: unable qck u.p over 1f out: wknd fnl f* **15/2**	64
46-0	7	5	**Colorado Gold**[15] 2834 3-9-2 **83** ... JohnFahy[(3)] 4 (Ed de Giles) *hld up in tch in midfield: rdn and fnd little wl over 1f out: sn struggling: wknd ent fnl f* **10/1**	57

1m 12.09s (-0.61) **Going Correction** +0.025s/f (Good)
WFA 3 from 4yo+ 7lb — **7** Ran SP% **110.9**
Speed ratings (Par 105): **105,103,101,99,98 97,91**
Tote Swingers: 1&2 £2.00, 1&3 £2.50, 2&3 £3.50 CSF £8.42 CT £36.58 TOTE £3.00: £1.60, £1.40; EX 6.00.
Owner The Dreaming Squires **Bred** Whitsbury Manor Stud **Trained** Lambourn, Berks

FOCUS
Not many of these came into this in great form, so not strong form for the grade. The winner is basically rated back to his best.

3352 HOMELEIGH TIMBER & BUILDING SUPPLIES H'CAP — 1m 7f 92y

4:15 (4:15) (Class 5) (0-75,73) 4-Y-O+ — **£2,661** (£785; £393) **Stalls** High

Form				RPR
44-2	1		**Addwaitya**[168] 81 6-9-6 **72** ... FergusSweeney 5 (Laura Mongan) *hld up in rr: swtchd lft and effrt jst over 2f out: rdn and hdwy to chse ldr jst over 1f out: led ins fnl f: r.o wl: rdn out* **16/1**	79+

0213 **2** ¾ **My Valley (IRE)**[50] 1839 9-9-3 **69**.................................. IanMongan 3 75
(Pat Phelan) *hld up in last trio: gd hdwy on outer over 3f out: rdn to ld jst over 2f out: drvn over 1f out: hdd and no ex ins fnl f* **11/4**[1]

-106 **3** 4 **Warne's Way (IRE)**[7] 3120 8-9-7 **73**.............................(v) GeorgeBaker 4 74
(Brendan Powell) *chsd ldr tl pushed along to ld 4f out: drvn and hdd jst over 2f out: styd on same pce fr over 1f out* **9/2**[3]

5-54 **4** 1 **Corr Point (IRE)**[59] 1596 4-9-3 **69**.............................. FrankieMcDonald 1 69
(Jamie Osborne) *in tch in midfield: nt clr run and shuffled bk 3f out: rallied and hdwy on inner 2f out: drvn and styd on same pce fr over 1f out* **7/1**

430- **5** 2½ **Astrovenus**[138] 7388 4-7-13 **54** oh6.............................. SimonPearce(3) 7 50
(Mark H Tompkins) *hld up in tch in last trio: hdwy over 3f out: chsd ldrs and unable qck u.p 2f out: no imp after* **66/1**

-306 **6** 11 **Albeed**[25] 2552 4-9-6 **72**.. TedDurcan 8 54
(John Dunlop) *chsd ldrs: n.m.r over 2f out: rdn and fnd nil 2f out: wknd over 1f out: eased ins fnl f* **4/1**[2]

2-54 **7** 1½ **Swordsman (GER)**[18] 2758 9-8-10 **62**.......................(vt) SamHitchcott 2 42
(Chris Gordon) *dwlt: rdn along early: hdwy to chse ldrs after 2f: losing pl and rdn whn short of room and hmpd over 2f out: wknd 2f out: wl bhd and eased ins fnl f* **25/1**

535- **8** 13 **Uncle Keef (IRE)**[27] 5564 5-8-4 **56**.................................(b) ChrisCatlin 6 19
(Nicky Henderson) *dwlt and early reminders: hdwy and in tch in midfield after 2f: rdn and lost pl 3f out: wknd jst over 2f out: wl bhd and eased ins fnl f: t.o* **11/2**

2-20 **9** 24 **Indochina**[14] 2892 4-9-0 **69**...................................... AdamBeschizza(3) 9 —
(David Simcock) *led tl 4f out: rdn and wknd over 1f out: wl bhd over 1f out: eased fnl f: t.o* **11/2**

3m 28.08s (-1.62) **Going Correction** -0.025s/f (Good) **9** Ran SP% **119.3**
Speed ratings (Par 103): **103,102,100,99,98 92,91,85,72**
Tote Swingers: 1&2 £5.50, 1&3 £9.60, 2&3 £4.30 CSF £62.02 CT £242.22 TOTE £20.40: £4.40, £1.80, £2.20; EX 42.10.
Owner Mrs P J Sheen **Bred** L McLaughlin **Trained** Epsom, Surrey

FOCUS
Just ordinary handicap form, but the gallop looked decent and the field were quite well strung out by the time they turned for home. The winner is a bit better than the bare form.
Albeed Official explanation: jockey said filly had no more to give

3353 HELPFORHEROES.ORG.UK H'CAP 1m 4f
4:45 (4:45) (Class 6) (0-60,60) 4-Y-0+ **£1,910** (£564; £282) **Stalls** High

Form RPR

/60- **1** **Steady Gaze**[438] 1262 6-8-1 **47** oh1 ow1.......................... LukeRowe(7) 1 52+
(Richard Rowe) *chsd ldr tl led after 1f: sn hdd: grad stdd and hld up in last trio 8f out: stl only 6th and effrt in centre over 1f out: rdn and str run fnl f to ld last strides* **33/1**

3063 **2** hd **Barbirolli**[18] 2759 9-8-5 **47**.. AdamBeschizza(3) 5 52
(William Stone) *hld up in tch in last pair: hdwy to chse ldrs and rdn 2f out: drvn and ev ch over 1f out: led ins fnl f: kpt on tl hdd last strides* **8/1**

6215 **3** 1½ **Astroleo**[11] 2991 5-8-12 **51**... ChrisCatlin 7 54
(Mark H Tompkins) *chsd ldrs tl wnt 2nd over 8f out: led 4f out: rdn over 2f out: hrd drvn over 1f out: hdd and one pce ins fnl f* **3/1**[2]

0-55 **4** 1¾ **Motarjm (USA)**[16] 2820 7-8-8 **50**...............................(t) SimonPearce(3) 4 50
(Lydia Pearce) *broke wl: led for 1f: stdd and hld up in midfield after: hdwy to press ldr 3f out: ev ch and drvn wl over 1f out: no ex and btn jst ins fnl f* **7/1**[3]

0/0 **5** shd **Beech View (IRE)**[46] 819 6-8-7 **46** oh1............................. MartinLane 8 46
(Martin Bosley) *in tch in last trio: gd hdwy on outer over 4f out: chsd ldrs and drvn 2f out: swtchd lft and styd on same pce fr over 1f out* **16/1**

000 **6** 6 **Satwa Sunrise (FR)**[28] 2457 4-9-7 **60**................................ GeorgeBaker 3 50
(Ed Dunlop) *chsd ldrs: rdn and ev ch 2f out: drvn and unable qck wl over 1f out: btn 1f out: wknd fnl f* **11/10**[1]

1305 **7** nk **Mister Frosty (IRE)**[13] 2923 5-9-0 **58**.................... MatthewCosham(5) 6 48+
(George Prodromou) *hld up in last pair: pushed along whn nt clr run and hmpd wl over 2f out: lost any ch and wl btn ent fnl 2f: r.o ins fnl f: nvr trbld ldrs* **8/1**

050- **8** 68 **Casual Garcia**[18] 4223 6-9-7 **60**................................(b) FergusSweeney 2
(Mark Gillard) *dwlt: pushed along and hdwy to ld over 10f out: hdd and rdn 4f out: dropped out qckly 3f out: t.o and virtually p.u fr over 1f out* **50/1**

2m 45.16s (4.26) **Going Correction** -0.025s/f (Good) **8** Ran SP% **118.1**
Speed ratings (Par 101): **84,83,82,81,81 77,77,32**
Tote Swingers: 1&2 £17.40, 1&3 £2.10, 2&3 £24.50 CSF £279.36 CT £1047.19 TOTE £42.40: £10.10, £2.50, £1.10; EX 223.80.
Owner Miss Victoria Baalham **Bred** Juddmonte Farms Ltd **Trained** Sullington, W Sussex

FOCUS
A weak race in which the market expected improvement from handicap debutant Satwa Sunrise, but that wasn't forthcoming. Indeed she proved very disappointing. The gallop didn't appear overly vigorous, but the hold-up horses came to the fore in the closing stages. The form is rated around the second and third, with the winner overcoming being 9lb wrong.
Steady Gaze Official explanation: trainer said, regarding apparent improvement in form, that this was the gelding's first run for him, having had problems, but been free of these for the past five, six months
Mister Frosty(IRE) Official explanation: jockey said gelding ran in snatches

3354 LIPSCOMB.CO.UK H'CAP 1m 1f 149y
5:15 (5:15) (Class 5) (0-75,75) 3-Y-0+ **£2,661** (£785; £393) **Stalls** Centre

Form RPR

0020 **1** **Inef (IRE)**[22] 2649 4-9-13 **74**.. FergusSweeney 2 83
(Laura Mongan) *chsd ldr tl over 7f out: wnt 2nd again over 2f out: rdn and ev ch 2f out: led over 1f out: clr and in command ins fnl f: r.o wl* **17/2**

30-4 **2** 2 **Sally Friday (IRE)**[14] 2875 3-8-11 **70**................................ ChrisCatlin 1 74+
(Peter Winkworth) *dwlt: hld up in tch: rdn over 2f out: no imp tl hdwy u.p jst ins fnl f: swtchd lft and r.o to go 2nd towards fin: no threat to wnr* **7/2**[2]

50-4 **3** ¾ **Recalcitrant**[13] 2923 8-9-3 **67**...................................... SimonPearce(3) 7 69
(Simon Dow) *led: rdn and qcknd jst over 2f out: hdd over 1f out: nt pce of wnr and btn ins fnl f: styd on same pce: lost 2nd towards fin* **10/1**

-252 **4** ¾ **Shabak Hom (IRE)**[13] 2915 4-9-13 **74**................................ MartinLane 4 75
(David Simcock) *taken down early: t.k.h: hld up wl in tch: rdn and chsd ldrs 2f out: nt qckn u.p over 1f out: styd on same pce fnl f* **2/1**[1]

5-30 **5** 1¾ **Gallant Eagle (IRE)**[22] 2649 4-9-9 **73**............................ JohnFahy(3) 3 70
(Ed de Giles) *t.k.h: chsd ldng pair tl chsd ldr over 7f out tl over 2f out: unable qck and drvn 2f out: edgd rt u.p and btn 1f out* **4/1**[3]

0-00 **6** 1¾ **Sohcahtoa (IRE)**[22] 2649 5-10-0 **75**............................ SamHitchcott 5 68
(Robert Mills) *dwlt and pushed along early: in tch in last trio: hdwy 4f out: rdn and fnd little over 2f out: kpt on same pce u.p and wl hld fr over 1f out* **9/2**

-450 **7** 16 **Night Witch (IRE)**[11] 3002 3-8-9 **68**............................ EddieCreighton 6 28
(Edward Creighton) *hld up in last: rdn and effrt over 2f out: sn struggling and wknd wl over 1f: wl btn and eased ins fnl f* **50/1**

2m 5.14s (0.24) **Going Correction** -0.025s/f (Good)
WFA 3 from 4yo+ 12lb **7** Ran SP% **115.3**
Speed ratings (Par 103): **98,96,95,95,93 92,79**
Tote Swingers: 1&2 £2.70, 1&3 £6.30, 2&3 £7.70 CSF £38.82 TOTE £10.70: £5.60, £2.90; EX 41.90.
Owner Mrs P J Sheen **Bred** Fresi Marcello **Trained** Epsom, Surrey

FOCUS
A fair handicap run at a sound pace. The winner is rated back to her penultimate Sandown form.
T/Plt: £30.20 to a £1 stake. Pool:£56,450.65 - 1,360.62 winning tickets T/Qpdt: £7.60 to a £1 stake. Pool:£6,151.72 - 598.51 winning tickets SP

3313 NEWCASTLE (L-H)
Friday, June 24

OFFICIAL GOING: Good to soft (good in places; 7.0)
Wind: Slight, across Weather: Cloudy, dull

3355 COOPERS MARQUEES MAIDEN FILLIES' STKS 7f
6:20 (6:20) (Class 5) 3-Y-0+ **£2,525** (£751; £375; £187) **Stalls** Centre

Form RPR

350 **1** **Misrepresent (USA)**[12] 2960 3-8-12 0.......................... WilliamBuick 4 63+
(John Gosden) *trckd ldr: led 2f out: hung lft and rdn out ins fnl f* **4/11**[1]

4366 **2** 3 **Eilean Eeve**[7] 3128 5-9-7 48...(p) LeeNewman 6 55
(George Foster) *rrd s: sn trcking ldrs: effrt and pressed wnr over 1f out: no ex ins fnl f* **18/1**

5042 **3** 1½ **American Lover (FR)**[17] 2781 4-9-7 62............................ DavidNolan 1 51
(John Wainwright) *led to 2f out: sn drvn and kpt on same pce* **7/2**[2]

0 **4** 16 **Dream Of Wunders**[38] 2185 3-8-12 0.............................. TomQueally 3 —
(James Given) *in tch: rdn 1/2-way: wknd wl over 1f out* **25/1**

5 49 **Royal Playmate** 3-8-12 0.. PJMcDonald 5 —
(Keith Reveley) *s.s: bhd: lost tch fr 1/2-way: t.o* **16/1**[3]

1m 27.54s (-0.26) **Going Correction** -0.125s/f (Firm)
WFA 3 from 4yo+ 9lb **5** Ran SP% **110.5**
Speed ratings (Par 100): **101,97,95,77,21**
CSF £8.89 TOTE £1.30: £1.02, £6.90; EX 9.20.
Owner H R H Princess Haya Of Jordan **Bred** Arindel **Trained** Newmarket, Suffolk
■ Stewards' Enquiry : William Buick caution: careless riding.

FOCUS
Course at normal inner configuration. After a dry night, the ground was officially good to soft, soft in places. A weak fillies' maiden, and the winner has not gone on as expected.

3356 E B F "KHELEYF" HOPPINGS STKS (LISTED RACE) 1m 2f 32y
6:50 (6:50) (Class 1) 3-Y-0+
£17,031 (£6,456; £3,231; £1,611; £807; £405) **Stalls** Low

Form RPR

40-3 **1** **Principal Role (USA)**[34] 2290 4-9-5 106........................ TomQueally 10 100+
(Sir Henry Cecil) *hld up and bhd: stdy hdwy over 2f out: effrt and drvn over 1f out: led last 100yds: rdn out* **7/4**[1]

1104 **2** ¾ **Fanditha (IRE)**[49] 1851 5-9-5 90................................. HughBowman 9 98
(Mick Channon) *chsd clr ldng pair: effrt over 2f out: hdwy to ld 1f out to last 100yds: kpt on* **50/1**

-415 **3** nk **Piano**[11] 2994 4-9-5 90... WilliamBuick 1 97
(John Gosden) *hld up: rdn and hdwy over 2f out: kpt on towards fin* **3/1**[2]

-006 **4** 2¼ **Crystal Gal (IRE)**[11] 2994 4-9-5 96.............................. RobertWinston 6 93
(Lucy Wadham) *w ldr: rdn and led over 2f out to 1f out: kpt on same pce* **9/1**

-423 **5** 2¼ **Opera Gal (IRE)**[13] 2909 4-9-5 96..................................... LiamKeniry 12 88
(Andrew Balding) *taken early to post: led to over 2f out: sn rdn: rallied: one pce appr fnl f* **11/2**[3]

0-10 **6** nse **Plaisterer**[20] 2716 6-9-5 92.. GrahamGibbons 7 88
(Chris Wall) *prom: drvn and outpcd over 2f out: rallied fnl f: nvr able to chal* **16/1**

-126 **7** 3 **Cracking Lass (IRE)**[34] 2316 4-9-5 95............................ PaulHanagan 4 82
(Richard Fahey) *hld up: rdn along over 4f out: struggling 3f out: rdr dropped whip 1f out: plugged on: nvr on terms* **9/1**

2154 **8** ½ **Snow Dancer (IRE)**[21] 2676 7-9-5 83............................... PhillipMakin 2 81
(Hugh McWilliams) *hld up: drvn along fr 3f out: no imp fnl 2f* **66/1**

16-0 **9** ¾ **Matula (IRE)**[15] 2839 3-8-8 86 ow1.................................... JimCrowley 8 81
(Ralph Beckett) *hld up in midfield: rdn along 3f out: wknd fr 2f out* **14/1**

406- **10** 13 **Starkat**[230] 7349 5-9-5 85... TomEaves 11 54
(George Margarson) *hld up: drvn and outpcd 3f out: nvr on terms* **50/1**

-004 **11** 8 **Silver Grey (IRE)**[78] 1201 4-9-5 95......................(b[1]) MickyFenton 5 38
(Roger Ingram) *dwlt: t.k.h: hld up: rdn along and wandered fr 3f out: wknd* **40/1**

2m 9.13s (-2.77) **Going Correction** -0.125s/f (Firm)
WFA 3 from 4yo+ 12lb **11** Ran SP% **117.2**
Speed ratings (Par 111): **106,105,105,103,101 101,99,98,98,87 81**
Tote Swingers: 1&2 £11.90, 1&3 £3.40, 2&3 £43.20 CSF £114.23 TOTE £2.40: £1.10, £14.10, £1.80; EX 74.70.
Owner K Abdulla **Bred** Juddmonte Farms Inc **Trained** Newmarket, Suffolk

FOCUS
Just a fair contest by Listed standards. The winner didn't need to match her best, with the runner-up the key.

NOTEBOOK
Principal Role(USA), narrowly beaten when third against the colts at this level last time out, notched her second Listed success cleverly. She was given a confident ride, held up well off the pace in the early stages, and delivered her challenge late in the home straight towards the stands' side rail. She quickened up nicely, winning with a fraction in hand, and connections, who expect her to get further, will presumably now aim for black type at a higher level. (op 6-4 tchd 15-8 and 2-1 in places)
Fanditha(IRE), found wanting in a Chester Group 3 on her latest start, ran a cracker. Always in the leading trio, she was briefly outpaced when the winner swept to the front, but rallied gamely and was staying on at the finish. (op 40-1)
Piano, fifth over 1m3f in this grade on her latest start, was, like the winner, ridden patiently. She finished strongly and, with this run, has now attained the valuable black type her connections will have been chasing. (op 9-2, tchd 5-1 in a place)
Crystal Gal(IRE), third in a Leopardstown Group 3 in March 2010, chased the pace from the outset. She tired in the closing stages, but this was a sound effort and she should gain another place at this level when the cards fall for her. (tchd 8-1 and 10-1 in a place)
Opera Gal(IRE), third off an official mark of 94 in a Chester handicap 13 days earlier, helps set the level of the form. She led from the start and plugged on gamely when the principals quickened past her. (op 6-1 tchd 5-1)

Plaisterer, a Haydock handicap winner off 85 in May, raced in fourth until the final 2f. She was outpaced from there on, but still posted a highly commendable performance. (op 14-1)

3357 DELOITTE GOSFORTH PARK CUP (H'CAP) 5f

7:25 (7:26) (Class 2) (0-105,95) 3-Y-0+

£9,221 (£2,761; £1,380; £691; £344; £173) **Stalls** Centre

Form RPR

3103 **1** **Ancient Cross**[14] 2890 7-9-11 **95**.........................(t) GrahamGibbons 11 107
(Michael Easterby) *hld up towards rr: gd hdwy over 1f out: led ins fnl f: sn clr* **11/1**

532 **2** *1 ¾* **Noodles Blue Boy**[7] 3140 5-9-0 **84**............................ TomQueally 7 89
(Ollie Pears) *w ldrs: drvn 2f out: chsd wnr ins fnl f: r.o* **12/1**

1223 **3** *shd* **Verinco**[8] 3073 5-8-13 **83**...(v) TomEaves 12 88
(Bryan Smart) *led tl hdd ins fnl f: kpt on u.p* **12/1**

4300 **4** *nk* **Jamesway (IRE)**[13] 2934 3-8-12 **88**.......................... PaulHanagan 8 90+
(Richard Fahey) *blkd sn after s: bhd: drvn 1/2-way: hdwy over 1f out: r.o fnl f: nrst fin* **6/1**[2]

0-36 **5** *hd* **Racy**[20] 2727 4-9-6 **90**.. PhillipMakin 1 93
(Kevin Ryan) *in tch: n.m.r over 2f out: effrt on outside over 1f out: one pce fnl f* **6/1**[2]

-050 **6** *½* **Hazelrigg (IRE)**[20] 2727 6-9-0 **84**..............................(be) DavidAllan 6 85
(Tim Easterby) *hld up: hmpd sn after s: stdy hdwy over 1f out: pushed along and kpt on fnl f: nvr able to chal* **11/1**

1626 **7** *nk* **Cape Vale (IRE)**[20] 2717 6-9-4 **88**.......................... AndrewMullen 4 88
(David Nicholls) *w ldrs: rdn 2f out: kpt on same pce fnl f* **25/1**

1102 **8** *nk* **Mon Brav**[12] 2954 4-8-10 **85**.. DaleSwift(5) 5 84+
(Brian Ellison) *sn drvn towards rr: hdwy over 1f out: kpt on fnl f: nvr able to chal* **4/1**[1]

4402 **9** *1 ¾* **Confessional**[20] 2714 4-9-9 **93**..............................(e) RobertWinston 10 86
(Tim Easterby) *in tch: effrt over 2f out: one pce fnl f* **8/1**[3]

3112 **10** *shd* **Solemn**[12] 2959 6-9-5 **89**...(b) LiamKeniry 3 82
(Milton Bradley) *trckd ldrs: effrt and rdn over 2f out: wknd ins fnl f* **20/1**

0632 **11** *nk* **Ballista (IRE)**[6] 3181 3-8-12 **88**............................ RussKennemore 2 78
(Tom Dascombe) *cl up: drvn 1/2-way: wknd ent fnl f* **10/1**

2002 **12** *3* **Silaah**[41] 2117 7-9-9 **93**..(v[1]) AdrianNicholls 9 74
(David Nicholls) *plld hrd: sn midfield: drvn over 2f out: wknd appr fnl f* **11/1**

59.30 secs (-1.80) **Going Correction** -0.125s/f (Firm)
WFA 3 from 4yo+ 6lb **12** Ran SP% **117.8**
Speed ratings (Par 109): **109,106,106,105,105 104,103,103,100,100 100,95**
Tote Swingers: 1&2 £18.00, 1&3 £22.80, 2&3 £17.30 CSF £135.35 CT £1640.78 TOTE £12.20: £4.10, £3.60, £3.40; EX 164.00.
Owner Pete Bown,BackUp Technology & Steve Hull **Bred** Darley **Trained** Sheriff Hutton, N Yorks

FOCUS
A highly competitive sprint handicap in which few could be confidently discounted. The time was decent, suggesting the ground wasn't bad. The winner continues on the upgrade.

NOTEBOOK
Ancient Cross, third off this mark at York two weeks earlier, gave weight and a sound beating to the opposition. He raced in mid-division until halfway, but quickened smartly when asked and got to the front under strong driving just over 1f out. He soon shot clear and the rest never seemed remotely capable of cutting back his advantage. This trip with ease underfoot and a solid pace appears to suit him ideally. (op 12-1)
Noodles Blue Boy, narrowly beaten off this mark at Redcar a week earlier, seems a feasible guide to the form. He was always close to the pace and stayed on gamely, even though the winner comprehensively had his measure. (op 11-1)
Verinco, third off this mark at Beverley eight days earlier, disputed the lead from the outset. He too battled on bravely, but could not quicken in the closing stages.
Jamesway(IRE), dropped back in trip after a slightly below par 6f effort last time, looked far more at home over this distance. He did not exhibit the pace of the first three, but ran creditably enough. (op 8-1 tchd 5-1)
Racy, 1lb lower than when sixth at Musselburgh on his latest start, was always in the first half-dozen. He tried hard, but lacked the finishing zip of those ahead of him. (op 11-2 tchd 5-1)
Hazelrigg(IRE), dropping in the ratings but still 5lb higher than for his last win, ran his best race of the season so far. He lost ground at the start after rearing in the stalls, but plugged on gamely in the closing stages. Official explanation: jockey said gelding suffered interference at start (tchd 10-1 and 12-1)
Silaah Official explanation: jockey said gelding was unsuited by the good to soft (good in places) ground

3358 KB SHEET METAL & GDBS H'CAP 1m 3y(S)

7:55 (7:55) (Class 4) (0-85,85) 3-Y-0+ **£4,533** (£1,348; £674; £336) **Stalls** Centre

Form RPR

4521 **1** **Daring Dream (GER)**[7] 3112 6-9-2 **76** 6ex..................... GaryBartley(3) 5 86
(Jim Goldie) *hld up: stdy hdwy over 2f out: rdn to ld ins fnl f: kpt on wl* **11/4**[1]

0253 **2** *hd* **Reel Buddy Star**[17] 2783 6-10-0 **85**.............................. PJMcDonald 3 94
(George Moore) *pressed ldr: led over 2f out: sn rdn: hdd ins fnl f: rallied: jst hld* **7/2**[2]

6-12 **3** *4 ½* **Hernando Torres**[21] 2675 3-7-13 **66**........................... PatrickMathers 4 63
(Michael Easterby) *prom: niggled 1/2-way: drvn and effrt over 2f out: outpcd ent fnl f* **9/2**[3]

5000 **4** *1* **Keys Of Cyprus**[2] 3275 9-9-6 **77**................................ AdrianNicholls 9 73
(David Nicholls) *in tch: stdy hdwy over 2f out: sn drvn: no ex over 1f out* **9/1**

-216 **5** *2 ¼* **Jibaal (IRE)**[15] 2847 3-8-9 **76**.. PhillipMakin 7 65
(Mark Johnston) *in tch: rdn and hung lft over 2f out: sn no imp* **9/2**[3]

0060 **6** *¾* **Rasselas (IRE)**[17] 2783 4-9-6 **77**............................... AndrewMullen 1 66
(David Nicholls) *hld up in tch: drvn and outpcd over 2f out: n.d after* **14/1**

1-56 **7** *2* **Out Of Nothing**[10] 3026 8-9-0 **78**.............................. JustinNewman(7) 6 63
(Kevin M Prendergast) *led to over 2f out: rdn and wknd over 1f out* **25/1**

-260 **8** *21* **Lakeman (IRE)**[8] 3088 5-8-9 **66** oh1...............................(b) TomEaves 2 —
(Brian Ellison) *prom: drvn and outpcd over 3f out: sn struggling: t.o* **20/1**

1m 40.79s (-2.61) **Going Correction** -0.125s/f (Firm)
WFA 3 from 4yo+ 10lb **8** Ran SP% **110.5**
Speed ratings (Par 105): **108,107,103,102,100 99,97,76**
Tote Swingers: 1&2 £2.30, 1&3 £3.90, 2&3 £2.00 CSF £11.53 CT £37.74 TOTE £3.10: £1.10, £1.70, £2.70; EX 12.80.
Owner George Barclay & Graeme McGinlay **Bred** Gestut Auenquelle **Trained** Uplawmoor, E Renfrews

■ Stewards' Enquiry : P J McDonald one-day ban: used whip with excessive frequency (Jul 11)

FOCUS
An ordinary handicap, with the top-weight rated 85, and it looked open on paper. Small personal bests from the first two.

3359 FREEBETTING.CO.UK H'CAP 6f

8:25 (8:26) (Class 5) (0-75,74) 3-Y-0+ **£2,525** (£751; £375; £187) **Stalls** Centre

Form RPR

2451 **1** **Boy The Bell**[9] 3049 4-8-8 **61**.. DaleSwift(5) 10 74
(Brian Ellison) *w ldrs: rdn to ld appr fnl f: styd on wl* **6/1**[3]

0532 **2** *2* **Red Cape (FR)**[10] 3028 8-9-12 **74**................................ PJMcDonald 13 81
(Ruth Carr) *prom: effrt and drvn over 2f out: styd on fnl f: tk 2nd cl home* **4/1**[2]

-144 **3** *hd* **Arch Walker (IRE)**[15] 2845 4-8-11 **62**..................... PatrickDonaghy(3) 1 68
(Jedd O'Keeffe) *hld up: effrt on outside over 2f out: kpt on fnl f: no imp towards fin* **20/1**

-044 **4** *hd* **Feel The Heat**[20] 2732 4-9-2 **71**...........................(v[1]) JustinNewman(7) 8 76
(Bryan Smart) *dwlt: sn prom: hdwy to ld over 2f out to appr fnl f: kpt on same pce* **12/1**

1245 **5** *¾* **Italian Tom (IRE)**[17] 2794 4-9-9 **71**................................... JimCrowley 3 74
(Ronald Harris) *hld up: rdn and hdwy wl over 1f out: kpt on fnl f: nrst fin* **16/1**

0312 **6** *1* **Apache Ridge (IRE)**[11] 3000 5-9-12 **74**.....................(p) PaulHanagan 2 74
(Keith Dalgleish) *trckd ldrs: effrt and rdn over 2f out: one pce over 1f out* **7/2**[1]

1235 **7** *3 ½* **Ingleby Arch (USA)**[16] 2806 8-9-7 **69**........................ GrahamGibbons 5 58
(David Barron) *bmpd s: towards rr: rdn and hdwy over 1f out: nvr able to chal* **17/2**

0002 **8** *½* **Captain Royale (IRE)**[8] 3087 6-9-11 **73**...................(p) RobertWinston 9 60
(Colin Teague) *led to over 2f out: wknd over 1f out* **18/1**

2020 **9** *2* **Prince Of Vasa (IRE)**[9] 3036 4-9-8 **70**..................... AdrianNicholls 7 51
(Michael Smith) *prom: lost pl whn n.m.r over 3f out: rallied over 1f out: nvr rchd ldrs* **25/1**

0666 **10** *2* **Northern Bolt**[32] 2352 6-9-1 **63**..........................(b) PatrickMathers 14 37
(Ian McInnes) *bhd: drvn and struggling over 3f out: hdwy u.p over 1f out: nvr rchd ldrs* **33/1**

66-0 **11** *3 ½* **Leonid Glow**[48] 1907 6-9-10 **72**...................................... PhillipMakin 6 35
(Michael Dods) *hld up: stdy hdwy over 2f out: shkn up wl over 1f out: fnd little and sn btn* **33/1**

6-30 **12** *shd* **Burnwynd Boy**[22] 2633 6-8-13 **61**................................... LeeNewman 4 24
(Ian Semple) *prom: drvn over 2f out: wknd wl over 1f out* **12/1**

-000 **13** *2* **Durham Express (IRE)**[25] 2543 4-9-5 **67**....................(b[1]) TomEaves 12 23
(Michael Dods) *cl up tl rdn adnd wknd over 2f out* **25/1**

3611 **14** *6* **Choc'A'Moca (IRE)**[11] 2989 4-9-5 **67** 6ex....................(v) MickyFenton 15 —
(Paul Midgley) *racd alone stands' side: struggling after 2f: nvr on terms* **9/1**

1m 14.5s (-0.10) **Going Correction** -0.125s/f (Firm) **14** Ran SP% **121.9**
Speed ratings (Par 103): **95,92,92,91,90 89,84,84,81,78 74,74,71,63**
Tote Swingers: 1&2 £2.70, 1&3 £38.20, 2&3 £23.70 CSF £28.47 CT £469.51 TOTE £9.30: £3.20, £3.30, £7.70; EX 48.70.
Owner L S Keys **Bred** D J P Turner **Trained** Norton, N Yorks

FOCUS
Just a run-of-the-mill handicap with the top-weight being rated 74, but it presented punters with a tricky puzzle. The form looks sound enough.
Choc'A'Moca(IRE) Official explanation: trainer said, regarding running, that the race came too soon for the gelding

3360 KEVIN LEE MEMORIAL H'CAP 5f

9:00 (9:00) (Class 5) (0-75,71) 3-Y-0 **£2,525** (£751; £375; £187) **Stalls** Centre

Form RPR

2112 **1** **Rothesay Chancer**[7] 3126 3-9-3 **70**............................... GaryBartley(3) 5 80
(Jim Goldie) *in tch: effrt over 1f out: styd on wl fnl f: led towards fin* **9/4**[1]

2202 **2** *½* **Rylee Mooch**[7] 3136 3-8-11 **64**................................(e) RobertLButler(3) 6 72
(Richard Guest) *t.k.h: led: rdn over 1f out: edgd rt ins fnl f: kpt on: hdd towards fin* **13/2**[3]

1-06 **3** *2 ¼* **Black Annis Bower**[32] 2363 3-9-7 **71**........................ GrahamGibbons 8 71
(Michael Easterby) *prom: effrt and rdn 2f out: kpt on same pce fnl f* **6/1**[2]

-653 **4** *hd* **Pantella (IRE)**[8] 3075 3-8-13 **63**................................(p) PhillipMakin 4 62
(Kevin Ryan) *trckd ldrs: drvn over 2f out: one pce over 1f out* **13/2**[3]

4-50 **5** *2 ½* **Wandering Lad**[8] 3075 3-8-12 **62**................................... MickyFenton 1 52
(Paul Midgley) *s.i.s: bhd tl hdwy over 1f out: nvr able to chal* **40/1**

6140 **6** *nk* **Meandmyshadow**[16] 2798 3-8-13 **63**................................(p) TomEaves 3 52
(Alan Brown) *in tch: rdn 1/2-way: wknd over 1f out* **33/1**

1240 **7** *2* **Mini Bon Bon**[32] 2365 3-8-1 **56**..................................(v) JulieBurke(5) 9 38
(David O'Meara) *chsd main gp: rdn after 2f: nvr on terms* **16/1**

22-2 **8** *½* **Crystallus (IRE)**[32] 2365 3-9-4 **68**.............................. PaulHanagan 7 48
(Ann Duffield) *trckd ldrs tl rdn and wknd over 1f out* **9/4**[1]

61.07 secs (-0.03) **Going Correction** -0.125s/f (Firm) **8** Ran SP% **113.8**
Speed ratings (Par 99): **95,94,90,90,86 85,82,81**
CSF £17.75 CT £76.20 TOTE £3.10: £1.50, £2.10, £1.10; EX 10.50.
Owner Discovery Racing Club 2 **Bred** Mrs S R Kennedy **Trained** Uplawmoor, E Renfrews

FOCUS
A moderate finale, but the winner is progressive. The first two were both 3lb well in.
T/Plt: £29.00 to a £1 stake. Pool:£72,307.16 - 1,814.04 winning tickets T/Qpdt: £14.90 to a £1 stake. Pool:£5,762.16 - 286.08 winning tickets RY

3177 NEWMARKET (R-H)

Friday, June 24

OFFICIAL GOING: Good (good to firm in places) changing to good to firm after race 1 (6.00)
Wind: Light across Weather: Overcast

3361 NEWMARKET NIGHTS H'CAP 1m

6:00 (6:00) (Class 5) (0-75,75) 3-Y-0+ **£2,590** (£770; £385; £192) **Stalls** Low

Form RPR

0403 **1** **Master Mylo (IRE)**[13] 2917 4-10-0 **75**............................... ShaneKelly 12 84
(Dean Ivory) *free to post: hld up in tch: shkn up to ld wl ins fnl f: r.o* **9/1**

3510 **2** *1* **Qenaa**[14] 2883 3-9-3 **74**... RichardHills 16 79
(Mark Johnston) *chsd ldrs: led over 1f out: rdn and hdd wl ins fnl f* **11/2**[2]

00-5 **3** *1* **Proud Chieftain**[13] 2924 3-8-12 **69**................................ JamesDoyle 9 71
(Clifford Lines) *chsd ldrs: rdn over 1f out: hung lft ins fnl f: r.o* **12/1**

0-00 **4** *1 ¾* **Rio Tinto**[16] 2822 4-9-5 **66**... SaleemGolam 3 66
(Giles Bravery) *s.i.s: hld up: plld hrd: hdwy over 1f out: r.o: nt rch ldrs* **66/1**

0-00 **5** 3/4 **Marvo**[98] [799] 7-9-7 73 .... AshleyMorgan(5) 4 72
(Mark H Tompkins) *s.i.s: hld up: nt clr run over 2f out: hdwy over 1f out: styd on same pce ins fnl f* **20/1**

0552 **6** *shd* **Negotiation (IRE)**[14] [2887] 5-9-6 **67** .... JimmyFortune 10 65
(Michael Quinn) *chsd ldr: rdn over 2f out: no ex ins fnl f* **5/1**[1]

2104 **7** 1/2 **Broughtons Day**[31] [2381] 4-9-4 **65** .... StevieDonohoe 7 62
(Willie Musson) *hld up: rdn over 1f out: r.o ins fnl f: nvr nrr* **14/1**

4400 **8** *nk* **Eastern Gift**[7] [3130] 6-9-5 **66** .... MickaelBarzalona 2 63
(Gay Kelleway) *hld up: rdn over 1f out: r.o ins fnl f: nvr trbld ldrs* **25/1**

22 **9** 1/2 **Burning Stone (USA)**[29] [2419] 4-9-9 **70** .... NeilCallan 8 65
(Gay Kelleway) *hld up: hdwy 2f out: sn rdn: no ex ins fnl f* **6/1**[3]

3002 **10** 3 3/4 **Jungle Bay**[16] [2816] 4-9-4 **72** .... LewisWalsh(7) 5 59
(Jane Chapple-Hyam) *hld up: hdwy 1/2-way: rdn and wknd over 1f out* **11/2**[2]

/12- **11** *hd* **Matjar (IRE)**[80] [1161] 8-9-6 **67** .... DBDias 1 53
(Joseph Quinn, Ire) *hld up: rdn and hung lft over 2f out: nvr on terms* **12/1**

2-00 **12** 1 1/4 **Darcey**[14] [2876] 5-9-9 **70** .... HayleyTurner 15 53
(Amy Weaver) *led: rdn and hdd over 1f out: sn wknd* **40/1**

1-00 **13** 2 **Rasheed**[36] [2229] 3-9-1 **72** .... TadhgO'Shea 11 49
(John Gosden) *hld up: hdwy 1/2-way: hung rt and wknd over 1f out* **10/1**

15-6 **14** 5 **Private Joke**[66] [1460] 4-9-11 **72** .... MarcHalford 14 39
(Terry Clement) *prom: rdn over 2f out: wknd over 1f out* **33/1**

1m 38.66s (-1.34) **Going Correction** -0.075s/f (Good)
WFA 3 from 4yo+ 10lb **14** Ran SP% **118.3**
Speed ratings (Par 103): **103,102,101,99,98 98,97,97,97,93 93,91,89,84**
Tote Swingers: 1&2 £10.80, 1&3 £51.40, 2&3 £23.10 CSF £53.87 CT £623.23 TOTE £10.70: £2.70, £2.50, £4.70; EX 68.30.
Owner K Quinn/ C Benham/ I Saunders **Bred** David Eiffe **Trained** Radlett, Herts
■ Stewards' Enquiry : D B Dias one-day ban: used whip without giving gelding time to respond (Jul 8)

FOCUS
Stalls on far side of stands' side track except for 7.35 & 8.40, centre. No more than a fair handicap, though it was at least competitive for the level and there's no reason the form won't hold up. The winner is rated back to his best.

3362 E B F ARAAFA MAIDEN FILLIES' STKS 6f
6:30 (6:31) (Class 4) 2-Y-O **£4,533** (£1,348; £674; £336) **Stalls** Low

Form RPR

1 **Discourse (USA)** 2-9-0 0 .... AhmedAjtebi 4 88+
(Mahmood Al Zarooni) *hld up: hdwy over 2f out: rdn to chse ldr and hung lft over 1f out: r.o to ld post* **16/1**

2 **2** *shd* **Gamilati**[28] [2467] 2-9-0 0 .... MickaelBarzalona 10 88+
(Mahmood Al Zarooni) *led: rdn over 1f out: hdd post* **2/5**[1]

3 5 **Appointee (IRE)** 2-9-0 0 .... NickyMackay 11 73+
(John Gosden) *chsd ldrs: rdn and hung lft over 1f out: wknd fnl f* **10/1**[3]

4 2 1/2 **Traveller's Tales** 2-9-0 0 .... RyanMoore 5 65+
(Richard Hannon) *chsd ldrs: rdn over 2f out: wknd fnl f* **14/1**

5 *hd* **Cheworee** 2-9-0 0 .... NeilCallan 7 65+
(David Elsworth) *s.i.s: hld up: swtchd rt over 1f out: styd on ins fnl f: nvr trbld ldrs* **50/1**

4 **6** *shd* **Proud Pearl (USA)**[16] [2811] 2-9-0 0 .... MartinDwyer 1 64
(Brian Meehan) *chsd ldrs: rdn over 2f out: wknd ins fnl f* **7/2**[2]

7 1 3/4 **Plum Bay** 2-9-0 0 .... AndreaAtzeni 2 59
(David Elsworth) *s.i.s: in rr: rdn over 2f out: styd on ins fnl f: nvr on terms* **50/1**

8 1/2 **Superinjunction** 2-9-0 0 .... ShaneKelly 3 58
(Brian Meehan) *dwlt: hdwy 1/2-way: rdn over 2f out: wknd over 1f out* **25/1**

9 1/2 **Elbow Beach** 2-9-0 0 .... StevieDonohoe 6 56
(Dr Jon Scargill) *mid-div: rdn over 2f out: sn wknd* **50/1**

0 **10** 1/2 **Dine Out**[24] [2580] 2-8-9 0 .... AshleyMorgan(5) 9 55
(Mark H Tompkins) *chsd ldrs: rdn over 1f out: wknd fnl f* **25/1**

11 2 1/2 **Possibly** 2-9-0 0 .... JackMitchell 12 47
(Peter Chapple-Hyam) *hld up: sme hdwy whn hmpd over 1f out: nt rcvr* **66/1**

1m 13.62s (1.12) **Going Correction** -0.075s/f (Good) **11** Ran SP% **[illegible]**
Speed ratings (Par 92): **89,88,82,78,78 78,76,75,74,74 70**
Tote Swingers: 1&2 £3.10, 1&3 £8.10, 2&3 £1.50 CSF £25.06 TOTE £29.50: £5.10, £1.10, £2.70; EX 27.20.
Owner Godolphin **Bred** Darley **Trained** Newmarket, Suffolk

FOCUS
Form to view positively, at least in terms of the leading pair, stablemates who pulled well clear.

NOTEBOOK
Discourse(USA), a Street Cry half-sister to a US Grade 2 winner, made a highly promising start to her career, overcoming greenness to nail her stablemate on the line, really picking up once she got the hang of things. She has plenty of size about her and looks a smart prospect, one who should be up to making her presence felt in Listed/Pattern company before long. (op 20-1)
Gamilati's debut represents strong form and she'll be going one better before long, doing nothing wrong here, just unfortunate to bump into one. (op 8-15 tchd 4-7 in places and 8-13 in a place)
Appointee(IRE), an attractive daughter of Exceed And Excel, made an encouraging debut and should build on this, certainly showing signs of inexperience off the bridle (hung left). (tchd 9-1)
Traveller's Tales, a filly by Cape Cross, is on the small side so it remains to be seen if she's open to as much improvement as some, but this was clearly a fair introduction, sticking to her task in a manner which suggests she'll benefit from a step up to 7f. (op 16-1)
Cheworee was clearly green (started slowly) but shaped promisingly by the finish and could be up to going close at one of the smaller tracks next time with anything like normal improvement.
Proud Pearl(USA) hails from a yard whose inmates invariably come on for their first starts but she bucked the trend, this being nowhere near as promising as her debut at Haydock. It's still early days, though. (op 4-1)
Superinjunction didn't shape with any immediate promise but is entitled to come on for this initial experience.
Possibly, an Exceed And Excel half-sister to useful stayer Som Tala, was better than the result suggests on her debut, threatening to make some headway towards the rail when hampered over 1f out. She'll leave this bare form behind next time.

3363 DANWOOD CLAIMING STKS 1m
7:05 (7:05) (Class 5) 3-Y-O **£2,590** (£770; £385; £192) **Stalls** Low

Form RPR

1314 **1** **Certral**[23] [2615] 3-8-6 68 .... PaulPickard(3) 10 75
(Brian Ellison) *chsd ldrs: led 1f out: r.o wl* **7/4**[1]

3110 **2** 3 1/4 **Flying Phoenix**[15] [2850] 3-8-5 67 ow1 .... MartinDwyer 7 63
(William Haggas) *hmpd s: sn led: rdn: edgd rt and hdd 1f out: styd on same pce* **7/1**

21-2 **3** 2 1/4 **Janet's Pearl (IRE)**[20] [2728] 3-8-6 70 .... TadhgO'Shea 2 59
(Ann Duffield) *a.p: chsd ldr 3f out: rdn and ev ch over 1f out: no ex ins fnl f* **4/1**[2]

45-0 **4** 1 1/2 **Enlightening (IRE)**[35] [2256] 3-8-9 72 .... RyanMoore 6 58
(Richard Hannon) *s.i.s and hmpd s: hld up: plld hrd: hdwy over 2f out: rdn over 1f out: wknd ins fnl f* **7/1**

40-0 **5** 1 1/4 **Piccarello**[11] [3002] 3-8-11 69 .... KierenFallon 4 57
(Mark H Tompkins) *hld up in tch: rdn and hung rt over 2f out: wknd over 1f out* **16/1**

3-00 **6** 10 **Green Pearl (IRE)**[57] [1626] 3-8-9 72 .... StevieDonohoe 3 31
(Ralph Beckett) *s.i.s and hmpd s: hld up: rdn and wknd over 2f out* **16/1**

6516 **7** 2 1/4 **Malice Or Mischief (IRE)**[4] [3231] 3-9-5 80 .... NeilCallan 1 36
(Tony Carroll) *prom: rdn over 2f out: wknd over 1f out* **5/1**[3]

2203 **8** 24 **Back For Tea (IRE)**[11] [2418] 3-8-9 48 .... KirstyMilczarek 8 —
(Phil McEntee) *wnt rt s: chsd ldr 5f: sn rdn and wknd: eased over 1f out: t.o* **80/1**

40-0 **9** 17 **Dancerella**[42] [2068] 3-8-4 0 .... NickyMackay 5 —
(David Elsworth) *s.i.s and hmpd s: hld up: rdn 1/2-way: wknd over 2f out: eased over 1f out: t.o* **33/1**

1m 39.55s (-0.45) **Going Correction** -0.075s/f (Good) **9** Ran SP% **114.0**
Speed ratings (Par 99): **99,95,93,92,90 80,78,54,37**
Tote Swingers: 1&2 £3.60, 1&3 £2.80, 2&3 £5.50 CSF £14.49 TOTE £2.60: £1.50, £1.90, £1.40; EX 15.40.
Owner L S Keys **Bred** Whatton Manor Stud **Trained** Norton, N Yorks

FOCUS
A fair claimer. The runner-up was able to dictate what was probably no more than a modest gallop for much of the way. Doubts over the form but the winner rates a personal best.
Green Pearl(IRE) Official explanation: jockey said gelding lost its action
Back For Tea(IRE) Official explanation: trainer said gelding finished distressed

3364 PLASMOR BLOCKS BY RAIL SILVER ANNIVERSARY H'CAP 1m 5f
7:35 (7:37) (Class 4) (0-80,79) 3-Y-O **£4,533** (£1,348; £674; £336) **Stalls** Centre

Form RPR

003 **1** **Crimson Knight**[16] [2813] 3-8-11 **72** .... LouisBeuzelin(3) 3 83
(Brian Meehan) *hld up: hdwy over 3f out: led over 1f out: rdn out* **12/1**

0-32 **2** 3/4 **Starlight Walk**[32] [2360] 3-9-1 **73** .... RyanMoore 7 83
(Roger Charlton) *chsd ldr tl led 3f out: rdn and hdd over 1f out: styd on* **11/4**[1]

3321 **3** 2 **Cunning Act**[14] [2874] 3-9-4 **76** .... StephenCraine 10 83
(Jonathan Portman) *s.i.s: hld up: hdwy 6f out: rdn and ev ch over 1f out: hung lft ins fnl f: styd on same pce* **13/2**

0-34 **4** 1 **Monopolize**[13] [2930] 3-9-6 **78** .... IanMongan 2 84
(Sir Henry Cecil) *a.p: swtchd lft over 2f out: sn rdn: styd on same pce ins fnl f* **17/2**

-421 **5** 4 1/2 **Mokalif**[15] [2857] 3-8-3 **61** .... (v[1]) HayleyTurner 5 60+
(Michael Bell) *hld up: rdn over 3f out: nt clr run and outpcd over 2f out: styd on ins fnl f* **5/1**[3]

00-0 **6** 14 **Lejaam**[15] [2842] 3-8-8 **66** ow1 .... RichardHills 1 44
(John Dunlop) *chsd ldrs: rdn and ev ch over 2f out: wknd over 1f out* **16/1**

3114 **7** 13 **Szabo's Destiny**[21] [2695] 3-8-13 **71** .... JimmyFortune 4 30
(James Given) *led 10f: sn rdn: wknd and eased over 1f out: t.o* **8/1**

01-5 **8** 7 **Man Of God (IRE)**[35] [2253] 3-9-2 **74** .... (b[1]) NickyMackay 8 22
(John Gosden) *hld up: hdwy over 5f out: rdn over 2f out: wknd and eased over 1f out: t.o* **9/2**[2]

-220 **9** 41 **Prince Freddie**[42] [2076] 3-8-12 **70** .... NeilCallan 9 —
(Philip Kirby) *chsd ldrs: rdn over 4f out: wknd over 3f out: t.o* **16/1**

2m 44.77s (0.77) **Going Correction** -0.075s/f (Good) **9** Ran SP% **115.9**
Speed ratings (Par 101): **94,93,92,91,88 80,72,68,42**
Tote Swingers: 1&2 £10.50, 1&3 £20.30, 2&3 £2.10 CSF £45.35 CT £240.01 TOTE £15.50: £4.50, £1.60, £1.70; EX 84.70.
Owner W A Harrison-Allan **Bred** W A Harrison-Allan **Trained** Manton, Wilts
■ Louis-Philippe Beeuzelin's first winner of the season.

FOCUS
A fairly useful staying handicap. The gallop didn't look any better than modest for a long way but the field still finished quite well strung out. The form is rated on the positive side.
Man Of God(IRE) Official explanation: jockey said colt ran too free

3365 E B F PASTORAL PURSUITS FILLIES' CONDITIONS STKS 6f
8:05 (8:06) (Class 2) 3-Y-O+ **£7,447** (£2,216; £1,107; £553) **Stalls** Low

Form RPR

065- **1** **Puff (IRE)**[272] [6351] 4-8-12 105 .... StevieDonohoe 5 106
(Ralph Beckett) *mde all: hit rails sn after s: rdn and hung rt fr over 1f out: r.o wl* **11/8**[1]

-020 **2** 2 **Aneedah (IRE)**[34] [2298] 3-8-8 97 .... NickyMackay 1 101
(John Gosden) *awkward leaving stalls: a.p: rdn and ev ch over 1f out: styd on same pce ins fnl f* **5/2**[2]

102- **3** 3 1/2 **Wake Up Call**[252] [6887] 5-8-12 92 .... TedDurcan 2 88
(Chris Wall) *trckd ldrs: shkn up over 1f out: styd on same pce* **11/4**[3]

4-00 **4** 3 1/2 **Fleeting Echo**[41] [2099] 4-8-12 91 .... RyanMoore 4 77
(Richard Hannon) *chsd wnr: rdn and ev ch wl over 1f out: wknd and eased ins fnl f* **8/1**

1m 12.26s (-0.24) **Going Correction** -0.075s/f (Good)
WFA 3 from 4yo+ 7lb **4** Ran SP% **108.5**
Speed ratings (Par 104): **98,95,90,86**
CSF £5.06 TOTE £2.70; EX 5.00.
Owner Mr and Mrs David Aykroyd **Bred** Yeomanstown Stud **Trained** Kimpton, Hants

FOCUS
A useful conditions event but only 6lb faster than the earlier 2yo maiden. The winner dictated, sjowing her best form since last year's Fred Darling.

NOTEBOOK
Puff(IRE), whose reappearance had been delayed after suffering an injury in January, had proven her ability to go well fresh when landing the Fred Darling last season and outclassed her rivals on her return. Likely to prove best at up to 7f, she hasn't had much racing for a 4yo and is sure to be up to be making her presence felt back up in grade, at least amongst her own sex. (tchd 13-8)
Aneedah(IRE) wasted little time putting a poor run at Haydock behind her, though comfortably held by the winner after briefly looking a threat over 1f out. (op 11-4 tchd 9-4)
Wake Up Call's trainer felt she'd need her first outing in over eight months and she shaped that way, too, not knocked about once clearly held. She's five now but was still very much on the up last season and it's not out of the question there'll be more to come this time round (still lightly raced). (tchd 5-2)
Fleeting Echo has yet to find her best form this season. (op 7-1)

3366 NGK SPARK PLUGS H'CAP 1m 2f
8:40 (8:40) (Class 4) (0-80,83) 3-Y-O+
£4,361 (£1,306; £653; £326; £163; £81) **Stalls** Centre

Form RPR

3500 **1** **Ellemujie**[14] [2884] 6-10-0 **79** .... (p) ShaneKelly 6 88
(Dean Ivory) *hld up: hdwy over 2f out: swtchd rt over 1f out: led ins fnl f: rdn out* **5/1**[2]

-250 **2** 1 1/4 **Circus Star (USA)**[14] 2874 3-8-6 **69** .... MartinDwyer 4 75
(Brian Meehan) *led: rdn over 1f out: hdd and unable qck ins fnl f* **8/1**

5/ **3** 1/2 **Nobunaga**[86] 3365 6-9-7 **72** .... KierenFallon 7 77
(Venetia Williams) *chsd ldrs: rdn and ev ch fr over 1f out tl no ex wl ins fnl f* **10/1**

1411 **4** 1 3/4 **Ivan Vasilevich (IRE)**[9] 3044 3-8-13 **83** 6ex .... LewisWalsh(7) 9 85
(Jane Chapple-Hyam) *chsd ldr: rdn and ev ch over 2f out: styd on same pce fnl f* **5/1**[2]

0-20 **5** hd **Wiggy Smith**[22] 2649 12-9-8 **78** .... AmyScott(5) 3 79
(Henry Candy) *hld up: hdwy over 3f out: ev ch over 2f out: styd on same pce fnl f* **10/1**

14-3 **6** 3/4 **Indian Valley (USA)**[18] 2771 4-9-9 **74** .... NeilCallan 8 74
(Hugo Palmer) *a.p: rdn and hmpd over 1f out: styd on same pce* **13/2**[3]

-122 **7** 2 1/4 **Chain Of Events**[18] 2769 4-9-11 **76** .... HayleyTurner 2 71
(Neil King) *chsd ldrs: rdn over 2f out: styd on same pce fr over 1f out* **9/2**[1]

4256 **8** 9 **Black Pond (USA)**[21] 2664 3-8-9 **72** .... RichardHills 5 49
(Mark Johnston) *hld up: rdn over 3f out: wknd 2f out* **16/1**

40-0 **9** 11 **Farleigh House (USA)**[61] 235 7-10-0 **79** ....(v[1]) JackMitchell 12 34
(Neil King) *s.i.s: hld up: hdwy over 3f out: rdn and wknd 2f out* **50/1**

0/00 **10** 1 **Phonic (IRE)**[17] 2793 4-9-2 **67** .... JimmyFortune 10 20
(John Dunlop) *hld up: rdn over 3f out: wknd over 2f out* **14/1**

141 **11** 10 **Lord Theo**[146] 352 7-9-7 **77** .... RyanClark(5) 1 10
(Nick Littmoden) *hld up: swtchd rt over 3f out: rdn and wknd over 2f out: t.o* **12/1**

2m 4.30s (-1.20) **Going Correction** -0.075s/f (Good)
WFA 3 from 4yo+ 12lb 11 Ran SP% **116.3**
Speed ratings (Par 105): **101,100,99,98,98 97,95,88,79,78 70**
Tote Swingers: 1&2 £8.70, 1&3 £10.70, 2&3 £39.60 CSF £44.29 CT £386.81 TOTE £6.50: £2.10, £3.00, £3.90; EX 56.50.
Owner Mrs J A Cornwell **Bred** Mrs J A Cornwell **Trained** Radlett, Herts
■ Stewards' Enquiry : Shane Kelly one-day ban: careless riding (Jul 11)

FOCUS
A competitive race of its type. It was well run and there's no reason to doubt the form.
Lord Theo Official explanation: jockey said gelding never travelled

3367 TURFTV H'CAP — 5f
9:10 (9:10) (Class 4) (0-85,84) 3-Y-O+ **£6,476** (£1,927; £963; £481) **Stalls** Low

Form RPR

2041 **1** **Medici Time**[14] 2890 6-9-12 **84** ....(v) TedDurcan 2 95
(Tim Easterby) *hld up: hdwy over 1f out: r.o to ld wl ins fnl f* **7/2**[2]

-300 **2** nk **Lujeanie**[13] 2938 5-9-7 **79** ....(p) NeilCallan 4 89
(Dean Ivory) *trckd ldrs: led over 1f out: edgd rt: rdn and hdd wl ins fnl f* **13/2**

50-0 **3** 2 1/2 **Ryan Style (IRE)**[15] 2832 5-9-1 **76** .... LouisBeuzelin(3) 3 77
(Lisa Williamson) *s.s: hld up: nt clr run 2f out: edgd rt and hmpd over 1f out: sn rdn: styd on same pce* **20/1**

5051 **4** nse **Catfish (IRE)**[13] 2916 3-9-6 **84** .... ShaneKelly 1 83
(Brian Meehan) *hld up: hdwy 1/2-way: rdn and ev ch over 1f out: no ex ins fnl f* **10/3**[1]

2612 **5** 3 **Taurus Twins**[13] 2929 5-9-7 **84** ....(b) HarryBentley(5) 5 81+
(Richard Price) *chsd ldrs: rdn whn hmpd over 1f out: sn hung rt: styd on* **7/2**[2]

-521 **6** 1 3/4 **Chaussini**[15] 2852 4-9-7 **79** .... RoystonFfrench 8 63
(James Toller) *chsd ldrs: rdn over 1f out: wknd ins fnl f* **11/1**

2011 **7** 3/4 **Lucky Art (USA)**[8] 3087 5-9-1 **76** 6ex .... JamesSullivan(3) 7 57
(Ruth Carr) *led: rdn and hdd over 1f out: wknd ins fnl f* **4/1**[3]

0-54 **8** 11 **Cloth Ears**[34] 2303 5-8-0 **65** oh8 .... LeonnaMayor(7) 6 —
(Phil McEntee) *chsd ldr: rdn whn hmpd over 1f out: sn hung rt and wknd* **50/1**

58.70 secs (-0.40) **Going Correction** -0.075s/f (Good)
WFA 3 from 4yo+ 6lb 8 Ran SP% **115.9**
Speed ratings (Par 105): **100,99,95,95,90 87,86,69**
Tote Swingers: 1&2 £5.20, 1&3 £48.00, 2&3 £17.10 CSF £26.84 CT £396.55 TOTE £4.30: £1.40, £2.30, £3.90; EX 32.20.
Owner Mrs C A Hodgetts **Bred** Mrs Fiona Denniff **Trained** Great Habton, N Yorks

FOCUS
A fairly useful sprint. They went hard up front, setting it up for the winner.
T/Jkpt: Not won. T/Plt: £133.40 to a £1 stake. Pool:£61,495.25 - 336.41 winning tickets T/Qpdt: £18.30 to a £1 stake. Pool:£4,247.27 - 171.50 winning tickets CR

3368 - 3370a (Foreign Racing) - See Raceform Interactive

2698 CURRAGH (R-H)
Friday, June 24

OFFICIAL GOING: Yielding changing to soft after race 1 (6.00)

3371a IRISH DAILY MAIL INTERNATIONAL STKS (GROUP 3) — 1m 2f
7:30 (7:32) 3-Y-O+ **£33,642** (£9,849; £4,676; £1,573)

RPR

1 **Famous Name**[33] 2332 6-9-12 117 .... PJSmullen 1 123+
(D K Weld, Ire) *settled in 3rd: hdwy into 2nd under 2f out: pushed out to ld over 1f out: sn clr: easily* **4/5**[1]

2 6 **Jan Vermeer (IRE)**[9] 3031 4-9-9 113 .... JPO'Brien 2 108
(A P O'Brien, Ire) *trckd ldr in 2nd: rdn in 3rd 1 1/2f out: 2nd 1f out: no ch w wnr: kpt on same pce* **5/4**[2]

3 9 **Mid Mon Lady (IRE)**[6] 3197 6-9-6 99 ....(b) FMBerry 4 87+
(H Rogers, Ire) *hld up in rr: rdn and no imp 2f out: kpt on one pce into 3rd ins fnl f* **25/1**

4 4 **Last Crusade (IRE)**[7] 3147 3-8-12 95 ....(b[1]) SeamieHeffernan 3 86
(A P O'Brien, Ire) *led and sn clr: rdn ent st: reduced advantage under 2f out: hdd over 1f out: no ex and wknd* **16/1**[3]

2m 15.41s (1.11) **Going Correction** +0.275s/f (Good)
WFA 3 from 4yo+ 12lb 4 Ran SP% **109.7**
Speed ratings: **106,101,94,90**
CSF £2.11 TOTE £1.60; DF 2.00.
Owner K Abdulla **Bred** Juddmonte Farms Ltd **Trained** The Curragh, Co Kildare

FOCUS
The easy winner is rated to his best.

NOTEBOOK
Famous Name quickened up inside the final 2f impressively and had far too much class for his main market rival. Everything worked in his favour, but he had to take advantage and that he did without any fuss. The plan remains to try and win a Group 1. (op 4/6 tchd 9/10)
Jan Vermeer(IRE) was just totally out-matched the way the race was run. His best chance was to try and make something of a test of stamina about it, but the way the two principals just sat ten lengths off the pacemaker was only going to suit one horse. It was another case for whatever reason of pacemaking tactics being totally ineffective. (op 11/8 tchd 6/4)
Mid Mon Lady(IRE) was always likely to be ridden for third place, the best placing she was entitled to, and that worked.
Last Crusade(IRE) set the race up. (op 14/1 tchd 20/1)

3372 - 3374a (Foreign Racing) - See Raceform Interactive

3336 CHESTER (L-H)
Saturday, June 25

OFFICIAL GOING: Soft (6.1)
Wind: moderate 1/2 against Weather: overcast

3375 TRAFFORD CENTRE ALWAYS AHEAD NOVICE STKS — 5f 16y
2:05 (2:06) (Class 4) 2-Y-O **£4,533** (£1,348; £674; £336) **Stalls** Low

Form RPR

621 **1** **Red Art (IRE)**[12] 2997 2-9-5 0 .... RobertWinston 6 89+
(B W Hills) *trckd ldrs: effrt over 2f out: n.m.r over 1f out: styd on wl to ld fnl 75yds* **7/4**[2]

1305 **2** 3/4 **Signifer (IRE)**[9] 3064 2-8-13 0 .... MartinHarley(3) 4 83
(Mick Channon) *trckd ldr: led narrowly jst ins fnl f: hdd and no ex clsng stages* **6/4**[1]

5315 **3** 2 3/4 **Middleton Flyer (IRE)**[40] 2154 2-8-4 0 .... MatthewCosham(5) 7 66
(David Evans) *chsd ldrs on outside: outpcd 2f out: styd on to take 3rd clsng stages* **16/1**

0323 **4** 3/4 **Beau Mistral (IRE)**[5] 3237 2-8-6 0 .... PatrickDonaghy(3) 2 64
(Paul Green) *led: hdd jst ins fnl f: wknd clsng stages* **7/1**

4523 **5** 1 1/2 **Courtland King (IRE)**[14] 2907 2-9-0 0 ....(t) RoystonFfrench 1 63
(David Evans) *trckd ldrs: sn pushed along: wknd fnl f* **6/1**[3]

00 **6** 6 **Red Samantha (IRE)**[11] 3022 2-8-9 0 .... PatrickMathers 5 37
(Alan Berry) *sn outpcd and in rr: bhd fnl 2f* **100/1**

64.65 secs (3.65) **Going Correction** +0.725s/f (Yiel) 6 Ran SP% **110.0**
Speed ratings (Par 95): **99,97,93,92,89 80**
Tote Swingers: 1&2 £1.02, 1&3 £5.10, 2&3 £4.70 CSF £4.52 TOTE £2.40: £1.50, £1.40; EX 3.10.
Owner Des Anderson & R J Arculli **Bred** H Q Spooner **Trained** Lambourn, Berks

FOCUS
Rail out 9yds from 6f pole to 1.5f with a drop in at that point. Races of up to 7f increased by 28yds, 10f by 45yds, 11f by 53yds and 12f by 57yds. An interesting novice stakes in which the front pair drew clear close home. Straightforward form.

NOTEBOOK
Red Art(IRE) had shown some cut was no problem when second at Ayr previously and he stayed on strongly under a good ride to win with a bit in hand. This was a decent effort considering he was conceding 3lb or more all round. He's clearly progressing and ought to get an extra furlong. (op 6-4 tchd 15-8)
Signifer(IRE) looked the one to beat, especially in receipt of weight, but the winner proved far too strong in the final 50 yards. He gives the form a solid look. (op 15-8, tchd 9-4 in places)
Middleton Flyer(IRE), who had won a lowly seller two starts ago, had no trouble with the softer going here and kept on into third. (tchd 12-1)
Beau Mistral(IRE) got the lead but didn't have the class to see it out. (tchd 6-1 and 15-2)
Courtland King(IRE) found this tougher than the course maiden in which he was third last time. (tchd 13-2)

3376 TRAFFORD CENTRE HIGH HEEL H'CAP — 1m 4f 66y
2:35 (2:35) (Class 4) (0-85,85) 3-Y-O **£5,180** (£1,541; £770; £384) **Stalls** Low

Form RPR

1640 **1** **Gottany O'S**[21] 2711 3-8-10 **77** .... MartinHarley(3) 4 86
(Mick Channon) *in rr: hdwy on ins over 3f out: nt clr run and swtchd ins over 1f out: chal ins fnl f: led nr fin* **11/1**

1110 **2** hd **Lexi's Boy (IRE)**[21] 2726 3-8-7 **76** .... JulieBurke(5) 5 85
(Kevin Ryan) *chsd ldrs: chal over 2f out: led 1f out: hdd cl home* **11/1**

-363 **3** 1 3/4 **Unex Renoir**[13] 2956 3-9-1 **82** .... LouisBeuzelin(3) 2 88
(John Gosden) *in rr: hdwy over 2f out: styd on same pce fnl f: edgd lft nr fin* **8/1**

1-14 **4** 1 1/4 **Swift Alhaarth (IRE)**[21] 2726 3-9-5 **83** .... RobertWinston 1 88
(Mark Johnston) *trckd ldrs: effrt 2f out: sn upsides: kpt on same pce fnl f: hld whn hmpd nr fin* **4/1**[1]

0-12 **5** 4 1/2 **Area Fifty One**[17] 2819 3-8-9 **78** .... JamesRogers(5) 8 75
(William Muir) *led: hdd 1f out: sn wknd* **13/2**[3]

6-43 **6** 1 3/4 **Time To Work (IRE)**[35] 2287 3-9-3 **84** .... SimonPearce(3) 10 78
(Andrew Balding) *mid-div: drvn 5f out: kpt on fnl 2f: nvr a factor* **4/1**[1]

1-22 **7** 1/2 **Haylaman (IRE)**[37] 2230 3-9-7 **85** ....(p) SebSanders 3 78
(Ed Dunlop) *mid-div: hmpd and lost pl 8f out: hdwy on outside over 3f out: wknd fnl f* **9/2**[2]

-505 **8** 6 **Layla's King**[13] 2957 3-8-2 **66** .... AndrewHeffernan 6 49
(Richard Fahey) *in rr: hdwy 4f out: wknd over 2f out* **22/1**

14-6 **9** hd **Top Care (USA)**[16] 2833 3-8-13 **77** .... RoystonFfrench 9 60
(Mark Johnston) *chsd ldrs: lost pl 5f out: sn bhd* **25/1**

-624 **10** 69 **Oasis Storm**[30] 2435 3-8-12 **79** .... SeanLevey(3) 7 —
(Michael Dods) *chsd ldrs: drvn 6f out: sn lost pl and bhd: virtually p.u: t.o* **12/1**

2m 46.09s (7.59) **Going Correction** +0.725s/f (Yiel) 10 Ran SP% **115.2**
Speed ratings (Par 101): **103,102,101,100,97 96,96,92,92,46**
Tote Swingers: 1&2 £21.60, 1&3 £33.80, 2&3 £30.70 CSF £123.80 CT £1023.67 TOTE £12.90: £4.10, £2.40, £2.50; EX 179.60.
Owner Dr Marwan Koukash **Bred** Phil Jen Racing **Trained** West Ilsley, Berks
■ Stewards' Enquiry : Louis Beuzelin one-day ban: careless riding (Jul 11)

FOCUS
A decent middle-distance 3yo handicap but the ground was clearly a factor. The fourth helps with ths standard.
Time To Work(IRE) Official explanation: jockey said gelding was unsuited by the run of the race
Oasis Storm Official explanation: jockey said colt had no more to give

3377 TRAFFORD CENTRE A-LIST APP MAIDEN STKS — 1m 2f 75y
3:10 (3:10) (Class 4) 3-Y-O+ **£5,180** (£1,541; £770; £384) **Stalls** High

Form RPR

0 **1** **Aiken**[14] 2930 3-9-1 0 .... SebSanders 1 80+
(John Gosden) *dwlt: hdwy over 2f out: chsd ldr over 1f out: styd on strly to ld nr fin* **5/2**[1]

-342 **2** 1/2 **Number Theory**[16] 2835 3-8-8 69 .... LucyKBarry(7) 3 79
(John Holt) *led 2f: led over 7f out: qcknd 6f out: hdd nr fin* **7/2**[2]

0-4 **3** 4 **Quails Hollow (IRE)**[29] 2469 3-9-1 0 .... LiamJones 2 74+
(William Haggas) *s.i.s: sn trcking ldrs: hmpd over 3f out: nt clr run over 2f out: styd on to take 3rd nr fin* **5/2**[1]

54 **4** 1/2 **Mill Mick**[24] 2621 4-9-13 0 .... StephenCraine 6 70
(John Mackie) *hld up: hdwy 3f out: sn trckingd ldrs: on same pce fnl 2f* **14/1**

4-55 **5** *nk* **Musnad (USA)**[28] 2511 3-9-1 75 RobertWinston 4 69
(B W Hills) *hld up: hdwy to trck ldrs after 4f: wnt 2nd over 3f out: kpt on one pce over 1f out* **4/1**[3]
4-0 **6** *17* **Palagonia**[7] 3167 3-9-1 0 RoystonFfrench 5 35
(Mark Johnston) *w ldr: led after 2f: hdd over 7f out: drvn over 4f out: lost pl over 2f out: sn bhd* **11/1**

2m 20.12s (8.92) **Going Correction** +0.725s/f (Yiel)
WFA 3 from 4yo 12lb **6** Ran SP% **114.4**
Speed ratings (Par 105): **93,92,89,89,88 75**
Tote Swingers: 1&2 £3.30, 1&3 £1.80, 2&3 £3.10 CSF £11.90 TOTE £3.70: £2.00, £1.50; EX 14.90.
Owner George Strawbridge **Bred** George Strawbridge **Trained** Newmarket, Suffolk

FOCUS
A maiden that was there for the taking. A rather muddling race, with the form set around the runner-up. The winner and third are better than the bare form.
Quails Hollow(IRE) Official explanation: jockey said gelding was denied

3378 TRAFFORD CENTRE GIFT CARD H'CAP 7f 2y
3:45 (3:45) (Class 2) (0-100,92) 3-Y-**£12,616** (£3,776; £1,888; £944; £470) **Stalls** Low

Form RPR
3313 **1** **Bertiewhittle**[14] 2937 3-8-8 **79** GrahamGibbons 1 88+
(David Barron) *mid-div: hdwy over 2f out: led over 1f out: styd on wl* **4/1**[2]
-004 **2** *2* **Major Conquest (IRE)**[22] 2684 3-8-10 **81** ow3 SebSanders 2 83
(J W Hills) *trckd ldrs: drvn and dropped bk to rr after 2f: hdwy to chse ldrs whn bmpd over 1f out: kpt on wl ins fnl f* **16/1**
3211 **3** *shd* **Chosen Character (IRE)**[29] 2477 3-8-11 **82**(vt) RussKennemore 7 84
(Tom Dascombe) *dwlt: swtchd lft s: in rr: hdwy and nt clr run over 2f out: bmpd over 1f out: styd on wl fnl f* **17/2**
0421 **4** *3 1/4* **Kingscroft (IRE)**[8] 3134 3-9-0 **85** LiamJones 8 78
(Mark Johnston) *mid-div: hdwy 3f out: sn chsng ldrs: kpt on same pce over 1f out* **8/1**
0-60 **5** *3/4* **Waking Warrior**[14] 2934 3-8-12 **88** JulieBurke(5) 6 79
(Kevin Ryan) *led: hdd appr fnl f: wknd fnl 150yds* **20/1**
2061 **6** *nk* **Fred Willetts (IRE)**[14] 2908 3-9-2 **92**(v) MatthewCosham(5) 9 83
(David Evans) *w ldrs: edgd lft over 1f out: sn wknd* **11/1**
6-1 **7** *1 1/4* **Chilled**[26] 2568 3-8-11 **85** LouisBeuzelin(3) 3 72+
(Sir Michael Stoute) *trckd ldrs on ins: t.k.h: nt clr run: swtchd rt and hmpd over 1f out: nt rcvr: wknd ins fnl f* **5/4**[1]
6-31 **8** *42* **Power Punch (IRE)**[17] 2802 3-8-9 **80** RobertWinston 4 —
(B W Hills) *trckd ldrs: drvn over 3f out: sn lost pl: bhd and eased over 1f out: t.o* **7/1**[3]

1m 30.98s (4.48) **Going Correction** +0.725s/f (Yiel) **8** Ran SP% **117.6**
Speed ratings (Par 105): **103,100,100,96,96 95,94,46**
Tote Swingers: 1&2 £16.80, 1&3 £4.20, 2&3 £20.50 CSF £65.33 CT £524.85 TOTE £4.70: £1.40, £4.30, £2.90; EX 53.60.
Owner Norton Common Farm Racing **Bred** E Dafydd **Trained** Maunby, N Yorks
■ Stewards' Enquiry : Louis Beuzelin three-day ban: careless riding (Jul 12-14)

FOCUS
A good handicap in which it paid to come from off the pace. Ordinary form for the grade, with the favourite disappointing.

NOTEBOOK
Bertiewhittle struggled to go the gallop early but came strong in the straight and shot clear for a comfortable success.\n\x\x He hasn't been out of the first three in seven starts this season and had shown as a juvenile that a soft surface was no bother. Although 7lb higher than when winning at Musselburgh two starts ago, he's clearly progressing and is versatile ground-wise, suggesting he'll continue to give a good account. (tchd 7-2 and 9-2)
Major Conquest(IRE), who lost his early pitch, picked up again and stayed on well into second. He's on a career-low mark and can soon be back winning for a yard enjoying a good season. (op 20-1)
Chosen Character(IRE) was up another 6lb and couldn't cope with the drop to 7f, staying on without threatening to win. (op 8-1 tchd 10-1)
Kingscroft(IRE) goes well here and had recently won off 3lb lower at Newmarket. He kept on better than anything else that had been in the front half of the field early and may still have more to offer. (op 7-1 tchd 6-1)
Waking Warrior, trying 7f for the first time, took them along at too brisk a pace early and ultimately suffered. (op 10-1)
Fred Willetts(IRE) was unable to confirm last-time-out course form with Kingscroft. (tchd 12-1)
Chilled was too keen in tracking the early pace and found little once switched to challenge turning in, a notable bump not helping either. This effort can be ignored. (op 7-4, tchd 2-1in places)
Power Punch(IRE) was never travelling and failed to run his race, which was disappointing considering he has course form.

3379 TRAFFORD CENTRE SUMMER FASHION H'CAP 5f 16y
4:20 (4:20) (Class 3) (0-90,89) 3-Y-O-**£8,200** (£2,454; £1,227; £613; £305) **Stalls** Low

Form RPR
0630 **1** **Duchess Dora (IRE)**[15] 2890 4-9-3 **85** LeeTopliss(5) 7 96
(John Quinn) *wnt rt s: sn chsng ldrs: led jst ins fnl f: styd on wl* **15/2**
-000 **2** *1 3/4* **Foxy Music**[3] 3279 7-9-8 **85** SebSanders 4 90
(Eric Alston) *led: hdd jst ins fnl f: kpt on same pce* **13/2**[2]
0331 **3** *nk* **Lost In Paris (IRE)**[22] 2694 5-9-10 **87**(p) AndrewElliott 9 91+
(Tim Easterby) *chsd ldrs: outpcd over 2f out: styd on wl fnl f* **8/1**
1002 **4** *nse* **Oldjoesaid**[7] 3160 7-9-7 **84** StephenCraine 5 87
(Kevin Ryan) *dwlt: hld up in rr: hdwy 2f out: edgd rt: styd on same pce fnl f* **4/1**[1]
0400 **5** *1/2* **Baby Strange**[13] 2954 7-9-9 **89** SeanLevey(3) 2 91
(Derek Shaw) *hld up in rr: detached in last 3f out: hdwy and swtchd lft over 1f out: kpt on: nvr rchd ldrs* **7/1**[3]
0004 **6** *3/4* **Star Rover (IRE)**[13] 2954 4-9-5 **87**(v) MatthewCosham(5) 10 86
(David Evans) *swtchd rt after s: towards rr: hdwy over 1f out: keeping on same pce whn n.m.r nr fin* **10/1**
0130 **7** *1/2* **Tillys Tale**[7] 3166 4-8-12 **75** RussKennemore 3 72
(Paul Midgley) *chsd ldr: grad wknd fnl f* **16/1**
003 **8** *1* **Cruise Tothelimit (IRE)**[5] 3239 3-8-1 **73** ow1 LouisBeuzelin(3) 6 67
(Patrick Morris) *chsd ldrs: outpcd over 1f out: kpt on fnl 150yds* **33/1**
-150 **9** *nk* **Lucky Numbers (IRE)**[42] 2117 5-9-8 **88** PatrickDonaghy(3) 8 80
(Paul Green) *bmpd s: in rr: hdwy over 2f out: hmpd over 1f out: kpt on: nvr a factor* **18/1**
3045 **10** *1* **Whozthecat (IRE)**[13] 2954 4-9-6 **88**(v) NeilFarley(5) 1 77
(Declan Carroll) *sn chsng ldrs: chal on ins over 1f out: wknd last 150yds* **4/1**[1]
4205 **11** *2* **The Nifty Fox**[7] 3160 7-9-7 **84**(v) GrahamGibbons 11 66+
(Tim Easterby) *in rr: nvr a factor: eased towards fin* **16/1**

63.64 secs (2.64) **Going Correction** +0.725s/f (Yiel)
WFA 3 from 4yo+ 6lb **11** Ran SP% **117.8**
Speed ratings (Par 107): **107,104,103,103,102 101,100,99,98,97 93**
Tote Swingers: 1&2 £14.10, 1&3 £13.70, 2&3 £9.90 CSF £55.74 CT £412.94 TOTE £8.80: £2.80, £2.30, £2.50; EX 67.20.
Owner The Clay Family **Bred** Glending Bloodstock **Trained** Settrington, N Yorks
■ Stewards' Enquiry : Stephen Craine one-day ban: careless riding (Jul 11)

FOCUS
A typically open sprint handicap for the cours but few got involved. The winner took advantage of her reduced mark and is rated back to last year's form.

NOTEBOOK
Duchess Dora(IRE) hadn't won in 14 months, but her mark had dropped notably as a result and she fairly whizzed clear for a ready success. Although she'll go back up the weights, she's won and run well off marks in the mid-90s and should be capable of continuing to give a good account. (op 8-1)
Foxy Music was just 2lb higher than when winning over C&D on soft ground in September and it was no surprise to see him run up to something like his best. (op 6-1 tchd 7-1)
Lost In Paris(IRE) had gone up 7lb for winning at Musselburgh and did well considering he was moderately drawn and couldn't race as prominently as he likes. (op 13-2)
Oldjoesaid handles these conditions and was going on in the straight but never got close enough to challenge. (op 9-2)
Baby Strange was never likely to capitalise on his low draw, getting well back having struggled to go the gallop. He fairly flew home and will have caught the eye of many for next time. (op 15-2)
Star Rover(IRE), drawn wide, has still to win this season. (op 11-1 tchd 12-1)
Whozthecat(IRE) failed to capitalise on stall one and was disappointing. Official explanation: jockey said gelding ran flat (op 5-1)

3380 IGI WALLCOVERINGS CLAIMING STKS 1m 2f 75y
4:55 (4:56) (Class 5) 3-Y-O+ **£4,047** (£1,204; £601; £300) **Stalls** High

Form RPR
4040 **1** **Granny McPhee**[14] 2906 5-8-7 80 NatashaEaton(7) 6 69
(Alan Bailey) *dwlt: hld up: stdy hdwy over 3f out: str run on wd outside over 1f out: hung lft: styd on to ld last 75yds* **11/4**[2]
040 **2** *2* **Georgebernardshaw (IRE)**[35] 2282 6-9-0 85 LeeTopliss(5) 3 70
(David Simcock) *led: wnt clr over 2f out: hdd and no ex clsng stages* **5/4**[1]
5-32 **3** *2 3/4* **Lang Shining (IRE)**[33] 2359 7-9-3 79 SebSanders 2 62
(Jamie Osborne) *trckd ldrs: effrt 4f out: hung lft and styd on to take 3rd clsng stages* **3/1**[3]
465- **4** *1/2* **Bright Applause**[268] 6500 3-8-5 68 AndrewElliott 5 61
(Brian Baugh) *chsd ldr: drvn over 4f out: one pce over 1f out* **16/1**
00-0 **5** *2* **Grethel (IRE)**[14] 2912 7-8-7 35 DanielleMcCreery(5) 4 52?
(Alan Berry) *dwlt: hld up: outpcd 4f out: one pce fnl 2f* **50/1**
5643 **6** *3 3/4* **Dream Of Fortune (IRE)**[5] 3240 7-8-12 60(bt) MatthewCosham(5) 1 50
(David Evans) *chsd ldrs: drvn 4f out: wknd over 1f out* **10/1**

2m 22.3s (11.10) **Going Correction** +0.725s/f (Yiel)
WFA 3 from 5yo+ 12lb **6** Ran SP% **113.0**
Speed ratings (Par 103): **84,82,80,79,78 75**
Tote Swingers: 1&2 £1.10, 1&3 £2.50, 2&3 £1.50 CSF £6.70 TOTE £3.70: £1.70, £1.30; EX 7.00.

Owner Middleham Park Racing XXVI & Alan Bailey **Bred** Sugar Puss Corporation **Trained** Newmarket, Suffolk

FOCUS
An interesting claimer but muddling form. The winner did not need to match her recent best.

3381 CRUISE NIGHTSPOT H'CAP 1m 3f 79y
5:30 (5:31) (Class 4) (0-85,83) 4-Y-O+ **£5,180** (£1,541; £770; £384) **Stalls** Low

Form RPR
0-11 **1** **Kiama Bay (IRE)**[87] 1036 5-8-9 **80** LeeTopliss(5) 6 98+
(John Quinn) *hld up: hdwy over 4f out: sn chsng ldrs: qcknd on outside to ld 2f out: sn drvn wl clr: heavily eased last 75yds* **9/4**[1]
0-06 **2** *11* **Thin Red Line (IRE)**[24] 2604 5-9-0 **83** SeanLevey(3) 2 79
(Michael Dods) *sn trcking ldrs: drvn over 4f out: styd on over 1f out: tk modest 2nd last 75yds* **3/1**[2]
205 **3** *1/2* **High Figurine (IRE)**[22] 2676 4-9-1 **81** LiamJones 4 76
(William Haggas) *led: qcknd over 4f out: drvn 3f out: hdd 2f out: sn edgd lft: one pce fnl f* **9/4**[1]
0100 **4** *3/4* **Lovers Causeway (USA)**[43] 2071 4-9-1 **81**(v) AndrewElliott 1 75
(Mark Johnston) *trckd ldrs: drvn 6f out: nt clr run on ins over 1f out: kpt on one pce* **17/2**
0005 **5** *2 3/4* **Mister Angry (IRE)**[17] 2812 4-9-0 **83** LouisBeuzelin(3) 3 72
(Mark Johnston) *hld up: drvn over 4f out: one pce fnl 3f* **13/2**[3]

2m 35.1s (10.30) **Going Correction** +0.725s/f (Yiel) **5** Ran SP% **110.4**
Speed ratings (Par 105): **91,83,82,82,80**
CSF £9.28 TOTE £3.10: £1.80, £2.20; EX 9.70.
Owner Dr Marwan Koukash **Bred** Tipper House Stud **Trained** Settrington, N Yorks

FOCUS
This proved rather uncompetitive. Guessy form, with the progressive winner rated up 10lb which could underestimate.
T/Plt: £286.00 to a £1 stake. Pool:£70,875.14 - 180.90 winning tickets T/Qpdt: £46.30 to a £1 stake. Pool:£4,174.64 - 66.65 winning tickets WG

3342 DONCASTER (L-H)
Saturday, June 25

OFFICIAL GOING: Good to firm (6.7)
Wind: Moderate, against. Weather: Cloudy and sunny periods

3382 CROWNHOTEL-BAWTRY.COM MAIDEN STKS 7f
6:10 (6:11) (Class 5) 2-Y-O **£2,914** (£867; £433; £216) **Stalls** High

Form RPR
1 **Pearl Charm (USA)** 2-9-3 0 RobertWinston 8 84+
(Richard Hannon) *hld up: hdwy 3f out: swtchd rt and qcknd to ld 1 1/2f out: rn green ins fnl f: pushed out* **11/4**[1]
2 *1* **Sunnybridge Boy (IRE)** 2-9-3 0 AndrewHeffernan 5 83+
(Richard Fahey) *in tch: effrt whn n.m.r and rn green over 2f out: swtchd rt and rdn to chse wnr ent fnl f: sn wandered: kpt on towards fin* **10/1**
3 *6* **Hurricane Emerald (IRE)** 2-9-3 0 HughBowman 1 66+
(Mark Johnston) *chsd ldrs on outer: rdn along and outpcd 3f out: rn green but styd on fr over 1f out: edgd rt ins fnl f* **5/1**[2]
4 *1 1/4* **Magic Bounty** 2-9-3 0 DuranFentiman 10 62
(Tim Easterby) *trckd ldrs: hdwy 3f out: cl up 2f out: sn rdn and one pce fr over 1f out* **22/1**
5 *1* **Right Divine (IRE)** 2-9-3 0 EddieCreighton 7 60
(Brian Meehan) *trckd ldrs: effrt 3f out: rdn along 2f out and grad wknd* **25/1**
65 **6** *3/4* **Koalition (IRE)**[12] 2983 2-9-3 0 GregFairley 6 58
(Deborah Sanderson) *led: rdn along wl over 2f out: drvn and hdd 1 1/2f out: grad wknd: n.m.r ins fnl f* **9/1**
0 **7** *1 1/2* **Sir Elmo (IRE)**[12] 2983 2-9-3 0 RoystonFfrench 3 54
(Declan Carroll) *prom: rdn along wl over 2f out: sn wknd* **18/1**

8 *shd* **Catchy Tune (IRE)** 2-9-3 0 RichardMullen 4 54
(David Brown) *towards rr: effrt and sme hdwy 1/2-way: sn rdn along and wknd* **13/2**[3]

9 4 1/2 **Dark Celt (IRE)** 2-9-3 0 RobbieFitzpatrick 2 43
(Tim Pitt) *s.i.s: a bhd* **28/1**

10 4 1/2 **Sanad (IRE)** 2-9-3 0 TadhgO'Shea 9 32
(Brian Meehan) *prom: cl up 1/2-way: rdn along wl over 2f out: sn wknd* **5/1**[2]

11 2 **Beyond Hubris (IRE)** 2-9-3 0 MickyFenton 11 27
(Tom Tate) *a in rr* **10/1**

1m 30.58s (4.28) **Going Correction** +0.225s/f (Good) **11** Ran SP% **118.4**
Speed ratings (Par 93): **84,82,76,74,73 72,70,70,65,60 58**
Tote Swingers:1&2:£6.20, 2&3:£13.60, 1&3:£1.40 CSF £31.08 TOTE £3.20: £2.00, £3.70, £1.90; EX 26.90.
Owner Pearl Bloodstock Ltd **Bred** Kilroy Thoroughbred Partnership **Trained** East Everleigh, Wilts

FOCUS
Probably an up-to-scratch renewal of this maiden, with the first three home representing powerful stables. The initial pace was steady as the runners ignored the stands rail and raced more towards the centre. The first two were clear and their efforts have been rated positively.

NOTEBOOK
Pearl Charm(USA) ◆, who cost $155,000 as a yearling and is a brother to a Grade 3 winner in USA, made an impressive debut, soon in rear after getting impeded at the start but making very smooth headway at halfway and then coming clear under a hand ride despite looking noticeably green. He's sure to improve, and looks a useful prospect. (op 7-2)
Sunnybridge Boy(IRE), a half brother to the Irish 9.5f winner Born To Excel out of a mare that stayed 1m4f, made almost as promising a debut as the winner, losing his place at halfway but learning as he went along and gradually reducing the gap to the winner without seriously threatening to go one better. He ought to have little trouble winning a similar event in the North. (op 9-1 tchd 8-1 and 11-1)
Hurricane Emerald(IRE), a colt by Hurricane Run, shaped nicely on his debut despite looking extremely green, caught badly flat-footed when the pace increased at halfway when probably not helped by racing widest of all, but then steadily passing rival after rival looking something of a strong-galloping sort. He's another bound to improve. (op 11-2 tchd 7-1)
Magic Bounty, a gelding by Bahamian Bounty out of a mare still looking for her first winner, made an adequate debut for his in-form yard, albeit tending to spoil his effort by carrying his head to one side and tending to hang left. That said, it could have been greenness and he's entitled to improve. (tchd 20-1 and 25-1)
Right Divine(IRE), a gelding by Verglas and a brother to the 1m2f winner Silverglas, fetched 56,000 guineas as a yearling but right now looks one for the longer term, outpaced when the race began in earnest before keeping on in the closing stages. He's from a yard whose youngsters tend to improve, and he should do better next time. (op 40-1)
Koalition(IRE) hadn't shown a great deal in maidens at Beverley and Carlisle, and probably owed his finishing position up in trip here to being allowed to set a steady pace as much as anything else. His nursery mark might suffer as a result. (op 15-2 tchd 10-1)
Catchy Tune(IRE), a brother to the smart sprinter Sonny Red, was weak in the market and didn't obviously show much promise, losing his place badly once the tempo lifted and never any sort of threat thereafter. (op 9-2)
Sanad(IRE), who's by Red Clubs out of a Irish middle-distance winner, was very prominent in the betting for one from his yard first time up and travelled well until weakening so quickly from 2f out that there was probably more to it than any lack of race fitness. (op 11-2 tchd 6-1)

3383 SOVEREIGN HEALTH CARE H'CAP 6f
6:40 (6:42) (Class 4) (0-85,84) 3-Y-0+ **£3,885** (£1,156; £577; £288) **Stalls** High

Form RPR

3266 **1** **New Leyf (IRE)**[12] 3000 5-9-11 **81** (b[1]) HughBowman 2 93
(Jeremy Gask) *towards rr: hdwy over 2f out: swtchd rt and rdn wl over 1f out: str run to ld ins fnl f* **7/2**[2]

2021 **2** 2 **Grissom (IRE)**[17] 2806 5-9-12 **82** DuranFentiman 8 88
(Tim Easterby) *cl up: rdn to ld 2f out: drvn over 1f out: hdd and nt qckn ins fnl f* **3/1**[1]

3500 **3** 2 3/4 **Ocean Legend (IRE)**[35] 2300 6-9-7 **80** MichaelO'Connell(3) 9 77
(Tony Carroll) *cl up: effrt 2f out: sn rdn and ev ch tl drvn and one pce appr fnl f* **18/1**

-121 **4** 1 **Jack Rackham**[86] 1067 7-9-9 **79** (v) RoystonFfrench 5 73
(Bryan Smart) *trckd ldrs: effrt 2f out: sn rdn and no imp appr fnl f* **11/2**[3]

0603 **5** *nk* **Desert Strike**[9] 3078 5-9-0 **70** (p) RobertWinston 4 63
(Alan McCabe) *t.k.h: in tch: effrt over 2f out: sn rdn and no imp* **16/1**

055- **6** 2 **Cornus**[273] 6358 9-9-3 **76** (be) MartinHarley(3) 6 62
(Alan McCabe) *hld up: a towards rr* **18/1**

52 **7** 1 3/4 **Fantasy Explorer**[23] 2645 8-9-7 **77** MickyFenton 3 58
(John Quinn) *trckd ldrs: effrt over 2f out: sn rdn and wknd* **13/2**

0000 **8** 1/2 **Olynard (IRE)**[12] 3000 5-9-7 **80** JamesSullivan(3) 10 59
(Dr Richard Newland) *plld hrd: sn led: rdn along and hdd 2f out: sn wknd* **13/2**

-000 **9** 1 1/4 **Gap Princess (IRE)**[28] 2495 7-10-0 **84** DanielTudhope 7 59
(Geoffrey Harker) *s.i.s and bhd: hdwy and in tch over 2f out: sn rdn and wknd* **8/1**

1m 14.88s (1.28) **Going Correction** +0.225s/f (Good) **9** Ran SP% **116.8**
Speed ratings (Par 105): **100,97,93,92,91 89,86,86,84**
Tote Swingers:1&2:£3.30, 2&3:£15.10, 1&3:£17.50 CSF £14.64 CT £165.65 TOTE £4.70: £1.10, £1.90, £7.00; EX 18.30.
Owner James W Burdett **Bred** John Weld **Trained** Sutton Veny, Wilts

FOCUS
A fair handicap, with the majority of the runners near their recent best last time out, but it was muddling affair run at a steady gallop and the winner did very well in the circumstances. Once again the runners tended to ignore the stand rail. The form's rated around the second.

3384 HOWARD HUGHES MEMORIAL H'CAP 5f 140y
7:10 (7:11) (Class 4) (0-85,83) 3-Y-0 **£5,180** (£1,541; £770; £384) **Stalls** High

Form RPR

-130 **1** **Azzurra Du Caprio (IRE)**[29] 2468 3-9-7 **83** TomEaves 3 90
(Ben Haslam) *trckd ldng pair: pushed along and sltly outpcd over 2f out: rdn and hdwy to ld jst ins fnl f: drvn out* **5/1**[2]

3-41 **2** *nk* **Eland Ally**[21] 2710 3-8-13 **75** MickyFenton 4 81
(Tom Tate) *led: jnd and rdn along 2f out: drvn and hdd ins fnl f: rallied and kpt on towards fin* **10/11**[1]

0030 **3** 3 1/4 **Captain Kolo (IRE)**[30] 2411 3-9-0 **76** DuranFentiman 1 71
(Tim Easterby) *chsd ldrs on outer: rdn 2f out: sn drvn and kpt on same pce* **11/2**[3]

0050 **4** 3 1/2 **Jack Smudge**[10] 3052 3-8-13 **78** (b[1]) JamesSullivan(3) 7 61
(James Given) *in tch: hdwy on inner 1/2-way: chal over 2f out and ev ch tl rdn and wknd appr fnl f* **8/1**

1110 **5** 4 **Take Your Partner**[33] 2363 3-9-1 **80** (b) AmyRyan(3) 5 50
(Kevin Ryan) *chsd ldrs: rdn along 1/2-way: sn wknd* **8/1**

000- **6** 12 **Abzolutely (IRE)**[241] 7174 3-8-6 **68** AndrewHeffernan 2 —
(David O'Meara) *cl up: rdn along 1/2-way: sn wknd* **25/1**

1-60 **7** 15 **Look Who's Kool**[40] 2158 3-9-1 **77** GrahamGibbons 6 —
(Ed McMahon) *unruly in preliminaries: t.k.h and chsd ldrs for 2f: sn outpcd and bhd fr 1/2-way* **22/1**

1m 10.7s (1.90) **Going Correction** +0.225s/f (Good) **7** Ran SP% **114.9**
Speed ratings (Par 101): **94,93,89,84,79 63,43**
Tote Swingers:1&2:£1.50, 2&3:£2.30, 1&3:£3.10 CSF £10.06 TOTE £6.00: £3.50, £1.10; EX 12.40.
Owner Blue Lion Racing IX **Bred** Glending Bloodstock **Trained** Middleham Moor, N Yorks

FOCUS
A fairly useful handicap, though few came here either fully race fit or at their peak and it's not strong form for the grade despite the runners finishing well strung out with The action took place stand side this time.
Azzurra Du Caprio(IRE) Official explanation: trainer's rep said, regarding apparent improvement in form, that the filly was possibly suited by the softer ground.

3385 SOVEREIGN HEALTH CARE MAIDEN FILLIES' STKS 1m 2f 60y
7:45 (7:45) (Class 5) 3-Y-0+ **£2,914** (£867; £433; £216) **Stalls** Low

Form RPR

342 **1** **Stella Point (IRE)**[16] 2840 3-8-12 **92** HughBowman 7 88+
(Mick Channon) *hld up towards rr: hdwy over 3f out: swtchd rt and str run over 2f out: led wl over 1f out: sn clr* **8/11**[1]

2 6 **Word Power** 3-8-12 0 PatCosgrave 4 76
(Sir Henry Cecil) *trckd ldrs on inner: hdwy to ld 2 1/2f out: rdn and hdd wl over 1f out: drvn and kpt on fnl f: no ch w wnr* **8/1**

0 **3** 4 1/2 **Federation**[71] 1362 3-8-12 0 GrahamGibbons 12 67
(Roger Charlton) *trckd ldng pair: smooth hdwy and cl up 3f out: effrt 2f out and ev ch: sn rdn and one pce appr fnl f* **6/1**[3]

00 **4** 2 3/4 **Bollin Mandy**[7] 3167 3-8-12 0 RobertWinston 1 62
(Tim Easterby) *trckd ldrs: hdwy over 3f out: rdn along over 2f out: sn one pce* **33/1**

22- **5** 1 **Moonsail**[249] 7001 3-8-12 0 AhmedAjtebi 5 60
(Mahmood Al Zarooni) *in tch: hdwy on outer 4f out: chsd ldrs 3f out: rdn over 2f out and sn btn* **7/2**[2]

0 **6** *nk* **Convention**[16] 2840 3-8-12 0 RichardMullen 10 59+
(Ed Dunlop) *hld up in rr: hdwy over 3f out: swtchd ins and nt clr run over 2f out: no imp after* **25/1**

0 **7** *nk* **Sistine**[27] 2529 3-8-9 0 JamesSullivan(3) 11 58
(James Given) *hld up towards rr: effrt and sme hdwy on outer 3f out: sn rdn and n.d* **40/1**

- **8** 1 3/4 **Srimenanti** 3-8-12 0 PaddyAspell 3 55
(Brian Rothwell) *hld up towards rr: hdwy over 3f out: rdn to chse ldrs over 2f out: sn wknd* **100/1**

0 **9** 18 **Emsiyah (USA)**[16] 2836 3-8-12 0 TedDurcan 8 19
(Saeed Bin Suroor) *led: rdn clr over 4f out: hdd 2 1/2f out and sn wknd* **14/1**

00-0 **10** 1 1/2 **Hot Toddie**[18] 2781 3-8-12 **37** TomEaves 6 16
(James Given) *a bhd* **66/1**

0 **11** 2 3/4 **En Pointe**[39] 2185 3-8-12 0 AndrewHeffernan 9 10
(James Given) *cl up: rdn along over 4f out and sn wknd* **100/1**

2m 12.06s (2.66) **Going Correction** +0.225s/f (Good) **11** Ran SP% **124.9**
Speed ratings (Par 100): **98,93,89,87,86 86,86,84,70,69 66**
Tote Swingers:1&2:£1.40, 2&3:£7.60, 1&3:£1.30 CSF £8.25 TOTE £1.70: £1.02, £3.20, £2.50; EX 8.10.
Owner Jon and Julia Aisbitt **Bred** J Hanly, T Stewart & A Stroud **Trained** West Ilsley, Berks
■ A double for Australian rider Hugh Bowman, the first winners of his second stint in Britain.

FOCUS
Some powerful stables represented in a fillies' maiden run at just a fair gallop to the straight, but quite how much strength in depth there was remains to be seen. The winner did not need to match her best.

3386 GEOFF CLARKE MEMORIAL H'CAP 1m (R)
8:15 (8:15) (Class 4) (0-80,77) 4-Y-0+ **£3,561** (£1,059; £529; £264) **Stalls** Low

Form RPR

4050 **1** **Hawaana (IRE)**[10] 3042 6-9-4 **74** RobertWinston 1 82+
(Gay Kelleway) *hld up towards rr: hdwy 3f out: rdn to chse ldrs over 1f out: drvn ins fnl f: swtchd lft ins fnl 50yds and styd on strly to ld on line* **8/1**

4-00 **2** *nse* **Kerrys Requiem (IRE)**[17] 2806 5-9-4 **77** (p) SeanLevey(3) 10 85
(Tim Pitt) *hld up in tch: hdwy wl over 2f out: led wl over 1f out and sn rdn: drvn ins fnl f: edgd rt nr fin and hdd on line* **33/1**

3635 **3** *hd* **Elijah Pepper (USA)**[9] 3071 6-9-5 **75** GrahamGibbons 8 83
(David Barron) *trckd ldrs: hdwy over 3f out: rdn to chal over 2f out and ev ch tl drvn ins fnl f and nt qckn towards fin* **13/2**[3]

0440 **4** 3/4 **Fibs And Flannel**[26] 2545 4-9-0 **70** DuranFentiman 11 76
(Tim Easterby) *midfield: hdwy to trck ldrs 4f out: effrt 3f out: rdn over 2f out and ev ch tl drvn and one pce ins fnl f* **5/1**[1]

5006 **5** 3 1/2 **Ajdaad (USA)**[8] 3130 4-8-11 **70** MartinHarley(3) 5 68
(Alan McCabe) *hld up in rr: hdwy on outer wl over 2f out: rdn to chse ldrs whn hung lft over 1f out: sn no imp* **14/1**

0336 **6** 1 **Petomic (IRE)**[61] 1569 6-8-7 **63** RobbieFitzpatrick 2 58+
(Richard Guest) *hld up in rr: hdwy 3f out: rdn along over 2f out: styd on appr fnl f: nrst fin* **25/1**

0-64 **7** 1 1/4 **Christmas Light**[17] 2808 4-8-12 **68** SilvestreDeSousa 9 61
(David O'Meara) *trckd ldrs: hdwy 4f out: led 3f out: rdn and hdd wl over 1f out: grad wknd* **8/1**

1003 **8** 2 1/4 **Cono Zur (FR)**[13] 2955 4-9-3 **76** JamesSullivan(3) 4 63
(Ruth Carr) *cl up: effrt 3f out: sn rdn along and wknd over 2f out* **11/2**[2]

0060 **9** 1 3/4 **Aerodynamic (IRE)**[22] 2674 4-8-12 **68** PaddyAspell 6 51
(Clive Mulhall) *midfield: hdwy on inner to chse ldrs 3f out: sn rdn and wknd fnl 2f* **25/1**

5202 **10** 10 **White Diamond**[29] 2454 4-9-3 **73** TomEaves 7 33
(Malcolm Jefferson) *cl up on outer: rdn along over 3f out and sn wknd* **11/2**[2]

0100 **11** 3 1/2 **Global**[15] 2887 5-8-10 **66** RichardKingscote 3 18
(Brian Ellison) *led: rdn along and hdd 3f out: drvn and wknd over 2f out* **11/2**[2]

1m 40.36s (0.66) **Going Correction** +0.225s/f (Good) **11** Ran SP% **115.7**
Speed ratings (Par 105): **105,104,104,104,100 99,98,96,94,84 80**
Tote Swingers:1&2:£29.20, 2&3:£22.20, 1&3:£14.80 CSF £245.09 CT £1837.44 TOTE £10.70: £4.20, £6.60, £1.30; EX 115.70.
Owner E Jagger, Gay Kelleway, D Clarke **Bred** Norelands Bloodstock, J Hanly & H Lascelles **Trained** Exning, Suffolk
■ Stewards' Enquiry : Sean Levey two-day ban: used whip with excessive frequency (Jul 11-12)
Duran Fentiman two-day ban: used whip with excessive frequency (Jul 11-12)

FOCUS
An ordinary handicap that was run at a strong pace with the advantage very much with those held up. That said, few of the field came into this at the top of their game and it remains to be seen whether it proves strong form. The third and fourth help with the level.
Aerodynamic(IRE) Official explanation: trainer said gelding was unsuited by the good to firm ground
White Diamond Official explanation: jockey said filly ran flat
Global Official explanation: jockey said gelding had no more to give

3387 HOSPITAL HEARTBEAT APPEAL FILLIES' H'CAP 7f
8:50 (8:52) (Class 5) (0-70,68) 3-Y-O+ **£2,914** (£867; £433; £216) **Stalls** High

Form RPR

4325 **1** **Caelis**[17] [2821] 3-9-1 **64**..............................(v[1]) RichardKingscote 11 76
(Ralph Beckett) *trckd ldrs: hdwy to ld 2f out: rdn and edgd lft over 1f out: clr ins fnl f* **11/4**[1]

0255 **2** *4* **Alensgrove (IRE)**[18] [2781] 3-8-11 **60**..............................(p) MickyFenton 8 61
(Paul Midgley) *midfield: hdwy over 2f out: rdn to chse wnr over 1f out: drvn and edgd lft ent fnl f: sn one pce* **16/1**

0065 **3** *2 1/4* **Eternal Instinct**[7] [3162] 4-9-3 **60**.............................. GaryBartley(3) 13 58
(Jim Goldie) *hld up in rr: hdwy on stands' rail over 2f out: rdn wl over 1f out: kpt on ins fnl f* **10/1**

-033 **4** *hd* **Muroona (IRE)**[15] [2869] 3-8-13 **62**.............................. TadhgO'Shea 6 56
(Mark Johnston) *trckd ldrs: hdwy and cl up wl over 2f out: rdn wl over 1f out and kpt on same pce* **9/2**[3]

5-00 **5** *1/2* **Red Scintilla**[33] [2366] 4-9-9 **63**.............................. TomEaves 3 59
(Nigel Tinkler) *in tch: hdwy on outer over 2f out: sn rdn and kpt on same pce* **25/1**

0-00 **6** *1 1/4* **Luv U Noo**[17] [2799] 4-8-12 **52**.............................. RobertWinston 10 47
(Brian Baugh) *s.i.s and bhd: hdwy wl over 2f out: sn rdn and kpt on appr fnl f: nrst fin* **16/1**

655- **7** *6* **Evening Dress**[365] [3392] 3-9-4 **67**.............................. SilvestreDeSousa 1 40
(Mark Johnston) *midfield: rdn along 1/2-way: sn btn* **5/1**

0206 **8** *nk* **Sweet Possession (USA)**[5] [3234] 5-8-11 **54**.........(v) JamesSullivan(3) 4 30
(Pat Eddery) *racd wd: cl up tl led 1/2-way: rdn and hdd 2f out: drvn and wknd over 1f out* **10/1**

600- **9** *12* **Just Sam (IRE)**[285] [6040] 6-9-1 **62**.............................. ShaneBKelly(7) 9 —
(Ron Barr) *led to 1/2-way: sn rdn along and wknd* **20/1**

2022 **10** *8* **Sairaam (IRE)**[16] [2855] 5-9-9 **68**.............................. JulieBurke(5) 12 —
(Charles Smith) *chsd ldrs: rdn along over 2f out: sn wknd* **4/1**[2]

22-0 **11** *2* **Norton Girl**[28] [2493] 3-8-9 **61** ow1.............................. MichaelO'Connell(3) 7 —
(Michael Herrington) *in tch: rdn along bef 1/2-way: sn outpcd and bhd* **25/1**

-605 **12** *2* **Rattleyurjewellery**[19] [2765] 3-8-0 **49** oh4.............................. DuranFentiman 5 —
(David Brown) *a in rr: rdn along and bhd fr 1/2-way* **40/1**

1m 28.42s (2.12) **Going Correction** +0.225s/f (Good)
WFA 3 from 4yo+ 9lb **12** Ran SP% **126.4**
Speed ratings (Par 100): **96,91,88,88,88 86,79,79,65,56 54,52**
Tote Swingers:1&2:£13.20, 2&3:£29.50, 1&3:£4.60 CSF £52.23 CT £414.59 TOTE £4.00: £1.80, £4.50, £3.30; EX 47.10.
Owner Belmore Lane Stud Racing Partnership **Bred** S J And Mrs Pembroke **Trained** Kimpton, Hants

FOCUS
A run-of-the-mill fillies' handicap that looked to be run at quite a sound gallop. The runners stayed centre to stand side and the form is rated loosely around the second.
Sairaam(IRE) Official explanation: trainer said mare was unsuited by the good to firm ground
T/Plt: £64.70 to a £1 stake. Pool £82,193.56 - 927.06 winning tickets. T/Qpdt: £18.20 to a £1 stake. Pool £6,403.68 - 260.20 winning tickets. JR

[3171] LINGFIELD (L-H)
Saturday, June 25

OFFICIAL GOING: Turf course - good (good to firm in places, 0.4); all weather - standard
Wind: Moderate, half-behind. Weather: light cloud, bright spells

3388 BRITISH STALLION STUDS SUPPORTING BRITISH RACING E B F MAIDEN STKS (TURF) 5f
5:50 (5:50) (Class 5) 2-Y-O **£3,412** (£1,007; £504) **Stalls** High

Form RPR

1 **Pimpernel (IRE)** 2-8-5 0.............................. AntiocoMurgia(7) 7 73+
(Mahmood Al Zarooni) *in tch in midfield: swtchd lft 2f out: rdn and hdwy ent fnl f: r.o wl to ld wl ins fnl f: rdn out* **9/2**[3]

366 **2** *3/4* **Chillie Billie**[8] [3132] 2-9-3 0.............................. KirstyMilczarek 5 72
(Phil McEntee) *led for over 1f: chsd ldr after: rdn wl over 1f out: led ins fnl f tl hdd and no ex wl ins fnl f* **10/1**

0 **3** *1* **Princess Alessia**[15] [2880] 2-8-12 0.............................. AndreaAtzeni 4 63
(Terry Clement) *chsd ldrs: rdn wl over 1f out: chsd ldng pair fnl 100yds: kpt on same pce* **66/1**

4 *1 1/2* **Continuity (IRE)** 2-8-12 0.............................. StevieDonohoe 2 58
(Ralph Beckett) *dwlt: sn rcvrd and in tch in midfield: rdn and unable qck wl over 1f out: swtchd lft and kpt on fnl 150yds* **6/1**

054 **5** *nse* **Arabian Falcon**[37] [2214] 2-9-3 0..............................(b[1]) MartinDwyer 10 63
(Brian Meehan) *racd freely: chsd ldr tl led over 3f out: clr 1/2-way: rdn 1f out: drvn and hdd ins fnl f: sn fdd* **6/4**[1]

4 **6** *1 3/4* **Daunt (IRE)**[16] [2844] 2-9-3 0.............................. PatDobbs 9 57+
(Richard Hannon) *outpcd towards rr: rdn along and struggling 1/2-way: styd on fnl f: nvr trbld ldrs* **11/4**[2]

34 **7** *1* **Fairy Moss (IRE)**[26] [2563] 2-8-12 0.............................. FrankieMcDonald 6 48
(Richard Hannon) *outpcd towards rr: rdn and struggling 1/2-way: wandering u.p over 1f out: styd on fnl f: nvr trbld ldrs* **33/1**

8 *6* **Christopher Chua (IRE)** 2-9-3 0.............................. JackMitchell 3 31
(Simon Dow) *awkward leaving stalls and v.s.a: a outpcd in rr* **66/1**

9 *7* **Russian Bullet** 2-9-3 0.............................. FergusSweeney 1 6
(Jamie Osborne) *s.i.s: a struggling in rr* **50/1**

58.70 secs (0.50) **Going Correction** 0.0s/f (Good) **9** Ran SP% **116.1**
Speed ratings (Par 93): **96,94,93,90,90 87,86,76,65**
Tote Swingers:1&2:£8.50, 2&3:£59.00, 1&3:£40.10 CSF £46.64 TOTE £4.80: £1.50, £2.60, £7.20; EX 61.80.
Owner Godolphin **Bred** Peter Harris **Trained** Newmarket, Suffolk

FOCUS
On a warm evening the ground on the straight turf track had from the earlier description of good. A fair maiden with Arabian Falcon setting the standard but disappointing in first-time blinkers but a respectable time only 1.63 seconds outside the juvenile record. The second is the key to the level.

NOTEBOOK
Pimpernel(IRE) is an Invincible Spirit filly out of a half-sister to multiple 6f-1m 2fwinners, including the high-class performer Eagle Mountain and Prix Marcel Boussac winner Sulk, who earlier this year cost connections 135,000gns. She made a very taking debut in landing the spoils and, after being pulled wide for her effort, ran on well to score with something in hand. She caught the eye in the paddock and looks a smart recruit. (op 6-1)
Chillie Billie had shown considerable promise on debut but a little below that in two runs since. This was a far better effort and he lost little in defeat after battling away gamely from the front. He should get off the mark sooner rather than later if reproducing this effort. (op 8-1)
Princess Alessia stepped up considerably from her debut run and kept on well enough in the final furlong without ever quite managing to get upsides. She can only build on this and, if doing so, should find a maiden within her compass. (op 40-1)
Continuity(IRE), a 30,000gns purchase out of a 9f winner ran with plenty of promise and was staying on well in the latter stages. She will be seen to better effect over further in time but she showed enough speed to suggest she could be a force at this distance at present. (op 9-2)
Arabian Falcon was well-supported to open his account after some decent efforts in defeat but failed to justify the support after racing up with the pace, fading out in the latter stages. The headgear failed to have the desired effect and he can only be watched at present, albeit, with the ability to land one of these. (op 15-8 tchd 11-8 and 2-1 in places)
Daunt(IRE) could never find the pace to get involved. (op 10-3 tchd 7-2)

3389 CGGVERITAS H'CAP (TURF) 5f
6:20 (6:20) (Class 5) (0-75,74) 3-Y-O+ **£3,070** (£906; £453) **Stalls** High

Form RPR

1521 **1** **Miss Polly Plum**[14] [2920] 4-8-11 **59**..............................(p) AndreaAtzeni 3 75+
(Chris Dwyer) *mde all: sn crossed to r on stands' rail and clr thrght: wl in command and coasting fnl f: eased towards fin* **11/4**[3]

6022 **2** *4* **Grandmas Dream**[7] [3174] 3-9-6 **74**..............................(b) PaulDoe 8 72
(Jim Best) *dwlt: sn bustled along and chsd clr ldr: rdn and no imp on wnr over 1f out: plugged on same pce after* **2/1**[1]

0104 **3** *1 1/4* **Make My Dream**[14] [2903] 8-9-8 **70**.............................. IanMongan 7 65
(John Gallagher) *chsd ldng trio but nvr on terms w wnr: rdn wl over 1f out: kpt on fnl f to snatch 3rd cl home: nvr trbld wnr* **11/2**

6156 **4** *nk* **Rocker**[14] [2929] 7-9-7 **74**..............................(b) TobyAtkinson(5) 2 68
(Gary Moore) *disp 2nd bhd clr wnr: rdn and no imp over 1f out: wknd fnl 100yds* **12/1**

4123 **5** *6* **Speightowns Kid (USA)**[15] [2881] 3-9-5 **73**.............................. StevieDonohoe 4 43
(Matthew Salaman) *dwlt: sn rdn and a outpcd in detached last* **5/2**[2]

57.71 secs (-0.49) **Going Correction** 0.0s/f (Good)
WFA 3 from 4yo+ 6lb **5** Ran SP% **111.6**
Speed ratings (Par 103): **103,96,94,94,84**
CSF £8.82 TOTE £4.40: £2.30, £1.10; EX 9.50.
Owner Mrs J Hughes & Miss C Hughes **Bred** Brookfield Stud & Partners **Trained** Burrough Green, Cambs

FOCUS
With three defections this 56-75 sprint lost a lot of its competitive edge. The improved winner made all up the rail but this wasn't a strong race.
Speightowns Kid(USA) Official explanation: jockey said gelding never travelled

3390 BRITISH ARMED FORCES DAY FILLIES' H'CAP (TURF) 7f
6:50 (6:50) (Class 5) (0-75,75) 3-Y-O **£3,070** (£906; £453) **Stalls** High

Form RPR

30-6 **1** **Loving Thought**[27] [2528] 3-8-11 **65**.............................. IanMongan 8 70
(Sir Henry Cecil) *t.k.h: chsd ldr: rdn 2f out: led over 1f out: kpt on u.p fnl f: hld on wl cl home* **8/1**

130- **2** *hd* **Song Of The Siren**[266] [6563] 3-9-7 **75**.............................. FergusSweeney 11 79+
(Andrew Balding) *led: shkn up and hung lft 2f out: hdd over 1f out: styd pressing ldng pair: kpt on wl cl home: jst hld* **3/1**[1]

5-31 **3** *3/4* **Ma Quillet**[12] [2993] 3-9-2 **70**.............................. DaneO'Neill 5 72
(Henry Candy) *chsd ldrs: rdn and ev ch over 1f out: drvn 1f out: no ex and btn fnl 75yds* **7/2**[2]

0-50 **4** *3/4* **Silken Thoughts**[26] [2550] 3-8-10 **64**.............................. CathyGannon 7 64+
(John Berry) *hld up wl in tch: rdn and effrt over 1f out: chsd ldrs 1f out: kpt on u.p ins fnl f* **3/1**[1]

[illegible] **5** *nk* **Mawjoodah**[17] [2821] 3-8-13 **67**.............................. MartinDwyer 9 67
(Clive Brittain) [illegible] *midfield: rdn and chsd ldng trio over 1f out: unable qck and styd on same pce u.p fnl f* [illegible]

14-0 **6** *2* **Poyle Judy**[35] [2313] 3-9-4 **72**.............................. StevieDonohoe 3 66
(Ralph Beckett) *dwlt: hld up wl in tch in rr: nt clr run and swtchd lft wl over 1f out: hdwy 1f out and kpt on fnl f: nvr able to chal* **25/1**

3-46 **7** *hd* **Links Drive Lady**[115] [729] 3-8-12 **66**.............................. MarcHalford 6 60
(Mark Rimmer) *stdd s: hld up wl in tch in rr: rdn and effrt over 1f out: kpt on same pce and no imp ins fnl f* **40/1**

0-10 **8** *1/2* **Fettuccine (IRE)**[16] [2838] 3-9-2 **70**.............................. RobertHavlin 2 62
(John Gallagher) *stdd after s: t.k.h: hld up wl in tch: rdn and unable qck over 1f out: one pce and btn 1f out* **14/1**

24-0 **9** *3/4* **Map Of Heaven**[23] [2643] 3-9-2 **70**.............................. PatDobbs 10 60
(William Haggas) *chsd ldrs: pushed along jst over 2f out: lost pl and rdn wl over 1f out: one pce and no threat to ldrs ent fnl f* **10/1**

0-66 **10** *3/4* **Idiom (IRE)**[22] [2690] 3-9-2 **75**.............................. LauraPike(5) 4 63
(David Simcock) *stdd s: t.k.h: hld up wl in tch in rr: rdn and effrt in centre over 1f out: no hdwy and btn 1f out* **25/1**

1m 23.62s (0.32) **Going Correction** 0.0s/f (Good) **10** Ran SP% **122.6**
Speed ratings (Par 96): **98,97,96,96,95 93,93,92,91,90**
Tote Swingers:1&2:£5.50, 2&3:£5.60, 1&3:£7.10 CSF £33.44 CT £106.15 TOTE £12.40: £4.90, £1.10, £1.30; EX 25.40.
Owner Liam Sheridan **Bred** Peter Winkworth **Trained** Newmarket, Suffolk

FOCUS
A competitive fillies' handicap with the principals always at the head of affairs off a reasonable pace. Modest form and the runner-up should have won.
Song Of The Siren Official explanation: jockey said filly hung left

3391 SURREY ROYAL BRITISH LEGION 90TH ANNIVERSARY DAY (S) STKS 1m 4f (P)
7:25 (7:25) (Class 6) 3-Y-O+ **£1,706** (£503; £252) **Stalls** Low

Form RPR

3226 **1** **Eagle Nebula**[10] [3047] 7-9-5 64.............................. KierenFox(3) 3 69
(Brett Johnson) *in tch: jnd ldrs 3f out: rdn to ld over 1f out: kpt on and a holding rival ins fnl f* **9/2**[2]

0620 **2** *1/2* **Viewing**[10] [3054] 4-9-3 70.............................. PatDobbs 4 63
(James Given) *dwlt: flashed tail thrght: sn chsng ldr: ev ch 3f out: rdn and clr w wnr over 1f out: hung rt towards wnr and nt qckn ins fnl f: nvr looked like gng past* **2/1**[1]

0-3 **3** *11* **Cry Alot Boy**[62] [1538] 8-9-8 67..............................(t) JackMitchell 6 51
(Kevin Morgan) *stdd s: t.k.h: hld up in last: wnt 4th over 3f out: rdn and outpcd jst over 2f out: no ch over 1f out: wnt modest 3rd wl ins fnl f* **5/1**[3]

/U06 **4** *1 3/4* **Exotic Dream (FR)**[2] 3311 5-9-3 63 .... LukeMorris 1 43
(Ronald Harris) *led at stdy gallop: jnd and qcknd 3f out: rdn and hdd over 1f out: sn btn and fdd 1f out: lost 3rd wl ins fnl f* **14/1**

-113 **5** *18* **Dansilver**[80] 1181 7-9-13 66 .... PaulDoe 2 43
(Jim Best) *t.k.h: chsd ldng pair: rdn and dropped to last over 3f out: lost tch over 2f out: eased ins fnl f: t.o* **2/1**[1]

2m 37.88s (4.88) **Going Correction** +0.30s/f (Slow) **5** Ran SP% **108.2**
Speed ratings (Par 101): **95,94,87,86,74**
CSF £13.40 TOTE £3.30: £1.10, £1.50; EX 14.30.There was no bid for the winner.
Owner Tann Racing **Bred** Juddmonte Farms Ltd **Trained** Ashtead, Surrey

FOCUS
A seller run at just an ordinary pace with the front pair showing a good turn of foot to draw clear of the remainder when the race began in earnest turning in. The winner probably only had to run to his recent best.
Cry Alot Boy Official explanation: jockey said gelding ran too free
Dansilver Official explanation: vet said gelding finished lame right-hind

3392 POPPY SHOP - POPPYSHOP.ORG.UK MEDIAN AUCTION MAIDEN STKS 1m 2f (P)
7:55 (7:55) (Class 6) 3-4-Y-0 **£1,706** (£503; £252) **Stalls** Low

Form RPR
0 **1** **Chatterer (IRE)**[10] 3043 3-8-4 0 ....(t) KatiaScallan(7) 7 65+
(Marcus Tregoning) *dwlt: t.k.h: pushed rt bnd 9f out: chsd ldrs after 1f: pushed along and chal wl over 1f out: led ent fnl f: r.o wl* **20/1**

004 **2** *1/2* **Dare To Bare (IRE)**[37] 2231 3-9-2 71 .... PatDobbs 4 69
(Amanda Perrett) *led for over 1f: chsd ldrs after: pushed along over 3f out: rdn and ev ch 1f out: r.o u.p but a jst hld* **6/1**[3]

-0 **3** *3* **Steely**[14] 2924 3-9-2 0 .... PaulDoe 1 63
(Jim Best) *wl in tch in midfield: rdn and hung rt bnd 2f out: unable qck over 1f out: kpt on u.p fnl f* **33/1**

4-33 **4** *1* **Major Domo (FR)**[63] 1525 3-9-2 70 .... LukeMorris 8 61
(Harry Dunlop) *lef after 1f and set stdy gallop: rdn jst over 1f out: hdd ent fnl f: no ex and outpcd fnl 150yds* **4/1**[2]

50 **5** *shd* **Oculist**[12] 3001 3-9-2 0 .... FergusSweeney 3 61
(Jamie Osborne) *hld up in last trio: nudged along over 1f out: nt clr run jst ins fnl f: nudged along and kpt on fnl 100yds: nvr threatened ldrs* **28/1**

0 **6** *3/4* **Ibiza Sunset (IRE)**[21] 2723 3-9-2 0 .... IanMongan 6 59
(Peter Winkworth) *t.k.h: hld up in tch: wnt rt bnd 9f out: rdn and unable qck over 2f out: styd on same pce fr over 1f out* **8/1**

3 **7** *nk* **Deck Walk (USA)**[27] 2529 3-8-11 0 .... JackMitchell 5 54
(Roger Charlton) *chsd ldrs: wnt 2nd over 8f out: ev ch and shkn up 2f out: fnd nil and short of room over 1f out: rdn and nt qckn jst over 1f out: wknd fnl f* **8/13**[1]

8 *1/2* **Reggie Perrin** 3-8-11 0 .... JemmaMarshall(5) 2 58
(Pat Phelan) *stdd s: hld up wl in tch in last trio: rdn over 1f out: styd on same pce and no imp ins fnl f* **25/1**

2m 9.31s (2.71) **Going Correction** +0.30s/f (Slow) **8** Ran SP% **122.3**
Speed ratings (Par 101): **101,100,98,97,97 96,96,96**
Tote Swingers:1&2:£10.80, 2&3:£23.20, 1&3:£81.20 CSF £135.94 TOTE £22.10: £11.00, £1.10, £14.90; EX 144.00.
Owner Horne, Hoare, Gaskell & Partners **Bred** Airlie Stud And Sir Thomas Pilkington **Trained** Lambourn, Berks

FOCUS
An ordinary maiden with only a fair pace. The race is rated around the runner-up and the form is a little suspect.

3393 LINGFIELD MARRIOTT HOTEL & COUNTRY CLUB H'CAP 1m 4f (P)
8:25 (8:25) (Class 6) (0-60,60) 3-Y-O **£1,706** (£503; £252) **Stalls** Low

Form RPR
00-6 **1** **Final Liberation (FR)**[18] 2786 3-9-0 **53** .... StevieDonohoe 4 66+
(Sir Mark Prescott Bt) *mde all: rdn and qcknd 4f out: pressed by runner-up 2f out: styd on dourly and forged clr jst ins fnl f: rdn out* **8/1**

-403 **2** *3 3/4* **Breton Star**[7] 3175 3-9-1 **54** .... MartinLane 5 61
(David Simcock) *chsd wnr thrght: rdn whn pce qcknd 4f out: pressing wnr and drvn 2f out: no ex and btn jst ins fnl f: one pce after* **10/1**

4242 **3** *6* **Surprise (IRE)**[16] 2858 3-9-7 **60** .... MarcHalford 3 57
(Mark Rimmer) *hld up in tch: chsd ldng pair wl over 3f out: drvn and unable qck wl over 1f out: btn 1f out: wknd ins fnl f* **7/1**[3]

3622 **4** *1 1/4* **Sukhothai (USA)**[21] 2722 3-9-7 **60** .... JackMitchell 2 55+
(James Fanshawe) *hld up in midfield: rdn and effrt to chse clr ldng trio 3f out: drvn and no imp 2f out: wl btn but plugged on ins fnl f* **11/4**[1]

364 **5** *hd* **Delagoa Bay (IRE)**[14] 2904 3-8-11 **50** .... DaneO'Neill 8 45
(Sylvester Kirk) *stdd s: hld up in last trio: rdn and hdwy over 3f out: wnt poor 5th wl over 1f out: kpt on but no ch w ldrs* **12/1**

6506 **6** *5* **Beauchamp Zest**[40] 2166 3-8-12 **58** ....(t) MatthewLawson(7) 11 45
(Hans Adielsson) *stdd and dropped in bhd after s: hld up in last trio: stuck bhd a wall of horses whn pce qcknd 4f out: swtchd lft and wnt poor 8th jst over 2f out: kpt on but nvr on terms* **16/1**

0-00 **7** *1* **Handel's Messiah (IRE)**[25] 2596 3-8-0 **46** oh1 ....(v[1]) IanBurns(7) 9 31
(Michael Bell) *dwlt: sn rdn along: stuck wd and racd in last trio: rdn and immediately struggling whn pce qcknd 4f out: no ch fnl 3f* **20/1**

2434 **8** *3 1/2* **Revolutionary**[3] 3268 3-9-6 **59** .... FergusSweeney 10 39
(Jamie Osborne) *in tch in midfield: rdn and struggling whn pce qcknd 4f out: wl btn fnl 3f* **5/1**[2]

0-06 **9** *1 1/2* **Hurricane Spear**[35] 2307 3-8-7 **46** oh1 .... LukeMorris 6 23
(Gary Moore) *t.k.h: hld up in midfield: rdn and struggling whn pce qcknd 4f out: wl bhd over 2f out* **9/1**

0-65 **10** *27* **Dark And Dangerous (IRE)**[11] 3018 3-9-4 **57** ....(v) IanMongan 1 —
(Peter Winkworth) *chsd ldrs: lost pl qckly whn pce qcknd 4f out: t.o and virtually p.u fr over 1f out* **9/1**

-003 **11** *28* **Boston Court (IRE)**[9] 3077 3-9-0 **53** ....(b) MartinDwyer 7 —
(Brian Meehan) *chsd ldrs: reminders over 8f out: rdn and lost pl qckly whn pce qcknd 4f out: wl t.o 2f out: virtually p.u after* **20/1**

2m 32.73s (-0.27) **Going Correction** +0.30s/f (Slow) **11** Ran SP% **119.1**
Speed ratings (Par 97): **112,109,105,104,104 101,100,98,97,79 60**
Tote Swingers:1&2:£14.20, 2&3:£14.40, 1&3:£13.30 CSF £86.56 CT £587.34 TOTE £13.60: £3.40, £3.60, £4.50; EX 85.80.
Owner P Bamford **Bred** R & E Bamford Limited **Trained** Newmarket, Suffolk

FOCUS
There was a decent pace to this handicap and the bare time is good. The winner really got his act together.
Final Liberation(FR) Official explanation: trainer's rep said, regarding apparent improvement in form, that the gelding was suited by the better surface, step up in trip and change of tactics
Boston Court(IRE) Official explanation: jockey said gelding never travelled
T/Plt: £919.80 to a £1 stake. Pool £61,930.60 - 49.15 winning tickets. T/Qpdt: £163.90 to a £1 stake. Pool £7,487.24 - 33.80 winning tickets. SP

[3355] NEWCASTLE (L-H)
Saturday, June 25

OFFICIAL GOING: Good to soft (7.0)
Wind: Fresh, half-against. Weather: Cloudy, fine

3394 TOTESPORT.COM CHIPCHASE STKS (GROUP 3) 6f
2:00 (2:00) (Class 1) 3-Y-O+
£28,385 (£10,760; £5,385; £2,685; £1,345; £675) **Stalls** Centre

Form RPR
-100 **1** **Genki (IRE)**[7] 3154 7-9-3 110 ....(v) GeorgeBaker 8 114
(Roger Charlton) *missed break: hld up: stdy hdwy over 2f out: effrt and rdn over 1f out: led last 50yds: kpt on wl* **11/2**[3]

4003 **2** *hd* **Doncaster Rover (USA)**[28] 2502 5-9-3 106 .... SilvestreDeSousa 6 113
(David Brown) *trckd ldrs: drvn and outpcd over 2f out: rallied to ld appr fnl f: hdd last 50yds: kpt on* **9/1**

-522 **3** *2* **Regal Parade**[28] 2502 7-9-3 118 .... AdrianNicholls 5 107
(David Nicholls) *prom: rdn over 2f out: ev ch over 1f out: kpt on same pce ins fnl f* **5/6**[1]

22-5 **4** *1/2* **Eton Rifles (IRE)**[84] 1094 6-9-3 94 .... PaulHanagan 2 105
(Howard Johnson) *led tl hdd appr fnl f: kpt on same pce* **10/1**

2242 **5** *hd* **Waffle (IRE)**[7] 3155 5-9-3 107 .... PhillipMakin 7 105+
(David Barron) *hld up in tch: stdy hdwy whn nt clr run over 1f out: sn swtchd rt and rdn: no imp fnl f* **4/1**[2]

400/ **6** *nk* **Winker Watson**[728] 3398 6-9-3 0 .... HughBowman 3 104
(Mick Channon) *prom: drvn and outpcd over 2f out: rallied ent fnl f: nvr able to chal* **33/1**

-030 **7** *6* **Secret Witness**[21] 2717 5-9-3 93 ....(b) JimCrowley 1 85
(Ronald Harris) *trckd ldrs: drvn and ev ch over 1f out: wknd ent fnl f* **33/1**

0220 **8** *2 1/2* **Rain Delayed (IRE)**[45] 2005 5-9-3 105 .... TomEaves 4 77
(Michael Dods) *hld up bhd ldrs: hdwy and cl up 2f out: sn rdn and wknd* **25/1**

1m 13.76s (-0.84) **Going Correction** +0.05s/f (Good) **8** Ran SP% **118.8**
Speed ratings (Par 113): **107,106,104,103,103 102,94,91**
Tote Swingers:1&2:£4.80, 2&3:£2.50, 1&3:£2.30 CSF £53.36 TOTE £5.40: £1.70, £2.60, £1.10; EX 47.40 Trifecta £117.10 Pool £1,151.15 - 7.27 winning units..
Owner Ms Gillian Khosla **Bred** Rathbarry Stud **Trained** Beckhampton, Wilts
■ Stewards' Enquiry : Adrian Nicholls caution: used whip down shoulder in the forehand.
Silvestre De Sousa one-day ban: used whip in incorrect place (Jul 11)

FOCUS
Course at normal inner configuration and distances as advertised. They raced up the middle of the track. The pace was good - time 0.75 seconds faster than following Class 2 handicap - and this is solid Group-race form. The winner is rated to his best.

NOTEBOOK
Genki(IRE) was down in grade after running a bit than his eighth-place finish in the Golden Jubilee suggested (travelled well for long way, reported to have been unsuited by loose ground), and he was a game winner. He raced out the back after missing the break, but the good gallop helped him and he travelled strongly before battling on well. Considering there's so little between the top-end sprinters he's well worth his place back in a Group 1. The July Cup and Haydock Sprint Cup (third last year) are obvious targets, and he's versatile ground-wise. (op 5-1)
Doncaster Rover(USA) reversed recent Haydock form with the below-par Regal Parade, keeping on well having been flat out some way from this finish, and he was close to his best. (tchd 8-1)
Regal Parade had upwards of 8lb in hand on official figures and conditions were favourable, but he ran a laboured race, coming under pressure a fair way out. His very best form has come later in the year (top four RPRs from July 17 onwards), so he could yet return to form, but he'll still have a bit to prove next time. (op Evens tchd 11-10 in places)
Eton Rifles(IRE) could be used to hold the form down, but he had conditions to suit and is just the type to run a big race pitched into better company than he used to, as he's long looked more talented than his wins-to-runs ration (now 3-18) suggests. (op 16-1)
Waffle(IRE), runner-up in the Wokingham off 100 only seven days earlier, ran a bit better than result might indicate. He travelled just about as well as the winner, but was briefly denied a clear run at a crucial stage and couldn't build up sufficient momentum in the sticky ground.
Winker Watson, who won the 2007 Norfolk and July Stakes, has had his stud career interrupted for an apparently brief return to racing. His connections said he'd come on plenty for the run, so this rates a highly satisfactory comeback, although he could bounce if out again soon. (op 25-1)

3395 TOTESCOOP6 H'CAP 6f
2:30 (2:30) (Class 2) (0-100,99) 3-Y-O+
£12,462 (£3,732; £1,866; £934; £466; £234) **Stalls** Centre

Form RPR
1-30 **1** **Edinburgh Knight (IRE)**[43] 2075 4-9-6 **91** .... JimCrowley 7 100+
(Paul D'Arcy) *hld up towards rr: rdn and effrt over 1f out: qcknd to ld last 50yds: r.o* **15/2**

0260 **2** *1* **Everymanforhimself (IRE)**[35] 2288 7-8-13 **87** ....(b) AmyRyan(3) 1 93
(Kevin Ryan) *hld up: hdwy on outside of gp 2f out: led ins fnl f to last 50yds: kpt on* **33/1**

0000 **3** *nk* **Johannes (IRE)**[35] 2317 8-9-7 **92** .... PaulHanagan 6 97
(Richard Fahey) *midfield: rdn over 2f out: hdwy over 1f out: kpt on u.p fnl f* **9/1**

1101 **4** *shd* **Klynch**[7] 3162 5-8-11 **85** ....(b) JamesSullivan(3) 2 90
(Ruth Carr) *in tch: hdwy and ev ch over 1f out to ins fnl f: kpt on u.p* **6/1**[1]

-112 **5** *hd* **Singeur (IRE)**[9] 3073 4-9-12 **97** .... LeeNewman 5 101
(Robin Bastiman) *cl up: led over 2f out to ins fnl f: kpt on same pce* **10/1**

141 **6** *hd* **Ginger Ted (IRE)**[11] 3028 4-9-1 **89** ....(p) RobertLButler(3) 10 92+
(Richard Guest) *hld up: rdn and hdwy over 1f out: kpt on ins fnl f: nrst fin* **6/1**[1]

0-01 **7** *1 1/4* **Roker Park (IRE)**[22] 2668 6-9-0 **85** .... DanielTudhope 15 84+
(David O'Meara) *hld up: hdwy and swtchd lft over 1f out: kpt on fnl f: nvr able to chal* **7/1**[3]

0650 **8** *1* **Arganil (USA)**[24] 2620 6-9-1 **86** ....(p) PhillipMakin 4 82
(Kevin Ryan) *prom: effrt and rdn over 2f out: no ex 1f out* **16/1**

0-40 **9** *1 1/4* **My Kingdom (IRE)**[21] 2706 5-9-4 **89** .... HayleyTurner 13 81+
(David Nicholls) *hld up: hdwy on nr side of gp over 1f out: no imp fnl f* **20/1**

-050 **10** *2 1/4* **Rash Judgement**[42] 2116 6-9-2 **87** .... TedDurcan 9 72
(Eric Alston) *t.k.h: trckd ldrs: rdn over 2f out: wknd over 1f out* **25/1**

-000 **11** *2* **Tombi (USA)**[15] 2890 7-9-2 **87** ....(p) SilvestreDeSousa 12 66
(Geoffrey Harker) *in tch: rdn and outpcd over 2f out: n.d after* **6/1**[1]

31 **12** *3 1/2* **Marvellous Value (IRE)**[30] 2434 6-9-1 **86** .... TomEaves 8 53
(Michael Dods) *hld up: rdn over 2f out: wknd over 1f out* **13/2**[2]

0-00 **13** 1 1/4 **Amenable (IRE)**[24] 2620 4-9-2 **87**................................. AdrianNicholls 14 50
(David Nicholls) *led on nr side of gp to over 2f out: wknd over 1f out* **16/1**
1m 14.51s (-0.09) **Going Correction** +0.05s/f (Good) **13** Ran SP% **122.9**
Speed ratings (Par 109): **102,100,100,100,99 99,97,96,94,91 89,84,82**
Tote Swingers:1&2:£36.30, 2&3:£51.30, 1&3:£16.40 CSF £244.15 CT £2274.78 TOTE £8.70: £3.00, £9.50, £3.00; EX 238.30 Trifecta £781.70 Part won. Pool £1,056.45 - 0.30 winning units..
Owner Knights Racing **Bred** New England Stud Myriad Norelands **Trained** Newmarket, Suffolk
■ Stewards' Enquiry : Amy Ryan one-day ban: used whip down shoulder in the forehand (Jul 11)
Lee Newman caution: careless riding.

FOCUS
The field were spread out in the closing stages, but the main action unfolded up the middle of the track. This looked a pretty clean race for a big-field sprint and the form should be sound enough. The time was 0.75 seconds slower than the Group 3 Chipchase Stakes. A small step up from the winner.

NOTEBOOK
Edinburgh Knight(IRE) ◆ disappointed at York last time, but prior to that he'd finished a promising third on his reappearance at Ascot, one place behind subsequent Wokingham winner Deacon Blues. It was clear from some way out he was back in form as he travelled really smoothly and he was well ridden by Jim Crowley, a jockey doubtless high on confidence after landing a Group 1 sprint at Royal Ascot. The rider was patient on a horse evidently full of running and saved ground by challenging between rivals, at which point his mount quickened well. The winner's three previous victories had been gained on Polytrack, but this represented a career best and he did this in the style of horse who can reach quite a smart level in sprints. Official explanation: trainer said, regarding apparent improvement in form, that the gelding was better suited by having a 43-day break since its last run. (op 11-1)
Everymanforhimself(IRE) challenged widest, which might not have been ideal as he hasn't always found a great deal when in the clear. But in fairness he kept on well, with the winner's late challenge impossible to resist. (op 40-1)
Johannes(IRE) couldn't quite muster the finishing speed of the front two, but he kept on well on ground that his record suggests would have been easier than ideal. (op 12-1)
Klynch arrived on the scene going easily but didn't find quite enough. He had won four of his last five starts, but was up 9lb for his latest success and faced with better company. (op 8-1)
Singeur(IRE) ran with real credit considering his six wins to date have all been gained over 5f and, like the trip, the ground was also a question mark. (tchd 12-1)
Ginger Ted(IRE) was up 4lb for his recent Thirsk win and simply didn't find as much as some. However, he moved through the race like a horse who still has more to offer and might be worth another chance. (tchd 5-1)
Roker Park(IRE) was set a lot to do and had to be switched. He can probably do a bit better. Official explanation: jockey said he lost an iron in final furlong (op 6-1)
My Kingdom(IRE) ◆ raced more towards the near side than the eight runners who finished ahead of him and may have run quite a bit better than the result suggests. He's one to keep in mind.
Tombi(USA) may have been on slower ground than some, racing near side, but this was still a laboured performance. Quicker going might be more favourable. (tchd 11-2)

3396 JOHN SMITH'S NORTHUMBERLAND PLATE (HERITAGE H'CAP) 2m 19y
3:05 (3:05) (Class 2) 3-Y-0+

£92,475 (£27,840; £13,920; £6,945; £3,480; £1,755) **Stalls** Low

Form RPR
2363 **1** **Tominator**[17] 2812 4-8-5 **90**.. PaulPickard(3) 14 100+
(Reg Hollinshead) *stdd and swtchd lft s: t.k.h in rr: smooth hdwy over 2f out: led over 1f out: edgd lft: rdn and r.o strly* **25/1**
1032 **2** 1 3/4 **Montaff**[30] 2438 5-9-6 **102**................................ HughBowman 11 110
(Mick Channon) *hld up and bhd: hmpd on ins rail after 4f: gd hdwy over 2f out: chsd wnr appr fnl f: r.o* **18/1**
-644 **3** 2 1/2 **Deauville Flyer**[28] 2499 5-8-11 **93**.................................. TomEaves 16 98
(Tim Easterby) *hld up in midfield on ins: rdn over 3f out: hdwy and ev ch over 1f out: kpt on same pce fnl f* **8/1**[3]
30-4 **4** *shd* **Petara Bay (IRE)**[56] 1679 7-9-6 **102**............................... JimCrowley 21 107
(Robert Mills) *hld up: rdn over 3f out: styd on wl fr 2f out: nvr able to chal* **40/1**
-223 **5** 2 **Moyenne Corniche**[43] 2044 6-9-4 **100**.......................... GeorgeBaker 7 102+
(Brian Ellison) *hld up in midfield: smooth hdwy to trck ldrs over 1f out: sn rdn: kpt on same pce fnl f* **16/1**
10-1 **6** 1 1/2 **Overturn (IRE)**[52] 1808 7-9-5 **106**.......................... HenryBrooke(5) 2 107+
(Donald McCain) *led: qcknd over 3f out: edgd lft and hdd over 1f out: wknd ins fnl f* **7/1**[2]
-200 **7** 1 1/2 **Icon Dream (IRE)**[35] 2289 4-9-2 **98**.............................. PhillipMakin 17 97
(David Simcock) *dwlt: bhd: rdn over 3f out: styd on fnl 2f: nvr able to chal* **25/1**
-102 **8** 3/4 **High Office**[7] 3163 5-8-8 **90**....................................... PaulHanagan 12 88
(Richard Fahey) *midfield: drvn along over 3f out: effrt whn checked briefly 2f out: kpt on: no imp* **10/1**
0001 **9** 3/4 **My Arch**[6] 3205 9-8-5 **90** 5ex.................................. JamesSullivan(3) 22 87
(Ollie Pears) *hld up: stdy hdwy after 6f: rdn over 3f out: outpcd fr 2f out* **20/1**
00-4 **10** 5 **Prospect Wells (FR)**[35] 2316 6-9-1 **102**......................... DaleSwift(5) 9 93
(Howard Johnson) *t.k.h: trckd ldrs: rdn 3f out: wknd fr 2f out* **25/1**
0-00 **11** *nk* **La Vecchia Scuola (IRE)**[42] 2107 7-8-12 **94**.............. DanielTudhope 4 85
(Jim Goldie) *hld up in midfield on ins: effrt and hdwy over 2f out: wknd over 1f out* **25/1**
52-0 **12** 5 **Chock A Block (IRE)**[35] 2289 5-9-3 **99**.................. RichardMullen 10 84
(Saeed Bin Suroor) *midfield on ins: rdn along over 3f out: effrt and edgd lft over 2f out: sn wknd* **33/1**
14-3 **13** 7 **Mystery Star (IRE)**[52] 1808 6-8-11 **98**..................... AshleyMorgan(5) 15 74
(Mark H Tompkins) *hld up in midfield on outside: rdn over 4f out: wknd over 2f out* **33/1**
3-35 **14** 2 1/2 **Simenon (IRE)**[35] 2316 4-9-1 **97**.. LiamKeniry 1 70
(Andrew Balding) *trckd ldr: rdn over 3f out: wknd fr 2f out* **12/1**
1-21 **15** 1 **Harlestone Times (IRE)**[35] 2289 4-9-5 **101**.................. TedDurcan 5 73
(John Dunlop) *prom tl rdn and wknd over 2f out* **6/1**[1]
11-1 **16** 4 1/2 **Activate**[28] 2499 4-9-0 **96**.. HayleyTurner 18 63
(Michael Bell) *hld up: pushed along over 5f out: drvn over 3f out: sn btn: eased whn no ch fnl f* **7/1**[2]
0252 **17** *nse* **Nave (USA)**[35] 2289 4-8-9 **91**.. PJMcDonald 13 58
(Mark Johnston) *midfield on outside: struggling over 4f out: sn btn* **33/1**
3/1 **18** 8 **Investissement**[56] 1679 5-9-3 **99**................................... NickyMackay 3 56
(John Gosden) *t.k.h: trckd ldrs tl rdn and wknd over 2f out* **9/1**
5301 **19** 55 **English Summer**[35] 2285 4-8-10 **92**.................. SilvestreDeSousa 8 —
(Mark Johnston) *cl up tl rdn and wknd qckly fr 3f out* **12/1**
3m 29.48s (-9.92) **Going Correction** -0.275s/f (Firm) **19** Ran SP% **127.4**
Speed ratings (Par 109): **113,112,110,110,109 109,108,107,107,105 104,102,98,97,97 94,94,90,63**
Tote Swingers:1&2:£94.90, 2&3:£44.40, 1&3:£44.50 CSF £393.83 CT £3919.45 TOTE £32.90: £5.20, £3.40, £2.10, £8.30; EX 594.50 Trifecta £10317.50 Pool £79,472.63 - 5.70 winning units..
Owner Mrs Susy Haslehurst **Bred** Mrs S L Brimble **Trained** Upper Longdon, Staffs

FOCUS
The finish of this year's Northumberland Plate was dominated by those ridden patiently, indeed the winner, runner-up and fourth were all well behind for most of the way, and clearly Overturn, successful from the front in last season's edition, set an overly strong pace this time. The field tended to race up the middle of the track in the straight. Solid form.

NOTEBOOK
Tominator had only once tired further than 1m4f and had never previously gone beyond 1m6f, but he relished this stamina test, staying on really well having travelled strongly under a sensible ride from Paul Pickard. It's no surprise he found dramatic improvement for this trip considering his dam's only win came over 1m7f on soft ground and she's a sister to Goodwood Cup winner Tioman Island. Completely unexposed as a stayer, Tominator can defy a rise when faced with similar conditions and a race like the Cesarewitch is an obvious target.
Montaff found some early trouble but it didn't seem to cost him, and crucially he was well placed. He had to force his way through when looking for a run in the straight, but the winner was going better at that point and he was simply beaten by a better-handicapped rival. (op 25-1)
Deauville Flyer was 4lb higher than when fifth in this last year and didn't see his race out as well as the front two, but he deserves credit having sat a bit closer to the hot pace than that pair. (op 9-1)
Petara Bay(IRE) was another who benefited from the leaders going too fast and ran on past mainly beaten rivals. Lightly raced for his age, he's still capable of smart form, but plenty went his way.
Moyenne Corniche travelled strongly, but he was trying his furthest trip to date and didn't see his race out as well as some. The Ebor trip might suit better, although he may not be well enough handicapped. (op 14-1)
Overturn(IRE), up 7lb for his Chester Cup victory and 13lb higher than 12 months ago, got noticeably tired as the chasing pack began to close early in the straight, wandering and carrying his head to the side at one stage, but he kept on in typically gallant fashion. Those who raced close to him early were nowhere to be seen at the finish and it could take him a while to get over this. (op 15-2)
Icon Dream(IRE) conserved plenty of energy early but couldn't make it count. (op 28-1 tchd 33-1)
High Office failed to prove his stamina, not taking advantage of being 5lb well in. (tchd 12-1 and 16-1 in a place)
My Arch wasn't up to the task off 5lb higher than when winning a lesser race at Pontefract last time. (tchd 22-1)
Simenon(IRE) paid for chasing the overly strong gallop. (op 14-1)
Harlestone Times(IRE) was 6lb higher than when winning over 1m4f on quick going on his previous start and was trying this trip for the first time. Official explanation: trainer's rep said gelding may have failed to stay trip (op 7-1)
Activate had won his last three starts, including a 2m handicap off 5lb lower on his reappearance, but he ran flat. Official explanation: jockey said gelding never travelled (tchd 13-2 and 15-2 in places)
Investissement had Moyenne Corniche and Simenon behind when winning over 1m6f at Goodwood on his debut for this yard in April, and he was raised only 4lb, but this was poor even allowing for racing close the speed. (op 8-1)

3397 TOTESPORT 0800 221 221 H'CAP 7f
3:40 (3:44) (Class 2) (0-105,96) 3-Y-0+

£12,462 (£3,732; £1,866; £934; £466; £234) **Stalls** Centre

Form RPR
0000 **1** **Imperial Djay (IRE)**[2] 3315 6-9-3 **88**........................ JamesSullivan(3) 10 99
(Ruth Carr) *s.i.s: hld up: hdwy over 2f out: rdn to ld appr fnl f: sn pressed by 2nd: kpt on* **18/1**
2212 **2** 1/2 **Dubai Dynamo**[30] 2431 6-9-9 **91**.. PJMcDonald 1 101
(Ruth Carr) *hld up: gd hdwy 2f out: chal appr fnl f: kpt on: hld towards fin* **8/1**
046- **3** 2 **Don't Call Me (IRE)**[266] 6567 4-9-3 **88**.................. MichaelO'Connell(3) 4 92
(David Nicholls) *dwlt: in midfield: hdwy over 2f out: rdn to chal over 1f out: kpt on one pce fnl f* **22/1**
4005 **4** 3/4 **Dhaular Dhar (IRE)**[14] 2909 9-9-4 **86**.......................... DanielTudhope 12 88+
(Jim Goldie) *hld up: rdn over 2f out: hdwy over 1f out: kpt on fnl f: wnt 4th fnl 50yds: nvr threatened ldrs* **14/1**
0304 **5** 1/2 **Captain Ramius (IRE)**[8] 3134 5-9-5 **87**........................... JimCrowley 16 88
(Kevin Ryan) *hld up in tch: gd hdwy over 2f out: rdn and ev ch over 1f out: no ex ins fnl f: lost 4th fnl 50yds* **11/1**
6400 **6** 1 1/4 **Brae Hill (IRE)**[10] 3032 5-9-13 **95**..................................... DavidNolan 14 93+
(Richard Fahey) *in tch: rdn 2f out: one pce* **9/1**
6-61 **7** 1 1/2 **Xilerator (IRE)**[30] 2431 4-9-9 **91**............................. AdrianNicholls 2 84
(David Nicholls) *w ldr: rdn to ld over 1f out: sn hdd and edgd rt: wknd ins fnl f* **11/2**[1]
4110 **8** 3/4 **Masked Dance (IRE)**[8] 3134 4-9-6 **88**.........................(p) PhillipMakin 13 79
(Kevin Ryan) *prom: rdn and lost pl over 2f out: no imp fr over 1f out* **16/1**
3300 **9** 4 1/2 **Camerooney**[2] 3315 8-9-0 **87**.. DaleSwift(5) 15 66
(Brian Ellison) *prom: rdn over 3f out: wknd 2f out* **12/1**
1210 **10** 1 1/2 **Bawaardi (IRE)**[21] 2706 5-9-8 **90**.................................... PaulHanagan 7 65
(Richard Fahey) *midfield: rdn over 2f out: no imp: eased fnl 100yds* **15/2**[3]
0-00 **11** 1 1/4 **Mass Rally (IRE)**[14] 2927 4-9-11 **93**................................... TomEaves 8 65
(Michael Dods) *hld up: hdwy over 2f out: rdn 2f out: wknd ins fnl f* **25/1**
56-0 **12** 1/2 **Oratory (IRE)**[77] 1240 5-9-8 **90**................................ SilvestreDeSousa 11 61
(Geoffrey Harker) *midfield: rdn over 2f out: wknd over 1f out* **8/1**
2221 **13** 2 1/4 **Vito Volterra (IRE)**[2] 3315 4-9-4 **86** 6ex.......................... HayleyTurner 6 50
(Michael Smith) *sn led: rdn whn hdd over 1f out: sn wknd* **6/1**[2]
5000 **14** 2 **Osteopathic Remedy (IRE)**[14] 2933 7-9-10 **92**............... LiamKeniry 5 51
(Michael Dods) *in tch: pushed along over 3f out: wknd over 1f out* **14/1**
1m 27.4s (-0.40) **Going Correction** +0.05s/f (Good) **14** Ran SP% **122.4**
Speed ratings (Par 109): **109,108,106,105,104 103,101,100,95,93 92,91,89,87**
Tote Swingers:1&2:£40.70, 2&3:£27.60, 1&3:£67.50 CSF £158.08 CT £3285.30 TOTE £23.10: £7.70, £2.30, £7.20; EX 253.30 Trifecta £1084.50 Part won. Pool £1,465.65 - 0.62 winning units..
Owner Hollinbridge Partnership **Bred** D Veitch And Musagd Abo Salim **Trained** Huby, N Yorks
■ Stewards' Enquiry : Jim Crowley one-day ban: careless riding (Jul 11)
Phillip Makin two-day ban: careless riding (Jul 11-12)

FOCUS
A decent enough handicap run at a good pace, suiting those waited with. They raced up the middle of the track. Straightforward, solid form.

NOTEBOOK
Imperial Djay(IRE) wasn't at his best over 1m here two days previously, but prior to that he'd been going the right way and he returned to form with a game effort. Considering he made a big effort to get to the front before being challenged by his stable companion, he did well to keep on so strongly. There could be more to come. (op 20-1)
Dubai Dynamo achieved his sixth consecutive top-two finish, in the process reversing recent form with Xilerator. He was clear of the others and, like his successful stablemate, is one to keep on side for now. (op 9-1)
Don't Call Me(IRE) had been sold out of Bryan Smart's yard for £12,000 since last seen. He returned from a 266-day absence without his usual tongue-tie, but his new connections will surely be delighted with this reintroduction. (op 20-1)
Dhaular Dhar(IRE) ran a good race over a trip that is probably short enough for him these days, especially as he didn't get the clearest of runs through. (op 16-1)
Captain Ramius(IRE) ran okay without building on his recent Newmarket effort. (op 10-1)

Xilerator(IRE) couldn't dominate and wasn't at his best. He had Dubai Dynamo narrowly behind when winning over C&D on good ground last time, but he was well held off a 7lb higher mark after going plenty fast enough. Perhaps the going was easier than ideal. (op 5-1)
Bawaardi(IRE) Official explanation: jockey said gelding lost its action approaching line
Vito Volterra(IRE) was having his third start of the week after finishing second in the Carlisle Bell and then winning over 1m here and it seemingly came too soon. (op 7-1)

3398 IRISH E.B.F./TARMAC MAIDEN STKS 5f
4:15 (4:15) (Class 4) 2-Y-O £5,180 (£1,541; £770; £384) Stalls Centre

Form				RPR
0422	1		**Kool Henry (IRE)**[14] 2907 2-9-3 0 ... SilvestreDeSousa 4 (David O'Meara) *mde all: rdn and hrd pressed fr over 1f out: edgd lft ins fnl f: jst hld on* **2/1**[2]	75
0	2	*shd*	**Free Zone**[29] 2455 2-9-3 0 ... TomEaves 7 (Bryan Smart) *cl up: effrt and rdn over 1f out: disp ld ins fnl f: edgd lft: jst hld* **11/1**[3]	75
	3	*3/4*	**Satanic Beat (IRE)** 2-9-3 0 ... PJMcDonald 6 (Jedd O'Keeffe) *in tch: rdn and rn green 2f out: styd on wl fnl f: bttr for r* **20/1**	72
05	4	*2 1/4*	**Alnair (IRE)**[12] 2992 2-9-3 0 ... TedDurcan 9 (Declan Carroll) *t.k.h: hld up: hdwy over 1f out: kpt on fnl f: no imp* **12/1**	64
0	5	*3*	**Laffan (IRE)**[13] 2953 2-9-3 0 ... PhillipMakin 1 (Kevin Ryan) *prom: effrt and ev ch over 2f out: wknd appr fnl f* **11/8**[1]	53
	6	*1/2*	**I'll Be Good** 2-9-3 0 ... GeorgeBaker 10 (Robert Johnson) *s.i.s: hld up: shkn up and hdwy over 1f out: nvr nr ldrs* **14/1**	51
00	7	*2 1/2*	**Wake Up Sioux (IRE)**[6] 3200 2-8-12 0 ... HayleyTurner 5 (David C Griffiths) *in tch: rdn and outpcd over 2f out: n.d after* **33/1**	37
0	8	*5*	**Orrell Post**[9] 3092 2-8-12 0 ... PaulHanagan 3 (Richard Fahey) *in tch: drvn and outpcd over 2f out: btn over 1f out* **12/1**	19
	9	*21*	**Majestic Manannan (IRE)** 2-9-3 0 ... AdrianNicholls 2 (David Nicholls) *t.k.h: cl up tl rdn and wknd 2f out: t.o* **14/1**	—

62.27 secs (1.17) **Going Correction** +0.05s/f (Good) 9 Ran SP% **120.2**
Speed ratings (Par 95): **92,91,90,87,82 81,77,69,35**
Tote Swingers:1&2:£5.20, 2&3:£16.50, 1&3:£8.80 CSF £25.94 TOTE £3.10: £1.50, £2.80, £3.60; EX 24.40 Trifecta £497.20 Part won. Pool £672.01 - 0.70 winning units..
Owner Middleham Park Racing Equality Racing **Bred** Stephanie Hanly **Trained** Nawton, N Yorks

FOCUS
This went to the most exposed runner in the line, Kool Henry, who had achieved RPRs in the 70s on his last two goes, so just fair form. Improvement from the runner-up.

NOTEBOOK
Kool Henry(IRE) showed a good attitude and can make a nice enough handicapper. (op 15-8 tchd 7-4)
Free Zone stepped up a good deal on his Haydock debut, coping well with the drop back from 6f. He moved nicely for a long way and found for pressure, but the battle-hardened winner was just too strong. There should be a similar race in him. (op 12-1)
Satanic Beat(IRE) was going on at the finish and fared best of the three newcomers. His sales price increased from 34,000euros to £65,000 and he's a half-brother to a few fair winners, out of 1m Listed scorer. Clearly he's bred to win races and should do so.
Alnair(IRE) kept on without making a telling impression. He should find his level in nurseries. (tchd 11-1)
Laffan(IRE) again hinted at ability. (op 15-8)
I'll Be Good, whose sales price increased considerably to 20,000gns this year, made some minor late progress. (op 12-1)
Majestic Manannan(IRE), a 30,000euros purchase this year, was eased off before the race got serious and something looked to be amiss. Official explanation: jockey said colt lost its action (op 11-1)

3399 TRY TOTEQUICKPICK ON ALL TOTEPOOL BETS H'CAP 1m 2f 32y
4:45 (4:45) (Class 4) (0-85,83) 3-Y-O+ £5,180 (£1,541; £770; £384) Stalls Low

Form				RPR
0254	1		**Tres Coronas (IRE)**[7] 3164 4-9-12 **81** ... LeeNewman 8 (David Barron) *hld up: hdwy over 2f out: rdn over 1f out: led last 50yds: styd on wl* **9/2**[1]	92
0034	2	*1/2*	**San Cassiano (IRE)**[18] 2783 4-9-11 **80** ... PJMcDonald 1 (Ruth Carr) *led: rdn over 2f out: hdd last 50yds: kpt on* **12/1**	90
5564	3	*1 3/4*	**Jonny Lesters Hair (IRE)**[9] 3085 6-9-6 **75** ... DavidNolan 3 (Tim Easterby) *trckd ldrs: effrt and drvn over 2f out: kpt on same pce ins fnl f* **11/1**	82
-633	4	*nse*	**Grams And Ounces**[30] 2414 4-9-7 **76** ... HayleyTurner 6 (Amy Weaver) *t.k.h: hld up: smooth hdwy over 2f out: rdn and ev ch over 1f out: one pce ins fnl f* **8/1**	82
113	5	*1 1/2*	**Mcbirney (USA)**[26] 2544 4-9-9 **83** ... HarryBentley(5) 15 (Paul D'Arcy) *hld up: stdy hdwy and prom over 1f out: sn rdn: kpt on same pce fnl f* **5/1**[2]	86
0525	6	*1 1/4*	**Hakuna Matata**[2] 3319 4-8-12 **72** ... (b) DaleSwift(5) 14 (Brian Ellison) *s.i.s: hld up: rdn over 2f out: hdwy over 1f out: nvr rchd ldrs* **6/1**[3]	73
5-45	7	*1 1/4*	**Spirit Of A Nation (IRE)**[7] 3164 6-9-7 **76** ... (p) PaulHanagan 2 (James Moffatt) *prom: drvn and outpcd over 2f out: rallied fnl f: no imp* **20/1**	74
12-3	8	*2 1/4*	**Next Edition (IRE)**[26] 2572 3-9-1 **82** ... JimCrowley 5 (Howard Johnson) *cl up: rdn over 2f out: wknd appr fnl f* **10/1**	76
2052	9	*1 1/2*	**Doctor Zhivago**[7] 3164 4-10-0 **83** ... AdrianNicholls 11 (David Nicholls) *in tch: drvn and edgd rt over 2f out: edgd lft and wknd wl over 1f out* **13/2**	74
66-4	10	*1/2*	**Jewelled Dagger (IRE)**[20] 2260 7-8-7 **65** oh2 ... PaulPickard(3) 7 (Jim Goldie) *midfield: struggling over 2f out: sn n.d* **25/1**	55
01-0	11	*3/4*	**Best Prospect (IRE)**[43] 2059 9-9-8 **77** ... (vt) PhillipMakin 12 (Michael Dods) *s.i.s: hld up: shkn up 2f out: nvr nr ldrs* **16/1**	65
-000	12	*3*	**Golden Hinde**[28] 2506 3-8-10 **77** ... SilvestreDeSousa 13 (Mark Johnston) *midfield: drvn and outpcd wl over 2f out: sn struggling* **10/1**	59

2m 10.18s (-1.72) **Going Correction** -0.275s/f (Firm)
WFA 3 from 4yo+ 12lb 12 Ran SP% **122.3**
Speed ratings (Par 105): **95,94,93,93,91 90,89,88,86,86 85,83**
Tote Swingers:1&2:£13.90, 2&3:£27.80, 1&3:£12.80 CSF £61.02 CT £574.40 TOTE £5.20: £1.90, £4.30, £3.80; EX 66.20 Trifecta £436.60 Part won. Pool £590.03 - 0.70 winning units..
Owner J Cringan & D Pryde **Bred** Denis McDonnell **Trained** Maunby, N Yorks
■ Stewards' Enquiry : Lee Newman one-day ban: used whip in incorrect place (Jul 11)

FOCUS
A fair handicap, although the pace looked just ordinary. Solid form.

3400 TRY TOTEQUICKPICK IF YOU'RE FEELING LUCKY H'CAP 1m (R)
5:20 (5:20) (Class 4) (0-85,85) 3-Y-O £5,180 (£1,541; £770; £384) Stalls Low

Form				RPR
5503	1		**Weapon Of Choice (IRE)**[16] 2833 3-9-2 **80** ... SilvestreDeSousa 2 (David Simcock) *mde all: qcknd ordinary pce over 2f out: hld on wl fnl f* **6/1**	87
10-	2	*3/4*	**My Freedom (IRE)**[290] 5849 3-9-7 **85** ... TedDurcan 4 (Saeed Bin Suroor) *s.i.s: hld up: rdn and hdwy to chse wnr appr fnl f: kpt on* **9/4**[1]	90
-610	3	*nk*	**Yojimbo (IRE)**[28] 2506 3-8-13 **77** ... SamHitchcott 5 (Mick Channon) *hld up: rdn over 2f out: hdwy and edgd lft over 1f out: kpt on fnl f* **14/1**	81
-262	4	*2 3/4*	**Nicola's Dream**[10] 3038 3-8-6 **70** ... PaulHanagan 6 (Richard Fahey) *chsd wnr: rdn over 2f out: lost 2nd appr fnl f: no ex* **11/2**[3]	67
3331	5	*nk*	**Agiaal (USA)**[36] 2256 3-9-5 **83** ... NickyMackay 3 (John Gosden) *t.k.h: trckd ldrs: effrt over 2f out: one pce over 1f out* **4/1**[2]	80
4213	6	*1*	**Honest Deal**[42] 2092 3-9-0 **78** ... PJMcDonald 8 (Alan Swinbank) *prom: rdn over 2f out: wknd over 1f out* **10/1**	72
5-15	7	*nk*	**Youhavecontrol (IRE)**[37] 2215 3-8-10 **74** ... PhillipMakin 9 (Michael Dods) *hld up: pushed along and shortlived effrt appr 2f out: sn no imp* **4/1**[2]	68

1m 42.72s (-2.58) **Going Correction** -0.275s/f (Firm) 7 Ran SP% **116.2**
Speed ratings (Par 101): **101,100,99,97,96 95,95**
Tote Swingers:1&2:£4.80, 2&3:£7.90, 1&3:£9.40 CSF £20.56 CT £183.14 TOTE £6.30: £3.50, £1.90; EX 24.70 Trifecta £254.20 Pool £828.05 - 2.41 winning units..
Owner Dr Marwan Koukash **Bred** Stone Ridge Farm **Trained** Newmarket, Suffolk

FOCUS
A fair handicap 3-y-o handicap, although Weapon Of Choice was allowed an uncontested lead. He is rated back to his best, with the third the best guide.
T/Jkpt: Not won. T/Plt: £1,869.20 to a £1 stake. Pool £199,831.69 - 78.04 winning tickets.
T/Qpdt: £181.50 to a £1 stke. Pool £10,940.48 - 44.60 winning tickets. RY

3361 NEWMARKET (R-H)
Saturday, June 25

OFFICIAL GOING: Good to soft (good in places) changing to good after race 5 (3.55pm)
Wind: Fresh half-behind Weather: Overcast

3401 FEE GROUP PLC MAIDEN STKS 7f
1:45 (1:48) (Class 5) 2-Y-O £3,238 (£963; £481; £240) Stalls Low

Form				RPR
	1		**Rockinante (FR)** 2-9-3 0 ... RichardHughes 16 (Richard Hannon) *hld up: hdwy over 2f out: rdn over 1f out: r.o to ld wl ins fnl f: readily* **9/2**[2]	86+
	2	*nk*	**Burano (IRE)** 2-9-3 0 ... ShaneKelly 10 (Brian Meehan) *a.p: led over 1f out: rdn: edgd lft and hdd wl ins fnl f* **25/1**	85+
4	3	*3 3/4*	**Elkhart (IRE)**[16] 2831 2-9-3 0 ... RichardHills 5 (Mark Johnston) *a.p: rdn and ev ch over 1f out: styd on same pce ins fnl f* **20/1**	76
0	4	*3/4*	**Tudor Empire (IRE)**[8] 3132 2-9-3 0 ... WilliamBuick 15 (John Gosden) *chsd ldrs: rdn and ev ch over 1f out: no ex ins fnl f* **13/2**[3]	74
	5	*nk*	**Paladin (IRE)** 2-9-3 0 ... MickaelBarzalona 4 (Mahmood Al Zarooni) *a.p: rdn over 2f out: hung lft over 1f out: styd on same pce* **4/1**[1]	73
	6	*1/2*	**Fiscal** 2-9-3 0 ... SaleemGolam 9 (John Gosden) *hld up: hdwy over 2f out: rdn over 1f out: no imp fnl f* **20/1**	72+
	7	*1 3/4*	**Mister Music** 2-9-3 0 ... RyanMoore 1 (Richard Hannon) *s.i.s: hld up: hdwy and hung lft fr over 1f out: nvr trbld ldrs* **10/1**	68+
5	8	*1 1/4*	**Acer Diamonds (IRE)**[16] 2837 2-9-0 0 ... AdamBeschizza(3) 6 (Julia Feilden) *hld up: nt clr run over 2f out: sn rdn: nvr on terms* **9/1**	65
4	9	*nk*	**Flying Trader (USA)**[17] 2817 2-9-3 0 ... KierenFallon 12 (Jane Chapple-Hyam) *prom: rdn over 2f out: wknd fnl f* **9/2**[2]	64
	10	*1*	**Voodoo Rhythm (USA)** 2-9-3 0 ... EddieCreighton 11 (Brian Meehan) *sn pushed along in rr: styd on fr over 1f out: n.d* **80/1**	61
	11	*1 1/4*	**Palus San Marco (IRE)** 2-9-3 0 ... JackMitchell 8 (Peter Chapple-Hyam) *hld up: rdn over 2f out: sme hdwy over 1f out: sn wknd* **20/1**	58
	12	*2*	**Dollar Bill** 2-9-3 0 ... JimmyFortune 2 (Andrew Balding) *prom over 4f* **12/1**	53
	13	*2 3/4*	**Ocean Tempest** 2-9-3 0 ... KirstyMilczarek 3 (John Ryan) *s.i.s: hld up: wknd over 2f out* **100/1**	46
0	14	*2*	**Ooi Long**[42] 2109 2-9-3 0 ... MarcHalford 14 (Mark Rimmer) *led: rdn and hdd over 1f out: sn wknd* **200/1**	41
	15	*13*	**Like Clockwork** 2-9-3 0 ... NeilCallan 7 (Mark H Tompkins) *mid-div: rdn 1/2-way: wknd over 2f out* **66/1**	9

1m 26.78s (1.08) **Going Correction** -0.15s/f (Firm) 15 Ran SP% **118.8**
Speed ratings (Par 93): **87,86,82,81,81 80,78,77,76,75 74,71,68,66,51**
Tote Swingers: 1&2 £26.50, 1&3 £17.70, 2&3 £68.00 CSF £119.30 TOTE £5.40: £2.40, £9.70, £3.60; EX 188.00.
Owner Coriolan Links Partnership Iii **Bred** Azienda Agricola Il Tiglio **Trained** East Everleigh, Wilts
■ Stewards' Enquiry : Adam Beschizza three-day ban: careless riding (Jul 9,11,12)
Kirsty Milczarek two-day ban: careless riding (Jul 9,11)

FOCUS
Stalls on stands' side of stands' side track except for 2.45, 3.55 and 4.30 centre. The opening race hadn't produced any winners that went on to win lots of races at Group level, but it still looked an interesting contest, full of potentially nice types. The winner impressed and the first pair were clear.

NOTEBOOK
Rockinante(FR) ◆, a E90,000 second foal of a French 7f/1m winner, and seemingly the choice of Richard Hughes of the Hannon pair, showed a good attitude while under restraint before quickening really well to catch a horse who'd gained some lengths on him about 1f out. He looks a potentially very useful performer. (op 5-1 tchd 11-2 in a place)
Burano(IRE) ◆, an E82,000 half-brother to a 7f /1m winner, put up a terrific performance on his debut, and this son of Dalakhani should have little trouble going one better if kept to a realistic level.
Elkhart(IRE) didn't run too badly on his first start over 6f and appeared to run a shade better this time after being prominent throughout - his jockey reportedly thought he'd win at one point. The horse will have little trouble with 1m. (op 16-1)
Tudor Empire(IRE) was a well-beaten eighth at this course over 6f last time, but improved on that with a pleasing enough second effort. (op 7-1)
Paladin(IRE), who is entered in the Derby, was fancied in the betting but only put up a satisfactory first run. He may need further already. (op 9-2 tchd 7-2)

Fiscal, a half-brother to 6f 2-y-o winner Finoon, looked the stable's second string and made a promising start. (op 22-1 tchd 16-1)
Mister Music ◆, a half-brother to 7f AW winner Choral, was the biggest eyecatcher, as he looked green leaving the stalls and needed bustling along to get involved, but made good ground during the final stages, suggesting he'll be much straighter next time. Official explanation: jockey said colt was slowly away (op 9-1)
Acer Diamonds(IRE) ◆ showed promise on his first start at Newbury after attracting some market interest and kept on nicely here in the final furlong. (op 8-1 tchd 10-1)
Flying Trader(USA) showed promise at Kempton earlier this month but was most disappointing on his first try of turf. (tchd 5-1)
Ocean Tempest Official explanation: jockey said colt ran green and hung left

3402 TOTESPORT.COM EMPRESS STKS (LISTED RACE) 6f
2:15 (2:16) (Class 1) 2-Y-O
£12,205 (£4,626; £2,315; £1,154; £578; £290) **Stalls** Low

Form RPR
1135 **1** **Lily's Angel (IRE)**[8] 3104 2-8-12 0 .... RichardHughes 3 94
(Richard Fahey) *s.i.s: hld up: shkn up 1/2-way: hdwy: nt clr run and swtchd rt 1f out: r.o to ld towards fin: comf* **6/1[3]**
3 **2** ½ **Pearl Diva (IRE)**[14] 2914 2-8-12 0 .... JackMitchell 5 93
(Peter Chapple-Hyam) *a.p: rdn to ld ins fnl f: hdd towards fin* **5/1[2]**
5311 **3** *nk* **Misty Conquest (IRE)**[29] 2476 2-8-12 0 .... RichardKingscote 8 92
(Tom Dascombe) *led: rdn and hdd over 1f out: ev ch ins fnl f: unable qck* **10/1**
10 **4** 2½ **Worthington (IRE)**[11] 3014 2-8-12 0 .... TonyHamilton 4 84
(Richard Fahey) *hld up: pushed along over 2f out: r.o ins fnl f: nt rch ldrs* **10/1**
1 **5** *shd* **Hawfinch**[24] 2606 2-8-12 0 .... WilliamBuick 10 84
(John Gosden) *hld up: nt clr run and swtchd rt ins fnl f: r.o: nt rch ldrs* **7/1**
01 **6** *nk* **Red Larkspur (IRE)**[45] 1996 2-8-12 0 .... DaneO'Neill 7 83
(Roger Teal) *chsd ldr: led over 1f out: sn rdn hdd and no ex ins fnl f* **40/1**
1 **7** *shd* **The Clan Macdonald**[23] 2630 2-8-12 0 .... MickaelBarzalona 14 83
(David Barron) *s.i.s: hld up: rdn over 1f out: r.o ins fnl f: nt rch ldrs* **5/1[2]**
P2 **8** *nk* **Hidden Passion (USA)**[17] 2811 2-8-12 0 .... ShaneKelly 13 82
(Brian Meehan) *prom: rdn over 1f out: styd on same pce* **12/1**
222 **9** *nk* **Nayarra (IRE)**[21] 2718 2-8-12 0 ....(b[1]) JimmyFortune 6 81
(Mick Channon) *chsd ldrs: rdn over 1f out: no ex ins fnl f* **16/1**
14 **10** 2 **Queens Revenge**[31] 2404 2-8-12 0 .... RyanMoore 9 75
(Tim Easterby) *chsd ldrs: rdn and hung lft over 1f out: wknd fnl f* **4/1[1]**
0 **11** 7 **Weood (IRE)**[17] 2811 2-8-12 0 .... IvaMilickova 12 54
(Clive Brittain) *hld up: rdn and wknd over 1f out* **100/1**

1m 11.99s (-0.51) **Going Correction** -0.15s/f (Firm) **11** Ran SP% **115.3**
Speed ratings (Par 101): **97,96,95,92,92 92,91,91,91,88 79**
Tote Swingers: 1&2 £5.70, 1&3 £11.30, 2&3 £20.30 CSF £35.32 TOTE £5.60: £1.90, £2.30, £3.40; EX 53.60 Trifecta £277.00 Pool £681.44 - 1.82 winning units..
Owner Middleham Park Racing XLVIII **Bred** N And Mrs N Nugent **Trained** Musley Bank, N Yorks

FOCUS
This is usually a weak race for the grade and that looks the case again with the front nine covered by just over four lengths. It was thrown wide open when the likely favourite My Propeller, a 17l winner of a Pontefract maiden on her previous start, was taken out due to the easy ground.

NOTEBOOK
Lily's Angel(IRE) won her first three races, including the Lily Agnes at Chester, and has run well in the Hilary Needler at Beverley and Albany Stakes at Royal Ascot since, so looked the class act. After settling in behind, her jockey conjured a perfectly timed challenge to win with plenty to spare, giving connections plenty of hope for the coming weeks. (op 9-2)
Pearl Diva(IRE) travelled like a decent type and looked to have got everything right until mown down by the winner in the final stages. A maiden ought to be a formaility for her. (op 7-1 tchd 8-1 in a place)
Misty Conquest(IRE) came into this chasing a hat-trick since being stepped up to 6f and made a good fist of it having raced out in front. She helps to confirm the race to be up to scratch. (tchd 9-1)
Worthington(IRE) won a Carlisle maiden before finding the Windsor Castle Stakes at Royal Ascot a bit too hot for her just over a week previously. She looked to be going nowhere at the halfway stage, but appreciated the stiff finish and kept on well. (op 12-1)
Hawfinch ◆ still looked a bit green, despite having won on her debut, out the back before realising what was going on and stayed on strongly. She should be even better next time. (op 13-2 tchd 6-1)
Red Larkspur(IRE) looked an interesting outsider on form (her last win on the AW had received boosts by horses behind), and she ran really well until he stamina in this going seemed to give way. (op 33-1)
The Clan Macdonald made the perfect start to her career last time when beating a subsequent winner on her opening effort, but couldn't get into this until it was all too late. (op 6-1)
Queens Revenge finished behind Lily's Angel in the Hilary Needler (had excuses that day) and did so again, although she looked ill at ease on the going. Ryan Moore reported she hung left. Official explanation: jockey said filly hung left (tchd 9-2)

3403 TRY TIMEFORM.BETFAIR.COM ON YOUR SMARTPHONE FRED ARCHER STKS (LISTED RACE) 1m 4f
2:45 (2:47) (Class 1) 4-Y-O+
£17,031 (£4,843; £4,843; £1,611; £807; £405) **Stalls** Centre

Form RPR
004- **1** **Jukebox Jury (IRE)**[343] 4164 5-9-0 116 .... NeilCallan 5 115
(Mark Johnston) *mde all: rdn over 1f out: edgd lft: styd on* **11/2**
03-4 **2** ¾ **Cavalryman**[30] 2439 5-9-0 113 .... MickaelBarzalona 7 114
(Saeed Bin Suroor) *hld up: hdwy over 2f out: sn rdn: styd on* **10/3[1]**
1-65 **2** *dht* **Afsare**[30] 2439 4-9-0 112 .... KierenFallon 8 114
(Luca Cumani) *hld up in tch: plld hrd: rdn to chse wnr and hung lft fr over 1f out: styd on* **4/1[2]**
1-53 **4** 3½ **Verdant**[49] 1883 4-9-0 102 .... RyanMoore 1 108
(Sir Michael Stoute) *chsd ldrs: rdn over 2f out: no ex ins fnl f* **4/1[2]**
6-25 **5** *hd* **Sabotage (UAE)**[107] 826 5-9-0 105 .... WilliamBuick 4 108
(Saeed Bin Suroor) *chsd ldr: rdn over 2f out: styd on same pce appr fnl f* **20/1**
150- **6** 2¾ **Anmar (USA)**[455] 1026 5-9-0 107 .... RichardHills 2 104
(Ed Dunlop) *hld up: hdwy over 2f out: rdn and hung lft fr over 1f out: wknd fnl f* **14/1**
/40- **7** 3½ **Alwaary (USA)**[252] 6925 5-9-0 105 .... TadhgO'Shea 6 98
(John Gosden) *hld up: outpcd fr over 2f out* **16/1**
-423 **8** 6 **Allied Powers (IRE)**[20] 2753 6-9-0 111 .... RichardHughes 3 88
(Michael Bell) *prom: rdn over 3f out: wknd over 2f out* **9/2[3]**

2m 33.35s (0.45) **Going Correction** -0.15s/f (Firm) **8** Ran SP% **112.1**
Speed ratings (Par 111): **92,91,91,89,89 87,84,80**Place: Afsare £1.70 Cavalryman £1.60. Ex: JJ,A £18.10 JJ,C £11.30. CSF: JJ,A £13.29 JJ,C £11.58. Trifecta: JJ,A,C £58.90 JJ,C,A £63.80. Tote Swingers: 1&A £7.60, 1&C £3.80, 2&2 £3.80 TOTE £8.00: £2.10 TRIFECTA Pool £1,406.26 - 8.15 win27 Owner.

FOCUS
The field contained two Group 1 winners, but those wins came before 2009 and with doubts over most of these this was not a strong race for the grade. The time was slow and the form isn't rated too positively. The whole field entered the home straight as a group towards the centre but edged to the far side the further they went, and the early fractions looked far from being quick.

NOTEBOOK
Jukebox Jury(IRE) hadn't been out since finishing a close fourth in a German Group 1 last July. Officially the best of these on the figures, his trainer had reported before the race that his horse had been given a complete break and endured a couple of niggling issues, so this was a thoroughly likeable effort from a horse well known for giving his all. However, it remains to be seen whether he can produce the same sort of dominating performance next time after his lengthy break. Connections aren't ruling out a tilt at the King George at Ascot next for him. (tchd 6-1)
Cavalryman had been running well at mainly Group 1 level for some time since an exciting 3-y-o career, one that saw him finish third to the mighty Sea The Stars in the Prix de l'Arc de Triomphe, but hadn't managed a win. Well behind Workforce in the Brigadier Gerard on his seasonal debut, he made a threatening move as the tempo lifted but didn't really find anything more than one pace up the rail. This looks as good as he is now. (tchd 9-2)
Afsare had been a shade disappointing in a couple of Group 3s this season (both at Sandown) after an encouraging and progressive 3-y-o campaign. Luca Cumani had a two-from-three record in this race, and Afsare went very close to enhancing that record but wasn't quite able to get there. This was a much better effort and the trip seemed to be no problem. (tchd 9-2)
Verdant had been a little disappointing this season judged on market expectations, and although this was a bit better, he didn't look like winning. (op 5-1 tchd 7-2 and 11-2 in a place)
Sabotage(UAE) has looked a stayer, so was wisely ridden close to the pace. He wasn't beaten far and will surely be of more interest over a longer distance. (op 16-1)
Anmar(USA), absent since finishing a respectable 11th in the Shemma Classic in 2010 for Godolphin, never threatened but didn't shape without promise. (op 14-1)
Alwaary(USA) ◆ was so promising at three but failed to deliver last season after returning from an absence. Connections clearly think he can still show something, otherwise presumably he wouldn't be in training, and the way he kept on inside the final furlong does suggest ability is still there. (op 22-1)
Allied Powers(IRE) is a classy operator around Europe but this was a poor effort. Richard Hughes reported afterwards that his mount was unsuited by the slow pace. Official explanation: jockey said horse was unsuited by the slow pace (op 7-2)

3404 JOHN SUNLEY MEMORIAL CRITERION STKS GROUP 3 7f
3:20 (3:20) (Class 1) 3-Y-O+
£28,385 (£10,760; £5,385; £2,685; £1,345; £675) **Stalls** Low

Form RPR
-243 **1** **Libranno**[33] 2370 3-8-8 107 .... RyanMoore 1 112
(Richard Hannon) *racd stands' side: mde all: rdn over 1f out: r.o* **9/1**
2-14 **2** 1 **Pausanias**[30] 2440 3-8-8 106 .... RichardHughes 3 109
(Richard Hannon) *racd stands' side: sn chsng wnr: rdn over 1f out: styd on: 2nd of 5 in gp* **6/1[3]**
-153 **3** ½ **Beacon Lodge (IRE)**[13] 2980 6-9-3 109 .... GeraldMosse 4 111
(Clive Cox) *racd stands' side: a.p: rdn over 1f out: styd on: 3rd of 5 in gp* **7/1**
-221 **4** 2¾ **The Cheka (IRE)**[28] 2502 5-9-8 109 .... KierenFallon 7 108
(Eve Johnson Houghton) *swtchd to r stands' side over 5f out: prom: rdn over 1f out: no ex ins fnl f: 4th of 5 in gp* **5/1[2]**
0-36 **5** 2¾ **Awzaan**[21] 2713 4-9-3 109 .... RichardHills 9 96+
(Mark Johnston) *led centre: rdn over 2f out: wknd fnl f: 1st of 6 in gp* **14/1**
0-23 **6** *hd* **Redford (IRE)**[49] 1889 6-9-3 109 .... NeilCallan 2 95
(David Nicholls) *racd stands' side: hld up: rdn over 1f out: no imp: last of 5 in gp* **15/2**
0-24 **7** 1¾ **Field Of Dream**[27] 2541 4-9-3 105 ....(b[1]) J-PGuillambert 13 91+
(Luca Cumani) *racd centre: hld up: plld hrd: hdwy and hung lft over 2f out: wnt 2nd in gp fnl f: nvr trbld ldrs: 2nd of 6 in gp* **20/1**
-504 **8** 6 **Inler (IRE)**[28] 2502 4-9-3 104 .... ShaneKelly 10 75+
(Brian Meehan) *racd centre: hld up: effrt and hung lft over 2f out: nvr on terms: 3rd of 6 in gp* **10/1**
-220 **9** 1 **Kakatosi**[28] 2502 4-9-3 104 .... JimmyFortune 5 72+
(Andrew Balding) *racd centre: chsd ldr: rdn over 2f out: hung rt and wknd over 1f out: 4th of 6 in gp* **25/1**
3-12 **10** 2¾ **Flambeau**[19] 1002 1 0 0 107 .... DaneO'Neill 11 61+
(Henry Candy) *racd centre: chsd ldrs: rdn over 2f out: hung lft and wknd over 1f out: eased: 5th of 6 in gp* **4/1[1]**
0-40 **11** 4½ **Palace Moon**[7] 3154 6-9-3 105 ....(t) RichardKingscote 6 52+
(William Knight) *racd centre: hld up: rdn over 2f out: sn wknd: last of 6 in gp* **66/1**
0-00 **12** 8 **Shakespearean (IRE)**[28] 2502 4-9-3 110 ....(vt[1]) MickaelBarzalona 8 31
(Saeed Bin Suroor) *racd alone far side: prom 5f: eased* **25/1**

1m 23.56s (-2.14) **Going Correction** -0.15s/f (Firm)
WFA 3 from 4yo+ 9lb **12** Ran SP% **114.9**
Speed ratings (Par 113): **106,104,104,101,98 97,95,88,87,84 79,70**
Tote Swingers: 1&2 £12.20, 1&3 £7.10, 2&3 £10.10 CSF £57.59 TOTE £8.30: £3.50, £2.50, £2.60; EX 24.80 Trifecta £326.90 Pool £1,369.56 - 3.10 winning units..
Owner Mcdowell Racing **Bred** O McDowell **Trained** East Everleigh, Wilts

FOCUS
This looked bang up to the class you'd hope for a race of this nature at a specialist distance, but half the field had no chance as it turned out, because all the action unfolded down the stands' side, with the first four racing there. The form is not rated too positively.

NOTEBOOK
Libranno had been far from disgraced this season, and was trying 7f for the first time in his career. Ryan Moore quickly got his mount to the rail and made every yard under a canny ride. Whether he was the best horse on the day is debatable but he certainly made best use of a possible bias. The horse will possibly head to the Lennox Stakes at Goodwood. (tchd 10-1)
Pausanias came into this unbeaten at 7f, and wasn't at all disgraced last time (1m14yds) behind some decent types under a 5lb penalty for his Free Handicap success. He settled in and tracked his stablemate, going better it seemed, but couldn't force his way to the front. (op 8-1)
Beacon Lodge(IRE) finished behind The Cheka earlier in the season but appeared to produce a better effort last time when chasing down Byword in a French Group 3. He did manage to reverse that form, seemingly the penalty made the difference given the distances, but was no match for his younger rivals down their side. (op 6-1 tchd 11-2)
The Cheka(IRE) ran respectably under his penalty and is in great heart this season. (op 6-1)
Awzaan ◆ hadn't been disgraced in a couple of starts this year but had no chance towards the centre of the course. That said, he saw off his rivals on that side comfortably and there are definitely races to be won with him. (op 11-1)
Redford(IRE), given a short break since running well in a couple of good races in the spring, got outpaced on what was the favoured side before keeping on at the one pace. (op 6-1)
Field Of Dream was much too free early in the first-time blinkers and seemed sure to burn himself out. However, he gives the impression that he may be a bit of a character and he ran on quite well, despite not looking always the most co-operative. (op 16-1)

Flambeau had been given a little break since being beaten at odds on at Lingfield, and ran flat for some reason, albeit on the wrong side. Her jockey didn't subject her to a hard time in the final stages. Official explanation: jockey said filly never travelled (op 9-2)

3405 £150,000 TATTERSALLS MILLIONS 3-Y-O CUP 1m 2f

3:55 (3:55) (Class 2) 3-Y-O

£83,653 (£38,011; £15,214; £7,599; £4,571; £3,042) Stalls Centre

Form RPR

0-25 **1** **Dominant (IRE)**[42] 2100 3-9-3 94 .... NeilCallan 1 113
(Roger Varian) *a.p: racd keenly: led 2f out: rdn clr fnl f* **6/1**

1150 **2** *5* **Malthouse (GER)**[9] 3069 3-9-3 98 .... MickaelBarzalona 2 103
(Mark Johnston) *chsd clr ldr to 1/2-way: remained handy: rdn over 2f out: styd on same pce fr over 1f out: wnt 2nd post* **14/1**

5-35 **3** *hd* **Questioning (IRE)**[49] 1923 3-9-3 101 .... WilliamBuick 7 103
(John Gosden) *hld up: hdwy over 2f out: rdn to chse wnr over 1f out: no ex ins fnl f: lost 2nd post* **11/4**[1]

1-61 **4** *hd* **Chef**[21] 2705 3-9-3 102 .... JimmyFortune 10 102+
(Andrew Balding) *s.i.s: hld up: hdwy over 2f out: rdn over 1f out: styd on same pce* **8/1**

3-1 **5** *nk* **Lyric Street (IRE)**[44] 2019 3-9-3 90 .... KierenFallon 3 102
(Luca Cumani) *prom: racd keenly: chsd clr ldr 1/2-way: rdn and ev ch 2f out: styd on same pce fnl f* **11/2**[3]

1340 **6** *½* **Auld Burns**[9] 3068 3-9-3 104 .... RyanMoore 4 101+
(Richard Hannon) *hld up: hdwy over 1f out: styng on whn nt clr run towards fin: nvr trbld ldrs* **14/1**

-340 **7** *3 ¾* **Sergeant Ablett (IRE)**[21] 2711 3-9-3 90 .... RichardKingscote 8 93
(James Given) *chsd ldrs: rdn over 3f out: wknd over 1f out* **50/1**

-223 **8** *1* **Measuring Time**[49] 1895 3-9-3 104 .... RichardHughes 12 91
(Richard Hannon) *s.i.s: hld up: rdn over 1f out: n.d* **9/1**

0 **9** *1 ¾* **Siren's Song (IRE)**[22] 2682 3-8-12 102 .... GeraldMosse 5 83
(Mrs John Harrington, Ire) *s.i.s: hld up: hdwy 2f out: wknd and eased fnl f* **4/1**[2]

232 **10** *½* **Cala Santanyi**[15] 2875 3-8-12 75 .... ShaneKelly 11 82
(Gerard Butler) *hld up: rdn over 2f out: wknd over 1f out* **100/1**

-050 **11** *2* **Madawi**[9] 3067 3-9-3 92 .... RichardHills 9 83
(Clive Brittain) *hld up: rdn over 2f out: wknd over 1f out* **25/1**

0-05 **12** *23* **Stentorian (IRE)**[42] 2108 3-9-3 90 .... (b[1]) J-PGuillambert 6 37
(Mark Johnston) *sn led: clr 8f out tl wknd and hdd 2f out: t.o* **100/1**

2m 1.78s (-3.72) **Going Correction** -0.15s/f (Firm) **12** Ran SP% **118.6**
Speed ratings (Par 105): **108,104,103,103,103 103,100,99,97,97 95,77**
Tote Swingers: 1&2 £14.00, 1&3 £6.10, 2&3 £11.10 CSF £85.03 TOTE £7.20: £2.60, £4.50, £1.40; EX 110.50.
Owner Highclere Thoroughbred Racing(Isinglass) **Bred** Newhall Ltd **Trained** Newmarket, Suffolk
■ Stewards' Enquiry : William Buick caution: used whip without giving colt time to respond.

FOCUS
This valuable sales event looked a hard race to call, as it featured some unexposed types taking on a few that had already met in similar contests. The pace seemed to be good, although Stentorian, sporting blinkers for the first time, was largely ignored after going clear of the chasing pack. Nothing got involved from the rear but the form looks pretty solid, with the second setting a sound standard.

NOTEBOOK
Dominant(IRE) ◆ hadn't been out since disappointing in a fair race at Newbury after being an eyecatcher on his seasonal return at Sandown, but that didn't stop him putting up an impressive performance under a confident ride. A step up in class surely awaits and catching him fresh could be the key. Ease in the ground is also quite important to his chance. (op 5-1 tchd 9-2)
Malthouse(GER) was thrashed behind Brown Panther in the King George V Stakes last time, so this was a vastly better effort. He kept on really well, albeit without troubling the winner. (tchd 16-1)
Questioning(IRE), last seen running fifth in a 1m2f Group 2 at Saint-Cloud won by Derby hero Pour Moi from subsequent French Derby second Bubble Chic, threaded his way through to have every chance but didn't quite see it out. He should come on for the run and isn't one to give up on yet. (op 7-2 tchd 9-2)
Chef ran on quite well after being held up and continues on an upward curve. (op 13-2 tchd 6-1)
Lyric Street(IRE) ◆ was only having his third start but his form looked strong, as he met a potentially classy miler on debut and got the better of an exciting filly, making her debut, when winning his maiden. He was outpaced quite early and looked sure to drop away until keeping on again. This race will bring him on again and he will be interesting next time. (op 6-1)
Measuring Time, off since being beaten at a short price in the Lingfield Derby Trial, never got into it. (op 10-1 tchd 12-1)
Siren's Song(IRE) was disappointing after making her effort round the field. (op 7-2)

3406 AGORA CANCER CENTRE H'CAP 1m 2f

4:30 (4:34) (Class 2) (0-100,99) 3-Y-O+ £12,952 (£3,854; £1,926; £962) Stalls Centre

Form RPR

1/ **1** **Burj Nahar**[598] 7243 4-9-10 95 .... MickaelBarzalona 11 106+
(Saeed Bin Suroor) *hld up: hdwy over 3f out: rdn to ld ins fnl f: r.o wl* **11/2**[3]

-312 **2** *2 ¼* **Zain Shamardal (IRE)**[15] 2877 3-8-6 89 .... WilliamBuick 4 94+
(Brian Meehan) *edgd rt s: prom: lost pl over 4f out: rdn over 2f out: r.o ins fnl f: wnt 2nd post: nt rch wnr* **2/1**[1]

-231 **3** *nse* **Udabaa (IRE)**[17] 2810 4-9-7 92 .... (p) RichardHills 1 97
(Marcus Tregoning) *led: rdn over 1f out: edgd lft and hdd ins fnl f: styd on same pce* **4/1**[2]

12- **4** *½* **Alazan (IRE)**[57] 7084 5-9-2 87 .... RichardHughes 6 91
(Philip Hobbs) *chsd ldrs: pushed along over 2f out: outpcd over 1f out: r.o ins fnl f* **7/1**

60-0 **5** *3 ½* **Classic Punch (IRE)**[14] 2933 8-10-0 99 .... DaneO'Neill 10 96
(David Elsworth) *prom: chsd ldr 8f out: rdn and ev ch over 1f out: wknd ins fnl f* **16/1**

100- **6** *3 ¼* **Desert Kiss**[322] 4830 6-9-9 94 .... ShaneKelly 3 85
(Walter Swinburn) *hmpd s: hld up: hdwy over 2f out: rdn and wknd over 1f out* **25/1**

40-0 **7** *1 ¼* **Gritstone**[14] 2909 4-8-12 83 .... TonyHamilton 8 71
(Richard Fahey) *hld up: rdn over 2f out: sn wknd* **20/1**

53-5 **8** *1 ¼* **Status Symbol (IRE)**[35] 2292 6-9-9 94 .... (t) WilliamCarson 2 80
(Giles Bravery) *prom: hmpd and lost pl after 1f: hld up: effrt over 2f out: wknd over 1f out* **20/1**

50- **9** *33* **Seven Summits (IRE)**[85] 7084 4-9-5 90 .... JimmyFortune 5 —
(Barney Curley) *sn prom: rdn over 4f out: wknd 3f out: t.o* **66/1**

2m 3.15s (-2.35) **Going Correction** -0.15s/f (Firm)
WFA 3 from 4yo+ 12lb **9** Ran SP% **102.0**
Speed ratings (Par 109): **103,101,101,100,97 95,94,93,66**
Tote Swingers: 1&2 £2.90, 1&3 £2.80, 2&3 £2.10 CSF £12.88 CT £33.21 TOTE £6.20: £2.20, £1.10, £1.70; EX 11.90.
Owner Godolphin **Bred** Darley **Trained** Newmarket, Suffolk
■ Naqshabban was withdrawn (6/1, ref to ent stalls). Deduct 10p in the £ under R4.

FOCUS
There was a case to make for plenty of these runners on their best pieces of form so, although the ground should be much quicker in the coming weeks, this contest could prove one to follow. The winner has the potential to rate higher.

NOTEBOOK
Burj Nahar hadn't been on a racecourse since winning on his debut in a 2-y-o Nottingham maiden in November 2009. Of course, there was no way of accurately knowing how much ability he retained, and the betting market suggested a little weakness about him, so it was really pleasing to see him show a good attitude under pressure to keep going in good style to maintain his unbeaten record. It's quite possible that he needs some ease in the ground, connections more or less said that afterwards, and he's a half-brother to two heavy-ground winners in France, so it will be interesting to see how he is campaigned now, although it's highly unlikely that he'll be running in handicaps next time. (op 4-1)
Zain Shamardal(IRE) finished well when winning 1m maiden over the Rowley Mile last month (form looks sound) and only just lost out to the progressive Club Oceanic upped to this trip at Goodwood next time. Hard ridden well over 3f out, he stayed on but was never going to get to the winner. (op 5-2)
Udabaa(IRE) won easily at Haydock last time - up 9lb for that - when cheekpieces were tried for the first time and probably ran up to that sort of level again after dominating. (op 9-2 tchd 7-2 in places)
Alazan(IRE), last seen disappointing at Bangor in a handicap hurdle, ran a similar race to the runner-up and connections will surely be pleased with the effort. (op 12-1)
Classic Punch(IRE), a three-time course winner, had quite a few positives coming into this and shaped really well until getting tired in the final stages. He looks sure to win again is reproducing this sort of performance. (op 14-1)
Desert Kiss ◆, absent since August last year, found this company a bit too hot. That said, there was promise in the run and she is one to watch out for if eased in class next time. (tchd 33-1)
Gritstone made a highly promising return to the track when catching the eye at Chester but may need to run against lesser types to make a bigger impact. (op 16-1)

3407 CARTER CANCER CENTRE E B F FILLIES' H'CAP 1m

5:05 (5:08) (Class 3) (0-95,92) 3-Y-O+ £8,418 (£2,505; £1,251; £625) Stalls Low

Form RPR

411- **1** **Dark Promise**[192] 7881 4-9-8 86 .... NeilCallan 10 104+
(Roger Varian) *chsd ldr: led over 1f out: edgd rt ins fnl f: rdn out* **5/1**[3]

414- **2** *2 ¼* **Heavenly Dawn**[368] 3298 4-9-3 81 .... RyanMoore 5 93+
(Sir Michael Stoute) *hld up in tch: shkn up over 1f out: styd on to go 2nd wl ins fnl f: nt trble wnr* **2/1**[1]

11-1 **3** *1* **Wallis**[36] 2269 4-9-7 85 .... KierenFallon 9 95+
(Luca Cumani) *set stdy pce tl qcknd 3f out: rdn and hdd over 1f out: styd on same pce ins fnl f* **13/2**

-004 **4** *6* **Bahati (IRE)**[33] 2358 4-9-11 89 .... RichardKingscote 7 84
(Jonathan Portman) *chsd ldrs: rdn over 1f out: wknd fnl f* **33/1**

0150 **5** *1* **Emma's Gift (IRE)**[10] 3034 3-8-13 90 .... AdamBeschizza[(3)] 2 81
(Julia Feilden) *hld up: rdn over 2f out: wknd over 1f out* **20/1**

-346 **6** *2 ½* **Maid In Heaven (IRE)**[49] 1884 4-10-0 92 .... ShaneKelly 3 79+
(Walter Swinburn) *hld up: rdn over 2f out: nvr on terms* **12/1**

2500 **7** *½* **Cheers For Thea (IRE)**[14] 2933 6-9-2 85 .... (t) LanceBetts[(5)] 4 71
(Tim Easterby) *dwlt: hld up: rdn and wknd over 1f out* **16/1**

6- **8** *nk* **Rare Symphony (IRE)**[57] 6970 4-9-13 91 .... (bt) JimmyFortune 8 76
(Philip Hobbs) *chsd ldrs: rdn over 2f out: wknd over 1f out* **33/1**

1-31 **9** *3 ¾* **Watneya**[15] 2883 3-8-7 81 .... WilliamBuick 6 55
(William Haggas) *hld up: plld hrd: rdn over 2f out: wknd over 1f out* **5/2**[2]

1m 37.88s (-2.12) **Going Correction** -0.15s/f (Firm)
WFA 3 from 4yo+ 10lb **9** Ran SP% **116.1**
Speed ratings (Par 104): **104,101,100,94,93 91,90,90,86**
Tote Swingers: 1&2 £3.80, 2&3 £3.90 CSF £15.19 CT £64.85 TOTE £6.30: £1.80, £1.10, £2.40; EX 20.50.
Owner Lordship Stud **Bred** Lordship Stud **Trained** Newmarket, Suffolk

FOCUS
A race full of promising horses of different ages, and three pulled nicely clear. The form is rated slightly positively.

NOTEBOOK
Dark Promise ◆ enjoyed a good season at three and ended it with back-to-back victories at Lingfield over 1m2f. Unraced as a 2-y-o, there was always the chance she had plenty more to come and she oozed a bit of class as she chased the leader before going on and winning nicely. Connections will surely aim towards black type with her now. (op 6-1 tchd 9-2 and 13-2 in places)
Heavenly Dawn ◆, off since June of last year, was back down to a mile but gave the impression she needed a bit further here considering the way she kept finding for pressure. (op 9-4 tchd 5-2)
Wallis was chasing a four-timer after winning her last two races of the previous season and her return at the end of May. She proved troublesome to load but got away smartly and grabbed the stands' rail in front, but wasn't in the same league as the winner as she went past. (op 5-1 tchd 7-1)
Bahati(IRE) hadn't won since her racecourse debut and is a little frustrating.
Watneya, raised 7lb for winning a Sandown handicap on reappearance, looked to have plenty more to come considering her relative lack of experience, but she found nothing the moment her jockey went for her and something looked amiss. Official explanation: jockey said filly had no more to give (op 11-4)
T/Plt: £165.50 to a £1 stake. Pool:£121,947.17 - 537.77 winning tickets T/Qpdt: £16.90 to a £1 stake. Pool:£7,288.86 - 317.96 winning tickets CR

3228 WINDSOR (R-H)

Saturday, June 25

OFFICIAL GOING: Good (good to firm in places; 7.8) changing to good after race 1 (2.25)

Wind: Strong, behind Weather: Cloudy becoming fine

3408 BET ON TOTESCOOP6 AT TOTESPORT.COM MAIDEN STKS 6f

2:25 (2:26) (Class 5) 2-Y-O £2,914 (£867; £433; £216) Stalls Low

Form RPR

32 **1** **Right To Dream (IRE)**[25] 2584 2-9-3 0 .... MartinDwyer 9 88+
(Brian Meehan) *pressed ldr: pushed into ld over 1f out: r.o wl and sn clr* **4/6**[1]

6 **2** *5* **Breaking The Bank**[22] 2687 2-9-3 0 .... LukeMorris 5 73
(William Muir) *chsd clr ldng quartet after 2f: rdn over 2f out: prog to go 2nd ins fnl f: r.o but no ch w wnr* **12/1**

0 **3** *4 ½* **Pond Life (IRE)**[17] 2817 2-9-3 0 .... StevieDonohoe 1 60
(Amy Weaver) *pressed ldng pair: shkn up and outpcd 2f out: kpt on same pce after* **40/1**

02 **4** *3* **Macdonald Mor (IRE)**[35] 2291 2-9-3 0 .... JamieSpencer 6 51
(Paul Cole) *led: rdn and hdd over 1f out: hanging and wknd rapidly* **3/1**[2]

5 *¾* **Atlantis Crossing (IRE)** 2-9-3 0 .... PatCosgrave 11 48
(Jim Boyle) *s.i.s: prog fr last pair to go 6th after 2f: pushed along 2f out: nvr on terms but styd on steadily fnl f* **28/1**

05 **6** *1 1/4* **Kathryn Perry (IRE)**[8] [3117] 2-8-12 0 .... RobbieFitzpatrick 10 40
(Andrew Haynes) *chsd ldng pair: outpcd and rdn 2f out: hanging lft over 1f out: wknd qckly* **40/1**

00 **7** *6* **Calusa Bay (IRE)**[18] [2787] 2-8-12 0 .... IanMongan 4 22
(Pat Phelan) *towards rr and nvr on terms w ldrs: modest 7th over 1f out: eased last 75yds* **100/1**

8 *3/4* **Scouting For Girls** 2-9-3 0 .... RobertHavlin 2 24
(Jim Boyle) *nvr on terms w ldrs: wl off the pce 2f out: no prog* **33/1**

9 *nk* **Classy Strike (IRE)** 2-9-3 0 .... PatDobbs 8 23
(Richard Hannon) *s.s: rn green in last and early reminders: modest prog over 1f out: nvr a factor* **9/1**[3]

10 *2 1/2* **Lady Jane Grace (IRE)** 2-8-12 0 .... CathyGannon 3 11
(David Evans) *sn pushed along: a in rr: struggling fr 1/2-way* **20/1**

11 *10* **Distant Voyage** 2-9-3 0 .... FergusSweeney 7 —
(Michael Blanshard) *nvr on terms w ldrs: wknd over 2f out: t.o* **66/1**

1m 12.74s (-0.26) **Going Correction** 0.0s/f (Good) **11** Ran SP% **121.2**
Speed ratings (Par 93): **101,94,88,84,83 81,73,72,72,68 55**
Tote Swingers:1&2:£2.00, 2&3:£11.30, 1&3:£11.00 CSF £10.57 TOTE £1.70: £1.10, £2.80, £7.90; EX 8.80.

Owner Right Tack Partnership **Bred** Gigginstown House Stud **Trained** Manton, Wilts

FOCUS

Rails on inner line and distances as advertised. The ground was officially good, good to firm in places after 5.5 mm of overnight rain. An interesting juvenile maiden, featuring a couple with fair form and a clutch of nicely-bred newcomers. The field finished strung out and the winner impressed.

NOTEBOOK

Right To Dream(IRE), second behind the Coventry Stakes runner-up last time out, found these rivals far easier to deal with. Quickly away, he chased the pace for the first half-mile before easing alongside the leader. He hit the front at the 1f pole and drew clear under hands and heels. Improving with each run, he now looks ready to tackle something offering more prestige than a maiden, and the Richmond Stakes was mentioned. (op 10-11 tchd evens in places)

Breaking The Bank, sixth of eight at Goodwood on his only previous start, took a step forward here. Outpaced early on and only fifth with 2f left, he finished nicely and should land a small race at some stage. (tchd 11-1)

Pond Life(IRE), eighth of ten at Kempton on his debut, probably improved on his first effort. Always in the first four, he plugged on gamely and will be interesting off a lowish rating in nurseries later on.

Macdonald Mor(IRE), ahead of Right To Dream when second five weeks previously, was very disappointing. He led until the winner took over, but dropped away tamely in the closing stages and ought to have fared better than this. (op 11-4)

Atlantis Crossing(IRE), a first-time-out half-brother to a juvenile winner, showed a glimpse of ability. He will need to progress in order to win a maiden, but will stay longer trips than this and can be found easier opportunities. (op 25-1)

Kathryn Perry(IRE), fifth in a fair event at Goodwood last time out, did not match that performance in this. She chased the first two until 2f out but was left well behind once the winner quickened.

3409 BET ON IRISH DERBY AT TOTESPORT.COM STKS (REGISTERED AS THE MIDSUMMER STAKES) (LISTED RACE) 1m 67y

2:55 (2:57) (Class 1) 3-Y-0+

£17,031 (£6,456; £3,231; £1,611; £807; £405) **Stalls** Low

Form RPR

00-4 **1** **Nationalism**[21] [2713] 4-9-4 104 .... RobertHavlin 2 111+
(John Gosden) *dwlt: hld up in 4th: effrt 3f out: rdn to chse ldr wl over 1f out: chal fnl f: led post* **5/2**[2]

-642 **2** *nse* **The Rectifier (USA)**[26] [2558] 4-9-4 104 .... MickyFenton 6 111
(Jim Boyle) *led at gd pce: styd against nr side rail in st: jnd fnl f: styd on: jst pipped* **10/1**

132- **3** *hd* **Dux Scholar**[245] [7095] 3-8-8 105 .... JamieSpencer 5 109+
(Sir Michael Stoute) *hld up in last pair and wl off the pce: stl last over 2f out: prog after: hrd rdn and edgd rt over 1f out: chal last 150yds: nt qckn* **2/1**[1]

3-00 **4** *1 1/2* **Balducci**[8] [3107] 4-9-4 97 .... DavidProbert 1 107
(Andrew Balding) *trckd ldng pair: drvn to chse ldr wl over 2f out to wl over 1f out: one pce after* **11/2**[3]

-111 **5** *12* **Boom And Bust (IRE)**[18] [2783] 4-9-4 94 .... MartinDwyer 7 79
(Marcus Tregoning) *hld up in midfield: pushed along over 3f out: no prog 2f out: sn wknd qckly* **13/2**

-350 **6** *3 1/4* **Caymans (AUS)**[107] [828] 6-9-4 108 .... DarryllHolland 3 72
(Saeed Bin Suroor) *chsd ldr to wl over 2f out: sn wknd* **16/1**

215- **7** *3 1/2* **Al Khaleej (IRE)**[287] [5948] 7-9-4 102 .... MartinLane 4 64
(David Simcock) *s.s: hld up last and wl off the pce: effrt whn nt clr run and swtchd sharply lft wl over 2f out: sn wknd* **14/1**

1m 40.19s (-4.51) **Going Correction** -0.325s/f (Firm) course record
WFA 3 from 4yo+ 10lb **7** Ran SP% **112.3**
Speed ratings (Par 111): **109,108,108,107,95 92,88**
Tote Swingers:1&2:£5.30, 2&3:£5.10, 1&3:£1.10 CSF £25.94 TOTE £3.00: £2.30, £3.40; EX 27.10.

Owner George Strawbridge **Bred** George Strawbridge **Trained** Newmarket, Suffolk

FOCUS

A decent race of its type with all bar two of the runners officially rated in excess of 100. The early pace was strong. The front-running second sets the standard.

NOTEBOOK

Nationalism, a sound fourth at Group 3 level at Epsom three weeks earlier, just got the best of a three-way photo-finish. Patiently ridden, he began to make progress early in the home straight and joined the pacesetting runner-up approaching the 1f pole. He responded well to driving and scored on the nod. This was a game effort, and his rider was of the view that a gelding operation had done the winner some good. (op 3-1 tchd 9-4)

The Rectifier(USA), successful in this race in 2010 and second at Goodwood last time out, made a fast break and set a strong early gallop. His rider eased the pace on the home turn and, sticking close to the rail, tried to kick on again 2f out. He could never shrug off the second and third, though, and was just pipped at the post. (op 8-1)

Dux Scholar, beaten only a nose in a Newbury Group 3 on his final juvenile outing, looked as if this run would bring him on a little. He was given plenty of time to find his feet, racing in sixth in the early stages, but made progress with 2f to run. He tended to edge left when put under pressure and betrayed slight ring-rustiness in the closing stages, but went down fighting. There should be better to come. (op 15-8 tchd 7-4 and 5-2 in a place)

Balducci, who seemed not to stay 1m2f at Royal Ascot eight days earlier, looked much happier at this trip. He could not match the principals inside the final furlong, having raced in third from the start, but he was not beaten far and posted a creditable display. (op 17-2)

Boom And Bust(IRE), stepping up to this grade after notching a hat-trick in handicaps, was never closer than fourth. He does not look up to this level.

Caymans(AUS), twice below par since taking third in a Meydan Group 3 in January, was again disappointing. He chased the leader for six furlongs, but soon lost touch with the main protagonists. (op 11-1)

3410 BET ON LIVE TENNIS AT TOTESPORT.COM H'CAP 6f

3:30 (3:30) (Class 2) (0-105,99) 3-Y-0+

£18,693 (£5,598; £2,799; £1,401; £699; £351) **Stalls** Low

Form RPR

1240 **1** **Norville (IRE)**[13] [2954] 4-9-3 94 ....(b) CathyGannon 15 104
(David Evans) *pressed ldrs: drvn on outer 2f out: prog to ld 1f out and c to nr side rail: styd on* **14/1**

2003 **2** *1* **Medicean Man**[13] [2954] 5-9-3 94 ....(p) ClareLindop 16 101
(Jeremy Gask) *hld up in rr: stdy prog on outer fr over 2f out: rdn to go 2nd jst ins fnl f: nt qckn* **15/2**[2]

10-0 **3** *1* **R Woody**[42] [2099] 4-9-1 92 .... IanMongan 13 96
(Dean Ivory) *taken down early: hld up towards rr: prog on outer over 2f out: rdn and nt qckn over 1f out: kpt on same pce* **20/1**

-241 **4** *hd* **Addictive Dream (IRE)**[24] [2620] 4-9-7 98 .... JamieSpencer 9 101
(Walter Swinburn) *trckd ldrs: waiting for room fr 2f out: prog over 1f out and cl enough: shkn up and nt qckn: kpt on* **10/3**[1]

5540 **5** *3/4* **Lui Rei (ITY)**[7] [3155] 5-9-5 99 ....(p) JohnFahy(3) 12 100
(Robert Cowell) *settled in midfield: rdn over 2f out: prog to chse ldrs 1f out: one pce after* **8/1**[3]

-334 **6** *1 3/4* **Captain Carey**[15] [2890] 5-9-1 92 .... LukeMorris 3 87+
(Malcolm Saunders) *hld up in midfield: pushed along over 2f out: trapped bhd wkng rival jst over 1f out against rail: swtchd lft and kpt on one pce* **15/2**[2]

0-20 **7** *3/4* **Global City (IRE)**[114] [755] 5-9-5 96 ....(t) PatCosgrave 1 89
(Saeed Bin Suroor) *taken down early: racd against nr side rail: pressed ldrs: led 1/2-way: hdd & wknd 1f out* **25/1**

000- **8** *1/2* **Edge Closer**[259] [6735] 7-9-4 95 .... RobertHavlin 14 86
(David Arbuthnot) *w ldrs: upsides jst over 1f out: wknd fnl f* **33/1**

1606 **9** *3/4* **Fathsta (IRE)**[7] [3155] 6-9-5 96 .... MartinDwyer 8 94+
(David Simcock) *taken down early: hld up in midfield: pushed along 2f out: trying to make prog whn squeezed out jst ins fnl f: no ch after* **11/1**

000 **10** *1 1/4* **Cheveton**[7] [3155] 7-8-11 93 .... RyanClark(5) 2 78
(Richard Price) *prom: lost pl over 2f out: no ch in rr whn short of room fnl f* **11/1**

-301 **11** *hd* **Crown Choice**[35] [2288] 6-9-6 97 .... DarryllHolland 7 81+
(Walter Swinburn) *taken down early: a wl in rr: swtchd lft and drvn 2f out: no great prog* **15/2**[2]

0041 **12** *3 1/4* **Sohraab**[13] [2959] 7-9-1 92 .... PatDobbs 5 66
(Hughie Morrison) *trckd ldrs: rdn over 2f out: sn lost pl: no ch whn crowded for room fnl f* **14/1**

-030 **13** *8* **Vitznau (IRE)**[14] [2927] 7-9-0 91 ....(p) MartinLane 11 39
(Robert Cowell) *dwlt: a struggling in rr: t.o* **50/1**

160- **14** *nk* **Arthur's Edge**[406] [2119] 7-9-4 95 .... FergusSweeney 4 42
(Christopher Mason) *led to 1/2-way: wknd qckly: t.o* **40/1**

-020 **F** **Mon Cadeaux**[14] [2927] 4-9-4 95 .... DavidProbert 10 —
(Andrew Balding) *hld up towards rr: pushed along and in tch whn clipped heels and fell over 2f out* **10/1**

10-0 **U** **Little Garcon (USA)**[105] [848] 4-9-4 95 .... AndreaAtzeni 6 —
(Marco Botti) *hld up: stl wl in rr whn bdly hmpd and uns rdr over 2f out* **33/1**

1m 11.59s (-1.41) **Going Correction** 0.0s/f (Good) **16** Ran SP% **127.5**
Speed ratings (Par 109): **109,107,106,106,105 102,101,101,100,98 98,93,83,82,— —**
Tote Swingers:1&2:£11.50, 2&3:£27.50, 1&3:£83.70 CSF £112.89 CT £1340.49 TOTE £17.00: £3.20, £2.50, £2.20, £1.80; EX 202.20.

Owner Raymond N R Auld **Bred** R N Auld **Trained** Pandy, Monmouths

■ Stewards' Enquiry : Cathy Gannon one-day ban: careless riding (Jul 11); two-day ban: used whip with excessive frequency (Jul 12-13)

FOCUS

A good-quality handicap, with the top weight rated 99, and it looked very competitive. The time was only ordinary but the form is taken at face value.

NOTEBOOK

Norville(IRE), already a five-time winner this year, notched another game success. Always in the first four, he got a decent position close to the rail and hit the front approaching the final furlong. The runner-up challenged strongly, but he always looked to be doing just enough to collect. He wasn't suited by the soft ground at Doncaster last time but conditions were far more suitable here. His rating has rocketed this term and he seems likely to take another nudge up the handicap after this. (op 16-1)

Medicean Man, refitted with cheekpieces after his fast-finishing third at Doncaster last time, ran a cracker in defeat. In rear early on, he put in a determined late effort and almost got alongside Norville in the final furlong. He deserves a change of luck. (op 8-1 tchd 10-1)

R Woody, progressive last season but overly keen on his previous start this term, showed he is still going the right way. He is not going to be that easy to place profitably off his current mark, but should remain competitive in this sort of event.

Addictive Dream(IRE), 7lb higher than when scoring at Ripon 24 days earlier, found that rise too much to overcome. He travelled well throughout, close to the pace from the start, but could not quicken in the closing stages. (op 3-1 tchd 7-2 in places)

Lui Rei(ITY), a solid ninth from a poor draw in Royal Ascot's Wokingham, ran another sound race. His profile is beginning to suggest his rating is a bit high, though, as he continues to run well without getting his head in front. (op 10-1)

Captain Carey, whose six wins prior to this had all been registered over 5f, seemed to stay this trip well enough. He never threatened to collect, however, and is another whose official mark may be a little too taxing. (op 8-1)

3411 BET ON WIMBLEDON AT TOTESPORT.COM H'CAP 1m 3f 135y

4:00 (4:02) (Class 2) (0-100,95) 3-Y-0+ **£12,952** (£3,854; £1,926; £962) **Stalls** Centre

Form RPR

-000 **1** **Sirvino**[26] [2573] 6-9-2 89 .... LMcNiff(5) 10 104
(David Barron) *trckd ldrs: wnt 2nd over 3f out: led jst over 2f out: sn pushed clr: in n.d and cruising fnl f* **13/2**[3]

4-40 **2** *7* **Magicalmysterytour (IRE)**[14] [2931] 8-9-0 82 .... StevieDonohoe 1 85
(Willie Musson) *hld up off the pce towards rr: prog 3f out: rdn to chse wnr over 1f out: no ch* **12/1**

-340 **3** *1/2* **Life And Soul (IRE)**[7] [3156] 4-9-10 92 .... DarryllHolland 6 94
(Amanda Perrett) *hld up off the pce in midfield: prog 3f out: rdn to dispute 2nd over 1f out: no ch w wnr* **6/1**[2]

0-62 **4** *1 3/4* **Berling (IRE)**[21] [2716] 4-9-8 90 .... PatDobbs 11 89
(John Dunlop) *hld up in last pair: sme prog over 2f out: rdn and kpt on same pce fr over 1f out* **7/4**[1]

100 **5** *1/2* **Nice Style (IRE)**[45] [2002] 6-9-11 93 .... ClareLindop 9 91
(Jeremy Gask) *hld up off the pce in midfield: gng wl enough and sme prog fr 3f out: rdn over 1f out: sn wknd* **11/1**

0-20 **6** *6* **Albaqaa**[10] 3032 6-9-8 **90**.. PatCosgrave 13 78
(P J O'Gorman) *hld up last and wl off the pce: effrt 3f out: hrd rdn and wl btn in 6th over 1f out* **33/1**

411 **7** *2 1/2* **Uphold**[13] 2958 4-9-8 **90**..(e) CathyGannon 7 74
(Gay Kelleway) *mde most at decent pce to jst over 2f out: sn wknd* **11/1**

-465 **8** *2 3/4* **Apprimus (IRE)**[27] 2540 5-9-6 **95**..........................(tp) AntiocoMurgia(7) 2 74
(Marco Botti) *dwlt: rapid prog to join ldr after 2f: rdn and wknd qckly over 3f out* **12/1**

0-00 **9** *1 3/4* **Treble Jig (USA)**[45] 2002 4-9-4 **86**.............................. JamieSpencer 12 62
(Sir Michael Stoute) *w ldr 2f: settled to trck ldrs after: rdn on outer 3f out: sn wknd* **9/1**

600/ **10** *3 1/2* **First Avenue**[113] 7293 6-9-4 **86**.. RobertHavlin 4 56
(Gary Moore) *hld up in rr: shkn up and no prog 3f out* **66/1**

30-4 **11** *2 3/4* **Sea Of Galilee**[59] 1622 4-9-2 **84**............................. FergusSweeney 3 50
(Henry Candy) *prom: rdn over 3f out: sn wknd qckly* **7/1**

2m 26.51s (-2.99) **Going Correction** -0.325s/f (Firm) **11** Ran SP% **123.0**
Speed ratings (Par 109): **96,91,91,89,89 85,83,82,80,78 76**
Tote Swingers:1&2:£27.70, 2&3:£27.60, 1&3:£5.00 CSF £85.81 CT £503.34 TOTE £9.90: £2.50, £3.60, £2.40; EX 105.00.
Owner Theo Williams and Charles Mocatta **Bred** Allan Perry **Trained** Maunby, N Yorks

FOCUS
Another competitive handicap in which few could be confidently discounted. The winner impressed and is rated back near his old form.

NOTEBOOK
Sirvino lined up without a victory since July 2009, but took this impressively. Always in the leading quartet, he went to the front 2f from home and was clear by the 1f marker. The winner was entitled to go well here on the strength of his John Smith's Cup victory almost two years previously, but had seemingly been out of form recently. Glorious Goodwood is up next, but the official handicapper will obviously take note of his massively improved display. (op 7-1 tchd 8-1)
Magicalmysterytour(IRE), second in this event in 2009 and sixth last season, again made a plucky bid to land the prize. In rear early on, he made eyecatching progress in the home straight and was third 2f out. He ran on gamely, but was always chasing the winner's shadow. (op 10-1)
Life And Soul(IRE) had posted two solid efforts before disappointing at Royal Ascot and looked much like his old self here. Never far off the pace, he battled on bravely in the closing stages without threatening to make a more significant impact. (op 13-2 tchd 7-1 in a place)
Berling(IRE), 2lb higher than when second in a decent event at Epsom last time out, never really got into contention. Held up in rear in the early stages, he was asked to make progress in the home straight, but failed to quicken sufficiently to make the first three. He is no easy ride. (op 11-4)
Nice Style(IRE), 1lb lower than when scoring at Lingfield in January, posted his best performance since that success. Another in touch from the outset, he got as close as second at one point, before proving one paced inside the final furlong. (op 14-1)
Albaqaa, second in a claimer on his reappearance and outclassed at Royal Ascot last time, was held up in the early stages and, although he made up some of the forfeited ground, never looked capable of making the progress needed to trouble the winner. He is difficult to predict. (op 20-1)

3412 BET TOTEPOOL ON ALL UK RACING H'CAP 6f
4:35 (4:37) (Class 5) (0-70,70) 3-Y-O+ **£2,914** (£867; £433; £216) **Stalls** Low

Form RPR

00-1 **1** **Questionnaire (IRE)**[15] 2869 3-9-2 **65**.............................. LukeMorris 1 80+
(Nicky Vaughan) *mde all against nr side rail: clr over 1f out: comf* **11/4**[1]

0404 **2** *2 1/2* **Desert Icon (IRE)**[17] 2806 5-9-9 **65**.................................. MartinLane 2 72
(David Simcock) *taken down early: chsd ldrs: rdn bef 1/2-way: wnt 2nd 2f out: no imp on wnr* **15/2**

4160 **3** *1* **Memphis Man**[18] 2794 8-9-2 **61** ow1.......................... RichardEvans(3) 6 64
(David Evans) *taken down early: sn pushed along in rr: prog over 2f out: wnt 3rd jst over 1f out: kpt on* **14/1**

5-40 **4** *1 1/2* **Adventure Story**[37] 2222 4-9-5 **61**.............................. FergusSweeney 9 60
(Peter Makin) *taken down early: chsd ldrs: rdn and nt qckn over 2f out: effrt again over 1f out: kpt on* **20/1**

3003 **5** *1 3/4* **Hereford Boy**[5] 3217 7-9-9 **68**..(b) PatrickHills(3) 11 61
(Dean Ivory) *settled in rr: effrt on outer 2f out: kpt on: no threat* **17/2**

0-00 **6** *nk* **Tubby Isaacs**[33] 2369 7-10-0 **70**.....................................(p) IanMongan 10 62
(Dean Ivory) *taken down early: stdd s: hld up in rr: nvr on terms: kpt on fnl f* **14/1**

0300 **7** *1 1/2* **Danzoe (IRE)**[24] 2609 4-9-6 **67**.. RyanClark(5) 7 54
(Christine Dunnett) *taken down early: a same pl and nvr on terms: rdn on outer over 2f out: no prog* **20/1**

-060 **8** *nk* **Putin (IRE)**[5] 3230 3-8-8 **57**..(b[1]) NeilChalmers 5 41
(Derek Haydn Jones) *trckd ldng pair: rdn over 2f out: sn wknd* **25/1**

3-42 **9** *nk* **C'Mon You Irons (IRE)**[15] 2879 6-9-5 **64**...................(b) KierenFox(3) 15 49
(Mark Hoad) *pressed wnr: rdn 1/2-way: wknd 2f out* **5/1**[3]

0260 **10** *4 1/2* **Tourist**[70] 1394 6-8-13 **55**..(t) JamieSpencer 14 26
(Ian Williams) *stdd s: hld up in detached last: nvr a factor* **7/2**[2]

2020 **11** *1 3/4* **Play The Blues (IRE)**[15] 2870 4-9-6 **67**..........................(t) RyanPowell(5) 13 32
(Mark Allen) *a in rr: rdn and no prog sn after 1/2-way* **16/1**

1500 **12** *6* **Replicator**[14] 2920 6-8-7 **52**.....................................(e) AshleyHamblett(3) 4 —
(Patrick Gilligan) *chsd ldrs: rdn over 2f out: sn wknd* **33/1**

1m 12.37s (-0.63) **Going Correction** 0.0s/f (Good)
WFA 3 from 4yo+ 7lb **12** Ran SP% **123.4**
Speed ratings (Par 103): **104,100,99,97,95 94,92,92,91,85 83,75**
Tote Swingers:1&2:£22.40, 2&3:£10.40, 1&3:£5.10 CSF £23.66 CT £257.77 TOTE £4.60: £2.00, £3.10, £2.20; EX 38.70.
Owner Gordon Kendrick **Bred** Pheroze Sorabjee **Trained** Helshaw Grange, Shropshire

FOCUS
A modest event, weakened by a raft of non-runners, but several had similar claims on paper. the winner more than confirmed her Chepstow improvement.

3413 BET TOTEPOOL ON ALL IRISH RACING FILLIES' H'CAP 1m 67y
5:10 (5:10) (Class 5) (0-75,73) 3-Y-O+ **£2,914** (£867; £433; £216) **Stalls** Low

Form RPR

6-12 **1** **Epernay**[26] 2548 4-8-12 **62**..(vt[1]) RyanClark(5) 5 73+
(Ian Williams) *hld up in midfield: prog over 2f out: clsd on ldrs over 1f out: cajoled along to ld ins fnl f: styd on* **11/4**[1]

3463 **2** *1 1/4* **Miss Bootylishes**[12] 2999 6-9-8 **70**.................................. JohnFahy(3) 3 78
(Paul Burgoyne) *sn restrained bhd ldng pair: rdn to go 2nd 2f out: led 1f out: hdd and nt qckn ins fnl f* **10/1**

4026 **3** *hd* **Very Well Red**[14] 2912 8-9-11 **70**.................................. DarryllHolland 7 77
(Peter Hiatt) *led: drvn and hdd 1f out: nt qckn* **14/1**

5-00 **4** *1 3/4* **Arctic Maiden**[16] 2838 3-8-3 **58**.............................. AdrianMcCarthy 8 62
(Willie Musson) *hld up in 7th: rdn and sme prog fr over 2f out: kpt on fr over 1f out: nvr able to chal* **14/1**

-242 **5** *3* **Duquesa (IRE)**[1] 3337 3-8-9 **64**.......................................(v) CathyGannon 6 62
(David Evans) *t.k.h early: trckd ldng trio: rdn over 2f out: fdd over 1f out* **9/2**[3]

632- **6** *1* **Madonna Dell'Orto**[309] 5265 4-10-0 **73**.......................... JamieSpencer 1 69
(Walter Swinburn) *hld up in last pair: effrt on outer over 2f out: shkn up and nt qckn wl over 1f out: fdd* **4/1**[2]

1-56 **7** *6* **Leelu**[50] 1867 5-9-1 **60**.. RobertHavlin 10 44
(David Arbuthnot) *mostly chsd ldr to 2f out: wknd and eased* **8/1**

1641 **8** *3 1/2* **Shamardal Phantom (IRE)**[22] 2663 4-9-13 **72**................ MartinLane 4 57
(David Simcock) *stdd s: hld up in last: swtchd to outer over 2f out: no prog over 1f out: sn eased* **6/1**

1530 **9** *2* **Cat Hunter**[26] 2566 4-9-9 **68**... LukeMorris 2 41
(Ronald Harris) *hld up in midfield: pushed along sn after 1/2-way: wknd 2f out* **16/1**

1m 41.92s (-2.78) **Going Correction** -0.325s/f (Firm)
WFA 3 from 4yo+ 10lb **9** Ran SP% **118.6**
Speed ratings (Par 100): **100,98,98,96,93 92,86,83,81**
Tote Swingers:1&2:£4.20, 2&3:£24.10, 1&3:£5.80 CSF £32.56 CT £337.24 TOTE £3.70: £1.50, £2.50, £3.90; EX 40.10.
Owner Mr & Mrs G Middlebrook **Bred** Mr & Mrs G Middlebrook **Trained** Portway, Worcs

FOCUS
Just a run-of-the-mill fillies' handicap but won in good style by an improving type. The time was good and the form is rated slightly positively.
T/Plt: £130.80 to a £1 stake. Pool £77,842.20 - 434.16 winning tickets. T/Qpdt: £35.40 to a £1 stake. Pool £5,096.47 - 106.49 winning tickets. JN

3414 - 3415a (Foreign Racing) - See Raceform Interactive

3368 CURRAGH (R-H)
Saturday, June 25

OFFICIAL GOING: Yielding to soft (yielding in places) changing to good to yielding after race 6 (4.40)

3416a GRANGECON STUD STKS (GROUP 3) (FILLIES) 6f
3:00 (3:00) 2-Y-O **£29,418** (£8,599; £4,073; £1,357) **Stalls** High

RPR

1 **Experience (IRE)**[10] 3055 2-9-0 .... WMLordan 4 99+
(David Wachman, Ire) *trckd ldrs: cl 5th 1/2-way: chal on outer over 1f out: rdn to ld ins fnl f: kpt on wl* **1/1**[1]

2 *1 3/4* **Somasach (USA)**[10] 3033 2-9-0 .... KJManning 5 93
(J S Bolger, Ire) *prom: cl 4th 1/2-way: rdn 2f out: stl cl-up u.p 1f out: no imp on wnr ins fnl f: kpt on same pce* **5/1**[3]

3 *shd* **Naseem Sea (IRE)**[19] 2777 2-9-0 .... WJSupple 2 93
(P D Deegan, Ire) *prom on outer: disp after 1/2-way: rdn and slt advantage over 1f out: no imp whn hdd by wnr ins fnl f: kpt on one pce* **6/1**

4 *hd* **Aaraas**[15] 2893 2-9-0 .... DPMcDonogh 1 92+
(Kevin Prendergast, Ire) *in rr: drvn along 1/2-way: kpt on wl u.p ins fnl f: nrest at fin* **8/1**

5 *shd* **Dam Beautiful**[9] 3092 2-9-0 .... PJSmullen 6 92
(Kevin Ryan) *prom on stands' side rail: cl 3rd 1/2-way: sn rdn to dispute: hdd over 1f out and no imp on wnr ins fnl f: kpt on one pce u.p* **4/1**[2]

6 *7* **Muckle Bahoochie (IRE)**[35] 2322 2-9-0 .... KLatham 3 71
(G M Lyons, Ire) *led: jnd over 2f out: sn hdd and no ex fr over 1f out: eased whn btn fnl f* **16/1**

1m 12.36s (-2.64) **Going Correction** -0.425s/f (Firm) **6** Ran SP% **117.9**
Speed ratings: **100,97,97,97,97 87**
CSF £7.08 TOTE £1.90: £1.40, £2.00; DF 7.30.
Owner Derrick Smith **Bred** Whisperview Trading Ltd **Trained** Goolds Cross, Co Tipperary

FOCUS
A compressed finish to this but the form has been rated a bit more positively than might have been. The winner has more to offer.

NOTEBOOK
Experience(IRE) registered quite an impressive victory. Confidently ridden and displaying a high cruising speed early on, she was waited with until a furlong out and then showed a taking turn of foot to cut down her main rivals inside the final furlong. She looks likely to step up in trip and is undoubtedly a smart and progressive filly. (op 15/8)
Somasach(USA), for whom the ground was presumed to be responsible for her disappointing performance at Ascot, was on ground which wouldn't have been too dissimilar, indeed it was probably tackier here, but she ran a much better race. She did have every chance and stuck it out well up the hill but was outclassed. It's highly likely though that quicker ground would see her in a better light, but that's undoubtedly true of the winner as well. (op 6/1)
Naseem Sea(IRE) has form lines with a few good fillies and ran another very sound race. Produced on the outside with her challenge over a furlong out, she just wasn't quite good enough to cope with the winner. She does deserve to get her head in front in a race of this nature. (op 5/1)
Aaraas's performance was interesting. Declan McDonogh said she was flat out the whole way and she seemed beaten two furlongs out, but it was a combination of her staying on and a couple of others stopping in front of her which saw her come home well. She looks certain to step up in trip now. (op 7/1)
Dam Beautiful found this a bit more taxing than the Warwick maiden she contested previously but she ran well, travelling nicely next to the rail until the pace increased. She ran a broadly similar race to Somasach and Naseem Sea. (op 11/4)
Muckle Bahoochie(IRE) set a decent enough clip but couldn't last it out.

3417a STOBART IRELAND PRETTY POLLY STKS (GROUP 1) (F&M) 1m 2f
3:35 (3:35) 3-Y-O+
£103,448 (£32,758; £15,517; £5,172; £3,448; £1,724) **Stalls** High

RPR

1 **Misty For Me (IRE)**[22] 2682 3-8-12 **114**.................... SeamieHeffernan 4 119+
(A P O'Brien, Ire) *mde all: set a stdy pce tl qcknd ent st: asserted 2f out: rdn out and in command fr over 1f out: kpt on wl* **10/3**[2]

2 *6* **Midday**[22] 2680 5-9-10 .... TomQueally 7 107+
(Sir Henry Cecil) *trckd ldrs in 3rd: wnt 2nd early st: rdn over 2f out and sn no imp: no ch w wnr fr wl over 1f out: kpt on one pce* **1/3**[1]

3 *4 1/2* **Chrysanthemum (IRE)**[34] 2334 3-8-12 **104**...................... WMLordan 5 98+
(David Wachman, Ire) *trckd ldrs on inner in 4th: pushed along early st: sn no ch w wnr: mod 3rd 1f out: kpt on one pce* **16/1**[3]

4 *3/4* **Claiomh Solais (IRE)**[8] 3106 3-8-12 **109**......................... KJManning 3 97
(J S Bolger, Ire) *trckd ldr in 2nd: rdn early st and dropped to 3rd: sn no imp u.p: mod 4th fr 1f out* **33/1**

5 *3 1/2* **Aoife Alainn (IRE)**[244] 7109 4-9-10 **111**......................... PShanahan 6 90+
(Tracey Collins, Ire) *towards rr: nvr a factor: no imp in 7th early st: kpt on one pce fr over 1f out wout threatening* **20/1**

6 *shd* **Obama Rule (IRE)**[35] 2325 4-9-10 **103**......................... PJSmullen 2 89+
(Ms Joanna Morgan, Ire) *hld up towards rr on inner: 6th in tch ent st: sn rdn and no ex fr 2f out* **50/1**

7 22 **Empowering (IRE)**[55] 1719 3-8-12 103 .... CO'Donoghue 8 45+
(A P O'Brien, Ire) *trckd ldrs in 5th: rdn early st and sn no ex: eased whn btn over 1f out* **40/1**

2m 13.37s (-0.93) **Going Correction** +0.175s/f (Good)
WFA 3 from 4yo+ 12lb **7** Ran SP% **116.1**
Speed ratings: **110,105,101,101,98 98,80**
CSF £4.87 TOTE £3.60: £1.60, £1.10; DF 8.10.
Owner Michael Tabor, Mrs John Magnier & Derrick Smith **Bred** March Thoroughbreds **Trained** Ballydoyle, Co Tipperary

FOCUS
This rates the best performance by a 3yo filly this season and the best in this race in the last decade, although the ground exaggerated the distances and the time was 0.6sec slower than the maiden.

NOTEBOOK
Misty For Me(IRE) put up a fine performance under a textbook front-running ride from Seamus Heffernan. He dictated a gradually increasing pace and when she quickened early in the straight the favourite simply couldn't live with her. It was a performance that confirms her as a top-class filly over 1m to 1m2f, although whether she'll prove effective over the extra couple of furlongs of an Irish Oaks remains to be seen. The way she was ridden here suggests that connections won't regard the extra distance as a problem. (op 7/2 tchd 3/1)
Midday's trainer had no complaints. It was disappointing that she failed to pick up in the straight, and as the filly with the confirmed stamina, perhaps more use could have been made of her. The way it turned out, though, she was no match for the winner and different tactics wouldn't have made the slightest difference. (op 4/11)
Chrysanthemum(IRE) looks as though she falls short at this level and her sights would need to be lowered. Tracking the pace most of the way, she couldn't respond when the winner quickened on and this is probably about as good as she is.
Claiomh Solais(IRE) was stepping up in trip and the evidence is probably not that conclusive. She was ridden reasonably positively, tracking the winner most of the way, but found wanting when matters heated up in the straight. She just falls short in Group 1 company anyway and more evidence is needed about how well she gets this trip.
Aoife Alainn(IRE) was never a factor, but improvement can be expected from her first run of the season. (op 16/1)
Obama Rule(IRE) isn't up to this level. (op 66/1 tchd 40/1)
Empowering(IRE) dropped out very tamely in the straight. Official explanation: jockey said filly lost her action in running (op 20/1)

3418a AT THE RACES CURRAGH CUP (GROUP 3) 1m 6f
4:10 (4:10) 3-Y-0+
£32,327 (£10,237; £4,849; £1,616; £1,077; £538) **Stalls** High

RPR
1 **Red Cadeaux**[6] 3204 5-9-11 .... TomMcLaughlin 2 114+
(Ed Dunlop) *trckd ldrs in 4th: hdwy to chal early st and c over to stands' side: led 2f out: rdn to assert 1f out: drew clr fnl f* **7/2**[2]
2 9 **Zerashan (IRE)**[8] 3147 4-9-11 100 .... ShaneFoley 7 101
(M Halford, Ire) *towards rr: hdwy on inner appr st: chal early st and c over to stands' side: rdn and no imp on wnr in 2nd fr wl over 1f out: kpt on one pce* **11/1**
3 nk **Admiral Of The Red (IRE)**[48] 1925 3-8-10 98 .... CO'Donoghue 6 103
(A P O'Brien, Ire) *led: hung lft appr st: strly pressed and brought over to stands' side early st: hdd 2f out and sn no imp in 3rd: no ch w wnr fr over 1f out* **7/2**[2]
4 6 **Address Unknown**[56] 1705 4-9-11 105 ....(bt) PJSmullen 3 93
(D K Weld, Ire) *chsd ldrs mainly 5th: pushed along ent st: c over to stands' side and 4th 2f out: sn no imp u.p: no ex fnl f* **7/1**[3]
5 21 **Penthesilea Eile (USA)**[19] 2779 5-9-8 80 ....(p) WJSupple 8 60
(Brendan W Duke, Ire) *a towards rr: nvr a factor: no threat fr early st: t.o* **66/1**
6 7 **Admiral Barry (IRE)**[6] 2534 6-9-11 99 .... DPMcDonogh 5 53
(Eoin Griffin, Ire) *trckd ldrs in 3rd: rdn ent st and sn no ex: eased whn btn wl over 1f out: t.o* **14/1**
7 9 **Nebula Storm (IRE)**[27] 2534 4-9-11 102 .... JMurtagh 4 41
(John M Oxx, Ire) *trckd ldr in 2nd: drvn along ent st: sn no ex and wknd 2f out: eased: t.o* **11/8**[1]

3m 5.82s (-3.58) **Going Correction** +0.175s/f (Good)
WFA 3 from 4yo+ 17lb **7** Ran SP% **115.5**
Speed ratings: **117,111,111,100,90 [illegible]**
CSF £40.70 TOTE £3.60: £3.00, £3.70; DF 61.90.
Owner R J Arculli **Bred** Foursome Thoroughbreds **Trained** Newmarket, Suffolk

FOCUS
A weaker than average renewal but the winner is up to scratch.

NOTEBOOK
Red Cadeaux, for whom the tacky ground was apparently perfect, proved a class apart over a fairly substandard field for this particular contest. Once going on early in the straight, he continued to build up momentum and the further they went the further clear he pulled. It was a good performance no doubt, one he would need to very much improve on if he's to contest a race such as the Irish St Leger, but it's a performance that entitles him to take his place should connections be so inclined. (op 7/2 tchd 10/3)
Zerashan(IRE) ran up to his mark of 100, and being by Azamour one would suspect that the ground was probably against him. He was patiently ridden and delivered with a chance early in the straight but the winner outclassed him. With his rating he could be quite a difficult horse to place but he's consistent and will continue to run his race, winning one or two could be a different story. (op 10/1)
Admiral Of The Red(IRE), on whom Colm O'Donoghue had to use his whip from some way out to try to prevent the colt from hanging, had no extra when challenged and looked a far from easy ride. (op 4/1)
Address Unknown, for whom the trip shouldn't have been a problem, was held up a little bit off the pace. It was disappointing in the light of that when he made no progress of any sort in the straight. In fairness to him he's a more effective operator on better ground. (op 7/1 tchd 8/1)
Penthesilea Eile(USA) is rated 80 and probably ran up to that sort of mark.
Admiral Barry(IRE) dropped away disappointingly in the straight. Official explanation: jockey said gelding hung badly in the closing stages (op 11/1)
Nebula Storm(IRE) made a move to challenge entering the straight, but dropped away fairly quickly inside the final two furlongs. He was found to be blowing hard post race. Official explanation: jockey said colt weakened very quickly in the straight; vet said colt was found to be blowing hard post-race (op 13/8 tchd 5/4)

3420a LONDON SOUTHEND AIRPORT EUROPEAN BREEDERS FUND H'CAP 2m
5:15 (5:15) (60-100,92) 4-Y-0+ **£14,568** (£4,258; £2,017; £672) **Stalls** Far side

RPR
1 **Silk Hall (UAE)**[41] 2031 6-8-13 78 .... CDHayes 86
(J J Lambe, Ire) *chsd clr ldr: clsr in 5th 1/2-way: gd hdwy to ld ent st: sn rdn to assert: kpt on wl: reduced advantage clsng stages* **25/1**
2 1 1/4 **Cry For The Moon (USA)**[15] 2896 5-8-10 78 .... ShaneFoley[(3)] 84
(J H Culloty, Ire) *hld up in rr of mid-div: 8th ent st: prog into 2nd 2f out: kpt on wl u.p ins fnl f wout rching wnr* **14/1**
3 4 1/2 **Dearest Girl (IRE)**[7] 3196 4-8-10 75 .... DPMcDonogh 76
(Charles O'Brien, Ire) *hld up in rr: 11th ent st: wnt 5th 2f out: mod 3rd u.p 1f out: no imp and kpt on one pce* **20/1**
4 1 1/2 **Oneeightofamile (IRE)**[14] 2946 6-9-4 83 .... PJSmullen 83
(John E Kiely, Ire) *chsd clr ldr: hdwy to ld 6f out: hdd ent st: sn drvn along and no imp: mod 5th over 1f out: kpt on one pce* **9/4**[1]
5 1 1/2 **Darenjan (IRE)**[587] 5054 8-8-5 70 .... WJSupple 68
(John Joseph Hanlon, Ire) *chsd clr ldr in 2nd: clsr fr 1/2-way: pushed along ent st: dropped to 3rd and no imp 2f out: no ex* **8/1**
6 1/2 **Idarah (USA)**[41] 5933 8-9-6 85 .... BACurtis 83
(Paul Cashman, Ire) *in rr of mid-div: 10th ent st: swtchd lft over 2f out: kpt on u.p ins fnl f* **16/1**
7 1/2 **Bahrain Storm (IRE)**[37] 1262 8-9-10 92 ....(b) JPO'Brien[(3)] 89
(Patrick J Flynn, Ire) *mid-div: 9th 4f out: no ex fr early st: kpt on one pce* **10/1**
8 3/4 **La Estrella (USA)**[11] 3013 8-9-9 88 .... JMurtagh 84
(Don Cantillon) *chsd clr ldr in 3rd: clsr 1/2-way: 7th ent st: sn rdn and no imp* **5/1**[2]
9 shd **Jawad (IRE)**[47] 5977 10-8-8 73 .... RPCleary 69
(Ms Joanna Morgan, Ire) *towards rr: hdwy 1/2-way: wnt 5th briefly ent st: sn rdn and no ex* **25/1**
10 1 **Virgil Earp**[12] 3005 4-7-13 69 ....(b) LFRoche[(5)] 64
(Noel Meade, Ire) *chsd clr ldr: clsr in 6th 1/2-way: 4th appr st: rdn over 2f out and sn no ex: wknd* **6/1**[3]
11 1 **Greenbelt Star**[27] 2535 5-8-10 75 ....(p) FMBerry 69
(Mrs John Harrington, Ire) *mid-div: hdwy into 3rd after 1/2-way: rdn and no ex early st: wknd* **5/1**[2]
12 24 **Bobs Pride (IRE)**[273] 731 9-9-11 90 ....(t) PShanahan 57
(D K Weld, Ire) *a in rr: in tch ent st: sn no ex: eased whn btn: t.o* **20/1**
13 dist **Spinning Wings (IRE)**[311] 5225 5-9-6 92 ....(tp) KatherineSO'Brien[(7)] —
(T Hogan, Ire) *led racing keenly and sn clr: reduced ld 1/2-way: hdd 6f out and sn wknd: completely t.o* **25/1**

3m 33.0s **Going Correction** +0.175s/f (Good) **13** Ran SP% **132.2**
Speed ratings: **107,106,104,103,102 102,102,101,101,101 100,88,—**
CSF £348.10 CT £6989.45 TOTE £61.00: £8.80, £3.50, £5.30; DF 516.10.
Owner James Callow **Bred** Darley **Trained** Dungannon, Co. Tyrone

NOTEBOOK
Silk Hall(UAE), twice a winner over 1m6f on the all-weather in England where he also scored twice over hurdles for Alan King, was having his first run on the Flat for Jimmy Lambe after a couple of outings over hurdles. Sent to the front into the straight, he kept on quite well under pressure. (op 20/1)
Cry For The Moon(USA) was up 8lb for his two-length win over a slightly shorter trip on quicker ground at Navan 15 days previously. He was held up and began to close before the straight. Second from 2f out, he tried hard to peg back the winner and kept on, although held towards the finish. (op 12/1)
Dearest Girl(IRE) was taking a big step up in trip having won a 1m2f handicap off 76 on fast ground at Roscommon last month before making little impact in the 1m5f Ulster Derby. She seemed to stay the distance and, after being held up out the back, she closed turning for home and kept on steadily without holding a winning chance.
Oneeightofamile(IRE) was up 10lb for his four-length win over the trip on quicker ground at Limerick two weeks previously. He led from 6f out until the straight, but was unable to raise his effort under pressure from almost 2f out. (op 5/2 tchd 2/1)
Darenjan(IRE), a triple winner including twice over this trip on quicker ground, was having his first run since November and raced in second place for much of the journey. Still prominent into the straight, he was soon under pressure and could make little impression.
La Estrella(USA) failed to make any impression. (op 9/2)

3419 - 3421a, 3423a (Foreign Racing) - See Raceform Interactive

HAMBURG (R-H)
Saturday, June 25

OFFICIAL GOING: Turf: good

3422a FRANZ-GUNTHER VON GAERTNER-GEDACHTNISRENNEN (HAMBURGER MEILE) (GROUP 3) (3YO+) (TURF) 1m
6:45 (12:00) 3-Y-0+
£27,586 (£9,482; £4,741; £2,586; £1,724; £1,293)

RPR
1 **Alianthus (GER)**[23] 2657 6-9-6 0 .... ADeVries 2 113
(J Hirschberger, Germany) *broke wl: sent to the ld: set gd pce: r.o wl in st: nvr threatened: wnt clr: easily* **1/1**[1]
2 2 **Le Big (GER)**[48] 7-9-2 0 .... AHelfenbein 7 104
(U Stoltefuss, Germany) *hld up towars rr: looked threatening coming out of the fnl turn: r.o wl in st wout threatening wnr* **196/10**
3 2 1/2 **Sanjii Danon (GER)**[48] 5-9-2 0 .... APietsch 5 98
(W Hickst, Germany) *bkmarker fr s: looked btn early in st but responded to press and r.o wl ins fnl f* **132/10**
4 1 1/2 **Emerald Commander (IRE)**[266] 6593 4-9-2 0 .... THellier 3 95
(Saeed Bin Suroor) *broke wl to r cl bhd ldr initially then dropped bk: u.p arnd fnl turn: failed to qckn in st: no imp on ldrs* **19/10**[2]
5 6 **Rose Danon (GER)**[34] 2338 3-8-10 0 .... ASuborics 6 83
(P Schiergen, Germany) *broke wl: settled in 3rd: threatened briefly in st but sn rdn and btn* **43/5**
6 nk **Neatico (GER)**[23] 2657 4-9-2 0 .... AStarke 4 80
(P Schiergen, Germany) *racd freely fr outset: a.p in 4th down bkst: rdn but no ex in st* **71/10**
7 7 **Earl Of Fire (GER)**[17] 6-9-2 0 .... DominiqueBoeuf 1 64
(W Baltromei, Germany) *broke wl to r in 2nd: rdn but no ex arnd fnl furn: sn fdd* **66/10**[3]

1m 34.88s (94.88)
WFA 3 from 4yo+ 10lb **7** Ran SP% **132.3**
WIN (incl. 10 euro stake): 20. PLACES: 13, 35, 25. SF: 785.
Owner Baron G Von Ullmann **Bred** Gestut Karlshof **Trained** Germany

NOTEBOOK
Emerald Commander(IRE), whose rider reported that the colt ran very flat and found nothing at all in the straight, had been a bit free early on, and might have needed this seasonal reappearance.

3287 SALISBURY (R-H)

Sunday, June 26

OFFICIAL GOING: Good to firm (good in places; 8.2)

Wind: virtually nil Weather: sunny and very warm

3424 BRITISH STALLION STUDS SUPPORTING BRITISH RACING E B F BLAGRAVE MAIDEN STKS (DIV I) 6f 212y

2:00 (2:01) (Class 4) 2-Y-O **£3,917** (£1,165; £582; £291) **Stalls** Centre

Form RPR

6 1 **Graphic (IRE)**[17] 2837 2-9-3 0 WilliamBuick 2 86+
(Richard Hannon) *trckd ldr: led 3f out: sn rdn whn hrd pressed: r.o wl to assert fnl 100yds* **8/1**

3324 2 ½ **Esentepe (IRE)**[8] 3152 2-8-12 0 PatDobbs 3 80
(Richard Hannon) *trckd ldr: jnd wnr 2f out: sn rdn: ev ch ins fnl f: kpt on but no ex fnl 100yds* **6/4**[1]

43 3 3¾ **Bronze Angel (IRE)**[23] 2687 2-9-3 0 TadhgO'Shea 8 76+
(Marcus Tregoning) *mid-div: hdwy 3f out: rdn to dispute 3rd 2f out: nt pce to chal: styd on* **11/4**[2]

6 4 ¾ **Whinging Willie (IRE)**[16] 2880 2-9-3 0 GeorgeBaker 5 74
(Gary Moore) *mid-div: hdwy 3f out: sn rdn: nt pce to chal: kpt on tl no ex fnl 75yds* **11/2**[3]

5 1 **Drummond** 2-9-3 0 LukeMorris 11 71+
(Clive Cox) *hld up bhd: swtchd to centre whn rdn and stdy prog fr 2f out: styd on: nvr trbld ldrs* **33/1**

6 3¾ **Jasie Jac (IRE)** 2-9-3 0 IanMongan 1 62
(Robert Mills) *chsd ldrs: rdn 3f out: nvr gng pce to chal: wknd ins fnl f* **16/1**

0 7 ½ **Merv (IRE)**[20] 2767 2-9-3 0 FrankieMcDonald 6 60
(Henry Candy) *mid-div: rdn 3f out: fdd ins fnl f* **20/1**

8 4½ **Lunar Deity** 2-9-3 0 CathyGannon 7 49
(Eve Johnson Houghton) *s.i.s: hmpd after 1f: a towards rr* **40/1**

050 9 1 **Samasana (IRE)**[14] 2953 2-8-12 0 (v[1]) LiamKeniry 10 42
(Ian Wood) *led: rdn and hdd 3f out: sn hung rt: wknd 2f out* **150/1**

10 ½ **Ballyheigue (IRE)** 2-9-3 0 MartinDwyer 9 45
(Brian Meehan) *a towards rr* **20/1**

11 6 **Clowance Keys** 2-9-3 0 DarryllHolland 4 30
(Rod Millman) *sn pushed along in midfield: wknd 2f out: hmpd and hung lft sn after* **66/1**

1m 27.72s (-0.88) **Going Correction** -0.10s/f (Good) 11 Ran SP% **116.1**
Speed ratings (Par 95): **101,100,96,95,94 89,89,84,83,82 75**
Tote Swingers: 1&2 £3.10, 1&3 £4.00, 2&3 £1.90 CSF £19.10 TOTE £10.80: £2.90, £1.02, £1.70; EX 21.10.
Owner The Royal Ascot Racing Club **Bred** Kevin & Meta Cullen **Trained** East Everleigh, Wilts

FOCUS

False rail in place 20ft off permanent far-side rail between 6f and winning post. A number of subsequent Pattern-race winners have taken a division of this maiden in recent years, namely Passing Glance (2001), Norse Dancer (2002), Perfectperformance (2004) and Lord Zenith (2009). Hand times make this maiden just under a second faster than the next leg and this is fairly useful form. The second and third were both 5lb off their recent level.

NOTEBOOK

Graphic(IRE) stepped up a good deal on the form of his Newbury debut, taking this in the manner of a useful colt. He doesn't look Pattern material yet, but could progress in nurseries. (op 9-1)
Esentepe(IRE) ran okay without giving the Chesham form a boost, this being her first start since finishing fourth at Royal Ascot. She's now had fives goes, but she can still win a maiden before going back up in class. (op 5-4)
Bronze Angel(IRE) ran an improved race in fair company at Goodwood last time, but he failed to build on that on this rise in trip. Still, he ran to a pretty fair level in defeat and, seeing as he didn't get much cover early on, he could yet do a bit better. (op 3-1 tchd 5-2 and 7-2 in a place)
Whinging Willie(IRE) showed ability over 5f on his debut at Sandown and did so again, plugging on at the one pace. (op 7-1 tchd 5-1)
Drummond is bred to stay well on the dam's side of his pedigree and was under pressure a fair way out, but he kept on steadily. He has ability.

3425 BRITISH STALLION STUDS SUPPORTING BRITISH RACING E B F BLAGRAVE MAIDEN STKS (DIV II) 6f 212y

2:35 (2:37) (Class 4) 2-Y-O **£3,917** (£1,165; £582; £291) **Stalls** Centre

Form RPR

1 **Shamrocked (IRE)** 2-9-3 0 HughBowman 4 80+
(Mick Channon) *trckd ldrs: led 2f out: sn idled and rdn: won w plenty in hand* **6/4**[1]

0 2 2 **Maccabees**[26] 2584 2-9-3 0 JamesMillman 3 73
(Rod Millman) *prom: rdn whn outpcd over 2f out: styd on ins fnl f: wnt 2nd nr fin* **12/1**

3 hd **Cavaleiro (IRE)** 2-9-3 0 TadhgO'Shea 9 73
(Marcus Tregoning) *in tch: rdn 3f out: no imp tl styd on fnl f: wnt 3rd nr fin* **7/1**[3]

4 4 ½ **King's Ciel**[14] 2962 2-9-0 0 MatthewDavies(3) 10 71
(George Baker) *led: rdn and hdd 2f out: kpt chsng wnr tl no ex and lost 2 pls nring fin* **15/2**

00 5 1 **Plym**[19] 2787 2-8-12 0 WilliamBuick 2 65+
(Richard Hannon) *hld up: outpcd over 2f out: styng on at same pce whn little short of room on far rails fnl 100yds* **10/1**

6 nk **Art Law (IRE)** 2-9-3 0 ShaneKelly 7 68+
(Brian Meehan) *hld up but in tch: rdn 3f out: kpt on but nvr gng pce to threaten* **14/1**

7 hd **Gold Sceptre (FR)** 2-9-3 0 PatDobbs 1 68+
(Richard Hannon) *s.i.s: racd green in rr: swtchd lft u.p over 2f out: sme late prog: nvr a factor* **4/1**[2]

8 16 **Itsonlymakebelieve (IRE)** 2-8-12 0 JamesDoyle 6 23
(Ian Wood) *trckd ldrs: rdn 3f out: wknd wl over 1f out* **33/1**

1m 28.61s (0.01) **Going Correction** -0.10s/f (Good) 8 Ran SP% **110.7**
Speed ratings (Par 95): **95,92,92,91,90 90,90,71**
Tote Swingers: 1&2 £5.90, 1&3 £2.90, 2&3 £11.00 CSF £19.88 TOTE £3.00: £1.40, £4.10, £2.30; EX 23.80.
Owner Box 41 **Bred** Lodge Park Stud **Trained** West Ilsley, Berks

FOCUS

Hand times have this maiden at just under a second slower than the first division, but the race can produce a few winners. The field was compressed and it's hard to rate the form any higher.

NOTEBOOK

Shamrocked(IRE) ◆, a sizeable individual, made a thoroughly pleasing introduction. A 72,000euros purchase, his entry in the Group 1 National Stakes gave a clue to the regard in which he's held and he took this with a lot to spare, having his ears pricked when clear inside the final furlong. We might not see the best of him until he fully strengthens up, but he rates a smart prospect. (op 7-4)
Maccabees improved on a moderate debut over 6f. He ran into a nice type and might find a lesser maiden, but nurseries will be easier after one more run. (op 14-1)
Cavaleiro(IRE), a 78,000gns purchase from the first crop of the trainer's Derby winner Sir Percy, made a respectable debut and can improve. (op 6-1)
King's Ciel showed ability over 6f on soft ground here first time up and this was another respectable effort, although he didn't improve as much as one might have hoped over the longer trip. (op 17-2)
Plym ◆ could have finished second had she enjoyed a better trip and been given a more vigorous ride. She still looked green tucked away towards the inside rail, perhaps shying away a touch from taking a narrow gap between the fence and her rivals, but she wasn't subjected to a hard ride and crossed the line with something left. She is a nice nursery prospect. (op 9-1)
Art Law(IRE), a 42,000gns purchase who has already been gelded, ran green but has ability. (tchd 16-1)
Gold Sceptre(FR), a 62,000euros purchase, was solid enough in the market considering the strength of the favourite, but he started slowly and made no progress. He can probably do a lot better considering how much some Richard Hannon juveniles are improving for a run this year. (op 7-2 tchd 10-3)

3426 K J PIKE & SONS LTD H'CAP 1m 1f 198y

3:05 (3:05) (Class 5) (0-70,69) 4-Y-O+ **£2,590** (£770; £385; £192) **Stalls** Low

Form RPR

1340 1 **Sasheen**[18] 2816 4-9-2 **64** (p) DarryllHolland 10 71
(Jeremy Gask) *mde all: rdn over 2f out: sn edgd off far rails: styd on gamely: drvn out* **7/1**

0-56 2 1¾ **Oriental Girl**[16] 2872 6-9-6 **68** (p) LiamKeniry 1 72
(Jonathan Geake) *in tch: rdn whn swtchd lft 2f out: sn chsng wnr: styd on same pce fnl f* **6/1**[3]

5303 3 ½ **Chief Exec**[15] 2900 9-8-4 **52** (v) LukeMorris 5 55
(Jeremy Gask) *in tch: nt clr run on far rails over 2f out: rdn whn gap appeared sn after: styd on same pce ins fnl f* **8/1**

2500 4 2¼ **The Blue Dog (IRE)**[15] 2923 4-9-0 **62** (v) WilliamCarson 2 60
(Michael Wigham) *trckd wnr: rdn and edgd lft over 2f out: lost 2nd over 1f out: no ex fnl f* **11/1**

060- 5 7 **Penchesco (IRE)**[77] 7548 6-9-6 **68** PatDobbs 7 52
(Amanda Perrett) *in tch: effrt whn swtchd lft over 2f out: fdd ins fnl f* **4/1**[2]

00-0 6 ½ **George Thisby**[34] 2354 5-9-1 **63** JamesMillman 4 46
(Rod Millman) *trckd wnr tl rdn over 2f out: grad fdd* **16/1**

3052 7 ¾ **Free Tussy (ARG)**[23] 2685 7-9-4 **66** (bt) GeorgeBaker 8 48
(Gary Moore) *hld up in last pair: rdn over 2f out: nvr any imp* **4/1**[2]

0404 8 ¾ **Red Somerset (USA)**[9] 3130 8-9-2 **64** MartinDwyer 9 44
(Mike Murphy) *dwlt: hdwy 3f out: sn rdn: nvr a danger: fdd fnl f* **7/2**[1]

2m 8.05s (-1.85) **Going Correction** -0.10s/f (Good) 8 Ran SP% **114.3**
Speed ratings (Par 103): **103,101,101,99,93 93,92,92**
Tote Swingers: 1&2 £6.50, 1&3 £8.40, 2&3 £5.30 CSF £48.21 CT £343.28 TOTE £9.90: £4.00, £1.10, £1.20; EX 59.00.
Owner Sashay Partnership **Bred** Edward J G Young **Trained** Sutton Veny, Wilts

FOCUS

A modest handicap.
Free Tussy(ARG) Official explanation: vet said gelding returned lame left-fore

3427 K J PIKE & SONS LTD SENIORS' SPRINT H'CAP 5f

3:35 (3:35) (Class 4) (0-80,80) 6-Y-O+ **£4,533** (£1,348; £674; £336) **Stalls** Low

Form RPR

2365 1 **Maze (IRE)**[13] 3000 6-8-10 **76** LucyKBarry(7) 5 85+
(Tony Carroll) *squeezed up sn after s: last: hdwy whn swtchd to centre over 2f out: led ent fnl f: r.o: pushed out* **5/1**[3]

1105 2 1¼ **Steelcut**[14] 2959 7-9-2 **75** (p) CathyGannon 8 79
(David Evans) *chsd ldrs: rdn over 2f out: kpt on ins fnl f: wnt 2nd nr fin* **13/2**

2210 3 hd **Wooden King (IRE)**[15] 2929 6-9-3 **76** TomMcLaughlin 2 79+
(Malcolm Saunders) *sn pushed into ld: rdn 2f out: hdd enterin g fnl f: kpt on but no ex: lost 2nd nr fin* **10/3**[1]

6001 4 1¾ **Alfresco**[27] 2557 7-9-2 **75** (b) LukeMorris 1 72
(John Best) *chsd ldrs: rdn over 2f out: kpt on same pce* **9/2**[2]

4640 5 ½ **Brandywell Boy (IRE)**[15] 2903 8-8-10 **69** JamesDoyle 4 64
(Dominic Ffrench Davis) *squeezed up sn after s: in last pair but in tch: rdn 3f out: nvr gng pce to get involved* **6/1**

0040 6 ¾ **Bertoliver**[22] 2714 7-9-7 **80** JackMitchell 6 72
(Stuart Williams) *prom: rdn over 2f out: ev ch tl fdd fnl f* **5/1**[3]

1310 7 ½ **Kyllachy Storm**[14] 2959 7-8-4 **68** HarryBentley(5) 3 59
(Ron Hodges) *chsd ldrs tl lost pl whn squeezed up after 2f: in tch: rdn 3f out: nvr gng pce to get bk on terms* **10/1**

60.13 secs (-0.87) **Going Correction** -0.10s/f (Good) 7 Ran SP% **111.3**
Speed ratings: **102,100,99,96,96 94,94**
Tote Swingers: 1&2 £6.50, 1&3 £5.10, 2&3 £3.90 CSF £34.67 CT £118.82 TOTE £5.30: £2.10, £2.20; EX 44.80.
Owner Centaur Global Partnership I **Bred** Millsec Limited **Trained** Cropthorne, Worcs

FOCUS

A sprint for 6-y-os and above, so not obviously strong form. The pace was predictably fast.

3428 H S LESTER MEMORIAL H'CAP 1m 6f 21y

4:10 (4:12) (Class 4) (0-85,86) 4-Y-O+ **£4,533** (£1,348; £674; £336) **Stalls** Far side

Form RPR

0604 1 **Sherman McCoy**[39] 2190 5-9-2 **80** JamesMillman 6 87
(Rod Millman) *mde all: styd on wl: drvn out* **9/1**

00-3 2 1½ **Mildoura (FR)**[14] 2958 6-9-8 **86** IanMongan 4 91
(Laura Mongan) *hld up in tch: tk clsr order 6f out: rdn over 2f out: wnt 2nd ins fnl f: styd on but no ex* **12/1**

-416 3 hd **Arab League (IRE)**[15] 2931 6-9-0 **78** ShaneKelly 2 83
(Richard Price) *trckd wnr: rdn 3f out: nvr able to chal: styd on: lost 2nd narrowly ins fnl f* **6/1**

/-22 4 1¾ **Tappanappa (IRE)**[30] 2458 4-9-1 **79** LiamKeniry 1 82
(Andrew Balding) *hld up: rdn 3f out: hdwy sn after: styd on w out threatening ldrs* **3/1**[2]

4-52 5 1½ **Sunny Future (IRE)**[38] 2224 5-8-9 **73** LukeMorris 9 73
(Malcolm Saunders) *hld up in last pair: rdn in last over 3f out: swtchd lft and rdr nrly dropped whip over 1f out: styd on: nrst fin* **11/2**[3]

5310 6 ¾ **High On A Hill (IRE)**[15] 2931 4-9-2 **80** JamesDoyle 11 79
(Sylvester Kirk) *trckd ldrs: rdn over 3f out: one pce fnl f* **10/1**

/5-0 7 nk **Kazzene (USA)**[15] 2931 4-9-1 **79** (tp) AndreaAtzeni 5 78
(David Pipe) *hld up in tch: hdwy over 3f out: sn rdn: no ex fnl f* **22/1**

433 8 hd **Trovare (USA)**[29] 2512 4-9-7 **85** (p) PatDobbs 12 84
(Amanda Perrett) *trckd ldrs: rdn over 3f out: one pce fnl 2f* **5/2**[1]

322/ **9** *nse* **Souter Point (USA)**[45] [6571] 5-9-5 **83**............................ CathyGannon 8 82
(Tony Carroll) *kicked at s: hld up in tch: effrt 3f out: one pce fnl 2f* **20/1**
3m 7.06s (-0.34) **Going Correction** -0.10s/f (Good) **9** Ran SP% **119.1**
Speed ratings (Par 105): **96,95,95,94,93 92,92,92,92**
Tote Swingers: 1&2 £13.10, 1&3 £10.70, 2&3 £12.00 CSF £113.44 CT £707.63 TOTE £15.10: £3.70, £2.70, £3.00; EX 125.50.
Owner Mustajed Partnership **Bred** Horizon Bloodstock Limited **Trained** Kentisbeare, Devon

FOCUS
A few runners broke the tape ahead of the first intended start, but they were soon gathered in. This looked a fair handicap, but the well-ridden Sherman McCoy was allowed a soft lead and the form needs treating with a bit of caution.

3429 K J PIKE & SONS LTD AUCTION STKS (CONDITIONS RACE) 6f
4:45 (4:47) (Class 3) 2-Y-O **£6,476** (£1,927; £963; £481) **Stalls** Low

Form RPR
1 **1** **Eureka (IRE)**[40] [2181] 2-8-10 0.. PatDobbs 3 100+
(Richard Hannon) *trckd ldrs: rdn to ld wl over 1f out: fnd plenty whn briefly chal ent fnl f: r.o strly* **10/3**[2]
1 **2** *2 ¼* **Sir Glanton (IRE)**[27] [2559] 2-8-8 0.................................... LiamKeniry 1 90
(Amanda Perrett) *hld up: rdn and hdwy wl over 2f out: chsd wnr and briefly flattered ent fnl f: nt pce of wnr fnl 140yds* **7/2**[3]
532 **3** *2 ½* **Minal**[4] [3288] 2-8-0 0... RyanPowell(5) 4 80
(Richard Hannon) *hld up: pushed along and stdy hdwy fr over 2f out: rdn over 1f out: wnt 3rd sn after: styd on wout threatening* **15/2**
21 **4** *2 ½* **Travis County (IRE)**[25] [2617] 2-8-4 0............................. PaulPickard(3) 9 74
(Brian Ellison) *prom: led over 3f out: rdn over 2f out: hdd wl over 1f out: fdd ins fnl f* **4/1**
2341 **5** *1 ½* **Choice Of Remark (IRE)**[50] [1913] 2-8-5 0...................... CathyGannon 6 68
(David Evans) *led early: chsd ldrs: rdn over 2f out: fdd fnl f* **14/1**
31 **6** *½* **Blackdown Fair**[19] [2787] 2-7-12 0.................................... AndreaAtzeni 8 59
(Rod Millman) *fly-leapt leaving stalls: sn led: hdd over 3f out: rdn over 2f out: sn hld: fdd fnl f* **11/4**[1]
7 *27* **Il Pazzo** 2-7-11 0.. HarryBentley(5) 7 —
(Mike Murphy) *s.i.s: sn pushed along in last: hung lft u.p 3f out: wknd 2f out: t.o* **28/1**
1m 13.87s (-0.93) **Going Correction** -0.10s/f (Good) **7** Ran SP% **113.8**
Speed ratings (Par 97): **102,99,95,92,90 89,53**
Tote Swingers: 1&2 £3.40, 1&3 £4.50, 2&3 £4.60 CSF £15.28 TOTE £4.10: £1.80, £1.20; EX 16.80.
Owner Noodles Racing **Bred** Jerry Murphy **Trained** East Everleigh, Wilts

FOCUS
A race with an impressive roll of honour in recent years, winners including Milk It Mick (later won Dewhurst), Sir Percy (Dewhurst and Derby), Classic Blade (July Stakes), Orpen Grey (runner-up July Stakes) and most recently Crown Prosecutor (runner-up Gimcrack). This looked an up-to-scratch renewal and the winner showed Listed-class form. The pace was overly strong.

NOTEBOOK
Eureka(IRE) ◆ was sent off 16-1 when narrowly defeating the smart Burwaaz (subsequently even better than fourth-place finish in Norfolk indicates) for a successful debut at Nottingham and he proved that was no fluke with a very useful performance. Having travelled well enough, he briefly looked set for a serious race when the runner-up got close, but he readily put that rival away. A horse with plenty of size, he has a lot of speed - his trainer nominated the Super Sprint as his next target - but he saw out this 6f really well and there's plenty of stamina on the dam's side of his pedigree, so it will be a surprise if he doesn't stay at least 7f. Whatever, he looks Group class. (op 3-1)
Sir Glanton(IRE) looked useful prospect when a rare debut winner for this yard at odds of 40-1 in a decent Goodwood maiden and confirmed that promise with a good second. He was simply beaten by a smart type but gave the impression he'll come on again for this. (op 9-2)
Minal was only just behind Sir Glanton two starts ago, before suffering another narrow defeat on soft ground over this C&D. Turned out only four days later, he ran well but is not at progressive as the front two. (op 6-1 tchd 8-1)
Travis County(IRE) ◆, a Ripon maiden winner, deserves credit for finishing so close considering he was taken on for the lead. (op 9-2)
Choice Of Remark(IRE) deserves credit as he had been off for 50 days and raced up with the hot pace. (op 10-1 tchd 18-1)
Blackdown Fair did too much too soon, taking on Travis County for the lead, and this was a lot tougher than the weak C&D maiden she won. (op 10-3 tchd 5-2)

3430 JOLLY PROPERTY SERVICES MAIDEN STKS 1m 1f 198y
5:15 (5:15) (Class 5) 3-Y-O+ **£2,914** (£867; £433; £216) **Stalls** Low

Form RPR
2 **1** **Gatewood**[13] [3001] 3-9-0 0.. WilliamBuick 9 85+
(John Gosden) *prom: led over 3f out: sn rdn and hrd pressed: styd on strly to assert ent fnl f* **4/9**[1]
0 **2** *3 ¾* **Anatolian**[17] [2848] 3-8-7 0.. AntiocoMurgia(7) 10 78+
(Mahmood Al Zarooni) *trckd ldrs: rdn to press wnr 3f out: ev ch tl wandered and no ex ent fnl f* **25/1**
63 **3** *3 ¼* **Hawridge Song**[17] [2848] 3-9-0 0.................................... JamesMillman 7 71
(Rod Millman) *racd keenly: led tl over 3f out: sn rdn: styd on same pce* **12/1**
36 **4** *½* **Kleitomachos (IRE)**[13] [3001] 3-9-0 0................................ IanMongan 4 70+
(Stuart Kittow) *racd keenly in mid-div: hdwy to trck ldrs 5f out: pushed along 3f out: styd on same pce* **11/1**[3]
5 *2* **The Calling Curlew** 3-9-0 0..................................... FrankieMcDonald 1 66+
(Henry Candy) *in tch: rdn 3f out: kpt on same pce fnl 2f* **40/1**
6 *1 ¼* **Charlie Fable (IRE)** 3-9-0 0.. TravisBlock 3 64
(Hughie Morrison) *nvr bttr than mid-div* **40/1**
0 **7** *1* **Proof (IRE)**[13] [3001] 3-9-0 0.. AhmedAjtebi 6 62
(Mahmood Al Zarooni) *nvr bttr than mid-div* **15/2**[2]
-04 **8** *½* **Another Whisper (IRE)**[23] [2689] 3-8-9 0................................ PatDobbs 2 56
(Richard Hannon) *trckd ldrs: rdn 3f out: wknd over 1f out* **12/1**
00 **9** *1 ¾* **Bright Abbey**[24] [2648] 3-9-0 0...................................... DarryllHolland 12 57
(Walter Swinburn) *a towards rr* **40/1**
10 *¾* **Perfect Rapture** 3-8-9 0.. LukeMorris 8 51
(Clive Cox) *rdn over 5f out: a towards rr* **20/1**
0 **11** *6* **Brunello**[38] [2231] 3-9-0 0... LiamKeniry 5 44
(Walter Swinburn) *a towards rr* **66/1**
2m 8.99s (-0.91) **Going Correction** -0.10s/f (Good) **11** Ran SP% **122.2**
Speed ratings (Par 103): **99,96,93,93,91 90,89,89,87,87 82**
Tote Swingers: 1&2 £4.10, 1&3 £2.80, 2&3 £36.40 CSF £24.13 TOTE £1.70: £1.02, £5.80, £2.60; EX 15.80.
Owner George Strawbridge **Bred** George Strawbridge **Trained** Newmarket, Suffolk

FOCUS
A race won two years ago by subsequent Breeders' Cup Turf hero Dangerous Midge. Just an ordinary maiden - the time was 0.94 seconds slower than the earlier Class 5 handicap - but the winner is a nice prospect.

3431 AXMINSTER CARPETS RACING EXCELLENCE APPRENTICE H'CAP (WHIPS SHALL BE CARRIED BUT NOT USED) 1m
5:45 (5:48) (Class 6) (0-60,59) 3-Y-O **£1,942** (£578; £288; £144) **Stalls** Low

Form RPR
-031 **1** **Camberley Two**[5] [3253] 3-9-3 **59** 6ex......................... CharlesBishop(3) 7 72+
(Roger Charlton) *a.p: led 3f out: sn drifted to far rail: in command fr 2f out: pushed out* **4/6**[1]
12-4 **2** *3 ¼* **Salvationist**[55] [1769] 3-9-5 **58**.................................... MatthewLawson 12 64
(John Dunlop) *hld up towards rr: pushed along and hdwy fr over 3f out: chsd wnr over 1f out: kpt on but a being hld* **8/1**[3]
0642 **3** *4* **Oliver's Gold**[6] [3226] 3-8-8 **52**.................................... JustinNewman(5) 6 49
(Amanda Perrett) *mid-div: pushed along and hdwy over 3f out: chsd ldng pair sn after: styd on same pce fnl 2f* **4/1**[2]
0055 **4** *7* **Bedibyes**[37] [2243] 3-8-11 **55**.. IanBurns(5) 5 36
(Richard Mitchell) *prom tl squeezed out over 3f out: sn pushed along: edgd rt and one pce fnl 2f* **40/1**
5350 **5** *1 ¾* **Magical Star**[6] [3226] 3-7-13 **45**.. RichardOld(7) 8 22
(Michael Wigham) *chsd ldrs: one pce fnl 2f* **50/1**
0-05 **6** *1 ¼* **Little Book**[11] [3039] 3-9-3 **56**..(v[1]) LucyKBarry 2 30
(Edward Vaughan) *chsd ldrs: losing pl whn nt clr run on far rails and swtchd lft 3f out: rdr sn used whip but nvr any danger after* **12/1**
0-00 **7** *3 ½* **Kalgoolie**[6] [3226] 3-8-11 **55**.. NoelGarbutt(5) 1 21
(Rae Guest) *led tl 3f out: grad fdd* **40/1**
0004 **8** *7* **Blazing Apostle (IRE)**[26] [2598] 3-8-1 **45**........................ DanielHarris(5) 9 —
(Christine Dunnett) *chsd ldrs: pushed along over 3f out: wknd wl over 1f out* **33/1**
0-00 **9** *4* **Ollywood**[36] [2311] 3-8-4 **46**....................................... GeorgeDowning(3) 11 —
(Tony Carroll) *a towards rr* **40/1**
0060 **10** *1 ¼* **A B Celebration**[4] [3289] 3-8-9 **51**.. JakePayne(3) 3 —
(John Bridger) *prom tl wknd over 2f out* **66/1**
0-40 **11** *5* **Invent**[17] [2858] 3-8-11 **57**... StephanieThewlis(7) 4 —
(Sir Mark Prescott Bt) *chsd ldrs tl wknd 3f out* **14/1**
-050 **12** *5* **Soldiers Point**[6] [3220] 3-8-6 **50**...................................(b[1]) LewisWalsh(5) 10 —
(Jane Chapple-Hyam) *s.i.s: hdwy to sit promly after 3f: wknd 3f out* **25/1**
06-0 **13** *19* **Rather Cool**[19] [2792] 3-8-13 **52**.. CharlesEddery 13 —
(John Bridger) *sn swtchd rt: a bhd* **40/1**
1m 42.88s (-0.62) **Going Correction** -0.10s/f (Good) **13** Ran SP% **125.5**
Speed ratings (Par 97): **99,95,91,84,83 81,78,71,67,66 61,56,37**
Tote Swingers: 1&2 £3.10, 1&3 £1.30, 2&3 £2.50 CSF £6.83 CT £17.73 TOTE £1.70: £1.10, £2.50, £1.30; EX 8.50.
Owner H R H Sultan Ahmad Shah **Bred** Barry Walters Farms **Trained** Beckhampton, Wilts
■ Stewards' Enquiry : Lucy K Barry seven-day ban: used whip (Jul 11,12,14,15,17,18,20)

FOCUS
The field were strung out behind the well-handicapped favourite. These apprentices were not allowed to use their whips. They raced towards the far side of the track.
T/Plt: £2,133.10 to a £1 stake. Pool £59,172.00 - 20.25 winning tickets. T/Qpdt: £316.70 to a £1 stake. Pool £3,510.00 - 8.20 winning tickets. TM

3408 WINDSOR (R-H)
Sunday, June 26

OFFICIAL GOING: Good (7.8)
Wind: Almost nil Weather: Sunny, very warm

3432 TOTEPLACEPOT WIN WITHOUT BACKING A WINNER H'CAP 1m 67y
2:25 (2:25) (Class 5) (0-70,70) 3-Y-O **£2,525** (£751; £375; £187) **Stalls** Low

Form RPR
2605 **1** **Uncle Dermot (IRE)**[16] [2885] 3-9-2 **65**.............................. KierenFallon 6 71
(Brendan Powell) *t.k.h: hld up in midfield: prog 3f out: edgd lft but drvn to ld over 1f out: styd on wl* **6/1**[2]
6-06 **2** *¾* **Blue Maisey**[18] [2821] 3-9-0 **63**... SebSanders 12 67
(Peter Makin) *t.k.h: hld up in midfield: clsd on ldrs over 2f out: styd on to take 2nd ins fnl f: unable to chal* **12/1**
3620 **3** *¾* **Whodathought (IRE)**[17] [2838] 3-9-7 **70**......................(b) JimmyFortune 2 73
(Richard Hannon) *trckd ldrs: prog over 2f out: rdn to chal over 1f out and upsides: kpt on same pce* **8/1**
-565 **4** *2 ¼* **Countess Ellen (IRE)**[30] [2478] 3-9-2 **65**..........................(p) NeilCallan 8 62
(Gerard Butler) *pressed ldr: led 5f out: drvn and hdd over 1f out: fdd* **10/1**
4500 **5** *1 ¼* **Night Witch (IRE)**[2] [3354] 3-9-1 **64**................................ EddieCreighton 9 59
(Edward Creighton) *hld up in 11th: sme prog fr 3f out: shkn up and kpt on fr over 1f out: nvr rchd ldrs* **7/1**
4635 **6** *½* **Arctic Mirage**[9] [3122] 3-9-3 **66**.. TedDurcan 1 59
(Michael Blanshard) *hld up towards rr: crept clsr to ldrs 3f out: shkn up and edgd lft fnl 2f but kpt on: eased last 75yds* **7/1**[3]
33-6 **7** *½* **Thank You Joy**[171] [60] 3-9-2 **65**.. JimCrowley 4 57
(J R Jenkins) *hld up in last trio: stl there 3f out: reminders and sme prog 2f out: more reminders and hanging lft 1f out: styd on: nrst fin* **40/1**
1346 **8** *nk* **Beach Babe**[14] [2964] 3-9-0 **63**.. NickyMackay 13 55
(Jonathan Portman) *hld up towards rr: taken wdst of all over 3f out and nt on terms: rdn and kpt on: n.d* **11/1**
0-30 **9** *7* **Full Footage**[27] [2568] 3-9-3 **66**... HayleyTurner 7 41
(Roger Charlton) *slowest away: hld up in last trio: rdn over 3f out: no prog* **16/1**
00-0 **10** *½* **Last Act (IRE)**[24] [2637] 3-8-2 **51** oh3........................... AdrianMcCarthy 10 25
(Mark Hoad) *led 3f: rdn over 3f out: sn wknd* **50/1**
0500 **11** *7* **Warbond**[27] [2550] 3-8-3 **55**.. SimonPearce(3) 3 13
(Michael Madgwick) *a wl in rr and nvr appeared to be gng wl* **66/1**
60-3 **12** *4* **Valeo Si Vales (IRE)**[55] [1749] 3-8-13 **62**......................... FergusSweeney 11 11
(Jamie Osborne) *prom: carried lft bnd 6f out: wknd over 2f out* **8/1**
-002 **13** *2* **Zaheeb**[26] [2599] 3-8-6 **58**.. AdamBeschizza(3) 5 —
(Dave Morris) *prom: hung lft bnd 6f out: wknd over 2f out* **9/2**[1]
0-66 **14** *3 ¼* **My Ruby (IRE)**[39] [2192] 3-9-6 **69**.. PaulDoe 14 —
(Jim Best) *hld up in midfield: hanging lft bnd 6f out: bustled along 4f out: dropped to rr over 2f out: eased fnl f* **7/1**[3]
1m 42.65s (-2.05) **Going Correction** -0.325s/f (Firm) **14** Ran SP% **119.0**
Speed ratings (Par 99): **97,96,95,93,92 91,91,90,83,83 76,72,70,66**
Tote Swingers: 1&2 £17.50, 1&3 £6.60, 2&3 £19.80 CSF £73.91 CT £600.84 TOTE £7.30: £2.80, £6.40, £3.30; EX 99.40 Trifecta £277.30 Part won. Pool: £374.82 - 0.20 winning units..
Owner K Rhatigan **Bred** Ballyhane Stud **Trained** Upper Lambourn, Berks

FOCUS
Rails on inner line and distances as advertised. A low-grade handicap.

Zaheeb Official explanation: trainer said gelding lost its right-fore shoe and did not handle the bend

3433 TRY TOTEQUICKPICK ON ALL TOTEPOOL BETS H'CAP 5f 10y
2:55 (2:57) (Class 5) (0-70,71) 3-Y-O **£2,525** (£751; £375; £187) **Stalls** Low

Form RPR
3211 **1** **Albany Rose (IRE)**[3] 3321 3-9-13 **71** 12ex.......................... TedDurcan 4 85+
(Rae Guest) *hld up in 6th: nt clr run fr 2f out tl swtchd lft over 1f out: r.o to ld jst ins fnl f: shkn up and drew rt away* **5/6**[1]
2543 **2** *5* **Johnny Hancocks (IRE)**[3] 3321 3-9-3 **61**........................ KierenFallon 2 57
(Linda Stubbs) *disp ld: narrow advantage 2f out: edgd lft and hdd jst ins fnl f: outpcd after* **4/1**[2]
-103 **3** *2 ¼* **Best Be Careful (IRE)**[23] 2660 3-9-4 **62**........................ HayleyTurner 7 50
(Mark Usher) *disp ld to 2f out: stl pressing ldr 1f out: fdd* **7/1**[3]
000- **4** *2 ¾* **Elusive Diva (IRE)**[193] 7879 3-8-9 **53**........................(b[1]) EddieCreighton 5 31
(Edward Creighton) *s.i.s: pushed along in last and struggling: kpt on to take 4th fnl f: eased last 75yds* **50/1**
5500 **5** *hd* **Acclamatory**[26] 2598 3-8-7 **56**.. RyanClark(5) 1 33
(Stuart Williams) *disp ld to 1/2-way: wknd over 1f out* **12/1**
000- **6** *1 ¾* **Cliffords Reprieve**[251] 6986 3-8-10 **59** ow3.................. LeeNewnes(5) 3 30
(Eric Wheeler) *disp ld to 1/2-way: sn lost pl: wknd over 1f out* **20/1**
-323 **7** *4 ½* **Abadejo**[30] 2453 3-9-7 **65**... FergusSweeney 6 20
(J R Jenkins) *hld up in tch: shkn up on outer 2f out: wknd qckly over 1f out* **9/1**

59.87 secs (-0.43) **Going Correction** -0.10s/f (Good) **7** Ran SP% **111.5**
Speed ratings (Par 99): **99,91,87,83,82 79,72**
Tote Swingers: 1&2 £1.90, 1&3 £2.50, 2&3 £2.80 CSF £4.10 TOTE £1.50: £1.10, £2.80; EX 4.00.

Owner E P Duggan **Bred** Blue Bloodstock Ltd **Trained** Newmarket, Suffolk

FOCUS
A moderate sprint handicap that was all about one horse.
Elusive Diva(IRE) Official explanation: jockey said filly lost right-fore shoe

3434 TRY TOTEQUICKPICK IF YOU'RE FEELING LUCKY H'CAP 1m 3f 135y
3:25 (3:25) (Class 4) (0-80,80) 4-Y-O+ **£3,561** (£1,059; £529; £264) **Stalls** Centre

Form RPR
/44- **1** **Samsons Son**[162] 7337 7-9-5 **78**.................................. JimmyFortune 11 86
(Alan King) *hld up in rr: prog 4f out gng strly: rdn to press ldr 2f out: drvn into narrow ld ins fnl f: hld on* **6/1**[2]
16- **2** *hd* **Jivry**[316] 5083 4-9-7 **80**.. FergusSweeney 2 88
(Henry Candy) *prom: wnt 2nd over 3f out: rdn to ld over 2f out: hrd pressed over 1f out: hdd ins fnl f: kpt on wl: jst hld* **9/1**
-046 **3** *1 ½* **Significant Move**[24] 2649 4-9-3 **76**................................ NeilCallan 7 81
(Stuart Kittow) *t.k.h: hld up towards rr: shkn up 4f out: taken to outer and prog over 2f out u.p: tried to cl on ldng pair over 1f out: one pce* **7/4**[1]
061- **4** *¾* **Foxhaven**[265] 6639 9-9-7 **80**.................................(v) KierenFallon 1 84
(Patrick Chamings) *hld up in last pair: gd prog on inner over 3f out to press ldrs over 2f out: sn rdn and nt qckn: kpt on same pce after* **13/2**[3]
1240 **5** *8* **Where's Susie**[27] 2552 6-8-12 **71**................................ KirstyMilczarek 4 61
(Michael Madgwick) *trckd ldrs: rdn and outpcd over 2f out: nvr on terms after* **20/1**
3-31 **6** *½* **Ghufa (IRE)**[23] 2696 7-8-8 **70**...................................... SimonPearce(3) 10 59
(Lydia Pearce) *hld up in last pair: shuffled along over 3f out: modest late prog: nvr nr ldrs* **12/1**
-535 **7** *1 ½* **Countess Comet (IRE)**[15] 2906 4-9-4 **77**......................(p) JimCrowley 6 64
(Ralph Beckett) *led at decent pce: shkn up and hdd over 2f out: pushed along and fdd* **11/1**
124/ **8** *8* **Mick's Dancer**[112] 6546 6-9-4 **77**.................................. MartinLane 3 50
(Richard Phillips) *trckd ldrs: rdn over 3f out: wknd over 2f out* **40/1**
103- **9** *4 ½* **Tenessee**[235] 7293 4-9-7 **80**.. SebSanders 9 45
(Peter Makin) *prom: rdn 4f out: sn lost pl and struggling: wkng w rdr looking down 2f out* **16/1**
0330 **10** *1 ¾* **Urban Space**[20] 2769 5-8-11 **70**.................................. HayleyTurner 8 33
(Conor Dore) *chsd ldr to over 3f out: sn wknd* **11/1**
5-03 **R** **Aspro Mavro (IRE)**[20] 2769 5-9-4 **77**............................. PaulDoe 5 —
(Jim Best) *ref to r: tk no part* **16/1**

2m 24.68s (-4.82) **Going Correction** -0.325s/f (Firm) **11** Ran SP% **117.3**
Speed ratings (Par 105): **103,102,101,101,96 95,94,89,86,85** —
Tote Swingers: 1&2 £10.80, 1&3 £3.20, 2&3 £4.10 CSF £58.95 CT £134.01 TOTE £7.70: £2.10, £3.10, £1.20; EX 88.10 Trifecta £413.90 Part won. Pool: £559.39 - 0.90 winning units..
Owner M Folan **Bred** John Best **Trained** Barbury Castle, Wilts
■ Stewards' Enquiry : Fergus Sweeney one-day ban: used whip with excessive frequency down shoulder in the forehand in incorrect place (Jul 11)

FOCUS
A race that concerned only four down the straight and it was the pair who raced nearer the rail that prevailed.

3435 E B F "WINKER WATSON" FILLIES' CONDITIONS STKS 5f 10y
4:00 (4:01) (Class 2) 2-Y-O
£9,034 (£2,705; £1,352; £677; £337; £169) **Stalls** Low

Form RPR
141 **1** **Betty Fontaine (IRE)**[15] 2902 2-8-12 0.......................... SamHitchcott 1 71+
(Mick Channon) *settled off the pce in last trio: pushed along to cl 1/2-way: drvn over 1f out: r.o to ld last 100yds: won narrowly but decisively* **10/3**[2]
0221 **2** *nk* **Aquasulis (IRE)**[13] 2998 2-8-9 0.................................. RoystonFfrench 5 67
(David Evans) *mostly chsd ldr: rdn over 1f out: upsides ent fnl f: kpt on but a jst hld nr fin* **8/1**
461 **3** *shd* **My Lucky Liz (IRE)**[12] 3016 2-8-12 0.............................. MartinLane 4 70
(David Simcock) *settled off the pce in last trio: rdn 2f out: prog and squeezed through wl ins fnl f: jst hld* **6/1**[3]
316 **4** *1 ¼* **Guru Girl**[20] 2777 2-8-12 0.. AndrewElliott 3 65
(Mrs K Burke) *pressed ldrs: lost pl sltly over 1f out: renewed effrt fnl f on outer: one pce* **3/1**[1]
1 **5** *½* **Pressure Drop (IRE)**[13] 2992 2-8-9 0............................ MarkLawson 6 60
(Jo Hughes) *swvd lft s: hanging lft thrght: sn w ldrs: trying to chal 1f out: nt qckn last 150yds* **3/1**[1]
0 **6** *½* **Bookiesindexdotnet**[88] 1042 2-8-9 0............................ FergusSweeney 7 58
(J R Jenkins) *led against nr side rail: drvn over 1f out: hdd & wknd last 100yds* **50/1**
33 **7** *24* **Finalist**[18] 2817 2-8-9 0... KierenFallon 2 —
(Dean Ivory) *sn last: nudged along and nt gng wl after 2f: allowed to coast home after* **15/2**

60.16 secs (-0.14) **Going Correction** -0.10s/f (Good) **7** Ran SP% **112.2**
Speed ratings (Par 96): **97,96,96,94,93 92,54**
Tote Swingers: 1&2 £5.40, 1&3 £3.70, 2&3 £7.20 CSF £28.28 TOTE £4.20: £1.60, £8.80; EX 37.90.

Owner Billy Parish **Bred** Tony And Mary McKiernan **Trained** West Ilsley, Berks

FOCUS
Something of a bunch finish for this fillies' conditions race. The form is rated on the positive side through the race averages.

NOTEBOOK
Betty Fontaine(IRE), well on top at the finish when landing the spoils at Bath last time, again saw it out strongly, winning with more in hand than the official margin of victory suggests. A good gallop is key to her at this distance and she may even be helped by a return to 6f. She's declared to run at Pontefract the following day. (op 3-1 tchd 11-4)
Aquasulis(IRE), winner of a 6f course seller last time, stepped up on that form and is clearly just as effective at this shorter trip. (op 9-1)
My Lucky Liz(IRE) stayed on well close home having been held up, but was never getting there. (op 4-1)
Guru Girl bounced back from a disappointing effort when clearly below her best at Naas, showing good speed before keeping on again. (op 9-2)
Pressure Drop(IRE), well on top towards the finish when scoring at Warwick on debut, went left coming out the gate and continued to hang that way. She ran a reasonable race considering. Official explanation: jockey said filly hung left (tchd 9-4)
Bookiesindexdotnet showed her debut running to be all wrong, making a good fist of it against the near-side rail. She can surely be found a small race. (op 40-1 tchd 33-1)

3436 TOTEEXACTA BETTER VALUE FORECAST H'CAP 1m 67y
4:35 (4:42) (Class 3) (0-90,90) 3-Y-O+ **£6,670** (£1,984; £991; £495) **Stalls** Low

Form RPR
6312 **1** **Jewelled**[26] 2597 5-8-10 **72**.. SebSanders 3 82
(Lady Herries) *hld up in 8th: prog against rail over 2f out: fnd gap and sn through to ld over 1f out: hanging lft and cajoled along: sn in command* **8/1**
-300 **2** *1 ¼* **Moynahan (USA)**[16] 2884 6-9-8 **84**..............................(b) PaulDoe 2 91
(Paul Cole) *wl in tch in 6th: rdn over 2f out: styd on u.p over 1f out: tk 2nd last stride* **11/1**
5420 **3** *nse* **Audemar (IRE)**[127] 615 5-9-9 **85**................................ MartinLane 9 92
(Edward Vaughan) *chsd ldng trio: drvn 3f out: clsd and ch over 1f out: styd on same pce* **11/1**
420- **4** *¾* **Woodcote Place**[218] 7522 8-9-10 **86**............................ NickyMackay 1 91
(Patrick Chamings) *trckd ldng pair: rdn over 2f out: chal and upsides over 1f out: one pce after* **16/1**
5501 **5** *3 ¾* **Norman Orpen (IRE)**[24] 2647 4-9-11 **87**...................... KierenFallon 13 84
(Jane Chapple-Hyam) *s.i.s: hld up in 9th: prog on wd outside over 2f out: drvn and nt qckn over 1f out: eased whn no ch last 150yds* **11/4**[1]
4-05 **6** *¾* **Directorship**[24] 2647 5-9-9 **85**.................................... JimCrowley 12 80
(Patrick Chamings) *chsd ldrs in 5th: rdn and nt qckn over 2f out: steadily fdd* **4/1**[2]
6-50 **7** *2* **Conciliatory**[13] 2994 4-9-8 **84**...................................... NeilCallan 10 74
(Rae Guest) *chsd ldr to over 2f out: wkng whn n.m.r over 1f out: eased* **12/1**
-434 **8** *¾* **Guilded Warrior**[31] 2428 8-9-7 **83**............................... FergusSweeney 4 71
(Stuart Kittow) *led: rdn and hdd over 1f out: wknd* **6/1**[3]
013- **9** *4 ½* **Spectait**[179] 8009 9-9-9 **85**.. HayleyTurner 6 63
(Jonjo O'Neill) *blindfold off sltly late and then v s.i.s: hld up in detached last: pushed along firmly 4f out: no prog* **10/1**
55-6 **10** *1 ¼* **Wisecraic**[15] 2937 4-9-0 **76**...................................... RoystonFfrench 8 51
(J S Moore) *settled in 7th: rdn over 3f out: sn struggling in last pair* **20/1**

1m 40.63s (-4.07) **Going Correction** -0.325s/f (Firm) course record **10** Ran SP% **116.2**
Speed ratings (Par 107): **107,105,105,104,101 100,98,97,93,91**
Tote Swingers: 1&2 £10.10, 1&3 £10.90, 2&3 £16.60 CSF £91.88 CT £990.57 TOTE £8.00: £1.80, £5.10, £4.20; EX 85.30 Trifecta £238.90 Pool: £878.15 - 2.72 winning units..
Owner Lady Herries **Bred** Wyck Hall Stud Ltd **Trained** Patching, W Sussex

FOCUS
A decent handicap.

NOTEBOOK
Jewelled, who had done all her previous winning at Bath, hugged the inside rail in the straight and, despite not looking overly straightforward, did more than enough to secure the win. This is the highest mark she's won off, so more will be required if she's to follow up.
Moynahan(USA) fared better with the blinkers back on, staying on to edge second. (op 12-1)
Audemar(IRE) ran well on this return from 127 days off. (op 12-1)
Woodcote Place remains 4lb above his last winning mark, but should improve on this first outing in 218 days. (op 20-1)
Norman Orpen(IRE), only 2lb higher than when winning at Sandown, wasn't the best away and was forced to challenge wide, which cost him his chance.
Guilded Warrior briefly tried to make a fight of it when headed, but ended up well held. (op 5-1)

3437 TOTESWINGER MORE WAYS TO WIN MAIDEN FILLIES' STKS 1m 67y
5:05 (5:09) (Class 5) 3-5-Y-O **£2,525** (£751; £375; £187) **Stalls** Low

Form RPR
02-2 **1** **Electra Star**[14] 2960 3-8-10 77.................................... KierenFallon 7 81+
(William Haggas) *t.k.h: prom: pushed along over 2f out: wnt 2nd over 1f out: led jst ins fnl f: pushed out fnl 100yds* **6/4**[1]
-204 **2** *1 ½* **Lucky Legs (IRE)**[22] 2735 3-8-10 72............................ JimCrowley 5 77
(B W Hills) *led: drvn 2f out: hdd and one pce jst ins fnl f* **7/1**[3]
0-0 **3** *½* **Regal Salute**[62] 1568 3-8-7 0...................................... JohnFahy(3) 6 76
(Jeremy Noseda) *prom: rdn to chse ldr over 2f out to over 1f out: kpt on same pce* **12/1**
0 **4** *2* **Eastern Breeze (IRE)**[14] 2960 3-8-10 0.......................... TedDurcan 8 71
(Saeed Bin Suroor) *chsd ldr to over 2f out: hrd rdn and nt qckn* **8/1**
5 *1* **Indian Mist (IRE)** 3-8-10 0... NeilCallan 1 69+
(Roger Varian) *s.s: sn in 8th: prog over 3f out: tried to cl on ldrs fr 2f out: one pce after* **2/1**[2]
0 **6** *4 ½* **Graceful Act**[22] 2723 3-8-10 0..................................... RoystonFfrench 9 59
(James Toller) *in tch: rdn 3f out: grad wknd fnl 2f* **66/1**
5-0 **7** *nk* **Renoir's Lady**[24] 2648 3-8-10 0..................................... HayleyTurner 3 58
(Simon Dow) *hld up in tch: effrt 3f out and cl enough over 2f out: shkn up and fdd* **33/1**
45 **8** *5* **Tiger Tess**[40] 2175 3-8-7 0..[1] AdamBeschizza(3) 2 47
(Jonathan Portman) *rrd s: mostly in last pair: nvr a factor* **66/1**
00 **9** *12* **Dansette**[43] 2097 3-8-10 0.. FergusSweeney 4 40
(Jim Boyle) *hld up in 7th: sltly hmpd 3f out: jst hld together after and sn dropped away: eased over 1f out* **40/1**
10 *15* **Lady Valtas** 3-8-10 0.. NickyMackay 10 —
(Robert Eddery) *s.s: a in last pair: reminder 1/2-way: t.o* **66/1**

1m 41.56s (-3.14) **Going Correction** -0.325s/f (Firm) **10** Ran SP% **114.5**
Speed ratings (Par 100): **102,100,100,98,97 92,92,87,75,60**
Tote Swingers: 1&2 £35.40, 1&3 £13.80, 2&3 £47.60 CSF £12.26 TOTE £2.80: £1.20, £2.50, £2.70; EX 11.00 Trifecta £43.80 Pool: £868.73 - 14.65 winning units..
Owner Mohamed Obaida **Bred** Rabbah Bloodstock Limited **Trained** Newmarket, Suffolk

FOCUS
A relatively modest fillies' maiden.

T/Plt: £217.20 to a £1 stake. Pool £79,677.00 - 267.68 winning tickets. T/Qpdt: £38.40 to a £1 stake. Pool £5,309.00 - 102.10 winning tickets. JN

3438 - (Foreign Racing) - See Raceform Interactive

[3414]CURRAGH (R-H)

Sunday, June 26

OFFICIAL GOING: Good (good to yielding in places on straight course)

3439a DUBAI DUTY FREE RAILWAY STKS (GROUP 2) 6f

2:10 (2:10) 2-Y-O **£49,267** (£15,560; £7,370; £2,456; £1,508) **Stalls** High

RPR

1 **Lilbourne Lad (IRE)**[20] 2776 2-9-1 .... RichardHughes 2 111
(Richard Hannon) *a.p: disp ld fr bef 1/2-way: rdn over 1f out: edgd rt u.p ins fnl f: led and kpt on best fnl 100yds* **9/4**[3]

2 3/4 **Tough As Nails (IRE)**[36] 2322 2-9-1 .... GFCarroll 1 109
(Michael Mulvany, Ire) *a.p: disp ld fr bef 1/2-way: drvn along fr wl over 1f out: kpt on wl u.p and carried sltly rt ins fnl f: hdd and no ex fnl 100yds* **15/8**[1]

3 4 1/2 **French Emperor (IRE)**[20] 2776 2-9-1 .... WMLordan 5 95
(Edward Lynam, Ire) *towards rr: 4th fr 1/2-way: pushed along 2f out and sn no imp on ldng pair: kpt on one pce* **33/1**

4 1 **Choir (IRE)**[46] 2010 2-9-1 .... RyanMoore 3 92
(A P O'Brien, Ire) *chsd ldrs: pushed along in 3rd 1/2-way: no imp on ldng pair fr wl over 1f out: kpt on one pce* **2/1**[2]

5 7 **Vault (IRE)**[23] 2698 2-9-1 .... CO'Donoghue 4 71
(A P O'Brien, Ire) *led early: rdn along and dropped to rr bef 1/2-way: no ex fr 2f out: wknd* **12/1**

1m 13.56s (-1.44) **Going Correction** -0.20s/f (Firm) 5 Ran SP% **109.5**

Speed ratings: **101,100,94,92,83**

CSF £6.80 TOTE £3.00: £1.30, £1.20; DF 5.50.

Owner Andrew Russell **Bred** Swordlestown Little **Trained** East Everleigh, Wilts

FOCUS

A small field but right up to scratch. The form looks sound with the front pair clear.

NOTEBOOK

Lilbourne Lad(IRE) was a smart winner of a Listed race at Naas early in the month, looking like a feasible Coventry Stakes contender in the process. The decision to miss Royal Ascot for this was thoroughly vindicated. The National Stakes could now be on his agenda, and with the second providing a form-link with the Coventry winner Power, he is right up there with the best of his age-group. The winner came off the rail and drifted towards Tough As Nails in the closing stages, but the runner-up, who had hung sharply to the right and was demoted from first place in the first juvenile race of the season, was also drifting right at the same time, and any marginal interference did not influence the outcome, which was confirmed after a stewards' inquiry. (op 2/1 tchd 5/2)

Tough As Nails(IRE), tackling this trip for the first time after running second to the Coventry winner in the Marble Hill, lost nothing in defeat and is proving a credit to his trainer. He can continue to hold his own at a high level as the season progresses, though it would obviously be a help if his drifting tendency could be corrected. (op 9/4)

French Emperor(IRE), who had been beaten more than six lengths when third to Lilbourne Lad at Naas, got just a bit closer this time and was able to take advantage of below-par displays by the O'Brien pair to secure the same placing again. (op 28/1)

Choir(IRE) came under pressure around half-way and was soon fighting a losing battle as the contest developed into a duel. As a son of Danehill Dancer, one would not have expected the ground to pose a major problem and it was\n\x\x disappointing that he failed to make more of an impact. (op 15/8 tchd 7/4)

Vault(IRE) was struggling before halfway. (op 10/1)

3440a PADDY POWER SPRINT (PREMIER H'CAP) 6f 63y

2:40 (2:41) 3-Y-O+ **£43,965** (£13,922; £6,594; £2,198; £1,465; £732) **Stalls** High

RPR

1 **Six Of Hearts**[16] 2894 7-9-7 102 .... (b) SHJames(5) 30 109
(Cecil Ross, Ire) *chsd ldrs: 8th 1/2-way: hdwy to go 3rd 1f out: led over 100yds out and kpt on wl u.p* **16/1**

2 1 1/4 **Cheviot (USA)**[71] 1421 5-9-3 93 .... (p) NGMcCullagh 24 96
(Reginald Roberts, Ire) *a.p: disp ld: hdd briefly over 2f out: sn led and kpt on u.p: no ex and hdd over 100yds out* **14/1**

3 shd **Collingwood (IRE)**[20] 2775 9-8-12 88 .... (bt) WMLordan 27 91
(T M Walsh, Ire) *mid-div: nt clr after 1/2-way: styd on wl u.p fr over 1f out: nrest at fin* **14/1**

4 shd **Rock Jock (IRE)**[64] 1533 4-9-5 102 .... DJBenson(7) 7 104+
(Tracey Collins, Ire) *prom in centre of crse: 4th over 1f out: kpt on same pce u.p fnl f* **25/1**

5 hd **Roicead (USA)**[23] 2703 4-8-9 85 .... (t) WJSupple 14 87
(Brendan W Duke, Ire) *a.p: led briefly over 2f out: sn hdd but kpt on u.p: lost 2nd fnl 100yds* **14/1**

6 nk **Maarek**[2] 3372 4-8-9 85 5ex .... MCHussey 25 86
(David Peter Nagle, Ire) *in rr of mid-div: drvn along 1/2-way: swtchd lft to stands' side rail: kpt on u.p fr over 1f out* **14/1**

7 1/2 **The Confessor**[15] 2927 4-8-11 87 .... DaneO'Neill 3 86+
(Henry Candy) *chsd ldrs in centre: 7th over 1f out: no imp fnl f* **8/1**[1]

8 1 3/4 **Tajneed (IRE)**[22] 2717 8-9-13 103 .... AdrianNicholls 10 97+
(David Nicholls) *prom in centre: no imp fr over 1f out* **10/1**[2]

9 shd **Snaefell (IRE)**[36] 2323 7-9-10 103 .... (tp) ShaneFoley(3) 15 96+
(M Halford, Ire) *chsd ldrs: no imp in 8th 1f out: kpt on one pce* **20/1**

10 nk **Colonel Mak**[8] 3155 4-9-6 96 .... FMBerry 22 88+
(David Barron) *chsd ldrs: 9th 2f out: no imp fr over 1f out* **10/1**[2]

11 shd **Bay Knight (IRE)**[11] 3057 5-9-9 99 .... DPMcDonogh 16 91+
(K J Condon, Ire) *in rr of mid-div: nt clr run after 1/2-way: kpt on fr over 1f out wout threatening* **25/1**

12 shd **Croisultan (IRE)**[36] 2323 5-9-11 104 .... JPO'Brien(3) 28 96
(Liam McAteer, Ire) *chsd ldrs on stands' side: 5th 1/2-way: no ex fr over 1f out* **25/1**

13 3/4 **Toufan Express**[36] 2326 9-8-7 83 .... CDHayes 8 72+
(Adrian McGuinness, Ire) *mid-div: kpt on one pce fr over 1f out* **40/1**

14 shd **Moonreach (IRE)**[9] 3109 4-9-4 94 .... GFCarroll 4 83+
(James J Hartnett, Ire) *prom in centre: cl 10th under 2f out: no imp fnl f* **20/1**

15 nk **Anderiego (IRE)**[73] 1347 3-7-13 87 oh1 .... LFRoche(5) 2 73+
(D K Weld, Ire) *prom on far side: 6th over 1f out: no ex fnl f* **12/1**[3]

16 hd **Lechevalier Choisi (IRE)**[14] 2967 3-7-10 89 .... MMMonaghan(10) 26 74
(James Bernard McCabe, Ire) *chsd ldrs on stands' side: 7th 1/2-way: no ex fr over 1f out* **16/1**

17 1/2 **Tornadodancer (IRE)**[16] 2894 8-8-9 85 .... (b) BACurtis 29 71
(T G McCourt, Ire) *chsd ldrs on stands' side: 6th 1/2-way: no ex fr over 1f out: wknd* **40/1**

18 1 **Queenie Keen (IRE)**[23] 2703 4-8-3 86 .... CPHoban(7) 21 69
(M Halford, Ire) *prom and disp ld: hdd after 1/2-way: no ex fr under 2f out: wknd* **16/1**

19 1 1/2 **Rodrigo De Torres**[64] 1533 4-9-12 102 .... SeamieHeffernan 18 80
(James J Hartnett, Ire) *nvr a factor* **50/1**

20 nk **Truly Genius (IRE)**[46] 2011 3-8-1 87 oh2 .... SMGorey(3) 20 62+
(C P Donoghue, Ire) *nvr a factor* **33/1**

21 1 1/4 **Still Point (IRE)**[30] 2482 4-8-4 80 .... SilvestreDeSousa 1 53+
(Noel Meade, Ire) *mid-div best on far side: nvr a factor* **14/1**

22 1 **Sean Og Coulston (IRE)**[71] 1422 7-8-10 86 .... PJSmullen 13 56+
(John J Coleman, Ire) *nvr a factor* **16/1**

23 1 1/4 **Blue Dahlia (IRE)**[14] 2967 4-8-13 96 .... SAGray(7) 12 62+
(T Stack, Ire) *nvr a factor* **25/1**

24 4 1/2 **Glor Na Mara (IRE)**[14] 2967 3-9-5 102 .... (t) KJManning 19 51
(J S Bolger, Ire) *chsd ldrs on stands' side: pushed along in 10th 2f out: sn no ex: eased whn btn fnl f* **14/1**

25 1 1/4 **Money Trader (IRE)**[8] 3195 4-8-6 82 .... RPCleary 5 29+
(J T Gorman, Ire) *a towards rr* **50/1**

26 2 **Knock Stars (IRE)**[17] 2861 3-8-12 95 .... PBBeggy 9 34+
(Patrick Martin, Ire) *nvr a factor* **14/1**

27 2 **Whipless (IRE)**[64] 1533 3-8-5 95 .... RPWhelan(7) 6 27+
(J S Bolger, Ire) *in rr of mid-div on far side: nvr a factor* **25/1**

U **Thats A Fret (IRE)**[16] 2894 5-7-11 80 oh1 .... (b[1]) RADoyle(7) 11 —
(Liam McAteer, Ire) *sddle slipped and uns rdr after 1f* **33/1**

1m 16.05s (-2.55) **Going Correction** -0.20s/f (Firm)

WFA 3 from 4yo+ 7lb 28 Ran SP% **150.6**

Speed ratings: **109,107,107,107,106 106,105,103,103,102 102,102,101,101,101 100,100,98,96,96 94,93,91,85,84 8**

CSF £225.71 TOTE £23.60: £5.50, £3.20, £3.60, £8.90; DF 378.00.

Owner Round Tower Syndicate **Bred** Castlemartin Stud And Skymarc Farm **Trained** Mullingar, Co Westmeath

NOTEBOOK

Six Of Hearts was drawn closest to the rail, and while it was the eventual runner-up who held the initiative on the inside for a long way, apprentice Sam James also had the Cecil Ross-trained gelding well placed, and he asserted inside the last half-furlong to run out a worthy winner of this ultra-competitive handicap under a big burden.

Cheviot(USA), who began his career in Britain with Michael Jarvis, made a gallant attempt to supplement the win that he gained on his seasonal debut at Naas in April. Trainer Reggie Roberts already had this race in mind for him at that stage, and his decision to send him here relatively fresh nearly paid handsome dividends. Like the winner he is a dependable type.

Collingwood(IRE) appeared to meet some traffic problems and had to come from a fair way back in the field. He really needs a bit further than this and he came home strongly to take third in a tight battle for the minor money

Rock Jock(IRE) has only a Down Royal maiden win to his name as a two-year-old, but should be able to rectify matters. After showing good speed to take up a prominent mid-course position he maintained his effort well. This was his second run back in Ireland after running a few good races in Dubai during the winter and he seems to be hitting peak form. (op 25/1 tchd 33/1)

Roicead(USA) is proving a good standard bearer for Brendan Duke, who has relocated to Ireland.

Maarek proved that he is a tough sort, turning out under a penalty for a win over 5f on Friday evening

The Confessor put in a solid effort from a disadvantageous low draw, finishing best of the British raiders. (op 8/1 tchd 7/1)

Tajneed(IRE) raced prominently towards the favoured side but didn't quicken.

Bay Knight(IRE) ◆ appeared to meet traffic problems and might be worth looking out for in the coming weeks.

Queenie Keen(IRE) Official explanation: jockey said filly was found to be in season post-race

Glor Na Mara(IRE), a smart juvenile last season, continues to disappoint and was eased after his chance had gone. (op 16/1)

Thats A Fret(IRE) Official explanation: jockey said gelding jumped awkwardly leaving the stalls and unseated him as a result

3441a WOODIES D.I.Y. SAPPHIRE STKS (GROUP 3) 5f

3:10 (3:11) 3-Y-O+ **£32,327** (£10,237; £4,849; £1,616; £1,077; £538) **Stalls** High

RPR

1 **Invincible Ash (IRE)**[17] 2861 6-9-4 111 .... (tp) GFCarroll 3 110
(M Halford, Ire) *settled in rr: swtchd rt over 1f out and sn wnt 4th: styd on wl u.p on outer to ld fnl 50yds* **3/1**[3]

2 1 **Hamish McGonagall**[21] 2754 6-9-7 .... DavidAllan 4 110
(Tim Easterby) *a.p: disp bef 1/2-way: led 2f out: kpt on u.p: hdd fnl 50yds* **11/4**[2]

3 1 **Move In Time**[15] 2928 3-9-1 .... TomEaves 1 103
(Bryan Smart) *chsd ldrs: 3rd 1/2-way: drvn along fr wl over 1f out: kpt on same pce u.p* **13/2**

4 nk **Inxile (IRE)**[14] 2967 6-9-10 .... (p) AdrianNicholls 6 107
(David Nicholls) *led: jnd bef 1/2-way: drvn along and hdd 2f out: no imp u.p and dropped to 4th fnl f* **6/4**[1]

5 shd **Arctic (IRE)**[12] 3010 4-9-7 109 .... PJSmullen 5 104
(Tracey Collins, Ire) *chsd ldrs mainly 5th: drvn along fr 1/2-way: kpt on u.p fnl f* **8/1**

6 5 1/2 **Calm Bay (IRE)**[14] 2967 5-9-7 92 .... (bt) KJManning 2 84
(H Rogers, Ire) *awkward leaving stalls: chsd ldrs: 4th 1/2-way: no ex fr over 1f out: wknd* **33/1**

60.13 secs (-2.37) **Going Correction** -0.20s/f (Firm)

WFA 3 from 4yo+ 6lb 6 Ran SP% **112.2**

Speed ratings: **110,108,106,106,106 97**

CSF £17.21 TOTE £5.90: £2.10, £1.80; DF 17.70.

Owner P J Condron **Bred** Mrs Sandra Maye **Trained** Doneany, Co Kildare

FOCUS

The first three ran close to their recent form.

NOTEBOOK

Invincible Ash(IRE), given a fine hold-up ride by Gary Carroll, picked up well on the outside, taking advantage of the fact that the leaders had gone a bit quick for their own good. Winner of the valuable handicap on the same card during a highly successful campaign last year, Invincible Ash had shown smart form in Dubai during the winter, notably when taking fourth place behind J J The Jet Plane, and here she showed the benefit of her first run back in Ireland at Leopardstown earlier in the month. It looked as if the two market leaders cut each other's throats. (op 4/1)

Hamish McGonagall, who had run creditably in a Group 2 event at Chantilly earlier in the month, maintained his effort in game fashion to take second place. (op 3/1)

Move In Time has continued to prosper this term after ending last season with a fine second in the Cornwallis, and he did well to grab third spot. (op 8/1)

Inxile(IRE) had made hay on previous visits to Ireland this season. He often manages to burn off the opposition, but with Hamish McGonagall persistent in pursuit he was unable to dictate on this occasion. This was a rare blot on his overseas record. (op 6/4 tchd 11/8)

Arctic(IRE), having only his second run of the season, shaped as if he might benefit from going up to 6f again. (op 9/1)

Calm Bay(IRE) found this too demanding. (op 25/1)

3442a DUBAI DUTY FREE IRISH DERBY (GROUP 1) (ENTIRE COLTS & FILLIES) 1m 4f

3:50 (3:50) 3-Y-0

£625,000 (£204,741; £96,982; £32,327; £21,551; £10,775) **Stalls** High

RPR

1 **Treasure Beach**[22] 2715 3-9-0 119 .... CO'Donoghue 8 122
(A P O'Brien, Ire) *settled in 4th: clsr in 3rd appr st: pushed along to chal over 1f out: styd on best u.p to ld fnl 100yds* **7/2**[2]

2 ¾ **Seville (GER)**[22] 2715 3-9-0 115 .... SeamieHeffernan 1 121
(A P O'Brien, Ire) *trckd ldr in 2nd: rdn to ld early st: strly pressed and kpt on wl u.p: hdd and no ex fnl 100yds* **5/1**[3]

3 1 **Memphis Tennessee (IRE)**[22] 2715 3-9-0 117 .... JPO'Brien 3 119
(A P O'Brien, Ire) *led: pushed along ent st: hdd over 2f out: 3rd fr over 1f out but kpt on wl u.p* **10/1**

4 nk **Carlton House (USA)**[22] 2715 3-9-0 118 .... RyanMoore 7 119
(Sir Michael Stoute) *settled in 6th: hdwy to go 4th ent st: sn rdn along: no imp over 1f out: kpt on same pce u.p fnl f* **5/4**[1]

5 3 **Dunboyne Express (IRE)**[36] 2324 3-9-0 111 .... DPMcDonogh 2 114
(Kevin Prendergast, Ire) *settled on inner in 5th: rdn early st: no ex fr over 1f out: kpt on one pce* **33/1**

6 5 **Roderic O'Connor (IRE)**[21] 2751 3-9-0 119 .... WMLordan 6 106
(A P O'Brien, Ire) *hld up in rr: pushed along early st: no threat fr 2f out: kpt on one pce* **20/1**

7 nk **Native Khan (FR)**[22] 2715 3-9-0 116 .... JMurtagh 5 105
(Ed Dunlop) *hld up on inner mainly 7th: swtchd lft and drvn along early st: no ex fr 2f out* **8/1**

8 3 ½ **Notable Graduate (IRE)**[17] 2865 3-9-0 104 .... PJSmullen 4 100
(D K Weld, Ire) *trckd ldrs in 3rd: rdn ent st: sn no ex* **12/1**

2m 33.26s (-5.24) **Going Correction** -0.075s/f (Good) **8** Ran SP% **118.9**
Speed ratings: **114,113,112,112,110 107,107,104**
CSF £22.38 TOTE £5.10: £1.60, £2.50, £2.00; DF 26.30.
Owner D Smith, Mrs J Magnier, M Tabor **Bred** Ashley House Stud **Trained** Ballydoyle, Co Tipperary

■ A sixth successive Irish Derby for Aidan O'Brien, and a fourth 1-2-3. Colm O'Donoghue's first Irish Classic, & a 1-2 for Galileo.

■ Stewards' Enquiry : Seamie Heffernan two-day ban: used whip with excessive frequency and without giving mount time to respond (July 10-11)

FOCUS

Easy form to rate with the winner and third to their Epsom marks. It was not a strong renewal, but matches Cape Blanco's effort last year.

NOTEBOOK

Treasure Beach has established himself at the forefront with a performance that validated the Derby form. Handily placed throughout in a race in which the pace was perfectly controlled, he got the better of the gallant runner-up inside the last furlong. The improvement made by Treasure Beach since winning a Galway nursery off a mark of 84 has no precedent in the modern history of the race. The King George and the Grand Prix de Paris are among possible options. (op 7/2 tchd 4/1)

Seville(GER) went a long way towards erasing the memory of an insipid Derby run. The Dante runner-up, positively ridden behind the pacesetter, reversed form with Carlton House in emphatic style, making a determined bid after the front-running Memphis Tennessee began to feel the heat. (op 11/2)

Memphis Tennessee(IRE)'s Derby fourth looked a more serious aberration than Treasure Beach's second, but that notion was firmly put to bed by another smart display which confirmed the one-time 94-rated Dundalk maiden winner as one of the best of his generation. There are so many permutations among the options for Ballydoyle's middle-distance squad that speculation will be merely idle until running plans are confirmed, but the St Leger is a possibility.

Carlton House(USA) appeared to find everything go to plan here until the vital moment when he was asked to quicken. His rider had taken a perfect tracking position, but the response was minimal. Following a break, it looks inevitable that his next run will be over a shorter trip, but there is now a question mark about his ability to win a Group 1 race. (op 5/4 tchd 11/8)

Dunboyne Express(IRE) emerged with some credit and will benefit from dropping back in trip.

Roderic O'Connor(IRE) didn't stay the trip.

Native Khan(FR) gave a disappointingly lacklustre display, not in keeping with his Epsom run. He'll be given a break before dropping in trip. (op 10/1)

Notable Graduate(IRE) was out of his depth as the official ratings suggested. (op 14/1)

3444a DUBAI DUTY FREE FULL OF SURPRISES CELEBRATION STKS (LISTED RACE) 1m

5:00 (5:01) 3-Y-0+ **£28,017** (£8,189; £3,879; £1,293) **Stalls** High

RPR

1 **Pirateer (IRE)**[274] 6380 3-8-13 96 .... RyanMoore 3 104
(A P O'Brien, Ire) *mde all: pressed and rdn early st: kpt on wl u.p fnl f* **5/1**[3]

2 ¾ **Ezalli (IRE)**[215] 7546 4-9-6 92 .... WMLordan 6 101
(Edward Lynam, Ire) *trckd ldrs: 5th ent st: rdn to go 2nd 1f out: no imp on wnr fnl f* **25/1**

3 nk **One Spirit (IRE)**[10] 3098 3-8-10 .... NGMcCullagh 4 98
(F Dunne, Ire) *settled in rr of mid-div: 6th early st: sn pushed along: kpt on wl ins fnl f: nrest at fin* **14/1**

4 nk **Ask Jack (USA)**[10] 3100 7-9-12 104 ....(p) CDHayes 9 106
(Joseph G Murphy, Ire) *mid-div: 6th ent st: rdn 2f out: kpt on wl u.p ins fnl f* **6/1**

5 hd **Penitent**[48] 1948 5-9-12 .... RichardHughes 2 105+
(William Haggas) *a.p: 3rd on inner 1/2-way: pushed along wl over 1f out: short of room ins fnl f* **13/8**[1]

6 ½ **Luisant**[44] 2078 8-9-12 106 .... FMBerry 8 104
(J A Nash, Ire) *towards rr early: hdwy on outer into 4th 1/2-way: 3rd early st: sn rdn and no imp over 1f out: kpt on one pce* **16/1**

7 shd **Asheerah**[11] 3057 3-8-10 98 .... DPMcDonogh 10 96
(Kevin Prendergast, Ire) *prom: 2nd 1/2-way: rdn to chal briefly early st: no ex u.p ins fnl f* **25/1**

8 ½ **Hujaylea (IRE)**[20] 2774 8-9-9 105 ....(p) ShaneFoley 5 100
(M Halford, Ire) *towards rr: rdn on outer fr early st: no imp over 1f out: kpt on same pce u.p fnl f* **8/1**

9 2 **Barack (IRE)**[10] 3100 5-9-12 103 ....(bt) BACurtis 1 98
(Francis Ennis, Ire) *chsd ldrs on inner: 6th 1/2-way: rdn and no ex over 1f out* **12/1**

10 nk **Creekside**[10] 3099 3-8-13 104 ....(p) JMurtagh 7 92
(John M Oxx, Ire) *a in rr: rdn along and no imp early st* **7/2**[2]

1m 38.7s (-7.30) **Going Correction** -0.475s/f (Firm)
WFA 3 from 4yo+ 10lb **10** Ran SP% **130.3**
Speed ratings: **117,116,115,115,115 114,114,114,112,112**
CSF £133.35 TOTE £5.60: £1.90, £5.80, £2.80; DF 157.30.
Owner Mrs John Magnier **Bred** Churchtown House Stud **Trained** Ballydoyle, Co Tipperary

FOCUS

They finished in a bunch but the first three posted personal bests.

NOTEBOOK

Pirateer(IRE) ◆, who accounted for earlier Irish Derby hero Treasure Beach in a Listowel nursery last year, made most to win this under an inspired Ryan Moore ride. The winner was having his first start back for nine months, so it wasn't surprising the dual winner from last season was easy to back on his return. He didn't lack courage at the business end when he kept responding to his riders urgings. He should be sharper with this run behind him and the Desmond Stakes at Leopardstown on August 11 is a possible target. (op 4/1)

Ezalli(IRE) was another returning from a lengthy absence and ran well in the circumstances. She tried hard to reel in the front-runner, but the lack of a recent run told in the end.

One Spirit(IRE), one of three fillies in the field, performed with much credit. This was a big step up in class for the Leopardstown maiden winner over this trip, but she acquitted herself well. (op 12/1)

Ask Jack(USA) had shown a return to his best form in a similar contest at Leopardstown and she ran a similar race, but never looked like imposing his presence entering the final furlong. (op 10/1)

Penitent, a three-time winner over this trip, hung in running and was denied a clear run up the inner after the race unfolded in the straight when responding to pressure. It probably cost the 2010 Lincoln winner a place or two as it certainly hindered some momentum at a crucial time. Richard Hughes said Penitent hung throughout and had to check for a stride in the closing stages. Official explanation: jockey said gelding hung throughout and had to check for a stride in the closing stages (op 13/8 tchd 7/4)

Luisant raced close up into the straight, but was soon struggling to keep on terms on this contrasting surface.

Creekside, winner of a four-runner handicap at Leopardstown, was stepping up in class but he proved a big disappointment after racing off the pace throughout. (op 7/1)

3445a DUBAI DUTY FREE TENNIS CHAMPIONSHIP H'CAP (PREMIER HANDICAP) 1m

5:30 (5:31) 3-Y-0+

£31,034 (£9,827; £4,655; £1,551; £1,034; £517) **Stalls** High

RPR

1 **Moran Gra (USA)**[20] 2775 4-9-4 98 ....(p) RPWhelan(7) 15 104
(Ms Joanna Morgan, Ire) *a.p in centre of crse: 3rd 1/2-way: rdn to ld narrowly 1f out: kpt on wl u.p: hld on* **14/1**

2 nk **Northgate (IRE)**[20] 2775 6-9-3 90 .... CDHayes 3 95
(Joseph G Murphy, Ire) *mid-div: hdwy into 4th over 1f out: kpt on u.p fnl f: nt rch wnr* **14/1**

3 ½ **Casela Park (IRE)**[14] 2971 6-8-4 77 .... BACurtis 10 81
(Jaclyn Tyrrell, Ire) *mid-div in centre of crse: 7th 3f out: kpt on wl u.p ins fnl f* **20/1**

4 1 **Boynagh Joy (IRE)**[20] 2774 6-9-11 98 .... SeamieHeffernan 4 100
(James Halpin, Ire) *settled in mid-div: 8th 3f out: hdwy to go 2nd 1f out: rdn and no ex ins fnl f* **25/1**

5 ¾ **Winning Impact (IRE)**[247] 7075 4-7-13 77 oh1 ....(t) LFRoche(5) 1 77
(J G Coogan, Ire) *prom on far side: 4th 1/2-way: led narrowly 2f out: sn rdn and hdd 1f out: no ex ins fnl f* **20/1**

6 1 ½ **Toraidhe (IRE)**[44] 2082 5-9-7 94 ....(tp) KJManning 6 91
(J S Bolger, Ire) *chsd ldrs: 5th 1/2-way: rdn 2f out: no imp fr over 1f out* **14/1**

7 2 **Back Burner (IRE)**[14] 2969 3-8-9 92 .... FMBerry 9 82
(Mrs John Harrington, Ire) *trckd ldrs: 6th 1/2-way: rdn and no ex fr over 1f out* **3/1**[1]

8 ¾ **Estithmaar (IRE)**[10] 3099 3-8-6 89 .... WJSupple 2 77
(Kevin Prendergast, Ire) *towards rr: hdwy after 1/2-way: wnt 6th under 2f out: sn pushed along and no ex ins fnl f* **13/2**[2]

9 1 **Spirit Of Xaar (IRE)**[20] 2775 5-8-11 84 .... CO'Donoghue 13 72
(David Marnane, Ire) *towards rr: 15th and drvn along over 1f out: kpt on ins fnl f* **13/2**[2]

10 ½ **Douze Points (IRE)**[38] 2217 5-9-0 87 ....(b) PatCosgrave 12 74
(Ed de Giles) *mid-div best: nvr a factor* **14/1**

11 hd **Bold Thady Quill (IRE)**[14] 2970 4-8-7 83 .... ShaneFoley(3) 5 69
(K J Condon, Ire) *towards rr: kpt on wout threatening* **14/1**

12 3 **Keep It Cool (IRE)**[28] 2535 7-8-0 83 ....(t) RossCoakley(10) 8 63
(P F O'Donnell, Ire) *prom and disp ld far side: hdd after 1/2-way: no ex under 2f out: wknd* **12/1**

13 3 ½ **Banna Boirche (IRE)**[11] 3057 5-9-12 99 .... JMurtagh 16 71
(M Halford, Ire) *a towards rr: nvr a factor* **8/1**[3]

14 3 **Elusive Award (USA)**[36] 2326 4-8-11 84 ....(b) DPMcDonogh 11 49
(Andrew Oliver, Ire) *trckd ldrs on far side: 10th 3f out: no ex fr wl over 1f out* **8/1**[3]

15 ½ **Libano (IRE)**[20] 2775 5-9-7 94 .... PShanahan 14 57
(D K Weld, Ire) *chsd ldrs in centre: 8th 1/2-way: no threat fr under 2f out* **33/1**

16 3 **Jembatt (IRE)**[20] 2775 4-9-1 91 .... JPO'Brien(3) 7 48
(Edward Lynam, Ire) *prom and disp ld far side: led narrowly 3f out: hdd 2f out and sn no ex: wknd* **16/1**

17 1 ¼ **Triple Eight (IRE)**[17] 2865 3-8-13 96 ....(b) PJSmullen 17 48
(D K Weld, Ire) *mid-div in centre: 9th 1/2-way: no ex fr 2f out: wknd* **14/1**

1m 40.22s (-5.78) **Going Correction** -0.475s/f (Firm)
WFA 3 from 4yo+ 10lb **17** Ran SP% **143.8**
Speed ratings: **109,108,108,107,106 104,102,102,101,100 100,97,94,91,90 87,86**
Daily double: 360.50euros to a 5euro stake. Pick six: Not won CSF £220.50 CT £4111.82 TOTE £13.10: £2.80, £4.00, £6.10, £9.60; DF 237.80.
Owner D T Breen **Bred** Airlie Stud & Robert N Clay **Trained** Ballivor, Co Meath

NOTEBOOK

Moran Gra(USA) lasted home well to confirm form with Northgate who finished seventh in the same Naas event on his first outing of the season. (op 12/1)

Northgate(IRE) stayed on well but didn't quite get there.

Casela Park(IRE), who has made headlines for the wrong reasons in the past, ran a solid race to suggest that he may be capable of adding to the wins that he obtained at Dundalk for his current trainer's father. (op 16/1)

Boynagh Joy(IRE) coped admirably with a big weight, dropped in class here after having her first two outings of the season at Listed and Group 3 level. She is a tough mare who seems to have maintained the dramatic improvement made last year.

Winning Impact(IRE) ◆ looks one to watch out for next time. (op 25/1)

Toraidhe(IRE) hinted at a return to the level of form that yielded a second placing in the Irish Lincoln.

Back Burner(IRE), well fancied for his handicap debut after a Cork maiden win, found the competition a bit hot but should be able to build on this experience. (op 9/2 tchd 5/2)

T/Jkpt: @2,812.50. Pool of @15,000.00 - 4 winning units. T/Plt: @144.50. Pool of @32,381.40 - 168 winning units. II

3422 HAMBURG (R-H)
Sunday, June 26

OFFICIAL GOING: Turf: good

3446a GROSSER PREIS VON LOTTO HAMBURG - HANSA-PREIS (GROUP 2) (3YO+) (TURF) 1m 4f
4:20 (12:00) 3-Y-0+

£36,206 (£14,224; £6,034; £3,879; £2,586; £1,724)

RPR
1 **Lucas Cranach (GER)**[32] 2408 4-9-6 0....................(b) EFrank 4 118
(S Smrczek, Germany) *broke wl: plld hrd early: settled towards rr: a travelling smoothly: swung wd into st: shkn up and qcknd wl: led 1 1/2f out: r.o strly: easily* **14/5**[2]
2 *3 1/2* **Durban Thunder (GER)**[21] 2749 5-9-6 0.................... THellier 7 112
(T Mundry, Germany) *broke fast: led: set mod pce: led into st: r.o wl: hdd 1 1/2f out: r.o to chse wnr home* **91/10**
3 *1 1/4* **Sir Lando**[26] 2601 4-9-6 0.................... EddieAhern 8 110
(Wido Neuroth, Norway) *settled 4th: two l off ldrs: mde promising move coming out of turn: rdn and r.o wl wout threatening first two* **33/10**[3]
4 *1 1/2* **Flamingo Fantasy (GER)**[28] 2538 6-9-6 0.................... ASuborics 1 108
(S Smrczek, Germany) *settled towards rr: rdn and r.o in st: passed btn horses fnl f* **56/10**
5 *1 1/2* **Val Mondo (GER)**[21] 2749 4-9-6 0.................... AHelfenbein 6 105
(Uwe Ostmann, Germany) *a.p on ins: racing freely: rdn early in st but fnd no ex: fdd* **94/10**
6 *3/4* **Seventh Sky (GER)**[15] 4-9-6 0.................... AStarke 5 104
(P Schiergen, Germany) *settled midfield: nvr a threat* **13/1**
7 *3* **Russian Tango (GER)**[21] 2749 4-9-6 0.................... EPedroza 2 99
(A Wohler, Germany) *settled midfield on ins: failed to settle down bk st: threatened briefly ent st: sn wknd* **5/2**[1]
8 *9* **Solidaro (GER)**[27] 4-9-6 0.................... ADeVries 9 85
(J Hirschberger, Germany) *racd midfield: already u.p bef fnl turn: hrd rdn but sn btn in st: t.o* **79/10**

2m 29.22s (-5.33) **8** Ran SP% **131.2**
WIN (incl. 10 euro stake): 38. PLACES: 18, 23, 17. SF: 382.
Owner Frau E Muller **Bred** Gestut Graditz **Trained** Germany

2484 SAINT-CLOUD (L-H)
Sunday, June 26

OFFICIAL GOING: Turf: good to soft

3447a ABU DHABI PRIX DE MALLERET (GROUP 2) (3YO FILLIES) (TURF) 1m 4f
1:30 (12:00) 3-Y-0 **£73,706** (£28,448; £13,577; £9,051; £4,525)

RPR
1 **Testosterone (IRE)**[21] 2750 3-8-11 0.................... StephanePasquier 2 110
(P Bary, France) *sn led: qcknd to go wl clr end of bk st: stl clr ent fnl f: u.p fnl 100yds: appeared to be wkng: jst hld on* **2/1**[1]
2 *nk* **Campanillas (IRE)**[21] 2750 3-8-11 0.................... OlivierPeslier 1 110
(C Laffon-Parias, France) *settled clr 2nd: rdn early in st to chse clr ldr: r.o wl fnl f and fin strly to almost catch ldr and hld on wl for 2nd* **18/1**
3 *nse* **Shankardeh (IRE)**[34] 3-8-11 0.................... Christophe-PatriceLemaire 6 109
(M Delzangles, France) *settled 3rd: rdn ent st to chse first two: qcknd wl ent fnl f: r.o strly ins fnl 100yds: jst failed to take 2nd* **11/2**
4 *nk* **Adventure Seeker (FR)**[50] 1922 3-8-11 0.......... ChristopheSoumillon 7 109
(A De Royer-Dupre, France) *settled 6th: u.p 2f out: picked up and r.o wl: fin strly fnl 100yds* **10/3**[2]
5 *3/4* **Danedream (GER)**[28] 2539 3-9-2 0.................... MaximeGuyon 8 113
(P Schiergen, Germany) *settled towards rr: swung wd ent st: rdn and proged fnl 1 1/2f out: styd on wl* **13/2**
6 *1 1/2* **Avongrove**[21] 2750 3-8-11 0.................... MickaelBarzalona 4 105
(A Fabre, France) *settled 4th on ins: rdn but no ex fr 1 1/2f out: styd on one pce fnl f* **8/1**
7 *6* **Chegei Has (FR)**[21] 2750 3-8-11 0.................... IoritzMendizabal 3 96
(J-P Gallorini, France) *settled 5th: rdn but no ex in st: sn btn* **12/1**
8 *5* **Pagera (FR)**[24] 2658 3-8-11 0.................... FranckBlondel 5 88
(Y Fouin, France) *settled towasrds rr: u.p early in st: no ex: wknd qckly* **28/1**

2m 28.6s (-11.80) **8** Ran SP% **112.6**
WIN (incl. 1 euro stake): 2.80. PLACES: 1.50, 4.90, 2.50. DF: 18.10. SF: 33.00 CSF: 39.32.
Owner Ecurie La Boetie **Bred** S C E A La Poterie **Trained** Chantilly, France

NOTEBOOK
Testosterone(IRE) ◆, who appreciated a positive ride when successful at Chantilly last time, was soon sent to the front and held a ten-length lead entering the back straight. Although her rider was hard at work 2f from home, she responded well and narrowly held off the closing pack. She'll be given a break now before being brought back for the Prix Vermeille. (op 5/2)

3448a GRAND PRIX DE SAINT-CLOUD (GROUP 1) (4YO+) (TURF) 1m 4f
2:45 (12:00) 4-Y-0+ **£197,034** (£78,827; £39,413; £19,689; £9,862)

RPR
1 **Sarafina (FR)**[34] 2373 4-8-13 0.................... Christophe-PatriceLemaire 4 120+
(A De Royer-Dupre, France) *3rd: racd freely: settled at rr down bk st: last ent st: rdn and qcknd wl on outside fr 1 1/2f out: r.o strly fnl f to catch ldr cl home: comf* **4/9**[1]
2 *nk* **Cirrus Des Aigles (FR)**[13] 3008 5-9-2 0.................... FranckBlondel 3 121
(Mme C Barande-Barbe, France) *led: set mod pce: qcknd down bk st: rdn and qcknd clr early in st: stl wl clr 1f out: r.o wl but ct cl home* **4/1**[2]
3 *1 1/2* **Silver Pond (FR)**[21] 2753 4-9-2 0.................... OlivierPeslier 1 119
(C Laffon-Parias, France) *settled in 2nd: rdn to chse ldr early in st: styd on wl but no threat to ldng pair ins fnl 1 1/2f* **13/2**[3]
4 *3/4* **Zack Hall (FR)**[52] 1842 4-9-2 0.................... ChristopheSoumillon 5 117?
(M Delzangles, France) *settled in 4th: rdn early in st to chse ldrs: styd on wl wout threatening* **16/1**
5 *4* **Indian Days**[23] 2680 6-9-2 0.................... TomQueally 2 111
(James Given) *in rr: grad moved forwards to go 3rd at end of bk st: swtchd early in st: styd on fnl 2f wout threatening to take part in fin* **33/1**

2m 34.4s (-6.00) **5** Ran SP% **111.4**
WIN (incl. 1 euro stake): 1.40. PLACES: 1.10, 1.20. SF: 2.40 CSF: 2.65.
Owner H H Aga Khan **Bred** H H Aga Khan **Trained** Chantilly, France

FOCUS
A race that has been won by the likes of Montjeu, Helissio, El Condor Pasa, Pride and Alkaased in recent seasons, but this year's running looked decidedly below par. This was the smallest field since Montjeu got the better of three rivals in 2000 and, with the exception of Sarafina, none of them had won at Group 1 level. Indeed, only one of them, Cirrus Des Aigles, had previously finished in the frame at the highest level. Sarafina did well to overcome a slow pace.

NOTEBOOK
Sarafina(FR) made no mistake here despite the race being run at a crawl, which would have hardly suited the come-from-behind tactics deployed. After pulling ridiculously hard in the opening part of the race, she was settled at the rear and was still at the back of the five-strong field a furlong from home. Indeed, she wasn't asked to pick up until inside the final furlong, something she did in good fashion, winning a tad comfortably. The Grand-Prix/Arc double has not been completed since Helissio in 1996, although this race has been responsible for plenty of placed horses at Longchamp in October, including two of the last five runners-up, and quotes of around 12-1 for the Arc seem fair at this point. However, with the competition certain to be in a different class to this she may add to the list of nearly horses who have gone on from this race. (op 1/2)
Cirrus Des Aigles(FR) had already finished second in Group 1 company twice this season. He tried to make all upped in trip, kicking for home fully 2f out and only got caught in the final strides. The dubious pace helped him get this longer trip and connections mentioned he could now drop back to a more familiar distance in the Juddmonte International. (op 7/2)
Silver Pond(FR) has been brought along slowly this year, claiming the scalp of Bekhabad last time. This is the second race in a row where he has been unruly in the preliminaries. He looks one to swerve for the time being as there are obvious concerns about his temperament. (tched 7/1 and 6/1)
Zack Hall(FR) progressed throughout last year. He finished second in a Group 3 on his reappearance last time. That looks more his level. (op 18/1)
Indian Days is getting hard to place. A talented individual, Group 1s look a bit beyond him and, having attempted to make a challenge as they raced down the straight, he was out of contention at the business end. Even though it was a warm day, it was noticeable how much he was sweating up during the race. This run is probably best forgotten. (op 28-1)

3212 SAN SIRO (R-H)
Sunday, June 26

OFFICIAL GOING: Turf: good

3449a PREMIO MARIO INCISA DELLA ROCHETTA (GROUP 3) (3YO FILLIES) (TURF) 1m 2f
4:15 (4:44) 3-Y-0 **£43,103** (£18,965; £10,344; £5,172)

RPR
1 **Navarra Queen**[21] 3-8-11 0.................... MircoDemuro 3 105
(P Schiergen, Germany) *trckd ldrs in 5th: smooth hdwy 2f out: qcknd to ld ent fnl f: r.o wl* **37/10**[2]
2 *nk* **Don't Hurry Me (IRE)**[35] 2342 3-9-0 0.............. Jean-BernardEyquem 8 107
(J-C Rouget, France) *sn led: rdn 1 1/2f out: hdd ins fnl f: kpt on wl u.p* **4/5**[1]
3 *2 1/2* **Oeuvre D'Art (IRE)**[28] 2539 3-8-11 0.................... CristianDemuro 4 99
(B Grizzetti, Italy) *racd in midfield: hdwy on outside 3f out: disputing 2nd ins fnl 2f: kpt on u.p: no ex fnl f* **157/10**
4 *nk* **Pocket A Pound (IRE)**[357] 3-8-11 0.................... UmbertoRispoli 10 98
(S Botti, Italy) *w.w towards rr: prog on outside over 2f out: styd on u.p fnl f: nvr nrr* **227/10**
5 *2 1/2* **Good Karma (ITY)**[28] 2539 3-8-11 0.................... FabioBranca 2 93
(S Botti, Italy) *led early but sn settled in 3rd: effrt to press ldr 2 1/2f out: sn rdn: wknd fnl 1 1/2f* **4/1**[3]
6 *shd* **Omkara**[49] 3-8-11 0.................... SSulas 7 93
(E Borromeo, Italy) *chsd ldng gp: one pce fnl 2f* **153/10**
7 *1* **Senza Rete (IRE)**[28] 2539 3-8-11 0.................... MKolmarkaj 1 85
(M Gasparini, Italy) *racd in btn on rail: rdn 2f out: wknd fnl f* **109/10**
8 *2* **Rivabella (FR)**[39] 3-8-11 0.................... GCroogovic 9 81
(S Bietolini, Italy) *hld up towards rr: rdn and mod hdwy 3f out: one pce fr 2f out* **66/1**
9 *3/4* **Jojo Bonita (FR)**[39] 3-8-11 0.................... MEsposito 6 80
(L Polito, Italy) *settled in midfield: rdn and btn fr 2f out* **138/10**
10 *1* **Reyal (ITY)** 3-8-11 0.................... CColombi 5 78
(S Botti, Italy) *w.w in fnl 3rd: no imp fr 2f out* **226/10**
11 *5* **Kapitale (GER)** 3-8-11 0.................... JBojko 12 68
(A Wohler, Germany) *trckd ldr: rdn and wknd fnl 2 1/2f* **31/1**
12 *8* **Zamindowa**[21] 3-8-11 0.................... DarioVargiu 11 52
(B Grizzetti, Italy) *nvr in contention* **28/1**
13 *6* **Fedemartina (ITY)**[49] 3-8-11 0....................(b) StefanoLandi 13 40
(S Botti, Italy) *racd on heels of ldrs: rdn and wknd over 2f out* **25/1**

1m 59.2s (-7.50) **13** Ran SP% **144.5**
PARI-MUTUEL (all including 1 euro stakes): WIN 4.69; PLACE 1.70, 1.31, 2.42; DF 10.77.
Owner Gestut Ammerland **Bred** Gestut Ammerland **Trained** Germany

3123 MUSSELBURGH (R-H)
Monday, June 27

OFFICIAL GOING: Good (good to soft in places on straight; 6.4)
Wind: Virtually nil Weather: Overcast and drizzle

3450 DELOITTE H'CAP FOR GENTLEMAN AMATEUR RIDERS 2m
6:55 (6:55) (Class 6) (0-65,63) 4-Y-0+ **£1,873** (£581; £290; £145) **Stalls** Low

Form RPR
1-65 **1** **Los Nadis (GER)**[10] 3127 7-10-13 **62**.................... MrStevenFox(7) 2 74
(Jim Goldie) *hld up towards rr: smooth hdwy 4f out: n.m.r and swtchd to inner over 3f out: led over 2f out: sn pushed clr: styd on wl* **7/2**[2]
0- **2** *3 1/2* **Soprano (GER)**[108] 409 9-9-13 **48**....................(p) MrMAllan(7) 1 55
(Jim Goldie) *hld up towards rr: hdwy on outer 4f out: effrt over 2f out: rdn to chse wnr wl over 1f out: no imp* **20/1**
00-3 **3** *1 1/4* **Strikemaster (IRE)**[11] 3072 5-10-3 **52**....................(t) MrAaronJames(7) 5 58
(Lee James) *dwlt and bhd: stdy hdwy 3f out: rdn over 2f out: styd on appr fnl f: nrst fin* **12/1**

/002 **4** *8* **Westlin' Winds (IRE)**[23] 2733 5-11-7 **63** MrSWalker 8 59
(Brian Ellison) *trckd ldrs: pushed along and sltly outpcd over 5f out: rdn to chse ldrs over 3f out: drvn over 2f out and sn one pce* **13/8**[1]
0-61 **5** *shd* **Zefooha (FR)**[9] 3187 7-11-3 **59** (p) MrMSeston 7 55
(Tim Walford) *prom: effrt over 3f out: rdn and ch over 2f out: sn drvn and grad wknd* **5/1**[3]
334- **6** *4* **Park's Prodigy**[20] 6028 7-11-2 **63** (t) MrGRSmith(5) 3 54
(David Thompson) *trckd ldrs on inner: hdwy 5f out: led briefly 3f out: sn rdn and hdd over 2f out: grad wknd* **33/1**
600- **7** *11* **French Seventyfive**[14] 3614 4-9-13 **46** MrARawlinson(5) 6 24
(Tim Walford) *midfield: hdwy to trck ldrs 7f out: rdn along 3f out: sn wknd* **25/1**
-304 **8** *8* **Rare Coincidence**[26] 1218 10-10-10 **52** (p) MrSDobson 9 20
(Alan Berry) *cl up: led after 2f: rdn along 4f out: hdd 3f out and sn wknd* **18/1**
9 *3* **Via Archimede (USA)**[16] 3647 6-10-5 **54** (b1) MrCNichol(7) 4 19
(Lucinda Russell) *led 2f: cl up: rdn along 5f out: wknd over 3f out* **33/1**
4010 **10** *16* **Dechiper (IRE)**[4] 3316 9-10-4 **49** MrMEnnis(3) 10 —
(Robert Johnson) *chsd ldrs: rdn along 6f out: sn wknd and bhd fnl 3f* **16/1**
4540 **11** *4 ½* **Silent Lucidity (IRE)**[15] 2952 7-10-5 **50** (b1) MrJHamer(3) 11 —
(Peter Niven) *a in rr: bhd fnl 3f* **20/1**

3m 33.12s (-0.38) **Going Correction** +0.025s/f (Good) **11** Ran SP% **115.1**
Speed ratings (Par 101): **101,99,98,94,94 92,87,83,81,73 71**
Tote Swingers: 1&2 £8.60, 1&3 £4.20, 2&3 £26.10 CSF £75.90 CT £745.84 TOTE £4.20: £2.10, £6.10, £5.40; EX 71.60.
Owner Ian G M Dalgleish **Bred** Stiftung Gestut Fahrhof **Trained** Uplawmoor, E Renfrews
■ The first winner under rules on just his second ride for Steven Fox, 16.
■ Stewards' Enquiry : Mr S Dobson three-day ban: careless riding (tbn)

FOCUS
The bottom bend was moved out three metres, adding 24 metres to all races on the round course. A dry weekend but, after 1mm of evening rain, the ground was eased slightly to good, good to soft in places in the straight. Exposed performers in a low-key opener. An ordinary gallop steadied before halfway before picking up again early in the straight and the time was over 8sec outside Racing Post standard. It was the only race on the card where hold-up horses got involved. The winner is rated back to the sort of form he showed when winning this last year.

3451 MATRIX GROUP H'CAP 5f
7:25 (7:26) (Class 6) (0-65,64) 4-Y-0+ **£1,942** (£578; £288; £144) **Stalls** High

Form RPR
3150 **1** **Ridley Didley (IRE)**[13] 3027 6-9-7 **64** AdrianNicholls 7 73
(Noel Wilson) *qckly away: mde all: rdn ent fnl f: styd on wl* **14/1**
0464 **2** *1 ¾* **Wicked Wilma (IRE)**[11] 3087 7-8-12 **55** PatrickMathers 2 58
(Alan Berry) *trckd ldrs: hdwy over 2f out: rdn to chse wnr wl over 1f out: drvn and edgd lft ins fnl f: one pce* **9/2**[3]
4160 **3** *2* **Dower Glen**[19] 2803 4-8-12 **55** (v) TomEaves 10 51
(Keith Dalgleish) *chsd ldrs: rdn along wl over 1f out: kpt on ins fnl f* **15/2**
0552 **4** *½* **Lees Anthem**[13] 3027 4-9-1 **58** PhillipMakin 5 52
(Colin Teague) *midfield: hdwy 2f out: sn rdn and kpt on ins fnl f* **4/1**[2]
6030 **5** *½* **Spirit Of Coniston**[24] 2667 8-8-6 **56** DavidSimmonson(7) 4 48
(Paul Midgley) *prom: rdn along 2f out: grad wknd over 1f out* **16/1**
5050 **6** *2* **Sandwith**[25] 2632 8-9-3 **60** (v) LeeNewman 6 45
(George Foster) *chsd ldrs on inner: rdn along 2f out: sn drvn and wknd over 1f out* **8/1**
0-00 **7** *½* **Blown It (USA)**[28] 2543 5-8-9 **52** PaulHanagan 11 35
(Keith Dalgleish) *a towards rr* **7/2**[1]
00-0 **8** *1* **Future Gem**[14] 2990 5-7-11 **45** (p) DanielleMcCreery(5) 9 24
(David Thompson) *awkward s: a towards rr* **66/1**
0000 **9** *¾* **Ya Boy Sir (IRE)**[19] 2803 4-8-3 **46** DuranFentiman 3 23
(Ian Semple) *towards rr: hdwy to chse ldrs 1/2-way: rdn along 2f out: sn wknd* **33/1**
0430 **10** *hd* **Distant Sun (USA)**[12] 3036 7-8-11 **54** FrederikTylicki 8 30
(Linda Perratt) *a in rr* **7/1**

59.54 secs (-0.86) **Going Correction** -0.125s/f (Firm) **10** Ran SP% **112.8**
Speed ratings (Par 101): **101,98,95,94,93 90,89,87,86,86**
Tote Swingers: 1&2 £13.90, 1&3 £12.80, 2&3 £7.20 CSF £73.49 CT £524.66 TOTE £14.70: £6.10, £2.40, £3.10; EX 78.80.
Owner Frank Tobin & Nicola Wilson **Bred** Peter Molony **Trained** Sandhutton, N Yorks

FOCUS
Another very ordinary handicap but, although the gallop was decent, very few figured and those held up were at a disadvantage. Paul Hanagan reported the ground was "near enough good to soft", though the time was only just over a second outside the Racing Post standard. The form is rated around the winner.
Future Gem Official explanation: jockey said mare missed the break

3452 BRITISH STALLION STUDS SUPPORTING BRITISH RACING E B F MAIDEN STKS 5f
7:55 (7:56) (Class 5) 2-Y-0 **£3,238** (£963; £481; £240) **Stalls** High

Form RPR
1 **Hot Sugar (USA)** 2-9-3 0 PhillipMakin 8 71+
(Kevin Ryan) *mde all: rdn over 1f out: drvn ins fnl f: kpt on wl* **3/1**[2]
0442 **2** *nk* **First Fast Now (IRE)**[10] 3125 2-8-12 0 PaulHanagan 5 65+
(Nigel Tinkler) *trckd ldrs: hdwy wl over 1f out: rdn to chal ent fnl f: sn drvn and ev ch tl no ex towards fin* **9/2**[3]
0 **3** *3* **Hopes Rebellion**[14] 2983 2-9-3 0 AndrewElliott 3 59
(Declan Carroll) *cl up: rdn along wl over 1f out: drvn and one pce ent fnl f* **9/1**
4 *6* **Mantuana (IRE)** 2-8-12 0 DanielTudhope 1 33
(David O'Meara) *prom: rdn along 2f out: drvn and wknd appr fnl f* **8/1**
5 *2* **Lowtherwood** 2-9-3 0 TomEaves 2 30
(Bryan Smart) *chsd ldrs: rdn along over 2f out: sn outpcd* **11/5**[1]
6 *1* **Professor Tim (IRE)** 2-8-12 0 SladeO'Hara(5) 4 27
(Patrick Morris) *in tch: rdn along 1/2-way: sn outpcd* **14/1**
7 *7* **Lollypop Lady** 2-8-12 0 FrederikTylicki 6 —
(Linda Perratt) *sn outpcd and a bhd* **16/1**
8 *48* **Burnwynd Spirit (IRE)** 2-9-3 0 TonyHamilton 7 —
(Ian Semple) *green and lost many l s: a wl bhd* **20/1**

60.90 secs (0.50) **Going Correction** -0.125s/f (Firm) **8** Ran SP% **112.9**
Speed ratings (Par 93): **91,90,85,76,72 71,60,—**
Tote Swingers: 1&2 £1.50, 1&3 £3.60, 2&3 £6.60 CSF £16.47 TOTE £5.70: £1.90, £1.02, £3.10; EX 10.70.
Owner The C H F Partnership **Bred** Winchester Farm **Trained** Hambleton, N Yorks

FOCUS
The gallop was sound but the time was nearly a second and a half slower than the previous handicap over this trip. Fairly weak form, and the winner did not have to rate too highly.

NOTEBOOK
Hot Sugar(USA) ◆, from a yard with a strong hand in the juvenile department, has winners up to 1m5f in his pedigree but he showed plenty of foot and a good attitude to get off the mark at the first time of asking to justify market support. He'll be equally well suited by 6f and, although this bare form is no more than modest, he's the type to improve again. (op 7-2)
First Fast Now(IRE), warm and edgy and a market drifter beforehand, is the most experienced of these but ran as well as she ever has done. She should be able to pick up a small race, but is likely to remain vulnerable to the better types in this grade. (op 9-4)
Hopes Rebellion had been soundly beaten on his racecourse debut but attracted support and fared a good deal better dropped to this trip. Low-grade nurseries are likely to provide him with his best chance of success. (op 16-1 tchd 17-2)
Mantuana(IRE), a half-sister to 1m2f selling winner Orthology, showed ability at a moderate level and, although entitled to improve for the experience, she is another likely to remain vulnerable in this type of race. (tchd 9-1)
Lowtherwood, a Green Desert half-brother to dual Group 1 winning sprinter Reverence, who was left behind in the last quarter mile. Presumably he had been showing a fair bit at home and will almost certainly be worth another chance. (op 11-4 tchd 7-2 in a place)

3453 RACING UK H'CAP 1m 4f 100y
8:25 (8:25) (Class 5) (0-70,69) 4-Y-0+ **£2,266** (£674; £337; £168) **Stalls** Low

Form RPR
126- **1** **Amazing King (IRE)**[22] 5868 7-9-7 **69** RussKennemore 6 77+
(Philip Kirby) *trckd ldr: effrt 3f out: led 2f out: sn rdn and edgd rt over 1f out: kpt on* **5/1**
4015 **2** *½* **King's Counsel (IRE)**[12] 3054 5-9-6 **68** (b) DanielTudhope 8 73
(David O'Meara) *led: rdn along 3f out: hdd 2f out: swtchd lft and drvn ins fnl f: kpt on towards fin* **9/2**[3]
0434 **3** *1 ¾* **Beneath**[10] 3129 4-8-12 **60** (b) PhillipMakin 1 62
(Kevin Ryan) *chsd ldng pair: pushed along and sltly outpcd over 3f out: rdn over 2f out: drvn over 1f out: kpt on u.p fnl f: nrst fin* **3/1**[1]
5-50 **4** *5* **Parc Des Princes (USA)**[24] 2696 5-9-1 **63** TomEaves 2 58
(Nicky Richards) *in tch: hdwy over 3f out: sn rdn and plugged on same pce fnl 2f* **8/1**
4040 **5** *2 ¼* **Birkside**[10] 3129 8-8-8 **56** TonyHamilton 5 47
(Linda Perratt) *dwlt and towards rr: hdwy 4f out: rdn along 3f out: plugged on same pce fnl 2f* **20/1**
6/4- **6** *9* **Grandad Bill (IRE)**[72] 7054 8-8-12 **60** PaulHanagan 4 37
(Jim Goldie) *a in rr* **7/2**[2]
-060 **7** *11* **Mainland (USA)**[39] 2213 5-9-3 **68** PaulPickard(3) 7 28
(Tracy Waggott) *s.i.s: a bhd* **11/1**
246- **8** *13* **Barliffey (IRE)**[14] 7275 6-9-7 **69** FrederikTylicki 3 —
(Lucinda Russell) *hld up: stdy hdwy 1/2-way: chsd ldr briefly over 3f out: sn drvn and wknd qckly* **14/1**

2m 43.14s (1.14) **Going Correction** +0.025s/f (Good) **8** Ran SP% **112.9**
Speed ratings (Par 103): **97,96,95,92,90 84,77,68**
Tote Swingers: 1&2 £3.40, 1&3 £4.20, 2&3 £2.80 CSF £26.99 CT £77.79 TOTE £8.40: £1.80, £2.30, £2.20; EX 34.60.
Owner The New Venture Partnership **Bred** Kraemer Partnership **Trained** Castleton, N Yorks
■ Stewards' Enquiry : Russ Kennemore caution: used whip without giving gelding time to respond.

FOCUS
A modest handicap in which an ordinary gallop steadied after half a mile before picking up again approaching the straight. Those held up were at a disadvantage and the first three finished clear. The winner is rated basically in line with last year's Flat form.
Grandad Bill(IRE) Official explanation: jockey said gelding never travelled
Barliffey(IRE) Official explanation: jockey said gelding lost its action

3454 MORRISON BOWMORE DISTILLERS TROPHY H'CAP 1m
8:55 (8:56) (Class 6) (0-65,60) 3-Y-0+ **£1,942** (£578; £288; £144) **Stalls** Low

Form RPR
5312 **1** **Thinking**[6] 3245 4-9-11 **57** DuranFentiman 1 66
(Tim Easterby) *prom: effrt on inner 2f out: rdn to ld over 1f out: drvn ins fnl f: styd on wl* **9/4**[1]
0604 **2** *1 ¼* **Glenluji**[12] 3038 6-9-10 **56** PaulHanagan 2 62
(Jim Goldie) *trckd ldrs: hdwy 3f out: effrt 2f out and sn rdn: drvn to chse wnr ent fnl f: no imp towards fin* **5/2**[2]
4123 **3** *1 ½* **Shunkawakhan (IRE)**[10] 3128 8-9-8 **54** (p) PhillipMakin 6 57
(Linda Perratt) *led: rdn along over 2f out: sn jnd and drvn: hdd over 1f out: kpt on u.p fnl f* **10/1**
0000 **4** *1 ¾* **Northern Flyer (GER)**[30] 2487 5-10-0 **60** (v) TonyHamilton 9 59
(John Quinn) *prom: effrt 3f out: rdn over 2f out and ev ch tl drvn and one pce appr fnl f* **16/1**
0050 **5** *1 ¾* **Rosbertini**[10] 3110 5-8-12 **47** GaryBartley(3) 5 42
(Linda Perratt) *hld up towards rr: hdwy over 3f out: rdn and n.m.r 2f out: sn swtchd rt and kpt on u.p fnl f: nrst fin* **33/1**
5500 **6** *1 ¾* **Walleyd (IRE)**[24] 2692 4-8-13 **52** RossSmith(7) 13 43
(Linda Perratt) *hld up in rr: hdwy 3f out: rdn and in tch 2f out: sn edgd rt and wknd* **80/1**
0060 **7** *½* **Mr Emirati (USA)**[19] 2804 4-9-2 **48** (p) TomEaves 7 37
(Bryan Smart) *chsd ldrs: rdn along 3f out: drvn and wknd 2f out* **16/1**
-003 **8** *¾* **Coolella (IRE)**[10] 3110 4-8-8 **47** JustinNewman(7) 8 35
(John Weymes) *hld up: hdwy 3f out: rdn to chal and ev ch over 2f out: sn drvn and wknd wl over 1f out* **12/1**
03-6 **9** *nk* **Broughtons Silk**[4] 3306 6-8-7 **46** GarryWhillans(7) 10 33
(Alistair Whillans) *hld up towards rr: gd hdwy on wd outside 3f out: rdn to chse ldrs over 2f out: drvn and wknd wl over 1f out* **14/1**
0051 **10** *¾* **Drive Home (USA)**[10] 3128 4-9-9 **55** (p) AdrianNicholls 12 40
(Noel Wilson) *trckd ldrs: hdwy 3f out: rdn to chal over 2f out and ev ch tl drvn wl over 1f out and sn wknd* **7/1**[3]
-000 **11** *1* **Cold Quest (USA)**[10] 3110 7-9-4 **50** FrederikTylicki 4 33
(Linda Perratt) *dwlt: a bhd* **33/1**

1m 41.59s (0.39) **Going Correction** +0.025s/f (Good) **11** Ran SP% **114.2**
Speed ratings (Par 101): **99,97,96,94,92 91,90,89,89,88 87**
Tote Swingers: 1&2 £1.80, 1&3 £3.50, 2&3 £6.70 CSF £7.48 CT £43.89 TOTE £2.90: £1.10, £1.30, £2.60; EX 6.80.
Owner Habton Farms **Bred** L T Roberts **Trained** Great Habton, N Yorks

FOCUS
A moderate handicap in which the gallop was a modest one. Again few got involved, and the form is rated around the runner-up.

3455 SCOTTISH RACING YOUR BETTER BET H'CAP 7f 30y
9:25 (9:25) (Class 6) (0-55,54) 3-Y-0 **£1,942** (£578; £288; £144) **Stalls** Low

Form RPR
0000 **1** **Twennyshortkid**[12] 3039 3-8-9 **45** (v1) TonyHamilton 2 55
(Paul Midgley) *trckd ldrs on inner: hdwy to chse ldr 2f out: drvn to chal and edgd rt ins fnl f: kpt on to ld nr fin* **15/2**

6-00 **2** *nk* **Cannon Bolt (IRE)**[20] 2782 3-8-9 **45**............................(b[1]) LeeNewman 3 54
(Robin Bastiman) *led: rdn along 2f out: drvn ent fnl f: n.m.r whn hdd and no ex nr fin* **50/1**

-000 **3** *7* **Formidable Girl (USA)**[12] 3039 3-9-3 **53**......................(tp) PhillipMakin 1 43
(Kevin Ryan) *dwlt: sn in tch: hdwy to chse ldrs 3f out: rdn along over 2f out: kpt on same pce u.p appr fnl f* **16/1**

0400 **4** *3 3/4* **Love For Love**[20] 2786 3-9-0 **50**.................................... DanielTudhope 7 30
(David O'Meara) *chsd ldr: rdn along 3f out: drvn 2f out and grad wknd* **6/1**

4413 **5** *2 1/4* **See The Storm**[10] 3142 3-8-12 **53** ow1......................... SladeO'Hara(5) 9 27
(Patrick Morris) *hld up towards rr: hdwy over 2f out: sn rdn and no imp fr wl over 1f out* **4/1**[3]

000- **6** *2 1/4* **Henry Chettle (IRE)**[291] 5878 3-8-9 **45**................................ TomEaves 6 13
(David O'Meara) *nvr nr ldrs* **12/1**

-004 **7** *hd* **Face East (USA)**[24] 2697 3-8-9 **45**............................ PatrickMathers 10 12
(Alan Berry) *in rr: sme hdwy over 2f out: sn rdn and wknd* **33/1**

5-30 **8** *9* **Diamond Sunrise (IRE)**[136] 505 3-9-1 **51**.................. AdrianNicholls 8 —
(Noel Wilson) *in tch: rdn along over 3f out: sn drvn and wknd* **25/1**

-020 **9** *4* **Ryedale Dancer (IRE)**[20] 2782 3-9-2 **52**.................... DuranFentiman 4 —
(Tim Easterby) *dwlt: a in rr* **7/2**[2]

-044 **10** *20* **Inside**[12] 3039 3-9-4 **54**..(p) PaulHanagan 5 —
(Richard Fahey) *prom whn hmpd: rn wd and lost action bnd over 5f out: bhd after* **10/3**[1]

1m 29.14s (0.14) **Going Correction** +0.025s/f (Good) **10** Ran SP% **113.7**
Speed ratings (Par 97): **100,99,91,87,84 82,82,71,67,44**
Tote Super 7: Win: Not won. Place: £423.50 - 3 winning units. CSF £323.34 CT £3598.95 TOTE £11.80: £3.40, £16.60, £6.40; EX 270.50.
Owner A Turton & T Shepherd **Bred** John Hussey And Stephen Hillen **Trained** Westow, N Yorks

FOCUS
A very moderate handicap in which the two market leaders disappointed but, although the gallop was soon sound, those held up were at a disadvantage. The first two pulled clear, but this was a weak race and the form isn't taken at face value.
Inside Official explanation: jockey said filly hung left final bend and bit slipped through its mouth
T/Plt: £607.60 to a £1 stake. Pool £70,089.00 - 84.20 winning tickets. T/Qpdt: £43.90 to a £1 stake. Pool £5,498.00 - 92.60 winning tickets. JR

3200 PONTEFRACT (L-H)
Monday, June 27

OFFICIAL GOING: Good to firm (good in places; 8.0)
Wind: almost nil Weather: sunny, hot

3456 PONTEFRACT LADIES' H'CAP (LADY AMATEUR RIDERS) 1m 2f 6y
2:15 (2:15) (Class 5) (0-75,71) 3-Y-O+ **£2,186** (£677; £338; £169) **Stalls** Low

Form RPR
133- **1** **Fujin Dancer (FR)**[73] 7679 6-10-1 **70**.......................... MissHBethell(5) 3 82
(Brian Ellison) *hld up in rr: hdwy over 2f out: switchd rt over 1f out: hung lft and led wl ins fnl f: drvn clr* **9/2**[2]

2156 **2** *3 3/4* **Amazing Blue Sky**[13] 3023 5-10-5 **69**...................... MissSBrotherton 13 73
(Ruth Carr) *edgd lft after s: trckd ldrs: led over 2f out: hdd and no ex last 75yds* **4/1**[1]

4551 **3** *nk* **Entrance**[18] 2850 3-8-6 **61**... MissSBirkett(7) 5 64
(Julia Feilden) *dwlt: in rr: gd hdwy and swtchd rt 1f out: fin wl* **14/1**

0424 **4** *6* **Amir Pasha (UAE)**[4] 3301 6-9-6 **61**..............................(v) MissRSmith(5) 2 52
(Micky Hammond) *t.k.h: w ldr: led after 2f: hdd over 2f out: wknd over 1f out* **13/2**

0326 **5** *1 1/2* **Rub Of The Relic (IRE)**[10] 3129 6-8-11 **54**...............(b) MissHDukes(7) 1 42
(Paul Midgley) *trckd ldrs: t.k.h: outpcd and lost pl over 2f out: kpt on fnl f* **14/1**

1551 **6** *3/4* **Visions Of Johanna (USA)**[7] 3240 6-10-6 **70** 6ex.....(p) MrsCBartley 14 57
(Richard Guest) *chsd ldrs: drvn over 2f out: one pce* **12/1**

0-00 **7** *3/4* **Blue Spinnaker (IRE)**[74] 1324 12-9-4 **59**......... MissJoannaMason(5) 12 44
(Michael Easterby) *swtchd lft after s: in rr: kpt on fnl 2f: nvr nr ldrs* **50/1**

002 **8** *1 1/4* **Tropical Bachelor (IRE)**[344] 4170 5-10-3 **70**
MissPernillaHermansson(4) 6 53
(Richard Ford) *mid-div: drvn over 3f out: hung lft and wknd over 1f out* **33/1**

2266 **9** *3/4* **Zaplamation (IRE)**[19] 2800 6-10-4 **68**......................... MissGAndrews 11 49
(John Quinn) *mid-div: hdwy to chse ldrs 5f out: wknd over 1f out* **10/1**

-606 **10** *hd* **Tropical Duke (IRE)**[11] 3086 5-9-4 **54**............................ MissADeniel 7 35
(Ron Barr) *mid-div: drvn 3f out: nvr a factor* **12/1**

0122 **11** *2* **Strike Force**[6] 3244 7-10-4 **71**...........................(t) MissALHutchinson(3) 9 48
(Clifford Lines) *s.s: sme hdwy on wd outside over 2f out: sn wknd* **6/1**[3]

4340 **12** *14* **Bajan Pride**[4] 3306 7-9-3 **56**.................................... MissWGibson(3) 4 —
(Paul Midgley) *led 2f: w ldrs: wknd 2f out: sn bhd* **20/1**

13 *5* **Street Legal**[306] 5431 6-9-11 **61**.. MissZoeLilly 10 —
(Alan McCabe) *sn chsng ldrs: lost pl over 2f out: sn bhd* **33/1**

2m 13.97s (0.27) **Going Correction** -0.025s/f (Good)
WFA 3 from 5yo+ 12lb **13** Ran SP% **116.2**
Speed ratings (Par 103): **97,94,93,88,87 87,86,85,84,84 83,72,68**
Tote Swingers: 1&2 £4.00, 1&3 £13.70, 2&3 £12.10 CSF £21.22 CT £233.45 TOTE £6.30: £2.20, £1.90, £4.50; EX 19.90 Trifecta £41.40 Pool: £299.08 - 5.33 winning units..
Owner W A Bethell **Bred** Loughtown Stud Ltd **Trained** Norton, N Yorks
■ Harriet Bethell's first Flat winner.
■ Stewards' Enquiry : Miss A Deniel caution: used whip when out of contention

FOCUS
There was a false rail in place over the final 6f, dolled out 15ft from the inside rail. The pace was good as usual for this type of race and the winner looks back to his best.

3457 MONTY HEMPTON - A LIFETIME IN RACING FILLIES' H'CAP 1m 4y
2:45 (2:46) (Class 5) (0-70,66) 3-Y-O+ **£2,266** (£674; £337; £168) **Stalls** Low

Form RPR
/001 **1** **Qeethaara (USA)**[4] 3326 7-10-0 **66**.................................... ShaneKelly 4 74+
(Mark Brisbourne) *hld up in mid-div: wnt 2nd over 2f out: hung lft and led appr fnl f: hld on towards fin* **4/1**[2]

3131 **2** *1/2* **Mini's Destination**[15] 2964 3-9-3 **65**........................... NickyMackay 8 69
(John Holt) *mid-div: drvn over 3f out: chsd ldrs over 2f out: styd on fnl f: no ex towards fin* **11/2**[3]

0550 **3** *nk* **Generous Genella**[18] 2858 3-8-2 **50** oh2 ow3..............(t) FrannyNorton 1 54
(Julia Feilden) *trckd ldrs on inner: styd on same pce ins fnl f* **33/1**

5530 **4** *2* **Lady Excel (IRE)**[11] 3074 5-9-0 **52**............................ AndrewHeffernan 3 53
(Brian Rothwell) *led: hdd appr fnl f: one pce* **20/1**

0503 **5** *2 1/4* **Wiseman's Diamond (USA)**[11] 3088 6-9-2 **54**...........(b) MickyFenton 5 50
(Paul Midgley) *trckd ldrs: t.k.h: effrt and edgd lft over 1f out: kpt on same pce* **13/2**

1304 **6** *1* **Spavento (IRE)**[16] 2912 5-9-8 **60**.. KierenFallon 7 54
(Eric Alston) *s.i.s: in rr: hdwy over 2f out: kpt on nvr rchd ldrs* **4/1**[2]

555- **7** *12* **Alioonagh (USA)**[290] 5925 4-9-13 **65**................................ RyanMoore 9 31
(Peter Chapple-Hyam) *hld up in rr: effrt over 3f out: wknd over 2f out* **7/2**[1]

0-04 **8** *1/2* **Whats For Pudding (IRE)**[8] 3202 3-7-12 **51**.............(b[1]) NeilFarley(5) 10 14
(Declan Carroll) *gave problems at s: chsd ldrs on outside: lost pl 2f out* **33/1**

006- **9** *1* **Gee Ceffyl Bach**[286] 6062 7-8-6 **47** oh2.......................... BillyCray(3) 2 9
(Garry Woodward) *hld up in rr: drvn over 3f out: hung rt and lost pl over 1f out* **100/1**

5660 **10** *11* **Sennockian Storm (USA)**[11] 3088 4-9-3 **55**........... SilvestreDeSousa 6 —
(Mark Johnston) *trckd ldrs: wnt lft over 1f out: sn lost pl: heavily eased towards fin* **17/2**

1m 45.96s (0.06) **Going Correction** -0.025s/f (Good)
WFA 3 from 4yo+ 10lb **10** Ran SP% **113.1**
Speed ratings (Par 100): **98,97,97,95,92 91,79,79,78,67**
Tote Swingers: 1&2 £4.20, 1&3 £18.40, 2&3 £16.30 CSF £24.44 CT £638.46 TOTE £5.00: £1.40, £2.20, £8.30; EX 26.70 Trifecta £203.00 Pool: £466.45 - 1.70 winning units..
Owner Mark Brisbourne **Bred** Shadwell Farm LLC **Trained** Great Ness, Shropshire

FOCUS
A moderate fillies' handicap. The third is a slight doubt but the winner travelled a bit better than the bare form.
Gee Ceffyl Bach Official explanation: jockey said mare hung right

3458 SPINDRIFTER CONDITIONS STKS 6f
3:15 (3:15) (Class 2) 2-Y-O **£6,476** (£1,927) **Stalls** Low

Form RPR
10 **1** **Sans Loi (IRE)**[11] 3064 2-8-12 0.................................... RobertWinston 2 88+
(Alan McCabe) *trckd ldr: t.k.h: chal over 2f out: shkn up to ld 1f out: nudged out* **2/5**[1]

1025 **2** *3 3/4* **Princess Banu**[23] 2712 2-8-7 0.............................. SilvestreDeSousa 3 72
(Mick Channon) *led: qcknd 3f out: sn drvn: hdd 1f out: no ch w wnr* **15/8**[2]

1m 19.45s (2.55) **Going Correction** -0.025s/f (Good) **2** Ran SP% **106.2**
Speed ratings (Par 99): **82,77**
TOTE £1.50.
Owner Mrs Z Wentworth **Bred** Joan Murphy & Lawman Syndicate **Trained** Averham Park, Notts

FOCUS
A poor turnout. Two of the three declared by Mick Channon didn't take part, with the previous day's Windsor winner Betty Fontaine found to be lame. The form could be worth more but the time was slow.

NOTEBOOK
Sans Loi(IRE), who made such an impressive debut over this trip prior to finishing well beaten over 5f at Royal Ascot, was able to get back on track, tanking his way into the lead and readily drawing clear. A fine, strong sort, he clearly has plenty of speed, but 6f looks his trip for the moment at least and he'll go back up in grade now. (op 1-2)
Princess Banu did little more than give a lead to the classier winner. (op 13-8)

3459 BRITISH STALLION STUDS E.B.F./ PARK SUITE FILLIES' H'CAP 6f
3:45 (3:46) (Class 3) (0-90,90) 3-Y-O+
£7,165 (£2,145; £1,072; £537; £267; £134) **Stalls** Low

Form RPR
2025 **1** **Sioux Rising (IRE)**[52] 1854 5-9-8 **89**................................ LeeTopliss(5) 2 98
(Richard Fahey) *dwlt: in rr: hdwy on inner over 2f out: styd on to ld fnl stride* **10/1**

6-02 **2** *hd* **Desert Poppy (IRE)**[24] 2690 4-9-11 **87**.............................. ShaneKelly 12 95+
(Walter Swinburn) *chsd ldrs: led last 100yds: hdd post* **9/1**

4405 **3** *hd* **Favourite Girl (IRE)**[9] 3158 5-9-9 **90**..........................(p) LanceBetts(5) 9 97
(Tim Easterby) *led: qcknd clr over 1f out: hdd ins fnl f: no ex nr fin* **18/1**

1-01 **4** *1* **Entitled**[16] 2938 4-9-11 **87**.. RyanMoore 11 91+
(Sir Michael Stoute) *dwlt: in rr on outer: hdwy over 2f out: chsng ldrs appr fnl f: kpt on same pce* **11/4**[1]

1-32 **5** *3 3/4* **Blanche Dubawi (IRE)**[31] 2468 3-8-13 **82**........................ TomQueally 7 72+
(Noel Quinlan) *dwlt: swtchd lft after s: bhd tl kpt on fnl 2f: styd on wl last 100yds: nt rch ldrs* **4/1**[2]

3-11 **6** *1/2* **Mosaicist (IRE)**[19] 2818 3-9-1 **84**...................................... KierenFallon 6 73
(James Fanshawe) *mid-div: effrt over 2f out: nvr trbld ldrs* **13/2**[3]

0-46 **7** *shd* **Mango Music**[9] 3160 8-8-6 **75**.. LauraBarry(7) 8 65+
(Richard Fahey) *mid-div: stdy hdwy on outside 2f out: kpt on steadily fnl f: nt rch ldrs* **25/1**

-000 **8** *5* **Who's Shirl**[32] 2434 5-9-6 **82**.. KellyHarrison 4 66
(Chris Fairhurst) *mid-div: sn drvn along: lost pl over 1f out* **22/1**

040- **9** *2* **Ishiadancer**[284] 6113 6-9-5 **81**.................................... RobertWinston 5 49
(Eric Alston) *chsd ldrs: wknd appr fnl f* **100/1**

0-10 **10** *3 1/4* **Pepper Lane**[26] 2620 4-9-7 **83**.............................. SilvestreDeSousa 1 40
(David O'Meara) *hld up on ins: outpcd over 2f out: no ch after* **11/1**

3000 **11** *19* **Breedj (IRE)**[30] 2508 3-9-7 **90**.................................... PhilipRobinson 10 —
(Clive Brittain) *w ldrs: wknd 2f out: eased ins fnl f: t.o* **50/1**

13-0 **12** *26* **Amitola (IRE)**[37] 2298 4-10-0 **90**.................................. JamieSpencer 3 —
(David Barron) *in rr: drvn over 2f out: sn lost pl: heavily eased ins fnl f: t.o* **8/1**

1m 16.07s (-0.83) **Going Correction** -0.025s/f (Good)
WFA 3 from 4yo+ 7lb **12** Ran SP% **114.9**
Speed ratings (Par 104): **104,103,103,102,97 96,96,89,87,82 57,22**
Tote Swingers: 1&2 £10.00, 1&3 £16.70, 2&3 £18.10 CSF £90.89 CT £1615.70 TOTE £10.00: £3.10, £2.60, £5.00; EX 85.30 TRIFECTA Not won..
Owner Mrs Una Towell **Bred** N And Mrs N Nugent **Trained** Musley Bank, N Yorks
■ Stewards' Enquiry : Laura Barry ten-day ban: failed to obtain best possible placing (Jul 11-20)

FOCUS
A typically competitive sprint handicap and good form for a fillies' race, rated around the third.

NOTEBOOK
Sioux Rising(IRE) made it 3-4 at the course with a last-gasp success. Much of the credit goes to Lee Topliss, riding the mare for the first time, but this was the highest mark she has won off by some way and she'll life a lot tougher now, for all she'll again warrant respect when returning here. (op 12-1)
Desert Poppy(IRE), runner-up off this mark at Goodwood, made her way to the front inside the final furlong, only to be robbed of victory on the line. She deserves to win again. (op 12-1)
Favourite Girl(IRE) gave it a good go from the front, but the final climb to the line proved too much. (op 22-1)
Entitled did well as she wasn't the best away and was then forced to race wide. She'd closed to a challenging position by the turn, but the kick she produced to win at York previously was missing this time. Still a respectable effort, she remains capable of better at this trip, with a return to a straight track also a possible help. (op 5-2)
Blanche Dubawi(IRE) was noted making good late headway, having been the slowest away. This was a credible effort for a 3-y-o and she can pick up a race off this mark returned to her own age-group. (op 5-1 tchd 7-2)
Mosaicist(IRE) lacked the speed to throw down a serious challenge when coming under pressure. The 10lb she'd gone up for winning at Kempton may have proved too much. (op 4-1 tchd 7-1)

Mango Music came wide and was doing her best to run on close home. Official explanation: jockey said, regarding runing and riding, that her orders were to settle the mare early stages as it has been too keen previously, it had been bustled midway, resulting in being too far back; trainer confirmed instructions but was not satisfied with the ride. (op 20-1)

Pepper Lane was trying to come with a run when short for room on the inner. (op 12-1)

3460 WAYNE CONWAY MEMORIAL H'CAP 1m 4f 8y

4:15 (4:16) (Class 5) (0-70,70) 3-Y-O **£2,266** (£674; £337; £168) **Stalls** Low

Form RPR

6535 **1** **Bradbury (IRE)**[28] 2571 3-8-10 **59** ow1 (p) JamieSpencer 5 71
(James Bethell) *s.i.s: hld up in rr: effrt and nt clr run 3f out: chsd ldr over 1f out: hrd rdn and styd on to ld last strides* **7/2**[2]

1110 **2** *hd* **Memorabilia**[16] 2925 3-9-7 **70** SilvestreDeSousa 8 81
(Mark Johnston) *led: pushed 5 l clr 2f out: hdd towards fin* **6/1**

4035 **3** *10* **Commander Veejay**[10] 3116 3-8-2 **51** oh6 (p) AndrewHeffernan 7 46
(Brian Rothwell) *in rr: hdwy on outer over 4f out: wnt 3rd over 2f out: one pce* **40/1**

0-50 **4** *3 ¼* **Geminus (IRE)**[45] 2058 3-8-7 **59** MichaelO'Connell(3) 3 49
(Jedd O'Keeffe) *dwlt: mid-div: reminders 6f out: sn lost pl: kpt on fnl 2f: tk modest 4th nr fin* **12/1**

-353 **5** *2* **Residence And Spa (IRE)**[33] 2407 3-9-5 **68** RobertWinston 6 55
(Tim Easterby) *mid-div: wnt 2nd over 2f out: fdd fnl f: sddle slipped* **4/1**[3]

2564 **6** *7* **Paco Belle (IRE)**[10] 3141 3-8-11 **60** ShaneKelly 1 35
(Andrew Crook) *trckd ldrs: outpcd over 2f out: lost pl over 1f out* **25/1**

-602 **7** *33* **Around The Clock (USA)**[13] 3018 3-9-1 **64** TomQueally 4 —
(Amanda Perrett) *trckd ldrs: drvn over 4f out: lost pl 3f out: bhd whn eased ins fnl f: virtually p.u: wl t.o* **3/1**[1]

43-0 **8** *28* **Dictate**[17] 2874 3-9-6 **69** KierenFallon 9 —
(Mark H Tompkins) *w ldr: drvn over 3f out: sn wknd: eased over 1f out: virtually p.u: wl t.o* **9/1**

5-40 **9** *2 ¼* **Geronimo Chief (IRE)**[12] 3039 3-8-6 **55** PJMcDonald 2 —
(Ben Haslam) *in rr: reminders 5f out: lost pl over 3f out: t.o whn eased ins fnl f: virtually p.u: wl t.o* **10/1**

2m 39.07s (-1.73) **Going Correction** -0.025s/f (Good) **9** Ran SP% **114.6**

Speed ratings (Par 99): **104,103,97,95,93 89,67,48,46**

Tote Swingers: 1&2 £4.20, 1&3 £13.70, 2&3 £17.00 CSF £24.64 CT £707.41 TOTE £4.20: £1.40, £2.10, £6.60; EX 28.00 Trifecta £212.00 Pool: £538.67 - 1.88 winning units..

Owner Clarendon Thoroughbred Racing **Bred** Pat Harnett **Trained** Middleham Moor, N Yorks

FOCUS

The front two drew 10l clear in this modest middle-distance handicap. The winner is rated back to last year's nursery best, with the third offering perspective.

Residence And Spa(IRE) Official explanation: jockey said saddle slipped

Around The Clock(USA) Official explanation: jockey said colt ran flat

3461 WILFRED UNDERWOOD MEMORIAL CLASSIFIED STKS 6f

4:45 (4:46) (Class 5) 3-Y-O **£2,266** (£674; £337; £168) **Stalls** Low

Form RPR

3212 **1** **York Glory (USA)**[41] 2180 3-9-0 75 JamieSpencer 4 80
(Kevin Ryan) *trckd ldrs: led wl over 1f out and c wd: hrd rdn fnl f: all out* **5/6**[1]

-200 **2** *nk* **Defence Council (IRE)**[45] 2074 3-9-0 75 FrannyNorton 8 79
(Mel Brittain) *trckd ldrs: effrt over 2f out: wnt 2nd 1f out: hrd rdn and no ex nr fin* **25/1**

-036 **3** *3* **Breezolini**[12] 3052 3-9-0 75 RobertWinston 6 69
(Richard Whitaker) *sn drvn along: outpcd and lost pl over 2f out: kpt on wl to take 3rd last 100yds* **9/2**[2]

4222 **4** *8* **Moral Issue**[10] 3111 3-8-11 74 MichaelO'Connell(3) 3 44
(Jedd O'Keeffe) *led: hdd wl over 1f out: hung lft and wknd fnl f* **9/2**[2]

4-55 **5** *10* **Eshoog (IRE)**[7] 3222 3-9-0 74 PhilipRobinson 2 12
(Clive Brittain) *s.i.s: sn chsng ldrs: drvn over 2f out: wknd over 1f out* **16/1**

1-00 **6** *27* **Kinlochrannoch**[16] 2911 3-9-0 75 PJMcDonald 7 —
(Ben Haslam) *w ldr: wknd over 1f out: eased ins fnl f* **66/1**

1306 **7** *4 ½* **Golden Taurus (IRE)**[10] 3122 3-9-0 72 (p) KierenFallon 5 —
(J W Hills) *s.v.s: a detached in last: eased 2f out* **10/1**[3]

1m 17.35s (0.45) **Going Correction** -0.025s/f (Good) **7** Ran SP% **111.2**

Speed ratings (Par 99): **96,95,91,80,67 31,25**

Tote Swingers: 1&2 £5.50, 1&3 £1.80, 2&3 £7.00 CSF £24.39 TOTE £1.90: £1.80, £5.00; EX 21.30 Trifecta £119.40 Pool: £881.70 - 5.46 winning units..

Owner Salman Rashed **Bred** Paget Bloodstock & Horse France **Trained** Hambleton, N Yorks

■ Stewards' Enquiry : Franny Norton caution: used whip with excessive frequency

Philip Robinson caution: used whip down shoulder in the forehand

FOCUS

This proved much harder than the market suggested it would for York Glory, who has yet to really progress from his Southwell win. The form is rated around the runner-up.

Moral Issue Official explanation: jockey said gelding moved poorly throughout

Eshoog(IRE) Official explanation: jockey said filly lost a shoe

3462 BEST UK RACECOURSES ON TURFTV H'CAP 1m 4y

5:15 (5:15) (Class 5) (0-75,75) 3-Y-O+ **£2,266** (£674; £337; £168) **Stalls** Low

Form RPR

0011 **1** **Regimental (IRE)**[10] 3124 3-9-4 **75** SilvestreDeSousa 7 82+
(Ann Duffield) *hld up in midfield: effrt over 2f out: led over 1f out: edgd lft: drvn out* **9/2**[2]

0023 **2** *1* **Desert Hunter (IRE)**[14] 2985 8-8-9 **56** oh3 KellyHarrison 8 61
(Micky Hammond) *trckd ldng pair: led over 2f out: hdd over 1f out: swtchd rt ins fnl f: kpt on* **12/1**

3130 **3** *1 ¼* **Violent Velocity (IRE)**[17] 2887 8-9-3 **71** ShaneBKelly(7) 1 73
(John Quinn) *trckd ldrs: effrt on ins over 2f out: n.m.r ins fnl f: kpt on same pce* **7/1**

4021 **4** *2 ½* **Classic Descent**[11] 3088 6-9-0 **61** (bt) JamesSullivan 6 57
(Ruth Carr) *hld up in rr: hdwy over 4f out: c wd over 1f out: kpt on same pce* **10/1**

2011 **5** *hd* **Unknown Rebel (IRE)**[12] 3038 3-8-11 **71** AmyRyan(3) 5 65
(Kevin Ryan) *w ldr: led after 2f: hdd over 2f out: one pce over 1f out* **3/1**[1]

0214 **6** *½* **Ra Junior (USA)**[14] 2985 5-9-6 **67** MickyFenton 4 62
(Paul Midgley) *hld up in rr: drvn over 3f out: one pce fnl 2f* **6/1**

-410 **7** *5* **Royal Reverie**[18] 2838 3-9-4 **75** KierenFallon 9 56
(Walter Swinburn) *hld up in rr: effrt over 3f out: c wd 2f out: sn wknd: eased towards fin* **5/1**[3]

0060 **8** *7* **Aussie Blue (IRE)**[14] 2985 7-9-0 **61** RobertWinston 3 28
(Richard Whitaker) *stdd s: in rr: drvn over 3f out: nvr on terms: eased ins fnl f* **16/1**

0200 **9** *13* **Hab Reeh**[10] 3133 3-8-13 **70** RoystonFfrench 2 —
(Clive Brittain) *led 2f: chsd ldrs: lost pl over 1f out: heavily eased towards fin* **50/1**

1m 46.46s (0.56) **Going Correction** -0.025s/f (Good)

WFA 3 from 5yo+ 10lb **9** Ran SP% **111.3**

Speed ratings (Par 103): **96,95,93,91,91 90,85,78,65**

Tote Swingers: 1&2 £7.40, 1&3 £6.30, 2&3 £9.40 CSF £53.64 CT £362.32 TOTE £5.10: £2.20, £2.10, £1.60; EX 53.60 Trifecta £207.70 Pool: £729.86 - 2.60 winning units..

Owner I Farrington & R Chapman **Bred** Deer Forest Stud **Trained** Constable Burton, N Yorks

FOCUS

A fairly ordinary handicap rated around the second and third. the winner looked a bit better than the bare form.

T/Plt: £303.50 to a £1 stake. Pool £74,450.00 - 179.03 winning tickets. T/Qpdt: £78.00 to a £1 stake. Pool £4,197.00 - 39.80 winning tickets. WG

3432 WINDSOR (R-H)

Monday, June 27

OFFICIAL GOING: Good (good to firm in places; 7.8)

Wind: Almost nil Weather: Hot, humid, cloudy

3463 BET ON TOTEPLACEPOT AT TOTESPORT.COM FILLIES' MEDIAN AUCTION MAIDEN STKS 5f 10y

6:40 (6:41) (Class 5) 2-Y-O **£2,266** (£674; £337; £168) **Stalls** Low

Form RPR

52 **1** **Amis Reunis**[14] 2997 2-9-0 0 RyanMoore 3 77
(Richard Hannon) *chsd ldng pair: wnt 2nd over 2f out: rdn and looked hld over 1f out: styd on fnl f: led last strides* **5/4**[1]

04 **2** *hd* **Royal Red**[11] 3092 2-9-0 0 JimCrowley 8 76
(Ralph Beckett) *led against nr side rail: pushed along and looked in command over 1f out: rdn fnl f: hdd last strides* **5/2**[2]

44 **3** *4 ½* **Kyllasie**[56] 1765 2-9-0 0 DaneO'Neill 1 60+
(Richard Hannon) *in tch: prog 1/2-way: pushed along to take 3rd over 1f out: no imp on ldng pair: kpt on* **6/1**[3]

0 **4** *3 ¾* **Poker Hospital**[15] 2962 2-9-0 0 TonyCulhane 6 46+
(George Baker) *hld up in tch: carried hd high whn pushed along fr 1/2-way: kpt on to take 4th fnl f* **22/1**

063 **5** *1 ¾* **River Nova**[28] 2556 2-8-11 0 MatthewDavies(3) 9 40
(Alan Jarvis) *chsd ldr to over 2f out: wknd over 1f out* **66/1**

6 *shd* **Alupka (IRE)** 2-9-0 0 PatDobbs 2 40
(Richard Hannon) *chsd ldrs: outpcd fr 1/2-way: nt on terms after* **14/1**

7 *3* **Sudden Wish (IRE)** 2-9-0 0 PaulDoe 5 29
(Jim Best) *s.i.s: sn pushed along in 7th: nvr on terms* **33/1**

8 *3 ¼* **Two Bridges** 2-9-0 0 JimmyFortune 7 17
(Gary Moore) *slowly away: sn t.o in last: nvr a factor* **16/1**

9 *6* **Auntie Kathryn (IRE)** 2-9-0 0 SaleemGolam 4 —
(Stuart Williams) *slowest away: rn green in last pair: nvr on terms: wknd over 1f out* **25/1**

60.09 secs (-0.21) **Going Correction** -0.20s/f (Firm) **9** Ran SP% **112.5**

Speed ratings (Par 90): **93,92,85,79,76 76,71,66,56**

Tote Swingers: 1&2 £1.10, 1&3 £1.50, 2&3 £2.80 CSF £3.99 TOTE £2.10: £1.10, £1.40, £2.10; EX 5.00 Trifecta £16.90 Pool: £8,597.95 - 374.57 winning units..

Owner Mrs J Wood **Bred** Paddock Space **Trained** East Everleigh, Wilts

FOCUS

Rail on inner line and distances as advertised. After a dry night, the going was changed to good, good to firm in places on a watered track. A modest race for the track, in which the two experienced market leaders pulled clear. Both stepped forward on their previous form.

NOTEBOOK

Amis Reunis got a bit upset in the stalls and never got to grips with a fellow joint-favourite here two weeks ago, but she had decent claims on that form and justified strong support by finding a sustained run to just reel in her main market rival. A £30,000 half-sister to six winners, she should continue to progress and shapes like a move to 6f will suit. (op 6-5 tchd 11-10)

Royal Red showed similar form when beaten around 4l in two previous maiden fillies' events. A solid second favourite, she attacked against the stands' rail but was just worn down. This was a likeable effort from a scopey daughter of Holy Roman Emperor who is well connected, being at out of a dual 5f winning sister to high-class 5f-7f winner Galeota. (op 3-1, tchd 7-2 in places)

Kyllasie was turned over at long odds-on in April on debut and was never dangerous at Warwick last time. She had similar form claims to her stablemate Amis Reunis, but couldn't land a blow from off the pace. (op 13-2 tchd 11-2)

Poker Hospital didn't show much on soft ground when a springer in a Salisbury maiden on debut. She ran very green and looked a bit awkward here but showed a bit of ability staying on late switched to fast ground. Official explanation: vet said filly had been struck into (op 25-1)

River Nova came up short in a Goodwood seller last time and found things tough back in a maiden.

Alupka(IRE), the third of Richard Hannon's trio, was never really involved on debut but she should have learned something and is out of a 1m1f winner, so should be suited by further in due course. (tchd 16-1)

3464 FREE RACING POST FORM AT TOTESPORT.COM (S) STKS 6f

7:10 (7:11) (Class 6) 3-Y-O+ **£1,619** (£481; £240; £120) **Stalls** Low

Form RPR

0022 **1** **Efistorm**[3] 3350 10-9-8 73 HayleyTurner 2 78
(Conor Dore) *chsd ldrs: effrt 2f out: rdn to ld 1f out: styd on and sn in command* **9/4**[1]

3244 **2** *1 ¾* **Miss Firefly**[7] 3217 6-8-7 57 (p) HarryBentley(5) 7 62
(Ron Hodges) *chsd ldr: clsd to chal jst over 1f out: nt qckn w wnr: kpt on* **7/1**[2]

0260 **3** *1 ½* **Dvinsky (USA)**[21] 2756 10-9-8 61 (b) JimmyFortune 1 67
(Michael Squance) *chsd ldrs: pushed along 1/2-way: kpt on one pce fr over 1f out: tk 3rd nr fin* **20/1**

-116 **4** *nk* **The Jailer**[41] 2167 8-8-12 65 (p) RyanPowell(5) 5 61
(John O'Shea) *racd against nr side rail: led: rdn 2f out: hdd & wknd 1f out* **9/1**[3]

4524 **5** *nk* **Fawley Green**[16] 2920 4-8-12 57 (v) JamesRogers(5) 8 60
(William Muir) *settled in last pair: effrt 2f out: kpt on fr over 1f out: nt pce to threaten* **7/1**[2]

353- **6** *1* **Dear Maurice**[219] 7525 7-8-10 73 (t) CharlesBishop(7) 4 57
(Tobias B P Coles) *dwlt: t.k.h: hld up in last pair: effrt on outer 1/2-way: no prog over 1f out* **9/4**[1]

6500 **7** *8* **Griffin Point (IRE)**[16] 2921 4-8-12 50 MartinDwyer 10 26
(William Muir) *towards rr: effrt on outer over 2f out: sn no prog and wknd* **14/1**

0645 **8** *6* **Veuveveuvevoom**[3] 3350 3-8-2 36............................(p) SimonPearce(3) 3 —
(Gerry Enright) *hung lft thrght and racd in centre bef 1/2-way: nvr on terms after* **100/1**

1m 12.83s (-0.17) **Going Correction** -0.20s/f (Firm)
WFA 3 from 4yo+ 7lb **8** Ran SP% **109.0**
Speed ratings (Par 101): **93,90,88,88,87 86,75,67**
Tote Swingers: 1&2 £3.90, 1&3 £11.70, 2&3 £18.00 CSF £17.15 TOTE £2.80: £1.30, £2.20, £3.70; EX 15.90 Trifecta £92.10 Pool: £5,129.44 - 41.18 winning units..There was no bid for the winner.
Owner Sean J Murphy **Bred** E Duggan And D Churchman **Trained** Cowbit, Lincs

FOCUS
A reasonable seller in which a 73-rated joint-favourite scored in gritty style from off the decent pace. The form makes some sense at face value.

3465 BET ON LIVE TENNIS AT TOTESPORT.COM MAIDEN STKS 6f
7:40 (7:44) (Class 5) 3-4-Y-O **£2,266** (£674; £337; £168) **Stalls** Low

Form RPR
23-3 **1** **Midnight Feast**[16] 2924 3-9-3 82.. LukeMorris 8 79+
(Peter Winkworth) *trckd ldr: led over 2f out: drvn over 1f out: styd on wl* **7/4**[1]
2 *1 3/4* **Passing Stranger (IRE)** 3-8-12 0.............................. JimmyFortune 9 68+
(Jeremy Noseda) *s.s and lost several l: prog fr rr 1/2-way: rdn to chse wnr wl over 1f out: styd on but no imp* **7/4**[1]
0 **3** *1 1/2* **Festival Dance**[11] 3091 3-8-9 0.................................. MatthewDavies(3) 1 64
(Ron Hodges) *s.i.s: sn wl in tch: rdn to dispute 2nd 2f out: one pce over 1f out* **100/1**
0-44 **4** *hd* **Tiberius Claudius (IRE)**[59] 1654 3-9-3 77...................... SebSanders 6 68
(George Margarson) *t.k.h: hld up in rr: taken out wd over 1f out: pushed along and styd on steadily: nrst fin* **12/1**
02 **5** *hd* **Crew Cut (IRE)**[23] 2710 3-9-3 0.................................... RobertHavlin 12 67
(Jeremy Gask) *trckd ldrs: pushed along 2f out: outpcd sn after: kpt on steadily* **9/1**[3]
6 *1 1/4* **Hollie** 3-8-12 0.. FergusSweeney 3 58+
(Peter Makin) *hld up in rr: gng wl 2f out: shuffled along and kpt on steadily: fair debut* **66/1**
-200 **7** *nk* **Mixed Emotions (IRE)**[39] 2223 3-8-12 70............................ PatDobbs 7 57+
(Richard Hannon) *taken down early: pushed along in 10th after 2f and in danger of tailing off: sed to run on 2f out: nt clr run sn after: swtchd out wd and kpt on* **40/1**
402 **8** *1 1/2* **Rafaaf (IRE)**[52] 1865 3-9-3 72..................................... AndreaAtzeni 2 58+
(Robert Eddery) *hld up in tch: gng wl enough 2f out: lost pl and squeezed out over 1f out: eased* **8/1**[2]
04 **9** *3* **Adaeze (IRE)**[11] 3091 3-8-12 0.................................. StephenCraine 11 43
(Jonathan Portman) *prom: disp 2nd 2f out: shkn up and wknd over 1f out* **50/1**
0 **10** *11* **Grayfriars**[38] 2266 3-9-3 0....................................... SaleemGolam 4 13
(J R Jenkins) *bolted 1/2-way to post then dismntd and led rest of way: racd freely: led to over 2f out: wknd rapidly* **100/1**
11 *14* **Jeewana** 3-8-12 0.. DaneO'Neill 5 —
(Henry Candy) *s.i.s: outpcd and sn t.o* **10/1**

1m 13.64s (0.64) **Going Correction** -0.20s/f (Firm) **11** Ran SP% **118.5**
Speed ratings (Par 103): **87,84,82,82,82 80,80,78,74,59 40**
Tote Swingers: 1&2 £1.50, 1&3 £26.50, 2&3 £24.90 CSF £4.44 TOTE £3.20: £1.70, £1.10, £11.60; EX 7.90 Trifecta £308.20 Pool: £3,390.53 - 8.14 winning units..
Owner Rupert Williams **Bred** Whitsbury Manor Stud **Trained** Chiddingfold, Surrey
■ Stewards' Enquiry : Jimmy Fortune one-day ban: careless riding (Jul 11)

FOCUS
The leading form contender held off a heavily backed newcomer in this interesting maiden. Modest form, with the winner not needing to match his best.

3466 MORE WIMBLEDON BETTING AT TOTESPORT.COM H'CAP 1m 2f 7y
8:10 (8:13) (Class 4) (0-80,77) 3-Y-O+ **£3,561** (£1,059; £529; £264) **Stalls** Centre

Form RPR
0-01 **1** **Broughtons Swinger**[6] 3256 4-8-12 64................... AdamBeschizza(3) 4 70
(Willie Musson) *trckd ldr 4f: cl up after in modly run contest: squeezed through to ld 2f out: rdn and a holding rivals ins fnl f* **3/1**[2]
2100 **2** *nk* **Edgewater (IRE)**[28] 2047 4-10-0 77..................................... DaneO'Neill 1 82+
(John Akehurst) *hld up in last pair: stl last over 1f out: looking for room after: squeezed through ins fnl f: r.o to press wnr nr fin* **7/1**
4-01 **3** *nk* **Aldwick Bay (IRE)**[24] 2688 3-9-1 76............................... RyanMoore 2 80
(Richard Hannon) *hld up in 5th: looking for room and swtchd rt over 1f out: drvn and r.o fnl f: nt quite able to chal* **5/2**[1]
46-5 **4** *hd* **Royal Etiquette (IRE)**[21] 2771 4-9-1 64......................... HayleyTurner 3 68
(Lawney Hill) *hld up in last pair: effrt towards outer 2f out: squeezed through jst over 1f out: styd on but a hld* **11/1**
5 *1* **Charmeur (USA)**[12] 4-9-13 76.................................(bt) SebSanders 6 78?
(Philip Hobbs) *led at mod pce: hdd and nt qckn 2f out: kpt on same pce fnl f* **33/1**
565 **6** *2 1/2* **Trend Line (IRE)**[52] 1845 3-9-0 75............................... JackMitchell 7 72
(Peter Chapple-Hyam) *prom: chsd ldr after 4f to 2f out: stl on terms over 1f out: wknd ins fnl f* **8/1**
-310 **7** *3 3/4* **May Be Some Time**[18] 2835 3-8-12 73............................ LiamKeniry 5 63
(Stuart Kittow) *trckd ldrs in 4th: cl up wl over 1f out: sn rdn and nt qckn: wknd fnl f* **7/2**[3]

2m 8.11s (-0.59) **Going Correction** -0.20s/f (Firm)
WFA 3 from 4yo 12lb **7** Ran SP% **110.7**
Speed ratings (Par 105): **94,93,93,93,92 90,87**
Tote Swingers: 1&2 £4.80, 1&3 £1.20, 2&3 £4.30 CSF £22.30 CT £55.31 TOTE £4.50: £2.60, £3.90; EX 33.10 Trifecta £91.50 Pool: £514.88 - 4.16 winning units..
Owner Broughton Thermal Insulation **Bred** Michael E Broughton **Trained** Newmarket, Suffolk
■ Stewards' Enquiry : Adam Beschizza two-day ban: careless riding (Jul 14-15)

FOCUS
There was a tight four-way finish to this steadily run handicap. Very ordinary form.

3467 TOTEPOOL SUPPORTS CLIC SARGENT FILLIES' H'CAP 1m 3f 135y
8:40 (8:43) (Class 5) (0-70,70) 3-Y-O+ **£2,266** (£674; £337; £168) **Stalls** Centre

Form RPR
5-03 **1** **Undulant Way**[16] 2904 3-8-11 67.. PatDobbs 8 78
(Amanda Perrett) *prom: effrt 3f out: led 2f out: rdn and forged clr fnl f* **11/2**[2]
-441 **2** *3 1/2* **Choral Festival**[14] 3003 5-9-2 63............................. HarryBentley(5) 12 68
(John Bridger) *hld up in midfield: prog gng wl fr 3f out: chal 2f out: outpcd jst over 1f out* **6/1**[3]
2313 **3** *1/2* **Broughtons Paradis (IRE)**[14] 3003 5-9-9 65........... StevieDonohoe 11 69
(Willie Musson) *hld up in 8th: stdy prog on outer fr 3f out: rdn and nt qckn over 1f out: one pce after* **6/1**[3]
-010 **4** *nse* **Miss Topsy Turvy (IRE)**[18] 2850 3-8-8 64......................... TedDurcan 9 68+
(John Dunlop) *s.s: hld up in last trio: rdn over 3f out: prog on outer 2f out: styd on: unable to chal* **4/1**[1]
6003 **5** *1 1/2* **Corvette**[18] 2850 3-8-5 61.. AdrianMcCarthy 2 62
(J R Jenkins) *trckd ldrs: cl enough 2f out: sn rdn and nt qckn: one pce after* **16/1**
-453 **6** *nk* **Glyn Ceiriog**[15] 2957 3-8-12 68...................................... TonyCulhane 4 69
(George Baker) *pressed ldr: led after 4f to over 5f out: led again 4f out to 2f out: shuffled along and fdd* **9/1**
2635 **7** *1 3/4* **Woop Woop (IRE)**[8] 3202 3-8-13 69................................. SebSanders 1 69+
(Stef Higgins) *hld up in last trio: prog on inner 3f out: trying to cl whn nt clr run over 1f out: nt rcvr* **12/1**
0430 **8** *1 3/4* **Commerce**[24] 2685 4-9-9 65... RyanMoore 10 60
(Gary Moore) *walked to post rdrless: hld up last: shkn up over 2f out: kpt on but nvr on terms* **12/1**
0-33 **9** *1 3/4* **Diverting**[37] 2307 3-8-5 61.. LukeMorris 6 53
(William Jarvis) *chsd ldrs: rdn 3f out: lost pl wl over 1f out: steadily wknd* **14/1**
00-2 **10** *2* **Geblah (IRE)**[31] 2463 3-8-6 65................................. MartinHarley(3) 7 54
(David Simcock) *a towards rr: rdn 4f out: sn struggling* **16/1**
060 **11** *1 1/4* **Compassion**[18] 2840 3-9-0 70...................................... HayleyTurner 3 56
(Michael Bell) *nt that wl away but sn pushed up to go prom: led over 5f out to 4f out: wknd qckly 2f out* **20/1**
6004 **12** *6* **It's Dubai Dolly**[14] 3003 5-8-12 54............................... MartinDwyer 5 30
(Alastair Lidderdale) *led 4f: lost pl 4f out: wknd over 2f out* **20/1**

2m 27.07s (-2.43) **Going Correction** -0.20s/f (Firm)
WFA 3 from 4yo+ 14lb **12** Ran SP% **117.3**
Speed ratings (Par 100): **100,97,97,97,96 96,94,93,92,91 90,86**
Tote Swingers: 1&2 £6.30, 1&3 £6.10, 2&3 £8.10 CSF £38.07 CT £144.55 TOTE £5.50: £1.70, £2.30, £2.30; EX 40.00 Trifecta £122.90 Pool: £745.89 - 4.49 winning units..
Owner Mrs Alexandra J Chandris **Bred** Mrs J Chandris **Trained** Pulborough, W Sussex

FOCUS
This looked a competitive fillies' handicap but a relatively unexposed type was a runaway winner. The form looks pretty solid.
Woop Woop(IRE) Official explanation: jockey said filly was denied a clear run
It's Dubai Dolly Official explanation: jockey said mare had no more to give

3468 BET TOTEPOOL ON 0800 221221 H'CAP 1m 67y
9:10 (9:11) (Class 5) (0-70,70) 3-Y-O+ **£2,266** (£674; £337; £168) **Stalls** Low

Form RPR
0062 **1** **Hip Hip Hooray**[19] 2829 5-9-6 62...................................... IanMongan 8 71+
(Luke Dace) *hld up in midfield: prog on outer 3f out: chsd ldr wl over 1f out: clsd to ld last 75yds: shade cleverly* **15/2**
6214 **2** *nk* **Catchanova (IRE)**[11] 3071 4-9-8 64........................... FergusSweeney 4 72
(Eve Johnson Houghton) *trckd ldr: led over 5f out: clr over 2f out: kpt on: hdd and hld last 75yds* **4/1**[2]
5540 **3** *1 1/2* **Ilie Nastase (FR)**[10] 3130 7-9-7 63.........................(b) HayleyTurner 12 68
(Conor Dore) *t.k.h and hld up in rr: coaxed along 3f out: no prog tl r.o over 1f out on outer: tk 3rd last 100yds* **12/1**
4005 **4** *1 1/2* **Starwatch**[17] 2879 4-8-12 59.................................... HarryBentley(5) 10 60
(John Bridger) *trckd ldrs: effrt to dispute 2nd 2f out: nt qckn over 1f out: readily hld after* **16/1**
3053 **5** *2 3/4* **Regal Rave (USA)**[13] 3017 4-9-2 58................................. DaneO'Neill 11 53
(Mouse Hamilton-Fairley) *hld up wl in rr: effrt on outer 3f out: drvn and kpt on same pce fnl 2f: no threat* **20/1**
153 **6** *nk* **Foxley (IRE)**[7] 3219 3-9-1 67...................................... MartinDwyer 1 59
(Brian Meehan) *led to over 5f out: chsd ldr to 2f out: grad wknd* **9/2**[3]
30-0 **7** *1* **Point Du Jour (FR)**[10] 3133 3-9-4 70............................ SebSanders 9 60
(Ian Wood) *stdd s: hld up last: taken to outer over 3f out: sme prog 2f out: pushed along and nvr on terms* **16/1**
2640 **8** *1/2* **Prince Of Thebes (IRE)**[28] 2561 10-8-9 56..................... MarkCoumbe(5) 5 47
(Michael Attwater) *s.s: mostly in last trio: no prog over 2f out:modest hdwy fnl f* **28/1**
-514 **9** *hd* **Prince Of Sorrento**[14] 2999 4-9-9 70........................ NathanAlison(5) 7 60
(John Akehurst) *t.k.h: trckd ldrs: awkward bnd 6f out and snatched up: no prog 2f out: fdd* **11/4**[1]
2660 **10** *2* **Pipers Piping (IRE)**[10] 3130 5-8-12 61...................(p) LauraSimpson(7) 2 47
(Michael Squance) *t.k.h: prom: steadily wknd on inner fr over 2f out* **40/1**
31-0 **11** *5* **Scottish Glen**[19] 2822 5-10-0 70.. JimCrowley 13 44
(Patrick Chamings) *prom: rdn over 2f out: wknd wl over 1f out* **10/1**
030- **12** *1/2* **Formidable Guest**[299] 5663 7-9-1 57............................... RobertHavlin 6 30
(Jamie Poulton) *hld up in midfield: lost pl totally bhd rivals over 3f out and sn last: no ch after* **33/1**

1m 43.32s (-1.38) **Going Correction** -0.20s/f (Firm)
WFA 3 from 4yo+ 10lb **12** Ran SP% **118.8**
Speed ratings (Par 103): **98,97,96,94,91 91,90,90,89,87 82,82**
Tote Swingers: 1&2 £7.30, 1&3 £15.70, 2&3 £12.10 CSF £36.14 CT £369.50 TOTE £9.10: £2.60, £1.70, £3.30; EX 44.90 Trifecta £567.20 Part won. Pool: £766.53 - 0.90 winning units..
Owner M C S D Racing Partnership **Bred** Mrs R S Evans **Trained** Five Oaks, W Sussex

FOCUS
An ordinary handicap. The pace was fairly steady and the performance of the winner can be marked up because she came from some way back to catch the long-time leader, but overall the form is not rated too positively.
Prince Of Thebes(IRE) Official explanation: jockey said gelding was slowly away
Prince Of Sorrento Official explanation: jockey said gelding was unable to handle the bend
T/Jkpt: £1,098.50 to a £1 stake. Pool £126,537.00 - 81.78 winning tickets. T/Plt: £28.70 to a £1 stake. Pool £128,363.00 - 3,261.24 winning tickets. T/Qpdt: £17.60 to a £1 stake. Pool £6,765.00 - 283.10 winning tickets. JN

3234 WOLVERHAMPTON (A.W) (L-H)
Monday, June 27

OFFICIAL GOING: Standard
Wind: Fresh behind Weather: Overcast

3469 32 ONLINE CASINO MEDIAN AUCTION MAIDEN STKS 1m 4f 50y(P)
2:30 (2:30) (Class 6) 3-4-Y-O **£1,706** (£503; £252) **Stalls** Low

Form RPR
25-2 **1** **A Boy Named Suzi**[21] 2764 3-9-0 76.................................. LukeMorris 1 79
(James Eustace) *hld up: hdwy over 2f out: chsd ldr over 1f out: r.o u.p to ld towards fin* **7/4**[2]
-562 **2** *nk* **Hidden Valley**[41] 2175 3-8-9 74...................................... LiamKeniry 2 73
(Andrew Balding) *chsd ldrs: led 2f out: sn rdn: hdd towards fin* **8/11**[1]
0 **3** *4 1/2* **Princesse Gaelle**[12] 3043 3-8-9 0................................. AndreaAtzeni 3 66
(Marco Botti) *a.p: led over 2f out: sn hdd: no ex fnl f* **33/1**

06 **4** ¾ **Tanmawy (IRE)**[23] 2723 3-9-0 0 TadhgO'Shea 5 70
(Ed Dunlop) *hld up: hdwy over 1f out: sn rdn and hung lft: styd on same pce* **10/1**[3]

0-0 **5** 11 **Sulliman**[15] 2956 4-10-0 0 SebSanders 6 52
(George Margarson) *chsd ldr after 1f: led 3f out: sn rdn and hdd: wknd over 1f out* **50/1**

50 **6** 39 **Chlodan**[31] 2457 4-9-9 0 DaleSwift(5) 4 —
(Ollie Pears) *led at stdy pce tl hdd 3f out: sn rdn and wknd: t.o* **50/1**

2m 42.26s (1.16) **Going Correction** -0.05s/f (Stan)
WFA 3 from 4yo 14lb **6** Ran SP% **110.2**
Speed ratings (Par 101): **94,93,90,90,82 56**
Tote Swingers: 1&2 £1.30, 1&3 £4.60, 2&3 £5.10 CSF £3.20 TOTE £2.90: £1.70, £1.10; EX 3.90.

Owner Greenstead Hall Racing Ltd **Bred** Greenstead Hall Racing **Trained** Newmarket, Suffolk

FOCUS
There seemed to be a bit more kickback than usual. The first two finishers both came into this with official marks in the mid-70s and this was just an ordinary maiden. The pace was modest and the time was over six seconds above standard. The first two may not have been at their best in a muddling race.

3470 32 FOR SLOTS H'CAP 5f 216y(P)
3:00 (3:00) (Class 6) (0-65,65) 3-Y-O **£1,706** (£503; £252) **Stalls** Low

Form RPR

0251 **1** **Roodee Queen**[21] 2756 3-9-5 **63** LiamKeniry 13 71
(Milton Bradley) *chsd ldr 5f out: led over 1f out: drvn out* **15/2**

6432 **2** ¾ **Abeer (USA)**[17] 2869 3-9-5 **63** (p) TadhgO'Shea 9 68
(Ed Dunlop) *hld up: hdwy over 1f out: r.o: wnt 2nd post: nt rch wnr* **4/1**[2]

4244 **3** nse **Climaxfortackle (IRE)**[11] 3079 3-9-4 **62** (v[1]) RobbieFitzpatrick 7 67
(Derek Shaw) *trckd ldrs: rdn to chse wnr over 1f out: styd on: lost 2nd post* **11/2**

235 **4** 2½ **Piccoluck**[41] 2186 3-9-6 **64** WilliamBuick 11 61
(Amy Weaver) *s.i.s: hld up: rdn over 2f out: r.o wl ins fnl f: nvr nrr* **7/2**[1]

5536 **5** hd **Merrjanah**[9] 3180 3-9-6 **64** ChrisCatlin 3 60
(Clive Brittain) *in rr: rdn over 2f out: hdwy over 1f out: r.o: nt rch ldrs* **5/1**[3]

2065 **6** 6 **Reachtothestars (USA)**[16] 2918 3-9-1 **59** (t) NeilCallan 6 36
(Noel Quinlan) *led: rdn and hdd over 1f out: wknd fnl f* **8/1**

0126 **7** shd **Loves Theme (IRE)**[21] 2770 3-8-12 **63** (v) MissAlexOwen(7) 12 40
(Alan Bailey) *chsd ldrs: rdn over 2f out: wknd over 1f out* **14/1**

0304 **8** 1 **Passing Moment**[14] 2993 3-8-4 **48** MartinLane 5 22
(Brian Baugh) *sn pushed along in rr: hdwy over 2f out: wknd over 1f out* **14/1**

-026 **9** 44 **Ezzles (USA)**[4] 3321 3-9-2 **65** KieranO'Neill(5) 2 —
(Alan McCabe) *chsd ldrs tl wknd over 2f out: eased over 1f out: t.o* **16/1**

1m 15.05s (0.05) **Going Correction** -0.05s/f (Stan) **9** Ran SP% **116.4**
Speed ratings (Par 97): **97,96,95,92,92 84,84,82,24**
Tote Swingers: 1&2 £6.70, 1&3 £10.80, 2&3 £4.00 CSF £37.89 CT £181.65 TOTE £9.30: £3.30, £1.70, £2.00; EX 32.90.
Owner T A Godbert **Bred** Tom & Evelyn Yates **Trained** Sedbury, Gloucs

FOCUS
A modest handicap and they didn't seem to go that quick for a sprint. Nothing was progressive and the winner is rated to her 2yo best.
Ezzles(USA) Official explanation: vet said gelding pulled up lame

3471 32 FOR BLACKJACK (S) STKS 5f 20y(P)
3:30 (3:30) (Class 6) 3-Y-O+ **£1,706** (£503; £252) **Stalls** Low

Form RPR

2440 **1** **Grudge**[18] 2845 6-9-5 63 (b) HayleyTurner 4 71
(Conor Dore) *mde all: rdn over 1f out: r.o* **6/1**

4506 **2** 1½ **Atlantic Beach**[18] 2832 6-9-5 68 LiamKeniry 9 66+
(Milton Bradley) *hld up: hung lft and r.o u.p ins fnl f: wnt 2nd post: nt rch wnr* **8/1**

1550 **3** nse **Mottley Crewe**[28] 2543 4-9-10 72 JamesDoyle 6 70
(Michael Dods) *prom: rdn 1/2-way: r.o* **3/1**[2]

3252 **4** 1½ **Decider (USA)**[7] 3216 8-9-10 64 (b) LukeMorris 2 65
(Ronald Harris) *prom: chsd wnr 3f out: rdn over 1f out: hung lft and no ex ins fnl f* **4/1**[3]

00-6 **5** 3¾ **Lady Vivien**[25] 2655 5-8-9 47 (p) DaleSwift(5) 5 42
(George Foster) *prom: rdn 1/2-way: wknd over 1f out* **33/1**

00-0 **6** ½ **Flaxen Lake**[169] 102 4-9-5 50 ChrisCatlin 7 45
(Milton Bradley) *chsd wnr 2f: sn rdn: wknd over 1f out* **50/1**

6432 **7** 1¾ **Jigajig**[21] 2766 4-9-0 69 (p) JulieBurke(5) 3 38
(Kevin Ryan) *hld up: rdn over 1f out: nvr on terms* **15/8**[1]

61.63 secs (-0.67) **Going Correction** -0.05s/f (Stan) **7** Ran SP% **110.1**
Speed ratings (Par 101): **103,100,100,98,92 91,88**
Tote Swingers: 1&2 £3.50, 1&3 £3.80, 2&3 £6.10 CSF £47.67 TOTE £5.90: £3.20, £3.10; EX 41.10.There was no bid for the winner. Mottley Crewe was claimed by Mr S. Arnold for £6,000.
Owner Mrs Jennifer Marsh **Bred** D H Brailsford **Trained** Cowbit, Lincs

FOCUS
An ordinary seller rated around the front-running winner.

3472 BRITISH STALLION STUDS SUPPORTING BRITISH RACING E B F MAIDEN STKS 7f 32y(P)
4:00 (4:01) (Class 5) 2-Y-O **£3,238** (£963; £481; £240) **Stalls** High

Form RPR

1 **Ghostwriting (USA)** 2-9-3 0 WilliamBuick 1 76+
(John Gosden) *led 1f: chsd ldrs: outpcd 1/2-way: hdwy over 1f out: hmpd ins fnl f: r.o to ld nr fin: readily* **4/1**[2]

4 **2** nk **Juno The Muffinman (IRE)**[11] 3076 2-9-3 0 RichardKingscote 8 75
(Tom Dascombe) *trckd ldrs: rdn to ld ins fnl f: hung rt: hdd nr fin* **5/1**[3]

3 **3** 2¾ **Repeater**[11] 3076 2-9-3 0 SebSanders 9 68
(Sir Mark Prescott Bt) *prom: chsd ldr over 5f out: rdn and ev ch fr over 1f out: sn hung rt: no ex wl ins fnl f* **2/1**[1]

00 **4** ¾ **Moon Trip**[33] 2395 2-9-3 0 NeilCallan 5 66
(Mark Johnston) *led 6f out: rdn over 1f out: hdd ins fnl f: nt clr run sn after: styd on same pce* **16/1**

34 **5** 4 **Rock Canyon (IRE)**[17] 2882 2-9-3 0 RobertHavlin 2 56
(Robert Mills) *hld up in tch: rdn over 1f out: wknd fnl f* **2/1**[1]

0 **6** 13 **Milwr**[46] 2017 2-9-3 0 AndreaAtzeni 7 25
(Chris Dwyer) *s.i.s: hld up: rdn over 2f out: sn wknd* **33/1**

00 **7** 3 **Hiding In The Open (IRE)**[39] 2214 2-9-0 0 LouisBeuzelin(3) 3 17
(Brian Meehan) *hld up: rdn and wknd over 2f out* **66/1**

00 **8** 2¾ **Street Angel (IRE)**[16] 2914 2-8-12 0 LiamJones 4 5
(Alan Bailey) *hld up: rdn and wknd over 2f out* **100/1**

9 11 **Red Hot Penny (IRE)** 2-9-3 0 MartinDwyer 6 —
(Brian Meehan) *s.s: outpcd* **25/1**

1m 29.69s (0.09) **Going Correction** -0.05s/f (Stan) **9** Ran SP% **118.5**
Speed ratings (Par 93): **97,96,93,92,88 73,69,66,54**
Tote Swingers: 1&2 £3.00, 2&3 £2.90 CSF £24.38 TOTE £5.00: £1.20, £1.90, £1.10; EX 28.50.
Owner H R H Princess Haya Of Jordan **Bred** Darley **Trained** Newmarket, Suffolk
■ The first winner in Britain as a sire for brilliant 2004 Breeders' Cup Classic winner Ghostzapper.

FOCUS
A decent maiden for the course, rated around the race averages. The pace was overly strong and the third and fourth-placed finishers, Repeater and Moon Trip, were poorly ridden. They were eyeballing each other from well before halfway and unsurprisingly they were picked off in the straight. There should be better to come from both.

NOTEBOOK
Ghostwriting(USA) ◆ was given a smart ride by William Buick, being settled just off the pace for an educational introduction. He lost his place quite badly around the final bend (touched 80 on Betfair in running), but was given time to hit full stride and looked likely to get there from over a furlong out, with the leaders getting tired. The race unfolded in his favour, but he's value for further as he was bumped near the line and wasn't given a hard ride. This was very much the kind of introduction he can be expected to improve considerably from and he's related to some smart types in the US, so he rates a pretty useful prospect. (tchd 7-1)
Juno The Muffinman(IRE) hung right when he got the front, but it looked just greenness and he wouldn't have beaten the winner anyway. This was an improvement on his debut, where he finished behind todays' third, and he can step forward again. (tchd 7-2)
Repeater had too much use made of him, taking on the fourth, but can do better. (tchd 13-8)
Moon Trip did too much and he can do better in nurseries.
Rock Canyon(IRE) was in the right place early considering how the race unfolded, which makes the absence of a finishing kick all the more disappointing. He had shown plenty of ability on his first two starts on turf, so it's too early to write him off. (op 11-4)

3473 32 FOR POKER APPRENTICE CLAIMING STKS 7f 32y(P)
4:30 (4:30) (Class 6) 4-Y-O+ **£1,706** (£503; £252) **Stalls** High

Form RPR

4210 **1** **Fleetwoodsands (IRE)**[63] 1558 4-8-11 69 (t) DaleSwift 8 71
(Ollie Pears) *led 6f out: rdn over 1f out: edgd lft ins fnl f: jst hld on* **10/3**[2]

4315 **2** ½ **Jordaura**[3] 3348 5-9-5 76 LucyKBarry(3) 2 81+
(Tony Carroll) *hld up: r.o ins fnl f: wnt 2nd nr fin: nt rch wnr* **11/4**[1]

6323 **3** ½ **Could It Be Magic**[60] 1634 4-9-1 72 (b) JakePayne(5) 4 77
(Bill Turner) *s.i.s: sn prom: chsd wnr over 2f out: rdn over 1f out: hung lft ins fnl f: r.o: lost 2nd nr fin* **8/1**

-060 **4** ½ **Whispering Spirit (IRE)**[12] 3038 5-8-11 78 (p) JulieBurke 3 67
(Ann Duffield) *prom: pushed along 1/2-way: rdn and hung lft fr over 1f out: styng on whn n.m.r nr fin* **5/1**

0006 **5** 3¾ **Lady Florence**[4] 3326 6-8-3 58 ClaireMurray(7) 5 56
(David C Griffiths) *chsd ldr over 4f: sn rdn: hmpd and no ex ins fnl f* **25/1**

0606 **6** 2¼ **Salerosa (IRE)**[12] 3036 6-8-12 79 RosieJessop(3) 7 55
(Ann Duffield) *prom: racd keenly: rdn over 2f out: wknd fnl f* **8/1**

2261 **7** 17 **Grand Piano (IRE)**[26] 2605 4-8-11 68 (v) ThomasBrown(5) 1 10
(Andrew Balding) *s.i.s: outpcd* **4/1**[3]

1m 29.29s (-0.31) **Going Correction** -0.05s/f (Stan) **7** Ran SP% **112.5**
Speed ratings (Par 101): **99,98,97,97,93 90,71**
Tote Swingers: 1&2 £2.60, 1&3 £3.80, 2&3 £3.30 CSF £12.49 TOTE £4.00: £2.20, £1.50; EX 15.20.Fleetwoodsands claimed by Mr J. M. Bradley for £5,500.
Owner Ollie Pears **Bred** Gary O'Reilly **Trained** Norton, N Yorks
■ Stewards' Enquiry : Jake Payne one-day ban: careless riding (Jul 11)

FOCUS
A modest claimer and they didn't seem to go that quick. The winner did not quite need to match his best.

3474 WOLVERHAMPTON-RACECOURSE.CO.UK H'CAP 1m 4f 50y(P)
5:00 (5:00) (Class 4) (0-80,79) 3-Y-O **£3,238** (£963; £481; £240) **Stalls** Low

Form RPR

1102 **1** **Lexi's Boy (IRE)**[2] 3376 3-8-13 **76** JulieBurke(5) 5 81
(Kevin Ryan) *mde all: pushed along over 4f out: drvn out* **15/8**[1]

01-0 **2** 1¾ **Quiz Mistress**[24] 2695 3-9-4 **76** (p) NeilCallan 2 78
(Gerard Butler) *hld up in tch: chsd wnr over 1f out: sn shkn up and hung rt: nt run on* **7/2**[3]

-461 **3** 2¼ **Mojolika**[28] 2571 3-8-9 **67** (e) GrahamGibbons 1 65
(Tim Easterby) *chsd wnr: chal over 4f out tl rdn over 2f out: no ex fnl f* **9/4**[2]

0-45 **4** shd **Hollow Tree**[39] 2228 3-8-12 **70** LiamKeniry 4 68
(Andrew Balding) *prom: rdn over 3f out: outpcd over 2f out: styd on ins fnl f* **4/1**

2m 39.16s (-1.94) **Going Correction** -0.05s/f (Stan) **4** Ran SP% **107.8**
Speed ratings (Par 101): **104,102,101,101**
CSF £8.32 TOTE £2.20; EX 6.40.
Owner Mrs Margaret Forsyth **Bred** R S Cockerill (farms) Ltd & Peter Dodd **Trained** Hambleton, N Yorks
■ Stewards' Enquiry : Julie Burke caution: used whip with excessive frequency.

FOCUS
A disappointing turnout numerically, although the prize money fell £1,300 below the tariff set by the Horsemen's Group. The winner set a fair pace and probably didn't have to improve on his latest Chester form.

3475 32 FOR BINGO H'CAP 1m 141y(P)
5:30 (5:30) (Class 6) (0-60,59) 3-Y-O+ **£1,706** (£503; £252) **Stalls** Low

Form RPR

0005 **1** **Justcallmehandsome**[7] 3235 9-9-6 **58** (v) LucyKBarry(7) 5 67
(Dominic Ffrench Davis) *hld up: hdwy 2f out: rdn to ld ins fnl f: r.o* **8/1**

4652 **2** ½ **Kyle Of Bute**[7] 3235 5-10-0 **59** (p) J-PGuillambert 6 67
(Brian Baugh) *hld up: hdwy over 1f out: rdn ins fnl f: r.o* **3/1**[1]

5321 **3** ½ **Pie Poudre**[77] 1273 4-9-11 **56** (b[1]) WilliamCarson 8 63
(Roy Brotherton) *hld up: hdwy u.p over 1f out: hung lft: r.o* **7/1**[3]

-066 **4** 2 **William Van Gogh**[73] 1372 4-10-0 **59** (b[1]) DavidNolan 12 61
(Michael Easterby) *hld up: r.o ins fnl f: nrst fin* **20/1**

0-00 **5** nse **Peter Tchaikovsky**[7] 3235 5-9-5 **55** DaleSwift(5) 1 57
(Ian McInnes) *led: rdn over 1f out: hdd and no ex ins fnl f* **66/1**

1350 **6** nse **Diddums**[6] 3256 5-8-12 **50** KatiaScallan(7) 10 52
(Alastair Lidderdale) *hld up: hdwy over 1f out: styd on* **13/2**[2]

5023 **7** 1¼ **Aggbag**[5] 3280 7-8-9 **47** GeorgeDowning(7) 2 46
(Tony Carroll) *chsd ldrs: pushed along over 2f out: no ex fnl f* **15/2**

-060 **8** 3¾ **Smart Step**[12] 3039 3-8-11 **53** NeilCallan 7 43
(Mark Johnston) *chsd ldr: rdn over 2f out: wknd ins fnl f* **7/1**[3]

00/1 **9** 1¾ **Dannios**[19] 2828 5-9-3 **55** (t) HayleyBurton(7) 4 41
(Ed Walker) *s.s: outpcd* **7/1**[3]

1400 **10** 1¾ **Pilgrim Dancer (IRE)**[7] 3235 4-9-9 **59** (v) BrianToomey(5) 9 41
(Patrick Morris) *prom: rdn over 2f out: wknd over 1f out* **25/1**

/-56 **11** ½ **Missprint**[77] 1277 4-9-2 **52**.. JemmaMarshall(5) 3 33
(Brian Baugh) *chsd ldrs: rdn over 2f out: wknd over 1f out* **50/1**

1234 **12** 1 ¼ **Charlietoo**[25] 2655 5-9-1 **51**..(p) RyanClark(5) 11 29
(Edward Bevan) *chsd ldrs: rdn 3f out: wknd over 1f out* **12/1**

1m 50.62s (0.12) **Going Correction** -0.05s/f (Stan)
WFA 3 from 4yo+ 11lb 12 Ran SP% **118.5**
Speed ratings (Par 101): **97,96,96,94,94 94,93,89,88,86 86,85**
Tote Swingers: 1&2 £7.50, 1&3 £11.90, 2&3 £4.40 CSF £31.14 CT £181.32 TOTE £10.70: £2.60, £1.70, £2.60; EX 27.50.
Owner Mrs J E Taylor **Bred** Mrs J E Taylor **Trained** Lambourn, Berks

FOCUS
A modest handicap run at a fair pace. Straightforward form.
T/Plt: £165.80 to a £1 stake. Pool £73,009.00 - 321.31 winning tickets. T/Qpdt: £59.10 to a £1 stake. Pool £4,090.00 - 51.20 winning tickets. CR

3249 BRIGHTON (L-H)

Tuesday, June 28

OFFICIAL GOING: Good (good to firm in places) changing to good after race 2 (3.00)
Wind: light half behind Weather: thunder storms

3476 HARDINGS CATERING H'CAP 5f 213y
2:30 (2:31) (Class 6) (0-55,58) 3-Y-0+ **£1,619** (£481; £240; £120) **Stalls** Low

Form RPR

2043 **1** **Interakt**[14] 3019 4-9-1 **54**.. HarryBentley(5) 11 62
(Joseph Tuite) *chsd ldng pair: rdn over 1f out: styd on u.p to go 2nd and clsng on ldr ins fnl f: led fnl 75yds: kpt on* **7/2**[1]

5542 **2** *nk* **Talamahana**[17] 2921 6-9-6 **54**..(v) ChrisCatlin 1 61
(Andrew Haynes) *racd off the pce in midfield: rdn over 2f out: hdwy u.p over 1f out: ev ch fnl 50yds: kpt on* **8/1**[3]

0050 **3** 1 ¼ **What Katie Did (IRE)**[43] 2162 6-8-12 **46** oh1.......(p) RussKennemore 13 49
(Milton Bradley) *led and sn clr: stl clr and rdn over 1f out: tiring u.p ins fnl f: hdd fnl 75yds: wknd towards fin* **16/1**

05-6 **4** ¾ **Heavenly Pursuit**[77] 1284 3-8-11 **55**........................ MatthewDavies(3) 4 54
(Jim Boyle) *chsd clr ldr: rdn wl over 1f out: drvn and clsng on ldr 1f out: lost 2nd and styd on same pce ins fnl f* **20/1**

5240 **5** ½ **Dancing Welcome**[17] 2921 5-9-5 **53**..(b) LiamKeniry 9 52
(Milton Bradley) *racd off the pce in midfield: rdn and swtchd rt 2f out: styd on u.p ins fnl f: nt rch ldrs* **7/2**[1]

5052 **6** ½ **Bold Ring**[7] 3253 5-9-5 **53**.. EddieCreighton 8 50
(Edward Creighton) *stdd s: racd wl off the pce in last trio: rdn and effrt over 2f out: hdwy u.p jst over 1f out: kpt on ins fnl f: nt rch ldrs* **8/1**[3]

646 **7** 3 ¼ **Kate Skate**[10] 3190 4-9-2 **53**..(b[1]) KierenFox(3) 5 40
(Gay Kelleway) *v.s.a: wl bhd in rr: effrt on inner over 2f out: rdn and kpt on fr over 1f out: nvr trbld ldrs* **18/1**

4161 **8** 1 **Athaakeel (IRE)**[7] 3254 5-9-10 **58** 6ex........................(b) CathyGannon 3 42
(Ronald Harris) *taken down early: midfield whn barging match w rival and lost pl after 1f: racd off the pce towards rr after: rdn and effrt in centre over 2f out: drvn and plugged on fr over 1f out: nvr trbld ldrs* **4/1**[2]

6-00 **9** ¾ **Gazamali (IRE)**[112] 798 4-8-10 **51**.. DavidKenny(7) 7 32
(Michael Scudamore) *a wl off the pce in last trio: n.d* **12/1**

0050 **10** 7 **The Wonga Coup (IRE)**[7] 3253 4-9-2 **50**........................(b[1]) IanMongan 2 9
(Pat Phelan) *taken down early: midfield whn barging match w rival sn after s: rdn and struggling over 2f out: wknd 2f out: wl bhd and eased ins fnl f* **25/1**

3605 **11** ¾ **Fairy Tales**[7] 3254 3-9-0 **55**.. EddieAhern 6 10
(John Bridger) *a wl off the pce towards rr: rdn and no hdwy in centre over 2f out: wl bhd and eased ins fnl f* **20/1**

69.37s (0.63) **Going Correction** -0.05s/f (Good)
WFA 3 from 4yo+ 7lb 11 Ran SP% **118.9**
Speed ratings (Par 101): **102,101,99,98,98 97,93,91,90,81 80**
toteswingers:1&2:£6.70, 2&3:£14.50, 1&3:£13.30 CSF £31.36 CT £407.67 TOTE £3.40: £1.10, £3.20, £5.20; EX 33.70 Trifecta £402.20 Part won. Pool of £543.57 - 0.60 winning units..
Owner Heart Of The South Racing **Bred** P C Hunt **Trained** Great Shefford, Berkshire
■ The first training success for Joseph Tuite.
■ Stewards' Enquiry : Chris Catlin one-day ban: used whip with excessive frequency without giving mare time to respond (Jul 12)

FOCUS
Course at inner configuration and distances as advertised. A low-grade sprint handicap. Straightforward but weak form.
Kate Skate Official explanation: jockey said filly was slowly away

3477 BRIGHTON RACECOURSE CAR BOOT EVERY SUNDAY H'CAP 7f 214y
3:00 (3:00) (Class 5) (0-70,70) 4-Y-0+ **£2,266** (£674; £337; £168) **Stalls** Low

Form RPR

4-23 **1** **Phluke**[33] 2420 10-8-10 **59**.. CathyGannon 3 67
(Eve Johnson Houghton) *w ldr tl led over 4f out: rdn ent fnl 2f: narrowly hdd over 1f out: led again ins fnl f: kpt on wl fnl 100yds: rdn out* **5/1**[1]

0431 **2** ¾ **Mandhooma**[14] 3019 5-9-0 **63**.. ChrisCatlin 5 69
(Peter Hiatt) *hld up in midfield: rdn and effrt in centre over 2f out: kpt on u.p to chse wnr wl ins fnl f: no imp fnl 50yds* **11/2**[2]

6003 **3** 1 ¾ **Pytheas (USA)**[17] 2922 4-8-8 **57**.. KierenFallon 9 59
(Michael Attwater) *chsd ldng pair: wnt 2nd over 3f out: rdn to chal 2f out: led narrowly over 1f out: hdd ins fnl f: no ex and btn fnl 100yds* **7/1**

0022 **4** *hd* **Ivory Lace**[7] 3250 10-8-13 **67**.. HarryBentley(5) 2 69
(Steve Woodman) *chsd ldrs: cl 3rd and rdn whn n.m.r over 1f out: kpt on same pce u.p ins fnl f* **6/1**[3]

-344 **5** 2 ¾ **Intiqaal (IRE)**[20] 2815 4-9-4 **67**..(t) TadhgO'Shea 4 62
(Ed Dunlop) *stdd s: hld up in last trio: rdn and effrt whn swtchd rt wl over 1f out: styd on same pce and no imp ins fnl f* **13/2**

2304 **6** 3 **Integria**[5] 3326 5-9-5 **68**..(bt) TonyCulhane 1 57
(George Baker) *dwlt: bustled along early: racd in last trio: rdn 5f out: c centre over 3f out: no imp fnl 2f* **12/1**

0606 **7** *nk* **Kavachi (IRE)**[12] 3081 8-9-7 **70**..(b[1]) GeorgeBaker 10 58
(Gary Moore) *in tch in midfield: effrt jst over 2f out: rdn and fnd little over 1f out: btn ent fnl f* **15/2**

3506 **8** *shd* **Diddums**[1] 3475 5-8-5 **61**.. KatiaScallan(7) 7 49
(Alastair Lidderdale) *a in rr: pushed along and effrt whn nt clr run and swtchd lft 2f out: no imp after* **17/2**

4-32 **9** 44 **Rich Boy**[14] 3017 4-8-6 **58**..(p) SimonPearce(3) 6 —
(Laura Mongan) *racd freely: led tl over 4f out: dropped away qckly over 2f out: wl bhd and eased ins fnl f: t.o* **8/1**

1m 34.84s (-1.16) **Going Correction** -0.05s/f (Good) 9 Ran SP% **113.3**
Speed ratings (Par 103): **103,102,100,100,97 94,94,94,50**
toteswingers:1&2:£4.60, 2&3:£7.40, 1&3:£9.00 CSF £31.56 CT £191.87 TOTE £8.00: £2.20, £2.00, £2.70; EX 25.90 Trifecta £391.40 Pool: £581.83 - 1.10 winning units..
Owner Mrs R F Johnson Houghton **Bred** Mrs R F Johnson Houghton **Trained** Blewbury, Oxon
■ Stewards' Enquiry : Cathy Gannon one-day ban: used whip with excessive frequency (Jul 14)

FOCUS
A modest handicap. It's two years since the winner rated this high.
Rich Boy Official explanation: trainer said gelding bled from the nose

3478 DAVID ASHFORTH "I THINK I'VE CRACKED IT" MAIDEN STKS 1m 1f 209y
3:30 (3:30) (Class 5) 3-Y-0+ **£2,266** (£674; £337; £168) **Stalls** High

Form RPR

4-3 **1** **Misty Isles**[19] 2836 3-8-9 0.. EddieAhern 4 75+
(Heather Main) *chsd ldr tl led over 6f out: mde rest: pushed along and readily drew clr 2f out: in command after: eased wl ins fnl f: easily* **8/11**[1]

5450 **2** 6 **Informed Award**[11] 3118 3-9-0 71.. WilliamBuick 5 65
(John Gosden) *chsd ldrs: wnt 2nd over 4f out: rdn and unable qck w wnr 2f out: no ch w wnr but kpt on u.p to hold 2nd ins fnl f* **9/2**[3]

5 **3** *shd* **Munaawib**[25] 2691 3-9-0 0..(b[1]) TadhgO'Shea 1 65
(Marcus Tregoning) *in tch in last pair: rdn and hung rt over 2f out: stl last and racing awkwardly over 1f out: no ch but fnlly styd on ins fnl f: pressing for 2nd cl home* **10/1**

0 **4** 1 ¾ **Cordillera**[13] 3043 3-8-9 0.. KierenFallon 3 56
(Luca Cumani) *hld up in last pair: rdn and effrt over 2f out: disputing 2nd but no threat to wnr over 1f out: no ex ins fnl f* **7/2**[2]

44 **5** 13 **Miss Excel**[22] 2760 4-9-7 0.. EddieCreighton 2 30
(Edward Creighton) *sn pushed along to ld: hdd over 6f out: rdn and lost 2nd over 4f out: wknd u.p jst over 2f out: wl bhd ins fnl f* **40/1**

2m 2.45s (-1.15) **Going Correction** -0.05s/f (Good)
WFA 3 from 4yo 12lb 5 Ran SP% **109.8**
Speed ratings (Par 103): **102,97,97,95,85**
CSF £4.40 TOTE £2.00: £1.70, £1.10; EX 3.60.
Owner Donald M Kerr **Bred** Barry Walters **Trained** Kingston Lisle, Oxon

FOCUS
A heavy downpour after race two led to the ground easing to good, and runners started to head stands' side. An uncompetitive maiden, weakened by the absence of morning favourite Polperro. The winner probably did not need to improve much on her reappearance.

3479 JANES SOLICITORS H'CAP 1m 3f 196y
4:00 (4:03) (Class 5) (0-70,74) 3-Y-0+ **£2,266** (£674; £337; £168) **Stalls** High

Form RPR

4254 **1** **Lemon Drop Red (USA)**[18] 2874 3-8-8 **62**........................ WilliamBuick 1 76
(Ed Dunlop) *hld up in tch: hdwy to chse ldrs 4f out: led gng best 2f out: sn rdn clr: in command 1f out: eased towards fin* **9/2**[2]

1351 **2** 6 **Achalas (IRE)**[8] 3233 3-9-6 **74** 6ex.. KierenFallon 5 78
(Heather Main) *hld up in tch: hdwy to press ldrs 4f out: led wl over 2f out: sn rdn: hdd and nt qckn w wnr 2f out: one pce and btn whn edgd lft jst over 1f out: hld on for 2nd wl ins fnl f* **5/6**[1]

4142 **3** ½ **Penang Cinta**[7] 3252 8-9-7 **61**.. CathyGannon 7 64
(David Evans) *chsd ldrs: jnd ldr over 4f out: rdn 3f out: drvn and outpcd jst over 2f out: no ch w wnr whn swtchd lft 1f out: kpt on ins fnl f* **9/2**[2]

3400 **4** *nse* **Soundbyte**[57] 1750 6-9-5 **59**.. ChrisCatlin 6 62
(John Gallagher) *hld up in last trio: hdwy to chse ldng quartet: rdn and no imp over 2f out: no ch w wnr but kpt on fnl f* **20/1**

0060 **5** 12 **Ringstead Bay (FR)**[15] 3002 3-8-4 **58**........................(b[1]) RichardThomas 4 42
(Ralph Beckett) *chsd ldrs: rdn and lost pl 5f out: lost tch u.p 3f out: wl bhd fnl 2f* **20/1**

56-0 **6** 1 **Herschel (IRE)**[14] 2308 5-9-13 **67**.. GeorgeBaker 2 49
(Gary Moore) *led tl 3f out: sn rdn: wknd 2f out: wl btn ent fnl f* **14/1**[3]

05-0 **7** 24 **Silent Applause**[38] 2312 8-9-7 **61**..(v) LiamKeniry 3 —
(Dr Jon Scargill) *chsd ldr tl over 4f out: rdn and lost tch 3f out: t.o and eased ins fnl f* **16/1**

2m 34.51s (1.01) **Going Correction** +0.175s/f (Good)
WFA 3 from 5yo+ 14lb 7 Ran SP% **112.0**
Speed ratings (Par 103): **100,96,95,95,87 86,70**
toteswingers:1&2:£1.50, 2&3:£1.40, 1&3:£1.60 CSF £8.43 TOTE £3.40: £1.10, £1.40; EX 13.20.

Owner R J Arculli **Bred** Nancy M Leonard Living Trust **Trained** Newmarket, Suffolk

FOCUS
A low-grade middle-distance handicap and it was no surprise to see the 3-y-os come to the fore. The winner franked the form of his Goodwood run.
Ringstead Bay(FR) Official explanation: jockey said gelding lost its action

3480 DAVID ASHFORTH BRIGHTON ROCK WINNER H'CAP 1m 1f 209y
4:30 (4:32) (Class 6) (0-55,54) 4-Y-0+ **£1,619** (£481; £240; £120) **Stalls** High

Form RPR

6400 **1** **Royal Defence (IRE)**[10] 3184 5-9-2 **54**.. PatCosgrave 10 63
(Michael Quinn) *chsd ldrs: wnt 2nd over 4f out: led 3f out: rdn over 2f out: drvn and styd on wl 1f out: drew clr fnl 100yds: eased towards fin* **11/2**[3]

0000 **2** 3 ¼ **Excellent Vision**[18] 2869 4-8-13 **51**..(t) LiamKeniry 1 54
(Milton Bradley) *stdd s: t.k.h: hld up in rr: hdwy and pushed lft over 1f out: sn rdn: chsd clr wnr fnl 100yds: no imp* **33/1**

0060 **3** 1 **Corlough Mountain**[25] 2685 7-8-7 **45**.. CathyGannon 5 46
(Paddy Butler) *hld up in midfield: rdn 3f out: hdwy u.p to chse wnr and hung rt over 1f out: no ex and btn fnl 150yds: lost 2nd fnl 100yds* **50/1**

4603 **4** 1 ¼ **Hault**[35] 2385 5-8-12 **50**.. WilliamBuick 4 48
(Gary Moore) *stdd and stmbld s: hld up in rr: hdwy 3f out: sn rdn: chsd ldrs and drvn over 1f out: no ex 1f out: wknd fnl 100yds* **9/2**[2]

0000 **5** ½ **Guildenstern (IRE)**[8] 3235 9-8-6 **49**.. AmyScott(5) 8 46
(Alastair Lidderdale) *hld up in rr: pushed along and effrt in centre over 2f out: chsd ldrs and drvn over 1f out: no ex 1f out: wknd fnl 100yds* **25/1**

00/0 **6** *shd* **Petito (IRE)**[21] 2793 8-8-5 **46**..(b) SimonPearce(3) 12 43
(Mark Gillard) *t.k.h: chsd ldr tl over 4f out: rdn and unable qck over 1f out: wknd u.p jst over 1f out* **14/1**

0446 **7** 3 ¼ **Tt's Dream**[17] 2905 4-8-8 **46**..(v[1]) RobertHavlin 7 36
(Alastair Lidderdale) *t.k.h: hld up in midfield: effrt and n.m.r 2f out: sn pushed lft and drvn over 1f out: fnd little and btn 1f out: wknd ins fnl f* **11/2**[3]

0130 **8** 3 **Major Eradicator (USA)**[7] 3256 4-8-11 **49**........................(b[1]) EddieAhern 2 33
(Alastair Lidderdale) *led: clr tl over 4f out: hdd and rdn 3f out: hung rt u.p 2f out: wknd over 1f out* **4/1**[1]

0P40 **9** *17* **Dawson Creek (IRE)**[14] 3017 7-8-4 **45**........................ SophieDoyle(3) 6 —
(Mark Hoad) *chsd ldr tl over 4f out: sn rdn and struggling 4f out: wknd jst over 2f out: wl bhd and eased fnl 75yds* **8/1**

3461 **10** *7* **Sunset Boulevard (IRE)**[10] 3176 8-9-0 **52**........................(b) PaulDoe 11 —
(Jim Best) *t.k.h: hld up in tch in midfield: rdn and nt qckning wl over 2f out: wknd 2f out: wl bhd and eased ins fnl f: t.o* **9/2**[2]

00-0 **11** *70* **Chill Out Charley**[12] 3094 4-8-4 **45**........................ KierenFox(3) 9 —
(Ronald Harris) *t.k.h: hld up in last quartet: rdn and dropped out qckly over 4f out: wl t.o and eased fnl 2f* **100/1**

2m 5.95s (2.35) **Going Correction** +0.175s/f (Good) **11** Ran SP% **114.6**
Speed ratings (Par 101): **97,94,93,92,92 92,89,87,73,67 11**
toteswingers:1&2:£23.60, 2&3:£86.20, 1&3:£48.00 CSF £174.26 CT £7893.39 TOTE £9.40: £3.30, £8.50, £10.80; EX 196.20 TRIFECTA Not won..
Owner M Quinn **Bred** Joseph Rogers **Trained** Newmarket, Suffolk

FOCUS
A weak handicap, the winner taking advantage of a big drop in the weights and the third 11lb wrong.
Dawson Creek(IRE) Official explanation: trainer's rep said gelding was unsuited by the good ground
Chill Out Charley Official explanation: jockey said gelding ran too free

3481 DIGIBET.COM H'CAP 6f 209y
5:00 (5:00) (Class 5) (0-70,70) 3-Y-O **£2,266** (£674; £337; £168) **Stalls** Low

Form RPR

0311 **1** **Camberley Two**[2] 3431 3-8-5 **59** 6ex........................ KieranO'Neill(5) 7 67
(Roger Charlton) *t.k.h: led: sn hdd and chsd ldr: clsd and pressed ldr jst over 2f out: rdn to ld over 1f out: hdd 1f out: drvn ins fnl f: r.o u.p to ld again cl home* **1/4**[1]

-406 **2** *shd* **Hawk Moth (IRE)**[21] 2792 3-8-11 **60**........................ CathyGannon 2 68
(John Spearing) *stdd s: t.k.h: hld up in last: hdwy to join ldrs 2f out: rdn and qckn clr w wnr over 1f out: drvn to ld narrowly 1f out: r.o u.p: hdd cl home* **7/1**[2]

3360 **3** *5* **His Grace (IRE)**[11] 3122 3-9-2 **65**........................ RobertHavlin 8 60
(Andrew Haynes) *awkward leaving stalls and dwlt: t.k.h: sn led: clr over 5f out: jnd jst over 2f out: hdd over 1f out: outpcd and rdn over 1f out: hung lft 1f out and sn wknd* **33/1**

0561 **4** *9* **Russian Ice**[8] 3223 3-8-10 **59** 6ex........................(b) AdrianMcCarthy 4 29
(Dean Ivory) *chsd ldrs: rdn over 4f out: drvn and dropped to last over 2f out: hung lft and wknd over 1f out: wl btn and eased wl ins fnl f* **17/2**[3]

1m 24.65s (1.55) **Going Correction** +0.175s/f (Good) **4** Ran SP% **106.0**
Speed ratings (Par 99): **98,97,92,81**
CSF £2.31 TOTE £1.20; EX 1.70.
Owner H R H Sultan Ahmad Shah **Bred** Barry Walters Farms **Trained** Beckhampton, Wilts

FOCUS
A race decimated by four non-runners and very nearly a major upset. The time was slow and it's doubtful the winner matched either of his previous wins.
Russian Ice Official explanation: jockey said filly never travelled

3482 JOHN SMITHS RACEDAY HERE 3RD AUGUST H'CAP 5f 59y
5:30 (5:30) (Class 5) (0-70,70) 3-Y-O+ **£2,266** (£674; £337; £168) **Stalls** Low

Form RPR

5303 **1** **Welsh Inlet (IRE)**[7] 3255 3-8-13 **63**........................ CathyGannon 3 69
(John Bridger) *led tl 3f out: styd w ldr: rdn to ld jst over 1f out: edgd rt jst ins fnl f: styd on wl and in command fnl 100yds* **4/1**[3]

0062 **2** *2 1/4* **Do More Business (IRE)**[7] 3254 4-8-3 **52**........................ JemmaMarshall(5) 2 52
(Pat Phelan) *chsd ldrs: wnt 3rd over 3f out: rdn over 2f out: drvn and styd on fr over 1f out: chsd wnr ins fnl f: no imp and btn fnl 100yds* **11/2**

5511 **3** *1/2* **Stonecrabstomorrow (IRE)**[7] 3255 8-8-9 **58** 6ex..(v) MarkCoumbe(5) 6 56
(Michael Attwater) *sn rdn and outpcd in last: stl last but hdwy u.p jst over 1f out: styd on ins fnl f: no threat to wnr* **7/2**[2]

0235 **4** *1 3/4* **Billy Red**[17] 2903 7-9-10 **68**........................(b) JimCrowley 5 60
(J R Jenkins) *chsd wnr tl led 3f out: rdn and hdd jst over 1f out: wknd ins fnl f* **3/1**[1]

0025 **5** *6* **Kinigi (IRE)**[8] 3217 5-9-9 **70**........................(b) JohnFahy(3) 7 41
(Ronald Harris) *dwlt: pushed along early: in tch: rdn and effrt 2f out: hung lft and no hdwy over 1f out: wknd ins fnl f* **7/2**[2]

6010 **6** *6* **Gothic Chick**[17] 2918 3-7-13 **54**........................(p) KieranO'Neill(5) 1 —
(Alan McCabe) *chsd ldng pair tl over 3f out: drvn and struggling over 2f out: wknd u.p wl over 1f out* **16/1**

62.68 secs (0.30) **Going Correction** +0.175s/f (Good)
WFA 3 from 4yo+ 6lb **6** Ran SP% **110.7**
Speed ratings (Par 103): **103,99,98,95,86 76**
Tote Super 7: Win: Not won. Place: Not won. CSF £24.71 TOTE £6.00: £3.20, £3.20; EX 31.30.
Owner J J Bridger **Bred** Patrick Gleeson **Trained** Liphook, Hants

FOCUS
Few got into this. Weak handicap form.
T/Plt: £128.90 to a £1 stake. Pool of £80,021.21 - 453.12 winning tickets. T/Qpdt: £28.10 to a £1 stake. Pool of £5,155.63 - 135.50 winning tickets. SP

3300 HAMILTON (R-H)
Tuesday, June 28

OFFICIAL GOING: Good (good to soft in places; 7.8)
Wind: Breezy, across Weather: Cloudy, bright

3483 WEATHERBYS BANK MAIDEN STKS 6f 5y
2:15 (2:15) (Class 5) 2-Y-O **£2,729** (£806; £403) **Stalls** High

Form RPR

33 **1** **Vassaria (IRE)**[24] 2709 2-8-12 0........................ FrederikTylicki 6 71+
(Michael Dods) *w ldr: led 2f out: drifted rt and pushed clr ins fnl f* **1/6**[1]

2 *3 1/4* **Shomberg** 2-9-3 0........................ NickyMackay 3 66+
(Mark H Tompkins) *dwlt: rn green in rr: hdwy over 1f out: chsd (clr) wnr ins fnl f: kpt on: bttr for r* **16/1**[3]

03 **3** *nk* **Angel Of Hope (IRE)**[11] 3125 2-8-12 0........................ TomEaves 1 60
(Bryan Smart) *led to 2f out: sn rdn and carried rt: edgd lft and kpt on same pce ins fnl f* **8/1**[2]

00 **4** *1 1/2* **Spoken Words**[25] 2672 2-8-12 0........................ DavidAllan 5 56
(Hugh McWilliams) *trckd ldrs: drvn over 2f out: nt qckn over 1f out* **50/1**

5 *27* **Villa Reigns** 2-9-3 0........................ AndrewMullen 4 —
(John Weymes) *t.k.h: prom: rn green and outpcd wl over 3f out: sn lost tch* **33/1**

1m 13.69s (1.49) **Going Correction** +0.075s/f (Good) **5** Ran SP% **107.6**
Speed ratings (Par 93): **93,88,88,86,50**
CSF £3.83 TOTE £1.30: £1.02, £5.00; EX 3.30.
Owner Andrew Tinkler **Bred** Celbridge Estates Ltd **Trained** Denton, Co Durham

FOCUS
Rail realignment reduced advertised distances on Round course by 8yds. The betting suggested this would be a one-horse race and the hot favourite duly obliged, but it wasn't complete plain sailing. She was the pre-race form choice.

NOTEBOOK
Vassaria(IRE) had finished third in her first two starts and the form of her second outing at Doncaster has been boosted by the subsequent successes of the fourth and fifth, but this slightly shorter trip may not have helped her, even on such a stiff track. Having hit the front over a furlong out, she had to come off the bridle to make sure of it and hung away to the centre of the track as she asserted. She doesn't look anything special, but will appreciate a return to further. (op 1-5 tchd 1-4 in a place early)
Shomberg proved green at the back of the field early, but was staying on nicely towards the end and this half-brother to a winner at up to 1m4f looks sure to make his mark in time. (op 18-1)
Angel Of Hope(IRE) seemed to improve for the drop to 5f at Musselburgh on her second start and set the pace until over a furlong from home. A return to the minimum trip may help and nurseries might be a better option for her. (op 7-1)
Spoken Words, beaten a long way in her first two starts, raced in touch for over half a mile but she may not have improved that much on her previous efforts.
Villa Reigns, a £9,000 2-y-o out of a winner over 1m4f, proved too green to do himself justice.

3484 SCOTTISH RACING CLAIMING STKS 5f 4y
2:45 (2:45) (Class 6) 3-5-Y-O **£2,047** (£604; £302) **Stalls** Centre

Form RPR

-153 **1** **Saucy Brown (IRE)**[10] 3162 5-9-13 **79**........................ AdrianNicholls 4 80
(David Nicholls) *t.k.h: cl up: rdn and sltly outpcd over 1f out: styd on wl ins fnl f: led cl home* **9/4**[3]

0-31 **2** *hd* **Sands Of Dee (USA)**[13] 3040 4-9-4 **71**........................ BillyCray(3) 2 73
(David Nicholls) *led: rdn along 2f out: kpt on ins fnl f: hdd cl home* **11/5**[2]

3522 **3** *2* **Tro Nesa (IRE)**[11] 3114 3-8-12 **75**........................ SilvestreDeSousa 3 61
(Ann Duffield) *cl up: rdn and ev ch over 1f out: one pce wl ins fnl f* **11/8**[1]

6034 **4** *2* **Running Water**[11] 3143 3-8-7 **43** ow1........................(bt) DavidAllan 6 49
(Hugh McWilliams) *dwlt: prom: effrt and drvn 2f out: edgd rt: kpt on same pce ins fnl f* **40/1**

60.55 secs (0.55) **Going Correction** +0.075s/f (Good)
WFA 3 from 4yo+ 6lb **4** Ran SP% **106.6**
Speed ratings (Par 101): **98,97,94,91**
CSF £7.25 TOTE £2.30; EX 5.50.
Owner D Nicholls **Bred** Churchtown House Stud **Trained** Sessay, N Yorks
■ Stewards' Enquiry : Adrian Nicholls caution: used whip down shoulder in the forehand.

FOCUS
A weak sprint claimer and effectively a three-horse race. It resulted in a 1-2 for the David Nicholls yard.

3485 WEATHERBYS BANK H'CAP 1m 65y
3:15 (3:15) (Class 5) (0-70,69) 3-Y-O **£2,914** (£867; £433; £216) **Stalls** Low

Form RPR

-600 **1** **Cuckney Bear**[26] 2650 3-8-9 **57**........................ RichardMullen 4 67+
(Ed McMahon) *hld up in tch: hdwy over 2f out: effrt and chsd ldr over 1f out: edgd lft and styd on wl ins fnl f: led last stride* **4/1**[2]

0-01 **2** *shd* **Save The Bees**[13] 3039 3-8-10 **63**........................ NeilFarley(5) 7 73+
(Declan Carroll) *prom: hdwy to ld 2f out: sn rdn: kpt on wl u.p ins fnl f: hdd last stride* **5/2**[1]

3525 **3** *2 1/2* **Carrowbeg (IRE)**[13] 3038 3-9-7 **69**........................(b[1]) SilvestreDeSousa 5 73
(Mark Johnston) *t.k.h: stdd in rr: hdwy on outside 3f out: effrt and chsd ldrs over 1f out: edgd rt: kpt on same pce fnl f* **9/2**[3]

224 **4** *1 3/4* **Dr Red Eye**[16] 2957 3-9-6 **68**........................ AdrianNicholls 2 68
(David Nicholls) *led 2f: trckd ldrs: rdn and outpcd over 2f out: kpt on fnl f: no imp* **11/2**

3466 **5** *1 3/4* **Sabratha (IRE)**[11] 3124 3-9-0 **62**........................ PaulHanagan 6 58
(Linda Perratt) *t.k.h: prom: hdwy to ld briefly over 2f out: wknd over 1f out* **11/1**

3-00 **6** *shd* **Reason To Believe (IRE)**[45] 2119 3-9-1 **63**........................ PJMcDonald 1 59
(Ben Haslam) *in tch on ins: effrt and rdn over 2f out: no imp fr over 1f out* **10/1**

55-0 **7** *5* **Cat Island**[20] 2827 3-8-8 **56**........................ NickyMackay 3 40
(Mark H Tompkins) *hld up: rdn along over 3f out: nvr on terms* **50/1**

1241 **8** *2* **Goal (IRE)**[8] 3235 3-9-7 **69** 6ex........................ TomEaves 8 49
(Richard Guest) *led after 2f: rdn and hdd over 2f out: wknd over 1f out* **15/2**

1m 48.5s (0.10) **Going Correction** +0.075s/f (Good) **8** Ran SP% **113.3**
Speed ratings (Par 99): **102,101,99,97,95 95,90,88**
toteswingers:1&2:£5.00, 2&3:£3.90, 1&3:£6.10 CSF £14.15 CT £45.27 TOTE £4.80: £1.20, £2.30, £2.50; EX 23.80.
Owner Premspace Ltd **Bred** D R Botterill **Trained** Lichfield, Staffs

FOCUS
A fair handicap and a gamble landed. The least exposed pair dominated.
Cuckney Bear Official explanation: trainer's rep said, regarding apparent improvement in form, that the gelding was suited by the softer ground.
Goal(IRE) Official explanation: jockey said colt hung left-handed throughout

3486 WEATHERBYS BLOODSTOCK INSURANCE H'CAP 1m 1f 36y
3:45 (3:46) (Class 5) (0-75,75) 3-Y-O+ **£3,561** (£1,059; £529; £264) **Stalls** Low

Form RPR

3366 **1** **Petomic (IRE)**[3] 3386 6-8-11 **63**........................ RobertLButler(3) 1 71
(Richard Guest) *hld up in last pl: hdwy over 2f out: effrt appr fnl f: styd on wl to ld nr fin* **11/1**

5423 **2** *hd* **Just Five (IRE)**[7] 3244 5-9-6 **69**........................ TomEaves 5 76
(John Weymes) *prom: effrt over 2f out: sn rdn: led over 1f out: kpt on ins fnl f: hdd nr fin* **13/2**[3]

0-10 **3** *4* **Pandoro De Lago (IRE)**[39] 2253 3-9-1 **75**........................ PaulHanagan 3 73
(Richard Fahey) *dwlt: rcvrd and led after 1f: rdn and hdd appr fnl f: outpcd ins fnl f* **10/1**

3461 **4** *3/4* **Casino Night**[5] 3303 6-9-1 **71** 6ex........................ ShaneBKelly(7) 4 68
(Barry Murtagh) *trckd ldrs: ev ch over 3f out: rdn and outpcd over 2f out: n.d after* **5/2**[2]

41 **5** *1 1/4* **Circle Of Angels**[13] 3037 3-9-1 **75**........................ SilvestreDeSousa 2 68
(Mark Johnston) *t.k.h: led 1f: cl up: ev ch and drvn over 2f out: wandered and wknd appr fnl f* **1/1**[1]

1m 59.78s (0.08) **Going Correction** +0.075s/f (Good)
WFA 3 from 5yo+ 11lb **5** Ran SP% **109.3**
Speed ratings (Par 103): **102,101,98,97,96**
CSF £70.69 TOTE £16.20: £5.10, £1.10; EX 82.40.
Owner Johnson Racing **Bred** Neil McGrath **Trained** Stainforth, S Yorks

FOCUS
Despite the small field, the pace seemed solid enough and this was a race of changing fortunes. The first two came from the rear and the winner posted a length personal best.

3487 RACING UK SKY 432 H'CAP — 1m 4f 17y
4:15 (4:15) (Class 6) (0-65,65) 3-Y-O — £1,942 (£578; £288; £144) Stalls High

Form — RPR
-503 **1** **Getabuzz**[25] [2677] 3-9-7 **65** .... DavidAllan 10 — 82+
(Tim Easterby) *hld up: smooth hdwy over 3f out: rdn to ld over 1f out: kpt on strly* **10/3**[2]
00-2 **2** *3* **Fire Fighter (IRE)**[26] [2635] 3-9-5 **63** .... StevieDonohoe 5 — 75+
(Sir Mark Prescott Bt) *trckd ldrs: led 3f out: sn rdn and veered lft: hdd over 1f out: plugged on same pce* **7/4**[1]
-242 **3** *2 ¾* **Silver Tigress**[5] [3301] 3-8-3 **47** .... PatrickMathers 3 — 55
(George Moore) *hld up: hdwy 3f out: chsd ldrs over 1f out: kpt on same pce ins fnl f* **6/1**[3]
255 **4** *7* **Body Language (IRE)**[20] [2813] 3-9-7 **65** .... PaulHanagan 7 — 62
(Ann Duffield) *midfield: drvn and outpcd over 3f out: styd on ins fnl f: nvr able to chal* **6/1**[3]
06-0 **5** *1* **Colzium**[19] [2857] 3-8-2 **46** .... NickyMackay 11 — 41
(Mark H Tompkins) *midfield on outside: rdn and hung rt over 2f out: wknd wl over 1f out* **80/1**
-003 **6** *4 ½* **Henrys Gift (IRE)**[11] [3116] 3-9-1 **59** .... FrederikTylicki 4 — 47
(Michael Dods) *hld up in tch: drvn along 3f out: wknd fnl 2f* **22/1**
0-60 **7** *3* **Nay Secret**[5] [3301] 3-8-3 **47** .... AndrewMullen 8 — 30
(Jim Goldie) *hld up: drvn along over 4f out: sn n.d* **100/1**
55-0 **8** *5* **Miss Villefranche**[50] [1958] 3-9-5 **63** ....(v) HayleyTurner 6 — 38
(Michael Bell) *led: stdd 1/2-way: hdd 3f out: rdn and wknd 2f out* **14/1**
4-03 **9** *2 ¼* **Kian's Delight**[26] [2635] 3-8-11 **58** .... MichaelO'Connell(3) 1 — 30
(Jedd O'Keeffe) *prom tl rdn and wknd fr 3f out* **18/1**
1440 **10** *6* **Investment World (IRE)**[27] [2613] 3-9-2 **60** .... SilvestreDeSousa 9 — 22
(Mark Johnston) *trckd ldrs: rdn and ev ch over 3f out: wknd over 2f out* **16/1**
000 **11** *10* **Right Credentials**[21] [2781] 3-7-11 **46** oh1 .... NeilFarley(5) 2 — —
(Bruce Hellier) *bhd: struggling over 4f out: sn btn* **150/1**

2m 38.22s (-0.38) **Going Correction** +0.075s/f (Good) — 11 Ran SP% **113.1**
Speed ratings (Par 97): **104,102,100,95,94 91,89,86,85,81 74**
toteswingers:1&2:£2.60, 2&3:£3.20, 1&3:£4.60 CSF £8.97 CT £31.48 TOTE £5.10: £2.40, £1.10, £2.70; EX 12.80.
Owner Langham Hall Stud Three **Bred** Peter Botham **Trained** Great Habton, N Yorks

FOCUS
A moderate middle-distance handicap for 3-y-os, but the first three pulled well clear of the others and the front pair showed above-average form for the grade. They can both do better.

3488 WEATHERBYS BETTRENDS.CO.UK H'CAP — 5f 4y
4:45 (4:45) (Class 5) (0-75,75) 3-Y-O+ — £2,914 (£867; £433; £216) Stalls Centre

Form — RPR
5020 **1** **Mandalay King (IRE)**[14] [3028] 6-9-3 **66** ....(p) PJMcDonald 7 — 79
(Marjorie Fife) *prom: smooth hdwy 2f out: shkn up to ld ins fnl f: sn clr* **14/1**
0223 **2** *2* **Ingleby Star (IRE)**[19] [2832] 6-9-3 **69** ....(p) GaryBartley(3) 5 — 75
(Ian McInnes) *led: rdn over 1f out: hdd ins fnl f: kpt on same pce* **7/2**[2]
6413 **3** *¾* **Hinton Admiral**[13] [3036] 7-9-9 **72** .... TomEaves 3 — 75
(Keith Dalgleish) *hld up: swtchd lft 2f out: hdwy over 1f out: sn rdn: kpt on same pce ins fnl f* **4/1**[3]
2234 **4** *1* **Sharp Bullet (IRE)**[10] [3166] 5-8-9 **58** ....(p) SilvestreDeSousa 2 — 58
(Bruce Hellier) *in tch on outside: hdwy 1/2-way: rdn over 1f out: sn no ex* **3/1**[1]
5604 **5** *shd* **Northern Dare (IRE)**[13] [3040] 7-9-2 **65** ....(b) PaulHanagan 4 — 64
(Richard Fahey) *prom: drvn and outpcd wl over 1f out: kpt on ins fnl f: no imp* **12/1**
-053 **6** *1 ½* **Go Go Green (IRE)**[10] [3160] 5-9-12 **75** .... DanielTudhope 1 — 69
(Jim Goldie) *wnt rt s: sn niggled in rr: effrt on outside over 1f out: edgd rt: nvr able to chal* **4/1**[3]
31-5 **7** *1* **Tadalavil**[5] [3305] 6-9-5 **68** .... FrederikTylicki 6 — 61
(Linda Perratt) *cl up tl rdn and wknd appr fnl f* **7/1**

59.90s (0.01) **Going Correction** +0.075s/f (Good) — 7 Ran SP% **114.1**
Speed ratings (Par 103): **103,99,98,97,96 94,92**
toteswingers:1&2:£7.80, 2&3:£3.30, 1&3:£10.70 CSF £61.92 TOTE £18.70: £5.80, £2.00; EX 97.30.
Owner R W Fife **Bred** Forenaghts Stud And Dermot Cantillon **Trained** Stillington, N Yorks
■ Stewards' Enquiry : Gary Bartley two-day ban: careless riding (Jul 12-13)

FOCUS
An ordinary sprint handicap and a surprise result. The winner is rated back to his best.
Mandalay King(IRE) Official explanation: trainer said, regarding apparent improvement in form, that the gelding benefited from the better start and the reapplication of cheek pieces.

3489 FAMILY NIGHT WITH THE STARS FROM XFACTOR H'CAP — 6f 5y
5:15 (5:17) (Class 6) (0-65,62) 3-Y-O+ — £2,047 (£604; £302) Stalls Centre

Form — RPR
-144 **1** **Blues Jazz**[11] [3128] 5-8-13 **54** .... GarryWhillans(7) 4 — 64
(Ian Semple) *hld up towards rr: hdwy over 1f out: led ins fnl f: kpt on strly* **9/1**
-531 **2** *1* **Hayek**[20] [2803] 4-10-0 **62** ....(b) DavidAllan 2 — 69
(Tim Easterby) *bhd: rdn and hdwy on outside 2f out: edgd rt: chsd wnr ins fnl f: r.o* **6/1**[3]
40-2 **3** *½* **I Got You Babe (IRE)**[9] [3207] 3-9-5 **60** .... PaulHanagan 1 — 63
(Richard Guest) *midfield on outside: hdwy over 1f out: led briefly ent fnl f: kpt on same pce* **9/4**[1]
2006 **4** *2 ¼* **Forzarzi (IRE)**[15] [2990] 7-8-9 **46** ....(p) GaryBartley(3) 9 — 44
(Hugh McWilliams) *bhd tl swtchd lft and hdwy over 1f out: kpt on fnl f: nrst fin* **25/1**
0542 **5** *nk* **Tahitian Princess (IRE)**[15] [2990] 3-8-10 **51** ....(p) SilvestreDeSousa 6 — 46
(Ann Duffield) *in tch: effrt over 2f out: kpt on same pce ins fnl f* **9/2**[2]
0551 **6** *1* **Unwrapit (USA)**[7] [3248] 3-9-0 **55** ....(p) TomEaves 7 — 47
(Bryan Smart) *towards rr: rdn and edgd rt thrght: effrt and swtchd lft over 2f out: nvr able to chal* **6/1**[3]
0030 **7** *2* **Suddenly Susan (IRE)**[19] [2845] 3-9-2 **60** ....(b) BillyCray(3) 5 — 45+
(David Nicholls) *led to over 2f out: wknd appr fnl f* **16/1**
0000 **8** *1 ¼* **Hold On Tiger (IRE)**[15] [2989] 4-8-4 **45** .... ShirleyTeasdale(7) 3 — 28
(Nicky Richards) *chsd ldrs: drvn over 2f out: sn wknd* **80/1**
-000 **9** *shd* **Blown It (USA)**[1] [3451] 5-9-4 **52** .... FrederikTylicki 12 — 35
(Keith Dalgleish) *t.k.h: cl up: led over 2f out to ent fnl f: kpt on same pce* **10/1**
15-0 **10** *3* **Adam De Beaulieu (USA)**[56] [1803] 4-9-9 **57** ....(t) PJMcDonald 8 — 30
(Ben Haslam) *bhd: pushed along 1/2-way: nvr on terms* **20/1**
0-00 **11** *17* **Craicattack (IRE)**[69] [1498] 4-8-10 **47** ....(p) MichaelO'Connell(3) 11 — —
(Sharon Watt) *chsd ldrs: drvn 1/2-way: wknd over 2f out: t.o* **50/1**
0/00 **12** *2* **Rue Soleil**[15] [2989] 7-8-11 **45** .... AndrewMullen 10 — —
(John Weymes) *in tch: drvn and outpcd over 3f out: sn btn: t.o* **100/1**

1m 13.16s (0.96) **Going Correction** +0.075s/f (Good)
WFA 3 from 4yo+ 7lb — 12 Ran SP% **115.3**
Speed ratings (Par 101): **96,94,94,91,90 89,86,84,84,80 58,55**
toteswingers:1&2:£5.10, 2&3:£4.10, 1&3:£5.30 CSF £58.01 CT £156.30 TOTE £8.20: £2.70, £1.10, £1.60; EX 55.70.
Owner Robert Reid **Bred** David Sugars And Bob Parker **Trained** Carluke, S Lanarks

FOCUS
Quite a competitive, if modest, sprint handicap and those drawn low came to the fore with the first three home starting from the four far-side stalls. It was strong run and the winner built on last month's C&D win.
T/Plt: £202.00 to a £1 stake. Pool of £49,191.30 - 177.75 winning tickets. T/Qpdt: £78.80 to a £1 stake. Pool: of 4,078.96 - 38.30 winning tickets. RY

2650 SOUTHWELL (L-H)
Tuesday, June 28

OFFICIAL GOING: Standard
Wind: Light across Weather: Cloudy

3490 E B F PHILLIP SMALLEY 65TH BIRTHDAY CELEBRATION MAIDEN STKS — 6f (F)
6:00 (6:00) (Class 5) 2-Y-O — £3,238 (£963; £481; £240) Stalls Low

Form — RPR
0 **1** **Four Richer**[8] [3229] 2-9-3 0 .... FergusSweeney 7 — 71+
(Jamie Osborne) *trckd ldrs: wd st: smooth hdwy to ld 2f out: rdn over 1f out and styd on wl ins fnl f* **14/1**
2 *4* **Scrooby Doo** 2-8-5 0 .... LeonnaMayor(7) 10 — 54
(David Nicholls) *towards rr: hdwy whn hung lft over 2f out: flashed tail: styd on to chse wnr over 1f out: one pce ins fnl f* **16/1**
0 **3** *hd* **Rano Pano (USA)**[34] [2404] 2-8-9 0 .... PaulPickard(3) 9 — 53
(Brian Ellison) *chsd ldrs: wd st and rdn along wl over 2f out: drvn and sltly outpcd wl over 1f out: edgd lft and kpt on u.p ins fnl f* **5/1**
4 *1 ¼* **Fresa** 2-8-12 0 .... LukeMorris 6 — 52+
(Sir Mark Prescott Bt) *hamperd s: green and sn rdn along in rr: hdwy 2f out: sn rdn and swtchd lft over 1f out: kpt on ins fnl f: nrst fin* **7/2**[2]
5 *4* **Lord Buffhead** 2-9-3 0 .... J-PGuillambert 5 — 42+
(Richard Guest) *wnt rt s: sn rdn along and a bhd* **20/1**
3306 **6** *nk* **Lord Ali McJones**[15] [2997] 2-9-3 0 .... RichardKingscote 2 — 41
(Tom Dascombe) *led: wd st: rdn along and hdd 2f out: sn drvn and edgd rt wl over 1f out: wknd* **3/1**[1]
00 **7** *nse* **Man Of My Word**[18] [2886] 2-9-3 0 .... MickyFenton 8 — 41
(David Nicholls) *chsd ldr: rdn along 3f out: wd st and wknd over 2f out* **9/1**
8 *hd* **Remember Rocky** 2-9-3 0 .... MartinLane 1 — 41+
(Steve Gollings) *in tch: rdn along 1/2-way: sn outpcd* **22/1**
9 *1 ½* **Vociferous (USA)** 2-8-12 0 .... RoystonFfrench 3 — 31
(Mark Johnston) *sn rdn along and outpcd in rr: bhd fr 1/2-way* **9/2**[3]

1m 18.08s (1.58) **Going Correction** +0.075s/f (Slow) — 9 Ran SP% **113.7**
Speed ratings (Par 93): **92,86,86,84,79 79,78,78,76**
toteswingers:1&2:£34.40, 2&3:£16.40, 1&3:£11.90 CSF £209.48 TOTE £23.10: £4.20, £3.70, £1.70; EX 269.90.
Owner Mr & Mrs J Wilson C Woollett & P Hearn **Bred** Redmyre Bloodstock & Gareth Jones Bloodstock **Trained** Upper Lambourn, Berks

FOCUS
A modest juvenile maiden and after four broke clear at halfway they bunched up in the end. The form is rated around the time and race averages.

NOTEBOOK
Four Richer, whose pedigree is a mixture of speed and stamina, has clearly learned plenty from his debut effort two weeks earlier. He forged clear in the end and will no doubt ply his trade in nursery company now. There may be even better to come. (op 22-1)
Scrooby Doo, from the family of the owner's Dewhurst winner Milk It Mick, was very green and swerved badly left once in line for home. Despite swishing her tail she stuck on in willing fashion and looks sure to improve and find a race. (op 14-1)
Rano Pano(USA), who made her debut in a Class 2 event at Beverley, shaped well for a long way and will improve again for the outing. (op 7-1)
Fresa, who was badly hampered and lost ground at the start, was outpaced and clueless. She picked up once in line for home and will be a different proposition next time over 7f. (op 9-2)
Lord Buffhead, a cheap buy, took the eye, staying on nicely under a considerate ride from way off the pace. (op 16-1)
Lord Ali McJones, having his fifth run, already looks fully exposed. He is not progressing and, after taking them along, dropped away tamely. He may have to descend to claimers or sellers now. (op 10-3 tchd 7-2)
Vociferous(USA), out of a Cheveley Park winner, was green early. She did pick up late and can do much better with more experience. (op 7-2)

3491 LADBROKES.COM CLAIMING STKS — 6f (F)
6:30 (6:31) (Class 6) 2-Y-O — £1,706 (£503; £252) Stalls Low

Form — RPR
0221 **1** **Pint Size**[21] [2784] 2-8-6 0 .... PaulPickard(3) 4 — 81+
(Brian Ellison) *mde all: rdn clr 2f out: easily* **4/6**[1]
5321 **2** *7* **Flying Pickets (IRE)**[11] [3137] 2-8-3 0 .... JamesSullivan 1 — 54
(David C Griffiths) *trckd ldrs: hdwy 1/2-way: rdn to chse wnr 2f out: sn drvn and no imp* **9/1**[3]
4363 **3** *½* **Reina Sofia**[29] [2563] 2-8-1 0 .... LukeMorris 5 — 51
(Tony Carroll) *in tch: hdwy to chse ldrs 1/2-way: rdn 2f out and sn one pce* **4/1**[2]
0 **4** *2 ¼* **Johnson's Cat (IRE)**[13] [3050] 2-8-7 0 .... RobbieFitzpatrick 6 — 50
(Richard Guest) *sn rdn along and outpcd in rr tl sme hdwy fnl 2f: nvr a factor* **25/1**
0214 **5** *4 ½* **Arcticality (IRE)**[18] [2889] 2-8-3 0 .... AndrewHeffernan 8 — 32
(Richard Fahey) *in tch: rdn along bef 1/2-way: sn outpcd and bhd* **4/1**[2]
663 **6** *8* **Sophar**[11] [3137] 2-8-5 0 ow2 .... AndrewElliott 7 — 10
(Jason Ward) *chsd wnr: rdn along 1/2-way: drvn 2f out and sn wknd* **40/1**
5 **7** *8* **Lady Cresta (IRE)**[53] [1863] 2-7-9 0 .... AmyBaker(3) 2 — —
(Ronald Harris) *sltly hmpd s: in tch: rdn along 1/2-way: sn wknd and bhd* **66/1**

6543 **8** *9* **The Coulbeck Kid**[28] 2595 2-8-3 0................................(b) AndreaAtzeni 3 —
(Des Donovan) *wnt lft s: sn rdn along and outpcd in rr: a bhd* **25/1**

1m 17.04s (0.54) **Going Correction** +0.075s/f (Slow) **8** Ran SP% **121.6**
Speed ratings (Par 91): **99,89,89,86,80 69,58,46**
toteswingers:1&2:£2.40, 2&3:£5.00, 1&3:£1.50 CSF £8.59 TOTE £2.10: £1.20, £2.80, £1.70; EX 8.50.Flying Pickets was claimed by T. R. Pearson for £5000. Pint Size was claimed by G Kelleway for £11000.
Owner Koo's Racing Club **Bred** Bambi Bloodstock **Trained** Norton, N Yorks

FOCUS
This turned out to be a one-horse race and with the time good Pint Size is given full credit for this.

NOTEBOOK
Pint Size was claimed for £6,000 after an easy win in a claimer at Redcar. Making his Fibresand debut, he was put in here to be claimed for £11,000. Racing with bags of enthusiasm, he went clear once in line for home and scored in easy fashion. He may lack size but looks sure to make his mark in nursery company. He was claimed by Gay Kelleway. (op 10-11)
Flying Pickets(IRE), winner of a seller at Redcar, had finished 13 lengths behind Pint Size when third in the Redcar claimer. He was claimed here for £5,000.
Reina Sofia, down in grade and up in trip, was fast closing down the runner-up at the line on her fifth start. She should win a seller over seven. (op 7-2)
Johnson's Cat(IRE), a cheap purchase, showed a fraction more than on his debut in maiden company.
Arcticality(IRE) was run off her feet before halfway and this regressive filly seems to need 7f-plus already. (tchd 9-2)
Sophar Official explanation: trainer said colt had been struck into
The Coulbeck Kid Official explanation: jockey said colt never travelled

3492 GOT THE FEELING GET TO LADBROKES H'CAP — 2m (F)
7:00 (7:00) (Class 6) (0-60,60) 4-Y-0+ **£1,706** (£503; £252) **Stalls** Low

Form RPR
5320 **1** **Trojan Gift (USA)**[34] 2400 4-9-7 **60**................................(p) TonyHamilton 1 67
(Julie Camacho) *led 2f: cl up tl led again 7f out: rdn over 2f out: drvn over 1f out: kpt on gamely* **9/4**[2]
2056 **2** *1 1/4* **Bring Sweets (IRE)**[12] 3072 4-8-11 **53**.......................... PaulPickard(3) 5 59
(Brian Ellison) *hld up in rr: smooth hdwy 6f out: trckd wnr over 3f out: effrt over 2f out: sn rdn and ev ch tl drvn and one pce ins fnl f* **15/8**[1]
0100 **3** *9* **Blazing Buck**[6] 3281 5-8-13 **52**.. FrannyNorton 6 47
(Tony Carroll) *reminders early and pushed along to ld after 2f: hdd 7f out and sn rdn: drvn along over 3f out and sn btn* **7/2**[3]
0030 **4** *38* **Jackson (BRZ)**[22] 2762 9-8-7 **46** oh1......................(be) RoystonFfrench 3 —
(Richard Guest) *rdn along early: hdwy to chse ldng pair after 4f: rdn along 1/2-way: sn wknd and bhd* **11/1**
-006 **5** *55* **Fifty Moore**[20] 2804 4-9-2 **55**...................................(b) AndrewElliott 2 —
(Jedd O'Keeffe) *chsd ldng pair: rdn along 6f out: drvn and outpcd over 4f out: sn bhd and t.o whn eased 2f out* **8/1**

3m 46.49s (0.99) **Going Correction** +0.075s/f (Slow) **5** Ran SP% **107.2**
Speed ratings (Par 101): **100,99,94,75,48**
CSF £6.48 TOTE £2.90: £1.90, £2.20; EX 5.50.
Owner Axom (XIX) **Bred** River Bend Farm **Trained** Norton, N Yorks

FOCUS
A low-grade 46-60 stayers' handicap run at a sound pace and only the first two in serious contention in the home straight. The winner is rated in line with his previous form here.

3493 LADBROKES MOBILE H'CAP — 5f (F)
7:30 (7:31) (Class 5) (0-75,75) 3-Y-0+ **£2,266** (£674; £337; £168) **Stalls** High

Form RPR
2543 **1** **Sleepy Blue Ocean**[10] 3166 5-9-6 **69**...........................(p) MartinLane 10 79
(John Balding) *prom: hdwy to chal 2f out: rdn to ld appr fnl f: drvn out* **6/1**
0-03 **2** *nk* **Boogie Waltzer**[42] 2179 4-9-1 **69**..................................(t) RyanClark(5) 3 78
(Stuart Williams) *trckd ldrs: sltly outpcd 1/2-way: hdwy wl over 1f out and sn rdn: drvn to chse wnr ins fnl f: edgd rt and kpt on wl towards fin: jst hld* **9/2**[2]
103 **3** *2 1/4* **Spic 'n Span**[14] 3015 6-9-2 **65**...(b) LukeMorris 4 66
(Ronald Harris) *led: jnd and rdn along 2f out: drvn and hdd appr fnl f: kpt on same pce* **11/2**[3]
0000 **4** *5* **Ace Of Spies (IRE)**[26] 2653 6-9-4 **67**.........................(b[1]) JamesSullivan 5 50
(Conor Dore) *prom: rdn along 2f out: sn drvn and one pce appr fnl f* **16/1**
0060 **5** *2 1/2* **Bookiesindex Boy**[42] 2179 7-9-10 **73**...................(bt) StephenCraine 8 47
(J R Jenkins) *trckd ldrs gng wl: effrt 2f out: rdn wl over 1f out: sn wknd* **17/2**
1300 **6** *1 3/4* **Tillys Tale**[3] 3379 4-9-5 **75**.............................. DavidSimmonson(7) 2 43
(Paul Midgley) *chsd ldrs on inner: rdn along 1/2-way: sn wknd* **9/1**
-600 **7** *1 3/4* **Egyptian Lord**[91] 1029 8-8-7 **56** oh11.......................(b) KirstyMilczarek 6 17
(Peter Grayson) *a in rr* **80/1**
1400 **8** *1 1/4* **Fantasy Fry**[41] 2199 3-8-13 **75**.. BenWilliams(7) 1 30
(Tom Dascombe) *s.i.s: a bhd* **16/1**
6122 **9** *1* **Shawkantango**[12] 3078 4-9-6 **69**.............................(v) RobbieFitzpatrick 7 22
(Derek Shaw) *s.i.s: sn rdn along and a bhd* **4/1**[1]

59.87 secs (0.17) **Going Correction** +0.20s/f (Slow) **9** Ran SP% **101.4**
WFA 3 from 4yo+ 6lb
Speed ratings (Par 103): **106,105,101,93,89 87,84,82,80**
toteswingers:1&2:£4.40, 2&3:£4.20, 1&3:£4.60 CSF £25.84 CT £109.54 TOTE £4.90: £1.10, £2.10, £1.70; EX 32.30.
Owner Tykes And Terriers Racing Club **Bred** Exors Of The Late N Ahamad & P C Scott **Trained** Scrooby, Notts
■ Six Wives was withdrawn (13/2, broke out of stalls). Deduct 10p in the £ under R4.

FOCUS
Seven horses with 23 C&D wins to their credit in this modest but highly competitive sprint handicap run, at a furious pace. Pretty solid form.

3494 PLAY ROULETTE AT LADBROKES.COM MEDIAN AUCTION MAIDEN STKS — 5f (F)
8:00 (8:00) (Class 6) 3-4-Y-0 **£1,706** (£503; £252) **Stalls** High

Form RPR
24 **1** **Triviality (IRE)**[31] 2493 3-8-11 0.................................. FergusSweeney 4 69+
(Jamie Osborne) *dwlt: trckd ldrs: swtchd lft and hdwy to ld after 2f: pushed clr appr fnl f: kpt on* **4/9**[1]
063 **2** *2 1/2* **These Dreams**[10] 3192 3-8-6 51.................................. RoystonFfrench 8 52
(Richard Guest) *chsd ldrs: hdwy 2f out: rdn to chse wnr over 1f out: edgd lft and no imp ins fnl f* **8/1**[3]
5- **3** *4 1/2* **Bint Alakaaber (IRE)**[298] 5719 3-8-6 0............................ FrannyNorton 7 36
(J R Jenkins) *led 2f: cl up tl rdn along wl over 1f out and sn one pce* **3/1**[2]
4 *1/2* **Lizzy's Dream** 3-8-11 0.. LeeNewman 2 39
(Robin Bastiman) *trckd ldrs: hdwy to chse wnr 1/2-way: rdn along wl over 1f out: grad wknd* **33/1**
00 **5** *3* **Lord Sun**[89] 1065 3-8-11 0.. RobbieFitzpatrick 6 28
(Peter Grayson) *prom: rdn along bef 1/2-way: sn wknd* **100/1**
6-00 **6** *4* **Gessabelle**[12] 3090 4-8-12 36...................................(t) KirstyMilczarek 5 —
(Phil McEntee) *prom: rdn along and lost pl after 2f: sn bhd* **50/1**
00 **7** *3 3/4* **Bop Till Dawn (IRE)**[21] 2790 3-8-6 0................................. LukeMorris 3 —
(Harry Dunlop) *prom: rdn along and lost pl after 1 1/2f: edgd lft and drvn in rr 1/2-way: sn bhd and eased* **33/1**

61.06 secs (1.36) **Going Correction** +0.20s/f (Slow)
WFA 3 from 4yo 6lb **7** Ran SP% **114.2**
Speed ratings (Par 101): **97,93,85,85,80 73,67**
toteswingers:1&2:£1.30, 2&3:£1.50, 1&3:£1.10 CSF £4.94 TOTE £1.50: £1.10, £2.80; EX 2.20.
Owner J A Osborne **Bred** Denis A McCarthy **Trained** Upper Lambourn, Berks

FOCUS
A very weak sprint maiden. The winner did not need to improve much on his CD debut.
Bint Alakaaber(IRE) Official explanation: jockey said filly ran too free
Gessabelle Official explanation: jockey said filly was outpaced

3495 MEMBERSHIP OF SOUTHWELL GOLF CLUB H'CAP — 7f (F)
8:30 (8:33) (Class 6) (0-65,65) 3-Y-0+ **£1,706** (£503; £252) **Stalls** Low

Form RPR
000 **1** **Tenancy (IRE)**[29] 2547 7-8-9 **51**........................... DanielleMcCreery(5) 9 61
(Shaun Harris) *mde virtually all: rdn wl over 1f out: drvn ent fnl f: hld on gamely* **66/1**
1315 **2** *1/2* **Jonnie Skull (IRE)**[20] 2829 5-9-6 **57**...........................(vt) KirstyMilczarek 1 65
(Phil McEntee) *prom on inner: effrt over 2f out: rdn to chse wnr ent fnl f: sn drvn and kpt on same pce towards fin* **8/1**
0500 **3** *hd* **Avec Moi**[20] 2829 4-8-2 **46** oh1.. DanielHarris(7) 4 53
(Christine Dunnett) *cl up: pushed along and sltly outpcd 1/2-way: hdwy over 2f out: rdn to chal wl over 1f out and ev ch tl no ex wl ins fnl f* **66/1**
3560 **4** *1 1/4* **Ubenkor (IRE)**[29] 2543 6-9-5 **63**.................................. JustinNewman(7) 7 67+
(Michael Herrington) *s.i.s and bhd: hdwy 2f out: swtchd rt and rdn over 1f out: kpt on ins fnl f: nrst fin* **5/1**[2]
6635 **5** *2 3/4* **Elusive Warrior (USA)**[40] 2237 8-8-11 **55**..................(p) NoraLooby(7) 11 52
(Alan McCabe) *prom: rdn along wl over 2f out: drvn wl over 1f out: one pce appr fnl f* **7/1**[3]
4064 **6** *3 3/4* **Exceedingly Good (IRE)**[7] 3248 5-9-2 **58**...................... RyanClark(5) 10 45
(Roy Bowring) *cl up: rdn along 2f out: drvn over 1f out and grad wknd* **10/1**
4500 **7** *shd* **Vanilla Rum**[25] 2674 4-10-0 **65**...................................(p) MickyFenton 8 52
(John Mackie) *dwlt and in rr tl sme late hdwy* **8/1**
3105 **8** *1 1/4* **Bold Diva**[8] 3241 6-9-6 **57**..(v) LukeMorris 5 40
(Tony Carroll) *in tch: rdn along over 2f out: sn drvn and wknd wl over 1f out* **8/1**
-022 **9** *3 1/2* **Baby Driver**[15] 2984 3-9-5 **65**.. RichardKingscote 2 39
(Tom Dascombe) *in tch: rdn along wl over 2f out: sn wknd* **7/1**[3]
1512 **10** *4 1/2* **Zarius**[104] 869 4-9-10 **61**.. JackMitchell 6 23
(Chris Wall) *towards rr: rdn along 1/2-way: drvn over 2f out: eased over 1f out* **9/4**[1]

1m 31.5s (1.20) **Going Correction** +0.075s/f (Slow)
WFA 3 from 4yo+ 9lb **10** Ran SP% **117.8**
Speed ratings (Par 101): **96,95,95,93,90 86,86,84,80,75**
toteswingers:1&2:£75.90, 2&3:£35.40, 1&3:£75.90 CSF £536.40 CT £30976.08 TOTE £51.40: £12.80, £2.60, £9.70; EX 362.60.
Owner Wilf Hobson **Bred** G A E And J Smith Bloodstock Ltd **Trained** Carburton, Notts

FOCUS
A modest 46-65 handicap and few got involved. A shock winner but no fluke. He's rated back to his post-3yo best.
Zarius Official explanation: trainer's rep said, regarding running, that the gelding did not face the kickback.

3496 GOLF AND RACING AT SOUTHWELL H'CAP — 1m (F)
9:00 (9:01) (Class 6) (0-55,55) 3-Y-0+ **£1,706** (£503; £252) **Stalls** Low

Form RPR
6033 **1** **Eastern Hills**[55] 1814 6-9-7 **55**...................................(p) MartinHarley(3) 7 69
(Alan McCabe) *cl up: led after 2f: qcknd clr wl over 2f out: rdn over 1f out: kpt on wl ins fnl f* **13/2**[3]
20-3 **2** *3* **Master Of Song**[20] 2828 4-9-7 **52**..................................(p) PaulQuinn 11 59
(Roy Bowring) *in tch: hdwy to trck ldrs over 3f out: rdn to chse wnr wl over 1f out: sn drvn and no imp fnl f* **7/1**
0005 **3** *3* **Amtired**[11] 3110 5-9-3 **51**...(be) PaulPickard(3) 10 51+
(Brian Ellison) *in rr: hdwy 3f out: rdn over 2f out: styd on u.p appr fnl f: nrst fin* **12/1**
6325 **4** *4 1/2* **St Ignatius**[14] 3019 4-9-8 **53**...(p) JamesDoyle 4 43
(Michael Appleby) *chsd ldrs: rdn along wl over 2f out: sn drvn and kpt on same pce* **17/2**
3542 **5** *1* **Goodmanyourself**[21] 2786 3-8-5 **46**............................ JamesSullivan 6 32
(Paul Midgley) *trckd ldrs: hdwy to chse wnr wl over 2f out: rdn wl over 1f out: sn drvn and wknd* **11/4**[1]
-032 **6** *3* **Jamarjo (IRE)**[49] 1979 4-9-7 **52**...................................(b) MartinLane 14 33
(Steve Gollings) *trckd ldrs: effrt 3f out: rdn over 2f out: sn drvn and btn* **9/2**[2]
0/55 **7** *1/2* **Can Can Dancer**[20] 2828 6-9-1 **46**............................ RobbieFitzpatrick 9 26
(Charles Smith) *towards rr: sme hdwy over 2f out: nvr a factor* **50/1**
3-60 **8** *1 1/2* **Richo**[5] 3317 5-9-2 **52**..(b) DanielleMcCreery(5) 5 28
(Shaun Harris) *s.i.s: a in rr* **20/1**
4002 **9** *6* **Herecomethegirls**[20] 2820 5-9-3 **53**...........................(b) KylieManser(5) 12 15
(Olivia Maylam) *a towards rr* **20/1**
0-30 **10** *12* **Kathindi (IRE)**[7] 3243 4-9-7 **52**.. KellyHarrison 3 —
(Michael Chapman) *midfield: rdn along bef 1/2-way: sn wknd* **66/1**
30-0 **11** *2 1/4* **Catawollow**[5] 3317 4-9-1 **49**..(e) RobertLButler(3) 8 —
(Richard Guest) *dwlt: a towards rr* **20/1**
0004 **12** *4 1/2* **Fly By Nelly**[14] 3017 5-9-2 **47**... WilliamCarson 1 —
(Mark Hoad) *led 2f: prom tl rdn along 1/2-way and sn wknd* **20/1**
0/-5 **13** *6* **Ocarito (GER)**[151] 340 10-9-4 **49**.. TonyHamilton 2 —
(Elliott Cooper) *a towards rr: bhd fr 1/2-way* **10/1**

1m 43.69s (-0.01) **Going Correction** +0.075s/f (Slow)
WFA 3 from 4yo+ 10lb **13** Ran SP% **120.5**
Speed ratings (Par 101): **103,100,97,92,91 88,88,86,80,68 66,61,55**
toteswingers:1&2:£9.10, 2&3:£20.70, 1&3:£16.60 CSF £46.87 CT £543.67 TOTE £9.30: £2.10, £1.50, £6.70.
Owner Charles Wentworth **Bred** Azienda Agricola Patrizia **Trained** Averham Park, Notts

FOCUS
A rock bottom 46-55 handicap and again the pace was sound. The time was decent and the winner is rated back to his winter best.
Richo Official explanation: jockey said gelding was slowly away
T/Plt: £404.40 to a £1 stake. Pool of £60,485.44 - 109.18 winning tickets. T/Qpdt: £30.80 to a £1 stake. Pool of £6,864.86 - 164.90 winning tickets. JR

3497 - 3503a (Foreign Racing) - See Raceform Interactive

2665 CATTERICK (L-H)

Wednesday, June 29

OFFICIAL GOING: Good to firm (9.0)

Wind: light 1/2 against Weather: overcast

3504 EBF "MULLIONMILEANHOUR" MAIDEN FILLIES' STKS 5f

2:30 (2:31) (Class 5) 2-Y-O **£3,238** (£963; £481; £240) **Stalls** Low

Form RPR

324 **1** **Almond Branches**[57] 1797 2-9-0 0................................ PJMcDonald 12 75+
(George Moore) *sn chsng ldrs on outside: hdwy over 1f out: styd on wl to ld last strides* **15/2**

42 **2** *shd* **Excelette (IRE)**[11] 3165 2-9-0 0................................ TomEaves 4 75
(Bryan Smart) *led: rdn 2f out: kpt on wl fnl f: hdd nr fin* **7/2**[1]

34 **3** *3* **Rougini (IRE)**[30] 2542 2-9-0 0................................ AndrewElliott 8 64
(Mrs K Burke) *w ldrs: styd on same pce appr fnl f* **16/1**

4 *3/4* **Kyllachy Dancer** 2-9-0 0................................ FrannyNorton 1 64+
(John Quinn) *mid-div: swtchd rt and kpt on wl appr fnl f* **11/2**

4 **5** *2* **Blue Belle Lady**[15] 3021 2-9-0 0................................ TonyHamilton 11 54+
(Richard Fahey) *in rr: hdwy on outer 2f out: kpt on: nt rch ldrs* **28/1**

0303 **6** *nk* **See Clearly**[7] 3273 2-9-0 0................................ DavidAllan 7 53
(Tim Easterby) *w ldrs: wknd ins fnl f* **5/1**[3]

66 **7** *1 1/2* **Lady Caprice**[7] 3273 2-9-0 0................................ PaulHanagan 3 48
(Ann Duffield) *chsd ldrs: one pce fnl 2f* **14/1**

0 **8** *1* **Elusive Bonus (IRE)**[7] 3273 2-9-0 0................................ DanielTudhope 2 44
(David O'Meara) *w ldrs: wknd appr fnl f* **16/1**

9 *hd* **Al Doha** 2-9-0 0................................ PhillipMakin 6 50+
(Kevin Ryan) *dwlt: a towards rr* **9/2**[2]

0 **10** *10* **Blue Ridges (IRE)**[19] 2886 2-9-0 0................................ SilvestreDeSousa 5 —
(Geoffrey Harker) *chsd ldrs: lost pl after 2f: sn bhd* **7/1**

11 *6* **Dapper's Dancer** 2-9-0 0................................ RobertWinston 10 —
(David O'Meara) *s.i.s: a in rr: bhd fnl 2f: eased clsng stages* **50/1**

60.12 secs (0.32) **Going Correction** -0.175s/f (Firm) **11** Ran SP% **120.6**

Speed ratings (Par 90): **90,89,85,83,80 80,77,76,75,59 50**

toteswingers:1&2:£7.10, 2&3:£8.10, 1&3:£21.80 CSF £34.80 TOTE £9.60: £3.40, £1.40, £3.50; EX 25.90 Trifecta £105.10 Pool: £525.96 - 3.70 winning units..

Owner J A And M A Knox **Bred** J A And Mrs M A Knox **Trained** Middleham Moor, N Yorks

FOCUS

Back straight and top bend moved in 3yds. A modest maiden in which those with the best form and experience dominated. The runners stayed far side. The winner built on her early-season promise.

NOTEBOOK

Almond Branches put a modest latest effort behind her and probably showed a bit of improvement in the process, running down the pacemaker close home and probably deserving a bit of extra credit in that she did it from the widest draw. There's plenty of speed in her pedigree, but she shaped here as though she'll stay 6f and her future almost certainly lies in nurseries. (op 6-1)

Excelette(IRE) has bags of pace and will always be best kept to a sharp 5f. Her future too lies in nurseries, but she is probably up to winning a similar event in the north given similarly fast conditions. (op 5-2)

Rougini(IRE) looks something of a short runner for now, and didn't see her race out anywhere near as strongly as it looked likely she would 2f out.

Kyllachy Dancer ◆, a half-sister to the useful sprinting 2-y-o BA Foxtrot, was a springer in the market and left the impression that she'll do a fair bit better with this run under her belt, getting behind early as her inexperience showed but catching the eye in keeping on well without being knocked about. (op 12-1)

Blue Belle Lady ◆ stepped up on her debut form in a 6f Thirsk seller while leaving the impression she found this drop in trip all against her. She might be one her shrewd connections are bringing along with nurseries in mind.

See Clearly had shown improved form on a softer surface over a stiffer 5f last time, and looked to be done for pace on this sharper track. (op 6-1 tchd 13-2)

Al Doha, whose sales price rose to 30,000gns as a yearling, looked all at sea on the undulations after missing the break, but the penny started to drop close home and she looks sure to improve next time, not least at 6f. (tchd 4-1)

3505 YORKSHIRE-OUTDOORS.CO.UK MEDIAN AUCTION MAIDEN STKS 5f 212y

3:00 (3:01) (Class 5) 2-Y-0 **£2,072** (£616; £308; £153) **Stalls** Low

Form RPR

0 **1** **Sinai (IRE)**[18] 2936 2-8-12 0................................ SilvestreDeSousa 11 69+
(Geoffrey Harker) *chsd ldrs: outpcd over 3f out: hdwy on outer over 2f out: r.o to ld last 100yds* **6/1**[3]

0602 **2** *2 1/2* **Beechey's Beauty**[15] 3021 2-9-3 0................................(p) DavidNolan 8 64
(Ann Duffield) *w ldrs: led over 3f out: edgd lft over 1f out: hdd jst ins fnl f: no ex* **20/1**

3 *3* **Stormy Whatever (FR)** 2-9-3 0................................ JamesSullivan 9 55+
(James Given) *sn trcking ldrs: chal over 1f out: wknd fnl 75yds* **10/1**

00 **4** *nk* **Lady Gadfly**[29] 2587 2-8-12 0................................ FrederikTylicki 6 49
(Micky Hammond) *mid-div: outpcd and lost pl over 3f out: kpt on wl ins fnl f* **100/1**

2522 **5** *shd* **Superplex**[14] 3050 2-9-3 0................................ PJMcDonald 1 54
(John Quinn) *chsd ldrs: pushed lft over 1f out: kpt on same pce* **13/8**[1]

44 **6** *nk* **Armiger**[23] 2767 2-9-3 0................................ PaulHanagan 3 53
(William Muir) *led: hdd over 3f out: hmpd and lost pl over 1f out: kpt on towards fin* **2/1**[2]

7 *1* **Docs Legacy (IRE)** 2-9-3 0................................ TonyHamilton 7 50
(Richard Fahey) *s.i.s: in rr tl styd on fnl 2f* **18/1**

50 **8** *3* **Egyptian Cross**[53] 1890 2-9-3 0................................(t) TomEaves 4 41
(John Weymes) *had front shoe removed at s: in rr: outpcd over 3f out: sme hdwy 2f out: nvr nr ldrs* **50/1**

550 **9** *1 1/2* **Kodiac King (IRE)**[32] 2485 2-9-3 0................................(b[1]) PhillipMakin 2 36
(Kevin Ryan) *t.k.h: trckd ldrs: wknd over 1f out* **14/1**

10 *12* **Thunder Bullet** 2-9-3 0................................ AndrewElliott 5 —
(Andrew Crook) *s.i.s: sn bhd: t.o 2f out* **50/1**

1m 12.52s (-1.08) **Going Correction** -0.30s/f (Firm) **10** Ran SP% **116.4**

Speed ratings (Par 93): **95,91,87,87,87 86,85,81,79,63**

toteswingers:1&2:£8.60, 2&3:£12.70, 1&3:£5.50 CSF £115.81 TOTE £9.30: £2.40, £3.10, £3.80; EX 79.20 Trifecta £396.60 Part won. Pool of £535.98 - 0.60 winning units..

Owner Mr & Mrs H Nensey, Saif Nensey **Bred** Con Marnane **Trained** Thirkleby, N Yorks

FOCUS

Modest fare again with the proximity of the fourth certainly calling the form into question, but the winner promises to rate higher and the third also shaped well. The pace looked a fair one.

NOTEBOOK

Sinai(IRE) had shaped well in a stronger maiden than this on her debut at York and belied market weakness to run out convincing winner, albeit only really putting her seal on things well inside the last, in the process giving her yard their first juvenile winner since 2008. She'll improve again and leaves impression she'll have no trouble staying 7f. (op 5-1 tchd 7-1)

Beechey's Beauty had been second in a seller last time, but that was his best effort to date and he looks to have improved again, being never far away and keeping on well to finish clear of the rest. He'd be up to winning a seller if he was to be risked at that level again. (op 18-1)

Stormy Whatever(FR), who cost 40,000euros at the sales this year, shaped well on his debut, looking to be travelling strongly early in the straight but ultimately running as if he needed the race to put him straight. Youngsters from his yard generally improve for the run and he may be up to winning a small race. (op 14-1)

Lady Gadfly had been well held in both starts to date, but turned in an improved effort which was all the more creditable considering she had a shoe removed at the start. That said, she's blown her cover with regards to nurseries now.

Superplex just about set the standard on his 5f form, but his pedigree is all speed and he was found wanting for stamina trying this trip for the first time. He's always going to be vulnerable in maidens from now on. (op 15-8 tchd 6-4)

Armiger's main undoing was a basic lack of speed, but in his defence he didn't get a clear run soon after being headed in the straight. He was coming back at the finish and like his recent equine namesake, looks in need of a stiffer test of stamina. (tchd 7-4)

Docs Legacy(IRE), a colt by Ad Valorem out of a German middle-distance winner, was weak in the market and never threatened after a slowish start, but there were signs late on he was getting the hang of things and he'll improve with time and distance. (op 16-1 tchd 20-1)

3506 PIN POINT RECRUITMENT H'CAP 7f

3:30 (3:31) (Class 4) (0-80,80) 3-Y-0+ **£4,209** (£1,252; £625; £312) **Stalls** Low

Form RPR

5-50 **1** **Orpsie Boy (IRE)**[18] 2938 8-9-10 **78**................................ SilvestreDeSousa 1 89
(Ruth Carr) *trckd ldrs: led on ins jst ins fnl f: kpt on wl: readily* **9/1**

2101 **2** *2* **Pelmanism**[15] 3025 4-9-4 **72**................................(b) PhillipMakin 9 78+
(Kevin Ryan) *hmpd s: in rr: gd hdwy on outside 2f out: styd on wl ins fnl f: tk 2nd post* **9/1**

0106 **3** *nse* **My Gacho (IRE)**[13] 3071 9-9-7 **75**................................(v) AndrewMullen 11 80
(David Nicholls) *hdwy on outer to ld over 4f out: hdd jst ins fnl f: no ex* **28/1**

3020 **4** *1 1/4* **Carambola**[18] 2938 5-9-3 **71**................................ RobertWinston 6 73
(Mel Brittain) *chsd ldrs: kpt on same pce appr fnl f* **12/1**

1202 **5** *1/2* **Dazeen**[11] 3169 4-9-7 **75**................................ TonyCulhane 7 76+
(Paul Midgley) *s.i.s: hdwy over 2f out: swtchd rt over 1f out: kpt on wl: nt rch ldrs* **6/1**[2]

0023 **6** *nk* **Sacrosanctus**[18] 2916 3-9-0 **77**................................ GrahamGibbons 14 74
(David Nicholls) *mid-div: hdwy on outside 2f out: kpt on same pce appr fnl f* **14/1**

0210 **7** *1* **Not My Choice (IRE)**[13] 3071 6-9-12 **80**................................(t) PJMcDonald 3 77
(David C Griffiths) *led tl over 4f out: kpt on same pce ins fnl f* **14/1**

0-52 **8** *3/4* **Last Sovereign**[18] 2917 7-9-9 **77**................................ TomEaves 2 72+
(Ollie Pears) *s.v.s: gd hdwy on inner whn nt clr run over 2f out: chsng ldrs whn nt clr run over 1f out: nt rcvr* **5/1**[1]

0-06 **9** *nk* **Horatio Carter**[14] 3038 6-9-5 **73**................................(p) PaulHanagan 4 67
(Michael Smith) *chsd ldrs: effrt over 2f out: wknd ins fnl f* **9/1**

1300 **10** *1* **Mujaadel (USA)**[22] 2783 6-9-9 **80**................................(p) MichaelO'Connell[(3)] 10 72+
(David Nicholls) *s.i.s: swtchd lft after s: hdwy over 2f out: one pce whn nt clr run appr fnl f* **11/1**

3064 **11** *3 1/4* **Malcheek (IRE)**[15] 3028 9-9-11 **79**................................ DavidAllan 15 62
(Tim Easterby) *trckd ldrs on outer: wknd over 1f out* **8/1**[3]

0606 **12** *19* **Glenridding**[16] 2995 7-9-10 **78**................................(p) FrederikTylicki 5 10
(James Given) *mid-div: lost pl over 4f out: sn bhd: t.o 3f out: virtually p.u* **20/1**

-162 **13** *2 1/2* **George Benjamin**[57] 1793 4-9-12 **80**................................ AdrianNicholls 12 —
(David Nicholls) *trckd ldrs: effrt over 2f out: sn lost pl: bhd whn heavily eased ins fnl f: virtually p.u: t.o* **8/1**[3]

1m 23.91s (-3.09) **Going Correction** -0.30s/f (Firm)

WFA 3 from 4yo+ 9lb **13** Ran SP% **120.7**

Speed ratings (Par 105): **105,102,102,101,100 100,99,98,97,96 93,71,68**

toteswingers:1&2:£21.20, 2&3:£30.60, 1&3:£58.80 CSF £88.64 CT £2267.32 TOTE £11.10: £4.10, £3.80, £12.70; EX 99.00 TRIFECTA Not won..

Owner Miss Vanessa Church **Bred** Minch Bloodstock **Trained** Huby, N Yorks

FOCUS

A competitive handicap, though not one that was run at the breakneck gallop that seemed likely beforehand, given the number of usual front runners up against each other.

Last Sovereign Official explanation: jockey said gelding missed the break

Mujaadel(USA) Official explanation: jockey said gelding was denied a clear run

3507 RACING AGAIN NEXT WEDNESDAY H'CAP 1m 7f 177y

4:00 (4:00) (Class 5) (0-75,73) 4-Y-0+ **£2,072** (£616; £308; £153) **Stalls** Low

Form RPR

65-0 **1** **Tillietudlem (FR)**[17] 2952 5-8-9 **61**................................ LeeNewman 1 67
(Jim Goldie) *s.i.s: hld up in rr: hdwy 6f out: effrt on ins over 3f out: chsd ldr appr fnl f: edgd lft styd on to ld towards fin: all out* **4/1**[1]

4-64 **2** *hd* **Mason Hindmarsh**[40] 2262 4-8-12 **64**................................ PaulHanagan 8 70
(Karen McLintock) *mid-div: hdwy 6f out: sn chsng ldrs: slipped bnd over 3f out: styd on wl ins fnl f* **9/2**[2]

1053 **3** *hd* **Capable Guest (IRE)**[26] 2666 9-8-8 **60**................................ PJMcDonald 7 65
(George Moore) *in rr div: hdwy 6f out: rdn and outpcd over 3f out: styd on wl appr fnl f: fin wl* **16/1**

0002 **4** *nk* **Drop The Hammer**[28] 2618 5-8-2 **54**................................(b) SilvestreDeSousa 4 59
(David O'Meara) *led 1f: w ldr: led over 4f out: 3 l clr over 1f out: hdd: crowded and no ex nr fin* **8/1**

5-61 **5** *1 1/4* **Spiders Star**[13] 3072 8-8-10 **65**................................ PaulPickard[(3)] 9 68
(Simon West) *hld up in rr: gd hdwy over 2f out: styng on wl whn nt clr run nr fin* **13/2**[3]

2-00 **6** *3/4* **Danceintothelight**[15] 3023 4-8-12 **64**................................ KellyHarrison 11 66
(Micky Hammond) *hld up in mid-div: t.k.h: hdwy on outer over 2f out: kpt on same pce fnl f* **10/1**

5-22 **7** *2 1/4* **Jeu De Roseau (IRE)**[13] 3072 7-8-12 **64**................................ JamieSpencer 10 63
(Chris Grant) *hld up towards rr: rdn and outpcd over 3f out: hdwy on outer over 2f out: kpt on same pce: nvr nr ldrs* **4/1**[1]

1413 **8** *8* **Relative Strength (IRE)**[57] 1792 6-9-4 **70**................................(p) StephenCraine 5 59
(Jennie Candlish) *trckd ldng pair: jnd ldrs 7f out: wnt 2nd over 4f out: hung lft and wknd fnl f: eased towards fin* **14/1**

2504 **9** *8* **Valdan (IRE)**[11] 3185 7-8-7 **59**................................(bt[1]) FrannyNorton 3 38
(Maurice Barnes) *t.k.h: sn trcking ldrs: wknd over 2f out* **10/1**

/3-0 **10** *10* **Alhaque (USA)**[11] 3170 5-9-0 **66**................................ TonyCulhane 6 32
(Paul Midgley) *in rr: bhd and drvn 8f out* **50/1**

5-20 **11** *7* **My Mate Max**[13] 3095 6-9-7 **73**................................(b[1]) GrahamGibbons 2 30
(Reg Hollinshead) *reminders after s: led after 1f: hdd over 4f out: lost pl over 2f out: sn bhd: eased towards fin* **16/1**

3m 26.26s (-5.74) **Going Correction** -0.30s/f (Firm) **11** Ran SP% **118.0**

Speed ratings (Par 103): **102,101,101,101,101 100,99,95,91,86 83**

toteswingers:1&2:£4.90, 2&3:£18.70, 1&3:£21.90 CSF £21.83 CT £262.36 TOTE £6.00: £2.50, £2.20, £4.90; EX 23.60 TRIFECTA Not won..

Owner Phoenix Horse Racing Club Ltd **Bred** Bernard Ducasse **Trained** Uplawmoor, E Renfrews
■ Stewards' Enquiry : Lee Newman one-day ban: used whip in incorrect place (Jul 13)

FOCUS
An ordinary staying handicap run at a good pace and whose complexion changed completely in the closing stages.
Mason Hindmarsh Official explanation: jockey said gelding slipped on bend turn for home
Valdan(IRE) Official explanation: jockey said gelding became unbalanced bend turn into home straight

3508 GO RACING IN YORKSHIRE CLASSIFIED STKS — 7f
4:30 (4:32) (Class 6) 3-Y-0+ — **£2,729** (£806; £403) **Stalls** Low

Form — RPR

3-34 **1** **Al Burkaan (IRE)**[36] 2392 3-8-12 70 ... JamieSpencer 2 — 74
(Ed Dunlop) *in rr: hdwy on inner over 3f out: styd on to ld last 50yds: kpt on* **9/4**[2]

-300 **2** *nk* **Azimuth (USA)**[8] 3245 4-9-7 70 ... PaulHanagan 7 — 76
(Ann Duffield) *hld up in mid-div: hdwy over 2f out: led 1f out: hdd and no ex wl ins fnl f* **10/1**[3]

1002 **3** *2 ¾* **No Quarter (IRE)**[15] 3024 4-9-7 63 ... FrannyNorton 5 — 69
(Tracy Waggott) *hld up in rr: hdwy on ins over 2f out: n.m.r over 1f out: styd on to take 3rd last 100yds* **12/1**

01-0 **4** *2 ¼* **Dan's Martha**[33] 2466 3-8-12 70 ... (t) PJMcDonald 3 — 60
(Ben Haslam) *trckd ldrs: outpcd over 3f out: styd on to chse ldrs over 1f out: one pce* **14/1**

-000 **5** *¾* **Adorable Choice (IRE)**[16] 2986 3-8-12 70 ... (vt[1]) RichardKingscote 1 — 58
(Tom Dascombe) *s.i.s: sn trcking ldrs: wnt 2nd over 4f out: wknd 1f out* **20/1**

60-4 **6** *nk* **Johannesgray (IRE)**[177] 22 4-9-2 64 ... NeilFarley(5) 4 — 60
(Noel Wilson) *sn led: edgd rt over 1f out: hdd 1f out: sn wknd* **33/1**

5425 **7** *¾* **Coax**[5] 3337 3-8-12 70 ... SilvestreDeSousa 6 — 55
(Mark Johnston) *stmbld s: led early: chsd ldrs: drvn over 4f out: wknd appr fnl f* **5/4**[1]

-050 **8** *7* **En Fuego**[35] 2398 4-9-4 70 ... (p) MichaelO'Connell(3) 8 — 39
(Geoffrey Harker) *chsd ldrs: rn v wd and lost pl bnd over 3f out: sn bhd* **12/1**

1m 24.25s (-2.75) **Going Correction** -0.30s/f (Firm)
WFA 3 from 4yo 9lb — **8** Ran SP% **114.1**
Speed ratings (Par 101): **103,102,99,96,96 95,94,86**
toteswingers:1&2:£4.20, 2&3:£6.80, 1&3:£4.30 CSF £24.84 TOTE £3.70: £1.70, £2.00, £3.30; EX 22.80 Trifecta £131.40 Pool: £872.34 - 4.91 winning units..
Owner Ahmad Al Shaikh **Bred** Old Carhue Stud **Trained** Newmarket, Suffolk

FOCUS
An ordinary classified event into which few came on the back of a good recent effort, so not form to go overboard about for all the winner is unexposed. The pace seemed a decent one.
Coax Official explanation: trainer's rep had no explanation for the poor form shown
En Fuego Official explanation: jockey said gelding failed to handle bend

3509 CATTERICKBRIDGE.CO.UK H'CAP (DIV I) — 1m 3f 214y
5:00 (5:00) (Class 6) (0-65,65) 4-Y-0+ — **£1,364** (£403; £201) **Stalls** Low

Form — RPR

3243 **1** **Golden Future**[12] 3129 8-8-12 56 ... TomEaves 1 — 63
(Peter Niven) *trckd ldr: effrt on ins over 2f out: styd on to ld jst ins fnl f: all out* **10/3**[2]

-002 **2** *hd* **Rubi Dia**[14] 3041 4-9-4 62 ... (v[1]) AndrewHeffernan 6 — 69
(Kevin M Prendergast) *hld up in mid-div: hdwy over 2f out: styd on wl ins fnl f: edgd lft: jst hld* **5/1**

0440 **3** *1 ½* **Lady Norlela**[28] 2622 5-8-2 53 ... ShaneBKelly(7) 11 — 57
(Brian Rothwell) *hld up in rr: outpcd over 4f out: hdwy over 2f out: styd on to take 3rd nr fin* **8/1**

100 **4** *nk* **Boa**[34] 2436 6-9-6 64 ... GrahamGibbons 3 — 68
(Reg Hollinshead) *trckd ldrs: upsides 6f out: hung lft and led over 1f out: hdd jst ins fnl f: hmpd and no ex* **4/1**[3]

0340 **5** *4 ½* **Monkton Vale (IRE)**[19] 2892 4-9-7 65 ... PaulHanagan 2 — 62
(Richard Fahey) *led: hdd over 1f out: sn wknd* **3/1**[1]

0065 **6** *nk* **Quaestor (IRE)**[11] 3185 4-7-13 46 oh1 ... (p) DeclanCannon(3) 4 — 42
(Andrew Crook) *t.k.h in mid-div: outpcd over 4f out: chsng ldrs over 2f out: sn wknd* **16/1**

6415 **7** *3 ¾* **Dimashq**[12] 3129 9-8-6 50 ... KellyHarrison 9 — 40
(Paul Midgley) *s.s: hld up in rr: hdwy over 4f out: hung lft and wknd over 2f out* **7/1**

2m 35.98s (-2.92) **Going Correction** -0.30s/f (Firm) — **7** Ran SP% **114.2**
Speed ratings (Par 101): **97,96,95,95,92 92,89**
toteswingers:1&2:£3.40, 2&3:£8.60, 1&3:£3.50 CSF £20.20 CT £121.72 TOTE £3.50: £2.00, £2.90; EX 15.10 Trifecta £94.30 Pool: £539.60 - 4.23 winning units..
Owner The Little Ice Club **Bred** Larksborough Stud Limited **Trained** Barton-le-Street, N Yorks
■ Stewards' Enquiry : Andrew Heffernan three-day ban: careless riding (Jul 13-15)

FOCUS
A modest handicap run at a fair pace.

3510 CATTERICKBRIDGE.CO.UK H'CAP (DIV II) — 1m 3f 214y
5:30 (5:30) (Class 6) (0-65,64) 4-Y-0+ — **£1,364** (£403; £201) **Stalls** Low

Form — RPR

3066 **1** **Light The City (IRE)**[28] 2618 4-8-2 45 ... JamesSullivan 2 — 57+
(Ruth Carr) *trckd ldrs: wnt 2nd 4f out: led over 2f out: hung lft and sn clr: readily* **8/1**

2501 **2** *3 ¾* **Eijaaz (IRE)**[12] 3141 10-8-13 59 ... (p) MichaelO'Connell(3) 3 — 64
(Geoffrey Harker) *hld up in mid-div: effrt over 3f out: styd on to take 2nd last 100yds: no imp* **7/2**[2]

0-53 **3** *1* **Folk Tune (IRE)**[32] 2492 8-9-6 63 ... (v[1]) PhillipMakin 8 — 66
(John Quinn) *s.i.s: sn chsng ldrs: drvn over 4f out: wnt 2nd over 1f out: kpt on same pce* **8/1**

030- **4** *4* **San Deng**[34] 4648 9-8-4 47 ... (p) PaulHanagan 6 — 44
(Micky Hammond) *mid-div: drvn over 5f out: one pce fnl 3f* **11/2**[3]

2145 **5** *2 ½* **Magic Haze**[106] 859 5-9-1 58 ... SilvestreDeSousa 1 — 51
(Sally Hall) *sn trcking ldrs: drvn over 4f out: one pce fnl 2f* **10/1**

045- **6** *1* **Bijou Dan**[357] 3772 10-9-5 62 ... PJMcDonald 5 — 53
(George Moore) *in rr div: drvn over 5f out: outpcd over 3f out: kpt on fnl 2f* **18/1**

260- **7** *¾* **Follow The Sun (IRE)**[20] 7475 7-8-7 50 ... (p) TomEaves 10 — 40
(Peter Niven) *in rr div: drvn over 4f out: outpcd over 3f out: kpt on fnl 2f: no threat* **33/1**

-024 **8** *5* **Spahi (FR)**[6] 3317 5-8-12 55 ... (b[1]) DanielTudhope 11 — 37
(David O'Meara) *t.k.h: trckd ldr: led over 4f out: hdd over 2f out: wknd over 1f out* **10/3**[1]

1200 **9** *3* **Dazakhee**[21] 2815 4-9-7 64 ... TonyCulhane 4 — 41
(Paul Midgley) *hld up in rr: nvr on terms* **10/1**

02-0 **10** *10* **Flora's Pride**[30] 1039 7-8-9 52 ... FrederikTylicki 7 — 13
(Keith Reveley) *stmbld s: a in rr: bhd fnl 3f* **12/1**

00-0 **11** *8* **Fourlanends**[34] 2415 4-8-2 45 ... PaulQuinn 9 — —
(Noel Wilson) *t.k.h: led: hdd over 4f out: wknd over 2f out: sn bhd* **100/1**

2m 35.04s (-3.86) **Going Correction** -0.30s/f (Firm) — **11** Ran SP% **118.0**
Speed ratings (Par 101): **100,97,96,94,92 91,91,88,86,79 74**
toteswingers:1&2:£6.40, 2&3:£9.30, 1&3:£12.80. Tote Super 7: Win: Not won. Place: £742.00 CSF £36.22 CT £236.68 TOTE £10.20: £3.30, £1.10, £3.10; EX 50.90 Trifecta £462.00 Part won. Pool of £624.43 - 0.20 winning units..
Owner Atkins Legal Services **Bred** Rabbah Bloodstock Limited **Trained** Huby, N Yorks

FOCUS
A more strongly-run handicap than the first division with the two pacesetters ultimately paying the price, but overall weak-looking form.
Flora's Pride Official explanation: jockey said mare stumbled leaving stalls
T/Jkpt: Not won. T/Plt: £2,478.90 to a £1 stake. Pool of £67,372.85 - 19.84 winning tickets.
T/Qpdt: £104.60 to a £1 stake. Pool of £5,091.04 - 36.00 winning tickets. WG

3214 CHEPSTOW (L-H)
Wednesday, June 29

OFFICIAL GOING: Good (good to soft in places; 7.3)
Wind: Mild against Weather: Cloudy with sunny periods

3511 BRITISH STALLION STUDS SUPPORTING BRITISH RACING EBF MAIDEN STKS — 6f 16y
6:10 (6:11) (Class 5) 2-Y-O — **£3,238** (£963; £481; £240) **Stalls** High

Form — RPR

62 **1** **Avon Pearl**[17] 2962 2-9-3 0 ... DaneO'Neill 6 — 74+
(Henry Candy) *prom: rdn 2f out: led ent fnl f: kpt on strly towards fin: won gng away* **9/2**[2]

4 **2** *1* **Tango Sky (IRE)**[86] 1136 2-9-3 0 ... PatCosgrave 2 — 71
(Ralph Beckett) *prom: led over 3f out: rdn 2f out: narrowly hdd ent fnl f: kpt on but no ex towards fin* **14/1**

60 **3** *¾* **Maroosh**[30] 2559 2-9-3 0 ... ShaneKelly 5 — 69
(Brian Meehan) *trckd ldrs: rdn 2f out: kpt on but nt quite pce to chal* **12/1**[3]

2 **4** *1 ½* **Moustache (IRE)**[20] 2837 2-9-3 0 ... JimmyFortune 8 — 65
(Richard Hannon) *trckd ldrs: rdn 2f out: nt pce to chal: hung rt and squeezed up whn hld fnl f* **1/3**[1]

45 **5** *5* **Gypsy Rider**[22] 2787 2-9-3 0 ... CathyGannon 9 — 49
(Bryn Palling) *led tl over 3f out: sn rdn: wknd over 1f out* **50/1**

6 **6** *3* **Littlecote Lady**[21] 2817 2-8-12 0 ... LiamKeniry 1 — 35
(Mark Usher) *s.i.s: in tch: rdn 2f out: wknd over 1f out* **66/1**

7 *13* **Ionwy** 2-8-12 0 ... NeilChalmers 4 — —
(Derek Haydn Jones) *broncho'd for 1st f: wl bhd and nvr any ch but sme prog on gp fr over 1f out* **100/1**

1m 12.24s (0.24) **Going Correction** -0.125s/f (Firm) — **7** Ran SP% **112.0**
Speed ratings (Par 93): **93,91,90,88,82 78,60**
toteswingers: 1&2 £3.10, 1&3 £3.10, 2&3 £5.30. CSF £55.18 TOTE £4.80: £1.70, £4.20; EX 37.20.
Owner Pearl Bloodstock Ltd **Bred** Park Farm Racing **Trained** Kingston Warren, Oxon

FOCUS
After a dry day the going was changed to good, good to soft in places. Richard Hannon's hot odds-on favourite was disappointing in this maiden in which there was not much separating the first three.

NOTEBOOK
Avon Pearl showed some improvement when beating all except a well-fancied newcomer when favourite on soft ground at Salisbury last time. He had something to find but was always well positioned and showed some battling qualities to win going away at the finish. An Avonbridge colt whose sales price rose considerably to £52,000 as a yearling, he should be open to further progress and shapes like 7f will be within range this season. (tchd 4-1)
Tango Sky(IRE) showed good speed before fading on his Windsor debut, but this time he stayed in the firing line in an improved effort. Out of a 6f juvenile scorer, he is bred to make a sprinting 2-y-o and is capable of further progress for a yard whose youngsters have been relatively slow to come to hand this season. (op 12-1)
Maroosh, a Kyllachy colt who is out of a triple 1m winner, failed to build on his debut form at Goodwood last time, but that may have come too soon and he took a step forward this time, staying on well out wide to finish just behind the front pair. (tchd 14-1)
Moustache(IRE) was no match for a well-regarded newcomer when favourite in a 6.5f Newbury maiden on debut, but that form is beginning to work out well and he set a clear standard on this second outing. Tucked away, he had to wait for a gap but when he found a run he couldn't make any inroads on the leaders in a lacklustre effort. (op 2-5 tchd 4-9 in a place)
Ionwy was bucking and kicking when exiting the stalls and was quickly tailed off on debut.

3512 MAILADOC HYBRID MAIL SOLUTIONS H'CAP — 6f 16y
6:40 (6:42) (Class 6) (0-65,65) 3-Y-0+ — **£1,050** (£1,050; £240; £120) **Stalls** High

Form — RPR

2624 **1** **Bermondsey Bob (IRE)**[8] 3255 5-9-7 61 ... CathyGannon 7 — 75
(John Spearing) *racd centre and overall ldr: rdn 2f out: sn 2 l clr: all out whn jnd fnl stride* **6/1**[2]

-330 **1** *dht* **Euroquip Boy (IRE)**[18] 2921 4-9-1 55 ... JamieGoldstein 1 — 69
(Michael Scudamore) *chsd ldrs in centre: rdn over 2f out: chsd ldr over 1f out: kpt on ins fnl f: dead-heated fnl stride* **12/1**

-001 **3** *2 ½* **Royal Box**[9] 3216 4-9-1 55 6ex ... (p) SamHitchcott 6 — 61
(Dai Burchell) *racd centre: in tch: rdn over 3f out: wnt 3rd over 1f out: styd on same pce fnl f* **16/1**

2162 **4** *¾* **Emiratesdotcom**[9] 3217 5-9-9 63 ... LiamKeniry 12 — 67+
(Milton Bradley) *in tch on stands' side: rdn over 2f out: kpt on ins fnl f but nvr gng pce to get on terms* **5/1**[1]

12-6 **5** *1 ¾* **Delaware Dancer (IRE)**[20] 2845 4-9-8 62 ... JamesMillman 14 — 60+
(Jeremy Gask) *hld up towards rr on stands' side: rdn and hdwy fr 2f out: styd on wout threatening fnl f* **8/1**

0405 **6** *nse* **Chinese Democracy (USA)**[30] 2555 4-9-0 54 ... (v) TomMcLaughlin 9 — 52
(David Evans) *towards rr on stands' side: hdwy whn rdn and swtchd lft fr 2f out: styd on fnl f* **25/1**

0-20 **7** *1 ¾* **Cwmni**[131] 589 5-9-5 59 ... LukeMorris 11 — 51
(Bryn Palling) *racd in centre: nvr bttr than mid-div* **16/1**

6043 **8** *1* **Abacist (IRE)**[11] 3173 3-9-1 62 ... PatCosgrave 4 — 49
(Ralph Beckett) *hld up towards rr of centre gp: rdn and stdy prog on far side fr over 1f out: nvr trbld ldrs* **28/1**

3333 **9** *2* **Witchry**[18] 2903 9-9-2 63 ... DavidKenny(7) 13 — 46
(Tony Newcombe) *hld up towards rr on stands' side: sme late prog: nvr a factor* **7/1**[3]

35-0 **10** ½ **Babich Bay (IRE)**[16] 2993 3-9-2 **63**............................(b[1]) DarryllHolland 2 42
(Jo Hughes) *chsd ldr in centre: rdn over 2f out: wknd fnl f* **33/1**

6060 **11** *shd* **Gwilym (GER)**[28] 2609 8-9-4 **58**.......................(p) DaneO'Neill 15 39
(Derek Haydn Jones) *chsd ldrs on stands' side tl wknd over 1f out* **33/1**

0-45 **12** 1¼ **Holiday Snap**[6] 3322 5-9-9 **63**..............................(t) TravisBlock 10 40
(Mary Hambro) *sn prom on stands' side: rdn 3f out: wknd 2f out* **7/1**[3]

0002 **13** 1 **Caldermud (IRE)**[34] 2412 4-9-5 **59**..........................(t) RoystonFfrench 17 33
(Olivia Maylam) *a towards rr on stands' side* **11/1**

0205 **14** 1¼ **Defector (IRE)**[28] 2610 5-9-11 **65**............................ FrankieMcDonald 16 35
(David Bourton) *a towards rr on stands' side* **33/1**

46 **15** *nk* **Boragh Jamal (IRE)**[8] 3261 4-9-7 **64**......................(b) LouisBeuzelin(3) 5 33
(Brian Meehan) *chsd ldrs in centre gp: rdn over 2f out: wknd ent fnl f* **25/1**

01/0 **16** 4 **Half A Crown (IRE)**[20] 2845 6-9-1 **55**...........................(vt) JimmyFortune 3 —
(Noel Quinlan) *mid-div of centre gp: rdn over 2f out: sn wknd* **28/1**

0043 **17** 5 **Lutine Charlie (IRE)**[7] 3266 4-9-7 **64**...........................(p) JohnFahy(3) 8 —
(Ronald Harris) *sn pushed into ld on stands' side but 5 l down on centre gp: rdn over 2f out: sn wknd* **14/1**

1m 11.3s (-0.70) **Going Correction** -0.125s/f (Firm)
WFA 3 from 4yo+ 7lb **17** Ran SP% **124.9**
Speed ratings (Par 101): **99,99,95,94,92 92,89,88,85,85 85,83,82,80,80 74,68**WIN: BB £3.60, EB £9.60. PL: BB £2.00, EB £6.10, RB £5.90, Emiratesdotcom £1.10. CSF: BB & EB £35.69, EB & BB £38.76. TRICAST: BB, EB & RB £552.23. EB, BB, RB £586.79, EX: BB/EB £86.90, EB/BB £69.50.swingers: BB & EB £18.80, BB & RB £13.60, EB & RB £97.1027 CSF £Owner CT £A A Campbell TOTE £Bred: £Pier House Stud, £Trained, £Kinnersley, Worcs.
Owner Ted Bennett **Bred** Gerard And Yvonne Kennedy **Trained** Bromsash, Herefordshire

FOCUS
An ordinary sprint handicap. The field raced centre to stands' side and the clear, dead-heating first two raced down the middle.

3513 UHY PEACHEYS MEDIAN AUCTION MAIDEN STKS 7f 16y
7:10 (7:11) (Class 6) 3-4-Y-O **£1,706** (£503; £252) **Stalls** High

Form RPR

22 **1** **Outsmart**[18] 2924 3-9-0 0.. AhmedAjtebi 2 80+
(Mahmood Al Zarooni) *trckd ldrs: shkn up to ld over 1f out: rdn clr fnl f: readily* **1/1**[1]

04 **2** 2¾ **Lady Bayside**[9] 3218 3-8-9 0.. TomMcLaughlin 1 67
(Malcolm Saunders) *hld up: hdwy 3f out: rdn to chse ldrs 2f out: styd on to go 2nd 1f out: a readily hld by wnr* **20/1**

53-4 **3** 1¼ **Alshazah**[30] 2568 3-9-0 75.. JamesMillman 7 69
(Rod Millman) *led: rdn 2f out: hdd over 1f out: kpt on same pce* **7/2**[2]

05 **4** ¾ **Budley**[9] 3236 3-9-0 0.. CathyGannon 8 67
(Bill Turner) *chsd ldrs: rdn over 3f out: styd on same pce fnl 2f* **33/1**

2-30 **5** 2½ **Les Verguettes (IRE)**[7] 3283 3-8-9 71............................ PatCosgrave 10 55
(Stef Higgins) *prom: rdn over 2f out: sn one pce* **12/1**

06 **6** 1¼ **Concrete Jungle (IRE)**[6] 3324 3-9-0 0............................ DaneO'Neill 3 57
(Andrew Haynes) *towards rr: pushed along over 3f out: nvr a factor* **66/1**

7 5 **Winged Diva (IRE)** 3-8-9 0.. LiamKeniry 5 38
(Andrew Balding) *s.i.s: rdn over 2f out: a towards rr* **11/2**[3]

8 1 **Top Design** 3-9-0 0.. DarryllHolland 9 41
(Karen George) *in tch tl wknd 2f out* **33/1**

9 *hd* **Lechlade Lass** 3-8-9 0.. NeilChalmers 6 35
(Adrian Chamberlain) *slowly away whn rrd leaving stalls: a towards rr* **66/1**

4 **10** 10 **Long Live Love (USA)**[99] 937 3-9-0 0............................ RoystonFfrench 4 13
(Mark Johnston) *trckd ldrs: hung lft 3f out: rdn and wknd tamely sn after* **12/1**

1m 22.99s (-0.21) **Going Correction** -0.125s/f (Firm) **10** Ran SP% **116.6**
Speed ratings (Par 101): **96,92,91,90,87 86,80,79,79,67**
toteswingers: 1&2 £3.70, 1&3 £1.50, 2&3 £9.40. CSF £29.36 TOTE £1.90: £1.10, £4.00, £1.40; EX 17.30.
Owner Godolphin **Bred** Rabbah Bloodstock Limited **Trained** Newmarket, Suffolk

FOCUS
A useful maiden, in which the favourite scored with plenty in hand.
Lechlade Lass Official explanation: jockey said filly was slowly away

3514 DIGIBET.COM H'CAP 1m 14y
7:40 (7:41) (Class 5) (0-75,75) 3-Y-O+ **£2,266** (£674; £337; £168) **Stalls** High

Form RPR

2/0- **1** **Pat's Legacy (USA)**[182] 8003 5-9-4 73 .... MarkLawson(3) 1 [illegible]
(Jo Hughes) *trckd ldrs: rdn to ld wl over 2f out: kpt on wl fnl f: drvn out* **25/1**

4632 **2** ¾ **Miss Bootylishes**[4] 3413 6-9-6 **70**.................................. JohnFahy(3) 1 78
(Paul Burgoyne) *mid-div: hdwy to trck ldrs over 3f out: rdn to chse wnr over 2f out: styd on to cl on wnr ins fnl f but a being hld* **7/2**[1]

6022 **3** 1¾ **Dr Wintringham (IRE)**[57] 1789 5-9-11 **72**........................ DarryllHolland 5 76
(Karen George) *mid-div: hdwy over 3f out: rdn over 2f out: styd on but nt pce to mount chal* **11/2**[2]

3502 **4** ½ **Urban Kode (IRE)**[13] 3089 3-8-6 **63**.............................(v) CathyGannon 3 64
(David Evans) *hld up towards rr: hdwy whn nt clr run over 2f out: sn rdn: styd on fnl f: nt rch ldrs* **17/2**

-010 **5** ¾ **Bidable**[25] 2719 7-9-12 **73**.. LukeMorris 7 74
(Bryn Palling) *mid-div tl lost pl over 4f out: hdwy over 3f out: sn rdn: styd on same pce fnl 2f* **16/1**

124- **6** 4½ **Cotswold Village (AUS)**[334] 4533 5-9-3 **71**.................. LucyKBarry(7) 9 62
(Adrian Chamberlain) *racd keenly: trckd ldrs: squeezed up over 2f out and lost pl: styd on same pce fnl f but nvr able to get bk on terms* **12/1**

-000 **7** *nk* **Skyfire**[16] 2999 4-9-12 **73**.. PatCosgrave 2 63
(Ed de Giles) *stdd s: bhd: styd on past btn horses fnl f: nvr nrr* **12/1**

-220 **8** ½ **My Vindication (USA)**[14] 3044 3-9-4 **75**........................ DaneO'Neill 6 62
(Richard Hannon) *mid-div: hdwy to trck ldrs over 3f out: rdn over 2f out: wknd over 1f out* **6/1**[3]

-606 **9** 1¾ **Mishrif (USA)**[16] 2999 5-9-10 **71**.................................. LiamKeniry 11 56
(J R Jenkins) *mid-div: pushed along after 2f: rdn over 3f out: wknd jst over 1f out* **17/2**

3451 **10** 2 **Kentish (USA)**[83] 1195 4-9-9 **70**.................................. ShaneKelly 12 50
(Noel Quinlan) *prom: rdn 3f out: wknd over 1f out* **20/1**

366- **11** 3½ **Gallego**[257] 6479 9-8-10 **60**.. SophieDoyle(3) 13 32
(Richard Price) *hld up: racd alone on stands' side fnl 2f: a towards rr* **16/1**

043- **12** 10 **Cross Culture (IRE)**[285] 6158 3-9-4 **75**........................ JimmyFortune 8 22
(Andrew Balding) *led tl rdn wl over 2f out: sn wknd* **13/2**

5600 **13** 4½ **Home Office**[11] 3168 3-8-13 **70**...............................(b) RoystonFfrench 10 —
(Mark Johnston) *prom tl rdn wl over 3f out: sn wknd* **33/1**

1m 34.56s (-1.64) **Going Correction** -0.125s/f (Firm)
WFA 3 from 4yo+ 10lb **13** Ran SP% **125.0**
Speed ratings (Par 103): **103,102,100,100,99 94,94,93,92,90 86,76,72**
toteswingers: 1&2 £43.20, 1&3 £20.80, 2&3 £2.80. CSF £113.72 CT £478.32 TOTE £42.20: £9.30, £1.50, £3.10; EX 208.30.
Owner Mrs Joanna Hughes **Bred** Brereton C Jones **Trained** Lambourn, Berks

FOCUS
A fair handicap in which the first five pulled clear. The pace wasn't very strong and the field raced down the middle of the course.
Cross Culture(IRE) Official explanation: jockey said gelding ran too free

3515 SJH MACHINERY KUBOTA DEALER H'CAP 1m 2f 36y
8:10 (8:17) (Class 6) (0-65,65) 4-Y-O+ **£1,619** (£481; £240; £120) **Stalls** Low

Form RPR

4322 **1** **Corrib (IRE)**[13] 3094 8-8-6 **50**.......................................(p) CathyGannon 5 60
(Bryn Palling) *in tch: hdwy over 3f out: led wl over 1f out: rdn clr: styd on strly* **9/2**[1]

106- **2** 2½ **Cuckoo Rock (IRE)**[143] 7912 4-9-2 **60**.......................... JimmyFortune 7 65
(Jonathan Portman) *chsd ldrs: rdn over 2f out: styd on ins fnl f to go 2nd towards fin: no ch w wnr* **25/1**

40-2 **3** ½ **Daneside (IRE)**[7] 3266 4-8-2 **49** ow1................................. JohnFahy(3) 2 53
(Gary Harrison) *in tch: hdwy over 3f out: led over 2f out: rdn and hdd wl over 1f out: no ex whn lost 2nd ins fnl f* **5/1**[2]

600 **4** 3½ **La Belle Au Bois (IRE)**[19] 2871 5-8-3 **50**...................... LouisBeuzelin(3) 12 47
(Nick Lampard) *unsettled in stalls after long wait: towards rr: hdwy over 4f out: rdn to chse ldrs over 2f out: kpt on same pce fnl f* **16/1**

4040 **5** ¾ **Chik's Dream**[31] 2530 4-8-13 **57**.................................. DaneO'Neill 1 53
(Derek Haydn Jones) *s.i.s: in rr: stdy hdwy u.p in centre fr over 2f out: styd on: nrst fin* **20/1**

1132 **6** ½ **Angelena Ballerina (IRE)**[44] 2144 4-9-7 **65**...............(v) DarryllHolland 9 60
(Karen George) *mid-div: rdn 4f out: styd on same pce fnl 2f* **7/1**[3]

355 **7** 2¼ **Waahej**[16] 2996 5-9-3 **61**.. TomMcLaughlin 11 51
(Peter Hiatt) *s.i.s: towards rr: stdy prog u.p fr over 2f out: styd on: nvr trbld ldrs* **8/1**

0066 **8** 7 **Libre**[13] 3094 11-8-2 **46** oh1.. AdrianMcCarthy 4 22
(Violet M Jordan) *mid-div: rdn 3f out: wknd over 1f out* **50/1**

-400 **9** 1½ **Ledgerwood**[103] 896 6-8-3 **47** oh1 ow1..........................(p) NeilChalmers 8 20
(Adrian Chamberlain) *sn led: 4 l clr 4f out: sn rdn: hdd over 2f out: wknd* **50/1**

50-0 **10** 4 **Gypsy Boy (USA)**[119] 727 4-8-13 **60**.........................(t) MarkLawson(3) 10 25
(Jo Hughes) *s.i.s: a towards rr* **12/1**

03-1 **11** 5 **Command Marshal (FR)**[16] 2996 8-9-5 **63**.................... PatCosgrave 13 18
(Ed de Giles) *chsd ldrs: rdn 3f out: wknd over 1f out* **8/1**

04-0 **12** ½ **Stef And Stelio**[147] 387 4-7-13 **46** oh1.....................(b) SimonPearce(3) 14 —
(David Pipe) *mid-div tl wknd 3f out* **16/1**

2m 9.38s (-1.22) **Going Correction** -0.125s/f (Firm) **12** Ran SP% **101.6**
Speed ratings (Par 101): **99,97,96,93,93 92,91,85,84,81 77,76**
toteswingers: 1&2 £15.70, 1&3 £2.10, 2&3 £31.90. CSF £90.25 CT £359.91 TOTE £4.60: £1.40, £6.40, £2.40; EX 69.50.
Owner Bryn Palling **Bred** Dr John Waldron **Trained** Tredodridge, Vale Of Glamorgan

FOCUS
A competitive handicap for the grade. It was run at a fast pace and they were well strung out early on. Yensi (5/1) and Hint Of Honey (20/1) both reared over backwards and hit the stalls in a couple of nasty incidents at the start, and both were withdrawn. Deduct 15p in the £ under R4.

3516 LINDLEY CATERING H'CAP 1m 4f 23y
8:40 (8:43) (Class 6) (0-60,58) 4-Y-O+ **£1,619** (£481; £240; £120) **Stalls** Low

Form RPR

6004 **1** **Turjuman (USA)**[11] 3184 6-9-4 **58**.............................. AdamBeschizza(3) 7 66
(Willie Musson) *hld up towards rr: hdwy 4f out: rdn to chse ldr 2f out: chalng whn edgd lft jst ins fnl f: tk narrow ld towards fin: all out* **10/3**[1]

0062 **2** *hd* **Oak Leaves**[26] 2659 4-8-11 **48**.................................... DarryllHolland 5 56
(Nikki Evans) *prom: led after 5f: rdn 3f out: kpt on gamely u.str.p: edgd rt jst ins fnl f: narrowly hdd towards fin* **15/2**

/00- **3** 2¼ **Captain Oats (IRE)**[321] 4987 8-8-5 **49**........................ RachealKneller(7) 4 53
(Pam Ford) *hld up towards rr: hdwy fr over 2f out: sn rdn: styd on to go 3rd jst ins fnl f: nt rch ldrs* **66/1**

P315 **4** 3 **Maydream**[14] 3047 4-8-12 **49**.. FrankieMcDonald 1 48
(Jimmy Fox) *hld up towards rr: hdwy 4f out: sn rdn: styd on fnl 2f* **10/1**

2123 **5** *hd* **Wrecking Crew (IRE)**[16] 2991 7-9-7 **58**........................ JamesMillman 12 57
(Rod Millman) *mid-div: hdwy to trck ldrs 4f out: rdn wl over 2f out: styd on same pce* **4/1**[3]

-432 **6** 8 **Outland (IRE)**[11] 3184 5-9-7 **58**.................................... PatCosgrave 3 44
(J R Jenkins) *in tch: hdwy to join ldr over 3f out: rdn over 2f out: wknd ent fnl f* **7/2**[2]

4010 **7** 1¼ **Zagarock**[18] [illegible] 4-9-0 61.. NeilChalmers 11 [illegible]
(Bryn Palling) *broke wl: led for 5f: sn dropped to mid-div: rdn over 3f out: nvr a threat after* **14/1**

/460 **8** 1¾ **Shesha Bear**[16] 3003 6-9-5 **56**....................................(b) JimmyFortune 6 37
(Jonathan Portman) *trckd ldrs: rdn over 3f out: wknd ent fnl f* **17/2**

436 **9** ½ **Madame Boot (FR)**[16] 2996 4-9-7 **58**.............................. LukeMorris 2 38
(Peter Makin) *mid-div: rdn over 3f out: wknd over 1f out* **12/1**

604/ **10** 7 **Rock Peak (IRE)**[584] 502 6-9-2 **53**...........................(b[1]) TomMcLaughlin 8 22
(Bernard Llewellyn) *a towards rr* **22/1**

65-0 **11** 25 **Robbmaa (FR)**[13] 3094 6-8-5 **45**................................(b) AmyBaker(3) 13 —
(Tony Carroll) *chsd ldrs tl wknd 4f out: t.o* **66/1**

2m 38.04s (-0.96) **Going Correction** -0.125s/f (Firm) **11** Ran SP% **118.4**
Speed ratings (Par 101): **98,97,96,94,94 88,88,86,86,81 65**
toteswingers: 1&2 £5.60, 1&3 £41.20, 2&3 £65.90. CSF £28.68 CT £1382.44 TOTE £5.60: £2.00, £2.30, £14.40; EX 33.00.
Owner King & Prince **Bred** Shadwell Farm LLC **Trained** Newmarket, Suffolk

FOCUS
A modest middle-distance handicap run. It was run at a fair pace and there was a tight finish.
T/Plt: £74.70 to a £1 stake. Pool of £68,274.25 - 666.77 winning tickets. T/Qpdt: £6.40 to a £1 stake. Pool of £7,731.78 - 887.00 winning tickets. TM

3280 KEMPTON (A.W) (R-H)
Wednesday, June 29

OFFICIAL GOING: Standard
Wind: Moderate, half against Weather: Fine

3517 FREE ENTRY FOR BETDAQ MEMBERS APPRENTICE H'CAP 6f (P)
6:20 (6:22) (Class 5) (0-75,81) 4-Y-O+ **£2,266** (£674; £337; £168) **Stalls** Low

Form RPR

1631 **1** **Mymumsaysimthebest**[9] 3222 6-9-13 **81** 6ex................. HarryBentley 3 96+
(Gary Moore) *settled in 6th: prog over 2f out: chsd ldr over 1f out: clsd to ld jst ins fnl f: wl in command after* **8/11**[1]

5-50 **2** 1 ½ **Paphos**[11] 3172 4-8-8 **62**....(v) RyanClark 2 69
(Stuart Williams) *sn urged along in 9th and early reminders: struggling tl fnlly picked up and gd prog over 1f out: wnt 2nd last 100yds: no imp on wnr after but styd on wl* **10/1[2]**

-065 **3** 4 **Peter Island (FR)**[34] 2422 8-8-10 **67**....(b) AntiocoMurgia(3) 6 61
(John Gallagher) *led: clr after 2f: hdd & wknd jst ins fnl f: clung on for 3rd* **16/1**

0-30 **4** ½ **Dies Solis**[30] 2554 4-8-1 **58**.... RaulDaSilva(3) 10 51
(Jeremy Gask) *chsd ldr to over 1f out: wknd ins fnl f* **14/1**

5005 **5** 1 ½ **Fantasy Fighter (IRE)**[18] 2920 6-8-13 **67**.... LeeTopliss 8 55
(John Quinn) *in tch: rdn over 2f out: kpt on same pce fr over 1f out: no threat* **12/1[3]**

1000 **6** ¾ **Tislaam (IRE)**[81] 1239 4-8-12 **69**....(p) NoraLooby(3) 1 55
(Alan McCabe) *sn off the pce towards rr: rdn over 2f out: plugged on same pce: no threat* **10/1[2]**

0000 **7** 2 **Picansort**[18] 2929 4-8-10 **69**....(t) AccursioRomeo(5) 9 48
(Brett Johnson) *awkward s: hld up and swtchd to inner fr wd draw: virtually t.o after 1f: nvr on terms after* **16/1**

0640 **8** 1 ½ **Primo De Vida (IRE)**[18] 2903 4-9-1 **72**....(p) NathanAlison(3) 4 46
(Jim Boyle) *chsd ldng pair to 2f out: sn wknd* **14/1**

5200 **9** 2 ½ **Freddie's Girl (USA)**[48] 2027 4-9-0 **71**.... MatthewLawson(3) 5 37
(Seamus Durack) *chsd ldrs to 2f out: wknd* **33/1**

40-0 **10** ½ **Angel Of Fashion (IRE)**[50] 1989 4-7-13 **56**.... RosieJessop(3) 7 21
(Peter Charalambous) *chsd ldrs to 2f out: wknd qckly* **40/1**

1m 13.42s (0.32) **Going Correction** +0.10s/f (Slow) **10** Ran SP% **114.3**
Speed ratings (Par 103): **101,99,93,93,91 90,87,85,82,81**
toteswingers: 1&2 £2.80, 1&3 £4.40, 2&3 £31.20. CSF £8.48 CT £65.90 TOTE £1.50: £1.10, £3.20, £4.60; EX 9.90.
Owner Mrs M J George **Bred** Bearstone Stud **Trained** Lower Beeding, W Sussex

FOCUS
There was a shortage of in-form runners.
Primo De Vida(IRE) Official explanation: jockey said gelding never travelled

3518 LAY BACK AND WIN AT BETDAQ.COM H'CAP 1m 4f (P)
6:50 (6:51) (Class 6) (0-65,65) 3-Y-O **£1,619** (£481; £240; £120) **Stalls** Centre

Form RPR

3000 **1** **Strewth (IRE)**[40] 2253 3-9-7 **65**.... GeorgeBaker 11 76
(John Best) *hld up in last trio: sme prog 1/2-way: pushed along and hdwy in 7th over 3f out: clsd to ld narrowly over 1f out: drvn and asserted last 100yds* **22/1**

2124 **2** ¾ **Watered Silk**[26] 2677 3-9-5 **63**.... MartinDwyer 2 73+
(Marcus Tregoning) *hld up in last trio: only 9th and plenty to do 3f out: nt clr run briefly over 2f out: gd prog wl over 1f out: clsng whn stuck bhd ldng pair last 50yds: tk 2nd post* **10/3[2]**

0-40 **3** shd **Ministry**[27] 2637 3-8-12 **56**.... HayleyTurner 10 66
(John Best) *racd on outer: wnt prom 7f out: rdn in 4th over 3f out: prog to ld briefly wl over 1f out: kpt pressing wnr tl no ex last 100yds: lost 2nd post* **16/1**

6-21 **4** 6 **Nutshell**[25] 2722 3-9-3 **61**.... RyanMoore 1 61
(Harry Dunlop) *sn settled in midfield: rdn in 8th over 3f out: prog over 1f out: no ch w ldrs* **8/1**

0-61 **5** 3 ¼ **Final Liberation (FR)**[4] 3393 3-9-1 **59** 6ex.... StevieDonohoe 3 54
(Sir Mark Prescott Bt) *prom: led after 4f: kicked on 4f out: drvn and hdd wl over 1f out: wknd* **9/4[1]**

454 **6** nse **Dark Spirit (IRE)**[29] 2591 3-9-2 **60**.... RobertHavlin 6 55
(Tim Pitt) *wl in tch: gng bttr than most in 5th over 3f out: rdn and nt qckn over 2f out: fdd* **25/1**

0-60 **7** ¾ **Kambis**[33] 2469 3-9-2 **60**.... J-PGuillambert 9 54
(Luca Cumani) *s.s and rousted along to get in tch in last trio: effrt u.p over 3f out: plugged on one pce: no ch* **25/1**

2200 **8** 3 ¼ **Gower Rules (IRE)**[21] 2819 3-9-1 **62**.... SeanLevey(3) 8 50
(John Bridger) *trckd ldr 3f: styd prom: rdn in 3rd over 3f out: wknd 2f out* **25/1**

5131 **9** ¾ **Westhaven (IRE)**[9] 3220 3-9-3 **61** 6ex....(b) NickyMackay 12 48
(David Elsworth) *hld up in last trio: prog on outer over 6f out: drvn in 6th over 3f out: wknd over 2f out* **9/2[3]**

3300 **10** 20 **Warrant**[12] 3131 3-9-3 **61**.... NeilCallan 4 16
(Jane Chapple-Hyam) *pushed up to ld: hdd after 4f: drvn in 2nd over 3f out: wknd rapidly over 2f out: t.o* **28/1**

506 **11** 15 **Dakar (GER)**[11] 3183 3-9-6 **64**.... IanMongan 5 —
(Pat Phelan) *nvr on terms: dropped to last and struggling 1/2-way: wl t.o* **40/1**

0-24 **12** 46 **Toucan Tango (IRE)**[20] 2858 3-9-3 **61**....(b[1]) JackMitchell 7 —
(Peter Chapple-Hyam) *a towards rr: reminder over 7f out: wknd 4f out: hopelessly t.o* **16/1**

2m 35.86s (1.36) **Going Correction** +0.10s/f (Slow) **12** Ran SP% **116.7**
Speed ratings (Par 97): **99,98,98,94,92 92,91,89,89,75 65,35**
toteswingers: 1&2 £6.20, 1&3 £32.10, 2&3 £15.20. CSF £87.20 CT £1241.33 TOTE £34.30: £8.20, £2.00, £6.30; EX 171.10.
Owner Simon Malcolm & John Foulger **Bred** John Yarr **Trained** Hucking, Kent

FOCUS
This looked a good, competitive handicap for the grade, and it was run at a solid pace. It's likely to throw up a few winners.

3519 BETDAQ.COM EXCHANGE PRICE MULTIPLES MAIDEN STKS 1m 4f (P)
7:20 (7:24) (Class 5) 3-Y-O+ **£2,266** (£674; £337; £168) **Stalls** Centre

Form RPR

-343 **1** **El Mansour (USA)**[21] 2819 3-8-12 78.... AdamKirby 12 84
(Clive Cox) *mde all: shkn up over 2f out: drvn wl over 1f out and briefly pressed sn after: styd on wl* **2/1[1]**

24 **2** 1 ½ **Keys (IRE)**[21] 2813 4-9-12 0....(b[1]) GeorgeBaker 2 82
(Roger Charlton) *trckd ldng trio: rdn to chse wnr 2f out: tried to cl over 1f out: nt qckn after: styd on* **5/1[2]**

04 **3** 6 **Tarkeeba (IRE)**[20] 2836 3-8-7 0.... RichardHills 13 67
(Roger Varian) *chsd wnr to jst over 2f out: sn wl outpcd in 4th: plugged on fnl f* **13/2**

3- **4** hd **Hawawi**[246] 7152 3-8-12 0.... TedDurcan 1 72+
(David Lanigan) *trckd ldng pair: rdn to dispute 2nd 2f out: nt qckn over 1f out: fdd* **8/1**

0 **5** ½ **Asterism**[27] 2648 3-8-8 0 ow1.... TomQueally 11 67+
(Sir Henry Cecil) *chsd ldng quartet: pushed along over 4f out: nt on terms w them over 2f out: kpt on fnl f* **6/1[3]**

6 4 ½ **Epic Storm (IRE)** 3-8-12 0.... RyanMoore 8 64+
(Jeremy Noseda) *hung lft bnd over 9f out in last pair: nvr gng that wl: 9th and no ch over 3f out: kpt on* **10/1**

06 **7** nse **All My Heart**[9] 3224 3-8-8 0 ow1.... StevieDonohoe 7 60+
(Sir Mark Prescott Bt) *settled in last pair: pushed along 4f out: 11th and wl bhd over 3f out: shkn up and kpt on steadily fnl 2f: nvr nr ldrs* **40/1**

8 15 **Dawn Story** 3-8-7 0.... NickyMackay 6 35
(Hughie Morrison) *difficult to load into stalls: towards rr: pushed along 8f out: nt gng wl in 8th over 3f out: t.o* **50/1**

9 3 ½ **Manarola** 3-8-5 0.... AntiocoMurgia(7) 5 34
(Mahmood Al Zarooni) *s.s: sn midfield: drvn in 6th over 3f out: sn wknd: t.o* **16/1**

6 **10** 7 **Oasis Memory (IRE)**[14] 3043 3-8-7 0.... WilliamBuick 3 18
(John Gosden) *settled in rr: pushed along 4f out: wl off the pce in 10th over 3f out: t.o* **16/1**

3 **11** 1 ¼ **Notabadlad**[53] 1897 4-9-12 0.... NeilCallan 10 21
(Simon Dow) *s.s: in tch in midfield: drvn in 7th over 3f out: wknd over 2f out: t.o* **25/1**

50 **12** 6 **Gilt (USA)**[13] 3080 3-8-7 0.... ChrisCatlin 4 —
(Ed Dunlop) *a in rr: tailing off in last over 3f out* **66/1**

2m 34.8s (0.30) **Going Correction** +0.10s/f (Slow)
WFA 3 from 4yo 14lb **12** Ran SP% **119.3**
Speed ratings (Par 103): **103,102,98,97,97 94,94,84,82,77 76,72**
toteswingers: 1&2 £3.70, 1&3 £4.30, 2&3 £4.40. CSF £11.25 TOTE £3.60: £1.50, £1.10, £2.60; EX 14.30.
Owner H E Sheikh Sultan Bin Khalifa Al Nahyan **Bred** Sultan Bin Khalifa Al Nahyan **Trained** Lambourn, Berks

FOCUS
No more than a fair maiden.
Notabadlad Official explanation: jockey said gelding hung left

3520 BETDAQ MOBILE APPS BRITISH STALLION STUDS E B F MAIDEN FILLIES' STKS 7f (P)
7:50 (7:53) (Class 5) 2-Y-O **£3,238** (£963; £481; £240) **Stalls** Low

Form RPR

4 **1** **Gooseberry Fool**[9] 3237 2-9-0 0.... StevieDonohoe 9 75+
(Sir Mark Prescott Bt) *settled in last trio: pushed along over 2f out and no prog: swtchd out wd jst over 1f out: r.o wl fnl f: led last strides* **8/1**

542 **2** ½ **Iceni Girl**[19] 2882 2-9-0 0.... WilliamBuick 1 74
(John Gosden) *led: kicked on 2f out and looked in command: idled fnl f and drvn: hdd last strides* **11/8[1]**

22 **3** ½ **Costa Del Fortune (IRE)**[30] 2563 2-9-0 0.... PatDobbs 2 73
(Richard Hannon) *pressed ldr: rdn and nt qckn 2f out: styd on again fnl f but lost 2nd nr fin* **3/1[2]**

4 nk **Parley (USA)** 2-9-0 0.... ChrisCatlin 4 72+
(Mahmood Al Zarooni) *difficult to load into stalls: pushed along in midfield fr 1/2-way: no prog u.p 2f out: styd on fnl f* **6/1[3]**

5 2 **Accustomed** 2-9-0 0.... JamesDoyle 8 67+
(Sylvester Kirk) *sn in last pair: pushed along 3f out: no prog 2f out: picked up quite wl last 100yds and styng on at fin* **50/1**

6 nk **Gypsy Ballad** 2-8-7 0.... AntiocoMurgia(7) 7 66+
(Mahmood Al Zarooni) *dwlt and rn green early: sn in midfield: pushed along over 2f out: tried to cl over 1f out: fdd ins fnl f* **14/1**

7 ½ **Catherine Laboure (IRE)** 2-9-0 0.... MartinDwyer 6 65
(David Arbuthnot) *rn green and sn wl detached in last: prog on wd outside 3f out: disp 3rd briefly 2f out: sn wknd* **50/1**

0 **8** 2 ½ **Make Up**[7] 3287 2-9-0 0.... RyanMoore 5 58
(Richard Hannon) *chsd ldng pair: wknd over 1f out* **12/1**

0 **9** 22 **Reemeya (USA)**[16] 2983 2-9-0 0.... NeilCallan 3 —
(Mark Johnston) *dwlt: chsd ldng pair to over 2f out: wknd rapidly: t.o* **25/1**

1m 28.67s (2.67) **Going Correction** +0.10s/f (Slow) **9** Ran SP% **114.6**
Speed ratings (Par 90): **88,87,86,86,84 83,83,80,55**
toteswingers 1&2 £2.20 1&3 £3.90, 2&3 £1.30. CSF £19.10 TOTE £12.10: £2.90, £1.10, £1.10; EX 27.50.
Owner Denford Stud **Bred** Denford Stud Ltd **Trained** Newmarket, Suffolk

FOCUS
An ordinary maiden.

NOTEBOOK
Gooseberry Fool finished strongest down the outside to claim the prize. She was showing marked improvement from her debut at Wolverhampton and, although there's not much of her, she's very well bred, being closely related to Aussie Rules out of high-class filly Last Second, and there's surely more to come. The extra furlong really suited her. (op 9-1)
Iceni Girl couldn't really be faulted as she was holding the third and fourth in the closing stages and just couldn't do anything about the winner's strong finish down the outside. She should find a race sooner or later. (op 5-4 tchd 6-4 in places)
Costa Del Fortune(IRE) had every chance in the straight but couldn't get by the leader. She got the longer trip alright, though, and will now have the nursery option. (op 11-4)
Parley(USA) was being pushed along at halfway but she did respond and was going on at the finish. Her dam was a dual Grade 1 winner on turf in the US and she should improve for this experience. (op 9-1)
Accustomed, out the back early, was green but kept on at the finish and looks more of a longer-term project.
Gypsy Ballad travelled a lot better than her stablemate but found less off the bridle. Bred to make a middle-distance 3yo, she should derive plenty from this debut. (tchd 12-1)

3521 IRISH NIGHT AT KEMPTON 03.08.11 H'CAP (LONDON MILE QUALIFIER) 1m (P)
8:20 (8:20) (Class 4) (0-85,84) 3-Y-O+ **£4,079** (£1,214; £606; £303) **Stalls** Low

Form RPR

2200 **1** **Islesman**[11] 3178 3-8-12 **78**.... WilliamBuick 2 85
(Heather Main) *trckd ldng pair: led wl over 1f out and edgd lft v briefly: hrd pressed and drvn fnl f: hld on: fin 1st: disqualified and plcd 2nd* **16/1**

3103 **2** shd **Loyalty**[7] 3285 4-9-9 **79**....(v) RobbieFitzpatrick 6 88
(Derek Shaw) *settled in midfield: prog whn checked v sltly wl over 1f out: str chal fnl f: jst hld: fin 2nd: promoted to 1st* **8/1[3]**

404 **3** ¾ **Merchant Of Medici**[14] 3045 4-9-11 **81**.... MartinDwyer 5 88
(William Muir) *dwlt: sn in midfield: prog on inner to chal wl over 1f out: nt qckn fnl f* **5/2[1]**

4455 **4** ¾ **Sonoran Sands (IRE)**[49] 2003 3-9-4 **84**.... RyanMoore 4 87
(Peter Chapple-Hyam) *pressed ldr: chal and upsides jst over 2f out to over 1f out: nt qckn fnl f* **13/2[2]**

-116 **5** 1 ½ **Nahab**[40] 2269 4-9-13 **83**.... TedDurcan 9 85
(David Lanigan) *dwlt: hld up in rr: nt clr run briefly over 2f out: prog over 1f out: jst pushed along and kpt on same pce: nvr nr ldrs* **8/1[3]**

1000 **6** ¾ **Big Bay (USA)**[16] 2999 5-9-11 **81**.... NeilCallan 3 81
(Jane Chapple-Hyam) *nvr gng that wl in midfield: hrd rdn and nt qckn 2f out: kpt on again fnl f* **20/1**

-130 **7** *1 ½* **Stirling Bridge**[41] 2216 3-8-11 **77** .... RobertHavlin 10 72
(William Jarvis) *stdd s: hld up in last: pushed along 2f out: sme prog 1f out: rdn and kpt on: nvr nr ldrs* **33/1**

4-12 **8** *shd* **Taqaat (USA)**[36] 2389 3-9-3 **83** .... RichardHills 1 77
(Mark Johnston) *led: rdn and hdd wl over 1f out: losing pl whn sltly short of room and eased 1f out* **13/2**[2]

/34- **9** *½* **Latansaa**[422] 1769 4-9-11 **81** .... TadhgO'Shea 12 76
(Marcus Tregoning) *hld up in rr: rdn on outer over 2f out: carried hd to one side and nt qckn: n.d after: keeping on at fin* **12/1**

0356 **10** *1 ¾* **Sir George (IRE)**[21] 2814 6-9-12 **82** .... TomQueally 11 73
(Ollie Pears) *heavily restrained leaving stalls: racd wd and hld up in last pair: stl there and reminders over 1f out: nvr nr ldrs* **12/1**

0501 **11** *1* **Willow Dancer (IRE)**[11] 3172 7-9-10 **80** ....(p) AdamKirby 7 69
(Walter Swinburn) *chsd ldng pair: rdn over 2f out: wknd over 1f out* **8/1**[3]

1m 40.36s (0.56) **Going Correction** +0.10s/f (Slow)
WFA 3 from 4yo+ 10lb **11** Ran SP% **117.5**
Speed ratings (Par 105): **101,100,100,99,97 97,95,95,95,93 92**
toteswingers: 1&3 £37.30, 1&3 £7.90, 2&3 £28.90. CSF £128.13 CT £414.16 TOTE £8.70: £2.00, £6.90, £1.90; EX 145.90.
Owner Donald M Kerr **Bred** Barry Walters **Trained** Kingston Lisle, Oxon

FOCUS
Following a successful objection by Robbie Fitzpatrick, who rode Loyalty to finish second, the result was amended and Derek Shaw's gelding was awarded the race, on account of Islesman having taken his ground and forced him to check slightly approaching the final furlong.

3522 PETER ANDRE HERE NEXT WEDNESDAY H'CAP 2m (P)
8:50 (8:50) (Class 3) (0-90,89) 4-Y-0+ **£5,310** (£1,580; £789; £394) **Stalls** Low

Form RPR

-551 **1** **Captain John Nixon**[41] 2224 4-9-4 **86** .... ChrisCatlin 1 103
(Pat Eddery) *mde all: set reasonable pce: turned the screw fr 4f out: drew rt away over 2f out: galloped all the way to the line: impressive* **13/2**

-114 **2** *10* **Seaside Sizzler**[32] 2512 4-8-12 **80** ....(bt) StevieDonohoe 4 85
(Ralph Beckett) *chsd wnr: rdn over 3f out: clr of rest but lft wl bhd over 2f out: no ch after* **3/1**[2]

2-11 **3** *4* **Danvilla**[22] 2793 4-8-8 **76** .... WilliamCarson 5 76
(Paul Webber) *hld up in tch: outpcd fr 3f out: kpt on to take modest 3rd 2f out: no ch* **5/1**[3]

5126 **4** *3 ¾* **Rosewood Lad**[10] 3205 4-8-4 **72** ow1 ....(b[1]) TadhgO'Shea 8 68
(J S Moore) *mostly in last and nvr gng that wl: wl bhd 3f out: plugged on to take remote 4th nr fin* **20/1**

0-02 **5** *1 ¼* **Regal Park (IRE)**[18] 2931 4-9-4 **86** ....(p) AdamKirby 2 80
(Marco Botti) *hld up in last pair: rdn and sme prog 3f out: disp modest 3rd briefly over 2f out: wknd over 1f out* **2/1**[1]

0/50 **6** *11* **Harry Tricker**[12] 3120 7-9-4 **86** ....(p) RyanMoore 3 67
(Gary Moore) *hld up in tch: outpcd whn effrt to dispute modest 3rd over 2f out: sn wknd* **16/1**

-510 **7** *12* **Dark Ranger**[19] 2888 5-8-2 **70** oh1 .... NickyMackay 6 36
(Tim Pitt) *prom: rdn wl over 3f out: wknd over 2f out* **11/1**

1003 **8** *12* **Phoenix Flight (IRE)**[15] 3013 6-9-7 **89** .... FergusSweeney 7 41
(James Evans) *racd wd 1st 6f: prom: drvn 4f out: sn lost pl and bhd: t.o* **8/1**

3m 27.38s (-2.72) **Going Correction** +0.10s/f (Slow) **8** Ran SP% **118.4**
Speed ratings (Par 107): **110,105,103,101,100 95,89,83**
toteswingers: 1&2 £6.00, 1&3 £4.80, 2&3 £5.20. CSF £27.37 CT £107.99 TOTE £3.70: £1.60, £2.40, £2.30; EX 31.70.
Owner Paul Dean **Bred** Patrick Eddery Ltd **Trained** Nether Winchendon, Bucks

FOCUS
The winner had the run of the race, but still thrashed his rivals in the style of an ultra-progressive type.

NOTEBOOK
Captain John Nixon, only 3lb higher than when a game winner over 1m6f at Salisbury last time, ran out an impressive winner on this step up to 2m. It's true that he was given a good front-running ride, but he drew clear so easily in the straight and won by such a wide margin that he was clearly by far the best horse in the race. Equally effective on turf and Polytrack, he's a progressive stayer, and this has earned him a crack at a decent prize, perhaps at Goodwood. (op 6-1)
Seaside Sizzler tried to go with the winner from the turn in but the chase was in vain. Despite being beaten ten lengths it was probably still a good effort off a career-high mark versus a well-handicapped rival. (op 4-1)
Danvilla, chasing a hat-trick and up half a mile in distance, allowed the first two to get first run on her but she was staying on at the finish. The trip didn't seem to be a problem and there remains room for improvement. (op 9-2 tchd 11-2)
Rosewood Lad, trying blinkers for the first time, didn't really take to them and put in a laboured effort. (op 25-1)
Regal Park(IRE), who had the cheekpieces back on for his AW debut, wasn't best placed in a race dominated from the front, but it was disappointing not to see him stay on stronger at the finish. (op 5-2 tchd 11-4 in a place)
Phoenix Flight(IRE), who won this race last year off 8lb lower, was under pressure and going backwards from the turn in. Official explanation: jockey said gelding ran flat (op 13-2)

3523 RACING AT SKYSPORTS.COM H'CAP 6f (P)
9:20 (9:21) (Class 5) (0-75,75) 3-Y-0 **£2,266** (£674; £337; £168) **Stalls** Low

Form RPR

-315 **1** **King Ferdinand**[23] 2763 3-9-7 **75** .... WilliamBuick 8 88+
(Andrew Balding) *gd spd fr wd draw: mde all: rdn and qckly drew clr over 1f out: in n.d after: eased last 75yds* **11/8**[1]

60 **2** *3* **Hoover**[12] 3122 3-9-2 **70** .... StephenCraine 2 70
(Jim Boyle) *chsd wnr 2f: styd cl up: outpcd over 1f out: styd on to take 2nd again last strides* **8/1**

6000 **3** *nk* **My Love Fajer (IRE)**[6] 3307 3-7-12 **57** .... KieranO'Neill(5) 1 56
(Alan McCabe) *hld up in tch: prog on inner over 2f out: drvn to chse wnr over 1f out: no imp: lost 2nd last strides* **13/2**[3]

5030 **4** *1 ¼* **Karate (IRE)**[74] 1400 3-8-6 **60** .... ChrisCatlin 4 55
(Hans Adielsson) *chsd ldrs: drvn and nt qckn over 2f out: sn outpcd: kpt on again fnl f* **33/1**

-005 **5** *1 ¾* **Jeeran**[12] 3136 3-8-10 **64** ....(b) PhilipRobinson 6 53
(Clive Brittain) *chsd wnr after 2f: outpcd and lost 2nd over 1f out: wknd* **20/1**

-625 **6** *1 ½* **Catalinas Diamond (IRE)**[13] 3091 3-8-13 **67** .... RobertHavlin 3 52
(Pat Murphy) *blindfold off sltly late and dwlt: hld up in rr: shkn up 2f out: sn outpcd: n.d after* **14/1**

4020 **7** *½* **Rafaaf (IRE)**[2] 3465 3-9-4 **72** .... AndreaAtzeni 7 55
(Robert Eddery) *sltly impeded s: hld up in last pair: rdn and outpcd 2f out: no prog after* **10/3**[2]

-225 **8** *6* **Court Applause (IRE)**[36] 2375 3-8-10 **64** ....(b[1]) MartinDwyer 5 28
(William Muir) *wnt lft s: t.k.h: prom and wd: wknd wl over 1f out: eased* **9/1**

1m 13.57s (0.47) **Going Correction** +0.10s/f (Slow) **8** Ran SP% **114.0**
Speed ratings (Par 99): **100,96,95,93,91 89,88,80**
toteswingers: 1&2 £4.00, 1&3 £3.50, 2&3 £7.50. CSF £13.30 CT £54.23 TOTE £2.60: £1.10, £3.30, £2.10; EX 16.90.
Owner Thurloe Thoroughbred XXVII **Bred** Farleigh Court Racing Partnership **Trained** Kingsclere, Hants

FOCUS
This didn't take much winning.
T/Plt: £22.60 to a £1 stake. Pool of £54,323.72 - 1,747.18 winning tickets. T/Qpdt: £5.20 to a £1 stake. Pool of £5,116.33 - 724.00 winning tickets. JN

3524 - 3526a (Foreign Racing) - See Raceform Interactive

FAIRYHOUSE (R-H)
Wednesday, June 29

OFFICIAL GOING: Good

3527a IRISH STALLION FARMS EUROPRAN BREEDERS FUND BROWNSTOWN STKS (GROUP 3) (F&M) 7f
7:30 (7:31) 3-Y-0+ **£43,426** (£12,693; £6,012; £2,004)

RPR

1 **Emulous**[39] 2325 4-9-12 112 .... PJSmullen 6 112+
(D K Weld, Ire) *trckd ldrs: 4th 1/2-way: rdn to ld 1f out: kpt on wl fnl f* **9/4**[1]

2 *1* **Claiomh Solais (IRE)**[4] 3417 3-8-12 109 .... KJManning 2 100+
(J S Bolger, Ire) *mid-div: 6th 1/2-way: rdn in 5th 2f out: 3rd 1f out: kpt on to go 2nd ins fnl f: nt rch wnr* **8/1**

3 *¾* **Rose Bonheur**[23] 2774 3-8-12 105 .... DPMcDonogh 7 98
(Kevin Prendergast, Ire) *chsd ldrs: 3rd 1/2-way: 2nd 2f out: rdn to ld 1 1/2f out: hdd 1f out: no ex ins fnl f: kpt on same pce* **6/1**

4 *nk* **Dawn Eclipse (IRE)**[4] 3419 6-9-7 92 .... BACurtis 1 100
(T G McCourt, Ire) *hld up towards rr: hdwy into 7th 2f out: rdn in 6th 1f out: kpt on same pce fnl f* **66/1**

5 *nk* **History Note (IRE)**[38] 2334 3-8-12 108 .... JMurtagh 8 96
(John M Oxx, Ire) *chsd ldrs: 5th 1/2-way: rdn in 6th 2f out: 4th 1f out: no ex ins fnl f: kpt on same pce* **4/1**[2]

6 *shd* **Peahen**[20] 2861 3-8-12 96 .... NGMcCullagh 3 96
(G M Lyons, Ire) *hld up towards rr: rdn 2f out: hdwy into 5th 1f out: no ex ins fnl f: kpt on same pce* **33/1**

7 *2 ½* **Blaze Brightly (IRE)**[23] 2774 4-9-7 101 .... ShaneFoley 10 92
(Mrs John Harrington, Ire) *mid-div: 7th 1/2-way: rdn and no ex over 2f out: 8th 1f out: kpt on one pce* **25/1**

8 *4 ½* **Sharnberry**[45] 2137 3-8-12 .... KierenFallon 9 77
(Ed Dunlop) *hld up towards rr: 8th 1/2-way: rdn 2f out: no imp in 7th 1f out: kpt on one pce* **11/2**[3]

9 *10* **Agony And Ecstasy**[88] 1104 4-9-7 ....(t) JimCrowley 4 50
(Ralph Beckett) *sn led: rdn and hdd 1 1/2f out: wknd* **16/1**

10 *8* **Future Generation (IRE)**[4] 3419 3-8-12 96 .... KLatham 5 29
(G M Lyons, Ire) *disp early: sn chsd ldr in 2nd: rdn in 3rd 2f out: sn wknd* **6/1**

1m 29.53s (-0.97)
WFA 3 from 4yo+ 9lb **10** Ran SP% **120.0**
CSF £21.81 TOTE £2.50: £1.50, £2.00, £2.00; DF 25.40.
Owner K Abdulla **Bred** Juddmonte Farms Ltd **Trained** The Curragh, Co Kildare

FOCUS
The winner, third and sixth have been rated close to their marks.

NOTEBOOK
Emulous ◆ was giving weight away all round and looks to be a filly that's still improving. It isn't a race where everything went perfectly either. She was a little bit keen until the pace of the race really quickened after initially being steady enough, but she took command readily inside the final furlong and a half and, once getting there, idled a bit and kept the others in it. The winner's approaching the highest class and deserves to take her chance against Group 1 fillies later in the year, which seems likely. She'll probably have a little break now and then come back for the Group 1 Matron Stakes and later the Sun Chariot Stakes. (op 5/2)
Claiomh Solais(IRE), who was thrown into Group 1 level very quickly just over a month previously, had acquitted herself well but looks more likely to win at this sort of level. She was dropping back in trip as well and 1m is likely to be more suitable as she stayed on well inside the last having been outpaced briefly in the straight. (op 10/1)
Rose Bonheur seemed to get home well enough here having been ridden quite prominently but just wasn't quite good enough. That's not a disgrace against fillies of this calibre and considering what was behind her. (op 7/1)
Dawn Eclipse(IRE) has taken the step up in class quite well this year and kept on well from mid-division. It slightly belied her mark of 90 and what the handicapper does may or may not make up connections' minds as to what they'll be doing for the rest of the season.
History Note(IRE) did threaten briefly just over a furlong out but couldn't quite quicken enough.
Peahen isn't always the easiest filly to assess despite what looks like consistent form figures, but she ran on to decent enough effect towards the outside late in the day.
Blaze Brightly(IRE) couldn't get involved.
Sharnberry was held up off the pace but was unable to get into the race in any meaningful way. (op 9/2)

3528 - 3530a (Foreign Racing) - See Raceform Interactive

3446 HAMBURG (R-H)
Wednesday, June 29

OFFICIAL GOING: Turf: good

3531a PREIS DER BESITZERVEREINIGUNG FUR VOLLBLUTZUCHT UND RENNEN E.V. (FLIEGER TROPHY) (GROUP 3) (TURF) 6f
5:55 (12:00) 3-Y-0+
£27,586 (£9,482; £4,741; £2,586; £1,724; £1,293)

RPR

1 **Walero (GER)**[25] 5-9-2 0 .... KClijmans 8 109
(Uwe Ostmann, Germany) *broke wl: settled bhd ldrs in mid-trck: pursued eventual 3rd into st: swtchd to outside: picked up wl: fin strly to get up in fnl strides* **175/10**

2 *shd* **Calrissian (GER)**[29] 7-9-2 0 .... RafaelSchistl 9 109
(Fredrik Reuterskiold, Sweden) *a.p in ldng gp: settled on ins rail: qcknd wl in st: r.o strly to overcome eventual 3rd wl ins fnl f: ct fnl strides* **36/1**

3 *shd* **Smooth Operator (GER)**[25] 5-9-4 0 (b) THellier 11 110
(Mario Hofer, Germany) *racd promly in ldng gp: swung wd into st: r.o wl to chal and take ld jst under 2f out: r.o wl: ct wl ins fnl f* **4/1**[2]

4 *1* **Aslana (IRE)**[25] 4-9-1 0 AStarke 2 104
(P Schiergen, Germany) *settled bhd ldng gp: shkn up ent st: slow to pick up then r.o wl fnl f* **102/10**

5 *nk* **Clairvoyance (IRE)**[25] 4-8-13 0 FilipMinarik 3 101
(H-A Pantall, France) *settled towards rr: proged into st: r.o wl but no threat to ldrs* **59/10**

6 *½* **Alcohuaz (CHI)**[29] 6-9-2 0 JacobJohansen 1 103
(Lennart Reuterskiold Jr, Sweden) *broke fast: a.p: tk ld down bk st: stl in front ent st: rdn but no ex fr under 2f out* **14/5**[1]

7 *¾* **Konig Concorde (GER)**[25] 6-9-4 0 DPorcu 4 102
(C Sprengel, Germany) *a.p in ldng gp: picked up wl early in st: rdn but sn btn 2f out* **128/10**

8 *2 ½* **Exciting Life (IRE)**[32] 2520 3-8-11 0 MSrnec 5 92
(Adam Wyrzyk, Poland) *broke fast to ld: then settled amongst ldng gp: threatened briefly ent st: rdn but no ex: fdd* **67/10**

9 *2 ½* **Murcielago (GER)**[25] 4-9-0 0 AHelfenbein 6 82
(M Keller, Germany) *prom fr s: rdn and picked up wl ent st but sn wknd and fdd towards rr* **34/1**

10 *6* **Ferro Sensation (GER)**[25] 5-9-0 0 ADeVries 10 63
(J Pubben, Holland) *broke wl: settled bhd ldrs: threatened briefly ent st: no ex* **54/10**[3]

11 *1* **Govinda (USA)**[25] 4-9-4 0 EPedroza 7 64
(A Wohler, Germany) *broke wl: racd promy: rdn bef st: nvr figured thereafter* **58/10**

1m 11.38s (-1.31)
WFA 3 from 4yo+ 7lb **11** Ran SP% **131.3**
WIN (incl. 10 euro stake): 185. PLACES: 44, 85, 21. SF: 5,851.
Owner H Schroer-Dreesmann **Bred** H Schroer-Dreesmann **Trained** Germany

2711 EPSOM (L-H)

Thursday, June 30

OFFICIAL GOING: Good to firm (overall 8.6; far side 8.5; stands' side; 8.8)
Wind: virtually nil Weather: dry now, black clouds threatening rain

3533 BROTHERS PEAR CIDER H'CAP — 1m 4f 10y

6:20 (6:26) (Class 5) (0-75,74) 4-Y-0+ **£2,590** (£770; £385; £192) **Stalls** Centre

Form RPR

-305 **1** **Goldtrek (USA)**[23] 2791 4-9-7 **74** (p) SteveDrowne 12 81
(Roger Charlton) *mde all: rdn and edgd rt fr jst over 2f out: styd on wl ins fnl f and in command fnl 100yds* **6/1**[3]

1113 **2** *1* **Filun**[23] 2793 6-9-5 **72** LiamKeniry 1 76
(Anthony Middleton) *hld up in tch in midfield: hdwy 3f out: swtchd rt and hdwy to chse wnr travelling wl 2f out: rdn ent fnl f: unable qck and styd on same pce ins fnl f* **8/1**

-105 **3** *nk* **Gloucester**[23] 2793 8-8-10 **70** DavidKenny(7) 7 74
(Michael Scudamore) *s.i.s: hld up in rr: effrt on outer over 2f out: rdn and hdwy over 1f out: styd on wl ins fnl f: nt rch ldrs* **20/1**

3006 **4** *¾* **Goodlukin Lucy**[9] 3256 4-8-12 **70** (p) HarryBentley(5) 5 73
(Pat Eddery) *t.k.h: hld up in tch: rdn and unable qck whn sltly short of room 2f out: rallied u.p 1f out: kpt on but nt gng pce to rch ldrs* **8/1**

-030 **5** *½* **Cornish Beau (IRE)**[18] 2952 4-8-11 **67** JohnFahy(3) 10 69
(Mark H Tompkins) *hld up in last trio: rdn and effrt 2f out: hdwy jst ins fnl f: styd on strly fnl 100yds: nt rch ldrs* **16/1**

2124 **6** *shd* **Miss Bounty**[31] 2562 6-8-5 **61** (v) KierenFox(3) 9 63
(Jim Boyle) *t.k.h: hld up in tch in midfield: rdn and effrt jst over 2f out: drvn over 1f out: kpt on u.p ins fnl f* **14/1**

0-30 **7** *shd* **Rodrigo De Freitas (IRE)**[17] 3003 4-8-8 **61** (v) MartinDwyer 13 63
(Jim Boyle) *hld up in last quartet: nt clr run jst over 2f out: hdwy u.p jst over 1f out: kpt on but nt gng pce to chal ldrs* **18/1**

3100 **8** *½* **Admirable Duque (IRE)**[13] 3120 5-9-5 **72** JamesDoyle 8 73
(Dominic Ffrench Davis) *in tch: rdn 4f out: hdwy u.p to chse ldrs 2f out: unable qck and struggling over 1f out: one pce and hld ins fnl f* **25/1**

0-05 **9** *2 ½* **Maybe I Wont**[26] 2708 6-8-10 **63** (p) CathyGannon 2 60
(Lucinda Featherstone) *stdd after s: hld up in last trio: hdwy and nt clr run over 2f out: swtchd lft and drvn 2f out: wknd jst ins fnl f* **5/1**[2]

0005 **10** *3 ½* **Sand Skier**[13] 3120 4-9-7 **74** ChrisCatlin 11 65
(Mark Johnston) *chsd ldrs: rdn 4f out: wkng and towards rr whn n.m.r ent fnl 2f: bhd and wl btn over 1f out* **9/2**[1]

5140 **11** *nse* **Mons Calpe (IRE)**[23] 2793 5-9-5 **72** (p) JimmyFortune 6 63
(Paul Cole) *chsd ldr: rdn over 3f out: lost 2nd and dropping away 2f out: wknd and wl btn 1f out* **11/1**

2454 **12** *nk* **Potentiale (IRE)**[18] 2958 7-9-3 **73** (p) PatrickHills(3) 4 64
(J W Hills) *stdd after s: hld up in rr: effrt on inner and rdn 3f out: nt clr run and swtchd rt 2f out: sn drvn and no hdwy: wl hld 1f out* **10/1**

2m 38.61s (-0.29) **Going Correction** -0.05s/f (Good) **12** Ran SP% **115.2**
Speed ratings (Par 103): **98,97,97,96,96 96,96,95,94,91 91,91**
toteswingers:1&2:£5.40, 2&3:£44.40, 1&3:£49.40 CSF £51.84 CT £899.99 TOTE £7.10: £2.30, £2.40, £7.40; EX 44.60.
Owner AXOM (XVII) **Bred** Kenneth Lejeune & Charles Simon **Trained** Beckhampton, Wilts

FOCUS
Course at normal inner configuration distances as advertised. This moderate handicap was run at something of an uneven pace and there was a bunched finish for the places. The form makes sense at face value with the winner rated back to her 3yo best.

3534 BRITISH STALLION STUDS SUPPORTING BRITISH RACING E B F MEDIAN AUCTION MAIDEN STKS — 7f

6:50 (6:55) (Class 5) 2-Y-0 **£3,885** (£1,156; £577; £288) **Stalls** Low

Form RPR

0 **1** **Captain Cardington (IRE)**[20] 2882 2-9-3 0 CathyGannon 1 71
(Mick Channon) *hld up in last pair: clsd qckly and rn into heels od runner-up and lost pl 2f out: rdn and rallied to chse ldrs over 1f out: led ins fnl f: r.o wl* **14/1**

0 **2** *¾* **Siouxperhero (IRE)**[12] 3171 2-9-3 0 (b[1]) MartinDwyer 3 69
(William Muir) *chsd ldng trio: swtchd rt and hdwy to chal 2f out: ev ch after tl nt gng pce of wnr fnl 100yds: kpt on* **40/1**

6 **3** *3 ¼* **Poetic Lord**[20] 2882 2-9-3 0 JimmyFortune 6 61
(Richard Hannon) *led: rdn ent fnl 2f: hanging lft and hdd jst ins fnl f: continued to hang down camber and sn btn: eased towards fin* **5/2**[2]

53 **4** *6* **Khazium (IRE)**[12] 3171 2-9-3 0 (v[1]) ChrisCatlin 4 45
(Pat Eddery) *racd freely: hdwy to press ldr after 1f: ev ch and rdn ent fnl 2f: nt qckn and sn struggling: wknd over 1f out: fdd ins fnl f* **11/8**[1]

5 *2 ½* **Alborz (IRE)** 2-9-3 0 NeilCallan 5 39+
(Mark Johnston) *chsd ldrs: pushed along and racing awkwardly on downhill run wl over 3f out: wknd 2f out: wl bhd ins fnl f* **4/1**[3]

6 *2* **Lady Bellatrix** 2-8-12 0 SaleemGolam 2 29
(Mark H Tompkins) *s.i.s: a in rr: rdn and effrt over 2f out: wknd wl over 1f out: wl bhd ins fnl f* **12/1**

1m 23.65s (0.35) **Going Correction** -0.05s/f (Good) **6** Ran SP% **107.5**
Speed ratings (Par 93): **96,95,91,84,81 79**
CSF £291.78 TOTE £13.30: £6.60, £7.90; EX 295.80.
Owner Nick & Olga Dhandsa & John & Zoe Webster **Bred** Brian Williamson **Trained** West Ilsley, Berks

FOCUS
A modest juvenile maiden, run at a decent pace. The form is pitched at the lesser end of the race averages, with much-improved efforts from the first two.

NOTEBOOK
Captain Cardington(IRE), who didn't go unbacked, got on top near the finish under his substitute jockey to win going away. He bided his time out the back and the solid pace suited. He picked up from halfway but lost momentum when running into the back of the runner-up 2f out. Once getting reorganised he motored, though, and has clearly improved a bundle for his debut run 20 days earlier. Returning to a stiffer track over this trip should prove ideal and it will be interesting to see how he is handled by connections. (op 22-1 tchd 25-1)
Siouxperhero(IRE), distinctly green on his debut 12 days previously, was equipped with first-time blinkers and showed vastly improved form switched to quicker ground. He just paid for doing too much early on and should learn again for this experience, but there is always a slight worry about second-time headgear on juveniles so he's not certain to build on it. (op 33-1)
Poetic Lord ◆, whose yard was bidding for a fourth win in the race, broke a lot better than had been the case on his debut at Sandown, when in front of the winner. He made a bold bid but got taken on out in front and was made to pay from the furlong marker. He is better than the bare form and can improve on a flatter track. (op 9-4 tchd 7-4)
Khazium(IRE) probably should have won at Lingfield last time, when he thrashed Siouxperhero, and it wasn't surprising to see headgear installed. He got far too lit up through the first half, however, and it's a case of back to the drawing board with him. (op 11-10 tchd 6-4)
Alborz(IRE) was making his debut over a suitable trip on pedigree and showed up well from the gates. He dropped away tamely in the home straight but should improve and enjoy a more conventional track. (op 5-1 tchd 11-2)
Lady Bellatrix was well backed at long odds ahead of this racecourse debut, but proved too green to do herself justice. (op 22-1)

3535 TRY TOTEQUICKPICK ON ALL TOTEPOOL BETS H'CAP — 6f

7:25 (7:26) (Class 3) (0-95,93) 3-Y-0+ **£6,670** (£1,984; £991; £495) **Stalls** High

Form RPR

4504 **1** **Mac Gille Eoin**[12] 3179 7-9-2 **81** IanMongan 12 92
(John Gallagher) *in tch in midfield on outer tl lost pl and dropped in rr 4f out: rdn and hdwy wl over 2f out: swtchd rt 2f out: styd on wl to chal 1f out: led fnl 50yds: r.o wl* **8/1**

0661 **2** *1* **Another Try (IRE)**[31] 2557 6-8-10 **80** HarryBentley(5) 9 88
(Alan Jarvis) *hld up in tch: clsd to trck ldrs 2f out: rdn to chal 1f out: led ins fnl f: hdd and outpcd by wnr fnl 50yds* **8/1**

-10 **3** *1 ½* **Free For All (IRE)**[13] 3109 4-9-10 **89** JamesDoyle 3 92
(Sylvester Kirk) *dwlt: rcvrd and hdwy on inner to ld over 4f out: rdn 2f out: hdd ins fnl f: btn fnl 100yds: wknd towards fin* **4/1**[1]

6035 **4** *½* **Hamoody (USA)**[20] 2890 7-9-3 **85** MichaelO'Connell(3) 8 87
(David Nicholls) *s.i.s: bhd: clsd and wl in tch 2f out: rdn and edgd lft over 1f out: kpt on same pce ins fnl f* **8/1**

0511 **5** *nk* **We Have A Dream**[6] 3351 6-9-10 **89** 6ex MartinDwyer 4 90
(William Muir) *led tl over 4f out: chsd ldrs after: rdn and pressing ldr 2f out: drvn and outpcd over 1f out: plugged on same pce ins fnl f* **10/1**

-200 **6** *1* **Avonmore Star**[33] 2508 3-9-2 **93** KieranO'Neill(5) 2 88
(Richard Hannon) *dwlt: towards rr: rdn and hdwy on inner over 2f out: nt clr run 2f out: styd on same pce ins fnl f* **7/1**[3]

2112 **7** *nk* **Collect Art (IRE)**[19] 2938 4-9-6 **85** StevieDonohoe 7 81+
(Andrew Haynes) *in tch on outer: pushed along and outpcd jst over 2f out: rdn over 1f out: kpt on ins fnl f but nvr gng pce to threaten ldrs* **7/1**[3]

0-03 **8** *3* **Fireback**[26] 2717 4-9-13 **92** JimmyFortune 5 79+
(Andrew Balding) *chsd ldrs: rdn and unable qck over 2f out: wknd jst over 1f out* **9/2**[2]

5000 **9** *2* **Below Zero (IRE)**[13] 3109 4-9-7 **86** NeilCallan 11 66
(Mark Johnston) *prom for 2f: lost pl and bhd over 3f out: rdn and no prog wl over 2f out: n.d after* **20/1**

68.79 secs (-0.61) **Going Correction** -0.05s/f (Good)
WFA 3 from 4yo+ 7lb **9** Ran SP% **110.4**
Speed ratings (Par 107): **102,100,98,98,97 96,95,91,89**
toteswingers:1&2:£9.40, 2&3:£5.00, 1&3:£6.70 CSF £65.26 CT £280.03 TOTE £9.60: £1.80, £1.70, £1.90; EX 63.50.
Owner M C S D Racing Partnership **Bred** M C S D Racing Ltd **Trained** Chastleton, Oxon

FOCUS
A good sprint handicap that was always likely to be run at a frantic pace, and so it played out with five abreast up front going into the home bend. Sound form.

NOTEBOOK
Mac Gille Eoin, drawn widest of all, relished the way the race panned out and, getting a lovely split from the furlong marker, ran on strongly to end a losing run that dated back to success in this race two years earlier. He proved inconsistent in 2010 and hadn't been at his best this year in four previous spins, but was a stone lower than when last winning. His form figures here now read 12101 and this should serve his confidence well, so a return to Goodwood (dual course winner) for the Stewards' Cup next month is likely to figure. However, he would very likely have to win again to avoid dropping into the consolation race once more.
Another Try(IRE) was well backed to follow up his Goodwood dead-heat last month and turned in a solid effort off his 5lb higher mark, despite not settling. He's evidently in the form of his life. (op 14-1)
Free For All(IRE) ◆, bogged down on soft in the Buckingham Palace Stakes 13 days earlier, tanked to the front and bagged the inside on the bend. He gave his all and ran well, but the drop back in trip on this sharp track found him out. He remains capable of better on a quick surface. (op 9-2 tchd 5-1)
Hamoody(USA) ◆ was trying to get to the front prior to getting tightened up inside the final furlong and is a little better than this bare form. His turn looks to be nearing again and is one to side with when returning to Goodwood next month. (op 6-1)
We Have A Dream ran a bold race in this quest for the hat-trick, but paid for his early exertions nearing the furlong marker. (op 15-2)
Avonmore Star may not have enjoyed this track that much and didn't get the best of runs under pressure, but still looks to need respite in the weights. (op 8-1)
Collect Art(IRE), having a first run at this course, was done no favours on the bend and had to race widest of all in the home straight. This run is best forgiven. Steve Donohoe later reported his mount hung left in the home straight. (op 5-1)

Fireback was forced wide into the home turn and as a result never looked like capitalising on this drop in grade. (op 11-2)

3536 TOTEPOOL A BETTER WAY TO BET H'CAP 7f
7:55 (7:56) (Class 4) (0-85,84) 3-Y-0+ **£4,079** (£1,214; £606; £303) **Stalls** Low

Form RPR

4060 **1** **Space Station**[27] 2679 5-9-11 **81**..(b) NeilCallan 5 94
(Simon Dow) *t.k.h: hld up in tch: chsd ldng pair 4f out: swtchd lft and chsd ldr 2f out: pushed ahd over 1f out: clr and rdn 1f out: r.o wl: comf* **11/4**[1]

0350 **2** *3 ¾* **Nezami (IRE)**[20] 2876 6-8-13 **72**....................................(b[1]) KierenFox(3) 9 75
(John Akehurst) *rdn along early: hdwy to join ldr 5f out: led over 3f out: rdn and hung rt 2f out: hdd over 1f out: no ch w wnr ins fnl f: hung rt again nr fin* **14/1**

-133 **3** *hd* **Rondeau (GR)**[26] 2719 6-9-7 **77**.. LiamKeniry 11 79
(Patrick Chamings) *stdd s: hld up in last pair: rdn and effrt on outer 2f out: styd on wl ins fnl f to press for 2nd cl home: no ch w wnr* **13/2**[3]

3003 **4** *1* **Chilli Green**[13] 3121 4-9-11 **81**.. JimmyFortune 10 81
(John Akehurst) *racd in midfield: rdn and no real imp over 2f out: no ch w wnr but kpt on ins fnl f: short of room and hmpd nr fin* **11/2**[2]

-365 **5** *½* **Proper Charlie**[20] 2875 3-7-12 **68**.. HarryBentley(5) 8 63
(William Knight) *stdd after s: hld up in last trio: rdn and hdwy into midfield jst over 2f out: no threat to wnr but plugged on ins fnl f* **16/1**

6-00 **6** *1 ¼* **Moretta Blanche**[15] 3045 4-9-12 **82**.. StevieDonohoe 7 77
(Ralph Beckett) *taken down early: stdd s: hld up in last pair: stl last and pushed along 2f out: rdn jst over 1f out: r.o fnl 150yds: n.m.r nr fin: n.d* **8/1**

33-0 **7** *½* **Plume**[27] 2690 4-9-7 **80**.. JohnFahy(3) 4 74
(Roger Teal) *chsd ldr tl over 5f out: chsd ldrs after: outpcd over 3f out: shkn up and effrt jst over 2f out: styd on same pce and n.d fr over 1f out* **12/1**

-130 **8** *nk* **Bassett Road (IRE)**[12] 3178 3-9-2 **84**.. RossAtkinson(3) 3 74
(Tom Dascombe) *led: hdd but clr w rival over 3f out: rdn and hanging lft into rail jst over 2f out: 3rd and wkng whn continued to hang and faltered over 1f out: n.d after* **7/1**

4-50 **9** *1 ¾* **Micky P**[15] 3045 4-8-9 **65** oh1..(t) SaleemGolam 1 53
(Stuart Williams) *racd in midfield tl over 4f out: outpcd and towards rr over 3f out: rdn and no prog jst over 2f out* **10/1**

0640 **10** *8* **Ghostwing**[17] 2995 4-9-10 **80**..(v) ChrisCatlin 13 46
(John Gallagher) *chsd ldrs after 2f: rdn and struggling 3f out: wknd over 2f out: wl btn fnl f* **16/1**

1m 21.97s (-1.33) **Going Correction** -0.05s/f (Good)
WFA 3 from 4yo+ 9lb **10** Ran SP% **114.2**
Speed ratings (Par 105): **105,100,100,99,98 97,96,96,94,85**
toteswingers:1&2:£10.40, 2&3:£11.50, 1&3:£5.60 CSF £43.18 CT £233.66 TOTE £3.50: £1.70, £4.50, £1.50; EX 42.40.
Owner Mr & Mrs Chua, Moore & Jurd **Bred** Juddmonte Farms Ltd **Trained** Epsom, Surrey

FOCUS
Despite being run at an okay early pace it proved an advantage to race handily in this fair handicap. The winner rates a length personal best.

3537 PIPER HEIDSIECK CHAMPAGNE CLAIMING STKS 1m 114y
8:30 (8:30) (Class 5) 3-Y-0+ **£2,590** (£770; £385; £192) **Stalls** Low

Form RPR

1211 **1** **Song To The Moon (IRE)**[24] 2768 4-8-10 70......(b) MatthewDavies(3) 4 77
(Jim Boyle) *stdd s: hld up in tch: rdn and effrt on outer over 2f out: led and hung lft fr over 1f out: kpt on fnl 100yds* **9/2**

0120 **2** *½* **Avon River**[20] 2884 4-9-12 87..(b) JimmyFortune 7 89
(Richard Hannon) *rdn along early: chsd ldrs: rdn and effrt 3f out: hrd drvn and ev ch fr wl over 1f out: carried lft 1f out tl fnl 75yds: no ex towards fin* **11/4**[1]

-000 **3** *3 ¼* **Dream Lodge (IRE)**[46] 2123 7-9-9 87........................ MichaelO'Connell(3) 6 82
(David Nicholls) *chsd ldrs: t.k.h whn pce stdd: drvn and effrt on inner 3f out: outpcd and n.m.r over 1f out: no ch w ldng pair but kpt on to go 3rd towards fin* **4/1**[3]

0-00 **4** *1* **Beauchamp Xerxes**[17] 0100 [illegible] (tb) NeilCallan [illegible] 81
(Gerard Butler) *racd keenly: chsd ldr: wnt upsides 3f out: rdn to ld 2f out: drvn and hdd over 1f out: edgd lft and outpcd 1f out: no ch w ldng pair ins fnl f: lost 3rd towards fin* **3/1**[2]

0-46 **5** *shd* **Norse Wing**[21] 2849 3-7-12 60..(v[1]) CathyGannon 1 61
(Ralph Beckett) *sn led: racd keenly tl stdd pce 6f out: jnd 3f out: hdd and rdn 2f out: 4th and struggling whn short of room and hmpd jst over 1f out: no ch w ldrs after* **9/1**

-323 **6** *nk* **Lang Shining (IRE)**[5] 3380 7-9-6 79.. SophieDoyle(3) 3 75
(Jamie Osborne) *hld up in tch: shkn up: racd awkwardly and outpcd over 2f out: rdn and styd on same pce fnl 2f* **9/1**

1040 **7** *21* **Silly Billy (IRE)**[9] 3259 3-8-0 70.. JemmaMarshall(5) 2 19
(Sylvester Kirk) *a IN last: lost tch over 2f out* **20/1**

1m 44.14s (-1.96) **Going Correction** -0.05s/f (Good)
WFA 3 from 4yo+ 11lb **7** Ran SP% **114.6**
Speed ratings (Par 103): **106,105,102,101,101 101,82**
toteswingers:1&2:£2.30, 2&3:£2.60, 1&3:£3.30 CSF £17.38 TOTE £6.70: £3.30, £2.60; EX 19.70.
Owner Sean O'Connell **Bred** Michael Woodlock & Seamus Kennedy **Trained** Epsom, Surrey

FOCUS
A decent race of its type, but the usual doubts over the form. It was run at a solid pace and the first pair came clear.

3538 BEACH BOYS LIVE AT EPSOM 7/7/11 H'CAP 1m 2f 18y
9:00 (9:05) (Class 4) (0-80,80) 3-Y-0+ **£4,079** (£1,214; £606; £303) **Stalls** Low

Form RPR

01 **1** **Street Secret (USA)**[28] 2639 3-8-11 **75**.. NeilCallan 5 84
(Roger Varian) *in tch: chsd ldng pair over 3f out: jnd ldrs and rdn over 2f out: led over 1f out: kpt on gamely ins fnl f* **6/1**[3]

3066 **2** *½* **Ramona Chase**[26] 2716 6-9-12 **78**........................(t) RobbieFitzpatrick 4 86
(Michael Attwater) *t.k.h: chsd ldrs: 4th and rdn over 2f out: swtchd rt and drvn wl over 1f out: edging lft ins fnl f: styd on fnl 100yds and pressing wnr cl home* **7/2**[1]

0-1 **3** *½* **Gold Mine**[59] 1751 3-8-8 **72**..(t) LiamKeniry 8 79
(Andrew Balding) *dwlt: sn rcvrd and chsd ldr: rdn and ev ch over 2f out: stl ev ch and n.m.r ins fnl f: styd on same pce fnl 100yds* **15/2**

0-64 **4** *hd* **If I Were A Boy (IRE)**[24] 2771 4-9-2 **68**........................(p) JamesDoyle 7 75
(Dominic Ffrench Davis) *led: jnd and rdn over 2f out: battled on wl u.p: hdd over 1f out: n.m.r ins fnl f: styd on same pce fnl 100yds* **10/1**

0306 **5** *2* **Dahaam**[22] 2810 4-9-9 **75**.. StevieDonohoe 1 78
(David Simcock) *stdd after s: hld up in last trio: rdn and effrt wl over 2f out: hdwy and wnt modest 5th over 1f out: swtchd rt 1f out: kpt on wl fnl f but nvr gng to rch ldrs* **12/1**

3524 **6** *6* **Tasfeya**[21] 2833 3-9-2 **80**.. JimmyFortune 6 71
(Mark Johnston) *wl in tch in midfield: rdn and fnd little 3f out: outpcd and wl btn fnl 2f* **11/2**[2]

4402 **7** *2 ¼* **Arashi**[7] 3311 5-8-9 **61** oh2..(v) CathyGannon 3 47
(Lucinda Featherstone) *stdd after s: t.k.h: hld up in midfield: rdn and unable qck over 2f out: wandering and wknd 2f out* **15/2**

10-1 **8** *3* **Halyard (IRE)**[41] 2245 4-9-4 **73**..(v) JohnFahy(3) 9 53
(Walter Swinburn) *dwlt: in tch: rdn and outpcd wl over 2f out: n.d fnl 2f* **8/1**

406- **9** *shd* **Goodwood Starlight (IRE)**[57] 6437 6-9-8 **79**..........(t) HarryBentley(5) 2 59
(Jim Best) *t.k.h: hld up in tch towards rr: rdn and short-lived effrt 3f out: sn outpcd and n.d fnl 2f* **7/1**

0202 **10** *3 ¾* **Ede's Dot Com (IRE)**[34] 2450 7-8-4 **61** oh1.......... JemmaMarshall(5) 10 33
(Pat Phelan) *awkward leaving stalls and s.i.s: t.k.h: hld up in rr: rdn and effrt on outer 3f out: sn struggling: wl btn fnl 2f* **25/1**

2m 7.27s (-2.43) **Going Correction** -0.05s/f (Good)
WFA 3 from 4yo+ 12lb **10** Ran SP% **119.7**
Speed ratings (Par 105): **107,106,106,106,104 99,97,95,95,92**
toteswingers:1&2:£8.00, 2&3:£7.20, 1&3:£1.60 CSF £28.08 CT £163.75 TOTE £7.40: £3.20, £1.80, £3.10; EX 40.20.
Owner Saif Ali **Bred** Adena Springs **Trained** Newmarket, Suffolk

FOCUS
Not a bad handicap, and sound enough run, but again racing handily was a must. Improvement from the unexposed winner.

T/Jkpt: Not won. T/Plt: £3,849.30 to a £1 stake. Pool of £81,732.18 - 15.50 winning tickets. T/Qpdt: £16.30 to a £1 stake. Pool of £8,806.12 - 397.78 winning tickets. SP

3165 HAYDOCK (L-H)
Thursday, June 30

OFFICIAL GOING: Good to firm (watered; 5f & 6f 7.6, 7f & further 7.4)
Wind: Light, half-against Weather: Sunny intervals

3539 FLOAT GLASS INDUSTRIES MAIDEN AUCTION STKS 5f
2:30 (2:30) (Class 5) 2-Y-0 **£2,266** (£674; £337; £168) **Stalls** Centre

Form RPR

062 **1** **Musical Valley**[19] 2901 2-8-6 0..(t) FrannyNorton 2 74+
(Tom Dascombe) *a gng wl: chsd ldr to 3f out: wnt 2nd again 2f out: led jst over 1f out and r.o ins fnl f: a in command* **4/1**[2]

22 **2** *2 ¾* **Excavator**[29] 2602 2-9-0 0.. PaulHanagan 4 72
(Roger Charlton) *led: rdn and hdd jst over 1f out: hung lft u.p whn nt pce of wnr ins fnl f: wl hld* **30/100**[1]

0000 **3** *5* **Come To Mind**[14] 3082 2-8-6 0.. PatrickMathers 5 46
(Alan Berry) *chsd ldrs: dropped to last 3f out: pushed along 2f out: wnt 3rd over 1f out but one pce and no ch w ldrs* **100/1**

2054 **4** *1* **Triggerlo**[9] 3249 2-8-9 0..(v[1]) SamHitchcott 1 45
(Mick Channon) *restless in stalls: s.i.s: in rr and racd keenly: hdwy to chse ldr 3f out: lost 2nd 2f out: outpcd and last fr over 1f out* **12/1**[3]

63.21 secs (2.41) **Going Correction** +0.55s/f (Yiel) **4** Ran SP% **105.6**
Speed ratings (Par 93): **104,99,91,90**
CSF £5.56 TOTE £4.50; EX 5.80.
Owner The MHS 4x10 Partnership **Bred** Millsec Limited **Trained** Malpas, Cheshire

FOCUS
Sprints on inner home straight. Races on round course on outer home straight and distances on round course increased by 51yds. Not the most inspiring of maidens and a nasty shock for long odds-on punters, but the form makes sense.

NOTEBOOK
Musical Valley seemed to improve for a change to more patient tactics when narrowly beaten at Bath last time, so was more than happy to get a lead from the favourite. It was obvious from some way out that he was travelling much the better and had little difficulty in picking off the market leader. He seems to be improving and shapes as though an extra furlong wouldn't bother him. (op 7-2)
Excavator had by far the best credentials even though he had been turned over at odds-on at Kempton last time, with the form of his Bath debut working out so well. However, despite being able to bowl along in what seemed a comfortable lead, the resistance he put up when challenged by the winner over a furlong out was minimal. His Bath effort now seems to flatter him and he seems to be going backwards. (op 4-11)
Come To Mind had shown nothing in four previous outings so the only surprise was that he didn't finish last. (op 66-1)
Triggerlo, tried in a visor, fluffed the start then carted himself into contention mid-race before emptying. He hasn't built on early promise and looks exposed. (op 9-1)

3540 BOHLE BRITISH STALLION STUDS E B F NOVICE STKS 6f
3:00 (3:00) (Class 4) 2-Y-0 **£4,857** (£1,445; £722) **Stalls** Centre

Form RPR

1 **1** **Ralphy Boy (IRE)**[27] 2665 2-9-5 0.. AdrianNicholls 1 88
(David Nicholls) *mde all: shkn up whn pressed fr 2f out: rdn over 1f out: r.o gamely ins fnl f: hld on wl at fin* **14/1**[3]

10 **2** *nk* **Silverheels (IRE)**[14] 3064 2-9-5 0.. PaulHanagan 4 87
(Paul Cole) *racd keenly: chsd wnr tl rdn and outpcd fr jst over 2f out: r.o fnl 75yds: clsd and pressed wnr at fin: jst hld* **8/11**[1]

3 **3** *¾* **Electric Qatar**[7] 3314 2-9-0 0.. JamieSpencer 2 80
(Tom Dascombe) *plld hrd early: hld up: moved upsides to chal 2f out: rdn over 1f out: continued to press wnr tl no ex fnl 50yds* **11/8**[2]

1m 17.97s (4.17) **Going Correction** +0.55s/f (Yiel) **3** Ran SP% **106.7**
Speed ratings (Par 95): **92,91,90**
CSF £24.51 TOTE £7.00; EX 10.10.
Owner Frank Lowe **Bred** Frank Lowe **Trained** Sessay, N Yorks

FOCUS
Only three runners, but a fascinating race. The early tempo was very modest, however. Tricky form to assess, rated through the form of the runner-up's debut.

NOTEBOOK
Ralphy Boy(IRE) couldn't be given away in the market, but he had proved game when winning narrowly on his Catterick debut and repeated the feat here having been allowed to bowl along in front at his own pace. He kept on finding more for pressure and obviously has a decent attitude, but he will probably be forced to take on better company now. (op 13-2)
Silverheels(IRE) found everything happening too quickly for him when sent off favourite for the Norfolk, so this extra furlong ought to have suited, but the slow pace wasn't ideal and he got tapped for foot over 2f from before running on again towards the line. A stronger pace or a step up to 7f may help. (op 5-4 tchd 11-8 in places)

Electric Qatar was very well backed to make a winning debut at Newcastle, but didn't get home after looking likely to score. He compromised his chances here by taking a strong hold early, and although he looked dangerous when delivered towards the far side of the winner entering the last 2f, again faltered in the closing stages and went left. He remains a horse of potential, but will need to deliver fairly soon. (op 6-5 tchd 11-10, evens in places)

3541 DISTINCTION DOORS H'CAP 6f
3:30 (3:30) (Class 4) (0-80,80) 3-Y-0+ **£4,209** (£1,252; £625; £312) **Stalls** Centre

Form RPR

0-03 **1** **Ryan Style (IRE)**[6] 3367 5-9-10 **76** TomEaves 9 87
(Lisa Williamson) *hld up in rr: hdwy 2f out: rdn to ld ent fnl f: r.o and in control fnl 100yds* **12/1**

0005 **2** 1 3/4 **Invincible Force (IRE)**[6] 3339 7-9-11 **77** (b) SilvestreDeSousa 7 82
(Paul Green) *dwlt: in tch: effrt to chse ldrs over 2f out: led over 1f out: hdd ent fnl f: kpt on: hld fnl 100yds* **15/2**

3210 **3** 1 1/4 **Kylladdie**[10] 3222 4-10-0 **80** (b) JamieSpencer 8 81
(Steve Gollings) *hld up: hdwy to chse ldrs 1/2-way: rdn and nt qckn over 1f out: kpt on same pce ins fnl f* **14/1**

-043 **4** hd **Tyfos**[7] 3322 6-9-12 **78** PaulHanagan 6 78
(Brian Baugh) *led: rdn and hdd over 1f out: kpt on same pce fnl 100yds* **7/2**[2]

1-00 **5** 2 3/4 **Piddie's Power**[19] 2938 4-9-8 **74** GrahamGibbons 1 66
(Ed McMahon) *prom: rdn over 1f out: one pce fnl 150yds* **9/1**

5306 **6** 2 1/2 **Red Roar (IRE)**[12] 3166 4-8-10 **62** PatrickMathers 3 46
(Alan Berry) *midfield: u.p 2f out: no imp and outpcd fnl f* **20/1**

5322 **7** 1 1/4 **Red Cape (FR)**[6] 3359 8-9-11 **77** PJMcDonald 5 57
(Ruth Carr) *dwlt: prom after 1f: rdn over 2f out: wknd over 1f out* **9/4**[1]

0065 **8** 3 **Al Muheer (IRE)**[12] 3169 6-9-11 **77** (b) JamesSullivan 2 47
(Ruth Carr) *prom: rdn over 1f out: sn wknd* **6/1**[3]

0/0- **9** 25 **Enjoyment**[307] 5474 4-8-13 **65** RobertWinston 4 —
(Alan McCabe) *hld up: u.p over 2f out: wl bhd ins fnl f: eased* **20/1**

1m 16.02s (2.22) **Going Correction** +0.55s/f (Yiel) **9** Ran SP% **112.9**
Speed ratings (Par 105): **105,102,101,100,97 93,92,88,54**
toteswingers:1&2:£10.00, 1&3:£9.40, 2&3:£9.20 CSF £96.13 CT £890.38 TOTE £13.10: £3.30, £2.50, £2.60; EX 109.10.
Owner Bluegrass Racing Ltd **Bred** Johnny Kent **Trained** Saighton, Cheshire

FOCUS
A decent sprint handicap with the first three home starting from the three highest stalls. The winner is rated back to his best.
Piddie's Power Official explanation: trainers rep had no explanation for the poor form shown
Red Cape(FR) Official explanation: jockey said gelding ran flat
Enjoyment Official explanation: jockey said filly slipped leaving stalls and appeared to lose its action

3542 TUFFX CONSERVATORY ROOF GLASS H'CAP 1m
4:00 (4:01) (Class 3) (0-95,95) 3-Y-0+ **£7,123** (£2,119; £1,059; £529) **Stalls** Low

Form RPR

1000 **1** **Crown Counsel (IRE)**[14] 3067 3-8-8 **85** SilvestreDeSousa 6 98
(Mark Johnston) *chsd ldrs: led over 2f out: r.o wl and in command fnl 150yds: eased cl home* **10/1**

5363 **2** 2 1/4 **First Post (IRE)**[28] 2647 4-8-13 **80** RobertWinston 4 90
(Derek Haydn Jones) *hld up: pushed along over 3f out: swtchd rt and hdwy over 2f out: hung lft u.p and chsd wnr fr over 1f out: no imp fnl 150yds* **9/1**

0342 **3** 3/4 **San Cassiano (IRE)**[5] 3399 4-8-13 **80** PJMcDonald 3 88
(Ruth Carr) *chsd ldr tl rdn over 2f out: nt qckn over 1f out: styd on same pce ins fnl f* **4/1**[2]

0-66 **4** 1 3/4 **Classic Colori (IRE)**[33] 2509 4-9-7 **88** (v[1]) KierenFallon 8 92
(Tom Dascombe) *s.i.s: bhd: pushed along over 4f out: styd on ins fnl f: gng on at fin: nt rch ldrs* **11/1**

0310 **5** nk **Balcarce Nov (ARG)**[19] 2933 6-10-0 **95** JamieSpencer 1 99
(Tom Tate) *hld up: shkn up and hdwy over 1f out: chsd ldrs ins fnl f: one pce and no imp fnl 100yds* **9/2**[3]

0305 **6** 3/4 **Space War**[26] 2706 4-9-10 **91** JamesSullivan 7 93
(Michael Easterby) *midfield: shkn up whn n.m.r and hmpd wl over 1f out: one pce and no imp fnl f* **8/1**

0442 **7** 1 1/4 **Vainglory (USA)**[8] 3290 7-9-4 **90** LauraPike[(5)] 5 89
(David Simcock) *hld up: u.p fr over 3f out: nvr able to chal* **10/3**[1]

00-0 **8** 7 **Caldercruix (USA)**[50] 2002 4-9-1 **82** MickyFenton 9 65
(Tom Tate) *led: hdd over 2f out: wknd qckly over 1f out: eased whn wl btn fnl 100yds* **25/1**

0061 **9** nk **Ezdeyaad (USA)**[35] 2428 7-9-1 **87** LeeTopliss[(5)] 2 69
(Ed Walker) *chsd ldrs: rdn over 2f out: wknd over 1f out* **10/1**

1m 44.24s (1.34) **Going Correction** +0.35s/f (Good)
WFA 3 from 4yo+ 10lb **9** Ran SP% **112.7**
Speed ratings (Par 107): **107,104,104,102,101 101,99,92,92**
toteswingers:1&2:£11.70, 1&3:£7.00, 2&3:£7.40 CSF £93.32 CT £419.37 TOTE £10.20: £3.20, £2.40, £2.10; EX 100.20.
Owner Sheikh Hamdan Bin Mohammed Al Maktoum **Bred** Gerrardstown House Stud **Trained** Middleham Moor, N Yorks

FOCUS
A decent handicap and they went a rapid pace. The form's rated around the second.

NOTEBOOK
Crown Counsel(IRE) was bidding to give his trainer a hat-trick in this race, but had been disappointing in his last three starts, albeit he contested the Britannia last time. Close to the strong pace from the off, he was set alight over 2f from home and was never going to be caught once in front. The only 3-y-o in the field, he didn't see the racecourse until February, so may still have some improvement left. He is in the sales. (op 12-1)
First Post(IRE), still 6lb above his last winning mark, did best of those who were held up well off the early pace, but he veered sharply away to his left when brought to challenge 2f out and looked awkward inside the last furlong. He has now hung badly in his last three starts, so has to be treated with caution. (op 10-1)
San Cassiano(IRE) was always there or thereabouts and kept staying on, but he was already due to go up 3lb following his improved effort stepped up to 1m2f at Newcastle five days earlier, which won't make his life any easier. (tchd 7-2)
Classic Colori(IRE) was back down in trip having run over 1m2f in his last four outings and had a visor on for the first time. Slowly away, he ran on to take fourth late on, but may merely have been running on past beaten horses, so more evidence is needed that he is on the way back. (op 12-1 tchd 10-1)
Balcarce Nov(ARG) was taking on lesser company than he normally meets and has winning form over this C&D, but he could only make limited late progress. (tchd 5-1 in places)
Space War was back up to his optimum trip and was travelling better than anything over 2f from home, but he was then badly hampered by the hanging First Post and there was no way back. He is better than this. (op 7-1)
Vainglory(USA), who needs his run timing to perfection, saw plenty of daylight on the wide outside up the home straight and never threatened to take a hand. He was reportedly never travelling. (op 4-1)
Caldercruix(USA), apparently in as a pacemaker for Balcarce Nov, soon tore off in front and stayed there until over 2f from home. (op 18-1)
Ezdeyaad(USA) was reported to have lost his action on the home bend. Official explanation: jockey said gelding lost action on the bend and found nothing in the home straight (op 9-1)

3543 PLANITHERM MAIDEN STKS 1m
4:30 (4:30) (Class 5) 3-Y-0+ **£2,266** (£674; £337; £168) **Stalls** Low

Form RPR

232- **1** **Mujrayaat (IRE)**[294] 5893 3-9-0 79 RichardHills 11 84+
(Roger Varian) *racd keenly: trckd ldrs: forced wd after 2f: led wl over 1f out: rdn ins fnl f: r.o: in command at fin* **11/8**[1]

2 1 **Garud (IRE)** 3-8-9 0 TobyAtkinson[(5)] 2 82+
(Marco Botti) *s.i.s: plld hrd: wnt rt after 1f: in tch after 2f: effrt 2f out: rn green: chsd wnr over 1f out: tried to chal ins fnl f: nt qckn and hld fnl 75yds* **40/1**

-422 **3** 1 **Uppercut**[31] 2568 3-9-0 78 FergusSweeney 4 79
(Stuart Kittow) *chsd ldr: swtchd rt after 2f: led over 2f out: hdd wl over 1f out: sn hung lft: kpt on u.p ins fnl f but hld* **4/1**[3]

65- **4** 2 1/2 **Figaro**[251] 7058 3-9-0 0 KierenFallon 1 73
(William Haggas) *chsd ldrs: rdn over 2f out: nt qckn: styd on same pce ins fnl f* **11/4**[2]

5 1 1/4 **Maloof** 3-9-0 0 TomEaves 14 70+
(Roger Varian) *hld up: pushed along over 4f out: nt clr run jst over 1f out: styd on ins fnl f: gng on at fin: promising* **20/1**

6 **6** hd **Come Here Yew (IRE)**[34] 2457 3-9-0 0 DavidAllan 10 69+
(Declan Carroll) *hld up: pushed along over 2f out: swtchd lft over 1f out: sn nt clr run briefly: kpt on ins fnl f: no imp on ldrs: promising* **50/1**

-5 **7** 3/4 **Rockerfellow**[10] 3232 3-9-0 0 PaulHanagan 5 67
(J W Hills) *midfield: pushed along and hdwy to chse ldrs over 1f out: one pce ins fnl f* **66/1**

0 **8** 2 3/4 **Highland Colori (IRE)**[44] 2185 3-9-0 0 RobertWinston 6 61
(Tom Dascombe) *in tch: forced wd after 2f: effrt over 1f out: no imp fnl f* **25/1**

0 **9** 1/2 **Shopping Oasis**[61] 1693 3-9-0 0 SilvestreDeSousa 15 60
(Mark Johnston) *led: pushed along 3f out: hdd over 2f out: wknd fnl f* **33/1**

-050 **10** 3/4 **Reset To Fit**[21] 2845 4-9-10 50 GrahamGibbons 9 60
(Eric Alston) *hld up: pushed along over 2f out: nvr a threat* **100/1**

0 **11** nse **The Buska (IRE)**[7] 3320 3-8-9 0 NeilFarley[(5)] 3 58
(Declan Carroll) *midfield: rdn over 2f out: no imp* **100/1**

4-4 **12** nk **Guisho (IRE)**[33] 2511 3-9-0 0 JamieSpencer 13 58
(Brian Meehan) *in tch: forced wd after 2f: racd on outer: rdn over 2f out: wknd ins fnl f* **13/2**

0 **13** 5 **Price Of Retrieval**[64] 1605 4-9-10 0 FrannyNorton 12 46
(Peter Chapple-Hyam) *hld up: pushed along over 4f out: edgd lft over 2f out: no imp: eased whn wl btn ins fnl f* **100/1**

4 **14** 10 **Fiftynotout (IRE)**[76] 1370 4-9-10 0 PatrickMathers 7 22
(Alan Berry) *s.i.s: bhd: rdn over 2f out: nvr on terms* **100/1**

15 1 **Riczar** 3-8-9 0 RoystonFfrench 8 14
(Tom Dascombe) *s.i.s: in rr: struggling over 2f out: nvr on terms* **80/1**

1m 44.98s (2.08) **Going Correction** +0.35s/f (Good)
WFA 3 from 4yo 10lb **15** Ran SP% **124.7**
Speed ratings (Par 103): **103,102,101,98,97 97,96,93,93,92 92,91,86,76,75**
toteswingers:1&2:£20.30, 1&3:£2.90, 2&3:£31.50 CSF £82.43 TOTE £2.80: £1.20, £10.10, £1.60; EX 68.70.
Owner Hamdan Al Maktoum **Bred** Lady Richard Wellesley **Trained** Newmarket, Suffolk
■ Stewards' Enquiry : Fergus Sweeney three-day ban: careless riding (Jul 14-16)
David Allan three-day ban: careless riding (29th-31st July)

FOCUS
Plenty of dead wood in this maiden and something of a rough race with Uppercut switching right after 2f and causing interference to the winner, Highland Colori and Guisho.
Guisho(IRE) Official explanation: jockey said colt hung right

3544 RITEC 30TH ANNIVERSARY H'CAP 1m 3f 200y
5:00 (5:01) (Class 4) (0-85,84) 4-Y-0+ **£4,209** (£1,252; £625; £312) **Stalls** Centre

Form RPR

0152 **1** **Warlu Way**[18] 2958 4-9-7 **84** PhillipMakin 6 96+
(John Dunlop) *hld up: hdwy 3f out: led over 1f out: r.o ins fnl f: in command fnl 100yds* **5/1**[3]

014 **2** 2 3/4 **Butler (IRE)**[28] 2649 4-9-3 **80** KierenFallon 4 89+
(Luca Cumani) *trckd ldrs: effrt 2f out: keeping on whn n.m.r over 1f out: wnt 2nd ins fnl f: no imp fnl 100yds* **11/4**[1]

2-36 **3** 3 **Maoi Chinn Tire (IRE)**[24] 2762 4-8-5 **68** (p) PaulHanagan 8 71
(Jennie Candlish) *midfield: clsd over 4f out: led over 2f out: rdn and hdd over 1f out: styd on same pce fnl 100yds* **7/1**

1260 **4** 1 3/4 **Scamperdale**[96] 994 9-9-6 **83** KellyHarrison 2 83
(Brian Baugh) *hld up in midfield: nt qckn 2f out: hdwy over 1f out: kpt on but no imp on ldrs ins fnl f* **40/1**

1624 **5** 2 3/4 **Ubi Ace**[26] 2708 5-9-4 **81** GrahamGibbons 7 77
(Tim Walford) *trckd ldrs: ev ch over 2f out: wknd ins fnl f* **7/1**

2621 **6** 3/4 **Oriental Cavalier**[26] 2708 5-9-3 **80** (v) DavidAllan 5 75
(Mark Buckley) *hld up: rdn over 2f out: nvr able to chal* **6/1**

-262 **7** 1 3/4 **Hydrant**[55] 1874 5-8-13 **76** GregFairley 10 68
(Peter Salmon) *chsd ldr tl over 4f out: rdn and stl in tch over 2f out: wknd ins fnl f* **16/1**

00-0 **8** 1 1/4 **Epic (IRE)**[19] 2932 4-9-4 **81** (b) SilvestreDeSousa 9 71
(Mark Johnston) *s.i.s: bhd: u.p over 4f out: nvr on terms* **16/1**

0-30 **9** 2 1/4 **Beat The Rush**[20] 2888 4-9-4 **81** TomEaves 1 67
(Julie Camacho) *led: rdn and hdd over 2f out: wknd over 1f out* **9/2**[2]

2m 32.81s (-1.19) **Going Correction** +0.05s/f (Good) **9** Ran SP% **115.0**
Speed ratings (Par 105): **105,103,101,100,98 97,96,95,94**
toteswingers:1&2:£4.20, 1&3:£7.60, 2&3:£6.90. Tote Super 7: Win: Not won. Place: £98.40 CSF £19.06 CT £95.89 TOTE £5.50: £1.50, £1.80, £2.20; EX 11.70.
Owner The Earl Cadogan **Bred** The Earl Cadogan **Trained** Arundel, W Sussex

FOCUS
Not a bad middle-distance handicap and the front pair look progressive. The form is rated on the positive side.

3545 GLASS TIMES H'CAP 1m 2f 95y
5:30 (5:31) (Class 5) (0-70,69) 3-Y-0+ **£2,266** (£674; £337; £168) **Stalls** Centre

Form RPR

06-6 **1** **Hot Spice**[21] 2838 3-8-11 **64** PhillipMakin 3 75+
(John Dunlop) *racd keenly: hld up: swtchd lft and hdwy over 2f out: chsd ldrs over 1f out: styd on to ld fnl 100yds* **10/3**[2]

/060 **2** *1* **Burza**[20] 2887 5-9-5 **60**.. PaulHanagan 2 67
(John Mackie) *in tch: effrt to chal over 2f out: led narrowly 1f out: hdd fnl 100yds: styd on for press but hld cl home* **11/1**
1562 **3** *hd* **Amazing Blue Sky**[3] 3456 5-10-0 **69**........................ JamesSullivan 4 76
(Ruth Carr) *led: rdn over 2f out: hdd narrowly 1f out: stl ev ch ins fnl f: kpt on u.p: hld cl home* **2/1**[1]
304- **4** *2 ¾* **Muwalla**[256] 6961 4-9-8 **63**.. KierenFallon 6 64
(James Bethell) *s.i.s: hld up: hdwy to chse ldrs over 3f out: rdn over 1f out: one pce fnl f* **15/2**[3]
3433 **5** *¾* **Star Addition**[21] 2851 5-8-10 **51**........................ RobertWinston 10 51
(Eric Alston) *hld up: rdn and hdwy to chse ldrs over 1f out: sn edgd lft: one pce fnl 100yds* **14/1**
-000 **6** *2 ¼* **Think Its All Over (USA)**[18] 2952 4-9-8 **63**........................ TomEaves 5 58
(Julie Camacho) *trckd ldrs: wnt 2nd 6f out: lost 2nd over 2f out: sn n.m.r and checked: wknd 1f out* **16/1**
-003 **7** *1 ¾* **Oldmeldrum (IRE)**[21] 2835 3-8-6 **59** ow1........................ GregFairley 1 51
(Peter Salmon) *chsd ldr to 6f out: remained handy: u.p 3f out: wknd over 2f out: hung rt whn btn over 1f out* **40/1**
0536 **8** *1 ½* **Lord Lansing (IRE)**[15] 3054 4-9-11 **66**........................ AndrewElliott 7 55
(Mrs K Burke) *hld up: effrt on outer over 1f out: no imp* **14/1**
441- **9** *1 ¾* **Rockweiller**[279] 6326 4-9-6 **66**........................(v) LeeTopliss[(5)] 8 51
(Steve Gollings) *in tch: effrt to chal and hung lft over 2f out: wknd over 1f out* **8/1**

2m 15.22s (-0.78) **Going Correction** +0.05s/f (Good)
WFA 3 from 4yo+ 12lb **9** Ran SP% **109.3**
Speed ratings (Par 103): **105,104,104,101,101 99,98,96,95**
toteswingers:1&2:£7.60, 1&3:£2.80, 2&3:£4.30 CSF £35.92 CT £81.42 TOTE £2.90: £1.10, £3.20, £1.90; EX 35.50.
Owner David & Jennifer Sieff & Partner **Bred** J L Dunlop **Trained** Arundel, W Sussex

FOCUS
An ordinary handicap won by the least-exposed runner in the field.
Hot Spice ◆ Official explanation: trainer said, regarding apparent improvement in form, that the gelding had possibly benefited by the step up in trip.
Lord Lansing(IRE) Official explanation: jockey said gelding hung right
T/Plt: £1,059.40 to a £1 stake. Pool:£49,606.95 - 34.18 winning tickets T/Qpdt: £51.40 to a £1 stake. Pool:£5,661.02 - 81.50 winning tickets DO

3256 NEWBURY (L-H)
Thursday, June 30

OFFICIAL GOING: Good to firm (good in places; 6.9)
Wind: virtually nil Weather: sunny

3546 RUNDLES.ORG.UK APPRENTICE H'CAP — 1m 3f 5y
6:35 (6:35) (Class 5) (0-70,70) 4-Y-O+ **£2,266** (£674; £337; £168) **Stalls** Low

Form RPR
610 **1** **Amana (USA)**[7] 3300 7-9-0 **65**........................ RachealKneller[(5)] 6 76
(Mark Brisbourne) *travelled wl in mid-div: swtchd to centre and gd hdwy fr 4f out: led 3f out: sn pushed clr: styd on wl: comf* **8/1**[3]
-000 **2** *2 ¾* **Rock With You**[22] 2816 4-8-10 **59**........................ DarylByrne[(3)] 4 65
(Pat Phelan) *s.i.s: towards rr: rdn and hdwy fr over 3f out: chsd wnr over 1f out: styd on* **40/1**
3211 **3** *2 ¾* **Transfer**[14] 3094 6-9-5 **65**........................ RyanClark 3 66
(Richard Price) *trckd ldrs: rdn and ev ch 3f out: kpt on same pce: jst hld on for 3rd* **13/8**[1]
4442 **4** *shd* **Edgeworth (IRE)**[9] 3256 5-9-3 **70**........................(p) JoshBaudains[(7)] 5 71
(David Bridgwater) *hld up towards rr: hdwy 3f out: sn rdn: styd on same pce fnl 2f: nvr trbld ldrs: jst failed to snatch 3rd* **11/2**[2]
400- **5** *6* **Two Kisses (IRE)**[96] 3478 4-8-11 **57**........................ MatthewCosham 2 47
(Brendan Powell) *led tl rdn 3f out: one pce fnl 2f* **11/2**[2]
0350 **6** *3* **Lunar River (FR)**[12] 3176 8-8-11 **57**........................(t) JamesRogers 8 42
(David Pinder) *hld up towards rr: rdn and sme prog fr 3f out: nvr threatened ldrs* **22/1**
-540 **7** *13* **Bin End**[21] 2846 5-9-2 **67**........................ GeorgeDowning[(5)] 10 28
(Barry Brennan) *w ldr tl rdn 3f out: sn wknd* **12/1**
-360 **8** *2* **Meglio Ancora**[24] 2769 4-9-7 **67**........................(b[1]) RyanPowell 7 25
(Jonathan Portman) *s.i.s: sn mid-div: rdn 3f out: wknd over 1f out* **11/1**
3335 **9** *2 ¼* **Striding Edge (IRE)**[9] 3256 5-9-2 **65**........................(b[1]) MatthewLawson[(3)] 9 19
(Hans Adielsson) *trckd ldrs: rdn over 3f out: sn wknd* **12/1**
310- **10** *81* **Venir Rouge**[271] 6578 7-9-4 **67**........................ AntiocoMurgia[(3)] 1 —
(Matthew Salaman) *a bhd: t.o fnl 5f* **16/1**

2m 20.95s (-0.25) **Going Correction** +0.075s/f (Good) **10** Ran SP% **116.4**
Speed ratings (Par 103): **103,101,99,98,94 92,82,81,79,20**
toteswingers:1&2:£41.30, 2&3:£24.60, 1&3:£5.00 CSF £269.48 CT £772.18 TOTE £10.50: £2.10, £5.40, £1.10; EX 499.10.
Owner Mark Brisbourne **Bred** Shadwell Farm LLC **Trained** Great Ness, Shropshire
■ Stewards' Enquiry : Antioco Murgia jockey said gelding never travelled; vet said gelding was found to have an irregular heart beat.

FOCUS
Course at normal configuration. No more than a modest apprentice handicap but it was run at a good pace and the principals came from off the gallop. Amana built on her Warwick win.

3547 MPS GLOBAL SECURITIES E B F MAIDEN FILLIES' STKS — 6f 8y
7:05 (7:08) (Class 4) 2-Y-O **£4,403** (£1,310; £654; £327) **Stalls** Centre

Form RPR
3 **1** **Ballyea (IRE)**[9] 3258 2-9-0 0........................ DaneO'Neill 14 80
(Richard Hannon) *trckd ldrs: rdn wl over 1f out: led ent fnl f: hld on: all out* **11/8**[1]
2 *hd* **Lady Gorgeous** 2-9-0 0........................ HughBowman 1 79+
(Mick Channon) *mid-div: rdn wl over 1f out: r.o wl ent fnl f: drifted rt: jst failed* **9/2**[2]
3 *1 ¾* **Ligurian Sea** 2-9-0 0........................ ShaneKelly 8 74+
(Walter Swinburn) *mid-div: rdn whn swtchd lft ent fnl f: r.o wl* **28/1**
0 **4** *hd* **Miss Astragal (IRE)**[55] 1846 2-9-0 0........................ PatDobbs 3 74
(Richard Hannon) *in tch: rdn 2f out: kpt on ins fnl f* **16/1**
5 *nk* **Rock On Candy** 2-9-0 0........................ TravisBlock 15 73+
(Sylvester Kirk) *in tch: rdn over 2f out: kpt on same pce ins fnl f* **50/1**
52 **6** *nk* **Alice's Dancer (IRE)**[13] 3117 2-8-9 0........................ JamesRogers[(5)] 16 72
(William Muir) *led: rdn 2f out: hdd ent fnl f: no ex* **8/1**
7 *¾* **Zaahya (IRE)** 2-9-0 0........................ TadhgO'Shea 2 70+
(John Dunlop) *s.i.s: in rr and sn pushed along: styd on ins fnl f: improve* **12/1**
00 **8** *½* **Solfilia**[18] 2962 2-9-0 0........................ FrankieMcDonald 9 69
(Hughie Morrison) *in tch: rdn over 2f out: kpt on same pce ins fnl f* **50/1**
9 *nk* **Camrock Star (IRE)** 2-9-0 0........................ MartinLane 11 67
(William Knight) *little slowly away: towards rr: rdn 2f out: kpt on but nt gng pce to threaten* **20/1**
10 *½* **Lovage** 2-9-0 0........................ TedDurcan 7 66+
(Roger Charlton) *dwlt bdly: bhd: kpt on but nvr able to get on terms: improve* **10/1**
46 **11** *¾* **Sister Guru**[15] 3046 2-8-9 0........................ RyanClark[(5)] 13 63
(Peter Hedger) *trckd ldr: rdn over 2f out: fdd fnl f* **66/1**
6 **12** *20* **More Is To Come (USA)**[29] 2606 2-9-0 0........................ JimCrowley 12 —
(Ralph Beckett) *trckd ldrs: rdn over 2f out: sn wknd* **5/1**[3]
13 *3 ½* **The Boomingbittern** 2-9-0 0........................ EddieCreighton 5 —
(Edward Creighton) *sn pushed along in rr: nvr a factor* **100/1**

1m 13.98s (0.98) **Going Correction** +0.075s/f (Good) **13** Ran SP% **125.3**
Speed ratings (Par 92): **96,95,93,93,92 92,91,90,90,89 88,61,57**
toteswingers:1&2:£4.50, 2&3:£50.90, 1&3:£13.50 CSF £7.43 TOTE £2.70: £1.10, £2.00, £8.40; EX 11.60.
Owner Denis J Barry **Bred** L Mulryan & M C Fahy **Trained** East Everleigh, Wilts
■ Stewards' Enquiry : Hugh Bowman caution: used whip without giving filly time to respond.

FOCUS
Not a strong maiden for the track with little good public form among those who had run and few of the newcomers appealing on breeding. The pace was strong, though, and for all the runners were soon strung out, they passed the post in something of a heap. Several of these showed promise.

NOTEBOOK
Ballyea(IRE) extended the good run of her yard in this event, this their fourth win in its last five runnings. She didn't have much in hand at the line with her experience proving vital in the closing stages, but considering she tracked the strong gallop she's probably a bit better than the result makes her look. That said, she doesn't promise to be much out of the ordinary for now. (op 2-1)
Lady Gorgeous has winners in her immediate pedigree and shaped well enough to suggest she would beat the winner were they to meet again, making her ground steadily from a position well back but tending to run around close home. She'll stay 7f and should find a similar event. (op 11-2 tchd 6-1)
Ligurian Sea, by Medicean and out of a mare who won at 1m4f, also shaped promisingly considering she was notably green for much of the way (also hung left late on) but she was doing some good work late on under an educational ride and is sure to appreciate a step up in trip before long. (op 20-1)
Miss Astragal(IRE) shaped better than she had on her debut at Ascot, clearly helped by the longer trip as her pedigree suggested she would be, though it's doubtful she possesses the scope for further progress of some of those around her.
Rock On Candy, who is from the family of Oaks winner Imagine and Derby winner Generous, fared well considering her stable's youngsters first time out usually need the experience badly.
Alice's Dancer(IRE) probably improved further on her Goodwood form, looking all speed and clearly much better suited by these faster conditions than on the soft ground then. A drop to 5f will see her in an even better light. (op 13-2 tchd 6-1)
Zaahya(IRE) comes from a yard that gets few first-time-out winners any more but this Shamardal filly half-sister to the 6f AW winner Waabel shaped promisingly, very slowly away and greener than most for a long way but finding the penny dropping strongly close home. She'll improve a lot. (tchd 14-1)
Solfilia stepped up on her previous form but never really threatened, albeit she'd have been a bit closer had she not run into trouble late on. (op 33-1)
Lovage ◆, by Exceed And Excel out of the Rockfel winner Name Of Love, would probably have gone very close had she broken on terms, detached early and on the back foot thereafter but finishing with a flourish when the race was all but over over (op 9-1 tchd 11-1)
More Is To Come(USA) was well supported to improve on her debut form but was the first beaten. (op 11-1)

3548 ABN AMRO CLEARING BANK CONDITIONS STKS — 7f (S)
7:35 (7:39) (Class 4) 3-Y-O+
£5,296 (£1,586; £793; £396; £198; £99) **Stalls** Centre

Form RPR
3-00 **1** **Yaa Wayl (IRE)**[133] 587 4-9-3 110........................(v) TedDurcan 1 107
(Saeed Bin Suroor) *trckd ldrs: led wl over 2f out: rdn over 1f out: hdd ins fnl f: rallied wl u.str.p: led fnl strides* **3/1**[2]
546- **2** *hd* **Mia's Boy**[208] 7689 7-9-0 97........................ AndreaAtzeni 2 103
(Chris Dwyer) *hld up bhd ldrs: tk clsr order 2f out: rdn to chal ent fnl f: sn led: no ex whn hdd fnl strides* **7/2**[3]
-603 **3** *2 ¾* **Angel's Pursuit (IRE)**[96] 986 4-9-0 104........................ PatDobbs 6 96
(Richard Hannon) *hld up bhd ldrs: clsd 2f out: sn rdn: kpt on but nt gng pce to chal* **11/4**[1]
0-00 **4** *1 ¼* **King Of Dixie (USA)**[13] 3109 7-9-0 103........................ JimCrowley 5 [illegible]
(William Knight) *trckd ldr: rdn over 2f out: kpt on but nt gng pce to chal* **7/1**
1-1 **5** *12* **Retainer (IRE)**[91] 1059 3-8-12 105........................ DaneO'Neill 4 64
(Richard Hannon) *stdd s: racd v keenly bhd ldrs: clsd whn short of room 2f out: sn rdn: wknd over 1f out* **3/1**[2]
0- **6** *10* **Simpulse**[242] 7248 3-8-2 0 ow2........................ FrankieMcDonald 3 27
(Norma Twomey) *led: rdn 3f out: sn hdd and btn* **150/1**

1m 25.72s (0.02) **Going Correction** +0.075s/f (Good)
WFA 3 from 4yo+ 9lb **6** Ran SP% **112.1**
Speed ratings (Par 105): **102,101,98,97,83 72**
toteswingers:1&2:£2.90, 2&3:£2.20, 1&3:£3.70 CSF £13.78 TOTE £2.70: £1.10, £3.00; EX 15.00.
Owner Godolphin **Bred** Ballylinch Stud **Trained** Newmarket, Suffolk

FOCUS
A useful minor event but most came here with something to prove, and with the pace very steady until 2f out the strength of the form is debatable. The runner-up is perhaps the best guide.

3549 FORSTERS LLP FILLIES' H'CAP — 7f (S)
8:10 (8:10) (Class 4) (0-80,80) 3-Y-O+ **£4,079** (£1,214; £606; £303) **Stalls** Centre

Form RPR
-314 **1** **Bakoura**[10] 3219 3-8-9 **70**........................ TadhgO'Shea 1 76+
(John Dunlop) *hld up in tch: swtchd rt and gd hdwy over 1f out: led ins fnl f: r.o wl: rdn out* **9/2**[2]
-056 **2** *1 ¼* **Primo Lady**[29] 2615 3-9-5 **80**........................(b[1]) DavidProbert 2 83
(Gay Kelleway) *trckd ldrs: rdn to ld over 1f out: hdd ins fnl f: kpt on but nt gng pce of wnr* **8/1**
2115 **3** *¾* **Wishformore (IRE)**[16] 3017 4-8-7 **64**........................(p) RyanPowell[(5)] 9 68
(J S Moore) *in tch: swtchd rt 2f out: sn rdn: kpt on ins fnl f to snatch 3rd line* **9/1**
-341 **4** *nse* **Queen Of Cash (IRE)**[28] 2643 3-9-2 **77**........................ JimCrowley 10 78
(Hughie Morrison) *trckd ldr: rdn and ev ch over 1f out: kpt on same pce fnl f: lost 3rd line* **4/1**[1]
-025 **5** *½* **Red Yarn**[14] 3079 4-9-8 **74**........................(b) GeorgeBaker 4 77
(Gary Moore) *sn led: rdn whn hrd pressed 2f out: sn hdd: no ex ins fnl f* **9/1**
0501 **6** *1 ¾* **Polar Annie**[20] 2870 6-9-1 **67**........................ HughBowman 5 65
(Malcolm Saunders) *trckd ldrs: rdn and ch 2f out: one pce sn after* **9/2**[2]

-663 **7** *1 ½* **Sakhee's Pearl**22 2822 5-9-11 **77**....................................(b) DaneO'Neill 6 71
(Jo Crowley) *in tch: nt clrest of runs bhd horses 2f out: swtchd lft: sn rdn: nt gng pce to get involved* **11/2**3

1-05 **8** *3 ¼* **Malpas Missile (IRE)**12 3168 3-9-0 **75**......................... StephenCraine 3 57
(Tom Dascombe) *hld up in tch: rdn over 2f out: nt pce to get involved: wknd ins fnl f* **11/1**

433- **9** *nk* **Requisite**196 7892 6-9-9 **75**...(v) MartinLane 7 59
(Ian Wood) *hld up in tch: rdn 2f out: nt pce to threaten: wknd ins fnl f* **20/1**

1m 25.72s (0.02) **Going Correction** +0.075s/f (Good)
WFA 3 from 4yo+ 9lb **9** Ran SP% **116.0**
Speed ratings (Par 102): **102,100,99,99,99 97,95,91,91**
toteswingers:1&2:£10.40, 2&3:£12.70, 1&3:£8.60 CSF £40.38 CT £313.58 TOTE £4.80: £1.70, £2.90, £2.90; EX 39.70.
Owner Hamdan Al Maktoum **Bred** Shadwell Estate Company Limited **Trained** Arundel, W Sussex

FOCUS
No more than a fair handicap and one run at no more than a steady pace initially with the runners once again sticking to the centre of the track. The form makes a fair bit of sense.

3550 STUDENTRACING.CO.UK MAIDEN STKS 1m 4f 5y
8:40 (8:40) (Class 5) 3-Y-O+ **£2,914** (£867; £433; £216) **Stalls** Low

Form RPR
04 **1** **Korabushka**18 2956 3-8-9 0...(p) ShaneKelly 7 81
(Jeremy Noseda) *s.i.s: sn trcking ldr: chal 3f out: led 2f out: rdn jst over 1f out: kpt on: drvn out* **4/1**3

230 **2** *2* **End Or Beginning**13 3108 3-9-0 87.............................. JamieSpencer 1 83
(Paul Cole) *led: rdn 3f out: hdd 2f out: styd on same pce whn hld sn after* **8/11**1

-020 **3** *1 ¾* **Sirius Superstar**31 2551 3-9-0 78................................ HughBowman 5 80
(Andrew Balding) *chsd ldrs: rdn 3f out: drifted to far rail: styd on same pce* **3/1**2

0 **4** *15* **Etheldreda (IRE)**15 3043 3-8-9 0....................................... TadhgO'Shea 3 51
(Clive Cox) *racd in 4th: rdn 4f out: wknd 2f out* **22/1**

5 *4 ½* **Delight Of The Eye** 3-8-9 0.. PatDobbs 4 44
(Alastair Lidderdale) *s.i.s: in last: rdn wl over 3f out: nvr any imp: wknd 2f out* **40/1**

0- **6** *13* **Classical Air**286 6155 3-8-9 0.. TedDurcan 8 23
(John Dunlop) *hld up in last pair: rdn 4f out: nvr any imp: wknd 2f out: eased ins fnl f* **16/1**

2m 33.46s (-2.04) **Going Correction** +0.075s/f (Good) **6** Ran SP% **115.6**
Speed ratings (Par 103): **109,107,106,96,93 84**
toteswingers:1&2:£1.90, 2&3:£1.10, 1&3:£1.20 CSF £7.64 TOTE £3.40: £1.10, £1.40; EX 9.00.
Owner Cheveley Park Stud **Bred** Cheveley Park Stud Ltd **Trained** Newmarket, Suffolk

FOCUS
A strongly run race for a six-runner maiden and probably the right result on the day, for all the runner-up didn't run quite up to the form he appeared to show at Royal Ascot last time. Decent maiden form from the first three.

3551 STAN JAMES H'CAP 1m 4f 5y
9:10 (9:12) (Class 4) (0-85,85) 3-Y-O **£4,079** (£1,214; £606; £303) **Stalls** Low

Form RPR
14 **1** **Western Prize**22 2819 3-8-13 **77**.. JimCrowley 2 84+
(Ralph Beckett) *trckd ldr: led narrowly travelling wl over 3f out: rdn 2f out: styd on wl ins fnl f: drvn out* **9/2**3

6415 **2** *¾* **Manifestation**67 1550 3-9-4 **82**.. WilliamBuick 4 88
(John Gosden) *reluctant to load: trckd ldrs: rdn wl over 3f out: nt gng pce to chal: edgd rt ent fnl f: styng on whn edgd lft towards fin: wnt 2nd fnl stride* **10/1**

002 **3** *shd* **Shamacam**14 3080 3-8-7 **74**... LouisBeuzelin(3) 5 80
(Sir Michael Stoute) *trckd ldrs: rdn over 2f out: chsd wnr ent fnl f: styd on but a being hld: lost 2nd fnl stride* **20/1**

0-06 **4** *1 ¾* **State Opera**47 2100 3-9-7 **85**.................................... SilvestreDeSousa 3 88
(Mark Johnston) *led: rdn and narrowly hdd wl over 3f out: rallied gamely and ev ch tl no ex ent fnl f* **8/1**

0-12 **5** *1 ¼* **Four Nations (USA)**21 2842 3-9-0 **78**................................. PatDobbs 9 79+
(Amanda Perrett) *mid-div: rdn over 3f out: nt pce to chal: styd on ins fnl f* **7/2**2

63-0 **6** *½* **Secret Edge**20 2885 3-8-3 **70**.. SimonPearce(3) 6 70
(Alan King) *mid-div: rdn over 3f out: nt gng pce to chal: styd on ins fnl f* **25/1**

2136 **7** *1 ¼* **Viking Storm**40 2295 3-8-13 **77**...................................... JamieSpencer 1 77+
(Harry Dunlop) *hld up: sme hdwy u.p 3f out: nvr gng pce to trble ldrs* **7/1**

4-51 **8** *1 ¾* **Schism**20 2871 3-8-11 **75**.. DaneO'Neill 7 70
(Henry Candy) *hld up towards rr: rdn over 3f out: nvr any imp on ldrs* **14/1**

4111 **9** *3 ½* **Anton Dolin (IRE)**21 2842 3-9-2 **80**................................... TedDurcan 8 70
(John Dunlop) *mid-div: rdn 3f out: wknd ins fnl f* **5/2**1

2m 38.71s (3.21) **Going Correction** +0.075s/f (Good) **9** Ran SP% **117.0**
Speed ratings (Par 101): **92,91,91,90,89 89,88,87,84**
toteswingers:1&2:£18.60, 2&3:£25.80, 1&3:£19.30 CSF £49.24 CT £819.90 TOTE £6.90: £2.70, £2.60, £3.80; EX 62.90.
Owner J C Smith **Bred** Littleton Stud **Trained** Kimpton, Hants

FOCUS
Several progressive sorts in opposition in an interesting finale, but it turned into something of a tactical affair in which those prominent throughout were favoured. The unexposed winner rates a clear personal best, with the fourth setting the standard.
T/Plt: £128.80 to a £1 stake. Pool of £6,397.74 - 364.94 winning units. T/Qpdt: £31.40 to a £1 stak. Pool of £5,399.35 - 127.05 winning units. TM

2852YARMOUTH (L-H)
Thursday, June 30

OFFICIAL GOING: Good to firm (7.8)
Wind: moderate behind Weather: bright and breezy but a bit overcast

3552 BRITISH STALLION STUDS SUPPORTING BRITISH RACING E B F MAIDEN STKS (DIV I) 6f 3y
2:10 (2:13) (Class 5) 2-Y-O **£3,238** (£963; £481; £240) **Stalls** High

Form RPR
022 **1** **Apostle (IRE)**40 2318 2-9-3 0... HayleyTurner 8 85
(Michael Bell) *mde all: rdn 2f out: strly pressed and jnd 1f out: drvn ahd to assert fnl 25yds* **1/3**1

0 **2** *hd* **Hazaz (IRE)**12 3182 2-9-3 0.. PhilipRobinson 3 84
(Clive Brittain) *t.k.h: chsd ldr: pushed along 2f out: drvn to chal wl over 1f out: sustained effrt to join ldr 1f out: tl no ex fnl 25yds* **10/1**

3 *3 ½* **Vital Gold** 2-9-3 0.. RyanMoore 5 74+
(William Haggas) *s.i.s: in last trio early: pushed along 3f out: hdwy 2f out: pushed out to take 3rd ins fnl f: should improve* **16/1**

5 **4** *2* **Invincible Dream (IRE)**8 3288 2-9-3 0............................. TomQueally 2 68
(Robert Mills) *dwlt: sn in midfield: pushed along to chse ldrs 2f out: sn no imp on ldng pair: lost 3rd ins fnl f* **13/2**3

5 *hd* **Aim Higher** 2-9-3 0.. WilliamBuick 4 67+
(John Gosden) *t.k.h: midfield: pushed along 4f out and sn hanging rt: kpt on ins fnl f: should improve* **6/1**2

6 **6** *5* **Selbaar**30 2594 2-9-3 0... DarryllHolland 10 52
(Chris Dwyer) *midfield: pushed along over 2f out: outpcd ins fnl 2f and sn wknd* **100/1**

0 **7** *4 ½* **Our Boy Billy**28 2640 2-9-3 0.. RichardMullen 1 39
(Robert Cowell) *prom: rdn over 3f out: wknd and hung rt 2f out: wl btn fnl 1f* **80/1**

8 *hd* **Flashbak (IRE)** 2-8-5 0... NatashaEaton(7) 7 33
(Alan Bailey) *hld up: t.k.h: pushed along and effrt over 2f out: no imp and wknd ins fnl f* **66/1**

9 *5* **The Mighty Lohan (IRE)** 2-9-3 0..................................... PatCosgrave 9 23
(Amy Weaver) *s.i.s: in rr: running green and dropped last over 2f out: sn btn* **125/1**

1m 12.26s (-2.14) **Going Correction** -0.525s/f (Hard) **9** Ran SP% **122.1**
Speed ratings (Par 93): **93,92,88,85,85 78,72,72,65**
toteswingers:1&2:£2.30, 1&3:£3.10, 2&3:£7.50 CSF £5.85 TOTE £1.50: £1.02, £3.30, £3.30; EX 5.80 Trifecta £35.00 Pool: £762.77 - 16.12 winning units..
Owner Highclere Thoroughbred Racing - Jackson **Bred** Mrs Eleanor Kent **Trained** Newmarket, Suffolk

FOCUS
A middling juvenile maiden that was made slightly more interesting by a clutch of well-bred newcomers. The form has quite a sound feel with the first pair clear.

NOTEBOOK
Apostle(IRE), second in Class 3 events at York on his last two starts, broke his duck at the fourth attempt. It was a close run thing, though, as after disputing the lead for much of the race, he was strongly challenged by Hazaz through the final furlong. The runner-up may just have got his head in front at one stage, but the winner fought hard and was edging away at the finish. (op 4-9)
Hazaz(IRE), seventh of 15 at Newmarket first time out, took a marked step forward from that run. Just outgunned in the dying strides, he should go one better at some stage. (op 12-1)
Vital Gold, a debutant half-brother to a two-year-old sprint winner, posted an encouraging first effort. He stayed on nicely in the final furlong and should improve for this run. (tchd 14-1)
Invincible Dream(IRE), an encouraging fifth on his only previous outing, did not really build on that initial display. He was never nearer than fourth and will need to progress significantly to land an average maiden. (tchd 7-1)
Aim Higher, a first-time-out half-brother to 1,000 Guineas third Super Sleuth, was green throughout. Racing apart from the others, he repeatedly changed his legs and was never on a completely even keel. Given that, he seems sure to show improvement next time. (op 11-2 tchd 5-1)
Selbaar, sixth of seven here on her first appearance, showed speed for more than half the journey. She was left well behind, however, once the first two got down to their final-furlong battle. (tchd 80-1)

3553 BRITISH STALLION STUDS SUPPORTING BRITISH RACING E B F MAIDEN STKS (DIV II) 6f 3y
2:40 (2:42) (Class 5) 2-Y-O **£3,238** (£963; £481; £240) **Stalls** High

Form RPR
1 **Saigon** 2-9-3 0.. KirstyMilczarek 4 86+
(James Toller) *s.i.s: pushed into midfield and racd on outer: rdn to chse ldrs 2f out: led 1f out: kpt on u.p hld on wl* **12/1**

3 **2** *hd* **Justineo**29 2612 2-9-3 0.. RyanMoore 1 85+
(William Haggas) *prom: pushed along to chse ldr 2f out: drvn to ld ins fnl 2f: hdd 1f out: responded wl to press ins fnl f: jst hld* **4/9**1

0 **3** *6* **Vinnie Jones**65 1583 2-9-3 0... WilliamBuick 8 67
(John Gosden) *taken lft and sltly hmpd after s: midfield: pushed along ins fnl 2f: drvn along to chse ldrs over 1f out: wnt 3rd ins fnl f* **5/1**2

30 **4** *3 ½* **Thorpe Bay**75 1396 2-9-3 0...(be1) MarcHalford 2 56
(Mark Rimmer) *chsd ldr: hmpd after 1f: led 4f out: pushed along and jnd 2f out: sn hdd and outpcd by ldng pair: lost 3rd ins fnl f* **80/1**

65 **5** *2 ¾* **Reve Du Jour (IRE)**14 3092 2-8-7 0.............................. KieranO'Neill(5) 5 42
(Alan McCabe) *t.k.h: led: swvd after 100yds: hdd 4f out: remained prom tl rdn and grad wknd ins fnl 2f* **8/1**3

6 *½* **Lucky Money** 2-9-3 0.. StevieDonohoe 7 52+
(Sir Mark Prescott Bt) *s.i.s: green and woefully outpcd early: wl bhd 4f out: kpt on fr 2f out: nvr a threat* **12/1**

06 **7** *1 ¾* **Eagle Of Rome (IRE)**18 2962 2-9-3 0............................. TomMcLaughlin 3 40
(Nick Littmoden) *prom: rdn wl over 3f out: grad wknd ins fnl f* **25/1**

0 **8** *2 ¾* **My Guardian Angel**13 3132 2-8-12 0.............................. AshleyMorgan(5) 9 32
(Mark H Tompkins) *prom: lost pl and outpcd 4f out: rdn and no imp 2f out* **50/1**

0 **9** *11* **Festival Spirit**18 2953 2-9-3 0...................................... J-PGuillambert 10 —
(Mark Johnston) *urged along thrght: midfield: rdn along over 2f out: sn wknd* **40/1**

10 *2 ½* **Pack Of Cards (IRE)** 2-9-3 0... RobertHavlin 6 —
(Terry Clement) *in rr and clueless: rdn sn after s and clueless: t.o after 3f* **66/1**

1m 11.5s (-2.90) **Going Correction** -0.525s/f (Hard) **10** Ran SP% **123.4**
Speed ratings (Par 93): **98,97,89,85,81 80,78,74,60,56**
toteswingers:1&2:£3.30, 1&3:£7.80, 2&3:£2.00 CSF £18.77 TOTE £18.90: £3.10, £1.10, £1.60; EX 37.80 Trifecta £68.00 Pool: £611.28 - 6.65 winning units..
Owner P C J Dalby & R D Schuster **Bred** R Dollar, T Adams & G F Pemberton **Trained** Newmarket, Suffolk

FOCUS
On paper this looked weaker than the first division, but the time was fast and the first two were clear. The form could be rated up to 10lb better.

NOTEBOOK
Saigon, a half-brother to multiple sprint winner Tabaret, made an encouraging debut. Not the quickest away, he raced towards the inside rail and was off the pace in the early stages. He ran on well, though, and may stay another furlong in due course. Given his trainer's patient methods, improvement is likely. (op 20-1)
Justineo, third of four when second-favourite on his debut, was even more heavily backed here. He did his best to collect, racing in the first three throughout and leading 2f from home, but could not match the winner in the closing stages. (op 8-11 tchd 4-5 and 5-6 in a place)
Vinnie Jones, seventh of nine at Wolverhampton first time out, performed slightly better here. He plugged on late and did enough to suggest he may eventually be of interest in modest nurseries. (op 9-2)
Thorpe Bay, gelded since his last appearance, showed speed for more than 3f. He faded late on, though, and is clearly no great shakes. (op 100-1)
Reve Du Jour(IRE), fifth at Warwick on the second of her two previous runs, showed speed until beyond halfway. However, she was left well behind in the closing stages. (op 7-1 tchd 6-1)

Lucky Money, a newcomer out of a middle-distance Listed winner, was slowly away and adrift early on. He will probably fare better over longer distances and, after another couple of runs, in nurseries. (op 10-1)

3554 SEALIFE CENTRE GREAT YARMOUTH (S) STKS 6f 3y
3:10 (3:12) (Class 6) 2-Y-O **£1,619** (£481; £240; £120) **Stalls** High

Form RPR
3210 **1** **Selinda**[17] 2998 2-8-4 0 .... CharlesBishop(7) 8 56
(Mick Channon) *mde all: rdn and dashed 2 l clr over 1f out: pushed out ins fnl f: a holding on* **4/1**
2 **2** ½ **Artic Dancer (IRE)**[21] 2854 2-8-6 0 .... WilliamCarson 7 50
(Stuart Williams) *pressing ldr: rdn 3f out: drvn and outpcd by wnr 2f out: styd on again and swtchd lft ins fnl f: a looking hld* **7/2**[3]
60 **3** 1 ½ **One New Cat (IRE)**[29] 2617 2-8-11 0 .... TomMcLaughlin 4 50
(Ed Dunlop) *in rr: rdn 3f out: drvn along to chse ldng pair 2f out: kpt on wl ins fnl f* **3/1**[2]
5354 **4** 8 **Manderston**[21] 2854 2-8-11 0 .... J-PGuillambert 1 26
(Mark Johnston) *hld up: pushed along 4f out: wknd 2f out: nvr a threat* **9/1**
5 1 **Factor Three** 2-8-11 0 .... TomQueally 3 23
(George Margarson) *s.i.s: pushed along to chse ldng pair 4f out: drvn and no imp ins fnl 2f: wknd ins fnl f* **5/2**[1]
6 3 ¼ **Sleigh Bells** 2-8-2 0 ow1 .... AshleyMorgan(5) 6 12
(Mark H Tompkins) *in rr: racing green and sn outpcd: wl btn ins fnl 3f* **12/1**

1m 13.71s (-0.69) **Going Correction** -0.525s/f (Hard) **6** Ran SP% **113.5**
Speed ratings (Par 91): **83,82,80,69,68 64**
toteswingers:1&2:£2.80, 1&3:£3.40, 2&3:£3.10 CSF £18.56 TOTE £5.60: £1.80, £4.10; EX 11.20 Trifecta £47.00 Pool: £468.90 - 7.37 winning units..There was no bid for the winner.
Owner Dave and Gill Hedley **Bred** G Hedley & Mike Channon Bloodstock Limited **Trained** West Ilsley, Berks

FOCUS
A poor contest, even by selling-race standards. The winner is basically rated to his pre-race form.

NOTEBOOK
Selinda, winner of a weak C&D seller two starts back, added another Yarmouth victory to her tally. Quickly away, she raced close to the stands' rail and was always in the first two. Although the runner-up rallied in the closing stages, she was always doing just enough. (op 10-3 tchd 11-4)
Artic Dancer(IRE), second at this level over 7f here last time, appeared to need that extra distance in this contest. She showed early speed and was in front after more than 2f, but seemed to be caught flat-footed when the winner kicked on. (op 11-4 tchd 4-1)
One New Cat(IRE), midfield in modest maidens on his two previous outings, probably ran close to his debut form. (op 5-1)
Manderston, well behind Arctic Dancer last time out, never looked likely to reverse that form. (op 6-1)
Factor Three, a gelded newcomer out of a 7f winner, attracted some interest in the market. He was outpaced from halfway, though, and on this evidence will struggle to notch a victory. (op 7-2)
Sleigh Bells, a first-time-out filly whose dam was moderate, was always in the last pair. There was little encouragement in this performance. (op 16-1 tchd 18-1)

3555 AVENUE PUB BEATTY ROAD H'CAP 7f 3y
3:40 (3:43) (Class 5) (0-75,75) 3-Y-O+ **£2,266** (£674; £337; £168) **Stalls** High

Form RPR
4326 **1** **Rough Rock (IRE)**[12] 3179 6-9-6 69 .... HayleyTurner 12 77
(Chris Dwyer) *hld up: t.k.h: pushed along and swtchd rt over 2f out: gd hdwy to chse ldrs ins fnl f: surged home to ld fnl strides* **10/1**
3365 **2** hd **Cuthbert (IRE)**[38] 2354 4-9-0 68 ....(v[1]) MarkCoumbe(5) 8 75
(William Jarvis) *prom: led 2f out and sn rdn: drvn along and strly pressed ins fnl f: overhauled fnl strides* **20/1**
-110 **3** nk **Batgirl**[27] 2674 4-9-10 73 .... TomMcLaughlin 1 80
(John Berry) *hld up: hdwy over 2f out: rdn to chse ldrs ins fnl 2f: styd on to press ldr ins fnl f: no ex cl home* **11/2**[3]
-054 **4** 1 **Aleqa**[26] 2719 4-9-8 71 ....(p) GeorgeBaker 4 75
(Chris Wall) *hld up: hdwy to chse ldrs 2f out: pushed along to chse ldrs over 1f out: drvn and kpt on one pce ins fnl f* **6/1**
5-50 **5** ½ **Mudhish (IRE)**[17] [illegible] .... IvaMilickova 7 66
(Clive Brittain) *chsd ldr: urged along 2f out: [illegible] rdn and hung lft ins fnl f: no imp fnl 75yds* **33/1**
0-04 **6** 2 **Amoya (GER)**[21] 2855 4-9-8 74 ....(t) AdamBeschizza(3) 9 71
(Philip McBride) *t.k.h in rr: effrt into midfield 3f out: rdn and wknd 2f out* **66/1**
-365 **7** 1 **Tamareen (IRE)**[37] 2383 3-9-2 74 ....(t) RyanMoore 10 66
(Ed Dunlop) *t.k.h: midfield: pushed along 2f out: hdwy ins fnl 2f: drvn along 1f out: one pce ins fnl f* **9/2**[2]
2313 **8** hd **Magical Speedfit (IRE)**[22] 2826 6-9-9 75 .... SimonPearce(3) 3 69
(George Margarson) *t.k.h: midfield: ev ch and pushed along over 2f out: one pce ins fnl f* **11/1**
1514 **9** 1 **Bahia Emerald (IRE)**[13] 3122 3-9-0 72 .... DarryllHolland 5 60
(Jeremy Noseda) *hld up: lost pl and rdn 4f out: swtchd lft over 2f out: brief effrt over 1f out: no imp ins fnl f* **11/4**[1]
4166 **10** 1 ½ **Watch Chain (IRE)**[24] 2765 4-8-11 65 .... AshleyMorgan(5) 2 52
(Mark H Tompkins) *hld up: stl gng wl over 2f out: sn rdn and outpcd* **20/1**
06-0 **11** 7 **Elusive Hawk (IRE)**[73] 1444 7-9-7 70 .... TomQueally 6 38
(Barney Curley) *led tl rdn and hdd over 2f out: wknd rapidly* **20/1**

1m 25.41s (-1.19) **Going Correction** -0.075s/f (Good)
WFA 3 from 4yo+ 9lb **11** Ran SP% **110.7**
Speed ratings (Par 103): **103,102,102,101,100 98,97,97,95,94 86**
toteswingers:1&2:£25.40, 1&3:£10.20, 2&3:£25.90 CSF £175.80 CT £1063.51 TOTE £10.60: £2.70, £7.70, £2.40; EX 202.40 TRIFECTA Not won..
Owner M M Foulger **Bred** Mrs B Stroomer **Trained** Burrough Green, Cambs
■ Hobson was withdrawn (11/1, unruly in stalls & uns rdr). Deduct 5p in the £ under R4.

FOCUS
A run-of-the-mill event, with the top weight rated 75, but it looked competitive. Rain was falling as the runners went to post. Ordinary but sound form.

3556 EAST COAST TRUCKERS CHARITY H'CAP 5f 43y
4:10 (4:13) (Class 6) (0-60,60) 3-Y-O+ **£1,619** (£481; £240; £120) **Stalls** High

Form RPR
3242 **1** **The Tatling (IRE)**[16] 3015 14-9-10 60 .... HayleyTurner 4 69
(Milton Bradley) *stdd s: racd far side gp tl 4f out: niggled along 2f out: swtchd rt and styd on strly to chse ldrs ins fnl f: sustained chal to ld fnl 25yds* **7/2**[1]
/334 **2** 1 **Bobby's Doll**[14] 3090 4-9-2 55 .... AdamBeschizza(3) 5 60
(Terry Clement) *led far side gp tl crossed over to press ldr 4f out: rdn 2f out: shifted lft u.p ins fnl f: led 100yds out tl hdd fnl 25yds* **4/1**[2]
060- **3** ½ **Pocket's Pick (IRE)**[219] 7542 5-9-4 57 ....(b) RobertLButler(3) 8 60
(Jim Best) *taken to post early: led nr side gp and had overall advantage: rdn and chal 1f out: hdd fnl 100yds and lost 2 pls* **9/1**
040- **4** nk **Greek Secret**[237] 7334 8-9-6 56 ....(b) DarryllHolland 2 58+
(Deborah Sanderson) *racd in far side gp early: t.k.h in rr: swtchd lft and rdn over 1f out: styd on ins fnl f* **10/1**
625- **5** 1 ¾ **Clerical (USA)**[190] 7973 5-9-7 57 ....(p) RichardMullen 10 53
(Robert Cowell) *chsd ldr in stands' side gp: lost pl 3f out: drvn and outpcd over 2f out: styd on ins fnl f* **6/1**[3]
2204 **6** ¾ **Imaginary Diva**[7] 3307 5-9-2 52 .... TomQueally 9 45
(George Margarson) *racd nr side gp: hld up: swtchd lft over 2f out: rdn and kpt on one pce ins fnl f* **4/1**[2]
6000 **7** ½ **Canadian Danehill (IRE)**[19] 2920 9-8-9 52 ....(p) AmyScott(5) 3 41
(Robert Cowell) *reluctant to leave paddock and walked to s: chsd ldr far side gp: crossed over and chsng ldng pair wl over 3f out: rdn and wknd ins fnl 2f* **10/1**
0203 **8** 3 **Jemimaville (IRE)**[9] 3254 4-8-10 46 ....(v) WilliamCarson 7 27
(Giles Bravery) *racd far side gp early: in midfield: hrd rdn 2f out: wknd wl over 1f out* **10/1**
-600 **9** 3 ¼ **Macie (IRE)**[10] 3234 4-8-11 47 .... RobbieFitzpatrick 6 16
(Derek Shaw) *racd far side gp early: in midfield: rdn and effrt 2f out: wknd ins fnl f* **33/1**

62.30 secs (-0.40) **Going Correction** -0.075s/f (Good) **9** Ran SP% **116.7**
Speed ratings (Par 101): **100,98,97,97,94 93,92,87,82**
toteswingers:1&2:£4.10, 1&3:£6.20, 2&3:£7.90 CSF £17.75 CT £116.78 TOTE £4.50: £1.50, £2.70, £3.30; EX 22.70 Trifecta £128.10 Pool: £635.78 - 3.67 winning units..
Owner Darren Hudson-Wood **Bred** Patrick J Power **Trained** Sedbury, Gloucs

FOCUS
A modest event, with the top weight rated just 60, but it produced a hugely popular result. The Tatling is possibly the best guide to the form.

3557 DIGIBET.COM H'CAP 1m 1f
4:40 (4:40) (Class 4) (0-80,80) 3-Y-O **£3,974** (£1,189; £594; £297; £148) **Stalls** Low

Form RPR
5156 **1** **Arabian Star (IRE)**[26] 2711 3-9-2 78 .... MartinHarley(3) 11 86
(Mick Channon) *prom: led 3f out: rdn 2f out: strly chal ins fnl f: kpt finding for press: all out: gamely* **20/1**
-323 **2** ½ **Above All**[20] 2891 3-8-13 75 .... AdamBeschizza(3) 9 82
(William Haggas) *chsd ldr: pushed along over 3f out: drvn along and pressed wnr 2f out: sustained chal ins fnl f tl no ex cl home* **7/1**[3]
0-33 **3** ½ **Levitate**[21] 2838 3-9-3 76 ....(v[1]) RyanMoore 8 82+
(Sir Michael Stoute) *towards rr: nt travelled fluently thrght: dropped last 5f out: swtchd rt and rdn along 4f out: stl last 3f out: drvn along and styd on strly on outer to chse ldrs ins fnl f: hld fnl 50yds* **7/4**[1]
1-00 **4** 1 ¼ **Twice Bitten**[19] 2925 3-8-13 72 .... DarryllHolland 13 75
(James Toller) *led: rdn and hdd 3f out: kpt on one pce ins fnl 2f* **25/1**
1-20 **5** 2 **Prince Of Burma (IRE)**[29] 2607 3-9-7 80 .... RobertHavlin 4 79
(John Gosden) *midfield: rdn along 4f out: outpcd 3f out: drvn 2f out: kpt on ins fnl f* **5/1**[2]
6306 **6** 2 ½ **Planet Waves (IRE)**[19] 2925 3-9-4 77 .... PhilipRobinson 10 70
(Clive Brittain) *t.k.h in rr: pushed along over 3f out and outpcd: kpt on past btn horses ins fnl f* **25/1**
1-04 **7** 2 ¼ **Mantatisi**[27] 2675 3-8-12 71 .... PatCosgrave 2 59
(James Fanshawe) *midfield: pushed along 3f out: angled out for run 3f out: swtchd ins and ev ch over 2f out: rdn and outpcd over 1f out: no imp ins fnl f: could improve* **7/1**[3]
4-66 **8** 1 ¼ **Buckland (IRE)**[19] 2926 3-9-6 79 .... LiamJones 7 65
(Brian Meehan) *towards rr: rdn 5f out: no imp fnl 3f* **8/1**
2-00 **9** nse **Songsmith**[13] 3118 3-8-12 71 .... HayleyTurner 5 56
(Lucy Wadham) *midfield: rdn and brief effrt 3f out: wknd 2f out* **20/1**
-023 **10** ¾ **Labore**[14] 3081 3-9-1 74 .... J-PGuillambert 3 61
(Marco Botti) *prom: urged along 5f out: effrt to chse ldrs 3f out: ev ch 2f out: wknd 1f out: eased cl home* **20/1**
544- **11** 7 **Cornish Quest**[259] 6859 3-8-4 68 .... AshleyMorgan(5) 12 36
(Mark H Tompkins) *hld up: pushed along over 3f out: no imp ins fnl 2f* **66/1**
464 **12** nk **Dervisher (IRE)**[21] [illegible] ....(h) TomQueally 1 39
(Sir Henry Cecil) *s.i.s: in rr: rdn over 4f out: wknd [illegible]* **16/1**

1m 53.99s (-1.81) **Going Correction** -0.075s/f (Good) **12** Ran SP% **118.5**
Speed ratings (Par 101): **105,104,104,103,101 99,97,95,95,95 88,88**
toteswingers:1&2:£21.10, 1&3:£13.40, 2&3:£3.30 CSF £142.28 CT £378.37 TOTE £27.80: £5.80, £2.00, £2.00; EX 308.10 TRIFECTA Not won..
Owner Jackie & George Smith **Bred** G A E And J Smith Bloodstock Ltd **Trained** West Ilsley, Berks

FOCUS
A wide-open contest in which the top weight was rated 80. Prominent racers were favoured and the form is not rated too positively.

3558 NORFOLK AND SUFFOLK ANIMAL TRUST H'CAP 1m 2f 21y
5:10 (5:12) (Class 5) (0-70,69) 3-Y-O+ **£2,266** (£674; £337; £168) **Stalls** Low

Form RPR
-154 **1** **Franciscan**[37] 2389 3-9-2 69 .... KirstyMilczarek 2 80+
(Luca Cumani) *midfield: rdn ins fnl 3f: swtchd rt 2f out and nt clr run: short of room wl over 1f out and swtchd ins to chal: str run to ld fnl 100yds* **11/8**[1]
032/ **2** ¾ **Flame Of Hestia (IRE)**[728] 3531 5-9-10 65 .... PatCosgrave 1 72
(James Fanshawe) *s.i.s: midfield: rdn 3f out: pressed ldrs over 2f out: styd on ins fnl f: grabbed 2nd on line* **5/1**[3]
440 **3** shd **Sciampin**[18] 2956 3-8-10 63 .... J-PGuillambert 3 70
(Marco Botti) *prom: chsd ldr 3f out: led 2f out: drvn along 1f out: hdd fnl 100yds: lost 2nd on line* **8/1**
-300 **4** 6 **Peira**[20] 2885 3-8-9 62 .... IvaMilickova 8 57
(Jane Chapple-Hyam) *t.k.h: chsd ldr: urged along to ld 3f out: rdn and hdd 2f out: wknd ins fnl f* **11/1**
0-20 **5** 4 ½ **Storm Runner (IRE)**[13] 3133 3-8-13 66 .... TomQueally 6 52
(George Margarson) *last pair: pushed along 5f out: no imp fnl 3f* **12/1**
3010 **6** 1 ¼ **Sail Home**[34] 2478 4-9-7 65 .... AdamBeschizza(3) 5 48
(Julia Feilden) *led: hdd 3f out: wknd fr over 1f out* **7/2**[2]
0660 **7** 47 **Gallantry**[13] 3130 9-9-9 64 .... DarryllHolland 4 —
(Michael Squance) *a in last: rdn and lost tch 4f out: t.o* **40/1**

2m 8.98s (-1.52) **Going Correction** -0.075s/f (Good)
WFA 3 from 4yo+ 12lb **7** Ran SP% **110.6**
Speed ratings (Par 103): **103,102,102,97,93 92,55**
toteswingers:1&2:£2.30, 1&3:£2.80, 2&3:£2.70 CSF £7.94 CT £35.79 TOTE £2.20: £1.20, £3.60; EX 7.80 Trifecta £27.20 Pool: £634.85 - 17.26 winning units..
Owner Fittocks Stud For Camilla Millbank **Bred** Fittocks Stud **Trained** Newmarket, Suffolk

FOCUS
A weakish handicap, with the top weight rated 65, but few could be confidently discounted. it was sound run and the first three finished clear.

3559 RACING WELFARE "HANDS AND HEELS" APPRENTICE SERIES H'CAP (PART OF RACING EXCELLENCE INITIATIVE) 1m 3f 101y
5:40 (5:40) (Class 6) (0-65,65) 4-Y-0+ **£1,619** (£481; £240; £120) **Stalls** Low

Form RPR
/000 **1** **Media Hype**[30] 2596 4-9-5 **63**.. TalibHussain(3) 3 76+
(Luca Cumani) *prom: chsng clr ldr 6f out: clsd on ldr 3f out: urged along to press ldr 2f out: pushed upsides and hung lft thrght fnl f: edgd to ld cl home: uns jubilant rdr after fin* **6/1**[3]
5-63 **2** *hd* **Miss Whippy**[21] 2856 4-8-2 **46**.. LewisWalsh(3) 5 53
(Michael Squance) *led: established clr advantage 5f out: rdn 2f out: strly pressed fr wl over 1f out: kpt trying valiantly tl hdd cl home* **9/1**
0311 **3** *8* **Art Scholar (IRE)**[19] 2900 4-9-5 **63**.......................... JustinNewman(3) 6 57
(Michael Appleby) *hld up: t.k.h: rdn and effrt to chse ldng pair over 2f out: no ex ins fnl f* **1/1**[1]
143- **4** *2 ½* **Hypnotic Gaze (IRE)**[4] 5765 5-9-10 **65**.........................(p) LucyKBarry 1 54
(Andrew Haynes) *hld up: hdwy 4f out: ev ch tl rdn and fnd little 2f out* **11/4**[2]
-300 **5** *2* **Royal Premier (IRE)**[14] 3086 8-8-7 **48**.......................... CharlesBishop 7 34
(Tom Keddy) *prom: chsng clr ldr 6f out: rdn and wknd 3f out* **8/1**
-000 **6** *29* **Carlcol Girl**[22] 2824 4-8-2 **46** oh1................................(v) DanielHarris(3) 2 —
(Christine Dunnett) *in rr: rdn and no imp 4f out: dropped away tamely over 2f out* **66/1**
2m 36.6s (7.90) **Going Correction** +0.375s/f (Good) **6** Ran SP% **113.6**
Speed ratings (Par 101): **86,85,80,78,76 55**
toteswingers:1&2:£5.20, 1&3:£2.30, 2&3:£3.20 CSF £55.24 TOTE £6.10: £3.80, £3.60; EX 48.30.
Owner Castle Down Racing **Bred** Meon Valley Stud **Trained** Newmarket, Suffolk
FOCUS
Heavy rain fell before and during this weak finale. It was slowly run with the second allowed a big lead, and he sets the standard. The winner is likely to be better than the bare form.
T/Plt: £30.40 to a £1 stake. Pool:£72,546.81 - 1,739.72 winning tickets T/Qpdt: £22.70 to a £1 stake. Pool:£3,550.97 - 115.68 winning tickets CS

3560 - 3566a (Foreign Racing) - See Raceform Interactive

980 DEAUVILLE (R-H)
Thursday, June 30
OFFICIAL GOING: Turf: good to soft; fibresand: standard

3567a PRIX YACOWLEF (LISTED RACE) (UNRACED 2YO) (TURF) 5f
12:30 (12:00) 2-Y-0 **£23,706** (£9,482; £7,112; £4,741; £2,370)

RPR
1 **Hi Molly (FR)** 2-9-2 0.. ThierryJarnet 6 96
(D Guillemin, France) **93/10**
2 *½* **Kortoba (USA)** 2-8-13 0.. JohanVictoire 3 91
(Mme C Head-Maarek, France) **13/10**[1]
3 *snk* **Barbayam** 2-8-13 0.. OlivierPeslier 7 91
(F Head, France) **7/2**[2]
4 *3* **Sunburnt** 2-8-13 0.. IoritzMendizabal 2 80
(E J O'Neill, France) **13/2**[3]
5 *5* **Funny Crazy (FR)** 2-8-13 0.......................... ChristopheSoumillon 5 62
(J E Hammond, France) **7/1**
6 *1* **Valerie Anne (IRE)** 2-8-13 0.............................. WilliamsSaraiva 1 58
(Mme J Bidgood, France) **20/1**
7 *nse* **Gung Ho Jack** 2-9-2 0.. LukeMorris 4 61
(John Best) *swvd rt exiting stalls: nrly uns rdr: racd in rr: swtchd to outside: rdn at 1/2-way: nt qckn: styd on fnl f* **9/1**
60.00 secs (2.50) **7** Ran SP% **116.0**
WIN (incl. 1 euro stake): 10.30. PLACES: 3.20, 1.60. SF: 28.20.
Owner Alain Morice **Bred** A Morice **Trained** France

NOTEBOOK
Gung Ho Jack got coltish beforehand, veered right exiting the stalls and struggled to get involved. Another furlong should suit him in time.

3568a PRIX DE PRE EN PAIL (CLAIMER) (4YO+) (FIBRESAND) 7f 110y
2:40 (12:00) 4-Y-0+ **£9,482** (£3,793; £2,844; £1,896; £948)

RPR
1 **Up And Coming (IRE)**[42] 7-9-4 0.................................. FlavienPrat 10 92
(J E Pease, France) **47/10**[1]
2 *1 ½* **Darling Pearl (FR)**[204] 4-8-0 0...................... ThomasHenderson(8) 11 78
(J-C Rouget, France) **9/1**
3 *hd* **Mount Berry (FR)**[115] 4-8-11 0..............................(b) FabienLefebvre 3 81
(D Sepulchre, France) **35/1**
4 *½* **Chico Del Sol (FR)**[9] 6-9-1 0......................................(p) TonyPiccone 8 84
(J Rossi, France) **10/1**
5 *hd* **Celtie Rod (IRE)**[42] 7-9-4 0.................................. GregoryBenoist 13 86
(X Nakkachdji, France) **13/1**
6 *½* **Bacarrita (FR)**[25] 6-9-2 0.. JohanVictoire 14 83
(L A Urbano-Grajales, France) **44/5**[3]
7 *1 ½* **Tagar Bere (FR)**[244] 4-9-4 0.................................. FranckBlondel 16 81
(M Pimbonnet, France) **10/1**
8 *nk* **Vantage Point (FR)**[21] 8-8-13 0.............................. AlexisAchard(5) 5 80
(Mlle C Cardenne, France) **11/1**
9 *2* **Hi Shinko**[42] 5-8-11 0.. FredericSpanu 2 68
(Mme G Rarick, France) **47/1**
10 *¾* **El Pib D'Oro (IRE)**[15] 5-9-1 0................................ MaximeGuyon 7 70
(Mlle S-V Tarrou, France) **11/1**
0 **Something (IRE)**[90] 1122 9-8-11 0.......................... IoritzMendizabal 1 —
(P Monfort, France) **6/1**[2]
0 **Cape Velvet (IRE)**[25] 7-8-8 0.................................. WilliamsSaraiva 4 —
(Mme J Bidgood, France) **12/1**
0 **Lisselan Muse (USA)**[22] 7-8-11 0.............................. SylvainRuis 15 —
(Mme J Bidgood, France) **19/1**
0 **I Am That (IRE)**[361] 4-9-3 0.......................... AnthonyCaramanolis(3) 12 —
(Mme L Braem, Belgium) **32/1**
0 **Hecton Lad (USA)**[22] 2816 4-9-10 0.............................(b) LukeMorris 6 —
(John Best) *broke wl to r 3rd: sent to ld at 1/2-way: led into st: sn u.p: hdd 2f out: qckly fdd* **27/1**
1m 30.2s (90.20) **15** Ran SP% **118.2**
WIN (incl. 1 euro stake): 5.70. PLACES: 2.40, 3.60, 9.50. DF: 34.40. SF: 47.40.
Owner Mme S Seymour & Mme R M Pease **Bred** Henry Seymour & The Hon Mrs Pease **Trained** Chantilly, France

NOTEBOOK
Hecton Lad(USA) was up against it in this company and dropped out after racing prominently to 2f out.

3242 BEVERLEY (R-H)
Friday, July 1
OFFICIAL GOING: Good to firm (8.4)
Wind: Light behind Weather: Sunny periods

3569 HAPPY 50TH BIRTHDAY BERTIE BEADLE (S) STKS 7f 100y
6:30 (6:30) (Class 6) 3-Y-0+ **£1,811** (£539; £269; £134) **Stalls** Low

Form RPR
2460 **1** **Opus Maximus (IRE)**[9] 3275 6-9-3 78.........................(p) StephenCraine 11 61
(Jennie Candlish) *stdd s: hld up and bhd: hdwy over 2f out: swtchd lft and rdn over 1f out: styd on wl to ld last 75yds* **11/2**[3]
-306 **2** *¾* **Eeny Mac (IRE)**[10] 3245 4-8-10 43............................ TerenceFury(7) 10 59?
(Neville Bycroft) *trckd ldrs: hdwy wl over 1f out: swtchd lft and rdn to ld ent fnl f: sn edgd rt: hdd and no ex last 75yds* **16/1**
225- **3** *2 ½* **Glenmuir (IRE)**[240] 7306 8-9-0 69.............................. DeclanCannon(3) 9 53
(John Quinn) *in tch: hdwy over 2f out: rdn to chse ldrs over 2f out: ch ent fnl f: kpt on same pce* **6/1**
4216 **4** *3* **Kipchak (IRE)**[11] 3235 6-9-1 65......................................(b) LucyKBarry(7) 2 50
(Conor Dore) *sn led: rdn along over 2f out: drvn and hdd wl over 1f out: kpt on same pce* **7/2**[2]
4206 **5** *1* **Handsome Falcon**[39] 2347 7-8-12 73...........................(p) LeeTopliss(5) 1 43
(Ollie Pears) *trckd ldng pair: hdwy over 2f out: rdn to ld wl over 1f out: sn drvn: hdd & wknd ent fnl f* **3/1**[1]
00-0 **6** *3* **Just Sam (IRE)**[6] 3387 6-8-5 62.................................. ShaneBKelly(7) 12 30
(Ron Barr) *cl up: rdn along over 2f out: sn drvn and wknd over 1f out* **20/1**
0-00 **7** *2 ¾* **Bold Indian (IRE)**[14] 3141 7-8-10 49............................ GarryWhillans(7) 3 28
(Mike Sowersby) *a towards rr* **100/1**
00-0 **8** *6* **Hogmaneigh (IRE)**[30] 2620 8-9-3 85............................ PaulHanagan 4 13
(Mark Johnston) *in tch: pushed along 3f out: rdn over 2f out: sn wknd* **3/1**[1]
0006 **9** *¾* **Blue Rum (IRE)**[10] 3248 4-9-3 43.................................. TomEaves 5 12
(Alan Kirtley) *a towards rr* **66/1**
050- **10** *1 ¼* **Loyal Knight (IRE)**[279] 3370 6-9-3 39.............................(t) MickyFenton 8 8
(Paul Midgley) *a towards rr* **100/1**
66-0 **11** *nk* **Saxby (IRE)**[42] 2249 4-9-0 57.............................(p) MichaelO'Connell(3) 7 8
(Geoffrey Harker) *a towards rr* **25/1**
000- **12** *8* **Govenor Eliott (IRE)**[352] 4014 6-8-10 40............... GeorgeChaloner(7) 6 —
(Alan Lockwood) *a towards rr* **100/1**
1m 30.72s (-3.08) **Going Correction** -0.35s/f (Firm) **12** Ran SP% **120.8**
Speed ratings (Par 101): **103,102,99,95,94 91,88,81,80,79 78,69**
toteswingers:1&2:£12.10, 1&3:£4.70, 2&3:£27.30 CSF £84.63 TOTE £7.30: £2.00, £4.70, £2.80; EX 93.10.There was no bid for the winner.
Owner Alan Baxter **Bred** Mrs Anne Marie Burns **Trained** Basford Green, Staffs
■ Stewards' Enquiry : Shane B Kelly two-day ban: careless riding (Jul 15-16)
FOCUS
The entire track has received 10mm of irrigation and, after a dry night, the back straight and bend were watered (5mm) to maintain in the morning. A fairly wide range of ability on show but the gallop was soon sound and the final time was less than a second outside Racing Post standard. Two riders described the ground as "fast, but with no jar".
Hogmaneigh(IRE) Official explanation: jockey said gelding never travelled

3570 BRITISH STALLION STUDS EBF WILLIAM JACKSON BAKERY NOVICE STKS 5f
7:00 (7:00) (Class 5) 2-Y-0 **£3,881** (£1,155; £577) **Stalls** Low

Form RPR
2153 **1** **Alejandro (IRE)**[27] 2725 2-9-5 0.................................. PaulHanagan 2 85+
(Richard Fahey) *mde all: rdn over 1f out: kpt on wl fnl f* **11/4**[2]
1 **2** *3 ¾* **Quite A Thing**[20] 2919 2-8-11 0.................................. SebSanders 3 64+
(Sir Mark Prescott Bt) *rrd and lost 3 l s: hdwy to chse wnr after 1 1/2f: effrt 2f out: rdn wl over 1f out: drvn ent fnl f and sn no imp* **1/4**[1]
6 **3** *20* **Brasingaman Espee**[22] 2831 2-9-0 0.............................. PJMcDonald 1 —
(George Moore) *chsd wnr 1 1/2f: rdn along bef 1/2-way: sn outpcd* **50/1**[3]
61.95 secs (-1.55) **Going Correction** -0.40s/f (Firm) **3** Ran SP% **108.6**
Speed ratings (Par 94): **96,90,58**
CSF £4.12 TOTE £3.10; EX 3.70.
Owner F L F S Ltd **Bred** Yeomanstown Stud **Trained** Musley Bank, N Yorks
FOCUS
A poor turnout and, with long odds-on favourite disappointing after missing the break, this was a straightforward task for the winner. He's rated back to his best pre-race figure.
NOTEBOOK
Alejandro(IRE)'s previous Musselburgh run has been very well advertised and he probably didn't have to improve to notch his second victory with his main market rival failing to build on her debut success. Nevertheless he's a useful and straightforward sort who should continue to give a good account. He will reportedly be aimed at the Super Sprint at Newbury. (tchd 5-2 and 3-1)
Quite A Thing, an impressive wide-margin debut turf winner, looked the one to beat in receipt of 8lb from her only serious challenger and was well supported at short odds, but she proved disappointing after getting edgy in the stalls and after rearing and missing the break. Although she isn't very big she's better than this bare form suggests and she is probably worth another chance. (op 2-7 tchd 1-3)
Brasingaman Espee, tailed off on his debut, showed plenty of knee action and was predictably outclassed behind two useful rivals. Low-grade nurseries will be the way forward with him in due course.

3571 AUNT BESSIE'S YORKSHIRE PUDDING H'CAP 7f 100y
7:30 (7:31) (Class 5) (0-75,74) 3-Y-0 **£2,522** (£750; £375; £187) **Stalls** Low

Form RPR
1350 **1** **Materialism**[17] 3024 3-9-1 **68**.................................. AdrianNicholls 8 77
(Mark Johnston) *led: pushed along over 2f out: sn rdn and hdd over 1f out: drvn ins fnl f: rallied gamely to ld nr fin* **9/2**[3]
2153 **2** *hd* **Abidhabidubai**[12] 3202 3-9-3 **70**.................................. TomEaves 4 79
(John Quinn) *trckd ldr: cl up 3f out: rdn to ld over 1f out: drvn ins fnl f: hdd and no ex nr fin* **5/2**[2]
2552 **3** *3* **Alensgrove (IRE)**[6] 3387 3-8-7 **60**...........................(p) MickyFenton 5 61
(Paul Midgley) *trckd ldng pair: hdwy wl over 2f out: rdn along wl over 1f out: drvn and one pce appr fnl f* **8/1**

0-23 **4** *1* **I Got You Babe (IRE)**[3] 3489 3-8-7 **60**..........................(p) PaulHanagan 2 59
(Richard Guest) *plld hrd: trckd ldng pair on inner: hdwy wl over 2f out: rdn along and n.m.r over 1f out: sn btn* **13/8**[1]

36-6 **5** *1 1/4* **Free Art**[23] 2802 3-9-4 **74**..........................(p) MichaelO'Connell(3) 1 69
(Geoffrey Harker) *hld up in tch: effrt 3f out: rdn along 2f out: sn btn* **15/2**

0-05 **6** *1 1/4* **Piccarello**[7] 3363 3-8-8 **66**.. AshleyMorgan(5) 6 58
(Mark H Tompkins) *hld up in tch: effrt wl over 2f out: sn rdn and btn* **20/1**

1m 34.84s (1.04) **Going Correction** -0.35s/f (Firm) **6** Ran SP% **112.5**
Speed ratings (Par 100): **80,79,76,75,73 72**
toteswingers:1&2:£2.20, 1&3:£3.70, 2&3:£4.30 CSF £16.21 CT £84.86 TOTE £5.50: £2.00, £1.40; EX 20.60.
Owner Sheikh Hamdan Bin Mohammed Al Maktoum **Bred** Darley **Trained** Middleham Moor, N Yorks

FOCUS
Exposed performers in an ordinary handicap but a race to treat with caution given the slow pace that only picked up turning for home. the winner is rated to his best.
I Got You Babe(IRE) Official explanation: jockey said filly hung right throughout
Piccarello Official explanation: jockey said gelding hung right throughout

3572 NATWEST AGRICULTURAL TEAM H'CAP 1m 1f 207y
8:00 (8:00) (Class 5) (0-75,75) 3-Y-O+ **£2,522** (£750; £375; £187) **Stalls** Low

Form RPR

4013 **1** **Judicious**[18] 2988 4-9-8 **72**.. MichaelO'Connell(3) 6 79
(Geoffrey Harker) *trckd ldrs: hdwy wl over 2f out: rdn to ld ent fnl f: sn edgd rt: rdn out* **10/3**[3]

-640 **2** *1* **Christmas Light**[6] 3386 4-9-7 **68**.. TomEaves 4 73
(David O'Meara) *trckd ldng pair: hdwy over 2f out: rdn over 1f out: styd on and ch ins fnl f: sn drvn and nt qckn towards fin* **8/1**

-251 **3** *nk* **Pinotage**[24] 2786 3-8-0 **58**.. PaulQuinn 5 62
(Richard Whitaker) *hld up in rr: pushed along and flashed tail over 2f out: hdwy towards inner whn nt clr run and swtchd to outer over 1f out: sn rdn and flashed tail: styd on wl towards fin* **7/1**

0-22 **4** *1 1/4* **Munaawer (USA)**[23] 2800 4-9-3 **64**.. PhilipRobinson 1 66
(James Bethell) *led 2f: cl up: rdn to chal over 2f out: led over 1f out: drvn and hdd ent fnl f: hld whn n.m.r last 100yds* **2/1**[1]

15-4 **5** *4 1/2* **Regal Kiss**[43] 2232 3-9-2 **74**.. PaulHanagan 2 67
(Mark Johnston) *cl up: led after 2f: rdn along over 2f out: hdd and drvn over 1f out: wknd ent fnl f* **9/4**[2]

2m 4.67s (-2.33) **Going Correction** -0.35s/f (Firm)
WFA 3 from 4yo+ 11lb **5** Ran SP% **110.8**
Speed ratings (Par 103): **95,94,93,92,89**
CSF £26.89 TOTE £4.90: £1.80, £4.00; EX 27.90.
Owner The Unique Partnership **Bred** Cheveley Park Stud Ltd **Trained** Thirkleby, N Yorks

FOCUS
Another run-of-the-mill handicap in which the gallop was a modest one until lifting early in the home straight. The winner confirmed C&D form with the favourite.

3573 FERGUSON FAWSITT ARMS H'CAP 5f
8:30 (8:33) (Class 6) (0-65,65) 3-Y-O+ **£1,811** (£539; £269; £134) **Stalls** Low

Form RPR

200 **1** **Time Medicean**[13] 3166 5-9-6 **62**.. MichaelO'Connell(3) 1 76
(Paul Midgley) *in tch: hdwy 2f out: swtchd lft over 1f out: sn rdn and styd on strly to ld last 100yds* **13/2**[3]

3005 **2** *1 3/4* **Galpin Junior (USA)**[72] 1493 5-9-0 **53**.. PJMcDonald 2 61
(Ruth Carr) *led: rdn along wl over 1f out: drvn clr ent fnl f: hdd and one pce last 100yds* **5/1**[2]

5000 **3** *3 1/2* **Kalahari Desert (IRE)**[10] 3248 4-8-8 **47**..........................(v1) PaulQuinn 3 42
(Richard Whitaker) *a.p: effrt 2f out: rdn to chal wl over 1f out and ev ch tl drvn and one pce ent fnl f* **33/1**

0400 **4** *nk* **King Of Swords (IRE)**[10] 3247 7-8-13 **52**..........................(p) PaulHanagan 4 46
(Nigel Tinkler) *trckd ldrs: effrt 2f out: sn rdn: drvn and kpt on same pce ent fnl f* **4/1**[1]

3040 **5** *1/2* **Ra[illegible] Night**[illegible] [illegible]..........................([illegible]1) LeeTopliss(5) 14 55
(Reg Hollinshead) *chsd ldrs: rdn along wl over 1f out: kpt on same pce fnl f* **11/1**

4040 **6** *1 1/4* **Sleights Boy (IRE)**[10] 3247 3-8-6 **50**..........................(b) PatrickMathers 16 36
(Ian McInnes) *towards rr: rdn along and hdwy on outer wl over 1f: kpt on ins fnl f: nrst fin* **33/1**

1503 **7** *nse* **Silvanus (IRE)**[25] 2766 6-9-12 **65**.. MickyFenton 5 53
(Paul Midgley) *hld up in rr: hdwy wl over 1f out: rdn and kpt on ins fnl f: nrst fin* **10/1**

1425 **8** *nk* **We'll Deal Again**[17] 3027 4-9-11 **64**..........................(b) DavidNolan 12 50
(Michael Easterby) *prom: rdn along 2f out: drvn and wknd over 1f out* **5/1**[2]

0-00 **9** *1 3/4* **Lady Lube Rye (IRE)**[72] 1493 4-8-7 **46** oh1.......................... AdrianNicholls 15 26
(Noel Wilson) *a towards rr* **25/1**

4003 **10** *nk* **Bossy Kitty**[10] 3248 4-9-1 **54**..........................(p) TomEaves 8 33
(Nigel Tinkler) *trckd ldrs: effrt wl over 1f out: sn rdn and hld whn n.m.r appr fnl f* **14/1**

5025 **11** *nk* **Green Warrior**[13] 3192 3-9-4 **62**..........................(p) SebSanders 9 38
(Ann Duffield) *nvr bttr than midfield* **9/1**

0000 **12** *nk* **Cheyenne Red (IRE)**[16] 3036 5-8-8 **54**..........................(b) ShaneBKelly(7) 13 31
(Michael Dods) *a in rr* **12/1**

540- **13** *nse* **Windjammer**[322] 5023 7-8-8 **50**..........................(b) DeclanCannon(3) 11 27
(Lawrence Mullaney) *a in rr* **33/1**

5-60 **14** *2 3/4* **Fair Bunny**[150] 375 4-8-7 **49**..........................(b) PaulPickard(3) 6 16
(Alan Brown) *cl up: rdn along 2f out: wkng whn n.m.r appr fnl f* **33/1**

0053 **15** *2* **Wotatomboy**[10] 3247 5-8-0 **46** oh1.......................... NoelGarbutt(7) 7 —
(Richard Whitaker) *dwlt: sn in midfield: rdn along 2f out: sn wknd* **14/1**

61.28 secs (-2.22) **Going Correction** -0.40s/f (Firm)
WFA 3 from 4yo+ 5lb **15** Ran SP% **130.7**
Speed ratings (Par 101): **101,98,92,92,91 89,89,88,85,85 85,84,84,80,76**
toteswingers:1&2:£8.50, 1&3:£36.50, 2&3:£23.10 CSF £40.23 CT £745.92 TOTE £8.90: £3.90, £1.80, £11.10; EX 48.80.
Owner G Sheehy **Bred** C A Cyzer **Trained** Westow, N Yorks
■ Stewards' Enquiry : Michael O'Connell three-day ban: careless riding (Jul 15-17)

FOCUS
A modest handicap run at a good gallop and one in which the draw was a significant factor given those berthed in stalls 1-4 filled the first four placings. The form of the first four is sound enough.
Windjammer Official explanation: jockey said blindfold became stuck on cups of blinkers and gelding was slowly away

3574 JOHN FORKIN MEMORIAL H'CAP (BEVERLEY MIDDLE DISTANCE SERIES) 1m 4f 16y
9:00 (9:00) (Class 6) (0-60,62) 3-Y-O+ **£2,911** (£866; £432; £216) **Stalls** Low

Form RPR

-403 **1** **Brasingaman Eric**[22] 2830 4-9-3 **53**.. PJMcDonald 10 61
(George Moore) *trckd ldrs: hdwy over 2f out: rdn over 1f out: styd on to ld ent fnl f: drvn out* **9/2**[3]

3460 **2** *1/2* **Grey Command (USA)**[29] 2654 6-9-0 **50**.. SebSanders 8 57
(Mel Brittain) *led: rdn along wl over 2f out: hdd briefly wl over 1f out: rallied and sn led again tl drvn and hdd ent fnl f: kpt on gamely u.p* **22/1**

2431 **3** *2 1/2* **Golden Future**[2] 3509 8-9-9 **62** 6ex.. DeclanCannon(3) 12 65
(Peter Niven) *chsd ldr: cl up 1/2-way: rdn to ld briefly wl over 1f out: sn drvn and hdd: kpt on same pce u.p fnl f* **4/1**[2]

-006 **4** *3/4* **Miss Wendy**[10] 3243 4-8-12 **53**.. AshleyMorgan(5) 3 55
(Mark H Tompkins) *trckd ldrs: hdwy over 3f out: rdn along 2f out: drvn and kpt on same pce appr fnl f* **16/1**

-004 **5** *1/2* **Hurlingham**[23] 2804 7-9-5 **55**..........................(b) PaddyAspell 9 56
(Michael Easterby) *hld up towards rr: hdwy 1/2-way: chsd ldrs wl over 2f out: sn rdn and sltly outpcd: styd on u.p fnl f* **20/1**

6-06 **6** *1 1/2* **Deferto Delphi**[16] 3041 4-8-9 **52**.. JustinNewman(7) 5 51
(Barry Murtagh) *hld up in rr: hdwy 3f out: rdn and styng on whn n.m.r over 1f out: swtchd rt and kpt on ins fnl f: nrst fin* **40/1**

44/3 **7** *nse* **Wood Fairy**[16] 3041 5-9-5 **55**.. PaulHanagan 7 54
(Richard Fahey) *t.k.h: hld up in tch: hdwy wl over 2f out: rdn wl over 1f out: drvn and no imp appr fnl f* **10/3**[1]

-003 **8** *1/2* **Simple Jim (FR)**[32] 2575 7-9-4 **54**.. TomEaves 11 52
(David O'Meara) *dwlt and in rr: effrt and sme hdwy over 2f out: sn rdn and n.d* **11/2**

3050 **9** *1 1/2* **Escape Artist**[15] 3072 4-9-0 **50**..........................(p) DavidNolan 6 45
(Tim Easterby) *trckd ldrs: hdwy to chse ldng pair 1/2-way: rdn along over 2f out: drvn wl over 1f out and grad wknd* **8/1**

0364 **10** *3 1/4* **Donna Elvira**[22] 2830 4-9-9 **59**..........................(p) AdrianNicholls 2 49
(Edwin Tuer) *chsd ldng pair on inner: rdn along wl over 2f out: drvn and wknd wl over 1f out* **8/1**

6403 **11** *1* **General Tufto**[15] 3074 6-9-2 **57**..........................(b) LeeTopliss(5) 4 46
(Charles Smith) *a in rr* **20/1**

/50- **12** *1/2* **Carmela Maria**[29] 5119 6-8-7 **50**.. GarryWhillans(7) 1 38
(Mike Sowersby) *hld up towards rr: effrt and sme hdwy on inner over 2f out: sn rdn and wknd* **50/1**

2m 38.42s (-1.38) **Going Correction** -0.35s/f (Firm) **12** Ran SP% **123.0**
Speed ratings (Par 101): **90,89,88,87,87 86,86,85,84,82 81,81**
toteswingers:1&2:£25.60, 1&3:£4.80, 2&3:£19.20 CSF £108.29 CT £439.52 TOTE £7.00: £2.00, £7.00, £2.00; EX 132.80.
Owner R Morgan **Bred** Mrs Heather Morgan **Trained** Middleham Moor, N Yorks
■ Stewards' Enquiry : P J McDonald two-day ban: careless riding (Jul 15-16)

FOCUS
A moderate handicap in which a modest gallop only picked up passing the 3f marker and those held up were at a disadvantage. The front-running second sets the standard.
T/Plt: £1,921.40 to a £1 stake. Pool:£52,406.36 - 19.91 winning tickets T/Qpdt: £98.30 to a £1 stake. Pool:£5,900.27 - 44.40 winning tickets JR

3382 DONCASTER (L-H)
Friday, July 1

OFFICIAL GOING: Good to firm (6.7)
Wind: light against Weather: Mixture of cloud and sunshine

3575 MICHAEL STOTHARD AND CHARLOTTE BOCZKARIW CARDSAVE MAIDEN STKS 7f
2:00 (2:01) (Class 5) 3-Y-O **£2,522** (£750; £375; £187) **Stalls** High

Form RPR

4-2 **1** **Easy Over (IRE)**[16] 3053 3-9-3 0.. SebSanders 6 76+
([illegible]) *[illegible] over 3f out: led over 1f out: edgd rt: pushed clr ins fnl f: comf* **[illegible]**

0-0 **2** *3 1/4* **Switchback**[13] 3177 3-9-3 0.. RichardMullen [illegible] [illegible]
(Sir Michael Stoute) *prom: rdn over 2f out: kpt on ins fnl f: no ch w wnr* **8/1**[3]

00- **3** *1 3/4* **Scottish Lake**[252] 7058 3-9-0 0.. PatrickDonaghy(3) 9 63
(Jedd O'Keeffe) *in tch: rdn and outpcd over 2f out: kpt on ins fnl f: wnt 3rd fnl 75yds* **66/1**

02-U **4** *1 1/4* **Numeral (IRE)**[11] 3232 3-9-3 0.. PatDobbs 4 59
(Richard Hannon) *led: rdn whn hdd over 1f out: wknd ins fnl f: lost 3rd fnl 75yds* **2/1**[2]

5- **5** *nk* **Sawahill**[261] 6850 3-8-12 0.. PhilipRobinson 2 53
(Clive Brittain) *hld up in tch: rdn over 2f out: kpt on fnl f: n.d* **12/1**

0 **6** *1 1/2* **Zee Zee Dan (IRE)**[14] 3135 3-9-3 0.. IanMongan 8 54
(Noel Quinlan) *t.k.h: in tch: pushed along over 3f out: lost pl over 2f out: no imp* **50/1**

0 **7** *shd* **Merito**[23] 2802 3-9-3 0.. PhillipMakin 5 54
(Kevin Ryan) *in tch: rdn over 3f out: wknd ins fnl f* **16/1**

8 *3 1/2* **Shirls Son Sam** 3-9-3 0.. KellyHarrison 7 45
(Chris Fairhurst) *dwlt: sn outpcd in rr: a bhd* **50/1**

1m 27.43s (1.13) **Going Correction** -0.075s/f (Good) **8** Ran SP% **118.0**
Speed ratings (Par 100): **90,86,84,82,82 80,80,76**
toteswingers:1&2:£2.60, 2&3:£26.20, 1&3:£10.60 CSF £9.30 TOTE £2.10: £1.10, £2.00, £23.50; EX 10.70.
Owner D J Allen S E Allen/ G A Weetman **Bred** Max Ervine **Trained** Lichfield, Staffs

FOCUS
Rail realignment added 54yds to distances on Round course. An ordinary, uncompetitive maiden and the time was the slowest of the three 7f races on the card. They raced stands' side, but the rail did not provide an advantage. The form is rated around the winner.

3576 BARRIE BAILY AND CHARLENE THORNBORROW CARDSAVE CLAIMING STKS 1m (S)
2:30 (2:30) (Class 5) 4-Y-O+ **£2,522** (£750; £375; £187) **Stalls** High

Form RPR

6401 **1** **High Five Society**[15] 3089 7-8-10 **72**..........................(b) RyanClark(5) 5 79
(Roy Bowring) *trckd ldr: pushed along over 2f out: swtchd lft over 1f out: sn drvn and hdwy: led fnl 120yds: kpt on* **12/1**

4636 **2** *2 1/4* **Charlie Cool**[8] 3315 8-9-6 **88**..........................(b) PJMcDonald 3 79
(Ruth Carr) *trckd ldr: led over 2f out: rdn over 1f out: hdd fnl 120yds: no ex* **5/6**[1]

-110 **3** *5* **Bolodenka (IRE)**[41] 2301 9-8-10 75................................ PaulHanagan 2 57
(Richard Fahey) *in tch: hdwy to chse ldr 2f out: sn drvn: wknd ins fnl f* **7/2**[2]

2560 **4** *3* **Ours (IRE)**[9] 3275 8-9-5 77...(p) FrederikTylicki 1 59
(John Harris) *sn outpcd in rr: kpt on ins fnl f: n.d* **6/1**[3]

06-0 **5** *11* **Gee Ceffyl Bach**[4] 3457 7-8-4 40.................................... KellyHarrison 4 19
(Garry Woodward) *hld up: pushed along over 3f out: a towards rr* **100/1**

-001 **6** *hd* **Spying**[13] 3190 4-9-6 75...(e) TomEaves 6 35
(Ann Duffield) *dwlt: sn led: rdn whn hdd over 2f out: sn wknd* **8/1**

1m 39.51s (0.21) **Going Correction** -0.075s/f (Good) **6** Ran SP% **110.9**
Speed ratings (Par 103): **95,92,87,84,73 73**
toteswingers:1&2:£3.10, 2&3:£1.02, 1&3:£2.00 CSF £22.28 TOTE £10.10: £5.00, £1.10; EX 32.20.
Owner S R Bowring **Bred** A C M Spalding **Trained** Edwinstowe, Notts

FOCUS
Most of these seemed to run below their best and this was just an ordinary claimer, although the pace was good. The form is not taken too literally. Again they raced stands' side but again the rail was not decisive.
Gee Ceffyl Bach Official explanation: trainer said mare finished lame

3577 EARL OF DONCASTER HOTEL MAIDEN FILLIES' STKS 7f
3:00 (3:01) (Class 5) 3-Y-O+ **£2,522** (£750; £375; £187) **Stalls** High

Form RPR

4-32 **1** **Panoptic**[28] 2673 3-8-12 76.. IanMongan 11 81+
(Sir Henry Cecil) *trckd ldrs: led wl over 2f out: clr over 1f out: rdn out fnl f: edgd lft ins fnl 100yds* **1/1**[1]

5 **2** *1 ½* **Crystal High**[33] 2529 3-8-12 0.. SebSanders 13 75
(Marco Botti) *w ldr: rdn over 2f out: kpt on: a hld by wnr ins fnl f* **16/1**

246 **3** *½* **Cheherazad (IRE)**[15] 3090 3-8-12 77................................. TomEaves 7 73
(Paul Cole) *midfield: hdwy to chse ldr over 2f out: sn rdn: kpt on ins fnl f* **8/1**

-423 **4** *2* **Swift Bird (IRE)**[99] 952 3-8-12 72................................... PhillipMakin 5 68
(Noel Quinlan) *t.k.h: led: rdn whn hdd wl over 2f out: sn outpcd: kpt on ins fnl f* **16/1**

5 *1* **Eclipseoftheheart** 3-8-12 0... PatCosgrave 8 65
(James Fanshawe) *dwlt: hld up: pushed along over 3f out: hdwy over 2f out: edgd rt over 1f out: kpt on one pce* **9/1**

2 **6** *1 ¼* **Rohlindi**[64] 1629 3-8-12 0... PatDobbs 2 62
(Clive Cox) *racd keenly: trckd ldrs: rdn over 2f out: wknd over 1f out* **13/2**[2]

7 *1 ½* **Bashama** 3-8-12 0.. PhilipRobinson 1 58+
(Clive Brittain) *s.i.s: hld up in rr: pushed along over 3f out: kpt on ins fnl f: n.d* **33/1**

8 *¾* **Cranworth Quest (IRE)** 3-8-9 0......................... MichaelO'Connell(3) 3 56
(Tim Etherington) *midfield: rdn over 2f out: edgd rt over 1f out: no imp* **100/1**

4 **9** *½* **Maharanee (USA)**[52] 1971 3-8-12 0................................ PaulHanagan 6 55
(Ann Duffield) *t.k.h: midfield: rdn over 2f out: wknd ins fnl f* **7/1**[3]

00 **10** *1 ¼* **Prices Lane**[13] 3167 4-9-6 0.. JamesSullivan 10 54?
(Michael Easterby) *hld up: pushed along 1/2-way: a towards rr* **100/1**

6 **11** *12* **Nafa (IRE)**[15] 3091 3-8-12 0... RichardMullen 9 19
(Michael Mullineaux) *in tch: rdn over 3f out: wknd over 2f out* **50/1**

12 *31* **Titch The Witch** 3-8-12 0.. RobbieFitzpatrick 14 —
(David C Griffiths) *hld up: a towards rr* **100/1**

1m 27.1s (0.80) **Going Correction** -0.075s/f (Good)
WFA 3 from 4yo 8lb **12** Ran SP% **116.6**
Speed ratings (Par 100): **92,90,89,87,86 84,83,82,81,80 66,31**
toteswingers:1&2:£7.10, 2&3:£28.70, 1&3:£3.20 CSF £19.61 TOTE £2.10: £1.10, £3.30, £1.70; EX 19.50.
Owner The Black Type Partnership **Bred** D R Tucker **Trained** Newmarket, Suffolk

FOCUS
The winner, third and fourth all came into this with official ratings in the 70s, so just a fair fillies' maiden, and nothing got involved from off the pace. They raced middle-to-stands' side, but all avoided the near rail. The time was slow.

3578 MARTIN FRANKS AND ADRIAN SMITH CARDSAVE H'CAP 7f
3:35 (3:35) (Class 3) (0-95,92) 3-Y-O+ **£7,439** (£2,213; £1,106; £553) **Stalls** High

Form RPR

2532 **1** **Reel Buddy Star**[7] 3358 6-9-7 85.................................. DanielTudhope 5 96
(George Moore) *prom: led 3f out: rdn whn hdd narrowly over 1f out: rallied to ld again ins fnl f: sn edgd rt: hld on towards fin* **7/1**[3]

1-62 **2** *½* **Webbow (IRE)**[27] 2706 9-9-9 90.............................. LouisBeuzelin(3) 4 99
(Mark Campion) *midfield: hdwy over 2f out: rdn to chse ldrs over 1f out: wnt 2nd fnl 120yds: kpt on: nt rch wnr* **7/1**[3]

0-0 **3** *1 ½* **Kajima**[28] 2679 4-10-0 92.. PatDobbs 6 97+
(Richard Hannon) *hld up: rdn over 2f out: hdwy over 1f out: kpt on ins fnl f: wnt 3rd post* **33/1**

0-00 **4** *nk* **Zero Money (IRE)**[35] 2470 5-9-10 88.........................(b[1]) SteveDrowne 3 92
(Roger Charlton) *in tch: hdwy to chse ldr over 2f out: rdn to ld narrowly over 1f out: hdd ins fnl f: wknd fnl 100yds: lost 3rd post* **10/1**

2122 **5** *4* **Dubai Dynamo**[6] 3397 6-9-13 91.................................... PJMcDonald 9 85+
(Ruth Carr) *midfield: rdn over 2f out: one pce* **3/1**[1]

-346 **6** *3* **My Single Malt (IRE)**[41] 2319 3-8-5 77........................ AndrewMullen 2 59
(Tom Tate) *dwlt: hld up: rdn over 2f out: kpt on ins fnl f: n.d* **16/1**

21 **7** *¾* **Flowing Cape (IRE)**[34] 2497 6-9-5 86........................ PaulPickard(3) 1 69
(Reg Hollinshead) *chsd ldrs: rdn over 2f out: wknd over 1f out* **10/1**

1-00 **8** *2* **Saint Pierre (USA)**[38] 2390 4-9-8 86........................ J-PGuillambert 11 64
(Luca Cumani) *in tch: rdn over 2f out: wknd over 1f out* **11/2**[2]

2240 **9** *½* **Advanced**[14] 3109 8-9-11 92.......................................(b) AmyRyan(3) 10 69
(Kevin Ryan) *dwlt: sn trckd ldr: rdn over 2f out: sn wknd* **15/2**

0100 **10** *27* **Follow The Flag (IRE)**[90] 1092 7-9-0 85......................(p) RyanTate(7) 7 —
(Alan McCabe) *sn pushed along towards rr: a bhd* **50/1**

0-23 **11** *5* **No Hubris (USA)**[35] 2470 4-10-0 92............................ PaulHanagan 8 —
(Paul Cole) *led: hdd 3f out: sn wknd* **8/1**

1m 24.45s (-1.85) **Going Correction** -0.075s/f (Good)
WFA 3 from 4yo+ 8lb **11** Ran SP% **117.2**
Speed ratings (Par 107): **107,106,104,104,99 96,95,93,92,61 56**
toteswingers:1&2:£9.40, 2&3:£28.70, 1&3:£72.40 CSF £55.19 CT £1519.02 TOTE £8.10: £2.40, £3.00, £6.80; EX 67.20.
Owner J W Armstrong & M J Howarth **Bred** M Pennell **Trained** Middleham Moor, N Yorks

FOCUS
A good handicap run at a solid pace and the time was much quicker than the two 7f maidens on the card. They raced middle-to-stands' side, but again the near rail looked best avoided. The form is worth taking at face value.

NOTEBOOK
Reel Buddy Star couldn't dominate outright, but he raced away from his nearest rival for the lead and this big horse was able to get into a good, free-flowing rhythm, as he likes to. In typical fashion, he stuck on most gamely and was taking advantage of being 2lb well in following his close second over 1m at Newcastle the previous week. This was his first win at 7f since he landed his maiden and he can remain competitive. (op 8-1 tchd 6-1)
Webbow(IRE) ran well off a 4lb higher mark than when runner-up over C&D on his debut for this yard. (tchd 13-2)
Kajima kept on gradually from off the pace, improving significantly on the form of his reappearance. There should be more to come again next time.
Zero Money(IRE) upped his recent level, seemingly helped by first-time blinkers, although his finishing effort was a bit tame even allowing for ending up towards the apparently unfavoured stands' rail. (op 8-1)
Dubai Dynamo couldn't make it seven consecutive top-two finishes. He probably wasn't helped by being asked to make his move towards the near rail, which may have been slower ground, and he never looked like taking advantage of being 4lb well in. (op 4-1)

3579 GAYE TURTON AND CHRIS BAILEY-STONALL CARDSAVE FILLIES' H'CAP 5f
4:10 (4:11) (Class 4) (0-80,79) 4-Y-O+ **£3,557** (£1,058; £529; £264) **Stalls** High

Form RPR

265 **1** **Hypnosis**[59] 1796 8-8-1 64.. NeilFarley(5) 5 72
(Noel Wilson) *mde all: rdn over 2f out: strly pressed fnl 100yds: hld on all out* **16/1**

1-14 **2** *hd* **Beauty Pageant (IRE)**[18] 2987 4-8-11 69..................... RichardMullen 6 76
(Ed McMahon) *trckd ldr: rdn over 1f out: pressed wnr fnl 100yds: kpt on: jst failed* **13/8**[1]

1602 **3** *¾* **Absa Lutte (IRE)**[13] 3166 8-8-12 70.................................. TomEaves 7 74
(Michael Mullineaux) *hld up: rdn over 2f out: hdwy over 1f out: chsd wnr ins fnl f: kpt on* **8/1**[3]

1203 **4** *2 ½* **Dispol Kylie (IRE)**[15] 3083 5-8-11 72................... MichaelO'Connell(3) 3 67
(Kate Walton) *hld up: rdn over 2f out: no imp tl kpt on ins fnl f: nrst fin* **8/1**[3]

0012 **5** *½* **Nomoreblondes**[31] 2590 7-8-10 68.............................(v) MickyFenton 4 62
(Paul Midgley) *awkward leaving stall: sn prom: rdn over 2f out: no ex ins fnl f* **8/1**[3]

1215 **6** *nk* **Athwaab**[44] 2193 4-8-3 68.. CharlesBishop(7) 1 60
(Noel Quinlan) *in tch on outer: rdn over 2f out: no imp* **16/1**

05-0 **7** *¾* **Atlantic Cycle (IRE)**[13] 3166 4-9-0 72...........................(t) AndrewElliott 9 62
(Mrs K Burke) *w ldr: rdn over 2f out: outpcd over 1f out: drvn and hung lft ent fnl f: no imp* **8/1**[3]

140- **8** *2* **High Spice (USA)**[184] 7998 4-9-7 79...........................(p) PatCosgrave 2 62
(Robert Cowell) *s.i.s: hld up in tch: rdn over 1f out: no imp* **16/1**

-060 **9** *1* **Mey Blossom**[22] 2832 6-9-4 76.. PaulHanagan 8 55
(Richard Whitaker) *hld up: rdn over 2f out: a towards rr* **6/1**[2]

59.85 secs (-0.65) **Going Correction** -0.075s/f (Good) **9** Ran SP% **114.5**
Speed ratings (Par 102): **102,101,100,96,95 95,94,90,89**
CSF £42.09 CT £234.46 TOTE £22.30: £5.20, £1.10, £2.50; EX 57.80.
Owner R W Snowden **Bred** Mrs V E Hughes **Trained** Sandhutton, N Yorks

FOCUS
An ordinary fillies' sprint for the class. The action unfolded up the centre of the track. A couple of the stalls opened fractionally sooner than the others, namely gates four and five. However, while Nomoreblondes (drawn four) ended up losing ground, the winner (five) got a slight head start and, considering the margin of victory, it's possible to argue it made the difference. The stewards didn't publicly announce an enquiry, though, and that's poor on their part.

3580 DIRECT TRAFFIC MANAGEMENT H'CAP 1m 4f
4:45 (4:46) (Class 4) (0-85,85) 3-Y-O+ **£4,528** (£1,347; £673; £336) **Stalls** Low

Form RPR

3-43 **1** **Leader Of The Land (IRE)**[35] 2475 4-9-11 82............. SteveDrowne 2 91+
(David Lanigan) *trckd ldrs: rdn over 2f out: led wl over 1f out: strly pressed fnl 100yds: kpt on* **10/1**

-225 **2** *½* **Incendo**[21] 2884 5-9-11 82..(t) PatCosgrave 4 90
(James Fanshawe) *hld up in tch: smooth hdwy over 2f out: chsd ldr over 1f out: rdn to chal fnl 120yds: sn edgd lft: edgd rt and hld towards fin* **4/1**[2]

4321 **3** *3* **Stagecoach Danman (IRE)**[12] 3206 3-9-0 84 6ex....... DarryllHolland 3 90+
(Mark Johnston) *trckd ldr: led 4f out: sn rdn: hdd over 1f out: keeping on in cl 3rd whn short of room 100yds out: eased* **4/5**[1]

1-34 **4** *1* **Istishaara (USA)**[24] 2791 3-8-4 77.......................... LouisBeuzelin(3) 7 79
(John Dunlop) *dwlt: hld up: pushed along over 3f out: kpt on ins fnl f: nvr threatened ldrs* **13/2**[3]

000- **5** *4 ½* **Royal Diamond (IRE)**[357] 3877 5-10-0 85...................... PaulHanagan 5 79
(Jonjo O'Neill) *in tch: rdn over 3f out: wknd over 1f out* **25/1**

5210 **6** *7* **Jeer (IRE)**[41] 2320 7-9-4 75...(b) JamesSullivan 1 58
(Michael Easterby) *led: hdd 4f out: sn rdn: wknd 2f out* **20/1**

1-00 **7** *17* **Music City (IRE)**[32] 2544 4-9-3 74................................ J-PGuillambert 6 30
(Mark Johnston) *hld up: pushed along over 4f out: sn wknd* **33/1**

2m 33.77s (-1.13) **Going Correction** +0.05s/f (Good)
WFA 3 from 4yo+ 13lb **7** Ran SP% **109.5**
Speed ratings (Par 105): **105,104,102,102,99 94,83**
toteswingers:1&2:£3.00, 2&3:£1.80, 1&3:£2.50 CSF £44.65 TOTE £11.10: £4.30, £2.80; EX 33.70.
Owner Saeed H Altayer **Bred** Rabbah Bloodstock Limited **Trained** Newmarket, Suffolk
■ Stewards' Enquiry : Pat Cosgrave two-day ban: careless riding (Jul 16-17)

FOCUS
A fair handicap, although things got a little messy late on. The time was 1.15 seconds quicker than the following Class 5 event. The winner posted a 3lb personal best, with the second basically to form.

3581 PLAND STAINLESS H'CAP 1m 4f
5:15 (5:15) (Class 5) (0-70,70) 4-Y-O+ **£2,522** (£750; £375; £187) **Stalls** Low

Form RPR

0211 **1** **Fossgate**[16] 3054 10-8-10 61.. AmyRyan(3) 3 69+
(James Bethell) *midfield on outer: hdwy over 3f out: rdn to ld over 2f out: kpt on* **9/4**[1]

302 **2** *1* **Harvey's Hope**[14] 3138 5-9-3 65.................................... PaddyAspell 2 71+
(Keith Reveley) *hld up in tch: rdn and hdwy over 1f out: wnt 2nd fnl 100yds: kpt on: nt rch wnr* **9/2**[3]

0001 **3** *2 ¾* **Buddy Holly**[11] 3225 6-9-6 68 6ex.................................. DarryllHolland 7 70
(Robert Eddery) *trckd ldr: led narrowly 3f out: hdd over 2f out: kpt on one pce* **11/2**

0-04 **4** *½* **Orpen Bid (IRE)**[29] 2654 6-7-11 50 oh5.......................... NeilFarley(5) 1 51
(Michael Mullineaux) *hld up: rdn over 3f out: hdwy over 1f out: kpt on ins fnl f: nvr threatened ldrs* **40/1**

0540 **5** *1 ¼* **Aegean Destiny**[19] 2952 4-8-9 **57**........................ FrederikTylicki 8 56
(John Mackie) *in tch: hdwy and ev ch over 2f out: drvn over 1f out: one pce* **7/2**[2]
0030 **6** *8* **Lure of The Night (IRE)**[19] 2952 4-8-9 **57**............... AndrewHeffernan 5 43
(Brian Rothwell) *midfield: rdn over 3f out: no imp: wknd over 1f out* **11/1**
5516 **7** *5* **Visions Of Johanna (USA)**[4] 3456 6-9-8 **70** 6ex(tp) RobbieFitzpatrick 6 48
(Richard Guest) *led: rdn whn hdd 3f out: wknd over 1f out* **13/2**
6-06 **8** *9* **Cabal**[20] 2906 4-9-4 **69**.. PaulPickard(3) 4 33
(Andrew Crook) *hld up in rr: a bhd* **22/1**
2m 34.92s (0.02) **Going Correction** +0.05s/f (Good) **8** Ran SP% **115.0**
Speed ratings (Par 103): **101,100,98,98,97 92,88,82**
toteswingers:1&2:£3.80, 2&3:£5.20, 1&3:£2.40. Tote Super 7: Win: Not won. Place: £313.60 CSF £12.73 CT £48.88 TOTE £3.30: £1.70, £2.00, £2.20; EX 16.60.
Owner Mrs James Bethell **Bred** Mrs P A Clark **Trained** Middleham Moor, N Yorks
FOCUS
The time was 1.15 seconds slower than the earlier Class 4 handicap, but this wasn't a bad race. The winner was basically to his recent form but the fourth is a doubt.
T/Plt: £103.70 to £1 stake. Pool of £63,017.68 - 443.60 winning tickets. T/Qpdt: £38.90 to a £1 stake. Pool of £4,927.24 - 93.50 winning tickets. AS

3539 HAYDOCK (L-H)

Friday, July 1

OFFICIAL GOING: Good to firm (watered; 5f & 6f 8.0, 7f & further 7.8)
Wind: light 1/2 against Weather: fine

3582 BETDAQ THE BETTING EXCHANGE APPRENTICE TRAINING SERIES H'CAP (RACING EXCELLENCE INITIATIVE) 5f
6:45 (6:46) (Class 5) (0-75,75) 3-Y-0+ **£2,587** (£770; £384; £192) **Stalls** Centre

Form RPR
3103 **1** **Your Gifted (IRE)**[8] 3305 4-9-4 **70**.............................. DarylByrne(3) 6 84
(Patrick Morris) *s.i.s: hld up: smooth hdwy over 2f out: led 1f out: pushed out* **6/1**[3]
6536 **2** *3* **Comptonspirit**[25] 2766 7-9-8 **71**.................................. JamesRogers 1 74
(Brian Baugh) *sn outpcd: hdwy 2f out: edgd rt and styd on to take 2nd ins fnl f* **10/1**
0352 **3** *nk* **Scarlet Rocks (IRE)**[25] 2770 3-9-7 **75**.................... MatthewCosham 8 75
(David Evans) *chsd ldrs: outpcd after 2f: hdwy 2f out: styd on fnl f* **9/1**
6624 **4** *nse* **Bosun Breese**[15] 3078 6-9-11 **74**.................................... RyanPowell 9 76
(David Barron) *led tl 2f out: rallied ins fnl f: kpt on* **7/2**[1]
4642 **5** *1 ¾* **Wicked Wilma (IRE)**[4] 3451 7-8-3 **57** oh1 ow1.... DavidSimmonson(5) 5 52
(Alan Berry) *w ldrs: hung lft and led 2f out: hdd 1f out: sn wknd* **7/1**
335 **6** *1* **Schoolboy Champ**[13] 3166 4-8-8 **57**................................ RyanClark 2 49
(Patrick Morris) *dwlt: sn outpcd: hdwy over 2f out: wknd over 1f out* **9/1**
0350 **7** *shd* **Chosen One (IRE)**[13] 3166 6-8-12 **66**.................. SophieSilvester(5) 7 57
(Ruth Carr) *hld up towards rr: effrt over 2f out: nvr a factor* **13/2**
64-4 **8** *shd* **Alis Aquilae (IRE)**[34] 2491 5-9-11 **74**.......................... BrianToomey 3 65
(Tim Etherington) *trckd ldrs: t.k.h: wkng whn n.m.r over 1f out* **4/1**[2]
61.95 secs (1.15) **Going Correction** +0.075s/f (Good)
WFA 3 from 4yo+ 5lb **8** Ran SP% **111.4**
Speed ratings (Par 103): **95,90,89,89,86 85,85,84**
toteswingers:1&2:£7.80, 1&3:£5.20, 2&3:£9.00 CSF £59.86 CT £525.33 TOTE £8.30: £2.50, £3.40, £2.80; EX 58.40.
Owner Mrs S Morris **Bred** Rathasker Stud **Trained** Tarporley, Cheshire
■ Stewards' Enquiry : David Simmonson caution: careless riding.
FOCUS
The going was good to firm on a watered track. The sprint races were run on the inner home straight, while the longer races were on the outer home straight. Races on Round course increased by 51yds. This looked a tight apprentice handicap, but the winner surged clear for a comfortable success, showing she wasn't entirelt flattered by her Thirsk win.

3583 BRITISH STALLION STUDS EBF MHA LIGHTING MAIDEN STKS 6f
7:15 (7:16) (Class 5) 2-Y-0 **£3,234** (£962; £481; £240) **Stalls** Centre

Form RPR
432 **1** *nse* **Letsgoroundagain (IRE)**[13] 3161 2-9-3 0.................... WilliamCarson 1 87
(B W Hills) *wnt rt s: chsd ldrs: chal 1f out: carried lft ins fnl f: jst failed: fin 2nd: awrdd the r* **5/1**[3]
20 **2** **Campanology**[17] 3012 2-9-3 0.. PatDobbs 8 87
(Richard Hannon) *trckd ldrs: smooth hdwy to ld over 1f out: rdr sn dropped whip: edgd lft ins fnl f: all out: fin 1st disqualified and plcd 2nd* **7/4**[1]
2 **3** *8* **Wolf Spirit (IRE)**[22] 2831 2-9-3 0.................................... PhillipMakin 7 63
(Kevin Ryan) *hld up: hdwy over 2f out: kpt on same pce over 1f out* **15/8**[2]
4 *shd* **Dorry K (IRE)** 2-8-12 0... LeeNewman 6 58+
(David Barron) *dwlt: hdwy over 2f out: kpt on same pce fnl f* **33/1**
62 **5** *3 ¾* **Cape Moss (IRE)**[20] 2902 2-9-3 0................................ SteveDrowne 9 51
(Tom Dascombe) *trckd ldrs: wknd over 1f out: fin lame* **9/1**
6 **6** *1 ¼* **Jay Kay**[18] 2983 2-9-3 0.. FrannyNorton 4 48
(Robert Wylie) *led: hdd over 1f out: sn wknd* **20/1**
7 *1 ½* **Flugelhorn (IRE)** 2-9-3 0.. RichardMullen 2 43
(Ed McMahon) *s.i.s: sn drvn along and wl outpcd: t.o 2f out: sme late hdwy* **14/1**
0 **8** *½* **Forster Street (IRE)**[30] 2617 2-9-3 0................................ DavidAllan 5 42
(Tim Easterby) *mid-div: effrt over 2f out: sn edgd lft and wknd* **80/1**
0 **9** *5* **M J Woodward**[13] 3165 2-9-3 0.................................... AndreaAtzeni 3 27
(Paul Green) *hld up in rr: hdwy over 2f out: hung lft and wknd over 1f out* **100/1**
1m 14.81s (1.01) **Going Correction** +0.075s/f (Good) **9** Ran SP% **114.4**
Speed ratings (Par 94): **93,94,83,83,78 76,74,73,67**
toteswingers:1&2:£3.20, 1&3:£7.60, 2&3:£7.90 CSF £13.76 TOTE £5.00: £1.70, £1.10, £1.30; EX 14.40.
Owner AEGIS Partnership **Bred** Lynn Lodge Stud **Trained** Lambourn, Berks
■ Stewards' Enquiry : Pat Dobbs one-day ban: careless riding (Jul 15)
FOCUS
The first two pulled a long way clear in this maiden, showing decent form, and after a stewards' enquiry the positions were reversed due to the first past the post carrying his rival to the left. The form could be underrated.
NOTEBOOK
Letsgoroundagain(IRE) put an odds-on reverse behind him with a close second in a decent small-field Ayr maiden on soft. A return to quicker ground was not a problem and he showed a gritty attitude to maintain a persistent challenge to a rival who was travelling much better than him with 2f to go. He looks tough and useful, and is a closely related to relentlessly progressive 11-time winner Spinning. (op 9-2 tchd 11-2)
Campanology made a promising start when second at Doncaster and shaped quite well out wide with a stiff task in the Coventry at Royal Ascot. This half-brother to the stable's high-class miler Dubawi Gold had decent form claims back in a maiden and travelled smoothly for a long way before showing some fighting spirit to finish first in a sustained duel in the final furlong. He eventually lost the race, but he should continue to progress and an entry in the Group 1 National Stakes suggests he is very highly regarded. (op 15-8 tchd 9-4 in places)
Wolf Spirit(IRE) travelled like the best horse for much of the way before showing signs of greenness and getting worn down in a C&D maiden on debut. He had solid claims and things seemed to be going well out wide for a long way but he was left behind when the first two quickened. (op 11-4 tchd 3-1 in places)
Dorry K(IRE), a half-sister to 7f-1m 3-y-o winner Buzz Bird, stayed on well to nearly snatch third on an encouraging debut at a big price. (op 25-1 tchd 40-1)
Cape Moss(IRE) finished second behind a subsequent winner in a fair Bath novice last month on his second start, but he had something to find and was one of the first under pressure and couldn't find a response. Official explanation: vet said gelding finished lame (op 15-2)
M J Woodward Official explanation: jockey said colt hung left

3584 SCISSOR SISTERS LIVE ON 16TH JULY (S) STKS 6f
7:45 (7:46) (Class 4) 2-Y-0 **£4,528** (£1,347; £673; £336) **Stalls** Centre

Form RPR
655 **1** **Faraway**[17] 3016 2-8-11 0... ShaneKelly 3 64
(William Haggas) *led: edgd rt after 150yds: racd towards stands' side rail: kpt on wl u.p fnl f* **9/2**[3]
63 **2** *1* **Stellar Express (IRE)**[14] 3117 2-8-6 0.......................... WilliamCarson 4 56
(B W Hills) *chsd ldrs: wnt 2nd 3f out: edgd lft over 1f out: kpt on same pce last 100yds* **7/2**[2]
0 **3** *2* **Storm Fairy**[74] 1434 2-8-6 0...................................... AndrewElliott 6 50+
(Mrs K Burke) *dwlt: swtchd lft and hdwy over 2f out: kpt on same pce fnl f* **25/1**
542 **4** *4 ½* **Emma Jean (IRE)**[18] 2998 2-8-1 0................................ RyanPowell(5) 1 37
(J S Moore) *chsd ldrs on outside: reminders after 1f: hung bdly lft 2f out: ended up racing far side: wknd ins fnl f* **6/4**[1]
0436 **5** *3 ½* **Adranian (IRE)**[41] 2283 2-8-11 0..............................(v) PhillipMakin 8 31
(David Evans) *hld up: hdwy on ins 3f out: wknd over 1f out* **11/1**
2251 **6** *8* **Rooknrasbryripple**[17] 3021 2-8-11 0.......................... SamHitchcott 7 7
(Mick Channon) *trckd ldrs: t.k.h: hmpd after 1f: drvn 3f out: lost pl over 1f out* **9/2**[3]
006 **7** *4* **Red Samantha (IRE)**[6] 3375 2-8-6 0............................ JamesSullivan 5 —
(Alan Berry) *trckd ldrs: hmpd after 1f: lost pl over 2f out: sn wl bhd* **100/1**
1m 15.39s (1.59) **Going Correction** +0.075s/f (Good) **7** Ran SP% **111.8**
Speed ratings (Par 96): **90,88,86,80,75 64,59**
toteswingers:1&2:£3.20, 1&3:£7.60, 2&3:£7.90 CSF £19.59 TOTE £6.80: £3.30, £2.90; EX 23.20.The winner was sold to Nick Shutts for 9,000gns.
Owner Mohammed Jaber **Bred** Stourbank Stud **Trained** Newmarket, Suffolk
■ Stewards' Enquiry : Shane Kelly four-day ban: careless riding (Jul 15-18)
FOCUS
A strong seller with a minimum claiming price of £20,000. The winner dominated against the stands' rail and the disappointing favourite moved sideways in the closing stages. The form makes sense.
NOTEBOOK
Faraway didn't find the anticipated improvement when fading into fifth of five in a Brighton maiden last time, but he had fair form claims dropped into a seller and put in a resolute front-running display after gabbing the near rail from stall three. (op 5-1 tchd 11-2)
Stellar Express(IRE) showed promise staying on late in a pair of 6f maidens. She showed a bit more tactical speed switched to this company and gave it a decent try. She should continue to progress and shapes like a stiffer test should suit. (op 4-1 tchd 9-2 in places)
Storm Fairy, unfancied when towards the rear in a 5f Redcar maiden auction on debut, showed some ability staying on strongly for third switched to a seller.
Emma Jean(IRE) was 10l clear of the third when just collared by the favourite in a Windsor seller last time, form which was boosted by the winner going close in a fillies' conditions event next time. She had leading form claims, but was marooned out wide for most of the way and veered badly left when struggling to get the grips with the front two in the closing stages. (op 11-8 tchd 11-10)
Rooknrasbryripple got off the mark on her second attempt in a seller when scoring readily at Thirsk last time but she was keen and cut out quickly in this disappointing follow up bid. She was reported to have lost her action. Official explanation: jockey said filly lost its action (tchd 4-1 and 5-1)

3585 HAPPY BIRTHDAY BOBBIE SUTTON H'CAP 1m 3f 95y
8:15 (8:18) (Class 4) (0-85,85) 3-Y-0+ **£4,528** (£1,347; £673; £336) **Stalls** Centre

Form RPR
-045 **1** **Watercourse (IRE)**[25] 2764 3-8-8 **76**............................ AndreaAtzeni 2 91+
(Roger Varian) *hld up in mid-div: hdwy over 3f out: n.m.r over 2f out: led wl over 1f out: rdn clr fnl 150yds* **9/2**[2]
131- **2** *3 ¾* **On Her Way**[318] 5181 4-9-10 **81**............................ J-PGuillambert 8 88
(Luca Cumani) *reluctant and led to s: trckd ldrs: t.k.h: drvn and outpcd over 4f out: hdwy to chse ldrs 3f out: carried hd high and edgd lft: wnt 2nd over 1f out: kpt on same pce fnl f* **12/1**
615 **3** *hd* **Voodoo Prince**[20] 2925 3-9-3 **85**.................................. PhillipMakin 7 92
(Ed Dunlop) *hld up in rr: hdwy on outside 3f out: wnt 3rd over 1f out: kpt on same pce* **9/4**[1]
4222 **4** *7* **Dolphin Rock**[15] 3085 4-10-0 **85**................................... LeeNewman 6 78
(David Barron) *led tl over 6f out: led 3f out: hdd wl over 1f out: sn wknd* **5/1**[3]
-000 **5** *shd* **Oriental Scot**[28] 2681 4-10-0 **85**.............................. SteveDrowne 4 80
(William Jarvis) *trckd ldrs: led over 6f out: hdd 3f out: wkng whn n.m.r 2f out* **10/1**
-410 **6** *½* **Kensei (IRE)**[9] 3276 4-9-9 **80**.................................. DanielTudhope 9 72
(David O'Meara) *mid-div: rdn over 3f out: one pce whn n.m.r over 2f out: hung lft and no threat after* **6/1**
2521 **7** *½* **Yes Chef**[21] 2872 4-9-8 **79**...................................... JamesMillman 5 70
(Rod Millman) *trckd ldrs: wknd over 1f out* **8/1**
3311 **8** *2 ¼* **Moody Tunes**[18] 2984 8-8-13 **77**.............................. BenWilliams(7) 3 63+
(Tom Dascombe) *awkward exit fr stalls: rdr lost iron after 2f: in rr: nvr on terms* **20/1**
4304 **9** *15* **The Galloping Shoe**[13] 3163 6-9-12 **83**.................... DarryllHolland 1 39
(Ian Semple) *hld up in mid-div: rdn over 2f out: sn wknd: bhd whn eased ins fnl f* **20/1**
2m 13.77s (-2.23) **Going Correction** -0.075s/f (Good)
WFA 3 from 4yo+ 11lb **9** Ran SP% **117.3**
Speed ratings (Par 105): **105,102,101,96,96 95,95,93,81**
toteswingers:1&2:£17.90, 1&3:£2.90, 2&3:£3.60 CSF £57.71 CT £149.99 TOTE £4.60: £1.30, £2.80, £1.50; EX 49.10.
Owner R Baines, S Dartnell & M Jarvis **Bred** Laundry Cottage Stud Farm **Trained** Newmarket, Suffolk

FOCUS
A decent handicap. It was run at a fair pace and won in good style by an unexpected 3-y-o improver who seems to have plenty of staying power. The first three were clear and the form is rated on the positive side.

3586 TURFTV.CO.UK FILLIES' H'CAP 1m
8:45 (8:46) (Class 5) (0-75,75) 3-Y-O £2,587 (£770; £384; £192) Stalls Low

Form RPR
10-5 1 **Luv U Too**[36] 2411 3-9-0 72 DarryllHolland 2 80
(Jo Hughes) *trckd ldr: led over 6f out: drvn and qcknd over 4f out: styd on wl* **10/1**
6415 2 3 1/4 **Maggie Mey (IRE)**[12] 3207 3-9-2 74 DanielTudhope 4 75
(David O'Meara) *led tl over 6f out: chsd wnr: rdn 3f out: one pce* **5/2**[1]
24 3 1 3/4 **Imaginary World (IRE)**[8] 3310 3-9-2 74 (be) ShaneKelly 1 71
(Alan McCabe) *dwlt: hld up: t.k.h: slipped bnd over 4f out: stdy hdwy over 2f out: wnt 3rd over 1f out: one pce* **11/4**[2]
6-26 4 1 1/4 **Fenella Fudge**[22] 2850 3-9-0 72 FrederikTylicki 5 66
(James Given) *stdd s: hld up: hdwy over 4f out: drvn over 3f out: wknd over 1f out* **5/1**[3]
0-21 5 hd **Royal Hush**[28] 2691 3-9-3 75 PhillipMakin 3 69
(Kevin Ryan) *dwlt: sn chsng ldrs: effrt over 2f out: hung lft and wknd over 1f out* **11/4**[2]
1m 45.37s (2.47) **Going Correction** -0.075s/f (Good) 5 Ran SP% **107.7**
Speed ratings (Par 97): **84,80,79,77,77**
CSF £33.20 TOTE £7.10: £3.30, £2.70; EX 19.40.
Owner 21C Telecom.co.uk **Bred** Richard Hunt **Trained** Lambourn, Berks

FOCUS
There was an open market for this minor fillies' handicap. It was won by a front-running outsider, but she set a decent pace for the others to aim at and there was no fluke about it. The winner has a hit-and-miss profile.
Imaginary World(IRE) Official explanation: jockey said filly slipped on the turn in
Royal Hush Official explanation: jockey said filly hung left-handed

3587 "KIKI" BY KIRSTY DOYLE H'CAP 1m 6f
9:15 (9:17) (Class 5) (0-70,69) 3-Y-O £2,587 (£770; £384; £192) Stalls Low

Form RPR
1625 1 **Dark Dune (IRE)**[15] 3084 3-9-7 69 DavidAllan 6 73
(Tim Easterby) *trckd ldrs: chal 4f out: led over 2f out: edgd lft over 1f out: styd on u.p: hld on wl* **11/1**
-324 2 2 **Veloce (IRE)**[43] 2228 3-9-1 63 ShaneKelly 2 64
(John Dunlop) *trckd ldrs: effrt over 3f out: styd on fnl f: tk 2nd post* **15/8**[1]
6101 3 nse **Tidal Run**[20] 2904 3-9-3 65 SamHitchcott 7 66
(Mick Channon) *t.k.h in mid-div: hdwy over 4f out: sn rdn: styd on fnl f: tk 2nd ins fnl f* **11/2**
-303 4 hd **C P Joe (IRE)**[30] 2613 3-8-13 61 FrannyNorton 1 62
(Paul Green) *t.k.h in mid-div: effrt over 3f out: sn rdn: kpt on same pce fnl f* **13/2**
4334 5 shd **Experimentalist**[11] 3233 3-9-7 69 HayleyTurner 4 70
(Hughie Morrison) *rrd s: sn swtchd lft and hld up: hdwy over 4f out: sn rdn: hung lft over 2f out: styd on ins fnl f* **5/1**[3]
0-00 6 nk **Princesse Fleur**[21] 2871 3-8-7 55 FrederikTylicki 9 55
(Michael Scudamore) *trckd ldr: chal over 4f out: led over 3f out: hdd over 2f out: one pce fnl f* **25/1**
0500 7 5 **Mountain Myst**[9] 3268 3-8-9 57 ow1 DarryllHolland 8 50
(William Muir) *led: drvn and qcknd pce over 4f out: hdd over 3f out: wknd over 1f out* **33/1**
0021 8 3 1/2 **Hal Of A Lover**[23] 2801 3-8-8 56 JamesSullivan 3 44
(David O'Meara) *t.k.h towards rr: effrt over 3f out: sn rdn: nvr a factor: wknd over 1f out* **9/2**[2]
3m 10.86s (9.66) **Going Correction** -0.075s/f (Good) 8 Ran SP% **113.5**
Speed ratings (Par 100): **69,67,67,67,67 67,64,62**
toteswingers:1&2:£4.90, 1&3:£12.80, 2&3:£4.20 CSF £31.59 CT £128.78 TOTE £13.40: £2.90, £1.60, £1.10; EX 39.10.
Owner Miss Betty Duxbury **Bred** P Turley **Trained** Great Habton, N Yorks

FOCUS
An ordinary staying handicap. The pace was very steady and several of the runners pulled hard early on. There was a bunch finish and it's hard to be positive about the bare form.
Hal Of A Lover Official explanation: jockey said gelding ran too freely
T/Plt: £133.00 to a £1 stake. Pool:£66,939.88 - 367.40 winning tickets T/Qpdt: £37.80 to a £1 stake. Pool:£5,483.32 - 107.30 winning tickets WG

2925 SANDOWN (R-H)
Friday, July 1

OFFICIAL GOING: Good (good to firm in places; rnd course 8.2, sprint course 8.0)
Wind: very light, half against Weather: light cloud, bright spells

3588 REWARDS4RACING.COM H'CAP 5f 6y
2:20 (2:23) (Class 4) (0-85,83) 3-Y-O+ £4,528 (£1,347; £673; £336) Stalls Low

Form RPR
111- 1 **Ritual (IRE)**[239] 7320 4-9-12 83 RyanMoore 6 93+
(Jeremy Noseda) *s.i.s: pushed along in last: clsd and in tch 3f out: hdwy on rail over 1f out: chsd ldr and swtchd lft jst ins fnl f: r.o strly to ld fnl 75yds: gng away at fin* **7/2**[2]
060 2 1 **Night Affair**[11] 3222 5-9-3 74 NeilCallan 1 80
(David Arbuthnot) *taken down early: dwlt: sn rcvrd to press ldr: rdn to ld over 1f out: drvn ins fnl f: hdd and no ex fnl 75yds* **14/1**
1161 3 1 1/2 **Doc Hay (USA)**[8] 3305 4-9-11 82 6ex TedDurcan 4 83+
(Keith Dalgleish) *hld up in tch: n.m.r 2f out: sn swtchd lft and rdn over 1f out: hanging rt and no imp 1f out tl r.o strly fnl 100yds: nvr gng to rch ldrs* **7/4**[1]
6-41 4 1 **Macdillon**[20] 2929 5-9-9 80 LiamKeniry 3 77
(Stuart Kittow) *broke wl: sn stdd and t.k.h: in tch: rdn and effrt jst over 1f out: styd on same pce u.p fnl f* **7/2**[2]
520 5 shd **Fantasy Explorer**[6] 3383 8-9-6 77 TomQueally 2 74
(John Quinn) *lw: t.k.h: led: hdd and rdn over 1f out: drvn and unable qck 1f out: wknd and lost 2 pls wl ins fnl f* **8/1**[3]
6035 6 2 3/4 **Desert Strike**[6] 3383 5-8-13 70 (p) RobertWinston 8 57
(Alan McCabe) *lw: taken down early: t.k.h and hld up in last pair: rdn 3f out: effrt whn pushed sltly lft over 1f out: hung bdly rt and wknd 1f out* **16/1**
0-03 7 3 **Brynfa Boy**[11] 3222 5-9-5 76 TonyCulhane 7 52
(Paul D'Arcy) *taken down early: t.k.h: chsd ldrs: rdn and fnd nil wl over 1f out: wknd jst over 1f out* **11/1**
61.27 secs (-0.33) **Going Correction** +0.075s/f (Good) 7 Ran SP% **112.8**
Speed ratings (Par 105): **105,103,101,99,99 94,90**
toteswingers:1&2:£6.10, 2&3:£6.50, 1&3:£1.70 CSF £47.08 CT £110.85 TOTE £3.60: £2.10, £4.30; EX 49.10 Trifecta £146.80 Pool: £1250.50 - 6.30 winning units..
Owner Highclere Thoroughbred Racing Churchill **Bred** Agricola Del Parco **Trained** Newmarket, Suffolk
■ Stewards' Enquiry : Ted Durcan one-day ban: careless riding (Jul 15)

FOCUS
The rails were dolled out three yards on the round course from 7f to 3f out, adding four yards to race distances, and the rail on the 5f course was dolled out three yards. The ground was riding as advertised, with no jar. An interesting sprint handicap, and fairly useful form. The progressive winner was helped by the rail but there looks more to come.

3589 BANK OF NEW YORK MELLON DRAGON STKS (LISTED RACE) 5f 6y
2:50 (2:53) (Class 1) 2-Y-O
£12,192 (£4,622; £2,313; £1,152; £578; £290) Stalls Low

Form RPR
3140 1 **Forevertheoptimist (IRE)**[15] 3064 2-9-2 0 KierenFallon 1 97
(Linda Stubbs) *swtg: chsd ldr tl disp ld and wnt on w runner-up after 1f: rdn and narrow ld over 1f out: drvn and hld on gamely thrght fnl f: all out* **9/1**[3]
315 2 hd **Kohala (IRE)**[16] 3033 2-8-11 0 GrahamGibbons 6 91
(David Barron) *chsd ldr tl led narrowly and wnt on w wnr after 1f: rdn and narrowly hdd over 1f out: kpt on gamely u.p ins fnl f: a jst hld* **2/1**[1]
215 3 1 **Bear Behind (IRE)**[17] 3014 2-9-2 0 RyanMoore 2 92
(Tom Dascombe) *broke fast and crossed to r on rail: hdd after 1f: chsd ldng pair after: pushed along 1/2-way: drvn over 1f out: switching lft ins fnl f: styd on u.p fnl 100yds* **2/1**[1]
10 4 2 1/2 **The Penny Horse (IRE)**[17] 3014 2-9-2 0 JamesDoyle 3 83
(J S Moore) *taken down early and led to s: chsd ldng trio: rdn jst over 2f out: no imp and edging rt over 1f out: styd on same pce u.p ins fnl f* **12/1**
110 5 2 **Jack Who's He (IRE)**[17] 3012 2-9-2 0 CathyGannon 4 76
(David Evans) *lw: chsd ldrs tl hmpd and lost pl after 1f: in last pair after: rdn and wandered 2f out: edgd rt and btn 1f out* **3/1**[2]
213 6 5 **Dawn Lightning**[65] 1598 2-8-11 0 RobertWinston 5 50
(Alan McCabe) *short of room and hmpd sn after s: a in rr: rdn 2f out: struggling and no imp whn unbalanced over 1f out: sn wknd* **40/1**
62.06 secs (0.46) **Going Correction** +0.075s/f (Good) 6 Ran SP% **111.8**
Speed ratings (Par 102): **99,98,97,93,89 81**
toteswingers:1&2:£3.90, 2&3:£1.10, 1&3:£2.20 CSF £27.23 TOTE £8.00: £2.70, £1.60; EX 30.50.
Owner G & T Bloodstock **Bred** Peter & Hugh McCutcheon **Trained** Norton, N Yorks
■ Stewards' Enquiry : Graham Gibbons three-day ban: careless riding (Jul 15-17)

FOCUS
Last year's scorer Zebedee, who retired unbeaten at the end of his 2-y-o season, was the best winner of this Listed event in the past decade. Five of the six runners this year were seen in action at Royal Ascot last month, contesting four different races at the meeting. Not strong form for the grade, the winner bouncing back to an effort in keeping with his previous win. The fourth is the long-term key to the form.

NOTEBOOK
Forevertheoptimist(IRE) had the rail to help and just prevailed after a good tussle, the pair matching strides from an early stage. Seventh to Bapak Chinta in the Norfolk at Ascot after a slow start, he was well away here and made good use of his favourable draw. He is likely to revert to 6f now. (tchd 11-1)
Kohala(IRE)'s Queen Mary fifth behind Best Terms looked the best form on offer. Upsides the winner for most of the way, she stuck to her guns bravely and just missed out. She has the right attitude and can win again back against her own sex. (op 9-4)
Bear Behind(IRE) ◆, by the same sire as the runner-up, had run well in the face of a poor draw in the Windsor Castle Stakes won by Frederick Engels. After breaking very well he claimed the lead against the rail, but soon found himself behind the front pair. He lacked the pace to get in a blow at them, but kept trying and was clawing them back near the finish. He ought to get another furlong and should be given another chance. (tchd 9-4 in places and 7-4 in places)
The Penny Horse(IRE) was in fourth position for most of the way and never really a factor, but did finish slightly closer to Bear Behind than he had at Ascot. (tchd 14-1)
Jack Who's He(IRE) finished eighth to Power in the Coventry Stakes, a creditable effort as apparently he was not trained for the race as he was on the verge of being sold. He disappointed down in trip, being forced to snatch up as Kohala went across him early on and never really on an even keel thereafter out wide. (tchd 11-4)
Dawn Lightning, off the track for two months, was found wanting at this elevated level. (op 33-1)

3590 BRITISH STALLION STUDS SUPPORTING BRITISH RACING EBF MAIDEN STKS 7f 16y
3:25 (3:26) (Class 5) 2-Y-O £3,881 (£1,155; £577; £288) Stalls Low

Form RPR
0 1 **Talwar (IRE)**[19] 2953 2-9-3 0 RyanMoore 4 85+
(Jeremy Noseda) *athletic: lw: broke fast: mde all: rdn and qcknd clr wl over 1f out: r.o strly and in n.d ins fnl f: eased towards fin* **4/1**[2]
2 4 **Gunner Will (IRE)** 2-9-0 0 MatthewDavies(3) 9 75
(George Baker) *w'like: str: b.bkwd: hld up in last quartet: rdn and hdwy in centre over 2f out: nt gng pce of wnr and edgd lft wl over 1f out: chsd wnr ins fnl f: kpt on but no threat to wnr* **33/1**
3 3 1/2 **Sehnsucht (IRE)**[14] 3132 2-9-3 0 RobertWinston 6 74
(Alan McCabe) *str: t.k.h: chsd ldrs: rdn and effrt on inner 2f out: outpcd and no threat to wnr over 1f out: kpt on u.p to go 3rd cl home* **11/4**[1]
4 nk **Nant Saeson (IRE)** 2-9-3 0 RichardHughes 8 74+
(Richard Hannon) *str: w wnr: rdn and unable qck w wnr wl over 1f out: btn 1f out: kpt on same pce and lost 2 pls fnl 150yds* **4/1**[2]
0 5 3/4 **Ex Oriente (IRE)**[13] 3182 2-9-3 0 RobertHavlin 10 71+
(John Gosden) *w'like: t.k.h: chsd ldrs: rdn: rn green and unable qck 2f out: styd on same pce and no threat to wnr fr over 1f out* **4/1**[2]
6 4 **Tigers Tale (IRE)** 2-9-3 0 KierenFallon 7 61
(Roger Teal) *w'like: leggy: t.k.h: hld up in midfield: rdn and outpcd jst over 2f out: styd on same pce and n.d fr wl over 1f out* **11/1**[3]
7 1 **Royal Academician (USA)** 2-9-3 0 TomQueally 5 59+
(Gary Moore) *unf: scope: s.i.s: hld up in rr: pushed along and sme hdwy over 2f out: no imp and wl hld fnl 2f* **28/1**
8 1 **Astraios (IRE)** 2-9-3 0 MartinDwyer 3 56+
(Brian Meehan) *str: wnt rt s: rn green in midfield: n.m.r over 2f out: sn rdn and outpcd: wl btn over 1f out* **16/1**
9 2 **Vergrigio (IRE)** 2-9-3 0 EddieCreighton 1 51
(Brian Meehan) *leggy: b.bkwd: hmpd s and s.i.s: rn green and a in rr: rdn and struggling over 3f out: wknd over 2f out* **50/1**

10 *hd* **Mcvicar** 2-9-3 0.. HughBowman 2 51
(Mick Channon) *s.i.s: a in last pair: pushed along and struggling 3f out: sn wknd* **18/1**

1m 31.62s (2.12) **Going Correction** -0.10s/f (Good) **10** Ran SP% **114.5**
Speed ratings (Par 94): **83,78,77,77,76 72,70,69,67,67**
toteswingers:1&2:£20.70, 2&3:£11.20, 1&3:£2.60 CSF £127.23 TOTE £5.60: £1.80, £6.00, £1.20; EX 110.90 Trifecta £376.10 Pool: £853.93 - 1.68 winning units..
Owner Vimal Khosla **Bred** Philip And Mrs Jane Myerscough **Trained** Newmarket, Suffolk

FOCUS
Zacinto, Scintillo and Mister Monet have all won this maiden in the past decade before going on to Group-race success.\n\x\x Only three of this field had previous racecourse experience and it's not easy to assess the worth of the form, but it looked an ordinary race for the track. The winner impressed though, showing big improvement from his debut.

NOTEBOOK
Talwar(IRE), the most expensive in the field at 140,000gns, was withdrawn at the stalls on his intended debut before finishing unplaced first time out at Doncaster. Making all this time, he stretched away in good style in the final furlong for an impressive victory. A nice prospect, he holds entries in the Group 1 Phoenix Stakes and several valuable sales races later in the season, but will need to improve a good bit on this bare form. (op 7-2)
Gunner Will(IRE)'s price rose to £48,000 at the breeze-ups. After meeting early interference he shaped with promise, running on down the outer despite edging to his left and racing a good way apart from the winner. He will learn from the experience.
Sehnsucht(IRE) ran a nice race on his debut at Newmarket and it's a little disappointing that he was unable to build on it. That said, he was running on well at the death and a maiden at this trip should come his way. (op 9-4)
Nant Saeson(IRE)'s stable had won two of the last half-dozen renewals, including with Scintillo. After showing up well for a long way, he was not knocked about when held inside the last. A drop back to 6f may suit him at this stage. Richard Hughes reported that his mount had jumped awkwardly. Official explanation: jockey said colt jumped off awkwardly (op 7-2)
Ex Oriente(IRE), down the field when joint favourite for his debut, travelled quite well but lacked the pace to get involved when let down. He is still learning. (op 5-1 tchd 11-2 in places)
Tigers Tale(IRE), a cheap buy this year who is bred to need further in time, came in for support. He ran as if in need of this debut experience. (op 25-1)
Royal Academician(USA) ◆ made a bit progress from the rear and can leave this debut running behind with the experience to call on. (op 33-1)

3591 AMBANT GALA STKS (LISTED RACE) 1m 2f 7y
4:00 (4:00) (Class 1) 3-Y-0+
£17,013 (£6,450; £3,228; £1,608; £807; £405) **Stalls** Low

Form RPR
24-2 **1** **Class Is Class (IRE)**[41] 2290 5-9-5 111..........................(v) RyanMoore 5 118
(Sir Michael Stoute) *chsd ldrs: rdn to chse ldr ent fnl 2f: drvn ahd over 1f out: styd on strly and clr ins fnl f: rdn out* **5/1**[3]
11-0 **2** *4* **Tazeez (USA)**[97] 1000 7-9-5 116.. RichardHills 1 110
(John Gosden) *led: rdn jst over 2f out: hdd over 1f out: nt gng pce of wnr and btn 1f out: kpt on for clr 2nd* **10/3**[1]
6-20 **3** *3* **Black Spirit (USA)**[36] 2439 4-9-5 110...............................(t) LukeMorris 8 104
(Clive Cox) *chsd ldr: rdn and outpcd by ldng pair 2f out: wnt 3rd but no threat to ldng pair jst over 1f out: no imp ins fnl f* **12/1**
256/ **4** *shd* **All The Aces (IRE)**[615] 7031 6-9-5 107................................ NeilCallan 7 104
(Roger Varian) *lw: hld up in midfield: rdn 3f out: outpcd over 2f out and no threat to ldng pair fnl 2f: kpt on u.p ins fnl f: nrly snatched 3rd* **25/1**
154- **5** *1* **Fallen Idol**[328] 4829 4-9-5 106.. RobertHavlin 4 103+
(John Gosden) *hld up in last pair: stl plenty to do and switching ins jst over 2f out: rdn along and hdwy over 1f out: kpt on and pressing for 3rd towards fin: nvr trbld ldrs* **9/1**
0-11 **6** *2* **Emirates Champion**[113] 824 5-9-5 108........................(t) MartinDwyer 2 98
(Saeed Bin Suroor) *hld up towards rr: rdn jst over 2f out: sn outpcd: n.d fr wl over 1f out: kpt on past btn horses ins fnl f* **12/1**
/43- **7** *nk* **Rasmy**[420] 1858 4-9-5 107... TadhgO'Shea 10 97
(Marcus Tregoning) *hld up towards rr: rdn and no prog 3f out: styd on same pce and wl btn ins fnl f* **40/1**
42-6 **8** *1/2* **Prince Siegfried (FR)**[41] 2290 5-9-5 109......................(v) TedDurcan 11 96
(Saeed Bin Suroor) *chsd ldr tl ent fnl 2f: sn drvn and outpcd: 3rd and wl btn over 1f out: fdd ins fnl f* **14/1**
6-12 **9** *1 1/4* **Jet Away**[41] 2292 4-9-5 113.. TomQueally 6 94
(Sir Henry Cecil) *s.i.s: hld up [illegible] rdn and effrt wl over 2f out: no hdwy: wl btn whn edgd rt over 1f out* **7/1**
-635 **10** *2* **Forte Dei Marmi**[41] 2290 5-9-5 110................................... KierenFallon 9 90
(Luca Cumani) *lw: racd in last trio: rdn and hdwy but hanging rt over 2f out: sme hdwy but no ch w ldrs 2f out: wknd ins fnl f* **9/2**[2]
15-0 **11** *20* **Vesuve (IRE)**[27] 2713 5-9-5 110.................................... RichardHughes 3 50
(Saeed Bin Suroor) *b: swtg: hld up in midfield: rdn and no hdwy over 2f out: in rr and wl btn over 1f out: virtually p.u ins fnl f: t.o* **12/1**

2m 6.95s (-3.55) **Going Correction** -0.10s/f (Good) **11** Ran SP% **116.5**
Speed ratings (Par 111): **110,106,104,104,103 101,101,101,100,98 82**
toteswingers:1&2:£3.30, 2&3:£11.00, 1&3:£9.00 CSF £21.75 TOTE £5.50: £2.00, £1.70, £3.00; EX 19.60 Trifecta £214.50 Pool: £1591.75 - 5.48 winning units..
Owner R Ahamad & P Scott **Bred** P And C Scott & Exors Of The Late N Ahamad **Trained** Newmarket, Suffolk

FOCUS
Another strong renewal of this Listed race and good form for the grade. Not many were able to get involved and the first two finished clear. There are doubts over the form as prominent runners were favoured.

NOTEBOOK
Class Is Class(IRE) settled better than at Goodwood and ran down the favourite before forging away to win decisively. A welcome winner for the yard ahead of Workforce's Eclipse bid, he is at the top of his game now and is well capable of winning in Group 3 company at this sort of trip. He handles easier ground too.
Tazeez(USA), who avoided a penalty for his Group 3 win last autumn, was the form pick on this first start since finishing down the field in the Dubai Duty Free in March. Attempting to make all, he could not hold off the winner but finished nicely clear of the others. He is effective at 1m4f too and there should be opportunities for him this season either at home or abroad. (op 7-2 tchd 3-1)
Black Spirit(USA) won a 1m handicap at this fixture 12 months ago and was just denied in the Gordon Richards Stakes over this C&D on his reappearance. He was well beaten behind Workforce here next time, but the easy ground was against him that night and he ran a solid race back on this sounder surface, albeit never a threat to the first two. (tchd 11-1)
All The Aces(IRE) ◆ stayed on well late in the day and would have caught his owner's other runner for third in another stride or two. He had been off since the autumn of 2009 following a leg injury and it's to be hoped that he can progress from this very pleasing return. This was his first run over this trip since his maiden win back in 2007, and he will be seen to better effect back at 1m4f. (op 33-1)
Fallen Idol was making a belated seasonal debut and had plenty on his plate at these weights. Last in the straight, he ran on nicely down the inside for fifth without threatening to pick up the leaders. This was promising, and he is lightly raced enough to have improvement in him, but he may not prove easy to place successfully. (op 12-1)
Emirates Champion, not seen since landing two Meydan handicaps on Tapeta earlier in the year, was never a factor but did beat his two stablemates. He remains somewhat unexposed on turf. (op 14-1 tchd 16-1)
Rasmy hadn't run since finishing third in last season's Dee Stakes, having had problems. He shaped as if retaining ability, but did look to hang a little.
Jet Away missed the break and could never get involved. This was disappointing, and he has not gone on from his defeat of Sri Putra in a muddling conditions race at Lingfield. (op 5-1)
Forte Dei Marmi, who missed Ascot because of the easy ground, was another who could not get into it from the back. He finished considerably further behind Class Is Class than he had at Goodwood. (op 5-1)
Vesuve(IRE) Official explanation: jockey said horse hung right throughout

3592 ODGERS BERNDTSON H'CAP 1m 2f 7y
4:35 (4:35) (Class 3) (0-95,91) 3-Y-0+ **£7,439** (£2,213; £1,106; £553) **Stalls** Low

Form RPR
0051 **1** **Oceanway (USA)**[7] 3338 3-8-11 85 6ex................................ NeilCallan 4 101
(Mark Johnston) *led tl over 8f out: chsd ldrs after: rdn to chse ldr jst over 2f out: drvn ahd over 1f out: styd on wl u.p fnl f* **8/1**[3]
1-10 **2** *3/4* **Chain Lightning**[15] 3067 3-9-3 91.............................. RichardHughes 6 105+
(Richard Hannon) *stdd after s: t.k.h: hld up in tch on outer: rdn and effrt over 2f out: drvn to chse ldng pair over 1f out: chsd wnr ins fnl f: kpt on but nvr quite getting to wnr* **11/8**[1]
0-00 **3** *2 1/2* **Absinthe (IRE)**[20] 2909 5-9-7 84.................................. KierenFallon 9 93
(Walter Swinburn) *chsd ldr tl led over 8f out: rdn over 2f out: hdd over 1f out: edgd lft u.p 1f out: lost 2nd ins fnl f: wknd wl ins fnl f* **7/1**[2]
-301 **4** *3 1/2* **The Only Key**[21] 2884 5-9-8 85.. LukeMorris 1 87
(Jane Chapple-Hyam) *hld up in tch: effrt u.p and edgd rt 2f out: no imp tl styd on ins fnl f: nvr gng pce to chal ldrs* **10/1**
1040 **5** *1 1/2* **Sweet Origin**[12] 3203 4-9-8 85.. TedDurcan 8 84
(Marco Botti) *t.k.h: chsd ldrs: rdn jst over 2f out: hung rt and nt qckn wl over 1f out: one pce and no threat to ldrs fnl f* **9/1**
4-03 **6** *1/2* **Diescentric (USA)**[12] 3203 4-9-8 85................................ TomQueally 10 83
(Sir Henry Cecil) *lw: t.k.h: hld up in midfield: grad stdd and in last trio 7f out: rdn and effrt jst over 2f out: hdwy u.p and edgd rt jst over 1f out: plugged on but no ch w ldrs* **9/1**
-000 **7** *1 3/4* **Gunner Lindley (IRE)**[16] 3032 4-9-12 89..................... RobertWinston 2 84
(B W Hills) *stdd s: hld up in last pair: rdn and effrt on inner jst over 2f out: styng on same pce and n.d whn squeezed for room and hmpd jst over 1f out* **20/1**
00-0 **8** *1 1/2* **Botanist**[45] 2178 4-9-0 77...(t) RyanMoore 5 69
(Sir Michael Stoute) *stdd s: hld up in last: rdn and effrt jst over 2f out: no hdwy: n.d* **12/1**
5003 **9** *6* **Totally Ours**[17] 3026 4-9-11 88.. MartinDwyer 3 68
(William Muir) *hld up in midfield: rdn and no hdwy over 2f out: plugging on same pce and n.d whn squeezed for room and hmpd jst over 1f out: wl bhd and eased wl ins fnl f* **33/1**
0300 **10** *1 1/4* **Tinshu (IRE)**[30] 2604 5-9-5 82..................................... RichardHills 11 59
(Derek Haydn Jones) *chsd ldrs: wnt 2nd over 7f out tl jst over 2f out: sn wknd u.p: wl bhd and eased towards fin* **25/1**

2m 7.73s (-2.77) **Going Correction** -0.10s/f (Good)
WFA 3 from 4yo+ 11lb **10** Ran SP% **114.0**
Speed ratings (Par 107): **107,106,104,101,100 100,98,97,92,91**
toteswingers:1&2:£4.10, 2&3:£3.10, 1&3:£5.90 CSF £18.47 CT £82.31 TOTE £5.50: £1.30, £1.10, £3.00; EX 23.00 Trifecta £115.10 Pool: £1954.78 - 12.56 winning units..
Owner Sheikh Hamdan Bin Mohammed Al Maktoum **Bred** Darley **Trained** Middleham Moor, N Yorks

FOCUS
A decent handicap, run only 0.78 secs slower than the Listed race, and solid form. Again it proved difficult to make ground from the rear but a positive view has been taken of the form.

NOTEBOOK
Oceanway(USA) followed up last week's Chester win with a battling victory, showing a most willing attitude to prevail. Officially 2lb well in here under her penalty, she is a filly on the upgrade since moving up in trip. (op 9-1)
Chain Lightning's April win here is looking good form now and he ran respectably in the Britannia at Royal Ascot. Back up in trip, he did well to finish finish where he did after being settled towards the rear on a day where it proved hard for hold-up horses, but after moving through into second he could not get by the tough winner. (op 6-4 tchd 13-8)
Absinthe(IRE) bounced back from a couple of below par efforts and only gave best going to the furlong pole. He is only a pound above his last winning mark and should find winning opportunities in the coming weeks. (op 13-2 tchd 6-1)
The Only Key did not look too harshly treated off a 4lb higher mark than when winning over C&D. She stayed on for fourth and remains in decent heart. (op 11-1)
Sweet Origin was keen again and raced awkwardly under pressure, perhaps feeling the ground. He's still to fully prove himself on turf, although he had excuses last time at Pontefract. Official explanation: jockey said gelding hung right-handed (op 8-1)
Diescentric(USA) made a little late progress without troubling the principals. (op 8-1)
Botanist, tried in a tongue tie and with his stamina to prove, was held up at the back and never looked like picking up the leaders. (tchd 14-1)

3593 HOUSE OF FRASER H'CAP 1m 6f
5:05 (5:08) (Class 4) (0-85,84) 3-Y-0+ **£4,528** (£1,347; £673; £336) **Stalls** Low

Form RPR
311- **1** **Beyond (IRE)**[107] 830 4-9-8 78...................................... RobertHavlin 7 87
(David Pipe) *lw: chsd ldr: drvn to chal wl over 1f out: led ins fnl f: forged ahd fnl 75yds: styd on wl* **4/1**[2]
1201 **2** *1 1/4* **Red Kestrel (USA)**[14] 3127 6-9-7 82................................ JulieBurke(5) 5 89
(Kevin Ryan) *lw: led: rdn ent fnl 2f: hdd ins fnl f: no ex fnl 75yds* **10/1**
6000 **3** *2 3/4* **Dynamic Drive (IRE)**[20] 2931 4-9-8 78.......................... RobertWinston 2 81
(Walter Swinburn) *hld up in midfield: effrt u.p to chse ldng trio over 2f out: drvn and kpt on same pce fr over 1f out: edgd rt 1f out: wnt 3rd ins fnl f* **10/1**
0-06 **4** *nk* **Baltimore Clipper (USA)**[19] 2958 4-9-5 75...................... TomQueally 4 78+
(Paul Cole) *swtg: hld up in last trio: nt clr run over 2f out: rdn and hdwy on inner 2f out: nt clr run and swtchd lft 1f out: styd on and pressing for 3rd nr fin* **25/1**
6061 **5** *3/4* **Simonside**[14] 3115 8-9-2 72.. GrahamGibbons 1 74
(Brian Ellison) *t.k.h: chsd ldrs: rdn and effrt jst over 2f out: drvn and unable qck over 1f out: plugged on same pce and lost 2 pls ins fnl f* **8/1**
-265 **6** *2 1/2* **Nibani (IRE)**[19] 2958 4-9-11 81.......................................(v[1]) RyanMoore 12 79
(Sir Michael Stoute) *t.k.h: chsd ldrs early: grad stdd and in last trio 10f out: hdwy on outer 3f out: drvn and no prog over 1f out: wknd ins fnl f* **11/2**[3]
432 **7** *2 1/2* **Lidar (FR)**[19] 2956 6-9-13 83.. JimmyFortune 13 78
(Alan King) *lw: hld up in last trio: rdn ent fnl 3f: drvn and no hdwy jst over 2f out: nvr trbld ldrs* **10/1**

20/0 **8** *1 ½* **Double Handful (GER)**[27] 2716 5-9-5 **75**.................... CathyGannon 10 68
(Venetia Williams) *t.k.h: hld up in midfield: rdn and short of room over 2f out: drvn and no hdwy 2f out* **22/1**

1-20 **9** *4 ½* **Kitty Wells**[23] 2812 4-10-0 **84**.. KierenFallon 11 70
(Luca Cumani) *t.k.h: chsd ldrs: rdn over 2f out: wknd wl over 1f out: eased wl ins fnl f* **7/2**[1]

3m 4.19s (-0.31) **Going Correction** -0.10s/f (Good) **9** Ran SP% **104.2**
Speed ratings (Par 105): **96,95,93,93,93 91,90,89,86**
toteswingers:1&2:£4.70, 2&3:£13.90, 1&3:£9.10 CSF £35.33 CT £268.23 TOTE £4.50: £2.00, £2.30, £3.00; EX 38.30 Trifecta £383.30 Pool: £631.95 - 1.22 winning units..
Owner R J H Geffen **Bred** Pat Fullam **Trained** Nicholashayne, Devon
■ Broughtons Point was withdrawn (13/2, ref to ent stalls). Deduct 10p in the £ under R4.
■ Stewards' Enquiry : Julie Burke two-day ban: used whip with excessive frequency (Jul 15-16)

FOCUS
The runner-up set a relatively steady pace in this fair handicap. Once again prominent racers seemed favoured so with that in mind the form is not rated as positively as it might have been. The winner was unexposed on the Flat.
T/Jkpt: Part won. £26,906.80 to a £1 stake. Pool of £37,896.95 - 0.50 winning units. T/Plt: £151.40 to a £1 stake. Pool of £80,462.07 - 387.78 winning tickets. T/Qpdt: £23.00 to a £1 stake. Pool of £6,527.77 - 209.63 winning tickets. SP

3320 WARWICK (L-H)

Friday, July 1

OFFICIAL GOING: Good to firm (good in places)
Wind: Light across Weather: Cloudy with sunny spells

3594 NICK BILL MEMORIAL FUND MAIDEN STKS — 7f 26y
2:10 (2:13) (Class 5) 3-4-Y-O **£2,587** (£770; £384; £192) **Stalls** Low

Form RPR

223 **1** **Moone's My Name**[24] 2790 3-8-12 76................................ JimCrowley 9 85+
(Ralph Beckett) *a.p: chsd ldr over 4f out: rdn to ld over 1f out: edgd rt ins fnl f: r.o wl* **5/4**[1]

32 **2** *3 ¾* **Escape To Glory (USA)**[13] 3173 3-9-3 0.......................... GeorgeBaker 7 80+
(Mikael Magnusson) *chsd ldr tl led 5f out: rdn and hdd over 1f out: styd on same pce* **7/2**[2]

5-0 **3** *7* **Queen's Choice (IRE)**[15] 3090 3-8-12 0.......................... StephenCraine 11 56
(Anabel K Murphy) *mid-div: hdwy 1/2-way: rdn over 2f out: styd on same pce: wnt 3rd ins fnl f: nvr trbld ldrs* **150/1**

22-6 **4** *4* **Chokidar (IRE)**[42] 2255 3-9-3 76.......................... DaneO'Neill 6 50
(David Nicholls) *led 2f: chsd ldrs: rdn over 2f out: wknd over 1f out* **13/2**[3]

260- **5** *¾* **Greek Islands (IRE)**[269] 6647 3-8-12 77...................... HarryBentley(5) 5 48
(Ed de Giles) *chsd ldrs: rdn over 2f out: wknd over 1f out* **12/1**

6 *shd* **Anrheg** 3-8-12 0.. FrannyNorton 13 43
(David Brown) *sn pushed along in rr: shkn up over 2f out: nvr on terms* **40/1**

0- **7** *6* **Alston**[198] 7880 3-9-3 0................................ FergusSweeney 12 32
(David Arbuthnot) *hld up: rdn over 2f out: sn wknd* **100/1**

0 **8** *hd* **Pastoral Jet**[13] 3173 3-8-10 0.......................... LukeRowe(7) 10 31
(Richard Rowe) *s.s: bhd: stl last 1/2-way: nvr nrr* **150/1**

9 *nk* **Outpost (IRE)** 3-9-3 0.. SamHitchcott 3 30
(Alan Bailey) *sn pushed along and a in rr: bhd fr 1/2-way* **50/1**

66- **10** *1 ¼* **Daa'Iman**[254] 7020 3-8-12 0.. ChrisCatlin 1 22
(Clive Brittain) *prom: rdn over 2f out: sn wknd* **12/1**

06 **11** *9* **Pagan Warrior (IRE)**[21] 2875 3-9-0 0.............................(t) JohnFahy(3) 8 —
(Clive Cox) *sn pushed along in rr: bhd fr 1/2-way* **28/1**

0 **12** *34* **Partly Pickled**[29] 2650 3-9-0 0.......................... BillyCray(3) 2 —
(David Nicholls) *s.i.s: sn pushed along and a in rr: bhd fr 1/2-way: t.o* **66/1**

1m 25.24s (0.64) **Going Correction** +0.125s/f (Good) **12** Ran SP% **107.0**
Speed ratings (Par 103): **101,96,88,84,83 83,76,76,75,74 64,25**
toteswingers:1&2:£1.30, 2&3:£30.60, 1&3:£24.50 CSF £4.29 TOTE £2.20: £1.10, £1.40, £16.90; EX 5.10.
Owner McDonagh Murphy And Nixon **Bred** Baroness Bloodstock & Tweenhills Stud **Trained** Kimpton, Hants
■ Sole Danser (11/1) was withdrawn after refusing to enter the stalls. Deduct 5p in the £ under R4.

FOCUS
A weakish maiden but the first pair were clear in a fair time. It was run at a sound pace and the form is straightforward enough, rated around the second.

3595 JOIN TODAY AT REWARDS4RACING.COM NOVICE AUCTION STKS — 7f 26y
2:40 (2:43) (Class 5) 2-Y-O **£2,587** (£770; £384; £192) **Stalls** Low

Form RPR

13 **1** **Percy Jackson**[21] 2868 2-8-13 0.......................... JohnFahy(3) 6 93+
(Denis Coakley) *chsd ldr: led over 1f out: rdn clr fnl f: easily* **5/2**[1]

5153 **2** *8* **Snowed In (IRE)**[21] 2889 2-8-13 0.......................... FergusSweeney 3 70
(J S Moore) *hld up: hdwy 1/2-way: rdn over 1f out: styd on u.p to go 2nd wl ins fnl f: no ch w wnr* **12/1**

41 **3** *¾* **Loyal Master (IRE)**[15] 3070 2-9-1 0.......................... LeeNewman 1 70
(George Foster) *chsd ldr: rdn over 2f out: hung rt over 1f out: wknd ins fnl f* **4/1**[3]

1634 **4** *1 ½* **Red Hearts (IRE)**[20] 2902 2-8-8 0.......................... AdamBeschizza(3) 4 62
(Julia Feilden) *led: clr 5f out: rdn and hdd over 1f out: sn hung rt and wknd* **12/1**

321 **5** *¾* **Grand Gold**[35] 2460 2-8-10 0.......................... MartinHarley(3) 5 63
(Mick Channon) *prom: rdn 1/2-way: outpcd over 2f out: n.d after* **3/1**[2]

51 **6** *shd* **Netley Marsh**[24] 2788 2-9-1 0.......................... DaneO'Neill 2 64
(Richard Hannon) *dwlt: pushed along and hdwy 6f out: sn drvn along and outpcd: n.d after* **9/2**

7 *11* **Diamond Marks (IRE)** 2-9-0 0.......................... ChrisCatlin 7 36
(John Gallagher) *s.s: outpcd* **50/1**

1m 26.13s (1.53) **Going Correction** +0.125s/f (Good) **7** Ran SP% **109.1**
Speed ratings (Par 94): **96,86,86,84,83 83,70**
toteswingers:1&2:£4.10, 2&3:£9.90, 1&3:£1.50 CSF £29.46 TOTE £3.20: £1.80, £6.10; EX 34.70.
Owner Count Calypso Racing **Bred** Clive Dennett **Trained** West Ilsley, Berks

FOCUS
This looked a fair novice event with all six with form being previous winners, three of them last time out. It was run at a strong pace and it saw an impressive winner. The second is probably the best guide.

NOTEBOOK
Percy Jackson, who was conceding weight all round, bumped into one in this class at Chepstow last time, but had won nicely on debut and this rates a clear personal-best effort up in trip. The strong pace was clearly right up his street, as was returning to a flatter track, and connections will rightly have to think about something more valuable for him now. A Listed race in Germany is likely to now figure on his agenda. (op 10-3)
Snowed In(IRE) locked horns with the winner near the stands' side from 2f out, but was firmly put in his place. He was beaten in a seller at York last time, but that was a valuable race of its type and this does rate his best effort so far. He got the extra furlong well enough and is a likely type for nurseries. (op 10-1)
Loyal Master(IRE), who got warm beforehand, was the proven stayer in the race and helps to set the level. He will probably struggle to win one of these, but also appeals as the sort to win a nursery. (op 10-3)
Red Hearts(IRE), having a first outing over this far, attained a clear lead and didn't hang about. She kept more towards the far side after straightening up and was done with 2f out. A drop back in trip looks on the cards.
Grand Gold comfortably beat Loyal Master when making it third time lucky at Newcastle in May. He never looked that happy up to this trip off a quick tempo and clearly has limitations. (op 7-2)
Netley Marsh won over 6f at Salisbury last time out and seemed sure to appreciate this extra furlong, but he was one of the first in trouble. Perhaps the track was not for him. (op 7-2)

3596 PREMIER PLANNING CAUTIOUSLY MANAGED (S) STKS — 1m 2f 188y
3:10 (3:11) (Class 6) 3-Y-O **£2,045** (£603; £302) **Stalls** Low

Form RPR

5024 **1** **Urban Kode (IRE)**[2] 3514 3-8-13 63.............................(v) KieranO'Neill(5) 10 66
(David Evans) *mde all: rdn over 1f out: edgd rt: r.o* **2/1**[1]

-550 **2** *¾* **Newby Lodge (IRE)**[9] 3268 3-8-8 55.......................... ShaneKelly 8 54
(William Haggas) *plld hrd: trckd wnr 9f out: rdn over 1f out: r.o* **9/2**[3]

3206 **3** *6* **Enriching (USA)**[14] 3131 3-8-13 67.............................(t) DaneO'Neill 7 48
(David Elsworth) *hld up: hdwy over 4f out: rdn over 2f out: styd on same pce fr over 1f out* **9/2**[3]

6044 **4** *1 ½* **Sing Alana Sing**[29] 2652 3-8-5 50.............................(t) KierenFox(3) 4 40
(Bill Turner) *chsd ldrs: rdn and hung lft over 3f out: wknd ins fnl f* **14/1**

600- **5** *1 ¼* **Romantic Girl (IRE)**[230] 7452 3-8-8 40.......................... LiamJones 9 38
(Alan Juckes) *hld up: plld hrd: hdwy over 2f out: rdn over 1f out: wknd ins fnl f* **66/1**

4510 **6** *3 ½* **Highlife Dancer**[17] 3018 3-9-4 62.......................... SamHitchcott 3 41
(Mick Channon) *hld up: nt clr run 3f out: shkn up over 1f out: nvr on terms* **3/1**[2]

0000 **7** *3* **Duchess Of Magenta (IRE)**[11] 3226 3-8-3 52.......................... AmyScott(5) 5 25
(Eve Johnson Houghton) *mid-div: rdn over 3f out: wknd over 2f out* **33/1**

-100 **8** *5* **Appyjack**[11] 3226 3-9-4 54.............................(t) FrannyNorton 2 26
(Tony Carroll) *mid-div: wknd over 3f out* **20/1**

6026 **9** *14* **Jane's Legacy**[23] 2801 3-8-8 45.......................... ChrisCatlin 1 —
(Reg Hollinshead) *chsd wnr 2f: remained handy: rdn over 3f out: wknd over 2f out: t.o* **33/1**

000- **P** **Tea And Sympathy**[263] 6811 3-8-5 0.............................(tp) AdamBeschizza(3) 6 —
(John Holt) *s.s: outpcd: t.o whn p.u over 1f out* **100/1**

2m 22.31s (1.21) **Going Correction** +0.125s/f (Good) **10** Ran SP% **114.5**
Speed ratings (Par 98): **100,99,95,94,93 90,88,84,74,—**
toteswingers:1&2:£2.50, 2&3:£3.70, 1&3:£2.20 CSF £10.57 TOTE £3.20: £1.20, £2.10, £1.80; EX 13.90.There was no bid for the winner. Newby Lodge was claimed by A. Bailey for £6000.
Owner Mrs B Grainger **Bred** Nils Koop **Trained** Pandy, Monmouths

FOCUS
A typically weak 3-y-o seller in which none of them had previously won over a distance this far. The first two were always the front pair.

3597 SUE HOWELLS ART FILLIES' H'CAP — 5f 110y
3:45 (3:47) (Class 5) (0-70,68) 3-Y-O+ **£2,587** (£770; £384; £192) **Stalls** Low

Form RPR

0055 **1** **Delira (IRE)**[11] 3230 3-8-8 **61**.......................... HarryBentley(5) 4 71
(Jonathan Portman) *chsd ldrs: outpcd 3f out: hdwy and swtchd lft over 1f out: r.o to ld nr fin* **11/2**

-404 **2** *nk* **Adventure Story**[6] 3412 4-9-5 **61**.......................... FergusSweeney 1 71
(Peter Makin) *s.i.s: hld up in tch: plld hrd: chsd ldr 2f out: rdn to ld ins fnl f: hdd nr fin* **4/1**[3]

-561 **3** *2 ½* **Bouncy Bouncy (IRE)**[10] 3261 4-9-5 **61** 6ex.................(t) HayleyTurner 2 62
(Michael Bell) *w ldr tl led over 3f out: rdn and edgd rt 2f out: hdd and no ex ins fnl f* **5/4**[1]

-422 **4** *1 ½* **Suzy Alexander**[41] 2303 4-9-4 **60**.......................... ChrisCatlin 6 56
(David Simcock) *edgd rt s: chsd ldrs: hmpd 2f out: sn rdn: styd on same pce ins fnl f* **11/4**[2]

00-0 **5** *13* **Thalia Grace**[20] 2920 4-8-11 **53**.......................... LeeNewman 3 —
(Les Hall) *led 2f: chsd ldr: rdn over 2f out: wknd over 1f out* **16/1**

67.15 secs (1.25) **Going Correction** +0.20s/f (Good)
WFA 3 from 4yo 5lb **5** Ran SP% **112.4**
Speed ratings (Par 100): **99,98,95,93,75**
CSF £27.01 TOTE £6.50: £2.60, £1.90; EX 27.40.
Owner Portlee Bloodstock **Bred** Carrigbeg Stud Ltd **Trained** Compton, Berks
■ Stewards' Enquiry : Hayley Turner two-day ban: careless riding (Jul 15-16)

FOCUS
A moderate sprint handicap for fillies. They didn't go that quick early on, resulting in most taking a keen hold, and the field came stands' side in the home straight. The winner is rated back to her best.

3598 AARCA SALES RECRUITMENT 10 YEAR ANNIVERSARY H'CAP — 6f
4:20 (4:21) (Class 4) (0-80,77) 3-Y-O **£6,469** (£1,925; £962; £481) **Stalls** Low

Form RPR

1115 **1** **Barkston Ash**[20] 2911 3-9-3 **75**.......................... DuranFentiman 5 80
(Eric Alston) *chsd ldrs: led over 2f out: rdn over 1f out: r.o* **9/2**[3]

3452 **2** *¾* **Restless Bay (IRE)**[9] 3269 3-9-5 **77**.............................(v) ChrisCatlin 8 79
(Reg Hollinshead) *s.i.s: sn prom: rdn over 1f out: r.o* **14/1**

1221 **3** *nk* **Close To The Edge (IRE)**[12] 3207 3-9-2 **77** 6ex......... MartinHarley(3) 1 78
(Alan McCabe) *chsd ldrs: rdn over 1f out: r.o* **4/1**[2]

0060 **4** *hd* **Penny's Pearl (IRE)**[16] 3048 3-9-0 **77**.......................... KieranO'Neill(5) 7 78
(David Evans) *s.i.s: hld up: hdwy over 1f out: nt clr run and swtchd lft ins fnl f: r.o: nvr able to chal* **28/1**

-605 **5** *shd* **Whipphound**[22] 2834 3-9-0 **72**.......................... TomMcLaughlin 3 72
(Mark Brisbourne) *hld up: hdwy over 1f out: sn rdn and edgd rt: r.o* **10/1**

1363 **6** *½* **Apollo D'Negro (IRE)**[21] 2878 3-8-13 **74**.............................(b) JohnFahy(3) 9 73
(Clive Cox) *sn rdn to ld: hdd over 2f out: no ex u.p wl ins fnl f* **7/2**[1]

0043 **7** *½* **Strictly Pink (IRE)**[14] 3114 3-9-5 **77**.......................... LiamJones 4 74
(Alan Bailey) *prom: rdn over 1f out: no ex wl ins fnl f* **14/1**

-201 **8** *12* **Da Ponte**[14] 3122 3-9-5 **77**.......................... ShaneKelly 2 36
(Walter Swinburn) *chsd ldrs: rdn over 2f out: wknd fnl f* **9/2**[3]

2662 **9** *4* **Roman Dancer (IRE)**[25] 2757 3-9-2 **74**...................... FergusSweeney 6 20
(John Gallagher) *w ldr tl rdn over 2f out: n.m.r over 1f out: sn wknd and eased* **12/1**

1m 12.65s (0.85) **Going Correction** +0.20s/f (Good) **9** Ran SP% **112.2**
Speed ratings (Par 102): **102,101,100,100,100 99,98,82,77**
toteswingers:1&2:£5.80, 2&3:£10.00, 1&3:£2.80 CSF £62.24 CT £270.27 TOTE £5.40: £2.50, £4.50, £1.10; EX 38.60.

Owner The Selebians **Bred** Jonathan Shack **Trained** Longton, Lancs

■ Stewards' Enquiry : Liam Jones caution: careless riding.

FOCUS
A competitive sprint handicap for the class and there was a very tight finish. There are one or two doubts over the form.

Da Ponte Official explanation: jockey said gelding never travelled

3599 C3 MIDLANDS DESIGN AND PRINT SOLUTIONS H'CAP 1m 6f 213y
4:55 (4:56) (Class 6) (0-65,64) 3-Y-0+ **£2,264** (£673; £336; £168) **Stalls** Low

Form RPR

320- **1** **Lastroseofsummer (IRE)**[33] 5963 5-10-0 **64**................. MartinLane 12 75
(Rae Guest) *chsd ldr tl led over 2f out: rdn over 1f out: jst hld on* **12/1**

4215 **2** *shd* **Mokalif**[7] 3364 3-8-8 **61**...(v) HayleyTurner 9 72
(Michael Bell) *a.p: racd keenly: rdn to chse wnr and hung lft fr over 1f out: styd on* **9/4**[1]

-252 **3** *8* **Dr Darcey**[20] 2904 3-8-5 **63**..(b) KieranO'Neill(5) 10 64
(Richard Hannon) *led: rdn and hdd over 2f out: wknd ins fnl f* **4/1**[2]

323- **4** *1* **Viviani (IRE)**[200] 6955 4-9-13 **63**....................................... GeorgeBaker 6 62
(Amanda Perrett) *hld up: drvn along 10f out: hdwy u.p over 2f out: nt rch ldrs* **9/1**

0545 **5** *hd* **Duar Mapel (USA)**[8] 3300 5-8-11 **50**..................(b) AdamBeschizza(3) 13 49
(Brian Baugh) *sn pushed along and prom: rdn over 2f out: wknd over 1f out* **33/1**

31-0 **6** *1* **Drawn Gold**[43] 2224 7-9-7 **64**... JackDuern(7) 5 62
(Reg Hollinshead) *mid-div: rdn over 3f out: nvr trbld ldrs* **25/1**

-613 **7** *1* **Ivanov (IRE)**[22] 2857 3-7-12 **51**.................................... AdrianMcCarthy 1 47
(Willie Musson) *hld up in tch: rdn over 3f out: wknd over 2f out* **5/1**[3]

0-05 **8** *2 1/4* **Jenny Soba**[10] 3243 8-8-11 **47**... DaneO'Neill 7 41
(Lucinda Featherstone) *dwlt: hld up: rdn over 2f out: n.d* **16/1**

14-4 **9** *2 3/4* **Foreign King (USA)**[33] 955 7-8-11 **52**....................(p) HarryBentley(5) 8 42
(Mike Hammond) *chsd ldrs: rdn over 4f out: wknd over 2f out* **25/1**

06-3 **10** *nk* **Haka Dancer (USA)**[13] 3187 8-8-4 **47** ow1................(p) DavidKenny(7) 2 37
(Philip Kirby) *s.i.s: hld up: wknd over 5f out* **22/1**

45-5 **11** *11* **The Composer**[21] 2873 9-8-9 **45**... ChrisCatlin 4 20
(Michael Blanshard) *in rr and pushed along thrght: wknd 3f out: t.o* **20/1**

0400 **12** *13* **Burnbrake**[23] 2820 6-9-3 **53**..(b) LiamJones 3 11
(Les Hall) *s.i.s: hld up: hdwy over 6f out: rdn and wknd over 2f out: t.o* **50/1**

-233 **13** *16* **Dove Cottage (IRE)**[28] 2659 9-9-5 **55**...................... FergusSweeney 11 —
(Stuart Kittow) *hld up in tch: racd keenly: rdn and wknd over 2f out: t.o* **9/1**

3m 21.16s (2.16) **Going Correction** +0.125s/f (Good)
WFA 3 from 4yo+ 17lb **13** Ran SP% **122.7**
Speed ratings (Par 101): **99,98,94,94,94 93,92,91,90,90 84,77,68**
toteswingers:1&2:£6.30, 2&3:£2.40, 1&3:£11.50 CSF £37.11 CT £135.89 TOTE £14.40: £2.50, £1.10, £1.70; EX 59.10.

Owner E P Duggan **Bred** Mount Coote Stud **Trained** Newmarket, Suffolk

FOCUS
Low-grade stuff, but it was competitive enough for the class. There was an uneven pace on and it proved an advantage to race handily, with the first pair dominating from 2f out. They both showed improvement and could be worth more at face value.

3600 [illegible] H'CAP 1m 4f 134y
5:25 (5:25) (Class 6) (0-60,55) 4-Y-0+ **£1,704** ([illegible]) [illegible]

Form RPR

0045 **1** **Lucky Diva**[20] 2900 4-8-6 **45**...(p) JakePayne(3) 10 53
(Bill Turner) *s.i.s: hld up: hdwy over 4f out: rdn to ld over 1f out: edgd rt ins fnl f: styd on* **16/1**

3523 **2** *3 1/2* **Naledi**[8] 3311 7-8-7 **48**... JacobButterfield(5) 3 51
(Richard Price) *chsd ldrs: rdn and ev ch whn hung lft fr over 1f out: styd on same pce ins fnl f* **3/1**[1]

40-U **3** *3/4* **Back To Paris (IRE)**[29] 630 9-8-12 **48**.......................(p) NatashaEaton 9 49
(Philip Kirby) *hld up in tch: rdn over 2f out: nt clr run and swtchd lft over 1f out: r.o* **25/1**

50-3 **4** *3 1/4* **Jocheski (IRE)**[20] 2905 7-9-2 **55**................................ ThomasBrown(3) 5 51
(Tony Newcombe) *led: hdd over 3f out: rdn and ev ch over 1f out: wknd ins fnl f* **7/2**[2]

20/2 **5** *2* **Ishismart**[32] 2569 7-8-6 **50**.. NicolaJackson(8) 6 43
(Reg Hollinshead) *chsd ldr: led over 3f out: rdn and hdd over 1f out: wknd ins fnl f* **11/2**

-300 **6** *3 3/4* **Crazy Bold (GER)**[52] 1987 8-8-8 **47**........................ GeorgeDowning(3) 7 34
(Tony Carroll) *s.i.s: hld up: rdn over 3f out: n.d* **5/1**[3]

056/ **7** *12* **Son Of Sophie**[1674] 615 9-8-9 **45**............................(v[1]) RachealKneller 4 14
(Christopher Kellett) *chsd ldr: rdn over 2f out: sn wknd* **12/1**

/0-0 **8** *2* **Pergamon (IRE)**[9] 1443 5-9-4 **54**......................................(t) NoraLooby 2 20
(Claire Dyson) *hld up: a in rr: wknd over 3f out* **25/1**

60-1 **9** *3 1/4* **Steady Gaze**[7] 3353 6-8-12 **51** 6ex.................................. LukeRowe(3) 8 12
(Richard Rowe) *hld up: bhd fnl 5f* **5/1**[3]

2m 45.75s (1.15) **Going Correction** +0.125s/f (Good) **9** Ran SP% **117.2**
Speed ratings (Par 101): **101,98,98,96,95 92,85,84,82**
toteswingers:1&2:£6.50, 2&3:£12.30, 1&3:£11.80 CSF £64.81 CT £1213.78 TOTE £12.50: £3.80, £1.10, £6.20; EX 74.80.

Owner Darren Coombes **Bred** Gracelands Stud **Trained** Sigwells, Somerset

FOCUS
A very moderate handicap, confined to apprentice riders, that was run at a suicidal early pace. The winner probably only needed to match her old turf mark.

T/Plt: £192.80 to a £1 stake. Pool of £44,824.22 - 169.71 winning tickets. T/Qpdt: £66.50 to a £1 stake. Pool of £3,721.86 - 41.40 winning tickets. CR

3601 - 3608a (Foreign Racing) - See Raceform Interactive

[3569]BEVERLEY (R-H)
Saturday, July 2

OFFICIAL GOING: Good to firm (firm in places; 8.4)
Wind: Light half behind Weather: Fine and dry

3609 AWARD WINNING COACHMAN CARAVANS MEDIAN AUCTION MAIDEN STKS 7f 100y
1:50 (1:51) (Class 6) 2-Y-0 **£2,181** (£644; £322) **Stalls** Low

Form RPR

43 **1** **Elkhart (IRE)**[7] 3401 2-9-3 0... DarrylHolland 5 83+
(Mark Johnston) *mde all: pushed clr over 2f out: rdn over 1f out: styd on strly* **4/1**[2]

44 **2** *3* **Badea**[15] 3123 2-9-3 0.. PaulHanagan 3 76
(Richard Fahey) *trckd ldng pair: hdwy on inner to chse wnr 1/2-way: rdn along 2f out: rdn wl over 1f out: sn no imp* **11/4**[1]

42 **3** *2* **Tidal Way (IRE)**[8] 3349 2-9-0 0..................................... MartinHarley(3) 9 70
(Mick Channon) *trckd ldrs: hdwy to chse ldng pair 3f out: rdn over 2f out: drvn and no imp fr over 1f out* **9/2**[3]

4 *3* **Daring Damsel (IRE)** 2-8-12 0.. PJMcDonald 8 58
(Paul Cole) *chsd wnr to 1/2-way: rdn along wl over 2f out: sn wknd* **20/1**

6 **5** *1* **Glad Eye Gladys**[12] 3229 2-8-12 0................................. FrederikTylicki 4 56
(David Nicholls) *in tch: rdn along 3f out: drvn wl over 1f out: sn one pce* **12/1**

6 *1/2* **Saffa Hill (IRE)** 2-9-3 0.. DavidAllan 1 60
(Tim Easterby) *midfield: hdwy on inner 2f out: swtchd lft and rdn over 1f out: kpt on same pce fnl f* **10/1**

3 **7** *1 1/4* **Rosie's Lady (IRE)**[13] 3201 2-8-12 0.......................... DanielTudhope 12 52
(David O'Meara) *in tch: hdwy on outer wl over 2f out: sn rdn and no imp fr wl over 1f out* **20/1**

8 *1 3/4* **Clare Island Boy (IRE)** 2-9-3 0.................................. RobertWinston 11 53+
(Richard Hannon) *bhd tl sme late hdwy* **11/2**

3430 **9** *2 3/4* **Sabusa (IRE)**[47] 2148 2-9-0 0... SeanLevey(3) 7 46
(Alan McCabe) *chsd ldrs: rdn along wl over 2f out: sn wknd* **22/1**

6 **10** *1/2* **Artistic Thread (IRE)**[8] 3349 2-9-3 0.......................... StevieDonohoe 6 45
(Sir Mark Prescott Bt) *a in rr* **50/1**

0 **11** *1/2* **Dazzlin Bluebell (IRE)**[10] 3273 2-8-12 0..................... TonyHamilton 10 39
(Tim Easterby) *a in rr* **14/1**

1m 32.46s (-1.34) **Going Correction** -0.35s/f (Firm) **11** Ran SP% **119.5**
Speed ratings (Par 92): **93,89,87,83,82 82,80,78,75,75 74**
toteswingers 1&2:£1.70, 1&3:£1.70, 2&3:£3.80 CSF £14.86 TOTE £4.30: £1.20, £1.50, £1.90; EX 10.30.

Owner Sheikh Hamdan Bin Mohammed Al Maktoum **Bred** Darley **Trained** Middleham Moor, N Yorks

FOCUS
A modest maiden and the front three in the betting dominated.

NOTEBOOK
Elkhart(IRE) built on his first two efforts, making all under an astute ride, with Darryl Holland gradually increasing the pace with 4f to run. He never looked in danger, appreciated this faster surface and will get further. He won a shade cosily and looks capable of stepping up in class. (op 3-1 tchd 11-4)

Badea came here with the best form of those who had run. In a noseband for the first time, he took a keen hold early on, which sapped his stamina. He battled on but couldn't quicken when the winner kicked. He is still improving, but is a big, backward horse, and there are races to be won with him. (tchd 3-1)

Tidal Way(IRE) ran on well past beaten horses, suggesting he will appreciate a stiffer test. He wasn't well drawn and did well in the circumstances. (op 4-1)

Daring Damsel(IRE), a half-sister to winners, knew her job and made an encouraging debut, despite having no chance with the winner. She has a future in this game, and will get this trip in time. (op 25-1)

Glad Eye Gladys didn't really improve from her first run over 6f at Windsor, not staying the longer trip. (op 16-1)

Saffa Hill(IRE) had the inside draw but found himself a little boxed in on the rail when the tempo [illegible] but he will have learned plenty. The stable's youngsters usually improve for their [illegible] enough for him. (op 14-1)

Clare Island Boy(IRE), a well-grown, scopey colt, looked fit enough to do himself justice on his debut, but ran a little green. (tchd 5-1 and 13-2)

Dazzlin Bluebell(IRE) attracted some money, but while this distance should have suited her, she failed to settle. Consequently, she didn't get the trip. (op 22-1)

3610 BRITISH STALLION STUDS E B F LEISURE FURNISHINGS MAIDEN STKS (DIV I) 5f
2:25 (2:27) (Class 5) 2-Y-0 **£2,911** (£866; £432; £216) **Stalls** Low

Form RPR

20 **1** **Springinmystep (IRE)**[18] 3014 2-9-3 0........................ FrederikTylicki 2 83+
(Michael Dods) *trckd ldrs: hdwy to ld over 1f out: sn rdn and kpt on strly fnl f* **15/8**[1]

2 *2 3/4* **Kimbali (IRE)** 2-8-13 0... PaulHanagan 4 69+
(Richard Fahey) *trckd ldrs on inner: effrt 2f out: rdn to chse wnr ent fnl f: no imp towards fin* **2/1**[2]

232 **3** *2 1/4* **Right Result (IRE)**[22] 2886 2-9-3 0............................... DarrylHolland 6 65
(Richard Hannon) *dwlt and towards rr: hdwy on inner and in tch 1/2-way: rdn wl over 1f out: styd on wl fnl f: nrst fin* **10/3**[3]

5 **4** *hd* **Baltic Bomber (IRE)**[17] 3050 2-9-3 0................................. PJMcDonald 1 64
(John Quinn) *cl up: led 1/2-way: rdn and hdd over 1f out: wknd* **28/1**

062 **5** *1* **Stepper Point**[19] 2992 2-9-3 0.. StevieDonohoe 5 61
(William Muir) *trckd ldrs: effrt and nt clr run over 1f out: swtchd lft and rdn ins fnl f: one pce* **12/1**

6 *1 1/4* **Trust Fund Babe (IRE)** 2-8-8 0.. DavidAllan 7 47+
(Tim Easterby) *dwlt and in rr: pushed along 1/2-way: rdn wl over 1f out: kpt on u.p fnl f: nrst fin* **66/1**

00 **7** *nk* **Elusive Bonus (IRE)**[3] 3504 2-8-12 0.......................... DanielTudhope 9 50
(David O'Meara) *in tch: rdn along over 2f out: sn drvn and wknd* **100/1**

8 *nse* **Dandy's Hero (IRE)** 2-8-13 0.. AndrewMullen 8 51
(David Nicholls) *led to 1/2-way: sn rdn along and wknd wl over 1f out* **50/1**

9 *1* **Lollina Paulina** 2-8-9 0 ow1.. StephenCraine 10 43
(Kevin Ryan) *a towards rr* **66/1**

10 *1 1/2* **Dark Ambition (IRE)** 2-8-13 0.. LiamJones 11 42
(William Haggas) *s.i.s: a in rr* **9/1**

11 7 **Hatsumomo (IRE)** 2-8-9 0 ow1 RobertWinston 3 13
(Tim Easterby) *a towards rr* **66/1**
61.81 secs (-1.69) **Going Correction** -0.35s/f (Firm) 11 Ran SP% **119.8**
Speed ratings (Par 94): **99,94,91,90,89 87,86,86,84,82 71**
toteswingers: 1&2 £2.10, 1&3 £1.20, 2&3 £2.50 CSF £5.90 TOTE £2.60: £1.10, £1.10, £1.10; EX 9.50.
Owner Andrew Tinkler **Bred** Dr D Harron **Trained** Denton, Co Durham

FOCUS
A decent maiden for the money.

NOTEBOOK
Springinmystep(IRE), dropped in class after running eighth in the Windsor Castle at Royal Ascot, was all the rage. Settled in third after breaking well, he was given plenty of daylight on the outside and asserted his authority just inside the final furlong, drawing away for a comfortable victory. He will get further on this evidence. (op 5-2)
Kimbali(IRE) made an eyecatching debut, having apparently been showing plenty of speed at home. He travelled well throughout, with the rail to help him, and was a clear second. His pedigree suggests he'll get 1m, although he may be better off over 6f for now. (tchd 9-4 and 15-8 in places)
Right Result(IRE) was slowly away and made plenty of headway up the rail late on. He's been in the frame on all four starts, and while you could not say he was unlucky here, surely his turn won't be far away. (tchd 3-1 and 7-2)
Baltic Bomber(IRE) appeared to have improved markedly from his Ripon debut and led them into the straight. He still looked a little green, but clearly has ability and stuck to his guns once the winner had passed him. (op 25-1)
Stepper Point appeared to be cruising in behind the leaders with 2f to go and didn't have a lot of room, but once the gap belatedly opened, he didn't really pick up. An easy 6f might be ideal for him. (op 9-1)
Trust Fund Babe(IRE) missed the break completely, but soon got going and made an reasonably encouraging debut, without looking threatening.

3611 BRITISH STALLION STUDS E B F LEISURE FURNISHINGS MAIDEN STKS (DIV II) 5f
3:00 (3:01) (Class 5) 2-Y-O **£2,911** (£866; £432; £216) **Stalls** Low

Form				RPR
6	**1**		**Ocean Myth**[10] 3270 2-8-12 0 LiamJones 8 (William Haggas) *wnt lft s: sn led and swtchd rt to inner rail: clr 2f out: rdn and kpt on strly fnl f* **4/1**[3]	70+
0420	**2**	2 ¾	**Red Shadow**[22] 2886 2-8-12 0 DarryllHolland 6 (Alan Brown) *sn chsng wnr: effrt 2f out: sn rdn and no imp fnl f* **8/1**	59
0	**3**	nk	**Zaffy (IRE)**[49] 2113 2-8-12 0 DavidAllan 1 (Tim Easterby) *s.i.s and towards rr: hdwy on inner 1/2-way: swtchd lft and rdn wl over 1f out: kpt on ins fnl f: nrst fin* **5/2**[1]	58+
0	**4**	3	**Our Boy Jack (IRE)**[91] 1095 2-9-3 0 PaulHanagan 5 (Richard Fahey) *hmpd s: in rr: pushed along and hdwy over 1f out: styd on ins fnl f: nrst fin* **11/4**[2]	52+
	5	¾	**True Bond** 2-8-8 0 AndrewHeffernan 3 (Geoffrey Oldroyd) *prom: rdn along over 2f out: grad wknd* **14/1**	41
	6	¾	**Uncle Timmy** 2-8-10 0 DeclanCannon(3) 2 (John Quinn) *chsd ldrs: rdn along wl over 1f out: sn drvn and wknd appr fnl f* **11/2**	43
00	**7**	5	**Mick Slates (IRE)**[19] 2983 2-8-12 0 NeilFarley(5) 4 (Declan Carroll) *in tch: rdn along 1/2-way: sn wknd* **40/1**	29
	8	1 ¾	**Precious Little** 2-8-5 0 BillyCray(3) 10 (David Nicholls) *a towards rr* **14/1**	14
	9	½	**Borley Ghost (FR)** 2-8-13 0 PJMcDonald 7 (John Quinn) *in tch: rdn along bef 1/2-way: sn outpcd* **25/1**	17

63.06 secs (-0.44) **Going Correction** -0.35s/f (Firm) 9 Ran SP% **121.4**
Speed ratings (Par 94): **89,84,84,79,78 76,68,66,65**
toteswingers: 1&2 £2.90, 1&3 £2.40, 2&3 £6.20 CSF £37.99 TOTE £4.00: £1.10, £2.90, £1.30; EX 23.20.
Owner Cheveley Park Stud **Bred** Mill House Stud **Trained** Newmarket, Suffolk

FOCUS
There appeared to be more dead wood in the second division of the 5f maiden than in the first and few got into a race that was run over a second and a half slower.

NOTEBOOK
Ocean Myth made a mockery of what looked, on paper at least, an open race. She had shown ability on her 5f Bath debut ten days ago, when a slowly away sixth of 11 to Responsive. Racing with enthusiasm, she responded well for a couple of cracks of the whip approaching the furlong pole and drew readily clear. It would not do to go overboard, but she will get further. (tchd 9-2)
Red Shadow had disappointed when upped in class at York, after a near miss in a Thirsk fillies' maiden on her penultimate start. Dropped back into a lower grade, she was quickly away and kept the winner company until she was found wanting with a furlong to run. She stuck to her task and simply bumped into a good one. She clearly has ability. (op 11-2)
Zaffy(IRE), having only her second start, had a decent draw, but as she had done at Thirsk she spoiled her chance with a tardy start, rearing in the stalls. She finished with aplomb, suggesting she might be better over a longer trip. Official explanation: jockey said filly reared as gates opened (op 3-1 tchd 10-3)
Our Boy Jack(IRE) had been well fancied on his debut in the Brocklesby at Doncaster on April 2 and was making his first start since flopping there. He looked green mid-race and didn't look an easy ride, but stayed on quite well. He will improve for the experience and once the penny drops, he will show his true ability. (op 5-2 tchd 3-1)
True Bond produced a pleasing display on her debut, staying on well from off the pace. Though beaten a long way, improvement is anticipated and she will get further than this. (op 16-1)
Uncle Timmy travelled well and only weakened in the closing stages. This was an encouraging start. (op 14-1)

3612 ELTHERINGTON STKS (H'CAP) 7f 100y
3:35 (3:35) (Class 5) (0-75,75) 4-Y-O+ **£3,234** (£962; £481; £240) **Stalls** Low

Form				RPR
6003	**1**		**Shadowtime**[14] 3188 6-9-4 72 AndrewMullen 5 (Colin Teague) *trckd ldr: hdwy to chal over 2f out: rdn to ld wl over 1f out: edgd rt ent fnl f: drvn out* **10/1**	82
3-03	**2**	2	**Ginger Grey (IRE)**[8] 3348 4-9-5 73 (b) DanielTudhope 6 (David O'Meara) *hld up towards rr: hdwy 3f out: chsd ldrs 2f out: effrt whn nt clr run on inner over 1f out: sn swtchd lft and rdn to chse wnr ins fnl f: kpt on* **7/2**[2]	78+
-032	**3**	1 ½	**Polish World (USA)**[14] 3188 7-9-7 75 MickyFenton 1 (Paul Midgley) *led: jnd and rdn along over 2f out: hdd wl over 1f out and sn drvn: hld whn n.m.r ent fnl f: edgd rt and kpt on towards fin* **11/4**[1]	76
5235	**4**	½	**Powerful Pierre**[11] 3245 4-8-11 68 (v) DeclanCannon(3) 8 (Ian McInnes) *chsd ldng pair: hdwy wl over 2f out: rdn wl over 1f out: drvn and one pce appr fnl f* **11/1**	68
4601	**5**	½	**Striker Torres (IRE)**[16] 3071 5-9-5 73 PaddyAspell 7 (Geoffrey Oldroyd) *hld up towards rr: hdwy over 2f out: rdn wl over 1f out: kpt on same pce appr fnl f* **9/2**[3]	72
5-65	**6**	2	**Saharia (IRE)**[21] 2910 4-9-7 75 (p) PaulHanagan 3 (Ollie Pears) *dwlt and hld up in rr: pushed along over 2f out: rdn and hdwy on inner over 1f out: styng on whn hmpd ins fnl f: no ch after* **7/1**	75+
025	**7**	1 ¼	**Master Of Dance (IRE)**[16] 3088 4-8-10 64 (p) GregFairley 2 (Peter Salmon) *in tch: hdwy 3f out: rdn along over 2f out: sn drvn and wknd* **16/1**	55
5623	**8**	½	**Jupiter Fidius**[9] 3306 4-8-2 63 (p) ShaneBKelly(7) 4 (Kate Walton) *in tch: rdn along wl over 2f out: sn wknd* **6/1**	52

1m 31.26s (-2.54) **Going Correction** -0.35s/f (Firm) 8 Ran SP% **117.2**
Speed ratings (Par 103): **100,97,96,95,94 92,91,90**
toteswingers: 1&2 £2.40, 1&3 £7.80, 2&3 £2.40 CSF £46.13 CT £126.12 TOTE £12.80: £3.20, £2.00, £1.10; EX 54.50.
Owner H Conlon **Bred** Darley **Trained** Station Town, Co Durham

FOCUS
A modest handicap run at a fair pace.
Saharia(IRE) Official explanation: jockey said gelding was denied a clear run

3613 COACHMAN CARAVANS QUALITY H'CAP 5f
4:05 (4:05) (Class 4) (0-85,85) 3-Y-O+ **£5,175** (£1,540; £769; £384) **Stalls** Low

Form				RPR
-000	**1**		**Master Rooney (IRE)**[10] 3279 5-9-7 80 RoystonFfrench 8 (Bryan Smart) *mde most: rdn 2f out: drvn ent fnl f: hld on gamely* **10/1**	90
0506	**2**	nk	**Hazelrigg (IRE)**[8] 3357 6-9-11 84 (be) DavidAllan 5 (Tim Easterby) *trckd ldrs: hdwy 2f out: rdn to chse ldng pair ent fnl f: drvn to chal last 100yds and ev ch whn put hd high and nt go past wnr towards fin* **4/1**[3]	93
5322	**3**	1	**Noodles Blue Boy**[8] 3357 5-9-9 85 MichaelO'Connell(3) 1 (Ollie Pears) *cl up: rdn 2f out: drvn over 1f out and ev ch tl no ex last 75yds* **2/1**[1]	90
0000	**4**	5	**Green Park (IRE)**[10] 3279 8-9-2 80 (b) NeilFarley(5) 6 (Declan Carroll) *chsd ldng pair: rdn along wl over 1f out: sn one pce* **25/1**	67
1431	**5**	2	**Another Wise Kid (IRE)**[14] 3189 3-9-3 81 MickyFenton 2 (Paul Midgley) *hld up in rr: effrt 2f out: sn rdn and n.d* **11/4**[2]	60
-404	**6**	1 ½	**Normandy Maid**[15] 3114 3-8-5 69 PaulHanagan 3 (Richard Fahey) *in tch: rdn along 1/2-way: n.d* **10/1**	42
0024	**7**	1 ¾	**Oldjoesaid**[7] 3379 7-9-11 84 StephenCraine 7 (Kevin Ryan) *dwlt: a in rr* **13/2**	53

61.04 secs (-2.46) **Going Correction** -0.35s/f (Firm)
WFA 3 from 5yo+ 5lb 7 Ran SP% **115.4**
Speed ratings (Par 105): **105,104,102,94,91 89,86**
toteswingers: 1&2 £5.20, 1&3 £2.20, 2&3 £10.50 CSF £50.23 CT £113.63 TOTE £12.50: £5.60, £1.40; EX 74.90.
Owner A Turton, P Langford & S Brown **Bred** Darley **Trained** Hambleton, N Yorks

FOCUS
A competitive sprint handicap run at a generous pace. The third has been rated close to his recent best in another race where few got involved.
Another Wise Kid(IRE) Official explanation: jockey said gelding never travelled

3614 C.G.I. H'CAP 1m 100y
4:40 (4:41) (Class 5) (0-75,74) 3-Y-O **£3,234** (£962; £481; £240) **Stalls** Low

Form				RPR
035-	**1**		**Groomed (IRE)**[216] 7610 3-9-7 74 LiamJones 1 (William Haggas) *trckd ldng pair: effrt over 2f out: rdn wl over 1f out: swtchd lft and drvn ent fnl f: styd on to ld last 75yds* **7/2**[2]	82+
1-45	**2**	1 ½	**Corsicanrun (IRE)**[22] 2891 3-9-5 72 PaulHanagan 3 (Richard Fahey) *led: rdn along 2f out: drvn over 1f out: hdd and no ex last 75yds* **3/1**[1]	77
-203	**3**	1 ½	**Pivot Bridge**[15] 3124 3-8-12 65 RobertWinston 4 (B W Hills) *hld up in rr: hdwy on outer 2f out: rdn to chal appr fnl f: sn drvn and kpt on same pce* **3/1**[1]	67+
2000	**4**	4 ½	**Falmouth Bay (USA)**[16] 3081 3-9-6 73 DarryllHolland 2 (Mark Johnston) *hld up in rr: hdwy over 2f out: n.m.r wl over 1f out: rdn and one pce appr fnl f* **9/1**	64
2300	**5**	1 ¾	**Rio Park (IRE)**[9] 3306 3-8-7 60 (p) RoystonFfrench 5 (Bryan Smart) *chsd ldrs: rdn along wl over 2f out: drvn 2f out and sn wknd* **7/1**	47
1335	**6**	¾	**Lady Gar Gar**[23] 2835 3-9-0 70 (p) DeclanCannon(3) 6 (Geoffrey Oldroyd) *chsd ldr: rdn over 2f out: drvn wl over 1f out: sn wknd* **4/1**[3]	55

1m 44.41s (-3.19) **Going Correction** -0.35s/f (Firm) 6 Ran SP% **114.7**
Speed ratings (Par 100): **101,99,98,93,91 91**
toteswingers: 1&2 £2.70, 1&3 £2.70, 2&3 £2.00 CSF £14.83 TOTE £5.20: £2.70, £2.10; EX 15.70.
Owner Scotney,Asplin,Symonds,Ball & Fisher **Bred** Rathbarry Stud **Trained** Newmarket, Suffolk

FOCUS
A generous pace for this ordinary handicap, the form of which is open to question. This has been rated around the front-running runner-up.
Falmouth Bay(USA) Official explanation: jockey said colt was denied a clear run

3615 POWERPART FILLIES' H'CAP 1m 1f 207y
5:10 (5:12) (Class 5) (0-70,69) 3-Y-O **£2,911** (£866; £432; £216) **Stalls** Low

Form				RPR
4-64	**1**		**Sleek Gold**[17] 3043 3-9-5 67 DarryllHolland 8 (Brian Meehan) *prom: led after 3f: rdn along over 2f out: drvn appr fnl f: kpt on gamely* **5/1**[3]	77
3-15	**2**	1	**Medaille D'Or**[15] 3131 3-9-6 68 AndreaAtzeni 3 (Roger Varian) *t.k.h: led 3f: trckd ldrs: effrt over 2f out: swtchd lft and rdn wl over 1f out: drvn to chse wnr ins fnl f: edgd rt and no ex towards fin* **11/4**[1]	76
00-3	**3**	1	**Sangar**[17] 3039 3-8-8 56 PaulHanagan 1 (Ollie Pears) *hld up in tch: pushed along 3f out: hdwy on inner wl over 1f out: sn rdn and kpt on fnl f: nrst fin* **11/4**[1]	62
-006	**4**	6	**May Burnett (IRE)**[40] 2350 3-8-2 50 oh5 (t) AndrewHeffernan 4 (Brian Rothwell) *hld up in rr: hdwy over 2f out: sn rdn and styd on ins fnl f* **40/1**	44
1334	**5**	hd	**Moonlight Rhapsody (IRE)**[9] 3325 3-9-7 69 RobertWinston 6 (B W Hills) *prom: chsd wnr after 4f: rdn along wl over 2f out: drvn wl over 1f out: grad wknd* **3/1**[2]	63
5040	**6**	2 ¼	**The Nifty Duchess**[17] 3039 3-7-13 50 oh4 (b[1]) DeclanCannon(3) 10 (Tim Easterby) *t.k.h: chsd ldrs: hdwy on outer 3f out: rdn to chal 2f out: drvn and wknd over 1f out* **20/1**	39
0400	**7**	4 ½	**Decadence**[15] 3138 3-8-2 50 AndrewMullen 7 (Eric Alston) *hld up towards rr: effrt and sme hdwy 3f out: sn rdn and wknd* **16/1**	30

2m 5.03s (-1.97) **Going Correction** -0.35s/f (Firm) 7 Ran SP% **108.1**
Speed ratings (Par 97): **93,92,91,86,86 84,81**
toteswingers: 1&2 £3.20, 1&3 £2.70, 2&3 £1.80 CSF £16.76 TOTE £4.70: £1.80, £1.60; EX 11.00.

Owner Jaber Abdullah **Bred** Rabbah Bloodstock Limited **Trained** Manton, Wilts
■ Syncopated Lady was withdrawn (17/2, unruly in stalls). Deduct 10p in the £ under R4.

FOCUS
The front three finished clear and the form looks okay.
Decadence Official explanation: jockey said filly ran too free

3616 COACHMAN MAIDEN STKS — 5f
5:40 (5:41) (Class 5) 3-Y-O+ — **£2,911** (£866; £432; £216) **Stalls** Low

Form — RPR

6534 **1** — **Pantella (IRE)**[8] 3360 3-8-12 63 ....(p) PaulHanagan 3 — 69+
(Kevin Ryan) *trckd ldrs whn n.m.r and hmpd after 1f: hdwy whn nt clr run and swtchd rt wl over 1f out: sn rdn and str run to ld ins fnl f: sn clr* **13/8**[1]

6-63 **2** 5 — **Dictionary**[8] 3343 3-9-3 64 ....(t) LiamJones 11 — 56
(William Haggas) *trckd ldrs on outer: hdwy 1/2-way: rdn to ld over 1f out: drvn ent fnl f: sn hdd and one pce* **11/4**[3]

-540 **3** ½ — **Media Jury**[15] 3143 4-9-5 42 ....(b[1]) DeclanCannon(3) 2 — 56
(John Wainwright) *chsd ldrs whn bmpd after 1f: sn cl up: rdn and ev ch over 1f out: sn drvn and one pce* **25/1**

6-33 **4** 1 ½ — **Guinea Seeker**[9] 3318 3-9-3 60 .... DavidAllan 4 — 49+
(Tim Easterby) *chsd ldrs: n.m.r and hmpd after 1f: pushed along and outpcd 1/2-way: hdwy whn nt clr run over 1f out: swtchd rt to inner and rdn: styd on ins fnl f* **9/4**[2]

0 **5** hd — **Missile Attack (IRE)**[16] 3075 3-9-0 0 .... PatrickDonaghy(3) 9 — 48+
(Ian Semple) *hld up towards rr: hdwy over 2f out: swtchd lft and rdn over 1f out: edgd rt and styd on u.p ins fnl f: nrst fin* **8/1**

400- **6** 1 ½ — **Cottam Stella**[290] 6075 3-8-5 51 .... JohnCavanagh(7) 6 — 37
(Mel Brittain) *hmpd s and in rr tl sme late hdwy* **28/1**

00 **7** 2 ¾ — **Lovely Lynn (IRE)**[8] 3343 3-8-7 0 .... NeilFarley(5) 8 — 28
(Declan Carroll) *led: rdn along 2f out: drvn and hdd over 1f out: sn wknd* **66/1**

0 **8** ½ — **Ingenti**[57] 1880 3-8-12 0 .... PaddyAspell 12 — 26
(Christopher Wilson) *t.k.h: chsd ldrs: rdn along 2f out: sn wknd* **100/1**

0 **9** 10 — **Donnywardsbird**[35] 2493 3-9-3 0 .... RobertWinston 1 — —
(Eric Alston) *t.k.h: chsd ldrs: rdn along bef 1/2-way and sn wknd* **40/1**

00-5 **10** ½ — **Indigo Sands (IRE)**[17] 3053 3-8-12 45 .... SladeO'Hara(5) 10 — —
(Alan Berry) *dwlt: a in rr: swtchd wd bef 1/2-way and sn bhd* **33/1**

00/0 **11** 1 — **Mrs Medley**[32] 2593 5-9-0 31 .... BillyCray(3) 5 — —
(Garry Woodward) *prom: rdn along bef 1/2-way: sn wknd* **100/1**

61.87 secs (-1.63) **Going Correction** -0.35s/f (Firm)
WFA 3 from 4yo+ 5lb — **11 Ran SP% 122.8**
Speed ratings (Par 103): **99,91,90,87,87 85,80,79,63,63 61**
toteswingers: 1&2 £2.20, 1&3 £10.80, 2&3 £11.70 CSF £6.48 TOTE £2.90: £1.20, £1.80, £4.00; EX 7.50.
Owner J Hanson **Bred** Rockfield Farm **Trained** Hambleton, N Yorks

FOCUS
A weak maiden sprint which the two market principals dominated. The winner didn't need to match her best with the moderate third limiting the form.
Guinea Seeker Official explanation: jockey said gelding was denied a clear run
T/Plt: £31.40 to a £1 stake. Pool: £60,398.16. 1,399.80 winning tickets. T/Qpdt: £26.20 to a £1 stake. Pool: £2,617.51. 73.80 winning tickets. JR

3273 CARLISLE (R-H)
Saturday, July 2

OFFICIAL GOING: Good (good to firm in places; 8.2)
Wind: Almost nil Weather: Hot, sunny

3617 TEXAS IN CONCERT TONIGHT APPRENTICE H'CAP — 5f 193y
6:00 (6:02) (Class 5) (0-75,75) 4-Y-O+ — **£2,658** (£785; £392) **Stalls** Low

Form — RPR

-212 **1** — **Needy McCredie**[19] 2989 5-8-5 **56** .... JulieBurke 11 — 69
(James Turner) *trckd ldr: pushed along to ld appr fnl f: edgd rt: kpt on wl* **2/1**[1]

-100 **2** 1 ¾ — **Bandstand**[35] 2497 5-9-2 **72** .... JustinNewman(5) 2 — 78
(Bryan Smart) *midfield: pushed along over 2f out: hdwy over 1f out: styd on fnl f to go 2nd nr fin: nt rch wnr* **7/1**

2013 **3** ¾ — **Clear Ice (IRE)**[9] 3307 4-8-11 **65** ....(b) CharlesEddery(3) 9 — 69
(Richard Guest) *led: rdn and hdd appr fnl f: kpt on same pce: lost 2nd nr fin* **7/1**[3]

0-00 **4** 1 ¾ — **Imjin River (IRE)**[14] 3179 4-8-11 **62** .... AshleyMorgan 7 — 60
(Mark H Tompkins) *hld up on outside: rdn 2f out: styd on fnl f: nvr able to chal* **25/1**

0030 **5** ½ — **Tasmeem (IRE)**[10] 3279 4-9-3 **75** ....(v) ShirleyTeasdale(7) 4 — 72
(David Nicholls) *in tch: effrt and pushed along 2f out: sn one pce* **10/1**

4020 **6** ½ — **Ryedane (IRE)**[10] 3279 9-9-1 **66** ....(b) LanceBetts 8 — 61
(Tim Easterby) *trckd ldrs tl rdn and no ex over 1f out* **7/1**[3]

3221 **7** 1 ¾ — **Volito**[22] 2879 5-9-1 **69** .... HenryBrooke(3) 3 — 59
(Anabel K Murphy) *hld up: n.m.r briefly over 2f out: sn rdn: no imp appr fnl f* **4/1**[2]

0 **8** 1 ¾ — **Welcome Approach**[56] 1912 8-8-5 **56** .... AdamCarter 5 — 40
(John Weymes) *in tch: drvn 1/2-way: wknd over 1f out* **16/1**

6004 **9** 9 — **Valentino Swing (IRE)**[33] 2554 8-8-7 **58** oh8 ow2 .... LeeTopliss 6 — 13
(Michael Appleby) *dwlt: sn drvn along towards rr: wknd fnl 2f* **25/1**

0000 **10** 5 — **Without Prejudice (USA)**[17] 3038 6-9-0 **70** .... DavidSimmonson(5) 1 — —
(Michael Easterby) *s.s: a wl bhd* **20/1**

1m 12.55s (-1.15) **Going Correction** -0.10s/f (Good) — **10 Ran SP% 118.3**
Speed ratings (Par 103): **103,100,99,97,96 96,93,91,79,72**
toteswingers: 1&2 £4.00, 1&3 £4.20, 2&3 £8.20 CSF £16.27 CT £82.96 TOTE £2.80: £1.60, £2.60, £2.70; EX 17.30.
Owner J R Turner **Bred** Mrs C M Brown **Trained** Norton-le-Clay, N Yorks

FOCUS
Rail on old Stable bend out further 3yds and continued up home straight adding 21yds to distances. New stable bend out 5yds adding 3yds. This has been rated around the third.
Without Prejudice(USA) Official explanation: jockey said gelding missed the break

3618 NORTHERN SECURITY MAIDEN AUCTION STKS — 5f 193y
6:30 (6:31) (Class 5) 2-Y-O — **£2,522** (£750; £375; £187) **Stalls** Low

Form — RPR

5232 **1** — **Haafkry**[9] 3302 2-8-9 0 .... JamesSullivan 8 — 69
(Linda Stubbs) *in tch on outside: hdwy to ld over 1f out: hld on wl fnl f* **9/4**[1]

2 ½ — **Star City (IRE)** 2-8-13 0 .... SeanLevey(3) 5 — 75+
(Michael Dods) *green in paddock: s.i.s: rn green in rr: hdwy whn nt clr run and swtchd to outside over 2f out: edgd rt over 1f out: kpt on to take 2nd nr fin: nt rch wnr* **8/1**[3]

3342 **3** ½ — **One Kool Dude**[16] 3082 2-8-7 0 ow1 .... LeeTopliss(5) 7 — 69
(Richard Fahey) *cl up: rdn and ev ch over 1f out: kpt on same pce fnl f* **9/4**[1]

020 **4** 3 ½ — **Louis Hull**[20] 2953 2-8-13 0 .... FrederikTylicki 6 — 60
(George Foster) *slt ld tl edgd rt and hdd over 1f out: sn no ex* **9/1**

4 **5** nk — **Medieval Bishop (IRE)**[19] 2983 2-8-11 0 .... TonyHamilton 2 — 57
(Howard Johnson) *t.k.h: disp ld to over 1f out: sn outpcd* **3/1**[2]

0 **6** shd — **Never In (IRE)**[10] 3273 2-8-4 0 .... PatrickMathers 3 — 49
(Alan Berry) *in tch: drvn 1/2-way: wknd over 1f out* **66/1**

00 **7** 1 — **Sir Elmo (IRE)**[7] 3382 2-8-11 0 .... PhillipMakin 4 — 53
(Declan Carroll) *in tch: drvn and outpcd wl over 1f out: n.d after* **16/1**

1m 14.38s (0.68) **Going Correction** -0.10s/f (Good) — **7 Ran SP% 115.0**
Speed ratings (Par 94): **91,90,89,85,84 84,83**
toteswingers: 1&2 £4.10, 1&3 £1.30, 2&3 £4.20 CSF £21.46 TOTE £3.20: £1.50, £4.50; EX 24.70.
Owner G & T Bloodstock **Bred** Southcourt Stud **Trained** Norton, N Yorks
■ Stewards' Enquiry : Patrick Mathers one-day ban: used whip down shoulder in the forehand (Jul 16)

FOCUS
A little interest was taken away from this auction maiden with Group 2 Gimcrack entry Sardanapalus not running, and overall the form is probably modest.

NOTEBOOK
Haafkry had gone close on varying ground in four runs to date and his experience held him in good stead here to get off the mark on his sixth attempt. He set the standard, and after making headway from 2f out, stayed on well to repel the late thrust of the runner-up. (tchd 2-1 and 11-4)
Star City(IRE) is a half-brother to several winners at up to 1m2f and looked the one to take out of the race. He missed the break and raced a little green early on, as he was entitled to, before staying on well from over a furlong out. (op 9-1 tchd 10-1)
One Kool Dude ran another solid race and did little wrong after holding every chance inside the final furlong. His turn will come and he looks an ideal type for nurseries as he is fairly well exposed in this company. (op 13-8)
Louis Hull cut out a solid pace but had no more to give when headed. He could be another for nurseries. (op 8-1)
Medieval Bishop(IRE) had been nicely supported after an encouraging debut, but after holding every chance over a furlong out, could not sustain his effort. (op 6-1)

3619 ANDERSONS DENTON HOLME LTD CLASSIFIED (S) STKS — 7f 200y
7:00 (7:06) (Class 6) 3-Y-O — **£1,908** (£563; £281) **Stalls** Low

Form — RPR

0200 **1** — **Ryedale Dancer (IRE)**[5] 3455 3-8-12 52 .... PJMcDonald 4 — 58
(Tim Easterby) *mde all: rdn 2f out: hld on wl fnl f* **13/2**

-300 **2** hd — **Sky Diamond (IRE)**[19] 3002 3-8-12 59 ....(b) JamesSullivan 1 — 58
(James Given) *t.k.h: trckd ldrs: rdn and outpcd 2f out: rallied 1f out: edgd lft and kpt on wl towards fin: jst hld* **7/2**[3]

0-23 **3** 2 ¼ — **Izzet**[9] 3309 3-8-7 60 .... AshleyMorgan(5) 7 — 52
(Mark H Tompkins) *t.k.h: in tch: effrt and edgd rt fr 2f out: blkd ins fnl f: one pce* **5/2**[2]

6422 **4** 1 ½ — **Chilledtothebone**[9] 3309 3-8-12 62 ....(v) TomEaves 6 — 49
(Linda Stubbs) *trckd wnr: drvn and edgd rt over 2f out: one pce whn hmpd ins fnl f* **6/4**[1]

0066 **5** 4 — **Ajaafa**[24] 2827 3-8-7 49 .... LeeTopliss(5) 5 — 40
(Michael Appleby) *loose bef s: missed break: t.k.h: hld up: rdn over 2f out: wknd over 1f out* **25/1**

300 **6** 2 ¼ — **Littlepromisedland (IRE)**[99] 967 3-8-5 38 .... CharlesEddery(7) 8 — 35
(Richard Guest) *plld hrd in rr: rdn along 3f out: btn over 1f out* **50/1**

1m 42.03s (2.03) **Going Correction** +0.125s/f (Good) — **6 Ran SP% 109.9**
Speed ratings (Par 98): **94,93,91,90,86 83**
toteswingers: 1&2 £4.20, 1&3 £1.50, 2&3 £1.90 CSF £27.88 TOTE £8.60: £3.40, £1.40; EX 34.40.There was no bid for the winner.
Owner Rapcalone **Bred** Max Morris **Trained** Great Habton, N Yorks
■ Stewards' Enquiry : Ashley Morgan caution: used whip down shoulder in the forehand.

FOCUS
An uncompetitive seller in which the third and fourth have been rated as below their recent best.

3620 STOBART SILVER CUP H'CAP — 7f 200y
7:30 (7:33) (Class 4) (0-80,80) 3-Y-O+ — **£7,762** (£2,310; £1,154; £577) **Stalls** Low

Form — RPR

4503 **1** — **M[illegible]bh (IRE)**[10] 3275 7-9-12 78 ....(b) PJMcDonald 9 — 90
(Ruth Carr) *midfield: hdwy over 2f out: swtchd [illegible] and qcknd to ld ins fnl f: sn clr* **7/1**

0144 **2** 3 ½ — **Euston Square**[29] 2674 5-9-11 77 .... TomEaves 4 — 81
(Alistair Whillans) *in tch: effrt and rdn over 2f out: styd on fnl f: wnt 2nd towards fin: no ch w wnr* **8/1**

-043 **3** hd — **Bella Noir**[15] 3112 4-9-4 70 ....(v[1]) AndrewElliott 1 — 73
(Mrs K Burke) *led: rdn over 2f out: hdd ins fnl f: kpt on same pce* **12/1**

-520 **4** 1 ½ — **Sunnyside Tom (IRE)**[10] 3276 7-9-9 80 .... LeeTopliss(5) 8 — 80
(Richard Fahey) *t.k.h: trckd ldrs: effrt over 2f out: kpt on same pce ins fnl f* **11/2**[2]

0210 **5** 2 — **Media Stars**[9] 3319 6-8-6 61 oh1 .... SeanLevey(3) 5 — 56
(Robert Johnson) *dwlt: hld up: rdn on outside over 2f out: kpt on fnl f: nvr able to chal* **33/1**

3040 **6** ½ — **Collateral Damage (IRE)**[9] 3315 8-9-9 80 ....(t) LanceBetts(5) 3 — 74
(Tim Easterby) *hld up: rdn over 2f out: hdwy over 1f out: kpt on: nrst fin* **15/2**

1141 **7** nk — **Fazza**[19] 2985 4-9-9 75 .... TonyHamilton 11 — 69
(Edwin Tuer) *in tch on outside: rdn over 2f out: sn no imp* **4/1**[1]

6466 **8** 1 — **Tartan Gunna**[16] 3085 5-10-0 80 ....(b) SilvestreDeSousa 13 — 71+
(Mark Johnston) *s.s: bhd: rdn and kpt on fnl 2f: nvr able to chal* **6/1**[3]

-005 **9** 2 ¼ — **Marvo**[8] 3361 7-9-0 71 .... AshleyMorgan(5) 12 — 57
(Mark H Tompkins) *hld up: rdn whn nt clr run briefly over 2f out: nvr able to chal* **12/1**

4-50 **10** 3 ¾ — **Christmas Carnival**[14] 3169 4-10-0 80 .... JamesSullivan 10 — 58
(Michael Easterby) *sn drvn along towards rr on outside: struggling 1/2-way: nvr on terms* **16/1**

02-0 **11** nk — **Captain Macarry (IRE)**[84] 1245 6-9-8 74 ....(v) WilliamCarson 2 — 51
(Stuart Williams) *hld up: drvn along 3f out: nvr on terms* **33/1**

440- **12** 2 ½ — **Touch Tone**[264] 6805 4-9-10 76 .... FrederikTylicki 7 — 47
(Michael Dods) *midfield: drvn and outpcd 3f out: sn btn* **20/1**

0 **13** 12 — **Born To Be Achamp (BRZ)**[20] 2955 5-9-12 78 .... PhillipMakin 6 — 21
(Geoffrey Harker) *w ldr to 1/2-way: rdn and wknd over 2f out* **40/1**

1m 39.9s (-0.10) **Going Correction** +0.125s/f (Good) — **13 Ran SP% 119.4**
Speed ratings (Par 105): **105,101,101,99,97 97,97,96,93,90 89,87,75**
toteswingers: 1&2 £6.60, 1&3 £31.10, 2&3 £23.20 CSF £59.60 CT £690.63 TOTE £7.40: £2.80, £3.20, £4.60; EX 68.00.
Owner Reach For The Moon & Mrs R Carr **Bred** Hascombe And Valiant Studs **Trained** Huby, N Yorks
■ Stewards' Enquiry : Lee Topliss one-day ban: used whip in incorrect place (Jul 16)

FOCUS
A competitive 61-80 handicap run at a strong pace. The winner looked back to something like last year's best.

Tartan Gunna Official explanation: jockey said gelding missed the break

Captain Macarry(IRE) Official explanation: jockey said gelding suffered interference in running

3621 LADIES' NIGHT ON 1ST AUGUST H'CAP — 6f 192y
8:00 (8:00) (Class 5) (0-70,68) 3-Y-O — **£2,522** (£750; £375; £187) **Stalls** Low

Form — RPR

604 **1** **Imperator Augustus (IRE)**[15] 3124 3-8-13 **65**......... ChrisDCogan(5) 12 — 77
(Patrick Holmes) *cl up: lft in ld bnd after 2f: rdn and hung lft over 2f out: edgd rt and kpt on strly fnl f* **12/1**

4-01 **2** *2 ¾* **Ted's Brother (IRE)**[9] 3318 3-9-0 **64**.......................... RobertLButler(3) 4 — 73+
(Richard Guest) *hld up: hdwy whn hmpd over 2f out: sn swtchd rt and nt clr run: swtchd lft and hdwy over 1f out: styd on to go 2nd nr fin: no ch w wnr* **11/4**[1]

0600 **3** *nk* **Cheylesmore (IRE)**[8] 3347 3-8-13 **60**.....................(e) WilliamCarson 11 — 64
(Stuart Williams) *chsd ldrs: wnt 2nd after 3f: effrt over 2f out: kpt on same pce fnl f: lost 2nd nr fin* **5/1**[3]

0440 **4** *1 ¾* **Inside**[5] 3455 3-8-7 **54**.. FrederikTylicki 9 — 53
(Richard Fahey) *bhd: struggling after 3f: hdwy on outside over 2f out: kpt on fnl f: no imp* **6/1**

543 **5** *2* **Magic Rhythm**[14] 3167 3-9-6 **67**.................................... AndrewElliott 10 — 61
(Mrs K Burke) *hld up on outside: rdn over 2f out: kpt on fnl f: nvr able to chal* **14/1**

3426 **6** *2* **Stilettoesinthemud (IRE)**[13] 3207 3-8-13 **60**.............. JamesSullivan 7 — 48
(James Given) *midfield: effrt on ins over 2f out: no imp wl over 1f out* **13/2**

350 **7** *5* **Ivy And Gold**[8] 3337 3-8-3 **50**....................................... PatrickMathers 1 — 25
(Alan Berry) *trckd ldrs tl rdn and wknd wl over 1f out* **80/1**

053 **8** *6* **Mandatori (IRE)**[16] 3091 3-9-1 **62**.............................(t) SilvestreDeSousa 5 — 21
(Nicky Vaughan) *t.k.h: hld up: nt handle bnd after 2f: effrt and edgd both ways 2f out: sn btn* **3/1**[2]

1106 **9** *4* **Finn's Rainbow**[15] 3114 3-9-5 **66**.. PhillipMakin 8 — 14
(Kevin Ryan) *plld hrd: cl up: hung lft and hdd bnd after 2f: wknd fr 3f out* **14/1**

1m 27.8s (0.70) **Going Correction** +0.125s/f (Good) **9** Ran SP% **118.2**
Speed ratings (Par 100): **101,97,97,95,93 90,85,78,73**
toteswingers: 1&2 £9.40, 1&3 £12.70, 2&3 £5.30 CSF £46.27 CT £194.80 TOTE £20.60: £4.80, £1.20, £2.40; EX 63.00.

Owner Foulrice Park Racing Limited **Bred** Western Bloodstock **Trained** Brandsby, N. Yorks

■ Patrick Holmes' first winner, and Chris Cogan's first for seven years after recently renewing his licence.

FOCUS
The pace was good for this average handicap. The third and fourth have been rated close to this year's turf form.

3622 WATCH RACING UK ON SKY 432 MAIDEN H'CAP — 2m 1f 52y
8:30 (8:30) (Class 6) (0-65,62) 4-Y-0+ — **£1,908** (£563; £281) **Stalls** Low

Form — RPR

0-00 **1** **Neptune Equester**[36] 2458 8-9-0 **55**.................................. TomEaves 4 — 66+
(Brian Ellison) *hld up: pushed along to improve over 5f out: n.m.r over 2f out: sn swtchd lft: hdwy to ld ins fnl f: styd on strly* **2/1**[1]

0-20 **2** *2 ¾* **Finellas Fortune**[14] 3187 6-8-11 **52**.......................... PJMcDonald 2 — 57
(George Moore) *in tch: hdwy and ev ch over 2f out: led briefly ent fnl f: kpt on same pce towards fin* **6/1**[3]

40/- **3** *¾* **Rawaaj**[33] 6975 5-9-2 **62**.. HenryBrooke(5) 9 — 66
(Donald McCain) *trckd ldrs: led over 3f out to ent fnl f: kpt on same pce* **10/1**

-254 **4** *4 ½* **Bandanaman (IRE)**[37] 2433 5-8-12 **60**...................... GarryWhillans(7) 5 — 59
(Alan Swinbank) *hld up: hdwy on outside 3f out: edgd rt 2f out: kpt on same pce appr fnl f* **6/1**[3]

5 *2 ½* **Nocturnal Knight**[15] 4126 8-8-5 **46**................................ JamesSullivan 1 — 42
(J J Lambe, Ire) *hld up in midfield: hdwy to trck ldrs whn hmpd and snatched up over 2f out: kpt on fnl f: no imp* **20/1**

6-50 **6** *hd* **Harsh But Fair**[14] 3185 5-8-4 **45**.................................. PatrickMathers 11 — 41
(Michael Easterby) *midfield: hdwy and prom over 3f out: one pce wl over 1f out* **12/1**

6-62 **7** *2 ½* **Word Of Warning**[14] 3185 7-8-9 **55**................................ LeeTopliss(5) 3 — 48
(Martin Todhunter) *hld up: effrt and c wd bnd ent st: sn no imp* **7/2**[2]

350/ **8** *8* **Mardood**[19] 2603 6-9-0 **55**..(v) TonyHamilton 6 — 39
(Chris Grant) *bhd: struggling over 4f out: sme late hdwy: nvr on terms* **18/1**

0-65 **9** *17* **Astromoon**[23] 2856 4-8-9 **55**.................................... AshleyMorgan(5) 10 — 21
(Mark H Tompkins) *cl up tl rdn and wknd over 2f out* **22/1**

0-65 **10** *shd* **Fantastic Storm**[31] 2618 4-8-5 **46** ow1..........................(v) LeeNewman 8 — 12
(Robin Bastiman) *cl up: led after 6f to over 3f out: wknd 2f out* **33/1**

0006 **11** *5* **Molannarch**[14] 3185 5-8-1 **45**.................................. NataliaGemelova(3) 13 — —
(Keith Reveley) *t.k.h: in tch: rdn whn hmpd 3f out: sn struggling* **20/1**

0 **12** *13* **Doberdan (USA)**[14] 3187 6-7-13 **45**............................(p) ChrisDCogan(5) 12 — —
(Patrick Holmes) *led 6f: cl up tl rdn and wknd over 3f out* **50/1**

0/46 **13** *dist* **Dynamic Rhythm (USA)**[142] 492 8-9-4 **59**............ RobbieFitzpatrick 7 — —
(David Thompson) *bhd: struggling 1/2-way: sn btn: eased whn no ch fnl 3f* **28/1**

3m 52.65s (-0.35) **Going Correction** +0.125s/f (Good) **13** Ran SP% **128.4**
Speed ratings (Par 101): **105,103,103,101,100 99,98,95,87,86 84,78,—**
toteswingers: 1&2 £5.10, 1&3 £8.00, 2&3 £20.90 CSF £14.08 CT £107.56 TOTE £3.90: £1.30, £2.80, £1.60; EX 22.60.

Owner Koo's Racing CLub II **Bred** Mrs Joanna Daniell **Trained** Norton, N Yorks

■ Stewards' Enquiry : Garry Whillans two-day ban: 1st incident careless riding (Jul 16-17); three-day ban: 2nd incident careless riding (Jul 18-20)

FOCUS
Not a bad race for a maiden handicap. Limited form that's been rated around the runner-up.

Neptune Equester Official explanation: trainer's rep said, regarding apparent improvement in form, that the gelding had benefited from a step up in distance.

T/Plt: £346.90 to a £1 stake. Pool: £65,537.40. 137.88 winning tickets. T/Qpdt: £58.10 to a £1 stake. Pool: £5,435.92. 69.20 winning tickets. RY

3582 HAYDOCK (L-H)
Saturday, July 2

OFFICIAL GOING: Good to firm (firm in places on 5f & 6f course) (5f & 6f 8.0, 1m & further 7.8)
Wind: Almost nil Weather: Fine and sunny

3623 BET365 H'CAP — 1m 3f 200y
2:15 (2:16) (Class 3) (0-95,94) 3-Y-O — **£8,409** (£2,502; £1,250; £625) **Stalls** Centre

Form — RPR

31 **1** **Highland Castle**[19] 3001 3-8-13 **86**................................ JamieSpencer 7 — 96+
(David Elsworth) *dwlt: in rr: detached and pushed along over 6f out: hdwy on outside over 3f out: edgd lft: led over 1f out: hung bdly lft ins fnl f: styd on* **6/1**[3]

-144 **2** *1 ½* **Swift Alhaarth (IRE)**[7] 3376 3-8-9 **82**...................... SilvestreDeSousa 6 — 90+
(Mark Johnston) *led: hdd over 1f out: 1/2 l down and keeping on wl whn bdly hmpd 100yds out* **9/2**[1]

3120 **3** *1 ½* **Reflect (IRE)**[16] 3069 3-9-2 **89**.. EddieAhern 5 — 92
(Richard Hannon) *trckd ldrs: keeping on same pce whn hmpd wl over 1f out swtchd rt and kpt on* **6/1**[3]

6411 **4** *hd* **Pintrada**[15] 3131 3-8-3 **76**... FrannyNorton 1 — 79
(James Bethell) *hld up towards rr: effrt 3f out: n.m.r and swtchd rt over 1f out: styd on ins fnl f* **9/2**[1]

01 **5** *3 ½* **Gosbeck**[23] 2836 3-8-13 **86**... DaneO'Neill 3 — 83
(Henry Candy) *hld up in mid-div: effrt over 4f out: one pce fnl 2f* **9/2**[1]

4-30 **6** *3 ¼* **Muqtarrib (IRE)**[20] 2956 3-8-11 **84**................................(b[1]) RichardHills 2 — 76
(Brian Meehan) *hld up in mid-div: drvn 4f out: one pce over 2f out* **20/1**

-011 **7** *6* **Good Boy Jackson**[23] 2835 3-8-10 **83**............................ PhillipMakin 9 — 65
(Kevin Ryan) *trckd ldrs: drvn over 3f out: lost pl over 1f out: bhd whn eased nr fin* **11/2**[2]

3400 **8** *7* **Sergeant Ablett (IRE)**[7] 3405 3-9-3 **90**.............................. TomQueally 8 — 61
(James Given) *chsd ldrs: drvn over 4f out: lost pl 2f out: bhd whn eased wl ins fnl f* **10/1**

2m 30.08s (-3.92) **Going Correction** -0.075s/f (Good) **8** Ran SP% **112.4**
Speed ratings (Par 104): **110,109,108,107,105 103,99,94**
toteswingers: 1&2 £6.50, 1&3 £4.80, 2&3 £3.80 CSF £31.87 CT £167.17 TOTE £7.60: £1.90, £1.40, £1.90; EX 35.30 Trifecta £70.00 Pool: £914.94 - 9.66 winning units..

Owner J Wotherspoon & W Harrison-Allan **Bred** John Wotherspoon **Trained** Newmarket, Suffolk

FOCUS
Races over 5f and 6f run on inner home straight. Races over 1m and further finished on the stands' side in the home straight. The first three races were actually run over 1m4f 38 yards, and the 5.30 over 1m 58 yards. A good handicap contested by some unexposed 3-y-os and a couple of improvers. It was run at a sound pace and has been rated on the positive side, around the third.

NOTEBOOK
Highland Castle was dropped in at the rear and was still last entering the home straight, having not looked to be going that well at one stage. He then made up his ground quickly down the outside in the straight, but edged to his left as he did so and inconvenienced a couple of rivals on his inside. He rolled to his left again inside the last and hampered the runner-up, but was the winner on merit. A nice prospect, he got the longer trip well and will get a bit further still on this evidence, but he is perhaps not straightforward. (op 13-2)

Swift Alhaarth(IRE) reverted to the tactics which brought him a win at Chester in May and went off in front. Headed at the furlong pole, he was battling on but perhaps just getting the worse of the argument when the winner tightened him up quite badly on the rail. This was a solid performance. (op 5-1)

Reflect(IRE) ran no sort of race behind Brown Panther in the King George V Handicap at Royal Ascot having earlier been second behind the same horse over this C&D. He bounced back to form here but lost momemtum when carried to his left by the winner not long after the two pole. Although sticking on for third, he gave the impression that some headgear may help him. (op 15-2)

Pintrada came here on a hat-trick, having been raised a further 7lb after taking a Newmarket classified stakes last time. He was squeezed up in a chain reaction caused by the winner and did not pick up immediately after, but was running on well at the death. (tchd 4-1)

Gosbeck, a Newbury maiden winner, promised to be suited by this step up in trip on her handicap debut but was being pushed along early in the straight and never really picked up. (tchd 4-1 and 5-1 in places)

Muqtarrib(IRE), fitted with first-time blinkers after a disappointing effort at Doncaster, was never a serious factor on this handicap debut. He has a bit to prove now and a confidence-booster in a maiden may prove the best course of action. (tchd 22-1)

Good Boy Jackson perhaps did too much on this first try at 1m4f and faded after chasing the leader. The stone rise for his romp over 1m2f here cannot have helped. (op 9-2)

Sergeant Ablett(IRE) has been running creditably off this sort of mark and this flatter track was expected to suit, but he was the first in trouble. The half-brother to Drill Sergeant had promised to be suited by this step up in trip. (op 11-1 tchd 12-1)

3624 BET365 LANCASHIRE OAKS (GROUP 2) (F&M) — 1m 3f 200y
2:50 (2:52) (Class 1) 3-Y-O+
£45,368 (£17,200; £8,608; £4,288; £2,152; £1,080) **Stalls** Centre

Form — RPR

50-1 **1** **Gertrude Bell**[63] 1677 4-9-5 104.................................. WilliamBuick 2 — 108
(John Gosden) *trckd ldr: wnt 2nd over 3f out: led 2f out: drvn out* **9/2**[2]

1-12 **2** *1 ¼* **Vita Nova (IRE)**[35] 2501 4-9-5 108.................................... TomQueally 3 — 110+
(Sir Henry Cecil) *hld up: t.k.h: hdwy 4f out: trcking ldrs whn sddle slipped over 1f out: rdr tk feet out of irons and almost uns ins fnl f: stuck on wl nr fin* **10/11**[1]

2213 **3** *nk* **Dorcas Lane**[16] 3065 3-8-6 100.. LukeMorris 6 — 106
(Lucy Wadham) *trckd ldrs: pushed along over 4f out: edgd lft over 2f out: styd on same pce fnl f: hmpd ins fnl f* **13/2**[3]

10-6 **4** *½* **Eleanora Duse (IRE)**[62] 1718 4-9-5 111........................ RichardMullen 1 — 105
(Sir Michael Stoute) *hmpd s: hld up: t.k.h: hdwy on ins over 4f out: sn chsng ldrs: styd on same pce fnl f* **7/1**

-224 **5** *nk* **Polly's Mark (IRE)**[20] 2968 5-9-5 106......................(v[1]) PhilipRobinson 7 — 104
(Clive Cox) *set stdy pce: qcknd over 4f out: hdd 2f out: kpt on same pce fnl f* **15/2**

4-30 **6** *18* **Fork Handles**[29] 2682 3-8-6 95..................................(b[1]) SamHitchcott 4 — 75
(Mick Channon) *hld up in rr: t.k.h: drvn 4f out: lost pl over 2f out: sn bhd* **33/1**

60-6 **7** *2 ¾* **Bilidn**[59] 1807 3-8-6 87.. SilvestreDeSousa 5 — 71
(Clive Brittain) *trckd ldr: t.k.h: drvn over 4f out: wkng whn n.m.r 2f out: hung lft and sn lost pl and bhd* **80/1**

2m 30.59s (-3.41) **Going Correction** -0.075s/f (Good)
WFA 3 from 4yo+ 13lb **7** Ran SP% **112.3**
Speed ratings (Par 115): **108,107,106,106,106 94,92**
toteswingers: 1&2 £2.80, 1&3 £4.20, 2&3 £1.02 CSF £8.66 TOTE £4.80: £2.40, £1.70; EX 12.90.

Owner Ms Rachel D S Hood **Bred** Ms Rachel Hood **Trained** Newmarket, Suffolk

The Form Book, Raceform Ltd, Compton, RG20 6NL

FOCUS
Not a strong renewal of the Lancashire Oaks, contested as it was by just one previous Group winner. The first five finished in a heap and the form is dubious. The pace was modest and the time was slightly slower than the earlier handicap.
NOTEBOOK
Gertrude Bell accounted for Polly's Mark when making a winning reappearance in a Listed race at Goodwood in May. She enjoyed a straightforward passage through the race and ran on willingly once edging to the front. Although luck was on her side here, she is a tough, genuine filly who may have further improvement in her as this was only the ninth race of her career. Slightly easier ground would suit. (op 7-2)
Vita Nova(IRE) was an unlucky loser. Held up and travelling well, she was looking for a run in the straight, rather hemmed in by Dorcas Lane on her outer, when Tom Queally's saddle began to slip at around the two pole. Struggling to retain his seat while keeping his mount in contention, he was nearly unseated inside the last but the filly ran on quite well once both his feet were out of the irons. A progressive filly, narrowly beaten by Ferdoos in a Listed race over C&D latest, she should be given a chance to atone for this luckless defeat. (op 11-8 tchd 6-4 in places)
Dorcas Lane, the Ribblesdale third, ran another good race, keeping on down the outside even though the unbalanced favourite was doing her no favours. She may get a bit further and the Park Hill Stakes at Doncaster looks a suitable target for later in the season. (op 15-2)
Eleanora Duse(IRE), a winner at this level last summer, was 3lb clear on official figures. Sticking to the inside in the straight, she ran her race with no apparent excuses and has yet to really fire this season. (op 11-2)
Polly's Mark(IRE) dictated the pace but perhaps raced a little keenly in the first-time visor. After quickening things up in the straight she could not hold off the challengers, but she was only beaten around two lengths. She's been a bit below her best in her last three starts and has been beaten in all seven Group races she has contested. (op 7-1 tchd 13-2)
Fork Handles, last in the Oaks on her previous start, was always in rear in the first-time blinkers. (op 28-1 tchd 25-1)
Bilidn was out of her depth and involved in buffeting as she dropped rapidly back through the field. (op 50-1)

3625 BET365 OLD NEWTON CUP (H'CAP) 1m 3f 200y
3:25 (3:27) (Class 2) 4-Y-0+
£37,350 (£11,184; £5,592; £2,796; £1,398; £702) **Stalls** Centre

Form RPR
6445 **1** **Halicarnassus (IRE)**[14] [3156] 7-8-13 **97**........................ HughBowman 7 107
(Mick Channon) *led 4f: trckd ldr: led 2f out: edgd lft: styd on strly: eased towards fin* **14/1**
-410 **2** *1 1/2* **Bourne**[28] [2716] 5-8-5 **89**.............................. KirstyMilczarek 14 96+
(Luca Cumani) *chsd ldrs: styd on fnl 2f: tk 2nd ins fnl f: no imp* **8/1**[2]
6446 **3** *hd* **Bowdler's Magic**[14] [3163] 4-8-2 **86**........... SilvestreDeSousa 17 92
(Mark Johnston) *w ldr: led 8f out tl 2f out: nt clr run and swtchd rt over 1f out: kpt on wl* **16/1**
0-14 **4** *1/2* **Mount Athos (IRE)**[59] [1808] 4-9-5 **103**........................ JamieSpencer 16 108+
(David Wachman, Ire) *hld up in rr: nt clr run and swtchd rt over 2f out: styd on wl fnl f: fin wl* **11/2**[1]
-132 **5** *1* **Granston (IRE)**[24] [2812] 10-8-6 **90**.............................. TomEaves 5 94
(James Bethell) *trckd ldrs: t.k.h: kpt on one pce fnl 2f* **40/1**
0-40 **6** *nk* **The Fonz**[50] [2071] 5-8-7 **91**.............................. EddieAhern 9 94+
(Sir Michael Stoute) *hdwy on ins to trck ldrs 7f out: effrt on ins and n.m.r 2f out: kpt on same pce* **9/1**[3]
4-01 **7** *nse* **Classic Vintage (USA)**[24] [2812] 5-8-11 **95**........................ TomQueally 12 98
(Amanda Perrett) *mid-div: effrt 3f out: kpt on over 1f out: nvr trbld ldrs* **20/1**
2-20 **8** *1 1/2* **Sharaayeen**[14] [3156] 4-9-0 **98**.............................. RichardHills 3 99+
(B W Hills) *hld up in rr: effrt on outside over 2f out: kpt on: nvr nr ldrs* **11/2**[1]
-206 **9** *shd* **Dansili Dancer**[24] [2812] 9-8-5 **89**.............................. LukeMorris 10 90
(Clive Cox) *trckd ldrs: one pce fnl 2f* **14/1**
0141 **10** *1/2* **Porgy**[11] [3243] 6-8-3 **87**.............................. CathyGannon 11 87+
(David Simcock) *s.i.s: sme hdwy over 2f out: kpt on fnl f: nvr a factor* **20/1**
0-00 **11** *1/2* **Very Good Day (FR)**[14] [3156] 4-8-7 **91**........................ SamHitchcott 6 90+
(Mick Channon) *in rr: drvn over 4f out: styd on fnl f* **22/1**
3010 **12** *1/2* **English Summer**[7] [3396] 4-8-8 **92**........................ FrannyNorton 15 90
(Mark Johnston) *chsd ldrs: wknd over 1f out* **33/1**
0001 **13** *1/2* **Sirvino**[7] [3411] 6-8-11 **100**.............................. LMcNiff(5) 4 98
([illegible]) *[illegible] ldrs on inner: hmpd and lost pl bnd over 4f out: no threat after* **10/1**
3212 **14** *hd* **War Poet**[28] [2708] 4-8-2 **86**.............................. JamesSullivan 1 83+
(David O'Meara) *in rr: drvn and swtchd rt over 2f out: nvr a factor* **8/1**[2]
5 **15** *3 1/4* **Kidnapped (AUS)**[149] [417] 5-9-10 **108**........................ WilliamBuick 8 100
(Saeed Bin Suroor) *mid-div: hmpd and lost pl on bnd over 4f out: sn bhd* **25/1**
0013 **16** *3/4* **Bay Willow (IRE)**[114] [824] 4-9-7 **105**........................ RichardMullen 2 96
(Saeed Bin Suroor) *mid-div: hmpd and lost pl bnd over 4f out: sn bhd* **20/1**
5301 **17** *1/2* **Crackentorp**[21] [2932] 6-8-4 **88**.............................. DuranFentiman 13 78
(Tim Easterby) *in rr: drvn 4f out: sn lost pl* **25/1**

2m 32.08s (-1.92) **Going Correction** -0.075s/f (Good) **17** Ran SP% **125.0**
Speed ratings (Par 109): **103,102,101,101,100 100,100,99,99,99 98,98,98,98,95 95,95**
toteswingers: 1&2 £35.60, 1&3 £18.60, 2&3 £45.30 CSF £109.27 CT £1846.25 TOTE £15.50: £2.30, £2.40, £3.40, £2.10; EX 106.90 Trifecta £1002.10 Pool: £4,062.72 - 3.00 winning units..
Owner Mrs Begum Atman Karatas **Bred** Yeomanstown Lodge Stud **Trained** West Ilsley, Berks

FOCUS
A typically open renewal of this prestigious race, although it's no longer classed as a heritage handicap and the first prize was the best part of £19,000 down on last year's, when it went to subsequent Breeders' Cup Turf winner Dangerous Midge. The pace was not especially strong and it proved difficult to get involved from the rear. It was the slowest of the three C&D times.
NOTEBOOK
Halicarnassus(IRE) was a good fifth in the Duke of Edinburgh Handicap at Royal Ascot and he confirmed that form with a couple of these rivals. Never out of the first two, he won rather comfortably in the end. This smart and consistent performer deserves his place at stud at the end of the season.
Bourne disappointed at Epsom on Derby Day but the trip was clearly not to blame there as he stayed it well here. Indeed, there could be more to come from him over further. His trainer Luca Cumani has a fine record in this event with three winners and two seconds now in the last eight runnings. (op 7-1)
Bowdler's Magic has not been given much help by the handicapper and remains 2lb above his last winning mark, which came a year ago. Overcoming his wide draw, he ran a bold race from the front, sticking on willingly once headed by the winner.
Mount Athos(IRE) ◆ was caught up in trouble on the home turn before running on strongly down the outside for fourth. The Irish raider, who was again unlucky with the draw here, finds this trip a bare minimum and definitely has more improvement still in him over further. A big handicap should come his way. (op 6-1 tchd 13-2 in places)
Granston(IRE) was never far from the pace and continues to run consistently well this season. (op 33-1)
The Fonz was always well placed but lacked any extra pace at the business end.
Classic Vintage(USA), a neck in front of Granston over C&D last time and a pound worse off now, was closing on the leaders at the finish. (op 16-1)
Sharaayeen, down the field in the Duke of Edinburgh, ran a little better back on this faster ground and was running on late without threatening the principals. He remains capable of better. (op 15-2 tchd 5-1 and 8-1 in places)
Dansili Dancer, who won this event in 2007 when it was run in August, has been given a chance by the handicapper on turf and ran creditably. (op 11-1)
Sirvino, raised 11lb for his Windsor win, was the chief sufferer of the trouble on the bend. (op 12-1)
War Poet was another who met interference and should be kept on the right side.
Kidnapped(AUS) Official explanation: jockey said gelding suffered interference in running

3626 BET365.COM CONDITIONS STKS 6f
3:55 (3:57) (Class 3) 3-Y-0+
£8,092 (£2,423; £1,211; £605; £302; £152) **Stalls** Centre

Form RPR
5620 **1** **High Standing (USA)**[14] [3155] 6-8-11 105..................... JamieSpencer 5 104
(William Haggas) *hmpd sn after s: hld up: effrt over 2f out: edgd lft over 1f out: styd on to ld jst ins fnl f: drvn out* **5/2**[2]
4440 **2** *3/4* **Atlantic Sport (USA)**[15] [3109] 6-8-12 100 ow1.............. HughBowman 3 103
(Mick Channon) *hld up: effrt over 2f out: chsng ldrs over 1f out: styd on same pce to take 2nd last 75yds* **13/2**
0501 **3** *3/4* **Fitz Flyer (IRE)**[15] [3140] 5-8-11 90.................................(v) TomEaves 2 100
(Bryan Smart) *led: rdn and hung rt appr fnl f: sn hdd: kpt on same pce* **12/1**
2401 **4** *2 1/4* **Norville (IRE)**[7] [3410] 4-8-11 99.................................(b) CathyGannon 4 92
(David Evans) *chsd ldr centre: drvn 3f out: one pce whn bmpd over 1f out* **2/1**[1]
6000 **5** *2* **Prime Defender**[14] [3155] 7-9-5 99.............................. SebSanders 1 94
(B W Hills) *wnt far side and racd alone: upsides and sn drvn along: wknd fnl f* **5/1**[3]
-000 **6** *2 1/4* **Blue Jack**[14] [3155] 6-9-2 100.....................................(t) RichardKingscote 6 84
(Tom Dascombe) *hld up: effrt over 2f out: chsng ldrs over 1f out: sn wknd* **6/1**

1m 11.92s (-1.88) **Going Correction** 0.0s/f (Good) **6** Ran SP% **113.9**
Speed ratings (Par 107): **110,109,108,105,102 99**
toteswingers: 1&2 £3.30, 1&3 £3.90, 2&3 £28.20 CSF £19.04 TOTE £3.40: £1.30, £4.10; EX 21.70.
Owner Tony Bloom **Bred** Dr Melinda Blue **Trained** Newmarket, Suffolk

FOCUS
This conditions race has been won by some smart sprinters in the past decade. The first two came from the back of the field and, as is often the case for this type of race, the form is a little muddling. The runner-up has been rated as close to his best from the past two years.
NOTEBOOK
High Standing(USA) was 5lb clear on BHA figures and he bounced back after some lacklustre efforts this season. Running on to pick up the leaders entering the last furlong, this was his first win since he took a Listed race over 5f here early last season. (tchd 3-1)
Atlantic Sport(USA), who is back with his original trainer, is without a win since September 2008. This trip is on the sharp side for him and he came through late from the back of the field for second. He's not going to prove easy to place. (op 8-1 tchd 9-1 in places)
Fitz Flyer(IRE), a Redcar handicap winner last time, again displayed bags of pace in the visor, leading the main group of the field down the centre. He hung to his left when the pressure was on and could not hold off the closers, but this was a decent effort at the weights. (op 10-1 tchd 9-1)
Norville(IRE) has made terrific improvement this year but was stepping up in grade here. He was being chased along from an early stage and never really looked like adding to his six wins this season. (tchd 7-4 and 9-4 in places)
Prime Defender, not well in on these terms, showed pace racing alone against the far rail before fading. (op 7-1 tchd 8-1)
Blue Jack had been behind High Standing and Prime Defender when all three were unplaced in the Wokingham at Ascot. In a reapplied tongue-tie but without any headgear, he was disappointing. (tchd 11-2)

3627 BET365.COM H'CAP 6f
4:30 (4:32) (Class 3) (0-95,95) 3-Y-0+ **£8,409** (£2,502; £1,250; £625) **Stalls** Centre

Form RPR
5104 **1** **Piazza San Pietro**[15] [3140] 5-9-1 **88**.............................. JamieSpencer 17 98+
(Andrew Haynes) *dwlt and swtchd lft sn after s: in rr: gd hdwy 2f out: [illegible] drvn out* **10/1**
4046 **2** *3/4* **Lutine Bell**[20] [2954] 4-9-4 **91**..(b) HughBowman [illegible] [illegible]
(Mike Murphy) *swtchd rt s: hld up in rr: hdwy and edgd lft over 2f out: kpt on same pce fnl f: tk 2nd towards fin* **8/1**
0300 **3** *1/2* **Secret Witness**[7] [3394] 5-9-5 **92**.................................(b) TomMcLaughlin 4 98
(Ronald Harris) *hld up in mid-div on outer: hdwy over 2f out: led over 1f out: hdd and no ex ins fnl f* **12/1**
2400 **4** *2 1/2* **Secret Asset (IRE)**[34] [2525] 6-9-6 **93**........................ LukeMorris 3 91
(Jane Chapple-Hyam) *wnt rt s: chsd ldrs: kpt on same pce fnl f* **28/1**
-000 **5** *nk* **Swilly Ferry (USA)**[14] [3155] 4-9-8 **95**........................ WilliamCarson 8 92+
(B W Hills) *mid-div: effrt and nt clr run over 2f out: styd on fnl f* **16/1**
3004 **6** *1 3/4* **Beat The Bell**[14] [3160] 6-9-2 **89**.............................. LeeNewman 6 81
(David Barron) *chsd ldrs: one pce fnl f* **12/1**
0000 **7** *1/2* **Barney McGrew (IRE)**[14] [3155] 8-9-5 **92**........................ TomEaves 12 82
(Michael Dods) *in rr: drvn over 2f out: kpt on fnl f* **15/2**[3]
0-01 **8** *1/2* **Novellen Lad (IRE)**[49] [2099] 6-9-3 **90**........................ EddieAhern 13 79+
(Willie Musson) *hld up towards rr: hdwy over 2f out: nt clr run over 1f out: kpt on ins fnl f* **4/1**[1]
-050 **9** *1 1/4* **Noverre To Go (IRE)**[31] [2620] 5-9-5 **92**..................(t) RichardKingscote 9 77
(Tom Dascombe) *mid-div: effrt and nt clr run over 2f out: swtchd rt and kpt on fnl f* **12/1**
2600 **10** *2 1/2* **Love Delta (USA)**[14] [3155] 4-9-8 **95**........................ SilvestreDeSousa 7 72
(Mark Johnston) *mid-div: effrt on outside over 2f out: nvr nr ldrs* **16/1**
1500 **11** *hd* **Lucky Numbers (IRE)**[7] [3379] 5-9-0 **87**........................ CathyGannon 1 63
(Paul Green) *chsd ldrs: wknd 2f out* **25/1**
0-40 **12** *3/4* **Taajub (IRE)**[42] [2317] 4-9-8 **95**.....................................(v[1]) RichardHills 14 69
(William Haggas) *hld up towards rr: effrt over 2f out: wknd jst ins fnl f* **11/1**
0006 **13** *shd* **Judd Street**[24] [2826] 9-9-1 **88**.....................................(v) TomQueally 5 61
(Eve Johnson Houghton) *led: hdd over 1f out: sn wknd* **20/1**
5100 **14** *2 1/4* **Discanti (IRE)**[22] [2890] 6-9-0 **87**.................................(t) DuranFentiman 15 53
(Tim Easterby) *chsd ldrs: wknd 2f out* **22/1**
11-0 **15** *23* **Kuanyao (IRE)**[56] [1888] 5-9-6 **93**.............................. SebSanders 10 —
(Peter Makin) *chsd ldrs: lost pl over 2f out: bhd and heavily eased over 1f out: t.o* **13/2**[2]

1m 12.34s (-1.46) **Going Correction** 0.0s/f (Good) **15** Ran SP% **124.9**
Speed ratings (Par 107): **107,106,105,102,101 99,98,97,96,92 92,91,91,88,57**
toteswingers: 1&2 £11.60, 1&3 £25.10, 2&3 £4.50 CSF £86.02 CT £1015.45 TOTE £11.00: £2.80, £2.70, £3.20; EX 87.80.
Owner K Corke **Bred** T E Pocock **Trained** Limpley Stoke, Bath

FOCUS
A fair handicap but the great majority of these were fully exposed. The first two came from the very back of the field and the principals ended up on the far side of the track. The winner has been rated as running a length personal best.

NOTEBOOK
Piazza San Pietro, drawn right on the stands' side of the field, burst through from the rear to win comfortably despite drifting across to his left. He has made a lot of progress in the last year and is a good advertisement for his trainer's talents. (op 11-1)
Lutine Bell was drawn on the opposite flank to the winner but they ended up alongside each other. He made good headway from right out the back after missing the break and was unfortunate to run into one too good on the day. He's suited by a strong pace. (tchd 17-2)
Secret Witness burst to the front but might have been ahead too soon and was cut down. His losing run extends to 17 races now, but he has been second or third in 11 of them and is still 17lb higher than when last winning. (op 11-1)
Secret Asset(IRE) ran a solid race in fourth but remains without a win on turf for nearly four years. (op 25-1)
Swilly Ferry(USA) ◆ has eased 5lb in the weights this term. This was a much more encouraging run and he could be ready to strike again soon. William Carson reported that he had been denied a clear run. Official explanation: jockey said colt was denied a clear run
Beat The Bell chased the pace all the way but is perhaps too consistent for his own good. (op 16-1)
Barney McGrew(IRE) is 16lb lower than this stage last year and he was keeping on quite well at the end. (op 7-1)
Novellen Lad(IRE), 4lb higher than at Newbury, did not enjoy a trouble-free passage but can't be counted as unlucky. Official explanation: jockey said gelding was denied a clear run (op 5-1 tchd 11-2)
Kuanyao(IRE) dropped right away after chasing the pace. Seb Sanders reported his mount had become very upset in the stalls. Official explanation: jockey said gelding became very upset in stalls (op 11-2 tchd 5-1)

3628 CASINO AT BET365.COM H'CAP — 5f
5:00 (5:01) (Class 5) (0-75,78) 3-Y-O — £3,234 (£962; £481; £240) Stalls Centre

Form				RPR
1020	1		**Gottcher**[28] 2724 3-9-7 **75** ... LeeNewman 8	83
			(David Barron) *trckd ldrs: led over 1f out: kpt on wl: all out* **7/2**[3]	
-412	2	*shd*	**Eland Ally**[7] 3384 3-9-10 **78** ... HughBowman 4	85
			(Tom Tate) *dwlt: hld up in rr: effrt over 2f out: upsides 1f out: no ex nr fin* **13/8**[1]	
4511	3	*¾*	**Royal Bajan (USA)**[12] 3239 3-9-1 **69** ... TomQueally 6	75+
			(James Given) *trckd ldrs: n.m.r over 1f out: nt clr run and swtchd rt jst ins fnl f: styd on* **10/3**[2]	
1-36	4	*1 ¾*	**Ice Trooper**[14] 3189 3-9-7 **75** ... DuranFentiman 5	73
			(Linda Stubbs) *trckd ldrs: effrt over 2f out: upsides over 1f out: wknd last 100yds* **25/1**	
56-0	5	*nse*	**Ballinargh Girl (IRE)**[19] 2986 3-9-5 **73** ... LukeMorris 3	70
			(Robert Wylie) *trckd ldrs: effrt over 2f out: n.m.r: swtchd rt and kpt on fnl f* **16/1**	
-100	6	*2*	**Melodize**[43] 2265 3-8-4 **58** ... SilvestreDeSousa 2	48
			(David O'Meara) *led 1f: chsd ldrs: wknd fnl f* **12/1**	
1140	7	*1 ¾*	**Mandy's Hero**[50] 2074 3-9-4 **72** ...(p) JamieSpencer 7	56
			(Ian Williams) *sn drvn along: led after 1f: edgd lft: hdd over 1f out: sn wknd: eased ins fnl f* **8/1**	

61.04 secs (0.24) **Going Correction** 0.0s/f (Good) 7 Ran SP% **111.9**
Speed ratings (Par 100): **99,98,97,94,94 91,88**
toteswingers: 1&2 £1.10, 1&3 £3.70, 2&3 £1.10 CSF £9.18 CT £18.88 TOTE £5.50: £3.10, £1.10; EX 11.80.
Owner Twinacre Nurseries Ltd **Bred** Peter Webb **Trained** Maunby, N Yorks
FOCUS
Modest handicap form. The field gravitated to the far rail. The winner and runner-up have been rated as improving.
Ballinargh Girl(IRE) Official explanation: jockey said filly was denied a clear run

3629 GET MOBILE AT MOBILE.BET365.COM H'CAP — 1m
5:30 (5:31) (Class 5) (0-75,73) 3-Y-O+ — £3,234 (£962; £481; £240) Stalls Low

Form				RPR
1121	1		**Powerful Presence (IRE)**[29] 2671 5-9-12 **71** ... SilvestreDeSousa 1	85+
			(David O'Meara) *hld up: hdwy on ins to trck ldrs over 5f out: swtchd lft over 2f out: led and edgd rt over 1f out: hld on wl* **5/4**[1]	
6110	2	*¾*	**Dysios (IRE)**[23] 2838 3-9-5 **73** ... J-PGuillambert 6	81
			(Luca Cumani) *trckd ldrs: pushed along 4f out: styd on to chse wnr 1f out: edgd rt: kpt on same pce* **7/2**[2]	
3120	3	*2 ¾*	**Bussa**[8] 3340 3-9-4 **72** ... CathyGannon 4	73
			(David Evans) *trckd ldrs: effrt over 2f out: sn n.m.r: one pce appr fnl f* **16/1**	
3161	4	*2*	**Bold Marc (IRE)**[24] 2815 9-9-13 **72** ... HughBowman 3	71
			(Mrs K Burke) *led hdd over 1f out: wknd last 100yds* **9/2**[3]	
-001	5	*8*	**Orchid Street (USA)**[9] 3309 3-9-4 **72** ... TomQueally 2	49
			(Ann Duffield) *hld up: hdwy and n.m.r over 2f out: rdn and wknd over 1f out* **8/1**	
4335	6	*7*	**Star Addition**[2] 3545 5-8-9 **54** oh3 ... DuranFentiman 5	17
			(Eric Alston) *sn upsides ldr: wknd over 1f out: sn bhd* **10/1**	

1m 43.57s (0.67) **Going Correction** -0.075s/f (Good)
WFA 3 from 5yo+ 9lb 6 Ran SP% **110.9**
Speed ratings (Par 103): **93,92,89,87,79 72**
toteswingers: 1&2 £1.80, 1&3 £10.30, 2&3 £15.00 CSF £5.63 TOTE £2.10: £1.30, £2.30; EX 6.10.
Owner The Lawton Bamforth Partnership **Bred** Corduff Stud **Trained** Nawton, N Yorks
FOCUS
They went a decent pace in this ordinary handicap. This has been rated on the positive side around the third.
T/Plt: £221.00 to a £1 stake. Pool: £136,646.22. 451.23 winning tickets. T/Qpdt: £44.80 to a £1 stake. Pool: £7,545.08. 124.60 winning tickets. WG

3307 LEICESTER (R-H)
Saturday, July 2

OFFICIAL GOING: Good (good to firm in places; watered; 7.7)
Wind: Cloudy with sunny spells Weather: Nil

3630 PENTAGON VAUXHALL EAST MIDLANDS FILLIES' H'CAP — 5f 218y
2:10 (2:11) (Class 5) (0-70,71) 3-Y-O — £2,911 (£866; £432; £216) Stalls High

Form				RPR
0052	1		**Millyluvstobougie**[10] 3283 3-9-1 **71** ... LucyKBarry(7) 10	78
			(Clive Cox) *hld up in tch: hung rt fr over 2f out: led over 1f out: jst hld on* **2/1**[1]	
2163	2	*hd*	**Shes Rosie**[10] 3269 3-9-4 **67** ... RussKennemore 5	73
			(John O'Shea) *led 1f: chsd ldrs: rdn and ev ch fr over 1f out: r.o* **5/1**[3]	
0332	3	*2*	**Cool In The Shade**[14] 3191 3-8-5 **54** ...(p) MartinLane 1	54
			(Paul Midgley) *s.i.s: hld up: hdwy over 2f out: rdn and ev ch over 1f out: styd on same pce ins fnl f* **13/2**	
2-10	4	*4*	**Lady Kildare (IRE)**[32] 2592 3-8-13 **65** ... PatrickDonaghy(3) 8	52
			(Jedd O'Keeffe) *chsd ldrs: led over 3f out: rdn and hdd over 1f out: wknd ins fnl f* **9/1**	
6035	5	*1 ¾*	**Alkhawarah (USA)**[15] 3114 3-8-13 **62** ... AdrianNicholls 2	44
			(Mark Johnston) *chsd ldrs: rdn over 2f out: edgd lft and wknd over 1f out* **16/1**	
0-00	6	*4*	**Azzoom (IRE)**[45] 2200 3-9-2 **65** ... ChrisCatlin 4	34
			(Clive Brittain) *mid-div: rdn over 3f out: wknd over 2f out* **22/1**	
001	7	*hd*	**Pinch Of Posh (IRE)**[16] 3091 3-9-5 **68** ... JimCrowley 3	36
			(Paul Cole) *s.i.s: outpcd* **4/1**[2]	
	8	*15*	**Style Margi (IRE)**[78] 1376 3-9-6 **69** ... PatCosgrave 6	—
			(Ed de Giles) *s.i.s: rcvrd to ld 5f out: hdd over 3f out: wknd 2f out* **8/1**	
0106	9	*3 ¾*	**Gothic Chick**[4] 3482 3-7-12 **54** ...(v[1]) NoraLooby(7) 7	—
			(Alan McCabe) *s.i.s: rdn over 3f out: wknd over 2f out* **40/1**	

1m 11.9s (-1.10) **Going Correction** -0.25s/f (Firm) 9 Ran SP% **117.1**
Speed ratings (Par 97): **97,96,94,88,86 81,80,60,55**
toteswingers: 1&2 £1.70, 1&3 £1.70, 2&3 £3.80 CSF £12.34 CT £55.60 TOTE £3.50: £1.50, £1.10, £2.40; EX 12.90.
Owner Ken Lock Racing **Bred** Ken Lock Racing **Trained** Lambourn, Berks
FOCUS
Just an ordinary fillies' handicap. Winner looks back to her best with the runner-up the standard.
Pinch Of Posh(IRE) Official explanation: vet said filly finished distressed

3631 SLIDEROBES (S) STKS — 5f 218y
2:45 (2:52) (Class 6) 2-Y-O — £2,070 (£616; £307; £153)

Form				RPR
24	1		**That's Dangerous**[60] 1785 2-8-6 0 ... KieranO'Neill(5) 4	72+
			(Roger Charlton) *chsd ldr tl led over 3f out: rdn over 1f out: styd on wl* **2/1**[2]	
240	2	*2*	**Artists Corner**[22] 2889 2-8-6 0 ... BarryMcHugh 2	62+
			(Richard Fahey) *hmpd s: sn prom: chsd wnr 1/2-way: rdn over 1f out: styd on same pce ins fnl f* **11/8**[1]	
0635	3	*5*	**River Nova**[5] 3463 2-8-1 0 ... HarryBentley(5) 1	45
			(Alan Jarvis) *prom: rdn over 2f out: wknd over 1f out* **7/1**[3]	
0	4	*4*	**June Thirteen (IRE)**[19] 2998 2-8-11 0 ... PatDobbs 6	38
			(Richard Hannon) *led: hdd over 3f out: sn rdn: wknd wl over 1f out* **9/1**	
503	5	*nk*	**Aljosan**[19] 2998 2-8-6 0 ... MartinLane 7	32
			(David Evans) *prom: rdn 1/2-way: wknd over 2f out* **9/1**	
46	6	*12*	**Jaci Uzzi (IRE)**[40] 2362 2-8-6 0 ... AdrianNicholls 3	—
			(David Evans) *sn pushed along and prom: rdn over 3f out: wknd 2f out* **12/1**	

1m 12.2s (-0.80) **Going Correction** -0.25s/f (Firm) 6 Ran SP% **115.6**
Speed ratings (Par 92): **95,92,85,80,79 63**
toteswingers:1&2:£1.20, 1&3:£6.60, 2&3:£1.20 CSF £5.38 TOTE £2.80: £2.10, £1.10; EX 5.70.The winner was bought in for 9,500gns.
Owner D Carter and P Inglett **Bred** Mrs G Sainty **Trained** Beckhampton, Wilts
FOCUS
Godber (7/1) broke the stalls when bursting out and running loose, so this race had to be run from a flag start. Deduct 10p in the £ under R4. New market formed.
NOTEBOOK
That's Dangerous found plenty out in front and was always holding off Artists Corner. The step up to 6f appeared to help the winner, whose two previous outings had been over the minimum trip. The way he saw this out suggests he'll probably go a bit further in time and he's a colt with scope for further progress. (old market op 9-4 tchd 5-2)
Artists Corner took quite a heavy broadside from River Nova at the start, which meant she wasn't the sharpest away. She posted a really good effort to finish 5l clear of the rest given what happened to him at the start. She has shown enough to suggest she can go one better at this level. (old market op 9-4 tchd 13-8)
River Nova failed to improve for the step up to 6f. (old market op 12-1 tchd 14-1 and 17-2)

3632 BRITISH STALLION STUDS E.B.F./EAST MIDLANDS AIRPORT FILLIES' H'CAP — 1m 1f 218y
3:20 (3:20) (Class 4) (0-80,80) 3-Y-O+ — £5,175 (£1,540; £769; £384)

Form				RPR
1161	1		**Apache Glory (USA)**[23] 2849 3-9-1 **78** ... PatDobbs 6	86+
			(Richard Hannon) *a.p: chsd ldr over 2f out: rdn to ld and edgd lft over 1f out: r.o* **6/1**	
23-1	2	*1 ½*	**Ken's Girl**[26] 2769 7-10-0 **80** ... PatCosgrave 4	85
			(Stuart Kittow) *led: rdn and hdd over 1f out: styd on same pce ins fnl f* **11/2**[3]	
00-2	3	*nk*	**Hayaku (USA)**[35] 2511 3-8-10 **73** ...(t) JimCrowley 8	77
			(Ralph Beckett) *hld up: rdn over 2f out: hdwy u.p fr over 1f out: r.o: nt rch ldrs* **5/1**[2]	
-004	4	*nk*	**Sing Sweetly**[17] 3042 4-9-6 **77** ... TobyAtkinson(5) 7	81+
			(Gerard Butler) *hld up: hdwy over 2f out: rdn over 1f out: styd on* **10/1**	
0-36	5	*2 ¼*	**Cosmic Moon**[29] 2695 3-8-8 **71** ... BarryMcHugh 2	70
			(Richard Fahey) *mid-div: hdwy over 3f out: rdn over 1f out: styd on same pce ins fnl f* **12/1**	
0324	6	*1 ¼*	**Bollin Dolly**[21] 2906 8-9-8 **74** ... DavidNolan 10	71
			(Tim Easterby) *hld up: hdwy over 3f out: rdn over 2f out: styd on: nt trble ldrs* **4/1**[1]	
2030	7	*nse*	**Night Lily (IRE)**[30] 2647 5-9-13 **79** ... TonyCulhane 12	76+
			(Paul D'Arcy) *hld up: swtchd rt over 2f out: hdwy over 1f out: r.o: nt rch ldrs* **15/2**	
04-0	8	*5*	**Gale Green**[20] 2956 4-8-13 **70** ... AmyScott(5) 3	57
			(Henry Candy) *chsd ldrs: rdn over 2f out: wknd ins fnl f* **33/1**	
10-0	9	*5*	**Golden Delicious**[58] 1837 3-9-3 **80** ... ChrisCatlin 11	57
			(Hughie Morrison) *hld up in tch: racd keenly: rdn over 2f out: wknd over 1f out* **14/1**	
6-60	10	*11*	**Ashkalara**[22] 2872 4-8-5 **62** ... RyanClark(5) 9	17
			(Stuart Howe) *hld up: a in rr: rdn and wknd over 2f out* **25/1**	
100-	11	*3 ¾*	**Balletlou (IRE)**[324] 5008 4-9-4 **73** ... KierenFox(3) 5	20
			(John Best) *hld up: stmbld 6f out: effrt over 3f out: sn wknd* **20/1**	
55-0	12	*2 ¼*	**Evening Dress**[7] 3387 3-8-4 **67** ... AdrianNicholls 1	10
			(Mark Johnston) *chsd ldr tl rdn over 2f out: sn wknd* **20/1**	

2m 4.80s (-3.10) **Going Correction** -0.25s/f (Firm)
WFA 3 from 4yo+ 11lb 12 Ran SP% **117.9**
Speed ratings (Par 102): **102,100,100,100,98 97,97,93,89,80 77,75**
toteswingers:1&2:£5.10, 1&3:£13.60, 2&3:£11.80 CSF £36.61 CT £179.40 TOTE £6.80: £2.80, £2.30, £2.00; EX 30.50.
Owner Malih Lahej Al Basti **Bred** Malih Al Basti **Trained** East Everleigh, Wilts

The Form Book, Raceform Ltd, Compton, RG20 6NL

FOCUS
Another flip start. Only fillies' form and it has not been rated too positively, though it's arguably worth a bit more at face value. The one-two were always prominent.
Balletlou(IRE) Official explanation: jockey said filly stumbled and lost its action

3633 STORMCLAD HOME IMPROVEMENTS RATING RELATED MAIDEN STKS 7f 9y
3:50 (3:50) (Class 5) 3-Y-O **£2,911** (£866; £432; £216)

Form RPR
-452 **1** **Icebuster**[15] 3133 3-9-1 70 .... JamesMillman 11 69
(Rod Millman) *a.p: chsd ldr over 2f out: rdn over 1f out: r.o to ld post* **7/2**[2]
3-34 **2** *shd* **Red Marling (IRE)**[47] 2147 3-9-1 70 .... MichaelHills 7 69+
(B W Hills) *plld hrd and prom: rdn over 2f out: led wl ins fnl f: hdd post* **3/1**[1]
40-0 **3** *½* **Makheelah**[32] 2596 3-8-12 65 .... ChrisCatlin 4 64
(Clive Brittain) *mid-div: hdwy over 2f out: rdn to ld and hung lft ins fnl f: sn hdd and unable qck* **16/1**
256- **4** *2* **Phoenix Flame**[186] 7990 3-8-7 60 .... KieranO'Neill(5) 9 59
(Alan McCabe) *hld up: hdwy and n.m.r wl over 1f out: sn rdn: styd on same pce ins fnl f* **40/1**
500 **5** *1 ¾* **Brio**[24] 2802 3-9-1 62 ....(p) TonyCulhane 10 57
(Alan McCabe) *led: rdn and edgd rt fr over 1f out: hdd and no ex ins fnl f* **80/1**
-026 **6** *½* **Mister Ben Vereen**[23] 2853 3-9-1 63 ....(b1) JimCrowley 1 56
(Eve Johnson Houghton) *hld up: plld hrd: rdn over 2f out: hdwy over 1f out: r.o: nt rch ldrs* **16/1**
363 **7** *nk* **To The Spring**[29] 2691 3-8-12 70 .... ShaneKelly 6 52
(William Haggas) *dwlt: hld up: rdn over 2f out: hdwy over 1f out: nt trble ldrs* **7/2**[2]
56-0 **8** *3 ¾* **Jahanara (IRE)**[11] 3259 3-8-12 65 .... PatDobbs 5 42
(Richard Hannon) *s.i.s: hld up: rdn over 2f out: nt clr run over 1f out: nvr on terms* **25/1**
504 **9** *5* **Faith And Hope (IRE)**[34] 2529 3-8-12 70 ....(t) PatCosgrave 8 28
(James Fanshawe) *trckd ldrs: rdn over 2f out: wknd over 1f out* **12/1**
3-50 **10** *1 ½* **Too Many Questions (IRE)**[16] 3093 3-9-1 67 .... MartinLane 3 27
(David Evans) *plld hrd: w ldr tl rdn 1/2-way: wknd over 2f out* **12/1**
5202 **11** *10* **Tinaheely (IRE)**[12] 3219 3-8-9 70 .... AdamBeschizza(3) 2 —
(Jonathan Portman) *s.s: hdwy over 4f out: sn rdn and wknd* **7/1**[3]

1m 25.0s (-1.20) **Going Correction** -0.25s/f (Firm) **11** Ran SP% **116.6**
Speed ratings (Par 100): **96,95,95,93,91 90,90,85,80,78 66**
toteswingers:1&2:£1.80, 1&3:£29.30, 2&3:£25.10 CSF £14.09 TOTE £3.30: £1.10, £1.50, £3.90; EX 10.60.
Owner The Links Partnership **Bred** Cheveley Park Stud Ltd **Trained** Kentisbeare, Devon
FOCUS
Again a flip start which, for a maiden, was far from ideal. A fairly ordinary maiden, with the third to fifth-placed finishers limiting the form.

3634 ROYAL CENTRE NOTTINGHAM H'CAP 7f 9y
4:25 (4:25) (Class 4) (0-85,85) 3-Y-O+ **£6,301** (£1,886; £943; £472; £235)

Form RPR
4245 **1** **Tevez**[10] 3285 6-9-7 81 .... MartinHarley(3) 11 96+
(Des Donovan) *s.i.s: hld up: hdwy over 2f out: led and hung rt fr over 1f out: r.o: easily* **9/2**[1]
5664 **2** *2 ½* **Barista (IRE)**[12] 3231 3-8-3 75 .... CharlesBishop(7) 3 76
(Mick Channon) *s.s: bhd: hdwy over 1f out: r.o to go 2nd wl ins fnl f: nt trble wnr* **22/1**
2400 **3** *1 ½* **Masai Moon**[19] 2995 7-9-12 83 ....(b) JamesMillman 1 83
(Rod Millman) *chsd ldrs: led 4f out: rdn and hdd over 1f out: styd on same pce* **12/1**
0531 **4** *¾* **Elusive Sue (USA)**[10] 3278 4-9-2 73 .... BarryMcHugh 2 71
(Richard Fahey) *hld up: nt clr run over 2f out: hdwy over 1f out: sn rdn* **11/1**
1456 **5** *2 ¼* **Yair Hill (IRE)**[22] 2878 3-8-12 77 .... MartinLane 8 66
(John Dunlop) *hld up: hdwy 1/2-way: rdn over 1f out: no ex* **6/1**[3]
0142 **6** *hd* **Hail Promenader (IRE)**[20] 2955 5-9-9 80 .... MichaelHills 9 71
(B W Hills) *prom: rdn 1/2-way: outpcd over 2f out: n.d after* **8/1**
-000 **7** *3* **Linnens Star (IRE)**[10] 3290 4-9-11 82 ....(v1) JimCrowley 7 65
(Ralph Beckett) *led over 5f out: hdd 4f out: rdn over 2f out: wknd over 1f out* **10/1**
0014 **8** *2 ¼* **Kakapuka**[8] 3348 4-9-6 77 .... RussKennemore 10 54
(Anabel K Murphy) *mid-div: lost pl over 4f out: n.d after* **16/1**
-320 **9** *1 ¾* **Sir Bruno (FR)**[42] 2300 4-9-6 77 ....(p) TonyCulhane 12 49
(Bryn Palling) *led: hdd over 5f out: pushed along 4f out: rdn and wknd over 1f out* **11/1**
4214 **10** *8* **Kingscroft (IRE)**[7] 3378 3-9-6 85 .... PatCosgrave 4 33
(Mark Johnston) *chsd ldrs: rdn over 2f out: wknd over 1f out: eased* **5/1**[2]
4-05 **11** *¾* **Cloud Rock**[29] 2684 3-9-5 84 .... RobertHavlin 6 30
(Peter Chapple-Hyam) *chsd ldrs tl rdn and wknd over 2f out* **7/1**

1m 25.2s (-1.00) **Going Correction** -0.25s/f (Firm)
WFA 3 from 4yo+ 8lb **11** Ran SP% **116.4**
Speed ratings (Par 105): **95,92,90,89,87 86,83,80,78,69 68**
toteswingers:1&2:£47.80, 1&3:£47.80, 2&3:£30.40 CSF £102.39 CT £1134.30 TOTE £5.90: £1.70, £7.30, £3.70; EX 126.70.
Owner River Racing **Bred** P A And Mrs D G Sakal **Trained** Newmarket, Suffolk
FOCUS
A flip start again. This had the look of a fairly open handicap on paper, and it has been rated around the runner-up to this year's form.
Masai Moon Official explanation: jockey said gelding hung left

3635 FENWICK OF LEICESTER H'CAP 5f 2y
4:55 (4:55) (Class 5) (0-70,72) 3-Y-O **£2,911** (£866; £432; £216) **Stalls** High

Form RPR
-322 **1** **Volcanic Dust (IRE)**[12] 3239 3-9-4 72 .... RyanClark(5) 3 78
(Milton Bradley) *w ldrs: led over 3f out: rdn over 1f out: jst hld on* **5/1**[2]
245 **2** *shd* **Porthgwidden Beach (USA)**[12] 3223 3-7-11 51 oh2(t) KieranO'Neill(5) 8 57
(Stuart Williams) *chsd ldrs: rdn over 1f out: r.o* **11/1**
2443 **3** *1* **Climaxfortackle (IRE)**[5] 3470 3-8-13 62 ....(v) RobbieFitzpatrick 4 64
(Derek Shaw) *sn outpcd: r.o ins fnl f: nt rch ldrs* **7/1**[3]
4240 **4** *½* **Pineapple Pete (IRE)**[23] 2845 3-8-12 64 ....(tp) MartinHarley(3) 6 64
(Alan McCabe) *s.i.s: hdwy 1/2-way: rdn over 1f out: styd on* **8/1**
0513 **5** *½* **Madame Kintyre**[15] 3136 3-9-2 65 .... JamesMillman 7 63
(Rod Millman) *chsd ldrs: rdn over 1f out: styd on same pce ins fnl f* **4/1**[1]
4-52 **6** *1 ¾* **Aristeia**[15] 3122 3-9-5 68 .... PatDobbs 2 60
(Richard Hannon) *hld up: pushed along 1/2-way: running on wl whn nt clr run ins fnl f: nvr able to chal* **5/1**[2]
0003 **7** *nk* **Whoateallthepius (IRE)**[10] 3292 3-9-4 67 ....(p) ShaneKelly 9 58
(Dean Ivory) *led: hdd over 3f out: rdn 1/2-way: styd on same pce fnl f* **5/1**[2]
5256 **8** *2 ¼* **Vicona (IRE)**[15] 3136 3-9-3 66 ....(p) JimCrowley 5 49
(Paul Cole) *prom: rdn 1/2-way: wknd ins fnl f* **11/1**
0255 **9** *22* **Take Root**[12] 3239 3-9-4 67 ....(p) ChrisCatlin 1 —
(Reg Hollinshead) *s.i.s: sn prom: rdn and wknd 1/2-way* **14/1**

59.90 secs (-0.10) **Going Correction** -0.25s/f (Firm) **9** Ran SP% **116.9**
Speed ratings (Par 100): **90,89,88,87,86 83,83,79,44**
toteswingers:1&2:£7.70, 1&3:£5.40, 2&3:£7.40 CSF £59.03 CT £389.56 TOTE £5.40: £2.30, £3.80, £1.20; EX 92.80.
Owner Miss Diane Hill **Bred** Top Of The Form Syndicate **Trained** Sedbury, Gloucs
FOCUS
The front two have rated as having improved, with the third and fourth close to their marks.

3636 TAYLOR WIMPEY HOMES H'CAP 1m 60y
5:25 (5:27) (Class 6) (0-65,65) 3-Y-O+ **£2,070** (£616; £307; £153)

Form RPR
2326 **1** **Fault**[18] 3019 5-10-0 65 ....(t) PatCosgrave 2 73+
(Stef Higgins) *hld up: hdwy over 1f out: rdn: hung rt and r.o to ld wl ins fnl f* **4/1**[1]
-466 **2** *½* **Tanforan**[24] 2815 9-9-1 52 .... KellyHarrison 9 59
(Brian Baugh) *plld hrd: led after 1f and set stdy pce tl qcknd 3f out: rdn over 1f out: hdd wl ins fnl f* **16/1**
5403 **3** *1 ¾* **Ilie Nastase (FR)**[5] 3468 7-9-12 63 ....(b) RobertHavlin 8 67
(Conor Dore) *chsd ldrs: rdn over 1f out: nt clr run ins fnl f: r.o* **5/1**[2]
5340 **4** *nk* **Kheskianto (IRE)**[11] 3245 5-8-4 46 ....(bt) HarryBentley(5) 13 48
(Michael Chapman) *hld up: hdwy over 2f out: rdn over 1f out: styng on same pce whn nt clr run wl ins fnl f* **16/1**
2320 **5** *½* **Muftarres (IRE)**[24] 2799 6-10-0 65 .... TonyCulhane 6 66
(Paul Midgley) *hld up: hdwy over 3f out: chsd wnr over 1f out: sn rdn and ev ch: no ex ins fnl f* **5/1**[2]
5-34 **6** *2* **Scorn (USA)**[67] 1587 4-9-13 64 .... PatDobbs 11 61
(Richard Hannon) *s.i.s: hld up: rdn over 2f out: hdwy over 1f out: styd on* **8/1**
4006 **6** *dht* **Tortilla (IRE)**[12] 3230 3-8-12 61 .... MartinHarley(3) 3 56
(Des Donovan) *chsd ldrs: rdn over 2f out: styd on same pce fnl f* **16/1**
00-0 **8** *¾* **Cils Blancs (IRE)**[24] 2820 5-8-9 46 ....(b1) IvaMilickova 12 41
(Jane Chapple-Hyam) *hld up in tch: plld hrd: styd on same pce appr fnl f* **16/1**
060- **9** *½* **Distant Waters**[240] 7315 4-9-5 56 .... JimCrowley 5 50
(Alan Jarvis) *chsd ldrs: rdn over 2f out: no ex fnl f* **16/1**
6-06 **10** *3* **Polish Sunset**[12] 3223 3-8-7 53 .... MartinLane 1 38
(Amy Weaver) *led 1f: chsd ldr tl rdn over 3f out: wknd over 1f out* **16/1**
05-4 **11** *¾* **My Jeanie (IRE)**[16] 3096 7-8-4 46 oh1 .... KieranO'Neill(5) 14 31
(Jimmy Fox) *hld up: plld hrd: rdn over 2f out: n.d* **10/1**
-000 **12** *2* **Warden Bond**[12] 3223 3-8-3 52 .... AdamBeschizza(3) 10 30
(William Stone) *hld up: rdn over 2f out: n.d* **40/1**
0064 **13** *3 ½* **Vezere (USA)**[11] 3253 4-8-9 46 oh1 ....(b) ShaneKelly 4 18
(Simon Dow) *prom: rdn over 2f out: wknd over 1f out* **7/1**[3]

1m 48.4s (3.30) **Going Correction** -0.25s/f (Firm)
WFA 3 from 4yo+ 9lb **13** Ran SP% **123.8**
Speed ratings (Par 101): **73,72,70,70,69 67,67,67,66,63 62,60,57**
toteswingers:1&2:£21.80, 1&3:£7.80, 2&3:£8.90 CSF £73.62 CT £349.16 TOTE £4.00: £1.90, £4.70, £2.90; EX 70.40.
Owner David Gilbert **Bred** Mrs A M Vestey **Trained** Lambourn, Berks
FOCUS
A flip start for this weak handicap. There was no pace on and the race has been rated around the front-running runner-up to recent form.
Ilie Nastase(FR) Official explanation: jockey said gelding was denied a clear run
T/Plt: £67.50 to a £1 stake. Pool:£61,757.48 - 667.62 winning tickets T/Qpdt: £45.20 to a £1 stake. Pool:£4,144.01 - 67.70 winning tickets CR

2844 NOTTINGHAM (L-H)
Saturday, July 2
OFFICIAL GOING: Good to firm (7.3)
Wind: Almost nil Weather: Fine

3637 AJA LADIES' FEGENTRI WORLD CHAMPIONSHIP INVITATION H'CAP (FOR LADY AMATEUR RIDERS) 1m 2f 50y
6:10 (6:11) (Class 6) (0-60,60) 3-Y-O+ **£1,996** (£619; £309; £154) **Stalls** Low

Form RPR
0-U3 **1** **Back To Paris (IRE)**[1] 3600 9-9-9 48 ....(p) MissMMullineaux 2 59
(Philip Kirby) *led after 2f: mde rest: rdn 3f out: clr over 1f out: kpt on ins fnl f* **14/1**
0-36 **2** *4* **Chantilly Dancer (IRE)**[32] 2600 5-9-7 46 oh1 .... MissVictoriaAllers 7 49
(Michael Quinn) *hld up: rdn and gd hdwy on outer 2f out: wnt 2nd jst ins fnl f: kpt on: no ch w wnr* **25/1**
5340 **3** *1* **Market Puzzle (IRE)**[21] 2900 4-9-7 46 oh1 .... MlleJessicaMarcialis 5 47
(Mark Brisbourne) *hld up: swtchd to outer 4f out: rdn and gd hdwy 2f out: wnt 3rd jst ins fnl f: kpt on* **10/1**
4343 **4** *2 ¾* **Beneath**[5] 3453 4-10-7 60 ....(b) MrsCBartley 6 56
(Kevin Ryan) *midfield: rdn 3f out: hdwy to chal for 2nd over 1f out: wknd ins fnl f* **15/8**[1]
6315 **5** *¾* **Dragon Slayer (IRE)**[23] 2851 9-10-7 60 .... MissKJHarrison 8 54
(John Harris) *trckd ldrs: rdn to chal 3f out: stl 2nd over 1f out: wknd ins fnl f* **15/2**[3]
00-0 **6** *2 ½* **Apurna**[34] 2530 6-9-7 46 oh1 ....(b1) MlleDelphineGarcia-Dubois 9 35
(John Harris) *slowly away: hld up: rdn over 3f out: bhd tl kpt on ins fnl f: n.d* **50/1**
10-0 **7** *½* **Hurricane Thomas (IRE)**[19] 2991 7-10-4 57 .... MissPhillipaTutty 11 45
(Karen Tutty) *led for 2f: trckd ldrs: rdn 3f out: wknd over 1f out* **12/1**
0204 **8** *shd* **Bussell Along (IRE)**[21] 2905 5-9-7 46 oh1 .... MlleJadeyPietrasiewicz 3 34
(Pam Ford) *midfield on outer: rdn over 3f out: no imp* **20/1**
6200 **9** *7* **Professor John (IRE)**[23] 2851 4-10-5 58 ....(b) MmeBeritWeber 4 32
(Ian Wood) *midfield: rdn over 3f out: sn no imp: wknd over 1f out* **14/1**
0310 **10** *2 ½* **Iguacu**[11] 3256 7-9-13 52 ....(p) MissSBrotherton 10 21
(George Baker) *prom: rdn over 3f out: wknd over 1f out* **11/4**[2]

2m 16.03s (4.33) **Going Correction** +0.175s/f (Good)
WFA 3 from 4yo+ 11lb **10** Ran SP% **113.9**
Speed ratings (Par 101): **89,85,85,82,82 80,79,79,74,72**
toteswingers: 1&2 £29.10, 1&3 £11.50, 2&3 £19.60 CSF £309.27 CT £3603.82 TOTE £14.80: £5.30, £10.10, £2.90; EX 169.40.
Owner Julie Haughton,Mark Cooper,Philip Kirby **Bred** P Bolger **Trained** Castleton, N Yorks

FOCUS
All races on outer course. Rail out 2m on stands' bend and 5m on bottom bend, adding 16yds to distances. A modest ladies' invitation event and the level is set around the moderate runner-up.

3638 WINNING WAY WITH DG CARS (S) STKS 6f 15y
6:40 (6:42) (Class 6) 3-4-Y-O £2,070 (£616; £307; £153) Stalls High

Form RPR
03 1 **Gertmegalush (IRE)**[23] 2845 4-9-2 58 BarryMcHugh 6 68
(John Harris) *chsd ldrs: hdwy to ld over 2f out: rdn clr over 1f out: kpt on fnl f* 11/2[3]
2024 2 3 ½ **Finefrenzyrolling (IRE)**[13] 3207 3-8-5 65 (bt) MartinLane 2 51
(Mrs K Burke) *hld up in tch: rdn 2f out: hdwy to go 2nd over 1f out: kpt on: no ch w wnr* 13/8[1]
4400 3 6 **Prophet In A Dream**[8] 3337 3-8-7 68 MartinHarley(3) 1 37
(Mick Channon) *prom: rdn 3f out: sn outpcd: no imp over 1f out* 15/8[2]
-000 4 ½ **Craicattack (IRE)**[4] 3489 4-9-2 47 (p) KellyHarrison 5 36
(Sharon Watt) *hld up: rdn over 2f out: kpt on fnl f: nvr threatened* 50/1
6-05 5 11 **Turn The Tide**[32] 2581 3-8-5 70 PaulQuinn 4 —
(Mike Hammond) *s.i.s: hld up: a towards rr* 15/2
0-60 6 2 ¾ **Love Club**[9] 3321 3-8-10 46 SaleemGolam 3 —
(Brian Baugh) *pressed ldr: rdn over 2f out: sn wknd* 66/1
460 7 16 **Kate Skate**[4] 3476 4-8-8 53 (v[1]) AdamBeschizza(3) 7 —
(Gay Kelleway) *sn led: rdn whn hdd over 2f out: sn wknd: t.o* 14/1

1m 15.88s (0.98) **Going Correction** +0.175s/f (Good)
WFA 3 from 4yo 6lb 7 Ran SP% **110.1**
Speed ratings (Par 101): **100,95,87,86,72 68,47**
toteswingers: 1&2 £2.20, 1&3 £2.30, 2&3 £1.30 CSF £13.77 TOTE £7.00: £2.80, £1.10; EX 20.90.There was no bid for the winner.
Owner Peter Smith P C Coaches Limited **Bred** Kildare Racing Syndicate **Trained** Eastwell, Leics

FOCUS
A moderate seller in which the whole field raced towards the stands' side.

3639 GOLDEVA MAIDEN AUCTION FILLIES' STKS 5f 13y
7:10 (7:10) (Class 5) 2-Y-O £2,911 (£866; £432; £216) Stalls High

Form RPR
2 1 **Impassive**[16] 3092 2-8-8 0 RichardMullen 3 76+
(Ed McMahon) *mde all: rdn 2f out: strly pressed jst ins fnl f: kpt on: asserted nr fin* 1/4[1]
343 2 1 **Rougini (IRE)**[3] 3504 2-7-13 0 HarryBentley(5) 4 67
(Mrs K Burke) *prom: rdn 2f out: chal strly jst ins fnl f: kpt on: hld nr fin* 5/1[2]
406 3 4 **Phoenix Clubs (IRE)**[22] 2886 2-8-4 0 MartinLane 1 53
(Paul Midgley) *prom: rdn 2f out: sn hung lft: one pce and no ch w ldng pair appr fnl f* 12/1[3]
0 4 2 **Empressive**[10] 3270 2-8-1 0 PaulPickard(3) 7 46
(William Muir) *chsd ldrs: rdn and outpcd over 2f out: no imp over 1f out* 33/1
040 5 1 ¼ **Nude (IRE)**[15] 3117 2-8-1 0 SophieDoyle(3) 5 41
(Sylvester Kirk) *hld up: rdn and outpcd over 2f out: nvr threatened* 20/1
6 nse **Colourful Event (IRE)** 2-8-4 0 FrankieMcDonald 6 41+
(David Arbuthnot) *slowly away: sn outpcd and green in rr: nvr threatened* 33/1

62.12 secs (1.12) **Going Correction** +0.175s/f (Good) 6 Ran SP% **115.0**
Speed ratings (Par 91): **98,96,90,86,84 84**
toteswingers: 1&2 £1.10, 1&3 £1.50, 2&3 £2.50 CSF £2.01 TOTE £1.30: £1.02, £2.00; EX 2.20.
Owner J C Fretwell **Bred** Fittocks Stud **Trained** Lichfield, Staffs

FOCUS
A run-of-the-mill juvenile fillies' maiden.

NOTEBOOK
Impassive, runner-up in a fair event at Warwick on her debut, was heavily backed to break her duck. Victory was secured only in the dying strides as the runner-up gave her a real fight. This was therefore an unimpressive victory, but she should stay a longer trip and be competitive in nurseries. (op 3-10 tchd 1-3 and 4-11 in places)
Rougini(IRE), third at Catterick on her latest start, seemed to improve on this stiffer track. That said, after making the winner work hard from the 2f marker, she faltered and stumbled slightly in the dying strides. She too can make a mark in nurseries. (tchd 11-2)
Phoenix Clubs(IRE), hampered when sixth in a decent York contest last time, was third throughout. She tried to stay with the first two until beyond halfway but was brushed aside in the closing stages. (tchd 14-1)
Empressive, last of 11 on her only previous start, took a small step forward. She will need to do a great deal better, however, to win a maiden.
Nude(IRE) had looked limited on her three previous outings and underlined that impression here. She was never closer than fifth. (op 16-1)
Colourful Event(IRE), a debutante half-sister to a 1m winner, reared at the start and was always playing unavailing catch-up thereafter. (tchd 50-1 in places)

3640 FOR YOUR COMFORT DG CARS 01159500500 H'CAP 5f 13y
7:40 (7:42) (Class 5) (0-70,70) 3-Y-O+ £2,911 (£866; £432; £216) Stalls High

Form RPR
0-15 1 **Baby Queen (IRE)**[28] 2720 5-9-4 62 J-PGuillambert 8 74+
(Brian Baugh) *mde all: rdn clr appr fnl f: comf* 9/2[2]
0050 2 4 **Divertimenti (IRE)**[14] 3179 7-9-10 68 (b) RussKennemore 7 66
(Roy Bowring) *hld up: rdn over 2f out: hdwy over 1f out: kpt on to go 2nd fnl 75yds: no ch w wnr* 11/2
535- 3 1 ½ **Star Twilight**[247] 7193 4-9-1 64 (v) HarryBentley(5) 9 56
(Derek Shaw) *chsd wnr: rdn over 2f out: kpt on one pce* 5/1[3]
21-0 4 1 ½ **Bertie Southstreet**[26] 2766 8-9-12 70 (v) RichardMullen 6 57
(Paul Midgley) *prom: rdn over 2f out: sn outpcd by wnr: no ex ins fnl f* 12/1
-261 5 shd **Musical Bridge**[21] 2913 5-9-10 68 (b) AndrewHeffernan 4 54
(Lisa Williamson) *in tch: rdn over 2f out: one pce* 4/1[1]
0-30 6 ½ **Liberty Ship**[32] 2585 6-8-7 56 (b) KieranO'Neill(5) 3 41
(Mark Buckley) *chsd ldr towards outer: rdn over 2f out: hung lft over 1f out: wknd fnl 100yds* 8/1
-140 7 2 ¾ **Bilash**[32] 2585 4-9-10 68 TonyCulhane 2 43
(Reg Hollinshead) *hld up: sn outpcd in rr: nvr threatened* 9/1
3000 8 6 **Danzoe (IRE)**[7] 3412 4-9-7 65 (v) SaleemGolam 5 18
(Christine Dunnett) *hld up: rdn over 2f out: wknd over 1f out* 16/1
303/ 9 25 **Lady Royal Oak (IRE)**[694] 4746 4-9-4 65 AshleyHamblett(3) 1 —
(Peter Chapple-Hyam) *wnt bdly lft s: racd keenly: hld up in tch on outer: lost pl over 2f out: sn bhd: eased ins fnl f* 8/1

61.13 secs (0.13) **Going Correction** +0.175s/f (Good) 9 Ran SP% **116.0**
Speed ratings (Par 103): **105,98,96,93,93 92,88,78,38**
toteswingers: 1&2 £7.10, 1&3 £4.90, 2&3 £5.50 CSF £29.63 CT £117.46 TOTE £5.60: £1.80, £2.60, £1.80; EX 33.30.
Owner G B Hignett **Bred** Gainsborough Stud Management Ltd **Trained** Audley, Staffs

FOCUS
Just a moderate sprint handicap with the top-weight rated 70 and several could be fancied. The first four raced nearest the rail, though not in finishing order. The winner has been rated a length personal best.

3641 YOUR RELIABLE BET 01159500500 DG CARS H'CAP 1m 2f 50y
8:10 (8:10) (Class 4) (0-80,78) 3-Y-O+ £5,175 (£1,540; £769; £384) Stalls Low

Form RPR
3113 1 **Art Scholar (IRE)**[2] 3559 4-8-13 63 NeilChalmers 9 80+
(Michael Appleby) *hld up: smooth hdwy 3f out: chsd ldr 2f out: led 1f out: pushed clr: comf* 6/1
4565 2 5 **Standpoint**[29] 2674 5-9-11 75 GrahamGibbons 5 84+
(Reg Hollinshead) *dwlt: sn in midfield: gd hdwy on inner over 3f out: led wl over 2f out: rdn whn hdd 1f out: sn no ch w wnr: eased fnl 75yds* 4/1[2]
21 3 2 ½ **Lady Chloe**[32] 2591 3-8-8 72 PaulPickard(3) 6 74
(Philip Kirby) *midfield on outer: rdn and hdwy over 2f out: one pce fr over 1f out* 7/2[1]
0306 4 2 ¾ **Champagne Style (USA)**[10] 3275 4-9-12 76 (p) PatDobbs 7 73
(Richard Guest) *hld up: rdn 3f out: hdwy over 1f out: kpt on one pce: nvr threatened* 11/1
-321 5 1 **Golden Waters**[11] 3251 4-9-6 70 CathyGannon 3 65
(Eve Johnson Houghton) *led after 1f: rdn whn hdd wl over 2f out: wknd appr fnl f* 11/2[3]
0020 6 5 **Marjury Daw (IRE)**[10] 3275 5-10-0 78 BarryMcHugh 2 63
(James Given) *led for 1f: trckd ldrs: rdn over 3f out: wknd over 1f out* 17/2
2444 7 7 **Saint Thomas (IRE)**[18] 3023 4-9-9 73 StephenCraine 8 44
(John Mackie) *trckd ldrs: rdn over 3f out: sn wknd* 14/1
-030 8 18 **King Zeal (IRE)**[22] 2892 7-9-13 77 RussKennemore 10 12
(Barry Leavy) *prom: rdn over 3f out: sn wknd* 8/1
4110 9 27 **Strong Vigilance (IRE)**[58] 1826 4-9-11 75 (p) JamieSpencer 4 —
(Michael Bell) *dwlt: hld up in rr: drvn 4f out: sn lost tch: t.o* 14/1

2m 12.1s (0.40) **Going Correction** +0.175s/f (Good)
WFA 3 from 4yo+ 11lb 9 Ran SP% **115.2**
Speed ratings (Par 105): **105,101,99,96,96 92,86,72,50**
toteswingers: 1&2 £3.20, 1&3 £2.00, 2&3 £4.10 CSF £30.15 CT £96.88 TOTE £8.90: £2.90, £2.60, £1.50; EX 36.30.
Owner D J Lewin **Bred** John Ramsbottom **Trained** Danethorpe, Notts

FOCUS
A fair handicap in which the top-weight was rated 78 and it produced a decisive winner. This has been rated around the runner-up to his recent best.
Strong Vigilance(IRE) Official explanation: jockey said gelding was slowly away and never travelled

3642 WINNING NUMBERS 01159500500 DG CARS H'CAP 1m 2f 50y
8:40 (8:41) (Class 5) (0-75,75) 3-Y-O £2,911 (£866; £432; £216) Stalls Low

Form RPR
3-31 1 **Set To Music (IRE)**[20] 2957 3-9-7 75 JamieSpencer 6 87
(Michael Bell) *trckd ldr: led 3f out: rdn clr over 1f out: kpt on: eased nr fin: comf* 5/2[1]
1152 2 4 ½ **Amistress**[9] 3325 3-9-0 68 CathyGannon 1 71
(Eve Johnson Houghton) *midield: hdwy over 3f out: rdn to go 2nd 2f out: kpt on: no ch w wnr fnl f* 5/2[1]
626 3 1 ½ **Diptimat**[16] 3080 3-9-5 73 (b) AdamKirby 5 73
(Marco Botti) *trckd ldr: chal 3f out: sn drvn and one pce* 12/1
-230 4 1 ¼ **Madrasa (IRE)**[22] 2874 3-9-2 70 RichardMullen 9 68
(Ed McMahon) *led: rdn whn hdd 3f out: sn dropped to 4th: one pce* 10/1[3]
1366 5 1 ½ **Tijori (IRE)**[24] 2819 3-9-4 72 PatDobbs 8 67
(Richard Hannon) *hld up: rdn over 3f out: one pce: nvr threatened* 11/1
35-4 6 13 **Mr Dream Maker (IRE)**[32] 2582 3-8-6 65 RyanClark(5) 4 34
(Ian Williams) *hld up: rdn over 3f out: sn no hdwy: wknd over 1f out* 11/4[2]
30-0 7 26 **Jaridh (USA)**[54] 1947 3-9-3 71 (v[1]) TedDurcan 7 —
(Saeed Bin Suroor) *in tch: rdn over 3f out: sn wknd: eased* 16/1

2m 14.34s (2.64) **Going Correction** +0.175s/f (Good) 7 Ran SP% **114.8**
Speed ratings (Par 100): **96,92,91,90,89 78,57**
toteswingers: 1&2 £1.70, 1&3 £2.90, 2&3 £2.60 CSF £9.13 CT £60.07 TOTE £2.80: £1.30, £2.10; EX 8.50.
Owner The Queen **Bred** His Highness The Aga Khan's Studs S C **Trained** Newmarket, Suffolk

FOCUS
An ordinary 3-y-o handicap.
Mr Dream Maker(IRE) Official explanation: trainer had no explanation for the poor form shown

3643 RAINBOW INTERNATIONAL FIRE AND FLOOD RESTORATION H'CAP 1m 75y
9:10 (9:11) (Class 5) (0-70,69) 3-Y-O+ £2,911 (£866; £432; £216) Stalls Centre

Form RPR
5133 1 **You've Been Mowed**[12] 3215 5-9-9 69 RyanClark(5) 3 82+
(Richard Price) *mde all: rdn over 2f out: clr over 1f out: kpt on: comf* 11/4[1]
4135 2 3 ¼ **See The Storm**[5] 3455 3-7-11 52 KieranO'Neill(5) 4 54
(Patrick Morris) *trckd wnr in 2nd: rdn over 2f out: outpcd over 1f out: kpt on fnl f* 12/1
-060 3 ½ **Joe Strummer (IRE)**[19] 3002 3-8-13 63 (v[1]) JamieSpencer 2 64
(Michael Bell) *trckd ldng pair: rdn over 2f out: hung lft over 1f out: kpt on one pce fnl f* 8/1
1024 4 1 ¼ **Mr Chocolate Drop (IRE)**[24] 2809 7-9-3 58 (t) AdamKirby 8 62+
(Mandy Rowland) *hld up in rr: rdn 3f out: sn hdwy on inner: keeping on whn short of room towards rail fnl 100yds: eased* 7/1
0022 5 3 ¼ **Bentley**[9] 3306 7-8-12 58 (p) LMcNiff(5) 1 51
(Brian Baugh) *trckd ldng pair: rdn and outpcd over 2f out: wknd fnl f* 6/1[3]
0065 6 2 ¾ **Ajdaad (USA)**[7] 3386 4-9-10 68 (p) MartinHarley(3) 6 54
(Alan McCabe) *midfield: rdn over 3f out: sn no imp* 11/2[2]
206- 7 6 **Rising Kheleyf (IRE)**[263] 6826 5-9-11 66 (p) BarryMcHugh 7 38
(John Harris) *hld up: rdn over 3f out: no imp* 25/1
3611 8 2 ¼ **Flying Applause**[23] 2845 6-9-12 67 (bt) RussKennemore 5 34
(Roy Bowring) *awkward leaving stalls: hld up: rdn over 3f out: a towards rr* 11/4[1]

1m 47.51s (1.91) **Going Correction** +0.175s/f (Good)
WFA 3 from 4yo+ 9lb 8 Ran SP% **118.2**
Speed ratings (Par 103): **97,93,93,92,88 86,80,77**
toteswingers: 1&2 £15.40, 1&3 £3.10, 2&3 £15.50 CSF £39.93 CT £240.72 TOTE £4.30: £1.70, £4.60, £3.70; EX 51.10.
Owner Mrs K Oseman **Bred** T E Pocock **Trained** Ullingswick, H'fords

FOCUS
A modest finale, with the top-weight rated 69, but run at a fair pace. A small personal best for thr winner, with the runner-up and third close to their marks.
Joe Strummer(IRE) Official explanation: jockey said gelding hung left

Mr Chocolate Drop(IRE) Official explanation: jockey said gelding was denied a clear run
Flying Applause Official explanation: jockey said gelding juumped off awkwardly
T/Plt: £595.00 to a £1 stake. Pool: £58,120.32. 71.30 winning tickets. T/Qpdt: £5.30 to a £1 stake. Pool: £5,830.67. 812.90 winning tickets. AS

3588 SANDOWN (R-H)

Saturday, July 2

OFFICIAL GOING: Sprint course - good to firm (good in places); round course - good (good to firm in back straight)
Wind: Almost nil Weather: Fine, warm

3644 CORAL CHARGE (REGISTERED AS THE SPRINT STKS) (GROUP 3) 5f 6y

2:00 (2:00) (Class 1) 3-Y-O+

£28,355 (£10,750; £5,380; £2,680; £1,345; £675) **Stalls** Low

Form RPR

-114 **1** **Night Carnation**[21] 2928 3-8-9 108 JimmyFortune 2 110
(Andrew Balding) *lw: trckd ldng pair against rail: rdn to ld jst ins fnl f: styd on wl* **11/2**

5-64 **2** 1 3/4 **Beyond Desire**[23] 2861 4-9-0 92 NeilCallan 3 106
(Roger Varian) *led against rail: hdd and outpcd jst ins fnl f* **9/1**

0015 **3** 1/2 **Humidor (IRE)**[34] 2525 4-9-3 93 (t) MatthewDavies 1 107
(George Baker) *swtg: walked to post: hld up in midfield against rail: prog 2f out: tk 3rd fnl f: styd on* **25/1**

3411 **4** 1 3/4 **Margot Did (IRE)**[14] 3158 3-8-9 112 HayleyTurner 10 96+
(Michael Bell) *lw: chsd ldng pair: disp 2nd 2f out: fdd fnl f* **5/1**[3]

-052 **5** 1 **Triple Aspect (IRE)**[28] 5-9-3 108 JMurtagh 5 97
(William Haggas) *hld up in midfield: rdn 2f out: no prog* **9/2**[2]

-260 **6** 1/2 **Kingsgate Native (IRE)**[14] 3154 6-9-3 115 (v[1]) RyanMoore 9 95+
(Sir Michael Stoute) *t.k.h: racd wd in midfield: rdn and no prog 2f out* **4/1**[1]

10-0 **7** *hd* **Broox (IRE)**[63] 1686 3-8-12 112 MartinDwyer 8 93
(E J O'Neill, France) *slowest away: hld up in last trio: rdn 2f out: no prog* **20/1**

1-13 **8** *shd* **Pastoral Player**[14] 3155 4-9-3 103 GeorgeBaker 6 94
(Hughie Morrison) *lw: hld up in last trio: shkn up over 1f out: sme late prog* **13/2**

1-00 **9** 1 3/4 **Astrophysical Jet**[18] 3010 4-9-0 109 GrahamGibbons 7 85
(Ed McMahon) *s.i.s: a bhd* **15/2**

0010 **10** 5 **Burning Thread (IRE)**[14] 3155 4-9-3 98 TedDurcan 4 70
(Tim Etherington) *chsd ldr to 2f out: wknd qckly* **40/1**

59.68 secs (-1.92) **Going Correction** -0.05s/f (Good)
WFA 3 from 4yo+ 5lb **10** Ran SP% **116.4**
Speed ratings (Par 113): **113,110,109,106,105 104,103,103,100,92**
toteswingers:1&2:£18.20, 1&3:£25.10, 2&3:£37.20 CSF £52.52 TOTE £7.70: £2.40, £2.50, £5.90; EX 57.90 Trifecta £309.10 Pool: £1,503.96 - 3.60 winning units..
Owner George Strawbridge **Bred** George Strawbridge **Trained** Kingsclere, Hants

FOCUS
Round Course at normal inner configuration and distances as advertised. Sprint course rail dolled out 3yds. A strongly run Group 3 sprint in which it paid to be handy, whilst the draw also played its part with the first three home berthed closest to the far rail. The third has been rated as producing a length personal best, though he may be flattered.

NOTEBOOK
Night Carnation had 7l to find with Margot Did on last month's C&D running on an easier surface, but she was badly drawn there whilst the winner had a great draw and the roles were reversed this time. She was always travelling well in stalking the leader against the rail and quickened up smartly to hit the front well inside the last furlong. Her trainer had feared the ground drying up too much, so she can be marked up for this and she looks just the type to go on to even better things, provided the surface isn't too quick. (op 6-1)
Beyond Desire, having only her second try over the minimum trip, is only rated 92 so had plenty on at this level, but she benefited from being given a positive ride from her good draw and, with her stamina guaranteed, managed to hold off all bar the winner. (op 10-1 tchd 8-1)
Humidor(IRE) knows how to win, but he was worst in on official ratings so this was a cracking effort. Having been led to post, he was held up in the pack once under way and, having been switched left passing the furlong pole, finished with a flourish and very nearly got up for second. However, what this performance will do to his handicap mark remains to be seen. (op 20-1)
Margot Did(IRE) had developed a habit of finding one or two too good after winning her first two starts as a juvenile, but came here at the top of her game following wins in Listed events over this C&D and at Ayr. However, unlike when beating Night Carnation here last month, she had the worst of the draw this time and could never quite get on terms with the principals. (op 13-2, tchd 7-1 in places)
Triple Aspect(IRE) came into this with a record of 3-4 over C&D including this race last year, but he could never get himself involved this time once coming under pressure. (op 5-1 tchd 6-1)
Kingsgate Native(IRE), who was successful the last time he raced in Group 3 company, wore cheekpieces when only tenth in the Golden Jubilee and was tried in a visor here, but he saw plenty of daylight on the outside and never threatened to get involved. (op 5-1 tchd 7-2)
Broox(IRE) was back to sprinting after finishing a tailed-off last in the 2,000 Guineas on his return, but he gave away ground at the start which was fatal in a race like this. (tchd 16-1)
Pastoral Player has developed into a most progressive handicapper and was well worth a go at this level, but this was his first try over the minimum trip and he found everything happening too quickly. (op 5-1)

3645 CORAL CHALLENGE (H'CAP) 1m 14y

2:35 (2:36) (Class 2) 3-Y-O+

£43,575 (£13,048; £6,524; £3,262; £1,631; £819) **Stalls** Low

Form RPR

0532 **1** **Highland Knight (IRE)**[29] 2679 4-8-9 89 (t) DavidProbert 8 102
(Andrew Balding) *trckd ldr after 2f: led over 2f out and kicked clr: drvn out: unchal* **10/1**

-436 **2** 1 3/4 **Start Right**[17] 3032 4-9-5 99 KierenFallon 12 108+
(Luca Cumani) *hld up towards rr: plld out and prog 2f out: drvn to chse wnr jst ins fnl f: hung rt and styd on: nvr cl enough to chal* **11/2**[1]

-020 **3** 1 1/2 **Sooraah**[17] 3032 4-8-12 92 RyanMoore 1 98+
(William Haggas) *lw: hld up in midfield on inner: effrt over 2f out: prog wl over 1f out: styd on to take 3rd fnl f* **15/2**[2]

-664 **4** 3/4 **Pendragon (USA)**[17] 3032 8-8-11 91 GrahamGibbons 6 95
(Brian Ellison) *lw: hld up in midfield: shkn up over 2f out: prog over 1f out: styd on to take 4th ins fnl f* **8/1**[3]

2-01 **5** 1/2 **Duster**[19] 2995 4-8-8 88 HayleyTurner 7 91
(Hughie Morrison) *led 1f: chsd ldng pair: hrd rdn and outpcd fr 2f out: one pce after* **25/1**

12-0 **6** 1/2 **Man Of Action (USA)**[42] 2284 4-9-2 96 (v[1]) TedDurcan 3 98
(Saeed Bin Suroor) *lw: chsd ldrs and a abt same pl: nt qckn 2f out: kpt on same pce* **20/1**

4251 **7** *shd* **Leviathan**[10] 3290 4-8-12 92 CO'Donoghue 5 93+
(Tony Newcombe) *hld up in last pair: stl there 2f out: swtchd out wd and gd prog over 1f out: too much to do* **15/2**[2]

-144 **8** 1/2 **Decent Fella (IRE)**[15] 3109 5-8-12 92 (v) LiamKeniry 4 92
(Andrew Balding) *prom: gng strly 3f out: shkn up over 2f out: chsd clr wnr over 1f out: nt qckn and no imp: wknd ins fnl f* **9/1**

542- **9** 3/4 **Emerald Wilderness (IRE)**[484] 821 7-8-8 91 JohnFahy[(3)] 11 90+
(Robert Cowell) *dwlt: t.k.h: hld up in rr: prog over 2f out: no hdwy fr midfield over 1f out: wl hld whn nt clr run briefly jst over 1f out* **66/1**

30-0 **10** *nk* **Circumvent**[15] 3107 4-9-10 104 JMurtagh 15 102
(Paul Cole) *swtchd fr wd draw to inner: hld up in last pair: stl there and pushed along 2f out: sed to run on jst over 1f out: nvr any ch and eased last 100yds* **18/1**

2510 **11** 1/2 **Benandonner (USA)**[29] 2679 8-8-11 91 ow1 SeamieHeffernan 17 88
(Mike Murphy) *t.k.h: hld up wl in rr: no prog 2f out: kpt on ins fnl f: no threat* **50/1**

-535 **12** 3/4 **Toolain (IRE)**[42] 2296 3-9-1 104 (p) NeilCallan 10 101
(Roger Varian) *trckd ldrs: effrt over 2f out: ch of pl over 1f out: hanging rt and fnd nil: sltly impeded and heavily eased ins fnl f* **9/1**

-000 **13** 1/2 **Harrison George (IRE)**[21] 2933 6-9-1 102 GeorgeChaloner[(7)] 2 96
(Richard Fahey) *awkward s: a towards rr on inner: rdn and no prog over 2f out* **25/1**

5-41 **14** 4 **Dunn'o (IRE)**[37] 2441 6-9-4 98 AdamKirby 14 83
(Clive Cox) *taken down early: spd fr wd draw: led after 1f and crossed over: hdd over 2f out: lost 2nd over 1f out: wknd rapidly fnl f* **9/1**

0100 **15** 5 **Kyllachy Star**[17] 3032 5-9-3 97 JimmyFortune 13 70
(Richard Fahey) *lw: racd wd in midfield: no prog over 2f out: wknd rapidly wl over 1f out* **25/1**

0100 **16** 2 3/4 **Light From Mars**[21] 2909 6-9-6 100 SteveDrowne 9 67
(David Nicholls) *prom tl wknd rapidly fr 2f out* **22/1**

-145 **P** **Trade Storm**[16] 3067 3-8-10 99 TadhgO'Shea 16 —
(John Gallagher) *stmbld bdly leaving stalls and p.u* **20/1**

1m 39.61s (-3.69) **Going Correction** -0.175s/f (Firm)
WFA 3 from 4yo+ 9lb **17** Ran SP% **123.2**
Speed ratings (Par 109): **111,109,107,107,106 106,105,105,104,104 103,103,102,98,93 90,—**
toteswingers:1&2:£9.10, 1&3:£19.80, 2&3:£8.10 CSF £57.27 CT £464.01 TOTE £13.30: £3.20, £1.80, £2.40, £2.30; EX 55.60 Trifecta £686.90 Pool: £22,596.18 - 24.34 winning units..
Owner J C Smith **Bred** Littleton Stud **Trained** Kingsclere, Hants

FOCUS
A red-hot handicap, as it should be for the money, and run in a time just over half a second outside the course record. Again the winner benefited from racing handily. The winner and runner-up have been rated as producing personal bests, with the third, fourth and fifth setting the standard.

NOTEBOOK
Highland Knight(IRE) was put up 2lb after chasing home the subsequent Hunt Cup second Dance And Dance at Epsom last time, but it made little difference as he won this well under a nicely judged ride. He was always close to the pace, and being sent for home over 2f out as the leader faded proved to be a race-winning move. This was his first handicap success, but surely not his last. (op 11-1 tchd 9-1)
Start Right was by no means disgraced when sixth in the Hunt Cup, but hasn't enjoyed the best of luck and was drawn wider than ideal here. Having travelled well enough in midfield, he had to be switched wide coming to the last 2f and, although finishing powerfully, there was no way he was ever going to catch the winner. He deserves a change of luck, but is now 11lb higher than for his last win and is unlikely to be dropped for this. (op 6-1, tchd 13-2 in a place)
Sooraah found herself drawn on the wrong side in the Hunt Cup, but had previously run a subsequent winner close at Ascot and this was more indicative of her ability. She finished well against the inside rail from over 1f out and should be up to winning a nice handicap. (op 7-1 tchd 8-1 and 17-2 in a place)
Pendragon(USA) had three of today's rivals behind him when fourth in the Hunt Cup off 2lb lower and he again stayed on well, but may benefit from a return to further. (op 10-1)
Duster, raised 5lb for last month's Warwick success, was always handy and ran really well considering this was much tougher company than he normally keeps.
Man Of Action(USA), who flopped on his debut for Godolphin at Chester in May, had been gelded since and had a first-time visor on for this step up from 7f. Never far away, he kept staying on and this was much better, so he is far from a lost cause. (op 16-1)
Leviathan ◆, 3lb higher than when scrambling home at Salisbury ten days earlier, can be rated much better than his finishing position as he was in a poor position against the inside rail with nothing behind him over 2f out, but he took off when switched out wide and finished like a train. He may still be better on easier ground. (op 8-1)
Decent Fella(IRE) was close enough 2f out, but seemed to empty inside the last furlong and may be best at 7f. (op 10-1)
Toolain(IRE), one of only two three-year-olds in the field, had cheekpieces on for the first time but, despite making a promising effort passing the 2f pole, then carried his head to one side and didn't look keen. (tchd 8-1)
Dunn'o(IRE) was given an inspired ride when gaining his third C&D success in May, but was 4lb higher here. He had to do a lot of running in order to get across and lead from his wide draw and his efforts in doing so had told by the time he reached the 2f pole. (op 10-1 tchd 17-2)
Trade Storm, beaten less than 2l into fifth in the Britannia on his first attempt at the trip, went down on his haunches exiting the stalls and that was race over. Official explanation: jockey said colt stumbled badly leaving stalls (op 16-1)

3646 CORAL-ECLIPSE (BRITISH CHAMPIONS' SERIES) (GROUP 1) 1m 2f 7y

3:10 (3:12) (Class 1) 3-Y-O -Y-O+ **£226,840** (£86,000; £43,040; £21,440; £10,760) **Stalls** Low

Form RPR

-112 **1** **So You Think (NZ)**[17] 3031 5-9-7 126 SeamieHeffernan 3 129
(A P O'Brien, Ire) *lw: trckd ldng pair: wnt 2nd over 2f out: shkn up to cl over 1f out: r.o determinedly to ld last 150yds: rdn out* **4/6**[1]

51-1 **2** 1/2 **Workforce**[37] 2439 4-9-7 128 RyanMoore 2 128
(Sir Michael Stoute) *lw: trckd ldr: led 1/2-way: kicked on 3f out: drvn and 2 l clr 2f out: hdd last 150yds: styd on wl but readily hld* **7/4**[2]

0-23 **3** 5 **Sri Putra**[17] 3031 5-9-7 116 NeilCallan 5 118
(Roger Varian) *hld up in last pair: rdn over 2f out: outpcd but wnt 3rd over 1f out: no imp* **33/1**

411- **4** 3 3/4 **Snow Fairy (IRE)**[202] 7854 4-9-4 120 JMurtagh 4 108
(Ed Dunlop) *hld up in last pair: outpcd over 2f out: no imp on ldrs fnl 2f* **10/1**[3]

54-1 **5** 23 **Confront**[21] 2933 6-9-7 107 JimmyFortune 1 65
(Sir Michael Stoute) *led to 1/2-way: lost 2nd over 2f out: wknd rapidly over 1f out: t.o* **80/1**

2m 4.77s (-5.73) **Going Correction** -0.175s/f (Firm) **5** Ran SP% **109.6**
Speed ratings (Par 117): **115,114,110,107,89**
CSF £2.03 TOTE £1.90: £1.10, £1.50; EX 2.70.
Owner Smith/Magnier/Tabor/Dato Tan/Tunku Yahaya **Bred** M J Moran & Piper Farm Ltd **Trained** Ballydoyle, Co Tipperary

FOCUS
As was the case in 1997, 2002 and 2010, just five horses went to post for this famous old feature, the co-smallest field since Pebbles defeated three rivals in 1985. Nevertheless, despite the lack of any 3-y-os this was one of the most anticipated Eclipses for years, featuring two colts that have made a big impression at the top level at opposite ends of the globe, together with a dual Classic-winning filly. The 'big three' had already collected 12 Group/Grade 1 victories between them coming into this and this was a race that lived up to its billing. This has been rated slightly positively - the third is a possible limit but he did run a personal best in the race last year.

NOTEBOOK
So You Think(NZ) barely had a race in winning a Group 3 and the Group 1 Tattersalls Gold Cup in his first two starts for Ballydoyle, so his defeat by Rewilding in the Prince Of Wales's Stakes at Royal Ascot last time was a big shock to many. However, his trainer was inclined to blame himself for not having the horse fit enough for Ascot, and it is true that he would have been used to a much more punishing schedule in his native Australia. In addition, the Ascot race was something of a messy contest and, unlike then, the stable didn't employ a pacemaker on this occasion. The colt normally likes to race handily, but this time he was content to get a lead from the Sir Michael Stoute pair and his rider seemed happy to slipstream Workforce for as long as possible in the home straight before making his effort. Despite sticking his tongue out and taking a few strides to find top gear after being pulled out from behind his rival, the favourite produced a telling turn of foot to go past well inside the last furlong and he was well on top at the line. This was a much more accurate demonstration of just how good he is than we had seen in Europe so far and he will have to be feared in whichever of the big Group 1 races he contests between now and the end of the season. It's hoped to send him back to Australia to bid for a third Cox Plate in October, but quarantine regulations may scupper that plan. (op 5-6, tchd Evens in places)

Workforce's weakness in the betting market in the days leading up to the race was more to do with the form of his yard as much as anything else, with the stable without a winner for three weeks until the drought ended here the previous day. Last year's Derby and Arc winner had warmed up for this with a workmanlike victory over Poet (to whom he was conceding 7lb) in the Brigadier Gerard over C&D last month, but although the runner-up has done nothing for the form in two outings since, his trainer had warned that the race would be badly needed and the run should have put Workforce spot-on for this much tougher assignment. Content to sit just off his pacemaker, he was sent to the front rounding the home bend, presumably in an attempt to draw the sting from So You Think. Gradually winding up the pace, he gave absolutely everything but had to concede inside the last furlong that he was up against a rival with a superior turn of foot. The feeling is that he is probably better over 1m4f, whilst his main rival relishes this trip, so if he does head for the King George next he must take all the beating. His main target though, is the Arc. (op 13-8, tchd 2-1 in places)

Sri Putra has developed a habit of running way above himself in Group 1 company, getting within half a length of Twice Over in this race last year and finishing a 6l third behind Rewilding and So You Think in the Prince Of Wales's at odds of 66-1. However, this year's Eclipse was a much stronger renewal than in 2010 and, as was the case at Ascot, he was put firmly in his place. (op 25-1)

Snow Fairy(IRE), bidding to become the first filly to win the Eclipse since Kooyonga in 1992, looked fit enough but was the disappointment of the race. She was scheduled to make her reappearance in the Sheema Classic in Dubai in March, but was injured a week before that race and plans to run her in the Pretty Polly Stakes at the Curragh the previous weekend were scrapped when the ground threatened to become too soft for her. Having been switched off in last place, she was close enough starting up the home straight, but when her rider got after her coming to the last 2f the response was muted. She was entitled to need the run and she still holds entries in the King George, Juddmonte International and Irish Champion Stakes, but it's hard to imagine her turning the tables on the two colts and, if she is to win again at Group 1 level, it's likely to be back against her own sex in something like the Nassau and/or Yorkshire Oaks. (op 8-1)

Confront, who was here to act as pacemaker for Workforce, did his job well until moving off the rail to enable his stable companion to pass him on his inside half a mile from home. (op 66-1)

3647 CORAL MARATHON (REGISTERED AS THE ESHER STKS) (LISTED RACE) 2m 78y

3:40 (3:41) (Class 1) 4-Y-0+

£17,013 (£6,450; £3,228; £1,608; £807; £405) **Stalls** Low

Form				RPR
-041	**1**		**Chiberta King**[15] 3120 5-9-0 98 ... JimmyFortune 3 (Andrew Balding) *chsd ldr 4f: styd prom: rdn 2f out: r.o fnl f to chal last 100yds: drvn ahd post* **6/1**	109
-540	**2**	*nse*	**Aaim To Prosper (IRE)**[16] 3066 7-9-0 106 ... LouisBeuzelin 6 (Brian Meehan) *lw: hld up in 6th: quick prog to go 2nd 7f out: rdn 3f out: dropped bk to 3rd briefly over 1f out: rallied fnl f to ld last 100yds: hdd post* **5/1**[3]	109
40-0	**3**	*2*	**Electrolyser (IRE)**[50] 2072 6-9-0 111 ... AdamKirby 11 (Clive Cox) *chsd ldr after 4f to 7f out: dropped bk to 4th sn after: rdn and prog to ld over 1f out: hdd and one pce last 100yds* **9/2**[2]	107
52-4	**4**	*½*	**Ship's Biscuit**[49] 2098 4-8-9 99 ... RyanMoore 1 (Sir Michael Stoute) *lw: settled in midfield: hanging and nt qckn over 2f out: styd on wl over 1f out: clsd on ldrs fnl f: one pce last 100yds* **3/1**[1]	101
5230	**5**	*1 ¾*	**Akmal**[37] 2438 5-9-0 105 ... TadhgO'Shea 4 (John Dunlop) *led at gd pce: hdd over 1f out: fdd fnl f* **6/1**	104
36-0	**6**	*6*	**Sentry Duty (FR)**[59] 1808 9-9-0 100 ... KierenFallon 7 (Nicky Henderson) *hld up in 7th: prog and threatened briefly jst over 2f out: effrt sn fizzled out* **8/1**	97
00-0	**7**	*6*	**Shimmering Surf (IRE)**[35] 2501 4-8-9 99 ... FergusSweeney 5 (Peter Winkworth) *settled in midfield: in tch over 3f out: sn wknd* **12/1**	85
0-40	**8**	*12*	**Desert Sea (IRE)**[18] 3013 8-9-0 90 ... MartinDwyer 2 (David Arbuthnot) *rrd bdly s and lost at least 10 l: given time to rcvr and in tch by 1/2-way: wknd over 2f out: eased* **14/1**	82

3m 31.41s (-7.29) **Going Correction** -0.175s/f (Firm) **8** Ran SP% **113.9**
Speed ratings (Par 111): **111,110,109,109,108 105,102,96**
toteswingers:1&2:£5.50, 1&3:£7.00, 2&3:£3.70 CSF £35.61 TOTE £7.80: £2.00, £1.90, £1.70; EX 35.40 Trifecta £173.60 Pool: £1,867.50 - 7.96 winning units..
Owner The Pink Hat Racing Partnership **Bred** Watership Down Stud **Trained** Kingsclere, Hants

FOCUS
A fair staying Listed race. There were doubts over a few of these, but they went a solid gallop and the form has been rated through the runner-up, with the winner producing a 5lb personal best.

NOTEBOOK
Chiberta King, successful in a Goodwood handicap last time, was well beaten in his only previous try at this level and didn't seem to stay in his only attempt at this trip, but he removed any doubts over his class or his stamina and would have been an unlucky loser. He didn't have much room to play with on the inside over 2f out, but stayed on really well when switched and sustained his effort to lead right on the line. This was a good effort as he had quite a bit to find with the placed horses at the weights. (op 8-1)

Aaim To Prosper(IRE) hasn't been able to make much impact in three tries in Group company since winning last year's Cesarewitch, but performed much better at this slightly lower level. Having moved into a handy position after halfway, he looked beaten at various stages up the home straight, but kept on coming back for more and, having got himself to the front inside the last furlong, had the race snatched from him on the line. (tchd 6-1)

Electrolyser(IRE), who has winning form at this level, had run poorly in his last two starts though he scoped badly following his reappearance in the Yorkshire Cup. His prospects didn't look good before the end of the back straight as he was seriously off the bridle but, rather like the runner-up, he kept on coming back and was in front over 1f out. However, once there he couldn't make it count and was run out of it by the front pair. This was effectively his seasonal reappearance, so he can be expected to come on for it. (op 4-1 tchd 5-1)

Ship's Biscuit ran a strange race when just behind Akmal on her Newbury reappearance, and this step up to 2m didn't bring about much improvement. She appeared to be hanging after being pulled out for her effort inside the last 2f and has a bit to prove.

Akmal found the ground had gone against him when running poorly in the Henry II over C&D last time, but he had no such excuses this time and, despite being allowed an uncontested lead, was comfortably picked off from over 1f out. (op 11-2 tchd 13-2)

Sentry Duty(FR) had questions to answer after finishing tailed off in the Chester Cup on his return to the Flat, and he was inclined to race on and off the bridle on this occasion. (tchd 15-2)

Shimmering Surf(IRE) has run poorly since a narrow defeat at Newbury last August, and didn't see out the longer trip. (op 14-1 tchd 10-1)

Desert Sea(IRE) gained his last win in this race two years ago, but he was by far worst in on official ratings and he made a difficult task impossible by completely fluffing the start. Official explanation: jockey said gelding reared leaving stalls (op 16-1)

3648 CORAL DISTAFF (LISTED RACE) (FILLIES) 1m 14y

4:15 (4:15) (Class 1) 3-Y-O

£17,013 (£6,450; £3,228; £1,608; £807; £405) **Stalls** Low

Form				RPR
-11	**1**		**Nahrain**[23] 2833 3-8-12 102 ... NeilCallan 3 (Roger Varian) *w'like: lw: sltly awkward s: hld up in 4th: clsd on ldrs over 2f out: pushed into ld over 1f out: shkn up and sn in command: readily* **4/6**[1]	107+
1-44	**2**	*1 ½*	**Primevere (IRE)**[50] 2073 3-8-12 92 ... SteveDrowne 6 (Roger Charlton) *trckd ldr: chal and upsides over 2f out to over 1f out: styd on but no match for wnr* **16/1**	102
-004	**3**	*2 ¼*	**Cape Dollar (IRE)**[17] 3034 3-9-7 103 ... RyanMoore 5 (Sir Michael Stoute) *lw: t.k.h: hld up in last pair: pushed along and no prog over 2f out: styd on fr over 1f out: tk 3rd last 75yds* **11/2**[3]	106
-122	**4**	*1 ¼*	**Dubai Queen (USA)**[17] 3034 3-8-12 95 ... KierenFallon 2 (Luca Cumani) *lw: trckd ldng pair: effrt to ld over 2f out: hdd over 1f out: wknd fnl f* **10/3**[2]	94
62-6	**5**	*3 ½*	**Cochabamba (IRE)**[77] 1404 3-8-12 104 ... TedDurcan 4 (Roger Teal) *hld up in last pair: shkn up and nt qckn 2f out: wl btn after* **12/1**	86
1-16	**6**	*3*	**Cloud Illusions (USA)**[35] 2506 3-8-12 81 ... JMurtagh 1 (Heather Main) *led to over 2f out: sn wknd* **50/1**	79

1m 41.83s (-1.47) **Going Correction** -0.175s/f (Firm) **6** Ran SP% **114.0**
Speed ratings (Par 105): **100,98,96,95,91 88**
toteswingers:1&2:£4.00, 1&3:£2.10, 2&3:£4.80 CSF £14.12 TOTE £1.80: £1.10, £4.90; EX 16.50.
Owner Sheikh Ahmed Al Maktoum **Bred** Darley **Trained** Newmarket, Suffolk

FOCUS
They went just a fair gallop in this fillies' Listed event, but it was won by a most progressive sort. The runner-up has been rated 6lb higher than in the Pretty Polly, with the third close to her mark.

NOTEBOOK
Nahrain ◆ was unbeaten in her first two starts and was up in grade after bolting up off 87 in a Haydock handicap, but she took the step up in class in her stride and quickened up nicely from off the pace to lead 1f out. Her pedigree suggests she may get a bit further and she is unlikely to have reached the end of her potential. (op 8-11, tchd 4-5 in places)

Primevere(IRE) has already twice been found out at this level, but this represented a solid effort and she never stopped trying. A return to further may see her winning again. (op 12-1)

Cape Dollar(IRE) was unlucky not to do even better than fourth in the Sandringham at Royal Ascot last time and would have finished a lot closer to the runner-up Dubai Queen with a clear run, but her 9lb Group 2 penalty left her with a big task against some unexposed fillies. Having been held up, she took far too long in engaging top gear and, by the time she did, it was far too late. (op 7-1)

Dubai Queen(USA) had been improving and ran her best race yet when runner-up in the Sandringham, but she took quite a grip early on here and, though in front over 2f out, she couldn't get away and had run her race a furlong later. (op 4-1)

Cochabamba(IRE) didn't make much impression from off the pace, and doesn't seem to have trained on. (op 9-1)

Cloud Illusions(USA) was easily picked off over 2f out after making much of the running. (op 40-1)

3649 WIN MORE WITH CORAL.CO.UK GREEN TICK H'CAP 7f 16y

4:50 (4:52) (Class 3) (0-95,93) 3-Y-O

£8,092 (£2,423; £1,211; £605; £302; £152) **Stalls** Low

Form				RPR
6-10	**1**		**Chilled**[7] 3378 3-8-13 **85** ... RyanMoore 3 (Sir Michael Stoute) *lw: trckd ldrs: prog over 2f out: wnt 2nd over 1f out: sn clsd and led 1f out: drvn out* **9/2**[1]	98+
2222	**2**	*¾*	**Elusivity (IRE)**[8] 3346 3-8-10 **82** ... MartinDwyer 1 (Brian Meehan) *hld up in midfield: gng strly whn nt clr run wl over 1f out: prog after: chsd wnr ins fnl f: r.o and clsd but a hld* **17/2**	93+
36-2	**3**	*½*	**Aerial Acclaim (IRE)**[12] 3218 3-8-3 **78** ... JohnFahy(3) 2 (Clive Cox) *lw: s.i.s: settled in last trio: nt clr run briefly over 2f out: prog over 1f out: drvn and r.o to take 3rd ins fnl f: clsd but unable to chal* **13/2**	88+
-424	**4**	*2 ¾*	**Local Singer (IRE)**[21] 2926 3-8-7 **82** ... LouisBeuzelin(3) 8 (Malcolm Saunders) *led at gd clip: drew clr after 3f: hrd rdn and hdd 1f out: fdd* **7/1**	84
12-	**5**	*1*	**Try The Chance**[285] 6254 3-8-12 **87** ... MatthewDavies(3) 5 (Mick Channon) *dwlt: hld up in rr: rdn on outer 2f out: prog over 1f out: styd on but n.d* **20/1**	87
4-15	**6**	*1*	**Dimension**[35] 2506 3-9-2 **88** ... KierenFallon 4 (James Fanshawe) *lw: hld up towards rr: pushed along and nt the clrest of runs fr 2f out: kpt on fnl f: n.d* **6/1**[3]	85+
4610	**7**	*2*	**May's Boy**[21] 2926 3-8-4 **76** ... (p) DavidProbert 11 (Mark Usher) *hld up in rr and racd wd: drvn and effrt over 2f out: no prog tl kpt on fnl f* **20/1**	67
012-	**8**	*nk*	**Morache Music**[222] 7534 3-9-7 **93** ... SteveDrowne 7 (Peter Makin) *trckd ldrs: rdn over 2f out: in contention wl over 1f out: sn wknd: eased* **20/1**	86
6-41	**9**	*¾*	**Muzdahi (USA)**[23] 2841 3-8-8 **80** ... TadhgO'Shea 12 (John Dunlop) *hld up in last: bustled along 3f out and nt gng wl: nvr a factor* **10/1**	69
4-00	**10**	*2 ¾*	**Catalyze**[16] 3067 3-8-11 **83** ... (t) JimmyFortune 6 (Andrew Balding) *t.k.h: chsd ldr to over 1f out: wknd qckly fnl f* **8/1**	64
-211	**11**	*2*	**Johnny Castle**[14] 3178 3-9-6 **92** ... NickyMackay 9 (John Gosden) *t.k.h: chsd ldng pair: disp 2nd wl over 1f out: wknd qckly and eased fnl f* **11/2**[2]	73

2200 **12** *3 1/2* **City Legend**[29] 2684 3-8-4 **76**.................................(bt) HayleyTurner 10 42
(Alan McCabe) *rn in snatches: racd wd: prom tl wknd and hanging 2f out* **33/1**

1m 27.57s (-1.93) **Going Correction** -0.175s/f (Firm) **12** Ran SP% **121.6**
Speed ratings (Par 104): **104,103,102,99,98 97,94,94,93,90 88,84**
toteswingers:1&2:£9.40, 1&3:£8.10, 2&3:£10.60 CSF £41.54 CT £211.44 TOTE £5.60: £2.30, £3.00, £2.10; EX 58.40 Trifecta £548.90 Pool: £2,440.48 - 3.29 winning units..

Owner Cheveley Park Stud **Bred** Cheveley Park Stud Ltd **Trained** Newmarket, Suffolk

■ Stewards' Enquiry : Jimmy Fortune caution: failed to take all reasonable and permissable measures to obtain best possible placing.

FOCUS
A decent handicap in which a few were unlucky and the race should produce winners. It has been rated around the exposed fourth to his recent C&D form.

NOTEBOOK
Chilled didn't find things panning out in his favour when a disappointing favourite on his handicap debut at Chester seven days earlier, but everything went his way here as he got the gap just when he needed it over 1f out, whilst his two nearest rivals were finding trouble. He still has scope for further improvement and will not take up his entry in the sales next week. (op 7-1, tchd 15-2 in a place)

Elusivity(IRE) has been enduring a frustrating run of seconds, but has been creeping up the weights in doing so and was another 3lb higher here. Unfortunately luck wasn't on his side again, as after having sat on the tail of the winner his rival got the gap when he needed it, whilst Elusivity ran into a dead end, and by the time he was extracted it was too late. It's hard to know what he has to do in order to get his head back in front. (op 9-1)

Aerial Acclaim(IRE) ◆ was making his handicap debut after finishing runner-up in a Chepstow maiden last month on his return from a lengthy absence. His race was basically lost at the start as a tardy exit left him in a poor position starting up the home straight, and his rider was forced to try and thread him through the eye of a needle in order to get him to finish where he did. It's only a matter of time before he breaks his duck. (op 11-2)

Local Singer(IRE) met plenty of trouble when fourth over C&D last time, but the way he was aggressively ridden here made a repeat impossible. Considering how fast he went off, he did remarkably well to keep on for fourth. (op 14-1)

Try The Chance ◆ made up a lot of late ground from well off the pace and should come on for this first start in 285 days. (op 25-1)

Dimension ◆ had shown his best previous form on Polytrack, but he was repeatedly stopped in his run from over 2f out and is better than he showed here. (op 5-1)

May's Boy reportedly missed the break. Official explanation: jockey said colt missed the break

Morache Music Official explanation: jockey said colt had no more to give

Muzdahi(USA) was reported to have never been travelling. Official explanation: jockey said colt never travelled (op 8-1, tchd 11-1 in places)

Johnny Castle reportedly ran flat. Official explanation: jockey said colt ran flat (op 4-1)

3650 GREEN TICK FOR BETTER ODDS AT CORAL.CO.UK H'CAP — 1m 2f 7y
5:20 (5:25) (Class 4) (0-85,85) 3-Y-O — **£5,175** (£1,540; £769; £384) Stalls Low

Form / RPR

135 **1** **Cool Macavity (IRE)**[21] 2908 3-8-8 **79**.................. MatthewLawson(7) 9 88
(B W Hills) *hld up in last quartet: stdy prog on wd outside fr 3f out: sustained effrt to ld 1f out: r.o wl* **16/1**

-604 **2** *3/4* **Mr Perceptive (IRE)**[9] 3312 3-8-11 **75**........................ JimmyFortune 12 82
(Richard Hannon) *hld up towards rr: prog over 2f out: drvn and r.o fr over 1f out: wnt 2nd last 100yds: unable to chal* **16/1**

-311 **3** *1/2* **Grumeti**[22] 2885 3-9-3 **81**.. HayleyTurner 11 87
(Michael Bell) *lw: trckd ldng pair: effrt gng strly 2f out: c to chal 1f out: r.o but outpcd* **11/2[2]**

1-13 **4** *1/2* **Parlour Games**[49] 2108 3-9-0 **85**............................. AntiocoMurgia(7) 10 90
(Mahmood Al Zarooni) *hld up in midfield: rdn over 2f out: prog over 1f out: chsd ldrs fnl f: styd on: unable to chal* **13/2[3]**

-125 **5** *1/2* **Area Fifty One**[7] 3376 3-8-4 **73**............................. JamesRogers(5) 13 77
(William Muir) *lw: led at gd pce: kpt on wl whn hrd pressed 2f out: hdd 1f out: steadily outpcd* **15/2**

-506 **6** *3/4* **Mattoral**[23] 2842 3-8-10 **74**..................................(b1) SteveDrowne 14 77
(Peter Makin) *t k h: pressed ldr to jst over 2f out: hanging and nt qckn* [illegible]

-100 **7** *1/2* **Harry Luck (IRE)**[21] 2925 3-9-2 **80**.............................. FergusSweeney 2 82
(Henry Candy) *hld up towards rr: rdn over 2f out: no prog and struggling in rr over 1f out: styd on wl fnl f: nrst fin* **14/1**

1-34 **8** *2 1/4* **Rastaban**[49] 2100 3-8-13 **77**.. JMurtagh 8 76
(William Haggas) *hld up in last quartet: effrt on outer 3f out: sn drvn and limited prog: kpt on fnl f* **4/1[1]**

0054 **9** *shd* **Orientalist**[12] 3231 3-9-2 **80**... KierenFallon 3 77
(Eve Johnson Houghton) *trckd ldng pair: rdn over 2f out: lost pl and wl btn over 1f out: one pce fnl f* **11/1**

015 **10** *3/4* **Doricemay (IRE)**[31] 2615 3-9-0 **78**.................................... AdamKirby 16 73
(Clive Cox) *prom: rdn wl over 2f out: steadily wknd over 1f out* **16/1**

0333 **11** *hd* **Standout**[12] 3233 3-8-10 **74**..(b) RyanMoore 1 69
(Richard Hannon) *trckd ldrs: prog on inner to go 2nd jst over 2f out: rdn and nt qckn whn n.m.r wl over 1f out: wknd* **13/2[3]**

-610 **12** *1 1/4* **Miss Chicane**[25] 2791 3-8-7 **74**.. JohnFahy(3) 15 66
(Walter Swinburn) *rel to r and drvn in last early: in tch after 2f: brief effrt on inner over 2f out: sn no prog* **25/1**

24-6 **13** *4 1/2* **Another Laugh**[29] 2688 3-8-8 **72**.. LiamKeniry 7 55
(Alan King) *hld up in midfield: rdn over 2f out: sn lost pl and btn* **33/1**

451- **14** *5* **For What (USA)**[203] 7830 3-9-4 **82**.. TedDurcan 5 55
(David Lanigan) *dwlt: hld up in last pair: rdn wl over 2f out: no prog and sn btn* **20/1**

2m 8.49s (-2.01) **Going Correction** -0.175s/f (Firm) **14** Ran SP% **123.9**
Speed ratings (Par 102): **101,100,100,99,99 98,98,96,96,95 95,94,90,86**
toteswingers:1&2:£90.10, 1&3:£20.50, 2&3:£30.00. Tote Super 7: Win: Not won. Place: £184.50 CSF £251.87 CT £1606.82 TOTE £21.00: £5.40, £6.10, £2.20; EX 423.90 Trifecta £1654.90 Part won. Pool: £2,236.38 - 0.40 winning units..

Owner Triermore Stud **Bred** C O P Hanbury **Trained** Lambourn, Berks

FOCUS
A competitive handicap and a race of changing fortunes. Personal bests from the front two, with the third and fourth to their marks.

Rastaban Official explanation: jockey said gelding was slowly away

T/Jkpt: Not won. T/Plt: £100.20 to a £1 stake. Pool: £187,438.94. 1,364.35 winning tickets. T/Qpdt: £11.30 to a £1 stake. Pool: £11,183.13. 732.30 winning tickets. JN

3531 HAMBURG (R-H)
Saturday, July 2

OFFICIAL GOING: Turf: good

3651a GROSSER PREIS DER MERCEDES-BENZ NIEDERLASSUNG HAMBURG (HAMBURGER STUTENPREIS) (GROUP 3) (FILLIES) — 1m 3f
4:10 (12:00) 3-Y-O
£27,586 (£9,482; £4,741; £2,586; £1,724; £1,293)

RPR

1 **Karsabruni (FR)**[42] 3-9-2 0.. FabriceVeron 4 100
(H-A Pantall, France) *racd 4th on outside: powerful move arnd fnl turn: sn chal: led 1 1/2f out: chal ins fnl f but a in control* **11/2**

2 *nk* **Labrice**[27] 3-9-2 0.. THellier 6 100
(T Mundry, Germany) *bkmarker fr s: shkn up in st: mde str move over 1 1/2f out: clsd fast on ldr ins fnl f: narrowly failed* **69/10**

3 *6* **Alkhana (IRE)**[20] 2981 3-9-2 0.. FilipMinarik 7 89
(P Schiergen, Germany) *broke wl to ld then settled in 2nd: r.o wl in st wout ever threatening ldrs* **171/10**

4 *1* **Julie's Love**[20] 2981 3-9-2 0... ASuborics 1 87
(Manfred Hofer, Germany) *racd midfield: r.o wl in st but no threat to ldrs* **3/1[2]**

5 *2* **Aigrette Garzette (IRE)**[13] 3209 3-9-2 0............................. AStarke 3 84
(P Schiergen, Germany) *settled 3rd: sn rdn in st but failed to qckn and fdd* **17/10[1]**

6 *2* **Paragua (GER)**[20] 2981 3-9-2 0... EPedroza 5 80
(A Wohler, Germany) *settled towards rr: nvr figured* **7/2[3]**

7 *2 1/2* **Kellemoi De Pepita**[20] 2981 3-9-2 0.................................... ADeVries 2 76
(R Dzubasz, Germany) *broke wl: t.k.h: led bk st and set gd pce: stl led into st: rdn and qckly wknd* **63/10**

2m 26.29s (1.59) **7** Ran SP% **131.5**
WIN (incl. 10 euro stake): 65. PLACES: 21, 22, 29. SF: 548..
Owner Horst Rapp **Bred** Chevotel De La Hauquerie **Trained** France

3652 - 3655a See RI

3008 LONGCHAMP (R-H)
Saturday, July 2

OFFICIAL GOING: Turf: good

3653a PRIX DAPHNIS (GROUP 3) (3YO) (TURF) — 1m 1f 55y
1:30 (12:00) 3-Y-O **£34,482** (£13,793; £10,344; £6,896; £3,448)

RPR

1 **Ziyarid (IRE)**[46] 3-8-11 0.. MichaelPoirier 2 110
(A De Royer-Dupre, France) *set pce for Valiyr: sn wnt wl clr: extended ld bef st: rdn 2f out: r.o wl fnl f: jst hld on* **16/1**

2 *nk* **Valiyr (IRE)**[36] 2484 3-8-11 0.............. Christophe-PatriceLemaire 4 109
(A De Royer-Dupre, France) *racd 3rd on settling: rdn ent st to pursue pcemaker: r.o wl fnl f: jst failed* **1/1[1]**

3 *2 1/2* **Absolutly Yes (FR)**[27] 2751 3-9-1 0.......................... FabienLefebvre 7 108
(Y-M Porzier, France) *racd 2nd on settling: rdn early in st to chse ldr: u.p fnl 1 1/2f: styd on wl* **7/2[2]**

4 *1/2* **Slow Pace (USA)**[20] 2978 3-8-11 0.................................. OlivierPeslier 1 103
(F Head, France) *settled 4th on rail: rdn but nt qckn 2f out: styd on wl fnl f* **7/2[2]**

5 *3* **Nobel Winner (FR)**[27] 2751 3-8-11 0............................ MaximeGuyon 3 97
(J-M Beguigne, France) *bkmarker fr s: rdn early in st: no ex: styd on* **44/5[3]**

6 *nk* **Lustre (FR)**[56] 1923 3-8-11 0.. IoritzMendizabal 5 96
(Y De Nicolay, France) *settled towards rr: rdn but no ex fnl 2f* **17/1**

7 *4* **Staros (IRE)**[54] 1965 3-8-11 0........................... Pierre-CharlesBoudot 6 88
(E Lellouche, France) *settled 5th: rdn but no ex in st: nvr figured* **25/1**

1m 53.04s (-2.26) **7** Ran SP% **119.9**
WIN (incl. 1 euro stake): 1.00 [illegible]
Owner H H Aga Khan **Bred** His Highness The Aga Khan's Studs S C **Trained** Chantilly, France

NOTEBOOK
Ziyarid(IRE) was in the race as a pacemaker for Valiyr but he soon built up a decent gap and, turning into the straight, still held a sizeable advantage over his field. He was closed down by his stable companion close home but was always just holding on.

Valiyr(IRE), settled in third, was given too much to do in chasing down his pacemaking stablemate and the line was always coming just too soon.

3654a PRIX DE LA PORTE MAILLOT (GROUP 3) (3YO+) (TURF) — 7f
2:40 (12:00) 3-Y-O+ **£34,482** (£13,793; £10,344; £6,896; £3,448)

RPR

1 **Moonlight Cloud**[28] 2744 3-8-8 0.................................... ThierryJarnet 8 108
(F Head, France) *racd 2nd fr s but sn sent to ld: rdn clr at 1/2-way: r.o wl: hld on wl fnl 100yds* **6/5[1]**

2 *hd* **African Story**[28] 2744 4-9-2 0.................................... MaximeGuyon 10 110
(A Fabre, France) *settled midfield: rdn 2f out: qcknd wl ent fnl f: fin strly: jst failed* **6/1[2]**

3 *1/2* **Evaporation (FR)**[28] 2744 4-8-13 0............................... OlivierPeslier 5 106
(C Laffon-Parias, France) *settled 4th: rdn 2f out: fin wl fnl f* **8/1**

4 *3/4* **Marchand D'Or (FR)**[27] 2754 8-9-2 0.................................. DavyBonilla 11 107
(M Delzangles, France) *racd wd fr s: settled towards rr: qcknd wl at 1/2-way: r.o wl fr 2f out but no ex fnl 100yds* **44/5**

5 *1 1/2* **Myasun (FR)**[23] 4-9-2 0... JohanVictoire 6 103
(C Baillet, France) *in rr fr s: swtchd to outside and finshed wl fnl 1 1/2f* **7/1[3]**

6 *hd* **Glad Sky**[28] 5-9-2 0... AnthonyCrastus 9 102
(W Gulcher, Germany) *w.w towards rr: rdn 2f out: fin wl fnl f* **76/1**

7 *snk* **Eightfold Path (USA)**[33] 4-9-2 0........................ StephanePasquier 3 102
(P Bary, France) *racd 3rd fr s: then settled 5th: rdn 2 1/2f out: nt qckn: styd on one pce fnl 1 1/2f* **14/1**

8 *snk* **Blue Panis (FR)**[20] 2980 4-9-2 0................ Christophe-PatriceLemaire 2 101
(F Chappet, France) *led fr s then settled in 2nd: rdn 2 1/2f out: r.o but no ex fnl f* **26/1**

9 *1* **Thai Haku (IRE)**[135] 586 4-8-13 0................................ GregoryBenoist 1 96
(M Delzangles, France) *racd midfield: short of room in st: no ex: fdd* **29/1**

10 *hd* **Salto (IRE)**[48] 2139 3-8-8 0.................................. MickaelBarzalona 4 95
(F Head, France) *bkmarker: rdn but no ex in st: nvr figured* **28/1**

11 **Baiadera (GER)**[17] 4-8-13 0 ChristopheSoumillon 7 —
(T Potters, Germany) *racd 3rd and stl prom 2f out: rdn but no ex: qckly wknd* **22/1**

1m 20.23s (-0.47)
WFA 3 from 4yo+ 8lb **11** Ran SP% **116.4**
WIN (incl. 1 euro stake): 2.20. PLACES: 1.30, 1.60, 1.90. DF: 6.20. SF: 8.20..
Owner George Strawbridge **Bred** George Strawbridge **Trained** France

3158 AYR (L-H)

Sunday, July 3

OFFICIAL GOING: Good to firm (9.1)
Wind: Breezy, half against Weather: Hot, sunny

3656 FRIENDS OF BOB STIRLING MEDIAN AUCTION MAIDEN STKS 7f 50y
2:15 (2:15) (Class 5) 2-Y-O **£2,328** (£693; £346; £173) **Stalls** High

Form RPR
1 **Nemushka** 2-8-12 0 PaulHanagan 3 71+
(Richard Fahey) *s.i.s: t.k.h in tch: hdwy to ld over 1f out: edgd lft: rdn out* **11/4**[2]

3422 2 *1 ½* **Joshua The First**[11] 3274 2-9-3 0 (v[1]) PhillipMakin 6 72
(Keith Dalgleish) *led at modest gallop: rdn and hdd over 1f out: kpt on same pce* **5/4**[1]

3 *nk* **Rasputin (IRE)** 2-9-3 0 FrederikTylicki 4 71+
(Michael Dods) *in tch: effrt on outside over 2f out: edgd lft over 1f out: kpt on: nt pce of first two* **6/1**[3]

4 *3* **Curtain Patch (USA)** 2-8-12 0 TomEaves 2 59
(Bryan Smart) *in tch: rn green and outpcd after 3f: no imp tl sme late hdwy: nvr rchd ldrs* **11/1**

3424 5 *nse* **Latte**[9] 3345 2-9-3 0 DarryllHolland 1 64
(Linda Stubbs) *dwlt: t.k.h and chsd ldr after 1f: rdn over 2f out: edgd lft and wknd over 1f out* **8/1**

65 6 *nk* **Dansili Dutch (IRE)**[14] 3201 2-8-12 0 LeeNewman 5 58
(David Barron) *chsd ldr 1f: cl up tl rdn and wknd over 1f out* **14/1**

1m 33.57s (0.17) **Going Correction** -0.125s/f (Firm) **6** Ran SP% **111.5**
Speed ratings (Par 94): **94,92,91,88,88 88**
toteswingers: 1&2 £1.50, 1&3 £2.30, 2&3 £1.90 CSF £6.49 TOTE £3.80: £2.70, £1.10; EX 8.00.
Owner The G-Guck Group **Bred** Avenue Farm Stud **Trained** Musley Bank, N Yorks

FOCUS
Back straight out 2m, home bend out 4m, home straight out 5m adding 12yds to 7f, 8f and 1m1f races and 24yds to 1m5f race. The leading form contender was comfortably overhauled by a newcomer after trading at 1.32 in running.

NOTEBOOK
Nemushka looked a bit keen and inexperienced but she travelled when into contention and forged past the favourite in the closing stages to make a winning debut. A Sakhee filly, she is out of a dam who started off winning at 1m but later developed into a useful sprinter. (tchd 5-2)
Joshua The First had improved in each of his four previous starts and finished a close second at Hamilton and Carlisle on his last two runs. This well backed favourite set the standard stepped up to 7f and had the run of the race in a first-time visor, but it was a bit disappointing that he was a sitting duck in the closing stages. He could continue to be vulnerable to anything above average in maidens. (op 11-8 tchd 6-4)
Rasputin(IRE) looked inexperienced before showing some promise, staying on late on debut. His price jumped to £45,000 last year and he is a first foal of a 7f winning half-sister to fairly useful quadruple AW winner Gaily Noble. (op 9-2 tchd 4-1)
Curtain Patch(USA), a $50,000 half-sister to a dual winner in US, ran green and was slightly detached halfway up the straight before rallying on debut. (op 9-1)
Latte ran respectably when not beaten far in a small-field novice event last time, but he came up some way short back in a maiden and looks exposed after seven starts. (op 12-1)

3657 BET ON WIMBLEDON FINAL AT TOTESPORT.COM H'CAP 7f 50y
2:45 (2:46) (Class 5) (0-70,70) 3-Y-0+ **£2,328** (£693; £346; £173) **Stalls** High

Form RPR
0204 1 **Frequency**[15] 3162 4-10-0 **70** (b) PhillipMakin 7 78
(Keith Dalgleish) *s.i.s: hld up: nt clr run and swtchd lft wl over 1f out: hdwy to ld ins fnl f: pushed out* **15/2**[3]

1034 2 *nk* **Music Festival (USA)**[16] 3113 4-9-10 **66** DanielTudhope 8 73
(Jim Goldie) *t.k.h in midfield: effrt over 2f out: ev ch ins fnl f: kpt on* **5/2**[1]

1332 3 *½* **Beckermet (IRE)**[9] 3348 9-9-3 **66** ShaneBKelly[(7)] 9 72
(Ruth Carr) *prom: hdwy to ld over 1f out: hdd ins fnl f: kpt on: hld nr fin* **7/2**[2]

-300 4 *1* **Burnwynd Boy**[9] 3359 6-9-2 **58** LeeNewman 1 61
(Ian Semple) *in tch: hdwy and ev ch over 1f out: kpt on same pce ins fnl f* **16/1**

5005 5 *¾* **Whispered Times (USA)**[15] 3190 4-9-5 **64** (p) PaulPickard[(3)] 5 65
(Tracy Waggott) *hld up: rdn over 2f out: hdwy on outside over 1f out: nvr able to chal* **18/1**

0000 6 *1 ½* **Chambers (IRE)**[36] 2494 5-8-13 **55** DavidAllan 11 52
(Eric Alston) *led tl rdn and hdd over 1f out: kpt on same pce* **22/1**

0400 7 *½* **Balance On Time (IRE)**[16] 3128 5-8-9 **51** oh6 AndrewHeffernan 12 47
(Linda Perratt) *towards rr: rdn over 2f out: no imp fr 2f out* **66/1**

1233 8 *hd* **Shunkawakhan (IRE)**[6] 3454 8-8-9 **54** (p) GaryBartley[(3)] 2 49
(Linda Perratt) *chsd ldrs: rdn over 2f out: no ex over 1f out* **17/2**

000- 9 *nk* **Chicamia**[341] 4454 7-8-2 **51** oh2 JosephYoung[(7)] 6 45
(Michael Mullineaux) *hld up: rdn and sme hdwy wl over 1f out: nvr able to chal* **66/1**

4355 10 *3 ¼* **Hellbender (IRE)**[16] 3128 5-9-4 **60** (p) PaulHanagan 10 45
(George Foster) *t.k.h: trckd ldr tl rdn and wknd over 1f out* **9/1**

3002 11 *¾* **Berbice (IRE)**[16] 3128 6-9-9 **65** FrederikTylicki 3 48
(Linda Perratt) *t.k.h: in tch: nt clr run briefly 2f out: sn rdn and wknd* **11/1**

1030 12 *1* **Master Leon**[20] 2985 4-9-0 **56** (v) TomEaves 4 37
(Bryan Smart) *dwlt: bhd: drvn over 2f out: nvr on terms* **11/1**

1m 31.95s (-1.45) **Going Correction** -0.125s/f (Firm) **12** Ran SP% **118.2**
Speed ratings (Par 103): **103,102,102,100,100 98,97,97,97,93 92,91**
toteswingers: 1&2 £4.30, 1&3 £5.40, 2&3 £3.10 CSF £26.11 CT £78.77 TOTE £7.50: £2.20, £1.10, £2.10; EX 31.90 Trifecta £62.80 Pool: £596.60 - 7.03 winning units..
Owner Mrs Francesca Mitchell **Bred** Manor Farm Stud (rutland) **Trained** Carluke, South Lanarkshire

FOCUS
A minor handicap run at a decent pace. The winner has been rated as a length personal best, with the runner-up and third close to solid recent marks.

Hellbender(IRE) Official explanation: jockey said gelding hung right throughout

3658 BET ON LIVE TENNIS AT TOTESPORT.COM H'CAP 1m 1f 20y
3:15 (3:15) (Class 6) (0-65,67) 4-Y-O+ **£1,704** (£503; £251) **Stalls** Low

Form RPR
3046 1 **Spavento (IRE)**[6] 3457 5-9-4 **60** DavidAllan 1 69+
(Eric Alston) *in tch: smooth hdwy to ld 2f out: sn rdn and edgd lft: kpt on wl fnl f* **11/4**[1]

0450 2 *3* **Dean Iarracht (IRE)**[10] 3319 5-8-12 **57** (p) PaulPickard[(3)] 5 59
(Tracy Waggott) *missed break: bhd: hdwy on outside over 2f out: chsd (clr) wnr ins fnl f: r.o* **15/2**

0-05 3 *hd* **Grethel (IRE)**[8] 3380 7-8-3 **45** PatrickMathers 9 47
(Alan Berry) *s.i.s: bhd: rdn over 2f out: hdwy and hung lft over 1f out: kpt on wl fnl f* **28/1**

6000 4 *2 ¾* **Pictures (IRE)**[10] 3317 4-8-0 **45** NataliaGemelova[(3)] 11 41
(Ron Barr) *s.i.s: hdwy into midfield 1/2-way: hdwy to chse wnr over 1f out to ins fnl f: one pce* **22/1**

06-0 5 *3* **Wind Shuffle (GER)**[17] 3086 8-9-3 **59** PaulHanagan 7 48
(Richard Fahey) *led: rdn and hdd 2f out: btn fnl f* **7/2**[2]

605 6 *1* **Crocodile Bay (IRE)**[19] 3025 8-8-9 **51** (be) RobbieFitzpatrick 6 38
(Richard Guest) *t.k.h: hld up in tch: effrt over 1f out: no imp over 1f out* **11/1**

006 7 *1* **Bunacurry**[20] 2984 6-8-7 **49** ow1 BarryMcHugh 13 34
(Barry Murtagh) *in tch: rdn over 2f out: wknd over 1f out* **66/1**

000- 8 *¾* **Captain Peachey**[293] 6029 5-7-12 **45** NeilFarley[(5)] 10 28
(Alistair Whillans) *t.k.h early: hld up towards rr: rdn over 2f out: nvr on terms* **16/1**

0505 9 *2 ¼* **Rosbertini**[6] 3454 5-8-5 **47** JamesSullivan 2 25
(Linda Perratt) *in tch tl rdn and wknd over 1f out* **16/1**

-544 10 *6* **Let's Face Facts**[10] 3303 4-8-12 **57** GaryBartley[(3)] 3 22
(Jim Goldie) *hld up: rdn over 2f out: nvr on terms* **8/1**

0304 11 *shd* **Mangham (IRE)**[20] 2988 6-9-7 **63** LeeNewman 8 33
(George Foster) *cl up: rdn over 2f out: wknd over 1f out: eased whn no ch fnl f* **6/1**[3]

1m 56.14s (-1.36) **Going Correction** -0.125s/f (Firm) **11** Ran SP% **115.4**
Speed ratings (Par 101): **101,98,98,95,93 92,91,90,88,83 83**
toteswingers: 1&2 £6.10, 1&3 £17.50, 2&3 £31.70 CSF £22.86 CT £473.36 TOTE £4.00: £1.50, £2.60, £12.20; EX 22.10 Trifecta £278.50 Part won. Pool: £376.45 - 0.60 winning units..
Owner Whitehills Racing Syndicate **Bred** E Prosser, J Singh, & N & E Kent **Trained** Longton, Lancs

FOCUS
An ordinary handicap. The pace was fair and it was won in good style by the favourite.

3659 CAMPBELTOWN BAR STEWART SCOTT MEMORIAL H'CAP 1m
3:45 (3:45) (Class 4) (0-85,80) 3-Y-O+ **£4,528** (£1,347; £673; £336) **Stalls** Low

Form RPR
3310 1 **Munsarim (IRE)**[11] 3275 4-9-7 **77** PaulHanagan 4 86
(Keith Dalgleish) *in tch: hdwy to ld over 1f out: drvn out fnl f* **5/1**[3]

0030 2 *1 ¾* **Cono Zur (FR)**[8] 3386 4-9-5 **75** JamesSullivan 6 80
(Ruth Carr) *led at stdy gallop: rdn and hdd over 1f out: kpt on same pce ins fnl f* **7/2**[1]

2600 3 *1 ¾* **Northern Fling**[11] 3276 7-9-5 **78** GaryBartley[(3)] 8 79
(Jim Goldie) *hld up in tch: rdn 2f out: kpt on fnl f: nvr able to chal* **6/1**

2000 4 *1* **Bowmaker**[9] 3339 4-9-10 **80** (b[1]) AdrianNicholls 7 79
(Mark Johnston) *t.k.h: prom on outside: rn wd bnd ent st: hung lft and chal over 1f out: sn edgd both ways: one pce fnl f* **12/1**

2006 5 *1* **High Resolution**[11] 3276 4-9-2 **77** DaleSwift[(5)] 3 73
(Linda Perratt) *t.k.h: hld up in tch: effrt and rdn over 1f out: nt pce to chal* **5/1**[3]

3064 6 *hd* **Champagne Style (USA)**[1] 3641 4-9-6 **76** (p) TomEaves 2 72
(Richard Guest) *trckd ldr: rdn and ev ch over 2f out: no ex over 1f out* **4/1**[2]

06-0 7 *½* **Hawdyerwheesht**[15] 3159 3-9-0 **79** DarryllHolland 5 72
(Mark Johnston) *hld up: rdn 3f out: no imp fr 2f out* **8/1**

60-0 8 *1 ½* **Stags Leap (IRE)**[15] 3164 4-8-9 **72** GarryWhillans[(7)] 1 63
(Alistair Whillans) *trckd ldrs tl rdn and wknd over 1f out* **20/1**

1m 42.62s (-1.18) **Going Correction** -0.125s/f (Firm)
WFA 3 from 4yo+ 9lb **8** Ran SP% **113.4**
Speed ratings (Par 105): **100,98,96,95,94 94,93,92**
toteswingers: 1&2 £2.90, 1&3 £6.10, 2&3 £4.90 CSF £22.46 CT £106.69 TOTE £5.40: £2.80, £1.10, £3.60; EX 20.10 Trifecta £143.40 Pool: £579.67 - 2.99 winning units..
Owner Joseph Leckie & Sons Ltd **Bred** Shadwell Estate Company Limited **Trained** Carluke, South Lanarkshire

■ Stewards' Enquiry : Adrian Nicholls caution: used whip with excessive frequency without giving gelding time to respond.

FOCUS
An ordinary handicap - most of the runners had been beaten 9l-plus on their latest start.

3660 BET ON LIVE CRICKET AT TOTESPORT.COM H'CAP 1m 5f 13y
4:15 (4:15) (Class 5) (0-70,75) 4-Y-O+ **£2,328** (£693; £346; £173) **Stalls** Low

Form RPR
40-4 1 **Forrest Flyer (IRE)**[16] 3115 7-9-4 **66** PhillipMakin 2 75+
(Jim Goldie) *chsd ldrs: effrt over 2f out: sn chsng ldr and drvn: kpt on wl u.p fnl f: led nr fin* **2/1**[1]

26-1 2 *¾* **Amazing King (IRE)**[6] 3453 7-9-6 **75** 6ex DavidKenny[(7)] 1 82
(Philip Kirby) *hld up in tch: hdwy on outside to ld over 2f out: sn rdn and hung lft: kpt on fnl f: hdd nr fin* **2/1**[1]

0523 3 *13* **Sharp Sovereign (USA)**[18] 3054 5-9-1 **68** LMcNiff[(5)] 6 55
(David Barron) *cl up: rdn and hung lft over 2f out: plugged on fr over 1f out: no ch w first two* **9/4**[2]

-504 4 *4 ½* **Parc Des Princes (USA)**[6] 3453 5-9-1 **63** (b) TomEaves 5 44
(Nicky Richards) *chsd ldr after 3f: led and qcknd over 6f out: hdd over 2f out: wknd over 1f out* **13/2**[3]

0005 5 *46* **Wing N Prayer (IRE)**[16] 3141 4-8-2 **50** oh5 (t) PatrickMathers 3 —
(Alan Berry) *in tch: stdy hdwy 1/2-way: rdn and wknd fr over 3f out: t.o* **66/1**

2m 54.03s (0.03) **Going Correction** -0.125s/f (Firm) **5** Ran SP% **112.3**
Speed ratings (Par 103): **94,93,85,82,54**
toteswingers: 1&2 £3.60 CSF £6.53 TOTE £2.10: £1.10, £2.50; EX 2.70.
Owner Mrs Camille Macdonald **Bred** Philip Lau **Trained** Uplawmoor, E Renfrews

■ Stewards' Enquiry : David Kenny one-day ban: careless riding (Jul 17); caution: used whip with excessive frequency.

FOCUS
There was an open market for this staying handicap. The early pace was steady but it quickened at halfway and it was a race of changing fortunes in the closing stages.

3661 BET ON LIVE GOLF AT TOTESPORT.COM H'CAP — 6f
4:45 (4:48) (Class 6) (0-60,61) 3-Y-O — £1,704 (£503; £251) Stalls Low

Form	Pos	Btn	Horse / Trainer / Comment	Jockey / SP	RPR
-001	1		**Monel**[39] 2396 3-9-4 **57** (Jim Goldie) *dwlt: hld up: gd hdwy to ld appr fnl f: edgd lft and kpt on strly last 100yds*	DanielTudhope 2 **4/1**[1]	66+
5305	2	¾	**Brave Battle**[33] 2588 3-9-6 **59** (David Nicholls) *hld up: hdwy over 2f out: ev ch appr fnl f: kpt on: hld towards fin*	(b) AdrianNicholls 4 **9/1**	63
3440	3	1 ¾	**Winning Draw (IRE)**[14] 3207 3-8-13 **52** (Paul Midgley) *led tl hung rt and hdd appr fnl f: kpt on same pce u.p*	(v[1]) BarryMcHugh 8 **10/1**	50
0026	4	¾	**Catallout (IRE)**[20] 2986 3-9-0 **58** (Declan Carroll) *hld up: hdwy over 1f out: kpt on fnl f: nrst fin*	NeilFarley(5) 10 **6/1**	54
00-6	5	1 ¾	**Kwik Time**[17] 3075 3-8-13 **52** (Robin Bastiman) *chsd ldrs: rdn over 2f out: kpt on same pce over 1f out*	LeeNewman 5 **14/1**	42
0560	6	¾	**Vintage Grape (IRE)**[16] 3143 3-8-8 **47** (Eric Alston) *chsd ldrs tl rdn and no ex over 1f out*	(b[1]) DavidAllan 7 **16/1**	35
0006	7	2 ¾	**Country Waltz**[31] 2631 3-8-12 **56** (Linda Perratt) *disp ld to appr fnl f: sn outpcd*	DaleSwift(5) 6 **16/1**	35
5516	8	2 ½	**Unwrapit (USA)**[5] 3489 3-9-1 **61** (Bryan Smart) *hld up: drvn along 1/2-way: nvr able to chal*	(p) JustinNewman(7) 12 **9/2**[2]	32
-305	9	2 ½	**Roman Ruler (IRE)**[58] 1880 3-9-4 **57** (Chris Fairhurst) *prom tl rdn and wknd over 1f out*	PhillipMakin 13 **11/2**[3]	20
-460	10	¾	**Georgian Silver**[71] 1514 3-8-7 **46** oh1 (George Foster) *prom: drvn over 2f out: wknd over 1f out*	(p) PaulHanagan 9 **25/1**	7
503	11	1	**Crabbies Ginger**[34] 2574 3-9-1 **54** (Lisa Williamson) *chsd ldrs tl rdn and wknd fr 2f out*	TomEaves 3 **16/1**	12
0040	12	½	**Face East (USA)**[6] 3455 3-8-7 **46** oh1 (Alan Berry) *midfield: struggling 1/2-way: btn over 1f out*	PatrickMathers 1 **33/1**	—
06-5	13	17	**Tinzo (IRE)**[15] 3191 3-8-4 **46** oh1 (Alan Berry) *dwlt: bhd: struggling fr 1/2-way: t.o*	PaulPickard(3) 11 **80/1**	—

1m 13.45s (1.05) **Going Correction** -0.125s/f (Firm) — **13** Ran SP% **119.3**
Speed ratings (Par 98): **96,95,92,91,89 88,84,81,78,77 75,75,52**
toteswingers: 1&2 £7.30, 1&3 £8.90, 2&3 £15.00 CSF £39.57 CT £352.39 TOTE £5.70: £2.80, £3.80, £2.40; EX 31.20 Trifecta £386.70 Part won. Pool: £522.64 - 0.04 winning units..
Owner A L Gregg **Bred** Frank Brady And Brian Scanlon **Trained** Uplawmoor, E Renfrews

FOCUS
A weak 3-y-o handicap, rated around the runner-up and third with the winner probably a bit better than the bare result.
Vintage Grape(IRE) Official explanation: jockey said filly hung both ways

3662 MORE LIVE SPORT BETTING AT TOTESPORT.COM AMATEUR RIDERS' H'CAP — 5f
5:15 (5:18) (Class 6) (0-60,67) 4-Y-O+ — £1,646 (£506; £253) Stalls Low

Form	Pos	Btn	Horse / Trainer / Comment	Jockey / SP	RPR
0653	1		**Eternal Instinct**[8] 3387 4-11-0 **60** (Jim Goldie) *hld up: hdwy over 1f out: led ins fnl f: pushed out*	MrsCBartley 5 **10/1**	71
-330	2	1 ½	**Arriva La Diva**[30] 2694 5-10-7 **60** (Linda Perratt) *led: rdn over 2f out: hdd ins fnl f: kpt on same pce*	MrSFeeney(7) 7 **11/1**	66
4511	3	nk	**Boy The Bell**[9] 3359 4-11-2 **67** (Brian Ellison) *prom: rdn 2f out: kpt on wl fnl f: nrst fin*	MissHBethell(5) 8 **7/2**[1]	72
0522	4	¾	**Royal Blade (IRE)**[12] 3248 4-10-0 **46** (Alan Berry) *trckd ldrs: rdn 2f out: kpt on same pce fnl f*	MissSBrotherton 3 **4/1**[2]	48
6004	5	nk	**Sea Salt**[15] 3190 8-10-9 **60** (Ron Barr) *in tch: rdn over 2f out: kpt on same pce ins fnl f*	MissVBarr(5) 2 **14/1**	61
[illegible]	6	½	**Tournedos (IRE)**[20] 2087 9-10-5 **58** (Ruth Carr) *dwlt: bhd tl hdwy and swtchd rt appr fnl f: kpt on wl: nrst fin*	(h) MrBHowe(7) 10 **10/1**	57+
-000	7	1 ¼	**Argentine (IRE)**[20] 2987 7-10-5 **56** (George Foster) *dwlt: hld up: hdwy on outside 1/2-way: no imp fnl f*	(v[1]) MrGBWatters(5) 16 **18/1**	51
6632	8	½	**Two Turtle Doves (IRE)**[10] 3307 5-10-12 **61** (Michael Mullineaux) *prom: rdn over 2f out: kpt on same pce ins fnl f*	MissMMullineaux(3) 9 **15/2**	54
0404	9	1	**Boga (IRE)**[12] 3247 4-9-9 **46** oh1 (Karen Tutty) *trckd ldrs tl rdn and no ex over 1f out*	MissPhillipaTutty(5) 6 **28/1**	35
-050	10	hd	**Mujahope**[45] 2233 6-9-9 **46** oh1 (Colin Teague) *in tch: pushed along over 2f out: kpt on same pce over 1f out*	(v) LucyAlexander(5) 12 **33/1**	35
600-	11	2 ½	**Andrasta**[345] 4324 6-9-7 **46** oh1 (Alan Berry) *towards rr: pushed along 1/2-way: sn no imp*	MissJGillam(7) 14 **66/1**	26
4051	12	shd	**Dispol Grand (IRE)**[10] 3307 5-10-8 **57** (Paul Midgley) *in tch tl rdn and wknd over 1f out*	(v) MissWGibson(3) 4 **7/1**[3]	36
55-0	13	1	**Weetentherty**[10] 3306 4-9-7 **46** oh1 (Linda Perratt) *bhd: pushed along 1/2-way: nvr rchd ldrs*	MrJHamilton(7) 13 **40/1**	22
00-0	14	1 ¾	**Classlin**[38] 2412 4-9-7 **46** oh1 (Jim Goldie) *dwlt: bhd and pushed along: nvr on terms*	MissMKeegan(7) 11 **33/1**	15
00-5	15	shd	**Autocracy**[58] 1861 4-10-4 **55** (Eric Alston) *trckd ldrs tl rdn and wknd over 1f out*	MrNdeBoinville(5) 1 **14/1**	24
00-0	16	1 ½	**Royal Premium**[16] 3142 5-9-7 **46** (Bruce Hellier) *hld up in tch: struggling 2f out: sn btn*	(v) MissNStead(7) 15 **66/1**	9

60.75 secs (1.35) **Going Correction** -0.125s/f (Firm) — **16** Ran SP% **126.4**
Speed ratings (Par 101): **89,86,86,84,84 83,81,80,79,78 74,74,73,70,70 67**
toteswingers: 1&2 £19.20, 1&3 £11.20, 2&3 £7.20 CSF £114.49 CT £472.94 TOTE £13.70: £2.50, £2.20, £1.40, £1.60; EX 90.30 Trifecta £353.00 Pool: £691.84 - 1.45 winning units..
Owner Johnnie Delta Racing **Bred** Jim Goldie **Trained** Uplawmoor, E Renfrews

FOCUS
An ordinary sprint handicap for amateur riders. The runner-up sets the standard with the third and fourth close to their recent marks.

T/Jkpt: £18,596.30 to a £1 stake. Pool: £65,480.02. 2.50 winning tickets. T/Plt: £13.10 to a £1 stake. Pool: £79,457.85. 4,394.81 winning tickets. T/Qpdt: £8.00 to a £1 stake. Pool: £5,528.88. 509.70 winning tickets. RY

3663 -3668a - (Foreign Racing) - See Raceform Interactive

3062 CHANTILLY (R-H)
Sunday, July 3

OFFICIAL GOING: Turf: good

3669a PRIX DU BOIS (GROUP 3) (2YO) (TURF) — 5f
1:00 (12:00) 2-Y-O — £34,482 (£13,793; £10,344; £6,896; £3,448)

Pos	Btn	Horse / Trainer / Comment	Jockey / SP	RPR
1		**Family One (FR)**[44] 2-8-11 0 (Y Barberot, France) *racd 2nd on rail: proged to chal 2f out: led 1 1/2f out: sn clr: easily*	IoritzMendizabal 1 **5/1**	109
2	2	**Boomerang Bob (IRE)**[17] 3064 2-8-11 0 (J W Hills) *racd 4th on rail: qcknd to go 2nd 1 1/2f out: r.o wl fnl f: no threat to wnr*	SebSanders 2 **15/8**[1]	102
3	2 ½	**Pyman's Theory (IRE)**[17] 3064 2-8-8 0 (Tom Dascombe) *led fr s: chal 2f out: hdd 1 1/2f out: u.p to hold 3rd on line*	Christophe-PatriceLemaire 5 **6/1**	90
4	nse	**Bay Shore (IRE)**[30] 2-8-9 0 ow1 (J-C Rouget, France) *at rr: rdn 2f out: r.o wl fnl f: jst missed 3rd*	ChristopheSoumillon 3 **5/2**[2]	91
5	3	**Murano (IRE)**[24] 2-8-11 0 (B De Montzey, France) *settled 3rd on outer: rdn 2f out: nt qckn: fdd fnl f*	PhilippeSogorb 4 **9/2**[3]	82

57.58 secs (-0.72) **Going Correction** -0.025s/f (Good) — **5** Ran SP% **112.5**
Speed ratings: **104,100,96,96,91**
WIN (incl. 1 euro stake): 4.70. PLACES: 1.90, 1.40. SF: 17.70.
Owner Ecurie Ascot **Bred** Ecurie Ascot **Trained** France

NOTEBOOK
Family One(FR) provided Yann Berberot with his first Group winner as a trainer. He quickened up well to win by 2l, and will now be aimed at the Prix Robert Papin. (op 4/1 tchd 9/2)
Boomerang Bob(IRE), runner-up in the Norfolk, couldn't cope with the winner but ran a solid race in defeat, and apparently connections are keen to reoppose the winner in the Robert Papin.
Pyman's Theory(IRE), ninth in the Norfolk, showed her usual pace but didn't see her race out.

3670a PRIX JEAN PRAT (GROUP 1) (3YO COLTS & FILLIES) (TURF) — 1m
2:45 (12:00) 3-Y-O — £197,034 (£78,827; £39,413; £19,689; £9,862)

Pos	Btn	Horse / Trainer / Comment	Jockey / SP	RPR
1		**Mutual Trust**[21] 2978 3-9-2 0 (A Fabre, France) *racd 2nd: qcknd 2f out to share ld: led 1f out: hdd 100yds out: rallied strly to get up on line*	MaximeGuyon 6 **5/2**[2]	119
2	hd	**Zoffany (IRE)**[19] 3011 3-9-2 0 (A P O'Brien, Ire) *settled 4th: wnt 3rd 2f out: rdn and qcknd on outside 1f out: r.o strly fnl f: jst failed*	RyanMoore 5 **6/4**[1]	119+
3	nse	**Strong Suit (USA)**[18] 3029 3-9-2 0 (Richard Hannon) *sn led: setting slow pce: shared ld 2f out: hdd 1f out: rallied to ld again 100yds out: hdd cl home*	RichardHughes 1 **9/2**[3]	118
4	1 ½	**Glorious Sight (IRE)**[21] 2977 3-8-13 0 (Robert Collet, France) *racd 3rd tl st whn relegated to 4th: rdn and r.o wl fr 2f out: no threat to ldrs fnl f*	OlivierPeslier 2 **8/1**	112
5	nse	**Venomous**[21] 2978 3-9-2 0 (T Clout, France) *racd towards rr: rdn 2f out: r.o wl fnl f: no threat to ldrs fnl f*	FlavienPrat 7 **20/1**	115
6	2 ½	**Neebras (IRE)**[19] 3011 3-9-2 0 (Mahmood Al Zarooni) *s.i.s: racd in rr: rdn ent st: no ex fnl f*	MickaelBarzalona 3 **16/1**	109
P		**Temps Au Temps (IRE)**[49] 2139 3-9-2 0 (M Delzangles, France) *exited stalls v slowly: ref to r: sn p.u*	GregoryBenoist 4 **13/1**	—

1m 40.45s (2.45) **Going Correction** +0.675s/f (Yiel) — **7** Ran SP% **115.7**
Speed ratings: **114,113,113,112,112 109,—**
WIN (incl. 1 euro stake): 3.10. PLACES: 1.60, 1.60. SF: 6.40.
Owner K Abdulla **Bred** Juddmonte Farms **Trained** Chantilly, France

FOCUS
The seventh running of the Prix Jean Prat as a Group 1 over a mile and one that unusually had very little Guineas form on show with just the second from the Pouliches and third from the Poulains lining up. Added to that there was just a single Group 1 winner in the race in the shape of Zoffany, whose sole success at the highest level came as a juvenile. As is often the case in French races, particularly those with small fields, they went no pace at all early on and, with a number of the field unsuited by that, it is probably worth treating the form with a degree of caution.

NOTEBOOK
Mutual Trust was the most lightly raced of these having had just the three starts, two over this C&D, since making his debut on May 2. He had handled the gradual progression through the grades with no problems and, even though this may not have been the toughest Group 1, it was a step up from what he had been competing in before. He was in an ideal position throughout, sat just off the leader and, having disputed three out, he was shaken up two from home before being driven to take the lead in the final strides. He gave the impression that he would have no problem stepping up in trip and has shown in his brief career that he does not mind a bit of cut. With four runs coming in a short space of time he could be set for a break now. Races such as the Prix du Moulin and the Prix Jacques le Marois are his obvious targets, which are likely to be governed by where Frankel, who is in the same ownership, goes.
Zoffany(IRE) won five times as a juvenile but has now finished second on each of his three starts this season. As was the case at Ascot last time, when he got within three-quarters of a length of Frankel, his best work was coming in the closing stages. However, he once again showed a tendency to throw his head to the left and he looked a particularly tricky ride. He may not be one to trust at the moment. Connections will now decide whether to persevere with racing over a mile or drop him back in trip. The Prix Maurice de Gheest was mentioned afterwards as a possible target for this July Cup entry.
Strong Suit(USA), the Jersey Stakes winner, pulled hard early on this first try over a mile. Having been challenged for the lead by the winner three out, he responded to his rider's urgings well before losing second on the line. He may well have been beaten by two very good horses as opposed to the longer trip, although he is likely to drop back to 7f for the Lennox Stakes for his next outing. (op 4/1)
Glorious Sight(IRE), the only filly in the field, was dropping back in trip having finished third in the Prix De Diane last time. Although she was not taking on her own sex this time, with two Classic places to her name, she could have been expected to have been more of a factor in this. She was never able to get in a challenging position though, and swished her tail late on. (op 9/1)
Venomous, third in the Poulains two outings previously, finished a similar distance behind Mutual Trust as when the pair met in a Group 3 here last time. He was the only horse to come through late on from off the pace. This looked a respectable effort on his favoured quicker surface.
Neebras(IRE) jumped away slowly. He has posted a couple of solid performances this year, including when finishing two places behind Zoffany in the St James's Palace Stakes last time. This, though, was not one of them and he never looked like figuring.

Temps Au Temps(IRE) lost all chance when walking out the stalls and then virtually pulling himself up. He was probably out of his depth here anyway.

3671a PRIX CHLOE (GROUP 3) (3YO FILLIES) (TURF) — 1m 1f

3:20 (12:00) 3-Y-0 **£34,482** (£13,793; £10,344; £6,896; £3,448)

RPR

1 **Beatrice Aurore (IRE)**[30] 2682 3-8-11 0 .... OlivierPeslier 2 110
(John Dunlop) *settled 3rd: relegated to 4th bef st: rdn 2f out: picked up wl 1f out: r.o strly to ld 100yds out: comf* **9/2**[2]

2 *1* **Peinture Abstraite**[28] 2752 3-8-11 0 .... ChristopheSoumillon 5 108
(A De Royer-Dupre, France) *racd 2nd: rdn to ld 1f out: hdd 100yds out: r.o wl* **2/1**[1]

3 *3/4* **Dream Peace (IRE)**[46] 2208 3-8-11 0 .... ThomasHuet 4 106
(Robert Collet, France) *racd towards rr: picked up wl 1 1/2f out: r.o wl ins fnl f to take 3rd on line* **6/1**

4 *shd* **Margravine (USA)**[26] 3-8-11 0 .... MickaelBarzalona 6 106
(A Fabre, France) *racd 5th: rdn 2f out: r.o wl fnl f to go 3rd 100yds out: lost 3rd on line* **11/2**[3]

5 *3/4* **Dalarua (IRE)**[42] 2342 3-8-11 0 .... ThierryThulliez 1 105
(S Wattel, France) *racd 3rd on rail: full of running but short of room 1 1/2f out: unable to mount chal ins fnl f: unlucky* **8/1**

6 *nk* **Malicia (USA)**[36] 3-8-11 0 .... IoritzMendizabal 3 104
(X Thomas-Demeaulte, France) *led fr s and stl in front over 1 1/2f out: rdn but fnd no ex and fdd ins fnl f* **8/1**

7 *1/2* **Coutances**[34] 3-8-11 0 .... Christophe-PatriceLemaire 7 103
(M Delzangles, France) *settled towards rr: rdn early in st: nt qckn: styd on wl fnl f* **7/1**

1m 55.53s (4.43) **Going Correction** +0.675s/f (Yiel) **7** Ran SP% **115.9**
Speed ratings: **107,106,105,105,104 104,103**
WIN (incl. 1 euro stake): 5.90. PLACES: 2.00, 1.40. SF: 14.10.
Owner Benny Andersson **Bred** Chess Racing Ab **Trained** Arundel, W Sussex

NOTEBOOK
Beatrice Aurore(IRE), sixth in the Oaks last time out, picked up well and finished her race off strongly to secure her third win of the campaign. Never too far off the steady early pace, she picked up impressively when asked to quicken, and deserves to return to better company now.

3651 HAMBURG (R-H)

Sunday, July 3

OFFICIAL GOING: Turf: heavy

3672a IDEE 142. DEUTSCHES DERBY (GROUP 1) (3YO COLTS & FILLIES) (TURF) — 1m 4f

4:35 (12:00) 3-Y-0 **£258,620** (£86,206; £51,724; £25,862; £8,620)

RPR

1 **Waldpark (GER)**[31] 3-9-2 0 .... JBojko 10 115+
(A Wohler, Germany) *hld up in midfield: gd prog through field to join ldng gp under 2f out: qcknd to ld over 1f out: r.o wl to go clr fnl 100yds: comf* **12/1**

2 *2* **Earl Of Tinsdal (GER)**[42] 2345 3-9-2 0 .... EPedroza 3 112
(A Wohler, Germany) *prom bhd ldrs fr s: travelling wl: mde move early in st: r.o wl u.p: led briefly 2f out: hdd over 1 1/2f out: battled on gamely* **16/1**

3 *2* **Saltas (GER)**[20] 3007 3-9-2 0 .... AStarke 15 109
(P Schiergen, Germany) *settled in midfield: began move down bk st: rdn patiently ent st: asked for effrt 1 1/2f out: r.o wl: got up for 3rd almost on line* **25/1**

4 *hd* **Mawingo (GER)**[42] 2345 3-9-2 0 .... ADeVries 11 108
(J Hirschberger, Germany) *midfield: patiently rdn early in st: mde move whn in clr: r.o wl: ct for 3rd cl home* **8/1**

5 *shd* **Brown Panther**[17] 3069 3-9-2 0 .... RichardKingscote 2 108
(Tom Dascombe) *sent to ld fr s: set gd pce: r.o wl in st: failed to qckn whn hdd 2f out: styd on wl* **7/4**[1]

6 *1 1/2* **Tahini (GER)**[31] 3-9-2 0 .... MCadeddu 13 106
(J Hirschberger, Germany) *settled towards rr: short of room ent st: r.o wl whn clr* **66/1**

7 *2 1/2* **Lindenthaler (GER)**[49] 2136 3-9-2 0 .... WilliamBuick 8 102
(P Schiergen, Germany) *settled in 6th: mde prog down bk st: jnd ldrs ent st: rdn but failed to qckn: styd on at same pce* **20/1**

8 *6* **Ibicenco (GER)**[21] 2979 3-9-2 0 .... TomQueally 7 92
(J Hirschberger, Germany) *racd bhd ldrs on ins rail: rdn and r.o early in st: styd on at one pce* **11/1**

9 *nse* **Silvaner (GER)**[42] 2345 3-9-2 0 .... THellier 6 92
(P Schiergen, Germany) *settled in midfield on ins: short of room ent st: rdn and styd on* **33/1**

10 *1 1/2* **Gereon (GER)**[20] 3007 3-9-2 0 .... JMurtagh 16 90
(C Zschache, Germany) *settled in midfield: rdn early in st: styd on but no ex* **7/1**[3]

11 *11* **Ametrin (IRE)**[20] 3007 3-9-2 0 .... FilipMinarik 18 72
(J Hirschberger, Germany) *broke wl fr outside draw: qckly swtchd to join ldr on ins: settled in 2nd: shkn up early in st: fnd no ex and sn wknd* **18/1**

12 *1/2* **Mi Senor (GER)**[14] 3-9-2 0 .... StefanieHofer 5 71
(A Wohler, Germany) *settled in midfield: rdn and r.o early in st: fdd fnl 2f* **100/1**

13 *hd* **Sommernachtstraum (GER)**[31] 3-9-2 0 .... StephanePasquier 14 71
(W Hickst, Germany) *settled bhd ldng gp: rdn early in st but fnd no ex: fdd* **16/1**

14 *shd* **Appleby (GER)**[14] 3-9-2 0 .... DPorcu 1 71
(S Smrczek, Germany) *prom early: pulling freely in 5th: r.o ent st: fdd fnl 2f* **66/1**

15 *5* **Theo Danon (GER)**[20] 3007 3-9-2 0 .... ASuborics 9 63
(P Schiergen, Germany) *nvr moving wl: settled towards rr: mde no imp in st* **50/1**

16 *nk* **Ordensritter (GER)**[20] 3007 3-9-2 0 .... DavyBonilla 17 62
(H Steinmetz, Germany) *sweating profusely bef s: settled towards rr and nvr figured* **100/1**

17 *8* **Hoseo (GER)**[14] 3-9-2 0 .... HenkGrewe 12 50
(Frau E Mader, Germany) *a bhd and nvr figured* **300/1**

18 *nk* **Arrigo (GER)**[20] 3007 3-9-2 0 .... KierenFallon 4 49
(J Hirschberger, Germany) *settled in midfield: hrd rdn bef fnl turn: wknd qckly in st* **9/2**[2]

2m 40.29s (5.74) **18** Ran SP% **130.0**
WIN (incl. 10 euro stake): 115. PLACES: 37, 34, 42. SF: 1,041.
Owner Gestut Ravensberg **Bred** Gestut Ravensberg **Trained** Germany

NOTEBOOK
Waldpark(GER), who travelled well off the pace and quickened past Earl Of Tinsdal approaching the final furlong, led home a one-two for his trainer Andreas Wohler. (op 11-1)
Brown Panther, stepping up in class following his handicap success at Royal Ascot, found himself in front soon after the gates opened and, rather than forfeiting his position, Kingscote decided to make the most of it and set about making every yard. He led them into the straight but got tired in the closing stages and lost a couple of places in the final yards. This competition was tougher than anything he'd encountered before, and he remains capable of better. (op 2-1)

3476 BRIGHTON (L-H)

Monday, July 4

OFFICIAL GOING: Good to firm (good in places) changing to good to firm after race 1 (2.30)
Wind: Moderate, against Weather: Sunny and warm

3673 BRITISH STALLION STUDS SUPPORTING BRITISH RACING E B F MEDIAN AUCTION MAIDEN STKS — 5f 213y

2:30 (2:30) (Class 5) 2-Y-0 **£3,169** (£943; £471; £235) **Stalls** Low

Form RPR

240 **1** **Pride And Joy (IRE)**[20] 3012 2-9-3 0 .... FergusSweeney 4 78+
(Jamie Osborne) *broke wl: t.k.h and stdd into 4th: effrt and eased outside to ld jst ins fnl 2f: drvn out* **5/4**[1]

3 **2** *nk* **Tones (IRE)**[20] 3016 2-9-3 0 .... RyanMoore 3 77+
(Richard Hannon) *sn outpcd in rr: hdwy 2f out: drvn to chal fnl f: r.o: jst hld nr fin* **5/4**[1]

0 **3** *17* **Picura**[12] 3270 2-8-12 0 .... MartinDwyer 7 21
(William Muir) *cl 3rd: sn pushed along: carried rt over 2f out: sn wknd* **25/1**

4230 **4** *1/2* **Copper Falls**[20] 3014 2-8-12 0 .... KierenFallon 5 20
(Brendan Powell) *led tl jst ins fnl 2f: hrd rdn: sn wknd* **9/1**[2]

0 **5** *1 1/4* **Get The Trip**[18] 3092 2-8-12 0 .... KirstyMilczarek 2 16
(James Toller) *stdd s: sn chsng ldr: wknd wl over 1f out* **16/1**[3]

69.96 secs (-0.24) **Going Correction** -0.10s/f (Good) **5** Ran SP% **108.6**
Speed ratings (Par 94): **97,96,73,73,71**
CSF £2.85 TOTE £2.10: £1.10, £1.30; EX 3.40.
Owner Miss J Kask **Bred** R P Ryan **Trained** Upper Lambourn, Berks

FOCUS
Rail dolled out 4yds from 4.5f to 3.5f increasing distances by 8yds. A more interesting maiden than it may have looked with a couple of these having run at Royal Ascot. The first two pulled a very long way clear of the others and the form's rated around the winner's pre-race mark.

NOTEBOOK
Pride And Joy(IRE) met trouble in running when well beaten in the Coventry, but his maiden form in the spring was good enough to win a race like this. He kept on well to withstand the late challenge of the runner-up and his trainer expects him to keep on improving and get another furlong. (tchd 11-8 and 13-8 in a place)
Tones(IRE), third of five when joint-favourite for his debut over C&D last month, failed to go the early gallop and was pulled very wide over 2f from home. He tried hard and finished miles clear of the third, but the winner proved too professional. (tchd 11-10 and 11-8 in a place)
Picura was keen early and didn't look happy on the track coming to the last quarter-mile. (op 33-1)
Copper Falls had made the frame in three maidens before beating just two home in the Windsor Castle. Soon in front, she was comfortably picked off over a furlong from home and dropped right away. She looks to be going backwards. (op 8-1 tchd 10-1)

3674 REA MABEY 21ST BIRTHDAY CELEBRATION H'CAP — 6f 209y

3:00 (3:00) (Class 5) (0-75,74) 3-Y-0+ **£2,264** (£673; £336; £168) **Stalls** Low

Form RPR

6003 **1** **Cheylesmore (IRE)**[2] 3621 3-8-6 **60** .... (v[1]) WilliamCarson 4 66
(Stuart Williams) *mde all: hrd drvn fnl f: all out* **8/1**[3]

4312 **2** *1/2* **Mandhooma**[6] 3477 5-9-4 **64** .... ChrisCatlin 1 71
(Peter Hiatt) *stdd s: hld up towards rr: rdn over 2f out: gd hdwy over 1f out: pressed wnr fnl 75yds: jst hld* **11/4**[1]

0-31 **3** *1* **Patavium Prince (IRE)**[117] 810 8-9-13 **73** .... FergusSweeney 6 78
(Jo Crowley) *hld up in tch: chsd wnr ins fnl 2f: drvn to chal 1f out: one pce ins fnl f* **5/4**[1]

2430 **4** *3/4* **Khajaaly (IRE)**[18] 3093 4-9-2 **65** .... AdamBeschizza[(3)] 3 68
(Julia Feilden) *t.k.h: in tch on rail: rdn to chse ldrs ins fnl 2f: one pce* **16/1**

0224 **5** *1/2* **Ivory Lace**[6] 3477 10-9-2 **67** .... HarryBentley[(5)] 5 68
(Steve Woodman) *chsd ldrs: outpcd and n.m.r over 1f out: kpt on ins fnl f* **7/2**[2]

05-6 **6** *1/2* **My Learned Friend (IRE)**[30] 2719 7-9-7 **74** .... ThomasBrown[(7)] 9 74
(Andrew Balding) *towards rr: effrt on outer 2f out: no ex 1f out* **8/1**[3]

5-00 **7** *3/4* **Silver Alliance**[26] 2818 3-9-4 **72** .... EddieAhern 8 67
(Walter Swinburn) *chsd ldrs tl hrd rdn and wknd over 1f out* **9/1**

1206 **8** *3* **Buxton**[48] 2169 7-10-0 **74** .... (t) TomQueally 2 64
(Roger Ingram) *stdd s: hld up in last: hrd rdn 2f out: nvr a factor* **11/1**

0-23 **9** *14* **Screenprint**[30] 2728 3-9-2 **70** .... (t) HayleyTurner 7 19
(Michael Bell) *t.k.h: chsd wnr tl wknd 2f out: eased whn no ch fnl f* **8/1**[3]

1m 22.23s (-0.87) **Going Correction** -0.10s/f (Good)
WFA 3 from 4yo+ 8lb **9** Ran SP% **113.1**
Speed ratings (Par 103): **100,99,98,97,96 96,95,92,76**
Tote Swingers: 1&2 £5.60, 1&3 £16.80, 2&3 £4.20 CSF £29.64 CT £305.65 TOTE £12.00: £2.50, £1.40, £3.70; EX 35.60 Trifecta £221.50 Pool: £518.04 - 1.73 winning units..
Owner Keith & Meta Pryce **Bred** John Cullinan **Trained** Newmarket, Suffolk

FOCUS
An ordinary handicap, rated around the second with a turf best from the winner.

3675 SPORTING SIGNS MAIDEN STKS — 7f 214y

3:30 (3:30) (Class 5) 3-Y-0 **£2,264** (£673; £336; £168) **Stalls** Low

Form RPR

0-42 **1** **Starbound (IRE)**[14] 3236 3-8-12 76 .... RyanMoore 2 61
(William Haggas) *led for 3f: led again 2f out: narrow ld after: idled: drvn out* **1/3**[1]

0266 **2** *1* **Mister Ben Vereen**[2] 3633 3-9-3 63 .... (b) CathyGannon 3 63
(Eve Johnson Houghton) *cl up: led 5f out tl 2f out: kpt on u.p: jst hld fnl 50yds* **9/1**[3]

03 **3** *1 1/2* **Powder Keg**[19] 3053 3-9-3 .... KierenFallon 5 59
(Mark Johnston) *dwlt: in tch in rr: rdn to chse ldrs on outer 2f out: hung bdly lft and one pce appr fnl f* **5/1**[2]

00- **4** *3* **My Mate Les (IRE)**[290] 6159 3-9-0 .... KierenFox[(3)] 6 52
(John Best) *cl up: rdn 3f out: outpcd fnl 2f* **16/1**

00 **5** *5* **Habsburg**[51] 2103 3-9-3 .... FrankieMcDonald 4 40
(Paul Fitzsimons) *sed awkwardly and wnt rt: in tch tl wknd wl over 1f out* **100/1**

6 2¾ **Magic Maid (GER)** 3-8-12 .... TomQueally 1 28
(Barney Curley) *in tch in rr: pushed along 4f out: wknd 2f out: lame after r: fatally injured* **33/1**

1m 34.96s (-1.04) **Going Correction** -0.10s/f (Good) **6** Ran SP% **111.5**
Speed ratings (Par 100): **101,100,98,95,90 87**
Tote Swingers: 1&2 £1.60, 1&3 £1.60, 2&3 £1.40 CSF £4.24 TOTE £1.40: £1.10, £2.10; EX 3.30.

Owner Cheveley Park Stud **Bred** Lodge Park Stud **Trained** Newmarket, Suffolk

FOCUS
A moderate and uncompetitive maiden which proved hard work for the long odds-on favourite. She didn't match her AW latest.

3676 DIGIBET.COM H'CAP 1m 1f 209y
4:00 (4:05) (Class 5) (0-70,69) 3-Y-O **£2,264** (£673; £336; £168) **Stalls** High

Form RPR

6-05 **1** **Plattsburgh (USA)**^{68} [1609] 3-9-6 **68** .... KierenFallon 2 72
(Mark Johnston) *prom: pushed along over 4f out: outpcd over 1f out: rallied u.str.p to ld fnl strides* **7/1**

364 **2** *nk* **Clarion Call**^{54} [1998] 3-9-6 **68** .... CathyGannon 3 71
(Eve Johnson Houghton) *t.k.h: in tch: effrt and nt clr run fr 2f out: drvn into narrow ld ins fnl f: kpt on: hdd fnl strides* **28/1**

00-6 **3** *1¼* **Wom**^{17} [3133] 3-8-11 **59** ....(b^{1}) RyanMoore 6 60
(William Haggas) *sn led and set modest pce: hrd rdn and hdd ins fnl f: no ex* **7/2**^{2}

03-3 **4** *1* **U A E Storm (USA)**^{26} [2808] 3-9-4 **69** .... AdamBeschizza$^{(3)}$ 1 68
(David Simcock) *t.k.h in rr: hdwy on outer to press ldrs over 2f out: hrd rdn over 1f out: one pce* **7/1**

655 **5** *nk* **Maricopa**^{17} [3135] 3-8-13 **68** ....(vt^{1}) AntiocoMurgia$^{(7)}$ 7 66
(Mahmood Al Zarooni) *t.k.h: in tch: rdn to chal over 2f out: no ex fnl f* **13/2**^{3}

01-5 **6** *19* **Spanish Pride (IRE)**^{24} [2883] 3-9-5 **67** .... EddieAhern 5 27
(John Dunlop) *t.k.h: prom tl wknd 2f out: eased: b.b.v* **1/1**^{1}

2m 2.46s (-1.14) **Going Correction** -0.10s/f (Good) **6** Ran SP% **114.0**
Speed ratings (Par 100): **100,99,98,97,97 82**
Tote Swingers: 1&2 £6.90, 1&3 £2.40, 2&3 £4.50 CSF £139.33 TOTE £6.60: £2.90, £6.60; EX 67.80.

Owner Sheikh Hamdan Bin Mohammed Al Maktoum **Bred** Mr & Mrs Bertram R Firestone **Trained** Middleham Moor, N Yorks

FOCUS
A modest 3-y-o handicap and slightly suspect form.

Spanish Pride(IRE) Official explanation: trainer's rep said filly bled from the nose

3677 BRIGHTONANDHOVEJOBS.COM H'CAP 7f 214y
4:30 (4:32) (Class 6) (0-65,65) 3-Y-O+ **£1,617** (£481; £240; £120) **Stalls** Low

Form RPR

-320 **1** **Fire King**^{17} [3142] 5-9-11 **60** ....(p) TomQueally 8 69
(Andrew Haynes) *hld up in 2nd last: smooth hdwy to ld wl over 1f out: shkn up: readily* **7/2**^{2}

0-32 **2** *1½* **Love Nest**^{14} [3227] 3-8-9 **53** .... EddieAhern 7 55
(John Dunlop) *in tch: rdn over 3f out: drvn to chse wnr ins fnl f: a hld* **3/1**^{1}

-231 **3** *hd* **Phluke**^{6} [3477] 10-9-11 **65** 6ex .... AmyScott$^{(5)}$ 4 69
(Eve Johnson Houghton) *prom: drvn to chal ins fnl 2f: one pce fnl f* **7/2**^{2}

4033 **4** *1¾* **Ilie Nastase (FR)**^{2} [3636] 7-10-0 **63** ....(b) HayleyTurner 1 63
(Conor Dore) *led over 1f: rejnd ldrs 2f out: no ex 1f out* **4/1**^{3}

6400 **5** *¾* **Prince Of Thebes (IRE)**^{7} [3468] 10-9-2 **56** .... MarkCoumbe$^{(5)}$ 2 54
(Michael Attwater) *s.s: bhd: hrd rdn 2f out: nvr rchd ldrs* **20/1**

0640 **6** *2* **Vezere (USA)**^{2} [3636] 4-8-7 **45** ....(b) SimonPearce$^{(3)}$ 5 39
(Simon Dow) *prom: led 6f out tl wl over 1f out: sn wknd* **12/1**

4016 **7** *1¾* **Inquisitress**^{13} [3253] 7-9-5 **54** .... CathyGannon 3 44
(John Bridger) *chsd ldrs: rdn over 2f out: wknd over 1f out* **11/1**

0340 **8** *5* **Rainsborough**^{47} [2201] 4-8-13 **48** ....(e) DaneO'Neill 6 26
(Peter Hedger) *hld up in 6th: rdn and wknd over 2f out* **16/1**

1m 34.93s (-1.07) **Going Correction** -0.10s/f (Good)
WFA 3 from 4yo+ 9lb **8** Ran SP% **116.1**
Speed ratings (Par 101): **101,99,99,97,96 94,93,88**
Tote Swingers: 1&2 £3.40, 1&3 £3.80, 2&3 £2.70 CSF £14.73 CT £39.14 TOTE £4.90: £2.00, £1.30, £1.40; EX 19.50 Trifecta £119.40 Pool: £682.75 - 4.23 winning units..

Owner T Suttle & Miss S Wicks **Bred** Dr J M Leigh **Trained** Limpley Stoke, Bath

FOCUS
A moderate handicap which was sound run. The winner posted a 3lb personal best.

3678 SIS LIVE H'CAP 5f 59y
5:00 (5:01) (Class 6) (0-55,55) 3-Y-O+ **£1,617** (£481; £240; £120) **Stalls** Low

Form RPR

3342 **1** **Bobby's Doll**^{4} [3556] 4-9-2 **55** .... AdamBeschizza$^{(3)}$ 4 67
(Terry Clement) *prom: narrow ld 2f out: rdn clr over 1f out: comf* **2/1**^{1}

5422 **2** *3* **Talamahana**^{6} [3476] 6-9-4 **54** ....(v) ChrisCatlin 3 55
(Andrew Haynes) *in rr: rdn over 2f out: styd on to take 2nd fnl 100yds: no ch w wnr* **5/2**^{2}

033 **3** *2½* **Spic 'n Span**^{6} [3493] 6-9-2 **52** ....(b) TomMcLaughlin 2 44
(Ronald Harris) *led to s: pressed ldrs after 2f: one pce appr fnl f* **7/2**^{3}

0605 **4** *1¾* **Bookiesindex Boy**^{6} [3493] 7-9-1 **51** ....(bt) TomQueally 6 37
(J R Jenkins) *hdwy to join ldrs after 2f: outpcd by wnr over 1f out* **6/1**

5064 **5** *8* **Triskaidekaphobia**^{49} [2164] 8-8-12 **48** ....(t) FrankieMcDonald 7 —
(Paul Fitzsimons) *sn led: hdd 2f out: hrd rdn and wknd over 1f out* **17/2**

00-0 **6** *6* **Michelle (IRE)**^{13} [3253] 5-8-7 **46** oh1 ....^{1} JohnFahy$^{(3)}$ 1 —
(Paddy Butler) *broke on terms: sn outpcd and struggling to stay in tch* **40/1**

61.90 secs (-0.40) **Going Correction** -0.10s/f (Good) **6** Ran SP% **111.4**
Speed ratings (Par 101): **99,94,90,87,74 65**
Tote Swingers: 1&2 £1.50, 1&3 £2.00, 2&3 £2.40 CSF £7.15 CT £14.46 TOTE £3.30: £2.10, £1.10; EX 4.70 Trifecta £12.50 Pool: £752.58 - 44.20 winning units..

Owner Ms Sarah Jensen **Bred** Peter Balding **Trained** Newmarket, Suffolk

FOCUS
A moderate sprint handicap. The winner probably didn't need to improve much on her latest form.

T/Plt: £30.00 to a £1 stake. Pool: £66,688.00. 1,618.23 winning tickets. T/Qpdt: £9.20 to a £1 stake. Pool: £359.56. 4,497.00 winning tickets. LM

3082 RIPON (R-H)
Monday, July 4

OFFICIAL GOING: Good (good to firm in places; 8.5)
Wind: Light behind Weather: Fineand dry

3679 BUY YOUR TICKETS ON-LINE @RIPON-RACES.CO.UK CLASSIFIED (S) STKS 1m 1f 170y
6:50 (6:50) (Class 6) 3-Y-O **£2,045** (£603; £302) **Stalls** Low

Form RPR

1-23 **1** **Janet's Pearl (IRE)**^{10} [3363] 3-8-12 67 .... PaulHanagan 5 66
(Ann Duffield) *mde all: pushed along over 3f out: rdn over 2f out: drvn and wandered over 1f out: styd on wl fnl f* **10/11**^{1}

2410 **2** *2¾* **Goal (IRE)**^{6} [3485] 3-9-3 68 .... RobbieFitzpatrick 2 65
(Richard Guest) *dwlt: hld up in rr: hdwy on outer 3f out: rdn to chse wnr wl over 1f out: sn edgd rt: drvn and no imp fnl f* **11/2**

65-4 **3** *1½* **Bright Applause**^{9} [3380] 3-8-12 68 ....(p) AndrewElliott 1 57
(Brian Baugh) *chsd ldng pair: rdn along wl over 3f out: drvn and one pce fnl 2f* **9/2**^{3}

0-20 **4** *¾* **Geblah (IRE)**^{7} [3467] 3-8-12 65 .... MartinLane 7 55
(David Simcock) *trckd ldrs: hdwy on outer 4f out: effrt to chal over 3f out: rdn and edgd rt over 2f out: sn drvn and one pce* **7/2**^{2}

000 **5** *36* **Miss Emily (IRE)**^{17} [3138] 3-8-12 43 .... PJMcDonald 6 —
(George Moore) *chsd wnr: rdn along 4f out: wknd 3f out: sn bhd* **80/1**

2m 5.38s (-0.02) **Going Correction** -0.10s/f (Good) **5** Ran SP% **109.4**
Speed ratings (Par 98): **96,93,92,92,63**
Tote Swingers: 1&2 £5.70 CSF £6.35 TOTE £2.00: £1.50, £2.40; EX 5.80.The winner was bought in for £6,500. Bright Applause was claimed by Miss T. Waggott for £6,000.

Owner Middleham Park Racing XL **Bred** Roundhill Stud & Gleadhill House Stud Ltd **Trained** Constable Burton, N Yorks

FOCUS
Rail on bend from back straight to home straight moved out 3m adding 7yds to distances on Round course. After a warm, dry day the ground had quickened a tad but after the opener it was still described as 'good'. A run-of-the-mill classified selling race. The winner probably didn't need to improve on this year's form.

3680 RACING AGAIN SATURDAY 16TH JULY MAIDEN AUCTION FILLIES' STKS 6f
7:20 (7:20) (Class 5) 2-Y-O **£2,328** (£693; £346; £173) **Stalls** High

Form RPR

43 **1** **Imelda Mayhem**^{23} [2901] 2-8-10 0 .... NeilCallan 5 76+
(J S Moore) *trckd ldrs: hdwy to ld 2f out: sn rdn and edgd lft: drvn and kpt on wl fnl f* **11/4**^{1}

3 **2** *1* **Van Der Art**^{23} [2919] 2-8-7 0 .... PaulHanagan 7 70+
(Alan Jarvis) *cl up: led 1/2-way: rdn and hdd 2f out: drvn and rallied ent fnl f: ev ch tl no ex last 100yds* **3/1**^{2}

2 **3** *6* **Alice Rose (IRE)**^{11} [3308] 2-8-10 0 .... MartinLane 6 55
(Rae Guest) *towards rr: hdwy and edgd lft over 2f out: sn rdn and ch tl drvn and one pce ent fnl f* **7/2**^{3}

4 *1* **Moment In The Sun** 2-8-4 0 .... FrannyNorton 2 49+
(William Muir) *s.i.s and bhd: stdy hdwy over 2f out: styd on ins fnl f: nrst fin* **9/2**

00 **5** *¾* **Dylan's Dream (IRE)**^{12} [3274] 2-8-4 0 .... KellyHarrison 8 44
(Tim Easterby) *led: pushed along and hdd 1/2-way: rdn over 2f out and sn one pce* **33/1**

2 **6** *¾* **Delia Mary**^{15} [3201] 2-8-4 0 .... JamesSullivan 1 42
(Jedd O'Keeffe) *chsd ldrs: rdn along whn n.m.r over 2f out: sn wknd* **9/1**

0 **7** *9* **Lady Advocate (IRE)**^{16} [3186] 2-8-7 0 ....(b^{1}) DavidAllan 3 18
(Tim Easterby) *dwlt: a in rr* **16/1**

30 **8** *4½* **Keyhole Kate**^{21} [2983] 2-8-7 0 .... DuranFentiman 9 4
(Tim Walford) *trckd ldrs on inner: rdn along 1/2-way: sn wknd* **17/2**

0 **9** *2* **Nadia's Place**^{15} [3201] 2-8-7 0 .... TomEaves 4 —
(Nigel Tinkler) *cl up: rdn along 1/2-way: sn wknd* **100/1**

1m 13.00s (0.00) **Going Correction** 0.225s/f (Firm) **9** Ran SP% **122.4**
Speed ratings (Par 91): **86,84,76,75,74 73,61,55,52**
Tote Swingers: 1&2 £2.30, 1&3 £1.50, 2&3 £2.60 CSF £12.08 TOTE £5.10: £1.70, £1.90, £1.80; EX 23.70.

Owner Mrs E O'Leary & J S Moore **Bred** Mrs R Wilson **Trained** Upper Lambourn, Berks

FOCUS
No strength in depth in this ordinary fillies' auction maiden. The first two finished well clear and the form is rated around the front three and the race averages.

NOTEBOOK
Imelda Mayhem, who has a speedy pedigree, was tackling 6f for the first time on her third start. With the running rail to help she did just enough to get the better of the runner-up. Nurseries presumably now beckon. (op 3-1 tchd 7-2)

Van Der Art, third on her debut at Lingfield in a race that has nor worked out, went on at halfway and went down fighting. She had clearly learnt plenty from her debut effort and deserves to go one better. (tchd 11-4 and 10-3)

Alice Rose(IRE), runner-up in a similar event first time at Leicester, was left trailing by the first two and will be suited by a step up to 7f. Official explanation: jockey said filly hung left (tchd 3-1)

Moment In The Sun, well supported, fell out of the traps. She put in some eyecatching late work and will be a lot sharper next time. (op 10-1)

Dylan's Dream(IRE) showed a good deal more than on her first two outings. (op 50-1)

Delia Mary had finished runner-up first time at Pontefract, beaten 17 lengths by a Cherry Hinton entry. (tchd 8-1 and 10-1)

3681 TOTEEXACTA H'CAP 1m 4f 10y
7:50 (7:50) (Class 4) (0-80,78) 3-Y-O **£4,204** (£1,251; £625; £312) **Stalls** Low

Form RPR

-101 **1** **Dragonera**^{24} [2891] 3-9-7 **78** .... NeilCallan 6 86+
(Ed Dunlop) *hld up in rr: smooth hdwy 3f out: chal 2f out and sn led: rdn clr appr fnl f: edgd lft and styd on wl towards fin* **5/4**^{1}

5050 **2** *2* **Layla's King**^{9} [3376] 3-8-4 **61** .... FrannyNorton 2 64
(Richard Fahey) *chsd wnr to 1/2-way: rdn along and sltly outpcd over 3f out: drvn wl over 1f out: styd on to chse wnr ins fnl f: no imp towards fin* **9/2**^{3}

2-23 **3** *4½* **She's Got The Luck (IRE)**^{15} [3206] 3-8-13 **70** .... PaulHanagan 4 66
(Richard Fahey) *trckd ldng pair: hdwy to chse ldr 1/2-way: pushed along over 3f out: rdn to ld wl over 2f out: drvn and hdd wl over 1f out: sn one pce* **5/2**^{2}

-063 **4** *4* **Cape Of Dance (IRE)**[11] 3303 3-8-5 **62**........................ AdrianNicholls 5 51
(Mark Johnston) *led: pushed along and qckn d over 4f out: rdn over 3f out: hdd and drvn wl over 2f out: sn wknd* **11/2**

2m 37.14s (0.44) **Going Correction** -0.10s/f (Good) **4** Ran SP% **106.6**
Speed ratings (Par 102): **94,92,89,87**
Tote Swingers: 1&2 £4.70 CSF £6.76 TOTE £2.00; EX 6.60.

Owner J Weatherby, Champneys **Bred** Preston Lodge Stud **Trained** Newmarket, Suffolk

FOCUS
A depleted field for this 61-78 3yo handicap and the pace was very steady until once in line for home. The winner is progressing but may not have needed to improve much here.

3682 FOLLOW @ATTHERACES ON TWITTER H'CAP 6f
8:20 (8:21) (Class 3) (0-90,87) 3-Y-O **£6,616** (£1,980; £990; £495; £246) **Stalls** High

Form RPR

0204 **1** **El Viento (FR)**[19] 3052 3-9-7 **87**....................................(b) PaulHanagan 2 96
(Richard Fahey) *trckd ldrs: hdwy 1/2-way: chal and edgd lft over 2f out: rdn to ld ent fnl f: drvn out* **13/2**

4000 **2** *1 3/4* **Julius Geezer (IRE)**[23] 2908 3-9-6 **86**...................... RichardKingscote 7 89
(Tom Dascombe) *towards rr: hdwy whn n.m.r wl over 2f out: sn rdn: styd on ins fnl f: tk 2nd on line* **12/1**

0202 **3** *hd* **Indian Ballad (IRE)**[19] 3052 3-9-6 **86**......................... GrahamGibbons 6 89
(Ed McMahon) *led: hdd briefly 1/2-way: sn led again: rdn over 2f out: drvn and hdd ent fnl f: no ex towards fin: lost 2nd on line* **7/2**[2]

2002 **4** *2* **Defence Council (IRE)**[7] 3461 3-8-9 **75**........................ FrannyNorton 4 71
(Mel Brittain) *cl up: rdn 2f out and ev ch tl drvn and wknd ent fnl f* **13/2**

-460 **5** *3 3/4* **Mappin Time (IRE)**[23] 2934 3-9-6 **86**..........................(p) DavidAllan 1 70
(Tim Easterby) *hld up in rr: gd hdwy on outer and cl up 1/2-way: rdn over 2f out: drvn wl over 1f out and grad wknd* **9/1**

0001 **6** *5* **Serena's Pride**[11] 3322 3-8-11 **77**... NeilCallan 3 45
(Alan Jarvis) *hld up towards rr: effrt 1/2-way: sn rdn along and n.d* **6/1**[3]

-110 **7** *1 3/4* **Elusive Prince**[23] 2934 3-9-5 **85**.. LeeNewman 5 59
(David Barron) *trckd ldrs: pushed along whn n.m.r wl over 2f out: sn rdn and btn* **2/1**[1]

1m 10.38s (-2.62) **Going Correction** -0.325s/f (Firm) **7** Ran SP% **114.2**
Speed ratings (Par 104): **104,101,101,98,93 87,84**
Tote Swingers: 1&2 £28.20, 1&3 £3.50, 2&3 £13.70 CSF £76.41 TOTE £7.80: £3.30, £2.00; EX 75.10.

Owner John Nicholls Ltd/David Kilburn **Bred** Ballykilbride Stud **Trained** Musley Bank, N Yorks

FOCUS
A competitive 75-87 3yo sprint handicap but two of the seven runners were well below form. The form is rated around the winner and third, who ran in a good race over C&D previously.

NOTEBOOK
El Viento(FR), just behind Indian Ballad when they were second and fourth over course and distance 19 days earlier when he met trouble at the start, enjoyed a 1lb pull. Best in blinkers, he enjoyed first run and was always doing just enough. (op 7-1 tchd 11-2)

Julius Geezer(IRE), dropped 11lb after running over further on his two previous, stayed on to snatch second. Seven may yet prove his optimum trip. (tchd 14-1)

Indian Ballad(IRE), who won four times in nursery company at two, had to give best to his old rivals this time, seemingly with no excuses. (op 4-1 tchd 9-2)

Defence Council(IRE) is very much in and out and he was not at his very best here after racing keenly. (op 8-1)

Mappin Time(IRE), in first-time cheekpieces, has not reproduced his juvenile form so far at three. (tchd 17-2)

Serena's Pride, 4lb higher than her Warwick success, ran poorly. Official explanation: jockey said filly did not handle the track (op 11-2 tchd 13-2)

Elusive Prince, twice a C&D winner before coming up short in a Class 2 at York, dropped right away and was heavily eased. He was reported to have lost his action. Official explanation: jockey said gelding lost its action (tchd 15-8 and 9-4)

3683 YORKSHIRE RACING SUMMER FESTIVAL COMING SOON H'CAP 1m
8:50 (8:50) (Class 5) (0-70,69) 3-Y-O+ **£4,095** (£1,225; £612; £306; £152) **Stalls** Low

Form RPR

5035 **1** **Wiseman's Diamond (USA)**[7] 3457 6-8-13 **54**..........(b) MickyFenton 6 63
(Paul Midgley) *in tch: hdwy on inner 3f out: rdn 2f out: swtchd lft and drvn ent fnl f: styd on wl to ld last 75 yds* **8/1**

-406 **2** *1/2* **Seldom (IRE)**[39] 2413 5-9-3 **58**...................................... RobertWinston 1 66
(Mel Brittain) *led: rdn along and hdd 3f out: rallied to ld again 2f out and sn drvn: hdd and no ex last 75 yds* **6/1**[3]

-212 **3** *3/4* **Petsas Pleasure**[17] 3139 5-9-4 **59**.................................. PaulHanagan 12 65+
(Ollie Pears) *hld up in rr: stdy hdwy on wd outside over 3f out: rdn to chse ldrs and edgd rt over 1f out: drvn and ev ch ent fnl f: no ex towards fin* **9/2**[2]

0232 **4** *3/4* **Desert Hunter (IRE)**[7] 3462 8-8-12 **53**......................(p) KellyHarrison 13 58
(Micky Hammond) *in tch: hdwy to chse ldrs 1/2-way: rdn along wl over 2f out: drvn over 1f out and ev ch whn hmpd ent fnl f: no ex after* **6/1**[3]

4404 **5** *2* **Fibs And Flannel**[9] 3386 4-10-0 **69**..............................(b[1]) DavidAllan 2 69
(Tim Easterby) *keen: cl up: disp ld 4f out:led 3f out: rdn and hdd 2f out: sn drvn and ev ch tl no ex ins fnl f* **9/4**[1]

555 **6** *2 1/4* **Fairy Mist (IRE)**[18] 3075 4-9-5 **60**..................................... PaddyAspell 9 55
(Brian Rothwell) *hld up towards rr: hdwy over 3f out: rdn to chse ldrs 2f out: kpt on same pce* **20/1**

3440 **7** *1/2* **Ad Vitam (IRE)**[11] 3325 3-8-0 **57**...........................(p) LeonnaMayor(7) 3 50
(David C Griffiths) *in rr: sme late hdwy: nvr a factor* **16/1**

20 **8** *hd* **Carlitos Spirit (IRE)**[26] 2799 7-8-12 **58**.....................(v) LeeTopliss(5) 10 51
(Ian McInnes) *towards rr: rdn and sme hdwy 3f out: n.d* **14/1**

0065 **9** *2 1/4* **Lady Florence**[7] 3473 6-9-1 **63**................................ ClaireMurray(7) 14 51
(David C Griffiths) *racd wd: cl up: effrt wl over 3f out:.rdn along over 2f out: drvn and wknd wl over 1f out* **50/1**

6060 **10** *1 3/4* **Tropical Duke (IRE)**[7] 3456 5-8-6 **54**....................(v[1]) ShaneBKelly(7) 8 38
(Ron Barr) *nvr bttr than midfield* **16/1**

0003 **11** *44* **Into Mac**[27] 2785 5-8-2 **50** oh1... TerenceFury(7) 7 —
(Neville Bycroft) *t.k.h: chsd ldrs to 1/2-way: sn lost pl and bhd* **66/1**

1m 39.98s (-1.42) **Going Correction** -0.10s/f (Good)
WFA 3 from 4yo+ 9lb **11** Ran SP% **115.3**
Speed ratings (Par 103): **103,102,101,101,99 96,96,96,93,92 48**
Tote Swingers: 1&2 £6.30, 1&3 £8.70, 2&3 £7.20 CSF £53.50 CT £247.13 TOTE £10.10: £2.50, £2.70, £2.30; EX 41.60.

Owner D I Perry **Bred** Hatta Bloodstock International **Trained** Westow, N Yorks

FOCUS
A modest 57-69 handicap. The gallop was unrelenting and few became seriously involved, with prominent racers favoured. The form is rated around the second and third.

3684 SIS LIVE MAIDEN STKS 1m
9:20 (9:21) (Class 5) 3-Y-O+ **£2,328** (£693; £346; £173) **Stalls** Low

Form RPR

3 **1** **Shalloon (IRE)**[11] 3304 3-9-3 0.. NeilCallan 3 84+
(Mark Johnston) *trckd ldrs: smooth hdwy 3f out: led 2f out: sn clr: comf* **4/6**[1]

2 *6* **Eagle Rock (IRE)** 3-9-3 0... AndrewMullen 6 65+
(Tom Tate) *towards rr: hdwy on inner 3f out: rdn to chse ldrs wl over 1f out: kpt on fnl f: no ch w wnr* **7/1**

3 *2 1/2* **Lord Emerson** 3-8-12 0.. LeeTopliss(5) 2 59
(Richard Fahey) *dwlt: sn trcking ldrs on inner: hdwy to ld 3f out: rdn and hdd 2f out: sn drvn and one pce* **28/1**

0 **4** *2* **Morning Air (IRE)**[15] 3206 3-8-12 0.................................. FrannyNorton 8 50+
(Ann Duffield) *towards rr: hdwy 3f out: rdn over 2f out: kpt on appr fnl f: nrst fin* **50/1**

06 **5** *nk* **Kool Shuffle (GER)**[13] 3246 3-9-3 0................................. MickyFenton 5 54
(Tom Tate) *keen: chsd ldrs: lost pl 1/2-way: rdn 3f out: styd on appr fnl f* **6/1**[3]

6 *1/2* **Andiamo Via** 4-9-12 0.. LeeNewman 7 55
(Michael Smith) *led: rdn along over 3f out: sn hdd and grad wknd fnl 2f* **22/1**

0- **7** *6* **Lady Intrigue (IRE)**[269] 6704 3-8-12 0.............................. PaulHanagan 4 34
(Richard Fahey) *in tch: sme hdwy 4f out: rdn along over 3f out and sn wknd* **11/2**[2]

0-0 **8** *19* **Al Raqi**[75] 1496 3-9-3 0.. TomEaves 9 —
(Bryan Smart) *s.i.s: a in rr* **22/1**

04 **9** *1 1/4* **Dream Of Wunders**[10] 3355 3-8-12 0............................ FrederikTylicki 1 —
(James Given) *cl up: rdn along wl over 3f out: sn wknd* **66/1**

1m 41.06s (-0.34) **Going Correction** -0.10s/f (Good)
WFA 3 from 4yo 9lb **9** Ran SP% **117.8**
Speed ratings (Par 103): **97,91,88,86,86 85,79,60,59**
Tote Swingers: 1&2 £2.00, 1&3 £11.30, 2&3 £27.20 CSF £5.69 TOTE £1.60: £1.02, £2.50, £8.10; EX 5.20.

Owner Sheikh Hamdan Bin Mohammed Al Maktoum **Bred** Gigginstown House Stud & Lynn Lodge Stud **Trained** Middleham Moor, N Yorks

FOCUS
A weak maiden run in a relatively slow time, but a clearcut winner of some potential. It is hard to know just what he achieved.
T/Plt: £48.10 to a £1 stake. Pool: £67,818.82. 1,028.60 winning tickets. T/Qpdt: £50.00 to a £1 stake. Pool: £5,192.74. 76.82 winning tickets. J

3463 WINDSOR (R-H)
Monday, July 4

OFFICIAL GOING: Good to firm (8.2)
Wind: Nil Weather: Fine but cloudy, humid

3685 SPORTINGBET.COM APPRENTICE H'CAP 6f
6:40 (6:41) (Class 5) (0-75,75) 4-Y-O+ **£2,264** (£673; £336; £168) **Stalls** Low

Form RPR

50-2 **1** **Titus Gent**[23] 2903 6-8-13 **69**... RaulDaSilva(5) 1 77
(Jeremy Gask) *mde virtually all: rdn over 1f out: edgd lft but hld on wl nr fin* **9/2**[2]

00-3 **2** *shd* **Our Piccadilly (IRE)**[16] 3179 6-9-3 **68**.......................... LouisBeuzelin 10 75
(Stuart Kittow) *trckd ldng pair gng strly: rdn wl over 1f out: wnt 2nd fnl f: chal last 150yds: nt qckn* **6/1**[3]

-551 **3** *1/2* **Maryolini**[13] 3247 6-8-3 **59**... CharlesBishop(5) 9 64
(Tom Keddy) *hld up towards rr: prog over 2f out: rdn to chal fnl f: nt qckn last 100yds* **14/1**

-530 **4** *3/4* **Super Duplex**[32] 2649 4-9-1 **66**.. KierenFox 8 69+
(Pat Phelan) *hld up in last pair: stdy prog on wd outside fr 1/2-way: cl up and rdn 1f out: kpt on same pce* **7/1**

0034 **5** *3/4* **Diamond Johnny G (USA)**[10] 3350 4-8-7 **65**....(t) JenniferFerguson(7) 5 65
(Edward Creighton) *taken down early: w wnr: rdn over 2f out: lost 2nd 1f out: fdd* **25/1**

0-44 **6** *shd* **Silvee**[12] 3293 4-8-2 **56** oh5.. KieranO'Neill(3) 6 56
(John Bridger) *hld up in midfield: pushed along over 2f out: no prog over 1f out: rdn and styd on fnl f: unable to chal* **20/1**

1603 **7** *1 1/4* **Memphis Man**[9] 3412 8-8-6 **60**.................................. MatthewCosham(3) 2 56
(David Evans) *taken down early: wl in tch: shkn up over 2f out: outpcd over 1f out: kpt on* **8/1**

3413 **8** *3/4* **Commandingpresence (USA)**[23] 2920 5-8-3 **57**..... HarryBentley(3) 11 51
(John Bridger) *sweating: in tch on outer: effrt over 2f out: cl enough over 1f out: wknd fnl f* **13/2**

0000 **9** *6* **The Scorching Wind (IRE)**[63] 1760 5-8-5 **59**..............(t) RyanClark(3) 4 33
(Stuart Williams) *prom: drvn over 2f out: lost pl over 1f out: wknd qckly* **7/2**[1]

1300 **10** *3 1/4* **Dream Number (IRE)**[18] 3079 4-8-10 **64**.................... JamesRogers(3) 3 28
(William Muir) *sn towards rr: dropped away tamely fnl 2f* **20/1**

1000 **11** *3* **Diriculous**[21] 3000 7-9-3 **75**.....................................(v[1]) DanielCremin(7) 7 29
(Robert Mills) *s.i.s: a in last pair: hung bdly lft whn rdn over 1f out: wknd: t.o* **20/1**

1m 12.7s (-0.30) **Going Correction** -0.15s/f (Firm) **11** Ran SP% **116.4**
Speed ratings (Par 103): **96,95,95,94,93 93,91,90,82,78 74**
Tote Swingers: 1&2 £2.50, 1&3 £11.80, 2&3 £16.10 CSF £29.21 CT £355.59 TOTE £4.80: £1.70, £1.60, £4.80; EX 20.70 Trifecta £223.60 Pool: £2,931.92 - 9.70 winning units..

Owner The Nobles **Bred** Heather Raw **Trained** Sutton Veny, Wilts

■ A first winner in Britain on only his third ride for Brazilian apprentice Raul Da Silva.

FOCUS
Stands' rail dolled out 6yds at 6f and 2yds at winning post. Top bend out 3yds from normal configuration, adding 14yds to races of 1m and over. A modest but competitive apprentice handicap. The winner was the first of four on the card to make all and it's doubtful he had to improve much.

3686 BRITISH STALLION STUDS E B F SPORTINGBET.COM MAIDEN STKS 6f
7:10 (7:11) (Class 5) 2-Y-O **£3,299** (£981; £490; £245) **Stalls** Low

Form RPR

52 **1** **Radiomarelli (USA)**[17] 3132 2-9-3 0.............................. StevieDonohoe 4 83+
(Ralph Beckett) *mde virtually all: pressed 2f out: shkn up and drew clr jst over 1f out: readily* **9/2**[2]

	2	2 ¼	**Dutch Rose (IRE)** 2-8-12 0 .... SebSanders 14 (Ralph Beckett) *in tch in midfield: prog on outer over 2f out: styd on wl to take 2nd last 100yds: no ch w wnr* **14/1**	71+
4	3	1 ¼	**Tidy Affair (IRE)**[12] 3288 2-9-3 0 .... KierenFallon 1 (Richard Hannon) *in tch in midfield: pushed along bef 1/2-way: no prog tl drvn and r.o fnl f to take 3rd last strides* **7/2**[1]	73+
0	4	¾	**Red Senor (IRE)**[12] 3288 2-9-3 0 .... MichaelHills 13 (B W Hills) *trckd ldrs: effrt 2f out: wnt 2nd 1f out: no imp on wnr: fdd last 100yds* **8/1**[3]	70
	5	3 ½	**Captain Kendall (IRE)** 2-9-3 0 .... CathyGannon 10 (David Evans) *sn off the pce: 10th and nt on terms bef 1/2-way: pushed along and styd on steadily fnl 2f: nrst fin* **100/1**	60
3	6	shd	**Billyrayvalentine (CAN)**[21] 2997 2-9-3 0 .... TonyCulhane 12 (George Baker) *prom gng wl: wnt 2nd 1/2-way: jnd wnr over 2f out to over 1f out: wknd fnl f* **9/2**[2]	59
	7	nk	**Golden Valley** 2-8-12 0 .... JamesMillman 2 (Rod Millman) *pressed ldrs: outpcd 2f out: n.d after: keeping on at fin* **100/1**	54
	8	¾	**Jubilance (IRE)** 2-9-3 0 .... GeorgeBaker 7 (Jeremy Noseda) *pressed wnr to 1/2-way: steadily wknd fr 2f out* **11/1**	56+
	9	1	**Stepturn** 2-9-3 0 .... RyanMoore 5 (Sir Michael Stoute) *settled midfield: pushed along 1/2-way: no prog but kpt on one pce fnl 2f* **9/2**[2]	53
	10	3 ¼	**Venetian View (IRE)** 2-9-3 0 .... PatDobbs 6 (Gary Moore) *prom 2f: sn lost pl and pushed along: outpcd in midfield 2f out: fdd* **66/1**	44+
	11	6	**Journalistic (USA)** 2-9-3 0 .... TadhgO'Shea 3 (Marcus Tregoning) *s.s: nvr on terms: 13th bef 1/2-way and wl bhd: no prog* **20/1**	26+
	12	3 ¼	**Charitable Act (FR)** 2-9-3 0 .... MartinDwyer 16 (William Muir) *s.s and then bdly hmpd: t.o tl latched on to bkmarkers 1/2-way: no prog after but nt disgracd* **100/1**	16+
	13	4 ½	**Ventus D'Or** 2-9-0 0 .... LouisBeuzelin(3) 9 (Walter Swinburn) *dwlt: nvr on terms: 11th and off the pce 1/2-way: no prog* **40/1**	—
0	14	3 ¼	**Lady Jane Grace (IRE)**[9] 3408 2-8-7 0 .... MatthewCosham(5) 8 (David Evans) *sn drvn in rr: struggling in 12th bef 1/2-way: no prog* **100/1**	—
	15	1 ¼	**Inniscastle Boy** 2-9-3 0 .... HayleyTurner 15 (William Muir) *dwlt and veered bdly lft s: hopelessly t.o after: r.o last 100yds* **66/1**	—
	16	7	**Justbookies Dotnet** 2-9-0 0 .... KierenFox(3) 11 (Louise Best) *s.s: a in rr: hung violently lft 1/2-way towards far rail: t.o after* **100/1**	—

1m 12.82s (-0.18) **Going Correction** -0.15s/f (Firm) 16 Ran SP% **118.0**
Speed ratings (Par 94): **95,92,90,89,84 84,84,83,81,77 69,65,59,54,53 43**
Tote Swingers: 1&2 £13.70, 1&3 £2.40, 2&3 £12.10 CSF £61.03 TOTE £4.70: £1.10, £6.60, £1.60; EX 73.60 Trifecta £656.80 Pool: £1,331. - 1.50 winning units..
Owner Speedlic Racing **Bred** Ben Lengacher **Trained** Kimpton, Hants

FOCUS
A few interesting types from decent stables, but plenty of them were soon struggling and needed the experience. The time was a highly respectable 0.12 seconds slower than the earlier Class 5 handicap for older horses.

NOTEBOOK
Radiomarelli(USA) ◆ put his experience to good use, leading at a decent pace against the near rail, and there was much to like about the way he kept on, looking every bit as strong at the line as he did a furlong out. It's fair to say the track was favouring front-runners, but he still looked pretty useful and could be one for a decent nursery at a big meeting, maybe Glorious Goodwood. It's possible, however, that he'll go for a Listed race in Italy. (op 7-2)
Dutch Rose(IRE) ◆ made a promising start. Drawn wider than ideal, she was one of those who lost a bit of ground at the start and was under pressure by halfway, but she produced a sustained challenge. The first foal of a dual 5f winner, she should make her mark. (op 12-1)
Tidy Affair(IRE) ◆ confirmed the ability he showed on his debut at Salisbury, but he was in need in of this further experience. The ground was a lot quicker this time and that might explain why he didn't travel that well, but he ran on nicely. There should be more to come. (tchd 4-1)
Red Senor(IRE) ◆ was caught a bit wide from a less than ideal draw and didn't see his race out after briefly looking a big threat halfway up the straight. Still, he showed plenty of ability, building on his first [illegible] (tchd 17-2)
Captain Kendall(IRE) cost only 4,500gns earlier this year, but he fared second best of the newcomers, finishing nicely after getting behind.
Billyrayvalentine(CAN) had shown ability over 5f here on his debut, but this looked a better race. (op 11-2 tchd 4-1)
Golden Valley showed ability on her debut.
Jubilance(IRE) can be expected to improve. (op 10-1)
Stepturn is from a really smart family (dam won Queen Mary and Cheveley Park), but was well held on this debut. Chris Richardson, of Cheveley Park Stud, was quoted beforehand as saying: "His work in the spring was good and we do like him, but the last couple of times he's worked he's just been a little flat." (op 5-1 tchd 11-2 in places)
Venetian View(IRE) ◆ needed the experience, but he showed up okay early on and has ability.
Charitable Act(FR) ◆ missed the break and was virtually taken out of the race when hampered by stablemate Inniscastle on leaving the stalls. He lost at least 8l, but latched onto the back of the main group before understandably getting tired. There should be a lot better to come.
Ventus D'Or Official explanation: jockey said colt missed the break
Justbookies Dotnet Official explanation: jockey said colt hung badly left

3687 TRAILFINDERS, TAILORMADE TRAVEL WORLDWIDE H'CAP 5f 10y
7:40 (7:40) (Class 4) (0-85,84) 3-Y-0+ **£3,881** (£1,155; £577; £288) **Stalls** Low

Form				RPR
0-04	1		**Living It Large (FR)**[69] 1584 4-9-4 79 .... JohnFahy(3) 8 (Ed de Giles) *mde all and crossed to nr side rail fr outside draw: rdn over 1f out: styd on wl fnl f* **12/1**	88
-200	2	¾	**Diamond Charlie (IRE)**[82] 1322 3-9-1 78 .... SebSanders 6 (Simon Dow) *stdd s: t.k.h and hld up in rr: prog on outer fr 1/2-way: chsd wnr jst over 1f out: chal fnl f: styd on but a hld* **16/1**	82
004	3	1 ¼	**Kingsgate Choice (IRE)**[14] 3222 4-9-11 83 ....(b) LukeMorris 3 (John Best) *settled in last pair: urged along and stl there over 1f out: drvn and r.o fnl f to take 3rd nr fin* **7/2**[2]	85+
000-	4	1	**Caledonia Princess**[279] 6446 5-9-4 76 .... DarryllHolland 7 (Jo Hughes) *trckd ldrs: effrt 2f out: rdn and cl enough jst over 1f out: fdd last 150yds* **8/1**	74
6125	5	1 ¼	**Taurus Twins**[10] 3367 5-9-7 84 ....(b) HarryBentley(5) 1 (Richard Price) *prom: rdn over 2f out: sn outpcd: one pce and n.d over 1f out* **5/2**[1]	78
-334	6	1	**Osiris Way**[22] 2959 9-9-12 84 .... GeorgeBaker 5 (Patrick Chamings) *chsd wnr: rdn and nt qckn 2f out: lost 2nd and wknd jst over 1f out* **4/1**[3]	74
2010	7	1 ½	**Style And Panache (IRE)**[22] 2959 3-9-0 77 .... CathyGannon 2 (David Evans) *chsd ldrs: rdn 2f out: no prog over 1f out: fdd* **14/1**	60
20-6	8	6	**Avrilo**[22] 2959 5-8-11 69 .... TomMcLaughlin 4 (Malcolm Saunders) *in tch in rr tl wknd u.p wl over 1f out* **10/1**	32

59.64 secs (-0.66) **Going Correction** -0.15s/f (Firm)
WFA 3 from 4yo+ 5lb 8 Ran SP% **111.2**
Speed ratings (Par 105): **99,97,95,94,92 90,88,78**
Tote Swingers: 1&2 £29.40, 1&3 £8.10, 2&3 £12.30 CSF £169.89 CT £800.32 TOTE £10.10: £3.70, £5.40, £1.60; EX 144.40 Trifecta £2229.60 Pool: £4,218.25 - 1.40 winning units..
Owner T Gould **Bred** Sunny Days Limited **Trained** Ledbury, Herefordshire
■ Stewards' Enquiry : Seb Sanders caution: used whip without giving gelding time to respond

FOCUS
An ordinary handicap, and form to treat with a bit of caution as Living It Large became the third winner from only three races on the straight track to make just about all, and that's despite being drawn widest.

3688 TRAILFINDERS TRAVEL EXPERTS H'CAP 1m 67y
8:10 (8:11) (Class 5) (0-70,70) 3-Y-O **£2,264** (£673; £336; £168) **Stalls** Low

Form				RPR
-062	1		**Blue Maisey**[8] 3432 3-9-0 63 .... SebSanders 12 (Peter Makin) *mde all: drvn and hrd pressed over 1f out: hd to one side but battled on wl* **7/2**[1]	72
-202	2	hd	**Empress Charlotte**[26] 2821 3-8-12 61 .... HayleyTurner 4 (Michael Bell) *trckd ldrs: prog to chse wnr wl over 1f out and edgd rt: sn chalng: outbattled fnl f* **8/1**	69
-600	3	3	**Marie Rose**[17] 3118 3-9-4 67 ....(p) MartinDwyer 5 (Brian Meehan) *taken down early and ponied to post: chsd wnr 3f: styd prom: drvn over 2f out: outpcd over 1f out* **14/1**	68
-125	4	1	**Elvira Delight (IRE)**[48] 2184 3-9-3 66 .... GeorgeBaker 6 (Jeremy Noseda) *prom: chsd wnr after 3f to wl over 1f out: sltly hmpd sn after: fdd fnl f* **13/2**[3]	65
0-00	5	1 ¼	**Conjuror's Bluff**[17] 3133 3-9-2 70 .... KieranO'Neill(5) 8 (Richard Hannon) *hld up last: u.p bef 1/2-way and gng nowhere: gd prog 3f out: chsd ldrs over 1f out but nt on terms: one pce after* **40/1**	66
0-02	6	1	**Ride The Wind**[25] 2853 3-9-0 63 .... EddieAhern 2 (Chris Wall) *hld up towards rr: jst pushed along fr 3f out: kpt on but nvr nr ldrs* **13/2**[3]	57
2425	7	hd	**Duquesa (IRE)**[9] 3413 3-9-2 65 ....(v) CathyGannon 7 (David Evans) *hld up in midfield: drvn 3f out: no imp on ldrs over 1f out: fdd* **8/1**	58
03-0	8	2 ½	**Elegant Muse**[44] 2313 3-9-4 67 .... KierenFallon 3 (Walter Swinburn) *wl in tch in midfield: rdn over 2f out: nt qckn wl over 1f out: fdd* **20/1**	55
0-06	9	½	**Heezararity**[27] 2790 3-9-6 69 .... FergusSweeney 1 (Stuart Kittow) *hld up in last quartet: pushed along over 2f out: no prog and nvr nr ldrs* **12/1**	55
1450	10	½	**Red Zeus (IRE)**[14] 3235 3-8-11 60 ....(p) LiamKeniry 9 (J S Moore) *hld up in last quartet: rdn 3f out: no prog* **33/1**	45
6203	11	½	**Whodathought (IRE)**[8] 3432 3-9-7 70 ....(b) RyanMoore 11 (Richard Hannon) *hld up in last quartet: shkn up and no prog over 2f out: wknd fnl f* **9/2**[2]	54
0600	12	10	**Putin (IRE)**[9] 3412 3-8-5 54 ....(b) NeilChalmers 10 (Derek Haydn Jones) *t.k.h: hld up in tch and racd wd: effrt 3f out: wknd rapidly over 2f out: t.o* **40/1**	15

1m 43.36s (-1.34) **Going Correction** -0.15s/f (Firm) 12 Ran SP% **116.2**
Speed ratings (Par 100): **100,99,96,95,94 93,93,90,90,89 89,79**
Tote Swingers: 1&2 £5.00, 1&3 £16.40, 2&3 £37.70 CSF £29.78 CT £349.70 TOTE £4.10: £2.30, £2.70, £4.40; EX 31.40 Trifecta £370.80 Part won. Pool: £501.18 - 0.94 winning units..
Owner Lady O'Brien **Bred** Worksop Manor Stud **Trained** Ogbourne Maisey, Wilts

FOCUS
The first race of the evening on the round course, but like on the sprint track, speed was holding up well, indeed Blue Maisey became the fourth straight winner on the card to make just about all. The time was good for the grade and the form makes a fair bit of sense.
Elvira Delight(IRE) Official explanation: jockey said filly suffered interference in running
Elegant Muse Official explanation: jockey said filly had no more to give

3689 SAVILLS IRISH GUARDS MAIDEN FILLIES' STKS 1m 67y
8:40 (8:43) (Class 5) 3-4-Y-O **£2,264** (£673; £336; £168) **Stalls** Low

Form				RPR
60-6	1		**Blessed Biata (USA)**[19] 3034 3-9-0 93 .... RyanMoore 7 (William Haggas) *trckd ldr: shkn up to ld over 2f out: hrd pressed fnl f: drvn out and hld on wl* **1/7**[1]	77+
	2	nk	**Garbah (IRE)** 3-9-0 0 .... PhilipRobinson 8 (Clive Brittain) *difficult to load in stalls: trckd ldng pair: pushed along to take 2nd wl over 1f out: rdn to chal fnl f: r.o but a jst hld* **16/1**	76
0	3	7	**Little Cottonsocks**[22] 2960 3-9-0 0 ....(t) LukeMorris 4 (Clive Cox) *trckd ldng pair: shkn up and outpcd 2f out: n.d after: kpt on* **25/1**	60
	4	3 ¼	**Fairling** 3-9-0 0 .... SteveDrowne 3 (Hughie Morrison) *dwlt: rn green in last pair: wl off the pce 1/2-way: kpt on fnl 2f: no ch* **7/1**[2]	52+
00	5	2	**Funny Enough**[22] 2960 3-9-0 0 ....(t) MartinDwyer 1 (George Baker) *led to over 2f out: edgd lft and wknd over 1f out* **12/1**[3]	48
	6	3 ¾	**Beckfield Dancer** 3-9-0 0 .... WilliamCarson 2 (Stuart Williams) *a in rr: struggling fr 1/2-way: wl bhd after* **25/1**	39
00-	7	10	**Kublahara (IRE)**[229] 7478 3-9-0 0 .... LiamKeniry 6 (Martin Bosley) *sweating: s.s: chsd ldng quartet: wknd 3f out* **33/1**	16
0	8	dist	**Present Laughter**[18] 3090 3-8-11 0 .... MatthewDavies(3) 10 (Ron Hodges) *last after 2f: sn wl t.o* **50/1**	—

1m 43.11s (-1.59) **Going Correction** -0.15s/f (Firm) 8 Ran SP% **126.2**
Speed ratings (Par 100): **101,100,93,90,88 84,74,—**
Tote Swingers: 1&2 £2.40, 1&3 £3.60, 2&3 £9.10 CSF £5.66 TOTE £1.10: £1.02, £2.40, £4.60; EX 5.30 Trifecta £34.40 Pool: £485.27 - 10.43 winning units..
Owner Bernard Kantor **Bred** Wentworth Racing Pty Ltd **Trained** Newmarket, Suffolk

FOCUS
Almost a shock result with 1-7 shot Blessed Biata all out to win what had looked an uncompetitive maiden. However, while the favourite was clearly below form, it might be unwise to be too negative. The time was 0.25 seconds faster than the earlier Class 5 handicap, and the winner, who had already given the impression of being an idle type, pulled a long way clear with a newcomer.

3690 TRAILFINDERS AWARD WINNING SERVICE H'CAP 1m 3f 135y
9:10 (9:11) (Class 6) (0-60,60) 3-Y-0+ **£1,704** (£503; £251) **Stalls** Centre

Form				RPR
2000	1		**Gower Rules (IRE)**[5] 3518 3-8-10 60 .... HarryBentley(5) 6 (John Bridger) *prom: chsd ldr over 2f out: clsd to ld over 1f out: in command after: readily* **9/1**	67

4-36 **2** *1 ½* **Lauberhorn**[25] 2856 4-9-11 **57**......(b) KierenFallon 7 61
(Eve Johnson Houghton) *hld up in midfield: prog fr 4f out: drvn and styd on to take 2nd 1f out: no imp wnr* **10/1**

06S2 **3** *1 ¾* **Aine's Delight (IRE)**[16] 3176 5-9-8 **57**...... SimonPearce(3) 13 58
(Andy Turnell) *led after 2f: kicked on over 3f out: hdd and one pce over 1f out* **6/1**[3]

-035 **4** *½* **Fleeting Tiger**[24] 2874 3-8-9 **54**...... EddieAhern 12 55+
(John Dunlop) *hld up wl in rr: plenty to do in last pair 4f out: prog 3f out: styd on to take 4th ins fnl f: hopeless task* **5/2**[1]

0-00 **5** *2* **Rowan Ridge**[28] 2760 3-8-12 **60**......(p) MatthewDavies(3) 5 57
(Jim Boyle) *prom: chsd ldr 1/2-way to over 2f out: fdd over 1f out* **40/1**

0000 **6** *shd* **What About Now**[14] 3220 3-8-12 **57**......(p) SebSanders 16 54
(J W Hills) *awkward s and rousted along to go prom: drvn 3f out: one pce and no hdwy fnl 2f* **50/1**

0-00 **7** *1* **Fastada (IRE)**[12] 3268 3-8-9 **54**......(v[1]) FergusSweeney 9 49
(Jonathan Portman) *hld up in midfield: effrt on wd outside 3f out: no prog fnl 2f* **28/1**

6510 **8** *3* **Galiotto (IRE)**[21] 2991 5-9-12 **58**......(b) RyanMoore 14 51+
(Gary Moore) *hld up in midfield: pushed along and lost pl over 3f out: effrt fr rr whn nt clr run 2f out: no ch whn nt clr run 1f out* **4/1**[2]

00 **9** *hd* **Dhampas**[12] 3268 3-8-1 **46** oh1...... DavidProbert 3 36
(Jim Boyle) *towards rr: effrt and sme prog into midfield over 2f out: no hdwy after* **14/1**

-365 **10** *3 ¾* **Thymesthree (IRE)**[25] 2858 3-9-0 **59**...... HayleyTurner 4 43
(Chris Wall) *trckd ldrs: shkn up 3f out: steadily wknd* **16/1**

00 **11** *11* **Valdaw**[22] 2964 3-9-0 **59**...... TadhgO'Shea 1 24
(Joseph Tuite) *hld up in last quartet: brief effrt on outer 3f out: sn btn* **66/1**

0-05 **12** *¾* **Caledonia Prince**[34] 2583 3-8-1 **46** oh1...... CathyGannon 8 10
(Jo Hughes) *stdd s: hld up wl in rr: drvn and struggling 4f out: sn no ch* **12/1**

0600 **13** *4 ½* **Folio (IRE)**[86] 1233 11-9-4 **50**...... StevieDonohoe 10 —
(Willie Musson) *hld up wl in rr: pushed along and no prog 3f out: wknd* **16/1**

0-00 **14** *8* **Dixie Land Band**[14] 3220 3-8-2 **47** oh1 ow1...... RichardThomas 11 —
(Paul Burgoyne) *nvr beyond midfield: wknd over 3f out: eased* **100/1**

600- **15** *½* **Annacaboe (IRE)**[406] 2398 4-9-9 **55**...... GeorgeBaker 15 —
(Martin Bosley) *led 2f: chsd ldr to 1/2-way: wknd wl over 2f out: eased* **66/1**

300/ **16** *3 ¼* **Tricky Trev (USA)**[583] 7572 5-9-0 **46** oh1......(t) JamesDoyle 2 —
(Joanna Davis) *a wl in rr: last and wl bhd 4f out* **40/1**

2m 29.36s (-0.14) **Going Correction** -0.15s/f (Firm)
WFA 3 from 4yo+ 13lb **16** Ran SP% **122.3**
Speed ratings (Par 101): **94,93,91,91,90 90,89,87,87,84 77,76,73,68,68 66**
Tote Swingers: 1&2 £10.40, 1&3 £13.70, 2&3 £9.30 CSF £93.31 CT £595.14 TOTE £5.80: £1.10, £2.30, £2.10, £1.20; EX 130.60 TRIFECTA Not won..
Owner Mrs Liz Gardner **Bred** Michael O'Mahony **Trained** Liphook, Hants

FOCUS
A moderate handicap.
Galiotto(IRE) Official explanation: jockey said gelding was denied a clear run
Caledonia Prince Official explanation: jockey said gelding had no more to give
Annacaboe(IRE) Official explanation: jockey said filly lost its action
T/Plt: £54.20 to a £1 stake. Pool: £101,862.90. 1,370.36 winning tickets. T/Qpdt: £21.00 to a £1 stake. Pool: £6,962.37. 245 winning tickets. JN

3004 ROSCOMMON (R-H)
Monday, July 4

OFFICIAL GOING: Good to firm

3695a LENEBANE STKS (LISTED RACE) 1m 4f
8:00 (8:00) 3-Y-O+ **£22,413** (£6,551; £3,103; £1,034)

RPR

1 **Quest For Peace (IRE)**[85] 1260 3-8-10 99...... CO'Donoghue 5 108+
(A P O'Brien, Ire) *trckd ldrs: clsr in 4th under 2f out: styd on wl u.p fnl f to ld nr fin* **3/1**[2]

2 *1 ¼* **Haziyna (IRE)**[12] 3297 3-8-7 97...... NGMcCullagh 6 103
(John M Oxx, Ire) *sn trckd ldrs: chal and led under 2f out: styd on wl u.p fnl f: ct nr fin* **5/1**[3]

3 *1* **Banksters Bonus (IRE)**[16] 3196 3-8-10 106...... FMBerry 2 104
(Mrs John Harrington, Ire) *trckd ldrs: chal and on terms under 2f out: sn hdd: no imp and kpt on same pce ins fnl f* **5/2**[1]

4 *1 ¼* **Unity (IRE)**[17] 3147 4-9-6 98......(p) WMLordan 7 99
(David Wachman, Ire) *trckd ldrs: 5th under 2f out: kpt on wout threatening u.p fnl f* **10/1**

5 *½* **Address Unknown**[9] 3418 4-9-9 104......(bt) PJSmullen 3 102
(D K Weld, Ire) *led and disp: hdd under 2f out: sn no imp u.p: kpt on same pce* **10/1**

6 *nk* **Zerashan (IRE)**[9] 3418 4-9-9 100...... JMurtagh 8 101
(M Halford, Ire) *towards rr: sltly hmpd after 5f: kpt on wout threatening u.p fr 2f out* **5/1**[3]

7 *2* **Why (IRE)**[22] 2968 3-8-7 94......(p) DavidMcCabe 1 95
(A P O'Brien, Ire) *towards rr: short of room and hit rail after 5f: kpt on same pce u.p st* **22/1**

8 *3 ½* **Priomhbhean (IRE)**[12] 3297 4-9-6 95......(p) KJManning 4 89
(J S Bolger, Ire) *cl up and disp ld at times: no ex fr under 2f out* **25/1**

9 *9* **Rising Wind (IRE)**[12] 3297 3-8-7 95...... DPMcDonogh 9 75
(Kevin Prendergast, Ire) *towards rr: sltly hmpd after 5f: no imp u.p st* **16/1**

2m 32.93s (-10.37)
WFA 3 from 4yo 13lb **9** Ran SP% **119.2**
CSF £19.23 TOTE £2.60: £1.02, £1.60, £1.60; DF 24.00.
Owner Mrs John Magnier **Bred** Macquarie **Trained** Ballydoyle, Co Tipperary
■ Stewards' Enquiry : C O'Donoghue two-day ban: careless riding (Jul 18, 20)
N G McCullagh caution: careless riding

FOCUS
A competitive Listed contest that turned into a rough race. It produced a likeable winner and has been rated around the fourth down to the seventh.

NOTEBOOK
Quest For Peace(IRE) avoided most of the trouble and won in the manner of a real staying type. Nicely positioned in midfield throughout, he was pulled out to challenge well into the straight and kept galloping to get up close home. This colt was described as "still a baby" by his rider after the race. What is certain is that he will stay further than this and there is every chance he will be a live Irish Leger candidate come the day. (op 3/1 tchd 7/2)
Haziyna(IRE) has been remarkably progressive and still is. She travelled kindly, came to win her race and was basically beaten by an improving and better rival. The obvious aim for her connections will be a Listed success and she must have every chance. (op 5/1 tchd 4/1)
Banksters Bonus(IRE) was perfectly placed throughout and the 106-rated gelding had every chance. He battled on gamely under pressure and ran a similar race relative to the runner-up as he did two runs back at Leopardstown. He has developed into a reliable performer. (op 3/1 tchd 10/3)
Unity(IRE) was one of the victims of the scrimmaging in the straight and her rider felt it cost her a placing. She already has a Listed placing and is a solid type at around this trip. (op 7/1)
Address Unknown looked to have the run of the race and no excuses. This seems as good as he is. (op 10/1 tchd 12/1)
Zerashan(IRE) was another who had a rough enough ride. He is better than this. (op 6/1)
Why(IRE) looked a bit outclassed but she was snatched up early on. (op 16/1)
Rising Wind(IRE) Official explanation: jockey said filly suffered interference on bend past stands

3691 - 3694a, 3696 - 3699a (Foreign Racing) - See Raceform Interactive

3456 PONTEFRACT (L-H)
Tuesday, July 5

OFFICIAL GOING: Good to firm (good in places; 7.9)
Wind: light 1/2 against Weather: overcast, light showers after race 1

3700 DIANNE NURSERY 6f
2:30 (2:30) (Class 4) 2-Y-O **£3,428** (£1,020; £509; £254) **Stalls** Low

Form RPR

6035 **1** **Xinbama (IRE)**[32] 2661 2-8-11 **64**...... SebSanders 11 68
(J W Hills) *t.k.h in rr: hdwy on outside over 2f out: chal 1f out: styd on to ld towards fin* **16/1**

501 **2** *nk* **Indepub**[20] 3035 2-9-7 **74**...... PhillipMakin 8 77+
(Kevin Ryan) *1/2 rrd s: in rr: sn pushed along: hdwy over 2f out: led 1f out: hdd nr fin* **7/1**[2]

4225 **3** *¾* **Auntie Joy**[14] 3242 2-8-10 **63**...... JamesSullivan 9 64
(Michael Easterby) *in rr: sn pushed along: hdwy on outside 2f out: styd on ins fnl f* **25/1**

01 **4** *2* **Lady Victory (IRE)**[45] 2302 2-9-6 **73**...... HughBowman 6 68
(Mick Channon) *dwlt: swtchd lft s: hld up in rr: hdwy 2f out: swtchd outside over 1f out: styd on wl* **15/2**[3]

433 **5** *1 ¾* **Maltease Ah**[20] 3050 2-9-4 **71**...... PaulHanagan 12 61+
(Richard Fahey) *w ldrs: fdd last 150yds* **8/1**

01 **6** *1* **Pendle Lady (IRE)**[29] 2761 2-8-13 **66**...... FrannyNorton 10 53
(Mark Brisbourne) *mid-div: effrt over 2f out: nt clr run over 1f out: kpt on wl ins fnl f* **12/1**

3153 **7** *1 ¾* **Middleton Flyer (IRE)**[10] 3375 2-9-5 **72**...... NeilCallan 7 53+
(David Evans) *chsd ldrs: wknd ins fnl f* **16/1**

2212 **8** *¾* **Aquasulis (IRE)**[9] 3435 2-8-12 **65**...... CathyGannon 4 44+
(David Evans) *led: hdd 1f out: sn wknd* **9/2**[1]

10 **9** *1 ½* **Chevanah (IRE)**[41] 2404 2-9-5 **72**...... SilvestreDeSousa 2 47
(Ann Duffield) *mid-div: effrt on ins and nt clr run 2f out: sn wknd* **10/1**

431 **10** *½* **Fayr Fall (IRE)**[50] 2160 2-9-2 **69**...... DavidAllan 1 42+
(Tim Easterby) *trckd ldrs: effrt over 2f out: wknd appr fnl f* **9/2**[1]

0031 **11** *¾* **Nameitwhatyoulike**[25] 2889 2-9-4 **71**......(b) DavidNolan 5 42+
(Michael Easterby) *w ldrs: wknd appr fnl f* **9/1**

01 **12** *10* **Seven Year Itch (IRE)**[83] 1301 2-8-5 **58**...... RoystonFfrench 3 —
(James Bethell) *chsd ldrs: lost pl 2f out: sn bhd: eased clsng stages* **16/1**

1m 19.22s (2.32) **Going Correction** +0.05s/f (Good) **12** Ran SP% **120.0**
Speed ratings (Par 96): **86,85,84,81,79 78,75,74,72,72 71,57**
toteswingers:1&2:£20.30, 2&3:£24.80, 1&3:£35.20 CSF £125.49 CT £2808.54 TOTE £26.30: £6.80, £2.60, £6.60; EX 133.60 TRIFECTA Not won..
Owner Xinbama Partnership **Bred** P Heffernan **Trained** Upper Lambourn, Berks
■ The 'official' ratings shown next to each horse are estimated and for information purposes only.

FOCUS
False rail in place over last 6f about 15ft from inside rail. The first nursery of the season, so not that easy to gauge the strength of the form, though it did look competitive beforehand, with nine of the 12 being previous winners. The leaders went off too hard, setting it up for those coming from behind, with the front four all being well off the pace at halfway.

NOTEBOOK
Xinbama(IRE)'s profile didn't look as obviously progressive as some in the line-up, but he's undoubtedly improved to get off the mark, the step up to a stiff 6f looking the key as it was only late on that he got his head in front. A half-brother to the useful, if quirky, Scotty's Future, he may do better still, with 7f likely to suit him before long. (op 25-1)
Indepub emerges with plenty credit in only narrowly failing to defy top weight and appeals as the type to keep on progressing. His awkward start didn't do him any harm the way things developed, but it's to be hoped it doesn't become a habit. (op 8-1)
Auntie Joy didn't seem to get home over 7.5f at Beverley last time but looks well worth another try over further on this evidence, finishing strongly. She's evidently starting out off a fair mark. (op 33-1)
Lady Victory(IRE)'s maiden win didn't come in a strong race and she probably improved on that form here, staying on from out the back. This was just her third start so it'll be a surprise if there's not a bit more to come from her. (op 6-1)
Maltease Ah can be rated better than the bare result, faring best of those who forced the pace. She's starting out on a fair mark and is one to bear in mind for a similar event, with an easier 6f perhaps ideal for her at this stage. (op 17-2 tchd 9-1)
Pendle Lady(IRE)'s maiden win may not amount to a great deal and she needs a bit of help from the assessor on this evidence, not making any real impression from midfield. Official explanation: jockey said filly was denied a clear run (op 14-1)
Aquasulis(IRE) had looked consistent prior to this and probably remains in form, simply paying for going too hard in front. (tchd 5-1)
Fayr Fall(IRE) had beaten Auntie Joy in a maiden last time but was nowhere near that form on this occasion, despite the market very much speaking in his favour. (op 7-1)
Nameitwhatyoulike didn't get home. (op 13-2)

3701 YORKSHIRE RACING SUMMER FESTIVAL H'CAP 1m 2f 6y
3:00 (3:01) (Class 5) (0-75,75) 3-Y-O+ **£4,204** (£1,251; £625; £312) **Stalls** Low

Form RPR

4123 **1** **King Kurt (IRE)**[18] 3131 3-9-3 **75**...... PhillipMakin 8 90+
(Kevin Ryan) *chsd ldr: led over 2f out: edgd lft 1f out: drvn clr* **6/1**[3]

0030 **2** *3 ½* **Hidden Glory**[13] 3277 4-9-13 **74**...... TomQueally 10 82+
(James Given) *swtchd lft s: in rr: hdwy and swtchd outside 2f out: styd on to take 2nd nr fin* **20/1**

5623 **3** *nk* **Amazing Blue Sky**[5] 3545 5-9-8 **69**...... JamesSullivan 2 76
(Ruth Carr) *led: hdd over 2f out: kpt on same pce* **9/4**[1]

3-01 **4** *6* **Eltheeb**[14] 3244 4-9-12 **73**...... PJMcDonald 5 68
(George Moore) *hld up in mid-div: drvn 3f out: nt clr run and hmpd over 1f out tl jst ins fnl f: r.o to take modest 4th nr fin* **5/1**[2]

0060 **5** *1* **Satin Love (USA)**[18] 3131 3-8-7 **65**...... SilvestreDeSousa 6 58
(Mark Johnston) *t.k.h: trckd ldrs: lost pl and drvn after 4f: hdwy on outer 2f out: kpt on same pce ins fnl f* **16/1**

5500 **6** *1* **Idealism**[22] 2988 4-8-10 **57**...... FrederikTylicki 3 48
(Micky Hammond) *trckd ldrs: t.k.h: n.m.r over 1f out: one pce* **25/1**

The Form Book, Raceform Ltd, Compton, RG20 6NL

5600 **7** *nse* **Gold Rules**[13] 3277 4-9-6 **74**...............................(tp) DavidSimmonson(7) 1 65
(Michael Easterby) *t.k.h: trckd ldrs: wknd 1f out* **14/1**
3-05 **8** *5* **Daaweitza**[43] 2364 8-10-0 **75**......................................(b) TomEaves 4 56
(Brian Ellison) *t.k.h towards rr: effrt over 2f out: nt clr run over 1f out: sn wknd* **12/1**
5400 **9** *1 1/4* **Desert Vision**[25] 2887 7-9-9 **70**.......................................(vt) DavidNolan 7 48
(Michael Easterby) *chsd ldrs: drvn over 2f out: wknd over 1f out* **40/1**
5210 **10** *2 1/4* **Adlington**[24] 2935 3-9-0 **72**.. PaulHanagan 9 46
(Richard Fahey) *hld up in mid-div: drvn 3f out: wknd over 1f out* **8/1**
3426 **11** *31* **Prince Apollo**[13] 3286 6-9-13 **74**................................(t) HughBowman 11 —
(Gerard Butler) *hdwy on outside to join ldrs after 2f: wknd 2f out: bhd whn heavily eased 1f out: virtually p.u: t.o* **7/1**

2m 13.3s (-0.40) **Going Correction** +0.05s/f (Good)
WFA 3 from 4yo+ 11lb **11** Ran SP% **116.6**
Speed ratings (Par 103): **103,100,99,95,94 93,93,89,88,86 61**
toteswingers:1&2:£12.50, 2&3:£7.90, 1&3:£3.20 CSF £120.31 CT £350.34 TOTE £6.30: £1.60, £5.10, £1.70; EX 119.40 Trifecta £243.50 Pool: £411.39 - 1.25 winning units..
Owner Matthew Taylor **Bred** Hong Kong Breeders Club **Trained** Hambleton, N Yorks

FOCUS
A fair handicap. The gallop looked on the steady side and not that many got in a blow, the performance of the second, who was held up out the back, definitely worth marking up. The form is rated around the second.
Eltheeb Official explanation: jockey said gelding was denied a clear run

3702 JEFF AND MARGARET SMITH MEMORIAL H'CAP 5f
3:30 (3:31) (Class 5) (0-75,75) 3-Y-O **£2,264** (£673; £336; £168) **Stalls** Low

Form RPR
-052 **1** **Lady Royale**[17] 3189 3-9-7 **75**..................................(b) SilvestreDeSousa 4 86
(Geoffrey Oldroyd) *mid-div: hdwy over 2f out: styd on wl to ld last 50yds* **4/1**[2]
2101 **2** *1* **Irish Boy (IRE)**[18] 3126 3-8-9 **63**................................... DuranFentiman 9 70
(Noel Wilson) *w ldrs: led over 2f out: hdd and no ex wl ins fnl f* **5/2**[1]
-155 **3** *1 3/4* **Mr Mo Jo**[17] 3189 3-8-13 **67**.. PaulHanagan 2 68
(Lawrence Mullaney) *led: hdd over 2f out: kpt on same pce ins fnl f* **15/2**
2220 **4** *hd* **Rhal (IRE)**[53] 2062 3-9-3 **71**.. TomEaves 7 71
(Bryan Smart) *trckd ldrs: kpt on same pce ins fnl f* **8/1**
632 **5** *1 3/4* **These Dreams**[7] 3494 3-8-2 **56** oh5................................ AndrewMullen 3 50
(Richard Guest) *in rr: hdwy 2f out: kpt on same pce: nvr trbld ldrs* **12/1**
0344 **6** *1* **Running Water**[7] 3484 3-8-2 **56** oh11.......................(bt) FrannyNorton 10 46
(Hugh McWilliams) *rn wout declared tongue strap: dwlt: swtchd lft after s: hdwy on ins whn nt clr run over 1f out: nvr a threat* **50/1**
06 **7** *2 1/4* **Celtic Sixpence (IRE)**[19] 3079 3-9-5 **73**........................(p) TomQueally 5 55
(Noel Quinlan) *in rr: effrt on outer 2f out: nvr on terms* **8/1**
4505 **8** *3 3/4* **Je Suis Unrockstar**[110] 875 3-8-7 **64**............................(p) BillyCray(3) 8 32
(David Nicholls) *mid-div on outer: sn drvn along: lost pl over 2f out* **20/1**
6504 **9** *1/2* **Lady Del Sol**[11] 3347 3-9-0 **68**................................(be1) DanielTudhope 6 35
(Marjorie Fife) *trckd ldrs: swtchd rt 1f out: sn wknd* **9/2**[3]
0060 **10** *1 1/4* **Bellemere**[19] 3087 3-8-5 **59**.. JamesSullivan 1 21
(Michael Easterby) *mid-div: effrt over 2f out: hung lft over 1f out: sn wknd* **40/1**

63.87 secs (0.57) **Going Correction** +0.05s/f (Good) **10** Ran SP% **117.6**
Speed ratings (Par 100): **97,95,92,92,89 87,84,78,77,75**
toteswingers:1&2:£3.20, 2&3:£4.00, 1&3:£6.50 CSF £14.30 CT £74.20 TOTE £5.00: £1.10, £1.80, £2.70; EX 14.30 Trifecta £171.70 Pool: £491.97 - 2.12 winning units..
Owner R C Bond **Bred** Bond Thoroughbred Corporation **Trained** Brawby, N Yorks

FOCUS
Just a run-of-the-mill 3-y-o sprint. The gallop was a sound one. The winner is rated back to her 2yo best.

3703 WEATHERBYS BLOODSTOCK INSURANCE PIPALONG STKS (LISTED RACE) (F&M) 1m 4y
4:00 (4:01) (Class 1) 4-Y-0+
£17,013 (£6,450; £3,228; £1,608; £807; £405) **Stalls** Low

Form RPR
-411 **1** **Law Of The Range**[24] 2927 4-8-12 94....................... SilvestreDeSousa 7 106
(Marco Botti) *led: swtchd lft after 1f: shkn up and qcknd over 2f out: styd on gamely* **6/1**[3]
-350 **2** *1 3/4* **Fontley**[20] 3030 4-8-12 99.. TomQueally 1 102
(Eve Johnson Houghton) *chsd ldrs: effrt over 2f out: styd on to take 3rd 1f out: kpt on wl to snatch 2nd post* **5/1**[3]
-235 **3** *nse* **Off Chance**[54] 2031 5-8-12 100...................................... DuranFentiman 6 102+
(Tim Easterby) *dwlt: hld up in rr: effrt on outer 3f out: hunt lft and wnt 4th: 1f out: styd on wl towards fin: tk 3rd post* **7/2**[2]
11-1 **4** *shd* **Dark Promise**[10] 3407 4-8-12 95.. NeilCallan 3 102
(Roger Varian) *trckd wnr: chal over 1f out: wknd last 75yds* **6/4**[1]
6316 **5** *5* **Gobama**[16] 3213 4-8-12 93.. SebSanders 8 90
(J W Hills) *hld up in rr: drvn over 2f out: nvr nr ldrs* **33/1**
3-61 **6** *1 1/4* **Folly Bridge**[39] 2470 4-8-12 99....................................... SteveDrowne 5 87
(Roger Charlton) *sn trcking ldrs on outer: drvn 3f out: wkng whn checked appr fnl f* **8/1**
4030 **7** *nk* **Kinky Afro (IRE)**[18] 3109 4-8-12 98.................................. LukeMorris 2 87
(J S Moore) *dwlt: sme hdwy over 2f out: wknd over 1f out* **33/1**
1540 **8** *3/4* **Snow Dancer (IRE)**[11] 3356 7-8-12 86............................ PhillipMakin 4 85
(Hugh McWilliams) *hld up in rr: effrt over 2f out: wknd over 1f out* **66/1**

1m 44.68s (-1.22) **Going Correction** +0.05s/f (Good) **8** Ran SP% **114.0**
Speed ratings (Par 111): **108,106,106,106,101 99,99,98**
toteswingers:1&2:£3.70, 2&3:£4.30, 1&3:£2.90 CSF £29.50 TOTE £6.80: £2.20, £1.90, £1.50; EX 34.10 Trifecta £171.30 Pool: £979.71 - 4.23 winning units..
Owner Christopher McHale **Bred** Brookside Breeders Club **Trained** Newmarket, Suffolk

FOCUS
Not the strongest of Listed races by any means, the form ordinary for the grade. The winner had the advantage of being able to dictate what was no more than a modest gallop. She's accorded a 6lb personal best.

NOTEBOOK
Law Of The Range is an uncomplicated filly who just keeps on getting better. She had a tactical advantage here, and things will get tougher from now on, but her excellent attitude is sure to continue to hold her in good stead. There is a Group 3 at Goodwood later this month on her agenda. (op 6-1)
Fontley had a more realistic chance back down at Listed level and ran well, particularly as a stronger gallop would have suited better, the fact a 13lb turnaround in the weights wasn't enough to see her reverse Ascot form with Law Of The Range from earlier in the season more an indication of how much the winner has improved since. (op 13-2 tchd 9-2)
Off Chance did win this race last season but her hold-up style is probably better suited to big-field handicaps where they tend to go a stronger gallop. She kept on well at the death here but was never going to reach the winner. (op 11-4 tchd 4-1)
Dark Promise certainly wasn't discredited, as this was a step up in class after all, but she didn't really see her race out after moving comfortably in the winner's slipstream for a long way. There's just a chance she found this coming a little quick ten days on from her reappearance win, and she's worth another chance at this level. (op 13-8)
Folly Bridge's Newmarket handicap win looked to give her decent claims and she might have been expected to do a lot better, certainly being beaten before stamina should have been an issue. (op 9-1)

3704 KING RICHARD III H'CAP 6f
4:30 (4:31) (Class 3) (0-90,87) 3-Y-0+
£6,411 (£1,919; £959; £479; £239; £120) **Stalls** Low

Form RPR
1401 **1** **Thunderball**[20] 3045 5-9-5 **87**.......................................(b) LeonnaMayor(7) 8 99
(David Nicholls) *hld up: hdwy on outer over 3f out: sn trcking ldrs: led appr fnl f: kpt on strly* **9/1**
1014 **2** *2* **Klynch**[10] 3395 5-9-10 **85**...(b) JamesSullivan 5 90
(Ruth Carr) *mid-div on outside: hdwy over 2f out: wnt 2nd: jst ins fnl f: styd on same pce* **5/1**[2]
-400 **3** *2* **My Kingdom (IRE)**[10] 3395 5-9-12 **87**.........................(t) AdrianNicholls 2 86
(David Nicholls) *towards rr: hdwy over 2f out: sn chsng ldrs: wnt 3rd jst ins fnl f: kpt on same pce* **8/1**
0400 **4** *2* **Jack My Boy (IRE)**[31] 2706 4-9-11 **86**.......................... CathyGannon 12 79
(David Evans) *chsd ldrs: drvn over 2f out: sn outpcd: kpt on clsng stages* **7/1**[3]
55-6 **5** *nk* **Cornus**[10] 3383 9-8-10 **74**...(be) MartinHarley(3) 10 66
(Alan McCabe) *chsd ldr: one pce appr fnl f* **10/1**
0500 **6** *1/2* **Summer Dancer (IRE)**[19] 3071 7-9-2 **77**............................ MickyFenton 6 67
(Paul Midgley) *chsd ldrs: drvn over 2f out: one pce over 1f out* **16/1**
-064 **7** *1 3/4* **Mr Wolf**[29] 2766 10-8-7 **71**..(p) AmyRyan(3) 4 55
(John Quinn) *led: hdd appr fnl f: sn wknd* **16/1**
0-00 **8** *nk* **Haadeeth**[21] 3028 4-8-13 **74**.. PaulHanagan 14 57
(Richard Fahey) *hld up towards rr: edgd lft over 2f out: kpt on ins fnl f* **18/1**
10 **9** *shd* **Flowing Cape (IRE)**[4] 3578 6-9-8 **86**............................ PaulPickard(3) 3 69
(Reg Hollinshead) *sn chsng ldrs: lost pl over 1f out* **9/2**[1]
6500 **10** *5* **Arganil (USA)**[10] 3395 6-9-9 **84**.. PhillipMakin 7 51
(Kevin Ryan) *stmbld s: in rr: sme hdwy 2f out: nvr nr ldrs: eased nr fin* **8/1**
0000 **11** *1* **Haajes**[25] 2890 7-9-4 **79**.. TonyCulhane 13 43
(Paul Midgley) *in rr on wd outside: sme hdwy over 2f out: nvr on terms* **16/1**
1305 **12** *7* **Dickie Le Davoir**[18] 3140 7-9-7 **85**.......................(b) RobertLButler(3) 1 27
(Richard Guest) *dwlt: in rr: bhd fnl 2f* **14/1**
0100 **13** *8* **Thrust Control (IRE)**[23] 2954 4-8-13 **81**.................. ShaneBKelly(7) 9 —
(Tracy Waggott) *chsd ldrs: lost pl over 2f out* **33/1**

1m 16.42s (-0.48) **Going Correction** +0.05s/f (Good) **13** Ran SP% **121.2**
Speed ratings (Par 107): **105,102,99,97,96 95,93,93,93,86 85,75,65**
toteswingers:1&2:£8.40, 2&3:£4.60, 1&3:£12.80 CSF £54.30 CT £397.79 TOTE £10.30: £3.10, £1.70, £3.20; EX 62.20 Trifecta £196.50 Pool: £1075.73 - 4.05 winning units..
Owner Paul J Dixon & Brian Morton **Bred** Mrs Yvette Dixon **Trained** Sessay, N Yorks
■ Stewards' Enquiry : Leonna Mayor one-day ban: used whip in incorrect place (Jul 19)

FOCUS
A fairly useful sprint. Confirmed front-runner Mr Wolf took them along but didn't blast off as hard as he often does. The form is rated around the runner-up.

NOTEBOOK
Thunderball has thrived for Dandy Nicholls, this his fourth win of the season, and he has the potential to do better as he's totally unexposed as a sprinter, this being the first time he's dropped down to 6f since his debut. He's always had plenty of speed and, having loomed upsides around halfway, was always in control after hitting the front over 1f out. (op 10-1)
Klynch, like so many from his yard, is at the very top of his game and will continue to give a good account, going down only to a thriving rival. (op 9-2)
My Kingdom(IRE), a stablemate of the winner, is probably ready to strike for his new yard before long, certainly impressing with how he travelled for a long way in a refitted tongue-tie (all wins come in one). Four of his five successes have come at 7f but he certainly doesn't lack for speed.
Jack My Boy(IRE) has edged back down the weights and this was more like it, without necessarily suggesting he's a winner in waiting. (op 9-1 tchd 13-2)
Cornus, who won this last year off a 7lb higher mark, has taken a while to make it the track this term and left the impression he still needed the run ten days on from his reappearance, finding no extra having been eased up. He's well handicapped and should be sharper next time. (op 11-1)
Summer Dancer(IRE) wasn't discredited, particularly as he's probably better over 7f. (op 14-1)
Haadeeth hasn't been with his excellent new yard long and was better than the result here, travelling strongly under restraint and not being unduly knocked about. He'll come down a bit more in the weights for this and is probably in better heart than his form figures might suggest. (op 16-1)
Flowing Cape(IRE) still figures on a fair mark but has now been below his best on his last two starts. (op 5-1)
Arganil(USA)'s yard could hardly be in much better form but he continues to struggle despite a sliding mark. Official explanation: jockey said gelding had a breathing problem (op 9-1)

3705 SUNDAY RACEDAY BBQ PACKAGE MAIDEN STKS 1m 4f 8y
5:00 (5:00) (Class 5) 3-Y-0+ **£2,264** (£673; £336; £168) **Stalls** Low

Form RPR
0-22 **1** **Thubiaan (USA)**[27] 2813 3-8-13 82................................. RichardHills 6 87+
(William Haggas) *led: pushed along and increased pce over 3f out: drvn clr over 1f out: styd on strly: eased towards fin* **30/100**[1]
2 *4* **Tiny Temper (IRE)** 3-8-8 0.. PaulHanagan 3 73+
(Richard Fahey) *s.i.s: hld up in last: effrt over 3f out: styd on to chse wnr jst ins fnl f* **20/1**
-206 **3** *2 1/4* **Kadoodd (IRE)**[16] 3206 3-8-13 75...................................... HughBowman 1 74
(Mick Channon) *hld up in mid-div: effrt over 2f out: kpt on one pce to take 3rd last 100yds* **14/1**
-232 **4** *1 1/4* **Star Commander**[16] 3206 3-8-13 75..................................... KierenFallon 7 72
(Mark H Tompkins) *trckd wnr: drvn over 3f out: wknd last 150yds* **4/1**[2]
0 **5** *9* **Sugar Apple**[18] 3138 3-8-8 0... FrederikTylicki 8 53
(James Given) *trckd ldrs: effrt over 3f out: wknd over 1f out* **50/1**
00-0 **6** *7* **Business Bay (USA)**[22] 2991 4-9-12 50.............................. MarcHalford 2 46
(Patrick Clinton) *trckd ldrs: drvn over 3f out: wknd 2f out* **100/1**
7 *7* **Jacob McCandles**[24] 4-9-7 0...................................... LMcNiff(5) 4 35
(David Barron) *hld up towards rr: effrt over 2f out: sn wknd* **33/1**
8 *2 1/2* **Afrikaans (IRE)** 3-8-13 0.. SilvestreDeSousa 5 31
(Mark Johnston) *in rr: sn drvn along: reminders over 3f out: sn outpcd and bhd* **9/1**[3]

2m 40.15s (-0.65) **Going Correction** +0.05s/f (Good)
WFA 3 from 4yo 13lb **8** Ran SP% **124.2**
Speed ratings (Par 103): **104,101,99,99,93 88,83,82**
toteswingers:1&2:£4.20, 2&3:£9.70, 1&3:£2.60 CSF £14.55 TOTE £1.50: £1.10, £4.40, £2.50; EX 15.00 Trifecta £65.20 Pool: £1075.60- 12.19 winning units..
Owner Hamdan Al Maktoum **Bred** Shadwell Farm LLC **Trained** Newmarket, Suffolk

FOCUS
A simple task in the end for the odds-on favourite, particularly with the third and fourth not at their best.

3706 RED SHIRT NIGHT ON FRIDAY 15TH JULY H'CAP 1m 4y
5:30 (5:30) (Class 5) (0-70,70) 3-Y-O £2,264 (£673; £336; £168) Stalls Low

Form RPR
3024 **1** **Byron Bear (IRE)**[18] 3142 3-8-2 **51** oh1 PaulQuinn 3 58
(Paul Midgley) *rrd s: last and drvn 4f out: hdwy over 2f out: styd on to ld wl ins fnl f: won gng away* **5/1**
5253 **2** 2 1/4 **Carrowbeg (IRE)**[7] 3485 3-9-6 **69** (v[1]) SilvestreDeSousa 7 71
(Mark Johnston) *chsd ldrs: drvn and wnt 2nd over 2f out: hung lft and led over 1f out: hdd and no ex last 50yds* **3/1**[1]
-040 **3** 1 1/4 **Chadford**[57] 1945 3-8-2 **51** oh1 (p) DuranFentiman 5 50
(Tim Walford) *mid-div: effrt 3f out: kpt on same pce over 1f out* **20/1**
1456 **4** 2 1/2 **Ventura Sands (IRE)**[11] 3337 3-9-6 **69** PaulHanagan 8 62
(Richard Fahey) *trckd ldrs: led over 6f out: drvn and increased pce over 2f out: hdd over 1f out: sn crowded: fdd ins fnl f* **9/2**[3]
4300 **5** 1/2 **Deep Applause**[12] 3318 3-8-8 **57** TomEaves 2 49
(Michael Dods) *hld up in mid-div: effrt and swtchd ins over 1f out: sn hmpd and swtchd rt: kpt on fnl 150yds* **12/1**
-525 **6** 1 1/4 **Phair Winter**[14] 3246 3-8-2 **51** JamesSullivan 6 40
(Alan Brown) *hld up towards rr: effrt over 2f out: swtchd rt over 1f out: kpt on same pce: nvr threatened* **8/1**
4-06 **7** 26 **Palagonia**[10] 3377 3-9-0 **63** NeilCallan 4 —
(Mark Johnston) *led tl over 6f out: drvn 3f out: wknd 2f out: bhd whn eased: t.o* **10/1**
0232 **8** 3/4 **Maxamillion Bounty**[20] 3037 3-9-2 **70** LeeTopliss(5) 9 —
(Michael Dods) *racd wd: sn trcking ldrs: lost pl 2f out: eased whn bhd: t.o* **7/2**[2]

1m 46.91s (1.01) **Going Correction** +0.05s/f (Good) **8** Ran SP% **114.7**
Speed ratings (Par 100): **96,93,92,90,89 88,62,61**
toteswingers:1&2:£4.30, 2&3:£14.20, 1&3:£12.40 CSF £20.49 CT £275.64 TOTE £7.30: £2.60, £1.40, £11.70; EX 22.10 Trifecta £550.40 Part won..
Owner Mad 4 Fun Syndicate **Bred** R Riordan **Trained** Westow, N Yorks

FOCUS
Hard to escape the conclusion that this was no more than an ordinary 3-y-o handicap, only one of the eight having won a race previously, and none looked obviously progressive. The gallop was at least a sound one, though. The form's rated around the second and third.
Maxamillion Bounty Official explanation: trainer's rep had no explanation for the poor form shown
T/Jkpt: Not won. T/Plt: £108.50 to a £1 stake. Pool of £90,538.22 - 608.97 winning tickets. T/Qpdt: £12.70 to a £1 stake. Pool of £7,305.82 - 424.46 winning tickets. WG

3490 SOUTHWELL (L-H)
Tuesday, July 5

OFFICIAL GOING: Standard
Wind: Light across Weather: overcast and showers

3707 BRITISH STALLION STUDS SUPPORTING BRITISH RACING EBF MAIDEN STKS 5f (F)
6:40 (6:40) (Class 5) 2-Y-O £3,408 (£1,006; £503) Stalls High

Form RPR
1 **Al Shaqab (IRE)** 2-9-3 0 PhillipMakin 4 70+
(Kevin Ryan) *cl up: effrt 2f out: rdn to ld over 1f out: green and edgd lft ins fnl f: hld on wl* **11/10**[1]
4 **2** nk **Mantuana (IRE)**[8] 3452 2-8-12 0 DanielTudhope 1 64
(David O'Meara) *prom: hdwy 2f out: rdn to chal ent fnl f: sn drvn and ev ch: jst hld* **9/1**
04 **3** 1 1/2 **Molly Jones**[13] 3270 2-8-12 0 AndreaAtzeni 2 59
(Derek Haydn Jones) *dwlt: sn chsng ldrs: rdn along and sltly outpcd wl over 1f out: kpt on u.p fnl f* **16/1**
4 3/4 **Samba Night (IRE)** 2-9-3 0 RichardMullen 3 61+
(Ed McMahon) *trckd ldrs: green: rdn along and outpcd after 1f: swtchd lft to outer 3f out: sn rdn and kpt on appr fnl f* **4/1**[3]
422 **5** 2 1/2 **Banksy**[15] 3221 2-9-3 0 RoystonFfrench 6 52
(John Gosden) *led: rdn along over 2f out: drvn and hdd over 1f out: sn wknd* **9/4**[2]
6 **6** 18 **Professor Tim (IRE)**[8] 3452 2-9-3 0 StephenCraine 5 —
(Patrick Morris) *prom: rdn along bef 1/2-way: sn outpcd and bhd* **80/1**

62.35 secs (2.65) **Going Correction** +0.325s/f (Slow) **6** Ran SP% **115.5**
Speed ratings (Par 94): **91,90,88,86,82 54**
toteswingers:1&2:£3.40, 2&3:£8.50, 1&3:£5.10 CSF £12.85 TOTE £2.50: £2.00, £5.10; EX 15.20.
Owner Mubarak Al Naimi **Bred** J Hanly **Trained** Hambleton, N Yorks

FOCUS
A maiden not without interest despite the small field, but a bunch finish and and a slow time so probably just modest form.

NOTEBOOK
Al Shaqab(IRE), a half-brother by Amadeus Wolf out of a 6f winner, was strong in the market and made a winning debut, albeit only narrowly from one that hadn't shown much first time out. He'll improve and it'll be a surprise if he's not a lot better than this, with nurseries an obvious route in the circumstances. (op 6-4)
Mantuana(IRE) left her debut form on turf behind, probably stripping fitter on this occasion, and would have to be of interest next time if chanced in slightly weaker grade than this. (op 14-1 tchd 16-1)
Molly Jones probably wasn't far behind the form she showed at Bath last time down in trip and might just find a bit more improvement back up at 6f in nurseries. (tchd 14-1 and 20-1)
Samba Night(IRE), a half-brother to three winners from a yard that does well with their youngsters, wasn't obviously strong in the market and shaped no more than adequately but is entitled to improve. (op 6-1)
Banksy set the standard, but he's starting to prove expensive to follow with this being the third time he's been beaten when either favourite or second favourite. It might not be wise to blame the change of surface. (op 13-8)

3708 SOUTHWELL RACECOURSE SUPPORTING MACMILLAN CANCER CARE (S) STKS 5f (F)
7:10 (7:11) (Class 6) 2-Y-O £1,704 (£503; £251) Stalls High

Form RPR
05 **1** **Very First Blade**[36] 2556 2-8-11 0 FrannyNorton 1 57
(Mark Brisbourne) *in tch on outer: hdwy to chse ldng pair 1/2-way: rdn wl over 1f out: styd on ent fnl f to ld last 75yds* **9/2**[2]
000 **2** 1 1/2 **Roy's Legacy**[12] 3314 2-8-11 0 (b[1]) RobbieFitzpatrick 2 52
(Shaun Harris) *cl up: led after 2f: rdn wl over 1f out: drvn and edgd rt ent fnl f: hdd & wknd last 75yds* **33/1**
5 **3** 1 **Miss Medici (IRE)**[33] 2651 2-8-6 0 CathyGannon 4 43
(Des Donovan) *led 2f: cl up: rdn 2f out: drvn over 1f out: kpt on same pce* **13/2**[3]
00 **4** 8 **Joli Colourful (IRE)**[28] 2788 2-8-4 0 DavidKenny(7) 3 20
(Tony Newcombe) *dwlt: sn in tch: hdwy to chse ldrs 3f out: rdn wl over 2f out: sn drvn and one pce* **12/1**
500 **5** 1 **Egyptian Cross**[6] 3505 2-8-11 0 (t) LukeMorris 8 16
(John Weymes) *in tch: rdn along over 2f out: sn drvn and wknd* **9/1**
0060 **6** 4 1/2 **Red Samantha (IRE)**[4] 3584 2-8-6 0 PatrickMathers 10 —
(Alan Berry) *prom: rdn along after 2f: sn wknd* **66/1**
335 **7** 4 **Nannerl (IRE)**[18] 3125 2-8-3 0 AmyRyan(3) 7 —
(Kevin Ryan) *chsd ldrs: rdn along bef 1/2-way: sn wknd* **5/2**[1]
600 **8** 1/2 **Metal Dealer (IRE)**[36] 2570 2-8-11 0 (tp) LeeNewman 9 —
(George Foster) *dwlt: a towards rr* **20/1**
0 **9** 4 **Gabrial's Girl (IRE)**[61] 1823 2-8-6 0 AndreaAtzeni 6 —
(Ian Williams) *a in rr: bhd fr 1/2-way* **9/2**[2]
0 **10** 5 **Dapper's Dancer**[6] 3504 2-8-6 0 SilvestreDeSousa 5 —
(David O'Meara) *a in rr: bhd fr 1/2-way* **9/1**

61.87 secs (2.17) **Going Correction** +0.325s/f (Slow) **10** Ran SP% **115.2**
Speed ratings (Par 92): **95,92,91,78,76 69,63,62,55,47**
toteswingers:1&2:£13.30, 2&3:£30.70, 1&3:£6.70 CSF £142.84 TOTE £4.50: £1.50, £10.70, £1.40; EX 129.30.There was no bid for the winner.
Owner L R Owen **Bred** L R Owen **Trained** Great Ness, Shropshire

FOCUS
A very weak race even by selling standards with recent form of any merit very thin on the ground, but it was quicker than the maiden. Little behind the first three ever threatened.

NOTEBOOK
Very First Blade had already been beaten in a seller, albeit one won by an above-average sort for the grade at Goodwood, so his win limits the form to some degree but he clearly improved, possibly for the change of surface and might be even more effective at 6f given the manner in which he stayed strongly. (op 6-1)
Roy's Legacy had been tailed off in all his runs in maidens but first-time headgear, a drop in grade and the switch to Fibresand all clearly paid some part in an improved effort, briefly looking the winner inside the last despite drifting right. (op 22-1)
Miss Medici(IRE) had finished well beaten on her debut here in a 6f maiden. This is clearly her grade but she doesn't look to have much scope and, an ungainly mover, she might need some give in the ground back on turf. (op 6-1 tchd 11-2)
Joli Colourful(IRE) isn't really entitled to show much at 5f being by Tiger Hill but at least improved on earlier efforts in maidens. (op 11-1)
Egyptian Cross was always about the same place and, like those behind him, is going to be difficult to place. (op 11-1)
Nannerl(IRE) looked to set the standard such as it was but was soon struggling to hold her place and clearly isn't progressing. (tchd 9-4 and 11-4)
Gabrial's Girl(IRE) didn't face the kickback on her debut for her new yard and was soon in arrears. (tchd 5-1)

3709 JAMIE HEMPSALL INTERIORS MACMILLAN CENTENARY MAIDEN H'CAP 1m (F)
7:40 (7:41) (Class 6) (0-60,60) 3-Y-O+ £1,704 (£503; £251) Stalls Low

Form RPR
6-05 **1** **Patriotic (IRE)**[18] 3111 3-9-0 **57** SilvestreDeSousa 13 73+
(Mark Johnston) *chsd ldrs on outer: cl up 1/2-way: led 3f out: rdn over 2f out: edgd rt over 1f out: sn clr* **11/2**[2]
0-32 **2** 2 1/4 **Master Of Song**[7] 3496 4-9-4 **52** (p) PaulQuinn 4 61
(Roy Bowring) *trckd ldrs: hdwy 3f out: sn chsng wnr: rdn to chal 2f out: drvn over 1f out and sn one pce* **15/8**[1]
-046 **3** 3 **Like A Boy**[24] 2904 3-9-0 **57** SebSanders 1 57
(Peter Makin) *cl up on inner: led after 3f: rdn along over 3f out: sn hdd: drvn 2f out and kpt on same pce* **10/1**
0-42 **4** 5 **Dubai Gem**[18] 3110 5-9-0 **48** CathyGannon 7 39
(Olivia Maylam) *chsd ldrs: rdn along over 3f out: drvn over 2f out and sn one pce* **15/2**[3]
-506 **5** 1 1/2 **Snow Ridge**[49] 2186 3-9-0 **57** MartinLane 11 42
(Andrew Haynes) *in rr: hdwy 3f out: sn rdn and kpt on fnl2f: nt rch ldrs* **12/1**
200- **6** 8 **Mad Millie (IRE)**[255] 7082 4-9-7 **55** DanielTudhope 8 24
(David O'Meara) *led 3f: chsd ldrs: rdn along 3f out: grad wknd* **25/1**
6032 **7** 3 3/4 **Valley Tiger**[15] 3223 3-8-11 **59** JamesRogers(5) 2 17
(William Muir) *dwlt and towards rr: sme hdwy over 3f out: nvr a factor* **8/1**
0326 **8** 1 3/4 **Jamarjo (IRE)**[7] 3496 4-9-4 **52** (v[1]) PhillipMakin 10 8
(Steve Gollings) *dwlt: a towards rr* **14/1**
-003 **9** 5 **Viking Rose (IRE)**[21] 3018 3-9-2 **59** LukeMorris 9 —
(James Eustace) *a towards rr* **9/1**
6-06 **10** 5 **Grecian Goddess (IRE)**[40] 2418 3-9-2 **59** KirstyMilczarek 3 —
(John Ryan) *a towards rr* **50/1**
0500 **11** 5 **Imperial Fong**[71] 1566 3-8-7 **50** KellyHarrison 6 —
(Chris Dwyer) *prom: rdn along 1/2-way: sn wknd* **33/1**
034/ **12** 11 **Golden Emperor (IRE)**[44] 6461 4-9-7 **55** PaulHanagan 5 —
(Keith Dalgleish) *chsd ldrs: rdn along after 3f: sn lost pl and bhd fr 1/2-way* **14/1**

1m 43.65s (-0.05) **Going Correction** +0.10s/f (Slow)
WFA 3 from 4yo+ 9lb **12** Ran SP% **121.9**
Speed ratings (Par 101): **104,101,98,93,92 84,80,78,73,68 63,52**
toteswingers:1&2:£6.10, 2&3:£9.50, 1&3:£13.30 CSF £16.36 CT £106.79 TOTE £9.00: £2.50, £1.80, £4.10; EX 20.90.
Owner Sheikh Hamdan Bin Mohammed Al Maktoum **Bred** Darley **Trained** Middleham Moor, N Yorks

FOCUS
A weak maiden handicap in which few were ever seen with a winning chance and most were well beaten by the home turn, but the winner did it well and promises to rate higher.
Patriotic(IRE) Official explanation: trainer's rep said, regarding apparent improvement in form, that this was the colt's first run in a handicap, in what appeared to be a poor race.

3710 SOUTHWELL-RACECOURSE.CO.UK CLAIMING STKS 1m (F)
8:10 (8:12) (Class 6) 3-Y-O £1,704 (£503; £251) Stalls Low

Form RPR
321- **1** **Golden Creek (USA)**[88] 1227 3-9-9 **73** LukeMorris 1 72
(Mrs K Burke) *trckd ldrs: hdwy 3f out: rdn to chse ldng pair over 2f out: drvn to chse ldr over 1f out: styd on to ld last 75yds* **5/2**[2]
060 **2** 3/4 **Fluctuation (IRE)**[17] 3177 3-8-11 **57** PaulHanagan 8 58
(William Haggas) *cl up: effrt 3f out: led wl over 2f out: rdn and hung rt wl over 1f out: hung lft ent fnl f: sn drvn and hung rt again: hdd and no ex last 75yds* **9/4**[1]
5234 **3** 5 **So Is She (IRE)**[12] 3309 3-8-4 **62** (v) CathyGannon 4 40
(Alan Bailey) *chsd ldrs: rdn along 3f out: sn outpcd: drvn and styd on fr over 1f out to take 3rd nr fin* **11/4**[3]

23 **4** *1* **Precocious Kid (IRE)**[84] 1288 3-9-1 0 ... NeilCallan 2 48
(Chris Wall) *led: rdn along over 3f out: hdd wl over 2f out: drvn and wknd over 1f out* **6/1**

-400 **5** *11* **Endaxi Mana Mou**[37] 2527 3-8-10 65 ... RichardMullen 6 18
(Noel Quinlan) *chsd ldrs: rdn along 3f out: sn wknd* **10/1**

6 *15* **Leonverre (IRE)** 3-9-1 0 ... SilvestreDeSousa 7 —
(David O'Meara) *prom: hmpd and stmbld after 1 1/2f: sn in rr* **16/1**

66 **7** *8* **Tuscany Red**[98] 1027 3-8-12 0 ... (e[1]) RobertLButler(3) 3 —
(Richard Guest) *dwlt: sn outpcd and a bhd* **100/1**

1m 44.7s (1.00) **Going Correction** +0.10s/f (Slow) **7** Ran SP% **116.3**
Speed ratings (Par 98): **99,98,93,92,81 66,58**
toteswingers:1&2:£2.00, 2&3:£2.80, 1&3:£2.50 CSF £8.88 TOTE £3.50: £1.50, £1.70; EX 9.50.Fluctuation was claimed by Ian Williams for £6000.
Owner M Gittins & Mrs E Burke **Bred** Overbrook Farm **Trained** Middleham Moor, North Yorks

FOCUS
An uncompetitive claimer run at just a fair pace.

3711 MEMBERSHIP OF SOUTHWELL GOLF CLUB H'CAP 6f (F)
8:40 (8:41) (Class 5) (0-70,70) 3-Y-0+ **£2,113** (£624; £312) **Stalls** Low

Form RPR

52 **1** **Equuleus Pictor**[14] 3261 7-9-12 70 ... (p) CathyGannon 12 80
(John Spearing) *chsd ldrs: hdwy on outer 1/2-way: chal 2f out: rdn to ld wl over 1f out: kpt on strly* **13/2[3]**

0004 **2** *1 1/4* **Ace Of Spies (IRE)**[7] 3493 6-9-9 67 ... (b) JamesSullivan 2 73
(Conor Dore) *prom: effrt wl over 2f out: rdn to chal wl over 1f out: drvn and ev ch ent fnl f: kpt on same pce* **33/1**

5350 **3** *1/2* **Elhamri**[29] 2765 7-9-10 68 ... JamesDoyle 3 72
(Conor Dore) *in tch: hdwy on inner to chse ldrs over 2f out: rdn wl over 1f out: drvn and kpt on ins fnl f* **16/1**

5454 **4** *shd* **Bonnie Prince Blue**[19] 3083 8-9-5 68 ... (b) DaleSwift(5) 13 72
(Ian McInnes) *sn outpcd and wl bhd 1/2-way: rdn along and hdwy wl over 1f out: swtchd rt and str run ins fnl f: fin fast* **22/1**

0133 **5** *1/2* **Clear Ice (IRE)**[3] 3617 4-9-4 65 ... (b) RobertLButler(3) 9 67
(Richard Guest) *in tch: hdwy to chse ldrs over 2f out: swtchd rt and rdn wl over 1f out: drvn and one pce ins fnl f* **9/2[1]**

12-0 **6** *1 1/2* **Hidden Destiny**[28] 2794 4-9-9 67 ... (p) SebSanders 4 65
(Peter Makin) *led: rdn along over 2f out: drvn and hdd wl over 1f out: grad wknd ins fnl f* **11/1**

6010 **7** *hd* **Premier League**[14] 3261 4-8-13 60 ... (p) AdamBeschizza(3) 10 57+
(Julia Feilden) *towards rr: sme hdwy 2f out: sn rdn and kpt on appr fnl f: nrst fin* **8/1**

41 **8** *nk* **Gracie's Games**[15] 3217 5-8-13 60 ... SophieDoyle(3) 5 56
(Richard Price) *towards rr: hdwy over 2f out: sn rdn and kpt on: nrst fin* **16/1**

2436 **9** *3 1/4* **Mata Hari Blue**[12] 3307 5-8-11 62 ... LucyKBarry(7) 7 48
(John Holt) *in rr: sme hdwy over 2f out: swtchd lft and styd on appr fnl f: nvr nr ldrs* **17/2**

0632 **10** *1 3/4* **Dancing Freddy (IRE)**[20] 3040 4-9-5 63 ... (p) RichardMullen 6 43
(Richard Guest) *nvr nr ldrs* **13/2[3]**

1420 **11** *2 1/4* **Steel City Boy (IRE)**[12] 3322 8-9-0 58 ... KellyHarrison 14 31
(Garry Woodward) *cl up: rdn along 3f out: wknd over 2f out* **22/1**

4000 **12** *4 1/2* **Takajan (IRE)**[11] 3341 4-9-9 67 ... FrannyNorton 1 25
(Mark Brisbourne) *midfield: rdn along bef 1/2-way: sn wknd* **12/1**

5630 **13** *5* **Stamp Duty (IRE)**[20] 3036 3-9-4 68 ... PaulHanagan 11 9
(Ollie Pears) *swtchd to outer sn after s: a in rr: bhd fr 1/2-way* **11/2[2]**

1m 17.68s (1.18) **Going Correction** +0.10s/f (Slow)
WFA 3 from 4yo+ 6lb **13** Ran SP% **121.3**
Speed ratings (Par 103): **96,94,93,93,92 90,90,90,85,83 80,74,67**
toteswingers:1&2:£22.70, 2&3:£63.00, 1&3:£16.00 CSF £212.90 CT £3402.98 TOTE £5.90: £1.90, £11.30, £8.10; EX 178.60.
Owner Masonaires **Bred** A J And Mrs L Brazier **Trained** Kinnersley, Worcs

FOCUS
The highlight of a modest card but few were ever in contention, partly on account of some severe kickback on the home turn.
Gracie's Games Official explanation: jockey said mare suffered interference at start
Stamp Duty(IRE) Official explanation: jockey said gelding never travelled

3712 TICKETS ON LINE AT SOUTHWELL-RACECOURSE.CO.UK H'CAP 1m 6f (F)
9:10 (9:11) (Class 6) (0-65,63) 4-Y-0+ **£1,704** (£503; £251) **Stalls** Low

Form RPR

0661 **1** **Light The City (IRE)**[6] 3510 4-8-9 51 6ex ... JamesSullivan 5 62
(Ruth Carr) *hld up towards rr: stdy hdwy over 4f out: trckd ldng trio 3f out: led 2f out and sn rdn: drvn ent fnl f and styd on wl* **5/2[1]**

1/24 **2** *2* **Im Spartacus**[19] 3072 9-9-1 62 ... RyanClark(5) 4 70
(Ian Williams) *trckd ldng pair: hdwy over 4f out: chal over 3f out: sn rdn and ev ch tl drvn and one pce ent fnl f* **3/1[2]**

51- **3** *7* **Rhyton (IRE)**[33] 3242 4-9-7 63 ... (p) PaulHanagan 8 61
(Donald McCain) *hld up in rr: hdwy 3f out: rdn over 2f out: styd on appr fnl f: tk 3rd nr fin* **11/1**

4023 **4** *2* **Dr Finley (IRE)**[13] 3281 4-9-1 60 ... SimonPearce(3) 10 56
(Lydia Pearce) *in tch: effrt to chse ldrs over 4f out: rdn along and outpcd wl over 2f out: drvn and kpt on appr fnl f* **9/2[3]**

00-0 **5** *1* **Merrion Tiger (IRE)**[32] 2696 6-8-8 50 ... LeeNewman 7 44
(George Foster) *prom: led 1/2-way: rdn along over 3f out: drvn and hdd 2f out: grad wknd* **10/1**

-061 **6** *1* **Denison Flyer**[17] 3185 4-8-4 49 ... (b) DeclanCannon(3) 2 42
(Lawrence Mullaney) *chsd ldrs on inner: rdn along over 5f out: drvn over 3f out: grad wknd* **8/1**

U064 **7** *26* **Exotic Dream (FR)**[10] 3391 5-8-12 54 ... LukeMorris 6 10
(Ronald Harris) *trckd ldrs: hdwy over 4f out: cl up 3f out: sn rdn and wknd* **40/1**

5300 **8** *nk* **L'Homme De Nuit (GER)**[20] 3047 7-9-1 60 ... (p) RobertLButler(3) 12 16
(Jim Best) *a in rr* **20/1**

343- **9** *9* **Pobs Trophy**[2] 6038 4-8-8 50 ... (p) RobbieFitzpatrick 3 —
(Richard Guest) *led to 1/2-way: rdn along over 4f out: sn wknd and bhd* **28/1**

0-50 **10** *15* **Pyjoma**[23] 2956 4-8-5 50 ... AdamBeschizza(3) 11 —
(Julia Feilden) *s.i.s: a bhd* **16/1**

3m 9.60s (1.30) **Going Correction** +0.10s/f (Slow) **10** Ran SP% **116.8**
Speed ratings (Par 101): **100,98,94,93,93 92,77,77,72,63**
toteswingers:1&2:£1.50, 2&3:£2.80, 1&3:£4.70 CSF £9.76 CT £68.70 TOTE £3.60: £1.30, £2.00, £2.50; EX 12.90.
Owner Atkins Legal Services **Bred** Rabbah Bloodstock Limited **Trained** Huby, N Yorks

FOCUS
Just a modest finale but the first two in the betting drew clear and it is probably reasonable form for the grade.
Exotic Dream(FR) Official explanation: jockey said mare had no more to give

T/Plt: £266.20 to a £1 stake. Pool of £68,889.91 - 188.90 winning tickets. T/Qpdt: £37.90 to a £1 stake. Pool of £7,280.23 - 141.95 winning tickets. JR

3469 WOLVERHAMPTON (A.W) (L-H)
Tuesday, July 5

OFFICIAL GOING: Standard
Wind: Light behind Weather: Overcast

3713 SPONSOR A RACE BY CALLING 01902 390000 CLASSIFIED CLAIMING STKS 5f 216y(P)
2:15 (2:16) (Class 6) 3-Y-0+ **£1,704** (£503; £251) **Stalls** Low

Form RPR

6020 **1** **Whiskey Junction**[12] 3307 7-8-8 63 ... LiamJones 7 70
(Michael Quinn) *sn chsng ldr: rdn over 2f out: r.o u.p to ld wl ins fnl f* **20/1**

3110 **2** *1/2* **Cavitie**[20] 3045 5-8-12 66 ... (p) DarryllHolland 1 72
(Andrew Reid) *hld up: hdwy over 1f out: sn rdn: r.o* **3/1[1]**

2000 **3** *hd* **Co Dependent (USA)**[21] 3019 5-8-10 70 ... FergusSweeney 2 69
(Jamie Osborne) *dwlt: hld up: nt clr run over 1f out: r.o ins fnl f: wnt 3rd post: nrst fin* **17/2**

5062 **4** *shd* **Atlantic Beach**[8] 3471 6-9-2 68 ... LiamKeniry 6 75
(Milton Bradley) *chsd ldrs: rdn over 1f out: r.o* **6/1[3]**

2/02 **5** *nk* **Enigma Code (UAE)**[102] 974 6-9-0 70 ... (t) BACurtis 3 72
(James McAuley, Ire) *sn led: rdn over 1f out: hdd wl ins fnl f* **13/2**

0221 **6** *1* **Efistorm**[8] 3464 10-8-12 65 ... KirstyMilczarek 4 67
(Conor Dore) *prom: rdn over 2f out: no ex towards fin* **4/1[2]**

0405 **7** *2 1/4* **Rainy Night**[4] 3573 5-8-9 62 ... (v) DaleSwift(5) 5 62
(Reg Hollinshead) *hld up: hdwy over 1f out: no ex ins fnl f* **8/1**

5340 **8** *2 3/4* **Hand Painted**[25] 2870 5-9-0 64 ... TravisBlock 8 53
(Peter Makin) *chsd ldrs: rdn 1/2-way: wknd ins fnl f* **8/1**

U000 **9** *13* **Cinderella**[13] 3293 4-8-5 32 ... (p) JohnFahy(3) 9 —
(Lucinda Featherstone) *s.i.s: in rr: rdn and wknd over 2f out* **200/1**

1m 13.22s (-1.78) **Going Correction** -0.125s/f (Stan) **9** Ran SP% **110.6**
Speed ratings (Par 101): **106,105,105,104,104 103,100,96,79**
toteswingers:1&2:£11.60, 2&3:£5.50, 1&3:£13.50 CSF £74.68 TOTE £23.90: £6.30, £1.10, £2.20; EX 76.50.
Owner Steven Astaire **Bred** Mrs I A Balding **Trained** Newmarket, Suffolk
■ Stewards' Enquiry : Fergus Sweeney one-day ban: careless riding (Jul 19)

FOCUS
A couple of recent winners but no more than a modest classified claimer and one in which the gallop was reasonable (time 0.22s above RP standard). The winner raced centre-to-far-side in the straight.

3714 WOLVERHAMPTON-RACECOURSE.CO.UK H'CAP 5f 216y(P)
2:45 (2:46) (Class 6) (0-60,61) 3-Y-0+ **£1,567** (£462; £231) **Stalls** Low

Form RPR

0020 **1** **Almaty Express**[27] 2803 9-9-5 55 ... (b) DarryllHolland 9 62
(John Weymes) *mde virtually all: rdn over 1f out: jst hld on* **16/1**

301 **2** *shd* **Avonlini**[50] 2161 5-9-2 52 ... GrahamGibbons 2 59
(Brian Baugh) *a.p: rdn to chse wnr 2f out: r.o* **7/1**

6-46 **3** *3/4* **Katy's Secret**[29] 2756 4-9-6 56 ... DaneO'Neill 7 60
(William Jarvis) *s.i.s: hld up: hdwy over 1f out: r.o: nt rch ldrs* **20/1**

-304 **4** *1/2* **Dies Solis**[6] 3517 4-9-8 58 ... WilliamBuick 10 61+
(Jeremy Gask) *hld up: rdn over 1f out: hung lft and r.o ins fnl f: nrst fin* **9/2[3]**

3301 **5** *nse* **Euroquip Boy (IRE)**[6] 3512 4-9-4 61 6ex ... DavidKenny(7) 4 64
(Michael Scudamore) *hld up: rdn over 2f out: hdwy over 1f out: r.o* **4/1[2]**

0663 **6** *nk* **Itsthursdayalready**[15] 3234 4-9-10 60 ... ShaneKelly 3 62
(Mark Brisbourne) *hld up: rdn over 1f out: r.o ins fnl f: nvr nrr* **17/2**

4466 **7** *nk* **Simple Rhythm**[25] 2879 5-8-11 52 ... (p) RyanPowell(5) 11 53
(John Ryan) *prom: rdn over 1f out: styd on* **25/1**

0000 **8** *1/2* **Dingaan (IRE)**[24] 2922 8-9-0 55 ... SladeO'Hara(5) 8 54
(Peter Grayson) *s.i.s: sn pushed along in rr: nt clr run and swtchd rt ins fnl f: r.o: nt rch ldrs* **100/1**

01[illegible] **9** *3/4* **Tell Halaf**[15] 3234 4-9-10 60 ... JamieSpencer 12 57
(Noel Quinlan) *trckd ldrs: rdn over* [illegible] *whn btn wl ins fnl f* **7/2[1]**

6060 **10** *1 1/2* **Vhujon (IRE)**[24] 2920 6-9-3 53 ... RobbieFitzpatrick 6 45
(Peter Grayson) *sn pushed along in rr: rdn over 2f out: styng on whn eased fnl 100yds* **50/1**

2340 **11** *1 1/2* **Charlietoo**[8] 3475 5-8-12 51 ... (p) KierenFox(3) 5 38
(Edward Bevan) *hld up: rdn over 2f out: wknd ins fnl f* **11/1**

-040 **12** *2 1/2* **Crimson Queen**[36] 2555 4-9-8 58 ... AndrewHeffernan 13 37
(Roy Brotherton) *w wnr tl pushed along 1/2-way: rdn and wknd ins fnl f* **20/1**

3300 **U** **Pinball (IRE)**[14] 3248 5-8-9 50 ... (b) DaleSwift(5) 1 —
(Lisa Williamson) *rrd and uns rdr as the stalls opened* **33/1**

1m 14.02s (-0.98) **Going Correction** -0.125s/f (Stan) **13** Ran SP% **116.9**
Speed ratings (Par 101): **101,100,99,99,99 98,98,97,96,94 92,89,—**
toteswingers:1&2:£15.20, 2&3:£21.90, 1&3:£32.20 CSF £112.31 CT £2321.94 TOTE £18.00: £5.10, £2.30, £4.60; EX 81.90.
Owner Highmoor Racing 4 & Tag Racing **Bred** P G Airey **Trained** Middleham Moor, N Yorks

FOCUS
A moderate handicap run at a reasonable gallop. Those held up were at a disadvantage and winner raced against the inside rail throughout.

3715 NEAL WOOD SECOND ANNIVERSARY MEMORIAL H'CAP 1m 4f 50y(P)
3:15 (3:15) (Class 5) (0-75,75) 3-Y-0+ **£1,940** (£577; £288; £144) **Stalls** Low

Form RPR

2541 **1** **Lemon Drop Red (USA)**[7] 3479 3-8-8 68 6ex ... WilliamBuick 5 73+
(Ed Dunlop) *prom: rdn to chse ldr over 1f out: led ins fnl f: styd on u.p* **8/11[1]**

-500 **2** *1/2* **Pertemps Networks**[21] 3023 7-9-7 68 ... GrahamGibbons 1 72
(Michael Easterby) *led: clr over 6f out: hdd ins fnl f: styd on* **10/1[3]**

34-0 **3** *1/2* **Dynamic Idol (USA)**[53] 2055 4-10-0 75 ... (b[1]) GeorgeBaker 2 78
(Mikael Magnusson) *chsd ldr: rdn over 2f out: styd on* **5/1[2]**

10 **4** *3/4* **Merton Lady**[26] 2849 3-8-6 66 ... WilliamCarson 7 68?
(John Flint) *s.i.s: hld up: racd keenly: hdwy over 2f out: rdn over 1f out: styd on* **18/1**

4-10 **5** *2 1/4* **Mr Plod**[125] 733 6-8-11 58 ... (p) DarryllHolland 6 56
(Andrew Reid) *hld up: hdwy u.p over 1f out: styd on: nt trble ldrs* **16/1**

1 **6** *3 1/2* **Time Travel**[67] 1667 6-9-3 64 ... (bt) BACurtis 4 57
(James McAuley, Ire) *hld up: hdwy over 1f out: sn rdn: wknd ins fnl f* **16/1**

0605 **7** *1* **Ringstead Bay (FR)**[7] 3479 3-8-6 66 ... (p) DavidProbert 3 57
(Ralph Beckett) *chsd ldrs: rdn over 2f out: wknd over 1f out* **25/1**

25 **8** *3* **Rainy Champion (USA)**[48] 2203 3-8-10 **75**................ KieranO'Neill(5) 8 61
(Gerard Butler) *s.s: hld up: hdwy over 4f out: sn rdn: wknd over 2f out*
10/1[3]

2m 37.37s (-3.73) **Going Correction** -0.125s/f (Stan)
WFA 3 from 4yo+ 13lb **8** Ran SP% **113.6**
Speed ratings (Par 103): **107,106,106,105,104 102,101,99**
toteswingers:1&2:£4.00, 2&3:£5.00, 1&3:£1.70 CSF £8.99 CT £22.95 TOTE £1.70: £1.10, £2.60, £1.60; EX 8.50.
Owner R J Arculli **Bred** Nancy M Leonard Living Trust **Trained** Newmarket, Suffolk

FOCUS
A fair handicap in which the gallop was an ordinary one. The principals came down the centre in the straight.

3716 STAY AT THE WOLVERHAMPTON HOLIDAY INN (S) STKS 1m 141y(P)
3:45 (3:46) (Class 6) 3-Y-0+ **£1,567** (£462; £231) **Stalls** Low

Form RPR

0604 **1** **Whispering Spirit (IRE)**[8] 3473 5-9-3 78.................(v) DarrylHolland 11 62
(Ann Duffield) *a.p: rdn to ld ins fnl f: r.o* **11/4**[2]

2605 **2** *3/4* **Cloudy Bay (USA)**[20] 3051 4-9-8 69.............................(p) AndrewElliott 1 65
(Mrs K Burke) *racd keenly: trckd ldr over 2f: remained handy: wnt 2nd again over 2f out: led over 1f out: rdn and hdd ins fnl f: kpt on* **2/1**[1]

0435 **3** *1* **Cobo Bay**[9] 2656 6-10-0 73...............................(b) JamieSpencer 6 69
(Conor Dore) *led: rdn and hdd over 1f out: styd on same pce ins fnl f* **7/2**[3]

1253 **4** *1* **Unlimited**[14] 3250 9-10-0 75... LiamJones 4 67
(Tony Carroll) *a.p: rdn over 2f out: styd on same pce ins fnl f* **4/1**

00 **5** *1 3/4* **Ossie Ardiles (IRE)**[17] 3167 3-8-12 0............................... NeilChalmers 5 56
(Michael Appleby) *hld up: hdwy over 2f out: sn rdn: styng on same pce whn hung rt ins fnl f* **100/1**

6-60 **6** *2 3/4* **Smart Violetta (IRE)**[36] 2571 3-8-7 41.......................(t) TadhgO'Shea 10 44
(Ann Duffield) *s.i.s: sn prom: rdn 4f out: wknd over 1f out* **50/1**

0- **7** *4* **Kiss N Kick**[292] 6115 5-9-8 0.. DaneO'Neill 7 41
(Lucinda Featherstone) *prom: chsd ldr 6f out tl rdn over 2f out: wknd over 1f out* **22/1**

00 **8** *2 3/4* **Phlorian**[12] 3320 5-9-3 0..(t) KieranO'Neill(5) 8 35
(Ian Patrick Browne, Ire) *s.i.s: rdn over 3f out: a in rr* **100/1**

/0-5 **9** *hd* **Almowj**[36] 2569 8-9-1 41.. LucyKBarry(7) 9 34
(George Jones) *s.s: rdn over 3f out: a in rr* **100/1**

10 *3 3/4* **Fortunelini**[148] 6-9-3 0..(t) J-PGuillambert 3 21
(Ian Patrick Browne, Ire) *s.i.s: a in rr: rdn over 3f out: sn lost tch* **40/1**

1m 49.94s (-0.56) **Going Correction** -0.125s/f (Stan)
WFA 3 from 4yo+ 10lb **10** Ran SP% **113.9**
Speed ratings (Par 101): **97,96,95,94,93 90,87,84,84,81**
toteswingers:1&2:£2.00, 2&3:£2.50, 1&3:£2.50 CSF £8.21 TOTE £2.60: £1.10, £1.70, £2.30; EX 10.40.The winner was bought in for 6,250gns. Cloudy Bay was claimed by J. L. Flint for £6000.
Owner Middleham Park Racing XLII **Bred** David Barry **Trained** Constable Burton, N Yorks

FOCUS
A couple of fair sorts in an ordinary seller. The gallop was a moderate one and the proximity of the fifth and sixth holds the form down. The winner edged towards the far side in the closing stages.

3717 ENJOY THE PARTY PACK GROUP OFFER MEDIAN AUCTION MAIDEN STKS 1m 141y(P)
4:15 (4:15) (Class 6) 3-4-Y-O **£1,704** (£503; £251) **Stalls** Low

Form RPR

-523 **1** **Trumpington Street (IRE)**[15] 3236 3-9-3 78.................. WilliamBuick 1 75+
(John Gosden) *led: hdd over 7f out: chsd ldr tl led again over 1f out: sn hung lft: rdn ins fnl f: r.o* **10/11**[1]

6-03 **2** *shd* **Miss Exhibitionist**[25] 2883 3-8-12 72.......................... DaneO'Neill 3 70+
(James Eustace) *a.p: swtchd lft and chsd wnr ins fnl f: sn rdn and ev ch: r.o* **5/2**[2]

25 **3** *6* **Fog Cutter (IRE)**[81] 1376 3-9-3 0...................................(t) BACurtis 4 61
(James McAuley, Ire) *led over 7f out: rdn and hdd over 1f out: wknd ins fnl f* **28/1**

4 *1* **Spanish Plume** 3-9-3 0... GrahamGibbons 5 59
(Reg Hollinshead) *hld up: r.o ins fnl f: wnt 4th nr fin: nvr nrr* **33/1**

0-23 **5** *1/2* **Daddyow**[31] 2723 3-9-3 75.. DavidProbert 6 58
(Bryn Palling) *chsd ldrs: rdn over 2f out: hung lft and wknd ins fnl f* **11/2**[3]

-000 **6** *3 1/4* **Ollywood**[9] 3431 3-9-3 46.. LiamJones 2 50?
(Tony Carroll) *chsd ldrs: rdn over 2f out: wknd over 1f out* **150/1**

7 *nse* **Sister Andrea** 3-8-12 0.. ShaneKelly 8 45
(James Fanshawe) *s.i.s: swished tail and rn green in rr: shkn up over 2f out: sn wknd* **14/1**

0 **8** *6* **Patricias Pride**[27] 2813 4-9-8 0.................................... KieranO'Neill(5) 7 37
(Lucinda Featherstone) *sn pushed along in rr: rdn over 3f out: wknd 2f out* **150/1**

1m 50.23s (-0.27) **Going Correction** -0.125s/f (Stan)
WFA 3 from 4yo 10lb **8** Ran SP% **110.7**
Speed ratings (Par 101): **96,95,90,89,89 86,86,80**
toteswingers:1&2:£1.60, 2&3:£9.40, 1&3:£5.40 CSF £3.01 TOTE £2.10: £1.10, £1.20, £6.90; EX 3.90.
Owner Bailey, Hall & Hood **Bred** Eimear Mulhern J Flynn & Abbeville Stud **Trained** Newmarket, Suffolk

FOCUS
An uncompetitive maiden run at an ordinary gallop and one in which the two market leaders pulled clear in the closing stages. The winner raced towards the centre in the straight.

3718 GREAT OFFERS AT WOLVERHAMPTON-RACECOURSE.CO.UK MAIDEN AUCTION STKS 7f 32y(P)
4:45 (4:45) (Class 5) 2-Y-O **£2,045** (£603; £302) **Stalls** High

Form RPR

0 **1** **Meanwhile (IRE)**[28] 2787 2-8-4 0.. LiamJones 6 62
(William Knight) *in rr: hdwy u.p over 1f out: led ins fnl f: r.o* **10/1**

2 *1 3/4* **Lady Tycoon** 2-7-13 0.. KieranO'Neill(5) 2 57+
(Mark Brisbourne) *w ldr tl led 3f out: rdn and hdd ins fnl f: styd on same pce* **16/1**

5 **3** *5* **Bit A Craic**[12] 3302 2-8-4 0.. KirstyMilczarek 8 45
(John Ryan) *sn prom: outpcd 1/2-way: hdwy over 1f out: styd on: nt trble ldrs* **12/1**

06 **4** *3/4* **Ernest Speak (IRE)**[17] 3171 2-8-9 0..............................(p) KierenFox(3) 7 51
(Bill Turner) *chsd ldrs: rdn over 2f out: styd on same pce appr fnl f* **50/1**

5 *2 1/2* **Path Finder (FR)** 2-8-13 0.. GrahamGibbons 11 46
(Reg Hollinshead) *s.s: hld up: styd on ins fnl f: nvr nr to chal* **12/1**

5 **6** *1/2* **Tweet Lady**[20] 3046 2-8-8 0.. JamesMillman 9 40
(Rod Millman) *prom: rdn over 2f out: sn wknd* **9/2**[2]

23 **7** *3 3/4* **Goal Hanger**[11] 3336 2-8-8 0.. RussKennemore 4 31
(Tom Dascombe) *led 4f: sn rdn: wknd ins fnl f* **1/1**[1]

8 *6* **Our Monica (IRE)** 2-8-8 0 ow1.. DarrylHolland 3 16
(Ann Duffield) *hdwy over 5f out: rdn over 2f out: wknd over 1f out* **7/1**[3]

1m 29.89s (0.29) **Going Correction** -0.125s/f (Stan) **8** Ran SP% **113.0**
Speed ratings (Par 94): **93,91,85,84,81 81,76,69**
toteswingers:1&2:£20.60, 2&3:£18.50, 1&3:£9.20 CSF £147.21 TOTE £6.20: £1.40, £6.00, £2.80; EX 288.20.
Owner Red & White Racing **Bred** Gerard & Anne Corry **Trained** Patching, W Sussex

FOCUS
No more than a modest maiden and one that took less winning than had seemed likely beforehand, with the short-priced market leader disappointing. The gallop was only fair and the winner came down the centre.

NOTEBOOK
Meanwhile(IRE), who hinted at ability, despite greenness, on her debut, turned in an improved effort upped in trip on this AW bow. This wasn't much of a race and she isn't very big but should stay further (dam a dual 1m2f winner) and she may do better in run-of-the-mill nurseries. (tchd 12-1)
Lady Tycoon, a half-sister to a couple of 1m4f winners, showed ability at a modest level on this racecourse debut. Low-grade handicaps over further will provide her with her best chance of success in due course. (op 50-1)
Bit A Craic, who hinted at ability in a race that has already been franked on her debut at Hamilton, stepped up on that form over this longer trip on this different surface. She is another that may have more of a chance once qualified for a mark. (tchd 10-1)
Ernest Speak(IRE)'s proximity (tried in first-time cheekpieces) confirms this form is modest at best but he has a bit of physical scope and may do a bit better in handicaps over further. (op 40-1)
Path Finder(FR), a half-brother to a French 1m-1m2f winner, hinted at ability after a tardy start on this racecourse debut and should do better over further, though he'll have to improve significantly to win a similar event. (op 22-1)
Goal Hanger failed by a long chalk to reproduce her fair Chester run after racing with the choke out on this all-weather debut. She's better than this and may do better back on turf but wouldn't be one to go in head-down for next time after this tame effort. Official explanation: jockey said filly ran too freely (op 8-13)
Our Monica(IRE) Official explanation: jockey said filly ran too freely

3719 RINGSIDE CONFERENCE SUITE - 700 THEATRE STYLE H'CAP (DIV I) 7f 32y(P)
5:15 (5:15) (Class 6) (0-60,60) 3-Y-0+ **£1,363** (£402; £201) **Stalls** High

Form RPR

3010 **1** **Fortunate Bid (IRE)**[59] 1911 5-9-7 **57**......................(p) TonyHamilton 4 64+
(Linda Stubbs) *hld up: r.o u.p ins fnl f: led post* **7/1**

0-40 **2** *shd* **Meia Noite**[25] 2869 4-9-10 **60**.. GeorgeBaker 11 67
(Chris Wall) *led 6f out: sn hdd: remained w ldr tl led over 2f out: rdn over 1f out: hdd post* **13/2**[3]

5-00 **3** *nse* **Talent Scout (IRE)**[76] 1493 5-9-5 **55**.............................(b) LiamKeniry 3 62
(Tim Walford) *a.p: rdn over 1f out: r.o* **5/1**[2]

0033 **4** *3/4* **Pytheas (USA)**[7] 3477 4-9-2 **57**................................. MarkCoumbe(5) 2 62
(Michael Attwater) *chsd ldrs: rdn over 1f out: r.o* **5/1**[2]

6231 **5** *1/2* **This Ones For Eddy**[15] 3241 6-9-9 **59**.......................... GrahamGibbons 5 63+
(John Balding) *hld up: rdn over 1f out: hdwy over 1f out: r.o: nt rch ldrs* **3/1**[1]

4000 **6** *3/4* **Pilgrim Dancer (IRE)**[8] 3475 4-9-1 **58**.......................... DarylByrne(7) 10 60
(Patrick Morris) *led over 5f out: rdn and hdd over 2f out: no ex ins fnl f* **16/1**

-005 **7** *1 1/2* **Gazboolou**[12] 3326 7-9-10 **60**.. FergusSweeney 7 58
(David Pinder) *prom: rdn and ev ch over 2f out: no ex ins fnl f* **12/1**

020- **8** *1* **My Name Is Bert**[228] 7502 5-9-7 **57**..................................... DaneO'Neill 8 52
(Lucinda Featherstone) *led 1f: chsd ldrs: rdn over 2f out: no ex ins fnl f* **8/1**

0-R0 **9** *shd* **Erfaan (USA)**[35] 2593 4-9-0 **50**.. BarryMcHugh 6 47
(Julie Camacho) *s.i.s: hld up: hdwy over 2f out: sn rdn: no ex ins fnl f* **66/1**

-560 **10** *8* **Yes We Can**[24] 2920 4-9-0 **55**.................................(p) KieranO'Neill(5) 1 28
(Jeremy Gask) *hld up: rdn 1/2-way: wknd 2f out* **12/1**

1m 28.92s (-0.68) **Going Correction** -0.125s/f (Stan) **10** Ran SP% **118.0**
Speed ratings (Par 101): **98,97,97,96,96 95,93,92,92,83**
toteswingers:1&2:£9.00, 2&3:£4.70, 1&3:£6.40 CSF £52.66 CT £257.00 TOTE £11.10: £2.80, £2.50, £2.50; EX 55.20.
Owner Mrs L Stubbs **Bred** E O'Leary **Trained** Norton, N Yorks

FOCUS
A modest handicap run at just an ordinary gallop and one in which the first five finished in a heap. The winner raced centre-to-far side in the straight.
Erfaan(USA) Official explanation: trainer's rep said gelding suffered interference in running

3720 RINGSIDE CONFERENCE SUITE - 700 THEATRE STYLE H'CAP (DIV II) 7f 32y(P)
5:45 (5:46) (Class 6) (0-60,60) 3-Y-0+ **£1,363** (£402; £201) **Stalls** High

Form RPR

0000 **1** **Ensnare**[60] 1868 6-9-5 **55**.. StevieDonohoe 6 69
(Noel Quinlan) *chsd ldr tl led over 2f out: rdn clr ins fnl f: comf* **11/2**[2]

0-00 **2** *2 3/4* **Istiqdaam**[85] 1276 6-9-10 **60**......................................(b) GrahamGibbons 8 69+
(Michael Easterby) *hld up in tch: hmpd 2f out: rdn to chse wnr fnl f: no imp* **4/1**[1]

6-00 **3** *1 1/2* **Annes Rocket (IRE)**[13] 3293 6-9-4 **59**......................... KieranO'Neill(5) 4 62
(Jimmy Fox) *s.i.s: hld up: hdwy over 1f out: r.o: nt rch ldrs* **14/1**

206 **4** *1 1/4* **Tudor Prince (IRE)**[90] 1177 7-9-7 **57**............................... DavidProbert 9 57
(Tony Carroll) *prom: rdn over 2f out: no ex ins fnl f* **11/1**

2230 **5** *1* **Gold Story**[56] 1979 4-9-7 **57**..(p) LiamKeniry 5 54
(Chris Gordon) *prom: rdn over 1f out: no ex* **28/1**

100 **6** *3 3/4* **El Libertador (USA)**[25] 2870 5-9-9 **59**.........................(b) GeorgeBaker 12 46
(Jeremy Gask) *hld up: hdwy 2f out: sn rdn: wknd ins fnl f* **8/1**[3]

0-26 **7** *3/4* **Breezed Well (IRE)**[52] 1380 4-9-5 **55**................................(t) BACurtis 10 40
(James McAuley, Ire) *hld up: rdn over 2f out: nvr on terms* **20/1**

0000 **8** *3* **Bishopbriggs (USA)**[15] 3241 6-9-1 **58**............................ AntiocoMurgia(7) 11 35
(K F Clutterbuck) *hld up: rdn over 2f out: n.d* **40/1**

2004 **9** *1/2* **Lily Wood**[15] 3241 5-9-0 **50**...(p) LiamJones 3 25
(James Unett) *chsd ldrs: led 3f out: sn rdn and hdd: wknd over 1f out* **14/1**

4665 **10** *1/2* **The Name Is Frank**[13] 3293 6-9-7 **57**..........................(t) FergusSweeney 1 31
(Mark Gillard) *a in rr* **16/1**

0-05 **11** *1 1/2* **Ari Gold (IRE)**[40] 2419 3-9-0 **58**..................................(p) RussKennemore 7 28
(Tom Dascombe) *chsd ldrs: rdn over 3f out: wknd over 1f out* **8/1**[3]

4601 **12** *11* **Meydan Style (USA)**[15] 3234 5-9-1 **51**.......................... WilliamBuick 2 —
(Bruce Hellier) *led: rdn and hdd 3f out: wknd 2f out* **4/1**[1]

1m 27.82s (-1.78) **Going Correction** -0.125s/f (Stan)
WFA 3 from 4yo+ 8lb **12** Ran SP% **115.8**
Speed ratings (Par 101): **105,101,100,98,97 93,92,89,88,87 86,73**
toteswingers:1&2:£5.10, 2&3:£14.20, 1&3:£19.80 Tote Super 7: Win: Not won. Place: Not won. CSF £26.40 CT £293.25 TOTE £6.70: £1.70, £2.10, £4.00; EX 35.10.
Owner C Owen **Bred** Cheveley Park Stud Ltd **Trained** Newmarket, Suffolk

FOCUS
Division two of a modest handicap in which the best backed runners finished first and second. The gallop was fair and the winner raced centre-to-far-side.
Ensnare ◆ Official explanation: trainer's rep said, regarding apparent improvement in form, that the gelding appears to have benefited from a two-month break, first-time blindfold in stalls, which helped it gain a prominent position from the outset and racing over a shorter distance.
The Name Is Frank Official explanation: jockey said gelding reared as stalls opened
T/Plt: £182.50 to a £1 stake. Pool of £64,402.62 - 257.50 winning units. T/Qpdt: £24.50 to a £1 stake. Pool £6,029.18 - 181.41 winning units. CR

3266 BATH (L-H)
Wednesday, July 6

OFFICIAL GOING: Firm (9.9)
Wind: Strong across Weather: Sunny periods and showers

3721 DIGIBET.COM H'CAP — 5f 11y
2:10 (2:10) (Class 6) (0-65,60) 3-Y-0+ — **£1,617** (£481; £240; £120) **Stalls** Centre

Form — RPR

-30 **1** **Jolly Ranch**[119] 812 5-9-0 **48**........ SteveDrowne 10 — 62
(Tony Newcombe) *chsd ldrs: drvn to ld 1f out: styd on strly clsng stages* **8/1**[3]

0-0 **2** *1 3/4* **My Meteor**[109] 912 4-9-0 **48**........ DaneO'Neill 11 — 56
(Tony Newcombe) *chsd ldrs: rdn 2f out: kpt on to go 2nd ins fnl f but no imp on wnr clsng stages* **33/1**

4-00 **3** *1 1/4* **Ridgeway Sapphire**[37] 2554 4-8-11 **45**........(v) RobertHavlin 3 — 48
(Mark Usher) *in rr tl pushed along and hdwy over 1f out: styd on ins fnl f to take 3rd clsng stages but no ch w ldng duo* **11/1**

-000 **4** *3/4* **Madam Isshe**[16] 3216 4-9-5 **53**........ TomMcLaughlin 12 — 54
(Malcolm Saunders) *a chsng ldrs: drvn along 2f out: styd on ins fnl f and gng on clsng stages but nvr a threat to ldng duo* **20/1**

0-06 **5** *3/4* **Flaxen Lake**[9] 3471 4-9-0 **48**........ CathyGannon 7 — 46
(Milton Bradley) *broke wl: outpcd 1/2-way: styd on u.p over 1f out: kpt on cl home* **16/1**

4222 **6** *1/2* **Talamahana**[2] 3678 6-9-6 **54**........ ChrisCatlin 13 — 50
(Andrew Haynes) *bmpd s: in rr and stl plenty to do appr fnl f: r.o wl clsng stages: gng on cl home* **9/2**[1]

5-43 **7** *1/2* **Lisselton Cross**[103] 958 3-9-2 **55**........ GeorgeBaker 5 — 47
(Martin Bosley) *bmpd s: sn in tch: hdwy 2f out: chsd ldrs over 1f out: one pce ins fnl f* **10/1**

6-00 **8** *nse* **Best One**[163] 276 7-9-4 **52**........(b) DavidProbert 2 — 46
(Ronald Harris) *chsd ldr: led briefly over 1f out: sn hdd: wknd ins fnl f* **16/1**

5043 **9** *nk* **Bateleur**[22] 3020 7-9-12 **60**........ HughBowman 8 — 53
(Mick Channon) *chsd ldrs: rdn and no imp fr 2f out: wknd ins fnl f* **5/1**[2]

0653 **10** *2* **Lithaam (IRE)**[16] 3216 7-8-12 **46**........(tp) RussKennemore 4 — 32
(Milton Bradley) *chsd ldrs tl wknd appr fnl f* **11/1**

2524 **11** *1/2* **Decider (USA)**[9] 3471 8-9-9 **57**........(b) KirstyMilczarek 9 — 41
(Ronald Harris) *sn led: hdd over 1f out: sn btn* **5/1**[2]

-040 **12** *3 3/4* **Perlachy**[164] 269 7-9-12 **60**........(v) KellyHarrison 1 — 30
(Ronald Harris) *outpcd* **11/1**

62.09 secs (-0.41) **Going Correction** -0.075s/f (Good)
WFA 3 from 4yo+ 5lb — **12** Ran SP% **116.2**
Speed ratings (Par 101): **100,97,95,94,92 92,91,91,90,87 86,80**
toteswingers:1&2:£31.00, 2&3:£61.20, 1&3:£19.30 CSF £236.11 CT £2924.29 TOTE £9.20: £3.20, £13.50, £4.50; EX 220.70 TRIFECTA Not won..
Owner Joli Racing **Bred** C G Reid **Trained** Yarnscombe, Devon

FOCUS
An ordinary sprint handicap and a one-two for Tony Newcombe. Whether the forecast was landed, possibly one of the last avenues still left open for a successful gamble, is unknown, but both the winner and runner-up, who had missed several engagements for various reasons over the past few months and rocked up here having not run since March, looked interesting in this company on the best of their form.

3722 BRITISH STALLION STUDS SUPPORTING BRITISH RACING E B F MAIDEN STKS — 5f 11y
2:40 (2:41) (Class 5) 2-Y-0 — **£2,911** (£866; £432; £216) **Stalls** Centre

Form — RPR

P20 **1** **Hidden Passion (USA)**[11] 3402 2-8-12 0........(t) ShaneKelly 2 — 82+
(Brian Meehan) *hld up in bhd ldrs: qcknd on inner 1f out: led gng wl fnl 120yds: easily* **4/11**[1]

2 *1 1/2* **Blanc De Chine (IRE)** 2-8-12 0........ SteveDrowne 8 — 72
(Peter Makin) *sn led: rdn and kpt on ins fnl f tl hdd and readily outpcd by wnr fnl 120yds* **18/1**[3]

4 **3** *2 3/4* **Thirsty Bear**[19] 3132 2-9-3 0........ J-PGuillambert 9 — 67
(Rebecca Curtis) *chsd ldr: hrd drvn over 1f out: outpcd by ldng duo ins fnl f* **7/2**[2]

00 **4** *1/2* **Mister Musicmaster**[26] 2880 2-9-3 0........ JamesMillman 7 — 65+
(Rod Millman) *in rr: rdn 1/2-way: hdwy 1f out and sn swtchd lft to inner: kpt on clsng stages to take 4th cl home but nvr a danger* **40/1**

5 *3/4* **Mae Rose Cottage (IRE)** 2-8-5 0........ JacobMoore(7) 4 — 58
(Hughie Morrison) *chsd ldrs: pushed along over 1f out: nt qckn ins fnl f and lost 4th cl home* **28/1**

6 *6* **Royal Trix** 2-8-5 0........ KatiaScallan(7) 1 — 35
(Marcus Tregoning) *in rr and detached after 2f and green: sme prog ins fnl f* **25/1**

00 **7** *1/2* **Jawim**[51] 2143 2-8-12 0........ TomMcLaughlin 5 — 34
(Malcolm Saunders) *led briefly early: styd prom tl wknd ins fnl 2f* **100/1**

00 **8** *19* **Doctor Banner**[14] 3288 2-9-3 0........ HughBowman 3 — —
(Mick Channon) *a in rr: lost tch 2f out: eased whn no ch fnl f* **20/1**

62.00 secs (-0.50) **Going Correction** -0.075s/f (Good) — **8** Ran SP% **116.3**
Speed ratings (Par 94): **101,98,94,93,92 82,81,51**
toteswingers:1&2:£3.40, 2&3:£4.70, 1&3:£1.10 CSF £8.34 TOTE £1.40: £1.10, £3.40, £1.10; EX 13.00 Trifecta £18.50 Pool: £359.22 - 14.31 winning units..
Owner Andrew Rosen **Bred** Andrew Rosen **Trained** Manton, Wilts
■ Emerald Smile (12/1) was withdrawn after refusing to enter the stalls. Deduct 5p in the 3 under R4.

FOCUS
Not a bad maiden, but the classy winner was too good for the rest.

NOTEBOOK
Hidden Passion(USA), having travelled smoothly, she had no trouble quickening up and beating this lot. She did no more than her previous form in better company suggested she should, and whether the first-time tongue tie had any beneficial effect is moot. (op 4-9 tchd 1-2 in places)
Blanc De Chine(IRE), a newcomer by Dark Angel, ran a perfectly satisfactory race against a rival whose last two RPRs were in the 80s. She should come on for the run. (op 20-1)
Thirsty Bear, a solid fourth on her debut over 6f at Newmarket, found the drop back to the minimum against him. (tchd 4-1)
Mister Musicmaster, having his third run, still looked green. Nurseries will offer him better opportunities. (op 50-1)
Mae Rose Cottage(IRE) is out of a 5f winner but she'll probably want further than this as she's by Dylan Thomas. Not knocked about by her inexperienced rider, she should come on plenty for the experience.

3723 VISIT BATH H'CAP — 5f 161y
3:10 (3:10) (Class 5) (0-75,74) 3-Y-0 — **£2,264** (£673; £336; £168) **Stalls** Centre

Form — RPR

216 **1** **Redvers (IRE)**[21] 3048 3-9-7 **74**........ JimCrowley 1 — 83+
(Ralph Beckett) *hld up in tch: travelling wl but nt clr run fr ins fnl 2f and stl n.m.r ins fnl f: drvn and qcknd between horses fnl 120yds: edgd lft: led last strides: readily* **7/4**[1]

0252 **2** *hd* **Sarangoo**[14] 3272 3-8-5 **58**........ NickyMackay 4 — 64
(Malcolm Saunders) *trckd ldrs: rdn and hdwy over 1f out: chal ins fnl f and slt ld fnl 120yds: hdd last strides* **10/3**[2]

1-62 **3** *1/2* **Yasmeena (USA)**[14] 3271 3-9-2 **69**........ TadhgO'Shea 5 — 73
(B W Hills) *s.i.s: in rr and t.k.h: hdwy fr 2f out: drvn to chal fnl 100yds: no ex cl home* **9/2**[3]

-103 **4** *1 1/4* **Swendab (IRE)**[14] 3271 3-8-13 **66**........ DarryllHolland 6 — 66
(John O'Shea) *sn led: rdn over 1f out: kpt slt advantage tl hdd fnl 120yds: edgd rt and wknd cl home* **9/1**

0-43 **5** *nse* **Thunda**[13] 3324 3-9-1 **68**........ CathyGannon 3 — 68
(Eve Johnson Houghton) *chsd ldrs: chal 1f out and stl upsides fnl 100yds: one pce whn hmpd cl home* **9/2**[3]

-040 **6** *1* **Diamond Vine (IRE)**[25] 2916 3-9-5 **72**........(p) TomMcLaughlin 2 — 68
(Ronald Harris) *chsd ldrs tl outpcd fnl f* **12/1**

1m 10.94s (-0.26) **Going Correction** -0.075s/f (Good) — **6** Ran SP% **113.5**
Speed ratings (Par 100): **98,97,97,95,95 94**
toteswingers:1&2:£1.90, 2&3:£2.10, 1&3:£1.80 CSF £7.96 TOTE £2.50: £1.80, £2.90; EX 9.90.
Owner R A Pegum **Bred** Peter Jones And G G Jones **Trained** Kimpton, Hants

FOCUS
Quite a tight little handicap on paper and, while there was quite a bunched finish, Redvers won with a lot more in hand than the margin suggests.

3724 BATH CHRONICLE H'CAP — 5f 161y
3:40 (3:45) (Class 6) (0-55,56) 3-Y-0 — **£1,617** (£481; £240; £120) **Stalls** Centre

Form — RPR

1053 **1** **Dreams Of Glory**[14] 3272 3-8-7 **46**........ DavidProbert 11 — 55
(Ron Hodges) *mde all: drvn over 1f out: styd on strly ins fnl f* **5/1**[2]

3200 **2** *1 3/4* **Cathcart Castle**[16] 3223 3-9-2 **55**........(v[1]) HughBowman 1 — 58
(Mick Channon) *trckd ldrs on ins: rdn to chse wnr ins fnl f: kpt on for clr 2nd but no imp clsng stages* **6/1**[3]

3005 **3** *4 1/2* **Local Diktator**[13] 3309 3-9-2 **55**........ TomMcLaughlin 12 — 43
(Ronald Harris) *in rr: hdwy 2f out: styd on to chse ldng duo fnl f but nvr any ch* **28/1**

0000 **4** *shd* **Lady Excellentia (IRE)**[14] 3272 3-8-7 **46** oh1........ ChrisCatlin 16 — 34+
(Ronald Harris) *s.i.s: in rr: hdwy 2f out: kpt on fnl f to press for 4th cl home but no ch w ldrs* **66/1**

0005 **5** *2 1/2* **Crazy In Love**[15] 3248 3-8-7 **46** oh1........(b) NickyMackay 3 — 26
(Olivia Maylam) *reluctant to load: disp 2nd and rdn 3f out: one pce fr over 1f out* **33/1**

5514 **6** *1/2* **Chester Deelyte (IRE)**[18] 3192 3-8-13 **52**........(v) JimCrowley 4 — 30+
(Lisa Williamson) *in rr: hdwy 2f out: nvr rchd ldrs and wknd ins fnl f* **14/1**

000 **7** *1 1/4* **Hertford Street**[29] 2790 3-9-0 **53**........ SteveDrowne 2 — 27+
(Peter Makin) *s.i.s: in rr: swtchd to outside fr 2f out: sme prog ins fnl f* **11/1**

545 **8** *nse* **Bambika**[18] 3173 3-9-2 **55**........ DaneO'Neill 7 — 29
(Jo Crowley) *chsd ldrs: rdn 3f out: wknd: appr fnl f* **12/1**

450 **9** *1 1/4* **Celestial Flyer (IRE)**[16] 3227 3-8-0 **46** oh1........ CharlesBishop(7) 5 — 16
(Tor Sturgis) *s.i.s: hdwy on inner 2f out: nvr rchd ldrs and no ch fnl f* **18/1**

000- **10** *3/4* **Arakova (IRE)**[350] 4254 3-8-12 **56** ow3........ LeeNewnes(5) 9 — 23
(Matthew Salaman) *chsd ldrs: rdn 1/2-way: wknd wl over 1f out* **20/1**

050 **11** *3 1/2* **Mistress Quick**[20] 3090 3-8-8 **50**........ JohnFahy(3) 6 — —
(Ben De Haan) *in tch: rdn 2f out: sn btn* **17/2**

-002 **12** *3/4* **Cannon Bolt (IRE)**[9] 3455 3-8-7 **46** oh1........(b) CathyGannon 8 — —
(Robin Bastiman) *pressed ldrs:* [illegible] **7/2**[1]

00-0 **13** *3 1/4* **Zartina (IRE)**[14] 3289 3-9-1 **54**........ LiamKeniry 14 — —
(Sylvester Kirk) *a struggling to go pce* **25/1**

5666 **14** *1 1/4* **Silca Conegliano (IRE)**[14] 3272 3-8-11 **50**........ SamHitchcott 17 — —
(Mick Channon) *in rr: sme hdwy on outside over 2f out: sn btn* **14/1**

0000 **15** *1/2* **Heart Felt**[57] 1985 3-8-7 **46** oh1........(b) AndrewHeffernan 10 — —
(Roy Brotherton) *chsd ldrs on outside 1/2-way: sn wknd* **33/1**

600 **16** *2 1/2* **Elite Syncopations**[61] 1865 3-8-12 **51**........ RobertHavlin 13 — —
(Andrew Haynes) *chsd ldrs on outside to 1/2-way* **20/1**

1m 11.37s (0.17) **Going Correction** -0.075s/f (Good) — **16** Ran SP% **122.5**
Speed ratings (Par 98): **95,92,86,86,83 82,80,80,79,78 73,72,68,66,65 62**
toteswingers:1&2:£7.60, 2&3:£30.20, 1&3:£24.80 CSF £32.09 CT £815.53 TOTE £6.80: £2.10, £1.50, £6.00, £7.90; EX 29.20 Trifecta £379.80 Part won. Pool of £513.24 - 0.20 winning units..
Owner P E Axon **Bred** P E Axon **Trained** Charlton Mackrell, Somerset

FOCUS
An ordinary sprint but probably solid enough form for the level.
Chester Deelyte(IRE) Official explanation: jockey said filly was denied a clear run
Cannon Bolt(IRE) Official explanation: jockey said gelding never travelled

3725 BATH ABBEY H'CAP — 2m 1f 34y
4:10 (4:10) (Class 4) (0-80,77) 4-Y-0+ — **£2,587** (£770; £384; £192) **Stalls** Centre

Form — RPR

61/0 **1** **Praxiteles (IRE)**[14] 3277 7-9-5 **75**........(tp) J-PGuillambert 1 — 83+
(Rebecca Curtis) *trckd ldr after 5f: led over 2f out: sn clr: v easily* **2/1**[1]

-525 **2** *4* **Sunny Future (IRE)**[10] 3428 5-9-3 **73**........ TomMcLaughlin 4 — 74
(Malcolm Saunders) *in rr but in tch: pushed along 4f out: styd on towards outside over 2f out: wnt 2nd appr fnl f but nvr any ch w v easy wnr* **11/4**[2]

000- **3** *1 1/2* **Callisto Moon**[39] 6715 7-9-7 **77**........(v[1]) DarryllHolland 3 — 76
(Jo Hughes) *led: quite keen but under control: qcknd 5f out: hdd over 2f out: sn no ch w wnr: lost 2nd appr fnl f and kpt on same pce* **3/1**[3]

06 **4** *6* **Emrani (USA)**[60] 1901 4-9-7 **77**........(p) EddieAhern 7 — 70
(Donald McCain) *chsd ldr 5f: styd wl there and drvn to dispute 2nd again over 4f out: wknd u.p over 2f out* **10/1**

2530 **5** *22* **Stormy Morning**[26] 2873 5-8-8 **64**........(p) LiamKeniry 5 — 41
(J S Moore) *in rr but in tch: hdwy into 4th 1/2-way: rdn and wknd over 3f out: eased whn no ch appr fnl f* **11/2**

3m 52.17s (0.27) **Going Correction** -0.075s/f (Good) — **5** Ran SP% **109.5**
Speed ratings (Par 105): **96,94,93,90,80**
CSF £7.65 TOTE £3.40: £1.70, £3.00; EX 9.70.

Owner Los Amigos **Bred** Ballymacoll Stud Farm Ltd **Trained** Newport, Dyfed
FOCUS
Two of these were unexposed over this sort of trip on the Flat and they filled the first two places.

3726 BATH TOURISM PLUS H'CAP — 1m 2f 46y
4:40 (4:41) (Class 6) (0-65,65) 3-Y-0+ — **£1,617** (£481; £240; £120) **Stalls** Low

Form — RPR
-046 **1** **Monicalew**[44] 2349 3-9-3 **65** .... EddieAhern 7 — 75
(Walter Swinburn) *wl there and chsd ldrs fr 3f out: rdn to go 2nd ins fnl 2f: styd on u.p ins fnl f to ld cl home* **4/1**[2]
0000 **2** *nk* **Tegan (IRE)**[36] 2583 3-8-0 **47** ow1 .... FrankieMcDonald 6 — 57+
(Richard Hannon) *in rr and hmpd bnd ins fnl 5f: hdwy 3f out: styd on and nt clr whn hanging lft fr over 1f out: stl hanging ins fnl f: styd on cl home to take 2nd but nt rch wnr* **16/1**
6113 **3** *1/2* **Miss Blink**[13] 3301 4-9-12 **63** .... CathyGannon 10 — 72+
(Robin Bastiman) *in rr and sltly hmpd bnd ins fnl 5f: hdwy over 3f out: chal 2f out: led sn after but hanging lft u.p ins fnl f: stmbld fnl 160yds: no ex and hdd cl home* **10/3**[1]
0100 **4** *6* **Zagarock**[7] 3516 4-9-0 **51** .... (p) NeilChalmers 2 — 47
(Bryn Palling) *chsd ldr 3f: styd wl there and lft in 2nd bnd ins fnl 5f: led 4f out: hdd ins fnl 2f: wknd over 1f out* **9/1**
4434 **5** *3* **Goose Green (IRE)**[2] 2900 7-9-1 **52** .... (t) GeorgeBaker 1 — 42
(Ron Hodges) *sn wl there: chsd ldrs over 3f out: wknd wl over 1f out* **9/1**
0002 **6** *10* **Excellent Vision**[8] 3480 4-9-0 **51** .... (t) LiamKeniry 3 — 21
(Milton Bradley) *in rr: hdwy 4f out and chsd ldrs sn after: wknd 2f out* **16/1**
000 **7** *23* **Mistress Shy**[41] 2420 4-8-2 **46** oh1 .... (t) SophieSilvester(7) 8 — —
(Robin Dickin) *broke wl: in rr whn sltly hmpd bnd ins fnl 5f* **100/1**
40-0 **8** *24* **Transeggselence**[21] 3043 4-9-1 **55** .... MarkLawson(3) 5 — —
(Gary Harrison) *plld hrd: sn chsng ldr and led 7f out: hdd & wknd rapidly 4f out* **66/1**
0225 **S** **Aviso (GER)**[19] 3130 7-9-9 **63** .... RichardEvans(3) 9 — —
(David Evans) *led tl hdd 7f out: stl cl 2nd whn slipped up bnd ins fnl 5f* **9/2**[3]
3406 **B** **Leitzu (IRE)**[16] 3228 4-9-11 **62** .... HughBowman 4 — —
(Mick Channon) *mid-div whn hmpd and b.d bnd ins fnl 5f* **11/2**

2m 9.95s (-1.05) **Going Correction** -0.075s/f (Good)
WFA 3 from 4yo+ 11lb — **10 Ran SP% 110.9**
Speed ratings (Par 101): **101,100,100,95,93 85,66,47,—,—**
toteswingers:1&2:£16.00, 2&3:£10.90, 1&3:£3.90 CSF £61.87 CT £224.47 TOTE £6.20: £2.50, £6.50, £1.70; EX 67.00 Trifecta £332.70 Part won. Pool of £449.63 - 0.20 winning units..
Owner Mrs Doreen M Swinburn **Bred** Genesis Green Stud Ltd **Trained** Aldbury, Herts
FOCUS
The incident on the bend with over 4f to run in which Aviso lost his footing and fell, sending his rider crashing to the ground and in turn causing Hugh Bowman to be unseated from Leitzu, resulted in the final race on the card being abandoned on safety grounds.

3727 ROMAN BATHS H'CAP — 1m 5y
() (Class 5) (0-75,) 3-Y-0+ — £

T/Plt: £160.40 to a £1 stake. Pool of £66,031.82 - 300.47 winning tickets. T/Qpdt: £9.80 to a £1 stake. Pool of £5,897.15 - 443.75 winning tickets. ST

3504 CATTERICK (L-H)
Wednesday, July 6

OFFICIAL GOING: Good to firm (good in places; 8.5)
Wind: light 1/2 behind Weather: overcast, showers at first, becoming fine and sunny

3728 YORKSHIRE-OUTDOORS.CO.UK CLAIMING STKS — 5f
2:20 (2:21) (Class 6) 2-Y-0 — **£1,704** (£503; £251) **Stalls** Low

Form — RPR
660 **1** **Lady Caprice**[7] 3504 2-8-7 0 .... (b[1]) SilvestreDeSousa 6 — 57
(Ann Duffield) *mde all: swtchd lft after 1f: kpt on wl ins fnl f: unchal* **4/1**[2]
660 **2** *1 1/4* **Sonko (IRE)**[26] 2889 2-8-7 0 ow2 .... (p) SeanLevey(3) 10 — 56
(Tim Pitt) *sn chsng ldrs: wnt 2nd over 1f out: no imp* **25/1**
045 **3** *2 1/2* **Justine Time (IRE)**[22] 3021 2-8-6 0 .... (b[1]) LeeNewman 2 — 43
(David Barron) *chsd ldrs: outpcd over 1f out: styd on fnl 150yds* **9/1**
00 **4** *3/4* **Cooldine Cat (IRE)**[14] 3273 2-9-1 0 .... (v[1]) TomEaves 8 — 49
(John Quinn) *chsd ldrs: kpt on same pce over 1f out* **11/1**
5613 **5** *3/4* **The Dancing Lord**[25] 2902 2-8-11 0 .... JakePayne(7) 3 — 54
(Bill Turner) *chsd ldrs: stmbld after 1f: unbalanced and wandered over 1f out: sn wknd* **8/11**[1]
050 **6** *nk* **Only Orsenfoolsies**[29] 2780 2-8-10 0 .... FrederikTylicki 5 — 40
(Micky Hammond) *mid-div: stmbld over 2f out: kpt on ins fnl f* **40/1**
7 *1* **Lady Jourdain (IRE)** 2-8-11 0 .... AndrewElliott 11 — 37+
(Mrs K Burke) *wnt rt s: in rr: kpt on ins fnl f* **20/1**
00 **8** *6* **Ruskins View (IRE)**[22] 3021 2-8-7 0 .... PatrickMathers 7 — 12
(Alan Berry) *s.i.s: a towards rr* **200/1**
0 **9** *1 1/4* **Come On Dave (IRE)**[22] 3021 2-8-12 0 .... AdrianNicholls 9 — 12
(David Nicholls) *chsd ldrs: wknd over 1f out* **17/2**[3]
500 **10** *2 1/4* **Maria Anna (IRE)**[13] 3302 2-8-7 0 .... (p) RoystonFfrench 1 — —
(Ann Duffield) *s.i.s: in rr: bhd fnl 2f* **66/1**
00 **11** *5* **Low Pastures**[16] 3237 2-9-0 0 .... JamesSullivan 4 — —
(Michael Easterby) *dwlt: in rr: bhd fnl 2f* **125/1**

60.88 secs (1.08) **Going Correction** +0.025s/f (Good) — **11 Ran SP% 120.6**
Speed ratings (Par 92): **92,90,86,84,83 83,81,71,69,66 58**
toteswingers:1&2:£7.50, 2&3:£19.80, 1&3:£3.20 CSF £103.26 TOTE £3.30: £1.30, £5.10, £2.80; EX 78.10.
Owner Mrs A Cantillon **Bred** Lady Betambeau Partnership **Trained** Constable Burton, N Yorks
FOCUS
It rained in the hours before racing and riders in the first suggested that it was just starting to get into the ground. The time for the opener was only just over two seconds outside standard though, suggesting that conditions were still relatively quick at this stage. A weak claimer, contested by just one previous winner, the odds-on favourite. With him disappointing the race took little winning.
NOTEBOOK
Lady Caprice looked the main threat to the favourite on the figures and she stepped up on her previous efforts, breaking well and making just about all. The first-time blinkers helped, but it remains to be seen if they work as well again. (op 6-1 tchd 13-2 in a place)
Sonko(IRE), whose rider could only claim a pound of his 3lb allowance, was tried in cheekpieces for the first time. This half-sister to prolific sprinter Gone'N'Dunnett was not well drawn but came through for second without looking like getting to the winner. She is clearly moderate but may improve a bit further. (op 28-1)
Justine Time(IRE) plugged on for third but in truth was well held by the front pair. Connections had swapped cheekpieces for blinkers. (op 10-1 tchd 11-1)
Cooldine Cat(IRE), another in first-time headgear, was not discredited down in grade and is now eligible for nurseries. (op 9-1)
The Dancing Lord had two wins to his name and had an obvious form chance. He was well drawn too, but slipped after a furlong, hitting the rail, and was again unbalanced as he chased the leaders heading to the furlong pole. Relegated two places late on, he has an inconsistent profile. He was reported to have lost his action. Official explanation: jockey said gelding lost its action (op 10-11 tchd Evens)
Lady Jourdain(IRE) ◆, a half-sister to three minor sprint winners, shaped with a little promise. She looked green early but came home quite well from the back and will know a lot more next time. There could be a seller for her. (op 18-1 tchd 16-1)
Come On Dave(IRE) came in for support down in trip, but after chasing the pace he faded badly late on. At least there was no repeat of the hanging he displayed on his debut. (op 8-1 tchd 9-1)

3729 BOOK TICKETS ON-LINE AT CATTERICKBRIDGE.CO.UK H'CAP — 7f
2:50 (2:50) (Class 5) (0-75,74) 3-Y-0 — **£2,070** (£616; £307; £153) **Stalls** Low

Form — RPR
45-0 **1** **Ingleby Exceed (IRE)**[36] 2592 3-8-11 **64** .... SilvestreDeSousa 2 — 74
(David O'Meara) *in rr: reminders after 1f: hdwy and swtchd rt over 2f out: styd on wl to ld last 75yds: readily* **5/1**[3]
0242 **2** *2 1/2* **Finefrenzyrolling (IRE)**[4] 3638 3-8-9 **65** .... (bt) PatrickDonaghy(3) 1 — 68
(Mrs K Burke) *trckd ldrs: wnt 2nd over 2f out: upsides ins fnl f: no ex* **5/2**[1]
0031 **3** *2 1/2* **Cheylesmore (IRE)**[2] 3674 3-8-13 **66** 6ex .... (v) GrahamGibbons 3 — 62
(Stuart Williams) *led over 5f out: sent 3 l clr over 2f out: hdd ins fnl f: sn wknd: eased nr fin* **11/4**[2]
-035 **4** *6* **In Babylon (GER)**[61] 1869 3-8-6 **64** .... (p) DaleSwift(5) 6 — 44
(Ann Duffield) *trckd ldrs: drvn and outpcd over 2f out: hung rt: one pce* **15/2**
-020 **5** *3 3/4* **Rapturous Applause**[53] 2119 3-8-8 **61** .... TomEaves 4 — 31
(Micky Hammond) *led over 1f: chsd ldrs: wknd over 1f out* **20/1**
3004 **6** *3 1/2* **Prince Of Passion (CAN)**[13] 3318 3-8-12 **65** .... (b) FrederikTylicki 7 — 25
(Michael Dods) *sn chsng ldrs on outer: lost pl over 2f out: sn bhd* **15/2**
6-65 **7** *1 1/4* **Free Art**[5] 3571 3-9-7 **74** .... (p) TonyHamilton 5 — 31
(Geoffrey Harker) *in rr: lost pl over 2f out: sn bhd* **8/1**

1m 26.6s (-0.40) **Going Correction** +0.025s/f (Good) — **7 Ran SP% 111.3**
Speed ratings (Par 100): **103,100,97,90,86 82,80**
CSF £16.93 TOTE £5.70: £1.80, £1.70; EX 23.60.
Owner Dave Scott **Bred** Dave Scott **Trained** Nawton, N Yorks
FOCUS
A very modest handicap, run at a brisk pace. The form is best rated around the runner-up.

3730 TURMERIC H'CAP — 1m 7f 177y
3:20 (3:20) (Class 4) (0-85,82) 3-Y-0+ — **£4,204** (£1,251; £625; £312) **Stalls** Low

Form — RPR
0012 **1** **Rosewin (IRE)**[13] 3316 5-9-5 **78** .... JulieBurke(5) 3 — 89
(Ollie Pears) *s.s: hld up in rr: hdwy 4f out: chal on ins over 1f out: edgd rt ins fnl f: led nr fin* **9/2**[1]
-651 **2** *hd* **Los Nadis (GER)**[9] 3450 7-9-0 **68** 6ex .... LeeNewman 7 — 78
(Jim Goldie) *trckd ldrs: drvn over 4f out: ed over 2f out: edgd rt: edgd lft ins fnl f: no ex and hdd nr fin* **7/1**
0060 **3** *6* **Cat O' Nine Tails**[19] 3115 4-9-5 **73** .... SilvestreDeSousa 5 — 75
(Mark Johnston) *sn chsng ldrs: chal over 2f out: one pce over 1f out* **5/1**[2]
-006 **4** *2 1/4* **Danceintothelight**[7] 3507 4-8-10 **64** .... FrederikTylicki 9 — 63
(Micky Hammond) *trckd ldrs: effrt over 2f out: one pce* **5/1**[2]
0152 **5** *2 3/4* **King's Counsel (IRE)**[9] 3453 5-9-0 **68** .... (b) DanielTudhope 10 — 64
(David O'Meara) *led: hdd over 2f out: wknd appr fnl f* **11/2**[3]
-543 **6** *11* **Puy D'Arnac (FR)**[19] 3115 8-8-12 **66** .... TomEaves 2 — 47
(George Moore) *mid-div: effrt over 3f out: drvn and outpcd over 2f out: nvr a factor* **8/1**
0616 **7** *2 1/2* **Jackday (IRE)**[19] 3127 6-9-2 **70** .... (p) DavidAllan 4 — 48
(Tim Easterby) *in rr: hdwy over 4f out: drvn and outpcd over 2f out: sn wknd* **8/1**
/03- **8** *6* **Sonara (IRE)**[161] 6028 7-8-11 **70** .... DaleSwift(5) 8 — 40
(Howard Johnson) *chsd ldrs: drvn over 6f out: lost pl over 3f out: sn bhd* **20/1**
00-0 **9** *1 3/4* **Rangefinder**[10] 1412 7-9-11 **82** .... SeanLevey(3) 6 — 50
(Andrew Crook) *mid-div: drvn 7f out: lost pl over 3f out: sn bhd* **25/1**
00/0 **10** *3 1/4* **Ladies Best**[18] 3157 7-9-7 **75** .... (v) JamesSullivan 1 — 39
(James Given) *sn chsng ldrs: reminders over 8f out: hung lft and lost pl over 3f out: sn bhd* **33/1**

3m 31.06s (-0.94) **Going Correction** +0.025s/f (Good) — **10 Ran SP% 113.2**
Speed ratings (Par 105): **103,102,99,98,97 91,90,87,86,85**
toteswingers:1&2:£3.20, 2&3:£7.40, 1&3:£3.30 CSF £33.88 CT £161.43 TOTE £5.70: £1.80, £2.50, £1.70; EX 27.50.
Owner Major P H K Steveney **Bred** E A Bourke M R C V S **Trained** Norton, N Yorks
■ Stewards' Enquiry : Lee Newman one-day ban: used whip in incorrect place (Jul 20)
Julie Burke two-day ban: used whip with excessive frequency (Jul 20-21)
FOCUS
An ordinary stayers' handicap run at no more than a reasonable pace. The time was seven seconds outside the standard. The first pair were clear, with another step up from the winner.
Ladies Best Official explanation: jockey said gelding hung left back straight

3731 TONY'S 60TH BIRTHDAY H'CAP — 5f 212y
3:50 (3:51) (Class 5) (0-75,73) 3-Y-0 — **£2,070** (£616; £307; £153) **Stalls** Low

Form — RPR
3133 **1** **Fast Shot**[12] 3347 3-8-13 **65** .... DavidAllan 7 — 72
(Tim Easterby) *chsd ldrs: drvn over 2f out: sn chsng ldr: styd on wl ins fnl f: led cl home* **11/8**[1]
-050 **2** *nk* **Bay Of Fires (IRE)**[13] 3318 3-9-4 **70** .... SilvestreDeSousa 3 — 76
(David O'Meara) *led: drvn 2 l clr over 1f out: hdd and no ex nr fin* **7/2**[2]
-332 **3** *3 1/2* **Bilko Pak (IRE)**[16] 3238 3-9-2 **73** .... (p) DaleSwift(5) 5 — 68
(Ann Duffield) *dwlt: sn outpcd and drvn along: hdwy 3f out: 3rd and kpt on one pce over 1f out* **4/1**[3]
-150 **4** *3 3/4* **Silver Turn**[89] 1214 3-9-6 **72** .... TomEaves 2 — 55
(Bryan Smart) *dwlt: in rr: hdwy 3f out: edgd rt and one pce over 1f out* **12/1**
0320 **5** *1 1/2* **Mazovian (USA)**[16] 3230 3-8-6 **63** .... AmyScott(5) 1 — 41
(Michael Chapman) *sn outpcd: bhd and drvn over 4f out: kpt on fnl 2f* **7/1**
1060 **6** *6* **Finn's Rainbow**[4] 3621 3-9-0 **66** .... PhillipMakin 4 — 25
(Kevin Ryan) *chsd ldr: wknd over 1f out: eased nr fin* **16/1**
3560 **7** *9* **Bygones For Coins (IRE)**[18] 3192 3-8-0 **55** oh5 ow1 DeclanCannon(3) 6 — —
(Alan Berry) *chsd ldrs: wknd 2f out: sn bhd: eased ins fnl f* **66/1**

1m 13.47s (-0.13) **Going Correction** +0.025s/f (Good) — **7 Ran SP% 111.9**
Speed ratings (Par 100): **101,100,95,90,88 80,68**
toteswingers:1&2:£2.50, 2&3:£2.70, 1&3:£1.10 CSF £6.02 TOTE £2.00: £1.40, £2.90; EX 6.90.

Owner Ontoawinner & Partners **Bred** Whitsbury Manor Stud & Pigeon House Stud **Trained** Great Habton, N Yorks

FOCUS
A modest handicap run at a good pace. There were doubts over most of these but not the winner, who posted a length personal best.

3732 YORKSHIRE RACING SUMMER FESTIVAL H'CAP (DIV I) 7f
4:20 (4:23) (Class 6) (0-65,65) 3-Y-O+ **£1,363** (£402; £201) **Stalls** Low

Form RPR
4040 **1** **Boga (IRE)**[3] 3662 4-8-9 **46** oh1 BarryMcHugh 4 55
(Karen Tutty) *chsd ldrs: wnt clr 3rd over 2f out: hung lft and styd on to ld last 50yds* **10/1**
0-05 **2** ¾ **Nufoudh (IRE)**[33] 2671 7-9-11 **65** PaulPickard(3) 1 72
(Colin Teague) *w ldrs: led over 5f out: drvn 3 l clr 2f out: hrd rdn: hdd and no ex towards fin* **3/1**[1]
026- **3** 4 ½ **He's A Humbug (IRE)**[327] 5045 7-9-8 **59** MickyFenton 11 54+
(Paul Midgley) *stmbld s: in rr: swtchd lft after s: hdwy on outside over 2f out: tk modest 4th over 1f out: edgd lft and kpt on to take 3rd nr fin* **7/1**[3]
0000 **4** ½ **Real Diamond**[15] 3248 5-8-13 **50** PhillipMakin 10 43
(Ollie Pears) *racd wd: led: edgd lft and hdd over 5f out: chsd ldr: one pce fnl 2f* **7/1**[3]
-050 **5** 5 **Come And Go (UAE)**[22] 3025 5-9-8 **64** (v[1]) DaleSwift(5) 12 44
(Ian McInnes) *in rr: sn drvn along: sme hdwy over 2f out: nvr a factor* **4/1**[2]
-000 **6** 8 **Dream Express (IRE)**[23] 2989 6-8-9 **46** StevieDonohoe 5 —
(David Thompson) *chsd ldrs: outpcd over 2f out: sn lost pl: eased nr fin* **16/1**
6-05 **7** 2 **Peppercorn Rent (IRE)**[23] 2984 3-8-1 **46** oh1 (e) PaulQuinn 3 —
(Tracy Waggott) *chsd ldrs: drvn over 3f out: sn outpcd* **12/1**
0030 **8** 1 ¾ **Coolella (IRE)**[9] 3454 4-8-5 **47** ChrisDCogan(5) 6 —
(John Weymes) *in rr: sme hdwy over 2f out: nvr on terms* **8/1**
-000 **9** 3 **Stardust Dancer**[70] 1615 4-8-9 **46** oh1 (v[1]) TomEaves 2 —
(Paul Green) *dwlt: hld up in rr: nvr on terms* **25/1**
000- **10** 6 **Olympic Ceremony**[279] 6494 4-9-3 **54** SilvestreDeSousa 8 —
(Tracy Waggott) *chsd ldrs: outpcd over 3f out: lost pl over 2f out: eased ins fnl f* **16/1**
0-00 **11** 3 ¼ **Baby Judge (IRE)**[98] 1037 4-8-7 **49** AmyScott(5) 9 —
(Michael Chapman) *chsd ldrs: lost pl over 3f out: sn bhd* **50/1**

1m 27.33s (0.33) **Going Correction** +0.025s/f (Good)
WFA 3 from 4yo+ 8lb **11** Ran SP% **115.5**
Speed ratings (Par 101): **99,98,93,92,86 77,75,73,69,63 59**
toteswingers:1&2:£9.60, 2&3:£4.40, 1&3:£13.20 CSF £37.68 CT £203.81 TOTE £15.50: £4.60, £1.10, £2.20; EX 67.90.
Owner N D Tutty **Bred** Cathal Ennis **Trained** Osmotherley, N Yorks
■ Karen Tutty's first Flat winner.
■ Stewards' Enquiry : Paul Pickard two-day ban: used whip without giving gelding time to respond (Jul 20-21)

FOCUS
The first division of this low-grade handicap, and the slower of the pair by a second. The pace seemed solid and very few got into it. They finished well strung out and the first two are rated close to their best.
He's A Humbug(IRE) Official explanation: jockey said gelding stumbled leaving stalls

3733 YORKSHIRE RACING SUMMER FESTIVAL H'CAP (DIV II) 7f
4:50 (4:50) (Class 6) (0-65,64) 3-Y-O+ **£1,363** (£402; £201) **Stalls** Low

Form RPR
0000 **1** **Hot Rod Mamma (IRE)**[28] 2803 4-8-12 **48** DuranFentiman 7 67
(Dianne Sayer) *hld up in midfield: effrt over 2f out: chsd wnr over 1f out: r.o to ld last 50yds: styd on strly* **16/1**
4155 **2** 2 ¾ **North Central (USA)**[12] 3341 4-10-0 **64** (p) DanielTudhope 2 76
(Jim Goldie) *sn chsng ldrs: led 3f out: 3 l clr and rdn over 1f out: hung lft and hdd wl ins fnl f* **4/1**[1]
U041 **3** 9 **Viking Warrior (IRE)**[22] 3024 4-9-10 **60** FrederikTylicki 4 47
(Michael Dods) *chsd ldrs: wnt 2nd 2f out: kpt on same pce* **9/2**[2]
5304 **4** *shd* **Lady Excel (IRE)**[9] 3457 5-8-13 **52** SeanLevey(3) 8 39
(Brian Rothwell) *mid-div: sn drvn along: reminders 3f out: kpt on one pce fnl 2f* **7/1**
3-00 **5** 3 ¾ **Handicraft (IRE)**[126] 731 3-8-1 **45** SilvestreDeSousa 9 19
(Kevin Ryan) *chsd ldrs: drvn over 3f out: one pce* **13/2**[3]
0055 **6** *nk* **Whispered Times (USA)**[3] 3657 4-9-11 **64** (p) PaulPickard(3) 12 40
(Tracy Waggott) *in rr: sme hdwy 2f out: nvr nr ldrs* **8/1**
-005 **7** 3 ¾ **Peter Tchaikovsky**[9] 3475 5-8-9 **50** DaleSwift(5) 3 16
(Ian McInnes) *mid-div: sn drvn along: lost pl over 2f out* **11/1**
-000 **8** 3 **Flyjack (USA)**[21] 3041 4-8-9 **45** (v) BarryMcHugh 1 —
(Lisa Williamson) *hld up in rr: effrt over 2f out: nvr on terms* **66/1**
5450 **9** 1 ½ **Isle Of Ellis (IRE)**[36] 2593 4-8-4 **47** ShaneBKelly(7) 5 —
(Ron Barr) *s.i.s: in rr and sn drvn along: nvr on terms* **28/1**
1024 **10** 1 **Dhhamaan (IRE)**[22] 3024 6-9-8 **58** (b) JamesSullivan 6 —
(Ruth Carr) *led: hdd 3f out: wknd over 1f out* **4/1**[1]
0-00 **11** 5 **Future Gem**[9] 3451 5-8-4 **45** (p) JulieBurke(5) 10 —
(David Thompson) *chsd ldrs: wknd 2f out* **66/1**
6006 **12** *shd* **Moon Lightning (IRE)**[48] 2233 5-8-9 **45** (b) TomEaves 11 —
(Tina Jackson) *mid-div: sn drvn along: lost pl over 3f out: wknd 2f out* **33/1**

1m 26.33s (-0.67) **Going Correction** +0.025s/f (Good)
WFA 3 from 4yo+ 8lb **12** Ran SP% **118.7**
Speed ratings (Par 101): **104,100,90,90,86 85,81,78,76,75 69,69**
toteswingers:1&2:£16.80, 2&3:£4.70, 1&3:£15.60 CSF £77.85 CT £350.38 TOTE £23.10: £4.10, £1.10, £3.80; EX 120.60.
Owner A Slack **Bred** Philip Hore Jnr **Trained** Hackthorpe, Cumbria

FOCUS
Another weak handicap, but it was run a full second quicker than the first division and the first pair produced decent form for the grade, although this was not a race to take too literally. It was similar race to division 1 in that very few were able to get involved.
Hot Rod Mamma(IRE) Official explanation: trainer said, regarding apparent improvement in form, that the filly was better suited by a return to the track having previously won over course and distance.
Dhhamaan(IRE) Official explanation: trainer said gelding was unsuited by the good to firm (good in places) ground

3734 RACING AGAIN WEDNESDAY 13TH JULY MEDIAN AUCTION MAIDEN STKS 1m 3f 214y
5:20 (5:20) (Class 5) 3-4-Y-O **£2,070** (£616; £307; £153) **Stalls** Low

Form RPR
5-44 **1** **Memory Lane**[27] 2857 3-8-9 66 StevieDonohoe 1 78+
(Sir Mark Prescott Bt) *mde all: drvn 4f out: forged 4 l clr over 2f out: sn wnt further clr: eased last 100yds* **4/1**[3]
2 8 **Far Flung (IRE)**[273] 6687 4-9-8 0 SilvestreDeSousa 4 62
(Jim Best) *chsd ldng pair: shkn up bnd after 3f: drvn 6f out: reminders over 3f out: kpt on to take modest 2nd 1f out* **1/1**[1]
3535 **3** 8 **Residence And Spa (IRE)**[9] 3460 3-9-0 68 DavidAllan 3 54
(Tim Easterby) *trckd wnr: drvn 4f out: outpcd over 2f out: wknd appr fnl f* **9/4**[2]
00 **4** 8 **Leah's Angel (IRE)**[48] 2218 3-8-2 0 JosephYoung(7) 2 36
(Michael Mullineaux) *dwlt: last and sn pushed along: detached and reminders over 7f out: poor 5th over 2f out: tk modest 4th last 100yds* **150/1**
-020 **5** 6 **White Fusion**[13] 3318 3-8-9 57 DaleSwift(5) 7 32
(Howard Johnson) *trckd ldrs: t.k.h: effrt over 5f out: sn outpcd: wknd over 2f out* **9/1**
0-66 **6** 10 **Good Faith**[20] 3084 3-9-0 50 TomEaves 6 16
(George Moore) *in rr: drvn over 6f out: lost pl over 4f out: bhd whn hung rt over 2f out* **40/1**

2m 39.12s (0.22) **Going Correction** +0.025s/f (Good)
WFA 3 from 4yo 13lb **6** Ran SP% **113.9**
Speed ratings (Par 103): **100,94,89,84,80 73**
Tote Super 7: Win: Not won. Place: 41.60. toteswingers:1&2:£1.50, 2&3:£1.30, 1&3:£1.80 CSF £8.65 TOTE £4.90: £2.40, £1.60; EX 8.90.
Owner Miss K Rausing **Bred** Miss K Rausing **Trained** Newmarket, Suffolk

FOCUS
A modest maiden lacking strength in depth. The winner set a good pace but it's doubtful how much she had to improve. She rates value for a bit extra.
T/Plt: £59.00 to a £1 stake. Pool of £50,826.48 - 627.91 winning tickets. T/Qpdt: £5.40 to a £1 stake. Pool of £4,285.12 - 581.64 winning tickets. WG

3517 KEMPTON (A.W) (R-H)
Wednesday, July 6

OFFICIAL GOING: Standard
Wind: Fresh, half behind Weather: Fine

3735 BETDAQ.COM EVERY WEDNESDAY AT KEMPTON PARK APPRENTICE H'CAP 7f (P)
6:20 (6:20) (Class 5) (0-70,70) 4-Y-O+ **£2,264** (£673; £336; £168) **Stalls** Low

Form RPR
-502 **1** **Paphos**[7] 3517 4-9-2 **62** (v) RyanClark 6 71+
(Stuart Williams) *hld up in midfield: plld out and prog over 2f out: led over 1f out: drvn and styd on wl* **3/1**[1]
-006 **2** 1 **Tubby Isaacs**[11] 3412 7-9-7 **67** (p) HarryBentley 9 74
(Dean Ivory) *hld up in last trio: gd prog on outer 2f out: chsd wnr jst over 1f out: styd on but a hld* **7/1**[3]
0043 **3** 1 **Abriachan**[43] 2382 4-9-7 **67** TobyAtkinson 7 71
(Noel Quinlan) *hld up in last trio: prog over 2f out: rdn to chal over 1f out: styd on same pce after* **11/1**
-100 **4** 1 ¼ **Woolston Ferry (IRE)**[20] 3093 5-9-2 **65** DavidKenny(3) 2 68
(David Pinder) *hld up in midfield: effrt and hanging over 2f out: squeezed out sn after: prog over 1f out: styd on: unable to chal* **14/1**
0-24 **5** 4 ½ **Yanbu (USA)**[22] 3019 6-8-5 **51** AshleyMorgan 10 39
(Tobias B P Coles) *racd wd: hld up in midfield: nt qckn over 2f out and struggling: kpt on fnl f* **20/1**
3321 **6** 1 **Anjomarba (IRE)**[41] 2426 4-9-8 **68** KieranO'Neill 11 54
(Brett Johnson) *hld up in last trio: rdn and no prog over 2f out: modest late hdwy* **12/1**
4060 **7** 1 **Exceedingly Bold**[26] 2870 4-9-2 **65** (t) MatthewLawson(3) 1 48
(Jo Crowley) *trckd ldng pair: tried to chal on inner wl over 1f out: sn wknd* **7/1**[3]
0000 **8** 1 **Valmina**[20] 3093 4-8-12 **61** (t) LucyKBarry(3) 5 41
(Tony Carroll) *t.k.h: trckd ldrs tl wknd wl over 1f out* **10/1**
3221 **9** 7 **Foxtrot Alpha (IRE)**[15] 3250 5-9-10 **70** JamesRogers 3 31
(Peter Winkworth) *led: rdn over 2f out: hdd over 1f out: wknd rapidly: eased* **7/2**[2]
0-05 **10** 3 ¾ **Towy Boy (IRE)**[15] 3261 6-9-7 **67** (bt) LeeTopliss 4 18
(Ian Wood) *chsd ldr to 2f out: wknd rapidly* **20/1**

1m 26.45s (0.45) **Going Correction** +0.05s/f (Slow) **10** Ran SP% **113.5**
Speed ratings (Par 103): **99,97,96,95,90 89,87,86,78,74**
toteswingers: 1&2 £4.00, 1&3 £5.60, 2&3 £14.50 CSF £23.54 CT £198.28 TOTE £3.20: £1.20, £2.80, £3.00; EX 17.50 Trifecta £47.90 Pool: £5,231.40 - 80.80 winning units..
Owner Stuart C Williams **Bred** L Ellinas And Old Mill Stud Ltd **Trained** Newmarket, Suffolk

FOCUS
A modest handicap run at an ordinary gallop. The first four finished clear and the winner edged towards the far rail in the closing stages.

3736 BRITISH STALLION STUDS SUPPORTING BRITISH RACING E B F MAIDEN FILLIES' STKS 6f (P)
6:50 (6:51) (Class 5) 2-Y-O **£3,169** (£943; £471; £235) **Stalls** Low

Form RPR
0 **1** **Mahkama (USA)**[28] 2811 2-9-0 0 TedDurcan 5 82+
(Saeed Bin Suroor) *racd freely early: mde virtually all: pushed clr over 2f out: 4 l up 1f out: pushed out to the fin* **11/8**[1]
4 **2** 1 ¾ **Al Mahmeyah**[12] 3342 2-9-0 0 DaneO'Neill 2 76+
(Richard Hannon) *s.s: sn trckd ldrs: prog over 2f out: chsd clr wnr wl over 1f out: styd on wl fnl f but nvr any ch* **3/1**[2]
3 2 **By Invitation (USA)** 2-9-0 0 JimCrowley 4 70+
(Ralph Beckett) *settled in midfield: nt clr run briefly over 2f out: prog after: pushed along and styd on to take 3rd ins fnl f* **11/1**
0 **4** 1 ¼ **White Spirit (IRE)**[20] 3092 2-9-0 0 AdamKirby 1 66
(Marco Botti) *sn restrained bhd ldrs: effrt to go 2nd over 2f out to wl over 1f out: fdd* **14/1**
0 **5** *nse* **Fire And Sparks**[32] 2718 2-9-0 0 JamieSpencer 6 66
(David Simcock) *hld up in midfield: prog 2f out: chal for a pl 1f out: effrt petered out* **33/1**
0 **6** 3 ¼ **Superinjunction**[12] 3362 2-9-0 0 KierenFallon 3 56
(Brian Meehan) *rn green and sn dropped towards rr: pushed along over 3f out: sme prog 2f out: no threat to ldrs: fdd fnl f* **12/1**
4 **7** *hd* **Fresa**[8] 3490 2-9-0 0 SebSanders 8 56
(Sir Mark Prescott Bt) *rn green in rr: pushed along over 3f out: awkward bnd sn after: last over 1f out: styd on fnl f* **9/1**[3]
0 **8** ¾ **Wrapped Up**[30] 2767 2-9-0 0 WilliamBuick 7 53+
(Heather Main) *dwlt: detached in last early: wd bnd 3f out: sme prog over 2f out: no hdwy over 1f out* **80/1**
9 3 ½ **Siberian Belle (IRE)** 2-9-0 0 PaulHanagan 9 43
(Richard Fahey) *a in rr: shkn up and no prog 2f out: no ch after* **25/1**

10 2 ¼ **Compton Bird** 2-9-0 0 JamesDoyle 11 36
(Hans Adielsson) *prom: chsd wnr over 3f out to over 2f out: wknd qckly* **66/1**

5 11 4 ½ **Pindrop**[14] 3270 2-9-0 0 ShaneKelly 10 23
(Walter Swinburn) *chsd wnr to over 3f out: wknd rapidly over 2f out* **10/1**

1m 13.93s (0.83) **Going Correction** +0.05s/f (Slow) **11** Ran SP% **118.4**
Speed ratings (Par 91): **96,93,91,89,89 84,84,83,79,76 70**
toteswingers: 1&2 £1.60, 1&3 £4.90, 2&3 £8.70 CSF £5.16 TOTE £2.50: £1.50, £1.60, £2.70; EX 7.00 Trifecta £35.30 Pool: £5,888.45 - 123.34 winning units..
Owner Godolphin **Bred** Mt Brilliant Farm LLC **Trained** Newmarket, Suffolk

FOCUS
A couple of decent sorts won this race in the previous two years and, although this lacked strength-in-depth, this year's winner looks a useful prospect. The gallop was no more than fair and the winner came down the centre in the straight.

NOTEBOOK
Mahkama(USA) ♦, who showed ability before tiring on easy ground on her debut, raced with the choke out but showed much-improved form on this quicker surface on this all-weather debut. She is value for more than the winning margin suggests and this speedy sort should be able to win again. (op 6-4 tchd 13-8 in places)
Al Mahmeyah was no match for the ready winner but duly stepped up on the form shown on her debut at Doncaster. She will be suited by the step up to 7f and should be able to pick up a run-of-the-mill maiden on this surface or on turf. (tchd 10-3)
By Invitation(USA) ♦, who cost 50,000gns and is a half-sister to Group 3 winner Sahara Star, is another to take from the race. She has a bit of size and scope, wasn't unduly knocked about and can be expected to come on a fair bit for this experience. (op 14-1 tchd 16-1)
White Spirit(IRE) bettered the form of her debut run at Warwick and should do better once qualified for a nursery mark.
Fire And Sparks was soundly beaten on firm ground on her debut but fared better on this first run on an artificial surface. She'll be better suited by 7f and already looks more of a nursery type. (op 25-1)
Fresa, whose dam was Listed placed up to 1m1f abroad, again shaped as though she will be suited by a much stiffer test of stamina and the eventual switch to handicap company. (op 12-1)

3737 BETDAQ.COM EXCHANGE PRICE MULTIPLES H'CAP 6f (P)
7:20 (7:20) (Class 4) (0-80,81) 3-Y-0+ **£4,075** (£1,212; £606; £303) **Stalls** Low

Form RPR
-100 1 **Great Acclaim**[12] 3346 3-9-0 **75** EddieAhern 4 85+
(James Fanshawe) *w.w in midfield: shkn up over 2f out: r.o jst over 1f out to ld fnl 120yds: pushed out* **16/1**

0356 2 1 **Desert Strike**[5] 3588 5-9-8 **77** (p) ShaneKelly 12 84
(Alan McCabe) *patiently rdn in rr: prog 2f out: drvn and r.o fnl f to take 2nd last strides* **33/1**

10-0 3 nk **Zip Lock (IRE)**[21] 3045 5-9-9 **78** KierenFallon 1 84
(David Elsworth) *trckd ldrs: effrt on inner 2f out: drvn to chal and upsides fnl f: nt qckn last 100yds* **14/1**

6-05 4 hd **Quasi Congaree (GER)**[44] 2369 5-9-6 **75** (t) GeorgeBaker 10 80
(Ian Wood) *led: rdn 2f out: hdd and no ex last 120yds* **20/1**

3151 5 1 **King Ferdinand**[7] 3523 3-9-6 **81** 6ex DavidProbert 7 82+
(Andrew Balding) *dwlt: nvr in gd position in rr: tried to make prog over 2f out: styd on fnl f: nvr able to land a blow* **11/10**[1]

163- 6 ¾ **Dominium (USA)**[442] 1453 4-9-7 **76** SteveDrowne 2 78+
(Jeremy Gask) *hld up wl in rr: prog on inner over 2f out: tried to cl on ldrs over 1f out: one pce fnl f* **16/1**

650- 7 nk **Safari Mischief**[287] 6280 8-9-0 **74** HarryBentley(5) 8 73
(Peter Winkworth) *prom: chsd ldr over 2f out to over 1f out: fdd* **12/1**[3]

4413 8 nk **Firstknight**[21] 3048 3-9-1 **76** AdamKirby 6 73
(Marco Botti) *towards rr: drvn over 2f out: kpt on fr over 1f out: nvr gng pce to threaten* **11/2**[2]

16-5 9 1 ½ **Squires Gate (IRE)**[47] 2255 3-9-2 **77** MichaelHills 3 69
(B W Hills) *settled in midfield: effrt over 2f out: shuffled along and no imp over 1f out: eased ins fnl f* **16/1**

0311 10 4 **Lord Of The Reins (IRE)**[84] 1309 7-9-3 **72** (t) WilliamBuick 11 52
(P J O'Gorman) *rrd s and lost several l: ct up in last pair after 2f: shuffled along fnl 2f: nvr nr ldrs* **14/1**

032 11 2 **Night Trade (IRE)**[21] 3036 4-9-4 **78** (v[1]) NeilFarley(5) 9 52
(Deborah Sanderson) *racd wd: prom but hanging lft: wknd rapidly 2f out* **25/1**

0142 12 3 ¾ **Dream Catcher (FR)**[25] 2910 3-9-4 **79** FergusSweeney 5 40
(David Pinder) *chsd ldr to over 2f out: wknd rapidly* **14/1**

1m 13.03s (-0.07) **Going Correction** +0.05s/f (Slow)
WFA 3 from 4yo+ 6lb **12** Ran SP% **119.9**
Speed ratings (Par 105): **102,100,100,100,98 97,97,96,94,89 86,81**
toteswingers: 1&2 £49.80, 1&3 £70.60, 2&3 £29.70 CSF £469.13 CT £7489.83 TOTE £27.20: £8.20, £9.70, £2.40; EX 1418.50 TRIFECTA Not won..
Owner Norman Brunskill **Bred** Mr & Mrs A E Pakenham **Trained** Newmarket, Suffolk

FOCUS
A fair handicap but one in which the well-backed market leader proved a shade disappointing. The gallop was a reasonable one (9/10ths of a second quicker than the preceding maiden over this trip) and the winner raced centre-to-far side in the straight.
Lord Of The Reins(IRE) Official explanation: jockey said gelding reared on leaving stalls

3738 LAY BACK AND WIN AT BETDAQ.COM H'CAP 2m (P)
7:50 (7:50) (Class 5) (0-75,75) 4-Y-0+ **£2,264** (£673; £336; £168) **Stalls** Low

Form RPR
0024 1 **Red Courtier**[25] 2931 4-9-7 **75** (p) JimmyFortune 4 84
(Paul Cole) *trckd ldr: led 5f out: kicked on 3f out: hrd rdn and edgd lft fnl f: hld on* **5/2**[1]

-644 2 nk **Penangdouble O One**[20] 3095 4-9-3 **71** (tp) JimCrowley 13 79
(Ralph Beckett) *hld up in midfield in abt 8th: effrt over 3f out: drvn over 2f out: clsd on ldrs over 1f out: styd on to chal and carried sltly lft ins fnl f: jst hld* **11/1**

0421 3 nk **Kavaloti (IRE)**[14] 3281 7-9-2 **70** (b) GeorgeBaker 9 78
(Gary Moore) *hld up in midfield in 9th: prog over 3f out: cajoled along fr 2f out: clsd to chal and looked likely wnr ins fnl f: n.g.t* **7/1**[2]

1250 4 nk **Storm Hawk (IRE)**[20] 3095 4-8-13 **67** (p) WilliamBuick 3 75
(Pat Eddery) *prom: lost pl sltly over 4f out on inner: prog to chse wnr wl over 2f out: cl enough over 1f out but nt qckn: swtchd rt fnl f: kpt on but lost 2 pls* **10/1**[3]

6411 5 3 **Money Money Money**[21] 3047 5-9-1 **69** JamesMillman 5 74+
(Rod Millman) *trckd ldrs on inner disputing 6th: trapped bhd wkng rival and dropped to last pair over 3f out: prog on inner over 2f out: styd on: nvr rchd ldrs* **10/1**[3]

4004 6 1 ¼ **Soundbyte**[8] 3479 6-8-5 **59** ChrisCatlin 11 62
(John Gallagher) *settled in 11th: nt gng wl bef 1/2-way: shoved along 6f out: struggling after: rallied 3f out: styd on: nrst fin* **25/1**

2254 7 7 **Blackstone Vegas**[17] 3205 5-8-9 **63** RobbieFitzpatrick 12 57
(Derek Shaw) *hld up in 12th: hld up wl outpcd fr over 3f out: rdn and sme prog over 2f out: no ch and wknd fnl f* **10/1**[3]

-120 8 3 ½ **Spice Fair**[24] 2958 4-8-12 **71** LeeNewnes(5) 10 61
(Mark Usher) *dropped in fr wd draw and hld up in 13th: rapid prog fr 7f out and plld way through to chse wnr over 4f out: lost 2nd wl over 2f out: sn wknd* **10/1**[3]

1-05 9 7 **Saggiatore**[20] 3095 4-9-6 **74** SebSanders 14 56
(William Muir) *racd wd: prom: rdn to dispute 2nd briefly over 4f out: wknd u.p over 2f out* **14/1**

0050 10 12 **Boston Blue**[26] 2892 4-9-6 **74** (v) JamieSpencer 8 41
(Tim Etherington) *hld up in 10th: rdn on outer 3f out: no real prog: wknd 2f out: t.o* **10/1**[3]

-650 11 4 **Gaselee (USA)**[18] 3157 5-9-4 **72** MartinLane 2 34
(Rae Guest) *led to 5f out: wknd rapidly: t.o* **25/1**

0434 12 7 **William's Way**[51] 2159 9-9-1 **69** (t) PaulHanagan 1 23
(Ian Wood) *hld up in detached last: briefest of effrt to dispute 12th 4f out: sn shkn up and wknd: eased: t.o* **33/1**

540- 13 4 **Grey Granite (IRE)**[310] 5611 5-9-2 **70** DaneO'Neill 7 19
(Warren Greatrex) *trckd ldrs disputing 6th: wknd 4f out: t.o* **14/1**

1020 14 29 **Coda Agency**[65] 1761 8-9-1 **69** NeilCallan 6 —
(David Arbuthnot) *prom: rdn after 5f: under maximum press sn after 1/2-way: kpt in tch tl wknd rapidly 4f out: t.o* **25/1**

3m 28.17s (-1.93) **Going Correction** +0.05s/f (Slow) **14** Ran SP% **122.7**
Speed ratings (Par 103): **106,105,105,104 103,99,98,94,88 86,83,81,66**
toteswingers: 1&2 £8.90, 1&3 £4.80, 2&3 £13.90 CSF £29.89 CT £180.08 TOTE £3.90: £1.10, £5.20, £2.40; EX 63.10 Trifecta £156.00 Pool: £527.14 - 2.50 winning units..
Owner C Shiacolas **Bred** Pegasus Racing Ltd **Trained** Whatcombe, Oxon
■ Stewards' Enquiry : Jimmy Fortune caution: careless riding.

FOCUS
Mainly exposed performers in no more than a fair handicap in which the gallop was an ordinary one. The first four pulled clear and the winner hung into the centre late on.
Coda Agency Official explanation: jockey said gelding never travelled

3739 BETDAQ MOBILE APPS H'CAP 1m 3f (P)
8:20 (8:22) (Class 4) (0-80,80) 3-Y-0+ **£4,075** (£1,212; £606; £303) **Stalls** Low

Form RPR
06-1 1 **Making Eyes (IRE)**[24] 2960 3-9-2 **80** IanMongan 11 90+
(Hugo Palmer) *hld up in 7th: smooth prog 3f out to chse ldr over 2f out: rdn to ld over 1f out: drvn and a holding on fnl f* **15/8**[1]

64-4 2 ¾ **Alfouzy**[60] 1915 3-8-8 **72** NeilCallan 4 80
(Roger Varian) *cl up: rdn wl over 2f out and nudged rival: drvn to chal over 1f out: pressed wnr after but a hld* **7/2**[2]

5500 3 nk **Elmfield Giant (USA)**[13] 3319 4-8-12 **64** PaulHanagan 1 71
(Richard Fahey) *trckd ldr: led 1/2-way: drvn over 2f out: hdd over 1f out: styd on but a hld* **9/1**

0323 4 3 **Beat Route**[16] 3225 4-8-13 **70** JemmaMarshall(5) 8 72
(Michael Attwater) *hld up in tch: effrt whn carried wd bnd 3f out: prog over 2f out and cl enough in 4th: nt qckn sn after: one pce over 1f out* **10/1**

-400 5 3 ¼ **Conducting**[18] 3178 3-8-13 **77** (b) ShaneKelly 6 73
(Brian Meehan) *cl up: rdn whn carried wd bnd 3f out: sn lost pl and btn* **14/1**

55-0 6 3 ¼ **Myboyalfie (USA)**[36] 2596 4-9-3 **69** JimCrowley 3 59
(J R Jenkins) *settled in last pair: pushed along 4f out: outpcd wl over 2f out: n.d after* **8/1**[3]

4-00 7 1 ¾ **True To Form (IRE)**[29] 2793 4-9-5 **71** TonyCulhane 10 58
(George Baker) *t.k.h: racd wd: cl up: wd bnd after 2f: sing to lose grnd whn carrried v wd bnd 3f out: wknd* **14/1**

-156 8 hd **Adoyen Spice**[49] 2204 4-8-11 **63** MartinLane 2 50
(Mike Murphy) *dwlt: hld up last rdn 3f out: hd to one side and reluctant over 2f out: sn btn* **16/1**

030 9 32 **Spyder**[16] 3233 3-8-9 **73** TedDurcan 9 —
(Jane Chapple-Hyam) *led to 1/2-way: rn wd bnd 3f out: gave up and t.o* **14/1**

-03R R **Aspro Mavro (IRE)**[10] 3434 5-9-11 **77** PaulDoe 5 —
(Jim Best) *ref to r: tk no part* **20/1**

2m 20.58s (-1.32) **Going Correction** +0.05s/f (Slow)
WFA 3 from 4yo+ 12lb **10** Ran SP% **117.9**
Speed ratings (Par 105): **106,105,105,103,100 98,97,96,73,—**
toteswingers: 1&2 £2.50, 1&3 £4.20, 2&3 £9.80 CSF £8.17 CT £47.08 TOTE £3.80: £1.30, £2.10, £2.30; EX 12.20 Trifecta £93.30 Pool: £304.05 - 2.41 winning units..
Owner Starter For Ten Partnership **Bred** F Dunne **Trained** Newmarket, Suffolk

FOCUS
A fair handicap in which the two handicap newcomers filled the first two places. The early gallop soon steadied and the winner came down the centre in the straight.

3740 SILVER BLAZE WESSEX CUP H'CAP (LONDON MILE QUALIFIER) 1m (P)
8:50 (8:50) (Class 4) (0-85,84) 3-Y-0+ **£4,075** (£1,212; £606; £303) **Stalls** Low

Form RPR
-055 1 **Snow Magic (IRE)**[22] 3026 4-9-7 **77** KierenFallon 5 87
(James Fanshawe) *trckd ldrs: prog to go 3rd over 2f out: clsd and rdn to ld over 1f out: in command fnl f: readily* **5/1**[2]

1165 2 1 **Nahab**[7] 3521 4-9-13 **83** TedDurcan 3 91
(David Lanigan) *hld up in rr: prog over 2f out: hrd rdn over 1f out: wnt 2nd ins fnl f: no imp on wnr but styd on* **11/2**[3]

4000 3 ¾ **Douze Points (IRE)**[10] 3445 5-9-4 **77** (b) JohnFahy(3) 11 83
(Ed de Giles) *s.s: hld up in last trio: gd prog on inner over 2f out: drvn to chal over 1f out: hld by wnr fnl f and lost 2nd: kpt on* **10/1**

340- 4 2 ¼ **Be A Devil**[329] 4956 4-9-3 **73** NeilCallan 1 74
(William Muir) *in tch in midfield: rdn wl over 2f out and nt pce of others making prog: drvn and styd on fr over 1f out: nvr able to chal* **14/1**

12-0 5 1 ¼ **Frances Stuart (IRE)**[60] 1884 4-9-8 **78** JimmyFortune 9 76
(Andrew Balding) *t.k.h: trckd ldr to 2f out: nt qckn over 1f out: fdd fnl f* **9/2**[1]

-323 6 1 ¾ **Amazing Star (IRE)**[18] 3169 6-9-4 **79** NeilFarley(5) 12 73
(Declan Carroll) *hld up in last trio: shkn up 3f out: sn outpcd: drvn and styd on fr over 1f out: nrst fin* **13/2**

0-45 7 1 ¼ **Mr Hichens**[120] 799 6-9-12 **82** DarryllHolland 4 73
(Karen George) *prom: rdn and nt qckn over 2f out: steadily wknd over 1f out* **20/1**

210- 8 nk **Rock Anthem (IRE)**[282] 6430 7-9-1 **71** MartinLane 8 62
(Mike Murphy) *led to over 1f out: wknd* **20/1**

15 9 ½ **Protractor (IRE)**[54] 2064 3-8-2 **74** MatthewLawson(7) 7 61
(B W Hills) *sn in midfield: outpcd fr 3f out: pushed along and nvr on terms after* **7/1**

41-0 **10** 3 3/4 **Irons On Fire (USA)**[21] 3045 3-8-12 **77**.......................... TonyCulhane 6 56
(George Baker) *stdd s: hld up in last trio: rowed along over 2f out: nvr nr ldrs* **33/1**

0-50 **11** 3/4 **Beauchamp Yorker**[53] 2105 4-10-0 **84**.......................... JamesDoyle 14 63
(Hans Adielsson) *racd wd: prom: lost pl and outpcd wl over 2f out: sn bhd* **25/1**

01-1 **12** 1/2 **Mcconnell (USA)**[183] 38 6-9-9 **79**.......................... GeorgeBaker 10 57+
(Gary Moore) *racd v wd: in tch to 3f out: sn wknd* **8/1**

1m 39.63s (-0.17) **Going Correction** +0.05s/f (Slow)
WFA 3 from 4yo+ 9lb **12** Ran SP% **119.2**
Speed ratings (Par 105): **102,101,100,98,96 95,93,93,92,89 88,87**
toteswingers: 1&2 £7.10, 1&3 £13.10, 2&3 £20.20 CSF £31.07 CT £273.15 TOTE £5.00: £1.80, £2.00, £3.80; EX 38.50 Trifecta £291.30 Part won. Pool: £393.74 - 0.10 winning units..
Owner Nigel & Carolyn Elwes **Bred** Aylesfield Farms Stud Ltd **Trained** Newmarket, Suffolk

FOCUS
A useful and competitive handicap in which the pace was an ordinary one. The winner came down the centre in the straight.

3741 HOTHOUSE FLOWERS HERE 03.08.11 H'CAP — 1m (P)
9:20 (9:20) (Class 6) (0-58,61) 3-Y-0+ **£1,617** (£481; £240; £120) **Stalls** Low

Form RPR

0000 **1** **Focail Eile**[19] 3130 6-9-2 **58**.......................... KierenFallon 13 72
(John Ryan) *hld up bhd ldrs: prog over 2f out: burst through to ld over 1f out: sn rdn clr: in n.d fnl f* **14/1**

4532 **2** 2 1/4 **Fitz**[14] 3293 5-9-2 **58**.......................... WilliamBuick 4 66
(Matthew Salaman) *hld up on inner: grad dropped to rr of field by 1/2-way: gd prog on inner over 2f out: drvn to chse wnr jst over 1f out: no imp* **4/1**[1]

3100 **3** 3/4 **Ermyntrude**[18] 3176 4-9-1 **57**.......................... IanMongan 5 64+
(Pat Phelan) *hld up towards rr and racd wd: shkn up over 2f out and no prog: drvn and r.o over 1f out: wnt 3rd last strides* **15/2**[3]

0054 **4** nse **Starwatch**[9] 3468 4-8-11 **58**.......................... HarryBentley(5) 9 65
(John Bridger) *settled in midfield: effrt over 2f out: rdn over 1f out: styd on fnl f: jst lost out in battle for 3rd* **13/2**[2]

0331 **5** 1 **Eastern Hills**[8] 3496 6-9-2 **61** 6ex.......................... (p) MartinHarley(3) 3 65
(Alan McCabe) *wl plcd bhd ldrs: effrt over 2f out: drvn and nt qckn wl over 1f out: one pce after* **4/1**[1]

4031 **6** 1 **Kielty's Folly**[14] 3280 7-8-10 **57**.......................... JamesRogers(5) 12 59
(Brian Baugh) *t.k.h: pressed ldr to 2f out: steadily fdd* **9/1**

3203 **7** 1 **Abigails Angel**[18] 3176 4-9-2 **58**.......................... (p) AdamKirby 7 58
(Brett Johnson) *snatched up sn after s: hld up towards rr: nt clr run briefly over 2f out: prog over 1f out: shkn up and fdd fnl f* **8/1**

2060 **8** 3/4 **Sweet Possession (USA)**[11] 3387 5-9-0 **56**.......................... (p) NeilCallan 2 54
(Pat Eddery) *led to over 1f out: wknd fnl f* **14/1**

6500 **9** 1 1/4 **Spinning Ridge (IRE)**[22] 3017 6-9-0 **56**.......................... (b) DavidProbert 11 51
(Ronald Harris) *slowly away and snatched up sn after s: a in rr* **14/1**

6-06 **10** 3/4 **Bell's Ocean (USA)**[13] 3303 4-9-0 **56**.......................... KirstyMilczarek 1 49
(John Ryan) *prom: pushed along and wknd 2f out* **33/1**

0006 **11** 2 1/2 **Having A Ball**[14] 3266 7-9-1 **57**.......................... ChrisCatlin 6 45
(Jonathan Portman) *stdd after s: hld up in rr and racd v wd: nvr a factor* **25/1**

21-0 **12** 3 **Gadobout Dancer**[89] 1216 4-8-9 **56**.......................... NeilFarley(5) 8 37
(Declan Carroll) *s.i.s: pushed up on outer to go prom after 2f: wknd over 2f out* **14/1**

1m 39.78s (-0.02) **Going Correction** +0.05s/f (Slow) **12** Ran SP% **119.7**
Speed ratings (Par 101): **102,99,99,98,97 96,95,95,93,93 90,87**
toteswingers: 1&2 £6.90, 1&3 £35.40, 2&3 £8.70 CSF £69.92 CT £472.72 TOTE £21.10: £5.30, £2.00, £4.30; EX 89.90 Trifecta £168.50 Pool: £369.02 - 1.62 winning units..
Owner Cathal Fegan **Bred** D Robb **Trained** Newmarket, Suffolk

FOCUS
A moderate handicap in which an ordinary gallop soon steadied. The winner edged towards the far rail late on.
Abigails Angel Official explanation: jockey said filly suffered interference at start
T/Jkpt: Not won. T/Plt: £863.40 to a £1 stake. Pool: £83,447.69. 70.55 winning tickets. T/Qpdt: £342.50 to a £1 stake. Pool: £6,064.07. 13.10 winning tickets. JN

3388 LINGFIELD (L-H)
Wednesday, July 6

OFFICIAL GOING: Turf course - good to firm; all-weather - standard
Wind: fresh, half behind Weather: dry, after showers earlier

3742 FUNCTION BUSINESS RELOCATION H'CAP (TURF) — 1m 1f
2:30 (2:31) (Class 6) (0-60,60) 3-Y-O **£1,704** (£503; £251) **Stalls** Low

Form RPR

0-32 **1** **Mystic Edge**[27] 2849 3-9-7 **60**.......................... JamieSpencer 2 73+
(Michael Bell) *mde all: rdn and edging rt over 2f out: drew clr ent fnl f: in command after: heavily eased fnl 50yds* **2/1**[1]

6423 **2** 3 3/4 **Oliver's Gold**[10] 3431 3-9-2 **55**.......................... PatDobbs 4 58
(Amanda Perrett) *dwlt: niggled along towards rr early: hdwy 3f out: drvn to chse wnr over 2f out: sn outpcd and no threat to wnr ins fnl f: plugged on* **7/1**[2]

-000 **3** 3/4 **Come On The Irons (USA)**[99] 1022 3-9-5 **58**.......................... JamieGoldstein 1 59
(Ralph Smith) *chsd ldrs: rdn wl over 2f out: no ch w wnr but kpt on u.p ins fnl f* **33/1**

5064 **4** 1 **Harry Lime**[22] 3018 3-9-3 **56**.......................... MartinDwyer 6 55
(William Jarvis) *chsd wnr: rdn wl over 2f out: lost 2nd 2f out: no ch w wnr and plugged on same pce after* **12/1**

5302 **5** 1/2 **Out Of The Storm**[15] 3251 3-9-1 **57**.......................... SimonPearce(3) 11 55
(Simon Dow) *chsd ldrs on outer: rdn and chsd wnr 2f out: sn hung rt and nt qckn: styd on same pce and no ch w wnr ins fnl f* **16/1**

0-51 **6** 1/2 **Hi Note**[16] 3227 3-8-11 **53**.......................... MartinHarley(3) 5 50
(Mick Channon) *in tch: rdn and unable qck over 2f out: outpcd and btn 2f out: plugged on same pce after* **8/1**[3]

046 **7** 3 **Don't Call Me Tiny (IRE)**[18] 3173 3-8-8 **47**.......................... AndreaAtzeni 12 37
(Don Cantillon) *dropped in bhd after s: hld up towards rr: rdn and no real hdwy over 3f out: no ch but plugged on past btn horses fnl f* **25/1**

3036 **8** 4 1/2 **Roman Flame**[22] 3018 3-9-3 **56**.......................... (v) SebSanders 7 36
(Michael Quinn) *chsd ldrs: rdn and struggling over 3f out: wknd u.p 2f out* **16/1**

0-04 **9** 1/2 **Pearl Opera**[49] 2196 3-9-4 **57**.......................... AdamKirby 3 36
(Denis Coakley) *hld up towards rr: rdn and no hdwy over 2f out: nvr trbld ldrs* **7/1**[2]

6203 **10** 6 **Lady Mango (IRE)**[16] 3223 3-9-3 **56**.......................... LukeMorris 13 22
(Ronald Harris) *t.k.h: hld up in rr: rdn and effrt jst over 2f out: no hdwy and wl btn over 1f out* **25/1**

00-0 **11** 2 1/2 **Notify**[49] 2192 3-8-6 **50**.......................... HarryBentley(5) 8 —
(Patrick Chamings) *hld up in tch towards rr: rdn and struggling wl over 2f out: sn wknd* **50/1**

000- **12** 25 **Burst Of Applause (IRE)**[244] 7309 3-9-7 **60**.......................... IanMongan 10 —
(Noel Quinlan) *wnt rt s and s.i.s: a detached in last and nvr travelling: lost tch 3f out: virtually p.u fnl f: t.o* **33/1**

2m 0.54s (3.94) **Going Correction** +0.40s/f (Good) **12** Ran SP% **104.4**
Speed ratings (Par 98): **98,94,94,93,92 92,89,85,85,79 77,55**
toteswingers: 1&2 £2.40, 2&3 £31.30, 1&3 £17.50 CSF £10.67 CT £203.68 TOTE £2.60: £1.10, £1.30, £12.30; EX 13.60.
Owner Herts And Hinds Racing Syndicate **Bred** F D Harvey **Trained** Newmarket, Suffolk

FOCUS
The ground was changed to Good to Firm, Good in places after rain had fallen, but the jockeys in the first considered it was somewhat easier than that and one suggested there were some soft patches. A moderate handicap weakened further when Ishikawa, one of only two previous winners in the contest, had to be withdrawn after bursting his stall (9/2, deduct 15p in the £ under R4). It was a major advantage to race close to the pace.
Burst Of Applause(IRE) Official explanation: jockey said filly jumped out awkwardly and never travelled

3743 BLACKBERRY LANE (S) STKS (TURF) — 1m 2f
3:00 (3:01) (Class 6) 3-Y-O+ **£1,704** (£503; £251) **Stalls** Low

Form RPR

1-6 **1** **Country Road (IRE)**[16] 3240 5-9-6 68.......................... (be) AdamKirby 3 71
(Tony Carroll) *chsd ldr untl rdn to ld 2f out: kpt on u.p whn pressed ins fnl f* **15/8**[2]

6202 **2** 1/2 **Viewing**[11] 3391 4-9-1 68.......................... PatDobbs 4 65
(James Given) *hld up in tch: hdwy to trck ldrs wl over 2f out: swtchd rt and rdn to chse wnr jst ins fnl f: pressed wnr fnl 100yds but flashed tail u.p and a hld* **6/4**[1]

1-00 **3** 2 1/2 **Fly By White (IRE)**[33] 2688 3-7-13 70.......................... KieranO'Neill(5) 5 60
(Richard Hannon) *racd keenly: led: rdn and hdd 2f out: no ex a1f out: wknd ins fnl f* **11/4**[3]

00 **4** 6 **Milton Hill**[20] 3080 4-9-6 0.......................... JamesDoyle 6 53?
(Dominic Ffrench Davis) *dwlt: sn rcvrd to chse ldng pair: rdn 3f out: edgd lft u.p and wknd over 1f out* **100/1**

0 **5** 20 **Insidious**[25] 2924 3-8-9 0.......................... MartinDwyer 1 13
(William Jarvis) *dwlt: a in last pair: in tch: reminder 5f out: rdn and lost tch over 2f out* **12/1**

0504 **6** 1/2 **Battle Axe (FR)**[15] 3252 6-8-8 42.......................... [1] CharlotteJenner(7) 2 —
(Laura Mongan) *taken down early: s.i.s: racd wd and a in last pair: lost tch over 2f out* **50/1**

2m 14.78s (4.28) **Going Correction** +0.40s/f (Good)
WFA 3 from 4yo+ 11lb **6** Ran SP% **112.1**
Speed ratings (Par 101): **98,97,95,90,74 74**
toteswingers: 1&2 £1.10, 2&3 £1.80, 1&3 £1.10 CSF £5.05 TOTE £2.30: £1.50, £1.30; EX 4.30. There was no bid for the winner. Viewing was claimed by A. G. Newcombe for £6000.
Owner S Hussain & P O'Neill **Bred** Brittas House Stud & Lynch Bages & Samac **Trained** Cropthorne, Worcs

FOCUS
A moderate seller and not form to get carried away with.

3744 HENRY STREETER FILLIES' H'CAP (TURF) — 1m 3f 106y
3:30 (3:30) (Class 5) (0-70,73) 3-Y-0+ **£2,385** (£704; £352) **Stalls** High

Form RPR

1522 **1** **Amistress**[4] 3642 3-9-2 **68**.......................... SebSanders 1 74+
(Eve Johnson Houghton) *mde virtually all: set stdy gallop: rdn and fnd ex 2f out: clr ins fnl f: styd on wl: pushed out* **13/8**[2]

-031 **2** 2 1/2 **Undulant Way**[9] 3467 3-9-7 **73** 6ex.......................... PatDobbs 2 75+
(Amanda Perrett) *chsd wnr: rdn and effrt wl over 2f out: drvn to chse wnr and edgd rt 1f out: no imp after* **8/11**[1]

33-0 **3** 2 1/2 **Phase Shift**[16] 3228 3-8-12 **64**.......................... MartinDwyer 3 62
(William Muir) *t.k.h: chsd wnr: rdn wl over 2f out: nt pce of wnr 2f out: [illegible]* **12/1**[3]

04-0 **4** 2 **Melancholy Hill (IRE)**[illegible] [illegible] [illegible] 1 [illegible]
(Alan King) *stdd s: hld up in last: rdn over 2f out: kpt on same pce and no imp* **25/1**

2m 40.19s (8.69) **Going Correction** +0.40s/f (Good) **4** Ran SP% **107.5**
Speed ratings (Par 100): **84,82,80,78**
CSF £3.14 TOTE £2.40; EX 2.70.
Owner Mrs P Robeson **Bred** Southcourt Stud **Trained** Blewbury, Oxon

FOCUS
This became tactical with no-one wanting to lead early and the order hardly changed during the contest.

3745 AIREY MILLER PARTNERSHIP NURSERY — 5f (P)
4:00 (4:00) (Class 5) 2-Y-O **£2,726** (£805; £402) **Stalls** High

Form RPR

51 **1** **Piranha (IRE)**[16] 3221 2-9-5 **78**.......................... WilliamBuick 4 81+
(Ed Dunlop) *hld up in tch: rdn and qcknd to chal 1f out: led jst ins fnl f: r.o wl: rdn out* **11/10**[1]

604 **2** nk **Gin Twist**[18] 3165 2-7-13 **63**.......................... HarryBentley(5) 2 65
(Tom Dascombe) *chsd ldrs: rdn and effrt 2f out: ev ch fnl f: r.o wl u.p* **9/1**

444 **3** 3/4 **Balm**[33] 2661 2-8-2 **66**.......................... KieranO'Neill(5) 6 65
(Richard Hannon) *chsd ldr: rdn wl over 1f out: drvn and ev ch 1f out: styd on same pce fnl 100yds* **7/1**[3]

104 **4** 3 1/4 **I'm Still The Man (IRE)**[14] 3284 2-8-12 **74**.......................... KierenFox(3) 3 62
(Bill Turner) *racd in last pair: shkn up and hdwy on outer 4f out: chsd ldrs and rdn 2f out: wknd u.p ent fnl f* **12/1**

421 **5** 3/4 **Dark Ages (IRE)**[38] 2523 2-9-0 **73**.......................... JamieSpencer 1 58
(Noel Quinlan) *hld up in tch: swtchd to outer 3f out: rdn and effrt whn hung lft wl over 1f out: sn struggling and btn ent fnl f* **3/1**[2]

0615 **6** 2 **Powerful Wind (IRE)**[41] 2437 2-9-6 **79**.......................... LukeMorris 5 57
(Ronald Harris) *led: rdn 2f out: drvn over 1f out: hdd jst ins fnl f: fdd fnl 150yds* **14/1**

60.09 secs (1.29) **Going Correction** +0.175s/f (Slow) **6** Ran SP% **109.5**
Speed ratings (Par 94): **96,95,94,89,87 84**
toteswingers: 1&2 £1.60, 2&3 £5.10, 1&3 £1.40 CSF £11.25 TOTE £2.70: £1.30, £3.10; EX 7.30.
Owner St Albans Bloodstock LLP **Bred** Epona Bloodstock Ltd **Trained** Newmarket, Suffolk
■ The 'official' ratings shown next to each horse are estimated and for information purposes only.

FOCUS
A fair nursery run at a good pace.

NOTEBOOK
Piranha(IRE) had looked progressive when winning easily over this trip at Kempton last time and was all the rage to follow up. Having travelled smoothly behind the leaders, she had to battle much harder than it appeared she would need to when produced through the gap a furlong out, but she always looked as though she was going to get there. She should continue to progress. (op 10-11)
Gin Twist showed some ability in three turf maidens and was presented with an inviting gap against the inside rail once into the straight. She may even have hit the front for a few strides inside the last furlong and made the favourite battle all the way to the line. She should be up to winning a similar event. (op 8-1 tchd 7-1)
Balm had finished fourth in all three starts in turf maidens and improved a place here having been up there throughout and holding every chance. (op 8-1 tchd 17-2 and 13-2)
I'm Still The Man(IRE) had excuses for two defeats since winning at 25-1 on his Sandown debut, being outclassed in the Windsor Castle and not improving for the extra furlong at Kempton. He had his chance, but lost ground on the outside turning into the straight and there was no way back. (op 16-1)
Dark Ages(IRE) had shown progressive form in three starts on turf culminating in her Nottingham success, but she didn't seem to take to the surface and didn't handle the home bend too well. She was reported to have been slowly away and it's probably best to forgive her this. Official explanation: jockey said filly was slowly away (op 7-2 tchd 4-1)
Powerful Wind(IRE) was totally out of his depth in Listed company last time, but had previously made all to win his maiden over this trip at Kempton. He attempted the same tactics here, but stopped quickly once headed inside the last furlong. (op 12-1 tchd 11-1)

3746 GOT THE FEELING? GET TO LADBROKES MAIDEN AUCTION STKS 6f (P)
4:30 (4:35) (Class 6) 2-Y-O £1,704 (£503; £251) **Stalls** Low

Form RPR
340 **1** **Crowning Star (IRE)**[22] 3014 2-9-1 0 (t) LukeMorris 2 74
(J S Moore) *mde all: rdn clr over 1f out: in command and pushed out ins fnl f* **5/2**[1]
0 **2** *2* **King Of Wing (IRE)**[16] 3229 2-8-12 0 PatDobbs 12 65
(Richard Hannon) *in tch on outer: lost pl end 2f out: drvn and effrt over 1f out: chsd wnr ins fnl f: no imp* **6/1**[3]
3 *nk* **Emirates Art** 2-8-10 0 JamieSpencer 5 62+
(David Simcock) *hmpd and dropped to rr sn after s: hld up in last: c wd wl over 1f out: stl last and pushed along over 1f out: r.o wl ins fnl f: gng on fin* **13/2**
054 **4** *½* **Flosse**[20] 3070 2-8-4 0 AndreaAtzeni 11 55+
(Ed Walker) *stdd s: t.k.h: hld up wl in tch: short of room 4f out: rdn and effrt over 1f out: chsd wnr and hld hd awkwardly 1f out: styd on same pce ins fnl f* **12/1**
55 **5** *nk* **Purple Affair (IRE)**[18] 3171 2-8-7 0 RyanPowell(5) 6 62+
(J S Moore) *t.k.h: chsd ldrs: lost pl bnd 2f out: rallied 1f out: kpt on ins fnl f: no threat to wnr* **11/1**
20 **6** *¾* **Mystery Cool (IRE)**[18] 3171 2-8-4 0 WilliamCarson 1 51
(Stuart Williams) *led rdrless to s: chsd ldrs: effrt u.p wl over 1f out: unable qck 1f out: styd on same pce after* **25/1**
7 *¾* **Raffinn** 2-8-12 0 JamesDoyle 3 57+
(Sylvester Kirk) *hld up wl in tch in last trio: rdn and effrt on inner over 1f out: styd on same pce and no imp ins fnl f* **50/1**
0 **8** *½* **Russian Bullet**[11] 3388 2-8-12 0 FergusSweeney 9 56
(Jamie Osborne) *chsd ldrs: wnt 2nd 2f out: rdn and unable qck w wnr over 1f out: lost 2nd 1f out and wknd ins fnl f* **66/1**
0 **9** *1½* **Best In Show**[25] 2901 2-9-1 0 SebSanders 4 54+
(J W Hills) *hld up in last pair: nt clr run 4f out: rdn and effrt towards inner over 1f out: no imp: nvr trbld ldrs* **4/1**[2]
10 *1¼* **Bareback (IRE)** 2-9-1 0 AdamKirby 8 50
(John Best) *chsd wnr: rdn 3f out: lost 2nd 2f out and sn struggling: wknd over 1f out* **15/2**
0 **11** *½* **Melting Pot**[46] 2291 2-9-1 0 IanMongan 10 49
(Hugo Palmer) *broke wl: sn stdd and t.k.h and hld up in tch towards rr: rn green and lost pl bnd 2f out: n.d after* **12/1**

1m 14.08s (2.18) **Going Correction** +0.175s/f (Slow) 11 Ran SP% 119.0
Speed ratings (Par 92): **92,89,88,88,87 86,85,85,83,81 80**
toteswingers:1&2:£4.60, 2&3:£6.50, 1&3:£3.00 CSF £17.67 TOTE £2.90: £1.30, £1.60, £2.80; EX 19.50.
Owner Ray Styles & J S Moore **Bred** Summerhill Bloodstock **Trained** Upper Lambourn, Berks

FOCUS
A modest maiden, but with a couple of eye-catchers.

NOTEBOOK
Crowning Star(IRE) was out of his depth in the Windsor Castle last time, but had run well to make the frame in his first two starts and won this well under a positive ride. Soon in front, he injected a bit of pace as he was angled off the rail after turning in and was never going to be caught from that point. He should be able to build on this. (op 2-1 tchd 15-8)
King Of Wing(IRE) didn't get home on the easy ground when second-favourite for his Windsor debut, but ran much better here especially as he took a wide course throughout. A routine maiden should come his way. (tchd 13-2)
Emirates Art ◆ was slowly away and was still in last place passing the furlong pole having come extremely wide off the home bend, but she finished like a train. A 19,000gns 2-y-o out of a winner at up to 1m2f, she is one to keep onside especially when upped in trip. She was reported to have suffered interference shortly after the start. Official explanation: jockey said filly suffered interference shortly after start (op 15-2)
Flosse didn't seem to see out the extended 7f at Beverley on her third start and ran better here, staying on well down the home straight, but she has had a few chances now. (op 8-1)
Purple Affair(IRE) showed a little ability in his first two starts and again ran creditably without suggesting he is moving forward. (op 9-1)
Mystery Cool(IRE) was never far away and had her chance, but she had proved very awkward before the start and had to be walked to post. She doesn't seem to be improving. (op 14-1)
Best In Show attracted plenty of support in the market, but he never threatened to take a hand. (op 9-1 tchd 10-1)

3747 LADBROKES.COM MEDIAN AUCTION MAIDEN STKS 6f (P)
5:00 (5:04) (Class 6) 3-4-Y-O £1,704 (£503; £251) **Stalls** Low

Form RPR
02 **1** **Bravo King (IRE)**[41] 2427 3-9-3 0 PaulDoe 11 83+
(Jim Best) *broke fast and crossed to rail: mde all: clr after 1f: rdn and drew wl clr 2f out: eased wl ins fnl f: unchal* **7/2**[2]
564 **2** *4* **Arabian Heights**[25] 2924 3-9-3 73 SebSanders 5 70+
(Sir Mark Prescott Bt) *dwlt: towards rr: bustled along and hdwy into midfield 4f out: rdn and hung lft over 1f out: wnt 2nd ins fnl f: no ch w wnr* **11/8**[1]
4-60 **3** *3½* **Wong Again**[16] 3223 3-8-9 57 KierenFox(3) 1 56
(J W Hills) *chsd ldng pair: rdn to chse clr wnr over 1f out: no imp and lost 2nd iside fnl f* **8/1**
4 *nk* **Cahala Dancer (IRE)** 3-8-12 0 JamesDoyle 8 55+
(Roger Teal) *s.i.s: bhd: rdn and rn green 2f out: stl running green but styd on past btn horses ins fnl f: nvr trbld ldrs* **8/1**

0000 **5** *3* **Sailing North (USA)**[14] 3272 3-9-3 62 LukeMorris 6 52
(Ronald Harris) *chsd clr wnr: drvn and no hdwy over 3f out: lost 2nd 2f out and sn wl btn: wknd over 1f out* **14/1**
5-3 **6** *nk* **Bint Alakaaber (IRE)**[8] 3494 3-8-12 0 PatDobbs 4 46
(J R Jenkins) *t.k.h: prom in main gp: rdn and struggling over 2f out: wl btn fr wl over 1f out* **6/1**[3]
7 *1¼* **Boblini** 3-8-12 0 FergusSweeney 12 43
(Mark Usher) *s.i.s: hld up wl off the pce in rr: rn green bnd 2f out: nvr on terms* **33/1**
0 **8** *hd* **Reggie Perrin**[11] 3392 3-9-3 0 IanMongan 7 47
(Pat Phelan) *s.i.s: a in rr: n.d* **14/1**
00- **9** *3¼* **Disco Doll**[399] 2641 3-8-12 0 WilliamCarson 3 34
(Patrick Chamings) *dwlt: sn midfield and t.k.h: rdn and wknd over 2f out: wl bhd fnl 2f: eased wl ins fnl f* **16/1**
10 *½* **Mucky Molly** 3-8-12 0 MarcHalford 9 32
(Olivia Maylam) *prom in main gp on outer: rdn and struggling 3f out: wknd over 2f out: wl bhd and eased ins fnl f* **28/1**

1m 12.91s (1.01) **Going Correction** +0.175s/f (Slow) 10 Ran SP% 126.4
Speed ratings (Par 101): **100,94,90,89,85 85,83,83,78,78**
toteswingers:1&2:£2.20, 2&3:£3.70, 1&3:£4.00 CSF £9.52 TOTE £5.80: £2.40, £1.10, £3.10; EX 12.20.
Owner M&R Refurbishments Ltd **Bred** Celbridge Estates Ltd **Trained** Lewes, E Sussex

FOCUS
A modest maiden which was basically won in the first furlong.
Disco Doll Official explanation: jockey said filly hung right on bend
T/Plt: £12.10 to a £1 stake. Pool of £49,866.55 - 2,990.52 winning tickets. T/Qpdt: £7.00 to a £1 stake. Pool of £3,145.80 - 329.60 winning tickets. SP

3748 - 3753a (Foreign Racing) - See Raceform Interactive

[3575]DONCASTER (L-H)
Thursday, July 7

OFFICIAL GOING: Good to firm (watered; 7.8)
Wind: Light against Weather: Sunny with cloudy periods

3754 AMATEUR JOCKEYS ASSOCIATION H'CAP (FOR AMATEUR RIDERS) 2m 110y
6:30 (6:31) (Class 6) (0-65,65) 4-Y-O+ £2,634 (£810; £405) **Stalls** Low

Form RPR
00-3 **1** **Sendali (FR)**[27] 1794 7-10-1 52 MissLHorner 4 66
(Chris Grant) *hld up in midfield: stdy hdwy 6f out: trckd ldrs 4f out: cl up 3f out: led over 2f out: rdn clr wl over 1f out: sn edgd lft and styd on strly* **5/1**[1]
6103 **2** *7* **Heart Of Dubai (USA)**[19] 3185 6-9-13 55 (p) MissRSmith(5) 9 61
(Micky Hammond) *trckd ldrs: hdwy over 4f out: led 3f out: sn rdn and hdd over 2f out: drvn over 1f out and kpt on same pce* **13/2**[3]
-615 **3** *1½* **Spiders Star**[8] 3507 8-10-7 65 MissCarlyFrater(7) 6 69
(Simon West) *hld up and bhd: hdwy on wd outside 4f out: rdn to chse ldng pair over 2f out: sn hung lft and no imp* **6/1**[2]
0-33 **4** *3½* **Strikemaster (IRE)**[10] 3450 5-9-8 52 (t) MrAaronJames(7) 12 52
(Lee James) *dwlt and in rr: hdwy on wd outside 4f out: rdn along over 2f out: styd on appr fnl f: nvr nr ldrs* **7/1**
34-6 **5** *2¾* **Park's Prodigy**[10] 3450 7-10-7 63 (t) MrGRSmith(5) 1 60
(David Thompson) *in tch: effrt and hdwy 4f out: rdn to chse ldrs 3f out: sn no imp* **33/1**
5020 **6** *5* **Leaving Alone (USA)**[40] 2496 4-10-3 54 (p) MissSBrotherton 3 45
(Edwin Tuer) *trckd ldr: cl up 1/2-way: led over 4f out: rdn along and hdd 3f out: grad wknd* **5/1**[1]
5455 **7** *3* **Duar Mapel (USA)**[6] 3599 5-9-7 49 (b) MissHCuthbert(5) 5 36
(Brian Baugh) *trckd ldr: led after 7f: rdn along over 5f out: hdd over 4f out: grad wknd fr over 2f out* **22/1**
4012 **8** *¾* **Mustajed**[17] 3240 10-10-4 60 MrPMillman(5) 11 46
(Rod Millman) *hld up in tch: hdwy over 4f out: rdn and hung lft 3f out: sn wknd* **8/1**
-050 **9** *¾* **Hi Dancer**[21] 3086 8-10-2 58 MissCharlotteHolmes(5) 7 43
(Ben Haslam) *hld up towards rr: sme hdwy over 3f out: sn rdn and n.d* **14/1**
60-0 **10** *3¼* **Follow The Sun (IRE)**[8] 3510 7-9-13 50 (p) MissGAndrews 2 31
(Peter Niven) *hld up: hdwy over 5f out: swtchd rt and rdn over 3f out: sn no hdwy* **25/1**
5/62 **11** *5* **Ritsi**[14] 3300 8-9-5 49 MissNHayes(7) 10 24
(Marjorie Fife) *a in rr* **9/1**
255- **12** *11* **Sand Repeal (IRE)**[370] 3641 9-9-13 53 MrRBirkett(3) 14 15
(Julia Feilden) *led: pushed along and hdd after 7f: rdn 5f out: sn wknd* **20/1**

3m 41.68s (1.28) **Going Correction** -0.05s/f (Good) 12 Ran SP% 117.1
Speed ratings (Par 101): **94,90,90,88,87 84,83,82,82,81 78,73**
toteswingers:1&2:£6.20, 1&3:£6.00, 2&3:£10.10 CSF £34.50 CT £200.83 TOTE £3.70: £1.10, £2.70, £2.70; EX 29.30.
Owner Elliott Brothers And Peacock **Bred** Sarl Haras Du Taillis Et Al **Trained** Newton Bewley, Co Durham
■ Stewards' Enquiry : Miss N Hayes caution: used whip when out of contention.

FOCUS
Inside rail on Round course moved out 6yds which added 76yds to 2m race, 57yds to 1m 4f race and 28yds to 1m race. The Town Moor had escaped the showers and on a bright, sunny evening the ground was reckoned to be on the 'fast side of good. A low-grade amateur riders' handicap run at a sound pace. The first two were closely matched on Catterick May form.
Duar Mapel(USA) Official explanation: vet said gelding finished lame left-fore

3755 HAPPY BIRTHDAY DANIEL CALOW MAIDEN STKS 6f
7:00 (7:08) (Class 5) 2-Y-O £2,264 (£673; £336; £168) **Stalls** High

Form RPR
1 **Al Khan (IRE)** 2-9-3 0 JimmyFortune 7 82+
(Peter Chapple-Hyam) *trckd ldrs: smooth hdwy 2f out: rdn to ld jst over 1f out: kpt on strly* **16/1**
0 **2** *2¼* **The Blue Banana (IRE)**[19] 3182 2-9-3 0 MartinDwyer 11 75
(Brian Meehan) *prom: cl up 1/2-way: led 2f out: sn rdn and hdd jst over 1f out: drvn ent fnl f and kpt on same pce* **20/1**
54 **3** *1* **Commanche**[14] 3314 2-9-3 0 TomEaves 4 72
(Bryan Smart) *prom: effrt and cl up 1/2-way: rdn and ev ch over 2f out: tl drvn appr fnl f and kpt on same pce* **8/1**[3]
4 *¾* **Bartolomeu** 2-9-3 0 AndreaAtzeni 6 70+
(Marco Botti) *hld up in midfield: effrt and hdwy whn n.m.r 2f out: sn rdn: kpt on ins fnl f: nrst fin* **9/4**[2]

Form	Pos	Dist	Horse	Jockey	RPR
	5	*1 ½*	**O'Gorman** 2-9-3 0 (Kevin Ryan) *s.i.s and bhd: t.k.h: gd hdwy into midfield 1/2-way: chsd ldrs 2f out: sn rdn and one pce* **5/4**[1]	PhillipMakin 14	66+
4	**6**	*½*	**Magic Bounty**[12] 3382 2-8-12 0 (Tim Easterby) *hmpd s and bhd: swtchd rt over 2f out: gd hdwy over 1f out: r.o strly fnl f: nrst fin* **25/1**	LanceBetts(5) 2	64+
5	**7**	*½*	**Electrickery**[15] 3274 2-8-12 0 (Mark Johnston) *chsd ldrs: rdn along over 2f out: grad wknd* **10/1**	AdrianNicholls 12	58
0	**8**	*1*	**Angel Warrior (IRE)**[22] 3035 2-9-3 0 (Ben Haslam) *wnt lft s: in tch on outer: rdn along wl over 2f out: no imp* **100/1**	BarryMcHugh 3	60
	9	*¾*	**Divine Success (IRE)** 2-9-3 0 (Richard Fahey) *dwlt and towards rr: pushed along and sme hdwy over 2f out: n.d* **33/1**	TonyHamilton 8	57
55	**10**	*½*	**Look Here's Lady**[17] 3237 2-8-12 0 (Ed McMahon) *in tch on outer: hdwy to chse ldrs over 2f out: sn rdn and wknd over 1f out* **100/1**	GrahamGibbons 16	51
5	**11**	*2 ½*	**Keep Swinging (IRE)**[19] 3186 2-9-3 0 (Tom Tate) *cl up: led 1/2-way: rdn and hdd 2f out: sn drvn and wknd over 1f out* **10/1**	JamieSpencer 10	48
	12	*nk*	**Methaen (USA)** 2-9-3 0 (Ed Dunlop) *nvr bttr than midfield* **33/1**	TadhgO'Shea 13	47
0	**13**	*3*	**On The Hoof**[15] 3274 2-9-3 0 (Michael Easterby) *dwlt: a towards rr* **80/1**	JamesSullivan 15	38
04	**14**	*shd*	**Johnson's Cat (IRE)**[9] 3491 2-9-0 0 (Richard Guest) *a in rr* **100/1**	RobertLButler(3) 1	38
	15	*2 ¾*	**Copp The Lot (USA)** 2-9-3 0 (David Nicholls) *slt ld to 1/2-way: cl up tl rdn over 2f out and sn wknd* **25/1**	AndrewMullen 5	30

1m 13.49s (-0.11) **Going Correction** -0.05s/f (Good) **15** Ran SP% **132.9**
Speed ratings (Par 94): **98,95,93,92,90 90,89,88,87,86 83,82,78,78,74**
toteswingers:1&2:£28.20, 1&3:£9.30, 2&3:£9.90 CSF £313.33 TOTE £24.60: £5.80, £6.90, £2.80; EX 211.60.
Owner Ziad A Galadari **Bred** Galadari Sons Stud Company Limited **Trained** Newmarket, Suffolk

FOCUS
Probably a fair juvenile maiden.

NOTEBOOK
Al Khan(IRE), a well-made newcomer, is a homebred and, a bit above himself, he gave a problem or two in the paddock. He travelled strongly on the heels of the leaders and after being put about his job he was firmly in command at the line. He looks a decent prospect. (op 14-1 tchd 20-1)
The Blue Banana(IRE), stoutly bred on his dam's side, had picked up late on his debut over 7f. He was bang in the firing line throughout and can certainly go one better possibly returned to seven. (op 16-1)
Commanche, having his third run, travelled strongly towards the far side. He has improved with each outing and looks a likely nursery type. (op 12-1 tchd 7-1)
Bartolomeu, a good-bodied newcomer, carried plenty of support. After racing in midfield he put in some eyecatching late work. His stable's youngsters generally improve a good deal for their first outing. (op 11-4 tchd 2-1)
O'Gorman, who cost 63,000 euros, is a half-brother to the smart youngster and Mill Reef winner Temple Meads. Not that big, he was all the rage in the market. After having to have a hind shoe attended to at the start, he missed the break completely. He made smooth headway on to the heels of the leaders soon after halfway but in the end ran out of petrol. Clearly well regarded from a stable with a powerful hand in the 2yo division, he must be given another chance. (op 13-8 tchd 9-4)
Magic Bounty, who made his debut over 7f, stayed on nicely after being last at halfway. He needs another outing for a nursery mark and a step back up in distance.
Electrickery, who showed ability on her debut at Carlisle, was soon flat out and needs a stiffer test. (op 12-1 tchd 8-1)
Keep Swinging(IRE) Official explanation: jockey said colt hung right throughout

3756 CROWNHOTEL-BAWTRY.COM MAIDEN STKS 6f

7:35 (7:38) (Class 5) 3-Y-O+ **£2,385** (£704; £352) **Stalls** High

Form	Pos	Dist	Horse	Jockey	RPR
00	**1**		**My Own Way Home**[13] 3343 3-8-9 0 [illegible] *[illegible] ldrs 2f out: styd on to ld jst ins fnl f: sn drvn and jst hld on* [illegible]	MartinHarley(3) 2	65
0-22	**2**	*shd*	**Vizean (IRE)**[21] 3090 3-8-12 74 (Ed McMahon) *prom and sn swtchd rt to r on stands' rail: chsd ldng pair: hdwy wl over 1f out: sn rdn: drvn to chal ins fnl f: kpt on wl: jst hld* **1/1**[1]	RichardMullen 8	65
	3	*2 ¼*	**Green Howard** 3-9-3 0 (Robin Bastiman) *dwlt and bhd: swtchd rt and hdwy wl over 1f out: sn rdn and styd on strly ins fnl f* **25/1**	DanielTudhope 7	63
0	**4**	*nk*	**Saktoon (USA)**[83] 1362 3-8-12 0 (Clive Brittain) *chsd ldrs on outer: rdn along over 2f out: drvn over 1f out: kpt on ins fnl f* **8/1**	PhilipRobinson 1	57
	5	*1*	**Needwood Park** 3-9-3 0 (David Barron) *midfield: hdwy over 2f out: sn rdn and kpt on u.p appr fnl f: nrest fnish* **12/1**	GrahamGibbons 6	59
0-0	**6**	*½*	**Valentine's Gift**[29] 2802 3-9-3 0 (Neville Bycroft) *bhd: rdn along 2f out: swtchd lft to outer and styd on wl fnl f: nrst fin* **100/1**	AndrewElliott 10	57
550-	**7**	*1 ½*	**Sulis Minerva (IRE)**[356] 4090 4-8-11 68 (Jeremy Gask) *chsd clr ldr: rdn along 2f out: led briefly appr fnl f: sn drvn and hdd: wknd* **9/1**	RaulDaSilva(7) 5	48
0-00	**8**	*1*	**Stella Marris**[30] 2781 4-9-4 37 (Christopher Wilson) *towards rr: rdn and sme hdwy over 2f out: n.d* **100/1**	PaddyAspell 12	45?
0-	**9**	*½*	**Da'Quonde (IRE)**[391] 2936 3-8-12 0 (Bryan Smart) *in rr: rdn along and hdwy 2f out: drvn over 1f out and n.d* **20/1**	TomEaves 13	42
-540	**10**	*2 ¾*	**Amhran (IRE)**[28] 2841 3-9-3 72 (Brian Meehan) *racd alone centre: led and sn clr at str pce: rdn along wl over 1f out: wknd qckly and hdd appr fnl f: dropped away rapidly* **9/2**[2]	(b[1]) MartinDwyer 3	39
60	**11**	*28*	**Langtoon Lass**[22] 3053 3-8-12 0 (David Nicholls) *in tch: rdn along 1/2-way: sn wknd and bhd* **40/1**	AdrianNicholls 11	—

1m 13.71s (0.11) **Going Correction** -0.05s/f (Good)
WFA 3 from 4yo 6lb **11** Ran SP% **122.5**
Speed ratings (Par 103): **97,96,93,93,92 91,89,88,87,83 46**
toteswingers:1&2:£3.40, 1&3:£18.60, 2&3:£10.20 CSF £14.58 TOTE £10.30: £2.10, £1.10, £5.60; EX 17.10.
Owner L Audus **Bred** Theresa Fitsall **Trained** Newmarket, Suffolk
■ Stewards' Enquiry : Richard Mullen caution: used whip with excessive frequency.

FOCUS
A modest sprint maiden run at a breakneck pace. The second possibly paid for racing a bit more prominently than the rest of the first six home and some of these may be flattered.

Amhran(IRE) Official explanation: jockey said colt ran too free

3757 DC TRAINING AND DEVELOPMENT SERVICES LTD FILLIES' H'CAP 1m (R)

8:10 (8:10) (Class 4) (0-85,83) 3-Y-O+ **£4,294** (£1,268; £634) **Stalls** High

Form	Pos	Dist	Horse	Jockey	RPR
0-41	**1**		**Submission**[36] 2615 3-9-5 83 (Luca Cumani) *hld up towards rr: smooth hdwy to trck ldrs over 2f out: effrt and nt clr run over 1f out: swtchd lft and rdn ent fnl f: qcknd wl to ld last 50yds* **4/6**[1]	KierenFallon 7	95+
10	**2**	*1*	**Gracefield (USA)**[28] 2839 3-9-2 80 (Mahmood Al Zarooni) *trckd ldrs: smooth hdwy on outer 3f out: cl up 2f out: rdn to chal over 1f and ev ch tl drvn and nt qckn last 50yds* **9/1**[3]	AhmedAjtebi 8	86
5-06	**3**	*½*	**Mazamorra (USA)**[29] 2822 4-9-6 75 (Marco Botti) *trckd ldr: hdwy and cl up 2f out: rdn to ld over 1f out: drvn ent fnl f: hdd and nt qckn last 50yds* **25/1**	AndreaAtzeni 3	82
6402	**4**	*1 ¾*	**Christmas Light**[6] 3572 4-8-9 64 (David O'Meara) *trckd ldrs: hdwy 3f out: rdn over 2f out: drvn and n.m.r over 1f out: one pce ent fnl f* **6/1**[2]	TomEaves 5	67
-002	**5**	*nk*	**Kerrys Requiem (IRE)**[12] 3386 5-9-5 77 (Tim Pitt) *hld up in rr: hdwy 3f out: trckd ldrs 2f out: swtchd lft and rdn ent fnl f: one pce* **10/1**	(p) SeanLevey(3) 6	79
0-03	**6**	*½*	**Makheelah**[5] 3633 3-8-1 65 (Clive Brittain) *trckd ldng pair: hdwy 3f out and sn cl up: rdn to chal 2f out and ev ch tl drvn and wknd ent fnl f* **12/1**	FrannyNorton 1	64
1630	**7**	*hd*	**Adaria**[26] 2935 3-9-1 79 (David C Griffiths) *led: rdn along 2f out: drvn and edgd lft over 1f out: sn hdd and grad wknd* **14/1**	RichardMullen 4	77
5000	**8**	*10*	**Cheers For Thea (IRE)**[12] 3407 6-9-9 83 (Tim Easterby) *hld up towards rr: effrt and sme hdwy 3f out: rdn along 2f out: sn outpcd and eased over 1f out* **20/1**	(t) LanceBetts(5) 2	59

1m 39.64s (-0.06) **Going Correction** -0.05s/f (Good)
WFA 3 from 4yo+ 9lb **8** Ran SP% **116.3**
Speed ratings (Par 102): **98,97,96,94,94 93,93,83**
toteswingers:1&2:£2.10, 1&3:£6.70, 2&3:£17.30 CSF £7.89 CT £84.36 TOTE £1.70: £1.10, £2.10, £4.50; EX 8.00.
Owner Pearl Bloodstock Ltd **Bred** Fittocks Stud Ltd **Trained** Newmarket, Suffolk

FOCUS
There was a heavy rainstorm ahead of this fillies' handicap. The pace was not strong and they raced in one group towards the centre in the home straight. The first pair were unexposed and the winner can do better.

3758 ATTEYS H'CAP 1m 4f

8:45 (8:46) (Class 4) (0-80,80) 3-Y-O+ **£4,075** (£1,212; £606; £303) **Stalls** Low

Form	Pos	Dist	Horse	Jockey	RPR
04-0	**1**		**Royal Trooper (IRE)**[23] 3023 5-9-11 77 (James Given) *hld up in rr: hdwy 3f out: cl up over 1f out: rdn to ld ent fnl f: kpt on wl* **9/1**	FrederikTylicki 3	88
41-3	**2**	*¾*	**Sense Of Pride**[35] 2649 4-9-11 77 (John Gosden) *trckd ldrs on outer: pushed along over 4f out: hdwy and cl up 3f out: led wl over 2f out: jnd and rdn over 1f out: hdd and drvn ent fnl f: sn edgd lft: kpt on* **11/8**[1]	RobertHavlin 12	87
-133	**3**	*9*	**Ollon (USA)**[31] 2764 3-8-2 67 (Richard Fahey) *hld up in rr: hdwy over 3f out: chsd ldng pair wl over 1f out: sn rdn and one pce appr fnl f* **7/2**[2]	PaulHanagan 9	62
0030	**4**	*2*	**Green Lightning (IRE)**[27] 2892 4-9-6 72 (Mark Johnston) *trckd ldng pair: hdwy over 3f out: sn cl up: rdn over 2f out: drvn and wknd appr fnl f* **8/1**	(b) AdrianNicholls 2	64
3541	**5**	*5*	**Patavium (IRE)**[20] 3129 8-9-7 73 (Edwin Tuer) *hld up in tch: hdwy on inner 3f out: rdn and cl up wl over 2f out: sn rdn and wknd over 1f out* **9/1**	JamesSullivan 7	57
03P-	**6**	*8*	**Ugalla**[350] 4304 4-9-10 76 (Jane Chapple-Hyam) *led: rdn along over 3f out: hdd wl over 2f out: sn drvn and wknd* **20/1**	GrahamGibbons 1	47
0006	**7**	[illegible]	[illegible][13] [illegible] [illegible] 79 (John Mackie) *trckd ldr: effrt 4f out: rdn along 3f out: [illegible] 2f* **6/1**[3]	StephenCraine 4	36

2m 32.58s (-2.32) **Going Correction** -0.05s/f (Good)
WFA 3 from 4yo+ 13lb **7** Ran SP% **114.5**
Speed ratings (Par 105): **105,104,98,97,93 88,82**
toteswingers:1&2:£3.70, 1&3:£7.40, 2&3:£1.70 CSF £21.99 CT £53.14 TOTE £14.50: £4.10, £1.20; EX 32.60.
Owner J Barson **Bred** Western Bloodstock **Trained** Willoughton, Lincs

FOCUS
More rain ahead of this depleted 67-79 handicap, run at just a steady pace until the final half-mile. The first pair pulled clear, with a 6lb step up from the winner.

3759 ARTSIGN H'CAP 5f

9:15 (9:15) (Class 5) (0-75,74) 3-Y-O+ **£4,204** (£1,251; £625; £312) **Stalls** High

Form	Pos	Dist	Horse	Jockey	RPR
0201	**1**		**Mandalay King (IRE)**[9] 3488 6-9-10 72 6ex (Marjorie Fife) *towards rr: hdwy on outer 2f out: rdn to ld ent fnl f: kpt on wl* **11/2**	(p) DanielTudhope 2	82
4000	**2**	*1 ½*	**Go Nani Go**[14] 3322 5-9-10 72 (Ed de Giles) *hld up in tch: swtchd lft and hdwy 2f out: effrt to chse ldrs over 1f out: n.m.r ent fnl f: sn rdn and kpt on to take 2nd nr line* **16/1**	PatCosgrave 5	77
2232	**3**	*shd*	**Ingleby Star (IRE)**[9] 3488 6-9-4 69 (Ian McInnes) *stmbld s: in tch: hdwy 2f out: rdn and ev ch jst over 1f out: drvn and one pce ins fnl f: lost 2nd nr line* **7/1**	(p) GaryBartley(3) 3	74
6244	**4**	*1*	**Bosun Breese**[6] 3582 6-9-7 74 (David Barron) *led early: trckd ldrs on stands rail: effrt and nt clr run 2f out: sn swtchd lft: drvn to chal and ev ch whn n.m.r ent fnl f: sn drvn and carried rt: one pce last 75 yds* **4/1**[2]	LMcNiff(5) 9	75
5320	**5**	*shd*	**Crimson Cloud**[19] 3166 3-9-4 71 (Richard Fahey) *veered bdly lft jst after s and sn bhd: rdn and hdwy wl over 1f out: kpt on ins fnl f: nrst fin* **11/4**[1]	PaulHanagan 1	70
30-0	**6**	*2 ½*	**Milton Of Campsie**[37] 2590 6-9-8 70 (John Balding) *trckd ldrs: hdwy to ld 2f out: sn rdn: hdd and drvn ent fnl f: sn edgd rt and wknd* **10/1**	MartinLane 4	63
6600	**7**	*5*	**Garstang**[17] 3222 8-8-9 57 (John Balding) *cl up: disp ld 1/2-way: rdn 2f out: wkng whn n.m.r on inner ent fnl f* **16/1**	(b) GrahamGibbons 6	34

5211 **8** *10* **Miss Polly Plum**[12] 3389 4-9-12 **74**............................(p) AndreaAtzeni 7 19
(Chris Dwyer) *sn led: rdn along 1/2-way: hdd 2f out: sn wknd and bhd whn eased over 1f out* **9/2**[3]

59.94 secs (-0.56) **Going Correction** -0.05s/f (Good)
WFA 3 from 4yo+ 5lb **8** Ran SP% **113.6**
Speed ratings (Par 103): **102,99,99,97,97 93,85,69**
toteswingers:1&2:£9.40, 1&3:£7.00, 2&3:£14.40 CSF £84.41 CT £619.64 TOTE £5.10: £1.50, £4.50, £1.60; EX 132.30.
Owner R W Fife **Bred** Forenaghts Stud And Dermot Cantillon **Trained** Stillington, N Yorks

FOCUS
A modest 57-74 sprint handicap run at a strong pace. The winner is rated better than ever.
Ingleby Star(IRE) Official explanation: jockey said gelding slipped leaving stalls
Garstang Official explanation: jockey said gelding ran too free
Miss Polly Plum Official explanation: trainer said, regarding running, that the filly was unsuited by not being able to dominate.
T/Plt: £34.70 to a £1 stake. Pool:£75,010.58 - 1,574.42 winning tickets T/Qpdt: £6.60 to a £1 stake. Pool:£8,359.44 - 928.70 winning tickets JR

3533 EPSOM (L-H)
Thursday, July 7

OFFICIAL GOING: Good to soft (soft in places; overall 7.7; home straight: far side 8.0, stands' side 8.3)
Wind: Strong, across towards stands Weather: Fine but cloudy

3760 DOWNLOAD THE EPSOM IPHONE APP NOW APPRENTICE H'CAP 1m 2f 18y
6:20 (6:21) (Class 5) (0-75,75) 4-Y-0+ **£2,587** (£770; £384; £192) **Stalls** Low

Form RPR
0501 **1** **Hawaana (IRE)**[12] 3386 6-9-10 **75**.............................. DeclanCannon 7 84+
(Gay Kelleway) *hld up in 7th: gng wl whn trapped bhd rivals against nr side rail 3f out: hmpd 2f out and looked to have no ch: rallied strly over 1f out: r.o wl to ld last strides* **4/1**[1]

4540 **2** *½* **Potentiale (IRE)**[7] 3533 7-9-8 **73**.............................. PatrickHills 3 78
(J W Hills) *hld up in 6th: sltly impeded in melee over 2f out: plld wd and prog to ld over 1f out: hung rt to rail fnl f: hdd last strides* **9/1**

1246 **3** *hd* **Miss Bounty**[7] 3533 6-8-5 **61**..............................(v) NathanAlison(5) 10 66+
(Jim Boyle) *dwlt: hld up in last: hmpd over 2f out in melee: prog over 1f out: styd on fnl f but nt as qckly as wnr* **8/1**

0610 **4** *nk* **Effigy**[31] 2769 7-9-5 **75**.............................. AmyScott(5) 1 79
(Henry Candy) *hld up in 8th: clr run on outer in st and chal fr 2f out: upsides fnl f: no ex nr fin* **15/2**[3]

0-43 **5** *2 ¾* **Recalcitrant**[13] 3354 8-9-2 **67**.............................. SimonPearce 8 66
(Simon Dow) *prom: 4th st: avoided melee and led over 2f out to over 1f out: wknd ins fnl f* **14/1**

6101 **6** *5* **Amana (USA)**[7] 3546 7-9-1 **71** 6ex.............................. RachealKneller(5) 9 60+
(Mark Brisbourne) *dwlt: sn prom and racd wd: 3rd st: trapped bhd wkng rivals over 2f out: hmpd sn after: nt rcvr and wknd* **4/1**[1]

-621 **7** *nk* **Megalala (IRE)**[16] 3252 10-9-1 **66**.............................. KierenFox 2 54
(John Bridger) *led: rdn and pressed 4f out: hdd & wknd over 2f out* **17/2**

0263 **8** *2* **Very Well Red**[12] 3413 8-9-2 **70**.............................. TobyAtkinson(3) 5 54
(Peter Hiatt) *pressed ldr: rdn to chal 4f out: upsides against rail over 2f out: sn wknd* **14/1**

1023 **9** *1 ¾* **Bubbly Braveheart (IRE)**[16] 3256 4-8-10 **66**.............................. DarylByrne(5) 4 47
(Pat Phelan) *trckd ldrs: 5th st: nt clr run in melee over 2f out: sn wknd* **13/2**[2]

2m 12.59s (2.89) **Going Correction** +0.375s/f (Good) **9** Ran SP% **110.1**
Speed ratings (Par 103): **103,102,102,102,100 96,95,94,92**
toteswingers:1&2:£8.20, 1&3:£4.40, 2&3:£17.80 CSF £37.45 CT £254.02 TOTE £4.80: £2.20, £2.50, £2.80; EX 37.60.
Owner E Jagger, Gay Kelleway, D Clarke **Bred** Norelands Bloodstock, J Hanly & H Lascelles **Trained** Exning, Suffolk
■ Stewards' Enquiry : Toby Atkinson three-day ban: careless riding (Jul 21,22,24)

FOCUS
Rail dolled out up to 4yds from 1m to winning post, adding approximately 6yds to advertised distances. According to the clerk of the course there had been nearly an inch of rain in the 12 hours before racing, easing conditions appreciably. The rail had been dolled out up to four yards from the 1m start to the winning post adding approximately six yards to race distances. A run-of-the-mill opener but even though the pace wasn't as strong as might have been expected with several front-runners in the field, the principals all came from off the pace in what was a rough race with plenty of scrimmaging as the riders tried to secure a position on the rail. Hawaana did well to win but the bare form is modest.

3761 JUNIPER HILL MAIDEN AUCTION STKS 6f
6:50 (6:50) (Class 5) 2-Y-O **£3,234** (£962; £481; £240) **Stalls** High

Form RPR
230 **1** **Bayleyf (IRE)**[23] 3014 2-8-11 0.............................. LukeMorris 2 83
(John Best) *mde all: led field across to nr side in st: drvn over 1f out: hld on wl* **7/4**[2]

6 **2** *¾* **Chapter Seven**[25] 2953 2-8-8 0.............................. LeeTopliss(5) 8 83
(Richard Fahey) *chsd ldrs in 5th: rdn over 2f out: styd on u.p over 1f out: tk 2nd last strides* **6/1**[3]

3242 **3** *nk* **Esentepe (IRE)**[11] 3424 2-8-11 0.............................. DaneO'Neill 3 80
(Richard Hannon) *trckd ldrs in 4th: effrt on outer over 2f out: chsd wnr over 1f out: kpt on but hld fnl f: lost 2nd last strides* **11/8**[1]

40 **4** *3* **Tidal's Baby**[38] 2559 2-8-11 0.............................. RobbieFitzpatrick 5 71
(Noel Quinlan) *chsd ldrs in 6th: clr of rest 3f out: rdn and kpt on fnl 2f: nvr able to chal* **66/1**

0 **5** *2 ¾* **Possibly**[13] 3362 2-8-4 0.............................. SilvestreDeSousa 1 56
(Peter Chapple-Hyam) *chsd wnr to over 1f out: wknd* **18/1**

6 *2 ½* **Chrissycross (IRE)** 2-8-4 0.............................. DavidProbert 10 48+
(Roger Teal) *hld up in last trio: 9th st and wl off the pce: pushed along and kpt on steadily fnl 2f* **25/1**

0 **7** *½* **Intomist (IRE)**[50] 2194 2-8-8 0.............................. MatthewDavies(3) 9 54
(Jim Boyle) *nvr on terms: 7th and off the pce st: rdn over 2f out: one pce* **80/1**

03 **8** *nse* **Hi There (IRE)**[14] 3308 2-8-11 0.............................. SebSanders 11 53+
(J W Hills) *hld up in last trio: 10th st: wl off the pce 3f out: pushed along and kpt on fnl 2f* **12/1**

0 **9** *4* **King's Future**[17] 3229 2-8-6 0.............................. KierenFox(3) 4 39
(John Akehurst) *chsd ldng pair to 2f out: wknd* **80/1**

0 **10** *nk* **Stag Hill (IRE)**[30] 2788 2-8-10 0 ow1.............................. PatDobbs 6 40
(Sylvester Kirk) *a in rr: 8th and off the pce st: rdn over 2f out: no prog* **33/1**

00 **11** *2 ¼* **Love Grows Wild (USA)**[16] 3257 2-8-8 0.............................. EddieAhern 7 31
(Michael Bell) *mostly in last: detached 1/2-way: nvr a factor* **33/1**

1m 11.31s (1.91) **Going Correction** +0.375s/f (Good) **11** Ran SP% **119.4**
Speed ratings (Par 94): **102,101,100,96,92 89,88,88,83,83 80**
toteswingers:1&2:£2.50, 1&3:£1.10, 2&3:£3.30 CSF £12.43 TOTE £2.40: £1.10, £2.50, £1.10; EX 15.30.
Owner Graham Jones & Partners **Bred** Marchwood Aggregates **Trained** Hucking, Kent

FOCUS
A fair contest by maiden auction standards and both the second and third were unlucky to bump into a horse with as good credentials as the winner had for a race like this. The pace wasn't strong and the runners again came up the stand rail.

NOTEBOOK
Bayleyf(IRE) was taking a step down in grade having found 5f inadequate in the Windsor Castle last time, but even so looked to have a bit to find on form with the eventual third. Well away, however, he was able to dictate once unharried in front and was always doing enough to keep the rest at bay, seeing the trip out well enough. His nursery mark won't be a lenient one, though, and it's doubtful he's quite good enough for Listed races just yet, even at this trip. (op 2-1)

Chapter Seven had shaped well in a Doncaster maiden that's thrown up a couple of winners and he improved markedly on that effort, throwing down a sustained challenge inside the last 2f that took him into second close home. He'll improve again, will stay 7f and can win a similar event. (op 7-1 tchd 8-1)

Esentepe(IRE)'s yard usually aren't wide of the mark bringing their youngsters back in trip, but they might in hindsight wish this one had been made more use of given she was good enough to finish fourth in the Chesham, handing the initiative to the more enterprisingly-ridden winner very early on and never threatening to peg him back. She's beginning to look exposed but remains good enough to win one of these. (tchd 6-5 and 6-4)

Tidal's Baby was presumably all the better for a five-week break and will step up on this again when put over 7f (dam won at 1m4f) but in finishing so close up he's rather blown his cover so far as his nursery mark is concerned. (op 100-1)

Possibly improved on her debut running at Newmarket where she was hampered, fading only late on, but her pedigree is a rare mixture of speed and stamina and it's not easy to know what her ideal trip will be. (op 25-1)

Chrissycross(IRE), a cheaply bought daughter of Cape Cross, was doing all her best work at the finish and should improve.

Hi There(IRE) is now eligible for nurseries. She compounded a poor draw with a sloppy start and was soon too far back to ever promise to get involved. (op 11-1)

3762 MERLAND RISE H'CAP 1m 4f 10y
7:25 (7:26) (Class 4) (0-80,80) 4-Y-O+ **£4,075** (£1,212; £606; £303) **Stalls** Centre

Form RPR
-543 **1** **Dancing Storm**[19] 3184 8-8-2 **61**.............................. LukeMorris 4 68
(Stuart Kittow) *s.s: hld up in last pair: prog and grabbed nr side rail in st: led over 2f out: drvn and styd on wl fr over 1f out* **7/2**[2]

0662 **2** *1* **Ramona Chase**[7] 3538 6-9-5 **78**..............................(t) RobbieFitzpatrick 3 83+
(Michael Attwater) *trckd ldng pair: effrt on outer over 2f out: chsd wnr wl over 1f out: nt qckn and hld fnl f* **9/4**[1]

2-15 **3** *½* **New Code**[34] 2686 4-9-6 **79**.............................. GeorgeBaker 6 84
(Gary Moore) *hld up in 4th: gng easily but dropped to 5th 3f out: effrt 2f out: rdn to dispute 2nd over 1f out: nt qckn* **5/1**[3]

3125 **4** *6* **Pelham Crescent (IRE)**[29] 2810 8-9-5 **78**.............................. DavidProbert 7 73
(Bryn Palling) *trckd ldr: chal and upsides over 3f out to over 2f out: wknd over 1f out* **9/1**

-046 **5** *1 ¼* **Silverglas (IRE)**[22] 3042 5-8-11 **70**.............................. ShaneKelly 2 63
(William Knight) *stdd s: hld up in last pair: detached in last over 2f out: hanging and no prog* **8/1**

0055 **6** *3 ½* **Mister Angry (IRE)**[12] 3381 4-9-7 **80**.............................. SilvestreDeSousa 5 67
(Mark Johnston) *led: rdn over 3f out: hdd over 2f out: sn wknd* **7/2**[2]

2m 46.32s (7.42) **Going Correction** +0.375s/f (Good) **6** Ran SP% **113.0**
Speed ratings (Par 105): **90,89,89,85,84 81**
toteswingers:1&2:£1.70, 1&3:£3.10, 2&3:£3.60 CSF £11.98 TOTE £3.00: £2.30, £1.60; EX 12.00.
Owner M E Harris **Bred** D R Tucker **Trained** Blackborough, Devon

FOCUS
Just an ordinary handicap for the grade and one run at as steady a gallop as seemed likely beforehand given the absence of a regular front runner. The winner is rated to his best form in the past year or so.

3763 TOTEPOOL FLEXI BETTING H'CAP 1m 114y
8:00 (8:00) (Class 4) (0-85,91) 3-Y-O+ **£7,115** (£2,117; £1,058; £529) **Stalls** Low

Form RPR
4301 **1** **Salient**[15] 3266 7-8-12 **69**.............................. J-PGuillambert 4 77
(Michael Attwater) *mde all: grabbed nr side rail in st: drvn and styd on wl fnl 2f* **14/1**

0001 **2** *1* **Crown Counsel (IRE)**[7] 3542 3-9-10 **91** 6ex.............................. SilvestreDeSousa 1 96
(Mark Johnston) *pressed wnr: tried to chal over 2f out to over 1f out: nt qckn and readily hld fnl f* **11/8**[1]

0201 **3** *1 ½* **Inef (IRE)**[13] 3354 4-9-9 **80**.............................. IanMongan 5 83
(Laura Mongan) *trckd ldng pair: cl up but hanging 2f out: nt qckn after: kpt on fnl f* **11/2**[3]

0-20 **4** *1 ¾* **Young Dottie**[131] 703 5-8-8 **70**.............................. JemmaMarshall(5) 3 69
(Pat Phelan) *taken down early: t.k.h: mostly in 4th: effrt on outer over 2f out: nt qckn wl over 1f out: one pce after* **10/1**

1622 **5** *2 ¾* **She's A Character**[23] 3026 4-9-6 **82**.............................. LeeTopliss(5) 6 74
(Richard Fahey) *t.k.h: hld up in 5th: outpcd 3f out: rdn and no prog 2f out* **9/2**[2]

2111 **6** *¾* **Song To The Moon (IRE)**[7] 3537 4-9-2 **76** 6ex...(b) MatthewDavies(3) 2 66
(Jim Boyle) *dwlt: hld up in 6th: prog on outer over 2f out: wknd wl over 1f out* **9/2**[2]

4510 **7** *3 ¼* **Kentish (USA)**[8] 3514 4-8-13 **70**.............................. ShaneKelly 7 53
(Noel Quinlan) *taken down early: restless stalls: t.k.h: hld up in last: shkn up and no prog over 2f out* **28/1**

1m 48.32s (2.22) **Going Correction** +0.375s/f (Good)
WFA 3 from 4yo+ 10lb **7** Ran SP% **113.1**
Speed ratings (Par 105): **105,104,102,101,98 98,95**
toteswingers:1&2:£3.30, 1&3:£17.30, 2&3:£1.10 CSF £33.17 TOTE £15.80: £5.10, £1.70; EX 41.00.
Owner Canisbay Bloodstock **Bred** Hesmonds Stud Ltd **Trained** Epsom, Surrey

FOCUS
A fair handicap run at a steady pace initially, but though the winner dictated and the order barely changed throughout, he still left the impression he was the best horse on the day. This was his best form since last summer.

3764 BROTHERS STRAWBERRY CIDER CLAIMING STKS — 1m 2f 18y
8:35 (8:37) (Class 5) 3-Y-0+ — £2,587 (£770; £384; £192) Stalls Low

Form — RPR
1/11 **1** **Troopingthecolour**[22] 3042 5-9-7 89 ... MatthewLawson(7) 5 — 95
(Steve Gollings) *trckd ldr: led wl over 2f out: edgd lft over 1f out but styd on strly* **1/1**[1]
1202 **2** 3 1/4 **Avon River**[7] 3537 4-9-5 87 ... (b) KieranO'Neill(5) 1 — 85
(Richard Hannon) *trckd ldng pair: chsd wnr over 2f out: rdn and sn readily outpcd* **5/2**[2]
3236 **3** 5 **Lang Shining (IRE)**[7] 3537 7-9-5 77 ... SophieDoyle(3) 4 — 73
(Jamie Osborne) *hld up in last: effrt over 2f out: wnt 3rd wl over 1f out: no imp* **7/1**
2-40 **4** 12 **Hermes**[26] 2930 3-8-8 73 ... (p) JimCrowley 2 — 46
(Ralph Beckett) *racd keenly: led: kicked on 4f out: hdd & wknd wl over 2f out* **5/1**[3]

2m 14.59s (4.89) **Going Correction** +0.375s/f (Good)
WFA 3 from 4yo+ 11lb — 4 Ran SP% **107.7**
Speed ratings (Par 103): **95,92,88,78**
CSF £3.70 TOTE £1.60; EX 3.80.
Owner Northern Bloodstock Racing **Bred** Meon Valley Stud **Trained** Scamblesby, Lincs

FOCUS
A fair range of abilities on show but with the minimum BHA rating among the runners being 73, not a bad contest for the grade. The pace was steady but the result was very much the right one. Not form to take too literally though.

3765 TOTEPOOL A BETTER WAY TO BET H'CAP — 6f
9:05 (9:05) (Class 4) (0-80,80) 3-Y-0+ — £4,075 (£1,212; £606; £303) Stalls High

Form — RPR
-000 **1** **Baldemar**[23] 3028 6-9-6 **79** ... LeeTopliss(5) 4 — 90
(Richard Fahey) *prom: trckd ldr st: led over 1f out: drvn and hld on nr fin* **5/1**[3]
3145 **2** 1/2 **Perfect Pastime**[22] 3048 3-9-2 **76** ... EddieAhern 11 — 84+
(Walter Swinburn) *trckd ldr over 2f: styd cl up: gap appeared against rail over 1f out but tk time to go through it: r.o to chse wnr last 100yds: clsng at fin* **6/1**
4501 **3** 2 **Aye Aye Digby (IRE)**[13] 3350 6-9-11 **79** ... GeorgeBaker 5 — 82
(Patrick Chamings) *led: edgd off nr side rail over 1f out and hdd: one pce* **10/3**[2]
1430 **4** 1 **Clear Praise (USA)**[67] 1720 4-9-12 **80** ... SebSanders 7 — 80
(Simon Dow) *stdd s: t.k.h: hld up in 7th: effrt 2f out: hanging lft and nt qckn: kpt on fnl f* **13/2**
5542 **5** 1/2 **Seek The Fair Land**[19] 3179 5-9-9 **80** ... (b) MatthewDavies(3) 8 — 78
(Jim Boyle) *chsd ldrs: 5th st: rdn 2f out: sn outpcd and btn* **5/2**[1]
5630 **6** 1 1/4 **Saucy Buck (IRE)**[78] 1483 3-8-6 **66** ... JamieGoldstein 2 — 59
(Ralph Smith) *hld up in tch: 4th st: pushed along 2f out: steadily wknd* **14/1**
5113 **7** 1 1/4 **Stonecrabstomorrow (IRE)**[9] 3482 8-8-7 **61** oh2(v) RobbieFitzpatrick 1 — 51
(Michael Attwater) *s.i.s: a in last trio: rdn over 2f out: no prog whn rdr dropped whip over 1f out* **14/1**
3150 **8** 5 **Mary's Pet**[14] 3322 4-8-4 **61** ... SimonPearce(3) 6 — 35
(John Akehurst) *s.i.s and then checked: detached in last thrght: nvr a factor* **25/1**

1m 11.15s (1.75) **Going Correction** +0.375s/f (Good)
WFA 3 from 4yo+ 6lb — 8 Ran SP% **113.1**
Speed ratings (Par 105): **103,102,99,98,97 96,94,87**
toteswingers:1&2:£9.70, 1&3:£4.90, 2&3:£2.80 CSF £34.04 CT £113.50 TOTE £6.00: £1.90, £1.80, £1.60; EX 29.50.
Owner A Rhodes Haulage And P Timmins **Bred** Hellwood Stud Farm **Trained** Musley Bank, N Yorks

FOCUS
A fair sprint handicap that wasn't strongly run and it paid to be handy once again. The winner is rated back to his latter form of last year.
T/Plt: £48.40 to a £1 stake. Pool:£68,743.41 - 1,036.14 winning tickets T/Qpdt: £23.40 to a £1 stake. Pool:£4,857.83 - 153.60 winning tickets JN

3349 FOLKESTONE (R-H)
Thursday, July 7

OFFICIAL GOING: Good to firm (good in places; 8.1)
Wind: fresh, across Weather: dry and breezy

3766 ENHANCED WIN ODDS FROM NOON AT CORAL.CO.UK MEDIAN AUCTION MAIDEN STKS — 7f (S)
2:05 (2:09) (Class 6) 3-Y-0 — £1,704 (£503; £251) Stalls High

Form — RPR
3-6 **1** **Celestyna**[48] 2266 3-8-5 0 ... CharlesEddery(7) 5 — 72
(Sir Henry Cecil) *taken down early: stdd s: hld up in tch: effrt and hmpd wl over 1f out: swtchd rt and hdwy u.p 1f out: r.o wl to ld wl ins fnl f* **10/1**[3]
00 **2** 3/4 **Semmsu (IRE)**[28] 2848 3-9-3 0 ... J-PGuillambert 1 — 75
(Luca Cumani) *chsd ldrs: rdn wl over 2f out: chal 1f out: led fnl 100yds tl hdd and no ex wl ins fnl f* **3/1**[2]
3-5 **3** nse **Perfect Cracker**[68] 1682 3-9-3 0 ... AdamKirby 2 — 75
(Clive Cox) *pressed ldr: rdn jst over 2f out: drvn to ld over 1f out: hrd drvn 1f out: hdd and one pce fnl 100yds* **6/5**[1]
4234 **4** 2 **Swift Bird (IRE)**[6] 3577 3-8-12 72 ... DaneO'Neill 4 — 65
(Noel Quinlan) *led: rdn ent fnl 2f: hdd over 1f out: wknd ins fnl f: btn and eased towards fin* **3/1**[2]
0-05 **5** 14 **Trust Me Boy**[86] 1284 3-9-0 45 ... (v) NataliaGemelova(3) 6 — 32
(John E Long) *sn bustled along and toiling bdly in rr: lost tch 1/2-way* **150/1**
0- **6** 1 **Samanda (IRE)**[244] 7335 3-8-10 0 ... HayleyBurton(7) 3 — 29
(Luca Cumani) *dwlt: sn totally outpcd in rr: virtually t.o 4f out* **22/1**
00-4 **7** 1 3/4 **Elusive Diva (IRE)**[11] 3433 3-8-12 53 ... (b) EddieCreighton 7 — 19
(Edward Creighton) *chsd ldrs: rdn wl over 2f out: wknd u.p over 1f out: tired and fdd rapidly fnl f* **100/1**

1m 26.62s (-0.68) **Going Correction** -0.10s/f (Good) — 7 Ran SP% **110.5**
Speed ratings (Par 98): **99,98,98,95,79 78,76**
toteswingers:1&2:£2.40, 2&3:£1.80, 1&3:£2.90 CSF £37.18 TOTE £13.80: £4.30, £2.50; EX 26.60.
Owner Lady Cecil & Partners **Bred** Gestut Ammerland **Trained** Newmarket, Suffolk

FOCUS
Not much solid form to go on, but probably a fair maiden.

3767 BRITISH STALLION STUDS SUPPORTING BRITISH RACING E B F MAIDEN FILLIES' STKS — 5f
2:40 (2:40) (Class 5) 2-Y-0 — £3,169 (£943; £471; £235) Stalls High

Form — RPR
32 **1** **Pearl Diva (IRE)**[12] 3402 2-9-0 0 ... JackMitchell 2 — 84+
(Peter Chapple-Hyam) *racd in midfield: pushed along over 2f out: chsd ldr 2f out: led over 1f out: sn in command: v easily* **1/16**[1]
00 **2** 4 1/2 **Dine Out**[13] 3362 2-9-0 0 ... SebSanders 4 — 65+
(Mark H Tompkins) *sn pushed along in last pair: styd on jst over 1f out: wnt 2nd fnl 75yds: no ch w wnr* **9/1**[2]
06 **3** 3/4 **Monessa (IRE)**[16] 3249 2-9-0 0 ... EddieCreighton 6 — 61
(Edward Creighton) *sn pushed along: chsd ldr over 3f out tl 2f out: outpcd and no ch w wnr whn hung rt 1f out* **50/1**
0 **4** 3/4 **Especially Red (IRE)**[24] 2992 2-9-0 0 ... AdamKirby 1 — 58
(Lisa Williamson) *led and sn clr: rdn and hdd over 1f out: sn no ch w wnr: wknd and lost 2 pls ins fnl f* **16/1**
60 **5** 6 **Misred Melissa (IRE)**[15] 3270 2-9-0 0 ... IanMongan 3 — 36
(John Gallagher) *chsd ldr tl over 3f out: rdn and wknd over 1f out: fdd ins fnl f* **12/1**[3]
6 7 **Almirah** 2-8-7 0 ... JenniferFerguson(7) 5 — 10
(Edward Creighton) *s.i.s: a wl bhd* **16/1**

60.11 secs (0.11) **Going Correction** -0.10s/f (Good) — 6 Ran SP% **125.5**
Speed ratings (Par 91): **95,87,86,85,75 64**
toteswingers:1&2:£1.70, 2&3:£6.00, 1&3:£4.10 CSF £2.80 TOTE £1.10: £1.02, £2.20; EX 2.20.
Owner John C Davies **Bred** Brian Wallace **Trained** Newmarket, Suffolk

FOCUS
Nothing more than a routine victory.

NOTEBOOK
Pearl Diva(IRE) was by far and away the form selection. None of her rivals should have caused her any problems and so it proved with a fluent and ultimately easy victory, despite a couple of worrying moments when her jockey made her go on. It's an important win under her belt and it remains to be seen how ambitious connections will be with her now. (tchd 1-20)

Dine Out got outpaced over 2f out but ran on strongly to catch the eye to some extent. It appears she'll want at least another furlong. (tchd 8-1)

Monessa(IRE) was shoved along from quite some way out and, judged on previous efforts, she is either flattered by this or the favourite ran some way below her best. (op 33-1)

Especially Red(IRE) got away sharply and bagged the stands' rail easily. She showed quite a bit of pace for a long time and may easily be good enough to win a low-grade handicap or seller over a sharp 5f.

3768 BETTER WIN PRICES EVERY RACE AT CORAL.CO.UK H'CAP — 5f
3:15 (3:15) (Class 5) (0-70,69) 3-Y-0+ — £2,385 (£704; £352) Stalls High

Form — RPR
2615 **1** **Musical Bridge**[5] 3640 5-9-11 **68** ... (b) AdamKirby 5 — 76
(Lisa Williamson) *led: rdn ent fnl 2f: drvn and hdd over 1f out: rallied u.p fnl 100yds: led again nr fin* **4/1**[2]
1031 **2** hd **Your Gifted (IRE)**[6] 3582 4-9-4 **68** ... DarylByrne(7) 1 — 75+
(Patrick Morris) *wnt rt s: t.k.h: hdwy to chse wnr 3f out: led over 1f out: pushed along ins fnl f: fnd little and hdd nr fin* **10/11**[1]
4130 **3** 1 1/2 **Commandingpresence (USA)**[3] 3685 5-8-11 **57** ... KierenFox(3) 4 — 59
(John Bridger) *in tch in last pair: rdn and effrt wl over 1f out: styd on same pce u.p ins fnl f* **4/1**[2]
1043 **4** 3/4 **Make My Dream**[12] 3389 8-9-12 **69** ... (v) IanMongan 6 — 68
(John Gallagher) *chsd wnr tl 3f out: drvn wl over 1f out: styd on same pce u.p ins fnl f* **10/1**[3]
0045 **5** 3 3/4 **Durgan**[26] 2921 5-8-9 **52** ... (tp) SteveDrowne 3 — 38
(Linda Jewell) *in tch in last pair: wknd u.p over 1f out* **14/1**

59.34 secs (-0.66) **Going Correction** -0.10s/f (Good) — 5 Ran SP% **108.1**
Speed ratings (Par 103): **101,100,98,97,91**
CSF £7.85 TOTE £6.40: £3.00, £1.50; EX 8.90.
Owner John Conway **Bred** John Starbuck **Trained** Dalghton, Cheshire

FOCUS
Modest stuff but most of these could be given a chance, so the form ought to be reliable for the level.

3769 CLAYDON HORSE EXERCISERS H'CAP — 1m 7f 92y
3:45 (3:45) (Class 6) (0-60,59) 4-Y-0+ — £1,704 (£503; £251) Stalls High

Form — RPR
6032 **1** **Kadouchski (FR)**[15] 3281 7-8-11 **56** ... HannahNunn(7) 3 — 66
(John Berry) *in tch: swtchd rt and effrt on inner over 1f out: rdn to ld ins fnl f: r.o wl: comf* **5/2**[2]
30-5 **2** 3 1/2 **Astrovenus**[13] 3352 4-8-10 **48** ... SebSanders 2 — 53
(Mark H Tompkins) *chsd ldrs: rdn to ld over 1f out: drvn ent fnl f: hdd ins fnl f: nt gng pce of wnr* **9/4**[1]
/046 **3** 1 3/4 **Appointment**[15] 3281 6-8-10 **48** ... JamieGoldstein 4 — 51
(Ralph Smith) *led for 1f: chsd ldr after: rdn to press ldr 2f out: unable qck ent fnl f: wknd ins fnl f* **8/1**
-540 **4** 3 3/4 **Swordsman (GER)**[13] 3352 9-9-7 **59** ... (bt) DaneO'Neill 7 — 57
(Chris Gordon) *dwlt: bustled along to ld after 1f: rdn 4f out: drvn and hdd over 1f out: wknd 1f out* **4/1**[3]
0-0 **5** 2 **Whitcombe Spirit**[19] 3184 6-8-10 **48** ... (b) SteveDrowne 8 — 43
(Jamie Poulton) *in tch in last trio: clsd on ldrs 3f out: drvn and no imp fnl 2f* **14/1**
0045 **6** 34 **Illuminative (USA)**[35] 2638 5-8-5 **46** ... (p) KierenFox(3) 6 — —
(Zoe Davison) *hld up in last pair: rdn 6f out: lost tch over 2f out: t.o* **22/1**
0630 **7** 19 **King Kieren (IRE)**[22] 3047 6-8-12 **50** ... (tp) IanMongan 1 — —
(Linda Jewell) *a in last pair: rdn and lost tch wl over 2f out: eased fr over 1f out: t.o* **10/1**

3m 27.5s (-2.20) **Going Correction** -0.10s/f (Good) — 7 Ran SP% **110.6**
Speed ratings (Par 101): **101,99,98,96,95 77,66**
toteswingers:1&2:£2.20, 2&3:£5.20, 1&3:£5.50 CSF £7.94 CT £33.83 TOTE £3.60: £1.50, £2.20; EX 9.40.
Owner John Berry **Bred** Henrietta Charlet & Danny Charlesworth **Trained** Newmarket, Suffolk
■ Hannah Nunn's first winner.

FOCUS
A very ordinary contest in which it was impossible to fancy any of the runners with confidence.

King Kieren(IRE) Official explanation: jockey said gelding never travelled

3770 LIPSCOMB.CO.UK H'CAP — 1m 4f
4:20 (4:20) (Class 5) (0-70,70) 3-Y-O — **£2,385** (£704; £352) **Stalls** High

Form				RPR
0-22	**1**		**Fire Fighter (IRE)**[9] 3487 3-9-0 **63** ... SebSanders 4 (Sir Mark Prescott Bt) *bustled along leaving stalls and sn chsng ldr: rdn to ld over 2f out: idling and rn green over 1f out: a doing enough and rdn out hands and heels ins fnl f* **8/13**[1]	80+
4-05	**2**	*1 ¼*	**Astromagick**[14] 3325 3-8-12 **61** ... SteveDrowne 1 (Mark H Tompkins) *chsd ldrs: rdn and effrt jst over 2f out: drvn to chse wnr over 1f out: kpt on* **11/1**[3]	72+
-235	**3**	*7*	**Drumadoon (IRE)**[15] 3268 3-8-8 **57** ... DaneO'Neill 3 (John Dunlop) *in tch in last pair: rdn 4f out: c wd and drvn jst over 2f out: plugged on same pce and no imp over 1f out* **3/1**[2]	59
0042	**4**	*3 ¾*	**Dare To Bare (IRE)**[12] 3392 3-9-7 **70** ... PatDobbs 2 (Amanda Perrett) *led tl over 2f out: wknd u.p over 1f out* **14/1**	64
0-20	**P**		**Brezza Di Mare (IRE)**[36] 2613 3-9-7 **70** ... ShaneKelly 5 (Brian Meehan) *mounted on crse and taken down early: in tch in last pair: rdn and dropped to last over 5f out: eased over 4f out and sn p.u: dismntd: b.b.v* **14/1**	—

2m 39.39s (-1.51) **Going Correction** -0.10s/f (Good) — 5 Ran SP% **108.6**
Speed ratings (Par 100): **101,100,95,93,—**
CSF £8.08 TOTE £1.40: £1.10, £4.60; EX 7.30.
Owner J Fishpool - Osborne House **Bred** Airlie Stud And Sir Thomas Pilkington **Trained** Newmarket, Suffolk

FOCUS
This has produced one or two decent winners in the past.
Brezza Di Mare(IRE) Official explanation: trainer's rep said gelding bled from the nose

3771 ROMAN ROAD FILLIES' H'CAP — 1m 1f 149y
4:50 (4:50) (Class 5) (0-70,68) 3-Y-O+ — **£2,385** (£704; £352) **Stalls** Centre

Form				RPR
452	**1**		**Full Bloom**[132] 684 3-9-1 **66** ... (p) SteveDrowne 2 (Gerard Butler) *led tl over 7f out: chsd ldrs after tl rdn to ld over 1f out: hrd drvn and hld on wl ins fnl f* **9/1**	72
40-0	**2**	*hd*	**Sweet Secret**[24] 2999 4-9-12 **66** ... AdamKirby 6 (Jeremy Gask) *chsd ldr tl led over 7f out: drvn and hdd over 1f out: rallied u.p ins fnl f: jst hld* **11/1**	71
01	**3**	*3 ¾*	**Chatterer (IRE)**[12] 3392 3-8-9 **67** ... (t) KatiaScallan(7) 1 (Marcus Tregoning) *v.s.a: detached in last: clsd and in tch 7f out: hdwy on outer to chse ldrs over 2f out: edgd rt and no hdwy 1f out* **7/2**[2]	64
4412	**4**	*2*	**Choral Festival**[10] 3467 5-9-9 **63** ... PatDobbs 7 (John Bridger) *dwlt: in tch: rdn 4f out: drvn to chse ldrs 2f out: no ex and btn 1f out* **2/1**[1]	56
-430	**5**	*3 ¼*	**Lady Barastar (IRE)**[17] 3228 3-8-12 **63** ... (p) ShaneKelly 4 (Walter Swinburn) *chsd ldrs: wnt 2nd 7f out tl 2f out: sn wknd u.p* **9/2**[3]	49
6350	**6**	*8*	**Woop Woop (IRE)**[10] 3467 3-9-3 **68** ... SebSanders 3 (Stef Higgins) *hld up in last pair: rdn and effrt on inner 2f out: no prog and wl btn over 1f out* **7/2**[2]	38

2m 3.77s (-1.13) **Going Correction** -0.10s/f (Good)
WFA 3 from 4yo+ 11lb — 6 Ran SP% **114.3**
Speed ratings (Par 100): **100,99,96,95,92 86**
toteswingers:1&2:£8.00, 2&3:£7.90, 1&3:£3.90 CSF £94.57 TOTE £9.70: £3.80, £5.40; EX 57.90.
Owner Shoreham Stud **Bred** Heather Raw **Trained** Newmarket, Suffolk

FOCUS
This isn't form to take to seriously mainly because the pace set by the leader was thoroughly uneven, and the fancied Tregoning runner ruined her chance even before the race got serious.
Woop Woop(IRE) Official explanation: trainer had no explanation for the poor form shown
T/Plt: £154.90 to a £1 stake. Pool of £40,283.96 - 189.80 winning tickets. T/Qpdt: £15.20 to a £1 stake. Pool of £3,817.62 - 185.60 winning tickets. SP

3401 NEWMARKET (R-H)
Thursday, July 7

OFFICIAL GOING: Good
The July meeting was held from Thursday-Saturday for the first time.
Wind: Fresh across Weather: Overcast

3772 BAHRAIN TROPHY (GROUP 3) — 1m 5f
1:20 (1:20) (Class 1) 3-Y-O
£28,355 (£10,750; £5,380; £2,680; £1,345; £675) **Stalls** Centre

Form				RPR
-510	**1**		**Masked Marvel**[33] 2715 3-9-0 109 ... JimmyFortune 1 (John Gosden) *chsd ldr after 1f: led at stdy pce 9f out: qcknd over 3f out: rdn and hung lft fr over 1f out: jst hld on* **2/1**[1]	114
1-12	**2**	*hd*	**Census (IRE)**[21] 3069 3-9-0 97 ... RyanMoore 2 (Richard Hannon) *chsd ldr 1f: remained handy: pushed along and hung lft over 4f out: rdn to chse wnr over 2f out: hung lft over 1f out: nt clr run ins fnl f: r.o wl* **2/1**[1]	113
1105	**3**	*4*	**Zain Al Boldan**[21] 3065 3-8-11 104 ... HughBowman 4 (Mick Channon) *hld up: outpcd over 3f out: hdwy to go 3rd over 1f out: styd on same pce ins fnl f* **11/1**[3]	104
2200	**4**	*1 ¾*	**Hurricane Higgins (IRE)**[20] 3105 3-9-0 103 ... NeilCallan 6 (Mark Johnston) *led at stdy pce tl hdd 9f out: chsd wnr tl rdn over 2f out: edgd lft and no ex over 1f out* **16/1**	105
212	**5**	*2 ¾*	**Solar Sky**[20] 3108 3-9-0 102 ... TomQueally 5 (Sir Henry Cecil) *chsd ldrs: rdn over 2f out: sn hung lft: wknd over 1f out* **11/4**[2]	101
0031	**6**	*13*	**Crimson Knight**[13] 3364 3-9-0 78 ... LouisBeuzelin 3 (Brian Meehan) *s.i.s: hld up: hdwy over 4f out: rdn and wknd over 2f out* **50/1**	83

2m 49.74s (5.74) **Going Correction** +0.225s/f (Good) — 6 Ran SP% **109.5**
Speed ratings (Par 110): **91,90,88,87,85 77**
toteswingers:1&2:£1.30, 2&3:£3.50, 1&3:£3.30 CSF £5.89 TOTE £3.00: £1.70, £1.50; EX 6.90.
Owner B E Nielsen **Bred** Newsells Park Stud **Trained** Newmarket, Suffolk

FOCUS
Far side track used which had not been used since August 2010. Stalls on far side except 1.20, 2.25 & 3.00 centre. Bend into home straight repositioned, adding 16m to 1.20, 2.25 and 3.00. This was the third running of the Bahrain Trophy as a Group 3, and since the distance was reduced by nearly a quarter of a mile in 2006, it has been won by some classy types such as Youmzain, Tranquil Tiger, Kite Wood and Corsica, the last two going on to be placed in the St Leger. The early pace was by no means strong and didn't quicken up until around 3f from home. A combination of the modest tempo, a strong headwind and the rain resulted in a slow time. The runners came up the centre of the track once into the straight. This was an up-to-scratch renewal and the winner was another to frank the Derby form.

NOTEBOOK
Masked Marvel had the highest BHA rating in this field following his eighth in the Derby, whilst his previous defeat of Namibian at Goodwood looked better when the runner-up went on to take the Queen's Vase. His rider wasn't satisfied with the early pace and sent him to the front after half a mile, from which point he travelled comfortably. Gradually winding things up around 3f out, he soon had his rivals off the bridle and seemed likely to win by a decent margin, but he hung away to his left in the final furlong as he lost concentration and was being closed down at the line. He is likely to head straight for the St Leger now for which he is a top-priced 16-1. (op 9-4)
Census(IRE) was up in grade after chasing home Brown Panther at a respectful distance in the King George V Handicap at Royal Ascot. Always close to the pace, he seemed to shy and falter when the winner ran across him a furlong out, but he ran on again once straightened and was eating into his advantage at the line. He certainly has a Pattern race in him and may also end up in the St Leger, for which he is a top-priced 20-1. (tchd 5-2 in places)
Zain Al Boldan won her first three starts including the Lingfield Oaks Trial, but was found wanting in both the Oaks and Ribblesdale. Held up from the start, she was probably not in the ideal position in last place when the winner quickened from the front 3f out, and although she stayed on to the line, she could never get anywhere near the front pair. The extra furlong and a half of the Park Hill could be right up her street. (op 12-1)
Hurricane Higgins(IRE) looked a nice prospect earlier in the year, but poor efforts in a French Listed race and especially in the King Edward VII when blinkered for the first time left him with questions to answer. In front for the first half-mile, he remained close to the winner until coming off the bridle and fading from over 2f out. He seems likely to remain hard to place. (op 14-1 tchd 12-1)
Solar Sky didn't see the racecourse until April and ran really well to go down narrowly to Namibian in the Queen's Vase, but a line through the winner gave him something to find with Masked Marvel. He was close enough 3f out, but found nothing once off the bridle and although the drop back in trip wasn't in his favour, especially in view of the modest early pace, this was a bit disappointing. (op 5-2)
Crimson Knight, successful off 72 in a C&D handicap last time, had upwards of 19lb to find with his rivals and was duly put in his place. (tchd 66-1)

3773 TNT JULY STKS (GROUP 2) (C&G) — 6f
1:50 (1:51) (Class 1) 2-Y-O
£34,026 (£12,900; £6,456; £3,216; £1,614; £810) **Stalls** High

Form				RPR
2211	**1**		**Frederick Engels**[23] 3014 2-8-12 0 ... EddieAhern 6 (David Brown) *a.p: pushed along and hung lft over 1f out: rdn to ld ins fnl f: r.o wl* **7/4**[2]	111
612	**2**	*1*	**Roman Soldier (IRE)**[23] 3012 2-8-12 0 ... RyanMoore 8 (Jeremy Noseda) *chsd ldr: rdn and hung lft over 1f out: styd on* **6/4**[1]	108
1126	**3**	*nk*	**Bannock (IRE)**[21] 3064 2-8-12 0 ... SilvestreDeSousa 4 (Mark Johnston) *led: rdn over 2f out: edgd lft and hdd ins fnl f: styd on* **10/1**	107
210	**4**	*4*	**North Star Boy (IRE)**[23] 3012 2-8-12 0 ... JimmyFortune 5 (Richard Hannon) *dwlt: hdwy over 4f out: rdn over 1f out: no ex ins fnl f* **11/1**	95
43	**5**	*nk*	**Kenny Powers**[14] 3313 2-8-12 0 ... (t) RichardKingscote 1 (Tom Dascombe) *chsd ldrs: rdn over 1f out: no ex ins fnl f* **50/1**	94
101	**6**	*7*	**Sans Loi (IRE)**[10] 3458 2-8-12 0 ... RobertWinston 2 (Alan McCabe) *hld up: plld hrd: hdwy 1/2-way: rdn and ev ch wl over 1f out: wknd ins fnl f* **25/1**	73
1	**7**	*7*	**Church Music (IRE)**[27] 2886 2-8-12 0 ... RichardMullen 3 (Kevin Ryan) *hld up: rdn over 2f out: wknd over 1f out* **7/1**[3]	52

1m 13.76s (1.26) **Going Correction** +0.225s/f (Good) — 7 Ran SP% **112.1**
Speed ratings (Par 106): **100,98,98,92,92 83,73**
toteswingers:1&2:£1.40, 2&3:£2.90, 1&3:£3.70 CSF £4.52 TOTE £2.60: £1.80, £1.40; EX 5.10 Trifecta £29.00 Pool: £5659.42 - 144.38 winning units..
Owner Pearl Bloodstock Ltd **Bred** Peter Baldwin **Trained** Averham Park, Notts

FOCUS
This historic Group 2 juvenile contest looked a strong race for the grade and the form seems rock-solid with three proven Pattern performers coming clear in a tight finish. There was a sound enough pace on and the runners unsurprisingly stuck towards the far side. The time was 0.20 seconds quicker than the highly promising Harbour Watch recorded in the later conditions race, although by then the ground would have deteriorated somewhat. Frederick Engels progressed from the Windsor Castle, with Roman Soldier rated to his Coventry form.

NOTEBOOK
Frederick Engels continued his rise up the ladder by landing the hat-trick in ready fashion on this debut in Group company. David Brown's son of Iceman landed a huge public gamble when comfortably winning the Listed Windsor Castle Stakes at Royal Ascot last month and the trainer was of the firm belief stepping up to 6f was now required. The colt looked in great nick in the preliminaries, but once jumping out of the gates he appeared to be going that bit faster than his new jockey Eddie Ahern ideally wanted. He settled nicely after a couple of furlongs, however, and once the gap opened for him at the furlong pole there was only going to be one winner. There was plenty to like about his attitude when pressed near the finish and he obviously improved for this stiffer test. That was not totally assured looking at his breeding as his dam's side of the pedigree is about speed, but his late sire has thrown up winners over middle distances.Connections were keen to refrain from putting up any immediate targets, but he was the only one of these to hold a Group 1 entry, in the Phoenix Stakes at the Curragh next month. One possible target could be the Gimcrack at York's Ebor meeting as the track at York would likely be right up his street, but the 3lb penalty might be a stumbling block. He could also bid to emulate Arcano, who won this in 2009 before following up in the Group 1 Prix Morny at Deauville (also next month). Indeed now well may be the time to have a crack at the top level as he is clearly thriving and it's most unlikely we have seen the best of him, so he firmly remains one to follow. (op 15-8)
Roman Soldier(IRE) ran a massive race when touched off over this trip in a battling finish by Aidan O'Brien's Power in the Coventry last month, where he finished a clear second-best, and that form entitled him to be market leader here. He got a positive ride and settled fine, but as the tempo became serious he didn't appear too happy and looked somewhat uneasy on the ground. He got reorganised when meeting the rising finish and deserves credit for coming back as he did, but probably ran a little below his previous level. He could now take in the Gimcrack, but whether a quick 6f is now suitable for him is up for some debate. Indeed, he may now prefer a stiffer test. (op 7-4)
Bannock(IRE) had twice proved himself in Listed company before a below-par sixth in the Norfolk Stakes last month and proved easy to back on this debut in Group company returned to quicker ground. He returned to his best with a gutsy effort in defeat and, as could have been expected beforehand, appreciated this greater test of stamina. He rates a solid benchmark and fully deserves to find an opening in this sort of class. (op 17-2)

North Star Boy(IRE) was beaten around 6l by the runner-up in the Coventry on his previous outing. He got fractious in the stalls just before they opened and made a tardy start, but recovered to make his bid on the far rail from halfway. He lacked the tactical speed to stay with the principals, but still ran a fair race and is another who helps to give substance to the form. (op 14-1 tchd 10-1)
Kenny Powers was facing a stiff task, but is clearly well thought of and, while never threatening, posted a pleasing effort. He deserves a confidence boost in a maiden and looks a decent handicapper in the making. (op 66-1)
Sans Loi(IRE), who took time to settle, made a positive move around halfway but looked pay for his early exertions when meeting the rising finish. This was too hot for him. (op 16-1)
Church Music(IRE) looked a very useful colt when winning his maiden at York last month. This was obviously much tougher, but he is bred to appreciate this extra furlong as a 2-y-o and the past two winners of this race had been won by once-raced maiden winners. He proved far too keen early on, however, and it was clear 3f out he was in trouble. Surely he's capable of better again down the line, but does now have something to prove. (tchd 8-1)

3774 SPORTINGBET.COM H'CAP — 1m 2f
2:25 (2:26) (Class 2) (0-105,98) 3-Y-O

£31,125 (£9,320; £4,660; £2,330; £1,165; £585) **Stalls** Centre

Form — RPR

-035 **1** — **Fulgur**[20] 3105 3-8-12 **89** .... KierenFallon 3 — 106
(Luca Cumani) *hld up: hdwy over 2f out: rdn to ld ins fnl f: sn hung lft: r.o* **7/1**[2]

2-14 **2** *1* **Mijhaar**[20] 3105 3-9-5 **96** .... NeilCallan 9 — 111
(Roger Varian) *hld up: hdwy over 3f out: led over 2f out: sn hung rt: rdn and hdd ins fnl f: edgd lft: styd on* **13/8**[1]

1-42 **3** *2 ¾* **Labarinto**[54] 2100 3-9-1 **92** .... RyanMoore 16 — 101+
(Sir Michael Stoute) *hld up: nt clr run 2f out: swtchd rt and hdwy over 1f out: rdn and hung lft ins fnl f: r.o: nt rch ldrs* **11/1**

1502 **4** *½* **Malthouse (GER)**[12] 3405 3-9-7 **98** .... SilvestreDeSousa 7 — 106
(Mark Johnston) *hld up: hdwy over 3f out: rdn over 1f out: no ex ins fnl f* **16/1**

3613 **5** *2 ¼* **Well Sharp**[21] 3069 3-9-0 **91** .... PhillipMakin 10 — 95
(Michael Dods) *hld up: hdwy over 2f out: rdn over 1f out: styd on same pce* **12/1**

-303 **6** *1 ¼* **Star Surprise**[26] 2925 3-8-13 **90** .... JamieSpencer 13 — 91
(Michael Bell) *hld up: hdwy over 2f out: rdn over 1f out: styd on same pce* **25/1**

-213 **7** *hd* **Seelo (USA)**[22] 3044 3-9-3 **94** .... NickyMackay 5 — 95
(John Gosden) *dwlt: hld up: hdwy over 3f out: rdn over 2f out: no ex fr over 1f out* **22/1**

01-3 **8** *½* **Rain Mac**[57] 2008 3-8-10 **87** .... RobertHavlin 11 — 87
(John Gosden) *dwlt: hld up: shkn up over 1f out: nvr nr to chal* **12/1**

1-12 **9** *3 ½* **Tullius (IRE)**[26] 2925 3-8-11 **88** .... LukeMorris 6 — 81
(Peter Winkworth) *prom: racd keenly: rdn and ev ch over 2f out: wknd over 1f out* **20/1**

311 **10** *½* **Club Oceanic**[27] 2877 3-9-3 **94** ....(p) MickaelBarzalona 14 — 86
(Jeremy Noseda) *hld up: rdn over 2f out: nvr nrr* **9/1**[3]

2220 **11** *3 ½* **Mica Mika (IRE)**[21] 3069 3-8-7 **84** .... PaulHanagan 8 — 69
(Richard Fahey) *prom: rdn over 2f out: wknd over 1f out* **40/1**

2310 **12** *2 ¾* **Glencadam Gold (IRE)**[20] 3105 3-9-4 **95** .... TomQueally 2 — 74
(Sir Henry Cecil) *hld up in tch: rdn over 2f out: wknd wl over 1f out* **22/1**

-126 **13** *½* **Fadhaa (IRE)**[15] 3291 3-8-6 **83** .... RichardHills 18 — 61
(B W Hills) *prom: led 3f out: rdn and hdd over 2f out: wknd over 1f out* **20/1**

01-2 **14** *1 ¼* **Swindy**[91] 1194 3-8-0 **77** .... DavidProbert 1 — 53
(Paul Cole) *chsd ldrs: rdn and ev ch over 2f out: wknd over 1f out* **33/1**

3230 **15** *2 ½* **Azrael**[28] 2847 3-8-13 **93** .... MartinHarley(3) 12 — 64
(Alan McCabe) *hld up: rdn over 3f out: wknd over 2f out* **100/1**

-140 **16** *3 ½* **Discoteca**[21] 3069 3-8-13 **90** ....(v[1]) JimmyFortune 17 — 54
(Andrew Balding) *chsd ldrs: rdn and ev ch over 2f out: wknd over 1f out* **40/1**

-003 **17** *1* **Waltz Darling (IRE)**[26] 2935 3-8-10 **87** .... TonyHamilton 15 — 49
(Richard Fahey) *prom: hmpd and lost pl over 8f out: hdwy 5f out: rdn and wknd over 2f out* **40/1**

1442 **18** *13* **Swift Alhaarth (IRE)**[5] 3623 3-8-5 **82** .... MartinLane 4 — 18
(Mark Johnston) *led: rdn and hdd 3f out: sn hung lft and wknd* **18/1**

2m 6.26s (0.76) **Going Correction** +0.225s/f (Good) — **18** Ran SP% **128.8**
Speed ratings (Par 106): **105,104,102,101,99 98,98,98,95,95 92,90,89,88,86 83,83,72**
toteswingers:1&2:£5.50, 2&3:£7.80, 1&3:£10.90 CSF £17.12 CT £138.07 TOTE £8.10: £2.30, £1.20, £2.70, £4.10; EX 23.30 Trifecta £148.90 Pool of £2415.15 - 12.00 winning units..
Owner Scuderia Rencati Srl **Bred** Azienda Agricola Francesca **Trained** Newmarket, Suffolk

FOCUS
A red-hot handicap and a tough race for favourites with only one market leader successful in the last ten years, whilst within the past six years there have been winners at 20-1, 25-1 and 40-1. As in the opener on the round course, the field came down the centre in the straight. The first two probably improved on their Ascot form and will probably soon be back in pattern races. The fifth and sixth set the standard.

NOTEBOOK
Fulgur had finished just over 4l behind Mijhaar in the King Edward VII Stakes at Royal Ascot when not enjoying the clearest of runs and enjoyed a 7lb pull, so there wasn't much between them. It may be that Fulgur was the better suited of the pair by this shorter trip for, having been held up well off the pace, he produced a smart turn of foot inside the last 2f and, despite hanging away to his left towards his rival, was always doing enough to force his head in front and was going away at the line. He can probably improve further and is well worth another crack at Pattern company. (op 13-2)
Mijhaar ◆ was making his handicap debut and was sent off at very skinny odds for a race like this. It seemed likely that his supporters would collect as he was still on the bridle when joining in with the leaders passing the 2f pole and he soon went over a length clear, but he was inclined to run about once in front and despite battling hard, was just run out of it. This was only his fourth start and he certainly has enough ability to still make the grade. (tchd 9-4 in places)
Labarinto ◆ was put up 5lb despite only finishing second at Newbury in his previous start. Given plenty to do, though in truth no more than the winner, he made his move at around the same time, but he was briefly stopped in his run when trying for a gap between Fulgur and Seelo 2f out, and although he ran on again once in the clear, it was too late. He still has a nice prize in him. (op 10-1)
Malthouse(GER) ran well in a valuable sales race over C&D last month and this was another fine effort. He remains 9lb higher than when winning on the Rowley Mile in May and isn't going to get any respite after this, so his best chance of another win may be back in a conditions events.
Well Sharp was just 1lb higher than when a fine third of 18 behind Brown Panther in the King George V Handicap at Royal Ascot and this return to 1m2f looked to be in his favour. He looked likely to play a part when moving into contention approaching the last quarter-mile, but then couldn't find any more. (op 10-1)
Star Surprise, up a furlong in trip, made some late progress towards the far side of the track, but seems to reserve his best for Sandown. (op 33-1)
Seelo(USA) looked progressive before flopping when long odds-on for a handicap on the Kempton Polytrack last time and was up another 8lb here, but this was probably a better effort and he was right there with a chance passing the 2f pole. He still has some scope, but will need to improve to defy this sort of mark. (tchd 25-1)
Rain Mac ran on over the last 2f without ever looking like getting involved. He remains unexposed and may be worth a try over further.
Tullius(IRE) was up another 5lb having been consistent in his previous five starts, but although disputing the advantage coming to the last 2f he then didn't seem to get home over this extra furlong. (op 18-1)
Club Oceanic had responded well to the application of cheekpieces with two narrow successes and was bidding for a hat-trick off a 6lb higher mark, but he was being niggled along in last place fully half a mile from home and could never make any impression from then on. (tchd 17-2 and 10-1)

3775 PRINCESS OF WALES'S SPORTINGBET.COM STKS (GROUP 2) — 1m 4f
3:00 (3:05) (Class 1) 3-Y-O+

£45,368 (£17,200; £8,608; £4,288; £2,152; £1,080) **Stalls** Centre

Form — RPR

10-4 **1** — **Crystal Capella**[40] 2501 6-8-13 115 .... RyanMoore 4 — 121
(Sir Michael Stoute) *hld up: racd centre turning for home: hdwy and edgd lft over 3f out: led over 2f out: shkn up: edgd rt and clr over 1f out: r.o wl* **4/1**[2]

32-2 **2** *8* **Redwood**[103] 1001 5-9-2 116 .... MichaelHills 9 — 112
(B W Hills) *prom: racd centre turning for home: edgd lft over 3f out: rdn and ev ch over 2f out: styd on same pce appr fnl f* **2/1**[1]

-123 **3** *6* **Buthelezi (USA)**[33] 2707 3-8-3 104 .... NickyMackay 1 — 103
(John Gosden) *sn led: wnt far side to r alone over 6f out: rdn and hdd over 3f out: wknd ins fnl f* **12/1**

-652 **4** *5* **Afsare**[12] 3403 4-9-2 112 .... KierenFallon 7 — 96
(Luca Cumani) *hld up in tch: racd keenly: racd centre turning for home: edgd lft over 3f out: rdn over 2f out: wknd over 1f out* **6/1**

-425 **5** *9* **Campanologist (USA)**[19] 3153 6-9-2 116 .... MickaelBarzalona 8 — 82
(Saeed Bin Suroor) *prom: racd centre tunring for home: edgd lft over 3f out: hmpd and lost pl wl over 2f out: sn wknd* **10/1**

-101 **6** *8* **Dordogne (IRE)**[61] 1895 3-8-3 105 .... SilvestreDeSousa 5 — 73
(Mark Johnston) *s.i.s: hdwy to chse ldr over 9f out: racd centre turning for home: lft in ld of that gp over 6f out: rdn to ld overall and edgd lft over 3f out: hdd over 2f out: sn wknd: t.o* **10/1**

-454 **7** *18* **Laaheb**[19] 3153 5-9-2 113 .... RichardHills 3 — 64
(Roger Varian) *chsd ldrs: racd centre turning for home: edgd lft over 3f out: rdn over 2f out: wknd and eased wl over 1f out: t.o* **5/1**[3]

12-0 **8** *1 ¼* **Myplacelater**[56] 2029 4-8-13 110 .... PaulHanagan 10 — 38
(David Elsworth) *dwlt: a in rr: racd centre turning for home: lost tch fnl 5f: t.o* **25/1**

2m 31.57s (-1.33) **Going Correction** +0.225s/f (Good)
WFA 3 from 4yo+ 13lb — **8** Ran SP% **114.0**
Speed ratings (Par 115): **113,107,103,100,94 89,77,76**
CSF £12.34 TOTE £4.60: £1.40, £1.20, £4.20; EX 13.70 Trifecta £198.30 Pool of: 10119.73 - 37.76 winning units..
Owner Sir Evelyn De Rothschild **Bred** Southcourt Stud **Trained** Newmarket, Suffolk

FOCUS
A solid Group 2 line up. The early pace didn't appear that strong and the field bunched right up 3f from the finish, but they still finished strung out. Once again the near side was shunned in the home straight. Crystal Capella is a high-class mare on her day and this rates a personal best. Only the first three showed anything like their form.

NOTEBOOK
Crystal Capella's trainer has a fine record in this contest and his dual Pride Stakes winner further enhanced it with a most taking success. She has been dogged with shin splints throughout her career to date and reportedly had a few niggles going into her comeback run at Haydock in May, when running below par. Providing she was back to her best she looked to have a decent chance in this company, though, and the showers prior to racing were much in her favour. Ryan Moore gave her a confident ride and, as the runners came together nearing 3f out, it was apparent she was cantering all over her rivals. She came right away when asked to win the race shortly afterwards and this does rate a career-best effort from the 6-y-o, as the runner-up is a decent benchmark. Her season will now rightly be geared around finding an elusive success at the top level and the Group 1 Yorkshire Oaks next month should be right up her street as she was successful on her previous outing on the Knavesmire. Her trainer mentioned that race as her likely port of call, but added connections would now have a good think about her future targets. (tchd 9-2)
Redwood was made to look pretty slow by the winner and had to settle for second place once again. He has proved consistent since finding Sans Frontieres too strong in this last season and his previous second to Rewilding at Meydan back in March was well advertised at Royal Ascot last month. Well backed to go one better on this ease in class, he had to be re-plated down at the start and caused a delay to the scheduled off time. He was a little free once jumping out, but held every chance in the home straight and looked to run his race. It's hard to know how much his chance was compromised at the start, but it's unlikely he would have coped with the winner whatever. No doubt he deserves to get his had back in front. (op 5-2 tchd 15-8 and 11-4 in places)
Buthelezi(USA) fared best of the two 3-y-os. He set out to make all and took time to settle. It wasn't that surprising to see him sent over to the far rail once straightening for home considering he has markedly hung in the past, but he looked in trouble when coming under pressure around 4f out. To his credit he kept on gamely once headed and he should be up to winning a Listed race at least before the season's end. Official explanation: jockey said colt hung left to rail 6f out (op 20-1)
Afsare registered a career-best on his first attempt over this trip in Listed company here 12 days earlier, but could have done without the rain falling beforehand and probably had a harder race that day than connections might have realised. He can do better again when reverting to a genuinely quick surface. (op 9-2 tchd 4-1)
Campanologist(USA), who flopped in this event in 2009, travelled well enough but proved laboured under pressure and again ran below his best. He's become hard to get right. (op 8-1)
Dordogne(IRE) came into this having won the Lingfield Derby trial in May. Coltish beforehand, he came under pressure at the top of the home straight and failed to see the race out. This wasn't his day. (op 11-1 tchd 12-1)
Laaheb had work to do to reverse Meydan form with Redwood, but had finished one place ahead of Campanologist at Royal Ascot last time and is a C&D winner. He faded tamely once put under pressure and something may well have gone amiss. (op 11-2)
Myplacelater was never in the hunt from out the back and has now run below par in two outings since resuming this year. (tchd 28-1)

3776 EARL OF EUSTON E B F CONDITIONS STKS — 6f
3:35 (3:35) (Class 3) 2-Y-O — **£7,762** (£2,310; £1,154; £577) **Stalls** High

Form — RPR

1 **1** — **Harbour Watch (IRE)**[25] 2962 2-9-1 0 .... RyanMoore 5 — 110+
(Richard Hannon) *trckd ldrs: racd keenly: led wl over 1f out: sn hdd: rallied to ld ins fnl f: r.o strly* **2/1**[2]

214 **2** *4 ½* **Burwaaz**[21] 3064 2-8-13 0 .... RichardHills 1 — 95
(Ed Dunlop) *hld up in tch: rdn 2f out: led over 1f out: sn hung lft: hdd and no ex ins fnl f* **11/8**[1]

1 **3** 4 1/2 **Hadaj**[20] 3132 2-9-1 0 PhilipRobinson 2 83
(Clive Brittain) *chsd ldrs: rdn over 1f out: wknd ins fnl f* **4/1**[3]

1 **4** 3 1/2 **Citizen's Charter (USA)**[14] 3314 2-8-13 0 MickaelBarzalona 4 71
(Mahmood Al Zarooni) *chsd ldr tl rdn over 2f out: wknd ins fnl f* **8/1**

2136 **5** 3 **Dawn Lightning**[6] 3589 2-8-6 0 ow1 MartinHarley(3) 3 58
(Alan McCabe) *led: rdn and hdd wl over 1f out: sn wknd* **66/1**

1m 13.96s (1.46) **Going Correction** +0.225s/f (Good) 5 Ran SP% **108.0**
Speed ratings (Par 98): **99,93,87,82,78**
CSF £4.92 TOTE £3.10: £1.50, £1.30; EX 4.70.
Owner H Robin Heffer **Bred** T Molan **Trained** East Everleigh, Wilts

FOCUS
This was an intriguing clash between three colts who had won their only previous starts and one who had already run well in Group company. Despite the rain appearing to slow the ground up as the meeting progressed, the winning time was only 0.2 seconds slower than the July Stakes which suggests this is strong form. The winner is arguably the most exciting 2yo we've seen to date this year.

NOTEBOOK
Harbour Watch(IRE) ◆ was impressive when beating a subsequent winner on his Salisbury debut last month and he confirmed the impression he made there with a big effort. Held up early, he made his way through the gap to lead 2f out and it looked as though he would face a real battle when the favourite was produced on his outside, but he dismissed him relatively comfortably and one couldn't help but be impressed by the way he stuck his neck out and ran like an arrow to the line. There is enough stamina on the dam's side of his pedigree to suggest he will stay further and he looks a very nice prospect indeed. The Prix Morny or Gimcrack may be next. (op 15-8 tchd 7-4)
Burwaaz 'won' the race on his side when fourth in the Norfolk and was sent off favourite to gain compensation. Held up early, he was being niggled along to take closer order on the outside of the field coming to the last 2f and once in a challenging position, started to hang away to his left. His finishing effort was tame when compared to the attitude of the winner and he has questions to answer now. (tchd 5-4 and 6-4)
Hadaj was impressive when beating a subsequent winner on his debut over C&D last month, but he didn't find a lot off the bridle coming to the last quarter-mile on this occasion. Perhaps the race he won here wasn't that strong after all. (op 9-2)
Citizen's Charter(USA) wasn't expected to make a winning debut at Newcastle last month judging by the market, so that must have been a pleasant surprise, but he was in trouble against the inside rail over 2f from home and found this task well beyond him. (op 15-2)
Dawn Lightning, the most exposed in the field, was well beaten in Listed company last time and this was her first try at 6f. She made the early running, but was easily picked off a quarter of a mile from home.

3777 PORTLAND PLACE PROPERTIES CONDITIONS STKS 1m
4:05 (4:05) (Class 3) 3-Y-O **£8,092** (£2,423; £1,211; £605; £302) **Stalls** High

Form RPR

3450 **1** **Bridgefield (USA)**[21] 3067 3-8-12 98 MickaelBarzalona 2 105+
(Mahmood Al Zarooni) *hld up in tch: led over 2f out: rdn and hung lft over 1f out: r.o wl* **9/1**[3]

-466 **2** 2 3/4 **Casual Glimpse**[34] 2683 3-9-3 95 PaulHanagan 4 102
(Richard Hannon) *chsd ldrs: nt clr run over 2f out to over 1f out: r.o to go 2nd wl ins fnl f: nvr able to chal* **40/1**

1232 **3** nk **Cai Shen (IRE)**[21] 3067 3-9-1 105 RyanMoore 3 99
(Richard Hannon) *led at stdy pce tl qcknd over 3f out: hdd over 2f out: sn rdn: styd on same pce ins fnl f* **13/8**[2]

-400 **4** 2 **Slim Shadey**[21] 3068 3-8-12 98 (b1) LukeMorris 1 92
(J S Moore) *trckd ldr: rdn and ev ch over 2f out: edgd rt over 1f out: no ex ins fnl f* **16/1**

1-52 **5** 6 **Fury**[42] 2440 3-9-3 106 KierenFallon 5 83
(William Haggas) *hld up: swtchd rt over 3f out: hdwy over 2f out: wknd over 1f out* **5/6**[1]

1m 44.54s (4.54) **Going Correction** +0.225s/f (Good) 5 Ran SP% **111.0**
Speed ratings (Par 104): **86,83,82,80,74**
CSF £161.96 TOTE £9.50: £3.60, £5.20; EX 98.60.
Owner Godolphin **Bred** B M Kelley **Trained** Newmarket, Suffolk

FOCUS
This decent little conditions 3-y-o event essentially looked to be a match between the two clear market leaders, but it was run at a steady early pace and there was a turn-up. Messy form with the winner reversing Britannia form with the third.

NOTEBOOK
Bridgefield(USA) bounced back with a clear-cut success. He ran well without scoring in three runs at Meydan after resuming at three earlier this year, but was comfortably held in the Britannia Handicap at Royal Ascot on his British return last month and had a fair bit to prove. He ran somewhat freely early on, but obviously enjoyed the way the race unfolded as he sprinted clear of rivals when the dash for home developed nearing 2f out. He was well on top inside the final furlong and this should boost his confidence no end. He's entered in the Totesport Mile at Goodwood later this month, but connections hinted at finding him a possible opening in Listed company next. (op 14-1)
Casual Glimpse has not won since landing the preceding conditions race as a juvenile on this card last year and was the second-string from his yard. He never threatened the winner, but finished nicely and rates better than the bare form as he appeared the chief sufferer off the uneven pace. He looks well worth another try over this longer trip. (op 25-1)
Cai Shen(IRE) was well ahead of the winner when finishing second under top weight at Royal Ascot last time out and was well backed here. He raced from the front and had the run of things, but lacked any sort of a turn of foot when the sprint for home was on. This will disappoint some, but he needs much more of a test at this trip and deserves another chance to show his true colours. (op 15-8 tchd 2-1 in places)
Slim Shadey was somewhat lit up by the first-time blinkers, but was still going well as the tempo began to lift. He couldn't quicken for pressure and is in danger of becoming disappointing, but he too needs more of a test over 1m. (op 12-1)
Fury looked to have lots in his favour, but it was a tame effort from him. He pulled off the uneven pace, but still looked a player when switched to the outside for his effort. His response when it mattered was flat, however, and for all that this was a falsely run affair, it does leave him with a fair amount to prove. Official explanation: jockey said colt was unsuited by the slow early pace (op 4-5 tchd 10-11 and evens in places)

3778 THREE CHIMNEYS H'CAP 5f
4:40 (4:40) (Class 3) (0-95,91) 3-Y-O+ **£8,409** (£2,502; £1,250; £625) **Stalls** High

Form RPR

205- **1** **Murura (IRE)**[7] 3563 4-8-10 75 (b1) MickaelBarzalona 6 90
(James J Hartnett, Ire) *hld up: hdwy to ld over 1f out: hung lft: r.o wl* **12/1**

0450 **2** 2 3/4 **Whozthecat (IRE)**[12] 3379 4-9-8 87 (v) RobertWinston 5 92
(Declan Carroll) *prom: rdn and ev ch whn hung lft over 1f out: styd on same pce ins fnl f* **12/1**

3002 **3** shd **Lujeanie**[13] 3367 5-9-4 83 (p) NeilCallan 3 88+
(Dean Ivory) *hld up: 1/2-way: nt clr run over 1f out: r.o* **13/2**[3]

-216 **4** 3 **Apace (IRE)**[19] 3181 3-9-2 86 RyanMoore 8 78
(Sir Michael Stoute) *sn pushed along in rr: swtchd rt over 1f out: r.o wl towards fin: nvr nrr* **9/2**[2]

0-03 **5** 1/2 **La Fortunata**[33] 2714 4-9-2 81 TonyCulhane 10 73
(Mike Murphy) *led: hdd over 3f out: rdn 1/2-way: edgd rt over 1f out: wknd ins fnl f* **9/1**

-045 **6** 1/2 **Fol Hollow (IRE)**[33] 2727 6-9-0 86 ShirleyTeasdale(7) 4 77
(David Nicholls) *chsd ldr: rdn over 1f out: wknd ins fnl f* **16/1**

3004 **7** nk **Jamesway (IRE)**[13] 3357 3-9-4 88 PaulHanagan 1 76
(Richard Fahey) *wnt rt s: sn pushed along in rr: rdn over 1f out: nvr on terms* **7/2**[1]

10-0 **8** shd **Perfect Blossom**[33] 2714 4-9-9 91 AmyRyan(3) 2 80
(Kevin Ryan) *chsd ldrs: led over 3f out: rdn: hmpd and hdd over 1f out: wknd ins fnl f* **8/1**

0406 **9** 1 **Bertoliver**[11] 3427 7-9-1 80 (t) HughBowman 9 66
(Stuart Williams) *chsd ldrs: rdn over 1f out: wknd ins fnl f* **20/1**

4003 **10** nk **Five Star Junior (USA)**[20] 3140 5-9-11 90 KierenFallon 7 78
(Linda Stubbs) *sn pushed along in rr: hdwy over 1f out: btn whn nt clr run and eased ins fnl f* **9/2**[2]

58.99 secs (-0.11) **Going Correction** +0.225s/f (Good)
WFA 3 from 4yo+ 5lb 10 Ran SP% **119.1**
Speed ratings (Par 107): **109,104,104,99,98 98,97,97,95,95**
toteswingers:1&2:£24.80, 2&3:£15.60, 1&3:£13.20 CSF £149.58 CT £1027.61 TOTE £14.40: £3.80, £3.80, £2.40; EX 203.30 Trifecta £1060.30 Part won. Pool of £1432.89 - 0.63 winning units..
Owner Seamus D Fitzpatrick **Bred** Corrin Stud **Trained** Duleek, Co Meath
■ A first winner in Britain for James Hartnett.

FOCUS
A strongly run sprint handicap with a three-way battle for the early lead, but they merely set it up for the closers. Ordinary form for the grade.

NOTEBOOK
Murura(IRE) was 0-9 on turf before this, but he was tried in blinkers for the first time after becoming disappointing in cheekpieces and the jockey booking was most eyecatching. The key to this victory also was the rapid pace, as he settled nicely at the back of the field in the early stages. Creeping closer over 2f from home, he settled the issue with a smart turn of foot over a furlong from home and he quickly established an unassailable lead. He would be interesting if turned out again before being reassessed provided the headgear works again. (op 16-1)
Whozthecat(IRE) emerges with plenty of credit as he was never too far off the contested lead and kept on all the way to the line. His best form has come on flat tracks, so this was a good effort. (op 14-1 tchd 16-1)
Lujeanie was put up 4lb for last month's narrow defeat over C&D. Another to stay on well from off the pace after having to be switched over a furlong from home, all four of his career successes have come over 6f. (op 15-2)
Apace(IRE) was a disappointing favourite off 1lb higher over C&D last month and ran better here, but she became outpaced at a crucial stage and was last coming to the final furlong. By the time she found her stride again up the hill, the front three had gone well beyond recall. (tchd 5-1)
La Fortunata ◆, one of the trio who forced the issue, fared best in hanging on for fifth so her performance should be marked up. (op 8-1 tchd 10-1)
Jamesway(IRE) hasn't won in over a year, but had been running well in stronger handicaps recently and was sent off favourite. He gave away ground at the start by swerving right exiting the stalls, which wasn't in itself fatal given the way the race was run, and the winner was racing alongside him, but he took an age to find his stride after coming off the bridle and never had a prayer of making his presence felt. Official explanation: jockey said gelding never travelled (tchd 4-1)
Five Star Junior(USA) Official explanation: jockey said gelding was denied a clear run
T/Jkpt: Not won. T/Plt: £282.80 to a £1 stake. Pool of £128,937.76 - 332.75 winning tickets. T/Qpdt: £99.50 to £1 stake. Pool of £7,266.29 - 54.00 winning tickets. CR

3594 WARWICK (L-H)
Thursday, July 7

OFFICIAL GOING: Good
Wind: Moderate across Weather: Sunny intervals

3779 BRITISH STALLION STUDS SUPPORTING BRITISH RACING E B F MEDIAN AUCTION MAIDEN STKS (DIV I) 7f 26y
2:15 (2:15) (Class 5) 2-Y-O **£2,975** (£885; £442; £221) **Stalls** Low

Form RPR

33 **1** **Red Alpha (IRE)**[35] 2640 2-9-3 0 DarryllHolland 9 75+
(Jeremy Noseda) *led after 1f: hdd over 3f out: led again 2f out: pushed along fnl f: comf* **9/2**[3]

4 **2** 1 1/4 **Royal Majestic**[13] 3336 2-8-12 0 SamHitchcott 12 66
(Mick Channon) *in rr: hdwy on outside3f out and c wd into st to r on stands' side wl over 2f out: styd on wl u.p ins fnl f to take 2nd fnl 120yds: no ch w wnr* **4/1**[2]

0 **3** 3/4 **Dickens Rules (IRE)**[15] 3288 2-9-3 0 JamesDoyle 8 69
(Sylvester Kirk) *chsd ldrs: rdn and c wd into st to r towards stands' side: kpt on wl fnl f to press for 2nd fnl 120yds: nvr any ch w wnr and one pce into 3rd cl home* **15/2**

4 **4** 1 3/4 **Ashpan Sam**[14] 3308 2-9-3 0 LiamJones 1 65
(John Spearing) *chsd ldrs: wnt 2nd ins fnl 2f but nvr any ch w wnr: wknd into 4th fnl 120yds* **7/1**

0 **5** 6 **Fugitive Motel (IRE)**[24] 2997 2-9-3 0 CathyGannon 4 50+
(Richard Hannon) *led 1f: styd w wnr and led again over 3f out: hdd and edgd rt u.p 2f out: veered sharply rt sn after and cannoned into rival: no ch after but kpt on clsng stages* **13/2**

6 shd **Always Eager** 2-9-3 0 AdrianNicholls 7 54+
(Mark Johnston) *chsd ldrs: rdn and keeping on one pce whn bdly bmpd by rival and lost considerable momentum: no ch after* **14/1**

7 nse **Fu Fic Fas** 2-8-12 0 FrankieMcDonald 6 44+
(Paul Fitzsimons) *s.i.s: in rr: styd on fr over 1f out: kpt on wl clsng stages* **100/1**

0 **8** 1 1/4 **Cool Light**[16] 3258 2-8-7 0 HarryBentley(5) 11 43+
(Alan Jarvis) *in rr and pushed along 1/2-way: edgd lft and green over 2f out: nvr in contention* **33/1**

9 3/4 **My Boy Ginger** 2-9-3 0 JamesMillman 10 44
(Rod Millman) *s.i.s: in rr: mod late prog* **33/1**

0 **10** 8 **Jungle**[16] 3257 2-8-12 0 WilliamCarson 3 19
(B W Hills) *s.i.s: sn rcvrd: rdn over 2f out and hung rt towards stands' side: wknd qckly* **7/2**[1]

000 **11** 3/4 **Arbeejay**[15] 3288 2-8-12 0 RichardThomas 2 18
(Paul Burgoyne) *early spd: bhd fnl 3f* **250/1**

12 9 **Parque Atlantico** 2-9-3 0 LiamKeniry 5 —
(Andrew Balding) *s.i.s: a in rr* **18/1**

1m 27.39s (2.79) **Going Correction** +0.275s/f (Good) 12 Ran SP% **117.2**
Speed ratings (Par 94): **95,93,92,90,83 83,83,82,81,72 71,61**
toteswingers:1&2:£3.80, 2&3:£14.60, 1&3:£9.80 CSF £22.30 TOTE £3.70: £1.80, £2.00, £2.70; EX 21.60.
Owner Mrs Susan Roy **Bred** Paul Denis Houlihan **Trained** Newmarket, Suffolk

The Form Book, Raceform Ltd, Compton, RG20 6NL

FOCUS
This looked no better than an ordinary juvenile maiden.
NOTEBOOK
Red Alpha(IRE), third over 5f and 6f on Polytrack on his two previous starts, stepped up on those efforts. The second and third were closing at the line, but he always looked likely to hold on. (op 7-2)
Royal Majestic, an encouraging fourth despite greenness over this trip on her Chester debut, built on that display. Drawn wide and held up early on, she had made progress by halfway and, racing near the stands' rail, finished strongly. She ought to be able to find an ordinary maiden. (tchd 9-2)
Dickens Rules(IRE), beaten just over 5l when seventh on his first appearance, attracted decent support. He showed why in the race, too, staying on nicely near the stands' rail in the closing stages. Like the second, he should win a modest maiden event. (op 16-1)
Ashpan Sam, a staying-on fourth over 6f on his only previous outing, did not entirely convince that this extra distance is in his favour, appearing to get tired inside the last. (op 13-2 tchd 15-2)
Fugitive Motel(IRE), tenth of 12 over 5f at Windsor on debut, led until 3f out, but swerved wildly right - then left - and lost much of his forward momentum. He ran better than his finishing position suggests, but seemingly has steering problems to overcome in order to fulfil his potential. (op 10-1)
Always Eager, a first-time-out half-brother to a 1m juvenile winner, showed a little promise and improvement seems likely. (op 11-1)

3780 BRITISH STALLION STUDS SUPPORTING BRITISH RACING E B F MEDIAN AUCTION MAIDEN STKS (DIV II) 7f 26y
2:50 (2:50) (Class 5) 2-Y-O £2,975 (£885; £442; £221) Stalls Low

Form RPR

1 **Crius (IRE)** 2-9-3 0 .... CathyGannon 4 75+
(Richard Hannon) *s.i.s: in tch and t.k.h: hdwy fr 2f out: drvn to chal between horse fnl 100yds: r.o wl to ld fnl 30yds* **7/1**[3]

2 ½ **Niceofyoutotellme** 2-9-3 0 .... JimCrowley 1 74+
(Ralph Beckett) *hmpd s: in rr: drvn and hdwy 2f out: styd on wl to chal fnl 100yds: kpt on wl clsng stages but nt gng pce of wnr* **9/4**[1]

0 3 ½ **Emperors Pearl (IRE)**[33] [2709] 2-8-12 0 .... WilliamCarson 9 68+
(B W Hills) *led: c rt and grabbed stands' rail wl over 2f out whn 3 l clr: sn hrd drvn: jnd fnl 100yds: hdd and no ex fnl 30yds: dropped to 3rd cl home* **15/2**

562 4 3¾ **Alabanda (IRE)**[20] [3123] 2-8-12 0 .... DuranFentiman 11 58
(Tim Easterby) *prom: c over to stands' rail and chsd clr ldr over 2f out: no imp and styd on same pce fr over 1f out* **5/2**[2]

602 5 1 **Dovils Date**[19] [3171] 2-9-3 0 .... JamesMillman 10 61
(Rod Millman) *in tch: drvn and outpcd over 3f out: pushed along and kpt on again ins fnl f* **9/1**

6 2 **Tingo In The Tale (IRE)** 2-9-3 0 .... JamesDoyle 5 56
(David Arbuthnot) *in rr: pushed along over 2f out: styd on fr over 1f out and kpt on ins fnl f but nvr a threat* **66/1**

0256 7 2½ **Fromthestables Com (IRE)**[30] [2788] 2-9-3 0 .... ChrisCatlin 3 49
(J W Hills) *chsd ldrs: rdn 3f out: wknd over 1f out* **20/1**

00 8 ¾ **Nifty Shiftin**[20] [3132] 2-9-3 0 .... LiamKeniry 8 48
(David Elsworth) *toodk t.k.h: stdd in rr: nvr gng pce to rch ldrs fnl 2f but sme prog clsng stages* **33/1**

05 9 nk **Clean Bowled (IRE)**[15] [3282] 2-9-3 0 ....(b[1]) DarryllHolland 6 47
(Brian Meehan) *stmbld s: sn chsng ldrs: wknd 2f out* **33/1**

0 10 5 **Sudden Wish (IRE)**[10] [3463] 2-8-12 0 .... PaulDoe 7 29
(Jim Best) *chsd ldrs: drvn 3f out: wknd 2f out* **50/1**

006 11 7 **Coach Montana (IRE)**[15] [3282] 2-9-3 0 .... TedDurcan 2 17
(Jane Chapple-Hyam) *wnt lft s: sn chsng ldrs: wknd quicky ins fnl 2f* **14/1**

1m 26.77s (2.17) **Going Correction** +0.275s/f (Good) 11 Ran SP% **114.4**
Speed ratings (Par 94): **98,97,96,92,91 89,86,85,85,79 71**
toteswingers:1&2:£4.00, 2&3:£5.80, 1&3:£10.00 CSF £21.46 TOTE £7.90: £3.00, £1.10, £3.70; EX 25.90.
Owner Titan Assets **Bred** Oak Lodge Bloodstock **Trained** East Everleigh, Wilts
FOCUS
Seemingly less depth to this second division of the 2-y-o maiden, the finish of which was fought out between two newcomers.
[illegible]
Crius(IRE), a newcomer out of a [illegible] winner in [illegible], notched a game win. He battled on bravely for pressure and was edging away from the second at the post. (op [illegible])
Niceofyoutotellme, a newcomer out of a sprint winner in the US, was last early on. Still only ninth at halfway, he threw down a decent challenge inside the last 2f, but could not quite match the winner's finishing drive. (op 11-4 tchd 2-1)
Emperors Pearl(IRE), eighth of 11 on her Doncaster debut, improved a fair bit on that effort. She led from the outset and, after turning into the straight, made for the stands' rail. She was still in front over 1f out, but was tiring when the principals closed her down. (op 8-1)
Alabanda(IRE), a sound second over this trip at Musselburgh last time out, looks a feasible marker for the form. She raced in second from the start and, although she was once-paced in the closing stages, seemed to try her best. (op 11-4)
Dovils Date, runner-up over this distance at Lingfield last time, was obliged to race wide in the early stages, which obviously was not in his favour. He plugged on gamely in the last couple of furlongs, though, and was not far below the best of his previous form. (op 7-1)
Tingo In The Tale(IRE), a first-time-out half-sister from a family of 5f-7f winners, showed a hint of promise. Towards the rear early on, he made up some ground in the closing stages, when others were dropping away.
Coach Montana(IRE) Official explanation: vet said gelding finished lame

3781 SILVER FOX CHALLENGE MAIDEN STKS 1m 2f 188y
3:25 (3:26) (Class 5) 3-Y-0+ £2,587 (£770; £384; £192) Stalls Low

Form RPR

3-4 1 **Star In Flight**[15] [3267] 4-9-12 0 .... DarryllHolland 4 86
(Brian Meehan) *t.k.h: hanging rt whn hdwy 1m out: trckd ldr 7f out: chal ins fnl 3f tl drvn to ld wl over 1f out: styd on strly* **9/1**

-200 2 3¼ **Canna (IRE)**[68] [1689] 3-9-0 79 .... WilliamCarson 5 80+
(B W Hills) *hld up in rr: hdwy over 3f out and sn drvn: styd on u.p ins fnl f to take 2nd in theclsng stages: no ch w wnr* **10/3**[3]

45- 3 ½ **Mungo Park**[246] [7303] 3-9-0 0 .... AdrianNicholls 8 79+
(Mark Johnston) *chsd ldrs: drvn along fr 5f out: styd on u.p fnl 2f to chse wnr briefly fnl 100yds but no imp: one pce into 3rd clsng stages* **5/1**

232 4 3¼ **Lady Elsie**[17] [3224] 3-8-9 75 .... LiamJones 6 68
(William Haggas) *led: rdn and jnd 3f out: hdd wl over 1f out: wknd ins fnl f* **3/1**[2]

062 5 ½ **Brick Dust (IRE)**[14] [3324] 3-9-0 76 .... KirstyMilczarek 7 72+
(Luca Cumani) *t.k.h: chsd ldr to over 7f out: shkn up one styd on same pce fnl 3f* **7/4**[1]

6 6 13 **Charlie Fable (IRE)**[11] [3430] 3-9-0 0 .... TravisBlock 3 48
(Hughie Morrison) *chsd ldrs: rdn 4f out: wknd ins fnl f* **28/1**

0 7 2¼ **Farmers Hill**[24] [3001] 3-9-0 0 .... ChrisCatlin 2 44
(Mark Hoad) *t.k.h in rr and wl off pce: r.o through btn horses ins fnl f* **100/1**

0 8 7 **Manarola**[8] [3519] 3-8-7 0 .... AntiocoMurgia(7) 9 31
(Mahmood Al Zarooni) *in tch whn carried rt 1m out: styd chsng ldrs tl wknd 4f out* **25/1**

00 9 24 **Astroverdi**[19] [3177] 3-9-0 0 .... TedDurcan 10 —
(Mark H Tompkins) *a in rr: t.o* **200/1**

0 10 37 **Greyemkay**[17] [3218] 3-9-0 0 .... JamesDoyle 1 —
(Richard Price) *sn bhd: t.o* **200/1**

2m 23.28s (2.18) **Going Correction** +0.275s/f (Good)
WFA 3 from 4yo 12lb 10 Ran SP% **120.4**
Speed ratings (Par 103): **103,100,100,97,97 88,86,81,63,37**
toteswingers:1&2:£4.50, 2&3:£4.20, 1&3:£5.80 CSF £39.92 TOTE £11.40: £2.30, £2.10, £2.00; EX 46.40.
Owner J H Widdows **Bred** J H Widdows **Trained** Manton, Wilts
■ Stewards' Enquiry : Adrian Nicholls caution: careless riding.
FOCUS
An average maiden in which only a few had obvious chances. Typically muddling for Warwick but the winner showed improvement.
Brick Dust(IRE) Official explanation: jockey said gelding ran too free

3782 BRITISH STALLION STUDS E B F FILLIES' H'CAP 7f 26y
3:55 (3:58) (Class 4) (0-80,80) 3-Y-0+ £5,175 (£1,540; £769; £384) Stalls Low

Form RPR

3414 1 **Queen Of Cash (IRE)**[7] [3549] 3-9-3 77 .... DarryllHolland 4 85
(Hughie Morrison) *mde all: hrd drvn over 1f out: styd on wl and in command ins fnl f* **7/2**[1]

0142 2 ¾ **No Poppy (IRE)**[15] [3278] 3-9-6 80 .... DuranFentiman 5 85
(Tim Easterby) *t.k.h and chsd ldrs: drvn along ins fnl 3f: styd on u.p fnl f to take 2nd nr fin: gng on last strides but a hld by wnr* **6/1**[3]

-356 3 ¾ **Saskia's Dream**[37] [2582] 3-8-10 70 .... TedDurcan 1 73
(Jane Chapple-Hyam) *chsd wnr: rdn fr 2f out: no imp fnl f and lost 2nd nr fin* **12/1**

1424 4 1 **Ellie In The Pink (IRE)**[29] [2821] 3-7-12 63 .... HarryBentley(5) 6 63
(Alan Jarvis) *in tch: hdwy 2f out: pushed along and one pce fr over 1f out* **5/1**[2]

4-06 5 3 **Poyle Judy**[12] [3390] 3-8-10 70 .... JimCrowley 2 62
(Ralph Beckett) *t.k.h in rr: styd on fnl 2f but nvr gng pce to get into contention* **12/1**

-303 6 1¾ **Camache Queen (IRE)**[24] [2986] 3-8-13 76 .... JohnFahy(3) 3 63
(Denis Coakley) *t.k.h and in tch: chsd ldrs fr 4f out: rdn: hung lft and wknd over 1f out* **7/2**[1]

6-52 7 nse **Mrs Greeley**[15] [3292] 3-8-8 68 .... CathyGannon 8 55
(Eve Johnson Houghton) *chsd ldrs: effrt and wd into st bnd 3f out: hung lft and btn 2f out* **5/1**[2]

-000 8 11 **Herminella**[16] [3259] 3-8-4 64 .... FrannyNorton 7 22
(William Muir) *tightened up s: a in last: lost tch ins fnl 3f* **20/1**

1m 26.06s (1.46) **Going Correction** +0.275s/f (Good) 8 Ran SP% **112.2**
Speed ratings (Par 102): **102,101,100,99,95 93,93,81**
toteswingers:1&2:£2.20, 2&3:£5.80, 1&3:£6.60 CSF £23.76 CT £223.50 TOTE £4.80: £1.90, £2.00, £2.90; EX 15.90.
Owner Hugh Scott-Barrett And Partners **Bred** Grangemore Stud **Trained** East Ilsley, Berks
■ Stewards' Enquiry : John Fahy caution: careless riding.
FOCUS
A fair fillies' handicap, with the top weight rated 80, and it looked competitive. Not many got involved and the form's rated around the first three.
Herminella Official explanation: jockey said filly suffered interference leaving stalls

3783 PERRYS PEUGEOT OF MILTON KEYNES H'CAP 7f 26y
4:30 (4:31) (Class 5) (0-70,70) 3-Y-0 £2,587 (£770; £384; £192) Stalls Low

Form RPR

0-35 1 **Oetzi**[28] [2841] 3-8-8 62 .... HarryBentley(5) 10 70+
(Alan Jarvis) *stdd s: hld up towards rr: rdn and hdwy over 1f out: styd on to ld fnl 120yds: kpt on wl and in command cl home* **4/1**[1]

6356 2 2 **Arctic Mirage**[11] [3432] 3-9-3 66 .... LiamKeniry 6 69
(Michael Blanshard) *trckd ldrs: rdn and styd on fnl 2f: r.o u.p to take 2nd clsng stages but no imp on wnr* **10/1**

0100 3 shd **Spirit Of Grace**[30] [2782] 3-9-4 67 .... JamesDoyle 13 70
([illegible]) *racd wd early and led: c over to take stands' rail over 2f out: sn hrd drvn: [illegible] lost 2nd clsng stages* **[illegible]**

40-3 4 2¾ **Minety Lass**[14] [3320] 3-8-10 66 .... LucyKBarry(7) 11 61
(Adrian Chamberlain) *sn chsng ldr: rdn over 2f out and ev ch 1f out: wknd ins fnl f* **22/1**

2662 5 1 **Mister Ben Vereen**[3] [3675] 3-9-0 63 ....(b) CathyGannon 8 56
(Eve Johnson Houghton) *chsd ldrs and disp 2nd early: t.k.h over 4f out: rdn over 2f out: wknd* **5/1**[2]

1610 6 ½ **Cadmium Loch**[13] [3337] 3-8-13 62 .... RussKennemore 5 53
(Reg Hollinshead) *chsd ldrs: rdn 2f out: wknd ins fnl f* **8/1**[3]

0004 7 ¾ **Watts Up Son**[13] [3337] 3-9-2 70 ....(t) NeilFarley(5) 1 59
(Declan Carroll) *in rr: rdn and sme prog fr 2f out: nvr rchd ldrs and btn appr fnl f* **8/1**[3]

0304 8 shd **Karate (IRE)**[8] [3523] 3-9-0 63 .... ChrisCatlin 4 52
(Hans Adielsson) *in rr: drvn along 3f out: mod prog ins fnl f* **33/1**

1260 9 ¾ **Loves Theme (IRE)**[10] [3470] 3-9-0 63 .... LiamJones 12 50
(Alan Bailey) *rdn in rr 5f out: nvr gng pce to get into contention* **66/1**

6150 10 ½ **Spirit Of Oakdale (IRE)**[30] [2792] 3-8-9 61 ....(p) JohnFahy(3) 14 47
(Walter Swinburn) *in rr and c rwd into st: a bhd* **20/1**

-055 11 1½ **Khaleeji**[31] [2772] 3-9-7 70 .... DarryllHolland 7 52
(J W Hills) *chsd ldrs: rdn 3f out: wknd appr fnl 2f* **28/1**

4200 12 2 **Avalon Bay**[50] [2197] 3-8-12 64 ....(v[1]) SeanLevey(3) 2 40
(Pat Eddery) *rdn 3f out: a bhd* **10/1**

1m 26.37s (1.77) **Going Correction** +0.275s/f (Good) 12 Ran SP% **99.9**
Speed ratings (Par 100): **100,97,97,94,93 92,91,91,90,90 88,86**
toteswingers:1&2:£7.00, 2&3:£13.10, 1&3:£13.90 CSF £27.36 CT £303.17 TOTE £4.80: £1.70, £3.60, £3.70; EX 31.90.
Owner Allen B Pope & Jarvis Associates **Bred** Jarvis Associates **Trained** Twyford, Bucks
■ Hawk Moth was withdrawn (7/2F, refused to enter stalls). Deduct 20p in the £ under R4.
FOCUS
A modest handicap, in which the top weight was rated 70. Again few got involved. The winner is rated up 6lb.

3784 SISK GROUP CONSTRUCTION H'CAP 6f
5:00 (5:00) (Class 4) (0-85,85) 3-Y-0+ £4,528 (£1,347; £673; £336) Stalls Low

Form RPR

-501 1 **Orpsie Boy (IRE)**[8] [3506] 8-9-6 84 6ex .... DaleSwift(5) 4 96
(Ruth Carr) *in tch: drvn and hdwy over 1f out chsd ldr ins fnl f: kpt on u.p to ld fnl 100yds* **3/1**[2]

1120 **2** *1 ¼* **Collect Art (IRE)**[7] 3535 4-9-5 **85** LucyKBarry(7) 8 93
(Andrew Haynes) *sn trcking ldr: slt ld and edgd lft 2f out: drvn and hung lft ins fnl f: hdd and no ex fnl 100yds* **5/2**[1]
01 **3** *1* **Barons Spy (IRE)**[26] 2903 10-9-9 **82** JamesDoyle 5 87
(Richard Price) *in rr: drvn and hdwy over 1f out: styd on wl fnl f to take 3rd fnl 120yds but no imp on ldng duo* **12/1**
1052 **4** *1* **Steelcut**[11] 3427 7-9-2 **75** (p) CathyGannon 7 77
(David Evans) *in rr tl hdwy over 1f out: kpt on ins fnl f but nvr gng pce to get into contention* **8/1**
5003 **5** *2 ¼* **Ocean Legend (IRE)**[12] 3383 6-9-3 **79** MichaelO'Connell(3) 2 73
(Tony Carroll) *chsd ldrs: drvn to chal 2f out: wknd u.p ins fnl f* **14/1**
2505 **6** *1 ¼* **Shifting Star (IRE)**[27] 2876 6-9-7 **83** (p) JohnFahy(3) 9 73
(Walter Swinburn) *in rr: hdwy on outside bnd over 2f out: no imp on ldrs ins fnl f* **6/1**[3]
210/ **7** *1 ¾* **Fabreze**[727] 3795 6-9-10 **83** (e[1]) JimCrowley 6 68
(Peter Makin) *s.i.s: in rr: pushed along 1/2-way: mod prog ins fnl f* **20/1**
412- **8** *3* **Seneschal**[308] 5678 10-9-2 **80** JamesRogers(5) 3 55
(Adrian Chamberlain) *chsd ldrs tl wknd over 1f out* **50/1**
100- **9** *3* **Spanish Acclaim**[279] 6524 4-9-0 **73** NeilChalmers 10 39
(Andrew Balding) *chsd ldrs tl wknd wl over 1f out* **20/1**
35-0 **10** *8* **Westwood**[98] 1067 6-8-12 **71** WilliamCarson 1 11
(Derek Haydn Jones) *led tl hdd and sltly hmpd 2f out: wknd sn after* **10/1**

1m 12.1s (0.30) **Going Correction** +0.175s/f (Good) **10** Ran SP% **113.9**
Speed ratings (Par 105): **105,103,102,100,97 96,93,89,85,75**
toteswingers:1&2:£3.00, 2&3:£6.20, 1&3:£7.50 CSF £10.31 CT £75.23 TOTE £5.40: £1.80, £1.40, £4.40; EX 9.10.
Owner Miss Vanessa Church **Bred** Minch Bloodstock **Trained** Huby, N Yorks

FOCUS
A competitive handicap featuring several established front-runners, and the pace was strong. Sound form.
Westwood Official explanation: vet said gelding bled from the nose

3785 ELIZA DOOLITTLE AFTER RACING ON AUGUST 23RD H'CAP 5f
5:35 (5:36) (Class 5) (0-75,75) 3-Y-O **£2,587** (£770; £384; £192) **Stalls** Low

Form RPR
04-1 **1** **Farlow (IRE)**[21] 3075 3-9-3 **71** JimCrowley 8 80+
(Ralph Beckett) *chsd ldrs: c rt to grab stands' rail over 2f out: drvn to chal 1f out: led sn after: styd on wl and won gng away* **2/1**[1]
3302 **2** *1 ¼* **Whitecrest**[14] 3321 3-8-13 **67** CathyGannon 5 71
(John Spearing) *wnt rt s: sn led: rdn 2f out: jnd 1f out: hdd sn after: kpt on but nt gng pce of wnr* **3/1**[2]
2-24 **3** *½* **Midnight Rider (IRE)**[119] 818 3-9-5 **73** (p) TedDurcan 6 75+
(Chris Wall) *s.i.s and crossed s: in rr tl drvn and hdwy over 1f out: kpt on to take 3rd cl home and clsng on 2nd but no ch w wnr* **6/1**
3523 **4** *nk* **Scarlet Rocks (IRE)**[6] 3582 3-9-2 **75** MatthewCosham(5) 2 76
(David Evans) *chsd ldrs: rdn over 2f out: ev ch over 1f out: styd on one pce ins fnl f* **8/1**
2452 **5** *4 ½* **Porthgwidden Beach (USA)**[5] 3635 3-7-11 **56** oh7(t) HarryBentley(5) 1 41
(Stuart Williams) *chsd ldrs: rdn over 2f out: wknd over 1f out* **9/2**[3]
020 **6** *2 ½* **Brian Sprout**[15] 3272 3-7-12 **57** ChrisDCogan(5) 3 33
(John Weymes) *s.i.s: a struggling towards rr* **16/1**
2106 **7** *1* **Sugar Beet**[15] 3269 3-9-7 **75** ChrisCatlin 7 47
(Ronald Harris) *a outpcd* **33/1**
5440 **8** *10* **Liberty Green (IRE)**[82] 1391 3-9-4 **72** JamesDoyle 4 —
(Alan McCabe) *chsd ldrs to 1/2-way: sn btn* **40/1**

60.59 secs (0.99) **Going Correction** +0.175s/f (Good) **8** Ran SP% **113.2**
Speed ratings (Par 100): **99,97,96,95,88 84,82,66**
toteswingers:1&2:£2.40, 2&3:£3.40, 1&3:£2.80. Tote Super 7: Win: Not won. Place: Not won. CSF £7.88 CT £28.71 TOTE £4.10: £1.90, £1.80, £1.10; EX 10.00.
Owner Lawrence, Deal & Carolyn Thornton **Bred** Patrick J Monahan **Trained** Kimpton, Hants

FOCUS
An interesting finale and it looked wide-open on paper. The whole field made for the stands' rail in the straight. The winner was unexposed and the form is rated around the second and fourth.
Liberty Green(IRE) Official explanation: jockey said filly lost its action
T/Plt: £55.80 to a £1 stake. Pool of £43,424.43 - 567.31 winning tickets. T/Qpdt: £14.40 to a £1 stake. Pool of £3,777.97 - 193.10 winning tickets. ST

3786 - 3792a (Foreign Racing) - See Raceform Interactive

3152 ASCOT (R-H)
Friday, July 8

OFFICIAL GOING: Good to firm (good in places) changing to good after race 2 (2.50)
Wind: fresh, half against Weather: early rain, then dry and breezy

3793 HELICAL BAR E B F MAIDEN STKS 6f
2:15 (2:15) (Class 3) 2-Y-O **£7,762** (£2,310; £1,154; £577) **Stalls** High

Form RPR
1 **Moon Pearl (USA)** 2-9-3 0 AdamKirby 2 80+
(Ralph Beckett) *swtchd lft after s: hld up in tch: rdn and effrt wl over 1f out: swtchd rt ent fnl f: r.o strly fnl 150yds to ld towards fin* **11/1**
2 *½* **Gerfalcon** 2-9-3 0 ShaneKelly 1 78
(Brian Meehan) *t.k.h: pressed ldrs: shkn up and ev ch wl over 1f out: led ins fnl f: rn green fnl 100yds: hdd and no ex towards fin* **14/1**
3 *½* **Nawwaar (USA)** 2-9-3 0 IanMongan 5 77
(John Dunlop) *s.i.s: rn green thrght and hld up in tch: hdwy to chse ldrs 3f out: rdn 2f out: ev ch over 1f out: kpt on same pce fnl 100yds* **6/1**[2]
4 *hd* **Sequoia** 2-9-3 0 RobertWinston 6 76+
(B W Hills) *trckd ldrs on stands' rail: rdn and effrt whn short of room over 1f out: sn swtchd lft: rallied ins fnl f and styd on wl fnl 100yds* **8/1**[3]
2 **5** *½* **Poole Harbour (IRE)**[56] 2049 2-9-3 0 PatDobbs 4 75
(Richard Hannon) *t.k.h: led and grad crossed to r against stands' rail: rdn and edgd rt over 1f out: hdd ins fnl f: no ex and btn fnl 75yds* **4/7**[1]
6 *5* **Rock Of Monet** 2-9-3 0 ChrisCatlin 7 59
(David Simcock) *in tch in rr: rdn 3f out: struggling and outpcd whn edgd rt over 2f out: no threat to ldrs fnl 2f* **20/1**
7 *shd* **Aussie Guest (IRE)** 2-9-0 0 MatthewDavies(3) 3 58
(Mick Channon) *sn w ldr: rdn 2f out: unable qck and outpcd jst over 1f out: wknd qckly fnl 100yds* **25/1**

1m 17.64s (3.24) **Going Correction** +0.25s/f (Good) **7** Ran SP% **112.7**
Speed ratings (Par 98): **88,87,86,86,85 79,78**
Tote Swingers: 1&2 £10.30, 1&3 £7.00, 2&3 £7.90 CSF £138.27 TOTE £14.10: £5.70, £6.30; EX 210.00.
Owner Pearl Bloodstock Ltd **Bred** Dream With Me Stables Inc Et Al **Trained** Kimpton, Hants

FOCUS
Round course rail moved 3-4 yds from 1m4f start to home straight when rail moved 8yds to past winning post. 2m race increased by circa 25yds, 1m2f by 20yds and Round (Old) mile by 10yds. The favourite failed to confirm the promise of his debut, and a steady early pace helped result in a bunch finish so not obviously strong form, but the race ought to produce winners. Three of these are entered in the Gimcrack. They raced towards the stands'-side rail.

NOTEBOOK
Moon Pearl(USA), a 92,000euros half-brother to French 7.5f-1m winner Shaheen Hawk, has already been gelded but proved up to making a winning debut. From a stable in good form, he picked up best of all when switched out wide having travelled nicely, and gave the impression there's better to come. (op 16-1)
Gerfalcon, like the winner, has already been gelded, but he's one of those in the Gimcrack. A £35,000 half-brother some decent sprinters out of a dual 5f winner, he showed good speed and kept on quite well. Provided he goes the right way he should find a similar race. (op 16-1 tchd 18-1)
Nawwaar(USA), having missed the break, was taken wider than ideal without cover for a lot of the way and was too green. Out of a useful 6f-7f winner, he can be expected to come on plenty. (op 10-1)
Sequoia was going well enough when becoming short of room and having to switch to the near rail late on, and he ran out of time to build up sufficient momentum. This 55,000gns purchase, who has been given an entry in the Gimcrack, should improve plenty. (op 11-1)
Poole Harbour(IRE) showed a deal of ability when a close second in a hot Newbury maiden on his debut and he's been given a Gimcrack entry, but it was disconcerting that he'd been off for 56 days. He was simply too keen and will have a bit to prove next time. (op 4-11)
Rock Of Monet was badly in need of the experience, coming under pressure a fair way out, but he made minor late progress. There should be a lot better to come in time. (op 22-1)

3794 ICAP H'CAP 2m
2:50 (2:50) (Class 3) (0-95,90) 3-Y-O+
£7,158 (£2,143; £1,071; £535; £267; £134) **Stalls** Low

Form RPR
3-6P **1** **Colloquial**[41] 2499 10-9-13 **89** (v) FergusSweeney 7 98
(Henry Candy) *chsd ldr for over 1f: chsd ldng trio tl rdn to chse ldr again 3f out: upsides ldr and drvn over 2f out: ears pricked and finding little for press tl consented to go by and led wl ins fnl f: rdn out* **14/1**
1-03 **2** *½* **Mountain Hiker (IRE)**[28] 2888 4-10-0 **90** (p) ShaneKelly 6 98
(Jeremy Noseda) *led: rdn and hrd pressed 2f out: drvn and hld on to ld tl hdd and no ex wl ins fnl f* **4/1**[1]
2-22 **3** *1 ¾* **Plato (JPN)**[21] 3120 4-9-10 **86** IanMongan 10 92
(Sir Henry Cecil) *hld up in last trio: rdn and hdwy on outer over 4f out: drvn to chse ldrs and hung rt 2f out: 3rd and kpt on same pce fr wl over 1f out* **4/1**[1]
1-1 **4** *10* **Roberto Pegasus (USA)**[20] 3184 5-9-2 **78** DaneO'Neill 4 72+
(Pat Phelan) *hld up in last trio: hdwy and hung lft bnd wl over 2f out: wnt modest 5th and hung rt 2f out: no imp and no ch after: wnt 4th ins fnl f* **6/1**[3]
6-54 **5** *3 ½* **Alsadaa (USA)**[16] 3286 8-9-9 **85** AdamKirby 9 75
(Laura Mongan) *dwlt: pushed along and hdwy to chse ldr over 14f out: upsides ldr 10f out tl rdn 3f out: 4th and btn over 1f out: fdd bdly fnl f* **10/1**
-000 **6** *4 ½* **Herostatus**[20] 3157 4-9-4 **80** J-PGuillambert 3 65
(Mark Johnston) *hld up in last trio: bhd and wall of horses 3f out: stl plenty to do and switching lft over 2f out: no real hdwy: n.d* **20/1**
0-30 **7** *7* **Baddam**[19] 3205 9-8-10 **72** (v) MartinLane 2 48
(Ian Williams) *rdn along early: chsd ldrs: rdn over 5f out: lost pl over 4f out: no ch fr over 2f out* **50/1**
3106 **8** *11* **High On A Hill (IRE)**[12] 3428 4-9-4 **80** JamesDoyle 5 43
(Sylvester Kirk) *t.k.h: hld up in midfield: rdn and no prog 3f out: sn wknd: wl bhd fr wl over 1f out: t.o* **25/1**
20 **9** *3 ¼* **Sunwise (USA)**[24] 3013 5-9-11 **90** (b) JohnFahy(3) 1 49
(William Haggas) *in tch: shkn up and reminders 10f out: rdn and btn 3f out: wl bhd fnl 2f* **6/1**[3]
6342 **10** *nk* **Dazinski**[19] 3205 5-9-12 **88** PhilipRobinson 8 47
(Mark H Tompkins) *in tch towards rr: hdwy to chse ldrs 6f out: rdn and wknd over 3f out: bhd and wl btn whn sltly hmpd jst over 2f out: t.o* **9/2**[2]

3m 33.66s (4.66) **Going Correction** +0.475s/f (Yiel) **10** Ran SP% **113.1**
Speed ratings (Par 107): **107,106,105,100,99 96,93,87,86,86**
Tote Swingers: 1&2 £21.90, 1&3 £15.40, 2&3 £3.30 CSF £65.90 CT £269.43 TOTE £22.80: £4.80, £1.80, £1.90; EX 95.70.
Owner Mrs David Blackburn & M Blackburn **Bred** Mrs M J Blackburn **Trained** Kingston Warren, Oxon
■ Stewards' Enquiry : James Doyle two-day ban: careless riding (Jul 22,24)

FOCUS
The runners seemed to finish tired - they were strung out behind the front three and the time was over 11 seconds above standard. Following the race the ground was changed to good all over, but the impression was that the round course was on the soft side. The form is rated around the winner.

NOTEBOOK
Colloquial was reported to have finished distressed on his previous start, but he bounced back in no uncertain terms. He was off the same mark as when winning over C&D in this month last year and was just persuaded to go through with his challenge, eventually grabbing the long-time leader in something of a slow-motion finish. A rise in the weights might find him out, but he'll be worthy of respect if returned to Ascot. (op 16-1 tchd 12-1)
Mountain Hiker(IRE) was mulish beforehand, his jockey having to lead him some of the way to the start, but in the race itself he was content in a soft enough lead. There was no obvious excuse. (op 9-2 tchd 11-2)
Plato(JPN), upped to this trip for the first time, raced further back than the front two and made his bid widest of all. He can be given another chance. (op 7-2)
Roberto Pegasus(USA) had won his first two starts, including a 1m5f handicap on good to soft on his reappearance, but this was disappointing off 4lb higher. He hung left off the final bend and continued to wander under pressure in the straight, and it's possible he got unbalanced on this tight track. (op 4-1)
Alsadaa(USA) likes to dominate, but a sluggish start meant he couldn't do so this time and he's probably best excused. (tchd 11-1)
Sunwise(USA) ran as though something was amiss and is one to tread carefully with next time. (op 7-1 tchd 5-1)
Dazinski probably didn't appreciate ground a lot easier than the official description. (op 13-2)

3795 BOURNE CAPITAL NOVICE STKS 6f 110y
3:25 (3:25) (Class 4) 2-Y-O **£6,469** (£1,925; £962; £481) **Stalls** High

Form RPR
1 **1** **Red Seventy**[16] 3288 2-9-5 0 PatDobbs 4 89+
(Richard Hannon) *stdd s: hld up wl in tch in last: rdn and nt clr run 2f out: hdwy between horses jst over 1f out: qcknd wl u.p to ld fnl 75yds: sn in command* **2/1**[2]

146 **2** *1* **Sixx**[28] 2868 2-9-5 0................................ DaneO'Neill 1 86
(Richard Hannon) *wnt rt s: t.k.h: led and grad crossed to r against stands' rail: rdn and qcknd wl over 1f out: hdd fnl f 75yds: nt pce of wnr towards fin* **9/1**[3]

31 **3** *3/4* **Poetic Dancer**[48] 2309 2-8-8 0................................ JohnFahy(3) 2 76
(Clive Cox) *in tch: rdn and effrt ent fnl 2f: pressed ldr over 1f out: no ex and styd on same pce ins fnl f* **10/11**[1]

0 **4** *3 3/4* **Abshir Zain (IRE)**[20] 3182 2-9-0 0................................ PhilipRobinson 3 69
(Clive Brittain) *pressed ldr: rdn and sltly outpcd wl over 1f out: btn whn hung lft 1f out: wknd ins fnl f* **22/1**

1 **5** *3 3/4* **Bellechance**[34] 2731 2-8-11 0................................ HayleyTurner 5 56
(Nigel Tinkler) *trckd ldrs on stands' rail: n.m.r 2f out: sn rdn and unable qck: wknd jst over 1f out* **11/1**

1m 23.45s (2.65) **Going Correction** +0.25s/f (Good) **5** Ran SP% **108.4**
Speed ratings (Par 96): **94,92,92,87,83**
CSF £17.73 TOTE £2.90: £1.50, £3.00; EX 15.20.

Owner Terry Neill **Bred** Sir Eric Parker **Trained** East Everleigh, Wilts

FOCUS
A novice event that has gone to smart types in recent seasons, namely Where Or When, Norse Dancer, Il Warrd and The Cheka, albeit the race was staged over 7f in those years. It was run at this unusual distance last term, though, and went to subsequent 2,000 Guineas fourth Slim Shadey. They raced towards the stands' rail and the pace didn't seem that strong.

NOTEBOOK
Red Seventy ◆, who was sent off at 14-1 when denying a much shorter-priced stable companion on his debut at Salisbury (6f, soft), did well to follow up as he had to wait for a clear run and the useful Sixx, another Hannon inmate, had been allowed a relatively soft time on the lead. The winner doesn't yet look as good some juveniles from this yard, but his pedigree suggests he should continue to progress with time and distance and he's not to be underestimated. (op 15-8 tchd 9-4, 5-2 in places)

Sixx was reported to have run too free last time and admittedly was a bit keen again, but he was getting away with setting an ordinary gallop. (tchd 10-1)

Poetic Dancer will be worth another chance as she was caught wide without cover for much of the way, which was not ideal, especially for a 2-y-o. (op 11-10 tchd 5-6, 11-8 in places and 5-4 in places)

Abshir Zain(IRE) stepped up a good deal on the form of his debut. (tchd 16-1)

Bellechance, a winner over 6f on quick ground on her first start at Newcastle, struggled badly on this rise in class. (op 8-1)

3796 JAMES TAYLOR GROUP H'CAP — 6f
4:00 (4:03) (Class 3) (0-90,90) 3-Y-O+ **£7,439** (£2,213; £1,106; £553) **Stalls** High

Form RPR

0-02 **1** **Kanaf (IRE)**[30] 2826 4-9-11 **89**................................ ChrisCatlin 17 101+
(Ed Dunlop) *stdd s: hld up towards rr: swtchd rt and effrt 2f out: gd hdwy in centre to ld jst over 1f out: edgd lft 1f out: r.o wl and in command ins fnl f* **14/1**

0000 **2** *1 1/2* **Bravo Echo**[16] 3290 5-9-4 **82**................................ J-PGuillambert 13 89
(Michael Attwater) *in tch: rdn over 3f out: kpt on u.p and chsng ldrs whn edgd rt over 1f out: chsd wnr ins fnl f: kpt on but no imp* **25/1**

1150 **3** *3/4* **King Of Eden (IRE)**[26] 2954 5-9-9 **87**................................ ShaneKelly 14 91+
(Eric Alston) *hld up in rr: rdn and effrt on stands' rail over 1f out: styd on wl ins fnl f: nt rch ldrs* **12/1**

0-04 **4** *3/4* **Oil Strike**[30] 2826 4-9-9 **87**................................ IanMongan 2 89+
(Peter Winkworth) *stdd and swtchd lft s: hld up in last pair: hdwy and switching lft 2f out: chsd ldrs whn nt clr run and swtchd rt 1f out: chsd ldng pair ins fnl f: styd on same pce fnl 100yds* **13/2**[1]

3-60 **5** *1 1/4* **Dorback**[26] 2954 4-9-10 **88**................................ DaneO'Neill 10 86
(Henry Candy) *towards rr: rdn and hdwy over 2f out: drvn and chsd ldrs over 1f out: styd on same pce ins fnl f* **7/1**[2]

043 **6** *1/2* **Kingsgate Choice (IRE)**[4] 3687 4-9-5 **83**................(b) RobertWinston 9 79
(John Best) *t.k.h early: in tch in midfield: rdn and hdwy 2f out: drvn and chsng ldrs over 1f out: no ex and btn fnl 100yds* **9/1**

[illegible] **7** *1 [illegible]* **[illegible]** [illegible] .... LucyKBarry(7) 15 80
(Hugo Palmer) *led: rdn and [illegible]* **12/1**
fnl f

1-20 **8** *1/2* **Tagula Night (IRE)**[26] 2954 5-9-9 **90**................(vt) JohnFahy(3) 8 80
(Walter Swinburn) *in tch: rdn and effrt jst over 2f out: drvn to chse ldr briefly over 1f out: unable qck and struggling whn bmpd 1f out: wknd ins fnl f* **14/1**

-540 **9** *3/4* **Yer Woman (IRE)**[55] 2099 4-9-4 **87**................................ KieranO'Neill(5) 4 75+
(Richard Hannon) *stdd and swtchd lft after s: hld up in last pair: swtchd rt and effrt in centre over 2f out: no imp u.p fr over 1f out* **16/1**

0004 **10** *1/2* **Silver Wind**[15] 3322 6-8-9 **76**................(b) MichaelO'Connell(3) 6 62
(Alan McCabe) *chsd ldr tl over 1f out: struggling u.p whn pushed rt 1f out: sn wknd* **20/1**

0000 **11** *1 1/2* **Elna Bright**[118] 844 6-9-6 **84**................................ PatDobbs 18 65
(Brett Johnson) *broke wl enough: t.k.h: chsd ldrs early but grad stdd into midfield: rdn and effrt whn n.m.r 2f out: keeping on but stl plenty to do whn hmpd over 1f out: styd on same pce after* **20/1**

2431 **12** *5* **Ivory Silk**[20] 3179 6-9-7 **85**................(b) AdamKirby 19 50
(Jeremy Gask) *chsd ldrs: drvn and unable qck wl over 1f out: wknd ent fnl f: eased wl ins fnl f* **15/2**[3]

0000 **13** *3/4* **Olynard (IRE)**[13] 3383 5-8-13 **77**................................ MartinLane 12 40
(Dr Richard Newland) *in tch towards rr: rdn and no hdwy whn hung rt 2f out: nvr trbld ldrs* **25/1**

2661 **14** *2 3/4* **New Leyf (IRE)**[13] 3383 5-9-10 **88**................(b) SteveDrowne 16 42
(Jeremy Gask) *in tch towards rr: rdn and no rspnse 2f out: wl bhd fnl f* **9/1**

1-32 **15** *8* **Reposer (IRE)**[35] 2684 3-8-10 **80**................................ JimmyQuinn 11 —
(John Best) *chsd ldrs: wkng whn hmpd 2f out: wl bhd and eased ins fnl f* **9/1**

1m 14.74s (0.34) **Going Correction** +0.25s/f (Good)
WFA 3 from 4yo+ 6lb **15** Ran SP% **119.4**
Speed ratings (Par 107): **107,105,104,103,101 100,98,98,97,96 94,87,86,83,72**
Tote Swingers: 1&2 £82.40, 1&3 £30.00, 2&3 £75.60 CSF £331.52 CT £4253.02 TOTE £15.10: £4.40, £9.50, £4.80; EX 446.20.

Owner Hamdan Al Maktoum **Bred** Catcher Equine Ltd **Trained** Newmarket, Suffolk

■ Stewards' Enquiry : Ian Mongan three-day ban: careless riding (Jul 22,24,25)

FOCUS
The stands' rail did not look particularly advantageous, yet all 15 runners congregated towards the near side of the track, before fanning out towards the middle late on. This looked a good, quite competitive sprint handicap, but Kanaf was much the best. He produced a 5lb personal best.

NOTEBOOK
Kanaf(IRE) was a major eyecatcher under a tender ride when well behind on his comeback at Goodwood (track may not have suited), and again wasn't given a particularly hard time when going a lot closer at Yarmouth on his latest start, but he stepped up on those efforts to confirm the promise of his 3-y-o campaign. The return to this more level course and forgiving surface probably helped, and he won well. He's in the Stewards' Cup, but is not sure to make the cut even with a penalty, and anyway he would have something to prove on the course, albeit his previous run at Goodwood came over 5f. (op 10-1)

Bravo Echo had lost his way a bit lately, but he's a smart type when at his best (ex-John Gosden and really looks the part) and returned to form on this drop back to sprinting. His very best form is on Polytrack. (op 40-1)

King Of Eden(IRE) was poorly placed around 2f out, being just about last of all when briefly having to wait for a run towards the near rail, but he produced a sustained bid to pass most of the field. His progression seemed to have levelled out, but that's not the case. (op 14-1)

Oil Strike, behind Kanaf at Yarmouth last time, didn't look desperately unlucky but he might have been a bit closer with a better trip as he was going well when racing behind the winner for much of the way and didn't get as clear a run as that rival. (op 8-1)

Dorback, reported to have lost his action last time, fared better on this occasion without ever really looking likely to justify his position towards the head of the market. (tchd 8-1)

Kingsgate Choice(IRE) had been shaping as though well worth a step back up to this trip, but he wasn't good enough after being a bit keen early. (op 12-1)

Elna Bright shaped better than his finishing position suggests. He travelled well, but was denied a clear run on a couple of occasions in the closing stages and then got a bit tired late on, which is understandable considering he was having his first start for the best part of four months. (op 28-1)

3797 CLOSE PROPERTY FINANCE H'CAP — 1m (R)
4:35 (4:37) (Class 3) (0-90,87) 3-Y-O+ **£7,439** (£2,213; £1,106; £553) **Stalls** High

Form RPR

0212 **1** **Rave (IRE)**[20] 3159 3-9-2 **87**................................ PatrickHills(3) 11 101+
(J W Hills) *racd in midfield on outer: hdwy to ld over 1f out: sn rdn and qcknd clr: r.o strly: readily* **9/2**[1]

3031 **2** *3 3/4* **El Wasmi**[29] 2838 3-9-0 **82**................(b) PhilipRobinson 6 87
(Clive Brittain) *chsd ldr: rdn to ld 2f out: hdd and nt pce of wnr over 1f out: no ch w wnr but kpt on to hold 2nd fnl f* **8/1**

-001 **3** *1* **Dunhoy (IRE)**[21] 3133 3-8-12 **80**................................ JimmyQuinn 5 83
(Stef Higgins) *v.s.a: bhd and pushed along: rdn and effrt on outer over 2f out: hdwy to chse ldng pair over 1f out: edgd rt u.p jst over 1f out: kpt on but no ch w wnr* **17/2**

1-30 **4** *hd* **Primaeval**[42] 2470 5-9-13 **86**................(v) HayleyTurner 9 90+
(James Fanshawe) *stdd s: hld up in last pair: clsd 5f out: nt clr run and swtchd lft wl over 1f out: hdwy and pushed rt jst over 1f out: kpt on ins fnl f: no ch w wnr* **11/2**[3]

5646 **5** *1/2* **Fantasy Gladiator**[16] 3290 5-9-3 **79**................(p) AdamBeschizza(3) 2 84+
(Robert Cowell) *t.k.h: hld up in midfield: shuffled bk to rr and nt clr run over 2f out: switching lft after: fnlly clr run on outer and styd on ins fnl f: n.d* **16/1**

-001 **6** *1 1/2* **Watch Amigo (IRE)**[22] 3081 5-9-10 **86**................................ JohnFahy(3) 10 86
(Walter Swinburn) *led and set stdy gallop: clr tl over 5f out: hdd and rdn 2f out: wknd jst over 1f out* **5/1**[2]

0000 **7** *1/2* **Hacienda (IRE)**[23] 3032 4-9-4 **84**................................ DarylByrne(7) 8 82
(Mark Johnston) *hld up in midfield: swtchd rt and effrt on inner 2f out: plugging on same pce and no threat to wnr whn nt clr run jst over 1f out* **9/1**

-000 **8** *3/4* **South Cape**[16] 3290 8-9-10 **83**................................ FergusSweeney 4 81
(Gary Moore) *hld up in midfield: effrt and rdn jst over 2f out: styng on same pce and btn whn hmpd jsut over 1f out: n.d after* **28/1**

-000 **9** *nse* **Fremont (IRE)**[37] 2604 4-9-10 **83**................................ PatDobbs 7 81
(Richard Hannon) *in tch on outer: chsd ldrs over 3f out: drvn and unable qck 2f out: one pce and btn whn squeezed for room and eased 1f out: n.d after* **11/1**

0-14 **10** *3* **Nelson's Bounty**[55] 2105 4-9-13 **86**................................ TonyCulhane 1 84+
(Paul D'Arcy) *t.k.h: hld up in tch: effrt on inner whn nt clr run and hmpd 2f out: nvr enough room and no ch after* **11/2**[3]

1m 44.88s (4.18) **Going Correction** +0.475s/f (Yiel)
WFA 3 from 4yo+ 9lb **10** Ran SP% **114.9**
[illegible] (Par 107): **98,94,93,93,92, 91,90,89,89,86**
Tote Swingers: 1&2 £6.30, 1&3 £5.00, [illegible] TOTE £4.60: £1.90, £2.70, £3.20; EX 22.40.

Owner Gary And Linnet Woodward **Bred** P E Banahan **Trained** Upper Lambourn, Berks

■ Stewards' Enquiry : Daryl Byrne two-day ban: careless riding (Jul 22,24)
Jimmy Quinn two-day ban: careless riding (Jul 22,24)

FOCUS
Some of these found trouble, but the manner of Rave's success suggests the best horse won. Muddling form, with the runner-up setting the standard.

NOTEBOOK
Rave(IRE) ◆ couldn't follow up his Newmarket maiden victory (1m, good) when runner-up at Ayr last time, but it was soft ground that day and judging by how well he quickened this time, the return to a better surface was surely the key. He was impressive relative to the grade and his change of pace can see him progress to a smart level. (op 11-2 tchd 4-1)

El Wasmi was behind Rave in that aforementioned Newmarket race before winning a Newbury handicap in first-time blinkers. Up 7lb, he ran well, but was no match at all for his old rival. (op 6-1)

Dunhoy(IRE), up 6lb for winning at Newmarket, was being niggled along in last place turning into the straight, but he stuck out dourly. (op 8-1 tchd 9-1)

Primaeval, trying a trip this far for the first time, didn't get the best of runs but was essentially one-paced. A strongly run 7f might suit best. (op 5-1 tchd 6-1)

Fantasy Gladiator didn't have much room to make a move for most of the straight, at which point it was notable he was being just cajoled along, and while he made some progress albeit all too late when finally in the open, it's not certain he would have been significantly closer with one clear run. He has only ever won on Fibresand and Polytrack. (op 22-1)

Watch Amigo(IRE) was held off 3lb higher than when winning at Leicester last time. (tchd 9-2 and 11-2)

Nelson's Bounty, who attracted support during the day, is significantly better than he showed as he was continually denied a clear run against the inside rail in the straight. There's no way of knowing where he could have finished with a better trip, and the winner would have been extremely tough to match, but he probably wouldn't have been that far away. Official explanation: jockey said gelding was denied a clear run (op 9-2 tchd 6-1)

3798 DELANCEY APPRENTICE H'CAP — 7f
5:10 (5:10) (Class 4) (0-85,83) 3-Y-O **£6,145** (£1,828; £913; £456) **Stalls** High

Form RPR

-114 **1** **Lightning Cloud (IRE)**[34] 2729 3-9-7 **80**................................ AmyRyan 9 91
(Kevin Ryan) *t.k.h: hld up in midfield: hdwy and edgd lft 2f out: drvn to ld jst over 1f out: in command and r.o wl ins fnl f* **9/2**[1]

-244 **2** *1 ¾* **Majestic Dream (IRE)**[36] 2646 3-9-10 **83** .... JohnFahy 5 88
(Walter Swinburn) *bhd: swtchd rt and hdwy u.p wl over 1f out: styd on to chse wnr wl ins fnl f* **5/1**[2]

43 **3** *1 ¼* **Konstantin (IRE)**[35] 2675 3-8-3 **69** .... KatiaScallan(7) 2 71
(Marcus Tregoning) *chsd ldr: rdn 2f out: unable qck jst over 1f out: styd on same pce ins fnl f* **10/1**

51 **4** *½* **Above Standard (IRE)**[15] 3324 3-9-0 **78** .... MatthewLawson(5) 1 79
(B W Hills) *chsd ldrs tl led 3f out: rdn jst over 2f out: hdd jst over 1f out: wknd ins fnl f* **5/1**[2]

4-03 **5** *hd* **Cocohatchee**[21] 3122 3-8-9 **73** .... LucyKBarry(5) 11 73
(Pat Phelan) *chsd ldrs: rdn jst over 2f out: unable qck u.p over 1f out: styd on same pce ins fnl f* **8/1**

4-06 **6** *5* **Silenzio**[29] 2841 3-8-8 **70** .... KieranO'Neill(3) 10 68
(Richard Hannon) *towards rr: niggled along 4f out: sme hdwy u.p over 1f out: swtchd rt 1f out: styng on but no threat to wnr whn swtchd rt again ins fnl f: sddle slipped and sn eased* **7/1**

-204 **7** *1 ¼* **Perfect Mission**[15] 3324 3-9-2 **75** .... (v[1]) SimonPearce 4 58
(Andrew Balding) *in tch: rdn and effrt jst over 2f out: edgd rt and no imp over 1f out: wknd jst ins fnl f* **20/1**

-531 **8** *2* **My Son Max**[27] 2937 3-9-4 **80** .... RyanPowell(3) 3 58
(Richard Hannon) *racd off the pce towards rr: rdn and effrt 2f out: edgd lft and no hdwy over 1f out: nvr trbld ldrs* **6/1**[3]

0042 **9** *1 ¼* **Major Conquest (IRE)**[13] 3378 3-9-8 **81** .... PatrickHills 8 55
(J W Hills) *towards rr: rdn 3f out: sme hdwy over 2f out: sn drvn: wknd over 1f out* **15/2**

0502 **10** *15* **Royal Opera**[17] 3259 3-8-11 **70** .... (v) AdamBeschizza 7 —
(Rod Millman) *sn led: hdd 3f out: wknd and hung rt jst over 2f out: wl bhd over 1f out* **16/1**

1m 28.11s (0.91) **Going Correction** +0.25s/f (Good) **10** Ran SP% **120.9**
Speed ratings (Par 102): **104,102,100,100,99 94,92,90,88,71**
Tote Swingers: 1&2 £4.40, 1&3 £9.20, 2&3 £9.50 CSF £27.97 CT £223.90 TOTE £5.90: £2.30, £1.60, £3.60; EX 33.60.
Owner Hambleton Racing Ltd XVIII **Bred** John Cullinan **Trained** Hambleton, N Yorks

FOCUS
A fair apprentice handicap run at a good pace. They raced towards the stands' side. The second and third set a sound standard.
Silenzio Official explanation: jockey said saddle slipped
T/Plt: £2,810.80 to a £1 stake. Pool:£68,538.00 - 17.80 winning tickets T/Qpdt: £87.10 to a £1 stake. Pool:£7,766.00 - 65.95 winning tickets SP

3511 CHEPSTOW (L-H)
Friday, July 8

OFFICIAL GOING: Good to soft (6.6)
Wind: mild across Weather: cloudy with sunny periods

3799 BETFAIR RACING EXCELLENCE APPRENTICE TRAINING SERIES H'CAP — 1m 4f 23y
6:30 (6:30) (Class 5) (0-70,69) 4-Y-O+ **£2,522** (£750; £375; £187) **Stalls** Low

Form RPR

2400 **1** **Resplendent Light**[53] 2159 6-9-1 **65** .... (t) ThomasBrown(5) 8 73
(Bernard Llewellyn) *cl up: led over 3f out: in command fr over 1f out: styd on wl* **4/1**[1]

105- **2** *3 ¼* **Picot De Say**[12] 2923 9-8-4 **54** .... NoelGarbutt(5) 4 57
(Bernard Llewellyn) *cl up: wnt 2nd 2f out: sn rdn: styd on same pce: a being hld* **5/1**[2]

-U60 **3** *2* **Holden Eagle**[67] 1756 6-9-1 **60** .... DavidKenny 3 60
(Tony Newcombe) *hld up in last but in tch: pushed along and stdy prog fr over 2f out: rdn in 3rd ent fnl f: hung rt and no further imp* **4/1**[1]

10-3 **4** *2 ½* **Gremlin**[22] 1050 7-9-7 **69** .... GeorgeDowning(3) 9 65
(Bernard Llewellyn) *hld up in tch: rdn to chse ldrs 2f out: sn one pce* **13/2**[3]

060- **5** *3* **Silvermine Bay (IRE)**[361] 3960 4-8-5 **50** oh5 .... NathanAlison 7 41
(Pat Eddery) *trckd ldr: rdn 4f out: wknd over 1f out* **7/1**

4006 **6** *¾* **Swords**[98] 1080 9-8-2 **50** oh5 .... (v) RaulDaSilva(3) 2 40
(Ray Peacock) *led at crawl for 3f: prom: led 5f out: rdn and hdd over 3f out: wknd over 1f out* **33/1**

3600 **7** *½* **Quinsman**[40] 2526 5-9-5 **67** .... JakePayne(3) 6 56
(J S Moore) *hld up: rdn over 2f out: nvr any imp on ldrs* **4/1**[1]

04/0 **8** *1 ¼* **Rock Peak (IRE)**[9] 3516 6-8-3 **53** .... (b) LukeRowe(5) 1 40
(Bernard Llewellyn) *trckd ldr: led after 3f: hdd 5f out: rdn over 3f out: wknd 2f out* **11/1**

2m 45.58s (6.58) **Going Correction** +0.10s/f (Good) **8** Ran SP% **113.8**
Speed ratings (Par 103): **82,79,78,76,74 74,74,73**
toteswingers:1&2:£2.00, 1&3:£2.90, 2&3:£10.20 CSF £23.83 CT £83.77 TOTE £5.00: £1.50, £1.50, £1.60; EX 28.80.
Owner B J Llewellyn **Bred** Usk Valley Stud **Trained** Fochriw, Caerphilly
■ Stewards' Enquiry : Raul Da Silva seven-day ban: used whip in contrary to race conditions (Jul 22,23,25,28-30)

FOCUS
After 10mm of rain overnight the going was changed to good to soft. There was an open market for this apprentice handicap. The early pace was very steady and Bernard Llewellyn trained three of the first four home. The time was over 11 seconds slower than standard.

3800 BRITISH STALLION STUDS SUPPORTING BRITISH RACING E B F NOVICE STKS — 5f 16y
7:00 (7:02) (Class 4) 2-Y-O **£4,528** (£1,347; £673) **Stalls** High

Form RPR

6156 **1** **Powerful Wind (IRE)**[2] 3745 2-9-2 0 .... TomMcLaughlin 4 83
(Ronald Harris) *mde all: qcknd clr over 1f out: rdn fnl f: unchal* **20/1**[3]

001 **2** *6* **Fanrouge (IRE)**[27] 2901 2-8-11 0 .... SaleemGolam 1 59
(Malcolm Saunders) *chsd wnr: rdn 2f out: nvr gng pce to get on terms* **8/1**[2]

31 **3** *6* **Ballyea (IRE)**[8] 3547 2-9-0 0 .... DaneO'Neill 2 41
(Richard Hannon) *chsd wnr tl rdn over 2f out: sn hld* **13/8**[1]

61.43 secs (2.13) **Going Correction** +0.10s/f (Good) **3** Ran SP% **54.0**
Speed ratings (Par 96): **86,76,66**
CSF £22.26 TOTE £5.90; EX 5.60.
Owner Anthony Cooke **Bred** Miss Ciara Doyle **Trained** Earlswood, Monmouths
■ Stewards' Enquiry : Tom McLaughlin caution: used whip when clearly winning.

FOCUS
The hot favourite Quite A Thing (4/6) got very agitated in the stalls before being withdrawn from this novice event (deduct 55p in the £ under R4. That seemed to leave the door open for Richard Hannon's Ballyea but she was very disappointing behind a front-running outsider.

NOTEBOOK
Powerful Wind(IRE) faded into 7l last of six off a mark of 76 on nursery debut at Lingfield on Wednesday and looked to have plenty of work to do here, but he set a strong pace and ran his rivals into complete submission on this quick reappearance. It is very hard to rate the form but there was quite a lot to like about his blazing display and he may have improved on his Kempton maiden win in May. A patchy profile casts some doubt whether he will repeat this next time but he clearly handles soft ground well and is speedy. (op 12-1 tchd 11-1 and 25-1)
Fanrouge(IRE) took a big step forward when springing 33-1 surprise in ordinary 5f Bath maiden auction last month. That form was boosted by placed horses both winning next time but he couldn't near the all-the-way winner in this contest. (tchd 7-1 and 10-1)
Ballyea(IRE) was an encouraging debut third in 7f Newbury maiden before showing plenty of speed and some battling qualities to justify strong support over 6f at same track last time. She had leading form claims after the withdrawal of the favourite, but was never really travelling and a drop in trip and switch to slower ground probably caused her downfall. (op 2-1 tchd 5-2)

3801 TAYLOR WIMPEY BRISTOL H'CAP — 7f 16y
7:35 (7:35) (Class 4) (0-85,83) 3-Y-O+ **£3,234** (£962; £481; £240) **Stalls** High

Form RPR

5016 **1** **Polar Annie**[8] 3549 6-8-12 **67** .... DaneO'Neill 2 81
(Malcolm Saunders) *mde all: pushed clr over 1f out: unchal* **5/2**[1]

4110 **2** *5* **Frognal (IRE)**[16] 3276 5-9-7 **79** .... (b) RobertLButler(3) 6 80
(Richard Guest) *hld up bhd ldrs: smooth hdwy over 2f out: rdn to chse wnr jst over 1f out: nvr gng pce to get on terms* **8/1**

0223 **3** *5* **Dr Wintringham (IRE)**[9] 3514 5-9-3 **72** .... SebSanders 4 60
(Karen George) *chsd ldrs: rdn to chse wnr 2f out tl jst over 1f out: fdd* **5/2**[1]

-315 **4** *6* **Frozen Over**[27] 2916 3-8-10 **73** .... PatDobbs 5 45
(Stuart Kittow) *chsd wnr tl rdn 2f out: wknd over 1f out* **7/1**[3]

0310 **5** *1* **Galatian**[42] 2470 4-10-0 **83** .... JamesMillman 1 53
(Rod Millman) *chsd ldrs: rdn over 3f out: sn btn: wknd over 1f out* **3/1**[2]

0606 **6** *12* **Mujood**[28] 2876 8-9-9 **83** .... (v) AmyScott(5) 3 22
(Eve Johnson Houghton) *reluctant and dwlt v bdly: a wl bhd* **12/1**

1m 23.75s (0.55) **Going Correction** +0.10s/f (Good)
WFA 3 from 4yo+ 8lb **6** Ran SP% **113.4**
Speed ratings (Par 105): **100,94,88,81,80 66**
toteswingers:1&2:£3.40, 1&3:£1.10, 2&3:£3.00 CSF £22.83 TOTE £3.80: £2.00, £3.50; EX 29.70.
Owner Lockstone Business Services Ltd **Bred** Cobhall Court Stud **Trained** Green Ore, Somerset

FOCUS
Not the strongest handicap for the grade but the winner is rated back to something like her best. She put in a dominant display and they were well strung out behind.
Galatian Official explanation: jockey said gelding never travelled and lost a shoe

3802 PLAY MECCA BINGO ON YOUR IPHONE H'CAP — 1m 14y
8:05 (8:07) (Class 2) (0-100,100) 3-Y-O+ **£8,086** (£2,406; £1,202; £601) **Stalls** High

Form RPR

5203 **1** **Shavansky**[16] 3290 7-9-3 **89** .... JamesMillman 2 99
(Rod Millman) *trckd ldrs: rdn to ld ent fnl f: styd on wl* **9/2**[2]

-015 **2** *2* **Duster**[6] 3645 4-9-2 **88** .... RobertHavlin 5 93
(Hughie Morrison) *prom: led over 2f out: rdn whn hdd ent fnl f: no ex* **5/1**[3]

6-14 **3** *4* **Belgian Bill**[22] 3067 3-9-2 **100** .... (t) MatthewDavies(3) 4 94
(George Baker) *cl up: rdn 2f out: nvr able to chal: kpt on same pce* **6/4**[1]

3002 **4** *½* **Moynahan (USA)**[12] 3436 6-8-12 **84** .... (b) PaulDoe 3 79
(Paul Cole) *cl up: rdn over 2f out: styd on for press but nvr threatened ldrs* **10/1**

/0-1 **5** *14* **Pat's Legacy (USA)**[9] 3514 5-8-6 **81** 6ex oh2 .... (b[1]) MarkLawson(3) 6 44
(Jo Hughes) *led tl rdn over 2f out: wknd over 1f out* **8/1**

-622 **6** *½* **Kingsdine (IRE)**[23] 3045 4-8-13 **85** .... DaneO'Neill 1 47
(Malcolm Saunders) *prom: rdn over 2f out: wknd over 1f out* **6/1**

05-0 **7** *12* **Mahadee (IRE)**[27] 2927 6-9-5 **91** .... (b) DavidProbert 7 25
(Ed de Giles) *s.i.s: in last but in tch: rdn over 3f out: wknd 2f out* **33/1**

1m 35.15s (-1.05) **Going Correction** +0.10s/f (Good)
WFA 3 from 4yo+ 9lb **7** Ran SP% **112.3**
Speed ratings (Par 109): **109,107,103,102,88 88,76**
toteswingers:1&2:£2.70, 1&3:£1.30, 2&3:£1.20 CSF £25.95 TOTE £6.40: £2.80, £2.50; EX 29.30.
Owner John Southway & Andrew Hughes **Bred** George Strawbridge **Trained** Kentisbeare, Devon

FOCUS
A useful handicap. The pace was not very strong and they raced up the centre of the track. It was the pick of the C&D times and the winner is rated back to his best.

NOTEBOOK
Shavansky can often start slowly but he had posted a series of creditable efforts in 1m-1m2f handicaps on fast and slow ground recently. Well backed, he kept the leaders in his sights before finding a surging run to win with authority. This run can be marked up because this dual winning hurdler has registered all of his previous Flat wins at 1m2f, and is ideally suited by more of an emphasis on stamina. His mark will re-enter the 90s after this but he is a genuine and reliable type who should continue to go well. (op 6-1)
Duster was always handy and put in a second creditable effort since a 7f Warwick win off 5lb lower last month. He should continue to be competitive but his personal duel with the handicapper looks finely balanced. (op 11-2 tchd 9-2)
Belgian Bill started this campaign with a 1m Doncaster win before running a cracking race when a close fourth in the Britannia at Royal Ascot last time. Racing off 3lb higher, he looked a big danger when switched towards the stands' side but he lugged in behind a rival and his effort flattened out. This was a slight setback but he is still very lightly raced and this track may not have suited him. (op 11-8 tchd 5-4)
Moynahan(USA) is 3lb lower than last win, and a second with blinkers reapplied at Windsor last time was a reminder of what he can do when in the mood, but he couldn't make an impact in this stronger grade and has modest strike-rate of 2-34 for a horse of his ability. (op 9-1 tchd 11-1)
Pat's Legacy(USA) scored on his second start back in Britain when winning over C&D on return for a new yard after six-months off last week. However, he had more to do under a penalty and from out of the weights, and sweated up before racing too keenly and dropping out under a prominent ride. (tchd 9-1)
Kingsdine(IRE) was just caught close home after trading at 1.01 in running at Newmarket in May and was a closing second behind a front-runner who was given too much rope in a 7f Kempton handicap last month. He was interesting back at the secne of his 7f win on good to soft during this month last year but h didn't find much before dropping away quickly.\n (op 13-2 tchd 15-2)

3803 PIMM'S FILLIES' H'CAP — 1m 14y
8:40 (8:45) (Class 5) (0-70,70) 3-Y-O **£2,522** (£750; £375; £187) **Stalls** High

Form RPR

-535 **1** **Abergeldie (USA)**[39] 2550 3-9-3 **66** .... (v[1]) DavidProbert 3 77+
(Andrew Balding) *trckd ldrs: led over 3f out: rdn clr over 1f out: comf* **11/4**[2]

3-33 **2** *3 ¼* **Destiny Of Dreams**[17] 3259 3-9-4 **67** .... RobertHavlin 10 70
(Jo Crowley) *hld up: rdn and stdy hdwy fr over 2f out: styd on to go 2nd ins fnl f: no ch w wnr* **7/2**[3]

0103 **3** *4* **Sienna Blue**[26] 2963 3-8-13 **62** SaleemGolam 8 56
(Malcolm Saunders) *trckd ldrs: rdn and ev ch over 2f out: hld by wnr over 1f out: no ex whn lost 2nd ins fnl f* **11/1**

-300 **4** *½* **Obiter Dicta**[21] 3122 3-9-5 **68** DaneO'Neill 12 61
(Henry Candy) *towards rr: rdn and hdwy over 2f out: nvr threatened ldrs: styd on same pce* **5/2**[1]

2020 **5** *nk* **Tinaheely (IRE)**[6] 3633 3-9-4 **70** AdamBeschizza(3) 9 62
(Jonathan Portman) *trckd ldrs: rdn over 3f out: one pce fnl 2f* **9/1**

530 **6** *2¼* **Waterbury Girl**[22] 3090 3-8-0 **54** (p) NathanAlison(5) 4 41
(Bryn Palling) *t.k.h: prom: led 4f out tl jst over 3f out: sn rdn: wknd over 1f out* **22/1**

0554 **7** *1¾* **Bedibyes**[12] 3431 3-8-1 **55** JamesRogers(5) 2 38
(Richard Mitchell) *prom tl 3f out: wknd over 1f out* **14/1**

0-60 **8** *17* **Burst Of Stardust**[29] 2848 3-8-3 **55** LouisBeuzelin(3) 5 —
(Bryn Palling) *led tl rdn over 3f out: sn wknd* **12/1**

1m 37.86s (1.66) **Going Correction** +0.10s/f (Good) **8** Ran SP% **114.5**
Speed ratings (Par 97): **95,91,87,87,86 84,82,65**
toteswingers:1&2:£3.10, 1&3:£18.00, 2&3:£6.90 CSF £12.89 CT £89.42 TOTE £3.80: £1.30, £2.00, £3.90; EX 12.20.
Owner The Queen **Bred** Darley **Trained** Kingsclere, Hants

FOCUS
A minor fillies' handicap run at a fairly steady pace, but they finished well strung out. A personal best for the winner.

3804 FESTIVAL RACING H'CAP 1m 14y
9:10 (9:11) (Class 5) (0-70,70) 3-Y-0+ **£2,522** (£750; £375; £187) **Stalls** High

Form RPR

6322 **1** **Miss Bootylishes**[9] 3514 6-9-7 **70** DarylByrne(7) 6 78+
(Paul Burgoyne) *cl up: led wl over 2f out: rdn over 1f out: sn hung lft: fin on far rails: drvn out* **2/1**[1]

0003 **2** *¾* **Advertise**[16] 3293 5-8-13 **58** MatthewDavies(3) 1 63
(Joseph Tuite) *trckd ldrs: rdn over 2f out: styd on ins fnl f: wnt 2nd fnl 100yds* **8/1**

5322 **3** *shd* **Fitz**[2] 3741 5-8-9 **54** AdamBeschizza(3) 8 59
(Matthew Salaman) *s.i.s: towards rr: hdwy over 4f out: rdn over 2f out: racd alone in centre and styd on fnl f* **11/4**[2]

6-06 **4** *shd* **No Larking (IRE)**[67] 1768 3-9-0 **65** DaneO'Neill 2 69+
(Henry Candy) *led tl rdn wl over 2f out: kpt chsng wnr: carried lft over 1f out: 1 l down whn snatched up whn short of room fnl 120yds: sn lost 2nd: nt rcvr* **9/1**

0330 **5** *½* **Mr Udagawa**[16] 3293 5-9-4 **60** (p) JamesMillman 10 63
(Bernard Llewellyn) *trckd ldr: rdn over 2f out: styd on same pce: edgd lft fnl f* **14/1**

5243 **6** *5* **Danceyourselfdizzy (IRE)**[22] 3089 3-9-2 **67** PatDobbs 3 57
(Richard Hannon) *in tch: hung lft to far side rails over 4f out: racd alone: rdn over 2f out: wknd fnl f* **6/1**[3]

5000 **7** *6* **Bobbyow**[18] 3216 3-8-0 **51** oh1 DavidProbert 9 27
(Bryn Palling) *in tch: rdn over 3f out: wknd over 2f out* **16/1**

40-0 **8** *2* **Fair Breeze**[27] 2922 4-8-11 **53** RobertHavlin 7 26
(Richard Phillips) *trckd ldr tl rdn over 3f out: wknd over 2f out* **28/1**

1063 **9** *1¼* **Aflaam (IRE)**[126] 761 6-9-13 **69** TomMcLaughlin 5 40
(Ronald Harris) *trckd ldrs: effrt over 2f out: wknd over 1f out* **20/1**

1m 38.02s (1.82) **Going Correction** +0.10s/f (Good)
WFA 3 from 4yo+ 9lb **9** Ran SP% **116.2**
Speed ratings (Par 103): **94,93,93,93,92 87,81,79,78**
toteswingers:1&2:£2.50, 1&3:£1.50, 2&3:£5.90 CSF £19.09 CT £44.84 TOTE £4.10: £1.60, £3.00, £1.10; EX 21.40.
Owner Mrs Helen Adams **Bred** T P Young And D Hanson **Trained** Shepton Montague, Somerset

FOCUS
There was not much separating the first five in this steadily run handicap. The winner did not need to repeat her recent best.
T/Plt: £877.20 to a £1 stake. Pool:£49,441.03 - 41.14 winning tickets T/Qpdt: £28.20 to a £1 stake. Pool:£5,632.30 - 147.70 winning tickets TM

3375 CHESTER (L-H)
Friday, July 8

OFFICIAL GOING: Good to soft (good in places; 7.0) changing to good (good to soft in places) after race 4 (7.45pm)
Wind: moderate 1/2 against Weather: overcast, light rain race 5 onwards

3805 BARBARA ALLYSON SUTTON MEMORIAL H'CAP (FOR LADY AMATEUR RIDERS) 7f 122y
6:10 (6:12) (Class 5) (0-75,75) 4-Y-0+ **£4,116** (£1,266; £633) **Stalls** Low

Form RPR

4321 **1** **Kingswinford (IRE)**[27] 2910 5-10-2 **75** MissHBethell(5) 2 85
(Brian Ellison) *trckd ldrs: wnt 2nd over 2f out: styd on to ld last 100yds* **5/2**[1]

1404 **2** *1* **Tewin Wood**[38] 2597 4-10-6 **74** MissMMullineaux 11 81
(Alan Bailey) *swtchd lft after s: led: drvn 3f out: hdd and no ex ins fnl f* **12/1**

6042 **3** *2½* **Glenluji**[11] 3454 6-9-2 **56** MrsCBartley 10 57+
(Jim Goldie) *1/2 rrd s: hld up towards rr: hdwy over 2f out: styd on to take 3rd last 50yds* **5/1**[2]

4502 **4** *1¼* **Lockantanks**[14] 3341 4-10-0 **68** MissLMasterton 7 66
(Michael Appleby) *trckd ldrs: effrt over 2f out: kpt on one pce* **13/2**[3]

5053 **5** *¾* **Just The Tonic**[17] 3245 4-9-2 **61** MissNHayes(5) 8 57
(Marjorie Fife) *hld up in mid-div: effrt on outside over 2f out: kpt on same pce* **12/1**

1-16 **6** *nk* **Foreign Rhythm (IRE)**[46] 2365 6-9-8 **67** MissVBarr(5) 4 62
(Ron Barr) *chsd ldrs: drvn 3f out: one pce* **20/1**

5312 **7** *nk* **Hayek**[10] 3489 4-9-3 **62** (b) MissJGillam(5) 3 56
(Tim Easterby) *s.s: in rr: nt clr run over 1f out: kpt on fnl f* **13/2**[3]

4060 **8** *¾* **Fishforcompliments**[16] 3275 7-10-1 **74** MissPhillipaTutty(5) 9 66
(Richard Fahey) *1/2 rrd s: sn mid-div: effrt over 2f out: kpt on fnl f: nvr a factor* **10/1**

0400 **9** *¾* **King Bertolini (IRE)**[20] 3191 4-9-2 **56** oh9 MissWGibson 1 47
(Alan Berry) *mid-div: effrt on inner over 2f out: nvr nr ldrs* **100/1**

6030 **10** *1¼* **Memphis Man**[4] 3685 8-9-1 **60** MissCHJones(5) 6 47
(David Evans) *hld up in mid-div: lost pl and nt clr run over 1f out: swtchd outside: nvr a factor* **20/1**

/6-0 **11** *2* **July Days (IRE)**[30] 2814 5-10-2 **75** MissHCuthbert(5) 13 57
(Brian Baugh) *in rr: rn wd bnd 2f out: nvr on terms* **40/1**

4020 **12** *¾* **The Big Haerth (IRE)**[14] 3341 5-10-4 **72** MissEJJones 5 53
(David Evans) *trckd ldrs: t.k.h: effrt over 2f out: wknd over 1f out: eased ins fnl f* **16/1**

1m 34.56s (0.76) **Going Correction** +0.05s/f (Good) **12** Ran SP% **115.2**
Speed ratings (Par 103): **98,97,94,93,92 92,91,91,90,89 87,86**
toteswingers:1&2:£7.80, 1&3:£2.60, 2&3:£9.50 CSF £32.00 CT £142.43 TOTE £3.20: £1.20, £3.10, £1.70; EX 34.30.
Owner L S Keys **Bred** J Costello **Trained** Norton, N Yorks

FOCUS
Rail at inner (normal) configuration and distances as advertised. A dry night but, after 2mm of rain fell during the day, the going was eased to "good to soft, good in places" before the first. Experienced amateur Carol Bartley reported the ground, that had soaked up 20mm of rain in the past three days, to be "on the soft side."Exposed performers but a couple of previous winners in an ordinary handicap. The gallop was sound but the first two pulled clear and those held up were at a disadvantage. The first pair are rated to their best.

3806 GO-STYLE.CO.UK H'CAP 7f 2y
6:40 (6:42) (Class 5) (0-70,70) 3-Y-0+ **£4,043** (£1,203; £601; £300) **Stalls** Low

Form RPR

0020 **1** **Jungle Bay**[14] 3361 4-9-11 **69** TedDurcan 1 79
(Jane Chapple-Hyam) *dwlt: sn trcking ldrs: swtchd rt over 1f out: edgd lft and sn led: drvn out: hld on wl towards fin* **5/1**[2]

4441 **2** *1* **Gemma's Delight (IRE)**[14] 3341 4-9-2 **60** (p) LiamJones 8 67
(James Unett) *reluctant and led rdrless to post: hld up in rr: t.k.h: hdwy on ins 2f out: styd on strly fnl f: tk 2nd last 100yds: nt rch wnr* **9/2**[1]

-604 **3** *2¼* **Ishetoo**[20] 3188 7-9-12 **70** FrannyNorton 4 71
(Ollie Pears) *chsd ldrs: effrt over 2f out: kpt on to take 3rd towards fin* **7/1**[3]

0546 **4** *½* **Mount Hollow**[14] 3348 6-8-7 **58** (v) JackDuern(7) 5 58
(Reg Hollinshead) *chsd ldrs: effrt over 2f out: one pce over 1f out* **11/1**

5035 **5** *1* **Cyflymder (IRE)**[14] 3341 5-9-9 **67** (v[1]) CathyGannon 14 64+
(Declan Carroll) *s.i.s: wnt rt s: swtchd lft after s: hld up in rr: hdwy 2f out: kpt on fnl f: nt rch ldrs* **10/1**

-052 **6** *2* **Nufoudh (IRE)**[2] 3732 7-9-4 **65** PaulPickard(3) 2 57
(Colin Teague) *led: hdd and crowded appr fnl f: fdd last 150yds* **9/2**[1]

-000 **7** *5* **Rowan Spirit (IRE)**[14] 3337 3-9-1 **67** PaulQuinn 6 42
(Mark Brisbourne) *mid-div: effrt and nt clr run over 2f out: one pce* **16/1**

-433 **8** *3½* **Hoppy's Flyer (FR)**[14] 3337 3-9-2 **68** (p) MickyFenton 13 34
(Paul Midgley) *in rr-div: sme hdwy 2f out: nvr on terms* **10/1**

0006 **9** *1¼* **Pilgrim Dancer (IRE)**[3] 3719 4-9-0 **58** StephenCraine 3 23
(Patrick Morris) *dwlt: sn trcking ldr: rdn over 2f out: wknd 1f out* **22/1**

2202 **10** *¾* **Silly Gilly (IRE)**[19] 3202 7-9-1 **59** JamesSullivan 9 22
(Ron Barr) *chsd ldrs: rdn over 2f out: wknd wl over 1f out* **8/1**

1660 **11** *¾* **Downhill Skier (IRE)**[109] 928 7-9-3 **61** PatrickMathers 11 22
(Mark Brisbourne) *in rr: sn drvn along: wd outside over 2f out: nvr a factor* **28/1**

1m 26.55s (0.05) **Going Correction** +0.05s/f (Good)
WFA 3 from 4yo+ 8lb **11** Ran SP% **116.8**
Speed ratings (Par 103): **101,99,97,96,95 93,87,83,82,81 80**
toteswingers:1&2:£4.10, 1&3:£6.70, 2&3:£4.20 CSF £27.58 CT £161.52 TOTE £5.70: £1.70, £1.60, £2.60; EX 33.60.
Owner Simon Brewster **Bred** Stowell Hill Ltd & Major & Mrs R B Kennard **Trained** Dalham, Suffolk

FOCUS
A modest handicap run at a reasonable pace that again went to a low-drawn, prominent, racer. The time suggested the ground wasn't as slow as the official going suggested. The winner's best run since coming to Britain.
Gemma's Delight(IRE) Official explanation: jockey said filly was denied a clear run

3807 IG MARKETS H'CAP 5f 16y
7:10 (7:10) (Class 3) (0-95,94) 3-Y-0 **£7,246** (£2,168; £1,084; £542; £270) **Stalls** Low

Form RPR

-150 **1** **Shoshoni Wind**[48] 2298 3-9-0 **92** JulieBurke(5) 7 97
(Kevin Ryan) *swtchd lft after s: led: jnd appr fnl f: kpt on: all out* **5/1**[3]

3050 **2** *nse* **Bathwick Bear (IRE)**[27] 2934 3-9-5 **92** SilvestreDeSousa 6 97
(David Evans) *chsd ldrs: upsides appr fnl f: jst failed* **5/1**[3]

-000 **3** *2¼* **Marine Commando**[27] 2934 3-9-3 **90** BarryMcHugh 1 87+
(Richard Fahey) [illegible] *detached in last: hdwy and nt clr run on ins over 2f out: styd on to take 3rd ins fnl f* [illegible]

3543 **4** *2* **Crimson Knot (IRE)**[34] 2724 3-8-5 **78** PatrickMathers 4 68
(Alan Berry) *chsd ldrs: hmpd and lost pl after 1f: hdwy over 2f out: one pce over 1f out* **6/1**

2226 **5** *shd* **Bold Bidder**[20] 3158 3-9-0 **87** CathyGannon 3 76
(Kevin Ryan) *chsd ldrs: rdn over 2f out: one pce over 1f out* **2/1**[1]

0514 **6** *1½* **Catfish (IRE)**[14] 3367 3-8-10 **83** LiamJones 9 67
(Brian Meehan) *sn w wnr: wknd over 1f out* **9/2**[2]

60.52 secs (-0.48) **Going Correction** +0.05s/f (Good) **6** Ran SP% **111.6**
Speed ratings (Par 104): **105,104,101,98,97 95**
toteswingers:1&2:£3.30, 1&3:£5.80, 2&3:£6.70 CSF £28.97 CT £170.07 TOTE £6.50: £2.80, £2.80; EX 32.30.
Owner Hambleton Racing Ltd XVI **Bred** Mrs A F Tullie **Trained** Hambleton, N Yorks
■ Stewards' Enquiry : Julie Burke caution: used whip with excessive frequency.

FOCUS
A third of the field (including the two likely market leaders) were taken out in the morning, leaving very few progressive or bang in-form sorts in what had looked a decent handicap. The gallop was a decent one and the final time again suggested the ground was close to good. The form's rated around the second.

NOTEBOOK
Shoshoni Wind, having her first run in a handicap, returned to form back over 5f to confirm herself a very useful sprinter when setting and sustaining a decent gallop. She has a good attitude and should continue to give a good account, especially away from progressive or well-handicapped sorts. (op 9-2)
Bathwick Bear(IRE), was nibbled at in the market with Silvestre De Sousa replacing an apprentice and, after edging down the weights, ran as well as he has done all year returned to 5f. He's a very useful sprinter, but he'll be up in the weights for this and may remain difficult to place. (op 7-1 tchd 9-2)
Marine Commando has been essentially disappointing since winning last year's Windsor Castle, but confirmed he retains plenty of ability dropped to 5f for the first time since that win. He looks a bit better than the bare form after rearing at the start and meeting a bit of trouble and, given he isn't fully exposed, is worth another chance back over 6f. (op 13-2)
Crimson Knot(IRE) doesn't win very often, but she has been a model of consistency and is a bit better than the bare form after being squeezed out after less than a furlong. She wasn't disgraced and should continue to give it her best shot. (op 8-1)
Bold Bidder, a stable-companion of the winner, was again below the pick of her earlier-season efforts returned to handicap company. She will have to show a bit more before she is a solid betting proposition. (tchd 5-2)

Catfish(IRE), whose two wins have been when making most of the running over 6f, wasn't helped by being taken on for the lead and wasn't at her best. She may do better back over that longer trip. (op 4-1 tchd 7-2)

3808 TETLEY'S BITTER CONDITIONS STKS 5f 16y
7:45 (7:45) (Class 2) 2-Y-O £8,506 (£2,546; £1,273; £637) Stalls Low

Form RPR
1220 1 **Vocational (USA)**[23] 3033 2-8-9 0 SilvestreDeSousa 5 94
(Mark Johnston) *mde all: shkn up over 1f out: styd on strly: v readily* 10/11[1]
016 2 2 **Luv U Forever**[21] 3104 2-8-9 0 TadhgO'Shea 1 87
(Jo Hughes) *trckd ldrs: effrt over 2f out: chsd wnr over 1f out: no imp* 5/2[2]
1230 3 5 **Redair (IRE)**[56] 2070 2-8-9 0 CathyGannon 2 69
(David Evans) *chsd ldrs: sn drvn along: outpcd and lost pl 2f out: kpt on to take 3rd nr fin* 6/1
2310 4 ¾ **Bubbly Ballerina**[23] 3033 2-8-6 0 LiamJones 6 63
(Alan Bailey) *wnt rt s: sn w wnr: hung rt bnd 2f out: wknd appr fnl f* 11/2[3]
60.68 secs (-0.32) **Going Correction** +0.05s/f (Good) 4 Ran SP% **110.6**
Speed ratings (Par 100): **104,100,92,91**
CSF £3.55 TOTE £1.80; EX 3.30.
Owner Sheikh Hamdan Bin Mohammed Al Maktoum **Bred** Darley **Trained** Middleham Moor, N Yorks

FOCUS
Several smart colts have taken this since 2001, notably triple Group 3 scorer Majestic Missile (2003) and dual Listed/Group 3 winner Captain Gerrard (2007) but, although this year's renewal (run at a sound pace) was effectively a fillies-only race, the winner is a very useful sprinter. The time was less than a second outside Racing Post Standard and the ground was changed to "good, good to soft in places" following this race.

NOTEBOOK
Vocational(USA), far from disgraced in last month's Queen Mary, found this company much more to her liking and, although she raced with the choke out for much of the way, confirmed herself a very useful sprinter. There are more races to be won with her granted a suitable test of speed. (op 11-10)
Luv U Forever, who showed useful form in the Albany last month, got a good tow into the race on this first run for her new stable and ran up to her best down in trip against a very useful sort. There is a bit of a worry that she may not be the easiest to place but she should continue to give it her best shot. (op 9-4)
Redair(IRE), who showed useful early season form, had her limitations exposed in this company on this first run since mid-May. There will be easier opportunities than this one and she is the type to win again for this yard. (op 8-1)
Bubbly Ballerina finished last in the Queen Mary and was again much further behind today's winner than when the pair clashed at York in May. She is better than this but has plenty to prove at present. (op 9-2 tchd 6-1)

3809 EDGE WORLDWIDE LOGISTICS H'CAP 1m 2f 75y
8:15 (8:16) (Class 4) (0-85,84) 3-Y-O £4,851 (£1,443; £721; £360) Stalls High

Form RPR
4022 1 **Calaf**[14] 3340 3-8-12 74 BarryMcHugh 2 84
(Richard Fahey) *trckd ldrs: squeezed through between horses over 1f out: sn upsides: led last 75yds: drvn out* 9/4[1]
4114 2 ½ **Ivan Vasilevich (IRE)**[14] 3366 3-9-7 83 FrannyNorton 5 92
(Jane Chapple-Hyam) *drvn to ld: sn stdd pce: increased gallop over 3f out: hrd rdn and hdd wl ins fnl f: no ex* 4/1
-042 3 3 ¼ **El Torbellino (IRE)**[28] 2891 3-9-1 77 SilvestreDeSousa 3 80
(David O'Meara) *trckd ldrs: t.k.h: chal over 3f out: hung lft over 1f out: kpt on to take 3rd nr fin* 7/2[3]
31- 4 ½ **Umseyat (USA)**[286] 6360 3-9-7 83 TadhgO'Shea 4 85
(John Gosden) *hld up: effrt 3f out: wnt one pce 3rd 1f out: lost 3rd nr fin* 3/1[2]
5402 5 3 ½ **Persian Herald**[21] 3118 3-8-11 73 RichardMullen 7 68
(William Muir) *dwlt: sn trcking ldrs: t.k.h: drvn 3f out: wknd over 1f out* 14/1
-123 6 4 **Hernando Torres**[14] 3358 3-8-4 66 JamesSullivan 6 53
(Michael Easterby) *hld up: hdwy over 3f out: sn drvn: lost pl 2f out* 10/1
2m 13.66s (2.46) **Going Correction** +0.05s/f (Good) 6 Ran SP% **113.7**
Speed ratings (Par 102): **92,91,89,88,85 82**
toteswingers:1&2:£2.50, 1&3:£2.20, 2&3:£1.70 CSF £11.86 TOTE £3.40: £1.70, £2.40; EX 8.90.
Owner Dr Marwan Koukash **Bred** Norcroft Park Stud **Trained** Musley Bank, N Yorks
■ Stewards' Enquiry : Franny Norton one-day ban: used whip with excessive frequency (Jul 22)

FOCUS
A useful handicap but, with a steady pace to the home turn, the bare form looks unreliable. The level revolves around the runner-up.
Persian Herald Official explanation: jockey said colt ran too freely

3810 ASTBURY WREN NURSERY 6f 18y
8:50 (8:51) (Class 4) 2-Y-O £4,851 (£1,443; £721; £360) Stalls Low

Form RPR
6326 1 **Silvas Romana (IRE)**[14] 3336 2-7-12 61 PaulQuinn 1 65
(Mark Brisbourne) *chsd ldr: led on ins after 2f: hld on towards fin: all out* 25/1
323 2 nk **Tight Lipped (IRE)**[20] 3161 2-8-10 73 RichardMullen 3 76
(David Brown) *trckd ldrs on ins: nt clr run over 1f out: styd on wl ins fnl f: jst hld* 5/2[1]
2120 3 ½ **Aquasulis (IRE)**[3] 3700 2-8-2 65 CathyGannon 9 67
(David Evans) *led 2f: chsd ldrs: kpt on same pce fnl 100yds* 15/2
1620 4 ½ **Cravat**[22] 3064 2-9-5 82 SilvestreDeSousa 10 82+
(Mark Johnston) *chsd ldrs: effrt over 2f out: edgd lft over 1f out: kpt on same pce fnl 150yds* 7/1[3]
623 5 ¾ **Pitt Rivers**[57] 2023 2-8-11 74 TedDurcan 2 72
(Mick Channon) *s.i.s: in rr: hdwy over 2f out: chsng ldrs whn n.m.r 1f out: kpt on same pce* 5/1[2]
0621 6 hd **Musical Valley**[8] 3539 2-8-10 73 6ex (t) RichardKingscote 6 72+
(Tom Dascombe) *dwlt: hld up in rr: hdwy over 2f out: chsng ldrs whn nt clr run over 1f out and ins fnl f: kpt on* 15/2
1530 7 10 **Middleton Flyer (IRE)**[3] 3700 2-8-9 72 SamHitchcott 7 39+
(David Evans) *mid-div: hdwy on outside over 2f out: sn chsng ldrs: wknd over 1f out* 33/1
016 8 1 **Pendle Lady (IRE)**[3] 3700 2-8-3 66 FrannyNorton 8 30+
(Mark Brisbourne) *chsd ldrs on outer: lost pl after 1f and sn drvn along: bhd fnl 3f* 14/1
053 9 ¾ **Clarkson (IRE)**[18] 3221 2-8-0 66 SophieDoyle(3) 5 28
(Jamie Osborne) *mid-div: drvn over 2f out: sn lost pl* 11/1
5165 10 73 **He's So Cool (IRE)**[14] 3345 2-9-7 84 TadhgO'Shea 4 —
(Bill Turner) *s.v.s: hacked rnd t.o in last* 15/2
1m 15.11s (1.31) **Going Correction** +0.05s/f (Good) 10 Ran SP% **114.8**
Speed ratings (Par 96): **93,92,91,91,90 90,76,75,74,—**
toteswingers:1&2:£32.90, 1&3:£48.20, 2&3:£2.40 CSF £85.98 CT £547.30 TOTE £31.50: £5.00, £1.60, £2.60; EX 116.80.
Owner The Bourne Connection **Bred** Limetree Stud **Trained** Great Ness, Shropshire
■ The 'official' ratings shown next to each horse are estimated and for information purposes only.

FOCUS
A fair nursery in which over half the field were winners. The handicap marks are estimated and for official purposes only. The gallop wasn't overly strong and those held up were at a disadvantage. The first six pulled clear.

NOTEBOOK
Silvas Romana(IRE), dropped in trip, had the run of the race against the inside rail from the plum draw but showed a good attitude to get off the mark on the fifth attempt over this shorter trip. Everything went right but she isn't fully exposed and may do a little better. (op 22-1)
Tight Lipped(IRE) is a steadily progressive sort who was ideally placed from his good draw close to the inside rail but he may well have won had he not been checked briefly turning for home. He should be able to make amends. (op 11-4)
Aquasulis(IRE), the most experienced of these, had gone off too quickly earlier in the week but that wasn't the case here and she returned to something like her best after attracting support. She is capable of picking up one of these when allowed her own way in front. (op 10-1)
Cravat, who looked in tremendous condition, could be a bit better than the bare facts of this nursery debut given he raced three deep for much of the way from his draw. He's capable of winning a similar event when more favourably berthed. (op 8-1)
Pitt Rivers is a better than the bare facts of this nursery debut given he was ridden with more restraint than the four that finished ahead of him and that he met trouble in the closing stages. This trip seemed to suit and he's capable of winning a race. (op 9-2)
Musical Valley ◆ raced with the choke out in the early stages but who had to sit and suffer as the gaps closed around him in the straight. He will be worth another chance back at a more conventional course. (op 6-1 tchd 11-2)
Pendle Lady(IRE) Official explanation: jockey said filly lost its action
He's So Cool(IRE) Official explanation: jockey said colt was slowly away having put its head over adjoining stall as gates opened

3811 EXECUTIVE NETWORK LEGAL H'CAP 1m 4f 66y
9:20 (9:20) (Class 5) (0-75,75) 3-Y-O+ £4,043 (£1,203; £601; £300) Stalls Low

Form RPR
5351 1 **Bradbury (IRE)**[11] 3460 3-8-4 64 6ex TadhgO'Shea 7 72
(James Bethell) *hld up in mid-div: reminders 6f out: hdwy 4f out: wnt cl 3rd over 1f out: led jst ins fnl f: jst hld on* 7/2[2]
3-50 2 nse **Shernando**[24] 3023 4-10-0 75 SilvestreDeSousa 8 85+
(Mark Johnston) *chsd ldrs: drvn 4f out: nt clr run over 1f out: styd on wl ins fnl f: upsides nr fin: jst failed* 9/2[3]
1525 3 2 ½ **King's Counsel (IRE)**[2] 3730 5-9-7 68 (b) DanielTudhope 3 72
(David O'Meara) *led: hdd jst ins fnl f: kpt on same pce* 3/1[1]
0245 4 nk **The Lock Master (IRE)**[25] 3003 4-9-5 66 CathyGannon 4 69
(Michael Appleby) *trckd ldrs: drvn over 3f out: nt clr run and swtchd rt ins fnl f: kpt on* 8/1
3434 5 nk **Beneath**[6] 3637 4-8-8 60 (b) JulieBurke(5) 2 63
(Kevin Ryan) *trckd ldr: stmbld bnd after 4f: upsides 6f out: chal strly over 1f out: wknd clsng stages* 11/2
0452 6 ½ **Straversjoy**[27] 2912 4-8-10 60 PaulPickard(3) 6 62
(Reg Hollinshead) *dwlt: hld up in rr: hdwy over 3f out: chsng ldrs over 1f out: kpt on one pce* 11/2
6014 7 8 **Magnitude**[22] 3094 6-8-6 58 oh7 (p) LMcNiff(5) 5 47
(Brian Baugh) *in rr: bhd and drvn 6f out: sme hdwy over 2f out: wknd over 1f out* 20/1
2m 41.8s (3.30) **Going Correction** +0.05s/f (Good)
WFA 3 from 4yo+ 13lb 7 Ran SP% **112.0**
Speed ratings (Par 103): **91,90,89,89,88 88,83**
toteswingers:1&2:£4.50, 1&3:£2.70, 2&3:£1.80 CSF £18.70 CT £50.74 TOTE £3.40: £1.90, £2.30; EX 18.40.
Owner Clarendon Thoroughbred Racing **Bred** Pat Harnett **Trained** Middleham Moor, N Yorks

FOCUS
A modest handicap run at a stop-start gallop and this bare form doesn't look entirely reliable, although it does make sense. The first two pulled clear in the closing stages and the runner-up looked unlucky.
T/Plt: £316.70 to a £1 stake. Pool:£61,104.42 - 140.82 winning tickets T/Qpdt: £95.00 to a £1 stake. Pool:£3,982.64 - 31.00 winning tickets WG

3546 NEWBURY (L-H)
Friday, July 8

OFFICIAL GOING: Good (7.6)
Wind: Moderate ahead Weather: Cloudy

3812 CHRISTAL MANAGEMENT E B F MAIDEN FILLIES' STKS (DIV I) 7f (S)
5:50 (5:55) (Class 4) 2-Y-O £5,175 (£1,540; £769; £384) Stalls Centre

Form RPR
4 1 **Arsaadi (IRE)**[23] 3046 2-8-9 0 HarryBentley(5) 10 83+
(Ed Dunlop) *chsd ldrs: led ins fnl 2f: pushed clr fnl f: comf* 4/1[2]
2 1 ¾ **Na Zdorovie** 2-9-0 0 RobertWinston 13 77+
(B W Hills) *s.i.s: in rr: hdwy over 2f out: swtchd rt wl over 1f out: styd on to chse wnr fnl 120yds but nvr any ch* 20/1
25 3 1 ½ **Dare To Dream**[30] 2811 2-9-0 0 ChrisCatlin 12 73
(Richard Hannon) *chsd ldrs: drvn: hung lft and nt clr run ins fnl 2f: kpt on to chse wnr fnl f: no imp and one pce into 3rd fnl 120yds* 5/1[3]
6 4 1 **Savanna Days (IRE)**[30] 2811 2-9-0 0 HughBowman 8 70
(Mick Channon) *led tl hdd ins fnl 2f: wknd ins fnl f* 11/4[1]
5 ¾ **Idyllic Star (IRE)** 2-9-0 0 LiamKeniry 7 69
(J S Moore) *in tch: rdn and outpcd 3f out: drvn and styd on again ins fnl f: kpt on cl home* 100/1
6 nse **Perfect Delight** 2-9-0 0 LukeMorris 3 68+
(Clive Cox) *t.k.h: chsd ldrs early: drvn along and one pce 3f out: rdn and kpt on again ins fnl f* 8/1
7 nse **Viola Da Gamba (IRE)** 2-9-0 0 ShaneKelly 11 68+
(William Knight) *stdd s: hld up towards rr: pushed along and hdwy over 1f out: kpt on fnl f: nvr a threat* 16/1
8 2 ¾ **Saint Irene** 2-9-0 0 FrankieMcDonald 9 61
(Michael Blanshard) *mid-div: rdn over 3f out: kpt on fnl f: nvr a threat* 100/1
9 4 **Tiger Cub** 2-9-0 0 SteveDrowne 4 51
(Roger Charlton) *in tch: rdn along over 2f out: no ch after* 16/1

10 ½ **Gold Coin** 2-9-0 0 .... DarryllHolland 2 50
(J W Hills) *in rr: mod prog fnl f* **16/1**

11 4 **Joyful Spirit (IRE)** 2-9-0 0 .... IanMongan 6 40
(John Dunlop) *green and in rr thrght* **40/1**

5 12 *hd* **Accustomed**[9] 3520 2-9-0 0 .... JamesDoyle 1 40
(Sylvester Kirk) *chsd ldrs: wknd 2f out: hung rt fnl f and eased whn no ch* **16/1**

04 13 ¾ **Damask (IRE)**[27] 2914 2-9-0 0 .... J-PGuillambert 5 38
(Richard Hannon) *chsd ldr: rdn: hung lft and wknd qckly 2f out: eased fnl f* **7/1**

1m 27.29s (1.59) **Going Correction** +0.20s/f (Good) **13** Ran SP% **119.7**
Speed ratings (Par 93): **98,96,94,93,92 92,92,89,84,83 79,79,78**
toteswingers:1&2:£17.20, 1&3:£3.10, 2&3:£19.10 CSF £87.35 TOTE £6.60: £2.20, £7.10, £2.40; EX 124.60.
Owner Sultan Ali **Bred** Rabbah Bloodstock Limited **Trained** Newmarket, Suffolk

FOCUS
Rail out from 1m from 5f to 3f, adding 26yds to distances on Round course. The first division of an interesting juvenile fillies' maiden (1.85secs quicker than the second division) and it was one of the five with previous experience who triumphed.

NOTEBOOK
Arsaadi(IRE) readily confirmed the promise of last month's Kempton debut. Slowly away and green that day, her trainer Ed Dunlop is in much better form now and, having travelled nicely, she picked up really well to assert. She's in numerous valuable sales races, but it'll first be interesting to see what mark she's given by the handicapper. (op 7-2)
Na Zdorovie ◆ was weak in the market on this racecourse debut and soon found herself at the back. She began to pick up well from over 2f out though, and created a good impression in taking second, suggesting she ought to go one better with the experience behind her. (op 14-1)
Dare To Dream returned to the sort of form shown on debut, having disappointed last time, and looks a nursery type. (tchd 11-2 in a place)
Savanna Days(IRE) was backed beforehand and had the run of things in front, therefore it was disappointing to see her so readily brushed aside. She holds a Group 1 entry, which now seems unrealistic. (op 4-1)
Idyllic Star(IRE) ◆, half-sister to two hurdles winners, shaped with a good deal of promise considering newcomers from the yard often come on for a run.
Perfect Delight, whose Group3-winning half-sister Perfect Tribute won on debut, was too keen early and can do better with this run behind her. (op 9-1)
Viola Da Gamba(IRE), who's related to a couple of very decent winners, should improve. (op 66-1)
Accustomed failed to build on a promising debut Official explanation: jockey said filly ran too free and hung right (op 20-1)
Damask(IRE) took a big step backwards. The way she dropped out suggests something may have been amiss. Official explanation: jockey said filly moved poorly closing stages (op 6-1 tchd 11-2)

3813 CHRISTAL MANAGEMENT E B F MAIDEN FILLIES' STKS (DIV II) 7f (S)
6:20 (6:25) (Class 4) 2-Y-O **£5,175** (£1,540; £769; £384) **Stalls** Centre

Form RPR

1 **Zingana** 2-9-0 0 .... FergusSweeney 11 79+
(Eve Johnson Houghton) *chsd ldrs: pushed along: green and hung lft 2f out: stl green but kpt on strly ins fnl f: led cl home: readily* **100/1**

53 2 ¾ **Self Centred**[20] 3152 2-9-0 0 .... RobertWinston 12 77
(B W Hills) *chsd ldrs: chal 2f out: led wl over 1f out: drvn ins fnl f: hdd and no ex cl home* **1/1**[1]

3 *nk* **Gifted Girl (IRE)** 2-9-0 0 .... LukeMorris 10 76+
(Paul Cole) *towards rr but in tch: hdwy 2f out: sn drvn and green: kpt on ins fnl f: fin wl and gng on nr fin* **8/1**[3]

04 4 ¾ **Miss Astragal (IRE)**[8] 3547 2-9-0 0 .... AdamKirby 7 74
(Richard Hannon) *led: jnd 2f out: hdd over 1f out: styd chsng ldr tl dropped two pls clsng stages* **5/1**[2]

5 *hd* **Petaluma** 2-9-0 0 .... HughBowman 6 74+
(Mick Channon) *in tch: drvn and hdwy fr 2f out: styd on ins fnl f but nvr gng pce to press ldrs* **5/1**[2]

04 6 ¾ **Zuzu Angel (IRE)**[21] 3117 2-9-0 0 .... ShaneKelly 9 72
(William Knight) *chsd ldrs: drvn 2f out: outpcd ins fnl f* **16/1**

7 6 **La Confession** 2-9-0 0 .... HayleyTurner 13 57
(J W Hills) *in rr: rdn over 2f* [illegible] *ldrs over 1f out* **20/1**

8 6 **The Giving Tree (IRE)** 2-9-0 0 .... LiamKeniry 5 42
(Sylvester Kirk) *chsd ldrs: rdn over 2f out: wknd appr fnl 2f* **66/1**

9 3 ½ **Farleaze** 2-9-0 0 .... DarryllHolland 3 33+
(Brian Meehan) *a bhd* **40/1**

10 3 ½ **Better Be Mine (IRE)** 2-9-0 0 .... MartinLane 8 25+
(John Dunlop) *in rr and green a bhd* **33/1**

1m 29.14s (3.44) **Going Correction** +0.20s/f (Good) **10** Ran SP% **113.0**
Speed ratings (Par 93): **88,87,86,85,85 84,78,71,67,63**
toteswingers:1&2:£21.30, 1&3:£217.90, 2&3:£1.20 CSF £193.22 TOTE £76.20: £14.20, £1.10, £2.80; EX 223.00.
Owner Lord Astor,Lady Lewinton,R Morgan-Jones **Bred** Rockcliffe Stud **Trained** Blewbury, Oxon

FOCUS
This appeared to be the less competitive division and there was a shock result.

NOTEBOOK
Zingana, half-sister to a couple of Flat maidens, is from a yard whose first-time-out winners are few and far between, so it was easy to see why she was so readily dismissed in the market. However, having made ready enough headway into a challenging position, she moved alongside the favourite and asserted once getting her head down. Still green, she should improve and deserves a chance to prove this wasn't a fluke. (op 80-1)
Self Centred stood out on the form of her two previous starts, especially her Ascot third, and she looked all over the winner when going on over 1f out, but couldn't get away and was ultimately claimed. This was disappointing, but she can surely pick up a race at some stage. (op 4-5 tchd 11-10)
Gifted Girl(IRE) ◆ finished well, having not been the best away and will have gone into many a notebook. For all that her trainer can get one ready, she ought to improve and should have no trouble winning a maiden, with 1m likely to suit. (tchd 7-1)
Miss Astragal(IRE) appears to be improving with each run and looks a likely type for nurseries. (op 8-1)
Petaluma holds a Group 2 entry in Ireland next month, and she shaped promisingly in fifth, keeping on as though 1m would suit. (op 15-2 tchd 8-1)
Zuzu Angel(IRE) now looks ready for the step into nurseries.

3814 AXMINSTER CARPETS H'CAP 1m 2f 6y
6:50 (6:53) (Class 5) (0-70,70) 4-Y-O+ **£3,234** (£962; £481; £240) **Stalls** Low

Form RPR

0524 1 **One Hit Wonder**[16] 3266 4-9-0 **63** .... LiamKeniry 6 73
(Jonathan Portman) *in tch: stdy hdwy over 2f out: chal ins fnl f: rdn to ld fnl 120yds: on top cl home* **10/1**

204- 2 ¾ **Pennfield Pirate**[263] 6993 4-8-12 **61** .... DarryllHolland 1 69
(Hughie Morrison) *led: drvn wl over 2f out: sn strly chal but kpt slt advantage tl hdd fnl 120yds: no ch w wnr but kpt on wl for clr 2nd cl home* **11/2**[2]

4300 3 1 ½ **Commerce**[11] 3467 4-9-2 **65** .... FergusSweeney 5 70
(Gary Moore) *sn chsng ldr: rdn to chal fr over 2f out: nt get past ldr: no ex fnl 120yds: wknd cl home* **12/1**

01-1 4 *hd* **Two Certainties**[21] 3130 4-8-10 **64** .... RyanClark(5) 10 69
(Stuart Williams) *in rr: hdwy on outside fr over 2f out: kpt on ins fnl f: nt gng pce to rch ldrs* **4/1**[1]

-300 5 1 ¼ **Rodrigo De Freitas (IRE)**[8] 3533 4-8-12 **61** ....(v) ShaneKelly 8 63
(Jim Boyle) *stdd s and swtchd lft: in rr: rdn over 2f out: kpt on ins fnl f but nvr gng pce to rch ldrs* **12/1**

3216 6D 3 ¼ **Byrd In Hand (IRE)**[27] 2923 4-8-5 **59** .... HarryBentley(5) 2 55
(John Bridger) *chsd ldrs: rdn 3f out: wknd appr fnl f: subs disq* **4/1**[1]

4-22 7 1 **Celestial Girl**[43] 2417 4-9-7 **70** .... ChrisCatlin 4 64
(Hughie Morrison) *t.k.h: in rr but in tch: rdn and hdwy on ins over 2f out: no imp on ldrs and wknd appr fnl f* **4/1**[1]

5610 8 1 ¾ **Catching Zeds**[28] 1052 4-8-11 **60** .... MartinLane 7 50
(Ian Williams) *in rr: rdn along 7f out: in tch 4f out: rdn 3f out and no ch after* **28/1**

404/ 9 7 **Nina Rose**[631] 6793 4-9-1 **64** .... AdamKirby 3 40
(Clive Cox) *s.i.s: sn chsng ldrs: rdn 3f out: sn btn* **7/1**[3]

2m 9.64s (0.84) **Going Correction** +0.20s/f (Good) **9** Ran SP% **115.8**
Speed ratings (Par 103): **104,103,102,102,101 98,97,96,90**
toteswingers:1&2:£12.10, 1&3:£22.50, 2&3:£7.10 CSF £64.17 CT £673.61 TOTE £15.50: £3.20, £2.90, £4.60; EX 79.60.
Owner More Money Than Sense Partnership **Bred** Elsdon Farms **Trained** Compton, Berks

FOCUS
A modest handicap run at a fair gallop. Byrd In Hand subs disq: prohibited substance in sample.

3815 MC SEAFOODS H'CAP 1m (S)
7:25 (7:27) (Class 4) (0-80,80) 3-Y-O+ **£4,528** (£1,347; £673; £336) **Stalls** Centre

Form RPR

4031 1 **Master Mylo (IRE)**[14] 3361 4-10-0 **80** .... ShaneKelly 6 89+
(Dean Ivory) *unruly in stalls: s.i.s: in rr: nt clr run and swtchd rt 2f out: str run ins fnl f to chse ldr fnl 120yds: led last stride* **11/1**

0-24 2 *nse* **Ssafa**[26] 2960 3-8-8 **68** ow1 .... DarryllHolland 9 76
(J W Hills) *sn pressing ldr: racd alone on stands'rail 5f out: and lost position: hdwy fr 3f out: drvn to chal 1f out: led fnl 120yds: hdd last stride* **11/1**

100- 3 1 ¼ **Compton Blue**[254] 7182 5-9-5 **76** ....(b) KieranO'Neill(5) 3 82
(Richard Hannon) *pressed ldrs tl slt ld over 2f out: jnd sn after and strly chal 1f out tl hdd fnl 120yds: no ex* **33/1**

-000 4 1 **Satwa Laird**[35] 2674 5-9-9 **75** .... KierenFallon 10 79
(Ed Dunlop) *in tch: nt clr run 2f out: rdn and hdwy appr fnl f: styd on but nvr quite gng pce to chal* **11/2**[2]

5565 5 1 ¼ **Franco Is My Name**[37] 2604 5-9-5 **76** ....(p) HarryBentley(5) 2 77
(Peter Hedger) *s.i.s: in rr: hdwy and hung lft fr over 1f out: styd on ins fnl f: sn one pce* **16/1**

-614 6 ¾ **Sergeant Troy (IRE)**[49] 2256 3-8-12 **73** .... SteveDrowne 11 70
(Roger Charlton) *sn chsng ldrs: ev ch ins fnl 2f: wknd ins fnl f* **4/1**[1]

-053 7 1 **On Khee**[18] 3228 4-9-5 **71** .... HayleyTurner 14 68
(Hughie Morrison) *s.i.s: in rr: hdwy fr 2f out: one pce ins fnl f* **17/2**

61 8 ½ **Stand To Reason (IRE)**[34] 2723 3-9-5 **80** .... LiamKeniry 13 74
(Mikael Magnusson) *s.i.s: sn in tch: rdn over 2f out: sn outpcd: sme prog again clsng stages* **7/1**[3]

0/04 9 3 ¼ **Billion Dollar Kid**[25] 2995 6-9-7 **73** ....(t) JamesDoyle 4 61
(Joanna Davis) *chsd ldrs fr 1/2-way and ev ch ins fnl 2f: wknd appr fnl f* **10/1**

2210 10 1 ¾ **Hugely Exciting**[35] 2684 3-9-1 **76** ....(p) LukeMorris 7 58
(J S Moore) *in tch: rdn 3f out: wknd 2f out* **28/1**

2142 11 *nk* **Catchanova (IRE)**[11] 3468 4-8-12 **64** .... FergusSweeney 8 47
(Eve Johnson Houghton) *mde most tl hdd over 2f out: wknd over 1f out* **8/1**

5102 12 4 ½ **Qenaa**[14] 3361 3-9-1 **76** .... J-PGuillambert 5 47
(Mark Johnston) *chsd ldrs: rdn and ev ch 2f out: eased whn no ch fnl f* **17/2**

1m 41.05s (1.35) **Going Correction** +0.20s/f (Good)
WFA 3 from 4yo+ 9lb **12** Ran SP% **118.1**
Speed ratings (Par 105): **101,100,99,98,97 96,95,95,91,90 89,85**
toteswingers:1&2:£47.50, 1&3:£32.10, 2&3:£107.50 CSF £125.90 CT £3881.47 TOTE £10.10: £3.00, £3.30, £8.00; EX 179.50.
Owner K Quinn/ C Benham/ I Saunders **Bred** David Eiffe **Trained** Radlett, Herts

FOCUS
A decent handicap.

3816 KKA - HIGHPOINT (S) STKS 6f 110y
7:55 (8:04) (Class 4) 2-Y-O **£5,175** (£1,540; £769; £384) **Stalls** Centre

Form RPR

03 1 **The New Black (IRE)**[17] 3249 2-8-4 0 .... KieranO'Neill(5) 15 60+
(Richard Hannon) *towards rr: hdwy 2f out: rdn and kpt on wl fnl f to ld fnl 50yds: hld on all out* **16/1**

0 2 *nk* **Mcvicar**[7] 3590 2-9-0 0 .... HughBowman 13 62
(Mick Channon) *s.i.s: in rr: hdwy over 2f out: rdn and rdr dropped whip sn after: styd on wl to ld ins fnl f but hanging rt: hdd fnl 50yds: nt qckn* **12/1**

3 2 ¼ **Titus Star (IRE)** 2-9-0 0 .... LukeMorris 10 56+
(J S Moore) *in rr: pushed along and green 1/2-way: hdwy fr 2f out: styd on wl to take 3rd fnl 120yds but no imp on ldng duo* **16/1**

5 4 1 ¼ **Lolita Lebron (IRE)**[51] 2187 2-8-9 0 .... FrankieMcDonald 16 47
(Richard Hannon) *chsd ldrs: led 2f out: rdn and hdd ins fnl f and hung rt: btn whn carried rt cl home* **5/1**[2]

5424 5 3 ¾ **Emma Jean (IRE)**[7] 3584 2-8-9 0 .... LiamKeniry 8 37
(J S Moore) *in tch 1/2-way: chsd ldrs fr 2f out: outpcd ins fnl f* **7/1**[3]

065 6 1 ¼ **Zigazag (IRE)**[22] 3076 2-9-0 0 .... JamesDoyle 12 39
(David Evans) *chsd ldrs: rdn over 2f out: one pce appr fnl f* **8/1**

7 3 ¼ **Holy Empress (IRE)** 2-8-9 0 .... HayleyTurner 11 25
(Michael Bell) *in tch: rdn 1/2-way: no imp: hung rt and btn over 1f out* **10/1**

3415 8 1 ¼ **Choice Of Remark (IRE)**[12] 3429 2-9-0 0 .... MatthewCosham(5) 7 31
(David Evans) *towards rr whn hmpd 4f out: rdn and hdwy to chse ldrs ins fnl 2f: wknd fnl f* **3/1**[1]

9 ¾ **King Kenobi (IRE)** 2-8-9 0 .... RyanPowell(5) 5 24
(J S Moore) *in rr: pushed along and sme prog fnl 2f: nvr a threat* **28/1**

5 10 3 **Our Cool Cat (IRE)**[17] 3249 2-9-0 0 ....(b[1]) FergusSweeney 6 16
(Gary Moore) *towards rr most of way* **25/1**

0 **11** *1 ¾* **Red Hot Penny (IRE)**[11] 3472 2-9-0 0 EddieCreighton 4 11
(Brian Meehan) *s.i.s: in rr: sme hdwy 3f out: wknd 2f out* **50/1**

000 **12** *3 ¾* **Hiding In The Open (IRE)**[11] 3472 2-9-0 0 (b[1]) ShaneKelly 1 —
(Brian Meehan) *led tl hdd 2f out: wknd over 1f out* **25/1**

06 **13** *½* **Milwr**[11] 3472 2-9-0 0 (v[1]) DarryllHolland 3 —
(Chris Dwyer) *chsd ldrs 4f* **22/1**

0 **14** *5* **Clone Devil (IRE)**[39] 2559 2-8-7 0 (p) KatiaScallan(7) 14 —
(Alastair Lidderdale) *chsd ldrs 4f* **40/1**

04 **15** *8* **June Thirteen (IRE)**[6] 3631 2-9-0 0 KierenFallon 9 —
(Richard Hannon) *spd to 1/2-way* **10/1**

1m 21.85s (2.55) **Going Correction** +0.20s/f (Good) **15** Ran SP% **122.8**
Speed ratings (Par 96): **93,92,90,88,84 82,79,77,76,73 71,67,66,60,51**
toteswingers:1&2:£44.70, 1&3:£96.70, 2&3:£67.90 CSF £183.61 TOTE £25.70: £6.90, £3.90, £8.10; EX 122.60.The winner was sold to Gay Kelleway for 6,400gns.
Owner Mrs J Wood **Bred** Tullamaine Castle Stud **Trained** East Everleigh, Wilts

FOCUS
An open juvenile seller in which they went a decent gallop. Not for the first time on the evening, those berthed in a high stall came out on top.

NOTEBOOK
The New Black(IRE) had previously shown moderate form in two starts over 6f, but the drop in grade was clearly a help, as was the extra half a furlong, and she was never stronger than at the finish. She appears to have a bit of scope, will stay further, and could make her mark in nurseries. The winner was sold to Gay Kelleway for 6,400gns. (op 12-1)
Mcvicar, last of ten in a 7f Sandown maiden a week earlier, was quickly dropped in grade and certainly knew more this time. He can go one better in something similar. Official explanation: jockey said he dropped his whip (tchd 11-1 and 14-1)
Titus Star(IRE) attracted support at big prices and, despite a sluggish start, came home well for a place. He can pick up a race at this level. (op 40-1)
Lolita Lebron(IRE) had her chance and probably didn't improve much on her debut effort. (tchd 9-2 and 11-2)
Emma Jean(IRE) doesn't look to be progressing. (op 11-2)
Zigazag(IRE) doesn't look to be progressing. (op 9-1 tchd 7-1)
Holy Empress(IRE) never posed a threat on debut. (tchd 12-1)
Choice Of Remark(IRE), who looked the one to beat, was slightly impeded and shuffled back early. He tried to get back into it, but had nothing more to give from 1f out. Official explanation: jockey said colt suffered interference shortly after start (tchd 7-2)
Red Hot Penny(IRE) Official explanation: jockey said colt was struck intoon way to post
Milwr Official explanation: jockey said colt hung
June Thirteen(IRE) was eased right down and, while better than this, he's clearly moderate. (op 9-1 tchd 8-1)

3817 SHREDDING FOR BEDDING H'CAP — 1m 5f 61y
8:30 (8:35) (Class 5) (0-75,81) 4-Y-0+ — **£3,234** (£962; £481; £240) **Stalls** Low

Form — RPR

-000 **1** **Kings Bayonet**[25] 2995 4-9-4 **72** HayleyTurner 9 81
(Alan King) *s.i.s: hld up in rr: swtchd rt to outside 3f out: stdy hdwy to ld over 1f out: drvn out* **14/1**

3034 **2** *¾* **Eshtyaaq**[31] 2793 4-9-1 **69** AdamKirby 7 77
(David Evans) *trckd ldrs: drvn to ld and hung lft 2f out: hdd over 1f out: kpt on: nt pce of wnr* **11/2**[2]

5-16 **3** *1 ¾* **Rockfella**[35] 2686 5-9-2 **73** JohnFahy(3) 12 78
(Denis Coakley) *sn led: hdd 11f out: led again 1m out: rdn 3f out: hdd 2f out: one pce fnl f: edgd lft clsng stages* **7/1**[3]

1-00 **4** *nse* **Spensley (IRE)**[34] 2708 5-9-3 **71** KierenFallon 4 76
(James Fanshawe) *hld up in rr: hdwy over 2f out: drvn and styd on to chse ldrs fnl f but no imp* **4/1**[1]

-405 **5** *nse* **Raktiman (IRE)**[29] 2830 4-8-13 **67** (p) SteveDrowne 1 72
(Tom Dascombe) *chsd ldrs: drvn to chal 2f out: one pce fnl f: edgd rt cl home* **16/1**

5-00 **6** *2* **Issabella Gem (IRE)**[39] 2552 4-8-11 **72** LucyKBarry(7) 3 76
(Clive Cox) *chsd ldrs: rdn over 2f out: one pce ins fnl f and readily hld whn hmpd cl home* **7/1**[3]

0002 **7** *2 ¾* **Rock With You**[8] 3546 4-8-0 **59** JemmaMarshall(5) 5 57
(Pat Phelan) *racd towards outside: on outer: shkn up3f out: rdn and styd on same pce fnl 2f* **14/1**

0305 **8** *3* **Cornish Beau (IRE)**[8] 3533 4-8-13 **67** JimmyQuinn 11 60
(Mark H Tompkins) *in rr: sme hdwy 3f out but nvr nr ldrs: no ch whn edgd lft ins fnl f* **8/1**

5-04 **9** *2 ¼* **Blazing Desert**[37] 2622 7-9-3 **71** HughBowman 8 61
(John Quinn) *led 11f out tl 1m out: styd trcking ldr: rdn 3f out: wknd over 2f out: no ch whn bmpd ins fnl f* **7/1**[3]

1000 **10** *20* **Admirable Duque (IRE)**[8] 3533 5-9-4 **72** JamesDoyle 2 32
(Dominic Ffrench Davis) *chsd ldrs on outside tl wknd fr 3f out* **16/1**

056/ **11** *12* **Katies Tuitor**[482] 5769 8-9-2 **70** LiamKeniry 10 12
(J S Moore) *chsd ldrs towards outside tl wknd 3f out* **14/1**

2m 55.36s (3.36) **Going Correction** +0.20s/f (Good) **11** Ran SP% **115.8**
Speed ratings (Par 103): **97,96,95,95,95 94,92,90,89,76 69**
toteswingers:1&2:£7.00, 1&3:£34.40, 2&3:£4.60 CSF £87.83 CT £593.62 TOTE £21.20: £6.00, £1.10, £3.00; EX 139.10.
Owner W H Ponsonby **Bred** Mickley Stud & C J Whiston **Trained** Barbury Castle, Wilts

FOCUS
Just an ordinary handicap.

3818 RIDGEWAY FILLIES' H'CAP — 7f (S)
9:00 (9:06) (Class 5) (0-75,78) 3-Y-O — **£3,234** (£962; £481; £240) **Stalls** Centre

Form — RPR

-233 **1** **Romantic Wish**[36] 2643 3-9-3 **74** SeanLevey(3) 10 91
(Robert Mills) *s.i.s: in rr: stdy hdwy fr over 2f out to ld appr fnl f sn drvn clr: easily* **9/1**[2]

3251 **2** *6* **Caelis**[13] 3387 3-9-4 **72** (v) StevieDonohoe 6 73
(Ralph Beckett) *chsd ldr: chal fr 2f out tl appr fnl f: chsd wnr sn after but nvr any ch* **4/1**[1]

21-4 **3** *1 ¼* **Zing Wing**[21] 3121 3-9-7 **75** ChrisCatlin 8 72
(Paul Cole) *t.k.h towards rr: drvn and hdwy over 1f out: kpt on wl fnl f to take 3rd clsng stages but nvr nr clr wnr* **10/1**[3]

0-51 **4** *1 ¼* **Luv U Too**[7] 3586 3-9-10 **78** 6ex DarryllHolland 11 72
(Jo Hughes) *led: jnd 2f out: hdd appr fnl f: wknd fnl 120yds* **4/1**[1]

51- **5** *nse* **Birdolini**[205] 7879 3-9-4 **72** FergusSweeney 12 66+
(Alan King) *in rr: pushed along 2f out: hdwy ins fnl f: gng on clsng stages* **12/1**

065 **6** *shd* **Amber Heights**[22] 3090 3-8-11 **65** LukeMorris 3 59
(David Pinder) *stdd s: in rr: swtchd lft to outer 2f out: sn hrd rdn: styd on same pce fnl f* **16/1**

01-6 **7** *nk* **Folly Drove**[17] 3259 3-8-12 **66** JamesDoyle 7 59
(Jonathan Portman) *chsd ldrs: rdn over 2f out: one pce fr over 1f out* **12/1**

6140 **8** *2 ¾* **Miss Dutee**[31] 2792 3-8-3 **62** KieranO'Neill(5) 2 47
(Richard Hannon) *outpcd most of way* **18/1**

511 **9** *5* **Dead Cool**[16] 3292 3-9-3 **71** KierenFallon 1 43
(Hughie Morrison) *in rr: hdwy towards outside over 2f out: nvr rchd ldrs and wknd appr fnl f* **4/1**[1]

-100 **10** *½* **Fettuccine (IRE)**[13] 3390 3-9-0 **68** HayleyTurner 9 39
(John Gallagher) *t.k.h: chsd ldrs to 1/2-way* **16/1**

6004 **11** *2 ¾* **One Cool Chick**[16] 3292 3-8-2 **56** oh6 RichardThomas 4 19
(John Bridger) *s.i.s: sn pulling hrd and chsng ldrs: wknd 1/2-way* **33/1**

-036 **12** *6* **Choose The Moment**[28] 2869 3-8-3 **60** (p) JohnFahy(3) 5 —
(Eve Johnson Houghton) *chsd ldrs over 3f* **16/1**

1m 26.12s (0.42) **Going Correction** +0.20s/f (Good) **12** Ran SP% **120.3**
Speed ratings (Par 97): **105,98,96,95,95 95,94,91,85,85 82,75**
toteswingers:1&2:£9.20, 1&3:£9.60, 2&3:£6.20 CSF £45.55 CT £377.98 TOTE £12.20: £3.30, £1.80, £2.70; EX 69.90.
Owner Miss J A Leighs **Bred** Mervyn Stewkesbury **Trained** Headley, Surrey

FOCUS
The field congregated stands' side in this 7f handcap.
One Cool Chick Official explanation: jockey said filly ran too free
T/Plt: £11,004.10 to a £1 stake. Pool:£47,483.68 - 3.15 winning tickets T/Qpdt: £1,087.90 to a £1 stake. Pool:£3,675.50 - 2.50 winning tickets ST

3772 NEWMARKET (R-H)
Friday, July 8

OFFICIAL GOING: Good (overall 8.0, far side 8.0, centre 8.1, stands' side 8.1)
Wind: Fresh across Weather: Overcast

3819 PIPER-HEIDSIECK CHAMPAGNE IRISH E B F FILLIES' H'CAP — 7f
1:20 (1:21) (Class 2) (0-100,93) 3-Y-O
£12,450 (£3,728; £1,864; £932; £466; £234) **Stalls** High

Form — RPR

1-13 **1** **Instance**[42] 2468 3-8-11 **83** WilliamBuick 10 99+
(Jeremy Noseda) *lw: hld up: nt clr run over 2f out: swtchd rt and hdwy over 1f out: rdn to ld 1f out: r.o* **5/2**[1]

1511 **2** *2 ¾* **Chokurei (IRE)**[15] 3310 3-8-9 **81** LukeMorris 3 87
(Clive Cox) *hld up: hdwy over 2f out: rdn over 1f out: styd on* **15/2**[3]

110- **3** *nk* **Ishbelle**[309] 5693 3-9-7 **93** StevieDonohoe 12 98
(Ralph Beckett) *s.i.s: hdwy over 5f out: rdn over 2f out: ev ch 1f out: saying on same pce whn hung rt wl ins fnl f* **12/1**

15- **4** *nk* **Tuscania**[258] 7098 3-9-4 **90** RyanMoore 9 95+
(Sir Michael Stoute) *hld up: swtchd lft over 2f out: hdwy over 1f out: styd on* **7/1**[2]

2220 **5** *hd* **Jade**[25] 2986 3-8-4 **76** PaulHanagan 7 80
(Ollie Pears) *s.i.s: hld up: r.o ins fnl f: nrst fin* **10/1**

3-02 **6** *2 ¼* **Sweetie Time**[15] 3323 3-9-1 **92** HarryBentley(5) 6 92
(Michael Bell) *b.hind: chsd ldrs: hmpd 2f out: sn rdn: styd on same pce fnl f* **8/1**

14 **7** *½* **Hezmah**[72] 1599 3-9-1 **87** RichardHills 4 84
(John Gosden) *chsd ldr tl led 3f out: hdd over 2f out: led again over 1f out: sn hung lft: hdd 1f out: wknd ins fnl f* **8/1**

0030 **8** *hd* **Sonning Rose (IRE)**[23] 3034 3-9-1 **87** HughBowman 13 83
(Mick Channon) *hld up: rdn over 1f out: r.o ins fnl f: nvr nrr* **16/1**

0644 **9** *4 ½* **Admirable Spirit**[20] 3178 3-8-9 **81** KierenFallon 1 65
(Richard Hannon) *lw: chsd ldrs: led over 2f out: rdn and hdd over 1f out: sn hung lft and wknd* **11/1**

-241 **10** *nk* **Psychic's Dream**[22] 3079 3-8-7 **79** AndreaAtzeni 2 62
(Marco Botti) *lw: hld up: rdn over 1f out: nvr on terms* **17/2**

150 **11** *6* **Mystic Dream**[56] 2073 3-8-13 **85** MichaelHills 5 52
(B W Hills) *led 4f: rdn whn hmpd 2f out: wknd over 1f out* **66/1**

1m 26.55s (0.85) **Going Correction** +0.15s/f (Good) **11** Ran SP% **118.1**
Speed ratings (Par 103): **101,97,97,97,96 94,93,93,88,88 81**
Tote Swingers: 1&2 £3.40, 1&3 £10.50, 2&3 £23.10 CSF £21.22 CT £195.73 TOTE £3.60: £1.60, £2.70, £4.40; EX 21.20 Trifecta £206.70 Pool: £1,181.64 - 4.23 winning units..
Owner The Hon William Vestey **Bred** T R G Vestey **Trained** Newmarket, Suffolk

FOCUS
Just the 1mm of rain during the morning, and the going remained good (GoingStick: 8.4 (far side 8.3, centre 8.7, stands' side 8.4). The far side course was again being used, while the positioning of the bend leading onto the far side course in the home straight increased distances of the 1m2f race by 16m. Although the top-weight was rated 7lb below the ceiling this still looked a decent handicap containing several potential improvers. It was well run. A clear best from the winner who rates slightly higher than the bare form.

NOTEBOOK
Instance promised to be very much suited by this extra furlong. Settled in midfield, she quickened once switched and stayed on really well to record her third win from four starts. She's a half-sister to a 1m4f winner, but gets plenty of speed from her sire Invincible Spirit and, while she might get a mile, she probably won't want any further. (op 11-4 tchd 3-1)
Chokurei(IRE), chasing a hat-trick following wins over this trip at Kempton and Leicester, showed she remains on the upgrade with a solid effort behind a well-handicapped rival. She should be able to win something similar off this sort of mark.
Ishbelle beat just one home, but was only 3l behind the winner in a Listed race on her final start last season and that had resulted in a 8lb rise in the handicap. Making her seasonal reappearance under top weight, she showed enough to suggest that with this run under her belt she can go close next time off this rating. (op 14-1)
Tuscania, another making her reappearance, was held up out the back and stayed on quite well once switched to the far-side rail to challenge. She very much looks the type who will benefit from a step up to a mile. (op 6-1)
Jade, who disappointed when sent off favourite at Carlisle last month, ran much better this time despite being 4lb higher. The suspicion is that the handicapper knows where he stands with her now, though. (op 14-1)
Sweetie Time looks handicapped right up to her best now. (op 15-2 tchd 7-1)
Hezmah remains capable of better, as she had plenty of use made of her here and will appreciate getting back on quicker ground.
Sonning Rose(IRE) is fully exposed. (op 20-1 tchd 22-1)
Psychic's Dream faced a much stiffer task off 9lb higher over this longer trip. (op 9-1 tchd 10-1)

3820 TOTESPORT.COM STKS (HERITAGE H'CAP) — 6f
1:50 (1:52) (Class 2) (0-105,104) 3-Y-O
£62,250 (£18,640; £9,320; £4,660; £2,330; £1,170) **Stalls** High

Form — RPR

-243 **1** **Coeus**[20] 3181 3-8-5 **88** DavidProbert 14 100
(Sir Mark Prescott Bt) *a.p: rdn over 1f out: r.o u.p to ld wl ins fnl f* **9/1**[3]

2101 **2** 1 ¼ **Lexi's Hero (IRE)**[27] 2934 3-9-3 **100**........................(b[1]) JamieSpencer 15 108
(Kevin Ryan) *lw: led: hung rt over 2f out: hrd rdn fr over 1f out: hung lft and hdd wl ins fnl f* **12/1**

-662 **3** ½ **Murbeh (IRE)**[27] 2911 3-8-12 **95**........................ RichardHills 16 101
(Brian Meehan) *chsd ldrs: rdn over 1f out: r.o* **16/1**

1-20 **4** ¾ **Desert Law (IRE)**[27] 2934 3-9-0 **97**........................ JimmyFortune 12 101+
(Andrew Balding) *mid-div: hdwy and hung rt over 1f out: r.o u.p* **12/1**

1-21 **5** hd **St Augustine (IRE)**[28] 2878 3-8-2 **85**........................ LukeMorris 6 88+
(John Best) *hld up: hdwy over 2f out: rdn over 1f out: r.o* **10/1**

-522 **6** nse **Cocktail Charlie**[27] 2934 3-8-11 **94**........................(p) DavidAllan 18 97
(Tim Easterby) *chsd ldrs: rdn over 1f out: styd on same pce ins fnl f* **11/1**

1011 **7** ½ **Barnet Fair**[23] 3048 3-8-6 **89**........................ WilliamBuick 4 91+
(Richard Guest) *hld up: rdn over 1f out: r.o wl ins fnl f: nt rch ldrs* **14/1**

2314 **8** hd **Swiss Dream**[27] 2934 3-8-7 **90**........................ RyanMoore 20 91+
(David Elsworth) *hld up: hdwy over 1f out: styd on* **6/1**[1]

0-40 **9** ¾ **Forjatt (IRE)**[27] 2934 3-9-2 **99**........................ FrankieDettori 1 98
(Roger Varian) *hld up: rdn over 1f out: r.o ins fnl f: nrst fin* **7/1**[2]

3-06 **10** 1 **New Planet (IRE)**[27] 2934 3-9-2 **104**........................ DaleSwift(5) 7 99
(John Quinn) *hld up: rdn over 1f out: r.o ins fnl f: nvr nrr* **14/1**

3-20 **11** hd **Dozy Joe**[27] 2934 3-8-6 **89**........................ MickaelBarzalona 11 84
(Ian Wood) *hld up: hdwy u.p over 1f out: nt trble ldrs* **25/1**

1-40 **12** nk **What About You (IRE)**[27] 2934 3-8-2 **85**........................ PaulHanagan 9 79
(Richard Fahey) *prom: rdn over 2f out: edgd rt and wknd over 1f out* **16/1**

-011 **13** ¾ **Steps (IRE)**[20] 3181 3-8-9 **92**........................ NeilCallan 13 83
(Roger Varian) *chsd ldr: rdn over 2f out: wkng whn hung lft ins fnl f* **11/1**

3540 **14** ½ **Face The Problem (IRE)**[20] 3181 3-8-9 **92**........................ MichaelHills 17 82
(B W Hills) *swtg: hld up: racd keenly: sme hdwy over 1f out: no ex ins fnl f* **50/1**

6320 **15** 1 **Ballista (IRE)**[14] 3357 3-8-8 **91**........................ RichardKingscote 3 78
(Tom Dascombe) *racd alone for much of the trip: prom: rdn over 1f out: wknd ins fnl f* **33/1**

0305 **16** ¾ **Arctic Feeling (IRE)**[27] 2928 3-8-12 **100**........................ LeeTopliss(5) 2 84
(Richard Fahey) *s.i.s and stmbld s: rdn over 1f out: n.d* **33/1**

-600 **17** 4 ½ **Majestic Dubawi**[27] 2934 3-9-2 **99**........................ HughBowman 8 69
(Mick Channon) *lw: hld up in tch: rdn over 2f out: wknd over 1f out* **11/1**

00-5 **18** 4 **Nasharra (IRE)**[85] 1326 3-8-0 **88**........................ JulieBurke(5) 5 45
(Kevin Ryan) *hld up: rdn over 2f out: wknd over 1f out* **66/1**

1m 12.38s (-0.12) **Going Correction** +0.15s/f (Good) **18** Ran SP% **124.5**
Speed ratings (Par 106): **106,104,103,102,102 102,101,101,100,99 98,98,97,96,95 94,88,83**
Tote Swingers: 1&2 £11.70, 1&3 £6.40, 2&3 £3.30 CSF £109.18 CT £1061.16 TOTE £11.90: £2.90, £2.60, £4.10, £3.00; EX 150.30 Trifecta £1201.40 Part won. Pool: £1,623.60 - 0.30 winning units..
Owner William Charnley & Richard Pegum **Bred** Lilac Bloodstock & Redmyre Bloodstock **Trained** Newmarket, Suffolk

FOCUS
This is always a competitive sprint handicap and a fertile source of winners. Recent scorers have included Total Gallery, who later won a Prix de l'Abbaye, and another high-class sprinter in Tax Free. The field tacked over towards the far rail, with the exeption of Ballista who raced alone and up with the pace before dropping away. High numbers seemed favoured, which just tempers enthusiasm for the form a little, but the form makes a fair bit of sense at face value. Improved efforts from the first three.

NOTEBOOK
Coeus had tried 5f and 7f on his last two starts, but this looks his optimum and he was only a pound higher than when second over this trip on the Rowley Mile in May. He travelled nicely behind the leaders and the way he picked up to strike the front augurs well for his future prospects. (op 11-1 tchd 12-1)
Lexi's Hero(IRE) had eight of these opponents behind when winning the Bond Tyres Trophy at York last month and confirmed the form despite going up 5lb. Showing bright pace, he edged across the track then wandered back over to his left and could not hold off the winner. The first-time blinkers worked well and he is a very smart performer. He is in the Stewards' Cup, and holds Group 1 entries in the Nunthorpe and the Betfred Sprint Cup. (op 10-1)
Murbeh(IRE) ran well back up in trip, travelling nicely and keeping on through the last furlong despite being carried to his left by the runner-up. (op 14-1)
Desert Law(IRE)'s trainer won this event in 2006 with the same owner's Dark Missile, a subsequent Wokingham winner, and in 2008 with Spanish Bounty who came back 12 months on to add the Bunbury Cup. This colt went just one home when starting favourite for Lexi's Hero's race at York, but that may have come a bit soon for him and he bounced back with a much better effort After drifting to his right, he was running on with gusto at the line. (op 10-1)
St Augustine(IRE), on his toes beforehand, hung two runs back and gave a little trouble before consenting to enter the stalls here. He is a progressive colt though, less exposed than the majority of his rivals, and was running on well for fifth on the wrong side of the pack. (tchd 9-1)
Cocktail Charlie dead-heated for second in the York race and he put in another solid performance upped 2lb and in first-time cheekpieces. This consistent gelding remains winless since his debut last year. (op 12-1)
Barnet Fair had won three of his last four but was another 5lb higher, a stone above his successful mark at Kempton in February. He finished well from the back, but his trademark slow start had left him with too much leeway to make up in such a warm race. This was a decent effort from an unfavourable draw.
Swiss Dream reverted to hold-up tactics and was never close enough in a race not run to suit closers. (op 9-1 tchd 10-1)
Forjatt(IRE), who had met trouble both at York and on the other track here, where he'd been two places behind Coeus, raced on the nearside of the pack from stall 1 and wasn't able to get in a challenge. He remains capable of better, quite possibly over 7f. (op 9-1)
New Planet(IRE) was rather too keen. (op 18-1)
Steps(IRE) was foiled in his hat-trick bid off a 5lb higher mark, weakening markedly through the final furlong after chasing the pace. He has won at this trip, but perhaps a stiff 5f is ideal. (op 9-1)

3821 IRISH THOROUGHBRED MARKETING CHERRY HINTON STKS (GROUP 2) (FILLIES) 6f

2:25 (2:26) (Class 1) 2-Y-O

£34,026 (£12,900; £6,456; £3,216; £1,614; £810) **Stalls** High

Form RPR

22 **1** **Gamilati**[14] 3362 2-8-12 0........................ FrankieDettori 7 107
(Mahmood Al Zarooni) *lw: hld up in tch: swtchd rt over 1f out: r.o to ld wl ins fnl f: readily* **14/1**

1 **2** 1 ½ **Russelliana**[27] 2914 2-8-12 0........................ RyanMoore 2 103
(Sir Michael Stoute) *lw: hld up: swtchd lft and hdwy ent fnl f: sn rdn and hung lft: r.o* **4/1**[2]

12 **3** nk **Shumoos (USA)**[23] 3033 2-8-12 0........................ MartinDwyer 9 102
(Brian Meehan) *trckd ldrs: racd keenly: led 1f out: sn rdn: edgd rt: hdd and unable qck wl ins fnl f* **5/2**[1]

12 **4** ¾ **Inetrobil (IRE)**[21] 3104 2-8-12 0........................ PhillipMakin 4 99
(Kevin Ryan) *chsd ldr: rdn over 1f out: styd on same pce ins fnl f* **13/2**

10 **5** ½ **Sajwah (IRE)**[21] 3104 2-8-12 0........................ RichardHills 8 98
(B W Hills) *awkward leaving stalls: hld up: hdwy over 1f out: sn rdn and hung lft: styd on same pce* **50/1**

13 **6** ¾ **Illaunglass (IRE)**[21] 3104 2-8-12 0........................ WilliamBuick 10 96
(Jeremy Noseda) *prom: rdn over 1f out: styd on same pce ins fnl f* **9/1**

1411 **7** 1 ¼ **Betty Fontaine (IRE)**[12] 3435 2-8-12 0........................ HughBowman 11 92
(Mick Channon) *hld up: hdwy over 1f out: no ex ins fnl f* **100/1**

53 **8** shd **Caledonia Lady**[23] 3033 2-8-12 0........................ DarryllHolland 3 92
(Jo Hughes) *hld up: outpcd over 1f out: r.o ins fnl f: nvr nrr* **12/1**

111 **9** 1 **Miss Work Of Art**[56] 2070 2-8-12 0........................ PaulHanagan 5 89
(Richard Fahey) *prom: rdn over 2f out: wknd over 1f out* **11/1**

01 **10** 1 ¼ **My Propeller (IRE)**[19] 3201 2-8-12 0........................ JamieSpencer 6 85
(Peter Chapple-Hyam) *lw: led: rdn and hdd 1f out: sn wknd* **5/1**[3]

41 **11** 6 **Pink Sapphire (IRE)**[16] 3287 2-8-12 0........................ JimmyFortune 1 67
(Richard Hannon) *hld up: a in rr: rdn and wknd over 1f out* **25/1**

1m 12.87s (0.37) **Going Correction** +0.15s/f (Good) **11** Ran SP% **118.1**
Speed ratings (Par 103): **103,101,100,99,98 97,96,96,94,93 85**
Tote Swingers: 1&2 £11.70, 1&3 £6.40, 2&3 £3.30 CSF £69.09 TOTE £13.40: £2.70, £2.00, £1.20; EX 88.70 Trifecta £397.40 Pool: £3,329.85 - 6.20 winning units..
Owner Godolphin **Bred** Darley **Trained** Newmarket, Suffolk

FOCUS
This promised to be an informative contest, with the placed fillies from the Queen Mary and Albany lining up against the unbeaten Richard Fahey-trained Miss Work Of Art and several unexposed rivals with interesting maiden form. The winning time was a very respectable 0.49sec slower than the heritage handicap earlier on the card.

NOTEBOOK
Gamilati ◆ may have arrived here a maiden, but she finished 5l clear of the rest when narrowly beaten by her stablemate Discourse last time, and her debut effort, when finishing in front of not only Albany winner Samitar but also Chesham third Self Centred and My Propeller, whom she re-opposed here, put her firmly in the picture. Always travelling well in midfield, she was going best when angled to the stands' side to take the leader' s measure and then stayed on well without being given anything like the full treatment to win a shade cosily. The first maiden to win this race since Sayyedati in 1992, she's a half-sister to a filly by Storm Cat who won at up to 7f in France, but she promises to stay further, being by Bernardini, and top quotes of 20-1 for the Guineas appear fair enough at this stage, as she looks sure to relish a step up to 7f and a mile in due course. That said, this success paid quite a compliment to her stablemate Discourse, who lacked the previous outing of Gamilati when edging her out here on her debut. She's clearly also a very smart filly, well worth her 20-1 quote for the Guineas, and it'll be interesting to see where she turns up next (reportedly been coughing recently, hence her absence from this race). Gamilati herself may well head to York next for the Lowther. (op 12-1)
Russelliana, well backed prior to making a winning debut at Leicester last month, had seen that form given a boost since. Again well supported on this big step up in class, she's clearly held in some regard, and went a long way to justifying that with a fine effort in second. By Medicean out of a half-sister to Notnowcato, she too should appreciate another furlong later in the season, but it wouldn't be a surprise if she reopposes the winner in the Lowther beforehand, as she was the least experienced in this line-up and is open to plenty of improvement. (op 6-1 tchd 13-2)
Shumoos(USA), on toes beforehand, won impressively on her debut and that form could not have worked out any better, but she was narrowly beaten in the Queen Mary and it was easy to pick holes in that form. Stepping up a furlong in distance, she was keen early and in the circumstances did well to keep on for third. She got the trip alright, but York might suit her better, and she deserves the chance to prove it in the Lowther. (op 3-1 tchd 10-3)
Inetrobil(IRE), who chased the clear leader, had every chance but didn't quite see it out as strongly as those ridden with a bit more patience. She ran close to her Albany form with the third at Ascot, Illaunglass. (op 6-1 tchd 11-2)
Sajwah(IRE), who was disappointing when only seventh in the Albany, wasn't best away and raced a shade keenly here, but she ran the placed horses from Ascot much closer this time, suggesting this was more her true form. (op 40-1)
Illaunglass(IRE) raced close to the winner in midfield and was just not good enough to match that one's turn of foot. She didn't finish much closer to Inetrobil than she did at Ascot. (op 10-1 tchd 12-1)
Betty Fontaine(IRE), the most experienced of these, had a lot more to do in this company and didn't run too badly in the circumstances.
Caledonia Lady, whose close third in the Queen Mary at 100-1 put something of a question mark over the value of that particular piece of form, failed to confirm that effort, and perhaps the Ascot run was something of a fluke after all. Official explanation: jockey said filly ran too free (op 14-1)
Miss Work Of Art, unbeaten in three previous starts, including in Listed company at York last time, was stepping up a furlong in distance and lines of form suggested she had a bit to find with one or two who ran at Royal Ascot. She never landed a blow and, while she might need quicker ground to be at her best, it didn't look a case of simply failing to get the trip. (op 8-1)
My Propeller(IRE) dotted up at Pontefract on her previous start and, while she beat nothing of note there, she showed tremendous speed. Sent to the front immediately, she was allowed a free hand in front, but she set a fair gallop and this isn't the easiest of tracks at which to make all. As soon as she hit the rising ground she cried enough. (op 9-2)
Pink Sapphire(IRE) was beaten a long way by Shumoos on her debut, but she was green that day and had since improved significantly, winning well at Salisbury subsequently. This was a step backwards, though, as she was always at the tail of the field and failed to pick up for pressure. This can't have been her true form. (op 18-1)

3822 ETIHAD AIRWAYS FALMOUTH STKS (BRITISH CHAMPIONS' SERIES) (GROUP 1) (F&M) 1m

3:00 (3:00) (Class 1) 3-Y-O+

£90,736 (£34,400; £17,216; £8,576; £4,304; £2,160) **Stalls** High

Form RPR

-341 **1** **Timepiece**[25] 2994 4-9-5 108........................ TomQueally 4 116
(Sir Henry Cecil) *trckd ldr tl led over 1f out: rdn and hung lft ins fnl f: styd on* **16/1**

13-1 **2** 1 ¼ **Sahpresa (USA)**[34] 2744 6-9-5 118........................ Christophe-PatriceLemaire 8 113+
(Rod Collet, France) *lw: hld up: hdwy over 1f out: sn rdn and edgd lft: r.o* **13/8**[1]

-623 **3** ½ **First City**[23] 3030 5-9-5 107........................ PaulHanagan 11 112
(David Simcock) *swtg: hld up in tch: rdn over 1f out: r.o* **40/1**

-216 **4** ½ **Joviality**[21] 3106 3-8-10 105........................ WilliamBuick 10 109
(John Gosden) *chsd ldrs: rdn over 2f out: styd on same pce ins fnl f* **12/1**

1262 **5** 1 ¼ **River Jetez (SAF)**[47] 2340 8-9-5 116........................ PatCosgrave 9 108+
(M F De Kock, South Africa) *hld up: hdwy over 1f out: nt trble ldrs* **14/1**

3-15 **6** 2 ¼ **I'm A Dreamer (IRE)**[23] 3030 4-9-5 110........................ JamieSpencer 3 103+
(David Simcock) *hld up: rdn and swtchd lft over 1f out: sn hung lft: nvr on terms* **9/1**

11-5 **7** 1 **Lily Of The Valley (FR)**[46] 2373 4-9-5 121........................ ChristopheSoumillon 1 100
(J-C Rouget, France) *hld up in tch: swtchd rt over 1f out: nvr trbld ldrs* **9/1**

-330 **8** 3 ¾ **Maqaasid**[54] 2137 3-8-10 110........................ RichardHills 5 89
(John Gosden) *hld up: a in rr* **8/1**[3]

02-1 **9** 7 **Antara (GER)**[35] 2678 5-9-5 116........................ FrankieDettori 6 74
(Saeed Bin Suroor) *lw: chsd ldrs: rdn over 2f out: wkng whn n.m.r over 1f out* **15/2**[2]

-633 **10** nk **Masaya**[15] 3323 3-8-10 96........................ NeilCallan 2 72
(Clive Brittain) *racd keenly: set stdy pce tl qcknd over 3f out: rdn and hdd over 1f out: wknd ins fnl f* **66/1**

6-00 **11** *dist* **Memory (IRE)**[21] 3106 3-8-10 111.. RyanMoore 7 —
(Richard Hannon) *lw: reluctant to s: eventually consented to leave the stalls but a t.o* **8/1**[3]

1m 41.06s (1.06) **Going Correction** +0.15s/f (Good)
WFA 3 from 4yo+ 9lb **11** Ran SP% **116.3**
Speed ratings (Par 117): **100,98,98,97,96 94,93,89,82,82** —
Tote Swingers: 1&2 £11.20, 1&3 £74.30, 2&3 £17.90 CSF £41.75 TOTE £25.10: £5.60, £1.10, £10.10; EX 62.40 Trifecta £3422.50 Pool: £10,776.29 - 2.33 winning units..
Owner K Abdulla **Bred** Juddmonte Farms Ltd **Trained** Newmarket, Suffolk

FOCUS

The eighth Falmouth Stakes since the race was elevated to Group 1 status, and not the strongest edition with only three of the field previously successful at the highest level, although another five had Group 2 or 3 wins to their name. It was an unsatisfactory race too as they dawdled along down the centre of the track. Several weren't able to show their best off the slow pace and the time was nearly five seconds outside the standard, underlining that this is form to treat with caution. Timepiece rates a small personal best.

NOTEBOOK

Timepiece was in the right position throghout in what was a tactical affair. Tom Queally kicked and the filly ran on strongly up the hill, never looking likely to be caught although she did edge to her left. Successful in the Warwickshire Oaks over 1m3f last time, her fourth success at Listed level, she had been found wanting in last year's Oaks on her one previous venture into Group 1 company and this race perhaps fell into her lap, but connections have always rated her. The Matron Stakes and Sun Chariot Stakes are likely aims, and the stiff mile of the latter could suit. (op 14-1)

Sahpresa(USA) warmed up for this with an easy win in a Longchamp Group 3 and looked just about the form pick. The rear of the field was not the place to be in such a falsely run race and although she came home nicely for second, the bird had flown. She can be forgiven this and will remain a force at this level, with a crack at a third successive Sun Chariot Stakes on the Rowley Mile in the autumn the obvious target. (op 2-1)

First City was ridden more prominently than is often the case and she ran on most willingly for third, showing her usual high head carriage. She has never won a Group race, but is well capable of putting that right and she still looks to be improving at the age of five. (op 33-1)

Joviality, the Musidora winner, did best of the 3-y-os, fighting on for fourth having never been too far from the pace. Easier ground may suit and connections have the option of stepping her back up to 1m2f.

River Jetez(SAF) is a genuine Group 1 mare, successful at that level in her native South Africa and runner-up in Singapore and in Dubai. It was reportedly a late decision to run her here and she wasn't fully tuned up, so in the circumstances she ran creditably enough. (tchd 16-1)

I'm A Dreamer(IRE) was another who had no chance ridden the way she was, but she did keep on at the end despite hanging towards the far rail. She is rated more highly than First City in the David Simcock yard and can be afforded another chance, although she may not be quite up to this level. The step up to 1m2f could suit and she may head for the Nassau Stakes next. (op 10-1 tchd 11-1)

Lily Of The Valley(FR), last year's Prix de l'Opera winner, disappointed on her seasonal return behind Sarafina in May and was never a factor here. A mile is probably too sharp for her these days and she prefers genuine cut in the ground. (op 8-1)

Maqaasid, who had no chance from a bad draw in the French Guineas, was tackling older fillies for the first time. She failed to pick up and it could be that 7f will prove her ideal trip. (op 9-1)

Antara(GER) had First City in second when winning the Princess Elizabeth Stakes at Epsom, but was below that form. Well enough placed but one of the first brought under pressure, she was twice runner-up in Group 1 company last year but has yet to win in five runs at the top level now. (op 7-1)

Masaya was allowed an easy lead but wasn't good enough to capitalise on it.

Memory(IRE) was an impressive winner of the Cherry Hinton on this day a year ago, but has not been able to add to that since. She gave no problems before the Coronation Stakes and ran encouragingly, but was back to her old tricks here, proving reluctant to enter the stalls then refusing to come out until the others had long gone. It remains to be seen if connections persevere with this talented filly. (tchd 9-1)

3823 WEATHERBYS E B F MAWATHEEQ MAIDEN STKS 7f

3:35 (3:36) (Class 4) 2-Y-O **£6,469** (£1,925; £962; £481) **Stalls** High

Form RPR

1 **Rougemont (IRE)** 2-9-3 0.. JimmyFortune 8 84+
(Richard Hannon) *athletic: scope: a.p: rdn to ld and hung rt ins fnl f: r.o wl* **25/1**

2 *2* **Sports Section** 2-9-3 0.. FrankieDettori 3 79+
(Mahmood Al Zarooni) *w'like: hld up: hdwy over 1f out: r.o to go 2nd wl ins fnl f: nt rch wnr* **8/1**[3]

3 *¾* **Mickdaam (IRE)** 2-9-3 0.. PaulHanagan 1 77+
(Richard Fahey) *unf: scope: lw: s.i.s: hld up: rdn over 2f out: hdwy over 1f out: r.o to go 3rd wl ins fnl f: nt rch ldrs* **25/1**

3 **4** *¾* **Right Regal (IRE)**[20] 3182 2-9-3 0........................ ChristopheSoumillon 4 75
(Marco Botti) *w'like: chsd ldrs: led over 1f out: edgd rt: rdn and hdd ins fnl f: hung lft and styd on same pce* **4/1**[2]

5 *1 ¼* **Strada Facendo (USA)** 2-9-3 0.. KierenFallon 13 74+
(Luca Cumani) *athletic: s.i.s: sn prom: swtchd rt wl over 1f out: styd on same pce ins fnl f: eased neat fin* **20/1**

6 *nk* **Almuftarris (USA)** 2-9-3 0.. RichardHills 2 71+
(Ed Dunlop) *lengthy: scope: s.i.s: hld up: r.o ins fnl f: nvr nrr* **25/1**

7 *1* **Balty Boys (IRE)** 2-9-3 0.. MichaelHills 11 69
(B W Hills) *strong: lw: led: rdn and hdd over 1f out: no ex ins fnl f* **10/1**

6 **8** *nk* **Fiscal**[13] 3401 2-9-3 0.. WilliamBuick 5 68
(John Gosden) *bit bkwd: hld up: rdn over 1f out: r.o ins fnl f: nrst fin* **8/1**[3]

9 *¾* **Menelik (IRE)** 2-9-3 0.. RichardKingscote 6 66+
(Tom Dascombe) *strong: lw: hld up: rdn over 1f out: r.o ins fnl f: nvr nrr* **33/1**

10 *1 ¾* **Net Whizz (USA)** 2-9-3 0.. RyanMoore 14 62
(Jeremy Noseda) *w'like: scope: prom: rdn over 2f out: wknd ins fnl f* **13/8**[1]

11 *1 ¼* **Police Force (USA)** 2-9-3 0.. MickaelBarzalona 9 59+
(Mahmood Al Zarooni) *w'like: scope: hld up in tch: rdn and hung lft over 2f out: wknd ins fnl f* **11/1**

3 **12** *1 ½* **Hurricane Emerald (IRE)**[13] 3382 2-9-3 0........................ NeilCallan 12 55
(Mark Johnston) *unf: scope: chsd ldr: rdn over 2f out: wknd over 1f out* **20/1**

13 *9* **Hawkino (IRE)** 2-9-3 0.. TomQueally 7 32
(Derek Shaw) *unf: s.s: in rr: wknd over 2f out* **125/1**

14 *23* **King Of Forces** 2-9-3 0.. StevieDonohoe 10 —
(Nick Littmoden) *w'like: prom: lost pl 1/2-way: sn bhd: t.o* **150/1**

1m 27.91s (2.21) **Going Correction** +0.15s/f (Good) **14** Ran SP% **123.2**
Speed ratings (Par 96): **93,90,89,89,87 87,86,85,84,82 81,79,69,43**
Tote Swingers: 1&2 £32.50, 1&3 £61.90, 2&3 £28.40 CSF £204.32 TOTE £33.90: £6.20, £2.90, £5.40; EX 188.50 Trifecta £683.00 Part won. Pool: £923.07 - 0.10 winning units..
Owner Mrs J Wood **Bred** Mrs Clodagh McStay **Trained** East Everleigh, Wilts

FOCUS

A maiden that has a history of throwing up good horses, with the last four winners (Rio De La Plata, Soul City, Elusive Pimpernel and Native Khan) all going on to win at Group level. The potential is there for that run to continue with Rougemont.

NOTEBOOK

Rougemont(IRE) ◆, who was green beforehand, was always nicely positioned tracking the leaders, picked up well when asked and stretched clear in the style of a useful-looking animal. He relished the uphill finish and, as his breeding suggests this trip will be the bare minimum for him - by Montjeu out of a mare by Spectrum who won at up to 1m4f - one suspects he will only improve when faced with a greater test of stamina. He was given a 33-1 quote by Hills for the Guineas and a 25-1 quote for the Derby, and while those prices make little appeal at the moment, the Epsom Classic looks by far the more suitable race on paper. Races like the Vintage, Acomb and Solario Stakes might come into consideration for him next, while connections, who hold him in some regard, apparently see him as a Racing Post Trophy candidate for later in the season. (op 22-1 tchd 20-1)

Sports Section ◆, an attractive half-brother to a 1m4f Grade 1 winning mare in the US and also to Italian Group 1 winner Ancient World, stayed on pleasingly for second and clearly has the pedigree to make up into a smart sort. A maiden should be a formality before he steps up in class. (tchd 15-2 and 9-1)

Mickdaam(IRE) ◆ shaped well considering he was a bit keen early. A half-brother to May Hill and Prix de l'Opera winner Kinnaird, he looks sure to come on plenty for the experience and shouldn't have too many problems getting off the mark.

Right Regal(IRE), who had the benefit of a previous outing, travelled well to 2f out and then edged over to the stands' rail. Given every chance, he simply didn't see out his race as well as the first three, but he was probably taking on some useful newcomers here and he can be found a race. (op 7-2 tchd 3-1)

Strada Facendo(USA) ◆, another who was a bit keen early, showed more than enough on this debut to suggest he has a future. Out of a sister to Prix de la Foret winner Toylsome, this $190,000 purchase looked in need of the outing beforehand and can only improve. (op 16-1)

Almuftarris(USA) ◆, green beforehand, was given an educational ride on his debut, stayed on steadily past beaten horses and hinted at much better to come. His pedigree suggests he'll improve for a mile this year and middle distances at three. (op 22-1 tchd 20-1)

Balty Boys(IRE), an attractive type, showed up well to 2f out before weakening. There's more speed in his pedigree than some of those he took on here and a sharper track might help him. (op 16-1)

Fiscal was another keeping on at the finish. He might be more of a nursery type after one more run. (op 11-1)

Menelik(IRE), who holds a Gimcrack entry, looked like the run would do him good.

Net Whizz(USA), an attractive type who holds the Group 2 entry at York, was disappointing, hanging under pressure and failing to pick up. He's surely capable of better than he showed here. (op 7-4 tchd 9-4)

Police Force(USA), whose jockey wore the Godolphin second colours, is a half-brother to top-class 2-y-o Dream Ahead. Having hung left towards the far-side rail, he ran green and weakened. He can do much better with this outing under his belt. (op 14-1)

Hurricane Emerald(IRE) was still green.

3824 THREE CHIMNEYS MAIDEN STKS 1m 2f

4:10 (4:10) (Class 4) 3-Y-O **£6,469** (£1,925; £962; £481) **Stalls** Centre

Form RPR

1 **Eagles Peak** 3-9-3 0.. RyanMoore 2 91+
(Sir Michael Stoute) *w'like: a.p: rdn to ld ins fnl f: r.o* **9/2**[2]

2-3 **2** *1 ¼* **Thimaar (USA)**[84] 1365 3-9-3 0.. RichardHills 12 88
(John Gosden) *chsd ldrs: led over 2f out: rdn over 1f out: hdd and unable qck ins fnl f* **8/13**[1]

3 *¾* **Dick Doughtywylie** 3-9-3 0.. WilliamBuick 4 87+
(John Gosden) *strong: lw: awkward leaving stalls: sn prom: ev ch wl over 1f out: sn rdn: styd on same pce ins fnl f* **12/1**

4 *1 ¼* **Risk Assessed (IRE)** 3-9-3 0.. FrankieDettori 9 84+
(Mahmood Al Zarooni) *w'like: strong: s.i.s: hld up: hdwy over 2f out: rdn over 1f out: styd on* **14/1**

5 *1 ¼* **Royal Peculiar** 3-9-3 0.. TomQueally 7 82+
(Sir Henry Cecil) *w'like: scope: hld up: hdwy over 3f out: rdn over 1f out: no ex ins fnl f* **12/1**

4 **6** *¾* **Sohar**[21] 3135 3-8-12 0.. KirstyMilczarek 10 75
(James Toller) *w'like: hld up: hdwy over 2f out: rdn over 1f out: no ex ins fnl f* **66/1**

7 *14* **Line of Sight (USA)** 3-9-3 0.. MickaelBarzalona 1 52
(Mahmood Al Zarooni) *lengthy: scope: plld hrd and prom: rdn over 2f out: wknd over 1f out* **22/1**

8 *3 ½* **Meshfi** 3-9-3 0.. NeilCallan 6 45
(Clive Brittain) *rangy: hld up: rdn over 3f out: wknd over 2f out* **50/1**

5305 **9** *4 ½* **Malanos (IRE)**[16] 3291 3-9-3 72.. JimmyFortune 3 36
(David Elsworth) *led over 7f: wknd over 1f out* **22/1**

10 *17* **Ascensive** 3-8-12 0.. StevieDonohoe 5 —
(Ralph Beckett) *mid-div: wknd 4f out: t.o* **40/1**

5 **11** *52* **Strategic Bid**[83] 1409 3-9-3 0..(t) JamieSpencer 11 —
(Paul Cole) *s.i.s: hld up: reins broke after 1f: hung lft: hdwy and hit rails sn after: racd alone far side fnl 8f: up w the pce tl wknd over 3f out: t.o* **11/1**[3]

2m 7.75s (2.25) **Going Correction** +0.15s/f (Good) **11** Ran SP% **125.1**
Speed ratings (Par 102): **97,96,95,94,93 92,81,78,75,61 20**
Tote Swingers: 1&2 £2.30, 1&3 £6.80, 2&3 £3.30 CSF £7.78 TOTE £5.20: £1.90, £1.20, £3.10; EX 11.90 Trifecta £99.40 Pool: £1,169.49 - 8.70 winning units..
Owner K Abdulla **Bred** Juddmonte Farms Ltd **Trained** Newmarket, Suffolk

FOCUS

More than half the field were newcomers in this maiden, an event that has not thrown up many star performers in the last decade or so. Yorkshire Cup winner Manifest, runner-up two years ago, was an exception. This looked a good edition though, with the second setting a high standard although he was short of that level.

Strategic Bid Official explanation: jockey said reins snapped on leaving stalls

3825 TURFTV H'CAP 1m

5:20 (5:23) (Class 3) (0-90,89) 3-Y-O+ **£8,409** (£2,502; £1,250; £625) **Stalls** High

Form RPR

-206 **1** **Albaqaa**[13] 3411 6-9-7 **82**.. PatCosgrave 3 93
(P J O'Gorman) *racd stands' side: hld up: hdwy 2f out: led that side 1f out: r.o to ld overall on post: 1st of 7 in gp* **50/1**

10-2 **2** *nse* **My Freedom (IRE)**[13] 3400 3-9-2 **86**.. FrankieDettori 12 97+
(Saeed Bin Suroor) *racd far side: hld up: hdwy over 2f out: led overall 2f out: sn rdn and hung rt: hdd post: 1st of 12 in gp* **4/1**[1]

00-4 **3** *1 ¼* **Markazzi**[28] 2884 4-9-10 **85**.. RichardHills 17 93
(Sir Michael Stoute) *racd far side: chsd ldrs: rdn over 1f out: r.o: 2nd of 12 in gp* **8/1**[3]

6203 **4** *nse* **Arabian Spirit**[15] 3315 6-9-9 **89**.. LeeTopliss(5) 4 97
(Richard Fahey) *racd stands' side: hld up: hdwy over 2f out: rdn over 1f out: r.o: 2nd of 7 in gp* **14/1**

01-0 **5** *2 ¼* **Capaill Liath (IRE)**[22] 3067 3-9-3 **87**........................(p) PaulHanagan 14 88
(Michael Bell) *racd far side: prom: rdn over 2f out: styd on same pce fnl f: 3rd of 12 in gp* **18/1**

1-01 **6** *nk* **Divine Call**[30] 2822 4-9-5 80........ RyanMoore 5 82+
(William Haggas) *led stands' side: rdn and hdd 1f out: styd on same pce: 3rd of 7 in gp* **7/1**[2]

1613 **7** *½* **Barney Rebel (IRE)**[20] 3159 3-9-3 87........ MichaelHills 8 86
(B W Hills) *racd stands' side: hld up: hdwy over 2f out: rdn and edgd lft over 1f out: styd on same pce: 4th of 7 in gp* **14/1**

0042 **8** *½* **Viva Vettori**[22] 3081 7-9-10 85........ NickyMackay 15 85
(David Elsworth) *dwlt: racd far side: hld up: hdwy over 1f out: rdn and hung rt over 1f out: styd on same pce ins fnl f: 4th of 12 in gp* **16/1**

-530 **9** *½* **Bronze Prince**[23] 3032 4-10-0 89........ WilliamBuick 2 88
(John Gosden) *racd stands' side: chsd ldrs: rdn over 2f out: no ex ins fnl f: 5th of 7 in gp* **11/1**

043 **10** *2* **Merchant Of Medici**[9] 3521 4-9-6 81........ NeilCallan 13 75
(William Muir) *racd far side: hld up: hdwy: nt clr run and swtchd rt over 2f out: rdn over 1f out: no ex ins fnl f: 5th of 12 in gp* **18/1**

0-03 **11** *¾* **Venutius**[30] 2814 4-9-7 87........ DaleSwift(5) 19 79
(Ed McMahon) *laced far side: overall ldr to 1/2-way: led again overall 3f out: sn rdn and hdd: wknd ins fnl f: 6th of 12 in gp* **14/1**

1314 **12** *1 ¾* **Veroon (IRE)**[16] 3276 5-9-8 83........(p) TomQueally 7 71
(James Given) *racd far side: hld up: hdwy over 2f out: rdn and hung rt over 1f out: sn wknd: 7th of 12 in gp* **28/1**

1160 **13** *1* **She Ain't A Saint**[63] 1843 3-8-11 81........ AlanMunro 1 65
(Jane Chapple-Hyam) *racd stands' side: chsd ldrs: rdn over 2f out: wknd fnl f: 6th of 7 in gp* **50/1**

1-46 **14** *1 ½* **John Biscuit (IRE)**[75] 1547 3-9-0 84........ JimmyFortune 6 65
(Andrew Balding) *racd stands' side: plld hrd: w ldr: rdn and hung lft over 1f out: sn wknd: last of 7 in gp* **25/1**

4221 **15** *6* **Whistle On By**[18] 3231 3-8-10 80........ MickaelBarzalona 18 47
(B W Hills) *racd far side: chsd ldrs: overall ldr over 2f out: sn rdn and hdd: wknd fnl f: 8th of 12 in gp* **11/1**

0033 **16** *1 ¾* **Marajaa (IRE)**[21] 3134 9-9-9 84........ StevieDonohoe 10 49
(Willie Musson) *racd far side: hld up: a in rr: 9th of 12 in gp* **16/1**

5140 **17** *6* **Prince Of Sorrento**[11] 3468 4-8-9 70........ RoystonFfrench 16 21
(John Akehurst) *racd far side: hld up in tch: rdn over 2f out: wknd over 1f out: 10th of 12 in gp* **40/1**

0054 **18** *1* **Dhaular Dhar (IRE)**[13] 3397 9-9-11 86........ KierenFallon 11 35
(Jim Goldie) *racd far side: chsd ldr tl overall ldr 1/2-way: hdd 3f out: sn rdn: wknd over 1f out: 11th of 12 in gp* **16/1**

1103 **19** *3 ¾* **Batgirl**[8] 3555 4-8-12 73........ AndreaAtzeni 9 —
(John Berry) *racd far side: hld up: a in rr: rdn over 2f out: sn wknd: last of 12 in gp* **40/1**

1m 40.27s (0.27) **Going Correction** +0.15s/f (Good)
WFA 3 from 4yo+ 9lb **19** Ran SP% **124.5**
Speed ratings (Par 107): **104,103,102,102,100 100,99,99,98,96 95,94,93,91,85 83,77,76,73**
Tote Swingers: 1&2 £35.90, 1&3 £63.30, 2&3 £6.30 CSF £235.00 CT £1881.12 TOTE £71.60: £10.60, £1.80, £2.40, £3.90; EX 416.00 Trifecta £1097.00 Part won. Pool: £1,482.53 - 0.20 winning units..
Owner Racing To The Max **Bred** C Eddington And Partners **Trained** Newmarket, Suffolk

FOCUS
They split into two groups here but neither side seemed to be at an advantage and there was a tight finish as My Freedom wandered under pressure once hitting the front and was caught on the line by Albaqaa. The form looks solid overall.

NOTEBOOK
Albaqaa was rated 98 when claimed on his reappearance, but following two heavy defeats in handicaps subsequently he got to race here off a 16lb lower mark here. Held up behind in the stands' side group, the good gallop suited him, he travelled and pick up well, and with the stands' rail to help in the closing stages he just got to the favourite on the line. He's just as effective over 1m2f.
My Freedom(IRE) ◆ went to the front approaching the furlong marker going easily, but as soon as he was asked to go on he began to hang, first right, then left, then right again, and in the end the ground covered left him vulnerable to the late challenge of the winner. Matched at 1.02 in running, he was clearly the best horse on the day, but looks the type that needs delivering as late as possible. (op 10-3 tchd 3-1)
Markazzi ran a promising race on his reappearance and this was another good run in defeat. He kept on solidly for pressure on the far side and will remain dangerous off this sort of mark in similar company. (op 7-1 tchd 11-2)
Arabian Spirit, second from the stands' side group, has been creeping up the weights but this was another solid effort. The handicapper might just be able to keep him in check, though. (tchd 16-1)
Capaill Liath(IRE), who finished in mid-division in the Britannia last time out when poorly drawn, showed what he can do here. This was only his second start for this stable and there could still be better to come. (op 20-1)
Divine Call, stepping up a furlong in distance, ran well for a long way but didn't get home. He can regain the winning thread back over seven. (op 9-1)
Barney Rebel(IRE) settled off this good gallop and ran a better race as a result. He might not want the ground any quicker than this. (op 11-1)
Viva Vettori likes a decent pace to run off, so this race was run to suit. He remains winless on turf, though. (op 18-1)
Bronze Prince again seemed to find the mile stretching him a bit, and a drop back to 7f might do the trick for him. (op 16-1)
Merchant Of Medici, 1lb well in at the weights, kept on from off the pace without really threatening the principals. He's probably more effective on Polytrack. (op 25-1)
Venutius got to race off the same mark as when second in this race last year, but he was given a far more positive ride this time around and the different tactics didn't work so effectively. (tchd 12-1 and 16-1)
John Biscuit(IRE) Official explanation: jockey said colt ran too free
T/Jkpt: Not won. T/Plt: £129.60 to a £1 stake. Pool:£144,026.00 - 810.78 winning tickets T/Qpdt: £22.70 to a £1 stake. Pool:£7,998.00 - 260.00 winning tickets CR

2932 YORK (L-H)
Friday, July 8

OFFICIAL GOING: Good (good to firm in places; 6.8) changing to good after race 6 (4.55)
Wind: Moderate behind Weather: Cloudy, sunny periods

3826 CAKEMARK E B F MAIDEN STKS 7f
2:05 (2:05) (Class 3) 2-Y-O **£6,469** (£1,925; £962; £481) **Stalls** Low

Form RPR

2 **1** **Rock Supreme (IRE)**[20] 3186 2-9-0 0........ SeanLevey(3) 12 81+
(Michael Dods) *a.p: effrt over 2f out: rdn to chal wl over 1f out: led ent fnl f: drvn and kpt on* **5/2**[1]

2 *nk* **Surfer (USA)** 2-9-3 0........ AhmedAjtebi 13 80+
(Mahmood Al Zarooni) *hld up in tch: hdwy on outer wl over 2f out: rdn to chse ldrs over 1f out: drvn to chal ins fnl f and ev ch tl no ex towards fin* **5/1**[3]

6 **3** *¾* **Saffa Hill (IRE)**[6] 3609 2-9-3 0........ DuranFentiman 7 78
(Tim Easterby) *led: rdn along wl over 2f out: drvn: edgd lft and hdd ent fnl f: kpt on u.p towards fin* **40/1**

3 **4** *nk* **Marching On (IRE)**[21] 3123 2-9-3 0........ StephenCraine 4 78
(Kevin Ryan) *prom: effrt and cl up over 2f out: sn rdn and edgd lft over 1f out: ev ch tl drvn and no ex fnl 100yds* **5/1**[3]

6 **5** *2 ½* **Thirkleby (IRE)**[20] 3161 2-9-3 0........ GrahamGibbons 8 71
(David Barron) *trckd ldrs: effrt wl over 2f out: sn rdn and kpt on same pce appr fnl f* **9/1**

4 **6** *¾* **Ventura Spirit**[27] 2936 2-9-3 0........ TonyHamilton 3 70
(Richard Fahey) *chsd ldrs: rdn along over 2f out: sn one pce* **9/2**[2]

7 *2 ¼* **Daddy Warbucks (IRE)** 2-9-3 0........ AdrianNicholls 10 64
(David Nicholls) *towards rr: pushed along 3f out: rdn and sme hdwy fnl 2f: n.d* **33/1**

50 **8** *5* **La Taniere**[18] 3237 2-9-3 0........ DavidNolan 11 51
(Michael Easterby) *a in rr* **100/1**

0 **9** *¾* **Knight Express**[16] 3274 2-9-3 0........ FrederikTylicki 6 50
(Richard Fahey) *t.k.h early: nvr bttr than midfield* **50/1**

4 **10** *½* **Ptolemaic**[15] 3302 2-9-3 0........ TomEaves 5 48+
(Bryan Smart) *s.i.s and wnt bdly lft s: a in rr* **16/1**

11 *4 ½* **Aliante** 2-8-12 0........ SilvestreDeSousa 1 32
(Mark Johnston) *dwlt: a towards rr* **9/1**

6 **12** *16* **I'll Be Good**[13] 3398 2-9-3 0........ GeorgeBaker 2 —
(Robert Johnson) *chsd ldrs on inner: rdn along 3f out: sn wknd* **40/1**

4 **U** **Margo Channing**[19] 3201 2-8-12 0........ PJMcDonald 9 —
(Micky Hammond) *in rr whn stmbld and uns rdr after 2f* **100/1**

1m 24.99s (-0.31) **Going Correction** -0.025s/f (Good) **13** Ran SP% **117.7**
Speed ratings (Par 98): **100,99,98,98,95 94,92,86,85,85 79,61,—**
Tote Swingers: 1&2 £4.40, 1&3 £16.50, 2&3 £34.20 CSF £14.05 TOTE £3.40: £1.40, £2.30, £6.90; EX 13.40.
Owner Andrew Tinkler **Bred** Tullamaine Castle Stud And Partners **Trained** Denton, Co Durham

FOCUS
Rail moved out 3m on home bend from 1m1f to entrance to straight, adding 7m to races of 1m and beyond. Probably not that strong a maiden by the course's standards, the form probably being no more than fair, and there weren't too many obvious eyecatchers.

NOTEBOOK
Rock Supreme(IRE) had shaped promisingly behind a useful sort at Redcar on his debut and probably didn't have to improve much to go one better. The way he saw things out suggests he'll be suited by 1m before much longer and he's the type to do better still. (tchd 11-4)
Surfer(USA), an American-bred colt, should be adding to his yard's juvenile tally before much longer, running a bit green at halfway but staying on well inside the last. (op 7-1)
Saffa Hill(IRE) improved a fair bit on his recent debut at Beverley and, a scopey sort, appeals as the type to progress with racing.
Marching On(IRE) confirmed he has ability without improving on his Musselburgh form, being one paced off the bridle.
Thirkleby(IRE), green on his debut, showed more here and, in good hands, is the type to improve with experience. Nurseries are an option for him after one more run. (op 15-2)
Ventura Spirit had shaped with a bit of encouragement here on his debut over 6f and might have been expected to make a bit more of an impact upped to a trip which promised to suit. It's still early days, though. (tchd 4-1)
Daddy Warbucks(IRE), a gelded son of Multiplex, showed ability and is likely to improve with this experience under his belt. (op 28-1 tchd 25-1)
Ptolemaic has more ability than his two starts to date suggest, once again missing the break and not being duly unpunished once clearly held. He's a likely type for nurseries later on.
Aliante didn't shape with any immediate promise, but is in good hands and will doubtless show more at some stage. (op 14-1)
I'll Be Good Official explanation: jockey said colt hung left throughout

3827 TYREGIANT.COM SUMMER STKS (GROUP 3) (F&M) 6f
2:35 (2:35) (Class 1) 3-Y-O+ **£29,600** (£11,195; £5,595; £2,795) **Stalls** Centre

Form RPR

5043 **1** **Ladies Are Forever**[20] 3158 3-8-10 98........ SilvestreDeSousa 8 111
(Geoffrey Oldroyd) *chsd ldrs: rdn along 2f out: hdwy to chal over 1f out: drvn ins fional f: kpt on gamely to ld nr line* **9/2**[2]

1-50 **2** *hd* **Dever Dream**[23] 3030 4-9-2 104........ EddieAhern 5 111
(William Haggas) *hld up towards rr: hdwy wl over 2f out: swtchd rt and chsd ldrs wl over 1f out: rdn to ld wl ins fnl f: hdd and no ex nr line* **4/1**[1]

-060 **3** *2* **Rose Blossom**[24] 3010 4-9-2 104........ TonyHamilton 7 105
(Richard Fahey) *led: rdn along wl over 1f out: drvn and edgd lft ent fnl f: hdd & wknd fnl 100yds* **8/1**[3]

65-1 **4** *3 ¼* **Puff (IRE)**[14] 3365 4-9-2 105........ JimCrowley 6 94
(Ralph Beckett) *trckd ldrs: hdwy 1/2-way: chsd ldr 2f out and sn rdn: drvn appr fnl f and kpt on same pce* **9/2**[2]

-060 **5** *hd* **Piccadilly Filly (IRE)**[33] 2754 4-9-2 104........ EddieCreighton 4 94
(Edward Creighton) *chsd ldr: rdn over 2f out: drvn wl over 1f out: kpt on same pce* **20/1**

4014 **6** *3 ½* **Anne Of Kiev (IRE)**[20] 3155 6-9-2 102........(t) GeorgeBaker 1 82
(Jeremy Gask) *swtchd rt s and hld up in rr: effrt and sme hdwy over 2f out: sn rdn and n.d* **9/2**[2]

0251 **7** *½* **Sioux Rising (IRE)**[11] 3459 5-9-2 89........ FrederikTylicki 10 81
(Richard Fahey) *chsd ldrs: rdn along 1/2-way: wknd over 2f out* **16/1**

5-52 **8** *7* **Dubai Media (CAN)**[48] 2298 4-9-2 91........ TomMcLaughlin 3 58
(Ed Dunlop) *hld up towards rr: effrt and sme hdwy 1/2-way: sn rdn and wknd* **14/1**

4031 **9** *8* **Show Rainbow**[41] 2500 3-8-10 98........ SamHitchcott 2 32
(Mick Channon) *chsd ldrs on outer: rdn along 1/2-way: sn outpcd and bhd fnl 2f* **12/1**

69.18 secs (-2.72) **Going Correction** -0.125s/f (Firm)
WFA 3 from 4yo+ 6lb **9** Ran SP% **110.7**
Speed ratings (Par 113): **113,112,110,105,105 100,100,90,80**
Tote Swingers: 1&2 £3.80, 1&3 £5.70, 2&3 £6.70 CSF £21.33 TOTE £5.50: £1.50, £1.80, £2.20; EX 30.90 Trifecta £138.90 Pool: £882.49 - 4.70 winning units..
Owner R C Bond **Bred** Bond Thoroughbred Corporation **Trained** Brawby, N Yorks

FOCUS
A few didn't perform up to expectations in the latest renewal of this Group 3 for fillies and mares, but that's not to take anything away from the leading pair who came clear off a sound pace, the field being well strung out in behind. Just an ordinary standard for the grade.

NOTEBOOK
Ladies Are Forever has taken a bit of time to fully confirm the promise of her close third in last year's Queen Mary, but probably even exceeded that level here, responding well to de Sousa's urgings to nail the runner-up on the line. She's always likely to be a force in races confined to her own sex. (op 6-1)
Dever Dream has a progressive profile bar her blip in the Windsor Forest and wasted no time getting back on track over this shorter trip, seeing off the rest comfortably. She was a dual listed winner last term and is likely to getting her head back in front before long if kept to this sort of level. (op 9-2)

Rose Blossom, successful in this last year, bettered her previous efforts this term without quite getting back to her very best, making the running but having nothing left late on. (op 6-1)
Puff(IRE) had made a winning return to action at Newmarket recently, but came unstuck in this stronger affair, having no obvious excuses save the fact this may have come a bit quick. (op 4-1)
Piccadilly Filly(IRE) wasn't totally discredited without reproducing her very best, and 5f probably suits her better in any case. (tchd 25-1)
Anne Of Kiev(IRE) has been a real success story in the past 12 months or so, but didn't fire on this occasion. She did win a Listed event a few starts back, but her hold-up style is arguably better suited to bigger fields than she'll often encounter in races of this type. Official explanation: jockey said mare was unsuited by the good (good to firm places) ground (op 4-1)
Show Rainbow was disappointing considering she had Ladies Are Forever behind her when winning at Haydock last time. (op 14-1)

3828 GLOBAL TRADING UK RESPONSIBLE PACKAGING STKS (H'CAP) 1m 6f

3:10 (3:10) (Class 4) (0-85,85) 3-Y-O+ £6,469 (£1,925; £962; £481) Stalls Low

Form RPR

6350 **1** **French Hollow**[35] 2696 6-8-9 **66** oh4 FrederikTylicki 7 78
(Tim Fitzgerald) *hld up towards rr: smooth hdwy on inner 4f out: trckd ldrs 3f out: led over 2f out: rdn over 1f out: styd on strly* **66/1**

4-00 **2** *3 ¾* **Bow To No One (IRE)**[27] 2931 5-9-6 **77** JimCrowley 12 83
(Alan Jarvis) *hld up in rr: gd hdwy on wd outside over 3f out: rdn to chse ldrs over 2f out: chse wnr ent fnl f: no imp* **10/1**

-103 **3** *1 ¾* **Bollin Greta**[14] 3344 6-9-7 **78** (t) GrahamGibbons 4 82
(Tim Easterby) *hld up towards rr: stdy hdwy 6f out: trckd ldrs gng wl 3f out: effrt over 2f out: sn rdn and one pce fr over 1f out* **9/1**

144/ **4** *½* **Spiekeroog**[631] 6803 5-9-2 **73** DanielTudhope 10 76
(David O'Meara) *hld up in rr: hdwy 3f out: effrt to chse ldrs and swtchd lft wl over 1f out: styd on ins fnl f: nrst fin* **28/1**

4063 **5** *shd* **Dazzling Light (UAE)**[21] 3127 6-9-5 **79** GaryBartley(3) 19 82
(Jim Goldie) *hld up and bhd: hdwy 4f out: rdn to chse ldrs wl over 1f out: swtchd lft and drvn ins fnl f: kpt on same pce* **12/1**

4232 **6** *3 ¼* **Hallstatt (IRE)**[29] 2846 5-8-13 **70** (t) EddieAhern 17 69+
(John Mackie) *hld up towards rr: hdwy 4f out: swtchd rt and effrt 3f out: rdn to chse ldrs over 2f out: sn drvn and no imp* **14/1**

1202 **7** *hd* **Lady Chaparral**[24] 3023 4-9-6 **77** PJMcDonald 2 75
(George Moore) *trckd ldng pair: smooth hdwy over 4f out: led briefly wl over 2f out: sn rdn and hdd: grad wknd* **7/1**[3]

1413 **8** *3 ¼* **Ravi River (IRE)**[16] 3277 7-9-6 **80** PaulPickard(3) 1 74
(Brian Ellison) *hld up in midfield: hdwy 4f out: rdn to chse ldrs 3f out: drvn over 2f out and no imp* **10/1**

0600 **9** *11* **Ejteyaaz**[16] 3277 4-9-0 **71** (t) TonyHamilton 9 49
(Richard Fahey) *hld up in midfield: hdwy 4f out: rdn along 3f out: n.d* **25/1**

0-14 **10** *7* **Red Fama**[14] 3344 7-9-2 **73** AndrewElliott 5 42
(Neville Bycroft) *midfield: effrt and sme hdwy 4f out: sn rdn and btn* **12/1**

-522 **11** *hd* **Defence Of Duress (IRE)**[22] 3084 3-8-9 **81** MickyFenton 11 49
(Tom Tate) *hld up in tch: smooth hdwy over 5f out: trckd ldrs 4f out: effrt over 3f out: sn rdn and btn over 2f out* **4/1**[1]

-642 **12** *2 ½* **Mason Hindmarsh**[9] 3507 4-8-9 **66** oh2 SamHitchcott 14 31
(Karen McLintock) *chsd ldrs: rdn along 4f out: sn drvn and grad wknd* **16/1**

0220 **13** *2 ½* **Dar Es Salaam**[36] 2262 7-8-13 **70** TomEaves 15 31
(Brian Ellison) *a towards rr* **22/1**

5040 **14** *2 ½* **Valdan (IRE)**[9] 3507 7-8-9 **66** oh7 (bt) AdrianNicholls 18 24
(Maurice Barnes) *a in rr* **66/1**

-203 **15** *5* **Sirgarfieldsobers (IRE)**[24] 3023 5-9-2 **78** NeilFarley(5) 3 29
(Declan Carroll) *chsd ldng pair: rdn along over 4f out: sn wknd* **20/1**

-064 **16** *2* **State Opera**[8] 3551 3-8-13 **85** SilvestreDeSousa 16 33
(Mark Johnston) *cl up: led wl over 3f out: rdn and hdd wl over 2f out: sn wknd* **6/1**[2]

2620 **17** *11* **Hydrant**[8] 3544 5-9-5 **76** GregFairley 8 —
(Peter Salmon) *led: rdn along over 4f out: hdd wl over 3f out and sn wknd* **33/1**

0506 **18** *20* **Why So Serious**[37] 2622 5-8-9 **66** oh16 AndrewMullen 13 —
(Peter Salmon) *in tch: rdn along 7f out: sn lost pl and bhd fnl 3f* **100/1**

2m 58.75s (-1.45) **Going Correction** +0.05s/f (Good)
WFA 3 from 4yo+ 15lb **18 Ran SP% 126.2**
Speed ratings (Par 105): **106,103,102,102,102 100,100,98,92,88 88,86,85,84,81 80,73,62**
Tote Swingers: 1&2 £87.90, 1&3 £73.70, 2&3 £28.10 CSF £622.20 CT £6445.06 TOTE £90.00: £10.90, £3.30, £1.80, £5.80; EX 1851.10.
Owner T J Fitzgerald **Bred** T J Fitzgerald **Trained** Norton, N Yorks

FOCUS

A fair staying handicap and competitive enough for the level. The pace was sound and there's no reason why the form won't hold up. The first six all came from the rear. A turf best from the winner, who was 4lb out of the handicap.
French Hollow Official explanation: trainer said, regarding apparent improvement in form, that the gelding settled better due to the stronger pace.
Defence Of Duress(IRE) Official explanation: trainer's rep said, regarding running, that the colt was unsuited by the good (good to firm places) ground

3829 CARAVAN CHAIRMAN'S CHARITY CUP (H'CAP) 1m 4f

3:45 (3:45) (Class 2) (0-100,98) 3-Y-O+ £11,450 (£3,407; £1,702; £851) Stalls Centre

Form RPR

1-00 **1** **Awsaal**[20] 3156 4-9-9 **93** TadhgO'Shea 3 104+
(John Dunlop) *hld up in rr: smooth hdwy 4f out: led 2f out: sn rdn and styd on wl fnl f* **6/1**[3]

3/2- **2** *½* **Waldvogel (IRE)**[50] 81 7-9-6 **90** TomEaves 1 100
(Nicky Richards) *hld up: hdwy 3f out: swtchd rt and rdn wl over 1f out: drvn to chse wnr ins fnl f: kpt on wl towards fin* **25/1**

0500 **3** *2 ¼* **Itlaaq**[27] 2933 5-9-3 **87** (t) GrahamGibbons 4 94
(Michael Easterby) *hld up in rr: hdwy over 3f out: cl up 2f out: sn rdn and one pce fnl f* **8/1**

2100 **4** *9* **Greyfriars Drummer**[22] 3069 3-8-3 **86** SilvestreDeSousa 7 78
(Mark Johnston) *prom: rdn along on inner 5f out: drvn and sltly outpcd over 3f out: rallied and cl up on outer over 2f out: sn one pce* **5/1**[2]

-042 **5** *3 ¼* **Kathleen Frances**[16] 3277 4-8-13 **83** EddieAhern 6 70
(Mark H Tompkins) *trckd ldrs: smooth hdwy 4f out: led 3f out: sn rdn: hdd 2f out and sn btn* **7/2**[1]

21-6 **6** *3* **Trip The Light**[27] 2932 6-8-13 **83** (v) TonyHamilton 10 65
(Richard Fahey) *trckd ldrs: hdwy and cl up over 3f out: rdn along wl over 2f out: grad wknd* **14/1**

-256 **7** *2 ¾* **Staff Sergeant**[20] 3164 4-8-11 **81** DanielTudhope 2 59
(Jim Goldie) *chsd ldrs on inner: rdn along 5f out: wknd 4f out* **8/1**

3423 **8** *11* **San Cassiano (IRE)**[8] 3542 4-8-13 **83** PJMcDonald 5 43
(Ruth Carr) *led: rdn along 4f out: sn hdd & wknd qckly 3f out* **10/1**

-224 **9** *1 ½* **Right Step**[21] 3107 4-10-0 **98** JimCrowley 9 56
(Alan Jarvis) *hld up in rr: hdwy over 3f out: rdn along wl over 2f out: n.d* **5/1**[2]

2520 **10** *2 ¼* **Nave (USA)**[13] 3396 4-9-6 **90** AdrianNicholls 8 44
(Mark Johnston) *prom: rdn along 4f out: wknd qckly and sn bhd* **9/1**

2m 31.07s (-2.13) **Going Correction** +0.05s/f (Good)
WFA 3 from 4yo+ 13lb **10 Ran SP% 121.7**
Speed ratings (Par 109): **109,108,107,101,99 97,95,87,86,85**
Tote Swingers: 1&2 £21.60, 1&3 £7.90, 2&3 £47.60 CSF £147.40 CT £1223.27 TOTE £8.00: £2.50, £4.90, £2.80; EX 117.70.
Owner Hamdan Al Maktoum **Bred** Meon Valley Stud **Trained** Arundel, W Sussex

FOCUS

A good handicap where they finished well strung out. The form is not rated as positively as it might have been, but the winner was back to his 3yo level.

NOTEBOOK

Awsaal has taken a couple of outings to get back on track after his injury enforced lay-off, but was better than ever here and clearly has the potential to do better still. This just his seventh outing after all. (op 8-1)
Waldvogel(IRE), who came here fit from hurdling, has been given a bit of a chance by the handicapper in relation to what he used to be capable of in this sphere and ran well enough to suggest he could strike at some stage, keeping on well. (op 20-1)
Itlaaq has steadily come down the weights since joining this yard and fared better in a first-time tongue tie, seeing off the rest comfortably. (op 11-1 tchd 12-1)
Greyfriars Drummer doesn't look one of the yard's progressive types at this stage, but there's no doubt he's going to prove fully effective at this trip, sticking to his task having been off the bridle a long way out. (tchd 9-2 and 11-2 in a place)
Kathleen Frances was better than the result, travelling strongly but being soon beaten off the bridle, and leaving the impression this may have come a bit quick after Carlisle. She's gone up 5lb for that, but went well enough for a long way to suggest it won't prove beyond her at some stage. Official explanation: jockey said filly ran flat (op 4-1 tchd 9-2)
Right Step came here in good form, but wasn't close to his best, being beaten too far out to blame lack of stamina. (tchd 11-2)
Nave(USA) dropped out quickly and presumably can't have been right. (op 8-1)

3830 WEWILLBUYYOURCAR.COM STKS (H'CAP) 7f

4:20 (4:23) (Class 3) (0-95,93) 3-Y-O £7,439 (£2,213; £1,106; £553) Stalls Low

Form RPR

231 **1** **Firebeam**[20] 3173 3-8-13 **85** EddieAhern 8 102+
(William Haggas) *mde all: pushed clr 2f out: easily* **7/4**[1]

5-15 **2** *4 ½* **Fityaan**[35] 2684 3-8-8 **80** TadhgO'Shea 7 80
(B W Hills) *a chsng wnr: rdn along 2f out: drvn over 1f out: kpt on: no ch w wnr* **7/1**[3]

0530 **3** *¾* **Rigolleto (IRE)**[22] 3067 3-8-12 **87** MartinHarley(3) 5 85
(Mick Channon) *hld up in rr: hdwy on outer wl over 2f out: sn rdn and styd on wl appr fnl f: nrst fin* **10/1**

1-26 **4** *shd* **Fieldgunner Kirkup (GER)**[32] 2763 3-8-10 **82** GrahamGibbons 1 80
(David Barron) *hld up towards rr: hdwy 1/2-way: rdn to chse ldrs over 2f out: sn drvn and one pce fr wl over 1f out* **8/1**

1450 **5** *1* **Ashva (USA)**[22] 3067 3-8-12 **84** TomEaves 3 79
(Michael Dods) *hld up in tch: hdwy 3f out: rdn along over 2f out: sn drvn and btn* **10/3**[2]

2-00 **6** *1 ½* **Robert The Painter (IRE)**[35] 2684 3-8-11 **83** TonyHamilton 6 74
(Richard Fahey) *trckd ldrs: hdwy on outer and cl up 3f out: sn rdn and wknd wl over 1f out* **12/1**

1335 **7** *3 ¼* **Iceblast**[27] 2935 3-8-3 **82** DavidSimmonson(7) 9 64
(Michael Easterby) *hld up in rr: effrt and sme hdwy wl over 2f out: sn rdn and n.d* **10/1**

2000 **8** *4* **City Legend**[6] 3649 3-8-1 **76** (vt) DeclanCannon(3) 4 47
(Alan McCabe) *hld up: a towards rr* **33/1**

1m 24.35s (-0.95) **Going Correction** -0.025s/f (Good) **8 Ran SP% 111.9**
Speed ratings (Par 104): **104,98,98,97,96 95,91,86**
Tote Swingers: 1&2 £2.60, 1&3 £4.00, 2&3 £6.80 CSF £13.91 CT £91.64 TOTE £2.60: £1.20, £2.20, £3.00; EX 11.20.
Owner Highclere Thoroughbred Racing-Blue Peter **Bred** Dukes Stud & Overbury Stallions Ltd **Trained** Newmarket, Suffolk

FOCUS

A most one-sided handicap, the field finishing in a bit of a heap behind the impressive winner who was value for 6l at least. The opposition was perhaps a bit limited.

NOTEBOOK

Firebeam is going to get hit hard by the handicapper, but it may not stop him as he's evidently a gelding very much on the up, quickening clear in ready fashion. Useful after just four starts, there's more to come and he could be making his mark outside handicaps before long. (op 9-4 tchd 5-2 in a place)
Fityaan put a below-par run at Epsom behind him, getting back to the form he showed when scoring at Warwick but being simply no match for a progressive rival. (op 9-1)
Rigolleto(IRE) is starting to look exposed, but at least found this easier than the Britannia. He needs a bit more help from the assessor, though. (op 14-1)
Fieldgunner Kirkup(GER) put a blip at Pontefract behind him, as expected being suited by the step up to 7f. He may still have more to offer. (op 11-2)
Ashva(USA) had been a bit better than the result in the Britannia, but didn't have any obvious excuse here, despite the market speaking in his favour. (op 3-1 tchd 11-4)
Robert The Painter(IRE) hasn't gone on as expected so far this term. (tchd 14-1)
Iceblast was below form despite being dropped back to a more suitable trip. (op 7-1)

3831 GEORGE AND PAULINE BLADES GOLDEN WEDDING STKS (CLAIMING STAKES) 1m 208y

4:55 (4:55) (Class 4) 3-Y-O+ £5,239 (£1,559; £779; £389) Stalls Low

Form RPR

6362 **1** **Charlie Cool**[7] 3576 8-9-2 87 (b) PJMcDonald 7 88
(Ruth Carr) *trckd ldrs: smooth hdwy 4f out: trckd ldrs 3f out: rdn to ld wl over 1f out and sn qcknd clr: styd on wl fnl f* **2/1**[2]

6164 **2** *1 ¾* **Extraterrestrial**[15] 3315 7-9-3 91 FrederikTylicki 2 85
(Richard Fahey) *hld up in tch: hdwy over 3f out and sn trcking ldrs: swtchd rt and rdn to chse wnr wl over 1f out: drvn edgd lft and no imp ins fnl f* **10/11**[1]

0456 **3** *6* **Lord Raglan (IRE)**[20] 3170 4-9-5 68 AndrewElliott 1 74
(Mrs K Burke) *led: rdn along and hdd 4f out: cl up and drvn over 2f out: kpt on same pce* **18/1**

-000 **4** *1 ½* **Scarab (IRE)**[49] 2259 6-8-7 59 (p) LukeStrong(7) 3 66?
(Tim Walford) *hld up in tch: hdwy 3f out: rdn over 2f out: sn drvn and one pce* **40/1**

2113 **5** *6* **Fremen (USA)**[30] 2807 11-9-0 77 AdrianNicholls 5 52
(David Nicholls) *trckd ldr: cl up 1/2-way: slt ld 4f out: rdn along 3f out: drvn jst over 2f out: sn hdd & wknd* **7/1**[3]

240 **6** *7* **Dabbers Ridge (IRE)**[16] 3275 9-8-11 73 GaryBartley(3) 4 37
(Ian McInnes) *a in rr* **25/1**

0460 **7** 3 ¾ **Tukitinyasok (IRE)**[84] 1373 4-9-0 **81**.................................... TomEaves 6 29
(Clive Mulhall) *chsd ldng pair: rdn along over 4f out: wknd over 3f out: sn bhd* **33/1**

1m 52.71s (0.71) **Going Correction** +0.05s/f (Good) **7** Ran SP% **112.7**
Speed ratings (Par 105): **98,96,91,89,84 78,74**
Tote Swingers: 1&2 £1.10, 1&3 £4.50, 2&3 £2.80 CSF £3.99 TOTE £2.40: £1.50, £1.30; EX 4.40.
Owner Middleham Park Racing Xxiv **Bred** Middle Park Stud Ltd **Trained** Huby, N Yorks

FOCUS
Pretty useful efforts from the leading pair who came well clear. They set a high standard but neither matched their recent best.

3832 WARBURTONS, BAKERS BORN & BRED APPRENTICE H'CAP 5f
5:30 (5:30) (Class 4) (0-80,80) 3-Y-0+ **£5,239** (£1,559; £779; £389) **Stalls** Centre

Form RPR
0125 **1** **Nomoreblondes**[7] 3579 7-8-12 **68**.....................................(v) LMcNiff[(2)] 9 79
(Paul Midgley) *cl up: led 1/2-way: rdn clr wl over 1f out: kpt on strly* **10/1**
-000 **2** 3 **Pavershooz**[38] 2590 6-9-12 **80**.. BrianToomey 8 80
(Noel Wilson) *chsd ldrs: hdwy 2f out: rdn to chse wnr ins fnl f: no imp* **14/1**
2-1 **3** 1 ¼ **Jamaican Bolt (IRE)**[80] 1465 3-9-0 **77**...................... JustinNewman[(4)] 5 71
(Bryan Smart) *trckd ldrs: hdwy over 2f out: rdn to chse wnr over 1f out: sn drvn and one pce* **2/1**[1]
1-50 **4** 1 ½ **Mayoman (IRE)**[28] 2890 6-9-12 **80**....................................(v) NeilFarley 10 70
(Declan Carroll) *in tch: hdwy over 2f out: sn rdn and kpt on same pce* **10/1**
0110 **5** 2 ½ **Lucky Art (USA)**[14] 3367 5-9-9 **79**................................ ShaneBKelly[(2)] 3 60
(Ruth Carr) *led: hdd 1/2-way: sn rdn along and wknd* **5/1**[2]
-063 **6** nk **Black Annis Bower**[14] 3360 3-8-7 **70**.................. DavidSimmonson[(4)] 2 48
(Michael Easterby) *racd wd: in tch: hdwy to chse ldrs 1/2-way: sn rdn and one pce fr wl over 1f out* **16/1**
0405 **7** ½ **Sonny Red (IRE)**[22] 3083 7-9-6 **80**.......................... ShirleyTeasdale[(6)] 4 58
(David Nicholls) *a towards rr* **14/1**
110 **8** hd **Sharp Shoes**[15] 3305 4-8-9 **67**.....................................(p) LauraBarry[(4)] 12 45
(Ann Duffield) *prom: rdn along over 2f out: sn wknd* **12/1**
6002 **9** ¾ **Mullglen**[25] 2987 5-9-1 **69**...(p) LanceBetts 6 44
(Tim Easterby) *in tch: rdn along 1/2-way: sn wknd* **13/2**[3]
46-0 **10** 1 ¼ **Commanche Raider (IRE)**[92] 1205 4-9-5 **75**.......... GarryWhillans[(2)] 11 46
(Michael Dods) *a in rr* **20/1**
1500 **11** ½ **Highland Warrior**[15] 3305 12-8-13 **71**..................... EdmondLinehan[(4)] 1 40
(Paul Midgley) *a in rr* **20/1**
0125 **12** 1 **Angelo Poliziano**[22] 3087 5-9-9 **79**...........................(v) RosieJessop[(2)] 7 44
(Ann Duffield) *dwlt: a bhd* **16/1**

58.02 secs (-1.28) **Going Correction** -0.125s/f (Firm)
WFA 3 from 4yo+ 5lb **12** Ran SP% **123.8**
Speed ratings (Par 105): **105,100,98,95,91 91,90,90,89,87 86,84**
Tote Swingers: 1&2 £15.40, 1&3 £6.80, 2&3 £5.80. Tote Super 7: Win: Not won. Place: Not won. CSF £148.33 CT £396.15 TOTE £15.60: £3.30, £4.00, £1.60; EX 206.30.
Owner Anthony D Copley **Bred** P John And Redmyre Bloodstock **Trained** Westow, N Yorks

FOCUS
A fair sprint in which few ever got competitive, the winner bolting up. Her run could rate higher if anything.
T/Plt: £171.20 to a £1 stake. Pool:£79,783.00 - 340.17 winning tickets T/Qpdt: £48.90 to a £1 stake. Pool:£4,814.00 - 72.80 winning tickets JR

3833 - 3839a (Foreign Racing) - See Raceform Interactive

3793 ASCOT (R-H)
Saturday, July 9

OFFICIAL GOING: Good (straight 10.1, round 9.5)
Wind: Moderate, across. Weather: Cloudy

3840 CENTRAL SAINT MARTINS DESIGN CHALLENGE STKS (H'CAP) 1m (R)
1:55 (1:57) (Class 4) (0-85,85) 3-Y-0+ **£5,175** (£1,540; £769; £384) **Stalls** High

Form RPR
-056 **1** **Directorship**[13] 3436 5-9-10 **84**.................................... FergusSweeney 10 93
(Patrick Chamings) *in rr: rapid hdwy on outside over 1f out: str run and hung rt thrght fnl f: led fnl 75yds: hld on all out* **16/1**
3046 **2** hd **Cruiser**[23] 3067 3-9-2 **85**.. LukeMorris 3 92
(William Muir) *in rr: hdwy on ins fr 2f out: str run to chal ins fnl f and stl upsides clsng stages: edgd lft and no ex last strides* **9/2**[1]
1121 **3** ¾ **Koo And The Gang (IRE)**[21] 3188 4-9-0 **77**..................... SeanLevey[(3)] 8 84
(Brian Ellison) *led: rdn over 2f out and kpt on wl to hold advantage tl hdd and no ex fnl 75yds: btn whn tightened up cl home* **8/1**
5626 **4** ½ **First Cat**[22] 3134 4-9-8 **82**.. PatDobbs 2 88
(Richard Hannon) *t.k.h: hld up in rr: hdwy 2f out: n.m.r over 1f out: styd on ins fnl f: nt gng pce to rch ldrs* **15/2**
-016 **5** 1 ¼ **Aciano (IRE)**[17] 3285 3-8-12 **81**.. ShaneKelly 9 82
(Brian Meehan) *chsd ldr: rdn 2f out: wknd fnl 120yds* **10/1**
1-56 **6** ¾ **Muntasib (USA)**[38] 2607 3-9-1 **84**..................................... TadhgO'Shea 1 83
(Marcus Tregoning) *chsd ldrs: rdn 2f out: n.m.r whn fading 1f out* **16/1**
5054 **7** 1 **Nazreef**[17] 3290 4-9-10 **84**..(t) TravisBlock 4 83
(Hughie Morrison) *chsd ldrs: rdn over 2f out: wknd ins fnl f* **5/1**[2]
0061 **8** ¾ **Shamir**[17] 3285 4-9-10 **84**... IanMongan 7 81
(Jo Crowley) *chsd ldrs towards outside: rdn over 2f out: wknd ins fnl f* **8/1**
3113 **9** 1 ½ **Sunset Kitty (USA)**[21] 3180 4-9-10 **84**.............................. AdamKirby 5 78
(Walter Swinburn) *trckd ldrs: n.m.r 2f out: sn rdn: wknd appr fnl f* **7/1**
0220 **10** ¾ **Tartan Trip**[28] 2933 4-9-10 **84**.......................................(b[1]) DavidProbert 6 76
(Andrew Balding) *sn in tch: nt clr run 2f out: sn rdn and btn* **13/2**[3]

1m 43.56s (2.86) **Going Correction** +0.225s/f (Good)
WFA 3 from 4yo+ 9lb **10** Ran SP% **115.5**
Speed ratings (Par 105): **94,93,93,92,91 90,89,88,87,86**
toteswingers:1&2:£15.30, 2&3:£7.10, 1&3:£34.90 CSF £85.88 CT £645.65 TOTE £21.20: £5.90, £2.00, £2.00; EX 123.50.
Owner Mrs R Lyon,Mrs P Hayton,P R Chamings **Bred** Mrs D O Joly **Trained** Baughurst, Hants
■ The jockeys wore specially designed 'fruit machine' silks in this race as part of a Racing For Change initiative.

FOCUS
Following a dry night the ground was given as good, and the winning jockey after the first race confirmed it as good, safe ground. The Round course rail was moved 3-4yds in from the 1m4f start to the home bend, where the rail was moved 8yds in to past the winning line, increasing distances by approx 2m - 25yds, 1m4f - 20yds, 1m -10yds. A competitive handicap but things got quite tight against the rail. The winner sets the standard.

Tartan Trip Official explanation: trainer said gelding had a breathing problem

3841 TOTEPOOL H'CAP 6f
2:30 (2:30) (Class 2) 3-Y-0+
£31,125 (£9,320; £4,660; £2,330; £1,165; £585) **Stalls** High

Form RPR
6000 **1** **Noble Citizen (USA)**[22] 3109 6-8-6 **87**...........................(b) MartinLane 18 98
(David Simcock) *s.i.s: in rr: hdwy on stands' rail 2f out: led appr fnl f: styd on wl u.p* **33/1**
0462 **2** ¾ **Lutine Bell**[7] 3627 4-8-11 **92**..(b) PatDobbs 11 101
(Mike Murphy) *towards rr: hdwy and nt clr run over 1f out: styd on strly ins fnl f: kpt on to chse wnr clsng stages but no imp* **16/1**
4-20 **3** 1 **Mac's Power (IRE)**[21] 3155 5-9-5 **100**...........................(t) PatCosgrave 16 105
(James Fanshawe) *s.i.s: in rr: hdwy 2f out: sn n.m.r: qckng fnl f and sn chsng wnr but no imp: one pce into 3rd clsng stages* **9/2**[2]
-365 **4** ½ **Racy**[15] 3357 4-8-9 **90**.. MichaelHills 17 94
(Kevin Ryan) *led: tended to edge rt over 3f out: rdn 2f out: hdd appr fnl f and styd on one pce* **16/1**
4-10 **5** 1 ¾ **Imperial Guest**[21] 3155 5-9-0 **98**.............................. AshleyHamblett[(3)] 13 96+
(George Margarson) *sn chsng ldrs: rdn and kpt on fnl f but no imp on ldng quartet* **12/1**
0000 **6** 1 **Below Zero (IRE)**[9] 3535 4-7-11 **83**............................... KieranO'Neill[(5)] 19 78
(Mark Johnston) *chsd ldrs: rdn over 2f out: wknd ins fnl f* **50/1**
-061 **7** 1 ¾ **Dungannon**[27] 2954 4-9-0 **95**.. DavidProbert 15 84
(Andrew Balding) *towards rr but in tch: hdwy fr 2f out: kpt on same pce ins fnl f* **8/1**[3]
4005 **8** 1 ½ **Baby Strange**[14] 3379 7-8-5 **89**...................................... KierenFox[(3)] 9 74
(Derek Shaw) *s.i.s: in rr: hdwy ins fnl 2f: nvr gng pce to rch ldrs* **25/1**
0-03 **9** ¾ **R Woody**[14] 3410 4-8-11 **92**.. ShaneKelly 6 74
(Dean Ivory) *chsd ldrs: rdn 2f out: outpcd ins fnl f* **22/1**
0003 **10** ¾ **Johannes (IRE)**[14] 3395 8-8-11 **92**.................................. RichardMullen 4 72
(Richard Fahey) *racd far side: chsd ldr and led that gp 2f out but nvr gng pce of main bunch: nvr any ch but fin first in gp* **25/1**
1125 **11** ¾ **Singeur (IRE)**[14] 3395 4-9-2 **97**.. LukeMorris 12 74
(Robin Bastiman) *in rr: hdwy over 1f out: nvr gng pce to rch ldrs* **20/1**
3003 **12** hd **Secret Witness**[7] 3627 5-8-11 **92**..........................(b) TomMcLaughlin 2 69
(Ronald Harris) *s.i.s: racd far side and sn in tch w that gp but nvr gng pce of main bunch: fin 2nd in gp* **18/1**
00-0 **13** 1 **Edge Closer**[14] 3410 7-8-12 **93**.. RobertHavlin 14 67
(David Arbuthnot) *chsd ldrs: rdn 2f out: wknd ins fnl f* **40/1**
1041 **14** nk **Piazza San Pietro**[7] 3627 5-8-12 **93**.................................. IanMongan 7 66
(Andrew Haynes) *in rr: rdn and hdwy 2f out: chsd ldrs over 1f out: wknd ins fnl f* **20/1**
0006 **15** 3 ¼ **Courageous (IRE)**[22] 3109 5-8-3 **89**............................ RyanClark[(5)] 5 51
(David Nicholls) *chsd ldrs tl wknd ins fnl 2f* **20/1**
-313 **16** 2 ¾ **L'Ami Louis (IRE)**[42] 2508 3-7-12 **85** oh2................ FrankieMcDonald 10 37
(Henry Candy) *chsd ldrs 4f* **11/1**
/0-5 **17** 4 **Tamagin (USA)**[63] 1891 8-9-10 **105**.........................(p) StevieDonohoe 3 46
(Lydia Pearce) *racd far side and led that gp tl 2f out: nvr any ch w main bunch and wknd sn after: fin 3rd in gp* **80/1**
1020 **18** 1 ¾ **Mon Brav**[15] 3357 4-8-4 **88** ow1.................................... SeanLevey[(3)] 1 23
(Brian Ellison) *racd far side: chsd ldrs that gp but nvr on terms w main bunch: no ch fr over 2f out: fin last of four in gp* **10/1**
11-1 **19** 4 ½ **Ritual (IRE)**[8] 3588 4-8-6 **90**....................................... JohnFahy[(3)] 8 —
(Jeremy Noseda) *pressed ldrs: rdn 2f out: sn btn* **4/1**[1]

1m 13.43s (-0.97) **Going Correction** +0.075s/f (Good)
WFA 3 from 4yo+ 6lb **19** Ran SP% **126.3**
Speed ratings (Par 109): **109,108,106,106,103 102,100,98,97,96 95,94,93,93,88 85,79,77,71**
toteswingers:1&2:£109.20, 2&3:£13.10, 1&3:£30.10 CSF £457.14 CT £2914.92 TOTE £31.00: £5.40, £4.50, £1.90, £4.40; EX 1081.70.
Owner Khalifa Dasmal **Bred** Don M Robinson **Trained** Newmarket, Suffolk

FOCUS
They split into two groups, with four racing towards the far rail and the majority coming up the stands' rail. The action developed on the stands' side. The winner was back to last year's International Handicap form.

NOTEBOOK
Noble Citizen(USA) is an Ascot specialist and, while the ground went against him at the Royal meeting, he showed what he was capable of in the Victoria Cup two starts earlier and got to race off a 5lb lower mark here. Dropping back to 6f for the first time in two years, he got a nice tow on the stands' side and was always holding his challengers once he hit the front. So much better here than at any other track, he'll always be of some interest in big-field events here. (op 28-1)
Lutine Bell travelled well out the back on the stands' side and came through to have his chance, but the winner kept pulling out more. He is building up a string of consistent efforts. (tchd 18-1)
Mac's Power(IRE), first on the wrong side in the Wokingham, had to make his challenge a bit further away from the rail than the first two, which may have been a disadvantage. He ran a respectable race in defeat once again and has one of these in him. (op 4-1)
Racy set the pace on the stands' side and took a bit of passing, showing he's just as effective over 6f as he is over the minimum trip. (op 18-1)
Imperial Guest, another with good form at this track, disappointed in the Wokingham but bounced back with a solid effort here. He has little room for manoeuvre off his current mark, though. (op 14-1)
Below Zero(IRE) had the stands' rail to help throughout, which looked to be quite an advantage. (op 66-1)
Dungannon ran a solid enough race off a 5lb higher mark but slightly easier ground might have suited him better. (op 9-1)
Ritual(IRE) saw plenty of daylight on the outer of the stands' side group but dropped out so tamely from 2f out that there must have been a problem as this was clearly not his true running. Official explanation: jockey said race came too soon (tchd 7-2)

3842 RUDDY NURSERY 6f
3:05 (3:05) (Class 4) 2-Y-0 **£6,469** (£1,925; £962; £481) **Stalls** High

Form RPR
01 **1** **Sovereign Debt (IRE)**[27] 2953 2-9-7 **81**............................ AdamKirby 4 86+
(Michael Bell) *in tch: hdwy on outside over 2f out: drvn to take narrow ld 1f out: edgd lft ins fnl f: rdn out* **5/4**[1]
61 **2** ¾ **Responsive**[17] 3270 2-9-6 **80**.. PatDobbs 2 83+
(Hughie Morrison) *hld up in rr: hdwy 2f out and sn chalng between horses to hold ev ch u.p fr 1f out: pushed mariginally lft clsng stages and one pce* **8/1**[3]
4613 **3** 1 **My Lucky Liz (IRE)**[13] 3435 2-8-13 **73**.............................. MartinLane 7 73
(David Simcock) *chsd ldrs: rdn and ev ch fr 2f out: pushed marginally lft clsng stages whn hld by ldng duo* **13/2**[2]
6551 **4** 2 **Faraway**[8] 3584 2-8-2 **67**.. KieranO'Neill[(5)] 9 61
(David Evans) *led tl narrowly hdd 2f out: styd pressing for ld and stl upsides 1f out: edgd lft into rail ins fnl f: hld whn hmpd cl home* **17/2**

052 **5** ½ **Brimstone Hill (IRE)**[41] 2523 2-9-3 **77** MichaelHills 6 70
(B W Hills) *hld up in rr: nt clr fr 2f out: and swtchd rt towards outside fnl f: kpt on but nvr gng pce to get into contention* **8/1**[3]

4301 **6** ¾ **Marygold**[18] 3249 2-9-0 **74** LukeMorris 3 66
(John Akehurst) *pressed ldr: chal 3f out tl slt ld 2f out: hdd 1f out but ev ch: btn whn crossed and hmpd wl ins fnl f* **16/1**

641 **7** 2¼ **My Solitaire (IRE)**[22] 3117 2-8-12 **75** JohnFahy(3) 8 59
(Clive Cox) *chsd ldrs: rdn over 2f out: wknd over 1f out* **9/1**

2101 **8** 8 **Selinda**[9] 3554 2-8-1 **61** DavidProbert 5 21
(Mick Channon) *chsd ldrs: ev ch 2f out: sn wknd* **25/1**

5224 **9** ½ **Night Angel (IRE)**[26] 2992 2-9-1 **75** (b) JamesMillman 1 33
(Rod Millman) *chsd ldrs: ev ch over 2f out: sn wknd* **22/1**

1m 15.19s (0.79) **Going Correction** +0.075s/f (Good) **9** Ran SP% **114.6**
Speed ratings (Par 96): **97,96,94,92,91 90,87,76,76**
toteswingers:1&2:£1.70, 2&3:£8.00, 1&3:£1.80 CSF £11.73 CT £48.32 TOTE £2.30: £1.10, £2.50, £1.80; EX 7.70.
Owner Lawrie Inman **Bred** Yeomanstown Stud **Trained** Newmarket, Suffolk
■ The 'official' ratings shown next to each horse are estimated and for information purposes only.
■ Stewards' Enquiry : Adam Kirby two-day ban: careless riding (Jul 24-25)

FOCUS
The market spoke in favour of the winner and it was a one-two for the top weights.

NOTEBOOK
Sovereign Debt(IRE) looked good winning his maiden at Doncaster last time and won a shade more cosily here than the margin suggests. He looks capable of scoring again in nursery company as the handicapper cannot punish him too much for landing this fairly narrowly. He'll get another furlong in time. (op 11-8 tchd 6-5 and 6-4 in a place)
Responsive, like the winner, came from off the pace to challenge late and landed the exacta for the two top weights. She holds a Lowther entry, and while that would be flying high, a similar race to this looks well within her grasp on this evidence. (op 15-2)
My Lucky Liz(IRE) battled on gamely for pressure and posted a solid effort. She has a fine attitude, which will stand her in good stead. (op 15-2)
Faraway, who had the rail to help, was tightened up inside the last when battling for third place. Winner of a seller last time out, it'll be a surprise if his new trainer doesn't find a race for him. (op 11-1 tchd 8-1)
Brimstone Hill(IRE) was denied a clear run approaching the final furlong and was switched out wider. He didn't make much progress from there, though, and proved slightly disappointing. There's probably better to come. (op 10-1 tchd 11-1)
Marygold had to be snatched up slightly when tightened up for room inside the last but was fighting a losing battle at the time. (op 14-1)

3843 TOTESPORT.COM SUMMER MILE STKS (GROUP 2) 1m (R)
3:45 (3:46) (Class 1) 4-Y-0+ **£56,710** (£21,500; £10,760; £5,360; £2,690) **Stalls** Low

Form RPR

-140 **1** **Dick Turpin (IRE)**[48] 2343 4-9-4 124 PatDobbs 4 123+
(Richard Hannon) *hld up 4th and trcking ldrs: smooth hdwy on outside fr 2f out to ld 1f out: rdn and styd on strly ins fnl f* **2/1**[2]

-231 **2** ¾ **Fanunalter**[35] 2713 5-9-1 110 AdamKirby 5 118
(Marco Botti) *hld up in cl 5th: stdy hdwy on outside fr 2f out to chse wnr fnl f: styd on wl u.p but no imp clsng stages* **9/1**

-311 **3** 2¼ **Side Glance**[61] 1948 4-9-1 115 DavidProbert 1 113+
(Andrew Balding) *t.k.h and trckd ldrs in cl 3rd: ct in pocket as pce qcknd over 2f out and sn edging rt: pushed along and nt clr run tl kpt on fnl f: tk 3rd clsng stages but nvr gng pce of ldng duo* **6/4**[1]

1-35 **4** ¾ **Red Jazz (USA)**[56] 2101 4-9-1 118 MichaelHills 3 111
(B W Hills) *trckd ldr: chal ins fnl 3f tl slt ld ins fnl 2f: hdd 1f out: sn outpcd and lost 3rd clsng stages* **7/2**[3]

2500 **5** 2½ **Fareer**[24] 3032 5-9-1 107 TadhgO'Shea 2 105
(Ed Dunlop) *sn led: jnd ins fnl 3f: hdd ins fnl 2f: wknd appr fnl f* **20/1**

1m 41.48s (0.78) **Going Correction** +0.225s/f (Good) **5** Ran SP% **110.3**
Speed ratings (Par 115): **105,104,102,101,98**
CSF £18.37 TOTE £2.50: £1.40, £3.40; EX 14.10.
Owner John Manley **Bred** John McEnery **Trained** East Everleigh, Wilts

FOCUS
Not the strongest Group 2 race, but the winner was the pick at the weights and won readily enough. He's rated back close to his best, although it was a bit of a messy race.

NOTEBOOK
Dick Turpin(IRE) was deposed as favourite by Side Glance on account of his poor effort in France last time and the fact that the ground wasn't as soft as connections had hoped for. Despite the negative vibes and a steady early pace, he travelled through the race like the best horse and picked up well once his rider went for him. Dobbs didn't have to get overly serious to maintain his advantage over the runner-up in the closing stages and, while the bare form certainly doesn't compare with Dick Turpin's best efforts, he got his season back on track. It wouldn't be a surprise if he's off on abroad again next in search of a soft-ground Group 1. (op 15-8 tchd 9-4)
Fanunalter had 11lb to find with Dick Turpin strictly on the ratings and, while the winner doesn't appear to have run to his best, this was probably still a career-best effort as he picked up well from the back of the field to chase the winner home. (op 17-2 tchd 8-1)
Side Glance was disappointing on the face of it but the steady early gallop didn't suit him and he raced far more keenly than ideal. He was also short of room in the straight and when the sprint for home began he was poorly positioned. He's better than this. (op 2-1 tchd 9-4 in places)
Red Jazz(USA) held the ideal position to the leader's outer but was in front only briefly before the winner took his measure. His best distance is 7f, so the Lennox Stakes looks a likely target again. (op 10-3)
Fareer, eighth in the Hunt Cup last time out, enjoyed the run of the race in front but wasn't anywhere near good enough to take advantage. (op 16-1)

3844 MITIE TOTAL SECURITY MANAGEMENT H'CAP 1m 2f
4:20 (4:20) (Class 3) (0-90,89) 3-Y-0+ **£8,409** (£2,502; £1,250; £625) **Stalls** Low

Form RPR

-622 **1** **All Action (USA)**[29] 2884 4-9-13 **88** IanMongan 6 105
(Sir Henry Cecil) *trckd ldrs: led ins fnl 2f: drvn clr appr fnl f: comf* **3/1**[1]

614 **2** 4½ **Mashaaref**[28] 2925 3-8-11 **83** TadhgO'Shea 5 91
(Roger Varian) *trckd ldrs: wnt 2nd 1f out: kpt on but nvr any ch w wnr* **3/1**[1]

01 **3** ½ **Arch Fire (USA)**[28] 2930 3-9-1 **87** (v) RichardMullen 14 94
(Sir Michael Stoute) *pushed along sn after s: in rr: hdwy fr 2f out: rdn and styd on wl thrght fnl f to cl on 2nd but nvr any ch w wnr* **5/1**[2]

2200 **4** 1¾ **Resentful Angel**[38] 2604 6-9-12 **87** PatDobbs 11 90
(Pat Eddery) *in tch: tk 4th ins fnl 2f and styd on same pce fnl f* **16/1**

5001 **5** ½ **Ellemujie**[15] 3366 6-9-10 **85** (p) ShaneKelly 2 87
(Dean Ivory) *in rr but in tch: hdwy 2f out: styd on fnl f but nvr gng pce to rch plcd horses* **14/1**

2-02 **6** ½ **Hurakan (IRE)**[29] 2872 5-8-12 **73** (t) TonyCulhane 4 74+
(George Baker) *in rr: hdwy and nt clr run over 2f out: styd on fnl f: nvr a threat* **25/1**

1602 **7** nk **Edgewater (IRE)**[12] 3466 4-9-0 **78** KierenFox(3) 13 78
(John Akehurst) *in rr: hdwy on outside over 2f out: styd on fnl f but nvr a danger* **16/1**

43/2 **8** shd **Vimiero (USA)**[30] 2848 4-9-6 **81** AdamKirby 1 81
(Walter Swinburn) *hld up in mid-div: hdwy on ins over 2f out: nvr rchd ldrs but shkn up and styd on clsng stages* **8/1**[3]

0305 **9** ¾ **Licence To Till (USA)**[20] 3203 4-9-10 **85** FergusSweeney 12 84
(Mark Johnston) *chsd ldr tl led ins fnl 3f: hdd ins fnl 2f: lost 2nd 1f out and sn wknd* **9/1**

0040 **10** 17 **Silver Grey (IRE)**[15] 3356 4-9-12 **87** (p) MartinLane 8 52
(Roger Ingram) *in rr: sme hdwy on outside over 3f out: sn wknd* **28/1**

6300 **11** 1 **Kidlat**[21] 3164 6-9-7 **82** PatCosgrave 9 45
(Alan Bailey) *sn led: hdd ins fnl 3f: wknd qckly 2f out* **66/1**

0301 **12** 59 **Denton (NZ)**[17] 3286 8-9-13 **88** (t) LukeMorris 7 —
(Jeremy Gask) *chsd ldrs tl wknd qckly over 2f out: virtually p.u ins fnl f* **16/1**

2m 7.35s (0.35) **Going Correction** +0.225s/f (Good)
WFA 3 from 4yo+ 11lb **12** Ran SP% **120.9**
Speed ratings (Par 107): **107,103,103,101,101 100,100,100,99,86 85,38**
toteswingers:1&2:£3.80, 2&3:£2.90, 1&3:£3.70 CSF £11.11 CT £44.64 TOTE £4.00: £1.70, £2.10, £1.80; EX 17.70.
Owner K Abdulla **Bred** Juddmonte Farms Inc **Trained** Newmarket, Suffolk

FOCUS
The two unexposed 3yos at the foot of the weights looked interesting on paper but in the end they could only fill the places behind runaway winner All Action, who posted a clear personal best. It was the pick of the round course times.

NOTEBOOK
All Action(USA), who had run well in defeat in his previous two starts, showed improved form on his first visit to Ascot. He is an American-bred son of Storm Cat and whether the track was the only reason for his improvement is debatable, but he will certainly be interesting whenever he returns here. (op 7-2)
Mashaaref, running in his first handicap and stepping up a furlong in distance, ran a perfectly respectable race but simply couldn't go with the winner from 2f out. There's better to come from him and he should be able to win a handicap off this sort of mark. (op 4-1)
Arch Fire(USA) flew home having been out the back early. He might not be the most straightforward (wore a visor again, as he did when winning his maiden second time out), but the ability is there and this well-related colt could yet improve again. (op 9-2 tchd 7-2)
Resentful Angel is a Polytrack specialist and is not the first to run well at this course having come here on the back of good AW form. (tchd 22-1 in a place)
Ellemujie, another with winning Polytrack form, did not run badly given that she had a 6lb higher mark to overcome in a better race.
Hurakan(IRE), five times a winner on Polytrack, did not get the clearest of runs 2f out but kept on fairly well and probably wasn't far off his best. (op 20-1)
Vimiero(USA) did not improve for the longer trip and, although it was 30 days since his reappearance and return from a lengthy layoff, perhaps it still came a bit soon for him. (op 9-1)
Denton(NZ) Official explanation: jockey said gelding stopped quickly

3845 TRANT ENGINEERING FILLIES' H'CAP 7f
4:55 (4:55) (Class 3) (0-90,87) 3-Y-0+ **£8,409** (£2,502; £1,250; £625) **Stalls** High

Form RPR

0-00 **1** **Golden Delicious**[7] 3632 3-8-2 **74** KieranO'Neill(5) 9 86+
(Hughie Morrison) *in rr and sn pushed along: t.k.h 3f out: swtchd rt and hdwy fr 2f out: drvn to ld ins fnl f: r.o wl clsng stages* **16/1**

-421 **2** 2¼ **Valencha**[22] 3121 4-9-5 **78** RobertHavlin 5 86
(Hughie Morrison) *s.i.s: in rr: hdwy fr 3f out: led over 1f out: hdd ins fnl f: kpt on but nt gng pce of wnr* **8/1**

1-54 **3** ¾ **Perfect Silence**[28] 2927 6-9-7 **87** LucyKBarry(7) 6 93
(Clive Cox) *led: rdn along fr 2f out: hdd over 1f out: outpcd by ldng duo ins fnl f but styd on wl to hold 3rd* **7/2**[1]

3141 **4** nk **Certral**[15] 3363 3-8-8 **78** SeanLevey(3) 3 80
(Brian Ellison) *chsd ldrs: rdn and edgd lft ins fnl 2f: rallied and kpt on u.p fnl f to cl on 3rd nr fin but no imp on ldng duo* **13/2**

2012 **5** ½ **Russian Rave**[22] 3121 5-9-9 **82** ShaneKelly 8 86
(Jonathan Portman) *in tch: rdn 2f out: kpt on fnl f but nvr gng pce to rch ldrs* **14/1**

-212 **6** shd **Bonnie Brae**[21] 3180 4-9-13 **86** AdamKirby 10 90+
(David Elsworth) *in rr tl hdwy and hmpd ins fnl 2f: swtchd rt and styd on wl fnl f: nt rch ldrs* **11/2**[3]

5124 **7** 2¾ **Sure Route**[29] 2883 3-9-2 **83** PatDobbs 11 76
(Richard Hannon) *chsd ldrs: rdn over 2f out: wknd ins fnl f* **9/2**[2]

-006 **8** 8 **Moretta Blanche**[9] 3536 4-9-7 **80** StevieDonohoe 4 55
(Ralph Beckett) *pressed ldrs: rdn 3f out: wknd ins fnl f* **10/1**

1003 **9** 3½ **Curtains**[15] 3351 4-9-12 **85** IanMongan 1 50
(Simon Dow) *t.k.h: in tch: hdwy on outside over 2f out: nvr rchd ldrs: pushed rt and wknd wl over 1f out* **20/1**

30-2 **10** 2¾ **Song Of The Siren**[14] 3390 3-8-10 **77** DavidProbert 7 32
(Andrew Balding) *chsd ldr: one pce whn bdly hmpd ins fnl 2f: eased and no ch after* **7/1**

1m 26.59s (-0.61) **Going Correction** +0.075s/f (Good)
WFA 3 from 4yo+ 8lb **10** Ran SP% **119.1**
Speed ratings (Par 104): **106,103,102,102,101 101,98,89,85,82**
toteswingers:1&2:£30.30, 2&3:£6.40, 1&3:£17.60 CSF £140.79 CT £559.89 TOTE £22.30: £4.30, £2.90, £1.60; EX 189.10.
Owner Nicholas Jones **Bred** Coln Valley Stud **Trained** East Ilsley, Berks

FOCUS
There wasn't much pace on early here, but the first two, both trained by Hughie Morrison, still came from behind. The winner was back to form with a bang.

NOTEBOOK
Golden Delicious had posted three poor performances since winning on her debut in soft ground at Newbury last autumn but had had excuses - outclassed second time out, ground too fast on reappearance, raced keenly over trip too far last time out. Back over 7f on safe ground off a handy mark, she did not look to be going that well early but eased into contention and, once switched to challenge down the outside, picked up in good style to win comfortably in the end. She could well win again, providing she can be found suitable ground.
Valencha travelled up strongly, looking the likeliest winner a furlong and a half out, and while she went through with her effort, her stablemate simply saw her race out better. (op 10-1)
Perfect Silence could have done with the ground being a bit softer but did not set a hectic gallop out in front and had her chance if good enough. (op 9-2 tchd 5-1)
Certral managed to get over to the rail and track the leaders and had every chance given the way the race worked out. This was a good effort considering she had gone up 10lb for winning a claimer last time out. (op 8-1 tchd 6-1)
Russian Rave, behind Valencha at Goodwood last time and another 4lb higher, is now 10lb higher than when winning narrowly at Leicester in May. (op 11-1)

Bonnie Brae, held up out the back, faced a wall of horses with 2f to run and instead of switching to the outside her rider waited for a gap to open up towards the inside. That was a mistake, and she got knocked by the weakening Song Of The Siren, and was then staying on all too late at the finish. She would have been placed with a clear run. Official explanation: jockey said filly was hampered closing stages (op 5-1 after 13-2 in places)
Sure Route was a bit keen early. (op 4-1 tchd 7-2)

3846 RITZ CLUB H'CAP — 5f
5:30 (5:33) (Class 2) (0-105,100) 3-Y-O+

£12,450 (£3,728; £1,864; £932; £466; £234) **Stalls** High

Form — RPR

0032 **1** **Medicean Man**[14] 3410 5-9-1 **96**....(p) RaulDaSilva(7) 7 — 107+
(Jeremy Gask) *in rr and t.k.h: stl pulling whn nt clr run 2f out and swtchd sharply rt to outside sn after: rapid hdwy fnl f to ld fnl 50yds: edge lft last strides: comf* **9/2**[2]

0410 **2** *½* **Sohraab**[14] 3410 7-8-11 **90**.... KieranO'Neill(5) 14 — 97
(Hughie Morrison) *pressed ldr tl slt advantage fr 3 f out: str chal but stl narrow ldr fnl f: hdd fnl 50yds and hung rt sn after* **15/2**

4020 **3** *nk* **Confessional**[15] 3357 4-9-4 **92**....(e) ShaneKelly 8 — 98
(Tim Easterby) *in tch: hdwy 2f out: drvn and styd on wl ins fnl f: kpt on clsng stages but nt rch ldng duo* **12/1**

0411 **4** *½* **Medici Time**[15] 3367 6-9-1 **89**....(v) RichardMullen 4 — 93
(Tim Easterby) *in rr but in tch: hdwy 2f out: str chal fnl f: one pce into 4th whn hmpd last strides* **10/1**

2414 **5** *1 ¼* **Addictive Dream (IRE)**[14] 3410 4-9-7 **98**.... JohnFahy(3) 6 — 98
(Walter Swinburn) *pressed ldrs: str chal fr over 3f out and stl upsides 1f out: wknd u.p fnl 120yds* **4/1**[1]

1202 **6** *½* **Collect Art (IRE)**[2] 3784 4-8-11 **85**.... StevieDonohoe 13 — 83
(Andrew Haynes) *in tch: drvn and hdwy over 1f out: styd on ins fnl f but nt pce to rch ldrs* **6/1**[3]

0000 **7** *4* **Cheveton**[14] 3410 7-8-11 **90**.... RyanClark(5) 9 — 73
(Richard Price) *in tch: drvn and outpcd 1/2-way: mod prog fnl f* **8/1**

5605 **8** *½* **Mister Manannan (IRE)**[43] 2456 4-9-12 **100**.... TadhgO'Shea 5 — 82
(David Nicholls) *chsd ldrs: chal fr 3f out to 2f out: wknd wl over 1f out* **25/1**

0200 **9** *5* **Befortyfour**[29] 2890 6-9-5 **93**.... TonyCulhane 11 — 57
(Richard Guest) *led 2f: styd chsng ldrs tl wknd over 2f out* **25/1**

1120 **10** *1 ¾* **Solemn**[15] 3357 6-8-12 **89**....(b) SeanLevey(3) 3 — 46
(Milton Bradley) *spd 3f* **22/1**

5405 **11** *2* **Lui Rei (ITY)**[14] 3410 5-9-9 **97**....(p) PatCosgrave 1 — 47
(Robert Cowell) *in rr but in tch: sme prog 1/2-way: sn wknd* **8/1**

60.08 secs (-1.12) **Going Correction** +0.075s/f (Good) — **11** Ran SP% **115.3**
WFA 3 from 4yo+ 5lb
Speed ratings (Par 109): **106,105,104,103,101 101,94,93,85,83 79**
toteswingers:1&2:£5.60, 2&3:£14.00, 1&3:£7.10 CSF £36.34 CT £380.28 TOTE £5.20: £2.00, £2.70, £3.90; EX 46.40.
Owner Stuart Dobb & Miss Kate Dobb **Bred** Barry Taylor **Trained** Sutton Veny, Wilts
■ Stewards' Enquiry : Raul Da Silva two-day ban: careless riding (Jul 24,26)

FOCUS
Plenty could be given a chance in this good handicap. The second and third set a sound standard.

NOTEBOOK
Medicean Man put up a good performance as things did not go entirely to plan. He ran up the back of rivals approaching the 2f pole and his rider initially looked like he might switch him left but then had a change of mind and switched him sharply right, to be brought with an uninterrupted run down the outside. It was a wise move and the gelding finished his race off strongly to record his second course success. Rider Raul Da Silva looks good value for his 7lb and has now partnered two winners in his first four rides over here. The winner coped well with the drop back to the minimum trip and one gets the impression that the faster the early pace the better it will be for him. The Stewards' Cup may come into consideration now. (op 5-1 tchd 11-2 in places)
Sohraab, back over his best trip, ran right up to his recent best but just came up a little short. (op 17-2 tchd 7-1)
Confessional has little room for error off his current mark and this sound effort will not help him on that score anytime soon.
Medici Time found the 5lb rise for his latest win just beyond him. He ran a perfectly decent race but [illegible] new mark. (op 11-1 tchd 12-1)
Addictive Dream(IRE) was a little disappointing. [illegible] well but he was behind Medicean Man at Windsor last time and, back in trip, dropped away inside the last, having been up there for most of the way. He has a bit to prove now but remains capable of better. (op 7-2)
Collect Art(IRE) keeps himself busy and ran a career-best at Warwick last time but could not quite match that effort on the back of just a two-day break. Things will not get easier once the handicapper has had his say. (op 8-1)
Cheveton is well handicapped on his best form from last season but ideally wants softer ground and usually comes good later in the year. (op 9-1)

3847 SALTMARSH PARTNERSHIP H'CAP — 5f
6:05 (6:05) (Class 4) (0-85,85) 3-Y-O+ — **£5,175** (£1,540; £769; £384) **Stalls** High

Form — RPR

3431 **1** **Ajjaadd (USA)**[21] 3174 5-9-0 **73**.... RichardMullen 3 — 83
(Ted Powell) *rrd stalls and s.i.s: in rr: hdwy 2f out: led 1f out: kpt on wl u.p* **5/1**[2]

2-21 **2** *1 ¼* **Admirable Duchess**[49] 2304 4-9-4 **80**.... KierenFox(3) 6 — 86
(Dominic Ffrench Davis) *mde most tl hdd 1f out: kpt on wl to hold 2nd but nt pce of wnr* **6/1**[3]

2103 **3** *1 ¼* **Wooden King (IRE)**[13] 3427 6-9-3 **76**.... TomMcLaughlin 8 — 77
(Malcolm Saunders) *in tch: rdn and outpcd 1/2-way: styd on again u.p fnl f: kpt on cl home but no imp on ldng duo* **7/1**

205 **4** *nk* **Fantasy Explorer**[8] 3588 8-8-11 **75**.... KieranO'Neill(5) 10 — 75
(John Quinn) *stdd s: in rr: swtchd rt to outside wl over 1f out: r.o ins fnl f: nt rch ldrs* **8/1**

40-0 **5** *hd* **High Spice (USA)**[8] 3579 4-9-4 **77**....(p) PatCosgrave 9 — 76
(Robert Cowell) *in rr and stl jst last over 1f out: drvn and hdwy ins fnl f: fin wl: nt rch ldrs* **20/1**

0312 **6** *hd* **Your Gifted (IRE)**[2] 3768 4-8-13 **79**.... DavidKenny(7) 7 — 77
(Patrick Morris) *pressed ldrs and stl ev ch over 1f out: wknd fnl 120yds* **8/1**

5660 **7** *2 ½* **Secret Millionaire (IRE)**[35] 2727 4-9-5 **85**.... LucyKBarry(7) 1 — 74
(Patrick Morris) *pressed ldrs: rdn and ev ch 2f out: wknd fnl f* **11/4**[1]

1255 **8** *¾* **Taurus Twins**[5] 3687 5-9-6 **84**....(b) RyanClark(5) 2 — 71
(Richard Price) *pressed ldrs to 1/2-way: sn outpcd* **6/1**[3]

0600 **9** *6* **Cape Royal**[23] 3078 11-8-9 **71**....(bt) SeanLevey(3) 5 — 36
(Milton Bradley) *pressed ldrs 3f: eased whn btn fnl f* **25/1**

61.36 secs (0.16) **Going Correction** +0.075s/f (Good) — **9** Ran SP% **115.2**
Speed ratings (Par 105): **96,94,92,91,91 90,86,85,76**
toteswingers:1&2:£2.90, 2&3:£4.80, 1&3:£8.60 CSF £34.94 CT £211.02 TOTE £6.50: £1.90, £2.00, £2.40; EX 22.50.
Owner Katy & Lol Pratt **Bred** Darley **Trained** Reigate, Surrey

FOCUS
The leaders went off too quick here and the winner came from off the pace. The winning time was a full 1.44sec slower than the class 2 handicap that preceded it. Esentially a reworking of race 2304 at Lingfield in May.
T/Plt: £77.20 to a £1 stake. Pool of £109,787.68 - 1,037.97 winning tickets. T/Qpdt: £10.20 to a £1 stake. Pool of £6,691.95 - 484.10 winning tickets. ST

3805 CHESTER (L-H)
Saturday, July 9

OFFICIAL GOING: Good (good to soft in places; 7.1)
Wind: Moderate, half-against. Weather: fine

3848 TOTEPLACEPOT H'CAP — 1m 2f 75y
2:15 (2:16) (Class 4) (0-80,80) 4-Y-O+ — **£5,175** (£1,540; £769; £384) **Stalls** High

Form — RPR

-321 **1** **Kenyan Cat**[28] 2912 4-9-2 **75**.... RoystonFfrench 5 — 86+
(Ed McMahon) *trckd ldrs: drvn 3f out: sn outpcd: hdwy and swtchd rt 1f out: r.o to ld wl ins fnl f* **7/2**[1]

5510 **2** *1 ¼* **Osgood**[18] 3244 4-9-4 **77**.... SamHitchcott 7 — 83
(Mick Channon) *trckd ldrs: upsides over 3f out: led over 1f out: hdd and no ex last 50yds* **20/1**

0401 **3** *1* **Granny McPhee**[14] 3380 5-9-0 **80**.... MissAlexOwen(7) 4 — 84
(Alan Bailey) *gave problems leaving paddock: s.i.s: hld up in rr: hdwy on outside over 4f out: chsng ldrs over 1f out: edgd lft: kpt on same pce last 150yds* **5/1**[2]

4123 **4** *1 ½* **Ay Tay Tate (IRE)**[16] 3317 5-8-6 **65**.... FrannyNorton 3 — 66
(David C Griffiths) *led: hdd over 1f out: kpt on same pce* **6/1**[3]

5510 **5** *¾* **Danderek**[49] 2320 5-9-6 **79**.... TonyHamilton 10 — 79
(Richard Fahey) *t.k.h in mid-div: effrt over 2f out: kpt on same pce: nvr trbld ldrs* **11/1**

6544 **6** *hd* **Rosbay (IRE)**[16] 3319 7-8-11 **70**....(p) DuranFentiman 11 — 69
(Tim Easterby) *s.i.s: hdwy on outside over 2f out: kpt on: nvr nr ldrs* **12/1**

1230 **7** *2* **Black Coffee**[92] 1222 6-8-10 **74**....(b) JamesRogers(5) 9 — 69
(Mark Brisbourne) *s.i.s: drvn 3f out: kpt on: nvr a factor* **25/1**

3110 **8** *1 ¾* **Moody Tunes**[8] 3585 8-9-1 **77**.... RossAtkinson(3) 1 — 69
(Tom Dascombe) *chsd ldrs: drvn 3f out: lost pl over 1f out* **9/1**

2542 **9** *nk* **One Scoop Or Two**[17] 3275 5-9-5 **78**.... RussKennemore 8 — 73
(Reg Hollinshead) *trckd ldrs: hmpd 1f out: sn lost pl* **5/1**[2]

1032 **10** *13* **Loyalty**[10] 3521 4-9-3 **76**....(v) RobbieFitzpatrick 2 — 41
(Derek Shaw) *mid-div: pushed along 6f out: lost pl over 2f out: sn bhd* **7/1**

2m 14.49s (3.29) **Going Correction** +0.225s/f (Good) — **10** Ran SP% **117.0**
Speed ratings (Par 105): **95,94,93,92,91 91,89,88,88,77**
Tote Swingers:1&2:£19.90, 2&3:£15.40, 1&3:£1.40 CSF £77.87 CT £352.88 TOTE £5.10: £1.90, £5.40, £1.40; EX 77.50.
Owner David Botterill & John Guest **Bred** D R Botterill **Trained** Lichfield, Staffs
■ Stewards' Enquiry : Royston Ffrench one-day ban: careless riding (Jul 24)

FOCUS
Rail out 3yds from 6f to top of home straight where there is a drop in. 5f increased by 3yds, 6 and 7f by 4yds and 1m2f and over by 5yds.A modest enough handicap that was run at a steady gallop. The form is rated around the runner-up.
Black Coffee Official explanation: jockey said gelding hung right-handed throughout

3849 TOTEEXACTA MAIDEN AUCTION STKS — 5f 16y
2:50 (2:50) (Class 5) 2-Y-O — **£4,043** (£1,203; £601; £300) **Stalls** Low

Form — RPR

422 **1** **Excelette (IRE)**[10] 3504 2-8-11 0.... RoystonFfrench 7 — 74
(Bryan Smart) *swvd rt s: sn drvn along: hdwy to chse ldrs over 2f out: sn outpcd: styd on wl down wd outside fnl f: led nr fin* **11/4**[1]

5 **2** *hd* **Tahnee Mara (IRE)**[15] 3342 2-8-11 0.... StephenCraine 1 — 73
(Kevin Ryan) *led: rdn fnl f: hdd cl home* **11/4**[1]

255 **3** *2 ¼* **Blodwen Abbey**[28] 2907 2-8-6 0.... LiamJones 5 — 60
(James Unett) *w ldr: chal over 1f out: kpt on same pce* **11/2**[3]

[illegible] **4** [illegible] **Dressed In Lace**[17] 3287 2-8-8 0.... LiamKeniry 3 — 62
(Andrew Balding) [illegible] *pce fnl f* **3/1**[2]

5 *3* **Al's Memory (IRE)** 2-9-2 0.... [illegible] — [illegible]
(David Evans) *sn outpcd and drvn along: sme hdwy over 1f out: nvr nr ldrs* **12/1**

3350 **6** *4* **Economic Crisis (IRE)**[28] 2907 2-8-4 0.... JamesSullivan 2 — 33
(Alan Berry) *rrd s and lost many l: sme hdwy over 2f out: sn wknd* **16/1**

03 **7** *14* **Hopes Rebellion**[12] 3452 2-8-9 0.... RobertWinston 4 — —
(Declan Carroll) *w ldrs on outer: wknd 2f out: sn bhd* **11/1**

62.22 secs (1.22) **Going Correction** +0.225s/f (Good) — **7** Ran SP% **115.6**
Speed ratings (Par 94): **99,98,95,94,90 83,61**
Tote Swingers:1&2:£2.10, 2&3:£2.50, 1&3:£2.40 CSF £10.88 TOTE £3.80: £2.10, £2.10; EX 14.60.
Owner Crossfields Racing **Bred** David John Brown **Trained** Hambleton, N Yorks
■ Stewards' Enquiry : Stephen Craine caution: used whip with excessive frequency.

FOCUS
An ordinary juvenile sprint maiden. Sound form with the front pair clear.

NOTEBOOK
Excelette(IRE), who had led on each of her last two runs, couldn't get to the lead from her wide draw, coming through late under Royston ffrench. The slight ease in the ground was clearly no inconvenience and she should have no trouble with 6f (a half-sister won over 1m2f). Nurseries will presumably come next. (tchd 9-4)
Tahnee Mara(IRE) had clearly improved from her debut effort and was driven to lead from stall one. She briefly looked the winner, but Excelette always had the momentum to get up once switched. A slightly more patient ride over 6f should see her off the mark. (op 9-2)
Blodwen Abbey was soon disputing it and kept on without matching the front pair. Nurseries should provide her with more of a chance. (op 8-1)
Dressed In Lace appeared to have a perfect tow through, but as it turned out she didn't have the pace to challenge. A return to 6f, possibly in nurseries, beckons. (op 9-4)
Al's Memory(IRE), a half-brother to a 5f 2-y-o winner, was going on at the finish, having been badly outpaced early, and should come on. (op 11-1 tchd 14-1)

3850 TOTEQUICKPICK H'CAP — 6f 18y
3:25 (3:26) (Class 3) (0-90,88) 3-Y-O+ — **£9,703** (£2,887; £1,443; £721) **Stalls** Low

Form — RPR

-010 **1** **Roker Park (IRE)**[14] 3395 6-9-9 **85**.... RobertWinston 10 — 95
(David O'Meara) *dwlt: in last: hdwy 2f out: swtchd rt appr fnl f: styd on wl to ld nr fin* **9/1**

0046 **2** *½* **Star Rover (IRE)**[14] 3379 4-9-10 **86**....(v) CathyGannon 11 — 94
(David Evans) *s.i.s: in rr: hdwy 2f out: edgd lft 1f out: disp ld last 100yds: hdd nr fin* **12/1**

0000 **3** *shd* **Corporal Maddox**[27] 2954 4-9-12 **88** .... FrannyNorton 6 96
(Jamie Osborne) *s.i.s: hdwy and nt clr run 2f out: disp ld last 100yds: hdd last strides* **16/1**
32-1 **4** *2* **Long Awaited (IRE)**[24] 3053 3-9-1 **83** .... AndreaAtzeni 8 83+
(Roger Varian) *trckd ldrs: hdwy to ld over 1f out: edgd lft: hdd last 100yds: no ex* **7/4**[1]
0212 **5** *1 1/4* **Grissom (IRE)**[14] 3383 5-9-7 **83** .... DuranFentiman 7 80+
(Tim Easterby) *chsd ldrs: kpt on same pce fnl f* **9/2**[2]
13 **6** *1* **Barons Spy (IRE)**[2] 3784 10-9-6 **82** .... RoystonFfrench 9 76
(Richard Price) *sn drvn along in rr: hdwy over 1f out: nvr rchd ldrs* **16/1**
0500 **7** *2 1/4* **Rash Judgement**[14] 3395 6-9-8 **84** .... AndrewHeffernan 5 71+
(Eric Alston) *chsd ldrs on ins: nt clr run over 2f out: keeping on same pce whn hmpd ins fnl f* **16/1**
0152 **8** *2 1/2* **Victorian Bounty**[26] 3000 6-9-6 **82** .... LiamKeniry 1 61
(Stef Higgins) *led: hdd appr fnl f: wkng whn hmpd ins fnl f* **5/1**[3]
0052 **9** *3/4* **Invincible Force (IRE)**[9] 3541 7-9-2 **78** ....(b) JamesSullivan 13 54
(Paul Green) *w ldr: wkng whn hmpd ins fnl f* **16/1**
6000 **10** *9* **Bahamian Lad**[15] 3339 6-8-9 **71** ....(p) SamHitchcott 14 19
(Reg Hollinshead) *sn drvn along in mid-div: lost pl over 2f out: sn bhd* **40/1**

1m 14.91s (1.11) **Going Correction** +0.225s/f (Good)
WFA 3 from 4yo+ 6lb **10** Ran SP% **114.9**
Speed ratings (Par 107): **101,100,100,97,95 94,91,88,87,75**
Tote Swingers:1&2:£12.10, 2&3:£11.70, 1&3:£20.50 CSF £109.59 CT £1743.61 TOTE £8.60: £2.70, £3.00, £3.70; EX 65.70.
Owner T Alderson **Bred** Dr Dean Harron **Trained** Nawton, N Yorks
■ Stewards' Enquiry : Franny Norton caution: used whip without giving gelding time to respond.
Andrea Atzeni one-day ban: careless riding (Jul 24)

FOCUS
An open sprint handicap that produced a tight three-way finish. They went quick early and coming from off the pace was a definite plus. The winner's best form since 2009.

NOTEBOOK
Roker Park(IRE), still 5lb higher than when winning at Catterick two starts ago, couldn't get involved at Newcastle last time when his jockey lost an iron, but this panned out well for him. He overcame a double-figure draw, from which he had to race well back, to get up close home. (op 12-1 tchd 14-1 in places)
Star Rover(IRE), racing off a career-low mark, came with a strong challenge in the straight and was only narrowly denied a first handicap win. (op 16-1)
Corporal Maddox had dropped 16lb in the handicap this year and it was only a matter of time before he returned to form. This was a good effort considering he was slow away and he will surely gain compensation soon. (op 18-1)
Long Awaited(IRE) moved up with a promising challenge before the straight, but he couldn't race on with the seasoned sprinters. He may have sat too close to the pace and remains capable of better as he gains experience. (op 15-8)
Grissom(IRE) was readily swallowed up by the closers. (op 4-1)
Rash Judgement would have been a good bit closer with anything like a clear run. He's working his way back to a fair mark. (op 14-1)
Victorian Bounty went too fast in front and had nothing left for the finish, being hampered late on. (op 9-2)

3851 TOTESWINGER H'CAP — 1m 7f 195y
4:00 (4:00) (Class 4) (0-85,84) 3-Y-0+ **£5,175** (£1,540; £769; £384) **Stalls** Low

Form RPR
-300 **1** **Colour Vision (FR)**[17] 3291 3-8-7 **82** .... SamHitchcott 1 93
(Mark Johnston) *dwlt: sn drvn to chse ldrs: wnt 2nd over 2f out: led 1f out: hung lft and drvn clr* **11/2**
-421 **2** *4 1/2* **Never Can Tell (IRE)**[28] 2906 4-10-0 **84** .... FrannyNorton 2 89
(Jamie Osborne) *led: hdd 1f out: kpt on same pce* **9/2**[2]
3435 **3** *2 3/4* **Descaro (USA)**[29] 2888 5-9-4 **74** ....(v[1]) StephenCraine 9 76
(David O'Meara) *hld up in rr: stdy hdwy over 3f out: wnt 3rd over 1f out: one pce* **9/1**
-464 **4** *4 1/2* **Beat The Shower**[22] 3127 5-8-10 **66** .... TonyHamilton 7 63
(Peter Niven) *hld up in rr: effrt over 4f out: n.m.r on inner over 2f out: one pce* **10/1**
-311 **5** *3/4* **Bollin Judith**[29] 2888 5-9-10 **80** ....(t) RobertWinston 8 76
(Tim Easterby) *hld up in rr: hdwy and swtchd outside over 2f out: wknd over 1f out* **4/1**[1]
2043 **6** *2 3/4* **Pittodrie Star (IRE)**[33] 2762 4-9-5 **75** .... LiamKeniry 5 67
(Andrew Balding) *trckd ldrs: effrt over 3f out: hung lft and wknd over 1f out* **5/1**[3]
0613 **7** *11* **Wells Lyrical (IRE)**[20] 3205 6-9-12 **82** .... RoystonFfrench 6 61
(Bryan Smart) *sn chsng ldrs: drvn over 3f out: wknd 2f out: eased whn bhd* **7/1**
-400 **8** *11* **Tobernea (IRE)**[23] 3072 4-8-11 **67** .... LiamJones 3 33
(Mark Johnston) *chsd ldr: drvn 5f out: lost pl 2f out: eased whn bhd* **20/1**
5220 **9** *9* **Dubara Reef (IRE)**[29] 2888 4-9-0 **70** ....(p) JamesSullivan 10 25
(Paul Green) *sn drvn along towards rr: reminders after 7f: lost pl 5f out: sn bhd: virtually p.u nr fin* **12/1**

3m 29.53s (1.53) **Going Correction** +0.225s/f (Good)
WFA 3 from 4yo+ 19lb **9** Ran SP% **114.3**
Speed ratings (Par 105): **105,102,101,99,98 97,91,86,81**
Tote Swingers:1&2:£5.20, 2&3:£13.50, 1&3:£5.20 CSF £30.11 CT £218.33 TOTE £7.70: £2.50, £1.30, £3.30; EX 34.90.
Owner Sheikh Hamdan Bin Mohammed Al Maktoum **Bred** Capricorn Stud **Trained** Middleham Moor, N Yorks

FOCUS
A decent staying handicap. A better run and a 4lb personal best from the winner.
Pittodrie Star(IRE) Official explanation: jockey said gelding hung left

3852 TOTEPOOL CITY PLATE (LISTED RACE) — 7f 2y
4:35 (4:37) (Class 1) 3-Y-0+
£17,013 (£6,450; £3,228; £1,608; £807; £405) **Stalls** Low

Form RPR
-150 **1** **Majestic Myles (IRE)**[24] 3029 3-8-8 **102** .... TonyHamilton 7 104
(Richard Fahey) *trckd ldrs: led 2f out: styd on strly* **7/1**
020F **2** *1 1/4* **Mon Cadeaux**[14] 3410 4-9-2 **95** .... LiamKeniry 4 104
(Andrew Balding) *wnt rt s: hld up in midfield: hdwy to chse wnr over 1f out: no imp* **16/1**
0455 **3** *3/4* **Capercaillie (USA)**[30] 2861 4-8-11 **91** .... RoystonFfrench 2 97
(Clive Cox) *led 2f: chsd ldrs: outpcd over 2f out: kpt on over 1f out* **16/1**
0032 **4** *3/4* **Doncaster Rover (USA)**[14] 3394 5-9-2 **106** .... RobertWinston 9 100+
(David Brown) *in rr: drvn over 3f out: kpt on fnl 2f: nt rch ldrs* **9/2**[2]
3120 **5** *shd* **Our Jonathan**[22] 3109 4-9-2 **102** .... FrannyNorton 6 100+
(Kevin Ryan) *hmpd s: swtchd lft after s: in rr: hdwy and n.m.r over 2f out: styd on wl fnl 100yds* **5/2**[1]
321- **6** *2 1/4* **Zenella**[264] 6982 3-8-3 **93** .... JamesSullivan 1 86
(Ann Duffield) *trckd ldrs: outpcd over 2f out: n.m.r 1f out: kpt on* **12/1**
4014 **7** *3/4* **Norville (IRE)**[7] 3626 4-9-2 **99** ....(b) CathyGannon 3 92
(David Evans) *hdwy on outer to chse ldrs after 2f: wknd fnl 150yds* **9/1**
100 **8** *2 3/4* **Not My Choice (IRE)**[10] 3506 6-9-2 **79** ....(t) AndrewHeffernan 11 84
(David C Griffiths) *stmbld s: hdwy on outside to ld after 2f: hdd 2f out: wknd fnl f* **66/1**
-365 **9** *3/4* **Awzaan**[14] 3404 4-9-2 **107** .... LiamJones 8 82
(Mark Johnston) *chsd ldrs: drvn 3f out: lost pl over 1f out* **13/2**[3]
0-53 **10** *1 3/4* **Oor Jock (IRE)**[27] 2967 3-8-8 **95** .... PShanahan 10 74
(Tracey Collins, Ire) *in rr: drvn over 2f out: nvr on terms* **28/1**
-200 **11** *12* **Rerouted (USA)**[25] 3011 3-8-8 **108** .... JamieMackay 5 42
(B W Hills) *carried rt s: in last and sn drvn along: bhd fnl 2f: eased towards fin* **8/1**

1m 26.67s (0.17) **Going Correction** +0.225s/f (Good)
WFA 3 from 4yo+ 8lb **11** Ran SP% **118.1**
Speed ratings (Par 111): **108,106,105,104,104 102,101,98,97,95 81**
Tote Swingers:1&2:£20.50, 2&3:£40.00, 1&3:£33.80 CSF £113.38 TOTE £9.10: £2.50, £4.90, £5.00; EX 133.00.
Owner James Gaffney **Bred** Arctic Tack Stud **Trained** Musley Bank, N Yorks

FOCUS
A thoroughly competitive Listed race run at a good clip. Ordinary form for the grade, rated around the winner.

NOTEBOOK
Majestic Myles(IRE) came out best, travelling up well to lead before the straight and quickening clear. This was a drop in grade after he had contested the Jersey Stakes last time, but he looks capable of mixing it back at Group 3 level over 6f/7f. (op 8-1 tchd 17-2 and 9-1 in places)
Mon Cadeaux arguably travelled just as well as the winner, but he'd been a bit keen early, and when asked for his winning effort he could only offer the one pace. He'd clipped heels and come down at Windsor on his last start, so this showed he's not feeling any after-effects. (op 22-1)
Capercaillie(USA) was always on the inner and kept on to register her first placing at Pattern level, which should prove valuable to her as a broodmare. (op 20-1 tchd 25-1)
Doncaster Rover(USA) is in good form and goes well here, so it was no surprise to see him run well, staying on from the rear. (tchd 4-1)
Our Jonathan was squeezed out at the start and could never recover, also being hampered when trying to gain ground. Official explanation: jockey said gelding suffered interference leaving stalls (op 3-1)
Zenella didn't shape badly. (tchd 11-1 and 14-1)
Awzaan dropped away in the straight and remains a disappointment. (op 6-1)
Rerouted(USA), who had been used as Frankel's pacemaker on his last two runs, was soon in trouble, not looking happy on the course, and is a horse with questions to answer. He was reported to have lost his action. (op 7-1 tchd 13-2)

3853 BET TOTEPOOL AT TOTESPORT.COM H'CAP — 6f 18y
5:10 (5:11) (Class 4) (0-80,80) 3-Y-O **£5,175** (£1,540; £769; £384) **Stalls** Low

Form RPR
-141 **1** **Louis The Pious**[33] 2763 3-9-7 **80** .... TonyHamilton 9 87+
(Kevin Ryan) *trckd ldrs: effrt over 2f out: led over 1f out: edgd lft: jst hld on* **9/2**[2]
6-05 **2** *nk* **Ballinargh Girl (IRE)**[7] 3628 3-8-13 **72** .... JamesSullivan 6 76
(Robert Wylie) *trckd ldrs: t.k.h: kpt on wl fnl f: no ex nr fin* **20/1**
-215 **3** *shd* **Muffraaj**[21] 3181 3-9-6 **79** .... LiamJones 4 83
(David Simcock) *led: hdd over 1f out: rallied ins fnl f: r.o towards fin* **4/1**[1]
0430 **4** *shd* **Strictly Pink (IRE)**[8] 3598 3-9-3 **76** ....(p) CathyGannon 1 79
(Alan Bailey) *chsd ldrs: swtchd lft over 1f out: styd on ins fnl f: no ex clsng stages* **7/1**
6055 **5** *3/4* **Whipphound**[8] 3598 3-8-8 **72** .... JamesRogers(5) 10 73
(Mark Brisbourne) *mid-div: effrt over 2f out: hdwy over 1f out: styd on fnl f: keeping on whn n.m.r nr fin* **20/1**
1121 **6** *1/2* **Rothesay Chancer**[15] 3360 3-9-0 **76** .... GaryBartley(3) 5 75
(Jim Goldie) *s.i.s: hdwy 3f out: chsng ldrs over 1f out: kpt on same pce ins fnl f* **11/2**[3]
-105 **7** *3 1/2* **Layla Jamil (IRE)**[28] 2937 3-9-5 **78** .... FrannyNorton 12 66
(Mick Channon) *mid-div on outside: effrt over 2f out: wl hld whn eased fnl 75yds* **9/1**
2020 **8** *1/2* **Crucis Abbey (IRE)**[15] 3337 3-7-13 **61** oh1 ....(v) AmyBaker(3) 2 48
(James Unett) *s.i.s: sme hdwy over 1f out: nvr on terms* **14/1**
0303 **9** *1* **Captain Kolo (IRE)**[14] 3384 3-9-2 **75** .... RobertWinston 8 58
(Tim Easterby) *sn trcking ldrs: t.k.h: wknd fnl f: eased nr fin* **14/1**
146- **10** *1 1/4* **Lady Paris (IRE)**[255] 7174 3-9-3 **76** .... RoystonFfrench 11 55
(Bryan Smart) *chsd ldrs on outside: wknd wl over 1f out* **16/1**
602 **11** *2* **Hoover**[10] 3523 3-8-11 **70** .... StephenCraine 13 43
(Jim Boyle) *in rr: sme hdwy 3f out: wknd over 1f out* **33/1**
0604 **12** *shd* **Penny's Pearl (IRE)**[8] 3598 3-8-11 **77** .... CharlesBishop(7) 7 50
(David Evans) *wnt lft s and s.s: sme hdwy 2f out: nvr on terms* **9/1**
14 **13** *5* **Twice Red**[19] 3239 3-8-13 **72** .... RobbieFitzpatrick 3 29
(Derek Shaw) *a towards rr: bhd fnl 2f* **16/1**

1m 15.56s (1.76) **Going Correction** +0.225s/f (Good) **13** Ran SP% **123.6**
Speed ratings (Par 102): **97,96,96,96,95 94,90,89,88,86 83,83,76**
Tote Swingers:1&2:£22.50, 2&3:£11.50, 1&3:£4.80 CSF £97.88 CT £400.51 TOTE £5.50: £2.00, £6.00, £2.30; EX 147.10.
Owner F Gillespie **Bred** Ashbrittle Stud **Trained** Hambleton, N Yorks

FOCUS
Just a fair 3-y-o sprint handicap but the winner, third and fourth give the form of substance. There was little between the front five at the line.
Captain Kolo(IRE) Official explanation: jockey said gelding ran too free
Penny's Pearl(IRE) Official explanation: jockey said filly jinked right on leaving stalls and was slowly away

3854 BET TOTEPOOL ON 0800 221221 APPRENTICE H'CAP — 7f 122y
5:45 (5:45) (Class 4) (0-80,80) 3-Y-O **£5,175** (£1,540; £769; £384) **Stalls** Low

Form RPR
-216 **1** **Roninski (IRE)**[56] 2092 3-8-8 **74** .... JustinNewman(7) 5 83+
(Bryan Smart) *hld up in mid-div: hdwy over 2f out: chsd ldr last 100yds: led nr fin* **7/1**
-012 **2** *nk* **Save The Bees**[11] 3485 3-8-9 **68** .... NeilFarley 3 76
(Declan Carroll) *chsd ldrs: squeezed through to ld over 1f out: no ex and hdd nr fin* **5/2**[1]
-001 **3** *3 3/4* **Isingy Red (FR)**[15] 3337 3-8-11 **73** .... NathanAlison(3) 1 72
(Jim Boyle) *dwlt: hld up in rr: sddle sn slipped: hdwy over 2f out: kpt on to take 3rd towards fin* **11/2**[3]
0006 **4** *hd* **First Class Favour (IRE)**[15] 3346 3-9-1 **74** .... LanceBetts 7 72
(Tim Easterby) *led and crossed to rail after 1f: hdd over 1f out: wknd towards fin* **12/1**
6642 **5** *2 3/4* **Barista (IRE)**[7] 3634 3-8-11 **75** .... CharlesBishop(5) 8 66
(Mick Channon) *rrd s: in rr: hdwy over 2f out: one pce* **4/1**[2]

2006 **6** *shd* **Barnum (USA)**[15] 3340 3-8-2 **61** oh1 .... AndrewHeffernan 4 52
(Mark Johnston) *mid-div: drvn 3f out: nvr a factor* **14/1**

-011 **7** *½* **Alluring Star**[26] 2986 3-8-5 **64** .... JamesSullivan 2 54
(Michael Easterby) *led: hdd and sltly hmpd after 1f: chsd ldrs: wknd fnl f* **4/1**[2]

1-0 **8** *17* **Tedsmore Dame**[16] 3310 3-9-7 **80** .... AmyBaker 6 27
(James Unett) *s.i.s: hdwy on outside to trck ldrs over 3f out: wknd over 2f out: sn bhd: eased* **40/1**

1m 35.32s (1.52) **Going Correction** +0.225s/f (Good) **8** Ran SP% **113.3**
Speed ratings (Par 102): **101,100,96,96,94 93,93,76**
Tote Tote Swingers:1&2:£5.50, 2&3:£3.60, 1&3:£7.20 CSF £24.40 CT £103.83 TOTE £7.60: £1.80, £1.20, £2.00; EX 34.40.
Owner Ron Hull **Bred** Peter Hodgson And Star Pointe Limited **Trained** Hambleton, N Yorks
■ Stewards' Enquiry : Lance Betts two-day ban: careless riding (Jul 24-25)

FOCUS
A fairly modest apprentice handicap. They probably went a bit too fast early and the form is ordinary for the grade.
Isingy Red(FR) Official explanation: jockey said saddle slipped
T/Plt: £2,752.40 to a £1 stake. Pool:£79,367.81. 21.05 winning tickets T/Qpdt: £240.70 to a £1 stake. Pool:£4,554.33. 14 winning tickets WG

[3483]HAMILTON (R-H)

Saturday, July 9

OFFICIAL GOING: Good (8.2)
Wind: Breezy, across Weather: Sunny, hot

3855 BRITISH STALLION STUDS SUPPORTING BRITISH RACING E B F MAIDEN STKS 5f 4y

6:00 (6:01) (Class 5) 2-Y-O **£3,234** (£962; £481; £240) **Stalls** High

Form RPR

2 **1** **Lesotho (IRE)**[15] 3342 2-8-12 0 .... PJMcDonald 6 74+
(Noel Quinlan) *mde all: shkn up and qcknd clr fnl f: comf* **4/11**[1]

2 *1 ¾* **Baltic Fizz (IRE)** 2-8-9 0 .... PatrickDonaghy(3) 7 68+
(Mrs K Burke) *dwlt: sn prom: effrt and chsd wnr fnl f: kpt on: no imp* **6/1**[2]

0 **3** *3 ¾* **Fifteentwo**[38] 2617 2-9-0 0 .... MichaelO'Connell(3) 4 60
(David Nicholls) *cl up: rdn 2f out: outpcd fnl f* **12/1**

0 **4** *2 ¾* **Well Wishes**[43] 2460 2-8-12 0 .... GregFairley 1 44
(Bryan Smart) *prom on outside: sn pushed along: outpcd 1/2-way: plugged on fnl f: no imp* **10/1**[3]

0003 **5** *1* **Come To Mind**[9] 3539 2-9-3 0 .... PatrickMathers 2 46
(Alan Berry) *chsd ldrs: rdn 2f out: wknd fnl f* **66/1**

6 *6* **Caymana Girl (IRE)** 2-8-12 0 .... KellyHarrison 3 19
(Micky Hammond) *chsd ldng gp: sn pushed along: struggling 1/2-way: nvr on terms* **20/1**

0 **7** *4 ½* **Burnwynd Spirit (IRE)**[12] 3452 2-9-3 0 .... PaddyAspell 5 8
(Ian Semple) *fly-jmpd s: bhd: struggling 1/2-way: sn btn* **50/1**

60.41 secs (0.41) **Going Correction** +0.025s/f (Good) **7** Ran SP% **112.6**
Speed ratings (Par 94): **97,94,88,83,82 72,65**
Tote Swingers:1&2:£1.60, 2&3:£3.50, 1&3:£1.50 CSF £2.86 TOTE £1.30: £1.10, £3.30; EX 3.60.
Owner Cillian S Ryan **Bred** Swordlestown Stud **Trained** Newmarket, Suffolk

FOCUS
Rail realignment added 8yds to distances on Round course. A weak maiden.

NOTEBOOK
Lesotho(IRE) had shaped well on her debut at Doncaster (6f) last month. As expected, the drop to 5f posed no problem for Noel Quinlan's filly and she was merely pushed out to make sure inside the last. She remains open to improvement and a sprint nursery will presumably be next on her agenda. (op 1-3)
Baltic Fizz(IRE), a daughter of Baltic King out of a mare who's related to plenty of winners, was no serious match for Lesotho, but this was a promising enough start, pulling well clear of the remainder by the finish. She should build on this. (op 17-2)
Fifteentwo is unlikely to be of any interest until he's contesting nurseries but this was at least a step up on his debut. (op 16-1)
Well Wishes hasn't achieved a great deal on her two starts to date and is another who's unlikely to really come into her own until qualified for handicaps. (op 11-1)
Come To Mind already looks very limited. (op 150-1)
Caymana Girl(IRE) didn't offer anything in the way of short-term promise.

3856 PAUL CAMPBELL-A LIFETIME IN RACING H'CAP (BETFAIR BONUS SCOTTISH RACING SPRINT FINAL QUALIFIER) 6f 5y

6:30 (6:33) (Class 5) (0-70,67) 3-Y-0+ **£4,204** (£1,251; £625; £312) **Stalls** High

Form RPR

1441 **1** **Blues Jazz**[11] 3489 5-8-12 **60** .... GarryWhillans(7) 7 71
(Ian Semple) *in tch stands' side gp: outpcd over 2f out: rallied to ld ins fnl f: r.o* **15/2**

331- **2** *hd* **Opus Dei**[194] 7987 4-9-8 **66** .... MichaelO'Connell(3) 9 76
(David Nicholls) *cl up: led stands' side over 1f out to ins fnl f: kpt on fin* **11/1**

2121 **3** *1 ¼* **Needy McCredie**[7] 3617 5-9-2 **62** .... JulieBurke(5) 5 68
(James Turner) *cl up on outside of stands' side gp: effrt 2f out: kpt on same pce ins fnl f* **3/1**[1]

15 **4** *hd* **Midnight Dynamo**[24] 3036 4-9-10 **65** .... AndrewMullen 8 70
(Jim Goldie) *in tch stands' side gp: outpcd over 2f out: styd on fnl f: no imp* **12/1**

0020 **5** *nk* **Berbice (IRE)**[6] 3657 6-9-10 **65** ....(b) KellyHarrison 6 69
(Linda Perratt) *plld hrd: hld up stands' side: smooth hdwy to chse ldrs over 1f out: one pce fnl f* **16/1**

2412 **6** *1* **Carrie's Magic**[16] 3305 4-9-5 **67** ....(b) ShaneBKelly(7) 13 68
(Alistair Whillans) *in tch stands' side: rdn over 2f out: kpt on same pce fnl f* **4/1**[2]

-500 **7** *hd* **Secret City (IRE)**[31] 2803 5-8-8 **54** ....(b) LMcNiff(5) 3 55
(Robin Bastiman) *trckd far side ldr: led that trio over 1f out: nt pce of stands' side gp* **33/1**

00-6 **8** *¾* **Angaric (IRE)**[25] 3025 8-9-5 **60** .... GregFairley 10 58
(Bryan Smart) *led stands' side gp to over 1f out: wknd ins fnl f* **16/1**

1541 **9** *1 ½* **Toby Tyler**[24] 3036 5-9-12 **67** ....(v) PJMcDonald 11 60
(Paul Midgley) *hld up stands' side: rdn over 2f out: kpt on fnl f: nvr able to chal* **11/2**[3]

1-50 **10** *1 ¾* **Tadalavil**[11] 3488 6-9-5 **67** .... RossSmith(7) 4 55
(Linda Perratt) *dwlt: sn prom on outside of stands' side gp: rdn over 2f out: wknd over 1f out* **28/1**

0-06 **11** *½* **Just Sam (IRE)**[8] 3569 6-9-0 **58** .... RobertLButler(3) 1 44
(Ron Barr) *led far side trio to over 1f out: btn fnl f* **28/1**

-002 **12** *¾* **Cawdor (IRE)**[21] 3190 5-9-5 **67** .... KristinStubbs(7) 2 51
(Linda Stubbs) *cl up far side: rdn and edgd lft 2f out: sn btn* **14/1**

1m 12.08s (-0.12) **Going Correction** +0.025s/f (Good) **12** Ran SP% **116.4**
Speed ratings (Par 103): **101,100,99,98,98 97,96,95,93,91 90,89**
Tote Swingers:1&2:£16.20, 2&3:£11.80, 1&3:£3.90 CSF £83.90 CT £303.14 TOTE £5.90: £1.10, £2.80, £2.20; EX 109.60.
Owner Robert Reid **Bred** David Sugars And Bob Parker **Trained** Carluke, S Lanarks

FOCUS
A fair handicap and a competitive enough event of its type. Those in the three lowest stalls raced far side but it was the bigger group who came centre to stands' side who held sway. There was no confirmed trailblazer in the line-up and, for a race of this nature, the gallop didn't appear overly strong through the early stages. Solid form rated through the third to her Carlisle effort and the fifth and sixth to their recent marks.
Toby Tyler Official explanation: jockey said gelding was denied a clear run

3857 RACING UK MAIDEN (S) STKS 6f 5y

7:00 (7:03) (Class 6) 3-Y-0+ **£2,249** (£664; £332) **Stalls** High

Form RPR

5-00 **1** **Weetentherty**[6] 3662 4-9-3 43 ....(p) DeclanCannon(3) 2 51
(Linda Perratt) *prom: effrt 2f out: led ins fnl f: r.o* **66/1**

46 **2** *nk* **The Fiery Cross**[22] 3111 4-8-13 0 .... GarryWhillans(7) 4 50
(Ian Semple) *cl up: led 2f out: hdd ins fnl f: r.o* **9/2**[2]

4000 **3** *¾* **King Bertolini (IRE)**[1] 3805 4-9-6 47 .... PatrickMathers 9 48
(Alan Berry) *towards rr: drvn 1/2-way: hdwy over 1f out: kpt on: nrst fin* **40/1**

3-00 **4** *1* **Deliberation (IRE)**[116] 855 3-9-0 65 .... PJMcDonald 8 44
(Ollie Pears) *t.k.h: hld up: rdn and hung rt over 2f out: styd on wl fnl f: nrst fin* **7/5**[1]

0200 **5** *½* **Chardonnay Star (IRE)**[21] 3191 4-9-1 46 ....(v) AndrewMullen 10 38
(Colin Teague) *towards rr: drvn and edgd rt 1/2-way: sme late hdwy: nvr rchd ldrs* **12/1**

000 **6** *¾* **Harmony Wold**[16] 3324 3-8-9 39 .... GregFairley 3 35
(Declan Carroll) *led tl hung rt and hdd 2f out: sn no ex* **66/1**

0300 **7** *2 ¾* **Coolella (IRE)**[3] 3732 4-8-10 46 ....(b[1]) ChrisDCogan(5) 6 27
(John Weymes) *cl up tl rdn and wknd over 1f out* **12/1**

5050 **8** *1 ¾* **Rosbertini**[6] 3658 5-9-6 45 .... PaddyAspell 7 26
(Linda Perratt) *towards rr: shortlived effrt over 2f out: wknd wl over 1f out* **14/1**

4 **9** *4 ½* **Goninodaethat**[16] 3304 3-8-9 0 .... JulieBurke(5) 5 11
(Jim Goldie) *dwlt: bhd: struggling over 2f out: nvr on terms* **6/1**

4000 **10** *½* **Balance On Time (IRE)**[6] 3657 5-8-12 43 .... AmyRyan(3) 1 —
(Linda Perratt) *midfield on outside: struggling over 2f out: sn btn* **5/1**[3]

1m 12.88s (0.68) **Going Correction** +0.025s/f (Good)
WFA 3 from 4yo+ 6lb **10** Ran SP% **118.3**
Speed ratings (Par 101): **96,95,94,93,92 91,87,85,79,78**
Tote Swingers:1&2:£17.90, 2&3:£16.10, 1&3:£51.20 CSF £349.01 TOTE £54.10: £7.50, £2.40, £8.00; EX 317.90.There was no bid for the winner. Deliberation was claimed by Kevin Ryan for £10,000.
Owner C & B Racing Club **Bred** New Hall Stud **Trained** East Kilbride, S Lanarks

FOCUS
Maiden sellers are seldom anything other than poor affairs and this looks no exception. It has been rated around the third to this year's form.
Harmony Wold Official explanation: jockey said filly hung right-handed throughout

3858 TURFTV H'CAP (QUALIFIER FOR THE BETFAIR BONUS SCOTTISH RACING STAYERS FINAL) 1m 3f 16y

7:35 (7:36) (Class 5) (0-75,73) 3-Y-0+ **£4,204** (£1,251; £625; £312) **Stalls** Low

Form RPR

-014 **1** **Eltheeb**[4] 3701 4-10-0 **73** .... AndrewMullen 1 87
(George Moore) *hld up in midfield: rdn over 3f out: hdwy 2f out: swtchd lft and qcknd to ld ent fnl f: edgd rt: sn clr* **10/3**[2]

0005 **2** *4 ½* **Full Speed (GER)**[29] 2892 6-10-0 **73** .... PJMcDonald 4 83+
(Alan Swinbank) *hld up: stdy hdwy on bit to trck ldrs whn no room fr over 2f out to ins fnl f: styd on wl to take 2nd nr fin: no ch w wnr* **9/1**

0115 **3** *nk* **Unknown Rebel (IRE)**[12] 3462 3-8-9 **71** .... JulieBurke(5) 6 76
(Kevin Ryan) *mde most tl rdn and hdd ent fnl f: kpt on same pce: lost 2nd nr fin* **3/1**[1]

4244 **4** *1 ¾* **Amir Pasha (UAE)**[12] 3456 6-9-1 **60** ....(p) KellyHarrison 5 62
(Micky Hammond) *prom: hdwy and cl up over 2f out: sn rdn and edgd rt: one pce fnl f* **8/1**

2161 **5** *5* **Jeu De Vivre (IRE)**[16] 3301 3-8-10 **70** .... AmyRyan(3) 7 63
(Mark Johnston) *disp ld: rdn over 2f out: wknd appr fnl f* **4/1**[3]

0-00 **6** *3 ¾* **Wicked Daze (IRE)**[17] 3277 8-9-7 **73** .... ShaneBKelly(7) 2 59
(Linda Perratt) *trckd ldrs: drvn and outpcd over 2f out: n.d after* **40/1**

6 **7** *1 ¼* **Morning Time (IRE)**[16] 3319 5-9-11 **70** .... JamieGoldstein 10 54
(Lucinda Russell) *trckd ldrs tl rdn and wknd fr 2f out* **25/1**

050- **8** *5* **Regent's Secret (USA)**[9] 6224 11-8-12 **57** ....(v) GregFairley 9 32
(Jim Goldie) *dwlt: sn pushed along in rr: rdn over 3f out: shortlived effrt wl over 1f out: nvr on terms* **18/1**

525- **9** *1 ¼* **Daytime Dreamer (IRE)**[99] 5355 7-9-4 **66** .... DeclanCannon(3) 3 39
(Martin Todhunter) *midfield: rdn 3f out: wknd 2f out* **28/1**

5000 **10** *4 ½* **Scented**[16] 3303 3-8-7 **64** ....(p[1]) DuranFentiman 11 29
(Ian Semple) *bhd: struggling over 3f out: sn btn* **50/1**

4345 **11** *66* **The Oil Magnate**[22] 3115 6-9-11 **73** .... PatrickDonaghy(3) 8 —
(Michael Dods) *in tch tl rdn and wknd over 3f out: virtually p.u over 1f out* **11/1**

2m 22.13s (-3.47) **Going Correction** -0.125s/f (Firm)
WFA 3 from 4yo+ 12lb **11** Ran SP% **114.5**
Speed ratings (Par 103): **107,103,103,102,98 95,94,91,90,87 39**
Tote Swingers:1&2:£4.00, 2&3:£5.70, 1&3:£2.20 CSF £31.15 CT £98.38 TOTE £4.80: £1.90, £2.60, £1.80; EX 31.90.
Owner Geoff & Sandra Turnbull **Bred** Bricklow Ltd **Trained** Middleham Moor, N Yorks

FOCUS
This looked a reasonable race for the grade and there's no reason to doubt the form, particularly with regards the front two, who look worth keeping on side. The winner has been rated a big improver and the third and fourth set the standard.

3859 TOTEPOOL A BETTER WAY TO BET H'CAP (QUALIFIER FOR THE BETFAIR BONUS SCOTTISH RACING MILE FINAL) 1m 65y

8:05 (8:07) (Class 5) (0-70,67) 3-Y-0+ **£4,204** (£1,251; £625; £312) **Stalls** Low

Form RPR

6352 **1** **Hits Only Jude (IRE)**[26] 2996 8-9-7 **60** ....(v) GregFairley 9 69
(Declan Carroll) *cl up: rdn to ld over 2f out: hld on wl u.p fnl f* **6/1**[3]

3121 **2** *shd* **Thinking**[12] 3454 4-9-9 **62** .... DuranFentiman 2 71
(Tim Easterby) *trckd ldrs: rdn over 2f out: styd on wl u.p fnl f: jst hld* **3/1**[1]

-446 **3** 1 ½ **Royal Straight**[57] 2059 6-9-6 **64**.. JulieBurke(5) 3 69
(Linda Perratt) *hld up: stdy hdwy over 2f out: chsng ldrs and rdn over 1f out: kpt on same pce fnl f* **7/1**

5611 **4** 2 ¼ **Botham (USA)**[16] 3306 7-9-10 **63**................................ AndrewMullen 11 63
(Jim Goldie) *in tch: pushed along and outpcd over 3f out: rallied 2f out: styd on fnl f* **9/2**[2]

0004 **5** ¾ **Northern Flyer (GER)**[12] 3454 5-9-2 **58**.................(v) DeclanCannon(3) 1 56
(John Quinn) *t.k.h: led to over 2f out: kpt on same pce fr over 1f out* **9/1**

-545 **6** ¾ **Jaldarshaan (IRE)**[26] 2985 4-9-8 **61**........................ PJMcDonald 8 58
(Alan Swinbank) *t.k.h: in tch: rdn and edgd lft 2f out: sn one pce* **13/2**

6006 **7** ¾ **Raleigh Quay (IRE)**[43] 2474 4-9-12 **65**........................(p) KellyHarrison 5 60
(Micky Hammond) *hld up: rdn over 2f out: hdwy over 1f out: nvr rchd ldrs* **14/1**

8 shd **Honest And True (IRE)**[58] 2039 4-9-3 **59**.............. PatrickDonaghy(3) 7 54
(Ian Semple) *hld up: rdn over 3f out: nvr able to chal* **18/1**

46-0 **9** 1 **Barliffey (IRE)**[12] 3453 6-10-0 **67**.......................... JamieGoldstein 4 59
(Lucinda Russell) *hld up: rdn 3f out: nvr rchd ldrs* **28/1**

33-6 **10** 6 **Social Rhythm**[22] 3113 7-10-0 **67**.............................. PaddyAspell 12 46
(Alistair Whillans) *s.i.s: bhd: rdn over 2f out: nvr on terms* **25/1**

6500 **11** hd **Abernethy (IRE)**[22] 3116 3-8-0 **48** oh1.......................... PatrickMathers 6 24
(Linda Perratt) *trckd ldrs: rdn over 2f out: wknd qckly appr fnl f* **25/1**

1m 47.69s (-0.71) **Going Correction** -0.125s/f (Firm)
WFA 3 from 4yo+ 9lb **11** Ran SP% **116.4**
Speed ratings (Par 103): **98,97,96,94,93 92,91,91,90,84 84**
Tote Swingers:1&2:£3.60, 2&3:£5.80, 1&3:£5.60 CSF £23.46 CT £131.90 TOTE £7.20: £1.80, £1.30, £2.40; EX 30.20.
Owner Dreams **Bred** Swordlestown Stud **Trained** Sledmere, E Yorks
■ Stewards' Enquiry : Greg Fairley caution: used whip with excessive frequency.

FOCUS
Another race on the card which looks to represent solid form for the level with some in-form horses fighting out the finish. The runner-up has been rated as running another personal best.

3860 JOHN SMITH'S FAIR FRIDAY NEXT WEEK H'CAP 5f 4y
8:40 (8:41) (Class 6) (0-65,65) 3-Y-O **£2,070** (£616; £307; £153) **Stalls** High

Form RPR

0603 **1** **Boundless Spirit**[24] 3040 3-9-4 **65**......................(t) MichaelO'Connell(3) 3 71+
(David Nicholls) *rrd and missed break: bhd: hdwy over 2f out: effrt and drvn over 1f out: led ins fnl f: jst hld on* **11/2**[3]

0106 **2** nse **Saxonette**[22] 3126 3-9-6 **64**.. PJMcDonald 6 70
(Linda Perratt) *hld up: hdwy on outside over 1f out: kpt on wl fnl f: jst hld* **28/1**

000 **3** 1 **Hardrock Diamond**[81] 1459 3-8-2 **46** oh1.................. DuranFentiman 7 48
(Ian Semple) *towards rr: drvn along 1/2-way: hdwy over 1f out: kpt on fnl f* **12/1**

2325 **4** 3 ¼ **Tancred Spirit**[22] 3143 3-8-1 **48**..............................(v[1]) DeclanCannon(3) 9 39
(Paul Midgley) *led tl rdn and hdd ins fnl f: sn btn* **4/1**[2]

-404 **5** hd **Bailadeira**[22] 3126 3-9-0 **58**.. GregFairley 4 48
(Tim Etherington) *prom: rdn and edgd lft over 1f out: kpt on same pce fnl f* **10/1**

2404 **6** 1 ¾ **Kassaab**[19] 3238 3-8-8 **59**..(b) ShirleyTeasdale(7) 5 43
(Jeremy Gask) *cl up: rdn and edgd lft 2f out: wknd appr fnl f* **18/1**

-520 **7** nk **Pizzarra**[36] 2697 3-8-11 **58**.. AmyRyan(3) 2 41
(James Given) *prom: effrt 2f out: wknd ins fnl f* **15/2**

3451 **8** ¾ **Dotty Darroch**[31] 2805 3-8-8 **57**.................................... JulieBurke(5) 8 37
(Robin Bastiman) *in tch: rdn and edgd rt over 2f out: sn no ex: btn fnl f* **7/4**[1]

0060 **9** 1 ½ **Country Waltz**[6] 3661 3-8-12 **56**.................................. KellyHarrison 1 31
(Linda Perratt) *midfield on outside: rdn 1/2-way: btn over 1f out* **22/1**

5600 **10** 3 ¼ **Bygones For Coins (IRE)**[3] 3731 3-8-5 **49**.................. PatrickMathers 10 12
(Alan Berry) *prom: drvn and outpcd 1/2-way: sn btn* **33/1**

60.17 secs (0.17) **Going Correction** +0.025s/f (Good) **10** Ran SP% **116.3**
Speed ratings (Par 98): **99,98,97,92,91 89,88,87,84,79**
Tote Swingers:1&2:£11.50, 2&3:£26.10, 1&3:£11.80 CSF £149.27 CT £1767.85 TOTE £7.50: £2.60, £6.30, £4.70; EX 118.10.
Owner Pinnacle Invincible Spirit Partnership **Bred** Silfield Bloodstock **Trained** Sessay, N Yorks
■ Stewards' Enquiry : Michael O'Connell two-day ban: used whip with excessive frequency (Jul 24-25)

FOCUS
A low-grade sprint. Tancred Spirit went hard in front, setting it up for those coming from behind. The form has been given a chance, with the runner-up the key.
T/Plt: £134.80 to a £1 stake. Pool:£45,940.69. 248.70 winning tickets T/Qpdt: £36.50 to a £1 stake. Pool:£4,383.45. 88.80 winning tickets RY

3819 NEWMARKET (R-H)
Saturday, July 9

OFFICIAL GOING: Good to firm (good in places; overall 8.5, far 8.3, stands' 8.6, centre 8.6)
Wind: Fresh, across. Weather: Overcast

3861 32RED.COM SUPERLATIVE STKS (GROUP 2) 7f
2:20 (2:21) (Class 1) 2-Y-O
£34,026 (£12,900; £6,456; £3,216; £1,614; £810) **Stalls** High

Form RPR

31 **1** **Red Duke (USA)**[21] 3186 2-9-0 0.................................... KierenFallon 11 107+
(John Quinn) *a.p: nt clr run and swtchd rt over 1f out: rdn to ld wl ins fnl f: r.o* **10/1**

10 **2** nk **Chandlery (IRE)**[25] 3012 2-9-0 0.................................... SteveDrowne 2 106
(Richard Hannon) *w ldr tl led over 1f out: rdn and hdd wl ins fnl f: r.o* **14/1**

102 **3** 4 **Silverheels (IRE)**[9] 3540 2-9-0 0.................................... HayleyTurner 6 96
(Paul Cole) *chsd ldrs: nt clr run and swtchd rt over 1f out: styd on same pce ins fnl f* **16/1**

21 **4** 1 ¼ **Pearl Mix (IRE)**[17] 3282 2-9-0 0.................................... SebSanders 8 93
(Ralph Beckett) *led: rdn and hdd over 1f out: no ex ins fnl f* **4/1**[2]

22 **5** nk **Fort Bastion (IRE)**[21] 3152 2-9-0 0.................................... OlivierPeslier 5 92
(Richard Hannon) *hld up: pushed along 1/2-way: hdwy u.p over 1f out: nvr rchd ldrs* **11/4**[1]

310 **6** 4 **Commissar**[25] 3012 2-9-0 0.................................... FrankieDettori 9 82
(Mahmood Al Zarooni) *hld up: rdn over 2f out: hung lft fnl f: n.d* **16/1**

1 **7** 1 **Ghostwriting (USA)**[12] 3472 2-9-0 0.................................... NickyMackay 4 79
(John Gosden) *hld up in tch: rdn and hung rt over 1f out: wknd fnl f* **10/1**

1 **8** nk **Sound Advice**[22] 3123 2-9-0 0.................................... HughBowman 3 78
(Keith Dalgleish) *s.i.s: hld up: styng on but nvr any ch whn hmpd ins fnl f: eased* **14/1**

12 **9** 5 **Sir Glanton (IRE)**[13] 3429 2-9-0 0.................................... JimmyFortune 1 65
(Amanda Perratt) *hld up: rdn 1/2-way: a in rr* **12/1**

33 **10** ¾ **Sehnsucht (IRE)**[8] 3590 2-9-0 0.................................... MartinHarley 10 63
(Alan McCabe) *racd keenly: trckd ldrs: hmpd and wknd over 2f out* **100/1**

1 **11** 1 ½ **John Lightbody**[29] 2882 2-9-0 0.................................... SilvestreDeSousa 7 59
(Mark Johnston) *s.i.s: racd keenly early in rr: pushed along over 4f out: wknd over 2f out: hung lft over 1f out* **11/2**[3]

1m 24.57s (-1.13) **Going Correction** -0.025s/f (Good) **11** Ran SP% **114.0**
Speed ratings (Par 106): **105,104,100,98,98 93,92,92,86,85 83**
Tote Swingers:1&2:£27.10, 2&3:£27.20, 1&3:£17.70 CSF £137.11 TOTE £11.10: £3.90, £10.40, £6.90; EX 230.80 Trifecta £3895.60 Part won. Pool 5,264.34 - 0.01 winning units..
Owner Maxilead Limited **Bred** B P Walden Jr & H Sexton **Trained** Settrington, N Yorks

FOCUS
Far side track used with stalls on far side except 1m4f centre. Bend into home straight repositioned, adding 16m to 1m4f race. The visual impression was that the pace only increased to a good tempo after around a couple of furlongs, and by that point the first four finishers were all positioned in the front five places with those further back facing a near impossible task to get involved. The time was a respectable 0.66 seconds slower than the Bunbury Cup, and unlike in that race where the winner was the sole runner against the stands' rail, all of these raced far side.

NOTEBOOK
Red Duke(USA) started off in a conditions event at Pontefract (6f, finished third), giving a clue of the regard in which he's held, before winning a 7f maiden at Redcar (runner-up won fair contest next time), and he proved himself a smart colt with a much-improved effort on this significant rise in class. He showed signs of greenness from some way out, but had the right partner to get him into a good racing rhythm and it was clear he had plenty to offer when Fallon began to look for room and switched out for a run inside the final 2f. John Quinn's runner didn't accelerate immediately, but was suited by the stiff finish and showed a good attitude. While more will be needed if the winner is to break through at the top level, further improvement is highly likely and his pedigree suggests he will stay 1m at the very least. He doesn't hold any big-race entries in Britain or Ireland, but it would be dangerous to underestimate him. The trainer is hopeful the horse could be a Guineas type. (tchd 11-1)
Chandlery(IRE) was allowed to go off a much bigger price than his stable companion Fort Bastion, but he outran his odds with a game effort in defeat, proving himself better than he showed when mid-division in the Coventry. He was a bit keen early but settled fine once the gallop increased and was in the right place. It was admirable how well he stuck on when headed by the winner and he'll be worth his place in something like the Vintage Stakes. (op 16-1)
Silverheels(IRE) is a January foal and hadn't progressed from a taking winning debut over 5f back in April, including when only second in a three-runner race over 6f last time, but he showed he's more than just an early-season juvenile with a respectable effort. The step up in trip suited, though he was well placed considering how the race unfolded and was still beaten a fair way. (op 14-1 tchd 12-1)
Pearl Mix(IRE) had his first two starts on the Kempton Polytrack, latterly when really impressive from the front in a 7f maiden, but dominating this field proved beyond him. He still ran well, especially as this came only 17 days after his big winning effort. (op 5-1)
Fort Bastion(IRE) couldn't build on his second-place finish to Maybe in the Chesham Stakes, and that's weak-looking form considering the third and fourth have since been beaten in maiden company. In fairness to the horse, though, he was poorly placed considering how the race unfolded having never recovered from a sluggish beginning. (op 9-4 tchd 15-8)
Commissar ran woefully in the Coventry on his first start since being bought out of Paul Cole's yard. This was better, but it didn't prove him up to the level. (op 10-1)
Ghostwriting(USA) overcame greenness to make a taking winning debut over this trip on Polytrack, but he ran like a horse who found this rise in class coming too soon. He wasn't too far off the pace, but was in trouble before halfway. It also remains to be seen whether turf is his best surface. (op 14-1)
Sound Advice, a Musselburgh maiden winner on his debut, was another who found this beyond him so soon in his career. He was still green, missing the break and coming off the bridle by halfway, but would have been a little closer with a better run late on. (op 16-1)
Sir Glanton(IRE) failed to advertise the form of Eureka, the horse he chased home over 6f at Salisbury last time. (op 14-1 tchd 16-1)
John Lightbody did not confirm the promise of his Sandown debut win, looking unsuited by the pace of the race, being keen early and then coming off the bridle once the tempo lifted, perhaps having been disappointed through the opening stages. (op 7-1)

3862 32RED BUNBURY CUP (H'CAP) 7f
2:55 (2:57) (Class 2) 3-Y-O+
£31,125 (£9,320; £4,660; £2,330; £1,165; £585) **Stalls** High

Form RPR

4006 **1** **Brae Hill (IRE)**[14] 3397 5-9-1 **93**.................................... BarryMcHugh 2 104
(Richard Fahey) *racd alone stands' side: w ldrs tl led over 4f out: rdn out* **11/1**

-102 **2** 1 ¾ **Excellent Guest**[22] 3109 4-9-2 **94**.................................... PhilipRobinson 18 102+
(George Margarson) *racd far side: prom: nt clr run and lost pl over 1f out: rallied and r.o to ld that gp wl ins fnl f: nt rch wnr* **11/1**

6060 **3** ¾ **Fathsta (IRE)**[14] 3410 6-9-2 **94**.................................... SilvestreDeSousa 12 98
(David Simcock) *racd far side: mid-div: hdwy 1/2-way: rdn to ld that gp over 1f out tl hdd wl ins fnl f* **18/1**

00-0 **4** nk **Mr David (USA)**[24] 3032 4-9-3 **95**.................................... HughBowman 14 98
(Jamie Osborne) *racd far side: hld up: hdwy over 1f out: edgd rt ins fnl f: r.o* **33/1**

3010 **5** ½ **Crown Choice**[14] 3410 6-9-5 **97**.................................... KierenFallon 13 99
(Walter Swinburn) *racd far side: hld up: hdwy over 1f out: r.o* **14/1**

6345 **6** ½ **Docofthebay (IRE)**[22] 3109 7-9-5 **97**........................(b) OlivierPeslier 7 98
(David Nicholls) *racd far side: hld up: swtchd rt over 1f out: sn hung rt: r.o: nt rch ldrs* **9/1**[3]

0130 **7** nk **Nasri**[21] 3155 5-9-5 **97**.................................... WilliamCarson 19 97
(David Nicholls) *racd far side: chsd ldrs: rdn over 1f out: styd on same pce ins fnl f* **18/1**

6033 **8** ¾ **Angel's Pursuit (IRE)**[9] 3548 4-9-10 **102**........................ CO'Donoghue 3 100
(Richard Hannon) *hld up: swtchd to r far side over 5f out: r.o ins fnl f: nt rch ldrs* **33/1**

15-0 **9** hd **Al Khaleej (IRE)**[14] 3409 7-9-7 **99**.................................... SteveDrowne 11 96+
(David Simcock) *s.i.s: racd far side: hld up: r.o ins fnl f: nrst fin* **20/1**

-030 **10** shd **Fireback**[9] 3535 4-8-13 **91**.................................... MaximeGuyon 4 88
(Andrew Balding) *swtchd to r far side over 5f out: prom: rdn and ev ch over 1f out: no ex ins fnl f* **20/1**

0-00 **11** ¾ **Reignier**[99] 1122 4-8-9 **90**.................................... MartinHarley(3) 10 85
(Mrs K Burke) *racd far side: hld up: hdwy and nt clr run over 2f out: sn lost pl: rdn over 1f out: nt clr run ins fnl f: r.o: nvr trbld ldrs* **50/1**

5503 **12** nk **Striking Spirit**[22] 3109 6-9-2 **94**.................................... SebSanders 1 88
(Tim Easterby) *swtchd to r far side over 5f out: hld up: rdn over 2f out: hdwy u.p over 1f out: no ex ins fnl f* **8/1**[2]

0001 **13** shd **Imperial Djay (IRE)**[14] 3397 6-9-2 **94**.................................... JackMitchell 8 88
(Ruth Carr) *racd far side: hld up: rdn and swtchd rt over 1f out: n.d* **22/1**

-222 **14** ½ **Red Gulch**[22] 3134 4-8-12 **90**.................................... J-PGuillambert 6 83
(Ed Walker) *racd far side: mid-div: hdwy over 2f out: wknd ins fnl f* **14/1**

-142 **15** *1 1/4* **King Of Jazz (IRE)**[49] [2296] 3-8-13 **99** .... JimmyFortune 17 88
(Richard Hannon) *racd far side: plld hrd and prom: rdn over 2f out: wknd and eased ins fnl f* **8/1**[2]

-505 **16** *1 3/4* **Lovelace**[63] [1889] 7-9-10 **102** .... AdrianNicholls 9 87
(David Nicholls) *racd far side: hld up: nt clr run and swtchd lft over 1f out: nvr on terms* **33/1**

0-20 **17** *hd* **Mont Agel**[24] [3032] 4-9-5 **97** .... HayleyTurner 5 81
(Michael Bell) *swtchd to r far side over 5f out: hld up: hdwy 1/2-way: wknd over 1f out* **14/1**

5/00 **18** *nse* **Shamandar (FR)**[24] [3030] 4-9-6 **98** .... RichardHills 15 82
(William Haggas) *racd far side: prom: plld hrd: nt clr run over 1f out: eased ins fnl f* **14/1**

3021 **19** *1/2* **Manassas (IRE)**[22] [3109] 6-9-9 **101** .... FrankieDettori 20 84
(Brian Meehan) *overall ldr far side tl over 4f out: continued to ld that gp tl rdn over 1f out: wknd ins fnl f* **13/2**[1]

-004 **20** *1* **King Of Dixie (USA)**[9] [3548] 7-9-3 **100** .... HarryBentley(5) 16 80
(William Knight) *racd far side: chsd ldrs: rdn: hung rt over 1f out: sn wknd* **40/1**

1m 23.91s (-1.79) **Going Correction** -0.025s/f (Good)
WFA 3 from 4yo+ 8lb **20** Ran SP% **126.5**
Speed ratings (Par 109): **109,107,106,105,105 104,104,103,103,103 102,101,101,101,99 97,97,97,96,95**
Tote Swingers:1&2:£25.80, 2&3:£55.40, 1&3:£61.40 CSF £115.78 CT £2232.56 TOTE £14.00: £4.00, £3.30, £5.60, £8.10; EX 222.70 Trifecta £2732.70 Part won. Pool 3,692.83 - 0.30 winning units..
Owner Dr Marwan Koukash **Bred** James Doyle **Trained** Musley Bank, N Yorks

FOCUS
One of the more historic handicaps in the racing calendar looked well up to scratch with all of the major races of this type at Royal Ascot represented. The pace was strong as could have been anticipated but, not for the first time this season, punters who backed horses drawn on one side of a course can feel aggrieved that their horses were taken across the track, even considering there was evidence that the stands' side the previous day was not a disadvantage. The really strange part was that those who chose to go across from a low stall appeared to follow French jockey Maxime Guyon, who hadn't ridden at the track. For that reason, this isn't an easy race to assess. The form is taken at face value for now.

NOTEBOOK
Brae Hill(IRE) wasn't beaten far in this last year off a 5lb higher mark despite an 11th place finish. He hadn't managed to get his head in front for some time and may well have won this from any position, but the fact he came alone up the stands' rail probably had a huge bearing on the outcome. He heads for the Totesport Mile next. (op 12-1)
Excellent Guest ◆, whose trainer won this race with Atavus in 2001, has been running well this year and was possibly the best horse in the race on the day as he comfortably won from the group that raced down the 'wrong' side, even though he was repeatedly stopped in his run.
Fathsta(IRE) has won plenty of races in his time but was only fairly treated for this at best. Well positioned to come with a clear run, he ran right up to his best and had no excuses. (op 16-1 tchd 20-1)
Mr David(USA) hasn't had a lot of racing and was disappointing for Jamie Osborne on his first run for him. However, this trip looked much more likely to suit and he shaped a lot better as a result. He looks the sort to run well in these types of races considering he was good enough to finish fourth in a Gimcrack as a juvenile.
Crown Choice dead-heated for fourth in this last year off a 4lb lower mark and looked set to do a bit better this time until finding only the one pace inside the final furlong. (tchd 11-1)
Docofthebay(IRE) has been extremely consistent over a range of trips this season but his run was proof that those who started from a low draw, then went over did the wrong thing, as he came home really strongly when angled, possibly due to hanging, back across. (tchd 8-1)
Nasri, back up in distance after running in the Wokingham Handicap, had every chance but lacked the pace to get involved. (op 16-1)
Angel's Pursuit(IRE) did all that could be expected under top weight and emerges with plenty of credit.
Al Khaleej(IRE) ◆ finished last in a Listed race on his seasonal comeback recently but that was probably a sharpener for this, and he ran much better than his final position suggests because he was forced to switch plenty of times to get a clear run. He clearly loves this course and is one to bear in mind if found another opportunity here under similar conditions.
Striking Spirit hadn't been tried over this trip until last time (second start for Tim Easterby) when beaten 1.5l by [illegible] improvement at the distance. However, along with a few others, he was switched from a potentially good draw to the main [illegible] making a brief effort about 2f out towards the centre of the course, he faded out of contention. (op 9-1)
King Of Jazz(IRE) looked by far the most interesting runner in the race, although he had a huge negative to overcome in that no 3yo had won this in the previous ten years. His form was more than good enough to be of serious interest against some mainly exposed rivals, but one got the impression he isn't quite battle-hardened enough against experienced campaigners, as although he wasn't beaten far, he didn't look like winning. (op 7-1)
Manassas(IRE) took the field along on the far side but stopped really quickly once his rivals caught up to him, as though something wasn't quite right. (op 8-1 tchd 6-1)

3863 DARLEY JULY CUP (BRITISH CHAMPIONS' SERIES AND GLOBAL SPRINT CHALLENGE) (GROUP 1) 6f
3:35 (3:35) (Class 1) 3-Y-O+

£226,840 (£86,000; £43,040; £21,440; £10,760; £5,400) **Stalls** High

Form RPR

15-5 **1** **Dream Ahead (USA)**[25] [3011] 3-8-13 126 .... HayleyTurner 2 124+
(David Simcock) *trckd ldrs: swtchd lft over 1f out: nt clr run and swtchd lft again ins fnl f: r.o to ld and hung lft wl ins fnl f: readily* **7/1**[3]

0115 **2** *1/2* **Bated Breath**[21] [3154] 4-9-5 113 .... SteveDrowne 9 122
(Roger Charlton) *trckd ldrs: rdn to ld over 1f out: hung rt ins fnl f: hdd wl ins fnl f* **8/1**

4410 **3** *1 1/2* **Hitchens (IRE)**[21] [3154] 6-9-5 109 .... SilvestreDeSousa 7 117
(David Barron) *chsd ldrs: rdn over 1f out: styd on same pce u.p ins fnl f* **28/1**

2431 **4** *1* **Libranno**[14] [3404] 3-8-13 112 .... SebSanders 1 113
(Richard Hannon) *led: rdn and hdd over 1f out: styd on* **12/1**

40-1 **5** *nse* **Delegator**[59] [2005] 5-9-5 112 .... FrankieDettori 17 114+
(Saeed Bin Suroor) *hld up: hdwy and nt clr run over 1f out: swtchd lft: r.o: nt rch ldrs* **11/2**[2]

1001 **6** *nse* **Genki (IRE)**[14] [3394] 7-9-5 110 .... (v) GeorgeBaker 5 114+
(Roger Charlton) *s.i.s: hld up: hdwy and nt clr run over 1f out: r.o ins fnl f: nvr able to chal* **20/1**

0125 **7** *1/2* **War Artist (AUS)**[25] [3010] 8-9-5 115 .... OlivierPeslier 14 112+
(Markus Klug, Germany) *hld up: hdwy on outside over 1f out: styd on same pce ins fnl f* **25/1**

-514 **8** *1/2* **Elzaam (AUS)**[21] [3154] 3-8-13 114 .... RichardHills 3 111
(Roger Varian) *chsd ldr tl rdn and hung lft over 1f out: no ex ins fnl f* **7/1**[3]

5223 **9** *1/2* **Regal Parade**[14] [3394] 7-9-5 114 .... AdrianNicholls 6 109+
(David Nicholls) *hld up: rdn over 1f out: r.o towards fin: nvr nrr* **20/1**

-023 **10** *hd* **Star Witness (AUS)**[21] [3154] 4-9-5 115 .... (t) StevenArnold 10 109
(Danny O'Brien, Australia) *prom: rdn over 2f out: no ex ins fnl f* **4/1**[1]

3-60 **11** *1/2* **Dalghar (FR)**[21] [3154] 5-9-5 111 .... JimmyFortune 13 107
(Andrew Balding) *hld up: plld hrd: r.o ins fnl f: nvr on terms* **25/1**

00/6 **12** *1 1/2* **Winker Watson**[14] [3394] 6-9-5 97 .... HughBowman 16 102
(Mick Channon) *half-rrd s: hld up: rdn over 1f out: n.d* **66/1**

0-34 **13** *1* **Oracle (IRE)**[24] [3029] 3-8-13 115 .... CO'Donoghue 12 99
(A P O'Brien, Ire) *mid-div: hdwy on outer over 1f out: no ex ins fnl f* **18/1**

3100 **14** *2 3/4* **Jimmy Styles**[21] [3154] 7-9-5 107 .... (p) PhilipRobinson 8 90
(Clive Cox) *hld up: plld hrd: hdwy over 4f out: wknd fnl f* **66/1**

/402 **15** *1* **Monsieur Chevalier (IRE)**[21] [3154] 4-9-5 116 .... KierenFallon 4 87
(Richard Hannon) *mid-div: sn pushed along: wknd over 1f out* **12/1**

0-16 **16** *2 1/4* **Amico Fritz (GER)**[21] [3154] 5-9-5 112 .... MaximeGuyon 11 80
(H-A Pantall, France) *chsd ldrs: rdn over 2f out: wknd fnl f* **16/1**

1m 10.66s (-1.84) **Going Correction** -0.025s/f (Good)
WFA 3 from 4yo+ 6lb **16** Ran SP% **121.7**
Speed ratings (Par 117): **111,110,108,107,106 106,106,105,104,104 103,101,100,96,95 92**
Tote Swingers:1&2:£14.40, 2&3:£44.60, 1&3:£63.30 CSF £56.73 CT £1553.11 TOTE £9.20: £3.20, £3.80, £14.80; EX 85.90 Trifecta £2053.90 Pool 11,296.96 - 4.07 winning units..
Owner Khalifa Dasmal **Bred** Darley **Trained** Newmarket, Suffolk
■ Hayley Turner is only the second female jockey to win a GB Group 1, after Alex Greaves (d-h in 1997 Nunthorpe on Ya Malak).

FOCUS
Following Brae Hill's solo effort against the stands' rail (quicker than far side according to GoingStick) in the Bunbury Cup, it was no surprise the entire field congregated towards the near-side fence and those drawn low were at an advantage, with five of the first six emerging from single-figure stalls. A prominent position was also essential. A field of 16 represented the largest turnout since Sakhee's Secret fared best of the 18 runners who lined up in 2007, but Dream Ahead was a class apart and this goes some way to vindicating his position as the joint-top rated two-year-old alongside Frankel in last season's World Thoroughbred Rankings. The form looks sound enough with Dream Ahead pretty much matching his 2yo best and stamping himself the best sprinter in Europe.

NOTEBOOK
Dream Ahead(USA) ◆ looks a rare top-class British-trained sprinter. It's true to say he benefited from a favourable draw, as well as being handily placed, but this big, powerful colt still won in a most taking manner. He travelled with supreme ease just in behind long-time leader Libranno against the rail, and he was only seriously racing with less than a furlong to run, having been steered around the hanging Bated Breath to get in the open. Once free of trouble he surged to the front without requiring pressure from the whip, and though he again hung left in the final strides, seemingly that's just him. A dual Group 1 winner over 6f as juvenile (Prix Morny and Middle Park), it's understandable he was tried over 1m this year with a view to his stud career, but a fifth-place finish (behind Frankel) in the St James's Palace Stakes on his belated return suggested he didn't stay and this drop in trip on a stiff track proved ideal. The fast ground was a bit of a concern as he has a knee action and had been at his most impressive on a soft surface, but David Simcock pointed out afterwards these conditions were no quicker than for his Morny win. Plus the uphill finish will have reduced the harshness of the going. A stronger-run race is almost sure to see him in an even better light, while should he ever get back on his favoured soft ground it will take an exceptional sprinter to match him. He can probably prove effective from 5f-7f (although Simcock is reluctant to drop him in trip) and has plenty of options, with the Prix Maurice de Gheest at Deauville the obvious target ahead of the Haydock Sprint Cup. (tchd 8-1)
Bated Breath was well ridden by Steve Drowne and had his chance. He hung slightly right once under maximum pressure, ending up tight against the rail late on, but was basically beaten by a far superior rival. This ground suited him better than the soft going he encountered when fifth in the Golden Jubilee.
Hitchens(IRE) was only 11th in the Golden Jubilee last time, but it wasn't a big surprise to see him fare better on this occasion as he was favourably drawn, is a horse who travels well, and had the ground to suit, unlike at Royal Ascot. (op 40-1)
Libranno, winner of the Group 3 Criterion Stakes over 7f here on an easy surface last time, kept on well when headed, even after being a bit short of room inside the final furlong. A return to further should suit, though he probably enjoyed as soft a lead as one could have hoped for in a race like this. (tchd 11-1)
Delegator hadn't been seen since winning the Duke of York in May, but he goes well fresh. The draw cost him his chance, though, and he deserves credit for finishing so close. Not only was he best of those berthed in a double-figure stall, but he was also the pick of the hold-up horses. (tchd 5-1 and 6-1)
Genki(IRE) was up in class after winning the Group 3 Chipchase Stakes, but he was probably unlucky not to finish [illegible] closer as he was going well when short of room at a crucial stage.
War Artist(AUS) is probably not at good as he once was (third in this in 2008), but he did well to finish so close as he was caught wide throughout from an unfavourable draw. (op 28-1)
Elzaam(AUS) had impressed in a Newbury Listed race before running fourth in the Golden Jubilee, but he struggled this time.
Regal Parade was disappointing behind Genki in the Chipchase last time, but this was more encouraging. The ground was faster than ideal and he ended up too far back when having to wait for a clear run, but he finished well. He could build on this if bidding to follow up last year's victory in the Prix Maurice de Gheest, although his connections will hope Dream Ahead goes elsewhere.
Star Witness(AUS) was expected to go well, but he underperformed. He was well enough placed early, but it didn't take much for him to lose his position and perhaps his recent exertions have taken their toll. (op 11-2)
Dalghar(FR) managed to get some cover early on, but still pulled too hard. He's talented, but seems quite highly strung these days (coltish ahead of below-par run in Golden Jubilee) and it's proving difficult to get the best out of him. Official explanation: jockey said horse ran too free (tchd 22-1 and 28-1)
Winker Watson never threatened after starting awkwardly from an unhelpful stall, but this was only his second run back after a spell at stud. (op 50-1)
Oracle(IRE) had to prove he was up to this level, but being caught wide throughout didn't help. (op 16-1 tchd 20-1)
Jimmy Styles ran too free. Official explanation: jockey said gelding ran too free
Monsieur Chevalier(IRE) couldn't match the form of his surprising second in the Golden Jubilee. The representative of Richard Hannon reported the colt was unsuited by the ground. Official explanation: trainer's rep said colt was unsuited by the good to firm (good in places) ground (op 9-1)
Amico Fritz(GER) probably found conditions too fast and failed to build on a fine run from a poor draw in the Golden Jubilee. (op 25-1)

3864 32RED CASINO H'CAP 1m
4:10 (4:10) (Class 2) (0-100,92) 3-Y-O

£12,450 (£3,728; £1,864; £932; £466; £234) **Stalls** High

Form RPR

2-1 **1** **Albaasil (IRE)**[39] [2596] 3-9-3 **88** .... RichardHills 5 104+
(Sir Michael Stoute) *hld up: swtchd lft and hdwy 2f out: led 1f out: rdn clr* **11/4**[1]

-156 **2** *3* **Dimension**[7] [3649] 3-9-2 **87** .... KierenFallon 3 96
(James Fanshawe) *chsd ldrs: led 2f out: rdn and hdd 1f out: styd on same pce* **6/1**[2]

5-00 **3** ½ **Baptist (USA)**23 3067 3-9-2 **87**........................ JimmyFortune 2 95
(Andrew Balding) *hld up: rdn and edgd lft over 1f out: r.o u.p ins fnl f: nt rch ldrs* **25/1**

1220 **4** *hd* **Tropical Beat**23 3067 3-9-1 **86**........................(v¹) NickyMackay 10 93+
(John Gosden) *dwlt: hld up: hdwy over 2f out: rdn and hung lft over 1f out: r.o ins fnl f* **6/1²**

-121 **5** *1* **Las Verglas Star (IRE)**21 3168 3-9-2 **87**........................ BarryMcHugh 1 92
(Richard Fahey) *chsd ldrs: rdn and ev ch over 1f out: edgd lft and no ex ins fnl f* **14/1**

101- **6** 1¼ **Roman Eagle (IRE)**280 6553 3-9-7 **92**........................ JackMitchell 9 94
(Roger Varian) *hld up: swtchd lft and hdwy over 1f out: styd on same pce ins fnl f* **7/1³**

10 **7** ½ **Buzz Law (IRE)**64 1843 3-7-13 **75**........................ HarryBentley(5) 4 76
(Mrs K Burke) *chsd ldrs: rdn over 1f out: no ex ins fnl f* **14/1**

22-5 **8** 1¼ **Seattle Drive (IRE)**30 2847 3-9-7 **92**........................ PhilipRobinson 6 90
(David Elsworth) *hld up: rdn over 2f out: nvr trbld ldrs* **16/1**

5020 **9** 1½ **Mubtadi**23 3067 3-9-0 **85**........................ SilvestreDeSousa 12 80
(David Simcock) *chsd ldrs: rdn and hung rt over 1f out: wknd fnl f* **11/1**

13-0 **10** *hd* **Zacynthus (IRE)**22 3134 3-9-6 **91**........................ FrankieDettori 7 85
(Mahmood Al Zarooni) *hld up in tch: rdn and hung lft over 1f out: wknd fnl f* **20/1**

1130 **11** *2* **Ektibaas**23 3067 3-9-2 **87**........................ SebSanders 11 77
(B W Hills) *prom: nt clr run over 2f out: wknd over 1f out* **16/1**

2113 **12** 1½ **Chosen Character (IRE)**14 3378 3-8-11 **82**.......(vt) RichardKingscote 8 68
(Tom Dascombe) *led: rdn and hdd 2f out: wknd over 1f out* **14/1**

5031 **13** 2¾ **Weapon Of Choice (IRE)**14 3400 3-8-12 **83**........................ SteveDrowne 13 63
(David Simcock) *chsd ldrs tl rdn and wknd over 1f out* **22/1**

1m 37.33s (-2.67) **Going Correction** -0.025s/f (Good) **13** Ran SP% **120.8**
Speed ratings (Par 106): **112,109,108,108,107 106,105,104,102,102 100,99,96**
Tote Swingers:1&2:£4.90, 2&3:£44.60, 1&3:£21.30 CSF £17.58 CT £299.82 TOTE £3.10: £1.70, £2.60, £7.20; EX 12.80 Trifecta £245.80 Pool 1,829.56 - 5.50 winning units..
Owner Hamdan Al Maktoum **Bred** Castlemartin Stud And Skymarc Farm **Trained** Newmarket, Suffolk
■ Stewards' Enquiry : Jimmy Fortune caution: careless riding.

FOCUS
A strong-looking contest in which all of the runners made a move towards the stands' side on leaving the stalls. This looks decent form and should produce quite a few winners, and the race has been rated positively.

NOTEBOOK
Albaasil(IRE) ◆ won a maiden known for throwing up Group performers at Yarmouth last time and was the least exposed in the line-up. He travelled like a smart type in behind and duly shot clear once given room to quicken. It would be a bit premature to get too carried away, he was getting weight from three rivals, but this contest has produced some classy horses recently (subsequent Group 3 winner Sea Lord won this last year) and he strongly gives the impression he can handle himself at a higher level if able to settle. (op 7-2)
Dimension returned to his best with a good performance, and while not good enough to hold off a classy looking winner, he did more than enough to claim second. The little bit of ease in the ground may have helped. (op 7-1)
Baptist(USA) ◆, who went to post early, promised plenty at two but hadn't come close to getting involved in a finish this season, so this was a lot better. He travelled like an above-average performer under restraint and eventually kept on well. If he now builds on this, he could be really interesting for a big-field handicap. (tchd 28-1)
Tropical Beat was noted as being unlucky in the Britannia at Ascot and connections reached for the visor in an attempt to sharpen him up. He made his effort wide of the field, closer to the centre of the track, and narrowly missed out on third. (op 5-1)
Las Verglas Star(IRE) had been raised 8lb for winning at Haydock last time, and that possibly told inside the final furlong as he lost a couple of places.
Roman Eagle(IRE) ◆, who was talked of as a possible German/Italian Guineas horse in the spring, had some good form at two and ended his season by winning a duel at Epsom. Connections will have been fairly pleased with this performance, but whether he'll be easy to place is a different matter.
Seattle Drive(IRE) ◆ made ground late on without being given a really hard time, and appeals as the sort to pop up in a nice handicap before the end of the year, possibly over further. (op 14-1)
Chosen Character(IRE) ran too free. Official explanation: jockey said gelding ran too free (op 16-1)
Weapon Of Choice(IRE) ran too free. Official explanation: jockey said colt ran too free (op 20-1)

3865 DE LA WARR RACING EBF MAIDEN FILLIES' STKS — 6f
4:45 (4:46) (Class 4) 2-Y-O **£6,469** (£1,925; £962; £481) **Stalls** High

Form RPR

1 **Desert Gazelle (USA)** 2-9-0 0........................ FrankieDettori 10 82+
(Saeed Bin Suroor) *trckd ldrs: led and hung rt over 1f out: shkn up and qcknd clr: impressive* **7/2²**

5 **2** *4* **Cheworee**15 3362 2-9-0 0........................ NickyMackay 12 70
(David Elsworth) *chsd ldrs: rdn and edgd rt over 1f out: styd on same pce ins fnl f* **20/1**

3 ½ **Ladyship** 2-9-0 0........................ KierenFallon 6 68+
(Sir Michael Stoute) *hld up in tch: racd keenly: shkn up over 1f out: styd on same pce ins fnl f* **9/4¹**

3 **4** ¾ **Lady Jameela**18 3257 2-9-0 0........................ HughBowman 13 66
(Mick Channon) *chsd ldrs: rdn over 1f out: styd on same pce fnl f* **7/1³**

5 ¾ **Hello Glory** 2-9-0 0........................ SilvestreDeSousa 3 64+
(David Simcock) *hld up: nt clr run: swtchd lft and hdwy over 1f out: rdn and hung lft ins fnl f: nt trble ldrs* **14/1**

0 **6** ½ **Caterina**50 2254 2-9-0 0........................ JimmyFortune 8 62+
(Richard Hannon) *chsd ldr: led over 3f out: qcknd over 2f out: rdn: edgd rt and hdd over 1f out: wknd wl ins fnl f* **25/1**

7 *1* **Cat Queen** 2-9-0 0........................ RichardKingscote 5 59
(Gay Kelleway) *chsd ldrs: rdn over 1f out: wknd ins fnl f* **40/1**

8 *1* **Flamborough Breeze** 2-9-0 0........................ JackMitchell 9 56
(Edward Vaughan) *hld up: hdwy over 1f out: hung lft and wknd ins fnl f* **100/1**

9 ½ **Silke Top** 2-9-0 0........................ AlanMunro 7 55
(William Jarvis) *s.i.s: hld up: nt clr run wl over 1f out: n.d* **66/1**

4 **10** ½ **Kune Kune**18 3257 2-9-0 0........................ SebSanders 2 59+
(Marco Botti) *chsd ldrs: nt clr run and lost pl over 1f out: nt rcvr* **7/2²**

0 **11** *shd* **Angel Cake (IRE)**21 3182 2-9-0 0........................ HayleyTurner 4 53
(Amy Weaver) *hld up: plld hrd: swtchd lft over 1f out: nvr on terms* **33/1**

422 **12** *2* **Midas Medusa (FR)**17 3270 2-9-0 0........................ RichardHills 1 53+
(Richard Hannon) *led at stdy pce tl hdd over 3f out: rdn and ev ch over 1f out: hmpd sn after: wknd fnl f* **10/1**

4 **13** ¾ **Absent Amy (IRE)**26 2997 2-9-0 0........................ PhilipRobinson 11 45
(Willie Musson) *s.i.s: hld up: rdn and wknd over 2f out* **20/1**

1m 13.47s (0.97) **Going Correction** -0.025s/f (Good) **13** Ran SP% **124.7**
Speed ratings (Par 93): **92,86,86,85,84 83,82,80,80,79 79,76,75**
Tote Swingers:1&2:£19.90, 2&3:£12.40, 1&3:£2.30 CSF £78.64 TOTE £4.60: £1.80, £6.20, £1.50; EX 88.70 Trifecta £433.60 Pool 2,525.65 - 4.31 winning units..
Owner Godolphin **Bred** W S Farish, Bcwt Ltd And Inwood Stable **Trained** Newmarket, Suffolk

FOCUS
A race with a mixed history of producing decent sorts, so it remains how high up the ladder Desert Gazelle can progress.

NOTEBOOK
Desert Gazelle(USA) ◆, a $400,000 yearling, was said to have been working as well as the stable's recent Kempton winner Mahkama, and was always prominent before lengthening nicely clear when Dettori asked her to go. There were signs of greenness when she hit the front, which should mean there is more to come. A flashy looker, she'll be worth her chance at a higher level amd bookies gave her a quote of between 16 and 33-1 for next year's 1,000 Guineas. (op 3-1 tchd 4-1)
Cheworee ◆ made her debut in a hot contest at this track, which contained Cherry Hinton winner Gamilati, and went a long way to proving that result wasn't a fluke with another solid effort. (op 16-1)
Ladyship ◆, the first foal of the top-class racemare Peeress, moved well just behind the leader and made a thoroughly pleasing debut. Her dam got better with age, although she was winning at a lower level earlier in her career, but one would expect to see this filly get a win under her belt soon before seeking black type. (op 5-2 tchd 11-4 in places)
Lady Jameela was one of a few to take a strong hold under restraint before keeping on, confirming the form with Kune Kune on their Newbury meeting. (op 8-1 tchd 13-2)
Hello Glory ◆ was given a really good introduction to racing and is definitely one that should be going much closer next time. Plenty of her relations have won at least one race and she looks like carrying on that tradition with normal progression. (op 16-1)
Kune Kune met all sorts of trouble up the rail and can be rated a good bit better than this run suggests. (op 13-2)

3866 JAGUAR XF NURSERY — 7f
5:20 (5:21) (Class 2) 2-Y-O **£9,703** (£2,887; £1,443; £721) **Stalls** High

Form RPR

41 **1** **Overpowered**23 3082 2-8-8 **79**........................ HayleyTurner 12 92+
(Paul Cole) *s.i.s: hld up: hdwy over 2f out: led 1f out: styd on wl* **8/1**

4101 **2** 3¾ **Wolfgang (IRE)**15 3345 2-8-11 **82**........................ JimmyFortune 8 85
(Richard Hannon) *hld up: hdwy over 1f out: sn rdn: r.o to go 2nd wl ins fnl f: no ch w wnr* **14/1**

51 **3** *nk* **Ladykin (IRE)**21 3161 2-8-3 **74**........................ JimmyQuinn 5 76
(Richard Fahey) *chsd ldrs: rdn and hung rt over 2f out: hung lft over 1f out: styd on* **5/1²**

210 **4** *3* **Falls Of Lora (IRE)**21 3152 2-9-7 **92**........................ FrankieDettori 7 87
(Mahmood Al Zarooni) *hld up: hdwy and hmpd over 2f out: styd on to go 4th nr fin: nvr nrr* **9/2¹**

3120 **5** ½ **Es Que Love (IRE)**25 3014 2-9-1 **86**........................ SilvestreDeSousa 9 79
(Mark Johnston) *led: rdn and hdd 1f out: sn wknd* **6/1³**

01 **6** 1½ **Democretes**42 2510 2-8-6 **77**........................ KierenFallon 11 66
(Richard Hannon) *chsd wnr tl rdn over 1f out: wknd fnl f* **9/2¹**

61 **7** 3¼ **Greatest Dancer (IRE)**37 2651 2-8-9 **80**........................ AlanMunro 6 61
(Jamie Osborne) *prom: rdn over 2f out: wknd over 1f out* **16/1**

522 **8** ½ **Sheila's Buddy**18 3242 2-8-0 **74** ow1........................ LouisBeuzelin(3) 10 54
(J S Moore) *prom: rdn and hung rt over 2f out: wknd over 1f out* **25/1**

413 **9** *hd* **Loyal Master (IRE)**8 3595 2-8-1 **75**........................ BillyCray(3) 1 54
(George Foster) *wnt rt s: hdwy over 4f out: sn rdn and hung lft: wknd over 2f out* **20/1**

510 **10** ¾ **Barolo Top (IRE)**25 3012 2-8-7 **78**........................ RichardKingscote 2 55
(Tom Dascombe) *hld up: rdn 1/2-way: wknd over 2f out* **8/1**

0330 **11** *2* **Yammos (IRE)**21 3152 2-8-0 **76**........................ HarryBentley(5) 4 48
(Mick Channon) *mid-div: sn pushed along: wknd over 2f out* **16/1**

1532 **12** *24* **Snowed In (IRE)**8 3595 2-8-4 **75**........................ AdrianNicholls 3 —
(J S Moore) *hld up: a in rr: wknd over 2f out: t.o* **33/1**

1m 25.19s (-0.51) **Going Correction** -0.025s/f (Good) **12** Ran SP% **119.5**
Speed ratings (Par 100): **101,96,96,92,92 90,86,86,86,85 83,55**
Tote Swingers:1&2:£15.50, 2&3:£15.00, 1&3:£9.00 CSF £112.53 CT £632.96 TOTE £8.30: £2.50, £4.20, £2.20; EX 113.30 Trifecta £839.20 Pool 2,120.73 - 1.87 winning units..
Owner Mrs Jill Haines & Jared Sullivan **Bred** Tafiya Syndicate **Trained** Whatcombe, Oxon
■ The 'official' ratings shown next to each horse are estimated and for information purposes only.

FOCUS
A deccent-looking contest.

NOTEBOOK
Overpowered ◆, whose stable won this last season, hadn't contested any big races but had some interesting form, especially his first start at York. Travelling strongly towards the rear, even though the gallop looked a fair one, it was far from certain he'd get home after those exertions, but he found quite a bit and won in the manner of a horse better than handicap grade. (tchd 15-2)
Wolfgang(IRE) was behind Es Que Love in the Windsor Castle but had already come out and won again since, over this trip. He held a similar position to the winner in the early stages but didn't have the class that one possessed to make the same mid-race move. That said, it was still a good performance to keep going after being a little keen early. (op 12-1)
Ladykin(IRE) had some really nice form in two previous starts and looked on a nice weight to get involved, but she took a while to hit top gear, hanging both left and right before duelling with the runner-up for that position. (op 9-2 tchd 4-1)
Falls Of Lora(IRE) got outpaced as the main body of the field tried to close in, before keeping on for pressure. (op 11-2)
Es Que Love(IRE), who had the misfortune to bump in to Frederick Engels on his last two starts, was up 2f in distance here and set a decent pace before tying up inside the final furlong. (tchd 13-2)
Democretes hadn't been out for a while but showed more than enough in May to suggest he was of interest here. However, after racing prominently, he didn't get home and may have needed this. (tchd 4-1)
Snowed In(IRE) was never travelling. Official explanation: jockey said gelding never travelled (tchd 28-1)

3867 EGERTON HOUSE STABLES H'CAP — 1m 4f
5:55 (5:57) (Class 3) (0-90,90) 3-Y-O+ **£8,409** (£2,502; £1,250; £625) **Stalls** Centre

Form RPR

4214 **1** **Tanfeeth**35 2711 3-9-1 **90**........................ RichardHills 16 101
(Ed Dunlop) *hld up: hdwy over 2f out: led over 1f out: sn rdn: hdd wl ins fnl f: rallied to ld post* **5/1²**

0-12 **2** *hd* **Spifer (IRE)**24 3044 3-8-7 **82**........................ KierenFallon 13 95+
(Luca Cumani) *stdd s: hld up: nt clr run: swtchd lft and hdwy over 2f out: rdn to ld wl ins fnl f: sn hung bdly lft: hdd post* **6/4¹**

1410 **3** ¾ **Porgy**7 3625 6-9-8 **84**........................ HughBowman 14 93
(David Simcock) *s.i.s: hld up: hdwy over 2f out: rdn over 1f out: styd on* **14/1**

1212 **4** *shd* **Hong Kong Island (IRE)**40 2544 4-9-5 **81**........................ SebSanders 10 89
(Micky Hammond) *a.p: rdn over 1f out: styd on* **9/1**

021 **5** 2¾ **Crassula**19 3224 3-8-2 **82**........................ HarryBentley(5) 8 86
(Terry Clement) *chsd ldrs: led over 2f out: rdn and hdd over 1f out: no ex ins fnl f* **13/2³**

3603 **6** *5* **Bedouin Bay**[29] 1651 4-8-12 **77** .... MartinHarley(3) 6 73
(Alan McCabe) *chsd ldrs tl led 1/2-way: rdn and hdd over 2f out: wknd fnl f* **66/1**

2100 **7** *¾* **Becausewecan (USA)**[25] 3013 5-9-12 **88** .... SilvestreDeSousa 1 83
(Mark Johnston) *chsd ldrs: lost pl over 5f out: rallied over 2f out: wknd fnl f* **14/1**

-402 **8** *11* **Magicalmysterytour (IRE)**[14] 3411 8-9-6 **82** .... PhilipRobinson 4 60
(Willie Musson) *hld up: swtchd lft over 2f out: shkn up and edgd rt over 1f out: nvr nr to chal* **12/1**

50-0 **9** *2 ¼* **Seven Summits (IRE)**[14] 3406 4-9-6 **82** .... JimmyQuinn 15 56
(Barney Curley) *prom: rdn over 3f out: wknd over 1f out* **66/1**

0-10 **10** *3* **Dance Tempo**[31] 2812 4-9-9 **85** .... HayleyTurner 3 54
(Hughie Morrison) *sn pushed along in rr: rdn over 4f out: n.d* **16/1**

0-00 **11** *1* **Chilly Filly (IRE)**[35] 2716 5-9-10 **86** .... RichardKingscote 7 54
(James Given) *led after 1f: hdd 1/2-way: rdn and wknd over 1f out: eased* **33/1**

3-50 **12** *shd* **Status Symbol (IRE)**[14] 3406 6-9-12 **88** .... (t) WilliamCarson 5 55
(Giles Bravery) *led 1f: chsd ldrs: rdn over 2f out: wknd over 1f out* **33/1**

450- **13** *3 ½* **Strategic Mount**[313] 5591 8-9-6 **82** .... FrankieDettori 9 44
(Paul Cole) *hld up: hdwy on outside over 2f out: wknd and eased fnl f* **25/1**

0013 **14** *36* **Buddy Holly**[8] 3581 6-8-11 **73** oh3 .... NickyMackay 11 —
(Robert Eddery) *chsd ldrs: n.m.r and wknd over 2f out: eased: t.o* **50/1**

2m 29.4s (-3.50) **Going Correction** -0.025s/f (Good)
WFA 3 from 4yo+ 13lb **14** Ran SP% **121.6**
Speed ratings (Par 107): **110,109,109,109,107 104,103,96,94,92 92,92,89,65**
Tote Swingers:1&2:£3.90, 2&3:£6.30, 1&3:£15.90 CSF £12.33 CT £102.31 TOTE £6.70: £2.20, £1.60, £4.50; EX 15.80 Trifecta £373.20 Pool 1,755.28 - 3.48 winning units..
Owner Hamdan Al Maktoum **Bred** Shadwell Estate Company Limited **Trained** Newmarket, Suffolk

FOCUS
A sound run handicap. A close finish, in which the runner-up have it away by hanging left when the race was at his mercy. The first two are both progressive 3yos and the form is set around the third.

NOTEBOOK
Tanfeeth, who was slightly disappointing on his handicap debut last time, albeit not disgraced, rallied well for Richard Hills, who never gave up on this step up in trip for the horse (something all punters want to see), which gave his mount the opportunity to pounce again. Lightly raced and clearly talented, he could easily land a big handicap over this sort of trip later in the season. (op 11-2 tchd 9-2)
Spifer(IRE) ◆ was as long as 3-1 in the morning. Things didn't look to be going according to plan over 2f out when he needed to be brought around runners, but he was manoeuvred into position to make a winning bid and seemed sure to collect when going to the front. However, the colt started to hang left shortly after hitting the front and was mugged on the line. If his jockey could have done anything different he would have used his whip in his other hand, something Luca Cumani suggested afterwards, but there is chance that the horse's eye was caught by what looked to be a camera positioned relatively close to the near-side rail, making him go left and away from it. Otherwise, there isn't a logical reason why he started to hang so badly, because he was described as being game when winning at Newbury and ran on strongly and straight at Kempton last time. He'll go up the weights for this but is open to more improvement. (op 7-4 tchd 5-4)
Porgy wasn't disgraced in the Old Newton Cup last time after landing a claimer at Beverley (retained by these connections) and travels like a Group horse when on the bridle. To be fair to him, he found quite a bit off it when push came to shove and is clearly in good heart. (op 12-1)
Hong Kong Island(IRE) had his momentum momentarily stopped and he was forced to sit and suffer for a few strides until getting in the clear. (op 12-1)
Crassula, making her handicap debut, came through to have her chance over 2f out but didn't quite get home in this class. (op 7-1 tchd 6-1)
Bedouin Bay won a novice hurdle the last time he was on the racecourse at Market Rasen, and shaped respectably here, although he was given a really hard ride.
Becausewecan(USA), down in trip after clearly not staying in the Ascot Stakes, needed plenty of driving and stayed on. (op 12-1)
Magicalmysterytour(IRE) was unsuited by the good to firm (good in places) ground. Official explanation: trainer said gelding was unsuited by the good to firm (good in places) ground (op 11-1)
T/Jkpt: Not won. T/Plt: £5,251.00 to a £1 stake. Pool:£174,795.94. 24.30 winning tickets. T/Qpdt: £35.90 to a £1 stake. Pool:£10,324.27. 212.45 winning tickets CR

3474 SALISBURY (R-H)
Saturday, July 9

OFFICIAL GOING: Good to firm (good in places)
Wind: Moderate, against Weather: sunny with some cloud

3868 BATHWICK TYRES SUPPORTS HEROS RE-HOMING RACEHORSES NOVICE AUCTION STKS — 6f
6:15 (6:15) (Class 5) 2-Y-O **£2,911** (£866; £432; £216) **Stalls** Low

Form RPR

1 **1** **Redact (IRE)**[37] 2640 2-8-9 0 .... RyanPowell(5) 6 88+
(Richard Hannon) *trckd ldr: led ent fnl f: pushed clr: easily* **4/6**[1]

01 **2** *5* **Son Du Silence (IRE)**[19] 3229 2-8-11 0 .... LukeMorris 7 70
(J S Moore) *led: rdn over 1f out: hdd ent fnl f: nt pce of wnr* **5/2**[2]

04 **3** *¾* **Mr Knightley (IRE)**[15] 3349 2-8-12 0 .... FrankieMcDonald 2 69
(Richard Hannon) *cl up: rdn over 2f out: no imp tl styd on ins fnl f: clsng on 2nd at fin* **11/1**[3]

06 **4** *3* **The Name Is Don (IRE)**[17] 3288 2-8-7 0 ow1 .... PatrickHills(3) 5 58
(Mark Gillard) *trckd ldrs: rdn over 2f out: nvr gng pce to chal: fdd ins fnl f* **50/1**

5 *3 ¼* **Loxton Lad (IRE)** 2-8-12 0 .... FergusSweeney 4 50
(Roger Charlton) *cl up: rdn over 2f out: wknd fnl f* **12/1**

6 *1* **Ishiamiracle** 2-8-4 0 .... NeilChalmers 3 39
(Andrew Balding) *s.i.s: racd green: sn pushed along in last but in tch: rdn over 2f out: no imp* **33/1**

1m 16.86s (2.06) **Going Correction** +0.225s/f (Good) **6** Ran SP% **109.5**
Speed ratings (Par 94): **95,88,87,83,79 77**
Tote Swingers:1&2:£1.10, 2&3:£2.70, 1&3:£2.60 CSF £2.34 TOTE £1.90: £1.10, £2.30; EX 2.60.
Owner Kennet Valley Thoroughbreds Iii **Bred** D And Mrs D Veitch **Trained** East Everleigh, Wilts

FOCUS
Rail erected up to 8yds off permanent far side rail between 6f and 2f. Following a dry night, the ground was officially good to firm. Watering had been carried out in the morning, with 2mm applied to the strip from the 2f pole and a similar amount between the 4f and 3f markers. Racing began with an interesting juvenile novice event in which Richard Hannon has a fine recent record, having won it with Dick Turpin in 2009 and Avonmore Star in 2010.

NOTEBOOK
Redact(IRE), easy winner of a Polytrack maiden on his only previous start, added to his stable's fine sequence in this contest. Quickly away, he was settled in second when the runner-up went on after a furlong and always travelling best. He went to the front approaching the 1f marker and drew clear despite still looking a little green. He is progressing, should win again, and the Super Sprint is the short-term target. (op 4-5)
Son Du Silence(IRE), successful over this trip at Windsor last time, showed decent speed to lead for half a mile, but was soon left behind when the winner changed gear. His future seems to be in moderate nurseries. (op 3-1)
Mr Knightley(IRE), a modest fourth over 7f at Folkestone last time, was held up in the early stages. He finished well, though, and appears to need a longer trip than this. He is now qualifies for nurseries and should not get a punitive mark. (op 9-1 tchd 8-1)
The Name Is Don(IRE), sixth of 11 over C&D 17 days earlier, raced in third for most of journey, but lost a place in the closing stages. He too now qualifies for nurseries, but may find life easier dropped into claiming grade. (op 28-1)
Loxton Lad(IRE), a newcomer by a first-season sire doing well, did not show enough to suggest he's an imminent future winner. He was never closer than fourth. (op 11-1)
Ishiamiracle, the only filly in the line-up, was green throughout. She should improve for this run, but will need to step forward a good deal in order to take a maiden. Official explanation: jockey said filly lost its action a furlong out (op 14-1)

3869 BATHWICK TYRES H'CAP — 6f
6:45 (6:45) (Class 5) (0-75,75) 3-Y-O+ **£2,911** (£866; £432; £216) **Stalls** Low

Form RPR

2455 **1** **Italian Tom (IRE)**[15] 3359 4-9-7 **70** .... LukeMorris 6 78
(Ronald Harris) *chsd ldrs: u.str.p 3f out: r.o to ld ent fnl f: kpt on wl: drvn out* **11/2**

-030 **2** *1 ¾* **Brynfa Boy**[8] 3588 5-9-9 **75** .... (t) MatthewDavies(3) 5 77
(Paul D'Arcy) *stdd s: last but in tch: rdn and hdwy whn hmpd ent fnl f: styd on to go 2nd sn after: hld nr fin* **10/1**

4042 **3** *½* **Desert Icon (IRE)**[14] 3412 5-9-2 **65** .... MartinLane 4 65
(David Simcock) *trckd ldrs: rdn over 2f out: nvr quite able to chal: kpt on same pce fnl f* **4/1**[3]

2-65 **4** *2 ¼* **Delaware Dancer (IRE)**[10] 3512 4-8-12 **61** .... JamesMillman 3 53
(Jeremy Gask) *prom: rdn 2f out: 1 l down whn hmpd ent fnl f: hld after: kpt on same pce* **10/3**[2]

-446 **5** *1 ¼* **Silvee**[5] 3685 4-8-7 **56** oh5 .... NeilChalmers 7 45+
(John Bridger) *trckd ldrs: rdn 2f out: looking hld whn bdly hmpd ent fnl f: no ch after* **16/1**

0524 **6** *1 ¾* **Steelcut**[2] 3784 7-9-7 **75** .... (p) MatthewCosham(5) 2 56
(David Evans) *led: hung lft u.p fr over 1f out: hdd ent fnl f: fdd* **5/2**[1]

0406 **7** *½* **Diamond Vine (IRE)**[3] 3723 3-9-3 **72** .... FergusSweeney 8 55+
(Ronald Harris) *trckd ldrs: rdn over 2f out: looking hld whn bdly squeezed out ent fnl f: no ch after* **12/1**

1m 15.72s (0.92) **Going Correction** +0.225s/f (Good)
WFA 3 from 4yo+ 6lb **7** Ran SP% **109.7**
Speed ratings (Par 103): **102,99,99,96,94 92,91**
Tote Swingers:1&2:£5.00, 2&3:£7.10, 1&3:£3.10 CSF £52.06 CT £224.20 TOTE £6.30: £3.00, £4.50; EX 52.30 Trifecta £157.30 Pool 4,555.74 - 21.42 winning units..
Owner S & A Mares **Bred** Tom Radley **Trained** Earlswood, Monmouths
■ Stewards' Enquiry : Matthew Cosham four-day ban: careless riding (Jul 24-26,28)

FOCUS
Just a run-of-the-mill handicap, with the top weight rated 75, but highly competitive on paper. The form's rated around the winner.
Steelcut Official explanation: jockey said gelding ran flat

3870 BATHWICK TYRES BRITISH STALLION STUDS E B F MAIDEN STKS — 6f 212y
7:20 (7:20) (Class 4) 2-Y-O **£4,528** (£1,347; £673; £336) **Stalls** Centre

Form RPR

1 **Bronterre** 2-9-3 0 .... PatDobbs 12 79+
(Richard Hannon) *a.p: led over 3f out: drifted lft fr 2f out: r.o wl to assert ins fnl f: pushed out* **9/2**[2]

2 *2* **Snooky** 2-9-3 0 .... FergusSweeney 9 74+
(Henry Candy) *trckd ldrs: rdn 2f out: nt pce to chal: r.o ins fnl f to snatch 2nd nr fin* **7/1**

3 *nk* **Eightfold** 2-9-3 0 .... DavidProbert 5 73+
(Richard Hannon) *mid-div: nt best of runs on rails over 2f out: pushed along and stdy hdwy fr wl over 1f out: styd on ins fnl f: snatched 3rd fnl stride: improve* **17/2**

3 **4** *nse* **Devdas (IRE)**[17] 3282 2-9-3 0 .... AdamKirby 6 73
(Clive Cox) *led tl over 3f out: kpt pressing wnr u.p: edgd lft 1f out: no ex and lost 2 pls fnl strides* **2/1**[1]

5 *1 ¾* **[illegible] (IRE)** 2-9-3 0 .... MatthewDavies(3) 11 70
(George Baker) *trckd ldrs: rdn over 2f out: styd on same pce* **20/1**

6 *2 ¾* **Mitch Rapp (USA)** 2-9-3 0 .... LukeMorris 8 63
(Harry Dunlop) *s.i.s: towards rr: rdn and styd on fr over 2f out but nvr rchd ldrs* **6/1**[3]

7 *½* **Amazing Storm (IRE)** 2-9-3 0 .... TadhgO'Shea 10 62
(Richard Hannon) *s.i.s: in rr: hdwy whn swtchd rt jst over 2f out: styd on but nvr threatened ldrs* **14/1**

8 *18* **Mount St Mistress** 2-8-12 0 .... TonyCulhane 2 11
(George Baker) *mid-div for 2f: sn pushed along in rr: wknd 2f out* **25/1**

9 *1* **Highly Likely (IRE)** 2-9-3 0 .... IanMongan 4 13
(John Dunlop) *little s.i.s: a towards rr: wknd 2f out* **20/1**

10 *1 ½* **Jambobo** 2-9-3 0 .... ShaneKelly 7 —
(William Knight) *trckd ldrs tl hung lft and wknd 2f out* **16/1**

0 **11** *nse* **Compton Monarch**[68] 1757 2-9-3 0 .... MartinLane 3 —
(Hans Adielsson) *trckd ldrs: rdn over 3f out: wknd 2f out* **40/1**

1m 31.19s (2.59) **Going Correction** +0.225s/f (Good) **11** Ran SP% **117.2**
Speed ratings (Par 96): **94,91,91,91,89 86,86,65,64,62 62**
Tote Swingers:1&2:£6.60, 2&3:£12.60, 1&3:£9.10 CSF £33.89 TOTE £6.60: £1.60, £3.40, £3.00; EX 43.10 Trifecta £558.70 Pool 3,699.52 - 4.90 winning units..
Owner Michael Pescod **Bred** Swettenham Stud & Lofts Hall Stud **Trained** East Everleigh, Wilts

FOCUS
Little worthwhile form to go on in this juvenile maiden, but it featured a clutch of nicely bred newcomers.

NOTEBOOK
Bronterre, a 110,000gns yearling whose dam won at this trip as a juvenile, made quite a promising start to his career. Always prominent and a little free in the early stages, he went to the front at the 2f marker and readily drew clear. His win was decisive and he ran slightly green when asked to quicken, but this does not look strong form and nurseries may prove his metier from now on. (op 4-1)
Snooky, a first-time-out son of out of a mare successful at this distance, was another who chased the pace from the start. He too stayed on nicely and, given his trainer's patient methods, is likely to come on for this run. (op 8-1)
Eightfold, a newcomer closely related to winners on the Flat and over hurdles, was always in the leading half-dozen. He plugged on towards the finish, without really quickening, and may well improve for this outing. Official explanation: jockey said colt was denied a clear run (op 10-1 tchd 8-1)
Devdas(IRE), beaten over 11 lengths when third on his Kempton debut, was an uneasy favourite. He led until the winner took over, but wandered when put under pressure and faded in the closing stages. This looked a step backwards. (op 15-8)

Piers Gaveston(IRE), a debutant half-brother to a winner in Italy, was towards the rear in the early stages. He made some late progress, but did not do enough to suggest a maiden win is just around the corner. (op 40-1)
Mitch Rapp(USA), a half-brother to a two-year-old winner in the US, was another some way back early on. He too plugged on late, without threatening to make a more significant impact.

3871 GORDON HOBBS MEMORIAL H'CAP 1m
7:50 (7:51) (Class 4) (0-85,85) 3-Y-O **£5,175** (£1,540; £769; £384) **Stalls** Low

Form RPR
5-21 **1** **Emilio Largo**[32] 2790 3-9-2 **80** IanMongan 2 93+
(Sir Henry Cecil) *trckd ldrs: led 2f out: sn rdn: idling but a doing enough to hold runner-up: rdn out* **11/8**[1]
55-1 **2** *1* **Maraheb**[21] 3183 3-9-7 **85** TadhgO'Shea 6 95+
(John Dunlop) *unsettled jst bef s and missed break: sn rcvrd to trck ldr: led briefly over 2f out: sn rdn: styd on but a being hld* **5/2**[2]
0-41 **3** *2* **Uptown Guy (USA)**[19] 3219 3-8-7 **71** (b) ShaneKelly 1 76
(William Haggas) *hld up in tch: trcking ldrs whn nt best of runs on rails over 2f out: rdn whn hung rt to far side rail wl over 1f out: styd on wout getting on terms* **9/1**
215- **4** *3 ¾* **Tick Tock Lover**[286] 6386 3-9-5 **83** FergusSweeney 5 79
(Jo Crowley) *led tl rdn over 2f out: hung lft whn no ex fnr over 1f out* **15/2**
0-10 **5** *3* **Chief Of Men**[51] 2229 3-8-7 **74** JohnFahy(3) 3 63
(Denis Coakley) *trckd ldrs: rdn 2f out: nt pce to chal: fdd ins fnl f* **20/1**
5232 **6** *nk* **Puttingonthestyle (IRE)**[19] 3232 3-8-13 **77** (b[1]) PatDobbs 4 65
(Richard Hannon) *hld up in tch: rdn 2f out: nt pce to get involved* **13/2**[3]

1m 44.46s (0.96) **Going Correction** +0.225s/f (Good) **6** Ran SP% **110.5**
Speed ratings (Par 102): **104,103,101,97,94 93**
Tote Swingers:1&2:£1.10, 2&3:£7.10, 1&3:£1.40 CSF £4.79 TOTE £2.20: £1.10, £1.70; EX 4.30.
Owner Malcolm C Denmark **Bred** Mrs M Chaworth-Musters **Trained** Newmarket, Suffolk

FOCUS
A decent handicap, with the top weight rated 85, and none could be confidently discounted. The early pace was steady. Muddling form but the first two are improving.

3872 PICADOR CHEVROLET H'CAP 1m 4f
8:25 (8:25) (Class 5) (0-75,74) 3-Y-O+ **£2,911** (£866; £432; £216) **Stalls** Low

Form RPR
3222 **1** **On The Feather**[19] 3215 5-9-7 **67** JamesMillman 2 75
(Rod Millman) *trckd ldrs: pushed along fr 2f out: led ins fnl f: styd on: pushed out* **4/1**[2]
-322 **2** *½* **Oneiric**[29] 2871 3-8-12 **71** JimCrowley 4 78
(Ralph Beckett) *a.p: rdn and ev ch fr 2f out: styd on but no ex nring fin* **7/2**[1]
1155 **3** *nk* **Dubai Glory**[19] 3233 3-9-1 **74** JamesDoyle 7 81
(Sheena West) *led: rdn and hrd pressed fr 2f out: hdd ins fnl f: styd on but no ex nring fin* **7/2**[1]
0-60 **4** *1 ¾* **Elrasheed**[37] 2648 3-8-13 **72** TadhgO'Shea 1 76
(John Dunlop) *in last pair: rn in snatches: rdn over 4f out: hdwy over 1f out: styd on same pce fnl f* **4/1**[2]
0-04 **5** *9* **Hoofprintinthesnow**[47] 2371 3-8-8 **67** LukeMorris 6 57
(Amanda Perrett) *trckd ldrs on outer: rdn 4f out: wknd over 1f out* **8/1**
6000 **6** *1 ¼* **Rio Prince**[18] 3256 4-8-11 **57** oh11 (vt[1]) RichardThomas 3 45
(John Bridger) *hld up in last pair: rdn 3f out: nvr any imp* **40/1**
6-23 **7** *6* **Maher (USA)**[138] 634 3-8-12 **71** MartinLane 5 49
(David Simcock) *awkward leaving stalls: trckd ldrs: rdn over 2f out: wknd over 1f out* **6/1**[3]

2m 39.35s (1.35) **Going Correction** +0.225s/f (Good)
WFA 3 from 4yo+ 13lb **7** Ran SP% **112.3**
Speed ratings (Par 103): **104,103,103,102,96 95,91**
Tote Swingers:1&2:£4.20, 2&3:£3.60, 1&3:£2.10 CSF £17.66 TOTE £6.60: £2.80, £1.60; EX 11.60.
Owner Mrs Jenny Willment **Bred** Mrs Jenny Willment **Trained** Kentisbeare, Devon

FOCUS
A modest handicap, in which the top weight was rated just 67, and the pace was not strong. The winner is rated in line with her Chester form.

3873 BRITISH STALLION STUDS E B F LADIES' EVENING FILLIES' H'CAP 1m
8:55 (8:58) (Class 3) (0-95,95) 3-Y-O
£9,337 (£2,796; £1,398; £699; £349; £175) **Stalls** Low

Form RPR
0-01 **1** **Azameera (IRE)**[39] 2582 3-8-12 **86** AdamKirby 4 91+
(Clive Cox) *in tch: rdn over 2f out: styd on wl to ld ins fnl f: drvn out* **9/4**[1]
1662 **2** *nk* **Belle Royale (IRE)**[30] 2833 3-9-1 **89** LukeMorris 7 93
(Mark Brisbourne) *in tch: rdn 2f out: str run ins fnl f: edgd rt: wnt 2nd towards fin: clsng fast on wnr* **10/1**
-043 **3** *1* **Byrony (IRE)**[30] 2847 3-8-9 **88** KieranO'Neill(5) 3 89
(Richard Hannon) *trckd ldr: rdn to ld over 1f out: hdd ins fnl f: no ex whn lost 2nd towards fin* **8/1**
41 **4** *1* **Thistle Bird**[41] 2528 3-8-10 **84** SteveDrowne 5 83+
(Roger Charlton) *in tch: squeezed up and dropped to last pair 4f out: sn nudged along: rdn 2f out: styd on fnl f* **9/2**[2]
20-0 **5** *nk* **Tipsy Girl**[28] 2926 3-8-2 **76** FrankieMcDonald 6 74
(Denis Coakley) *awkward leaving stalls: in last pair: swtchd rt and hdwy u.p 2f out: styd on same pce fnl f* **16/1**
2-30 **6** *nk* **Nordic Spruce (USA)**[49] 2319 3-8-12 **86** IanMongan 10 83
(Sir Henry Cecil) *racd keenly: trckd ldrs: rdn over 2f out: styng on same pce whn squeezed up briefly ins fnl f* **8/1**
-612 **7** *½* **Sylvestris (IRE)**[57] 2073 3-9-7 **95** JimCrowley 2 91
(Ralph Beckett) *led: rdn 2f out: hdd over 1f out: kpt on same pce* **11/2**[3]
2320 **8** *3 ¾* **Cala Santanyi**[14] 3405 3-8-2 **76** oh1 (p) DavidProbert 8 62
(Gerard Butler) *trckd ldr: rdn 2f out: wknd fnl f* **11/2**[3]

1m 45.42s (1.92) **Going Correction** +0.225s/f (Good) **8** Ran SP% **116.9**
Speed ratings (Par 101): **99,98,97,96,96 96,95,91**
Tote Swingers:1&2:£7.70, 2&3:£19.30, 1&3:£3.00 CSF £26.96 CT £157.08 TOTE £3.00: £1.10, £4.00, £2.80; EX 27.00 Trifecta £98.40 Pool 475.12 - 3.57 winning units..
Owner H E Sheikh Sultan Bin Khalifa Al Nahyan **Bred** P Byrne, Eimear Mulhern & B Grassick **Trained** Lambourn, Berks

FOCUS
All appeared to have a chance in this decent fillies' handicap, which was steadily-run in the early stages. Muddling form which has been taken at face value.

NOTEBOOK
Azameera(IRE) was up 8lb since her victory at Leicester six weeks earlier, but shrugged off that rise thanks to a strong-finishing victory. Keen in the early stages, when she was held up in fifth, she made progress approaching the 2f marker and quickened smartly. She will go up again for this success, but looks progressive and is bred to improve with age. (tchd 5-2)
Belle Royale(IRE), second to a good one off this mark at Haydock last time, ran another sound race. Held up off the pace early on, she too made good late progress, but could not quite get to the winner. She deserves another victory. (op 8-1)
Byrony(IRE), third off this mark at Nottingham a month earlier, seems a reasonable yardstick for the form. She was always in the first four and stayed on in the closing stages. She does not look especially well treated, but has now posted three sound efforts on the bounce. (op 11-1)
Thistle Bird, successful in a Nottingham maiden last time out, was unruly when first mounted and initially reluctant to go to post. She ran fairly creditably, staying on from the rear in the home straight, but obviously has the potential for showing temperament. (op 4-1 tchd 3-1)
Tipsy Girl, trying 1m for the first time, was held up at the back early on. She passed a few in the closing stages, but did not really prove that this trip is likely to bring about a marked improvement in what is now a 0-9 record.
Nordic Spruce(USA), on the sidelines for 49 days after a below-par effort at York last time, pulled hard early on and, probably as a consequence, was one-paced at the business end of the race. She may improve if this run has taken some of the freshness out of her. (op 10-1 tchd 12-1)
Sylvestris(IRE) has been raised 15lb since her Listed second at York in May and, on this evidence, her new mark is too high. She made a bold bid from the front and was still ahead 2f out, but was swamped in the closing stages. (op 6-1 tchd 5-1)
T/Plt: £77.60 to a £1 stake. Pool:£58,839.91. 553.34 winning tickets T/Qpdt: £16.40 to a £1 stake. Pool:£4,416.71. 198.80 winning tickets TM

3826 YORK (L-H)
Saturday, July 9

OFFICIAL GOING: Good
Wind: Moderate, across. Weather: Cloudy with sunny periods

3874 JOHN SMITH'S CITY WALLS STKS (LISTED RACE) 5f
2:05 (2:05) (Class 1) 3-Y-O+ **£17,760** (£6,717; £3,357; £1,677) **Stalls** Centre

Form RPR
-310 **1** **Masamah (IRE)**[35] 2714 5-9-0 106 PhillipMakin 13 113
(Kevin Ryan) *hld up in tch: gd hdwy wl over 1f out: rdn to chal ent fnl f: drvn and kpt on to ld last 100yds* **9/2**[2]
000- **2** *nk* **Amour Propre**[345] 4505 5-9-0 105 DaneO'Neill 6 112
(Henry Candy) *trckd ldrs: hdwy 2f out: rdn to chal over 1f out: ev ch tl drvn and nt qckn nr fin* **8/1**[3]
0042 **3** *nse* **Hamish McGonagall**[13] 3441 6-9-0 106 DavidAllan 4 112
(Tim Easterby) *led: rdn along wl over 1f out: drvn ent fnl f: hdd and no ex last 100yds* **7/2**[1]
20-0 **4** *2 ¼* **Golden Destiny (IRE)**[49] 2298 5-8-9 105 WilliamBuick 3 99
(Peter Makin) *swtg: racd wd: a.p: rdn and ev ch wl over 1f out: drvn ent fnl f and kpt on same pce* **25/1**
-050 **5** *shd* **Group Therapy**[25] 3010 6-9-0 108 JimCrowley 11 104
(David Barron) *hld up towards rr: hdwy on outer 2f out: sn rdn and styd on ins fnl f: nrst fin* **14/1**
-000 **6** *½* **Mister Hughie (IRE)**[21] 3155 4-9-0 100 TedDurcan 8 102
(Tim Easterby) *towards rr: hdwy 2f out: rdn over 1f out: kpt on ins fnl f: nrst fin* **33/1**
2200 **7** *nk* **Rain Delayed (IRE)**[14] 3394 5-9-0 104 RyanMoore 1 101
(Michael Dods) *bhd: hdwy wl over 1f out: rdn and kpt on ins fnl f: nrst fin* **11/1**
5013 **8** *nk* **Fitz Flyer (IRE)**[7] 3626 5-9-0 95 (v) TomEaves 5 100
(Bryan Smart) *trckd ldrs: effrt 2f out: sn rdn and wknd over 1f out* **22/1**
0-54 **9** *½* **Borderlescott**[49] 2297 9-9-0 112 NeilCallan 7 98
(Robin Bastiman) *bit bkwd: chsd ldrs: rdn along 2f out: grad wknd* **7/2**[1]
0041 **10** *nk* **Tax Free (IRE)**[23] 3073 9-9-0 94 AndrewMullen 10 97
(David Nicholls) *cl up: effrt 2f out and ev ch tl rdn and wknd over 1f out* **16/1**
1132 **11** *shd* **Liberty Lady (IRE)**[27] 2967 4-8-9 98 (t) JamesDoyle 12 91
(Des Donovan) *a towards rr* **16/1**
1124 **12** *2 ¼* **Doctor Parkes**[35] 2727 5-9-0 97 PaulHanagan 2 88
(Eric Alston) *a in rr* **12/1**
0100 **13** *nk* **Burning Thread (IRE)**[7] 3644 4-9-0 98 DaleSwift 9 87
(Tim Etherington) *in tch: rdn along 1/2-way: sn wknd* **66/1**

58.37 secs (-0.93) **Going Correction** +0.05s/f (Good) **13** Ran SP% **120.8**
Speed ratings (Par 111): **109,108,108,104,104 103,103,102,102,101 101,97,97**
toteswingers:1&2:£20.00, 2&3:£15.40, 1&3:£3.60 CSF £39.45 TOTE £5.30: £2.00, £3.60, £1.60; EX 81.30 Trifecta £449.00 Pool 1,225.67 - 2.02 winning units..
Owner Dr Marwan Koukash **Bred** Stanley Estate & Stud Co & Mount Coote Stud **Trained** Hambleton, N Yorks
■ This race has been moved from Chester, where it was known as the City Wall Stakes.

FOCUS
Rail moved out 3m on home bend from 1m1f to entrance to home straight, adding 7m to races of 1m and beyond. A strong Listed sprint. There was a tight three-way finish and the form is straightfoward and up to scratch for the grade.

NOTEBOOK
Masamah(IRE) bounced back to winning ways with a career-best effort and showed real guts in the process. He usually likes to stretch out from the front, as he did when winning a decent handicap off a mark of 100 over C&D on his penultimate outing, but wasn't able to gain the early lead as he wasn't best away from his high draw. That makes this success more meritorious and he has been a big improver so far this term. He has won over 6f, but is now looking a specialist over the minimum trip and a return here for the Group 1 Nunthorpe next month now looks on the cards. That will obviously represent another tougher test for him, but he wasn't disgraced on his previous outing in Group company last year and his liking for this venue would stand him in decent stead. He was available at 20-1 in the ante-post market with William Hill immediately after the race (op 6-1)
Amour Propre ◆, who looked fit for this reappearance, was making his belated seasonal bow with plenty to prove, but his yard is currently in decent form and he turned in a blinder. He quickened to throw down a strong challenge and was only just denied. It's hoped he can build on this. (tchd 9-1)
Hamish McGonagall likes this venue and proved popular after finishing second in a Group 3 at the Curragh on his previous outing. He was always up there and held every chance, going down fighting near the finish. He helps to set a decent standard and richly deserves to find another opening. (op 4-1)
Golden Destiny(IRE) ◆, racing without headgear, was quickly taken towards the far side from her low berth and raced pretty much solo. She lacked the required gear change, but kept on gamely to finish fourth and this was a much-improved effort. On this evidence, 5f is her minimum trip and it was only her second outing of the season so an end to her losing run may be imminent. (op 18-1)
Group Therapy was keeping on encouragingly late in the day and returned to the sort of form that saw him finish fifth in the Temple Stakes two runs back. He could build on this back on a stiffer track, but has become hard to catch right. (op 10-1)
Mister Hughie(IRE) was outpaced after a furlong or so and never threatened. However, he was doing his best work late on and it was his most encouraging effort for some time.
Rain Delayed(IRE) finished his race strongly, but this was not the first time he has done so and he's needs all to fall right in his races. (tchd 12-1)
Fitz Flyer(IRE) came into this in decent form and he posted a solid effort in defeat over a test sharp enough for his liking. (op 25-1)

Borderlescott came into this with course form figures reading 1116 and had to be of interest down in class. He was reported to have bruised a tendon when finishing fourth in the Temple Stakes when last seen, though, and he ran well below his best here. It may well be that he now wants a stiffer test and perhaps the run was needed, but it does leave him with a bit to prove.

Doctor Parkes was on his toes beforehand. (op 14-1)

3875 JOHN SMITH'S SILVER CUP (H'CAP) (LISTED RACE) 1m 6f

2:40 (2:40) (Class 1) (0-110,106) 3-Y-O+**£17,760** (£6,717; £3,357; £1,677) **Stalls** Low

Form				RPR
25-2	**1**		**Tactician**[56] 2107 4-9-5 **97**.......... EddieAhern 9 (Michael Bell) *lw: mde all: rdn along wl over 2f out: drvn over 1f out: kpt on gamely ins fnl f* **17/2**	108
6411	**2**	*1 ¼*	**Fox Hunt (IRE)**[21] 3156 4-10-0 **106**..........(v) NeilCallan 12 (Mark Johnston) *t.k.h early: chsd wnr: hdwy over 2f out: rdn wl over 1f out: drvn to chal ent fnl f: no ex last 100yds* **8/1**[3]	115
53	**3**	*2 ¼*	**Western Pearl**[22] 3120 4-9-0 **92** oh1.......... DaneO'Neill 13 (William Knight) *hld up towards rr: hdwy 4f out: swtchd rt and rdn to chse ldrs 2f out: drvn and styd on ins fnl f: nrst fin* **25/1**	98
6443	**4**	*1 ¾*	**Deauville Flyer**[14] 3396 5-9-2 **94**.......... TomEaves 20 (Tim Easterby) *stdd and swtchd lft to inner s: hld up towards rr: hdwy and wd st: effrt 3f out: rdn to chse ldrs 2f out: sn drvn and kpt on same pce* **12/1**	98+
1113	**5**	*nse*	**Eternal Heart (IRE)**[22] 3108 3-8-2 **95**.......... JimmyQuinn 14 (Mark Johnston) *in tch: hdwy to chse ldrs over 3f out: rdn along wl over 2f out: drvn wl over 1f out and kpt on same pce* **7/1**[2]	98
2000	**6**	*¾*	**Icon Dream (IRE)**[14] 3396 4-9-4 **96**.......... TedDurcan 10 (David Simcock) *lw: hld up towards rr: stdy hdwy 4f out: rdn 3f out: kpt on fnl 2f: nrst fin* **20/1**	98
-000	**7**	*hd*	**La Vecchia Scuola (IRE)**[14] 3396 7-9-0 **92** oh1.......... DanielTudhope 3 (Jim Goldie) *towards rr: hdwy over 3f out: rdn over 2f out: styd on wl appr fnl f: nrst fin* **25/1**	94+
3631	**8**	*½*	**Tominator**[14] 3396 4-9-5 **97**.......... PaulPickard 6 (Reg Hollinshead) *lw: hld up and bhd: gd hdwy on inner 3f out: rdn over 2f out: styd on: nrst fin* **14/1**	98+
-314	**9**	*4*	**Rock A Doodle Doo (IRE)**[21] 3156 4-9-5 **97**.......... PhillipMakin 18 (William Jarvis) *lw: hld up and bhd: hdwy 4f out: swtchd rt to stands' rails 3f out: effrt and n.m.r over 2f out: sn rdn and no imp* **5/1**[1]	93+
1020	**10**	*nk*	**High Office**[14] 3396 5-9-2 **94**.......... FrederikTylicki 5 (Richard Fahey) *chsd ldrs: rdn along wl over 3f out: drvn over 2f out and sn wknd* **20/1**	89
-255	**11**	*1 ½*	**Sabotage (UAE)**[14] 3403 5-9-13 **105**.......... MickaelBarzalona 19 (Saeed Bin Suroor) *in tch: hdwy to chse ldrs 4f out: rdn along 3f out: drvn over 2f out and grad wknd* **25/1**	98
10-3	**12**	*12*	**Vulcanite (IRE)**[20] 3204 4-9-11 **103**.......... JimCrowley 2 (Ralph Beckett) *lw: trckd ldng pair: rdn along 4f out: drvn 3f out and grad wknd* **8/1**[3]	80
-140	**13**	*¾*	**The Betchworth Kid**[23] 3066 6-9-11 **103**.......... AndrewElliott 1 (Alan King) *hld up: a towards rr* **28/1**	78
10-3	**14**	*2 ¾*	**Ajaan**[21] 3157 7-9-9 **101**..........(b) TomQueally 15 (Sir Henry Cecil) *midfield: rdn along over 6f out: sn wknd* **20/1**	73
00-5	**15**	*6*	**Total Command**[84] 1416 4-9-9 **101**.......... RyanMoore 8 (Sir Michael Stoute) *t.k.h early: trckd ldrs on inner: hdwy 4f out: rdn to chse ldrs 3f out: wknd over 2f out* **18/1**	64
0-62	**16**	*hd*	**Theology**[49] 2316 4-9-12 **104**.......... WilliamBuick 4 (Jeremy Noseda) *a towards rr* **8/1**[3]	67
1260	**17**	*2*	**Cracking Lass (IRE)**[15] 3356 4-9-2 **94**.......... PaulHanagan 11 (Richard Fahey) *a towards rr* **18/1**	54
001-	**18**	*23*	**Woolfall Treasure**[271] 6808 6-9-9 **101**.......... JamesDoyle 16 (Gary Moore) *in tch: rdn along on outer 6f out: wknd 4f out* **66/1**	29

2m 59.49s (-0.71) **Going Correction** +0.05s/f (Good)

WFA 3 from 4yo+ 15lb **18** Ran SP% **128.7**

Speed ratings (Par 111): **104,103,102,101,100 100,100,100,97,97 96,89,89,87,84 84,83,70**

toteswingers:1&2:£12.20, 2&3:£44.80, 1&3:£80.40 CSF £69.04 CT £1683.18 TOTE £10.90: [illegible] £0.30, £0.00, EX 06.70 TRIFECTA Not won

Owner The Queen **Bred** The Queen **Trained** Newmarket, Suffolk

FOCUS

An ultra-competitive Listed event, full of decent staying handicappers. There was a fair pace on, but making up ground from off the pace proved very difficult and it was a race in which it paid to race handily as the first pair were always in the firing line. The form is not rated as positively as it might have been.

NOTEBOOK

Tactician was allowed to dictate at the head of affairs and made all to open his account for the season at the second attempt. He had been a strong fancy for the Northumberland Plate a fortnight earlier only for to be pulled out of that on account of the soft ground and the drying surface here was much in his favour. He got the run of the race on a track that is well suited to prominent racers, but there was a lot to like about the way he fought off the progressive runner-up under pressure and he is clearly now peaking. This was his first handicap success and no doubt a return to the same C&D for the Ebor Handicap next month will now be on his agenda. He was cut into a general 12-1 in the ante-post betting for that and looks a big player as he will still be a relatively fresh horse going there. (op 10-1)

Fox Hunt(IRE) made it three wins for the year when readily landing the Duke of Edinburgh Handicap on soft ground at Royal Ascot last month, a clear personal-best effort. He got out early from his mid-draw to race near the early pace and that helped his cause, but in finishing a clear second-best off his big weight he no doubt posted another career-best in defeat. He was conceding 9lb to the winner and deserves another shot at him in next month's Ebor.

Western Pearl ◆ is another here that ran her best race to date. She took time to settle and was taken back off the pace as a result. She stayed on strongly inside the home straight and, despite just having a maiden win to her name, can surely add to her career tally before too long. (tchd 28-1)

Deauville Flyer was not done any favours by the outside draw and was another that had to come from well back, so he emerges with credit. He could have done with easier ground and is yet another likely Ebor candidate.

Eternal Heart(IRE), stablemate of the runner-up, was well fancied after running a decent race when third in the Queen's Vase over 2m last month. He was expected to enjoy the quicker ground and raced handily, but hit a marked flat spot turning for home. He was keeping on again inside the final furlong and remains capable of landing a big pot this year, most likely back over a stiffer test. (op 11-2)

Icon Dream(IRE) hasn't won since his debut in 2009, but he has been in good form of late and this was his best effort of the campaign. He's on a fair mark and deserves to get his head back in front. (op 25-1)

La Vecchia Scuola(IRE) stayed on dourly from off the pace to register her best effort of the season. She looks to be on the way back and is weighted to win again. (tchd 33-1)

Tominator ◆ was 7lb higher than when landing the Northumberland Plate on his previous outing and could have done without the ground drying up. He raced right out the back over this sharper test and, despite failing to confirm last-time-out form with three rivals that finished behind him at Newcastle, should be rated a good bit better than the bare form. Should it be riding on the easy side come Ebor time next month, he could well have a big say as he is evidently still capable of better as a stayer (op 11-1)

Rock A Doodle Doo(IRE) was an eyecatcher behind Fox Hunt at Royal Ascot last time and unsurprisingly got well backed. He raced well back on this step back up in trip and did his best to close in the home straight, but flattened out inside the final 2f. A more positive ride back down in trip looks required. Official explanation: jockey said colt hung right (op 13-2)

Theology Official explanation: jockey said gelding had no more to give

3876 52ND JOHN SMITH'S CUP (HERITAGE H'CAP) 1m 2f 88y

3:15 (3:18) (Class 2) 3-Y-O+ **£97,035** (£28,875; £14,430; £7,215) **Stalls** Low

Form				RPR
1-10	**1**		**Green Destiny (IRE)**[22] 3107 4-8-10 **99**.......... AdamBeschizza(3) 17 (William Haggas) *lw: hld up and bhd: gd hdwy 3f out: swtchd to outer over 2f out: led wl over 1f out: sn rdn clr and styd on strly* **6/1**[3]	115+
2-10	**2**	*3 ½*	**Modun (IRE)**[21] 3156 4-8-13 **99**.......... RyanMoore 8 (Sir Michael Stoute) *hld up: hdwy 3f out: effrt over 2f out: rdn wl over 1f out: chsd wnr ent fnl f: sn drvn and no imp* **11/2**[2]	108
0022	**3**	*1 ½*	**Lost In The Moment (IRE)**[22] 3107 4-9-4 **104**...(p) MickaelBarzalona 15 (Saeed Bin Suroor) *lw: hld up towards rr: hdwy wl over 2f out: rdn to chse ldrs wl over 1f out: kpt on u.p ins fnl f* **11/1**	112+
5231	**4**	*½*	**Beachfire**[22] 3107 4-9-3 **103** 5ex..........(b) WilliamBuick 11 (John Gosden) *lw: hld up in rr: hdwy 3f out: rdn along 2f out: styd on u.p fnl f: nrst fin* **8/1**	108
34-0	**5**	*½*	**Saptapadi (IRE)**[57] 2044 5-9-2 **105**.......... PaulPickard(3) 20 (Brian Ellison) *hld up and bhd: wd st: hdwy 3f out: bmpd 2f out: swtchd lft and rdn over 1f out: styd on ins fnl f: nrst fin* **33/1**	112+
4130	**6**	*nk*	**Kay Gee Be (IRE)**[24] 3032 7-8-7 **93**.......... PaulHanagan 3 (Richard Fahey) *trckd ldrs: hdwy 4f out: cl up 3f out and sn ev ch: rdn over 2f out and grad wknd* **20/1**	97
0-21	**7**	*nk*	**Constant Contact**[38] 2604 4-8-8 **97**..........(p) SimonPearce(3) 10 (Andrew Balding) *chsd ldrs: hdwy over 3f out: rdn along and n.m.r over 2f out: sn drvn and kpt on same pce* **22/1**	100
10-1	**8**	*1 ½*	**Tepmokea (IRE)**[57] 2071 5-8-6 **97**.......... LeeTopliss(5) 19 (Richard Fahey) *in tch on outer: wd st to stands' rail: n.m.r 3f out: nt clr run and swtchd lft and rdn 2f out: swtchd rt drvn through narrow gap on rails appr fnl f: kpt on: nt rch ldrs* **20/1**	97
-50	**9**	*1*	**Merchant Of Dubai**[40] 2573 6-8-13 **99**.......... LeeNewman 7 (Jim Goldie) *led 2f: cl up: rdn along over 3f out: sn drvn and wknd over 2f out* **33/1**	97
2235	**10**	*nk*	**Moyenne Corniche**[14] 3396 6-8-9 **100**.......... SHJames(5) 5 (Brian Ellison) *in tch: hdwy way to chse ldrs 3f out: rdn along over 2f out: grad wknd* **16/1**	97
0010	**11**	*hd*	**Smarty Socks (IRE)**[22] 3109 7-8-7 **93**.......... JimCrowley 12 (David O'Meara) *hld up in rr: smooth hdwy 4f out: led wl over 2f out: rdn: edgd rt and hdd wl over 1f out: sn wknd* **33/1**	90+
2240	**12**	*nk*	**Pintura**[24] 3032 4-8-9 **95**.......... TomQueally 18 (David Simcock) *nvr bttr than midfield* **28/1**	92
5501	**13**	*½*	**Nanton (USA)**[40] 2573 9-9-4 **104**.......... DanielTudhope 2 (Jim Goldie) *midfield on inner: effrt 3f out: sn rdn and btn* **25/1**	100
0064	**14**	*1 ¼*	**Crystal Gal (IRE)**[15] 3356 4-8-10 **96**.......... DaneO'Neill 14 (Lucy Wadham) *prom: wd to rail in home st: effrt and n.m.r 3f out: sn rdn and wknd* **40/1**	89
/1-1	**15**	*nse*	**Pekan Star**[59] 2002 4-8-9 **95**.......... NeilCallan 9 (Roger Varian) *lw: in tch: hdwy to trck ldrs 4f out: effrt to chal 3f out: rdn wl over 2f out and sn wknd* **3/1**[1]	88
044-	**16**	*nse*	**Demolition**[274] 6720 7-8-7 **93**.......... TomEaves 13 (Richard Fahey) *trckd ldrs: wd st towards stands' rail: effrt and n.m.r 3f out: rdn and nt clr run 2f out: sn wknd* **25/1**	86
2001	**17**	*1 ¾*	**Pleasant Day (IRE)**[23] 3085 4-8-7 **93** 5ex..........(b) FrederikTylicki 22 (Richard Fahey) *hld up towards rr: hdwy 4f out: effrt whn nt clr run over 2f [illegible] wknd after* **50/1**	83
-602	**18**	*9*	**Sarrsar**[28] 2933 4-8-10 **96**..........(t) TedDurcan 1 (Saeed Bin Suroor) *chsd ldrs: hdwy to ld 3f out: rdn and hdd over 2f out: sn drvn and wknd* **16/1**	68
6010	**19**	*3*	**Jutland**[21] 3156 4-9-0 **100**.......... DarryllHolland 6 (Mark Johnston) *lw: cl up: led after 2f: wd st to stands' rail: rdn along 4f out: hdd 3f out and sn wknd* **33/1**	66

2m 9.74s (-2.76) **Going Correction** +0.05s/f (Good) **19** Ran SP% **127.1**

Speed ratings (Par 109): **113,110,109,108,108 107,107,106,105,105 105,105,104,103,103 103,102,95,92**

toteswingers:1&2:£11.80, 2&3:£9.50, 1&3:£15.30 CSF £32.96 CT £370.83 TOTE £7.80: £2.20, £2.00, £2.00, £2.00; EX 47.60 Trifecta £853.80 Pool 30,518.59 - 26.45 winning units..

Owner Saleh Al Homaizi & Imad Al Sagar **Bred** Mubkera Syndicate **Trained** Newmarket, Suffolk

FOCUS

A cracking handicap. There was a solid pace set and those held up finished best, but surprisingly the leaders headed stands' side in the home straight. That caused a rough race inside the final 2f and those coming mid-track with their efforts proved at an advantage. The first two home, both Royal Ascot flops, dominated nearing the business end and both look Pattern performers in the making, so the form is strong.

NOTEBOOK

Green Destiny(IRE) ◆ was a huge public gamble when failing to fire in the Wolferton Handicap at Royal Ascot last month, but he was badly hampered early on there and better judged on his comeback success at Newmarket in April. If returning to that form there was every chance he was a very well handicapped horse and so it proved as he stormed home to run out an easy winner. Patiently ridden by his talented apprentice, he was produced widest of all when asked to improve from 3f out and displayed a proper turn of foot to seal the race. He was in no danger from the furlong pole and clearly relished this trip. This took his career record to 4-6 and a step up in class is now firmly on the cards. The ground was probably as quick as he ideally wants it too, so further success should be forthcoming towards the back-end of the campaign and it's hard to remember a more taking winner of this event. He will look very well handicapped in the Totesport Mile at Goodwood later this month and he was immediately cut into favouritism in the ante-post betting, with Coral going as short as 7-2, though he could be backed at 7-1. However, a run there would probably be ground dependant back down in trip and whether that test would really suit him is up for debate. (op 7-1 tchd 15-2)

Modun(IRE) ◆, on toes beforehand, was back down in trip and attracted strong support once again. He was patiently ridden and, while a more positive ride may have suited ideally over this trip as he lacked the same turn of foot of the winner, he wouldn't have beaten that rival. He still kept on to finish a clear second-best, enjoying this return to a sounder surface and looks well up to making his mark at a higher level before the season's end. (op 15-2)

Lost In The Moment(IRE) ◆ had finished second on his two previous outings, most recently to Beachfire in the Wolferton and he reversed form with that rival, was unlucky not to have finished closer to the front pair. He was denied a run towards the stands' side and finished strongly once seeing daylight. There is a nice prize waiting to be won with him. Official explanation: jockey said colt was denied a clear run (op 12-1 tchd 10-1)
Beachfire showed his true colours when trashing the winner on soft ground at Royal Ascot last time out and picked up a 5lb penalty for this. He too came from out the back and ran a decent race in defeat, giving the form a rock-solid look. (tchd 15-2)
Saptapadi(IRE) ◆, formerly owned by connections of the runner-up, was a big eyecatcher with next month's Ebor in mind. He has always looked a stayer in the making and, drawn wide, having to come from out the back over this shorter trip was never going to be for him. He was motoring inside the final furlong in the manner of a horse that will relish getting back over a longer distance and this was just his second outing for is current trainer, so improvement looks assured. He is a general 20-1 shot for the Ebor. Official explanation: jockey said gelding was denied a clear run
Kay Gee Be(IRE) had his chance and ran another solid race at a track he likes, helping to set the level. (op 18-1)
Constant Contact turned in an improved effort off his 7lb higher mark for winning on the AW last time out. (op 20-1)
Tepmokea(IRE) came into this having scored on his seasonal debut 57 days earlier and, 7lb higher, would have been a little closer with a better passage from 3f out. (op 16-1)
Pekan Star had registered his second win from three career outings when reappearing over C&D in May. He was 10lb higher, but appealed as a Pattern performer in the making and unsurprisingly headed the betting. He bustled his way into a share of the lead nearing 2f out, but hit a wall once put under maximum pressure and something may well have gone amiss. (tchd 10-3 in places)
Demolition ◆ deserves a mention as he travelled sweetly and didn't get a clear passage when trying to improve after straightening for home. He ought to come on plenty and is one to look out for next time. (op 33-1 tchd 20-1)

3877 JOHN SMITH'S RACING STKS (H'CAP) 1m
3:55 (3:55) (Class 3) (0-95,95) 3-Y-O+ £9,703 (£2,887; £1,443; £721) Stalls Low

Form				RPR
5015	1		**Norman Orpen (IRE)**[13] 3436 4-9-6 87 .... WilliamBuick 3 (Jane Chapple-Hyam) *lw: trckd ldrs: rdn over 2f out: led fnl 100yds: kpt on: all out* 14/1	97
1233	2	nk	**Snow Bay**[46] 2390 5-9-13 94 .... DaneO'Neill 8 (David Nicholls) *lw: led: rdn over 2f out: hdd fnl 100yds: kpt on* 12/1	103
0051	3	¾	**Barren Brook**[29] 2887 4-9-3 84 .... GrahamGibbons 20 (Michael Easterby) *midfield: rdn and hdwy over 2f out: chsd ldrs over 1f out: kpt on ins fnl f* 12/1	92
-111	4	½	**Mont Ras (IRE)**[21] 3169 4-9-5 86 .... DanielTudhope 13 (David O'Meara) *prom: rdn over 2f out: kpt on* 7/1[3]	92
1220	5	1	**Lord Aeryn (IRE)**[24] 3032 4-9-7 88 .... PaulHanagan 16 (Richard Fahey) *midfield: rdn over 2f out: hdwy over 1f out: swtchd lft appr fnl f: kpt on: nt rch ldrs* 12/1	92
0050	6	¾	**Kiwi Bay**[16] 3315 6-9-6 87 .... TomEaves 15 (Michael Dods) *hld up: rdn over 2f out: hdwy over 1f out: kpt on ins fnl f: nvr threatened ldrs* 40/1	89+
-230	7	nse	**Captain Bertie (IRE)**[23] 3067 3-8-12 88 .... EddieAhern 12 (B W Hills) *lw: hld up in midfield: hdwy over 2f out: short of room towards stands' rail appr fnl f: sn swtchd lft: kpt on* 5/1[1]	91+
5041	8	2	**Miami Gator (IRE)**[17] 3276 4-9-4 85 .... (v) AndrewElliott 17 (Mrs K Burke) *prom on outer: rdn over 2f out: wknd ins fnl f* 20/1	83
3056	9	½	**Space War**[9] 3542 4-9-9 90 .... DavidNolan 10 (Michael Easterby) *midfield: rdn over 2f out: one pce* 25/1	87
6031	10	½	**Amethyst Dawn (IRE)**[25] 3026 5-9-6 87 .... DavidAllan 14 (Tim Easterby) *trckd ldrs: rdn 3f out: one pce* 14/1	82
-150	11	1 ¾	**Mirrored**[28] 2909 5-9-9 90 .... TedDurcan 1 (Tim Easterby) *hld up: rdn over 2f out: kpt on ins fnl f: nvr threatened* 12/1	81
3000	12	hd	**Mujaadel (USA)**[10] 3506 6-8-11 78 .... (p) PhillipMakin 18 (David Nicholls) *s.i.s: hld up: nvr threatened* 50/1	69
3141	13	nk	**Quite Sparky**[17] 3275 4-9-3 84 .... (v) RyanMoore 2 (David O'Meara) *in tch: rdn over 2f out: no imp: wknd ins fnl f* 11/2[2]	74
402	14	1 ¾	**Georgebernardshaw (IRE)**[14] 3380 6-9-1 82 .... MickyFenton 6 (John Quinn) *in tch: rdn over 2f out: wknd over 1f out* 25/1	68
2451	15	hd	**Tevez**[7] 3634 6-9-1 89 .... DarylByrne(7) 9 (Des Donovan) *lw: dwlt: hld up: rdn 3f out: n.d* 10/1	75
-P00	16	1 ¼	**Capital Attraction (USA)**[24] 3032 4-9-11 92 .... (b) TomQueally 4 (Sir Henry Cecil) *lw: midfield: rdn over 2f out: no imp: wknd ins fnl f* 14/1	75
455-	17	2 ¾	**Clockmaker (IRE)**[284] 6447 5-9-7 88 .... DarryllHolland 11 (Tim Easterby) *hld up: a towards rr* 25/1	65
66-0	18	9	**Ordnance Row**[17] 3290 8-10-0 95 .... NeilCallan 7 (Roger Varian) *midfield: rdn over 2f out: wknd over 1f out* 33/1	51

1m 38.99s (0.19) **Going Correction** +0.05s/f (Good)
WFA 3 from 4yo+ 9lb **18 Ran SP% 128.1**
Speed ratings (Par 107): **101,100,99,99,98 97,97,95,95,94 92,92,92,90,90 89,86,77**
toteswingers:1&2:£151.60, 2&3:£37.70, 1&3:£68.30 CSF £165.89 CT £2169.82 TOTE £19.60: £4.20, £3.30, £4.00, £2.20; EX 309.50 TRIFECTA Not won..
Owner Gordon Li **Bred** Kevin Walsh **Trained** Dalham, Suffolk

FOCUS
This decent handicap looked wide open. The majority came stands' side in the home straight and it was yet another race where it paid to race handy. The form is sound among the principals.

NOTEBOOK
Norman Orpen(IRE) had won on his penultimate outing at Sandown and was better than the bare form off this mark at Windsor last time out. He bounced back with a game effort, racing handy from the off, and is evidently improving.
Snow Bay got his own way out in front and went down with all guns blazing towards the finish. This track very much suited his style, but he has now been placed on his last four outings since landing a hat-trick earlier this season and he rates a decent benchmark. (op 11-1)
Barren Brook ◆ was hiked up 8lb for winning here last time out and there is reason for thinking he was unfortunate not to have followed up. He proved best of those coming from off the pace and clearly found this test too sharp. He should gain compensation in the coming weeks. (op 11-1)
Mont Ras(IRE) proved easy to back in this quest for a four-timer off his 8lb higher mark. He was never far away and had every chance, but it would appear the handicapper now just has his measure. (op 11-2)
Lord Aeryn(IRE) was best forgiven his Ascot flop last time and this was more in keeping with his true form. He is a bit better than he showed here due to racing off the pace and may not be weighted out of winning again.
Kiwi Bay caught the eye finishing his race off well from off the pace and was unfortunate not to have improved on his fifth in the race last season. He could end his losing run if faced with easier ground next time.
Captain Bertie(IRE) ◆, the sole three-year-old, must be rated better than the bare form. He got too far back early and then found no sort of run when trying to improve on the stands' rail around the furlong marker. Official explanation: jockey said colt was denied a clear run (op 9-1 tchd 10-1 in places)
Quite Sparky, 6lb higher, faded when put under pressure and failed to give his true running. (op 6-1 tchd 5-1 and 13-2 in places)
Tevez Official explanation: jockey said gelding never travelled
Clockmaker(IRE) Official explanation: jockey said gelding ran too free

3878 JOHN SMITH'S MEDIAN AUCTION MAIDEN STKS 6f
4:25 (4:27) (Class 3) 2-Y-O £7,439 (£2,213; £1,106; £553) Stalls Centre

Form				RPR
	1		**Ladys First** 2-8-12 0 .... PaulHanagan 9 (Richard Fahey) *w'like: chsd ldrs: pushed along wl over 1f out: rdn appr fnl f: styd on wl to ld last 50yds* 11/2[3]	82+
2	2	1 ½	**Discression**[28] 2936 2-9-3 0 .... PhillipMakin 2 (Kevin Ryan) *lw: trckd ldr: cl up 1/2-way: chal 2f out and sn rdn: carried lft 1f out: sn drvn to take slt advantage: hdd and no ex last 50yds* 10/11[1]	83
42	3	1	**Choisan (IRE)**[67] 1797 2-9-3 0 .... DavidAllan 7 (Tim Easterby) *strong: lw: chsd ldng pair: rdn along 2f out: drvn over 1f out: kpt on ins fnl f* 12/1	80
43	4	nk	**Sunrise Dance**[35] 2718 2-8-12 0 .... AndrewElliott 3 (Alan Jarvis) *led: rdn along and edgd lft 1f out: drvn and hdd ins fnl f: wknd towards fin* 16/1	74
	5	nk	**Noble Silk** 2-9-3 0 .... DaneO'Neill 11 (Lucy Wadham) *w'like: leggy: towards rr: hdwy 2f out: sn rdn and kpt on ins fnl f: nrst fin* 25/1	78
64	6	1 ¾	**Whinging Willie (IRE)**[13] 3424 2-9-3 0 .... RyanMoore 12 (Gary Moore) *hld up in tch: effrt over 2f out: sn rdn and kpt on same pce* 5/1[2]	72
0	7	hd	**Dutch Heritage**[28] 2936 2-8-12 0 .... LeeTopliss(5) 6 (Richard Fahey) *chsd ldrs: rdn along over 2f out: sn wknd* 66/1	72
65	8	2 ¼	**Maria Medecis (IRE)**[55] 2120 2-8-12 0 .... FrederikTylicki 10 (Ann Duffield) *leggy: chsd ldrs: rdn along over 2f out: sn wknd* 50/1	60
0	9	2 ¼	**Dark Ambition (IRE)**[7] 3610 2-9-3 0 .... EddieAhern 4 (William Haggas) *w'like: strong: dwlt and in rr: hdwy to chse ldrs 1/2-way: rdn over 2f out and sn wknd* 16/1	58
	10	8	**Doyouknowwhoiam** 2-9-3 0 .... TomEaves 1 (Bryan Smart) *leggy: sn outpcd and a bhd* 10/1	34
06	11	¾	**Regal Acclaim (IRE)**[38] 2617 2-9-3 0 .... TedDurcan 8 (Tim Easterby) *w'like: scope: t.k.h: chsd ldrs to 1/2-way: sn wknd* 50/1	32

1m 11.7s (-0.20) **Going Correction** +0.05s/f (Good) **11 Ran SP% 122.2**
Speed ratings (Par 98): **103,101,99,99,98 96,96,93,90,79 78**
toteswingers:1&2:£2.90, 2&3:£4.10, 1&3:£10.20 CSF £11.10 TOTE £6.70: £2.00, £1.10, £2.90; EX 14.80.
Owner Mrs H Steel **Bred** Sparsholt Stud **Trained** Musley Bank, N Yorks

FOCUS
Not a bad maiden. It was run at a sound pace and again the main action developed down the centre of the track.

NOTEBOOK
Ladys First ◆, a good-bodied sort, hit top gear half a furlong out and ran on strongly to mow down rivals and score. She showed her inexperience early on and looked to hit something of a flat spot when the tempo got serious. However, once the penny dropped she motored and looks a very useful filly in the making. She should only improve for this debut experience and it will be interesting to see where turns up next. (op 5-1 tchd 9-2)
Discression was well backed to go one better than his debut second over C&D last month and was better away this time. He loomed up 3f out and his jockey seemed confident passing 2f out. However, he was done little favours when his main rival at that stage Sunrise Dance hung left and he took an age to find his full stride under pressure. Once he did so he was a sitting duck for the winner and this does look a missed opportunity. He deserves another chance, however, and remains a useful prospect. (op 5-4)
Choisan(IRE) got going late on this debut over 6f and ran just about his best race to date. He is now eligible for nurseries. (op 11-1 tchd 10-1)
Sunrise Dance proved keen up front and looked there for the taking when the runner-up ranged up to her. However, she kept responding, despite not helping her rider, and clearly has an engine. She too is now eligible for nurseries. (tchd 20-1 in places)
Noble Silk ◆ lacked the tactical pace to land a serious blow, but this was a pleasing debut effort and he looks certain to improve for the experience. Another furlong should also suit ideally. (op 20-1)
Whinging Willie(IRE), an athletic sort, travelled nicely enough in mid-field, but proved laboured once asked to quicken and looks in need of a stiffer test. He can make his mark in nurseries. (op 11-2 tchd 6-1)

3879 JOHN SMITH'S SPRINT (NURSERY) 5f
5:00 (5:01) (Class 3) 2-Y-O £7,439 (£2,213; £1,106; £553) Stalls Centre

Form				RPR
231	1		**Last Bid**[24] 3050 2-9-3 76 .... DavidAllan 6 (Tim Easterby) *trckd ldrs: cl up 1/2-way: rdn to ld 1 1/2f out: edgd lft ins fnl f: kpt on wl* 11/4[1]	82
4221	2	½	**Kool Henry (IRE)**[14] 3398 2-9-3 76 .... DanielTudhope 4 (David O'Meara) *led: rdn along over 2f out: hdd 1 1/2f out: drvn and rallied ins fnl f: no ex towards fin* 7/2[3]	80
510	3	3 ¼	**Rent Free**[25] 3014 2-9-5 78 .... PaulHanagan 5 (Nigel Tinkler) *trckd ldrs: hdwy over 2f out: rdn wl over 1f out: sn one pce* 3/1[2]	71
5610	4	hd	**Profile Star (IRE)**[59] 2007 2-9-7 80 .... LeeNewman 3 (David Barron) *lw: chsd ldr: rdn along over 2f out: drvn wl over 1f out: kpt on same pce* 10/1	72
1616	5	4	**Van Go Go**[45] 2404 2-8-6 72 .... LeonnaMayor(7) 7 (David Nicholls) *dwlt and awkward s: bhd: hdwy and in tch 1/2-way: rdn to chse ldrs wl over 1f out: sn wknd* 10/1	49
562	6	7	**Jimmy The Lollipop (IRE)**[47] 2346 2-9-4 77 .... (b) PhillipMakin 1 (Kevin Ryan) *chsd ldrs on outer: rdn along 1/2-way: sn wknd* 6/1	29
3662	7	2 ½	**Chillie Billie**[14] 3388 2-9-3 76 .... KirstyMilczarek 2 (Phil McEntee) *lw: chsd ldrs: rdn along 1/2-way: sn wknd* 15/2	19

59.19 secs (-0.11) **Going Correction** +0.05s/f (Good) **7 Ran SP% 118.1**
Speed ratings (Par 98): **102,101,96,95,89 78,74**
toteswingers:1&2:£2.60, 2&3:£2.90, 1&3:£2.90 CSF £13.40 CT £30.63 TOTE £3.80: £2.10, £2.40; EX 9.50.
Owner C H Stevens **Bred** Bearstone Stud **Trained** Great Habton, N Yorks
■ The 'official' ratings shown next to each horse are estimated and for information purposes only.

FOCUS
There was a cracking finish between the first pair in this modest maiden and the form looks sound.

NOTEBOOK
Last Bid followed up her Ripon maiden win on this first venture into handicap company and completed the task gamely. She had finished behind the runner-up on her penultimate outing so is clearly improving nicely and appeals as the sort her trainer will eke more improvement out of in this sphere. (op 5-2 tchd 3-1)
Kool Henry(IRE), on toes, just did enough to open his account at Newcastle last time, but got the worst of a battling finish on this nursery debut. He has to rate as somewhat unfortunate as he did most of the donkey work and finished clear of the rest, but compensation probably isn't far off. (op 4-1)
Rent Free, very well backed, was outclassed at Royal Ascot last time and he looked to find this too sharp. He has scope and should be able to better this over another furlong. (op 9-2)

Profile Star(IRE) was last seen finishing out the back over C&D in a decent contest in May, when he wore first-time blinkers. Gelded during his time off the track, he had his chance and left the impression he may benefit for the outing. (op 8-1 tchd 11-1)
Van Go Go blew her chance from the gates. (op 8-1)
Jimmy The Lollipop(IRE) Official explanation: jockey said gelding never travelled

3880 JOHN SMITH'S STKS (H'CAP) 6f

5:35 (5:35) (Class 4) (0-80,85) 3-Y-0+ **£7,439** (£2,213; £1,106; £553) **Stalls** Centre

Form RPR

1531 **1** **Saucy Brown (IRE)**[11] 3484 5-9-11 **79** .... PaulQuinn 16 88
(David Nicholls) *prom: effrt 2f out: rdn to chal over 1f out: drvn ins fnl f: led last 100yds* **10/1**[3]

0000 **2** ½ **Hotham**[15] 3339 8-9-7 **75** .... ChrisCatlin 13 84+
(Noel Wilson) *midfield: hdwy 2f out: swtchd rt and rdn ent fnl f: styd on strly: edgd rt and hld nr fin* **12/1**

1042 **3** *nse* **River Falcon**[21] 3162 11-9-9 **77** .... DanielTudhope 7 84
(Jim Goldie) *bhd: hdwy wl over 1f out: swtchd rt and rdn ent fnl f: fin strly* **7/1**[1]

3220 **4** *1* **Red Cape (FR)**[9] 3541 8-9-3 **76** .... DaleSwift(5) 11 80
(Ruth Carr) *cl up: led after 2f: rdn wl over 1f out: edgd rt and drvn ent fnl f: hdd and no ex last 100yds* **8/1**[2]

2354 **5** *nk* **Powerful Pierre**[7] 3612 4-8-13 **67** ....(b[1]) FrederikTylicki 18 70
(Ian McInnes) *midfield: hdwy on stands' rail 2f out: sn rdn and styd on ins fnl f: nrst fin* **25/1**

5603 **6** *nk* **Diman Waters (IRE)**[15] 3339 4-9-11 **79** .... DavidAllan 20 81
(Eric Alston) *trckd ldrs: hdwy 2f out: rdn over 1f out: drvn ins fnl f: hld whn n.m.r nr fin* **11/1**

0001 **7** 2 ¼ **Baldemar**[2] 3765 6-9-10 **85** 6ex .... GeorgeChaloner(7) 10 80
(Richard Fahey) *prom: effrt over 2f out and ev ch: rdn wl over 1f out and grad wknd* **8/1**[2]

-550 **8** *nk* **Bond Fastrac**[28] 2938 4-9-2 **70** ....(v[1]) DaneO'Neill 2 64
(Geoffrey Oldroyd) *towards rr: gd hdwy on wd outside to chse ldrs over 2f out: rdn wl over 1f out: sn one pce* **20/1**

6612 **9** 1 ¾ **Another Try (IRE)**[9] 3535 6-9-8 **83** .... MatthewLawson(7) 8 71
(Alan Jarvis) *in tch: rdn along 2f out: n.d* **10/1**[3]

0502 **10** *nk* **Divertimenti (IRE)**[7] 3640 7-8-13 **67** ....(b) RussKennemore 9 54
(Roy Bowring) *chsd ldrs: rdn along 1/2-way: kpt on same pce* **20/1**

-031 **11** *shd* **Ryan Style (IRE)**[9] 3541 5-10-0 **82** .... TomEaves 14 69
(Lisa Williamson) *dwlt: sn chsng ldrs: rdn along over 2f out and sn wknd* **8/1**[2]

0430 **12** ¾ **Illustrious Prince (IRE)**[25] 3028 4-9-10 **78** ....(v) EddieAhern 4 62
(Declan Carroll) *lw: cl up: rdn along over 2f out: sn wknd* **25/1**

0204 **13** *nk* **Caranbola**[10] 3506 5-9-3 **71** .... PhillipMakin 15 54
(Mel Brittain) *prom: rdn along over 2f out: grad wknd* **14/1**

5055 **14** ¾ **Another Citizen (IRE)**[15] 3346 3-8-13 **73** ....(b[1]) TedDurcan 3 53
(Tim Easterby) *rdn along and towards rr fr 1/2-way* **12/1**

6303 **15** *nse* **Dark Lane**[37] 2631 5-9-8 **76** ....(b) PaulHanagan 1 57
(Richard Fahey) *a towards rr* **16/1**

0463 **16** *nk* **Coolminx (IRE)**[22] 3113 4-9-7 **80** .... LeeTopliss(5) 5 60
(Richard Fahey) *a towards rr* **10/1**[3]

6110 **17** 4 ½ **Choc'A'Moca (IRE)**[15] 3359 4-8-13 **67** ....(v) MickyFenton 6 33
(Paul Midgley) *led 2f: prom tl rdn along over 2f out and sn wknd* **20/1**

1m 11.42s (-0.48) **Going Correction** +0.05s/f (Good)
WFA 3 from 4yo+ 6lb **17** Ran SP% **131.4**
Speed ratings (Par 105): **105,104,104,102,102 102,99,98,96,96 95,94,94,93,93 93,87**
toteswingers:1&2:£19.30, 2&3:£14.10, 1&3:£29.10 CSF £123.08 CT £948.77 TOTE £9.40: £2.30, £3.10, £2.20, £2.80; EX 153.30.
Owner D Nicholls **Bred** Churchtown House Stud **Trained** Sessay, N Yorks

FOCUS
A fair sprint handicap in which the field raced away from the far side and the form makes sense. The winner's best run since early last year.
T/Plt: £64.20 to a £1 stake. Pool of £177,053.58 - 2,012.45 winning tickets. T/Qpdt: £9.40 to a £1 stake. Pool of £8,404.09 - 660.68 winning tickets. JR

3881 - 3883a (Foreign Racing) - See Raceform Interactive

3337 TIPPERARY (L-H)

Saturday, July 9

OFFICIAL GOING: Yielding

3884a DANEHILL DANCER TIPPERARY STKS (LISTED RACE) 5f

3:40 (3:40) 2-Y-0 **£23,814** (£6,961; £3,297; £1,099)

RPR

1 **Requinto (IRE)**[33] 2776 2-9-1 .... WMLordan 5 104+
(David Wachman, Ire) *cl up: on terms travelling wl 2f out: rdn to ld and assert fr over 1f out: styd on wl to draw clr and swished tail ins fnl f: comf* **7/2**[2]

2 3 ½ **An Ghalanta (IRE)**[49] 2322 2-8-12 .... KJManning 4 88
(J S Bolger, Ire) *sn disp ld: hdd and no imp u.p fr over 1f out: kpt on same pce* **16/1**

3 1 ½ **Dam Beautiful**[14] 3416 2-8-12 .... DPMcDonogh 1 83
(Kevin Ryan) *sn disp ld: hdd and no imp fr over 1f out: sn 3rd and kpt on same pce* **8/1**[3]

4 1 ¼ **Experience (IRE)**[14] 3416 2-9-3 .... WJLee 2 84
(David Wachman, Ire) *w.w 4th of the 5: no imp u.p and kpt on same pce fr over 1f out* **8/15**[1]

5 *shd* **Naseem Sea (IRE)**[14] 3416 2-8-12 .... WJSupple 3 78
(P D Deegan, Ire) *sn struggling in rr: kpt on same pce u.p fr over 1f out* **11/1**

57.84 secs (-1.16) **5** Ran SP% **112.8**
CSF £45.02 TOTE £3.90: £1.70, £5.30; DF 49.10.
Owner Michael Tabor **Bred** Liberty Bloodstock **Trained** Goolds Cross, Co Tipperary

FOCUS
The stalls were on the far side but the five runners all came across to race on the stands' side where the ground was quicker.

NOTEBOOK
Requinto(IRE) is on the small side but he is quite smart and he left a disappointing run in a similar event at Naas behind him with an easy victory. He'd been held up over 6f at Naas, but being allowed to bowl along, as he did when winning his maiden over this trip at Cork clearly suits him well and he was always just about in front here before being sent about his business entering the final furlong. He quickened clear in good style. Official explanation: trainer said, regarding the apparent improvement in form shown, that colt won his maiden well when making all but at Naas last time they decided to drop him in and this may have worked against him; on this occasion they reverted to bouncing him out and making all and this may have brought about any apparent improvement. (op 4/1)
An Ghalanta(IRE), the only maiden in the line-up, had shown ability on her two previous starts and, although no match for the winner when things got serious, again acquitted herself well. (op 12/1)
Dam Beautiful, successful over the trip on her debut at Warwick before running respectably in a Group 3 over 6f at the Curragh, showed speed but was fighting a losing battle from over 1f out. (op 13/2)
Experience(IRE), a dual winner and stablemate of the winner, was carrying a 5lb penalty for her win in the same Group 3 6f event in which Dam Beautiful finished fifth. She was dropping back in trip here but that hardly accounted for her disappointing display and it is more likely that trainer David Wachman's view that the filly, who was having her fourth run in less than six weeks, "just ran flat" was about right. She is to have a break. Official explanation: jockey said filly may have been inconvenienced by today's shorter trip and easier ground (op 4/6 tchd 8/11)
Naseem Sea(IRE), third in the Group 3 event won by Experience, was first off the bridle and was struggling from halfway, although she did keep on in the closing stages. (op 9/1 tchd 12/1)

3885 - 3887a (Foreign Racing) - See Raceform Interactive

3423 BELMONT PARK (L-H)

Saturday, July 9

OFFICIAL GOING: Turf: good

3888a MAN O'WAR STKS (GRADE 1) (3YO+) (TURF) 1m 3f (T)

10:17 (10:19) 3-Y-0+

£230,769 (£76,923; £38,461; £19,230; £11,538; £7,692)

RPR

1 **Cape Blanco (IRE)**[25] 3009 4-8-8 0 .... JamieSpencer 6 121
(A P O'Brien, Ire) **61/20**[2]

2 2 ¼ **Gio Ponti (USA)**[28] 2949 6-8-8 0 .... RADominguez 5 117+
(Christophe Clement, U.S.A) **11/10**[1]

3 *1* **Boisterous (USA)**[48] 4-8-4 0 .... JRVelazquez 3 111
(Claude McGaughey III, U.S.A) **54/10**

4 1 ½ **Mission Approved (USA)**[28] 2949 7-8-11 0 .... JLEspinoza 1 115
(Naipaul Chatterpaul, U.S.A) **47/10**[3]

5 *5* **Al Khali (USA)**[28] 2949 5-8-6 0 .... EPrado 4 101
(William Mott, U.S.A) **101/10**

6 2 ¾ **Bearpath (USA)**[42] 5-8-4 0 .... FLenclud 2 94
(Ian Wilkes, U.S.A) **176/10**

2m 14.06s (-0.99) **6** Ran SP% **119.9**
PARI-MUTUEL (all including $2 stakes): WIN 8.10; PLACE (1-2) 4.10, 2.60; SHOW (1-2-3) 2.80, 2.10, 2.90; SF 18.20.
Owner Mrs F Hay,D Smith,Mrs J Magnier,M Tabor **Bred** Jack Ronan And Des Vere Hunt Farm Co **Trained** Ballydoyle, Co Tipperary

FOCUS
The pace was steady and Cape Blanco had to battle, so it's not certain he was back to his best.

NOTEBOOK
Cape Blanco(IRE), last season's Irish Derby/Irish Champion Stakes winner, hasn't looked at his this year, but this represented an easier assignment and he ran out a workmanlike winner. He'll now head for the Arlington Million and will probably take the beating.
Gio Ponti(USA), last year's winner, was ridden under restraint, but couldn't quicken sufficiently to challenge the winner.
Boisterous(USA) had his chance and ran well on this rise in grade.
Mission Approved(USA), winner of the Manhattan Handicap, had the run of things and still wasn't good enough.

3889 - 3896a & 3898a (Foreign Racing) - See Raceform Interactive

BREMEN

Sunday, July 10

OFFICIAL GOING: Turf: soft

3897a WALTHER J JACOBS STUTENMEILE (GROUP 3) (3YO+ FILLIES & MARES) (TURF) 1m

4:10 (12:00) 3-Y-0+

£27,586 (£9,482; £4,741; £2,586; £1,724; £1,293)

RPR

1 **Vanjura (GER)**[42] 2541 4-9-6 0 .... APietsch 5 109+
(R Dzubasz, Germany) *broke wl: sent to ld: set str pce: then settled in 2nd in bkst: qcknd wl early in st to chal: tk ld 2f out: r.o wl: a in command and eased fnl 100 yds* **1/2**[1]

2 ¾ **Rockatella (IRE)**[21] 3213 4-9-6 0 .... EFrank 3 107
(W Hefter, Germany) *settled towards rr: mde gd prog arnd fnl turn to be prom early in st: r.o wl and fin strly fnl f to chse wnr home* **136/10**

3 1 ½ **Magic Eye (IRE)**[38] 2657 6-9-6 0 .... AHelfenbein 1 104
(Andreas Lowe, Germany) *prom after s: shkn up early in st: r.o wl to pass btn horses* **165/10**

4 1 ¼ **Devilish Lips (GER)**[27] 4-9-4 0 .... MCadeddu 8 99
(Andreas Lowe, Germany) *bkmarker fr s: sn wl in rr: mde prog arnd fnl turn and r.o wl: fining strly fnl f* **211/10**

5 1 ¾ **Etive (USA)**[56] 2137 3-8-11 0 .... FabriceVeron 6 95
(H-A Pantall, France) *broke wl to be prom: r.o u.p ent st: threatened briefly but wknd fnl f* **26/5**[3]

6 2 ½ **Glady Romana (GER)**[52] 4-9-4 0 .... DPorcu 4 89
(W Baltromei, Germany) *broke slowly: moved through field on bkst: rdn but sn btn in st* **225/10**

7 *1* **Wolkenburg (GER)**[21] 3209 3-8-11 0 .... AStarke 2 87
(P Schiergen, Germany) *racd freely fr s then settled midfield: threatened briefly ent st: sn wknd* **17/5**[2]

8 1 ½ **Reine Vite (GER)**[21] 3209 3-8-11 0 .... KClijmans 7 83
(Uwe Ostmann, Germany) *broek wl to be prom: moved forward to take ld towards end of bkst: led into st: rdn and sn btn: wkng qckly* **145/10**

1m 35.9s (95.90)
WFA 3 from 4yo+ 9lb **8** Ran SP% **133.3**
WIN (incl. 10 euro stake): 15. PLACES: 11, 19, 23. SF: 65.
Owner M Barth **Bred** J-C Haimet & J-P Liberge **Trained** Germany

[3656]AYR (L-H)

Monday, July 11

OFFICIAL GOING: Good to firm (9.4)

Wind: Light, half against Weather: Sunny, hot

3899 BET WITH YOUR MOBILE AT VICTORCHANDLER.COM MEDIAN AUCTION MAIDEN STKS 6f

2:00 (2:02) (Class 5) 2-Y-O £2,328 (£693; £346; £173) **Stalls** Low

Form				RPR
6	**1**		**Bomber Jet**[18] 3314 2-9-3 0 PaulHanagan 3 (Nigel Tinkler) *dwlt: sn trcking ldrs: smooth hdwy over 2f out: shkn up to ld over 1f out: drvn out* **9/4**[2]	75+
242	**2**	*1 ½*	**Flambard House (IRE)**[18] 3314 2-8-12 0 DaleSwift(5) 1 (Howard Johnson) *led tl hdd over 1f out: kpt on same pce ins fnl f* **15/8**[1]	70
	3	*1 ¼*	**Bapak Pintar** 2-9-3 0 TomEaves 6 (Kevin Ryan) *trckd ldrs: pushed along 2f out: kpt on same pce fnl f* **10/3**[3]	66
0	**4**	*3*	**Koolgreycat (IRE)**[18] 3314 2-8-12 0 AdrianNicholls 2 (Noel Wilson) *t.k.h: trckd ldrs: effrt 2f out: outpcd fnl f* **50/1**	52
	5	*1 ½*	**Pitti Sing** 2-8-12 0 TonyHamilton 5 (Richard Fahey) *cl up tl rdn and wknd appr fnl f* **6/1**	47
	6	*15*	**Altnaharra** 2-9-3 0 LeeNewman 4 (Jim Goldie) *missed break and wl bhd: no ch fr 1/2-way* **11/1**	—

1m 13.43s (1.03) **Going Correction** -0.225s/f (Firm) **6** Ran SP% **113.2**

Speed ratings (Par 94): **92,90,88,84,82 62**

toteswingers:1&2:£1.60, 1&3:£2.20, 2&3:£2.20 CSF £7.02 TOTE £3.10: £1.90, £1.20; EX 8.00.

Owner Yan Wah Wu **Bred** Whitsbury Manor Stud **Trained** Langton, N Yorks

■ Stewards' Enquiry : Dale Swift one-day ban: used whip down shoulder in the forehand (Jul 25)

FOCUS

Back straight out 2m, home bend out 4m, home straight out 5m from innermost line adding 12yds to races over 7f and 24yds to 1m 5f race. Following this race winning rider Paul Hanagan described conditions as "quick but safe."

NOTEBOOK

Bomber Jet caught the eye staying on after a slow start when sixth on his debut at Newcastle, a race in which Flambard House was runner-up, and the Nigel Tinkler horse improved enough to reverse form in straightforward fashion. He should make a fair handicapper. (op 2-1 tchd 5-2)

Flambard House(IRE) seemed to become unbalanced for a few strides around 2f out, but he was basically beaten by a more progressive rival. (op 9-4)

Bapak Pintar's sales price increased from 3,000gns as a yearling to £24,000 this year. He plugged on for pressure without threatening and this was a respectable debut. (op 3-1 tchd 7-2)

Koolgreycat(IRE) was well behind today's one-two on her debut, and this was a little better. (op 40-1 tchd 66-1)

Pitti Sing was hard to fancy with the stable's first rider partnering Bomber Jet, and she duly shaped as though in need of this experience. (tchd 5-1 and 13-2)

3900 "DRUMMY'S 70TH" FILLIES' H'CAP 6f

2:30 (2:31) (Class 4) (0-85,75) 3-Y-0+ £4,204 (£1,251; £625; £312) **Stalls** Low

Form				RPR
-424	**1**		**Timeless Elegance (IRE)**[19] 3279 4-9-1 72 DaleSwift(5) 4 (Howard Johnson) *w ldr: led 1/2-way: sn rdn: hld on wl u.p fnl f* **9/4**[1]	80
-460	**2**	*¾*	**Mango Music**[14] 3459 8-9-9 75 PaulHanagan 3 (Richard Fahey) *prom: sn pushed along: hdwy over 1f out: chsd wnr ins fnl f: kpt on* **11/4**[2]	81
6531	**3**	*½*	**Eternal Instinct**[8] 3662 4-8-11 66 6ex GaryBartley(3) 1 (Jim Goldie) *hld up and bhd: hdwy and pushed along over 1f out: kpt on fnl f: hld nr fin* **7/2**[3]	70
5223	**4**	*hd*	**Tro Nesa (IRE)**[13] 3484 3-9-3 75 DavidNolan 5 (Ann Duffield) *trckd ldrs: rdn along 1/2-way: hdwy over 1f out: kpt on same pce fnl f* **7/1**	77
2301	**5**	*10*	**Mother Jones**[23] 3191 3-9-2 74 TomEaves 2 (Bryan Smart) *led to 1/2-way: wkng whn n.m.r over 1f out: sn btn* **5/1**	44

1m 11.88s (-0.52) **Going Correction** -0.225s/f (Firm)

WFA 3 from 4yo+ 6lb **5** Ran SP% **108.8**

Speed ratings (Par 102): **102,101,100,100,86**

CSF £8.46 TOTE £2.60: £2.00, £2.50; EX 8.30.

Owner Transcend Bloodstock LLP **Bred** Mrs M Togher **Trained** Billy Row, Co Durham

FOCUS

They went a strong pace and the field were soon strung out, yet they still finished in a bunch. The form looks straightforward rated around those in the frame behind the winner.

Mother Jones Official explanation: jockey said filly hung right throughout

3901 BEST ODDS GUARANTEED AT VICTOR CHANDLER H'CAP 5f

3:00 (3:01) (Class 6) (0-65,65) 3-Y-0+ £1,704 (£503; £251) **Stalls** Low

Form				RPR
3302	**1**		**Arriva La Diva**[8] 3662 5-9-7 60 PaulHanagan 5 (Linda Perratt) *mde all: rdn 2f out: hld on wl fnl f* **11/4**[2]	66
1603	**2**	*shd*	**Dower Glen**[14] 3451 4-9-1 54 (v) TomEaves 2 (Keith Dalgleish) *taken early to post: trckd ldrs: rdn and outpcd over 1f out: styd on fnl f: jst hld* **7/1**	59
00-0	**3**	*¾*	**Andrasta**[8] 3662 6-8-7 46 oh1 PatrickMathers 1 (Alan Berry) *sn bhd and pushed along: hdwy over 1f out: r.o fnl f: nrst fin* **66/1**	49
5524	**4**	*shd*	**Lees Anthem**[14] 3451 4-9-0 58 DaleSwift(5) 6 (Colin Teague) *prom: rdn 2f out: effrt appr fnl f: kpt on: hld nr fin* **15/8**[1]	60
3500	**5**	*½*	**Chosen One (IRE)**[10] 3582 6-9-12 65 JamesSullivan 4 (Ruth Carr) *w wnr: rdn 2f out: no ex ins fnl f* **9/2**[3]	65
3446	**6**	*shd*	**Running Water**[6] 3702 3-8-2 46 (bt) FrannyNorton 10 (Hugh McWilliams) *hld up on outside: hdwy and prom over 1f out: kpt on same pce fnl f* **11/1**	44
-600	**7**	*1 ¾*	**Micky Mac (IRE)**[27] 3027 7-9-0 53 FrederikTylicki 8 (Colin Teague) *in tch: drvn and outpcd 2f out: kpt on ins fnl f: nvr able to chal* **14/1**	47
0-00	**8**	*1*	**Classlin**[8] 3662 4-8-7 46 oh1 AndrewMullen 3 (Jim Goldie) *dwlt: bhd and sn pushed along: no imp fr over 1f out* **40/1**	36

59.53 secs (0.13) **Going Correction** -0.225s/f (Firm)

WFA 3 from 4yo+ 5lb **8** Ran SP% **111.1**

Speed ratings (Par 101): **95,94,93,93,92 92,89,88**

toteswingers:1&2:£3.40, 1&3:£20.00, 2&3:£26.40 CSF £20.92 CT £971.95 TOTE £3.60: £1.40, £1.80, £7.70; EX 10.70 Trifecta £130.10 Pool £383.54 - 2.18 winning units..

Owner Ken McGarrity **Bred** Mickley Stud, Stennett, Hillside Racing **Trained** East Kilbride, S Lanarks

FOCUS

A moderate sprint handicap with the form weak and the winner only having to run to previous course form to score.

3902 PLAY POKER AT VICTORCHANDLER.COM H'CAP (DIV I) 7f 50y

3:30 (3:30) (Class 6) (0-65,65) 3-Y-0+ £1,363 (£402; £201) **Stalls** High

Form				RPR
/56-	**1**		**Shayla**[402] 2725 4-9-13 64 PJMcDonald 9 (Alan Swinbank) *cl up: rdn and ev ch over 2f out: led ins fnl f: hld on wl* **12/1**	72
0205	**2**	*nk*	**Berbice (IRE)**[2] 3856 6-9-9 65 DaleSwift(5) 8 (Linda Perratt) *missed break: hld up gng wl: stdy hdwy on outside over 1f out: chsd wnr ins fnl f: kpt on: hld cl home* **4/1**[1]	72+
5530	**3**	*3*	**Newbury Street**[25] 3088 4-9-2 58 ChrisDCogan(5) 4 (Patrick Holmes) *trckd ldrs: led over 2f out to ins fnl f: no ex* **4/1**[1]	57
0265	**4**	*½*	**Hansomis (IRE)**[28] 2990 7-9-3 54 FrederikTylicki 1 (Bruce Mactaggart) *midfield: rdn whn blkd 2f out: sn outpcd: rallied appr fnl f: no imp* **4/1**[1]	52
0500	**5**	*hd*	**Rosbertini**[2] 3857 5-8-9 46 oh1 LeeNewman 6 (Linda Perratt) *hld up towards rr: hdwy whn blkd 2f out: kpt on same pce fnl f* **18/1**	43
0000	**6**	*¾*	**Balance On Time (IRE)**[2] 3857 5-8-9 46 oh1 TonyHamilton 10 (Linda Perratt) *hld up: rdn along over 2f out: no imp over 1f out* **18/1**	41
0560	**7**	*nse*	**Spread Boy (IRE)**[38] 2692 4-8-10 47 PatrickMathers 2 (Alan Berry) *prom: rdn over 2f out: wknd fnl f* **16/1**	42
0064	**8**	*1 ¾*	**Forzarzi (IRE)**[13] 3489 7-8-9 46 (p) FrannyNorton 5 (Hugh McWilliams) *t.k.h: in tch: rdn whn blkd 2f out: wknd fnl f* **7/1**[3]	36
-005	**9**	*7*	**Handicraft (IRE)**[5] 3733 3-8-1 46 oh1 PaulHanagan 7 (Kevin Ryan) *led tl rdn and hdd over 2f out: wknd over 1f out* **11/2**[2]	14

1m 31.92s (-1.48) **Going Correction** -0.225s/f (Firm)

WFA 3 from 4yo+ 8lb **9** Ran SP% **112.0**

Speed ratings (Par 101): **99,98,95,94,94 93,93,91,83**

toteswingers:1&2:£8.50, 1&3:£11.10, 2&3:£4.70 CSF £57.23 CT £228.84 TOTE £10.10: £3.40, £1.20, £2.30; EX 58.80 Trifecta £222.10 Part won. Pool £300.22 - 0.72 winning units..

Owner Panther Racing Ltd **Bred** Whitwell Bloodstock **Trained** Melsonby, N Yorks

FOCUS

A moderate contest run in a time 1.16 seconds slower than the second division. The winner could do better but the runner-up is rated just below last year's best backed up by the third.

Shayla Official explanation: trainer's rep said, regarding apparent improvement in form, that the filly had been breaking blood vessels and has benefited from 12 months off.

Handicraft(IRE) Official explanation: jockey said filly hung left throughout

3903 PLAY POKER AT VICTORCHANDLER.COM H'CAP (DIV II) 7f 50y

4:00 (4:00) (Class 6) (0-65,64) 3-Y-0+ £1,363 (£402; £201) **Stalls** High

Form				RPR
0510	**1**		**Drive Home (USA)**[14] 3454 4-9-5 55 (p) AdrianNicholls 9 (Noel Wilson) *trckd ldrs: led over 2f out: edgd lft over 1f out: drvn out* **6/1**[3]	65
0/40	**2**	*1 ¾*	**Billy Cadiz**[18] 3326 6-8-9 45 FrannyNorton 8 (Mark Campion) *in tch: hdwy to chse wnr over 1f out: r.o fnl f: nt rch wnr* **22/1**	50
2330	**3**	*3 ½*	**Shunkawakhan (IRE)**[8] 3657 8-9-4 54 (p) PaulHanagan 5 (Linda Perratt) *hld up: rdn over 2f out: hdwy over 1f out: kpt on fnl f: nrst fin* **6/1**[3]	50
1552	**4**	*shd*	**North Central (USA)**[5] 3733 4-10-0 64 (p) LeeNewman 7 (Jim Goldie) *stall opened fractionally early: t.k.h: mde most to over 2f out: no ex fr over 1f out* **6/4**[1]	59+
0004	**5**	*1*	**Craicattack (IRE)**[9] 3638 4-8-11 47 PJMcDonald 2 (Sharon Watt) *hld up: rdn and effrt over 2f out: no imp over 1f out* **28/1**	40
000-	**6**	*2 ¾*	**Sheedal (IRE)**[257] 7172 3-8-1 45 JamesSullivan 10 (Linda Perratt) *hld up in midfield: rdn over 2f out: one pce over 1f out* **33/1**	27
-005	**7**	*¾*	**Red Scintilla**[16] 3387 4-9-10 60 TomEaves 3 (Nigel Tinkler) *prom tl rdn and wknd over 1f out* **7/1**	43
-346	**8**	*1 ¼*	**Honest Buck**[41] 2593 4-9-2 52 FrederikTylicki 6 (Kate Walton) *bhd and sn detached: styd on fnl f: nvr on terms* **11/2**[2]	32
000-	**9**	*1 ¼*	**Anthemion (IRE)**[338] 4824 14-8-9 45 AndrewMullen 4 (Jean McGregor) *sn w ldr: rdn over 2f out: wknd wl over 1f out* **40/1**	21
5006	**P**		**Walleyd (IRE)**[14] 3454 4-8-13 49 TonyHamilton 1 (Linda Perratt) *hld up: outpcd 1/2-way: btn whn broke down over 2f out: fatally injured* **20/1**	—

1m 30.76s (-2.64) **Going Correction** -0.225s/f (Firm)

WFA 3 from 4yo+ 8lb **10** Ran SP% **114.4**

Speed ratings (Par 101): **106,104,100,99,98 95,94,93,91,—**

toteswingers:1&2:£16.50, 1&3:£5.50, 2&3:£8.20 CSF £128.51 CT £822.84 TOTE £6.60: £2.40, £4.00, £1.40; EX 171.90 TRIFECTA Not won..

Owner Wilson Downes Kennedy Tobin **Bred** Moyglare Stud **Trained** Sandhutton, N Yorks

■ Stewards' Enquiry : Adrian Nicholls one-day ban: careless riding (Jul 25)

FOCUS

The pace was strong and surprisingly few got involved from off the gallop. The winner is rated close to his early Irish form with the second confirming his recent improvement.

Drive Home(USA) Official explanation: trainer said, regarding apparent improvement in form, that the gelding may have failed to stay having been drawn wide on its previous run

3904 PLAY CASINO AT VICTORCHANDLER.COM H'CAP 1m

4:30 (4:33) (Class 4) (0-85,84) 3-Y-O £4,204 (£1,251; £625; £312) **Stalls** Low

Form				RPR
6134	**1**		**Shamdarley (IRE)**[23] 3159 3-9-0 77 FrederikTylicki 2 (Michael Dods) *hld up: effrt and rdn over 2f out: styd on wl fnl f: led nr fin* **2/1**[1]	86
51	**2**	*nk*	**Izzy The Ozzy (IRE)**[48] 2394 3-9-0 77 LeeNewman 6 (David Barron) *cl up: led over 2f out: sn rdn: kpt on fnl f: hdd nr fin* **11/4**[2]	85
2-30	**3**	*1 ½*	**Next Edition (IRE)**[16] 3399 3-8-11 79 DaleSwift(5) 1 (Howard Johnson) *led to over 2f out: kpt on same pce: hld whn n.m.r towards fin* **6/1**	85
6-16	**4**	*1 ½*	**The Mellor Fella**[23] 3168 3-9-7 84 PaulHanagan 3 (Richard Fahey) *in tch: effrt and rdn over 2f out: one pce fnl f* **6/1**	86
2136	**5**	*1*	**Honest Deal**[16] 3400 3-8-12 75 PJMcDonald 5 (Alan Swinbank) *unruly bef s: trckd ldrs: effrt over 2f out: one pce appr fnl f* **9/2**[3]	74
415	**6**	*13*	**Circle Of Angels**[13] 3486 3-8-10 73 AdrianNicholls 4 (Mark Johnston) *dwlt: sn pushed along towards rr: drvn over 3f out: wknd fnl 2f* **8/1**	42

1m 39.88s (-3.92) **Going Correction** -0.425s/f (Firm) **6** Ran SP% **117.9**

Speed ratings (Par 102): **102,101,100,98,97 84**

toteswingers:1&2:£2.10, 1&3:£2.80, 2&3:£3.40 CSF £8.31 TOTE £2.90: £1.70, £2.20; EX 10.10.

Owner Andrew Tinkler **Bred** D Veitch & R O'Brien **Trained** Denton, Co Durham

■ Stewards' Enquiry : Dale Swift one-day ban: careless riding (Jul 25)

FOCUS
A fair handicap run at a good pace and the form looks reasonable, with the placed horses setting the level.

3905 WEDDINGS AT WESTERN HOUSE H'CAP (QUALIFIER FOR THE BETFAIR BONUS SCOTTISH RACING MILE FINAL) 1m 2f
5:00 (5:01) (Class 5) (0-70,74) 3-Y-0+ **£4,204** (£1,251; £625; £312) **Stalls** Low

Form RPR
50 **1** **Sartingo (IRE)**[48] [2393] 4-9-10 **64**........................ PJMcDonald 4 73
(Alan Swinbank) *hld up in tch: effrt over 2f out: styd on wl fnl f: led nr fin* **9/1**
-521 **2** *hd* **Retreat Content (IRE)**[24] [3116] 3-8-9 **65**.................... DaleSwift(5) 7 73
(Linda Perratt) *chsd ldr: rdn to ld over 2f out: kpt on fnl f: hdd nr fin* **5/1**[2]
500- **3** *1* **Cadeaux Fax**[20] [3265] 6-9-3 **57**..............................(t) TomEaves 1 63
(Gordon Elliott, Ire) *taken early to post: hld up in tch: effrt and drvn over 1f out: kpt on fnl f: nrst fin* **7/1**
03/- **4** *½* **All For You (IRE)**[647] [6455] 5-9-7 **64**................... GaryBartley(3) 9 69
(Jim Goldie) *hld up: hdwy on outside over 2f out: sn rdn: kpt on same pce ins fnl f* **6/1**[3]
-544 **5** *2 ¼* **Purkab**[24] [3116] 3-8-5 **56**.. AndrewMullen 3 57
(Jim Goldie) *taken early to post: hld up towards rr: drvn over 2f out: styd on ins fnl f: nvr able to chal* **8/1**
0634 **6** *½* **Machir Bay**[24] [3110] 4-8-9 **49** oh4..........................(p) FrederikTylicki 6 49
(Keith Dalgleish) *led: rdn and hdd over 2f out: rallied: no ex fnl f* **12/1**
3405 **7** *1 ½* **Monkton Vale (IRE)**[12] [3509] 4-9-8 **62**.........................(v) PaulHanagan 8 59
(Richard Fahey) *prom: rdn over 2f out: one pce over 1f out: btn fnl f* **5/1**[2]
0406 **8** *17* **Colamandis**[24] [3142] 4-8-9 **49** oh4..............................(p) FrannyNorton 2 12
(Hugh McWilliams) *t.k.h: trckd ldrs tl rdn and wknd over 2f out* **33/1**
-051 **9** *33* **Plattsburgh (USA)**[7] [3676] 3-9-9 **74** 6ex......................... AdrianNicholls 5 —
(Mark Johnston) *j. off bhd ldrs: dropped in rr after 1f: lost tch after 2f: t.o: breastgirth c undone and sddle reportedly slipped* **7/2**[1]

2m 7.47s (-4.53) **Going Correction** -0.425s/f (Firm)
WFA 3 from 4yo+ 11lb **9** Ran SP% **114.1**
Speed ratings (Par 103): **101,100,100,99,97 97,96,82,56**
toteswingers:1&2:£10.30, 1&3:£15.20, 2&3:£8.40 CSF £52.83 CT £335.14 TOTE £9.20: £6.10, £1.50, £2.60; EX 61.40 Trifecta £223.40 Pool £706.60 - 2.34 winning units.
Owner Melvyn Robson **Bred** Lynch-Bages, Carhue Inv & Glenvale Stud **Trained** Melsonby, N Yorks

FOCUS
A modest handicap but well run and rated on the positive side, despite the level being a bit fluid.
Plattsburgh(USA) Official explanation: jockey said, regarding running and riding, that shortly after start, the saddle slipped.

3906 BET NOW AT VICTORCHANDLER.COM APPRENTICE H'CAP 1m 5f 13y
5:30 (5:30) (Class 6) (0-65,65) 3-Y-0+ **£1,704** (£503; £251) **Stalls** Low

Form RPR
6-40 **1** **Jewelled Dagger (IRE)**[16] [3399] 7-9-7 **61**................ EdmondLinehan(3) 3 69
(Keith Dalgleish) *mde all at stdy pce: qcknd clr 2f out: unchal* **7/2**[3]
0541 **2** *3 ½* **Terenzium (IRE)**[18] [3300] 9-9-4 **55**...........................(p) GarryWhillans 7 58
(Micky Hammond) *hld up: rdn and outpcd 4f out: rallied over 2f out: edgd lft: styd on fnl f: wnt 2nd nr fin: no ch w wnr* **8/1**
4035 **3** *hd* **Tasman Tiger**[25] [3086] 4-8-11 **48**.................................. ShaneBKelly 4 50
(Kate Walton) *hld up in tch: effrt on ins over 2f out: chsd (clr) wnr ins fnl f: lost 2nd nr fin* **17/2**
0656 **4** *2 ¼* **Quaestor (IRE)**[12] [3509] 4-8-4 **46** oh1..................(p) JacobButterfield(5) 1 45
(Andrew Crook) *trckd ldrs: effrt and chsd (clr) wnr over 1f out to ins fnl f: sn no ex* **20/1**
0-60 **5** *1* **Herrera (IRE)**[18] [3319] 6-9-10 **64**........................ GeorgeChaloner(3) 2 62
(Richard Fahey) *prom: drvn and outpcd 2f out: rallied ent fnl f: no imp* **3/1**[2]
6611 **6** *3 ½* **Light The City (IRE)**[6] [3712] 4-9-2 **58** 6ex............ DavidSimmonson(5) 5 50
(Ruth Carr) *cl up: rdn over 2f out: wknd appr fnl f* **13/8**[1]

2m 52.77s (-1.23) **Going Correction** -0.425s/f (Firm) **6** Ran SP% **111.7**
Speed ratings (Par 101): **86,83,83,82,81 79**
toteswingers:1&2:£2.90, 1&3:£6.50, 2&3:£2.70. Totesuper 7; Not won, Place; Not won. CSF £29.55 CT £214.46 TOTE £4.90: £3.70, £4.20; EX 31.00 Trifecta £149.70 Pool £394.57 - 1.95 [illegible]
Owner A R M Galbraith **Bred** [illegible]
■ Stewards' Enquiry : Edmond Linehan one-day ban: used whip in incorrect place (Jul 25)

FOCUS
Few got into this low-grade apprentice handicap, and with the front two in the market disappointing, the form probably needs treating with caution. The form is limited but the winner is rated to last summer's course mark.
Light The City(IRE) Official explanation: jockey said gelding ran flat
T/Plt: £57.00 to a £1 stake. Pool:£55,238.88 - 706.85 winning tickets T/Qpdt: £18.20 to a £1 stake. Pool:£4,142.02 - 167.68 winning tickets RY

1827 FFOS LAS (L-H)
Monday, July 11

OFFICIAL GOING: Good to firm (good in places; 8.3)
Wind: moderate against Weather: sunny

3907 AT THE RACES SKY 415 MAIDEN FILLIES' STKS 1m 4f (R)
2:20 (2:20) (Class 5) 3-Y-0+ **£2,264** (£673; £336; £168) **Stalls** Low

Form RPR
30 **1** **Lady of Burgundy**[83] [1474] 5-9-8 0........................... LeeNewnes(5) 8 74+
(Mark Usher) *stdd s: stl last 4f out: hdwy over 3f out: pressed ldr on bit 2f out: shkn up to ld ins fnl f* **80/1**
6 **2** *nk* **Fairy Pose**[32] [2836] 3-9-0 0.. JimmyQuinn 9 73
(Amanda Perrett) *chsng ldng pair: wnt 2nd 3f out: led ins fnl 2f: shkn up over 1f out: styd on same pce* **7/1**[2]
0-0 **3** *2* **Blazing Field**[66] [1845] 3-8-11 0............................... JohnFahy(3) 3 70
(Clive Cox) *midfield: rdn and outpcd 4f out: drvn to chse ldrs 2f out: sn one pce* **40/1**
54 **4** *4* **Handles For Forks (IRE)**[21] [3224] 3-9-0 0.................. HughBowman 1 64
(Mick Channon) *hld up: hdwy on outer to chse ldrs 3f out: sn rdn and one pce* **14/1**
0-30 **5** *4* **Mia Madonna**[52] [2253] 3-9-0 70..................................... LiamJones 2 57
(Brian Meehan) *led tl hdd after 1f: remained chsng ldr tl led again ins fnl 3f: hdd and grad wknd 2f out* **17/2**[3]
-322 **6** *14* **Starlight Walk**[17] [3364] 3-9-0 77............................... SteveDrowne 5 39
(Roger Charlton) *led: rdn and lost grnd qckly ins fnl 4f: sn btn: eased fnl 2f* **1/4**[1]
0 **7** *1 ¾* **Perfect Rapture**[15] [3430] 3-9-0 0.................................. DavidProbert 7 32
(Clive Cox) *hld up: pushed along 5f out: sn wknd and dropped last 3f out* **33/1**

2m 32.61s (-4.79) **Going Correction** -0.20s/f (Firm) course record
WFA 3 from 5yo 13lb **7** Ran SP% **116.3**
Speed ratings (Par 100): **105,104,103,100,98 88,87**
toteswingers:1&2:£14.50, 1&3:£21.10, 2&3:£11.20 CSF £561.46 TOTE £68.90: £9.20, £2.10; EX 301.80.
Owner Brian Rogan **Bred** Barkham Manor Stud **Trained** Upper Lambourn, Berks

FOCUS
After a dry night, and a warm and sunny morning, the ground had quickened up, officially being described as good to firm, good in places. The winning time was 2.39secs under standard, resulting in a course record. The form is hard to rate but is treated positively with the time good.
Starlight Walk Official explanation: vet said filly returned lame near-fore

3908 ATTHERACES.COM FREE RACE REPLAYS H'CAP 5f
2:50 (2:52) (Class 6) (0-65,62) 3-Y-0+ **£1,746** (£519; £259; £129) **Stalls** High

Form RPR
000- **1** **Just For Mary**[10] [3603] 7-9-6 **56**............................(be) AndreaAtzeni 7 68
(Daniel Mark Loughnane, Ire) *hld up: rdn and hdwy to chse ldrs 2f out: led 1f out: styd on wl* **4/1**[3]
300U **2** *1 ¼* **Pinball (IRE)**[6] [3714] 5-8-11 **50**.........................(p) RobertLButler(3) 3 57
(Lisa Williamson) *hld up: stl gng wl 2f out: pushed along wl over 1f out and swtchd lft: styd on wl to take 2nd fnl 50yds* **22/1**
3314 **3** *1 ½* **Liberal Lady**[21] [3230] 3-9-6 **61**.................................. SteveDrowne 9 61+
(Hughie Morrison) *prom: pushed along and pressed ldr 2f out: ev ch 1f out: kpt on same pce* **7/4**[1]
-650 **4** *1* **Kokojo (IRE)**[21] [3230] 3-9-5 **60**..............................(p) ChrisCatlin 8 56
(Brendan Powell) *in rr and outpcd early: hdwy 2f out: kpt on wl ins fnl f* **12/1**
1040 **5** *1 ½* **Francis Albert**[56] [2164] 5-8-11 **54**.......................(b) JosephYoung(7) 4 47
(Michael Mullineaux) *led at str pce: carried hd high and hdd 1f out: sn wknd* **20/1**
6634 **6** *¾* **Novabridge**[18] [3321] 3-9-7 **62**...............................(b) HughBowman 6 50
(Andrew Haynes) *chsd ldrs: pushed along 2f out: wknd ins fnl f* **7/2**[2]
050/ **7** *8* **Rare Bet**[672] [5716] 5-8-9 **45**.. DavidProbert 5 7
(John Panvert) *in rr: drvn and outpcd 3f out: sn struggling and btn* **40/1**
0000 **8** *½* **Hoh Hoh Hoh**[21] [3216] 9-9-2 **57**...............................(t) RyanClark(5) 1 17
(Richard Price) *midfield: rdn and outpcd 3f out: dropped away tamely ins fnl 2f* **11/2**

57.49 secs (-0.81) **Going Correction** +0.05s/f (Good)
WFA 3 from 4yo+ 5lb **8** Ran SP% **113.2**
Speed ratings (Par 101): **101,99,96,95,92 91,78,77**
toteswingers:1&2:£10.70, 1&3:£3.10, 2&3:£7.10 CSF £83.44 CT £205.83 TOTE £6.20: £1.50, £4.40, £1.10; EX 85.50.
Owner Andrew Doyle **Bred** Cheveley Park Stud Ltd **Trained** Trim, Co Meath

FOCUS
The winning time just dipped under standard, confirming that conditions were on the quick side. The form is best rated around the placed horses.

3909 WEATHERBYS BLOODSTOCK INSURANCE MAIDEN STKS 6f
3:20 (3:23) (Class 5) 3-Y-0+ **£2,264** (£673; £336; £168) **Stalls** High

Form RPR
1 **Miss Elegance** 3-8-12 0..(t) LiamJones 7 63+
(Brian Meehan) *t.k.h in rr: hdwy over 2f out: pushed along and hung lft u.p ins fnl 2f: led 1f out: r.o wl* **8/1**[3]
4 **2** *¾* **Dreams Of Dawn**[58] [2103] 3-9-3 0................................ HughBowman 6 68+
(Mick Channon) *t.k.h: chsd ldrs: gng wl and n.m.r 2f out: swtchd lft and drvn 1f out: eventually picked up for press: kpt on strly to take 2nd post* **1/5**[1]
-040 **3** *hd* **Dimaire**[83] [1463] 4-9-4 56.. AndreaAtzeni 1 60
(Derek Haydn Jones) *chsd ldr: urged along 2f out: drvn and ev ch 1f out: nt pce of wnr ins fnl f: lost 2nd post* **7/1**[2]
60 **4** *1 ¼* **Nafa (IRE)**[10] [3577] 3-8-5 0................................... JosephYoung(7) 8 55
(Michael Mullineaux) *t.k.h in rr: pushed along and wnt lft wl over 1f out: [illegible] ins fnl f* **25/1**
0-6 **5** *2 ¾* **Simpulse** [illegible] 46
(Norma Twomey) *led: rdn wl over 1f out: hdd 1f out: sn wknd and lost 4 pls* **28/1**
06 **6** *¾* **Zee Zee Dan (IRE)**[10] [3575] 3-9-3 0.......................... RobbieFitzpatrick 4 49
(Noel Quinlan) *hld up: rdn and hung lft over 2f out: btn 1f out* **16/1**
00- **7** *7* **Lucky Tricks**[370] [3769] 3-8-12 0................................. SteveDrowne 3 21
(Jeremy Gask) *in rr: effrt to midfield 3f out: rdn and fnd little 2f out: sn wl btn* **25/1**
8 *3 ½* **To Pack**[30] [2941] 4-9-9 0.. JimmyQuinn 5 16
(Daniel Mark Loughnane, Ire) *t.k.h: swtchd lft after 1f and chsd ldrs: rdn and lost grnd qckly 2f out: sn wl btn* **25/1**

1m 10.55s (0.55) **Going Correction** +0.05s/f (Good)
WFA 3 from 4yo 6lb **8** Ran SP% **127.8**
Speed ratings (Par 103): **96,95,94,93,89 88,79,74**
toteswingers:1&2:£2.50, 1&3:£1.80, 2&3:£2.10 CSF £11.06 TOTE £8.10: £1.80, £1.02, £1.40; EX 21.70.
Owner Mr & Mrs B Buckley & T G & Mrs M E Holdcroft **Bred** Bearstone Stud **Trained** Manton, Wilts

FOCUS
A modest maiden with the moderate third the guide to the form.

3910 WALTERS UK LTD H'CAP 1m 4f (R)
3:50 (3:52) (Class 6) (0-55,55) 3-Y-0+ **£1,746** (£519; £259; £129) **Stalls** Low

Form RPR
5014 **1** **Dancing Primo**[20] [3256] 5-9-1 **51**................................ RyanClark(5) 9 58
(Mark Brisbourne) *hld up: hdwy on outer 4f out: loomed up on bit to chse ldrs 3f out: shkn up to ld 1f out: r.o wl* **5/2**[1]
5645 **2** *¾* **Peachez**[21] [3228] 3-8-6 **55**......................................(p) AmyScott(5) 12 62+
(Alastair Lidderdale) *hld up: hdwy 4f out: short of room 3f out: styd on stoutly to chse ldng pair ins fnl f: wnt 2nd cl home* **7/1**[3]
0-06 **3** *¾* **Hawridge Knight**[21] [3226] 3-8-3 **47**............................ AndreaAtzeni 11 51
(Rod Millman) *prom: hdwy on outer to chse ldrs 4f out: drvn to go 3rd wl over 1f out: one pce ins fnl f* **14/1**
0622 **4** *nk* **Oak Leaves**[12] [3516] 4-9-6 **51**.................................... DavidProbert 7 55
(Nikki Evans) *led: rdn and carried hd on one side 2f out: hdd 1f out: lost 2 pls fnl 75yds* **9/2**[2]
5440 **5** *nk* **Disturbia (IRE)**[19] [3268] 3-8-2 **46** oh1......................... JimmyQuinn 3 50
(J W Hills) *hld up: rdn 4f out: stl plenty to do 2f out: swtchd rt ins fnl 2f: kpt on wl ins fnl f* **14/1**

645 **6** *2 ½* **Delagoa Bay (IRE)**[16] 3393 3-8-3 **47** oh1 ow1 .... ChrisCatlin 10 47
(Sylvester Kirk) *t.k.h: prom: chsd ldr after 3f: urged along 3f out and drifted lft: lost pl under driving 2f out* **10/1**

5232 **7** *½* **Naledi**[10] 3600 7-9-1 **49** .... SophieDoyle(3) 2 48
(Richard Price) *midfield: pushed along 4f out: effrt to chse ldrs over 2f out: sn outpcd: bdly hmpd 1f out: swtchd rt and kpt on again ins fnl f* **8/1**

2-05 **8** *¾* **Josephine Malines**[162] 355 7-9-5 **53** ....(tp) JohnFahy(3) 1 51
(John Flint) *chsd ldrs: rdn along and outpcd 4f out: drvn and lost pl 2f out: swtchd rt and one pce ins fnl f* **20/1**

-044 **9** *7* **Orpen Bid (IRE)**[10] 3581 6-8-9 **47** .... JosephYoung(7) 5 33
(Michael Mullineaux) *hld up: dropped to rr 3f out: sn btn* **33/1**

65 **10** *5* **Countess Salome (IRE)**[24] 3148 4-9-6 **51** .... RobbieFitzpatrick 8 29
(Muredach Kelly, Ire) *hld up: stl last 4f out: pushed along 3f out: no imp ins fnl 2f* **7/1**[3]

0060 **11** *20* **Hint Of Silver (IRE)**[19] 3268 3-8-7 **51** ow2 .... SamHitchcott 6 —
(Andrew Haynes) *midfield: lost pl 3f out and sn carrying hd v high: dropped last 2f out: wl bhd* **14/1**

2m 34.08s (-3.32) **Going Correction** -0.20s/f (Firm)
WFA 3 from 4yo+ 13lb **11** Ran SP% **119.7**
Speed ratings (Par 101): **101,100,100,99,99 97,97,97,92,89 75**
toteswingers:1&2:£6.70, 1&3:£10.70, 2&3:£21.00 CSF £20.51 CT £209.82 TOTE £3.90: £1.60, £3.70, £7.40; EX 30.20.
Owner L R Owen **Bred** L R Owen **Trained** Great Ness, Shropshire
■ Stewards' Enquiry : Chris Catlin one-day ban: careless riding (Jul 25)

FOCUS
A moderate handicap and the form is limited, with the fourth the best guide to the level.
Disturbia(IRE) Official explanation: jockey said filly suffered interference in running

3911 SUPER TERRAIN TYRE H'CAP 1m 6f (R)
4:20 (4:20) (Class 4) (0-85,82) 4-Y-O+ **£4,204** (£1,251; £625; £312) **Stalls** Low

Form RPR

1/01 **1** **Praxiteles (IRE)**[5] 3725 7-9-6 **81** 6ex ....(tp) J-PGuillambert 7 87+
(Rebecca Curtis) *t.k.h in last: rdn and hdwy wl over 2f out: surged past 4 rivals to ld ins fnl 100yds: won gng away* **11/8**[1]

1254 **2** *½* **Pelham Crescent (IRE)**[4] 3762 8-9-3 **78** .... DavidProbert 6 83
(Bryn Palling) *hld up: hdwy on outer to press ldrs 3f out: rdn to ld ins fnl 2f: drvn and idling ins fnl f: hdd fnl 100yds* **11/1**[3]

4300 **3** *1 ½* **Parhelion**[17] 3344 4-9-3 **78** .... AndreaAtzeni 4 81
(Derek Haydn Jones) *chsd ldr: rdn and ev ch 2f out: one pce ins fnl f* **16/1**

-023 **4** *nse* **Crocus Rose**[30] 2931 5-9-7 **82** .... JimmyQuinn 3 86+
(Harry Dunlop) *midfield: stl gng wl whn swtchd rt over 2f out: 6th and drvn 1f out: kpt on strly ins fnl f: nrly nabbed 3rd on line* **7/2**[2]

4163 **5** *1 ½* **Arab League (IRE)**[15] 3428 6-8-13 **79** .... RyanClark(5) 5 80
(Richard Price) *t.k.h: prom: rdn and outpcd 3f out: kpt on again ins fnl f: unable to rch ldrs* **7/2**[2]

/50- **6** *½* **Sansili**[34] 1578 4-7-9 **63** oh3 ....(v) NoelGarbutt(7) 8 63?
(Peter Bowen) *midfield on outer: rdn to press ldrs ins fnl 2f: outpcd ins fnl f* **28/1**

5 **7** *1 ¾* **Charmeur (USA)**[14] 3466 4-9-0 **75** ....(bt) ChrisCatlin 2 73
(Philip Hobbs) *led: rdn and hdd ins fnl 2f: fnd little and sn btn* **25/1**

0400 **8** *1* **Record Breaker (IRE)**[24] 3127 7-8-8 **76** ....(b) DarylByrne(7) 1 72
(Mark Johnston) *prom: lost pl 4f out: dropped away tamely fnl 3f* **12/1**

3m 8.62s (4.82) **Going Correction** -0.20s/f (Firm) **8** Ran SP% **115.8**
Speed ratings (Par 105): **78,77,76,76,75 75,74,74**
toteswingers:1&2:£3.90, 1&3:£5.90, 2&3:£8.80 CSF £19.04 CT £173.85 TOTE £2.60: £1.02, £3.90, £2.50; EX 15.90.
Owner Los Amigos **Bred** Ballymacoll Stud Farm Ltd **Trained** Newport, Dyfed

FOCUS
Unlike in the previous races, this was a slowly run affair, and as is often the case in that type of race, there were a couple of hard-luck stories. The form makes sense though, rated around the placed horses.
Crocus Rose Official explanation: jockey said mare was denied a clear run

3912 WEATHERBYS BANK H'CAP 1m 2f (R)
4:50 (4:51) (Class 5) (0-70,70) 3-Y-O+ **£2,264** (£673; £336; £168) **Stalls** Low

Form RPR

-433 **1** **Ice Nelly (IRE)**[29] 2964 3-8-9 **62** .... SteveDrowne 7 71
(Hughie Morrison) *hld up: pushed along over 2f out: styd on wl to chse ldr ins fnl f: sustained run to ld fnl strides* **15/8**[1]

2004 **2** *hd* **Madame Excelerate**[18] 3306 4-9-6 **62** .... ChrisCatlin 1 70
(Mark Brisbourne) *chsd ldrs: led 4f out: strly pressed 2f out: kpt finding plenty for press: hdd fnl strides* **9/1**

223 **3** *2* **Timocracy**[24] 3139 6-9-13 **69** .... SamHitchcott 5 73
(Andrew Haynes) *led: hdd 4f out: rdn 3f out: kpt battling on valiently to press ldr 2f out: wknd ins fnl f* **4/1**[2]

3221 **4** *1 ½* **Corrib (IRE)**[12] 3515 8-9-0 **56** ....(p) DavidProbert 4 57
(Bryn Palling) *prom: pushed along to chse ldng pair 2f out: drvn and one pce ins fnl f* **9/2**[3]

05-5 **5** *shd* **Rosairlie (IRE)**[19] 3289 3-9-3 **70** .... JimmyQuinn 3 71
(Harry Dunlop) *midfield: rdn 3f out: effrt to chse ldrs 2f out: wknd fnl f* **6/1**

0405 **6** *2 ½* **Chik's Dream**[12] 3515 4-8-13 **55** .... AndreaAtzeni 6 51
(Derek Haydn Jones) *hld up: pushed along and outpcd 3f out: no imp ins fnl f* **18/1**

15-0 **7** *2 ¾* **Noble Jack (IRE)**[29] 2973 5-9-12 **68** ....(p) RobbieFitzpatrick 9 59
(Muredach Kelly, Ire) *hld up: rdn 4f out: wknd and btn ins fnl 2f* **14/1**

1006 **8** *8* **Dubai Miracle (USA)**[21] 3215 4-9-6 **67** .... JamesRogers(5) 2 42
(Laura Young) *midfield: drvn along and dropped to rr 3f out: sn no ch* **20/1**

66-0 **9** *6* **Gallego**[12] 3514 9-8-11 **58** .... RyanClark(5) 8 21
(Richard Price) *t.k.h in rr: hung rt thrght: racd wd thrght: rdn and wknd fnl 4f* **25/1**

2m 7.22s (-2.18) **Going Correction** -0.20s/f (Firm)
WFA 3 from 4yo+ 11lb **9** Ran SP% **117.8**
Speed ratings (Par 103): **96,95,94,93,92 90,88,82,77**
toteswingers:1&2:£4.80, 1&3:£2.40, 2&3:£6.50 CSF £20.71 CT £62.78 TOTE £2.40: £1.30, £2.00, £1.50; EX 26.20.
Owner Lady Hardy **Bred** Lady Hardy **Trained** East Ilsley, Berks
■ Stewards' Enquiry : Steve Drowne two-day ban: used whip with excessive frequency (Jul 25-26)

FOCUS
Some well-established performers were taken on by a couple of improving 3-y-os in a competitive race for the grade. The form is ordinary with the third the best guide.
Gallego Official explanation: jockey said gelding hung right

3913 BETFAIR RACING EXCELLENCE APPRENTICE TRAINING SERIES H'CAP 1m (R)
5:20 (5:20) (Class 6) (0-65,64) 3-Y-O **£1,772** (£523; £261) **Stalls** Low

Form RPR

5664 **1** **Princess Gail**[21] 3226 3-8-6 **49** .... RachealKneller(3) 3 54
(Mark Brisbourne) *awkward leaving stalls: t.k.h: hld up: pushed along over 2f out: drvn to press ldr 1f out: styd on wl to ld fnl 50yds* **11/2**

-325 **2** *½* **Border Abby**[21] 3227 3-8-8 **53** .... NoelGarbutt(5) 1 57
(Rae Guest) *wnt lft fr stalls: hld up: rdn and swtchd rt to ld 2f out: kpt finding for press: hdd fnl 50yds* **11/4**[1]

055 **3** *1 ¾* **Joyful Sound (IRE)**[24] 3138 3-9-9 **63** .... MatthewCosham 5 63
(Andrew Haynes) *hld up: hdwy on outer 4f out: rdn and hung rt 2f out: kpt on ins fnl f: tk 3rd cl home* **9/2**[3]

0-30 **4** *½* **Valeo Si Vales (IRE)**[15] 3432 3-9-1 **62** ....(p) JohnLawson(7) 2 61
(Jamie Osborne) *midfield: hdwy to chse ldrs 2f out: drvn and lost 2 pls 1f out: wknd and lost 3rd cl home* **5/1**

0-55 **5** *6* **Madison Square (USA)**[75] 1623 3-9-8 **62** .... DarylByrne 6 47
(Mark Johnston) *prom: led briefly over 2f out: hdd & wknd 2f out* **3/1**[2]

-030 **6** *5* **Crabbies Bay**[21] 3227 3-8-9 **54** .... ThomasBrown(5) 8 28
(Lisa Williamson) *t.k.h: led: hdd over 2f out: sn wknd* **20/1**

6-10 **7** *5* **Henrys Air**[41] 2599 3-8-13 **56** .... GeorgeDowning(3) 7 18
(David Bridgwater) *prom: pushed along 4f out: struggling 3f out* **9/1**

1m 40.37s (-0.63) **Going Correction** -0.20s/f (Firm) **7** Ran SP% **116.7**
Speed ratings (Par 98): **92,91,89,89,83 78,73**
toteswingers:1&2:£3.20, 1&3:£4.00, 2&3:£3.00 CSF £21.76 CT £74.42 TOTE £5.70: £3.50, £1.10; EX 23.20.
Owner R Rickett **Bred** Ash Tree Farm Ltd **Trained** Great Ness, Shropshire

FOCUS
A modest but competitive apprentice handicap. The gallop was decent and the placed horses set the level.
T/Plt: £167.10 to a £1 stake. Pool:£60,912.63 - 265.99 winning tickets T/Qpdt: £6.80 to a £1 stake. Pool:£7,408.43 - 798.76 winning tickets CS

3685 WINDSOR (R-H)
Monday, July 11

OFFICIAL GOING: Good to firm (watered; 8.6)
Wind: Almost Nil Weather: Fine, warm

3914 RIPPLEFFECT.COM APPRENTICE H'CAP 5f 10y
6:10 (6:10) (Class 5) (0-75,76) 3-Y-O+ **£2,264** (£673; £336; £168) **Stalls** Low

Form RPR

030 **1** **Cruise Tothelimit (IRE)**[16] 3379 3-9-5 **70** .... KieranO'Neill 1 74
(Patrick Morris) *led against rail: rdn and hrd pressed 2f out: narrowly hdd fnl f: styd on to ld again last strides* **11/4**[2]

560 **2** *hd* **Even Bolder**[42] 2557 8-9-8 **70** .... DavidKenny(2) 3 75
(Eric Wheeler) *chsd ldrs: clsd fr 2f out: hung lft fr over 1f out: upsides nr fin: nt qckn* **9/1**

0345 **3** *shd* **Diamond Johnny G (USA)**[7] 3685 4-9-3 **65** ....(t) CharlesBishop(2) 2 70
(Edward Creighton) *pressed wnr: rdn 2f out: narrow ld fnl f: hdd and no ex last strides* **9/1**

3130 **4** *½* **Magical Speedfit (IRE)**[11] 3555 6-10-0 **74** .... RyanPowell 7 77
(George Margarson) *hld up last and sn wl outpcd: rdn 2f out: styd on wl fnl f: gaining fast fin* **6/1**[3]

521 **5** *1* **Equuleus Pictor**[6] 3711 7-10-0 **76** 6ex ....(p) LMcNiff(2) 5 76
(John Spearing) *awkward s: sn w ldrs: upsides over 1f out: sn rdn and nt qckn: fdd nr fin* **15/8**[1]

4525 **6** *1 ¾* **Porthgwidden Beach (USA)**[4] 3785 3-8-2 **55** oh1(vt[1]) NathanAlison(2) 4 46
(Stuart Williams) *chsd ldrs: rdn 2f out: no imp* **8/1**

6-00 **7** *7* **Pose (IRE)**[131] 725 4-9-3 **65** .... MatthewLawson(2) 6 33
(Roger Ingram) *outpcd in 6th and pushed along over 3f out: nvr on terms: wknd fnl f* **33/1**

61.20 secs (0.90) **Going Correction** +0.025s/f (Good)
WFA 3 from 4yo+ 5lb **7** Ran SP% **109.8**
Speed ratings (Par 103): **93,92,92,91,90 87,76**
toteswingers:1&2:£6.90, 1&3:£6.80, 2&3:£15.80 CSF £24.76 TOTE £3.90: £2.30, £5.70; EX 33.00.
Owner Odysian Ltd T/A Cruise Nightspot **Bred** D And Mrs D Veitch **Trained** Tarporley, Cheshire

FOCUS
Stands rail dolled out 6yds at 6f and 2yds at Winning Post. Top bend out 3yds from normal configuration adding 14yds to races of 1m and over. Just an ordinary sprint and the runners stuck mostly to the stand rail. The pace took a while to pick up, and the fourth looked a shade unlucky. The form is modest but looks sound enough.

3915 BRITISH STALLION STUDS E B F SPORTINGBET.COM MAIDEN STKS 5f 10y
6:40 (6:45) (Class 5) 2-Y-O **£3,234** (£962; £481; £240) **Stalls** Low

Form RPR

55 **1** **Chunky Diamond (IRE)**[71] 1721 2-9-3 0 .... JackMitchell 11 80
(Peter Chapple-Hyam) *pressed ldng pair: rdn to ld wl over 1f out: looked in command fnl f: drvn out to hold on* **13/2**

26 **2** *½* **Lemon Rock**[30] 2914 2-8-12 0 .... RyanMoore 4 73
(Noel Quinlan) *chsd ldng trio: hrd rdn over 1f out: r.o to take 2nd ins fnl f: clsd on wnr fin* **9/2**[3]

3 **3** *2 ¾* **School Fees**[19] 3287 2-8-12 0 .... DaneO'Neill 6 63
(Henry Candy) *pressed ldr to 2f out: rdn and outpcd over 1f out and dropped to 4th: plugged on again fnl f* **5/2**[2]

6 **4** *½* **Royal Award**[19] 3287 2-8-9 0 .... MartinHarley(3) 10 62
(Ian Wood) *led and sn crossed to rail fr wd draw: rdn and hdd wl over 1f out: wknd fnl f* **33/1**

3 **5** *2 ¾* **The Rising (IRE)**[23] 3165 2-9-3 0 .... StevieDonohoe 2 57
(Ed McMahon) *chsd ldng trio: shkn up and outpcd 2f out: n.d after* **9/4**[1]

6 *hd* **Full Support (IRE)** 2-9-3 0 ....(t) RichardMullen 1 56
(David Brown) *rousted along early and rn green: a in same pl: shkn up and no imp 2f out* **10/1**

7 *1* **Monymusk** 2-9-3 0 .... AdamKirby 8 52+
(David Elsworth) *s.s: wl off the pce in last: pushed along and modest prog 2f out: lost no further grnd: nt disgracd* **33/1**

8 *6* **Love Tale** 2-8-12 0 .... HayleyTurner 5 26
(Mark Rimell) *a in last trio: pushed along over 3f out: bhd fnl 2f* **80/1**

9 15 **Queens Sandridge (IRE)** 2-9-3 0 .... TomQueally 7 —
(Alan Bailey) *s.i.s: a in last trio: struggling bef 1/2-way: t.o* **25/1**

61.07 secs (0.77) **Going Correction** +0.025s/f (Good) **9** Ran SP% **110.9**
Speed ratings (Par 94): **94,93,88,88,83 83,81,72,48**
toteswingers:1&2:£3.70, 1&3:£3.60, 2&3:£2.60 CSF £31.58 TOTE £6.70: £1.90, £1.50, £1.90; EX 35.00 Trifecta £125.00 Pool £4,840.87 - 28.64 winning units.
Owner Rebel Racing **Bred** Mrs E Comer **Trained** Newmarket, Suffolk

FOCUS
No more than a fair maiden for the track and one in which those with experience and who were fast away held sway.

NOTEBOOK
Chunky Diamond(IRE) looked to have something to find on form having finished fifth at Newmarket when last seen in May, but there was no fluke about this success, soon to the fore and always holding the second at bay under a less vigorous ride. He's not short of speed, clearly, but his pedigree points to him being a better horse at 6f+. (op 8-1)
Lemon Rock holds an entry in the Lowther and 6f is clearly her trip right now rather than 5f, always finding things happening too quickly dropped in trip and enduring quite a hard race too in futile pursuit of the winner. There might be a bit more to come, but she's starting to look vulnerable in maidens. (tchd 10-3 and 5-1 in places)
School Fees ◆ seemed to step up a little on her debut run but, rather as at Salisbury, she left the impression she'll benefit from a step up to 6f, so she has the potential to do better again. (op 9-4 tchd 11-4)
Royal Award finished behind School Fees as she had last time but got much closer on this occasion and even led that one into the last furlong. She's quite speedy and will progress more as she starts to see her races out better.
The Rising(IRE) couldn't build on the promise of his Haydock debut, soon struggling to lay up and never promising to get into contention. He shouldn't be given up on yet, not least at 6f. (op 3-1 tchd 7-2)
Full Support(IRE), who's bred to be a sprinting 2-y-o, being by Acclamation out of a juvenile 6f winner, wasn't quite fully wound up judged by the market and ran as if he needed the experience to bring him on. (op 17-2 tchd 8-1 and 11-1)
Monymusk, a gelding by Norse Dancer and a half-brother to the 6f/1m winner Highland Quaich, was one of the more substantial types on looks but was taken off his feet after a slow start and is one for later in the season over further. (op 50-1 tchd 25-1)

3916 VESTRA WEALTH MANAGEMENT (S) STKS — 1m 3f 135y
7:10 (7:11) (Class 6) 3-4-Y-O — **£1,704** (£503; £251) **Stalls** Centre

Form — RPR

5301 **1** **Dew Reward (IRE)**[13] 3175 3-9-0 60 .... AdamKirby 1 63
(Bill Turner) *trckd ldr: shkn up over 3f out: chal over 2f out: drvn to ld over 1f out and edgd rt: styd on* **10/1**

2063 **2** 1/2 **Enriching (USA)**[10] 3596 3-8-10 60 ow1 .... (t) DaneO'Neill 3 58
(David Elsworth) *led at mod pce: tried to kick on 4f out: drvn and hdd over 1f out: styd on but a hld* **11/2**[3]

2030 **3** 2 1/2 **Abigails Angel**[5] 3741 4-9-3 58 .... IanMongan 6 47
(Brett Johnson) *t.k.h: hld up in last trio: effrt over 2f out: drvn and kpt on fr over 1f out to take 3rd last strides: nvr cl enough to threaten* **6/1**

3600 **4** hd **Meglio Ancora**[11] 3546 4-9-8 64 .... KierenFallon 7 52
(Jonathan Portman) *hld up bhd ldrs: drvn and effrt over 2f out: one pce and nvr able to chal* **85/40**[2]

6-00 **5** 1 1/4 **Rather Cool**[15] 3431 3-8-4 47 .... HayleyTurner 4 45
(John Bridger) *trckd ldng pair: rdn 3f out: nt qckn and no imp over 1f out* **20/1**

0241 **6** hd **Urban Kode (IRE)**[10] 3596 3-8-9 63 .... (v) KieranO'Neill(5) 9 55
(David Evans) *t.k.h: hld up in last trio: shkn up 4f out: effrt on outer over 2f out: no imp over 1f out: fdd* **2/1**[1]

54 **7** 10 **County Hotel (IRE)**[24] 3119 4-9-3 0 .... FrankieMcDonald 2 28
(Barry Brennan) *s.s: t.k.h: hld up in last trio: wknd over 2f out: eased over 1f out* **25/1**

2m 32.26s (2.76) **Going Correction** +0.025s/f (Good)
WFA 3 from 4yo 13lb **7** Ran SP% **112.7**
Speed ratings (Par 101): **91,90,89,88,88 87,81**
toteswingers:1&2:£6.90, 1&3:£6.80, 2&3:£6.30 CSF £61.06 TOTE £8.60: £2.50, £2.40; EX 26.10 Trifecta £118.30 Pool £4,940.63 - 30.89 winning units.The winner was bought in for £4,000. Enriching was claimed by Noel Quinlan for £5,000.
Owner Mrs Dorien Tucker **Bred** Tim Hyde Jnr **Trained** Sigwells, Somerset

FOCUS
A wide variety of abilities on show in a weak seller and probably muddling form too, with the race being run at a very steady pace that didn't pick up until 4f from home. The first two dominated throughout and the winner is the best guide to the form.

3917 CONOCOPHILLIPS MAIDEN STKS — 6f
7:40 (7:40) (Class 5) 2-Y-O — **£2,264** (£673; £336; £168) **Stalls** Low

Form — RPR

1 **Compton** 2-9-3 0 .... StevieDonohoe 7 81+
(Ralph Beckett) *trckd ldrs: effrt to ld wl over 1f out: rdn clr: readily* **4/1**[1]

2 2 1/2 **Rex Imperator** 2-9-3 0 .... GeorgeBaker 2 76+
(Roger Charlton) *trckd ldrs: nt clr run over 1f out and then hit over hd by rival's whip: shkn up and r.o fnl f to take 2nd nr fin* **12/1**

46 **3** nk **Daunt (IRE)**[16] 3388 2-9-3 0 .... RyanMoore 14 73
(Richard Hannon) *wl in tch: prog to chal 2f out: w wnr wl over 1f out: one pce after: lost 2nd nr fin* **6/1**[3]

4 1 **Storming Bernard (USA)** 2-9-3 0 .... TomQueally 13 70
(Alan Bailey) *awkward s: t.k.h: hld up in midfield: prog and nt clr run 2f out: rdn and kpt on same pce* **33/1**

33 **5** nse **Miss Lahar**[38] 2661 2-8-9 0 .... MartinHarley(3) 11 64
(Mick Channon) *dwlt: t.k.h and sn midfield: prog and eased off rail fr 2f out: rdn and hanging lft fr over 1f out: no hdwy after* **11/2**[2]

6 3 **Spunky** 2-9-3 0 .... KierenFallon 15 60+
(Luca Cumani) *racd wd towards rr: shuffled along in midfield 2f out: no further prog: nt disgracd* **13/2**

03 **7** 3/4 **Pond Life (IRE)**[16] 3408 2-9-3 0 .... HayleyTurner 6 58
(Amy Weaver) *settled towards rr: pushed along over 2f out: kpt on steadily fr over 1f out: may improve* **8/1**

8 3/4 **Zain Point (IRE)** 2-9-3 0 .... DaneO'Neill 1 56
(Gerard Butler) *pressed ldr: upsides 2f out: wknd over 1f out* **12/1**

9 4 1/2 **Showmepower (IRE)** 2-9-3 0 .... EddieAhern 10 45+
(John Dunlop) *slowest away: mostly last to 2f out: shuffled along and passed wkng rivals: do bttr* **25/1**

10 3 1/4 **Onebytheknows** 2-9-3 0 .... PatDobbs 4 33
(Richard Hannon) *settled in last pair: pushed along over 2f out: sme modest late prog* **10/1**

0 **11** 2 1/2 **Catchy Tune (IRE)**[16] 3382 2-9-3 0 .... RichardMullen 3 25
(David Brown) *a wl in rr and sn pushed along: rn green and hung lft over 1f out* **14/1**

04 **12** 1 3/4 **Illustrious Lad (IRE)**[39] 2640 2-9-3 0 .... PatCosgrave 8 20
(Jim Boyle) *mde most to wl over 1f out: wknd rapidly* **9/1**

0 **13** 1 1/4 **Inniscastle Boy**[7] 3686 2-9-3 0 .... JackMitchell 5 16
(William Muir) *sn lost midfield pl and rdn: struggling in rr fr 1/2-way* **50/1**

6 **14** 16 **Almirah**[4] 3767 2-8-12 0 .... EddieCreighton 12 —
(Edward Creighton) *pushed up to go prom: wknd rapidly over 2f out* **200/1**

1m 13.99s (0.99) **Going Correction** +0.025s/f (Good) **14** Ran SP% **124.5**
Speed ratings (Par 94): **94,90,90,88,88 84,83,82,76,72 69,66,65,43**
toteswingers:1&2:£25.90, 1&3:£6.80, 2&3:£23.40 CSF £54.71 TOTE £5.70: £2.90, £4.10, £1.80; EX 85.70 Trifecta £756.80 Pool £1,319.31 - 1.29 winning units.
Owner J H Richmond-Watson **Bred** Lawn Stud **Trained** Kimpton, Hants

FOCUS
Quite an interesting maiden featuring a host of unraced horses, several of whom are likely to improve a good deal next time.

NOTEBOOK
Compton ◆, by Compton Place and out of a 7f/1m winner who is a half-sister to the stable's Oaks winner Look Here, was well backed ahead of the race and made a promising debut, soon well positioned tracking the pace and asserting readily inside the last despite edging left. He's probably a fair bit better than this and a novice looks the obvious route with 7f unlikely to bother him before long. (op 13-2)
Rex Imperator ◆ who's a son of Royal Applause and the first foal of a 6f/1m winner, shaped really well too and seems sure to win a similar race given the improvement youngsters from this yard often make from their first run to their second. He was given a considerate introduction after being hit over the face with the whip 1f out, and looked to pass the post with plenty of running left in him. (op 10-1 tchd 14-1)
Daunt(IRE) almost certainly left his modest form behind back up at this trip, and might be one that will find more as he moves into nurseries now he's got his act together. However, he's blown his cover slightly in that regard with respect to his mark. (op 7-1 tchd 15-2)
Storming Bernard(USA), who was bought for 32,000 gns at the sales earlier this year, ran an encouraging first race considering his pedigree points to his needing a fair bit further in time, never far away and keeping on well. He'll improve. (op 40-1)
Miss Lahar didn't seem to give any trouble at the start on this occasion but her form looks to have hit a plateau, albeit not helped by being a bit keen early on and a bit short of room too. (tchd 5-1 and 6-1)
Spunky is a colt by Invincible Spirit out of a mare that stayed 1m4f. He wasn't best drawn and was always racing wide but this run was all about the future and he showed plenty of promise without being given anything like a hard time. (tchd 6-1 and 7-1)
Pond Life(IRE) wasn't up to this as expected and already looks to be crying out for either 7f or 1m in nurseries. (op 9-1 tchd 10-1)
Showmepower(IRE) is from a family that generally need time and distance, but this run after a slow start wasn't without promise and he'll be a different proposition once he gets handicapped.

3918 SPORTINGBET.COM FILLIES' H'CAP — 1m 67y
8:10 (8:10) (Class 4) (0-80,78) 3-Y-O+ — **£3,557** (£1,058; £529; £264) **Stalls** Low

Form — RPR

333 **1** **Totheendoftheearth (IRE)**[19] 3289 3-8-13 72 .... RyanMoore 3 78+
(Sylvester Kirk) *trckd ldrs: prog to ld over 2f out: hrd rdn and edgd lft fr over 1f out: hld on: all out* **2/1**[1]

2011 **2** 1/2 **Hurricane Lady (IRE)**[18] 3312 3-9-2 75 .... EddieAhern 6 80+
(Walter Swinburn) *squeezed out s: hld up in last pair: prog 3f out: chal 2f out: upsides after: nt qckn nr fin* **5/2**[2]

1102 **3** 1 **Flying Phoenix**[17] 3363 3-8-8 67 .... (b1) HayleyTurner 7 70
(Gay Kelleway) *hld up in last pair: sltly impeded bnd 5f out: stl last and shkn up over 2f out: prog and drvn over 1f out: wnt 3rd fnl f: clsng fin* **16/1**

1153 **4** 6 **Wishformore (IRE)**[11] 3549 4-8-9 64 .... (p) RyanPowell(5) 2 55
(J S Moore) *hld up in tch: rdn over 2f out: wknd over 1f out* **8/1**

140 **5** 2 1/4 **National Hope (IRE)**[56] 2147 3-8-9 71 .... (t) MatthewDavies(3) 4 55
(George Baker) *trckd ldrs: rdn 3f out: wknd 2f out* **22/1**

1-6 **6** hd **Pandorea**[18] 3310 3-9-5 78 .... DaneO'Neill 1 62
(Henry Candy) *led 1f: trckd ldr: upsides over 2f out: wknd wl over 1f out* **4/1**[3]

0255 **7** 9 **Red Yarn**[11] 3549 4-9-9 73 .... (b) GeorgeBaker 5 38
(Gary Moore) *hrd rdn to ld after 1f: hdd & wknd rapidly over 2f out: t.o* **8/1**

1m 43.8s (-0.90) **Going Correction** +0.025s/f (Good)
WFA 3 from 4yo 9lb **7** Ran SP% **114.4**
Speed ratings (Par 102): **105,104,103,97,95 95,86**
toteswingers:1&2:£1.10, 1&3:£6.10, 2&3:£6.10 CSF £7.22 TOTE [illegible] £1.80, £2.00; EX 5.20
Owner Mrs Barbara Facchino **Bred** Barouche Stud Ireland Ltd **Trained** Upper Lambourn, Berks

FOCUS
An ordinary fillies handicap run at a good pace and the winner looks open to a bit more improvement. The runner-up sets the level but the third limits the form.

3919 VESTRA WEALTH PRIVATE CLIENT H'CAP — 1m 2f 7y
8:40 (8:40) (Class 5) (0-75,75) 3-Y-O — **£2,264** (£673; £336; £168) **Stalls** Centre

Form — RPR

4-12 **1** **Lady Gabrielle (IRE)**[21] 3228 3-9-0 68 .... DaneO'Neill 6 77+
(David Elsworth) *trckd ldrs: rdn over 2f out: effrt to ld wl over 1f out: drvn out to hold on* **9/2**[2]

6-14 **2** 1/2 **Robin Hoods Bay**[24] 3118 3-9-7 75 .... PatCosgrave 4 83+
(Edward Vaughan) *hld up in tch: prog and nt clr run over 2f out: swtchd lft and effrt wl over 1f out: chsd wnr fnl f and chal: nt qckn last 100yds* **7/2**[1]

6-60 **3** 2 1/4 **Deny**[29] 2957 3-9-0 68 .... (v1) RyanMoore 9 71
(Sir Michael Stoute) *s.s: rushed up to ld after 1f: hdd 6f out: drvn 3f out: chal 2f out: nt qckn u.p* **13/2**[3]

21 **4** shd **Covert Decree**[131] 737 3-9-7 75 .... AdamKirby 7 78
(Clive Cox) *led 1f: styd handy: drvn 3f out: nt qckn 2f out: kpt on* **12/1**

-025 **5** 1 1/2 **Novel Dancer**[19] 3267 3-9-0 73 .... KieranO'Neill(5) 8 73
(Richard Hannon) *hld up in midfield: rdn over 3f out: nt qckn u.p 2f out: one pce* **8/1**

15-0 **6** nse **One Lucky Lady**[31] 2877 3-8-13 74 .... MatthewLawson(7) 3 74
(B W Hills) *hld up last: rdn and struggling 4f out: kpt on fnl 2f on outer: n.d* **10/1**

0001 **7** 6 **Gower Rules (IRE)**[7] 3690 3-8-10 64 6ex .... HayleyTurner 2 52
(John Bridger) *wl in tch: rdn over 3f out: no prog over 2f out: sn wknd* **14/1**

2502 **8** 3/4 **Circus Star (USA)**[17] 3366 3-9-3 71 .... KierenFallon 5 57
(Brian Meehan) *chsd ldr after 2f: led 6f out: kicked on 5f out: hdd & wknd qckly u.p wl over 1f out* **7/2**[1]

6100 **9** 11 **Miss Chicane**[9] 3650 3-9-6 74 .... (p) EddieAhern 1 38
(Walter Swinburn) *t.k.h: hld up in last pair: rdn over 3f out: wknd over 2f out: eased: t.o* **16/1**

2m 8.09s (-0.61) **Going Correction** +0.025s/f (Good) **9** Ran SP% **116.4**
Speed ratings (Par 100): **103,102,100,100,99 99,94,94,85**
toteswingers:1&2:£5.10, 1&3:£6.30, 2&3:£7.90 CSF £20.84 CT £102.23 TOTE £5.90: £2.10, £1.70, £1.80; EX 23.60 Trifecta £459.30 Part won. Pool £620.79 - 0.60 winning units..

Owner The Lady Gabrielle Partnership **Bred** Mount Coote Partnership **Trained** Newmarket, Suffolk
FOCUS
Just a fair handicap to finish off with but it was well run and provided a close finish. The form is fair for the grade with the fifth and sixth the best guides.
T/Jkpt: Not won. T/Plt: £345.50 to a £1 stake. Pool:£93,683.65 - 197.90 winning tickets T/Qpdt: £24.90 to a £1 stake. Pool:£8,313.91 - 246.20 winning tickets JN

3713 WOLVERHAMPTON (A.W) (L-H)
Monday, July 11

OFFICIAL GOING: Standard
Wind: Light across Weather: Cloudy with sunny spells

3920 RACING AND STATS AT INFORMRACING.COM (S) STKS 5f 20y(P)
6:20 (6:21) (Class 6) 3-4-Y-O £1,533 (£452; £226) Stalls Low

Form				RPR
4660	1		**Inde Country**28 2990 3-8-9 48 (t) JamesDoyle 2 (Nicky Vaughan) *w ldr tl led 2f out: drvn out* 22/1	56
5432	2	3/4	**Johnny Hancocks (IRE)**15 3433 3-9-0 60 RoystonFfrench 6 (Linda Stubbs) *led 3f: sn rdn: styd on u.p* 5/61	58
5005	3	3 1/4	**Justbookie Dot Com (IRE)**21 3238 3-9-0 62 (b1) SebSanders 7 (Louise Best) *chsd ldrs: rdn 1/2-way: styd on same pce fr over 1f out: wnt 3rd wl ins fnl f* 11/22	47
0600	4	3/4	**Lois Lane**21 3216 3-8-9 52 HarryBentley(5) 4 (Ron Hodges) *chsd ldrs: rdn over 1f out: wknd ins fnl f* 28/1	44
-055	5	1 1/4	**Turn The Tide**9 3638 3-8-9 65 PaulQuinn 3 (Mike Hammond) *sn pushed along and prom: rdn 1/2-way: styd on same pce fnl 2f* 8/13	34
2130	6	1 3/4	**Eternal Youth (IRE)**18 3309 3-9-5 65 (b) LukeMorris 5 (Ronald Harris) *s.i.s: outpcd* 11/22	38
-004	7	6	**Maggie's Treasure (IRE)**46 2421 3-9-0 54 (b1) TadhgO'Shea 1 (John Gallagher) *sn outpcd* 14/1	12

61.56 secs (-0.74) **Going Correction** -0.10s/f (Stan) 7 Ran SP% **110.9**
Speed ratings (Par 101): **101,99,94,93,91 88,79**
toteswingers:1&2:£6.20, 1&3:£12.10, 2&3:£1.50 CSF £38.93 TOTE £42.50: £11.20, £1.50; EX 39.00.There was no bid for the winner. Justbookie Dot Com was claimed by P D Evans for £6,000.
Owner Swanlow Stud **Bred** Swanlow Stud **Trained** Helshaw Grange, Shropshire
FOCUS
A very weak 3-y-o seller.

3921 INFORMRACING.COM HORSE RACING SPEED RATINGS MAIDEN AUCTION STKS 5f 216y(P)
6:50 (6:51) (Class 5) 2-Y-O £2,385 (£704; £352) Stalls Low

Form				RPR
40	1		**Balti's Sister (IRE)**17 3342 2-8-5 0 ow1 GrahamGibbons 3 (Michael Easterby) *s.i.s: hld up: nt clr run over 2f out: hdwy over 1f out: rdn and r.o to ld wl ins fnl f* 9/23	60
0	2	1/2	**Monty Fay (IRE)**21 3237 2-8-6 0 HarryBentley(5) 8 (Derek Haydn Jones) *led: rdn and hdd over 1f out: bmpd sn after: carried rt and led briefly wl ins fnl f: r.o* 33/1	64
54	3	shd	**Invincible Dream (IRE)**11 3552 2-9-1 0 JamieSpencer 2 (Robert Mills) *chsd ldr tl led over 1f out: sn rdn and hung rt: hdd wl ins fnl f* 9/42	68
03	4	1 1/4	**Fast On (IRE)**28 2983 2-8-11 0 SebSanders 6 (Ed McMahon) *chsd ldrs: rdn over 2f out: swtchd lft ins fnl f: styd on* 5/41	60
00	5	1 3/4	**Russian Bullet**5 3746 2-8-11 0 FergusSweeney 7 (Jamie Osborne) *hld up: edgd rt over 2f out: rdn over 1f out: r.o: nt rch ldrs* 12/1	54
0	6	1/2	**Liquid Sunshine**30 2919 2-8-4 0 MartinLane 5 (Sylvester Kirk) *hld up: rdn over 2f out: r.o: nvr trbld ldrs* 33/1	46
	7	20	**Dubar Way (IRE)** 2-8-4 0 LukeMorris 1 (Patrick Morris) *s.i.s: plld hrd and sn prom: rdn and wknd over 1f out* 16/1	—

1m 14.92s (-0.08) **Going Correction** -0.10s/f (Stan) 7 Ran SP% **112.9**
Speed ratings (Par 94): **96,95,95,93,91 90,63**
toteswingers:1&2:£15.30, 1&3:£1.90, 2&3:£12.10 CSF £113.25 TOTE £2.80: £1.70, £20.40; EX 111.80.
Owner Steve Hull & David Swales **Bred** P Monaghan, J Collins & G Dillon **Trained** Sheriff Hutton, N Yorks
■ Stewards' Enquiry : Harry Bentley caution: careless riding.
FOCUS
There was just an average pace on in this juvenile maiden, resulting in something of a bunched finish, and the form is modest.
NOTEBOOK
Balti's Sister(IRE) was on a recovery mission having flopped on her second outing at Doncaster last time and she proved easy to back. Patiently ridden, she overcame trouble 2f out and picked up nicely to get on top near the finish. She will stay further as she matures and ought to make her mark in nurseries. (op 3-1 tchd 5-1)
Monty Fay(IRE) was never in the hunt on his debut over C&D, but he had clearly improved a bundle for that as he was much more professional. Not beaten far, he could improve again for the experience.
Invincible Dream(IRE) was backed to return to something like his promising debut effort and he travelled in front. He ultimately paid for being taken on by the runner-up, however, as he hung right when tiring under maximum pressure. Nurseries are now an option. (op 11-4 tchd 3-1 in places)
Fast On(IRE), who fared best of those keeping stands' side at Carlisle on his previous outing, proved disappointing on this AW debut. It looked far too sharp for him, though, and he isn't one to write off when switching to nurseries. (op 13-8)

3922 INFORMRACING.COM ONLINE SINCE 2003 H'CAP 1m 5f 194y(P)
7:20 (7:22) (Class 6) (0-65,63) 3-Y-O £1,704 (£503; £251) Stalls Low

Form				RPR
05-0	1		**Susan Stroman**21 3228 3-9-5 61 JamieSpencer 10 (Ed Dunlop) *hld up: hdwy over 5f out: shkn up to ld over 1f out: rdn clr* 11/41	76
-455	2	4 1/2	**Golestan Palace (IRE)**30 2904 3-8-13 55 NickyMackay 4 (Ed Walker) *a.p: chsd ldr over 6f out: led over 2f out: rdn and hdd 1f out: sn outpcd* 12/1	63
6063	3	6	**Sum Satisfaction**19 3268 3-9-3 59 JamesDoyle 2 (Dominic Ffrench Davis) *s.i.s: sn pushed along and prom: led over 11f out: rdn and hdd over 2f out: wknd fnl f* 5/12	59
5000	4	8	**Mountain Myst**10 3587 3-8-9 51 DarryllHolland 7 (William Muir) *hld up: rdn 7f out: nvr nrr* 18/1	40
0004	5	nk	**Neighbourhood (USA)**82 1487 3-8-7 52 PaulPickard(3) 6 (James Evans) *hld up: rdn over 8f out: nvr on terms* 33/1	40
000-	6	1/2	**If What And Maybe**229 7552 3-9-0 59 MichaelO'Connell(3) 9 (John Ryan) *s.i.s: in rr: rdn over 7f out: n.d* 25/1	47
5050	7	1	**Laffraaj (IRE)**19 3268 3-8-9 56 (v) HarryBentley(5) 3 (Pat Eddery) *prom: rdn over 4f out: wknd over 3f out* 9/1	42
505	8	nk	**Oculist**16 3392 3-9-7 63 FergusSweeney 8 (Jamie Osborne) *mid-div: hdwy 7f out: rdn over 4f out: wknd wl over 2f out* 7/13	49
0-06	9	46	**Rasteau (IRE)**41 2586 3-8-3 45 LukeMorris 1 (Tom Keddy) *led: hdd over 11f out: chsd ldr to over 6f out: sn drvn along: wknd over 3f out: t.o* 50/1	—

3m 1.34s (-4.66) **Going Correction** -0.10s/f (Stan) 9 Ran SP% **87.5**
Speed ratings (Par 98): **109,106,103,98,98 97,97,97,70**
toteswingers:1&2:£4.10, 1&3:£1.90, 2&3:£3.30 CSF £20.00 CT £61.65 TOTE £5.80: £2.60, £3.80, £1.40; EX 38.20.
Owner Lord Lloyd-Webber **Bred** Watership Down Stud **Trained** Newmarket, Suffolk
FOCUS
The complexion of this moderate 3-y-o staying handicap completely changed when joint-favourite Final Liberation was withdrawn at the start. They went a fair enough pace and the first three had it to themselves leaving the back straight.
Oculist Official explanation: jockey said gelding had no more to give

3923 INFORMRACING.COM DISCOUNT SUBSCRIPTIONS AVAILABLE CLASSIFIED CLAIMING STKS 1m 4f 50y(P)
7:50 (7:50) (Class 6) 3-Y-O+ £1,704 (£503; £251) Stalls Low

Form				RPR
5035	1		**Colonel Sherman (USA)**21 3225 6-9-5 54 (t) JamieSpencer 9 (Philip Kirby) *prom: chsd ldr over 10f out: led over 2f out: rdn and hung rt fnl f: styd on* 5/12	63
430	2	3/4	**Thundering Home**50 1987 4-9-4 56 PaulPickard(3) 2 (Brian Ellison) *s.i.s: hld up: swtchd lft and hdwy over 1f out: wnt 2nd wl ins fnl f: nt rch wnr* 11/41	64+
4340	3	1 3/4	**Revolutionary**16 3393 3-8-4 57 SophieDoyle(3) 8 (Jamie Osborne) *sn led at stdy pce: hdd over 5f out: remained handy: rdn over 1f out: styd on* 5/12	60
0162	4	1 1/2	**Lytham (IRE)**21 3225 10-9-5 57 LukeMorris 7 (Tony Carroll) *hld up: racd keenly: hdwy over 3f out: sn drvn along: styd on same pce fnl f* 13/23	57
2365	5	hd	**Amical Risks (FR)**18 3317 7-8-11 54 JulieBurke(5) 1 (Ollie Pears) *hld up: rdn over 2f out: hdwy over 1f out: no ex ins fnl f* 13/23	53
0640	6	3 1/4	**Exotic Dream (FR)**6 3712 5-9-5 54 TomMcLaughlin 3 (Ronald Harris) *chsd ldrs: rdn over 2f out: styd on same pce fr over 1f out* 66/1	51
6436	7	2 1/4	**Dream Of Fortune (IRE)**16 3380 7-8-13 60 (bt) KevinLundie(7) 4 (David Evans) *s.i.s: hld up: plld hrd: rdn over 2f out: n.d* 18/1	48
05-4	8	1 1/4	**Summer Affair (IRE)**26 3047 6-9-4 51 ShaneKelly 5 (Ben Case) *prom: led over 5f out: rdn and hdd over 2f out: wknd fnl f* 11/1	44
2544	9	3/4	**Miles Of Sunshine**31 2873 6-9-1 54 HarryBentley(5) 6 (Ron Hodges) *hld up in tch: rdn and wknd wl over 1f out* 17/2	45

2m 40.94s (-0.16) **Going Correction** -0.10s/f (Stan)
WFA 3 from 4yo+ 13lb 9 Ran SP% **112.3**
Speed ratings (Par 101): **96,95,94,93,93 91,89,88,88**
toteswingers:1&2:£5.00, 1&3:£5.50, 2&3:£5.40 CSF £18.43 TOTE £4.60: £1.40, £1.90, £1.10; EX 26.30.Thundering Home was claimed by George Baker for £8,000.
Owner K Sivills, Preesall Garage & The Dublins **Bred** Fred M Allor **Trained** Castleton, N Yorks
FOCUS
A moderate claimer, run at an uneven pace.

3924 DANA ANDREWS 60TH BIRTHDAY CELEBRATION H'CAP 7f 32y(P)
8:20 (8:20) (Class 5) (0-75,75) 3-Y-O+ £2,385 (£704; £352) Stalls High

Form				RPR
3040	1		**Karate (IRE)**4 3783 3-8-0 58 SimonPearce(3) 3 (Hans Adielsson) *chsd ldrs: rdn to ld ins fnl f: r.o* 12/1	62
2010	2	shd	**All Right Now**17 3348 4-9-9 75 HarryBentley(5) 4 (Derek Haydn Jones) *chsd ldr: shkn up ins fnl f: r.o* 8/1	82
-421	3	hd	**Tamasou (IRE)**25 3093 6-9-13 74 GrahamGibbons 6 (Ed McMahon) *chsd ldrs: rdn over 2f out: r.o* 11/42	80
-341	4	shd	**Al Burkaan (IRE)**12 3508 3-9-1 70 JamieSpencer 7 (Ed Dunlop) *stdd s: hld up: rdn over 1f out: r.o towards fin: nt rch ldrs* 7/41	76+
0650	5	1/2	**Al Muheer (IRE)**11 3541 6-9-13 74 (b) SebSanders 2 (Ruth Carr) *hld up: rdn over 1f out: r.o* 7/23	79
-560	6	1/2	**Leelu**16 3413 5-9-4 65 LiamKeniry 5 (David Arbuthnot) *led: rdn and hdd ins fnl f: styd on same pce* 16/1	68

1m 27.97s (-1.63) **Going Correction** -0.10s/f (Stan)
WFA 3 from 4yo+ 8lb 6 Ran SP% **109.9**
Speed ratings (Par 103): **105,104,104,104,103 103**
toteswingers:1&2:£7.50, 1&3:£8.50, 2&3:£3.10 CSF £92.85 TOTE £22.10: £7.30, £2.40; EX 95.40.
Owner Erik Penser **Bred** C J Foy **Trained** Kingston Lisle, Oxon
FOCUS
With the first four being covered by about half a length at the finish, and the remaining pair hot on their heels, this is obviously muddling form.
All Right Now Official explanation: jockey said gelding hung left

3925 WOLVERHAMPTON-RACECOURSE.CO.UK MEDIAN AUCTION MAIDEN STKS 1m 1f 103y(P)
8:50 (8:51) (Class 6) 3-4-Y-O £1,704 (£503; £251) Stalls Low

Form				RPR
5642	1		**Arabian Heights**5 3747 3-9-3 73 SebSanders 5 (Sir Mark Prescott Bt) *hld up: hdwy over 3f out: led wl over 1f out: styd on wl* 5/41	78+
620	2	2 1/2	**Satwa Dream (IRE)**23 3164 4-9-13 77 JamieSpencer 2 (Ed Dunlop) *hld up in tch: rdn over 1f out: hung rt ins fnl f: styd on same pce* 9/42	74
03	3	shd	**Princesse Gaelle**14 3469 3-8-12 0 AndreaAtzeni 4 (Marco Botti) *chsd ldrs: rdn over 2f out: hmpd ins fnl f: styd on same pce* 9/13	68
-334	4	2 3/4	**Major Domo (FR)**16 3392 3-9-3 68 (p) LukeMorris 7 (Harry Dunlop) *prom: rdn over 1f out: no ex ins fnl f* 10/1	67
0	5	2 3/4	**Winged Diva (IRE)**12 3513 3-8-12 0 LiamKeniry 10 (Andrew Balding) *prom: chsd ldr over 6f out: ev ch 2f out: sn rdn: hmpd and wknd ins fnl f* 16/1	56
-060	6	1 1/2	**Grecian Goddess (IRE)**6 3709 3-8-9 59 MichaelO'Connell(3) 6 (John Ryan) *led at stdy pce: hdd wl over 1f out: wknd fnl f* 40/1	53?
4	7	2	**Spanish Plume**6 3717 3-9-3 0 GrahamGibbons 3 (Reg Hollinshead) *stdd s: hld up: racd keenly: nvr nr to chal* 11/1	54

0 **8** *3/4* **Haafhd Decent (IRE)**[55] 2174 3-8-12 0 .... DarryllHolland 1 47
(Karen George) *hld up: rdn over 3f out: n.d* **66/1**

9 *nse* **Magic Minstrel** 3-9-0 0 .... SimonPearce(3) 9 52
(Andrew Balding) *s.s: rn green and a in rr* **25/1**

2m 1.56s (-0.14) **Going Correction** -0.10s/f (Stan)
WFA 3 from 4yo 10lb **9** Ran SP% **116.3**
Speed ratings (Par 101): **96,93,93,91,88 87,85,85,84**
toteswingers:1&2:£1.60, 1&3:£2.40, 2&3:£6.00 CSF £4.06 TOTE £2.50: £1.20, £1.10, £1.80; EX 5.70.
Owner W E Sturt - Osborne House II **Bred** Biddestone Stud **Trained** Newmarket, Suffolk

FOCUS
Not a bad maiden.
Magic Minstrel Official explanation: jockey said gelding ran green

3926 TRY INFORMRACING.COM FOR WINNERS TODAY H'CAP 1m 141y(P)
9:20 (9:21) (Class 6) (0-60,60) 3-Y-0+ **£1,704** (£503; £251) **Stalls** Low

Form RPR
0316 **1** **Kielty's Folly**[5] 3741 7-9-6 **57** .... JamesRogers(5) 5 66
(Brian Baugh) *chsd ldrs: led over 5f out: rdn over 1f out: styd on gamely* **13/2**[3]

5000 **2** *hd* **Spinning Ridge (IRE)**[5] 3741 6-9-10 **56** ....(b) TomMcLaughlin 12 64
(Ronald Harris) *dwlt: hld up: hmpd wl over 2f out: hdwy over 1f out: sn rdn: r.o* **8/1**

6064 **3** *shd* **Belle Park**[48] 2385 4-9-4 **50** .... DarryllHolland 11 58
(Karen George) *hld up: hdwy over 2f out: rdn over 1f out: r.o* **16/1**

P234 **4** *1 1/4* **Signora Frasi (IRE)**[19] 3280 6-9-7 **60** .... DavidKenny(7) 3 65
(Tony Newcombe) *a.p: rdn over 1f out: styd on* **16/1**

3213 **5** *1 1/4* **Pie Poudre**[14] 3475 4-9-12 **58** ....(b) WilliamCarson 2 60
(Roy Brotherton) *hld up: hdwy over 3f out: nt clr run over 2f out: sn rdn: hung lft and no ex ins fnl f* **9/2**[2]

6660 **6** *nse* **Final Tune (IRE)**[68] 1814 8-9-2 **53** .... RyanClark(5) 7 55
(Mandy Rowland) *hld up: hdwy over 1f out: styd on* **25/1**

-050 **7** *3 1/2* **Trecase**[28] 3003 4-9-3 **49** .... JamesDoyle 4 43
(Tony Carroll) *mid-div: rdn over 1f out: nt trble ldrs* **16/1**

4350 **8** *3/4* **Lean Machine**[23] 3176 4-9-11 **57** ....(p) LukeMorris 9 49
(Ronald Harris) *hld up in tch: rdn and hung rt over 2f out: styd on same pce fr over 1f out* **10/1**

45-2 **9** *2 1/2* **Lujano**[24] 3142 6-9-5 **56** .... JulieBurke(5) 8 43
(Ollie Pears) *chsd ldrs: rdn over 2f out: wkng whn hung lft fnl f* **3/1**[1]

4004 **10** *1/2* **Lady Morganna (IRE)**[21] 3220 3-8-9 **56** ....(p) LauraPike(5) 10 41
(Olivia Maylam) *hld up: rdn over 1f out: n.d* **16/1**

0-00 **11** *3/4* **Gypsy Boy (USA)**[12] 3515 4-9-5 **54** .... MarkLawson(3) 6 38
(Jo Hughes) *led: hdd over 5f out: wknd over 1f out* **8/1**

0-00 **12** *43* **Go On The Badger**[30] 2924 3-9-0 **56** ....(v[1]) SebSanders 13 —
(James Toller) *prom: ct wd rnd the first bnd: rdn and wknd over 2f out: eased t.o* **33/1**

1m 49.14s (-1.36) **Going Correction** -0.10s/f (Stan)
WFA 3 from 4yo+ 10lb **12** Ran SP% **118.1**
Speed ratings (Par 101): **102,101,101,100,99 99,96,95,93,93 92,54**
toteswingers:1&2:£19.40, 1&3:£20.80, 2&3:£32.70 CSF £57.57 CT £816.80 TOTE £6.60: £2.20, £3.40, £5.20; EX 69.00.
Owner Saddle Up Racing **Bred** Stanneylands Livery **Trained** Audley, Staffs
■ Stewards' Enquiry : Tom McLaughlin two-day ban: used whip with excessive frequency (Jul 25-26)

FOCUS
A low-grade contest but it looked competitive for the class and there was a cracking finish.
Gypsy Boy(USA) Official explanation: trainer's rep said gelding had a breathing problem
T/Plt: £558.40 to a £1 stake. Pool:£67,929.71 - 88.80 winning tickets T/Qpdt: £106.90 to a £1 stake. Pool:£6,659.82 - 46.10 winning tickets CR

3927 - 3930a (Foreign Racing) - See Raceform Interactive

3609 BEVERLEY (R-H)
Tuesday, July 12

OFFICIAL GOING: Good to firm (8.4)
Wind: fresh 1/2 behind Weather: overcast

3931 TYREGIANT.COM SPRINT H'CAP (DIV I) 5f
1:30 (1:30) (Class 6) (0-60,60) 3-Y-0+ **£1,293** (£385; £192; £96) **Stalls** Low

Form RPR
0-52 **1** **Port Ronan (USA)**[21] 3247 5-8-10 **46** ....(p) BarryMcHugh 5 55
(John Wainwright) *swtchd rt after s: sn led: kpt on wl* **9/2**[2]

-060 **2** *2 1/2* **Commander Wish**[111] 950 8-8-13 **56** .... NoelGarbutt(7) 11 56
(Lucinda Featherstone) *chsd ldrs: wnt 2nd over 2f out: kpt on same pce fnl f* **40/1**

1406 **3** *shd* **Meandmyshadow**[18] 3360 3-9-5 **60** ....(p) SilvestreDeSousa 4 57
(Alan Brown) *chsd ldrs: kpt on wl ins fnl f* **13/2**[3]

4004 **4** *2* **King Of Swords (IRE)**[11] 3573 7-9-1 **51** ....(p) PaulHanagan 2 43
(Nigel Tinkler) *chsd ldr: one pce fnl 2f: rdr lost whip appr fnl f* **7/2**[1]

056 **5** *1 1/2* **Noels Princess**[18] 3343 4-8-10 **46** oh1 .... RobertWinston 9 33
(David O'Meara) *towards rr: rdn and hung lft over 2f out: nvr nr ldrs* **10/1**

6000 **6** *1* **Rio Sands**[21] 3247 6-8-5 **46** oh1 .... ChrisDCogan(5) 8 29
(Richard Whitaker) *mid-div: drvn over 2f out: nvr nr ldrs* **12/1**

3052 **7** *3/4* **Brave Battle**[9] 3661 3-9-4 **59** ....(b) AdrianNicholls 1 37
(David Nicholls) *led early: chsd ldrs: wknd over 1f out* **7/2**[1]

6-00 **8** *hd* **No Mean Trick (USA)**[36] 2765 5-9-10 **60** ....(v[1]) MickyFenton 10 40
(Paul Midgley) *t.k.h in rr: nvr on terms* **22/1**

5-60 **9** *shd* **Russian Winter**[18] 3343 3-8-11 **57** .... DaleSwift(5) 3 34
(Tim Etherington) *mid-div: drvn over 2f out: nvr nr ldrs* **16/1**

40-4 **10** *2 1/4* **Greek Secret**[12] 3556 8-9-6 **56** ....(b) DarryllHolland 7 27
(Deborah Sanderson) *a in rr* **8/1**

61.07 secs (-2.43) **Going Correction** -0.425s/f (Firm)
WFA 3 from 4yo+ 5lb **10** Ran SP% **116.5**
Speed ratings (Par 101): **102,98,97,94,92 90,89,89,88,85**
toteswingers:1&2:£26.80, 2&3:£32.00, 1&3:£5.90 CSF £159.98 CT £1197.80 TOTE £5.20: £1.50, £8.90, £2.30; EX 137.70.
Owner D R & E E Brown **Bred** Dr And Mrs M L Brosnan **Trained** Kennythorpe, N Yorks
■ Stewards' Enquiry : Robert Winston caution: used whip down shoulder in the forehand

FOCUS
Bottom bend moved out for fresh ground. This low-grade sprint handicap was run at a solid pace yet few landed a blow from off the pace. Fair form for the class with the third the best guide.
Noels Princess Official explanation: jockey said filly hung left throughout
Brave Battle Official explanation: jockey said gelding never travelled
Greek Secret Official explanation: jockey said gelding never travelled

3932 HAPPY 21ST BIRTHDAY RACHEL SHUBOTHAM MAIDEN AUCTION STKS 5f
2:00 (2:01) (Class 5) 2-Y-0 **£2,264** (£673; £336; £168) **Stalls** Low

Form RPR
3 **1** **Miss Rosie**[70] 1791 2-8-4 0 .... SilvestreDeSousa 2 66
(Mark Johnston) *stmbld s: led: narrowly hdd jst ins fnl f: kpt on to regain ld nr fin* **13/8**[1]

4422 **2** *hd* **First Fast Now (IRE)**[15] 3452 2-8-3 0 .... DeclanCannon(3) 7 67
(Nigel Tinkler) *wnt lft s: mid-div: hdwy on wd outside over 2f out: edgd rt over 1f out: slt ld jst ins fnl f: no ex and hdd nr fin* **6/1**[3]

3 *nk* **Byrama** 2-8-6 0 .... AndrewMullen 9 66
(Nigel Tinkler) *dwlt: mid-div: outpcd over 2f out: hdwy over 1f out: kpt on towards fin* **20/1**

4 *3 1/4* **Summer Lane (IRE)** 2-8-6 0 .... PaulHanagan 11 55+
(Richard Fahey) *s.i.s: in rr: outpcd over 2f out: styd on fnl f: tk 4th nr fin: will improve* **11/4**[2]

42 **5** *nk* **Mantuana (IRE)**[7] 3707 2-8-4 0 .... JamesSullivan 10 51
(David O'Meara) *stmbld bdly s: sn chsng ldrs: wknd ins fnl f* **7/1**

033 **6** *3/4* **Angel Of Hope (IRE)**[14] 3483 2-8-6 0 .... TomEaves 4 50
(Bryan Smart) *swvd rt s: chsd ldrs: wknd ins fnl f* **15/2**

6 **7** *1/2* **Tuibama (IRE)**[25] 3125 2-8-11 0 .... PJMcDonald 3 54
(Ben Haslam) *sn chsng ldrs: wknd over 1f out* **33/1**

8 *2* **Dream Walker (FR)** 2-8-9 0 .... PatrickMathers 8 44
(Ian McInnes) *dwlt: wl outpcd and bhd: nvr on terms* **66/1**

00 **9** *4* **Bertie Dancing (IRE)**[71] 1744 2-8-10 0 ow1 .... RobertWinston 5 31
(Nigel Tinkler) *hmpd s: sn chsng ldrs: wknd over 1f out* **40/1**

0 **10** *6* **Precious Little**[10] 3611 2-8-1 0 .... BillyCray(3) 6 3
(David Nicholls) *v free to post: hmpd s: sn wl outpcd and bhd* **40/1**

61.73 secs (-1.77) **Going Correction** -0.425s/f (Firm) **10** Ran SP% **117.4**
Speed ratings (Par 94): **97,96,96,91,90 89,88,85,78,69**
toteswingers:1&2:£3.00, 2&3:£17.00, 1&3:£10.90 CSF £11.49 TOTE £2.80: £1.30, £1.50, £5.10; EX 13.80.
Owner Greenland Park Stud **Bred** Greenland Park Ltd **Trained** Middleham Moor, N Yorks

FOCUS
Not a bad maiden which saw a tight three-way finish and it ought to produce winners. The runner-up sets the level.

NOTEBOOK
Miss Rosie just did enough to hold on in a tight three-way finish. Mark Johnston's filly was unsurprisingly well backed to go two better than on her debut at Catterick 70 days previously, as she had the best of the draw. She made that count, but wasn't given an easy time in front and looked vulnerable when briefly headed inside the final furlong. Her bang in-form jockey saved a little, however, and she forged back in front where it mattered. She ought to come on a little and make her mark in nurseries. (op 2-1 tchd 9-4 in a place)
First Fast Now(IRE) was having her sixth outing and proved easy to back. She responded strongly 1f out and edged to the front, but just failed to sustain her effort at the business end. She certainly deserves a change of fortune and rates a solid benchmark. (op 9-2)
Byrama ◆ was somewhat unlucky not to have made a winning debut. She was seemingly unfancied and her inexperience was greatly advertised as it took an age for the penny to drop. However, she motored home on the far side late on and would have prevailed in another few strides. A half-sister to last year's smart juvenile Klammer, she took time to pull up and it will be surprising if she doesn't collect next time out. (tchd 25-1)
Summer Lane(IRE) ◆ was representing connections who sent out a very useful-looking filly to win on her debut at York the previous weekend. She too proved too green to do herself justice from the outside stall, but was finishing strongly late in the day and ought to score when faced with a stiffer test. (op 4-1)
Mantuana(IRE), second at Southwell last time, was having her third outing and met support. She stumbled leaving the gates and, while she recovered to join the leaders, flattened out from the furlong marker. It looks worth giving her another chance and nurseries are now an option. Official explanation: jockey said filly stumbled at start (op 5-1)

3933 TYREGIANT.COM CLAIMING STKS 7f 100y
2:30 (2:30) (Class 5) 3-Y-0 **£2,264** (£673; £336; £168) **Stalls** Low

Form RPR
[illegible] **1** **[illegible] Mac**[21] [illegible] .... (h1) SilvestreDeSousa 2 69
(Neville Bycroft) *sn led: rdn over 1f out: all out* **11/1**

1532 **2** *hd* **Abidhabidubai**[11] 3571 3-8-12 **74** .... TomEaves 3 65
(John Quinn) *dwlt: sn trcking ldrs: effrt over 2f out: chsd wnr jst ins fnl f: no ex nr fin* **4/11**[1]

-000 **3** *3* **Spin A Wish**[35] 2782 3-8-1 **44** ow2 .... AmyRyan(3) 4 49?
(Richard Whitaker) *led early: chsd wnr: one pce over 1f out* **40/1**

-505 **4** *3/4* **Wandering Lad**[18] 3360 3-8-9 **60** .... MickyFenton 5 52
(Paul Midgley) *stdd s: hld up in last: hdwy to trck ldrs 3f out: one pce over 1f out* **16/1**[3]

1m 31.85s (-1.95) **Going Correction** -0.425s/f (Firm) **4** Ran SP% **108.3**
Speed ratings (Par 100): **94,93,90,89**
CSF £4.22 TOTE £3.90; EX 4.70.
Owner Mrs C M Whatley **Bred** Roger Ingram **Trained** Brandsby, N Yorks

FOCUS
A moderate claimer, run at an uneven pace. The winner looks the best guide.
Abidhabidubai Official explanation: caution: used whip without giving filly time to respond

3934 FINDING WINNERS AT IRISHBIGRACETRENDS.COM H'CAP 1m 100y
3:00 (3:00) (Class 4) (0-80,79) 3-Y-0+ **£4,204** (£1,251; £625; £312) **Stalls** Low

Form RPR
0-10 **1** **Toto Skyllachy**[20] 3276 6-10-0 **79** .... FrederikTylicki 2 87
(Ollie Pears) *hld up: hdwy on wd outside over 2f out: r.o to ld last 50yds* **4/1**[2]

3100 **2** *1 1/4* **Old English (IRE)**[97] 1176 3-8-8 **68** .... SilvestreDeSousa 6 71
(Mark Johnston) *sn led: qcknd pce over 3f out: hdd and no ex clsng stages* **7/1**

1111 **3** *2 1/4* **I Confess**[49] 2382 6-9-6 **71** ....(b) RobertWinston 3 71
(Geoffrey Harker) *led early: trckd ldrs: drvn 3f out: kpt on ins fnl f: tk 3rd towards fin* **7/1**

1103 **4** *nk* **Bolodenka (IRE)**[11] 3576 9-9-8 **73** .... PaulHanagan 8 72
(Richard Fahey) *trckd ldrs: chal 3f out: wknd last 100yds* **9/2**[3]

5040 **5** *2* **West End Lad**[20] 3275 8-9-8 **73** ....(b) RussKennemore 1 68
(Roy Bowring) *hld up: drvn over 2f out: nvr a threat* **14/1**

0031 **6** *2 1/2* **Shadowtime**[10] 3612 6-9-11 **76** .... AndrewMullen 5 65
(Colin Teague) *banged hd on stalls: t.k.h: trckd ldrs: effrt 3f out: wknd over 1f out* **13/8**[1]

0423 **7** *5* **American Lover (FR)**[18] 3355 4-8-11 **62**.......................... PaddyAspell 7 39
(John Wainwright) *t.k.h: hdwy to trck ldrs 4f out: drvn 3f out: wknd over 1f out* **16/1**

1m 43.64s (-3.96) **Going Correction** -0.425s/f (Firm)
WFA 3 from 4yo+ 9lb **7** Ran SP% **113.8**
Speed ratings (Par 105): **102,100,98,98,96 93,88**
toteswingers:1&2:£5.30, 2&3:£4.30, 1&3:£5.60 CSF £31.13 CT £188.34 TOTE £5.00: £1.90, £2.50; EX 39.50.
Owner Richard Walker **Bred** Mrs G Slater **Trained** Norton, N Yorks

FOCUS
The non-runner took something away from this handicap, but it was still competitive enough. There was a solid pace on and the form should work out with the placed horses setting the level.
Shadowtime Official explanation: trainer said gelding banged its head on front gate of stalls

3935 TYREGIANT.COM STAYERS H'CAP (REGISTERED AS THE 126TH YEAR OF THE WATT MEMORIAL) 2m 35y
3:30 (3:32) (Class 4) (0-85,73) 3-Y-O+ **£4,528** (£1,347; £673; £336) **Stalls** Low

Form RPR
4613 **1** **Mojolika**[15] 3474 3-8-3 **67**..(e) SilvestreDeSousa 1 81+
(Tim Easterby) *trckd ldr: led 3f out: drvn wl clr over 1f out: heavily eased last 50yds* **7/4**[1]

00-0 **2** *7* **Markington**[42] 1458 8-9-13 **72**..(b) PaulHanagan 5 75
(Peter Bowen) *trckd ldrs on outside: drvn over 5f out: rdn over 3f out: styd on to take modest 2nd last 100yds* **17/2**

6411 **3** *1 3/4* **John Forbes**[19] 3316 9-10-0 **73**.. TomEaves 2 74
(Brian Ellison) *led: hdd 3f out: one pce* **7/2**[3]

6153 **4** *1 3/4* **Spiders Star**[5] 3754 8-9-3 **65**.. PaulPickard(3) 3 64
(Simon West) *reluctant to load: sn trcking ldrs: drvn over 5f out: one pce fnl 2f* **9/2**

40/1 **5** *1 1/2* **Riptide**[26] 3095 5-9-8 **67**..(v) FrederikTylicki 4 64
(Michael Scudamore) *hld up detached in last: hdwy 7f out: drvn over 3f out: nvr a factor* **3/1**[2]

3m 31.23s (-8.57) **Going Correction** -0.425s/f (Firm)
WFA 3 from 5yo+ 19lb **5** Ran SP% **112.3**
Speed ratings (Par 105): **104,100,99,98,98**
CSF £16.72 TOTE £2.60: £1.20, £3.30; EX 13.80.
Owner A Brannon & Habton Farms **Bred** Miss K Rausing **Trained** Great Habton, N Yorks

FOCUS
This wasn't a strong race for the class with the top weight rated 12lb lower than the race ceiling. There was still an impressive winner, though, although doubts over those in behind.
Riptide Official explanation: jockey said gelding never travelled

3936 TYREGIANT.COM H'CAP 7f 100y
4:00 (4:01) (Class 5) (0-75,75) 3-Y-O+ **£2,425** (£721; £360; £180) **Stalls** Low

Form RPR
0323 **1** **Polish World (USA)**[10] 3612 7-10-0 **75**.......................... MickyFenton 1 86
(Paul Midgley) *mde all: wnt clr over 3f out: drvn out: unchal* **11/2**[2]

0535 **2** *1 1/4* **Just The Tonic**[4] 3805 4-9-0 **61**.. LeeNewman 2 69
(Marjorie Fife) *trckd ldrs: wnt 2nd 1f out: no imp* **7/1**

4062 **3** *nk* **Seldom (IRE)**[8] 3683 5-8-11 **58**.. RobertWinston 7 65
(Mel Brittain) *prom: effrt 3f out: styd on same pce ins fnl f* **6/1**[3]

1303 **4** *3/4* **Violent Velocity (IRE)**[15] 3462 8-9-2 **70**.................... ShaneBKelly(7) 12 75
(John Quinn) *mid-div: effrt 3f out: chsng ldrs over 1f out: kpt on one pce* **9/1**

0-00 **5** *1 1/2* **Our Boy Barrington (IRE)**[39] 2671 4-9-7 **68**...........(v) AdrianNicholls 10 70+
(David Nicholls) *s.s: in rr: hdwy on wd outside over 2f out: styd on ins fnl f* **33/1**

3062 **6** *nk* **Eeny Mac (IRE)**[11] 3569 4-8-2 **56** oh5.......................... TerenceFury(7) 8 57
(Neville Bycroft) *chsd wnr: one pce over 1f out* **10/1**

-656 **7** *1 3/4* **Saharia (IRE)**[10] 3612 4-9-9 **75**..(p) LeeTopliss(5) 11 71
(Ollie Pears) *hld up in midfield: effrt over 2f out: wknd ins fnl f* **10/1**

0600 **8** *1 1/4* **Aussie Blue (IRE)**[15] 3462 7-8-12 **59**.......................... RussKennemore 13 52
(Richard Whitaker) *mid-div: hdwy and swtchd lft over 2f out: r.o outer 3f out: wknd fnl 150yds* **33/1**

-452 **9** *1 3/4* **Corsicanrun (IRE)**[10] 3614 3-9-5 **74**.. PaulHanagan 9 60
(Richard Fahey) *chsd ldrs: drvn 4f out: wknd jst ins fnl f* **11/4**[1]

006 **10** *1 1/4* **Royal Deal**[24] 3167 4-9-3 **64**.. JamesSullivan 3 50
(Michael Easterby) *in rr: bhd 3f out: sme late hdwy* **33/1**

6015 **11** *nk* **Striker Torres (IRE)**[10] 3612 5-9-9 **73**.................... MichaelO'Connell(3) 6 58
(Geoffrey Oldroyd) *s.i.s: in rr: sme hdwy on outside over 2f out: wknd over 1f out* **7/1**

00-0 **12** *8* **Big Whitfield**[29] 2985 5-8-9 **56** oh4.. FrannyNorton 5 21
(Tracy Waggott) *t.k.h in rr: bhd fnl 3f* **50/1**

1m 29.98s (-3.82) **Going Correction** -0.425s/f (Firm)
WFA 3 from 4yo+ 8lb **12** Ran SP% **120.3**
Speed ratings (Par 103): **104,102,102,101,99 97,97,95,93,92 92,82**
toteswingers:1&2:£8.00, 2&3:£8.00, 1&3:£5.60 CSF £43.27 CT £247.82 TOTE £6.30: £1.90, £2.20, £2.30; EX 50.50.
Owner C R Green **Bred** Racehorse Management, Llc **Trained** Westow, N Yorks

FOCUS
A competitive handicap for the grade. It was run at a decent pace and there was another winner from the front. The runner-up and fourth set the standard.
Corsicanrun(IRE) Official explanation: jockey said gelding never travelled

3937 TYREGIANT.COM SPRINT H'CAP (DIV II) 5f
4:30 (4:30) (Class 6) (0-60,57) 3-Y-O+ **£1,293** (£385; £192; £96) **Stalls** Low

Form RPR
5403 **1** **Media Jury**[10] 3616 4-9-8 **55**..(v[1]) DavidNolan 9 61
(John Wainwright) *led: edgd lft 1f out: all out* **33/1**

0012 **2** *1/2* **Hambleton**[34] 2803 4-9-7 **54**.. TomEaves 2 58
(Bryan Smart) *sn trcking wnr: upsides 1f out: no ex nr fin* **9/2**[2]

0052 **3** *1/2* **Galpin Junior (USA)**[11] 3573 5-9-9 **56**.. PJMcDonald 3 58
(Ruth Carr) *chsd ldrs: kpt on wl ins fnl f* **6/4**[1]

-000 **4** *1 1/4* **Lady Lube Rye (IRE)**[11] 3573 4-8-12 **45**.......................... AdrianNicholls 7 43
(Noel Wilson) *hld up towards rr: hdwy on outside 2f out: kpt on ins fnl f* **20/1**

0003 **5** *nse* **Kalahari Desert (IRE)**[11] 3573 4-8-12 **45**..........................(v) PaulQuinn 5 43
(Richard Whitaker) *hmpd s: t.k.h: hdwy over 2f out: chsng ldrs appr fnl f: kpt on same pce: eased fnl strides and lost 4th post* **12/1**

1006 **6** *hd* **Duke Of Rainford**[21] 3247 4-9-1 **48**.. TonyHamilton 11 45
(Michael Herrington) *swtchd rt after s: mid-div: nt clr run and swtchd lft over 1f out: hung lft and kpt on down outside* **25/1**

0030 **7** *3/4* **Bossy Kitty**[11] 3573 4-9-5 **52**..(p) PaulHanagan 6 46
(Nigel Tinkler) *hld up towards rr: hdwy over 2f out: one pce over 1f out* **10/1**

0646 **8** *nk* **Exceedingly Good (IRE)**[14] 3495 5-9-5 **52**.................... RussKennemore 4 45
(Roy Bowring) *trckd ldrs: effrt and hung lft over 1f out: one pce: b.b.v* **8/1**[3]

0406 **9** *1 3/4* **Sleights Boy (IRE)**[11] 3573 3-8-12 **50**..........................(b) PatrickMathers 1 35
(Ian McInnes) *reminders and lost pl after 1f: sn bhd: sme late hdwy* **16/1**

060 **10** *4* **Sea Crest**[28] 3025 5-9-2 **49**.. FrannyNorton 10 21
(Mel Brittain) *wnt lft s: chsd ldrs: lost pl and hmpd: over 1f out* **10/1**

0-60 **11** *14* **Hitches Dubai (BRZ)**[34] 2798 6-9-10 **57**..........................(v[1]) RobertWinston 8 —
(Geoffrey Harker) *s.v.s: a wl detached in last: eased ins fnl f* **20/1**

61.54 secs (-1.96) **Going Correction** -0.425s/f (Firm)
WFA 3 from 4yo+ 5lb **11** Ran SP% **117.4**
Speed ratings (Par 101): **98,97,96,94,94 94,92,92,89,83 60**
toteswingers:1&2:£10.20, 2&3:£2.20, 1&3:£9.50 CSF £169.21 CT £379.30 TOTE £30.80: £5.40, £2.40, £1.50; EX 120.10.
Owner S Enwright **Bred** J S Wainwright **Trained** Kennythorpe, N Yorks
■ Stewards' Enquiry : Tony Hamilton one-day ban: careless riding (Jul 26)
Paul Quinn two-day ban: failed to ride out for 4th (Jul 26,28)

FOCUS
The second division of the 5f handicap and it was slightly weaker than the first. The form is rated negatively through the runner-up.
Exceedingly Good(IRE) Official explanation: trainer said mare bled from the nose
Hitches Dubai(BRZ) Official explanation: jockey said gelding did not face the visor

3938 DOROTHY LAIRD MEMORIAL TROPHY H'CAP (LADIES RACE) 1m 1f 207y
5:00 (5:00) (Class 6) (0-65,63) 3-Y-O+ **£1,617** (£481; £240; £120) **Stalls** Low

Form RPR
-405 **1** **Key Breeze**[25] 3112 4-10-0 **61**..(t) LucyAlexander(5) 17 70+
(Kevin Ryan) *s.i.s: swtchd rt after s: t.k.h in rr: gd hdwy over 2f out: r.o to ld last 75yds* **18/1**

1640 **2** *2* **Rowan Lodge (IRE)**[34] 2800 9-10-6 **62**..........................(b) JulieBurke 10 67
(Ollie Pears) *chsd ldrs: upsides 1f out: no ex* **10/1**

-U31 **3** *hd* **Back To Paris (IRE)**[10] 3637 9-9-12 **54**..............(p) MissMMullineaux 13 59
(Philip Kirby) *w ldr: led 6f out: hdd and no ex wl ins fnl f* **8/1**[3]

6522 **4** *shd* **Kyle Of Bute**[15] 3475 5-10-6 **62**.. MissSBrotherton 8 67
(Brian Baugh) *chsd ldrs: upsides 1f out: kpt on same pce* **7/2**[1]

3265 **5** *3/4* **Rub Of The Relic (IRE)**[15] 3456 6-9-5 **52**................(v) MissHDukes(5) 3 55
(Paul Midgley) *led tl 6f out: outpcd over 2f out: rallied over 1f out: kpt on one pce* **12/1**

-000 **6** *1/2* **Kingsdale Orion (IRE)**[43] 2544 7-10-7 **63**.......................... AmyRyan 1 65
(Brian Ellison) *in rr: hdwy on ins over 2f out: one pce over 1f out* **11/2**[2]

0600 **7** *3/4* **Tropical Duke (IRE)**[8] 3683 5-9-4 **51**..........................(p) MissVBarr(5) 16 52
(Ron Barr) *in rr div: hdwy over 2f out: kpt on one pce* **12/1**

0046 **8** *nk* **Child Of Our Time (IRE)**[19] 3317 4-9-3 **50**.......... DanielleMooney(5) 15 50
(Colin Teague) *chsd ldrs: one pce fnl 2f* **25/1**

3404 **9** *hd* **Kheskianto (IRE)**[10] 3636 5-8-13 **46**..........................(bt) CarolineKelly(5) 5 48+
(Michael Chapman) *s.s: in rr: effrt on ins and nt clr run over 2f out: kpt on ins fnl f* **28/1**

4504 **10** *2* **Lucayan Dancer**[26] 3074 11-9-2 **49**.. MissJWalker(5) 12 45
(David Nicholls) *t.k.h in mid-div: hdwy on wd outside over 2f out: nvr nr ldrs* **16/1**

0-55 **11** *1/2* **Royal Composer (IRE)**[34] 2800 8-9-0 **47**........... MissRRichardson(5) 7 42
(Tim Easterby) *in rr: sme hdwy on wd outside over 2f out: nvr nr ldrs* **17/2**

6-65 **12** *shd* **Harare**[22] 3240 10-9-7 **54**..(v) MissGTutty(5) 4 49
(Karen Tutty) *hld up towards rr: sme hdwy on ins over 2f out: lost pl over 1f out* **16/1**

0-00 **13** *1* **Hurricane Thomas (IRE)**[10] 3637 7-9-9 **56**.......... MissPhillipaTutty(5) 2 49
(Karen Tutty) *mid-div: hdwy on ins over 2f out: one pce* **12/1**

2600 **14** *5* **Lakeman (IRE)**[18] 3358 5-10-1 **62**..........................(b) MissHBethell(5) 14 45
(Brian Ellison) *sn chsng ldrs on outer: lost pl 2f out* **28/1**

00/0 **15** *6* **Amongst Amigos (IRE)**[19] 3317 10-8-12 **45**.........(b) NicolaJackson(5) 6 16
(Ian McInnes) *mid-div: effrt over 3f out: lost pl over 2f out: sn bhd* **16/1**

6-00 **16** *14* **Saxby (IRE)**[11] 3569 4-9-11 **53**.. MissADeniel 11 —
(Alan Lockwood) *in rr: drvn 4f out: sme hdwy on outside over 2f out: sn lost pl and bhd: eased* **50/1**

2m 3.97s (-3.03) **Going Correction** -0.425s/f (Firm) **16** Ran SP% **127.0**
Speed ratings (Par 101): **95,93,93,93,92 92,91,91,91,89 89,89,88,84,79 68**
toteswingers:1&2:£36.00, 2&3:£7.00, 1&3:£18.90 CSF £189.41 CT £1586.43 TOTE £37.50: £8.00, £2.70, £1.10, £1.60; EX 316.40.
Owner Allan Kerr Peter McGivney **Bred** Farmers Hill Stud **Trained** Hambleton, N Yorks
■ Stewards' Enquiry : Miss G Tutty two-day ban: careless riding (Jul 26,29)

FOCUS
A typically wide-open race of its type. It was run at a good pace and there were plenty of chances in the home straight. The form looks sound rest around those in the frame behind the winner.
T/Plt: £449.80 to a £1 stake. Pool of £55,439.70 - 89.96 winning tickets. T/Qpdt: £76.00 to a £1 stake. Pool of £4,715.49 - 45.90 winning tickets. WG

3673 BRIGHTON (L-H)
Tuesday, July 12

OFFICIAL GOING: Good to firm (8.0)
Wind: fresh, behind Weather: dry, overcast

3939 HARDINGSCATERING.CO.UK H'CAP 5f 59y
2:10 (2:10) (Class 6) (0-55,55) 3-Y-O+ **£1,681** (£500; £250; £125) **Stalls** Low

Form RPR
2046 **1** **Imaginary Diva**[12] 3556 5-9-1 **51**.. TomQueally 2 59
(George Margarson) *racd in midfield: rdn and hdwy 2f out: drvn to ld jst ins fnl f: in command and idling towards fin* **9/2**[3]

0622 **2** *1* **Do More Business (IRE)**[14] 3482 4-9-2 **52**.......................... IanMongan 8 56
(Pat Phelan) *dwlt: outpcd in last pair: drvn and hanging lft over 1f out: swtchd rt and hdwy 1f out: styd on wl ins fnl f: wnt 2nd on post: nt rch wnr* **4/1**[2]

6054 **3** *shd* **Bookiesindex Boy**[8] 3678 7-9-1 **51**..........................(vt) StephenCraine 1 55
(J R Jenkins) *hld up in midfield: clsd on ldrs 2f out: pressing ldrs and stl on bit 1f out: shkn up and fnd nil fnl 100yds: lost 2nd on post* **8/1**

0503 **4** *1* **What Katie Did (IRE)**[14] 3476 6-8-10 **46**..........................(p) NickyMackay 9 46
(Milton Bradley) *led: clr 1/2-way: pushed along over 1f out: drvn and hdd jst ins fnl f: no ex and wknd fnl 75yds* **7/2**[1]

-003 **5** *1 1/2* **Doctor Hilary**[21] 3261 9-9-5 **55**..(v) ChrisCatlin 6 50
(Mark Hoad) *sn outpcd in rr: c centre 3f out: rdn 1/2-way: no imp tl styd on ins fnl f: nt rch ldrs* **9/2**[3]

2500 **6** *1 1/4* **Ishipink**[19] 3307 4-8-5 **46** oh1.. HarryBentley(5) 5 37
(Ron Hodges) *taken down early: pressed ldrs for over 1f out: chsd ldrs after: rdn 2f out: wknd ins fnl f* **16/1**

-000 **7** 3 3/4 **Best One**[6] 3721 7-9-2 52....(b) TomMcLaughlin 4 29
(Ronald Harris) *chsd ldr: rdn jst over 2f out: wknd 1f out: fdd ins fnl f* **6/1**

-606 **8** 1 1/2 **Love Club**[10] 3638 3-8-5 46 oh1.... KellyHarrison 7 16
(Brian Baugh) *racd in midfield: rdn and struggling 1/2-way: bhd whn hung lft over 1f out* **25/1**

60.90 secs (-1.40) **Going Correction** -0.225s/f (Firm)
WFA 3 from 4yo+ 5lb **8** Ran SP% **113.7**
Speed ratings (Par 101): **102,100,100,98,96 94,88,85**
toteswingers:1&2:£4.20, 2&3:£5.10, 1&3:£6.70 CSF £22.57 CT £138.95 TOTE £5.60: £1.70, £1.20, £2.00; EX 24.10 Trifecta £157.20 Pool: £327.32 - 1.54 winning units..
Owner Graham Lodge Partnership **Bred** Norcroft Park Stud **Trained** Newmarket, Suffolk

FOCUS
Rail dolled out 4yds from 4.5f to 3.5f adding 8yds to distances. 8mm of water had been applied to maintain the good to firm going. There was a tailwind in the straight. A moderate sprint handicap best rated through the winner to last year's form.
Bookiesindex Boy Official explanation: vet said gelding lost a left-front shoe
What Katie Did(IRE) Official explanation: jockey said gelding lost a right-front shoe

3940 3663 FIRST FOR FOOD SERVICE H'CAP 5f 213y
2:40 (2:40) (Class 5) (0-70,70) 3-Y-0+ **£2,264** (£673; £336; £168) **Stalls** Low

Form RPR

6241 **1** **Bermondsey Bob (IRE)**[13] 3512 5-9-5 67.... KierenFox(3) 7 75
(John Spearing) *chsd clr ldr: rdn and rdr dropped whip 2f out: clsd on ldr over 1f out: led 1f out: all out cl home but a jst holding on* **7/2**[3]

-000 **2** *hd* **Comadoir (IRE)**[21] 3261 5-9-3 62....(p) DaneO'Neill 6 69
(Jo Crowley) *chsd ldng pair and clr of field: rdn over 2f out: styd on u.p 1f out: clsng on wnr cl home: nvr quite getting up* **20/1**

3122 **3** *nk* **Mandhooma**[8] 3674 5-9-6 65.... ChrisCatlin 8 71
(Peter Hiatt) *outpcd and wl off the pce in last trio: rdn 1/2-way: styd on wl u.p ins fnl f: clsng on wnr cl home: nvr quite getting up* **10/3**[2]

0-21 **4** 1 1/4 **Elsie's Orphan**[28] 3020 4-9-11 70.... LiamKeniry 5 72
(Patrick Chamings) *bmpd s: chsd ldng trio but wl off the pce: rdn over 2f out: styd on ins fnl f: nvr able to chal* **3/1**[1]

1130 **5** 1/2 **Stonecrabstomorrow (IRE)**[5] 3765 8-8-9 59....(v) MarkCoumbe(5) 4 59
(Michael Attwater) *racd wl off the pce in midfield: rdn 3f out: styd on u.p ins fnl f: nt rch ldrs* **17/2**

2421 **6** *nk* **The Tatling (IRE)**[12] 3556 14-9-6 65.... HayleyTurner 3 64
(Milton Bradley) *outpcd in last: rdn and hdwy over 1f out: styd on ins fnl f: nvr able to chal* **8/1**

0653 **7** 3/4 **Peter Island (FR)**[13] 3517 8-9-11 70....(b) TomQueally 2 67
(John Gallagher) *led: sn clr: rdn over 1f out: hdd 1f out: wknd ins fnl f* **8/1**

0445 **8** 5 **Highland Harvest**[21] 3255 7-9-3 62.... IanMongan 1 43
(Jamie Poulton) *a outpcd towards rr: rdn and no hdwy 2f out: wl btn and hung lft 1f out* **14/1**

68.63 secs (-1.57) **Going Correction** -0.225s/f (Firm) **8** Ran SP% **114.5**
Speed ratings (Par 103): **101,100,100,98,98 97,96,89**
toteswingers:1&2:£12.80, 2&3:£10.50, 1&3:£3.20 CSF £67.45 CT £230.47 TOTE £4.40: £2.20, £5.00, £1.40; EX 79.30 Trifecta £401.80 Part won..
Owner A A Campbell **Bred** Pier House Stud **Trained** Kinnersley, Worcs

FOCUS
This was always likely to be run at a good clip, thanks to the presence of Peter Island. The form looks pretty solid.
Highland Harvest Official explanation: jockey said gelding never travelled

3941 CATERING SERVICES INTERNATIONAL MEDIAN AUCTION MAIDEN STKS 5f 213y
3:10 (3:11) (Class 6) 2-Y-0 **£1,681** (£500; £250; £125) **Stalls** Low

Form RPR

44 **1** **Dixie's Dream (IRE)**[22] 3229 2-9-3 0.... PatDobbs 2 73+
(Richard Hannon) *chsd ldrs: rdn to ld over 1f out: drvn and asserted 1f out: wl in command and eased towards fin* **4/6**[1]

2 2 1/4 **Uncle Roger (IRE)** 2-9-3 0.... LiamKeniry 4 65
(Eve Johnson Houghton) *pressed ldr: rdn and ev ch wl over 1f out: nt pce of wnr and btn jst ins fnl f: no ch w wnr but kpt on to hold 2nd* **14/1**

0 **3** 1/2 **Two Bridges**[15] 3463 2-8-12 0.... DaneO'Neill 6 59
(Gary Moore) *chsd ldrs: rdn 2f out: styd on same pce and no threat to wnr fnl f* **25/1**

0 **4** 2 **Dutchman's Field**[26] 3076 2-9-3 0.... TomQueally 5 58
(Ed Dunlop) *s.i.s: rn green in rr: clsd and in tch after 2f: sme hdwy and hung lft over 1f out: plugged on but no ch w wnr fnl f* **12/1**[3]

06 **5** 2 1/2 **Lucifers Shadow (IRE)**[29] 2992 2-9-3 0.... JamesDoyle 1 50
(Sylvester Kirk) *led tl hdd and rdn over 1f out: wknd ent fnl f* **11/2**[2]

04 **6** 2 1/4 **Flying Kitty**[22] 3221 2-8-7 0.... HarryBentley(5) 3 39
(John Bridger) *rn green: bucking leaving stalls and veered lft after 100yds: a in last pair: clsd and in tch after 2f: hung lft and wknd over 1f out* **11/2**[2]

1m 10.04s (-0.16) **Going Correction** -0.225s/f (Firm) **6** Ran SP% **109.0**
Speed ratings (Par 92): **92,89,88,85,82 79**
toteswingers:1&2:£2.60, 2&3:£7.90, 1&3:£4.40 CSF £10.67 TOTE £1.80: £2.00, £5.70; EX 9.60.
Owner William Stobart **Bred** Miss Joan Murphy **Trained** East Everleigh, Wilts

FOCUS
A modest juvenile maiden that was won quite easily.

NOTEBOOK
Dixie's Dream(IRE) readily went to front 1f out and stayed on well. He's very much a nursery type, with 7f likely to be within range. (op 8-11 tchd 8-13 and 4-5 in places)
Uncle Roger(IRE), whose trainer had a first-time-out juvenile winner at Newbury last week, appeared to know his job and held on well for second. He can probably go one better, granted normal improvement. (op 12-1 tchd 16-1)
Two Bridges, soon tailed off on her Windsor debut, has clearly learnt a lot in a short space of time and she'll be winning minor races on this evidence. (op 16-1)
Dutchman's Field wasn't the best away and still looked green. He finished nicely, though, stepping up markedly on his debut effort, and will prove suited by 7f. (op 10-1)
Lucifers Shadow(IRE) again showed speed and will be of some interest switched to nurseries. (tchd 6-1)
Flying Kitty, who still has a bit to learn, also looking a likely type for handicaps. (op 7-1 tchd 8-1)

3942 3663.CO.UK FIRST FOR FOOD SERVICE H'CAP (DIV I) 6f 209y
3:40 (3:41) (Class 6) (0-55,55) 3-Y-0+ **£1,358** (£404; £202; £101) **Stalls** Low

Form RPR

0334 **1** **Olney Lass**[90] 1308 4-8-9 46.... SimonPearce(3) 4 55+
(Lydia Pearce) *hld up in last pair: stl plenty do and effrt on inner 2f out: rdn and gd hdwy over 1f out: chsd ldr ins fnl f: led fnl 50yds: r.o wl* **9/2**[2]

60-0 **2** 1/2 **Comrade Bond**[42] 2583 3-8-12 54.... TomQueally 5 59
(Mark H Tompkins) *chsd ldr: rdn to chal 2f out: led over 1f out: hdd and no ex fnl 50yds* **25/1**

2600 **3** 1 1/4 **Tourist**[17] 3412 6-9-4 52.... MartinLane 7 57
(Ian Williams) *chsd ldrs: rdn over 2f out: styd on same pce u.p ins fnl f* **5/1**[3]

-50 **4** 1 3/4 **My Flame**[66] 1911 6-9-5 53.... StephenCraine 13 53
(J R Jenkins) *led: rdn 2f out: hdd over 1f out: no ex and btn jst ins fnl f: wknd and edgd rt fnl 100yds* **8/1**

0205 **5** *nse* **Goodbye Cash (IRE)**[20] 3280 7-8-13 54.... MatthewLawson(7) 2 54
(Ralph Smith) *in tch in midfield: rdn and effrt over 2f out: no imp tl kpt on u.p ins fnl f* **8/1**

0606 **6** *nse* **Yakama (IRE)**[34] 2829 6-9-1 49....(v) HayleyTurner 8 49
(Christine Dunnett) *hld up towards rr: rdn and hdwy 2f out: drvn and styd on same pce ins fnl f* **14/1**

0500 **7** 1 3/4 **Ocean Rosie (IRE)**[21] 3253 4-8-12 46 oh1.... JimCrowley 9 41
(Tony Carroll) *in tch: rdn over 2f out: unable qck and drvn over 1f out: one pce ins fnl f* **33/1**

5300 **8** 1 1/4 **Titan Diamond (IRE)**[22] 3223 3-8-2 51....(p) RachealKneller(7) 6 40
(Mark Usher) *t.k.h: hld up in tch in midfield: swtchd rt and rdn 2f out: no imp and btn 1f out* **7/1**

3040 **9** 1 1/4 **Passing Moment**[15] 3470 3-8-4 46.... ChrisCatlin 3 31
(Brian Baugh) *t.k.h: chsd ldrs: rdn jst over 2f out: wknd u.p jst over 1f out: fdd ins fnl f* **14/1**

3254 **10** 10 **St Ignatius**[14] 3496 4-9-3 51....(p) JamesDoyle 12 12
(Michael Appleby) *s.i.s: nvr gng wl in rr: c wd and rdn 3f out: no prog and n.d: eased wl ins fnl f* **7/2**[1]

0000 **11** 7 **Millden**[22] 3241 4-8-12 46 oh1....(t) LiamKeniry 1 —
(Milton Bradley) *hld up in tch in midfield: rdn jst over 2f out: wkng whn nt clr run and hmpd over 1f out: wl bhd and eased wl ins fnl f* **50/1**

4400 **12** 2 1/4 **Lopinot (IRE)**[20] 3280 8-9-0 55....(v) DavidKenny(7) 11 —
(Martin Bosley) *hld up towards rr: rdn and no hdwy over 2f out: wl bhd and eased ins fnl f* **28/1**

1m 22.47s (-0.63) **Going Correction** -0.225s/f (Firm)
WFA 3 from 4yo+ 8lb **12** Ran SP% **117.3**
Speed ratings (Par 101): **94,93,92,90,89 89,87,86,85,73 65,63**
toteswingers:1&2:£25.50, 2&3:£26.60, 1&3:£5.50 CSF £117.48 CT £587.54 TOTE £5.50: £1.60, £6.50, £1.80; EX 172.80 TRIFECTA Not won..
Owner T H Rossiter **Bred** T H Rossiter **Trained** Newmarket, Suffolk

FOCUS
The first division of a weak 7f handicap. The winning time was 0.81secs slower than division two and the form looks shaky.
St Ignatius Official explanation: jockey said gelding hit the gates and was knocked back causing it to miss the break

3943 3663.CO.UK FIRST FOR FOOD SERVICE H'CAP (DIV II) 6f 209y
4:10 (4:10) (Class 6) (0-55,54) 3-Y-0+ **£1,358** (£404; £202; £101) **Stalls** Low

Form RPR

0526 **1** **Bold Ring**[14] 3476 5-9-3 53.... AlanCreighton(3) 1 63
(Edward Creighton) *in tch: rdn and effrt 2f out: led ent fnl f: edgd lft u.p jst ins fnl f: kpt on wl: drvn out* **9/1**

4464 **2** 1 3/4 **Avoncreek**[29] 2990 7-8-12 45....(v[1]) KellyHarrison 7 50
(Brian Baugh) *led tl over 4f out: rdn to ld again and edgd rt over 1f out: hdd ent fnl f: edgd lft u.p and hld hd high 1f out: hmpd and swtchd rt ins fnl f: styd on same pce after* **14/1**

2405 **3** *nk* **Dancing Welcome**[14] 3476 5-9-5 52....(b) LiamKeniry 5 56
(Milton Bradley) *chsd ldrs: rdn over 1f out: unable qck u.p over 1f out: kpt on again u.p fnl 100yds* **4/1**[1]

5020 **4** *nk* **Fedora (IRE)**[31] 2921 5-9-1 53....(t) LauraPike(5) 11 58
(Olivia Maylam) *stdd s: wl off the pce in last pair: hdwy on inner over 2f out: chsd ldrs 1f out: nt clr run and hmpd ins fnl f: kpt on fnl 75yds* **8/1**

0160 **5** 2 1/4 **Inquisitress**[8] 3677 7-9-2 54....(v) HarryBentley(5) 4 52
(John Bridger) *hld up in rr of main gp: hdwy over 2f out: chsd ldrs and styd on same pce ins fnl f* **13/2**

3403 **6** 1 1/4 **Set To Go**[22] 3241 4-8-13 46....(b) ChrisCatlin 9 40
(Tor Sturgis) *chsd ldr tl led over 4f out: rdn and hdd over 1f out: wknd ins fnl f* **9/2**[2]

00-6 **7** 3 3/4 **Raise All In (IRE)**[34] 2828 5-8-9 45.... NataliaGemelova(3) 3 29
(Ian McInnes) *in tch: rdn over 2f out: sn struggling: wknd wl over 1f out* **25/1**

[illegible] **8** 1/2 **Petito (IRE)**[14] 3480 [illegible] 45....(b) SimonPearce(3) 10 28
(Mark Gillard) *s.i.s: sn detached in last and nt travelling: sme hdwy fnl f: nvr on terms* **16/1**

2000 **9** 3/4 **Giulietta Da Vinci**[21] 3253 4-9-3 50....(b) HayleyTurner 12 31
(Steve Woodman) *chsd ldrs: rdn over 2f out: sn struggling: wknd 2f out* **16/1**

0230 **10** *hd* **Aggbag**[15] 3475 7-9-0 47.... JimCrowley 2 27
(Tony Carroll) *in tch: rdn and struggling over 2f out: sn wknd* **6/1**[3]

30-4 **11** 4 1/2 **Manasha**[21] 3254 3-8-6 47.... MartinLane 6 —
(John Dunlop) *in tch in rr of main gp: hung rt 3f out: rdn and c stands' side over 2f out: no prog: wl bhd fnl f* **16/1**

1m 21.66s (-1.44) **Going Correction** -0.225s/f (Firm)
WFA 3 from 4yo+ 8lb **11** Ran SP% **115.1**
Speed ratings (Par 101): **99,97,96,96,93 92,88,87,86,86 81**
toteswingers:1&2:£11.80, 2&3:£10.00, 1&3:£8.50 CSF £125.08 CT £594.79 TOTE £10.20: £4.00, £3.60, £1.10; EX 102.50 Trifecta £386.90 Pool: £559.50 - 1.07 winning units..
Owner Daniel Creighton **Bred** J A Pickering & T Pears **Trained** Wormshill, Kent
■ Stewards' Enquiry : Alan Creighton two-day ban: careless riding (Jul 26,28); caution: used whip with excessive frequency.

FOCUS
The winning time was 0.81secs faster than the first division. The third and fourth to recent form set the level.
Petito(IRE) Official explanation: jockey said gelding was slowly away

3944 HARDINGS CATERING SERVICES H'CAP 7f 214y
4:40 (4:41) (Class 6) (0-60,66) 3-Y-0+ **£1,681** (£500; £250; £125) **Stalls** Low

Form RPR

0000 **1** **Green Earth (IRE)**[31] 2920 4-9-9 58....(p) IanMongan 16 69
(Pat Phelan) *hld up in tch: rdn to ld 2f out: styd on wl u.p: ins fnl f* **10/1**

0030 **2** 1 1/4 **Indian Violet (IRE)**[49] 2385 5-9-9 58.... JamieGoldstein 14 66
(Ralph Smith) *in tch: rdn and effrt over 2f out: chsd wnr jst over 1f out: styd on same pce and no imp ins fnl f* **18/1**

-003 **3** 3/4 **Annes Rocket (IRE)**[7] 3720 6-9-10 59.... PatDobbs 10 65
(Jimmy Fox) *stdd s: hld up in rr: stl plenty to do jst over 2f out: hdwy towards inner wl over 1f out: chsd ldng pair ins fnl f: kpt on same pce fnl 100yds* **16/1**

5550 **4** 2 3/4 **Ocean Countess (IRE)**[21] 3251 5-9-6 55.... JimCrowley 8 55
(Tony Carroll) *hld up towards rr: swtchd rt and rdn over 2f out: kpt on u.p ins fnl f: nt rch ldrs* **28/1**

-006 **5** *hd* **Luv U Noo**17 3387 4-8-10 **50**........ HarryBentley(5) 2 49
(Brian Baugh) *s.i.s: sn rcvrd and in midfield: rdn and unable qck 2f out: kpt on again ins fnl f* **12/1**

4662 **6** *nk* **Tanforan**10 3636 9-9-5 **54**........ KellyHarrison 7 53
(Brian Baugh) *led tl hdd and rdn 2f out: edgd lft 1f out: wknd ins fnl f* **14/1**

2-42 **7** *2* **Salvationist**16 3431 3-8-7 **58**........ MatthewLawson(7) 1 53+
(John Dunlop) *chsd ldrs on inner: nt clr run 3f out: nvr enough room after tl over 1f out: rdn and hung lft and no hdwy 1f out: btn whn nt clr run again and eased fnl 100yds* **5/1**2

6034 **8** *½* **Hault**14 3480 5-9-0 **49**........(p) JamesDoyle 6 42
(Gary Moore) *hld up in midfield: rdn and effrt 2f out: kpt on ins fnl f: no threat to ldrs* **25/1**

100- **9** *1 ¼* **Sir Ike (IRE)**196 7996 6-9-11 **60**........(t) NeilChalmers 15 50
(Michael Appleby) *hld up in rr: rdn and effrt 2f out: sme hdwy and edgd rt ins fnl f: nvr trbld ldrs* **50/1**

-304 **10** *nk* **Loose Quality (USA)**22 3223 3-9-0 **58**........ LiamKeniry 12 45
(Chris Gordon) *chsd ldrs tl wknd qckly 2f out* **16/1**

3201 **11** *nk* **Fire King**8 3677 5-10-3 **66** 6ex........(p) TomQueally 11 55
(Andrew Haynes) *a towards rr: rdn and effrt in centre over 2f out: no hdwy: n.d* **9/2**1

50-2 **12** *½* **Genes Of A Dancer (AUS)**19 3326 5-9-1 **55**........ JamesRogers(5) 5 43
(Adrian Chamberlain) *chsd ldr tl over 2f out: wknd qckly wl over 1f out* **8/1**

1250 **13** *2 ¼* **Blue Charm**20 3280 7-9-3 **55**........ NataliaGemelova(3) 3 37
(Ian McInnes) *stdd s: t.k.h: hld up in rr: effrt on inner over 2f out: no real hdwy: nvr trbld ldrs* **33/1**

0334 **14** *1 ¼* **Pytheas (USA)**7 3719 4-9-8 **57**........ J-PGuillambert 13 37
(Michael Attwater) *chsd ldrs: rdn over 2f out: wknd over 1f out: wl btn whn hmpd ins fnl f* **11/2**3

0310 **15** *8* **Kenswick**20 3280 4-9-7 **56**........(v) DaneO'Neill 4 17
(Pat Eddery) *in tch in midfield: rdn and unable qck over 2f out: wknd over 1f out: wl bhd and eased ins fnl f* **11/1**

1m 33.94s (-2.06) **Going Correction** -0.225s/f (Firm)
WFA 3 from 4yo+ 9lb **15** Ran SP% **122.4**
Speed ratings (Par 101): **101,99,99,96,96 95,93,93,92,91 91,90,88,87,79**
toteswingers:1&2:£34.20, 2&3:£28.90, 1&3:£30.70 CSF £173.56 CT £2918.29 TOTE £14.60: £4.60, £6.00, £5.30; EX 157.50 Trifecta £226.60 Part won. Pool of £306.26 - 0.63 winning units..

Owner P Wheatley **Bred** Woodcote Stud Ltd **Trained** Epsom, Surrey

FOCUS

A very moderate yet competitive handicap. The form looks pretty solid rated around the placed horses.

Green Earth(IRE) Official explanation: trainer said, regarding apparent improvement in form, that the gelding had benefited from its lower Turf handicap mark and the application of cheek pieces.

Pytheas(USA) Official explanation: vet said gelding lost a right-front shoe

3945 BLAKES BUTCHER H'CAP — 1m 1f 209y

5:10 (5:15) (Class 6) (0-60,60) 3-Y-0+ **£1,940** (£577; £288; £144) **Stalls** High

Form RPR

0003 **1** **Come On The Irons (USA)**6 3742 3-9-1 **58**........(t) JamieGoldstein 3 67
(Ralph Smith) *dwlt and pushed along early: racd in midfield: rdn 4f out: pressed ldrs and drvn 2f out: led and edgd rt ins fnl f: forged ahd towards fin* **4/1**3

2000 **2** *¾* **Professor John (IRE)**10 3637 4-9-9 **55**........(v) JamesDoyle 10 62
(Ian Wood) *hld up off the pce towards rr: hdwy in centre 3f out: drvn to press ldrs over 1f out: ev ch and edgd lft ins fnl f: no ex towards fin* **16/1**

4001 **3** *2 ¾* **Royal Defence (IRE)**14 3480 5-10-0 **60**........ PatCosgrave 2 62+
(Michael Quinn) *dwlt: sn rdn along and sn led: rdn over 2f out: hrd drvn over 1f out: hdd ins fnl f: wknd towards fin* **11/4**1

00-0 **4** *2 ½* **Special Endeavour (IRE)**20 3268 3-8-11 **54**........ DaneO'Neill 5 51
(William Muir) *chsd ldr tl 5f out: chsd ldrs after: rdn over 2f out: no ex over 1f out: wknd ins fnl f* **16/1**

3025 **5** *3 ¾* **Out Of The Storm**6 3742 3-9-0 **57**........ PaulDoe 7 46+
(Simon Dow) *chsd ldrs: wnt 2nd 5f out: clr w ldr over 3f out: drvn wl over 1f out: wknd jst over 1f out: fdd ins fnl f* **3/1**2

0026 **6** *½* **Excellent Vision**6 3726 4-9-5 **51**........(t) LiamKeniry 9 39
(Milton Bradley) *stdd s: hld up in rr: hdwy over 4f out: rdn jst over 2f out: hung lft and wknd over 1f out* **8/1**

0006 **7** *¾* **Bahkov (IRE)**20 3293 5-8-11 **46**........(b) KierenFox(3) 6 33
(Eric Wheeler) *taken down early: sn detached in last: rdn 3f out: nvr on terms* **16/1**

P400 **8** *4* **Dawson Creek (IRE)**14 3480 7-9-0 **46** oh1........ ChrisCatlin 8 25
(Mark Hoad) *chsd ldrs: rdn 4f out: struggling whn bmpd over 3f out: wknd 2f out* **33/1**

5300 **9** *59* **Indian Wish (USA)**52 2307 3-8-9 **52**........ HayleyTurner 4 —
(Tim McCarthy) *taken down early: chsd ldrs tl lost pl and rdn 5f out: t.o and virtually p.u fnl 2f* **9/1**

2m 2.20s (-1.40) **Going Correction** -0.225s/f (Firm)
WFA 3 from 4yo+ 11lb **9** Ran SP% **113.4**
Speed ratings (Par 101): **96,95,93,91,88 87,87,84,36**
toteswingers:1&2:£11.40, 2&3:£9.80, 1&3:£3.60 CSF £63.61 CT £202.46 TOTE £5.90: £2.10, £5.50, £1.90; EX 40.80 Trifecta £405.60 Pool: £685.27 - 1.25 winning units..

Owner Mrs H J Fullerton **Bred** Tony Hancock & Rhonda Hancock **Trained** Epsom, Surrey

FOCUS

Another low-grade handicap. The form is taken at face value through the second.

Professor John(IRE) Official explanation: jockey said gelding hung both ways

3946 HARDINGS CATERING SERVICES APPRENTICE H'CAP — 1m 3f 196y

5:40 (5:42) (Class 6) (0-65,63) 4-Y-0+ **£1,681** (£500; £250; £125) **Stalls** High

Form RPR

6600 **1** **Sennockian Storm (USA)**15 3457 4-8-8 **52**........ DarylByrne(5) 5 62
(Mark Johnston) *chsd ldrs: rdn over 4f out: led over 1f out: forging ahd whn rdr dropped whip jst ins fnl f: pushed out and styd on wl after* **5/1**2

2153 **2** *3* **Astroleo**18 3353 5-8-6 **50**........ CharlesEddery(5) 7 55
(Mark H Tompkins) *chsd ldr: wnt 2nd over 6f out: rdn over 2f out: 3rd and unable qck u.p over 1f out: wnt 2nd fnl 100yds: no imp and eased towards fin* **6/1**3

5100 **3** *½* **Galiotto (IRE)**8 3690 5-9-2 **58**........(b) HarryBentley(3) 1 62
(Gary Moore) *hld up towards rr: clsd and in tch 6f out: rdn and nt qckn 2f out: styd on again ins fnl f: no threat to wnr* **10/3**1

3-10 **4** *1 ½* **Command Marshal (FR)**13 3515 8-9-10 **63**........ JohnFahy 9 65
(Ed de Giles) *chsd ldr untl led 7f out: rdn over 2f out: hdd and drvn over 1f out: btn and lost 2nd fnl 100yds: wknd towards fin* **16/1**

3640 **5** *1 ¼* **Olimamu (IRE)**19 3311 4-9-1 **54**........(t) SimonPearce 4 54
(Lydia Pearce) *hld up in last pair: clsd and in tch 6f out: nt clr run briefly over 3f out: sn rdn and no prog: plugged on same pce fr over 1f out* **14/1**

0632 **6** *1* **Barbirolli**18 3353 9-8-4 **48**........ MatthewLawson(5) 10 46
(William Stone) *in tch in midfield: hdwy to chse ldrs 6f out: drvn and nt qckn over 2f out: one pce and wl hld fr over 1f out* **12/1**

-060 **7** *5* **Tecktal (FR)**33 819 8-8-6 **45**........ KierenFox 2 35
(Pat Phelan) *stdd s: hld up in rr: clsd and in tch 6f out: c centre and rdn 3f out: sn wknd* **10/1**

0603 **8** *1 ¾* **Corlough Mountain**14 3480 7-8-1 **45**........ NathanAlison(5) 8 33
(Paddy Butler) *in tch: rdn and wknd over 2f out* **33/1**

0/05 **9** *51* **Beech View (IRE)**18 3353 6-8-2 **46** ow1........ DavidKenny(5) 3 —
(Martin Bosley) *in tch: rdn and hung rt 3f out: sn wknd: t.o and eased ins fnl f* **16/1**

2120 **P** **Gems**19 3311 4-9-5 **63**........ CharlesBishop(5) 6 —
(Peter Hiatt) *led tl 7f out: sn rdn and dropped to rr: lost tch rapidly 5f out: p.u 4f out* **10/3**1

2m 33.1s (0.40) **Going Correction** -0.225s/f (Firm) **10** Ran SP% **115.3**
Speed ratings (Par 101): **89,87,86,85,84 84,80,79,45,—**
Tote Super 7: WinL: Not won. Place: £660.20 CSF £34.67 CT £113.84 TOTE £8.40: £2.50, £2.00, £2.00; EX 53.00 Trifecta £357.00 Pool: £569.40 - 1.18 winning units..

Owner The Vine Accord **Bred** Overbrook Farm **Trained** Middleham Moor, N Yorks

FOCUS

Quite an open apprentice handicap rated through the runner-up and backed up by the third and fourth.

Gems Official explanation: jockey said filly lost its action and pulled up; vet said filly had an irregular heart rhythm

T/Plt: £395.80 to a £1 stake. Pool of £73,060.75 - 134.74 winning tickets. T/Qpdt: £90.00 to a £1 stake. Pool of £5,538.37 - 45.50 winning tickets. SP

3707 SOUTHWELL (L-H)

Tuesday, July 12

OFFICIAL GOING: Standard

Wind: Moderate across Weather: Cloudy and blustery

3947 BROAD APPEAL MAIDEN AUCTION STKS — 7f (F)

6:10 (6:11) (Class 5) 2-Y-0 **£2,264** (£673; £336; £168) **Stalls** Low

Form RPR

03 **1** **New Decade**19 3302 2-8-13 0........ SilvestreDeSousa 2 69+
(Mark Johnston) *trckd ldr: pushed along 1/2-way: swtchd rt and hdwy to chal whn edgd rt wl over 2f out: rdn to ld on stands' rail over 1f out: clr whn wandered lft ins fnl f: kpt on* **10/11**1

2 *3 ¾* **Behlul (IRE)** 2-8-13 0........ TedDurcan 1 59
(Gerard Butler) *green and sn pushed along: in tch: hdwy over 2f out: sn rdn: kpt on appr fnl f to take 2nd nr fin* **6/1**

2 **3** *½* **Scrooby Doo**14 3490 2-8-1 0........ LeonnaMayor(7) 4 53
(David Nicholls) *led: rdn along: flashed tail persistently and hung rt 2f out: sn wandered and hdd over 1f out: wknd ins fnl f and lost 2nd nr fin* **7/2**2

4 **4** *2 ¼* **Pearl Catcher (IRE)**21 3242 2-8-10 0........ DavidAllan 3 49
(Tim Easterby) *chsd ldng pair: rdn along 3f out: drvn over 2f out and sn one pce* **11/2**3

5 *22* **Brackendale** 2-8-11 0........ AndrewMullen 6 —
(John Weymes) *s.i.s and wnt rt s: green and sn outpcd in rr: bhd fr 1/2-way* **25/1**

5 **6** *2 ¾* **Elammato (IRE)**33 2831 2-8-11 0........ AndrewHeffernan 5 —
(Lisa Williamson) *sn rdn along and outpcd in rr: bhd fr 1/2-way* **40/1**

1m 31.95s (1.65) **Going Correction** +0.025s/f (Slow) **6** Ran SP% **110.6**
Speed ratings (Par 94): **91,86,86,83,58 55**
toteswingers:1&2:£1.30, 2&3:£1.60, 1&3:£1.30 CSF £6.76 TOTE £2.50: £2.10, £2.00; EX 5.80.

Owner Claire Riordan And Kieran Coughlan **Bred** Cheveley Park Stud Ltd **Trained** Middleham Moor, N Yorks

FOCUS

A modest maiden in which the winner and third-placed finisher both hung right in the straight, ending up stands' side.

NOTEBOOK

New Decade is a big colt who has plenty of maturing to do, but he was still able to confirm the improvement he showed on his latest outing. He was under strong pressure turning into the straight, at which point Scrooby Doo was going well in the lead, but he unsurprisingly proved by far the stronger stayer of the pair. Although he went sharply right when hit with the whip on his left side, his attitude was absolutely fine once he had the rail to help. The surface was no problem and he's progressing with each start. (op 6-5 tchd 5-4)

Behlul(IRE) was making his debut, but he'd reportedly already been around Southwell and that's something to keep in mind in future with Gerard Butler-trained runners having their first start at this track. A £12,000 purchase with a lot of stamina in his pedigree, he lacked the speed of the winner and third, but kept on gradually, going well clear after the line. He's going to want further, while a fast surface will probably be best avoided judging by his significant knee action. (op 9-2)

Scrooby Doo had wandered under pressure and flashed her tail when runner-up in a weak 6f maiden on her debut here, and she did so again. She has a lot of speed in her pedigree and it wasn't a surprise to see her run out of stamina, even allowing for her waywardness. (op 3-1 tchd 11-4)

Pearl Catcher(IRE) was never really travelling and may be more of a nursery prospect. (op 7-1 tchd 5-1)

3948 TEAM QUOTTER NURSERY — 5f (F)

6:40 (6:40) (Class 6) 2-Y-0 **£1,552** (£462; £230; £115) **Stalls** High

Form RPR

6602 **1** **Sonko (IRE)**6 3728 2-7-12 **53** oh1........(p) SilvestreDeSousa 5 61
(Tim Pitt) *dwlt sltly and sn pushed along to join ldrs: led after 2f: rdn and edgd rt wl over 1f out: drvn out* **4/1**3

2211 **2** *4* **Pint Size**14 3491 2-9-7 **83**........ AntiocoMurgia(7) 6 77
(Gay Kelleway) *cl up: rdn along to chse wnr over 2f out: drvn wl over 1f out: no imp* **11/4**2

026 **3** *3 ½* **Dicky Mint**31 2936 2-9-4 **73**........(t) GrahamGibbons 2 54
(Michael Easterby) *in tch: pushed along 1/2-way: rdn to chse ldng pair wl over 1f out: sn drvn and one pce* **13/8**1

560 **4** *1 ½* **Spring Daisy (IRE)**31 2907 2-7-9 **55**........ DanielleMcCreery(5) 1 31
(Tom Dascombe) *sn rdn along and outpcd in rr: bhd and hung rt to stands' rail 1/2-way: sme hdwy wl over 1f out: swtchd lft ent fnl f: plugged on: n.d* **14/1**

4300 **5** *½* **Sabusa (IRE)**10 3609 2-9-1 **70**........ DavidAllan 3 44
(Alan McCabe) *prom: rdn along bef 1/2-way: wknd over 2f out* **14/1**

0002 **6** *3 ¼* **Roy's Legacy**7 3708 2-7-8 **58** oh9 ow1........(b) NeilFarley(5) 7 16
(Shaun Harris) *led 2f: cl up on stands' rail: rdn along over 2f out and grad wknd* **8/1**

0506 **7** 2 3/4 **Only Orsenfoolsies**[6] 3728 2-7-12 **53** oh2 .... JamesSullivan 4 —
(Micky Hammond) *chsd ldrs: rdn along and lost pl over 3f out: bhd fr 1/2-way* **33/1**

62.14 secs (2.44) **Going Correction** +0.20s/f (Slow) **7** Ran SP% **112.1**
Speed ratings (Par 92): **88,81,76,73,72 67,63**
toteswingers:1&2:£2.90, 2&3:£1.90, 1&3:£2.20 CSF £14.80 TOTE £4.80: £7.80, £1.02; EX 15.50.

Owner Saintly Racing **Bred** Tally-Ho Stud **Trained** Newmarket, Suffolk

■ The 'official' ratings shown next to each horse are estimated and for information purposes only.

FOCUS
An ordinary nursery and nothing got seriously involved from off the pace.

NOTEBOOK
Sonko(IRE) wasn't best away and came under whip pressure over 3f out, but she responded well, eventually winning in decisive fashion. She had produced an improved performance when runner-up in a turf claimer on her previous start and stepped forward again, the surface clearly suiting. It remains to be seen whether she'll be as good back on grass, but she's at the right end of the handicap and should add to this. (op 7-2 tchd 10-3)

Pint Size had won 6f claimers on his last two starts, including here on his most recent outing, and he's already on his third trainer having joined this yard for £12,000. He showed speed and finished a clear second, suggesting the drop in trip wasn't a major inconvenience, but the concession of 23lb (allowing for Antioco Murgia's 7lb claimer) to an improving type unsurprisingly proved beyond him. (op 15-8 tchd 7-4 and 10-3)

Dicky Mint was having his first try on Fibresand so he can be given another chance. (op 11-4 tchd 6-4)

Spring Daisy(IRE) offered some encouragement. Her optimum trip is unclear as she went off too fast over 6f on her second outing, yet has now failed to produce the required speed in a couple of starts back at this trip, but she was going on at the finish. Perhaps the surface didn't suit. Official explanation: jockey said filly hung right throughout (op 12-1)

3949 ENHANCED WIN ODDS FROM NOON AT CORAL.CO.UK MAIDEN STKS 5f (F)
7:10 (7:11) (Class 5) 3-Y-O **£2,264** (£673; £336; £168) **Stalls** High

Form RPR

00 **1** **Highland Colori (IRE)**[12] 3543 3-9-3 0 .... RichardKingscote 1 81
(Tom Dascombe) *chsd ldng pair: hdwy on outer to chse ldr 2f out: rdn to ld over 1f out: clr whn edgd rt ins fnl f: kpt on strly* **11/4**[2]

322- **2** 5 **Supercharged (IRE)**[288] 6419 3-8-12 77 .... TedDurcan 5 58
(Chris Wall) *trckd ldr and n.m.r on inner after 1f: led 3f out: rdn along 2f out: hdd over 1f out: swtchd lft and drvn ent fnl f: one pce* **4/6**[1]

4 **3** 7 **Lizzy's Dream**[14] 3494 3-9-3 0 .... LeeNewman 7 38
(Robin Bastiman) *sn rdn along and outpcd in rr: hdwy wl over 1f out: styd on wl ins fnl f to take 3rd nr fin* **16/1**

4 nk **Boucher Garcon (IRE)** 3-9-3 0 .... DavidAllan 2 37
(Declan Carroll) *trckd ldng pair: hdwy to chse ldr 1/2-way: rdn along 2f out: sn one pce: lost poor 3rd nr fin* **8/1**[3]

5 1 3/4 **Femme Royale** 3-8-12 0 .... GrahamGibbons 3 26
(Robert Cowell) *in tch: rdn along 1/2-way: sn outpcd* **16/1**

50-0 **6** 4 **Sirens**[34] 2827 3-8-5 49 .... (be[1]) LeonnaMayor(7) 4 11
(Phil McEntee) *led: edgd rt after 1f: hdd 3f out: sn rdn along and wknd* **50/1**

0-50 **7** 3 **Indigo Sands (IRE)**[10] 3616 3-9-3 45 .... JamesSullivan 6 —
(Alan Berry) *sn rdn along in rr and sddle slipped: outpcd and bhd fr 1/2-way* **150/1**

60.64 secs (0.94) **Going Correction** +0.20s/f (Slow) **7** Ran SP% **112.2**
Speed ratings (Par 100): **100,92,80,80,77 71,66**
toteswingers:1&2:£2.00, 2&3:£1.40, 1&3:£3.00 CSF £4.68 TOTE £5.20: £2.30, £1.10; EX 9.10.

Owner Evan M Sutherland **Bred** Rathbarry Stud **Trained** Malpas, Cheshire

■ Stewards' Enquiry : Leonna Mayor two-day ban: careless riding (Jul 26,28)

FOCUS
Little strength in depth and hard to pinpoint the exact worth of the form. However, while the weak favourite Supercharged, who was making a belated reappearance, failed to match the pick of her efforts (RPR of 85 on second of three starts at two), there was still much to like about Highland Colori. The time was identical to the following 3-y-o claimer, although the winner of that race, Upper Lambourn, looks above average for the class. The form looks guessy.

Indigo Sands(IRE) Official explanation: jockey said saddle slipped

3950 MAXI MUSCLE CLAIMING STKS 5f (F)
7:40 (7:40) (Class 6) 3-Y-O **£1,567** (£462; £231) **Stalls** High

Form RPR

3 **1** **Upper Lambourn (IRE)**[150] 518 3-9-8 0 .... FergusSweeney 7 73
(Jamie Osborne) *cl up: rdn to ld 1 1/2f out: sn clr* **7/2**[3]

0600 **2** 4 **Rutterkin (USA)**[18] 3347 3-8-9 59 .... VictorSantos(7) 5 53
(Alan Berry) *in tch: hdwy over 2f out: rdn to chse ldrs over 1f out: kpt on to take 2nd nr fin* **14/1**

0000 **3** 3/4 **Pickled Pumpkin**[29] 2993 3-8-6 52 .... RyanClark(5) 8 45
(Olivia Maylam) *cl up on stands' rail: led after 2f: rdn along over 2f out: hdd 1 1/2f out: sn edgd lft and lost 2nd nr fin* **33/1**

3062 **4** 1 1/2 **Majestic Millie (IRE)**[34] 2805 3-8-7 46 .... SilvestreDeSousa 2 36
(David O'Meara) *chsd ldrs on outer: effrt 2f out: sn rdn and one pce* **3/1**[2]

0006 **5** 2 3/4 **Harmony Wold**[3] 3857 3-8-1 39 .... NeilFarley(5) 3 25
(Declan Carroll) *chsd ldng pair: rdn along 2f out: drvn wl over 1f out and grad wknd* **12/1**

3020 **6** 1 3/4 **Ever Roses**[21] 3248 3-8-9 54 ow1 .... (b) TonyCulhane 6 22
(Paul Midgley) *prom: rdn along after 2f: sn lost pl and bhd fnl 2f* **9/2**

7 5 **Two Bucks More** 3-8-9 0 .... JakePayne(7) 1 11
(Bill Turner) *chsd ldrs: rdn along over 2f out: sn wknd* **28/1**

00-6 **8** 19 **Abzolutely (IRE)**[17] 3384 3-8-7 65 .... GrahamGibbons 4 —
(David O'Meara) *led: hdd after 2f: wknd qckly and bhd whn eased fnl 2f* **5/2**[1]

60.64 secs (0.94) **Going Correction** +0.20s/f (Slow) **8** Ran SP% **114.7**
Speed ratings (Par 98): **100,93,92,90,85 82,74,44**
toteswingers:1&2:£8.20, 2&3:£37.50, 1&3:£19.40 CSF £50.29 TOTE £3.90: £1.02, £6.00, £7.50; EX 86.60.

Owner David Bramhill **Bred** Messrs Derek Gibbons & Peter Gibbons **Trained** Upper Lambourn, Berks

FOCUS
An uncompetitive claimer, but Upper Lambourn, who was conceding a good deal of weight all round, pulled clear in a time identical to the promising Highland Colori (carrying 5lb less) in the earlier maiden. The winner looks an improver but there are doubts over those in behind.

Rutterkin(USA) Official explanation: jockey said saddle slipped

Abzolutely(IRE) Official explanation: jockey said filly stopped quickly

3951 DAVID COLTMAN MEMORIAL H'CAP 1m 6f (F)
8:10 (8:10) (Class 6) (0-65,64) 4-Y-O+ **£1,567** (£462; £231) **Stalls** Low

Form RPR

3220 **1** **Shifting Gold (IRE)**[19] 3316 5-9-4 **64** .... (b) AmyRyan(3) 5 73
(Kevin Ryan) *hld up towards rr: stdy hdwy to trck ldrs 1/2-way: cl up 5f out: led 3f out: rdn over 2f out: hdd over 1f out: drvn and rallied to ld jst ins fnl f: kpt on gamely* **3/1**[2]

1455 **2** 2 **Magic Haze**[13] 3510 5-9-1 **58** .... SilvestreDeSousa 3 64
(Sally Hall) *hld up: stdy hdwy 6f out: trckd ldrs over 4f out: effrt to chse wnr 3f out: rdn to ld over 1f out: drvn: edgd rt and hdd jst ins fnl f: sn no ex* **11/2**[3]

/242 **3** 1 **Im Spartacus**[7] 3712 9-9-0 **62** .... RyanClark(5) 8 67
(Ian Williams) *hld up and bhd: pushed along after 6f: stdy hdwy over 5f out: chsd ldrs 3f out: rdn 2f out: drvn over 1f out: kpt on: tk 3rd nr fin* **2/1**[1]

0064 **4** hd **Goodlukin Lucy**[12] 3533 4-9-7 **64** .... (p) TedDurcan 4 69
(Pat Eddery) *trckd ldrs: smooth hdwy over 3f out: effrt and ev ch over 2f out: sn rdn and one pce appr fnl f: lost 3rd nr fin* **9/1**

0550 **5** 37 **Pinsplitter (USA)**[59] 2091 4-8-5 **53** .... (p) RosieJessop(5) 9 —
(Alan McCabe) *dwlt and in rr: hdwy after 6f: led 1/2-way: rdn along and hdd 3f out: sn wknd* **25/1**

05-0 **6** 11 **All Guns Firing (IRE)**[19] 3311 5-8-10 **53** .... (tp) RussKennemore 6 —
(Barry Leavy) *in tch: rdn along over 6f out: sn wknd* **20/1**

0306 **7** 1 3/4 **Lure of The Night (IRE)**[11] 3581 4-8-11 **54** .... MickyFenton 10 —
(Brian Rothwell) *prom: rdn along over 4f out: sn wknd* **28/1**

0 **8** 8 **Street Legal**[15] 3456 6-8-7 **57** .... RyanTate(7) 2 —
(Alan McCabe) *midfield: rdn along 6f out: sn wknd* **33/1**

0/00 **9** dist **Lord Wheathill**[33] 2830 4-8-2 **45** .... AndrewHeffernan 7 —
(Lisa Williamson) *led: rdn along and hdd 1/2-way: wknd qckly and sn bhd: t.o fr over 3f out* **66/1**

0-20 **P** **Black Tor Figarro (IRE)**[27] 3047 6-8-11 **54** .... RichardKingscote 1 —
(Lawney Hill) *prom: rdn along over 4f out: sn wknd: lost action and p.u wl over 1f out* **11/2**[3]

3m 8.32s (0.02) **Going Correction** +0.025s/f (Slow) **10** Ran SP% **115.6**
Speed ratings (Par 101): **100,98,98,98,77 70,69,65,—,—**
toteswingers:1&2:£3.30, 2&3:£4.40, 1&3:£2.90 CSF £18.29 CT £39.77 TOTE £3.20: £1.40, £3.50, £1.10; EX 20.00.

Owner Hambleton Racing Ltd VIII **Bred** Watership Down Stud **Trained** Hambleton, N Yorks

FOCUS
No unexposed improvers in this line-up, making for ordinary form. The winner is rated as running a small personal best.

Im Spartacus Official explanation: jockey said gelding did not face the kickback

3952 BETTER WIN PRICES EVERY RACE AT CORAL.CO.UK H'CAP 1m (F)
8:40 (8:42) (Class 5) (0-70,70) 3-Y-O+ **£2,264** (£673; £336; £168) **Stalls** Low

Form RPR

0141 **1** **Positivity**[21] 3245 5-9-7 **63** .... (p) TomEaves 8 75
(Bryan Smart) *chsd ldrs: rdn along 1/2-way: hdwy over 2f out: styd on to ld over 1f out: drvn ins fnl f and hld on gamely* **7/1**

0053 **2** nk **Amtired**[14] 3496 5-8-6 **51** oh1 .... (be) PaulPickard(3) 5 62
(Brian Ellison) *in rr and rdn along on inner after 2f: hdwy over 2f out: chsd ldrs over 1f out: nt clr run and swtchd rt ent fnl f: sn drvn and edgd lft: styd on and ev ch tl no ex nr fin* **10/1**

3315 **3** 6 **Eastern Hills**[6] 3741 6-9-3 **62** .... (p) AmyRyan(3) 4 60
(Alan McCabe) *led: rdn along wl over 2f out: drvn and hdd over 1f out: kpt on same pce* **5/1**[2]

3/01 **4** 3/4 **Invincible Hero (IRE)**[26] 3096 4-9-1 **62** .... (t) NeilFarley(5) 12 58
(Declan Carroll) *cl up: rdn to chal 3f out: ev ch over 2f out: drvn wl over 1f out and sn one pce* **8/1**

1331 **5** 2 **You've Been Mowed**[10] 3643 5-9-3 **64** .... RyanClark(5) 2 55
(Richard Price) *chsd ldng pair on inner: rdn along over 2f out: drvn wl over 1f out: grad wknd* **11/2**[3]

2000 **6** 1 1/2 **Dazakhee**[13] 3510 4-9-7 **63** .... TonyCulhane 14 51
(Paul Midgley) *dwlt and hld up in rr: wd st: hdwy 2f out: pushed along and kpt on appr fnl f: nrst fin* **12/1**

0506 **7** 1 1/2 **Lady Bridget** [illegible] .... FergusSweeney 1 44
(Mark Gillard) *bhd tl styd on fnl 2f* **66/1**

221- **8** 3 1/4 **Flying Power**[215] 7780 3-9-5 **70** .... (b[1]) TedDurcan 7 45
(David Lanigan) *chsd ldrs: rdn along 3f out: drvn 2f out and sn wknd* **3/1**[1]

5-60 **9** 7 **Private Joke**[18] 3361 4-9-11 **67** .... LeeNewman 10 28
(Terry Clement) *a towards rr* **25/1**

53-5 **10** 7 **Seamster**[21] 3250 4-9-8 **69** .... DaleSwift(5) 11 14
(Richard Ford) *in tch: rdn along 3f out: sn wknd* **33/1**

2-46 **11** 5 **Strike A Deal (IRE)**[43] 2548 4-9-6 **62** .... JackMitchell 13 —
(Chris Wall) *dwlt: a towards rr* **14/1**

000 **12** 1 1/4 **Valkov**[26] 3096 4-8-8 **53** ow2 .... MichaelO'Connell(3) 6 —
(Tony Carroll) *in tch: rdn along over 3f out: sn wknd* **50/1**

0-00 **13** 18 **Celtic Step**[60] 2057 7-9-2 **58** .... TonyHamilton 3 —
(Peter Niven) *in tch: rdn along 1/2-way: sn wknd* **50/1**

060- **14** 6 **Jobekani (IRE)**[359] 4168 5-8-9 **51** oh6 .... (p) SilvestreDeSousa 9 —
(Lisa Williamson) *a in rr: bhd fr 1/2-way* **50/1**

1m 43.27s (-0.43) **Going Correction** +0.025s/f (Slow)
WFA 3 from 4yo+ 9lb **14** Ran SP% **118.3**
Speed ratings (Par 103): **103,102,96,95,93 92,90,87,80,73 68,67,49,43**
toteswingers:1&2:£14.80, 2&3:£10.80, 1&3:£5.50 CSF £70.22 CT £385.40 TOTE £7.50: £2.50, £5.50, £2.50; EX 49.20.

Owner Mrs F Denniff **Bred** Mrs Fiona Denniff **Trained** Hambleton, N Yorks

■ Stewards' Enquiry : Neil Farley three-day ban: used whip with excessive frequency (Jul 26,28,29)

FOCUS
A competitive handicap for the class, but the pace looked overly strong. The winner is rated a length improver on her May C&D success.

Dazakhee ◆ Official explanation: jockey said filly hung left-handed

3953 MEMBERSHIP OF SOUTHWELL GOLF CLUB H'CAP 7f (F)
9:10 (9:12) (Class 5) (0-70,70) 3-Y-O+ **£2,264** (£673; £336; £168) **Stalls** Low

Form RPR

2315 **1** **This Ones For Eddy**[7] 3719 6-9-3 **59** .... GrahamGibbons 3 70
(John Balding) *chsd ldrs on inner: swtchd rt and rdn 2f out: led 1 1/2f out: drvn out* **9/2**[2]

6355 **2** 3/4 **Elusive Warrior (USA)**[14] 3495 8-8-4 **53** .... (p) NoraLooby(7) 6 62
(Alan McCabe) *cl up: rdn to ld 2f out: hdd 1 1/2f out and sn drvn: kpt on fnl f* **9/1**

4544 **3** 1 ½ **Bonnie Prince Blue**[7] 3711 8-9-7 **68**..............................(b) DaleSwift(5) 4 73
(Ian McInnes) *bhd: hdwy wl over 1f out: swtchd lft to inner and rdn ent fnl f: styd on strly* **11/2**[3]

3152 **4** ¾ **Jonnie Skull (IRE)**[14] 3495 5-9-2 **58**.....................(vt) SilvestreDeSousa 1 61
(Phil McEntee) *led: rdn along and hdd 2f out: sn drvn and kpt on same pce fnl f* **5/2**[1]

5-00 **5** nk **Babich Bay (IRE)**[13] 3512 3-8-10 **60**....................(v[1]) RobbieFitzpatrick 7 59
(Jo Hughes) *prom: rdn along over 2f out: drvn wl over 1f out and kpt on same pce appr fnl f* **16/1**

5005 **6** ¾ **Night Witch (IRE)**[16] 3432 3-9-2 **66**.............................. EddieCreighton 2 63
(Edward Creighton) *towards rr: hdwy over 2f out: sn rdn and kpt on appr fnl f: nrst fin* **25/1**

5604 **7** 1 ½ **Ubenkor (IRE)**[14] 3495 6-9-6 **62**...................................... TonyHamilton 8 58
(Michael Herrington) *in tch: effrt on outer over 2f out: rdn wl over 1f out and sn wknd* **9/2**[2]

0003 **8** 6 **Co Dependent (USA)**[7] 3713 5-10-0 **70**...................... FergusSweeney 9 50
(Jamie Osborne) *trckd ldrs on outer: smooth hdwy to chal 2f out: sn rdn and wknd appr fnl f* **7/1**

-505 **9** 3 ½ **Swish Dish (CAN)**[19] 3303 4-8-9 **51** oh3.........................(p) TomEaves 5 21
(Micky Hammond) *a in rr* **40/1**

1m 29.77s (-0.53) **Going Correction** +0.025s/f (Slow)
WFA 3 from 4yo+ 8lb **9** Ran SP% **115.0**
Speed ratings (Par 103): **104,103,101,100,100 99,97,90,86**
toteswingers:1&2:£7.00, 2&3:£20.20, 1&3:£4.50 CSF £44.19 CT £227.02 TOTE £7.00: £1.30, £6.10, £2.40; EX 38.00.
Owner Billy Herring **Bred** Broughton Bloodstock **Trained** Scrooby, Notts

FOCUS
A modest handicap run at a good pace. The form is rated positively through the runner-up.
T/Plt: £25.30 to a £1 stake. Pool of £59,869.11 - 1,723.27 winning tickets. T/Qpdt: £8.40 to a £1 stake. Pool of £5,191.27 - 454.60 winning tickets. JR

3552 YARMOUTH (L-H)
Tuesday, July 12

OFFICIAL GOING: Good to firm
Wind: blustery Weather: overcast and cool

3954 BRITISH STALLION STUDS E B F / 4HEAD MAIDEN STKS — 7f 3y
6:00 (6:01) (Class 5) 2-Y-O £3,557 (£1,058; £529; £264) **Stalls** High

Form RPR

53 **1** **Comical**[24] 3186 2-9-3 0.. NeilCallan 2 80+
(Mark Johnston) *mde virtually all: qcknd clr 2f out: rdn out: readily* **5/4**[1]

2 2 ½ **Croquembouche (IRE)** 2-9-3 0.. RyanMoore 4 74+
(Sir Michael Stoute) *midfield: rdn and hdwy over 2f out: chsd wnr fnl f: a hld but styng on stoutly* **5/1**[2]

00 **3** 3 ½ **My Guardian Angel**[12] 3553 2-9-3 0................................ SebSanders 10 65
(Mark H Tompkins) *chsd ldrs: rdn and outpcd by wnr over 2f out: kpt on one pce ins fnl f* **66/1**

0 **4** hd **Bewilder**[25] 3132 2-9-3 0.. WilliamBuick 11 65
(John Gosden) *prom but edging lft to 1/2-way: chsd wnr over 2f out tl rdn 1f out: no ex: jst lost duel for modest 3rd* **13/2**[3]

5 2 ½ **Perfect Gratitude (USA)** 2-9-3 0.................................. JamieSpencer 3 58+
(Ed Dunlop) *midfield: effrt 2f out: rdn and no imp whn edgd rt over 1f out* **8/1**

6 3 ½ **Grand Rapids (USA)** 2-9-3 0.. AhmedAjtebi 8 50
(Mahmood Al Zarooni) *v ungainly towards rr and hanging both ways: drvn over 2f out: no ch after* **5/1**[2]

U **7** 1 ¾ **Thecornishcockney**[45] 2510 2-9-3 0.........................(b[1]) StevieDonohoe 12 45
(John Ryan) *missed break: effrt to chse ldrs 1/2-way: sn rdn: wknd wl over 1f out* **80/1**

0 **8** 1 ½ **Carolingian (IRE)**[20] 3282 2-9-3 0.................................... ShaneKelly 6 41
(William Knight) *plld hrd: spd to 1/2-way: sn lost pl* **33/1**

0 **9** 6 **Like Clockwork**[17] 3401 2-9-3 0.................................... KierenFallon 1 26
(Mark H Tompkins) *coltish in paddock: prom tl drvn and wknd wl over 2f out: t.o* **40/1**

10 shd **Bountiful Catch** 2-9-3 0.. JimmyQuinn 9 26
(Pam Sly) *s.s: pushed along in rr: no ch fr 1/2-way: t.o* **40/1**

00 **11** 8 **Ooi Long**[17] 3401 2-9-3 0..(be[1]) MarcHalford 7 6
(Mark Rimmer) *plld v hrd: jnd wnr after 3f: stopped to nil 3f out: eased ins fnl f: t.o* **100/1**

1m 24.41s (-2.19) **Going Correction** -0.40s/f (Firm) **11** Ran SP% **113.8**
Speed ratings (Par 94): **96,93,89,88,86 82,80,78,71,71 62**
CSF £7.03 TOTE £2.00: £1.20, £1.40, £8.30; EX 8.90.
Owner Sheikh Hamdan Bin Mohammed Al Maktoum **Bred** Darley **Trained** Middleham Moor, N Yorks

FOCUS
A dry night and day with a strong wind behind the runners in the home straight. The jockeys reported the (watered) ground to be "on the good side of good to firm". Although last year's winner is only useful at best, several smart performers have taken this maiden, the clear pick being subsequent Group 1 Queen Elizabeth II/Grade 1 Breeders Cup Classic winner Raven's Pass in 2007. This race - run at just an ordinary gallop - didn't have much in the way of strength-in-depth and is held down by the proximity of the third but the first two look capable of holding their own in stronger company and this should also throw up other winners. The field came down the centre.

NOTEBOOK
Comical ◆'s latest Redcar form has been franked in no uncertain terms by the subsequent victories of the winner (Newmarket Group 2) and runner-up (fair York maiden) and this progressive sort, who had the run of the race, turned in his best effort to win in pleasing fashion. He'll have no problems with 1m, is in good hands and should be able to hold his own in a stronger grade. (op 6-5 tchd Evens)
Croquembouche(IRE) ◆, a half-brother to a 1m3f Fibresand winner out of a fair 1m4f Polytrack maiden scorer (herself from a good family) and from the stable that won this race last year, showed his inexperience but created a good impression without being knocked about on this racecourse debut against a more streetwise rival. He too should have no problems with 1m and be up to winning a similar event. (op 6-1)
My Guardian Angel had been soundly beaten on both previous starts over 6f but showed his first worthwhile form over this longer trip but, while this won't have done his handicap mark many favours, he's open to improvement and should benefit from the switch into nursery company. (op 80-1)
Bewilder, too green to do himself justice on his racecourse debut, fared a good deal better this time and, while again having his limitations exposed, has plenty of physical scope and he appeals as the sort to do better in handicaps and possibly on easier ground (showed plenty of knee action) further down the line. (tchd 15-2)
Perfect Gratitude(USA), who cost 100,000gns earlier this year and who is out of a high-class 1m-1m1f winner, showed ability without being knocked about on this racecourse debut. He's sure to come on for this experience and he should be able to pick up a race at some point. (op 7-1)
Grand Rapids(USA), a $325,000 half-brother to high-class US miler Miss Norman, never figured on debut proving noticeably green and should improve a fair bit for the experience. (op 6-1 tchd 13-2)

3955 DIOMED DEVELOPMENTS (S) NURSERY — 7f 3y
6:30 (6:30) (Class 6) 2-Y-O £1,617 (£481; £240; £120) **Stalls** High

Form RPR

046 **1** **Abercandy (IRE)**[44] 2523 2-7-10 **48**.............................. KieranO'Neill(5) 4 47
(David Evans) *mounted on crse: mde all and racd keenly: pushed along and a holding rival ins fnl f* **5/1**[3]

5035 **2** ¾ **Aljosan**[10] 3631 2-8-1 **48**.. SophieDoyle(3) 6 48
(David Evans) *chsd wnr: rdn 2f out: tried to get on terms fnl f: kpt on and clsng grad but a hld* **13/2**

2233 **3** 1 ¼ **Queen Of The Hop**[26] 3070 2-9-0 **57**.............................(p) LukeMorris 5 55
(J S Moore) *t.k.h early: hld up in midfield: effrt and shkn up 2f out: edgd lft: no imp under wild whip waving fnl f* **7/2**[2]

0544 **4** 4 **Triggerlo**[12] 3539 2-9-4 **64**.. MartinHarley(3) 1 52
(Mick Channon) *t.k.h towards rr: effrt and drvn 2f out: btn over 1f out* **10/3**[1]

4520 **5** ¾ **Ciara Boo (IRE)**[50] 2362 2-9-2 **59**...................................... JamieSpencer 2 45
(David Evans) *chsd ldng pair: rdn 2f out: btn whn fnd nil fnl f* **7/2**[2]

5005 **6** 11 **Egyptian Cross**[7] 3708 2-8-8 **51**...................................... JimmyQuinn 7 10
(John Weymes) *towards rr: rdn and btn over 2f out* **12/1**

056 **7** 47 **Vieira Da Silva (IRE)**[53] 2241 2-8-6 **52**.................... MatthewDavies(3) 3 —
(Mick Channon) *on her toes: s.i.s: bhd: rdn and struggling 1/2-way: hopelessly t.o and eased* **17/2**

1m 25.85s (-0.75) **Going Correction** -0.40s/f (Firm) **7** Ran SP% **115.7**
Speed ratings (Par 92): **88,87,85,81,80 67,14**
toteswingers:1&2:£10.50, 2&3:£4.70, 1&3:£6.10 CSF £37.58 TOTE £8.80: £4.00, £4.20; EX 54.20.There was no bid for the winner.
Owner Walters Plant Hire Ltd **Bred** R N Auld **Trained** Pandy, Monmouths
■ The 'official' ratings shown next to each horse are estimated and for information purposes only.

FOCUS
A low-grade selling nursery in which an ordinary gallop increased around halfway.

NOTEBOOK
Abercandy(IRE) achieved little in 5f maidens but turned in an improved effort on this nursery debut upped to 7f. She benefited from an enterprising ride at a meeting where the runners had a strong wind behind them but, although only small, could win again for this stable. (op 7-1)
Aljosan had also achieved very little in four previous starts but turned in her first worthwhile form in a race that suited the prominent-racers. She may do a bit better for this yard but this isn't a race to take many positives from. (op 8-1)
Queen Of The Hop, had shown ability up to 7f100yds and she looks the best guide to this form on this nursery debut. She pulled clear of the remainder but she lacks much in the way of physical scope and is going to have to improve to win in similar company. (tchd 3-1 and 4-1 in places)
Triggerlo, with the headgear left off for this nursery debut, attracted support but failed to improve for the step up to this trip. He's had a few chances and isn't one to take too short a price about. (op 5-1)
Ciara Boo(IRE) is related to a couple of 7f winners and to a hurdle scorer but she didn't get home upped to this trip for the first time on this nursery debut. She has plenty to prove at present. Official explanation: jockey said filly hung right (op 10-3)

3956 AEROPAK H'CAP — 6f 3y
7:00 (7:01) (Class 6) (0-60,60) 3-Y-O+ £1,617 (£481; £240; £120) **Stalls** High

Form RPR

-003 **1** **Captainrisk (IRE)**[34] 2829 5-9-7 **57**................................(v) SebSanders 4 67
(Christine Dunnett) *mde all: rdn over 2f out: fnd plenty fnl f: eased cl home* **15/2**

4200 **2** 1 **Steel City Boy (IRE)**[7] 3711 8-9-8 **58**...................... TomMcLaughlin 11 65
(Garry Woodward) *alone on stands' rails tl 1/2-way and t.k.h: prom: w wnr and rdn over 1f out: kpt on but a hld* **9/1**

-004 **3** ½ **Imjin River (IRE)**[10] 3617 4-9-10 **60**................................ KierenFallon 12 65
(Mark H Tompkins) *midfield: pushed along 1/2-way: rdn and effrt over 1f out: no imp fnl 100yds* **9/2**[1]

0055 **4** nse **Fantasy Fighter (IRE)**[13] 3517 6-8-11 **47**....................... JimmyQuinn 3 52
(John Quinn) *chsd ldrs: effrt over 1f out: reminder and waved tail 1f out: one pce fnl 100yds* **7/1**[3]

5-25 **5** 3 **Trojan Rocket (IRE)**[18] 3343 3-9-4 **60**.......................... WilliamBuick 9 55
(George Prodromou) *stdd and last away: rdn and outpcd 1/2-way: styd on ins fnl f: n.d* **9/1**

400- **6** hd **Cool Water Oasis**[194] 8011 3-9-1 **60**.......................... MartinHarley(3) 1 54
(Rae Guest) *w ldrs far side: rdn over 2f out: one pce and no threat after* **20/1**

356 **7** nse **Schoolboy Champ**[11] 3582 4-9-0 **55**........................ KieranO'Neill(5) 5 50
(Patrick Morris) *pressed ldrs: rdn over 2f out: btn over 1f out* **13/2**[2]

25-5 **8** 6 **Clerical (USA)**[12] 3556 5-9-6 **56**..................................(p) RichardMullen 8 32
(Robert Cowell) *w ldrs tl rdn and fdd over 2f out: eased cl home* **7/1**[3]

-030 **9** 1 **Atia**[43] 2549 3-9-2 **58**.. EddieAhern 2 29
(Jonathan Portman) *bhd: pushed along 1/2-way: struggling after* **7/1**[3]

0001 **10** hd **Rileys Crane**[34] 2829 4-9-3 **53**....................................(v) SaleemGolam 6 25
(Christine Dunnett) *rdn and struggling in rr fr 1/2-way: nt keen* **11/1**

1m 11.76s (-2.64) **Going Correction** -0.40s/f (Firm)
WFA 3 from 4yo+ 6lb **10** Ran SP% **113.9**
Speed ratings (Par 101): **101,99,99,98,94 94,94,86,85,85**
toteswingers:1&2:£14.50, 2&3:£5.80, 1&3:£6.00 CSF £71.28 CT £346.40 TOTE £10.00: £3.00, £4.10, £1.90; EX 93.70.
Owner P Fisher **Bred** B Walsh **Trained** Hingham, Norfolk

FOCUS
Largely exposed sorts in a moderate handicap. The gallop was reasonable and the field fanned from centre to stands side and this was the third winner in as many races to make all the running.
Clerical(USA) Official explanation: jockey said gelding had no more to give

3957 IBULEVE H'CAP — 5f 43y
7:30 (7:30) (Class 5) (0-70,69) 3-Y-O+ £2,264 (£673; £336; £168) **Stalls** High

Form RPR

0000 **1** **Danzoe (IRE)**[10] 3640 4-9-10 **62**...................................... SebSanders 4 71
(Christine Dunnett) *racd in last pl: shkn up 1/2-way and looked awkward: str burst ins fnl f: led 75yds out and dashed clr* **14/1**

0201 **2** 1 ¾ **Whiskey Junction**[7] 3713 7-10-3 **69** 6ex......................(v[1]) LiamJones 8 72
(Michael Quinn) *chsd ldrs: wnt lft 1/2-way: chal 1f out: hrd drvn and ev ch 75yds out: nt qckn w wnr* **13/2**

35-3 **3** ¾ **Star Twilight**[10] 3640 4-9-11 **63**....................................(v) NeilCallan 6 63
(Derek Shaw) *pressed ldr and keen: rdn to ld over 1f out: carried hd high: hdd and no ex fnl 75yds* **7/2**[2]

2225 **4** ½ **Paradise Place**[34] 2827 3-9-7 **64**.................................. RichardMullen 1 61
(Robert Cowell) *chsd ldrs: rdn 1/2-way: chal 1f out: nt qckn fnl 100yds* **15/2**

-600 **5** *1* **Wreningham**[19] 3307 6-9-4 **56**.................................... WilliamCarson 3 51
(Stuart Williams) *tk str hold in ld: rdn and hdd over 1f out: sn btn* **5/1**[3]
3421 **6** *9* **Bobby's Doll**[8] 3678 4-9-11 **63** 6ex................................ StevieDonohoe 2 26
(Terry Clement) *in last pair: rdn and no rspnse over 2f out: sn struggling bdly* **13/8**[1]

60.71 secs (-1.99) **Going Correction** -0.40s/f (Firm)
WFA 3 from 4yo+ 5lb **6** Ran SP% **108.7**
Speed ratings (Par 103): **99,96,95,94,92 78**
toteswingers:1&2:£10.90, 2&3:£2.30, 1&3:£9.60 CSF £90.60 CT £354.58 TOTE £14.50: £4.70, £3.30; EX 39.30.
Owner The Smart Syndicate **Bred** Miss Anne Ormsby **Trained** Hingham, Norfolk

FOCUS
No more than a modest handicap and one in which the market leader disappointed. The gallop was soon sound.
Bobby's Doll Official explanation: jockey said filly never travelled

3958 FREEDERM H'CAP 1m 1f
8:00 (8:00) (Class 6) (0-55,55) 3-Y-O **£1,617** (£481; £240; £120) **Stalls** Low

Form RPR
0-10 **1** **Dubawi Dancer**[30] 2964 3-8-13 **52**.................................... RyanMoore 1 67
(William Haggas) *t.k.h in midfield: prog far rails over 3f out: drvn to ld over 1f out: sn clr: v easily* **6/4**[1]
1352 **2** *4 1/2* **See The Storm**[10] 3643 3-8-8 **52**.................................. KieranO'Neill(5) 13 57
(Patrick Morris) *t.k.h: led 2f: pressed ldr tl led again over 3f out: drvn and hdd over 1f out: no ch w wnr but wl in command of rest* **15/2**[3]
-400 **3** *3 1/2* **Invent**[16] 3431 3-9-0 **53**... SebSanders 11 50
(Sir Mark Prescott Bt) *wnt prom after 2f: 3rd st: rdn and ev ch 2f out: sn outpcd: eased cl home* **8/1**
0003 **4** *1* **Scarborough Lily**[22] 3227 3-8-12 **51**.................................. LukeMorris 8 46
(Edward Vaughan) *in last pair: last 4f out: stl hopeless task over 2f out: rdn in 7th 1f out: styd on wl past btn horses* **16/1**
00-3 **5** *1 3/4* **Dolly Colman (IRE)**[34] 2825 3-8-9 **48** ow1................ StevieDonohoe 10 39
(Andrew Haynes) *chsd ldrs in midfield: rdn and effrt 3f out: btn over 2f out* **20/1**
5502 **6** *1* **Newby Lodge (IRE)**[11] 3596 3-8-10 **52**.........................(p) AmyBaker(3) 7 41
(Alan Bailey) *last early: hdwy to go 4th st: wknd over 2f out: sn drifting lft* **16/1**
3046 **7** *2* **Chillie Peppar**[19] 3309 3-8-13 **52**.................................... AndreaAtzeni 6 37
(George Prodromou) *t.k.h in midfield: rdn and effrt in centre of crse 3f out: btn over 2f out* **50/1**
-516 **8** *8* **Hi Note**[6] 3742 3-8-11 **53**.. MartinHarley(3) 5 20
(Mick Channon) *midfield: rdn 4f out: btn over 2f out: t.o* **9/1**
060 **9** *nse* **Daliana**[67] 1873 3-9-2 **55**.. JamieSpencer 3 22
(Michael Bell) *midfield: 6th st: rdn and wknd over 2f out: t.o* **5/1**[2]
0020 **10** *5* **Onlyfoalsandhorses (IRE)**[24] 3175 3-8-8 **52**...........(p) RyanPowell(5) 4 —
(J S Moore) *chsd ldrs: 5th st: rdn 3f out: nt keen and wnt lft and immediately btn: t.o* **25/1**
0-05 **11** *4* **Nettis**[29] 2993 3-9-2 **55**... KierenFallon 12 —
(George Prodromou) *t.k.h: led after 2f tl rdn and hdd over 3f out: lost pl qckly over 2f out: t.o* **33/1**
-060 **12** *6* **Polish Sunset**[10] 3636 3-9-0 **53**..(t) EddieAhern 2 —
(Amy Weaver) *bhd: rdn 4f out: no rspnse: bdly t.o* **40/1**
000- **13** *16* **Safe Haven (IRE)**[236] 7493 3-8-9 **48**.............................. RichardMullen 9 —
(Derek Shaw) *bhd: rdn and struggling 4f out: t.o 3f out: virtually p.u over 1f out* **40/1**

1m 53.01s (-2.79) **Going Correction** -0.40s/f (Firm) course record **13** Ran SP% **119.7**
Speed ratings (Par 98): **96,92,88,88,86 85,83,76,76,72 68,63,49**
toteswingers:1&2:£1.50, 2&3:£11.50, 1&3:£8.20 CSF £11.82 CT £74.28 TOTE £2.30: £1.10, £2.20, £3.10; EX 12.30.
Owner F W Golding, E Kirtland & N A Callaghan **Bred** Allan Munnis & Laurance Walwin **Trained** Newmarket, Suffolk

FOCUS
A couple of unexposed sorts in a moderate handicap. The gallop was no more than fair.
Dubawi Dancer ◆ Official explanation: trainer's rep said, regarding apparent improvement in form, that the filly was better suited by stronger riding and the better ground.

[illegible] [illegible] H'CAP 1m 2f 21y
8:30 (8:30) (Class 4) (0-80,80) [illegible] [illegible] **Stalls** Low

Form RPR
6-00 **1** **Agent Archie (USA)**[142] 628 4-10-0 **80**............................ LiamJones 8 97
(William Haggas) *prom: 3rd st: rdn to ld over 2f out: clr ins fnl f: easily* **12/1**
-610 **2** *3 3/4* **Destiny Blue (IRE)**[20] 3276 4-9-13 **79**............................... EddieAhern 1 88
(Jamie Osborne) *prom: 4th st: chsd wnr and rdn over 2f out: wl hld ins fnl f* **9/2**[2]
5526 **3** *1 1/2* **Negotiation (IRE)**[18] 3361 5-9-0 **66**............................... RichardMullen 9 72
(Michael Quinn) *led: drvn and hdd over 2f out: one pce and racing awkwardly fr over 1f out* **14/1**
-040 **4** *3/4* **Rutland Boy**[20] 3291 3-8-13 **76**....................................... JamieSpencer 6 81
(Ed Dunlop) *settled in midfield: effrt over 3f out: sn rdn: no imp fnl 2f* **8/1**
410 **5** *hd* **England Rules (IRE)**[31] 2925 3-9-2 **79**.........................(t) WilliamBuick 2 83
(Jeremy Noseda) *t.k.h towards rr: effrt over 2f out: no imp over 1f out and nvr posed a threat* **7/2**[1]
1-02 **6** *2 1/4* **Quiz Mistress**[15] 3474 3-8-12 **75**..................................(p) NickyMackay 4 75
(Gerard Butler) *t.k.h in rr: drvn 4f out: plugged on ins fnl f: nvr gng wl enough* **16/1**
6622 **7** *1 1/4* **Ferruccio (IRE)**[19] 3312 3-8-7 **70**..................................(t) KierenFallon 10 67
(James Fanshawe) *midfield: rdn 3f out: plugged on same pce and n.d after* **9/2**[2]
2-30 **8** *7* **Top Diktat**[31] 2924 3-8-11 **74**.. RyanMoore 5 64
(Sir Michael Stoute) *prom: 2nd st: drvn and hung lft and lost pl over 2f out: eased 1f out* **11/2**[3]
344- **9** *1/2* **Lyric Poet (USA)**[209] 7876 4-9-11 **77**............................ WilliamCarson 7 59
(Giles Bravery) *last away: a bhd: rdn 4f out: sn btn* **25/1**
0004 **10** *25* **Falmouth Bay (USA)**[10] 3614 3-8-10 **73**............................. NeilCallan 3 —
(Mark Johnston) *midfield: 5th st: rdn and wknd wl over 2f out: t.o and heavily eased fnl f* **16/1**

2m 6.00s (-4.50) **Going Correction** -0.40s/f (Firm)
WFA 3 from 4yo+ 11lb **10** Ran SP% **115.1**
Speed ratings (Par 105): **102,99,97,97,97 95,94,88,88,68**
toteswingers:1&2:£20.00, 2&3:£14.20, 1&3:£32.40 CSF £64.45 CT £773.25 TOTE £16.20: £3.80, £1.80, £3.80; EX 114.30.
Owner D Gorton **Bred** Earle I Mack **Trained** Newmarket, Suffolk

FOCUS
A few unexposed sorts in a fair handicap. The gallop was just an ordinary one to early in the home straight.
Ferruccio(IRE) Official explanation: jockey said gelding lost its action
Falmouth Bay(USA) Official explanation: jockey said colt moved poorly

3960 BAZUKA H'CAP 1m 6f 17y
9:00 (9:01) (Class 5) (0-70,68) 3-Y-O+ **£2,264** (£673; £336; £168) **Stalls** High

Form RPR
3005 **1** **Royal Premier (IRE)**[12] 3559 8-8-13 **53** oh8................(b1) SebSanders 5 65
(Tom Keddy) *dropped out last and declined frenetic gallop of ldrs tl st: str run on far rails 4f out: led over 3f out: sn drvn clr: 4 l ahd 1f out: hld on wl* **20/1**
600 **2** *1 1/2* **Native Colony**[54] 2231 3-8-9 **64**... NeilCallan 6 73
(Roger Varian) *hld up: wnt 4th and rdn st: chsd wnr but outpcd fr 3f out tl styd on wl fnl 100yds: a hld* **9/4**[1]
-256 **3** *8* **Locum**[24] 3184 6-9-3 **57**... WilliamBuick 3 56
(Mark H Tompkins) *midfield: 5th st: 3rd and rdn and outpcd 3f out: 8 l 3rd and wl btn 2f out* **6/1**[3]
006 **4** *11* **Green Future (USA)**[20] 3267 3-8-8 **63**............................ JimmyQuinn 1 45
(Amanda Perrett) *prom: 4th and rdn st: sn racing awkwardly: wl btn 3f out: t.o fnl 2f* **8/1**
-544 **5** *5* **Corr Point (IRE)**[18] 3352 4-10-0 **68**............................... KierenFallon 4 43
(Jamie Osborne) *led 1f: chsd ldr in fast r tl lost pl qckly over 3f out: t.o 2f out* **7/2**[2]
-632 **6** *38* **Miss Whippy**[12] 3559 4-8-13 **53** oh3.................................... EddieAhern 7 —
(Michael Squance) *flashing tail: bhd: rdn and struggling 4f out: sn t.o* **12/1**
3131 **7** *10* **Annelko**[33] 2856 4-9-7 **61**.. MartinLane 2 —
(Andrew Haynes) *set str gallop after 1f: hdd over 3f out and stopped to nil: hopelessly t.o and eased* **7/2**[2]

3m 2.16s (-5.44) **Going Correction** -0.40s/f (Firm)
WFA 3 from 4yo+ 15lb **7** Ran SP% **113.1**
Speed ratings (Par 103): **99,98,93,87,84 62,57**
toteswingers:1&2:£14.90, 2&3:£2.30, 1&3:£17.40 CSF £63.69 TOTE £20.70: £8.80, £1.40; EX 116.20.
Owner Maynard Durrant Partnership I **Bred** Mrs Anne Hughes **Trained** Newmarket, Suffolk

FOCUS
A modest handicap run at a reasonable gallop and one in which a couple of the fancied runners disappointed.
Annelko Official explanation: jockey said gelding moved poorly
T/Jkpt: Not won. T/Plt: £532.80 to a £1 stake. Pool of £78,738.60 - 107.87 winning tickets.
T/Qpdt: £42.20 to a £1 stake. Pool of £6,777.19 - 118.58 winning tickets. IM

3961 - 3971a (Foreign Racing) - See Raceform Interactive

3728 CATTERICK (L-H)
Wednesday, July 13

OFFICIAL GOING: Good (good to firm in places; 7.9)
Wind: Light half against Weather: Cloudy with sunny periods

3972 YORKSHIRE-OUTDOORS.CO.UK (S) STKS 5f 212y
2:20 (2:20) (Class 6) 3-Y-O+ **£1,704** (£503; £251) **Stalls** Low

Form RPR
4-10 **1** **Paper Dreams (IRE)**[24] 3207 3-8-6 60..........................(p) AmyRyan(3) 9 67
(Kevin Ryan) *hld up towards rr: hdwy on wd outside 2f out: rdn over 1f out: styd on ins fnl f to ld nr line* **14/1**
3323 **2** *shd* **Bilko Pak (IRE)**[7] 3731 3-8-8 73....................................(p) PaulHanagan 2 66
(Ann Duffield) *chsd ldrs: hdwy 2f out: swtchd lft and rdn ent fnl f: sn led: drvn and hung rt last 100yds: hdd nr line* **6/4**[1]
4601 **3** *2* **Opus Maximus (IRE)**[12] 3569 6-9-6 74....................(p) StephenCraine 5 67
(Jennie Candlish) *towards rr: hdwy 2f out: swtchd lft and rdn over 1f out: kpt on ins fnl f: nrst fin* **9/2**[3]
0-46 **4** *2 1/2* **Johannesgray (IRE)**[14] 3508 4-8-9 62............................ NeilFarley(5) 12 53
(Noel Wilson) *cl up: led 1/2-way: rdn clr 2f out: drvn over 1f out: hdd ins fnl f: wknd* **3/1**[2]
00-0 **5** *2* **Red River Boy**[54] 2247 6-9-0 51.. KellyHarrison 4 46
(Chris Fairhurst) *trckd ldrs: hdwy on inner over 1f out whn n.m.r over 1f out: sn swtchd rt and rdn: kpt on same pce* **22/1**
[illegible] **6** [illegible] [illegible][28] 3040 4-9-0 66..(b1) TomEaves 6 41
(Michael [illegible]) [illegible] *wknd over 1f out* **12/1**
0500 **7** *shd* **Mujahope**[10] 3662 6-8-9 40...(v) DaleSwift(5) 7 41
(Colin Teague) *s.i.s and bhd: hdwy 2f out: swtchd lft ent fnl f: nt rch ldrs* **150/1**
0040 **8** *1* **Piste**[30] 2990 5-8-9 41.. PJMcDonald 8 33
(Tina Jackson) *nvr bttr than midfield* **80/1**
0020 **9** *1 1/2* **Charles Parnell (IRE)**[48] 2412 8-9-0 60......................... AdrianNicholls 3 33
(Simon Griffiths) *s.i.s and bhd: sme hdwy on inner over 1f out: sn n.m.r and nvr a factor* **12/1**
0060 **10** *1/2* **Blue Rum (IRE)**[12] 3569 4-8-11 43................................. PaulPickard(3) 1 31
(Alan Kirtley) *chsd ldng pair on inner: rdn along 1/2-way: sn wknd* **50/1**
-000 **11** *6* **Future Gem**[7] 3733 5-8-9 41......................................(p) BarryMcHugh 10 —
(David Thompson) *chsd ldrs: rdn along wl over 2f out: sn wknd* **125/1**

1m 13.37s (-0.23) **Going Correction** +0.025s/f (Good)
WFA 3 from 4yo+ 6lb **11** Ran SP% **114.2**
Speed ratings (Par 101): **102,101,99,95,93 91,91,89,87,87 79**
toteswingers:1&2:£4.10, 2&3:£2.80, 1&3:£5.00 CSF £34.15 TOTE £18.50: £4.20, £1.60, £1.10; EX 35.30 Trifecta £357.30 Part won. Pool of £482.92 - 0.20 winning units..There was no bid for the winner. Bilko Pak was subject to a friendly claim.
Owner Opus Industrial Services Partnership **Bred** J Joyce **Trained** Hambleton, N Yorks
■ Stewards' Enquiry : Paul Hanagan one-day ban: careless riding (Jul 28)

FOCUS
A dry night and a fresh crosswind resulted in the ground drying out to Good, good to firm in places. Jockeys' opinions on the ground varied from good to quick. A wide mix of abilities in this seller but they went a good pace from the start and it resulted in a close finish.

3973 CATTERICKBRIDGE.CO.UK NOVICE AUCTION STKS 7f
2:50 (2:50) (Class 5) 2-Y-O **£2,070** (£616; £307; £153) **Stalls** Low

Form RPR
12 **1** **Piece By Piece**[20] 3313 2-9-2 0.. DavidAllan 4 86+
(Tim Easterby) *mde all: qcknd clr over 2f out: easily* **2/5**[1]
656 **2** *7* **Koalition (IRE)**[18] 3382 2-8-11 0...................................... GregFairley 5 61
(Deborah Sanderson) *in rr and pushed along 3f out: hdwy over 2f out: sn rdn and n.m.r over 1f out: swtchd rt and kpt on to take 2nd ins fnl f: no ch w wnr* **20/1**
10 **3** *4 1/2* **Judas Jo (FR)**[26] 3104 2-8-8 0....................................(t) RoystonFfrench 1 46+
(Gay Kelleway) *chsd ldng pair on inner: rdn along and outpcd wl over 2f out: kpt on u.p fnl f to take poor 3rd nr fin* **3/1**[2]

3212 **4** ½ **Flying Pickets (IRE)**[15] 3491 2-8-11 0 .... PaulHanagan 3 48
(Alan McCabe) *sn chsng wnr: rdn along over 2f out: drvn and edgd lft appr fnl f: sn wknd* **16/1**[3]

1m 26.93s (-0.07) **Going Correction** +0.025s/f (Good) **4** Ran SP% **107.1**
Speed ratings (Par 94): **101,93,87,87**
CSF £8.85 TOTE £1.90; EX 9.40.
Owner J Musgrave **Bred** M J Dawson **Trained** Great Habton, N Yorks

FOCUS
A small field for this novice auction stakes and it was turned into a procession. The runner-up is rated close to his previous form.

NOTEBOOK
Piece By Piece was a well-backed favourite who had scored on his debut and had given weight and a beating to a horse that subsequently finished fifth in a Group 2 when runner-up on his second start. He made all and had the race sewn up soon after straightening for home. The form is worth little but this should be a nice confidence booster before he goes on to better things. He has sales-race entries later in the year and will apparently be aimed at the St Leger Yearling Stakes at York next month. (op 4-7 tchd 8-13 in places)
Koalition(IRE) had shown only moderate form prior to this but was doing his best work late having been held up instead of leading this time. (op 18-1 tchd 16-1)
Judas Jo(FR), a winner here on her debut and bred to stay this far, had been well held in the Albany Stakes last time. However, she was ridden and failed to handle the home bend, which effectively ended her chance and made things easy for the favourite. Official explanation: jockey said filly was unsuited by the track (op 11-4 tchd 5-2)
Flying Pickets(IRE) whose win came in a seller, did his best to stay with the favourite but paid for his efforts in the closing stages. Official explanation: jockey said gelding hung left-handed in straight (op 9-1)

3974 RACINGUK.COM CLAIMING STKS — 1m 3f 214y
3:20 (3:21) (Class 6) 3-Y-O+ **£1,704** (£503; £251) **Stalls** Low

Form RPR

5012 **1** **Eijaaz (IRE)**[14] 3510 10-9-8 60 ....(p) SilvestreDeSousa 2 62
(Geoffrey Harker) *hld up towards rr: stdy hdwy wl over 3f out: chsd ldrs 2f out: rdn to chal over 1f out: edgd lft and kpt on wl to ld nr fin* **5/2**[2]

-153 **2** ½ **Hel's Angel (IRE)**[22] 3243 5-9-9 72 .... PaulHanagan 6 62
(Ann Duffield) *led: pushed along 3f out: rdn 2f out: drvn ent fnl f: edgd lft: hdd and no ex nr fin* **5/4**[1]

6010 **3** ¾ **Guga (IRE)**[34] 2851 5-9-3 61 ....(v) JulieBurke(5) 4 60
(John Mackie) *prom: effrt whn n.m.r over 1f out: swtchd rt and rdn to chal ent fnl f: drvn and ev ch whn n.m.r and bmpd wl ins fnl f: no ex nr fin* **11/1**

5040 **4** 1¼ **Lucayan Dancer**[1] 3938 11-9-6 49 .... AdrianNicholls 10 56
(David Nicholls) *trckd ldrs: hdwy 3f out: rdn to chal over 2f out: ev ch tl drvn ins fnl f and hld whn n.m.r and bmpd towards fin* **20/1**

4/0- **5** 8 **Hernando's Boy**[24] 7284 10-9-2 52 .... PhillipMakin 3 39
(Keith Reveley) *hld up towards rr: hdwy over 4f out: rdn to chse ldrs wl over 2f out: sn drvn and no imp* **25/1**

00/0 **6** 3¼ **Hada Men (USA)**[33] 2892 6-9-4 63 .... TomEaves 1 36
(Tina Jackson) *chsd ldrs: rdn along over 3f out and sn wknd* **25/1**

-000 **7** 5 **Charity Fair**[35] 2809 4-8-8 36 ....(v[1]) DaleSwift(7) 8 23
(Ron Barr) *midfield: rdn along over 4f out: sn outpcd* **200/1**

4130 **8** 5 **Relative Strength (IRE)**[14] 3507 6-9-10 67 ....(tp) StephenCraine 7 26
(Jennie Candlish) *prom: rdn along over 3f out: sn wknd* **13/2**[3]

-016 **9** 22 **Without Equal**[20] 3300 5-8-12 57 .... ShaneBKelly(7) 5 —
(David Thompson) *dwlt: a in rr: bhd fnl 4f* **16/1**

40 **10** 5 **Fiftynotout (IRE)**[13] 3543 4-9-6 0 .... BarryMcHugh 9 —
(Alan Berry) *s.i.s: a in rr: bhd fnl 4f* **125/1**

2m 39.21s (0.31) **Going Correction** +0.025s/f (Good) **10** Ran SP% **114.3**
Speed ratings (Par 101): **99,98,98,97,92 89,86,83,68,65**
toteswingers:1&2:£1.90, 2&3:£4.30, 1&3:£5.20 CSF £5.53 TOTE £4.40: £1.60, £1.10, £2.00; EX 6.60 Trifecta £38.20 Pool: £364.56 - 7.06 winning units..
Owner A S Ward **Bred** Shadwell Estate Company Limited **Trained** Thirkleby, N Yorks

FOCUS
An uncompetitive claimer judged on official ratings but another good finish.
Without Equal Official explanation: jockey said mare became upset in stalls and clipped heels on bend turning into back straight

3975 5TH REGIMENT ROYAL ARTILLERY H'CAP — 5f
3:50 (3:50) (Class 4) (0-85,82) 3-Y-O **£4,204** (£1,251; £625; £312) **Stalls** Low

Form RPR

3630 **1** **Cadeaux Pearl**[33] 2890 3-9-4 **82** ....(b) BillyCray(3) 1 89
(David Nicholls) *qckly away and sn clr: mde all: rdn over 1f out and kpt on* **6/1**

0502 **2** 1¾ **Bay Of Fires (IRE)**[7] 3731 3-8-9 **70** .... SilvestreDeSousa 4 71
(David O'Meara) *trckd ldrs: hdwy 1/2-way: rdn to chse wnr fr wl over 1f out: drvn and edgd lft ins fnl f: no imp towards fin* **5/2**[1]

5434 **3** 2½ **Crimson Knot (IRE)**[5] 3807 3-8-12 **78** .... JulieBurke(5) 8 70
(Alan Berry) *in rr: rdn along and hdwy over 2f out: kpt on u.p fr over 1f out: nrst fin* **8/1**

5113 **4** 2½ **Royal Bajan (USA)**[11] 3628 3-8-12 **73** .... PaulHanagan 5 56
(James Given) *towards rr: rdn along 1/2-way: sme late hdwy* **4/1**[2]

6-00 **5** 1¼ **Forty Proof (IRE)**[46] 2508 3-9-3 **78** ....(p) SebSanders 6 56
(William Knight) *dwlt: in tch: rdn along 1/2-way and sn one pce* **16/1**

0201 **6** *hd* **Gottcher**[11] 3628 3-9-5 **80** .... LeeNewman 7 57
(David Barron) *chsd ldng pair: effrt over 2f out: sn rdn and chsd wnr tl drvn: edgd lft and wknd wl over 1f out* **5/1**[3]

5044 **7** 4 **Berberana (IRE)**[32] 2911 3-9-1 **76** .... DavidAllan 2 39
(Tim Easterby) *chsd wnr: rdn along 1/2-way: sn wknd* **5/1**[3]

59.12 secs (-0.68) **Going Correction** -0.075s/f (Good) **7** Ran SP% **113.2**
Speed ratings (Par 102): **102,99,95,91,89 88,82**
toteswingers:1&2:£3.30, 2&3:£3.90, 1&3:£8.80 CSF £20.95 CT £119.67 TOTE £8.50: £3.50, £1.70; EX 27.70 Trifecta £226.40 Part won. Pool: £306.05 - 0.10 winning units..
Owner Paul J Dixon **Bred** Catridge Farm Stud Ltd **Trained** Sessay, N Yorks

FOCUS
A competitive-looking sprint handicap for 3-y-os but the winner made all and scored virtually unchallenged in comparatively the best time of the day.
Berberana(IRE) Official explanation: jockey said filly reared as stalls opened

3976 AUGUST 12TH IS LADIES EVENING H'CAP — 1m 3f 214y
4:20 (4:22) (Class 5) (0-70,72) 3-Y-O **£2,070** (£616; £307; £153) **Stalls** Low

Form RPR

-441 **1** **Memory Lane**[7] 3734 3-9-13 **72** 6ex .... SebSanders 9 82+
(Sir Mark Prescott Bt) *mde most: rdn along wl over 2f out: drvn over 1f out: kpt on wl* **2/1**[1]

00-0 **2** ¾ **Al Furat (USA)**[78] 1588 3-8-4 **52** .... PaulPickard(3) 2 58
(Ron Barr) *hld up in rr: hdwy 4f out: effrt on outer wl over 2f out: rdn and edgd lft: drvn to chse wnr over 1f out: sn hung lft: kpt on nt rch wnr* **40/1**

0210 **3** 3½ **Hal Of A Lover**[12] 3587 3-8-11 **56** .... SilvestreDeSousa 1 57+
(David O'Meara) *wnt bdly lft s: hld up towards rr: hdwy on inner 3f out: rdn along to chse ldrs whn swtchd rt to outer over 1f out: kpt on ins fnl f: tk 3rd nr fin* **5/2**[2]

0-05 **4** ½ **Torun City**[28] 3037 3-9-6 **65** .... PaulHanagan 7 65
(Richard Fahey) *prom: rdn along over 3f out: drvn wl over 1f out: kpt on same pce* **12/1**

004 **5** 4 **Bollin Mandy**[18] 3385 3-9-5 **64** .... DavidAllan 8 58
(Tim Easterby) *prom: chsd wnr after 3f: rdn along over 2f out: drvn and hung rt wl over 1f out: sn wknd* **14/1**

0064 **6** 2½ **May Burnett (IRE)**[11] 3615 3-8-2 **47** oh2 ....(t) JamesSullivan 4 37
(Brian Rothwell) *chsd ldrs: rdn along over 3f out: drvn over 2f out and sn one pce* **50/1**

6-06 **7** 1½ **Fimias (IRE)**[71] 1801 3-9-1 **60** .... DanielTudhope 5 47
(Geoffrey Harker) *bhd and rdn along 1/2-way: nvr a factor* **10/1**[3]

6300 **8** ½ **Subramaniam**[55] 2239 3-9-1 **60** .... PhillipMakin 6 46
(James Given) *chsd ldrs: rdn along over 4f out: sn wknd* **28/1**

302 **9** 4½ **Bella Montagna**[36] 2785 3-8-12 **57** .... TomEaves 3 36
(John Quinn) *midfield: rdn along 4f out: sn wknd* **12/1**

2m 40.37s (1.47) **Going Correction** +0.025s/f (Good) **9** Ran SP% **100.9**
Speed ratings (Par 100): **96,95,93,92,90 88,87,87,84**
toteswingers:1&2:£14.20, 2&3:£16.70, 1&3:£1.90 CSF £67.31 CT £129.98 TOTE £3.10: £1.10, £11.30, £1.10; EX 71.90 TRIFECTA Not won..
Owner Miss K Rausing **Bred** Miss K Rausing **Trained** Newmarket, Suffolk
■ Kodicil was withdrawn: broke out of stalls. Rule 4 applies, deduct 15p in the £.

FOCUS
A modest handicap which Sir Mark Prescott was won for the third time in the last ten years.

3977 YORKSHIRE RACING SUMMER FESTIVAL MEDIAN AUCTION MAIDEN STKS — 7f
4:50 (4:52) (Class 6) 3-Y-O **£2,726** (£805; £402) **Stalls** Low

Form RPR

2224 **1** **Moral Issue**[16] 3461 3-9-0 73 .... PatrickDonaghy(3) 5 69
(Jedd O'Keeffe) *mde all: rdn over 2f out: drvn over 1f out: styd on gamely fnl f* **15/8**[1]

0520 **2** 1 **Beechcraft Baron (IRE)**[23] 3230 3-9-3 65 .... PaulHanagan 7 66
(William Haggas) *cl up: effrt over 2f out and sn rdn: drvn over 1f out: kpt on* **9/4**[2]

4 **3** *hd* **Thatcherite (IRE)**[30] 1693 3-9-3 0 ....(t) StephenCraine 11 65
(Tony Coyle) *s.i.s and in rr: hdwy 3f out: rdn to chse ldrs wl over 1f out: nt clr run and swtchd lft jst ins fnl f: nrst fin* **16/1**

4266 **4** *nk* **Stilettoesinthemud (IRE)**[11] 3621 3-8-12 58 .... JamesSullivan 8 60
(James Given) *cl up on outer: effrt over 2f out and sn rdn: drvn over 1f out: kpt on u.p ins fnl f* **9/1**

00 **5** 1¼ **Merito**[12] 3575 3-9-3 0 .... PhillipMakin 9 62
(Kevin Ryan) *in tch on outer: hdwy to chse ldrs over 2f out: rdn wl over 1f out: kpt on same pce towards fin* **20/1**

6 1¾ **Chookie Royale** 3-8-12 0 .... DaleSwift(5) 3 61+
(Keith Dalgleish) *chsd ldrs: rdn along and edgd lft 2f out: grad wknd* **15/2**[3]

7 *nk* **Luck By Chance (IRE)** 3-8-12 0 .... TonyHamilton 1 51
(Richard Fahey) *chsd ldrs on inner: hdwy over 2f out: rdn wl over 1f out: wknd appr fnl f: fin lame* **9/1**

3005 **8** 1¼ **Deep Applause**[8] 3706 3-9-3 57 .... TomEaves 6 53
(Michael Dods) *in tch: hdwy to chse ldrs 1/2-way: rdn along wl over 2f out: sn drvn and wknd wl over 1f out* **12/1**

0-00 **9** 10 **Annalika**[26] 3138 3-8-9 33 .... PaulPickard(3) 4 21
(Colin Teague) *a in rr* **200/1**

1m 27.31s (0.31) **Going Correction** +0.025s/f (Good) **9** Ran SP% **116.2**
Speed ratings (Par 98): **99,97,97,97,95 93,93,92,80**
toteswingers:1&2:£2.00, 2&3:£9.50, 1&3:£7.90 . Tote Super 7: Win: Not won. Place: £4.60 CSF £6.24 TOTE £4.20: £1.60, £1.10, £4.00; EX 7.90 Trifecta £67.60 Pool: £558.27 - 6.11 winning units..
Owner Caron & Paul Chapman & Highbeck Racing **Bred** Redmyre Bloodstock Ltd **Trained** Middleham Moor, N Yorks

FOCUS
A modest 3-y-o maiden.
Luck By Chance(IRE) Official explanation: vet said filly finished lame left-fore
T/Plt: £5.80 to a £1 stake. Pool of £39,417.61 - 4,911.28 winning tickets. T/Qpdt: £4.30 to a £1 stake. Pool of £2,997.01 - 512.53 winning tickets. JR

3742 LINGFIELD (L-H)
Wednesday, July 13

OFFICIAL GOING: Turf course - good (good to firm in places; 8.3); all-weather - standard
Wind: modest, half against Weather: overcast, dry

3978 JACKSONS ESTATE AGENTS H'CAP — 2m
2:30 (2:32) (Class 5) (0-75,74) 3-Y-O+ **£2,385** (£704; £352) **Stalls** Low

Form RPR

4115 **1** **Money Money Money**[7] 3738 5-9-9 **69** .... JamesMillman 3 79
(Rod Millman) *hld up in tch in rr: swtchd rt and hdwy wl over 2f out: rdn to ld over 1f out: styd on strly and drew clr fnl f: comf* **7/1**[3]

3440 **2** 4 **Marcus Antonius**[34] 2856 4-8-12 **58** .... PatCosgrave 6 64
(Jim Boyle) *chsd ldr for 2f: styd handy: rdn to ld and edgd rt wl over 2f out: hdd over 1f out: styd on same pce fnl f* **14/1**

3533 **3** 1½ **Bow River Arch (USA)**[33] 2874 3-8-8 **73** ....(p) WilliamBuick 2 76
(Jeremy Noseda) *hld up in tch in last trio: swtchd rt and hdwy 3f out: nt clr run and swtchd lft over 2f out: drvn and ev ch over 1f out: outpcd by wnr 1f out: wknd ins fnl f* **5/2**[1]

-254 **4** *nk* **High Samana**[27] 3080 3-8-9 **74** .... JimCrowley 1 76
(Ralph Beckett) *chsd ldrs: rdn and effrt over 2f out: pressing ldrs and hrd drvn over 1f out: outpcd and btn 1f out: plugged on same pce fnl f* **10/3**[2]

23-4 **5** 9 **Viviani (IRE)**[12] 3599 4-9-2 **62** .... JimmyFortune 9 55
(Amanda Perrett) *dwlt: hdwy to chse ldr after 2f tl over 3f out: sn drvn and unable qck: wknd wl over 1f out: wl btn and hung lft 1f out* **8/1**

2330 **6** 3½ **Dove Cottage (IRE)**[12] 3599 9-8-9 **55** .... ChrisCatlin 8 43
(Stuart Kittow) *mounted on crse and taken down early: led tl rdn and hdd wl over 2f out: wknd 2f out* **18/1**

4213 **7** 7 **Kavaloti (IRE)**[7] 3738 7-9-10 **70** ....(b) GeorgeBaker 5 50
(Gary Moore) *dwlt: bustled along early: in tch in midfield after 2f: rdn and struggling over 3f out: lost tch over 2f out* **9/1**

00-5 **8** *16* **Cluain Alainn (IRE)**[54] 2259 5-9-5 65 ....(p) MartinLane 4 26
(Ian Williams) *in tch in last trio: pushed along 1/2-way: rdn and dropped to last over 5f out: lost tch 4f out: t.o* **33/1**

3m 36.81s (2.01) **Going Correction** +0.225s/f (Good)
WFA 3 from 4yo+ 19lb 8 Ran SP% **100.1**
Speed ratings (Par 103): **103,101,100,100,95 93,90,82**
toteswingers:1&2:£6.00, 2&3:£4.90, 1&3:£2.90 CSF £72.04 CT £197.27 TOTE £6.80: £1.60, £2.50, £1.30; EX 76.10.
Owner Mrs Jenny Willment **Bred** Mrs Jenny Willment **Trained** Kentisbeare, Devon

FOCUS
The times of the first two races were really slow, but that's indicative of the pace rather the ground as conditions were on the fast side of good. Last year's winner Ambrose Princess was withdrawn at the start, and the two 3-y-os in the line-up ran below market expectations, making for an ordinary staying handicap. They seemed to go just a modest tempo and the time was over nine seconds above standard.

3979 STARR COMPANIES H'CAP 1m 2f
3:00 (3:00) (Class 6) (0-65,65) 3-Y-O **£1,533** (£452; £226) **Stalls** Low

Form RPR
5106 **1** **Highlife Dancer**[12] 3596 3-8-12 59 .... MartinHarley(3) 3 66
(Mick Channon) *t.k.h: chse ldr for 2f: styd handy: jnd ldrs 4f out: rdn to ld over 2f out: drvn over 1f out: kpt on gamely ins fnl f* **7/1**

2213 **2** *3/4* **Whitby Jet (IRE)**[34] 2853 3-9-7 65 .... TedDurcan 6 71
(Edward Vaughan) *t.k.h: chsd ldrs: wnt 2nd 6f out tl unable qck and short of room 3f out: drvn and rallied to chse wnr 2f out tl wl over 1f out: kpt on same pce u.p and chsd wnr again wl ins fnl f* **11/4**[2]

-044 **3** *1 1/4* **Spade**[22] 3259 3-9-6 64 ....(b) DaneO'Neill 5 67
(David Elsworth) *stdd s: t.k.h: hld up in last pair: hdwy to trck ldrs 3f out: swtchd rt 2f out: trckd wnr gng wl over 1f out: fnd nil u.p and hung in bhd wnr ins fnl f: wknd cl home* **9/2**[3]

0305 **4** *1* **Sir Randolf (IRE)**[23] 3220 3-8-13 57 ....(t) JamesDoyle 7 58
(Sylvester Kirk) *in tch on outer: rdn and effrt over 2f out: styd on same pce u.p fr over 1f out* **16/1**

4645 **5** *2* **Midnight Trader (IRE)**[20] 3312 3-9-7 65 ....(t) TonyCulhane 9 62+
(Paul D'Arcy) *stdd s: t.k.h: hld up in tch in last: lost grnd on downhill run over 4f out: rdn 2f out: hung lft and hdd up on fnl f: nvr trbld ldrs* **8/1**

-425 **6** *3/4* **Swaninstockwell (IRE)**[26] 3118 3-9-5 63 .... IanMongan 2 59
(Pat Phelan) *t.k.h: chsd ldrs: wnt 2nd after 2f tl 6f out: rdn and effrt on inner to join ldrs 3f out: wknd 1f out* **13/8**[1]

0600 **7** *10* **A B Celebration**[17] 3431 3-8-6 50 ow2 .... NeilChalmers 1 26
(John Bridger) *led at stdy gallop: hdd and rdn over 2f out: wkng whn wandered u.p 2f out: sn bhd* **66/1**

2m 15.93s (5.43) **Going Correction** +0.225s/f (Good) 7 Ran SP% **113.9**
Speed ratings (Par 98): **87,86,85,84,83 82,74**
toteswingers:1&2:£4.20, 2&3:£2.60, 1&3:£4.80 CSF £26.37 CT £96.37 TOTE £8.90: £3.20, £1.60; EX 39.30.
Owner The Highlife Racing Club **Bred** Imperial & Mike Channon Bloodstock Ltd **Trained** West Ilsley, Berks

FOCUS
A really weak handicap run at a steady pace, resulting in a time almost nine seconds above standard.

3980 LADBROKES MOBILE MAIDEN STKS 1m 1f
3:30 (3:30) (Class 5) 3-4-Y-O **£2,385** (£704; £352) **Stalls** Low

Form RPR
-044 **1** **El Muqbil (IRE)**[34] 2847 3-9-2 83 ....(t) RichardHills 2 86
(Brian Meehan) *mde all: gng best wl over 2f out: rdn over 1f out: kpt on wl: comf* **6/5**[1]

-323 **2** *3 1/4* **Burj Hatta (USA)**[23] 3218 3-9-2 81 .... FrankieDettori 5 80
(Saeed Bin Suroor) *chsd ldng pair: rdn to chse wnr over 2f out: drvn and no imp 2f out: styd on same pce and wl hld after* **6/5**[1]

0 **3** *5* **Lupa Montana (USA)**[31] 2960 3-8-11 0 .... JimCrowley 8 63
(Ralph Beckett) *chsd wnr tl over 2f out: sn outpcd u.p: wl hld and edgd lft 1f out* **8/1**[2]

[illegible] **4** *9* **Galloping Queen (IRE)**[35] 2808 3-8-12 68 ow1 .... HughBowman 1 46
(Mick Channon) *[illegible] nvr on terms w ldng trio: rdn and no hdwy 3f out* **12/1**

00 **5** *7* **Aaranyow (IRE)**[25] 3173 3-9-2 0 .... DavidProbert 7 35
(Bryn Palling) *hld up off the pce in midfield: rdn and no hdwy 3f out: wl btn after* **50/1**

6 *5* **Avon Blaise** 4-9-7 0 .... DaneO'Neill 3 19
(Peter Hedger) *dwlt: a wl off the pce in last trio: wl bhd fnl 3f* **50/1**

0- **7** *4 1/2* **Pani Ash**[263] 7099 3-8-6 0 ....(t) JemmaMarshall(5) 4 9
(Pat Phelan) *stdd s: t.k.h: hld up wl off the pce in last trio: wl bhd over 3f out* **40/1**

8 *8* **Cinematique (IRE)** 3-9-2 0 .... IanMongan 6 —
(Laura Mongan) *s.i.s: rn green and sn pushed along: wl bhd fnl 4f: t.o* **33/1**

1m 56.9s (0.30) **Going Correction** +0.225s/f (Good)
WFA 3 from 4yo 10lb 8 Ran SP% **119.0**
Speed ratings (Par 103): **107,104,99,92,86 81,77,70**
toteswingers:1&2:£1.20, 2&3:£2.50, 1&3:£2.10 CSF £2.81 TOTE £1.70: £1.30, £1.10, £1.30; EX 3.00.
Owner Hamdan Al Maktoum **Bred** Yellow Bird Syndicate **Trained** Manton, Wilts

FOCUS
Not a great deal of strength in depth, but the front two have both shown useful form.
Cinematique(IRE) Official explanation: £450 fine: breach of rule (C)12 (failure to check the identity of horse)

3981 CAPITAL SPREADS BRITISH STALLION STUDS E B F MAIDEN FILLIES' STKS 6f (P)
4:00 (4:00) (Class 5) 2-Y-O **£3,169** (£943; £471; £235) **Stalls** Low

Form RPR
05 **1** **Fire And Sparks**[7] 3736 2-9-0 0 .... JamieSpencer 4 73
(David Simcock) *mde all: rdn and asserted ent fnl f: styd on wl* **6/1**

00 **2** *1 1/2* **Correct**[19] 3342 2-9-0 0 .... HayleyTurner 1 69
(Michael Bell) *chsd ldng pair: rdn and effrt on inner over 1f out: chsd wnr wl ins fnl f: kpt on* **18/1**

6 **3** *3/4* **Baltic Flyer (IRE)**[22] 3257 2-9-0 0 .... DarryllHolland 3 66
(Robert Eddery) *chsd ldng trio: rdn and effrt jst over 2f out: drvn and hanging lft over 1f out: styd on same pce ins fnl f: wnt 3rd towards fin* **4/1**[3]

04 **4** *nk* **White Spirit (IRE)**[7] 3736 2-9-0 0 .... AdamKirby 8 65
(Marco Botti) *chsd wnr: upsides and rdn 2f out: drvn and unable qck w wnr ent fnl f: no ex and lost 2 pls wl ins fnl f* **10/1**

4 **5** *1 3/4* **Continuity (IRE)**[18] 3388 2-9-0 0 .... JimCrowley 5 60
(Ralph Beckett) *awkward s and slowly away: rcvrd and hdwy into midfield over 4f out: rdn and outpcd 2f out: styd on same pce and no imp over 1f out* **5/2**[1]

4 **6** *1 1/4* **Musically**[22] 3258 2-9-0 0 .... HughBowman 6 56+
(Mick Channon) *hld up in tch in midfield: nudged along and lost pl jst over 2f out: kpt on but no threat to ldrs ins fnl f* **11/4**[2]

7 *2 1/4* **Country Wolf** 2-9-0 0 .... AndreaAtzeni 9 50
(Michael Wigham) *s.i.s: a in last trio: rdn and outpcd over 2f out: n.d after* **50/1**

0 **8** *2* **Ionwy**[14] 3511 2-9-0 0 .... NeilChalmers 2 44
(Derek Haydn Jones) *s.i.s: rn green and a in last trio: rdn and wknd over 2f out* **50/1**

9 *1/2* **Subtle Embrace (IRE)** 2-9-0 0 .... LukeMorris 7 42
(Harry Dunlop) *in tch: pushed along over 4f out: rdn and lost pl over 2f out: wl bhd over 1f out* **16/1**

1m 13.24s (1.34) **Going Correction** +0.075s/f (Slow) 9 Ran SP% **113.7**
Speed ratings (Par 91): **94,92,91,90,88 86,83,80,80**
toteswingers:1&2:£9.10, 2&3:£8.10, 1&3:£4.70 CSF £103.42 TOTE £7.20: £2.70, £6.60, £1.10; EX 75.60.
Owner Sultan Ali **Bred** D J Weston **Trained** Newmarket, Suffolk

FOCUS
The bare form looks ordinary, but this fillies' maiden should produce winners.

NOTEBOOK
Fire And Sparks improved on her debut performance when fifth at Kempton last time and she took another significant step forward to run out a ready winner. She had keen kept on honest up front, but still found plenty and looks the type to keep progressing with time and distance. (op 9-2 tchd 4-1)
Correct had hinted at ability on her debut before being beaten 43l next time (reported to have hung right throughout), but this was more like it. She could win a similar race and also now has the option of nurseries. (op 20-1 tchd 25-1)
Baltic Flyer(IRE) confirmed the ability she showed on her debut at Newbury without quite building on it as much as one might have expected. There may yet be better to come. (op 6-1 tchd 7-2)
White Spirit(IRE) ensured the winner didn't have it all her own way up front, but she did not quite see her race out. A half-sister to last year's very speedy juvenile Face The Problem, 5f might suit her better and handicaps are now an option. (op 8-1 tchd 15-2)
Continuity(IRE) again showed ability without really progressing from her debut. She didn't help herself with a slow start and also flashed her tail when hit with the whip. (op 15-8)
Musically didn't build on the form she showed over 7f on her introduction at Newbury, the drop in distance not appearing to suit. (op 7-2)
Country Wolf ♦'s sales price increased from 14,000gns last year to 48,000gns in April and she hinted at ability without being given too hard a time. (tchd 66-1)

3982 PAUL KELLEWAY MEMORIAL/BRITISH STALLION STUDS E B F CLASSIFIED STKS 1m (P)
4:30 (4:31) (Class 3) 3-Y-O+ **£5,498** (£1,636; £817; £408) **Stalls** High

Form RPR
3005 **1** **Layline (IRE)**[27] 3085 4-9-4 90 .... RobertWinston 8 94
(Gay Kelleway) *hld up in last pair: gd hdwy on outer over 3f out: rdn to ld ent fnl f: edgd lft but r.o wl ins fnl f* **5/1**[2]

110 **2** *1 1/2* **Uphold**[18] 3411 4-9-4 90 ....(b) DavidProbert 5 91
(Gay Kelleway) *led: rdn wl over 1f out: hdd ent fnl f: kpt on same pce ins fnl f* **15/2**[3]

0000 **3** *3/4* **Suited And Booted (IRE)**[21] 3290 4-8-11 87 .... LewisWalsh(7) 4 89
(Jane Chapple-Hyam) *in tch: rdn and effrt to chse ldrs on inner over 1f out: no ex and styd on same pce ins fnl f* **12/1**

1210 **4** *1 3/4* **Wilfred Pickles (IRE)**[67] 1898 5-9-4 82 .... DaneO'Neill 3 85
(Jo Crowley) *hld up in last quartet: rdn and effrt jst over 1f out: edgd lft and kpt on ins fnl f: nvr gng pce to rch ldrs* **15/2**[3]

55-0 **5** *1* **Hurricane Spirit (IRE)**[28] 3045 7-9-4 82 .... LukeMorris 6 83
(Terry Clement) *t.k.h: hld up in midfield: rdn and jostling match w rival 2f out: kpt on u.p ins fnl f: nvr gng pce to rch ldrs* **33/1**

42-0 **6** *hd* **Emerald Wilderness (IRE)**[11] 3645 7-9-4 90 ....(p) JimCrowley 1 82+
(Robert Cowell) *hld up in tch: rdn and effrt on inner over 1f out: styd on same pce and no imp fnl f* **5/2**[1]

0610 **7** *nse* **Ezdeyaad (USA)**[13] 3542 7-9-4 87 .... JackMitchell 9 82
(Ed Walker) *taken down early: in tch on outer: hdwy to join ldr over 2f out: rdn to ld narrowly over 1f out: hdd 1f out: wknd ins fnl f* **18/1**

-166 **8** *3/4* **Cloud Illusions (USA)**[11] 3648 3-8-7 81 ow1 .... EddieAhern 11 80
(Heather Main) *hld up in last pair: effrt on outer 2f out: styd on same pce and no imp fr over 1f out* **10/1**

0-05 **9** *1* **Cloudy Start**[31] 2955 5-9-4 90 ....(p) FergusSweeney 10 80
(Jamie Osborne) *chsd ldr tl over 2f out: rdn and unable qck wl over 1f out: btn 1f out: wknd ins fnl f* **8/1**

00-0 **10** *7* **Able Master (IRE)**[31] 2954 5-9-4 89 .... AdamKirby 2 62
(Jeremy Gask) *taken down early and ponied to s: chsd ldrs on inner: rdn over 3f out: lost pl and in rr whn nt clr run 2f out: sn bhd* **12/1**

0300 **11** *11* **Vitznau (IRE)**[18] 3410 7-8-13 87 ....(p) JamesRogers(5) 7 37
(Robert Cowell) *s.i.s: a in rr: rdn and lost tch over 2f out: wl bhd fnl 2f* **25/1**

1m 36.99s (-1.21) **Going Correction** +0.075s/f (Slow)
WFA 3 from 4yo+ 9lb 11 Ran SP% **116.4**
Speed ratings (Par 107): **109,107,106,105,104 103,103,103,102,95 84**
toteswingers:1&2:£7.80, 2&3:£17.30, 1&3:£15.00 CSF £41.93 TOTE £6.30: £2.50, £2.30, £3.20; EX 30.10.
Owner Whispering Winds & Partner **Bred** Mrs M E Slade **Trained** Exning, Suffolk

FOCUS
A race named in honour of former jockey/trainer Paul Kelleway and his daughter trained the one-two. This looked typically competitive for a classified event and the pace seemed reasonable.

NOTEBOOK
Layline(IRE), runner-up in this race last year when with Ralph Beckett, stepped up on his recent turf performances with a ready success. Prior to this his top six RPRs had been achieved on Polytrack. (op 9-2 tchd 11-2)
Uphold, the long-timer leader, looked likely to be swamped early in the straight, but he stuck on well, finding only his stable companion too strong. He's been racing over further recently and ran as though in need of more of a test, but whatever, he was a shrewd claim by this yard for £14,000 back in May. (op 8-1 tchd 7-1)
Suited And Booted(IRE), having his first start since leaving Richard Hannon, would have been 3lb better off with the front two in a handicap. This was much better than his four previous efforts this season. (op 10-1)
Wilfred Pickles(IRE) had quite a bit to find with the front three at the weights, but he's a strong-travelling horse who's just the type to run above himself in decent company. This was his first run for 67 days. (op 10-1)
Hurricane Spirit(IRE), a triple course winner, could have done with a bit more room in the straight, but he still stepped up on the form he showed on his debut for this yard on his recent return from the best part of a year off. (tchd 40-1)

Emerald Wilderness(IRE) was the subject of strong market support having shaped well on his return from a long absence at Sandown earlier in the month, but he didn't get the best of trips and was one-paced. He's not the most reliable, but could yet do a bit better considering this was only his second run back. (op 9-4 tchd 2-1)

3983 PLAY ROULETTE AT LADBROKES.COM H'CAP — 6f (P)

5:00 (5:00) (Class 5) (0-75,80) 3-Y-O — **£2,385** (£704; £352) **Stalls** Low

Form — RPR

161 **1** **Redvers (IRE)**[7] 3723 3-9-8 **80** 6ex................ HarryBentley(5) 4 — 87+
(Ralph Beckett) *chsd ldng trio: pushed along and hdwy over 1f out: rdn to ld ins fnl f: sn in command: comf* — **8/13**[1]

-500 **2** *1* **Wolf Slayer**[19] 3337 3-8-11 **64**................ RichardKingscote 5 — 68
(Tom Dascombe) *led: rdn wl over 1f out: drvn and hdd ins fnl f: kpt on same pce* — **15/2**[2]

36-5 **3** *1* **Zalano**[142] 636 3-8-12 **65**................ DaneO'Neill 7 — 66
(Derek Haydn Jones) *chsd ldr over 4f out: rdn 2f out: lost 2nd jst over 1f out and styd on same pce ins fnl f* — **16/1**

0024 **4** *1 1/4* **Pippa's Gift**[21] 3271 3-9-5 **72**................ HayleyTurner 1 — 69
(William Muir) *t.k.h early: chsd ldrs: rdn and effrt 2f out unable qck u.p over 1f out: btn whn swtchd rt wl ins fnl f* — **8/1**[3]

6306 **5** *2 3/4* **Saucy Buck (IRE)**[6] 3765 3-8-13 **66**................ JamieGoldstein 3 — 54
(Ralph Smith) *a in last trio: pushed along wl over 2f out: rdn and no imp fr over 1f out* — **16/1**

10-0 **6** *1 1/4* **Jolah**[50] 2383 3-9-7 **74**................(t) ChrisCatlin 6 — 58
(Clive Brittain) *stdd s: t.k.h: hld up in last trio: rdn and effrt wl over 1f out: no prog and nvr trbld ldrs* — **8/1**[3]

0400 **7** *6* **Silly Billy (IRE)**[13] 3537 3-8-12 **70**................ JemmaMarshall(5) 2 — 35
(Sylvester Kirk) *a outpcd in last: struggling bdly fr 1/2-way* — **22/1**

1m 12.56s (0.66) **Going Correction** +0.075s/f (Slow) — 7 Ran SP% **112.0**
Speed ratings (Par 100): **98,96,95,93,90 88,80**
toteswingers:1&2:£2.60, 2&3:£9.30, 1&3:£3.20 CSF £5.58 TOTE £2.00: £1.30, £2.20; EX 7.10.
Owner R A Pegum **Bred** Peter Jones And G G Jones **Trained** Kimpton, Hants

FOCUS
A modest sprint handicap.
T/Plt: £57.20 to a £1 stake. Pool of £58,597.22 - 747.77 winning tickets. T/Qpdt: £19.20 to a £1 stake. Pool of £3,250.48 - 124.80 winning tickets. SP

3644 SANDOWN (R-H)

Wednesday, July 13

OFFICIAL GOING: Good (good to firm in places; sprint 8.0; round 8.3)
Wind: Light, across Weather: Fine but cloudy

3984 FEDERATION OF BLOODSTOCK AGENTS MAIDEN STKS — 5f 6y

6:15 (6:17) (Class 5) 2-Y-O — **£2,264** (£673; £336; £168) **Stalls** Low

Form — RPR

44 **1** **Safari Storm (USA)**[77] 1619 2-9-3 0................(t) MartinDwyer 4 — 77+
(Brian Meehan) *racd off rail: pressed ldr: led after 2f: pushed along and in command whn edgd rt fnl f: sn clr* — **4/1**[3]

2 *3* **Hannibal Hayes (USA)** 2-9-3 0................ RyanMoore 1 — 67
(Jeremy Noseda) *racd against rail: led 2f: pressed wnr after: rdn 2f out: hld whn hmpd 150yds out and snatched up: kpt on* — **9/4**[2]

0 **3** *hd* **Elegant Flight**[60] 2113 2-8-12 0................ KierenFallon 3 — 60
(Alan Jarvis) *w ldng pair 2f: lost pl bdly and rdn sn after: rallied fnl f: styd on to take 3rd post* — **9/1**

3 **4** *hd* **Lana (IRE)**[30] 2992 2-8-12 0................ JamieSpencer 6 — 60
(Michael Bell) *trckd ldng trio: wnt 3rd 1/2-way: rdn towards outer 2f out: no imp after* — **6/4**[1]

6 **5** *1* **Colourful Event (IRE)**[11] 3639 2-8-12 0................ FrankieMcDonald 2 — 56
(David Arbuthnot) *racd against rail: in tch: green and light reminders over 3f out: outpcd fr 2f out: kpt on* — **25/1**

0 **6** *1 1/4* **The Wicked Lord**[23] 3229 2-9-3 0................ FergusSweeney 7 — 57+
(Stuart Kittow) *settled in rr: pushed along and no prog 2f out: one pce after* — **18/1**

0 **7** *5* **Welease Bwian (IRE)**[19] 3349 2-9-3 0................ SaleemGolam 5 — 39
(Stuart Williams) *stdd s: tk fierce hold and hld up: prog on wd outside after 2f: rdn 2f out: sn wknd* — **66/1**

00 **8** *2 1/4* **Our Boy Billy**[13] 3552 2-9-3 0................ JimCrowley 9 — 33+
(Robert Cowell) *dwlt and swvd lft s: a last: wl bhd fr 1/2-way* — **50/1**

62.51 secs (0.91) **Going Correction** +0.025s/f (Good) — 8 Ran SP% **113.3**
Speed ratings (Par 94): **93,88,87,87,85 83,75,72**
toteswingers:1&2:£2.20, 1&3:£5.40, 2&3:£2.60 CSF £13.16 TOTE £5.10: £1.40, £1.30, £1.30; EX 14.60.
Owner N Attenborough,Mrs L Mann,Mrs L Way **Bred** Sf Bloodstock **Trained** Manton, Wilts
■ Stewards' Enquiry : Martin Dwyer caution: careless riding.

FOCUS
As at the Coral Eclipse meeting, the round course was on the innermost configuration and the far rail on the sprint course was 3yds in. After a dry night and day the ground was changed to good, good to firm in places on both courses and the winning rider described the ground as "perfect, good ground". A very ordinary maiden by Sandown standards. The gallop was reasonable and the four behind the winner finished in a heap. The fourth is the best guide to the level.

NOTEBOOK
Safari Storm(USA), with the tongue-tie again fitted, had the run of the race on this first run since April and turned in his best effort to win an ordinary maiden with a fair bit in hand. He should prove equally effective over 6f and may do better in nurseries. (op 7-2)
Hannibal Hayes(USA), a £67,000 first foal of a sprint winner in Canada, held his place in the market and showed ability at an ordinary level. He would have finished a bit closer but for being checked in the closing stages, is in good hands and is entitled to improve for this experience. (op 2-1 tchd 5-2 and 11-4 in a place)
Elegant Flight, who was nibbled at a double-figure price, stepped up on her debut effort, in the process shaping as though the step up to 6f would be more to her liking. She is another that may progress once qualified for a mark. (op 12-1)
Lana(IRE) looked to have solid claims in an uncompetitive event but who failed to build on last month's debut run. She's likely to remain vulnerable in this type of event. (op 13-8 tchd 7-4)
Colourful Event(IRE) should be suited by 6f and may do better in run-of-the-mill nurseries in due course. (tchd 22-1)
The Wicked Lord wasn't unduly knocked over a trip that didn't look to suit about but is going to have to raise his game by some way to figure in maiden company. (op 25-1)

Welease Bwian(IRE) was soundly beaten after racing on the outside on only this second run but who has enough about him physically to suggest he can leave this bare form behind at some stage.

3985 SPINAL INJURIES ASSOCIATION H'CAP — 5f 6y

6:50 (6:50) (Class 4) (0-85,82) 3-Y-O — **£4,075** (£1,212; £606; £303) **Stalls** Low

Form — RPR

1-61 **1** **Manoori (IRE)**[42] 2611 3-9-4 **79**................ TedDurcan 1 — 88+
(Chris Wall) *racd against rail: hld up bhd ldrs in 4th: shkn up 2f out: eased out and squeezed through jst over 1f out: rdn to ld last 150yds: styd on wl* — **5/2**[2]

3-31 **2** *1* **Bless You**[27] 3090 3-9-7 **82**................ DaneO'Neill 6 — 88+
(Henry Candy) *chsd ldng pair and racd wd: rdn over 2f out: nudged by rival jst over 1f out: styd on but outpcd last 150yds* — **9/4**[1]

6214 **3** *3/4* **Alpha Delta Whisky**[21] 3269 3-9-1 **76**................ TomQueally 4 — 79
(John Gallagher) *racd off rail: led: rdn and edgd lft over 1f out: hdd and one pce last 150yds* — **6/1**

1554 **4** *3/4* **Chevise (IRE)**[21] 3283 3-8-13 **79**................ HarryBentley(5) 3 — 79
(Steve Woodman) *settled in 5th: rdn 2f out: no prog tl styd on last 150yds: nrst fin* — **8/1**

1154 **5** *1* **Rambo Will**[26] 3136 3-8-4 **65**................ DavidProbert 2 — 62
(J R Jenkins) *racd against rail: pressed ldr: rdn 2f out: wknd fnl f* — **8/1**

64-3 **6** *4* **Riverdale (IRE)**[88] 1391 3-9-2 **77**................ EddieAhern 5 — 59
(Nigel Tinkler) *a last: rdn over 3f out and struggling: sn btn* — **5/1**[3]

61.26 secs (-0.34) **Going Correction** +0.025s/f (Good) — 6 Ran SP% **112.5**
Speed ratings (Par 102): **103,101,100,99,97 91**
toteswingers:1&2:£1.10, 1&3:£3.30, 2&3:£2.90 CSF £8.61 TOTE £4.00: £2.10, £1.60; EX 7.30.
Owner Hassan Al Abdulmalik **Bred** T J Monaghan **Trained** Newmarket, Suffolk

FOCUS
A useful handicap in which the two progressive market leaders filled the first two placings. The gallop was sound and the time was 1.25s quicker than the opening maiden.

3986 SPINAL INJURIES ASSOCIATION MEDIAN AUCTION MAIDEN STKS — 7f 16y

7:20 (7:27) (Class 5) 2-Y-O — **£2,587** (£770; £384; £192) **Stalls** Low

Form — RPR

0 **1** **Mister Music**[18] 3401 2-9-3 0................ RyanMoore 7 — 82+
(Richard Hannon) *settled off the pce in 10th: gd prog on outer over 2f out: wnt 2nd over 1f out: rdn to ld last 150yds: sn clr* — **3/1**[1]

02 **2** *3 1/2* **Maccabees**[17] 3425 2-9-3 0................ JamesMillman 14 — 73
(Rod Millman) *led and sn clr: rdn over 2f out: hdd and one pce last 150yds* — **11/1**

40 **3** *1* **Flying Trader (USA)**[18] 3401 2-9-3 0................ LukeMorris 8 — 71
(Jane Chapple-Hyam) *fractious bef ent stalls: chsd ldrs in 5th: rdn wl over 2f out: styd on over 1f out: tk 3rd ins fnl f* — **20/1**

04 **4** *1 1/2* **Tudor Empire (IRE)**[18] 3401 2-9-3 0................(b[1]) WilliamBuick 5 — 67
(John Gosden) *chsd ldng trio: shkn up 3f out: nt pce to cl fr 2f out: plugged on* — **5/1**[2]

5 **5** *2 1/4* **Enjoying (IRE)**[26] 3132 2-9-3 0................ DaneO'Neill 6 — 61
(Richard Hannon) *dwlt: hld up in last quartet: sme prog over 2f out: shkn up over 1f out: styd on: nrst fin* — **15/2**

6 *1* **Spanish Wedding** 2-9-3 0................ AndreaAtzeni 1 — 59+
(Marco Botti) *chsd ldrs disputing 6th: pushed along over 2f out: no prog tl kpt on steadily fnl f* — **16/1**

0 **7** *hd* **Lunar Deity**[17] 3424 2-9-3 0................ TomQueally 16 — 58
(Eve Johnson Houghton) *a abt same pl: no imp on ldrs 2f out: kpt on fnl f: n.d* — **66/1**

62 **8** *nk* **Breaking The Bank**[18] 3408 2-9-3 0................ GeorgeBaker 13 — 57
(William Muir) *chsd clr ldr to over 1f out: wknd rapidly fnl f* — **11/2**[3]

9 *3/4* **Operation Tracer** 2-9-3 0................ JamieSpencer 12 — 56
(Michael Bell) *awkward to load into stalls: chsd ldrs disputing 6th: shkn up and no prog 2f out: n.d after* — **16/1**

10 *4 1/2* **Dont Take Me Alive** 2-9-3 0................ AdamKirby 2 — 44
(Clive Cox) *nvr beyond midfield: rdn over 2f out: wknd over 1f out* — **33/1**

11 *3/4* **Benzanno (IRE)** 2-9-3 0................ DavidProbert 3 — 45+
(Andrew Balding) *hld up in rr: pushed along over 2f out: no prog over 1f out: wknd* — **16/1**

12 *3/4* **Always A Sinner (USA)** 2-9-3 0................ ShaneKelly 4 — 41
(William Knight) *a in last quartet: shkn up and no prog 2f out* — **40/1**

13 *7* **Kingscombe (USA)** 2-9-3 0................ JimmyFortune 15 — 23
(Pat Eddery) *s.i.s: rn green in last pair: a wl bhd* — **16/1**

14 *3/4* **Kozmina Bay** 2-8-12 0................ EddieAhern 9 — 16
(Jonathan Portman) *s.s: rn green in last pair: a bhd* — **100/1**

1m 30.32s (0.82) **Going Correction** +0.025s/f (Good) — 14 Ran SP% **113.3**
Speed ratings (Par 94): **96,92,90,89,86 85,85,84,84,78 78,77,69,68**
toteswingers:1&2:£9.60, 2&3:£28.20, 1&3:£7.70 CSF £33.01 TOTE £3.80: £1.60, £2.10, £6.30; EX 40.50.
Owner Longview Stud & Bloodstock Ltd **Bred** Longview Stud & Bloodstock Ltd **Trained** East Everleigh, Wilts

FOCUS
No more than a fair maiden but the well-backed market leader turned in an improved effort. The gallop was sound and this form should prove reliable.

NOTEBOOK
Mister Music ◆ was well supported and duly stepped up a good deal on his debut in this truly run race and first start on a sound surface. The manner of this win coupled with his pedigree suggests the step up to 1m should suit even better and he's the sort to hold his own in slightly stronger company. (op 9-2)
Maccabees had shown fair form over this trip at Salisbury on his previous start and ran at least as well under a positive ride. He's likely to remain vulnerable to the better types in this grade but remains capable of picking up a small event at some point. (op 9-1)
Flying Trader(USA) turned in his best effort, despite finishing further behind the winner than he had done at Newmarket on his previous start. He should also be able to pick up a race over further when stepped into nurseries.
Tudor Empire(IRE) finished ahead of the winner and third at Newmarket on his previous start but failed to confirm those placings in the first-time blinkers. He looks a galloper and may be better suited by 1m. (tchd 9-2)
Enjoying(IRE) showed ability over 6f on his debut at Newmarket and bettered that effort over this longer trip after making up plenty of late ground on the outside. As with a few of these, he will be another to take into nursery company granted a stiffer test. (op 10-1)
Spanish Wedding, a 32,000gns yearling and brother to a 2m winner, showed ability, despite his inexperience, on this racecourse debut. He is in good hands and will be one to keep an eye on.
Breaking The Bank had shown improved form at Windsor on his previous run but didn't get home under a positive ride on his first run over this trip. He has a bit of physical scope and wouldn't be one to write off just yet. (op 5-1 tchd 6-1)

Operation Tracer, an 11,000gns half-brother to useful 7f winner Quadrant, proved difficult to load but hinted at ability and should come on a fair bit for this experience.

3987 SIS H'CAP — 1m 14y
7:55 (7:58) (Class 4) (0-85,85) 3-Y-0+ — **£4,075** (£1,212; £606; £303) **Stalls** Low

Form — RPR

631 **1** — **Stage Attraction (IRE)**[23] 3218 3-9-0 **82** .... DavidProbert 2 — 88+
(Andrew Balding) *trckd ldng pair: smooth prog to go 2nd over 2f out: shkn up to ld over 1f out: sn pressed: rdn and readily asserted fnl f* **9/4**[1]

-1 **2** 1 ½ **Galiando**[33] 2875 3-9-0 **82** .... JimmyFortune 1 — 85+
(Jeremy Noseda) *hld up in 5th: looking for room on inner over 2f out: nt clr run briefly wl over 1f out: rdn and styd on fnl f to take 2nd last 50yds* **7/2**[3]

-502 **3** ½ **Dukes Art**[21] 3285 5-9-9 **82** .... RobertHavlin 5 — 86
(James Toller) *hld up in 6th: prog on outer 2f out: rdn to chal jst over 1f out: outpcd fnl f: lost 2nd last 50yds* **3/1**[2]

2320 **4** ½ **Ethics Girl (IRE)**[106] 1030 5-9-4 **84** ....(t) HannahNunn(7) 3 — 87
(John Berry) *hld up in last: rdn and detached 2f out: styd on wl fr jst over 1f out: nrst fin* **20/1**

3031 **5** 2 **Moheebb (IRE)**[11] 3620 7-9-12 **85** ....(b) PJMcDonald 6 — 83
(Ruth Carr) *led to over 1f out: wknd fnl f* **6/1**

1200 **6** 2 ½ **Uncle Fred**[37] 2769 6-9-6 **79** .... JimCrowley 4 — 71
(Patrick Chamings) *t.k.h: hld up in 4th: rdn and nudged by rival 2f out: wknd over 1f out* **8/1**

-500 **7** 2 ¼ **Beauchamp Yorker**[7] 3740 4-9-11 **84** .... JamesDoyle 7 — 71
(Hans Adielsson) *racd wd 1st 2f: chsd ldr to over 2f out: sn wknd* **33/1**

1m 43.63s (0.33) **Going Correction** +0.025s/f (Good) — **7** Ran SP% **111.1**
WFA 3 from 4yo+ 9lb
Speed ratings (Par 105): **99,97,97,96,94 92,89**
toteswingers:1&2:£1.30, 2&3:£2.20, 1&3:£1.60 CSF £9.73 TOTE £2.90: £2.50, £1.90; EX 6.60.
Owner Miss A V Hill **Bred** Dermot Cantillon And Forenaghts Stud **Trained** Kingsclere, Hants
■ Stewards' Enquiry : David Probert one-day ban: careless riding (Jul 28)

FOCUS
A useful handicap in which the two unexposed handicap newcomers filled the first two places. The gallop was just an ordinary one but this race should throw up winners.

3988 ARBUTHNOT SECURITIES H'CAP — 1m 2f 7y
8:30 (8:31) (Class 4) (0-80,79) 3-Y-O — **£4,075** (£1,212; £606; £303) **Stalls** Low

Form — RPR

01 **1** — **Aiken**[18] 3377 3-9-2 **74** .... WilliamBuick 4 — 92+
(John Gosden) *hld up: racd awkwardly fr 4f out and stl looked green: prog to go 3rd over 1f out: rdn and picked up wl fnl f: clsd to ld last strides* **7/2**[3]

-340 **2** hd **Rastaban**[11] 3650 3-9-3 **75** .... JamieSpencer 5 — 92+
(William Haggas) *dwlt: sn trckd ldr: led over 7f out and increased tempo: drvn over 2f out: kpt on wl but hdd last strides* **3/1**[2]

-504 **3** 2 ¾ **Silken Thoughts**[18] 3390 3-8-6 **64** .... LukeMorris 6 — 75
(John Berry) *hld up in rr: smooth prog on inner to chse ldr 2f out: chal over 1f out: hld ent fnl f: wknd last 100yds* **14/1**

6042 **4** 4 ½ **Mr Perceptive (IRE)**[11] 3650 3-9-5 **77** .... RyanMoore 7 — 79
(Richard Hannon) *cl up: nt clr run briefly over 2f out: rdn and wknd over 1f out* **5/2**[1]

0540 **5** 4 **Orientalist**[11] 3650 3-9-5 **77** ....(p) FergusSweeney 3 — 71
(Eve Johnson Houghton) *cl up: chsd ldr over 3f out to 2f out: wknd over 1f out* **10/1**

4-31 **6** ¾ **Misty Isles**[15] 3478 3-9-7 **79** .... EddieAhern 2 — 72
(Heather Main) *wl in tch: shkn up over 2f out: wknd over 1f out: eased* **6/1**

4-40 **7** 2 ¾ **Guisho (IRE)**[13] 3543 3-9-1 **73** .... MartinDwyer 1 — 60
(Brian Meehan) *led at slow pce to over 7f out: lost 2nd over 3f out: wknd over 2f out* **9/1**

2m 10.16s (-0.34) **Going Correction** +0.025s/f (Good) — **7** Ran SP% **115.8**
Speed ratings (Par 102): **102,101,99,96,92 92,90**
toteswingers:1&2:£2.90, 2&3:£9.80, 1&3:£14.50 CSF £14.86 TOTE £4.20: £3.20, £1.80; EX [illegible]
Owner George Strawbridge **Bred** George Strawbridge **Trained** [illegible], Suffolk

FOCUS
A fair handicap but one in which a modest gallop only picked up turning for home. The first three finished clear but this bare form doesn't look entirely reliable.

3989 SCISSOR SISTERS HERE NEXT WEDNESDAY H'CAP — 1m 6f
9:00 (9:00) (Class 5) (0-75,70) 3-Y-O — **£2,587** (£770; £384; £192) **Stalls** Low

Form — RPR

-454 **1** — **Hollow Tree**[16] 3474 3-9-4 **67** .... JimmyFortune 5 — 78
(Andrew Balding) *mde all: rdn over 2f out: styd on stoutly to draw clr over 1f out: in n.d after* **13/2**

0022 **2** 4 ½ **May Contain Nuts**[34] 2857 3-9-2 **65** .... FergusSweeney 6 — 70
(Brendan Powell) *chsd wnr: rdn and cl enough over 2f out: nt qckn wl over 1f out: one pce after* **7/1**

0-00 **3** ½ **Strength And Stay (IRE)**[27] 3080 3-8-10 **59** .... EddieAhern 2 — 63
(Eve Johnson Houghton) *settled in 5th: reminder 6f out: rdn and struggling wl over 2f out: kpt on fr over 1f out: tk 3rd post* **12/1**

663 **4** hd **Golden City (IRE)**[33] 2871 3-9-7 **70** .... GeorgeBaker 3 — 74
(Chris Wall) *trckd ldng pair: looking for room over 2f out: rdn to dispute 2nd fr 2f out: no imp on wnr: one pce last 100yds* **4/1**[2]

00-2 **5** 2 ½ **Sea The Flames (IRE)**[21] 3268 3-8-6 **55** .... TadhgO'Shea 8 — 56
(Marcus Tregoning) *hld up last: rdn and struggling wl over 2f out: no real prog* **6/1**[3]

1-42 **6** 2 ¾ **Battery Power**[26] 3131 3-9-7 **70** .... KierenFallon 4 — 67
(Mark H Tompkins) *hld up in 4th: rdn and no prog 3f out: wknd over 1f out* **2/1**[1]

1140 **7** 8 **Szabo's Destiny**[19] 3364 3-9-7 **70** .... TomQueally 7 — 55
(James Given) *settled in 6th: pushed along over 4f out: rdn and btn over 2f out: wknd and hanging over 1f out* **8/1**

3m 5.50s (1.00) **Going Correction** +0.025s/f (Good) — **7** Ran SP% **112.3**
Speed ratings (Par 100): **98,95,95,95,93 92,87**
toteswingers:1&2:£6.40, 2&3:£14.00, 1&3:£10.20 CSF £48.18 CT £528.07 TOTE £7.10: £3.40, £2.40; EX 56.30.
Owner P A Brend **Bred** Mount Coote Stud **Trained** Kingsclere, Hants

FOCUS
A fair handicap run at no more than an ordinary gallop and one that saw those held up at a disadvantage. The two market leaders disappointed to varying degrees.
T/Jkpt: £17,126.80 to a £1 stake. Pool £24,122.31 - 1 winning ticket. T/Plt: £130.10 to a £1 stake. Pool £71,333.55 - 400.05 winning tickets. T/Qpdt: £78.00 to a £1 stake. Pool £5,264.88 - 49.90 winning tickets. JN

3990 - 3992a (Foreign Racing) - See Raceform Interactive

[3721] BATH (L-H)
Thursday, July 14

OFFICIAL GOING: Firm (9.1)
FIRM (9.1)
Wind: Moderate ahead Weather: Sunny early

3993 ASHTON GLASS NURSERY — 5f 11y
5:50 (5:52) (Class 5) 2-Y-O — **£2,587** (£770; £384; £192) **Stalls** Centre

Form — RPR

0012 **1** — **Fanrouge (IRE)**[6] 3800 2-9-6 **66** .... DaneO'Neill 3 — 71
(Malcolm Saunders) *in rr but in tch: nt clr run 2f out: qcknd 1f out: chsd ldrs fnl 120yds: drvn to ld cl home: readily* **9/2**

042 **2** ½ **Gin Twist**[8] 3745 2-9-0 **65** .... HarryBentley(5) 5 — 68
(Tom Dascombe) *chsd ldrs: drvn to ld ins fnl f: hdd and outpcd cl home* **3/1**[2]

0405 **3** 3 **Nude (IRE)**[12] 3639 2-8-10 **56** .... LiamKeniry 7 — 48
(Sylvester Kirk) *chsd ldr: rdn and ev ch fr 2f out: wknd fnl 120yds* **14/1**

000 **4** 1 ½ **Hawaiian Freeze**[22] 3270 2-8-5 **51** .... CathyGannon 6 — 38
(Richard Ford) *in rr but in tch: rdn 2f out: styd on same pce to take 4th wl ins fnl f* **20/1**

4443 **5** nse **Balm**[8] 3745 2-9-6 **66** .... SteveDrowne 4 — 52
(Richard Hannon) *led tl hdd ins fnl f: sn wknd* **7/2**[3]

000 **6** nse **Stans Deelyte**[47] 2504 2-8-0 **49** ow1 .... FrankieMcDonald 1 — 32
(Lisa Williamson) *chsd ldrs: rdn 2f out: wknd ins fnl f* **16/1**

15 **7** 1 ½ **Pressure Drop (IRE)**[18] 3435 2-9-7 **67** ....[1] J-PGuillambert 2 — 48
(Jo Hughes) *t.k.h: in rr but in tch: rdn and hdwy on outside to chse ldrs ins fnl 2f: wknd over 1f out* **9/4**[1]

62.93 secs (0.43) **Going Correction** 0.0s/f (Good) — **7** Ran SP% **113.5**
Speed ratings (Par 94): **96,95,90,88,87 87,85**
toteswingers: 1&2 £3.50, 1&3 £5.30, 2&3 £6.90. CSF £18.10 TOTE £5.70: £2.30, £2.10; EX 25.00.
Owner Chris Scott **Bred** Silk Fan Syndicate **Trained** Green Ore, Somerset
■ The 'official' ratings shown next to each horse are estimated and for information purposes only.

FOCUS
A modest but fairly competitive nursery contested solely by fillies. The winner more than confirmed her C&D form.

NOTEBOOK
Fanrouge(IRE) was easy in the market, despite the form of her penultimate win over C&D being franked by the second and third, and she had an excuse last time when really acting on the ground at Chepstow in a muddling three-runner affair. She had not encountered ground this fast, but handled it well. (op 5-1)
Gin Twist had previously been touched off by Piranha on the AW at Lingfield, showing improved form from her previous trio of runs in turf maidens. She ran to a similar level of form here on ground she would have found plenty quick enough. She is up to winning a similar race, simply finding one too good on this occasion. (tchd 11-4 and 7-2)
Nude(IRE) was in receipt of 10lb from the winner, who had beaten her a length and a half here last month. She was in contention until 1f out but was left looking one-paced. She does not appear to be progressing at this stage. (op 12-1)
Hawaiian Freeze was nibbled at in the market but never looked happy on this ground. She is struggling to find her niche. (op 33-1)
Balm helped set the pace but could not find another gear when asked. She appears genuine enough and is not one to write off yet. (op 10-3 tchd 4-1)
Stans Deelyte put up 1lb overweight, but it would not have made much difference. Having had a 47-day break after three very modest runs, she stuck to her guns and this was a big improvement on anything she'd previously achieved. (op 18-1 tchd 25-1)
Pressure Drop(IRE) had won on her debut when with Pat Murphy has not, as anticipated, amounted to much. Yet she had subsequently run well in defeat at Windsor for her new trainer Jo Hughes, despite hanging badly left. As a result, connections decided to equip her with first-time eye-shields here. She was truculent at the start and pulled very hard in restraint after breaking slowly. She was pulled wide to challenge but her rider was scrubbing away from a fair way out and she didn't appear to let herself down on this ground. (op 11-4)

3994 RG KELLY WINDOWS H'CAP — 5f 11y
[illegible] (Class 5) [illegible] — **£2,587** (£770; £384; £192) **Stalls** Centre

Form — RPR

2600 **1** — **Triple Dream**[35] 2832 6-9-3 **66** ....(tp) LiamKeniry 3 — 75
(Milton Bradley) *chsd ldrs: rdn to go 2nd 1f out: styd on u.p to ld fnl 30yds* **5/1**[3]

-151 **2** nk **Baby Queen (IRE)**[12] 3640 5-9-9 **72** .... J-PGuillambert 4 — 80
(Brian Baugh) *sn led: rdn along over 1f out: styd on u.p fnl f: hdd fnl 30yds* **7/2**[2]

6151 **3** 1 ¾ **Musical Bridge**[7] 3768 5-9-10 **73** 6ex ....(b) JimCrowley 1 — 75
(Lisa Williamson) *chsd ldr: rdn 2f out: lost 2nd 1f out: outpcd by ldng duo ins fnl f* **11/2**

1060 **4** 2 **Sugar Beet**[7] 3785 3-9-7 **75** .... ChrisCatlin 2 — 68
(Ronald Harris) *in rr but in tch: rdn and hdwy fr 2f out: nvr on terms w ldrs: no ch ins fnl f* **20/1**

6-63 **5** 3 ¼ **Dubai Affair**[26] 3174 3-8-11 **65** .... LukeMorris 5 — 46
(Ronald Harris) *s.i.s: rdn 1/2-way and a outpcd* **12/1**

3022 **6** 2 ¼ **Whitecrest**[7] 3785 3-8-13 **67** .... CathyGannon 6 — 40
(John Spearing) *chsd ldrs tl wknd fr 2f out* **5/4**[1]

61.62 secs (-0.88) **Going Correction** 0.0s/f (Good) — **6** Ran SP% **111.2**
WFA 3 from 5yo+ 5lb
Speed ratings (Par 103): **107,106,103,100,95 91**
toteswingers: 1&2 £3.40, 1&3 £3.00, 2&3 £2.70. CSF £22.12 TOTE £9.40: £3.20, £2.20; EX 26.10.
Owner J M Bradley **Bred** Hesmonds Stud Ltd **Trained** Sedbury, Gloucs
■ Stewards' Enquiry : Liam Keniry two-day ban: excessive use of whip (28th, 29th July)

FOCUS
An decent little sprint handicap for the money and the pace was true.
Whitecrest Official explanation: jockey said filly was never travelling.

3995 OAKLEY GREEN CONSERVATORIES H'CAP — 5f 161y
6:50 (6:50) (Class 4) (0-80,76) 3-Y-O+ — **£4,851** (£1,443; £721; £360) **Stalls** Centre

Form — RPR

0235 **1** — **Ebraam (USA)**[41] 2662 8-9-10 **74** .... LukeMorris 4 — 82
(Ronald Harris) *hld up towards rr but in tch: gng wl but nt clr run ins fnl 2f: rdn and hdwy over 1f out: hung lft ins fnl f: styd on u.p to ld last strides* **13/2**[3]

5362 **2** hd **Comptonspirit**[13] 3582 7-9-7 **71** .... J-PGuillambert 2 — 78
(Brian Baugh) *in tch: pushed along 3f out: chsd ldr fr 2f out: str chal fr 1f out tl slt ld clsng stages: hdd last strides* **13/2**[3]

1033 **3** ½ **Wooden King (IRE)**[5] 3847 6-9-12 **76** TomMcLaughlin 6 81
(Malcolm Saunders) *led: rdn and jnd appr fnl f: strly chal thrght fnl f: hdd: nt qckn and dropped to 3rd clsng stages* **15/8**[1]

3100 **4** 3¾ **Kyllachy Storm**[18] 3427 7-8-12 **67** HarryBentley(5) 1 60
(Ron Hodges) *chsd ldrs: rdn over 1f out: wknd jst ins fnl f* **5/1**[2]

5105 **5** 1¼ **Dualagi**[30] 3020 7-8-13 **63** DaneO'Neill 7 52
(Martin Bosley) *in rr but in tch: drvn along 3f out: outpcd wl over 1f out: styd on again fnl 120yds* **18/1**

1341 **6** 4½ **Indian Shuffle (IRE)**[22] 3271 3-9-2 **72** LiamKeniry 5 45
(Jonathan Portman) *chsd ldrs: ev ch wl over 1f out: sn btn: wknd fnl f* **5/1**[2]

3305 **7** 2¼ **Riflessione**[125] 833 5-9-1 **65** (p) ChrisCatlin 3 32
(Ronald Harris) *chsd ldrs to 2f out: sn btn* **9/1**

1m 10.62s (-0.58) **Going Correction** 0.0s/f (Good)
WFA 3 from 5yo+ 6lb **7** Ran SP% **110.0**
Speed ratings (Par 105): **103,102,102,97,95 89,86**
toteswingers: 1&2 £9.10, 1&3 £3.10, 2&3 £3.50. CSF £43.64 TOTE £8.50: £3.40, £2.80; EX 70.60.
Owner Robert & Nina Bailey **Bred** Shadwell Farm LLC **Trained** Earlswood, Monmouths

FOCUS
A weak handicap for the class but it was a true test.

3996 PREMIER CONSERVATORY ROOFS H'CAP 5f 161y
7:25 (7:25) (Class 3) (0-95,93) 3-Y-0+ **£6,663** (£1,982; £990; £495) **Stalls** Centre

Form RPR

-000 **1** **Drawnfromthepast (IRE)**[46] 2525 6-9-5 89 SophieDoyle(3) 2 95
(Ed Walker) *chsd ldrs: drvn to chal fr over 1f out: styd on u.p to take slt ld fnl 75yds: hld on wl* **17/2**

4522 **2** *nk* **Restless Bay (IRE)**[13] 3598 3-8-5 78 (v) ChrisCatlin 4 82
(Reg Hollinshead) *in tch: nt clr run over 1f out and swtchd rt: no room and wnt lft jst ins fnl f: str run between horses fnl 120yds to take 2nd cl home but nt rch wnr* **8/1**

1326 **3** *nk* **Yurituni**[28] 3078 4-8-11 78 (v) CathyGannon 1 82
(Eve Johnson Houghton) *chsd ldr: rdn to chal fr wl over 1f out tl slt ld ins fnl f: narrowly hdd fnl 75yds: lost 2nd last strides* **12/1**

3111 **4** *nse* **Pick A Little**[22] 3269 3-8-3 81 HarryBentley(5) 7 84
(Ron Hodges) *chsd ldrs: rdn on outside 2f out: styd on wl thrght fnl f: gng on cl home* **5/1**[3]

0410 **5** *nk* **Piazza San Pietro**[5] 3841 5-9-12 93 DaneO'Neill 6 96
(Andrew Haynes) *in rr: drvn and hdwy on outside over 1f out: styd on wl fnl 120yds: gng on clsng stages* **3/1**[2]

2026 **6** 1¾ **Collect Art (IRE)**[5] 3846 4-9-4 85 SteveDrowne 5 82
(Andrew Haynes) *led: jnd over 1f out: hdd ins fnl f: wknd qckly fnl 50yds* **5/2**[1]

00-4 **7** 2½ **Caledonia Princess**[10] 3687 5-8-9 76 (b) LukeMorris 3 65
(Jo Hughes) *trckd ldrs: rdn: ev ch and edgd rt over 1f out: wknd qckly ins fnl f* **9/1**

1m 10.05s (-1.15) **Going Correction** 0.0s/f (Good)
WFA 3 from 4yo+ 6lb **7** Ran SP% **109.6**
Speed ratings (Par 107): **107,106,106,106,105 103,100**
toteswingers: 1&2 £17.60, 1&3 £6.90, 2&3 £14.00. CSF £66.14 TOTE £13.40: £6.60, £2.10; EX 120.80.
Owner B Greenwood, T Walker, South Wind Racing **Bred** D And Mrs D Veitch **Trained** Newmarket, Suffolk

FOCUS
A generous pace for this decent handicap. They all finished in a heap and while the handicapper may well be pleased with himself, the form may not hold up.

NOTEBOOK
Drawnfromthepast(IRE) had shown precious little in three runs for his new yard in May and the 46-day break appeared to have freshened him up. While his confidence may have been restored, it would be a minor surprise if he can follow up. (op 9-1 tchd 8-1)
Restless Bay(IRE) appears to relish racing, having had 32 starts and he's still only in his second season. He is still without a win on the turf after 14 attempts, but he was finishing to great effect and only just failed, having been switched towards the rail with 1f to run. He was a shade unlucky. (op 15-2)
Yurituni had plenty on her plate here, despite getting the fast ground she loves. She continued to find more when the winner came past and this was another gallant effort.
Pick A Little has been in blinding form, having won four of his five previous starts and considering he had to come wide to deliver his challenge, he lost no caste in defeat. He was staying on at the finish and this trip may have been just too sharp on this ground. (op 9-2)
Piazza San Pietro had to come widest of all and was doing his best work at the finish. He wasn't beaten far and he should remain of interest. (op 11-4)
Collect Art(IRE) travelled well up with the pace, before fading late on. He has won six times this year and the handicapper appears to be taking a firm hold now. It wasn't a bad effort by any means and he is holding his form. (op 11-4 tchd 9-4)
Caledonia Princess had the blinkers back on and she ran well for a long while, but hung towards the far rail and didn't look an easy ride on this occasion. This was her second run in quick succession, having not been seen since September. She probably needed it and will be all the better for it next time. Official explanation: jockey said gelding was unsuited by firm ground. (op 10-1)

3997 MB FRAMES MAIDEN STKS 5f 161y
7:55 (7:55) (Class 5) 2-Y-0 **£2,264** (£673; £336; £168) **Stalls** Centre

Form RPR

1 **Waseem Faris (IRE)** 2-9-0 0 MartinHarley(3) 2 83+
(Mick Channon) *mde all: c clr fr 2f out: v easily* **8/11**[1]

50 **2** 8 **Sovereign Waters**[23] 3258 2-8-12 0 CathyGannon 5 52
(Eve Johnson Houghton) *wnt lft s and hung lft thrght: chsd wnr fr 2f outbut stl hanging bdly lft and nvr any ch* **5/1**[3]

3 4½ **Takeitfromalady (IRE)** 2-9-3 0 JimCrowley 3 42
(Ralph Beckett) *disp cl 2nd tl 2f out: fading whn crossed appr fnl f and dropped to 4th: styd on again to take mod 3rd fnl 120yds* **3/1**[2]

4 1½ **Purley Queen (IRE)** 2-8-12 0 LiamKeniry 4 32
(Sylvester Kirk) *pushed lft s: racd in 4th tl wnt n.d 3rd over 1f out: no ex and wknd bk into 4th fnl 120yds* **8/1**

1m 12.7s (1.50) **Going Correction** 0.0s/f (Good) **4** Ran SP% **110.7**
Speed ratings (Par 94): **90,79,73,71**
CSF £4.90 TOTE £1.40; EX 5.30.
Owner Jaber Abdullah **Bred** Rabbah Bloodstock Limited **Trained** West Ilsley, Berks

FOCUS
Probably no more than a modest sprint maiden which was run at a reasonable pace, but there was plenty to like about the way debutant Waseem Faris took the spoils. The form is pitched around the runner-up.

NOTEBOOK
Waseem Faris(IRE), a half-brother to Baby Queen, coasted away from his rivals suggests he has a bright future. He travelled kindly and asserted quickly when asked to go about his work. (op 4-5tchd 5-6 in places)
Sovereign Waters was the only one of the quartet who had any previous experience and she was taking a marked drop in trip, having run down the field over 7f at Newbury on her second start. She seems genuine enough, but she was made to look very one-paced - on ground she seemed to be hating - by a potentially decent colt. She is bred to appreciate much further and will be interesting in nurseries. Official explanation: jockey said filly hung left. (op 11-2 tchd 6-1)
Takeitfromalady(IRE) looked one of the stable's more backward juveniles and ran like the experience would do him good. He travelled well but dropped out tamely under a considerate ride.
Purley Queen(IRE) appears to have ability. She is speedily bred but looked badly in need of the experience. Though beaten a long way, she will be all the better for this debut. (op 10-1)

3998 K2 CONSERVATORIES MAIDEN FILLIES' STKS 5f 161y
8:30 (8:30) (Class 5) 3-Y-0+ **£2,385** (£704; £352) **Stalls** Centre

Form RPR

2522 **1** **Sarangoo**[8] 3723 3-8-12 58 DaneO'Neill 6 63
(Malcolm Saunders) *trckd ldrs: chal 2f out: drvn to ld wl over 1f out: jnd jst ins fnl f: forged clr fnl 120yds* **5/2**[2]

040 **2** 2 **Adaeze (IRE)**[17] 3465 3-8-7 57 HarryBentley(5) 3 56
(Jonathan Portman) *chsd ldrs: chal 2f out: pressed wnr jst ins fnl f: readily outpcd fnl 120yds* **12/1**

2463 **3** 1¼ **Cheherazad (IRE)**[13] 3577 3-8-12 75 ChrisCatlin 7 52
(Paul Cole) *wnt rt s: t.k.h towards rr but in tch: hdwy on outside to chse ldrs ins fnl 2f: styd on same pce ins fnl f* **5/4**[1]

6660 **4** 1 **Silca Conegliano (IRE)**[8] 3724 3-8-9 50 (v[1]) MartinHarley(3) 5 49
(Mick Channon) *in tch: drvn to chse ldrs over 1f out: no ex u.p ins fnl f* **33/1**

03 **5** 6 **Festival Dance**[17] 3465 3-8-12 0 LukeMorris 1 29
(Ron Hodges) *led tl hdd wl over 1f out: sn btn* **9/1**

6 **6** 16 **Hollie**[17] 3465 3-8-12 0 SteveDrowne 4 —
(Peter Makin) *chsd ldr: chal 2f out: wknd rapidly wl over 1f out: eased whn no ch* **9/2**[3]

1m 11.14s (-0.06) **Going Correction** 0.0s/f (Good) **6** Ran SP% **111.8**
Speed ratings (Par 100): **100,97,95,94,86 65**
toteswingers: 1&2 £8.20, 1&3 £1.10, 2&3 £4.90. CSF £29.66 TOTE £2.70: £1.80, £6.70; EX 25.00.
Owner Chris Scott **Bred** M S Saunders And Chris Scott **Trained** Green Ore, Somerset

FOCUS
An ordinary fillies' maiden and the pace was no more than fair early on.
Cheherazad(IRE) Official explanation: jockey said filly was unsuited by firm ground.
Hollie Official explanation: jockey said filly was unsuited by firm ground.

3999 KEN BRAITHWAITE MEMORIAL H'CAP 5f 161y
9:00 (9:02) (Class 6) (0-55,56) 3-Y-0+ **£1,617** (£481; £240; £120) **Stalls** Centre

Form RPR

-02 **1** **My Meteor**[8] 3721 4-9-0 48 DaneO'Neill 6 60
(Tony Newcombe) *in tch: hdwy on outside 2f out: drvn to chal ins fnl f: slt ld fnl 150yds: drvn out* **6/1**

-301 **2** *nk* **Jolly Ranch**[8] 3721 5-9-6 54 6ex SteveDrowne 8 65
(Tony Newcombe) *w ldr over 3f out: str chal fr 2f out tl slt ld ins fnl f: hdd fnl 150yds: no ex cl home* **5/1**[3]

0122 **3** 1½ **Running Mate (IRE)**[33] 2920 4-9-7 55 (t) LiamKeniry 3 61
(Jo Crowley) *chsd ldrs: chal ins fnl 3f tl slt ld ins fnl 2f: hdd ins fnl f: no ex clsng stages* **4/1**[2]

2002 **4** ¾ **Cathcart Castle**[8] 3724 3-8-12 55 (v) MartinHarley(3) 7 58
(Mick Channon) *chsd ldrs: rdn wl over 1f out: wknd ins fnl f* **10/3**[1]

00-6 **5** 1 **Cliffords Reprieve**[18] 3433 3-8-11 56 ow1 LeeNewnes(5) 5 55
(Eric Wheeler) *t.k.h: sn slt ld: jnd over 3f out: hdd ins fnl 2f: wknd over 1f out* **33/1**

0 **6** *hd* **Welcome Approach**[12] 3617 8-9-7 55 LukeMorris 4 55
(John Weymes) *hood removed late and s.i.s: in rr: hdwy on ins to cl on ldrs 2f out: nvr gng pce to chal and wknd fnl f* **8/1**

00U2 **7** 1¾ **Pinball (IRE)**[3] 3908 5-8-13 50 (p) RobertLButler(3) 9 44
(Lisa Williamson) *wnt rt s: in rr and t.k.h: hdwy on outside 2f out: nvr gng pce to chal and wknd 1f out* **9/1**

1m 11.86s (0.66) **Going Correction** 0.0s/f (Good)
WFA 3 from 4yo+ 6lb **7** Ran SP% **98.1**
Speed ratings (Par 101): **95,94,92,91,90 90,87**
toteswingers: 1&2 £5.00, 1&3 £6.00, 2&3 £5.20. CSF £25.30 CT £71.04 TOTE £5.10: £1.60, £3.40; EX 23.80.
Owner A G Newcombe **Bred** M P B Bloodstock Ltd **Trained** Yarnscombe, Devon

FOCUS
A dreadful handicap which lost a lot of the interest with the withdrawal of the favourite Miss Firelfly, who dumped her rider and got loose. The pace was not honest, it turned into something of a 2f sprint but produced a thrilling finish.
T/Plt: £571.30 to a £1 stake. Pool of £39,527.21 - 50.50 winning tickets. T/Qpdt: £60.10 to a £1 stake. Pool of £3,445.94 - 42.40 winning tickets. ST

3754 DONCASTER (L-H)
Thursday, July 14

OFFICIAL GOING: Good (good to firm in places; 7.6)
GOOD (Good to firm in places; 7.6)
Wind: Light half behind Weather: Cloudy with sunny periods

4000 BETA TECHNOLOGY APPRENTICE H'CAP 5f
6:30 (6:30) (Class 6) (0-65,64) 3-Y-0+ **£2,726** (£805; £402) **Stalls** High

Form RPR

-306 **1** **Liberty Ship**[12] 3640 6-9-1 **54** (t) EdmondLinehan(3) 1 65
(Mark Buckley) *hld up in rr: smooth hdwy 2f out: nt clr run over 1f out: effrt to chse ldr ent fnl f: shkn up and qcknd to ld last 100yds* **9/2**[2]

5224 **2** 1 **Royal Blade (IRE)**[11] 3662 4-8-3 **46** DanielleMooney(7) 6 53
(Alan Berry) *cl up: led 2f out: rdn and edgd lft ent fnl f: hdd and one pce last 100yds* **7/2**[1]

0045 **3** 1½ **Sea Salt**[11] 3662 8-9-7 **60** RachealKneller(3) 7 62
(Ron Barr) *in tch: hdwy wl over 1f out: rdn and edgd lft ent fnl f: kpt on* **11/2**

3503 **4** *hd* **Elhamri**[9] 3711 7-10-0 **64** MatthewLawson 4 65
(Conor Dore) *chsd ldrs: rdn along wl over 1f out: one pce ent fnl f* **11/2**

0201 **5** 2¼ **Almaty Express**[9] 3714 9-9-8 **61** 6ex (b) JustinNewman(3) 2 54
(John Weymes) *chsd ldrs on outer: rdn along wl over 1f out: wknd appr fnl f* **8/1**

4660 **6** ½ **Simple Rhythm**[9] 3714 5-9-3 **53** (p) RosieJessop 5 44
(John Ryan) *led: rdn along and hdd 2f out: sn wknd* **5/1**[3]

0044 **7** *1 1/4* **King Of Swords (IRE)**[2] 3931 7-8-10 **51**..........(p) DavidSimmonson[(5)] 3 37
(Nigel Tinkler) *trckd ldrs: effrt over 2f out: rdn wl over 1f out: sn wknd* **13/2**

59.58 secs (-0.92) **Going Correction** -0.10s/f (Good) **7** Ran SP% **112.3**
Speed ratings (Par 101): **103,101,99,98,95 94,92**
toteswingers: 1&2 £5.40, 1&3 £6.70, 2&3 £4.70. CSF £19.79 TOTE £7.40: £3.20, £2.90; EX 19.40.
Owner David Lockwood & Fred Lockwood **Bred** Mrs R D Peacock **Trained** Castle Bytham, Stanford

FOCUS
Inside rail on Round course moved out 6yds which added 57yds to 1m2f60yds races. A modest opener on what looked well-watered ground but at least it was well run and the result looked the right one. the winner was up a length on this year's form.

4001 LAURIE BOLGER HAPPY BIRTHDAY MEMORIAL NOVICE STKS 6f
7:00 (7:00) (Class 5) 2-Y-O **£3,234** (£962; £481) **Stalls** High

Form RPR
2212 **1** **Stonefield Flyer**[30] 3014 2-9-2 0.. TomEaves 2 100
(Keith Dalgleish) *qckly away: mde all: pushed along 2f out: rdn wl over 1f out: styd on strly* **1/4**[1]

1 **2** *4* **Pimpernel (IRE)**[19] 3388 2-9-0 0.................................... FrankieDettori 1 86
(Mahmood Al Zarooni) *trckd wnr: effrt over 2f out: rdn wl over 1f out: no imp fnl f* **3/1**[2]

041 **3** *11* **Lady Nickandy (IRE)**[36] 2823 2-8-6 0......................... KieranO'Neill[(5)] 4 50
(Alan McCabe) *chsd ldng duo: rdn along bef 1/2-way: sn outpcd* **28/1**[3]

1m 12.7s (-0.90) **Going Correction** -0.10s/f (Good) **3** Ran SP% **108.4**
Speed ratings (Par 94): **102,96,82**
CSF £1.36 TOTE £1.30; EX 1.20.
Owner G R Leckie **Bred** Ian Crawford And Gordon Leckie **Trained** Carluke, South Lanarkshire

FOCUS
An uncompetitive minor event that went the way of the horse with easily the best form in a race that was still something of a tactical affair despite a fair gallop. Stonefield Flyer still matched his pre-race figure.

NOTEBOOK
Stonefield Flyer gave the Windsor Castle form another boost, not as if it was in need of it, with a fairly bloodless success much as expected, soon in front after a lightning break and always having things well under control on the rail, the runner-up accepting things inside the last. He's bags of pace and if he goes to Goodwood as the trainer intends, there's a good chance he'll be seen to better effect in the Molecomb rather than the Richmond. (op 4-9 tchd 1-2)
Pimpernel(IRE) hadn't won much of a race at Lingfield on her debut but she'd done it well and gave it her best shot without ever looking from halfway as if she could give the winner a race. For all she was eased, the winning margin doesn't flatter the winner and she'll probably have to cope with a tough handicap mark if she doesn't prove up to winning a similar event, perhaps back among her own sex. Her pedigree suggests 7f will suit better. (op 2-1)
Lady Nickandy(IRE) hadn't gone into the stalls for the Windsor Castle but if she had she'd have clearly finished a long way behind Stonefield Flyer, struggling here before halfway to hold her position. Ordinary nurseries are where she fits in. (op 20-1)

4002 E B F LIGHT DRAGOONS COLONEL'S APPEAL MAIDEN FILLIES' STKS 7f
7:35 (7:36) (Class 5) 2-Y-O **£3,476** (£1,026; £513) **Stalls** High

Form RPR
6 **1** **Elbe**[48] 2467 2-9-0 0.. TomQueally 4 85+
(Sir Henry Cecil) *trckd ldrs: smooth hdwy to ld 1 1/2f out: green and edgd rt ent fnl f: kpt on* **1/1**[1]

2 *1 1/4* **Arley Hall** 2-9-0 0.. TonyHamilton 10 80+
(Richard Fahey) *in tch: hdwy 3f out: chsd ldrs over 2f out: rdn wl over 1f out: kpt on ins fnl f* **40/1**

3 *hd* **Vezzali (USA)** 2-9-0 0.. FrankieDettori 6 79+
(Mahmood Al Zarooni) *dwlt: sn in tch: hdwy wl over 2f out: rdn to chal over 1f out: drvn and one pce ins fnl f* **13/2**[2]

4 *3* **Scarlet Whispers** 2-9-0 0.. MickyFenton 9 71+
(Pam Sly) *s.i.s and in rr: stdy hdwy 1/2-way: in tch over 2f out: rdn: green and edgd lft over 1f out: kpt on fnl f* **16/1**

0 **5** *3/4* **Jumeirah Palm Star**[25] 3201 2-9-0 0................................. EddieAhern 5 70
(Richard Hannon) *led 2f: cl up tl led again 1/2-way: rdn along 2f out: hdd 1 1/2f out: sn edgd rt and grad wknd* **20/1**

0 **6** *nk* **Perfect Paradise** 2-9-0 0.. WilliamBuick 7 69+
(John Gosden) *towards rr: hdwy 1/2-way: rdn to chse ldrs wl over 1f out: edgd lft and one pce ent fnl f* **13/2**[2]

30 **7** *4* **Bedlam**[22] 3274 2-9-0 0.. DavidAllan 13 58
(Tim Easterby) *midfield: hdwy on outer to trck ldrs 1/2-way: sn cl up: rdn along 2f out: grad wknd* **15/2**[3]

8 *1 3/4* **Small Steps (IRE)** 2-9-0 0... RichardMullen 8 54
(Ed McMahon) *trckd ldrs: pushed along 3f out: rdn over 2f out: grad wknd* **28/1**

9 *nk* **Champagne Valley** 2-8-11 0.................................. MichaelO'Connell[(3)] 2 53
(Sharon Watt) *a towards rr* **100/1**

00 **10** *5* **Emley Moor**[21] 3314 2-9-0 0... KellyHarrison 11 40
(Chris Fairhurst) *cl up: led after 2f: hdd 1/2-way: sn rdn along and wknd* **200/1**

11 *2 1/2* **Sweet Fairnando** 2-9-0 0.. DuranFentiman 1 34
(Tim Easterby) *s.i.s: sn outpcd and bhd* **100/1**

03 **12** *hd* **Angel Kiss (IRE)**[44] 2587 2-9-0 0................................ DanielTudhope 12 33
(David O'Meara) *cl up: pushed along 1/2-way: sn rdn and wknd* **25/1**

13 *13* **Party Line** 2-9-0 0.. KierenFallon 3 —
(Mark Johnston) *chsd ldrs on outer: rdn along over 3f out: sn wknd* **12/1**

1m 25.92s (-0.38) **Going Correction** -0.10s/f (Good) **13** Ran SP% **119.0**
Speed ratings (Par 91): **98,96,96,92,92 91,87,85,84,79 76,76,61**
toteswingers: 1&2 £17.30, 1&3 £2.70, 2&3 £111.10. CSF £67.30 TOTE £2.10: £1.20, £11.50, £1.90; EX 54.40.
Owner K Abdulla **Bred** Juddmonte Farms Ltd **Trained** Newmarket, Suffolk

FOCUS
Probably no more than a fair fillies maiden overall and one run at no more than a fair pace initially with the runners tending to avoid the stand rail. The winner looks decent though and there is more to come.

NOTEBOOK
Elbe's debut sixth at Newmarket had been franked in no uncertain fashion since (second went on to win the Cherry Hinton, the third the Albany) and she wasn't hard pressed to get off the mark without looking quite up to that class herself yet, still clearly plenty to learn as she changed her legs and ran very green in front. While there's probably a fair bit more to come, it was noticeable she showed quite a round action and it may be she'll prove best this year in the autumn as the ground softens. (op 10-11)
Arley Hall ◆, a filly by Excellent Art out of a 2yo 6f winner and daughter of a US Grade 2 8.5f winner, made a promising debut and looks sure to win a similar event, taking a while for the penny to drop and never travelling with the same fluency as the winner but sticking to her task well close home. (op 50-1)
Vezzali(USA), by Medalgia d'Oro and the third foal of a winning US sprinter, also shaped well, almost getting upsides the winner with over 1f to run but unable to sustain her run and losing second close home. (tchd 6-1)
Scarlet Whispers has plenty of stamina in her pedigree, being by Sir Percy out of a 2yo 1m winner, and she shaped well on her debut, keeping on without being given a hard time. Her stable know a good filly when they see one, and she seems sure to progress and win a race. (tchd 25-1)
Jumeirah Palm Star was another not given a hard time once beaten, but she had the run of things in front dictating the pace so doesn't need too many excuses with her already having had a run. That said, her stable usually know what they're doing when they bring youngsters back in trip and it will be interesting to see if she's returned to 6f next time. (op 25-1)
Perfect Paradise, by Giant's Causeway out of a mare that stayed 1m4f and is a sister to three Oaks-placed fillies, couldn't quite muster the pace to get to the leaders but she was looked after late on and will surely leave this form behind in due course later this year as her stamina is tested more. (op 8-1)
Bedlam hasn't gone on since her debut but looks a filly with something about her and isn't one to give up on if she's given a break. (op 8-1)
Small Steps(IRE), by Acclamation and out of a 7f/9f winner, wasn't obviously strong in the market and didn't show much immediate promise but is entitled to improve. (op 33-1)

4003 ESQUIRES COFFEE WHEATLEY RETAIL PARK CONDITIONS STKS 1m (S)
8:05 (8:05) (Class 3) 4-Y-O+ **£6,663** (£1,982; £990; £495) **Stalls** High

Form RPR
214- **1** **Secrecy**[257] 7234 5-8-12 110.. FrankieDettori 5 112
(Saeed Bin Suroor) *hld up in rr: hdwy over 3f out: rdn to ld over 1f out and sn edgd rt: styd on* **7/4**[1]

4003 **2** *1 3/4* **Invisible Man**[29] 3032 5-8-9 107.......................................(b) TedDurcan 2 105
(Saeed Bin Suroor) *trckd ldng pair: hdwy to ld 2f out: sn rdn and hdd over 1f out: kpt on same pce fnl f* **9/4**[2]

40-0 **3** *2 1/2* **Lord Zenith**[78] 1600 4-8-9 109.. KierenFallon 1 99
(Andrew Balding) *t.k.h: cl up tl led after 1 1/2f and sn swtchd rt to stands' rail: pushed along 3f out: rdn and hdd 2f out: hld whn n.m.r over 1f out* **5/1**

/36- **4** *5* **Palavicini (USA)**[409] 2593 5-8-9 111..................................... EddieAhern 4 88
(John Dunlop) *hld up in rr: hdwy to take clsr order 1/2-way: rdn to chse ldrs over 2f out: wknd wl over 1f out* **7/2**[3]

-400 **5** *12* **Colonial (IRE)**[140] 682 4-8-12 109................................. RichardMullen 3 63
(Saeed Bin Suroor) *led 1 1/2f: cl up tl rdn along over 2f out and sn wknd* **14/1**

1m 36.99s (-2.31) **Going Correction** -0.10s/f (Good) **5** Ran SP% **112.7**
Speed ratings (Par 107): **107,105,102,97,85**
CSF £6.18 TOTE £2.50: £1.60, £2.40; EX 3.30.
Owner Godolphin **Bred** Whatton Manor Stud **Trained** Newmarket, Suffolk

FOCUS
Little between the runners on official ratings but an uncompetitive event with a couple clearly below their best. The pace picked up after 2f or so, having been steady initially, the runners sticking more to the stand rail this time. The winner is probably the best guide to the form.

NOTEBOOK
Secrecy looked the Godolphin stable pick with his record in these sort of races in mind, a good record fresh and Dettori electing to ride him ahead of their other two runners. He wasn't hard pressed to gain a cosy success, getting to the readily and never pressed seriously by his stable mate under hands and heels, and something like the Group 3 Sovereign Stakes at Salisbury in which he was third last year might be on the agenda again next month. (op 13-8 tchd 15-8 tchd 2-1 in places)
Invisible Man came here after an excellent effort in the Hunt Cup but the tempo of that race was totally different to this one and his lack of tactical speed was laid bare by his winning stable companion, his rider accepting second from some way out. Presumably he'll head next for the totesport Mile in which he was second last year off a mark of 101. (op 2-1 tchd 5-2 in places)
Lord Zenith is being held back by his keen nature (early to post again) but the ability is there and he'd have finished closer had not been crossed by the winner late on, and perhaps too had his stride been used earlier, as he still looked to have some running left in him passing the line. (op 17-2 tchd 9-1)
Palavicini(USA) ran some way below his best on his first run since May last year but this isn't really a race to judge him on, for all he still looks to possess some of his free-going nature. (op 4-1 tchd 10-3)
Colonial(IRE) ended up the early pacemaker but the manner in which he dropped out on his debut here was hardly auspicious for one that won three Listed races in France, the latest most as most recently as last autumn. Official explanation: jockey said colt had no more to give. (op 10-1 tchd 20-1)

4004 LILYWHITES H'CAP 1m 2f 60y
8:40 (8:41) (Class 4) (0-85,84) 4-Y-O+ **£4,075** (£1,212; £606; £303) **Stalls** Low

Form RPR
1131 **1** **Art Scholar (IRE)**[12] 3641 4-8-10 **73**................................ NeilChalmers 7 83+
(Michael Appleby) *hld up in rr: swtchd rt and gd hdwy 3f out: rdn to ld over 1f out: kpt on wl* **6/1**[2]

5652 **2** *1* **Standpoint**[12] 3641 5-9-0 **77**.. GrahamGibbons 5 84
(Reg Hollinshead) *hld up: hdwy 4f out: rdn to chse ldrs over 1f out: styd on wl u.p ins fnl f* **15/2**

2604 **3** *3/4* **Scamperdale**[14] 3544 9-9-4 **81**.. KellyHarrison 10 87
(Brian Baugh) *hld up in rr: hdwy wl over 2f out: rdn wl over 1f out: styd on ins fnl f: nrst fin* **14/1**

1435 **4** *hd* **Count Bertoni (IRE)**[22] 3276 4-9-2 **79**........................... DanielTudhope 2 85
(David O'Meara) *in tch: hdwy 4f out: chsd ldrs and n.m.r 2f out: rdn and ev ch ent fnl f: sn edgd lft and one pce* **11/2**[1]

6216 **5** *4* **Oriental Cavalier**[14] 3544 5-9-2 **79**............................(v) RoystonFfrench 8 77
(Mark Buckley) *trckd ldrs: hdwy over 3f out: rdn 2f out: drvn over 1f out and kpt on same pce* **14/1**

0-00 **6** *1 1/4* **Jo'Burg (USA)**[25] 3203 7-9-7 **84**.. PhillipMakin 6 79
(Ollie Pears) *in tch: effrt 3f out: rdn along over 2f out: nt clr run wl over 1f out: kpt on same pce* **7/1**[3]

0-03 **7** *nk* **Solicitor**[22] 3286 4-9-4 **81**... KierenFallon 11 76
(Mark Johnston) *trckd ldr: effrt and cl up over 3f out: rdn 2f out and ev ch tl drvn and wknd over 1f out* **8/1**

1114 **8** *1 1/4* **Frontline Phantom (IRE)**[36] 2810 4-8-3 **73**.......... MatthewLawson[(7)] 3 65
(Mrs K Burke) *set stdy pce: qcknd over 3f out: rdn over 2f out: drvn and hdd over 1f out: wknd* **6/1**[2]

0/0- **9** *nk* **Stevie Thunder**[67] 2640 6-8-12 **80**.................................. RyanClark[(5)] 4 72
(Ian Williams) *trckd ldng pair: hdwy on inner 3f out: chal over 2f out: sn rdn and ev ch tl drvn and wknd over 1f out* **16/1**

22-5 **10** *hd* **Silvery Moon (IRE)**[73] 1746 4-8-7 **70**............................... DavidAllan 12 61
(Tim Easterby) *dwlt: t.k.h in rr: effrt and sme hdwy over 3f out: sn rdn along and nvr a factor* **6/1**[2]

1000 11 8 **Follow The Flag (IRE)**[13] 3578 7-9-1 **83**..................(v) KieranO'Neill(5) 9 59
(Alan McCabe) *hld up: a towards rr* **40/1**
2m 12.69s (3.29) **Going Correction** +0.30s/f (Good) **11** Ran SP% **115.3**
Speed ratings (Par 105): **98,97,96,96,93 92,92,91,90,90 84**
toteswingers: 1&2 £5.00, 1&3 £12.00, 2&3 £11.40. CSF £49.48 CT £603.68 TOTE £7.30: £2.70, £3.20, £4.50; EX 59.70.
Owner D J Lewin **Bred** John Ramsbottom **Trained** Danethorpe, Notts

FOCUS
A fair handicap but one run at a steady pace and possibly muddling form, though there's little doubt the winner was the right one. He can do better still.
Silvery Moon(IRE) Official explanation: jockey said gelding ran too free.

4005 BALACLAVA H'CAP 1m 2f 60y
9:10 (9:10) (Class 5) (0-70,70) 3-Y-O **£3,749** (£1,107; £553) **Stalls** Low

Form RPR
0-33 **1** **Sangar**[12] 3615 3-8-7 **56**.. TomEaves 8 72
(Ollie Pears) *t.k.h early: trckd ldrs: hdwy 3f out: effrt 2f out: rdn to ld over 1f out: drvn ins fnl f and kpt on gamely* **6/1**[3]
4403 **2** ½ **Sciampin**[14] 3558 3-9-0 **63**.. AdamKirby 1 78
(Marco Botti) *trckd ldrs on inner: hdwy 3f out: rdn 2f out and ev ch: drvn ins fnl f: no ex towards fin* **3/1**[2]
060- **3** *nk* **Lordofthehouse (IRE)**[260] 7178 3-8-8 **57**.......................... EddieAhern 5 71+
(William Haggas) *s.i.s and in rr: hdwy 3f out: chsd ldrs whn n.m.r and hit over hd by opponents whip: drvn and styd on ins fnl f* **5/2**[1]
4102 **4** 5 **Goal (IRE)**[10] 3679 3-9-0 **68**.............................. RyanClark(5) 6 73
(Richard Guest) *hld up in rr: gd hdwy on wd outside 4f out: led wl over 2f out and sn rdn: drvn and hdd over 1f out: kpt on same pce* **10/1**
3100 **5** 2 **Tapis Libre**[21] 3318 3-9-4 **67**.. JamesSullivan 9 68
(Michael Easterby) *hld up towards rr: hdwy 3f out: swtchd rt and rdn 2f out: kpt on: nvr nr ldrs* **11/1**
0020 **6** 6 **Zaheeb**[18] 3432 3-8-9 **58**.. RichardMullen 2 47
(Dave Morris) *led: rdn along 3f out and sn hdd: grad wknd* **10/1**
62 **7** 1 ¼ **Celani**[35] 2850 3-9-5 **68**.. GrahamGibbons 3 55
(Tim Walford) *trckd ldr: effrt 3f out: sn rdn and wknd wl over 1f out* **7/1**
0646 **8** *nk* **May Burnett (IRE)**[1] 3976 3-7-13 **51** oh6.................(t) DeclanCannon(3) 7 37
(Brian Rothwell) *chsd ldrs on inner: rdn along over 3f out and sn wknd* **80/1**
53-6 **9** ¾ **Syncopated Lady (IRE)**[48] 2465 3-8-3 **52**...........(e[1]) DuranFentiman 10 37
(David O'Meara) *chsd ldrs on outer: pushed along over 4f out: rdn along over 3f out and sn wknd* **11/1**
2m 12.39s (2.99) **Going Correction** +0.30s/f (Good) **9** Ran SP% **116.4**
Speed ratings (Par 100): **100,99,99,95,93 88,87,87,87**
toteswingers: 1&2 £2.60, 1&3 £3.80, 2&3 £1.60. CSF £24.57 CT £56.96 TOTE £5.80: £1.50, £2.10, £2.10; EX 15.10.
Owner Timothy O'Gram **Bred** L C And Mrs A E Sigsworth **Trained** Norton, N Yorks

FOCUS
An ordinary handicap to end proceedings and again it turned into something of a test of finishing speed. The first three came clear and the form is sound enough.
Celani Official explanation: trainer was unable to offer a reason as to poor run.
T/Plt: £30.80 to a £1 stake. Pool of £53,497.36 - 1,265.17 winning tickets. T/Qpdt: £4.70 to a £1 stake. Pool of £4,721.75 - 732.78 winning tickets. JR

3760 EPSOM (L-H)
Thursday, July 14

OFFICIAL GOING: Good (good to firm in places)
GOOD (Good to firm in places)
Wind: Moderate, against Weather: Fine, warm

4006 BETFAIR SUPPORTS RACING WELFARE CLAIMING STKS 7f
6:10 (6:11) (Class 5) 3-Y-O+ **£2,587** (£770; £384; £192) **Stalls** Low

Form RPR
4340 **1** **Guilded Warrior**[18] 3436 8-9-2 82....................................... IanMongan 2 84
(Stuart Kittow) *mde all: shkn up over 2f out: hrd pressed and looked vulnerable over 1f out: battled on wl nr fin* **11/4**[2]
20-4 **2** *shd* **Woodcote Place**[18] 3436 8-9-12 86................................ GeorgeBaker 4 94
(Patrick Chamings) *trckd ldng pair: wnt 2nd 2f out gng wl: rdn to chal fnl f and upsides: outbattled last strides* **5/2**[1]
1102 **3** 1 ½ **Frognal (IRE)**[6] 3801 5-8-12 79................................(b) RobertLButler(3) 6 79
(Richard Guest) *t.k.h: hld up in 5th: wnt 3rd over 1f out gng easily: asked to go through gap between ldng pair fnl f: fnd nil* **5/1**
3502 **4** 3 ½ **Nezami (IRE)**[14] 3536 6-9-0 72..(b) NeilCallan 7 69
(John Akehurst) *chsd ldng trio: rdn and nt qckn over 2f out: no imp over 1f out* **8/1**
5055 **5** 5 **Bunce (IRE)**[26] 3179 3-8-13 78...................................... JamieSpencer 5 59
(Richard Hannon) *chsd wnr to 2f out: wknd qckly* **10/3**[3]
-005 **6** *shd* **Ancient Greece**[40] 2719 4-9-3 72..........................(t) MatthewDavies(3) 3 61
(George Baker) *sn in 6th: drvn and struggling to stay in tch 1/2-way: sn no ch* **20/1**
006 **7** 29 **Gessabelle**[16] 3494 4-8-0 35..(t) LeonnaMayor(7) 1 —
(Phil McEntee) *sn last: t.o bef 1/2-way* **125/1**
1m 22.96s (-0.34) **Going Correction** 0.0s/f (Good)
WFA 3 from 4yo+ 8lb **7** Ran SP% **111.7**
Speed ratings (Par 103): **101,100,99,95,89 89,56**
toteswingers: 1&2 £1.20, 1&3 £3.20, 2&3 £2.70. CSF £9.56 TOTE £3.50: £1.40, £3.10; EX 9.90.Guilded Warrior was claimed by P Butler for £10,000. Frognal was claimed by Conor Dore for £9,000.
Owner The Racing Guild **Bred** Manor Farm Packers Ltd **Trained** Blackborough, Devon

FOCUS
Rail dolled out up to 6yds from 1m to 7f, and 6f to Winning Post adding approximately 10yds to advertised distances. After a dry and warm day course officials changed the going description. This was a fair event for the class and the form is straightforward enough. The winner did not need to match this year's best.

4007 PLAY THE RACING LOTTERY E B F MAIDEN STKS 7f
6:40 (6:41) (Class 5) 2-Y-O **£3,881** (£1,155; £577; £288) **Stalls** Low

Form RPR
33 **1** **Repeater**[17] 3472 2-9-3 0.. StevieDonohoe 13 78
(Sir Mark Prescott Bt) *trckd ldrs: 4th st: prog to chal 2f out: narrow ld over 1f out: drvn to assert fnl f: jst hld on* **4/1**[1]
50 **2** *nse* **Goldoni (IRE)**[26] 3152 2-9-3 0.. DavidProbert 6 78+
(Andrew Balding) *chsd ldrs: hmpd 5f out: 7th st: rdn over 2f out: prog on outer over 1f out: styd on strly fnl f: jst failed* **5/1**[3]
32 **3** ¾ **Tones (IRE)**[10] 3673 2-9-3 0.. PatDobbs 2 76
(Richard Hannon) *cl up bhd ldr: disp ld 1/2-way: narrow advantage over 2f out: hdd over 1f out: kpt pressing wnr tl no ex last 100yds* **9/2**[2]
423 **4** 1 **Tidal Way (IRE)**[12] 3609 2-9-3 0...................................... SamHitchcott 5 74
(Mick Channon) *chsd ldrs: 5th st: rdn over 2f out: styd on fnl 2f but nvr quite gng pce to chal* **10/1**
0 **5** *hd* **Royal Academician (USA)**[13] 3590 2-9-3 0..................... GeorgeBaker 4 73+
(Gary Moore) *hld up: 8th st and last of those in tch: nt clr run over 2f out: sme prog but hanging lft after: styd on wl fnl f: gaining at fin* **12/1**
2 **6** 4 **Halling Dancer**[24] 3229 2-9-3 0...................................... DarryllHolland 10 63
(John Akehurst) *pressed ldr: disp ld 1/2-way to jst over 2f out: wknd over 1f out* **5/1**[3]
6 **7** *nse* **Tigers Tale (IRE)**[13] 3590 2-9-3 0..................................... JamieSpencer 1 66+
(Roger Teal) *hld up: hmpd 5f out: 10th and wl off the pce st: jst pushed along fr over 2f out and kpt on steadily: nrst fin* **15/2**
0 **8** 4 ½ **Scouting For Girls**[19] 3408 2-9-3 0.............................. StephenCraine 8 52
(Jim Boyle) *prom: v awkward downhill 5f out and lost pl: 6th st: hanging lft and no prog 2f out: fdd* **50/1**
0 **9** ½ **Ice Loch**[22] 3288 2-9-3 0.. WilliamCarson 11 50
(Michael Blanshard) *towards rr: nt handle downhill wl: rdn in 9th st and nt on terms: no prog* **100/1**
10 3 ¾ **Fox's Ambers (FR)** 2-8-12 0.. NeilCallan 12 36
(Richard Hannon) *s.s: a wl in rr: pushed along in 11th st: no prog* **16/1**
0 **11** 3 ¾ **Voodoo Rhythm (USA)**[19] 3401 2-9-3 0.......................... MartinDwyer 7 32
(Brian Meehan) *v restless stalls: dwlt: a wl in rr: last and wl bhd st* **14/1**
5 **12** 3 ¼ **Mr Hendrix**[24] 3221 2-8-12 0...................................... MarkCoumbe(5) 3 24
(Brett Johnson) *led to 1/2-way: sn wknd qckly* **100/1**
1m 25.16s (1.86) **Going Correction** 0.0s/f (Good) **12** Ran SP% **116.6**
Speed ratings (Par 94): **89,88,88,86,86 82,82,76,76,72 67,64**
toteswingers: 1&2 £6.30, 1&3 £5.80, 2&3 £4.80. CSF £23.32 TOTE £3.60: £1.10, £2.20, £2.70; EX 29.40.
Owner Cheveley Park Stud **Bred** W & R Barnett Ltd & Balmerino B'Stock **Trained** Newmarket, Suffolk

FOCUS
A competitive juvenile maiden and it saw tight finish. The third and fourth set the standard, with improvement from the winner.

NOTEBOOK
Repeater, despite being drawn widest of all, forged to the front half a furlong out and, just holding off the fast-finishing runner-up at the business end, opened his account at the third attempt. He was produced 2f out, but didn't look in love with the undulations and took time to hit full stride. This progressive son of Montjeu rates better than the bare form and his success added to his bang in-form trainer's excellent record at this course. (op 9-2)
Goldoni(IRE) ◆, ninth in the Chesham at Royal Ascot last month, took an age to get organised under pressure but finished strongly and was in front a stride after the line. This rangy colt is well up to winning an average maiden and looks a nice staying prospect for next year. (tchd 9-2)
Tones(IRE), who held every chance, has now improved with each of his three outings to date and sets the level. He just found this a touch too stiff and now qualifies for nurseries, where he should make his mark. (op 10-3)
Tidal Way(IRE) has now made the frame on each of his four career outings. He travelled nicely into contention, but lacked an immediate turn of foot and was just held. He looks likely to peak this year when faced with 1m. (tchd 8-1)
Royal Academician(USA) ◆ would have probably pushed the first pair really close had he broke better from the gates. He also fell out of the stalls on his debut so needs to iron that out, but is in decent hands and should be winning before long. (op 16-1 tchd 20-1 in a place)
Halling Dancer clearly failed to last out the extra furlong under such positive tactics.
Tigers Tale(IRE) ◆ was representing the same connections of last year's winner Surrey Star and met support to improve on his debut at Sandown, where he finished once place ahead of Royal Academican. However, his jockey took him back after breaking well and that ultimately cost him any chance. He will come on again for this and looks one to side with next time out. (op 8-1)

4008 BETFAIR SUPPORTS THE PRIDE OF RACING H'CAP 1m 4f 10y
7:15 (7:16) (Class 4) (0-80,80) 4-Y-O+ **£4,528** (£1,347; £673; £336) **Stalls** Centre

Form RPR
2053 **1** **High Figurine (IRE)**[19] 3381 4-9-5 **78**.......................... JamieSpencer 2 87
(William Haggas) *hld up in last: crept clsr over 2f out: plld out over 1f out: cajoled along and wl-timed run to ld last 75yds: won gng away* **9/2**[2]
-644 **2** 1 ¼ **If I Were A Boy (IRE)**[14] 3538 4-8-11 **70**.....................(p) JamesDoyle 6 77
(Dominic Ffrench Davis) *led: kicked on over 3f out: drvn over 2f out: edgd rt over 1f out: kpt on wl but hdd and outpcd last 75yds* **7/1**
-153 **3** 2 ½ **New Code**[7] 3762 4-9-6 **79**.. GeorgeBaker 4 83
(Gary Moore) *patiently rdn: 6th st: prog over 2f out: chsd ldr over 1f out and sn chalng: nt qckn fnl f: lost 2nd and btn whn checked last 100yds* **9/2**[2]
6622 **4** *hd* **Ramona Chase**[7] 3762 6-9-7 **80**.............................(t) RobbieFitzpatrick 3 83
(Michael Attwater) *wl in tch: 5th and rdn st: disp 2nd over 2f out to over 1f out: nt qckn u.p* **4/1**[1]
61-4 **5** ¾ **Foxhaven**[18] 3434 9-9-7 **80**..(v) DavidProbert 5 81
(Patrick Chamings) *cl up: 4th st: disp 2nd fr 3f out: hanging lft after: lost pl and sltly impeded over 1f out: sn btn* **5/1**[3]
-262 **6** 10 **Marju King (IRE)**[31] 3003 5-8-8 **67**............................(b) HayleyTurner 1 52
(Stuart Kittow) *t.k.h: cl up: 3rd st: chsd ldr 3f out to 2f out: wknd qckly* **5/1**[3]
0-00 **7** 10 **Epic (IRE)**[14] 3544 4-9-7 **80**...(v[1]) NeilCallan 8 49
(Mark Johnston) *chsd ldr to 3f out: wknd u.p: t.o* **8/1**
2m 38.35s (-0.55) **Going Correction** 0.0s/f (Good) **7** Ran SP% **113.3**
Speed ratings (Par 105): **101,100,98,98,97 91,84**
toteswingers: 1&2 £3.90, 1&3 £4.70, 2&3 £5.40. CSF £34.49 CT £148.08 TOTE £6.40: £3.40, £2.30; EX 65.30.
Owner D I Scott **Bred** D I Scott **Trained** Newmarket, Suffolk
■ Stewards' Enquiry : Jamie Spencer one day ban: careless riding (28th July)

FOCUS
A competitive handicap in which there was plenty of course form on offer. It was run at an uneven pace and plenty had their chance. The winner is rated back to her French 2yo form.

4009 BETFAIR SUPPORTS RACING'S BACKBONE H'CAP 1m 2f 18y
7:45 (7:47) (Class 4) (0-80,77) 3-Y-O **£4,528** (£1,347; £673; £336) **Stalls** Low

Form RPR
-321 **1** **Mystic Edge**[8] 3742 3-8-11 **67** 6ex.................................. JamieSpencer 1 77+
(Michael Bell) *led 150yds: trckd ldr after: poised to chal and jst nudged along over 2f out: led over 1f out: pressed and drvn fnl f: drifted rt but clung on* **6/4**[1]
1-20 **2** *nk* **Swindy**[7] 3774 3-9-7 **77**.. NeilCallan 3 84
(Paul Cole) *hld up in last pair: prog to go 3rd over 2f out: drvn and r.o to chse wnr ins fnl f: sn chalng: hung rt nr fin: jst hld* **7/2**[2]

4-00 **3** *4* **Bloodsweatandtears**[22] 3291 3-9-7 **77**......................(b[1]) HayleyTurner 7 76
(William Knight) *pushed up to ld after 150yds: urged along over 2f out: hdd and hanging over 1f out: one pce* **6/1**

-064 **4** *1* **Misk Khitaam (USA)**[41] 2664 3-9-2 **72**.............................. MartinLane 2 69
(John Dunlop) *cl up: disp 3rd st: rdn 3f out: outpcd 2f out: plugged on* **15/2**

-202 **5** *4 1/2* **Barathea Dancer (IRE)**[34] 2883 3-9-4 **77**...................... SeanLevey(3) 4 65
(Roger Teal) *cl up: disp 3rd st: rdn wl over 2f out: wknd wl over 1f out* **9/2**[3]

2510 **6** *hd* **Classic Voice (IRE)**[27] 3133 3-9-1 **71**........................(p) WilliamCarson 6 59
(Roy Brotherton) *in tch in last pair but nt gng wl after 4f: rdn over 3f out: sn btn* **20/1**

2m 9.12s (-0.58) **Going Correction** 0.0s/f (Good) **6** Ran SP% **111.2**
Speed ratings (Par 102): **102,101,98,97,94 94**
toteswingers: 1&2 £1.02, 1&3 £2.90, 2&3 £2.30. CSF £6.79 TOTE £2.10: £2.40, £1.30; EX 4.60.
Owner Herts And Hinds Racing Syndicate **Bred** F D Harvey **Trained** Newmarket, Suffolk

FOCUS
A tight 3yo handicap. It was run at a fair early pace and the form looks solid with the first pair coming clear. The winner looks better than the bare form.

4010 RACING WELFARE HELP FOR RACING'S PEOPLE H'CAP 7f
8:20 (8:20) (Class 4) (0-80,80) 3-Y-O+ **£4,528** (£1,347; £673; £336) **Stalls** Low

Form RPR

1333 **1** **Rondeau (GR)**[14] 3536 6-9-11 **77**.................................... GeorgeBaker 7 87
(Patrick Chamings) *hld up: 8th st but wl in tch: prog over 2f out: rdn to ld 1f out: drvn and styd on wl* **13/2**

5300 **2** *1* **Cat Hunter**[19] 3413 4-8-13 **65**...................................... KirstyMilczarek 11 72
(Ronald Harris) *in tch on outer: 6th st: rdn and effrt on outer over 2f out: styd on to press wnr ins fnl f: no ex last 100yds* **20/1**

-000 **3** *1/2* **Catalyze**[12] 3649 3-9-6 **80**...(t) DavidProbert 4 83
(Andrew Balding) *pressed ldr: gng strly over 2f out: shkn up to ld over 1f out: hdd 1f out: one pce* **7/2**[2]

6060 **4** *hd* **Glenridding**[15] 3506 7-9-10 **76**.. HayleyTurner 1 81
(James Given) *led: rdn and hdd over 1f out: kpt on fnl f: a hld* **8/1**

626- **5** *hd* **Elspeth's Boy (USA)**[226] 7637 4-9-11 **77**........................ JamieSpencer 5 82+
(William Haggas) *stdd s: hld up last: stl only 8th and pushed along over 1f out: styd on wl fnl f: no ch to chal* **3/1**[1]

5162 **6** *3/4* **Ree's Rascal (IRE)**[24] 3231 3-9-3 **77**........................... StephenCraine 3 77
(Jim Boyle) *trckd ldrs: 5th st: rdn over 2f out: cl up but hld whn n.m.r over 1f out: kpt on* **4/1**[3]

10 **7** *2 3/4* **Leadenhall Lass (IRE)**[68] 1898 5-9-1 **67**........................ IanMongan 2 62
(Pat Phelan) *prom: 3rd st: rdn over 2f out: stl cl up over 1f out: wknd fnl f* **17/2**

4465 **8** *1/2* **Silvee**[5] 3869 4-8-6 **61** oh10... SeanLevey(3) 6 55
(John Bridger) *wl in tch: 7th st: stl cl up on inner over 2f out: wknd fnl f* **28/1**

1226 **9** *12* **Fivefold (USA)**[154] 483 4-9-3 **69**.............................(p) DarryllHolland 10 30
(John Akehurst) *chsd ldrs: 4th st: sn rdn: wknd over 2f out: t.o* **20/1**

1m 24.01s (0.71) **Going Correction** 0.0s/f (Good)
WFA 3 from 4yo+ 8lb **9** Ran SP% **115.2**
Speed ratings (Par 105): **95,93,93,93,92 91,88,88,74**
toteswingers: 1&2 £20.10, 1&3 £6.00, 2&3 £5.00. CSF £125.45 CT £531.14 TOTE £8.70: £2.30, £5.20, £1.90; EX 189.70.
Owner The Foxford House Partnership **Bred** Ippotour Stud **Trained** Baughurst, Hants

FOCUS
A modest handicap, run at a fair pace. The form is rated around the runner-up, with a personal best from the winner.

Elspeth's Boy(USA) Official explanation: jockey said gelding was unsuited by track.

Fivefold(USA) Official explanation: jockey said colt was unsuited by good ground.

4011 JOCKEY CLUB SUPPORTS RACING WELFARE H'CAP 1m 114y
8:50 (8:50) (Class 5) (0-75,75) 3-Y-O **£2,587** (£770; £384; £192) **Stalls** Low

Form RPR

43-0 **1** **Cross Culture (IRE)**[15] 3514 3-9-5 **73**........................... DavidProbert 8 80
(Andrew Balding) *taken down early: tk fierce hold early: mde all: kicked on over 3f out: drvn and pressed fnl f: styd on wl* **16/1**

-540 **2** *1* **High On The Hog (IRE)**[23] 3259 3-8-11 **65**.................. JamieSpencer 4 70
(John Dunlop) *trckd ldrs in 4th: prog over 2f out: rdn to chse wnr wl over 1f out: tried to cl fnl f: a hld* **8/1**

-633 **3** *1/2* **Orthodox Lad**[20] 3346 3-9-3 **71**....................................... DarryllHolland 3 74
(John Best) *trckd ldng pair: shkn up over 2f out: nt qckn wl over 1f out: styd on same pce* **7/2**[2]

6051 **4** *1 1/4* **Uncle Dermot (IRE)**[18] 3432 3-9-1 **69**............................ GeorgeBaker 7 70
(Brendan Powell) *hld up in 6th: gng easily 3f out: prog 2f out: rdn and nt qckn over 1f out: one pce after* **15/2**

2022 **5** *nk* **Empress Charlotte**[10] 3688 3-8-7 **61**............................. HayleyTurner 1 66+
(Michael Bell) *hld up in 5th: nt clr run briefly on inner over 2f out: jst pushed along fnl 2f: kpt on but nvr nr to chal* **9/4**[1]

-660 **6** *1 1/4* **Buckland (IRE)**[14] 3557 3-9-7 **75**..................................(p) MartinDwyer 2 72
(Brian Meehan) *hld up in 7th: rdn wl over 2f out: kpt on fnl 2f but nvr gng pce to rch ldrs* **9/2**[3]

5654 **7** *6* **Countess Ellen (IRE)**[18] 3432 3-8-11 **65**..........................(p) NeilCallan 6 48
(Gerard Butler) *t.k.h: chsd wnr to wl over 1f out: wknd qckly: eased last 100yds* **16/1**

4-00 **8** *26* **Sylas Ings**[35] 2841 3-8-13 **67**..(vt[1]) IanMongan 5 —
(Pat Phelan) *nvr gng wl: mostly in last: rdn over 3f out: wknd: t.o and eased* **14/1**

1m 46.66s (0.56) **Going Correction** 0.0s/f (Good) **8** Ran SP% **112.5**
Speed ratings (Par 100): **97,96,95,94,94 93,87,64**
toteswingers: 1&2 £33.20, 1&3 £14.90, 2&3 £5.90. CSF £131.20 CT £557.13 TOTE £12.80: £3.80, £2.10, £2.10; EX 138.00.
Owner Favourites Racing XIX **Bred** Rathbarry Stud **Trained** Kingsclere, Hants

FOCUS
This was a moderate 3yo handicap and it was a race in which it proved hard to make up ground from off the pace. The winner had an easy lead and is rated in line with his final 2yo start.

Orthodox Lad Official explanation: jockey said colt was denied a run and hung left

T/Plt: £252.60 to a £1 stake. Pool of £52,006.79 - 150.25 winning tickets. T/Qpdt: £68.80 to a £1 stake. Pool of £4,129.65 - 44.40 winning tickets. JN

[3855]HAMILTON (R-H)
Thursday, July 14

OFFICIAL GOING: Good (good to firm in places)
Wind: Light, half behind Weather: Hot, sunny

4012 BRITISH STALLION STUDS SUPPORTING BRITISH RACING E B F MAIDEN STKS 6f 5y
2:00 (2:01) (Class 5) 2-Y-O **£3,749** (£1,107; £553) **Stalls** High

Form RPR

1 **Sardanapalus** 2-9-3 0.. PhillipMakin 4 78+
(Kevin Ryan) *noisy in paddock: slowly away: hld up: swtchd outside and smooth hdwy 1/2-way: rdn to ld ins fnl f: r.o* **5/4**[1]

4222 **2** *nk* **Joshua The First**[11] 3656 2-9-3 0...............................(v) PaulHanagan 2 69
(Keith Dalgleish) *cl up: rdn to ld over 1f out: hdd ins fnl f: kpt on* **9/4**[2]

50 **3** *2* **Electrickery**[7] 3755 2-8-12 0....................................... SilvestreDeSousa 6 58
(Mark Johnston) *led: rdn over 2f out: hdd over 1f out: kpt on same pce ins fnl f* **7/1**[3]

4 *3/4* **Elusive Island (USA)** 2-9-3 0.. FrannyNorton 1 61
(Ann Duffield) *t.k.h: prom: effrt and ev ch over 1f out: kpt on same pce ins fnl f* **9/1**

56 **5** *3 3/4* **Chorister Girl**[49] 2430 2-8-7 0.. DaleSwift(5) 7 45
(Howard Johnson) *w ldr: rdn over 2f out: wknd appr fnl f* **20/1**

50 **6** *3/4* **In A Jiffy (IRE)**[28] 3082 2-8-12 0.. LeeNewman 8 42
(David Barron) *trckd ldrs: rdn over 2f out: wknd over 1f out* **33/1**

7 *7* **Celestrial (IRE)** 2-9-3 0... TomEaves 5 26
(Bryan Smart) *noisy in paddock: s.i.s: rn green in rr: nvr on terms* **9/1**

0 **8** *1/2* **Flashbak (IRE)**[14] 3552 2-8-7 0....................................... LeeTopliss(5) 9 20
(Alan Bailey) *t.k.h: prom tl rdn and wknd over 2f out* **40/1**

9 *11* **Brian's Best** 2-9-3 0.. RichardKingscote 3 —
(Bruce Hellier) *in tch: drvn 1/2-way: sn struggling* **100/1**

1m 12.2s **Going Correction** -0.15s/f (Firm) **9** Ran SP% **118.8**
Speed ratings (Par 94): **94,93,90,89,84 83,74,73,59**
toteswingers:1&2:£1.50, 2&3:£2.10, 1&3:£3.20 CSF £4.17 TOTE £2.80: £1.30, £1.10, £2.00; EX 5.50 Trifecta £34.40 Pool: £568.46 - 12.21 winning units..
Owner J Nixon **Bred** Rosyground Stud **Trained** Hambleton, N Yorks

FOCUS
All races over distances beyond 6f measured 8yds further than the official distances, owing to the rail configuration on the Round course where fresh ground was provided. Jockeys in the first agreed the ground was quick, but with no jar. This was a modest maiden, run in a time 2.4 seconds outside the standard. The runners raced near the stands' rail. Sound form and an impressive winner, but the runner-up limits the rating.

NOTEBOOK
Sardanapalus ◆, who was well supported, came from last to first after appearing to have forfeited his chance at the start. After cruising up on the outside, he was carried to his right by the fourth before knuckling down well to see off the runner-up. A half-brother to Wave Aside, who was Listed-placed as a juvenile, he had been notably green in the parade ring and he looks certain to improve on the bare form of this debut victory. (tchd 6-4 and 13-8 in places)
Joshua The First set a fair standard and had every chance on this drop back in trip, but had to settle for a fourth successive second-place finish. His turn will come one day, but he is likely to remain opposable. (op 11-4)
Electrickery, from the yard on target in this race a year ago, ran a solid race and made up a couple of lengths on Joshua The First from their meeting at Carlisle last month. A step up to 7f and switch to nurseries should prove beneficial. (op 8-1 tchd 11-2)
Elusive Island(USA), a half-brother to a smart winner in the USA, was a bit free early and edged to his right under pressure, but was keeping on determinedly at the end. He should pay his way. (op 14-1)
Chorister Girl helped set the pace again before dropping out. (op 25-1 tchd 18-1)
In A Jiffy(IRE) was found wanting again but at least she didn't finish last this time.
Celestrial(IRE) is a half-brother to Distinctive, who won the Firth Of Clyde Stakes for the Smart stable in 2009. Green in the paddock, he was slowly away in the race and never figured, but he can surely improve on this with the experience to call on. (tchd 8-1)

4013 TOTEQUICKPICK H'CAP 6f 5y
2:30 (2:30) (Class 4) (0-80,80) 3-Y-O+ £5,175 (£1,540; £769; £384) **Stalls** Centre

Form RPR

5206 **1** **Jarrow (IRE)**[30] 3028 4-9-8 **76**.. AdrianNicholls 3 83+
(David Nicholls) *hld up: effrt and gd hdwy over 1f out: led wl ins fnl f: pushed out* **11/2**[3]

-662 **2** *1/2* **Sunrise Safari (IRE)**[28] 3071 8-9-7 **80**.........................(v) LeeTopliss(5) 6 85
(Richard Fahey) *trckd ldrs: effrt and rdn over 1f out: chsd wnr wl ins fnl f: r.o* **10/1**

0000 **3** *1/2* **Greyfriarschorista**[22] 3285 4-9-4 **72**.......................... SilvestreDeSousa 2 76
(Mark Johnston) *w ldr: rdn and led over 1f out: hdd and no ex wl ins fnl f* **8/1**

2204 **4** *2* **Red Cape (FR)**[5] 3880 8-9-3 **76**... DaleSwift(5) 8 73
(Ruth Carr) *led: rdn over 2f out: hdd over 1f out: kpt on same pce* **11/4**[1]

0000 **5** *1 1/4* **Solar Spirit (IRE)**[22] 3275 6-9-9 **77**................................. FrannyNorton 1 70
(Tracy Waggott) *in tch: shkn up and outpcd 2f out: no imp fnl f* **14/1**

4133 **6** *2 1/4* **Hinton Admiral**[16] 3488 7-9-4 **72**....................................... PaulHanagan 7 58
(Keith Dalgleish) *hld up in tch: rdn over 2f out: btn over 1f out* **9/2**[2]

2011 **7** *hd* **Mandalay King (IRE)**[7] 3759 6-9-10 **78** 6ex.................(p) PJMcDonald 5 64
(Marjorie Fife) *s.i.s: hld up: rdn over 2f out: nvr on terms* **8/1**

154 **8** *7* **Midnight Dynamo**[5] 3856 4-8-11 **65**............................. DanielTudhope 4 28
(Jim Goldie) *t.k.h: trckd ldrs tl edgd rt and wknd fr 2f out* **6/1**

1m 10.42s (-1.78) **Going Correction** -0.15s/f (Firm) **8** Ran SP% **112.5**
Speed ratings (Par 105): **105,104,103,101,99 96,96,86**
toteswingers:1&2:£8.80, 2&3:£14.60, 1&3:£9.90 CSF £56.14 CT £436.99 TOTE £7.70: £1.80, £2.60, £2.90; EX 65.90 Trifecta £289.20 Part won. Pool of £390.91 - 0.50 winning units..
Owner Dab Hand Racing **Bred** Derek Veitch **Trained** Sessay, N Yorks

FOCUS
An ordinary handicap, run in a time just under two seconds quicker than the juvenile maiden. In contrast to that race, the action took place down the centre of the track, although the winner did race on the stands' side of the group. He's rated back to his 3yo summer form with the runner-up setting the standard.

4014 ALWAYS TRYING MAIDEN STKS 1m 3f 16y
3:05 (3:05) (Class 5) 3-Y-O+ **£3,234** (£962; £481; £240) **Stalls** High

Form RPR

45-3 **1** **Mungo Park**[7] 3781 3-9-2 0.. SilvestreDeSousa 7 84+
(Mark Johnston) *hmpd s: prom: rdn to chal 3f out: led over 1f out: styd on wl: edgd lft nr fin* **15/8**[2]

4020 **2** *hd* **Sunday Bess (JPN)**[28] [3065] 3-8-11 83..................(v) RichardKingscote 3 79
(Tom Dascombe) *led at ordinary gallop: rdn and hrd pressed fr 3f out: hdd over 1f out: rallied: jst hld* **6/4**[1]

0 **3** *2* **Cape Rising (IRE)**[48] [2458] 4-9-9 0.................................. PJMcDonald 2 75
(Alan Swinbank) *t.k.h: trckd ldrs: effrt and swtchd lft over 2f out: rdn and kpt on steadily fnl f* **9/1**

06 **4** *2 ¼* **Convention**[19] [3385] 3-8-11 0.................................. PaulHanagan 1 71
(Ed Dunlop) *hld up in tch: rdn 3f out: hdwy over 1f out: no imp fnl f* **6/1**[3]

0 **5** *3 ¼* **Rose Of Sarratt (IRE)**[24] [3224] 3-8-11 0.................................. PhillipMakin 6 66
(Rae Guest) *hmpd s: hld up: hdwy on outside 3f out: edgd rt and wknd over 1f out* **10/1**

6 *16* **Snare**[33] 4-9-9 0.................................. DavidNolan 8 37
(Ann Duffield) *checked s: chsd ldr: rdn over 3f out: edgd rt: wknd over 2f out* **200/1**

7 *16* **Apassionforfashion** 3-8-11 0.................................. TomEaves 5 —
(Bryan Smart) *dived lft s: t.k.h in rr: lost tch fr 4f out: t.o* **50/1**

2m 25.19s (-0.41) **Going Correction** -0.15s/f (Firm)
WFA 3 from 4yo 12lb **7** Ran SP% **110.6**
Speed ratings (Par 103): **95,94,93,91,89 77,66**
toteswingers:1&2:£1.90, 2&3:£2.40, 1&3:£3.10 CSF £4.67 TOTE £3.20: £2.20, £2.10; EX 5.80 Trifecta £17.40 Pool: £828.76 - 35.20 winning units..
Owner Sheikh Hamdan Bin Mohammed Al Maktoum **Bred** Newsells Park Stud Limited **Trained** Middleham Moor, N Yorks

FOCUS
Just a fair maiden, lacking in depth and run at a modest pace. Three horses were hampered at the start as Apassionforfashion swerved leaving the stalls, amongst them the winner. The form makes a fair bit of sense, rated around the runner-up.

4015 TOTEPOOL GLASGOW STKS (LISTED RACE) 1m 3f 16y
3:40 (3:40) (Class 1) 3-Y-O **£23,680** (£8,956; £4,476; £2,236) **Stalls** High

Form RPR

2-10 **1** **Hunter's Light (IRE)**[28] [3068] 3-9-3 100.................................. PhillipMakin 5 107
(Saeed Bin Suroor) *t.k.h: stdd in tch: smooth hdwy to ld over 2f out: sn rdn and edgd rt: drvn out ins fnl f* **2/1**[2]

5024 **2** *nk* **Malthouse (GER)**[7] [3774] 3-9-3 98.................................. SilvestreDeSousa 6 106
(Mark Johnston) *cl up: wnt 2nd after 3f: rdn to chal over 2f out: kpt on up ins fnl f: hld nr fin* **5/4**[1]

210 **3** *5* **Albaraka**[35] [2839] 3-8-12 85.................................. SebSanders 7 92
(Sir Mark Prescott Bt) *led: rdn and hdd over 2f out: kpt on same pce fr over 1f out* **14/1**

3421 **4** *3 ¾* **Stella Point (IRE)**[19] [3385] 3-8-12 92.................................. HughBowman 4 85
(Mick Channon) *hld up in tch: hdwy to chse ldrs over 2f out: rdn and wknd over 1f out* **5/1**[3]

1104 **5** *10* **Palm Pilot (IRE)**[35] [2839] 3-8-12 90..................(p) PaulHanagan 3 67
(Ed Dunlop) *hld up: outpcd and hung rt 4f out: sn struggling: no ch after* **16/1**

-125 **6** *2 ¼* **Calypso Magic (IRE)**[26] [3159] 3-9-3 89.................................. FrederikTylicki 1 68
(Howard Johnson) *trckd ldrs tl rdn and wknd fr 3f out* **16/1**

2m 21.67s (-3.93) **Going Correction** -0.15s/f (Firm) **6** Ran SP% **112.9**
Speed ratings (Par 108): **108,107,104,101,94 92**
toteswingers:1&2:£1.60, 2&3:£2.50, 1&3:£3.10 CSF £4.93 TOTE £2.50: £1.20, £1.50; EX 4.70.
Owner Godolphin **Bred** Darley **Trained** Newmarket, Suffolk
■ Stewards' Enquiry : Silvestre De Sousa caution: excessive use of whip.

FOCUS
Run at York before switching to this venue in 2006, and previously held in May and regarded as a Derby trial, this was the first running at this time of year and fillies are now eligible. None of the runners had previously been successful at this level, but the first two, who came clear, showed good form for the grade. The winner is rated up 7lb. The pace was reasonable and the time was more than three seconds quicker than the preceding maiden.

NOTEBOOK
Hunter's Light(IRE)'s yard won this three years running from 2001-3. Easy winner of a decent Newmarket maiden, the colt was held on rain-softened ground in the Tercentenary Stakes at Ascot, where he failed to settle, and he was again keen early on here. At home on this faster surface, he travelled up well but took time to get the better of a determined rival, with his stamina for this longer trip perhaps beginning to wane late on. This was only his fourth run and he may have further improvement in him. He is worth a try in Group 3 company. (op 9-4)
Malthouse(GER)'s trainer won the last four May runnings of this event, most recently with St Leger third Corsica, and went close to extending the sequence. Reappearing just a week after his good fourth in a hot handicap at the Newmarket July festival, the Great Voltigeur entry fought on well but went down narrowly after a lively tussle. He had no problem with the longer trip and is well up to winning a race at this level. (op 7-4)
Albaraka, who needed a rug for stalls entry, made the running and stuck on for third once the first pair had kicked away. She had been well beaten in this grade at Newbury last month, but secured some invaluable black type here. (op 10-1)
Stella Point(IRE) was a good fourth to Oaks principals Izzi Top and Dancing Rain in a warm Listed race at Newbury before breaking her maiden at Doncaster. The Nassau Stakes entry was in fourth spot for much of the long straight without making any telling inroads and hinted that she'd appreciate a return to 1m2f. (op 9-2 tchd 4-1)
Palm Pilot(IRE) had Albaraka behind when missing black type by a nose at Newbury. This cleverly named filly has looked less than straightforward at times and confirmed that impression here as she hung with her jockey at the back of the field, looking a hard ride. She is very useful, but one to be wary of. (op 12-1)
Calypso Magic(IRE) gets 1m1f well but this extra quarter-mile found him out and he weakened badly. (tchd 14-1 and 18-1)

4016 HAMILTON-PARK.CO.UK CLAIMING STKS 6f 5y
4:15 (4:18) (Class 6) 3-Y-O+ **£1,940** (£577; £288; £144) **Stalls** Centre

Form RPR

-501 **1** **Zomerlust**[28] [3083] 9-9-6 85..................(v) PhillipMakin 2 87
(John Quinn) *mde all: pushed along 2f out: kpt on ins fnl f* **15/8**[2]

4050 **2** *2* **Sonny Red (IRE)**[6] [3832] 7-8-10 80.................................. ShirleyTeasdale(7) 4 78
(David Nicholls) *chsd wnr: edgd rt over 2f out: effrt over 1f out: kpt on fnl f: nt gng pce of wnr* **6/1**

0200 **3** *3* **Prince Of Vasa (IRE)**[20] [3359] 4-8-13 67.................................. PaulHanagan 3 64
(Michael Smith) *taken early to post: trckd ldrs: effrt and drvn 2f out: kpt on same pce fnl f* **9/2**[3]

2234 **4** *½* **Tro Nesa (IRE)**[3] [3900] 3-8-4 75..................(p) SilvestreDeSousa 5 59
(Ann Duffield) *in tch: effrt over 2f out: edgd rt and wknd over 1f out* **6/4**[1]

40 **5** *11* **Goninodaethat**[5] [3857] 3-8-9 0.................................. AndrewMullen 6 29
(Jim Goldie) *in tch tl rdn and wknd over 2f out* **66/1**

1m 10.88s (-1.32) **Going Correction** -0.15s/f (Firm)
WFA 3 from 4yo+ 6lb **5** Ran SP% **108.7**
Speed ratings (Par 101): **102,99,95,94,80**
CSF £12.53 TOTE £2.70: £1.90, £3.10; EX 13.70.
Owner Dawson And Quinn **Bred** The Lavington Stud **Trained** Settrington, N Yorks

FOCUS
A routine claimer, and probably not form to treat too literally. The winner didn't need to be at his best.

4017 BILL AND DAVID MCHARG MEMORIAL H'CAP 5f 4y
4:50 (4:51) (Class 6) (0-60,58) 3-Y-O+ **£1,940** (£577; £288; £144) **Stalls** Centre

Form RPR

6425 **1** **Wicked Wilma (IRE)**[13] [3582] 7-9-7 55.................................. PatrickMathers 10 65
(Alan Berry) *cl up stands' side: led over 1f out: drvn out* **7/1**

0000 **2** *1 ¼* **Argentine (IRE)**[11] [3662] 7-9-8 56..................(b) PaulHanagan 8 62
(George Foster) *taken early to post: dwlt: hdwy on outside of that gp over 1f out: styd on to go 2nd nr fin: nt rch wnr* **9/1**

5606 **3** *shd* **Vintage Grape (IRE)**[11] [3661] 3-8-8 47..................(b) AndrewMullen 1 50
(Eric Alston) *cl up centre: rdn over 2f out: kpt on u.p ins fnl f* **22/1**

300/ **4** *1* **Here Now And Why (IRE)**[43] [2626] 4-8-11 50.................................. DaleSwift(5) 4 52
(Ian Semple) *cl up centre: rdn and edgd rt over 2f out: kpt on same pce fnl f* **9/2**[2]

2344 **5** *½* **Sharp Bullet (IRE)**[16] [3488] 5-9-9 57..................(b) RichardKingscote 7 57
(Bruce Hellier) *cl up stands' side: rdn over 2f out: edgd rt over 1f out: kpt on same pce* **7/2**[1]

0605 **6** *nk* **Mandarin Spirit (IRE)**[29] [3040] 11-9-9 57..................(b) SilvestreDeSousa 5 56
(Linda Perratt) *led and sn swtchd to stands' rail: hdd over 1f out: kpt on same pce* **14/1**

3130 **7** *½* **Sparking**[30] [3027] 4-9-10 58.................................. LeeNewman 3 55
(David Barron) *cl up centre tl rdn and no ex over 1f out* **11/2**[3]

0-50 **8** *2 ¾* **Autocracy**[11] [3662] 4-9-7 55.................................. HughBowman 9 42
(Eric Alston) *hld up in tch centre: pushed along over 2f out: no imp over 1f out* **20/1**

6356 **9** *hd* **Tournedos (IRE)**[11] [3662] 9-9-10 58..................(b) PJMcDonald 6 44
(Ruth Carr) *prom stands' side: rdn over 2f out: wknd over 1f out* **11/2**[3]

00-0 **10** *9* **Olympic Ceremony**[8] [3732] 4-9-6 54..................(p) FrannyNorton 2 —
(Tracy Waggott) *dwlt: hld up in tch centre: rdn over 2f out: sn wknd* **40/1**

59.70 secs (-0.30) **Going Correction** -0.15s/f (Firm)
WFA 3 from 4yo+ 5lb **10** Ran SP% **111.9**
Speed ratings (Par 101): **96,94,93,92,91 90,90,85,85,71**
toteswingers:1&2:£9.20, 2&3:£23.10, 1&3:£14.40 CSF £63.44 CT £1325.36 TOTE £7.80: £2.50, £3.50, £4.10; EX 42.90 Trifecta £557.30 Part won. Pool of £753.12 - 0.63 winning units..
Owner Mrs Thelma White **Bred** Gerry O'Sullivan **Trained** Cockerham, Lancs

FOCUS
Few came into this low-grade sprint handicap in much form. Four of the field, the winner included, came over to race on the stands' side, with the remainder staying down the centre. The latter are perhaps a bit better than the bare form.

4018 HAMILTON PARK LADIES NIGHT H'CAP 1m 65y
5:20 (5:21) (Class 6) (0-65,64) 3-Y-O **£1,940** (£577; £288; £144) **Stalls** Low

Form RPR

-606 **1** **Smart Violetta (IRE)**[9] [3716] 3-8-2 45..................(t) FrannyNorton 7 49
(Ann Duffield) *hld up last but in tch: rdn and edgd rt 3f out: rallied 2f out: styd on wl ins fnl f: led nr fin* **8/1**

3204 **2** *nk* **Crown Ridge (IRE)**[72] [1790] 3-9-3 60.................................. HughBowman 1 63
(Mick Channon) *trckd ldrs: rdn to ld over 1f out: kpt on fnl f: hdd nr fin* **4/1**

0425 **3** *1 ¼* **Philharmonic Hall**[21] [3318] 3-9-2 64.................................. LeeTopliss(5) 5 64
(Richard Fahey) *hld up in tch: hdwy to chse ldrs over 2f out: sn rdn: kpt on ins fnl f* **5/2**[1]

0600 **4** *1 ¼* **Smart Step**[17] [3475] 3-8-7 50.................................. SilvestreDeSousa 2 48
(Mark Johnston) *led tl rdn and hdd over 1f out: kpt on same pce fnl f* **3/1**[3]

000- **5** *5* **Oakwell (IRE)**[265] [7058] 3-8-2 45.................................. PaulHanagan 4 31
(Sally Hall) *t.k.h early: prom: rdn 3f out: wknd over 1f out* **11/4**[2]

0000 **6** *21* **Right Credentials**[16] [3487] 3-7-11 45.................................. NeilFarley(5) 6 —
(Bruce Hellier) *trckd ldr to over 3f out: sn rdn and wknd: t.o* **100/1**

1m 47.82s (-0.58) **Going Correction** -0.15s/f (Firm) **6** Ran SP% **112.3**
Speed ratings (Par 98): **96,95,94,93,88 67**
toteswingers:1&2:£5.50, 2&3:£1.60, 1&3:£3.60 CSF £39.24 TOTE £14.90: £8.10, £1.40; EX 45.50.
Owner Six Iron Partnership **Bred** Peter Byrne **Trained** Constable Burton, N Yorks

FOCUS
A very weak handicap, rated around the second and third.
Smart Violetta(IRE) Official explanation: trainer said regarding apparent improvement in form, filly had improved since being fitted with a tongue strap.
T/Plt: £57.70 to a £1 stake. Pool of £42,898.04 - 542.23 winning tickets. T/Qpdt: £17.90 to a £1 stake. Pool of £3,098.81 - 127.90 winning tickets. RY

3630 LEICESTER (R-H)
Thursday, July 14

OFFICIAL GOING: Good to firm (good in places; 7.9)
Wind: Fresh behind Weather: Cloudy with sunny spells

4019 PADDOCK NURSERY 5f 218y
2:10 (2:10) (Class 6) 2-Y-O **£1,617** (£481; £240; £120) **Stalls** High

Form RPR

3334 **1** **Red Mischief (IRE)**[26] [3171] 2-8-12 65.................................. KierenFallon 3 69
(Harry Dunlop) *mde all: rdn over 1f out: jst hld on* **13/2**

241 **2** *shd* **That's Dangerous**[12] [3631] 2-8-13 71.................................. KieranO'Neill(5) 2 75
(Roger Charlton) *a.p: rdn over 2f out: chsd wnr over 1f out: r.o* **11/4**[1]

0351 **3** *3 ¼* **Xinbama (IRE)**[9] [3700] 2-9-3 70 6ex.................................. MichaelHills 8 64
(J W Hills) *hld up: rdn and hung rt fr over 2f out: hdwy over 1f out: nt rch ldrs* **5/1**[3]

330 **4** *1 ¼* **Worth**[42] [2641] 2-8-13 66.................................. MartinDwyer 1 57
(Brian Meehan) *chsd ldrs: rdn over 1f out: no ex ins fnl f* **10/3**[2]

0544 **5** *2 ¾* **Flosse**[8] [3746] 2-8-4 57.................................. AndreaAtzeni 5 39
(Ed Walker) *prom: rdn over 2f out: wknd over 1f out* **12/1**

545 **6** *¾* **Sweet Ovation**[22] [3287] 2-8-1 53.................................. JimmyQuinn 6 34
(Mark Usher) *hld up: hdwy 2f out: wknd ins fnl f* **10/1**

0204 **7** *8* **Louis Hull**[12] [3618] 2-8-13 66.................................. TonyHamilton 7 22
(George Foster) *sn pushed along in rr: rdn over 2f out: wknd over 1f out* **12/1**

406 **8** *½* **Arachis Bow**[29] [3050] 2-8-5 58.................................. JamesSullivan 4 13
(Michael Easterby) *chsd ldrs: rdn over 2f out: sn wknd* **33/1**

554 **9** *4 ½* **First Rebellion**[31] [2998] 2-8-0 52.................................. NickyMackay 9 —
(Tony Carroll) *prom: rdn and hung rt fr over 4f out: wknd over 2f out* **12/1**

1m 13.02s (0.02) **Going Correction** -0.075s/f (Good) **9** Ran SP% **114.9**
Speed ratings (Par 92): **96,95,91,89,86 85,74,73,67**
toteswingers:1&2:£2.60, 2&3:£3.00, 1&3:£3.40 CSF £24.58 CT £97.55 TOTE £6.90: £2.20, £1.10, £2.70; EX 19.10.

Owner Harry Dunlop Racing Partnership **Bred** C Farrell **Trained** Lambourn, Berks
■ The 'official' ratings shown next to each horse are estimated and for information purposes only.

FOCUS

A run-of-the-mill nursery. The front two were clear and the winner was back to his debut form.

NOTEBOOK

Red Mischief(IRE), dropped back in trip after a disappointing 7f run a month earlier, just edged a driving finish. Always prominent, she was in front at halfway, before being joined by the runner-up at the 1f pole. She fought back gamely, racing closest to the stands' rail, and possibly had a fraction more in hand than the winning margin suggests. (op 15-2 tchd 8-1)

That's Dangerous, winner of a C&D seller on his last start, was not the quickest away. He had edged into contention by halfway, however, and was sharing second 2f out. He may narrowly have got his head in front inside the last, but could not cope with the winner's brave rally. (tchd 5-2 and 3-1)

Xinbama(IRE), carrying a 6lb penalty for a Ponterfract nursery win nine days previously, never looked likely to register a follow-up. He was ridden with restraint early on and third was the best position he ever held. (op 9-2 tchd 4-1 and 11-2)

Worth, twice placed in 5f turf maidens before a below-par Polytrack effort over 6f, showed early speed to chase the pace. She faded inside the final furlong, though, and it appears she is better at the minimum distance. (op 7-2 tchd 3-1)

Flosse, too keen when fourth over this trip on Polytrack last time out, settled marginally better here. She was never too far off the pace, but could not quicken with the principals and faded late on. (tchd 16-1)

Sweet Ovation, stepping up in trip after three runs in 5f maidens, was off the pace in the early stages. She had improved her position slightly at halfway, but soon tired and did not threaten to make a more significant impact. (op 11-1 tchd 14-1)

4020 WELCOMM COMMUNICATIONS H'CAP — 7f 9y

2:40 (2:40) (Class 4) (0-80,80) 3-Y-O+ — **£4,075** (£1,212; £606; £303) **Stalls** High

Form — RPR

1141 **1** — **Lightning Cloud (IRE)**[6] 3798 3-9-3 **80** .... AmyRyan[(3)] 9 — 88
(Kevin Ryan) *hld up: plld hrd: hdwy over 4f out: rdn to ld ins fnl f: styd on* **11/10**[1]

-000 **2** *¾* **Big Noise**[27] 3134 7-10-0 **80** .... (p) TedDurcan 2 — 89
(Dr Jon Scargill) *hld up: rdn over 1f out: r.o ins fnl f: nt rch wnr* **7/1**[3]

0061 **3** *nse* **The Guru Of Gloom (IRE)**[23] 3246 3-8-12 **72** .... MartinDwyer 4 — 78
(William Muir) *a.p: led over 1f out: sn rdn and hung lft: hdd and unable qck ins fnl f* **14/1**

-520 **4** *2 ½* **Last Sovereign**[15] 3506 7-9-6 **77** .... KieranO'Neill[(5)] 3 — 79
(Ollie Pears) *hld up in tch: rdn over 1f out: no ex ins fnl f* **9/2**[2]

3066 **5** *shd* **Planet Waves (IRE)**[14] 3557 3-9-0 **74** .... PhilipRobinson 8 — 73
(Clive Brittain) *led: rdn: hung rt and hdd over 2f out: outpcd over 1f out: styd on towards fin* **8/1**

-005 **6** *1 ¼* **Piddie's Power**[14] 3541 4-9-6 **72** .... GrahamGibbons 7 — 70
(Ed McMahon) *s.i.s: hld up: r.o ins fnl f: nt trble ldrs* **18/1**

20-0 **7** *1 ¼* **Flameoftheforest (IRE)**[28] 3081 4-9-8 **77** .... JohnFahy[(3)] 1 — 72
(Ed de Giles) *s.i.s: hdwy over 4f out: rdn over 1f out: wknd ins fnl f* **25/1**

6-00 **8** *½* **Elusive Hawk (IRE)**[14] 3555 7-9-2 **68** .... TomQueally 6 — 62
(Barney Curley) *chsd ldr tl led over 2f out: rdn and hdd over 1f out: wknd ins fnl f* **50/1**

24-6 **9** *15* **Cotswold Village (AUS)**[15] 3514 5-8-13 **70** .... JamesRogers[(5)] 5 — 23
(Adrian Chamberlain) *prom: rdn over 2f out: wknd wl over 1f out* **25/1**

1m 24.66s (-1.54) **Going Correction** -0.075s/f (Good)
WFA 3 from 4yo+ 8lb — **9** Ran SP% **111.0**
Speed ratings (Par 105): **105,104,104,101,101 99,98,97,80**
toteswingers:1&2:£2.90, 2&3:£6.00, 1&3:£2.50 CSF £8.45 CT £64.40 TOTE £2.10: £1.30, £2.30, £3.40; EX 7.20.

Owner Hambleton Racing Ltd XVIII **Bred** John Cullinan **Trained** Hambleton, N Yorks
■ Stewards' Enquiry : James Rogers one-day ban: careless rising (28th July)

FOCUS

A fair handicap, with the top weight rated 80, and few could be confidently discounted. The unpenalised winner did not need to match his Ascot form with the second rated back towards last year's form.

4021 GLEBE (S) STKS — 5f 2y

3:15 (3:15) (Class 6) 2-Y-O — **£1,617** (£481; £240; £120) **Stalls** High

Form — RPR

5235 **1** — **Courtland King (IRE)**[19] 3375 2-8-11 0 .... (t) KierenFallon 8 — 70
(David Evans) *hld up: hdwy to ld over 1f out: pushed out* **4/7**[1]

00 **2** *3* **Flirty Gerty (IRE)**[22] 3273 2-8-6 0 .... (p) LiamJones 4 — 53
(Tom Dascombe) *w ldr tl rdn 1/2-way: styd on u.p* **16/1**[3]

50 **3** *1 ¾* **Ave Sofia**[33] 2914 2-8-6 0 .... AndreaAtzeni 6 — 47
(John Holt) *chsd ldrs: rdn over 1f out: no ex ins fnl f* **11/2**[2]

46 **4** *2 ½* **J Cunningham**[33] 2919 2-8-1 0 .... RyanPowell[(5)] 2 — 38
(Mark Usher) *chsd ldrs: rdn 1/2-way: wknd ins fnl f* **25/1**

051 **5** *¾* **Very First Blade**[9] 3708 2-8-11 0 .... KieranO'Neill[(5)] 1 — 45
(Mark Brisbourne) *led: rdn and hdd over 1f out: wknd ins fnl f* **11/2**[2]

050 **6** *1 ¼* **Purple Angel**[33] 2901 2-8-6 0 .... NickyMackay 7 — 31
(Jonathan Portman) *prom: rdn 1/2-way: wknd over 1f out* **50/1**

7 *14* **Symphony Of Space** 2-8-6 0 .... KellyHarrison 5 — —
(Dai Burchell) *s.i.s: sn outpcd* **33/1**

61.36 secs (1.36) **Going Correction** -0.075s/f (Good) — **7** Ran SP% **109.1**
Speed ratings (Par 92): **86,81,78,74,73 71,48**
toteswingers:1&2:£3.40, 2&3:£3.60, 1&3:£1.40 CSF £10.05 TOTE £1.60: £1.40, £4.90; EX 11.30.The winner was bought in for 10,000gns.

Owner Bathwick Gold Partnership **Bred** Henry O'Callaghan **Trained** Pandy, Monmouths

FOCUS

A modest juvenile seller in which few had obvious chances. The winner replicated his penultimate Chester form for an easy win.

NOTEBOOK

Courtland King(IRE), dropped markedly in class after a fifth in a novice stakes last time, made this opposition look very pedestrian. Held up in the early stages, he was switched right before making progress at halfway and then eased to the front approaching the final furlong. No great effort was required for him to go clear and he is well above this weak company. (op 8-13 tchd 4-6)

Flirty Gerty(IRE), fitted with first-time cheekpieces for this drop in grade, led early on and battled on dourly when the winner shot past. She held her head slightly to one side in the last furlong, suggesting she has more to give if consenting, yet was still too good for the rest. (op 12-1)

Ave Sofia, seventh in a warm 6f maiden here a month earlier, was never closer than at the finish. This is her level and now that she has had three runs, selling nurseries will be available to her. (op 8-1)

J Cunningham had shown little in two auction maidens before this but, not surprisingly, found these rivals less taxing. He was always close to the pace and, as this was his third run, he too now qualifies for two-year-old handicaps. (op 14-1)

Very First Blade, successful in a Southwell seller nine days earlier, was prominent from the start and in front briefly 2f out. He dropped away tamely, though, when the winner swept past. (op 5-1)

Purple Angel had beaten just one home in three previous starts and doubled that tally here. She never threatened to do more, however. (op 66-1 tchd 40-1)

4022 MELTON MOWBRAY CONDITIONS STKS — 1m 1f 218y

3:50 (3:50) (Class 3) 3-Y-O — **£6,301** (£1,886; £943) **Stalls** Low

Form — RPR

3406 **1** — **Auld Burns**[19] 3405 3-9-7 102 .... RichardHughes 3 — 102
(Richard Hannon) *mde all: clr 8f out: shkn up over 1f out: easily* **4/9**[1]

44-5 **2** *9* **Fanny May**[35] 2839 3-8-12 92 .... KierenFallon 1 — 81
(Denis Coakley) *chsd wnr thrght: rdn over 2f out: outpcd fr over 1f out* **9/4**[2]

1203 **3** *31* **Bussa**[12] 3629 3-8-10 71 .... KevinLundie[(7)] 2 — 49
(David Evans) *s.i.s: hld up: rdn over 2f out: sn wknd and eased* **25/1**[3]

2m 4.51s (-3.39) **Going Correction** -0.125s/f (Firm) — **3** Ran SP% **103.9**
Speed ratings (Par 104): **108,100,76**
CSF £1.59 TOTE £1.30; EX 1.80.

Owner P A Byrne **Bred** Simon Tindall **Trained** East Everleigh, Wilts

FOCUS

A disappointing turn-out and, as most punters suspected beforehand, easy pickings for the very short-priced favourite. The time was decent and Auld Burns is rated around his latest form.

NOTEBOOK

Auld Burns, a Listed fourth in May and officially rated 102, routed these from the front. Quickly away, he was perhaps 5l ahead after a couple of furlongs and still three clear turning into the home straight. He kicked again with 2f left and soon established a comfortable advantage. This told us little new about him, but it was a decent prize to collect before, presumably, he steps back up in grade. (op 2-5 tchd 1-2)

Fanny May, well beaten when fifth of nine in a Listed event last time out, was always second. Ridden patiently in the early stages, she was asked to make ground turning into the home straight and briefly made a little progress. She was soon struggling, though, and seemed to find this trip beyond her. Dropping to 1m appears to make sense now. (op 5-2 tchd 15-8)

Bussa, third off a mark of 72 in a Haydock handicap last time, was predictably outclassed. He was awkward leaving the stalls, which obviously did not help his cause, but then niggled along to stay in touch 3f out, before dropping away tamely. (op 20-1)

4023 O2 MAIDEN STKS — 1m 1f 218y

4:25 (4:25) (Class 5) 3-4-Y-O — **£2,264** (£673; £336; £168) **Stalls** Low

Form — RPR

2- **1** — **Laatafreet (IRE)**[274] 6844 3-8-13 0 .... FrankieDettori 9 — 99+
(Saeed Bin Suroor) *chsd ldrs: led 1/2-way: shkn up over 1f out: r.o wl: eased nr fin* **1/2**[1]

432 **2** *3 ¾* **Polperro (USA)**[33] 2930 3-8-13 82 .... WilliamBuick 11 — 91
(John Gosden) *chsd ldrs: led over 8f out: hung lft and hdd 1/2-way: remained handy: chsd wnr over 2f out: rdn and hung rt fr over 1f out: nt run on* **2/1**[2]

5 **3** *4 ½* **Qahriman**[33] 2930 3-8-13 0 .... KierenFallon 6 — 82+
(Luca Cumani) *sn prom: outpcd over 3f out: n.d after* **7/1**[3]

4 *12* **Ecossaise** 3-8-8 0 .... RobertWinston 12 — 53
(Mark Johnston) *sn prom: chsd wnr over 3f out to over 2f out: sn wknd* **20/1**

00 **5** *7* **Price Of Retrieval**[14] 3543 4-9-10 0 .... JackMitchell 7 — 44
(Peter Chapple-Hyam) *chsd ldrs tl rdn and wknd over 3f out* **80/1**

00-6 **6** *7* **Misefi**[24] 3232 3-8-5 0 .... JohnFahy[(3)] 5 — 25
(Martin Bosley) *sn pushed along in rr: bhd fr 1/2-way: t.o* **100/1**

4 **7** *1* **Knowe Head (NZ)**[26] 3167 4-9-8 0 .... LiamJones 8 — 26
(James Unett) *s.i.s: hdwy 6f out: rdn and wknd over 2f out: t.o* **33/1**

8 *½* **Miracle Play (IRE)** 3-8-8 0 .... (t) BarryMcHugh 10 — 22
(David Evans) *hld up and a in rr: lost tch fnl 4f: t.o* **50/1**

00 **9** *1 ½* **Patricias Pride**[9] 3717 4-9-5 0 .... KieranO'Neill[(5)] 3 — 24
(Lucinda Featherstone) *sn pushed along and a in rr: bhd fnl 4f: t.o* **150/1**

6 **10** *10* **Ballina Blue**[24] 3214 3-8-13 0 .... TadhgO'Shea 4 — —
(John Gallagher) *led: hdd over 8f out: rdn and wknd over 2f out* **100/1**

2m 4.75s (-3.15) **Going Correction** -0.125s/f (Firm)
WFA 3 from 4yo 11lb — **10** Ran SP% **126.0**
Speed ratings (Par 103): **107,104,100,90,85 79,78,78,77,69**
toteswingers:1&2:£1.10, 2&3:£2.30, 1&3:£2.00 CSF £1.94 TOTE £1.50: £1.02, £1.10, £1.90; EX 2.40.

Owner Godolphin **Bred** Shadwell Estate Company Limited **Trained** Newmarket, Suffolk

FOCUS

A potentially interesting maiden featuring a handful with fair form in the book and a clutch of nicely-bred newcomers, but turned into a procession by the well-backed odds-on favourite. The runner-up set a good standard.

4024 GREAT GLEN H'CAP — 1m 3f 183y

5:00 (5:01) (Class 6) (0-65,65) 4-Y-O+ — **£1,617** (£481; £240; £120) **Stalls** Low

Form — RPR

04-4 **1** — **Muwalla**[14] 3545 4-9-4 **62** .... KierenFallon 2 — 71
(James Bethell) *chsd ldrs: rdn to ld 1f out: styd on* **5/2**[1]

4020 **2** *1 ½* **Arashi**[14] 3538 5-9-3 **64** .... (p) JohnFahy[(3)] 7 — 70
(Lucinda Featherstone) *hld up: hdwy over 2f out: rdn over 1f out: r.o to go 2nd nr fin: nt rch wnr* **13/2**

004 **3** *hd* **Boa**[15] 3509 6-9-3 **64** .... PaulPickard[(3)] 3 — 70
(Reg Hollinshead) *chsd ldr: rdn to ld wl over 1f out: hdd 1f out: styd on same pce* **4/1**[2]

250/ **4** *½* **Reset City**[641] 6698 5-9-7 **65** .... (t) RobertHavlin 10 — 70
(David Pipe) *s.i.s: hdwy over 10f out: rdn over 1f out: styd on* **7/1**

0451 **5** *4 ½* **Lucky Diva**[13] 3600 4-8-0 **51** .... (p) JakePayne[(7)] 11 — 49
(Bill Turner) *s.i.s: hld up: hdwy over 1f out: nt trble ldrs* **12/1**

2150 **6** *nk* **Kingaroo (IRE)**[66] 1956 5-8-13 **60** .... BillyCray[(3)] 1 — 58
(Garry Woodward) *led: rdn and hdd wl over 1f out: wknd ins fnl f* **16/1**

-362 **7** *shd* **Lauberhorn**[10] 3690 4-8-13 **57** .... (b) TomQueally 4 — 54
(Eve Johnson Houghton) *chsd ldrs: rdn over 2f out: styd on same pce* **11/2**[3]

640- **8** *8* **Tom Wade (IRE)**[61] 5923 4-8-8 **52** ow1 .... BarryMcHugh 6 — 37
(John Harris) *hld up: hdwy over 3f out: wknd over 1f out* **28/1**

3-00 **9** *4 ½* **Alhaque (USA)**[15] 3507 5-9-2 **60** .... TonyCulhane 5 — 37
(Paul Midgley) *hld up: bhd 8f out: nvr a factor* **33/1**

5-00 **10** *2 ¾* **Silent Applause**[16] 3479 8-9-1 **59** .... TedDurcan 9 — 32
(Dr Jon Scargill) *mid-div: rdn and wknd over 2f out* **11/1**

2m 31.87s (-2.03) **Going Correction** -0.125s/f (Firm) — **10** Ran SP% **118.1**
Speed ratings (Par 101): **101,100,99,99,96 96,96,90,87,86**
toteswingers:1&2:£4.00, 2&3:£6.60, 1&3:£3.50 CSF £19.39 CT £64.18 TOTE £3.70: £2.10, £3.10, £1.10; EX 22.50.

Owner Elliott Brothers And Peacock **Bred** S P Burke **Trained** Middleham Moor, N Yorks

FOCUS

A modest handicap in which the top weight was rated just 65. Straightfoward form.

Silent Applause Official explanation: jockey said gelding had no more to give.

4025 HIGHFIELDS APPRENTICE H'CAP 5f 218y
5:30 (5:30) (Class 6) (0-65,65) 3-Y-O+ £1,617 (£481; £240; £120) **Stalls** High

Form RPR

-002 1 **Istiqdaam**[9] 3720 6-9-9 **60**...(b) NathanAlison 13 72
(Michael Easterby) *sn pushed along in rr: hdwy u.p over 1f out: r.o to ld post* **7/2**[1]

4360 2 *nk* **Mata Hari Blue**[9] 3711 5-9-8 **62**... GeorgeDowning(3) 3 73
(John Holt) *chsd ldrs: led over 3f out: rdn and edgd rt fr over 1f out: hdd post* **10/1**

0431 3 *1 1/2* **Interakt**[16] 3476 4-9-7 **58**... CharlesBishop 4 64
(Joseph Tuite) *hld up in tch: rdn over 1f out: styd on* **11/2**[2]

5003 4 *nk* **Avec Moi**[16] 3495 4-8-6 **46**... DanielHarris(3) 16 51
(Christine Dunnett) *chsd ldrs: rdn over 2f out: styd on* **25/1**

5513 5 *3* **Maryolini**[10] 3685 6-9-8 **59**... CharlesEddery 12 55
(Tom Keddy) *hld up: swtchd rt and hdwy over 1f out: nt rch ldrs* **10/1**

2164 6 *1 1/2* **Kipchak (IRE)**[13] 3569 6-9-8 **62**...(b) SophieSilvester(3) 2 53
(Conor Dore) *led: hdd over 3f out: sn rdn: styd on same pce fr over 1f out* **12/1**

3002 7 *hd* **Errigal Lad**[43] 2609 6-9-2 **53**... AmyScott 15 43
(Garry Woodward) *s.i.s: hld up: hdwy over 2f out: no ex ins fnl f* **15/2**

0160 8 *hd* **Fathey (IRE)**[36] 2829 5-8-9 **49**... JakePayne(3) 11 39
(Charles Smith) *chsd ldrs: rdn 1/2-way: styng on same pce whn hung rt fr over 1f out* **33/1**

4056 9 *4* **Chinese Democracy (USA)**[15] 3512 4-8-13 **53**...(v) KevinLundie(3) 14 30
(David Evans) *chsd ldrs: rdn over 3f out: wknd over 1f out* **20/1**

0663 10 *1* **Boldinor**[20] 3350 8-9-8 **59**... ShaneBKelly 9 33
(Martin Bosley) *hld up: hdwy u.p over 1f out: wknd ins fnl f* **10/1**

0130 11 *2 1/4* **Cape Kimberley**[34] 2870 4-9-9 **60**... DavidKenny 8 26
(Tony Newcombe) *hld up: rdn over 2f out: nvr on terms* **7/1**[3]

0042 12 *1 1/4* **Ace Of Spies (IRE)**[9] 3711 6-9-11 **65**...(b) NoelGarbutt(3) 10 27
(Conor Dore) *chsd ldrs tl rdn and wknd over 1f out* **16/1**

050 13 *1 1/2* **Rattleyurjewellery**[19] 3387 3-7-12 **46** oh1... ClaireMurray(5) 1 —
(David Brown) *chsd ldr to over 3f out: wknd over 1f* **66/1**

354 14 *3 1/4* **Piccoluck**[17] 3470 3-9-5 **62**...(b[1]) DarylByrne 6 —+
(Amy Weaver) *s.i.s and rdr lost iron s: outpcd: kicked other leg out of iron over 3f out: a bhd* **12/1**

1m 12.76s (-0.24) **Going Correction** -0.075s/f (Good)
WFA 3 from 4yo+ 6lb **14** Ran SP% **123.5**
Speed ratings (Par 101): **98,97,95,95,91 89,88,88,83,82 79,77,75,71**
toteswingers:1&2:£15.00, 2&3:£16.50, 1&3:£3.60 CSF £38.59 CT £201.45 TOTE £4.30: £1.30, £7.20, £3.10; EX 78.00.
Owner Two Old Pals **Bred** Cheveley Park Stud Ltd **Trained** Sheriff Hutton, N Yorks

FOCUS
A modest finale, but plenty of runners and it looked competitive. Those nearer the stands' rail appeared to have an advantage. The form is rated around the second and third.
Boldinor Official explanation: jockey said gelding hung right.
Piccoluck Official explanation: jockey lost iron leaving stalls.
T/Plt: £5.40 to a £1 stake. Pool of £47,051.52 - 6,307.30 winning tickets. T/Qpdt: £3.60 to a £1 stake. Pool of £2,338.78 - 479.70 winning tickets. CR

4026 - 4030a (Foreign Racing) - See Raceform Interactive

3786 LEOPARDSTOWN (L-H)
Thursday, July 14

OFFICIAL GOING: Good

4031a SILVER FLASH STKS (GROUP 3) (FILLIES) 7f
6:45 (6:46) 2-Y-O £26,616 (£7,780; £3,685; £1,228)

RPR

1 **Maybe (IRE)**[26] 3152 2-9-1 ow3... JPO'Brien 4 106
(A P O'Brien, Ire) *trckd ldr in 2nd: led under 2f out: sn rdn and kpt on wl fr over 1f out* **2/7**[1]

2 *nk* **La Collina (IRE)**[33] 2939 2-8-12... DPMcDonogh 3 102
(Kevin Prendergast, Ire) *trckd ldrs: 4th 1/2-way: 3rd ent st and sn rdn: wnt 2nd ins fnl f and kpt on wl u.p wout rching wnr* **10/1**[3]

3 *2 1/2* **Gooseberry Fool**[15] 3520 2-8-12... PJSmullen 1 96
(Sir Mark Prescott Bt) *racd in 5th: drvn along early st: wnt 4th 1f out: kpt on same pce u.p* **12/1**

4 *2* **Somasach (USA)**[19] 3416 2-8-12... KJManning 2 91
(J S Bolger, Ire) *led: strly pressed and hdd under 2f out: no ex ins fnl f* **7/1**[2]

5 *1/2* **Miss Dylan (IRE)** 2-8-12... RPCleary 5 90
(J S Bolger, Ire) *prom and t.k.h: 3rd on inner 1/2-way: rdn early st and no ex fr over 1f out* **50/1**

6 *6* **Maid To Master (IRE)** 2-8-12... FMBerry 6 75
(Mrs John Harrington, Ire) *dwlt and a towards rr: pushed along appr st: no ex fr 2f out* **20/1**

1m 31.47s (2.77) **Going Correction** +0.225s/f (Good) **6** Ran SP% **113.8**
Speed ratings: **93,92,89,87,86 80**
CSF £4.43 TOTE £1.30: £1.10, £2.20; DF 4.50.
Owner Michael Tabor **Bred** Epona Bloodstock Ltd **Trained** Ballydoyle, Co Tipperary

FOCUS
She wasn't that visually impressive but considering she was carrying 3lb more than she should have and that the race probably wasn't run to suit her, Maybe did well. She improved, but her win was below the recent standard of this race.

NOTEBOOK
Maybe(IRE), whose rider put up 3lb overweight, got to the front well over a furlong out and was never really doing any more than what she had to. It was a performance that confirms her as probably the best juvenile filly around, although the runner-up did its bit to stake her claim. Winning rider Joseph O'Brien: "She wasn't doing a stroke in front. They went slow and it turned into a sprint which wouldn't have suited her but she still won very easily. She's as good a filly as we have." (op 3/10)
La Collina(IRE) ◆ created a good impression when winning at Limerick previously and did much better here. Held up just off the early pace, she was caught slightly flat-footed early in the straight but when she picked up she did so in good style and was unfortunate to come up against one as good as the winner. The way she put distance between herself and the remainder was impressive though and she looks certain to win a good race.
Gooseberry Fool was held up just off the pace and did some good late work without threatening. The pace of the race didn't seem to play to her strengths and she should appreciate further. (op 12/1 tchd 10/1)
Somasach(USA) was beaten fairly quickly once headed.
Miss Dylan(IRE) ◆ was keen and quite green and wasn't disgraced while giving the impression that there will be plenty more to come. (op 33/1 tchd 66/1)

4035a CHALLENGE STKS (LISTED RACE) 1m 6f
8:55 (8:56) 3-Y-O+ £22,413 (£6,551; £3,103; £1,034)

RPR

1 **Sense Of Purpose (IRE)**[32] 2968 4-9-6 98... PJSmullen 2 101
(D K Weld, Ire) *mde all: drvn along fr early st: kpt on wl u.p fnl f to hold on* **5/1**[3]

2 *nk* **Bob Le Beau (IRE)**[27] 3147 4-9-12 110... FMBerry 5 107
(Mrs John Harrington, Ire) *trckd ldrs in 4th: hdwy to go 2nd over 1f out: kpt on wl u.p: nt rch wnr* **13/8**[1]

3 *1/2* **Fictional Account (IRE)**[28] 3066 6-9-9 103... GFCarroll 3 103+
(V C Ward, Ire) *hld up in rr: rdn on outer fr early st: wnt 3rd ins fnl f: kpt on wl u.p* **9/2**[2]

4 *nk* **Kalabaya (IRE)**[27] 3149 3-8-7... NGMcCullagh 7 102+
(John M Oxx, Ire) *settled towards rr: 5th 1/2-way: clsr ent st: sn rdn and no imp: kpt on wl u.p ins fnl f* **5/1**[3]

5 *3* **Why (IRE)**[10] 3695 3-8-7 94...(p) WMLordan 4 98
(A P O'Brien, Ire) *trckd ldrs in 3rd: 2nd and rdn early st: no ex early fnl f: wknd* **14/1**

6 *1 3/4* **Zerashan (IRE)**[10] 3695 4-9-9 100... ShaneFoley 6 96
(M Halford, Ire) *trckd wnr in 2nd: pushed along appr st: 3rd 2f out: rdn and no ex fr 1f out* **9/2**[2]

7 *1 1/2* **Drumfire (IRE)**[242] 5314 7-9-9 104...(b[1]) KJManning 1 94
(Eoin Griffin, Ire) *a towards rr: rdn and no imp appr st: kpt on one pce fr over 1f out* **20/1**

3m 1.82s (0.82) **Going Correction** +0.225s/f (Good)
WFA 3 from 4yo+ 15lb **7** Ran SP% **119.2**
Speed ratings: **106,105,105,105,103 102,101**
Daily Double: 45.50 euros to a five euro stake. CSF £14.43 TOTE £3.70: £2.10, £1.80; DF 10.40.
Owner Moyglare Stud Farm **Bred** Moyglare Stud Farm Ltd **Trained** The Curragh, Co Kildare

FOCUS
The form is rated around the winner and seventh.

NOTEBOOK
Sense Of Purpose(IRE) made all under the rider who is the best around at executing these tactics, keeping up Dermot Weld's remarkable record in this race with his sixth win in the last ten runnings and his fourth in succession. This filly enjoyed herself in front, Smullen kept plenty in reserve for the challenges that were sure to emerge in the straight. She didn't disappoint and kept on strongly to hold off her adversaries in the style of a tough and genuine filly. Winning trainer Dermot Weld: "She had run an excellent race against Banimpire at Cork last time trying to give plenty of weight away and I thought that form was good enough to win this. The Park Hill Stakes at Doncaster looks a logical race for her and she'll be entered in the Melbourne Cup although she's not guaranteed to run in it."
Bob Le Beau(IRE) was tackling this trip for the first time and came through the test well without quite being good enough. Racing in mid-division, he delivered his challenge over a furlong out and kept chipping away without quite being able to get on terms. He gets the trip and this will open up more options for him. (op 2/1)
Fictional Account(IRE) is a hold-up mare but she was just asked to do a bit too much here. Travelling very well turning out of the back straight, she just was caught for a bit of tactical speed before the straight and picked up too slowly to get to the winner, stay on well though she did inside the last. Two miles is probably her trip but it may well have been wiser to keep her a few lengths closer to the pace here. (op 4/1)
Kalabaya(IRE) ◆ ran a fine race one run out of winning a maiden. Just fractionally outpaced before the straight, she kept going well although she never really looked like getting on terms. There's probably still improvement in her and there should be more to come. (op 6/1)
Why(IRE) ran well for a long way and just left the impression she didn't stay. (op 12/1)
Zerashan(IRE) came off the bridle before they turned in, wasn't beaten all that far but she's probably a shade better than this. (op 4/1)
Drumfire(IRE) was the one horse in the race who was never in a challenging position.
T/Jkpt: @78.10. Pool of @5,000.00 - 48 winning units. T/Plt: @22.60. Pool of @11,424.98 - 378.31 winning units. II

4032 - 4035a (Foreign Racing) - See Raceform Interactive

3653 LONGCHAMP (R-H)
Thursday, July 14

OFFICIAL GOING: Turf: good to soft

4036a PRIX ROLAND DE CHAMBURE (LISTED RACE) (2YO) (TURF) 7f
5:05 (12:00) 2-Y-O £23,706 (£9,482; £7,112; £4,741; £2,370)

RPR

1 **American Devil (FR)**[50] 2-8-11 0... RonanThomas 3 99
(J Van Handenhove, France) **11/5**[2]

2 *1 1/2* **Aesop's Fables (USA)**[23] 2-8-11 0... MaximeGuyon 1 95
(A Fabre, France) **13/10**[1]

3 *1 1/2* **Vizir Bere (FR)**[30] 2-8-11 0... Christophe-PatriceLemaire 6 92
(D Prod'Homme, France) **78/10**

4 *2* **Lady Orpen (FR)** 2-8-8 0... StephanePasquier 5 84
(Y Durepaire, Spain) **14/1**

5 *2 1/2* **Misty Conquest (IRE)**[19] 3402 2-8-8 0... DavyBonilla 2 77
(Tom Dascombe) *broke wl and disp ld on outside of Aesop's Fables: hdd narrowly after 1 1/2f: remained cl 2nd: shkn up to retain position over 1 1/2f out: hrd rdn and nt qckn over 1f out: wknd ins fnl 150yds* **58/10**[3]

6 *1* **Vital Wave (IRE)**[14] 2-8-11 0... IoritzMendizabal 4 78
(E J O'Neill, France) **12/1**

1m 21.1s (0.40) **6** Ran SP% **115.2**
WIN (incl. 1 euro stake): 3.20. PLACES: 1.50, 1.30. SF: 7.00.
Owner Ecurie Haras de Quetieville **Bred** Ecurie Haras De Quetieville **Trained** France

NOTEBOOK
Misty Conquest(IRE), third in the Empress Stakes last time out, found the seventh furlong beyond her here and will be suited by a return to sprint distances.

4036b PRIX DE THIBERVILLE (LISTED RACE) (3YO FILLIES) (TURF) 1m 4f
5:40 (12:00) 3-Y-O £23,706 (£9,482; £7,112; £4,741; £2,370)

Form RPR

0 1 **Shareta (IRE)**[32] 2977 3-8-11 0... Christophe-PatriceLemaire 3 102
(A De Royer-Dupre, France) **9/5**[1]

0 2 *1 1/2* **Mourasana**[39] 2750 3-8-11 0... JohanVictoire 2 99
(C Lerner, France) **38/1**

3 *snk* **Miss Crissy (IRE)**[36] 3-8-11 0... GregoryBenoist 9 99
(M Delzangles, France) **58/10**

4 *1/2* **La Pomme D'Amour**[23] 3-8-11 0... MaximeGuyon 1 98
(A Fabre, France) **7/2**[3]

5 **5** *1 1/2* **Aspasia De Mileto** 3-8-11 0.. OlivierPeslier 5 96
(C Laffon-Parias, France) **13/1**

5 **6** *hd* **Andromeda Galaxy (FR)**[32] 2977 3-8-11 0........ ChristopheSoumillon 6 95
(E Lellouche, France) **5/2**[2]

50 **7** *2* **Bernieres (IRE)**[39] 2750 3-8-11 0..........................(p) MickaelBarzalona 4 92
(Mme Pia Brandt, France) **40/1**

2421 **8** *15* **Galivant (IRE)**[24] 3214 3-8-11 0.. RyanMoore 8 68
(J W Hills) *racd in 2nd on outside of ldr's quarters: pushed along and pressed ldr appr fnl 2 1/2f: rdn and wknd over 2f out: eased fnl f* **17/1**

2m 28.69s (-1.71) **8** Ran SP% **118.9**
WIN (incl. 1 euro stake): 2.80. PLACES: 1.50, 5.10, 1.90. DF: 35.30. SF: 61.40.
Owner H H Aga Khan **Bred** His Highness The Aga Khan's Studs S C **Trained** Chantilly, France

4037a PRIX MAURICE DE NIEUIL (GROUP 2) (4YO+) (TURF) 1m 6f

6:15 (12:00) 4-Y-0+ **£63,879** (£24,655; £11,767; £7,844; £3,922)

RPR

1 **Watar (IRE)**[70] 1842 6-8-11 0.. DavyBonilla 4 112
(F Head, France) *led early: sn hdd and settled in 3rd on rail: travelling wl but no room to chal fr 2f out: 3rd whn rdn and qcknd as gap appeared ins fnl f: r.o wl to ld 50yds out* **9/1**

2 *snk* **Times Up**[54] 2316 5-8-11 0.. RyanMoore 1 112
(John Dunlop) *w.w in midfield: 5th and travelling strly 4f out: short of room whn shkn up over 2f out: in clr ins fnl 300yds: r.o wl fnl f* **6/1**[3]

3 *hd* **Shamanova (IRE)**[29] 3063 4-8-8 0........... Christophe-PatriceLemaire 10 109
(A De Royer-Dupre, France) *hld up towards rr: pushed along and hdwy on outside appr 2f out: styd on wl fnl f: jst failed to get up for 2nd* **5/1**[2]

4 *3/4* **Ted Spread**[25] 3204 4-8-11 0... OlivierPeslier 5 110
(Mark H Tompkins) *sn led: shkn up and qcknd over 2 1/2f out: r.o wl fnl f: hdd 50yds out: no ex* **14/1**

5 *hd* **Allied Powers (IRE)**[19] 3403 6-8-11 0....................... IoritzMendizabal 3 110
(Michael Bell) *racd in 6th: pushed along 3f out: sltly hmpd and swtchd outside Tres Rock Danon 2 1/2f out: sn rdn and nt qckn instantly 1 1/2f out: styd on u.p fnl 110yds* **14/1**

6 *1* **Ley Hunter (USA)**[39] 2753 4-8-11 0.......................... MickaelBarzalona 2 109
(A Fabre, France) *racd keenly in midfield: rdn and nt qckn 2f out: styd on fnl f: nvr in contention* **4/1**[1]

7 *shd* **Mores Wells**[25] 3211 7-8-11 0.................................(b) GregoryBenoist 11 109
(M Delzangles, France) *w.w towards rr: 10th over 2 1/2f out: sn rdn: styd on fnl f: n.d* **9/1**

8 *snk* **Tres Rock Danon (FR)**[46] 2538 5-9-2 0............................. ASuborics 6 113
(W Hickst, Germany) *racd in 4th: rdn and nt qckn 2f out: one pce fnl f: eased cl home* **16/1**

9 *shd* **Diamond Boy (FR)**[29] 3063 5-8-11 0............................ GeraldMosse 12 108
(F Doumen, France) *trckd ldr: rdn 2f out: wknd u.p ins fnl f* **16/1**

10 *snk* **Kasbah Bliss (FR)**[28] 3066 9-8-11 0............................ ThierryThulliez 9 108
(F Doumen, France) *hld up next to last: mod late progrsss: nvr plcd to chal* **9/1**

0 **Marinous (FR)**[53] 2344 5-9-2 0... ThierryJarnet 8 —
(F Head, France) *dwlt: settled in last pl: rdn and no imp ins fnl 2f* **8/1**

0 **Talgado**[50] 2408 4-8-11 0.................................... MariaMagdalenaRossak 7 —
(F Neuberg, Czech Republic) *hld up towards rr: rdn and no imp fr 2f out* **66/1**

3m 6.04s (186.04) **12** Ran SP% **118.7**
WIN (incl. 1 euro stake): 7.10. PLACES: 2.10, 2.70, 2.00. DF: 32.70. SF: 61.60.
Owner Hamdan Al Maktoum **Bred** Haras Du Mezeray **Trained** France

NOTEBOOK

Watar(IRE) appreciated the greater test of stamina he faced here and picked up well when the gap appeared to win narrowly. His trainer suggested he would go for either the Prix Kergolay or Grand Prix de Deauville next.

Times Up finished very well after not getting the clearest of runs. He remains progressive and a stronger pace and return to quicker ground will help in future. He could reoppose the winner in the [illegible]

Ted Spread was always on the front end and was in prime position to kick for home in the straight. He was only caught well inside the last and probably ran right up to his best on this step up in class.

Allied Powers(IRE) was keeping on at the finish and he too might have done better with a stronger pace to chase.

4038a JUDDMONTE GRAND PRIX DE PARIS (GROUP 1) (3YO COLTS & FILLIES) (TURF) 1m 4f

6:50 (12:00) 3-Y-0 **£295,551** (£118,241; £59,120; £29,534; £14,793)

RPR

1 **Meandre (FR)**[53] 2341 3-9-2 0.. MaximeGuyon 7 123+
(A Fabre, France) *racd in 3rd: 6 l off ldr 2 1/2f out: rdn appr 2f out: 4 l down but styng on u.p 1 1/2f out: swtchd outside Treasure Beach and r.o strly fnl f: led under 100yds out: eased cl home* **10/1**

2 *1 1/2* **Seville (GER)**[18] 3442 3-9-2 0.................................. SeamieHeffernan 5 120
(A P O'Brien, Ire) *led: pushed along 2 1/2f out: rdn over 1 1/2f out: 2 l clr ent fnl f: strly rdn and hdd under 100yds out: no ex* **9/2**[3]

3 *3* **Reliable Man**[39] 2751 3-9-2 0.. GeraldMosse 4 115+
(A De Royer-Dupre, France) *settled in 4th: 6 l off ldr over 2f out: styd on fnl 1 1/2f: tk 3rd cl home: nvr able to chal* **2/1**[1]

4 *snk* **Treasure Beach**[18] 3442 3-9-2 0.................................... CO'Donoghue 2 115
(A P O'Brien, Ire) *trckd ldr: 1 l down in 2nd whn rdn over 2f out: hrd rdn 1 1/2f out: one pce fnl f: lost 3rd cl home* **5/2**[2]

5 *4* **Bubble Chic (FR)**[39] 2751 3-9-2 0.......................... StephanePasquier 6 109
(G Botti, Italy) *disp 5th: styd on at one pce fnl 2f: nvr threatened* **15/2**

6 *2* **Marksmanship (IRE)**[28] 3068 3-9-2 0................................ RyanMoore 3 105
(A P O'Brien, Ire) *disp 5th pl: 6th and rdn over 3f out: no imp u.p ins fnl 2f* **14/1**

7 *4* **Kreem**[32] 2979 3-9-2 0... MickaelBarzalona 1 99
(A Fabre, France) *slowly away: a bhd: nvr in contention* **22/1**

2m 26.63s (-3.77) **7** Ran SP% **112.0**
WIN (incl. 1 euro stake): 6.50. PLACES: 3.60, 6.40. SF: 76.00.
Owner Rothschild Family **Bred** Famille Rothschild **Trained** Chantilly, France

FOCUS

This important Group 1 had plenty of interest as it featured the winners and runners-up in both the French and Irish Derbys. However, all three were beaten by a clearly progressive and talented performer. Meandre has been a real improver since going up in trip. The pace and time were decent.

NOTEBOOK

Meandre(FR) had not been seen since narrowly winning a C&D Listed race in May. However, he was supplemented for this so his master trainer clearly held him in high regard. He chased the good pace set by the O'Brien pair but had a fair amount of ground to make up when asked around 2f from home. However, he picked up in good style and, although it may have been made to look more impressive by the leaders tiring, he significantly increased his advantage over Reliable Man, who was around a length behind when making his effort at the same time. He was quoted at between 7-1 and 14-1 for the Arc, and on this showing looks sure to figure in that race, although Fabre also has the Derby winner Pour Moi, the current favourite.

Seville(GER) set out to make all the running and looked as though he might succeed having beaten off his stable companion entering the final furlong, only for the winner to sweep past late on. He has yet to win at a Group race but has finished second in three Group 1s now and deserves to win a race at this level.

Reliable Man, the winner of the Prix du Jockey Club, was stepping up in trip. Held up in fourth, he was just behind the winner at around 2f from home but could not pick up as well as that rival, despite running on. He is bred to stay and it will be interesting to see if connections persevere or drop him back to 1m2f.

Treasure Beach, the Irish Derby winner, got a good lead from his stable companion but began to weaken entering the last furlong and was just run out of the places. His trainer thought this may have come too soon after hard races at Epsom and the Curragh, and he is likely to give the colt a break now.

Bubble Chic(FR), runner-up on his last six starts, was tackling 1m4f for the first time and was below the form he showed behind Reliable Man in the French Derby.

Marksmanship(IRE) had been beaten in a Group 3 at Royal Ascot but was allowed to take his chance at the top level over this longer trip. However, after being held up, he failed to make any headway in the straight.

4012 HAMILTON (R-H)

Friday, July 15

OFFICIAL GOING: Good to firm (good in places; 8.7)
Wind: Fresh, across Weather: Cloudy, light rain

4039 ANYA'S PAPA JOE'S 50TH BIRTHDAY APPRENTICE SERIES H'CAP (RND 3 HAMILTON PARK APPRENTICE SERIES) 1m 65y

6:10 (6:10) (Class 6) (0-60,66) 4-Y-0+ **£2,045** (£603; £302) **Stalls** Low

Form RPR

0300 **1** **Master Leon**[12] 3657 4-8-12 **56**..............................(p) JustinNewman(3) 1 64
(Bryan Smart) *t.k.h: cl up: chal over 3f out: led over 1f out: kpt on wl* **6/1**[3]

0423 **2** *1/2* **Glenluji**[7] 3805 6-9-0 **58**... GeorgeDowning(3) 2 65
(Jim Goldie) *hld up: stdy hdwy to chse ldrs over 3f out: rdn over 2f out: chsd wnr ins fnl f: r.o* **11/4**[1]

5600 **3** *2 1/4* **Spread Boy (IRE)**[4] 3902 4-7-13 **47**......................... DanielleMooney(7) 5 49
(Alan Berry) *prom: rdn and outpcd over 2f out: rallied over 1f out: kpt on fnl f* **12/1**

3521 **4** *nk* **Hits Only Jude (IRE)**[6] 3859 8-9-4 **66** 6ex..............(v) MichaelKenny(7) 7 67
(Declan Carroll) *t.k.h early: trckd ldrs: led over 3f out: edgd rt and hdd over 1f out: no ex ins fnl f* **11/4**[1]

00 **5** *10* **Carlitos Spirit (IRE)**[11] 3683 7-9-3 **58**........................(v) GarryWhillans 6 36
(Ian McInnes) *led to over 3f out: rdn and wknd over 2f out* **7/2**[2]

0-40 **6** *12* **Second Reef**[28] 3128 9-8-8 **49**... DavidKenny 4 —
(Thomas Cuthbert) *hld up in tch: rdn and outpcd 3f out: sn btn* **50/1**

056 **7** *3 1/2* **Crocodile Bay (IRE)**[12] 3658 8-8-10 **51**......................(be) JamesRogers 3 —
(Richard Guest) *s.i.s: hld up: rdn over 3f out: wknd fnl 2f* **8/1**

1m 46.9s (-1.50) **Going Correction** -0.20s/f (Firm) **7** Ran SP% **110.6**
Speed ratings (Par 101): **99,98,96,95,85 73,70**
Tote Swingers:1&2:£4.60, 2&3:£8.00, 1&3:£9.40 CSF £21.32 TOTE £8.00: £2.80, £1.80; EX 30.20.
Owner Alan Zheng **Bred** Ms R A Myatt **Trained** Hambleton, N Yorks

FOCUS

Rail realignment added 8yds to distances on round course. Most of these find winning difficult and [illegible]

4040 JOHN SMITH'S EXTRA SMOOTH MAIDEN AUCTION STKS 5f 4y

6:45 (6:45) (Class 5) 2-Y-0 **£2,726** (£805; £402) **Stalls** High

Form RPR

1 **Irrational** 2-8-9 0... TomEaves 1 64+
(Bryan Smart) *wnt rt s and sn outpcd: hdwy on outside 2f out: styd on wl fnl f: led cl home* **8/1**[3]

2 **2** *nk* **Half A Billion (IRE)**[23] 3273 2-9-0 0.............................. FrederikTylicki 5 68
(Michael Dods) *led: rdn over 1f out: kpt on fnl f: hdd nr fin* **1/4**[1]

66 **3** *2 3/4* **Jay Kay**[14] 3583 2-8-11 0.. GregFairley 4 55
(Robert Wylie) *t.k.h: disp ld tl ins fnl f: kpt on same pce* **7/1**[2]

06 **4** *shd* **Never In (IRE)**[13] 3618 2-8-4 0.................................... AndrewMullen 3 48
(Alan Berry) *in tch: sn pushed along: outpcd 1/2-way: kpt on fnl f: nrest at fin* **33/1**

00 **5** *3/4* **Burnwynd Spirit (IRE)**[6] 3855 2-8-7 0................... PatrickDonaghy(3) 2 51
(Ian Semple) *cl up: rdn 2f out: kpt on same pce fnl f* **80/1**

5 **6** *shd* **Lord Buffhead**[17] 3490 2-8-10 0..................................... J-PGuillambert 6 51
(Richard Guest) *dwlt: bhd and outpcd: styd on fnl f: nrest at fin* **20/1**

60.14 secs (0.14) **Going Correction** -0.20s/f (Firm) **6** Ran SP% **112.5**
Speed ratings (Par 94): **90,89,85,84,83 83**
Tote Swingers:1&2:£1.10, 2&3:£1.50, 1&3:£1.90 CSF £10.74 TOTE £6.40: £2.30, £1.10; EX 11.50.
Owner Crossfields Racing **Bred** Sir Eric Parker **Trained** Hambleton, N Yorks

FOCUS

The race can't be rated any higher but the winner should go forward from this bare form.

NOTEBOOK

Irrational ◆ is related to plenty of winners but she was noticeably inexperienced through the initial stages of the contest. The further she went though the more she got the hang of things and she stormed up the hill to nail the favourite and become the first winning debutant from her stable this year. She could be useful. (op 7-1)

Half A Billion(IRE), for whom this looked a straightforward opportunity, was sent off at long odds-on after a very promising debut, but he was collared late in the day by the only debutant in the line-up. He had to work quite hard to shake off Jay Kay towards the stands' rail but he began to assert in the final furlong only to succumb to another rival. It's debatable whether he improved on his debut effort and he didn't look entirely straightforward in hanging to his right, but still appears more than capable of going one better. (op 2-7 tchd 30-100 after early 1-3)

Jay Kay fared a little better than on his first two starts and this trip might suit better. He is qualified for handicaps now and he'll be allotted a fairly modest mark. (op 15-2)

Never In(IRE) kept on from off the pace to post arguably her best effort so far. (op 28-1)

Lord Buffhead looks one to keep an eye on over longer trips down the line. (op 25-1)

4041 BOOK NOW FOR LADIES NIGHT (S) H'CAP 6f 5y
7:15 (7:15) (Class 6) (0-65,65) 3-5-Y-O **£2,045** (£603; £302) **Stalls** Centre

Form RPR

5425 **1** **Tahitian Princess (IRE)**[17] 3489 3-8-6 **51**.................(p) PaulHanagan 10 59
(Ann Duffield) *in tch: rdn 1/2-way: hdwy to ld ins fnl f: r.o* **4/1**[2]

1443 **2** 1 ¼ **Arch Walker (IRE)**[21] 3359 4-9-7 **63**......................... PatrickDonaghy(3) 5 68
(Jedd O'Keeffe) *trckd ldrs: led 1/2-way: sn rdn: hdd ins fnl f: r.o* **3/1**[1]

-001 **3** *nk* **Weetentherty**[6] 3857 4-8-9 **51** 6ex.......................(p) DeclanCannon(3) 8 55
(Linda Perratt) *hld up in tch: hdwy to press ldr 1/2-way: sn rdn and edgd rt: kpt on same pce ins fnl f* **12/1**

1335 **4** 1 ½ **Clear Ice (IRE)**[10] 3711 4-9-9 **65**...............................(b) RobertLButler(3) 2 64
(Richard Guest) *dwlt: bhd: hdwy over 1f out: styd on fnl f: no imp* **4/1**[2]

0520 **5** 6 **Brave Battle**[3] 3931 3-9-0 **59**.......................................(v[1]) AndrewMullen 9 38
(David Nicholls) *w ldrs: drvn and outpcd 2f out: sn btn* **5/1**[3]

1-00 **6** 2 **Blue Noodles**[48] 2487 5-9-4 **57**......................................(p) PaddyAspell 3 31
(John Wainwright) *led to 1/2-way: sn rdn: wknd over 1f out* **16/1**

-360 **7** 1 ½ **Ballinargh Boy**[30] 3039 3-8-7 **52** ow2.............................(p) GregFairley 7 20
(Robert Wylie) *t.k.h: cl up: n.m.r and lost pl 1/2-way: n.d after* **5/1**[3]

0000 **8** 10 **Ya Boy Sir (IRE)**[18] 3451 4-8-7 **46** oh1............................. LeeNewman 6 —
(Ian Semple) *s.i.s: hld up: hdwy after 2f: rdn and wknd 2f out* **40/1**

1m 10.47s (-1.73) **Going Correction** -0.20s/f (Firm)
WFA 3 from 4yo+ 6lb **8** Ran SP% **114.3**
Speed ratings (Par 101): **103,101,100,98,90 88,86,72**
Tote Swingers:1&2:£2.50, 2&3:£8.10, 1&3:£3.90 CSF £16.43 CT £130.74 TOTE £5.20: £1.40, £1.40, £3.00; EX 20.10.There was no bid for the winner. Clear Ice was claimed by Miss Gay Kelleway for £7,000.
Owner Mr & Mrs David & Carole McMahon **Bred** Roger K Lee **Trained** Constable Burton, N Yorks

FOCUS
Low-grade stuff, but the form looks sound.
Brave Battle Official explanation: jockey said gelding hung right throughout.

4042 JOHN SMITH'S SCOTTISH STEWARDS' CUP (H'CAP) 6f 5y
7:45 (7:46) (Class 2) (0-105,102) 3-Y-O+
£20,542 (£6,151; £3,075; £1,537; £768; £386) **Stalls** Centre

Form RPR

0-61 **1** **Quest For Success (IRE)**[27] 3160 6-9-7 **97**.................. PaulHanagan 2 107
(Richard Fahey) *cl up: rdn 2f out: led ins fnl f: drvn out* **9/1**

0000 **2** 1 ½ **Colonel Mak**[19] 3440 4-9-4 **94**... LeeNewman 16 99
(David Barron) *led: rdn 2f out: hdd ins fnl f: kpt on same pce towards fin* **11/2**[2]

0101 **3** ¾ **Roker Park (IRE)**[6] 3850 6-9-1 **91** 6ex............................ DavidNolan 10 94
(David O'Meara) *in tch: drvn along over 2f out: kpt on ins fnl f: nrst fin* **10/1**

0-10 **4** *hd* **Enderby Spirit (GR)**[63] 2075 5-9-2 **92**............................ TomEaves 15 94
(Bryan Smart) *racd alone stands' side: rdn over 2f out: kpt on u.p ins fnl f* **11/1**

0020 **5** *nk* **Tajneed (IRE)**[19] 3440 8-9-12 **102**................................ AndrewMullen 11 103
(David Nicholls) *midfield: rdn over 2f out: kpt on ins fnl f: nrst fin* **16/1**

5115 **6** ½ **We Have A Dream**[15] 3535 6-8-7 **88**........................ JamesRogers(5) 8 88
(William Muir) *cl up: rdn over 2f out: kpt on same pce fnl f* **16/1**

4300 **7** ½ **Brave Prospector**[55] 2284 6-9-10 **100**......................... FrederikTylicki 7 98
(Richard Fahey) *hld up: pushed along over 2f out: hdwy over 1f out: kpt on: nrst fin* **20/1**

2602 **8** *hd* **Everymanforhimself (IRE)**[20] 3395 7-8-12 **88**..........(b) PhillipMakin 13 85
(Kevin Ryan) *s.i.s: bhd tl hdwy over 1f out: kpt on fnl f: nvr able to chal* **16/1**

-000 **9** *nk* **Irish Heartbeat (IRE)**[34] 2927 6-8-11 **92**...................... LeeTopliss(5) 12 88
(Richard Fahey) *hld up: rdn and effrt over 2f out: no imp appr fnl f* **15/2**

3050 **10** *nk* **Lowther**[28] 3109 6-9-3 **100**.....................................(be) MissAlexOwen(7) 3 95
(Alan Bailey) *midfield: drvn and outpcd over 3f out: edgd rt 2f out: kpt on fnl f: nvr able to chal* **18/1**

3050 **11** 1 ¾ **Dickie Le Davoir**[10] 3704 7-8-9 **85**............................(b) AndrewElliott 14 75
(Richard Guest) *hld up: rdn over 2f out: no imp over 1f out* **40/1**

1000 **12** *shd* **Evens And Odds (IRE)**[27] 3155 7-9-5 **102**............ MatthewLawson(7) 4 92+
(David Nicholls) *cl up: drvn along over 2f out: no ex over 1f out* **16/1**

1613 **13** ½ **Doc Hay (USA)**[14] 3588 4-8-9 **85**.................................. GregFairley 5 73+
(Keith Dalgleish) *dwlt and bmpd s: sn in tch: rdn over 2f out: wknd over 1f out* **5/1**[1]

416 **14** 1 ½ **Ginger Ted (IRE)**[20] 3395 4-8-13 **89**.........................(p) J-PGuillambert 6 72
(Richard Guest) *midfield: drvn and outpcd over 2f out: n.d after* **7/1**[3]

69.52 secs (-2.68) **Going Correction** -0.20s/f (Firm) **14** Ran SP% **119.7**
Speed ratings (Par 109): **109,107,106,105,105 104,104,103,103,102 100,100,99,97**
Tote Swingers:1&2:£15.20, 2&3:£9.60, 1&3:£16.20 CSF £57.45 CT £527.37 TOTE £11.50: £3.40, £3.00, £3.90; EX 89.70.
Owner S & G Clayton **Bred** Desmond Monaghan **Trained** Musley Bank, N Yorks

FOCUS
A hot sprint handicap. The winner posted a length personal best, with the second's best run since the Ayr Silver Cup.

NOTEBOOK
Quest For Success(IRE), winner of the race in 2009, scored with a deal of authority and looks right at the top of his game. Having returned to form in a warm race at Ayr last time, he laughed off a 3lb rise, powering clear in the final furlong. He seems equally effective at 5f or 6f, all ground seems to come alike (although connections are of the opinion that he is a better horse with ease in the ground), and he will be targeted at races like the Stewards' Cup, Great St Wilfrid, and Ayr Gold Cup, but he'll probably be pushed up to something approaching a career-high mark on the back of this, so it will be tough for him in those races. (tchd 10-1 in places)
Colonel Mak ◆ hasn't been at his best this season but he returned to form with a bang here, running a blinder down the middle of the track. He looks ready to cash in his falling mark and it's worth remembering he was at his best in the second half of last season. (op 13-2 tchd early 8-1 in places tchd 5-1)
Roker Park(IRE)'s penalty meant he was racing off a 3lb higher mark than he would be in future handicaps, but he's won off higher in the past and this was a solid effort. He remains in excellent form. (op 9-1)
Enderby Spirit(GR) raced alone up the stands' rail and was upsides for most of the way, but he had to give best in the final half furlong. This wasn't a bad run but he seems better suited by flatter tracks. (op 12-1)
Tajneed(IRE), whose main target will surely be another crack at the Great St Wilfrid at his beloved Ripon, warmed up for that with a promising run, keeping on well from off the pace. The downside is he is much higher in the weights this year so it's going to be tough. (op 14-1)
Doc Hay(USA) lost his place early and used up too much energy working his way back into contention. (tchd 11-2 and 6-1 in places)

Ginger Ted(IRE) was in trouble a long way out and proved disappointing. Official explanation: jockey said gelding was unsuited by good to firm ground. (op 6-1 tchd 5-1)

4043 JOHN SMITH'S STAYERS H'CAP 1m 5f 9y
8:20 (8:20) (Class 4) (0-85,84) 3-Y-O+ **£5,175** (£1,540; £769; £384) **Stalls** High

Form RPR

3501 **1** **French Hollow**[7] 3828 6-8-12 **68** 6ex............................... PaulHanagan 2 76
(Tim Fitzgerald) *hld up: hdwy and in tch over 4f out: rdn fr 3f out: kpt on wl fnl f: led cl home* **11/4**[1]

-055 **2** ½ **Comedy Act**[26] 3205 4-10-0 **84**... AndrewElliott 3 91
(Mark Johnston) *chsd ldrs: chal over 3f out: sn rdn: led ins fnl f: hdd nr fin* **8/1**

0-00 **3** ¾ **Union Island (IRE)**[23] 3276 5-9-0 **75**............................... LeeTopliss(5) 1 81
(Brian Ellison) *hld up in tch: rdn and outpcd 3f out: rallied over 1f out: kpt on towards fin* **11/2**

4-01 **4** ¾ **Royal Trooper (IRE)**[8] 3758 5-9-13 **83** 6ex................... FrederikTylicki 7 88
(James Given) *hld up in midfield: hdwy to ld over 2f out: hdd ins fnl f: kpt on same pce* **4/1**[2]

0305 **5** ½ **Gordonsville**[27] 3163 8-9-10 **80**..................................... DanielTudhope 9 84
(Jim Goldie) *hld up: rdn 3f out: styd on fnl f: nvr able to chal* **5/1**[3]

5233 **6** 3 ¼ **Sharp Sovereign (USA)**[12] 3660 5-8-12 **68**.................... LeeNewman 8 67
(David Barron) *led: rdn and hdd over 2f out: wknd ins fnl f* **10/1**

-006 **7** 7 **Wicked Daze (IRE)**[6] 3858 8-9-3 **73**.............................. PhillipMakin 5 62
(Linda Perratt) *trckd ldrs: rdn 3f out: wknd over 1f out* **20/1**

3040 **8** 8 **The Galloping Shoe**[14] 3585 6-9-10 **80**............................ TomEaves 6 57
(Ian Semple) *t.k.h: hld up: rdn over 3f out: btn fnl 2f* **20/1**

25- **9** 14 **Golden Blaze**[266] 7059 3-7-12 **68**.................................. AndrewMullen 10 24
(James Moffatt) *t.k.h: in tch: rdn and wknd fr 3f out* **20/1**

2m 49.78s (-4.12) **Going Correction** -0.20s/f (Firm)
WFA 3 from 4yo+ 14lb **9** Ran SP% **113.2**
Speed ratings (Par 105): **104,103,103,102,102 100,96,91,82**
Tote Swingers:1&2:£3.70, 2&3:£5.40, 1&3:£3.10 CSF £23.85 CT £110.73 TOTE £3.40: £1.70, £2.10, £2.20; EX 18.90.
Owner T J Fitzgerald **Bred** T J Fitzgerald **Trained** Norton, N Yorks

FOCUS
Quite a competitive staying handicap in which the pace was generous thanks to Sharp Sovereign, but that played into the hands of the hold-up performers. The winner backed uo his York form.

4044 WESTLIFE LIVE NEXT SATURDAY H'CAP 1m 4f 17y
8:50 (8:50) (Class 6) (0-65,63) 3-Y-O **£1,940** (£577; £288; £144) **Stalls** High

Form RPR

-260 **1** **Downtown Boy (IRE)**[31] 3024 3-8-6 **48**......................... AndrewMullen 1 55
(Tom Tate) *in tch: effrt and swtchd lft 2f out: led and hung rt ins fnl f: drvn and kpt on wl* **8/1**

2103 **2** 2 **Hal Of A Lover**[2] 3976 3-9-0 **56**.................................... DanielTudhope 3 59
(David O'Meara) *led at stdy gallop: rdn over 3f out: hdd ins fnl f: kpt on same pce* **6/4**[2]

0-01 **3** 1 ¼ **Cotton Grass**[36] 2858 3-9-7 **63**...................................... PaulHanagan 5 64
(Mark H Tompkins) *trckd ldr: rdn and ev ch over 3f out: kpt on same pce over 1f out* **11/8**[1]

244 **4** 2 ¾ **Brook Star (IRE)**[30] 3037 3-8-12 **54**............................. FrederikTylicki 2 51
(Michael Dods) *trckd ldrs: rdn over 2f out: kpt on same pce over 1f out* **6/1**[3]

2m 38.22s (-0.38) **Going Correction** -0.20s/f (Firm) **4** Ran SP% **107.5**
Speed ratings (Par 98): **93,91,90,89**
CSF £20.11 TOTE £11.30; EX 31.00.
Owner T P Tate **Bred** Eclipse Thoroughbreds Inc **Trained** Tadcaster, N Yorks
■ Stewards' Enquiry : Andrew Mullen one-day ban: excessive use of whip (29th July)

FOCUS
A weak handicap and a muddling race which has been rated a shade negatively.

4045 JOHN BANKS MEMORIAL H'CAP 1m 1f 36y
9:20 (9:20) (Class 5) (0-75,75) 3-Y-O+ **£2,587** (£770; £384; £192) **Stalls** High

Form RPR

-210 **1** **Abdicate (IRE)**[24] 3260 3-9-4 **75**................................... PaulHanagan 5 79
(Richard Fahey) *mde all at stdy pce: qcknd over 2f out: kpt on strly fnl f* **11/4**[2]

3661 **2** 2 ¼ **Petomic (IRE)**[17] 3486 6-9-3 **67**.............................. RobertLButler(3) 3 67
(Richard Guest) *dwlt: t.k.h: hld up in tch on ins: n.m.r briefly 3f out: hdwy over 1f out: chsd wnr ins fnl f* **10/1**

6114 **3** ¾ **Botham (USA)**[6] 3859 7-9-2 **63**...................................... DanielTudhope 6 61
(Jim Goldie) *hld up in tch: rdn and outpcd 3f out: rallied over 1f out: r.o fin* **5/1**[3]

0302 **4** 1 ½ **Hidden Glory**[10] 3701 4-9-8 **74**.................................... LeeTopliss(5) 2 69+
(James Given) *dwlt: hld up: rdn along 3f out: hdwy on outside over 1f out: kpt on ins fnl f: nrst fin* **12/5**[1]

0050 **5** ½ **Marvo**[13] 3620 7-9-7 **68**... TomEaves 1 62
(Mark H Tompkins) *trckd ldrs: stdy hdwy 3f out: chsd wnr over 1f out to ins fnl f: no ex* **9/1**

0400 **6** *nk* **So Bazaar (IRE)**[32] 2988 4-8-7 **61**............................. GarryWhillans(7) 7 54
(Alan Swinbank) *chsd wnr 1f: cl up: rdn and outpcd over 2f out: no imp fnl f* **5/1**[3]

2-00 **7** 1 **Edas**[28] 3129 9-9-3 **64**.. GregFairley 4 55
(Thomas Cuthbert) *dwlt: t.k.h and chsd wnr after 1f: rdn over 2f out: wknd over 1f out* **16/1**

2m 0.18s (0.48) **Going Correction** -0.20s/f (Firm)
WFA 3 from 4yo+ 10lb **7** Ran SP% **114.4**
Speed ratings (Par 103): **89,87,86,85,84 84,83**
Tote Swingers:1&2:£5.40, 2&3:£9.90, 1&3:£1.70 CSF £29.52 CT £130.41 TOTE £4.50: £2.30, £4.30; EX 34.50.
Owner Highclere Thoroughbred Racing Lady Salsa **Bred** Ceka Ireland Ltd **Trained** Musley Bank, N Yorks

FOCUS
An unsatisfactory race from a form perspective as it was very steadily run, the winner making all. The form is taken at face value.
Edas Official explanation: jockey said gelding hung right throughout.
T/Plt: £343.60 to £1 stake. Pool £44,098.76 - 93.68 winning units. T/Qpdt: £131.40 to a £1 stake. Pool £3,588.29 - 20.20 winning units RY

[3623]HAYDOCK (L-H)

Friday, July 15

OFFICIAL GOING: Good to firm (firm in places; 8.0)

Wind: light 1/2 against Weather: fine and sunny, becoming overcast with light shower after race 2

4046 MELLER BRAGGINS 175TH ANNIVERSARY H'CAP — 5f

2:20 (2:20) (Class 4) (0-80,79) 3-Y-O+ **£4,528** (£1,347; £673; £336) **Stalls** Centre

Form RPR

3126 **1** **Your Gifted (IRE)**[6] 3847 4-9-5 **79** .... DarylByrne(7) 1 89
(Patrick Morris) *dwlt: hld up: shkn up to ld 1f out: r.o wl* **4/1**[3]

1251 **2** *1* **Nomoreblondes**[7] 3832 7-8-10 **68** .... (v) LMcNiff(5) 6 74
(Paul Midgley) *led after 1f: hdd 1f out: no ex* **5/6**[1]

156 **3** *2 ½* **Athwaab**[14] 3579 4-9-0 **67** .... PaulHanagan 7 64
(Noel Quinlan) *chsd ldrs: drvn over 1f out: one pce* **10/1**

0520 **4** *4* **Invincible Force (IRE)**[6] 3850 7-9-11 **78** .... (b) SilvestreDeSousa 4 61
(Paul Green) *led 1f: sn drvn along: wknd fnl f* **3/1**[2]

59.82 secs (-0.98) **Going Correction** -0.10s/f (Good)
WFA 3 from 4yo+ 5lb **4** Ran SP% **108.6**
Speed ratings (Par 105): **105,103,99,93**
CSF £7.95 TOTE £5.10; EX 7.90.

Owner Mrs S Morris **Bred** Rathasker Stud **Trained** Tarporley, Cheshire

FOCUS
It had been dry since the weekend and the watered ground was given as good to firm, firm in places, with a GoingStick reading of 8.0. Races over 5f & 6f were run on the Inner sprint course. Races over 7f & further finished in the outer home straight, adding 37yds to the distances of those races. A disappointing turnout for this sprint handicap, with half the original field declared non-runners. Another surprise best from the winner.

4047 E B F HAPPY 60TH BIRTHDAY MARGARET FORSYTH MAIDEN STKS — 6f

2:50 (2:51) (Class 5) 2-Y-O **£3,234** (£962; £481; £240) **Stalls** Centre

Form RPR

1 **Chooseday (IRE)** 2-9-3 0 .... PhillipMakin 3 72+
(Kevin Ryan) *s.i.s: smooth hdwy over 2f out: n.m.r over 1f out: sn led: pushed out* **8/13**[1]

2 *½* **Magic Destiny** 2-8-12 0 .... AndrewElliott 8 61
(Mrs K Burke) *w ldrs: led over 2f out: edgd lft over 1f out: sn hdd: no ex clsng stages* **14/1**

0 **3** *nk* **Vociferous (USA)**[17] 3490 2-8-12 0 .... SilvestreDeSousa 9 61
(Mark Johnston) *w ldrs: effrt over 2f out: kpt on same pce fnl 150yds* **7/1**[2]

4 *1 ¼* **Rapid Heat Lad (IRE)** 2-9-0 0 .... PaulPickard(3) 7 62
(Reg Hollinshead) *sn drvn along and outpcd in rr: kpt on fnl 2f* **33/1**

0 **5** *1 ¼* **Docs Legacy (IRE)**[16] 3505 2-9-3 0 .... PaulHanagan 4 59
(Richard Fahey) *mid-div: drvn over 2f out: kpt on one pce: nvr a threat* **7/1**[2]

6 *nk* **New Romantic** 2-8-12 0 .... TonyHamilton 6 52
(Julie Camacho) *dwlt: in rr: styd on fnl f* **25/1**

500 **7** *1 ½* **La Taniere**[7] 3826 2-9-3 0 .... DavidNolan 2 53
(Michael Easterby) *chsd ldrs: drvn and outpcd 3f out: one pce* **20/1**

8 *½* **Time To Excel** 2-9-0 0 .... SeanLevey(3) 5 51
(Michael Dods) *chsd ldrs: hmpd over 1f out: sn wknd* **9/1**[3]

00 **9** *7* **M J Woodward**[14] 3583 2-9-3 0 .... CathyGannon 1 30
(Paul Green) *led: hdd over 2f out: hung lft and lost pl over 1f out* **100/1**

1m 14.28s (0.48) **Going Correction** -0.10s/f (Good) **9** Ran SP% **116.1**
Speed ratings (Par 94): **90,89,88,87,85 85,83,82,73**
Tote Swingers: 1&2 £5.00, 1&3 £3.00, 2&3 £3.50 CSF £10.56 TOTE £1.50: £1.10, £3.70, £1.90; EX 13.50.

Owner Mrs S J Barker **Bred** Jerry O'Sullivan **Trained** Hambleton, N Yorks

FOCUS
Not many with experience in this maiden. The bare form is only modest but the winner can do better.

NOTEBOOK
Chooseday(IRE) ♦, who the market spoke heavily in favour of, delivered in good style despite hitting a bit of a flat spot 1 1/2f out and having to squeeze between rivals to get a run. While he idled once in front, he'd travelled through the race like the best horse in the race and left the impression that he'll improve for this debut effort. A late foal and brother to Wokingham winner Laddies Poker Two, he looks to have a future. (op 5-6)
Magic Destiny, a half-sister to four-time winner at up to 1m Magic Cat, showed pace for a long way and, despite showing signs of greenness, kept on to finish second. She'll improve for this. (op 16-1)
Vociferous(USA), whose dam was a high-class 2yo, had the benefit of a previous outing (on Fibresand) and showed much more for that debut effort switched to turf. (op 8-1)
Rapid Heat Lad(IRE), a half-brother to five winners, only cost 4,000gns. He ran green early but kept on well and looks the type to pay his way in handicaps in time. (op 25-1)
Docs Legacy(IRE) again hinted he has ability, but there's plenty of stamina on the dam's side of his pedigree and he's going to be suited by further in time. (op 13-2 tchd 6-1)
New Romantic, by Singspiel out of a half-sister to Soviet Song, is another who's bred to be suited by a greater test of stamina. (op 16-1)
Time To Excel, an already gelded May foal, is a half-brother to a couple of winners over 7f and 8.4f, but is by a sire that injects more speed, so this trip looked likely to suit on his debut. Having shown early speed he dropped out, but he can be expected to build on this next time. (tchd 10-1)

4048 PARRY & CO SOLICITORS ANNUAL H'CAP — 6f

3:25 (3:26) (Class 4) (0-85,84) 3-Y-O **£4,528** (£1,347; £673; £336) **Stalls** Centre

Form RPR

1-01 **1** **Cinderkamp**[41] 2736 3-9-2 **79** .... JamieSpencer 1 100+
(Edward Vaughan) *wnt lft s: swtchd rt sn after s: hld up: nt clr run and swtchd rt over 1f out: str run to ld last 50yds* **13/2**[3]

2121 **2** *½* **York Glory (USA)**[18] 3461 3-9-1 **78** .... (b[1]) PhillipMakin 5 97
(Kevin Ryan) *trckd ldr: led over 2f out: hdd and no ex clsng stages* **9/2**[2]

3131 **3** *3 ½* **Thirteen Shivers**[30] 3052 3-9-6 **83** .... DavidNolan 9 91
(Michael Easterby) *mid-div: hdwy to chse ldrs over 2f out: kpt on same pce fnl f* **4/1**[1]

0555 **4** *2 ½* **Whipphound**[6] 3853 3-8-9 **72** .... FrannyNorton 10 72
(Mark Brisbourne) *t.k.h in rr: kpt on fnl 2f: nvr nr ldrs* **15/2**

1-0 **5** *1 ½* **Above The Stars**[97] 1241 3-9-0 **82** .... LeeTopliss(5) 6 77
(Richard Fahey) *hld up: hdwy to trck ldrs 3f out: sn drvn: one pce* **16/1**

1151 **6** *5* **Barkston Ash**[14] 3598 3-9-2 **79** .... DuranFentiman 8 58
(Eric Alston) *chsd ldrs: drvn over 2f out: fdd fnl f* **13/2**[3]

6040 **7** *3 ½* **Penny's Pearl (IRE)**[6] 3853 3-9-0 **77** .... CathyGannon 7 45
(David Evans) *s.v.s: reminders after s: sn t.k.h: sme hdwy over 2f out: sn wknd* **20/1**

0100 **8** *¾* **Style And Panache (IRE)**[11] 3687 3-9-0 **77** .... RoystonFfrench 2 42
(David Evans) *led tl over 2f out: hung rt and sn wknd* **50/1**

0-20 **9** *¾* **Tom Sawyer**[101] 1152 3-9-7 **84** .... TonyHamilton 4 47
(Julie Camacho) *chsd ldrs: wknd over 1f out* **33/1**

5022 **10** *9* **Bay Of Fires (IRE)**[2] 3975 3-8-7 **70** .... SilvestreDeSousa 3 —
(David O'Meara) *w ldrs: wknd 2f out: sn bhd* **9/2**[2]

1m 12.3s (-1.50) **Going Correction** -0.10s/f (Good) **10** Ran SP% **110.3**
Speed ratings (Par 102): **104,103,98,95,93 86,82,81,80,68**
Tote Swingers: 1&2 £7.90, 1&3 £5.50, 2&3 £2.90 CSF £33.09 CT £126.90 TOTE £8.20: £2.30, £1.90, £2.20; EX 48.30.

Owner Ali Saeed **Bred** Baron F Von Oppenheim **Trained** Newmarket, Suffolk

FOCUS
They didn't seem to go an overly strong early gallop here but the winner came from behind. The form is rated on the positive side with the winner nicely progressive.
Penny's Pearl(IRE) Official explanation: jockey said filly missed the beak
Style And Panache(IRE) Official explanation: jockey said filly hung right
Bay Of Fires(IRE) Official explanation: jockey said filly was never travelling.

4049 NATIONWIDEVEHICLECONTRACTS.CO.UK WELSH EMPEROR CONDITIONS STKS — 7f

4:00 (4:00) (Class 3) 3-Y-O+ **£7,439** (£2,213; £1,106; £553) **Stalls** Low

Form RPR

-000 **1** **Reignier**[6] 3862 4-8-12 **90** .... MartinHarley(3) 2 101
(Mrs K Burke) *stdd s: hld up: stdy hdwy over 2f out: sn nt clr run: shkn up to ld 1f out: drvn out* **20/1**

2200 **2** *1 ¾* **Kakatosi**[20] 3404 4-9-1 **104** .... DavidProbert 4 96
(Andrew Balding) *w ldrs: rdn to ld over 2f out: hdd 1f out: kpt on same pce* **7/4**[1]

/000 **3** *1 ½* **Shamandar (FR)**[6] 3862 4-8-10 **98** .... SilvestreDeSousa 3 87
(William Haggas) *t.k.h: trckd ldrs: drvn over 3f out: upsides 2f out: kpt on same pce fnl f* **5/2**[2]

0140 **4** *hd* **Norville (IRE)**[6] 3852 4-9-1 **99** .... (b) CathyGannon 6 92
(David Evans) *trckd ldrs: sn t.k.h: jnd ldrs after 2f: led over 3f out: hdd over 2f out: kpt on same pce* **6/1**[3]

0010 **5** *2* **Imperial Djay (IRE)**[6] 3862 6-9-1 **94** .... FrannyNorton 7 86
(Ruth Carr) *swtchd lft after s: hld up in last: effrt over 2f out: kpt on fnl f: nvr a factor* **8/1**

20 **6** *6* **Mahubo (SAF)**[141] 682 5-9-1 **100** .... JamieSpencer 1 76
(Tom Tate) *led: hdd over 3f out: lost pl over 1f out: eased towards fin* **6/1**[3]

1m 28.49s (-2.41) **Going Correction** -0.10s/f (Good) **6** Ran SP% **109.4**
Speed ratings (Par 107): **109,107,105,105,102 95**
Tote Swingers: 1&2 £3.80, 1&3 £5.30, 2&3 £1.50 CSF £52.84 TOTE £31.20: £10.00, £1.10; EX 63.40.

Owner Philip Richards **Bred** Sean Gollogly **Trained** Middleham Moor, North Yorks

FOCUS
Not a strong conditions race - only two of the runners boasted a three-figure official mark. Typical conditions form which shouldn't be taken too literally.

NOTEBOOK
Reignier would have been 14lb better off with the runner-up had this been a handicap and the fact that he won probably says more about the quality of the race than any improvement he has found. He didn't have much go right for him in the Bunbury Cup, but settled in this smaller field, unlike some of his rivals, and saw the trip out well (previously unproven over the distance). He's now likely to run in the 7f heritage handicap at Ascot next weekend under a penalty. Official explanation: trainer's rep said, regarding the apparent improvement in form shown, gelding was unexposed at the trip (op 25-1)
Kakatosi was the pick of the weights but he'd been well beaten in Group 3 company on his previous two starts and, while he ran better race on this drop in class, he's clearly not at his best at the moment. (tchd 13-8 and 15-8 in a place)
Shamandar(FR) didn't run badly in the Victoria Cup on her reappearance, but she'd failed to build on that in two starts since and she didn't settle here, or handle the bend. She might have been feeling the ground, though, and it's too early to write her off. (tchd 9-4, 11-4 and 3-1 in a place)
Norville(IRE), who has done all his winning over 6f but was beaten only a nose by Imperial Djay over this trip at Chester earlier in the year, was another who failed to settle in the early stages, and he eventually pulled himself to the front on the turn in. Unsurprisingly he didn't have much left in the tank for the finish. (tchd 13-2)
Imperial Djay(IRE), who finished two places behind Reignier in the Bunbury Cup, was on the back throughout and proved disappointing. (op 17-2 tchd 9-1)
Mahubo(SAF), who was having his first run for Tom Tate having won in Dubai for Mike de Kock over the winter, led them into the straight but dropped out soon afterwards in the manner of a horse who needed the run badly. (op 11-2 tchd 13-2)

4050 REWARDS4RACING.COM H'CAP — 1m 6f

4:35 (4:35) (Class 4) (0-85,88) 3-Y-O **£5,822** (£1,732; £865; £432) **Stalls** Low

Form RPR

3001 **1** **Colour Vision (FR)**[6] 3851 3-9-13 **88** 6ex .... SilvestreDeSousa 2 105+
(Mark Johnston) *trckd ldr: drvn 5f out: led over 3f out: clr 2f out: heavily eased clsng stages* **13/8**[1]

6251 **2** *10* **Dark Dune (IRE)**[14] 3587 3-8-11 **72** .... DavidAllan 3 72
(Tim Easterby) *trckd ldr: chal over 3f out: kpt on same pce fnl 2f* **9/1**

-454 **3** *4* **Argocat (IRE)**[62] 2108 3-9-5 **80** .... JamieSpencer 4 74
(Tom Tate) *hld up: drvn 5f out: outpcd over 2f out: kpt on fnl f: tk modest 3rd fnl strides* **6/1**[3]

2-16 **4** *hd* **Captain Brown**[41] 2726 3-9-5 **80** .... StevieDonohoe 1 74
(Sir Mark Prescott Bt) *dwlt: t.k.h: effrt over 3f out: kpt on to take modest 3rd over 2f out: one pce* **7/4**[2]

321 **5** *17* **Emperor Of Rome (IRE)**[28] 3138 3-8-9 **73** .... SeanLevey(3) 5 51
(Michael Dods) *led: hdd over 3f out: wknd 2f out: bhd whn eased last 100yds* **10/1**

3m 0.93s (-0.27) **Going Correction** -0.10s/f (Good) **5** Ran SP% **107.8**
Speed ratings (Par 102): **96,90,88,87,78**
CSF £14.83 TOTE £2.80: £2.20, £2.20; EX 11.00.

Owner Sheikh Hamdan Bin Mohammed Al Maktoum **Bred** Capricorn Stud **Trained** Middleham Moor, N Yorks

FOCUS
The early pace was pretty steady but it picked up rounding the turn into the straight, and once in line for home. the winner improved again and the form is rated around the runner-up.

4051 BETDAQ BETTING EXCHANGE APPRENTICE TRAINING SERIES H'CAP (RACING EXCELLENCE INITIATIVE) — 1m

5:05 (5:05) (Class 5) (0-75,73) 4-Y-O+ **£2,587** (£770; £384; £192) **Stalls** Low

Form RPR

1614 **1** **Bold Marc (IRE)**[13] 3629 9-9-6 **72** .... LMcNiff(3) 4 81
(Mrs K Burke) *led: wnt clr over 5f out: kpt on fnl 2f: drvn out: unchal* **5/1**[3]

4353 **2** 4 ½ **Bold Cross (IRE)**[22] 3326 8-9-4 67 .... MatthewCosham 7 66
(Edward Bevan) *s.i.s: t.k.h in rr: hdwy over 3f out: kpt on to take 2nd nr fin* **8/1**

0011 **3** *hd* **Qeethaara (USA)**[18] 3457 7-9-6 69 .... RyanClark 3 67
(Mark Brisbourne) *rrd s: chsd wnr: hung rt over 1f out: kpt on same pce* **13/8**[1]

0461 **4** 1 ¾ **Spavento (IRE)**[12] 3658 5-9-0 66 6ex .... DarylByrne(3) 9 60
(Eric Alston) *chsd ldrs: drvn over 3f out: one pce fnl 2f* **9/2**[2]

60-0 **5** 8 **Island Chief**[42] 2671 5-8-13 67 .... GeorgeChaloner(5) 2 43
(Michael Easterby) *rrd s: t.k.h towards rr: wknd over 2f out* **25/1**

-032 **6** 7 **Ginger Grey (IRE)**[13] 3612 4-9-10 73 ....(b) BrianToomey 6 33
(David O'Meara) *dwlt: hld up in rr: stmbld bdly bnd over 4f out: lost pl over 3f out: sn bhd* **5/1**[3]

-604 **7** 6 **Timber Treasure (USA)**[21] 3341 7-8-3 55 ....(b) RosieJessop(3) 8 —
(Paul Green) *rrd s: hld up in rr: lost pl 3f out: sn bhd* **14/1**

1m 42.93s (0.03) **Going Correction** -0.10s/f (Good) 7 Ran SP% **111.2**
Speed ratings (Par 103): **95,90,90,88,80 73,67**
CSF £40.87 CT £88.56 TOTE £6.10: £3.00, £3.80; EX 15.60.
Owner Aricabeau Racing Limited **Bred** Eamon D Delany **Trained** Middleham Moor, North Yorks

FOCUS
A modest apprentices' handicap. Not form to take too literally with the winner allowed an easy lead. He could be rated higher on face value.
Qeethaara(USA) Official explanation: jockey said mare hung right-handed
T/Plt: £281.10 to a £1 stake. Pool of £49,718.00 - 129.10 winning tickets. T/Qpdt: £28.60 to a £1 stake. Pool of £3,975.00 - 102.58 winning tickets. WG

3812 NEWBURY (L-H)
Friday, July 15

OFFICIAL GOING: Good to firm (8.2)
Wind: Virtually nil Weather: Sunny spells

4052 HIGHCLERE THOROUGHBRED RACING E B F MAIDEN FILLIES' STKS 6f 8y
1:55 (1:56) (Class 4) 2-Y-O **£4,560** (£1,357; £678; £339) **Stalls** Centre

Form RPR

2 **1** **Lady Gorgeous**[15] 3547 2-9-0 0 .... HughBowman 7 85+
(Mick Channon) *broke wl and led 1f: stdd to trck ldrs: pushed along and qcknd to ld over 1f out: shkn up and styd on strly fnl 120yds* **4/1**[2]

2 **2** 1 ¼ **Tickled Pink (IRE)**[34] 2914 2-9-0 0 .... TomQueally 3 81+
(Sir Henry Cecil) *trckd ldrs: carried sltly lft 2f out: pushed along and qcknd to press wnr 1f out: ev ch ins fnl f tl outpcd fnl 120yds* **8/15**[1]

3 2 ¼ **Dance Company** 2-9-0 0 .... JimCrowley 18 74+
(William Knight) *mid-div: pushed along: green and one pce over 2f out: drvn and styd on wl fnl f to take 3rd last strides: nt rch ldng duo* **40/1**

45 **4** *shd* **Tina's Spirit (IRE)**[44] 2606 2-8-9 0 .... KieranO'Neill(5) 17 74
(Richard Hannon) *pressed ldrs: rdn and ev ch 2f out: chsd ldng duo ins fnl f but no imp and dropped to 4th last strides* **28/1**

0 **5** 1 **Gifted Dancer**[46] 2559 2-9-0 0 .... DaneO'Neill 10 71
(Henry Candy) *led after 1f: rdn and kpt on whn chal over 2f out: hdd over 1f out: wknd fnl 120yds* **50/1**

6 4 ½ **Ice Missile** 2-9-0 0 .... LiamKeniry 16 57+
(Sylvester Kirk) *in tch: rdn over 2f out: kpt on fnl f: nvr a threat* **50/1**

6 **7** 1 **Iced Opal**[41] 2718 2-9-0 0 .... LukeMorris 11 54
(Michael Blanshard) *mid-div: pushed along and green over 2f out: styd on same pce fnl f* **100/1**

8 1 **City Dazzler (IRE)** 2-9-0 0 .... WilliamBuick 13 51+
(Richard Hannon) *in rr: c to r stands over 2f out and stl bhd: pushed along and styd on ins fnl f: nvr a threat* **50/1**

9 ½ **Idols Eye** 2-9-0 0 .... RyanMoore 8 50+
(Richard Hannon) *in rr: rdn and styd on fr over 1f out: nvr in contention* **22/1**

10 1 ½ **Periwinkle Way** 2-9-0 0 .... JamesDoyle 14 45
(Sylvester Kirk) *mid-div: pushed along 1/2-way: nvr gng pce to rch ldrs* **66/1**

11 ½ **Refreshestheparts (USA)** 2-8-11 0 .... MatthewDavies(3) 9 44
(George Baker) *pressed ldrs: rdn: green and hung lft 2f out: sn btn* **40/1**

12 ¾ **Tamima (USA)** 2-9-0 0 .... MartinDwyer 1 42
(Brian Meehan) *broke wl: sn rr: drvn and sme hdwy fr 3f out: nvr rchd ldrs and wknd ins fnl 2f* **50/1**

0 **13** *nk* **Shannon Spree**[23] 3287 2-9-0 0 .... RichardHughes 5 41
(Richard Hannon) *chsd ldrs tl wknd over 2f out* **16/1**[3]

0 **14** 2 ¼ **Compton Bird**[9] 3736 2-9-0 0 .... AdamKirby 2 34
(Hans Adielsson) *in tch tl wknd over 2f out* **100/1**

15 1 **Manbaa (USA)** 2-9-0 0 .... RichardHills 15 31
(John Dunlop) *wnt rt s and slowly away: sn rdn and green: a struggling in rr* **33/1**

16 1 **Amphora** 2-9-0 0 .... JimmyFortune 4 28
(Andrew Balding) *in tch: rdn 3f out: green and wknd over 2f out* **16/1**[3]

1m 12.95s (-0.05) **Going Correction** +0.175s/f (Good) 16 Ran SP% **123.9**
Speed ratings (Par 93): **107,105,102,102,100 94,93,92,91,89 88,87,87,84,83 81**
Tote Swingers: 1&2 £2.20, 1&3 £4.40, 2&3 £3.50 CSF £5.96 TOTE £5.20: £1.50, £1.10, £10.80; EX 9.40 Trifecta £357.50 Part won. Pool: £483.13 - 0.82 winning units..
Owner Jaber Abdullah **Bred** Newsells Park Stud **Trained** West Ilsley, Berks

FOCUS
Rail realignment added 26m to advertised distances on Round course. A headwind in the straight appeared to have an effect on the race times. A decent fillies' race in which the best recent scorer was subsequent Prix Morny winner Silca's Sister. Plenty of debutantes were taking on a couple of fillies with form in the book and the market suggested the race only involved the latter pair. That proved to be the case, although the result was not quite as the betting suggested.

NOTEBOOK
Lady Gorgeous ◆, out of a 1m1f Listed winner, had shaped well when runner-up to a more experienced rival over C&D on her debut. She broke well but was settled off the pace, then found plenty when asked to challenge. She will presumably be aimed at something better now, and was given a 50-1 quote for the 1,000 Guineas. (op 5-1)
Tickled Pink(IRE), out of the high-class sprinter Cassandra Go, had been runner-up on her debut to a filly who went on to finish second in the Cherry Hinton. As a result of that she was sent off at odds on and appeared to have every chance, but the winner proved strongest in the last furlong. She was clear of the rest and her turn should not be far away. (op 4-7)
Dance Company ◆, a half-sister to three winners at 6f-7f from the family of Misraah, caught the eye staying on steadily in the closing stages and should be much sharper for the outing. (op 33-1)
Tina's Spirit(IRE) had shown modest form in two starts in maidens on fast ground and Polytrack but ran better this time. She helps set the level and now qualifies for a mark.
Gifted Dancer had started slowly and ran green on her debut but had clearly learnt from that and showed good pace until tiring in the closing stages. She can win an ordinary maiden. (tchd 66-1)
Ice Missile, a half-sister to Wokingham winner Dark Missile amongst others, showed signs of ability on this debut.
Refreshestheparts(USA), a 35,000euros daughter of a useful miler, displayed plenty of speed but stopped quite quickly in the closing stages. (op 50-1 tchd 33-1)

4053 HIGHCLERE THOROUGHBRED RACING E B F MAIDEN STKS (DIV I) 7f (S)
2:30 (2:30) (Class 4) 2-Y-O **£4,237** (£1,260; £630; £315) **Stalls** Centre

Form RPR

1 **Ektihaam (IRE)** 2-9-3 0 .... RichardHills 2 87+
(Roger Varian) *wnt lft s: t.k.h and sn rcvrd to trck ldrs: drvn to ld appr fnl f: edgd rt and styd on strly fnl 120yds* **8/1**[3]

2 1 ½ **Harvard N Yale (USA)** 2-9-3 0 .... GeorgeBaker 7 84+
(Jeremy Noseda) *in tch: pushed along and green 2f out: shkn up and styd on strly ins fnl f: tk 2nd last strides but nt rch wnr* **9/2**[2]

201 **3** *hd* **Campanology**[14] 3583 2-9-3 0 .... RichardHughes 3 82
(Richard Hannon) *led: drvn and edgd rt 2f out: hdd appr fnl f: hung bdly rt sn after: no imp on wnr fnl 120yds: lost 2nd last strides* **11/8**[1]

2 **4** 1 ¼ **Gunner Will (IRE)**[14] 3590 2-9-3 0 .... MatthewDavies(3) 6 80
(George Baker) *in tch: rdn to chse ldrs whn bmpd wl over 1f out: styd on same pce ins fnl f* **11/1**

5 4 **Martin Chuzzlewit (IRE)** 2-9-3 0 .... RyanMoore 10 69+
(Sir Michael Stoute) *in rr but in tch: drvn along over 2f out: styd on fnl f: nt rch ldrs* **9/2**[2]

6 2 ¼ **Producer** 2-9-3 0 .... WilliamBuick 5 63
(Richard Hannon) *chsd ldrs: pushed along and green 2f out: outpcd fnl f* **16/1**

7 1 ¾ **Alvitude (USA)** 2-9-3 0 .... SteveDrowne 1 59+
(Roger Charlton) *slowly away: in rr: pushed along and hdwy over 2f out: nvr rchd ldrs and one pce fr over 1f out* **33/1**

8 ½ **Beau Duke (IRE)** 2-9-3 0 .... JimmyFortune 9 58
(Andrew Balding) *rdn and bhd fnl 3f* **40/1**

5 **9** 1 ¾ **Drummond**[19] 3424 2-9-3 0 .... AdamKirby 8 53
(Clive Cox) *chsd ldrs over 4f* **20/1**

10 6 **Welsh Nayber** 2-9-3 0 .... JimCrowley 11 38
(Amanda Perrett) *chsd ldrs over 4f* **66/1**

11 13 **Kula Kangri (IRE)** 2-9-3 0 .... TomQueally 4 6
(Rebecca Curtis) *spd to 1/2-way* **66/1**

1m 26.74s (1.04) **Going Correction** +0.175s/f (Good) 11 Ran SP% **116.9**
Speed ratings (Par 96): **101,99,99,97,93 90,88,87,85,79 64**
Tote Swingers: 1&2 £5.20, 1&3 £3.40, 2&3 £3.50 CSF £41.93 TOTE £10.30: £2.70, £2.10, £1.10; EX 53.70 Trifecta £353.30 Part won. Pool: £477.52 - 0.88 winning units..
Owner Hamdan Al Maktoum **Bred** Bernard Cooke **Trained** Newmarket, Suffolk

FOCUS
A fair maiden in which the best recent winner was the dual subsequent Group 2 winner Emerald Commander.

NOTEBOOK
Ektihaam(IRE) ◆, a 250,000gns son of a 1m and 1m4f winner from the family of Awaasif, is by sire who gets precocious stock and that enabled him to make a winning debut. He jumped awkwardly from the gate and was a little keen early, but then came through to take the favourite and score with something in reserve. A big, imposing sort, he looks capable of going on from this and was given a quote of 33-1 for next year's 2,000 Guineas. (op 13-2)
Harvard N Yale(USA) ◆, a half-brother to a smart US performer and with a Group 1 entry, had a noseband on for this debut. He travelled well off the pace but could not pick up immediately when the first two went for home, although he stayed on in good style to snatch second near the line. He should have learnt a lot from this and a similar contest looks a formality. (tchd 6-1)
Campanology, whose trainer had been responsible for three winners of this in the last ten years, had already had three starts, and had been disqualified after he narrowly scored at Haydock on his previous outing. He made the running but faded in the closing stages and might have found the extra furlong too far. (op 13-8 tchd 5-4)
Gunner Will(IRE) had made a promising debut in a decent 7f fast ground maiden at Sandown, but the third had been well beaten since and he was easy to back. He tracked the pace before coming through to challenge, but rather ran into the back of the favourite under a right-handed drive over a furlong out before keeping on again. He can win races, possibly at one of the smaller tracks. (op 12-1)
Martin Chuzzlewit(IRE), a 420,000euros son of an unraced half-sister to a French Oaks second, was well backed against the favourite but was being niggled along from an early stage. He ran on in the closing stages and looks sure to appreciate a longer trip in future. (op 6-1)
Producer, a £28,000 half-brother to three winners including Kabis Amigos, showed good pace before fading. He was not given a hard time once his chance had gone and should last much better next time. (op 20-1)
Alvitude(USA), a half-brother to four winners at 1m-1m6f from the family of Sanglamore, totally missed the break on his debut but showed signs of ability, staying on steadily in the latter stages. (op 25-1)

4054 HIGHCLERE THOROUGHBRED RACING E B F MAIDEN STKS (DIV II) 7f (S)
3:05 (3:05) (Class 4) 2-Y-O **£4,237** (£1,260; £630; £315) **Stalls** Centre

Form RPR

1 **Jungle Beat (IRE)** 2-9-3 0 .... WilliamBuick 6 83+
(John Gosden) *trckd ldrs: slt ld appr fnl 2f: drvn and green fnl f and edgd rt: kpt on strly* **9/4**[1]

2 2 **Farhaan (USA)** 2-9-3 0 .... RichardHills 4 76+
(John Dunlop) *stdd in tch: pushed along and hdwy fr 2f out: styd on ins fnl f: tk 2nd last strides* **14/1**

0 **3** *hd* **Gold Sceptre (FR)**[19] 3425 2-9-3 0 .... RichardHughes 8 75
(Richard Hannon) *sn led: narrowly hdd appr fnl 2f: styd pressing wnr tl over 1f out: styng on same pce whn swtchd lft ins fnl f: lost 2nd last strides* **11/4**[2]

5 **4** *hd* **Opera Buff**[33] 2962 2-9-3 0 .... LiamKeniry 9 75
(Sylvester Kirk) *chsd ldrs: drvn along over 2f out: styd on thrght fnl f: gng on cl home but no ch w wnr* **13/2**[3]

5 ¾ **Rugged Cross** 2-9-3 0 .... DaneO'Neill 10 73+
(Henry Candy) *in rr: pushed along and gd hdwy over 1f out: styd on wl thrght fnl f: gng on cl home but no ch w wnr* **8/1**

0 **6** 3 ½ **Vergrigio (IRE)**[14] 3590 2-9-3 0 .... MartinDwyer 5 65+
(Brian Meehan) *s.i.s: in rr: drvn over 2f out: styd on fnl f but nvr gng pce to rch ldrs* **33/1**

7 9 **Hidden Justice (IRE)** 2-9-3 0 .... JimCrowley 7 41
(Amanda Perrett) *chsd ldrs: rdn 3f out: hung lft: green and wknd 2f out* **14/1**

8 5 **Next Cry (USA)** 2-9-3 0 .... RyanMoore 2 29
(Richard Hannon) *pressed ldrs 4f: wknd qckly fr 2f out* **15/2**

9 2 1/4 **Compton Target (IRE)** 2-9-3 0.. JamesDoyle 3 23
(Hans Adielsson) *t.k.h: chsd ldrs tl wknd qckly fr 2f out* **66/1**

1m 27.15s (1.45) **Going Correction** +0.175s/f (Good) **9** Ran SP% **111.4**
Speed ratings (Par 96): **98,95,95,95,94 90,80,74,71**
Tote Swingers: 1&2 £6.40, 1&3 £2.20, 2&3 £8.20 CSF £33.40 TOTE £2.70: £1.10, £2.50, £1.60; EX 22.90 Trifecta £50.80 Pool: £606.69 - 8.83 winning units..
Owner Michael Tabor, Mrs John Magnier & Derrick Smith **Bred** Flamingo Guitar Syndicate **Trained** Newmarket, Suffolk

FOCUS
The second division of this maiden was run 0.41secs slower than the first and resulted in another taking debut.

NOTEBOOK
Jungle Beat(IRE) ◆, the first foal of a 7f winner from a good US family, was well backed and was always travelling on this debut for a trainer with a good record in similar contests here. He eased to the front over 2f out going well and, despite showing signs of greenness, came away to win decisively. He has a Derby entry and connections are likely to be looking to step him up in grade after this. (op 3-1)
Farhaan(USA) ◆, the fourth foal of a Listed winner from the family of Shadayid and related to winners at 6f-1m1f, is another with a Derby entry but was easy in the market. He was held up before keeping on steadily under hands-and-heels riding, and should come on a good deal for the experience. (op 10-1)
Gold Sceptre(FR) was sent off favourite for his debut but started slowly and ran green. Again well supported, he was always up with the pace but failed to hold off the winner, although he was done no favours by that rival over a furlong out. He will have easier tasks. (op 9-4)
Opera Buff, a half-brother to a 1m2f-1m3f winner from the family of Night Shot and Grey Shot, had been slowly away but showed signs of ability on his debut and was sharper this time. He looked a threat when coming through to challenge, but suffered a little in the concertina effect caused by the winner and had no more to offer in the closing stages. (op 12-1)
Rugged Cross ◆, a 55,000gns half-brother to eight winners including Blue Monday and Lundy's Lane, is yet another Derby entry. He raced on the flank of his field nearest the stands' side, before making progress to finish on the heels of the placed horses under considerate handling. He is another who can be expected to benefit from the experience. (op 13-2)
Vergrigio(IRE), who was a long price and ran green on his debut, ran on from out the back and drew clear of the remainder. He should win a race in due course, possibly when there is ease in the ground.

4055 ROSE BOWL STKS - SPONSORED BY COMPTON BEAUCHAMP ESTATES LTD (LISTED RACE) 6f 8y
3:40 (3:40) (Class 1) 2-Y-O
£12,192 (£4,622; £2,313; £1,152; £578; £290) **Stalls** Centre

Form RPR
1 **1** **Saigon**[15] 3553 2-9-0 0.. KirstyMilczarek 3 102+
(James Toller) *hld up in rr: drvn and str run appr fnl f whn pushed rt: fin wl to ld last strides* **6/1**[3]
1243 **2** *nk* **Caspar Netscher**[31] 3014 2-9-0 0.. RobertWinston 6 101
(Alan McCabe) *in rr: drvn and hdwy 2f out: hung rt u.p appr fnl f: kpt on to ld fnl 120yds: hdd last strides* **9/2**[2]
11 **3** *1 3/4* **Factory Time (IRE)**[35] 2868 2-9-0 0.. HughBowman 10 96
(Mick Channon) *t.k.h: trckd ldr and wnt lft towards far side over 3f out: drvn over 1f out: kpt on to take 3rd clsng stages but no imp on ldng duo* **4/1**[1]
2104 **4** *nk* **North Star Boy (IRE)**[8] 3773 2-9-0 0.. RichardHughes 9 95
(Richard Hannon) *led: wnt lft to far rail over 3f out: rdn and kpt on fnl 2f: hdd fnl 120yds: sn no ex and lost 3rd clsng stages* **13/2**
516 **5** *1/2* **Telwaar**[27] 3152 2-9-0 0.. JimmyFortune 2 93
(Peter Chapple-Hyam) *chsd ldrs towards far rail: swtchd rt over 1f out and kpt on ins fnl f: nvr gng pce to get into contention* **16/1**
0116 **6** *1/2* **B Fifty Two (IRE)**[31] 3012 2-9-0 0.. SebSanders 7 92
(J W Hills) *in rr: hdwy and carried rt over 1f out: kpt on u.p: nvr gng pce to rch ldrs* **15/2**
0120 **7** *1 1/4* **Bling King**[27] 3152 2-9-0 0.. DaneO'Neill 5 88
(Eve Johnson Houghton) *in rr: pushed along over 2f out: styd on fnl f but nvr gng pce to get into contention* **66/1**
[illegible] [illegible] [illegible] **[illegible] (IRE)**[14] 3580 2-9-0 0.. RyanMoore 1 78
(David Evans) *chsd ldrs: rdn over 2f out: sn outpcd: [illegible] fnl f* **16/1**
11 **9** *2 1/4* **Wise Venture (IRE)**[45] 2594 2-9-0 0.. JimCrowley 4 72
(Alan Jarvis) *chsd ldrs tl wknd fr ins fnl 2f* **4/1**[1]
5120 **10** *1 3/4* **Evervescent (IRE)**[31] 3012 2-9-0 0.. LiamKeniry 8 66
(J S Moore) *t.k.h: chsd ldrs 4f* **50/1**

1m 13.74s (0.74) **Going Correction** +0.175s/f (Good) **10** Ran SP% **112.8**
Speed ratings (Par 102): **102,101,99,98,98 97,95,91,88,86**
Tote Swingers: 1&2 £5.00, 1&3 £6.70, 2&3 £5.70 CSF £31.99 TOTE £7.10: £2.30, £1.90, £1.70; EX 39.30 Trifecta £131.60 Pool: £912.62 - 5.13 winning units..
Owner P C J Dalby & R D Schuster **Bred** R Dollar, T Adams & G F Pemberton **Trained** Newmarket, Suffolk

FOCUS
A decent Listed sprint which has produced a couple of subsequent Group 2 winners (Deportivo and Assertive) in recent seasons. The runners crossed to the inside rail at about halfway but the first two race on the outside of the pack and came more towards the centre in the closing stages. The time was 0.79secs slower than the earlier fillies' maiden.

NOTEBOOK
Saigon, a half-brother to multiple sprint winner Tabaret, had beaten an odds-on shot on his debut on fast ground. He raced on the outside of his field here and came through with the runner-up, then managed to overcome interference from that rival to edge ahead near the finish. He still looked inexperienced and may have more to offer. (tchd 13-2)
Caspar Netscher, a 5f winner on fast ground, had finished a good third in the Windsor Castle, and the winner of that race had since taken the Group 2 July Stakes. He came through on the outside of the field to take the lead but edged right under pressure towards the winner and lost the advantage near the finish. He might appreciate a return to the minimum. (op 4-1)
Factory Time(IRE) had won both previous starts, including beating Bling King at Chepstow, and came through to challenge the leader near the far rail, but was unable to cope with the pair up the centre. (op 10-3)
North Star Boy(IRE), a 5f winner but only half-a length behind B Fifty Two in the Coventry, then fourth in the July Stakes, was dropping in grade and made the running. He took the field to the far side but could not resist the late challenges. (op 8-1)
Telwaar had Bling King behind when sixth in the Chesham having hung right throughout. He got rather locked away when the field went to the far rail and was unable to get close enough to mount a challenge. (op 18-1 tchd 20-1)
B Fifty Two(IRE), a dual winner at 5f-6f on fast ground, raced with the principals up the centre before weakening in the last furlong. (op 7-1 tchd 13-2)
Bling King, a 6f fast-ground winner and placed at that trip, had finished well behind in the Chesham.
Wise Venture(IRE), previously 2-2, showed up early if racing a little keenly, but was the first one beaten. (op 9-2 tchd 7-2)

4056 SMITH & WILLIAMSON FILLIES' H'CAP 1m 2f 6y
4:15 (4:15) (Class 4) (0-80,76) 3-Y-O **£4,528** (£1,347; £673; £336) **Stalls** Low

Form RPR
1224 **1** **Sacred Shield**[24] 3260 3-9-6 **75**.. TomQueally 12 82+
(Sir Henry Cecil) *trckd ldrs: drvn to ld appr fnl f: rdn and styd on strly fnl 120yds* **10/3**[2]
0-00 **2** *3/4* **Sugar Hiccup (IRE)**[35] 2885 3-8-5 **63**.. JohnFahy(3) 5 68
(Clive Cox) *chsd ldrs: rdn along 4f out: outpcd 2f out: styd on again over 1f out: fin wl to take 2nd cl home but no imp on wnr* **25/1**
0-42 **3** *1/2* **Sally Friday (IRE)**[21] 3354 3-9-2 **71**.. LukeMorris 11 75
(Peter Winkworth) *chsd ldr over 7f out: str chal fr 3f out and stl upsides w wnr over 1f out: no ex fnl 120yds: lost 2nd cl home* **8/1**
5-15 **4** *1/2* **Countermarch**[27] 3180 3-9-6 **75**.. DaneO'Neill 4 78
(Richard Hannon) *in rr: rdn and hdwy towards outside fr 2f out: styd on u.p fnl f: gng on cl home but no rch ldrs* **16/1**
2-53 **5** *1* **Lucy Limelites**[36] 2849 3-9-3 **72**..(b) SteveDrowne 7 73
(Roger Charlton) *led: rdn to hold slt advantage whn jnd fr 3f out: hdd over 1f out: wknd fnl 120yds* **8/1**
2123 **6** *nk* **Mrs Neat (IRE)**[106] 1057 3-8-5 **65**.. KieranO'Neill(5) 6 65
(Sylvester Kirk) *chsd ldrs: rdn 3f out: styd on same pce fr over 1f out* **40/1**
025- **7** *hd* **Ninfea (IRE)**[261] 7165 3-9-2 **71**.. LiamKeniry 8 71
(Sylvester Kirk) *stdd in rr s: drvn 2f out: pushed along and hdwy ins fnl f: kpt on clsng stages* **40/1**
6341 **8** *3/4* **Zamina (IRE)**[25] 3228 3-9-1 **70**.. JamesDoyle 10 69
(Sylvester Kirk) *in rr: pushed along over 2f out: sme prog ins fnl f* **15/2**[3]
5622 **9** *shd* **Hidden Valley**[18] 3469 3-9-4 **73**..(p) JimmyFortune 9 73+
(Andrew Balding) *in tch: pushed along and sme hdwy 2f out: nvr rchd ldrs: eased whn wl hld clsng stages* **11/1**
01-4 **10** *1/2* **Tameen**[27] 3180 3-9-6 **75**.. RichardHills 2 72+
(John Dunlop) *hld up in mid-div: hdwy on ins and nt clr run over 2f out edgd lft after and lost position: styd on again clsng stages* **11/4**[1]
-204 **11** *9* **Shewalksinbeauty (IRE)**[30] 3044 3-9-7 **76**.. RyanMoore 1 55
(Richard Hannon) *in rr: sme hdwy on ins fr 3f out: nvr in contention: wknd fr 2f out* **9/1**

2m 8.66s (-0.14) **Going Correction** -0.175s/f (Firm) **11** Ran SP% **116.7**
Speed ratings (Par 99): **93,92,92,91,90 90,90,89,89,89 82**
Tote Swingers: 1&2 £21.10, 1&3 £6.00, 2&3 £44.30 CSF £86.46 CT £616.99 TOTE £3.70: £1.70, £9.40, £3.60; EX 109.40 TRIFECTA Not won..
Owner K Abdulla **Bred** Juddmonte Farms Ltd **Trained** Newmarket, Suffolk

FOCUS
A dry night resulted in the ground firming up on the round course, and the rail was set out so that races were run over 26m further than advertised. A fair but competitive fillies' handicap, but the pace was not that strong and the first three were always in the leading group. Probably ordinary fillies' form overall.
Hidden Valley Official explanation: jockey said filly was unsuited by good to firm ground.
Tameen Official explanation: jockey said filly hung right throughout.

4057 DOWNLOAD THE BLUE SQUARE BET APP H'CAP 5f 34y
4:45 (4:45) (Class 5) (0-70,70) 3-Y-O+ **£2,587** (£770; £384; £192) **Stalls** Centre

Form RPR
1234 **1** **Rebecca Romero**[24] 3261 4-8-12 **56**.. RichardHughes 4 67
(Denis Coakley) *trckd ldrs: drvn and hung lft fr over 1f out: led fnl 150yds: pushed out and in command clsng stages* **9/2**[2]
602 **2** *1 1/2* **Even Bolder**[4] 3914 8-9-9 **70**.. KierenFox(3) 11 76
(Eric Wheeler) *in rr: hdwy fnl f: styd on wl: edgd lft and tk 2nd cl home but no ch w wnr* **8/1**
0430 **3** *1* **Bateleur**[9] 3721 7-8-13 **60**.. MatthewDavies(3) 3 62
(Mick Channon) *in rr: rdn and hdwy over 1f out: styd on u.p ins fnl f to take 3rd clsng stages but nvr any ch w ldng duo* **14/1**
6256 **4** *hd* **Catalinas Diamond (IRE)**[16] 3523 3-9-2 **65**.. SteveDrowne 10 65
(Pat Murphy) *bmpd s: sn in tch: hdwy to trck ldrs 2f out: str chal ins fnl f: one pce clsng stages* **16/1**
[illegible] [illegible] [illegible] **[illegible] (IRE)**[25] 3238 3-9-7 **70**..(tp) RyanMoore 12 65
(Sylvester Kirk) *s.i.s: in rr: drvn hdwy and hung rt ins fnl [illegible]* **11/2**[3]
6050 **6** *nk* **Fairy Tales**[17] 3476 3-7-11 **51** oh1.. RyanPowell(5) 5 45
(John Bridger) *mid-div: hdwy over 1f out: n.m.r ins fnl f and swtchd lft: nvr gng pce to press ldrs* **66/1**
3453 **7** *nk* **Diamond Johnny G (USA)**[4] 3914 4-9-4 **65**..........(t) AlanCreighton(3) 9 60
(Edward Creighton) *chsd ldrs: drvn and hung bdly lft fr 2f out: stl hanging whn styng on fnl f: nt rcvr* **9/1**
0333 **8** *1* **Spic 'n Span**[11] 3678 6-8-8 **52**..(b) LukeMorris 7 43
(Ronald Harris) *led and racd alone 3f: c towards main gp fr 2f out: hdd & wknd fnl 150yds* **14/1**
0-32 **9** *4 1/2* **Our Piccadilly (IRE)**[11] 3685 6-9-7 **68**.. LouisBeuzelin(3) 1 43
(Stuart Kittow) *in rr: rdn and sme hdwy fr 2f out: nvr rchd ldrs and wknd fnl f* **11/4**[1]
2-06 **10** *1* **Hidden Destiny**[10] 3711 4-9-6 **64**..(b[1]) SebSanders 8 36
(Peter Makin) *chsd ldr tl hung lft and wknd wl over 1f out* **8/1**

61.87 secs (0.47) **Going Correction** +0.175s/f (Good)
WFA 3 from 4yo+ 5lb **10** Ran SP% **113.2**
Speed ratings (Par 103): **103,100,99,98,96 96,95,94,86,85**
Tote Swingers: 1&2 £7.20, 1&3 £11.20, 2&3 £14.00 CSF £39.07 CT £471.12 TOTE £4.90: £2.10, £2.50, £3.70; EX 47.60 Trifecta £510.40 Pool: £703.62 - 1.02 winning units..
Owner Keepers Racing Ii **Bred** D W Armstrong **Trained** West Ilsley, Berks

FOCUS
A modest sprint handicap in which Spic 'N Span ensured a good gallop. The level is set around the runner-up.
Diamond Johnny G(USA) Official explanation: jockey said gelding was unsuited by good to firm ground.

4058 SHADWELL "STANDING FOR SUCCESS" H'CAP 1m 2f 6y
5:20 (5:28) (Class 3) (0-95,93) 3-Y-O+
£7,158 (£2,143; £1,071; £535; £267; £134) **Stalls** Low

Form RPR
3000 **1** **Tinshu (IRE)**[14] 3592 5-9-0 **79**.. DaneO'Neill 6 90
(Derek Haydn Jones) *hld up in rr: hdwy on outside fr 3f out: rdn to ld appr fnl f: drvn out* **20/1**
2461 **2** *1 1/4* **Suits Me**[26] 3203 8-9-12 **91**.. MickyFenton 3 99
(David Barron) *led: jnd fr over 3f out but kpt slt advantage: rdn: hung rt and hdd appr fnl f: nt gng pce of wnr but wl clr of 3rd* **17/2**

-116 **3** *6* **Sud Pacifique (IRE)**[29] 3069 3-9-2 **92**......................(p) RichardHughes 1 88
(Jeremy Noseda) *hld up in rr: rdn along 4f out: hdwy to chse ldrs 2f out: no further prog u.p and styd on one pce for wl-hld 3rd ins fnl f* **11/8**[1]
00-6 **4** *1* **Desert Kiss**[20] 3406 6-9-12 **91**...................... AdamKirby 2 85
(Walter Swinburn) *chsd ldrs: drvn to chal 2f out: wknd qckly over 1f out* **14/1**
2313 **5** *1 1/2* **Udabaa (IRE)**[20] 3406 4-9-13 **92**......................(p) RichardHills 5 83
(Marcus Tregoning) *chsd ldr: chal 3f out to 2f out: sn btn* **7/2**[2]
3300 **6** *shd* **Bikini Babe (IRE)**[46] 2573 4-9-10 **89**...................... DarrylIHolland 4 80
(Mark Johnston) *in tch: rdn 4f out: btn over 2f out: styd on again clsng stages* **20/1**
4300 **7** *1/2* **Breakheart (IRE)**[30] 3032 4-9-9 **88**......................(v[1]) LiamKeniry 8 78
(Michael Dods) *trckd ldrs: chal travelling wl fr 3f out: wknd qckly fr 2f out* **9/2**[3]

2m 5.17s (-3.63) **Going Correction** -0.175s/f (Firm)
WFA 3 from 4yo+ 11lb 7 Ran SP% **109.2**
Speed ratings (Par 107): **107,106,101,100,99 99,98**
Tote Swingers: 1&2 £18.80, 1&3 £6.90, 2&3 £2.80 CSF £157.77 CT £361.14 TOTE £28.50: £6.40, £2.20; EX 149.90 TRIFECTA Not won..
Owner Llewelyn, Runeckles **Bred** Mrs M L Parry & P M Steele-Mortimer **Trained** Efail Isaf, Rhondda C Taff

FOCUS
A good and very competitive handicap but in the end the first two came clear and the time was almost 3.5secs faster than the earlier fillies' handicap. The winner is rated to her turf best.

NOTEBOOK
Tinshu(IRE) has struggled in recent races but had dropped a few pounds as a result so that she was 3lb below her last winning turf rating. Held up at the back, she got a clear run down the outside in the straight and, despite tending to edge left, managed to get past the game runner-up. She should not go up much for this. (op 22-1 tchd 25-1)
Suits Me, up 4lb for his last success, did not get an uncontested lead this time but battled away in his usual fashion and drew away from the rest. (op 7-1 tchd 9-1)
Sud Pacifique(IRE), a dual winner at this trip earlier in the season before appearing not to stay 1m4f at Royal Ascot, had cheekpieces on for the first time. He was short of room early in the straight but was soon ridden and had nothing more to offer once in the clear over a furlong out. (op 7-4)
Desert Kiss, having just her second outing of the season, ran reasonably and only needs to drop a couple of pounds to be back to her last winning mark. (op 12-1 tchd 16-1)
Udabaa(IRE) kept the leader company for a long way but, once under pressure, found little. This was disappointing. (op 3-1)
Bikini Babe(IRE) has been struggling for form this season and even a declining mark has failed to inspire a revival. (op 16-1)
Breakheart(IRE), who was wearing a first-time visor, was replated before the start. He travelled well in the race and looked the most likely winner halfway up the straight, only to find virtually nothing off the bridle. Maybe he did too much early and cheekpieces might not fire him up as much.

4059 OAKLEY COACHBUILDERS APPRENTICE H'CAP 1m 3f 5y
5:55 (5:56) (Class 5) (0-75,75) 4-Y-0+ **£2,587** (£770; £384; £192) **Stalls** Low

Form RPR
-502 **1** **Shernando**[7] 3811 4-9-10 **75**...................... EdmondLinehan 6 85
(Mark Johnston) *stdd towards rr but in tch: hdwy fr 2f out: trckd ldr 1f out: shkn up to ld fnl 75yds: comf* **15/8**[1]
3005 **2** *2* **Rodrigo De Freitas (IRE)**[7] 3814 4-8-2 **60**..............(v) DanielCremin[(7)] 1 66
(Jim Boyle) *s.i.s: sn rcvrd to chse ldrs: rdn to ld appr fnl 2f: hrd rdn fnl f: hdd and no ex fnl 75yds* **9/1**
6-12 **3** *4 1/2* **Amazing King (IRE)**[12] 3660 7-9-4 **74**...................... DavidSimmonson[(5)] 4 72
(Philip Kirby) *chsd ldr: rdn and no imp 2f out: wknd ins fnl f* **5/2**[2]
-036 **4** *1 1/2* **Rosco Flyer (IRE)**[39] 2769 5-9-5 **73**...................... LewisWalsh[(3)] 2 68
(Roger Teal) *in rr: rdn along 3f out: mod prog fnl f* **15/2**
6210 **5** *5* **Megalala (IRE)**[8] 3760 10-9-1 **66**...................... JakePayne 3 52
(John Bridger) *led: clr over 5f out: rdn 3f out: hdd over 2f out: sn btn* **12/1**
4001 **6** *3 3/4* **Resplendent Light**[7] 3799 6-9-3 **71** 6ex..................(t) ThomasBrown[(3)] 7 50
(Bernard Llewellyn) *rdn along 3f out: a in rr* **11/2**[3]

2m 21.64s (0.44) **Going Correction** -0.175s/f (Firm) 6 Ran SP% **108.2**
Speed ratings (Par 103): **91,89,86,85,81 78**
Tote Swingers: 1&2 £4.40, 1&3 £1.30, 2&3 £4.20. Tote Super 7: Win: not won. Place: not won. CSF £17.44 TOTE £2.40: £1.30, £4.90; EX 17.20.
Owner The Originals **Bred** Miss K Rausing **Trained** Middleham Moor, N Yorks

FOCUS
An ordinary apprentices' handicap which was sound run. The winner probably only needed to match his unlucky Chester second.
T/Jkpt: Part won. £7,100.00 to a £1 stake. Pool: £12,503.03 - 0.50 winning units. T/Plt: £25.90 to a £1 stake. Pool of £63,962.00 - 1,802.77 winning tickets. T/Qpdt: £18.40 to a £1 stake. Pool of £3,565.00 - 143.05 winning tickets. ST

3861 NEWMARKET (R-H)
Friday, July 15

OFFICIAL GOING: Good to firm (8.0)
Wind: Light across Weather: Overcast

4060 TURFTV H'CAP 1m 2f
5:50 (5:51) (Class 5) (0-70,70) 3-Y-0+ **£2,587** (£770; £384; £192) **Stalls** Centre

Form RPR
0-53 **1** **Proud Chieftain**[21] 3361 3-9-2 **69**...................... JamesDoyle 5 80+
(Clifford Lines) *s.i.s: hdwy over 7f out: rdn to ld ins fnl f: r.o* **7/2**[1]
4603 **2** *2 3/4* **Focail Maith**[28] 3133 3-9-3 **70**...................... MichaelHills 11 75
(John Ryan) *hld up: swtchd lft and hdwy over 1f out: r.o to go 2nd post: nt rch wnr* **12/1**
30-0 **3** *nse* **Formidable Guest**[18] 3468 7-8-8 **55**...................... HarryBentley[(5)] 13 60
(Jamie Poulton) *hld up: hdwy over 3f out: led over 1f out: rdn and hdd ins fnl f: styd on same pce* **33/1**
-004 **4** *1/2* **Twice Bitten**[15] 3557 3-9-3 **70**...................... PatDobbs 16 74
(James Toller) *chsd ldrs: rdn and ev ch over 2f out: edgd rt and styd on same pce ins fnl f* **4/1**[2]
036- **5** *nk* **Jamhoori**[378] 3631 3-9-1 **68**...................... PhilipRobinson 10 71
(Clive Brittain) *mid-div: hdwy 1/2-way: led over 2f out: rdn and hdd over 1f out: styd on same pce ins fnl f* **6/1**[3]
-043 **6** *2 1/2* **Kalendar Girl (IRE)**[22] 3312 3-8-10 **63**...................... EddieAhern 7 61
(Willie Musson) *led early: chsd ldr tl led 3f out: rdn and hdd over 2f out: hmpd and wknd ins fnl f* **7/2**[1]
2040 **7** *1 3/4* **Laconicos (IRE)**[27] 3176 9-9-0 **61**......................(t) LauraPike[(5)] 15 56
(William Stone) *hld up: hdwy 6f out: jnd ldrs over 2f out: sn rdn: styd on same pce appr fnl f* **20/1**
0-33 **8** *hd* **Cry Alot Boy**[20] 3391 8-9-6 **62**...................... JackMitchell 12 56
(Kevin Morgan) *stdd s: hld up: hdwy 2f out: sn rdn: wknd ins fnl f* **25/1**
2-66 **9** *26* **Alternative Choice (USA)**[126] 839 5-8-9 **58**...................... RichardOld[(7)] 8 —
(Nick Littmoden) *s.i.s: hmpd sn after s: a in rr: wknd over 2f out: t.o* **40/1**
1312 **10** *3* **Mini's Destination**[18] 3457 3-8-13 **66**...................... NickyMackay 14 —
(John Holt) *chsd ldrs: rdn over 2f out: wknd over 1f out: t.o* **7/1**
0400 **11** *1 1/4* **Varlak**[83] 1526 3-7-12 **51** oh2......................(v) JamieMackay 1 —
(K F Clutterbuck) *plld hrd and prom: wknd over 2f out: t.o* **40/1**
500 **12** *11* **Kindlelight Soleil (FR)**[22] 3324 4-9-4 **60**..............(b) TomMcLaughlin 3 —
(Nick Littmoden) *sn led: rdn over 4f out: hdd & wknd 3f out: t.o* **50/1**

2m 4.86s (-0.64) **Going Correction** 0.0s/f (Good)
WFA 3 from 4yo+ 11lb 12 Ran SP% **117.3**
Speed ratings (Par 103): **102,99,99,99,99 97,95,95,74,72 71,62**
Tote Swingers:1&2:£14.50, 2&3:£66.40, 1&3:£27.60 CSF £42.12 CT £1195.04 TOTE £5.00: £1.90, £3.40, £9.20; EX 52.90.
Owner Prima Racing Partnership **Bred** John James **Trained** Exning, Suffolk

FOCUS
Stands side track used with stalls on Far side except 5.50 race: centre. The going was good to firm. A minor handicap in which the top four in the weights were all non-runners. The early pace was decent but it slackened at halfway, and relatively unexposed 3yos filled five of the first six places. Another clear best from the winner, with the fourth setting a sound standard.
Mini's Destination Official explanation: jockey said filly ran flat.

4061 TYRRELL & COMPANY MAIDEN FILLIES' STKS 7f
6:20 (6:22) (Class 5) 2-Y-O **£3,234** (£962; £481; £240) **Stalls** High

Form RPR
1 **Kunooz (IRE)** 2-9-0 0...................... AhmedAjtebi 9 80+
(Mahmood Al Zarooni) *chsd ldrs: rdn to ld over 1f out: jst hld on* **14/1**
2 *shd* **Fragonard** 2-9-0 0...................... TomQueally 7 80+
(Sir Henry Cecil) *hld up: hdwy over 2f out: shkn up over 1f out: r.o wl: nt quite get up* **6/1**[2]
4 **3** *1 1/2* **Parley (USA)**[16] 3520 2-9-0 0...................... FrankieDettori 13 76
(Mahmood Al Zarooni) *chsd ldrs: rdn and ev ch over 1f out: styd on same pce ins fnl f* **7/2**[1]
4 *1 3/4* **Gathering (USA)** 2-9-0 0...................... WilliamBuick 10 71
(John Gosden) *sn led: hdd over 1f out: shkn up and edgd lft: no ex ins fnl f* **7/2**[1]
5 *1 1/2* **My Queenie (IRE)** 2-9-0 0...................... PatDobbs 2 68+
(Richard Hannon) *prom: rdn over 2f out: outpcd over 1f out: styd on towards fin* **25/1**
5 **6** *nk* **Protect**[27] 3182 2-9-0 0...................... RyanMoore 12 67
(Sir Michael Stoute) *chsd ldr: rdn over 2f out: sn ev ch: no ex ins fnl f* **7/2**[1]
7 *hd* **Travelling** 2-9-0 0...................... MichaelHills 6 66+
(J W Hills) *hld up: pushed along over 2f out: styd on: nt trble ldrs* **66/1**
6 **8** *2* **Madame St Clair (IRE)**[24] 3258 2-9-0 0...................... EddieCreighton 3 61
(Brian Meehan) *s.i.s: sn mid-div: rdn 1/2-way: hung lft and wknd over 1f out* **10/1**[3]
0 **9** *3 1/2* **Plum Bay**[21] 3362 2-9-0 0...................... AndreaAtzeni 14 52
(David Elsworth) *prom: rdn over 2f out: wknd over 1f out* **14/1**
10 *1 3/4* **Balady (IRE)** 2-9-0 0...................... PhilipRobinson 8 47+
(John Dunlop) *s.i.s: hld up: hdwy over 2f out: shkn up over 1f out: nt knocked abt and sn lost pl* **25/1**
11 *8* **Looks Like Rain** 2-9-0 0...................... EddieAhern 1 27
(Michael Bell) *s.i.s: hld up and a in rr* **33/1**
12 *10* **Tresabella** 2-9-0 0...................... JamesDoyle 5 —
(Michael Appleby) *prom over 4f: t.o* **80/1**

1m 27.37s (1.67) **Going Correction** 0.0s/f (Good) 12 Ran SP% **116.7**
Speed ratings (Par 91): **90,89,88,86,84 84,83,81,77,75 66,55**
Tote Swingers:1&2:£17.80, 2&3:£4.40, 1&3:£10.70 CSF £90.54 TOTE £25.10: £5.10, £2.30, £1.70; EX 151.70.
Owner Godolphin **Bred** Darley **Trained** Newmarket, Suffolk
■ Stewards' Enquiry : Philip Robinson £140 fine: Entered parade ring after signal to mount had been given.

FOCUS
A fascinating fillies' maiden in which the Godolphin second-string just held on from a big eye-catcher.

NOTEBOOK
Kunooz(IRE) attracted some support at biggish prices and showed a good turn of foot to hit the front before holding off a fast finisher on debut. She looks a nice prospect and has an international pedigree, being by a 7f Grade 1 US performer, out of a top-class 1m2f winner in Argentina. (op 20-1)
Fragonard took a while to get the hang of things but finished well and was just denied. This was a highly promising debut from a 400,000euros half-sister to French Derby winner Blue Canari (9f winner at two). (op 11-2 tchd 7-1)
Parley(USA), a Street Cry filly out of a US multiple Grade 1 9f winner, ran green before staying on strongly for a close fourth behind three experienced rivals in a 7f Kempton maiden on debut. She set the standard and looked a lot more streetwise, but was just outgunned by two promising newcomers. (op 11-4 tchd 5-2)
Gathering(USA), a half-sister to four winners, out of 6f 2yo Group 3/US Grade 3 9f winner, moved well up with the pace for a long way and kept battling on debut, despite looking inexperienced when pressure was applied. (op 4-1 tchd 9-2)
My Queenie(IRE), a 26,000gns half-sister to French 2yo winner Pull The Plug and US 9f winner Pure White, got caught out when the pace increased before staying on well on a promising debut.
Protect was supported in the morning but couldn't sustain her effort as well as the others in the firing line on this second start. (op 9-2)
Balady(IRE), out of a well related dam who has already produced lightly raced/progressive 3yo 9.7f maiden winner Junoob, crept into contention out wide before fading. She shaped a bit better than her finishing position suggests and should improve for the experience. Official explanation: jockey said saddle slipped (op 20-1)

4062 WALKER TRANSPORT H'CAP 7f
6:55 (6:55) (Class 4) (0-85,85) 3-Y-O **£4,528** (£1,347; £673; £336) **Stalls** High

Form RPR
0236 **1** **Sacrosanctus**[16] 3506 3-8-12 **76**...................... TomQueally 8 86
(David Nicholls) *chsd ldrs: led 1f out: rdn and edgd rt ins fnl f: r.o* **22/1**
2331 **2** *1 3/4* **Romantic Wish**[7] 3818 3-9-2 **80** 6ex...................... JimCrowley 5 86+
(Robert Mills) *s.i.s: hld up: hdwy over 1f out: rdn and hung lft ins fnl f: r.o to go 2nd wl ins fnl f: nt rch wnr* **9/4**[1]
2-64 **3** *1* **Chokidar (IRE)**[14] 3594 3-8-6 **73**...................... BillyCray[(3)] 1 76
(David Nicholls) *w ldr tl led over 2f out: rdn and hdd 1f out: styd on same pce* **33/1**
2222 **4** *1 3/4* **Elusivity (IRE)**[13] 3649 3-9-7 **85**...................... FrankieDettori 6 83+
(Brian Meehan) *hld up: swtchd rt and hdwy over 1f out: sn rdn: no ex ins fnl f* **9/4**[1]
2232 **5** *1/2* **Roman Strait**[21] 3347 3-8-4 **68**...................... LukeMorris 9 65
(Michael Blanshard) *hld up: hdwy over 1f out: no imp fnl f* **15/2**[3]

3205 **6** *1* **Mazovian (USA)**[9] 3731 3-7-9 **66** oh3 .... NoelGarbutt(7) 7 60
(Michael Chapman) *chsd ldrs: rdn over 2f out: styd on same pce fr over 1f out* **66/1**

5-62 **7** *9* **Red Riverman**[36] 2852 3-8-8 **72** .... (b[1]) RyanMoore 10 42
(William Haggas) *hld up: rdn over 1f out: n.d* **7/1[2]**

0000 **8** *5* **Shafgaan**[34] 2926 3-9-1 **79** .... (b[1]) PhilipRobinson 4 35
(Clive Brittain) *led over 4f: wknd over 1f out* **14/1**

4304 **9** *2 1/4* **Strictly Pink (IRE)**[6] 3853 3-8-12 **76** .... (p) LiamJones 3 26
(Alan Bailey) *chsd ldrs: rdn over 2f out: wknd over 1f out* **14/1**

414- **10** *7* **Gentleman Is Back (USA)**[249] 7379 3-9-2 **80** .... EddieAhern 2 —
(Ed de Giles) *mid-div: rdn over 2f out: wknd over 1f out* **20/1**

1m 24.82s (-0.88) **Going Correction** 0.0s/f (Good) **10** Ran SP% **112.7**
Speed ratings (Par 102): **105,103,101,99,99 98,87,82,79,71**
Tote Swingers:1&2:£6.40, 2&3:£19.10, 1&3:£52.40 CSF £67.26 CT £1732.85 TOTE £20.90: £3.90, £1.50, £5.60; EX 79.30.
Owner Paul J Dixon **Bred** Worksop Manor Stud **Trained** Sessay, N Yorks

FOCUS
A decent handicap. The pace looked strong and they were well strung out in the early stages, but two of the prominent runners kept on well and the two market leaders couldn't land a blow from some way back. The form is rated around the winner.
Strictly Pink(IRE) Official explanation: trainers representative said filly finished distressed
Gentleman Is Back(USA) Official explanation: jockey said gelding was never travelling.

4063 NGK SPARK PLUGS CONDITIONS STKS 5f

7:25 (7:25) (Class 3) 3-Y-O+
£7,158 (£2,143; £1,071; £535; £267; £134) **Stalls** High

Form RPR

-332 **1** **Dinkum Diamond (IRE)**[34] 2928 3-8-6 106 ow1 .... WilliamBuick 1 103
(Henry Candy) *trckd ldrs: racd keenly: wnt 2nd over 1f out: rdn to ld and edgd lft ins fnl f: r.o* **1/1[1]**

0030 **2** *1 1/4* **Five Star Junior (USA)**[8] 3778 5-8-10 90 .... KierenFallon 4 99
(Linda Stubbs) *sn pushed along in rr: swtchd lft and hdwy over 1f out: rdn to chse wnr wl ins fnl f: r.o* **9/1**

0605 **3** *1/2* **Piccadilly Filly (IRE)**[7] 3827 4-8-5 104 .... (v[1]) EddieCreighton 5 92
(Edward Creighton) *led and sn clr: rdn over 1f out: hdd and unable qck ins fnl f* **6/1[3]**

3-05 **4** *2* **Darajaat (USA)**[63] 2054 3-8-0 97 .... JimmyQuinn 6 83
(Marcus Tregoning) *a.p: chsd ldr 3f out tl rdn over 1f out: no ex ins fnl f* **8/1**

-301 **5** *nk* **Poppy Seed**[42] 2690 4-8-7 92 ow2 .... RyanMoore 3 86
(Richard Hannon) *chsd ldrs: rdn 1/2-way: no ex ins fnl f* **10/3[2]**

0-50 **6** *3 1/2* **Belle Bayardo (IRE)**[48] 2500 3-8-5 87 .... LukeMorris 2 74
(Ronald Harris) *sn outpcd* **66/1**

0-50 **7** *1/2* **Tamagin (USA)**[6] 3841 8-8-10 105 .... (p) JimCrowley 8 75
(Lydia Pearce) *chsd ldr 2f: wknd over 1f out* **25/1**

58.55 secs (-0.55) **Going Correction** 0.0s/f (Good)
WFA 3 from 4yo+ 5lb **7** Ran SP% **113.8**
Speed ratings (Par 107): **104,102,101,98,97 91,91**
Tote Swingers:1&2:£2.80, 2&3:£8.80, 1&3:£1.30 CSF £11.27 TOTE £2.10: £1.40, £3.30; EX 12.70.
Owner Eight Star Syndicate **Bred** Ms H W Topping **Trained** Kingston Warren, Oxon

FOCUS
A useful conditions event won by the strong favourite, who didn't need to match his best.

NOTEBOOK
Dinkum Diamond(IRE) had a few juvenile highlights, which included a Listed Sandown win, a creditable seventh in the Nunthorpe and a narrow defeat in the Flying Childers. Placed in three Listed events this season, he had strong form claims dropped in class and found a sustained run out wide to justify favouritism. His hold-up style can depend on luck in bigger fields but he has a good turn of foot at 5f/6f and his versatility regarding ground will be a useful asset as the season progresses. Connections are now considering another tilt at the Nunthorpe. (op 11-10, tchd 5-4 in places and 11-8 in a place)
Five Star Junior(USA), a close third off a mark of 90 two runs back, ran a big race with plenty to find on official figures back outside handicap company. (op 10-1)
Piccadilly Filly(IRE) had decent claims on her close sixth in a Group 3 at Longchamp in May and a cracking third in the Nunthorpe last August. She was a little revved up in a first-time visor but did quite well to hang on for third after setting a blazing pace. An inconsistent profile makes her a bit risky but she is very speedy and has shown enough in two of her five starts this year to suggest she could pick up a good prize this season. (op 13-2 tchd 6-1)
Darajaat(USA) had not fired in two runs in Group 3/Listed company this year and she couldn't find a decisive finishing kick back at 5f, but things didn't really pan out because she was a bit short of room when the winner attacked out wide. She rates a bit better than the form. (tchd 9-1)
Poppy Seed took advantage of a return to handicap company when winning off 88 at Goodwood last month. This progressive filly was prominent in the betting, but she couldn't find an effective response when things got serious and seemed to find this company a bit too hot. (tchd 3-1)

4064 NOVAE BLOODSTOCK INSURANCE H'CAP 6f

7:55 (7:55) (Class 4) (0-80,78) 4-Y-O+ **£4,528** (£1,347; £673; £336) **Stalls** High

Form RPR

0434 **1** **Tyfos**[15] 3541 6-9-6 **77** .... TomMcLaughlin 5 89
(Brian Baugh) *mde all: rdn over 1f out: hung rt ins fnl f: jst hld on* **7/2[1]**

-054 **2** *nse* **Quasi Congaree (GER)**[9] 3737 5-9-4 **75** .... (t) RyanMoore 7 87
(Ian Wood) *awkd s: hld up: hdwy over 1f out: rdn and r.o wl ins fnl f: jst failed* **5/1[3]**

5320 **3** *1 1/4* **Ongoodform (IRE)**[27] 3172 4-9-0 **74** .... JohnFahy(3) 3 82
(Paul D'Arcy) *a.p: swtchd rt and chsd wnr over 1f out: sn rdn: nt run on* **5/1[3]**

0000 **4** *3* **Diriculous**[11] 3685 7-9-4 **75** .... JimCrowley 2 73
(Robert Mills) *chsd ldrs: rdn over 1f out: styd on same pce fnl f* **28/1**

1524 **5** *hd* **Jonnie Skull (IRE)**[3] 3953 5-8-2 **59** oh1 .... (vt) KirstyMilczarek 4 57
(Phil McEntee) *chsd wnr tl rdn over 1f out: no ex ins fnl f* **10/1**

00-0 **6** *3 3/4* **Spitfire**[27] 3179 6-9-7 **78** .... KierenFallon 1 64
(J R Jenkins) *hld up: rdn over 1f out: wknd ins fnl f* **5/1[3]**

32 **7** *2 1/2* **Basle**[29] 3079 4-9-2 **73** .... TomQueally 9 51+
(Gay Kelleway) *broke out of stalls sltly early w blindfold stl on: stmbld after s: hld up: rdn over 2f out: wknd fnl f* **8/1**

0-21 **8** *2 1/4* **Titus Gent**[11] 3685 6-8-5 **69** .... RaulDaSilva(7) 8 40+
(Jeremy Gask) *hood removed late: s.s: wl bhd: rdn and wknd over 1f out* **9/2[2]**

1m 12.45s (-0.05) **Going Correction** 0.0s/f (Good) **8** Ran SP% **114.1**
Speed ratings (Par 105): **101,100,99,95,95 90,86,83**
Tote Swingers:1&2:£3.00, 2&3:£5.50, 1&3:£5.00 CSF £21.00 CT £85.94 TOTE £5.00: £1.90, £1.80, £2.00; EX 16.80.
Owner J Tomlinson/G Williams **Bred** J Tomlinson And G Williams **Trained** Audley, Staffs
■ Stewards' Enquiry : Tom McLaughlin one-day ban: careless riding (31st July)

FOCUS
There was an extremely ragged start and this is form to treat with caution.

Spitfire Official explanation: jockey said gelding moved poorly

4065 THANK YOU RON WALLWORK MAIDEN STKS 1m

8:30 (8:31) (Class 5) 3-Y-O **£3,234** (£962; £481; £240) **Stalls** High

Form RPR

4-0 **1** **Red Eyes**[32] 3001 3-9-3 0 .... NeilCallan 4 89
(Brian Meehan) *w ldr tl led over 3f out: rdn and hung lft over 1f out: hung rt and hdd ins fnl f: rallied to ld post* **6/1**

03 **2** *nse* **Federation**[20] 3385 3-8-12 0 .... SteveDrowne 10 84
(Roger Charlton) *a.p: chsd wnr over 1f out: sn hung lft: rdn to ld and hung rt ins fnl f: hdd post* **4/1[2]**

3 *9* **Fruehling (IRE)** 3-9-3 0 .... RyanMoore 14 68+
(Sir Michael Stoute) *hld up: hdwy over 2f out: wnt 3rd 1f out: nvr trbld ldrs* **11/2[3]**

6 **4** *1 3/4* **Tamara Bay**[27] 3177 3-8-9 0 .... GilmarPereira(3) 6 59
(William Haggas) *s.i.s: sn chsng ldrs: pushed along over 2f out: rdn: hung lft and wknd over 1f out* **16/1**

52 **5** *1/2* **Roy The Boy (USA)**[27] 3177 3-9-3 0 .... LukeMorris 1 63
(Jane Chapple-Hyam) *trckd ldrs: rdn over 2f out: wknd over 1f out* **7/2[1]**

3 **6** *3 1/2* **Carinya (IRE)**[27] 3177 3-8-12 0 .... TomQueally 2 50
(Amy Weaver) *led over 4f: sn rdn: wknd wl over 1f out* **6/1**

0-0 **7** *2 1/4* **Cantor**[27] 3183 3-9-3 0 .... WilliamCarson 8 50
(Giles Bravery) *hld up: rdn 1/2-way: sme hdwy over 2f out: hung lft and wknd sn after* **50/1**

0 **8** *3 1/2* **Lady Valtas**[19] 3437 3-8-12 0 .... AndreaAtzeni 12 37
(Robert Eddery) *mid-div: rdn 1/2-way: wknd over 2f out* **66/1**

9 *5* **Isometric (USA)** 3-9-3 0 .... FrankieDettori 13 30
(Mahmood Al Zarooni) *s.s: hld up: hdwy over 2f out: sn wknd* **4/1[2]**

0-00 **10** *42* **Generous Pursuit**[37] 2825 3-8-12 0 .... KirstyMilczarek 9 —
(Phil McEntee) *chsd ldrs: rdn over 3f out: wknd over 2f out* **100/1**

1m 39.74s (-0.26) **Going Correction** 0.0s/f (Good) **10** Ran SP% **116.5**
Speed ratings (Par 100): **101,100,91,90,89 86,83,80,75,33**
Tote Swingers:1&2:£4.50, 2&3:£4.40, 1&3:£7.10 CSF £30.17 TOTE £6.50: £2.10, £1.60, £2.00; EX 35.80.
Owner Jaber Abdullah **Bred** Roger Charlton And Floors Farming **Trained** Manton, Wilts
■ Stewards' Enquiry : Steve Drowne one-day ban: careless riding (29th July)

FOCUS
There was a open market for this maiden but the first two had a good duel and finished a long way clear of the rest. With the favourite disappointing there's a doubt over what they achieved.
Fruehling(IRE) Official explanation: jockey said colt hung right.

4066 CARRS MINI H'CAP 7f

9:00 (9:00) (Class 5) (0-75,75) 4-Y-O+ **£2,587** (£770; £384; £192) **Stalls** High

Form RPR

2110 **1** **George Baker (IRE)**[53] 2354 4-9-2 **70** .... FrankieDettori 8 81+
(George Baker) *hld up in tch: swtchd rt over 2f out: rdn over 1f out: r.o to ld nr fin* **9/2[2]**

-350 **2** *nk* **Mingun Bell (USA)**[39] 2771 4-9-3 **71** .... LukeMorris 14 81
(Ed de Giles) *chsd ldrs: led 2f out: rdn over 1f out: hdd nr fin* **12/1**

020 **3** *1 1/4* **Aspectus (IRE)**[23] 3285 8-9-4 **75** .... (b) SophieDoyle(3) 10 82
(Jamie Osborne) *chsd ldrs: led over 3f out: hdd 2f out: styd on u.p* **12/1**

3113 **4** *1/2* **Dashwood**[35] 2879 4-9-7 **75** .... (t) WilliamCarson 7 81
(Giles Bravery) *chsd ldrs: rdn and ev ch 2f out: styd on same pce ins fnl f* **7/1**

-046 **5** *2* **Amoya (GER)**[15] 3555 4-8-13 **72** .... (t) AshleyMorgan(5) 6 72+
(Philip McBride) *hld up: nt clr run over 2f out: sn swtchd lft: hdwy over 1f out: r.o: nt rch ldrs* **40/1**

220 **6** *3/4* **Burning Stone (USA)**[21] 3361 4-9-0 **68** .... TomQueally 3 66
(Gay Kelleway) *prom: outpcd 1/2-way: r.o ins fnl f* **6/1[3]**

0400 **7** *3* **Sumbe (USA)**[25] 3235 5-8-9 **63** .... AndreaAtzeni 13 53
(Michael Wigham) *hld up: hdwy 1/2-way: rdn over 1f out: wknd ins fnl f* **22/1**

-063 **8** *2 1/4* **Mazamorra (USA)**[8] 3757 4-9-7 **75** .... AdamKirby 12 59
(Marco Botti) *led 1f: chsd ldrs: rdn over 2f out: wknd fnl f* **4/1[1]**

-000 **9** *3* **Darcey**[21] 3361 5-8-11 **65** .... MickyFenton 1 41
(Amy Weaver) *led 6f out: hdd over 3f out: wknd wl over 1f out* **25/1**

5-66 **10** *2 1/2* **My Learned Friend (IRE)**[11] 3674 7-9-3 **74** .... SimonPearce(3) 11 43
(Andrew Balding) *chsd ldrs: rdn over 2f out: wknd wl over 1f out* **20/1**

0063 **11** *nk* **Tubby Isaacs**[9] 3735 7-8-8 **67** .... (p) HarryBentley(5) 2 35
(Dean Ivory) *s.i.s: hdwy over 4f out: wknd over 2f out* **[illegible]**

5021 **12** *16* **Paphos**[9] 3735 4-8-5 **59** .... (v) NickyMackay 4 —
(Stuart Williams) *hld up: rdn 1/2-way: wknd over 2f out* **7/1**

1m 25.02s (-0.68) **Going Correction** 0.0s/f (Good) **12** Ran SP% **119.4**
Speed ratings (Par 103): **103,102,101,100,98 97,94,91,88,85 84,66**
Tote Swingers:1&2:£10.80, 2&3:£33.50, 1&3:£15.40 CSF £54.80 CT £623.89 TOTE £4.50: £2.00, £5.20, £4.80; EX 75.00.
Owner George Baker & Partners **Bred** Mull Enterprises Ltd **Trained** Whitsbury, Hants

FOCUS
They were tightly grouped for a long way in this fair handicap and there was another close finish. Sound form, with improvement from the winner.
T/Plt: £148.60 to a £1 stake. Pool £51,004.36 - 250.53 winning units. T/Qpdt: £45.10 to £1 stake. Pool £4,869.64 - 79.75 winning units. CR

3637 NOTTINGHAM (L-H)

Friday, July 15

OFFICIAL GOING: Good to firm (7.5)
Wind: Light half against Weather: Fine and dry

4067 CORPORATE CHOICE DG CARS H'CAP 6f 15y

2:10 (2:10) (Class 5) (0-70,70) 3-Y-O **£2,522** (£750; £375; £187) **Stalls** Centre

Form RPR

2511 **1** **Roodee Queen**[18] 3470 3-8-13 **67** .... RyanClark(5) 2 76
(Milton Bradley) *cl up: led 2f out: rdn ent fnl f: kpt on wl* **10/3[1]**

4-00 **2** *1 1/4* **Map Of Heaven**[20] 3390 3-9-4 **67** .... (b[1]) LiamJones 7 72
(William Haggas) *hld up in tch: hdwy over 2f out: rdn to chse wnr ins fnl f: sn drvn and no imp towards fin* **9/2**

-000 **3** *3/4* **Brave Dream**[21] 3347 3-8-13 **62** .... NeilCallan 4 65
(Kevin Ryan) *led 1f: trckd ldrs: effrt 2f out: sn chsng wnr: rdn ent fnl f and kpt on same pce* **7/2[2]**

0055 **4** *3* **Jeeran**[16] 3523 3-8-7 **61** .... (t) JemmaMarshall(5) 1 54
(Alastair Lidderdale) *in tch on outer: hdwy wl over 2f out: sn rdn to chse ldrs: drvn over 1f out and no imp* **16/1**

5-05 **5** *1 1/4* **Magic Stella**[165] 364 3-9-7 **70**............ KierenFallon 9 59
(Alan Jarvis) *dwlt sltly: sn trcking ldrs: effrt 1/2-way: rdn along over 2f out and sn btn* **4/1**[3]

0030 **6** *1 1/2* **Stravsambition**[32] 2993 3-8-2 **58**............ JackDuern(7) 5 42
(Reg Hollinshead) *a towards rr* **33/1**

-360 **7** *9* **Consistant**[45] 2592 3-8-9 **58**............ JackMitchell 6 13
(Brian Baugh) *prom: effrt 1/2-way: sn rdn along: wknd 2f out and sn eased* **9/1**

0003 **8** *4 1/2* **My Love Fajer (IRE)**[16] 3523 3-8-7 **56**............(p) MartinLane 8 —
(Alan McCabe) *cl up: led after 1f: pushed along 1/2-way: rdn and hdd 2f out: sn wknd and eased* **7/1**

1m 16.15s (1.25) **Going Correction** -0.075s/f (Good) 8 Ran SP% **114.8**
Speed ratings (Par 100): **88,86,85,81,79 77,65,59**
Tote Swingers: 1&2 £1.30, 1&3 £3.60, 2&3 £3.70 CSF £18.75 CT £55.10 TOTE £4.10: £1.30, £1.30, £1.70; EX 18.60.
Owner T A Godbert **Bred** Tom & Evelyn Yates **Trained** Sedbury, Gloucs

FOCUS
All races on Outer course, Inner rail out 2m on stands' bend and 5m on bottom bend. A modest sprint handicap run in a slow time of four just over seconds outside standard on ground described as good to firm. The form is rated a little negatively.
Consistant Official explanation: jockey said gelding stopped quickly

4068 BRITISH STALLION STUDS SUPPORTING BRITISH RACING E B F MAIDEN STKS 6f 15y
2:40 (2:40) (Class 5) 2-Y-O **£3,234** (£962; £481; £240) **Stalls** Centre

Form RPR

0 **1** **Sanad (IRE)**[20] 3382 2-9-3 0............ TadhgO'Shea 6 70+
(Brian Meehan) *cl up: led wl over 2f out: pushed clr wl over 1f out: comf* **5/1**[2]

0U **2** *1 1/4* **Berlusca (IRE)**[25] 3237 2-9-3 0............ LiamJones 1 66
(William Jarvis) *chsd ldrs: pushed along whn n.m.r and swtchd rt 2f out: sn rdn and styd on wl fnl f to take 2nd on line* **28/1**

3 *nse* **Frog Hollow** 2-9-3 0............ MartinLane 2 66+
(Ralph Beckett) *dwlt: sn in tch: gd hdwy on outer 1/2-way: rdn to chse wnr wl over 1f out: one pce ins fnl f: lost 2nd on line* **6/1**[3]

4 *1 3/4* **Whatyoucallit (IRE)** 2-9-3 0............ TedDurcan 3 61+
(David Lanigan) *in rr: gd hdwy over 2f out: rdn wl over 1f out: kpt on wl fnl f: nrst fin* **12/1**

5 *3 1/2* **Archers Prize (IRE)** 2-9-3 0............ RichardMullen 4 50
(Ed McMahon) *cl up: effrt wl over 2f out: rdn wl over 1f out and sn one pce* **10/1**

42 **6** *1 1/2* **Juno The Muffinman (IRE)**[18] 3472 2-9-3 0....(v[1]) RichardKingscote 11 46
(Tom Dascombe) *wnt rt s: racd alone stands' rail and sn led: pushed along 1/2-way: swtchd towards centre: rdn: hdd wl over 2f out: sn btn and eased over 1f out* **10/11**[1]

7 *3/4* **Welsh Royale** 2-9-3 0............ NeilCallan 5 44
(William Muir) *chsd ldrs: rdn along 1/2-way: sn wknd* **25/1**

0 **8** *1/2* **Remember Rocky**[17] 3490 2-9-3 0............ IanMongan 9 42
(Steve Gollings) *chsd ldrs: rdn along 1/2-way: sn wknd* **40/1**

0 **9** *nk* **Spirit Of The Law (IRE)**[23] 3282 2-9-3 0............ ChrisCatlin 7 41
(Ed Dunlop) *towards rr tl sme late hdwy* **16/1**

00 **10** *16* **Clone Devil (IRE)**[7] 3816 2-8-10 0............(p) KatiaScallan(7) 8 —
(Alastair Lidderdale) *a towards rr* **125/1**

11 *18* **Miss Bloom** 2-8-9 0............ BillyCray(3) 10 —
(Garry Woodward) *dwlt: sn chsng ldrs: rdn along bef 1/2-way and sn wknd* **100/1**

1m 15.67s (0.77) **Going Correction** -0.075s/f (Good) 11 Ran SP% **117.5**
Speed ratings (Par 94): **91,89,89,86,82 80,79,78,78,56 32**
Tote Swingers: 1&2 £8.10, 1&3 £7.10, 2&3 £14.00 CSF £139.28 TOTE £5.80: £1.90, £13.20, £3.00; EX 109.30.
Owner Hamdan Al Maktoum **Bred** Holborn Trust Co **Trained** Manton, Wilts

FOCUS
Probably just an ordinary maiden, but they went a fair pace and the time was respectable.

NOTEBOOK
Sanad(IRE) was disappointing on debut, showing good early speed before dropping out over 7f, although he wasn't given a hard time. The experience stood him in good stead and the drop back in trip was beneficial. Leading the majority in the centre of the field, he found plenty when asked to put the race to bed and should go on from this. (op 11-2 tchd 9-2)
Berlusca(IRE) can be forgiven for unseating his rider when the saddle slipped last time and this was a step forward judged on his debut. He will be seen in a better light when stepped up in distance as he was staying on in the closing stages.
Frog Hollow is a half-brother to several winners and made an encouraging debut. He could never quite reel in the winner but kept on well enough and he should be going one better before long with his stable in good form. (op 15-2)
Whatyoucallit(IRE), a half-brother to Chesham winner Big Audio, shaped with promise on this debut. (op 10-1)
Archers Prize(IRE) is a half-brother to the useful Masta Plasta and has plenty of speed in his pedigree. He travelled well upsides the winner before fading and this was a respectable debut. (op 5-1)
Juno The Muffinman(IRE) set the standard on his two runs to date, but it was a bit disconcerting the visor had now been reached for. He raced alone on the stands'-side rail after going right on leaving the stalls, and although showing speed, he did not look straightforward, hanging under pressure. Official explanation: jockey said colt hung badly left (op 11-8)

4069 FIRST PAST POST DG CARS NURSERY 6f 15y
3:15 (3:16) (Class 5) 2-Y-O **£2,522** (£750; £375; £187) **Stalls** Centre

Form RPR

000 **1** **Solfilia**[15] 3547 2-9-2 **69**............ KierenFallon 5 78+
(Hughie Morrison) *trckd ldrs: cl up 1/2-way: led over 2f out: rdn and edgd rt over 1f out: clr ent fnl f: kpt on* **7/2**[2]

450 **2** *3 3/4* **Cataract**[23] 3273 2-7-12 **51** oh2............(b[1]) JamesSullivan 2 49
(John Weymes) *awkward s and towards rr: hdwy 1/2-way: rdn 2f out: chsd wnr over 1f out: drvn and no imp fnl f* **20/1**

0656 **3** *2* **Zigazag (IRE)**[7] 3816 2-8-13 **66**............(t) RichardMullen 8 58+
(David Evans) *s.i.s and swtchd lft s: in rr tl hdwy 1/2-way: rdn to chse ldrs 2f out: drvn and kpt on same pce fnl f* **20/1**

61 **4** *2 3/4* **Ocean Myth**[13] 3611 2-9-4 **71**............ LiamJones 3 55
(William Haggas) *led: rdn along 1/2-way: hdd over 2f out: sn drvn and outpcd* **5/2**[1]

5514 **5** *nk* **Faraway**[6] 3842 2-9-0 **67**............ JackMitchell 4 50
(David Evans) *in tch: rdn along and outpcd wl over 2f out: styd on appr fnl f* **7/2**[2]

4030 **6** *1/2* **Always Ends Well (IRE)**[35] 2886 2-8-11 **64**............ NeilCallan 1 45
(Mark Johnston) *cl up: ev ch over 2f out: sn rdn and wknd over 1f out* **9/1**

6216 **7** *7* **Musical Valley**[7] 3810 2-9-7 **74**............(t) RichardKingscote 7 34
(Tom Dascombe) *trckd ldrs: smooth hdwy 1/2-way: rdn along 2f out: sn drvn and btn* **6/1**[3]

000 **P** **Bertorella (IRE)**[34] 2901 2-8-0 **53** ow2............ MartinLane 6 —
(Ralph Beckett) *unruly stalls: chsd ldrs: rdn along bef 1/2-way: sn wknd and bhd: p.u fnl f* **16/1**

1m 15.22s (0.32) **Going Correction** -0.075s/f (Good) 8 Ran SP% **112.7**
Speed ratings (Par 94): **94,89,86,82,82 81,72,—**
Tote Swingers: 1&2 £30.40, 1&3 £13.70, 2&3 £21.70 CSF £65.36 CT £1219.28 TOTE £4.50: £1.50, £5.70, £5.40; EX 69.30.
Owner Swire, Scott, Margadale **Bred** Stonethorn Stud Farms Ltd **Trained** East Ilsley, Berks
■ The 'official' ratings shown next to each horse are estimated and for information purposes only.
■ Stewards' Enquiry : Liam Jones one-day ban: careless riding (29th July).

FOCUS
A fairly uncompetitive nursery run at a decent clip, and the time was the quickest of the three 6f races.

NOTEBOOK
Solfilia had failed to trouble the judge on her three runs to date but had run into some trouble last time and possessed a progressive profile. On her first crack at a nursery she attracted support, racing off an estimated mark of 66, and her backers were duly rewarded with a comfortable success. There should be more to come. Official explanation: trainer's rep said, regarding the apparent improvement in form shown, filly was a weak filly who had been progressive on her previous runs (op 4-1 tchd 10-3)
Cataract had been beaten in three modest maidens but had a chance off an estimated mark of 48 if the first-time headgear had the desired effect. She stayed on to chase the winner without ever looking to threaten. (op 28-1)
Zigazag(IRE), in a first-time tongue-tie, missed the break and was being pushed along in the early stages, but stayed on when switched out with over a furlong to run. He was well beaten in a seller last time so casts a shadow over the form. (op 25-1)
Ocean Myth, a winner over 5f last time, showed good pace to take them along but, just as on her debut, failed to see out the extra furlong. (tchd 11-4)
Musical Valley was disappointing as he was in a good enough position when asked to go about his business but failed to pick up. Official explanation: jockey said gelding ran flat (op 4-1 tchd 7-2)
Bertorella(IRE) went down in the stalls beforehand and can be given another chance as she ran as though something might have been amiss, being eased right down when beaten. Official explanation: jockey said filly reared and slipped leaving stalls and never travelled thereafter (op 12-1)

4070 CARTWRIGHT KING SOLICITORS H'CAP 1m 75y
3:50 (3:53) (Class 4) (0-85,85) 3-Y-O+ **£4,528** (£1,347; £673; £336) **Stalls** Centre

Form RPR

0300 **1** **Night Lily (IRE)**[13] 3632 5-9-6 **78**............ LiamJones 3 84
(Paul D'Arcy) *hld up towards rr: hdwy 3f out: chsd ldrs over 1f out: swtchd rt and rdn ent fnl f: styd on u.p to ld nr line* **3/1**[1]

0302 **2** *shd* **Cono Zur (FR)**[12] 3659 4-9-3 **75**............ JamesSullivan 2 80
(Ruth Carr) *led: qcknd 3f out: rdn wl over 1f out: drvn ent fnl f: hdd and no ex nr line* **4/1**[2]

0206 **3** *3/4* **Marjury Daw (IRE)**[13] 3641 5-8-13 **76**............ DaleSwift(5) 8 79
(James Given) *trckd ldrs: hdwy over 2f out: rdn to chse ldr over 1f out: drvn and ev ch ent fnl f: no ex fnl 100yds* **9/1**

0005 **4** *1/2* **Oriental Scot**[14] 3585 4-9-12 **84**............ RichardMullen 9 86+
(William Jarvis) *hld up in rr: hdwy 3f out: effrt and n.m.r over 1f out: sn rdn and kpt on ins fnl f: nrst fin* **4/1**[2]

13-0 **5** *3/4* **Spectait**[19] 3436 9-9-13 **85**............ RichardKingscote 6 85
(Jonjo O'Neill) *dwlt and hld up in rr: hdwy on inner over 2f out: rdn to chse ldrs over 1f out: drvn and one pce fnl f* **11/1**

3560 **6** *1 1/2* **Sir George (IRE)**[16] 3521 6-9-7 **79**............ BarryMcHugh 7 76
(Ollie Pears) *trckd ldrs: hdwy 3f out: rdn along 2f out: sn drvn and kpt on same pce* **13/2**[3]

4011 **7** *5* **High Five Society**[14] 3576 7-8-7 **72**............(b) CharlesEddery(7) 1 57
(Roy Bowring) *sn trcking ldrs: hdwy and cl up 1/2-way: rdn along 3f out: drvn 2f out and grad wknd* **7/1**

3/10 **8** *13* **Ivory Jazz**[71] 1826 4-9-10 **82**............ TonyCulhane 5 38
(Richard Guest) *cl up: rdn along over 3f out: sn wknd* **22/1**

1m 46.48s (0.88) **Going Correction** +0.25s/f (Good) 8 Ran SP% **113.5**
Speed ratings (Par 105): **105,104,104,103,102 101,96,83**
CSF £14.78 CT £94.49 TOTE £3.90: £1.60, £1.90, £3.40; EX 17.60.
Owner K Snell **Bred** Keith Wills **Trained** Newmarket, Suffolk

FOCUS
A fair pace for this 66-85 handicap. Ordinary for, with the second setting the standard.
High Five Society Official explanation: trainer said gelding was unsuited by good to firm ground.

4071 CORPORATE RELIABILITY DG CARS (S) STKS 1m 2f 50y
4:25 (4:25) (Class 6) 3-Y-O **£1,811** (£539; £269; £134) **Stalls** Low

Form RPR

2416 **1** **Urban Kode (IRE)**[4] 3916 3-9-0 63............(v) KierenFallon 1 68
(David Evans) *mde all: rdn along wl over 2f out: drvn over 1f out: kpt on wl* **6/5**[1]

3-03 **2** *3/4* **Phase Shift**[9] 3744 3-8-4 64............ MartinLane 2 56
(William Muir) *trckd ldng pair: hdwy on inner to chse wnr 4f out: rdn to chal wl over 2f out: drvn and edgd lft over 1f out: kpt on u.p fnl f* **5/2**[3]

0052 **3** *23* **Take A Spin**[29] 3077 3-8-9 63............ ChrisCatlin 4 15
(Paul Cole) *trckd wnr: pushed along 4f out: rdn 3f out and sn outpcd* **2/1**[2]

50 **4** *16* **Sally Anne**[35] 2871 3-8-4 0............ JamesSullivan 3 —
(John Harris) *sn rdn along and outpcd in rr: bhd fr 1/2-way: t.o whn hung bdly rt to stands' rail wl over 2f out* **50/1**

2m 12.99s (1.29) **Going Correction** +0.25s/f (Good) 4 Ran SP% **109.3**
Speed ratings (Par 98): **104,103,85,72**
CSF £4.59 TOTE £1.40; EX 4.20.There was no bid for winner. Phase Shift was claimed by Dan Gilbert for £6,000.
Owner Mrs B Grainger **Bred** Nils Koop **Trained** Pandy, Monmouths

FOCUS
A poor turnout for this seller, so a tactical affair was on the cards. Weak form and the favourite probably won by default.
Take A Spin Official explanation: vet said colt lost near fore shoe.
Sally Anne Official explanation: jockey said filly hung right

4072 FOR YOUR COMFORT DG CARS 01159500500 MAIDEN FILLIES' STKS 1m 2f 50y
4:55 (4:55) (Class 5) 3-Y-O **£2,522** (£750; £375; £187) **Stalls** Low

Form RPR

0 **1** **Jiwen (CAN)**[43] 2648 3-9-0 0............ NeilCallan 9 75
(Roger Varian) *trckd ldrs: hdwy on outer over 3f out: chal over 2f out: rdn to ld over 1f out: drvn ins fnl f: jst hld on* **4/1**[3]

6-2 **2** *nse* **Whispered**[43] 2639 3-9-0 0 .... KierenFallon 8 76+
(Sir Michael Stoute) *trckd ldrs: hdwy over 3f out: chsd ldrs 2f out: rdn and sltly outpcd and n.m.r over 1f out: swtchd rt and styd on strly nr fin: jst failed* **10/3**[2]
3-3 **3** *1/2* **Shuhra (IRE)**[30] 3043 3-9-0 0 .... TadhgO'Shea 2 74
(William Haggas) *hld up in tch: hdwy over 3f out: rdn to chse ldrs wl over 1f out: drvn and ch ins fnl f: nt qckn towards fin* **2/1**[1]
5 **4** *nk* **Elraabeya (CAN)**[92] 1343 3-9-0 0 .... RichardMullen 3 73
(Sir Michael Stoute) *sn led: rdn along wl over 2f out: drvn and hdd over 1f out: kpt on* **4/1**[3]
5 *1 1/4* **Shaqira** 3-9-0 0 .... MartinLane 14 71
(Marcus Tregoning) *hld up in tch: hdwy 3f out: rdn to chse ldrs 2f out: drvn and one pce ins fnl f* **20/1**
6 *1/2* **Viva Diva** 3-9-0 0 .... TedDurcan 12 70
(David Lanigan) *in tch: hdwy to chse ldrs on inner over 3f out: rdn 2f out: drvn and kpt on same pce fnl f* **16/1**
04 **7** *10* **Morning Air (IRE)**[11] 3684 3-9-0 0 .... RussKennemore 11 50
(Ann Duffield) *a towards rr* **100/1**
40 **8** *2 1/2* **Maharanee (USA)**[14] 3577 3-9-0 0 .... FrankieMcDonald 13 45
(Ann Duffield) *a towards rr* **40/1**
00 **9** *1* **Heart Of Dixie (IRE)**[25] 3224 3-9-0 0 .... ChrisCatlin 7 43
(Paul Cole) *cl up: rdn along 3f out: drvn 2f out: sn wknd* **66/1**
0035 **10** *6* **Corvette**[18] 3467 3-9-0 61 .... AdrianMcCarthy 5 31
(J R Jenkins) *a towards rr* **20/1**
-0 **11** *2 1/4* **Srimenanti**[20] 3385 3-9-0 0 .... RobbieFitzpatrick 1 26
(Brian Rothwell) *dwlt: a bhd* **125/1**

2m 13.07s (1.37) **Going Correction** +0.25s/f (Good) **11** Ran SP% **117.5**
Speed ratings (Par 97): **104,103,103,103,102 101,93,91,91,86 84**
Tote Swingers: 1&2 £4.40, 1&3 £2.30, 2&3 £2.20 CSF £16.82 TOTE £5.50: £2.00, £2.00, £1.10; EX 23.30.
Owner Hamdan Al Maktoum **Bred** Adena Springs **Trained** Newmarket, Suffolk

FOCUS
A strongly contested fillies' maiden with big yards being well represented and the form should work out with the fancied runners filling the right places. The time only comes out as the same for the seller, but the form is rated around the race averages.
T/Plt: £146.30 to a £1 stake. Pool of £37,759.00 - 188.33 winning tickets. T/Qpdt: £29.20 to a £1 stake. Pool of £2,584.00 - 65.40 winning tickets. JR

3700 PONTEFRACT (L-H)
Friday, July 15

OFFICIAL GOING: Good to firm (good in places; 7.8)
Wind: Light, half behind Weather: Cloudy, drizzle after race 3, steady rain after race 5

4073 COUNTRYWIDE FREIGHT MAIDEN AUCTION STKS 6f
6:35 (6:37) (Class 4) 2-Y-O **£3,881** (£1,155; £577; £288) **Stalls** Low

Form RPR
3 **1** **Vital Gold**[15] 3552 2-8-13 0 .... SilvestreDeSousa 7 85+
(William Haggas) *w ldr: rdn to ld narrowly over 1f out: strly pressed ins fnl f: kpt on: jst hld on* **2/1**[1]
4 **2** *nse* **Byronic Hero**[23] 3273 2-8-9 0 .... TonyHamilton 3 81+
(Jedd O'Keeffe) *led narrowly: rdn whn hdd over 1f out: remained upsides: kpt on: jst failed* **5/2**[2]
3 **3** *10* **Sunny Side Up (IRE)**[39] 2761 2-8-4 0 .... PatrickMathers 11 46
(Richard Fahey) *racd keenly: trckd ldrs: rdn over 2f out: sn wnt 3rd: kpt on one pce: no ch ldng pair* **14/1**
45 **4** *1 1/2* **Medieval Bishop (IRE)**[13] 3618 2-8-9 0 .... JamesSullivan 2 46+
(Howard Johnson) *midfield on inner: rdn over 2f out: kpt on ins fnl f: wnt 4th post* **20/1**
32 **5** *hd* **Miss Conduct**[24] 3249 2-8-4 0 .... CathyGannon 5 41
(John Spearing) *trckd ldrs: rdn over 2f out: sn one pce: lost 4th post* **7/1**[3]
02 **6** *1* **Mcvicar**[7] 3816 2-8-9 0 .... SamHitchcott 12 43
(Mick Channon) *midfield: rdn over 2f out: kpt on one pce* **8/1**
7 *4 1/2* **After Timer (IRE)** 2-8-2 0 ow1 .... PaulPickard(3) 8 25
(Julie Camacho) *hld up in midfield towards inner: pushed along 1/2-way nvr threatened* **50/1**
8 *3* **Hareby (IRE)** 2-8-11 0 .... DuranFentiman 1 22
(Tim Easterby) *slowly away: hld up towards inner: pushed along over 2f out: nvr threatened* **25/1**
9 *5* **Allegri (IRE)** 2-8-9 0 .... RoystonFfrench 9 —
(Ann Duffield) *green in midfield: nvr threatened* **50/1**
26 **10** *3/4* **Delia Mary**[11] 3680 2-8-4 0 .... PaulQuinn 6 —
(Jedd O'Keeffe) *in tch: rdn over 2f out: sn wknd* **50/1**
11 *1 1/2* **Chorister Sport (IRE)** 2-8-8 0 .... DaleSwift(5) 15 —
(Howard Johnson) *hld up towards outer: rdn over 2f out: a towards rr* **40/1**
12 *nk* **Only A Round (IRE)** 2-8-9 0 .... BarryMcHugh 13 —
(Micky Hammond) *slowly away: hld up: a in rr* **100/1**
0 **13** *18* **Tallula (IRE)**[87] 1455 2-8-4 0 .... KellyHarrison 10 —
(Micky Hammond) *midfield on outer: rdn and hung rt on bnd over 2f out: sn wknd* **66/1**
3 **14** *1* **Quiet Appeal (IRE)**[26] 3200 2-8-11 0 .... AdrianNicholls 17 —
(Mark Johnston) *prom on outer: rdn over 2f out: sn lost pl and wknd* **11/1**
15 *3 3/4* **Eastlands Lad (IRE)** 2-8-10 0 .... GaryBartley(3) 14 —
(Micky Hammond) *dwlt: sn outpcd in rr: a wl bhd* **100/1**
U **Mistress Of Rome** 2-8-4 0 .... FrannyNorton 16 —
(Michael Dods) *wnt rt and uns rdr leaving stalls* **25/1**

1m 15.41s (-1.49) **Going Correction** -0.175s/f (Firm) **16** Ran SP% **124.8**
Speed ratings (Par 96): **102,101,88,86,86 85,79,75,68,67 65,64,40,39,34** —
Tote Swingers:1&2:£3.90, 2&3:£12.70, 1&3:£5.80 CSF £6.43 TOTE £2.70: £1.20, £1.60, £3.70; EX 8.80.
Owner Ian and Christine Beard **Bred** Bearstone Stud **Trained** Newmarket, Suffolk

FOCUS
The temporary rail in place from the 6f bend to the finish since May 27 had been removed; fresh ground for this meeting. A reasonable median auction maiden, and quite competitive being a Racing Post Yearling Bonus race. Very few became involved, with only five at most holding any type of chance turning for home, and it soon became two as the first pair pulled well clear. They showed decent form for the grade and the time was only 0.42sec outside the standard, confirming that the ground was quick.

NOTEBOOK
Vital Gold, who was well backed, turned for home perhaps a neck down on the runner-up before just getting the better of an extended tussle. More streetwise than when a promising third on his debut at Yarmouth, he is a decent type physically who should pay his way in nurseries. He scored despite being ill at ease on the track's undulations. (op 9-4 tchd 6-4)

Byronic Hero showed a similar standard of form as the winner did on his debut, when catching the eye at Carlisle. He attempted to make all and had the benefit of the rails position, but lost out on the nod. The sixth furlong posed him no problems and he should quickly make amends if kept at a realistic level. (op 3-1 tchd 7-2)

Sunny Side Up(IRE) was quickly outpaced by the first two once they had swung in. A strong filly who had been third on her debut over C&D in a much smaller field, she is probably ready for 7f now and should find a race this year.

Medieval Bishop(IRE), carrying the second colours of his owner/trainer Howard Johnson, stayed on late for a never threatening fourth, probably running to a similar level as on his first two starts. Nurseries will be available to him now. (op 16-1 tchd 14-1)

Miss Conduct, placed on her first two starts, was close enough on the approach to the bend before the principals drew away. This was slightly disappointing. (tchd 8-1)

Mcvicar finished second in a decent seller at Newbury last time and although he was never a threat at the front end here, he confirmed he has some ability by staying on when it was all over. He had been coltish in the paddock. (op 15-2 tchd 7-1)

After Timer(IRE), whose trainer doesn't run many juveniles these days, proved best of the newcomers. (op 66-1)

Hareby(IRE) did quite well to finish where he did after a very slow start. (op 16-1)

Quiet Appeal(IRE) was badly drawn again and she dropped away after showing initial speed. (op 14-1)

4074 TOTEPOOL FILLIES' H'CAP 1m 4f 8y
7:05 (7:05) (Class 5) (0-75,75) 3-Y-O+ **£2,587** (£770; £384; £192) **Stalls** Low

Form RPR
0-42 **1** **Parvana (IRE)**[23] 3267 3-9-1 **75** .... SilvestreDeSousa 2 88
(William Haggas) *mde all: drvn over 1f out: kpt on fnl f* **11/8**[1]
0104 **2** *1* **Miss Topsy Turvy (IRE)**[18] 3467 3-8-4 **64** .... FrannyNorton 4 75
(John Dunlop) *dwlt: sn in tch: rdn over 2f out: wnt 2nd over 1f out: kpt on fnl f: hld towards fin* **2/1**[2]
1104 **3** *13* **Laverre (IRE)**[36] 2846 4-9-6 **72** .... DaleSwift(5) 3 63
(Lucy Wadham) *trckd ldr: rdn and ev ch over 2f out: lost 2nd over 1f out: sn wknd* **13/2**
100- **4** *6* **Miss Ferney**[280] 6707 7-8-8 **58** .... PaulPickard(3) 5 39
(Alan Kirtley) *t.k.h: hld up: pushed along over 3f out: a towards rr* **20/1**
4001 **5** *1 3/4* **No Time For Tears (IRE)**[47] 2526 4-8-7 **57** oh4 .... SeanLevey(3) 6 35
(Lucinda Featherstone) *in tch: pushed along over 4f out: wknd 2f out* **11/2**[3]

2m 36.32s (-4.48) **Going Correction** -0.175s/f (Firm)
WFA 3 from 4yo+ 13lb **5** Ran SP% **108.9**
Speed ratings (Par 100): **107,106,97,93,92**
CSF £4.26 TOTE £1.90: £1.40, £1.30; EX 2.90.
Owner Cheveley Park Stud **Bred** Epona Bloodstock Ltd **Trained** Newmarket, Suffolk

FOCUS
No more than a fair fillies' handicap, in which the first two came a long way clear.

4075 BETFRED H'CAP 5f
7:35 (7:39) (Class 3) (0-95,92) 3-Y-O+
£7,158 (£2,143; £1,071; £535; £267; £134) **Stalls** Low

Form RPR
6301 **1** **Duchess Dora (IRE)**[20] 3379 4-9-6 **91** .... DaleSwift(5) 4 105
(John Quinn) *trckd ldrs: effrt on outer over 1f out: led jst ins fnl f: kpt on strly* **13/2**[3]
3223 **2** *2 1/4* **Noodles Blue Boy**[13] 3613 5-9-5 **85** .... FrannyNorton 2 91
(Ollie Pears) *prom: rdn and ev ch over 1f out: kpt on fnl f: no ch w wnr* **7/1**
4502 **3** *nse* **Whozthecat (IRE)**[8] 3778 4-9-7 **87** ....(v) DavidAllan 6 93
(Declan Carroll) *hld up in tch: rdn and hdwy over 1f out: edgd rt ent fnl f: kpt on strly to go 3rd towards fin: nrly snatched 2nd* **7/1**
111 **4** *1/2* **Albany Rose (IRE)**[19] 3433 3-9-1 **86** .... TedDurcan 1 88
(Rae Guest) *in tch on inner: rdn over 1f out: chsd ldng pair jst ins fnl f: kpt on: lost 3rd towards fin* **11/2**[1]
4053 **5** *3/4* **Favourite Girl (IRE)**[18] 3459 5-9-6 **91** ....(p) LanceBetts(5) 9 92
(Tim Easterby) *led narrowly: rdn over 1f out: hdd jst ins fnl f: sn wknd* **6/1**[2]
0002 **6** *3 1/2* **Hotham**[6] 3880 8-8-9 **75** .... BarryMcHugh 8 64
(Noel Wilson) *reluctant to load in stalls: s.i.s: hld up: rdn over 1f out: mod late hdwy: nvr threatened* **11/2**
0552 **7** *1* **Magical Macey (USA)**[35] 2890 4-9-1 **81** ....(b) JamieSpencer 5 66
(David Barron) *hld up and t.k.h: hung lft over 2f out: mod late hdwy: nvr threatened* **7/1**
0001 **8** *1 1/4* **Master Rooney (IRE)**[13] 3613 5-9-4 **84** .... RoystonFfrench 3 65
(Bryan Smart) *w ldr: rdn over 1f out: sn wknd* **9/1**
4004 **9** *1/2* **Secret Asset (IRE)**[13] 3627 6-9-12 **92** .... SilvestreDeSousa 10 71
(Jane Chapple-Hyam) *slowly away: hld up: a towards rr* **10/1**
0000 **10** *2 1/4* **Tabaret**[55] 2299 8-8-12 **78** .... TonyHamilton 7 49
(Richard Whitaker) *midfield on outer: rdn 2f out: sn wknd* **33/1**

61.53 secs (-1.77) **Going Correction** -0.175s/f (Firm)
WFA 3 from 4yo+ 5lb **10** Ran SP% **117.9**
Speed ratings (Par 107): **107,103,103,102,101 95,94,92,91,87**
Tote Swingers:1&2:£7.10, 2&3:£14.70, 1&3:£11.30 CSF £52.08 CT £332.02 TOTE £8.00: £2.60, £2.30, £2.70; EX 69.30.
Owner The Clay Family **Bred** Glending Bloodstock **Trained** Settrington, N Yorks

FOCUS
A good, competitive sprint handicap, run at a warm pace and in a time slightly inside the standard.

NOTEBOOK
Duchess Dora(IRE) returned to winning ways at Chester last month and followed up off this 6lb higher mark, swooping down the outside. She is versatile with regard to her ground requirements, the Chester win having been on soft, and there could be a bit more to come yet from this in-form filly. (op 7-1)

Noodles Blue Boy was always towards the fore from a favourable draw and had every chance. He is running right up to form currently, and the handicapper is unlikely to drop him. (op 15-2)

Whozthecat(IRE) flashed home late and would have been second in another stride. He is in fine heart at the moment and is feasibly handicapped. (op 10-1)

Albany Rose(IRE) was ideally berthed in stall one but lacked the pace to go through a gap up the rail. She was no less than 27lb higher than for the first leg of her five-day hat-trick last month and the handicapper looks to have caught up. (op 6-1 tchd 5-1)

Favourite Girl(IRE) ran a bold race from an outside draw before fading up the hill. She is still 3lb higher than when last winning a year ago. (op 13-2)

Hotham took concerted efforts to force him into his stall, but the track specialist was a little slowly away from his wide draw and was never a factor. He was 2lb well in following his good second at York. (op 4-1)

Master Rooney(IRE) had Noodles Blue Boy back in third when winning at Beverley. Now 4lb higher, he showed bright pace for a long way but was going backwards in the final furlong. (op 10-1 tchd 11-1)

4076 COLSTROPE CUP H'CAP — 1m 4y

8:05 (8:05) (Class 5) (0-70,68) 3-Y-O+ — **£2,587** (£770; £384; £192) **Stalls** Low

Form — RPR

43-0 **1** **Carragold**[98] 1216 5-8-9 **49** ... RobertWinston 2 — 60
(Mel Brittain) *midfield: hdwy over 2f out: rdn to chal over 1f out: led jst ins fnl f: edgd lft: kpt on* **8/1**[3]

000- **2** *1 3/4* **Motafarred (IRE)**[244] 6724 9-9-6 **65** ... DaleSwift(5) 7 — 72
(Micky Hammond) *hld up on inner: pushed along over 2f out: hdwy over 1f out: wnt 2nd fnl 100yds: kpt on* **7/1**[2]

6000 **3** *1 1/4* **Aussie Blue (IRE)**[3] 3936 7-9-5 **59** ... RussKennemore 10 — 63
(Richard Whitaker) *hld up: swtchd to inner over 2f out: sn hdwy: chsd ldrs over 1f out: kpt on* **12/1**

5-20 **4** *3 1/4* **Lujano**[4] 3926 6-9-2 **56** ... TonyHamilton 3 — 53
(Ollie Pears) *trckd ldr: rdn to ld narrowly over 1f out: hdd jst ins fnl f: wknd* **4/1**[1]

0600 **5** *1* **El Dececy (USA)**[21] 3348 7-9-12 **66** ...(t) TonyCulhane 1 — 60
(Richard Guest) *led: drvn whn hdd over 1f out: wknd fnl f* **7/1**[2]

06-0 **6** *2 1/2* **Rising Kheleyf (IRE)**[13] 3643 5-9-11 **65** ...(p) BarryMcHugh 8 — 53
(John Harris) *hld up: rdn over 2f out: sme late hdwy: nvr threatened* **25/1**

5000 **7** *1 3/4* **Vanilla Rum**[17] 3495 4-9-8 **62** ...(p) StephenCraine 4 — 46
(John Mackie) *midfield: rdn over 2f out: wknd over 1f out* **10/1**

0351 **8** *3 3/4* **Wiseman's Diamond (USA)**[11] 3683 6-9-0 **59** 6ex ...(b) LMcNiff(5) 9 — 35
(Paul Midgley) *sn trckd ldr: rdn over 2f out: wknd over 1f out* **4/1**[1]

00-0 **9** *hd* **Sir Ike (IRE)**[3] 3944 6-9-6 **60** ...(t) NeilChalmers 5 — 35
(Michael Appleby) *dwlt: hld up in midfield: rdn over 2f out: wknd over 1f out* **12/1**

5555 **10** *9* **Hard Rock City (USA)**[31] 3024 11-10-0 **68** ... DavidAllan 6 — 23
(Declan Carroll) *midfield towards outer: drvn over 2f out: sn wknd* **7/1**[2]

1m 43.46s (-2.44) **Going Correction** -0.175s/f (Firm) **10** Ran SP% **116.9**
Speed ratings (Par 103): **105,103,102,98,97 95,93,89,89,80**
Tote Swingers:1&2:£11.50, 2&3:£12.00, 1&3:£25.60 CSF £63.13 CT £688.46 TOTE £10.10: £2.30, £3.50, £2.80; EX 86.80.
Owner Mel Brittain **Bred** Darley **Trained** Warthill, N Yorks

FOCUS
The pace was brisk in this modest handicap. Not many came into it in much form.
Wiseman's Diamond(USA) Official explanation: jockey said mare lost her action
Hard Rock City(USA) Official explanation: jockey said gelding hung right.

4077 GEORGE V WMC GLASSHOUGHTON MAIDEN H'CAP — 1m 2f 6y

8:40 (8:40) (Class 5) (0-70,70) 3-Y-O+ — **£2,587** (£770; £384; £192) **Stalls** Low

Form — RPR

0500 **1** **Reset To Fit**[15] 3543 4-8-13 **55** ... DavidAllan 5 — 63
(Eric Alston) *hld up in tch: hdwy over 2f out: rdn to ld over 1f out: sn edgd lft: kpt on: hld on towards fin* **11/1**

4403 **2** *nk* **Lady Norlela**[16] 3509 5-8-11 **53** ... BarryMcHugh 7 — 60
(Brian Rothwell) *hld up: hdwy over 2f out: sn chsd ldrs: wnt 2nd 1f out: kpt on: jst hld* **7/1**[3]

000- **3** *2 3/4* **Tricky Situation**[224] 7678 5-9-0 **56** ... RobertWinston 3 — 58
(David Brown) *dwlt: hld up and t.k.h: rdn and hdwy on outer over 2f out: chsd ldr over 1f out: one pce fnl f* **9/2**[2]

35 **4** *2 3/4* **Minsky Mine (IRE)**[151] 539 4-9-13 **69** ... NeilChalmers 1 — 65
(Michael Appleby) *trckd ldrs: rdn to ld 2f out: hdd over 1f out: wknd ins fnl f* **7/1**[3]

2624 **5** *3 1/4* **Nicola's Dream**[20] 3400 3-9-2 **69** ... TonyHamilton 4 — 59
(Richard Fahey) *in tch: lost pl 3f out: sn rdn: rallied to chse ldrs over 1f out: wknd fnl f* **15/8**[1]

000 **6** *5* **Strong Knight**[31] 3024 4-9-4 **60** ... DuranFentiman 8 — 40
(Tim Walford) *trckd ldr: rdn to ld wl over 2f out: hdd 2f out: sn wknd* **25/1**

000- **7** *22* **The Midshipmaid**[262] 7149 4-8-6 **51** oh6 ... SeanLevey(3) 11 — —
(Lucinda Featherstone) *led: rdn whn hdd wl over 2f out: sn wknd* **33/1**

-303 **8** *2 3/4* **Mayan Flight (IRE)**[37] 2801 3-7-12 **51** ... PaulQuinn 9 — —
(Richard Whitaker) *hld up: rdn over 2f out: sn wknd* **10/1**

5006 **9** *4 1/2* **Idealism**[10] 3701 4-8-10 **57** ... DaleSwift(5) 10 — —
(Micky Hammond) *in tch on outer: rdn over 2f out: sn wknd* **8/1**

2m 12.09s (-1.61) **Going Correction** -0.175s/f (Firm)
WFA 3 from 4yo+ 11lb **9** Ran SP% **113.3**
Speed ratings (Par 103): **99,98,96,94,91 87,70,67,64**
Tote Swingers:1&2:£12.20, 2&3:£9.70, 1&3:£13.20 CSF £83.76 CT £398.61 TOTE £15.50: £3.40, £1.80, £2.50.
Owner Lancashire Lads Partnership **Bred** Capt J H Wilson **Trained** Longton, Lancs

FOCUS
There was a little rain after the fourth race but not enough to affect the ground. The contestants in this maiden handicap had run 87 times between them without reward, and it was obviously a weak race. The leaders went off quick and the principals came from off the pace.
Nicola's Dream Official explanation: trainers representative was unable to offer any explanation as to poor run.

4078 YORKSHIRE RACING SUMMER FESTIVAL H'CAP — 6f

9:10 (9:10) (Class 5) (0-75,77) 3-Y-O+ — **£2,587** (£770; £384; £192) **Stalls** Low

Form — RPR

3545 **1** **Powerful Pierre**[6] 3880 4-9-0 **67** ...(b) DaleSwift(5) 7 — 75
(Ian McInnes) *in tch: rdn and hdwy over 1f out: led narrowly appr fnl f: kpt on: hld on all out* **9/2**[2]

5-65 **2** *shd* **Cornus**[10] 3704 9-9-9 **74** ...(be) MartinHarley(3) 6 — 82
(Alan McCabe) *dwlt: hld up in tch: rdn and hdwy over 1f out: chal ins fnl f: kpt on: jst failed* **7/1**

0006 **3** *1/2* **Chambers (IRE)**[12] 3657 5-8-7 **55** ... DavidAllan 5 — 61
(Eric Alston) *midfield on inner: rdn and hdwy over 1f out: ev ch ins fnl f: kpt on* **10/1**

4-11 **4** *nk* **Farlow (IRE)**[8] 3785 3-9-9 **77** 6ex ... StevieDonohoe 10 — 81
(Ralph Beckett) *midfield on outer: rdn and hdwy over 1f out: ev ch ins fnl f: kpt on* **3/1**[1]

0000 **5** *1 1/4* **Pearly Wey**[70] 1861 8-8-4 **55** oh1 ... PaulPickard(3) 11 — 56
(Ian McInnes) *slowly away: hld up and t.k.h: hdwy over 1f out: sltly short of room 1f out: kpt on: nt rch ldrs* **33/1**

0640 **6** *1 3/4* **Mr Wolf**[10] 3704 10-9-9 **71** ...(p) TonyHamilton 9 — 67
(John Quinn) *led: rdn whn hdd appr fnl f: sn wknd* **12/1**

0046 **7** *3* **Accamelia**[32] 2989 5-8-7 **55** oh1 ...(v[1]) SilvestreDeSousa 1 — 41
(Chris Fairhurst) *trckd ldrs: rdn over 1f out: losing pl whn sltly short of room 1f out: wknd fnl f* **15/2**

031 **8** *7* **Gertmegalush (IRE)**[13] 3638 4-9-4 **66** ... BarryMcHugh 8 — 30
(John Harris) *hld up: rdn over 2f out: sn no imp: eased ins fnl f* **7/1**

3600 **9** *26* **Besty**[129] 794 4-9-5 **67** ... AdrianNicholls 3 — —
(David Nicholls) *trckd ldr: rdn over 2f out: wknd over 1f out: eased* **5/1**[3]

1m 16.08s (-0.82) **Going Correction** -0.175s/f (Firm)
WFA 3 from 4yo+ 6lb **9** Ran SP% **116.3**
Speed ratings (Par 103): **98,97,97,96,95 92,88,79,44**
Tote Swingers:1&2:£3.70, 2&3:£15.40, 1&3:£5.80 CSF £36.25 CT £300.32 TOTE £6.00: £2.30, £2.20, £3.80; EX 33.10.
Owner Richard Mustill **Bred** Hedsor Stud **Trained** Catwick, E Yorks

FOCUS
A tight finish to this ordinary sprint handicap.
Besty Official explanation: jockey said gelding had no more to give.
T/Plt: £1,176.40 to a £1 stake. Pool £42,949.14 - 26.65 winning units T/Qpdt: £506.90 to a £1 stake. Pool £3,767.55 - 5.50 winning units. AS

4046 HAYDOCK (L-H)

Saturday, July 16

OFFICIAL GOING: Good to soft (good in places; 8.5)
Wind: Light, against Weather: Fine

4079 HATTONS BUSINESS SERVICES NURSERY — 5f

6:40 (6:41) (Class 5) 2-Y-O — **£2,911** (£866; £432; £216) **Stalls** Centre

Form — RPR

01 **1** **Roger Sez (IRE)**[39] 2780 2-9-0 **75** ... DavidAllan 6 — 83
(Tim Easterby) *squeezed out s: in rr: pushed along 1/2-way: rdn and hdwy over 1f out: led ins fnl f: r.o and edgd lft: in command towards fin* **5/1**

530 **2** *1* **Lupo D'Oro (IRE)**[32] 3014 2-8-8 **71** ... LukeMorris 1 — 73
(John Best) *led: rdn over 1f out: sn hung rt: hdd ins fnl f: hld towards fin* **11/2**

326 **3** *2 1/4* **Sea Odyssey (IRE)**[61] 2148 2-8-6 **74** ... MatthewLawson(7) 3 — 70
(B W Hills) *in tch: pushed along 2f out: rdn and nt qckn over 1f out: no imp and styd on same pce ins fnl f* **4/1**[2]

4215 **4** *2 1/4* **Dark Ages (IRE)**[10] 3745 2-8-11 **72** ... PaulHanagan 7 — 60
(Noel Quinlan) *w ldr tl rdn and nt qckn over 1f out: no ex ins fnl f* **9/2**[3]

213 **5** *2 3/4* **Amadeus Denton (IRE)**[32] 3022 2-9-7 **82** ... FrederikTylicki 2 — 60
(Michael Dods) *in tch: effrt over 1f out: nvr able to chal: one pce fnl f* **11/4**[1]

030 **6** *3 3/4* **Hopes Rebellion**[7] 3849 2-7-13 **62** ... SilvestreDeSousa 5 — 25
(Declan Carroll) *chsd ldrs: rdn 1/2-way: wknd over 1f out* **20/1**

6165 **7** *4 1/2* **Van Go Go**[7] 3879 2-8-7 **71** ... BillyCray(3) 4 — 20
(David Nicholls) *missed break: pushed along 1/2-way: a bhd* **8/1**

63.06 secs (2.26) **Going Correction** +0.325s/f (Good) **7** Ran SP% **112.8**
Speed ratings (Par 94): **96,94,90,87,82 76,69**
toteswingers:1&2:£6.70, 2&3:£7.40, 1&3:£2.40 CSF £31.22 CT £118.91 TOTE £4.60: £2.70, £3.40; EX 41.40.
Owner R Sidebottom **Bred** B Kennedy **Trained** Great Habton, N Yorks
■ The 'official' ratings shown next to each horse are estimated and for information purposes only.

FOCUS
Sprints on Inner home straight. Races on Round course used outer home straight and distances increased by 37yds.\n\x\x Fair form in a nursery which was run at a sound pace.

NOTEBOOK
Roger Sez(IRE) is very much going the right way and will continue to be of interest, particularly back at 6f, needing most of this shorter trip to prevail having been off the bridle before most. (op 7-2 tchd 10-3)
Lupo D'Oro(IRE) ran well on his nursery bow, showing plenty of speed and worn down only by one ahead of her mark. He may do better still. (op 10-1)
Sea Odyssey(IRE) ran close to the pick of his form in maidens without suggesting he's going to improve a great deal now handicapping, though he is worth trying at 6f before long. (op 3-1)
Dark Ages(IRE) has yet to reproduce her winning maiden form in two tries in nurseries, fading having helped force the pace. (op 11-2)
Amadeus Denton(IRE) was sent off favourite on his nursery bow but didn't find a great deal after travelling comfortably for a long way. It's still early days, and it's possible the easy ground may have been against him, but this isn't the first time he hasn't delivered quite as much as looked likely off the bridle. (op 10-3)
Van Go Go has yet to show her form for her new yard.

4080 HATTONS ACCIDENT COMPENSATION MAIDEN STKS — 7f

7:10 (7:13) (Class 5) 2-Y-O — **£2,911** (£866; £432; £216) **Stalls** Low

Form — RPR

1 **Now My Sun** 2-9-3 0 ... AndrewElliott 4 — 72+
(Mrs K Burke) *ref to settle: in tch: rdn and clsd over 1f out: edgd lft and r.o ins fnl f: led fnl stride* **5/1**[3]

6 **2** *shd* **Not Bad For A Boy (IRE)**[37] 2844 2-9-0 0 ... SeanLevey(3) 10 — 72
(Richard Hannon) *trckd ldrs: led 4f out: rdn over 1f out: hdd fnl stride* **20/1**

6 **3** *2* **Art Law (IRE)**[20] 3425 2-9-0 0 ... LouisBeuzelin(3) 1 — 67
(Brian Meehan) *trckd ldr tl over 4f out: remained handy: rdn over 1f out: styd on u.p ins fnl f: nt quite pce of front 2* **7/2**[2]

4 *1/4* **Double Cee** 2-9-3 0 ... BarryMcHugh 11 — 66+
(Richard Fahey) *hld up: effrt over 3f out: n.m.r and hmpd wl over 2f out: sn lost pl and rdn: clsd over 1f out: edgd lft and kpt on ins fnl f* **33/1**

5 *1* **Trail Blaze (IRE)** 2-9-3 0 ... PhillipMakin 5 — 64+
(Kevin Ryan) *racd keenly in midfield: rdn over 2f out: kpt on same pce ins fnl f: no imp* **12/1**

6 *3* **Fine Altomis** 2-9-3 0 ... FrederikTylicki 7 — 56
(Michael Dods) *hld up: rdn over 1f out: nvr able to chal* **40/1**

7 *1/2* **Double Bass (USA)** 2-8-10 0 ... AntiocoMurgia(7) 2 — 55
(Mahmood Al Zarooni) *led: hdd 4f out: remained prom: rdn 2f out: wknd 1f out* **10/1**

5 **8** *2 3/4* **Gabrial's Princess (IRE)**[22] 3336 2-8-12 0 ... TomEaves 8 — 43
(Bryan Smart) *chsd ldrs on outer: rdn over 2f out: wknd over 1f out* **8/1**

9 *2 3/4* **Bollin Tommy** 2-9-3 0 ... DavidAllan 3 — 41
(Tim Easterby) *v.s.a: pushed along over 3f out: a bhd* **33/1**

10 *nk* **Pembrey** 2-9-3 0 ... PaulHanagan 9 — 41
(Mahmood Al Zarooni) *missed break: in rr: toiling fnl 3f* **7/4**[1]

1m 32.75s (1.85) **Going Correction** +0.025s/f (Good) **10** Ran SP% **116.2**
Speed ratings (Par 94): **90,89,87,87,86 82,82,79,75,75**
toteswingers:1&2:£40.80, 2&3:£11.30, 1&3:£6.00 CSF £101.07 TOTE £5.80: £1.40, £4.90, £1.70; EX 127.90.
Owner Ray Bailey **Bred** Ray Bailey **Trained** Middleham Moor, North Yorks

FOCUS
Not that easy to gauge the strength of this maiden with previous form rather thin on the ground, though the majority of the newcomers left the impression they'll do better with this behind them. The pace was on the steady side until the straight.

NOTEBOOK

Now My Sun's debut success clearly wasn"t unexpected given his prominent position in the market. There should be more to come as he did show signs of inexperience, keen enough early on and taking a bit of time of time to respond to pressure but picking up well by the finish. A son of Notnowcato, he's bred to be suited by 1m+ in due course. (op 4-1 tchd 6-1)

Not Bad For A Boy(IRE) was much more clued up than his debut and duly showed plenty of improvement up in trip, caught only on the line having been in front rank throughout. It"s doubtful he figures that high up his powerful yard's juvenile pecking order but he should pick up a similar event at some stage. (op 25-1)

Art Law(IRE) stepped up a little on his debut form in all probability and could be the type to progress steadily with racing. His dam won over 1m4f, so he should stay a bit further. (op 4-1)

Double Cee, a brother by Haafhd to the useful 7f winner Infiraad showed ability and, in top hands, can be expected to build on this, squeezed out just the race was really starting in earnest but keeping on nicely by the finish. (op 25-1 tchd 20-1)

Trail Blaze(IRE), a son of Tagula, suggested he has a future, running green on his debut but sticking to his task. He's sure to do better. (op 11-1 tchd 14-1)

Fine Altomis never seriously threatened but should be sharper with this behind him. (op 25-1)

Double Bass(USA) faded after cutting out the running. (op 8-1)

Gabrial's Princess(IRE) failed to improve as expected, soon beaten once the race began in earnest. (tchd 13-2)

Pembrey was sent off a short-priced favourite for a yard enjoying a good year with its juveniles but he never looked like winning after missing the break, clearly needing this first experience a lot more than anticipated. We should get a better idea about him next time. (op 3-1 tchd 13-8)

4081 HATTONS ACCESS TO JUSTICE H'CAP — 1m

7:40 (7:41) (Class 5) (0-75,75) 3-Y-O — **£2,911** (£866; £432; £216) **Stalls** Low

Form — RPR

4564 **1** — **Ventura Sands (IRE)**[11] 3706 3-8-13 **67** .... PaulHanagan 11 — 73
(Richard Fahey) *racd keenly in midfield: rdn and hdwy 2f out: r.o ins fnl f: got up to ld post* — **8/1**

244 **2** *nse* **Dr Red Eye**[18] 3485 3-8-10 **67** .... BillyCray(3) 2 — 73
(David Nicholls) *led: rdn and pressed 2f out: hd post* — **13/2**[3]

5-01 **3** *nk* **Ingleby Exceed (IRE)**[10] 3729 3-9-2 **70** .... SilvestreDeSousa 12 — 75
(David O'Meara) *restless in stalls: wnt rt s: hld up: hdwy over 2f out: rn to chal ins fnl f: hld fnl strides* — **9/2**[1]

2200 **4** *1 1/4* **My Vindication (USA)**[17] 3514 3-9-2 **73** .... SeanLevey(3) 1 — 75
(Richard Hannon) *midfield: hdwy over 3f out: chalng fr over 2f out: no ex fnl strides* — **9/1**

6003 **5** *1 1/2* **Marie Rose**[12] 3688 3-8-13 **67** ....(p) LiamJones 9 — 66
(Brian Meehan) *hld up in rr: rdn and hdwy over 1f out: chsd ldrs ins fnl f: styd on same pce* — **9/1**

-000 **6** *1* **Crabbies Gold (IRE)**[31] 3039 3-8-2 **56** oh1 .... LukeMorris 7 — 53
(Lisa Williamson) *midfield: rdn over 2f out: kpt on u.p ins fnl f: nvr able to chal ldrs: one pce fnl 75yds* — **40/1**

5435 **7** *1* **Magic Rhythm**[14] 3621 3-8-11 **65** .... AndrewElliott 8 — 61+
(Mrs K Burke) *prom: effrt over 2f out: keeping on same pce whn n.m.r and hmpd over 1f out: no imp after* — **16/1**

1514 **8** *1/2* **Shadow Catcher**[28] 3168 3-9-7 **75** .... FrederikTylicki 4 — 68
(Michael Dods) *midfield: rdn over 2f out: wknd over 1f out* — **5/1**[2]

0040 **9** *1 3/4* **Watts Up Son**[9] 3783 3-9-1 **69** ....(t) DavidAllan 3 — 58
(Declan Carroll) *trckd ldrs tl rdn and wknd over 1f out* — **11/1**

06-0 **10** *2* **Spartan King (IRE)**[22] 3337 3-8-10 **64** .... GregFairley 6 — 49
(Ian Williams) *plld hrd: chsd ldr tl over 3f out: wknd over 1f out* — **9/1**

060 **11** *19* **Desert Chieftain**[39] 2790 3-8-5 **59** .... KirstyMilczarek 10 — —
(Luca Cumani) *in rr: pushed along over 3f out: nvr on terms* — **11/1**

2410 **12** *9* **Bountiful Guest**[37] 2835 3-9-0 **68** .... PhillipMakin 5 — —
(Brian Baugh) *hld up: u.p over 2f out: nvr on terms* — **40/1**

1m 44.92s (2.02) **Going Correction** +0.025s/f (Good) — **12** Ran SP% **116.7**

Speed ratings (Par 100): **90,89,89,88,86 85,84,84,82,80 61,52**

toteswingers:1&2:£10.00, 2&3:£4.70, 1&3:£11.20 CSF £58.30 CT £266.05 TOTE £7.60: £2.00, £3.50, £3.30; EX 64.10.

Owner Keith Denham **Bred** J Jamgotchian **Trained** Musley Bank, N Yorks

FOCUS

A modest but competitive 3-y-o handicap, if one devoid of obviously progressive types. The gallop didn't look strong in the early stages and that probably contributed to a number still being in with every chance entering the final furlong.

4082 HATTONS 10 YEAR ANNIVERSARY H'CAP — 1m 6f

8:10 (8:10) (Class 4) (0-85,79) 4-Y-O+ — **£5,175** (£1,540; £769; £384) **Stalls** Low

Form — RPR

-450 **1** — **Spirit Of A Nation (IRE)**[21] 3399 6-9-1 **73** .... PhillipMakin 8 — 80
(James Moffatt) *midfield: lost pl and outpcd over 3f out: swtchd rt and rallied ent fnl f: styd on to ld fnl 75yds: wl on top at fin* — **9/1**

542 **2** *1 1/4* **The Caped Crusader (IRE)**[31] 3054 4-9-5 **77** .... BarryMcHugh 7 — 82
(Ollie Pears) *in tch: pushed along over 2f out: styd on to chal ins fnl f: pce of wnr cl home* — **5/4**[1]

-120 **3** *nse* **Rare Ruby (IRE)**[22] 3344 7-9-5 **77** .... StephenCraine 6 — 82
(Jennie Candlish) *trckd ldrs: wnt 2nd 6f out: led over 3f out: pressed fr over 1f out: hdd fnl 75yds: hld cl home* — **9/1**

03-0 **4** *nse* **Tropical Bachelor (IRE)**[19] 3456 5-8-6 **67** .... JohnFahy(3) 5 — 72
(Richard Ford) *hld up: hdwy gng wl over 2f out: rdn to chal fr over 1f out: hld cl home* — **20/1**

1-06 **5** *3/4* **Drawn Gold**[15] 3599 7-8-5 **63** .... LukeMorris 3 — 67
(Reg Hollinshead) *prom: rdn and outpcd 3f out: rallied to chal for press ins fnl f: no ex fnl 75yds* — **11/1**

/205 **6** *4 1/2* **Advisor (FR)**[35] 2931 5-9-7 **79** .... PaulHanagan 4 — 79
(Michael Bell) *led: hdd over 3f out: rdn over 2f but stl wl there tl fdd and eased fnl 75yds* — **7/2**[2]

6160 **7** *3* **Jackday (IRE)**[10] 3730 6-8-11 **69** ....(b[1]) DavidAllan 2 — 62
(Tim Easterby) *hld up in rr: rdn over 5f out: struggling over 3f out: nvr a danger* — **17/2**[3]

3m 7.04s (5.84) **Going Correction** +0.025s/f (Good) — **7** Ran SP% **110.3**

Speed ratings (Par 105): **84,83,83,83,82 80,78**

toteswingers:1&2:£2.50, 2&3:£5.30, 1&3:£6.10 CSF £19.32 CT £98.90 TOTE £13.20: £5.00, £1.80; EX 28.80.

Owner Mr & Mrs Gordon Grant **Bred** J P Hardiman **Trained** Cartmel, Cumbria

■ Stewards' Enquiry : Luke Morris two-day ban: used whip with excessive frequency (Jul 31, Aug 1)

John Fahy one-day ban: used whip with excessive frequency (Jul 31)

FOCUS

A fairly useful handicap, rated around the front three. The gallop was on the steady side, not quickening until the home turn, and that resulted in six of the seven still holding every chance inside the final furlong.

4083 HATTONS SUPPORTING SAINTS H'CAP — 1m 2f 95y

8:40 (8:40) (Class 5) (0-75,79) 3-Y-O+ — **£2,911** (£866; £432; £216) **Stalls** Centre

Form — RPR

3422 **1** — **Number Theory**[21] 3377 3-8-8 **71** .... LucyKBarry(7) 4 — 80
(John Holt) *hld up: rdn and hdwy 2f out: edgd rt and led over 1f out: all out cl home* — **4/1**[3]

4563 **2** *shd* **Lord Raglan (IRE)**[8] 3831 4-9-9 **69** .... AndrewElliott 5 — 78
(Mrs K Burke) *led: rdn and hung lft whn hdd over 1f out: stl ev ch ins fnl f: rallied nr fin: jst hld* — **6/1**

3246 **3** *1 3/4* **Bollin Dolly**[14] 3632 8-9-13 **73** .... DavidAllan 2 — 78
(Tim Easterby) *racd keenly: trckd ldrs: lost pl 6f out: in tch: rdn and hdwy over 2f out: chsd ldrs over 1f out: styd on same pce fnl 100yds* — **11/2**

-041 **4** *nk* **Pandorica**[29] 3118 3-9-1 **74** .... JohnFahy(3) 1 — 79
(Clive Cox) *racd keenly: prom: pushed along over 3f out: rdn over 1f out: styd on same pce fnl 100yds* — **10/3**[1]

544 **5** *1* **Mill Mick**[21] 3377 4-9-8 **68** .... StephenCraine 8 — 71
(John Mackie) *hld up: hdwy over 2f out: hung lft and chsd ldrs over 1f out: one pce ins fnl f* — **16/1**

5/3 **6** *1 1/4* **Nobunaga**[22] 3366 6-9-13 **73** .... PaulHanagan 9 — 73
(Venetia Williams) *in tch: wnt prom 6f out: rdn over 2f out: one pce and no imp fnl f* — **7/2**[2]

00-0 **7** *34* **Balletlou (IRE)**[14] 3632 4-9-11 **71** .... LukeMorris 10 — —
(John Best) *in rr: u.p 5f out: eased whn wl btn over 1f out* — **20/1**

-050 **8** *7* **Daaweitza**[11] 3701 8-9-11 **71** ....(b) TomEaves 7 — —
(Brian Ellison) *racd keenly in midfield: impr to trck ldrs 6f out: rdn and wknd over 2f out* — **16/1**

2m 15.39s (-0.61) **Going Correction** +0.025s/f (Good)

WFA 3 from 4yo+ 10lb — **8** Ran SP% **111.5**

Speed ratings (Par 103): **103,102,101,101,100 99,72,66**

toteswingers:1&2:£5.40, 2&3:£6.60, 1&3:£2.90 CSF £26.62 CT £127.49 TOTE £4.90: £1.70, £2.10, £1.80; EX 31.60.

Owner Mohan Fonseka **Bred** R Haim **Trained** Peckleton, Leics

■ Stewards' Enquiry : John Fahy one-day ban: careless riding (Aug 1)

FOCUS

A fair handicap which was run at a fair gallop. The form looks sound.

4084 HATTONS INDUSTRIAL CLAIMS H'CAP — 1m 3f 200y

9:10 (9:10) (Class 5) (0-75,74) 3-Y-O — **£2,911** (£866; £432; £216) **Stalls** Centre

Form — RPR

1541 **1** — **Franciscan**[16] 3558 3-9-5 **72** .... KirstyMilczarek 7 — 82+
(Luca Cumani) *chsd ldrs: wnt 2nd over 6f out: led ent fnl 2f: rdn over 1f out: wl on top fnl 75yds* — **2/1**[1]

364 **2** *1/2* **Kleitomachos (IRE)**[20] 3430 3-9-3 **70** .... PaulHanagan 6 — 79
(Stuart Kittow) *hld up: hdwy to chse ldrs over 3f out: rdn and chalng over 1f out: nt qckn fnl 75yds* — **5/1**[2]

2666 **3** *3* **Lunar Phase (IRE)**[25] 3260 3-9-7 **74** .... LukeMorris 8 — 78
(Clive Cox) *hld up: effrt to chse ldrs over 3f out: rdn and chalng over 1f out: no ex fnl 100yds* — **5/1**[2]

5031 **4** *1/2* **Getabuzz**[18] 3487 3-9-7 **74** .... DavidAllan 3 — 77
(Tim Easterby) *chsd ldr: led after 4f: rdn and hdd ent fnl 2f: stl ev ch over 1f out: one pce ins fnl f* — **2/1**[1]

0030 **5** *14* **Oldmeldrum (IRE)**[16] 3545 3-7-13 **55** oh1 .... BillyCray(3) 4 — 36
(Peter Salmon) *racd keenly: chsd ldrs: lost pl 5f out: struggling over 3f out: n.d after* — **25/1**

005- **6** *2* **Jossy Johnston (IRE)**[405] 2785 3-8-9 **62** .... AndrewElliott 2 — 40
(Eric Alston) *led: hdd after 4f: rdn and wknd over 3f out* — **14/1**[3]

2m 39.55s (5.55) **Going Correction** +0.025s/f (Good) — **6** Ran SP% **110.5**

Speed ratings (Par 100): **82,81,79,79,70 68**

toteswingers:1&2:£2.80, 2&3:£2.00, 1&3:£3.10 CSF £12.17 CT £39.67 TOTE £3.00: £2.30, £2.70; EX 13.60.

Owner Fittocks Stud For Camilla Millbank **Bred** Fittocks Stud **Trained** Newmarket, Suffolk

FOCUS

A steadily run handicap and the fourth was a bit disappointing but probably still best to view the form in a positive light, the front two both progressive.

Oldmeldrum(IRE) Official explanation: jockey said filly hung right.

T/Plt: £243.10 to a £1 stake. Pool £81,998.82 - 246.14 winning tickets. T/Qpdt: £12.10 to a £1 stake. Pool £7,981.85 - 21.30 winning tickets. DO

3978 LINGFIELD (L-H)

Saturday, July 16

OFFICIAL GOING: Turf course - good (8.5) all-weather - standard

Wind: fresh, half behind Weather: showers, overcast

4085 CROWHURST NURSERY (TURF) — 6f

6:25 (6:26) (Class 5) 2-Y-O — **£3,067** (£905; £453) **Stalls** High

Form — RPR

043 **1** — **Molly Jones**[11] 3707 2-8-2 **65** .... AndreaAtzeni 2 — 70
(Derek Haydn Jones) *chsd ldrs: wnt 2nd over 4f out: led 2f out: drvn over 1f out: edgd lft u.p but styd on wl fnl f* — **11/1**

1650 **2** *3/4* **He's So Cool (IRE)**[8] 3810 2-9-4 **84** .... KierenFox(3) 1 — 87
(Bill Turner) *in tch on outer: chsd wnr wl over 1f out: sn drvn and unable qck: styd on same pce and a hld fnl f* — **11/1**

553 **3** *3 1/2* **Leenavesta (USA)**[30] 3092 2-8-4 **72** .... KieranO'Neill(5) 8 — 64
(Richard Hannon) *in tch: rdn and effrt 2f out: sn outpcd by ldng pair: plugged on to go 3rd ins fnl f: no ch w ldrs* — **11/4**[1]

555 **4** *1/2* **Purple Affair (IRE)**[10] 3746 2-7-8 **62** .... RyanPowell(5) 5 — 53
(J S Moore) *dwlt: hld up in tch: rdn and outpcd jst over 2f out: no ch w ldrs but plugged on fnl f* — **9/2**[2]

1203 **5** *1 1/2* **Aquasulis (IRE)**[8] 3810 2-8-4 **67** .... CathyGannon 3 — 53
(David Evans) *led and grad crossed to r against stands' rail hdd and rdn 2f out: sn outpcd by ldng pair and btn over 1f out: wknd fnl f* — **9/2**[2]

304 **6** *6* **Thorpe Bay**[16] 3553 2-7-12 **61** oh4 ....(be) JamieMackay 7 — 38+
(Mark Rimmer) *t.k.h: chsd ldr for over 1f: sddle slipped 4f out and rdr unable to give any assistance after: lost pl and btn 2f out* — **6/1**[3]

1105 **7** *6* **Miss Muga**[33] 2998 2-8-2 **65**.. JimmyQuinn 4 15
(Edward Creighton) *s.i.s: a struggling in rr: rdn and lost tch 2f out: sn wl bhd* **25/1**

1m 11.13s (-0.07) **Going Correction** -0.10s/f (Good) **7** Ran SP% **97.8**
Speed ratings (Par 94): **96,95,90,89,87 79,71**
toteswingers:1&2:£10.20, 2&3:£4.70, 1&3:£7.20 CSF £86.02 CT £269.20 TOTE £13.90: £5.00, £4.90; EX 67.60.
Owner North Cheshire Trading & Storage Ltd **Bred** Mrs M L Parry & P M Steele-Mortimer **Trained** Efail Isaf, Rhondda C Taff
■ The 'official' ratings shown next to each horse are estimated and for information purposes only.
■ Stewards' Enquiry : Andrea Atzeni caution: careless riding

FOCUS
An open-looking nursery lost a little lustre with the withdrawal of Alice's Dancer, who reared up twice before entering the stalls, unshipping Chris Catlin. The pace was true, few got into it and the front two drew well clear.

NOTEBOOK
Molly Jones, up in trip after showing improvement at Southwell over 5f 11 days ago, was making her handicap debut. Prominent throughout, she readily went about her work when asked the question 2f out. She drifted markedly left under a right-hand drive, possibly intimidating the runner-up. She won a shade cosily in the end, has improved with every run and shows a willing attitude. She may get a little further in time. (tchd 12-1)
He's So Cool(IRE), with seven runs and two victories under his belt, had experience on his side which was negated a little by an awkward draw and he raced wide. Giving the winner 19lb, he travelled very well and ran on for pressure. He'd missed the break at Chester last week, but was better away here and game in defeat, this was a another solid effort. He remains consistent. (op 12-1 tchd 14-1)
Leenavesta(USA) was aiming to give trainer Richard Hannon his third consecutive victory in the race. She had not been beaten far in maidens and this easy 6f should have suited her, but she produced a tame effort. (op 7-2)
Purple Affair(IRE) had raced up with the pace in 6f/7f maidens but a change of tactics didn't seem to help. Held up, he raced widest of all and looked one-paced. He looks tripless at present. (op 4-1)
Aquasulis(IRE) was a close third at Chester last week when had met He's So Cool, but the tables were well and truly turned. She had a decent draw but ran flat and she may have felt the toll of four quick runs in succession.
Thorpe Bay needed the race and blew up behind Saigon at Yarmouth when equipped with blinkers and eyeshields for the first time. They were back on again, but his saddle slipped and this effort is best ignored. Official explanation: jockey said saddle slipped. (op 8-1)

4086 SANDRA D'URSO BIRTHDAY CELEBRATION H'CAP (TURF) 6f
6:55 (6:57) (Class 6) (0-65,68) 3-Y-O+ **£1,533** (£452; £226) **Stalls** High

Form RPR
3330 **1** **Witchry**[17] 3512 9-9-9 **62**.. DaneO'Neill 8 70
(Tony Newcombe) *stdd s: hld up in rr: stl plenty to do and swtchd lft over 1f out: str run ins fnl f to ld fnl 75yds: sn in command and eased nr fin* **9/2**[2]
0560 **2** *1* **Chinese Democracy (USA)**[2] 4025 4-9-0 **53**...........(v) CathyGannon 13 58
(David Evans) *t.k.h: hld up in midfield: sltly hmpd wl over 4f out: rdn and effrt over 1f out: drvn and styd on ins fnl f: snatched 2nd on line* **7/1**[3]
1303 **3** *nse* **Commandingpresence (USA)**[9] 3768 5-8-13 **57**....... KieranO'Neill(5) 3 62
(John Bridger) *chsd ldrs: wnt 2nd 2f out: rdn to ld over 1f out: hdd and nt pce of wnr fnl 75yds: lost 2nd on post* **10/1**
4053 **4** *1 3/4* **Dancing Welcome**[4] 3943 5-8-13 **52**............................(b) LiamKeniry 10 51
(Milton Bradley) *hld up in midfield: sltly hmpd wl over 4f out: rdn and effrt wl over 1f out: hdwy to chse ldrs 1f out: styd on same pce ins fnl f* **7/2**[1]
0530 **5** *3/4* **Little Perisher**[47] 2554 4-8-8 **50**.............................(b) KierenFox(3) 14 47
(Karen George) *chsd ldrs: rdn and hanging lft 4f out: rdn and outpcd 2f out: rallied and styd on ins fnl f: no threat to ldrs* **11/1**
0420 **6** *1* **Ace Of Spies (IRE)**[2] 4025 6-9-10 **68**......................(b) HarryBentley(5) 6 61
(Conor Dore) *led and grad crossed to r against stands' rail: rdn and hdd over 1f out: lost 2nd and wknd ins fnl f* **10/1**
4P-0 **7** *nk* **Into The Wind**[24] 3293 4-9-4 **57**.. JamesMillman 7 49
(Rod Millman) *s.i.s: outpcd in rr: styd on and edgd rt ins fnl f: nvr trbld ldrs* **12/1**
0040 **8** *1* **One Cool Chick**[8] 3818 3-8-1 **50**................................... RyanPowell(5) 12 38
(John Bridger) *awkward s and v.s.a: bhd: hdwy 1/2-way: nt clr run and swtchd lft over 1f out: styd on same pce u.p fnl f* **16/1**
5034 **9** *2 3/4* **Elhamri**[2] 4000 7-9-11 **64**.. JamesSullivan 9 44
(Conor Dore) *chsd ldrs: stmbld on path wl over 4f out: rdn wl over 2f out: wknd wl over 1f out* **8/1**
0066 **10** *1 3/4* **Tortilla (IRE)**[14] 3636 3-8-10 **57**................................... SophieDoyle(3) 11 31
(Des Donovan) *s.i.s: struggling and outpcd in rr: sme hdwy and swtchd rt over 1f out: nvr trbld ldrs* **14/1**
4-00 **11** *11* **Private Olley**[26] 3216 4-9-1 **54**.......................................(b¹) JamesDoyle 5 —
(Harry Dunlop) *taken down early and led to s: chsd ldr tl 2f out: sn wknd u.p: in rr whn hmpd 1f out: eased ins fnl f* **33/1**

1m 12.15s (0.95) **Going Correction** -0.10s/f (Good)
WFA 3 from 4yo+ 5lb **11** Ran SP% **113.7**
Speed ratings (Par 101): **89,87,87,85,84 82,82,81,77,75 60**
toteswingers:1&2:£7.60, 2&3:£12.70, 1&3:£7.70 CSF £34.79 CT £303.30 TOTE £4.80: £2.50, £1.70, £2.40; EX 29.00.
Owner White Swan Racing & A G Newcombe **Bred** Darley **Trained** Yarnscombe, Devon
■ Stewards' Enquiry : James Sullivan two-day ban: careless riding (Jul 31-Aug 1)

FOCUS
A modest race and the time was slower than the nursery. The winner is probably the best guide.
Elhamri Official explanation: jockey said gelding lost its action early on.
Tortilla(IRE) Official explanation: jockey said filly missed the break.

4087 BRITISH STALLION STUDS SUPPORTING BRITISH RACING E B F MAIDEN STKS (TURF) 7f
7:25 (7:26) (Class 5) 2-Y-O **£3,340** (£986; £493) **Stalls** High

Form RPR
5323 **1** **Minal**[20] 3429 2-8-12 0.. KieranO'Neill(5) 3 80
(Richard Hannon) *travelled wl: chsd ldr tl jst over 2f out: rdn to ld over 1f out: kpt on wl fnl f: rdn out* **9/2**[2]
0 **2** *1* **Freddy Q (IRE)**[38] 2817 2-9-3 0.. DaneO'Neill 12 78+
(Richard Hannon) *hld up in tch: rdn and effrt wl over 1f out: chsd wnr jst over 1f out: kpt on but a hld fnl f* **14/1**
3 *3 3/4* **Sunley Valentine** 2-8-12 0... SamHitchcott 9 63
(Mick Channon) *hld up in tch: rdn and effrt wl over 1f out: chsd ldrs jst over 1f out: outpcd by ldng pair ins fnl f but plugged on for clr 3rd* **50/1**
4 *5* **Parisian Princess (IRE)** 2-8-9 0......................... MatthewDavies(3) 10 51
(George Baker) *hld up in tch: rdn: outpcd and rn green over 1f out: no ch w ldrs but plugged on to go modest 4th ins fnl f* **40/1**

03 **5** *3 1/2* **Emperors Pearl (IRE)**[9] 3780 2-8-12 0............................ MichaelHills 7 42
(B W Hills) *led and grad crossed to r against stands' rail: hdd over 1f out: sn hung lft and btn: eased ins fnl f* **6/1**[3]
6 *1 1/4* **Harrier Hill (USA)** 2-9-3 0.. AhmedAjtebi 6 44
(Mahmood Al Zarooni) *chsd ldrs: pushed along and hung lft ent fnl 2f: wknd over 1f out* **10/1**
7 *1/2* **Cash Injection** 2-9-0 0.. KierenFox(3) 8 43
(Karen George) *v.s.a: rn green and pushed along in rr: sme modest late hdwy: nvr on terms* **80/1**
0 **8** *3/4* **My Scat Daddy (USA)**[24] 3282 2-9-3 0..............................(t) IanMongan 4 41
(Brett Johnson) *a towards rr: rdn and struggling 3f out: no ch fnl 2f* **100/1**
9 *1 3/4* **Northern Territory (IRE)** 2-9-3 0..................................... GeorgeBaker 2 36
(Jim Boyle) *s.i.s: a in rr and rn green: n.d* **66/1**
10 *1/2* **Abhaath (USA)** 2-9-3 0.. FrankieDettori 11 35
(Saeed Bin Suroor) *chsd ldrs: jnd ldr 2f out: rdn and fnd nil over 1f out: sn btn and wknd qckly ent fnl f: eased fnl 100yds* **4/6**[1]
11 *13* **Cold Blow Den** 2-9-3 0.. NickyMackay 5 3
(Jim Boyle) *awkward leaving stalls: rn green and sn pushed along in rr: wl bhd fnl 3f: t.o* **100/1**

1m 24.77s (1.47) **Going Correction** -0.10s/f (Good) **11** Ran SP% **117.3**
Speed ratings (Par 94): **87,85,81,75,71 70,69,69,67,66 51**
toteswingers:1&2:£6.80, 2&3:£33.40, 1&3:£27.40 CSF £60.80 TOTE £5.10: £1.60, £2.90, £11.10; EX 67.80.
Owner B Bull **Bred** Poulton Stud **Trained** East Everleigh, Wilts

FOCUS
An ordinary maiden and the pace was solid for the conditions. Richard Hannon farmed this race in the past couple of years and completed a hat-trick of victories, saddling the first two home for good measure.

NOTEBOOK
Minal had the most experience, as this was his fifth run. In the frame on his last three starts, he was always up with the pace and five wide from the stands' rail, he readily drew clear from the 2f marker for an impressive victory. This was the first time he had encountered good ground and he idled a little in front, so the victory was all the more meritorious. The extra furlong was a big help, and he looks progressive. (tchd 5-1 in a place)
Freddy Q(IRE) had a similar profile to the winner, having been all at sea on his AW debut last month before looking a much different proposition on his second start. He was catching the winner late on, suggesting he will get a little further. (op 16-1)
Sunley Valentine ran a blinder, despite being a little green. She is bred to stay further than this and will be better for the experience.
Parisian Princess(IRE) was beaten a long way but also made a pleasing debut. The stable's juveniles always seem to improve for their first run and it would be a surprise if this was not the case.
Emperors Pearl(IRE) held every chance, but her jockey was looking down as if something was amiss a furlong from home. This run is consequently best written off. She had a progressive profile beforehand and remains of interest. Official explanation: jockey said filly hung left and lost her action. (op 9-2)
Harrier Hill(USA), a half-brother to a champion 2yo filly in Argentina, dropped away tamely, suggesting he was in need of the run. He was green and the run should bring him on. (op 12-1)
Northern Territory(IRE) Official explanation: jockey said colt ran green.
Abhaath(USA), a $400,000 colt from the first crop of 2007 Kentucky Derby and Breeders' Cup Classic runner-up Hard Spun, and a half-brother to a Grade 1 2yo winner in the States, was all the rage in the market. He was Frankie Dettori's only ride of the meeting but the Italian may have wished he'd stayed at home. The colt travelled well enough until the 2f pole, where he emptied quickly. This was a very ordinary debut for such a well-bred individual. There were no apparent excuses. (op 8-11 tchd 4-5 in places)

4088 HEART BREAKFAST SHOW'S JACK THE LAD CLASSIFIED (S) STKS 1m 2f (P)
7:55 (7:55) (Class 6) 3-Y-O+ **£1,533** (£452; £226) **Stalls** Low

Form RPR
0151 **1** **Stand Guard**[61] 2159 7-9-11 **70**... AdamKirby 5 77
(Noel Quinlan) *trckd ldng pair: rdn to chse ldr over 2f out: drvn to ld 1f out: in command ins fnl f: eased towards fin* **5/2**[1]
2022 **2** *1 3/4* **Viewing**[10] 3743 4-9-5 **64**.. SteveDrowne 6 67
(Tony Newcombe) *in tch in midfield: effrt to chse ldng pair and c wd bnd 2f out: rdn and edgd lft over 1f out: chsd wnr fnl 100yds: no imp* **7/2**[3]
-311 **3** *1 3/4* **Carlton Scroop (FR)**[42] 2721 8-9-11 **70**................................ PaulDoe 4 70
(Jim Best) *sn bustled up to ld: drvn and qcknd 3f out: drvn and hrd pressed 2f out: hdd 1f out: styd on same pce fnl f* **3/1**[2]
4360 **4** *5* **Dream Of Fortune (IRE)**[5] 3923 7-9-2 **60**.............(bt) RichardEvans(3) 3 54
(David Evans) *pushed along early: in tch in midfield: rdn and effrt on inner to chse ldng trio 2f out: edgd rt and wknd fnl f* **6/1**
-000 **5** *6* **Control Chief**[26] 3220 3-8-9 **55**... JimCrowley 1 42
(Ralph Beckett) *broke wl: stdd and t.k.h in last pair: rdn and outpcd jst over 2f out: sn wl btn* **7/1**
50-4 **6** *hd* **Alqaahir (USA)**[101] 1172 9-9-2 **65**.............................(p) RobertLButler(3) 2 41
(Paddy Butler) *stdd after s: hld up in last pair: rdn and outpcd over 2f out: sn wl btn* **40/1**
460- **7** *7* **Until The Man (IRE)**[200] 7992 4-9-5 **58**..........................(p) IanMongan 7 27
(Jim Best) *t.k.h: chsd ldr tl wl over 2f out: wknd qckly 2f out: sn bhd* **14/1**

2m 8.19s (1.59) **Going Correction** +0.175s/f (Slow)
WFA 3 from 4yo+ 10lb **7** Ran SP% **111.7**
Speed ratings (Par 101): **100,98,97,93,88 88,82**
toteswingers:1&2:£2.40, 2&3:£3.00, 1&3:£1.40 CSF £10.95 TOTE £3.00: £2.40, £3.40; EX 11.20.There was no bid for the winner.
Owner C Owen **Bred** Juddmonte Farms Ltd **Trained** Newmarket, Suffolk

FOCUS
A modest seller with the market proving a good guide, as the top three in the betting fought out the finish. The winner only had to run to this year's form.

4089 LADBROKES MOBILE CLAIMING STKS 1m (P)
8:25 (8:25) (Class 6) 3-5-Y-O **£2,181** (£644; £322) **Stalls** High

Form RPR
5020 **1** **Come On Safari (IRE)**[53] 2376 4-8-8 **68**...............(b) CharlesBishop(7) 9 61
(Joseph Tuite) *dwlt: t.k.h: sn rcvrd and chsd ldr after 1f: led wl over 3f out: rdn and clr over 1f out: idled and drvn out ins fnl f: eased towards fin* **8/1**
-060 **2** *1* **Bell's Ocean (USA)**[10] 3741 4-8-6 **54**.................................. JimmyQuinn 3 50
(John Ryan) *in tch: drvn and unable qck wl over 1f out: styd on u.p fnl 100yds: wnt 2nd towards fin* **20/1**
4504 **3** *nk* **Jackie Love (IRE)**[26] 3227 3-7-12 **50**..........................(b¹) NickyMackay 7 47
(Olivia Maylam) *dwlt: sn rcvrd and chsng ldrs: pressed ldrs over 2f out: drvn over 1f out: chsd wnr and kpt on same pce ins fnl f: lost 2nd towards fin* **25/1**

6000 **4** *nk* **Putin (IRE)**[12] 3688 3-8-5 49 .... AndreaAtzeni 8 53
(Derek Haydn Jones) *led: hdd and hung rt bnd wl over 3f out: drvn and unable qck over 1f out: edgd rt and one pce 1f out* **33/1**

6425 **5** *½* **Barista (IRE)**[7] 3854 3-8-11 75 .... SamHitchcott 1 58
(Mick Channon) *in tch: rdn wl over 2f out: effrt on inner and pressing for 2nd 1f out: styd on same pce after* **7/2**[2]

6224 **6** *2¼* **Lastkingofscotland (IRE)**[25] 3250 5-9-3 75 ....(b) GeorgeBaker 6 53
(Conor Dore) *t.k.h: chsd ldr for 1f: chsd ldrs after: rdn and unable qck over 1f out: wknd ins fnl f* **11/10**[1]

004 **7** *1½* **Artisan**[26] 3232 3-8-13 0 .... JamieMackay 2 52
(Willie Musson) *stdd s: t.k.h: hld up in tch in rr: rdn and unable qck over 2f out: styd on same pce and no threat to ldrs fnl 2f* **6/1**[3]

-460 **8** *8* **Minortransgression (USA)**[10] 3253 4-8-13 62 ....(p) CathyGannon 5 27
(H Edward Haynes) *sn niggled along but in tch in rr: rdn and struggling wl over 2f out: wknd 2f out* **20/1**

1m 39.34s (1.14) **Going Correction** +0.175s/f (Slow)
WFA 3 from 4yo+ 8lb **8** Ran SP% **111.5**
Speed ratings (Par 101): **101,100,99,99,98 96,95,87**
toteswingers:1&2:£8.60, 2&3:£24.90, 1&3:£19.10 CSF £139.99 TOTE £6.10: £1.10, £3.50, £3.50; EX 120.60.Artisan was claimed by L. S. Keys for £14,000.
Owner Montagu Racing **Bred** J Quigley **Trained** Great Shefford, Berkshire

FOCUS
Modest fare and not truly run. The form is dubious and has been rated negatively.
Minortransgression(USA) Official explanation: jockey said gelding was slow away.

4090 GOT THE FEELING? GET TO LADBROKES FILLIES' H'CAP 1m 2f (P)
8:55 (8:55) (Class 5) (0-75,75) 3-Y-0+ **£3,067** (£905; £453) **Stalls** Low

Form RPR

2162 **1** **Fashionable Gal (IRE)**[28] 3170 4-10-0 **75** .... AdamKirby 12 84+
(Neil King) *in tch: rdn and effrt between horses jst over 1f out: led jst ins fnl f: sn drvn clr: r.o wl* **5/1**[2]

13 **2** *1* **Libritish**[71] 1862 3-8-11 **73** ....(b[1]) TobyAtkinson(5) 11 79
(Marco Botti) *stdd after s: t.k.h: hld up in tch in last quartet: rdn and hdwy to chse ldrs 2f out: unable qck over 1f out: chsd wnr ins fnl f: styd on* **14/1**

5656 **3** *1½* **Trend Line (IRE)**[19] 3466 3-9-2 **73** .... JackMitchell 8 76
(Peter Chapple-Hyam) *hld up in tch in last quartet: pushed along and hdwy on outer wl over 3f out: rdn to ld 2f out: drvn and hdd jst ins fnl f: styd on same pce after* **10/1**

-220 **4** *1¼* **Celestial Girl**[8] 3814 4-9-4 **70** .... KieranO'Neill(5) 9 71
(Hughie Morrison) *hld up in tch: nt clr run and swtchd rt over 1f out: styd on ins fnl f: no threat to wnr* **11/2**[3]

1003 **5** *hd* **Ermyntrude**[10] 3741 4-8-5 **57** .... JemmaMarshall(5) 5 57+
(Pat Phelan) *hld up wl in tch in midfield: nt clr run and shuffled bk over 2f out: swtchd rt over 1f out: r.o wl ins fnl f: no threat to wnr* **14/1**

006- **6** *1¼* **Secoya**[221] 7733 3-8-5 **62** .... CathyGannon 4 60
(Ralph Beckett) *stdd s: hld up in rr: stl disputing last and c wd bnd 2f out: styd on ins fnl f: nvr trbld ldrs* **14/1**

1-45 **7** *nk* **Tenby Lady (USA)**[43] 2664 3-9-1 **72** .... SebSanders 3 69+
(Sir Mark Prescott Bt) *wl in tch in midfield on inner: nt clr run and shuffled bk to last trio over 2f out: stl bhd and no ch but switching rt 1f out: pushed along and styd on ins fnl f: hmpd towards fin: nvr able to chal* **15/8**[1]

5666 **8** *½* **Kathleen Kennet**[25] 3251 11-8-4 **56** .... RyanPowell(5) 6 52
(Jonathan Geake) *fly-jmpd leaving stalls: t.k.h: chsd ldrs tl wnt 2nd 8f out: led over 2f out: rdn and hdd 2f out: fdd ins fnl f* **66/1**

31- **9** *1¼* **Yensi**[247] 7413 4-9-1 **65** .... MatthewDavies(3) 1 59
(George Baker) *t.k.h: chsd ldr for 2f: nt clr run jst over 2f out: rdn and unable qck over 1f out: drvn and styd on same pce fnl f* **8/1**

0106 **10** *1¾* **Sail Home**[16] 3558 4-9-0 **64** .... AdamBeschizza(3) 7 54
(Julia Feilden) *led tl over 2f out: rdn and unable qck 2f out: wknd u.p over 1f out* **25/1**

00-4 **10** *dht* **Toballa**[53] 2386 6-8-9 **56** oh11 ....(t) JimmyQuinn 13 46
(Clifford Lines) *stdd and swtchd sharply lft after s: t.k.h: hld up in tch in last quartet: rdn: racd awkwardly and no imp wl over 1f out* **66/1**

5-36 **12** *10* **Heavenly Music (IRE)**[60] 2175 3-8-3 **60** .... DavidProbert 10 30
(Sylvester Kirk) *chsd ldrs on outer: rdn to chse ldr over 2f out: ev ch 2f out: wknd qckly ent fnl f* **10/1**

2m 6.86s (0.26) **Going Correction** +0.175s/f (Slow)
WFA 3 from 4yo+ 10lb **12** Ran SP% **119.7**
Speed ratings (Par 100): **105,104,103,102,101 100,100,100,99,97 97,89**
toteswingers:1&2:£6.80, 2&3:£29.90, 1&3:£12.40 CSF £73.00 CT £680.67 TOTE £5.40: £1.70, £3.00, £6.30; EX 57.30.
Owner John Webb & Dr Clive Layton **Bred** B D Burnett **Trained** Newmarket, Suffolk

FOCUS
A reasonable fillies' handicap for the money and the pace was just fair. Sound enough form amongst the principals.
Secoya Official explanation: jockey said filly was slowly away
T/Plt: £9,957.00 to a £1 stake. Pool £80,474.00 - 5.90 winning tickets. T/Qpdt: £277.30 to a £1 stake. Pool £7,982.00 - 21.30 winning tickets. SP

4052 NEWBURY (L-H)
Saturday, July 16

OFFICIAL GOING: Good
Wind: Moderate ahead Weather: Overcast

4091 TRAILFINDERS CONDITIONS STKS 7f (S)
1:45 (1:48) (Class 4) 2-Y-O **£4,668** (£1,398; £699; £349; £174) **Stalls** Centre

Form RPR

21 **1** **Coupe De Ville (IRE)**[28] 3182 2-8-13 0 .... RichardHughes 2 90+
(Richard Hannon) *stdd s: t.k.h: hld up in tch: hdwy and hung lft over 2f out: wnt rt over 1f out and sn chalng: led fnl 120yds: drvn out* **5/4**[1]

1 **2** *shd* **Leqqaa (USA)**[30] 3076 2-8-13 0 .... RichardHills 3 90+
(Mark Johnston) *disp cl 2nd: rdn and hung lft ins fnl 3f: chal over 1f out: led ins fnl f: hdd and hung lft again fnl 120yds: kpt on wl: nt quite pce of wnr* **9/4**[2]

1 **3** *2½* **Shamrocked (IRE)**[20] 3425 2-8-13 0 .... HughBowman 5 84
(Mick Channon) *led: pushed along whn chal ins fnl 2f: hdd ins fnl f: hld whn sltly hmpd fnl 120yds* **5/1**[3]

4322 **4** *½* **Letsgoroundagain (IRE)**[15] 3583 2-8-13 0 .... MichaelHills 1 83
(B W Hills) *disp 2nd: rdn along 3f out: outpcd over 1f out: kpt on again clsng stages* **9/1**

5 **8** **Expense Claim (IRE)** 2-8-7 0 .... FrannyNorton 4 57
(Andrew Balding) *t.k.h: in tch tl pushed along and wknd fr 2f out* **12/1**

1m 29.23s (3.53) **Going Correction** +0.425s/f (Yiel) **5** Ran SP% **109.6**
Speed ratings (Par 96): **96,95,93,92,83**
CSF £4.24 TOTE £2.10: £1.10, £1.70; EX 3.20.
Owner Coupe de Ville Partnership **Bred** Flor Ryan **Trained** East Everleigh, Wilts

FOCUS
The rail was moved in overnight to give fresh ground from 1m to 5f out on the round course. The course was 20m longer than standard. Rain from mid-morning meant a total of 7mm had fallen between the last race on Friday and Saturday's opener, and the reference to good to firm in the official going description had gone before racing. Riders in the first described the ground as good to soft and loose on top, and the time, over six seconds outside standard, seemed to confirm that it was riding on the easy side. There was also quite a stiff breeze in the horses' faces.\nThis was an interesting conditions event contested by four previous winners. The runners raced in a bunch down the centre.

NOTEBOOK
Coupe De Ville(IRE) gave Richard Hannon his third successive victory in this race. Travelling smoothly, the colt drifted out to his left when first let down before coming back in again once Hughes switched his whip, and had to battle to edge out the runner-up. Already proven in easy conditions but well at home on fast ground too, he is well regarded and will be worth a try in Listed company now. He is not the biggest. (op 6-4 tchd 6-5)
Leqqaa(USA), an easy Leicester winner, stepped up on that form and was just denied after holding every chance. The easy ground may have been more of a hindrance than a help and he remains a colt of potential, with improvement to come as he accrues experience. He still betrayed signs of greenness here. (op 5-2 tchd 2-1)
Shamrocked(IRE), successful on his debut at Salisbury, holds National Stakes and Derby entries. A little keen going down to post, he settled well in front but was just held when he was leaned into by the runner-up late on. This was a creditable effort. (op 4-1 tchd 6-1)
Letsgoroundagain(IRE) lacked the pace of the principals when they really began racing but was keeping on again close home, suggesting that the extra furlong was fine for him. (op 10-1 tchd 8-1)
Expense Claim(IRE) faced a tough task for a debutant and was duly found wanting. A 95,000gns buy, he was green in the preliminaries and should benefit from the introduction. (op 10-1 tchd 14-1)

4092 SHADWELL STKS (REGISTERED AS THE HACKWOOD STAKES) (GROUP 3) 6f 8y
2:20 (2:20) (Class 1) 3-Y-O+
£28,355 (£10,750; £5,380; £2,680; £1,345; £675) **Stalls** Centre

Form RPR

0-21 **1** **Deacon Blues**[28] 3155 4-9-3 107 .... FrankieDettori 5 121
(James Fanshawe) *hld up in tch: stdy hdwy on bit to ld jst ins fnl f: sn drvn to assert: c clr: easily* **5/2**[1]

1-00 **2** *2¾* **Markab**[56] 2297 8-9-3 118 .... DaneO'Neill 9 112
(Henry Candy) *led: pushed along and qcknd ins fnl 2f: hdd jst ins fnl f and sn outpcd by wnr but kpt on wl for 2nd* **6/1**

1000 **3** *1¼* **Jimmy Styles**[7] 3863 7-9-3 107 ....(p) AdamKirby 2 108
(Clive Cox) *in rr: rdn and hdwy over 1f out: styd on u.p fnl f to take 3rd clsng stages but no imp on ldng duo* **12/1**

2230 **4** *¾* **Regal Parade**[7] 3863 7-9-3 112 .... AdrianNicholls 10 106
(David Nicholls) *chsd ldrs: rdn in 3rd over 1f out and no imp: dropped to 4th clsng stages* **10/3**[2]

-130 **5** *1¼* **Pastoral Player**[14] 3644 4-9-3 103 .... RyanMoore 7 102
(Hughie Morrison) *s.i.s: in rr but in tch: rdn and effrt fr 2f out but nvr gng pce to rch ldrs* **5/1**[3]

4402 **6** *nk* **Atlantic Sport (USA)**[14] 3626 6-9-3 100 .... HughBowman 1 101
(Mick Channon) *in rr: pushed along 2f out: styd on ins fnl f: nt pce to rch ldrs* **25/1**

-320 **7** *1¾* **Cape To Rio (IRE)**[35] 2934 3-8-12 99 .... JamieSpencer 8 94
(Richard Hannon) *s.i.s: in rr: rdn ins fnl 2f: sn hung lft: no ch* **33/1**

0330 **8** *¾* **Angel's Pursuit (IRE)**[7] 3862 4-9-3 101 ....(b) RichardHughes 4 93
(Richard Hannon) *stdd in tch and t.k.h: clsd on ldrs 1/2-way: sn rdn: wknd ins fnl 2f* **16/1**

-630 **9** *hd* **Royal Rock**[28] 3154 7-9-3 103 .... GeorgeBaker 3 91
(Chris Wall) *chsd ldrs tl wknd qckly over 1f out* **16/1**

1-15 **10** *13* **Retainer (IRE)**[16] 3548 3-8-12 103 .... JimmyFortune 6 50
(Richard Hannon) *[illegible] and hung lft ins fnl 2f: wknd qckly: eased whn no ch* **[illegible]**

1m 13.51s (0.51) **Going Correction** +0.425s/f (Yiel)
WFA 3 from 4yo+ 5lb **10** Ran SP% **113.2**
Speed ratings (Par 113): **113,109,107,106,105 104,102,101,101,83**
toteswingers:1&2:£3.70, 2&3:£12.40, 1&3:£6.90 CSF £16.70 TOTE £3.10: £1.70, £2.00, £2.80; EX 15.10 Trifecta £229.70 Pool: £1,484.16 - 4.78 winning units..
Owner Jan & Peter Hopper & Michelle Morris **Bred** Mr & Mrs K W Grundy, Mr & Mrs P Hopper **Trained** Newmarket, Suffolk

FOCUS
An up-to-scratch edition of the Hackwood Stakes, which was elevated to Group 3 status in 2006. Deacon Blues progressed again from the Wokingham and a literal reading of this form would put him on terms with the best domestic sprinters.

NOTEBOOK
Deacon Blues ◆ has made big strides over the last year or so and the 9lb rise for his Wokingham success at the Royal meeting took him to a mark of 107, so he looked well worth this first try in Group company. Always travelling strongly, he quickened up smartly for a most impressive win and his stable, which already houses Golden Jubilee Stakes winner Society Rock, looks to contain another potential sprinting star. Dream Ahead would be a stumbling block, but he looks worth aiming at the Betfred Sprint Cup at Haydock in September. Somnus completed the Hackwood-Sprint Cup double in 2003. Deacon Blues picks up a 6lb penalty for the Stewards' Cup for this but won't run now. (op 11-4)
Markab escaped a penalty for his Betfred Sprint Cup win last autumn and was 6lb best in on BHA figures, but he was a disappointing favourite in this last year and had not been at his best in two runs in the spring. He showed his customary bright pace and stuck on for second, but the winner was much too good on the day. (tchd 11-2)
Jimmy Styles was back down to a more realistic level and he ran well, coming through for third without threatening the first two. This was a good effort on ground that was going against him. (tchd 14-1)
Regal Parade, last year's winner, went on to take the Prix Maurice De Gheest, but was unpenalised here for that Group 1 win. He showed more than he had in last weekend's July Cup, but was one of the first off the bridle and is not quite operating at his best. (op 4-1)
Pastoral Player, the Wokingham third, was back up to 6f, having been taken off his feet at Sandown, and ran only respectably. His trainer believes him to be more suited by smaller fields. (tchd 11-2)
Atlantic Sport(USA) ran on late, confirming that this trip is a minimum for him these days. (op 22-1 tchd 20-1)
Cape To Rio(IRE), who was never a factor, had the least chance on official figures. (op 28-1)
Angel's Pursuit(IRE) was also well beaten in this last year. (op 18-1)

Royal Rock has not built on his third to Bated Breath and Society Rock at Haydock. (op 12-1)

4093 AON EBF "AQLAAM" FILLIES' STKS (H'CAP) 1m (S)
2:55 (2:55) (Class 3) (0-95,91) 3-Y-O+

£8,092 (£2,423; £1,211; £605; £302; £152) **Stalls** Centre

Form RPR

14-2 **1** **Heavenly Dawn**[21] 3407 4-9-8 **85**........ RyanMoore 8 100+
(Sir Michael Stoute) *trckd ldr: rdn over 2f out: led appr fnl f: drvn clr* **6/5**[1]

43 **2** *4* **Imaginary World (IRE)**[15] 3586 3-7-11 **73**........(be) KieranO'Neill(5) 5 77
(Alan McCabe) *stdd in rr s and t.k.h: hdwy fr 2f out: styd on u.p fnl f to take 2nd last strides but nvr any ch w wnr* **20/1**

-310 **3** *hd* **Watneya**[21] 3407 3-8-10 **81**........ SilvestreDeSousa 3 84
(William Haggas) *led: rdn over 2f out: hdd appr fnl f: sn no ch w wnr: lost 2nd last strides* **5/1**[2]

4-02 **4** *1 ¾* **Al Mayasah (IRE)**[51] 2432 3-8-8 **79**........ JamieSpencer 10 78+
(David Simcock) *hld up in rr: hdwy over 2f out: shkn up: carried hd high and to one side over 1f out: styd on one pce* **9/1**[3]

6622 **5** *1 ¼* **Belle Royale (IRE)**[7] 3873 3-9-6 **91**........ FrannyNorton 4 87
(Mark Brisbourne) *chsd ldrs: rdn over 2f out: styd on same pce fnl f* **9/1**[3]

0300 **6** *hd* **Sonning Rose (IRE)**[8] 3819 3-9-0 **85**........ HughBowman 1 81
(Mick Channon) *in rr but in tch: rdn and styd on fr over 2f out: sn no imp on ldrs and one pce fnl f* **20/1**

0044 **7** *6* **Bahati (IRE)**[21] 3407 4-9-10 **87**........ RichardKingscote 11 71
(Jonathan Portman) *in rr: rdn: hung lft and sme prog over 2f out but nvr gng pce to get into contention* **33/1**

0-55 **8** *14* **Rosedale**[33] 2999 4-8-9 **72** oh2........ LiamKeniry 2 24
(James Toller) *chsd ldrs: rdn 3f out: wknd 2f out* **16/1**

0150 **9** *4* **Doricemay (IRE)**[14] 3650 3-8-6 **77**........ LukeMorris 6 18
(Clive Cox) *t.k.h: in rr but in tch: rdn 3f out: no ch after* **33/1**

0433 **10** *3* **Byrony (IRE)**[7] 3873 3-9-3 **88**........ RichardHughes 7 22
(Richard Hannon) *in tch: pushed along and effrt 3f out: nvr rchd ldrs and wknd 2f out* **12/1**

6-00 **11** *30* **Matula (IRE)**[22] 3356 3-9-1 **86**........(p) GeorgeBaker 9 —
(Ralph Beckett) *in rr: sme prog 3f out: nvr beyond mid-div and wknd qckly over 2f out: eased whn no ch* **11/1**

1m 40.8s (1.10) **Going Correction** +0.425s/f (Yiel)
WFA 3 from 4yo 8lb **11** Ran SP% **115.3**
Speed ratings (Par 104): **111,107,106,105,103 103,97,83,79,76 46**
toteswingers:1&2:£9.40, 2&3:£22.90, 1&3:£2.60 CSF £33.17 CT £92.56 TOTE £2.00: £1.30, £4.60, £2.10; EX 30.50 Trifecta £140.30 Pool: £1,701.71 - 8.97 winning units..
Owner Cheveley Park Stud **Bred** Cheveley Park Stud Ltd **Trained** Newmarket, Suffolk

FOCUS
A decent fillies' handicap which was won last year by First City, who has been placed at the top level this season. The runners gravitated towards the stands' side. The winner stepped forward and recorded a 6lb personal best.

NOTEBOOK
Heavenly Dawn ◆ is an improving filly and she shrugged off a 4lb rise after her Newmarket second. She required some stoking up to get to the leader, but stayed on strongly once in front. The rain was a plus, and she gives the impression that she will get 1m2f if needed. The intention will no doubt be to pick up some black type with her, and she looks well up to the task. (op 11-10 tchd Evens)
Imaginary World(IRE) made the frame once again, running on late to snatch second, and is capable of adding to her sole win if things go right. A solid pace will help her in that respect. (op 28-1)
Watneya momentarily had the favourite in trouble when kicking from the front, but was quickly worn down. She finished a lot closer to Heavenly Dawn than she had at Newmarket, where she failed to give her running. (op 6-1)
Al Mayasah(IRE) was one of two fillies to race slightly apart from the others, nearer to the rail. She was brought to have her chance, but carried her head awkwardly and failed to knuckle down. She is clearly tricky.
Belle Royale(IRE) was 2lb higher than when runner-up on her latest two starts. She ran her race, but lacked what was necessary to mount a challenge. Franny Norton reported that she hung right. Official explanation: jockey said filly hung right throughout. (op 8-1)
Sonning Rose(IRE) continues to look high enough in the weights. (op 16-1)
Rosedale showed promise at Windsor last time but she was 2lb out of the weights here and she checked out rather quickly.
Matula(IRE) Official explanation: jockey said filly stopped quickly.

4094 WEATHERBYS SUPER SPRINT 5f 34y
3:30 (3:35) (Class 2) 2-Y-0

£98,360 (£41,820; £19,680; £11,800; £7,860; £5,900) **Stalls** Centre

Form RPR

610 **1** **Charles The Great (IRE)**[30] 3064 2-8-11 0........ JimmyFortune 5 102
(Andrew Balding) *racd towards far side: disp ld tl led 2f out: hung rt u.p ins fnl f: all out* **25/1**

1351 **2** *shd* **Lily's Angel (IRE)**[21] 3402 2-8-3 0........ PaulHanagan 6 94
(Richard Fahey) *in rr: rousted along 1/2-way: gd hdwy over 1f out: str run ins fnl f: fin strly: jst failed* **4/1**[1]

12 **3** *½* **Nagham (IRE)**[32] 3022 2-8-1 0........ KieranO'Neill 21 90
(Kevin Ryan) *in rr towards stands' side: hdwy and rdn over 1f out: styd on ins fnl f: nt rch ldng duo* **28/1**

11 **4** *½* **Redact (IRE)**[7] 3868 2-8-8 0........ RyanMoore 15 95+
(Richard Hannon) *racd towards far side and outpcd: rdn and hdwy over 1f out: str run fnl f: fin strly* **13/2**[2]

11 **5** *1 ½* **Eureka (IRE)**[20] 3429 2-8-8 0........ RichardHughes 4 90
(Richard Hannon) *in tch towards far side: rdn 2f out: styd on fnl f but nvr gng pce to press ldrs* **4/1**[1]

02 **6** *¾* **Orders From Rome (IRE)**[36] 2880 2-8-11 0........ FrankieDettori 22 90
(Eve Johnson Houghton) *racd towards stands' side and outpcd: drvn along 2f out: r.o wl fnl f: gng on cl home* **20/1**

1341 **7** *nk* **Ponty Acclaim (IRE)**[32] 3022 2-7-12 0........ DuranFentiman 20 76
(Tim Easterby) *sn chsng ldrs stands' side: rdn and kpt on same pce ins fnl f* **14/1**

5103 **8** *1 ½* **Pyman's Theory (IRE)**[13] 3669 2-9-2 0........ JamieSpencer 14 90
(Tom Dascombe) *racd towards middle: in tch: drvn over 2f out: styd on fnl f: hmpd fnl 120yds: nt rch ldrs* **28/1**

130 **9** *hd* **On The Dark Side (IRE)**[31] 3033 2-8-1 0........ FrannyNorton 13 73
(Kevin Ryan) *chsd ldrs towards centre: one pce fnl f* **16/1**

33 **10** *½* **Electric Qatar**[16] 3540 2-9-3 0........ RichardKingscote 11 87
(Tom Dascombe) *wnt rt s: towards rr in centre of crse: rdn 1/2-way: styd on fnl f: nt rch ldrs* **33/1**

31 **11** *½* **Airborne Again (IRE)**[65] 2023 2-9-1 0........ DaneO'Neill 2 84
(Richard Hannon) *pressed ldrs far side: wknd ins fnl f* **40/1**

1236 **12** *hd* **Hamza (IRE)**[32] 3014 2-8-9 0........ PhillipMakin 8 77
(Kevin Ryan) *in tch towards far side: drvn and hdwy over 1f out: kpt on fnl f: nt rch ldrs* **14/1**

41 **13** *nk* **Mention (IRE)**[25] 3257 2-8-3 0........ SilvestreDeSousa 3 72
(Brian Meehan) *chsd ldrs towards far side: rdn 1/2-way: one pce and hld whn hmpd ins fnl f* **14/1**

1531 **14** *½* **Alejandro (IRE)**[15] 3570 2-8-9 0........ TonyHamilton 24 74
(Richard Fahey) *sn pushed along towards stands' side: hung lft 1/2-way: styd on fnl f* **25/1**

3052 **15** *½* **Signifer (IRE)**[21] 3375 2-8-6 0........ MatthewDavies 12 69
(Mick Channon) *bmpd s: sn in tch: chsd ldrs towards centre crse over 1f out: wknd and hung lft fnl 120yds* **33/1**

3140 **16** *2 ¼* **Sweet Chilli (IRE)**[29] 3104 2-7-12 0........ CathyGannon 7 53
(David Barron) *chsd ldrs towards centre: wknd fnl f* **11/1**[3]

2 **17** *nse* **Blanc De Chine (IRE)**[10] 3722 2-8-0 0........ HarryBentley 17 55
(Peter Makin) *mde most towards centre: narrowly hdd 2f out: styd chalng tl wknd 1f out* **33/1**

21 **18** *1 ¾* **Impassive**[14] 3639 2-7-13 0........ NickyMackay 18 48
(Ed McMahon) *racd towards centre: spd 3f* **16/1**

6104 **19** *nk* **Profile Star (IRE)**[7] 3879 2-8-4 0........ WilliamCarson 19 51
(David Barron) *chsd ldrs towards stands' side: hung lft and wknd wl over 1f out* **80/1**

331 **20** *1 ¼* **Pen Bal Crag (IRE)**[24] 3273 2-8-6 0........ LukeMorris 9 49
(Richard Fahey) *racd towards centre: outpcd most of way* **40/1**

2323 **21** *4* **Right Result (IRE)**[14] 3610 2-8-9 0........ JimmyQuinn 10 38
(Richard Hannon) *hrd drvn 1/2-way in centre: sn bhd* **50/1**

10 **22** *2 ¾* **Ebony Clarets**[31] 3033 2-8-1 0........ JamesSullivan 16 20
(Richard Fahey) *bhd fr 1/2-way* **50/1**

02 **23** *¾* **Free Zone**[21] 3398 2-8-8 0........ TomEaves 25 24
(Bryan Smart) *racd stands' rail: bhd fr 1/2-way* **66/1**

5626 **24** *3 ¾* **Jimmy The Lollipop (IRE)**[7] 3879 2-8-9 0........(p) NeilCallan 23 11
(Kevin Ryan) *racd towards stands' side: sn outpcd* **100/1**

0252 **25** *4* **Princess Banu**[19] 3458 2-8-7 0........ AndrewHeffernan 1 —
(Mick Channon) *early spd far side: sn wknd* **100/1**

63.53 secs (2.13) **Going Correction** +0.425s/f (Yiel) **25** Ran SP% **135.1**
Speed ratings (Par 100): **99,98,98,97,94 93,93,90,90,89 88,88,88,87,86 82,82,79,79,77 71,66,65,59,53**
toteswingers:1&2:£33.40, 2&3:£36.10, 1&3:£229.90 CSF £116.27 TOTE £37.60: £9.60, £2.10, £15.50; EX 267.90 TRIFECTA Not won..
Owner Kennet Valley Thoroughbreds V **Bred** Michael Woodlock & Seamus Kennedy **Trained** Kingsclere, Hants

FOCUS
The 20th running of this valuable sales race and another highly competitive edition. The field spread across the course but the principals ended up near the stands' rail.

NOTEBOOK
Charles The Great(IRE) was always either in front or disputing the lead, and he held on well despite edging across the track from his low draw. A tough sort, he lost a shoe when tenth in the Norfolk at Ascot and turned around that form with both Signifer and Pyman's Theory. He would get another furlong if necessary, but clearly is blessed with more than his share of speed. (op 28-1)
Lily's Angel(IRE) almost became the twelfth filly to win this race. She emerged as the last threat to the winner but needed a couple more strides. Her recent Listed win in Newmarket's Empress Stakes came over 6f, but she is clearly effective over the minimum provided the ground is not riding fast. (op 5-1 tchd 6-1)
Nagham(IRE), one of four runners in the race for Kevin Ryan, ran on late nearest the fence and for a moment looked set to claim the winner, but she had to settle for third in the end. Her apprentice rider was unable to claim his usual 5lb. (op 25-1)
Redact(IRE)'s trainer saddled four in a bid for an eighth Super Sprint and this one, in the the same ownership as the winner, proved the best of them. Unbeaten in two starts, both over 6f, he ran on strongly from the back of the field on the far side of the track and will be suited by a step back up in trip. (op 8-1)
Eureka(IRE), the choice of Richard Hughes, took a lot of persuasion to enter the stalls which cannot have helped his demeanour. In the circumstances he ran a solid race, and this Gimcrack entry should be borne in mind back at 6f. (op 9-2 tchd 11-2 and 6-1 in places)
Orders From Rome(IRE) ◆ did best of the half-dozen maidens in the line-up despite getting rather buzzed up going to post. He should soon get off the mark, probably over 6f given the way he finished off his race. (op 25-1)
Ponty Acclaim(IRE) had Nagham back in second when winning at Thirsk and although she could not confirm her superiority over that filly, she still ran respectably. (op 16-1 tchd 12-1)
Pyman's Theory(IRE) ran well under her big weight and would have finished a shade closer had she not been hampered late on. (op 33-1)
On The Dark Side(IRE), second best of the Ryan quartet, again raced prominently. (tchd 14-1)
Electric Qatar, a big colt who was conceding weight all round, may not be entirely straightforward but should not remain a maiden for long.
Mention(IRE) was another to meet with trouble but she looked held at the time. She'll be suited by a return to 6f and, a Lowther Stakes entry, is probably capable of better. (op 16-1 tchd 12-1)
Sweet Chilli(IRE) looked a real player off bottomweight, but her Ascot run had been a little underwhelming and she was found wanting again despite abandoning hold-up tactics.
Blanc De Chine(IRE), runner-up in her one previous start, was the least experienced runner in the race. She showed up well for a long way under her apprentice, who couldn't claim, but looked green under pressure. She is better than the bare form.

4095 SHADWELL BEECH HOUSE STUD STKS (REGISTERED AS THE STEVENTON STAKES) (LISTED RACE) 1m 2f 6y
4:05 (4:05) (Class 1) 3-Y-O+

£17,013 (£6,450; £3,228; £1,608; £807; £405) **Stalls** Low

Form RPR

32-3 **1** **Dux Scholar**[21] 3409 3-8-7 105........ RyanMoore 13 115
(Sir Michael Stoute) *stdd s: hld up in rr: pushed along and qcknd fr 3f out to ld over 2f out: drvn out fnl f* **4/1**[2]

246- **2** *1 ¼* **Hot Prospect**[266] 7096 4-9-3 110........ NeilCallan 3 112
(Roger Varian) *in rr but in tch: hdwy fr 2f out: rdn and styd on fnl f: tk 2nd fnl 50yds and kpt on but no imp on wnr* **11/2**

50-6 **3** *½* **Anmar (USA)**[21] 3403 5-9-3 104........ RichardHills 9 111
(Ed Dunlop) *chsd ldrs: rdn to chse wnr ins fnl 2f but no imp: styd on same pce fnl f and lost 2nd fnl 50yds* **25/1**

453- **4** *½* **Shimraan (FR)**[272] 6974 4-9-3 116........ GeraldMosse 6 110
(A De Royer-Dupre, France) *hld up in rr: pushed along whn pce qcknd over 2f out: hdwy over 1f out: styd on fnl f but nvr gng pce to chal* **11/4**[1]

5-36 **5** *3 ½* **Elusive Pimpernel (USA)**[51] 2439 4-9-3 115........ RichardHughes 11 103
(John Dunlop) *t.k.h: trckd ldrs: rdn and styd on whn pce qcknd over 2f out and edgd lft: sn one pce: wknd ins fnl f* **6/1**

-203 **6** *2 ¼* **Black Spirit (USA)**[15] 3591 4-9-3 110........(t) LukeMorris 10 99
(Clive Cox) *in tch: hdwy to chse ldrs 3f out: rdn 2f out: pushed lft and n.m.r after: wknd u.p fnl f* **12/1**

1042 **7** *1 1/4* **Fanditha (IRE)**[22] 3356 5-8-12 101 .... HughBowman 2 91
(Mick Channon) *in rr but in tch: hdwy 3f out: rdn and no imp 2f out: sn wknd* **40/1**

-123 **8** *hd* **Spring Of Fame (USA)**[128] 827 5-9-3 112 .... SilvestreDeSousa 4 96
(Saeed Bin Suroor) *chsd ldrs: rdn and hung lft 2f out: sn btn* **20/1**

2322 **9** *3/4* **Enak (ARG)**[128] 829 5-9-3 111 .... (t) FrankieDettori 8 94
(Saeed Bin Suroor) *led tl hdd over 2f out: sn wknd* **9/2**[3]

5-00 **10** *hd* **Wealthy (IRE)**[148] 608 4-9-3 107 .... (t) PaulHanagan 7 94
(Saeed Bin Suroor) *t.k.h: a towards rr* **25/1**

2m 10.18s (1.38) **Going Correction** +0.225s/f (Good)
WFA 3 from 4yo+ 10lb **10** Ran SP% **117.1**
Speed ratings (Par 111): **103,102,101,101,98 96,95,95,94,94**
toteswingers:1&2:£5.70, 2&3:£15.70, 1&3:£12.80 CSF £25.06 TOTE £4.40: £1.80, £2.40, £5.40; EX 35.20 Trifecta £614.90 Part won. Pool: £831.08 - 0.54 winning units..
Owner K Abdulla **Bred** Juddmonte Farms Ltd **Trained** Newmarket, Suffolk

FOCUS
Subsequent Arc winner Sakhee is the biggest name on the roll of honour for the past deacde. This looked a warm race for the grade with plenty having form at a higher level. The winner built on his reappearance effort. It was the first race of the afternoon on the round course and the runners came down the centre in the home straight.

NOTEBOOK
Dux Scholar, the only 3yo in the line-up, showed a taking turn of foot from off the pace and was always holding on once in front. He was clearly sharper for his reappearance at Windsor and, placed in two Group 3s last autumn, is well up to winning at that level provided he has a bit of ease in the ground. This longer trip was not a problem to him. (op 3-1)
Hot Prospect, who has been waiting for suitable conditions underfoot, was another to come from off the pace, staying on for second. He has more to offer and should get 1m4f in time. (op 5-1 tchd 6-1)
Anmar(USA) improved on what he showed on his recent debut for the yard and is clearly up to this level. He won't mind a return to 1m4f. (tchd 20-1 and 28-1)
Shimraan(FR), winner of the Group 2 Prix Eugene Adam last year and unpenalised for that, has reportedly been gelded since his last appearance in the autumn. Racing on the near-side of the bunch up the straight, he just lacked a quickening touch. (op 7-2 tchd 4-1)
Elusive Pimpernel(USA) took a bit of a tug behind the leaders than lacked the pace of the principals when the race began to develop. He kept on and seemed to see out the trip well enough. (op 5-1)
Spring Of Fame(USA) (tchd 16-1)
Enak(ARG), who made the running, ended up well beaten. Like his two stablemates, who also finished down the field, he had not run since the Dubai Carnival. (op 6-1)

4096 SHADWELL "NUNNERY STUD" CONDITIONS STKS 7f (S)
4:35 (4:35) (Class 4) 3-Y-O **£6,536** (£1,957; £978; £489) **Stalls** Centre

Form RPR

0130 **1** **Chilworth Lad**[30] 3067 3-8-9 98 .... JamieSpencer 4 104
(Mick Channon) *hld up in last pl: hdwy 2f out: led ins fnl f: hrd drvn: asserted clsng stages* **4/1**[3]

1420 **2** *3/4* **King Of Jazz (IRE)**[7] 3862 3-8-9 99 .... RichardHughes 3 102
(Richard Hannon) *led: rdn and edgd rt over 1f out: hdd ins fnl f: no ex u.p fnl 120yds* **7/2**[2]

-365 **3** *3* **Eucharist (IRE)**[23] 3323 3-7-13 98 .... KieranO'Neill(5) 2 89
(Richard Hannon) *trckd ldrs: in 3rd: pushed along over 2f out: carried rt over 1f out: rdn and no ch w ldng duo sn after* **7/1**

-525 **4** *10* **Fury**[9] 3777 3-8-12 106 .... RyanMoore 1 70
(William Haggas) *chsd ldr: rdn over 2f out: wknd wl over 1f out: eased whn no ch* **5/6**[1]

1m 27.98s (2.28) **Going Correction** +0.425s/f (Yiel) **4** Ran SP% **109.3**
Speed ratings (Par 102): **103,102,98,87**
CSF £16.83 TOTE £5.00; EX 16.20.
Owner 7Rus **Bred** Phil Jen Racing **Trained** West Ilsley, Berks
■ Stewards' Enquiry : Jamie Spencer caution: use of whip

FOCUS
A fair conditions race, but the pace was only steady and this is perhaps not form to take too literally. With Fury disappointing the form is tricky to pin down.
Fury Official explanation: trainer was unable to offer any explanation as to poor run.

4097 SHADWELL "DUBAI SUMMER FESTIVAL" H'CAP 2m
5:10 (5:10) (Class 4) (0-80,80) 4-Y-O+ **£5,175** (£1,540; £769; £384) **Stalls** Low

Form RPR

242 **1** **Keys (IRE)**[17] 3519 4-9-5 78 .... (b) JamieSpencer 11 100+
(Roger Charlton) *hld up in rr: smooth hdwy on ins fr 3f out: trckd ldr 2f out: sn chalng on bit: led 1f out: canter* **7/4**[1]

-113 **2** *3 3/4* **Danvilla**[17] 3522 4-9-3 76 .... WilliamCarson 10 87
(Paul Webber) *chsd ldrs: rdn 3f out: styd on u.p to take 2nd clsng stages but no ch w cantering wnr* **8/1**[3]

00-5 **3** *nk* **Royal Diamond (IRE)**[15] 3580 5-9-7 80 .... GeorgeBaker 9 90
(Jonjo O'Neill) *led: jnd 2f out: hdd 1f out and no ch w cantering wnr: lost 2nd cl home* **14/1**

-064 **4** *1* **Baltimore Clipper (USA)**[15] 3593 4-9-2 75 .... JimmyFortune 1 84
(Paul Cole) *mid-div: hdwy 3f out: kpt on to go one pce 4th ins fnl f* **18/1**

4-21 **5** *3 1/2* **Addwaitya**[22] 3352 6-9-4 77 .... IanMongan 3 82
(Laura Mongan) *in rr: hdwy on outside over 2f out: kpt on fnl f but nvr any ch* **18/1**

-510 **6** *2 1/4* **Cosimo de Medici**[27] 3205 4-9-7 80 .... (t) RichardHughes 12 82
(Hughie Morrison) *mid-div: hdwy 4f out: sn rdn to chse ldrs: wknd over 1f out* **8/1**[3]

6160 **7** *3 1/4* **Momkinzain (USA)**[28] 3157 4-9-7 80 .... HughBowman 7 78
(Mick Channon) *in rr: drvn and sme prog 3f out: nvr rchd ldrs and no ch fnl 2f* **12/1**

0003 **8** *1 1/2* **Dynamic Drive (IRE)**[15] 3593 4-9-5 78 .... AdamKirby 4 74
(Walter Swinburn) *chsd ldrs: wnt 2nd 3f out sn rdn: wknd over 1f out* **10/1**

150- **9** *4 1/2* **Yemeni Princess (IRE)**[307] 5996 5-9-0 73 .... RobertHavlin 13 64
(Brendan Powell) *in rr: sme prog 3f out: sn wknd* **13/2**[2]

030/ **10** *3 1/4* **Raslan**[24] 6851 8-9-7 80 .... (vt) NeilCallan 5 67
(David Pipe) *chsd ldr to 3f out: wknd over 2f out* **20/1**

03-0 **11** *4 1/2* **Tenessee**[20] 3434 4-9-6 79 .... RyanMoore 14 61
(Peter Makin) *chsd ldrs tl wknd fr 3f out* **20/1**

00-3 **12** *2 1/2* **Callisto Moon**[10] 3725 7-9-0 76 .... (v) MarkLawson(3) 8 55
(Jo Hughes) *in tch: rdn over 3f out: sn btn* **22/1**

3m 33.46s (1.46) **Going Correction** +0.225s/f (Good) **12** Ran SP% **119.8**
Speed ratings (Par 105): **105,103,102,102,100 99,97,97,94,93 91,89**
toteswingers:1&2:£4.60, 2&3:£15.40, 1&3:£7.40 CSF £15.28 CT £155.97 TOTE £2.70: £1.30, £2.20, £4.20; EX 20.60 Trifecta £448.60 Pool: £897.34 - 1.48 winning units..
Owner Seasons Holidays **Bred** B Hurley **Trained** Beckhampton, Wilts

FOCUS
A fair staying handicap run at a solid pace. The very easy winner has been rated value for 10l, but that could underestimate him and he is potentially a smart stayer.

T/Plt: £203.70 to a £1 stake. Pool £129,781.56 - 465.02 winning tickets. T/Qpdt: £98.40 to a £1 stake. Pool £5,856.32 - 44.02 winning tickets. ST

4060 NEWMARKET (R-H)
Saturday, July 16

OFFICIAL GOING: Good changing to good to soft after race 1 (2.00)
Wind: Fresh across Weather: Raining

4098 LETTERGOLD MAIDEN STKS 6f
2:00 (2:00) (Class 4) 2-Y-O **£4,528** (£1,347; £673; £336) **Stalls** Low

Form RPR

3 **1** **Diamondhead (IRE)**[24] 3288 2-9-3 0 .... MartinDwyer 5 82+
(Brian Meehan) *mde all: rdn and hung lft fr over 1f out: r.o* **10/11**[1]

2 *3/4* **Grizzle** 2-9-3 0 .... AhmedAjtebi 2 80+
(Mahmood Al Zarooni) *trckd ldr: plld hrd: rdn and ev ch whn carried lft fr over 1f out: unable qck towards fin* **10/3**[2]

3 *3 1/2* **Heeraat (IRE)** 2-9-3 0 .... TadhgO'Shea 3 69+
(William Haggas) *prom: outpcd 1/2-way: r.o ins fnl f* **16/1**

4 *1/2* **Firestarter** 2-9-3 0 .... KierenFallon 4 68
(David Elsworth) *s.s: hdwy over 3f out: rdn and hung lft fr over 1f out: styd on same pce* **6/1**[3]

5 *1* **Money Never Sleeps** 2-9-3 0 .... WilliamBuick 1 65
(John Gosden) *chsd ldrs: pushed along and edgd lft over 2f out: styd on same pce appr fnl f* **7/1**

1m 17.07s (4.57) **Going Correction** +0.225s/f (Good) **5** Ran SP% **108.1**
Speed ratings (Par 96): **78,77,72,71,70**
CSF £3.97 TOTE £1.90: £1.20, £2.20; EX 4.60.
Owner Sir Robert Ogden **Bred** J Joyce **Trained** Manton, Wilts

FOCUS
Stands side track used with stalls on stand side except 1m2f and 1m4f Centre. The ground was good to firm after a dry night but the rain arrived in the morning and it was officially changed to good before the first race. The ground was changed to good to soft after the race. A small field for this maiden and only one with previous experience but a number of recent winners were making their debuts, including the subsequent 2000 Guineas winner Cockney Rebel. The pace was steady until it quickened from around the 2f pole. The field raced up the stands' rail but the first two ended up near the far side. The form does not look particularly strong at first sight.

NOTEBOOK
Diamondhead(IRE), a 50,000euros colt out of a half-sister to three winners at up to 1m1f, made a promising debut in a Salisbury maiden in which the winner had scored since. He made the running but hung severely under pressure and as a result had to survive a stewards' enquiry. (op 8-11 tchd 8-13)
Grizzle, a half-brother to winners at 7f-1m2f out of a Listed juvenile winner, was making his debut but was well backed against the favourite. He had his chance and was done no favours as he was carried right across the track in the closing stages. He was clear of the rest and should gain compensation before long. (op 13-2 tchd 7-1)
Heeraat(IRE), a 140,000gns son of a half-sister to high-class sprinter Malhub, looked as if the race would bring him on a good deal and was a market drifter. He did not fare too badly and the experience should not be lost on him. (op 10-1)
Firestarter, an 80,000gns half-brother to three winners at 6f-1m whose sire won this on his debut, was slowly away but was able to catch up as the early pace was so modest. He was not good enough to go with the principals in the closing stages but should come on for the outing. (op 11-2 tchd 5-1)
Money Never Sleeps, a first foal of a half-sister to a winner at up to 1m from the family of Fly To The Stars, was keen early before settling but could not keep up in the latter stages. He should also do better with this behind him. (tchd 13-2 and 15-2)

4099 NEWSELLS PARK STUD STKS (REGISTERED AS THE APHRODITE STAKES) (LISTED RACE) (F&M) 1m 4f
2:35 (2:35) (Class 1) 3-Y-O+
£22,684 (£8,600; £4,304; £2,144; £1,076; £540) **Stalls** Centre

Form RPR

21 **1** **Wild Coco (GER)**[38] 2813 3-8-6 90 ow2 .... EddieAhern 4 114+
(Sir Henry Cecil) *s.i.s: sn prom: chsd clr ldr over 4f out: led over 1f out: hung lft ins fnl f: pushed out: comf* **4/5**[1]

00 0 **2** *1/2* **Meeznah (USA)**[49] 2501 4-9-2 109 .... TedDurcan 7 111
(David Lanigan) *a.p: rdn over 3f out: chsd wnr fnl f: styd on u.p* **9/2**[2]

4235 **3** *10* **Opera Gal (IRE)**[22] 3356 4-9-2 95 .... DavidProbert 2 95
(Andrew Balding) *led and sn wl clr: rdn and hdd over 1f out: wknd fnl f* **16/1**

132 **4** *1 3/4* **Imperial Pippin (USA)**[37] 2839 3-8-4 93 .... MartinDwyer 9 92
(John Gosden) *hld up: rdn over 3f out: nvr on terms* **8/1**[3]

50-0 **5** *16* **Never Forget (FR)**[49] 2501 4-9-2 105 .... KierenFallon 10 67
(Luca Cumani) *hld up: hdwy over 3f out: wknd over 2f out: eased* **14/1**

41-2 **6** *15* **Charleston Lady**[76] 1722 3-8-4 96 .... MartinLane 11 43
(Ralph Beckett) *hld up: a in rr: rdn over 4f out: sn lost tch: t.o* **8/1**[3]

0461 **7** *shd* **Monicalew**[10] 3726 3-8-4 69 .... (p) JohnFahy 5 42
(Walter Swinburn) *hld up: a in rr: rdn over 4f out: sn lost tch: t.o* **100/1**

-106 **8** *11* **Plaisterer**[22] 3356 6-9-2 92 .... WilliamBuick 3 25
(Chris Wall) *chsd clr ldr tl rdn over 4f out: wknd over 3f out: eased: t.o* **33/1**

2m 31.56s (-1.34) **Going Correction** +0.225s/f (Good)
WFA 3 from 4yo+ 12lb **8** Ran SP% **112.4**
Speed ratings (Par 111): **113,112,106,104,94 84,84,76**
toteswingers:1&2:£1.90, 2&3:£5.40, 1&3:£4.80 CSF £4.40 TOTE £1.70: £1.10, £1.60, £3.30; EX 4.20 Trifecta £42.10 Pool: £1,470.33 - 25.82 winning units..
Owner Gestut Rottgen **Bred** Gestut Rottgen **Trained** Newmarket, Suffolk
■ Stewards' Enquiry : William Buick one-day ban & 140 fine: failed to ride out (Jul 31)

FOCUS
A fillies and mares' listed race in which several recent winners have gone on to win Group races, the best known of which was the multiple Group 1 scorer Dar Re Mi. Three withdrawals resulted in a short-priced favourite but they seemed to go a decent gallop in the driving rain and the field finished well strung out in the easing ground.

NOTEBOOK
Wild Coco(GER) ◆ had been impressive in spreadeagling her field in a maiden at Haydock on her previous start, and with both placed horses in that race scoring since, she was odds-on for this step up in grade. She was held up in the pack and her rider, who put up 2lb overweight, took a confident look around for dangers while still having several lengths to make up on the leader. She closed that gap without too much fuss but then had to fight to hold off the runner-up, although she scored with something in hand in the end. The Lillie Langtry at Goodwood or the Galtres Stakes at York or the could be her next target, followed by the Park Hill later on. (op 10-11 tchd 8-11)
Meeznah(USA) had failed to build on her subsequently disqualified second in last year's Oaks, but she might be getting her act together judged on this effort. She came through with the progressive winner and made that rival pull out extra, coming well clear of the rest in the process. She should be able to pick up a similar contest on this evidence. (op 4-1)

Opera Gal(IRE) made the running and soon opened up a clear lead. It looked for a moment over 2f out as if she might not come back, but she was quickly collared in the Dip and had no more to give. She kept on for third to earn valuable black type.

Imperial Pippin(USA) appeared to get the longer trip but was struggling a good way from home on her first try on ground this soft.

Never Forget(FR) made good headway around half a mile from home but was beaten and eased over 2f out as if something was amiss. (op 11-1)

Charleston Lady, the Pretty Polly runner-up, was always at the back and probably did not handle the ground. (tchd 10-1)

4100 UKUNPUBLISHED.CO.UK H'CAP 1m

3:10 (3:11) (Class 2) (0-105,102) 3-Y-0+

£15,562 (£4,660; £2,330; £1,165; £582; £292) **Stalls** Low

Form				RPR
4-06	**1**		**Namecheck (GER)**[35] [2927] 4-9-7 **95** .... AhmedAjtebi 5 (Mahmood Al Zarooni) *hld up: hdwy over 2f out: led 1f out: rdn and hung lft ins fnl f: r.o* **20/1**	107
5100	**2**	1 ½	**Benandonner (USA)**[14] [3645] 8-9-1 **89** .... MartinLane 10 (Mike Murphy) *a.p: rdn to chse ldr over 2f out: ev ch 1f out: styd on same pce* **20/1**	97
1225	**3**	1 ½	**Dubai Dynamo**[15] [3578] 6-9-7 **95** .... SebSanders 13 (Ruth Carr) *hld up: hdwy over 1f out: sn rdn: styd on same pce ins fnl f* **11/1**	100
2034	**4**	1 ¾	**Arabian Spirit**[8] [3825] 6-9-2 **90** .... DavidNolan 15 (Richard Fahey) *hld up: hdwy over 2f out: rdn over 1f out: styd on same pce* **7/1**	91
2332	**5**	½	**Snow Bay**[7] [3877] 5-9-9 **97** .... SamHitchcott 12 (David Nicholls) *led: rdn and hung rt over 1f out: sn hdd: wknd ins fnl f* **9/1**	97
0-00	**6**	1 ½	**Circumvent**[14] [3645] 4-10-0 **102** .... WilliamBuick 8 (Paul Cole) *s.i.s: hdwy 6f out: rdn and hung lft fr over 1f out: wknd fnl f* **6/1**[2]	98
-540	**7**	hd	**World Heritage**[29] [3107] 5-9-10 **98** .... AndreaAtzeni 7 (Robert Eddery) *prom: rdn over 1f out: wknd fnl f* **33/1**	94
-041	**8**	7	**Viva Ronaldo (IRE)**[22] [3339] 5-8-13 **87** .... BarryMcHugh 9 (Richard Fahey) *s.i.s: hld up: hdwy rdn over 2f out: n.d* **14/1**	67
/103	**9**	4 ½	**Desert Romance (IRE)**[47] [2573] 5-9-4 **92** .... DanielTudhope 1 (David O'Meara) *chsd ldr tl rdn over 2f out: wknd over 1f out* **14/1**	61
-140	**10**	1 ½	**Nelson's Bounty**[8] [3797] 4-8-12 **86** .... DarryllHolland 2 (Paul D'Arcy) *hld up: rdn over 2f out: wknd over 1f out* **10/1**	52
211-	**11**	17	**Give Your Verdict (USA)**[309] [5917] 4-8-13 **87** .... KierenFallon 16 (Sir Michael Stoute) *in rr and sn pushed along: sme hdwy over 2f out: wknd over 1f out: eased* **13/2**[3]	14
0-03	**12**	nk	**Kajima**[15] [3578] 4-9-4 **92** .... PatDobbs 3 (Richard Hannon) *prom: rdn over 3f out: wknd over 2f out: t.o* **16/1**	18
0-10	**13**	1 ¾	**Bahceli (IRE)**[30] [3067] 3-8-10 **92** .... SteveDrowne 4 (Richard Hannon) *mid-div: sn pushed along: n.m.r and lost pl 6f out: rdn and bhd fr 1/2-way: t.o* **11/2**[1]	12
-100	**14**	3 ½	**Wannabe King**[43] [2679] 5-9-10 **98** .... (b) TedDurcan 6 (David Lanigan) *mid-div: rdn over 2f out: sn wknd: t.o* **12/1**	12

1m 41.25s (1.25) **Going Correction** +0.225s/f (Good)
WFA 3 from 4yo+ 8lb **14** Ran SP% **122.3**
Speed ratings (Par 109): **102,100,99,97,96 95,95,88,83,82 65,64,63,59**
toteswingers:1&2:£123.70, 2&3:£38.50, 1&3:£34.00 CSF £368.76 CT £4689.21 TOTE £29.30: £6.90, £8.10, £4.00; EX 455.50 TRIFECTA Not won..
Owner Godolphin **Bred** Darley **Trained** Newmarket, Suffolk
■ Stewards' Enquiry : William Buick one-day ban: used whip down shoulder (2nd August)

FOCUS

A high-class, competitive mile handicap with some relatively unexposed types taking on battle-hardened performers. The market was volatile though and in the end there was a surprise result. The winner is rated up 9lb, and the second ran his best race for two years.

NOTEBOOK

Namecheck(GER), relatively lightly raced, had shown signs of a revival dropped back to 7f last time and came through from off the pace to score in good style. He will go up a few pounds for this, which may mean he has to contest Listed races or the top handicaps in the short term. (op 28-1)

Benandonner(USA) had a good spring and put behind him a couple of lesser efforts on ground that his record suggested was not entirely suitable. He seems well suited to these big field, straight-track handicaps. (op 22-1 tchd 33-1 in a place)

Dubai Dynamo has been in mainly fine form this season and bounced back from a slightly below-par effort last time on this easier surface. However, he has gone up 10lb since his last success and will not find it easy to add to his score off his current mark. (op 12-1 tchd 10-1)

Arabian Spirit has form on soft ground and he followed up a couple of decent recent efforts by running well again. He does not have the best strike-rate and is 15lb above his last winning mark, but still looks as if he can win a decent handicap before long. (op 9-1)

Snow Bay made the running but was given no peace and faded in the closing stages. He is admirably consistent but is ideally suited by a turning track. (tchd 8-1)

Circumvent, who normally races up with the pace, was soon rushed up to chase the leaders but could make no impression in the last quarter-mile. His rider picked up a one-day ban for misuse of the whip to add to the two days he got for dropping his hands on Plaisterer in the preceding race. (op 8-1)

World Heritage has slipped down the ratings since joining his current yard from France and the drop back to 1m seemed to suit, as he was noted staying on steadily in the closing stages. (tchd 50-1)

Nelson's Bounty Official explanation: jockey said gelding was unsuited by the good to soft ground

Give Your Verdict(USA) opened up as favourite on this return to action, but had never run on ground softer than good and was a big drifter in the minutes before the off. He chased the pace early but was unable to make an impression and was eased when beaten. (op 11-2 tchd 7-1, 8-1 in places)

Bahceli(IRE), whose best form has been on fast going, seemed to handle easy ground at Ascot on his previous start but was soon struggling on the rain-softened ground here. Official explanation: jockey said gelding never travelled (op 6-1)

4101 EBF "EQUIANO" FILLIES' H'CAP 6f

3:40 (3:41) (Class 3) (0-95,95) 3-Y-0+

£8,715 (£2,609; £1,304; £652; £326; £163) **Stalls** Low

Form				RPR
-022	**1**		**Desert Poppy (IRE)**[19] [3459] 4-9-6 **89** .... EddieAhern 5 (Walter Swinburn) *chsd ldrs: rdn to ld and hung lft over 1f out: r.o wl* **10/3**[2]	101
0125	**2**	2 ¼	**Russian Rave**[7] [3845] 5-8-13 **82** .... SebSanders 12 (Jonathan Portman) *chsd ldrs: rdn over 1f out: sn outpcd: r.o ins fnl f: wnt 2nd towards fin: nt trble wnr* **15/2**	87
0-20	**3**	½	**Cloud's End**[62] [2122] 4-8-6 **78** .... JohnFahy(3) 10 (Robert Cowell) *chsd ldr tl led over 2f out: rdn and hdd over 1f out: styd on same pce ins fnl f* **33/1**	81
2006	**4**	1 ¾	**Glas Burn**[23] [3323] 3-8-13 **90** .... AdamBeschizza(3) 4 (Jonathan Portman) *prom: rdn over 1f out: sn hung lft: styd on same pce* **16/1**	86
1-01	**5**	hd	**Guided Missile (IRE)**[47] [2553] 3-8-4 **78** .... (v) DavidProbert 8 (Andrew Balding) *hld up: rdn over 1f out: styd on ins fnl f: nt rch ldrs* **3/1**[1]	74
3-34	**6**	¾	**Carrignavar (USA)**[23] [3323] 3-9-0 **88** .... JimCrowley 3 (Ralph Beckett) *hld up: rdn over 1f out: hung lft and styd on ins fnl f: nt trble ldrs* **11/2**[3]	81
4310	**7**	1 ¾	**Ivory Silk**[8] [3796] 6-8-9 **85** .... (b) RaulDaSilva(7) 7 (Jeremy Gask) *chsd ldrs: rdn over 1f out: wkng whn nt clr run and swtchd rt ins fnl f* **7/1**	74
1036	**8**	½	**Button Moon (IRE)**[35] [2928] 3-9-7 **95** .... (p) MartinLane 6 (Ian Wood) *led over 3f: sn rdn: wknd ins fnl f* **22/1**	81
6-00	**9**	2 ½	**Tallahasse (IRE)**[70] [1902] 3-9-2 **90** .... KierenFallon 13 (Alan Swinbank) *prom tl wknd and eased over 1f out* **12/1**	68
-004	**10**	1	**Fleeting Echo**[22] [3365] 4-9-6 **89** .... PatDobbs 1 (Richard Hannon) *s.s: hld up: rdn and wknd over 1f out* **16/1**	65

1m 13.59s (1.09) **Going Correction** +0.225s/f (Good)
WFA 3 from 4yo+ 5lb **10** Ran SP% **114.5**
Speed ratings (Par 104): **101,98,97,95,94 93,91,90,87,86**
toteswingers:1&2:£6.50, 2&3:£76.70, 1&3:£42.60 CSF £28.10 CT £708.30 TOTE £4.20: £1.70, £2.40, £7.20; EX 21.70.
Owner Oasis Dreamers **Bred** Kildaragh Stud **Trained** Aldbury, Herts

FOCUS

A good fillies' sprint handicap in which four of the seven previous winners went on to score at Listed level, including Frankel's dam Kind. The pace did not look that strong and it paid to not be far off the lead. A 5lb personal best from the winner, rated around the third.

NOTEBOOK

Desert Poppy(IRE) hit form on her return in July last year but had already shown herself in good heart this season. There was a doubt about the ground, as she had not handled soft last season, but this going was just on the easy side and she won well, despite hanging when hitting the front. (op 3-1 tchd 11-4)

Russian Rave, who has been running over 7f this season, ran pretty well dropped in trip on ground she has handled in the past. She stayed on as if the extra furlong is her ideal these days. (op 8-1 tchd 7-1)

Cloud's End, who had been given a break since disappointing last time, helped set the pace and stuck on pretty well, although no match for the winner.

Glas Burn had put up arguably her best previous effort on easy ground and ran well again, having been close up all the way. Her only previous success was on her only try at 5f, and she may be worth trying back at that trip when the ground is on the soft side.

Guided Missile(IRE) was held up on the outside of the field but, despite staying on, she never got close enough to make a challenge. (op 7-2 tchd 4-1)

Carrignavar(USA) had form on soft ground last year as a juvenile but had been running well on fast ground this time. Held up early, she could never land a blow at the leaders. (op 5-1 tchd 6-1)

Button Moon(IRE) helped make the running and still looked to be going well 2f out but faded quickly coming out of the Dip. (op 25-1 tchd 20-1)

4102 BURTS CHIPS NATURALLY DELICIOUS MAIDEN STKS 7f

4:15 (4:15) (Class 5) 3-Y-O **£3,881** (£1,155; £577; £288) **Stalls** Low

Form				RPR
5-	**1**		**Lay Time**[317] [5692] 3-8-12 0 .... DavidProbert 7 (Andrew Balding) *chsd ldrs: rdn to ld ins fnl f: r.o wl: comf* **7/4**[1]	83
3202	**2**	3	**Danehill Dante (IRE)**[28] [3183] 3-9-3 77 .... PatDobbs 3 (Richard Hannon) *led: rdn over 1f out: hdd and unable qck ins fnl f* **11/4**[2]	80
	3	1 ½	**Awjila** 3-8-12 0 .... JimCrowley 2 (Ralph Beckett) *a.p: rdn and ev ch over 1f out: no ex ins fnl f* **7/1**	71
0-	**4**	5	**Encore Un Fois**[288] [6532] 3-9-0 0 .... MichaelGeran(3) 5 (Luca Cumani) *plld hrd and prom: rdn and wknd over 1f out* **11/2**[3]	62
0-	**5**	7	**Grandad Mac**[260] [7202] 3-9-3 0 .... MartinDwyer 4 (Jane Chapple-Hyam) *s.s: a in rr: rdn over 2f out: sn wknd* **12/1**	43
-0	**6**	1 ¼	**Diamond Run**[76] [1724] 3-8-12 0 .... SebSanders 6 (J W Hills) *s.i.s: hld up: plld hrd: rdn and wknd over 1f out* **12/1**	35
	7	hd	**Prana (USA)** 3-8-12 0 .... SteveDrowne 1 (Jeremy Gask) *chsd ldrs: rdn over 2f out: wknd over 1f out* **33/1**	35

1m 28.28s (2.58) **Going Correction** +0.225s/f (Good) **7** Ran SP% **109.2**
Speed ratings (Par 100): **94,90,88,83,75 73,73**
toteswingers:1&2:£1.70, 2&3:£4.00, 1&3:£3.10 CSF £5.98 TOTE £2.40: £1.70, £1.70; EX 5.60.
Owner R Barnett **Bred** W And R Barnett Ltd **Trained** Kingsclere, Hants

FOCUS

An ordinary 3yo maiden that fell to the subsequent Lincoln and Listed winner Penitent in 2009. The form is rated around the second.

Diamond Run Official explanation: jockey said filly ran too free.

4103 ATKINSON BOLTON H'CAP (IN MEMORY OF REG DAY) 1m 2f

4:45 (4:45) (Class 3) (0-95,91) 3-Y-O

£8,715 (£2,609; £1,304; £652; £326; £163) **Stalls** Centre

Form				RPR
3-11	**1**		**Halfsin (IRE)**[78] [1652] 3-9-4 **88** .... SebSanders 6 (Marco Botti) *sn led: hdd over 8f out: styd stands' side to r alone turning for home: led again overall 7f out: rdn and hung lft fr over 2f out: styd on gamely* **15/2**	106+
2-01	**2**	1	**Kirthill (IRE)**[28] [3177] 3-9-2 **86** .... KierenFallon 2 (Luca Cumani) *s.i.s: hld up: racd centre turning for home: hdwy over 2f out: rdn to chse wnr over 1f out: sn hung lft: styd on* **3/1**[2]	102+
4554	**3**	4 ½	**Sonoran Sands (IRE)**[17] [3521] 3-9-0 **84** .... TadhgO'Shea 5 (Peter Chapple-Hyam) *hld up: racd centre turning for home: hdwy u.p over 1f out: wnt 3rd ins fnl f: nt trble ldrs* **20/1**	91
0423	**4**	1	**El Torbellino (IRE)**[8] [3809] 3-8-7 **77** .... MartinDwyer 7 (David O'Meara) *chsd ldr tl led over 8f out: wnt centre turning for home: hdd overall 7f out but continued to ld that gp tl hdd over 2f out: no ex fnl f* **11/1**	82
-212	**5**	½	**Trojan Nights (USA)**[42] [2711] 3-9-5 **89** .... EddieAhern 8 (William Haggas) *prom: racd centre turning for home: rdn and hung rt over 2f out: styd on same pce fr over 1f out* **7/2**[3]	93
12-1	**6**	12	**Tahaamah**[22] [3340] 3-8-13 **83** .... TedDurcan 1 (Saeed Bin Suroor) *prom: wnt centre turning for home: chsd ldr of that gp tl led those over 2f out: hung rt and hdd over 1f out: sn wknd* **13/8**[1]	63
-050	**7**	41	**Stentorian (IRE)**[21] [3405] 3-8-11 **81** .... DarryllHolland 3 (Mark Johnston) *chsd ldrs: wnt far side to r alone turning for home: up w the pce tl rdn 4f out: wknd wl over 2f out: eased* **28/1**	—

2m 6.58s (1.08) **Going Correction** +0.225s/f (Good) **7** Ran SP% **113.6**
Speed ratings (Par 104): **104,103,99,98,98 88,56**
toteswingers:1&2:£3.10, 2&3:£13.00, 1&3:£7.60 CSF £29.83 CT £432.30 TOTE £7.10: £2.90, £2.50; EX 28.80.

Owner Giuliano Manfredini **Bred** Glending Bloodstock **Trained** Newmarket, Suffolk

FOCUS

A good, competitive handicap featuring several progressive types, but they spread across the track in the straight before two came clear up the hill. The favourite was disappointing but still looks good form.

NOTEBOOK

Halfsin(IRE) was bidding for a hat-trick but had been given a good break since a hard-fought success at Doncaster in April. He helped make the running and was the only one to stick to the stands' side rail in the straight. He wandered about in the Dip but responded well for pressure to hold off the runner-up, as the pair drew away from the rest. He is clearly still improving and has the right attitude. (op 8-1 tchd 7-1)

Kirthill(IRE), who won his maiden over a mile here on easy ground, looked to have every chance going into the Dip but drifted left under pressure up the hill, and was always being held. He came clear of the rest so it is hard to say he didn't stay. (op 11-4 tchd 5-2)

Sonoran Sands(IRE) has handled soft ground in the past but, despite running on, never got competitive having been held up at the back.

El Torbellino(IRE) heped make the running and led the main group up the centre but was too keen early and was struggling over 2f from home. (op 10-1 tchd 9-1)

Trojan Nights(USA) has shown progressive form this season on fast turf but looked less effective on this going. (op 3-1 tchd 4-1)

Tahaamah gained his recent handicap success on easy ground and appeared to travel well enough but dropped away quickly under pressure. He was 9lb higher than for his Chester success in a better race, but it may also be he prefers a flat track. Official explanation: jockey said colt stopped quickly. (op 2-1 tchd 9-4 in a place)

Stentorian(IRE) tracked the pace until going to the far side in the straight but was in trouble a good way from home. (op 33-1 tchd 25-1)

4104 HOME OF RACING H'CAP 5f

5:20 (5:22) (Class 3) (0-95,92) 3-Y-O+ **£9,056** (£2,695; £1,346; £673) **Stalls** Low

Form					RPR
0-00	**1**		**Swiss Franc**[56] 2317 6-9-5 **89**	WilliamBuick 10	99
			(David Elsworth) *a.p: rdn over 1f out: r.o to ld wl ins fnl f*	**6/1**	
0050	**2**	¾	**Baby Strange**[7] 3841 7-9-3 **87**	JimCrowley 6	94
			(Derek Shaw) *chsd ldr: rdn to ld 1f out: hdd wl ins fnl f*	**7/2**[1]	
-044	**3**	1	**Judge 'n Jury**[52] 2397 7-9-4 **88**	TomMcLaughlin 9	91
			(Ronald Harris) *led: rdn and hdd 1f out: styd on same pce*	**4/1**[2]	
-050	**4**	6	**Fathom Five (IRE)**[28] 3160 7-9-6 **90**	MartinDwyer 8	72
			(David Nicholls) *chsd ldrs: rdn over 1f out: wknd ins fnl f*	**5/1**[3]	
2000	**5**	1	**Befortyfour**[7] 3846 6-9-6 **90**	RobbieFitzpatrick 5	68
			(Richard Guest) *prom: pushed along 1/2-way: hung lft and wknd over 1f out*	**14/1**	
-400	**6**	3 ¾	**Taajub (IRE)**[14] 3627 4-9-8 **92**	(b[1]) SebSanders 3	57
			(Brett Johnson) *hld up: rdn and hung lft fr 1/2-way: sn wknd*	**14/1**	

59.78 secs (0.68) **Going Correction** +0.225s/f (Good) **6** Ran SP% **86.5**

Speed ratings (Par 107): **103,101,100,90,89 83**

toteswingers:1&2:£2.80, 2&3:£2.20, 1&3:£3.30 CSF £15.74 CT £35.80 TOTE £4.90: £2.50, £2.20; EX 17.00.

Owner Lordship Stud **Bred** Lordship Stud **Trained** Newmarket, Suffolk

■ Hazelrigg (3-1f) withdrawn (unruly in stalls): Rule 4 applies: deduct 25p in the £ from all bets.

■ Stewards' Enquiry : William Buick caution: used whip down shoulder

FOCUS

A decent, tightly knit sprint handicap but three non-runners and the withdrawal of the favourite Hazelrigg reduced much of the interest. Nevertheless, it produced a good finish. An ordinary handicap for the grade.

NOTEBOOK

Swiss Franc has had a truncated career since his busy 2-y-o season, and missed a whole year before returning in May. He had been given a break since two quick runs that month, and appreciated the easy ground, as he gained his sole previous success on it. He was never far away and, although his rider started to get animated going into the Dip, he did not ask for everything until meeting the rising ground, from which point his mount found plenty. He could have more to offer if he remains in one piece. (op 13-2 tchd 11-2)

Baby Strange has dropped a little in the weights since returning to turf and looked as if he might score when delivering his challenge. However, he just found the winner too strong up the hill and is probably ideally suited by a flatter track. (op 4-1)

Judge 'n Jury has not won for nearly two years but has now dropped to a 10lb lower mark than for his last success. He made the running and stuck on well but could not resist the challengers on either side. (op 10-3 tchd 3-1)

Fathom Five(IRE) chased the leaders but could not go with the first three up the hill. He handles cut in the ground but seems to reserve his best for Epsom. (tchd [illegible] and [illegible])

Befortyfour who has handled soft ground in the distant past, has been a bit hit and miss this season after a long absence and was unable to go the pace here. (op 10-1)

Taajub(IRE), who might have been hit when the favourite lashed out in the stalls, was passed fit to race by the vet but was soon struggling at the rear. (tchd 12-1 and 16-1)

T/Jkpt: Not won. T/Plt: £214.20 to a £1 stake. Pool £101,167.00 - 334.78 winning tickets. T/Qpdt: £136.50 to a £1 stake. Pool £5,353.17 - 29 winning tickets. CR

3679 RIPON (R-H)

Saturday, July 16

OFFICIAL GOING: Good (good to soft in places) changing to good to soft after race 1 (1.40)

Wind: Virtually nil Weather: Heavy cloud and rain

4105 WELCOME TO YORKSHIRE HAVE A BRILLIANT YORKSHIRE (S) STKS 6f

1:40 (1:41) (Class 6) 2-Y-O **£2,587** (£770; £384; £192) **Stalls** High

Form					RPR
0	**1**		**Lady Jourdain (IRE)**[10] 3728 2-8-6 0	AndrewElliott 7	55
			(Mrs K Burke) *dwlt and towards rr: pushed along and hdwy whn nt clr run and swtchd rt 2f out: sn rdn and styd on to ld ent fnl f: sn edgd lft: drvn out*	**14/1**	
0453	**2**	1 ¼	**Justine Time (IRE)**[10] 3728 2-8-6 0	(b) LeeNewman 6	51
			(David Barron) *chsd ldrs: rdn along to ld 2f out: drvn and hdd ent fnl f: kpt on same pce*	**14/1**	
004	**3**	5	**Cooldine Cat (IRE)**[10] 3728 2-8-8 0	DeclanCannon(3) 9	41
			(John Quinn) *midfield: hdwy 1/2-way: rdn along to chse ldrs over 1f out: kpt on ins fnl f: nrest at fin*	**8/1**[3]	
000	**4**	3 ½	**Bertie Dancing (IRE)**[4] 3932 2-8-11 0	(p) RobertWinston 4	31
			(Nigel Tinkler) *in tch: pushed along 1/2-way: effrt whn n.m.r 2f out: sn rdn and kpt on same pce*	**33/1**	
613	**5**	nk	**First Bid**[32] 3021 2-9-2 0	RichardMullen 2	35
			(Kevin Ryan) *chsd ldrs: rdn along 1/2-way: drvn 2f out: sn edgd rt and btn*	**1/1**[1]	
	6	8	**Needwood Rose** 2-8-6 0	PaulQuinn 8	1
			(David Nicholls) *s.i.s: a bhd*	**20/1**	
	7	½	**Bea Persuasive** 2-8-4 0 ow1	PaulPickard(3) 3	—
			(Shaun Harris) *s.i.s: a bhd*	**66/1**	
00	**8**	4	**Come On Dave (IRE)**[10] 3728 2-8-11 0	AndrewMullen 5	—
			(David Nicholls) *qckly away and sn clr: rdn along over 2f out: sn hdd & wknd*	**33/1**	
405	**9**	3 ¾	**Tyre Giant Dot Com**[28] 3161 2-8-11 0	(b[1]) FrederikTylicki 1	—
			(Geoffrey Oldroyd) *chsd ldrs on outer: rdn along 1/2-way: sn drvn and wknd over 2f out*	**2/1**[2]	

1m 15.43s (2.43) **Going Correction** +0.275s/f (Good) **9** Ran SP% **119.9**

Speed ratings (Par 92): **94,92,85,81,80 69,69,63,58**

toteswingers:1&2:£27.10, 2&3:£14.90, 1&3:£11.90 CSF £181.17 TOTE £20.20: £3.20, £2.50, £2.20; EX 225.00.There was no bid for the winner.

Owner Mrs Elaine M Burke **Bred** Tally-Ho Stud **Trained** Middleham Moor, North Yorks

■ Stewards' Enquiry : Andrew Elliott two-day ban: excessive use of whip (31st July-1st August)

FOCUS

Rail from back straight to home straight moved out 3m adding about 7yds to distances on round course. The pace of this opening contest seemed overly strong and the form of an already modest-looking contest needs treating with caution. They raced near side.

NOTEBOOK

Lady Jourdain(IRE) improved on the form she showed over 5f on quick ground at Catterick on her debut, although the race set up well for her. She found herself in the right place after missing the break and simply stayed on best as the pace horses got tired. (op 10-1)

Justine Time(IRE) ◆, who had Lady Jourdain behind last time, emerges with a deal of credit. She chased the hot gallop and was left in front sooner than ideal when the early leader faded, only to be picked off by a rival who had raced much further back. (op 11-1)

Cooldine Cat(IRE), without the visor this time, was never really going and probably didn't achieve much. (op 7-1)

First Bid paid for chasing the strong gallop and floundered in the ground, so can be given another chance. (op 13-8)

Come On Dave(IRE) took them along against the near rail and was clear by a couple of lengths or so at halfway, but he had little hope of sustaining the gallop. (op 22-1)

Tyre Giant Dot Com was another who was a bit too close to the quick pace, but he was beaten over 2f out and dropped right away. He seemed to go okay on a soft surface last time, but perhaps he didn't face the first-time blinkers on this occasion. (op 11-4)

4106 BRITISH STALLION STUDS E B F STOWE FAMILY LAW MAIDEN STKS 5f

2:15 (2:16) (Class 4) 2-Y-O **£4,851** (£1,443; £721; £360) **Stalls** High

Form					RPR
3036	**1**		**See Clearly**[17] 3504 2-8-12 0	RobertWinston 2	72
			(Tim Easterby) *qckly away: sn swtchd lft to stands' rail: mde all: rdn and qcknd clr appr fnl f: kpt on strly*	**16/1**	
2	**2**	1 ¾	**Kimbali (IRE)**[14] 3610 2-8-12 0	LeeTopliss(5) 10	71
			(Richard Fahey) *trckd ldrs: hdwy to chse wnr over 1f out: sn rdn: drvn ins fnl f and no imp*	**8/11**[1]	
6	**3**	2 ¼	**Trust Fund Babe (IRE)**[14] 3610 2-8-12 0	DavidAllan 4	58
			(Tim Easterby) *cl up: effrt 2f out: sn rdn and one pce appr fnl f*	**8/1**[2]	
04	**4**	¾	**Our Boy Jack (IRE)**[14] 3611 2-9-3 0	FrederikTylicki 11	60+
			(Richard Fahey) *hld up towards rr: hdwy on inner wl over 1f out: styd on ins fnl f: nrst fin*	**8/1**[2]	
044	**5**	¾	**Busy Bimbo (IRE)**[27] 3200 2-8-12 0	StevieDonohoe 6	52
			(Alan Berry) *chsd ldrs: rdn along 2f out: drvn and wknd over 1f out*	**18/1**	
	6	1 ¾	**Lady Hello (IRE)** 2-8-9 0	MartinHarley(3) 9	46
			(Mick Channon) *trckd ldrs: pushed along 2f out: n.d*	**12/1**	
4202	**7**	6	**Red Shadow**[14] 3611 2-8-12 0	AndrewElliott 1	24
			(Alan Brown) *cl up on outer: rdn along 1/2-way: sn wknd*	**14/1**	
	8	1 ¾	**Show Of Faith (IRE)** 2-8-12 0	RichardMullen 3	18
			(Ed McMahon) *prom: rdn along over 2f out: sn wknd*	**10/1**[3]	
	9	1	**Heidi's Delight (IRE)** 2-8-7 0	DaleSwift(5) 8	14
			(Ann Duffield) *a bhd*	**20/1**	

61.11 secs (0.41) **Going Correction** +0.275s/f (Good) **9** Ran SP% **119.5**

Speed ratings (Par 96): **107,104,100,99,98 95,85,83,81**

toteswingers:1&2:£4.30, 2&3:£2.70, 1&3:£6.50 CSF £29.20 TOTE £18.70: £3.10, £1.10, £2.50; EX 39.00.

Owner Ryedale Partners No 4 **Bred** Rabbah Bloodstock Limited **Trained** Great Habton, N Yorks

■ Stewards' Enquiry : Robert Winston one-day ban: careless riding (31st July)

FOCUS

An ordinary maiden and few were seriously competitive. The action unfolded near side.

NOTEBOOK

See Clearly was already having her sixth start, but her experience was an asset and it was utilised by Robert Winston. The winner showed good speed from the off and was gradually edged across to the near rail, allowing her something of a head start on the favourite. She kept on strongly, evidently handling conditions well, and her natural pace should see her getting competitive in nurseries. (tchd 14-1)

Kimbali(IRE) had shown plenty of ability when runner-up on his debut on quick ground at Beverley, but he couldn't build on that after compromising his chance with a sluggish start. It took him too long to get organised, meaning he could never get on terms with the front-running winner, but he saw his race out reasonably well and can be given another chance in similar company. (op Evens)

Trust Fund Babe(IRE) had the assistance of the trainer's first-choice jockey, but she couldn't build sufficiently on the form of her Beverley debut. This still represents improvement, however. (op 9-1)

Our Boy Jack(IRE) ◆ was soon behind and never threatened at any stage, but he kept on gradually. He very much looks the type to progress in nurseries. (op 9-1 tchd 10-1)

4107 TYREGIANT.COM H'CAP 1m

2:50 (2:50) (Class 4) (0-85,84) 3-Y-O+ **£5,355** (£1,603; £801; £401; £199) **Stalls** Low

Form					RPR
2025	**1**		**Dazeen**[17] 3506 4-9-5 **75**	TonyCulhane 13	84
			(Paul Midgley) *hld up in rr: hdwy wl over 2f out: chsd ldrs over 1f out: swtchd rt to inner ins fnl f and styd on to ld nr fin*	**5/1**[3]	
0064	**2**	nk	**First Class Favour (IRE)**[7] 3854 3-8-8 **72**	KellyHarrison 6	78
			(Tim Easterby) *led: rdn along and jnd over 2f out: hdd 1 1/2f out: drvn and rallied to ld ent fnl f: hdd and no ex nr fin*	**7/1**	
4300	**3**	2	**Illustrious Prince (IRE)**[7] 3880 4-9-6 **76**	(v) RichardMullen 10	80
			(Declan Carroll) *in tch: hdwy over 3f out: rdn to chal 2f out: sn led: drvn and hdd ent fnl f: sn edgd rt and one pce*	**18/1**	
10-5	**4**	2 ¾	**Scrapper Smith (IRE)**[24] 3275 5-9-8 **78**	FrederikTylicki 8	75
			(Alistair Whillans) *s.i.s and bhd: hdwy on outer over 3f out: rdn to chse ldrs 2f out: kpt on fnl f: nrst fin*	**9/2**[2]	
0-00	**5**	nk	**Lucky Windmill**[63] 2112 4-9-3 **78**	DaleSwift(5) 1	75
			(Alan Swinbank) *midfield: rdn along and sltgly outpcd 3f out: hdwy wl over 1f out: kpt on same pce fnl f*	**6/1**	
020	**6**	6	**Georgebernardshaw (IRE)**[7] 3877 6-9-6 **79**	MartinHarley(3) 11	62
			(John Quinn) *trckd ldr: cl up 4f out: rdn along over 3f out: sn drvn and wknd*	**9/2**[2]	

510 **7** *8* **J R Hartley**[56] 2319 3-9-0 **78** .... RoystonFfrench 7 40
(Bryan Smart) *in tch: rdn along over 3f out: drvn over 2f out and sn wknd* **16/1**

1-11 **8** *10* **Rustic Deacon**[33] 2999 4-9-6 **76** .... StevieDonohoe 5 17
(Willie Musson) *trckd ldng pair: hdwy and cl up 3f out: rdn over 2f out: sn drvn and wknd* **10/3**[1]

1m 42.53s (1.13) **Going Correction** +0.275s/f (Good)
WFA 3 from 4yo+ 8lb **8** Ran SP% **114.0**
Speed ratings (Par 105): **105,104,102,99,99 93,85,75**
toteswingers:1&2:£10.50, 2&3:£10.10, 1&3:£5.70 CSF £39.25 CT £581.95 TOTE £6.10: £1.70, £2.80, £4.10; EX 57.80.
Owner Darren & Annaley Yates **Bred** Bond Thoroughbred Corporation **Trained** Westow, N Yorks

FOCUS
The favourite disappointed and this was just an ordinary handicap, although the pace seemed fair enough, suiting all running styles. A length best from the winner.
Rustic Deacon Official explanation: jockey said gelding lost its action.

4108 RIPON BELL-RINGER H'CAP 1m 4f 10y
3:25 (3:28) (Class 2) (0-100,95) 3-Y-O
£12,450 (£3,728; £1,864; £932; £466; £234) **Stalls** Low

Form RPR

-630 **1** **Bridle Belle**[42] 2726 3-8-10 **84** .... FrederikTylicki 7 95
(Richard Fahey) *hld up in midfield: hdwy to trck ldrs 4f out: cl up 3f out: rdn to ld wl over 1f out: drvn and edgd rt ins fnl f: kpt on wl* **9/1**

-431 **2** *2 1/4* **King Of The Celts (IRE)**[43] 2669 3-8-2 **76** oh1 .... KellyHarrison 2 83
(Tim Easterby) *led 3f: prom: effrt to ld again over 3f out: sn rdn and hdd wl over 1f out: rallied ent fnl f: one pce last 100yds* **10/1**

-120 **3** *1 1/2* **Ittirad (USA)**[29] 3108 3-8-13 **87** .... JackMitchell 9 92
(Roger Varian) *hld up in tch: hdwy to trck ldrs 3f out: effrt 2f out: sn rdn and kpt on same pce fnl 2f* **7/2**[2]

3-21 **4** *8* **Lady Amakhala**[30] 3084 3-8-4 **78** .... AndrewMullen 1 70
(George Moore) *chsd ldrs: rdn along and sltly outpcd over 4f out: styd on fnl 2f: n.d* **7/1**

2-12 **5** *12* **Motivado**[43] 2695 3-9-1 **89** .... StevieDonohoe 10 62
(Sir Mark Prescott Bt) *dwlt: sn pushed along to join ldrs after 1f: cl up tl led wl over 4f out: rdn along over 3f out: sn drvn and hdd: wknd 2f out* **3/1**[1]

-306 **6** *3* **Fork Handles**[14] 3624 3-9-4 **95** .... MartinHarley(3) 3 63
(Mick Channon) *in tch: smooth hdwy to trck ldrs over 4f out: effrt and cl up over 3f out: sn rdn and wknd over 2f out* **20/1**

0210 **7** *18* **The Bells O Peover**[30] 3069 3-8-13 **87** .... RoystonFfrench 6 26
(Mark Johnston) *trckd ldrs on outer: rdn along over 4f out: sn outpcd* **20/1**

41-0 **8** *18* **Stansonnit**[104] 1113 3-8-9 **83** .... RobertWinston 5 —
(Alan Swinbank) *midfield: rdn along over 4f out: n.d* **33/1**

051 **9** *20* **Midnight Oil**[30] 3080 3-8-11 **85** .... J-PGuillambert 4 —
(Luca Cumani) *cl up: led after 3f: pushed along and hdd wl over 4f out: rdn along wl over 3f out and wknd qckly: sn wl bhd* **5/1**[3]

2m 37.66s (0.96) **Going Correction** +0.275s/f (Good) **9** Ran SP% **107.9**
Speed ratings (Par 106): **107,105,104,99,91 89,77,65,51**
toteswingers::1&2:£17.30, 2&3:£13.40, 1&3:£11.80 CSF £76.58 CT £281.10 TOTE £13.10: £3.30, £2.50, £1.60; EX 189.50.
Owner Mrs H Steel **Bred** Mrs C R Philipson & Mrs H G Lascelles **Trained** Musley Bank, N Yorks
■ Kinyras was withdrawn (8/1, ref to ent stalls). Deduct 10p in the £ under R4.
■ Stewards' Enquiry : Jack Mitchell one-day ban: careless riding (31st July)

FOCUS
The form is not as strong as it might have been, with Kinyras withdrawn at the start and a couple of the other fancied runners, Motivado and Midnight Oil, soon taking each other on up front. The form is rated around the third.

NOTEBOOK
Bridle Belle was disappointing on quick ground last time and these conditions were more favourable. However, she was well placed considering how the race unfolded and a rise in the weights will make things tougher. (op 14-1)
King Of The Celts(IRE) was soon racing just in behind the duelling leaders and then had his chance. Racing from 1lb out of the handicap, this was a good effort on his first start since winning a fast-ground maiden. (op 12-1)
Ittirad(USA), who was probably stretched by 2m and outclassed in the Queen's Vase on his previous outing, had much more realistic claims this time but was a bit disappointing. The race set up well for him (held up, main rivals underperformed), but he didn't find as much as had looked likely. In fairness, he didn't look comfortable on the track, being inclined to edge right under pressure. (tchd 4-1)
Lady Amakhala couldn't defy a 6lb rise for her recent C&D success and was a bit disappointing. (op 8-1 tchd 13-2)
Motivado had excuses. Having got a bit warm between his back legs, he was reluctant to load (has given trouble at the start before), then played up in his stall when finally consenting to go forward. In the race itself he was not given a particularly shrewd ride, being rushed up to try to recover from a slow start, and consequently being caught about five-wide on the first bend before eyeballing Midnight Oil. All things considered it was no surprise he had little left in the straight, and he might be worth another chance, although he will have a bit to prove next time. (op 4-1)
Midnight Oil was off the bridle along way out, even allowing for facing pace pressure, and J-P Guillambert was looking down when easing his mount off in the straight. Official explanation: jockey said gelding moved poorly throughout. (op 4-1 tchd 7-2)

4109 SKY BET SUPPORTING THE YORKSHIRE RACING SUMMER FESTIVAL H'CAP 1m 1f 170y
3:55 (3:55) (Class 4) (0-85,84) 3-Y-O+ **£5,355** (£1,603; £801; £401; £199) **Stalls** Low

Form RPR

1442 **1** **Euston Square**[14] 3620 5-9-2 **77** .... DaleSwift(5) 11 86
(Alistair Whillans) *hld up in rr: stdy hdwy over 3f out: swtchd outside and effrt 2f out: rdn to chal and edgd rt ent fnl f: sn led and styd on wl* **13/2**[3]

0-06 **2** *1 3/4* **Fastnet Storm (IRE)**[27] 3203 5-10-0 **84** .... LeeNewman 15 89
(David Barron) *cl up: led over 3f out: rdn 2f out: drvn ent fnl f: sn hdd and one pce* **7/1**

0311 **3** *1/2* **Quanah Parker (IRE)**[23] 3319 5-9-9 **79** .... RobertWinston 2 83
(Richard Whitaker) *hld up: hdwy and in tch 1/2-way: swtchd lft over 2f out and sn chsng ldng pair: rdn wl over 1f out: n.m.r ent fnl f: kpt on towards fin* **4/1**[1]

2030 **4** *1/2* **Sirgarfieldsobers (IRE)**[8] 3828 5-9-0 **75** .... NeilFarley(5) 1 78
(Declan Carroll) *hld up towards rr: hdwy wl over 2f out: rdn wl over 1f out: styd on appr fnl f: nrst fin* **16/1**

5102 **5** *1 1/2* **Osgood**[7] 3848 4-9-5 **78** .... MartinHarley(3) 10 78
(Mick Channon) *cl up: effrt 3f out: chal 2f out: sn rdn and ev ch tl drvn and wknd ent fnl f* **11/2**[2]

204F **6** *7* **Embsay Crag**[35] 2932 5-9-9 **79** .... KellyHarrison 6 65
(Kate Walton) *s.i.s and bhd: hdwy 3f out: rdn 2f out: kpt on appr fnl f: nrst fin* **11/1**

5643 **7** *2 1/2* **Jonny Lesters Hair (IRE)**[21] 3399 6-9-5 **75** .... DavidAllan 14 55
(Tim Easterby) *sn led: rdn along over 4f out: hdd over 3f out: sn drvn and wknd over 2f out* **4/1**[1]

0200 **8** *6* **Call Of Duty (IRE)**[43] 2671 6-8-13 **69** .... AndrewElliott 9 37
(Dianne Sayer) *hld up towards rr: hdwy over 4f out: chsd ldrs over 3f out: sn rdn and grad wknd fnl 2f* **16/1**

240 **9** *4 1/2* **Oasis Storm**[21] 3376 3-8-9 **78** .... SeanLevey(3) 7 37
(Michael Dods) *trckd ldrs: pushed along 4f out: rdn over 3f out and sn wknd* **14/1**

2300 **10** *4* **Sharakti (IRE)**[36] 2887 4-9-0 **73** .... DeclanCannon(3) 5 24
(Alan McCabe) *in tch: hdwy to chse ldrs 4f out: rdn along over 3f out and sn wknd* **22/1**

0-00 **11** *4* **Aktia (IRE)**[43] 2676 4-9-13 **83** .... J-PGuillambert 3 26
(Luca Cumani) *chsd ldrs on inner: rdn along over 4f out: sn wknd and bhd* **7/1**

0600 **12** *44* **Mainland (USA)**[19] 3453 5-8-6 **65** oh1 ....(p) PaulPickard(3) 13 —
(Tracy Waggott) *dwlt and towards rr: hdwy on outer to chse ldrs 7f out: rdn along 4f out: sn wknd and wl bhd fnl 2f* **33/1**

2m 6.99s (1.59) **Going Correction** +0.275s/f (Good)
WFA 3 from 4yo+ 10lb **12** Ran SP% **127.8**
Speed ratings (Par 105): **104,102,102,101,100 95,93,88,84,81 78,43**
toteswingers:1&2:£14.20, 2&3:£10.90, 1&3:£6.70 CSF £55.88 CT £214.18 TOTE £9.90: £2.70, £3.50, £1.90; EX 89.10.
Owner Granite City Racing **Bred** Juddmonte Farms Ltd **Trained** Newmill-On-Slitrig, Borders

FOCUS
A fair handicap run at a solid pace. A step up from the winner over this longer trip.
Embsay Crag Official explanation: jockey said gelding missed the break
Sharakti(IRE) Official explanation: jockey said gelding was unsuited by good to soft ground

4110 DOBSONS GASKETS MAIDEN H'CAP 6f
4:30 (4:30) (Class 5) (0-70,66) 3-Y-O+ **£2,911** (£866; £432; £216) **Stalls** High

Form RPR

-250 **1** **Spinatrix**[33] 2986 3-8-9 **57** .... SeanLevey(3) 2 68
(Michael Dods) *a cl up: led 1/2-way: rdn wl over 1f out: drvn and edgd rt ins fnl f: kpt on* **15/2**[3]

-500 **2** *3/4* **Bahamian Jazz (IRE)**[51] 2412 4-8-12 **52** .... LeeNewman 8 62
(Robin Bastiman) *led to 1/2-way: styd prom: swtchd rt and rdn to chse wnr fr wl over 1f out: drvn ins fnl f: one pce towards fin* **10/1**

0626 **3** *4* **Eeny Mac (IRE)**[4] 3936 4-8-4 **51** .... TerenceFury(7) 4 48
(Neville Bycroft) *midfield: hdwy and in tch 1/2-way: rdn along over 2f out: kpt on ins fnl f* **7/2**[2]

2303 **4** *1 1/4* **Lady Platinum Club**[26] 3238 3-9-0 **62** ....(b[1]) DeclanCannon(3) 10 54
(Geoffrey Oldroyd) *dwlt: sn trcking ldrs: rdn over 2f out: chsd wnr wl over 1f out: drvn and wknd fnl f* **8/1**

-634 **5** *3/4* **Blue Deer (IRE)**[36] 2869 3-9-4 **66** .... MartinHarley(3) 12 55
(Mick Channon) *prom on stands' rail: effrt 1/2-way: rdn along 2f out: sn one pce* **10/3**[1]

500 **6** *3/4* **Ivy And Gold**[14] 3621 3-8-2 **47** .... AndrewMullen 3 34
(Alan Berry) *in rr tl sme late hdwy* **40/1**

2-42 **7** *3/4* **Arrivaderci**[30] 3075 3-9-6 **65** .... RobertWinston 7 50
(Richard Whitaker) *dwlt: a towards rr* **7/2**[2]

00-6 **8** *nk* **Cottam Stella**[14] 3616 3-8-1 **51** .... NeilFarley(5) 11 35
(Mel Brittain) *a towards rr* **20/1**

000 **9** *6* **Gambatte**[30] 3091 4-9-0 **54** .... LiamJones 1 19
(Tony Carroll) *chsd ldrs: rdn along 1/2-way: wknd 2f out* **20/1**

-000 **10** *1/2* **Grazeon Again (IRE)**[29] 3124 3-8-8 **53** ow1 ....(v) StevieDonohoe 6 16
(John Quinn) *dwlt: a towards rr* **16/1**

1m 14.42s (1.42) **Going Correction** +0.275s/f (Good)
WFA 3 from 4yo 5lb **10** Ran SP% **117.3**
Speed ratings (Par 103): **101,100,94,93,92 91,90,89,81,80**
toteswingers:1&2:£22.10, 2&3:£15.20, 1&3:£6.00 CSF £77.91 CT £318.34 TOTE £9.80: £2.80, £3.70, £1.60; EX 86.30.
Owner Mrs J W Hutchinson & Mrs P A Knox **Bred** T K & Mrs P A Knox **Trained** Denton, Co Durham
■ Stewards' Enquiry : Lee Newman caution: used whip down shoulder.

FOCUS
A typically moderate maiden handicap, although the winner may have more to offer. The majority of these raced towards the near side, although the rail was not an advantage and the front two drifted towards the far side late on. Limited form, rated around the winner.
Arrivaderci Official explanation: jockey said filly was never travelling.

4111 BET BRITISH WITH TOTEPOOL H'CAP (DIV I) 1m 1f 170y
5:05 (5:05) (Class 6) (0-60,62) 3-Y-O+ **£2,264** (£673; £336; £168) **Stalls** Low

Form RPR

0001 **1** **Hot Rod Mamma (IRE)**[10] 3733 4-9-5 **56** .... LeeTopliss(5) 5 73
(Dianne Sayer) *hld up in rr: hdwy over 3f out: swtchd lft to outer jst over 2f out: rdn to ld wl over 1f out: sn clr: styd on strly* **6/1**[2]

3-66 **2** *4 1/2* **Royal Bonsai**[22] 2407 3-8-13 **58** .... SeanLevey(3) 2 66
(John Quinn) *in tch: hdwy on outer to chse ldrs whn sltly hmpd over 2f out and sn rdn: drvn and styng on whn edgd rt ins fnl f: kpt on: no ch w wnr* **10/1**

0000 **3** *2* **Politbureau**[80] 1615 4-9-7 **53** .... PaddyAspell 4 57
(Michael Easterby) *trckd ldrs: effrt 3f out: rdn over 2f out: drvn and kpt on to take 3rd ins fnl f* **28/1**

-032 **4** *1* **Damascus Symphony**[29] 3116 3-9-1 **60** .... MartinHarley(3) 8 62
(James Bethell) *led: qcknd clr over 3f out: rdn over 2f out: hdd wl over 1f out: drvn and wl hld whn n.m.r ins fnl f* **9/2**[1]

3403 **5** *5* **Market Puzzle (IRE)**[14] 3637 4-8-9 **46** oh1 .... RyanClark(5) 10 38
(Mark Brisbourne) *hld up and bhd: hdwy on inner and in tch whn hmpd wl over 2f out and again 2f out: taken bk and swtchd lft to outer over 1f out: rdn and styd on ins fnl f: nrst fin* **9/1**

2035 **6** *1/2* **Inca Blue**[29] 3124 3-8-11 **53** .... KellyHarrison 7 44
(Tim Easterby) *hld up: hdwy over 3f out: rdn to chse ldrs wl over 2f out: sn drvn and wknd* **9/1**

-004 **7** *1 1/4* **Arctic Maiden**[21] 3413 3-9-0 **56** .... StevieDonohoe 12 44
(Willie Musson) *stdd and swtchd rt to inner s: hld up in rr: sme hdwy 3f out: rdn over 2f out: nvr a factor* **6/1**[2]

0004 **8** *1 3/4* **Scarab (IRE)**[8] 3831 6-9-11 **62** ....(p) DaleSwift(5) 9 46
(Tim Walford) *trckd ldr: rdn along wl over 3f out: drvn over 2f out: grad wknd* **8/1**

-402 **9** *7* **Tobrata**[52] 2401 5-9-12 **58** .... RobertWinston 6 28
(Mel Brittain) *chsd ldrs on outer: rdn along over 4f out: sn wknd* **13/2**[3]

0436 **10** *9* **Highland Love**[30] 3074 6-9-8 **54** .... TonyCulhane 1 —
(Jedd O'Keeffe) *trckd ldng pair on inner: effrt 3f out: sn rdn along and wknd over 2f out* **9/1**

0000 **11** *20* **Warden Bond**[14] 3636 3-8-7 **49**.. LiamJones 11 —
(William Stone) *a in rr: outpcd and bhd fr wl over 2f out* **50/1**

2m 7.66s (2.26) **Going Correction** +0.275s/f (Good)
WFA 3 from 4yo+ 10lb **11** Ran SP% **115.7**
Speed ratings (Par 101): **101,97,95,95,91 90,89,88,82,75 59**
toteswingers:1&2:£14.70, 2&3:£54.80, 1&3:£9.20 CSF £63.61 CT £1551.05 TOTE £7.70: £2.90, £2.40, £7.50; EX 76.60.
Owner A Slack **Bred** Philip Hore Jnr **Trained** Hackthorpe, Cumbria
■ Stewards' Enquiry : Lee Topliss one-day ban: careless riding (31st July)

FOCUS
They finished strung out behind the improving winner in this lowly handicap. The time was 0.90 seconds faster than the second division. Modest form, but a clear personal best from the winner.
Highland Love Official explanation: jockey said gelding was never travelling.

4112 BET BRITISH WITH TOTEPOOL H'CAP (DIV II) 1m 1f 170y
5:40 (5:40) (Class 6) (0-60,59) 3-Y-O+ **£2,264** (£673; £336; £168) **Stalls** Low

Form RPR

0505 **1** **Playful Girl (IRE)**[39] 2786 3-8-4 **45**.................................(b) KellyHarrison 8 53
(Tim Easterby) *mde all: rdn along wl over 2f out: jnd and drvn wl over 1f out: kpt on gamely ins fnl f* **12/1**

-000 **2** *1 1/4* **Celtic Step**[4] 3952 7-9-0 **50**.. LeeTopliss(5) 11 55
(Peter Niven) *a.p: effrt 3f out: chal 2f out: drvn ent fnl f: ev ch tl no ex last 75yds* **14/1**

2460 **3** *1 1/2* **Hathaway (IRE)**[35] 2912 4-9-1 **51**...................................... RyanClark(5) 4 53
(Mark Brisbourne) *trckd ldrs: hdwy 3f out: swtchd lft and effrt to chse ldng trio wl over 2f out: rdn wl over 1f out: drvn and kpt on fnl f: nrst fin* **11/2**[3]

5556 **4** *3* **Fairy Mist (IRE)**[12] 3683 4-9-13 **58**.................................... PaddyAspell 9 54
(Brian Rothwell) *prom: cl up 4f out: rdn along wl over 2f out: drvn and n.m.r over 1f out: kpt on same pce* **12/1**

-666 **5** *3 1/4* **Twisted**[13] 2985 5-9-7 **59**....................................(b) DavidSimmonson(7) 12 48
(Michael Easterby) *midfield: on outer: hdwy 3f out: sn rdn along and plugged on same pce fnl 2f* **10/1**

015 **6** *1* **Marino Prince (FR)**[29] 3139 6-9-11 **56**.............................. TonyCulhane 3 43
(Paul Midgley) *hld up in rr on inner: pushed along over 3f out: swtchd lft and rdn wl over 2f out: nvr a factor* **11/2**[3]

2513 **7** *2 3/4* **Pinotage**[15] 3572 3-9-3 **58**.. RobertWinston 7 39
(Richard Whitaker) *hld up in rr: hdwy 3f out: rdn along over 2f out: sn drvn and n.d* **3/1**[1]

000- **8** *3 1/2* **Ptolomeos**[171] 7330 8-9-1 **53**.. DavidKenny(7) 10 27
(Sean Regan) *in tch: effrt on outer over 3f out: rdn along wl over 2f out: sn wknd* **28/1**

666 **9** *1* **Good Faith**[10] 3734 3-8-5 **46**... AndrewMullen 5 18
(George Moore) *a towards rr* **22/1**

0066 **10** *3/4* **Barnum (USA)**[7] 3854 3-8-7 **55**.. DarylByrne(7) 6 26
(Mark Johnston) *a towards rr* **9/2**[2]

0/-5 **11** *7* **Revolving World (IRE)**[44] 450 8-8-9 **45**........................... DaleSwift(5) 2 —
(Lee James) *s.i.s: a in rr* **25/1**

000- **12** *6* **Melody Belle (IRE)**[242] 7470 3-8-11 **52**.......................(t) StevieDonohoe 1 —
(Tobias B P Coles) *chsd ldrs on inner: rdn along 4f out: sn wknd* **20/1**

2m 8.56s (3.16) **Going Correction** +0.275s/f (Good)
WFA 3 from 4yo+ 10lb **12** Ran SP% **121.5**
Speed ratings (Par 101): **98,97,95,93,90 90,87,85,84,83 78,73**
toteswingers:1&2:£41.30, 2&3:£36.40, 1&3:£14.00 CSF £163.07 CT £1041.93 TOTE £11.80: £2.50, £4.30, £1.90; EX 196.40.
Owner Peter C Bourke **Bred** D Veitch **Trained** Great Habton, N Yorks

FOCUS
It paid to be prominent - the time slowest of three races at the trip.
Playful Girl(IRE) Official explanation: trainer had no explanation for the apparent improvement in form shown
T/Plt: £1,624.90 to a £1 stake. Pool £67,891.23 - 30.50 winning tickets. T/Qpdt: £184.30 to a £1 stake. Pool £5,753.32 - 23.10 winning tickets. JR

4113 - 4115a (Foreign Racing) - See Raceform Interactive

3438 CURRAGH (R-H)
Saturday, July 16

OFFICIAL GOING: Good changing to yielding after race 2 (2.40)

4116a MINSTREL STKS (GROUP 3) 7f
3:40 (3:40) 3-Y-O+ **£32,219** (£9,418; £4,461; £1,487)

RPR

1 **Across The Rhine (USA)**[29] 3109 5-9-8 103..................... PShanahan 5 111
(Tracey Collins, Ire) *mde all: rdn and kpt on wl fnl f* **12/1**

2 *1* **Future Generation (IRE)**[17] 3527 3-8-12 102...................... JMurtagh 8 102+
(G M Lyons, Ire) *chsd ldr in 2nd: rdn over 1f out: no ex ins fnl f: kpt on same pce* **8/1**[3]

3 *3/4* **Hujaylea (IRE)**[20] 3444 8-9-8 105......................................(p) CPHoban 1 106
(M Halford, Ire) *settled bhd ldrs: 5th 1/2-way: rdn into 3rd 1f out: no ex ins fnl f: kpt on same pce* **12/1**

4 *3/4* **The Cheka (IRE)**[21] 3404 5-9-11.. TomQueally 7 107
(Eve Johnson Houghton) *trckd ldrs: 3rd 1/2-way: pushed along 2f out: rdn in 4th and no ex 1f out: kpt on same pce* **4/5**[1]

5 *1/2* **Seeharn (IRE)**[55] 2334 3-8-12 97................................... DPMcDonogh 3 97
(Kevin Prendergast, Ire) *hld up: rdn and no imp 2f out: kpt on same pce fr over 1f out* **10/1**

6 *3 1/2* **Duff (IRE)**[6] 3892 8-9-8 102.. KJManning 2 93
(Edward Lynam, Ire) *hld up in rr: clsr in 6th 2f out: rdn and no imp in 5th 1f out: kpt on same pce* **12/1**

7 *hd* **Six Of Hearts**[20] 3440 7-9-8 109..(b) FMBerry 6 93
(Cecil Ross, Ire) *settled bhd ldrs: 4th 1/2-way: rdn in 5th 2f out: no ex over 1f out* **11/2**[2]

8 *4* **Snaefell (IRE)**[20] 3440 7-9-11 100....................................(tp) ShaneFoley 4 85
(M Halford, Ire) *hld up: 6th 1/2-way: rdn in rr 2f out: no imp* **16/1**

1m 27.6s (-3.20) **Going Correction** -0.425s/f (Firm)
WFA 3 from 5yo+ 7lb **8** Ran SP% **120.1**
Speed ratings: **101,99,99,98,97 93,93,88**
CSF £107.56 TOTE £23.10: £3.90, £2.00, £3.20; DF 275.20.
Owner Thistle Bloodstock Ltd **Bred** Dr & Mrs J K Griggs **Trained** The Curragh, Co Kildare

FOCUS
The winner is rated back to his 2010 best, although the time was slow compared with the earlier handicap.

NOTEBOOK
Across The Rhine(USA) made all and stuck to his task well having raced alone, towards the far side of the track, for much of the journey. The ground had been changed to yielding after the second race and winning trainer Tracey Collins thought conditions were no worse than that. "He much prefers fast ground but he got through it okay and it musn't be any worse than yielding," Collins said. (op 12/1 tchd 11/1)
Future Generation(IRE), a dual handicap winner this season and one of only two three-year-olds in the line-up, had finished last of ten in a similar event over the trip at Fairyhouse on her previous start. She appears adaptable in terms of ground and she produced a much better effort here, racing prominently all the way and keeping on gamely although always being held by the winner. (op 10/1)
Hujaylea(IRE) ran an honest race on ground, which was slower than ideal for him. He went third over 1f out and kept on without finding enough to pose a serious threat. (op 10/1)
The Cheka(IRE) raced prominently but was being driven along over 2f out and failed to pick up to any significant degree. (op 1/1 tchd 8/11)
Seeharn(IRE) raced alone on the stands-side rail from soon after half-way and kept on steadily to be nearest at the finish. (op 15/2)
Duff(IRE) made headway in the centre of the course over 2f out but was struggling over 1f out. (op 10/1)
Six Of Hearts had a slight setback when winning a valuable handicap here last month and that, as well as the rain-softened ground, probably accounted for this below par performance. (op 5/1)

4117 - 4119a (Foreign Racing) - See Raceform Interactive

3898 MAISONS-LAFFITTE (R-H)
Saturday, July 16

OFFICIAL GOING: Turf: good

4120a PRIX MESSIDOR (GROUP 3) (3YO+) (TURF) 1m (S)
2:40 (12:00) 3-Y-O+ **£34,482** (£13,793; £10,344; £6,896; £3,448)

RPR

1 **Vagabond Shoes (IRE)**[34] 2980 4-9-1 0........... ChristopheSoumillon 5 108
(Y Durepaire, Spain) *led: set mod pce: rdn 2f out: qcknd wl: r.o wl fnl f to gamely hold off chals on all sides* **51/10**[3]

2 *nk* **Biondetti (USA)**[252] 7363 3-8-7 0.............................. MickaelBarzalona 8 105
(Mahmood Al Zarooni) *settled 2nd: rdn 2f out: lost 2nd 1f out: rallied wl u.p fnl 100yds to threaten ldr: a being hld* **15/2**

3 *hd* **Polytechnicien (USA)**[76] 1740 5-9-5 0............................ OlivierPeslier 1 111
(A Fabre, France) *settled towards rr on stands' rail: swtchd to outside over 1 1/2f out: rdn and r.o wl fnl 100yds* **5/2**[2]

4 *shd* **One Clever Cat (IRE)**[33] 3008 5-8-11 0.............................. FlavienPrat 6 103
(T Clout, France) *settled bhd ldrs on stands' rail: u.p 2f out: r.o wl fnl f: fin strly* **68/10**

5 *nk* **Sir Oscar (GER)**[34] 2980 4-9-1 0.. ASuborics 7 106
(T Potters, Germany) *settled 4th on outside: wnt 2nd 2f out: hrd rdn 1f out: styd on wl fnl f* **19/1**

6 *nk* **Shamalgan (FR)**[20] 4-9-1 0................................. IoritzMendizabal 2 105
(A Savujev, Czech Republic) *bkmarker fr s: stl in rr 1f out: hrd rdn and fin wl fnl 50yds wout threatening: clst at fin* **13/2**

7 *3* **Sandagiyr (FR)**[41] 2751 3-8-7 0.................. Christophe-PatriceLemaire 3 96
(A De Royer-Dupre, France) *settled towards rr: rdn 2f out: fnd no ex: nt in contention fnl f* **23/10**[1]

1m 39.5s (-2.80)
WFA 3 from 4yo+ 8lb **7** Ran SP% **118.2**
WIN (incl. 1 euro stake): 6.10. PLACES: 2.00, 2.90, 1.60. DF: 27.90. SF: 58.40.
Owner Javier Martinez Salmean **Bred** Almagro De Actividades Comerci **Trained** Spain

FOCUS
A real bunch finish.

NOTEBOOK
Vagabond Shoes(IRE) enjoyed the run of things out in front and was able to just about dominate throughout. His trainer believes he'll get another 2f and.
Biondetti(USA), tracked the leader before coming under pressure 2f out, but he rallied well to regain second and looks sure to come on a good deal for this first start since finishing fourth in the Breeders' Cup Juvenile last November.

4121a PRIX DE RIS-ORANGIS (GROUP 3) (3YO+) (TURF) 6f (S)
3:10 (12:00) 3-Y-O+ **£34,482** (£13,793; £10,344; £6,896; £3,448)

RPR

1 **Time Prisoner (USA)**[72] 1841 4-9-0 0........................ MaximeGuyon 10 109
(A Fabre, France) *racd cl up bhd ldrs: qcknd wl to ld 1f out: r.o wl* **44/5**[3]

2 *nk* **Fred Lalloupet**[22] 3374 4-9-0 0.................................. OlivierPeslier 11 108
(D Smaga, France) *sn prom: rdn and r.o wl fnl f* **23/1**

3 *3/4* **Smooth Operator (GER)**[17] 3531 5-9-4 0.........................(b) THellier 2 110
(Mario Hofer, Germany) *settled towards rr: had trble finding daylight to chal: fin wl whn in clr* **68/10**[2]

4 *snk* **Tertio Bloom (SWE)**[28] 6-9-0 0............................... MickaelBarzalona 1 105
(Fredrik Reuterskiold, Sweden) *sn prom: r.o but no ex ins fnl 100yds* **28/1**

5 *shd* **Split Trois (FR)**[41] 2754 3-8-9 0................. Christophe-PatriceLemaire 3 104
(Y De Nicolay, France) *racd midfield: short of room ent fnl f: r.o wl whn fnd daylight* **12/1**

6 *1/2* **Dam D'Augy (FR)**[22] 3374 6-8-10 0..............................(b) ThierryJarnet 8 99
(Mlle S-V Tarrou, France) *racd bhd ldrs: failed to qckn fnl 1 1/2f: styd on* **19/1**

7 *1* **Golden Eagle**[20] 5-9-0 0... DavidBreux 9 100
(A Savujev, Czech Republic) *racd promly: rdn but no ex fr 1f out* **14/1**

8 *nk* **Spectacle Du Mars (FR)**[22] 3374 4-9-0 0................... GregoryBenoist 5 99
(X Nakkachdji, France) *w.w: short of room whn trying to chal fnl 1 1/2f: nvr in contention* **194/1**

9 *3/4* **Green Dandy (IRE)**[33] 4-8-10 0.. FergalLynch 7 93
(E J O'Neill, France) *w.w on outer fr s: rdn but no ex fnl 1 1/2f* **59/1**

10 *15* **Blu Constellation (ITY)**[88] 3-9-1 0.................................. MircoDemuro 6 54
(Vittorio Caruso, Italy) *qckly fdd on wd outside fr 2f out: eased* **1/1**[1]

1m 10.4s (-3.00)
WFA 3 from 4yo+ 5lb **10** Ran SP% **102.2**
WIN (incl. 1 euro stake): 9.80. PLACES: 2.90, 5.50, 2.40. DF: 59.00. SF: 138.60.
Owner Godolphin SNC **Bred** Darley Stud Management Co Ltd **Trained** Chantilly, France

FOCUS
Another race where they finished in a heap.

NOTEBOOK
Time Prisoner(USA), a winner over 1m two starts back, coped well with the drop back to sprinting (related to lots of sprint winners) and got up narrowly in something of a bunch finish.

3185 **REDCAR** (L-H)

Sunday, July 17

OFFICIAL GOING: Good to firm (good in places) changing to good after race 1 (2.05) changing to good to soft after race 2 (2.35)

Wind: Fresh, half behind Weather: Overcast, outbreaks of rain, brighter after race 6

4122 E B F WIN A VIP DAY OUT @ REDCARRACING.CO.UK MAIDEN STKS 7f

2:05 (2:08) (Class 5) 2-Y-O **£2,975** (£885; £442; £221) **Stalls** High

Form RPR

1 **Asatir (USA)** 2-9-3 0 .... TedDurcan 11 79+
(Saeed Bin Suroor) *midfield: pushed along over 4f out: hdwy 2f out: drvn and r.o fnl f: led fnl 75yds* **7/2**[1]

520 2 ½ **Tip Top Gorgeous (IRE)**[30] [3104] 2-8-12 0 .... SilvestreDeSousa 8 73
(David O'Meara) *led for 2f: prom: rdn to ld again 2f out: hdd fnl 75yds* **13/2**[3]

3 *nk* **Beyond Conceit (IRE)** 2-9-3 0 .... JamieSpencer 9 77+
(Tom Tate) *dwlt: sn in tch: rdn over 2f out: edgd lft jst ins fnl f: kpt on: wnt 3rd towards fin* **7/2**[1]

6 4 1 ¾ **Lucky Money**[17] [3553] 2-9-3 0 .... SebSanders 3 72
(Sir Mark Prescott Bt) *hld up: hdwy after 2f: trckd ldrs: rdn to chal over 2f out: drvn appr fnl f: no ex fnl 100yds: lost 3rd towards fin* **4/1**[2]

4 5 6 **Fine Kingdom**[29] [3186] 2-9-0 0 .... SeanLevey(3) 5 57
(Michael Dods) *prom: led after 2f: rdn whn hdd 2f out: wknd fnl f* **11/1**

4U 6 *hd* **Margo Channing**[9] [3826] 2-8-12 0 .... PJMcDonald 10 51
(Micky Hammond) *in tch: rdn over 3f out: no imp: wknd over 1f out* **100/1**

7 3 **Istan Star (USA)** 2-9-3 0 .... BarryMcHugh 7 48
(Julie Camacho) *dwlt: hld up: rdn over 3f out: no imp* **66/1**

8 1 **Crossley** 2-9-3 0 .... PhillipMakin 2 46
(Geoffrey Oldroyd) *midfield: rdn over 2f out: sn wknd:* **80/1**

9 1 **Swift Encounter (IRE)** 2-9-3 0 .... DavidNolan 12 43
(Ann Duffield) *hld up: rdn over 3f out: a towards rr* **66/1**

4 10 6 **Curtain Patch (USA)**[14] [3656] 2-8-12 0 .... TomEaves 14 23
(Bryan Smart) *trckd ldrs: rdn over 3f out: sn lost pl: wknd 2f out* **10/1**

11 *nk* **Catramis** 2-9-0 0 .... NataliaGemelova(3) 6 27
(Geoffrey Oldroyd) *slowly away: a bhd* **66/1**

6 12 17 **Dubai Destiny**[29] [3186] 2-9-3 0 .... DavidAllan 13 —
(Tim Easterby) *midfield: rdn over 3f out: sn lost pl: bhd fnl 2f* **20/1**

1m 24.86s (0.36) **Going Correction** -0.10s/f (Good) **12** Ran SP% **106.7**
Speed ratings (Par 94): **93,92,92,90,83 83,79,78,77,70 70,50**
toteswingers: 1&2 £5.00, 1&3 £2.30, 2&3 £4.00 CSF £19.80 TOTE £4.60: £1.80, £1.20, £1.50; EX 22.60 Trifecta £100.60 Pool: £280.19 - 2.06 winning units..
Owner Godolphin **Bred** Robert Raphaelson **Trained** Newmarket, Suffolk

FOCUS

It was raining, but the time suggests conditions were at least good. This maiden was weakened by the late withdrawal of Yeomanoftheguard, who refused to enter the stalls (9/2, deduct 15p in the £ under R4), but there were still some promising types on show and the form looks at least fair.

NOTEBOOK

Asatir(USA) ◆, a $260,000 brother to two winners, notably smart 6f-1m dirt performer Elusive Warning (won Group 3 in Dubai), was a significant drifter, but he overcame inexperience to make a successful start. He was being pushed along by around halfway, but gradually responded, showing a good attitude. A horse with plenty of scope, he should have learned a lot and can improve significantly. (op 2-1)

Tip Top Gorgeous(IRE) failed to beat a rival when outclassed in the Albany last time, but this was probably her best effort so far. She was simply outstayed by the winner on this step up in distance, having been keen early, but she'll get the trip better if settling. (op 9-1)

Beyond Conceit(IRE) ◆, a 250,000gns purchase, is out of Lingfield Oaks Trial winner Baraka (half-sister to Pilsudski) and he really took the eye in the paddock, being a sizeable and scopey colt. In the race itself he showed ability, travelling well before becoming outpaced and then keeping on. There should be a lot better to come granted more time and distance. (op 5-1 tchd 10-3)

Lucky Money was badly in need of the experience over 6f on his debut, but he clearly learnt plenty. He didn't quite see his race out after briefly looking a major player, but he's likely to keep improving. (op 13-2)

Fine Kingdom's debut fourth over C&D has worked out extremely well (front three all successful next time, notably Red Duke in the Superlative Stakes), but he failed to build on that effort. Time will probably show he again bumped into some decent types, however, and he should find his level once handicapped. (op 18-1)

4123 REDCAR CRICKET CLUB H'CAP (DIV I) 1m 1f

2:35 (2:39) (Class 6) (0-60,60) 3-Y-O+ **£1,293** (£385; £192; £96) **Stalls** Low

Form RPR

0500 1 **Escape Artist**[16] [3574] 4-9-0 **48** ....(p) DavidAllan 3 56
(Tim Easterby) *hld up: rdn and hdwy over 2f out: chsd ldrs over 1f out: kpt on fnl f: led post* **6/1**[3]

65-5 2 *shd* **Obara D'Avril (FR)**[31] [3074] 9-8-12 **46** oh1 .... PhillipMakin 2 53
(Simon West) *in tch: rdn and hdwy over 2f out: led over 1f out: kpt on: hdd post* **16/1**

0560 3 3 ½ **Crocodile Bay (IRE)**[2] [4039] 8-8-13 **50** ....(be) RobertLButler(3) 12 49
(Richard Guest) *hld up: hdwy over 2f out: rdn over 1f out: kpt on fnl f: wnt 3rd post* **16/1**

2324 4 *shd* **Desert Hunter (IRE)**[13] [3683] 8-9-10 **58** ....(p) KellyHarrison 10 57
(Micky Hammond) *trckd ldrs: rdn over 3f out: one pce: lost 3rd post* **6/1**[3]

3401 5 3 ¾ **Broctune Papa Gio**[30] [3142] 4-9-1 **52** .... DeclanCannon(3) 11 43
(Keith Reveley) *midfield: rdn and hdwy over 3f out: chsd ldrs over 2f out: wknd ins fnl f* **9/2**[2]

/3P0 6 1 **Moonlight Fantasy (IRE)**[29] [3176] 8-8-8 **49** .... NoelGarbutt(7) 9 38
(Lucinda Featherstone) *led after 2f: clr 6f out tl over 2f out: hdd over 1f out: wknd ins fnl f* **20/1**

4502 7 1 ¾ **Dean Iarracht (IRE)**[14] [3658] 5-9-9 **57** ....(p) SilvestreDeSousa 1 42
(Tracy Waggott) *dwlt: sn midfield: rdn over 3f out: no imp* **7/2**[1]

600 8 4 **Jack's Rocket**[31] [3074] 4-8-12 **46** oh1 ....(e) PaulHanagan 5 22
(Richard Guest) *led for 2f: trckd ldr: rdn and hung lft over 2f out: sn lost pl: wknd over 1f out* **25/1**

0004 9 5 **Pictures (IRE)**[14] [3658] 4-8-9 **46** oh1 .... NataliaGemelova(3) 8 11
(Ron Barr) *midfield: rdn over 3f out: wknd over 2f out* **8/1**

/00- 10 ½ **Princess Neenee (IRE)**[288] [6579] 4-8-12 **46** oh1..... AndrewHeffernan 4 10
(Paul Green) *midfield: rdn over 4f out: wknd over 3f out* **100/1**

-000 11 *shd* **Bold Indian (IRE)**[16] [3569] 7-8-13 **47** .... TomEaves 7 11
(Mike Sowersby) *hld up: a towards rr* **40/1**

2105 12 ¾ **Media Stars**[15] [3620] 6-9-7 **60** .... LeeTopliss(5) 6 22
(Robert Johnson) *hld up: rdn over 3f out: a towards rr* **8/1**

1m 55.64s (2.64) **Going Correction** +0.20s/f (Good) **12** Ran SP% **115.0**
Speed ratings (Par 101): **96,95,92,92,89 88,86,83,78,78 78,77**
toteswingers: 1&2 £23.50, 1&3 £11.50, 2&3 £40.50 CSF £90.43 CT £1469.46 TOTE £5.60: £2.10, £6.20, £3.30; EX 107.20 TRIFECTA Not won..
Owner Habtons Baggie Rams **Bred** Sarah J Leigh And Robin S Leigh **Trained** Great Habton, N Yorks

FOCUS

It continued to rain and after this race the ground was changed to good to soft. Phillip Makin said: "It's on the easy side, but it's not soft." This was a moderate contest. They were soon going a good pace courtesy of Moonlight Fantasy, who opened up a clear lead, and those who raced off the speed were favoured. The winner is rated back to his best.

Dean Iarracht(IRE) Official explanation: jockey said gelding had a breathing problem.
Jack's Rocket Official explanation: jockey said gelding hung left.

4124 SKYBET SUPPORTING THE YORKSHIRE RACING SUMMER FESTIVAL H'CAP 5f

3:05 (3:06) (Class 5) (0-70,70) 3-Y-O **£3,493** (£1,039; £519; £259) **Stalls** High

Form RPR

1 1 **Little Jimmy Odsox (IRE)**[23] [3343] 3-9-4 **67** .... DavidAllan 8 77+
(Tim Easterby) *dwlt: midfield: rdn over 2f out: hdwy over 1f out: kpt on: led towards fin* **3/1**[1]

2631 2 ½ **Mecca's Team**[30] [3143] 3-8-11 **63** .... SeanLevey(3) 6 71
(Michael Dods) *wnt lft s: led: rdn over 2f out: kpt on: hdd towards fin* **4/1**[2]

5146 3 ½ **Chester Deelyte (IRE)**[11] [3724] 3-8-2 **51** ....(v) PaulHanagan 7 57
(Lisa Williamson) *midfield: rdn over 2f out: hdwy over 1f out: ev ch jst ins fnl f: kpt on* **12/1**

1006 4 2 ¼ **Melodize**[15] [3628] 3-8-7 **56** .... SilvestreDeSousa 9 54
(David O'Meara) *hld up: pushed along 1/2-way: hdwy over 1f out: kpt on fnl f: nt rch ldrs* **7/1**

1553 5 *shd* **Mr Mo Jo**[12] [3702] 3-8-12 **66** ....(p) LanceBetts(5) 2 64
(Lawrence Mullaney) *w ldr: rdn over 2f out: wknd ins fnl f* **4/1**[2]

3335 6 1 ¼ **Hootys Agogo**[24] [3321] 3-8-0 **54** ....(b[1]) NeilFarley(5) 1 47
(Declan Carroll) *prom: rdn over 2f out: wknd fnl f* **6/1**[3]

604 7 1 **See Vermont**[32] [3053] 3-8-6 **55** ow2 .... LeeNewman 5 44
(Robin Bastiman) *dwlt and bmpd s: hld up: a towards rr* **20/1**

1545 8 2 **Morermaloke**[94] [1323] 3-9-2 **70** .... LeeTopliss(5) 4 52
(Ian McInnes) *wnt rt s: hld up: a towards rr* **33/1**

-104 9 ¾ **Lady Kildare (IRE)**[15] [3630] 3-8-10 **62** .... PatrickDonaghy(3) 10 42
(Jedd O'Keeffe) *dwlt: midfield: rdn over 2f out: wknd over 1f out* **9/1**

58.10 secs (-0.50) **Going Correction** -0.10s/f (Good) **9** Ran SP% **117.2**
Speed ratings (Par 100): **100,99,98,94,94 92,91,87,86**
toteswingers: 1&2 £4.10, 1&3 £5.60, 2&3 £8.70 CSF £15.23 CT £125.94 TOTE £3.60: £2.10, £1.70, £3.50; EX 13.20 Trifecta £93.90 Pool: £391.05 - 3.08 winning units..
Owner Reality Partnerships III **Bred** Dr D Crone & P Lafarge & P Johnston **Trained** Great Habton, N Yorks

■ Stewards' Enquiry : Sean Levey caution: used whip with excessive frequency

FOCUS

The time was only 0.90 seconds outside standard, suggesting conditions hadn't deteriorated too much on the straight course. There was a three-way battle for the lead, with Mecca's Team, Mr Mo Jo and Hootys Agogo taking each other on. The third limits this form and the winner can do better.

4125 WELCOME TO YORKSHIRE BACKING A WINNER CLAIMING STKS 1m 2f

3:40 (3:40) (Class 6) 3-Y-O+ **£1,704** (£503; £251) **Stalls** Low

Form RPR

0520 1 **Doctor Zhivago**[22] [3399] 4-9-10 83 .... AdrianNicholls 3 79
(David Nicholls) *mde all: rdn over 2f out: jnd 1f out: kpt on gamely* **11/10**[1]

023 2 ¾ **The Osteopath (IRE)**[34] [2984] 8-9-11 79 .... PhillipMakin 4 79
(Michael Dods) *trckd ldng pair: rdn 3f out: chsd wnr over 1f out: upsides 1f out: no ex towards fin* **5/2**[2]

0500 3 7 **En Fuego**[18] [3508] 4-9-4 68 .... SilvestreDeSousa 10 58
(Geoffrey Harker) *t.k.h: hld up: rdn over 4f out: hdwy over 2f out: wnt 3rd appr fnl f: no threat ldng pair* **12/1**

00-0 4 *nk* **Maybeme**[175] [11] 5-8-6 47 .... TerenceFury(7) 9 52
(Neville Bycroft) *slowly away: hld up: rdn over 4f out: hdwy over 1f out: kpt on fnl f: nvr threatened ldrs* **50/1**

410 5 5 **Unex Goya (IRE)**[24] [3318] 3-8-4 63 ow1 ....(b[1]) SeanLevey(3) 7 46
(Michael Smith) *midfield: rdn over 3f out: no imp* **9/1**

360 6 ¾ **Lord Lansing (IRE)**[17] [3545] 4-9-5 64 ....(p) PatrickDonaghy(3) 5 50
(Mrs K Burke) *t.k.h: trckd wnr: rdn to chal 3f out: wknd over 1f out* **17/2**[3]

0060 7 2 ¼ **Yorksters Prince (IRE)**[121] [899] 4-9-4 39 .... StephenCraine 6 41
(Tony Coyle) *midfield: rdn over 4f out: wknd over 2f out* **100/1**

5 8 2 **Manager Mick (IRE)**[48] [2565] 3-8-12 0 ....(v[1]) PaddyAspell 1 41
(John Norton) *midfield: rdn over 3f out: sn wknd* **100/1**

60-0 9 11 **Smarty Sam (USA)**[72] [1857] 4-9-0 64 .... MickyFenton 8 11
(Paul Midgley) *trckd ldrs: rdn over 3f out: sn wknd* **20/1**

2m 9.23s (2.13) **Going Correction** +0.20s/f (Good)
WFA 3 from 4yo+ 10lb **9** Ran SP% **113.1**
Speed ratings (Par 101): **99,98,92,92,88 87,86,84,75**
toteswingers: 1&2 £1.20, 1&3 £4.50, 2&3 £5.40 CSF £3.66 TOTE £2.00: £1.10, £1.60, £2.00; EX 3.90 Trifecta £16.80 Pool: £583.72 - 25.62 winning units..The winner was claimed by Mr I W McInnes for £14,000.
Owner C Titcomb **Bred** Meon Valley Stud **Trained** Sessay, N Yorks

FOCUS

The pick of the weights, Doctor Zhivago, was allowed to set a steady pace through the early stages and those held up had little hope. The form pair were clear and none of the others counted.

4126 TYREGIANT.COM H'CAP 6f

4:15 (4:16) (Class 4) (0-85,84) 3-Y-O+ **£2,587** (£770; £384; £192) **Stalls** High

Form RPR

-100 1 **Pepper Lane**[20] [3459] 4-9-9 **81** .... SilvestreDeSousa 7 96
(David O'Meara) *led for 2f: trckd ldrs: led again over 2f out: sn rdn: kpt on* **11/2**[3]

0444 2 2 ½ **Feel The Heat**[23] [3359] 4-8-13 **71** ....(v) TomEaves 1 78
(Bryan Smart) *chsd ldrs: rdn to chal over 1f out: kpt on: hld ins fnl f* **5/1**[2]

-504 3 3 ½ **Mayoman (IRE)**[5] [3832] 6-9-6 **78** .... DavidAllan 11 74
(Declan Carroll) *prom: rdn over 2f out: one pce over 1f out* **13/2**

2034 4 3 ¼ **Dispol Kylie (IRE)**[16] [3579] 5-8-12 **70** .... PhillipMakin 2 55
(Kate Walton) *hld up in tch: rdn over 2f out: kpt on fnl f: nvr threatened* **17/2**

0000 5 1 ¾ **Who's Shirl**[20] [3459] 5-9-7 **79** .... KellyHarrison 8 59
(Chris Fairhurst) *hld up: rdn over 2f out: n.d* **14/1**

0005 6 2 **Solar Spirit (IRE)**[3] [4013] 6-9-2 **77** ....(p) PaulPickard(3) 3 50
(Tracy Waggott) *dwlt: led after 2f: rdn whn hdd over 2f out: wknd over 1f out* **13/2**

4241 **7** *1 1/2* **Timeless Elegance (IRE)**[6] 3900 4-9-1 **78** 6ex............. LeeTopliss(5) 6 47
(Howard Johnson) *dwlt: racd keenly: sn prom: rdn over 2f out: wknd over 1f out* **9/2**[1]

0500 **8** *1 1/4* **Dickie Le Davoir**[2] 4042 7-9-9 **84**............................(b) RobertLButler(3) 9 49
(Richard Guest) *hld up: a towards rr* **14/1**

000 **9** *3/4* **Not My Choice (IRE)**[8] 3852 6-9-7 **79**...............(b[1]) AndrewHeffernan 10 41
(David C Griffiths) *in tch: rdn over 2f out: sn wknd* **10/1**

-166 **10** *nk* **Foreign Rhythm (IRE)**[9] 3805 6-8-5 **66**.............. NataliaGemelova(3) 12 27
(Ron Barr) *midfield: rdn and outpcd 3f out: wknd over 1f out* **12/1**

1m 11.5s (-0.30) **Going Correction** -0.10s/f (Good) **10** Ran SP% **117.5**
Speed ratings (Par 105): **98,94,90,85,83 80,78,77,76,75**
toteswingers: 1&2 £4.20, 1&3 £6.50, 2&3 £5.10 CSF £33.47 CT £188.80 TOTE £5.90: £1.70, £1.40, £2.80; EX 34.40 Trifecta £171.20 Pool: £513.77 - 2.22 winning units..
Owner Mrs Lynne Lumley & K Nicholson **Bred** Conor J C Parsons & Brian M Parsons **Trained** Nawton, N Yorks

FOCUS
An ordinary sprint handicap and they finished strung out. Weakish form for the grade.
Pepper Lane Official explanation: trainer said, regarding the apparent improvement in form shown, filly was better suited by being able to dominate
Timeless Elegance(IRE) Official explanation: jockey said filly was unsuited by soft ground.

4127 HELP FOR HEROES AND YORKSHIRE REGIMENT FILLIES' H'CAP 1m
4:45 (4:45) (Class 5) (0-75,74) 3-Y-0+ **£1,940** (£577; £288; £144) **Stalls** High

Form RPR
0433 **1** **Bella Noir**[15] 3620 4-9-10 **70**...............................(v) AndrewElliott 3 79
(Mrs K Burke) *prom: rdn over 2f out: led fnl 100yds: kpt on: all out* **7/2**[2]

5- **2** *shd* **File And Paint (IRE)**[50] 2517 3-9-1 **74**.......................... LanceBetts(5) 1 81
(Lawrence Mullaney) *in tch: led 3f out: sn rdn: drvn and edgd lft ins fnl f: hdd fnl 100yds: kpt on: jst failed* **9/1**

4024 **3** *1 1/2* **Christmas Light**[10] 3757 4-9-8 **68**..................... SilvestreDeSousa 5 73
(David O'Meara) *dwlt: in tch: hdwy to chal 3f out: sn rdn: edgd lft 1f out: kpt on* **9/2**

443 **4** *2 1/2* **Chapter Five**[30] 3138 4-9-0 **60**................................ PaulHanagan 2 60
(Keith Reveley) *hld up: rdn and outpcd over 2f out: kpt on fnl f: nvr threatened ldrs* **10/1**

4614 **5** *1* **Spavento (IRE)**[2] 4051 5-9-6 **66**.............................. DavidAllan 6 63
(Eric Alston) *prom: rdn over 2f out: wknd ins fnl f* **4/1**[3]

2020 **6** *1 1/2* **Silly Gilly (IRE)**[9] 3806 7-8-6 **59**..........................(p) ShaneBKelly(7) 4 53
(Ron Barr) *t.k.h: led: hdd 3f out: wknd over 1f out* **17/2**

0113 **7** *6* **Qeethaara (USA)**[2] 4051 7-9-4 **69**............................ RyanClark(5) 7 49
(Mark Brisbourne) *hld up: rdn over 2f out: wknd over 1f out* **3/1**[1]

1m 39.4s (1.40) **Going Correction** -0.10s/f (Good)
WFA 3 from 4yo+ 8lb **7** Ran SP% **115.0**
Speed ratings (Par 100): **89,88,87,84,83 82,76**
toteswingers: 1&2 £6.10, 1&3 £4.30, 2&3 £7.40 CSF £34.33 CT £143.68 TOTE £5.30: £3.10, £4.00; EX 44.00 Trifecta £89.90 Pool: £613.72 - 5.05 winning units..
Owner John & Sally Kelsey-Fry **Bred** M E Broughton **Trained** Middleham Moor, North Yorks
■ Stewards' Enquiry : Lance Betts one-day ban: used whip with excessive frequency (Jul 31)

FOCUS
A modest fillies' handicap. The winner is rated back to the form of her maiden win.
Qeethaara(USA) Official explanation: jockey said mare was unsuited by soft ground

4128 REDCAR CRICKET CLUB H'CAP (DIV II) 1m 1f
5:15 (5:16) (Class 6) (0-60,60) 3-Y-0+ **£1,293** (£385; £192; £96) **Stalls** Low

Form RPR
4/30 **1** **Wood Fairy**[16] 3574 5-9-6 **54**.................................. PaulHanagan 7 69
(Richard Fahey) *trckd ldr: led 4f out: rdn clr over 1f out: eased towards fin: comf* **10/3**[1]

3044 **2** *5* **Lady Excel (IRE)**[11] 3733 5-9-0 **51**.......................... SeanLevey(3) 2 55
(Brian Rothwell) *trckd ldrs: rdn to chse wnr 3f out: no imp fr over 1f out* **10/1**

3356 **3** *3 3/4* **Star Addition**[15] 3629 5-9-2 **50**.............................. RobertWinston 1 46
(Eric Alston) *midfield: hdwy over 3f out: wnt 3rd 2f out: no imp after* **8/1**

0241 **4** *7* **Byron Bear (IRE)**[12] 3706 3-9-0 **57**.......................... MickyFenton 4 37
(Paul Midgley) *hld up: rdn over 3f out: hdwy over 1f out: nvr threatened ldrs* **11/2**[3]

0400 **5** [illegible] ...(p) DuranFentiman 12 23
(Tim Walford) *trckd ldrs: rdn over 3f out: wknd over 1f out* **14/1**

4153 **6** *1/2* **Sinatramania**[24] 3319 4-9-9 **60**.............................. PaulPickard(3) 8 32
(Tracy Waggott) *hld up: rdn and hdwy over 3f out: wknd over 1f out* **4/1**[2]

0600 **7** *3 1/4* **Mr Emirati (USA)**[20] 3454 4-8-12 **46**...........................(p) TomEaves 5 10
(Bryan Smart) *midfield: hdwy on outer 4f out: sn rdn: wknd 2f out* **16/1**

0000 **8** *6* **Stardust Dancer**[11] 3732 4-8-12 **46** oh1................. SilvestreDeSousa 10 —
(Paul Green) *in tch: rdn over 4f out: wknd over 2f out: eased* **33/1**

0000 **9** *1/2* **Flyjack (USA)**[11] 3733 4-8-12 **46** oh1.......................... BarryMcHugh 9 —
(Lisa Williamson) *hld up: hdwy over 3f out: rdn over 2f out: sn wknd* **100/1**

-061 **10** *6* **Pattern Mark**[24] 3317 5-9-4 **57**.............................. LeeTopliss(5) 6 —
(Ollie Pears) *slowly away: hld up: rdn over 4f out: a bhd* **4/1**[2]

/000 **11** *24* **Hair Of The Dog**[24] 3317 7-8-12 **46** oh1.............(bt) AndrewHeffernan 11 —
(George Charlton) *sn led: hdd 4f out: wknd qckly: t.o* **33/1**

1m 55.09s (2.09) **Going Correction** +0.20s/f (Good)
WFA 3 from 4yo+ 9lb **11** Ran SP% **118.1**
Speed ratings (Par 101): **98,93,90,84,80 80,77,72,71,66 45**
toteswingers: 1&2 £12.20, 1&3 £4.20, 2&3 £8.50 CSF £37.60 CT £257.01 TOTE £3.60: £2.00, £2.90, £2.70; EX 39.00 Trifecta £313.70 Part won. Pool: £423.93 - 0.62 winning units..
Owner Mrs P B E P Farr **Bred** Worksop Manor Stud **Trained** Musley Bank, N Yorks

FOCUS
A moderate contest, but a well-handicapped winner. It was a bit quicker than division I but the form is obviously limited.
Pattern Mark Official explanation: jockey said gelding missed break and never travelled thereafter.

4129 BETFAIR RACING EXCELLENCE APPRENTICE JOCKEYS TRAINING SERIES H'CAP 1m 6f 19y
5:45 (5:45) (Class 5) (0-70,70) 4-Y-0+ **£1,940** (£577; £288; £144) **Stalls** Low

Form RPR
3022 **1** **Harvey's Hope**[16] 3581 5-9-8 **68**.............................. ShaneBKelly 12 79+
(Keith Reveley) *hld up in midfield: rdn and hdwy over 3f out: led 2f out: styd on wl* **3/1**[1]

2444 **2** *3* **Amir Pasha (UAE)**[8] 3858 6-8-13 **59**.....................(p) EdmondLinehan 10 65
(Micky Hammond) *midfield: hdwy over 3f out: chal 2f out: kpt on one pce fnl f* **9/2**[3]

4313 **3** *nk* **Golden Future**[16] 3574 8-8-11 **60**..................... GeorgeChaloner(3) 8 66
(Peter Niven) *midfield: rdn and hdwy 3f out: chsd ldng pair over 1f out: kpt on one pce* **10/1**

0240 **4** *3* **Spahi (FR)**[18] 3510 5-8-2 **53**....................................(e[1]) LukeRowe(5) 7 55
(David O'Meara) *hld up: smooth hdwy fr over 5f out: rdn and ev ch 2f out: wknd ins fnl f* **9/2**[3]

000/ **5** *6* **Seven Stars**[494] 6217 6-8-2 **51** oh4.......................... LeonnaMayor(3) 9 44
(Mike Sowersby) *hld up: rdn over 3f out: hdwy over 2f out: nvr trbld ldrs* **66/1**

0-64 **6** *4 1/2* **Ferney Boy**[29] 3187 5-8-2 **53** oh2 ow2......................... LewisWalsh(5) 14 40
(Chris Fairhurst) *sn led: rdn whn hdd 2f out: sn wknd* **12/1**

11-3 **7** *3/4* **Andorn (GER)**[37] 2183 7-9-6 **69**.............................. JustinNewman(3) 3 55
(Philip Kirby) *midfield: rdn and hdwy over 3f out: chsd ldrs 2f out: wknd over 1f out* **4/1**[2]

0/06 **8** *5* **Hada Men (USA)**[4] 3974 6-9-3 **63**.............................. HenryBrooke 4 42
(Tina Jackson) *hld up: a towards rr* **25/1**

-615 **9** *nk* **Zefooha (FR)**[20] 3450 7-8-8 **59**...........................(p) DavidSimmonson(5) 6 38
(Tim Walford) *trckd ldrs: rdn over 3f out: wknd over 2f out* **11/1**

0616 **10** *3* **Denison Flyer**[12] 3712 4-8-5 **51** oh2..........................(b) MatthewLawson 2 25
(Lawrence Mullaney) *trckd ldr: rdn 4f out: wknd over 1f out* **14/1**

50-0 **11** *1 3/4* **Carmela Maria**[15] 3574 6-8-2 **51** oh6.............................. JakePayne(3) 5 23
(Mike Sowersby) *a towards rr* **100/1**

06/0 **12** *8* **Alltheclews**[39] 2813 6-8-5 **54** oh4 ow3.................. GeorgeDowning(3) 13 15
(Lucinda Featherstone) *trckd ldrs: rdn over 4f out: sn wknd* **28/1**

3m 6.32s (1.62) **Going Correction** +0.20s/f (Good) **12** Ran SP% **122.9**
Speed ratings (Par 103): **103,101,101,99,95 93,92,90,89,88 87,82**
toteswingers: 1&2 £3.60, 1&3 £5.20, 2&3 £10.20; totesuper7: Win: Not won; Place: Not won CSF £16.69 CT £125.00 TOTE £4.90: £1.90, £2.20, £3.00; EX 17.50 Trifecta £117.70 Pool: £432.88 - 2.72 winning units..
Owner The Home & Away Partnership **Bred** Chevington Stud **Trained** Lingdale, Redcar & Cleveland

FOCUS
An ordinary apprentices' staying handicap and they went a good pace.
Andorn(GER) Official explanation: jockey said horse was unsuited by good to soft ground.
T/Jkpt: £11,899.70 to a £1 stake. Pool: £16,760.15. 1.00 winning tickets. T/Plt: £101.90 to a £1 stake. Pool: £75,860.07. 543.15 winning tickets. T/Qpdt: £12.40 to a £1 stake. Pool: £4,535.29. 269.00 winning tickets. AS

4130 - (Foreign Racing) - See Raceform Interactive

4113 CURRAGH (R-H)
Sunday, July 17

OFFICIAL GOING: Round course - yielding; straight course - yielding to soft

4131a JEBEL ALI STABLES & RACECOURSE ANGLESEY STKS (GROUP 3) 6f 63y
2:40 (2:40) 2-Y-O **£29,137** (£8,517; £4,034; £1,344)

RPR
1 **Fire Lily (IRE)**[32] 3033 2-8-12 100.. WMLordan 3 103
(David Wachman, Ire) *chsd ldrs: 4th 1/2-way: 3rd 2f out: rdn to ld 1f out: kpt on wl fnl f* **11/4**[1]

2 *2 1/2* **After (IRE)**[21] 3438 2-8-12 .... RyanMoore 8 96
(A P O'Brien, Ire) *hld up in rr: hdwy into 4th 2f out: rdn into 3rd 1f out: styd on into 2nd fnl f: kpt on same pce* **3/1**[2]

3 *1/2* **Boris Grigoriev (IRE)**[63] 2127 2-9-1 ....(b[1]) JPO'Brien 1 97
(A P O'Brien, Ire) *chsd ldrs: 3rd 1/2-way: 2nd 2f out: led 1 1/2f out: rdn and hdd 1f out: no ex and kpt on same pce* **12/1**

4 *1 3/4* **Ishvana (IRE)**[85] 1531 2-8-12 .... SeamieHeffernan 4 89
(A P O'Brien, Ire) *settled bhd ldrs: 5th 1/2-way: rdn 2f out: 4th 1f out: no ex ins fnl f: kpt on same pce* **10/1**

5 *4 1/2* **Fulbright**[33] 3012 2-9-1 .... FrankieDettori 7 78
(Mark Johnston) *chsd ldr in 2nd: led over 2f out: rdn and hdd 1 1/2f out: no ex in 5th 1f out: kpt on one pce* **4/1**[3]

6 *11* **Zip Top (IRE)**[38] 2860 2-9-1 .... KJManning 6 45
(J S Bolger, Ire) *dwlt: towards rr: pushed along in 6th 1/2-way: no imp over 2f out: wknd* **3/1**[2]

7 *9* **Cheerful Giver (IRE)**[30] 3145 2-9-1 80.................................. RPCleary 2 18
(J S Bolger, Ire) [illegible] **50/1**

1m 15.81s (-2.79) **Going Correction** -0.325s/f (Firm) **7** Ran SP% **115.4**
Speed ratings: **105,101,101,98,92 78,66**
CSF £11.58 TOTE £3.50: £1.90, £2.70; DF 14.50.
Owner Michael Tabor **Bred** Beauty Is Truth Syndicate **Trained** Goolds Cross, Co Tipperary

FOCUS
This Group 3 has gone to some smart performers such as Oratorio and One Cool Cat. Ballydoyle had no outstanding candidate this time but it was still very much a worthy Group 3. The pace was strong.

NOTEBOOK
Fire Lily(IRE) ◆ was the one to beat on the balance of form but there is no doubt but that she improved for the extra furlong - and quite possibly due to the ease in the ground. By Dansili out of a Pivotal mare, the rain was less of a concern for her than others and she travelled strongly, one of the last off the bridle. What was particularly impressive was how she knuckled down when strongly challenged in the final furlong and a half and, at the finish, she was entirely in command. (op 5/2 tchd 3/1)
After(IRE) had looked no star in maidens but the market suggested he would show more here and he burst through to deliver his challenge, which briefly looked a winning one, over a furlong out. (op 9/2)
Boris Grigoriev(IRE) was the surprise of the race and he moved powerfully throughout. He has plenty of raw speed but, like at Navan last time, he had no more to give when it really mattered. That said, he seemed to battle on His trip is probably 5f. (op 12/1 tchd 14/1)
Ishvana(IRE) was not disgraced in a good Cork contest last time and did her connections proud here, despite failing to get black-type placing. She will presumably be trained for that and has the ability to achieve it. (op 16/1)
Fulbright had questions to deal with after the Coventry. In his defence, he was not given a soft time of it up front but he looks a bit limited at Group level. (op 9/2 tchd 5/1)
Zip Top(IRE) was not good at the start and was one of the first horses beaten. He was the subject of plenty of hype around his maiden win but the jury is out after this, for all that he is worth another chance and perhaps the ground was against him. Official explanation: jockey said colt never travelled (op 9/4)

4132a KILBOY ESTATE STKS (GROUP 3) (F&M) 1m 1f
3:10 (3:12) 3-Y-O+ **£36,422** (£10,646; £5,043; £1,681)

RPR
1 **Manieree (IRE)**[38] 2865 3-8-12 100............................(b) NGMcCullagh 11 105
(John M Oxx, Ire) *sn led and clr: reduced advantage bef 1/2-way: kicked clr again over 3f out: rdn 2f out: reduced advantage over 1f out: kpt on wl fnl f* **7/1**[3]

2 *1 3/4* **Kirinda (IRE)**[77] 1734 3-8-12 98 .... JMurtagh 2 102+
(John M Oxx, Ire) *hld up towards rr: mod 10th travelling wl 2f out: rdn into 8th 1f out: r.o wl fnl f to 2nd cl home* **7/1**[3]

3 *1/2* **Claiomh Solais (IRE)**[18] 3527 3-8-12 109 .... KJManning 4 100
(J S Bolger, Ire) *chsd ldrs: 3rd 1/2-way: pushed along over 3f out: rdn in 3rd 2f out: 2nd 1f out: no imp on ldr: kpt on same pce fnl f* **5/1**[2]

4 *nk* **Look At Me (IRE)**[31] 3065 3-8-12 95 .... CO'Donoghue 5 99+
(A P O'Brien, Ire) *hld up towards rr: mod 9th 2f out: rdn into 7th 1f out: kpt on fnl f* **8/1**

5 *1 3/4* **Eirnin (IRE)**[35] 2968 3-8-12 91 .... SeamieHeffernan 9 96
(A P O'Brien, Ire) *chsd ldr in 2nd: pushed along over 3f out: rdn 2f out: no ex in 3rd 1f out: kpt on same pce* **25/1**

6 *hd* **Blaze Brightly (IRE)**[18] 3527 4-9-7 101 .... FMBerry 1 96
(Mrs John Harrington, Ire) *mid-div: 8th 1/2-way: rdn into mod 6th 2f out: no imp and kpt on one pce* **14/1**

7 *1* **Wild Wind (GER)**[31] 3100 3-8-12 106 .... (b[1]) RyanMoore 13 93+
(A P O'Brien, Ire) *chsd ldrs: 4th 1/2-way: rdn 2f out: kpt on: no ex ins fnl f* **2/1**[1]

8 *3 1/2* **Fontley**[12] 3703 4-9-7 .... TomQueally 7 87
(Eve Johnson Houghton) *mid-div: 6th 1/2-way: rdn into mod 5th 2f out: wknd over 1f out* **8/1**

9 *3 1/2* **Asheerah**[21] 3444 3-8-12 98 .... DPMcDonogh 10 78
(Kevin Prendergast, Ire) *chsd ldrs: 5th 1/2-way: rdn in 6th 3f out: no ex and wknd 2f out* **16/1**

10 *2* **Obama Rule (IRE)**[22] 3417 4-9-10 101 .... PJSmullen 6 78
(Ms Joanna Morgan, Ire) *mid-div: 7th 1/2-way: rdn 3f out: wknd 2f out* **16/1**

11 *5 1/2* **Ballybacka Lady (IRE)**[56] 2334 3-9-1 102 .... WJSupple 3 66
(P A Fahy, Ire) *a towards rr* **12/1**

2m 1.53s (6.63) **Going Correction** +0.675s/f (Yiel)
WFA 3 from 4yo 9lb **11** Ran SP% **127.2**
Speed ratings: **97,95,95,94,93 93,92,89,85,84 79**
CSF £60.18 TOTE £9.70: £2.50, £1.80, £1.80; DF 61.50.
Owner Maxwell Morris **Bred** Max Morris **Trained** Currabeg, Co Kildare

FOCUS
This was a good Group 3 which produced a John Oxx one-two, the respective rides given to each arguably deciding the result of the race. The form is rated around the second.

NOTEBOOK
Manieree(IRE) had become a little disappointing but she got her own way in front here to a large degree, slowed it at the right time and Niall McCullagh had left enough to keep the rest at bay in the final two furlongs. She can be rated a lucky winner, but her jockey is having a superb season and he won the race for her. Manieree has probably had her cup final here and the soft ground seems important for her. Certainly making the pace with her seems to suit too.
Kirinda(IRE) ◆ has more natural ability than the winner and she was very unfortunate here. Having looked tricky in previous races, she is not an easy ride and Johnny Murtagh was at pains to restrain her for as long as he could. She was a bit keen, as she often is. That said, she had virtually no chance of winning after finding trouble around two furlongs out, yet Murtagh still bided his time before asking any question. She showed a remarkable burst of pace to finish as close as she did. (op 13/2)
Claiomh Solais(IRE) was niggled a long way out and she had no excuses, as she was in the right place throughout. This is probably as good as she is and there is nothing wrong with her attitude. (op 9/2)
Look At Me(IRE) was finishing better than everything other than the runner-up and ran a good race. Her ideal trip is probably around 1m2f and this was a solid effort; indeed, she should really have finished closer too.
Eirnin(IRE) battled on gamely to run above herself. She was probably the intended pacemaker and will continue to struggle at this level.
Blaze Brightly(IRE) is pretty exposed and had every chance over a trip that may stretch her a little.
Wild Wind(GER) was bitterly disappointing and it was hard to think of an obvious excuse. (op 11/4)

4133a DARLEY IRISH OAKS (GROUP 1) (FILLIES) 1m 4f
3:45 (3:47) 3-Y-0

£212,500 (£69,612; £32,974; £10,991; £7,327; £3,663)

RPR

1 **Blue Bunting (USA)**[44] 2682 3-9-0 .... FrankieDettori 3 115+
(Mahmood Al Zarooni) *mid-div: mod 7th 1/2-way: hdwy into 5th 3f out: rdn 2f out: swtchd to outer over 1f out: r.o wl fnl f to ld on line* **5/2**[2]

2 *shd* **Banimpire (IRE)**[31] 3065 3-9-0 110 .... KJManning 5 114
(J S Bolger, Ire) *settled bhd ldrs: mod 5th 1/2-way: hdwy into 3rd 3f out: led 2f out: rdn over 1f out: strly pressed and kpt on fnl f: hdd on line* **8/1**

3 *1/2* **Wonder Of Wonders (USA)**[44] 2682 3-9-0 111 .... RyanMoore 6 113
(A P O'Brien, Ire) *settled bhd ldrs: mod 6th 1/2-way: hdwy into 4th 3f out: impr to chal 2f out: rdn 1 1/2f out: kpt on and ev ch ins fnl f: no ex cl home* **5/4**[1]

4 *shd* **Laughing Lashes (USA)**[56] 2334 3-9-0 111 .... FMBerry 4 113
(Mrs John Harrington, Ire) *hld up towards rr: hdwy in 6th 3f out: rdn in 4th 2f out: rdr lost whip over 1f out: styd on to chal and ev ch ins fnl f: no ex cl home* **15/2**

5 *1 3/4* **Dancing Rain (IRE)**[44] 2682 3-9-0 .... JMurtagh 7 110
(William Haggas) *settled bhd ldrs: mod 4th 1/2-way: hdwy in 2nd 3f out: led over 2 1/2f out: rdn and hdd 2f out: no ex in 4th 1f out: kpt on same pce* **5/1**[3]

6 *3* **Gemstone (IRE)**[35] 2968 3-9-0 98 .... (b[1]) CO'Donoghue 2 105
(A P O'Brien, Ire) *hld up towards rr: hdwy into 7th 3f out: rdn in 6th 2f out: no imp over 1f out: kpt on same pce* **80/1**

7 *23* **Rumh (GER)**[31] 3065 3-9-0 .... PJSmullen 9 69
(Saeed Bin Suroor) *chsd ldrs in 3rd: impr to ld over 3f out: rdn and hdd over 2 1/2f out: no ex and wknd: t.o* **33/1**

8 *26* **Hurricane Havoc (IRE)**[38] 2865 3-9-0 97 .... RPCleary 1 27
(J S Bolger, Ire) *sn disp: 2nd 1/2-way: led 5f out: rdn and hdd over 3f out: sn wknd: completely t.o* **100/1**

9 *11* **Amazing Beauty (IRE)**[35] 2968 3-9-0 96 .... JPO'Brien 8 9
(A P O'Brien, Ire) *led and disp: rdn 1/2-way: hdd 5f out: wknd 4f out: completely t.o* **66/1**

2m 42.97s (4.47) **Going Correction** +0.675s/f (Yiel) **9** Ran SP% **119.2**
Speed ratings: **112,111,111,111,110 108,93,75,68**
CSF £23.26 TOTE £3.70: £1.40, £2.20, £1.02; DF 26.50.
Owner Godolphin **Bred** B M Kelley **Trained** Newmarket, Suffolk

FOCUS
A spell-binding finish to a fine race in which Frankie Dettori timed it just right on the winner. The first three were pretty much ignored and it tuned into something of a sprint, so that is the main proviso about this form. The sixth also limits it, but Blue Bunting is rated closer to her Guineas form.

NOTEBOOK
Blue Bunting(USA) was held up worse than midfield, had every chance once they turned in to the straight, but looked as though she was struggling to pick up around two furlongs out. She then finally kicked into gear, powered home in the final furlong and got up in the shadow of the post to credit Dettori with another victory in this race. She conclusively stayed the trip and talk of the Leger is not surprising. She flashes her tail and has the odd quirk - she seemed to be going nowhere here until Dettori pulled her out. It hardly looks a vintage St Leger and she would be a contender. (op 7/2)

Banimpire(IRE) has been a remarkable improver and one had to feel sorry for her. Quite whether a mile and a half on easy ground is entirely ideal for her is still questionable, but she showed just how good she is and looked to have mastered her rivals, until the winner's dramatic late burst.

Wonder Of Wonders(USA) was noticeably easy in the market, though one could also argue - and plenty did - that she was underpriced all week. The big question was how the Kingmambo filly would handle conditions and, perhaps, it cost her the race. Ryan Moore never looked entirely happy on her and, though she got to dispute the lead a long way out and rallied under pressure, she never quite looked like getting there. No doubt she will get another chance to prove that she can win a Group 1. (op 6/4)

Laughing Lashes(USA) ◆ was the revelation of the race, the rider's loss of the whip perhaps costing her a place. She stayed the trip, or at least virtually all of it, and this gives connections new options. (op 7/1)

Dancing Rain(IRE) ran a respectable race, her Oaks victory denied the credit it would usually get due to the brilliance of the ride, and she was never going to have it so easy here. She handles an ease but her stamina is probably stretched over this trip when conditions are soft. (op 4/1)

Gemstone(IRE) ran another good race and has possibilities at a lesser level over this trip. She goes well on easy ground. (op 100/1)

4135a BRADY'S MERCEDES BENZ ROCKINGHAM H'CAP (PREMIER HANDICAP) 5f
4:50 (4:52) 3-Y-0+

£41,379 (£13,103; £6,206; £2,068; £1,379; £689)

RPR

1 **Captain Carey**[22] 3410 5-9-2 92 .... FMBerry 3 100
(Malcolm Saunders) *prom on outer: cl 3rd 1/2-way: disp 2f out: rdn to ld narrowly last 100yds: all out cl home* **5/1**[1]

2 *hd* **Cheviot (USA)**[21] 3440 5-9-5 95 .... (p) NGMcCullagh 8 102+
(Reginald Roberts, Ire) *mid-div: hdwy in 7th 2f out: rdn into 4th 1f out: styd on wl fnl f: jst failed* **13/2**[3]

3 *1 3/4* **Your Gifted (IRE)**[2] 4046 4-8-4 82 5ex .... KieranO'Neill[(5)] 4 86
(Patrick Morris) *prom and disp: cl 2nd 1/2-way: led 2f out: sn disp: rdn and hdd last 100yds: no ex and kpt on same pce* **14/1**

4 *nk* **Empirico (FR)**[5] 3961 5-8-4 80 oh3 .... ShaneFoley 5 80
(David Marnane, Ire) *chsd ldrs: rdn in 4th 2f out: 3rd 1f out: no ex ins fnl f: kpt on same pce* **16/1**

5 *shd* **Maarek**[21] 3440 4-8-11 87 .... SeamieHeffernan 15 86
(David Peter Nagle, Ire) *chsd ldrs: rdn in 6th 2f out: 5th 1f out: no ex ins fnl f: kpt on same pce* **5/1**[1]

6 *1/2* **Tornadodancer (IRE)**[7] 3893 8-8-4 80 .... (b) BACurtis 10 77
(T G McCourt, Ire) *chsd ldrs: rdn in 5th 2f out: no ex in 6th 1f out: kpt on same pce* **16/1**

7 *3* **Collingwood (IRE)**[21] 3440 9-9-0 90 .... (bt) WMLordan 13 77
(T M Walsh, Ire) *towards rr: rdn 2f out: sme late hdwy fnl f* **8/1**

8 *nk* **Kolokol (IRE)**[346] 4773 4-9-12 102 .... DaneO'Neill 9 88
(Henry Candy) *in rr of mid-div: rdn and no imp 2f out: kpt on same pce* **14/1**

9 *1 3/4* **Confessional**[8] 3846 4-9-3 93 .... (b) PJSmullen 12 72
(Tim Easterby) *towards rr: rdn into 7th 1f out: no ex fnl f* **6/1**[2]

10 *1 1/4* **Look Busy (IRE)**[51] 2480 6-9-4 94 .... (p) CDHayes 7 69
(P J Prendergast, Ire) *mid-div best: rdn and no imp 2f out* **8/1**

11 *1* **Airspace (IRE)**[23] 3372 5-8-4 87 .... CPHoban[(7)] 11 58
(M Halford, Ire) *led: rdn and hdd 2f out: no ex and wknd* **7/1**

12 *nk* **Anadolu (IRE)**[63] 2128 3-9-4 98 .... (b) MCHussey 2 67
(Tracey Collins, Ire) *mid-div best: rdn and no ex 2f out* **33/1**

13 *20* **Patrickswell (IRE)**[14] 3665 7-8-3 84 .... (p) LFRoche[(5)] 6 —
(Marcus Callaghan, Ire) *mid-div: rdn and wknd 2f out: eased fnl f and t.o* **20/1**

59.63 secs (-2.87) **Going Correction** -0.325s/f (Firm)
WFA 3 from 4yo+ 4lb **13** Ran SP% **128.5**
Speed ratings: **109,108,105,105,105 104,99,99,96,94 92,92,60**
CSF £39.77 CT £449.34 TOTE £5.80: £2.00, £2.40, £3.60; DF 46.50.

Owner M S Saunders **Bred** Barry Walters **Trained** Green Ore, Somerset

FOCUS
A seventh win for Captain Carey and the first on slow ground for the 5yo all of whose wins have been achieved over the minimum trip.

NOTEBOOK
Captain Carey came up the centre of the track and was always in the firing line, disputing the lead from 2f out and edging ahead inside the final furlong. He was being reeled in late on but held on. (op 13/2)

Cheviot(USA), up 2lb since finishing second in a valuable 6f handicap here last month, made headway 2f out and ran on well for pressure inside the final furlong. He was closing all the way to the line and the drop back in trip probably wasn't ideal on this ground. (op 6/1 tchd 11/2)

Your Gifted(IRE) was making a quick reappearance having scored over the trip at Haydock only two days previously. A six-time winner, all at this distance, she probably wasn't ideally suited by the ground but she showed plenty of dash and disputed the lead before edging ahead 2f out. She gave best inside the final furlong. (op 14/1 tchd 12/1)

Empirico(FR) ran his best race for some time. Soon close up, he came under pressure under 2f out and could raise no extra in the closing stages. (op 33/1)

Maarek, bidding for his third win of the season and suited by ease, has been creeping up the ratings. He chased the front runners and kept on for pressure from 2f out without getting to the leaders. (op 5/1 tchd 11/2)

Patrickswell(IRE) Official explanation: jockey said gelding became upset in the stalls, missed the break and returned with a cut on his face

4134a, 4136 - 4137a (Foreign Racing) - See Raceform Interactive

3209 DUSSELDORF (R-H)

Sunday, July 17

OFFICIAL GOING: Turf: soft

4138a GRAFENBERGER MEILEN TROPHY (GROUP 2) (3YO+) (TURF) — 1m

4:00 (12:00) 3-Y-0+

£34,482 (£13,362; £5,603; £3,448; £2,155; £1,293)

RPR

1 — **Alianthus (GER)**[22] [3422] 6-9-6 0 .... ADeVries 1 — 117
(J Hirschberger, Germany) *broke fast to ld: set only stdy pce: qckndd down bk st to go 4 l clr: r.o wl in st: rdn hands and heels to fin: comf* **4/5**[1]

2 ¾ **Emerald Commander (IRE)**[22] [3422] 4-9-6 0 .... MickaelBarzalona 2 — 115
(Saeed Bin Suroor) *broke wl: settled bhd ldr: swung wd ent st then wandered off st crse down st: r.o wl fnl f* **21/10**[2]

3 1 ¼ **Set The Trend**[48] [2558] 5-9-6 0 .... LiamKeniry 4 — 112
(Andrew Balding) *settled in 3rd: rdn to chal early in st: threatened briefly but no real danger to first two ins fnl f* **113/10**

4 4 **Le Big (GER)**[22] [3422] 7-9-6 0 .... AHelfenbein 6 — 103
(U Stoltefuss, Germany) *bkmarker fr s: rdn early in st but no threat to ldrs: only passing btn horses* **144/10**

5 nk **Lips Poison (GER)**[28] [3209] 3-8-9 0 .... DavyBonilla 5 — 98
(Andreas Lowe, Germany) *broke wl to r 4th: pulling freely: rdn early in st but sn fdd* **47/10**[3]

6 hd **Nice Danon**[35] 3-8-13 0 .... ASuborics 3 — 101
(A Wohler, Germany) *racd midfield: nvr proged in st* **97/10**

7 2 **Sanjii Danon (GER)**[22] [3422] 5-9-6 0 .... APietsch 7 — 97
(W Hickst, Germany) *settled towards rr and nvr threatened in st* **218/10**

1m 38.78s (-2.38)
WFA 3 from 4yo+ 8lb — 7 Ran SP% **133.7**
WIN (incl. 10 euro stake): 18. PLACES: 10, 10, 11. SF: 37.
Owner Baron G Von Ullmann **Bred** Gestut Karlshof **Trained** Germany

NOTEBOOK
Emerald Commander(IRE) stepped up on his reappearance effort at Hamburg but didn't help his rider by continually hanging. He would have given the winner more to think about had he kept straight, and the plan is to look for a similar race for him now.
Set The Trend, a Listed winner at Goodwood last time out, ran well on this step up in class, keeping on well for third and well clear of the rest. He could well return to Germany for a mile race at Baden-Baden.

3899 AYR (L-H)

Monday, July 18

OFFICIAL GOING: Good to soft (good in places; 8.6)
Wind: Slight, half behind Weather: Cloudy, bright

4140 BRITISH STALLION STUDS SUPPORTING BRITISH RACING E B F MAIDEN STKS — 7f 50y

2:30 (2:31) (Class 4) 2-Y-O — £4,463 (£1,328; £663; £331) Stalls High

Form — RPR

40 1 — **Fresa**[12] [3736] 2-8-12 0 .... StevieDonohoe 6 — 68+
(Sir Mark Prescott Bt) *t.k.h: hld up in tch: rdn 2f out: hdwy: drifted lft and led ins fnl f: styd on strly* **10/1**

2222 2 1 ¼ **Joshua The First**[4] [4012] 2-9-3 0 .... (v) TomEaves 8 — 70
(Keith Dalgleish) *trckd ldrs: rdn: edgd lft and ev ch over 1f out: wnt 2nd towards fin: nt rch wnr* **10/3**[2]

3 3 ½ **Rasputin (IRE)**[15] [3656] 2-9-3 0 .... FrederikTylicki 7 — 69
(Michael Dods) *trckd ldr: led over 2f out to ins fnl f: kpt on same pce: lost 2nd towards fin* **4/1**[3]

4 2 ¼ **Sygnature** 2-9-3 0 .... PJMcDonald 1 — 63+
(Alan Swinbank) *s.i.s: t.k.h: hld up: effrt and swtchd rt wl over 1f out: styd on fnl f: nrst fin* **6/1**

0 5 2 ¾ **Eraada**[40] [2811] 2-8-12 0 .... TadhgO'Shea 4 — 51
(Mark Johnston) *hld up in tch: rdn over 3f out: edgd lft and styd on fnl f: no imp* **5/2**[1]

6 6 1 ½ **Altnaharra**[7] [3899] 2-9-3 0 .... DanielTudhope 3 — 53
(Jim Goldie) *sn pushed along in rr: rdn 3f out: sme late hdwy: nvr on terms* **50/1**

00 7 2 **Blue Ridges (IRE)**[19] [3504] 2-8-9 0 .... MichaelO'Connell(3) 2 — 43
(Geoffrey Harker) *led: rdn and hdd over 2f out: wknd appr fnl f* **33/1**

6 8 ¾ **Nayef Flyer**[33] [3035] 2-8-12 0 .... LeeTopliss(5) 5 — 46
(Richard Fahey) *trckd ldrs: rdn over 2f out: wknd over 1f out* **8/1**

9 46 **Endangered Species** 2-9-3 0 .... TonyHamilton 9 — —
(John Weymes) *dwlt: rn green in rr: sn lost tch: t.o* **66/1**

1m 35.22s (1.82) **Going Correction** +0.20s/f (Good) — 9 Ran SP% **112.5**
Speed ratings (Par 96): **97,95,95,92,89 87,85,84,31**
Tote Swingers: 1&2 £4.00, 1&3 £6.20, 2&3 £1.70 CSF £41.95 TOTE £12.20: £3.20, £1.30, £1.50; EX 32.60.
Owner Miss K Rausing **Bred** Miss K Rausing **Trained** Newmarket, Suffolk

FOCUS
Back straight out 4m, home bend out 6m, and home straight out 8m from innermost line adding 18yds to races over 7f and beyond. A bright, sunny day but after 30mm of rain over the previous days the ground rode on the dead side. Quite an interesting 7f juvenile maiden and straightforward form with the runner-up and third setting the standard.

NOTEBOOK
Fresa, whose first two outings were over 6f on the all-weather, is a well-made filly with some size and scope. After taking a bump at the start, she had to be switched round the errant Joshua The First to make her final effort. She was firmly in command at the line and, likely to improve again, will be even better suited by a mile. (op 14-1 tchd 8-1)
Joshua The First, having his seventh start, finished runner-up for the fifth time in succession. Wearing a visor for the third time, he ducked right under pressure but stuck on to snatch second spot near the line. He does not look entirely straightforward, but must surely break his duck at some stage. (op 7-2 tchd 4-1)
Rasputin(IRE), a neck behind Joshua The First when they were second and third over this C&D, took it up over a furlong out but could not see it out. They ran their form to a pound. (op 11-4)
Sygnature, one of the first crop of Authorised, was slow to find stride. He put in some solid late work and will improve a good deal, especially if stepped up to a mile. (op 9-1 tchd 10-1)
Eraada, closely related to a Dubai World Cup winner, still looks immature. Checked in her stride over a furlong out, she will be suited by a mile and with her pedigree would be very interesting if tried on Polytrack. (op 9-4)
Altnaharra struggled to go the pace, but picked up very late on. He needs another outing to qualify for a handicap mark and he too will be suited by a step up to a mile. (tchd 66-1)
Blue Ridges(IRE) was much too keen in front and stopped to nothing in the final furlong. (op 25-1)
Nayef Flyer came in for support, but if anything went backwards after showing limited promise on his debut behind Joshua The First at Hamilton. (op 14-1)

4141 POLYFLOR H'CAP (QUALIFIER FOR BETFAIR BONUS SCOTTISH RACING MILE FINAL) — 7f 50y

3:00 (3:01) (Class 5) (0-75,75) 3-Y-0+ — £4,204 (£1,251; £625; £312) Stalls High

Form — RPR

4665 1 — **Sabratha (IRE)**[20] [3485] 3-8-3 62 ow3 .... JulieBurke(5) 3 — 74
(Linda Perratt) *hld up: hdwy and squeezed through wl over 1f out: kpt on wl fnl f: led nr fin* **6/1**[2]

0240 2 shd **Dhhamaan (IRE)**[12] [3733] 6-8-11 58 .... (b) PJMcDonald 9 — 72
(Ruth Carr) *led: rdn 2f out: kpt on wl u.p: hdd nr fin* **14/1**

2052 3 5 **Berbice (IRE)**[7] [3902] 6-9-3 64 .... TonyHamilton 5 — 65
(Linda Perratt) *hld up in midfield on ins: hdwy over 2f out: rdn over 1f out: one pce fnl f* **17/2**[3]

40-0 4 nk **Touch Tone**[16] [3620] 4-9-13 74 .... FrederikTylicki 8 — 74
(Michael Dods) *hld up: hdwy on outside over 2f out: kpt on fnl f: no imp* **20/1**

3120 5 nk **Hayek**[10] [3805] 4-9-4 65 .... (b) DavidAllan 11 — 64
(Tim Easterby) *s.i.s: bhd: hdwy on wd outside 2f out: kpt on u.p fnl f: nvr able to chal* **6/1**[2]

0342 6 nk **Music Festival (USA)**[15] [3657] 4-9-7 68 .... DanielTudhope 1 — 66
(Jim Goldie) *in tch: effrt and rdn over 2f out: no ex fr over 1f out* **9/2**[1]

5352 7 2 ½ **Just The Tonic**[6] [3936] 4-9-0 61 .... DuranFentiman 2 — 53
(Marjorie Fife) *sn cl up: rdn over 2f out: wknd over 1f out* **6/1**[2]

045- 8 1 ¼ **Benny The Bear**[261] [7225] 4-8-8 58 oh1 ow2 .... PatrickDonaghy(3) 10 — 46
(Linda Perratt) *stdd s: t.k.h in rr: rdn over 2f out: nvr on terms* **33/1**

4-01 9 1 **Spes Nostra**[31] [3111] 3-9-7 75 .... LeeNewman 6 — 58
(David Barron) *trckd ldrs tl rdn and wknd wl over 1f out* **9/2**[1]

3-60 10 1 ¾ **Social Rhythm**[9] [3859] 7-9-1 65 .... MichaelO'Connell(3) 4 — 46
(Alistair Whillans) *hld up: rdn over 2f out: nvr on terms* **33/1**

-000 11 5 **Haadeeth**[13] [3704] 4-9-4 70 .... (b) LeeTopliss(5) 14 — 37
(Richard Fahey) *cl up tl rdn and wknd qckly* **14/1**

-060 12 shd **Horatio Carter**[19] [3506] 6-9-10 71 .... (p) TomEaves 12 — 38
(Michael Smith) *prom tl rdn and wknd fr 2f out* **14/1**

1m 34.13s (0.73) **Going Correction** +0.20s/f (Good)
WFA 3 from 4yo+ 7lb — 12 Ran SP% **120.4**
Speed ratings (Par 103): **103,102,97,96,96 96,93,91,90,88 83,82**
Tote Swingers: 1&2 £16.10, 1&3 £12.70, 2&3 £25.10 CSF £86.34 CT £727.25 TOTE £7.40: £2.10, £4.40, £2.40; EX 124.90.
Owner Shatin Racing Group **Bred** Adrian Purvis **Trained** East Kilbride, S Lanarks

FOCUS
A modest 7f handicap run at a sound pace thanks to the runner-up. The runner-up is rated in line with his best turf form.
Spes Nostra Official explanation: trainer's representative was unable to offer any explanation for the poor performance shown

4142 AYRSHIRE POST H'CAP (QUALIFIER FOR BETFAIR SCOTTISH RACING MILE FINAL) — 1m 2f

3:30 (3:30) (Class 5) (0-70,70) 3-Y-0+ — £4,204 (£1,251; £625; £312) Stalls Low

Form — RPR

-033 1 — **Persian Peril**[46] [2656] 7-9-12 68 .... PJMcDonald 2 — 77
(Alan Swinbank) *trckd ldrs: smooth hdwy over 2f out: led over 1f out: rdn out fnl f* **7/1**[2]

6032 2 1 ¼ **Focail Maith**[3] [4060] 3-9-4 70 .... StevieDonohoe 10 — 76
(John Ryan) *prom: effrt and hdwy over 2f out: ev ch over 1f out: kpt on ins fnl f* **5/2**[1]

-650 3 ½ **Free Art**[12] [3729] 3-9-1 70 .... MichaelO'Connell(3) 1 — 75
(Geoffrey Harker) *in tch: effrt and chsd ldrs over 1f out: sn drvn: kpt on u.p ins fnl f* **33/1**

-401 4 nk **Jewelled Dagger (IRE)**[7] [3906] 7-9-5 61 .... TomEaves 4 — 65
(Keith Dalgleish) *led: rdn over 2f out: hdd over 1f out: kpt on same pce fnl f* **5/2**[1]

052 5 nk **Grethel (IRE)**[4] [3658] 7-8-9 51 oh6 .... PatrickMathers 3 — 66?
(Alan Berry) *dwlt: hld up: effrt and drvn along over 2f out: edgd lft and kpt on ins fnl f* **66/1**

-230 6 ¾ **Grand Diamond (IRE)**[19] [2887] 7-9-10 66 .... (p) DanielTudhope 7 — 68
(Jim Goldie) *t.k.h in midfield: rdn over 2f out: kpt on fnl f: nvr able to chal* **14/1**

4463 7 2 ¼ **Royal Straight**[9] [3859] 6-9-3 64 .... JulieBurke(5) 6 — 62
(Linda Perratt) *s.i.s: hld up: rdn over 2f out: kpt on: nvr rchd ldrs* **7/1**[2]

2200 8 2 **Dar Es Salaam**[10] [3828] 7-9-7 68 .... (v) LeeTopliss(5) 5 — 62
(Brian Ellison) *hld up: hdwy in to midfield after 4f: rdn over 2f out: sn no imp* **14/1**

5214 9 3 ½ **Hits Only Jude (IRE)**[3] [4039] 8-9-3 64 .... (v) NeilFarley(5) 11 — 51
(Declan Carroll) *sn bhd: drvn over 2f out: nvr on terms* **11/1**[3]

0-00 10 3 ½ **Stags Leap (IRE)**[15] [3659] 4-9-11 67 .... TonyHamilton 9 — 47
(Alistair Whillans) *chsd ldr: rdn 3f out: wknd over 1f out* **28/1**

00-6 11 14 **Sheedal (IRE)**[7] [3903] 3-7-13 51 oh6 .... DuranFentiman 8 — —
(Linda Perratt) *plld hrd: hld up: rdn along 3f out: sn struggling: t.o* **80/1**

2m 13.28s (1.28) **Going Correction** +0.20s/f (Good)
WFA 3 from 4yo+ 10lb — 11 Ran SP% **112.9**
Speed ratings (Par 103): **102,101,100,100,100 99,97,96,93,90 79**
Tote Swingers: 1&2 £4.70, 1&3 £17.10, 2&3 £24.20 CSF £23.30 CT £537.71 TOTE £8.70: £2.30, £1.40, £6.70; EX 23.60.
Owner Mrs J Porter **Bred** Mrs P Lewis **Trained** Melsonby, N Yorks
■ Stewards' Enquiry : Neil Farley one-day ban: used whip when out of contention (1 Aug)

FOCUS
A modest 1m2f handicap run at a strong pace. The form is rated at face value although there are some doubts.

4143 HAMILTON ADVERTISER H'CAP (QUALIFIER FOR BETFAIR SCOTTISH RACING MILE) — 1m

4:00 (4:00) (Class 6) (0-65,63) 3-Y-0+ — £2,587 (£770; £384; £192) Stalls Low

Form — RPR

5000 1 — **Abernethy (IRE)**[9] [3859] 3-8-2 45 .... DuranFentiman 9 — 53
(Linda Perratt) *hld up: nt clr run briefly over 2f out: hdwy on outside wl over 1f out: led ins fnl f: drvn out* **40/1**

0001 2 nk **Focail Eile**[12] [3741] 6-10-0 63 .... StevieDonohoe 2 — 72
(John Ryan) *in tch: nt clr run over 3f out to over 2f out: hdwy over 1f out: pressed wnr ins fnl f: kpt on but a hld* **3/1**[2]

4232 **3** 2 3/4 **Glenluji**[3] 4039 6-9-9 **58** .... DanielTudhope 5 61
(Jim Goldie) *in tch: hdwy to ld over 1f out: hdd ins fnl f: kpt on same pce* **15/8**[1]

0214 **4** 7 **Classic Descent**[21] 3462 6-9-11 **60** ....(bt) PJMcDonald 4 47
(Ruth Carr) *hld up: hdwy over 2f out: rdn and rdr dropped whip wl over 1f out: sn no imp* **11/2**[3]

3-60 **5** 3/4 **Broughtons Silk**[21] 3454 6-8-10 **45** .... TonyHamilton 12 30
(Alistair Whillans) *led: rdn over 2f out: hdd over 1f out: wknd fnl f* **25/1**

1-00 **6** 3/4 **Gadobout Dancer**[12] 3741 4-9-1 **55** .... NeilFarley(5) 11 38
(Declan Carroll) *midfield on outside: effrt and drvn over 2f out: wknd over 1f out* **14/1**

0 **7** 8 **Honest And True (IRE)**[9] 3859 4-9-5 **57** .... PatrickDonaghy(3) 1 22
(Ian Semple) *chsd ldr tl rdn and wknd over 2f out* **12/1**

3303 **8** 3/4 **Shunkawakhan (IRE)**[7] 3903 8-8-13 **53** ....(p) LeeTopliss(5) 10 16
(Linda Perratt) *t.k.h: cl up tl rdn and wknd 2f out* **8/1**

5005 **9** 7 **Rosbertini**[7] 3902 5-8-10 **45** .... LeeNewman 13 —
(Linda Perratt) *s.i.s: bhd: rdn over 2f out: btn over 1f out* **20/1**

0000 **10** nk **Cold Quest (USA)**[21] 3454 7-8-12 **47** .... TomEaves 8 —
(Linda Perratt) *cl up tl rdn and wknd over 2f out* **40/1**

1m 46.79s (2.99) **Going Correction** +0.20s/f (Good)
WFA 3 from 4yo+ 8lb **10** Ran SP% **114.1**
Speed ratings (Par 101): **93,92,89,82,82 81,73,72,65,65**
Tote Swingers: 1&2 £33.10, 1&3 £16.70, 2&3 £2.40 CSF £150.33 CT £347.93 TOTE £32.40: £8.10, £2.00, £1.30; EX 275.30.
Owner Ken McGarrity **Bred** Glenlogan Park Stud **Trained** East Kilbride, S Lanarks

FOCUS
The rain arrived ahead of this low-grade mile handicap. There was a shock result, although the placed form makes sense.
Abernethy(IRE) Official explanation: trainer said, regarding the apparent improvement of form, that the gelding benefitted from being held up in this race

4144 RUTHERGLEN REFORMER H'CAP (QUALIFIER FOR BETFAIR BONUS SCOTTISH RACING SPRINT FINAL) 5f
4:30 (4:30) (Class 6) (0-65,65) 3-Y-O+ **£2,587** (£770; £384; £192) **Stalls** High

Form RPR

4251 **1** **Wicked Wilma (IRE)**[4] 4017 7-9-8 **61** 6ex.... PatrickMathers 8 71
(Alan Berry) *trckd ldrs: effrt and drvn over 1f out: edgd lft: led ins fnl f: r.o wl* **5/1**[3]

1430 **2** 1 1/2 **Ballarina**[39] 2832 5-9-9 **62** .... DavidAllan 5 67
(Eric Alston) *disp ld: rdn 2f out: kpt on ins fnl f: nt pce of wnr* **4/1**[1]

0000 **3** 3/4 **Grand Stitch (USA)**[34] 3027 5-9-4 **62** ....(v) NeilFarley(5) 9 64
(Declan Carroll) *trckd ldrs: rdn over 2f out: kpt on ins fnl f* **16/1**

0000 **4** hd **Blown It (USA)**[20] 3489 5-8-10 **49** .... TomEaves 7 50
(Keith Dalgleish) *slt ld tl rdn and hdd ins fnl f: kpt on same pce* **9/2**[2]

625/ **5** 1 1/4 **Glenlini**[742] 3678 5-9-4 **60** .... GaryBartley(3) 10 57
(Jim Goldie) *hld up: pushed along and hdwy over 1f out: kpt on fnl f: nvr able to chal* **8/1**

-000 **6** 1/2 **Classlin**[7] 3901 4-8-7 **46** oh1.... AndrewMullen 11 41
(Jim Goldie) *dwlt: bhd and pushed along: hdwy over 1f out: no imp fnl f* **25/1**

5005 **7** 5 **Chosen One (IRE)**[7] 3901 6-9-12 **65** .... PJMcDonald 4 42
(Ruth Carr) *prom: rdn along 1/2-way: struggling fnl 2f* **5/1**[3]

135- **8** 1/2 **Embra (IRE)**[250] 7390 6-9-2 **58** .... MichaelO'Connell(3) 2 33
(Tim Etherington) *dwlt: sn pushed along in rr: struggling fr 1/2-way* **8/1**

0506 **9** 2 **Sandwith**[21] 3451 8-9-5 **58** ....(v) LeeNewman 6 26
(George Foster) *in tch: rdn and hung lft over 2f out: sn btn* **9/1**

60.47 secs (1.07) **Going Correction** +0.075s/f (Good) **9** Ran SP% **113.5**
Speed ratings (Par 101): **100,97,96,96,94 93,85,84,81**
Tote Swingers: 1&2 £3.40, 1&3 £12.00, 2&3 £19.30 CSF £24.83 CT £296.23 TOTE £4.90: £2.00, £2.10, £5.10; EX 16.80.
Owner Mrs Thelma White **Bred** Gerry O'Sullivan **Trained** Cockerham, Lancs

FOCUS
A low-grade sprint handicap and modest form rated around the first three.
Sandwith Official explanation: jockey said gelding anticipated the start and hit his nose on the gates

4145 PAISLEY DAILY EXPRESS H'CAP (QUALIFIER FOR BETFAIR BONUS SCOTTISH RACING SPRINT FINAL) 6f
5:00 (5:01) (Class 5) (0-70,68) 3-Y-O+ **£4,204** (£1,251; £625; £312) **Stalls** High

Form RPR

2242 **1** **Royal Blade (IRE)**[4] 4000 4-8-2 **49** oh3.... JulieBurke(5) 3 61
(Alan Berry) *mde all: pushed along over 1f out: kpt on wl fnl f* **9/1**

3323 **2** 1 **Beckermet (IRE)**[15] 3657 9-9-11 **67** .... PJMcDonald 12 76
(Ruth Carr) *cl up: rdn over 2f out: chsd wnr fnl f: r.o* **11/2**[2]

2350 **3** 2 **Ingleby Arch (USA)**[24] 3359 8-9-6 **67** .... LMcNiff(5) 9 70
(David Barron) *rdr slow to remove blindfold: sn chsng ldng gp: effrt over 1f out: styd on fnl f: nrst fin* **7/1**

5500 **4** shd **Bond Fastrac**[9] 3880 4-9-12 **68** ....(v) FrederikTylicki 2 70
(Geoffrey Oldroyd) *in tch on outside: drvn over 2f out: edgd rt and styd on fnl f* **6/1**[3]

6045 **5** 2 **Northern Dare (IRE)**[20] 3488 7-9-2 **63** ....(b) LeeTopliss(5) 7 59
(Richard Fahey) *trckd ldrs: rdn over 2f out: no ex over 1f out* **16/1**

3004 **6** 3/4 **Burnwynd Boy**[15] 3657 6-9-1 **57** .... LeeNewman 11 50
(Ian Semple) *cl up tl rdn and wknd over 1f out* **8/1**

0020 **7** nk **Mullglen**[10] 3832 5-9-11 **67** ....(p) DavidAllan 8 60
(Tim Easterby) *bhd: effrt and swtchd to outside over 2f out: nvr rchd ldrs* **12/1**

5313 **8** 3/4 **Eternal Instinct**[7] 3900 4-9-6 **65** .... GaryBartley(3) 10 55
(Jim Goldie) *hld up: pushed along 2f out: sn no imp* **10/1**

0011 **9** 3/4 **Monel**[15] 3661 3-9-2 **63** .... DanielTudhope 5 50
(Jim Goldie) *bhd: pushed along 1/2-way: shortlived effrt 2f out: sn btn* **3/1**[1]

-500 **10** 6 **Tadalavil**[9] 3856 6-9-6 **65** .... TomEaves 4 34
(Linda Perratt) *cl up tl rdn and wknd wl over 1f out* **16/1**

5040 **11** 12 **Lady Del Sol**[13] 3702 3-9-5 **66** ....(be) StevieDonohoe 6 —
(Marjorie Fife) *chsd ldng gp: rdn 1/2-way: wknd 2f out* **33/1**

1m 13.59s (1.19) **Going Correction** +0.075s/f (Good)
WFA 3 from 4yo+ 5lb **11** Ran SP% **119.8**
Speed ratings (Par 103): **103,101,99,98,96 95,94,93,92,84 68**
Tote Swingers: 1&2 £5.20, 1&3 £11.50, 2&3 £7.60 CSF £59.02 CT £379.93 TOTE £10.60: £3.60, £1.90, £2.80; EX 59.20.
Owner A B Parr **Bred** Miss Sarah Sands **Trained** Cockerham, Lancs

FOCUS
Another low-grade sprint handicap and the form is a bit shaky, being best rated around the placed horses.
Ingleby Arch(USA) Official explanation: jockey said that he was unable to remove the blindfold on his first attempt due to the gelding being restless
Monel Official explanation: jockey said that the gelding was never travelling

4146 EAST KILBRIDE NEWS H'CAP (QUALIFIER FOR BETFAIR BONUS SCOTTISH RACING SPRINT FINAL) 6f
5:30 (5:32) (Class 6) (0-60,63) 3-Y-O **£2,587** (£770; £384; £192) **Stalls** High

Form RPR

2501 **1** **Spinatrix**[2] 4110 3-9-10 **63** 6ex.... FrederikTylicki 10 77+
(Michael Dods) *mde all: pushed along and qcknd clr 2f out: kpt on strly: unchal* **5/2**[2]

0003 **2** 9 **Hardrock Diamond**[9] 3860 3-8-8 **47** .... DuranFentiman 2 32
(Ian Semple) *bhd: swtchd rt after 2f: effrt and hdwy over 1f out: styd on to take 2nd cl home: no ch w wnr* **11/2**[3]

6-50 **3** nk **Tinzo (IRE)**[15] 3661 3-8-7 **46** oh1.... PatrickMathers 3 30
(Alan Berry) *dwlt: bhd and sn pushed along: hdwy 2f out: chsd (clr) wnr ins fnl f: lost 2nd cl home* **50/1**

45-0 **4** 2 1/2 **Myjestic Melody (IRE)**[29] 3207 3-8-11 **53** .... MichaelO'Connell(3) 11 29
(Noel Wilson) *cl up tl rdn and no ex over 1f out* **7/1**

6002 **5** 5 **Rutterkin (USA)**[6] 3950 3-8-13 **59** .... VictorSantos(7) 5 19
(Alan Berry) *in tch: shkn up whn n.m.r over 1f out: sn no imp* **14/1**

-040 **6** 3 3/4 **Whats For Pudding (IRE)**[21] 3457 3-8-5 **49** ....(b) NeilFarley(5) 4 —
(Declan Carroll) *in tch: drvn 1/2-way: wknd wl over 1f out* **11/1**

0600 **7** 8 **Country Waltz**[9] 3860 3-9-0 **53** ....(p) TonyHamilton 9 —
(Linda Perratt) *walked to post: prom: drvn 1/2-way: wknd fr 2f out* **18/1**

206 **8** 3/4 **Brian Sprout**[11] 3785 3-9-2 **55** .... PJMcDonald 6 —
(John Weymes) *towards rr: drvn and edgd lft 1/2-way: sn btn* **14/1**

-334 **9** 2 1/2 **Guinea Seeker**[16] 3616 3-9-7 **60** .... DavidAllan 1 —
(Tim Easterby) *cl up: sn rdn along: wknd over 1f out: eased whn btn fnl f* **2/1**[1]

1m 14.04s (1.64) **Going Correction** +0.075s/f (Good) **9** Ran SP% **118.7**
Speed ratings (Par 98): **100,88,87,84,77 72,61,60,57**
Tote Swingers: 1&2 £3.60, 1&3 £9.30, 2&3 £10.30. Tote Super 7: Win: Not won. Place: £1,631.00. CSF £17.42 CT £555.26 TOTE £2.90: £1.40, £2.70, £10.20; EX 17.90.
Owner Mrs J W Hutchinson & Mrs P A Knox **Bred** T K & Mrs P A Knox **Trained** Denton, Co Durham
■ Stewards' Enquiry : Frederik Tylicki one-day ban: excessive use of whip (31th July)

FOCUS
A low-grade 3-y-os-only sprint, but a wide-margin winner. The form could rate higher if taken literally but the level looks weak.
Rutterkin(USA) Official explanation: jockey said colt was denied a clear run
Guinea Seeker Official explanation: trainer's representative was unable to offer any explanation for the poor performance shown
T/Plt: £99.70 to a £1 stake. Pool £73,943.99 - 541.01 winning units T/Qpdt: £14.90 to a £1 stake. Pool £5,830.90 - 288.84 winning units RY

3931 BEVERLEY (R-H)
Monday, July 18
OFFICIAL GOING: Good (good to soft in places)
Wind: fresh across Weather: overcast

4147 WELCOME TO YORKSHIRE DELICIOUS TRAILS CLAIMING STKS 5f
6:30 (6:31) (Class 5) 2-Y-O **£2,385** (£704; £352) **Stalls** Low

Form RPR

1 **Class Monitor** 2-8-12 0.... AndrewElliott 7 60+
(Mrs K Burke) *s.i.s: chsd ldrs after 1f: rdn 2f out: led ent fnl f: kpt on: rdn out* **11/4**[2]

6022 **2** 1 1/2 **Beechey's Beauty**[19] 3505 2-9-5 0....(p) SilvestreDeSousa 6 62
(Ann Duffield) *led for 2f: prom: rdn to ld again jst over 1f out: hdd ent fnl f: kpt on same pce* **9/4**[1]

0 **3** 3/4 **Wish Again (IRE)**[33] 3050 2-9-2 0.... AdrianNicholls 5 56+
(David Nicholls) *s.i.s: chsd ldrs after 1f: rdn whn outpcd 2f out: styd on ins fnl f: wnt 3rd fnl stride* **25/1**

0 **4** hd **Dandy's Hero (IRE)**[16] 3610 2-9-0 0.... BarryMcHugh 3 54
(David Nicholls) *led after 2f: rdn 2f out: sn hdd: ev ch ent fnl f: kpt on same pce* **7/2**[3]

5 1/2 **No More Games** 2-9-5 0.... PhillipMakin 2 57+
(Kevin Ryan) *dwlt: outpcd and detached: styd on ent fnl f: nrst fin* **7/1**

6 **6** 1 1/4 **Uncle Timmy**[16] 3611 2-9-5 0.... PaulHanagan 1 52
(John Quinn) *prom: rdn to ld briefly over 1f out: ev ch ent fnl f: fdd fnl 120yds* **6/1**

360 **7** 1 1/4 **Rhianna Brianna (IRE)**[30] 3165 2-8-11 0.... JamesSullivan 4 40
(Michael Easterby) *little slowly away: sn chsng ldrs: c centre over 2f out: sn rdn and hung lft to nr-side rails but hld ch: wknd ent fnl f* **16/1**

65.74 secs (2.24) **Going Correction** +0.05s/f (Good) **7** Ran SP% **116.2**
Speed ratings (Par 94): **84,81,80,80,79 77,75**
Tote Swingers: 1&2 £1.80, 1&3 £12.60, 2&3 £13.20 CSF £9.71 TOTE £3.30: £2.90, £1.10; EX 11.40.Class Monitor was subject to a friendly claim. Dandy's Hero was claimed by Claes Bjorling for £10,000.
Owner Leydens Farm Stud **Bred** Leydens Farm Stud **Trained** Middleham Moor, North Yorks

FOCUS
Bottom bend moved out for fresh ground but impact on distances not advised. They stayed towards the far side, but the main action unfolded away from the rail. There was a three-way contest for the early lead, with Beechey's Beauty, Dandy's Hero and Uncle Timmy going off quickly. The runner-up looks the best guide to the level.

NOTEBOOK
Class Monitor, a well-backed debutante (around 10-1 in the morning) from an in-form yard, stayed on best having held a good position. There wasn't a great deal to go on pedigree-wise, but she travelled like a horse a bit better than this level and found enough for pressure, despite understandably looking green off the bridle. She looks a nice type for nurseries as she ought to start off at a manageable level. (op 5-2)
Beechey's Beauty was runner-up for the third consecutive race, but he didn't do much wrong, faring best of those who contested the early lead. (tchd 5-2)
Wish Again(IRE), beaten a long way in a maiden on his debut, shaped better this time but just took too long to pick up. He might be worth a try over 6f. (op 20-1)
Dandy's Hero(IRE) ◆ showed speed but he stuck more towards the far rail than the front three and gradually faded. An easier 5f might help. (op 5-1)
No More Games, an £8,000 purchase out of a 6f winner, made a sluggish start and struggled for most of the way, but he kept on reasonably well. He should learn from this and can win a race. (op 6-1)
Uncle Timmy didn't step up as expected on his debut effort, but he did plenty of racing early and also stuck closest to the far rail, so he might be worth another chance. (op 8-1)

 The Form Book, Raceform Ltd, Compton, RG20 6NL

Rhianna Brianna(IRE) Official explanation: jockey said that the filly hung left

4148 JOANNA STEVENSON MEMORIAL H'CAP 1m 1f 207y
7:00 (7:01) (Class 5) (0-75,73) 3-Y-O+ £2,264 (£673; £336; £168) Stalls Low

Form RPR
6233 1 **Amazing Blue Sky**[13] 3701 5-9-11 **70** JamesSullivan 2 79
(Ruth Carr) *led for 3f: trckd ldr: led over 2f out: styd on strly fnl f: pushed out* 11/4[1]
41-0 2 4 **Rockweiller**[18] 3545 4-9-5 **64** (v) RobertWinston 3 65
(Steve Gollings) *trckd ldr for 3f: cl 3rd: rdn 3f out: chsd wnr 2f out: styd on same pce* 5/1
0505 3 1 ½ **Come And Go (UAE)**[12] 3732 5-8-12 **60** PaulPickard(3) 5 58
(Ian McInnes) *hld up: hdwy fr 3f out: sn rdn: wnt 3rd ent fnl f: styd on wout threatening ldrs* 16/1
-224 4 ¾ **Munaawer (USA)**[17] 3572 4-9-4 **63** PhillipMakin 8 60
(James Bethell) *in tch: rdn over 3f out: disp 3rd over 1f out: no ex fnl f* 7/2[3]
4300 5 4 **Prime Mover**[38] 2885 3-9-1 **70** PaulHanagan 7 59
(Ed Dunlop) *plld v hrd: led after 3f: rdn 3f out: sn hdd: wknd ent fnl f* 3/1[2]
3234 6 nse **Beat Route**[12] 3739 4-9-5 **69** JemmaMarshall(5) 6 57
(Michael Attwater) *in tch: rdn 3f out: wknd 1f out* 7/1
0064 7 7 **Baltimore Jack (IRE)**[40] 2800 7-8-13 **58** GrahamGibbons 4 32
(G P Kelly) *s.i.s: sn pushed along in last: nvr any imp* 22/1

2m 7.19s (0.19) **Going Correction** 0.0s/f (Good)
WFA 3 from 4yo+ 10lb 7 Ran SP% **113.3**
Speed ratings (Par 103): **99,95,94,94,90 90,85**
Tote Swingers: 1&2 £2.50, 1&3 £11.90, 2&3 £7.30 CSF £16.54 CT £180.49 TOTE £3.70: £1.70, £2.70; EX 22.10.
Owner Graham Scruton **Bred** Hong Kong Breeders Club **Trained** Huby, N Yorks

FOCUS
A modest handicap run at a steady pace. The winner is rated back to his best.
Prime Mover Official explanation: jockey said that the gelding ran too free
Baltimore Jack(IRE) Official explanation: jockey said that the gelding ran in snatches

4149 SKY BET SUPPORTING THE YORKSHIRE RACING SUMMER FESTIVAL H'CAP 7f 100y
7:30 (7:30) (Class 6) (0-65,62) 3-Y-O £1,811 (£539; £269; £134) Stalls Low

Form RPR
0-60 1 **Last Destination (IRE)**[54] 2406 3-9-3 **58** SilvestreDeSousa 1 68
(Nigel Tinkler) *mid-div: rdn and stdy hdwy fr wl over 2f out: sn hung rt: led ent fnl f: drifted rt: kpt on wl* 3/1[1]
0-60 2 3 **Cottam Stella**[2] 4110 3-8-10 **51** RobertWinston 6 54
(Mel Brittain) *hld up: rdn 3f out: no imp tl styd on wl fr over 1f out: fin strly to snatch 2nd fnl stride* 8/1
0001 3 hd **Twennyshortkid**[21] 3455 3-8-10 **51** (v) BarryMcHugh 7 53
(Paul Midgley) *trckd ldrs: rdn 3f out: styd on to chal ent fnl f: sn hld by wnr: no ex whn lost 2nd fnl stride* 10/3[2]
0046 4 2 ¼ **Prince Of Passion (CAN)**[12] 3729 3-9-7 **62** PaulHanagan 8 58
(Michael Dods) *led: rdn and hrd pressed fr 3f out: kpt on tl hdd ent fnl f: hmpd sn after: no ex* 7/1
5-03 5 1 ½ **Queen's Choice (IRE)**[17] 3594 3-8-13 **54** StephenCraine 5 47
(Anabel K Murphy) *hld up: rdn over 2f out: styd on fr over 1f out: nvr trbld ldrs* 9/2[3]
600 6 ¾ **Langtoon Lass**[11] 3756 3-8-11 **52** AdrianNicholls 4 43
(David Nicholls) *trckd ldrs: rdn 3f out: nt pce to get on terms: fdd ins fnl f* 20/1
0003 7 6 **Formidable Girl (USA)**[21] 3455 3-8-10 **51** (tp) PhillipMakin 9 27
(Kevin Ryan) *sn trcking ldr: rdn to chal 3f out tl jst over 1f out: fdd* 6/1
1464 8 18 **Slatey Hen (IRE)**[148] 620 3-9-2 **60** RobertLButler(3) 3 —
(Richard Guest) *mid-div tl wknd over 2f out* 20/1

1m 34.73s (0.93) **Going Correction** 0.0s/f (Good) 8 Ran SP% **113.7**
Speed ratings (Par 98): **94,90,90,87,86 85,78,57**
Tote Swingers: 1&2 £9.70, 1&3 £2.00, 2&3 £5.70 CSF £27.07 CT £82.72 TOTE £3.60: £2.00, £2.00, £1.90; EX 21.70.
Owner A Killoran **Bred** Pier House Stud **Trained** Langton, N Yorks

FOCUS
A moderate handicap and the pace was a bit too quick. The third looks the best guide to the level.
Last Destination(IRE) Official explanation: trainer said regarding the apparent improvement of form, that the gelding appreciated the drop in drip

4150 TYREGIANT.COM H'CAP 1m 100y
8:00 (8:00) (Class 5) (0-75,74) 3-Y-O+ £2,587 (£770; £384; £192) Stalls Low

Form RPR
0623 1 **Seldom (IRE)**[6] 3936 5-9-0 **60** RobertWinston 9 68
(Mel Brittain) *trckd ldrs: rdn 2f out: led jst over 1f out: kpt on wl* 7/2[1]
5604 2 1 **Ours (IRE)**[17] 3576 8-10-0 **74** (p) BarryMcHugh 6 80
(John Harris) *hld up in last 4: pushed along and hdwy fr over 2f out: rdn over 1f out: styd on ins fnl f: wnt 2nd nr fin* 5/1[2]
3011 3 hd **Salient**[11] 3763 7-10-0 **74** J-PGuillambert 2 79
(Michael Attwater) *trckd ldr: pushed into ld over 2f out: edgd rt u.p and hdd jst over 1f out: kpt on but no ex* 7/2[1]
5-43 4 shd **Bright Applause**[14] 3679 3-8-5 **62** PaulPickard(3) 1 65
(Tracy Waggott) *trckd ldrs: rdn over 2f out: swtchd off rails whn nt clr run over 1f out: styd on fnl f* 7/1
05 5 4 **Carlitos Spirit (IRE)**[3] 4039 7-8-11 **57** SilvestreDeSousa 7 53
(Ian McInnes) *pushed into early ld: rdn 3f out: hdd over 2f out: kpt chsng ldr tl no ex ent fnl f* 5/1[2]
406 6 1 **Dabbers Ridge (IRE)**[10] 3831 9-9-10 **70** PaulHanagan 3 64
(Ian McInnes) *hld up last: pushed along and sme hdwy over 2f out: sn rdn: styd on same pce: nvr a threat* 11/2[3]
000 7 4 ½ **Prices Lane**[17] 3577 4-8-11 **57** JamesSullivan 5 40
(Michael Easterby) *hld up: pushed along and hdwy over 3f out: rdn over 2f out: nvr rchd ldrs: wknd fnl f* 33/1
5000 8 20 **Unbreak My Heart (IRE)**[131] 806 6-9-8 **71** (p) RobertLButler(3) 8 —
(Richard Guest) *hld up: rdn over 3f out: wknd over 2f out: t.o* 14/1

1m 46.99s (-0.61) **Going Correction** 0.0s/f (Good)
WFA 3 from 4yo+ 8lb 8 Ran SP% **115.3**
Speed ratings (Par 103): **103,102,101,101,97 96,92,72**
Tote Swingers: 1&2 £3.40, 1&3 £1.90, 2&3 £3.70 CSF £21.38 CT £65.32 TOTE £5.70: £1.20, £3.20, £1.10; EX 21.80.
Owner Mel Brittain **Bred** Stephen Moloney **Trained** Warthill, N Yorks

FOCUS
A competitive handicap and the pace was strong. The form looks reasonable, rated around the first four.

Carlitos Spirit(IRE) Official explanation: jockey said that the gelding hung right throughout

4151 YORKSHIRE POST MAIDEN H'CAP 2m 35y
8:30 (8:30) (Class 6) (0-65,62) 3-Y-O £1,617 (£481; £240; £120) Stalls Low

Form RPR
0605 1 **Mina's Boy**[47] 2613 3-8-12 **53** RoystonFfrench 5 61
(Ed Dunlop) *awkward leaving stalls: sn trcking ldrs: lost pl whn outpcd over 3f out: styd on u.str.p fr over 1f out: fin strly to ld nr fin* 4/1[3]
2554 2 ½ **Body Language (IRE)**[20] 3487 3-9-7 **62** SilvestreDeSousa 2 69
(Ann Duffield) *trckd ldrs: led over 6f out: rdn over 2f out: jst over 3 l clr ent fnl f: no ex whn hdd fnl strides* 7/2[2]
0462 3 3 ¼ **Market Maker (IRE)**[24] 2801 3-8-11 **52** (b) RobertWinston 4 55
(Tim Easterby) *hld up in last pair: hdwy to chse ldr 3f out: sn rdn: styng on at same pce and hld in 3rd whn sltly hmpd ins fnl f* 11/4[1]
0353 4 hd **Commander Veejay**[21] 3460 3-8-4 **45** (p) AndrewHeffernan 6 48
(Brian Rothwell) *hld up last: hdwy over 3f out: sn rdn to chse ldng pair: styd on same pce fnl 2f* 17/2
-504 5 18 **Geminus (IRE)**[21] 3460 3-9-1 **56** PhillipMakin 7 37
(Jedd O'Keeffe) *prom: hmpd 10f out: reminders sn after: rdn 6f out: wknd over 2f out: eased fnl f* 7/2[2]
-536 6 7 **Hartforth**[47] 2613 3-9-5 **60** (p) GrahamGibbons 1 33
(James Bethell) *led: looked at path and rn wd on stable bnd 10f out: rdn over 3f out: wknd over 2f out: eased fnl f* 7/1

3m 39.74s (-0.06) **Going Correction** 0.0s/f (Good) 6 Ran SP% **114.1**
Speed ratings (Par 98): **100,99,98,98,89 85**
Tote Swingers: 1&2 £2.30, 1&3 £4.00, 2&3 £1.80 CSF £18.68 TOTE £3.00: £1.10, £1.30; EX 16.60.
Owner P A Deal, G Lowe & M J Silver **Bred** Hermes Services Ltd **Trained** Newmarket, Suffolk

FOCUS
A proper test for these 3-y-os in this maiden handicap. The form is sound but moderate, although the winner can rate higher.
Mina's Boy ◆ Official explanation: trainer's representative said, regarding the apparent improvement in for, that he had been gelded since his last run, having run well last time, and he was suited by the step up in trip.
Geminus(IRE) Official explanation: jockey said that the gelding was never travelling

4152 CHARLY CHUCKLEBUS H'CAP 5f
9:00 (9:02) (Class 5) (0-75,74) 3-Y-O+ £2,264 (£673; £336; £168) Stalls Low

Form RPR
3066 1 **Red Roar (IRE)**[18] 3541 4-8-12 **60** RoystonFfrench 10 70
(Alan Berry) *a.p: rdn 2f out: slt advantage ent fnl f: kpt on: all out* 9/1
2040 2 nk **Caranbola**[9] 3880 5-9-8 **70** SilvestreDeSousa 7 79
(Mel Brittain) *a.p: rdn 2f out: ev ch thrght fnl f: kpt on* 11/4[2]
2323 3 nk **Ingleby Star (IRE)**[11] 3759 6-9-4 **69** (p) PaulPickard(3) 9 77
(Ian McInnes) *led w narrow advantage: rdn 2f out: hdd ent fnl f: rallied gamely and ev ch tl no ex nr fin* 15/2[3]
135 4 ¾ **Electioneer (USA)**[56] 2352 4-9-2 **64** GrahamGibbons 12 69
(Michael Easterby) *chsd ldrs: rdn over 2f out: nt quite upsides 1f out: kpt on same pce* 9/1
0523 5 3 **Galpin Junior (USA)**[6] 3937 5-8-8 **56** JamesSullivan 5 50
(Ruth Carr) *chsd ldrs: rdn 2f out: nt pce to chal: no ex ins fnl f* 5/2[1]
50-0 6 1 ½ **Avertuoso**[35] 2987 7-9-0 **69** (v) JustinNewman(7) 2 58
(Bryan Smart) *slowly away: towards rr: sme hdwy u.p 2f out: no further imp fr over 1f out* 18/1
3562 7 1 ¾ **Desert Strike**[12] 3737 5-9-6 **68** (p) RobertWinston 8 51
(Alan McCabe) *wnt rt and sltly hmpd leaving stalls: sn chsng ldrs: rdn over 2f out: wknd fnl f* 14/1
0206 8 shd **Ryedane (IRE)**[16] 3617 9-8-12 **65** (b) LanceBetts(5) 1 47
(Tim Easterby) *a towards rr: nvr pce to get involved* 8/1
6-00 9 hd **Commanche Raider (IRE)**[10] 3832 4-9-10 **72** PhillipMakin 3 54
(Michael Dods) *cl up whn hmpd ins 1st f: sn towards rr and nvr able to get bk on terms* 20/1
1-04 10 1 ¾ **Bertie Southstreet**[16] 3640 8-9-7 **69** (v) MickyFenton 4 44
(Paul Midgley) *chsd ldrs: rdn 2f out: wknd ent fnl f* 20/1

63.26 secs (-0.24) **Going Correction** +0.05s/f (Good) 10 Ran SP% **119.6**
Speed ratings (Par 103): **103,102,102,100,96 93,90,90,90,87**
Tote Swingers: 1&2 £3.40, 1&3 £1.90, 2&3 £3.70 CSF £34.89 CT £197.92 TOTE £12.00: £4.10, £1.70, £1.90; EX 46.90.
Owner Sporting Kings **Bred** Tally-Ho Stud **Trained** Cockerham, Lancs

FOCUS
The impression throughout the evening that the far rail was best avoided was borne out here, with the three runners from the widest stalls all finishing in the top four. The form is rated around the placed horses.
T/Plt: £40.10 to a £1 stake. Pool £60,925.60 - 1,108.14 winning units T/Qpdt: £14.50 to a £1 stake. Pool £5,343.02 - 271.66 winning units TM

3914 WINDSOR (R-H)
Monday, July 18

OFFICIAL GOING: Good
Wind: Light, behind Weather: Cloudy with occasional showers

4153 CHRIS DAGLEY MEMORIAL CLASSIFIED (S) STKS 1m 3f 135y
6:10 (6:11) (Class 6) 3-Y-O+ £1,617 (£481; £240; £120) Stalls Centre

Form RPR
2261 1 **Eagle Nebula**[23] 3391 7-9-8 64 KierenFox(3) 4 65
(Brett Johnson) *hld up in rr: plenty to do whn prog over 3f out: wnt 2nd 2f out: rdn to cl 1f out: styd on u.p to ld nr fin* 11/2[3]
4161 2 nk **Urban Kode (IRE)**[3] 4071 3-8-8 63 (v) KieranO'Neill(5) 3 64
(David Evans) *led: clr w one rival 4f out: kicked on and taken to far rail 3f out: hdd u.p nr fin* 11/4[1]
450 3 1 **Tiger Tess**[22] 3437 3-8-8 53 NeilChalmers 8 58
(Jonathan Portman) *fractious preliminaries: awkward s: hld up last pair: plenty to do whn prog over 3f out: wnt 3rd wl over 1f out: cl enough 1f out but nt qckn: kpt on* 22/1
0006 4 10 **What About Now**[14] 3690 3-8-8 53 (p) MartinDwyer 2 41
(J W Hills) *chsd ldr: clr w him 4f out: drvn and lost 2nd 2f out: wkng whn hmpd sn after* 11/2[3]
3011 5 3 ½ **Dew Reward (IRE)**[7] 3916 3-8-13 60 (p) AdamKirby 6 40
(Bill Turner) *chsd ldng pair: pushed along 5f out: sn outpcd: lost 3rd over 2f out: wknd* 3/1[2]
6004 6 2 ¾ **Meglio Ancora**[7] 3916 4-9-6 64 (p) EddieAhern 7 30
(Jonathan Portman) *hld up in rr: brief effrt and limited prog 3f out: no hdwy and wl btn 2f out* 6/1

0006 **7** *27* **Rio Prince**[9] 3872 4-9-6 46..............................(vt) CathyGannon 1 —
(John Bridger) *trckd ldrs: pushed along 5f out: sn lost pl and btn: t.o and eased over 1f out* **33/1**

1624 **8** *23* **Lytham (IRE)**[7] 3923 10-9-11 57.. LukeMorris 5 —
(Tony Carroll) *t.k.h: hld up in rr: struggling over 3f out: eased whn no ch 2f out: t.o* **14/1**

2m 31.07s (1.57) **Going Correction** +0.10s/f (Good)
WFA 3 from 4yo+ 12lb **8** Ran SP% **110.7**
Speed ratings (Par 101): **98,97,97,90,88 86,68,52**
Tote Swingers: 1&2 £3.50, 1&3 £8.60, 2&3 £10.00 CSF £19.62 TOTE £6.20: £2.40, £1.20, £5.30; EX 29.00 Trifecta £420.90 Pool: £6,052.38 - 10.64 winning units..The winner was bought in for £4,800. Urban Kode waas claimed by Ollie Pears for £5,000.
Owner Tann Racing **Bred** Juddmonte Farms Ltd **Trained** Ashtead, Surrey

FOCUS
Stands rail dolled out 12yds at 6f and 6yds at Winning Post. Top bend out 3yds from normal configuration adding 17yds to races of 1m and over. The going had eased a tad, being changed to good, from good to firm, before the opening race. Although there was no soft in the description, the field ventured far side for this seller. The form is weak and a bit fluid, so is rated negatively.
Dew Reward(IRE) Official explanation: jockey said that the gelding hung right and was unsuited by the Good ground
Meglio Ancora Official explanation: jockey said that the gelding hung left

4154 NATIONAL BRAIN APPEAL AND ASOS H'CAP 1m 2f 7y
6:40 (6:41) (Class 5) (0-70,69) 3-Y-0+ **£2,264** (£673; £336; £168) **Stalls** Centre

Form RPR
5241 **1** **One Hit Wonder**[10] 3814 4-9-11 **66**.. LiamKeniry 10 74+
(Jonathan Portman) *prom: waiting to chal fr 3f out gng easily: produced fnl f: drvn ahd last 100yds and fnd enough* **11/2**[1]

2304 **2** *½* **Kishanda**[35] 3002 3-8-5 **61**.. KieranO'Neill(5) 1 68
(Hughie Morrison) *settled in midfield: prog on outer over 2f out: hanging lft u.p over 1f out: styd on fnl f to take 2nd nr fin* **11/2**[1]

52-0 **3** *nk* **Green Wadi**[184] 174 6-9-11 **66**.. GeorgeBaker 9 73
(Gary Moore) *hld up in midfield: stdy prog 3f out: gng strly over 2f out: rdn to ld over 1f out: hdd and nt qckn last 100yds* **10/1**

-562 **4** *1 ¼* **Oriental Girl**[22] 3426 6-10-0 **69**..............................(p) SteveDrowne 2 73
(Jonathan Geake) *hld up in last pair: pushed along 4f out: gd prog on outer over 2f out: tried to cl on ldrs fnl f: nt qckn* **10/1**

5-64 **5** *1* **Supa Seeker (USA)**[35] 2996 5-9-8 **63**.. AdamKirby 13 65
(Tony Carroll) *hld up in last trio: reminder 4f out: prog over 2f out: chsd ldrs and hrd rdn over 1f out: one pce* **15/2**[3]

3401 **6** *shd* **Sasheen**[22] 3426 4-10-0 **69**..............................(p) DarryllHolland 12 71
(Jeremy Gask) *led: drvn over 2f out: hdd over 1f out: fdd fnl f* **9/1**

64-0 **7** *2 ½* **Present Story**[33] 3042 4-8-13 **57**.. MarkLawson(3) 7 54
(Gary Harrison) *cl up: drvn to press ldr against far rail over 2f out: wknd over 1f out* **66/1**

1605 **8** *1 ½* **Inquisitress**[6] 3943 7-8-12 **53**..............................(v) CathyGannon 6 47
(John Bridger) *settled in last pair: cajoled along fr 3f out: plugged on fnl 2f: nvr a threat* **25/1**

2166 **9** *nk* **Byrd In Hand (IRE)**[10] 3814 4-9-0 **58**.. SeanLevey(3) 8 51
(John Bridger) *hld up towards rr: gng wl enough 3f out: sltly impeded over 2f out: drvn and no imp on ldrs over 1f out: fdd* **12/1**

4511 **10** *7* **Gud Day (IRE)**[32] 3077 3-9-3 **68**.. LukeMorris 3 47
(Ronald Harris) *mostly in midfield: in tch over 2f out: hung lft and fnd nil after: sn btn* **8/1**

40-2 **11** *7* **Frederick William**[35] 3002 3-9-4 **69**.. FergusSweeney 11 34
(Peter Makin) *racd wd in midfield: no prog over 2f out: wknd wl over 1f out* **6/1**[2]

40-0 **12** *43* **Fidler Bay**[31] 3130 5-9-4 **64**.. AmyScott(5) 4 —
(Henry Candy) *prom: rdn 1/2-way: sn lost pl: t.o* **40/1**

-005 **13** *2 ¼* **Conjuror's Bluff**[14] 3688 3-9-4 **69**.. RichardHughes 5 —
(Richard Hannon) *chsd ldrs: wknd rapidly jst over 2f out: sn virtually p.u: t.o* **14/1**

2m 9.93s (1.23) **Going Correction** +0.10s/f (Good)
WFA 3 from 4yo+ 10lb **13** Ran SP% **118.2**
Speed ratings (Par 103): **99,98,98,97,96 96,94,93,93,87 81,47,45**
Tote Swingers: 1&2 £9.00, 1&3 £5.90, 2&3 £21.50 CSF £34.01 CT £298.74 TOTE £5.40: £2.00, £3.30, £4.60; EX 49.90 Trifecta £632.90 Pool: £3113.55 - 3.64 winning units..
Owner More Money Than Sense Partnership **Bred** Elsdon Farms **Trained** Compton, Berks

FOCUS
A modest handicap in which the field again raced far side in the straight, suggesting the ground was slower than the official description. The form looks sound with the winner confirming his latest Newbury form, and the fourth and sixth close to recent Salisbury efforts.
Gud Day(IRE) Official explanation: jockey said that the gelding hung left
Conjuror's Bluff Official explanation: jockey said that the colt lost his action

4155 BRITISH STALLIONS STUDS E B F SPORTINGBET.COM MAIDEN FILLIES' STKS 6f
7:10 (7:11) (Class 5) 2-Y-0 **£3,557** (£1,058; £529; £264) **Stalls** Low

Form RPR
1 **Free Verse** 2-9-0 0.. RichardHughes 4 82+
(Richard Hannon) *mde all: wl in command over 1f out: shkn up fnl f: comf* **9/2**[2]

0 **2** *1 ½* **Elusive Flame**[52] 2467 2-9-0 0.. DavidProbert 7 77
(David Elsworth) *hld up in midfield: prog 2f out: rdn over 1f out: styd on fnl f: tk 2nd post* **11/2**[3]

3 *nse* **Salford Art (IRE)** 2-9-0 0.. DaneO'Neill 8 76+
(David Elsworth) *dwlt: sn wl in tch in midfield: prog 1/2-way: rdn to chse wnr jst over 1f out: no imp: lost 2nd post* **14/1**

0 **4** *3* **Lovage**[18] 3547 2-9-0 0.. SteveDrowne 1 67
(Roger Charlton) *mostly chsd wnr: rdn and no imp 2f out: lost 2nd and fdd jst over 1f out* **3/1**[1]

6 **5** *nk* **Guava**[31] 3117 2-9-0 0.. PatDobbs 6 66
(Richard Hannon) *prom: rdn to dispute 2nd 2f out: no imp over 1f out: fdd fnl f* **14/1**

0230 **6** *1 ½* **Meloneras**[32] 3092 2-9-0 0.. JamesMillman 12 62
(Rod Millman) *prom: rdn over 2f out: no imp over 1f out: wknd fnl f* **13/2**

7 *1 ¾* **Emmuska** 2-8-9 0.. KieranO'Neill(5) 3 57
(Richard Hannon) *dwlt: sn in tch: effrt on outer over 2f out: no imp on ldrs over 1f out* **25/1**

8 *nk* **Semayyel (IRE)** 2-9-0 0.. PhilipRobinson 2 56
(Clive Brittain) *s.s: sn in tch in rr: effrt on outer over 2f out: no imp over 1f out* **7/1**

9 *1 ¾* **Remix (IRE)** 2-9-0 0.. DarryllHolland 13 51
(J W Hills) *a towards rr: in tch but pushed along 1/2-way: no prog after* **40/1**

0 **10** *1 ¼* **Anginola (IRE)**[32] 3092 2-9-0 0.. EddieCreighton 10 47
(Joseph Tuite) *dwlt: hld up in rr: shkn up and no prog 2f out: wl hld after* **66/1**

11 *shd* **Diamond Belle** 2-9-0 0.. TomQueally 14 47
(Noel Quinlan) *a in rr: in tch over 2f out: no prog after* **14/1**

12 *hd* **Heartsong (IRE)** 2-9-0 0.. FergusSweeney 15 46
(John Gallagher) *s.s and wnt lft: sn in tch in rr: no prog 2f out: wl hld after* **100/1**

0 **13** *½* **Auntie Kathryn (IRE)**[21] 3463 2-9-0 0.. SaleemGolam 5 44
(Stuart Williams) *chsd ldrs: wl in tch jst over 2f out: shkn up and wknd wl over 1f out* **80/1**

06 **14** *½* **Superinjunction**[12] 3736 2-9-0 0.. MartinDwyer 11 43
(Brian Meehan) *in tch in rr: no prog 2f out: wl hld after* **20/1**

1m 14.07s (1.07) **Going Correction** +0.10s/f (Good) **14** Ran SP% **119.2**
Speed ratings (Par 91): **100,98,97,93,92 91,89,88,86,84 84,84,83,83**
Tote Swingers: 1&2 £7.10, 1&3 £9.30, 2&3 £24.50 CSF £27.66 TOTE £3.30: £1.30, £2.40, £5.00; EX 37.80 Trifecta £822.40 Part won. Pool: £1,111.45 - 0.70 winning units..
Owner The Queen **Bred** The Queen **Trained** East Everleigh, Wilts

FOCUS
Runners eventually worked their way over to the far side. The winner can do better and the placed horses ran pleasing races.

NOTEBOOK
Free Verse certainly knew her job and led throughout. A daughter of Danehill Dancer whose dam was a 1m2f winner, she always seemed to be readily holding her rivals and won with a fair bit in hand, suggesting she'll be well worth her place in a better grade. (op 11-4)
Elusive Flame, well held in a good Newmarket maiden on her debut, showed much-improved form with that run under her belt. She had clearly learned a lot from that initial effort and can win a maiden, with 7f expected to suit. (op 10-1)
Salford Art(IRE) ◆ wasn't the best away and showed signs of greenness but made an encouraging mid-race move, suggesting she has a good deal of ability. It will be disappointing if she doesn't go close next time. (op 16-1)
Lovage probably ran to a similar level as on her debut, holding every chance this time and simply not looking good enough. Perhaps the slight ease in the going was against her. (tchd 10-3 in a place)
Guava stepped up on her initial effort and looks a likely type for handicaps. (op 20-1)
Meloneras is probably best switched to nurseries. (op 15-2)
Emmuska, a daughter of Sir Percy, showed a bit of ability on her debut and ought to be suited by 7f. (op 20-1)
Semayyel(IRE), a daughter of Green Desert, should leave this form behind now she's had a run. Official explanation: jockey said that the filly missed the break (op 10-1)

4156 SPORTINGBET.COM H'CAP 6f
7:40 (7:42) (Class 4) (0-85,82) 3-Y-0 **£3,557** (£1,058; £529; £264) **Stalls** Low

Form RPR
1-02 **1** **Sirius Prospect (USA)**[30] 3178 3-9-7 **82**.. JimCrowley 7 95
(Dean Ivory) *slowest away: rcvrd on wd outside to ld over 3f out: mde rest: drvn and in command over 1f out: styd on* **7/2**[1]

-105 **2** *1* **Sluggsy Morant**[26] 3269 3-9-1 **76**.. DaneO'Neill 4 86
(Henry Candy) *dwlt: hld up in last pair: shkn up over 2f out: prog over 1f out: r.o to take 2nd ins fnl f: clsd on wnr but nvr able to chal* **7/1**[3]

2413 **3** *2 ¼* **Palais Glide**[49] 2564 3-9-4 **79**.. RichardHughes 1 82
(Richard Hannon) *w ldr to over 3f out: styd handy: effrt 2f out: chsd wnr over 1f out: no imp: lost 2nd ins fnl f: fdd* **6/1**[2]

-063 **4** *1 ½* **Golden Tempest (IRE)**[26] 3283 3-9-4 **82**.. JohnFahy(3) 5 80
(Walter Swinburn) *in tch: shkn up over 2f out: nt qckn wl over 1f out: kpt on* **8/1**

025 **5** *¾* **Crew Cut (IRE)**[21] 3465 3-8-5 **73**.. RaulDaSilva(7) 10 69
(Jeremy Gask) *racd on outer early: sn prom: w wnr over 3f out: rdn over 2f out: fdd and lost 2nd over 1f out* **14/1**

3-31 **6** *hd* **Midnight Feast**[21] 3465 3-9-7 **82**.. LukeMorris 8 77
(Peter Winkworth) *in tch: rdn fr 1/2-way: nt qckn and btn 2f out* **7/2**[1]

0400 **7** *1 ¾* **Penny's Pearl (IRE)**[3] 4048 3-8-11 **77**..............................(t) KieranO'Neill(5) 9 66
(David Evans) *in tch: rdn over 2f out: no hdwy wl over 1f out: fdd* **25/1**

2213 **7** *dht* **Close To The Edge (IRE)**[17] 3598 3-8-13 **77**.............. MartinHarley(3) 3 66
(Alan McCabe) *rrng in stalls bef they opened: dwlt: sn chsd ldrs: rdn over 2f out: wknd over 1f out* **8/1**

6620 **9** *4 ½* **Roman Dancer (IRE)**[17] 3598 3-8-11 **72**.. TomQueally 2 47
(John Gallagher) *led to over 3f out: wknd over 2f out* **11/1**

41-0 **10** *10* **Premium Coffee**[37] 2926 3-9-5 **80**.. CathyGannon 6 23
(Joseph Tuite) *in tch: rdn and wknd over 2f out: t.o* **18/1**

1m 13.9s (0.90) **Going Correction** +0.20s/f (Good) **10** Ran SP% **117.6**
Speed ratings (Par 102): **102,100,97,95,94 94,92,92,86,72**
Tote Swingers: 1&2 £9.60, 1&3 £3.30, 2&3 £11.90 CSF £28.52 CT £146.79 TOTE £4.40: £1.30, £2.70, £1.80; EX 38.30 Trifecta £120.00 Pool: £3,081.67 - 19.00 winning units..
Owner Miss N Yarrow **Bred** Brookdale And Dr Ted Folkerth **Trained** Radlett, Herts

FOCUS
A decent handicap, in which the field headed down the centre in the straight. The time is nothing special compared with the earlier juvenile maiden and the form is not rated too positively, with the third the best guide.

4157 RONNIE SCOTT'S MAIDEN STKS 1m 2f 7y
8:10 (8:13) (Class 5) 3-4-Y-0 **£2,264** (£673; £336; £168) **Stalls** Centre

Form RPR
02 **1** **Anatolian**[22] 3430 3-9-3 0.. FrankieDettori 13 81+
(Mahmood Al Zarooni) *mde most: jnd 3f out: cajoled along and stl hrd pressed 1f out: rdn to narrowly assert last strides* **11/4**[2]

-0 **2** *hd* **Billy Buttons**[93] 1409 3-9-3 0.. LiamKeniry 15 80+
(Andrew Balding) *pressed wnr: chal and upsides fr over 2f out: drvn and stl rt on terms ins fnl f: jst hld nr fin* **14/1**

2 **3** *4 ½* **Word Power**[23] 3385 3-8-12 0.. TomQueally 12 66+
(Sir Henry Cecil) *trckd ldng pair: effrt to chal wl over 2f out: upsides after tl 1f out: wknd* **2/1**[1]

6 **4** *1* **Ashiri (IRE)**[95] 1338 3-9-3 0.. RichardMullen 16 69
(Sir Michael Stoute) *trckd ldrs: shkn up and outpcd over 2f out: rn green and kpt on same pce fnl f* **4/1**[3]

56 **5** *1 ¼* **Wordiness**[25] 3320 3-9-3 0.. FrankieMcDonald 6 66
(Barry Brennan) *t.k.h: hld up in 6th: shuffled along and outpcd over 2f out: shkn up and one pce after: nt disgrad* **33/1**

0 **6** *1 ¼* **Cardrona**[39] 2836 3-8-12 0.. RobertHavlin 10 59
(John Gosden) *chsd ldrs: rdn and outpcd over 2f out: hung lft wl over 1f out: wknd* **14/1**

66 **7** *4 ½* **Charlie Fable (IRE)**[11] 3781 3-9-3 0.. GeorgeBaker 7 55
(Hughie Morrison) *hld up towards rr: effrt on outer 3f out: drvn and sme hdwy 2f out: no prog over 1f out: fdd* **50/1**

00 **8** *shd* **Decana**[35] 3001 3-8-12 0............ TravisBlock 3 49
(Hughie Morrison) *sn restrained into last: nudged along fr 3f out: nvr nr ldrs: do bttr* **100/1**

5 **9** *2 1/4* **The Calling Curlew**[22] 3430 3-9-3 0............ DaneO'Neill 1 50
(Henry Candy) *dwlt: hld up in rr: shkn up 3f out: no prog* **18/1**

10 *nk* **Lily In Pink** 3-8-12 0............ EddieAhern 14 44
(Jonathan Portman) *in tch in midfield: pushed along over 2f out: steadily wknd* **66/1**

4 **11** *2 1/4* **Fairling**[14] 3689 3-8-12 0............ SteveDrowne 11 40
(Hughie Morrison) *nvr bttr than midfield: pushed along and steadily wknd fr over 2f out* **25/1**

0 **12** *4* **Tawseef (IRE)**[28] 3218 3-9-3 0............ WilliamCarson 8 37
(Roy Brotherton) *dwlt: hld up in rr: effrt over 3f out: sn shkn up and wknd* **100/1**

13 *40* **Father Martin (IRE)**[19] 4-9-13 0............ FergusSweeney 4 —
(Richard Phillips) *dwlt: in tch in rr to 4f out: sn wknd: t.o* **125/1**

2m 11.49s (2.79) **Going Correction** +0.10s/f (Good)
WFA 3 from 4yo 10lb **13** Ran SP% **111.6**
Speed ratings (Par 103): **92,91,88,87,86 85,81,81,79,79 77,74,42**
Tote Swingers: 1&2 £7.00, 1&3 £1.10, 2&3 £6.20 CSF £34.64 TOTE £3.40: £1.70, £3.10, £1.10; EX 49.60 Trifecta £48.90 Pool: £577.64 - 8.74 winning units..Palitana was withdrawn. Price at time of withdrawal 14-1. Rule 4 applies to all bets. Deduction - 5p in the pound.
Owner Godolphin **Bred** Darley **Trained** Newmarket, Suffolk

FOCUS
Few got into this ordinary maiden and the form is a bit muddling, and limited by the fifth. The front pair, who disputed the running throughout, drew clear against the far rail inside the final 100 yards.

4158 PENGUIN CLASSIC H'CAP 1m 67y
8:40 (8:41) (Class 5) (0-75,75) 3-Y-O+ £2,264 (£673; £336; £168) Stalls Low

Form RPR

0-03 **1** **Regal Salute**[22] 3437 3-9-2 71............ RichardHughes 6 89+
(Jeremy Noseda) *led 1f: trckd ldr: led again on outer over 2f out: in command whn drvn clr over 1f out: pushed out last 100yds: plenty in hand* **7/2**[1]

004 **2** *4* **Pegasus Again (USA)**[26] 3285 6-9-10 71............ JimCrowley 5 79
(Robert Mills) *hld up in midfield: prog on outer 3f out: chsd wnr jst over 2f out: hanging lft and no ch over 1f out: styd on* **6/1**

3221 **3** *3 1/4* **Miss Bootylishes**[10] 3804 6-9-9 73............ JohnFahy(3) 3 74
(Paul Burgoyne) *hld up in midfield: prog 3f out: chsd ldng pair 2f out: styd on but no match* **4/1**[2]

3-43 **4** *4 1/2* **Alshazah**[19] 3513 3-9-2 71............ JamesMillman 14 59
(Rod Millman) *prog on wd outside to ld after 1f and sn clr: hdd & wknd over 2f out* **9/2**[3]

4-05 **5** *1* **Only You Maggie (IRE)**[26] 3266 4-8-10 60............(v[1]) MarkLawson(3) 4 48
(Gary Harrison) *hld up in last trio: hrd rdn over 3f out and struggling: passed toiling rivals fnl 2f* **28/1**

4100 **6** *1* **Royal Reverie**[21] 3462 3-9-5 74............(v[1]) AdamKirby 9 58
(Walter Swinburn) *s.i.s: hld up in rr: effrt over 3f out: no real prog and btn 2f out* **11/1**

0-54 **7** *1* **Cool Hand Jake**[40] 2816 5-9-9 70............ FergusSweeney 10 53
(Peter Makin) *nvr bttr than midfield: rdn and no prog 3f out: wl btn fnl 2f* **12/1**

0105 **8** *1 3/4* **Bidable**[19] 3514 7-9-11 72............ DavidProbert 13 51
(Bryn Palling) *s.i.s: hld up in last trio: pushed along 1/2-way: no real prog whn rdn 2f out* **25/1**

12-0 **9** *1 1/2* **Crazy Chris**[55] 2378 6-9-11 75............ KierenFox(3) 1 51
(John Flint) *hld up in last trio: shkn up 3f out: sme prog 2f out: sn wknd* **8/1**

0630 **10** *5* **Aflaam (IRE)**[10] 3804 6-9-6 67............ LukeMorris 2 31
(Ronald Harris) *in tch in midfield: drvn 3f out: wknd 2f out* **28/1**

24/0 **11** *9* **Mick's Dancer**[22] 3434 6-9-10 71............ RobertHavlin 11 15
(Richard Phillips) *pressed ldrs: rdn 1/2-way: sn wknd and bhd* **28/1**

1m 44.73s (0.03) **Going Correction** +0.10s/f (Good)
WFA 3 from 4yo+ 8lb **11** Ran SP% **116.0**
Speed ratings (Par 103): **103,99,95,91,90 89,88,86,85,80 71**
Tote Swingers: 1&2 £2.70, 1&3 £2.90, 2&3 £3.10 CSF £23.08 CT £85.08 TOTE £4.50: £2.20, £1.10, £1.90; EX 16.50 Trifecta £13.60 Pool: £595.72 - 32.32 winning units..
Owner Cheveley Park Stud **Bred** Cheveley Park Stud Ltd **Trained** Newmarket, Suffolk

FOCUS
What had looked an open handicap was won quite impressively by Regal Salute. The form is rated at face value with the winner looking progressive, while the third is a pretty solid marker.
T/Plt: £67.40 to a £1 stake. Pool £95,592.87 - 1,034.87 winning units T/Qpdt: £9.80 to a £1 stake. Pool £7,787.31 - 587.56 winning units JN

3954 YARMOUTH (L-H)
Monday, July 18

OFFICIAL GOING: Soft (6.1)
Wind: fresh, across Weather: showers

4159 JACK ATHERTON LIFETIME IN RACING SERIES MEDIAN AUCTION MAIDEN STKS 7f 3y
2:15 (2:16) (Class 6) 2-Y-O £1,617 (£481; £240; £120) Stalls High

Form RPR

4 **1** **Rayvin Black**[30] 3182 2-9-3 0............ KierenFallon 3 76+
(Mark H Tompkins) *trckd ldr tl pushed ahd 2f out: sn readily drew clr: edgd lft but in command fr over 1f out: easily* **5/4**[1]

40 **2** *4 1/2* **Casa Bex**[51] 2510 2-9-0 0............(t) AdamBeschizza(3) 4 63
(Philip McBride) *chsd ldr: effrt and edgd lft over 2f out: chsd wnr ent fnl f: styd on same pce and no imp* **12/1**

00 **3** *1 1/4* **Melting Pot**[12] 3746 2-9-3 0............ IanMongan 1 60
(Hugo Palmer) *stdd s: t.k.h and hld up in rr: hdwy: swtchd rt and rn green over 1f out: kpt on to go 3rd ins fnl f: no ch w wnr* **50/1**

4 *1 1/2* **Tweedle Dee** 2-8-12 0............ RyanMoore 13 51
(Noel Quinlan) *chsd ldrs: rdn to chse clr wnr over 1f out: no imp and lost 2nd ent fnl f: wknd ins fnl f* **25/1**

60 **5** *1 3/4* **Artistic Thread (IRE)**[16] 3609 2-9-3 0............ SebSanders 6 56+
(Sir Mark Prescott Bt) *s.i.s: a bhd: rdn and outpcd over 2f out: no ch but plugged on again ins fnl f* **80/1**

6 *hd* **Gabrial's Gift (IRE)** 2-9-3 0............ JamieSpencer 9 51
(David Simcock) *stdd s: hld up in tch: pushed along and outpcd jst over 2f out: no ch but kpt on ins fnl f* **13/2**[3]

5 **7** *2 3/4* **Alborz (IRE)**[18] 3534 2-9-3 0............ NeilCallan 12 44
(Mark Johnston) *led tl 2f out: sn rdn and struggling: wknd over 1f out: fdd fnl f* **9/1**

8 *8* **Exning Halt** 2-9-3 0............ PatCosgrave 10 24
(James Fanshawe) *rn green in rr: j. path and unbalanced over 5f out: shkn up 1/2-way: lost tch ent fnl 2f* **15/2**

U **Equity Card (FR)** 2-8-12 0............ AhmedAjtebi 2 —
(Mahmood Al Zarooni) *swvd lft and uns rdr sn after s* **9/2**[2]

1m 30.76s (4.16) **Going Correction** +0.25s/f (Good) **9** Ran SP% **112.5**
Speed ratings (Par 92): **86,80,79,77,75 75,72,63,—**
Tote Swingers: 1&2 £4.00, 1&3 £12.00, 2&3 £39.30 CSF £17.41 TOTE £2.10: £1.20, £5.00, £10.50; EX 17.60 Trifecta £235.00 Part won. Pool: £317.68 - 0.40 winning units..
Owner R White & V J Walsh **Bred** Mystic Meg Limited **Trained** Newmarket, Suffolk

FOCUS
An average juvenile maiden in which they unsurprisingly raced more towards the centre of the track and the principals showed the benefit of their previous experience. The winner can do better but the form behind looks fluid.

NOTEBOOK
Rayvin Black ran a race full of promise on his debut at Newmarket last month and improved a good deal on that to run out an easy winner under a confident ride. He got a lovely tow through the race and soon had matters in control once asked for his effort. He drifted left late on, due to greenness, and would have won with greater authority had he kept a true line. From a family his trainer knows well, he should relish racing over middle distances next year and clearly enjoys cut underfoot. (op 11-8 tchd 6-5 and 6-4 in places)

Casa Bex was better than the bare form of his two previous outings at Newmarket, but was equipped with a first-time tongue tie on this return from a 51-day break and proved a market drifter. He ran a pleasing race, seeing out the extra furlong well enough, and shaped as though he would benefit for the run. Nurseries are now an option. (op 9-1)

Melting Pot had shown little in two previous spins, but her experience was a notable advantage here and stepping up in trip proved much more to her liking. She too is now qualified for nurseries.

Tweedle Dee, easy to back, fared best of the newcomers and should prove a good deal sharper next time out. (op 22-1)

Artistic Thread(IRE) ◆ was doing his best work late on under fairly considerate handling, and is one to keep an eye on now he can contest nurseries. (op 50-1)

Gabrial's Gift(IRE), stoutly bred on his dam's side, moved nicely through the early parts but hit a flat spot just as the winner wound up the tempo. He kept on under an educational ride thereafter and should learn plenty. (op 8-1)

Exning Halt, from a bang in-form stable, was expected to need this initial experience. He's a sizeable colt and didn't look happy on these undulations, so it's probably wise not to judge him too harshly on this. Official explanation: jockey colt ran green (op 17-2)

Equity Card(FR), solid enough in the betting, jinked jumping out and decanted her pilot in what appeared a pretty soft unseat. (op 4-1)

4160 M.R. KING PEUGEOT & SUZUKI LOWESTOFT H'CAP 7f 3y
2:45 (2:45) (Class 5) (0-75,75) 3-Y-O+ £2,264 (£673; £336; £168) Stalls High

Form RPR

3261 **1** **Rough Rock (IRE)**[18] 3555 6-9-11 72............ HayleyTurner 9 81
(Chris Dwyer) *t.k.h early: hld up in tch: travelling wl bhd a wall of horses over 1f out: gap opened and pushed along to chal ins fnl f: pushed into ld fnl 75yds: sn in command: eased towards fin* **6/1**[3]

1005 **2** *1* **Cativo Cavallino**[30] 3172 8-9-0 64............ NataliaGemelova(3) 8 70
(John E Long) *chsd ldr: rdn over 1f out: drvn to ld over 1f out: hdd and nt pce of wnr fnl 75yds* **14/1**

-444 **3** *2* **Tiberius Claudius (IRE)**[21] 3465 3-9-7 75............ SebSanders 10 73
(George Margarson) *hld up in tch in rr: rdn and effrt on stands' rail over 1f out: drvn to press ldrs jst ins fnl f: no ex and one pce fnl 150yds* **8/1**

1233 **4** *2* **Sammy Alexander**[30] 3172 3-9-3 71............ MartinLane 1 64
(David Simcock) *hld up in tch in last trio: hdwy over 2f out: rdn to chse ldrs and edgd rt over 1f out: wknd fnl 150yds* **10/3**[1]

0035 **5** *shd* **Hereford Boy**[23] 3412 7-9-7 68............(p) RobertHavlin 6 63
(Dean Ivory) *stdd after s: t.k.h: hld up in tch in rr: effrt and nt clr run over 1f out: swtchd lft jst over 1f out: no imp ins fnl f* **15/2**

-045 **6** *1 3/4* **Glass Mountain (IRE)**[32] 3093 3-9-1 69............ PatCosgrave 7 57
(James Fanshawe) *t.k.h: chsd ldrs: rdn and unable qck over 1f out: struggling and losing pl whn short of room over 1f out: wknd 1f out* **7/2**[2]

3652 **7** *2 1/2* **Cuthbert (IRE)**[18] 3555 4-9-4 70............(v) MarkCoumbe(5) 4 54
(William Jarvis) *led: rdn jst over 2f out: drvn and hdd over 1f out: wknd 1f out: fdd ins fnl f* **6/1**[3]

-505 **8** *1/2* **Mudhish (IRE)**[10] [illegible] 6-9-2 [illegible]............(b) IvaMilickova 5 46
(Clive Brittain) *chsd ldrs: rdn and effrt jst over 2f out: wknd ent fnl f* **14/1**

0-00 **9** *3 3/4* **Angel Of Fashion (IRE)**[19] 3517 4-8-6 56 oh3............ AdamBeschizza(3) 11 28
(Peter Charalambous) *taken down early: t.k.h: hld up in tch in rr: rdn 3f out: wknd wl over 1f out* **40/1**

1m 30.34s (3.74) **Going Correction** +0.25s/f (Good)
WFA 3 from 4yo+ 7lb **9** Ran SP% **112.5**
Speed ratings (Par 103): **88,86,84,82,82 80,77,76,72**
Tote Swingers: 1&2 £13.40, 1&3 £4.60, 2&3 £19.90 CSF £82.45 CT £669.58 TOTE £5.60: £2.30, £4.80, £3.50; EX 90.60 Trifecta £238.40 Pool: £799.06 - 2.48 winning units..
Owner M M Foulger **Bred** Mrs B Stroomer **Trained** Burrough Green, Cambs

FOCUS
A moderate handicap that turned into something of a dash from 2f out and the majority were closely covered at the furlong marker. The principals came clear thereafter and this time the main action developed towards the stands' side. The form is limited by the proximity of the runner-up.
Hereford Boy Official explanation: jockey said that the gelding was denied a clear run
Angel Of Fashion(IRE) Official explanation: trainer said the filly was unsuited by the soft ground

4161 J & H SIMPSON WELL BALANCED LEDGER H'CAP 1m 3y
3:15 (3:16) (Class 4) (0-85,84) 3-Y-O £4,075 (£1,212; £606; £303) Stalls High

Form RPR

6320 **1** **Robemaker**[31] 3133 3-9-2 79............ WilliamBuick 6 90
(John Gosden) *chsd ldrs tl wnt 2nd 1/2-way: rdn to ld over 1f out: edgd lft u.p ins fnl f: kpt on wl* **7/2**[2]

6421 **2** *1/2* **Arabian Heights**[7] 3925 3-9-2 79 6ex............ SebSanders 3 89+
(Sir Mark Prescott Bt) *stdd s: hld up in tch in rr: hdwy to chse ldrs jst over 2f out: rdn to chse wnr over 1f out: pushed lft and sltly hmpd ins fnl f: kpt on but a hld* **10/3**[1]

-152 **3** *7* **Wiqaaya (IRE)**[25] 3310 3-9-7 84............ RichardHills 5 78
(Ed Dunlop) *in tch in rr but nvr looked to be gng wl: rdn over 2f out: outpcd and no ch w ldng pair over 1f out: wnt modest 3rd ins fnl f* **7/2**[2]

3-21 **4** *1 1/4* **Set Me Free (IRE)**[41] 2785 3-8-13 76............ KierenFallon 4 67
(Luca Cumani) *wnt lft s: t.k.h: hld up in tch: rdn over 2f out: sn struggling: wknd over 1f out: wnt modest 4th ins fnl f* **7/2**[2]

-465 **5** *2 1/4* **Yahafedh Alaih**[55] 2389 3-8-4 67............ ChrisCatlin 1 53
(Clive Brittain) *led: rdn wl over 1f out: hdd over 1f out: 3rd and btn 1f out: wknd qckly fnl f* **16/1**

0-02 **6** 7 **Switchback**[17] 3575 3-8-9 72 .... RyanMoore 7 42
(Sir Michael Stoute) *t.k.h: chsd ldr tl 1/2-way: rdn and struggling over 2f out: sn bhd* **5/1**[3]

1m 42.63s (2.03) **Going Correction** +0.25s/f (Good) **6** Ran SP% **112.3**
Speed ratings (Par 102): **99,98,91,90,88 81**
Tote Swingers: 1&2 £2.70, 1&3 £3.80, 2&3 £2.30 CSF £15.48 TOTE £4.80: £2.00, £2.00; EX 24.20 TRIFECTA Not won..
Owner H R H Princess Haya Of Jordan **Bred** Cheveley Park Stud Ltd **Trained** Newmarket, Suffolk
■ Stewards' Enquiry : William Buick one-day ban: careless riding (3 Aug)

FOCUS
A fair little handicap. The first pair came clear in a tight finish and are rated as improvers.

4162 PLEASUREWOOD HILLS H'CAP — 6f 3y
3:45 (3:47) (Class 6) (0-55,55) 3-Y-O **£1,617** (£481; £240; £120) **Stalls** High

Form — RPR

-022 **1** **Golden Compass**[28] 3230 3-8-11 **50** .... WilliamCarson 4 60+
(Giles Bravery) *chsd overall ldr on far side: led 2f out: clr and switching to stands' rail 1f out: pressed and drvn fnl 100yds: a jst holding on* **5/1**[2]

005- **2** *nk* **Dixie Gwalia**[227] 7681 3-8-3 **47** oh1 ow1 .... LauraPike(5) 14 56+
(David Simcock) *bhd on stands' rail: rdn 1/2-way: hdwy against stands' rail wl over 1f out: chsd wnr and swtchd lft ins fnl f: pressed wnr fnl 100yds: kpt on and clsng on wnr cl home* **14/1**

-055 **3** *3 1/4* **Trust Me Boy**[11] 3766 3-8-7 **46** oh1 .... (v) KirstyMilczarek 1 45
(John E Long) *bhd on far side: rdn 4f out: hdwy u.p over 1f out: styd on to go 3rd fnl 50yds: nt rch ldrs* **66/1**

4606 **4** *1 1/2* **Ereka (IRE)**[28] 3227 3-8-11 **50** .... (v[1]) JimmyQuinn 3 44
(Murty McGrath) *chsd overall ldrs on far side: rdn jst over 2f out: chsd clr wnr jst over 1f out tl ins fnl f: wknd fnl 150yds* **20/1**

0460 **5** *nk* **Chillie Peppar**[6] 3958 3-8-10 **52** .... AmyBaker(3) 13 45
(George Prodromou) *racd in midfield towards stands' side: swtchd rt and rdn wl over 2f out: edgd lft and plugged on same pce ins fnl f* **12/1**

4060 **6** *1/2* **Sleights Boy (IRE)**[6] 3937 3-8-11 **50** .... (b) HayleyTurner 12 42
(Ian McInnes) *racd in midfield towards stands' side: rdn over 2f out: edgd lft and kpt on ins fnl f: nvr gng pce to rch ldrs* **16/1**

0600 **7** *1/2* **Microlight**[28] 3227 3-8-8 **50** .... (b) NataliaGemelova(3) 2 40
(John E Long) *racd towards far side and overall ldr: rdn and hdd 2f out: edgd rt 1f out: wknd ins fnl f* **40/1**

405 **8** *3 1/4* **Regal Bullet (IRE)**[26] 3272 3-8-13 **55** .... MatthewDavies(3) 6 35
(Dean Ivory) *dwlt: sn in midfield: rdn 1/2-way: no imp and wl hld over 1f out* **5/1**[2]

-604 **9** *5* **Alspritza**[40] 2827 3-8-7 **46** oh1 .... (p) NickyMackay 9 10
(Chris Wall) *prom towards stands' side: rdn 2f out: hung lft and wknd qckly over 1f out: wl btn and eased ins fnl f* **11/1**

-605 **10** *1* **Art Thief**[48] 2599 3-9-2 **55** .... RyanMoore 5 15
(Sylvester Kirk) *racd towards far side: sn outpcd in rr: rdn 4f out: nvr on terms: bhd and eased ins fnl f* **9/2**[1]

0-65 **11** *1 1/4* **Kwik Time**[15] 3661 3-8-11 **50** .... KierenFallon 8 —
(Robin Bastiman) *racd in midfield: rdn and no prog wl over 2f out: wknd over 1f out: bhd and eased ins fnl f* **7/1**[3]

5-64 **12** *2 1/4* **Heavenly Pursuit**[20] 3476 3-9-1 **54** .... PatCosgrave 10 —
(Jim Boyle) *chsd ldrs towards stands' side: drvn over 2f out: wknd over 1f out: bhd and eased ins fnl f* **15/2**

040- **13** *1 3/4* **Jamaica Grande**[250] 7395 3-8-7 **46** oh1 .... LiamJones 16 —
(Terry Clement) *prom on stands' side: rdn wl over 2f out: wknd wl over 1f out: bhd and eased ins fnl f* **14/1**

1m 16.07s (1.67) **Going Correction** +0.25s/f (Good) **13** Ran SP% **119.7**
Speed ratings (Par 98): **98,97,93,91,90 90,89,85,78,77 75,72,70**
Tote Swingers: 1&2 £20.20, 1&3 £18.10, 2&3 £36.10 CSF £72.22 CT £4239.43 TOTE £5.50: £2.20, £5.80, £8.00; EX 81.40.
Owner J P Carrington **Bred** Mrs F Bravery **Trained** Cowlinge, Suffolk

FOCUS
A weak 3-y-o handicap. The first two came clear against the stands' side. The form is modest and best rated around the third, fourth and sixth.
Kwik Time Official explanation: jockey said that the colt was never travelling

4163 VOLVO AT M.R. KING HALESWORTH MEDIAN AUCTION MAIDEN STKS — 1m 1f
4:15 (4:37) (Class 6) 3-5-Y-O **£1,617** (£481; £240; £120) **Stalls** Low

Form — RPR

-300 **1** **Top Diktat**[6] 3959 3-9-3 74 .... RyanMoore 13 79
(Sir Michael Stoute) *towards rr: pushed along and clsd 4f out: rdn and hdwy 3f out: led wl over 1f out: styd on wl u.p and drew clr ins fnl f: rdn out* **11/2**[2]

24-3 **2** *2 1/4* **Lion Court (IRE)**[33] 3037 3-9-3 72 .... SebSanders 11 74
(Sir Mark Prescott Bt) *led for 1f: swtchd rt and drvn 3f out: sn chsng ldr: pressing wnr wl over 1f out: no ex and one pce ins fnl f* **7/2**[1]

3 *2 1/2* **Gold Tobougg** 3-8-12 0 .... WilliamBuick 10 64
(David Simcock) *s.i.s: bhd: swtchd rt and hdwy 3f out: chsd ldrs and edgd lft over 1f out: no imp ins fnl f* **9/1**

4 **4** *nk* **John Louis**[31] 3138 3-9-0 0 .... AdamBeschizza(3) 5 68+
(Philip McBride) *t.k.h: hld up in midfield: hmpd after 2f: towards rr of ldng gp whn nt clr run over 2f out: unbalanced jst over 2f out: rdn and hdwy over 1f out: styd on to press for 3rd towards fin* **9/1**

00 **5** *6* **Dresden (IRE)**[51] 2511 3-9-3 0 .... KierenFallon 9 55
(Luca Cumani) *chsd ldr tl led over 3f out: rdn over 2f out: hdd wl over 1f out: btn jst over 1f out: wknd fnl f* **33/1**

0 **6** *1 1/2* **Famagusta**[28] 3224 4-9-2 0 .... (v) LauraPike(5) 1 47
(Peter Charalambous) *led after 1f tl hdd over 3f out: rdn 3f out: wknd wl over 1f out* **150/1**

5-0 **7** *2 1/2* **Five Hearts**[27] 3246 3-8-12 0 .... NeilCallan 8 41
(Mark H Tompkins) *in tch in midfield: rdn and effrt over 2f out: unable qck and drvn 2f out: wknd over 1f out* **16/1**

-560 **8** *8* **Shelovestobougie**[25] 3312 3-8-12 65 .... IanMongan 7 23
(Sir Henry Cecil) *in tch: rdn and fnd little over 2f out: sn struggling: wknd 2f out* **9/1**

223- **9** *1 1/4* **Handsome King**[222] 7767 4-9-12 63 .... (v[1]) JamesDoyle 3 25
(J R Jenkins) *in tch: rdn and lost pl qckly wl over 2f out: no ch fnl 2f* **28/1**

3 **10** *3 1/2* **Flaming Nora**[27] 3246 3-8-12 0 .... PatCosgrave 4 13
(James Fanshawe) *racd in midfield: niggled along 6f out: struggling and rdn over 2f out: sn btn: wl bhd and eased ins fnl f* **13/2**[3]

52 **11** *2* **Brinmore**[45] 2689 3-8-7 0 .... HarryBentley(5) 12 —
(William Knight) *hld up towards rr: hmpd and tack problems after 2f: bhd and rdr wout irons 5f out: no ch after* **7/2**[1]

12 *31* **Hot Tub** 3-8-10 0 .... DanielHarris(7) 2 —
(Christine Dunnett) *s.i.s: bhd: lost tch and t.o 4f out* **33/1**

1m 57.63s (1.83) **Going Correction** +0.25s/f (Good)
WFA 3 from 4yo 9lb **12** Ran SP% **119.0**
Speed ratings (Par 101): **101,99,96,96,91 89,87,80,79,76 74,46**
Tote Swingers: 1&2 £5.30, 1&3 £13.20, 2&3 £10.40 CSF £24.57 TOTE £6.30: £1.90, £2.10, £3.30; EX 28.60 Trifecta £590.60 Part won. Pool: £798.22 - 0.74 winning units..
Owner Mrs Denis Haynes **Bred** Wretham Stud **Trained** Newmarket, Suffolk

FOCUS
There was a delay of around half an hour before the off due to a flat tyre on one of the racecourse ambulances. A modest maiden, although the form looks sound enough.
Brinmore Official explanation: jockey said saddle slipped

4164 DIGIBET H'CAP — 1m 3f 101y
4:45 (5:04) (Class 6) (0-60,60) 3-Y-O+ **£1,617** (£481; £240; £120) **Stalls** Low

Form — RPR

302 **1** **Thundering Home**[7] 3923 4-9-3 **52** .... (t) MatthewDavies(3) 3 60
(George Baker) *hld up in tch in last trio: rdn and effrt on outer over 1f out: led ins fnl f: r.o wl* **9/4**[1]

0141 **2** *3/4* **Dancing Primo**[7] 3910 5-9-6 **57** 6ex .... RyanClark(5) 6 64
(Mark Brisbourne) *t.k.h: chsd ldrs: effrt to ld over 2f out: rdn and edgd rt wl over 1f out: hdd and styd on same pce ins fnl f* **9/2**[3]

4326 **3** *nk* **Outland (IRE)**[19] 3516 5-9-12 **58** .... RyanMoore 1 64
(J R Jenkins) *hld up in tch in last trio: rdn and hdwy 2f out: chsd ldrs and drvn ins fnl f: kpt on* **5/2**[2]

4/0- **4** *1 1/2* **Astrolibra**[269] 1012 7-9-8 **54** .... KierenFallon 4 58
(Mark H Tompkins) *hld up wl in tch: effrt and rdn to chse ldr 2f out: drvn and unable qck over 1f out: styd on same pce fnl f* **16/1**

2423 **5** *nk* **Surprise (IRE)**[23] 3393 3-9-3 **60** .... MarcHalford 8 63
(Mark Rimmer) *hld up in tch in midfield: rdn to chse ldrs wl over 1f out: unable qck jst over 1f out: styd on same pce fnl f* **9/1**

6405 **6** *2 1/4* **Olimamu (IRE)**[6] 3946 4-9-5 **54** .... (t) SimonPearce(3) 2 54
(Lydia Pearce) *hld up in tch: hdwy on inner over 3f out: chsd ldrs and rdn over 1f out: wknd ins fnl f* **22/1**

0644 **7** *16* **Harry Lime**[12] 3742 3-8-12 **55** .... LiamJones 9 27
(William Jarvis) *chsd ldr: rdn 4f out: drvn over 3f out: ev ch briefly 2f out: sn wknd: wl bhd and eased wl ins fnl f* **7/1**

0-06 **8** *2* **Apurna**[16] 3637 6-8-7 **46** oh1 .... (b) DavidKenny(7) 7 15
(John Harris) *hld up in tch in last trio: rdn and wknd 2f out: wl bhd and eased wl ins fnl f* **50/1**

0-06 **9** *9* **Business Bay (USA)**[13] 3705 4-9-0 **46** oh1 .... RussKennemore 5 —
(Patrick Clinton) *led tl over 2f out: wknd quiickly 2f out: wl bhd and eased ins fnl f* **33/1**

2m 33.85s (5.15) **Going Correction** +0.25s/f (Good)
WFA 3 from 4yo+ 11lb **9** Ran SP% **115.2**
Speed ratings (Par 101): **91,90,90,89,88 87,75,74,67**
Tote Swingers: 1&2 £4.00, 1&3 £2.60, 2&3 £2.90 CSF £12.50 CT £26.36 TOTE £4.30: £1.40, £1.70, £1.50; EX 17.30 Trifecta £23.70 Pool: £340.23 - 10.62 winning units..
Owner George Baker **Bred** Rabbah Bloodstock Limited **Trained** Whitsbury, Hants

FOCUS
An ordinary handicap, run at an average pace. The runner-up is progressing and the form looks reasonable with the third, fifth and sixth rated close to recent marks.

4165 TIME & TIDE MUSEUM APPRENTICE H'CAP — 1m 2f 21y
5:15 (5:23) (Class 6) (0-60,60) 4-Y-O+ **£1,617** (£481; £240; £120) **Stalls** Low

Form — RPR

0-30 **1** **Colinca's Lad (IRE)**[31] 3130 9-9-3 **56** .... RosieJessop 4 68
(Peter Charalambous) *mde all and sn clr: rdn over 2f out: kpt on: unchal* **4/1**[3]

2-00 **2** *7* **Saloon (USA)**[39] 2830 7-9-0 **60** .... (p) LauraSimpson(7) 5 60
(Jane Chapple-Hyam) *stdd s: hld up in last pair: hdwy on inner 4f out: pressing for 2nd but no ch w wnr whn n.m.r fr over 2f out tl ins fnl f: wnt 2nd nr fin* **16/1**

4035 **3** *nk* **Market Puzzle (IRE)**[2] 4111 4-8-4 **46** oh1 .... RachealKneller(3) 7 43
(Mark Brisbourne) *hld up in midfield: rdn to chse clr wnr over 3f out: hung lft u.p and no imp fr over 2f out: lost 2nd nr fin* **9/2**

2 **4** *7* **Far Flung (IRE)**[12] 3734 4-9-7 **60** .... CharlesEddery 8 43
(Jim Best) *stdd s: hld up in last: rdn over 4f out: no hdwy and nvr on terms: wnt modest 4th cl home* **9/4**[1]

0013 **5** *1/2* **Royal Defence (IRE)**[6] 3945 5-9-7 **60** .... MatthewLawson 6 42
(Michael Quinn) *chsd wnr tl over 3f out: sn drvn: 4th and wl btn over 1f out* **7/2**[2]

3155 **6** *12* **Dragon Slayer (IRE)**[16] 3637 9-9-5 **58** .... DavidKenny 1 16
(John Harris) *chsd ldrs tl over 3f out: sn struggling: wl bhd fnl 2f* **8/1**

2m 12.62s (2.12) **Going Correction** +0.25s/f (Good) **6** Ran SP% **108.2**
Speed ratings (Par 101): **101,95,95,89,89 79**
Tote Swingers: 1&2 £4.30, 1&3 £3.80, 2&3 £9.80 CSF £52.85 CT £260.90 TOTE £4.50: £2.90, £4.50; EX 59.70 Trifecta £100.60 Pool: £329.07 - 2.42 winning units..
Owner P Charalambous **Bred** Peter Charles **Trained** Newmarket, Suffolk
■ Stewards' Enquiry : Laura Simpson one-day ban: careless riding (1 Aug)

FOCUS
A weak handicap, confined to apprentice riders. Suspect form with a couple disappointing, and the winner to near his best looks the guide.
T/Jkpt: Not won. T/Plt: £72.80 to a £1 stake. Pool £83,387.22 - 835.42 winning units T/Qpdt: £23.00 to a £1 stake. Pool £7,145.33 - 229.10 winning units SP

4166 - 4169a (Foreign Racing) - See Raceform Interactive

3450 MUSSELBURGH (R-H)
Tuesday, July 19

OFFICIAL GOING: Good to soft (good in places; 6.3)
Wind: Breezy, half against Weather: Cloudy, fine

4170 TURFTV H'CAP — 1m 1f
2:30 (2:30) (Class 5) (0-70,68) 3-Y-O+ **£2,264** (£673; £336; £168) **Stalls** Low

Form — RPR

3040 **1** **Mangham (IRE)**[16] 3658 6-9-2 **60** .... (p) LeeNewman 2 71
(George Foster) *t.k.h: trckd ldrs: hdwy to ld wl over 1f out: pushed out fnl f* **8/1**

0505 **2** *2 3/4* **Marvo**[4] 4045 7-9-10 **68** .... TomEaves 3 73
(Mark H Tompkins) *hld up in tch: smooth hdwy over 2f out: rdn to chse wnr over 1f out: edgd rt and kpt on ins fnl f* **3/1**[2]

6612 **3** *1/2* **Petomic (IRE)**[4] 4045 6-9-6 **67** .... RobertLButler(3) 1 71
(Richard Guest) *hld up: hdwy over 2f out: edgd rt over 1f out: no imp fnl f* **3/1**[2]

2146 **4** *2* **Ra Junior (USA)**[22] 3462 5-9-8 **66**.. PhillipMakin 5 65
(Paul Midgley) *led at stdy gallop: rdn and hdd over 1f out: wknd ins fnl f* **7/2**[3]

3360 **5** *4 1/2* **Law To Himself (IRE)**[34] 3038 4-9-9 **67**............................ PJMcDonald 6 57
(Alan Swinbank) *fly-jmpd s: t.k.h: prom: rdn over 2f out: edgd rt and wknd wl over 1f out* **11/4**[1]

0-00 **6** *32* **Gumnd (IRE)**[37] 2955 4-9-7 **65**.. PaulHanagan 7 —
(Chris Grant) *cl up tl rdn and wknd over 2f out: sn lost tch: t.o* **28/1**

1m 55.16s (1.26) **Going Correction** +0.225s/f (Good) **6** Ran SP% **113.4**
Speed ratings (Par 103): **103,100,100,98,94 65**
Tote Swingers: 1&2 £5.30, 1&3 £3.00, 2&3 £2.30 CSF £32.54 CT £88.53 TOTE £10.60: £4.30, £1.60; EX 43.70.
Owner Ron Hull **Bred** Dr Dean Harron **Trained** Haddington, East Lothian

FOCUS
Bottom bend moved out 6m adding 18m to distances on Round course. A weak handicap run at an ordinary early pace. Straightforward form rated around the placed horses.
Mangham(IRE) Official explanation: trainer said, regarding the apparent improvement of form,that the gelding was better suited by the easier ground and the fitting of cheek pieces
Law To Himself(IRE) Official explanation: trainer's representative was unable to offer any explanation for the poor performance shown
Gumnd(IRE) Official explanation: jockey said that the gelding was never travelling

4171 BRITISH STALLION STUDS SUPPORTING BRITISH RACING E B F MAIDEN STKS 7f 30y
3:00 (3:00) (Class 5) 2-Y-O **£2,911** (£866; £432; £216) **Stalls** Low

Form RPR

543 **1** **Commanche**[12] 3755 2-9-3 0.. TomEaves 2 74
(Bryan Smart) *t.k.h: mde all: pushed clr over 1f out: kpt on wl fnl f* **5/4**[1]

0 **2** *2* **Daddy Warbucks (IRE)**[11] 3826 2-9-3 0.............................. AdrianNicholls 1 69
(David Nicholls) *t.k.h: chsd ldrs: effrt and chsd (clr) wnr over 1f out: kpt on fnl f: no imp* **11/4**[2]

30 **3** *5* **Rosie's Lady (IRE)**[17] 3609 2-8-12 0.............................. DanielTudhope 7 52
(David O'Meara) *pressed wnr: rdn over 2f out: lost 2nd and one pce over 1f out* **7/1**

6 **4** *1/2* **Karma Chameleon**[33] 3070 2-9-3 0.............................. PaulHanagan 6 55
(Richard Guest) *t.k.h: hld up: effrt and hdwy 2f out: kpt on fnl f: nvr rchd ldrs* **28/1**

5 *2* **Courtesy Call (IRE)** 2-9-3 0.. SilvestreDeSousa 4 50+
(Mark Johnston) *coltish and green in preliminaries: missed break: rn green in rr: hdwy over 2f out: sn no imp: improve* **9/2**[3]

5 **6** *1/2* **Villa Reigns**[21] 3483 2-9-3 0.. PhillipMakin 3 49
(John Weymes) *hld up in tch: stdy hdwy over 2f out: rdn and hung bdly lft wl over 1f out: sn btn* **100/1**

03 **7** *9* **Storm Fairy**[18] 3584 2-8-12 0.. AndrewElliott 5 22
(Mrs K Burke) *trckd ldrs: rdn over 2f out: sn wknd* **12/1**

1m 32.22s (3.22) **Going Correction** +0.225s/f (Good) **7** Ran SP% **113.9**
Speed ratings (Par 94): **90,87,82,81,79 78,68**
Tote Swingers: 1&2 £1.60, 1&3 £2.60, 2&3 £4.20 CSF £4.82 TOTE £1.90: £1.10, £3.30; EX 6.00.
Owner Andrew Tinkler **Bred** Paramount Bloodstock **Trained** Hambleton, N Yorks

FOCUS
An uncompetitive maiden but the winner is rated a slight improver with the third fitting in on previous form.

NOTEBOOK
Commanche made the most of an uncontested lead, despite racing a bit keenly and not really handling the bend into the straight. The step up in trip suited and he has progressed with each run so far, so he should be competitive in nurseries. (op 13-8)
Daddy Warbucks(IRE) had shown ability on his debut at York and did so again in this less competitive contest. (op 4-1)
Rosie's Lady(IRE) was always well placed and ran respectably. She should find her level now she can contest nurseries. (op 6-1 tchd 17-2)
Karma Chameleon, as on his debut, never threatened but he showed ability. He looks more of a nursery type. (tchd 33-1)
Courtesy Call(IRE), an 80,000euros purchase, out of a 1m Listed winner, showed a bit more than the beaten margin suggests. Coltish beforehand, he had little chance on this speed-favouring track after losing several lengths at the start, but he made a bit of progress halfway up the straight, briefly looking like he might get involved, before his exertions told. There should be a lot more to come. (op 7-2)
Villa Reigns Official explanation: jockey said the colt hung left handed in the straight

4172 SCOTTISH RACING H'CAP 5f
3:30 (3:30) (Class 6) (0-65,63) 3-Y-O **£1,617** (£481; £240; £120) **Stalls** High

Form RPR

0250 **1** **Green Warrior**[18] 3573 3-9-5 **61**..(p) PaulHanagan 9 68
(Ann Duffield) *t.k.h: trckd ldrs: effrt over 1f out: drvn to ld ins fnl f: r.o* **7/2**[3]

3254 **2** *1 3/4* **Tancred Spirit**[10] 3860 3-8-0 **47**..(v) JulieBurke(5) 6 48
(Paul Midgley) *led: rdn and hdd ins fnl f: kpt on same pce* **5/2**[1]

25 **3** *hd* **These Dreams**[14] 3702 3-8-9 **51**.. GrahamGibbons 5 51
(Richard Guest) *t.k.h: stdd in last pl: effrt over 1f out: kpt on same pce wl ins fnl f* **7/2**[3]

0624 **4** *1 1/4* **Majestic Millie (IRE)**[7] 3950 3-8-4 **46**.............................. SilvestreDeSousa 1 41
(David O'Meara) *cl up: rdn 2f out: kpt on same pce fnl f* **11/4**[2]

0400 **5** *2 3/4* **Face East (USA)**[16] 3661 3-8-3 **45**.............................. PatrickMathers 4 31
(Alan Berry) *sn drvn and outpcd towards rr: shortlived effrt on outside 1/2-way: edgd lft and no imp over 1f out* **25/1**

6000 **6** *3/4* **Bygones For Coins (IRE)**[10] 3860 3-7-13 **46**.............................. NeilFarley(5) 3 29
(Alan Berry) *cl up tl rdn and wknd over 1f out* **16/1**

61.01 secs (0.61) **Going Correction** +0.075s/f (Good) **6** Ran SP% **109.4**
Speed ratings (Par 98): **98,95,94,92,88 87**
Tote Swingers: 1&2 £1.90, 2&3 £3.60 CSF £11.98 CT £28.21 TOTE £4.10: £3.20, £1.60; EX 14.00.
Owner Sir Robert Ogden **Bred** Heather Raw **Trained** Constable Burton, N Yorks

FOCUS
A moderate sprint handicap contested solely by maidens. The form is weak, with the placed horses setting the level.

4173 TURFTV.CO.UK H'CAP (QUALIFIER FOR BETFAIR BONUS SCOTTISH RACING STAYERS FINAL) 1m 4f 100y
4:00 (4:00) (Class 5) (0-70,74) 4-Y-0+ **£4,204** (£1,251; £625; £312) **Stalls** Low

Form RPR

0331 **1** **Persian Peril**[1] 4142 7-9-12 **74** 6ex.. PJMcDonald 2 83
(Alan Swinbank) *trckd ldrs: gng wl over 2f out: led over 1f out: drvn out* **5/1**[3]

-561 **2** *2* **Dane Cottage**[26] 3317 4-8-4 **52**.. PaulHanagan 8 58
(Brian Ellison) *trckd ldrs: rdn and led over 2f out: hdd over 1f out: kpt on same pce ins fnl f* **4/1**[2]

1026 **3** *nse* **Madamlily (IRE)**[26] 3316 5-9-4 **66**.. TomEaves 10 72
(John Quinn) *midfield: effrt over 2f out: sn rdn: kpt on wl fnl f: nrst fin* **14/1**

0045 **4** *1 3/4* **Hurlingham**[18] 3574 7-8-6 **54** ow1..(b) GrahamGibbons 11 57
(Michael Easterby) *hld up: hdwy and in tch 2f out: sn rdn: one pce fnl f* **10/1**

2111 **5** *3* **Fossgate**[18] 3581 10-8-13 **66**.. JulieBurke(5) 7 65
(James Bethell) *hld up: hdwy on outside over 4f out: hung rt fr over 2f out: kpt on fnl f: nvr rchd ldrs* **8/1**

5446 **6** *nk* **Rosbay (IRE)**[10] 3848 7-9-2 **69**.. LanceBetts(5) 6 67
(Tim Easterby) *t.k.h: hld up: rdn 3f out: styd on fnl f: no imp* **12/1**

-030 **7** *3* **Magic Millie (IRE)**[26] 3319 4-8-8 **56**.............................. SilvestreDeSousa 9 49
(David O'Meara) *cl up: rdn 3f out: edgd rt and wknd wl over 1f out* **16/1**

-132 **8** *2 1/4* **Pokfulham (IRE)**[32] 3115 5-9-3 **65**.. DanielTudhope 5 55
(Jim Goldie) *hld up: rdn over 5f out: no imp fr 3f out* **5/2**[1]

0562 **9** *2 1/4* **Bring Sweets (IRE)**[21] 3492 4-8-6 **54**.. AdrianNicholls 3 40
(Brian Ellison) *led at stdy pce: rdn and hdd over 2f out: sn wknd* **20/1**

0405 **10** *11* **Birkside**[22] 3453 8-8-5 **53**.. LeeNewman 1 22
(Linda Perratt) *dwlt: hld up: hdwy on ins over 3f out: wknd 2f out* **16/1**

0-05 **11** *12* **Merrion Tiger (IRE)**[14] 3712 6-7-11 **50** oh4.............................. ChrisDCogan(5) 4 —
(George Foster) *t.k.h: towards rr: hdwy to chse ldrs after 4f: rdn and wknd fr 4f out* **40/1**

2m 45.04s (3.04) **Going Correction** +0.225s/f (Good) **11** Ran SP% **118.8**
Speed ratings (Par 103): **98,96,96,95,93 93,91,89,88,80 72**
Tote Swingers: 1&2 £5.40, 1&3 £12.70, 2&3 £10.40 CSF £25.59 CT £267.15 TOTE £7.90: £2.20, £2.30, £5.40; EX 34.60.
Owner Mrs J Porter **Bred** Mrs P Lewis **Trained** Melsonby, N Yorks

FOCUS
A modest handicap in which the runner-up is the best guide and the form appears to make sense.
Pokfulham(IRE) Official explanation: trainer was unable to offer any explanation for the poor performance shown

4174 SCOTTISH RACING YOUR BETTER BET CLAIMING STKS 5f
4:30 (4:30) (Class 6) 3-Y-0+ **£1,617** (£481; £240; £120) **Stalls** High

Form RPR

5-00 **1** **Atlantic Cycle (IRE)**[18] 3579 4-8-12 69.............................. AndrewElliott 6 75
(Mrs K Burke) *mde all: rdn over 1f out: hld on gamely fnl f* **9/2**

-200 **2** *3/4* **Strike Up The Band**[45] 2714 8-9-6 87.............................. AdrianNicholls 5 80
(David Nicholls) *cl up: rdn 1/2-way: effrt over 1f out: ev ch ins fnl f: one pce towards fin* **11/8**[1]

1250 **3** *3 1/4* **Angelo Poliziano**[11] 3832 5-9-6 77.............................(p) SilvestreDeSousa 4 69
(Ann Duffield) *trckd ldrs: rdn 1/2-way: effrt over 1f out: no imp fnl f* **5/2**[2]

5060 **4** *3* **Sandwith**[1] 4144 8-9-1 58..(v) LMcNiff(5) 3 58
(George Foster) *in tch: drvn and outpcd 2f out: n.d after* **40/1**

1501 **5** *1 1/4* **Ridley Didley (IRE)**[22] 3451 6-8-12 69.............................. NeilFarley(5) 2 50
(Noel Wilson) *trckd ldrs: rdn 1/2-way: wknd appr fnl f* **4/1**[3]

60.12 secs (-0.28) **Going Correction** +0.075s/f (Good) **5** Ran SP% **111.3**
Speed ratings (Par 101): **105,103,98,93,91**
CSF £11.36 TOTE £7.00: £2.40, £1.80; EX 16.70.Atlantic Cycle was claimed by Mr J. M. Bradley for £7,000.
Owner R Kent **Bred** Iona Equine **Trained** Middleham Moor, North Yorks

FOCUS
A modest claimer, the form held down by the 58-rated Sandwith, who had plenty to find at the weights.
Ridley Didley(IRE) Official explanation: jockey said that the gelding had a breathing problem

4175 RACING UK THE UK'S BEST RACECOURSES LIVE H'CAP 1m 5f
5:00 (5:00) (Class 6) (0-65,63) 3-Y-O **£1,940** (£577; £288; £144) **Stalls** Low

Form RPR

1032 **1** **Hal Of A Lover**[4] 4044 3-9-0 **56**.. SilvestreDeSousa 2 63
(David O'Meara) *trckd ldr: led over 2f out: drvn out fnl f* **5/4**[1]

2423 **2** *2 1/4* **Silver Tigress**[21] 3487 3-8-7 **49**.. PJMcDonald 3 53+
(George Moore) *rt rein snapped and veered bdly lft leaving stalls: sn corrected and chsd ldrs: effrt and hdwy to chse wnr over 1f out: edgd rt ins fnl f: one pce* **15/8**[2]

-013 **3** *1 1/2* **Cotton Grass**[4] 4044 3-9-7 **63**.. TomEaves 1 64
(Mark H Tompkins) *led at ordinary gallop: rdn and hdd over 2f out: kpt on same pce over 1f out* **9/2**[3]

5445 **4** *12* **Purkab**[8] 3905 3-9-0 **56**.. DanielTudhope 4 45
(Jim Goldie) *carried bdly lft s: hld up in tch: effrt and rdn over 2f out: sn btn: eased whn no ch fnl f* **8/1**

2m 54.7s (2.70) **Going Correction** +0.225s/f (Good) **4** Ran SP% **108.5**
Speed ratings (Par 98): **100,98,97,90**
CSF £3.88 TOTE £2.40; EX 3.40.
Owner Glenn Briers & The Dreamers **Bred** Genesis Green Stud Ltd **Trained** Nawton, N Yorks

FOCUS
Very moderate form that needs treating with caution, although the unfortunate runner-up is rated to form.

4176 WATCH RACING UK ON SKY 432 H'CAP 7f 30y
5:30 (5:30) (Class 5) (0-70,68) 3-Y-0+ **£2,264** (£673; £336; £168) **Stalls** Low

Form RPR

6651 **1** **Sabratha (IRE)**[1] 4141 3-9-4 **65** 6ex.. PaulHanagan 1 74
(Linda Perratt) *t.k.h early: mde all: rdn 2f out: hld on wl fnl f* **5/1**[3]

0021 **2** *nk* **Istiqdaam**[5] 4025 6-9-6 **60**..(b) GrahamGibbons 6 71
(Michael Easterby) *in tch: effrt and rdn over 2f out: kpt on wl fnl f: jst hld* **5/4**[1]

-005 **3** *1/2* **Our Boy Barrington (IRE)**[7] 3936 4-10-0 **68**...........(v) AdrianNicholls 3 77
(David Nicholls) *prom: effrt and ev ch over 1f out to ins fnl f: kpt on same pce towards fin* **12/1**

0355 **4** *8* **Cyflymder (IRE)**[11] 3806 5-9-7 **66**..(v) NeilFarley(5) 5 54
(Declan Carroll) *hld up: rdn over 2f out: hdwy over 1f out: nvr able to chal* **13/2**

3662 **5** *3 1/4* **Eilean Eeve**[25] 3355 5-9-1 **55**..(p) LeeNewman 4 34
(George Foster) *trckd ldrs: rdn over 2f out: wknd over 1f out* **33/1**

1002 **6** *shd* **Old English (IRE)**[7] 3934 3-9-7 **68**.............................. SilvestreDeSousa 2 47
(Mark Johnston) *t.k.h: pressed wnr: rdn over 2f out: outpcd whn short of room over 1f out: sn btn* **9/4**[2]

1m 30.34s (1.34) **Going Correction** +0.225s/f (Good)
WFA 3 from 4yo+ 7lb **6** Ran SP% **115.8**
Speed ratings (Par 103): **101,100,100,90,87 87**
Tote Swingers: 1&2 £1.80, 1&3 £4.00, 2&3 £3.30. Tote Super 7: Win: Not won. Place: £188.50. CSF £12.27 TOTE £4.90: £1.60, £1.30; EX 15.20.
Owner Shatin Racing Group **Bred** Adrian Purvis **Trained** East Kilbride, S Lanarks
■ Stewards' Enquiry : Adrian Nicholls two-day ban: careless riding (2-3 Aug)
Paul Hanagan one-day ban: used whip in the incorrect place (2 Aug)

FOCUS
An ordinary handicap with the winner improving and the form rated slightly positively.

Cyflymder(IRE) Official explanation: jockey said that the gelding bled from the nose
T/Plt: £136.50 to a £1 stake. Pool: £65,700.73 - 351.13 winning tickets. T/Qpdt: £45.70 to a £1 stake. Pool: £6,637.59 - 107.32 winning tickets. RY

[3947] SOUTHWELL (L-H)

Tuesday, July 19

OFFICIAL GOING: Standard

Wind: Light behind Weather: Cloudy

4177 DINE IN THE PANTRY RESTAURANT H'CAP — 1m 3f (F)

6:00 (6:00) (Class 6) (0-65,65) 3-Y-0+ — **£1,704** (£503; £251) **Stalls** Low

Form — RPR

0006 **1** **Think Its All Over (USA)**[19] [3545] 4-9-7 **58** .... MickyFenton 9 — 69
(Julie Camacho) *in tch on inner: swtchd outside and hdwy over 3f out: rdn to chal wl over 1f out: drvn and styd on ins fnl f to ld last 100yds* **9/2**[2]

0-04 **2** *1* **Mighty Mambo**[26] [3311] 4-9-12 **63** .... DarrylHolland 3 — 72
(George Margarson) *led: pushed along over 3f out: rdn over 2f out: drvn over 1f out: edgd rt ins fnl f: hdd and no ex last 100yds* **5/1**[3]

04-2 **3** *3 ¼* **Pennfield Pirate**[11] [3814] 4-9-11 **62** .... SteveDrowne 7 — 65
(Hughie Morrison) *cl up: effrt over 2f out: sn rdn and ev ch tl drvn and wknd appr fnl f* **5/2**[1]

550 **4** *1 ¾* **Waahej**[20] [3515] 5-9-3 **59** .... LauraPike(5) 2 — 59
(Peter Hiatt) *towards rr: hdwy 4f out: rdn to chse ldrs 2f out: sn drvn and no imp appr fnl f* **8/1**

/550 **5** *7* **Can Can Dancer**[21] [3496] 6-8-9 **46** oh1 .... RobbieFitzpatrick 11 — 33
(Charles Smith) *in rr: hdwy 4f out: rdn along to chse ldrs on inner 2f out: sn drvn and no further prog* **50/1**

6-05 **6** *nse* **Colzium**[21] [3487] 3-7-12 **46** oh1 .... NickyMackay 12 — 33
(Mark H Tompkins) *trckd ldrs: effrt over 3f out: rdn along over 2f out: drvn wl over 1f out and sn wknd* **20/1**

4232 **7** *2* **Carnac (IRE)**[126] [859] 5-8-13 **57** ....(p) NoraLooby(7) 10 — 41
(Alan McCabe) *trckd ldrs: rdn along over 3f out: drvn over 2f out and grad wknd* **10/1**

/060 **8** *12* **Hardanger (IRE)**[52] [451] 6-8-9 **46** oh1 ....(t[1]) BarryMcHugh 1 — 8
(Tim Fitzgerald) *sn pushed along to chse ldrs on inner: rdn along over 4f out: drvn over 3f out and sn wknd* **50/1**

5630 **9** *3 ¼* **Camps Bay (USA)**[34] [3047] 7-9-4 **62** .... SophieSilvester(7) 6 — 18
(Conor Dore) *a in midfield* **16/1**

1236 **10** *hd* **Hernando Torres**[11] [3809] 3-9-3 **65** .... JamesSullivan 13 — 21
(Michael Easterby) *dwlt: a in rr* **14/1**

2-13 **11** *2 ¼* **Castle Myth (USA)**[99] [374] 5-10-0 **65** ....(be) PaulDoe 8 — 17
(Jim Best) *midfield: rdn along over 4f out: sn bhd* **8/1**

4-05 **12** *4 ½* **River Ardeche**[52] [2492] 6-9-6 **60** .... PatrickDonaghy(3) 5 — —
(Ben Haslam) *a in rr* **20/1**

450/ **13** *72* **Millers Crossing**[759] [3175] 5-9-4 **55** ....(p) CathyGannon 4 — —
(Michael Squance) *a towards rr: rdn along and lost pl 7f out: sn bhd and t.o fnl 3f* **33/1**

2m 25.49s (-2.51) **Going Correction** -0.15s/f (Stan)
WFA 3 from 4yo+ 11lb — **13** Ran SP% **123.7**
Speed ratings (Par 101): **103,102,99,98,93 93,92,83,80,80 79,75,23**
toteswingers: 1&2 £5.70, 1&3 £3.80, 2&3 £3.40. CSF £26.73 CT £70.10 TOTE £6.00: £2.30, £2.40, £2.10; EX 34.20.
Owner Terry Warner **Bred** B Wayne Hughes **Trained** Norton, N Yorks

FOCUS

A modest opener lacking in-form horses. It was a run at a reasonable gallop but, as usual, few horses got into the race from off the pace. The first two are on good marks while the third is rated 4lb below his latest Newbury form.

Castle Myth(USA) Official explanation: jockey said that the gelding ran flat
Millers Crossing Official explanation: jockey said that the gelding had no more to give

4178 SOUTHWELL CLAIMING STKS — 6f (F)

6:30 (6:30) (Class 6) 2-Y-0 — **£1,704** (£503; £251) **Stalls** Low

Form — RPR

2112 **1** **Pint Size**[7] [3948] 2-8-13 0 .... AntiocoMurgia(7) 1 — 84
(Gay Kelleway) *mde all: shkn up and wnt clr wl over 1f out: pushed along* **8/13**[1]

53 **2** *12* **Miss Medici (IRE)**[14] [3708] 2-8-5 0 .... LukeMorris 2 — 33
(Des Donovan) *trckd ldng pair: hdwy to chse wnr 3f out: rdn over 2f out: drvn and one pce fr wl over 1f out* **12/1**

5604 **3** *1 ¼* **Spring Daisy (IRE)**[7] [3948] 2-8-10 0 .... RichardKingscote 5 — 34
(Tom Dascombe) *cl up: rdn along 1/2-way: drvn and one pce fr wl over 2f out* **16/1**

5205 **4** *6* **Ciara Boo (IRE)**[7] [3955] 2-8-5 0 ....(v[1]) CathyGannon 6 — 11
(David Evans) *dwlt: sn rdn along and a in rr* **10/1**[3]

2253 **5** *1* **Auntie Joy**[14] [3700] 2-9-0 0 .... JamesSullivan 4 — 17
(Michael Easterby) *chsd ldrs: rdn along bef 1/2-way and sn outpcd* **3/1**[2]

1m 16.35s (-0.15) **Going Correction** -0.15s/f (Stan) — **5** Ran SP% **109.6**
Speed ratings (Par 92): **95,79,77,69,68**
toteswinger: 1&2 £5.70. CSF £8.99 TOTE £1.70: £1.40, £1.40; EX 8.20.
Owner Whispering Winds **Bred** Bambi Bloodstock **Trained** Exning, Suffolk

FOCUS

An uncompetitive claimer won as easily by the favourite as the betting suggested it would be. The form is hard to rate but this was probably the winner's best effort yet.

NOTEBOOK

Pint Size had an outstanding chance at the weights and won well under a sensible no-nonsense ride, taken straight to the front and dictating to the others instead of being dictated to. His trainer reported beforehand that she doubted he'd win a nursery right now and she's almost certainly right with the official assessor nearly always inclined to take an overly cautious view of early-season wide-margin claiming/selling race winners. (op 4-7 tchd 8-15)

Miss Medici(IRE) was a bit keen early on and probably paid in the end for being the only one able to chase the winner when that horse upped the tempo. Never a threat to Pint Size, she was well clear of the third for much of the straight and deserves to be rated as such. (op 10-1)

Spring Daisy(IRE) well behind the winner in a nursery here on their most recent run, had next to no chance of reversing form on considerably worse terms and was left behind as soon as the pace increased. There's a small possibility 7f will suit her better, being out of a Celtic Swing mare. (tchd 14-1)

Ciara Boo(IRE) showed no promise (tchd 12-1)

Auntie Joy ran no sort of race on her surface debut. (op 4-1)

4179 MEMBERSHIP OF SOUTHWELL GOLF CLUB H'CAP — 1m (F)

7:00 (7:02) (Class 6) (0-60,60) 3-Y-0+ — **£1,704** (£503; £251) **Stalls** Low

Form — RPR

15 **1** **On The Cusp (IRE)**[26] [3306] 4-9-8 **59** ....(p) MartinHarley(3) 9 — 70
(Richard Guest) *mde all: rdn wl over 1f out: drvn and edgd rt ins fnl f: jst hld on* **5/1**[2]

0532 **2** *nse* **Amtired**[7] [3952] 5-8-13 **50** .... PaulPickard(3) 1 — 61
(Brian Ellison) *dwlt and sn pushed along in rr: hdwy on inner whn n.m.r 3f out: drvn to chse wnr wl over 1f out: sn edgd lft: styd on ins fnl f: jst failed* **5/2**[1]

0-06 **3** *7* **George Thisby**[23] [3426] 5-9-12 **60** ....(b[1]) JamesMillman 4 — 55
(Rod Millman) *sn rdn along and outpcd in rr: wd st and hdwy 2f out: drvn wl over 1f out: kpt on: nrst fin* **9/1**

0-65 **4** *3 ¾* **Sopran Nad (ITY)**[64] [2162] 7-8-12 **46** oh1 .... JamesDoyle 3 — 32
(Frank Sheridan) *trckd wnr: cl up 3f out: rdn over 2f out and sn one pce* **11/2**[3]

0004 **5** *6* **Putin (IRE)**[3] [4089] 3-8-7 **49** .... LukeMorris 5 — 19
(Derek Haydn Jones) *chsd ldrs: rdn along over 3f out: drvn wl over 2f out and sn one pce* **5/1**[2]

0506 **6** *9* **King Columbo (IRE)**[40] [2843] 6-9-7 **58** ....(e[1]) AdamBeschizza(3) 2 — 10
(Julia Feilden) *chsd ldrs on inner: rdn along wl over 2f out: drvn wl over 1f out and grad wknd* **16/1**

6066 **7** *2 ¾* **Yakama (IRE)**[7] [3942] 6-9-1 **49** ....(v) ChrisCatlin 10 — —
(Christine Dunnett) *dwlt: sn chsng ldrs on outer: effrt 3f out: rdn wl over 2f out and grad wknd* **25/1**

0000 **8** *6* **Vibration**[29] [3233] 3-8-9 **51** .... NickyMackay 6 — —
(Hughie Morrison) *prom: rdn along over 3f out and sn wknd* **10/1**

2500 **9** *½* **Blue Charm**[7] [3944] 7-9-4 **55** .... GaryBartley(3) 11 — —
(Ian McInnes) *s.i.s: a in rr* **20/1**

0-00 **10** *½* **Swing Door (IRE)**[27] [3289] 3-9-2 **58** .... AndreaAtzeni 7 — —
(Robert Eddery) *a towards rr* **9/1**

1m 42.08s (-1.62) **Going Correction** -0.15s/f (Stan)
WFA 3 from 4yo+ 8lb — **10** Ran SP% **120.9**
Speed ratings (Par 101): **102,101,94,91,85 76,73,67,66,66**
toteswingers: 1&2 £3.00, 1&3 £5.20, 2&3 £8.10. CSF £18.61 CT £115.72 TOTE £5.80: £2.00, £1.10, £2.50; EX 12.90.
Owner Rakebackmypoker.com **Bred** J Stan Cosgrove **Trained** Stainforth, S Yorks

FOCUS

An ordinary handicap and one in which few horses ever threatened to make an impact. The runner-up is rated to his best course form.

Swing Door(IRE) Official explanation: jockey said that the filly was never travelling.

4180 SOUTHWELL MEDIAN AUCTION MAIDEN STKS — 1m 4f (F)

7:30 (7:32) (Class 5) 3-5-Y-0 — **£2,385** (£704; £352) **Stalls** Low

Form — RPR

63 **1** **Cluain Dara (IRE)**[29] [3214] 3-8-10 0 .... DarrylHolland 3 — 77+
(Mark Johnston) *trckd ldr: led over 5f out: pushed clr over 2f out: rdn wl over 1f out: edgd rt ent fnl f: kpt on wl* **6/1**[3]

0-43 **2** *7* **Quails Hollow (IRE)**[24] [3377] 3-9-1 70 .... LiamJones 1 — 71+
(William Haggas) *rn in snatches: bhd and pushed along after 3f: hdwy 5f out: rdn along 4f out: drvn to chse ldng pair 3f out: plugged on same pce to take poor 2nd ins fnl f: no ch w wnr* **2/5**[1]

4-04 **3** *1 ¾* **Zenarinda**[31] [3170] 4-9-8 65 .... NickyMackay 5 — 63
(Mark H Tompkins) *trckd ldrs: hdwy to chse wnr over 4f out: effrt 3f out: sn rdn and one pce* **4/1**[2]

5 **4** *8* **Delight Of The Eye**[19] [3550] 3-8-10 0 .... SteveDrowne 2 — 50
(Alastair Lidderdale) *chsd ldrs: rdn along wl over 3f out: sn drvn and outpcd* **20/1**

4 **5** *13* **Frolic Along (IRE)**[98] [1285] 4-9-8 0 .... StephenCraine 8 — 29
(J R Jenkins) *dwlt and in rr: sme hdwy over 3f out: sn rdn and nvr a factor* **33/1**

-0 **6** *14* **Seawood**[26] [3324] 5-9-13 0 .... PaulQuinn 6 — 12
(Roy Bowring) *prom: rdn along 4f out: drvn over 3f out and sn wknd* **100/1**

7 *18* **Miss Kessie**[55] 5-9-8 0 .... MickyFenton 9 — —
(Paul Midgley) *led: rdn along 1/2-way: sn hdd & wknd: bhd fnl 3f* **66/1**

8 *3 ¼* **Fair Dinkum (IRE)** 3-9-1 0 .... FergusSweeney 4 — —
(Jamie Osborne) *dwlt: a in rr: bhd fnl 3f* **7/1**

006- **9** *2 ¼* **Micky's Bird**[469] [1145] 4-9-8 36 .... RobbieFitzpatrick 7 — —
(Richard Guest) *a towards rr: bhd fnl 3f* **66/1**

2m 38.52s (-2.48) **Going Correction** -0.15s/f (Stan)
WFA 3 from 4yo+ 12lb — **9** Ran SP% **129.9**
Speed ratings (Par 103): **102,97,96,90,82 72,60,58,57**
toteswingers: 1&2 £1.20, 1&3 £2.30, 2&3 £1.70. CSF £9.95 TOTE £8.00: £1.80, £1.02, £1.40; EX 13.80.
Owner Mrs Joan Keaney **Bred** Mrs Joan Keaney **Trained** Middleham Moor, N Yorks

FOCUS

A weak median auction maiden run at a fair gallop but once again only a handful ever threatened to get competitive. The clear winner is rated close to his turf form.

Zenarinda Official explanation: jockey said that the filly hung right

4181 DINE IN THE PANTRY H'CAP — 2m (F)

8:00 (8:00) (Class 6) (0-65,60) 3-Y-0 — **£1,704** (£503; £251) **Stalls** Low

Form — RPR

0210 **1** **Captain Bellamy (USA)**[40] [2842] 3-9-7 **60** .... SteveDrowne 5 — 71
(Hughie Morrison) *trckd ldng pair: hdwy to ld 3f out: rdn wl over 1f out: drvn out* **10/11**[1]

3403 **2** *4 ½* **Revolutionary**[8] [3923] 3-9-1 **57** .... SophieDoyle(3) 1 — 62
(Jamie Osborne) *led: rdn along 4f out: hdd 3f out: drvn wl over 1f out: kpt on same pce u.p fnl f* **11/4**[2]

00-6 **3** *17* **If What And Maybe**[8] [3922] 3-9-3 **59** .... MichaelO'Connell(3) 2 — 44
(John Ryan) *cl up: rdn along over 3f out: drvn and wknd wl over 2f out* **12/1**

6456 **4** *11* **Delagoa Bay (IRE)**[8] [3910] 3-8-9 **48** .... LiamKeniry 4 — 20
(Sylvester Kirk) *in rr: sme hdwy and in tch 1/2-way: rdn along over 5f out: sn outpcd and bhd fnl 3f* **9/2**[3]

004 **5** *21* **Leah's Angel (IRE)**[13] [3734] 3-8-6 **45** ....(p) PaulQuinn 3 — —
(Michael Mullineaux) *in tch: rdn along 1/2-way: sn outpcd and wl bhd fnl 3f* **25/1**

000- **P** **Henry Bond**[9] [6676] 3-8-1 **45** .... DanielleMcCreery(5) 6 — —
(Shaun Harris) *trckd ldrs: rdn along 1/2-way: sn wknd and in rr whn p.u 5f out* **33/1**

3m 47.74s (2.24) **Going Correction** -0.15s/f (Stan) — **6** Ran SP% **111.7**
Speed ratings (Par 101): **88,85,77,71,61** —
toteswingers: 1&2 £1.10, 1&3 £1.60, 2&3 £2.80. CSF £3.57 TOTE £1.80: £1.10, £1.80; EX 4.20.

Owner A C Pickford & G J Parrott **Bred** Brereton C Jones **Trained** East Ilsley, Berks

FOCUS

A very uncompetitive handicap that featured only the first three from a long way out. With all the runners trying the trip for the first time the pace was not surprisingly moderate. The winner is rated to form.

Henry Bond Official explanation: jockey said that the gelding lost action

4182 JOLLY JUNGLE PLAYLAND H'CAP 5f (F)

8:30 (8:30) (Class 5) (0-70,70) 3-Y-O+ **£3,234** (£962; £481; £240) **Stalls** High

Form RPR

3153 **1** **Eastern Hills**[7] 3952 6-9-1 **62**.......................(p) MartinHarley(3) 2 79
(Alan McCabe) *cl up: led wl over 1f out: rdn clr ent fnl f: edgd lft and kpt on strly* **7/2**[1]

4530 **2** *3 1/4* **Diamond Johnny G (USA)**[4] 4057 4-9-3 **64**..........(t) AlanCreighton(3) 4 69
(Edward Creighton) *led: rdn along 2f out: sn hdd: drvn and kpt on fnl f* **9/1**

0100 **3** *3/4* **Premier League**[14] 3711 4-9-1 **59**.......................(p) RoystonFfrench 6 62
(Julia Feilden) *in tch: hdwy wl over 1f out: sn rdn and kpt on ins fnl f: nrst fin* **10/1**

0543 **4** *2 3/4* **Bookiesindex Boy**[7] 3939 7-9-12 **70**.......................(bt) StephenCraine 9 63
(J R Jenkins) *trckd ldrs: effrt over 1f out: sn rdn and one pce* **7/1**[3]

-000 **5** *1/2* **No Mean Trick (USA)**[7] 3931 5-9-2 **60**....................... MickyFenton 7 51
(Paul Midgley) *in tch 1f: sn outpcd and in rr tl styd on u.p fr over 1f out: n.d* **33/1**

3143 **6** *3/4* **Liberal Lady**[8] 3908 3-8-13 **61**....................... SteveDrowne 5 49
(Hughie Morrison) *chsd ldrs: effrt and cl up 1/2-way: sn rdn and wknd wl over 1f out* **4/1**[2]

3330 **7** *3/4* **Spic 'n Span**[4] 4057 6-9-6 **64**.......................(b) LukeMorris 1 50
(Ronald Harris) *rrd and plunged s and rdr lost iron: a in rr* **7/2**[1]

6005 **8** *3/4* **Wreningham**[7] 3957 6-8-12 **56**.......................(t) WilliamCarson 8 39
(Stuart Williams) *cl up: rdn along bef 1/2-way: sn wknd* **8/1**

0030 **9** *2 1/2* **Co Dependent (USA)**[7] 3953 5-9-12 **70**................(b[1]) FergusSweeney 3 44
(Jamie Osborne) *chsd ldrs: rdn along 1/2-way: sn wknd* **14/1**

58.46 secs (-1.24) **Going Correction** -0.15s/f (Stan)
WFA 3 from 4yo+ 4lb **9** Ran SP% **116.8**
Speed ratings (Par 103): **103,97,96,92,91 90,89,87,83**
toteswingers: 1&2 £2.70, 1&3 £5.00, 2&3 £10.30. CSF £36.04 CT £291.52 TOTE £4.10: £1.30, £2.40, £3.60; EX 42.50.

Owner Charles Wentworth **Bred** Azienda Agricola Patrizia **Trained** Averham Park, Notts

FOCUS

A fair handicap turned into a procession by one previously considered a miler who proved a revelation on his first run at the minimum trip. The winner is rated to his best with the runner-up the best guide to his recent marks.

4183 BOOK TICKETS ON LINE SOUTHWELL-RACECOURSE.CO.UK H'CAP 7f (F)

9:00 (9:03) (Class 6) (0-60,60) 3-Y-O+ **£1,704** (£503; £251) **Stalls** Low

Form RPR

3050 **1** **Norcroft**[85] 1570 9-8-5 **46** oh1.......................(p) DanielHarris(7) 5 55
(Christine Dunnett) *chsd ldrs: swtchd rt and hdwy over 2f out: rdn over 1f out: styd on ins fnl f to ld on line* **20/1**

3552 **2** *nse* **Elusive Warrior (USA)**[7] 3953 8-9-5 **53**.......................(p) JamesDoyle 11 62
(Alan McCabe) *cl up: chal wl over 1f out and sn rdn: drvn ent fnl f: led last 100yds: hdd and no ex nr line* **9/4**[1]

10-2 **3** *1* **Clever Omneya (USA)**[166] 397 5-9-9 **57**....................... StephenCraine 3 63
(J R Jenkins) *led: rdn wl over 1f out: drvn ent fnl f: hdd and one pce last 100yds* **6/1**[2]

-005 **4** *6* **Babich Bay (IRE)**[7] 3953 3-9-5 **60**.......................(v) DarryllHolland 4 47
(Jo Hughes) *prom whn n.m.r and squeezed out after 1f: swtchd rt and sn chsng ldrs: rdn along wl over 2f out: no imp* **6/1**[2]

0000 **5** *3/4* **Spacecraft (IRE)**[38] 2900 4-8-9 **46** oh1.......................(b) PaulPickard(3) 13 34
(Christopher Kellett) *s.i.s and bhd: rdn along bef 1/2-way: styd on fnl 2f: nrst fin* **50/1**

3040 **6** *3 1/4* **Loose Quality (USA)**[7] 3944 3-8-10 **58**....................... BrendanPowell(7) 6 34
(Chris Gordon) *cl up: rdn along wl over 2f out: drvn wl over 1f out and grad wknd* **8/1**

0000 **7** *3 1/2* **Realt Na Mara (IRE)**[27] 3293 8-8-5 **46** oh1....................... JacobMoore(7) 1 16
(Hughie Morrison) *awkward s: a towards rr* **6/1**[2]

2-00 **8** *3/4* **Norton Girl**[24] 3387 3-8-12 **56**....................... MichaelO'Connell(3) 8 21
(Michael Herrington) *midfield: rdn along over 2f out: n.d* **14/1**

0000 **9** *2 1/2* **Bishopbriggs (USA)**[14] 3720 6-9-8 **56**....................... FrankieMcDonald 12 17
(K F Clutterbuck) *a towards rr* **28/1**

3400 **10** *8* **Bajan Pride**[22] 3456 7-9-5 **53**.......................(b) MickyFenton 10 —
(Paul Midgley) *in tch: rdn along wl over 2f out: sn wknd* **14/1**

0000 **11** *6* **Scintillating (IRE)**[50] 2569 4-8-12 **46** oh1.......................(p) RoystonFfrench 9 —
(Ray Peacock) *midfield: rdn along bef 1/2-way: sn wknd and bhd* **50/1**

4003 **12** *22* **Invent**[7] 3958 3-8-12 **53**.......................(t) AndreaAtzeni 7 —
(Robert Eddery) *dwlt and a in rr: lost action and bhd after 2f: t.o and virtually p.u fnl 2f* **13/2**[3]

1m 29.78s (-0.52) **Going Correction** -0.15s/f (Stan)
WFA 3 from 4yo+ 7lb **12** Ran SP% **123.5**
Speed ratings (Par 101): **96,95,94,87,87 83,79,78,75,66 59,34**
toteswingers: 1&2 £10.40, 1&3 £34.70, 2&3 £5.90. CSF £66.07 CT £328.29 TOTE £25.50: £8.10, £1.30, £2.90; EX 59.30.

Owner Mrs Christine Dunnett **Bred** Norcroft Park Stud **Trained** Hingham, Norfolk

FOCUS

A modest finale in which once again it paid to adopt a handy position from the off. The form looks sound at face value, rated around the placed horses.

Invent Official explanation: jockey said gelding's saddle slipped

T/Plt: £19.40 to a £1 stake. Pool: £65,708.58 - 2,463.12 winning tickets. T/Qpdt: £8.70 to a £1 stake. Pool: £6,265.65 - 532.22 winning tickets. JR

[4159]YARMOUTH (L-H)

Tuesday, July 19

OFFICIAL GOING: Soft (6.1)

Wind: fairly light, medium against Weather: sunny, light cloud, light rain for final two races

4184 SPIFFING CRABBIE'S ALCOHOLIC GINGER BEER MAIDEN AUCTION STKS 6f 3y

2:15 (2:22) (Class 5) 2-Y-O **£2,264** (£673; £336; £168) **Stalls** High

Form RPR

3 **1** **Emirates Art**[13] 3746 2-8-11 0....................... JamieSpencer 4 76
(David Simcock) *chsd ldrs: rdn and effrt 2f out: chsd ldr and drvn over 1f: kpt on under hands and heels fnl f to ld fnl 50yds: hld on cl home* **4/5**[1]

45 **2** *shd* **My Sharona**[28] 3257 2-7-13 0....................... KieranO'Neill(5) 2 69
(Sylvester Kirk) *led: rdn ent fnl 2f: drvn and hrd pressed 1f out: hdd fnl 50yds: rallied gamely cl home* **9/4**[2]

404 **3** *4* **Tidal's Baby**[12] 3761 2-8-12 0....................... AdamKirby 3 66
(Noel Quinlan) *t.k.h: chsd ldr: rdn ent fnl 2f: drvn and lost 2nd over 1f out: wknd fnl f* **9/2**[3]

0 **4** *2 3/4* **Levi Draper**[26] 3308 2-8-9 0....................... PatCosgrave 5 54
(James Fanshawe) *t.k.h: hld up wl in tch: shkn up and nt clr run over 2f out: sn rdn: wknd over 1f out* **7/1**

1m 16.81s (2.41) **Going Correction** +0.30s/f (Good) **4** Ran SP% **117.0**
Speed ratings (Par 94): **95,94,89,85**
CSF £3.29 TOTE £1.70; EX 3.20.

Owner M M Racing **Bred** David Elsworth & Matthew Green **Trained** Newmarket, Suffolk

FOCUS

The front pair drew a little way clear in what was a modest juvenile maiden. The form is rated through the runner-up to her Newbury mark.

NOTEBOOK

Emirates Art caught the eye when a promising third over this trip on her recent Lingfield debut and probably made harder work of landing this than expected. She can improve for a step up to 7f, though, and should make her mark in nurseries. (op 8-11 tchd 10-11)

My Sharona briefly looked to have the winner in trouble, but it was inevitable from 1f out she was going to be denied. Clear of the third, she too is a likely type for nurseries. (op 3-1)

Tidal's Baby was unable to race on with the front pair and looks likely to benefit from further. (op 11-2 tchd 7-2)

Levi Draper still looked immature and it's doubtful he'll be winning a maiden, but as a close relation of Soar and Feet So Fast, it'll be disappointing if he can't make an impact in handicaps at some stage. (op 11-1 tchd 13-2)

4185 STANLEY THREADWELL MEMORIAL FILLIES' H'CAP 1m 3y

2:45 (2:46) (Class 5) (0-70,76) 3-Y-O+ **£2,264** (£673; £336; £168) **Stalls** High

Form RPR

26-6 **1** **Complexion**[37] 2960 3-9-4 **68**....................... RyanMoore 10 86+
(Sir Michael Stoute) *stdd and dropped in bhd after s: hld up in rr: swtchd lft and hdwy over 2f out: rdn to ld and edgd rt over 1f out: rdn clr fnl f: styd on wl: comf* **5/2**[1]

0042 **2** *5* **Madame Excelerate**[8] 3912 4-9-6 **62**....................... TomMcLaughlin 2 70
(Mark Brisbourne) *in tch: hdwy to press ldrs over 3f out: rdn to ld 2f out: hdd and edgd rt over 1f out: no ex and btn 1f out: wknd ins fnl f* **10/3**[2]

0030 **3** *4* **Viking Rose (IRE)**[14] 3709 3-8-8 **58**....................... LukeMorris 9 55
(James Eustace) *chsd ldrs: rdn and ev ch 2f out: wandered u.p wl over 1f out: wknd 1f out* **10/1**

5-00 **4** *2* **Miss Villefranche**[21] 3487 3-8-10 **60**.......................(v) HayleyTurner 8 52
(Michael Bell) *led: hdd and rdn 2f out: wknd u.p jst over 1f out: fdd fnl f* **14/1**

4344 **5** *10* **But Beautiful (IRE)**[31] 3172 4-9-13 **69**....................... EddieAhern 7 40
(Robert Mills) *hld up in tch in last pair: hdwy over 3f out: rdn and wknd over 1f out: wl btn and eased ins fnl f* **5/1**[3]

4203 **6** *shd* **Exopuntia**[32] 3130 5-9-1 **57**....................... TonyCulhane 1 28
(Julia Feilden) *chsd ldrs: rdn and struggling wl over 2f out: wknd 2f out: wl bhd and eased ins fnl f* **11/2**

000 **7** [illegible] [illegible] The Light [illegible]
(Garry Woodward) *dwlt: sn in tch: rdn and wknd over 2f out: wl bhd fnl f* **66/1**

-036 **8** *20* **Makheelah**[12] 3757 3-9-0 **64**....................... PhilipRobinson 3 —
(Clive Brittain) *chsd ldr tl lost pl qckly over 3f out: wl bhd and virtually p.u fnl 2f: t.o* **8/1**

400 **9** *17* **Gay Gallivanter**[38] 2916 3-8-12 **62**....................... PatCosgrave 5 —
(Michael Quinn) *taken down early: t.k.h: chsd ldrs tl rdn and wknd wl over 3f out: wl bhd and virtually p.u fnl 2f: t.o* **50/1**

1m 43.62s (3.02) **Going Correction** +0.30s/f (Good)
WFA 3 from 4yo+ 8lb **9** Ran SP% **114.0**
Speed ratings (Par 100): **96,91,87,85,75 74,74,54,37**
Tote Swingers: 1&2 £2.80, 1&3 £6.40, 2&3 £8.30 CSF £10.65 CT £68.62 TOTE £2.70: £1.10, £1.70, £3.50; EX 10.70 Trifecta £93.00 Pool: £645.19 - 5.13 winning units..
Owner K Abdulla **Bred** Juddmonte Farms Ltd **Trained** Newmarket, Suffolk

FOCUS

A fairly moderate fillies' handicap with the second the best guide to the level.

Exopuntia Official explanation: traine said the mare had a breathing problem

Makheelah Official explanation: trainer's representative said that the filly was unsuited by the soft ground

4186 MRKING.CO.UK MAIDEN STKS 7f 3y

3:15 (3:21) (Class 5) 3-4-Y-O **£2,264** (£673; £336; £168) **Stalls** High

Form RPR

0-20 **1** **Our Gal**[31] 3183 3-8-12 75....................... RyanMoore 7 76
(Noel Quinlan) *t.k.h: hld up in tch: rdn and effrt 2f out: drvn to chal 1f out: kpt on u.p to ld wl ins fnl f* **4/1**[3]

52 **2** *hd* **Crystal High**[18] 3577 3-8-12 0....................... AdamKirby 8 75
(Marco Botti) *racd alone on stands' rail: w ldrs tl led over 3f out: rdn 2f out: drvn and hrd pressed 1f out: kpt on tl hdd and no ex wl ins fnl f* **3/1**[2]

00 **3** *3* **Llewellyn**[31] 3183 3-9-3 0....................... PatCosgrave 1 73
(James Fanshawe) *stdd s: t.k.h: hld up in tch: rdn 3f out: hdwy u.p over 1f out: ev ch 1f out: wknd fnl 75yds* **11/1**

02 **4** *3/4* **Noverton**[27] 3289 3-8-12 0....................... DaneO'Neill 4 66
(James Eustace) *led tl over 3f out: rdn 2f out: ev ch 1f out: wknd fnl 100yds* **11/4**[1]

5 *10* **Lifetime (IRE)** 3-9-3 0....................... NeilCallan 3 45
(Mark Johnston) *chsd ldrs: rdn 3f out: wknd u.p 2f out: wl bhd fnl f* **7/1**

U 6 13 **Kantata**[38] 2924 3-8-12 0 .... KirstyMilczarek 5 —
(James Toller) *restless in stalls: in tch tl 3f out: sn lost tch: t.o fnl f* **33/1**

1m 30.79s (4.19) **Going Correction** +0.30s/f (Good) **6** Ran SP% **95.4**
Speed ratings (Par 103): **88,87,84,83,72 57**
Tote Swingers: 1&2 £1.80, 1&3 £4.60, 2&3 £5.20 CSF £11.54 TOTE £4.10: £1.70, £1.70; EX 14.30 Trifecta £85.30 Pool: £386.20 - 3.35 winning units..
Owner G Wilding **Bred** G Wilding **Trained** Newmarket, Suffolk

FOCUS
A moderate maiden best rated through the winner.

4187 NELSON MUSEUM H'CAP 6f 3y
3:45 (3:45) (Class 6) (0-60,63) 3-Y-0+ **£1,617** (£481; £240; £120) **Stalls** High

Form RPR

-463 **1** **Katy's Secret**[14] 3714 4-9-6 **56** .... DaneO'Neill 10 65
(William Jarvis) *hld up in tch in rr: rdn and hdwy jst over 2f out: rdn to chse ldr over 1f out: led fnl 100yds: r.o wl* **10/1**

2002 **2** *1* **Steel City Boy (IRE)**[7] 3956 8-9-7 **57** .... KellyHarrison 7 63
(Garry Woodward) *racd keenly: led: rdn over 1f out: hdd and no ex fnl 100yds* **5/1**[3]

0020 **3** *hd* **Caldermud (IRE)**[20] 3512 4-9-9 **59** ....(t) IanMongan 5 64+
(Olivia Maylam) *taken down early: t.k.h: hld up in tch in last pair: swtchd lft over 2f out: rdn and effrt 2f out: chsd ldrs 1f out: kpt on wl u.p fnl 100yds* **11/2**

0031 **4** *1 ¼* **Captainrisk (IRE)**[7] 3956 5-9-13 **63** 6ex ....(v) SebSanders 8 64
(Christine Dunnett) *chsd ldrs: rdn and swtchd lft 2f out: drvn over 1f out: styd on same pce fnl f* **7/2**[2]

6636 **5** *4 ½* **Itsthursdayalready**[14] 3714 4-9-4 **54** .... TomMcLaughlin 4 41
(Mark Brisbourne) *taken down early: in tch: pushed along over 3f out: rdn and effrt to chse ldrs jst over 2f out: wknd over 1f out* **6/1**

-402 **6** *1 ¼* **Meia Noite**[14] 3719 4-9-10 **60** .... GeorgeBaker 3 43
(Chris Wall) *taken down early: chsd ldr: rdn and fnd little 2f out: lost 2nd over 1f out: wknd ent fnl f* **3/1**[1]

0300 **7** *3* **Memphis Man**[11] 3805 8-9-6 **59** .... RichardEvans(3) 1 32
(David Evans) *taken down early: chsd ldrs: rdn over 3f out: wknd and bhd 2f out* **8/1**

0600 **8** *9* **Bird Dog**[31] 3173 5-8-10 **46** oh1 ....(v[1]) KirstyMilczarek 2 —
(Phil McEntee) *in tch: hdwy to chse ldrs after 2f: rdn and wkng whn sltly hmpd 2f out: sn wl bhd: t.o* **66/1**

1m 17.13s (2.73) **Going Correction** +0.30s/f (Good)
WFA 3 from 4yo+ 5lb **8** Ran SP% **115.3**
Speed ratings (Par 101): **93,91,91,89,83 82,78,66**
Tote Swingers: 1&2 £6.50, 1&3 £11.80, 2&3 £8.40 CSF £59.55 CT £306.50 TOTE £9.10: £3.10, £1.20, £2.30; EX 35.40 Trifecta £241.80 Pool: £895.31 - 2.74 winning units..
Owner Miss S E Hall **Bred** Miss S E Hall **Trained** Newmarket, Suffolk

FOCUS
A fairly low-grade sprint handicap rated around the first two.

4188 TAKE A TEST DRIVE WITH M.R. KING H'CAP 6f 3y
4:15 (4:15) (Class 4) (0-85,85) 3-Y-0+ **£4,075** (£1,212; £606; £303) **Stalls** High

Form RPR

0006 **1** **Below Zero (IRE)**[10] 3841 4-9-8 **81** .... KierenFallon 8 91
(Mark Johnston) *chsd ldrs: swtchd lft and rdn jst over 2f out: led over 1f out: hld on wl fnl f* **8/1**[2]

6/0- **2** *nk* **Capone (IRE)**[346] 4832 6-9-9 **82** .... IanMongan 7 91
(David Nicholls) *t.k.h: hld up in tch: swtchd lft and hdwy 2f out: ev ch and drvn jst ins fnl f: kpt on* **16/1**

5000 **3** *1 ½* **Cardinal**[31] 3179 6-9-1 **74** .... HayleyTurner 4 78
(Robert Cowell) *in tch: shkn up and effrt over 1f out: ev ch and rdn jst ins fnl f: no ex and btn fnl 75yds* **12/1**

2-10 **4** *5* **Chiefdom Prince (IRE)**[73] 1888 4-9-11 **84** .... RyanMoore 6 72
(Sir Michael Stoute) *stdd after s: t.k.h: hld up in last pair: rdn over 2f out: swtchd lft and hrd drvn over 1f out: no imp* **4/9**[1]

4004 **5** *1* **Jack My Boy (IRE)**[14] 3704 4-9-9 **85** ....(v[1]) RichardEvans(3) 2 70
(David Evans) *led tl hdd and drvn over 1f out: wknd 1f out* **10/1**[3]

1-00 **6** *2 ¼* **Indian Emperor (IRE)**[38] 2916 3-8-9 **73** ....(p) NeilCallan 1 50
(Roger Varian) *taken down early: chsd ldrs: rdn over 2f out: sn struggling: wknd wl over 1f out* **11/1**

1m 15.36s (0.96) **Going Correction** +0.30s/f (Good)
WFA 3 from 4yo+ 5lb **6** Ran SP% **111.4**
Speed ratings (Par 105): **105,104,102,95,94 91**
Tote Swingers: 1&2 £6.30, 1&3 £2.70, 2&3 £7.80 CSF £106.30 CT £1480.98 TOTE £9.20: £3.10, £5.50; EX 98.80 Trifecta £163.70 Pool: £896.27 - 4.05 wiining units..
Owner Sheikh Hamdan Bin Mohammed Al Maktoum **Bred** Darley **Trained** Middleham Moor, N Yorks

FOCUS
Not the result many were expecting, with red-hot favourite Chiefdom Prince flopping in fourth, making it a fairly weak race for the grade.
Chiefdom Prince(IRE) Official explanation: trainer's representative was unable to offer any explanation for the poor performance shown

4189 DIGIBET H'CAP 5f 43y
4:45 (4:45) (Class 6) (0-60,60) 4-Y-0+ **£1,617** (£481; £240; £120) **Stalls** High

Form RPR

5613 **1** **Bouncy Bouncy (IRE)**[18] 3597 4-9-7 **60** ....(t) HayleyTurner 3 69
(Michael Bell) *t.k.h: hld up wl off the pce in last trio: hdwy 1/2-way: rdn to chse clr ldrs wl over 1f out: drvn and styd on to chal ins fnl f: led fnl 75yds: kpt on wl* **5/2**[2]

3061 **2** *nk* **Liberty Ship**[5] 4000 6-8-8 **54** ....(t) EdmondLinehan(7) 6 62+
(Mark Buckley) *hld up wl off the pce in last trio: nt clr run and swtchd lft 2f out: hdwy on bit jst over 1f out: chsd ldrs and nudged along ins fnl f: pressed wnr and rdn fnl 50yds: kpt on but too much to do* **6/4**[1]

6456 **3** *¾* **Shakespeares Excel**[64] 2164 4-8-7 **46** .... JimmyQuinn 5 51
(Derek Shaw) *racd off the pce in midfield: rdn 1/2-way: clsd u.p jst over 1f out: led ins fnl f: hdd and one pce fnl 75yds* **9/1**

2030 **4** *3 ¼* **Jemimaville (IRE)**[19] 3556 4-8-7 **46** ....(v) WilliamCarson 4 39
(Giles Bravery) *dwlt: short of room and squeezed out sn after s: bhd: edging lft and rdn over 2f out: styd on same pce fnl f: nvr trbld ldrs* **16/1**

-540 **5** *2* **Cloth Ears**[25] 3367 5-9-2 **55** ....(be[1]) KirstyMilczarek 2 41
(Phil McEntee) *led and sn clr w one rival: rdn and forged ahd over 1f out: hdd ins fnl f: fdd bdly fnl 100yds* **25/1**

0/00 **6** *3* **Mrs Medley**[17] 3616 5-8-7 **46** oh1 .... KellyHarrison 1 21
(Garry Woodward) *chsd clr ldrs: rdn and struggling 1/2-way: no ch whn nt clr run and sltly hmpd jst over 1f out* **100/1**

60-3 **7** *2* **Pocket's Pick (IRE)**[19] 3556 5-9-5 **58** ....(b) IanMongan 8 26
(Jim Best) *taken down early: w ldr and sn clr: rdn wl over 1f out: wknd and lost 2nd over 1f out: fdd bdly 1f out* **5/1**[3]

0000 **8** *6* **Takajan (IRE)**[14] 3711 4-8-12 **51** .... TomMcLaughlin 7 —
(Mark Brisbourne) *taken down early: chsd clr ldrs: rdn 3f out: sn lost pl and bhd whn drvn 2f out: sn lost tch* **10/1**

65.27 secs (2.57) **Going Correction** +0.30s/f (Good) **8** Ran SP% **115.0**
Speed ratings (Par 101): **91,90,89,84,80 76,72,63**
Tote Swingers: 1&2 £1.90, 2&3 £3.50 CSF £6.67 CT £26.57 TOTE £3.10: £1.10, £1.20, £2.80; EX 7.10 Trifecta £36.90 Pool: £898.19 - 17.99 winning units..
Owner Mrs A Scotney Mrs D Asplin A Symonds **Bred** Ms Adelaide Foley & Roger O'Callaghan **Trained** Newmarket, Suffolk
■ Stewards' Enquiry : Edmond Linehan three-day ban: weighed in 2lb heavier

FOCUS
The market leaders came to the fore late on in this ordinary handicap, although there's little doubt Liberty Ship should have won. He is rated to his Doncaster form with the winner recording a slight personal-best.
Liberty Ship Official explanation: jockey said, regarding the running and riding, that his instructions were to ride him with plenty of confidence but the horse found little off the bridle; he also reported at the Scales that he was denied a clear run. The trainer stated that these were his instructions.

4190 NELSONS JOURNEY CHARITY H'CAP 1m 3f 101y
5:15 (5:15) (Class 6) (0-65,67) 3-Y-0 **£1,617** (£481; £240; £120) **Stalls** Low

Form RPR

0-60 **1** **Snow Hill**[37] 2956 3-9-6 **64** .... JackMitchell 4 82
(Chris Wall) *chsd ldr tl led over 2f out: rdn clr and hung lft wl over 1f out: stl hanging but in command after: styd on wl fnl f* **8/1**

-052 **2** *4* **Astromagick**[12] 3770 3-9-7 **65** .... KierenFallon 8 77
(Mark H Tompkins) *bhd and niggled along: rdn and hdwy over 3f out: drvn to chse clr wnr 2f out: edgd lft and no imp over 1f out* **10/3**[2]

5-01 **3** *2 ¾* **Susan Stroman**[8] 3922 3-9-9 **67** 6ex .... JamieSpencer 6 76
(Ed Dunlop) *racd in last pair: hdwy on outer over 3f out: rdn to dispute 2nd whn edgd lft 2f out: no prog: 3rd and wl btn whn eased wl ins fnl f* **6/5**[1]

0606 **4** *8* **Grecian Goddess (IRE)**[8] 3925 3-8-13 **57** .... KirstyMilczarek 7 50
(John Ryan) *sn led: rdn and hdd over 2f out: wknd wl over 1f out: 4th and wl btn fnl f* **28/1**

005 **5** *1* **Talbot Green**[33] 3080 3-9-7 **65** .... HayleyTurner 1 57
(William Muir) *in tch in midfield: rdn over 3f out: wknd u.p over 2f out: no ch fnl 2f* **12/1**

-045 **6** *9* **Hoofprintinthesnow**[10] 3872 3-9-7 **65** .... RyanMoore 2 41
(Amanda Perrett) *in tch in midfield: pushed along over 3f out: rdn and wknd over 2f out: wl bhd fnl f* **11/2**[3]

4400 **7** *½* **Investment World (IRE)**[21] 3487 3-8-9 **53** .... NeilCallan 3 29
(Mark Johnston) *chsd ldrs tl wknd u.p over 2f out: wl bhd and eased wl ins fnl f* **14/1**

2m 34.07s (5.37) **Going Correction** +0.30s/f (Good) **7** Ran SP% **112.8**
Speed ratings (Par 98): **92,89,87,81,80 74,73**
Tote Swingers: 1&2 £3.60, 1&3 £3.80, 2&3 £1.50 CSF £33.78 CT £53.91 TOTE £12.40: £5.00, £1.60; EX 18.20 Trifecta £79.80 Pool: £691.74 - 6.41 winning units..
Owner Mollers Racing **Bred** Old Mill Stud **Trained** Newmarket, Suffolk

FOCUS
An interesting middle-distance handicap for 3-y-os. The first two are rated improvers in a fair race for the level.
Snow Hill Official explanation: trainer's representative said regarding the apparent improvement of form, that the gelding benefited from a drop in class and the yard picking up after having been out of form
Astromagick Official explanation: jockey said that the filly hung badly left
T/Jkpt: Part won. £10,124.10 to a £1 stake. T/Plt: £184.90 to a £1 stake. Pool: £78,081.81 - 308.12 winning tickets. T/Qpdt: £45.70 to a £1 stake. Pool: £6,637.59 - 107.32 winning tickets.
SP

4191a - (Foreign Racing) - See Raceform Interactive

3972 CATTERICK (L-H)
Wednesday, July 20

OFFICIAL GOING: Soft (6.8)
Wind: Light, half against Weather: Rain races 1, 2 & 7

4192 BRITISH STALLION STUDS SUPPORTING BRITISH RACING E B F MAIDEN STKS 5f 212y
2:10 (2:11) (Class 5) 2-Y-0 **£3,234** (£962; £481; £240) **Stalls** Low

Form RPR

3 **1** **Stormy Whatever (FR)**[21] 3505 2-9-3 0 .... FrederikTylicki 1 77
(James Given) *w ldr: led over 4f out: styd on to forge clr fnl f* **11/4**[1]

3235 **2** *3 ¾* **Blue Shoes (IRE)**[51] 2570 2-8-12 0 .... DavidAllan 7 61
(Tim Easterby) *led tl over 4f out: chsd wnr: kpt on same pce fnl f* **5/1**[3]

3 *¾* **Indego Blues** 2-9-3 0 .... AdrianNicholls 8 64+
(David Nicholls) *pushed along to chse ldrs on wd outside after 1f: kpt on same pce appr fnl f* **6/1**

65 **4** *½* **Valley Of Hope**[61] 2261 2-9-3 0 .... TonyHamilton 10 62
(Richard Fahey) *mid-div: hdwy over 2f out: kpt on: nvr nr to chal* **6/1**

0 **5** *2* **Siberian Belle (IRE)**[14] 3736 2-8-12 0 .... PaulHanagan 2 51+
(Richard Fahey) *chsd ldrs: outpcd over 3f out: kpt on fnl 2f* **10/1**

00 **6** *nk* **Angel Warrior (IRE)**[13] 3755 2-9-3 0 .... PJMcDonald 9 57+
(Ben Haslam) *outpcd and lost pl over 4f out: sn bhd: hdwy over 2f out: kpt on fnl f* **16/1**

64 **7** *¾* **Drummoyne (USA)**[76] 1835 2-9-3 0 .... SilvestreDeSousa 11 53
(Mark Johnston) *chsd ldrs: drvn 4f out: wknd over 1f out* **7/2**[2]

00 **8** *7* **On The Hoof**[13] 3755 2-9-3 0 .... JamesSullivan 4 32
(Michael Easterby) *s.i.s: bhd 4f out: nvr on terms* **50/1**

9 *4* **Point At Issue (IRE)** 2-9-0 0 .... MichaelO'Connell(3) 3 20
(David Nicholls) *s.i.s: bhd fnl 4f* **14/1**

6 **10** *1* **Caymana Girl (IRE)**[11] 3855 2-8-12 0 .... KellyHarrison 5 12
(Micky Hammond) *sn outpcd: bhd fnl 4f* **100/1**

0 **11** *16* **Borley Ghost (FR)**[18] 3611 2-9-3 0 .... TomEaves 6 —
(John Quinn) *sn outpcd: bhd fnl 4f: t.o* **100/1**

1m 17.77s (4.17) **Going Correction** +0.675s/f (Yiel) **11** Ran SP% **119.7**
Speed ratings (Par 94): **99,94,93,92,89 89,88,78,73,72 50**
toteswingers: 1&2 £3.10, 1&3 £5.50, 2&3 £5.10 CSF £17.06 TOTE £4.80: £1.80, £1.10, £2.50; EX 18.90 Trifecta £176.30 Pool: £524.16 - 2.20 winning units..
Owner Simply Racing Limited **Bred** Deln Ltd **Trained** Willoughton, Lincs

FOCUS
This wasn't much of a race depth-wise and predictably, due to the easy ground, the field came to the stands' side on turning in. The winner looks improved with the second the best guide to the level.

NOTEBOOK
Stormy Whatever(FR) ◆ was back to the scene of his promising opening effort, albeit on different ground, and won in the manner of a useful sort in these conditions. He has the physical scope to keep improving and looks capable of more than holding his own in nurseries or novice company. (op 3-1)
Blue Shoes(IRE), up in distance, remains consistent but found the less exposed Stormy Whatever too good in the final stages. (op 6-1 tchd 4-1)
Indego Blues showed plenty of promise on his first racecourse start despite looking green at times. An already gelded £9,000 half-brother to winners, he looks capable of landing a race in time. (op 7-1 tchd 11-2)
Valley Of Hope ◆, returning after a short break, was a big eyecatcher in behind on his third start, and wasn't given a hard time in the final couple of furlongs. One would imagine handicaps are on the agenda now. (op 8-1 tchd 11-2)
Siberian Belle(IRE) kept on well. (op 11-1 tchd 12-1)
Angel Warrior(IRE) stayed on from the rear. (tchd 14-1 and 20-1)
Drummoyne(USA) weakened steadily inside the final furlong after rarely looking a threat once in the home straight. (op 3-1 tchd 11-4)

4193 ST TERESA'S HOSPICE (S) STKS 7f
2:40 (2:41) (Class 6) 2-Y-O **£1,704** (£503; £251) **Stalls** Low

Form RPR
01 **1** **Lady Jourdain (IRE)**[4] 4105 2-8-12 0 .... AndrewElliott 3 62+
(Mrs K Burke) *trckd ldrs: drvn over 3f out: rdn to ld over 1f out: drvn clr ins fnl f* **4/9**[1]
466 **2** *4 ½* **Jaci Uzzi (IRE)**[18] 3631 2-8-6 0 .... SilvestreDeSousa 5 45
(David Evans) *led: drvn over 3f out: hdd over 1f out: no ch w wnr* **6/1**[3]
5 **3** *5* **Brackendale**[8] 3947 2-8-11 0 .... PhillipMakin 4 38
(John Weymes) *trckd ldrs: drvn over 4f out: one pce fnl 2f* **25/1**
340 **4** *1* **Fortune Star (IRE)**[27] 3302 2-8-11 0 .... PaulHanagan 1 35
(Linda Perratt) *sn chsng ldrs: rdn and hung lft over 2f out: one pce* **7/2**[2]
40 **5** *6* **I'm Talking (IRE)**[51] 2556 2-8-6 0 .... CathyGannon 7 16
(David Evans) *hld up: hdwy over 3f out: sn drvn: edgd lft and lost pl over 1f out* **25/1**
00 **6** *14* **Dapper's Dancer**[15] 3708 2-8-6 0 ow3 .... SeanLevey[(3)] 2 —
(David O'Meara) *w ldr: styd centre over 2f out: sn lost pl and bhd* **66/1**
1m 33.11s (6.11) **Going Correction** +0.675s/f (Yiel) **6** Ran SP% **114.9**
Speed ratings (Par 92): **92,86,81,80,73 57**
toteswingers: 1&2 £1.30, 1&3 £4.30, 2&3 £6.70 CSF £3.91 TOTE £1.80: £2.10, £1.90; EX 4.60.There was no bid for the winner.
Owner Mrs Elaine M Burke **Bred** Tally-Ho Stud **Trained** Middleham Moor, North Yorks

FOCUS
A really poor contest, even by selling standards, although the winner is a fair type for the grade.

NOTEBOOK
Lady Jourdain(IRE) won a 6f seller four days previously at Ripon, so had at least proved she was capable of winning. There was a worrying moment for her supporters on turning in, when she seemed to lose her footing for a stride or two, and then had horses close in on her, but once in the clear, she soon put the race to bed and was well on top in the final stages. (op 4-6)
Jaci Uzzi(IRE), last of six on her previous start, was rushed up to lead and saw it out quite well under pressure, without ever causing the winner too many problems. (op 13-2 tchd 10-1)
Brackendale was well beaten at Southwell on his debut, so this was a little bit better.
Fortune Star(IRE) had shown bits and pieces in all three starts prior to this, including once at this level, but never got involved here while hanging. (op 4-1 tchd 9-2)

4194 PRODUCERS NURSERY 7f
3:10 (3:10) (Class 5) 2-Y-O **£2,264** (£673; £336; £168) **Stalls** Low

Form RPR
14 **1** **Act Your Shoe Size**[27] 3313 2-9-2 71 .... DavidAllan 11 75
(Keith Dalgleish) *chsd ldrs: wnt 3rd 2f out: styd on to ld towards fin* **6/1**[3]
3232 **2** *nk* **Tight Lipped (IRE)**[12] 3810 2-9-7 76 .... RichardMullen 7 79
(David Brown) *trckd ldrs: wnt 2nd over 2f out: led over 1f out: hdd and no ex nr fin* **4/1**[2]
656 **3** *2 ½* **Neil's Pride**[36] 3022 2-8-0 55 .... PatrickMathers 13 52+
(Richard Fahey) *rrd s: in rr and sn drvn along: hdwy over 2f out: kpt on fnl f: tk 3rd towards fin* **10/1**
004 **4** *¾* **Moon Trip**[23] 3472 2-8-10 65 .... SilvestreDeSousa 3 60
(Mark Johnston) *w ldr: led over 4f out: hdd over 1f out: one pce* **3/1**[1]
042 **5** *½* **Flurry Of Hands (IRE)**[34] 3070 2-8-3 58 .... AndrewHeffernan 10 52+
(Ann Duffield) [illegible]
302 **6** *1 ¾* **Al Jemailiya (IRE)**[26] 3336 2-9-0 69 .... PhillipMakin 8 59+
(Kevin Ryan) *in rr-div: drvn over 3f out: hdwy over 2f out: edgd lft: nvr nr ldrs* **4/1**[2]
051 **7** *hd* **Schmooze (IRE)**[41] 2854 2-8-7 62 ....(b) PJMcDonald 12 51
(Linda Perratt) *in rr-div: kpt on fnl 2f: nvr nr ldrs* **22/1**
346 **8** *3 ¼* **Devlin**[58] 2346 2-9-1 70 .... PaulHanagan 1 51
(Richard Fahey) *chsd ldrs: drvn 3f out: wknd over 1f out* **15/2**
040 **9** *9* **Come Hither**[27] 3314 2-8-9 64 .... GrahamGibbons 9 22
(Michael Easterby) *s.i.s: a bhd* **40/1**
4365 **10** *2 ½* **Adranian (IRE)**[19] 3584 2-8-4 59 ....(v) CathyGannon 5 11
(David Evans) *sn chsng ldrs: sn drvn along: lost pl over 2f out: sn bhd* **50/1**
13 **11** *12* **Beaumaris (IRE)**[26] 3345 2-9-7 76 .... TomEaves 2 —
(Ann Duffield) *in rr: sn drvn along: bhd fnl 2f: eased* **20/1**
064 **12** *10* **Ernest Speak (IRE)**[15] 3718 2-8-4 59 ....(p) DuranFentiman 6 —
(Bill Turner) *led: hdd over 4f out: lost pl over 2f out: sn bhd* **50/1**
1m 32.56s (5.56) **Going Correction** +0.675s/f (Yiel) **12** Ran SP% **120.4**
Speed ratings (Par 94): **95,94,91,90,90 88,88,84,74,71 57,46**
toteswingers: 1&2 £5.80, 1&3 £13.40, 2&3 £7.10 CSF £28.27 CT £243.70 TOTE £10.40: £3.10, £1.10, £3.70; EX 32.00 Trifecta £210.70 Pool: £484.16 - 1.70 winning units..
Owner Gordon McDowall **Bred** Gordon McDowall **Trained** Carluke, South Lanarkshire
■ The 'official' ratings shown next to each horse are estimated and for information purposes only.

FOCUS
Lots of these could be given a chance on their best pieces of form, albeit mainly on different ground, so this looked a decent contest. The winner scored slightly comfortably and is rated up a few lengths.

NOTEBOOK
Act Your Shoe Size, who won a seller on her first start, was due to take her chance in a Listed race last time at Newmarket before she was pulled out, so looked to have obvious credentials for this considering the faith connections seemingly had in her. Always thereabouts, she challenged late and won a shade comfortably. (op 11-2)
Tight Lipped(IRE) has been running consistently over 5f and 6f, including in another nursery, so his effort helps to give the race shape. Always close up, he looked set to collect when hitting the front a furlong out but wasn't able to hold off his final challenger. (op 7-2)
Neil's Pride ◆ stayed on well after being towards the rear early. She'll probably get 1m this season. (op 9-1 tchd 11-1)
Moon Trip didn't get home after racing prominently and may want quicker ground. (op 9-2 tchd 5-1 in a place)
Flurry Of Hands(IRE) ◆ was of some interest towards the foot of the weights and travelled strongly before weakening when off the bridle. He will be interesting in a similar race on better ground.
Al Jemailiya(IRE) had been steadily progressing but couldn't get involved from off the pace. (op 5-1 tchd 11-2)

4195 SKY BET SUPPORTING YORKSHIRE RACING SUMMER FESTIVAL H'CAP 5f
3:40 (3:56) (Class 4) (0-85,85) 3-Y-O+ **£4,204** (£1,251; £625; £312) **Stalls** Low

Form RPR
301 **1** **Cruise Tothelimit (IRE)**[9] 3914 3-8-7 70 .... PaulHanagan 8 77
(Patrick Morris) *chsd ldrs: outpcd over 2f out: edgd lft 1f out: styd on to ld clsng stages* **11/2**
1105 **2** *nk* **Lucky Art (USA)**[12] 3832 5-9-5 78 .... JamesSullivan 9 85
(Ruth Carr) *w ldr: led over 2f out: hdd and no ex towards fin* **13/2**
5000 **3** *¾* **Arganil (USA)**[15] 3704 6-9-9 82 ....(p) PhillipMakin 6 86
(Kevin Ryan) *sn outpcd: hdwy 2f out: n.m.r styd on ins fnl f* **4/1**[2]
6023 **4** *½* **Absa Lutte (IRE)**[19] 3579 8-8-13 72 .... TomEaves 3 75
(Michael Mullineaux) *outpcd and lost pl after 1f: hdwy 2f out: chsng ldrs 1f out: kpt on same pce ins fnl f* **12/1**
0002 **5** *nse* **Foxy Music**[25] 3379 7-9-12 85 .... GrahamGibbons 7 87
(Eric Alston) *led tl over 2f out: kpt on same pce fnl f* **7/2**[1]
2050 **6** *nk* **The Nifty Fox**[25] 3379 7-9-10 83 ....(v) DavidAllan 5 84
(Tim Easterby) *chsd ldrs: n.m.r 1f out: one pce* **9/2**[3]
3650 **7** *3 ½* **Tamareen (IRE)**[20] 3555 3-8-9 72 .... FrannyNorton 2 60
(Richard Fahey) *in rr: hdwy over 2f out: wknd fnl f* **9/2**[3]
61.17 secs (1.37) **Going Correction** +0.40s/f (Good)
WFA 3 from 4yo+ 4lb **7** Ran SP% **115.0**
Speed ratings (Par 105): **105,104,103,102,102 101,96**
toteswingers: 1&2 £4.40, 1&3 £5.10, 2&3 £5.80 CSF £40.63 CT £158.33 TOTE £7.00: £3.20, £5.50; EX 32.70 Trifecta £174.90 Pool: £917.25 - 3.88 winning units..
Owner Odysian Ltd T/A Cruise Nightspot **Bred** D And Mrs D Veitch **Trained** Tarporley, Cheshire

FOCUS
A decent sprint handicap and a bunched finish. Straightforward form.

4196 TYREGIANT.COM H'CAP 5f 212y
4:10 (4:43) (Class 6) (0-60,60) 3-Y-O+ **£1,617** (£481; £240; £120) **Stalls** Low

Form RPR
6660 **1** **Northern Bolt**[26] 3359 6-9-10 60 .... PatrickMathers 9 76
(Ian McInnes) *trckd ldrs on outside: led over 1f out: styd on wl to forge clr* **12/1**
1406 **2** *3 ¼* **Tombellini (IRE)**[46] 2732 4-9-7 57 .... AndrewMullen 12 63
(David Nicholls) *w ldr: led over 2f out: hdd over 1f out: kpt on same pce* **9/1**
-600 **3** *1 ¾* **Fair Bunny**[19] 3573 4-8-11 47 ....(b) AndrewElliott 4 47
(Alan Brown) *hmpd s: s.i.s: in rr: hdwy stands' side over 2f out: kpt on fnl f* **18/1**
4251 **4** *nk* **Tahitian Princess (IRE)**[5] 4041 3-9-2 57 6ex ....(p) SilvestreDeSousa 3 55+
(Ann Duffield) *s.i.s: bhd and reminders after 1f: hdwy far side over 2f out: hung rt over 1f out: kpt on: eased post* **3/1**[1]
00-6 **5** *1* **Mad Millie (IRE)**[15] 3709 4-9-5 55 .... DanielTudhope 1 51+
(David O'Meara) *chsd ldrs: styd towards far side in st: one pce fnl 2f* **12/1**
0122 **6** *shd* **Hambleton**[8] 3937 4-9-4 54 .... TomEaves 2 50
(Bryan Smart) *chsd ldrs: one pce fnl 2f* **7/2**[3]
3060 **7** *2 ¾* **Poppy's Rocket (IRE)**[29] 3247 3-8-9 50 .... DuranFentiman 7 36
(Marjorie Fife) *chsd ldrs: wknd fnl f* **33/1**
0004 **8** *2 ¾* **Real Diamond**[14] 3732 5-8-12 48 .... PaulHanagan 10 26
(Ollie Pears) *led: hdd over 2f out: wknd over 1f out* **10/3**[2]
0200 **9** *1 ½* **Charles Parnell (IRE)**[7] 3972 8-9-10 60 ....(p) AdrianNicholls 8 33
(Simon Griffiths) *s.s: hdwy over 3f out: lost pl over 1f out* **12/1**
04-3 **10** *1 ¼* **Be A Good Lady**[35] 3049 3-7-12 46 .... TerenceFury[(7)] 5 14
(Tony Coyle) *in rr: drvn 4f out: sn lost pl* **12/1**
1m 17.4s (3.80) **Going Correction** +0.675s/f (Yiel)
WFA [illegible]
Speed ratings (Par 101): **101,96,94,93,92 92,88,85,83,81**
toteswingers: 1&2 £20.50, 1&3 £36.80, 2&3 £31.30 CSF £117.70 CT £1983.26 TOTE £15.20: £4.90, £3.60, £5.30; EX 143.40 TRIFECTA Not won..
Owner Keith Brown Properties (hull) Ltd **Bred** Mrs C Regalado-Gonzalez **Trained** Catwick, E Yorks

FOCUS
A very moderate contest. The winner showed his best form since last autumn.

4197 WELCOME TO YORKSHIRE RAILWAY CHILDREN AT WATERLOO CLAIMING STKS 5f
4:40 (5:11) (Class 6) 3-Y-O+ **£1,704** (£503; £251) **Stalls** Low

Form RPR
0456 **1** **Fol Hollow (IRE)**[13] 3778 6-9-2 84 .... AdrianNicholls 4 73
(David Nicholls) *mde all: kpt on wl fnl f* **5/4**[1]
2466 **2** *1 ¼* **Patch Patch**[7] 3972 4-8-10 66 .... TomEaves 6 63
(Michael Dods) *hood removed v late: dwlt: sn trcking ldrs: styd on fnl f* **12/1**
-312 **3** *shd* **Sands Of Dee (USA)**[22] 3484 4-9-1 71 .... BillyCray[(3)] 7 70+
(David Nicholls) *sn outpcd: hdwy over 1f out: styd on ins fnl f* **9/4**[2]
0-00 **4** *shd* **Tongalooma**[55] 2412 5-8-7 51 ow2 .... PJMcDonald 3 59
(James Moffatt) *trckd ldrs: effrt over 2f out: kpt on same pce fnl f* **40/1**
-600 **5** *1 ¼* **Look Who's Kool**[25] 3384 3-8-10 73 ....(b[1]) RichardMullen 8 61
(Ed McMahon) *trckd ldrs: chal 2f out: wknd wl ins fnl f* **10/1**
100 **6** *3* **Sharp Shoes**[12] 3832 4-9-4 66 ....(p) PaulHanagan 2 55
(Ann Duffield) *chsd ldrs: chal over 2f out: hung lft and wknd fnl 100yds* **13/2**[3]
0066 **7** *shd* **Duke Of Rainford**[8] 3937 4-8-9 48 ....(p) TonyHamilton 1 45
(Michael Herrington) *dwlt: towards rr: hung rt over 1f out: nvr a factor* **22/1**
400- **8** *4 ½* **Evening In (IRE)**[347] 4848 3-8-2 47 ....(t) JamesSullivan 9 25
(Tony Coyle) *unruly s: chsd ldrs: outpcd over 2f out: sn lost pl* **50/1**
61.80 secs (2.00) **Going Correction** +0.40s/f (Good)
WFA 3 from 4yo+ 4lb **8** Ran SP% **114.1**
Speed ratings (Par 101): **100,98,97,97,95 90,90,83**
toteswingers: 1&2 £4.40, 1&3 £1.60, 2&3 £4.40 CSF £17.68 TOTE £2.70: £1.10, £2.60, £1.40; EX 15.50 Trifecta £89.80 Pool: £691.74 - 5.70 winning units..
Owner Middleham Park Racing Iii **Bred** Dan O'Brien **Trained** Sessay, N Yorks

FOCUS
A modest claimer judged by the proximity of the fourth, and the winner was nowhere near his best.

4198 YORKSHIRE RADIO APPRENTICE H'CAP — 1m 3f 214y
5:10 (5:40) (Class 6) (0-65,65) 4-Y-0+ — **£1,704** (£503; £251) **Stalls** Low

Form — RPR

4442 **1** **Amir Pasha (UAE)**[3] 4129 6-9-4 **59**....(p) ShaneBKelly 2 — 67
(Micky Hammond) *in rr-div: effrt over 4f out: chal 2f out: led jst ins fnl f: drvn out* **2/1**[1]

5-52 **2** ¾ **Obara D'Avril (FR)**[3] 4123 9-8-2 **46** oh1....(p) SophieSilvester(3) 6 — 52
(Simon West) *trckd ldrs: led over 6f out: hdd over 4f out: led over 2f out: hdd jst ins fnl f: kpt on wl towards fin* **7/1**[3]

0404 **3** 1 ¼ **Lucayan Dancer**[7] 3974 11-8-1 **49**.... ShirleyTeasdale(7) 8 — 53
(David Nicholls) *trckd ldrs: kpt on same pce appr fnl f* **6/1**[2]

/620 **4** 1 ½ **Ritsi**[13] 3754 8-8-8 **49**.... LMcNiff 7 — 51+
(Marjorie Fife) *hld up in rr: lost pl over 4f out: hdwy towards far side over 2f out: edgd rt: kpt on same pce over 1f out* **9/1**

00- **5** 2 ¼ **Ancient Times (USA)**[56] 7986 4-8-5 **51**.... DavidSimmonson(5) 9 — 49
(Philip Kirby) *t.k.h towards rr: wd bnd after 3f: hdwy over 3f out: one pce fnl 2f* **10/1**

43-0 **6** 3 **Pobs Trophy**[15] 3712 4-8-5 **46**....(p) CharlesEddery 10 — 42
(Richard Guest) *t.k.h: trckd ldrs: led after 2f: hdd over 6f out: wknd and heavily eased fnl 100yds* **12/1**

6564 **7** 4 ½ **Quaestor (IRE)**[9] 3906 4-8-2 **46** oh1....(p) LeonnaMayor(3) 1 — 32
(Andrew Crook) *s.v.s: t.k.h: gd hdwy to trck ldrs after 2f: outpcd 4f out: wknd fnl 2f* **20/1**

0304 **8** 3 ¾ **Jackson (BRZ)**[15] 3492 9-8-3 **49**....(b) LukeRowe(5) 11 — 29
(Richard Guest) *sn detached in rr: bhd and drvn over 5f out: styd far side in home st: nvr on terms* **12/1**

5160 **9** 2 ¼ **Visions Of Johanna (USA)**[19] 3581 6-9-7 **65**.... JakePayne(3) 4 — 42
(Richard Guest) *w ldrs: led over 4f out: hdd over 2f out: sn wknd* **9/1**

00-0 **10** 9 **Captain Peachey**[17] 3658 5-8-2 **46** oh1.... GeorgeChaloner(3) 5 — 8
(Alistair Whillans) *mid-div: sme hdwy over 3f out: sn wknd: eased clsng stages* **33/1**

25-0 **11** ½ **Daytime Dreamer (IRE)**[11] 3858 7-9-7 **62**.... HenryBrooke 3 — 24
(Martin Todhunter) *led 2f: chsd ldrs: lost pl over 3f out: sn bhd* **10/1**

2m 49.63s (10.73) **Going Correction** +0.675s/f (Yiel) **11** Ran SP% **121.4**
Speed ratings (Par 101): **91,90,89,88,87 85,82,79,78,72 71**
toteswingers: 1&2 £3.60, 1&3 £4.00, 2&3 £6.10. Totesuper 7: Win: Not won, Place: Not won. CSF £16.57 CT £75.84 TOTE £3.50: £1.90, £2.30, £3.00; EX 15.30 Trifecta £31.50 Pool: £673.28 - 15.80 winning units..
Owner Steven Kay **Bred** Darley **Trained** Middleham Moor, N Yorks

FOCUS
A moderate handicap but the market got it right and the form is probably solid enough for the level. The time was very slow.
Pobs Trophy Official explanation: jockey said that the gelding lost his action
T/Jkpt: Not won. T/Plt: £537.70 to a £1 stake. Pool: £56,400.43. 76.57 winning tickets. T/Qpdt: £188.80 to a £1 stake. Pool: £3,624.28. 14.20 winning tickets. WG

4019 LEICESTER (R-H)
Wednesday, July 20

OFFICIAL GOING: Good (good to soft in places; 7.3)
Wind: Light, behind Weather: Cloudy

4199 SIS LIVE KIMCOTE H'CAP — 5f 218y
6:15 (6:15) (Class 5) (0-70,69) 3-Y-0 — **£2,264** (£673; £336; £168) **Stalls** High

Form — RPR

2056 **1** **Mazovian (USA)**[5] 4062 3-8-7 **62**.... NoelGarbutt(7) 1 — 71
(Michael Chapman) *chsd ldrs: led over 4f out: styd on wl* **18/1**

-526 **2** 2 **Aristeia**[18] 3635 3-9-6 **68**.... RichardHughes 7 — 71
(Richard Hannon) *hld up: hdwy over 1f out: sn rdn: r.o to go 2nd wl ins fnl f: nt rch wnr* **5/1**[2]

0-31 **3** ¾ **Pearl Blue (IRE)**[30] 3230 3-9-7 **69**.... JackMitchell 6 — 70
(Chris Wall) *chsd ldrs: rdn over 1f out: styd on same pce ins fnl f* **5/4**[1]

2040 **4** 1 **Reginald Claude**[33] 3122 3-9-1 **68**....(v[1]) LeeNewnes(5) 3 — 65
(Mark Usher) *a.p: rdn over 1f out: hung lft ins fnl f: styd on same pce* **25/1**

6300 **5** ½ **Stamp Duty (IRE)**[15] 3711 3-9-4 **66**.... BarryMcHugh 2 — 62
(Ollie Pears) *hld up: rdn over 2f out: styd on fr over 1f out: nt trble ldrs* **12/1**

000 **6** 3 ¾ **Decadence**[18] 3615 3-8-2 **50** oh2.... KellyHarrison 5 — 34
(Eric Alston) *mid-div: rdn 1/2-way: wknd wl over 1f out* **40/1**

2-56 **7** 7 **Methayel (IRE)**[30] 3218 3-9-3 **65**.... PhilipRobinson 9 — 26
(Clive Brittain) *sn pushed along in rr: wknd over 2f out* **7/1**[3]

0200 **8** hd **Crucis Abbey (IRE)**[11] 3853 3-8-11 **59**....(v) LiamJones 8 — 20
(James Unett) *a in rr: rdn over 4f out: lost tch 1/2-way* **11/1**

2334 **9** 3 ½ **Captain Dimitrios**[111] 1056 3-9-4 **66**....(v) KierenFallon 4 — 16
(David Evans) *led: hdd over 4f out: rdn 1/2-way: wknd over 2f out* **12/1**

3024 **10** 2 **Look Twice**[28] 3272 3-8-10 **58**.... ChrisCatlin 10 — —
(Alex Hales) *chsd ldrs: rdn over 2f out: sn wknd* **14/1**

1m 12.04s (-0.96) **Going Correction** -0.15s/f (Firm) **10** Ran SP% **115.5**
Speed ratings (Par 100): **100,97,96,95,94 89,80,79,75,72**
toteswingers: 1&2 £19.10, 1&3 £7.60, 2&3 £2.60 CSF £104.76 CT £204.37 TOTE £34.70: £8.40, £1.10, £1.60; EX 180.90.
Owner Mrs M Chapman **Bred** Darley **Trained** Market Rasen, Lincs

FOCUS
2mm of overnight rain but a dry day and the ground was left at good, good to soft in places. Liam Jones said "It's quite loose on top but good under the top layer." A modest handicap run at a reasonable pace and one in which the principals came down the centre. The first five pulled clear and the form is rated around the second.

4200 OSBASTON (S) STKS — 1m 60y
6:45 (6:45) (Class 6) 3-Y-0 — **£1,617** (£481; £240; £120) **Stalls** Low

Form — RPR

0-35 **1** **Quite A Catch (IRE)**[38] 2964 3-8-8 58....(v[1]) JohnFahy(3) 7 — 62
(Jonathan Portman) *trckd ldrs: racd keenly: rdn to ld 1f out: sn hdd: rallied to ld towards fin* **8/1**

4224 **2** shd **Chilledtothebone**[18] 3619 3-8-11 62....(tp) KierenFallon 1 — 62
(Linda Stubbs) *led 1f: chsd ldrs: swtchd lft over 2f out: rdn to ld ins fnl f: hdd towards fin* **11/4**[1]

-003 **3** 1 ¼ **Fly By White (IRE)**[14] 3743 3-8-6 63.... FrankieMcDonald 2 — 54
(Richard Hannon) *hld up: plld hrd: hdwy over 1f out: r.o: nt rch ldrs* **5/1**

2042 **4** ½ **Crown Ridge (IRE)**[5] 4018 3-8-8 60.... MartinHarley(3) 5 — 58
(Mick Channon) *hld up: hdwy over 2f out: sn rdn: styd on same pce ins fnl f* **4/1**[3]

000 **5** 2 **Valdaw**[16] 3690 3-8-11 50....(b) TadhgO'Shea 9 — 53
(Joseph Tuite) *wnt lft s: rcvrd to ld at stdy pce over 7f out: qcknd over 3f out: rdn and hdd 1f out: no ex* **16/1**

60-0 **6** 8 **All In A Paddy**[30] 3226 3-8-11 53....(b[1]) ChrisCatlin 4 — 35
(Ed McMahon) *plld hrd and prom: rdn over 3f out: wknd over 2f out* **28/1**

00 **7** 9 **Voodoo Queen**[30] 3236 3-8-6 0.... AndreaAtzeni 6 — 9
(Marco Botti) *s.i.s: hld up: wknd over 2f out* **12/1**

2436 **8** 1 **Danceyourselfdizzy (IRE)**[12] 3804 3-8-11 65.... RichardHughes 8 — 12
(Richard Hannon) *trckd ldrs: rdn over 2f out: wknd and eased over 1f out* **10/3**[2]

1m 46.26s (1.16) **Going Correction** -0.15s/f (Firm) **8** Ran SP% **114.5**
Speed ratings (Par 98): **88,87,86,86,84 76,67,66**
toteswingers: 1&2 £3.60, 1&3 £7.60, 2&3 £3.80 CSF £30.40 TOTE £11.60: £3.80, £1.50, £1.60; EX 37.70.The winner was bought in for 5,200gns.
Owner J G B Portman **Bred** Yeomanstown Stud **Trained** Compton, Berks

FOCUS
A modest seller run at just an ordinary gallop and those up with the pace held the edge. The winner was back to his best.
Valdaw Official explanation: jockey said colt hung right
Voodoo Queen Official explanation: jockey said filly hung left

4201 MOTOWN IN MOTION MAIDEN AUCTION STKS — 7f 9y
7:20 (7:22) (Class 6) 2-Y-O — **£1,617** (£481; £240; £120) **Stalls** High

Form — RPR

0 **1** **Jubilance (IRE)**[16] 3686 2-8-12 0.... JohnFahy(3) 13 — 86+
(Jeremy Noseda) *s.i.s: sn prom: led over 2f out: hung lft over 1f out: comf* **10/3**[1]

0 **2** 2 ¾ **Benzanno (IRE)**[7] 3986 2-8-11 0.... NeilChalmers 17 — 75
(Andrew Balding) *chsd ldrs: hung lft over 2f out: rdn over 1f out: styd on same pce ins fnl f* **25/1**

02 **3** 5 **Siouxperhero (IRE)**[20] 3534 2-8-11 0....(b) FrannyNorton 18 — 63
(William Muir) *chsd ldrs: rdn over 2f out: styd on same pce fr over 1f out: edgd rt ins fnl f* **10/1**

4 **4** ½ **Daring Damsel (IRE)**[18] 3609 2-8-10 0.... ChrisCatlin 16 — 60
(Paul Cole) *led: rdn and hdd over 2f out: styd on same pce fr over 1f out* **22/1**

30 **5** nk **Hurricane Emerald (IRE)**[12] 3823 2-9-2 0.... KierenFallon 15 — 66
(Mark Johnston) *chsd ldrs: rdn and ev ch over 2f out: no ex fnl f* **9/2**[2]

05 **6** nk **Fugitive Motel (IRE)**[13] 3779 2-9-1 0.... RichardHughes 10 — 67+
(Richard Hannon) *hld up: hdwy over 1f out: n.m.r ins fnl f: nvr nr to chal* **8/1**[3]

42 **7** 1 **Royal Majestic**[13] 3779 2-8-6 0.... SamHitchcott 5 — 52
(Mick Channon) *mid-div: rdn 1/2-way: hdwy over 1f out: no imp fnl f* **9/2**[2]

8 nk **Philipstown** 2-9-2 0.... JimCrowley 11 — 62
(Richard Hannon) *prom: rdn over 1f out: wknd ins fnl f* **17/2**

0 **9** 1 ¾ **Astraios (IRE)**[19] 3590 2-9-1 0.... EddieCreighton 7 — 56
(Brian Meehan) *in rr and sn pushed along: styd on fr over 1f out: n.d* **28/1**

0 **10** ¾ **Il Pazzo**[24] 3429 2-8-10 0.... AndreaAtzeni 3 — 49
(Mike Murphy) *prom: rdn 1/2-way: wknd fnl f* **50/1**

11 hd **Shark In The Sea** 2-9-0 0.... LiamJones 4 — 53
(Brian Meehan) *sn drvn along in rr: nvr on terms* **50/1**

00 **12** 3 **High Five Prince (IRE)**[27] 3308 2-8-12 0....(p) RobertHavlin 8 — 43
(Mark Usher) *chsd ldrs: rdn over 2f out: wknd over 1f out* **100/1**

5 **13** 2 ¼ **Path Finder (FR)**[15] 3718 2-8-12 0.... GrahamGibbons 12 — 38
(Reg Hollinshead) *chsd ldrs over 3f* **50/1**

14 6 **Mexican Wave** 2-9-1 0.... JackMitchell 14 — 26
(Michael Bell) *sn outpcd* **16/1**

05 **15** 3 **Gadreel (IRE)**[27] 3308 2-8-9 0.... PatCosgrave 2 — 12
(Richard Hannon) *chsd ldrs: rdn over 2f out: wknd over 1f out: eased ins fnl f* **20/1**

16 3 ½ **Forest Edge (IRE)** 2-8-9 0.... CathyGannon 1 — 3
(David Evans) *sn pushed along in rr: bhd fr 1/2-way* **100/1**

17 25 **Emma Jean Boy** 2-8-11 0.... TadhgO'Shea 6 — —
(J S Moore) *s.i.s: outpcd: t.o* **100/1**

1m 25.39s (-0.81) **Going Correction** -0.15s/f (Firm) **17** Ran SP% **121.3**
Speed ratings (Par 92): **98,94,89,88,88 87,86,86,84,83 83,79,77,70,67 63,34**
toteswingers: 1&2 £38.90, 1&3 £10.90, 2&3 £59.50 CSF £96.28 TOTE £4.50: £1.50, £13.10, £5.20; EX 130.40.
Owner Miss Yvonne Jacques **Bred** Old Carhue & Graeng Bloodstock **Trained** Newmarket, Suffolk

FOCUS
Those with previous experience were no better than fair but the first two, who raced towards the stands' side away from the main group in the last quarter-mile, pulled clear of the remainder to show improved form. The gallop was reasonable and the first two came clear, with the previously raced third, fourth and fifth helping to set the level.

NOTEBOOK
Jubilance(IRE) ◆, who showed only moderate form on his debut, attracted support throughout the day and duly turned in a much improved effort over this longer trip, despite his greenness when asked for an effort. He holds several entries in sales races, is the type to rate more highly and it'll be a surprise if he doesn't win again. (op 4-1)
Benzanno(IRE), well beaten over this trip at Sandown on his debut, also stepped up considerably on that effort. He pulled clear of the remainder, should have no problems with 1m and should be able to pick up a similar event. (op 22-1)
Siouxperhero(IRE), who showed fair form in first-time blinkers at Epsom, failed to build on that but ran creditably against a couple of unexposed sorts. He remains worth a try over 1m and should be able to pick up a race. (op 9-1 tchd 17-2)
Daring Damsel(IRE), one of only two fillies in the race, stepped up on the form shown at Beverley on her debut. A stiffer test of stamina should suit and she should improve. (op 20-1 tchd 18-1)
Hurricane Emerald(IRE) has still to reproduce his debut form but he was by no means disgraced in easier company than he tackled at Newmarket last time. He has plenty of physical scope and will be of interest over 1m in ordinary nursery company in due course.
Fugitive Motel(IRE) ◆ ran creditably under a sympathetic ride on this third and qualifying run for a nursery mark. He has a bit to recommend him on looks and is one to keep a close eye on. (op 10-1 tchd 11-1 and 15-2)
Royal Majestic had shown form bordering on fair on both her previous starts but she was unable to build on those efforts this time. She's likely to remain vulnerable against the better sorts in this grade but should pick up a small event at some point. (op 4-1 tchd 7-2)

4202 BRITISH STALLION STUDS E B F WATERLOO FILLIES' H'CAP — 7f 9y
7:50 (7:51) (Class 4) (0-80,78) 3-Y-O — **£5,175** (£1,540; £769; £384) **Stalls** High

Form — RPR

2231 **1** **Moone's My Name**[19] 3594 3-9-5 **76**.... JimCrowley 2 — 82+
(Ralph Beckett) *a.p: hrd rdn fr over 1f out: led ins fnl f: styd on* **2/1**[1]

3141 **2** ¾ **Bakoura**[20] 3549 3-9-4 **75**.... RichardHills 9 — 79+
(John Dunlop) *s.i.s: hld up: hdwy over 1f out: sn rdn: styd on* **5/1**[2]

1050 **3** *½* **Layla Jamil (IRE)**[11] 3853 3-9-3 **77**.............................. MartinHarley(3) 8 80
(Mick Channon) *led: rdn and hung rt over 1f out: hdd and unable qck ins fnl f* **15/2**

1-43 **4** *1 ½* **Zing Wing**[12] 3818 3-9-3 **74**.............................. ChrisCatlin 7 73
(Paul Cole) *chsd ldrs: rdn over 2f out: styd on* **10/1**

521- **5** *1 ¾* **Mon Visage**[286] 6697 3-9-4 **75**.............................. JackMitchell 1 69
(Chris Wall) *hld up: hdwy 1/2-way: rdn over 1f out: no ex ins fnl f* **8/1**

-140 **6** *3 ¼* **Biaraafa (IRE)**[53] 2506 3-9-6 **77**.............................. JamieSpencer 5 62
(Michael Bell) *hld up: swtchd rt over 2f out: rdn over 1f out: wknd fnl f* **8/1**

6300 **7** *½* **Adaria**[13] 3757 3-9-7 **78**.............................. RobbieFitzpatrick 4 62
(David C Griffiths) *chsd ldrs: rdn over 2f out: wknd fnl f* **18/1**

0-61 **8** *2 ¼* **Loving Thought**[25] 3390 3-8-11 **68**.............................. IanMongan 3 46
(Sir Henry Cecil) *hld up in tch: rdn over 2f out: wknd fnl f* **7/1**[3]

4000 **9** *5* **Greenflash**[40] 2878 3-8-13 **70**.............................. RichardHughes 6 35
(Richard Hannon) *chsd ldr: rdn over 2f out: wknd over 1f out* **25/1**

1m 25.22s (-0.98) **Going Correction** -0.15s/f (Firm) **9** Ran SP% **114.7**
Speed ratings (Par 99): **99,98,97,95,93 90,89,87,81**
toteswingers: 1&2 £3.10, 1&3 £4.20, 2&3 £10.40 CSF £11.63 CT £61.42 TOTE £2.20: £1.10, £1.80, £1.50; EX 15.50.
Owner McDonagh Murphy And Nixon **Bred** Baroness Bloodstock & Tweenhills Stud **Trained** Kimpton, Hants

FOCUS
A fair fillies' handicap featuring several previous winners. The gallop was no more than fair and the whole field raced stands' side this time. The thirsd sets the standard.

4203 DINGLEY MAIDEN STKS 5f 218y
8:25 (8:29) (Class 5) 3-Y-O+ **£2,264** (£673; £336; £168) **Stalls** High

Form RPR

2-U4 **1** **Numeral (IRE)**[19] 3575 3-9-3 75.............................. RichardHughes 5 74+
(Richard Hannon) *led: hdd over 4f out: led again 1/2-way: shkn up and edgd rt fr over 1f out: clr fnl f: easily* **4/11**[1]

0 **2** *3 ¼* **Mucky Molly**[14] 3747 3-8-12 0.............................. IanMongan 3 51
(Olivia Maylam) *prom: rdn to chse wnr over 1f out: sn outpcd* **25/1**

0-0 **3** *3* **Poppet's Joy**[27] 3320 3-8-12 0.............................. ChrisCatlin 2 41
(Reg Hollinshead) *prom: rdn 1/2-way: no ex fnl f* **28/1**

0-0 **4** *3 ¾* **Kiss N Kick**[15] 3716 5-9-5 0.............................. JohnFahy(3) 1 34
(Lucinda Featherstone) *s.i.s: sn drvn along: led over 4f out: hdd 1/2-way: rdn and wknd over 1f out* **22/1**[3]

5 *3* **London Avenue (IRE)** 3-9-3 0.............................. PaddyAspell 4 24
(Dominic Ffrench Davis) *s.i.s: sn outpcd: hdwy over 3f out: wknd over 2f out* **14/1**[2]

1m 13.75s (0.75) **Going Correction** -0.15s/f (Firm)
WFA 3 from 5yo 5lb **5** Ran SP% **91.6**
Speed ratings (Par 103): **89,84,80,75,71**
toteswingers: 1&2 £4.20 CSF £5.65 TOTE £1.10: £1.02, £4.10; EX 4.40.
Owner Highclere Thoroughbred Racing-Flying Fox **Bred** Tinnakill Bloodstock & Forenaghts Stud **Trained** East Everleigh, Wilts

FOCUS
An uncompetitive maiden that was rendered one-sided when the second favourite A'Faal refused to enter the stalls. The gallop was an ordinary one. A weak race behind the winner.

4204 IBSTOCK H'CAP 1m 3f 183y
9:00 (9:00) (Class 5) (0-70,70) 4-Y-O+ **£2,264** (£673; £336; £168) **Stalls** Low

Form RPR

443- **1** **Pullyourfingerout (IRE)**[74] 4380 4-9-0 **63**.............................. (t) KierenFallon 2 74+
(Brendan Powell) *led after 1f and set stdy pce: qcknd over 3f out: rdn over 1f out: styd on wl* **5/2**[1]

5405 **2** *1 ½* **Aegean Destiny**[19] 3581 4-8-3 **55**.............................. DeclanCannon(3) 3 62
(John Mackie) *a.p: swtchd lft wl over 2f out: sn rdn to chse wnr: styd on* **7/1**

3050 **3** *1 ½* **Cornish Beau (IRE)**[12] 3817 4-9-2 **65**.............................. PhilipRobinson 4 70+
(Mark H Tompkins) *hld up: plld hrd: hdwy over 2f out: rdn over 1f out: styd on: nt rch ldrs* **8/1**

-260 **4** *½* **Eastern Magic**[38] 2952 4-9-1 **64**.............................. JackMitchell 6 68
(Reg Hollinshead) *led 1f: chsd wnr to over 3f out: hmpd and lost pl wl over 2f out: styd on ins fnl f* **9/2**[3]

0644 **5** *hd* **Goodlukin Lucy**[8] 3951 4-9-6 **69**.............................. (p) JimCrowley 5 73
[illegible] **7/1**

4055 **6** *1 ¼* **Raktiman (IRE)**[12] 3817 4-9-5 **68**.............................. (p) RussKennemore [illegible] [illegible]
(Tom Dascombe) *s.i.s: hld up: hrd rdn fr over 1f out: nvr trbld ldrs* **14/1**

6001 **7** *4 ½* **Sennockian Storm (USA)**[8] 3946 4-8-3 **52**.............................. AndrewElliott 10 46
(Mark Johnston) *prom: chsd wnr over 3f out tl rdn over 2f out: wknd fnl f* **10/3**[2]

2m 34.91s (1.01) **Going Correction** -0.15s/f (Firm) **7** Ran SP% **112.6**
Speed ratings (Par 103): **90,89,88,87,87 86,83**
toteswingers: 1&2 £3.80, 1&3 £7.80, 2&3 £8.50 CSF £19.77 CT £119.43 TOTE £2.40: £1.10, £5.60; EX 24.60.
Owner K Rhatigan **Bred** T Quayle **Trained** Upper Lambourn, Berks

FOCUS
A modest handicap in which the gallop was on the steady side and those held up were at a disadvantage. The winner was basically back to his old best.
T/Plt: £12.60 to a £1 stake. Pool: £63,120.61. 3,653.56 winning tickets. T/Qpdt: £6.50 to a £1 stake. Pool: £5,752.79. 648.44 winning tickets. CR

[4085] LINGFIELD (L-H)
Wednesday, July 20

OFFICIAL GOING: Standard
Wind: Modest, half behind Weather: Light rain

4205 B G INSURANCE MEDIAN AUCTION MAIDEN STKS 7f (P)
2:30 (2:31) (Class 6) 2-Y-O **£2,045** (£603; £302) **Stalls** Low

Form RPR

0 **1** **Bu Naaji (IRE)**[50] 2584 2-9-3 0.............................. NeilCallan 11 72
(Roger Varian) *t.k.h: chsd ldrs: rdn and effrt over 1f out: led ins fnl f: r.o wl* **5/1**[3]

03 **2** *1 ¾* **Dickens Rules (IRE)**[13] 3779 2-9-3 0.............................. JamesDoyle 5 67
(Sylvester Kirk) *chsd ldrs: rdn and unable qck over 2f out: no imp tl styd on wl u.p ins fnl f: snatched 2nd cl home* **4/1**[2]

3 *hd* **Long Lost Love** 2-8-12 0.............................. DarryllHolland 8 61
(Mark Johnston) *broke fast: led for 1f: chsd ldr after tl rdn to ld 2f out: drvn 1f out: hdd ins fnl f: styd on same pce after: lost 2nd cl home* **13/2**

6 **4** *2 ¼* **Stateos (IRE)**[32] 3182 2-9-3 0.............................. TomQueally 9 61+
(Sir Henry Cecil) *towards rr on outer: 6th and stl plenty to do and rdn jst over 2f out: hanging lft over 1f out: styd on fnl f: nvr gng pce to rch ldrs* **7/4**[1]

U0 **5** *shd* **Thecornishcockney**[8] 3954 2-9-3 0.............................. (b) StevieDonohoe 13 60
(John Ryan) *s.i.s: towards rr: rdn jst over 2f out: hdwy ent fnl f: r.o strly fnl 150yds: nt rch ldrs* **100/1**

6 *nk* **Zamarelle** 2-8-12 0.............................. SteveDrowne 4 55+
(Roger Charlton) *in tch in midfield: pushed along briefly over 4f out: lost pl and towards rr over 3f out: 9th and plenty to do jst over 2f out: hdwy over 1f out: styd on fnl f: nvr trbld ldrs* **8/1**

00 **7** *¾* **Carolingian (IRE)**[8] 3954 2-9-3 0.............................. (b[1]) ShaneKelly 12 58
(William Knight) *chsd ldr tl led after 1f: rdn and hdd 2f out: sn drvn: styd chsng ldrs tl wknd jst ins fnl f* **50/1**

8 *3* **Arrow Lake (FR)** 2-8-13 0 ow1.............................. AdamKirby 1 46
(Noel Quinlan) *t.k.h: chsd ldrs: effrt on inner and rdn wl over 1f out: btn 1f out: wknd qckly ins fnl f* **40/1**

9 *3 ½* **Hearts And Minds (IRE)** 2-9-3 0.............................. FergusSweeney 7 41
(Jamie Osborne) *dwlt: a towards rr: rdn and struggling 3f out: styd on same pce and n.d fnl 2f* **25/1**

0 **10** *3* **Distant Voyage**[25] 3408 2-9-3 0.............................. LiamKeniry 6 33
(Michael Blanshard) *in tch in midfield: rdn and outpcd over 2f out: wknd wl over 1f out* **150/1**

11 *2* **Pinseeker (IRE)** 2-9-3 0.............................. LukeMorris 10 28
(Peter Winkworth) *s.i.s: sn rdn along in rr: nvr on terms* **25/1**

0 **12** *2 ½* **Nic Nok**[41] 2837 2-9-3 0.............................. MartinDwyer 2 21
(Harry Dunlop) *in tch in midfield: rdn and struggling wl over 2f out: wknd jst over 2f out* **100/1**

13 *10* **Aunty Mavis (IRE)** 2-8-9 0.............................. KierenFox(3) 3 —
(Ronald Harris) *s.i.s: towards rr: hmpd bnd wl over 3f out: lost tch 3f out* **100/1**

1m 26.83s (2.03) **Going Correction** +0.15s/f (Slow) **13** Ran SP% **113.2**
Speed ratings (Par 92): **94,92,91,89,89 88,87,84,80,77 74,71,60**
toteswingers: 1&2 £4.60, 1&3 £6.90, 2&3 £6.10 CSF £22.83 TOTE £6.40: £2.00, £1.10, £2.10; EX 21.20.
Owner Sheikh Ahmed Al Maktoum **Bred** Darley **Trained** Newmarket, Suffolk

FOCUS
Not as strong a maiden as some on this track, but still a couple of interesting performances. The first three were prominent throughout. The first three look reasonable types, although the form is limited by the proximity of the fifth.

NOTEBOOK
Bu Naaji(IRE) ◆ was last of ten on his Leicester debut, but that turned out to be a useful maiden with the winner going on to finish runner-up in the Coventry and July Stakes. He was always close to the pace and produced a nice turn of foot to lead entering the last furlong before powering clear. A half-brother to four winners including the smart Mulaqat, he should appreciate further and seems likely to go on to better things. (op 11-2 tchd 9-2)
Dickens Rules(IRE) came off the bridle in a handy position at halfway, but eventually responded to the pressure and ran on to snatch second place close to the line. He now qualifies for nurseries and that appears to be where his future lies. (op 7-2)
Long Lost Love ◆, a half-sister to a winner over this trip out of a smart mare, led off the final bend but couldn't contain the winner from the furlong pole. She still fared much the best of the newcomers and should be able to go two better before too long. (op 7-1 tchd 8-1)
Stateos(IRE), a promising sixth on his debut in a Newmarket maiden last month that has worked out well, got outpaced coming to the home bend and left himself with too much to do. He is bred to appreciate further and this performance confirmed that a stiffer test is needed. Official explanation: jockey said that the colt was slowly away; vet said that the colt struck into itself in the stalls (op 2-1 tchd 13-8)
Thecornishcockney showed nothing on his second start after being gelded, but the way he finished here suggests that the operation may have had a positive effect after all.
Zamarelle, retained for 20,000gns as a yearling, proved a handful before the start and ran green during the race, but she also showed ability once in line for home and this half-sister to three winners at up to 1m2f, including the smart King's County, looks to have a future. (op 7-1)

4206 BIBBY FINANCIAL SERVICES H'CAP 6f (P)
3:00 (3:02) (Class 5) (0-70,70) 3-Y-O+ **£2,385** (£704; £176; £176) **Stalls** Low

Form RPR

4450 **1** **Highland Harvest**[8] 3940 7-9-4 **67**.............................. NeilCallan 6 73
[illegible] 1f out: hrd drvn ins fnl f: styd on fnl 100yds to ld last stride **20/1**

1102 **2** *shd* **Cavitie**[15] 3713 5-9-3 **66**.............................. (p) DarryllHolland 1 71
(Andrew Reid) *t.k.h: chsd ldrs: rdn ent fnl 2f: drvn and hdwy jst over 1f out: kpt on wl to ld towards fin: hdd last stride* **4/1**[1]

1610 **3** *nk* **Athaakeel (IRE)**[22] 3476 5-9-2 **65**.............................. (b) KirstyMilczarek 12 69
(Ronald Harris) *pressed ldrs on outer after 1f: ev ch and rdn 2f out: hung rt over 1f out: kpt on wl u.p tl no ex cl home* **12/1**

6020 **3** *dht* **Hoover**[11] 3853 3-9-2 **70**.............................. StephenCraine 10 73
(Jim Boyle) *pressed ldr: ev ch and drvn over 1f out: kpt on u.p: no ex cl home* **6/1**[2]

2050 **5** *hd* **Defector (IRE)**[21] 3512 5-9-7 **70**.............................. FrankieMcDonald 5 74
(Seamus Durack) *awkward s: sn rcvrd and led after 1f out: rdn ent 2f out: drvn over 1f out: battled on wl tl hdd and lost 4 pls towards fin* **25/1**

0006 **6** *½* **Tislaam (IRE)**[21] 3517 4-9-4 **67**.............................. (p) RobertWinston 8 69+
(Alan McCabe) *stdd s: t.k.h: hld up in last pair: hdwy jst over 1f out: switching rt and then lft ins fnl f: r.o wl fnl 100yds: nt quite rch ldrs* **7/1**

-500 **7** *nk* **Micky P**[20] 3536 4-9-0 **63**.............................. (vt[1]) WilliamCarson 4 64
(Stuart Williams) *sn pushed along in last trio: drvn over 2f out: styd wl on u.p ins fnl f: nt rch ldrs* **4/1**[1]

0554 **8** *hd* **Fantasy Fighter (IRE)**[8] 3956 6-9-1 **64**.............................. JimmyQuinn 2 64
(John Quinn) *hld up in tch in midfield: effrt on inner over 1f out: kpt on same pce ins fnl f* **8/1**

2603 **9** *1 ½* **Dvinsky (USA)**[23] 3464 10-9-7 **70**.............................. (b) TomMcLaughlin 3 66
(Michael Squance) *sn bustled along: in tch: short of room and lost pl bnd after 1f: rdn over 2f out: drvn and styd on same pce fr over 1f out* **20/1**

0043 **10** *4 ½* **Imjin River (IRE)**[8] 3956 4-9-7 **70**.............................. TomQueally 9 51
(Mark H Tompkins) *short of room sn after s: in tch in last pair: rdn over 2f out: swtchd rt and no imp wl over 1f out: wknd over 1f out* **13/2**[3]

0034 **11** *8* **Waterloo Dock**[63] 2205 6-9-3 **66**.............................. (v) MartinDwyer 7 22
(Michael Quinn) *in tch in midfield on outer: rdn and struggling 3f out: wknd jst over 2f out* **14/1**

1m 12.66s (0.76) **Going Correction** +0.15s/f (Slow)
WFA 3 from 4yo+ 5lb **11** Ran SP% **119.0**
Speed ratings (Par 103): **100,99,99,99,99 98,98,97,95,89 79**
PL: A £2.50, H £1.60; TRICAST: HH-C-A £523.23, HH-C-H £282.37; toteswingers: 1&2 £16.30, 1&3 (A) £19.60, 1&3 (H) £14.40, 2&3 (A) £3.70, 2&3 (H) £3.70 CSF £97.31 CT £523.23 TOTE £24.20: £6.50, £1.80, £2.50; EX 144.50.
Owner J Wotherspoon **Bred** John Wotherspoon **Trained** Telscombe, E Sussex

FOCUS
A modest sprint handicap, but incredibly competitive with only around 2l covering the first eight. The first five all raced prominently.

4207 EUROMONITOR H'CAP — 5f (P)
3:30 (3:30) (Class 6) (0-65,65) 3-Y-O+ — **£1,704** (£503; £251) **Stalls** High

Form — RPR

2625 **1** **Jimmy Ryan (IRE)**[85] 1581 10-9-4 **57**....(t) J-PGuillambert 2 — 64
(Tim McCarthy) *taken down early and led to s: t.k.h: chsd ldng pair: rdn to chal 1f out: drvn ahd fnl 100yds: hld on towards fin* **4/1**[2]

3400 **2** *shd* **Estonia**[49] 2603 4-9-11 **64**.... LukeMorris 5 — 71+
(Michael Squance) *taken down early: dwlt: in tch towards rr: rdn and hdwy on outer bnd 2f out: drvn and ev ch ins fnl f: kpt on but a jst hld towards fin* **3/1**[1]

5-33 **3** *1* **Star Twilight**[8] 3957 4-9-6 **59**....(v) AdamKirby 6 — 62
(Derek Shaw) *chsd ldr tl led 2f out: drvn over 1f out: hdd and no ex fnl 100yds* **4/1**[2]

6550 **4** *nk* **Rightcar**[39] 2921 4-8-7 **46** oh1....(b) RobbieFitzpatrick 4 — 48
(Peter Grayson) *led tl hdd and rdn 2f out: kpt on same pce u.p ins fnl f* **20/1**

-050 **5** *shd* **Towy Boy (IRE)**[14] 3735 6-9-12 **65**....(bt) NeilCallan 8 — 67
(Ian Wood) *in tch on outer: rdn and effrt over 1f out: styd on same pce ins fnl f* **8/1**[3]

0030 **6** *1 ½* **My Love Fajer (IRE)**[5] 4067 3-8-13 **56**.... RobertWinston 3 — 51
(Alan McCabe) *dwlt: t.k.h: hld up in last trio: rdn and effrt wl over 1f out: no imp* **3/1**[1]

400 **7** *2 ¼* **Rightcar Dominic**[65] 2161 6-8-7 **46** oh1.... KirstyMilczarek 1 — 34
(Peter Grayson) *dwlt: a towards rr: rdn over 2f out: styd on same pce and no imp fr over 2f out* **40/1**

-600 **8** *5* **Russian Winter**[8] 3931 3-9-0 **57**.... JamesDoyle 7 — 27
(Tim Etherington) *dwlt: sn rdn and a outpcd in last* **22/1**

59.66 secs (0.86) **Going Correction** +0.15s/f (Slow)
WFA 3 from 4yo+ 4lb — **8** Ran SP% **112.7**
Speed ratings (Par 101): **99,98,97,96,96 94,90,82**
toteswingers: 1&2 £3.40, 1&3 £2.90, 2&3 £4.00 CSF £15.73 CT £49.78 TOTE £4.50: £2.10, £1.20, £1.80; EX 15.40.
Owner Mrs D H McCarthy **Bred** Barronstown Stud And Orpendale **Trained** Godstone, Surrey

FOCUS
A weak sprint handicap. The winner is rated in line with his winter form.

4208 BRITISH ASSESSMENT BUREAU MAIDEN STKS — 1m 4f (P)
4:00 (4:00) (Class 5) 3-Y-O+ — **£2,385** (£704; £352) **Stalls** Low

Form — RPR

5 **1** **Royal Peculiar**[12] 3824 3-9-1 0.... TomQueally 4 — 85+
(Sir Henry Cecil) *hld up wl in tch: chsd ldrs and rdn 2f out: drvn to chse ldr and sltly hmpd jst ins fnl f: styd on wl fnl 100yds to ld last strides* **5/4**[1]

5- **2** *hd* **Jamr**[249] 7452 3-9-1 0....(v[1]) TedDurcan 5 — 84
(Saeed Bin Suroor) *dwlt: sn rcvrd and chsd ldrs: wnt 2nd over 5f out: drvn and ev ch 2f out: led jst over 1f out: edgd rt jst ins fnl f: edgd lft fnl 100yds: hdd last strides* **9/1**

2-20 **3** *3* **Ajeeb (USA)**[41] 2847 3-9-1 77.... JamieSpencer 6 — 79+
(David Simcock) *t.k.h: hld up in last trio: 8th and effrt but stl plenty to do 2f out: kpt on wl fnl f to snatch 3rd last stride* **12/1**

3633 **4** *shd* **Unex Renoir**[25] 3376 3-9-1 82.... WilliamBuick 12 — 79
(John Gosden) *chsd ldrs: wnt 2nd 10f out tl 6f out: chsd ldrs after: rdn and hanging lft over 1f out: swtchd rt and plugged on same pce fnl f* **7/2**[2]

2320 **5** *1* **Blaise Chorus (IRE)**[47] 2682 3-8-10 100.... MichaelHills 11 — 72
(B W Hills) *t.k.h: hld up wl in tch in midfield: hdwy to ld 6f out: rdn and hrd pressed 2f out: hdd jst over 1f out: wknd and lost 2 pls fnl 100yds* **9/2**[3]

6 *3 ¾* **Silent Ninja** 3-8-10 0.... SteveDrowne 10 — 66
(Hughie Morrison) *stdd s: t.k.h: hld up in midfield: rdn and outpcd over 2f out: plugged on same pce fnl 2f* **66/1**

00 **7** *6* **Sacred Sound (IRE)**[42] 2813 3-9-1 0.... HughBowman 9 — 62
(Mick Channon) *led at stdy gallop tl 6f out: styd chsng ldrs tl rdn and unable qck over 2f out: wknd 2f out* **50/1**

00 **8** *½* **Sharp Relief (IRE)**[51] 2551 3-8-10 0.... HayleyTurner 8 — 56
(Hughie Morrison) *t.k.h: hld up wl in tch towards rr: rdn and outpcd 3f out: n.d fnl 2f* **66/1**

0 **9** *3* **Himalayan Moon**[97] 1332 4-9-8 0.... MartinLane 7 — 51
(Ian Wood) *stdd s: t.k.h: hld up in tch in last trio: rdn and struggling over 3f out: sn lost tch* **150/1**

00 **10** *nse* **Brunello**[24] 3430 3-9-1 0.... AdamKirby 3 — 56
(Walter Swinburn) *hld up in tch towards rr: rdn and dropped to rr over 4f out: wknd over 3f out* **100/1**

66 **11** *1* **Momaris**[39] 2930 3-9-1 0.... NeilCallan 2 — 54
(Roger Varian) *chsd ldrs: rdn and lost pl 5f out: lost tch 3f out* **14/1**

30 **12** *15* **Notabadlad**[21] 3519 4-9-13 0.... SebSanders 1 — 30
(Simon Dow) *t.k.h: hld up in tch in last trio: swtchd to outer and hdwy over 8f out: rdn and wknd qckly 3f out: wl bhd fnl 2f: t.o* **66/1**

2m 33.77s (0.77) **Going Correction** +0.15s/f (Slow)
WFA 3 from 4yo 12lb — **12** Ran SP% **117.3**
Speed ratings (Par 103): **103,102,100,100,100 97,93,93,91,91 90,80**
toteswingers: 1&2 £4.40, 1&3 £5.00, 2&3 £6.00 CSF £13.98 TOTE £2.00: £1.30, £4.10, £2.90; EX 22.10.
Owner De La Warr Racing & Newsells Park Stud **Bred** Newsells Park Stud Limited **Trained** Newmarket, Suffolk
■ Stewards' Enquiry : Hugh Bowman one-day ban: careless riding (Aug 3)

FOCUS
Quite an interesting maiden, but the pace was modest so not the test of stamina it might have been.

4209 LADBROKES MOBILE H'CAP — 1m 4f (P)
4:30 (4:30) (Class 5) (0-75,75) 3-Y-O — **£2,045** (£603; £302) **Stalls** Low

Form — RPR

0-13 **1** **Gold Mine**[20] 3538 3-9-6 **74**....(t) LiamKeniry 4 — 81
(Andrew Balding) *chsd ldrs tl wnt 2nd over 7f out: led 4f out: rdn clr w runner-up and c centre bnd wl over 1f out: hld on gamely u.p fnl f* **13/8**[1]

1360 **2** *nk* **Viking Storm**[20] 3551 3-9-7 **75**.... JamieSpencer 5 — 82
(Harry Dunlop) *in tch in last pair: hdwy to chse ldr over 4f out: rdn and drew clr w wnr whn carried rt bnd wl over 1f out: kpt on wl but a jst hld fnl f* **2/1**[2]

3-00 **3** *4 ½* **Reillys Daughter**[41] 2840 3-9-2 **70**.... LukeMorris 3 — 70?
(J S Moore) *s.i.s and pushed along early: in tch in rr: rdn over 4f out: outpcd and looked wl btn over 2f out: kpt on u.p to go 3rd ins fnl f: no threat to ldrs* **25/1**

2304 **4** *3* **Madrasa (IRE)**[18] 3642 3-8-9 **68**.... KieranO'Neill[(5)] 1 — 63
(Ed McMahon) *led: hung rt bnd 9f out: hdd and rdn 4f out: drvn and outpcd over 2f out: 3rd and wl hld over 1f out* **9/2**[3]

104 **5** *2 ½* **Merton Lady**[15] 3715 3-8-11 **65**.... WilliamCarson 7 — 56
(John Flint) *t.k.h: w ldr tl over 7f out: chsd ldrs after: rdn and outpcd over 2f out: 4th and wl hld over 1f out* **13/2**

100- **6** *2 ½* **Lord Of The Storm**[282] 6795 3-8-6 **63**.... KierenFox[(3)] 2 — 50
(Bill Turner) *chsd ldrs: rdn and outpcd over 3f out: wl bhd* **40/1**

2m 34.79s (1.79) **Going Correction** +0.15s/f (Slow) — **6** Ran SP% **109.2**
Speed ratings (Par 100): **100,99,96,94,93 91**
toteswingers: 1&2 £1.90, 1&3 £4.20, 2&3 £4.30 CSF £4.81 TOTE £3.30: £1.80, £1.10; EX 3.90.
Owner Sir Gordon Brunton **Bred** Sir Gordon Brunton **Trained** Kingsclere, Hants

FOCUS
The early pace was more solid than in the maiden, but the winning time was over a second slower. This turned into a war of attrition with never more than a neck separating the front pair over the last half-mile. A 3lb best from the winner.
Reillys Daughter Official explanation: trainer's representative said that the filly bled from the nose

4210 PLAY ROULETTE AT LADBROKES.COM H'CAP — 7f (P)
5:00 (5:01) (Class 5) (0-75,75) 3-Y-O+ — **£2,045** (£603; £302) **Stalls** Low

Form — RPR

322 **1** **Escape To Glory (USA)**[19] 3594 3-9-5 **73**.... GeorgeBaker 12 — 85+
(Mikael Magnusson) *hld up in tch and a gng wl: smooth hdwy to join ldr 2f out: led wl over 1f out: rdn and readily c clr ins fnl f: comf* **6/4**[1]

1-00 **2** *2 ¼* **Scottish Glen**[23] 3468 5-9-9 **70**.... LiamKeniry 5 — 76
(Patrick Chamings) *hld up in midfield: rdn and effrt on outer bnd wl over 1f out: drvn 1f out: styd on wl to go 2nd wl ins fnl f: no ch w wnr* **8/1**[3]

3002 **3** *½* **Cat Hunter**[6] 4010 4-9-9 **70**.... KirstyMilczarek 6 — 75
(Ronald Harris) *t.k.h: hld up in midfield: rdn and hdwy 2f out: drvn to chse wnr jst over 1f out: kpt on but readily brushed aside ins fnl f: lost 2nd wl ins fnl f* **15/2**[2]

006 **4** *1* **Sunshine Always (IRE)**[32] 3172 5-9-4 **70**.... MarkCoumbe[(5)] 11 — 72
(Michael Attwater) *in tch in midfield: rdn and hdwy jst over 2f out: kpt on u.p fnl f: no ch w wnr* **10/1**

33-0 **5** *1* **Requisite**[20] 3549 6-10-0 **75**....(b) NeilCallan 4 — 75
(Ian Wood) *in tch: rdn and effrt over 1f out: unable qck u.p 1f out: styd on same pce fnl f* **14/1**

1004 **6** *½* **Woolston Ferry (IRE)**[14] 3735 5-8-12 **64**.... JamesRogers[(5)] 10 — 62
(David Pinder) *s.i.s: sn bustled along in rr: styd on past btn horses fnl f: nvr trbld ldrs* **12/1**

4000 **7** *shd* **Diplomatic (IRE)**[75] 1868 6-8-13 **60**....(p) AdamKirby 3 — 59+
(Michael Squance) *in tch: rdn and effrt whn hmpd and lost pl over 1f out: styd on ins fnl f: no ch w wnr* **25/1**

2060 **8** *¾* **Buxton**[16] 3674 7-9-7 **68**....(t) MartinLane 2 — 64
(Roger Ingram) *dwlt: sn niggled along towards rr: rdn 3f out: sme hdwy on inner over 1f out: no prog 1f out and n.d fnl f* **22/1**

0000 **9** *nk* **Picansort**[21] 3517 4-9-6 **67**....(t) SebSanders 9 — 62
(Brett Johnson) *stdd s: hld up in last trio: rdn and effrt over 1f out: no real hdwy: n.d* **25/1**

3110 **10** *2 ¼* **Lord Of The Reins (IRE)**[14] 3737 7-9-8 **72**....(t) SimonPearce[(3)] 7 — 61
(P J O'Gorman) *s.i.s: hld up in rr: rdn and hdwy on inner over 1f out: drvn and wknd ins fnl f* **25/1**

4600 **11** *nse* **Minortransgression (USA)**[4] 4089 4-9-1 **62**.... StevieDonohoe 14 — 51
(H Edward Haynes) *chsd ldr tl jst over 2f out: wkng whn short of room and hmpd over 1f out: n.d fnl f* **50/1**

2260 **12** *½* **Fivefold (USA)**[6] 4010 4-9-8 **69**....(p) J-PGuillambert 8 — 57
(John Akehurst) *chsd ldrs: drvn to press ldrs over 1f out: unable qck u.p and wknd ins fnl f* **20/1**

1003 **13** *2 ¾* **Spirit Of Grace**[13] 3783 3-8-13 **67**.... JamesDoyle 1 — 44
(Alan McCabe) *led tl wl over 1f out: sn drvn and wkng: wl bhd ins fnl f* **9/1**

1m 24.87s (0.07) **Going Correction** +0.15s/f (Slow)
WFA 3 from 4yo+ 7lb — **13** Ran SP% **118.9**
Speed ratings (Par 103): **105,102,101,100,99 99,98,98,97,95 95,94,91**
toteswingers: 1&2 £4.90, 1&3 £2.90, 2&3 £8.20 CSF £11.61 CT £74.53 TOTE £2.40: £1.10, £2.70, £2.30; EX 18.50.
Owner Eastwind Racing Ltd And Martha Trussell **Bred** Castleton Lyons **Trained** Upper Lambourn, Berks
■ Stewards' Enquiry : George Baker one-day ban: careless riding (Aug 3)

FOCUS
What had looked a competitive handicap was turned into a one-horse race and a successful gamble was landed. The bare form behind the winner is ordinary.
Lord Of The Reins(IRE) Official explanation: trainer said gelding ran in snatches
T/Plt: £20.20 to a £1 stake. Pool: £56,579.94. 2,041.76 winning tickets. T/Qpdt: £4.20 to a £1 stake. Pool: £4,507.50. 789.26 winning tickets. SP

3984 SANDOWN (R-H)
Wednesday, July 20

OFFICIAL GOING: Soft (good to soft in places on round course) (rnd 7.4, spr 7.3)
Wind: Light, half against Weather: Murky with rain

4211 BETFAIR TRAINING SERIES APPRENTICE H'CAP (PART OF THE RACING EXCELLENCE INITIATIVE) — 1m 2f 7y
6:05 (6:05) (Class 5) (0-75,75) 4-Y-O+ — **£2,264** (£673; £336; £168) **Stalls** Low

Form — RPR

4106 **1** **Rock The Stars (IRE)**[28] 3277 4-9-10 **75**.... DarylByrne 1 — 79+
(J W Hills) *trckd ldr and clr of rest: c alone to nr side in st: rdn over 2f out: nt quite on terms tl styd on last 100yds to ld fnl stride* **10/11**[1]

340- **2** *nse* **Croix Rouge (USA)**[293] 6502 9-8-5 **56** oh10.... MatthewLawson 8 — 60
(Ralph Smith) *sweating: led at gd pce: styd towards far side in st: rdn over 2f out: kpt on u.p: hdd post* **9/1**

60-5 **3** *nk* **Penchesco (IRE)**[24] 3426 6-8-11 **65**.... JustinNewman[(3)] 6 — 68
(Amanda Perrett) *trckd clr ldng pair but sn restrained off the pce: clsd on ldr 2f out: chal over 1f out: nt qckn last 100yds* **7/2**[2]

5060 **4** *6* **Diddums**[22] 3477 5-8-4 **60**.... KatiaScallan[(5)] 3 — 51
(Alastair Lidderdale) *dwlt: hld up in detached last trio: no prog over 2f out: tk modest 4th over 1f out* **10/1**

2363 **5** *6* **Lang Shining (IRE)**[13] 3764 7-9-2 **74**.... JohnLawson[(7)] 5 — 53
(Jamie Osborne) *s.i.s: hld up in detached last trio: shkn up and no prog over 2f out* **13/2**[3]

6-00 **6** *8* **Gallego**[9] 3912 9-8-7 **58**.. DavidKenny 7 21
(Richard Price) *stdd s: hld up in detached last trio: no prog over 2f out: sn bhd* **25/1**

2m 15.39s (4.89) **Going Correction** +0.625s/f (Yiel) **6** Ran SP% **110.9**
Speed ratings (Par 103): **105,104,104,99,95 88**
toteswingers: 1&2 £2.80, 1&3 £1.90, 2&3 £4.80 CSF £9.81 CT £19.23 TOTE £1.80: £1.40, £4.20; EX 8.50.
Owner David Cohen **Bred** Bernard Cooke **Trained** Upper Lambourn, Berks

FOCUS
Round course rail dolled out 3yds from inner line from 9f to 3f and 4yds up home straight adding 6yds to distances on Round course. Rail at full width on sprint course. This moderate handicap, confined to apprentice riders that had not ridden more than 20 winners previously, proved a lively betting heat. There was a frantic early pace on and the runners were expected to track stands' side once turning for home, but only the winner did. It was a messy race. With the runner-up 10lb wrong there is some doubt over the form.

4212 HCC MIND OVER RISK NURSERY — 5f 6y
6:35 (6:36) (Class 5) 2-Y-O **£2,587** (£770; £384; £192) **Stalls** Low

Form RPR
004 **1** **Mister Musicmaster**[14] 3722 2-9-2 **68**........................... JamesMillman 1 76
(Rod Millman) *racd against rail: led: rdn 2f out: hdd jst over 1f out: kpt on to ld again last 130yds: sn clr* **3/1**[2]
460 **2** *1 3/4* **Sister Guru**[20] 3547 2-8-4 **61**.. HarryBentley(5) 5 63
(Peter Hedger) *racd wd: pressed ldrs: clsd to ld jst over 1f out: wknd and hdd last 130yds* **8/1**
443 **3** *3/4* **Kyllasie**[23] 3463 2-9-0 **66**.. RyanMoore 6 65
(Richard Hannon) *sn pushed along in last: effrt u.p 2f out: kpt on fnl f: nvr able to chal* **2/1**[1]
422 **4** *hd* **Gin Twist**[6] 3993 2-8-13 **65**.............................. RichardKingscote 3 64
(Tom Dascombe) *racd against rail: in tch bhd ldrs: rdn and nt qckn 2f out: kpt on ins fnl f* **5/1**[3]
0625 **5** *8* **Stepper Point**[18] 3610 2-9-2 **68**.......................... MartinDwyer 2 44
(William Muir) *pressed wnr to wl over 1f out: wknd rapidly: eased* **3/1**[2]

65.21 secs (3.61) **Going Correction** +0.575s/f (Yiel) **5** Ran SP% **111.1**
Speed ratings (Par 94): **94,91,90,89,76**
toteswingers: 1&2 £27.30 CSF £24.50 TOTE £3.90: £1.30, £2.40; EX 38.60.
Owner Mrs Jan Fuller **Bred** Mrs J Fuller And S Dutfield **Trained** Kentisbeare, Devon
■ The 'official' ratings shown next to each horse are estimated and for information purposes only.

FOCUS
With the two at the top of the weights defecting this was a moderate little nursery and it paid to race handy. A fair lttle race given the ground.

NOTEBOOK
Mister Musicmaster shed his maiden tag at the fourth time of asking on this nursery debut and completed the task gamely. He got to the lead from his plum draw, but looked vulnerable as the runner-up challenged 1f out. Having the rail to race against was a big advantage, though, and he bravely found extra when asked for everything. He has now found his sort of level, but still looked somewhat green and could improve again back on a sounder surface in this sphere. (op 4-1)
Sister Guru pinged out from her wide stall, but was immediately taken back and took time to settle as a result. She improved going nicely nearing the final furlong, but the rising finish just found her out. She can build on this now she's shown her true colours.
Kyllasie was doing her best work towards the finish on this switch to a nursery and a stiffer test looks required. (op 11-4)
Gin Twist had narrowly found one too strong on both her previous outings in a nursery, including off this mark at Bath last week. She was faced with contrasting ground here, however, and proved friendless in the betting ring. It was apparent from halfway she was not that happy and, while she closed late on, a quicker surface is what she needs. (op 11-4 tchd 11-2)
Stepper Point was another having a first run on soft ground and he was well beaten off. He was later found to have scoped dirty. Official explanation: jockey said colt stopped quickly, trainer said colt scoped dirty post race (op 10-3 tchd 7-2)

4213 HCC INTERNATIONAL BRITISH STALLION STUDS EBF MAIDEN STKS — 7f 16y
7:10 (7:11) (Class 5) 2-Y-O **£3,881** (£1,155; £577; £288) **Stalls** Low

Form RPR
0 **1** **Clare Island Boy (IRE)**[18] 3609 2-9-3 0........................ HughBowman 4 79+
(Richard Hannon) *mde virtually all: jnd and pushed along 2f out: strly pressed and rdn fnl f: styd on wl* **14/1**
2 *3/4* **El Greco (IRE)** [illegible]
(Sir Michael Stoute) *hld up towards rr: prog over 2f out: rdn to go 2nd 1f out and sn chalng: styd on but outpcd last 75yds* **4/1**[2]
4 **3** *1 3/4* **Nant Saeson (IRE)**[19] 3590 2-9-3 0.................................. PatDobbs 7 73
(Richard Hannon) *trckd ldrs: nt qckn 2f out: rdn and styd on fr over 1f out: tk 3rd nr fin* **7/1**
4 *nk* **Sondeduro** 2-9-3 0.. FergusSweeney 13 72+
(Jamie Osborne) *hld up last: pushed along over 2f out: styd on quite takingly fnl f: nrst fin* **40/1**
5 *nk* **Greek War (IRE)** 2-9-3 0.. FrankieDettori 6 71
(Mahmood Al Zarooni) *pressed wnr: chal and upsides over 2f out to over 1f out: wknd and lost pls fnl f* **5/2**[1]
6 *nk* **Mr Maynard** 2-9-0 0... LouisBeuzelin(3) 1 71+
(Sir Michael Stoute) *trckd ldrs: shkn up over 2f out: sn outpcd: kpt on again fnl f* **20/1**
7 *1 1/2* **Holiday Reading (USA)** 2-9-3 0.................................. ShaneKelly 5 67
(Brian Meehan) *trckd ldrs: pushed along over 2f out: styd same pl tl fdd ins fnl f* **25/1**
0 **8** *1 1/4* **Dollar Bill**[25] 3401 2-9-3 0.. LiamKeniry 2 64
(Andrew Balding) *t.k.h: pressed ldng pair: shkn up and wknd 2f out* **15/2**
9 *nk* **Goodwood Atlantis (IRE)** 2-9-3 0................................ TedDurcan 10 63
(John Dunlop) *dwlt: settled in last trio: pushed along over 2f out: modest late hdwy* **28/1**
10 *3 1/2* **Lionrock (FR)** 2-9-3 0.. AhmedAjtebi 11 54+
(Mahmood Al Zarooni) *hld up in last trio and racd wd: brief effrt over 2f out: sn no prog and btn* **13/2**[3]
11 *1 3/4* **Songbird Blues** 2-8-12 0.. SteveDrowne 3 45
(Mark Usher) *dwlt: hld up in last trio: last whn n.m.r over 1f out: nudged along and no prog* **66/1**
5 **12** *1/2* **Right Divine (IRE)**[25] 3382 2-9-3 0.............................. MartinDwyer 9 49
(Brian Meehan) *awkward s: in tch towards rr: pushed along 1/2-way: wknd 2f out* **14/1**

1m 35.93s (6.43) **Going Correction** +0.625s/f (Yiel) **12** Ran SP% **115.5**
Speed ratings (Par 94): **88,87,85,84,84 84,82,80,80,76 74,74**
toteswingers: 1&2 £, 1&3 £, 2&3 £ CSF £64.02 TOTE £20.50: £4.20, £1.80, £2.20; EX 91.20.
Owner Middleham Park Racing Xiv **Bred** Norelands Bloodstock **Trained** East Everleigh, Wilts

FOCUS
The market suggested this juvenile maiden was an open heat and it saw numerous chances in the home straight, but the first pair dominated nearing the business end. Unsurprisingly these senior jockeys chose to come stands' side in the home straight. The third helps with the level.

NOTEBOOK
Clare Island Boy(IRE) stepped up greatly on the level of his debut effort and gamely opened his account at the second attempt. He was never far away and kept responding when asked to win the race. He has scope and will very likely come on again for the run, so it will be interesting to see where his leading yard sends him next. (op 16-1)
El Greco(IRE) ◆, entered in the Royal Lodge, had just about the most attractive pedigree in this line up and really should have made a winning debut. He got back in the pack after being tight for room early on, but made smooth headway into the home straight. He then got a little tapped for toe once the tempo became serious, before responding to go through horses and came with every chance on the stands' side. His jockey looked to get unbalanced near the finish, though, and he was just held. Considering he was the only one to make a serious impression from off the pace and he didn't get the strongest handling late on, he rates a sure-fire winner in the coming weeks and could be smart. (op 3-1)
Nant Saeson(IRE) was seemingly better fancied than his winning stablemate, but he is by a sire whose progeny have better success on faster ground and he couldn't quicken on this surface when asked for maximum effort. It was still an improved run, though, and he's going the right way. (op 9-2)
Sondeduro ◆ turned in an eye-catching debut display. He moved sweetly off the pace, but hit a flat spot when asked to quicken. This was a race where racing handy suited, though, and he motored home towards the finish. He's one to side with next time out. (op 50-1 tchd 33-1)
Greek War(IRE) ◆ is a half-brother to a soft-ground juvenile winner over 6f and was well backed to make a winning introduction. He raced professionally up with the pace and held every chance, but the rising finish proved too much for him at this stage of his career. A sharper test can see him off the mark. (op 7-2 tchd 2-1)
Mr Maynard, from a family his trainer knows very well, got outpaced before keeping on with promise late in the day. He will get another furlong without fuss already and is one to follow. (op 16-1)
Lionrock(FR) caught the eye in the paddock, but he needed this initial outing. (op 8-1)

4214 DEVINE HOMES H'CAP — 7f 16y
7:40 (7:43) (Class 3) (0-90,86) 3-Y-O **£6,663** (£1,982; £990; £495) **Stalls** Low

Form RPR
-211 **1** **Emilio Largo**[11] 3871 3-9-7 **86**.................................... TomQueally 4 94+
(Sir Henry Cecil) *hld up in 5th: prog to trck ldng pair 1/2-way: led wl over 1f out: rdn and a fending off chalr fnl f* **7/4**[1]
5303 **2** *1/2* **Rigolleto (IRE)**[12] 3830 3-9-6 **85**.......................... HughBowman 6 91
(Mick Channon) *pressed ldr: upsides 2f out: chsd wnr after: styd on but a hld fnl f* **11/1**
0420 **3** *1 1/2* **Major Conquest (IRE)**[12] 3798 3-9-2 **81**................... MartinDwyer 5 83
(J W Hills) *trckd ldng trio: pushed along and nt qckn over 2f out: rdn and styd on to take 3rd fnl f* **12/1**
0013 **4** *1 3/4* **Isingy Red (FR)**[11] 3854 3-8-8 **73**.......................... HayleyTurner 2 71
(Jim Boyle) *t.k.h: trckd ldng pair to 1/2-way: rdn and nt qckn over 2f out: plugged on* **8/1**
5013 **5** *1* **Silverware (USA)**[48] 2646 3-8-11 **76**.......................... RyanMoore 7 71
(Richard Hannon) *led: drvn and hdd wl over 1f out: fdd* **13/2**[3]
514 **6** *1* **Above Standard (IRE)**[12] 3798 3-8-13 **78**................... MichaelHills 3 70
(B W Hills) *stdd s: hld up in 6th: rdn 2f out: no imp on ldrs over 1f out: fdd fnl f* **7/2**[2]
4611 **7** *1* **Bajan Bear**[26] 3346 3-8-10 **75**.................................. LiamKeniry 1 65+
(Michael Blanshard) *s.s: a last: struggling 2f out* **8/1**

1m 33.3s (3.80) **Going Correction** +0.625s/f (Yiel) **7** Ran SP% **110.2**
Speed ratings (Par 104): **103,102,100,98,97 96,95**
toteswingers: 1&2 £3.10, 1&3 £5.10, 2&3 £13.30 CSF £20.40 TOTE £2.80: £1.10, £4.90; EX 23.00.
Owner Malcolm C Denmark **Bred** Mrs M Chaworth-Musters **Trained** Newmarket, Suffolk

FOCUS
A useful 3-y-o handicap, run at a fair enough pace. The field elected to shun the rail on the far side and again came over to the stands' side once straightening for home. Sound form, but not strong for the grade.

NOTEBOOK
Emilio Largo ◆ coped with the softest ground he had encountered to date and landed a hat-trick with another ready effort. He was well placed through the race and arrived to the leaders going easily around 2f out. He had to be kept up to his work once asked to seal the issue, but was always doing enough and this took his career record to 3-5. In the right hands to keep progressing, he looks well worth a shot at something more valuable. (tchd 13-8 and 2-1)
Rigolleto(IRE) ◆ down in the weights, acts well with cut in the ground. He duly posted a better effort, going down fighting on the stands' rail, [illegible]
Major Conquest(IRE) took time to get himself organised and never seriously threatened, but was doing some fair work late in the day. This was more like it again from him and he's on a competitive mark. (tchd 9-1)
Isingy Red(FR) came into this in decent form. He left the impression a greater test would have been ideal and still looks capable of success from this sort of mark. (op 17-2 tchd 9-1)
Silverware(USA) comes from a yard struggling for winners, but there's a chance this ground wasn't for him. (op 7-1)
Bajan Bear was bidding for a hat-trick off a 5lb higher mark. He spoilt his chance by falling out of the gates, but looked totally at sea on this softer ground when asked to improve and should show his true colours again when reverting to a sounder surface. Official explanation: jockey said gelding missed the break (op 11-2)

4215 CHILDREN'S TRUST H'CAP — 1m 14y
8:15 (8:16) (Class 4) (0-80,80) 3-Y-O+ **£4,075** (£1,212; £606; £303) **Stalls** Low

Form RPR
610 **1** **Stand To Reason (IRE)**[12] 3815 3-9-5 **79**...................... WilliamBuick 7 87
(Mikael Magnusson) *chsd clr ldr: rdn 3f out: wandered lft and rt after: clsd u.str.p to ld last 100yds* **15/2**
121 **2** *3/4* **Epernay**[25] 3413 4-9-0 **66**..(vt) RichardKingscote 8 75+
(Ian Williams) *hld up in 7th: rdn wl over 2f out: prog over 1f out: clsng whn nt clr run last 100yds: styd on to take 2nd nr fin* **5/1**[2]
5066 **3** *1/2* **Mattoral**[18] 3650 3-8-12 **72**...(b) SteveDrowne 9 77
(Peter Makin) *chsd ldng pair: rdn wl over 2f out: grad clsd fr over 1f out: styd on but nvr quite able to chal* **17/2**
0535 **4** *nk* **Huzzah (IRE)**[28] 3290 6-9-11 **77**.................................... MichaelHills 3 83
(B W Hills) *led and sn clr: 5 l clr whn styd towards centre in st: c badk to field over 1f out: hdd & wknd last 100yds* **8/1**
6-35 **5** *3* **Crystal Etoile**[69] 2026 3-9-0 **74**...................................... RyanMoore 12 71+
(Sir Michael Stoute) *hld up in last trio: shkn up and plenty to do 3f out: plugged on fr over 1f out: nvr rchd ldrs* **9/4**[1]
00-3 **6** *2 1/4* **Compton Blue**[12] 3815 5-9-5 **76**.............................(b) KieranO'Neill(5) 13 70
(Richard Hannon) *trckd ldrs: drvn over 2f out: nt qckn over 1f out: fdd ins fnl f* **16/1**
-504 **7** *3/4* **One Way Or Another (AUS)**[28] 3275 8-9-3 **76**........... RaulDaSilva(7) 1 69
(Jeremy Gask) *trckd ldrs: disp 2nd bhd clr ldr wl over 2f out to over 1f out: wknd* **7/1**[3]
334- **8** *1* **Rocky Rebel**[282] 6810 3-9-1 **75**.................................... StevieDonohoe 2 63
(Ralph Beckett) *prom: rdn 3f out: lost pl and struggling 2f out* **14/1**

3305 **9** *1* **Prohibition (IRE)**96 1353 5-8-4 61 oh3 AmyScott(5) 10 49
(Alastair Lidderdale) *hld up last: pushed along fr 3f out: nvr nr ldrs* **66/1**
10-0 **10** *6* **Rock Anthem (IRE)**14 3740 7-9-11 77 MartinLane 4 51+
(Mike Murphy) *s.v.s: a in rr: no great prog over 2f out: sn wknd* **20/1**
1-10 **11** *14* **Mcconnell (USA)**14 3740 6-9-13 79 (b) GeorgeBaker 6 21
(Gary Moore) *awkward s: a in rr: wknd over 2f out: eased and t.o* **25/1**
1m 47.19s (3.89) **Going Correction** +0.625s/f (Yiel)
WFA 3 from 4yo+ 8lb **11 Ran SP% 116.0**
Speed ratings (Par 105): **105,104,103,103,100 98,97,96,95,89 75**
toteswingers: 1&2 £7.40, 1&3 £13.40, 2&3 £9.40 CSF £43.31 CT £328.22 TOTE £9.30: £3.10, £2.00, £3.90; EX 59.00.
Owner B Nielsen & Eastwind Racing & M Trussell **Bred** Coleman Bloodstock Limited **Trained** Upper Lambourn, Berks

FOCUS
A competitive handicap, run at a sound enough pace and once again it proved an advantage to race prominently. The main action developed down the centre of the home straight. The winner is up 4lb on his maiden form.

4216 DEVINE HOMES - BRIDLEWAY EPSOM H'CAP 1m 6f
8:50 (8:50) (Class 4) (0-80,80) 4-Y-0+ **£4,075** (£1,212; £606; £303) **Stalls** Low

Form RPR
1200 **1** **Spice Fair**14 3738 4-8-12 71 RyanMoore 3 77
(Mark Usher) *hld up in 6th: swift move rt against nr side rail to ld over 1f out: drvn and styd on strly* **7/2**2
6-00 **2** *1 1/2* **Morar**32 3184 5-9-0 73 FergusSweeney 4 77
(Laura Mongan) *trckd ldr after 3f: rdn to ld over 2f out: hdd and outpcd over 1f out: kpt on* **11/1**
-212 **3** *1 1/2* **Mohanad (IRE)**76 1839 5-8-5 69 HarryBentley(5) 2 71+
(Sheena West) *hld up in 5th: outpcd once sprint sed and dropped to last 2f out: styd on wl fnl f to take 3rd nr fin* **5/1**
22/0 **4** *1* **Souter Point (USA)**24 3428 5-9-7 80 MartinLane 6 81
(Tony Carroll) *trckd ldr 3f: styd cl up: rdn over 2f out: one pce wl over 1f out* **20/1**
0001 **5** *1/2* **Kings Bayonet**12 3817 4-9-4 77 HayleyTurner 5 77
(Alan King) *hld up last: prog on outer 2f out: chsd ldrs over 1f out: no imp after: fdd fnl f* **4/1**3
5021 **6** *2* **Shernando**5 4059 4-9-6 79 NeilCallan 9 76
(Mark Johnston) *led at v stdy pce: tried to kick on 3f out: hdd over 2f out: wknd over 1f out* **5/2**1
0041 **7** *1/2* **Turjuman (USA)**21 3516 6-8-3 62 JamieMackay 8 58
(Willie Musson) *trckd ldng trio: rdn over 2f out on outer: nt qckn wl over 1f out: wknd* **8/1**
3m 24.18s (19.68) **Going Correction** +0.625s/f (Yiel) **7 Ran SP% 111.7**
Speed ratings (Par 105): **68,67,66,65,65 64,64**
toteswingers: 1&2 £9.40, 1&3 £3.10, 2&3 £8.30 CSF £37.96 CT £186.72 TOTE £4.90: £2.20, £4.10; EX 38.70.
Owner Saxon House Racing **Bred** Mrs D Hughes **Trained** Upper Lambourn, Berks

FOCUS
A modest staying handicap. It was run at an uneven pace and the field came right together nearing the final furlong, so the form is worth treating with some caution. The winner is rated to his best.
T/Plt: £2,408.90 to a £1 stake. Pool: £64,017.75. 19.40 winning units. T/Qpdt: £189.20 to a £1 stake. Pool: £6,701.77. 26.20 winning units. JN

4217 - 4222a (Foreign Racing) - See Raceform Interactive

VICHY
Wednesday, July 20

OFFICIAL GOING: Turf: very soft

4223a GRAND PRIX DE VICHY - AUVERGNE 7EME ETAPE DU DEFI DU GALOP (GROUP 3) (3YO+) (TURF) 1m 2f
8:25 (12:00) 3-Y-0+ **£34,482** (£13,793; £10,344; £6,896; £3,448)

RPR
1 **Cirrus Des Aigles (FR)**24 3448 5-9-6 0 FranckBlondel 2 123+
(Mme C Barande-Barbe, France) *settled 3rd on rail: travelling easily: rdn 2 1/2f out whn whole field swtchd to stands' rail: led 2f out: r.o wl: comf* **2/5**1
2 *3* **Agent Secret (IRE)**101 1266 5-9-2 0 Francois-XavierBertras 1 113
(F Rohaut, France) *led fr s: setting mod pce: stl in front 2 1/2f out: hdd 2f out: r.o wl fnl f* **10/1**3
3 *1/2* **Saga Dream (FR)**22 3532 5-9-2 0 StephanePasquier 7 112
(F Lemercier, France) *settled towards rr: hrd rdn 2f out: r.o wl fnl f: tk 3rd cl home* **20/1**
4 *1/2* **Announce**37 3008 4-9-3 0 MaximeGuyon 5 112
(A Fabre, France) *settled 2nd on outer: dropped bk to 4th whn field swtchd to stands' rail: rdn 2 1/2f out: nt qckn: styd on fnl f: wnt 4th on line* **5/1**2
5 *nse* **Zinabaa (FR)**22 3532 6-9-2 0 YannickLetondeur 4 111
(M Mace, France) *racd 4th on outer: rdn 2 1/2f out: r.o: no ex fnl 100yds* **10/1**3
6 *6* **Le Roi Mage (IRE)**22 3532 6-9-2 0 Christophe-PatriceLemaire 3 99
(T Lallie, France) *settled towards rr: rdn 2 1/2f out: nt qckn: fdd 1 1/2f out: eased ins fnl f* **12/1**
2m 14.0s (5.40) **6 Ran SP% 118.7**
WIN (incl. 1 euro stake): 1.40. PLACES: 1.10, 2.10. SF: 4.30.
Owner Jean-Claude-Alain Dupouy **Bred** Y Lelimouzin And B Deschamps **Trained** France

NOTEBOOK
Cirrus Des Aigles(FR), runner-up to Sarafina in the Grand Prix de Saint-Cloud, was down in class and back over his best trip. He won easily and, as he was entitled to, and the International at York could now be on his agenda.

3993 BATH (L-H)
Thursday, July 21

OFFICIAL GOING: Good (good to firm in places) changing to good (good to soft in places) after race 6 (4.20)
Another all-sprint card at Bath due to problems with the home bend.
Wind: fresh, partly against Weather: cloudy with sunny periods and occassional heavy showers

4224 BATH TOURISM PLUS H'CAP (DIV I) 5f 161y
1:30 (1:30) (Class 6) (0-65,65) 3-Y-0+ **£1,293** (£385; £192; £96) **Stalls** Centre

Form RPR
4313 **1** **Interakt**7 4025 4-9-0 58 HarryBentley(5) 11 69
(Joseph Tuite) *hld up in tch: hdwy fr over 2f out: rdn into narrow ld over 1f out: hrd pressed thrght fnl f: jst hld on: all out* **7/2**1
6650 **2** *nse* **The Name Is Frank**16 3720 6-9-4 60 (t) SimonPearce(3) 10 71
(Mark Gillard) *chsd ldrs: rdn to chal fr wl over 1f out: ev ch thrght fnl f: kpt on nr fin: jst failed* **9/1**
0004 **3** *3 1/2* **Lady Excellentia (IRE)**15 3724 3-7-11 46 oh1 KieranO'Neill(5) 7 44
(Ronald Harris) *hld up in tch: effrt 2f out: styd on fnl f* **22/1**
2060 **4** *1 1/2* **Trade Centre**166 432 6-8-13 52 LiamKeniry 8 47
(Milton Bradley) *chsd ldrs: rdn over 2f out: swtchd lft fr jst over 1f out: kpt on same pce* **20/1**
0-65 **5** *1* **Cliffords Reprieve**7 3999 3-8-11 55 EddieCreighton 3 45
(Eric Wheeler) *chsd ldrs: rdn to chal 2f out: ev ch ent fnl f: fdd* **33/1**
3050 **6** *3/4* **Riflessione**7 3995 5-9-12 65 (b) TomMcLaughlin 4 54
(Ronald Harris) *led: rdn over 2f out: hdd over 1f out: wknd ins fnl f* **12/1**
4303 **7** *nk* **Bateleur**6 4057 7-8-13 59 CharlesBishop(7) 6 47
(Mick Channon) *hmpd s: in tch: rdn and nt clrest of runs fr 2f out: nt pce to get on terms* **9/2**3
-003 **8** *7* **Ridgeway Sapphire**15 3721 4-8-8 47 oh1 ow1 (v) RobertHavlin 2 12+
(Mark Usher) *hld up in tch: rdn and stdy prog fr 2f out: styng on whn bdly squeezed out ent fnl f: no ch after: sn eased* **12/1**
0-06 **9** *6* **Safari Guide**48 2692 5-8-12 51 KellyHarrison 9 —
(Dai Burchell) *struggling over 3f out: a towards rr* **18/1**
3012 **10** *4 1/2* **Jolly Ranch**7 3999 5-9-2 55 FergusSweeney 5 —
(Tony Newcombe) *wnt rt s: chsd ldrs effrt 2f out: wkng whn short of room ent fnl f* **4/1**2
0403 **11** *1 3/4* **Dimaire**10 3909 4-9-3 56 CathyGannon 1 —
(Derek Haydn Jones) *chsd ldrs: rdn over 2f out: hld whn squeezed up on rails ent fnl f: eased whn no ch after* **8/1**
1m 11.28s (0.08) **Going Correction** +0.05s/f (Good)
WFA 3 from 4yo+ 5lb **11 Ran SP% 114.2**
Speed ratings (Par 101): **101,100,96,94,92 91,91,82,74,68 65**
toteswingers:1&2:£6.90, 1&3:£13.90, 2&3:£33.40 CSF £33.27 CT £597.05 TOTE £4.00: £1.50, £3.60, £7.10; EX 39.70.
Owner Heart Of The South Racing **Bred** P C Hunt **Trained** Great Shefford, Berkshire

FOCUS
The front pair drew a little way clear in what was the first division of a low-grade sprint handicap. It was the best time on the card and the form is taken at face value.
Riflessione Official explanation: jockey said that the gelding hung right handed
Jolly Ranch Official explanation: jockey said that the mare ran flat

4225 TRENT SERVICES/WOODLEY HALL MAIDEN AUCTION FILLIES' STKS 5f 161y
2:00 (2:01) (Class 6) 2-Y-0 **£1,617** (£481; £240; £120) **Stalls** Centre

Form RPR
1 **Mary Fildes (IRE)** 2-8-11 0 LiamKeniry 3 67+
(J S Moore) *bdly hmpd leaving stalls: chsd ldng trio: pushed along and hdwy to ld ent fnl f: drew clr: comf* **12/1**3
4245 **2** *4 1/2* **Emma Jean (IRE)**13 3816 2-8-11 0 LukeMorris 2 52
(J S Moore) *trckd ldng pair: rdn over 2f out: r.o ins fnl f: snatched 2nd fnl stride: no ch w wnr* **7/1**2
04 **3** *nse* **Empressive**19 3639 2-8-6 0 KieranO'Neill(5) 5 52
(William Muir) *led: rdn wl over 1f out: hdd ent fnl f: sn hld by wnr: no ex whn lost 2nd fnl stride* **18/1**
0 **4** *4* **Clodhopper (IRE)**30 3257 2-8-8 0 SophieDoyle(3) 4 39
(Jamie Osborne) *veered lft s: sn trcking ldr: rdn 2f out: fdd ent fnl f* **33/1**
34 **U** **Lady Jameela**12 3865 2-8-8 0 MartinHarley(3) 1 —
(Mick Channon) *veered sharply lft and uns rdr leaving stalls* **1/5**1
1m 12.98s (1.78) **Going Correction** +0.05s/f (Good) **5 Ran SP% 111.7**
Speed ratings (Par 89): **90,84,83,78,—**
CSF £82.77 TOTE £8.70: £3.40, £1.80; EX 32.30.
Owner Norton Common Farm Racing **Bred** Tally-Ho Stud **Trained** Upper Lambourn, Berks

FOCUS
High drama at the start of this moderate juvenile maiden, with red-hot 1-5 favourite Lady Jameela unseating Martin Harley leaving the stalls. This left a really weak race.

NOTEBOOK
Mary Fildes(IRE), from a speedy family, ran out a tidy winner, always travelling well and readily asserting. She displayed a ton of speed and would probably have given the favourite something to think about anyway. It'll be interesting to see how she progresses, with a rise in class inevitable. (op 11-1)
Emma Jean(IRE), who was much more experienced, had her chance but predictably wasn't quick enough on this drop in trip. (tchd 15-2)
Empressive ran her best race yet and may find a minor opening switched to nurseries. (tchd 16-1)
Clodhopper(IRE) still looked inexperienced and is probably one for nurseries over further later in the year. (tchd 40-1)
Lady Jameela veered sharply left leaving the stalls (the Monty Roberts rug probably spooking her as it slid off on exiting the gate) and gave Martin Harley little chance of staying aboard. This was an unfortunate incident, especially for those who took the prohibitive odds. (tchd 1-3 in places)

4226 TONY FOXWELL MEMORIAL NURSERY 5f 161y
2:35 (2:35) (Class 6) 2-Y-0 **£1,617** (£481; £240; £120) **Stalls** Centre

Form RPR
0121 **1** **Fanrouge (IRE)**7 3993 2-9-3 78 6ex KieranO'Neill(5) 3 84+
(Malcolm Saunders) *stdd s: trckd ldrs: pushed along whn swtchd lft over 1f out: led ent fnl f: r.o wl: readily* **3/1**2
3401 **2** *1 1/4* **Crowning Star (IRE)**15 3746 2-9-3 73 (t) LukeMorris 2 75
(J S Moore) *prom: led 2f out: sn rdn: hdd ent fnl f: no ex* **8/13**1
0530 **3** *5* **Clarkson (IRE)**13 3810 2-8-8 64 FergusSweeney 4 50
(Jamie Osborne) *trckd ldrs: rdn to chal over 2f out: nt pce of ldrs fr over 1f out* **7/1**3

1010 **4** *4* **Selinda**[12] 3842 2-8-3 59........................ CathyGannon 1 31
(Mick Channon) *led tl rdn 2f out: wknd ent fnl f* **10/1**
1m 12.89s (1.69) **Going Correction** +0.05s/f (Good) **4** Ran SP% **108.5**
Speed ratings (Par 92): **90,88,81,76**
CSF £5.37 TOTE £3.40; EX 4.60.

Owner Chris Scott **Bred** Silk Fan Syndicate **Trained** Green Ore, Somerset
■ The 'official' ratings shown next to each horse are estimated and for information purposes only.

FOCUS
Only two were expected to feature in what looked an ordinary nursery. The winner continues to progress.

NOTEBOOK
Fanrouge(IRE), already a dual course winner, came out much the best under a penalty, clicking into another gear when asked for maximum effort and scoring with a bit in hand. She's rapidly progressive and surely deserves a rise in class now. (op 2-1)

Crowning Star(IRE), who made all for a ready victory at Lingfield last time, surprisingly declined the lead and was ultimately done for speed by the winner. He'll be better ridden more forcefully over a stiff 6f. (op 11-10)

Clarkson(IRE) was again readily held and it surely won't be long before he's dropped to selling level. A step up to 7f may help him. (op 6-1 tchd 11-2)

Selinda has registered both wins this year in sellers, and she again wasn't up to competing in a tougher race. (op 8-1)

4227 LAS IGUANAS H'CAP 5f 11y
3:10 (3:10) (Class 5) (0-70,70) 3-Y-O **£2,264** (£673; £336; £168) **Stalls** Centre

Form RPR
0531 **1** **Dreams Of Glory**[15] 3724 3-8-1 **53**........................ SimonPearce(3) 5 62
(Ron Hodges) *mde all: shkn up ins fnl f: kpt on: hld on wl* **10/3**[2]

5221 **2** *1* **Sarangoo**[7] 3998 3-9-3 **66** 6ex........................ CathyGannon 1 71
(Malcolm Saunders) *trckd wnr: rdn over 1f out: kpt on but a being hld fnl f* **11/4**[1]

-623 **3** *¾* **Yasmeena (USA)**[15] 3723 3-9-7 **70**........................ TadhgO'Shea 3 73
(B W Hills) *wnt lft and bmpd leaving stalls: cl up: pushed along 2f out: rdn over 1f out: styd on ins fnl f* **11/4**[1]

3312 **4** *¾* **Juarla (IRE)**[57] 2396 3-9-4 **67**........................ LukeMorris 6 67
(Ronald Harris) *trckd wnr: rdn over 2f out: kpt on same pce fnl f* **11/2**[3]

0402 **5** *2 ¾* **Adaeze (IRE)**[7] 3998 3-8-3 **57**........................ HarryBentley(5) 2 47
(Jonathan Portman) *bmpd leaving stalls: trckd ldrs: rdn 2f out: fdd ins fnl f* **11/2**[3]

-635 **6** *½* **Dubai Affair**[7] 3994 3-9-2 **65**........................(p) TomMcLaughlin 4 53
(Ronald Harris) *little slowly away: trckd ldrs: effrt 2f out: fdd ins fnl f* **25/1**

62.38 secs (-0.12) **Going Correction** +0.05s/f (Good) **6** Ran SP% **111.0**
Speed ratings (Par 100): **102,100,99,98,93 92**
toteswingers:1&2:£1.60, 1&3:£2.30, 2&3:£3.00 CSF £12.59 TOTE £4.20: £2.60, £1.30; EX 14.00.

Owner P E Axon **Bred** P E Axon **Trained** Charlton Mackrell, Somerset

FOCUS
This Class 5 3-y-o sprint handicap was run in a heavy shower. The pace was sound and the winner is rated up a pound on his latest win here.

4228 BRITISH STALLION STUDS SUPPORTING BRITISH RACING E B F NOVICE STKS 5f 11y
3:45 (3:45) (Class 4) 2-Y-O **£4,463** (£1,328; £663; £331) **Stalls** Centre

Form RPR
521 **1** **Amis Reunis**[24] 3463 2-8-6 0........................ KieranO'Neill(5) 5 78
(Richard Hannon) *trckd ldr: pushed along over 2f out: rdn over 1f out: edgd lft but styd on to ld fnl 100yds: comf* **4/5**[1]

1561 **2** *1 ½* **Powerful Wind (IRE)**[13] 3800 2-9-7 0........................ TomMcLaughlin 3 83
(Ronald Harris) *led: rdn ent fnl f: no ex whn hdd fnl 100yds* **11/2**[3]

100 **3** *5* **Majestic Rose**[33] 3152 2-8-8 0........................ MartinHarley(3) 1 55
(Mick Channon) *awkward leaving stalls: chsd ldrs: pushed along over 3f out: rdn over 2f out: no ex fnl f* **8/1**

104 **4** *2 ½* **The Penny Horse (IRE)**[20] 3589 2-9-5 0........................ JamesDoyle 4 54
(J S Moore) *trckd ldr: rdn 2f out: wknd fnl f* **11/4**[2]

61.01 secs (0.71) **Going Correction** +0.05s/f (Good) **4** Ran SP% **108.7**
Speed ratings (Par 96): **97,94,86,82**
CSF £5.54 TOTE £1.70; EX 4.30.

Owner Mrs J Wood **Bred** Paddock Space **Trained** East Everleigh, Wilts

FOCUS
Hard to know what to make of this form, with Majestic Rose effectively losing her race at the start and The Penny Horse, who very much had the best form, clearly failing to give his running.

NOTEBOOK
Amis Reunis took her time to master the front-running Powerful Wind, from whom she was receiving 10lb (not including her rider's 5lb claim), but there's stamina on her dam's side of the pedigree and she looked a horse likely to appreciate 7f in time. (op 6-4 tchd 13-8)

Powerful Wind(IRE) had to concede weight all round, but as the only front-runner it was no surprise to see him go close in this small field. He'd beaten the highly progressive Fanrouge (winner of the 2.35) by 6l last time, and he himself is clearly on the up. (op 7-2)

Majestic Rose couldn't recover the lost momentum and may find life easier in minor nurseries. (op 13-2)

The Penny Horse(IRE), taken to post early, looked a big danger to the favourite judged on his last-time-out fourth in a 5f Listed race at Sandown, but he found little when asked and dropped away as though something may have been amiss. (op 2-1 tchd 3-1)

4229 BAILBROOK LODGE MEDIAN AUCTION MAIDEN STKS 5f 161y
4:20 (4:22) (Class 6) 2-Y-O **£1,617** (£481; £240; £120) **Stalls** Centre

Form RPR
5 **1** **Chandigarh (IRE)**[32] 3200 2-8-7 0........................ KieranO'Neill(5) 2 70
(Paul Fitzsimons) *disp ld tl over 1f out: sn hld: keeping on same pce lft in ld fnl 120yds* **15/2**

2 *1 ¼* **Silkee Supreme** 2-9-3 0........................ PatDobbs 4 71
(Richard Hannon) *s.i.s: chsd ldrs after 1f: rdn over 2f out: lft w wnr and ev ch whn hmpd fnl 120yds* **11/2**

44 **3** *3 ¾* **King's Ciel**[25] 3425 2-9-0 0........................ MatthewDavies(3) 7 59
(George Baker) *bmpd s: outpcd early: cl up after 1f: rdn wl over 2f out: lft 4th briefly fnl 120yds: styd on: nt gng pce to get involved* **5/2**[2]

5 **4** *1 ¼* **Courtland Avenue (IRE)**[31] 3229 2-8-12 0........................ HarryBentley(5) 1 54
(Jonathan Portman) *disp ld tl over 1f out: styng on at same pce whn lft 3rd briefly fnl 120yds: no ex* **9/4**[1]

03 **5** *13* **Two Bridges**[9] 3941 2-8-12 0........................ FergusSweeney 3 6
(Gary Moore) *disp ld tl wknd over 1f out* **25/1**

2 **U** **Uncle Roger (IRE)**[9] 3941 2-9-3 0........................ LiamKeniry 5 74+
(Eve Johnson Houghton) *prom: taken bk bhd ldrs after 1f: travelling best to ld over 1f out: sn rdn and drifted lft: wl in command whn jinked rt at half-f marker and uns rdr* **4/1**[3]

1m 14.27s (3.07) **Going Correction** +0.225s/f (Good) **6** Ran SP% **110.3**
Speed ratings (Par 92): **88,86,81,79,62** —
toteswingers:1&2:£5.90, 1&3:£4.70, 2&3:£3.40 CSF £44.93 TOTE £7.30: £2.70, £2.60; EX 55.80.

Owner Bal Sohal **Bred** Secret Justice Syndicate **Trained** Upper Lambourn, Berks

FOCUS
A modest juvenile maiden in which Uncle Roger was going clear and had the race sewn up when jinking right and causing Liam Keniry to be unshipped. The form could be rated a little higher.

NOTEBOOK
Chandigarh(IRE) capitalised on Uncle Roger's misfortune, stepping up markedly on her initial effort even if she was second best on the day. Her future will lie in ordinary handicaps. (op 16-1)

Silkee Supreme, from a top yard but whose breeding is nothing to be excited about, kept on nicely enough and ought to improve. (op 6-1 tchd 13-2)

King's Ciel is now qualified for nurseries and should fare better in that sphere, with a return to further likely to help. (op 9-4 tchd 11-4)

Courtland Avenue(IRE) was disappointing, fading out of it late on and failing to build on his initial effort. (op 3-1 tchd 2-1)

Two Bridges had little to find with Uncle Roger on Brighton form, so it's fairly safe to assume she didn't give her running. (op 12-1 tchd 10-1)

Uncle Roger(IRE) was going clear and had the race sewn up (traded for plenty at 1.01 on Betfair) when jinking right and causing Liam Keniry to be unshipped. Whether it was a slight kink in the rail or the fact he caught a glimpse of the fast-approaching half-furlong marker that caused it remains to be seen, but either way his rider will no doubt be wishing he'd changed his whip hand to try and prevent him drifting on to the rail. Compensation will surely be gained at some stage. (op 10-3 tchd 3-1)

4230 BATH TOURISM PLUS H'CAP (DIV II) 5f 161y
4:50 (4:51) (Class 6) (0-65,65) 3-Y-O+ **£1,293** (£385; £192; £96) **Stalls** Centre

Form RPR
-065 **1** **Flaxen Lake**[15] 3721 4-8-7 **46**........................ LukeMorris 3 55
(Milton Bradley) *towards rr: hrd rdn and hdwy over 1f out: swtchd rt ent fnl f: kpt on to ld fnl 120yds: hld on: all out* **7/1**

2442 **2** *hd* **Miss Firefly**[24] 3464 6-8-13 **55**........................(p) SimonPearce(3) 8 63
(Ron Hodges) *in tch: rdn whn nt clr run briefly 2f out: bmpd by wnr 1f out: kpt on to hold ev ch fnl 120yds: jst hld* **5/1**[2]

3200 **3** *1 ½* **Katmai River (IRE)**[50] 2605 4-9-4 **62**........................(v) LeeNewnes(5) 4 65
(Mark Usher) *sn pushed along towards rr: stdy prog fr 2f out: styd on fnl f: wnt 3rd nr fin* **11/2**[3]

0400 **4** *½* **Crimson Queen**[16] 3714 4-8-13 **52**........................ JamesDoyle 1 53+
(Roy Brotherton) *slipped leaving stalls: sn rcvrd: in tch: rdn to ld over 1f out: no ex whn hdd fnl 120yds* **14/1**

012 **5** *nk* **Avonlini**[16] 3714 5-9-1 **54**........................ SaleemGolam 6 54
(Brian Baugh) *trckd ldrs: rdn 2f out: ev ch over 1f out: kpt on same pce fnl f* **6/1**

021 **6** *½* **My Meteor**[7] 3999 4-9-3 **56** 6ex........................ FergusSweeney 7 55
(Tony Newcombe) *trckd ldrs: rdn to chal 2f out: ev ch ent fnl f: fdd fnl 120yds* **9/2**[1]

-500 **7** *¾* **Too Many Questions (IRE)**[19] 3633 3-9-7 **65**........................ CathyGannon 10 60
(David Evans) *led: rdn whn hrd pressed fr over 2f out: hdd over 1f out: no ex* **9/1**

034 **8** *8* **What Katie Did (IRE)**[9] 3939 6-8-7 **46**........................(p) LiamKeniry 9 16
(Milton Bradley) *trckd ldrs: rdn over 2f out: wknd over 1f out* **5/1**[2]

60-0 **9** *19* **Bold Argument (IRE)**[63] 2222 8-8-8 **50**........................ SophieDoyle(3) 2 —
(Nerys Dutfield) *v awkwardly away: a detached* **25/1**

1m 13.14s (1.94) **Going Correction** +0.225s/f (Good)
WFA 3 from 4yo+ 5lb **9** Ran SP% **114.2**
Speed ratings (Par 101): **96,95,93,93,92 92,91,80,55**
toteswingers:1&2:£6.60, 1&3:£8.20, 2&3:£6.30 CSF £41.37 CT £208.24 TOTE £7.90: £2.50, £2.00, £1.10; EX 10.60.

Owner Asterix Partnership **Bred** R Hollinshead And M Johnson **Trained** Sedbury, Gloucs

FOCUS
The more competitive of the two divisions, any number holding a chance from over 1f out, but it was slower than division I. The winner's best form since last autumn.

Crimson Queen Official explanation: jockey said that the filly slipped leaving the stalls

Bold Argument(IRE) Official explanation: jockey said that the gelding missed the break

4231 VISIT BATH FILLIES' H'CAP 5f 161y
5:20 (5:21) (Class 5) (0-75,75) 3-Y-O+ **£2,264** (£673; £336; £168) **Stalls** Centre

Form RPR
5111 **1** **Roodee Queen**[6] 4067 3-9-5 73 6ex........................ LiamKeniry 2 82
(Milton Bradley) *mde all: pushed clr over 1f out: rdn and r.o strly fnl f: comf* **3/1**[2]

0255 **2** *4* **Kinigi (IRE)**[23] 3482 5-9-0 68........................(b) KieranO'Neill(5) 3 65
(Ronald Harris) *trckd ldrs: effrt 2f out: chsd wnr over 1f out: a being hld: jst kpt 2nd* **9/2**[3]

3622 **3** *nse* **Comptonspirit**[7] 3995 7-9-7 70........................ J-PGuillambert 7 67
(Brian Baugh) *trckd ldrs: rdn wl over 1f out: kpt on same pce: nrly snatched 2nd fnl stride* **7/4**[1]

5234 **4** *2 ¼* **Scarlet Rocks (IRE)**[14] 3785 3-9-6 74........................ CathyGannon 4 62
(David Evans) *t.k.h: prom: rdn over 2f out: lost 2nd over 1f out: no ex fnl f* **9/2**[3]

2226 **5** *½* **Talamahana**[15] 3721 6-8-8 57 ow1........................(v) LukeMorris 1 45
(Andrew Haynes) *chsd ldrs: pushed along over 3f out: rdn over 2f out: nvr able to get on terms* **15/2**

1m 12.53s (1.33) **Going Correction** +0.225s/f (Good)
WFA 3 from 4yo+ 5lb **5** Ran SP% **109.5**
Speed ratings (Par 100): **100,94,94,91,90**
Totesuper 7: Win: Not won, Place: Not won. CSF £15.97 TOTE £3.60: £2.30, £1.60; EX 16.70.

Owner T A Godbert **Bred** Tom & Evelyn Yates **Trained** Sedbury, Gloucs

FOCUS
Another win for the rapidly progressive Roodee Queen. Pretty weak form, not taken too literally.

T/Plt: £3,131.20 to a £1 stake. Pool:£44,180.55 - 10.30 winning tickets T/Qpdt: £82.60 to a £1 stake. Pool:£4,041.08 - 36.20 winning tickets TM

4000 DONCASTER (L-H)

Thursday, July 21

OFFICIAL GOING: Good

Wind: Light, across Weather: Sunny periods

4232 TYREGIANT.COM MAIDEN AUCTION FILLIES' STKS 7f

6:20 (6:21) (Class 5) 2-Y-O **£2,264** (£673; £336; £168) **Stalls** High

Form RPR

0 **1** **Golden Valley**[17] 3686 2-8-4 0 AndreaAtzeni 11 74+
(Rod Millman) *cl up: led over 2f out: jnd and rdn over 1f out: drvn ins fnl f and kpt on strly* **5/1** 2

23 **2** 1 1/2 **Alice Rose (IRE)**[17] 3680 2-8-6 0 MartinLane 13 72
(Rae Guest) *trckd ldrs: swtchd lft and hdwy wl over 2f out: rdn to chal wl over 1f out and ev ch tl drvn ent fnl f and kpt on same pce* **10/1**

3 **3** 2 **Oddysey (IRE)**[27] 3342 2-8-6 0 TomEaves 5 67
(Michael Dods) *prom on outer: hdwy and cl up over 2f out: sn rdn and ev ch tl drvn and one pce appr fnl f* **7/4** 1

4 8 **Symphony Time (IRE)** 2-8-7 0 LiamJones 1 47
(Brian Meehan) *hld up towards rr: hdwy over 2f out: kpt on appr fnl f: nrst fin* **16/1**

5 2 3/4 **Dance For Georgie** 2-8-2 0 PatrickDonaghy(3) 9 38+
(Ben Haslam) *dwlt and towards rr: hdwy over 2f out: rdn and kpt on appr fnl f* **66/1**

4 **6** nk **Moment In The Sun**[17] 3680 2-8-4 0 FrannyNorton 12 36
(William Muir) *led: rdn along wl over 2f out: sn hdd and grad wknd* **6/1** 3

00 **7** 3/4 **Nadia's Place**[17] 3680 2-8-2 0 DeclanCannon(3) 6 35
(Nigel Tinkler) *prom: rdn along wl over 2f out: grad wknd* **100/1**

0 **8** 1/2 **Holy Empress (IRE)**[13] 3816 2-8-9 0 MickyFenton 2 38
(Michael Bell) *towards rr: pushed along and outpcd over 2f out: sme late hdwy* **22/1**

4 **9** 1/2 **Darling Lexi (IRE)**[49] 2630 2-8-7 0 PaulHanagan 4 35
(Richard Fahey) *midfield: rdn along 1/2-way: n.d* **5/1** 2

0 **10** 5 **Waterloo Girl**[30] 3258 2-8-1 0 BillyCray(3) 7 19
(Michael Blanshard) *prom: rdn along 3f out: sn wknd* **100/1**

11 1 **Iberian Rock** 2-8-7 0 FrederikTylicki 3 19
(Ann Duffield) *s.i.s: a in rr* **16/1**

0 **12** 3 **Hatsumomo (IRE)**[19] 3610 2-8-7 0 ow1 DavidAllan 8 11
(Tim Easterby) *chsd ldrs: rdn along 1/2-way: sn wknd* **50/1**

1m 27.02s (0.72) **Going Correction** -0.025s/f (Good) **12** Ran SP% **114.6**

Speed ratings (Par 91): **94,92,90,80,77 77,76,75,75,69 68,65**

toteswingers: 1&2 £8.40, 1&3 £2.70, 2&3 £4.80 CSF £50.63 TOTE £5.60 : £3.80, £4.40, £1.10; EX 72.10.

Owner R K Arrowsmith **Bred** Harts Farm Stud **Trained** Kentisbeare, Devon

FOCUS

Inside rail on Round course moved out 6yds which added 57yds to 1m2f race and 72yds to 1m4f race. Little strength in depth here but the winner did it well and the form could have been rated higher.

NOTEBOOK

Golden Valley, who was bought in for just £400 at the yearling sales, had shaped well when seventh on her debut over 6f at Windsor. She looked very professional here and took this in most decisive style. Nurseries presumably now beckon. (op 8-1)

Alice Rose (IRE), placed on her first two starts, was another stepping up to seven for the first time. She put a below par effort at Ripon, always a tricky course for an inexperienced runner, behind her. (op 8-1)

Oddysey (IRE), third over 6f here first time in a race that has worked out well, travelled strongly on the outside. She finished clear of the remainder and should have little trouble finding an opening (op 15-8 tchd 13-8)

Symphony Time (IRE), a daughter of Cape Cross, was expected to need the experience. She kept on towards the outside and this should have taught her something. (op 20-1)

Dance For Georgie, a 9,000gns yearling, is a half-sister to three winners. After a sluggish start she made significant headway from halfway and seems likely to improve a good deal for the experience. (tchd 100-1)

Moment In The Sun, who finished strongly after a slow break first time, led against the stands' side rail but dropped right away. (op 9-2 tchd 4-1)

4233 WELCOME TO YORKSHIRE ART OF YORKSHIRE GARDEN H'CAP 6f

6:50 (6:52) (Class 5) (0-70,70) 4-Y-O+ **£2,385** (£704; £352) **Stalls** High

Form RPR

4000 **1** **Kings 'n Dreams**[27] 3348 4-9-1 64 (b) KierenFallon 10 78
(Dean Ivory) *hld up in midfield: hdwy 2f out: sn n.m.r: rdn to chse ldr over 1f out: kpt on wl to ld last 100yds* **5/1** 2

5464 **2** 1 1/4 **Mount Hollow**[13] 3806 6-8-8 57 (v) GrahamGibbons 2 67
(Reg Hollinshead) *stdd and swtchd rt s: hld up in rr: hdwy over 2f out: swtchd rt and rdn to chse ldrs over 1f out: drvn and styd on wl fnl f* **11/2** 3

0453 **3** 1 **Sea Salt**[7] 4000 8-8-3 59 ShaneBKelly(7) 4 66
(Ron Barr) *cl up: led 1/2-way: rdn wl over 1f out and sn edgd lft: drvn and hung lft ins fnl f: hdd and no ex last 100yds* **8/1**

26-3 **4** 2 **He's A Humbug (IRE)**[15] 3732 7-8-10 59 MickyFenton 6 59
(Paul Midgley) *in tch: hdwy to chse ldrs 1/2-way: rdn along and hld whn nt clr run over 1f out: one pce after* **12/1**

0022 **5** 1 1/4 **Steel City Boy (IRE)**[2] 4187 8-8-5 57 BillyCray(3) 3 53
(Garry Woodward) *slt ld: hdd 1/2-way and sn pushed along: rdn 2f out and grad wknd* **6/1**

-404 **6** 1 1/4 **Nicholas Pocock (IRE)**[30] 3245 5-8-8 60 SeanLevey(3) 9 52
(Brian Ellison) *in rr: rdn along 1/2-way: styd on fnl 2f: n.d* **4/1** 1

1604 **7** 1/2 **Sir Nod**[61] 2286 9-9-7 70 PaulHanagan 11 61
(Julie Camacho) *cl up: effrt 2f out: sn rdn and hung lft over 1f out: sn wknd* **9/1**

0300 **8** nk **Bossy Kitty**[9] 3937 4-8-0 52 DeclanCannon(3) 12 42
(Nigel Tinkler) *chsd ldrs: rdn along over 2f out: sn wknd* **14/1**

2012 **9** 2 **Whiskey Junction**[9] 3957 7-9-1 64 LiamJones 7 47
(Michael Quinn) *prom: rdn along 1/2-way: sn wknd* **8/1**

0650 **10** 3 **Lady Florence**[17] 3683 6-8-5 61 ClaireMurray(7) 8 35
(David C Griffiths) *towards rr: sme hdwy on outer over 3f out: sn rdn and wknd* **33/1**

1m 12.99s (-0.61) **Going Correction** -0.025s/f (Good) **10** Ran SP% **115.9**

Speed ratings (Par 103): **103,101,100,97,95 94,93,92,90,86**

toteswingers: 1&2 £9.20, 1&3 £6.70, 2&3 £6.00 CSF £32.46 CT £221.47 TOTE £5.00 : £1.70, £1.20, £3.60; EX 39.20.

Owner Ian Gethin & Richard Gethin **Bred** P A Blows **Trained** Radlett, Herts

FOCUS

A modest sprint handicap run at a fast pace, but the time was slow suggesting they may have gone too quick. The winner is back to something like last summer's form.

Sir Nod Official explanation: jockey said that the gelding hung left

Whiskey Junction Official explanation: jockey said that the gelding was never travelling

4234 SKYBET SUPPORTING YORKSHIRE RACING SUMMER FESTIVAL H'CAP 6f

7:25 (7:25) (Class 4) (0-80,78) 3-Y-O **£3,557** (£1,058; £529; £264) **Stalls** High

Form RPR

1331 **1** **Fast Shot**[15] 3731 3-9-0 71 DavidAllan 4 85
(Tim Easterby) *trckd ldrs: hdwy 1/2-way: chsd ldr over 1f out: sn swtchd rt and rdn ent fnl f: styd on wl to ld last 50yds* **9/1**

1212 **2** 1 **York Glory (USA)**[6] 4048 3-9-7 78 (b) PhillipMakin 5 89
(Kevin Ryan) *cl up: led 1/2-way: pushed clr 2f out: rdn over 1f out: wknd ins fnl f: hdd and no ex last 50yds* **6/5** 1

341 **3** shd **Shesastar**[27] 3347 3-9-4 75 GrahamGibbons 1 85
(David Barron) *hld up: hdwy wl over 2f out: chsd ldrs over 1f out: swtchd rt and rdn 1f out: drvn and styd on wl fnl f* **7/2** 2

2560 **4** 1 1/2 **Maverik**[27] 3346 3-9-5 76 FrederikTylicki 2 81
(Michael Dods) *prom on outer: effrt over 2f out: sn rdn: drvn over 1f out and kpt on same pce* **10/1**

5222 **5** 8 **Restless Bay (IRE)**[7] 3996 3-9-7 78 (v) KierenFallon 6 58
(Reg Hollinshead) *towards rr: hdwy 1/2-way: rdn to chse ldrs 2f out: sn no imp* **8/1** 3

1605 **6** 1 1/2 **Dubaianswer**[29] 3283 3-9-7 78 AndreaAtzeni 3 53
(Marco Botti) *hld up and bhd: pushed along 1/2-way: rdn along 2f out: nvr a factor* **12/1**

321 **7** 1/2 **My Own Way Home**[14] 3756 3-9-0 74 SeanLevey(3) 9 47
(Des Donovan) *dwlt: a towards rr* **20/1**

4500 **8** 1 1/4 **Il Battista**[96] 1384 3-8-12 69 (p) RobertWinston 7 38
(Alan McCabe) *dwlt: sn chsng ldrs: rdn along 1/2-way: sn wknd* **50/1**

1134 **9** 2 1/4 **Royal Bajan (USA)**[8] 3975 3-9-2 73 PaulHanagan 8 35
(James Given) *led: hdd 1/2-way and sn pushed along: rdn over 2f out and sn wknd* **16/1**

1m 11.81s (-1.79) **Going Correction** -0.025s/f (Good) **9** Ran SP% **118.2**

Speed ratings (Par 102): **110,108,108,106,95 93,93,91,88**

toteswingers: 1&2 £3.50, 1&3 £4.70, 2&3 £2.50 CSF £20.71 CT £48.54 TOTE £10.40 : £2.10, £1.60, £1.60; EX 29.20.

Owner Ontoawinner & Partners **Bred** Whitsbury Manor Stud & Pigeon House Stud **Trained** Great Habton, N Yorks

FOCUS

A competitive 3yo sprint handicap and again there was no hanging about. The form is rated around the fourth with the first three all on the upgrade.

Dubaianswer Official explanation: jockey said that the filly was never travelling

4235 ESQUIRES COFFEE WHEATLEY RETAIL PARK FILLIES' H'CAP 7f

7:55 (7:59) (Class 3) (0-90,87) 3-Y-O+

£6,411 (£1,919; £959; £479; £239; £120) **Stalls** High

Form RPR

41 **1** **Gladys' Gal**[40] 2924 3-9-5 85 AndreaAtzeni 2 96+
(Roger Varian) *cl up: led 2f out: rdn ent fnl f: kpt on strly* **5/2** 1

1422 **2** 1 1/4 **No Poppy (IRE)**[14] 3782 3-9-0 80 DavidAllan 4 84
(Tim Easterby) *dwlt: gd hdwy to join ldrs 1/2-way: rdn to chal over 2f out: drvn over 1f out: kpt on u.p fnl f* **13/2**

62 **3** 1 1/4 **Primo Lady**[21] 3549 3-9-2 82 (b) RobertWinston 6 83
(Gay Kelleway) *hld up in tch: effrt wl over 2f out: swtchd lft to outer wl over 1f out and sn rdn: styd on ins fnl f: tk 3rd nr fin* **16/1**

-604 **4** nse **Jeannie Galloway (IRE)**[29] 3278 4-9-10 83 PaulHanagan 3 89+
(Richard Fahey) *plld hrd: chsd ldng pair: stdd and lost pl 3f out: hdwy whn n.m.r and swtchd lft wl over 1f out: sn rdn and styng on whn n.m.r nr line* **14/1**

2205 **5** 1/2 **Jade**[13] 3819 3-8-10 76 TomEaves 5 76
(Ollie Pears) *hld up: hdwy over 2f out: rdn to chse ldng pair over 1f out: one pce ins fnl f* **9/2** 3

102 **6** 2 **Gracefield (USA)**[14] 3757 3-9-4 84 AhmedAjtebi 1 78
(Mahmood Al Zarooni) *chsd ldrs: rdn along wl over 2f out: wkng whn n.m.r wl over 1f out* **6/1**

1-13 **7** nk **Wallis**[26] 3407 4-10-0 87 KierenFallon 7 83
(Luca Cumani) *led: pushed along 3f out: rdn and hdd 2f out: wkng whn n.m.r on inner wl over 1f out* **10/3** 2

1m 26.58s (0.28) **Going Correction** -0.025s/f (Good)

WFA 3 from 4yo 7lb **7** Ran SP% **110.0**

Speed ratings (Par 104): **97,95,94,94,93 91,90**

toteswingers: 1&2 £4.10, 1&3 £3.40, 2&3 £10.50 CSF £17.59 TOTE £3.60 : £2.20, £2.80; EX 14.80.

Owner Fishlake Commercial Motors Ltd **Bred** Mike Gosse **Trained** Newmarket, Suffolk

FOCUS

A 76-87 fillies' handicap but the pace was very steady until past the halfway mark. The winner looks a bit better than the bare form.

NOTEBOOK

Gladys' Gal ♦, who had five subsequent winners behind when opening her account at the second time of asking, was making her handicap bow on her turf debut. She travelled strongly in the wake of the leader but after taking charge edged towards the running rail. She did more than enough iand there should be even better to come. She should make the step up to Listed company in time. (op 3-1 tchd 7-2 and 9-4)

No Poppy (IRE), who had to descend to claiming company at Leicester in May to double her career score, is tough. Having her 21st career start, after giving an odd problem or two in the stalls she missed the break and had to make her effort on the wide outside. Hard as she tried she could not quite match the unexposed winner. (op 8-1 tchd 6-1)

Primo Lady, who took a Listed event at two, was fitted with blinkers for the second successive time. Raised 2lb after finishing runner-up at Newbury she is fully exposed and will continue to struggle in handicap company. (op 14-1)

Jeannie Galloway (IRE), very keen early on, is back on the same mark as when winning a nursery at Musselburgh last August, her fourth juvenile success. Below her best on three previous outings this time this was much more encouraging. (tchd 16-1)

Jade ran better than when behind No Poppy at Carlisle two outings ago but she is starting to look fully exposed. (op 13-2 tchd 7-1)

Gracefield (USA) was another to get a shade upset in the stalls. Down in trip and from a 4lb higher mark she was too keen due to the lack of any serious pace. (op 13-2 tchd 7-1 and 11-2)

Wallis, in a mulish mood for stalls entry, was soon taking them along against the stands' side rail but her chance had already gone when the winner went across her bows. Temperament seems to be getting the better of her. (op 2-1 tchd 15-8)

4236 ONE CALL INSURANCE H'CAP 1m 2f 60y

8:30 (8:30) (Class 5) (0-75,73) 3-Y-O **£2,264** (£673; £336; £168) **Stalls** Low

Form RPR

-101 **1** **Dubawi Dancer**[9] 3958 3-8-6 58 6ex PaulHanagan 5 73+
(William Haggas) *hld up: hdwy 4f out: chsd ldrs wl over 2f out: qcknd to ld wl over 1f out: sn rdn clr: kpt on strly* **4/5** 1

1-50 **2** 2 ¾ **Man Of God (IRE)**[27] 3364 3-9-7 **73**................................ RobertHavlin 2 80
(John Gosden) *hld up in rr: hdwy on inner wl over 2f out: rdn to chse wnr over 1f out: no imp* **7/2**[2]

3000 **3** 6 **Subramaniam**[8] 3976 3-8-8 **60**..(b[1]) TomEaves 6 55
(James Given) *trckd ldr: cl up 4f out: led wl over 2f out: sn rdn: hdd and drvn wl over 1f out: sn one pce* **50/1**

633 **4** 1 ¾ **Hawridge Song**[25] 3430 3-9-5 **71**.................................. JamesMillman 3 63
(Rod Millman) *trckd ldrs: hdwy 4f out: cl up 3f out and sn rdn: drvn wl over 1f out and sn one pce* **9/2**[3]

2100 **5** 7 **Adlington**[16] 3701 3-9-1 **70**.. LeeTopliss[(3)] 1 48
(Richard Fahey) *trckd ldng pair: effrt over 3f out: sn rdn and wknd wl over 2f out* **10/1**

300 **6** 25 **Spyder**[15] 3739 3-9-7 **73**.. KierenFallon 4 —
(Jane Chapple-Hyam) *set stdy pce: qcknd 4f out: rdn along 3f out: sn hdd & wknd* **16/1**

2m 12.93s (3.53) **Going Correction** +0.10s/f (Good) **6** Ran SP% **112.9**
Speed ratings (Par 100): **89,86,82,80,75 55**
toteswingers: 1&2 £1.10, 1&3 £5.10, 2&3 £21.30 CSF £3.96 TOTE £1.70: £1.50, £1.50; EX 4.50.

Owner F W Golding, E Kirtland & N A Callaghan **Bred** Allan Munnis & Laurance Walwin **Trained** Newmarket, Suffolk

FOCUS
A modest 3-y-o handicap. The winner was well in under her penalty and probably improved again. The first two were clear.

4237 NAPOLEONS CASINO SHEFFIELD H'CAP 1m 4f
9:00 (9:00) (Class 5) (0-75,74) 3-Y-O+ **£2,264** (£673; £336; £168) **Stalls** Low

Form RPR

0510 **1** **Plattsburgh (USA)**[10] 3905 3-9-0 **72**................................ KierenFallon 7 84
(Mark Johnston) *hld up in rr: hdwy 3f out: chsd ldrs and rdn along 2f out: swtchd lft over 1f out: styd on to ld ent fnl f: drvn clr* **4/1**[2]

0326 **2** 3 **Romeo Montague**[39] 2957 3-9-2 **74**......................(v[1]) TomMcLaughlin 5 81
(Ed Dunlop) *s.i.s and bhd: smooth hdwy wl over 3f out: trckd ldrs on bit 2f out: effrt and edgd lft over 1f out: sn rdn to chal and ev ch ent fnl f: sn drvn and one pce* **15/2**

0221 **3** shd **Harvey's Hope**[4] 4129 5-9-8 **68**.. PaulHanagan 1 75
(Keith Reveley) *hld up in tch: hdwy 4f out: effrt to chse ldr 3f out: rdn wl over 1f out and ev ch tl drvn ent fnl f and kpt on same pce* **11/8**[1]

0000 **4** 4 **Veiled Applause**[29] 3277 8-9-5 **72**................................ ShaneBKelly[(7)] 9 73
(John Quinn) *trckd ldrs: hdwy on outer over 4f out: led over 3f out: rdn over 2f out: drvn over 1f out: hdd ent fnl f: wknd* **18/1**

45-1 **5** 1 ½ **Dance For Julie (IRE)**[40] 1167 4-9-7 **70**............... PatrickDonaghy[(3)] 10 68
(Ben Haslam) *dwlt and towards rr: hdwy 4f out: chsd ldng pair wl over 2f out: drvn wl over 1f out and grad wknd* **8/1**

4-03 **6** 15 **Dynamic Idol (USA)**[16] 3715 4-9-12 **72**........................(b) PhillipMakin 4 46
(Mikael Magnusson) *trckd ldrs: effrt over 3f out: rdn along wl over 2f out: sn wknd* **6/1**[3]

6-60 **7** 8 **Fantino**[41] 2892 5-9-7 **67**.. StephenCraine 3 28
(John Mackie) *chsd ldng pair: rdn along over 3f out: sn wknd* **20/1**

00 **8** 1 ½ **Street Legal**[9] 3951 6-8-11 **57**....................................(p) RobertWinston 6 16
(Alan McCabe) *reminders s and sn chsng ldr: rdn along over 4f out: drvn over 3f out and sn wknd* **50/1**

2106 **9** 1 ½ **Jeer (IRE)**[20] 3580 7-10-0 **74**......................................(b) GrahamGibbons 8 31
(Michael Easterby) *led: rdn along over 4f out: hdd over 3f out and sn wknd* **22/1**

2m 34.95s (0.05) **Going Correction** +0.10s/f (Good)
WFA 3 from 4yo+ 12lb **9** Ran SP% **115.6**
Speed ratings (Par 103): **103,101,100,98,97 87,81,80,79**
toteswingers: 1&2 £7.40, 1&3 £2.20, 2&3 £3.90 CSF £33.00 CT £60.53 TOTE £6.50: £3.10, £3.10, £1.20; EX 38.30.

Owner Sheikh Hamdan Bin Mohammed Al Maktoum **Bred** Mr & Mrs Bertram R Firestone **Trained** Middleham Moor, N Yorks

FOCUS
A modest 57-74 handicap and the two clear leaders went off much too fast for their own good and were beaten some way. Fair form for the grade.
T/Plt: £29.20 to a £1 stake. Pool: £63,860.95. 1,592.87 winning tickets. T/Qpdt: £4.00 to a £1 stake. Pool: £5,286.40. 973.17 winning tickets. JR

4006 EPSOM (L-H)
Thursday, July 21

OFFICIAL GOING: Good to soft (soft in places on round course; good in places on sprint course) changing to soft after (race 3)
Wind: Light, across Weather: Dark, raining until Race 2

4238 DOWNLOAD EPSOM IPHONE APP NOW H'CAP 5f
6:10 (6:10) (Class 4) (0-80,80) 3-Y-O **£4,075** (£1,212; £606; £303) **Stalls** High

Form RPR

2002 **1** **Diamond Charlie (IRE)**[17] 3687 3-9-7 **80**...................... HayleyTurner 5 86
(Simon Dow) *mde all: jnd over 3f out: hung lft fr 1/2-way and ended in centre of crse: hrd rdn fnl f: hld on* **7/2**[3]

-035 **2** ½ **Cocohatchee**[13] 3798 3-9-0 **73**..(p) IanMongan 4 77
(Pat Phelan) *s.i.s and sn last: effrt 1/2-way but wanting to hang lft: r.o to take 2nd ins fnl f: clsd on wnr fin* **7/4**[1]

3221 **3** 2 **Volcanic Dust (IRE)**[19] 3635 3-9-0 **76**............................ RyanClark[(3)] 1 73
(Milton Bradley) *awkward s: t.k.h and jnd wnr over 3f out: drifted lft and carried lft fr 1/2-way: no ex ins fnl f* **10/3**[2]

2254 **4** 2 **Paradise Place**[9] 3957 3-8-7 **66** ow2............................... NeilChalmers 3 55
(Robert Cowell) *chsd ldrs: outpcd and rdn 2f out: nvr on terms after* **11/1**

5015 **5** 4 **Shostakovich (IRE)**[6] 4057 3-8-11 **70**...................(tp) RichardHughes 2 45
(Sylvester Kirk) *chsd wnr 1f: cl up tl shkn up and wknd over 1f out: eased* **9/2**

57.63 secs (1.93) **Going Correction** +0.45s/f (Yiel) **5** Ran SP% **108.2**
Speed ratings (Par 102): **102,101,98,94,88**
CSF £9.70 TOTE £2.80: £1.10, £1.80; EX 5.60.

Owner David & Stanley Adams **Bred** John Malone **Trained** Epsom, Surrey

FOCUS
Rail dolled out up to 6yds from 1m to 7f, and 6f to Winning Post adding approximately 10yds to advertised distances. There had been a heavy shower about 20 minutes before racing but the rain didn't look to have got into the ground significantly. As might have been expected with just five runners, the pace wasn't breakneck and the winner made virtually all. Modest form but a length personal best from the winner.

4239 TRY TOTEQUICKPICK ON ALL TOTEPOOL BETS H'CAP 5f
6:40 (6:41) (Class 4) (0-85,84) 4-Y-O+ **£4,528** (£1,347; £673; £336) **Stalls** High

Form RPR

-041 **1** **Living It Large (FR)**[17] 3687 4-9-4 **84**.............................. JohnFahy[(3)] 2 92
(Ed de Giles) *racd wd on terms w ldng trio for 1f then dropped in bhd: rdn and prog over 1f out: r.o to ld last 100yds* **9/2**

032 **2** 1 **Boogie Waltzer**[23] 3493 4-8-7 **73**....................................(t) RyanClark[(3)] 4 77
(Stuart Williams) *w ldr: led 2f out but wanting to hang lft: hdd and outpcd last 100yds* **4/1**[3]

00-0 **3** nk **Spanish Acclaim**[14] 3784 4-8-8 **71**.............................(b[1]) NeilChalmers 1 74
(Andrew Balding) *s.i.s: hld up in last pair fr wd draw: shkn up over 1f out and edgd lft: r.o last 100yds: gaining at fin: fin 4th: plcd 3rd* **12/1**

4304 **4** nk **Clear Praise (USA)**[14] 3765 4-9-1 **78**............................ HayleyTurner 5 80
(Simon Dow) *stdd s: hld up in last pair and off the pce: pushed along 1/2-way: effrt whn nt clr run briefly over 1f out: styd on fnl f: no ch: fin 5th: plcd 4th* **3/1**[2]

0015 **5** 1 **Bronze Beau**[51] 2590 4-9-6 **83**.......................................(t) JamesSullivan 3 81
(Linda Stubbs) *racd wd: w ldng pair: stl on terms over 1f out: wknd fnl f: fin 6th: plcd 5th* **7/1**

0310 **D** hd **Ryan Style (IRE)**[12] 3880 5-9-4 **81**........................... SilvestreDeSousa 6 85
(Lisa Williamson) *pushed up to ld against rail: rdn and hdd 2f out: kpt on u.p fnl f: a hld: fin 3rd, 1l, hd: disq: rdr failed to draw correct weight* **11/4**[1]

57.83 secs (2.13) **Going Correction** +0.45s/f (Yiel) **6** Ran SP% **110.0**
Speed ratings (Par 105): **100,98,97,97,95 98**
toteswingers: 1&2 £3.60, 1&3 £3.40, 2&3 £43.80 CSF £21.54 TOTE £4.40: £2.50, £2.70; EX 12.90.

Owner T Gould **Bred** Sunny Days Limited **Trained** Ledbury, Herefordshire

FOCUS
A fair handicap with little between the runners at the conclusion of a well-run race. The winner is rated back to his best.
Ryan Style(IRE) Official explanation: four-day ban: failed to draw correct weight (4-7 Aug)

4240 TOTEEXACTA BETTER VALUE FORECAST E B F MAIDEN STKS 6f
7:15 (7:15) (Class 5) 2-Y-O **£3,881** (£1,155; £577; £288) **Stalls** High

Form RPR

323 **1** **Tones (IRE)**[7] 4007 2-9-3 0.. RichardHughes 1 73+
(Richard Hannon) *mde all: pushed clr over 1f out: comf* **2/5**[1]

00 **2** 2 ½ **Dark Ambition (IRE)**[12] 3878 2-9-3 0....................... SilvestreDeSousa 3 61+
(William Haggas) *s.s: sn in tch in last: rdn over 2f out: styd on to take 2nd ins fnl f: no ch w wnr* **11/4**[2]

00 **3** 2 **Intomist (IRE)**[14] 3761 2-8-12 0.................................. NathanAlison[(5)] 6 55
(Jim Boyle) *t.k.h: chsd wnr: rdn and on terms 2f out: fdd and lost 2nd ins fnl f* **16/1**[3]

0 **4** 8 **Christopher Chua (IRE)**[26] 3388 2-9-3 0...................... HayleyTurner 2 31
(Simon Dow) *chsd wnr: rdn over 2f out: sn wknd* **25/1**

1m 14.19s (4.79) **Going Correction** +0.725s/f (Yiel) **4** Ran SP% **107.8**
Speed ratings (Par 94): **97,93,91,80**
toteswingers: 1&2 £1.70 CSF £1.74 TOTE £1.20.

Owner Ivan B Murphy **Bred** Whisperview Trading Ltd **Trained** East Everleigh, Wilts

FOCUS
Only four runners and not a true test with the pace only steady. The winner didn't need to match his pre-race mark.

NOTEBOOK
Tones(IRE) probably didn't need to repeat the form of his third last week to prevail as readily as the betting suggested. After being given a trademark stop-start Richard Hughes front-running ride, he was always in control. He's nothing out of the ordinary and it will be run-of-the-mill nurseries for him now. (op 4-9 tchd 1-2 in a place)
Dark Ambition(IRE) hadn't shown much so far and didn't help himself here with a slow start. He changed his legs early on, but left the impression he has more ability than this run suggested. He'll surely show it at 7f now he's qualified for nurseries. (op 3-1)
Intomist(IRE) threatened briefly when upsides the winner inside the penultimate furlong, but he couldn't sustain his run. He was flattered to finish as close as he did on account of the false pace. (op 10-1)
Christopher Chua(IRE) looks a poor mover and for all he might not have much ability anyway, didn't look at all at home on the track. (tchd 28-1)

4241 TOTESWINGER MORE WAYS TO WIN MAIDEN FILLIES' STKS 1m 2f 18y
7:45 (7:45) (Class 5) 3-Y-O+ **£2,587** (£770; £384; £192) **Stalls** Low

Form RPR

2 **1** **Neumark (GER)**[36] 3043 3-8-13 0...................................... TomQueally 1 89+
(Sir Henry Cecil) *led after 100yds: mde rest: easily drew clr fr 3f out* **4/9**[1]

0 **2** 6 **Deraasa (USA)**[42] 2848 3-8-13 0...................................... NeilCallan 4 70
(Saeed Bin Suroor) *chsd wnr after 1f to over 2f out: drvn into 3rd again over 1f out: no ch* **7/1**[3]

20 **3** 10 **Favorite Girl (GER)**[32] 3206 3-8-13 0............................. IanMongan 3 58
(Sir Henry Cecil) *hld up: last to 4f out: rdn to chse wnr over 2f out to over 1f out: wknd: heavily eased last 75yds* **10/3**[2]

6 **4** 9 **Beckfield Dancer**[17] 3689 3-8-13 0................................ HayleyTurner 2 32
(Stuart Williams) *led 100yds: chsd ldng pair to 4f out: sn wknd and wl bhd* **22/1**

2m 14.86s (5.16) **Going Correction** +0.725s/f (Yiel) **4** Ran SP% **109.2**
Speed ratings (Par 100): **108,103,95,88**
toteswingers: 1&2 £, 1&3 £, 2&3 £ CSF £4.19 TOTE £1.40; EX 3.70.

Owner G Schoeningh **Bred** Gestut Zoppenbroich **Trained** Newmarket, Suffolk

FOCUS
Another one-sided contest with the winner dictating as her rider wished, with the pace steady for a long way. WEak form behind the winner, and it's hard to know what she achieved.

4242 TOTEPOOL A BETTER WAY TO BET H'CAP 1m 4f 10y
8:20 (8:20) (Class 5) (0-70,67) 3-Y-O+ **£3,234** (£962; £481; £240) **Stalls** Centre

Form RPR

4600 **1** **Shesha Bear**[22] 3516 6-9-0 **53**...............................(p) RichardKingscote 9 64
(Jonathan Portman) *settled in last pair: pushed along and prog on outer over 2f out: rdn to ld over 1f out: styd on wl* **7/1**[3]

0-21 **2** 2 **Tanjung Agas (IRE)**[29] 3268 3-9-0 **65**.............................(b) NeilCallan 1 73+
(Roger Varian) *trckd ldng trio: effrt 3f out: rdn and cl enough 2f out: chsd wnr over 1f out: wandered bdly w hd at unattractive angle: nvr gng to chal* **5/2**[1]

2463 **3** *3 1/4* **Miss Bounty**[14] 3760 6-9-6 **62**....(v) MatthewDavies(3) 6 65
(Jim Boyle) *t.k.h: hld up in 6th: smooth prog 4f out to ld 3f out gng strly: rdn and hdd over 1f out: folded rather tamely* **11/2**[2]

100 **4** *3 1/4* **Robby Bobby**[31] 3225 6-9-1 **61**.... CharlotteJenner(7) 3 59
(Laura Mongan) *trckd ldr to over 3f out: rdn and one pce fr over 2f out* **20/1**

0052 **5** *5* **Rodrigo De Freitas (IRE)**[6] 4059 4-8-13 **59**....(v) DanielCremin(7) 5 49
(Jim Boyle) *hld up in last: effrt on outer over 2f out: drvn and no hdwy wl over 1f out: wknd* **8/1**

2523 **6** *8* **Dr Darcey**[20] 3599 3-8-12 **63**....(b) RichardHughes 2 40
(Richard Hannon) *chsd ldrs in 5th: shkn up over 3f out: sn struggling and btn* **5/2**[1]

1040 **7** *2 3/4* **Suhailah**[108] 1135 5-8-6 **50**.... MarkCoumbe(5) 4 23
(Michael Attwater) *led to 3f out: wknd* **33/1**

0002 **8** *6* **Professor John (IRE)**[9] 3945 4-9-2 **55**....(v) SilvestreDeSousa 8 18
(Ian Wood) *chsd ldng pair: tried to chal 4f out: sn rdn: wknd wl over 2f out* **8/1**

2m 49.25s (10.35) **Going Correction** +0.725s/f (Yiel)
WFA 3 from 4yo+ 12lb **8** Ran SP% **115.0**
Speed ratings (Par 103): **94,92,90,88,85 79,77,73**
toteswingers: 1&2 £5.10, 1&3 £12.60, 2&3 £3.10 CSF £25.05 CT £104.22 TOTE £9.90: £2.90, £1.60, £1.50; EX 32.10.
Owner RWH Partnership **Bred** Beechgrove Stud Farm Ltd & Catridge Farm Stud **Trained** Compton, Berks

FOCUS
An ordinary handicap in which the pace didn't look overly strong but in which the protagonists were ridden with varying degrees of restraint. The winner was still 5lb off her 2009 best.
Shesha Bear Official explanation: trainer said, regarding the apparent improvement of form, the gelding appeared better suited by the softer ground

4243 BLONDIE LIVE AT EPSOM 28.7.11 H'CAP 7f
8:50 (8:50) (Class 4) (0-85,85) 3-Y-0+ **£4,075** (£1,212; £606; £303) **Stalls** Low

Form RPR

2140 **1** **Kingscroft (IRE)**[19] 3634 3-9-6 **84**.... SilvestreDeSousa 1 92
(Mark Johnston) *mde all: rdn 2f out: strly pressed 1f out: styd on wl last 150yds* **4/1**[3]

-066 **2** *1 1/4* **Silenzio**[13] 3798 3-7-13 **68**.... KieranO'Neill(5) 9 72
(Richard Hannon) *dwlt: hld up in last pair: pushed along 1/2-way: prog on outer to chse wnr 2f out: chal fnl f: nt qckn last 100yds* **7/2**[2]

0003 **3** *1/2* **Catalyze**[7] 4010 3-9-2 **80**....(t) JimmyFortune 3 83
(Andrew Balding) *trckd ldng pair: chsd wnr 3f out to 2f out: kpt on same pce* **4/1**[3]

064 **4** *1/2* **Sunshine Always (IRE)**[1] 4210 5-8-8 **70**.... MarkCoumbe(5) 8 75
(Michael Attwater) *hld up in last pair: pushed along and no prog over 2f out: shkn up and styd on fnl f: nrst fin* **9/1**

-204 **5** *1 1/2* **Young Dottie**[14] 3763 5-8-11 **68**.... IanMongan 4 69
(Pat Phelan) *chsd ldng trio: shkn up over 2f out: no imp over 1f out: fdd ins fnl f* **5/1**

0604 **6** *17* **Glenridding**[7] 4010 7-9-5 **76**.... HayleyTurner 5 33
(James Given) *chsd wnr to 3f out: sn rdn and wknd: no ch whn hmpd over 1f out: t.o* **10/3**[1]

1m 27.43s (4.13) **Going Correction** +0.725s/f (Yiel)
WFA 3 from 5yo+ 7lb **6** Ran SP% **112.0**
Speed ratings (Par 105): **105,103,103,102,100 81**
toteswingers: 1&2 £2.60, 1&3 £1.50, 2&3 £1.70 CSF £18.11 CT £57.50 TOTE £5.10: £2.50, £1.50; EX 24.60.
Owner Dr Marwan Koukash **Bred** J Beckett **Trained** Middleham Moor, N Yorks

FOCUS
A fair handicap to end proceedings and one run at a decent pace as might have been expected with two front runners in the line-up. The form makes sense.
Glenridding Official explanation: jockey said that the gelding suffered interference in running
T/Plt: £78.20 to a £1 stake. Pool: £42,411.35. 395.75 winning tickets. T/Qpdt: £13.20 to a £1 stake. Pool: £3,367.94. 188.30 winning tickets. JN

3766 FOLKESTONE (R-H)
Thursday, July 21

OFFICIAL GOING: Good (6.5)
Wind: Virtually nil Weather: overcast

4244 ANNA BUSBRIDGE MEMORIAL H'CAP 7f (S)
6:00 (6:01) (Class 6) (0-65,65) 3-Y-O **£1,533** (£452; £226) **Stalls** High

Form RPR

-606 **1** **All Honesty**[29] 3292 3-9-4 **62**.... WilliamBuick 3 70
(William Knight) *trckd ldrs and a travelling wl: pushed along to ld and edgd lft over 1f out: rdn 1f out: r.o wl fnl 100yds: eased nr fin* **25/1**

-460 **2** *1 1/4* **Links Drive Lady**[26] 3390 3-8-13 **64**.... CharlesEddery(7) 10 68
(Mark Rimmer) *hld up in tch in midfield: rdn and swtchd rt over 1f out: hdwy 1f out: chsd wnr ins fnl f: no imp fnl 75yds* **20/1**

0320 **3** *1/2* **Valley Tiger**[16] 3709 3-8-10 **59**.... JamesRogers(5) 11 62
(William Muir) *s.i.s: hld up bhd: rdn and effrt 2f out: swtchd lft over 1f out: hdwy against stands' rail jst ins fnl f: r.o wl to go 3rd fnl 50yds: nt rch ldrs* **10/1**

0313 **4** *1 3/4* **Cheylesmore (IRE)**[15] 3729 3-9-5 **63**....(v) WilliamCarson 1 61
(Stuart Williams) *mounted on crse and taken down early: chsd ldr and sn crossed to r towards stands' rail: led and wandered 2f out: sn rdn: hdd and hmpd over 1f out: styd on same pce ins fnl f* **6/1**[2]

-064 **5** *1/2* **No Larking (IRE)**[13] 3804 3-9-7 **65**.... DaneO'Neill 13 62
(Henry Candy) *led tl hdd and bmpd 2f out: drvn and unable qck over 1f out: styd on same pce ins fnl f* **7/2**[1]

-446 **6** *1 1/2* **Adelina Patti**[32] 3202 3-9-4 **62**.... JimmyQuinn 4 55
(Walter Swinburn) *t.k.h: hld up in tch in midfield: pushed along and effrt 2f out: rdn and styd on same pce fr over 1f out* **13/2**[3]

0000 **7** *1 1/4* **Serial Sinner (IRE)**[42] 2841 3-9-2 **60**....(t) PaulDoe 5 50
(Paul Cole) *in tch in midfield on outer: hdwy to chse ldrs and rdn 2f out: unable qck over 1f out: wknd ins fnl f* **18/1**

0-05 **8** *3 1/4* **Goodwood Treasure**[27] 3351 3-9-6 **64**.... ChrisCatlin 6 45
(John Dunlop) *hld up in midfield: rdn and struggling over 2f out: sn wknd: wl bhd 1f out* **16/1**

0656 **9** *3/4* **Amber Heights**[13] 3818 3-9-2 **63**.... KierenFox(3) 14 42
(David Pinder) *s.i.s: hld up in rr: swtchd rt and hdwy on outer 3f out: rdn ent fnl 2f: wknd qckly over 1f out* **7/2**[1]

53-3 **10** *3 3/4* **Avon Supreme**[33] 3191 3-8-10 **57**.... AdamBeschizza(3) 7 26
(Gay Kelleway) *awkward leaving stalls and s.i.s: hld up towards rr on outer: rdn and effrt over 2f out: wknd 2f out: bhd fnl f* **16/1**

205 **11** *11* **Storm Runner (IRE)**[21] 3558 3-9-5 **63**....(b[1]) PhilipRobinson 12 —
(George Margarson) *sn bustled up to chse ldrs: pushed along and lost pl over 2f out: wl bhd over 1f out: eased ins fnl f* **9/1**

1m 28.14s (0.84) **Going Correction** +0.075s/f (Good) **11** Ran SP% **116.8**
Speed ratings (Par 98): **98,96,96,94,93 91,90,86,85,81 68**
toteswingers: 1&2 £62.60, 1&3 £40.60, 2&3 £18.10 CSF £445.97 CT £5313.03 TOTE £20.30: £6.50, £6.10, £4.40; EX 257.00.
Owner Bluehills Racing Limited **Bred** C J Murfitt **Trained** Patching, W Sussex

FOCUS
The going was good. A modest handicap. They leaders went off fast which played into the hands off those ridden off the pace.
All Honesty Official explanation: trainer said, regarding the apparent improvement of form
Amber Heights Official explanation: jockey said that the filly was slowly away

4245 BRITISH STALLION STUDS SUPPORTING BRITISH RACING E B F MAIDEN FILLIES' STKS 7f (S)
6:30 (6:30) (Class 5) 2-Y-O **£3,557** (£1,058; £529; £264) **Stalls** High

Form RPR

422 **1** **Iceni Girl**[22] 3520 2-9-0 0.... WilliamBuick 3 71
(John Gosden) *chsd ldr: jnd ldr 1/2-way: led over 2f out: hrd pressed and drvn over 1f out: forged ahd u.p fnl 75yds* **1/1**[1]

2 *1* **Roman Province (IRE)** 2-9-0 0.... DaneO'Neill 10 69+
(Roger Teal) *hld up towards rr: swtchd rt and hdwy on outer over 2f out: rdn to press wnr over 1f out: no ex u.p ins fnl f and btn fnl 50yds* **25/1**

3 *1 1/4* **Code Cracker** 2-9-0 0.... StevieDonohoe 1 65+
(Sir Mark Prescott Bt) *chsd ldrs: swtchd lft to r on stands' rail and effrt jst over 2f out: drvn over 1f out: chsd ldng pair ins fnl f: styd on same pce fnl 100yds* **11/2**[3]

U **4** *nk* **Equity Card (FR)**[3] 4159 2-8-7 0.... AntiocoMurgia(7) 6 65
(Mahmood Al Zarooni) *in tch in midfield: lost pl and sltly hmpd jst over 2f out: switching rt and hdwy over 1f out: kpt edging lft and styd on ins fnl f: nt pce to rch ldrs* **8/1**

0 **5** *1 1/2* **Fu Fic Fas**[14] 3779 2-9-0 0....(t) FrankieMcDonald 5 61
(Paul Fitzsimons) *dwlt: pushed along at times and in tch in midfield: rdn jst over 2f out: styd on same pce and no imp over 1f out* **40/1**

0 **6** *1 3/4* **Camrock Star (IRE)**[21] 3547 2-9-0 0.... JackMitchell 9 57
(William Knight) *t.k.h: chsd ldrs: jnd ldrs 1/2-way: pressed wnr over 2f out: rdn and unable qck over 1f out: hung rt and wknd ins fnl f* **11/4**[2]

0 **7** *8* **Better Be Mine (IRE)**[13] 3813 2-9-0 0.... ChrisCatlin 2 37
(John Dunlop) *s.i.s: a bhd: lost tch 2f out* **25/1**

00 **8** *4 1/2* **Leading Star**[29] 3282 2-9-0 0.... KirstyMilczarek 7 25
(Michael Madgwick) *led tl over 2f out: sn rdn and struggling: wknd qckly over 1f out: wl bhd and tired fnl f* **100/1**

1m 29.27s (1.97) **Going Correction** +0.075s/f (Good) **8** Ran SP% **114.3**
Speed ratings (Par 91): **91,89,88,88,86 84,75,70**
toteswingers: 1&2 £4.80, 1&3 £2.20, 2&3 £10.30 CSF £33.71 TOTE £1.50: £1.02, £7.70, £1.60; EX 27.70.
Owner Ms Rachel D S Hood **Bred** Rachel D S Hood **Trained** Newmarket, Suffolk

FOCUS
It was raining heavily before this fillies' maiden, in which the favourite had to work hard to fight off a big-priced newcomer. The winner is the best guide to this form.

NOTEBOOK
Iceni Girl was just caught by a subsequent Group 3-placed rival in a 7f Kempton maiden last time. She set a quite a decent standard but had to fight hard to cash in on a good opportunity in a race where there was not much separating the first four. (op 8-11)
Roman Province(IRE), closely related to four-time 1m-1m2f handicap winner Rock The Stars, was unfancied in the betting but she gave the form pick a big scare on this very promising debut run.
Code Cracker, a Medicean first foal of Confidential Lady, who was second in 1,000 Guineas and won the French Oaks, showed signs of inexperience before staying on late against the stands' rail on an encouraging debut. The market vibes were not very strong on this first assignment and she could improve significantly next time. (op 7-1)
Equity Card(FR) was 9-2 when swerving and unseating her rider soon after the start in 7f soft-ground Yarmouth maiden on debut on Monday. Sent off at a bigger price, she broke smoothly this time and stayed on quite well, despite running green. This was a decent effort from a first foal of an unplaced dam who is closely related to Derby/King George/Arc hero Lammtarra. (tchd 15-2)
Fu Fic Fas kept plugging on in an improved effort with a tongue tie applied on her second start. She hits the ground quite hard and may prove best on slow ground, like her smart 6f/7f winning half-brother Snow Kid. (op 50-1)
Camrock Star(IRE), a 4l ninth at 20-1 in a 7f Newbury maiden on debut, was a big market mover but she found a limited response after travelling well for the first 5f. (op 9-2 tchd 5-2)
Leading Star Official explanation: jockey said that the filly ran very green

4246 MATT HUDSON BIRTHDAY SURPRISE (S) STKS 6f
7:05 (7:05) (Class 6) 3-Y-O+ **£1,533** (£452; £226) **Stalls** High

Form RPR

2216 **1** **Efistorm**[16] 3713 10-9-6 70.... KirstyMilczarek 3 80
(Conor Dore) *sn niggled along in last pair: hdwy to chse ldr 2f out: rdn to ld over 1f out: pricking ears in front and sn drvn: kpt on and a doing enough fnl f* **3/1**[3]

3216 **2** *3/4* **Anjomarba (IRE)**[15] 3735 4-8-12 67.... KierenFox(3) 5 73
(Brett Johnson) *hld up in last pair: rdn and hdwy 2f out: drvn to chse ldng pair over 1f out: chsd wnr 1f out: kpt on but a hld after* **7/4**[1]

00-0 **3** *3 1/4* **For Life (IRE)**[47] 2719 9-8-11 72.... NataliaGemelova(3) 6 61
(John E Long) *taken down early: led: rdn: hld hd high and hdd over 1f out: lost 2nd 1f out: wknd ins fnl f* **7/1**

0600 **4** *13* **Sunrise Lyric (IRE)**[29] 3293 4-8-9 48....(p) ChrisCatlin 7 15
(Paul Cole) *awkward leaving stalls and slowly away: sn bustled along: chsd ldng trio after 1f: drvn and wknd qckly wl over 1f out: wl btn 1f out* **22/1**

0000 **5** *2 3/4* **Crystallize**[40] 2920 5-9-6 57.... StevieDonohoe 2 27
(Andrew Haynes) *chsd ldrs: rdn and effrt jst over 2f out: wknd qckly over 1f out: wl btn and eased wl ins fnl f* **20/1**

000- **6** *13* **Mambo Spirit (IRE)**[239] 7554 7-9-0 72.... DaneO'Neill 1 —
(Tony Newcombe) *pressed ldr tl jst over 2f out: sn wknd: t.o and eased ins fnl f* **11/4**[2]

1m 13.69s (0.99) **Going Correction** +0.25s/f (Good) **6** Ran SP% **109.6**
Speed ratings (Par 101): **103,102,97,80,76 59**
toteswingers: 1&2 £2.50, 1&3 £3.20, 2&3 £1.70 CSF £8.24 TOTE £2.90: £1.10, £2.20; EX 6.20.There was no bid for the winner. Anjomarba was claimed by C R Dore for £6,000.
Owner Sean J Murphy **Bred** E Duggan And D Churchman **Trained** Cowbit, Lincs

FOCUS
The ground seemed to be cutting up a bit following the earlier shower. The winner is rated to this year's form. A 70-rated performer held off the market leader in this fair seller.
Crystallize Official explanation: jockey said that the gelding lost its action

Mambo Spirit(IRE) Official explanation: jockey said that the gelding had no more to give

4247 LADBROKES.COM H'CAP — 6f

7:35 (7:37) (Class 5) (0-70,65) 3-Y-O — **£2,385** (£704; £352) **Stalls** High

Form — RPR

1545 **1** **Rambo Will**[8] 3985 3-9-7 **65** .... DaneO'Neill 5 — 69
(J R Jenkins) *w ldr tl led wl over 1f out: sn rdn and asserted: in command and styd on wl ins fnl f* **11/2**

540 **2** *1 3/4* **Piccoluck**[7] 4025 3-8-13 **62** .... (b) DarylByrne(5) 1 — 60
(Amy Weaver) *hld up in last pair: hdwy on outer jst over 2f out: rdn to chse wnr over 1f out: r.o for clr 2nd but readily hld by wnr fnl f* **5/1**[3]

0024 **3** *3 3/4* **Cathcart Castle**[7] 3999 3-8-13 **57** .... (v) HughBowman 2 — 43
(Mick Channon) *taken down early: chsd ldrs: rdn and unable qck 2f out: 3rd and outpcd by ldng pair 1f out: plugged on same pce and wl hld after* **5/2**[1]

4003 **4** *1/2* **Prophet In A Dream**[19] 3638 3-9-4 **65** .... RobertLButler(3) 6 — 50
(Paddy Butler) *chsd ldrs: rdn and unable qck wl over 1f out: outpcd and btn over 1f out: plugged on same pce and wl hld fnl f* **12/1**

5005 **5** *3/4* **Acclamatory**[25] 3433 3-8-9 **53** .... (t) WilliamCarson 7 — 35
(Stuart Williams) *taken down early: sn led: rdn and hdd wl over 1f out: drvn and lost 2nd over 1f out: sn outpcd and wl btn ins fnl f* **18/1**

600- **6** *nk* **Whitstable Native**[259] 7313 3-8-13 **60** .... KierenFox(3) 4 — 41
(John Best) *hld up in last pair: stuck bhd horses and nt clr run 2f out tl ins fnl f: no ch but no real imp after* **4/1**[2]

0506 **7** *shd* **Fairy Tales**[6] 4057 3-8-1 **50** .... RyanPowell(5) 3 — 31
(John Bridger) *in tch: rdn and effrt jst over 2f out: unable qck and outpcd wl over 1f out: hung rt and no ch w ldrs 1f out* **16/1**

1m 14.68s (1.98) **Going Correction** +0.25s/f (Good) — **7** Ran SP% **99.5**
Speed ratings (Par 100): **96,93,88,88,87 86,86**
toteswingers: 1&2 £4.50, 1&3 £2.70, 2&3 £1.40 CSF £24.30 CT £54.95 TOTE £5.70: £2.60, £1.10; EX 16.60.
Owner Mr & Mrs T H Bambridge **Bred** T H Bambridge **Trained** Royston, Herts

FOCUS
A trappy handicap, involving a majority of maidens. The pace was decent and the first two pulled clear. Weakish form, with doubts over plenty.
Whitstable Native Official explanation: jockey said that the gelding was denied a clear run

4248 LADBROKES.COM ON YOUR MOBILE H'CAP — 1m 4f

8:10 (8:10) (Class 6) (0-60,60) 3-Y-O — **£1,704** (£503; £251) **Stalls** High

Form — RPR

6452 **1** **Peachez**[10] 3910 3-8-11 **55** .... (p) AmyScott(5) 1 — 63+
(Alastair Lidderdale) *stdd s: hld up in last pair: clsd 4f out: hdwy on outer bnd over 2f out: chsd ldr jst over 1f out: rdn to ld ins fnl f: r.o wl* **9/2**[2]

4552 **2** *3/4* **Golestan Palace (IRE)**[10] 3922 3-9-2 **55** .... NickyMackay 4 — 62
(Ed Walker) *chsd ldr tl led 9f out: rdn jst over 2f out: drvn over 1f out: hdd and styd on same pce ins fnl f* **11/4**[1]

-005 **3** *1 3/4* **Rowan Ridge**[17] 3690 3-9-4 **57** .... (p) PatCosgrave 3 — 61
(Jim Boyle) *t.k.h early: chsd ldng trio: rdn over 2f out: hdwy u.p to chse ldr over 1f out tl jst over 1f out: styd on same pce fnl f* **16/1**

4235 **4** *1/2* **Surprise (IRE)**[3] 4164 3-9-7 **60** .... MarcHalford 2 — 63
(Mark Rimmer) *led tl 9f out: chsd ldr after tl 4f out: cl 3rd and rdn 2f out: n.m.r but unable qck wl over 1f out: styd on same pce fnl f* **9/2**[2]

0354 **5** *2 3/4* **Fleeting Tiger**[17] 3690 3-9-1 **54** .... TedDurcan 6 — 53
(John Dunlop) *chsd ldrs: disp 2nd 8f out tl chsd ldr 4f out: rdn and unable qck 2f out: lost 2nd over 1f out: wknd 1f out* **11/4**[1]

0-35 **6** *1* **Dolly Colman (IRE)**[9] 3958 3-8-9 **48** ow1 .... StevieDonohoe 9 — 45
(Andrew Haynes) *stdd and swtchd rt after s: t.k.h: hld up in rr: clsd and in tch over 3f out: rdn and no hdwy 2f out: wknd over 1f out* **25/1**

00-0 **7** *12* **Jam Maker**[163] 456 3-8-7 **46** oh1 .... AdrianMcCarthy 8 — 24
(J R Jenkins) *stdd s: hld up towards rr: clsd and in tch over 3f out: rdn and wknd 2f out: wl btn 1f out* **66/1**

0055 **8** *19* **Talkative Guest (IRE)**[42] 2853 3-9-5 **58** .... PhilipRobinson 5 — —
(George Margarson) *stdd s: hld up off the pce in midfield: clsd and in tch 4f out: hdwy on outer* [illegible] *eased ins fnl f* **17/2**[3]

2m 44.13s (3.23) **Going Correction** +0.20s/f (Good) — **8** Ran SP% **111.4**
Speed ratings (Par 98): **97,96,95,95,93 92,84,71**
toteswingers: 1&2 £5.30, 1&3 £4.50, 2&3 £4.80 CSF £16.37 CT £172.65 TOTE £6.50: £1.60, £1.20, £3.80; EX 19.50.
Owner The P And P Partnership **Bred** Mrs Sally Doyle **Trained** Eastbury, Berks

FOCUS
A low-grade handicap. The pace was fair and they were well strung out in the early stages. The form makes sense amongst the first four and could work out.
Talkative Guest(IRE) Official explanation: jockey said that the filly suffered interference in running

4249 LADBROKESPOKER.COM H'CAP — 1m 1f 149y

8:40 (8:40) (Class 5) (0-70,70) 3-Y-O+ — **£2,385** (£704; £352) **Stalls** Centre

Form — RPR

-152 **1** **Medaille D'Or**[19] 3615 3-9-4 **70** .... JackMitchell 9 — 80+
(Roger Varian) *chsd ldr: rdn to ld and edgd rt over 1f out: clr and in command 1f out: r.o wl: comf* **5/2**[1]

3400 **2** *2 1/2* **Blue Spartan (IRE)**[54] 2512 6-9-11 **70** .... LouisBeuzelin(3) 1 — 74
(Brian Meehan) *chsd ldrs: rdn jst over 2f out: swtchd lft and drvn over 1f out: styd on u.p ins fnl f to go 2nd fnl 50yds: no threat to wnr* **9/2**[3]

064 **3** *hd* **Tanmawy (IRE)**[24] 3469 3-9-2 **68** .... TadhgO'Shea 7 — 71
(Ed Dunlop) *hld up in midfield: hdwy on outer bnd over 2f out: disputing 2nd whn edgd rt u.p over 1f out: chsd clr wnr fnl 100yds: no imp and lost 2nd fnl 50yds* **5/1**

-435 **4** *1* **Recalcitrant**[14] 3760 8-9-3 **66** .... CharlesEddery(7) 5 — 67
(Simon Dow) *led: rdn and hdd over 1f out: unable qck w wnr and styd on same pce after: lost 2 pls fnl 100yds* **14/1**

1-06 **5** *1* **Jodawes (USA)**[155] 565 4-9-8 **64** .... TedDurcan 8 — 65+
(John Best) *hld up in last pair: rdn and outpcd over 2f out: rallied over 1f out: styng on but no threat to wnr whn nt clr run ins fnl f: swtchd lft towards fin* **22/1**

6455 **6** *1/2* **Midnight Trader (IRE)**[8] 3979 3-8-13 **65** .... (t) TonyCulhane 4 — 63
(Paul D'Arcy) *t.k.h: hld up in last pair: swtchd to outer over 2f out: rdn 2f out: no imp tl styd on ins fnl f: n.d* **10/1**

406B **7** *nk* **Leitzu (IRE)**[15] 3726 4-9-6 **62** .... HughBowman 2 — 59
(Mick Channon) *hld up in midfield: rdn and unable qck 2f out: swtchd lft jst over 1f out: plugged on but no ch fnl f* **11/1**

-004 **8** *1 1/4* **Rio Tinto**[27] 3361 4-9-9 **65** .... WilliamCarson 6 — 60
(Giles Bravery) *t.k.h: chsd ldrs: drvn and unable qck 2f out: wkng whn squeezed for room and hmpd ent fnl f: no ch after* **4/1**[2]

2m 6.01s (1.11) **Going Correction** +0.20s/f (Good)
WFA 3 from 4yo+ 10lb — **8** Ran SP% **111.9**
Speed ratings (Par 103): **103,101,100,100,99 98,98,97**
toteswingers: 1&2 £1.60, 1&3 £2.80, 2&3 £5.40 CSF £13.15 CT £49.86 TOTE £2.70: £1.20, £1.20, £1.10; EX 15.60.
Owner Miss K Rausing **Bred** Miss K Rausing **Trained** Newmarket, Suffolk
■ Stewards' Enquiry : Louis Beuzelin one-day ban: careless riding (4 Aug)

FOCUS
A relatively unexposed 3-y-o blew her rivals away in this minor handicap which was run at a fair pace. The winner is progressive.
Jodawes(USA) Official explanation: jockey said that the gelding was denied a clear run
T/Plt: £310.20 to a £1 stake. Pool: £49,210.29 115.80 winning tickets. T/Qpdt: £10.30 to a £1 stake. Pool: £4,803.26. 342.60 winning tickets. SP

4211 SANDOWN (R-H)

Thursday, July 21

OFFICIAL GOING: Soft (good to soft in places on round course; sprint 5.7 round 6.1)

Wind: Virtually nil Weather: White cloud

4250 BRITISH STALLION STUDS E B F LUBRICATORS MAIDEN STKS — 5f 6y

2:10 (2:12) (Class 5) 2-Y-O — **£3,881** (£1,155; £577; £288) **Stalls** Low

Form — RPR

04 **1** **Especially Red (IRE)**[14] 3767 2-9-0 0 ow2 .... AdamKirby 5 — 73
(Lisa Williamson) *mde all but pressed tl rdn and asserted appr fnl 2f: r.o strly fnl f* **8/1**

05 **2** *3 1/4* **Possibly**[14] 3761 2-8-12 0 .... JimmyFortune 4 — 59+
(Peter Chapple-Hyam) *chsd ldrs in 3rd: pushed along fr 2f out: styd on fnl f to take readily hld 2nd nr fin* **13/8**[1]

66 **3** *3/4* **Littlecote Lady**[22] 3511 2-8-12 0 .... DaneO'Neill 3 — 57
(Mark Usher) *pressed wnr tl rdn 1/2-way: outpcd fr 2f out: no ex and lost readily hld 2nd nr fin* **4/1**[3]

4 *1* **Key Addition (IRE)** 2-9-3 0 .... MartinDwyer 6 — 58
(William Muir) *pushed along and outpcd in 4th 1/2-way: styd on fnl f but nvr any ch* **8/1**

5 *2 3/4* **River Valley** 2-9-3 0 .... RyanMoore 2 — 48
(Gary Moore) *sn rdn along: a outpcd in last pl* **5/2**[2]

66.00 secs (4.40) **Going Correction** +0.75s/f (Yiel) — **5** Ran SP% **108.9**
Speed ratings (Par 94): **94,88,87,86,81**
CSF £21.08 TOTE £10.90: £3.50, £1.30; EX 19.00.
Owner D Goulding **Bred** Tally-Ho Stud **Trained** Saighton, Cheshire

FOCUS
Rail at full width on sprint course. Round course dolled out 3 yards from inner line from 1m1f to 3f pole, and 4 yards up the home straight, adding approximately 6 yards to round course distances. This event went to smart sprinter Triple Aspect in 2008, but this year's running was a weak race of its type for the track, particularly given it was a Racing Post Yearling Bonus event. The race was rendered even less competitive when leading contender Morning Muse was withdrawn after kicking her rider in the paddock (5/2, deduct 25p in the 3 under R4). The form is rated negatively.

NOTEBOOK
Especially Red(IRE) showed bright early pace when fourth at Folkestone on her second start but only recorded an RPR of 52 that day. Showing narrowly in front here, she did not have the help of the rail but still pulled clear in the last quarter mile for a comfortable win, despite flashing her tail. Her rider's 2lb overweight made no difference and this was an improved effort. She looks the sort for ordinary nurseries at this trip. (old market op 12-1)
Possibly tracked the leading pair and came through for second late on, but by that time the winner was away and clear. There is stamina on her dam's side and the drop back to 5f was against her. (old market tchd 11-4 new market op 7-4 tchd 6-4)
Littlecote Lady [illegible] before being put in her place. She is not really progressing, but is now eligible for nurseries. (old market op 10-1 new market tchd 7-2)
Key Addition(IRE) is a half-brother to winners at about 1m and should improve for the experience and an extra furlong. (old market tchd 12-1 new market op 7-1)
River Valley looked green in rear and may not have handled the ground. Official explanation: jockey said that the colt ran green (old market op 7-2 tchd 10-3 new market op 9-4)

4251 INKERMAN LONDON H'CAP — 1m 6f

2:45 (2:45) (Class 3) (0-90,85) 3-Y-O — **£6,663** (£1,982; £990; £495) **Stalls** Low

Form — RPR

4541 **1** **Hollow Tree**[8] 3989 3-8-9 **73** 6ex .... RichardHughes 6 — 90
(Andrew Balding) *led after 1f: pushed along over 3f out: rdn and styd on strly fnl f* **4/1**[2]

-434 **2** *1 3/4* **Slight Advantage (IRE)**[29] 3291 3-8-6 **73** .... JohnFahy(3) 1 — 88
(Clive Cox) *trckd ldrs: wnt 2nd 5f out: styd alone far side and pressing wnr on stands' side thrght fnl 2f: ev ch fnl f: one pce clsng stages* **5/1**[3]

060 **3** *4* **All My Heart**[22] 3519 3-8-4 **68** .... ChrisCatlin 8 — 77+
(Sir Mark Prescott Bt) *chsd ldrs: rdn and lost pl 4f out: rallied to chse wnr on stands' side 2f out: nvr on terms and styd on one pce into 3rd sn after* **10/1**

4152 **4** *6* **Manifestation**[21] 3551 3-9-7 **85** .... (p) WilliamBuick 5 — 86
(John Gosden) *chsd ldrs: rdn 3f out: wknd fr 2f out* **15/2**

6401 **5** *6* **Gottany O'S**[26] 3376 3-9-3 **81** .... HughBowman 3 — 74
(Mick Channon) *hld up in rr: stdy hdwy fr 4f out to chse ldrs ins fnl 3f: wknd 2f out* **6/1**

3213 **6** *3 3/4* **Stagecoach Danman (IRE)**[20] 3580 3-9-6 **84** .... SilvestreDeSousa 2 — 71
(Mark Johnston) *led 1f: chsd wnr to 5f out: wknd: hung lft and hit rail over 2f out* **7/2**[1]

015 **7** *1 1/4* **Gosbeck**[19] 3623 3-9-7 **85** .... DaneO'Neill 4 — 71
(Henry Candy) *in rr: rdn and hdwy fr 4f out: chsd ldrs 3f out: wknd qckly 2f out* **10/1**

041 **8** *28* **Korabushka**[21] 3550 3-9-5 **83** .... (p) RyanMoore 7 — 29
(Jeremy Noseda) *in rr: in tch fr 1/2-way: rdn and prog to chse ldrs 4f out: wknd quickly appr fnl 2f: eased whn no ch fnl f* **8/1**

3m 8.57s (4.07) **Going Correction** +0.475s/f (Yiel) — **8** Ran SP% **114.2**
Speed ratings (Par 104): **107,106,103,100,96 94,94,78**
toteswingers:1&2:£5.70, 1&3:£7.60, 2&3:£15.50 CSF £24.22 CT £184.73 TOTE £4.30: £1.70, £2.10, £2.70; EX 30.90 Trifecta £578.80 Part won. Pool: £782.27 - 0.74 winning units..
Owner P A Brend **Bred** Mount Coote Stud **Trained** Kingsclere, Hants

FOCUS
This handicap has been won by some decent stayers in the past decade, among them the likes of Warrsan, King Of Wands and Baddam. Some progressive types lined up. Led by the winner, the runners kept away from the rail down the back straight then crossed to the stands' side in the straight, except for the runner-up who stayed on the far side. The pace looked solid and it was a stern stamina test for these 3-y-os, run in a fair time. The form is rated positively.

NOTEBOOK
Hollow Tree made all here last week and was officially a pound well in under his penalty. Richard Hughes was keen to make the running and his mount had secured the lead going into the first bend. After leading the field over to the stands' side and claiming the rail, the gelding drew clear of his pursuers in the stands'-side bunch and was on top overall late on. He is progressing well. (op 9-2)
Slight Advantage(IRE) nipped through on the inside turning in and stayed on the far rail. She had nothing to race with, but looked to be in front overall at one stage before the winner on the opposite side took her measure. She's well at home in soft ground and this was a creditable effort over a longer trip. (op 9-1)
All My Heart was making her handicap and turf debuts after finishing unplaced in three Kempton maidens at 1m2f-1m4f. She ran a decent race over this longer trip, staying on after coming under pressure entering the straight. A well-bred filly out of a half-sister to Group 1 winners Alborada and Albanova, she should find a race at around this distance. (op 11-1 tchd 12-1)
Manifestation, tried in a change of headgear, ran no more than respectably but his pedigree suggests he is worth another try at 1m6f. (op 11-2)
Gottany O'S was proven in soft ground but was 4lb higher than when winning at Chester and tackling an extra 2f. He did not seem to get home. (op 8-1)
Stagecoach Danman(IRE) was unproven in soft conditions and could not get to the front this time. He was held when hitting the rail in the home straight. (op 11-4 tchd 5-2)
Gosbeck has twice been held in handicap company, with the ground and trip possible excuses here. (op 12-1 tchd 9-1)
Korabushka, a Newbury maiden winner, dropped right away with the ground and trip possible excuses. (op 15-2 tchd 13-2)

4252 WEATHERBYS VAT SERVICES STAR STKS (LISTED RACE) (FILLIES) 7f 16y
3:20 (3:20) (Class 1) 2-Y-O

£12,192 (£4,622; £2,313; £1,152; £578; £290) **Stalls** Low

Form RPR

21 **1** **Kinetica**[27] 3336 2-8-12 0 .... SebSanders 1 98+
(Sir Mark Prescott Bt) *mde all: styd alone on far side wl over 3f out: drvn and styd on wl fnl 2f: unchal* **7/2**[2]

41 **2** *2 ½* **Arsaadi (IRE)**[13] 3812 2-8-12 0 .... FrankieDettori 5 92
(Ed Dunlop) *in tch: drvn and hdwy to ld main gp on stands' side wl over 1f out: kpt on but no imp on lone wnr far side* **3/1**[1]

15 **3** *2 ¼* **Hawfinch**[26] 3402 2-8-12 0 .... WilliamBuick 8 86
(John Gosden) *hld up in rr: pushed along ins fnl 4f: c stands' side and chsd wnr of that gp over 1f out: nvr nr lone wnr far side and styd on same pce for 3rd* **3/1**[1]

104 **4** *¾* **Worthington (IRE)**[26] 3402 2-8-12 0 .... TonyHamilton 3 84
(Richard Fahey) *in rr: c w main gp stands' side: drvn and hdwy fr 2f out: nvr rchd ldrs and one pce fnl f* **8/1**

331 **5** *2 ¼* **Vassaria (IRE)**[23] 3483 2-8-12 0 .... TomQueally 7 79
(Michael Dods) *racd in 2nd 4f out: lft in ld of main gp whn wnr styd alone far side wl over 3f out: nvr quite on terms: hung rt 2f out: hdd for ld of main gp wl over 1f out: sn wknd* **16/1**

2 **6** *2 ¾* **Show Flower**[47] 2709 2-8-12 0 .... HughBowman 4 72
(Mick Channon) *chsd wnr 3f: styd chsng ldrs in main gp stands' side: rdn 3f out: wknd fr 2f out* **9/1**

410 **7** *3 ¼* **Pink Sapphire (IRE)**[13] 3821 2-8-12 0 .... RichardHughes 2 64
(Richard Hannon) *in tch: chsd ldrs in main gp stands' side tl wknd 2f out* **7/1**[3]

1m 33.25s (3.75) **Going Correction** +0.475s/f (Yiel) **7** Ran SP% **111.7**
Speed ratings (Par 99): **97,94,91,90,88 85,81**
toteswingers:1&2:£2.10, 1&3:£3.60, 2&3:£2.50 CSF £13.72 TOTE £4.70: £2.50, £2.20; EX 7.90 Trifecta £25.70 Pool: £1,160.77 - 33.32 winning units..
Owner Miss K Rausing **Bred** Miss K Rausing **Trained** Newmarket, Suffolk

FOCUS
Probably just an ordinary Listed race, with none of the runners successful or placed at this level previously. As with the preceding handicap, all bar one of the runners came over to the stands' side, and this time it was the exception who came out on top. The form is dubious but Kinetica did it well.

NOTEBOOK
Kinetica galloped on strongly after ploughing a lone furrow to win in good style. The runner-up in the 1m6f handicap had also raced alone on the inside rail and it may well have been a plus to race there, but this filly still deserves plenty of credit, seeing out the trip well and confirming that she is well at home in softish ground. Sir Mark Prescott sent out the best recent winner of this event, Confidential Lady who was second in the 1,000 Guineas and won the Prix de Diane in 2006, and while Kinetica has plenty more improvement to make to reach those heights she is a nice prospect. She has an entry for the Fillies' Mile, to be run at Newmarket this year, but something like the May Hill Stakes at Doncaster could be more suitable. In the meantime she could go for the Sweet Solera Stakes, in which Confidential Lady finished second after winning here. (tchd 10-3)
Arsaadi(IRE), successful in a Newbury maiden last time, 'won' the race amongst the half-dozen who tacked over on the home turn but was no match for the winner. Also entered in the Fillies' Mile, as well as several big sales races, she is very useful filly. (op 11-4)
Hawfinch was also entered for this Saturday's Princess Margaret Stakes, but the decision to step her up to 7f was vindicated as she stayed on into third, securing black type. She had previously been fifth at this level in the Empress Stakes at Newmarket, a place behind Worthington. (op 7-2 tchd 4-1)
Worthington(IRE) has now been held in three tries at this level at three different trips, but probably saw out this seventh furlong. (op 13-2)
Vassaria(IRE), who showed just fair form on her first three starts, led the runners over on entering the straight, but didn't see out the longer trip in the ground. (tchd 14-1)
Show Flower finished a place ahead of Vassaria when making her debut at Doncaster, and although that race has generally worked out well, the winner, Falls Of Lora, has been beaten in a nursery off 89 since. Show Flower weakened in the straight and the trip in this ground looked too much for her at this stage. (op 12-1 tchd 8-1)
Pink Sapphire(IRE) did not seem to get home over the longer trip, albeit she was racing on the worst ground. A small filly, she has failed to beat a rival on her last two starts and has something to prove now. (op 8-1)

4253 WISECALL CLAIMS ASSISTANCE H'CAP 1m 2f 7y
3:55 (3:55) (Class 4) (0-85,84) 3-Y-O+ **£4,075** (£1,212; £606; £303) **Stalls** Low

Form RPR

1-24 **1** **Mountain Range (IRE)**[48] 2688 3-8-9 75 .... JamieSpencer 1 86+
(John Dunlop) *in rr and rdn and hdwy fr 2f out: styd on strly u.p fnl f to go 2nd fnl 100yds: led last strides* **9/2**[2]

-003 **2** *nk* **Absinthe (IRE)**[20] 3592 5-10-0 84 .... AdamKirby 9 94
(Walter Swinburn) *chsd ldrs: chal ins fnl 3f: led 2f out: hung bdly rt into rails fr over 1f out but sn 2 l clr: hdd and no ex last strides* **11/4**[1]

0023 **3** *1 ½* **Shamacam**[21] 3551 3-8-11 77 .... RyanMoore 8 84
(Sir Michael Stoute) *chsd ldrs: rdn over 2f out: styd on to chse wnr over 1f out: no imp and styd on one pce to go 3rd fnl 100yds* **5/1**[3]

-013 **4** *1 ½* **Aldwick Bay (IRE)**[24] 3466 3-8-10 76 .... RichardHughes 11 80
(Richard Hannon) *hld up in rr: rdn and hdwy on outside 2f out: styd on same pce u.p fnl f* **8/1**

0400 **5** *hd* **Silver Grey (IRE)**[12] 3844 4-9-9 79 .... (p) JackMitchell 10 83
(Roger Ingram) *hld up in rr: swtchd to outside and hdwy fr 2f out: styd on u.p fnl f but nvr gng pce to rch ldrs* **50/1**

3050 **6** *4* **Licence To Till (USA)**[12] 3844 4-9-13 83 .... SilvestreDeSousa 13 79
(Mark Johnston) *towards rr: rdn over 3f out: hdwy over 2f out: no imp on ldrs and btn fnl f* **17/2**

5505 **7** *2 ¼* **Cashpoint**[29] 3277 6-9-8 78 .... ChrisCatlin 12 69
(Anthony Middleton) *led 2f: styd chsng ldr: led 3f out: hdd 2f out: styd chsng ldr tl wl over 1f out: wknd fnl f* **16/1**

1652 **8** *¾* **Nahab**[15] 3740 4-10-0 84 .... TedDurcan 5 74
(David Lanigan) *in rr: pushed along and kpt on into mid-div fr 3f out: no further prog and no ch fnl 2f* **14/1**

15-4 **9** *4 ½* **Tick Tock Lover**[12] 3871 3-9-2 82 .... IanMongan 6 63
(Jo Crowley) *chsd ldrs: rdn 3f out: wknd wl over 2f out* **9/1**

000/ **10** *8* **Serious Choice (IRE)**[454] 3734 6-9-0 70 .... (b) SebSanders 3 35
(Philip Hobbs) *s.i.s: in rr: hdwy and in tch over 3f out: wknd wl over 2f out* **25/1**

00/0 **11** *4* **First Avenue**[26] 3411 6-9-8 78 .... (p) GeorgeBaker 15 35
(Gary Moore) *chsd ldrs: rdn 3f out: wknd wl over 2f out* **50/1**

-120 **12** *25* **Allanit (GER)**[49] 2649 7-9-1 71 .... TomQueally 2 —
(Barney Curley) *led after 2f: hdd 3f out: wknd rapidly* **28/1**

2-03 **U** **Emeebee**[40] 2915 5-8-10 66 .... StevieDonohoe 14 —
(Willie Musson) *rrd and uns rdr s* **28/1**

2m 13.9s (3.40) **Going Correction** +0.475s/f (Yiel)
WFA 3 from 4yo+ 10lb **13** Ran SP% **120.4**
Speed ratings (Par 105): **105,104,103,102,102 99,97,96,93,86 83,63,—**
toteswingers:1&2:£4.40, 1&3:£5.40, 2&3:£4.70 CSF £16.50 CT £65.06 TOTE £5.10: £2.10, £1.70, £2.30; EX 17.30 Trifecta £89.90 Pool: £1,097.89 - 9.03 winning units..
Owner Sir Philip Wroughton **Bred** Holborn Trust Co **Trained** Arundel, W Sussex

FOCUS
A fair handicap and the form looks sound. This time the runners raced near to the rail in the back straight and they all remained on the inside once turning in. A 6lb personal best from the winner.
Allanit(GER) Official explanation: vet said gelding lost a shoe

4254 CB RICHARD ELLIS MAIDEN STKS 1m 14y
4:30 (4:43) (Class 5) 3-4-Y-O **£2,264** (£673; £336; £168) **Stalls** Low

Form RPR

3 **1** **Dare To Dance (IRE)**[85] 1605 3-9-2 0 .... RyanMoore 4 92+
(Jeremy Noseda) *hld up in rr: rdn 3f out: styd on u.p fr over 1f out: led fnl 120yds: kpt on wl clsng stages* **4/7**[1]

03 **2** *1 ¼* **West Brit (IRE)**[31] 3232 3-9-2 0 .... GeorgeBaker 8 89
(Ed Dunlop) *chsd ldrs: led over 2f out: kpt on u.p tl hdd and one pce fnl 120yds* **12/1**[3]

2 **3** *2 ¾* **Garud (IRE)**[21] 3543 3-9-2 0 .... AdamKirby 9 83
(Marco Botti) *sn led: hdd after 2f: styd chsng ldr and led again over 3f out: hdd over 2f out: one pce fnl 120yds* **9/4**[2]

5 **4** *3 ¼* **Eclipseoftheheart**[20] 3577 3-8-11 0 .... PatCosgrave 3 71
(James Fanshawe) *chsd ldrs: rdn 3f out: wknd fnl f* **12/1**[3]

5 *16* **Nuba (IRE)**[386] 3568 3-8-12 0 ow1 .... IanMongan 5 35
(Luke Dace) *a in rr: rdn and lost tch over 2f out* **100/1**

-50 **6** *5* **Rockerfellow**[21] 3543 3-9-2 0 .... SebSanders 7 27
(J W Hills) *led after 2f: hdd appr fnl 3f: wknd sn after* **25/1**

1m 48.18s (4.88) **Going Correction** +0.475s/f (Yiel) **6** Ran SP% **114.6**
Speed ratings (Par 103): **94,92,90,86,70 65**
toteswingers:1&2:£2.00, 1&3:£1.20, 2&3:£1.90 CSF £9.86 TOTE £1.70: £1.20, £3.10; EX 8.50 Trifecta £14.60 Pool: £1,088.58 - 55.11 winning units..
Owner R A Pegum **Bred** Round Hill Stud **Trained** Newmarket, Suffolk

FOCUS
There was a considerable delay to this maiden after Hope Point reared over behind the stalls and evaded capture for several minutes (100/1, withdrawn). The race lacked depth but the first three showed useful form.

4255 TOM JONES HERE NEXT WEDNESDAY H'CAP 7f 16y
5:00 (5:10) (Class 5) (0-75,74) 3-Y-O+ **£2,587** (£770; £384; £192) **Stalls** Low

Form RPR

33-0 **1** **Push Me (IRE)**[52] 2561 4-8-9 58 .... MichaelO'Connell(3) 2 67
(Jamie Poulton) *in tch: drvn to chal 2f out: sn led: rdn and styd on wl fnl f* **25/1**

0201 **2** *1 ¾* **Jungle Bay**[13] 3806 4-10-0 74 .... TedDurcan 9 78
(Jane Chapple-Hyam) *in tch: drvn and hdwy fr 2f out: styd on fnl f to take 2nd last stride: no imp on wnr* **5/1**[3]

/040 **3** *nse* **Billion Dollar Kid**[13] 3815 6-9-10 70 .... (bt[1]) RichardKingscote 1 74
(Joanna Davis) *chsd ldr: chal between horses 2f out: chsd wnr sn after but no imp fnl f: one pce and ct for 2nd last stride* **12/1**

-046 **4** *1 ¼* **Kingarrick**[28] 3312 3-9-7 74 .... RyanMoore 5 72
(Eve Johnson Houghton) *chsd ldrs: rdn along fr 3f out: styd on same pce fr over 1f out* **15/2**

12- **5** *2 ¾* **Junket**[271] 7082 4-9-13 73 .... GeorgeBaker 8 67+
(Dr Jon Scargill) *in rr: hdwy fr 2f out: styd on fnl f: nvr gng pce to rch ldrs: one pce clsng stages* **3/1**[1]

2-21 **6** *1 ¼* **Formal Demand**[49] 2650 3-9-5 72 .... JamieSpencer 10 59
(Edward Vaughan) *s.i.s: in rr: pushed along over 2f out: styd on fnl f but nvr a threat* **7/2**[2]

2213 **7** *½* **Miss Bootylishes**[3] 4158 6-9-10 73 .... JohnFahy(3) 11 62
(Paul Burgoyne) *chsd ldrs: rdn 3f out: sn edgd rt and btn* **6/1**

1500 **8** *9* **Mary's Pet**[14] 3765 4-8-12 58 .... IanMongan 4 24
(John Akehurst) *led tl hdd jst ins fnl 2f: wknd qckly wl over 1f out* **40/1**

150- **9** *3 ¾* **Whitechapel**[376] 3898 4-9-12 72 .... JimmyFortune 7 28
(Andrew Balding) *in tch tl wknd fr 3f out* **14/1**

2500 **10** *¾* **Tuxedo**[124] 908 6-9-10 70 .... SilvestreDeSousa 12 24
(Peter Hiatt) *in rr: rdn towards outside 3f out: no prog and sn wknd* **20/1**

1m 33.17s (3.67) **Going Correction** +0.475s/f (Yiel)
WFA 3 from 4yo+ 7lb **10** Ran SP% **115.3**
Speed ratings (Par 103): **98,96,95,94,91 89,89,79,74,73**
toteswingers:1&2:£25.00, 1&3:£35.10, 2&3:£13.30 CSF £141.76 CT £1641.73 TOTE £32.30: £8.20, £1.60, £4.00; EX 140.80 TRIFECTA Not won..
Owner Alex and Janet Card **Bred** Mrs Dolores Gleeson **Trained** Telscombe, E Sussex

FOCUS
Rain began to fall before this race. This was a modest handicap for the grade in which few were able to become involved, but the form makes some sense.
T/Jkpt: Not won. T/Plt: £57.10 to a £1 stake. Pool:£68,343.02 - 872.44 winning tickets T/Qpdt: £16.10 to a £1 stake. Pool:£5,137.61 - 236.10 winning tickets ST

4256 - (Foreign Racing) - See Raceform Interactive

4029 LEOPARDSTOWN (L-H)
Thursday, July 21

OFFICIAL GOING: Soft (yielding in places)

4257a KOREAN RACING AUTHORITY TYROS STKS (GROUP 3) 7f
6:25 (6:26) 2-Y-O £26,616 (£7,780; £3,685; £1,228)

RPR
1 **Remember Alexander**[61] 2321 2-8-12 .... JMurtagh 7 105+
(Mrs John Harrington, Ire) *hld up racing keenly in 4th: swtchd rt early st and brought over to stands' side: gd hdwy to ld early fnl f: kpt on wl: easily* **7/1**[3]
2 *4* **Parish Hall (IRE)**[102] 1256 2-9-1 .... KJManning 4 98
(J S Bolger, Ire) *trckd ldrs in 3rd: rdn to ld ent st: styd on far rail: hdd u.p early fnl f: kpt on one pce but no ch w wnr* **3/1**[2]
3 *2* **Tenth Star (IRE)**[21] 3562 2-9-1 108 .... JPO'Brien 6 93
(A P O'Brien, Ire) *trckd ldr in 2nd: 3rd ent st: sn pushed along in centre of crse: no imp u.p fr 1f out: kpt on one pce* **1/2**[1]
4 *2 ½* **Strait Of Zanzibar (USA)**[15] 3748 2-9-1 .... DPMcDonogh 2 87
(K J Condon, Ire) *chsd ldrs on inner: 5th 1/2-way: pushed along appr st: no imp in centre of crse fr over 1f out: kpt on one pce* **20/1**
5 *14* **Cheerful Giver (IRE)**[4] 4131 2-9-1 80 .... RPCleary 1 52
(J S Bolger, Ire) *led: edgd rt and hdd ent st: sn no ex: wknd* **66/1**
6 *½* **Orchestra Leader (USA)**[67] 2127 2-9-1 93 .... WMLordan 3 51
(David Wachman, Ire) *a in rr: drvn along appr st: no ex fr 2f out* **14/1**

1m 32.39s (3.69) **Going Correction** +0.625s/f (Yiel) **6 Ran SP% 117.1**
Speed ratings: **103,98,96,93,77 76**
CSF £29.52 TOTE £5.50: £2.20, £2.00; DF 21.50.
Owner Noel O'Callaghan **Bred** Wood Hall Stud Limited **Trained** Moone, Co Kildare

FOCUS
The easy winner is rated in line with this race's consistent averages.

NOTEBOOK
Remember Alexander was brought widest of all, and that decision proved a telling one as the daughter of Teofilo pulled right away on the better ground to register a comprehensive victory. Despite hanging in the closing stages, she got off the mark at her third attempt, clearly relishing the ease in the ground, and she is fully entitled to take her chance in the Moyglare on this evidence. (op 8/1)
Parish Hall(IRE) ◆ had made an encouraging winning debut over a furlong shorter at this venue in April in a race that worked out well. He was expected to put up a good display but the ease in the ground went against him. He took over up the inner after a gap opened entering the straight but began to struggle on the worst of the ground and soon had no more to offer. He is definitely worth another chance to confirm the favourable impression of his debut considering he made his bid on a part of the track that was much slower than the middle. (op 3/1 tchd 5/2)
Tenth Star(IRE) was a warm order to supplement his recent C&D maiden win. The ease in the ground was probably against him, but he proved most disappointing after holding every chance approaching the straight and his rating of 108 is flattering. (op 8/13 tchd 8/11)
Strait Of Zanzibar(USA) plugged on in the closing stages for a share of the minor honours and might be capable of winning a maiden on some nicer ground. (op 16/1)
Cheerful Giver(IRE) made the early running before he dropped away tamely. (op 66/1 tchd 100/1)
Orchestra Leader(USA), successful over shorter at his second attempt at Navan in May, was pushed along half a mile from home and never looked happy on this rain-softened surface. (op 14/1 tchd 12/1)

4259a JOCKEY CLUB OF TURKEY MELD STKS (GROUP 3) 1m 1f
[illegible] £32,219 (£9,418; £4,461; £1,487)

RPR
1 **Famous Name**[27] 3371 6-9-12 117 .... PJSmullen 5 123
(D K Weld, Ire) *chsd clr ldr in 3rd: clsr appr st: brought wd towards stands' side in st: led over 1f out: pushed out to stretch clr: comf* **4/9**[1]
2 *4 ½* **Dunboyne Express (IRE)**[25] 3442 3-9-3 112 .... DPMcDonogh 2 113
(Kevin Prendergast, Ire) *settled in rr: clsr and niggled along appr st: brought wd towards stands' side and rdn in 3rd early st: kpt on same pce fnl f but no ch w wnr* **7/2**[2]
3 *5 ½* **Creekside**[25] 3444 3-9-0 102 .... (p) JMurtagh 4 98
(John M Oxx, Ire) *chsd clr ldr in 2nd: clsr appr st: sn rdn and dropped to rr: no imp fr wl over 1f out* **16/1**
4 *1 ½* **Jan Vermeer (IRE)**[27] 3371 4-9-9 109 .... (b[1]) SeamieHeffernan 6 96
(A P O'Brien, Ire) *led racing keenly and clr bef 1/2-way: reduced advantage appr st: styd alone on far rail: hdd u.p over 1f out: no ex and wknd ins fnl f* **13/2**[3]

1m 56.71s (2.61) **Going Correction** +0.625s/f (Yiel)
WFA 3 from 4yo+ 9lb **4 Ran SP% 110.7**
Speed ratings: **113,109,104,102**
CSF £2.44 TOTE £1.80; DF 2.90.
Owner K Abdulla **Bred** Juddmonte Farms Ltd **Trained** The Curragh, Co Kildare

FOCUS
The winner was the clear form choice and has been rated to his mark.

NOTEBOOK
Famous Name closed the gap rounding the home turn and, when brought wide into the straight, easily got the better of the long-time leader over a furlong from home. Famous Name's only defeat this term came in the Tattersalls Gold Cup behind So You Think and Campanologist and his trainer has made no secret of the fact that he'd love to bag a Group 1 with his stable star. A trip to Munich is on the agenda now for the Group 1 Bayerisches Zuchtrennen on Sunday week. Ground conditions are likely to be in his favour and the yard won that race with Market Booster in 1993. (op 1/2)
Dunboyne Express(IRE), a creditable fifth behind Treasure Beach in the Dubai Duty Free Irish Derby, was one of just two 3yos in the field. The 2,000 Guineas Trial winner here in March was reported to be working well and the drop in trip and ground conditions looked ideal. He closed behind the winner into the straight but had no answer when asked for more. (op 10/3)
Creekside looked outclassed on figures and, after tracking the long-time leader for a time, struggled in the closing stages. (op 14/1)
Jan Vermeer(IRE) had finished half a dozen lengths behind the winner in the International Stakes last time. Seamie Heffernan elected to make the running and was several lengths clear leaving the back straight but the gap soon closed and he weakened as he kept to the inner of the course, a side not favoured on the night. (op 6/1)

4258 - 4262a (Foreign Racing) - See Raceform Interactive

3840 ASCOT (R-H)
Friday, July 22

OFFICIAL GOING: Straight course - good to soft changing to good; round course - soft (good to soft in places) changing to good to soft (good in places) after race 4 (3.55)
virtually nilbright spells, light cloud

4263 JOHN GUEST MAIDEN FILLIES' STKS 6f
2:10 (2:11) (Class 4) 2-Y-O £6,469 (£1,925; £962; £481) **Stalls** Centre

Form RPR
5 1 **Hello Glory**[13] 3865 2-9-0 0 .... JamieSpencer 6 89+
(David Simcock) *hld up in tch in last pair: gd hdwy to ld 2f out: sn rdn: r.o wl fnl f: readily* **11/4**[1]
5 2 *3 ¼* **Besito (IRE)**[41] 2914 2-9-0 0 .... KierenFallon 8 79
(William Jarvis) *wnt lft s: t.k.h and sn chsng ldrs: short of room briefly over 2f out: rdn and hdwy to chse wnr whn hung rt wl over 1f out: continued to hang and no imp on wnr fnl f* **3/1**[2]
3 *2 ¼* **I'm So Glad** 2-9-0 0 .... HughBowman 5 71+
(Mick Channon) *dwlt and flashed tail leaving stalls: in tch: outpcd and pushed along jst over 2f out: swtchd lft and rallied over 1f out: flashed tail u.p but styd on steadily fnl f: nt pce to threaten ldrs* **16/1**
4 *2* **Wahylah (IRE)** 2-9-0 0 .... PhilipRobinson 2 65
(Clive Brittain) *hld up in tch in last pair: hdwy over 2f out: rdn and unable qck w ldng pair over 1f out: 3rd and btn 1f out: plugged on same pce fnl f* **11/1**
06 5 *nk* **Caterina**[13] 3865 2-9-0 0 .... RyanMoore 1 64
(Richard Hannon) *chsd ldrs: rdn and unable qck w ldng pair over 1f out: plugged on same pce and wl hld fnl f* **8/1**
623 6 *shd* **Ivor's Princess**[30] 3270 2-9-0 0 .... JamesMillman 3 64+
(Rod Millman) *chsd ldr tl jst over 2f out: rdn and struggling to qckn whn squeezed for room and hmpd over 1f out: n.d after: swtchd lft 1f out: kpt on same pce fnl f* **9/2**[3]
5 7 *2* **Rain Dance**[31] 3258 2-9-0 0 .... RichardHughes 4 57
(Richard Hannon) *led tl hdd 2f out: sn rdn and carried rt: outpcd by ldng pair and btn over 1f out: wknd 1f out* **6/1**

1m 16.19s (1.79) **Going Correction** +0.45s/f (Yiel) **7 Ran SP% 109.5**
Speed ratings (Par 93): **106,101,98,96,95 95,92**
Tote Swingers: 1&2 £2.40, 1&3 £5.80, 2&3 £12.20 CSF £10.20 TOTE £3.30: £2.00, £1.90; EX 11.10 Trifecta £81.30 Pool: £829.65 - 7.54 winning units..
Owner A & A **Bred** Baydon House Stud **Trained** Newmarket, Suffolk

FOCUS
This maiden has been a good source of top-class juvenile fillies in the past ten years, with Carry On Katie, Silca's Sister and White Moonstone all going on to win Group 1s later in the season. The field raced up the centre of the track and the time suggested the ground was close to the official description. The winner looks well up to scratch and has the potential to rate a fair bit higher.

NOTEBOOK
Hello Glory caught the eye when just ahead of Caterina on her debut at Newmarket and was well supported. Held up at the back early, she made her effort soon after halfway and ran straight as an arrow to the line, in marked contrast to the runner-up. She looks sure to make her mark at a higher level, but quotes of 20-1 for next year's 1,000 Guineas do not look overly generous at this stage. (op 10-3)
Besito(IRE), fifth behind the subsequent Cherry Hinton runner-up in a Leicester maiden (form that had otherwise not worked out that well), went left as the stalls opened and then went right under pressure when challenging the winner. She has the ability to win races but is clearly not straightforward. (op 10-3 tchd 11-4)
I'm So Glad, a 26,000gns half-sister to two winning sprinters, was reported as a tail-swisher by her trainer. However, she showed a good measure of ability on this debut, despite being well beaten by the first two, as she was last around 2f out before running on quite nicely in the closing stages. (op 18-1)
Wahylah(IRE), a 32,000gns first foal of a half-sister to Fred Darling winner Sueboog, showed ability and can improve with this experience under her belt. (op 10-1 tchd 12-1)
Caterina had shown modest form in 6f maidens on a sound surface and never got involved on this [illegible] ground. She at least now qualifies for a handicap mark. (tchd 10-1)
Ivor's Princess, a half-sister to four-time winning [illegible] when placed in Bath maidens on her two previous starts, but looked out of her depth here. (op 5-1 tchd 11-2)
Rain Dance, who was dropping in trip after running over 7f on her debut, made the running but was brushed aside when the principals came to challenge. (op 4-1)

4264 SACO SERVICED APARTMENTS EBF MAIDEN STKS 7f
2:45 (2:46) (Class 3) 2-Y-O £6,469 (£1,925; £962; £481) **Stalls** Centre

Form RPR
430 1 **Caledonian Spring (IRE)**[38] 3014 2-9-3 0 .... KierenFallon 7 88
(Paul D'Arcy) *in tch: hdwy to press ldr 2f out: rdn to chal over 1f out: drvn ahd ins fnl f: r.o wl* **7/1**[3]
32 2 *1 ¼* **Mehdi (IRE)**[34] 3182 2-9-3 0 .... ShaneKelly 11 85
(Brian Meehan) *led: rdn over 2f out: hdd and drvn ins fnl f: styd on same pce fnl 100yds* **9/4**[1]
3 3 *1 ½* **Cavaleiro (IRE)**[26] 3425 2-9-3 0 .... PatDobbs 10 81
(Marcus Tregoning) *t.k.h early: hld up in tch: rdn and unable qck jst over 2f out: rallied ins fnl f: styd on steadily fnl 100yds* **8/1**
0 4 *2 ¼* **Police Force (USA)**[14] 3823 2-9-3 0 .... FrankieDettori 4 75+
(Mahmood Al Zarooni) *hld up in midfield: hdwy and switching rt jst over 2f out: rdn to press ldng pair and edgd lft over 1f out: btn ins fnl f: wknd fnl 100yds* **4/1**[2]
5 *1 ¼* **Strident Force** 2-9-3 0 .... RyanMoore 1 74+
(Sir Michael Stoute) *pushed rt s: hld up in tch on rr: pushed along 1/2-way: rdn and hdwy wl over 2f out: styd on same pce and no imp over 1f out* **7/1**[3]
6 *4 ½* **Johnno** 2-9-3 0 .... SebSanders 3 60+
(J W Hills) *wnt rt s: in tch in rr: rdn 1/2-way: hdwy into midfield over 2f out: wknd over 1f out* **33/1**
0 7 *3 ½* **Aussie Guest (IRE)**[14] 3793 2-9-3 0 .... HughBowman 5 51
(Mick Channon) *chsd ldrs: rdn and unable qck wl over 1f out: wknd jst over 1f out: fdd fnl f* **66/1**
8 *½* **Zavier (FR)** 2-9-3 0 .... AhmedAjtebi 8 50
(Mahmood Al Zarooni) *in tch towards rr: rdn over 2f out: sn wknd: wl bhd fnl f* **14/1**
9 *hd* **Youcouldbelucky (USA)** 2-9-3 0 .... SilvestreDeSousa 2 49
(Mark Johnston) *pushed rt s: in tch towards rr: pushed along 1/2-way: rdn and hdwy to chse ldrs over 2f out: wknd qckly over 1f out* **9/1**

55 **10** 2 1/4 **Enjoying (IRE)**[9] 3986 2-9-3 0 RichardHughes 6 44
(Richard Hannon) *stdd s: hld up in tch in rr: stl plenty to do and rdn whn hmpd 2f out: hung rt and sn wknd: wl bhd fnl f* **16/1**

11 1 **Topanga Canyon** 2-9-3 0 JimmyFortune 9 41
(Andrew Balding) *chsd ldr tl over 2f out: sn rdn and lost pl: bhd and rn green over 1f out: fdd 1f out* **20/1**

1m 30.21s (3.01) **Going Correction** +0.45s/f (Yiel) **11** Ran SP% **118.6**
Speed ratings (Par 98): **100,98,96,94,92 87,83,83,82,80 79**
Tote Swingers: 1&2 £3.40, 1&3 £6.80, 2&3 £4.00 CSF £22.90 TOTE £7.30: £1.80, £1.20, £2.60; EX 22.30 Trifecta £85.00 Pool: £953.09 - 8.29 winning units..

Owner Dr J S Kinnear **Bred** Patrick Cosgrove **Trained** Newmarket, Suffolk

FOCUS
A decent maiden whose best recent winner was the subsequent Royal Lodge scorer City Leader, while there have also been subsequent winners at Group 3 and Listed level. The race was dominated by two of the most experienced runners. The first three are all rated as progressing.

NOTEBOOK
Caledonian Spring(IRE) came through to get the better of the favourite in the closing stages. He had shown a fair level of ability when in the frame in fast-ground maidens before finishing well beaten in the Windsor Castle, and was stepping up in trip. He was settled early before coming through to collar the favourite and draw away for slightly comfortable success. There should be more to come at this trip. (op 9-1)

Mehdi(IRE) had finished third to the subsequent Coventry and July Stakes runner-up Roman Soldier on his debut before finishing second to a subsequent winner next time. He made the running but had no answer to the winner's challenge. He should find easier opportunities to get off the mark. (tchd 2-1 and 5-2 in places)

Cavaleiro(IRE), a 78,000gns purchase from the first crop of the trainer's Derby winner Sir Percy, had shown promise on his debut over 7f at Salisbury and did so again, tracking the leader and staying on to the line. He gives the impression he needs further already, but should be winning races before long. (op 11-1 tchd 12-1)

Police Force(USA), a half-brother to the top-class Dream Ahead, had run green behind Rougemont on his debut at Newmarket. He ran well this time and looked a big threat when coming through on the bridle around 2f out. However, he did not produce much before weakening in the closing stages. (tchd 9-2)

Strident Force, a half-brother to a 6f winner and related to other winners at up to 1m, was being pushed along over 2f out before staying on in encouraging fashion to hunt up those in the frame. He should come on a lot for the experience. (op 11-2)

Johnno, a half-brother to the high-class juvenile Russian Valour and several other winners, showed his inexperience on this debut but was noted keeping on quite well in the last furlong. He has Royal Lodge and Champagne Stakes entries, so is clearly well regarded, and should improve for the outing. (op 40-1)

4265 WOODCOTE STUD EBF "HALLING" VALIANT STKS (LISTED RACE) (F&M) 1m (R)

3:20 (3:21) (Class 1) 3-Y-O+

£17,013 (£6,450; £3,228; £1,608; £807; £405) **Stalls** Low

Form RPR

0203 **1** **Sooraah**[20] 3645 4-9-1 92 RyanMoore 7 82+
(William Haggas) *hld up in last pair: hdwy on outer wl over 2f out: rdn to chse ldr 2f out: ev ch over 1f out: kpt on wl u.p to ld nr fin* **5/2**[3]

-442 **2** hd **Primevere (IRE)**[20] 3648 3-8-7 100 SteveDrowne 1 80
(Roger Charlton) *led: rdn and qcknd over 2f out: hrd pressed and drvn over 1f out: kpt on gamely tl hdd and no ex nr fin* **9/4**[2]

-133 **3** 3/4 **Winter's Night (IRE)**[37] 3034 3-8-7 98 LukeMorris 6 78+
(Clive Cox) *stdd s: hld up in last pair: rdn and effrt over 2f out: nt clr run and switching lft over 1f out: clr run and edgd lft u.p 1f out: r.o wl ins fnl f: nt rch ldng pair* **13/8**[1]

6-56 **4** 2 1/4 **Ela Gonda Mou**[31] 3244 4-9-1 64 KirstyMilczarek 5 74
(Peter Charalambous) *chsd ldr tl 2f out: sn unable qck u.p: styd on same pce fnl f* **125/1**

432 **5** 1 3/4 **Imaginary World (IRE)**[6] 4093 3-8-7 73 (be) KierenFallon 4 67
(Alan McCabe) *t.k.h: chsd ldrs: rdn ent fnl 2f: unable qck u.p over 1f out: wknd ins fnl f* **16/1**

1505 **6** 2 **Emma's Gift (IRE)**[27] 3407 3-8-7 88 AdamBeschizza 3 62
(Julia Feilden) *chsd ldrs: rdn wl over 2f out: unable qck and n.m.r 2f out: wknd over 1f out* **16/1**

1m 41.69s (0.99) **Going Correction** +0.225s/f (Good)
WFA 3 from 4yo+ 8lb **6** Ran SP% **110.0**
Speed ratings (Par 111): **104,103,103,100,99 97**
Tote Swingers: 1&2 £1.60, 1&3 £1.50, 2&3 £1.40 CSF £8.17 TOTE £3.20: £1.60, £1.40; EX 8.90.

Owner Mohammed Jaber **Bred** C R Mason **Trained** Newmarket, Suffolk

■ Stewards' Enquiry : Steve Drowne four-day ban: used whip with excessive frequency in incorrect place (Aug 5-8)

FOCUS
A wide spread of ability in this fillies' Listed contest whose best recent winners were Echelon and Strawberrydaiquiri. The pace looked steady early and it developed into a sprint from the home turn, but the time was not that bad, suggesting the ground had dried out. The fourth is a big hole in the form and its doubtful if the front three were anywhere near their best in this steadily run race.

NOTEBOOK
Sooraah, a dual winner in July last year (her only successes), had been running creditably in handicaps since. Held up at the back, she picked up well down the outside to challenge in the straight and just got the better of the front-runner near the line. The black type earned will have increased her paddock value and she looks likely to continue to be campaigned at this level, although the return to handicaps remains an option.

Primevere(IRE), an AW winner on her debut, had put up fair efforts in Listed company since. She made the running, her rider dictating a steady gallop before kicking on but, despite doing nothing wrong, she was worn down near the finish. She is well capable of winning a race at this level. (op 11-4 tchd 3-1)

Winter's Night(IRE), a progressive filly who finished third in the Sandringham Handicap at the Royal meeting, was 2-3 at this track coming into this. She was held up at the back on the inside, and did not get a clear run when the leaders were quickening in the straight. She finished well but too late to reel in her market rivals, and surely would have gone close had she been ridden closer to the pace. (op 6-4 tchd 7-4)

Ela Gonda Mou had been well beaten in maidens and a handicap and, rated 64, had a very stiff task at the weights. She ran well, though, under a positive ride, although it could mean her handicap mark is blown if the assessor takes this seriously. (op 100-1)

Imaginary World(IRE), only out of the frame once in 13 starts since her last success, had plenty to do at the weights and, given she's well suited by fast ground, she may have found this surface against her. (tchd 14-1 and 20-1 in a place)

Emma's Gift(IRE), a useful juvenile and a dual winner at up to 1m, is another well suited by fast ground and could not pick up in the straight. (op 20-1 tchd 14-1)

4266 JOHN GUEST BROWN JACK H'CAP 2m

3:55 (3:55) (Class 2) (0-100,97) 3-Y-O+ **£14,231** (£4,235; £2,116; £1,058) **Stalls** Low

Form RPR

2421 **1** **Keys (IRE)**[6] 4097 4-9-1 84 6ex (b) JamieSpencer 2 95+
(Roger Charlton) *stdd s: hld up in last quartet: rdn and effrt over 2f out: swtchd lft and forced way out 2f out: edgd rt and drvn to chal over 1f out: led and edgd lft ins fnl f: styd on wl* **4/5**[1]

0011 **2** 3/4 **Colour Vision (FR)**[7] 4050 3-8-9 95 6ex SilvestreDeSousa 1 105+
(Mark Johnston) *chsd ldrs: rdn 3f out: swtchd lft and drvn to ld over 1f out: hdd 1f out: stl ev ch whn flashed tail u.p and veered lft ins fnl f: one pce and hld whn flashed tail and hung lft again cl home* **11/4**[2]

2012 **3** 5 **Red Kestrel (USA)**[21] 3593 6-8-11 85 JulieBurke(5) 6 89
(Kevin Ryan) *chsd ldr: rdn over 2f out: unable qck u.p over 1f out: 3rd and kpt on same pce fnl f* **25/1**

-032 **4** hd **Mountain Hiker (IRE)**[14] 3794 4-9-12 95 (v[1]) RyanMoore 3 99
(Jeremy Noseda) *led: rdn and qcknd wl over 2f out: drvn and hdd over 1f out: sn outpcd by ldng pair: battling for 3rd and no threat to ldng pair fnl f* **17/2**[3]

-000 **5** 1/2 **Very Good Day (FR)**[20] 3625 4-9-5 88 HughBowman 4 91
(Mick Channon) *in tch in midfield: rdn and effrt whn pushed rt 2f out: unable qck wl over 1f out: kpt on but no threat to ldrs fnl f* **20/1**

4020 **6** 3 1/2 **Magicalmysterytour (IRE)**[13] 3867 8-8-12 81 TonyCulhane 10 80
(Willie Musson) *stdd and dropped in bhd after s: hld up in rr: rdn and effrt jst over 2f out: no imp and wl btn over 1f out* **40/1**

06-5 **7** 1 **L Frank Baum (IRE)**[34] 3157 4-9-4 87 MartinDwyer 7 85
(Gay Kelleway) *hld up in tch: rdn 4f out: drvn and wknd wl over 1f out* **22/1**

010/ **8** 9 **Downhiller (IRE)**[807] 1790 6-9-11 94 TedDurcan 5 81
(John Dunlop) *hld up in last pair: rdn jst over 2f out: sn wknd* **50/1**

01-4 **9** 2 3/4 **Dayia (IRE)**[34] 3157 7-10-0 97 KierenFallon 9 81
(Lydia Pearce) *chsd ldrs: rdn 3f out: wknd qckly wl over 1f out: wl btn and eased ins fnl f* **14/1**

3m 34.68s (5.68) **Going Correction** +0.225s/f (Good)
WFA 3 from 4yo+ 17lb **9** Ran SP% **116.8**
Speed ratings (Par 109): **94,93,91,91,90 89,88,84,82**
Tote Swingers: 1&2 £11.20, 2&3 £6.80 CSF £2.81 CT £27.22 TOTE £1.90: £1.10, £1.30, £3.70; EX 3.60 Trifecta £25.80 Pool: £1,564.89 - 44.73 winning units..

Owner Seasons Holidays **Bred** B Hurley **Trained** Beckhampton, Wilts

■ Stewards' Enquiry : Jamie Spencer one-day ban: careless riding (Aug 5)

FOCUS
This handicap, named in honour of the great stayer of the 1930s, has been won in recent years by a mix of battle-hardened performers and progressive 3-y-os. The market was dominated by two penalised recent winners and they dominated the finish, coming right away from the rest. The early pace was steady and the time was very slow. The front pair were both well in and are rated to form at face value.

NOTEBOOK
Keys(IRE) had struggled to win in maidens before bolting in stepped up to 2m the previous week on his handicap debut. Carrying a 6lb penalty that still left him 10lb well in compared with his new mark, he travelled well towards the back of the field. He had to get out of a pocket as the pace was picking up in the straight, but he did so in plenty of time and ran on under pressure to beat his market rival, the pair clear. He looks progressive but will not find it easy to complete the hat-trick off his new mark, so connections might look for a Listed race for him instead. (op Evens tchd 11-10 in places)

Colour Vision(FR), whose trainer Mark Johnston had won this twice in the previous ten years, once with a similar type, is a progressive 3-y-o who had won his last two starts in the style of a real stayer. Raised 7lb for last success but due to be 6lb higher in future, the only doubt was his ability to act on soft ground. He had to be pushed along soon after leaving Swinley Bottom, but responded to his rider's urgings to hit the front well over a furlong out, only to be immediately challenged by the winner. He wandered about quite a bit under pressure and is clearly not straightforward, but there might still be more to come. (op 5-2 tchd 3-1)

Red Kestrel(USA), a progressive middle-distance/stayer who was having his first try at this trip on turf, had yet to prove his effectiveness on soft ground. He ran well, though, despite being no match for the principals. (op 22-1)

Mountain Hiker(IRE), narrowly beaten on both tries at this trip, including over C&D last time, was 5lb higher but wore cheekpieces then and had a visor for the first time. He made the running and his rider kicked clear rounding the turn, but his mount could not sustain the effort and was quickly done with when the first two arrived on the scene. (op 10-1)

Very Good Day(FR) had struggled since winning his maiden on good ground last summer and was stepping up in distance. He had dropped 10lb since his first start of this season and ran creditably, so is worth another try at the trip.

Dayia(IRE), the winner of a Saint-Cloud Listed race last November, had returned to run well in the Queen Alexandra at the Royal meeting, although she did not quite last home. Racing from 12lb above her last winning mark, and 6lb higher than she had run off before, she raced close behind the leaders but dropped away disappointingly in the straight. (op 12-1)

4267 NEWSMITH OCTOBER CLUB CHARITY H'CAP 1m 2f

4:30 (4:31) (Class 2) (0-100,100) 3-Y-O+

£11,205 (£3,355; £1,677; £838; £419; £210) **Stalls** Low

Form RPR

10-4 **1** **High Twelve (IRE)**[183] 242 4-9-7 100 AntiocoMurgia(7) 4 110
(Mahmood Al Zarooni) *hld up in midfield: smooth hdwy on outer over 3f out: rdn to chal over 1f out: led fnl 100yds: kpt on wl: rdn out* **20/1**

0511 **2** 1/2 **Oceanway (USA)**[21] 3592 3-8-9 91 SilvestreDeSousa 11 100
(Mark Johnston) *chsd ldrs: rdn to ld ent fnl 2f: hrd pressed and drvn over 1f out: hdd and no ex fnl 100yds* **4/1**[1]

0001 **3** 1 1/2 **Tinshu (IRE)**[7] 4058 5-8-8 85 6ex HarryBentley(5) 8 91
(Derek Haydn Jones) *stdd and dropped in towards rr after s: hld up in last quartet: rdn and effrt over 1f out: r.o wl to chse ldng pair ins fnl f: no imp fnl 75yds* **14/1**

-60 **4** nk **Pipette**[39] 2994 4-9-8 94 (t) JimmyFortune 2 99
(Andrew Balding) *hld up in last quartet: rdn 4f out: switching rt ent fnl 2f: hdwy u.p over 1f out: pressing for 3rd ins fnl f: no imp fnl 75yds* **8/1**

/111 **5** nk **Troopingthecolour**[15] 3764 5-9-4 90 JamieSpencer 9 95
(Steve Gollings) *chsd ldr: jnd ldr over 3f out: rdn and c wd bnd wl over 2f out: drvn and unable qck 2f out: styd on same pce and lost 2 pls ins fnl f* **14/1**

0-10 **6** 2 **Sam Sharp (USA)**[41] 2909 5-9-3 89 KierenFallon 5 90+
(Ian Williams) *stdd s: hld up in rr: stl last and nt clr run wl over 2f out: rdn jst over 2f out: swtchd lft and hdwy jst over 1f out: styd on wl ins fnl f: nvr able to chal* **16/1**

0-34 **7** nk **Dhaamer (IRE)**[33] 3203 4-9-1 87 RichardHills 3 87
(John Gosden) *in tch in midfield: rdn and unable qck over 2f out: styd on same pce and no imp fr wl over 1f out* **11/2**[3]

-406 **8** *8* **The Fonz**[20] 3625 5-9-4 **90**.. RyanMoore 10 74
(Sir Michael Stoute) *hld up in midfield: rdn and effrt over 2f out: drvn and no prog 2f out: wknd over 1f out* **11/2**[3]

4230 **9** *3/4* **San Cassiano (IRE)**[14] 3829 4-8-9 **81**.......................... JamesSullivan 6 64
(Ruth Carr) *chsd ldrs: swtchd lft and rdn over 2f out: wknd u.p over 1f out* **20/1**

4612 **10** *6* **Suits Me**[7] 4058 8-9-5 **91**.. MickyFenton 7 62
(David Barron) *led tl rdn and hdd ent fnl 2f: wknd jst over 1f out: virtually p.u fnl 150yds* **10/1**

-130 **11** *86* **Point North (IRE)**[37] 3032 4-9-4 **90**..........................(t) RichardHughes 1 —
(Jeremy Noseda) *t.k.h early: hld up in last quartet: rdn and no hdwy over 2f out: wknd 2f out: virtually p.u fnl f: t.o* **9/2**[2]

2m 6.79s (-0.21) **Going Correction** +0.225s/f (Good)
WFA 3 from 4yo+ 10lb **11** Ran SP% **117.9**
Speed ratings (Par 109): **109,108,107,107,106 105,105,98,98,93 24**
Tote Swingers: 1&2 £19.80, 1&3 £39.00, 2&3 £10.00 CSF £98.79 CT £1172.84 TOTE £28.30: £6.40, £1.70, £4.10; EX 163.10 Trifecta £1346.60 Part won. Pool: £1,819.85 - 0.08 winning units..

Owner Godolphin **Bred** Grangecon Stud **Trained** Newmarket, Suffolk

FOCUS
A good-class handicap run in a decent time, and the form looks solid.

NOTEBOOK
High Twelve(IRE), who was very useful for John Gosden last season, had not been seen since running fourth at Meydan in January. Racing off 8lb above his previous winning mark but with a claimer up, he was eased into contention rounding the home turn and, after challenging the favourite over 1f out, stuck on well to the line. He looks capable of making his mark at Listed level after this. (op 25-1 tchd 28-1)

Oceanway(USA) came through to lead around 2f out but was immediately challenged by the winner, and that rival proved too strong. (op 7-2)

Tinshu(IRE) bounced back to form when scoring from Suits Me at Newbury the previous week but had a 6lb penalty. She came from off the pace as usual and stayed on steadily, indicating that she will still be competitive off her new mark.

Pipette had struggled in two starts since returning from a year off in May but had the first-time tongue tie on for this handicap debut off 94. She stayed on well in the straight and might be on the way back. (tchd 9-1)

Troopingthecolour, a progressive type who had won his last four starts on the Flat on Polytrack and easy ground, had been raised just 1lb for his last success and showed up most of the way until finding no extra in the straight. (op 12-1)

Sam Sharp(USA) returned from over a year off to win at Haydock in May but possibly bounced next time and had been given a break since. Racing off 7lb above his last winning mark, he was noted staying on well from the back in the straight. (tchd 20-1 in a place)

Dhaamer(IRE), a useful sort at this trip on a sound surface, was well beaten on his only try on soft, admittedly over 1m4f, but was another who lacked an extra gear in the straight. (op 6-1)

The Fonz, a useful sort last summer, winning twice at around 1m4f, was dropping in trip but was unable to get competitive, having been held up. (op 7-1)

Point North(IRE) had progressed nicely over the winter and spring before finishing down the field in the Royal Hunt Cup. He was very keen early and then was done no favours by Pipette, before being eased right down in the straight. The rider reported the gelding stopped quickly. Official explanation: jockey said gelding stopped quickly (tchd 11-2 in a place)

4268 JOHN GUEST H'CAP 1m (S)
5:05 (5:07) (Class 4) (0-85,83) 3-Y-0+ **£5,175** (£1,540; £769; £384) **Stalls** Centre

Form RPR

3632 **1** **First Post (IRE)**[22] 3542 4-9-6 **80**.................................... HarryBentley(5) 1 88+
(Derek Haydn Jones) *hld up wl in tch: hdwy to trck ldr gng wl ent fnl 2f: led over 1f out: rdn to assert and hung lft ins fnl f: hld on u.p fnl 50yds* **5/2**[1]

6465 **2** *1/2* **Fantasy Gladiator**[14] 3797 5-9-7 **79**.....................(p) AdamBeschizza(3) 9 85
(Robert Cowell) *hld up in tch in rr: rdn and hdwy but edging rt 2f out: drvn to chse wnr and edgd lft ins fnl f: no ex fnl 50yds* **4/1**[2]

-450 **3** *1* **Mr Hichens**[16] 3740 6-10-0 **83**.. JimmyFortune 5 87
(Karen George) *hld up wl in tch in rr: hdwy over 2f out: rdn to chse ldrs over 1f out: drvn and kpt on same pce fnl 100yds* **14/1**

3022 **4** *1/2* **Cono Zur (FR)**[7] 4070 4-9-6 **75**....................................(b) JamesSullivan 2 78
(Ruth Carr) *led: rdn ent fnl 2f: drvn and hdd over 1f out: carried lft and styd on same pce ins fnl f* **7/1**

3130 **5** *1* **Diplomasi**[44] 2819 3-8-5 **68**.. SilvestreDeSousa 7 66
(Clive Brittain) *dwlt and short of room s: in tch: rdn and effrt 2f out: styng on same pce whn sltly hmpd and swtchd rt ins fnl f: no imp after* **13/2**

1020 **6** *5* **Qenaa**[14] 3815 3-8-13 **76**.. KierenFallon 6 63
(Mark Johnston) *chsd ldrs: wnt 2nd over 3f out: sn rdn: lost 2nd and unable qck u.p ent fnl 2f: wknd over 1f out* **9/2**[3]

5000 **7** *10* **Beauchamp Yorker**[9] 3987 4-9-3 **79**...........................(t) DavidKenny(7) 8 45
(Hans Adielsson) *wnt lft s: hld up in tch: rdn and lost pl 3f out: lost tch 2f out* **33/1**

12-0 **8** *1 3/4* **Seneschal**[15] 3784 10-9-4 **78**.. JamesRogers(5) 3 40
(Adrian Chamberlain) *chsd ldr tl over 3f out: rdn over 2f out: wknd qckly 2f out: wl bhd fnl f* **33/1**

001 **9** *9* **Islesman**[23] 3521 3-9-4 **81**.. ShaneKelly 4 20
(Heather Main) *in tch: rdn and struggling over 2f out: wknd 2f out and wl btn whn hung rt over 1f out: eased ins fnl f* **10/1**

1m 43.19s (2.59) **Going Correction** +0.45s/f (Yiel)
WFA 3 from 4yo+ 8lb **9** Ran SP% **114.2**
Speed ratings (Par 105): **105,104,103,103,102 97,87,85,76**
Tote Swingers: 1&2 £2.50, 1&3 £6.00, 2&3 £10.60 CSF £12.20 CT £111.30 TOTE £3.10: £1.10, £1.60, £3.50; EX 12.30 Trifecta £141.80 Pool: £1,646.70 - 8.59 winning units..

Owner Llewelyn, Runeckles **Bred** D Llewelyn & J Runeckles **Trained** Efail Isaf, Rhondda C Taff

FOCUS
A fair, competitive handicap that seemed to be run at a sound gallop, though the time was ordinary. The winner is rated slightly better than the bare form.

Islesman Official explanation: jockey said gelding hung right-handed and stopped quickly

T/Plt: £24.70 to a £1 stake. Pool:£95,985.86 - 2,831.02 winning tickets T/Qpdt: £8.90 to a £1 stake. Pool:£6,659.64 - 55.60 winning tickets SP

3799 CHEPSTOW (L-H)
Friday, July 22

OFFICIAL GOING: Good to soft (good in places) changing to soft after race 2 (6.50pm)
Wind: Virtually nil Weather: Raining first four races, overcast

4269 CHAIRMAN'S RESERVE FINE RUM MAIDEN AUCTION STKS 6f 16y
6:20 (6:21) (Class 5) 2-Y-0 **£2,522** (£750; £375; £187) **Stalls** Centre

Form RPR

02 **1** **The Blue Banana (IRE)**[15] 3755 2-8-11 0.................. EddieCreighton 2 76+
(Brian Meehan) *trckd ldrs: wnt 2nd 1/2-way: drvn to ld appr fnl f: styd on wl: comf* **8/11**[1]

2 *1 1/4* **Miss Purity Pinker (IRE)** 2-8-4 0.................................. CathyGannon 7 61
(David Evans) *chsd ldr to 1/2-way: styd disputing 2nd: ev ch appr fnl f: kpt on to retake 2nd again cl home but no ch w wnr* **10/1**[3]

02 **3** *nk* **King Of Wing (IRE)**[16] 3746 2-8-10 0 ow1............................ PatDobbs 5 66
(Richard Hannon) *in tch: rdn to chse ldrs 3f out: ev ch over 1f out: sn chsng wnr but no imp: one pce into 3rd cl home* **9/4**[2]

0 **4** *4* **Subtle Embrace (IRE)**[9] 3981 2-8-6 0................................ ChrisCatlin 4 49
(Harry Dunlop) *t.k.h: led: rdn and hdd appr fnl f: sn n.m.r and btn* **33/1**

5 *1 1/4* **The Noble Ord** 2-8-9 0.. LiamKeniry 6 48
(Sylvester Kirk) *s.i.s: in rr and green: pushed along 1/2-way: hdwy fnl f: gng on cl home but nvr a threat* **25/1**

6 *1/2* **Lady Heartbeat** 2-8-4 0... FrankieMcDonald 1 42
(Michael Blanshard) *v.s.a and v green: sn detached and rdn: styd on wl fnl f: gng on clsng stages but nvr a threat* **40/1**

7 *6* **Roman Senate (IRE)** 2-8-11 0................................. FergusSweeney 3 29
(Martin Bosley) *green and bhd: hdwy and in tch 1/2-way: wknd qckly 2f out* **16/1**

1m 13.87s (1.87) **Going Correction** +0.175s/f (Good) **7** Ran SP% **112.9**
Speed ratings (Par 94): **94,92,91,86,84 84,76**
Tote Swingers:1&2:£2.10, 2&3:£2.70, 1&3:£1.02 CSF £9.12 TOTE £1.90: £1.10, £3.20; EX 7.50.

Owner Lanesborough **Bred** Tally-Ho Stud **Trained** Manton, Wilts

FOCUS
The hot favourite had to work hard to get to the front but eventually scored with some authority in this maiden. Modest form.

NOTEBOOK
The Blue Banana(IRE) set a clear standard on his much improved 20-1 second of 15 behind a decent newcomer in a 6f Doncaster maiden on his second start. There were warning signs when he took a while to get to grips with the leader but he eventually grabbed the initiative before forging ahead to win with more in hand than the margin suggests. The form is hard to weigh up, but he has stacks of winners on his dam's side and is out of a mare who stayed 1m4f, so it is encouraging that he is showing speed at this early stage of his career. (op 5-6 tchd 10-11)

Miss Purity Pinker(IRE), a 10,000euros One Cool Cat half-sister to two fair 7f-1m winners, was always prominent and battled on gamely on a promising debut run. (op 9-1)

King Of Wing(IRE) left his debut form behind when second in a 6f Lingfield AW maiden auction and backed that up with a solid clear third behind the form pick switched back to turf. (tchd 2-1)

Subtle Embrace(IRE) dropped out when 16-1 last of nine on Lingfield AW debut, but she lasted a lot longer before fading late under a positive ride this time. (op 28-1)

The Noble Ord, an Indesatchel half-brother to useful prolific 6f-7f AW winner Benllech, looked inexperienced but showed a hint of promise staying on late on debut. (op 22-1)

4270 BRITISH STALLION STUDS SUPPORTING BRITISH RACING EBF FILLIES' H'CAP 7f 16y
6:50 (6:52) (Class 5) (0-70,64) 3-Y-0+ **£3,234** (£962; £481; £240) **Stalls** Centre

Form RPR

0534 **1** **Dancing Welcome**[6] 4086 5-9-2 **52**................................(b) LiamKeniry 9 59
(Milton Bradley) *pressed ldrs: str chal fr 2f out tl drvn to ld ins fnl f: drvn out* **7/1**

-654 **2** *1/2* **Delaware Dancer (IRE)**[13] 3869 4-9-9 **59**................(t) JamesMillman 14 65
(Jeremy Gask) *hld up in rr: gd hdwy fr 2f out: c towards stands' side and r.o wl fnl f to take 2nd clsng stages: nt rch wnr* **9/2**[1]

5602 **3** *hd* **Chinese Democracy (USA)**[6] 1000 [illegible]...............(v) CathyGannon 3 58
(David Evans) *plld hrd in rr early: hdwy to chse ldrs 1/2-way: led jst ins fnl 2f: sn hrd rdn: hdd ins fnl f: styd pressing wnr tl one pce and lost 2nd clsng stages* **6/1**[3]

3100 **4** *hd* **Kenswick**[10] 3944 4-9-6 **56**..(v) ChrisCatlin 12 61
(Pat Eddery) *in tch: hdwy fr 3f out: styd on u.p to press ldrs clsng stages: nt quite pce to get up* **16/1**

1-60 **5** *hd* **Folly Drove**[14] 3818 3-9-7 **64**.. LiamJones 7 65
(Jonathan Portman) *chsd ldrs: rdn and ev ch fr 2f out: nt qckn u.p ins fnl f* **9/1**

3-00 **6** *1 1/2* **Elegant Muse**[18] 3688 3-9-4 **64**...................................... JohnFahy(3) 1 61
(Walter Swinburn) *led: rdn 3f out: hdd jst ins fnl 2f: styd wl there tl wknd ins fnl f* **12/1**

200 **7** *hd* **Cwmni**[23] 3512 5-9-7 **57**.. NeilChalmers 5 56
(Bryn Palling) *in rr: rdn and hdwy over 2f out: styd on fnl f: nvr gng pce to rch ldrs* **7/1**

63-0 **8** *4 1/2* **Croeso Mawr**[73] 1989 5-9-2 **52**.................................... TomMcLaughlin 10 39
(John Spearing) *slowly away: in rr: hdwy and in tch 1/2-way: lost pl 3f out: no ch after but kpt on again ins fnl f* **14/1**

-346 **9** *1* **Scorn (USA)**[20] 3636 4-9-13 **63**... PatDobbs 2 48
(Richard Hannon) *chsd ldrs: rdn 2f out: sn btn* **10/1**

410 **10** *shd* **Gracie's Games**[17] 3711 5-9-5 **60**................................ RyanPowell(5) 13 44
(Richard Price) *racd alone stands' side: struggling to go pce and rdn 3f out: no ch fnl 2f* **5/1**[2]

505- **11** *1/2* **Mystica (IRE)**[277] 6986 3-8-13 **56**.............................(p) FergusSweeney 6 36
(Dominic Ffrench Davis) *chsd ldrs over 4f* **25/1**

2040 **12** *3/4* **Bussell Along (IRE)**[20] 3637 5-8-2 **45**...................... RachealKneller(7) 4 26
(Pam Ford) *s.i.s: rcvrd and in tch 4f out: btn ins fnl 3f* **25/1**

3-00 **13** *nk* **Iztaccihuatl**[36] 3090 3-8-10 **53**.................................... JamieGoldstein 11 30
(Michael Scudamore) *pressed ldrs over 4f* **50/1**

1m 26.52s (3.32) **Going Correction** +0.375s/f (Good)
WFA 3 from 4yo+ 7lb **13** Ran SP% **123.1**
Speed ratings (Par 100): **96,95,95,94,94 93,92,87,86,86 85,84,84**
Tote Swingers:1&2:£5.70, 2&3:£4.60, 1&3:£6.00 CSF £39.04 CT £213.90 TOTE £7.40: £2.70, £1.70, £2.90; EX 37.90.

Owner J M Bradley **Bred** The Hon Mrs E J Wills **Trained** Sedbury, Gloucs

FOCUS
An ordinary fillies' handicap in which most of the field raced up the centre of the track. The first seven finished in a bunch but were clear of the rest. The winner is rated to her turf best.

4271 GILES INSURANCE BROKERS BRISTOL H'CAP 7f 16y
7:20 (7:21) (Class 5) (0-75,72) 3-Y-0 £2,522 (£750; £375; £187) Stalls Centre

Form RPR
0430 1 **Abacist (IRE)**[23] 3512 3-8-9 **60** MartinLane 6 63
(Ralph Beckett) *led: rdn and hdd wl over 1f out: rallied u.p to chal fnl f: slt ld again fnl 100yds: all out* **10/1**[3]
3562 2 *shd* **Arctic Mirage**[15] 3783 3-9-1 **66** LiamKeniry 9 69
(Michael Blanshard) *pressed ldr: chal over 2f out: slt ld wl over 1f out: hrd pressed fnl f: hdd fnl 100yds: carried rt and styd chalng: jst failed* **4/1**[2]
042 3 *hd* **Lady Bayside**[23] 3513 3-9-3 **68** CathyGannon 7 72+
(Malcolm Saunders) *t.k.h: in rr: stl plenty to do whn swtchd rt to r on stands' rail over 1f out: rapid hdwy clsng stages: fin fast: nt quite get up* **4/1**[2]
51-5 4 *hd* **Birdolini**[14] 3818 3-9-7 **72** FergusSweeney 4 74
(Alan King) *in rr but in tch: hdwy 1/2-way: drvn to press ldrs fr over 1f out: ev ch thrght fnl f: nt qckn clsng stages* **4/1**[2]
4060 5 2 ¾ **Diamond Vine (IRE)**[13] 3869 3-9-4 **69** TomMcLaughlin 11 64
(Ronald Harris) *hld up in tch: chsd ldrs fr over 2f out: one pce u.p fnl f* **12/1**
-342 6 *shd* **Red Marling (IRE)**[20] 3633 3-9-4 **69** PatDobbs 3 64
(B W Hills) *trckd ldrs: pushed along over 2f out: nt qckn and styd on same pce* **5/2**[1]
0000 7 *nk* **Rowan Spirit (IRE)**[14] 3806 3-8-13 **64** ChrisCatlin 8 58
(Mark Brisbourne) *t.k.h: chsd ldrs: rdn over 2f out: no imp: styd on same pce* **10/1**[3]
4-30 8 3 ¼ **Monadreen Dancer**[37] 3058 3-8-10 **64**.........(t) AdamBeschizza(3) 5 49
(Daniel Mark Loughnane, Ire) *s.i.s: t.k.h in rr: rdn 3f out: sn btn* **25/1**

1m 25.88s (2.68) **Going Correction** +0.375s/f (Good) 8 Ran SP% **118.3**
Speed ratings (Par 100): **99,98,98,98,95 95,94,91**
Tote Swingers:1&2:£4.40, 2&3:£4.10, 1&3:£15.70 CSF £51.49 CT £191.31 TOTE £12.50: £2.50, £1.40, £1.90; EX 72.00.
Owner R Roberts **Bred** James Coen **Trained** Kimpton, Hants
■ Stewards' Enquiry : Martin Lane caution: careless riding.

FOCUS
After 3mm of rain in the last hour, the going was changed to soft. A minor handicap. It was run at a steady pace and the first four pulled clear for a close finish. The runner-up set the standard.

4272 GAYNOR & ROB JONES WEDDING CELEBRATION H'CAP 5f 16y
7:50 (7:50) (Class 5) (0-70,72) 3-Y-0+ £2,522 (£750; £375; £187) Stalls Centre

Form RPR
0U20 1 **Pinball (IRE)**[8] 3999 5-8-7 **51** oh1........................(p) MartinLane 10 59
(Lisa Williamson) *sn drvn along and bhd at 1/2-way: hrd drvn and styd on fr over 1f out: r.o strly clsng stages to ld last stride* **16/1**
0006 2 *nse* **Colourbearer (IRE)**[32] 3216 4-8-8 **52**..................(t) CathyGannon 7 60
(Milton Bradley) *chsd ldrs: styd on strly to chal fnl f: slt ld fnl 120yds: sn hrd pressed: hdd last stride* **8/1**
320 3 ½ **Dancing Freddy (IRE)**[17] 3711 4-9-4 **65**...........(tp) RobertLButler(3) 4 71
(Richard Guest) *chsd ldrs: led 1/2-way: rdn 2f out: hdd fnl 120yds: styd on one pce* **6/1**
6001 4 2 ¾ **Triple Dream**[8] 3994 6-10-0 **72** 6ex....................(tp) LiamKeniry 3 68
(Milton Bradley) *chsd ldrs: rdn 1/2-way: styd on same pce fnl f* **9/2**[2]
00-1 5 *hd* **Just For Mary**[11] 3908 7-9-1 **62** 6ex...............(be) AdamBeschizza(3) 6 57
(Daniel Mark Loughnane, Ire) *v.s.a and a struggling in rr: styd on u.p fnl f but nt rcvr* **3/1**[1]
0-05 6 2 ¾ **Aalsmeer**[32] 3216 4-8-9 **56** KierenFox(3) 8 41
(Karen George) *slt ld 1f: styd chsng ldrs tl wknd over 1f out* **10/1**
0000 7 ¾ **Best One**[10] 3939 7-8-7 **51** oh1........................(b) KirstyMilczarek 9 34
(Ronald Harris) *chsd ldrs: rdn 1/2-way: btn fnl 2f* **20/1**
0434 8 ½ **Make My Dream**[15] 3768 8-9-10 **68** ChrisCatlin 1 49
(John Gallagher) *in rr: sme hdwy over 1f out: nvr in contention* **15/2**
160- 9 3 ½ **Blessed Place**[354] 4659 11-8-7 **54** JohnFahy(3) 5 22
(Dominic Ffrench Davis) *chsd ldrs 3f* **25/1**
5400 10 4 **Amhran (IRE)**[15] 3756 3-9-8 **70**.......................(b) EddieCreighton 2 24
(Brian Meehan) *s.i.s: rcvrd to ld after 1f: hdd 1/2-way: wknd 2f out* **11/2**[3]

60.75 secs (1.45) **Going Correction** +0.375s/f (Good)
WFA 3 from 4yo+ 4lb 10 Ran SP% **119.3**
Speed ratings (Par 103): **103,102,102,97,97 93,91,91,85,79**
Tote Swingers:1&2:£13.20, 2&3:£20.60, 1&3:£7.30 CSF £140.99 CT £890.24 TOTE £20.20: £5.30, £2.70, £1.70; EX 139.60.
Owner D Manning, D Roycroft, P Kelly **Bred** John Morris **Trained** Saighton, Cheshire
■ Stewards' Enquiry : Cathy Gannon one-day ban: used whip with excessive frequency (Aug 5)

FOCUS
It was fast and furious in the testing conditions in this modest 5f handicap. Straightforward form.
Amhran(IRE) Official explanation: vet said colt finished lame

4273 CWMTILLERY GLASS CENTRE GWENT H'CAP 1m 4f 23y
8:20 (8:22) (Class 6) (0-65,65) 3-Y-0+ £1,811 (£539; £269; £134) Stalls Low

Form RPR
0-03 1 **Korngold**[35] 3118 3-9-0 **63** ChrisCatlin 2 72+
(John Dunlop) *trckd ldrs: led ins fnl 2f: styd on wl fnl f* **11/8**[1]
3006 2 2 ¼ **Crazy Bold (GER)**[21] 3600 8-8-9 **46** oh1 LiamJones 5 51
(Tony Carroll) *in tch: hdwy 4f out: styd on u.p fnl 2f: kpt on to take 2nd last strides but no imp on wnr* **25/1**
0/0- 3 *nk* **Sweet World**[33] 6518 7-9-5 **56** MartinLane 13 61
(Bernard Llewellyn) *in rr: rdn and hdwy on outer over 3f out: styd on wl fnl f to take 3rd last strides but nvr any ch w wnr* **25/1**
6-56 4 *shd* **James Pollard (IRE)**[36] 1750 6-9-10 **61**...............(t) CathyGannon 7 66
(Bernard Llewellyn) *towards rr: hdwy 4f out: styd on u.p to chse wnr fnl 120yds: no imp and dropped 2 pls last strides* **10/1**
06-2 5 ¾ **Cuckoo Rock (IRE)**[23] 3515 4-9-8 **62** JohnFahy(3) 3 66
(Jonathan Portman) *chsd ldr: led appr fnl 3f: hdd ins fnl 2f: lost 2nd fnl 120yds: one pce* **13/2**[3]
6 6 **Yourinthewill (USA)**[16] 3752 3-8-8 **60** AdamBeschizza(3) 6 54
(Daniel Mark Loughnane, Ire) *chsd ldrs: rdn over 3f out: no imp fnl 2f and sn btn* **25/1**
6430 7 1 ¾ **Shy**[39] 2991 6-9-7 **58** JamesMillman 8 49
(Rod Millman) *in tch: drvn and sme hdwy over 4f out: one pce fnl 3f* **4/1**[2]
-642 8 3 ½ **Captain Sharpe**[32] 3214 3-9-2 **65**........................(p) TomMcLaughlin 4 51
(Bernard Llewellyn) *led: sn 10 l clr: hdd appr fnl 3f: sn btn* **11/1**
5P-0 9 7 **Spring Stock**[39] 3003 4-9-3 **54** FergusSweeney 11 28
(Brendan Powell) *s.i.s: in rr: sme prog 4f out: nvr rchd ldrs: no ch fnl 3f* **25/1**
56/0 10 ½ **Katies Tuitor**[14] 3817 8-10-0 **65**..........................(tp) LiamKeniry 12 39
(J S Moore) *in rr: sme hdwy 6f out: wknd over 4f out* **12/1**
00-2 11 1 **Rosenblatt (GER)**[67] 173 9-8-10 **50** KierenFox(3) 10 22
(John Spearing) *a in rr* **16/1**

2m 41.34s (2.34) **Going Correction** +0.225s/f (Good)
WFA 3 from 4yo+ 12lb 11 Ran SP% **121.8**
Speed ratings (Par 101): **101,99,99,99,98 94,93,91,86,86 85**
Tote Swingers:1&2:£28.90, 2&3:£48.80, 1&3:£7.20 CSF £50.94 CT £604.08 TOTE £2.30: £1.10, £8.30, £5.40; EX 54.20.
Owner Benny Andersson **Bred** Highclere Stud **Trained** Arundel, W Sussex

FOCUS
A low-grade middle-distance handicap but it was run at a strong pace and won in good style by an unexposed improver. The bare form is only modest.

4274 DWJ METALS LTD H'CAP 2m 49y
8:55 (8:58) (Class 6) (0-60,59) 3-Y-0+ £1,811 (£539; £269; £134) Stalls Low

Form RPR
1003 1 **Blazing Buck**[24] 3492 5-9-7 **52** LiamJones 11 58
(Tony Carroll) *mde virtually all: rdn fr 4f out and kpt slt advantage whn strly chal fnl 3f: hld on wl u.p fnl f: all out* **17/2**
-006 2 ¾ **Princesse Fleur**[21] 3587 3-8-6 **54** JamieGoldstein 6 59
(Michael Scudamore) *chsd ldrs tl rdn and outpcd over 2f out: styd on wl fnl f and fin strly to take 2nd last strides: nt rch wnr* **11/1**
00-3 3 *shd* **Captain Oats (IRE)**[23] 3516 8-8-11 **49** RachealKneller(7) 4 54
(Pam Ford) *in rr tl hdwy to chse ldrs 10f out: str chal fr over 3f out tl ins fnl f: no ex and lost 2nd last strides* **14/1**
504 4 *nse* **Band Of Thunder**[32] 3214 3-8-6 **54**..........................(v[1]) LiamKeniry 9 59
(Andrew Balding) *chsd ldrs: rdn and one pce over 2f out: rallied and styd on fr over 1f out: styd on wl clsng stages to press for cl 3rd: nt rch wnr* **3/1**[1]
35-0 5 1 **Uncle Keef (IRE)**[28] 3352 5-9-3 **55** BrendanPowell(7) 1 59
(Brendan Powell) *in rr: hdwy on outside over 2f out: pushed along and styd on fnl f: nt quite rch ldrs* **16/1**
5440 6 4 ½ **Miles Of Sunshine**[11] 3923 6-9-6 **54** SimonPearce(3) 7 52
(Ron Hodges) *t.k.h: chsd ldrs: rdn over 2f out: outpcd fr over 1f out* **9/1**
05-2 7 2 **Picot De Say**[14] 3799 9-9-9 **54** MartinLane 10 50
(Bernard Llewellyn) *hld up towards rr: hdwy to get in bhd ldrs 3f out: rdn and no imp over 2f out* **7/2**[2]
3440 8 1 **Court Princess**[30] 3281 8-9-0 **48** AdamBeschizza(3) 5 43
(Richard Price) *mid-div: rdn and sme hdwy 3f out: nvr rchd ldrs and wknd 2f out* **12/1**
0-00 9 *shd* **Pergamon (IRE)**[21] 3600 5-9-5 **50** RussKennemore 3 45
(Claire Dyson) *chsd ldrs: rdn and btn 3f out* **33/1**
4/00 10 1 ¾ **Rock Peak (IRE)**[14] 3799 6-9-5 **50**......................(b) TomMcLaughlin 2 42
(Bernard Llewellyn) *in rr: rdn and sme hdwy on outside 3f out: nvr rchd ldrs and wknd 2f out* **25/1**
0500 11 10 **Laffraaj (IRE)**[11] 3922 3-8-4 **52** ow1..........................(p) ChrisCatlin 13 32
(Pat Eddery) *chsd ldr to 4f out: sn btn* **10/1**
5-40 12 ½ **Summer Affair (IRE)**[11] 3923 6-9-3 **51** JohnFahy(3) 12 31
(Ben Case) *mid-div: rdn and sme prog over 3f out: sn wknd* **8/1**[3]

3m 50.88s (11.98) **Going Correction** +0.225s/f (Good)
WFA 3 from 5yo+ 17lb 12 Ran SP% **123.3**
Speed ratings (Par 101): **79,78,78,78,78 75,74,74,74,73 68,68**
Tote Swingers:1&2:£28.90, 2&3:£30.40, 1&3:£12.60 CSF £102.64 CT £1316.30 TOTE £9.70: £3.00, £2.40, £5.30; EX 145.50.
Owner Mill House Racing Syndicate **Bred** Charlock Stud **Trained** Cropthorne, Worcs
■ Stewards' Enquiry : Liam Keniry one-day ban: used whip with excessive frequency (Aug 5)

FOCUS
A weak staying handicap, won in gritty style by a front-runner who set a modest pace. He probably didn't need to improve on his Ayr win in May.
Miles Of Sunshine Official explanation: jockey said gelding ran too free
T/Plt: £451.00 to a £1 stake. Pool £60,175.33 - 97.38 winning units. T/Qpdt: £144.70 to a £1 stake. Pool £4,656.85 - 23.80 winning units. ST

4098 NEWMARKET (R-H)
Friday, July 22

OFFICIAL GOING: Good
Wind: Light half-behind Weather: Cloudy with sunny spells

4275 NEWMARKETRACECOURSES.CO.UK FILLIES' H'CAP 1m 2f
5:40 (5:41) (Class 5) (0-70,70) 3-Y-0+ £2,587 (£770; £384; £192) Stalls Centre

Form RPR
3133 1 **Broughtons Paradis (IRE)**[25] 3467 5-9-9 **65** StevieDonohoe 5 77
(Willie Musson) *hld up: hdwy 2f out: led 1f out: rdn out* **11/1**
1212 2 *hd* **Epernay**[2] 4215 4-9-10 **66**................................(tp) TomQueally 2 78
(Ian Williams) *hld up: hdwy over 2f out: led appr fnl f: hdd 1f out: sn rdn and hung lft: r.o* **15/8**[1]
-365 3 3 ½ **Sixty Roses (IRE)**[39] 3002 3-8-11 **63**...........................(b[1]) NeilCallan 8 68
(John Dunlop) *hld up: hdwy and nt clr run over 1f out: r.o: nvr able to chal* **9/1**
-026 4 2 ¾ **Ride The Wind**[18] 3688 3-8-9 **61** JackMitchell 10 61+
(Chris Wall) *hld up: swtchd lft and hdwy over 1f out: r.o: nt trble ldrs* **16/1**
5004 5 1 ¾ **The Blue Dog (IRE)**[26] 3426 4-9-4 **60** WilliamCarson 7 56
(Michael Wigham) *prom: rdn over 1f out: wknd ins fnl f* **25/1**
0-02 6 1 **Sweet Secret**[15] 3771 4-9-13 **69** GeorgeBaker 13 63
(Jeremy Gask) *chsd ldrs: led over 7f out: rdn and hdd over 1f out: wknd ins fnl f* **25/1**
5513 7 ¾ **Entrance**[25] 3456 3-8-9 **61** HayleyTurner 12 54
(Julia Feilden) *hld up: hdwy over 3f out: rdn and edgd rt over 1f out: wknd ins fnl f* **8/1**[3]
0-03 8 3 ¾ **Formidable Guest**[7] 4060 7-8-13 **55** RobertHavlin 4 40
(Jamie Poulton) *half-rrd s: hld up: rdn over 2f out: wknd over 1f out* **16/1**
0602 9 *nk* **Burza**[22] 3545 5-9-5 **61** AdamKirby 9 45
(John Mackie) *chsd ldrs: rdn over 2f out: wknd over 1f out* **6/1**[2]
0443 10 1 ¼ **Spade**[9] 3979 3-8-12 **64**......................................(b) NickyMackay 3 46
(David Elsworth) *dwlt: hld up: rdn and wknd 2f out* **12/1**
4521 11 3 ½ **Full Bloom**[15] 3771 3-9-4 **70**................................(p) DaneO'Neill 11 45
(Gerard Butler) *chsd ldrs: rdn over 2f out: edgd rt and wknd over 1f out* **12/1**
-362 12 2 ¾ **Chantilly Dancer (IRE)**[20] 3637 5-8-9 **51** oh6............. AndreaAtzeni 14 20
(Michael Quinn) *s.i.s: hld up: rdn over 2f out: sn wknd* **40/1**

-033 **13** *2 ½* **Sanctum**[31] 3252 5-8-9 **51** oh6 ....(b) AdrianMcCarthy 1 15
(Dr Jon Scargill) *sn rdn to ld: hdd over 7f out: chsd ldrs tl rdn over 2f out: sn wknd* **50/1**

2m 7.29s (1.79) **Going Correction** +0.10s/f (Good)
WFA 3 from 4yo+ 10lb **13** Ran SP% **117.8**
Speed ratings (Par 100): **96,95,93,90,89 88,88,85,84,83 81,78,76**
Tote Swingers:1&2:£6.40, 2&3:£4.20, 1&3:£22.40 CSF £30.32 CT £203.07 TOTE £14.60: £4.00, £1.10, £3.60; EX 45.00.
Owner Broughton Thermal Insulation **Bred** Mount Coote Stud **Trained** Newmarket, Suffolk

FOCUS
Far-side track used with stalls on far side except 1m2f and 1m4f, centre. A modest contest and ordinary fillies form. A personal best from the winner, who was runner-up in this last year.
Burza Official explanation: jockey said mare stopped quickly
Chantilly Dancer(IRE) Official explanation: jockey said mare never travelled
Sanctum Official explanation: jockey said mare stopped quickly

4276 NEWMARKET NIGHTS MEDIAN AUCTION MAIDEN STKS 6f
6:10 (6:11) (Class 5) 2-Y-O **£3,234** (£962; £481; £240) **Stalls** Low

Form RPR
0 **1** **Gung Ho Jack**[22] 3567 2-9-3 0 .... AdamKirby 11 76
(John Best) *a.p: rdn over 1f out: led ins fnl f: drvn out* **16/1**
2 *hd* **Signor Sassi** 2-9-3 0 .... NeilCallan 2 76+
(Roger Varian) *hld up in tch: swtchd rt over 2f out: rdn over 1f out: r.o* **7/4**[1]
3 *hd* **Ruby Night (IRE)** 2-9-3 0 .... JamieSpencer 1 75+
(Michael Bell) *trckd ldrs: led over 1f out: hdd ins fnl f: r.o* **8/1**
4 *shd* **Thewinningmachine** 2-8-12 0 .... PatrickMathers 12 70+
(Richard Fahey) *mid-div: pushed along 1/2-way: hdwy over 2f out: swtchd lft over 1f out: sn rdn: r.o* **33/1**
5 *3* **Red Quartet (IRE)** 2-9-3 0 .... AndreaAtzeni 7 65
(Robert Eddery) *chsd ldrs: rdn and ev ch over 1f out: no ex ins fnl f* **66/1**
3 **6** *1 ½* **Eightfold**[13] 3870 2-9-3 0 .... RichardHughes 10 60
(Richard Hannon) *led over 4f: no ex ins fnl f* **11/4**[2]
00 **7** *½* **Angel Cake (IRE)**[13] 3865 2-8-12 0 .... HayleyTurner 4 54
(Amy Weaver) *hld up: shkn up over 1f out: nt clr run jst ins fnl f: r.o: nvr nr to chal* **66/1**
8 *1 ½* **Valiant Runner** 2-8-12 0 .... RyanMoore 13 49+
(Jeremy Noseda) *mid-div: pushed along 1/2-way: hung rt over 1f out: r.o ins fnl f: n.d* **12/1**
9 *nse* **Swing It** 2-9-3 0 .... DaneO'Neill 5 54+
(Richard Hannon) *dwlt: sn drvn along in rr: hung lft over 1f out: r.o ins fnl f: nvr nrr* **20/1**
0 **10** *¾* **Hawkino (IRE)**[14] 3823 2-9-3 0 .... RobbieFitzpatrick 8 51
(Derek Shaw) *mid-div: lost pl 1/2-way: sn bhd* **100/1**
6 **11** *1 ¾* **Rock Of Monet**[14] 3793 2-9-3 0 .... TomQueally 9 46
(David Simcock) *prom: rdn and ev ch over 1f out: hung lft and wknd ins fnl f* **9/2**[3]
66 **12** *5* **Selbaar**[22] 3552 2-9-3 0 .... SebSanders 14 30
(Chris Dwyer) *racd alone towards centre: prom tl edgd rt and wknd over 1f out* **100/1**
13 *4* **Ashkan** 2-9-3 0 .... GeorgeBaker 3 17
(William Haggas) *hld up: bhd fr 1/2-way* **25/1**

1m 13.9s (1.40) **Going Correction** +0.10s/f (Good) **13** Ran SP% **122.4**
Speed ratings (Par 94): **94,93,93,93,89 87,86,84,84,83 81,74,69**
Tote Swingers:1&2:£5.90, 2&3:£4.50, 1&3:£21.10 CSF £43.99 TOTE £22.70: £4.40, £1.60, £2.20; EX 81.70.
Owner John Fletcher **Bred** D R Tucker **Trained** Hucking, Kent

FOCUS
A neck covered the first four home, indicating this might prove to be among the weaker juvenile maidens staged at the track this summer. The form is rated around the race averages.

NOTEBOOK
Gung Ho Jack must have shown plenty of promise at home as he was relatively highly tried first time up, contesting a 5f Listed contest in France. He finished last on that occasion, but the experience clearly wasn't wasted on him. Stepped up to 6f, he got off the mark in gutsy style, revealing a real will to win when it came to a scrap with three others late on. (tchd 14-1)
Signor Sassi cost 140,000gns as a yearling and is a half-brother to three 2yo winners, including [illegible] The dam is a half sister to Gimcrack winner River Falls. Like his family members, he clearly possesses a fair amount of [illegible] and shouldn't have a problem breaking his maiden in the near future, granted some improvement from his debut for which he was well supported. (op 15-8 tchd 2-1 in places)
Ruby Night(IRE), a £34,000 breeze-up buy, has also been showing up well in his home work. He, too, is related to plenty of winners over sprint trips. This was an encouraging debut display and compensation for a narrow defeat surely awaits. (op 13-2)
Thewinningmachine is half-sister to the smart Italian filly March Madness, who made her mark over 7.5f and upwards. That makes this performance at 6f all the more promising as the likelihood is that the step up to 7f will suit her. Indeed, if the split had come for her, rather than having to be switched left at the business end of the race, she may have already lost her maiden tag. (op 40-1 tchd 50-1)
Red Quartet(IRE) was bought in the spring for £6,000 and looks a comparative bargain at the price. He showed up well on his racecourse bow and can win a maiden, albeit perhaps not at a track such as Newmarket.
Eightfold made the frame on his debut at Salisbury two weeks ago when the jockey reported his mount was denied a clear run. Here there were no such excuses available and it was may be a touch disappointing that he was unable to build on that first run, but it is far too soon to be writing him off. (op 9-4 tchd 3-1 in places)
Angel Cake(IRE) didn't have the hardest of races and it would be no surprise if an opportunity was found for her now she is qualified for nurseries. (op 50-1)
Swing It, from the same family as smart 2-y-os Majestic Desert and Atlantis Prince, was green as grass early on but the penny dropped in the closing strides and he should progress for this. (op 16-1)

4277 HOME OF RACING NURSERY 7f
6:40 (6:42) (Class 4) 2-Y-O **£3,881** (£1,155; £577; £288) **Stalls** Low

Form RPR
000 **1** **Nifty Shiftin**[15] 3780 2-7-12 **58** oh7 ....(b[1]) NickyMackay 2 65
(David Elsworth) *chsd ldrs: led over 2f out: rdn out* **14/1**
460 **2** *1 ¾* **Karuga**[39] 2997 2-7-11 **62** .... KieranO'Neill(5) 4 64
(Richard Hannon) *a.p: racd keenly: ev ch over 2f out: rdn over 1f out: hung lft ins fnl f: styd on same pce* **7/1**[3]
043 **3** *½* **Roedean (IRE)**[37] 3046 2-9-1 **75** .... RichardHughes 6 76
(Richard Hannon) *chsd ldr: rdn and ev ch over 2f out: sn hung lft: styd on same pce ins fnl f* **5/2**[1]
030 **4** *shd* **Hi There (IRE)**[15] 3761 2-8-4 **64** .... MartinDwyer 7 65+
(J W Hills) *hld up in tch: plld hrd: shkn up over 1f out: r.o: nt rch ldrs* **9/2**[2]
563 **5** *½* **Darnathean**[43] 2844 2-8-6 **66** ....(b) LukeMorris 1 65+
(Paul D'Arcy) *hld up: plld hrd: rdn over 1f out: r.o ins fnl f: nvr nrr* **14/1**
014 **6** *¾* **Lady Victory (IRE)**[17] 3700 2-8-12 **72** .... SamHitchcott 9 69
(Mick Channon) *set stdy pce tl hdd over 2f out: sn rdn: no ex ins fnl f* **10/1**
000 **7** *1 ¾* **Peters Pursuit (IRE)**[29] 3314 2-8-1 **61** .... PatrickMathers 8 53
(Richard Fahey) *trckd ldrs: racd keenly: rdn over 2f out: sn outpcd* **10/1**
000 **8** *12* **Street Angel (IRE)**[25] 3472 2-7-9 **58** oh10 ....(p) AmyBaker(3) 10 18
(Alan Bailey) *s.i.s: sn mid-div: rdn over 2f out: sn wknd* **50/1**

1m 29.2s (3.50) **Going Correction** +0.10s/f (Good) **8** Ran SP% **92.7**
Speed ratings (Par 96): **84,82,81,81,80 79,77,64**
Tote Swingers:1&2:£17.90, 2&3:£2.30, 1&3:£6.60 CSF £68.29 CT £173.34 TOTE £12.80: £2.70, £2.10, £1.20; EX 94.20.
Owner J Wotherspoon **Bred** D R C Elsworth **Trained** Newmarket, Suffolk
■ Maastricht was withdrawn after breaking out of the stalls. Deduct 20p in the £ under R4.

FOCUS
There was just a steady early pace and this is muddling form. It has been taken at face value. The 'official' ratings shown next to each horse are estimated and for information purposes only.

NOTEBOOK
Nifty Shiftin took this in relative comfort from 7lb outside the handicap. After not showing a great deal in his first three runs, he was sharpened by the application of first-time blinkers and won going away. He ran on to suggest that he'll get further, too. It would be no surprise if he continued to improve and the likelihood is there are more wins to come from him. Official explanation: trainer said, regarding apparent improvement in form, that the gelding had benefited from the first-time blinkers. (tchd 12-1)
Karuga had not made a great impression in her first three outings as her initial mark indicated, but the step up to 7f proved much more to her liking and an opportunity can be found for her in a similar sort of race. (op 17-2)
Roedean(IRE) had one useful piece of form to her name coming into this - she was fourth in a hot maiden behind two subsequent Group winners, but she didn't appear to be the most straightforward of rides, edging left in the closing exchanges. If she can put her best foot forward, she looks to have enough ability to pick up a race. (op 100-30 tchd 7-2 in places)
Hi There(IRE) was another trying 7f for the first time and it proved to be within his range without him ever really threatening to win. (op 11-2)
Darnathean appeared to have quite a hard race here. (op 17-2)
Lady Victory(IRE) may need some help from the handicapper having now twice been beaten in handicaps. (op 7-1)

4278 CARRS MINI H'CAP 1m
7:10 (7:10) (Class 5) (0-75,75) 4-Y-O+ **£2,587** (£770; £384; £192) **Stalls** Low

Form RPR
0200 **1** **Swiftly Done (IRE)**[39] 2985 4-8-13 **67** ....(b) SebSanders 13 76
(Declan Carroll) *racd stands' side: hld up: nt clr run fr over 1f out tl weaved through ins fnl f and r.o to ld towards fin: comf* **22/1**
-245 **2** *1 ½* **Yanbu (USA)**[16] 3735 6-8-2 **56** oh7 .... AndreaAtzeni 4 62
(Tobias B P Coles) *racd stands' side: chsd ldr: rdn to ld overall over 1f out: hdd towards fin* **66/1**
2036 **3** *¾* **Exopuntia**[3] 4185 5-8-3 **57** ....(t) HayleyTurner 9 61
(Julia Feilden) *wnt rt s: racd centre: led that pair: rdn and edgd rt over 1f out: unable qck towards fin* **14/1**
0000 **4** *nse* **Skyfire**[23] 3514 4-9-3 **71** .... LukeMorris 6 75
(Ed de Giles) *s.i.s: hld up: hdwy over 3f out: rdn and swtchd lft over 1f out: styd on* **10/1**
6060 **5** *1* **Kavachi (IRE)**[24] 3477 8-8-13 **67** .... RyanMoore 3 69
(Gary Moore) *racd stands' side: hld up: swtchd lft and hdwy over 1f out: no ex nr fin* **20/1**
1-50 **6** *shd* **Oh So Saucy**[53] 2545 7-9-7 **75** .... GeorgeBaker 14 76
(Chris Wall) *racd centre: chsd ldr: rdn and hung rt over 1f out: sn ev ch: styd on same pce ins fnl f* **16/1**
1-14 **7** *1* **Two Certainties**[14] 3814 4-8-10 **64** .... NeilCallan 12 63
(Stuart Williams) *racd stands' side: hld up: rdn over 1f out: styd on ins fnl f: nvr nrr* **9/2**[2]
40-4 **8** *½* **Be A Devil**[16] 3740 4-9-4 **72** .... MartinDwyer 2 70
(William Muir) *racd stands' side: chsd ldrs: rdn over 1f out: no ex ins fnl f* **8/1**
-224 **9** *2 ½* **Mashatu**[44] 2822 4-9-4 **72** ....(v[1]) PatCosgrave 7 64
(James Fanshawe) *hmpd s: racd stands' side: hld up: hdwy over 3f out: rdn over 2f out: wknd fnl f* **7/1**[3]
6141 **10** *1 ½* **Bold Marc (IRE)**[7] 4051 9-8-13 **72** .... LMcNiff(5) 1 61
(Mrs K Burke) *led overall on stands' side tl hdd over 1f out: wknd ins fnl f* [illegible]
203 **11** *1 ½* **Aspectus (IRE)**[7] 4066 8-9-4 **75** ....(b) SophieDoyle(3) 15 60
(Jamie Osborne) *racd alone far side: up w the pce tl wknd over 1f out* **10/1**
0012 **12** *7* **Focail Eile**[4] 4143 6-8-9 **63** ....(b) StevieDonohoe 11 32
(John Ryan) *racd stands' side: hld up: rdn over 2f out: wknd over 1f out* **7/1**[3]
056/ **13** *16* **Doncosaque (IRE)**[760] 3220 5-9-0 **68** ....(t) TedDurcan 5 —
(P J O'Gorman) *racd stands' side: chsd ldrs over 5f: t.o* **50/1**

1m 40.14s (0.14) **Going Correction** +0.10s/f (Good) **13** Ran SP% **119.8**
Speed ratings (Par 103): **103,101,100,100,99 99,98,98,95,94 92,85,69**
Tote Swingers:1&2:£175.80, 2&3:£123.80, 1&3:£74.20 CSF £1015.98 CT £19633.52 TOTE £26.40: £7.10, £20.80, £5.30; EX 1512.40.
Owner D Watts, Miss C King, J Syme & M Syme **Bred** Joe Fogarty **Trained** Sledmere, E Yorks

FOCUS
The form of the race may prove a little suspect with the second 7lb wrong, but the winner is rated back to his 3yo best. The front-runners went too quick early with all bar one of them falling away tamely. The other unsatisfactory factor was that Aspectus raced alone on the far side, two went up the middle, while the main cluster were bunched towards the stands' rail. The fast early pace played into the hands of the closers.
Swiftly Done(IRE) Official explanation: trainer's rep said, regarding apparent improvement in form, that the gelding had benefited from a well executed hold-up ride.
Bold Marc(IRE) Official explanation: trainer said gelding was unsuited by the straight track
Focail Eile Official explanation: trainer said gelding was unsuited by the good ground

4279 NGK SPARK PLUGS MAIDEN STKS 1m 4f
7:40 (7:43) (Class 5) 3-Y-O **£3,234** (£962; £481; £240) **Stalls** Centre

Form RPR
2-32 **1** **Thimaar (USA)**[14] 3824 3-9-3 **95** .... RichardHills 10 87+
(John Gosden) *mde all: shkn up to go clr over 1f out: styd on wl* **8/15**[1]
2 *2* **Cops And Robbers** 3-9-3 0 .... RyanMoore 13 84+
(Sir Michael Stoute) *dwlt: hld up: hdwy 5f out: rdn over 3f out: r.o to go 2nd wl ins fnl f: no ch w wnr* **8/1**[3]
034 **3** *¾* **Dawn Gale (IRE)**[56] 2458 3-8-12 **72** .... SteveDrowne 1 78
(Hughie Morrison) *a.p: rdn to chse wnr over 1f out tl ins fnl f: styd on same pce* **40/1**
0- **4** *8* **Midnight Moon**[278] 6953 3-9-3 0 ....(v[1]) TedDurcan 2 70
(Saeed Bin Suroor) *chsd ldrs: rdn over 2f out: wknd over 1f out* **22/1**

05 **5** *nk* **Astrantia**[32] 3224 3-8-12 0 TomQueally 11 65
(Sir Henry Cecil) *prom: pushed along over 2f out: wknd over 1f out* **16/1**
6 **6** *1 ¼* **Epic Storm (IRE)**[23] 3519 3-9-3 0 (p) RichardHughes 16 68
(Jeremy Noseda) *hld up: plld hrd: rdn over 3f out: nvr trbld ldrs* **7/1**[2]
0-3 **7** *½* **Warneford**[69] 2104 3-9-3 0 MartinDwyer 14 67
(Brian Meehan) *chsd wnr: rdn over 2f out: wknd over 1f out* **22/1**
0 **8** *4* **Ulla**[56] 2458 3-8-12 0 JackMitchell 4 56
(Chris Wall) *prom: rdn over 2f out: wknd over 1f out* **125/1**
04 **9** *nse* **Suzi's A Class Act**[39] 3001 3-8-12 0 LukeMorris 9 55
(James Eustace) *prom: rdn over 3f out: wknd 2f out* **12/1**
10 *2* **Palazzo Bianco** 3-9-3 0 RobertHavlin 15 57+
(John Gosden) *hld up: rdn over 2f out: sn wknd* **33/1**
11 *5* **Minnie Mambo (USA)** 3-8-12 0 JamieSpencer 7 44
(Michael Bell) *s.s: sn pushed along and a in rr* **33/1**
12 *20* **Raynell** 3-9-3 0 AdamKirby 8 17
(Noel Quinlan) *s.i.s: hdwy over 5f out: wknd over 2f out: t.o* **100/1**
03- **13** *¾* **Hurricane Guest**[290] 6653 3-9-3 0 PhilipRobinson 6 16
(George Margarson) *hld up: a in rr: wknd over 2f out: t.o* **80/1**
0- **14** *15* **Flo Motion (IRE)**[285] 6770 3-8-12 0 SebSanders 12 —
(J W Hills) *hld up: a in rr: wknd over 2f out: t.o* **50/1**

2m 35.32s (2.42) **Going Correction** +0.10s/f (Good) **14** Ran SP% **124.4**
Speed ratings (Par 100): **95,93,93,87,87 86,86,83,83,82 79,65,65,55**
Tote Swingers:1&2:£2.50, 2&3:£32.70, 1&3:£8.60 CSF £4.98 TOTE £1.50: £1.10, £2.30, £6.50; EX 6.10.
Owner Hamdan Al Maktoum **Bred** Shadwell Farm LLC **Trained** Newmarket, Suffolk

FOCUS
An uncompetitive maiden. The winner set a high standard and did not need to match his best. The third could be the long-term key to this form.

4280 CLUTTERBUCKS RESTAURANT AT WHEATSHEAF EXNING H'CAP 1m 4f
8:10 (8:14) (Class 3) (0-90,89) 3-Y-0+ **£7,439** (£2,213; £829; £829) **Stalls** Centre

Form RPR
61 **1** **Ithoughtitwasover (IRE)**[30] 3267 3-8-11 **84** NeilCallan 1 91+
(Mark Johnston) *chsd ldrs: rdn to ld ins fnl f: hung rt: r.o* **6/1**[3]
135 **2** *½* **Mcbirney (USA)**[27] 3399 4-9-7 **82** RyanMoore 3 88
(Paul D'Arcy) *hld up: hdwy and nt clr run over 1f out: chsd wnr and hmpd ins fnl f: r.o* **4/1**[1]
0-40 **3** *1* **Rajeh (IRE)**[28] 3344 8-9-8 **83** WilliamCarson 9 87
(John Spearing) *chsd ldr: rdn over 1f out: styd on* **20/1**
-025 **3** *dht* **Regal Park (IRE)**[23] 3522 4-9-11 **86** AdamKirby 5 90+
(Marco Botti) *hld up: nt clr run over 1f out: rdn and r.o ins fnl f: nt rch ldrs* **15/2**
1325 **5** *½* **Granston (IRE)**[20] 3625 10-10-0 **89** PhilipRobinson 2 93
(James Bethell) *plld hrd and prom: shkn up over 1f out: styd on same pce wl ins fnl f* **12/1**
1220 **6** *1 ½* **Chain Of Events**[28] 3366 4-9-1 **76** HayleyTurner 6 77
(Neil King) *hld up: nt clr run over 1f out: r.o ins fnl f: nvr able to chal* **11/1**
2124 **7** *hd* **Hong Kong Island (IRE)**[13] 3867 4-9-8 **83** SebSanders 10 84
(Micky Hammond) *hld up: hdwy over 1f out: sn rdn: no ex ins fnl f* **5/1**[2]
1-32 **8** *hd* **Sense Of Pride**[15] 3758 4-9-8 **83** RobertHavlin 8 84
(John Gosden) *led: rdn over 1f out: hdd and no ex ins fnl f* **4/1**[1]
0141 **9** *6* **Eltheeb**[13] 3858 4-9-5 **80** LukeMorris 11 71
(George Moore) *mid-div: hdwy over 2f out: rdn over 1f out: sn wknd* **9/1**
-220 **10** *31* **Rasam Aldaar**[70] 2076 3-7-12 **71** oh1 AndreaAtzeni 4 —
(Michael Wigham) *chsd ldrs: rdn over 2f out: wknd over 1f out: t.o* **20/1**

2m 38.42s (5.52) **Going Correction** +0.10s/f (Good)
WFA 3 from 4yo+ 12lb **10** Ran SP% **118.3**
Speed ratings (Par 107): **85,84,84,84,83 82,82,82,78,57**
Tote Swingers::1&2:£5.90, 2&3(RP):£2.90, 1&3(RP):£7.40, 2&3(R):£17.60, 1&3(R):£26.10 CSF £30.72 TOTE £5.10: £2.10, £1.90; EX 40.40 TRIFECTA PL 1.40 (RP), 3.10 (R); Tricast: 90.70 (RP), 223.84 (R).
Owner Crone Stud Farms Ltd **Bred** Stonethorn Stud Farms Ltd **Trained** Middleham Moor, N Yorks

FOCUS
The steady early pace favoured those who raced to the fore. Muddling form, but potential big improvement to come from the winner.

NOTEBOOK
Ithoughtitwasover(IRE) was making his handicap bow off what, on the face of it, looked a tough enough introductory mark of 84. He exceeded market expectations when winning a Bath maiden last month but this showed he is making up into a very useful performer. As well as travelling through his race smoothly, he revealed a turn of foot and a game attitude. (tchd 11-2 and 13-2)
Mcbirney(USA) ran a fine race and looked to have been hampered late on as Ithoughtitwasover edged right in front of him. (op 11-2 tchd 6-1)
Rajeh(IRE) was probably suited by the way the race unfolded, but this was his best run of the season to date. (op 17-2 tchd 7-1)
Regal Park(IRE) has looked in the grip of the handicapper so far this season. Back in trip, he gave a creditable account of himself without threatening a return to the winner's enclosure, but he is just 3lb above his best winning mark and it wouldn't need much relenting from the assessor to see him winning something similar. (op 17-2 tchd 7-1)
Granston(IRE) has been in fine form this season and wasn't beaten far when fifth in the Old Newton Cup at the beginning of July. This was another respectable display, although his current mark of 89 is 3lb higher than he has ever won from. (op 11-1)
Sense Of Pride went up 6lb for a second-place effort at Doncaster two weeks earlier and, while still unexposed, couldn't be recommended on the strength of this effort. (tchd 9-2)
Rasam Aldaar Official explanation: jockey said gelding stopped quickly

4281 NEWMARKETEXPERIENCE.CO.UK H'CAP 1m
8:45 (8:46) (Class 5) (0-75,75) 3-Y-0 **£2,587** (£770; £384; £192) **Stalls** Low

Form RPR
3414 **1** **Al Burkaan (IRE)**[11] 3924 3-9-2 **70** JamieSpencer 3 83+
(Ed Dunlop) *hld up: swtchd lft and hdwy over 1f out: rdn to ld and hung rt ins fnl f: r.o wl* **7/1**
-413 **2** *2 ¼* **Uptown Guy (USA)**[13] 3871 3-9-3 **71** (b) RyanMoore 4 79+
(William Haggas) *hld up: swtchd lft and hdwy over 1f out: styd on* **10/3**[1]
0603 **3** *1 ¾* **Joe Strummer (IRE)**[20] 3643 3-8-9 **63** (v) HayleyTurner 14 67
(Michael Bell) *chsd ldrs: rdn to ld ins fnl f: sn hdd and unable qck* **14/1**
2021 **4** *2 ¾* **Snow Trooper**[31] 3259 3-9-2 **70** AdamKirby 13 68
(Dean Ivory) *prom: rdn over 2f out: no ex ins fnl f* **6/1**[3]
0-00 **5** *1 ½* **Point Du Jour (FR)**[25] 3468 3-9-0 **68** NeilCallan 2 62
(Ian Wood) *hld up in tch: effrt and nt clr run over 1f out: nt rcvr* **20/1**
-000 **6** *½* **Songsmith**[22] 3557 3-8-11 **65** (b[1]) StevieDonohoe 6 58
(Lucy Wadham) *trckd ldr tl led over 1f out: sn rdn: hdd and no ex ins fnl f* **12/1**
2050 **7** *1* **Rojo Boy**[43] 2841 3-9-1 **69** (b) NickyMackay 8 60
(David Elsworth) *prom: rdn over 2f out: wknd over 1f out* **22/1**
60-5 **8** *¾* **Greek Islands (IRE)**[21] 3594 3-9-6 **74** PatCosgrave 15 63
(Ed de Giles) *hld up: nt clr run fr over 2f out tl r.o ins fnl f: nvr trbld ldrs* **22/1**
44-0 **9** *3 ½* **Cornish Quest**[22] 3557 3-8-11 **65** TomQueally 10 46
(Mark H Tompkins) *hld up: sme hdwy over 2f out: sn rdn: wknd over 1f out* **20/1**
0550 **10** *2 ¼* **Khaleeji**[15] 3783 3-8-11 **65** (p) RichardHills 11 41
(J W Hills) *hld up: nvr on terms* **28/1**
5-46 **11** *1* **Mr Dream Maker (IRE)**[20] 3642 3-8-9 **63** SteveDrowne 9 37
(Ian Williams) *hld up: plld hrd: hdwy 3f out: wknd over 1f out* **12/1**
-110 **12** *3 ¾* **Iron Step**[49] 2675 3-9-7 **75** LukeMorris 7 40
(Nicky Vaughan) *led: rdn and hdd over 1f out: sn wknd* **12/1**
-051 **13** *1 ¾* **Patriotic (IRE)**[17] 3709 3-8-10 **64** AndreaAtzeni 1 25
(Chris Dwyer) *prom: rdn 3f out: wknd and eased over 1f out* **11/2**[2]
000- **14** *21* **Welsh Dancer**[288] 6690 3-8-8 **62** MartinDwyer 12 —
(Marcus Tregoning) *prom: lost pl over 4f out: wknd over 1f out: eased: t.o* **20/1**

1m 40.71s (0.71) **Going Correction** +0.10s/f (Good) **14** Ran SP% **121.4**
Speed ratings (Par 100): **100,97,96,93,91 91,90,89,86,83 82,79,77,56**
Tote Swingers:1&2:£5.40, 2&3:£7.60, 1&3:£20.50. Totesuper 7: Win: Not won, Place: Not won. CSF £27.12 CT £336.92 TOTE £7.90: £2.60, £1.40, £3.20; EX 27.20.
Owner Ahmad Al Shaikh **Bred** Old Carhue Stud **Trained** Newmarket, Suffolk

FOCUS
This was run at an even tempo. There was no great depth to this ordinary race, but the winner is getting his act together.
Point Du Jour(FR) Official explanation: jockey said gelding was denied a clear run
T/Plt: £1,302.40 to a £1 stake. Pool £57,806.27 - 32.40 winning units T/Qpdt: £255.90 to a £1 stake. Pool £3,942.62 - 11.40 winning units. CR

3021 THIRSK (L-H)
Friday, July 22

OFFICIAL GOING: Good (8.6)
Wind: fresh across Weather: Cloudy

4282 SKYBET SUPPORTING THE YORKSHIRE RACING SUMMER FESTIVAL MAIDEN STKS (DIV I) 7f
1:30 (1:34) (Class 5) 3-Y-0+ **£2,587** (£770; £384; £192) **Stalls** Low

Form RPR
22- **1** **White Frost (IRE)**[294] 6532 3-9-3 0 MichaelHills 9 79+
(B W Hills) *trckd ldrs: led over 2f out: pushed clr over 1f out: rdn out fnl f* **10/11**[1]
3 **2** *1 ½* **Green Howard**[15] 3756 3-9-3 0 DanielTudhope 2 75
(Robin Bastiman) *midfield: rdn and hdwy over 2f out: wnt 2nd over 1f out: kpt on: nt rch wnr* **7/2**[2]
00 **3** *3 ¾* **Totally Trusted**[54] 2528 3-8-9 0 MichaelO'Connell(3) 6 60
(David Nicholls) *trckd ldrs: rdn over 2f out: kpt on same pce: no match ldng pair* **40/1**
6 **4** *4 ½* **Andiamo Via**[18] 3684 4-9-7 0 SeanLevey(3) 7 56
(Michael Smith) *prom: led wl over 2f out: sn hdd: one pce fr over 1f out* **16/1**
5 *2* **Isheforreal (IRE)**[24] 4-9-7 0 PaulPickard(3) 8 50+
(Brian Ellison) *s.i.s and swtchd lft s: hld up: pushed along over 2f out: kpt on fnl f: nrst fin* **80/1**
3 **6** *hd* **Lord Emerson**[18] 3684 3-9-3 0 PaulHanagan 3 47
(Richard Fahey) *in tch: rdn over 2f out: kpt on one pce* **11/2**[3]
7 *1 ¼* **Bond Blade** 3-9-3 0 TomEaves 10 43
(Geoffrey Oldroyd) *midfield: rdn over 2f out: kpt on one pce* **25/1**
44 **8** *½* **Stylistickhill (IRE)**[31] 3246 3-8-9 0 BillyCray(3) 4 37
(David Nicholls) *led: rdn whn hdd wl over 2f out: sn wknd* **7/1**
0 **9** *1 ¾* **Riczar**[22] 3543 3-8-12 0 RichardKingscote 11 32
(Tom Dascombe) *hld up: pushed along over 3f out: nvr threatened* **28/1**
00 **10** *½* **Ingenti**[20] 3616 3-8-12 0 PaddyAspell 5 31
(Christopher Wilson) *midfield: pushed along 2f out: n.d* **250/1**
11 *20* **Peteron** 3-9-3 0 AndrewHeffernan 1 —
(Colin Teague) *dwlt: hld up: a towards rr* **100/1**
P **Holtby (IRE)** 3-9-3 0 RobertWinston 12 —
(Mel Brittain) *hld up: pushed along and lost tch 5f out: p.u 4f out* **100/1**

1m 27.87s (0.67) **Going Correction** +0.175s/f (Good)
WFA 3 from 4yo 7lb **12** Ran SP% **121.7**
Speed ratings (Par 103): **103,101,97,91,89 89,87,87,85,84 61,—**
Tote Swingers: 1&2 £1.30, 1&3 £17.30, 2&3 £33.40 CSF £4.17 TOTE £2.00: £1.02, £1.80, £8.70; EX 5.80.
Owner Mr And Mrs J D Cotton **Bred** M Henochsberg & Mme D Hazan-Ades **Trained** Lambourn, Berks

FOCUS
An uncompetitive maiden and the winner did not need to match his 2yo best.
Peteron Official explanation: trainer said gelding had a breathing problem

4283 BRITISH STALLION STUDS SUPPORTING BRITISH RACING EBF MAIDEN STKS 5f
2:00 (2:03) (Class 5) 2-Y-0 **£3,234** (£962; £481; £240) **Stalls** High

Form RPR
5 **1** **O'Gorman**[15] 3755 2-9-3 0 PhillipMakin 7 86+
(Kevin Ryan) *trckd ldr: led on bit over 1f out: pushed clr fnl f: comf* **4/9**[1]
60 **2** *4* **I'll Be Good**[14] 3826 2-9-0 0 GaryBartley(3) 3 69
(Robert Johnson) *midfield towards outer: rdn and hdwy over 1f out: wnt 2nd ins fnl f: kpt on: no ch w wnr* **100/1**
04 **3** *¾* **Koolgreycat (IRE)**[11] 3899 2-8-12 0 BarryMcHugh 6 61
(Noel Wilson) *midfield: hdwy over 2f out: chsd ldr over 1f out: kpt on* **80/1**
4 *nk* **Citybell (IRE)** 2-8-12 0 PaulHanagan 10 60
(Richard Fahey) *led: rdn whn hdd over 1f out: no ex ins fnl f* **7/1**[2]
0 **5** *2 ½* **Duke Of Aricabeau (IRE)**[59] 2387 2-9-3 0 GrahamGibbons 1 56+
(Michael Easterby) *dwlt: wnt lft s: hld up: sn nudged along: hdwy over 1f out: kpt on fnl f: n.d* **14/1**
6 *1 ½* **Endless Applause** 2-8-12 0 MichaelHills 9 46
(Richard Whitaker) *dwlt: hld up: sn pushed along: edgd lft over 2f out: hdwy over 1f out: kpt on fnl f: nrst fin* **20/1**
3506 **7** *3* **Economic Crisis (IRE)**[13] 3849 2-8-12 0 TonyHamilton 5 35
(Alan Berry) *prom: rdn over 2f out: wknd over 1f out* **33/1**
8 *½* **My New Angel (IRE)** 2-8-12 0 TomEaves 4 33
(Paul Green) *outpcd in rr tl mod late hdwy* **33/1**
9 *1 ¼* **Brilliant Crystal** 2-8-12 0 AndrewElliott 12 28
(Mrs K Burke) *chsd ldrs: wknd over 1f out* **8/1**[3]

10 *shd* **Hareem Dancer** 2-8-9 0 .... BillyCray(3) 11 28
(David Nicholls) *s.i.s: sn pushed along into midfield: wknd over 1f out* **50/1**

03 11 *1 3/4* **Fifteentwo**[13] 3855 2-9-3 0 .... AdrianNicholls 8 27
(David Nicholls) *w ldr: rdn over 2f out: wknd over 1f out* **16/1**

12 *1 1/2* **Rusty Rocket (IRE)** 2-9-3 0 .... AndrewHeffernan 2 21
(Paul Green) *wnt lft s: a outpcd towards rr* **50/1**

60.88 secs (1.28) **Going Correction** +0.175s/f (Good) **12** Ran SP% **122.2**
Speed ratings (Par 94): **96,89,88,87,83 81,76,75,73,73 70,68**
Tote Swingers: 1&2 £22.00, 1&3 £19.40, 2&3 £72.40 CSF £116.66 TOTE £1.50: £1.02, £13.20, £11.20; EX 64.80.
Owner We Haven't Told The Wives Syndicate **Bred** Whitsbury Manor Stud **Trained** Hambleton, N Yorks

FOCUS
The odd interesting type lined up, but nothing could live with the well-backed winner who's potentially better than the bare form.

NOTEBOOK
O'Gorman ◆ confirmed the promise he showed over 6f on his debut at Doncaster with an impressive success. He again wasn't best away, but was soon moving strongly just off the pace and found plenty when asked for his effort. A half-brother to last year's Mill Reef winner Temple Meads, he has plenty of scope and looks up to contesting Group races at this trip, with something like the Flying Childers at Doncaster in September looking suitable. (op 8-15 tchd 4-7)
I'll Be Good was reported to have hung left throughout when well beaten over 7f at York last time, but he'd shown ability over this trip on his debut and did so again. He won't always run into such a decent type and might find an ordinary maiden, while nurseries are now an option and he could do okay in that sphere.
Koolgreycat(IRE) can now switch to nurseries and should find her level. (op 66-1)
Citybell(IRE), a May foal half-sister to a few winners, went unsold at £27,000 this April. She knew her job through the early stages, showing good pace against the near rail, before getting tired late on. Her natural speed should see her make her mark. (op 8-1)
Duke Of Aricabeau(IRE) ◆, who had been off the track since showing ability when in need of the experience at Ripon in May, again shaped nicely, keeping on without being subjected to a hard ride in the last furlong. There should be plenty more to come and appeals as one to keep on side in nursery/handicap company, although it would be dangerous to underestimate him next time. (tchd 10-1)
Endless Applause, a half-sister to a few winners, notably the same trainer's fair sprinter Mey Blossom, should be all the better for this first experience. (op 22-1 tchd 25-1)

4284 HABTON (S) H'CAP 1m
2:35 (2:36) (Class 6) (0-65,65) 3-Y-O **£2,587** (£770; £384; £192) **Stalls** Low

Form RPR

2001 **1** **Ryedale Dancer (IRE)**[20] 3619 3-9-5 **63** .... DavidAllan 9 69
(Tim Easterby) *mde all: rdn over 2f out: strly pressed over 1f out: hld on gamely fnl f* **8/1**

0050 **2** *1/2* **Deep Applause**[9] 3977 3-8-11 **55** .... (p) TomEaves 2 60
(Michael Dods) *in tch: smooth hdwy over 2f out: chal over 1f out: sn rdn: kpt on: hld towards fin* **9/1**

3-60 **3** *nk* **Syncopated Lady (IRE)**[8] 4005 3-8-5 **52** .... (e) SeanLevey(3) 11 56
(David O'Meara) *hld up in midfield: gd hdwy on outer over 3f out: rdn to chal over 1f out: one pce fnl f* **10/1**

0205 **4** *2 1/4* **Rapturous Applause**[16] 3729 3-9-1 **59** .... FrederikTylicki 8 58+
(Micky Hammond) *hld up in midfield: rdn and hdwy over 1f out: kpt on fnl f: nt rch ldng trio* **12/1**

-050 **5** *5* **Ari Gold (IRE)**[17] 3720 3-8-11 **55** .... (p) RichardKingscote 13 43
(Tom Dascombe) *midfield on outer: rdn over 3f out: one pce* **10/1**

6460 **6** *3/4* **May Burnett (IRE)**[8] 4005 3-8-4 **48** oh1 ow2 .... (t) AndrewHeffernan 10 34
(Brian Rothwell) *hld up: rdn over 3f out: sme late hdwy: nvr threatened* **50/1**

6641 **7** *1/2* **Princess Gail**[11] 3913 3-8-5 **49** .... TadhgO'Shea 3 34+
(Mark Brisbourne) *slowly away: hld up and bhd tl mod late hdwy* **11/2**[1]

456 **8** *4* **Dreamweaving (IRE)**[37] 3049 3-8-2 **46** oh1 .... KellyHarrison 12 22
(Nigel Tinkler) *t.k.h in midfield: rdn over 3f out: wknd over 1f out* **33/1**

3002 **9** *1* **Sky Diamond (IRE)**[20] 3619 3-9-4 **62** .... (b) PaulHanagan 14 35
(James Given) *racd keenly: hdwy on outer to trck ldr after 2f: rdn over 2f out: wknd over 1f out* **6/1**[2]

5256 **10** *nse* **Phair Winter**[17] 3706 3-8-5 **49** .... DuranFentiman 1 22
[illegible] *wknd over 2f out* **13/2**[3]

600- **11** *1* **Nippy Nikki**[254] 7393 3-8-2 **46** oh1 .... AndrewMullen 6 11
(John Norton) *hld up: a towards rr* **50/1**

0006 **12** *1/2* **Ollywood**[17] 3717 3-8-6 **50** .... FrannyNorton 4 20
(Tony Carroll) *midfield on inner: pushed along and outpcd over 3f out: n.d after: eased fnl 100yds* **16/1**

0403 **13** *18* **Fire Crystal**[32] 3226 3-8-7 **54** .... MartinHarley(3) 7 —
(Mick Channon) *trckd ldrs: rdn over 3f out: wknd over 2f out: eased* **6/1**[2]

1m 42.05s (1.95) **Going Correction** +0.175s/f (Good) **13** Ran SP% **117.0**
Speed ratings (Par 98): **97,96,96,93,88 88,87,83,82,82 81,81,63**
Tote Swingers: 1&2 £14.70, 1&3 £17.90, 2&3 £23.30 CSF £75.72 CT £752.87 TOTE £11.30: £3.30, £3.40, £3.00; EX 91.60.No bid for the winner.
Owner Rapcalone **Bred** Max Morris **Trained** Great Habton, N Yorks

FOCUS
A typically moderate selling handicap but further improvement from the winner.
Princess Gail Official explanation: jockey said filly reared as stalls opened
Fire Crystal Official explanation: vet said filly bled from the nose

4285 BRITISH STALLION STUDS SUPPORTING BRITISH RACING EBF MAIDEN FILLIES' STKS 7f
3:10 (3:10) (Class 4) 2-Y-O **£4,528** (£1,347; £673; £336) **Stalls** Low

Form RPR

5624 **1** **Alabanda (IRE)**[15] 3780 2-9-0 0 .... DavidAllan 8 77+
(Tim Easterby) *mde all: rdn clr over 1f out: kpt on: edgd rt fnl 100yds* **7/1**

2 *3* **Bountiful Girl** 2-9-0 0 .... PaulHanagan 2 69+
(Richard Fahey) *in tch: rdn and hdwy on inner over 1f out: kpt on: wnt 2nd fnl 100yds: no ch w wnr* **9/1**

3 *nk* **Lady Layla** 2-9-0 0 .... TomEaves 13 68+
(Bryan Smart) *wnt rt s: sn trckd ldr on outer: rdn over 2f out: kpt on one pce: lost 2nd fnl 100yds* **25/1**

65 **4** *2 1/4* **Glad Eye Gladys**[20] 3609 2-9-0 0 .... FrederikTylicki 3 64+
(David Nicholls) *hld up in midfield: rdn and hdwy over 2f out: short of room over 1f out: hmpd appr fnl f: kpt on: wnt 4th fnl 100yds* **10/1**

532 **5** *1 1/4* **Self Centred**[14] 3813 2-9-0 0 .... MichaelHills 1 59
(B W Hills) *midfield: rdn and hdwy on outer over 2f out: drvn over 1f out: sn one pce: lost 4th fnl 100yds* **2/1**[1]

6 *2 1/2* **Taro Tywod (IRE)** 2-9-0 0 .... DavidNolan 6 52
(Ann Duffield) *in tch: rdn 3f out: wknd ins fnl f* **66/1**

0 **7** *1* **Liesl (IRE)**[99] 1337 2-9-0 0 .... PhillipMakin 12 49
(Kevin Ryan) *trckd ldr: rdn over 2f out: bmpd appr fnl f: wknd* **14/1**

8 *3/4* **Martha's Way** 2-9-0 0 .... GrahamGibbons 7 47+
(Michael Easterby) *dwlt: sn midfield: hmpd over 2f out: sn pushed along: n.d* **100/1**

03 **9** *shd* **Vociferous (USA)**[7] 4047 2-9-0 0 .... DarryllHolland 4 47
(Mark Johnston) *trckd ldr: rdn and lost pl over 3f out: edgd rt over 2f out: n.d after* **5/1**[3]

0 **10** *1* **Bada Bing**[57] 2430 2-8-11 0 .... BillyCray(3) 5 44
(David Nicholls) *hld up: rdn over 3f out: nvr threatened* **100/1**

11 *6* **Annie Walker (IRE)** 2-9-0 0 .... AdrianNicholls 9 28
(David Nicholls) *hld up in midfield: pushed along over 3f out: sltly hmpd over 2f out: nvr threatened* **33/1**

12 *7* **Phoenician Blaze** 2-9-0 0 .... GregFairley 11 —
(Tim Etherington) *hld up: a towards rr* **200/1**

13 *21* **Hellenistic** 2-9-0 0 .... WilliamBuick 10 —
(Mahmood Al Zarooni) *slowly away: hld up: a towards rr: eased* **7/2**[2]

1m 28.99s (1.79) **Going Correction** +0.175s/f (Good) **13** Ran SP% **121.2**
Speed ratings (Par 93): **96,92,92,89,88 85,84,83,83,82 75,67,43**
Tote Swingers: 1&2 £12.30, 1&3 £46.80, 2&3 £18.20 CSF £67.68 TOTE £8.10: £2.20, £3.10, £6.30; EX 68.80.
Owner D A West **Bred** Yeomanstown Stud **Trained** Great Habton, N Yorks

FOCUS
The bare form of this fillies' maiden looks just fair, but a few interesting types lined up and the race should produce winners. Alabanda is probably the best guide to the form.

NOTEBOOK
Alabanda(IRE) got off the mark at the fifth attempt and put her experience to good use, going to the front (no bad thing on this card) and sustaining her effort well for a clear-cut success. She should be competitive in nurseries. (tchd 15-2)
Bountiful Girl, out of a triple 1m4f winner, made a pleasing introduction, showing a fair level of ability. Entitled to improve, she could be tough to beat in similar company next time. (op 8-1 tchd 10-1)
Lady Layla, a £28,000 purchase, out of a high-class multiple 1m2f-1m6f winner, hung left under pressure in the straight, but this was still a promising start. There really should be better to come. (op 33-1)
Glad Eye Gladys kept on nicely despite being a bit short of room in the closing stages. She gives the impression she can step forward again and nurseries are now an option. (op 25-1)
Self Centred hasn't gone on since finishing third in the Chesham, but she wasn't helped by the inside stall this time, proving unable to get a worthwhile position, and can be given another chance. (op 7-4)
Martha's Way Official explanation: jockey said filly suffered interference in running
Vociferous(USA) lost ground when not appearing to handle the bend into the straight all that well. She can now switch to nurseries and it's doubtful we've seen the best of her just yet. (op 9-2 tchd 4-1 and 11-2 in a place)
Hellenistic looked particularly interesting considering she was William Buick's only ride on the card, but she started slowly and was never going. The rider reported his mount ran green. Official explanation: jockey said filly ran green (op 11-2)

4286 SKYBET SUPPORTING THE YORKSHIRE RACING SUMMER FESTIVAL MAIDEN STKS (DIV II) 7f
3:45 (3:50) (Class 5) 3-Y-O+ **£2,587** (£770; £384; £192) **Stalls** Low

Form RPR

43 **1** **Thatcherite (IRE)**[9] 3977 3-9-3 0 .... (t) StephenCraine 10 72
(Tony Coyle) *in tch: rdn and hdwy on outer 4f out: drvn over 2f out: kpt on ins fnl f: led nr fin* **9/2**[2]

00 **2** *hd* **The Buska (IRE)**[22] 3543 3-9-3 0 .... DavidAllan 6 71
(Declan Carroll) *trckd ldr: rdn over 2f out: led over 1f out: drvn and edgd rt ins fnl f: hdd nr fin* **11/1**

3 *1 1/2* **Pulsatilla** 3-8-8 0 ow3 .... JustinNewman(7) 8 65+
(Bryan Smart) *midfield: pushed along and outpcd over 3f out: hdwy 2f out: rdn and kpt on ins fnl f: wnt 3rd post* **16/1**

04-3 **4** *shd* **Sole Danser (IRE)**[35] 3111 3-9-3 74 .... MichaelHills 4 67
(B W Hills) *led: rdn over 2f out: hdd over 1f out: one pce: lost 3rd post* **5/2**[1]

5 *1 1/2* **Swinger** 3-9-3 0 .... FrederikTylicki 1 63
(David Nicholls) *in tch: rdn over 2f out: kpt on one pce* **7/1**[3]

6 *8* **Upton Crystal** 3-8-12 0 .... GrahamGibbons 7 36
[illegible] **18/1**

7 *10* **Kyllachykov (IRE)** 3-9-3 0 .... LeeNewman 5 —
(Robin Bastiman) *dwlt: hld up: nvr threatened* **16/1**

8 *5* **Salik Tag (USA)** 3-9-3 0 .... AdrianNicholls 9 —
(David Nicholls) *slowly away: sn midfield: pushed along over 4f out: wknd over 2f out* **8/1**

004 **9** *1/2* **Toffee Nose**[34] 3191 4-9-3 46 .... ShaneBKelly(7) 11 —
(Ron Barr) *trckd ldrs: rdn and lost pl 4f out: wknd over 2f out* **100/1**

10 *6* **Shoulder Arms** 3-8-12 0 .... ChrisDCogan(5) 2 —
(John Weymes) *slowly away: a in rr* **50/1**

1m 29.39s (2.19) **Going Correction** +0.175s/f (Good)
WFA 3 from 4yo 7lb **10** Ran SP% **98.7**
Speed ratings (Par 103): **94,93,92,91,90 81,69,63,63,56**
Tote Swingers: 1&2 £8.10, 1&3 £11.90, 2&3 £11.30 CSF £36.14 TOTE £4.90: £1.50, £2.40, £5.30; EX 37.90.
Owner Brian Kerr & Tony Coyle **Bred** Taroka Equine Investments **Trained** Norton, N Yorks
■ The first winner as a trainer for former jump jockey Tony Coyle.
■ Stewards' Enquiry : Stephen Craine two-day ban: used whip with erxcessive frequency (Aug 5-6)
David Allan one-day ban: used whip with excessiv e frequency (Aug 5)

FOCUS
A modest maiden and not many got involved. The time was the slowest of the three races at this distance (1.52 seconds off first division), although the ground deteriorated a bit as the meeting progressed. The winner is rated up a length. Amazw was withdrawn (7/2, ref to ent stalls). Deduct 20p in the £ under R4.
Toffee Nose Official explanation: jockey said gelding stumbled on leaving stalls

4287 TYREGIANT.COM H'CAP 1m 4f
4:20 (4:21) (Class 4) (0-80,77) 3-Y-O **£4,528** (£1,347; £673; £336) **Stalls** Low

Form RPR

3402 **1** **Rastaban**[9] 3988 3-9-5 **75** .... MichaelHills 4 86+
(William Haggas) *trckd ldr: pushed along to ld over 2f out: sn rdn: kpt on fnl f* **4/6**[1]

-344 **2** *2 1/2* **Istishaara (USA)**[21] 3580 3-9-7 **77** .... TadhgO'Shea 1 84
(John Dunlop) *hld up: nudged along over 7f out: rdn 4f out: hdwy over 2f out: chal over 1f out: no ex fnl 100yds* **3/1**[2]

6-00 **3** *22* **Hawdyerwheesht**[19] 3659 3-9-5 **75** .... (b[1]) PaulHanagan 3 47
(Mark Johnston) *racd keenly: led: rdn whn hdd over 2f out: sn btn* **6/1**[3]

2560 4 33 **Black Pond (USA)**[28] 3366 3-8-12 **68** .... DarryllHolland 2 —
(Mark Johnston) *trckd ldrs: rdn and lost pl 4f out: sn bhd: t.o* **8/1**
2m 37.42s (1.22) **Going Correction** +0.175s/f (Good) 4 Ran SP% **110.4**
Speed ratings (Par 102): **102,100,85,63**
CSF £3.05 TOTE £1.60; EX 3.20.
Owner Abdulla Al Khalifa **Bred** Sheikh Abdullah Bin Isa Al-Khalifa **Trained** Newmarket, Suffolk
FOCUS
A disappointing turnout numerically for a race that met the Horseman's Group tariff, and half the field ran well below form. The pace was sound but it's doubtful if the winner had to improve on his latest form.

4288 WELCOME TO YORKSHIRE EVENTS & FESTIVALS FILLIES' H'CAP 6f
4:55 (4:56) (Class 5) (0-70,70) 3-Y-0+ **£2,911** (£866; £432; £216) **Stalls** High

Form RPR
003- 1 **Lizzie (IRE)**[291] 6619 3-9-3 **66** ....(b) DavidAllan 15 74
(Tim Easterby) *midfield towards rail: rdn and hdwy over 1f out: kpt on ins fnl f: led fnl 75yds* **4/1**[1]
0402 2 ½ **Caranbola**[4] 4152 5-9-12 **70** .... RobertWinston 2 77
(Mel Brittain) *prom on outer: rdn 2f out: led jst ins fnl f: edgd rt: hdd fnl 75yds* **5/1**[3]
0400 3 2¼ **Lady Del Sol**[4] 4145 3-9-3 **66** .... DanielTudhope 10 65
(Marjorie Fife) *dwlt and reminders early: sn midfield: rdn over 2f out: hdwy over 1f out: ev ch jst ins fnl f: kpt on* **14/1**
3323 4 ½ **Cool In The Shade**[20] 3630 3-8-5 **54** ....(p) PaulQuinn 7 51
(Paul Midgley) *led narrowly: rdn 2f out: hdd jst ins fnl f: one pce: sltly hmpd 100yds out* **11/1**
1213 5 nk **Needy McCredie**[13] 3856 5-9-4 **62** .... PaulHanagan 9 59
(James Turner) *midfield: rdn and hdwy over 1f out: ev ch jst ins fnl f: one pce* **9/2**[2]
1660 6 ¾ **Foreign Rhythm (IRE)**[5] 4126 6-9-1 **66** .... ShaneBKelly(7) 1 61
(Ron Barr) *hld up: pushed along and hdwy on outer over 2f out: kpt on one pce fnl f* **16/1**
0-03 7 nk **Andrasta**[11] 3901 6-8-4 **51** oh6 .... PaulPickard(3) 12 47
(Alan Berry) *chsd ldrs: short of room and lost pl 2f out: swtchd lft over 1f out: kpt on ins fnl f* **20/1**
-261 8 ½ **Forever's Girl**[102] 1279 5-9-12 **70** .... PhillipMakin 6 62
(Geoffrey Oldroyd) *chsd ldrs: rdn over 2f out: sn one pce* **13/2**
6-00 9 ¾ **Leonid Glow**[28] 3359 6-9-11 **69** .... FrederikTylicki 14 59
(Michael Dods) *hld up: pushed along and hdwy over 1f out: kpt on fnl f: nvr threatened* **10/1**
5160 10 2¾ **Unwrapit (USA)**[19] 3661 3-8-10 **59** ....(p) TomEaves 3 39
(Bryan Smart) *hld up: pushed along over 3f out: short of room 2f out and again over 1f out: nvr threatened* **25/1**
0600 11 6 **Bellemere**[17] 3702 3-8-6 **55** .... GrahamGibbons 13 16
(Michael Easterby) *prom: rdn and edgd lft over 1f out: wknd fnl f* **33/1**
-000 12 3½ **Stella Marris**[15] 3756 4-8-11 **55** .... PaddyAspell 4 —
(Christopher Wilson) *in tch: rdn over 2f out: wknd over 1f out* **66/1**
50 13 4½ **Lambrini Lace (IRE)**[50] 2632 6-8-7 **51** oh6............(b) RoystonFfrench 11 —
(Lisa Williamson) *w ldr: rdn over 2f out: wknd over 1f out* **50/1**
0065 14 shd **Harmony Wold**[10] 3950 3-8-2 **51** oh6............(b[1]) DuranFentiman 8 —
(Declan Carroll) *hld up: a towards rr* **80/1**
0-20 15 10 **Dream Dream Dream (IRE)**[52] 2593 4-8-10 **54**...... AndrewHeffernan 5 —
(Kevin M Prendergast) *midfield: lost pl over 2f out: sn wknd* **25/1**
1m 13.78s (1.08) **Going Correction** +0.175s/f (Good)
WFA 3 from 4yo+ 5lb 15 Ran SP% **118.2**
Speed ratings (Par 100): **99,98,95,94,94 93,92,92,91,87 79,74,68,68,55**
Tote Swingers: 1&2 £6.00, 1&3 £16.00, 2&3 £15.90 CSF £21.20 CT £263.49 TOTE £5.70: £2.60, £1.90, £2.40; EX 29.50.
Owner Mrs Jean P Connew **Bred** L Mulryan **Trained** Great Habton, N Yorks
■ Stewards' Enquiry : Robert Winston caution: careless riding.
FOCUS
A modest fillies' sprint handicap. The runner-up is probably the best guide to the form.
Andrasta Official explanation: jockey said mare was denied a clear run

4289 RACING AGAIN THIRSK NEXT FRIDAY "HANDS & HEELS" APPRENTICE SERIES H'CAP (RACING INITIATIVE) 5f
5:30 (5:30) (Class 5) (0-75,69) 3-Y-0+ **£2,911** (£866; £432; £216) **Stalls** High

Form RPR
0510 1 **Dispol Grand (IRE)**[19] 3662 5-8-10 **56** .... LukeStrong(3) 7 66
(Paul Midgley) *chsd ldrs: hdwy over 1f out: swtchd lft appr fnl f: led fnl 100yds: kpt on* **4/1**[2]
2421 2 ½ **Royal Blade (IRE)**[4] 4145 4-8-4 **52** 6ex............ DanielleMooney(5) 2 60
(Alan Berry) *stmbld s: sn prom: rdn to ld jst ins fnl f: hdd fnl 100yds: kpt on* **6/4**[1]
5620 3 1¾ **Desert Strike**[4] 4152 5-9-11 **68** ....(p) NoraLooby 4 70
(Alan McCabe) *hld up in tch: rdn and hdwy over 1f out: kpt on fnl f* **7/1**
5015 4 1¾ **Ridley Didley (IRE)**[3] 4174 6-9-12 **69** .... EdmondLinehan 5 64
(Noel Wilson) *led: rdn whn hdd jst ins fnl f: wknd fnl 100yds* **4/1**[2]
0-06 5 1¾ **Avertuoso**[4] 4152 7-9-12 **69** ....(v) LucyKBarry 3 58
(Bryan Smart) *rrd s: hld up: rdn over 1f out: nvr threatened* **5/1**[3]
500 6 4½ **Rattleyurjewellery**[8] 4025 3-7-12 **50** oh5............ ClaireMurray(5) 6 23
(David Brown) *in tch: rdn 2f out: sn wknd* **40/1**
60.88 secs (1.28) **Going Correction** +0.175s/f (Good)
WFA 3 from 4yo+ 4lb 6 Ran SP% **111.6**
Speed ratings (Par 103): **96,95,92,89,86 79**
Tote Swingers: 1&2 £1.80, 1&3 £3.20, 2&3 £2.60 CSF £10.34 TOTE £5.10: £2.50, £1.50.
Owner T W Midgley **Bred** Martyn J McEnery **Trained** Westow, N Yorks
FOCUS
A low-grade apprentices' sprint handicap. The winner's best form since last summer.
T/Plt: £293.80 to a £1 stake. Pool:£39,025.06 - 96.95 winning tickets T/Qpdt: £83.60 to a £1 stake. Pool:£2,577.80 - 22.80 winning tickets AS

3874 YORK (L-H)
Friday, July 22
OFFICIAL GOING: Good to soft (5.6)
Wind: Light against Weather: Cloudy

4290 FUTURE CLEANING SERVICES APPRENTICE H'CAP 1m
6:00 (6:00) (Class 4) (0-80,78) 3-Y-0 **£5,175** (£1,540; £769; £384) **Stalls** Low

Form RPR
-013 1 **Ingleby Exceed (IRE)**[6] 4081 3-9-2 **70** .... SeanLevey 2 80
(David O'Meara) *hld up: hdwy 3f out: swtchd lft and effrt 1 1/2f out: sn n.m.r: rdn and styd on strly ins fnl f to ld last 100yds* **5/1**[1]
4152 2 2 **Maggie Mey (IRE)**[21] 3586 3-9-6 **74** .... MichaelO'Connell 4 79
(David O'Meara) *led: rdn along 3f out: hdd 2f out: rallied to ld again jst over 1f out: drvn and edgd lft ins fnl f: hdd and no ex last 100yds* **10/1**
0 3 ½ **Buzz Law (IRE)**[13] 3864 3-9-1 **74** .... MatthewLawson(5) 1 78
(Mrs K Burke) *hld up: hdwy and in tch 1/2-way: effrt on inner to chse ldrs 3f out: rdn over 2f out: drvn and edgd lft ins fnl f: kpt on* **5/1**[1]
2161 4 1 **Roninski (IRE)**[13] 3854 3-9-4 **77** .... JustinNewman(5) 15 79
(Bryan Smart) *prom on outer: effrt to chal 3f out: rdn over 2f out and ev ch tl drvn and one pce ent fnl f* **5/1**[1]
6245 5 ¾ **Nicola's Dream**[7] 4077 3-8-12 **69** .... LeeTopliss(3) 10 69
(Richard Fahey) *towards rr: hdwy 3f out: rdn along over 2f out: drvn and kpt on ins fnl f: nrst fin* **10/1**
00-3 6 ¾ **Scottish Lake**[21] 3575 3-9-1 **69** .... PatrickDonaghy 9 68
(Jedd O'Keeffe) *hld up in rr: hdwy on wd outside wl over 2f out: sn rdn and kpt on same pce fnl f* **33/1**
0122 7 shd **Save The Bees**[13] 3854 3-8-13 **70** .... NeilFarley(3) 6 68
(Declan Carroll) *trckd ldrs: effrt wl over 2f out: sn rdn and grad wknd* **5/1**[1]
6103 8 1 **Yojimbo (IRE)**[27] 3400 3-9-9 **77** .... MartinHarley 12 73
(Mick Channon) *a in rr* **9/1**[3]
4330 9 hd **Hoppy's Flyer (FR)**[14] 3806 3-8-6 **67** .... DavidSimmonson(7) 8 63
(Paul Midgley) *cl up: rdn along over 3f out: wknd wl over 2f out* **20/1**
5231 10 nk **Trumpington Street (IRE)**[17] 3717 3-9-10 **78** .... LouisBeuzelin 7 73
(John Gosden) *trckd ldrs: hdwy over 3f out: led 2f out: sn rdn and hdd jst over 1f out: wknd* **7/1**[2]
5-0 11 26 **Golden Blaze**[7] 4043 3-8-7 **68** ....(p) NoelGarbutt(7) 11 —
(James Moffatt) *dwlt: sn chsng ldrs: cl up 1/2-way: rdn along and wknd wl over 3f out: sn bhd* **25/1**
1m 38.93s (0.13) **Going Correction** +0.075s/f (Good) 11 Ran SP% **118.9**
Speed ratings (Par 102): **102,100,99,98,97 97,96,95,95,95 69**
Tote Swingers:1&2:£6.30, 2&3:£13.00, 1&3:£6.70 CSF £55.36 CT £223.37 TOTE £6.70: £2.10, £2.70, £2.40; EX 56.30.
Owner Dave Scott **Bred** Dave Scott **Trained** Nawton, N Yorks
FOCUS
Rail moved in from 9f to entrance to home straight reducing distances of races of 1m and over by 27yds. A fair handicap in which the gallop was on the steady side in the first half of the race and, after racing in the centre down the straight, several - including the winner - edged towards the far rail late on. Solid form for the grade.

4291 SEDDON PROPERTY SERVICES H'CAP 6f
6:30 (6:31) (Class 4) (0-80,79) 4-Y-0+ **£5,175** (£1,540; £769; £384) **Stalls** Centre

Form RPR
5410 1 **Toby Tyler**[13] 3856 5-8-9 **67** ....(v) PJMcDonald 8 79
(Paul Midgley) *bhd: swtchd rt and hdwy 2f out: rdn over 1f out: str run to chal ins fnl f whn hung bdly lft: led last 100yds: sn clr* **9/1**
0026 2 2½ **Hotham**[7] 4075 8-9-5 **77** .... BarryMcHugh 11 82+
(Noel Wilson) *in tch: hdwy to chse clr ldr fr wl over 1f out: rdn ent fnl f: no imp whn hmpd last 100yds: kpt on for 2nd nr fin* **5/1**[2]
2512 3 ¾ **Nomoreblondes**[7] 4046 7-8-11 **76** ....(v) DavidSimmonson(7) 1 78
(Paul Midgley) *led and sn wl clr: rdn over 1f out: drvn and wknd ins fnl f: hdd whn sltly hmpd last 75yds* **9/1**
0004 4 shd **Green Park (IRE)**[20] 3613 8-9-1 **78** ....(b) NeilFarley(5) 13 79
(Declan Carroll) *towards rr: hdwy over 2f out: sn rdn and chsng ldrs whn n.m.r ins fnl f: no imp after* **16/1**
40-0 5 4 **Belinsky (IRE)**[76] 1907 4-8-5 **63** .... FrannyNorton 3 51
(Mark Campion) *chsd ldrs on outer: rdn along over 2f out: sn drvn and grad wknd* **12/1**
6036 6 ¾ **Diman Waters (IRE)**[13] 3880 4-9-6 **78** .... DavidAllan 2 64
(Eric Alston) *chsd clr ldr: rdn along over 2f out: drvn wl over 1f out: sn wknd* **4/1**[1]
20 7 1¼ **Night Trade (IRE)**[16] 3737 4-9-0 **75** ....(v) SeanLevey(3) 10 57
(Deborah Sanderson) *hld up: hdwy over 2f out: rdn wl over 1f out and sn no imp* **11/1**
0502 8 1¼ **Sonny Red (IRE)**[8] 4016 7-8-12 **77** .... ShirleyTeasdale(7) 5 55
(David Nicholls) *prom: rdn along over 2f out: sn wknd* **10/1**
3030 9 1¾ **Dark Lane**[13] 3880 5-9-2 **74** ....(b) TonyHamilton 7 46
(Richard Fahey) *a towards rr* **20/1**
2103 10 6 **Kylladdie**[22] 3541 4-9-7 **79** ....(b) FrankieDettori 12 32
(Steve Gollings) *a in rr: bhd fr 1/2-way* **6/1**[3]
0-03 11 4 **Zip Lock (IRE)**[16] 3737 5-9-6 **78** .... WilliamBuick 9 18
(David Elsworth) *chsd ldrs: rdn along wl over 2f out: sn wknd* **7/1**
1m 13.33s (1.43) **Going Correction** +0.375s/f (Good) 11 Ran SP% **119.2**
Speed ratings (Par 105): **105,101,100,100,95 94,92,90,88,80 75**
Tote Swingers:1&2:£8.70, 2&3:£10.00, 1&3:£12.40 CSF £54.36 CT £432.69 TOTE £11.20: £3.30, £2.00, £1.90; EX 75.70.
Owner Anthony D Copley **Bred** Whitsbury Manor Stud **Trained** Westow, N Yorks
■ Stewards' Enquiry : P J McDonald three-day ban: careless riding (Aug 5-7)
FOCUS
A modest sprint handicap run at a good pace. A length personal best from the winner.
Diman Waters(IRE) Official explanation: jockey said gelding lost a shoe
Kylladdie Official explanation: trainer had no explanation for the poor form shown
Zip Lock(IRE) Official explanation: jockey said gelding stopped quickly

4292 BATLEYS CASH AND CARRY STKS (MEDIAN AUCTION MAIDEN) 7f
7:00 (7:02) (Class 4) 2-Y-0 **£5,175** (£1,540; £577; £577) **Stalls** Low

Form RPR
24 1 **Holy Roman Warrior (IRE)**[34] 3161 2-9-3 0............ PaulHanagan 3 79+
(Richard Fahey) *led over 2f: cl up tl led again wl over 2f out: rdn clr over 1f out: drvn and edgd rt ins fnl f: hld on wl* **4/1**[3]
63 2 hd **Saffa Hill (IRE)**[14] 3826 2-9-3 0............ DavidAllan 6 78
(Tim Easterby) *trckd ldrs: hdwy over 3f out: effrt over 2f out: swtchd lft and rdn over 1f out: drvn and styd on wl fnl f: jst failed* **11/4**[2]
044 3 2¼ **Tudor Empire (IRE)**[9] 3986 2-9-3 0............(b) WilliamBuick 8 72
(John Gosden) *cl up: led over 4f out: rdn along and hdd wl over 2f out: edgd rt and sltly outpcd wl over 1f out: kpt on u.p fnl f* **9/2**
3 dht **Gulf Of Alaska** 2-9-3 0............ FrankieDettori 4 72+
(Mahmood Al Zarooni) *in tch: green and niggled along after 2f: pushed along 1/2-way: rdn and outpcd wl over 2f out: kpt on u.p appr fnl f* **9/4**[1]
0 5 5 **Amoure Medici**[34] 3182 2-9-3 0............ PJMcDonald 1 58+
(Noel Quinlan) *hld up: hdwy on inner 3f out: rdn to chal over 2f out and ev ch tl drvn and wknd over 1f out* **25/1**
6 11 **Bond Style** 2-9-3 0............ TomEaves 5 29
(Bryan Smart) *a towards rr* **10/1**
7 hd **Salutary** 2-9-3 0............ RobertWinston 7 28
(Nigel Tinkler) *a towards rr* **33/1**
8 2 **Mr Snoozy** 2-9-3 0............ GrahamGibbons 2 23
(Tim Walford) *prom: rdn along 1/2-way: sn wknd* **20/1**

The Form Book, Raceform Ltd, Compton, RG20 6NL

00 **9** *11* **Festival Spirit**[22] 3553 2-9-3 0.................................. DarryllHolland 9 —
(Mark Johnston) *chsd ldrs on outer: rdn along 3f out: sn wknd* **33/1**

1m 29.98s (4.68) **Going Correction** +0.375s/f (Good) **9** Ran SP% **119.2**
Speed ratings (Par 96): **88,87,85,85,79 66,66,64,51**
Tote Swingers:1&2:£2.90, 2&3:£1.40 (GA), 1&3 (GA):£1.00, 2&3:£1.60 (TE), 1&3:£2.20 (TE) CSF £15.31 TOTE £4.80: £1.70, £1.50; EX 14.90 TRIFECTA PL: 0.70 (GA), 0.80 (TE).
Owner Mrs J Penman **Bred** Epona Bloodstock Ltd And P A Byrne **Trained** Musley Bank, N Yorks

FOCUS
Probably an average juvenile maiden, rated around the second and third. It was slowly run.

NOTEBOOK
Holy Roman Warrior(IRE) brought some fair form to the table and turned in his best effort upped to 7f, in the process showing a good attitude to get off the mark on this third run. He's a highly regarded sort who should stay 1m and he appeals as the sort to win more races. (op 3-1)
Saffa Hill(IRE), who turned in an improved effort over this course-and-distance on his previous start, shaped as though a stiffer overall test would have suited but he probably ran to a similar level. He'll be suited by the step up to 1m and can win in ordinary company. (op 100-30)
Tudor Empire(IRE), with the blinkers again fitted, again underlined his vulnerability against the better sorts in this grade but he ran as well as he ever has done after racing with the choke out. He should stay 1m and is another that should be able to win a race at some stage. (op 5-1 tchd 11-2)
Gulf Of Alaska ◆, a half-brother to smart 1m4f-2m winner Veractity, to dual French 1m4f Listed winner and to a couple of other scorers up to 1m3f, was well supported and ran creditably, despite his apparent greenness on this racecourse debut. He will appreciate a mile plus in due course and should be able to pick up an ordinary maiden. (op 5-1 tchd 11-2)

4293 EBF "AUTHORIZED" LYRIC FILLIES' STKS (LISTED RACE) 1m 2f 88y
7:30 (7:30) (Class 1) 3-Y-0+
£19,848 (£7,525; £3,766; £1,876; £941; £472) **Stalls** Low

Form RPR
1-24 **1** **Sajjhaa**[37] 3030 4-9-4 111.. FrankieDettori 5 110+
(Saeed Bin Suroor) *led 2f: cl up on outer: effrt to ld wl over 2f out: rdn clr over 1f out: comf* **4/5**[1]
2-00 **2** *2* **Myplacelater**[15] 3775 4-9-4 109.. PaulHanagan 8 106
(David Elsworth) *hld up in rr: hdwy 3f out: swtchd lft and rdn wl over 1f out: sn chsng wnr: drvn ins fnl f and no imp towards fin* **12/1**
4-04 **3** *1 ½* **Contredanse (IRE)**[60] 2373 4-9-4 109..........................(v[1]) KierenFallon 4 103
(Luca Cumani) *trckd ldrs: hdwy over 3f out: rdn to dispute ld wl over 2f out: drvn and one pce fr wl over 1f out* **9/2**[2]
0420 **4** *2 ¾* **Fanditha (IRE)**[6] 4095 5-9-4 101.. FrannyNorton 1 98
(Mick Channon) *t.k.h: cl up: led after 2f: hdd 1/2-way: cl up and rdn along 3f out: drvn and grad wknd fnl 2f* **18/1**
3241 **5** *5* **Rainbow Springs**[35] 3119 3-8-8 90................................[1] WilliamBuick 3 88
(John Gosden) *t.k.h: hld up: hdwy on inner over 3f out: rdn to chal wl over 2f out: drvn and wknd wl over 1f out* **7/1**[3]
0415 **6** *3 ¼* **Bea Remembered**[35] 3107 4-9-4 99.................................... DarryllHolland 2 82
(Brian Meehan) *cl up: led 1/2-way: rdn along over 3f out: sn hdd and grad wknd fnl 2f* **9/1**
-130 **7** *24* **Wrekin Sunset**[37] 3034 3-8-8 88.. AndrewElliott 6 35
(Mrs K Burke) *t.k.h: trcking ldrs whn hmpd after 2f: in tch: rdn along 4f out: sn wknd and eased whn bhd fnl 2f* **50/1**

2m 11.3s (-1.20) **Going Correction** +0.075s/f (Good)
WFA 3 from 4yo+ 10lb **7** Ran SP% **111.2**
Speed ratings (Par 108): **107,105,104,102,98 95,76**
Tote Swingers:1&2:£1.20, 2&3:£4.70, 1&3:£1.30 CSF £11.23 TOTE £1.80: £1.50, £2.10; EX 8.90.
Owner Godolphin **Bred** Darley **Trained** Newmarket, Suffolk

FOCUS
Not the most competitive Listed event for fillies'. It was run at a muddling pace and the winner still has the potential to rate higher. It's doubtful if she had to match her reappearance form.

NOTEBOOK
Sajjhaa, who divided Henry Ceci's Group 1 winners Midday and Timepiece over C&D in May, faced nothing of that calibre this time and she didn't have to better that form to get off the mark for the year in fluent fashion in this muddling event. A better overall gallop would have suited and she appeals as the type to win more races around this trip. (op 5-6)
Myplacelater hadn't been anywhere near her best in two previous runs this term but fared a good deal better, even though she wouldn't have been suited by the way things unfolded. A more truly run race over this trip would have been to her liking and it will be interesting to see if this can be built on next time. (tchd 11-1)
Contredanse(IRE) also had a good chance at the weights and was far from disgraced after racing far too keenly in the first-time visor. As with many of these, she'll be suited by a stronger gallop but may not be the easiest to place successfully in Britain this season. (op 4-1)
Fanditha(IRE) had the run of the race and wasn't disgraced against three higher-rated rivals but she is another who may not be easy to place given she's plenty high enough in the weights for handicaps and doesn't look good enough for Listed or Group events. (op 16-1)
Rainbow Springs, who didn't look overly straightforward in the first-time hood, had plenty to find at the weights and had her limitations firmly exposed against several smart performers. She only has a maiden win to her name and doesn't look one for maximum faith. (op 8-1)

4294 SKYBET MOBILE SUPPORTING THE YORKSHIRE RACING FESTIVAL CLAIMING STKS 1m 4f
8:00 (8:02) (Class 4) 3-Y-0+ **£5,175** (£1,540; £769; £384) **Stalls** Centre

Form RPR
4650 **1** **Apprimus (IRE)**[27] 3411 5-9-7 93.. WilliamBuick 8 83
(Marco Botti) *trckd ldr: cl up 4f out: rdn to chal 3f out: slt ld whn edgd rt over 1f out: sn drvn and edgd lft jst ins fnl f: kpt on wl towards fin* **9/2**[3]
0005 **2** *½* **Overrule (USA)**[28] 3344 7-9-2 74................................ SeanLevey[(3)] 5 80
(Brian Ellison) *hld up in rr: hdwy over 3f out: effrt and nt clr run over 1f out: rdn and styng on whn hmpd jst ins fnl f: sn swtchd lft and drvn to chal and ev ch tl no ex nr fin* **12/1**
1-66 **3** *1 ½* **Trip The Light**[14] 3829 6-9-8 80....................................(v) PaulHanagan 7 81
(Richard Fahey) *trckd ldrs: hdwy on outer: effrt and cl up 3f out: rdn over 2f out and ev ch: drvn and outpcd over 1f out: rallied towards fin* **4/1**[2]
0552 **4** *¾* **Comedy Act**[7] 4043 4-9-8 84.. KierenFallon 2 80
(Mark Johnston) *hld up in rr: hdwy on outer 3f out: rdn to chal over 1f out: ev ch whn hung bdly rt jst ins fnl f: wknd* **6/4**[1]
6200 **5** *6* **Hydrant**[14] 3828 5-9-5 73.. AndrewMullen 6 69
(Peter Salmon) *led: rdn along 4f out: hdd over 2f out: drvn whn squeezed out ent fnl f: nt rcvr* **14/1**
-06 **6** *7* **Bavarian Nordic (USA)**[29] 3301 6-9-4 62......................... TonyHamilton 4 55
(Richard Whitaker) *trckd ldrs: effrt 3f out: rdn and ch 2f out: sn drvn and wknd over 1f out* **33/1**
0/ **7** *12* **Lil Ella (IRE)**[139] 6068 4-8-13 78.. ChrisDCogan[(5)] 1 36
(Patrick Holmes) *chsd ldrs on inner: rdn along 4f out: sn wknd* **25/1**

2m 32.96s (-0.24) **Going Correction** +0.075s/f (Good) **7** Ran SP% **99.3**
Speed ratings (Par 105): **103,102,101,101,97 92,84**
Tote Swingers:1&2:£5.70, 2&3:£5.30, 1&3:£1.50 CSF £39.62 TOTE £4.90: £2.50, £3.80; EX 41.50.
Owner Mrs L Botti **Bred** Larry And Billy Moran **Trained** Newmarket, Suffolk
■ Blizzard Blues (6/1) was withdrawn after proving unruly in the stalls. Deduct 10p in the £ under R4.
■ Stewards' Enquiry : William Buick one-day ban: careless riding (Aug 5)

FOCUS
A reasonable claimer but a muddling gallop and this bare form doesn't look reliable. The winner was best in and is rated a stone+ off his earlier Listed form.

4295 WELCOME TO YORKSHIRE ACTION PACKED OUTDOORS H'CAP 5f 89y
8:30 (8:31) (Class 4) (0-85,85) 3-Y-0 **£5,175** (£1,540; £769; £384) **Stalls** Centre

Form RPR
0440 **1** **Berberana (IRE)**[9] 3975 3-8-12 76.. RobertWinston 5 84
(Tim Easterby) *qckly away: mde all: rdn wl over 1f out: edgd rt and drvn ins fnl f: kpt on strly* **16/1**
1313 **2** *1 ½* **Thirteen Shivers**[7] 4048 3-9-5 83.. GrahamGibbons 10 86
(Michael Easterby) *in tch: hdwy 1/2-way: rdn to chse wnr over 1f out: drvn ins fnl f and ch tl one pce last 100yds* **9/4**[1]
4343 **3** *¾* **Crimson Knot (IRE)**[9] 3975 3-8-10 77.. LeeTopliss[(3)] 6 77
(Alan Berry) *in tch: rdn along over 2f out: drvn wl over 1f out: kpt on ins fnl f* **8/1**
3205 **4** *1 ¾* **Crimson Cloud**[15] 3759 3-8-6 70.. PaulHanagan 1 64
(Richard Fahey) *wnt rt s and in rr: hdwy 2f out: rdn to chse ldrs over 1f out: drvn and no imp ins fnl f* **6/1**[3]
1012 **5** *5* **Irish Boy (IRE)**[17] 3702 3-8-2 66.. DuranFentiman 7 42
(Noel Wilson) *chsd ldrs: effrt over 2f out: sn rdn and wknd over 1f out* **5/1**[2]
3030 **6** *1 ¾* **Captain Kolo (IRE)**[13] 3853 3-8-9 73.. DavidAllan 8 42
(Tim Easterby) *towards rr: sme hdwy wl over 1f out: sn rdn and nt d* **7/1**
0-15 **7** *6* **On The High Tops (IRE)**[55] 2505 3-9-4 82.................. AndrewMullen 2 30
(Tom Tate) *wnt rt s: sn chsng wnr: rdn along over 2f out and sn wknd* **15/2**
1416 **8** *3 ¼* **Even Stevens**[104] 1241 3-9-4 85.. BillyCray[(3)] 4 21
(David Nicholls) *dwlt: sn prom: rdn along over 2f out: sn drvn and wknd* **8/1**

65.95 secs (1.85) **Going Correction** +0.375s/f (Good) **8** Ran SP% **114.1**
Speed ratings (Par 102): **101,98,97,94,86 83,74,69**
Tote Swingers:1&2:£6.10, 2&3:£6.50, 1&3:£12.10 CSF £52.09 CT £321.34 TOTE £14.60: £3.10, £1.50, £2.90; EX 46.10.
Owner D A West **Bred** Patrick F Kelly And M J Foley **Trained** Great Habton, N Yorks

FOCUS
A fair sprint handicap for 3-y-os. The winner is rated back to her 2yo best.
T/Jkpt: Not won. T/Plt: £73.40 to a £1 stake. Pool £91,762.26 - 912.46 winning units T/Qpdt: £8.70 to a £1 stake. Pool £5,338.24 - 453.95 winning units JR

4296 - 4309a (Foreign Racing) - See Raceform Interactive

4263 ASCOT (R-H)
Saturday, July 23

OFFICIAL GOING: Good to soft (stands' side 7.9, centre 8.3, far side 7.8, round 7.3)
Arabian race at 5.05
Wind: fairly modest, across Weather: bright spells, light cloud

4310 LONGINES H'CAP (LADIES RACE) 7f
1:30 (1:31) (Class 3) (0-90,89) 3-Y-0+ **£8,110** (£2,515; £1,257; £629) **Stalls** Centre

Form RPR
3045 **1** **Captain Ramius (IRE)**[28] 3397 5-10-2 86............ MissHayleyMoore[(5)] 5 107
(Kevin Ryan) *chsd ldrs: wnt 2nd 3f out: led 2f out: sn clr and edgd lft u.p over 1f out: in command and styd on wl ins fnl f* **12/1**
1411 **2** *3* **Lightning Cloud (IRE)**[9] 4020 3-9-11 86............... LucyAlexander[(3)] 17 96
(Kevin Ryan) *in tch in midfield: rdn and effrt ent fnl 2f: drvn to chse clr wnr ent fnl f: r.o wl for clr 2nd but nvr a threat to wnr* **7/1**[3]
46-3 **3** *3 ½* **Don't Call Me (IRE)**[28] 3397 4-10-9 88.............. MrsAdeleMulrennan 15 91
(David Nicholls) *in tch: pushed along 2f out: rdn and kpt on steadily fr over 1f out: wnt 3rd wl ins fnl f: no ch w wnr* **17/2**
[illegible] **4** [illegible] **Ran's Gift (IRE)**[31] 3285 7-9-12 80...................(b) MissRachelKing[(3)] 21 83
(Clive Cox) *led: hdd 2f out: [illegible] lost 2nd ent fnl f: plugged on* **33/1**
0600 **5** *3 ¼* **Fishforcompliments**[15] 3805 7-9-7 72...........................(p) MissADeniel 6 66
(Richard Fahey) *awkward s and s.i.s: towards rr: hdwy to chse ldrs 1/2-way: outpcd wl over 1f out: rdn and fnd little over 1f out: wknd ins fnl f* **25/1**
6264 **6** *2 ¼* **First Cat**[14] 3840 4-10-2 81.. MsKWalsh 20 69
(Richard Hannon) *v.s.a: wl bhd: hdwy and swtchd lft over 2f out: v awkward hd carriage and sn outpcd: no ch but plugged on past btn horses fnl f* **7/1**[3]
-016 **7** *½* **Divine Call**[15] 3825 4-10-0 79.. MissNCarberry 12 65
(William Haggas) *in tch in midfield: rdn and effrt 2f out: sn drvn and outpcd by wnr: wknd over 1f out* **5/1**[1]
0234 **8** *½* **Absa Lutte (IRE)**[3] 4195 8-9-4 73........................(t) MissMMullineaux[(3)] 8 57
(Michael Mullineaux) *taken down early: hld up in tch: hdwy to chse ldrs 4f out: rdn and unable qck 2f out: wknd over 1f out* **33/1**
3152 **9** *1* **Jordaura**[26] 3473 5-9-5 75.. MissSallyRandell[(5)] 19 57
(Tony Carroll) *s.i.s: bhd: rdn 1/2-way: sme hdwy u.p over 2f out: no hdwy and no ch over 1f out: plugged on ins fnl f* **25/1**
3401 **10** *½* **Guilded Warrior**[9] 4006 8-9-12 82.. MissMBryant[(5)] 16 63
(Paddy Butler) *chsd ldrs: pushed along and struggling jst over 2f out: wknd wl over 1f out: no ch 1f out* **50/1**
2206 **11** *½* **Burning Stone (USA)**[8] 4066 4-9-5 71 oh4 ow1.. MrsEmmaLittmoden 1 50
(Gay Kelleway) *bhd: pushed along over 2f out: rdn wl over 1f out: plugged on but n.d* **40/1**
0-36 **12** *1* **Compton Blue**[3] 4215 5-9-6 76...................................(b) MissCWalton[(5)] 4 53
(Richard Hannon) *t.k.h: chsd ldrs: pushed along and struggling over 2f out: wknd 2f out: no ch over 1f out* **22/1**
-322 **13** *nk* **Suffolk Punch (IRE)**[29] 3339 4-9-11 79.............(v) MissLMasterton[(3)] 18 55
(Andrew Balding) *towards rr: hdwy wl over 2f out: rdn and no hdwy ent fnl 2f: sn wknd and no ch over 1f out* **12/1**
5006 **14** *½* **Summer Dancer (IRE)**[18] 3704 7-9-7 75.............. MissWGibson[(3)] 11 50
(Paul Midgley) *taken down early: bhd: niggled along after 2f: n.d* **25/1**
1201 **15** *¾* **April Fool**[46] 2789 7-9-12 82........................(b) MissPhillipaTutty[(5)] 9 55
(Ronald Harris) *chsd ldr tl 3f out: wknd wl over 1f out: edging rt u.p fr over 1f out: no ch 1f out* **16/1**
4510 **16** *1* **Tevez**[14] 3877 6-10-10 89.. MissZoeLilly 2 59
(Des Donovan) *in tch in midfield: rdn and hung rt over 2f out: wknd 2f out: wl bhd 1f out* **16/1**

0035 **17** *1 ½* **Ocean Legend (IRE)**[16] 3784 6-9-12 **77**...................... MissGAndrews 3 43
(Tony Carroll) *broke wl and t.k.h early: stdd and hld up in midfield after 1f: rdn and short-lived effrt 2f out: one pce and wl hld whn carried rt and hmpd over 1f out: no ch and swtchd lft sn after* **50/1**

3-26 **18** *5* **Discovery Bay**[73] 2008 3-9-8 **80**.............................. MissSBrotherton 7 30
(Roger Charlton) *racd freely: sn dashed up to chse ldrs: wknd qckly over 2f out: wl bhd over 1f out* **13/2**[2]

3000 **19** *18* **Vitznau (IRE)**[10] 3982 7-9-12 **82**.................. MissSallyAnnGrassick(5) 10 —
(Robert Cowell) *s.i.s: a in rr: lost tch 2f out: t.o and eased ins fnl f* **40/1**

50/0 **20** *16* **Rare Bet**[12] 3908 5-9-0 **70** oh25.................................. MissJoeyEllis(5) 13 —
(John Panvert) *midfield: struggling after 2f: bhd and lost tch 3f out: t.o and virtually p.u ins fnl f* **150/1**

1m 29.75s (2.55) **Going Correction** +0.425s/f (Yiel)
WFA 3 from 4yo+ 7lb **20** Ran SP% **123.9**
Speed ratings (Par 107): **102,98,94,94,90 87,87,86,85,85 84,83,83,82,81 80,78,73,52,34**
toteswingers:1&2:£62.90, 2&3:£2.60, 1&3:£57.50 CSF £82.83 CT £788.38 TOTE £16.60: £3.40, £2.10, £2.30, £6.50; EX 141.70 Trifecta £928.90 Pool of: £1280.39 - 1.02 winning units..
Owner Mrs Clodagh McStay **Bred** P G Lyons **Trained** Hambleton, N Yorks
■ Stewards' Enquiry : Miss Sally Randell three-day ban: used whip with excessive frequency out of contrention (Aug 11-13)

FOCUS
The runners in this ladies' contest were spread well across the track, although nothing raced close to either rail. With several established front-runners in opposition, a strong pace was assured and those that raced close to the pace appeared to be favoured. It resulted in a 1-2 for trainer Kevin Ryan. The winner's best form since he was a 2yo.

NOTEBOOK
Captain Ramius(IRE) appeared to have it to do in order to reverse last month's Newcastle running with Don't Call Me on just 1lb better terms, especially as that rival was making his seasonal reappearance, but unlike there this was a race where those that raced handily were at an advantage. Always up with the pace towards the far side of the field, he had established a sizeable advantage before the furlong pole and, despite hanging away to his left under pressure, was never in any danger of being caught. (op 14-1)
Lightning Cloud(IRE) ◆, winner of four of his five starts this year (all over this trip) and put up 6lb for his recent Leicester success, travelled noticeably well behind the leaders towards the nearside. He stayed on well once finally put under pressure, but his stable companion had got away and he was never going to reel him in. He remains in top form and may be capable of better still. (op 6-1)
Don't Call Me(IRE) ◆ ran a blinder on his debut for the yard when returning from a 266-day absence in that Newcastle contest last month (Captain Ramius back in fifth) and was another to travel particularly well behind the leaders. He ran on when finally put under pressure from over a furlong out, but didn't find as much as had seemed likely. He remains one to be interested in during the second-half of the season. (op 8-1 tchd 9-1)
Den's Gift(IRE) established his usual handy position towards the nearside of the field and stayed on well, but he is still to score on turf after 21 attempts.
Fishforcompliments, sixth when favourite for this race off 6lb higher last year, had every chance towards the far side of the group and performed creditably, but a record of 2-54 doesn't make him an attractive betting proposition.
First Cat seemed to struggle to go the early pace and was soon in a detached last. He did make some late headway, but was never going to win and is another that has become very hard to win with. (tchd 13-2)
Divine Call tried to stay on from off the pace over the last 2f, but it came to little and his best form so far has come on the all-weather. (op 11-2 tchd 6-1 in places)

4311 JAGUAR XKR-S WINKFIELD STKS (LISTED RACE) 7f
2:05 (2:05) (Class 1) 2-Y-O

£12,476 (£4,730; £2,367; £1,179; £591; £297) **Stalls** Centre

Form RPR
01 **1** **Talwar (IRE)**[22] 3590 2-9-2 0... JimmyFortune 2 105+
(Jeremy Noseda) *broke wl: sn stdd and in tch: led jst over 2f out: rdn wl over 1f out: drew clr w rival over 1f out: edgd lft ins fnl f: hld on wl* **9/2**[3]

310 **2** *shd* **Trumpet Major (IRE)**[39] 3012 2-9-2 0.............................. RyanMoore 5 105+
(Richard Hannon) *in tch: effrt to chal and edgd rt 2f out: drvn and clr w wnr over 1f out: kpt on wl but a jst hld ins fnl f* **5/1**

1050 **3** *6* **Jack Who's He (IRE)**[8] 4055 2-9-2 0........................... CathyGannon 6 89
(David Evans) *chsd ldr tl led 3f out: hdd and drvn jst over 2f out: ev ch and edgd rt 2f out: outpcd by ldng pair and btn over 1f out: 3rd and plugged on same pce ins fnl f* **14/1**

10 **4** *1* **Sound Advice**[14] 3861 2-9-2 0... DavidAllan 7 86
(Keith Dalgleish) *dwlt: sn rcvrd and in tch: rdn and unable qck ent fnl 2f: outpcd and btn over 1f out: styd on same pce ins fnl f* **7/1**

1 **5** *6* **Pearl Charm (USA)**[28] 3382 2-9-2 0............................ RichardHughes 3 70
(Richard Hannon) *stdd s: hld up in last pair: rdn and effrt over 2f out: no imp: rdn and wknd over 1f out* **7/4**[1]

531 **6** *3 ½* **Comical**[11] 3954 2-9-2 0.. FrankieDettori 4 60
(Mark Johnston) *led tl 3f out: sn rdn: drvn and wknd wl over 1f out* **4/1**[2]

60 **7** *5* **Tigers Tale (IRE)**[9] 4007 2-9-2 0.. LukeMorris 1 47
(Roger Teal) *a in rr and sn niggled along: drvn and wknd jst over 2f out* **66/1**

1m 30.17s (2.97) **Going Correction** +0.425s/f (Yiel) **7** Ran SP% **111.9**
Speed ratings (Par 102): **100,99,93,91,85 81,75**
toteswingers:1&2:£3.40, 2&3:£8.90, 1&3:£7.00 CSF £25.75 TOTE £5.70: £2.80, £2.80; EX 30.50.
Owner Vimal Khosla **Bred** Philip And Mrs Jane Myerscough **Trained** Newmarket, Suffolk

FOCUS
The sixth running of this Listed race. The best previous winner was Raven's Pass, who landed the Queen Elizabeth II Stakes and Breeders' Cup Classic, while in 2009 it went to the classy Polytrack performer Nideeb. This renewal looked up to the mark on paper, although none of the field had made an impact in stakes races previously and the first two in the betting disappointed. The runners raced down the centre, initially splitting into groups of four and three a short way apart before merging. The first two fought out a tight finish, finishing six lengths clear of the third, and the form fits with the race averages.

NOTEBOOK
Talwar(IRE) just about emerged on top. An impressive winner from the front at Sandown, he enjoyed a nice tow from Comical here before easing his way into the firing line. He edged to his left under pressure but stuck his neck out willingly and just prevailed. Well entered up, he is on the upgrade and will have no problem with a mile. (tchd 5-1)
Trumpet Major(IRE) was the choice of Richard Hughes in the Coventry, but failed to beat any of his three stable companions and finished only 14th, six places behind Jack Who's He. The stable second string here, he proved his class with a smart effort, challenging between horses and sticking on bravely despite being carried to his left slightly. The longer trip suited this Champagne Stakes and Royal Lodge entry. (op 9-2 tchd 11-2)
Jack Who's He(IRE) was initially reluctant to go down to the start. One of the first to be brought under pressure, he could not match the first pair for pace but stuck on for third and seemed to stay the 7f well enough. He has been beaten four times at this level and higher now, but at least earned black type here despite finishing well held. (op 11-1)
Sound Advice, dropped in class after contesting Newmarket's Grade 2 Superlative Stakes last time, was slow to break again but soon raced prominently. He could not quicken up when required and was readily held by the principals, but is probably still learning. The ground shouldn't have posed him a problem, as both his parents and his full sister won in easy conditions. (op 8-1)
Pearl Charm(USA) was the subject of favourable noises from connections and was expected to improve considerably on his Doncaster maiden win, having been markedly green that day. However, he failed to pick up and was beaten some way out. These different underfoot conditions may well have been a factor, but he could be expected to have done better than this. (op 9-4 tchd 13-8 and 5-2 in a place)
Comical, an all-the-way Yarmouth winner, attempted the same tactics but dropped away in disappointing fashion once tackled. The easy ground may have been against him. (op 7-2)
Tigers Tale(IRE) looked up against it, having been unplaced in both his maidens incuding the one won by Talwar at Sandown, and he was never seen with a chance. There was definite promise in his second run at Epsom though and he remains one to be interested in down in grade. (op 33-1)

4312 PRINCESS MARGARET JUDDMONTE STKS (GROUP 3) (FILLIES) 6f
2:40 (2:40) (Class 1) 2-Y-O

£28,355 (£10,750; £5,380; £2,012; £2,012; £675) **Stalls** Centre

Form RPR
1 **1** **Angels Will Fall (IRE)**[75] 1946 2-8-12 0........................ RobertWinston 1 104+
(B W Hills) *stdd s: t.k.h: hld up in rr: rdn and effrt 2f out: qcknd to ld ent fnl f: rdn to assert and edgd lft ins fnl f: r.o wl* **9/2**[3]

1 **2** *½* **Regal Realm**[57] 2467 2-8-12 0... JimmyFortune 5 103+
(Jeremy Noseda) *hld up in tch in last trio: rdn and effrt 2f out: edgd rt wl over 1f out: drvn to chse wnr ins fnl f: r.o wl* **5/2**[2]

35 **3** *2 ¼* **Miss Lahar**[12] 3917 2-8-12 0... HughBowman 6 96
(Mick Channon) *chsd ldr: rdn and ev ch over 1f out tl ins fnl f: wknd fnl 100yds* **100/1**

4110 **4** *1 ¾* **Betty Fontaine (IRE)**[15] 3821 2-8-12 0........................... FrannyNorton 3 90
(Mick Channon) *in tch: rdn ent fnl 2f: unable qck and outpcd over 1f out: no threat to ldrs but styd on again ins fnl f* **20/1**

0162 **4** *dht* **Luv U Forever**[15] 3808 2-8-12 0...................................... CathyGannon 4 90
(Jo Hughes) *led: rdn and qcknd jst over 2f out: hdd ent fnl f: wknd ins fnl f* **20/1**

12 **6** *7* **Russelliana**[15] 3821 2-8-12 0.. RyanMoore 2 73
(Sir Michael Stoute) *t.k.h: hld up in tch in last trio: rdn and effrt jst over 2f out: chsd ldrs over 1f out: no ex and btn 1f out: eased ins fnl f* **10/11**[1]

016 **7** *4* **Red Larkspur (IRE)**[28] 3402 2-8-12 0.......................... RichardHughes 7 59
(Roger Teal) *taken down early: stdd s: t.k.h: in tch: rdn and unable qck over 2f out: wkng whn short of room wl over 1f out: wl btn and eased ins fnl f* **33/1**

1m 16.8s (2.40) **Going Correction** +0.425s/f (Yiel) **7** Ran SP% **112.6**
Speed ratings (Par 101): **101,100,97,95,95 85,80**
toteswingers:1&2:£2.00, 2&3:£15.30, 1&3:£12.90 CSF £15.37 TOTE £5.20: £2.60, £2.20; EX 13.00.
Owner Mrs E O'Leary **Bred** Islanmore Stud **Trained** Lambourn, Berks

FOCUS
The race was ultimately fought out between two fillies that had won their only previous starts and, coincidentally, both were returning from short layoffs after suffering minor setbacks. Although the early pace was only fair, the front pair came from last and last but one. The favourite disappointed and the third is a big doubt, so this bare form is limited and rated to the bottom end of the race averages.

NOTEBOOK
Angels Will Fall(IRE) hadn't been seen since beating a subsequent winner impressively on her Windsor debut in May, with a pulled muscle forcing her to miss the Queen Mary. Having been held up last early, she was produced with a telling turn of foot towards the far side of the track to lead a furlong out and, despite understandably getting a bit tired, pulled out just enough to hold off the runner-up. This looks about as far as she wants to go and her pedigree is all about speed being by Acclamation out of a Listed-class sprinter. She holds some big entries in the coming months including the Cheveley Park, whilst the Lowther was immediately nominated as her next target. She would look a major player in those races on this evidence. She was immediately cut to a best-price 25-1 for the 1,000 Guineas, but with her stamina a major concern that doesn't look generous. (op 11-2)
Regal Realm's debut success at Newmarket in May had been boosted in the best-possible fashion with the runner-up going on to beat Russelliana in the Cherry Hinton and the third going on to take the Albany, but she hadn't been seen since then due to niggling problems. Also held up off the pace early, she made her effort towards the nearside of the field, on the opposite flank to the winner, but had every chance to pick her up. She couldn't quite find the speed to do so, but perhaps that was understandable given that, unlike her rival, her pedigree is much more about stamina, being by Medicean out of a Fantastic Light mare. She was also immediately quoted at 25-1 for the 1,000 Guineas, but would appear to have a better chance of getting the mile than her conqueror purely on breeding. (op 2-1)
Miss Lahar, who hadn't seemed to be progressing, could be considered to hold the form down, but she is held in high regard at home so perhaps this wasn't a great surprise to connections. She has the ability to win a nice race, although her confidence may be helped by trying to win a maiden with her first.
Betty Fontaine(IRE) had looked better over shorter before now and had around four lengths to find with Russelliana on Cherry Hinton running, but she ran something of a strange race here, getting outpaced over a furlong out before running on powerfully again near the line. (op 16-1 tchd 25-1)
Luv U Forever showed that she wasn't that far short of this class when sixth in the Albany and she showed good speed to take the field along to the furlong pole. The minimum trip may suit her better at the moment. (op 16-1 tchd 25-1)
Russelliana brought the classiest form into the race following her second to Gamilati in the Cherry Hinton, though strictly on form that gave her a bit to find with Regal Realm who had beaten the Godolphin filly on her debut. She was bitterly disappointing here, however, finding nothing off the bridle and looking particularly unhappy in the final furlong. Perhaps the ground wasn't too her liking, but this was still too bad to be true. Official explanation: jockey said filly hung left (op Evens tchd 11-10)
Red Larkspur(IRE) ran creditably when sixth in a Newmarket Listed event last time, but found this better company too much. (tchd 25-1)

4313 DELOITTE H'CAP 1m (S)
3:15 (3:16) (Class 2) 3-Y-O

£28,012 (£8,388; £4,194; £2,097; £1,048; £526) **Stalls** Centre

Form RPR
2121 **1** **Rave (IRE)**[15] 3797 3-9-3 **97**.. PatrickHills(3) 9 109+
(J W Hills) *hld up in rr: gd hdwy on bit 2f out: rdn to ld over 1f out: edgd rt 1f out: edgd lft u.p and r.o wl fnl f* **10/1**

2-11 **2** *1 ½* **Albaasil (IRE)**[14] 3864 3-9-7 **98**...................................... RichardHills 4 106+
(Sir Michael Stoute) *hld up in tch in rr: hdwy over 2f out: rdn to chse wnr over 1f out: r.o wl for clr 2nd but a hld by wnr fnl f* **11/4**[1]

6-23 **3** *2 ¾* **Aerial Acclaim (IRE)**[21] 3649 3-8-3 **80**............................... LukeMorris 1 82
(Clive Cox) *t.k.h: hld up wl in tch: rdn and effrt 2f out: drvn and outpcd by ldng pair 1f out: edgd lft u.p ins fnl f: kpt on one pce* **6/1**[3]

2-50 **4** *hd* **Seattle Drive (IRE)**^{14} 3864 3-8-12 **89**.......................... PhilipRobinson 3 91
(David Elsworth) *hld up in tch in rr: rdn and effrt 2f out: chsd ldrs and drvn jst over 1f out: outpcd by ldng pair 1f out: kpt on same pce after* **14/1**

2050 **5** *1 3/4* **Ahlaain (USA)**^{37} 3068 3-9-4 **95**....................................... WilliamBuick 2 93
(David Simcock) *chsd ldrs tl led jst over 2f out: sn rdn: drvn and hdd over 1f out: wknd and btn whn sltly hmpd ins fnl f* **25/1**

5351 **6** *1/2* **Abergeldie (USA)**^{15} 3803 3-7-9 **75** oh3.................(v) SimonPearce(3) 10 71+
(Andrew Balding) *t.k.h: hld up in tch: rdn and outpcd 2f out: keeping on but no threat to ldrs whn hung bdly rt ins fnl f* **28/1**

0-22 **7** *nk* **My Freedom (IRE)**^{15} 3825 3-8-13 **90**......................(v^{1}) FrankieDettori 11 86
(Saeed Bin Suroor) *stdd s: t.k.h: hld up in rr: rdn and hung bdly rt ent fnl f: sn bhd: styd on but no threat to ldrs ins fnl f* **4/1^{2}**

4441 **8** *1 1/4* **Mariachi Man**^{35} 3159 3-9-7 **98**.. DavidAllan 6 91
(Tim Easterby) *racd keenly: chsd ldr tl led after 1f: hdd and rdn 2f out: wknd u.p jst over 1f out* **6/1^{3}**

9 *1 3/4* **Alnashmy (FR)**^{14} 3883 3-9-1 **92**...................................... CO'Donoghue 5 81
(David Marnane, Ire) *chsd ldrs: rdn jst over 2f out: edgd lft u.p over 1f out: wknd ent fnl f* **25/1**

6311 **10** *nk* **Stage Attraction (IRE)**^{10} 3987 3-8-10 **87**..................... JimmyFortune 8 77+
(Andrew Balding) *chsd ldrs: rdn and unable qck 2f out: wkng and btn whn squeezed for room and hmpd 1f out* **9/1**

0012 **11** *7* **Crown Counsel (IRE)**^{16} 3763 3-9-2 **93**......................... RyanMoore 7 65
(Mark Johnston) *led for 1f: chsd ldr after tl jst over 2f out: sn struggling u.p: wknd over 1f out* **16/1**

1m 43.33s (2.73) **Going Correction** +0.425s/f (Yiel) **11** Ran SP% **118.0**
Speed ratings (Par 106): **103,101,98,98,96 96,96,94,93,92 85**
toteswingers:1&2:£4.40, 2&3:£5.30, 1&3:£16.30 CSF £36.99 CT £188.48 TOTE £9.60: £2.20, £1.60, £2.80; EX 38.80 Trifecta £309.40 Pool: £3617.58 - 8.64 winning units..
Owner Gary And Linnet Woodward **Bred** P E Banahan **Trained** Upper Lambourn, Berks

FOCUS
A classy and competitive handicap, and sound form amongst the first five. The pace did not appear to be overly strong, only lifting with under 3f to run, but even so the principals came from the back of the field. The runners raced down the centre and the main contenders emerged from the far side of the bunch, before the first two edged across the track late on.

NOTEBOOK
Rave(IRE) made rapid progress from the rear of the field to strike the front and then drifted markedly to his left, but was in command at that point. A rapidly improving colt, he shrugged off a 10lb rise for his win over the round mile here and this is unlikely to prove the limit of his progress. Likely to be tried in Listed or Group 3 company soon, he is still unexposed on a quick surface. (op 7-1)
Albaasil(IRE), an impressive winner at the Newmarket July festival, still looked fairly treated despite a 10lb rise. Held up again after being buffeted at the start, he picked up ground at the same time as the winner but could not quite match him for pace and was held when copying his rival and veering to his left late on. He was clear of the rest and remains on the upgrade. (op 10-3 tchd 7-2)
Aerial Acclaim(IRE), representing the connections of Dunelight, a previous winner of this race, was the only maiden in the line-up. After missing the break he was soon able to race prominently before sticking on at the same pace at the sharp end. He should find a race before long. (op 8-1 tchd 9-1 and 10-1 in places)
Seattle Drive(IRE)'s juvenile win came the last time he encountered easy ground and he was 13lb better off with Albaasil on their meeting at Newmarket. He was another to come from the rear, staying on without threatening the first two, and is probably ready for 1m2f now. He's settling better these days. (op 16-1)
Ahlaain(USA), running in his first handicap after contesting Group races earlier in the season, tracked the leaders before briefly edging ahead, but was unable to hold off challengers on both sides. He has no problem with softish conditions. (tchd 33-1)
Abergeldie(USA), the only filly in this field, showed improved form in a first-time visor at Chepstow but was effectively 9lb higher here, where she was 3lb out of the weights. She hung badly to her right when attempting to mount a challenge on the nearside of the bunch, but for which she would have finished closer. (op 25-1)
My Freedom(IRE), tried in a visor after hanging last time, settled well enough but was caught on heels when the pace lifted and could never get into it. He was beaten when hanging again late on. (op 7-2 tchd 3-1)
Mariachi Man's 9lb rise for his Ayr win left him with improvement to find, but he was still 3lb better off with Rave who was second that day. He had ground conditions to suit, but faded after showing ahead to the two pole. (op 8-1)
Stage Attraction(IRE) was already toiling on this hat trick bid when he was squeezed out. (op 8-1 tchd 15-2)
Crown Counsel(IRE) raced keenly and soon dropped away once the race developed. (op 14-1 tchd 12-1)

4314 BETFAIR SUMMER DOUBLE FIRST LEG INTERNATIONAL (HERITAGE H'CAP) 7f

3:50 (3:52) (Class 2) 3-Y-O+

£62,250 (£18,640; £9,320; £4,660; £2,330; £1,170) **Stalls** Centre

Form RPR

5300 **1** **Bronze Prince**^{15} 3825 4-8-6 **89**..................................... WilliamBuick 24 100
(John Gosden) *bhd: rdn jst over 2f out: stl plenty to do whn hung rt over 1f: swtchd lft ent fnl f: str run fnl 100yds to ld nr fin* **16/1**

5-30 **2** *1/2* **The Confessor**^{27} 3440 4-8-4 **87**...................................... CathyGannon 7 97
(Henry Candy) *chsd ldrs tl led 2f out: sn rdn: drvn and kpt on v gamely fr over 1f out: hdd and no ex nr fin* **10/1**

0001 **3** *hd* **Noble Citizen (USA)**^{14} 3841 6-8-7 **90** 3ex..................(b) MartinLane 19 99
(David Simcock) *hld up in tch in midfield: effrt 2f out: drvn to chse ldrs 1f out: kpt on wl u.p fnl 100yds* **12/1**

-110 **4** *hd* **Pravda Street**^{31} 3276 6-8-1 **84**... JimmyQuinn 2 93
(Brian Ellison) *in tch: rdn and effrt jst over 2f out: ev ch and drvn over 1f out: kpt on wl u.p: no ex towards fin* **40/1**

4026 **5** *1 1/4* **Atlantic Sport (USA)**^{7} 4092 6-9-3 **100**....................... HughBowman 13 106
(Mick Channon) *stdd s: hld up in rr: rdn and hdwy ent fnl 2f: drvn to chse ldrs over 1f out: kpt on same pce ins fnl f* **25/1**

1205 **6** *3/4* **Our Jonathan**^{14} 3852 4-9-5 **102**.................................... FrannyNorton 12 106
(Kevin Ryan) *stdd and wnt lft s: hld up in rr: rdn and hdwy over 1f out: r.o ins fnl f: nt rch ldrs* **11/1**

0400 **7** *1/2* **Castles In The Air**^{36} 3109 6-9-1 **98**........................... RichardHughes 8 100
(Richard Fahey) *stdd s: hld up in rr: rdn and hdwy jst over 1f out: r.o ins fnl f: nt rch ldrs* **16/1**

-105 **8** *1* **Imperial Guest**^{14} 3841 5-9-1 **98**.. SebSanders 21 97
(George Margarson) *hld up towards rr: hdwy over 2f out: rdn and styd on same pce fr over 1f out* **16/1**

0210 **9** *1/2* **Manassas (IRE)**^{14} 3862 6-9-4 **101**..................................... MartinDwyer 4 99
(Brian Meehan) *in tch: rdn over 2f out: edgd rt u.p 2f out: unable qck over 1f out: styd on same pce ins fnl f* **16/1**

0105 **10** *hd* **Imperial Djay (IRE)**^{8} 4049 6-8-11 **94**.......................... RobertWinston 6 92
(Ruth Carr) *stdd s: hld up in rr: rdn and edgd rt 2f out: kpt on ins fnl f: nvr trbld ldrs* **66/1**

2253 **11** *nse* **Dubai Dynamo**^{7} 4100 6-8-12 **95**..................................... JimmyFortune 9 92
(Ruth Carr) *t.k.h: hld up in tch in midfield: rdn and effrt ent fnl 2f: edgd rt u.p over 1f out: kpt on fnl f but nvr gng pce to rch ldrs* **22/1**

6505 **12** *3/4* **Al Muheer (IRE)**^{12} 3924 6-7-7 **81** oh4.......................(b) RyanPowell(5) 17 76
(Ruth Carr) *hld up in tch: rdn and unable qck 2f out: styd on same pce fr over 1f out* **33/1**

1022 **13** *1/2* **Excellent Guest**^{14} 3862 4-8-11 **94**............................... PhilipRobinson 3 88
(George Margarson) *hld up towards rr: swtchd rt and effrt over 2f out: rdn 2f out: no imp over 1f out: wknd ins fnl f* **8/1^{2}**

5030 **14** *hd* **Striking Spirit**^{14} 3862 6-8-11 **94**.. DavidAllan 18 88
(Tim Easterby) *in tch: rdn over 2f out: edgd rt u.p and unable qck over 1f out: wknd ins fnl f* **9/1^{3}**

0001 **15** *3/4* **Reignier**^{8} 4049 4-8-7 **93** 3ex.. MartinHarley(3) 10 85
(Mrs K Burke) *t.k.h: hld up in tch in midfield: rdn and unable qck jst over 2f out: outpcd wl over 1f out: styng on same pce and no threat to ldrs whn sltly hmpd ent fnl f* **16/1**

0-41 **16** *1 1/4* **Hawkeyethenoo (IRE)**^{77} 1885 5-9-4 **104**...................... GaryBartley(3) 5 92
(Jim Goldie) *hld up in tch: effrt 3f out: rdn and unable qck 2f out: wknd jst over 1f out* **6/1^{1}**

2400 **17** *2 1/4* **Advanced**^{22} 3578 8-8-4 **92**..(p) JulieBurke(5) 14 74
(Kevin Ryan) *chsd ldr tl jst over 2f out: wknd u.p over 1f out* **33/1**

00-0 **18** *nk* **Mirza**^{42} 2927 4-8-2 **85**.. LukeMorris 11 66
(Rae Guest) *stdd s: hld up towards rr: rdn and effrt 2f out: no imp whn n.m.r over 1f out: wknd ins fnl f* **66/1**

-105 **19** *7* **Joseph Henry**^{49} 2717 9-8-9 **92**.. RichardHills 16 63
(David Nicholls) *chsd ldrs: rdn 2f out: wknd over 1f out: eased ins fnl f* **50/1**

0061 **20** *1/2* **Brae Hill (IRE)**^{14} 3862 5-8-13 **96** 3ex............................. RyanMoore 23 57
(Richard Fahey) *hld up towards rr: rdn and effrt over 2f out: struggling and drvn wl over 1f out: sn wknd: eased ins fnl f* **8/1^{2}**

0061 **21** *1 1/2* **Below Zero (IRE)**^{4} 4188 4-8-6 **89** 3ex.............................. LiamJones 15 46
(Mark Johnston) *led tl 2f out: wknd qckly over 1f out: eased ins fnl f* **40/1**

1401 **22** *4* **Kingscroft (IRE)**^{2} 4243 3-7-12 **88** 3ex......................... JamieMackay 20 31
(Mark Johnston) *chsd ldrs: rdn over 2f out: wknd qckly wl over 1f out: eased ins fnl f* **33/1**

2510 **23** *2 1/4* **Leviathan**^{21} 3645 4-8-9 **92**.. CO'Donoghue 1 32
(Tony Newcombe) *wnt rt s: rcvrd and in midfield after 2f: rdn 1/2-way: wknd u.p wl over 1f out: eased jst ins fnl f* **12/1**

1m 28.6s (1.40) **Going Correction** +0.425s/f (Yiel)
WFA 3 from 4yo+ 7lb **23** Ran SP% **135.6**
Speed ratings (Par 109): **109,108,108,107,106 105,105,103,103,103 103,102,101,101,100 99,96,96,88,87 85,81,78**
toteswingers:1&2:£62.50, 2&3:£44.50, 1&3:£79.70 CSF £165.90 CT £2063.51 TOTE £22.20: £5.40, £3.10, £2.70, £11.40; EX 322.90 Trifecta £5041.70 Pool: £36247.45 - 5.32 winning units..

Owner Ali Saeed **Bred** Coln Valley Stud **Trained** Newmarket, Suffolk
■ Stewards' Enquiry : Cathy Gannon four-day ban: used whip with excessive frequency (Aug 6-9)

FOCUS
A fiercely competitive and valuable handicap and a race that has gone to a horse near the head of the handicap in recent years, with six of the seven previous winners officially rated 97 or above. However, this time it was a race for the lower weights with the first four home rated 90 or lower. The last two winners of the race lined up again and the entire field raced as a bunch down the middle of the track. The form seems sound enough with the winner up 5lb on his previous best.

NOTEBOOK
Bronze Prince hadn't got home over 1m in his previous two starts and he needed the ground to have dried up to take his chance here, so connections will have been glad that they allowed him to run. Given plenty to do at the back of the field having started from the stands'-side draw, he still only had two behind him passing the 2f pole, but once switched produced a devastating turn of foot to cut down the leaders and grab the race near the line, despite hanging away to his right. This was only his seventh start, so there is the possibility he could build on this.
The Confessor ◆ ran really well from a moderate draw dropped to 6f at the Curragh last time, but this is his best trip. Given a contrasting ride to the winner, he was at the sharp end from the start but had the close attentions of both Below Zero and Advanced. After shaking off that pair 2f from home, he kept battling hard and was unfortunate to have the prize snatched from him near the line. He deserves compensation for this. (tchd 9-1 and 11-1 in a place)
Noble Citizen(USA) picked up a 3lb penalty for his recent success over 6f here, but was still 2lb lower than when runner-up in this last year and 2lb well in compared to his revised mark. Held up early like the winner, he produced a dangerous looking challenge towards the nearside inside the last 2f and ran on to the line despite edging away to his right. (op 11-1)
Pravda Street didn't get home over 1m from a bad draw at Carlisle last time and proved much better suited by the return to this trip, holding a prominent position throughout and having every chance. Although 8lb above his last winning mark, he has won off 1lb higher in his time so isn't handicapped out of things just yet. (op 33-1)
Atlantic Sport(USA) ran on from off the pace to finish a highly creditable fifth and fared best of those near the head of the weights, but he is on a losing run of 17 and will remain difficult to place. (op 33-1)
Our Jonathan didn't enjoy the best of luck in his previous two starts, but didn't seem to have any excuses here though he still ran well and was doing all his best work late. He will still need to find improvement from somewhere to defy this sort of mark, however. (op 12-1 tchd 10-1)
Castles In The Air gained his last win off 2lb higher in the this race last year and was ridden with plenty of confidence. It looked as though he might sneak into a place inside the last 2f, but was making no impression on the leaders in the closing stages.
Imperial Guest ◆ 'won' the race on his side, though only seventh overall in this last year, and this was another creditable effort as he would have preferred quicker ground. Staying on well from off the pace over the last 2f, he is one to watch out for when getting his conditions.
Manassas(IRE) was no better off with Hawkeyethenoo having finished second to him in the Victoria Cup and had questions to answer following a poor effort in the Bunbury Cup. He was in a good position throughout, but found little once off the bridle.
Imperial Djay(IRE) ◆ had twice disappointed since winning off a 6lb lower at Newmarket last month and although only tenth here, was doing some good work late so is by no means a lost cause. (op 50-1)
Excellent Guest, runner-up to Manassas in the Buckingham Palace and Brae Hill in the Bunbury Cup, was 2lb well in compared to his revised mark and was close enough towards the far side over a furlong out, but didn't get home. (op 9-1)
Striking Spirit ◆ ran better than his finishing position would suggest as he was challenging for the lead over a furlong out before fading. The ground wouldn't have been ideal, so he is worth keeping an eye on. (op 11-1 tchd 12-1)
Reignier was strictly thrown in here as he would have had 11lb more to carry had the handicapper been able to include his recent success over higher-rated rivals in a Haydock conditions event, so after this it remains to be seen how he is campaigned. (op 20-1)
Hawkeyethenoo(IRE) was 8lb higher than when winning the Victoria Cup over C&D in May and a brief effort 2f from home amounted to little. He isn't going to be easy to place now and may need to switch to conditions events. (op 7-1 tchd 15-2)
Brae Hill(IRE)'s success in the Bunbury Cup was probably mainly due to a track bias, as he raced alone against the stands' rail, but he came nowhere near repeating that form here. He was reported to have run flat. Official explanation: jockey said gelding ran flat (op 9-1)

Leviathan wasn't ridden to best advantage last time, but was just plain disappointing here. (tchd 14-1)

4315 KING GEORGE VI AND QUEEN ELIZABETH STKS (SPONSORED BY BETFAIR) BRITISH CHAMPIONS' SERIES (GROUP 1) 1m 4f

4:30 (4:30) (Class 1) 3-Y-0+ **£611,123** (£236,137; £121,756; £64,246) **Stalls** Low

Form RPR

-121 **1** **Nathaniel (IRE)**[36] 3105 3-8-9 115 WilliamBuick 3 126
(John Gosden) *t.k.h: reluctant ldr and set slow pce for 2f: chsd ldr after: clsd on ldr over 3f out: rdn and qcknd to ld over 2f out: hung lft u.p 1f out: r.o strly* **11/2**

1-12 **2** *2 ¾* **Workforce**[21] 3646 4-9-7 128 RyanMoore 4 125+
(Sir Michael Stoute) *t.k.h: hld up in tch: allowed ldrs to go clr 8f out: clsd 4f out: rdn to chse wnr wl over 1f out: drvn and hung lft over 1f out: 1 l down 1f out: continued to hang across crse and lost all ch fnl f* **6/5**[1]

-311 **3** *1 ¼* **St Nicholas Abbey (IRE)**[50] 2680 4-9-7 123 JPO'Brien 2 120
(A P O'Brien, Ire) *t.k.h: hld up in tch: allowed ldrs to go clr 8f out: rdn and effrt jst over 2f out: kpt on same pce and no real imp on wnr* **7/2**[3]

-000 **4** *20* **Debussy (IRE)**[38] 3031 5-9-7 113 AhmedAjtebi 5 109
(Mahmood Al Zarooni) *t.k.h: w ldr tl led and crossed to rail 10f out: wnt clr 8f out: rdn and hdd 2f out: drvn and dropped to last over 1f out: btn and rdr looking arnd for stablemate 1f out: sn eased* **50/1**

6-11 **F** **Rewilding**[38] 3031 4-9-7 127 FrankieDettori 1 —
(Mahmood Al Zarooni) *stdd s: t.k.h: hld up in last: clsd over 3f out: disputing 4 l 4th and rdn whn broke leg and fell 2f out: fatally injured* **3/1**[2]

2m 35.07s (2.57) **Going Correction** +0.425s/f (Yiel)
WFA 3 from 4yo+ 12lb **5** Ran SP% **110.0**
Speed ratings (Par 117): **108,106,105,92,—**
CSF £12.69 TOTE £5.70: £2.20, £1.20; EX 12.50.
Owner Lady Rothschild **Bred** Kincorth Investments Inc **Trained** Newmarket, Suffolk

FOCUS

On paper this was another compelling edition of the midsummer highlight, first run 60 years ago, but it lacked a bit of depth and it was the smallest field since Aunt Edith beat four rivals in 1966. The winner was the sole three-year-old in the field, the Derby winner Pour Moi never even being considered for the race. He is being given a classic French prep for the Arc, worth the best part of four times as much these days as the King George, which has lost its status as Ascot's richest race to the Champion Stakes. That said, apart from the winner, all the runners had top-level wins to their name including last year's Derby and Arc and this season's Coronation Cup and Prince of Wales's Stakes. Unfortunately, it was a dramatic and messy race, marred by the death of Rewilding. It was run at a very sedate early pace and the time was slow. A cautious view has been taken of the form and Nathaniel is rated up 6lb on his Royal Ascot win and Workforce rated just off him, with St Nicholas Abbey 5lb below his best.

NOTEBOOK

Nathaniel(IRE) missed the Grand Prix de Paris because the ground was too quick, but conditions had come right for him here and he justified connections' decision to supplement him for £75,000. The colt sweated up in the paddock, as he tends to do, and was kept some distance from the other horses in the parade. William Buick was obliged to let him lead early as Debussy was reined back, but was happy to accept a lead when the pacemaker went on after a quarter of a mile. The colt was in the right place to strike entering the straight and ran on strongly, edging to his left as he did so but nothing like as much as his nearest pursuer, who threw away his winning chance. He's the first 3yo to win this since Alamshar in 2003 and the first of his age who had not run in an Epsom or Irish Derby since Ile De Bourbon in 1978. The last-named colt, like Nathaniel, came here after taking the King Edward VII Stakes at the Royal meeting. The unsatisfactory nature of the race means that there are doubts over this form, but Nathaniel is clearly a top-notch colt. The three horses who have beaten him include Classic winners Frankel and Treasure Beach and there is surely more progress to come as this was only the sixth start of his career. The St Leger is out now and the Arc is a realistic target, but he would need to be supplemented. He may go straight there, but also has the option of returning to Ascot for the Champion Stakes. He will almost certainly remain in training at four. (tchd 5-1 and 6-1 and 13-2 in places)

Workforce, following his record-breaking win at Epsom last year, was a bitterly disappointing fifth of six to stablemate Harbinger in this race 12 months ago, before atoning with a battling Arc victory. A very rare instance of a Derby winner contesting this race twice, he was strongly backed through the week with the softish ground looking sure to suit. Back at his optimum trip for the first time this year following his second to So You Think in the Eclipse, he settled well in fourth and went after Nathaniel in the straight. For a moment it looked as if he was going to get to him, but he then hung badly across the track and ended up near the stands' rail, despite Moore holding the whip in the correct hand. It would have been close, but he may well have won had he kept straight. It transpired that the colt had been struck into on the home turn, and returned with a cut to a leg. A rematch with the winner in the Arc would be on the cards provided he recovers fully and the most sensible route would be to give him a trial in the Prix Foy at Longchamp in early September. He has entries in the Juddmonte International, sponsored by his owner, and the Irish Champion Stakes, but they would both mean dropping back in trip and the former would come too soon. Official explanation: vet said colt was struck into (tchd 11-10 and 5-4 in places)

St Nicholas Abbey(IRE) came here on a roll after his Coronation Cup win and was bidding to emulate Harbinger, who won Chester's Ormonde Stakes en route to this race last year. He was in third position for much of the trip but had dropped back to fourth turning in and young Joseph O'Brien, who has ridden him a lot at home, did not get after him until passing the two pole, by which time Nathaniel and Workforce had already committed. The colt ran on, but was never going to bridge the gap. The slow-run nature of this race was against him, but his trainer was not offering excuses. He has plenty of options for the rest of the season. (op 10-3 tchd 4-1)

Debussy(IRE) was in to make the pace for Rewilding, but Ahmed Ajtebi did not let him go on immediately, perhaps mindful that he was very keen and might have gone too quick, and reined him back behind Nathaniel. Taking a keen hold, the 5yo was allowed to lead after two furlongs and increased the pace from halfway. Headed again turning in, he was eased when held. He has beaten just two horses in four runs for Godolphin, but now that Rewilding is no longer around, it is likely that connections will allow last year's Arlington Million winner to run on his own merits. (op 66-1 tchd 100-1 in places)

Rewilding, last year's Derby third and conqueror of So You Think in the Prince of Wales's Stakes at the Royal meeting last month, was attempting to pick up from the rear of the field when he snapped a cannon bone and fell with 2f to run. A sad end for a fine racehorse. (op 7-2)

4316 CANISBAY BLOODSTOCK H'CAP 1m 4f

5:40 (5:40) (Class 4) (0-85,85) 3-Y-O **£6,469** (£1,925; £962; £481) **Stalls** Low

Form RPR

011 **1** **Aiken**[10] 3988 3-9-2 80 WilliamBuick 2 92+
(John Gosden) *dwlt and pushed along early: clsd and in tch in rr after 2f: gd hdwy to chse ldrs 6f out: rdn to ld over 1f out: styd on strly fnl f* **15/8**[1]

-612 **2** *1 ¾* **Masaraat (FR)**[32] 3260 3-9-6 84 RichardHills 9 91
(John Dunlop) *stdd and dropped in bhd after s: hld up in midfield: rdn and effrt wl over 2f out: hdwy u.p over 1f out: edgd rt ins fnl f: chsd wnr fnl 75yds: kpt on* **9/2**[2]

4-15 **3** *1 ¾* **Mulaqen**[49] 2726 3-9-5 83 GeraldMosse 3 87
(Marcus Tregoning) *led: rdn jst over 2f out: hdd over 1f out: no ex and btn ins fnl f: kpt on same pce* **7/1**

-134 **4** *nk* **Parlour Games**[21] 3650 3-9-7 85 AhmedAjtebi 1 89+
(Mahmood Al Zarooni) *hld up in tch in midfield: shuffled bk and swtchd lft 3f out: rdn over 2f out: swtchd lft and drvn over 1f out: r.o wl ins fnl f: wnt 4th towards fin* **6/1**[3]

-436 **5** *½* **Time To Work (IRE)**[28] 3376 3-9-6 84 (v[1]) JimmyFortune 7 87
(Andrew Balding) *chsd ldrs: rdn over 2f out: unable qck u.p over 1f out: keeping on same pce whn sltly hmpd ins fnl f* **11/1**

4-10 **6** *1 ½* **Audacious**[57] 2471 3-9-6 84 RyanMoore 6 85
(Sir Michael Stoute) *chsd ldr: rdn over 2f out: drvn and ev ch 2f out tl over 1f out: wknd ins fnl f* **15/2**

3410 **7** *½* **Zamina (IRE)**[8] 4056 3-8-7 71 ow1 JamesDoyle 5 71
(Sylvester Kirk) *stdd s: hld up in last trio: rdn and effrt over 2f out: edgd rt and no imp over 1f out* **33/1**

1000 **8** *2 ¾* **Harry Luck (IRE)**[21] 3650 3-9-1 79 FergusSweeney 8 74
(Henry Candy) *hld up in tch in last trio: rdn and no prog jst over 2f out: nvr trbld ldrs* **14/1**

0001 **9** *57* **Strewth (IRE)**[24] 3518 3-8-8 72 ow1 RobertWinston 4 —
(John Best) *chsd ldrs: rdn over 3f out: wknd qckly over 2f out: virtually p.u fnl f: t.o* **12/1**

2m 36.41s (3.91) **Going Correction** +0.425s/f (Yiel) **9** Ran SP% **117.1**
Speed ratings (Par 102): **103,101,100,100,100 99,98,96,58**
toteswingers:1&2:£2.40, 2&3:£6.30, 1&3:£4.20 CSF £10.31 CT £48.72 TOTE £2.90: £1.30, £2.10, £2.60; EX 9.50 Trifecta £61.80 Pool: £3591.99 - 42.95 winning units..
Owner George Strawbridge **Bred** George Strawbridge **Trained** Newmarket, Suffolk

FOCUS

A decent 3-y-o handicap and a race notable for producing some high-class jumpers in the previous ten years with Contraband, Reveillez and Any Given Day all successful during that period. The pace was just fair and the winning time was 1.34 seconds slower than the King George. The form makes a lot of sense.

T/Jkpt: Not won. T/Plt: £462.30 to a £1 stake. Pool of £192,126.36 - 303.34 winning tickets. T/Qpdt: £47.70 to a £1 stake. Pool of £11,032.65 - 171.15 winning tickets. SP

4205 LINGFIELD (L-H)

Saturday, July 23

OFFICIAL GOING: Good

Wind: Almost nil Weather: Fine but cloudy

4317 ALMOND RESORTS, BARBADOS H'CAP 1m 2f

5:45 (5:45) (Class 6) (0-65,65) 3-Y-0+ **£2,181** (£644; £322) **Stalls** Low

Form RPR

1061 **1** **Highlife Dancer**[10] 3979 3-8-12 62 MartinHarley(3) 12 71
(Mick Channon) *pressed ldr: led jst over 3f out: kicked on but wanting to hang lft: drvn 2f out: styd on wl after* **7/1**[3]

0500 **2** *¾* **Trecase**[12] 3926 4-8-10 47 (t) FrannyNorton 10 54
(Tony Carroll) *trckd ldrs: rdn to go 2nd jst over 2f out: tried to chal after: a hld* **18/1**

0-21 **3** *3 ¼* **Ishikawa (IRE)**[68] 2166 3-8-9 56 NeilChalmers 7 57
(Alan King) *hld up in midfield: shkn up and nt qckn over 2f out: styd on fr over 1f out: tk 3rd nr fin* **9/2**[1]

-000 **4** *½* **Jinto**[40] 2991 4-9-4 55 PaulDoe 4 55
(David Elsworth) *rousted along early: rn in snatches in rr and also awkwardly: rdn 4f out: prog over 2f out: styd on fnl f: no ch* **10/1**

0001 **5** *hd* **Green Earth (IRE)**[11] 3944 4-9-12 63 IanMongan 13 62
(Pat Phelan) *t.k.h: hld up in midfield: prog 3f out: cl 3rd and rdn 2f out: sn outpcd: wknd fnl f* **8/1**

2214 **6** *½* **Corrib (IRE)**[12] 3912 8-9-5 56 (p) CathyGannon 5 54+
(Bryn Palling) *s.i.s: hld up: last 4f out: prog fr 3f out and nvr clrest of runs: styd on fnl f: nrst fin* **10/1**

-403 **7** *3 ½* **Ministry**[24] 3518 3-8-13 60 LukeMorris 6 51
(John Best) *led: rdn and hdd jst over 3f out: steadily wknd u.p* **9/2**[1]

3003 **8** *1 ¾* **Commerce**[15] 3814 4-9-8 64 HarryBentley(5) 8 52
(Gary Moore) *hld up in rr: 11th over 4f out but gng bttr than most: prog on inner over 2f out: no hdwy wl over 1f out: wknd* **6/1**[2]

1-40 **9** *3* **Slumbering Sioux**[66] 2196 3-9-0 61 AdamKirby 3 43
(Harry Dunlop) *trckd ldrs: shkn up over 2f out: steadily wknd* **16/1**

000 **10** *½* **Valkov**[11] 3952 4-8-12 49 LiamJones 9 30
(Tony Carroll) *a in rr: rdn over 4f out: no prog* **40/1**

0506 **11** *1* **Queenie's Star (IRE)**[35] 3176 4-8-6 46 KierenFox(3) 1 25
(Michael Attwater) *trckd ldng pair: rdn wl over 2f out: sn wknd* **18/1**

0020 **12** *11* **Herecomethegirls**[25] 3496 5-8-10 52 (b) RyanPowell(5) 2 —
(Olivia Maylam) *s.i.s: t.k.h: sn in midfield: wknd over 2f out: sn bhd* **25/1**

5600 **13** *28* **Fonterutoli (IRE)**[150] 647 4-9-7 65 HarryPoulton(7) 14 —
(Roger Ingram) *racd wd: hld up in rr: prog 1/2-way: wknd rapidly over 3f out: t.o and eased* **20/1**

2m 16.09s (5.59) **Going Correction** +0.60s/f (Yiel)
WFA 3 from 4yo+ 10lb **13** Ran SP% **119.9**
Speed ratings (Par 101): **101,100,97,97,97 96,94,92,90,89 89,80,57**
Tote Swingers:1&2:£19.80, 2&3:£29.70, 1&3:£5.60 CSF £123.62 CT £636.20 TOTE £6.10: £1.50, £7.50, £2.60; EX 272.10.
Owner The Highlife Racing Club **Bred** Imperial & Mike Channon Bloodstock Ltd **Trained** West Ilsley, Berks

FOCUS

Cloudy but dry conditions prevailed for this evening fixture. The going was changed to good following no further addition to 3mm of rain overnight, but Adam Kirby and Cathy Gannon reported after this opener that there were areas closer to soft, especially down the back straight. The winner's best form since his 2yo maiden win, with the first two clear.

Corrib(IRE) Official explanation: jockey said mare ran too free

Herecomethegirls Official explanation: trainer said mare failed to handle the downhill

4318 IT DOESN'T GET BETTER THAN BARBADOS H'CAP 2m

6:15 (6:15) (Class 5) (0-70,69) 3-Y-0+ **£3,067** (£905; £453) **Stalls** Low

Form RPR

2123 **1** **Mohanad (IRE)**[3] 4216 5-9-9 69 HarryBentley(5) 4 80+
(Sheena West) *trckd ldng pair: sltly outpcd over 4f out but stl gng wl enough: wnt 2nd over 2f out and sn clsd on ldr: shkn up to ld over 1f out: rdn and styd on wl* **6/4**[2]

5436 **2** *3 ½* **Vertueux (FR)**[60] 2377 6-9-0 55 LukeMorris 8 59
(Tony Carroll) *mostly in last trio: rdn sn after 1/2-way and struggling: fnlly responded and prog fr 3f out: styd on to take 2nd nr fin* **12/1**

00/5 **3** *1 ¼* **Dream Catcher (SWE)**[30] 3311 8-9-4 59 (p) AdamKirby 1 62
(Jonjo O'Neill) *led: kicked on over 3f out: drvn and hdd over 1f out: one pce after: lost 2nd nr fin* **7/1**[3]

50-0 **4** 3¾ **Winning Show**[19] 1582 7-8-2 **50** oh3......................(tp) BrendanPowell(7) 5 48
(Chris Gordon) *chsd ldrs in 5th: pushed along 6f out: outpcd over 4f out: plugged on fnl 2f: n.d* **25/1**

0-05 **5** 4½ **Whitcombe Spirit**[16] 3769 6-8-4 **50** oh4....................(b) NathanAlison(5) 3 43
(Jamie Poulton) *reminder sn after s: mostly last and nt gng wl: plugged on fr over 2f out: n.d* **25/1**

0060 **6** ½ **Rio Prince**[5] 4153 4-8-9 **50** oh4.......................................(t) NeilChalmers 7 42
(John Bridger) *trckd ldng trio: outpcd over 4f out: rdn and no prog 3f out: fdd* **50/1**

2152 **7** 2¼ **Mokalif**[22] 3599 3-8-5 **66**..(v) MartinHarley(3) 10 55
(Michael Bell) *trckd ldr: clr w him 4f out: drvn 3f out: fnd nil and sn wknd* **11/8**[1]

3000 **8** 60 **L'Homme De Nuit (GER)**[18] 3712 7-9-0 **55**........................(b) PaulDoe 6 —
(Jim Best) *dwlt and reminder sn after s: prog fr last pair to go prom 1/2-way: rdn and wknd 5f out: t.o and eased* **16/1**

3m 45.5s (10.70) **Going Correction** +0.60s/f (Yiel)
WFA 3 from 4yo+ 17lb **8** Ran SP% **117.8**
Speed ratings (Par 103): **97,95,94,92,90 90,89,59**
Tote Swingers:1&2:£2.20, 2&3:£6.30, 1&3:£4.10 CSF £20.15 CT £102.20 TOTE £2.70: £1.10, £1.80, £1.60; EX 15.40.
Owner Heart Of The South Racing **Bred** Ms Ashley O'Leary **Trained** Falmer, E Sussex

FOCUS
A very moderate marathon contest, which following defections contained only one runner, the winner, handicapped within 10lb of the ratings ceiling. He rates a personal best.

4319 VIRGIN HOLIDAYS ROCKSTAR MAIDEN AUCTION STKS 5f
6:45 (6:45) (Class 6) 2-Y-O **£2,181** (£644; £322) **Stalls** High

Form RPR

2 **1** **Baltic Fizz (IRE)**[14] 3855 2-8-6 0.. LukeMorris 1 72+
(Mrs K Burke) *w.w on outer: prog to chse ldr 2f out: sn rdn: styd on u.p to ld ins fnl f* **4/7**[1]

5 **2** 1¾ **Shout For Joy (IRE)**[81] 1785 2-8-7 0........................ FrankieMcDonald 2 67
(Richard Hannon) *t.k.h: mde most: crossed to nr side rail 1/2-way: drvn over 1f out: hdd and fdd ins fnl f* **6/1**[3]

046 **3** 2¾ **Flying Kitty**[11] 3941 2-7-13 0... RyanPowell(5) 5 54
(John Bridger) *pushed along in last over 3f out: taken to outer 1/2-way: rdn and kpt on to take 3rd over 1f out: no imp on ldng pair* **25/1**

0 **4** 2¾ **Arabian Flight**[68] 2153 2-8-6 0.. ChrisCatlin 6 46
(Ed Dunlop) *cl up against rail: outpcd fr 2f out and jst pushed along: nt on terms after* **11/2**[2]

50 **5** 1 **Ermyn Flyer**[32] 3257 2-7-13 0.................................. JemmaMarshall(5) 4 41
(Pat Phelan) *lost pl after 2f: shkn up in rr 2f out: fdd* **20/1**

50 **6** ½ **House Limit (IRE)**[30] 3308 2-9-0 0...................................... AdamKirby 3 49
(Harry Dunlop) *w ldr 2f: rdn and wknd fr 1/2-way* **8/1**

59.76 secs (1.56) **Going Correction** +0.15s/f (Good) **6** Ran SP% **113.0**
Speed ratings (Par 92): **93,90,85,81,79 79**
CSF £4.68 TOTE £1.60: £1.30, £2.70; EX 3.50.
Owner Mark James & Mrs Elaine Burke **Bred** Rocal Bloodstock **Trained** Middleham Moor, North Yorks

FOCUS
An unexceptional juvenile maiden auction stakes. The third sets the initial standard.

NOTEBOOK
Baltic Fizz(IRE) found this far from plain sailing. Unwilling to settle on the way to post, the Baltic King filly came under strong pressure a long way out and needed keeping right up to her work even once hitting the front inside the final furlong. \n\x\x Although this victory didn't look that impressive, it may be worth noting that while her immediate family's winning prowess is greater over the minimum distance, an intended engagement at Yarmouth four days earlier had been over 6f. It wouldn't be too surprising, therefore, if today's trip is already sharper than ideal. Connections also suggested she still has some maturing to do mentally.\n (op 8-13 tchd 4-6, 4-5 and 8-11 in a place)
Shout For Joy(IRE), absent since finishing both last and lame on debut nearly three months earlier, was too keen in the early stages but had stamina enough (as befitting a daughter of a 1m winner) to keep going, albeit at one pace late on. A step up in trip will do her no harm, so long as she can race more sparingly. (op 5-1)
[illegible] seventh in a 6f Salisbury event on debut, shaped with more promise than when set sharper assignments both starts since then, but [illegible] the minimum. (op 20-1)
Arabian Flight was not given a hard time once the leaders had taken flight. The profile of her damside suggests she won't come into his own until encountering at least a mile. (op 7-1)
House Limit(IRE) didn't see out this trip much better than the 6f of his two previous outings. (tchd 7-1)

4320 ALMOND RESORTS - FOR YOU, ABOUT YOU MEDIAN AUCTION MAIDEN STKS 7f
7:20 (7:23) (Class 6) 3-5-Y-O **£1,704** (£503; £251) **Stalls** High

Form RPR

332- **1** **Cape Rambler**[271] 7119 3-9-3 82.............................. FrankieMcDonald 7 72+
(Henry Candy) *mde virtually all and racd towards nr side rail: drvn and pressed over 1f out: hld on* **10/11**[1]

4 **2** ½ **Cahala Dancer (IRE)**[17] 3747 3-8-12 0.......................... JamesDoyle 6 66
(Roger Teal) *dwlt: racd against rail: trckd ldrs: prog to chse wnr over 1f out: sn chalng: jst hld nr fin* **9/2**[2]

06 **3** 1¾ **Ibiza Sunset (IRE)**[28] 3392 3-9-3 0................................ IanMongan 13 66+
(Peter Winkworth) *hld up wl in rr and racd against rail: prog over 2f out: drvn and styd on to take 3rd ins fnl f* **14/1**

60- **4** 1 **Omnipotent (IRE)**[289] 6689 3-8-12 0........................... HarryBentley(5) 2 63
(Richard Hannon) *wnt lft s: sn prom on outer: rdn and cl enough in 3rd over 1f out: one pce* **5/1**[3]

5 1½ **Harvest Mist (IRE)** 3-8-12 0... NeilChalmers 8 54
(Michael Blanshard) *dwlt: settled in midfield: nt clr run jst over 2f out: shkn up and styd on fr over 1f out* **66/1**

00- **6** 1½ **Teazel**[285] 6803 3-8-12 0... ChrisCatlin 11 50
(Dominic Ffrench Davis) *cl up: rdn wl over 2f out: steadily outpcd fnl 2f* **33/1**

05 **7** nk **Lightning Spirit**[78] 1865 3-8-9 0................................. MartinHarley(3) 14 49+
(Gary Moore) *wl in rr: rdn 2f out: sme late prog towards nr side: no ch* **9/1**

8 3¾ **Princess Willow** 3-8-12 0... RichardThomas 5 39
(John E Long) *s.i.s: wl in rr on outer and rn green: pushed along and sme prog fr 2f out* **66/1**

04 **9** 4½ **Dark Pegasus**[35] 3173 3-9-0 0..................................... KierenFox(3) 3 32
(Karen George) *spd fr wd draw to press wnr: rdn 3f out: wknd wl over 1f out* **33/1**

00 **10** 2½ **Reggie Perrin**[17] 3747 3-8-12 0............................. JemmaMarshall(5) 10 25
(Pat Phelan) *sn pushed along in last: nvr a factor* **40/1**

0- **11** 2 **Amun Ra (USA)**[303] 6308 3-9-3 0.. TravisBlock 1 20
(Jeremy Gask) *dwlt and sltly impeded s: hld up in midfield: effrt 3f out: wknd wl over 1f out* **33/1**

5 **12** 10 **Femme Royale**[11] 3949 3-8-12 0.. LukeMorris 4 —
(Robert Cowell) *t.k.h: prom: wknd wl over 2f out* **40/1**

00- **13** 5 **Key Impeller**[410] 2832 3-8-10 0.................................... JakePayne(7) 9 —
(Bill Turner) *dwlt: hld up in rr: racd awkwardly and wknd wl over 2f out* **100/1**

1m 26.17s (2.87) **Going Correction** +0.15s/f (Good) **13** Ran SP% **121.6**
Speed ratings (Par 101): **89,88,86,85,83 81,81,77,72,69 66,55,49**
Tote Swingers:1&2:£2.30, 2&3:£8.40, 1&3:£3.80 CSF £4.84 TOTE £1.90: £1.10, £1.60, £2.60; EX 5.60.
Owner Simon Broke & Partners II **Bred** Mrs A Savage **Trained** Kingston Warren, Oxon

FOCUS
There was little strength in depth and the winner did not need to match his 2yo best. The first three raced on the rail.

4321 BEAUTIFUL BARBADOS H'CAP 7f
7:55 (7:56) (Class 5) (0-70,70) 3-Y-O **£3,067** (£905; £453) **Stalls** High

Form RPR

3563 **1** **Saskia's Dream**[16] 3782 3-9-7 **70**......................................(p) AdamKirby 9 82
(Jane Chapple-Hyam) *cl up bhd ldrs: plld out over 2f out: rdn to ld wl over 1f out: styd on wl* **9/2**[3]

433 **2** 2¾ **Konstantin (IRE)**[15] 3798 3-9-6 **69**.................................. GeorgeBaker 6 74
(Marcus Tregoning) *trckd ldrs: rdn and effrt over 2f out: chsd wnr over 1f out: kpt on but no imp* **3/1**[2]

3-00 **3** 1¾ **Polar Auroras**[40] 2993 3-8-10 **59**................................ LukeMorris 11 59
(Tony Carroll) *towards rr: rdn bef 1/2-way: nt look keen but prog over 2f out: hanging lft over 1f out: kpt on to take 3rd nr fin* **20/1**

0034 **4** nk **Custom House (IRE)**[51] 2642 3-9-3 **69**.................. NataliaGemelova(3) 4 68
(John E Long) *in tch on outer: rdn wl over 2f out: chsd ldng pair jst over 1f out: fdd and lost 3rd nr fin* **20/1**

-332 **5** 1¼ **El Maachi**[46] 2792 3-9-4 **67**.. JamesDoyle 10 63
(Jim Best) *racd against rail: w ldr: rdn over 2f out: grad fdd fr over 1f out* **11/4**[1]

4033 **6** 2¾ **Full Shilling (IRE)**[33] 3230 3-8-3 **52**............................. CathyGannon 5 41
(John Spearing) *t.k.h early: hld up in rr: rdn over 2f out: sme modest late prog* **15/2**

2000 **7** 1¾ **Mixed Emotions (IRE)**[26] 3465 3-9-5 **68**............................. PatDobbs 3 52
(Richard Hannon) *settled in rr: rdn and struggling 3f out: no ch whn sltly hmpd over 1f out* **20/1**

4655 **8** ¾ **Yahafedh Alaih**[5] 4161 3-9-4 **67**... ChrisCatlin 1 49
(Clive Brittain) *narrow ldr and racd one off the rail: hdd & wknd qckly wl over 1f out* **14/1**

-000 **9** 11 **Sylas Ings**[9] 4011 3-8-11 **60**.. IanMongan 2 —
(Pat Phelan) *settled in rr: rdn and struggling 3f out: no prog* **11/1**

-660 **10** 10 **My Ruby (IRE)**[27] 3432 3-9-4 **67**.. PaulDoe 7 —
(Jim Best) *w ldrs to 1/2-way: sn wknd u.p: eased over 1f out: t.o* **14/1**

560- **11** 20 **Marmaduke**[323] 5709 3-7-11 **51** oh6............................ RyanPowell(5) 8 —
(John Bridger) *dropped to last bef 1/2-way: t.o* **100/1**

1m 24.66s (1.36) **Going Correction** +0.15s/f (Good) **11** Ran SP% **118.6**
Speed ratings (Par 100): **98,94,92,92,91 87,85,85,72,61 38**
Tote Swingers:1&2:£2.80, 2&3:£28.00, 1&3:£29.00 CSF £17.63 CT £253.35 TOTE £5.50: £1.60, £1.60, £8.70; EX 14.10.
Owner Peter Bottomley & Jane Chapple-Hyam **Bred** Psb Holdings Ltd **Trained** Dalham, Suffolk

FOCUS
Just 3lb separated the top seven in the weights of this tight-looking contest. The time was relatively good and the winner posted a clear personal best.
My Ruby(IRE) Official explanation: trainer said filly would be suited by faster ground

4322 VIRGIN HOLIDAYS ASK FOR WORLD H'CAP 7f 140y
8:25 (8:27) (Class 6) (0-65,65) 3-Y-O+ **£2,181** (£644; £322) **Stalls** Centre

Form RPR

0544 **1** **Starwatch**[17] 3741 4-9-3 **58**... SeanLevey(3) 6 71
([illegible]) *[illegible] ldrs and rcd wd: rdn to go 2nd 2f out: led 1f out: drew clr* [illegible]

3161 **2** 3¼ **Kielty's Folly**[12] 3926 7-9-3 **60**.................................. JamesRogers(5) 12 65
(Brian Baugh) *chsd ldr: led wl over 2f out: sn rdn: hdd and one pce 1f out* **8/1**[2]

0302 **3** 2¼ **Indian Violet (IRE)**[11] 3944 5-9-8 **60**......................... JamieGoldstein 13 59
(Ralph Smith) *trckd ldrs: rdn to chse ldng trio 2f out: nt qckn and wl hld after* **8/1**[2]

5-30 **4** 3½ **My Sister**[180] 278 4-9-3 **55**... PatDobbs 11 46
(Mark Usher) *chsd ldrs: rdn over 2f out: steadily outpcd after* **10/1**

3223 **5** ¾ **Fitz**[15] 3804 5-9-2 **54**..(b) AdamKirby 1 43
(Matthew Salaman) *racd on outer: in tch: rdn and prog wl over 2f out: cl enough wl over 1f out: wknd* **6/1**[1]

0604 **6** ¾ **Diddums**[3] 4211 5-9-1 **60**... KatiaScallan(7) 16 47+
(Alastair Lidderdale) *towards rr: rdn over 2f out: plugged on: nvr a threat* **10/1**

60-0 **7** hd **Distant Waters**[21] 3636 4-8-10 **53**............................. HarryBentley(5) 18 39
(Alan Jarvis) *wl in rr against rail: rdn over 3f out: sme late prog: nvr a factor* **11/1**

000 **8** ½ **Hector The Brave (IRE)**[46] 2790 4-9-0 **52**.................. RichardThomas 5 37
(John E Long) *pushed along in last trio over 4f out: struggling after: styd on fnl f* **50/1**

0000 **9** 1¼ **Valmina**[17] 3735 4-9-3 **55**..(t) LiamJones 10 37
(Tony Carroll) *wl in rr: rdn and sme prog fr 3f out: no hdwy and wl btn over 1f out* **16/1**

1646 **10** 1¼ **Kipchak (IRE)**[9] 4025 6-9-3 **62**.................................(b) DavidKenny(7) 8 41
(Conor Dore) *led and sn crossed to rail: hdd wl over 2f out: wknd* **10/1**

1-33 **11** 2 **Lend A Grand (IRE)**[108] 1178 7-9-13 **65**............................. IanMongan 2 39
(Jo Crowley) *dwlt: hld up in last pair and wl off the pce: swtchd out wd and effrt 3f out: sn no prog* **14/1**

-006 **12** 1 **Azzoom (IRE)**[21] 3630 3-9-0 **60**... ChrisCatlin 4 29
(Clive Brittain) *dwlt: wl off the pce in last pair: swtchd out wd over 2f out: no real prog* **25/1**

4550 **13** 28 **Sonny G (IRE)**[86] 1633 4-9-1 **53**....................................... LukeMorris 17 —
(John Best) *chsd ldrs and racd against rail: wknd 3f out: t.o* **6/1**[1]

60-0 **14** 4½ **Until The Man (IRE)**[7] 4088 4-9-8 **60**...............................(b) PaulDoe 9 —
(Jim Best) *rrd s: prom early: rdn and lost pl over 4f out: t.o* **33/1**

300- **P** **Jazacosta (USA)**[431] 2198 5-9-5 **57**................................. GeorgeBaker 7 —
(Jo Crowley) *hld up towards rr: p.u and dismntd 2f out* **12/1**

1m 33.14s (0.84) **Going Correction** +0.15s/f (Good)
WFA 3 from 4yo+ 8lb **15** Ran SP% **125.4**
Speed ratings (Par 101): **101,97,95,92,91 90,90,89,88,87 85,84,56,51,—**
Tote Swingers:1&2:£7.00, 2&3:£6.10, 1&3:£20.60 CSF £80.85 CT £629.87 TOTE £12.40: £3.50, £2.60, £3.30; EX 108.90.
Owner J J Bridger **Bred** Mrs J A Chapman **Trained** Liphook, Hants

FOCUS
A very congested market beforehand, with eight horses sent off between 6-1 (joint favourite) and 10-1. Not much got involved from the rear and the winner is rated back to his winter AW form.
My Sister Official explanation: vet said filly lost right-fore shoe
Lend A Grand(IRE) Official explanation: vet said gelding lost left-fore shoe
Jazacosta(USA) Official explanation: jockey said gelding lost its action
T/Plt: £34.60 to a £1 stake. Pool £62,143.68. 1,310.83 winning tickets. T/Qpdt: £7.70 to a £1 stake. Pool £6,082.34. 582.86 winning tickets. JN

3394 NEWCASTLE (L-H)
Saturday, July 23

OFFICIAL GOING: Good to soft (6.4)
Wind: Fresh, half-against. Weather: Cloudy

4323 TYNE TEES MODELS MAIDEN AUCTION STKS 7f
2:25 (2:25) (Class 4) 2-Y-O **£3,946** (£1,174; £586; £293) **Stalls** High

Form RPR

1 **Just Fabulous** 2-8-9 0................................. PJMcDonald 7 74+
(George Moore) *hld up in tch: gd hdwy over 2f out: led over 1f out: pushed clr* **7/1**[2]

2 4 **Rockntherunway (IRE)** 2-8-12 0................................. FrederikTylicki 1 67
(Michael Dods) *dwlt and wnt lft s: sn prom on outside: effrt over 2f out: chsd clr wnr ins fnl f: r.o* **8/1**[3]

3 nk **Shotley Music** 2-8-10 0................................. AndrewHeffernan 2 64
(Neville Bycroft) *dwlt: bhd: pushed along and rn green 1/2-way: styd on fnl 2f: nrst fin* **28/1**

34 **4** ½ **Marching On (IRE)**[15] 3826 2-8-13 0................................. PhillipMakin 3 66
(Kevin Ryan) *led: crossed to stands' rail over 4f out: rdn: edgd lft and hdd over 1f out: no ex and lost two pls ins fnl f* **4/7**[1]

0 **5** 16 **Allegri (IRE)**[8] 4073 2-8-10 0................................. TonyHamilton 4 21
(Ann Duffield) *cl up tl rdn and wknd over 2f out* **50/1**

44 **6** 2 ¾ **Pearl Catcher (IRE)**[11] 3947 2-8-10 0................................. DuranFentiman 6 14
(Tim Easterby) *prom: effrt 3f out: wknd 2f out* **11/1**

0 **7** 2 ¼ **Celestrial (IRE)**[9] 4012 2-9-0 0................................. TomEaves 5 —
(Bryan Smart) *trckd ldrs: lost pl 1/2-way: sn struggling* **9/1**

1m 30.55s (2.75) **Going Correction** +0.05s/f (Good) **7** Ran SP% **111.0**
Speed ratings (Par 96): **91,86,86,85,67 64,61**
Tote Swingers:1&2:£4.20, 2&3:£28.40, 1&3:£88.00 CSF £56.24 TOTE £9.80: £2.80, £2.20; EX 113.40.
Owner Sean P Graham **Bred** Palm Tree Thoroughbreds **Trained** Middleham Moor, N Yorks

FOCUS
Probably not a strong race considering the form horse was readily put in his place by three newcomers. The time was very slow and it's hard to know what the form is worth.

NOTEBOOK
Just Fabulous, a 40,000gns first foal of a half-sister to Listed juvenile winner Jira and to King Edward VII winner Plea Bargain, was certainly bred to be the part and she came home a most convincing winner from off the gallop. She can hold her own in novice company, especially with ease in the ground. (op 15-2, tchd 8-1 in a place)
Rockntherunway(IRE), an already gelded half-brother to winners, showed up all the way and kept on in pleasing style to take second. (op 5-1)
Shotley Music, the first foal of a three-time winner, took a little while to get organised but battled away for a game third. (op 25-1)
Marching On(IRE) hit the front going easily some way from home. However, his stride started to shorten quickly the moment he came under pressure and he was extremely disappointing. In hindsight, it probably would have been better to hold him up for much longer. (op 8-11, tchd 4-5 in places)

4324 PLAY MECCA BINGO ON YOUR IPHONE H'CAP 6f
2:55 (2:55) (Class 3) (0-90,84) 3-Y-O **£5,175** (£1,540; £769; £384) **Stalls** High

Form RPR

1411 **1** **Louis The Pious**[14] 3853 3-9-6 **83**................................. PhillipMakin 3 96+
(Kevin Ryan) *prom: effrt and rdn over 1f out: led wl ins fnl f: kpt on* **6/5**[1]

0550 **2** 1 ¼ **Another Citizen (IRE)**[14] 3880 3-8-8 **71**.......................(p) KellyHarrison 6 83+
(Tim Easterby) *led: qcknd over 1f out: hit rail: faltered and nrly uns rdr 100yds out: sn hdd and no ex* **8/1**

46-0 **3** 1 ¼ **Lady Paris (IRE)**[14] 3853 3-8-11 **74**................................. TomEaves 2 79
(Bryan Smart) *pressed ldr: rdn over 1f out: lost 2nd ins fnl f: one pce* **5/1**[3]

-114 **4** nk **Namwahjobo (IRE)**[29] 3346 3-9-7 **84**................................. DanielTudhope 1 88+
(Jim Goldie) *stdd in rr: effrt over 2f out: kpt on fnl f: nvr able to chal* **3/1**[2]

-200 **5** 7 **Tom Sawyer**[8] 4048 3-9-3 **80**................................. TonyHamilton 5 62
(Julie Camacho) *hld up in tch: rdn over 2f out: no imp over 1f out* **20/1**

4605 **6** 4 ½ **Mappin Time (IRE)**[19] 3682 3-9-6 **83**.......................(p) DuranFentiman 4 50
(Tim Easterby) *trckd ldrs: rdn over 2f out: wknd over 1f out* **10/1**

1m 15.23s (0.63) **Going Correction** +0.05s/f (Good) **6** Ran SP% **112.1**
Speed ratings (Par 104): **97,95,93,93,83 77**
Tote Swingers:1&2:£2.50, 2&3:£5.90, 1&3:£1.10 CSF £11.67 TOTE £2.10: £1.40, £3.90; EX 10.70.
Owner F Gillespie **Bred** Ashbrittle Stud **Trained** Hambleton, N Yorks

FOCUS
An unreliable result considering what happened to Another Citizen half a furlong out. The winner continues to progress.

NOTEBOOK
Louis The Pious was chasing his fourth win of the season and was closing in on Another Citizen at the time of the incident when handed the lead. One couldn't have been confident he would have got up had the runner-up not lost its momentum. (op 2-1)
Another Citizen(IRE) was showing no signs of stopping while leading up the stands' rail, but about half a furlong out, he touched the rail and jumped a couple of times, causing him to lose his footing. His rider displayed fine self-preservation skills to keep the partnership intact and finish second. (op 7-1)
Lady Paris(IRE) finished well behind Louis The Pious at Chester on her first start of the season from a wide stall, and was better off at the weights, but couldn't reverse the form after showing early speed. (op 9-2)
Namwahjobo(IRE), back down in trip after his hat-trick bid was thwarted at Doncaster, hit a flat spot and ran on when it was all too late. (op 11-4 tchd 7-2)
Mappin Time(IRE) has been edging down the weights after starting the year on a mark of 92 but doesn't look a winner waiting to happen considering this effort. (op 7-1)

4325 PIMMS BEESWING H'CAP 7f
3:30 (3:30) (Class 3) (0-95,91) 3-Y-O+ **£8,409** (£2,502; £1,250; £625) **Stalls** High

Form RPR

1100 **1** **Masked Dance (IRE)**[28] 3397 4-9-10 **87**.......................(p) PhillipMakin 13 96
(Kevin Ryan) *trckd stands' side ldrs: led over 2f out: hung lft over 1f out: hld on wl u.p fnl f* **10/1**

55-0 **2** ½ **Clockmaker (IRE)**[14] 3877 5-9-10 **87**................................. DuranFentiman 3 94
(Tim Easterby) *racd w one other centre: cl up: effrt and chsd wnr fnl f: r.o wl* **20/1**

1642 **3** 1 ½ **Extraterrestrial**[15] 3831 7-9-12 **89**................................. FrederikTylicki 11 92+
(Richard Fahey) *hld up: gd hdwy over 1f out: kpt on fnl f: no imp towards fin* **11/2**[1]

6300 **4** ½ **Silver Rime (FR)**[30] 3315 6-9-8 **85**................................. TomEaves 12 87
(Linda Perratt) *in tch stands' side: effrt and rdn over 1f out: kpt on same pce ins fnl f* **10/1**

200 **5** 1 ¼ **Askaud (IRE)**[51] 2634 3-8-11 **81**................................. AndrewMullen 1 77
(David Nicholls) *hld up on outside of stands' side gp: rdn and hdwy over 1f out: nrst fin* **20/1**

-555 **6** shd **Mr Rainbow**[35] 3188 5-9-10 **87**................................. PJMcDonald 5 85
(Alan Swinbank) *trckd stands' side ldrs: rdn over 2f out: kpt on same pce fnl f* **8/1**

0316 **7** ½ **Magic Cat**[35] 3169 5-9-9 **86**................................. AndrewElliott 10 83+
(Mrs K Burke) *hld up and bhd stands' side: hdwy over 1f out: kpt on: nvr able to chal* **13/2**[2]

6660 **8** 4 ½ **Damika (IRE)**[49] 2706 8-10-0 **91**................................. TonyHamilton 6 76
(Richard Whitaker) *midfield in stands' side gp: effrt over 2f out: btn appr fnl f* **12/1**

5211 **9** hd **Daring Dream (GER)**[29] 3358 6-8-13 **81**................................. DarylByrne(5) 7 65
(Jim Goldie) *fly-jmpd s: hld up stands' side: shortlived effrt on outside over 2f out: no ex over 1f out* **8/1**

2210 **10** 1 ¾ **Vito Volterra (IRE)**[28] 3397 4-9-6 **83**................................. MickyFenton 4 63
(Michael Smith) *racd w one other centre: cl up tl wknd appr fnl f* **7/1**[3]

25-0 **11** ½ **Piceno (IRE)**[107] 1202 3-8-3 **76**................................. BillyCray(3) 9 51
(David Nicholls) *led stands' side to over 2f out: rdn and wknd over 1f out* **20/1**

0111 **12** 1 ½ **Regimental (IRE)**[26] 3462 3-8-10 **80**................................. StephenCraine 8 51
(Ann Duffield) *in tch: rdn over 2f out: wknd wl over 1f out* **12/1**

1410 **13** 12 **Quite Sparky**[14] 3877 4-9-7 **84**.......................(v) DanielTudhope 2 26
(David O'Meara) *hld up in tch on outside of stands' side gp: struggling over 2f out: sn btn: eased whn no ch fnl f* **15/2**

1m 27.77s (-0.03) **Going Correction** +0.05s/f (Good)
WFA 3 from 4yo+ 7lb **13** Ran SP% **123.1**
Speed ratings (Par 107): **107,106,104,104,102 102,102,96,96,94 94,92,78**
Tote Swingers:1&2:£74.10, 2&3:£54.20, 1&3:£18.90 CSF £202.27 CT £1243.24 TOTE £15.30: £4.00, £6.70, £2.50; EX 271.20.
Owner Mrs J Ryan **Bred** Canice Farrell Jnr **Trained** Hambleton, N Yorks

FOCUS
A competitive handicap run at what looked a fair gallop. The field split into two reasonable sized groups early but most of the middle bunch edged stands' side after 1f, leaving two to come up the centre. A length personal best from the winner.

NOTEBOOK
Masked Dance(IRE) hadn't been running too badly this year, as a couple of wins in the spring proved, and collected another success after keeping towards the stands' rail until hanging away from it over a furlong out. His attitude was good under pressure but he will need to up his game again to follow up off what will be a career-high mark. (op 12-1)
Clockmaker(IRE) ◆, who hadn't run over 7f for quite a while, didn't show a lot on his first run for Tim Easterby (jockey reported that he ran too free) and was one of only two here that stayed towards the centre of the track. He too ran all the way to the line, leaving the other horse who raced with him well behind, and is worth following now he has blown all cobwebs away (op 16-1)
Extraterrestrial, beaten in a claimer last time, is capable of winning off his current rating and attracted market support. However, he didn't get going early enough and was never going to catch the winner, hard though he tried. (op 13-2 tchd 5-1)
Silver Rime(FR), the winner of this last season off a 2lb lower mark, had been beaten over 10l on his last two starts, and although he did run better, he never looked like lifting this prize again. (op 9-1)
Askaud(IRE) ◆ started this season well but had run badly on her two subsequent outings. Given a break, she was really hard ridden to make progress but stayed on nicely in the latter stages. She ought to be even better when stepped up to 1m again.
Magic Cat likes easy ground and had won at this course in the past (6f heavy ground), but was played too late from a rear position to cause the leaders any worries. (op 7-1)
Vito Volterra(IRE) Official explanation: jockey said gelding had no more to give
Regimental(IRE) was surprisingly easy to back considering he was chasing a fourth successive victory, even allowing for the rise in class. He failed to show much sparkle and the jockey reported the gelding was never travelling. Official explanation: jockey said gelding never travelled (op 10-1)
Quite Sparky finished in front of Clockmaker when they both finished well down the field at York, but ran a shocker here despite attracting market support. (op 11-1)

4326 MISS NEWCASTLE 2012 H'CAP 2m 19y
4:05 (4:05) (Class 5) (0-70,66) 4-Y-O+ **£2,911** (£866; £432; £216) **Stalls** Low

Form RPR

-220 **1** **Jeu De Roseau (IRE)**[24] 3507 7-9-4 **63**................................. PJMcDonald 11 74
(Chris Grant) *in tch: effrt over 2f out: led ins fnl f: styd on wl u.p* **8/1**

-252 **2** ½ **Falcun**[35] 3187 4-8-10 **55**.......................(p) TomEaves 3 65
(Micky Hammond) *t.k.h early: trckd ldrs: led gng wl over 2f out: sn rdn: hdd ins fnl f: rallied: hld towards fin* **11/2**[2]

5400 **3** 1 **Silent Lucidity (IRE)**[26] 3450 7-8-0 **48**.......................(p) DeclanCannon(3) 7 57
(Peter Niven) *hld up: hdwy on outside over 2f out: cl up fnl f: hld nr fin* **20/1**

5-01 **4** 3 ¼ **Tillietudlem (FR)**[24] 3507 5-9-5 **64**................................. DanielTudhope 4 69
(Jim Goldie) *midfield: effrt and rdn over 2f out: kpt on same pce ins fnl f* **11/2**[2]

334 **5** ½ **Strikemaster (IRE)**[16] 3754 5-8-6 **51**.......................(t) DuranFentiman 9 56
(Lee James) *hld up: hdwy on ins over 2f out: sn rdn: no imp tl styd on last 150yds: nt rch ldrs* **16/1**

0-00 **6** 1 **Follow The Sun (IRE)**[9] 3754 7-7-13 **47** oh1................................. BillyCray(3) 1 50
(Peter Niven) *hld up: hdwy on outside over 2f out: no imp over 1f out* **25/1**

3140 **7** ½ **Maid Of Meft**[30] 3316 4-9-4 **63**................................. FrederikTylicki 5 66
(Linda Perratt) *hld up: rdn along over 2f out: sn no imp* **5/1**[1]

2454 **8** 2 **The Lock Master (IRE)**[15] 3811 4-9-7 **66**................................. MickyFenton 8 66
(Michael Appleby) *prom: rdn over 2f out: wknd appr fnl f* **16/1**

0206 **9** 1 ½ **Leaving Alone (USA)**[16] 3754 4-8-7 **52**.......................(b) AndrewHeffernan 12 51
(Edwin Tuer) *midfield: pushed along over 3f out: wknd fr 2f out* **14/1**

The Form Book, Raceform Ltd, Compton, RG20 6NL

4000 **10** *2* **Tobernea (IRE)**[14] 3851 4-9-1 **65** .... DarylByrne(5) 2 — 61
(Mark Johnston) *led tl hdd over 2f out: wknd over 1f out* **7/1**[3]

0500 **11** *2 3/4* **Hi Dancer**[16] 3754 8-8-10 **55** .... PhillipMakin 6 — 48
(Ben Haslam) *hld up: rdn along 3f out: sn wknd* **10/1**

3201 **12** *74* **Trojan Gift (USA)**[25] 3492 4-9-1 **60** .... (p) TonyHamilton 13 — —
(Julie Camacho) *t.k.h: cl up tl rdn and wknd qckly over 3f out: eased fnl 2f* **15/2**

3m 36.17s (-3.23) **Going Correction** -0.125s/f (Firm) **12** Ran SP% **118.9**
Speed ratings (Par 103): **103,102,102,100,100 99,99,98,97,96 95,58**
Tote Swingers:1&2:£4.30, 2&3:£41.10, 1&3:£53.80 CSF £51.77 CT £862.37 TOTE £9.90: £2.90, £2.10, £8.60; EX 85.80.
Owner W Raw **Bred** P Connolly **Trained** Newton Bewley, Co Durham
■ Stewards' Enquiry : Declan Cannon caution: used whip down shoulder in the forehand.

FOCUS
Low-grade stuff in which the early gallop was far from exacting. The form seems sound enough.

4327 UTS CONNOR SADLER H'CAP — 5f
4:40 (4:40) (Class 4) (0-85,85) 3-Y-0+ — **£3,234** (£962; £481; £240) **Stalls** High

Form — RPR

2044 **1** **Red Cape (FR)**[9] 4013 8-9-2 **75** .... PJMcDonald 4 — 84
(Ruth Carr) *prom: effrt 2f out: led ins fnl f: drvn out* **7/1**[3]

0002 **2** *nk* **Pavershooz**[15] 3832 6-9-7 **80** .... DuranFentiman 1 — 88
(Noel Wilson) *racd centre: prom: led over 1f out to ins fnl f: kpt on: hld nr fin* **8/1**

600- **3** *1 1/2* **Rasaman (IRE)**[273] 7079 7-9-12 **85** .... DanielTudhope 5 — 87
(Jim Goldie) *hld up: swtchd rt and hdwy over 1f out: styd on fnl f: nt pce of first two* **20/1**

0000 **4** *nk* **Haajes**[18] 3704 7-8-10 **76** .... DavidSimmonson(7) 3 — 77
(Paul Midgley) *hld up: rdn and hdwy over 1f out: kpt on ins fnl f: nvr able to chal* **10/1**

0162 **5** *hd* **Bedloe's Island (IRE)**[31] 3279 6-9-4 **77** .... AndrewHeffernan 9 — 77
(Neville Bycroft) *in tch: effrt and hdwy over 1f out: rdn and kpt on same pce last 100yds* **8/1**

6130 **6** *nk* **Doc Hay (USA)**[8] 4042 4-9-11 **84** .... PhillipMakin 10 — 83
(Keith Dalgleish) *hld up: hdwy over 1f out: kpt on fnl f: nvr able to chal* **13/8**[1]

5000 **7** *2* **Rash Judgement**[14] 3850 6-9-8 **81** .... AndrewElliott 8 — 73
(Eric Alston) *chsd clr ldr stands' side: rdn over 2f out: one pce fnl f* **9/1**

5654 **8** *1 1/4* **Captain Scooby**[30] 3305 5-8-8 **67** .... TonyHamilton 2 — 55
(Richard Whitaker) *hld up in tch: hdwy and rdn and outpcd 2f out: n.d after* **13/2**[2]

5000 **9** *hd* **Nadeen (IRE)**[31] 3279 4-9-5 **78** .... TomEaves 6 — 65
(Michael Smith) *hld up: rdn over 2f out: nvr on terms* **14/1**

50-0 **10** *2* **Cayman Fox**[40] 2987 6-8-9 **68** .... FrederikTylicki 7 — 48
(Linda Perratt) *led and sn clr: rdn and hdd over 1f out: sn wknd* **22/1**

61.20 secs (0.10) **Going Correction** +0.05s/f (Good) **10** Ran SP% **121.0**
Speed ratings (Par 105): **101,100,98,97,97 96,93,91,91,88**
Tote Swingers:1&2:£16.60, 2&3:£10.90, 1&3:£15.90 CSF £64.33 CT £1085.81 TOTE £9.70: £2.40, £2.40, £5.40; EX 82.50.
Owner Middleham Park Racing LVI **Bred** Gilles And Mrs Forien **Trained** Huby, N Yorks

FOCUS
This was run at a strong pace thanks to Cayman Fox streaking down the stands' rail, so it wasn't a surprise to see quite a few who sat in behind finish off well. The winner deserved this after a string of good efforts.

4328 LA TAXIS H'CAP — 5f
5:15 (5:15) (Class 6) (0-60,60) 3-Y-0+ — **£2,070** (£616; £307; £153) **Stalls** High

Form — RPR

0660 **1** **Duke Of Rainford**[3] 4197 4-8-11 **47** .... TomEaves 1 — 56
(Michael Herrington) *dwlt: hld up: smooth hdwy 2f out: rdn to ld ins fnl f: r.o wl* **10/1**

5101 **2** *1/2* **Dispol Grand (IRE)**[1] 4289 5-9-6 **56** .... (v) MickyFenton 2 — 63
(Paul Midgley) *hld up: hdwy on outside 2f out: ev ch ins fnl f: kpt on fin* **9/2**[1]

3445 **3** *nse* **Sharp Bullet (IRE)**[9] 4017 5-9-6 **56** .... (p) FrederikTylicki 3 — 63
(Bruce Hellier) *in tch: hdwy to ld over 1f out: rdn and hdd ins fnl f: kpt on [illegible]* **5/1**[2]

5-06 **4** *3/4* **Cross Of Lorraine (IRE)**[illegible] [illegible] .... [illegible] — [illegible]
(Chris Grant) *bhd tl hdwy appr fnl f: kpt on: nrst fin* **11/1**

0330 **5** *3/4* **Mission Impossible**[32] 3248 6-8-11 **47** .... (p) AndrewMullen 8 — 48
(Colin Teague) *hld up: hdwy 2f out: rdn and no imp fnl f* **7/1**[3]

0004 **6** *nk* **Lady Lube Rye (IRE)**[11] 3937 4-8-10 **46** oh1 .... DuranFentiman 4 — 46
(Noel Wilson) *prom: rdn and outpcd 2f out: kpt on fnl f: nvr able to chal* **11/1**

0400 **7** *2* **Piste**[10] 3972 5-8-10 **46** oh1 .... AndrewHeffernan 11 — 39
(Tina Jackson) *trckd ldrs: rdn to ld briefly over 1f out: outpcd fnl f* **20/1**

-030 **8** *hd* **Andrasta**[1] 4288 6-8-10 **46** .... PhillipMakin 9 — 38
(Alan Berry) *prom: rdn over 2f out: btn ins fnl f* **7/1**[3]

0565 **9** *nk* **Noels Princess**[11] 3931 4-8-10 **46** oh1 .... DanielTudhope 13 — 37
(David O'Meara) *cl up: led over 2f out to over 1f out: btn fnl f* **12/1**

0001 **10** *3/4* **Tenancy (IRE)**[25] 3495 7-9-1 **56** .... (b) DanielleMcCreery(5) 14 — 45
(Shaun Harris) *led to 1/2-way: sn drvn along: no imp fnl 2f* **8/1**

5-00 **11** *2* **Ruler's Honour (IRE)**[32] 3247 4-9-3 **53** .... (be) AndrewElliott 6 — 34
(Tim Etherington) *s.i.s: bhd: pushed along 1/2-way: nvr on terms* **40/1**

5050 **12** *8* **Je Suis Unrockstar**[18] 3702 3-9-3 **60** .... BillyCray(3) 5 — 13
(David Nicholls) *chsd ldrs tl lost pl 1/2-way: sn struggling* **11/1**

62.03 secs (0.93) **Going Correction** +0.05s/f (Good)
WFA 3 from 4yo+ 4lb **12** Ran SP% **119.9**
Speed ratings (Par 101): **94,93,93,91,90 90,87,86,86,85 81,69**
Tote Swingers:1&2:£13.40, 2&3:£9.00, 1&3:£13.70 CSF £55.23 CT £219.86 TOTE £11.90: £4.10, £2.10, £2.00; EX 85.20.
Owner Stuart Herrington **Bred** Worksop Manor Stud **Trained** Cold Kirby, N Yorks

FOCUS
Like the preceding race over the same trip, the pace was good, meaning plenty had a chance of sorts. Straightforward form.
Tenancy(IRE) Official explanation: jockey said gelding was unsuited by the good to soft ground

4329 ROFLOW ENVIORNMENTAL ENGINEERING APPRENTICE H'CAP — 1m 2f 32y
5:50 (5:52) (Class 6) (0-60,60) 3-Y-0+ — **£2,070** (£616; £307; £153) **Stalls** Low

Form — RPR

3252 **1** **Border Abby**[12] 3913 3-8-10 **56** .... NoelGarbutt(4) 11 — 62
(Rae Guest) *t.k.h: cl up: led after 4f: qcknd over 1f out: kpt on fnl f: jst hld on* **3/1**[1]

4434 **2** *nse* **Chapter Five**[6] 4127 4-10-0 **60** .... GeorgeChaloner 10 — 66+
(Keith Reveley) *hld up in midfield on outside: rdn and outpcd 3f out: gd hdwy appr fnl f: kpt on wl: jst hld* **3/1**[1]

-006 **3** *1 1/4* **Reason To Believe (IRE)**[25] 3485 3-9-0 **60** .... JackDuern(4) 7 — 63
(Ben Haslam) *hld up in midfield: rdn and outpcd over 2f out: kpt on fnl f: nrst fin* **11/2**[2]

1050 **4** *1/2* **Media Stars**[6] 4123 6-9-12 **60** .... LauraBarry(2) 5 — 62
(Robert Johnson) *hld up in tch: hdwy over 2f out: effrt over 1f out: kpt on same pce ins fnl f* **16/1**

5 *1/2* **Desert Nova (IRE)**[953] 2381 9-8-12 **48** .... JacobButterfield(4) 2 — 49
(Mark Campion) *t.k.h: led 4f: cl up: rdn over 2f out: kpt on ins fnl f* **20/1**

156 **6** *shd* **Marino Prince (FR)**[7] 4112 6-9-5 **55** .... DavidSimmonson(4) 3 — 57+
(Paul Midgley) *missed break: t.k.h: hld up: rdn over 2f out: styd on fnl f: nvr able to chal* **11/2**[2]

-600 **7** *1* **Richo**[25] 3496 5-9-2 **48** .... (p) NoraLooby 6 — 47
(Shaun Harris) *missed break: bhd tl hdwy over 1f out: kpt on: nvr able to chal* **16/1**

0460 **8** *1/2* **Child Of Our Time (IRE)**[11] 3938 4-8-10 **48** .... DanielleMooney(6) 12 — 46
(Colin Teague) *t.k.h: w ldrs on outside: rdn 2f out: no ex fnl f* **8/1**[3]

55-0 **9** *2 3/4* **Lisbon Lion (IRE)**[24] 598 6-9-2 **48** .... JustinNewman 8 — 40
(Martin Todhunter) *t.k.h: cl up tl rdn and wknd over 1f out* **16/1**

2m 14.91s (3.01) **Going Correction** -0.125s/f (Firm)
WFA 3 from 4yo+ 10lb **9** Ran SP% **114.3**
Speed ratings (Par 101): **82,81,80,80,80 80,79,78,76**
Tote Swingers:1&2:£2.30, 2&3:£2.30, 1&3:£2.70 CSF £11.26 CT £45.70 TOTE £3.70: £1.40, £1.40, £1.90; EX 6.20.
Owner Beadle, Davies, Jennings & Drew **Bred** The Perfect Partnership **Trained** Newmarket, Suffolk
■ Stewards' Enquiry : David Simmonson one-day ban: careless riding (Aug 6)
Danielle Mooney caution: careless riding.
Jack Duern one-day ban: careless riding (Aug 6)

FOCUS
The early pace didn't look frenetic and plenty of these had a chance down the home straight. Weakish form, rated around the second and third.
T/Plt: £1,234.70 to a £1 stake. Pool £57,594.77. 34.05 winning tickets. T/Qpdt: £62.70 to a £1 stake. Pool £5,580.10. 65.80 winning tickets. RY

4275 NEWMARKET (R-H)
Saturday, July 23

OFFICIAL GOING: Good (7.1)
Wind: Fresh half-behind Weather: Cloudy

4330 BALLYGALLON STUD, IRELAND E B F MAIDEN STKS — 7f
1:45 (1:48) (Class 4) 2-Y-O — **£4,528** (£1,347; £673; £336) **Stalls** High

Form — RPR

1 **Entifaadha** 2-9-3 0 .... JMurtagh 18 — 90+
(William Haggas) *racd far side: chsd ldrs: rdn to ld ins fnl f: r.o* **15/2**[3]

4 **2** *2 3/4* **Storming Bernard (USA)**[12] 3917 2-9-3 0 .... SamHitchcott 15 — 83
(Alan Bailey) *overall ldr far side: rdn over 1f out: hdd ins fnl f: styd on same pce: 2nd of 7 in gp* **22/1**

3 *1* **Fencing (USA)** 2-9-3 0 .... RobertHavlin 3 — 80+
(John Gosden) *racd centre: s.i.s: hld up: racd centre: hdwy over 2f out: edgd lft fr over 1f out: led that gp ins fnl f: r.o: 1st of 13 in gp* **14/1**

2 **4** *1/2* **Burano (IRE)**[28] 3401 2-9-3 0 .... ShaneKelly 9 — 79
(Brian Meehan) *racd centre: hld up: hdwy over 3f out: rdn: hung lft and led that gp over 1f out: styd on same pce ins fnl f: 2nd of 13 in gp* **11/8**[1]

0 **5** *4* **Monymusk**[12] 3915 2-9-3 0 .... DaneO'Neill 5 — 68
(David Elsworth) *racd centre: hld up: hdwy over 1f out: edgd lft: styd on same pce ins fnl f: 3rd of 13 in gp* **50/1**

6 *1 3/4* **Goldream** 2-9-3 0 .... J-PGuillambert 8 — 63
(Luca Cumani) *racd centre: prom: rdn over 2f out: wknd over 1f out: 4th of 13 in gp* **50/1**

7 *hd* **Mubaraza (IRE)** 2-9-3 0 .... AdamKirby 6 — 63+
(John Dunlop) *s.i.s: hld up: racd centre: styd on fr over 1f out: n.d: 5th of 13 in gp* **16/1**

8 *hd* **Protanto (IRE)** 2-9-3 0 .... SteveDrowne 10 — 64+
(David Lanigan) *racd centre: hld up: styd on ins fnl f: nvr nrr: 6th of 13 in gp* **33/1**

9 *1 [illegible]* **[illegible]** 2-9-3 0 .... JamieSpencer 16 — 59+
(Mahmood Al Zarooni) *[illegible] 13 in gp* **10/1**

5 **10** *1 3/4* **Paladin (IRE)**[28] 3401 2-9-3 0 .... ChrisCatlin 11 — 54
(Mahmood Al Zarooni) *led centre tl rdn and hdd over 1f out: sn wknd: 8th of 13 in gp* **11/2**[2]

11 *5* **Cades Reef (IRE)** 2-9-3 0 .... LiamKeniry 20 — 41+
(Andrew Balding) *racd far side: prom: rdn over 2f out: sn wknd: 3rd of 7 in gp* **25/1**

12 *2 3/4* **Flight Connection** 2-9-3 0 .... KirstyMilczarek 12 — 33
(Clive Brittain) *racd centre: mid-div: rdn over 2f out: sn wknd: 9th of 13 in gp* **100/1**

0 **13** *1 3/4* **The Mighty Lohan (IRE)**[23] 3552 2-9-3 0 .... DarryllHolland 2 — 29
(Amy Weaver) *racd centre: prom tl rdn and wknd over 2f out: 10th of 13 in gp* **150/1**

0 **14** *3* **Highly Likely (IRE)**[14] 3870 2-9-3 0 .... IanMongan 17 — 20
(John Dunlop) *s.i.s: racd far side: sn pushed along and a in rr: 4th of 7 in gp* **50/1**

15 *1 3/4* **Endowing (IRE)** 2-9-3 0 .... PatDobbs 14 — 16
(Richard Hannon) *racd far side: s.i.s and sn outpcd: 5th of 7 in gp* **25/1**

16 *1 3/4* **Darrow (IRE)** 2-8-12 0 .... HarryBentley(5) 13 — 11
(William Knight) *racd far side: chsd ldrs: rdn over 2f out: sn wknd: 6th of 7 in gp* **50/1**

00 **17** *1 3/4* **Plum Bay**[8] 4061 2-8-12 0 .... NickyMackay 1 — —
(David Elsworth) *s.i.s: racd centre: a in rr: 11th of 13 in gp* **100/1**

18 *7* **Uprise** 2-9-3 0 .... RichardMullen 19 — —
(Sir Michael Stoute) *racd far side: sn pushed along and a in rr: last of 7 in gp* **25/1**

0 **19** *nk* **Jambobo**[14] 3870 2-9-3 0 .... GeorgeBaker 7 — —
(William Knight) *racd centre: prom tl rdn and wknd over 2f out: 12th of 13 in gp* **33/1**

6 **20** *3 1/4* **Echoes Of Joy**[77] 1890 2-9-3 0 .... TomMcLaughlin 4 — —
(David Evans) *racd centre: mid-div: rdn 1/2-way: sn wknd: last of 13 in gp* **66/1**

1m 25.61s (-0.09) **Going Correction** -0.10s/f (Good) **20** Ran SP% **124.6**
Speed ratings (Par 96): **96,92,91,91,86 84,84,84,82,80 74,71,69,66,64 62,60,52,52,48**
toteswingers:1&2:£24.90, 2&3:£42.50, 1&3:£15.80 CSF £168.33 TOTE £8.30: £2.60, £3.80, £3.40; EX 170.00.
Owner Hamdan Al Maktoum **Bred** Highclere Stud & Hmh Management **Trained** Newmarket, Suffolk

FOCUS
Far-side track used with stalls on far side except 1m2f and 1m5f, centre. Repositioning of bend into home straight added 20m to races of 1m2f and 1m5f. High numbers held sway here with Entifaadha and Storming Bernard breaking from stalls 18 and 15 respectively. The winning time was 2.71 seconds beyond standard and suggested the ground was riding a fraction on the slow side of the official description. This is usually a good maiden and it appeared so again. The first two were always prominent on the far side.

NOTEBOOK
Entifaadha cost 360,000gns and hails from a classy family with his half-brother being G1 winner Regal Parade. He holds an entry for the Champagne Stakes but connections indicated that the Group 3 Acomb Stakes at York may be a possibility unless they take in a conditions race before aiming for loftier targets. (op 8-1 tchd 7-1)
Storming Bernard(USA)'s performance was all the more credible given that he was exceptionally free to post. This was a definite step up on his debut fourth over 6f at Windsor and he should be able to pick up a maiden success before also making his mark in nurseries. (tchd 20-1)
Fencing(USA) ◆ was very much one to take from the race. A well-bred first foal out of a French Oaks winner, who herself was a half-sister to French Derby winner Lawman, his breeding indicates he'll be better over further in time. What makes his effort even more encouraging was that he was drawn away from the first and second and was very slowly into stride.
Burano(IRE) was only narrowly beaten over course and distance four weeks before this but found stiffer opposition this time around. A maiden should still come his way, but maybe at a smaller track. Official explanation: trainer said colt lost a shoe (op 11-10 tchd 6-4)
Monymusk put the experience of his previous run to good use and the step up in trip from 5f was also in his favour. He appeals as the type to come into his own when contesting nurseries later in the summer. (op 66-1)
Goldream has something of a mixed pedigree as he is by a champion sprinter out of a mare whose family have fared well over 1m2f and upwards. This respectable debut indicates that he'll be campaigned over further in time. (op 80-1)
Mubaraza(IRE) ◆, backed in from 100s, is bred to want much further than this and he shaped with some promise. (op 100-1)
Protanto(IRE), a first foal who cost 120,000gns, was another to offer some encouragement.

4331 BOYLESPORTS.COM H'CAP — 1m 2f

2:15 (2:18) (Class 3) (0-95,95) 3-Y-O+

£8,715 (£2,609; £1,304; £652; £326; £163) Stalls Centre

Form					RPR
110	1		**Club Oceanic**[16] 3774 3-9-3 **94** (p) JamieSpencer 10 (Jeremy Noseda) *hld up: hdwy 2f out: rdn to ld ins fnl f: r.o* 10/3[2]		100
3005	2	¾	**Tiger Reigns**[30] 3315 5-10-0 **95** JMurtagh 9 (Michael Dods) *hld up: rdn over 3f out: hdwy over 2f out: edgd rt ins fnl f: r.o* 12/1		99
44-0	3	hd	**Demolition**[14] 3876 7-9-8 **92** LeeTopliss(3) 8 (Richard Fahey) *a.p: rdn over 2f out: r.o* 15/2		96
0-05	4	1½	**Classic Punch (IRE)**[28] 3406 8-10-0 **95** DaneO'Neill 4 (David Elsworth) *led: rdn over 1f out: hdd and unable qck ins fnl f* 6/1[3]		96
00	5	4½	**Taqleed (IRE)**[35] 3156 4-9-12 **93** NickyMackay 5 (John Gosden) *chsd ldrs: rdn over 2f out: wknd fnl f* 5/2[1]		85
0-15	6	3¾	**George Adamson (IRE)**[57] 2475 5-8-10 **77** LiamKeniry 1 (Alan Swinbank) *prom: rdn over 2f out: wknd over 1f out* 9/1		62
4530	7	6	**Spa's Dancer (IRE)**[31] 3276 4-8-10 **77** DarryllHolland 3 (J W Hills) *dwlt: hld up: rdn over 1f out: sn wknd* 16/1		50
102	8	1¼	**Uphold**[10] 3982 4-9-9 **90** (b) SteveDrowne 2 (Gay Kelleway) *chsd ldrs: rdn over 3f out: wknd wl over 1f out* 16/1		60
1U-	9	19	**All Annalena (IRE)**[259] 7349 5-9-8 **89** (t) GeorgeBaker 7 (Lucy Wadham) *prom tl wknd 2f out* 14/1		21

2m 5.13s (-0.37) **Going Correction** -0.10s/f (Good)
WFA 3 from 4yo+ 10lb — 9 Ran SP% **113.8**
Speed ratings (Par 107): **97,96,96,95,91 88,83,82,67**
toteswingers:1&2:£5.90, 2&3:£16.90, 1&3:£7.30 CSF £42.00 CT £278.28 TOTE £4.00: £1.40, £2.80, £3.00; EX 37.50 Trifecta £327.90 Pool: £1028.22 - 2.32 winning units..
Owner Sir Robert Ogden **Bred** Card Bloodstock **Trained** Newmarket, Suffolk

FOCUS
This was run only at a steady gallop, as illustrated by the time, and they rather fanned out across the track. it was a bit muddling, but the second and third set the standard.

NOTEBOOK
Club Oceanic was able to get some cover, having been dropped out by Jamie Spencer from the stalls. This colt, who won twice in the early summer, regained his progressive profile after being easily beaten over C&D in a 1m2f handicap at the July festival. But he never managed to get into the race that day and deserved to be given another chance, and he showed a game attitude in getting the job done under a strong drive. Whether he can defy the handicapper again remains to be seen, but he has already paid his way for the season. (op 9-2)
Tiger Reigns may just appreciate going 1m2f these days, despite all his winning being done at 1m and less. This was a game effort but it may just have been that he was on the quickest ground towards the far side. (op 17-2)
Demolition faced a stiff task on his seasonal bow in the John Smith's Cup, where he showed up well for much of the race before understandably weakening in the closing exchanges. He was entitled to to be sharper for that experience and put in a stirring finish to suggest there are further wins in him, despite the fact that he is now seven. (tchd 7-1 and 8-1)
Classic Punch(IRE), a three-time course-and-distance winner who has come down the weights to just 1lb above the mark he took this race off a year earlier, gave a bold account of himself out in front, only being reined in during the final furlong. (tchd 5-1)
Taqleed(IRE) was progressive as a 3yo but hasn't quite lived up to expectations so far this season and this was another disappointing run. It was no surprise that connections opted to ease him back in trip after he apparently failed to see out 1m4f in a hot handicap at Royal Ascot, and this looked easier on paper without the depth of quality found in his three previous races. But he struggled to make an impression when push came to shove and has questions to answer now. (op 7-2)
George Adamson(IRE) is a largely consistent type and ran respectably upon his return from a near two-month break. (op 8-1)
Spa's Dancer(IRE) Official explanation: jockey said gelding hung left

4332 BOYLESPORTS EVERY SECOND COUNTS FILLIES' (H'CAP) — 7f

2:45 (2:46) (Class 2) (0-100,99) 3-Y-O+ £12,938 (£3,850; £1,924; £962) Stalls High

Form					RPR
2126	1		**Bonnie Brae**[14] 3845 4-9-1 **86** DaneO'Neill 12 (David Elsworth) *hld up in tch: rdn to ld ins fnl f: r.o* 11/1		94
-001	2	hd	**Golden Delicious**[14] 3845 3-7-11 **80** KieranO'Neill(5) 4 (Hughie Morrison) *hld up: swtchd lft and hdwy over 1f out: rdn and ev ch ins fnl f: r.o* 5/1[2]		85+
-543	3	nk	**Perfect Silence**[14] 3845 6-8-9 **87** LucyKBarry(7) 5 (Clive Cox) *led at stdy pce 6f out: qcknd over 2f out: hdd ins fnl f: r.o* 10/1[3]		94
10-3	4	1	**Ishbelle**[15] 3819 3-9-1 **93** StevieDonohoe 11 (Ralph Beckett) *hld up: hdwy over 1f out: rdn and hung lft ins fnl f: styd on* 11/1		94+
-616	5	½	**Folly Bridge**[18] 3703 4-10-0 **99** SteveDrowne 3 (Roger Charlton) *a.p: rdn over 1f out: styd on same pce ins fnl f* 14/1		102
2510	6	1	**Sioux Rising (IRE)**[15] 3827 5-9-4 **92** LeeTopliss(3) 8 (Richard Fahey) *s.i.s: hdwy over 5f out: rdn over 1f out: styd on same pce* 20/1		92
02-3	7	hd	**Wake Up Call**[29] 3365 5-9-7 **92** GeorgeBaker 1 (Chris Wall) *hld up: hdwy over 1f out: no ex ins fnl f* 14/1		92
-131	8	2¼	**Instance**[15] 3819 3-8-13 **91** JMurtagh 10 (Jeremy Noseda) *trckd ldrs: shkn up over 1f out: no ex ins fnl f* 10/11[1]		82
3006	9	hd	**Sonning Rose (IRE)**[7] 4093 3-8-4 **82** WilliamCarson 6 (Mick Channon) *hld up: plld hrd: rdn over 2f out: hdwy over 1f out: no ex ins fnl f* 25/1		72
0000	10	16	**Breedj (IRE)**[26] 3459 3-8-7 **85** ChrisCatlin 7 (Clive Brittain) *led at stdy pce tl hdd 6f out: chsd ldr tl rdn over 2f out: wknd over 1f out* 100/1		32
3653	11	hd	**Eucharist (IRE)**[7] 4096 3-9-4 **96** PatDobbs 2 (Richard Hannon) *hld up: rdn and wknd over 1f out* 33/1		42

1m 25.52s (-0.18) **Going Correction** -0.10s/f (Good)
WFA 3 from 4yo+ 7lb — 11 Ran SP% **120.7**
Speed ratings (Par 96): **97,96,96,95,94 93,93,90,90,72 72**
toteswingers:1&2:£10.30, 2&3:£8.50, 1&3:£20.20 CSF £64.79 CT £591.19 TOTE £14.10: £2.90, £1.90, £2.30; EX 82.10 Trifecta £355.20 Pool: £1296.19 - 2.70 winning units..
Owner Mrs T A Foreman **Bred** Rosyground Stud **Trained** Newmarket, Suffolk

FOCUS
The time was only fractionally quicker than the opening 2yo maiden staged over the same trip and that was as a consequence of the modest early pace. It was a bit of a messy race and the form isn't rated too positively.

NOTEBOOK
Bonnie Brae raced on the far side and was last off the bridle and just had enough up her sleeve to defeat Golden Delicious, who beat her at Ascot two weeks ago. As a result, there was a 6lb pull in the weights in favour of Bonnie Brae and that, combined with the way the race was run, saw her reverse the form. Connections are now planning to tackle the totesport Mile at Glorious Goodwood, where she'll need to improve again if she is to be competitive. But she has shown before that she stays a little further, so the step back up in trip holds no worries for her. (op 9-1)
Golden Delicious was raised 6lb for her Ascot success and only went down by a head here. She had every chance as she engaged in battle with the eventual winner, who proved just too good in the end. But this was another encouraging effort from the runner-up and there are more races to be won with her. (op 11-2)
Perfect Silence was third behind Golden Delicious in that Ascot handicap, so was entitled to be on the premises again. She took up the running early on with no confirmed front-runner among the field and didn't wilt, either, in the closing strides. But she is proving hard to win with this season and could probably do with a hand from the assessor.
Folly Bridge, eased back in class after contesting a Listed race last time, had no excuses. (op 11-1)
Instance proved something of a letdown after the impressive nature of her course-and-distance win a fortnight earlier. She was never travelling with the same fluency and may not have been helped by the lack of a true tempo. Indeed, she looked a shade keen early in the race and found nothing when asked for an effort. Maybe she had a harder race than appeared earlier in the month and it could be that a break would freshen her up for a productive autumn campaign. Official explanation: jockey said filly ran too free (op 6-4 tchd 13-8 in places)
Eucharist(IRE) Official explanation: jockey said filly lost its action

4333 BOYLESPORTS MOBILE H'CAP — 6f

3:20 (3:21) (Class 2) (0-105,101) 3-Y-O £29,110 (£8,662; £4,329; £2,164) Stalls High

Form					RPR
3140	1		**Swiss Dream**[15] 3820 3-8-10 **90** NickyMackay 3 (David Elsworth) *mde all: rdn and edgd lft over 1f out: r.o gamely* 8/1		101
0-60	2	1	**Pabusar**[42] 2928 3-9-7 **101** StevieDonohoe 8 (Ralph Beckett) *trckd ldrs: rdn over 1f out: edgd lft ins fnl f: r.o* 33/1		109
-011	3	½	**Cinderkamp**[8] 4048 3-8-6 **86** JamieSpencer 9 (Edward Vaughan) *hld up: swtchd lft and hdwy over 1f out: hrd rdn and edgd rt ins fnl f: r.o* 9/2[1]		92+
0110	4	¾	**Barnet Fair**[15] 3820 3-8-9 **89** LiamKeniry 4 (Richard Guest) *s.i.s: hdwy over 3f out: rdn over 1f out: hung lft ins fnl f: styd on* 12/1		93+
-400	5	shd	**What About You (IRE)**[15] 3820 3-8-3 **83** (b[1]) PatrickMathers 5 (Richard Fahey) *chsd wnr: rdn and ev ch over 1f out: styd on same pce ins fnl f* 20/1		86
1100	6	¾	**Elusive Prince**[19] 3682 3-8-4 **84** WilliamCarson 7 (David Barron) *hld up: swtchd rt to r alone on stands' side over 3f out: rdn over 1f out: r.o ins fnl f: nt rch ldrs* 25/1		85+
0-	7	hd	**The Reaper (IRE)**[43] 2894 3-9-1 **95** JMurtagh 2 (G M Lyons, Ire) *hld up: hdwy u.p and hung lft fr over 1f out: r.o: nt rch ldrs* 7/1[3]		95
3-20	8	¾	**Sadafiya**[30] 3323 3-8-5 **85** AdrianMcCarthy 19 (Ed Dunlop) *mid-div: hdwy 1/2-way: rdn over 1f out: styd on same pce ins fnl f* 25/1		83
1510	9	nk	**Mr Optimistic**[43] 2890 3-8-5 **85** RichardKingscote 18 (Richard Fahey) *mid-div: rdn over 2f out: hdwy over 1f out: nt rch ldrs* 25/1		82
3050	10	shd	**Arctic Feeling (IRE)**[15] 3820 3-9-0 **97** LeeTopliss(3) 17 (Richard Fahey) *hld up: hdwy over 2f out: rdn over 1f out: styd on same pce ins fnl f* 25/1		94
-110	11	1½	**Seal Rock**[42] 2934 3-9-2 **96** DaneO'Neill 14 (Henry Candy) *hld up: swtchd lft over 1f out: sn rdn: nt trble ldrs* 5/1[2]		88+
0616	12	shd	**Fred Willetts (IRE)**[28] 3378 3-8-7 **92** (v) MatthewCosham(5) 13 (David Evans) *prom: rdn over 2f out: styd on same pce appr fnl f* 50/1		84
5-04	13	¾	**Invincible Ridge (IRE)**[73] 2003 3-8-9 **94** KieranO'Neill(5) 20 (Richard Hannon) *prom: rdn over 1f out: hung rt and no ex ins fnl f* 11/1		83
-021	14	nk	**Sirius Prospect (USA)**[5] 4156 3-8-8 **88** 6ex ShaneKelly 15 (Dean Ivory) *s.i.s: sn prom: rdn over 1f out: no ex ins fnl f* 17/2		76
6000	15	4	**Majestic Dubawi**[15] 3820 3-9-3 **97** ChrisCatlin 12 (Mick Channon) *chsd ldrs: rdn 1/2-way: sn edgd rt and outpcd* 20/1		72
011-	16	½	**Loki's Revenge**[205] 8020 3-8-8 **88** SteveDrowne 11 (William Jarvis) *hld up: rdn over 2f out: nvr on terms* 25/1		62
2153	17	nk	**Muffraaj**[14] 3853 3-8-0 **80** AndreaAtzeni 6 (David Simcock) *chsd ldrs: rdn over 2f out: wknd over 1f out* 16/1		53
0502	18	1¾	**Bathwick Bear (IRE)**[15] 3807 3-8-12 **95** RyanClark(3) 10 (David Evans) *mid-div: rdn over 2f out: sn wknd* 40/1		62
2006	19	hd	**Avonmore Star**[23] 3535 3-8-11 **91** PatDobbs 1 (Richard Hannon) *s.s: a in rr* 40/1		58

1m 11.56s (-0.94) **Going Correction** -0.10s/f (Good) — 19 Ran SP% **129.4**
Speed ratings (Par 106): **102,100,100,99,98 97,97,96,96,96 94,93,92,92,87 86,86,83,83**
toteswingers:1&2:£151.80, 2&3:£40.50, 1&3:£10.80 CSF £260.86 CT £1362.40 TOTE £10.00: £2.50, £11.20, £1.70, £4.60; EX 422.80 TRIFECTA Not won..
Owner Lordship Stud **Bred** Lordship Stud **Trained** Newmarket, Suffolk
■ Stewards' Enquiry : Nicky Mackay three-day ban: used whip with excessive frequency (Aug 6-8)

FOCUS
A strong handicap. Plenty of these were renewing acquaintances after contesting a valuable course-and-distance handicap at the July festival. The winner made all on the stands' side, and six of the next seven raced there too.

NOTEBOOK
Swiss Dream, who has run solidly all season, was only beaten just over 3l on that occasion and consequently had to come into the equation for this. Connections went for a change of tactics here - instead of holding her up, she was allowed to bowl along in front. Perhaps a touch keen in the early strides, she proved game in defying all-comers. Next Saturday's Stewards' Cup looks probable for her and after that she is likely to be seen in stakes company in search of some black type. (op 10-1)
Pabusar gave a most encouraging performance under top weight, showing a willing attitude to battle into contention after being held up. He had been well held on his two previous starts this season, so this was very much a step back in the right direction. (op 50-1)
Cinderkamp has been a real star for his yard, winning four of his last five races, including at Haydock where he delivered a strong late challenge. This was undoubtedly his toughest assignment to date. He again gave a very creditable effort but looked to have quite a hard race here. (op 13-2)
Barnet Fair showed up well in that 6f handicap here two weeks earlier after back-to-back wins in the early summer. On this evidence he remains in good form, making up ground readily in his race after missing the break. Official explanation: jockey said gelding hung left (op 10-1)
What About You(IRE) has been running in seriously competitive handicaps this season - this being another. He responded well enough to the first-time blinkers and would be of interest if his sights were slightly lowered. Official explanation: jockey said gelding hung left (op 16-1)
Elusive Prince was last of seven at Ripon earlier in the month. He has quite useful bits of form to his name and his shrewd trainer is sure to find further winnable opportunities for him before the season is out. (op 20-1)
The Reaper(IRE) came into this off the back of two second-place efforts and was racing off a career-high mark of 95. He stayed on to pass rivals in the closing furlong and may be worth a try at 7f. (op 13-2)
Sadafiya benefited from being eased in class and trip after finishing last of seven in Listed company over 7f at Warwick a month earlier.
Seal Rock has gone up 11lb already this season after two wins on the Rowley Mile, but even so this was a shade disappointing. He'd been freshened up after running an acceptable race in a valuable 3yo handicap at York, but never threatened to play a part when the race got serious here. (op 13-2)
Avonmore Star Official explanation: jockey said colt was slowly away

4334 NSPCC E B F CONDITIONS STKS — 6f
3:55 (3:56) (Class 3) 2-Y-O — **£7,762** (£2,310; £1,154; £577) **Stalls** High

Form				RPR
1	**1**		**West Leake Diman (IRE)**[35] 3165 2-8-12 0.......... MatthewLawson(7) 3 (B W Hills) *w ldr tl led over 4f out: rdn and edgd lft ins fnl f: r.o* **14/1**	91
2230	**2**	½	**Magic City (IRE)**[39] 3014 2-9-5 0.......... PatDobbs 1 (Richard Hannon) *edgd rt s: hld up: hdwy over 2f out: rdn over 1f out: r.o* **5/1**	89
521	**3**	*hd*	**Radiomarelli (USA)**[19] 3686 2-9-5 0.......... StevieDonohoe 2 (Ralph Beckett) *edgd rt s: hld up: rdn over 1f out: r.o ins fnl f* **4/1**[3]	88
011	**4**	*hd*	**Sovereign Debt (IRE)**[14] 3842 2-9-3 0.......... JamieSpencer 4 (Michael Bell) *w ldrs: hrd rdn ins fnl f: unable qck towards fin* **15/8**[1]	86
201	**5**	5	**Springinmystep (IRE)**[21] 3610 2-9-5 0.......... JMurtagh 5 (Michael Dods) *prom: reminder 1/2-way: rdn over 1f out: wknd ins fnl f* **3/1**[2]	72
1420	**6**	8	**Monnoyer**[39] 3014 2-9-5 0.......... ShaneKelly 6 (Jeremy Noseda) *led: hdd over 4f out: remained w ldrs tl pushed along over 2f out: wknd and eased ins fnl f* **9/1**	56

1m 12.3s (-0.20) **Going Correction** -0.10s/f (Good) **6** Ran SP% **113.1**
Speed ratings (Par 98): **97,96,96,95,89 78**
toteswingers:1&2:£5.60, 2&3:£3.20, 1&3:£6.20 CSF £80.53 TOTE £12.00: £3.70, £2.40; EX 51.40.
Owner Henry Barton **Bred** Mr & Mrs G Middlebrook **Trained** Lambourn, Berks

FOCUS
A decent little conditions race, and sound form despite the small field.

NOTEBOOK
West Leake Diman(IRE) was the least experienced of these but showed the necessary resolve in a [illegible] 100 per cent record in a time that was 0.86 seconds slower than the preceding 3yo handicap staged over the same distance. [illegible] debut success at Haydock over 5f and took the step up in trip in his stride. His capable apprentice rider was claiming 7lb and that proved very useful in a close-fought finish. The colt wouldn't be out of place in Listed company, judged on this, and looks to be on the upgrade. (op 10-1 tchd 8-1)
Magic City(IRE) shaped as if he really appreciated the rise in distance. All of his previous racing had been done at 5f, including when finishing well down the field last time in Listed company at Royal Ascot. But he did all his best work late on here and it may be that he ends up getting a little further, too. (op 9-2)
Radiomarelli(USA) ran out a ready winner of a 6f Windsor maiden earlier this month and again ran well. He appeared to be outpaced for a stride or two but once organised he finished his race strongly and 7f is likely to be within his range, too. (tchd 9-2)
Sovereign Debt(IRE) had plenty to recommend him ahead of this and didn't lose much in defeat, going down by less than a length. But he has had four races within the last couple of months and may now benefit for a short break. (tchd 7-4 and 2-1)
Springinmystep(IRE), trying 6f for the first time, failed to convince that he gets the trip. In fact, he was niggled along quite early in the race and maybe this wasn't his running. Official explanation: trainer's rep said colt had a breathing problem (op 4-1 tchd 9-2 in places)
Monnoyer has not really progressed after an emphatic debut win at Wolverhampton in April. (op 12-1 tchd 14-1)

4335 NSPCC FAMILY DAY H'CAP — 1m
4:25 (4:25) (Class 3) (0-90,89) 3-Y-O
£8,715 (£2,609; £1,304; £652; £326; £163) **Stalls** High

Form				RPR
1-05	**1**		**Capaill Liath (IRE)**[15] 3825 3-9-4 **86**.......... (p) JamieSpencer 2 (Michael Bell) *chsd ldrs: rdn over 1f out: hung lft and r.o to ld nr fin* **6/1**[2]	94
1335	**2**	*hd*	**Little Black Book (IRE)**[43] 2877 3-8-5 **76**.......... (tp) SeanLevey(3) 12 (Gerard Butler) *led: rdn and hung rt over 1f out: carried lft and hdd nr fin* **15/2**[3]	84
4000	**3**	1¼	**Sergeant Ablett (IRE)**[21] 3623 3-9-7 **89**.......... RichardKingscote 6 (James Given) *chsd ldrs: rdn over 2f out: styd on same pce wl ins fnl f* **16/1**	94
2-13	**4**	*nk*	**Little Rocky**[35] 3168 3-9-5 **87**.......... LiamKeniry 11 (David Simcock) *hld up: hdwy over 1f out: sn rdn: styd on same pce wl ins fnl f* **8/1**	91+
31-4	**5**	*shd*	**Umseyat (USA)**[15] 3809 3-9-0 **82**.......... RobertHavlin 7 (John Gosden) *chsd ldrs: rdn and flashed tail fr over 1f out: no ex towards fin* **6/1**[2]	86
2130	**6**	8	**Amwell Pinot**[57] 2471 3-9-7 **89**.......... (v[1]) SamHitchcott 5 (Alan Bailey) *hld up in tch: rdn over 2f out: wknd over 1f out* **33/1**	75
-514	**7**	1	**Luv U Too**[15] 3818 3-8-10 **78**.......... DaneO'Neill 10 (Jo Hughes) *chsd ldrs: rdn over 1f out: sn wknd* **14/1**	61
2022	**8**	2¼	**Danehill Dante (IRE)**[7] 4102 3-8-9 **77**.......... PatDobbs 3 (Richard Hannon) *hld up in tch: rdn over 2f out: wknd ins fnl f* **14/1**	55
2-12	**9**	5	**Anoint**[42] 2926 3-9-4 **86**.......... JMurtagh 4 (William Haggas) *s.i.s: hld up: rdn over 2f out: wknd over 1f out* **15/8**[1]	53
0206	**10**	2½	**Mutajare (IRE)**[35] 3159 3-9-0 **82**.......... DarrylHolland 8 (Mark Johnston) *mid-div: rdn over 2f out: wknd over 1f out* **28/1**	43
5214	**11**	9	**Bosambo**[70] 2096 3-9-0 **82**.......... J-PGuillambert 1 (Alan Swinbank) *prom: rdn over 2f out: sn wknd* **16/1**	22

1m 38.24s (-1.76) **Going Correction** -0.10s/f (Good) **11** Ran SP% **117.7**
Speed ratings (Par 104): **104,103,102,102,102 94,93,90,85,83 74**
toteswingers:1&2:£7.50, 2&3:£20.00, 1&3:£20.00 CSF £50.62 CT £700.49 TOTE £6.30: £1.90, £2.60, £6.30; EX 47.40.
Owner D Hanafin **Bred** Stanley Estate & Stud Co & Mount Coote Stud **Trained** Newmarket, Suffolk
■ Stewards' Enquiry : Sean Levey three-day ban: used whip with excessive frequency (Aug 6-8)

FOCUS
There was a sensible, even gallop in this race and the time was just over two seconds beyond standard. Prominent racers fared best and the first five came clear.

NOTEBOOK
Capaill Liath(IRE) was not that far away when fifth in a similar race over course and distance at the July festival and, despite not looking the easiest of rides, did just enough to master Little Black Book. For a moment it appeared as if he might not want to go by his chief rival, but jockey Jamie Spencer managed to put his mount's head in front at exactly the right time. (op 5-1 tchd 9-2)
Little Black Book(IRE) had produced three fair efforts over further before coming back to 1m. On this evidence, it would seem sensible to stick to this trip for the time being. But the fact that less than 2l covered the first five home gives the overall form only an adequate appearance. (op 13-2 tchd 8-1)
Sergeant Ablett(IRE), well beaten in each of his last three starts, finished too close for comfort from a form perspective. That said, maybe he has appreciated the drop back in trip after being campaigned over middle distances. (op 14-1 tchd 20-1)
Little Rocky ran a fair race but may need a little respite from the handicapper. (op 15-2)
Umseyat(USA) was eased in trip for this and also ran adequately. She may find a little more improvement for this experience but is hard to build a strong case for in the immediate future. (op 15-2 tchd 8-1)
Anoint Official explanation: jockey said gelding lost its action
Bosambo Official explanation: jockey said gelding stopped quickly

4336 NSPCC H'CAP — 1m 5f
5:00 (5:01) (Class 4) (0-80,80) 3-Y-O — **£5,175** (£1,540; £769; £384) **Stalls** Centre

Form				RPR
-604	**1**		**Elrasheed**[14] 3872 3-8-12 **71**.......... DaneO'Neill 5 (John Dunlop) *a.p: rdn over 1f out: styd on to ld wl ins fnl f* **7/1**[3]	81
6-32	**2**	1¾	**Devoted (IRE)**[33] 3233 3-9-2 **75**.......... RichardKingscote 3 (Ralph Beckett) *chsd ldrs: led over 2f out: rdn and hung lft fr over 1f out: hdd wl ins fnl f* **4/1**[1]	84+
1242	**3**	½	**Watered Silk**[24] 3518 3-8-9 **68**.......... (p) PatDobbs 9 (Marcus Tregoning) *hld up: hdwy u.p and hung lft fr over 1f out: styd on: nrst fin* **4/1**[1]	74
-406	**4**	*hd*	**Wayward Glance**[41] 2956 3-9-7 **80**.......... ShaneKelly 1 (Michael Bell) *hld up: hdwy over 2f out: rdn over 1f out: styd on* **14/1**	86
-426	**5**	4½	**Battery Power**[10] 3989 3-8-11 **70**.......... NickyMackay 10 (Mark H Tompkins) *chsd ldr tl rdn over 2f out: wknd ins fnl f* **12/1**	69
3-06	**6**	2½	**Secret Edge**[23] 3551 3-8-9 **68**.......... LiamKeniry 8 (Alan King) *s.i.s: sn prom: rdn over 3f out: outpcd fr over 2f out* **14/1**	63
2122	**7**	1½	**Jacobs Son**[65] 2228 3-9-3 **79**.......... SeanLevey(3) 2 (Robert Mills) *led: rdn and hdd over 2f out: wknd ins fnl f* **5/1**[2]	72
6110	**8**	10	**L'Hermitage (IRE)**[36] 3108 3-9-2 **75**.......... (p) DarrylHolland 7 (Brian Meehan) *hld up: pushed along 6f out: hdwy over 3f out: sn rdn: wknd over 2f out* **10/1**	53
050	**9**	36	**Al Khawaneej**[42] 2930 3-8-7 **66**.......... JamieSpencer 4 (Ed Dunlop) *hld up: rdn 4f out: wknd wl over 2f out: eased: t.o* **5/1**[2]	—

2m 47.92s (3.92) **Going Correction** -0.10s/f (Good) **9** Ran SP% **115.9**
Speed ratings (Par 102): **83,81,81,81,78 77,76,70,47**
toteswingers:1&2:£6.90, 2&3:£4.10, 1&3:£7.10 CSF £35.29 CT £128.37 TOTE £8.30: £2.50, £1.60, £1.80; EX 40.30.
Owner Hamdan Al Maktoum **Bred** Shadwell Estate Company Limited **Trained** Arundel, W Sussex

FOCUS
There wasn't much pace on early and the [illegible] outside of standard.
Ordinary form, the winner building on is better run latest.
Jacobs Son Official explanation: jockey said gelding hung left
T/Plt: £1,262.60 to a £1 stake. Pool of £81,037.13 - 46.85 winning tickets. T/Qpdt: £104.30 to a £1 stake. Pool of £5,894.73 - 41.80 winning tickets. CR

[3868] SALISBURY (R-H)
Saturday, July 23

OFFICIAL GOING: Good to firm (good between 6f and 5f markers) changing to good after race 2 (6.30pm)
Wind: Moderate, against. Weather: sunny periods

4337 FERNDENE FARM "CARNARVON" H'CAP (FOR GENTLEMAN AMATEUR RIDERS) — 1m
6:00 (6:00) (Class 5) (0-75,70) 3-Y-O+ — **£2,807** (£870; £435; £217) **Stalls** Low

Form				RPR
-006	**1**		**Cultural Desert**[43] 2885 3-10-11 **70**.......... MrCharlieDuckworth(7) 5 (Ralph Beckett) *trckd ldrs: wnt 2nd 2f out: sn rdn and drifted lft: led ent fnl f: kpt on wl* **8/1**[3]	80
-063	**2**	1½	**George Thisby**[4] 4179 5-10-11 **60**.......... MrPMillman(5) 1 (Rod Millman) *led: rdn 3f out: hdd ent fnl f: kpt on but no ex* **8/1**[3]	69
0032	**3**	2	**Advertise**[15] 3804 5-10-9 **58**.......... MrARawlinson(5) 10 (Joseph Tuite) *stdd s: towards rr: hdwy fr 3f out: rdn 2f out: styd on fnl f: nt rch ldrs* **6/1**[2]	62
-006	**4**	3	**Gallego**[3] 4211 9-10-8 **57**.......... MrBJPoste(5) 3 (Richard Price) *stdd s: towards rr: hdwy over 3f out: rdn over 2f out: styd on same pce* **12/1**	55
0033	**5**	½	**Annes Rocket (IRE)**[11] 3944 6-10-10 **59**.......... MrFMitchell(5) 12 (Jimmy Fox) *s.i.s: bhd: hdwy fr 3f out: nt clr run whn swtchd lft 2f out: sn rdn: styd on same pce* **6/1**[2]	55
0-20	**6**	14	**Genes Of A Dancer (AUS)**[11] 3944 5-10-8 **55**.......... JamesBanks(3) 7 (Adrian Chamberlain) *chsd ldrs: rdn over 3f out: wknd 2f out* **12/1**	19
2064	**7**	13	**Lord Deevert**[156] 574 6-10-2 **53**.......... RyanWhile(7) 13 (Bill Turner) *in tch tl wknd over 2f out* **25/1**	—
50-0	**8**	*nk*	**Michael's Nook**[42] 2922 4-10-9 **53**.......... MrJMQuinlan 2 (Stuart Kittow) *trckd ldr: rdn over 3f out: hung lft and wknd 2f out* **18/1**	—

55-4 **9** ½ **Night Sky**[72] 2027 4-11-2 **60**.............................. MrSWalker 11 —
(Peter Makin) *awkwardly away: sn pushed along in mid-div: wknd 2f out* **9/2**[1]

3344 **10** 1 **Major Domo (FR)**[12] 3925 3-10-13 **68**........................(p) MrCMartin[(3)] 14 —
(Harry Dunlop) *rdn over 2f out: a towards rr* **14/1**

3305 **11** ½ **Mr Udagawa**[15] 3804 5-10-11 **60**..............................(p) MrRJWilliams[(5)] 4 —
(Bernard Llewellyn) *trckd ldr: rdn 3f out: wknd over 2f out* **16/1**

5060 **12** ½ **Lady Bridget**[11] 3952 3-10-2 **59**.............................. MrOGarner[(5)] 8 —
(Mark Gillard) *chsd ldrs for over 3f: sn bhd* **22/1**

1326 **13** ½ **Angelena Ballerina (IRE)**[24] 3515 4-11-0 **65**...........(v) MrLMichael[(7)] 9 —
(Karen George) *mid-div: rdn 3f out: wknd 2f out* **9/1**

1m 47.01s (3.51) **Going Correction** +0.40s/f (Good)
WFA 3 from 4yo+ 8lb **13** Ran SP% **120.4**
Speed ratings (Par 103): **98,96,94,91,91 77,64,63,63,62 61,61,60**
Tote Swingers:1&2:£9.80, 2&3:£10.80, 1&3:£8.70 CSF £71.23 CT £431.42 TOTE £11.20: £3.80, £3.30, £1.70; EX 87.80 Trifecta £1318.70 Part won. Pool 1,782.11 - 0.60 winning units..
Owner The Quick Fill Partnership **Bred** Mrs R D Peacock **Trained** Kimpton, Hants
■ The first winner for Charlie Duckworth, who is assistant to trainer Ralph Beckett.

FOCUS
Quite a competitive amateur riders' handicap on paper but few got into it in truth and the first two had it between them entering the final furlong. Ordinary form.
Night Sky Official explanation: jockey said filly ran flat

4338 DEREK BURRIDGE GOLF & RACING TROPHIES CLASSIFIED CLAIMING STKS 1m
6:30 (6:30) (Class 5) 3-4-Y-O **£2,911** (£866; £432; £216) **Stalls** Low

Form RPR

1140 **1** **Exchange**[30] 3318 3-8-11 66.............................. SteveDrowne 4 73
(Andrew Haynes) *hld up: stdy hdwy fr over 2f out: rdn whn drifted lft fr over 1f out: led jst ins fnl f: rdn out* **20/1**

2030 **2** 2 **Whodathought (IRE)**[19] 3688 3-8-7 70........................(bt) JimmyQuinn 8 64
(Richard Hannon) *trckd ldrs: rdn over 2f out: ev ch briefly ins fnl f: sn hld* **13/2**

4255 **3** ¾ **Barista (IRE)**[7] 4089 3-8-8 73 ow3.......................... MatthewDavies[(3)] 6 66
(Mick Channon) *in tch: rdn over 2f out: nt pce to chal: wnt 3rd ins fnl f* **11/2**[3]

1420 **4** 2¾ **Catchanova (IRE)**[15] 3815 4-8-10 67.............................. AmyScott[(5)] 7 58
(Eve Johnson Houghton) *s.i.s: towards rr: plugged on u.p fnl 2f: hung lft ins fnl f: nvr threatened* **4/1**[2]

5020 **5** hd **Royal Opera**[15] 3798 3-8-6 70..(v) JohnFahy[(3)] 2 57
(Rod Millman) *led: rdn whn lost action briefly 2f out: hdd jst ins fnl f: fdd* **10/1**

0255 **6** 6 **Novel Dancer**[12] 3919 3-8-9 71 ow1.............................. RichardHughes 1 44
(Richard Hannon) *in tch: reminders over 3f out: btn 2f: eased ins fnl f* **5/2**[1]

-465 **7** 3 **Norse Wing**[23] 3537 3-8-4 60..(v) MartinLane 5 32
(Ralph Beckett) *trckd ldrs tl rdn over 2f out: sn btn* **16/1**

-603 **8** 4½ **Deny**[12] 3919 3-9-2 67..(b[1]) SebSanders 3 33
(Sir Michael Stoute) *pushed along early: sn prom: rdn 3f out: btn 2f out* **11/2**[3]

1m 46.81s (3.31) **Going Correction** +0.40s/f (Good)
WFA 3 from 4yo 8lb **8** Ran SP% **112.4**
Speed ratings (Par 103): **99,97,96,93,93 87,84,79**
Tote Swingers:1&2:£20.60, 2&3:£4.80, 1&3:£23.60 CSF £137.97 TOTE £12.80: £3.00, £2.30, £2.30; EX 117.50 Trifecta £1857.90 Pool 6,779.14 - 2.70 winning units..
Owner G Gill **Bred** Southill Stud **Trained** Limpley Stoke, Bath

FOCUS
A modest claimer in which the first three home all came from off the pace, suggesting Royal Opera set a reasonable enough gallop. A clear personal best from the winner at face value, but there are doubts.

4339 PICADOR CHEVROLET MAIDEN STKS 6f
7:05 (7:07) (Class 5) 2-Y-O **£2,911** (£866; £432; £216) **Stalls** Low

Form RPR

2 **1** **Gerfalcon**[15] 3793 2-9-3 0.............................. MartinDwyer 8 85+
(Brian Meehan) *trckd ldr: led over 2f out: rdn and narrowly hdd over 1f out: regained ld jst ins fnl f: r.o: drifted lft fnl 75yds* **7/4**[2]

0 **2** ¾ **Charitable Act (FR)**[19] 3686 2-9-3 0.............................. HughBowman 6 83
(William Muir) *mid-div: hdwy whn nt clr run and swtchd lft 2f out: sn rdn: styd on fnl f: wnt 2nd nr fin* **33/1**

3 1¼ **Gusto** 2-8-12 0.............................. KieranO'Neill[(5)] 13 81+
(Richard Hannon) *trckd ldrs: rdn to chal 2f out: led over 1f out: hdd jst ins fnl f: hld whn short of room briefly nr fin* **17/2**[3]

4 nk **Sir Fredlot (IRE)** 2-9-3 0.............................. WilliamCarson 10 78+
(Peter Winkworth) *s.i.s: towards rr: swtchd lft and hdwy fr 2f out: wnt 4th and swtchd rt ent fnl f: styd on wl: nrst fin* **20/1**

00 **5** 8 **Best In Show**[17] 3746 2-9-3 0.............................. SebSanders 4 52
(J W Hills) *in tch: rdn over 2f out: sn one pce* **28/1**

6 2 **Peg Peg** 2-8-9 0.............................. JohnFahy[(3)] 3 41+
(Nerys Dutfield) *sn pushed along towards rr: rn green but styd on steadily fnl 2f: nvr threatened ldrs* **66/1**

5 **7** ¾ **Loxton Lad (IRE)**[14] 3868 2-9-3 0.............................. SteveDrowne 1 44
(Roger Charlton) *mid-div: rdn over 2f out: wkng whn edgd lft jst ins fnl f* **16/1**

0 **8** ½ **Ventus D'Or**[19] 3686 2-9-0 0.............................. MatthewDavies[(3)] 7 42
(Walter Swinburn) *led tl over 2f out: sn rdn: wknd over 1f out* **66/1**

9 hd **April Ciel** 2-9-3 0.............................. TomMcLaughlin 5 41+
(Andrew Haynes) *trckd ldrs: rdn 2f out: grad fdd* **50/1**

10 3 **Emirates Jack (IRE)** 2-9-3 0.............................. TonyCulhane 14 32
(George Baker) *a bhd* **22/1**

0 **11** 1¾ **Onebytheknows**[12] 3917 2-9-3 0.............................. RichardHughes 11 26
(Richard Hannon) *mid-div: rdn over 2f out: wknd over 1f out* **9/1**

0 **12** ¾ **Showmepower (IRE)**[12] 3917 2-9-3 0.............................. MartinLane 12 24
(John Dunlop) *tk v t.k.h on outer of mid-div: wknd over 2f out* **50/1**

2 **13** 5 **Dutch Rose (IRE)**[19] 3686 2-8-12 0.............................. StevieDonohoe 9 —
(Ralph Beckett) *chsd ldrs rdn over 2f out: wknd over 1f out: no ch whn nrly b.d jst ins fnl f: eased* **6/4**[1]

1m 18.12s (3.32) **Going Correction** +0.40s/f (Good) **13** Ran SP% **125.2**
Speed ratings (Par 94): **93,92,90,89,79 76,75,74,74,70 68,67,60**
Tote Swingers:1&2:£13.70, 2&3:£100.20, 1&3:£6.10 CSF £72.08 TOTE £2.80: £1.50, £10.10, £2.50; EX 92.20 TRIFECTA Not won..
Owner Michael Buckley **Bred** Enterprise B'Stock & Newsells Park Stud **Trained** Manton, Wilts
■ Stewards' Enquiry : Martin Dwyer caution: careless riding.

FOCUS
Quite an interesting maiden in which the first four finished a long way clear and the quartet all look to have bright futures.

NOTEBOOK
Gerfalcon ran a stormer at Ascot on debut, form which made her the one to beat here, even without the prospect of improvement, and he went one better despite edging to his right in the closing stages, causing the third placed horse to lose some momentum. A Gimcrack entry suggests the winner is rated quite highly by the Brian Meehan team and he is undoubtedly a colt of potential. (tchd 15-8)
Charitable Act(FR) left his debut run well behind with a rattling good performance in defeat, keeping on really well and shaping like a certain furture winner.
Gusto fared best of the newcomers and shaped with any amount of promise on debut. The winner edged across him in the closing stages, causing him to lose some momentum when he was still keeping on well. Given he's sure to benefit from this mentally, he looks sure to be a very warm order in similar company next time. (op 10-1)
Sir Fredlot(IRE) looked quite green early on but the further he went the more the penny dropped and he fairly flew home from a long way back. He goes down as a real eyecatcher and arguably shaped with as much promise as Gusto.
Dutch Rose(IRE) proved bitterly disappointing and was well beaten when badly hampered in the final furlong. This was a big step backwards from such a promising debut. Official explanation: jockey said filly suffered interference in running (op 13-8)

4340 ELLIE GRIMES BIRTHDAY CELEBRATION MAIDEN STKS 6f
7:35 (7:37) (Class 5) 3-Y-O+ **£2,911** (£866; £432; £216) **Stalls** Low

Form RPR

3-23 **1** **Cape Classic (IRE)**[35] 3178 3-9-3 73.............................. RichardHughes 1 78+
(William Haggas) *a.p: led 2f out: r.o to assert fnl f: pushed out* **1/2**[1]

-520 **2** 1 **Mrs Greeley**[16] 3782 3-8-12 67.............................. WilliamCarson 5 70
(Eve Johnson Houghton) *trckd ldrs: rdn to chal 2f out: kpt on but nt pce of wnr fnl f* **5/1**[2]

3 4 **Fabulouslyspirited** 3-8-12 0.............................. StevieDonohoe 12 59+
(Ralph Beckett) *swtchd rt s: bhd: pushed along over 2f out: swtchd lft over 1f out: styd on strly: nrst fin* **8/1**[3]

4 hd **Royal Selection (IRE)** 3-8-12 0.............................. TomMcLaughlin 2 59+
(Karen George) *towards rr: rdn over 2f out: hdwy fr wl over 1f out: sn swtchd rt: styd on fnl f: nrst fin* **66/1**

-40 **5** 1¾ **Ever The Optimist (IRE)**[33] 3232 3-9-3 0.............................. JimmyQuinn 4 59
(Stef Higgins) *led tl rdn 2f out: fdd ins fnl f* **18/1**

44-4 **6** 1 **Luisa Tetrazzini (IRE)**[58] 2424 5-8-12 54.............................. MarkCoumbe[(5)] 9 52
(Michael Attwater) *s.i.s: nvr bttr than mid-div* **33/1**

-06 **7** ½ **Diamond Run**[7] 4102 3-8-12 0..[1] SebSanders 11 50
(J W Hills) *t.k.h: hld up: rdn over 2f out: nvr a danger* **18/1**

60- **8** ½ **So Choosy**[367] 4253 3-8-13 0 ow1.............................. HughBowman 6 50
(Jeremy Gask) *mid-div: rdn over 2f out: no imp* **20/1**

9 1½ **Orpen'Arry (IRE)** 3-9-3 0.............................. MartinLane 3 49
(Andrew Haynes) *chsd ldrs tl rdn over 2f out: sn wknd* **50/1**

10 ¾ **Fleetwoodmaxi (USA)** 4-9-8 0.............................. SteveDrowne 8 48
(Peter Makin) *a towards rr* **25/1**

11 3½ **My Piccadill** 3-8-12 0.............................. FergusSweeney 10 33
(Stuart Kittow) *mid-div: hdwy over 3f out: rdn over 2f out: wknd over 1f out* **18/1**

1m 18.43s (3.63) **Going Correction** +0.40s/f (Good)
WFA 3 from 4yo+ 5lb **11** Ran SP% **125.2**
Speed ratings (Par 103): **91,89,84,84,81 80,79,79,77,76 71**
Tote Swingers:1&2:£2.70, 2&3:£4.40, 1&3:£2.40 CSF £3.41 TOTE £1.60: £1.02, £1.90, £2.20; EX 3.90 Trifecta £13.60 Pool 482.02 - 26.12 winning units..
Owner Bernard Kantor **Bred** Wentworth Racing **Trained** Newmarket, Suffolk

FOCUS
Not much depth to this maiden, which was slowly run. The first two were basically to form.

4341 FAMOUS GROUSE H'CAP 1m 6f 21y
8:10 (8:10) (Class 5) (0-75,76) 3-Y-O+ **£2,911** (£866; £432; £216) **Stalls** Far side

Form RPR

0644 **1** **Baltimore Clipper (USA)**[7] 4097 4-9-10 **76**.............................. KieranO'Neill[(5)] 6 88
(Paul Cole) *in tch tl lost pl 4f out: in rr but travelling wl whn nt clr run fr 3f out tl 2f out: sn swtchd rt: styd on strly on far rails to ld ins fnl f: rdn out* **9/2**[3]

0312 **2** 2½ **Undulant Way**[17] 3744 3-9-0 **75**.............................. SebSanders 8 83
(Amanda Perrett) *hld up towards rr: hdwy over 3f out: sn rdn: led over 2f out: hdd ins fnl f: no ex* **2/1**[1]

3-04 **3** 2¼ **Tropical Bachelor (IRE)**[7] 4082 5-9-3 **67**.............................. JohnFahy[(3)] 9 72
(Richard Ford) *hld up towards rr: hdwy over 2f out: sn rdn: chsd ldr briefly over 1f out: styd on same pce* **20/1**

4626 **4** 3½ **Now What**[43] 2873 4-9-2 **66**.............................. MatthewDavies[(3)] 2 66
(Jonathan Portman) *mid-div tl dropped to rr over 4f out: sn rdn: hdwy 3f out: chsd ldr briefly over 1f out: no ex fnl f* **14/1**

3P-6 **5** ¾ **Ugalla**[16] 3758 4-9-11 **72**.............................. HughBowman 4 71
(Jane Chapple-Hyam) *trckd ldrs: rdn over 3f out: hld whn bdly hmpd wl over 1f out: styd on past btn horses fnl f* **18/1**

-006 **6** 4½ **Issabella Gem (IRE)**[15] 3817 4-9-3 **71**.............................. LucyKBarry[(7)] 1 64
(Clive Cox) *trckd ldrs after 2f: rdn over 3f out: btn whn hmpd wl over 1f out* **9/1**

-065 **7** nk **Drawn Gold**[7] 4082 7-9-1 **62**.............................. RussKennemore 7 54
(Reg Hollinshead) *led for over 2f: trckd ldrs: rdn over 3f out: wknd over 1f out* **14/1**

3066 **8** 2¾ **Albeed**[29] 3352 4-9-8 **69**.............................. JimmyFortune 3 57
(John Dunlop) *hld up towards rr: hdwy over 3f out: sn rdn to chse ldrs: wknd ent fnl f* **12/1**

5252 **9** 1¼ **Sunny Future (IRE)**[17] 3725 5-9-12 **73**.............................. TomMcLaughlin 10 60
(Malcolm Saunders) *led after 2f: rdn whn hdd over 2f out: wknd over 1f out* **8/1**

50/4 **10** 26 **Reset City**[9] 4024 5-9-4 **65**..(t) RichardHughes 5 15
(David Pipe) *trckd ldrs early: mid-div after 3f: rdn to chse ldrs over 2f out: wkng whn hmpd wl over 1f out: eased fnl f* **3/1**[2]

3m 7.05s (-0.35) **Going Correction** +0.05s/f (Good)
WFA 3 from 4yo+ 14lb **10** Ran SP% **128.7**
Speed ratings (Par 103): **103,101,100,98,97 95,95,93,92,77**
Tote Swingers:1&2:£4.50, 2&3:£6.80, 1&3:£19.50 CSF £15.52 CT £178.31 TOTE £6.20: £1.90, £1.60, £5.00; EX 19.40 TRIFECTA Not won..
Owner Meyrick & Dunnington-Jefferson **Bred** Timothy Byrnes & Leah Byrnes **Trained** Whatcombe, Oxon
■ Stewards' Enquiry : Kieran O'Neill four-day ban: careless riding (Aug 6-8 and one-day remedial training)

FOCUS
An ordinary staying handicap, which was well run. Improved form from the first two.

4342 BETFAIR IPHONE AND ANDROID APP H'CAP 6f 212y
8:40 (8:40) (Class 4) (0-85,82) 3-Y-O **£5,175** (£1,540; £769; £384) **Stalls** Centre

Form RPR

1160 **1** **Flyn's Boy**[42] [2926] 3-9-0 **75** .... JimmyFortune 2 81
(Rae Guest) *trckd ldrs: rdn 2f out: led ent fnl f: r.o gamely* **15/2**

4244 **2** ½ **Local Singer (IRE)**[21] [3649] 3-9-7 **82** .... RichardHughes 6 87
(Malcolm Saunders) *restrained bhd ldrs: pushed along over 2f out: r.o whn swtchd rt jst over 1f out: ev ch ins fnl f: no ex towards fin* **10/11**[1]

4223 **3** ½ **Uppercut**[23] [3543] 3-9-3 **78** .... FergusSweeney 4 82
(Stuart Kittow) *trckd ldrs: rdn to ld 2f out: hdd ent fnl f: kpt on but no ex* **4/1**[3]

6-00 **4** 5 **Colorado Gold**[29] [3351] 3-9-0 **78** .... JohnFahy(3) 1 68
(Ed de Giles) *led tl rdn 2f out: fdd fnl f* **20/1**

0503 **5** ¾ **Layla Jamil (IRE)**[3] [4202] 3-9-2 **77** .... HughBowman 5 65
(Mick Channon) *prom: rdn and ev ch 2f out: sn short of room: fdd fnl f* **3/1**[2]

1m 30.94s (2.34) **Going Correction** +0.40s/f (Good) **5** Ran SP% **113.9**
Speed ratings (Par 102): **102,101,100,95,94**
CSF £15.63 TOTE £8.40: £2.20, £1.10; EX 14.50.
Owner C J Murfitt **Bred** C J Murfitt **Trained** Newmarket, Suffolk

FOCUS
The market suggested this was going to be the day for Local Singer but he was outbattled in the closing stages. The form is rated around the second and third.
T/Plt: £91.60 to a £1 stake. Pool £58,260.72. 464.02 winning tickets. T/Qpdt: £5.10 to a £1 stake. Pool £5,234.96. 745.50 winning tickets. TM

4290YORK (L-H)
Saturday, July 23

OFFICIAL GOING: Good (6.0)
Wind: Moderate, half-against. Weather: fine but breezy

4343 SKY BET MOBILE FOR IPHONE NURSERY 5f
2:00 (2:01) (Class 3) 2-Y-O **£7,439** (£2,213; £1,106; £553) **Stalls** Centre

Form RPR

2311 **1** **Last Bid**[14] [3879] 2-9-6 **80** .... TedDurcan 3 88
(Tim Easterby) *chsd ldng pair: hdwy 2f out: rdn to chal over 1f out: drvn and styd on ins fnl f to ld last 50yds* **7/2**[2]

2212 **2** nk **Kool Henry (IRE)**[14] [3879] 2-9-4 **78** .... SilvestreDeSousa 2 85
(David O'Meara) *led: rdn along wl over 1f out: jnd and drvn ins fnl f: hdd and no ex last 50yds* **3/1**[1]

5103 **3** 4 **Rent Free**[14] [3879] 2-9-0 **77** .... AdamBeschizza(3) 8 70
(Nigel Tinkler) *in tch: hdwy 1/2-way: chsd ldrs 2f out: sn rdn and kpt on fnl f* **8/1**

15 **4** ½ **Risky Art**[39] [3022] 2-9-5 **79** .... GrahamGibbons 7 70+
(Michael Easterby) *in rr: pushed along 1/2-way: swtchd lft and rdn wl over 1f out: styd on wl fnl f: nrst fin* **8/1**

4310 **5** ¾ **Fayr Fall (IRE)**[18] [3700] 2-8-10 **70** .... TadhgO'Shea 9 58
(Tim Easterby) *in rr: hdwy on wd outside over 2f out: sn rdn and kpt on ins fnl f: nrst fin* **18/1**

6021 **6** ½ **Sonko (IRE)**[11] [3948] 2-8-5 **65** .... (p) HayleyTurner 4 51
(Tim Pitt) *chsd ldr: rdn along 2f out: drvn wl over 1f out and grad wknd* **16/1**

0263 **7** ½ **Dicky Mint**[11] [3948] 2-8-10 **70** .... (t) PaddyAspell 5 55
(Michael Easterby) *chsd ldrs: rdn along wl over 1f out: grad wknd* **10/1**

3241 **8** hd **Almond Branches**[24] [3504] 2-9-3 **77** .... JamesSullivan 11 61
(George Moore) *in tch: rdn along over 2f out: sn drvn and wknd over 1f out* **8/1**

3423 **9** 1¼ **One Kool Dude**[21] [3618] 2-8-11 **71** .... PaulHanagan 12 50
(Richard Fahey) *midfield: rdn along over 2f out: sn drvn and n.m.r: nvr a factor* **6/1**[3]

650 **10** 8 **Maria Medecis (IRE)**[14] [3878] 2-8-5 **65** .... RoystonFfrench 1 15
(Ann Duffield) *in tch: rdn along 1/2-way: sn wknd* **33/1**

2351 **11** dist **Courtland King (IRE)**[9] [4021] 2-9-1 **75** .... (t) CDHayes 6 —
(David Evans) *v.s.a and virtually ref to r* **25/1**

60.58 secs (1.28) **Going Correction** +0.325s/f (Good) **11** Ran SP% **118.7**
Speed ratings (Par 98): **102,101,95,94,93 92,91,91,89,76** —
Tote Swingers:1&2:£1.10, 2&3:£7.40, 1&3:£4.00 CSF £14.57 CT £80.39 TOTE £4.00: £2.10, £1.60, £3.20; EX 7.20 Trifecta £45.90 Pool £876.26 - 14.11 winning units..
Owner C H Stevens **Bred** Bearstone Stud **Trained** Great Habton, N Yorks
■ The 'official' ratings shown next to each horse are estimated and for information purposes only.

FOCUS
Rail moved in from 9f to entrance to home straight by 3m reducing distances of races 1m and over by 27yds. This modest nursery was run at a strong early pace and they unsurprisingly raced mid-track. Straightforward form, with the same 1-2-3 as a similar race over C&D a fortnight ago.

NOTEBOOK
Last Bid was up to a mark of 77 here and thus 2lb worse off with her old rival Kool Henry, but her willing attitude won her the day again. Her stable is in top form and she looks just the sort the handicapper will have trouble fully getting to grips with. Another furlong could also bring out further improvement. (tchd 4-1 in places)
Kool Henry(IRE), 2lb higher, was well backed to gain revenge on the winner on 2lb better terms. He blazed the trail up front and, although unable to reverse previous C&D form, ran another blinder in defeat. He will go up a few pounds again, but is surely capable of going one better again at this level. (op 4-1)
Rent Free finished third behind the first pair over C&D on her previous outing and was dropped 1lb for that, so faced them again on decidedly better terms. He met support, but lacked the speed to land a serious blow last time and it was again the case here. He ought to find one of these when faced with a stiffer test. (op 11-1)
Risky Art ◆ got badly outpaced from halfway on this nursery debut. She caught the eye finishing well inside the final furlong, however, and looks a surefire winner of something similar over further.
Fayr Fall(IRE) was back down in trip and didn't help his cause with a tardy start. He was not surprisingly doing his best work late in the day and needs a stiffer test over this distance (op 20-1 tchd 25-1)

Sonko(IRE), off the mark at the fifth attempt at Southwell 11 days earlier, showed decent early speed but couldn't go with the first pair from the furlong marker. (op 11-1)

4344 SKY BET MOBILE E B F BERTOLINI FILLIES' H'CAP 1m 2f 88y
2:30 (2:30) (Class 3) (0-90,88) 3-Y-O+ **£9,703** (£2,887; £1,443; £721) **Stalls** Low

Form RPR

-450 **1** **Tenby Lady (USA)**[7] [4090] 3-8-1 **71** .... SilvestreDeSousa 8 81
(Sir Mark Prescott Bt) *led 1f: led 4f out: kpt on gamely fnl 2f: hld on towards fin* **7/2**[1]

3500 **2** ½ **Antigua Sunrise (IRE)**[31] [3277] 5-9-3 **77** .... PaulHanagan 6 86
(Richard Fahey) *mid-div: hdwy to chal over 2f out: no ex towards fin* **10/1**

1414 **3** 2½ **Certral**[14] [3845] 3-8-5 **78** .... PaulPickard(3) 2 82
(Brian Ellison) *mid-div: hdwy to chse ldrs over 2f out: kpt on same pce fnl f* **9/1**

410 **4** nk **Creme Anglaise**[37] [3065] 3-9-2 **86** .... HayleyTurner 11 89
(Michael Bell) *hld up in rr: effrt 4f out: hdwy over 2f out: styd on same pce ins fnl f* **8/1**

-212 **5** 2¾ **Baqaat (USA)**[67] [2184] 3-8-8 **78** .... KierenFallon 5 76
(Ed Dunlop) *mid-div: effrt 4f out: hdwy over 2f out: edgd lft over 1f out: one pce* **7/1**[3]

2004 **6** 1½ **Resentful Angel**[14] [3844] 6-9-13 **87** .... (p) NeilCallan 10 82
(Pat Eddery) *trckd ldrs: effrt over 2f out: one pce over 1f out* **14/1**

0635 **7** 2 **Dazzling Light (UAE)**[15] [3828] 6-9-5 **79** .... LeeNewman 9 70
(Jim Goldie) *s.i.s: swtchd lft after s: in rr: hdwy over 2f out: edgd rt over 1f out: nvr nr ldrs* **16/1**

0310 **8** 25 **Amethyst Dawn (IRE)**[14] [3877] 5-9-13 **87** .... TedDurcan 1 28
(Tim Easterby) *mid-div: hdwy over 3f out: wknd over 1f out* **12/1**

-211 **9** ¾ **Elmaam**[35] [3180] 3-8-12 **82** .... TadhgO'Shea 3 21
(William Haggas) *rrd s: s.s: effrt on ins 4f out: chsd ldrs over 2f out: wknd over 1f out: eased ins fnl f* **4/1**[2]

3 **10** 4½ **Love Over Gold (FR)**[46] [2791] 4-9-8 **82** .... PatCosgrave 7 12
(Ralph Beckett) *trckd ldrs: lost pl over 2f out* **7/1**[3]

50- **11** 1½ **Magic Echo**[364] [4389] 7-9-5 **79** .... GrahamGibbons 4 —
(Robert Johnson) *led after 1f: hdd 4f out: sn lost pl* **50/1**

2m 9.24s (-3.26) **Going Correction** -0.225s/f (Firm)
WFA 3 from 4yo+ 10lb **11** Ran SP% **119.6**
Speed ratings (Par 104): **104,103,101,101,99 97,96,76,75,72 70**
Tote Swingers:1&2:£8.00, 2&3:£65.80, 1&3:£16.30 CSF £39.98 CT £297.20 TOTE £4.40: £2.00, £2.70, £3.40; EX 32.90 Trifecta £362.80 Pool £784.50 - 1.60 winning units..
Owner David F O'Rourke **Bred** O'Rourke's Silver Springs Stud Farm Llc **Trained** Newmarket, Suffolk
■ Stewards' Enquiry : Paul Pickard caution: used whip without giving filly time to respond.

FOCUS
A decent fillies' handicap. It was run at a strong early pace and half the field got behind, but they closed right up around 3f out. Solid form.

NOTEBOOK
Tenby Lady(USA) got a very strong ride and bravely opened her account for the season at the fourth time of asking. She was never far from the decent early fractions and took it up nearing 2f out. Her attitude when hard pressed by the runner-up was spot on and this has to rate a personal-best effort. A likely rise may well not be enough to stop her from following up. (op 4-1 tchd 9-2 in places)
Antigua Sunrise(IRE) finished fifth in this race in 2009 and improved two placed on that last year. She was produced with every chance inside the final furlong and threw down a strong challenge, but the winner proved that bit too resolute. She deserves to go one better, but will likely go back up in the handicap for this. (tchd 9-1)
Certral ◆ ran another improved race in defeat. She appeals strongly as one to resume winning ways back down in grade. (tchd 10-1)
Creme Anglaise ◆ was making her handicap debut having bombed out in the Group 2 Ribblesdale at Royal Ascot last month. She must rate better than the bare form as being so heavily restrained over this shorter trip caught her out and she did well to finish so close. (op 9-1)
Baqaat(USA) was 3lb higher on her return from a 67-day break and wasn't at all disgraced considering the run just looked needed. (tchd 8-1)
Resentful Angel, yet to win on turf, ran well under a prominent ride but is in need of respite from the handicapper. (tchd 16-1)
Elmaam performed too bad to be true and was later reported to have lost her action. Official explanation: jockey said filly loost its action (op 5-1 tchd 11-2 in places)
Love Over Gold(FR) dropped away rather tamely under maximum pressure and disappointed. Official explanation: jockey said filly was unsuited by the good ground (op 11-2)

4345 SKY BET YORK STKS (GROUP 2) 1m 2f 88y
3:05 (3:06) (Class 1) 3-Y-O+
£56,710 (£21,500; £10,760; £5,360; £2,690; £1,350) **Stalls** Low

Form RPR

1065 **1** **Twice Over**[38] [3031] 6-9-5 123 .... TomQueally 1 120
(Sir Henry Cecil) *hld up towards rr: hdwy on inner wl over 2f out: rdn to ld ent fnl f: edgd rt and styd on wl* **5/2**[2]

-105 **2** 1¼ **Ransom Note**[39] [3009] 4-9-2 114 .... MichaelHills 6 115
(B W Hills) *prom: trckd ldr 1/2-way: effrt 3f out: rdn 2f out and sltly outpcd over 1f out: drvn and kpt on wl fnl f* **12/1**

-251 **3** shd **Dominant (IRE)**[28] [3405] 3-8-6 108 .... NeilCallan 2 115
(Roger Varian) *trckd ldrs: hdwy over 3f out: rdn over 1f out: and ev ch tl drvn and edgd rt ent fnl f: kpt on same pce* **2/1**[1]

4-21 **4** ¾ **Class Is Class (IRE)**[22] [3591] 5-9-2 115 .... (v) PaulHanagan 4 113
(Sir Michael Stoute) *plld hrd: prom: led wl over 2f out: rdn wl over 1f out: hdd and drvn ent fnl f: kpt on same pce* **4/1**[3]

4-05 **5** nk **Saptapadi (IRE)**[14] [3876] 5-9-2 105 .... PaulPickard 3 113+
(Brian Ellison) *hld up in rr: hdwy wl over 2f out: effrt and nt clr run over 1f out: swtchd lft and rdn ins fnl f: kpt on: nrst fin* **14/1**

0-64 **6** nk **Eleanora Duse (IRE)**[21] [3624] 4-8-13 108 .... SilvestreDeSousa 7 109
(Sir Michael Stoute) *dwlt: hld up towards rr: hdwy on outer over 4f out: chal 3f out and sn rdn: ev ch tl drvn and wknd ent fnl f* **12/1**

1-02 **7** 3 **Tazeez (USA)**[22] [3591] 7-9-2 113 .... TadhgO'Shea 5 106
(John Gosden) *set stdy pce: qcknd over 4f out: rdn and qcknd over 3f out: hdd wl over 2f out: grad wknd* **9/1**

2m 9.99s (-2.51) **Going Correction** -0.225s/f (Firm)
WFA 3 from 4yo+ 10lb **7** Ran SP% **114.0**
Speed ratings (Par 115): **101,100,99,99,99 98,96**
Tote Swingers:1&2:£6.60, 2&3:£6.60, 1&3:£1.10 CSF £31.13 TOTE £3.10: £2.00, £4.90; EX 22.70.
Owner K Abdulla **Bred** Juddmonte Farms Ltd **Trained** Newmarket, Suffolk

FOCUS
A fair Group 2, run at an uneven pace, that saw the penalised Twice Over show his true colours again. He is a class above these at his best. The level of the form is sound at face value.

NOTEBOOK

Twice Over had looked as good as ever when winning in Meydan earlier this year, but bombed out in the Dubai World Cup there next time and arrived here with plenty to prove after two lacklustre efforts back in Britain. His trainer Henry Cecil was adamant he was not right at Royal Ascot last time, reasoning he got distressed and had to be left at the course overnight. This dual Champion Stakes winner has lot his form mid-season in the past before taking advantage of a confidence booster down in class, and he once again proved he is still a true Group 1 performer by winning here under his penalty. He took command inside the final furlong and was never in serious danger thereafter. Considering he also had anything but the run of the race he has to rate value for further, plus he was likely idling somewhat in the last half furlong. His season will now gear totally around his bid to defend the Group 1 Champion Stakes in October, to be run at Ascot for the first time, and land that event for a third successive year. He will no doubt face a strong challenge again, but has shown a liking for that track and should make another bold bid. Perhaps connections will choose the Juddmonte International for him over this C&D beforehand, considering he finished a close second to Rip Van Winkle in it last season. (tchd 11-4)

Ransom Note was the only previous course winner in attendance and, like Twice Over, was dropping in class having been well held in Group 1s on his two previous outings. He raced close to the pace and gave his all in defeat, but never looked like emerging on top despite being in receipt of 3lb from the winner. He should be able to score in this class before the season's end. (tchd 14-1)

Dominant(IRE) hacked up in a Newmarket handicap off 94 on his previous outing 28 days earlier and, getting 13lb from Twice Over, was heavily backed on this debut in Group company. He too was produced with every chance, but wasn't able to quicken sufficiently when challenged by that rival and ultimately set the race up for him. This confirms him very much a Group 2 performer and there should be more to come, as he has few miles on the clock. (op 5-2 tchd 15-8 and 11-4 in places)

Class Is Class(IRE) sprang back to life when recording a career-best success in Listed company at Sandown 22 days earlier. He got warm beforehand here and didn't help his cause by refusing to settle through the early parts. He still gave his all once under pressure, however, and only just missed out on a place. There is very likely a Group race in him granted a more truly run race. (tchd 10-3)

Saptapadi(IRE) ◆ went into many a notebook when finishing strongly from a poor draw in the John Smith's Cup over C&D a fortnight previously. This was a stiff task for him and he was friendless in the betting, but ran a big race and would have probably placed had his rider attained a clear run with him nearing the final furlong. He looks bang on course for a crack at the Ebor back here next month, for which he was unsurprisingly promoted to near the top of the ante-post betting. That longer trip could be right up his street. (op 12-1 tchd 20-1)

Eleanora Duse(IRE) made a bold bid on the inside passing the 2f marker and ran her best race for a while. She can find another success back against her own sex. (tchd 11-1 and 14-1)

Tazeez(USA), second to Class Is Class on his return to action last time, had the run of the race out in front and dictated an uneven pace. He was a sitting duck when things got serious in the home straight, however, and has now failed to shine in two outings here (tchd 8-1 and 10-1)

4346 SKY BET DASH (H'CAP) 6f

3:40 (3:40) (Class 2) (0-105,105) 3-Y-O+ **£32,345** (£9,625; £4,810; £2,405) **Stalls** Centre

Form RPR

1-10 **1** **Hoof It**[35] 3155 4-9-10 **105** .... KierenFallon 7 119+
(Michael Easterby) *hld up in tch: swtchd lft and hdwy wl over 1f out: rdn to ld ins fnl f: kpt on wl* **3/1**[1]

0205 **2** *¾* **Tajneed (IRE)**[8] 4042 8-9-4 **102** .... MichaelO'Connell(3) 5 111
(David Nicholls) *hld up: hdwy wl over 1f out: rdn to chse wnr ins fnl f: drvn and no imp towards fin* **25/1**

4160 **3** *¾* **Ginger Ted (IRE)**[8] 4042 4-8-8 **89** .... (p) JamesSullivan 15 96+
(Richard Guest) *towards rr: hdwy on wd outside 2f out: rdn over 1f out: kpt on wl fnl f* **20/1**

0603 **4** *1 ¼* **Fathsta (IRE)**[14] 3862 6-8-13 **94** .... TomQueally 2 97+
(David Simcock) *towards rr: hdwy 2f out: nt clr run and swtchd rt over 1f out: rdn and styd on strly fnl f: nrst fin* **7/1**[3]

0502 **5** *nk* **Baby Strange**[7] 4104 7-8-8 **89** .... RobbieFitzpatrick 4 91
(Derek Shaw) *towards rr: hdwy 2f out: n.m.r: swtchd rt and rdn over 1f out: kpt on ins fnl f: nrst fin* **25/1**

0462 **6** *nk* **Star Rover (IRE)**[14] 3850 4-8-6 **87** .... (v) CDHayes 11 88
(David Evans) *cl up: rdn 2f out: drvn and led briefly appr fnl f: sn hdd & wknd* **28/1**

0535 **7** *¾* **Favourite Girl (IRE)**[8] 4075 5-8-5 **91** .... (p) LanceBetts(5) 14 89
(Tim Easterby) *led: rdn along over 2f out: drvn over 1f out: hdd appr fnl f: kpt on same pce* **25/1**

1013 **8** *1* **Roker Park (IRE)**[8] 4042 6-8-10 **91** .... SilvestreDeSousa 1 86
(David O'Meara) *bhd and rdn along 1/2-way: swtchd lft and hdwy over 1f out: styd on ins fnl f: nrst fin* **12/1**

0000 **9** *½* **Irish Heartbeat (IRE)**[8] 4042 6-8-9 **90** .... (p) PaulHanagan 20 83
(Richard Fahey) *chsd ldrs: rdn along 2f out: drvn wl over 1f out: sn one pce* **14/1**

3654 **10** *nk* **Racy**[14] 3841 4-8-9 **90** .... NeilCallan 8 83
(Kevin Ryan) *in tch: hdwy over 2f out: sn rdn and no imp* **8/1**

-014 **11** *1 ½* **Entitled**[26] 3459 4-8-3 **87** .... LouisBeuzelin(3) 19 75
(Sir Michael Stoute) *midfield: effrt and hdwy to chse ldrs over 2f out: sn rdn and wknd over 1f out* **13/2**[2]

0003 **12** *hd* **Corporal Maddox**[14] 3850 4-8-8 **89** .... RoystonFfrench 10 76
(Jamie Osborne) *towards rr: pushed along 1/2-way: swtchd rt 2f out: sn rdn and n.d* **20/1**

0005 **13** *nse* **Befortyfour**[7] 4104 6-8-6 **87** .... PaulQuinn 18 74
(Richard Guest) *midfield: effrt over 2f out: sn rdn and wkng whn n.m.r over 1f out* **50/1**

-030 **14** *½* **R Woody**[14] 3841 4-8-11 **92** .... HayleyTurner 16 77
(Dean Ivory) *chsd ldrs: rdn along 2f out: drvn and one pce fr over 1f out* **22/1**

1250 **15** *½* **Singeur (IRE)**[14] 3841 4-9-1 **96** .... LeeNewman 9 80
(Robin Bastiman) *a in rr* **22/1**

4114 **16** *1* **Medici Time**[14] 3846 6-8-8 **89** .... (v) GrahamGibbons 17 70
(Tim Easterby) *in tch: effrt over 2f out: sn rdn and wknd* **20/1**

0020 **17** *1 ¾* **Silaah**[29] 3357 7-8-12 **93** .... (p) AdrianNicholls 13 68
(David Nicholls) *cl up: rdn along 2f out: drvn and edgd lft wl over 1f out: wknd appr fnl f* **33/1**

0006 **18** *½* **Mister Hughie (IRE)**[14] 3874 4-9-5 **100** .... TedDurcan 6 73
(Tim Easterby) *a in rr* **25/1**

-056 **19** *3* **Midnight Martini**[63] 2298 4-8-10 **91** .... (t) TadhgO'Shea 12 55
(Tim Easterby) *cl up: rdn along wl over 2f out: sn wknd* **16/1**

0005 **20** *3 ¾* **Swilly Ferry (USA)**[21] 3627 4-8-13 **94** .... MichaelHills 3 46
(B W Hills) *chsd ldrs on outer: rdn along over 2f out: sn wknd* **20/1**

1m 12.49s (0.59) **Going Correction** +0.325s/f (Good) **20 Ran SP% 133.7**

Speed ratings (Par 109): **109,108,107,105,104 104,103,102,101,101 99,98,98,98,97 96,93,93,89,84**

Tote Swingers:1&2:£38.80, 2&3:£245.30, 1&3:£19.00 CSF £91.75 CT £1409.71 TOTE £3.40: £1.40, £8.10, £4.90, £2.10; EX 128.30 TRIFECTA Not won..

Owner A Chandler & L Westwood **Bred** Bond Thoroughbred Corporation **Trained** Sheriff Hutton, N Yorks

FOCUS

This was a typically competitive sprint handicap for the class. Solid form which reads well. The winner will make his mark in Group races before long.

NOTEBOOK

Hoof It failed to really see out the stiff 6f off this mark when favourite in the Wokingham at Royal Ascot last time, but he loves the Knavesmire and this was his third success from six outings at the course. He again travelled powerfully off the strong early pace and it looked 2f out as though he was going to bolt up. However, he had to switch over to the far side for his challenge and the manoeuvre cost him a length or so. That also enabled the fast-finishing Tajneed to throw down a strong challenge, but once getting organised there was only going to be one winner. He is now an intended runner in the Stewards' Cup at Glorious Goodwood next weekend and he will pick up a 6lb penalty for that (was due to carry 9st 8lb) which again puts him on top weight. He has never raced at the Sussex venue, but there is little reason why that test shouldn't suit him and he was cut to clear favouritism in the ante-post betting. (op 4-1 tchd 11-4 and 9-2 in places)

Tajneed(IRE), the second top-weight, tends to save his best for Ripon these days, but had shown a liking for this track in the past and he returned to his best with a cracking effort. He travelled beautifully before quickening up on the far rail and gave the winner a fright. He too is a likely runner in the Stewards' Cup and will be 9lb better off with the winner if renewing rivalry next weekend. (tchd 28-1)

Ginger Ted(IRE) ◆ made his challenge nearest to the stands' side, which was shunned by most, and thus emerges as slightly better than the bare form. It was a career-best effort in defeat from him. (op 16-1)

Fathsta(IRE) ◆, patiently ridden, hit a flat spot at a crucial stage but was motoring towards the finish and clearly found this drop back a furlong too sharp. He could take on the front pair again at Goodwood, but a slightly more positive ride will probably be required for him to have any chance of reversing this form. He can be backed at 33-1 for the Stewards' Cup. (op 8-1)

Baby Strange also came more towards the stands' side and finished strongly. He needs all to fall right, but surely his turn is nearing once more.

Star Rover(IRE) ran his best race for some time when runner-up at Chester eight days earlier and he backed that up with another solid effort, faring best of the pacesetters. (op 25-1)

Favourite Girl(IRE) helped force the pace and posted another decent run in defeat, but looks to be battling with the handicapper at present.

Racy Official explanation: jockey said gelding anticipated the start and hit its head on the gate

Entitled travelled nicely into contention more towards the stands' side, but found just the same pace when push came to shove. (op 8-1)

Corporal Maddox Official explanation: jockey said gelding hung right throughout

4347 SKY SPORTS MEDIAN AUCTION MAIDEN STKS 6f

4:10 (4:13) (Class 4) 2-Y-O **£6,016** (£1,790; £894; £447) **Stalls** Centre

Form RPR

3 **1** **Satanic Beat (IRE)**[28] 3398 2-9-3 0 .... TomQueally 6 82
(Jedd O'Keeffe) *chsd ldrs: outpcd over 2f out: styd on wl to ld nr fin* **7/1**

5202 **2** *1* **Tip Top Gorgeous (IRE)**[6] 4122 2-8-12 0 .... SilvestreDeSousa 12 74
(David O'Meara) *bmpd s: w ldrs centre: chsd ldr over 2f out: led last 75yds: hdd nr fin* **11/2**

3 *nse* **Lady Loch** 2-8-12 0 .... PaulHanagan 7 74+
(Richard Fahey) *dwlt: in rr: hdwy over 1f out: styd on strly towards fin: promising* **9/2**[3]

00 **4** *1 ¾* **Dutch Heritage**[14] 3878 2-9-3 0 .... DavidNolan 4 73
(Richard Fahey) *chsd ldrs: edgd rt and kpt on wl fnl f* **25/1**

000 **5** *nk* **On The Hoof**[3] 4192 2-9-3 0 .... JamesSullivan 8 72
(Michael Easterby) *chsd ldrs: outpcd over 2f out: kpt on fnl f* **40/1**

33 **6** *2 ¼* **Sunny Side Up (IRE)**[8] 4073 2-8-12 0 .... BarryMcHugh 10 60
(Richard Fahey) *chsd ldrs: wkng whn crowded jst ins fnl f* **25/1**

6 **7** *1 ½* **Bang Tidy (IRE)**[30] 3313 2-9-0 0 .... PaulPickard(3) 3 60
(Brian Ellison) *racd alone far side: overall ldr: clr 3f out: hdd & wknd last 150yds* **8/1**

8 *½* **Out Do** 2-9-3 0 .... KierenFallon 2 59+
(Luca Cumani) *dwlt: swtchd rt after 1f: sn trcking ldrs: edgd lft over 1f out: sn wknd* **3/1**[1]

423 **9** *5* **Choisan (IRE)**[14] 3878 2-9-3 0 .... TedDurcan 11 43
(Tim Easterby) *wnt rt s: a outpcd and bhd* **7/2**[2]

0 **10** *½* **Doyouknowwhoiam**[14] 3878 2-9-3 0 .... RoystonFfrench 5 41
(Bryan Smart) *chsd ldrs: wknd 2f out* **25/1**

11 *5* **Farzan (IRE)** 2-9-3 0 .... TadhgO'Shea 13 25
(Tim Easterby) *sn wl outpcd and bhd* **25/1**

1m 14.38s (2.48) **Going Correction** +0.325s/f (Good) **11 Ran SP% 122.2**

Speed ratings (Par 96): **96,94,94,92,91 88,86,86,79,78 72**

Tote Swingers:1&2:£4.60, 2&3:£5.30, 1&3:£7.70 CSF £44.09 TOTE £9.80: £2.20, £1.70, £2.10; EX 40.50.

Owner Caron & Paul Chapman **Bred** Patrick Gleeson **Trained** Middleham Moor, N Yorks

FOCUS

An average juvenile maiden in which the benefit of previous experience came to the fore. All bar one of the runners raced mid-track. The winner is rated up 9lb on his debut form.

NOTEBOOK

Satanic Beat(IRE) stuck his head down out where it mattered and readily opened his account at the second attempt. Third over 5f on his debut last month, he relished this extra furlong and showed a nice attitude under pressure. There should be improvement in him in nurseries. (tchd 15-2)

Tip Top Gorgeous(IRE) has now finished second in three of his four career outings, but there appears to be nothing wrong with his attitude. A stiffer 6f can see him go one better. (op 5-1)

Lady Loch ◆, out of a 5f juvenile winner, stayed on to fare best of the newcomers and looks the one to take from the race. She ought to prove a deal sharper next time and should take some beating. (op 4-1)

Dutch Heritage showed his best form to date and is now qualified for nurseries, where he can improve again.

On The Hoof, having his fourth outing, was doing some decent late work and is one to keep an eye on with a view to going handicapping.

Out Do, speedily bred, was immediately taken to the middle of the pack from his low draw. He improved to look a possible player 2f out, but ultimately ran too green to do himself full justice. (op 9-2 tchd 11-4)

Choisan(IRE) was bitterly disappointing and her rider later reported that she was never travelling. Official explanation: jockey said colt never travelled (op 10-3 tchd 9-2)

4348 SKY BET MOBILE FOR IPAD (H'CAP) 2m 88y

4:45 (4:45) (Class 3) (0-90,90) 4-Y-O+ **£8,409** (£2,502; £1,250; £625) **Stalls** Low

Form RPR

5003 **1** **Itlaaq**[15] 3829 5-9-5 **88** .... (t) GrahamGibbons 14 98+
(Michael Easterby) *hld up in rr: smooth hdwy over 2f out: sn trcking ldr: shkn up to ld jst ins fnl f: edgd lft all out* **16/1**

0342 **2** *hd* **Eshtyaaq**[15] 3817 4-8-4 **73** .... CDHayes 9 83
(David Evans) *hld up towards rr: hdwy over 3f out: led over 2f out: hdd jst ins fnl f: crowded and rdr dropped whip: carried lft nr fin: jst hld* **25/1**

0-12 **3** *4 ½* **Hawk Mountain (UAE)**[43] 2888 6-9-7 **90** .... NeilCallan 4 94
(John Quinn) *trckd ldrs: effrt over 3f out: edgd rt over 1f out: styd on same pce* **9/2**[1]

0615 **4** *hd* **Simonside**[22] 3593 8-8-3 **75** ow3 .... PaulPickard(3) 5 79
(Brian Ellison) *hld up in mid-div: hdwy on ins over 3f out: kpt on same pce fnl f* **12/1**

6000 **5** *2* **Ejteyaaz**[15] 3828 4-8-2 **71** oh1 .... PaulHanagan 8 73
(Richard Fahey) *mid-div: effrt over 3f out: kpt on: nvr trbld ldrs* **20/1**

44/4 **6** *½* **Spiekeroog**[15] 3828 5-8-4 **73** .... TadhgO'Shea 7 74
(David O'Meara) *hld up in rr: hdwy on outer over 3f out: hung lft: one pce whn hmpd ins fnl f* **12/1**

3115 **7** *1½* **Bollin Judith**[14] 3851 5-8-11 **80** .... (t) TedDurcan 3 79
(Tim Easterby) *chsd ldrs: wnt 2nd over 4f out: one pce whn short of room over 1f out: wknd towards fin* **13/2**

241 **8** *½* **Red Courtier**[17] 3738 4-8-10 **79** .... (p) TomQueally 11 78
(Paul Cole) *trckd ldrs: hung lft and outpcd over 2f out: kpt on fnl f* **15/2**

0121 **9** *1¼* **Rosewin (IRE)**[17] 3730 5-8-12 **84** .... MichaelO'Connell(3) 10 81
(Ollie Pears) *gave problems gng down: s.v.s: in rr: hdwy over 3f out: one pce fnl 2f* **17/2**

-102 **10** *nk* **Old Hundred (IRE)**[29] 3344 4-9-5 **88** .... (v) PatCosgrave 6 85
(James Fanshawe) *trckd ldrs: effrt over 3f out: wknd jst ins fnl f* **6/1**[3]

2504 **11** *6* **Storm Hawk (IRE)**[17] 3738 4-8-2 **71** oh3 .... (p) JamesSullivan 12 61
(Pat Eddery) *chsd ldrs: lost pl over 2f out* **33/1**

4501 **12** *17* **Spirit Of A Nation (IRE)**[7] 4082 6-8-6 **75** .... HayleyTurner 13 44
(James Moffatt) *in rr: bhd fnl 3f* **16/1**

1000 **13** *1* **Becausewecan (USA)**[14] 3867 5-9-4 **87** .... SilvestreDeSousa 1 55
(Mark Johnston) *led: clr after 6f: hdd over 2f out: wknd rapidly* **11/2**[2]

3m 33.32s (-1.18) **Going Correction** -0.225s/f (Firm) **13** Ran SP% **122.2**
Speed ratings (Par 107): **93,92,90,90,89 89,88,88,87,87 84,76,75**
Tote Swingers:1&2:£43.80, 2&3:£25.70, 1&3:£15.10 CSF £375.67 CT £2108.54 TOTE £21.90: £5.60, £6.90, £2.20; EX 495.80.
Owner Mrs Jean Turpin **Bred** Shadwell Estate Company Limited **Trained** Sheriff Hutton, N Yorks

FOCUS
A fair staying handicap, run at something of an uneven gallop and the first pair came clear in a battling finish. Sound form, with clear bests from the first two.

NOTEBOOK
Itlaaq improved going easily in the home straight and looked set to win pretty much as he pleased. His rider attempted to kid him to the front inside the final furlong, but the runner-up stuck with him and there was little in it at the finish. At no stage did the winner get hit by the whip, though, and he was always just doing enough. He didn't help the second when drifting left as his stamina ebbed away nearing the business end, but it wasn't really enough to affect the overall result. This was his first run beyond 1m4f and, while it may not have been a searching test over the trip, he is obviously open to further improvement as a stayer. (op 12-1)
Eshtyaaq set sail for home around 3f out and made a bold bid, but was always just looking held by the winner. His rider lost his whip late on, which probably didn't help and he was also not done any favours when carried left, so he has to rate as somewhat unfortunate. He was well clear of the rest and richly deserves to go one better. (op 20-1)
Hawk Mountain(UAE), 4lb higher, is another that would have ideally preferred more of a test. He goes well here and rates the benchmark. (tchd 5-1)
Simonside could have really done with more of a test. This was more like his true form again and he remains in good heart.
Spiekeroog emerged with every chance in the home straight, but his effort petered out. This was just his second outing for the yard, and his second run back from a layoff, so perhaps he will come on again for it. (op 10-1)
Red Courtier was 4lb higher than when winning on his first attempt over the trip at Kempton 17 days previously. He failed to see it out so well in this higher grade, though. (op 9-1 tchd 10-1)
Old Hundred(IRE), a winner on his previous outing at 2m last year, came under pressure shortly after straightening for home and disappointed. (tchd 11-2)

4349 SKY BET MOBILE FOR ANDROID STKS (H'CAP) 7f
5:20 (5:21) (Class 4) (0-80,80) 3-Y-O+ **£6,533** (£1,944; £971; £485) **Stalls** Low

Form RPR

3323 **1** **Karaka Jack**[45] 2806 4-9-8 **79** .... MichaelO'Connell(3) 1 90
(David Nicholls) *chsd ldrs: hmpd and dropped bk over 5f out: hdwy on ins 3f out: chal over 1f out: styd on to ld clsng stages* **5/1**[2]

1211 **2** *½* **Powerful Presence (IRE)**[21] 3629 5-9-8 **76** .... SilvestreDeSousa 11 86
(David O'Meara) *chsd ldrs: led over 2f out: hdd wl ins fnl f: no ex* **3/1**[1]

000[illegible] **3** *1¼* **Hereford Boy**[illegible] 7-9-11 [illegible] .... (b) TedDurcan 7 74
(Dean Ivory) *hmpd and s.s: swtchd lft and gd hdwy on inner over 2f out: kpt on fnl f* **25/1**

1012 **4** *½* **Pelmanism**[24] 3506 4-9-6 **74** .... CDHayes 4 79
(Brian Ellison) *chsd ldrs: kpt on same pce fnl f* **13/2**[3]

3003 **5** *½* **Illustrious Prince (IRE)**[7] 4107 4-9-2 **75** .... (v) NeilFarley(5) 15 78
(Declan Carroll) *in tch: effrt over 2f out: kpt on fnl f: nr rchd ldrs* **16/1**

01-0 **6** *2½* **Bond City (IRE)**[70] 2112 9-9-11 **79** .... DavidNolan 16 76
(Geoffrey Oldroyd) *mid-div: hdwy on outer over 2f out: kpt on: nvr nr ldrs* **40/1**

0001 **7** *1¼* **Legal Legacy**[29] 3348 5-9-5 **73** .... TomQueally 17 66
(Michael Dods) *hld up in rr: hdwy on outer over 2f out: kpt on: nvr nr ldrs* **16/1**

0316 **8** *1¾* **Shadowtime**[11] 3934 6-9-8 **76** .... RobbieFitzpatrick 20 64
(Colin Teague) *in rr: hdwy on outer over 2f out: kpt on: nvr nr ldrs* **16/1**

0025 **9** *¾* **Kerrys Requiem (IRE)**[16] 3757 5-9-9 **77** .... (b[1]) HayleyTurner 8 63
(Tim Pitt) *s.i.s: kpt on fnl 2f: nvr nr ldrs* **16/1**

5314 **10** *nse* **Elusive Sue (USA)**[21] 3634 4-9-5 **73** .... PaulHanagan 5 59
(Richard Fahey) *in rr: hdwy whn nt clr run over 1f out: kpt on ins fnl f* **10/1**

0606 **11** *nk* **Rasselas (IRE)**[29] 3358 4-9-5 **73** .... PaulQuinn 14 58
(David Nicholls) *mid-div: effrt over 2f out: sn wknd* **25/1**

40-0 **12** *shd* **Ishiadancer**[26] 3459 6-9-9 **77** .... PatCosgrave 10 62
(Eric Alston) *led: hdd 3f out: wknd over 1f out* **33/1**

3350 **13** *4½* **Iceblast**[15] 3830 3-9-5 **80** .... JamesSullivan 6 53
(Michael Easterby) *in rr: bhd fnl 2f* **14/1**

0505 **14** *nk* **Ghost (IRE)**[56] 2494 4-8-12 **73** .... ShirleyTeasdale(7) 2 45
(David Nicholls) *chsd ldrs: wknd 2f out* **25/1**

5204 **15** *hd* **Last Sovereign**[9] 4020 7-9-8 **76** .... NeilCallan 19 48
(Ollie Pears) *in tch on outer: effrt over 2f out: sn wknd* **16/1**

0040 **16** *¾* **Silver Wind**[15] 3796 6-9-7 **75** .... (v) RoystonFfrench 13 45
(Alan McCabe) *prom: effrt over 2f out: wkng whn hmpd over 1f out* **40/1**

5451 **17** *1* **Powerful Pierre**[8] 4078 4-9-1 **69** .... (b) BarryMcHugh 12 36
(Ian McInnes) *in tch on outer: lost pl over 2f out* **20/1**

1620 **18** *3* **George Benjamin**[24] 3506 4-9-10 **78** .... AdrianNicholls 9 37
(David Nicholls) *w ldrs: led 3f out: sn hdd: wknd rapidly and heavily eased jst ins fnl f* **20/1**

4600 **19** *7* **Tukitinyasok (IRE)**[15] 3831 4-9-9 **77** .... PaddyAspell 3 17
(Clive Mulhall) *dwlt: chsd ldrs: lost pl over 4f out: sn bhd* **50/1**

-500 **20** *50* **Christmas Carnival**[21] 3620 4-9-10 **78** .... (b) GrahamGibbons 18 —
(Michael Easterby) *in rr: bhd 3f out: t.o over 1f out: eased: virtually p.u* **25/1**

1m 26.6s (1.30) **Going Correction** +0.325s/f (Good)
WFA 3 from 4yo+ 7lb **20** Ran SP% **134.9**
Speed ratings (Par 105): **105,104,102,102,101 98,97,95,94,94 94,93,88,88,88 87,86,82,74,17**
Tote Swingers:1&2:£4.60, 2&3:£29.10, 1&3:£38.70 CSF £19.22 CT £384.25 TOTE £6.90: £2.20, £1.30, £7.00, £2.20; EX 26.60.
Owner M Mackay & S Bruce **Bred** Tarworth Bloodstock Investments Ltd **Trained** Sessay, N Yorks

FOCUS
A wide-open handicap, run at a solid pace and the first five came clear. Sound form, the winner close to his 3yo best.
Christmas Carnival Official explanation: vet said gelding finished distressed
T/Plt: £155.10 to a £1 stake. Pool £158,192.06. 744.18 winning tickets. T/Qpdt: £41.10 to a £1 stake Pool £6,824.35 122.80 w. tckts JR

4350 - 4351a - (Foreign Racing) - See RI

4310 ASCOT (R-H)
Sunday, July 24

OFFICIAL GOING: Good (stands' side 8.3, centre 8.7, far side 8.3, round 7.5)
Wind: virtualy nil Weather: bright and sunny

4352 ANDERS FOUNDATION E B F CROCKER BULTEEL MAIDEN STKS (C&G) 6f
2:15 (2:15) (Class 2) 2-Y-O **£12,938** (£3,850; £1,924; £962) **Stalls** Centre

Form RPR

1 **Zumbi (IRE)** 2-9-0 0 .... RyanMoore 3 84+
(Sir Michael Stoute) *in tch: rdn and effrt to chal over 1f out: carried rt fr 1f out: led wl ins fnl f: kpt on wl* **5/1**[3]

2 *nk* **Glen Moss (IRE)** 2-9-0 0 .... MichaelHills 2 83+
(B W Hills) *led: rdn wl over 1f out: sn hrd pressed: edgd rt 1f out: battled on wl tl hdd and no ex wl ins fnl f* **15/2**

3 *3½* **Mabaany** 2-9-0 0 .... RichardHills 4 71
(William Haggas) *in tch in last pair: rdn and hdwy 2f out: ev ch and carried rt 1f out: no ex and btn ins fnl f: wknd fnl 75yds* **7/2**[2]

4 *2¼* **Humungosaur** 2-9-0 0 .... NeilCallan 6 64
(Paul Cole) *wnt rt s: sn rcvrd and chsd ldr tl wl over 2f out: outpcd and btn wl over 1f out: no threat to ldrs but kpt on again ins fnl f* **14/1**

5 *1* **Confucius Elite** 2-9-0 0 .... PatCosgrave 1 61
(Jim Boyle) *wnt bdly rt s: rn green and sn t.k.h in tch: rdn and rn green over 2f out: wknd wl over 1f out* **40/1**

6 *7* **Blue Tiger** 2-9-0 0 .... JamieSpencer 5 49
(Saeed Bin Suroor) *bmpd s: t.k.h: sn chsng ldrs: swtchd away fr rivals and hdwy over 3f out: chsd ldr and rejnd rivals wl over 2f out: rdn and fnd nil 2f out: sn wknd: eased ins fnl f* **11/10**[1]

7 *2¼* **Young Prince (IRE)** 2-9-0 0 .... SeanLevey 7 31
(Robert Mills) *wnt lft s: hld up in tch in last pair: rdn and wknd jst over 2f out: wl bhd fnl f* **22/1**

1m 15.67s (1.27) **Going Correction** +0.25s/f (Good) **7** Ran SP% **111.7**
Speed ratings (Par 100): **101,100,95,92,91 82,79**
toteswingers:1&2:£3.20, 1&3:£2.50, 2&3:£3.70 CSF £39.16 TOTE £5.60: £2.80, £3.60; EX 20.30 Trifecta £66.70 Pool: £679.02 - 7.53 winning units..
Owner Lady Rothschild **Bred** Limetree Stud **Trained** Newmarket, Suffolk

FOCUS
An interesting juvenile maiden (time 0.82secs slower than the following 3-y-o handicap), with several well-bred runners from top yards being represented. No previous form to go on, the race before for unraced 2yos, and the form is set in the middle of the race averages.

NOTEBOOK
Zumbi(IRE) responded well to pressure to edge it close home. A 140,000gns foal, the son of Dubawi appeared to know his job well enough, but can be expected to come on a fair bit regardless, and he ought to benefit from an extra furlong (half-brother to a 1m winner). There was a lot to like about his performance, and perhaps a conditions race will be next. (tchd 11-2 and 13-2 in a place)
Glen Moss(IRE), who has a Champagne Stakes entry, is quite a late foal, but he certainly knew what was required and, having made most of the running, did well to try to fend off the winner (carrying him slightly right in the process). Normal progress should see him winning something similar. (op 7-1 tchd 6-1)
Mabaany ◆, another Champagne entrant, is a half-brother to a useful 1m winner and he shaped most promisingly, making ground from the rear before finding the front pair too pacey late on. With marked improvement anticipated, winning a maiden should prove straightforward. (op 10-3)
Humungosaur, who holds some notable entries (Champagne/Royal Lodge), is bred to stay further than this and he showed more than enough to suggest he'll be winning once granted a stiffer test. (op 10-1)
Confucius Elite, an already-gelded son of Bertolini, showed distinct signs of inexperience, veering right out of the stalls and not looking sure of what was required. Taking this into account, he made a very satisfactory debut, and ought to be found an opening. (op 33-1)
Blue Tiger, who is bred to make a 2-y-o, came in for strong market support and he travelled strongly a bit away from rivals under Spencer, despite having received a bump on exiting the gate. There was no response when asked to pick up, however, and it's hard to believe this is as good as he is. (op 11-8, tchd 6-4 in places)
Young Prince(IRE), already a gelding, is out of a 1m4f winner, and it was no surprise to see him struggle over this trip. (op 25-1 tchd 20-1)

4353 GL EVENTS OWEN BROWN H'CAP 6f
2:50 (2:50) (Class 4) (0-85,85) 3-Y-O **£5,175** (£1,540; £769; £384) **Stalls** Centre

Form RPR

-325 **1** **Blanche Dubawi (IRE)**[27] 3459 3-9-4 **82** .... RyanMoore 8 93
(Noel Quinlan) *stdd s: t.k.h: hld up in tch in rr: nt clr run 2f out: rdn and hdwy over 1f out: rdn to chal 1f out: edgd rt u.p ins fnl f: kpt on wl to ld wl ins fnl f* **2/1**[1]

1515 **2** *hd* **King Ferdinand**[18] 3737 3-9-7 **85** .... JamieSpencer 1 95
(Andrew Balding) *stdd and dropped in bhd after s: hld up in tch in rr: swtchd rt and hdwy over 2f out: rdn to ld over 1f out: edgd lft u.p 1f out: kpt on wl tl hdd and no ex wl ins fnl f* **9/2**[3]

-214 **3** *2½* **Foxtrot Hotel (IRE)**[48] 2763 3-9-4 **82** .... JimCrowley 4 84
(Peter Winkworth) *hld up in tch in midfield: hdwy to press ldrs gng wl jst over 2f out: rdn and ev ch wl over 1f out: one pce and struggling whn pushed rt ins fnl f: wknd towards fin* **7/2**[2]

6340 **4** *¾* **Remotelinx (IRE)**[57] 2508 3-9-7 **85** .... SebSanders 5 85
(J W Hills) *stdd after s: hld up in rr: rdn and hdwy wl over 1f out: chsd ldng trio 1f out: kpt on but no real imp fnl f* **14/1**

0-50 **5** *8* **Nasharra (IRE)**[16] 3820 3-8-13 **82** .... JulieBurke(5) 3 56
(Kevin Ryan) *led tl hdd wl over 1f out: sn rdn and edgd rt: btn jst over 1f out: wknd fnl f* **14/1**

3636 **6** *1 1/4* **Apollo D'Negro (IRE)**[23] 3598 3-8-9 **73**....................(p) PhilipRobinson 2 43
(Clive Cox) *chsd ldrs: pushed along to press ldr over 2f out: drvn and unable qck 2f out: wknd over 1f out* **6/1**

2010 **7** *1 1/2* **Da Ponte**[23] 3598 3-8-13 **77**....................(v[1]) ShaneKelly 9 43
(Walter Swinburn) *chsd ldr tl over 2f out: sn struggling u.p: wknd wl over 1f out* **16/1**

2110 **8** *1 3/4* **Clara Zetkin**[58] 2468 3-8-13 **77**.................... LiamKeniry 10 37
(J S Moore) *hld up in midfield: rdn and struggling over 2f out: bhd fnl 2f* **22/1**

1m 14.85s (0.45) **Going Correction** +0.25s/f (Good) **8** Ran SP% **111.6**
Speed ratings (Par 102): **107,106,103,102,91 90,88,85**
toteswingers:1&2:£2.80, 1&3:£2.40, 2&3:£3.20 CSF £10.54 CT £27.94 TOTE £2.40: £1.10, £1.80, £1.80; EX 12.20 Trifecta £23.00 Pool: £1,201.18 - 38.53 winning units..
Owner Burns Farm Racing **Bred** Burns Farm Stud **Trained** Newmarket, Suffolk

FOCUS
A decent 3-y-o sprint handicap run in a time 0.82secs quicker than the opening juvenile maiden. The form has been rated positively around the fourth.

4354 EAGLE ROCK STKS (H'CAP) 1m 4f
3:25 (3:25) (Class 2) (0-105,102) 3-Y-O+

£11,205 (£3,355; £1,677; £838; £419; £210) **Stalls** Low

Form RPR

22/0 **1** **Nehaam**[59] 2438 5-9-11 **99**.................... RichardHills 7 105+
(John Gosden) *hld up in last trio: hdwy on outer 2f out: hmpd and pushed lft over 1f out: led 1f out: edgd rt but sn in command: pushed out fnl 100yds* **20/1**

-111 **2** *1 1/2* **Kiama Bay (IRE)**[29] 3381 5-9-7 **95**.................... FrannyNorton 6 99
(John Quinn) *t.k.h: hld up in tch in midfield: rdn and effrt wl over 2f out: nt clr run over 2f out: hdwy u.p jst over 1f out: chsd wnr fnl 100yds: kpt on* **14/1**

2-00 **3** *1/2* **Chock A Block (IRE)**[29] 3396 5-9-7 **95**.................... HayleyTurner 9 98
(Saeed Bin Suroor) *chsd ldrs: rdn and effrt over 2f out: pushed lft and unable qck 2f out: keeping on same pce and n.m.r jst over 1f out: rallied and styd on wl ins fnl f* **11/1**

3-41 **4** *1/2* **Star In Flight**[17] 3781 4-8-10 **84**.................... ShaneKelly 3 86
(Brian Meehan) *t.k.h: led: rdn over 2f out: hung bdly lft over 1f out: hdd 1f out: styd on same pce after* **12/1**

1521 **5** *1/2* **Warlu Way**[24] 3544 4-9-3 **91**.................... RyanMoore 2 92+
(John Dunlop) *t.k.h: hld up in tch in midfield: rdn and effrt over 2f out: drvn and kpt on same pce fr over 1f out* **7/2[2]**

0100 **6** *nk* **English Summer**[22] 3625 4-9-4 **92**.................... NeilCallan 8 93
(Mark Johnston) *chsd ldr: rdn and ev ch whn carried bdly lft over 1f out: stl ev ch but unable qck whn squeezed for room and hmpd jst ins fnl f: kpt on same pce after* **16/1**

-300 **7** *1 3/4* **Prompter**[36] 3156 4-9-11 **99**.................... JamieSpencer 4 97
(Michael Bell) *stdd s: t.k.h: hld up in last trio: rdn and effrt on inner 2f out: drvn and hung lft over 1f out: no imp 1f out: wknd ins fnl f* **5/1[3]**

1/1 **8** *1* **Burj Nahar**[29] 3406 4-10-0 **102**.................... RichardMullen 1 99
(Saeed Bin Suroor) *t.k.h: chsd ldrs: looking to switch lft and trying to force way out 2f out: drvn and keeping on same pce whn nt clr run and swtchd rt 1f out: no imp after* **15/8[1]**

-325 **9** *1/2* **Aurorian (IRE)**[50] 2716 5-8-13 **87**.................... RichardHughes 5 83
(Richard Hannon) *stdd s: hld up in last trio: rdn and effrt over 2f out: nt clr run and swtchd rt over 1f out: no prog 1f out and no threat to ldrs fnl f* **12/1**

2m 35.86s (3.36) **Going Correction** +0.425s/f (Yiel) **9** Ran SP% **114.7**
Speed ratings (Par 109): **105,104,103,103,103 102,101,100,100**
toteswingers:1&2:£12.50, 1&3:£31.80, 2&3:£14.70 CSF £265.31 CT £3212.33 TOTE £23.50: £5.70, £2.80, £3.30; EX 148.60 Trifecta £976.40 Part won. Pool: £1,319.56 - 0.94 winning units..

Owner Hamdan Al Maktoum **Bred** Pollards Stables **Trained** Newmarket, Suffolk
■ Stewards' Enquiry : Shane Kelly caution: used whip above shoulder height.

FOCUS
The pace was an unsatisfactory one for this good-quality handicap and it was a bit of a messy race. The winner can do better than the bare form.

NOTEBOOK
Nehaam, held up at the rear on this drop down from 2m, picked up really well to win going away. From a yard that has enjoyed a golden King George meeting, this formerly progressive 3-y-o, who finished ahead of only one on his reappearance in the Henry II, was understandably weak in the market, but the handicapper had given him a chance, and he produced a telling burst widest of all from 1f out to win going away. On this evidence he'll be well worth his place returned to pattern-company, but would make some appeal in the Ebor first. (tchd 22-1)
Kiama Bay(IRE), hit with a 15lb rise for his 11l Chester romp, was keen in the second half of the field and would have preferred a better all-round gallop. He still managed to box on for second, but can expect another rise in the weights. (op 12-1)
Chock A Block(IRE) did well to rally and claim third, considering he seemed likely to be swamped at one stage. He's been given a chance by the handicapper and is another in the Ebor. (op 14-1)
Star In Flight, making his handicap debut, dictated the steady gallop and caused trouble in the straight by hanging left. He stuck on well, without suggesting he was thrown in off the mark, and should have more offer, being a brother to the same stable's useful handicapper Star Of Light.
Official explanation: jockey said ghelding hung left (op 10-1)
Warlu Way wouldn't have been suited by the way the race unfolded, and deserves a chance to show himself better than this. (tchd 4-1)
English Summer seemed ideally positioned to strike turning in, but having been carried left by the fourth, he became short of room and was interfered with when beaten. (tchd 20-1)
Prompter is coming down the weights, but not quickly enough. He wouldn't have been suited by the way things panned out. Jamie Spencer reported afterwards that his mount hung left. Official explanation: jockey said gelding hung left (op 7-1)
Burj Nahar, who looked a pattern performer in the making when winning off 7lb lower on last month's return from a lengthy absence, can be given another chance. The drying ground was probably against him, as was the steady pace which led to him racing keenly, and he was wisely not given a hard time once failing to find a clear run in the straight. (tchd 2-1 in a place)

4355 KELTBRAY H'CAP 1m 2f
4:00 (4:01) (Class 3) (0-90,87) 3-Y-O

£7,158 (£2,143; £1,071; £535; £267; £134) **Stalls** Low

Form RPR

1142 **1** **Ivan Vasilevich (IRE)**[16] 3809 3-9-6 **86**.................... MartinDwyer 4 93
(Jane Chapple-Hyam) *mde all: rdn and fnd ex 2f out: edgd lft wl over 1f out: hrd drvn and hld on v gamely fnl f: all out* **14/1**

3113 **2** *hd* **Grumeti**[22] 3650 3-9-2 **82**.................... JamieSpencer 7 89
(Michael Bell) *hld up in tch: rdn and effrt jst over 2f out: drvn and ev ch ins fnl f: r.o wl* **11/4[2]**

-566 **3** *1 1/4* **Muntasib (USA)**[15] 3840 3-9-2 **82**.................... RichardHills 5 86
(Marcus Tregoning) *t.k.h: hld up in last pair: swtchd lft and effrt over 2f out: hdwy u.p to chse ldrs 1f out: edgd rt and kpt on same pce fnl 100yds* **16/1**

21 **4** *1* **Gatewood**[28] 3430 3-9-7 **87**.................... RyanMoore 6 89
(John Gosden) *chsd wnr: rdn and unable qck 2f out: drvn and styd on same pce fr over 1f out* **6/4[1]**

-202 **5** *4 1/2* **Swindy**[10] 4009 3-9-1 **81**.................... NeilCallan 3 74
(Paul Cole) *stdd s: t.k.h: hld up in tch: rdn and effrt over 2f out: drvn and unable qck 2f out: wknd over 1f out* **15/2[3]**

1 **6** *4* **Val O'Hara (IRE)**[39] 3043 3-9-3 **83**.................... JimCrowley 1 68
(Peter Winkworth) *stdd s: hld up in rr: swtchd lft and rdn over 2f out: no prog: wl btn over 1f out* **8/1**

35-1 **7** *8* **Groomed (IRE)**[22] 3614 3-9-0 **80**.................... LiamJones 2 49
(William Haggas) *chsd ldrs: pushed along 3f out: drvn and unable qck over 2f out: wknd wl over 1f out* **8/1**

2m 9.26s (2.26) **Going Correction** +0.425s/f (Yiel) **7** Ran SP% **113.2**
Speed ratings (Par 104): **107,106,105,105,101 98,91**
toteswingers:1&2:£5.00, 1&3:£12.30, 2&3:£7.30 CSF £51.40 TOTE £12.80: £3.70, £2.00; EX 72.50.
Owner Chris Fahy **Bred** Liam Butler **Trained** Dalham, Suffolk

FOCUS
An intriguing handicap full of interesting prospects. It would be surprising if this doesn't prove to be a strong contest and the form is rated positively.

NOTEBOOK
Ivan Vasilevich(IRE) is incredibly consistent for a horse that races often, but was running off a 9lb higher mark than his last victory. Allowed to lead, his rider dictated all the right fractions and the horse battled on really strongly to hold off all challengers. (op 11-1)
Grumeti really came to life when running in handicaps, winning two of his four previous starts in them. 15lb higher than for his first success, he travelled strongly while chasing the pace and responded well to pressure, but couldn"t get past the resilient winner. Connections feel he'll be better with more ease in the ground, so he's one to watch out for in the autumn. (op 9-2, tchd 5-1 in a place)
Muntasib(USA), dropped 2lb since his last outing, which came at this course over 1m, hadn't been tried over this trip in the past but appeared to get home well enough. He is possibly not the most straightforward, however, as he tended to wander under pressure. (op 14-1)
Gatewood, who got warm beforehand, landed the short odds at Salisbury on his previous start, beating a subsequent winner, after a promising debut. Having his first run in handicap company, and weak in the market late on, he raced prominently, possibly a touch keen, before finding just the one pace under pressure. He should be allowed another chance. (op 11-8 tchd 5-4 and 2-1 in a place and 15-8 in places)
Swindy ran much better last time at Epsom than he had in a strong Newmarket handicap the time before, but never looked a danger this time. (tchd 7-1 and 8-1)
Val O'Hara(IRE) made the prefect start to her career on debut at Kempton last month. Starting at 25-1, she beat three horses (second, fourth and tenth) that won on their next outing, suggesting the form was strong. Making her handicap debut, she raced in rear and wasn't able to get involved. (tchd 10-1)
Groomed(IRE), who won on his handicap debut at Beverley on his seasonal return, needed pushing along on the home bend and was most disappointing. (tchd 7-1)

4356 JOHN MANDEVILLE MAIDEN FILLIES' STKS 1m (S)
4:35 (4:36) (Class 4) 3-Y-O **£5,175** (£1,540; £769; £384) **Stalls** Centre

Form RPR

5 **1** **Raasekha**[36] 3177 3-9-0 0.................... RichardHills 4 87
(B W Hills) *mde all: rdn wl over 1f out: kpt on wl fnl f* **8/1**

0520 **2** *1 1/4* **Nabah**[51] 2678 3-9-0 89.................... PhilipRobinson 5 84
(Clive Brittain) *stdd s: hld up in tch in last trio: hdwy over 2f out: chsd ldrs and hung rt over 1f out: chsd wnr ins fnl f: no imp fnl 100yds* **13/2[3]**

5-3 **3** *4* **Regal Heiress**[69] 2157 3-9-0 0.................... RyanMoore 6 74
(Sir Michael Stoute) *chsd ldrs: hdwy to chse wnr over 2f out: rdn wl over 1f out: drvn and unable qck over 1f out: wknd ins fnl f* **6/4[1]**

4 *2 1/2* **Interaction** 3-9-0 0.................... SebSanders 1 69
(John Gosden) *in tch: effrt to chse ldrs over 2f out: rdn and rn green 2f out: wknd ent fnl f* **8/1**

03 **5** *3/4* **Little Cottonsocks**[20] 3689 3-9-0 0....................(t) LukeMorris 3 67
(Clive Cox) *t.k.h: hld up in tch in rr: rdn and struggling over 2f out: wknd and wl btn over 1f out: plugged on fnl f* **25/1**

-242 **6** *1/2* **Ssafa**[16] 3815 3-8-11 72.................... PatrickHills(3) 2 66
(J W Hills) *chsd ldrs: rdn and unable qck ent fnl 2f: wknd u.p wl over 1f out* **12/1**

5 **7** *7* **Indian Mist (IRE)**[28] 3437 3-9-0 0.................... NeilCallan 7 50
(Roger Varian) *wnt lft s: chsd wnr tl over 2f out: sn rdn and wandered u.p: wknd 2f out* **3/1[2]**

1m 42.56s (1.96) **Going Correction** +0.20s/f (Good) **7** Ran SP% **112.1**
Speed ratings (Par 99): **98,96,92,90,89 89,82**
toteswingers:1&2:£5.70, 1&3:£3.80, 2&3:£2.70 CSF £55.39 TOTE £9.20: £3.30, £2.40; EX 56.00.
Owner Hamdan Al Maktoum **Bred** Shadwell Estate Company Limited **Trained** Lambourn, Berks

FOCUS
This hasn't proved to be a particularly strong maiden in the past, so it would be a surprise if there were any superstars hidden away in this field. The winner had a fairly easy lead but the form is taken at face value.
Nabah Official explanation: jockey said filly hung right

4357 CHRIS O'KEEFFE SPRINT STKS (H'CAP) 5f
5:10 (5:10) (Class 2) 3-Y-O+

£24,900 (£7,456; £3,728; £1,864; £932; £468) **Stalls** Centre

Form RPR

0321 **1** **Medicean Man**[15] 3846 5-9-5 **101**....................(p) HarryBentley(5) 13 112
(Jeremy Gask) *hld up in midfield: hdwy over 1f out: pushed along to chal and edgd rt ins fnl f: r.o wl to ld wl ins fnl f* **4/1[1]**

3011 **2** *1/2* **Duchess Dora (IRE)**[9] 4075 4-9-7 **98**.................... RyanMoore 11 107
(John Quinn) *chsd ldr: rdn wl over 1f out: drvn and kpt on 1f out: led ins fnl f tl hdd and no ex wl ins fnl f* **15/2**

-001 **3** *3/4* **Swiss Franc**[8] 4104 6-9-3 **94**.................... JamieSpencer 8 100+
(David Elsworth) *stdd s: hld up in rr: rdn and effrt over 1f out: edging rt but r.o wl ins fnl f: nt rch ldrs* **10/1**

0443 **4** *1* **Judge 'n Jury**[8] 4104 7-8-10 **87**.................... LukeMorris 12 90
(Ronald Harris) *led: rdn wl over 1f out: hdd ins fnl f: no ex fnl 75yds* **17/2**

05-1 **5** *1* **Murura (IRE)**[17] 3778 4-8-1 **83**....................(b) JulieBurke(5) 5 82+
(Kevin Ryan) *stdd s: bhd: pushed along and effrt whn nt clr run briefly wl over 1f out: styd on ins fnl f: nt rch ldrs* **9/2[2]**

2351 **6** *3/4* **Ebraam (USA)**[10] 3995 8-7-13 **76**.................... NickyMackay 6 72
(Ronald Harris) *t.k.h: hld up in midfield: effrt and pushed rt jst over 2f out: kpt on same pce u.p fnl f* **28/1**

1320 **7** ½ **Liberty Lady (IRE)**[15] 3874 4-9-4 **98**..........(t) MartinHarley(3) 9 — 93
(Des Donovan) *in tch: rdn and unable qck wl over 1f out: drvn and styd on one pce fr over 1f out* **28/1**

4102 **8** *nk* **Sohraab**[15] 3846 7-8-9 **91**.......... KieranO'Neill(5) 10 — 85
(Hughie Morrison) *midfield early: pushed along and lost pl after 2f: bhd and drvn 1/2-way: styd on ins fnl f: nvr trbld ldrs* **7/1**[3]

3015 **9** 1 **Poppy Seed**[9] 4063 4-9-1 **92**.......... RichardHughes 3 — 82
(Richard Hannon) *dwlt: rcvrd to chse ldrs over 3f out: rdn 2f out: wknd u.p ent fnl f* **12/1**

3110 **10** 3 ¼ **Swiss Cross**[36] 3155 4-9-6 **97**..........(t) NeilCallan 1 — 75
(Gerard Butler) *chsd ldrs tl wknd u.p over 1f out* **14/1**

0-00 **11** *hd* **Perfect Blossom**[17] 3778 4-8-9 **89**.......... AmyRyan(3) 7 — 67
(Kevin Ryan) *in tch: nt clr run and swtchd sharply rt jst over 2f out: sn rdn: wknd over 1f out* **16/1**

3313 **12** 1 ½ **Lost In Paris (IRE)**[29] 3379 5-8-10 **87**..........(p) HayleyTurner 4 — 59
(Tim Easterby) *hld up towards rr: shkn up over 2f out: no imp: wknd ent fnl f* **10/1**

61.25 secs (0.05) **Going Correction** +0.25s/f (Good) **12** Ran SP% **118.3**
Speed ratings (Par 109): **109,108,107,105,103 102,101,101,99,94 94,91**
toteswingers:1&2:£3.90, 1&3:£8.80, 2&3:£8.50. Totesuper 7: Win: Not won, Place: Not won. CSF £33.78 CT £281.99 TOTE £4.80: £2.00, £2.20, £3.60; EX 25.80 Trifecta £232.20 Pool: £2,043.44 - 6.51 winning units..
Owner Stuart Dobb & Miss Kate Dobb **Bred** Barry Taylor **Trained** Sutton Veny, Wilts
■ Stewards' Enquiry : Amy Ryan two-day ban: careless riding (Aug 7-8)

FOCUS
The final race was the most valuable event on the card. It was a competitive sprint but not too many got involved with a winning opportunity. The first four all raced towards the stands' side.

NOTEBOOK
Medicean Man, up 5lb for beating Sohraab over C&D last time, was on a career-high mark but that didn't stop him continuing his upward curve. Always travelling nicely, he kept on well for pressure to hold the runner-up and one would imagine that he'll head for the Stewards' Cup next Saturday, where he's already due to carry a penalty. (op 5-1 tchd 7-2)
Duchess Dora(IRE) was chasing a hat-trick off a 13lb higher mark than when she won two starts previously and made a good fist of it, only going down narrowly in a driving finish. (op 7-1)
Swiss Franc has made his own problems sometimes while being held up in behind runners but finally got back in the winner's enclosure (his last win came in May 2007) last time when finding a clear passage. Settled in rear, he didn't find any traffic this time but wasn't getting to the first two quickly enough to cause them a problem. (op 8-1)
Judge 'n Jury, who won this race in 2009 off a mark of 98, got to the lead quite easily and had his chance until weakening inside the final furlong. (op 10-1 tchd 11-1)
Murura(IRE) ◆ won for Irish connections last time when blinkers were tried for the first time, and had moved to the Kevin Ryan stable since. 8lb higher, he finished really well but would have been better served racing closer to the lead. (op 11-2)
Ebraam(USA) does most of his racing and winning on the AW but this was another perfectly good turf effort after his win at Bath last time. (tchd 25-1)
Sohraab wasn't beaten far into tenth in this last year off a pound lower mark but made no impression here after getting caught one paced when the tempo increased. (op 8-1)
Lost In Paris(IRE) looked to have a good chance of reversing form with Duchess Dora on Chester form for a couple of reasons, but for some reason he was dropped in almost from the start, which was strange for a horse that runs his best races when racing prominently. (op 17-2)
T/Plt: £332.70 to a £1 stake. Pool:£107,898.79 236.69 winning ticket T/Qpdt: £137.80 to a £1 stake. Pool:£9,182.72 49.30 winning tickets SP

3617 CARLISLE (R-H)
Sunday, July 24

OFFICIAL GOING: Good (8.1)
Wind: Light, half against Weather: Sunny, warm

4358 REBECCA FERGUSON LIVE AFTER RACING TODAY MAIDEN AUCTION STKS — 5f
1:50 (1:56) (Class 5) 2-Y-O — **£2,522** (£750; £375; £187) **Stalls** Low

Form — RPR

3 **1** **Byrama**[12] 3932 2-8-1 0.......... DeclanCannon(3) 8 — 79+
(Nigel Tinkler) *t.k.h: cl up: hdwy to ld over 1f out: edgd rt: [illegible] clr fnl f: readily* **2/1**[1]

2 4 **Key Ambition** 2-8-9 0.......... TomEaves 4 — 70
(Bryan Smart) *dwlt: sn trcking ldrs: effrt 2f out: chsd (clr) wnr ins fnl f: r.o* **12/1**

22 **3** *hd* **Half A Billion (IRE)**[9] 4040 2-8-12 0.......... FrederikTylicki 3 — 72
(Michael Dods) *led tl hdd over 1f out: kpt on same pce fnl f* **11/4**[2]

4 **4** 3 ½ **Summer Lane (IRE)**[12] 3932 2-8-4 0.......... PaulHanagan 5 — 51
(Richard Fahey) *chsd ldrs: rdn along and outpcd 2f out: kpt on same pce fnl f* **3/1**[3]

064 **5** 1 ½ **Never In (IRE)**[9] 4040 2-8-4 0.......... PatrickMathers 6 — 46
(Alan Berry) *cl up on outside: rdn over 2f out: no imp over 1f out* **40/1**

0 **6** ¾ **Simpson Millar**[39] 3050 2-8-9 0.......... GrahamGibbons 2 — 48
(Noel Wilson) *chsd ldng bunch: rdn and rn green over 2f out: no imp over 1f out* **28/1**

0 **7** 7 **Our Monica (IRE)**[19] 3718 2-8-7 0.......... LeeNewman 7 — 21
(Ann Duffield) *walked to post: dwlt: chsd ldng gp: shkn up and outpcd 2f out: btn fnl f* **66/1**

56 **8** 30 **Lord Buffhead**[9] 4040 2-8-9 0.......... J-PGuillambert 1 — —
(Richard Guest) *missed break: sn wl bhd: t.o fnl 2f* **7/1**

61.06 secs (0.26) **Going Correction** +0.05s/f (Good) **8** Ran SP% **112.6**
Speed ratings (Par 94): **99,92,92,86,84 83,71,23**
toteswingers:1&2:£10.10, 1&3:£1.10, 2&3:£5.20 CSF £26.20 TOTE £3.10: £1.10, £4.20, £1.30; EX 33.20.
Owner Yan Wah Wu **Bred** Ermyn Lodge Stud Limited **Trained** Langton, N Yorks

FOCUS
Rail realignment increased distances on round course by about 12yds. After a dry night the going was officially described as good. A modest maiden auction. The pace was decent and the winner was quite impressive. The form is rated around the third.

NOTEBOOK
Byrama took time to hit full stride but nearly caught an experienced pair when 20-1 in a 5f Beverley maiden on debut. She had a bit to find, but was well backed and powered past the leaders to win with plenty in hand, despite still showing signs of inexperience. The form is probably not very strong but she is closely related to smart 5f-1m winner Klammer, and could go on to better things. (op 11-4)
Key Ambition was a big drifter but he showed a decent cruising speed for long way before fighting to snatch second. He cost just £6,800 but this was an encouraging start from a colt who is out of a 6f winning half-sister to high-class sprinter Superior Premium. (op 8-1 tchd 14-1)
Half A Billion(IRE) ran an experienced rival close over C&D on debut but it was disappointing that he was caught close home when a hot odds-on favourite at Hamilton last time and he was comfortably overhauled here. (op 5-2 tchd 9-4)
Summer Lane(IRE) couldn't find an effective response when things got serious and was beaten quite a bit further by Byrama than she was on debut. (tchd 10-3)
Never In(IRE) was caught out when the pace increased and could only plug on out wide. She has shown a bit of ability in four starts and a switch to low-grade nurseries should broaden her horizons. (tchd 25-1 and 50-1)
Lord Buffhead looked like he was getting the hang of things when 4l behind Half A Billion at Hamilton on his second start. He was a huge market mover in the morning but was always trailing after a slow start before finishing tailed off. Official explanation: jockey said gelding missed the break and never travelled (op 6-1 tchd 11-2)

4359 LLOYD BMW H'CAP — 5f
2:25 (2:27) (Class 5) (0-70,70) 3-Y-O — **£2,522** (£750; £375; £187) **Stalls** Low

Form — RPR

2022 **1** **Rylee Mooch**[30] 3360 3-9-5 **68**..........(e) GrahamGibbons 5 — 74+
(Richard Guest) *mde all: rdn along over 1f out: kpt on strly fnl f* **10/3**[1]

1062 **2** ½ **Saxonette**[15] 3860 3-9-5 **68**.......... PJMcDonald 3 — 70
(Linda Perratt) *in tch: hdwy 1/2-way: effrt and ch over 1f out: kpt on fnl f* **17/2**[3]

6531 **3** 1 ¼ **Novalist**[36] 3192 3-8-5 **54**..........(b) LeeNewman 4 — 52
(Robin Bastiman) *cl up: rdn along 2f out: kpt on ins fnl f* **7/2**[2]

6031 **4** ¾ **Boundless Spirit**[15] 3860 3-9-0 **70**..........(t) ShirleyTeasdale(7) 1 — 65
(David Nicholls) *rrd s: t.k.h in rr: hdwy and swtchd lft over 2f out: sn rdn and edgd lft over 1f out: one pce fnl f* **10/3**[1]

4433 **5** 1 ¼ **Climaxfortackle (IRE)**[22] 3635 3-9-1 **64**..........(v) RobbieFitzpatrick 2 — 54
(Derek Shaw) *in tch: hdwy 1/2-way: sn rdn: one pce over 1f out* **10/3**[1]

4466 **6** 2 **Running Water**[13] 3901 3-7-11 **51** oh4..........(bt) NeilFarley(5) 7 — 34
(Hugh McWilliams) *hld up: effrt and rdn 2f out: btn ins fnl f* **25/1**

5006 **7** 5 **Ivy And Gold**[8] 4110 3-7-11 **51** oh6..........(b[1]) DanielleMcCreery(5) 6 — 16
(Alan Berry) *dwlt: sn pushed along in rr: hung rt and wknd fr 1/2-way* **40/1**

60.93 secs (0.13) **Going Correction** +0.05s/f (Good) **7** Ran SP% **108.3**
Speed ratings (Par 100): **100,99,97,96,94 90,82**
toteswingers:1&2:£1.10, 1&3:£3.40, 2&3:£5.20 CSF £27.93 CT £90.77 TOTE £3.60: £1.70, £3.90; EX 12.00.
Owner Katie Hughes,Julie McCarlie,Sheila White **Bred** Mrs Sheila White **Trained** Stainforth, S Yorks

FOCUS
A modest but competitive handicap, involving two last-time-out winners and three others who were placed on their latest run. The winner was value for a bit extra.

4360 STOBART LADIES' NORTHERN DERBY BOWL H'CAP (FOR LADY AMATEUR RIDERS) — 1m 3f 107y
3:00 (3:02) (Class 3) (0-90,88) 4-Y-O+ — **£7,486** (£2,322; £1,160; £580) **Stalls** High

Form — RPR

2020 **1** **Lady Chaparral**[16] 3828 4-9-10 **77**.......... MissLHorner 9 — 91
(George Moore) *chsd ldrs: led over 2f out: styd on strly fnl f* **15/2**[3]

0142 **2** 2 ¼ **Butler (IRE)**[24] 3544 4-9-10 **82**.......... MissFCumani(5) 17 — 92
(Luca Cumani) *t.k.h: hld up on outside: hdwy and plenty to do ent st: chsd wnr ins fnl f: r.o* **6/1**[1]

0052 **3** ¾ **Full Speed (GER)**[15] 3858 6-9-6 **76**.......... LucyAlexander(3) 6 — 85
(Alan Swinbank) *hld up: hdwy and swtchd rt over 1f out: styd on fnl f: nrst fin* **10/1**

-230 **4** 1 **Meetings Man (IRE)**[30] 3344 4-9-3 **75**.......... MissRSmith(5) 12 — 82
(Micky Hammond) *hld up: hdwy over 2f out: styd on fnl f: nvr nrr* **16/1**

5415 **5** 1 **Patavium (IRE)**[17] 3758 8-9-6 **73**.......... MissSBrotherton 3 — 78
(Edwin Tuer) *t.k.h in midfield: hdwy over 3f out: rdn and one pce fr over 1f out* **20/1**

-030 **6** ½ **Solicitor**[10] 4004 4-9-13 **80**.......... MissADeniel 2 — 84
(Mark Johnston) *in tch: effrt 3f out: nt qckn appr fnl f* **28/1**

-062 **7** *shd* **Thin Red Line (IRE)**[29] 3381 5-10-0 **81**.......... MissEJJones 15 — 85
(Michael Dods) *midfield: effrt and rdn over 2f out: kpt on same pce fr over 1f out* **16/1**

-003 **8** 1 ¼ **Union Island (IRE)**[9] 4043 5-9-4 **76**.......... MissNVorster(5) 5 — 78
(Brian Ellison) *midfield: stdy hdwy on ins whn nt clr run and swtchd lft over 1f out: nvr able to chal* **14/1**

33-1 **9** ½ **Fujin Dancer (FR)**[27] 3456 6-9-5 **77**.......... MissHBethell(5) 8 — 78
(Brian Ellison) *hld up on ins: hdwy over 3f out: no imp fnl 2f* **7/1**[2]

1225 **10** 1 **Houston Dynimo (IRE)**[31] 3316 6-8-12 **70**.......... MissJRRichards(5) 16 — 70
(Nicky Richards) *[illegible] led 1/2-way to over 2f out: wknd over 1f out* **20/1**

-663 **11** 7 **Trip The Light**[2] 4294 6-9-8 **80**..........(v) MissISyddall(5) 7 — 68
(Richard Fahey) *sddle slipped sn after s: prom tl wknd over 2f out* **16/1**

5212 **12** 1 **Zennor**[37] 3129 4-9-4 **78**.......... MissALMurphy(7) 14 — 64
(Tom Dascombe) *s.s: bhd: rdn and hung rt over 2f out: sn no imp* **7/1**[2]

3010 **13** 1 **Crackentorp**[22] 3625 6-10-7 **88**.......... MissJCoward 13 — 72
(Tim Easterby) *bhd: rdn along over 5f out: sme late hdwy: nvr on terms* **16/1**

2331 **14** *shd* **Amazing Blue Sky**[6] 4148 5-9-9 **76** 6ex.......... MrsAdeleMulrennan 11 — 60
(Ruth Carr) *led to 1/2-way: cl up tl wknd fr 2f out* **12/1**

16-0 **15** 3 **Graceful Descent (FR)**[36] 3163 6-9-10 **77**.......... MrsCBartley 4 — 56
(Jim Goldie) *s.s: bhd: pushed along over 4f out: nvr on terms* **25/1**

2/0- **16** ¾ **Worth A King'S**[19] 252 5-9-10 **80**.......... MissECSayer(3) 10 — 58
(Dianne Sayer) *bhd: rdn over 5f out: nvr on terms* **50/1**

2m 23.22s (0.12) **Going Correction** -0.10s/f (Good) **16** Ran SP% **116.8**
Speed ratings (Par 107): **95,93,92,92,91 91,90,90,89,88 83,83,82,82,80 79**
toteswingers:1&2:£15.70, 1&3:£32.10, 2&3:£8.50 CSF £45.81 CT £456.46 TOTE £10.00: £3.00, £2.20, £2.90, £4.50; EX 57.10.
Owner Geoff & Sandra Turnbull **Bred** Geoff & Sandra Turnbull **Trained** Middleham Moor, N Yorks

FOCUS
They went a good pace in this decent handicap for lady amateur riders. The time was close to two seconds faster than standard and the form looks sound. Sir Boss went down in the stalls and was withdrawn.

NOTEBOOK
Lady Chaparral travelled well for a long way but didn't seem to last the 1m6f trip at York last time. Never far away, she moved smoothly into the lead 2f out and was never in any serious danger dropped back in trip. She is a generally progressive filly who still has low mileage, and her good cruising speed should continue to be a valuable asset in middle-distance handicaps. (op 9-1 tchd 10-1)
Butler(IRE) had a tough draw to contend with, but stayed on well out wide behind the winner who got first run. He has improved with a win and three frame efforts in five starts since joining Luca Cumani and is still not fully exposed at this sort of trip. (tchd 11-2)
Full Speed(GER) weaved his way through the pack before staying on well against the far rail. He struggled initially this year but has recaptured form recently and could be close to a fourth career win. (op 8-1 tchd 15-2)
Meetings Man(IRE) stayed on strongly from an unpromising position to bounce back from a rare below-par run at Doncaster last time. (op 25-1)
Patavium(IRE) was a bit keen early on but got back somewhere near the form of his heavily-backed win in a similar race at Musselburgh last month. (tchd 18-1)

Solicitor ran a fair race, but he has found life tough since a runaway win off 5lb lower at Beverley last July and probably needs to drop further down the weights. (op 25-1)
Thin Red Line(IRE), supported at big prices, stayed on steadily but couldn't land a blow. (op 25-1)
Union Island(IRE) Official explanation: jockey said gelding was denied a clear run
Fujin Dancer(FR), a comfortable winner at Pontefract last time, couldn't get into a threatening position off 7lb higher in a race that didn't really pan out for the hold-up runners. (op 6-1)
Trip The Light had a feasible excuse because his saddle slipped. Official explanation: jockey said saddle slipped
Zennor, a strong finishing second behind Patavium in a similar race last time, was very laboured after a slow start. Official explanation: jockey said filly missed the break (op 6-1)
Graceful Descent(FR) Official explanation: jockey said mare missed the break

4361 LES TALLENTIRE MEMORIAL CLAIMING STKS 7f 200y
3:35 (3:35) (Class 6) 3-Y-0+ **£1,908** (£563; £281) **Stalls** Low

Form				RPR
0056	1		**Solar Spirit (IRE)**[7] 4126 6-9-0 75 ShaneBKelly(7) 2 *(Tracy Waggott) hld up on ins: hdwy 2f out: led ins fnl f: hld on wl* **16/1**	72
5204	2	*hd*	**Sunnyside Tom (IRE)**[22] 3620 7-9-12 79 PaulHanagan 1 *(Richard Fahey) led: rdn over 2f out: hdd ins fnl f: rallied: hld cl home* **2/1**[1]	77
-450	3	*shd*	**I'm Super Too (IRE)**[61] 2388 4-9-12 66 PJMcDonald 5 *(Alan Swinbank) hld up: rdn over 2f out: hdwy over 1f out: kpt on wl fnl f: jst hld* **33/1**	76
0253	4	1 ½	**Academy Blues (USA)**[36] 3190 6-9-9 82 PaulQuinn 3 *(David Nicholls) trckd ldrs on ins: effrt whn n.m.r over 2f out to ent fnl f: sn rdn: kpt on same pce* **10/1**[3]	70
6013	5	¾	**Opus Maximus (IRE)**[11] 3972 6-9-3 70 (p) StephenCraine 4 *(Jennie Candlish) hld up: smooth hdwy over 2f out: rdn over 1f out: kpt on u.p fnl f* **11/1**	62
232	6	2	**The Osteopath (IRE)**[7] 4125 8-9-12 79 TomEaves 7 *(Michael Dods) chsd ldr: rdn over 2f out: wknd ins fnl f* **4/1**[2]	67
0135	7	8	**Frontline Girl (IRE)**[30] 3338 5-9-5 75 AndrewElliott 8 *(Mrs K Burke) prom: rdn 3f out: wknd wl over 1f out* **2/1**[1]	41
0240	8	1 ½	**Carnival Dream**[31] 3317 6-8-4 44 (p) VictorSantos(7) 6 *(Hugh McWilliams) plld hrd: in tch tl wknd fr 3f out* **150/1**	30

1m 40.15s (0.15) **Going Correction** -0.10s/f (Good) **8** Ran SP% **113.6**
Speed ratings (Par 101): **95,94,94,93,92 90,82,80**
toteswingers:1&2:£7.70, 1&3:£26.90, 2&3:£16.70 CSF £47.79 TOTE £13.40: £2.60, £1.30, £7.00; EX 44.70.
Owner Christopher James Allan **Bred** Paul Hensey **Trained** Spennymoor, Co Durham
■ Stewards' Enquiry : P J McDonald one-day ban: careless riding (Aug 8)

FOCUS
A fair claimer. The pace was not very strong and there was a tight finish, as a revitalised performer ran down one of the market leaders. Muddling form, with the third the key.
Frontline Girl(IRE) Official explanation: trainer said mare was unsuited by the track

4362 EDINBURGH WOOLLEN MILL H'CAP 6f 192y
4:10 (4:10) (Class 5) (0-75,74) 3-Y-0+ **£2,522** (£750; £375; £187) **Stalls** Low

Form				RPR
560	1		**Schoolboy Champ**[12] 3956 4-8-10 **56** oh2 ow1 (v) DarryllHolland 5 *(Patrick Morris) early ldr: cl up: rdn to ld over 1f out: hld on wl fnl f* **18/1**	65
-150	2	½	**Youhavecontrol (IRE)**[29] 3400 3-9-6 **73** FrederikTylicki 8 *(Michael Dods) hld up: hdwy on outside to chse ldrs 2f out: sn rdn: kpt on ins fnl f* **11/4**[1]	78
1002	3	1 ¾	**Bandstand**[22] 3617 5-9-6 **73** JustinNewman(7) 4 *(Bryan Smart) dwlt: hld up: hdwy to ld over 2f out tl over 1f out: kpt on same pce ins fnl f* **9/2**[2]	76
-356	4	1	**Dubai Celebration**[31] 3318 3-9-2 **72** PatrickDonaghy(3) 3 *(Jedd O'Keeffe) hld up towards rr: effrt over 2f out: edgd rt over 1f out: kpt on fnl f: no imp* **8/1**	69
0523	5	3 ¼	**Berbice (IRE)**[6] 4141 6-9-7 **67** (p) LeeNewman 7 *(Linda Perratt) dwlt: t.k.h: hld up: hdwy over 2f out: rdn over 1f out: kpt on same pce* **7/1**	59
0023	6	2	**No Quarter (IRE)**[25] 3508 4-9-3 **63** PJMcDonald 2 *(Tracy Waggott) prom: drvn over 2f out: wknd appr fnl f* **6/1**[3]	49
0000	7	¾	**Durham Express (IRE)**[30] 3359 4-9-3 **63** TomEaves 9 *(Michael Dods) chsd ldrs: outpcd over 3f out: n.d after* **40/1**	47
0460	8	1	**Accamelia**[9] 4078 5-8-9 **55** oh2 RobertWinston 1 *(Chris Fairhurst) plld hrd: sn led: hdd over 2f out: wknd and eased over 1f out* **16/1**	39
4520	9	4 ½	**Corsicanrun (IRE)**[12] 3936 3-9-7 **74** (b1) PaulHanagan 6 *(Richard Fahey) sn bhd and pushed along: struggling 1/2-way: nvr on terms* **9/2**[2]	40

1m 27.59s (0.49) **Going Correction** -0.10s/f (Good)
WFA 3 from 4yo+ 7lb **9** Ran SP% **114.5**
Speed ratings (Par 103): **93,92,90,89,85 83,82,81,76**
toteswingers:1&2:£8.00, 1&3:£13.40, 2&3:£3.50 CSF £66.85 CT £271.10 TOTE £19.40: £4.10, £1.80, £2.20; EX 94.70.
Owner Chester Racing Club Ltd **Bred** Stephen Hillen And Hatta Bloodstock **Trained** Tarporley, Cheshire
■ Stewards' Enquiry : Justin Newman two-day ban: careless riding (Aug 7-8)
Frederik Tylicki one-day ban: used whip with excessive frequency (Aug 7)

FOCUS
A minor handicap run at a fast pace. Ordinary form.
Accamelia Official explanation: jockey said gelding failed to handle the bend and hung right in straight

4363 GET FREE BETS AT FREEBETTING.CO.UK MAIDEN STKS 1m 1f 61y
4:45 (4:46) (Class 5) 3-Y-0+ **£2,522** (£750; £375; £187) **Stalls** Low

Form				RPR
2	1		**Iulus**[33] 3246 3-9-3 0 TomEaves 1 *(John Quinn) midfield: rdn over 3f out: rallied over 2f out: led appr fnl f: drvn out* **5/1**[3]	79
2042	2	1 ¼	**Lucky Legs (IRE)**[28] 3437 3-8-12 72 RobertWinston 5 *(B W Hills) trckd ldrs: smooth hdwy to ld over 2f out: hdd appr fnl f: rallied: one pce last 75yds* **6/5**[1]	71
00	3	6	**Sistine**[29] 3385 3-8-12 0 FrederikTylicki 6 *(James Given) hld up: rdn 4f out: swtchd lft and hdwy 2f out: styd on to take 3rd towards fin: nt rch first two* **20/1**	58
	4	½	**Cairncross (IRE)** 3-8-12 0 DarryllHolland 2 *(Mark Johnston) trckd ldrs: flashed tail several times: effrt whn n.m.r briefly 2f out: one pce appr fnl f* **9/1**	57
-233	5	3 ½	**She's Got The Luck (IRE)**[20] 3681 3-8-12 67 PaulHanagan 4 *(Richard Fahey) early ldr: cl up: led over 3f out tl over 2f out: wknd over 1f out* **5/2**[2]	49
0-0	6	13	**Lady Intrigue (IRE)**[20] 3684 3-8-12 0 PatrickMathers 12 *(Richard Fahey) hld up: rdn along 1/2-way: nvr on terms* **40/1**	21
6	7	*hd*	**Snare**[10] 4014 4-9-7 0 DavidNolan 3 *(Ann Duffield) midfield: drvn along 1/2-way: wknd fr over 2f out* **150/1**	21
0	8	*nk*	**Shirls Son Sam**[23] 3575 3-9-0 0 PatrickDonaghy(3) 10 *(Chris Fairhurst) stdd s: hld up: rdn over 4f out: sn btn* **100/1**	25
0-	9	20	**Jack Bell (IRE)**[443] 1890 4-9-12 0 PJMcDonald 8 *(Alan Swinbank) sn led: rdn and hdd over 3f out: wknd fnl 2f* **25/1**	—
5-	10	5	**By Implication**[242] 7559 3-9-3 0 StephenCraine 11 *(Patrick Morris) bhd: drvn along over 4f out: nvr on terms* **66/1**	—

1m 57.1s (-0.50) **Going Correction** -0.10s/f (Good)
WFA 3 from 4yo 9lb **10** Ran SP% **114.9**
Speed ratings (Par 103): **98,96,91,91,88 76,76,76,58,53**
toteswingers:1&2:£2.80, 1&3:£9.20, 2&3:£5.60 CSF £10.88 TOTE £7.40: £1.80, £1.40, £3.10; EX 16.70.
Owner Mrs S Quinn **Bred** B & S Haynes **Trained** Settrington, N Yorks

FOCUS
There was not much strength in depth in this maiden. The strong favourite looked the likely winner 2f out but couldn't deal with a powerful finisher, who's rated up a stone. The first two pulled a long way clear.

4364 PAIJE RICHARDSON LIVE H'CAP 1m 1f 61y
5:20 (5:20) (Class 5) (0-70,67) 3-Y-0 **£2,522** (£750; £375; £187) **Stalls** Low

Form				RPR
1153	1		**One Pursuit (IRE)**[39] 3038 3-9-0 **67** ShirleyTeasdale(7) 3 *(David Nicholls) trckd ldrs: pushed along and led over 1f out: drew clr fnl f* **4/1**[1]	84+
-555	2	4	**Madison Square (USA)**[13] 3913 3-8-12 **58** DarryllHolland 6 *(Mark Johnston) hld up: hdwy on outside 3f out: chsd (clr) wnr ent fnl f: r.o* **14/1**	65
4253	3	7	**Philharmonic Hall**[10] 4018 3-9-4 **64** PaulHanagan 2 *(Richard Fahey) in tch: lost pl bnd over 4f out: sn pushed along: sme late hdwy: no ch w first two* **5/1**[3]	56
3522	4	½	**See The Storm**[12] 3958 3-8-1 **54** ShaneBKelly(7) 1 *(Patrick Morris) led: rdn over 2f out: hung rt and hdd over 1f out: sn btn* **9/2**[2]	45
5212	5	½	**Retreat Content (IRE)**[13] 3905 3-9-7 **67** (b) TomEaves 5 *(Linda Perratt) trckd ldrs: rdn and outpcd over 2f out: n.d after* **4/1**[1]	56
5353	6	1 ½	**Residence And Spa (IRE)**[18] 3734 3-9-5 **65** (p) PJMcDonald 4 *(Tim Easterby) trckd ldr: rdn over 2f out: wknd over 1f out* **7/1**	51
0324	7	6	**Damascus Symphony**[8] 4111 3-9-0 **60** AndrewElliott 7 *(James Bethell) hld up in tch: rdn along over 2f out: sn btn* **4/1**[1]	33

1m 56.62s (-0.98) **Going Correction** -0.10s/f (Good) **7** Ran SP% **114.0**
Speed ratings (Par 100): **100,96,90,89,89 88,82**
toteswingers:1&2:£6.40, 1&3:£5.30, 2&3:£9.50 CSF £56.58 TOTE £5.10: £2.20, £5.30; EX 63.90.
Owner Eamon Maher **Bred** Clougher Partnership **Trained** Sessay, N Yorks
■ Shirley Teasdale's first winner.
■ Stewards' Enquiry : Shirley Teasdale two-day ban: careless riding (Aug 7-8)

FOCUS
This looked a competitive handicap, but the winner powered away from a clear second in a strongly run race. He posted a clear best, but the form in behind is ordinary.
T/Plt: £77.50 to a £1 stake. Pool:£60,956.13 - 573.50 winning tickets T/Qpdt: £20.20 to a £1 stake. Pool:£4,117.33 - 150.60 winning tickets RY

4073 PONTEFRACT (L-H)
Sunday, July 24

OFFICIAL GOING: Good changing to good to firm after race 3 (3:15)
Wind: light 1/2 behind Weather: fine and sunny

4365 WELCOME TO YORKSHIRE THIS IS Y MAIDEN STKS 5f
2:05 (2:06) (Class 4) 2-Y-0 **£3,881** (£1,155; £577; £144; £144) **Stalls** Low

Form				RPR
	1		**Kylesku (IRE)** 2-8-12 0 PhillipMakin 5 *(Kevin Ryan) trckd ldr: led over 2f out: clr over 1f out: v readily* **8/1**	79+
655	2	4	**Reve Du Jour (IRE)**[24] 3553 2-8-12 0 (p) SteveDrowne 6 *(Alan McCabe) led tl over 2f out: kpt on same pce* **16/1**	63
	3	½	**Gabrial The King (USA)** 2-9-3 0 DavidAllan 9 *(Michael Bell) chsd ldrs: kpt on same pce over 1f out* **5/2**[1]	66
54	4	*hd*	**Baltic Bomber (IRE)**[22] 3610 2-9-3 0 TonyHamilton 10 *(John Quinn) chsd ldrs: kpt on same pce fnl 2f* **10/1**	65
0	4	*dht*	**Copp The Lot (USA)**[17] 3755 2-9-3 0 AndrewMullen 2 *(David Nicholls) chsd ldrs: kpt on same pce fnl 2f* **14/1**	65
0	6	2 ¼	**Minne Wa Wa**[46] 2811 2-8-12 0 SilvestreDeSousa 1 *(David Brown) s.i.s: in rr: hdwy over 2f out: fdd fnl f* **9/1**	52+
4	7	1 ¼	**Whatyoucallit (IRE)**[9] 4068 2-9-3 0 TedDurcan 4 *(David Lanigan) mid-div: hdwy 2f out: one pce* **5/1**[3]	53
0	8	*nk*	**Divine Success (IRE)**[17] 3755 2-9-0 0 LeeTopliss(3) 7 *(Richard Fahey) in rr: styd on fnl 2f: nvr a factor* **9/1**	52
	9	6	**Malvesi** 2-9-3 0 RoystonFfrench 8 *(Ann Duffield) s.i.s: outpcd and a bhd* **33/1**	30
	10	3 ¼	**Son Of May** 2-9-3 0 TadhgO'Shea 3 *(Jo Hughes) s.v.s: a detached in last* **9/2**[2]	19

63.44 secs (0.14) **Going Correction** -0.15s/f (Firm) **10** Ran SP% **119.1**
Speed ratings (Par 96): **92,85,84,84,84 80,78,78,68,63**
toteswingers:1&2:£18.50, 1&3:£4.40, 2&3:£8.20 CSF £129.70 TOTE £12.10: £3.20, £4.10, £1.70; EX 142.60.
Owner J M Birkett **Bred** R Lynch **Trained** Hambleton, N Yorks

FOCUS
An ordinary juvenile maiden but another impressive juvenile winner for Kevin Ryan. The form is rated around the second and fourth.

NOTEBOOK
Kylesku(IRE) clearly knew her job and fairly scooted clear once in line for home. A speedily bred daughter of Moss Vale, she'll presumably go up in class now and it'll be interesting to monitor her progress. (tchd 6-1)
Reve Du Jour(IRE) proved no match for the winner, but it was still her best effort yet in the first-time cheekpieces, and nurseries ought to be more her thing. (op 10-1)
Gabrial The King(USA), who cost £80,000 as a 2-y-o, became outpaced at a crucial stage before staying on to grab a place close home. He ought to come on appreciably for the experience and will benefit from 6f. (op 7-2)
Copp The Lot(USA) stepped up markedly on his initial effort and should be capable of winning races this year, with the probability of more to come. (op 22-1 tchd 12-1)
Baltic Bomber(IRE) is now qualified for a mark and ought to find an opening in that sphere. (op 22-1 tchd 12-1)
Whatyoucallit(IRE) failed to pick up on this drop to 5f. (op 9-2)

Son Of May blew the start and unsurprisingly failed to recover. He's clearly worth another chance. Official explanation: jockey said colt missed the break (op 5-1, tchd 6-1 in places)

4366 JOHN RANSOME ACCOUNTANCY SERVICES H'CAP 1m 4f 8y
2:40 (2:40) (Class 5) (0-70,68) 3-Y-O+ **£2,587** (£770; £384; £192) **Stalls** Low

Form RPR
-030 **1** **Kian's Delight**[26] 3487 3-8-3 **55**.................................... DuranFentiman 14 64
(Jedd O'Keeffe) *trckd ldr: upsides over 2f out: kpt on to ld towards fin* **25/1**
2336 **2** *hd* **Sharp Sovereign (USA)**[9] 4043 5-9-7 **66**......................... LMcNiff(5) 16 75
(David Barron) *led: jnd 3f out: hdd towards fin* **14/1**
0030 **3** *½* **Simple Jim (FR)**[23] 3574 7-9-0 **54**............................ SilvestreDeSousa 1 62+
(David O'Meara) *s.i.s: hld up in rr: gd hdwy and swtchd outside over 1f out: styd on wl towards fin* **11/2**[2]
4032 **4** *¾* **Lady Norlela**[9] 4077 5-9-1 **55**.. BarryMcHugh 12 62
(Brian Rothwell) *hld up in rr: hdwy on ins over 2f out: chsng ldrs appr fnl f: styd on same pce* **20/1**
4-41 **5** *2¾* **Muwalla**[10] 4024 4-9-12 **66**... PhillipMakin 6 68
(Chris Grant) *mid-div: drvn to chse ldrs over 2f out: one pce over 1f out* **13/2**[3]
4602 **6** *2¼* **Grey Command (USA)**[23] 3574 6-8-12 **52**........................ DavidAllan 2 51
(Mel Brittain) *chsd ldrs: drvn over 3f out: sn outpcd: hdwy on outside over 1f out: one pce* **9/1**
-605 **7** *¾* **Herrera (IRE)**[13] 3906 6-9-7 **61**.. TonyHamilton 3 59
(Richard Fahey) *in tch: effrt over 2f out: kpt on one pce over 1f out* **20/1**
4240 **8** *2* **Maslak (IRE)**[57] 2055 7-9-12 **66**....................................... MickyFenton 17 60
(Peter Hiatt) *hood removed late: slow into stride: swtchd lft after s: kpt on fnl 2f: nvr a factor* **20/1**
4031 **9** *2* **Brasingaman Eric**[23] 3574 4-9-3 **57**.......................... AndrewMullen 13 48
(George Moore) *prom: wkng whn hung lft and sltly hmpd over 1f out* **8/1**
6116 **10** *3½* **Light The City (IRE)**[13] 3906 4-9-2 **56**....................... JamesSullivan 15 42
(Ruth Carr) *chsd ldrs: wknd over 1f out* **14/1**
0051 **11** *5* **Royal Premier (IRE)**[12] 3960 8-9-1 **58**....................(b) SimonPearce(3) 8 36
(Tom Keddy) *s.i.s: in rr: drvn 7f out: nvr a factor* **20/1**
0064 **12** *7* **Danceintothelight**[18] 3730 4-9-9 **63**............................... KellyHarrison 11 29
(Micky Hammond) *mid-div: drvn over 4f out: lost pl over 2f out* **12/1**
-406 **13** *2¼* **Hail Bold Chief (USA)**[39] 3051 4-9-5 **66**........................ GarryWhillans(7) 10 29
(Alan Swinbank) *mid-div: drvn over 3f out: lost pl 2f out* **16/1**
314- **14** *9* **Master Nimbus**[302] 5681 11-9-6 **63**................................ LeeTopliss(3) 9 11
(John Quinn) *mid-div: sme hdwy 4f out: sn lost pl: bhd fnl 2f* **16/1**
3511 **15** *2½* **Bradbury (IRE)**[16] 3811 3-9-2 **68**..................................(p) TadhgO'Shea 5 12
(James Bethell) *s.i.s: sme hdwy on outer 4f out: wknd over 2f out* **9/2**[1]
-225 **16** *16* **Dunaskin (IRE)**[57] 2235 11-8-12 **55**........................(b) RobertLButler(3) 7 —
(Richard Guest) *t.k.h: trckd ldrs: lost pl over 3f out: sn bhd: t.o 2f out* **40/1**

2m 37.49s (-3.31) **Going Correction** -0.15s/f (Firm)
WFA 3 from 4yo+ 12lb **16** Ran SP% **126.1**
Speed ratings (Par 103): **105,104,104,104,102 100,100,98,97,95 91,87,85,79,78 67**
toteswingers:1&2:£79.00, 1&3:£38.30, 2&3:£23.40 CSF £325.13 CT £2227.71 TOTE £37.50: £5.90, £3.50, £2.00, £4.60; EX 524.80.
Owner Jenny & Ray Butler **Bred** Mrs J M Quy **Trained** Middleham Moor, N Yorks
■ Stewards' Enquiry : Silvestre De Sousa one-day ban: careless riding (Aug 8)
Duran Fentiman two-day ban: used whip with excessive frequency (Aug 7-8)

FOCUS
This moderate handicap was run at a fair enough pace, but this is a track where it very often pays to race handy and few got in a serious blow from off the pace. A clear personal best from the surprise winner.
Kian's Delight Official explanation: trainer's rep said, regarding apparent improvement in form, that the gelding enjoyed being ridden with the pace.
Maslak(IRE) Official explanation: jockey said blindfold became caught on bridle and was unable to remove it on first attempt.
Brasingaman Eric Official explanation: jockey said gelding hung left
Bradbury(IRE) Official explanation: jockey said gelding never travelled

4367 GRAHAM ROCK MEMORIAL H'CAP [illegible]
3:15 (3:15) (Class 5) (0-70,70) 3-Y-O+ **£2,587** (£770; £384; £192) **Stalls** Low

Form RPR
03-0 **1** **Betteras Bertie**[81] 1814 8-9-1 **57**................................(p) BarryMcHugh 4 67+
(Tony Coyle) *s.i.s: hld up in rr: hdwy on ins whn nt clr run over 2f out: styd on to ld last 150yds: all out* **28/1**
500 **2** *¾* **Singzak**[61] 2392 3-8-9 **61**.. JamesSullivan 14 70
(Michael Easterby) *prom: drvn along 6f out: swtchd rt over 2f out: hdwy on outside over 1f out: styd on wl ins fnl f: no ex clsng stages* **14/1**
1234 **3** *1¾* **Ay Tay Tate (IRE)**[15] 3848 5-9-7 **63**............................ AndrewHeffernan 2 68
(David C Griffiths) *dwlt: drvn to chse ldrs: led over 3f out: hdd jst ins fnl f: kpt on same pce* **8/1**[3]
4360 **4** *3½* **Highland Love**[8] 4111 6-8-11 **53**..................................... TonyCulhane 3 51
(Jedd O'Keeffe) *chsd ldrs: wnt 2nd 2f out: one pce* **20/1**
21-0 **5** *½* **Flying Power**[12] 3952 3-9-4 **70**.. TedDurcan 6 67
(David Lanigan) *towards rr: hmpd after 1f: hdwy over 2f out: kpt on same pce fnl f* **16/1**
0600 **6** *5* **Aerodynamic (IRE)**[29] 3386 4-9-9 **65**................................ PaddyAspell 1 52
(Clive Mulhall) *hld up in rr: hdwy on ins whn nt clr run over 2f out: swtchd rt: nvr rchd ldrs* **20/1**
-365 **7** *3* **Cosmic Moon**[22] 3632 3-9-1 **70**.. LeeTopliss(3) 8 51+
(Richard Fahey) *in rr whn hmpd after 1f: kpt on fnl 2f: nvr a factor* **8/1**[3]
6-61 **8** *1¾* **Hot Spice**[24] 3545 3-9-1 **67**... PhillipMakin 5 45+
(John Dunlop) *towards rr: hmpd after 1f: kpt on fnl 2f: nvr on terms* **7/4**[1]
01 **9** *2¼* **Sartingo (IRE)**[13] 3905 4-9-4 **67**..................................... GarryWhillans(7) 10 40
(Alan Swinbank) *hmpd sn after s: trckd ldrs: wknd over 1f out* **15/2**[2]
0220 **10** *17* **Nolecce**[31] 3311 4-9-6 **65**...(p) RobertLButler(3) 13 —
(Richard Guest) *hld up in rr: sme hdwy on outer over 3f out: wknd over 2f out* **20/1**
00-4 **11** *shd* **Miss Ferney**[9] 4074 7-8-9 **54**.. PaulPickard(3) 7 —
(Alan Kirtley) *in rr whn hmpd after 1f: nvr a factor* **33/1**
5623 **12** *nk* **Yossi (IRE)**[114] 1081 7-8-11 **53**.......................................(b) KellyHarrison 12 —
(Richard Guest) *edgd lft s: w ldrs: wknd over 1f out* **33/1**
00-3 **13** *8* **Tricky Situation**[9] 4077 5-8-12 **54**........................... SilvestreDeSousa 11 —
(David Brown) *hmpd after s: sn chsng ldrs: drvn over 3f out: wknd over 2f out: bhd whn eased over 1f out* **14/1**
1333 **14** *2½* **Ollon (USA)**[17] 3758 3-9-0 **66**.. TonyHamilton 9 —
(Richard Fahey) *in rr: bhd fnl 2f* **12/1**
50-0 **15** *45* **Loyal Knight (IRE)**[23] 3569 6-8-9 **51** ohб.......................(t) MickyFenton 15 —
(Paul Midgley) *led: hdd over 3f out: sn lost pl and bhd: t.o over 1f out: virtually p.u* **80/1**

2m 12.39s (-1.31) **Going Correction** -0.15s/f (Firm)
WFA 3 from 4yo+ 10lb **15** Ran SP% **122.1**
Speed ratings (Par 103): **99,98,97,94,93 89,87,86,84,70 70,70,63,61,25**
toteswingers:1&2:£65.30, 1&3:£41.40, 2&3:£16.20 CSF £358.58 CT £3428.95 TOTE £39.40: £11.50, £4.00, £2.80; EX 864.50.
Owner Mrs V C Sugden **Bred** Mrs V C Sugden **Trained** Norton, N Yorks
■ Stewards' Enquiry : Barry McHugh one-day ban: used whip with excessive frequency down shoulder in the forehand (Aug 7)

FOCUS
An ordinary handicap, run at an average pace and there was another tight finish. A return to form from the surprise winner.
Hot Spice Official explanation: jockey said gelding suffered interference in runing

4368 SKYBET SUPPORTING THE YORKSHIRE RACING SUMMER FESTIVAL POMFRET STKS (LISTED RACE) 1m 4y
3:50 (3:50) (Class 1) 3-Y-O+ **£17,013** (£6,450; £3,228) **Stalls** Low

Form RPR
3-42 **1** **Emerald Commander (IRE)**[7] 4138 4-9-1 110...............(t) TedDurcan 5 114+
(Saeed Bin Suroor) *trckd ldr: effrt over 2f out: led appr fnl f: r.o strly: eased towards fin* **2/1**[2]
1212 **2** *2¼* **St Moritz (IRE)**[50] 2713 5-9-5 107.................................. AdrianNicholls 3 112
(David Nicholls) *led: qcknd pce over 2f out: hdd appr fnl f: edgd lft: kpt on same pce* **6/5**[1]
2353 **3** *hd* **Off Chance**[19] 3703 5-8-10 99... DuranFentiman 6 103
(Tim Easterby) *hld up: trckd ldrs over 4f out: effrt over 2f out: keeping on same pce whn hmpd and swtchd rt jst ins fnl f: kpt on towards fin* **5/2**[3]

1m 43.97s (-1.93) **Going Correction** -0.15s/f (Firm)
WFA 3 from 4yo+ 8lb **3** Ran SP% **107.4**
Speed ratings (Par 111): **103,100,100**
CSF £4.69 TOTE £2.70; EX 3.90.
Owner Godolphin **Bred** Grangecon Stud **Trained** Newmarket, Suffolk

FOCUS
This Listed race was decimated by non-runners, most importantly Cityscape, who again found the ground go against him. Sound form.

NOTEBOOK
Emerald Commander(IRE) had previously shown his best form on softer ground, but the race was run perfectly for his needs and he ran out a ready enough winner. It was a deserved success, but he was very much entitled to win at the weights and this was probably his big day. This enhanced his trainer's decent record in the race. (op 7-4 tchd 13-8)
St Moritz(IRE) unsurprisingly dictated the pace and gave his all, but it was clear 1f out conceding 4lb to a rival rated 3lb his superior was beyond him. He has been a credit to his current yard and remains in decent form. (op 11-10 tchd 5-4)
Off Chance likes it here and looked a player turning for home. She was found out when the winner kicked for home, but would have been second had she not been hampered on the rail late on. (op 4-1)

4369 TYREGIANT.COM H'CAP 6f
4:25 (4:26) (Class 3) (0-90,90) 3-Y-O+
£7,158 (£2,143; £1,071; £535; £267; £134) **Stalls** Low

Form RPR
2125 **1** **Grissom (IRE)**[15] 3850 5-9-4 **82**... DavidAllan 9 95
(Tim Easterby) *w ldrs: chal over 1f out: kpt on to ld towards fin* **13/2**[3]
-004 **2** *nk* **Zero Money (IRE)**[23] 3578 5-9-10 **88**.............................(b) SteveDrowne 1 100
(Roger Charlton) *sn led: rdn over 1f out: hdd nr fin* **5/1**[1]
2436 **3** *1½* **Internationaldebut (IRE)**[50] 2706 6-9-9 **87**....................... TonyCulhane 2 94
(Paul Midgley) *s.i.s: hdwy on ins over 2f out: chsng ldng pair over 1f out: kpt on same pce ins fnl f* **11/2**[2]
10 **4** *4½* **Marvellous Value (IRE)**[29] 3395 6-9-7 **85**........................ TedDurcan 8 78
(Michael Dods) *mid-div: effrt on inner over 2f out: kpt on fnl f* **16/1**
-652 **5** *½* **Cornus**[9] 4078 9-8-8 **75**...(be) PaulPickard(3) 4 66
(Alan McCabe) *mid-div: hdwy 2f out: kpt on fnl f* **12/1**
5056 **6** *1* **Shifting Star (IRE)**[17] 3784 6-9-2 **80**............................(v[1]) MickyFenton 3 68
(Walter Swinburn) *chsd ldrs: one pce fnl 2f* **12/1**
[illegible] **7** [illegible] **Misplaced Fortune**[70] [illegible] [illegible]...................... SilvestreDeSousa 15 69+
(Nigel Tinkler) *in rr: swtchd rt over 1f out: kpt on: nvr nr ldrs* **10/1**
0240 **8** *¾* **Oldjoesaid**[22] 3613 7-9-5 **83**.. PhillipMakin 10 64
(Kevin Ryan) *chsd ldrs: wknd over 1f out* **20/1**
0-03 **9** *¾* **Bonnie Charlie**[51] 2668 5-9-3 **81**...................................... AdrianNicholls 16 59
(David Nicholls) *in rr whn swtchd lft after s: sme hdwy 2f out: nvr a factor* **16/1**
0142 **10** *1¼* **Klynch**[19] 3704 5-9-9 **87**..(b) JamesSullivan 11 61
(Ruth Carr) *in rr: effrt on outside over 2f out: nvr a factor* **11/1**
-000 **11** *½* **Amenable (IRE)**[29] 3395 4-9-6 **84**................................... AndrewMullen 12 57
(David Nicholls) *led early: w ldrs: wknd 2f out* **25/1**
2502 **12** *1½* **Stevie Gee (IRE)**[31] 3322 7-8-8 **75**................................... RyanClark(3) 17 43
(Ian Williams) *chsd ldrs on outer: wknd 2f out* **14/1**
0000 **13** *nk* **Barney McGrew (IRE)**[22] 3627 8-9-12 **90**...................... TonyHamilton 14 57
(Michael Dods) *in rr whn swtchd lft sn after s: hmpd over 1f out: nvr on terms* **20/1**
0000 **14** *3¼* **Olynard (IRE)**[16] 3796 5-8-10 **74**.......................................(b[1]) MartinLane 7 31
(Dr Richard Newland) *chsd ldrs: wknd over 2f out: in rr whn hung lft over 1f out* **22/1**
5011 **15** *1* **Orpsie Boy (IRE)**[17] 3784 8-9-5 **88**.................................... LMcNiff(5) 13 41
(Ruth Carr) *chsd ldrs on outer: effrt over 2f out: sn lost pl and bhd* **8/1**

1m 14.86s (-2.04) **Going Correction** -0.15s/f (Firm) **15** Ran SP% **125.5**
Speed ratings (Par 107): **107,106,104,98,97 96,94,93,92,90 90,88,87,83,82**
toteswingers:1&2:£8.30, 1&3:£7.00, 2&3:£6.60 CSF £38.04 CT £202.57 TOTE £8.20: £2.40, £2.40, £2.80; EX 39.40.
Owner Jim & Helen Bowers **Bred** Michael McGlynn **Trained** Great Habton, N Yorks

FOCUS
A good sprint handicap, but once again racing handily was a must. The third sets the level.

NOTEBOOK
Grissom(IRE) from a stable in hot form, helped force the pace and saw it out strongly inside the final furlong, landing some decent bets. This was his highest winning mark to date and so it rates a personal-best effort. He had yet to win on a genuinely quick surface just looked to be feeling the ground somewhat late on, so could well build on this when getting some cut underfoot again. (op 17-2)
Zero Money(IRE), awash with sweat, had the plum draw and he too cut out the early fractions. He pushed the winner all the way to the line, but ultimately giving that rival 6lb proved too much. He looks weighted to his best, but certainly deserves to go one better. (op 13-2)
Internationaldebut(IRE) fared best of those coming from off the pace and, not for the first time, ran an eye-catching race. He is a fiendishly difficult horse to actually win with, however. (op 13-2 tchd 5-1)

Marvellous Value(IRE) showed his Newcastle flop last time to be all wrong and returned to the sort of form that saw him winning at that venue back in May. He just looks held by the handicapper.
Stevie Gee(IRE), last year's winner, was 4lb higher and drawn out of making a serious bid this time around. (op 12-1)
Orpsie Boy(IRE) was another 4lb higher in this quest for the hat-trick and ultimately ran no sort of race.

4370 KEEPMOAT DELIVERING COMMUNITY REGENERATION MAIDEN STKS — 1m 4y
5:00 (5:02) (Class 5) 3-4-Y-O — **£2,587** (£770; £384; £192) **Stalls** Low

Form — RPR

2- **1** **Nordic Sky (USA)**[312] 6092 3-9-3 0 ... PhillipMakin 2 — 85
(William Haggas) *trckd ldrs: chal over 2f out: led 1f out: hld on towards fin* **6/5**[1]

04 **2** *nk* **Eastern Breeze (IRE)**[28] 3437 3-8-12 0 ... TedDurcan 4 — 80
(Saeed Bin Suroor) *hld up: hdwy to trck ldrs over 2f out: chal over 1f out: no ex towards fin* **4/1**[2]

3 *1 3/4* **Lady Sledmere (IRE)** 3-8-12 0 ... MickyFenton 7 — 76+
(Paul Midgley) *s.i.s: hdwy on inner over 2f out: chsng ldrs whn nt clr run 1f out: kpt on* **66/1**

66 **4** *2 1/2* **Come Here Yew (IRE)**[24] 3543 3-9-3 0 ... DavidAllan 3 — 75
(Declan Carroll) *mde most: hdd 1f out: grad wknd* **14/1**

2 **5** *1/2* **Eagle Rock (IRE)**[20] 3684 3-9-3 0 ... AndrewMullen 5 — 74
(Tom Tate) *mid-div: drvn and outpcd over 2f out: kpt on fnl f* **12/1**

4 **6** *16* **Ecossaise**[10] 4023 3-8-12 0 ... SilvestreDeSousa 6 — 32
(Mark Johnston) *sn trcking ldrs: wknd over 1f out* **7/1**

7 *5* **Wings Of Apollo (IRE)**[86] 1662 3-9-0 0 ... SimonPearce(3) 8 — 26
(Mrs K Burke) *s.i.s: sme hdwy over 1f out: nvr on terms* **33/1**

55-6 **8** *3 1/2* **Penderyn**[89] 1592 4-8-13 43 ... CharlesBishop(7) 9 — —
(Charles Smith) *w ldrs: wknd over 2f out* **100/1**

00- **9** *hd* **Bavarian Princess (USA)**[325] 5692 3-8-12 0 ... KellyHarrison 13 — —
(Mrs K Burke) *s.i.s: t.k.h in rr: nvr on terms* **33/1**

0 **10** *9* **Meshfi**[16] 3824 3-8-10 0 ... AntiocoMurgia(7) 10 — —
(Clive Brittain) *s.i.s: in rr: mid-div after 2f: lost pl over 2f out* **33/1**

-643 **11** *3 1/2* **Chokidar (IRE)**[9] 4062 3-9-0 73 ... BillyCray(3) 12 — —
(David Nicholls) *chsd ldrs: lost pl over 2f out* **13/2**[3]

12 *65* **Pronounce** 3-9-3 0 ... NeilChalmers 11 — —
(Michael Appleby) *s.i.s: sn trcking ldrs on outside: wknd over 3f out: t.o and virtually p.u 2f out* **40/1**

1m 44.33s (-1.57) **Going Correction** -0.15s/f (Firm)
WFA 3 from 4yo 8lb — 12 Ran SP% **119.4**
Speed ratings (Par 103): **101,100,98,96,95 79,74,71,71,62 58,—**
toteswingers:1&2:£2.20, 1&3:£20.00, 2&3:£41.40 CSF £5.57 TOTE £2.10: £1.20, £2.10, £11.10; EX 6.80.
Owner Paddy Twomey **Bred** Hawthorn Villa Stud **Trained** Newmarket, Suffolk

FOCUS
Little strength in depth here, but the first five came a long way clear in a fair time. The winner probably didn't match her 2yo debut form.
Chokidar(IRE) Official explanation: jockey said gelding moved poorly

4371 MOOR TOP FARM SHOP HEMSWORTH H'CAP — 5f
5:30 (5:31) (Class 5) (0-70,69) 3-Y-O+ — **£2,587** (£770; £384; £192) **Stalls** Low

Form — RPR

521 **1** **Port Ronan (USA)**[12] 3931 5-8-10 **53** ... (p) BarryMcHugh 5 — 62
(John Wainwright) *in rr-div: hdwy over 2f out: styd on to ld nr fin: jst hld on* **11/2**[3]

6406 **2** *nk* **Mr Wolf**[9] 4078 10-9-12 **69** ... (p) TonyHamilton 9 — 77
(John Quinn) *broke smartly: led and sn crossed over to rail: kicked 2 l clr over 1f out: hdd and no ex nr fin* **5/1**[2]

6203 **3** *nk* **Desert Strike**[2] 4289 5-9-4 **68** ... (p) RyanTate(7) 4 — 75
(Alan McCabe) *s.i.s: hld up in rr: hdwy over 1f out: str run ins fnl f: jst hld* **8/1**

5431 **4** *1 1/2* **Sleepy Blue Ocean**[26] 3493 5-9-12 **69** ... (p) MartinLane 3 — 71+
(John Balding) *chsd ldrs: kpt on same pce ins fnl f* **9/2**[1]

6000 **5** *1* **Besty**[9] 4078 4-9-8 **65** ... AndrewMullen 1 — 63
(David Nicholls) *s.i.s: sn trcking ldrs: wnt 2nd over 2f out: one pce fnl f* **8/1**

0440 **6** *2 1/4* **King Of Swords (IRE)**[10] 4000 7-8-7 **50** oh1 ... (p) SilvestreDeSousa 7 — 40
(Nigel Tinkler) *chsd ldrs: outpcd over 2f out: kpt on one pce fnl f* **11/2**[3]

5030 **7** *1 1/2* **Silvanus (IRE)**[23] 3573 6-9-8 **65** ... MickyFenton 6 — 49
(Paul Midgley) *mid-div: rdn and hung lft over 1f out: nvr a factor* **10/1**

5140 **8** *shd* **Mandurah (IRE)**[70] 2126 7-9-11 **68** ... AdrianNicholls 2 — 52
(David Nicholls) *chsd ldr: wknd appr fnl f* **7/1**

0602 **9** *1 3/4* **Commander Wish**[12] 3931 8-8-6 **56** ... NoelGarbutt(7) 11 — 34
(Lucinda Featherstone) *stmbld s: sme hdwy on outer over 1f out: edgd lft and sn wknd* **18/1**

000 **10** *14* **Gala Spirit (IRE)**[40] 3027 4-8-12 **55** ... WilliamCarson 8 — —
(Michael Wigham) *mid-div: lost pl over 2f out: bhd and eased 1f out* **25/1**

63.33 secs (0.03) **Going Correction** -0.15s/f (Firm) — 10 Ran SP% **118.5**
Speed ratings (Par 103): **93,92,92,89,88 84,82,81,79,56**
toteswingers:1&2:£7.20, 1&3:£10.10, 2&3:£6.60. CSF £33.79 CT £227.63 TOTE £4.60: £2.00, £2.20, £2.50; EX 26.70.
Owner D R & E E Brown **Bred** Dr And Mrs M L Brosnan **Trained** Kennythorpe, N Yorks

FOCUS
A moderate sprint handicap and yet again it suited those racing near the pace. Improved form from the winner, and the second's best run since last summer.
T/Jkpt: Not won. T/Plt: £5,068.80 to a £1 stake. Pool:£73,949.34 - 10.65 winning tickets T/Qpdt: £158.20 to a £1 stake. Pool:£5,068.58 - 23.70 winning tickets WG

3007 COLOGNE (R-H)
Sunday, July 24

OFFICIAL GOING: Turf: soft

4372a OPPENHEIM-RENNEN (LISTED RACE) (2YO) (TURF) — 7f
3:55 (4:13) 2-Y-O — **£11,206** (£3,448; £1,724; £862)

RPR

1 **Amaron** 2-8-11 0 ... AHelfenbein 6 — 91
(Andreas Lowe, Germany) **27/10**[2]

2 *1 1/4* **Percy Jackson**[23] 3595 2-9-2 0 ... JohnFahy 5 — 93
(Denis Coakley) *disp ld on outside: hdd over 2 1/2f out but remained cl 2nd: led 1 1/2f out: r.o u.p: hdd 110yds out: no ex cl home* **21/10**[1]

3 *1* **Amarillo (IRE)**[15] 2-9-2 0 ... JiriPalik 7 — 90
(P Schiergen, Germany) **39/10**

4 *hd* **Basantee**[30] 3345 2-8-8 0 ... SHellyn 3 — 82
(Tom Dascombe) *disp ld on rail: led over 2 1/2f out: sn rdn: hdd 1 1/2f out: kpt on tl nt qckn ins fnl f: lost 3rd cl home* **168/10**

5 *6* **Viola D'Amour (IRE)**[46] 2811 2-8-13 0 ... RichardKingscote 1 — 71
(Tom Dascombe) *racd in share of 3rd on rail: rdn and wknd fr over 1f out* **58/10**

6 *2 1/2* **Sun Of Jamaica** 2-8-13 0 ... THellier 2 — 65
(Mario Hofer, Germany) **7/2**[3]

7 *4 1/2* **Miss Coral (GER)** 2-8-13 0 ... HenkGrewe 4 — 53
(H-W Hiller, Germany) **109/10**

1m 29.5s (89.50) — 7 Ran SP% **130.6**
PARI-MUTUEL (all including 10 euro stakes): WIN 37; PLACE 15, 14, 14; SF 186.
Owner Gestut Winterhauch **Bred** Genesis Green Stud Ltd **Trained** Germany

NOTEBOOK
Percy Jackson, an 8l winner at Warwick last time, had softer ground to deal with this time and couldn't hold off the well-bred winner, who was making his racecourse debut.
Basantee faced a stiffer task in this company and didn't run badly in the circumstances.
Viola D'Amour(IRE) looked a promising sort when scoring on her debut at Haydock, but was a little disappointing on this step up in class against the colts.

2981 HOPPEGARTEN (R-H)
Sunday, July 24

OFFICIAL GOING: Turf: good

4373a INTERNATIONALES SUPER-HANDICAP (3YO+) (TURF) — 1m 1f
2:30 (2:43) 3-Y-O+
£34,482 (£15,517; £8,620; £5,172; £3,017; £2,155)

RPR

1 **Point Blank (GER)**[22] 3-8-0 **0** ... StefanieHofer 5 — 98
(Mario Hofer, Germany) **218/10**

2 *3/4* **Empire Storm (GER)**[21] 4-9-4 **0** ... EPedroza 2 — 106
(A Wohler, Germany) **29/10**[2]

3 *3/4* **Combat Zone (IRE)**[21] 5-8-10 **0** ... TomQueally 1 — 96
(Mario Hofer, Germany) **61/10**[3]

4 *2 1/2* **Lyssio (GER)**[14] 4-8-11 **0** ... AStarke 6 — 92
(P Schiergen, Germany) **89/10**

5 *1/2* **Freminius (GER)**[22] 7-8-5 **0** ... DominiqueBoeuf 3 — 85
(W Baltromei, Germany) **124/10**

6 *1/2* **Neatico (GER)**[29] 3422 4-9-5 **0** ... MaximeGuyon 8 — 98
(P Schiergen, Germany) **12/1**

7 *hd* **Indomito (GER)**[43] 5-9-0 **0** ... ASuborics 9 — 93
(A Wohler, Germany) **152/10**

8 *3/4* **Secrecy**[10] 4003 5-9-8 **0** ... MCadeddu 4 — 99
(Saeed Bin Suroor) *dwlt: racd in 7th running keenly: rdn 2 1/2f out: swtchd outside 2f out: nt pce to chal and n.d* **27/10**[1]

9 *1/2* **Amazing Beauty (GER)**[105] 1263 4-8-9 **0** ... EFrank 7 — 85
(M Figge, Germany) **36/1**

10 *2* **Wheredreamsare**[14] 4-8-8 **0** ... FilipMinarik 11 — 80
(W Figge, Germany) **43/5**

11 *1 1/4* **Beagle Boy (IRE)**[77] 4-8-2 **0** ow2 ... JBojko 12 — 71
(A Wohler, Germany) **28/1**

12 *7* **Zaungast (IRE)**[31] 3334 7-9-4 **0** ... APietsch 10 — 73
(W Hickst, Germany) **92/10**

1m 52.8s (112.80)
WFA 3 from 4yo+ 9lb — 12 Ran SP% **128.9**
PARI-MUTUEL (all including 10 euro stakes): WIN 228; PLACE 42, 15, 25; SF 1,016.
Owner Stall Antanando **Bred** F-P Von Auersperg & F Haffa **Trained** Germany

4374a GROSSER PREIS VON BERLIN (EX DEUTSCHLAND-PREIS) (GROUP 1) (3YO+) (TURF) — 1m 4f
3:40 (4:01) 3-Y-O+
£86,206 (£34,482; £17,241; £6,896; £3,879; £2,155)

RPR

1 **Danedream (GER)**[28] 3447 3-8-5 0 ... AStarke 7 — 119
(P Schiergen, Germany) *settled in midfield: 7th 5f out: hdwy on outside over 3f out: 3rd and styng on passing 2f marker: led ins fnl 300yds: sn rdn and qcknd clr fnl f: won gng away* **99/10**

2 *5* **Scalo**[42] 2982 4-9-6 0 ... MaximeGuyon 9 — 114
(A Wohler, Germany) *w.w towards rr: tk clsr order 5f out: 8th and pushed along 4f out: rdn 3f out: 8th and u.p 2 1/2f out: swtchd outside 2f out: styd on to take 2nd 75yds out: nrest at fin* **8/5**[1]

3 *nk* **Superstition (FR)**[28] 5-9-3 0 ... ASuborics 5 — 111
(Markus Klug, Germany) *racd in 5th: wnt 3rd appr 5f out: rdn and outpcd 2 1/2f out: styd on again ins fnl f to take 3rd cl home* **39/1**

4 *nse* **Night Magic (GER)**[49] 2749 5-9-3 0 ... FilipMinarik 2 — 111
(W Figge, Germany) *racd in 3rd running freely: qcknd on ins and led 5f out: rdn and one l up appr 2f out: hdd ins fnl 300yds: no ex last 100yds: lost two pls cl home* **59/10**

5 *hd* **Lucas Cranach (GER)**[28] 3446 4-9-6 0 ... (b) EFrank 6 — 114
(S Smrczek, Germany) *settled in last: stl last but swtchd outside and hdwy u.p ins fnl 2 1/2f: r.o fnl f: nvr nrr* **39/10**[2]

6 *3/4* **Sir Lando**[28] 3446 4-9-6 0 ... DominiqueBoeuf 3 — 112
(Wido Neuroth, Norway) *racd in 7th: rdn on ins 2 1/2f out: styd on ins fnl f: nt pce to chal* **28/1**

7 *1 1/2* **Dandino**[51] 2680 4-9-6 0 ... TomQueally 1 — 110
(James Given) *led after 1f: set stdy pce: hdd 5f out: remained 2nd: hrd rdn fr 2 1/2f out: 3rd and nt qckn 1f out: fdd fnl 100yds* **57/10**[3]

8 *4* **Solidaro (GER)**[28] 3446 4-9-6 0 ... MCadeddu 10 — 104
(J Hirschberger, Germany) *hld up towards rr: 9th and rdn 3f out: no imp* **43/1**

9 *nk* **Gereon (GER)**[21] 3672 3-8-8 0 ... EPedroza 4 — 103
(C Zschache, Germany) *racd in midfield: 6th 4f out: hdwy to chal for 3rd 2 1/2f out: sn rdn: wknd fnl 1 1/2f* **74/10**

10 *6* **Cavalryman**[29] 3403 5-9-6 0.. APietsch 8 94
(Saeed Bin Suroor) *dwlt and scrubbed along on outside to ld after 1f: sn hdd and settled in 2nd on outside of Dandino: dropped to 3rd 5f out: 4th and rdn 2 1/2f out: nt qckn fr 2f out: wknd fnl f* **84/10**

2m 33.5s (4.20)
WFA 3 from 4yo+ 12lb **10** Ran SP% **128.2**
PARI-MUTUEL (all including 10 euro stakes): WIN 109; PLACE 23, 14, 58; SF 314.
Owner Gestut Burg Eberstein **Bred** Gestut Brummerhof **Trained** Germany

FOCUS
It seems almost amazing that not one of the ten runners, mostly proven over the 1m4f trip, wanted to make this a test. Nothing fancied making the running, and this Group 1 turned into a sprint. Scalo, Lucas Cranach and Sir Lando should all have their efforts marked up.

NOTEBOOK
Danedream(GER), winner of the Italian Oaks and also placed in the Italian Derby, made full use of all of the allowances to win under a tactically astute ride. Supplemented for this race, she certainly had form good enough to be considered at Group 1 level, but was handed victory by some half asleep jockeys in behind. Winning trainer Peter Schiergen is now eyeing the Breeders' Cup Filly & Mare Turf for his filly. Her success also pays a handsome compliment to the progressive French filly Testosterone, who beat her last time in a Saint Cloud Group 2.
Scalo ◆ wasn't given the best of rides in the circumstances. Held up in what was a slowly run race, he passed six rivals once in the home straight but was never going to catch a lowly weighted, better positioned rival. It would be nice to see him go for the Arc, as at least he should have coniditons in his favour there (strongly run race, probably ease in the ground and long home straight). Connections really need to employ a pacemaker in the future to stop him being caught out.
Superstition(FR), who raced in third, had no obvious right to be finishing third in a Group 1, which only goes to show this result cannot be taken too seriously.
Night Magic(GER) is a solid marker in German Group races and her jockey finally gave up waiting for some pace at about halfway before kicking on into the lead. She merely set it up for others.
Lucas Cranach(GER) ◆'s jockey seemingly had no plan B, and remained in rear despite surely knowing the gallop wasn't strong enough to bring his mount's turn of foot into play. Nothing was finishing faster than him in the final furlong, and he is clearly up to Group 1 class.
Sir Lando was a bit unlucky not to finish closer as he was staying on well when short of room deep inside the final furlong. He looks the type that would do well across Europe in staying contests if connections ever took that route.
Dandino was left in the lead early before Night Magic went on, setting ordinary fractions. However, once given a lead he found only the one pace and probably didn't enjoy the sprint finish.
Cavalryman had every chance turning in but found nothing.

4120 MAISONS-LAFFITTE (R-H)
Sunday, July 24
OFFICIAL GOING: Turf: good to soft

4375a PRIX ROBERT PAPIN (GROUP 2) (2YO COLTS & FILLIES) (TURF) 5f 110y
1:30 (12:00) 2-Y-O **£63,879** (£24,655; £11,767; £7,844; £3,922)

RPR
1 **Family One (FR)**[21] 3669 2-9-2 0................................ IoritzMendizabal 1 108+
(Y Barberot, France) *trckd ldr: smooth prog to ld ins fnl f: pushed clr: comf* **5/6**[1]
2 *3* **Louve Rouge (FR)**[5] 4191 2-8-13 0................................ JohanVictoire 2 91
(C Boutin, France) *racd in last pl: hdwy over 2f out: chal on outside 1 1/2f out: led briefly 1f out: kpt on wout qckning fnl f: no ch w wnr* **12/1**
3 *snk* **Mac Row (IRE)**[51] 2-9-2 0.......................... Christophe-PatriceLemaire 5 93
(J-C Rouget, France) *reluctant to enter stalls: rrd and uns jockey: settled in 3rd: prog to press ldr 2 1/2f out: sn rdn: nt qckn fnl f* **5/2**[2]
4 *nse* **Bear Behind (IRE)**[23] 3589 2-9-2 0................................ WilliamBuick 4 93
(Tom Dascombe) *qckly away and led: rdn: outpcd and hdd 1f out: keeping on again cl home* **13/2**[3]
5 *2* **Kapitala (FR)**[45] 2-8-13 0.. DavyBonilla 3 83
(Andreas Lowe, Germany) *racd in 4th: rdn and rn green 2f out: kpt on wout qckning fnl f* **14/1**

67.20 secs (-0.10) **5** Ran SP% **110.8**
WIN (incl. 1 euro stake): 1.60. PLACES: 1.20, 2.00. SF: 8.10, CSF: 11.85.
Owner [illegible] **Bred** [illegible] **Trained** [illegible]

FOCUS
A weak renewal and the winner did not need to match his latest Group 3 form.

NOTEBOOK
Family One(FR) was always travelling well in behind the leader and, when asked to quicken, the response was immediate and he stretched clear to win easily. This was an impressive performance, although the form in behind isn't anything special, and he fully deserves to take his chance at the top level in the Prix Morny. (op evens)
Bear Behind(IRE), who faced a stiff task up in class, made the running but the impressive winner was always cruising in behind him and he was quickly put in his place when that one went on. (op 6-1)

4376a PRIX EUGENE ADAM (GRAND PRIX DE MAISONS-LAFFITTE) (GROUP 2) (3YO) (TURF) 1m 2f (S)
2:40 (12:00) 3-Y-O **£63,879** (£24,655; £11,767; £7,844; £3,922)

RPR
1 **Pisco Sour (USA)**[38] 3068 3-8-11 0.............................. JimmyFortune 1 112
(Hughie Morrison) *broke wl and led on ins rail: set stdy pce: qcknd ins fnl 3f: pushed along appr 2f out: r.o wl u.p fnl f: hld on wl cl home* **15/2**[3]
2 *3/4* **Glaswegian**[49] 2751 3-8-11 0.............................. StephanePasquier 8 111
(P Bary, France) *settled in 7th: hdwy on outside ins fnl 2f: r.o u.p fnl f: nrest at fin* **8/1**
3 *hd* **Colombian (IRE)**[49] 2751 3-8-11 0.............................. WilliamBuick 2 110
(John Gosden) *trckd ldr on rail in share of 3rd: travelling wl but no room to chal fr 1 1/2f out: moved off rail and bk ins bef gap appeared outside wnr 1f out: r.o ins fnl f* **5/2**[2]
4 *3/4* **Slow Pace (USA)**[22] 3653 3-8-11 0.............................. OlivierPeslier 4 109
(F Head, France) *trckd ldr on outside: chal ldr over 1 1/2f out: got cl w Colombian: sn rdn and nt qckn ins fnl f: short of room cl home* **12/1**
5 *hd* **Cool Dude (FR)**[39] 3-8-11 0.............................. JohanVictoire 7 108
(Mme C Head-Maarek, France) *w.w in rr: last and swtchd outside 1 1/2f out: styd on u.p: nvr plcd to chal* **12/1**
6 *1 1/2* **Valiyr (IRE)**[22] 3653 3-8-11 0.......................... Christophe-PatriceLemaire 3 105
(A De Royer-Dupre, France) *settled 6th: swtchd outside and rdn 1 1/2f out: nt qckn fnl f* **2/1**[1]
7 *nse* **Barocci (JPN)**[42] 2978 3-8-11 0.............................. AnthonyCrastus 6 105
(E Lellouche, France) *racd in share of 4th on rail: 4th and ev ch whn shkn up 1 1/2f out: sn nowhere to go and jockey stopped riding for a few strides as Colombian and Slow Pace edgd ins: sn rdn and no imp fnl 150yds* **14/1**
8 *1 1/2* **Absolutly Yes (FR)**[22] 3653 3-8-11 0.............................. FabienLefebvre 5 102
(Y-M Porzier, France) *racd in share of 3rd on outside of Colombian: rdn 1 1/2f out: nt qckn: fdd ins fnl f* **12/1**

2m 6.30s (3.90) **8** Ran SP% **114.5**
WIN (incl. 1 euro stake): 9.30. PLACES: 2.90, 2.30, 2.30. DF: 25.20. SF: 87.00 CSF: 65.22.
Owner Michael Kerr-Dineen **Bred** Hascombe Stud **Trained** East Ilsley, Berks

NOTEBOOK
Pisco Sour(USA) was given a fine, tactical front-running ride by Jimmy Fortune, so whether this will be a reliable guide in the future is debatable. That said, the horse has been really progressive this year and deserved to win a race of this nature after a solid performance at Royal Ascot, form that had already worked out. Connections revealed before the race that their horse is a rig, so intend operating on him over the winter to put that right, which should improve him again on whatever he does this season.
Glaswegian had been comfortably held in two French Classics but showed some of his earlier sparkle with a good staying-on effort after being held up.
Colombian(IRE) ◆, given a break since his fine fourth in the French Derby, looked a bit unlucky, as he didn't have a lot of room to manoeuvre when his jockey wanted to quicken after tracking Pisco Sour towards the rail. One would imagine that there's still more to come from him and he's capable of winning at this level at least.
Slow Pace(USA) sat just behind the winner but didn't have his acceleration when the pace quickened. He did at least reverse form with both Valiyr and Absolutly Yes on their clash last time at Longchamp.
Valiyr(IRE) was still open to improvement, despite being beaten by what looked to be his own pacemaker last time in a Group 3, but he failed by a long way to find what some thought he must have been capable of.
Barocci(JPN) made stealthy ground up the rail but almost predictably found trouble in a race that was run at uneven fractions. He didn't find a lot when out in the clear and may not be the most straightforward.

4140 AYR (L-H)
Monday, July 25
OFFICIAL GOING: Good to firm (9.3)
Wind: Breezy, half against Weather: Cloudy, bright

4377 BODOG BACKS AYR UNITED MEDIAN AUCTION MAIDEN STKS 6f
2:30 (2:30) (Class 5) 2-Y-O **£2,328** (£693; £346; £173) **Stalls** Centre

Form RPR
1 **Cafe Express (IRE)** 2-8-12 0.................................... TonyHamilton 1 75+
(Linda Perratt) *dwlt and wnt lft s: hld up in tch: effrt and hdwy 2f out: led ins fnl f: kpt on wl* **40/1**
4 2 *2* **Samba Night (IRE)**[20] 3707 2-9-3 0.............................. RichardMullen 2 74
(Ed McMahon) *led: rdn 2f out: hdd ins fnl f: kpt on* **9/2**[3]
2 3 *1/2* **Star City (IRE)**[23] 3618 2-9-3 0.............................. FrederikTylicki 4 72
(Michael Dods) *dwlt: sn chsng ldrs: effrt and rdn 2f out: kpt on same pce ins fnl f* **11/8**[1]
4 *7* **My Pearl (IRE)** 2-9-3 0.. PhillipMakin 5 50+
(Kevin Ryan) *green and coltish in preliminaries: sn prom: effrt and rn green 2f out: sn outpcd: bttr for r* **5/1**
04 5 *9* **Well Wishes**[16] 3855 2-8-12 0.................................... TomEaves 7 16
(Bryan Smart) *hld up: rdn and outpcd wl over 2f out: sn btn* **20/1**
0 6 *11* **Sonsie Lass**[32] 3314 2-8-12 0.............................. SilvestreDeSousa 6 —
(Mark Johnston) *t.k.h: prom tl rdn and wknd fr 2f out* **5/2**[2]
66 7 *8* **Professor Tim (IRE)**[20] 3707 2-9-3 0.............................. DanielTudhope 3 —
(Patrick Morris) *cl up: drvn and outpcd 1/2-way: sn btn* **150/1**

1m 13.87s (1.47) **Going Correction** -0.075s/f (Good) **7** Ran SP% **113.4**
Speed ratings (Par 94): **95,92,91,82,70 55,45**
toteswingers:1&2:£9.90, 2&3:£2.30, 1&3:£9.50 CSF £204.96 TOTE £30.40: £11.40, £3.50; EX 188.20.
Owner Mrs Seamus Burns **Bred** Lodge Park Stud **Trained** East Kilbride, S Lanarks

FOCUS
Back straight out 4m, home bend out 6m, and home straight out 10m from innermost line adding [illegible] a shock result and the field finished well spread out. The form is rated around the second and third.

NOTEBOOK
Cafe Express(IRE), whose trainer had a 40-1 winner at this track seven days earlier, repeated the feat here. A £5,000 half-sister to a couple of winners at up to 1m, she was slowly away and looked green early, but she got stronger as the race progressed and there was no fluke in the way she picked off her rivals and won going away. This was the stable's first 2-y-o winner in seven years and its first winning juvenile debutant in over ten years. (op 33-1)
Samba Night(IRE) looked green when fourth of six (just behind a subsequent winner) on his Southwell debut. He looked more professional here and tried to make every yard, but found the winner too good late on. He can win a race, but doesn't look anything special. (op 4-1 tchd 5-1)
Star City(IRE) raced green and met trouble in running when just beaten on his Carlisle debut, but although he had every chance here he was making hard work of it from over 2f and looked one-paced. This wasn't a step forwards. (op 6-4, tchd 13-8 in a place)
My Pearl(IRE), a £32,000 half-brother to three winners at up to 1m including Izmail and Bolodenka, showed up early but started to hang over 2f from home and was completely left behind by the leading trio. (op 7-2 tchd 3-1)
Sonsie Lass, who didn't get home over this trip on her Newcastle debut, attracted good market support but she came under strong pressure over 2f from home and fell in a hole. (op 5-1)

4378 SPORTEVENTAYRSHIRE.COM H'CAP (QUALIFIER FOR THE BETFAIR BONUS SCOTTISH RACING SPRINT FINAL) 6f
3:00 (3:01) (Class 5) (0-75,75) 3-Y-O+ **£4,204** (£1,251; £625; £312) **Stalls** Centre

Form RPR
4212 1 **Royal Blade (IRE)**[3] 4289 4-8-2 **56** 6ex oh1.................... JulieBurke(5) 6 68
(Alan Berry) *cl up: led over 2f out: rdn out ins fnl f* **9/2**[3]
3232 2 *1 1/2* **Beckermet (IRE)**[7] 4145 9-9-4 **67**.................................... PJMcDonald 7 74
(Ruth Carr) *prom: effrt over 2f out: chsd wnr ins fnl f kpt on* **3/1**[2]
0013 3 *1/2* **Weetentherty**[10] 4041 4-8-4 **56** oh6.....................(p) DeclanCannon(3) 9 61?
(Linda Perratt) *dwlt: hld up: hdwy to chse wnr over 1f out to fnl f: r.o* **20/1**
0063 4 *1 1/4* **Chambers (IRE)**[10] 4078 5-8-7 **56** oh1.................................... DavidAllan 5 57
(Eric Alston) *hld up: effrt and hdwy 2f out: kpt on fnl f: no imp* **10/1**
5524 5 *1/2* **North Central (USA)**[14] 3903 4-9-3 **66**....................(p) DanielTudhope 1 66
(Jim Goldie) *racd alone far side: cl up tl rdn and one pce appr fnl f* **9/1**
4300 6 *12* **Distant Sun (USA)**[28] 3451 7-8-7 **56** oh3..............(p) SilvestreDeSousa 3 17
(Linda Perratt) *prom: rdn over 2f out: sn wknd* **33/1**
00/- 7 *4* **Speed Dream (IRE)**[9] 4118 7-9-12 **75**.................................... PBBeggy 2 24
(Daniel Mark Loughnane, Ire) *hld up: hdwy on outside of gp over 2f out: wknd wl over 1f out* **25/1**

0-11 **8** 1 **Questionnaire (IRE)**[30] 3412 3-9-5 **73**.............................. LukeMorris 4 18
(Nicky Vaughan) *led: rdn and hdd over 2f out: sn lost pl and struggling: eased whn no ch* **9/4**[1]

3126 **9** 1 3/4 **Apache Ridge (IRE)**[31] 3359 5-9-12 **75**.........................(p) PhillipMakin 8 15
(Keith Dalgleish) *trckd ldrs: rdn over 2f out: wknd qckly wl over 1f out* **11/2**

1m 12.6s (0.20) **Going Correction** -0.075s/f (Good)
WFA 3 from 4yo+ 5lb **9** Ran SP% **120.0**
Speed ratings (Par 103): **103,101,100,98,98 82,76,75,73**
toteswingers:1&2:£2.50, 2&3:£9.30, 1&3:£7.80 CSF £18.79 CT £250.68 TOTE £6.10: £1.70, £1.90, £2.80; EX 17.90 Trifecta £410.70 Part won. Pool of £555.11 - 0.83 winning units..
Owner A B Parr **Bred** Miss Sarah Sands **Trained** Cockerham, Lancs
■ Stewards' Enquiry : Daniel Tudhope one-day ban: did not ride to draw (Aug 8)

FOCUS
A modest sprint handicap.
North Central(USA) Official explanation: jockey said, regarding appearing to drop hands before win post, that he felt he had already been past and the gelding was tired.
Questionnaire(IRE) Official explanation: jockey said filly hung right-handed throughout and lost right front shoe
Apache Ridge(IRE) Official explanation: trainer said gelding finished distressed

4379 WEDDINGS AT WESTERN HOUSE HOTEL H'CAP (QUALIFIER FOR BETFAIR BONUS SCOTTISH RACING MILE FINAL) 7f 50y
3:30 (3:30) (Class 6) (0-60,60) 3-Y-0+ **£2,587** (£770; £384; £192) **Stalls** High

Form RPR
2402 **1** **Dhhamaan (IRE)**[7] 4141 6-9-10 **58**..............................(b) PJMcDonald 12 70
(Ruth Carr) *mde all: qcknd 2f out: kpt on wl* **7/2**[1]

0046 **2** nk **Burnwynd Boy**[7] 4145 6-9-2 **57**.............................. GarryWhillans(7) 11 68
(Ian Semple) *hld up: stdy hdwy over 2f out: hdwy over 1f out: edgd lft and styd on wl ins fnl f* **7/1**[3]

-050 **3** 1 3/4 **Monsieur Pontaven**[38] 3142 4-9-3 **51**..........................(b) LeeNewman 8 57
(Robin Bastiman) *towards rr: pushed along after 3f: hdwy 2f out: kpt on ins fnl f* **16/1**

2654 **4** shd **Hansomis (IRE)**[14] 3902 7-9-2 **53**.............................. LeeTopliss(3) 5 59
(Bruce Mactaggart) *in tch: rdn over 2f out: hdwy over 1f out: kpt on same pce ins fnl f* **12/1**

45-0 **5** 1 3/4 **Benny The Bear**[7] 4141 4-9-7 **55**.............................. PhillipMakin 1 56
(Linda Perratt) *t.k.h in midfield: rdn over 2f out: styd on fnl f: no imp* **16/1**

-605 **6** 3/4 **Broughtons Silk**[7] 4143 6-8-12 **46** oh1.............................. TonyHamilton 3 45
(Alistair Whillans) *midfield: hdwy on ins over 1f out: kpt on same pce ins fnl f* **25/1**

7 2 **Charismas Birthday (IRE)**[16] 3882 3-8-11 **52**.................. PBBeggy 13 43
(Daniel Mark Loughnane, Ire) *prom tl rdn and outpcd wl over 1f out* **12/1**

413 **8** 1/2 **Viking Warrior (IRE)**[19] 3733 4-9-12 **60**...................... FrederikTylicki 10 52
(Michael Dods) *t.k.h: cl up tl wknd over 1f out* **6/1**[2]

5101 **9** shd **Drive Home (USA)**[14] 3903 4-9-11 **59**......................(p) DuranFentiman 2 51
(Noel Wilson) *t.k.h: cl up: rdn over 2f out: wknd over 1f out* **7/2**[1]

0050 **10** 2 **Rosbertini**[7] 4143 5-8-12 **46** oh1.............................. BarryMcHugh 9 33
(Linda Perratt) *dwlt: hld up: rdn over 2f out: nvr able to chal* **40/1**

0006 **11** 3/4 **Classlin**[7] 4144 4-8-12 **46** oh1.............................. DanielTudhope 7 31
(Jim Goldie) *hld up: rdn over 2f out: nvr on terms* **50/1**

6346 **12** shd **Machir Bay**[14] 3905 4-8-12 **46** oh1..............................(p) TomEaves 4 30
(Keith Dalgleish) *hld up in midfield on outside: struggling over 2f out: sn btn* **8/1**

00-0 **13** 8 **Anthemion (IRE)**[14] 3903 14-8-12 **46** oh1.............................. DavidAllan 6 —
(Jean McGregor) *in tch tl rdn and wknd over 2f out* **80/1**

1m 31.99s (-1.41) **Going Correction** -0.175s/f (Firm)
WFA 3 from 4yo+ 7lb **13** Ran SP% **119.0**
Speed ratings (Par 101): **101,100,98,98,96 95,93,92,92,90 89,89,80**
toteswingers:1&2:£8.90, 2&3:£15.90, 1&3:£10.70 CSF £27.15 CT £351.95 TOTE £4.20: £2.50, £4.00, £4.30; EX 33.60 Trifecta £273.70 Part won. Pool of £369.93 - 0.30 winning units..
Owner S B Clark **Bred** D Veitch And Musagd Abo Salim **Trained** Huby, N Yorks

FOCUS
A moderate handicap and an all-the-way winner. The winner ran to a similar level as he did over C&D last week.

4380 OVERTONES LIVE ON LADIES NIGHT H'CAP (QUALIFIER FOR BETFAIR BONUS SCOTTISH RACING MILE FINAL) 1m 1f 20y
4:00 (4:01) (Class 5) (0-75,75) 3-Y-0+ **£4,204** (£1,251; £625; £312) **Stalls** Low

Form RPR
5-06 **1** **Mariners Lodge (USA)**[89] 1624 3-9-3 **73**................ SilvestreDeSousa 1 87+
(Mark Johnston) *t.k.h: trckd ldr: led over 2f out: clr over 1f out: eased towards fin* **3/1**[2]

0065 **2** 2 **High Resolution**[22] 3659 4-9-7 **75**.............................. ShaneBKelly(7) 2 79
(Linda Perratt) *hld up: hdwy on outside over 2f out: chsd (clr) wnr ins fnl f: r.o: no imp* **12/1**

4630 **3** hd **Royal Straight**[7] 4142 6-8-12 **64**.............................. JulieBurke(5) 5 68
(Linda Perratt) *hld up: hdwy over 2f out: chsd (clr) wnr over 1f out to ins fnl f: one pce* **12/1**

2123 **4** 1 1/2 **Petsas Pleasure**[21] 3683 5-8-12 **59**.............................. TonyHamilton 3 60
(Ollie Pears) *hld up in tch: nt clr run over 2f out: effrt and rdn wl over 1f out: no imp ins fnl f* **7/1**

3426 **5** 1 **Music Festival (USA)**[7] 4141 4-9-7 **68**........................ DanielTudhope 6 67
(Jim Goldie) *prom: effrt over 2f out: edgd lft and outpcd over 1f out* **13/2**[3]

3/-4 **6** 2 1/4 **All For You (IRE)**[14] 3905 5-9-0 **64**.............................. GaryBartley(3) 8 58
(Jim Goldie) *t.k.h: hld up: rdn over 2f out: nvr able to chal* **15/2**

0400 **7** 1 1/2 **The Galloping Shoe**[10] 4043 6-10-0 **75**.............................. PhillipMakin 7 65
(Ian Semple) *t.k.h: hld up: stdy hdwy and in tch over 3f out: wknd wl over 1f out* **22/1**

1 **8** 2 3/4 **William Haigh (IRE)**[76] 1974 3-9-5 **75**.............................. PJMcDonald 9 58
(Alan Swinbank) *led: rdn and hdd over 2f out: wknd over 1f out* **11/4**[1]

1405 **9** 3/4 **Khandaq (USA)**[38] 3113 4-9-12 **73**.............................. TomEaves 4 56
(Keith Dalgleish) *trckd ldrs: rdn over 2f out: wknd over 1f out* **10/1**

1m 58.35s (0.85) **Going Correction** -0.175s/f (Firm)
WFA 3 from 4yo+ 9lb **9** Ran SP% **118.1**
Speed ratings (Par 103): **89,87,87,85,84 82,81,79,78**
toteswingers:1&2:£9.90, 2&3:£16.20, 1&3:£15.80 CSF £39.72 CT £384.78 TOTE £4.70: £2.50, £4.00, £2.80; EX 63.50 Trifecta £629.90 Part won. Pool of £851.31 - 0.71 winning units..
Owner Sheikh Hamdan Bin Mohammed Al Maktoum **Bred** Overbrook Farm **Trained** Middleham Moor, N Yorks

FOCUS
An ordinary handicap, but the pace looked solid and the winner looks progressive. He was value for 4l+. The favourite disappointed.

William Haigh(IRE) Official explanation: trainer's rep had no explanation for the poor form shown

4381 GLASGOW PRESTWICK AIRPORT H'CAP (QUALIFIER FOR BETFAIR BONUS SCOTTISH RACING MILE FINAL) 1m 2f
4:30 (4:30) (Class 6) (0-65,65) 3-Y-O **£2,587** (£770; £384; £192) **Stalls** Low

Form RPR
6001 **1** **Cuckney Bear**[27] 3485 3-9-7 **65**.............................. RichardMullen 5 75+
(Ed McMahon) *trckd ldrs: effrt over 2f out: led over 1f out: drvn and kpt on wl ins fnl f* **6/4**[1]

4454 **2** 2 3/4 **Purkab**[6] 4175 3-8-10 **54**..............................(p) DanielTudhope 1 57
(Jim Goldie) *pressed ldr: led over 2f to 1f out: rallied: kpt on same pce ins fnl f* **11/2**

0- **3** 1/2 **Ashgrove Nell (IRE)**[40] 3060 3-8-11 **55**.............................. PBBeggy 6 57
(Daniel Mark Loughnane, Ire) *hld up in tch: rdn 3f out: effrt and edgd lft 2f out: kpt on fnl f: no imp* **13/2**

0036 **4** 2 1/2 **Henrys Gift (IRE)**[27] 3487 3-9-1 **59**.............................. FrederikTylicki 2 56
(Michael Dods) *t.k.h: trckd ldrs: drvn and outpcd over 2f out: sn btn* **5/1**[3]

5051 **5** 1 1/2 **Playful Girl (IRE)**[9] 4112 3-8-6 **50**..............................(b) DavidAllan 7 44
(Tim Easterby) *led at stdy pce: rdn and hdd over 2f out: wknd over 1f out* **10/3**[2]

2m 11.36s (-0.64) **Going Correction** -0.175s/f (Firm) **5** Ran SP% **108.5**
Speed ratings (Par 98): **95,92,92,90,89**
CSF £9.66 TOTE £2.40: £1.10, £3.70; EX 10.80.
Owner Premspace Ltd **Bred** D R Botterill **Trained** Lichfield, Staffs

FOCUS
A moderate handicap lacking strength in depth. The winner is unexposed and the runner-up sets the standard.

4382 JOCKEY CLUB RESTAURANT H'CAP (QUALIFIER BETFAIR BONUS SCOTTISH RACING STAYERS FINAL) 1m 5f 13y
5:00 (5:00) (Class 5) (0-75,75) 3-Y-0+ **£4,204** (£1,251; £625; £312) **Stalls** Low

Form RPR
4014 **1** **Jewelled Dagger (IRE)**[7] 4142 7-9-0 **66**.............................. TomEaves 6 74+
(Keith Dalgleish) *mde all: rdn over 2f out: hld on gamely ins fnl f* **15/2**

0603 **2** hd **Cat O' Nine Tails**[19] 3730 4-9-7 **73**.............................. SilvestreDeSousa 3 80
(Mark Johnston) *hld up towards rr: pushed along over 5f out: hdwy on ins to chse wnr over 1f out: kpt on ins fnl f: jst hld* **5/1**[3]

1412 **3** 1 **Odin's Raven (IRE)**[38] 3127 6-9-4 **75**.............................. BrianToomey(5) 4 80
(Brian Ellison) *hld up: hdwy over 2f out: effrt and edgd lft over 1f out: kpt on ins fnl f* **9/2**[2]

0-41 **4** hd **Forrest Flyer (IRE)**[22] 3660 7-9-4 **70**.............................. PhillipMakin 9 75
(Jim Goldie) *hld up: rdn 4f out: hdwy 2f out: styd on ins fnl f* **6/1**

26-3 **5** 3 **Boss's Destination**[47] 2810 4-9-7 **73**.............................. PJMcDonald 2 73
(Alan Swinbank) *prom: effrt 3f out: sn rdn: outpcd over 1f out: n.d after* **4/1**[1]

6420 **6** 2 1/4 **Mason Hindmarsh**[17] 3828 4-9-0 **66**.............................. FrederikTylicki 7 63
(Karen McLintock) *hld up in tch: rdn over 2f out: sn outpcd: n.d after* **6/1**

0060 **7** 1/2 **Wicked Daze (IRE)**[10] 4043 8-8-7 **66**.............................. ShaneBKelly(7) 5 62
(Linda Perratt) *chsd ldr to 1/2-way: cl up tl rdn and wknd over 1f out* **15/2**

0/0- **8** 6 **Strobe**[25] 2060 7-9-0 **66**..............................(p) BarryMcHugh 8 53
(Lucy Normile) *cl up: wnt 2nd 1/2-way to over 1f out: sn wknd* **50/1**

2m 53.09s (-0.91) **Going Correction** -0.175s/f (Firm) **8** Ran SP% **108.9**
Speed ratings (Par 103): **95,94,94,94,92 90,90,86**
toteswingers:1&2:£6.60, 2&3:£4.60, 1&3:£4.50 CSF £40.35 CT £169.91 TOTE £9.90: £2.40, £2.10, £1.40; EX 41.10 Trifecta £148.30 Pool: £825.68 - 4.12 winning units..
Owner A R M Galbraith **Bred** Ballyhane Stud **Trained** Carluke, South Lanarkshire
■ Stewards' Enquiry : Tom Eaves caution: used his whip with excessive frequency.

FOCUS
An ordinary handicap, but they went a decent pace from the off. The winner will still be potentially well treated on his old form.

4383 SCOTTISH RACING APPRENTICE H'CAP (QUALIFIER FOR THE BETFAIR SCOTTISH RACING MILE FINAL) 1m
5:30 (5:31) (Class 6) (0-60,59) 3-Y-0+ **£2,587** (£770; £384; £192) **Stalls** Low

Form RPR
-004 **1** **Military Call**[38] 3112 4-9-10 **58**..............................(p) JustinNewman(3) 5 66
(Alistair Whillans) *trckd ldr: led over 2f out: edgd lft and drvn out ins fnl f* **5/1**[3]

5456 **2** 3/4 **Jaldarshaan (IRE)**[16] 3859 4-10-0 **59**.............................. GarryWhillans 3 65
(Alan Swinbank) *t.k.h: in tch: hdwy to chse wnr over 1f out: kpt on u.p ins fnl f* **5/2**[1]

0000 **3** 1 1/4 **Cold Quest (USA)**[7] 4143 7-8-11 **47**.............................. RossSmith(5) 4 50
(Linda Perratt) *rrd and missed break: hld up in tch: hdwy on ins over 2f out: kpt on ins fnl f* **33/1**

0-60 **4** hd **Sheedal (IRE)**[7] 4142 3-8-4 **46** ow1.......................... GeorgeChaloner(3) 7 47
(Linda Perratt) *hld up in tch: effrt on outside 2f out: kpt on ins fnl f* **20/1**

6003 **5** 1/2 **Spread Boy (IRE)**[10] 4039 4-8-10 **46**.................. DavidSimmonson(5) 2 48
(Alan Berry) *prom: rdn and outpcd over 2f out: kpt on ins fnl f* **6/1**

-000 **6** 1/2 **Emeralds Spirit (IRE)**[58] 2487 4-9-13 **58**.............................. LMcNiff 1 58
(John Weymes) *trckd ldrs: nt clr run over 2f out: effrt over 1f out: no imp whn n.m.r ins fnl f* **7/1**

0060 **7** 2 1/2 **Pilgrim Dancer (IRE)**[17] 3806 4-9-11 **56**........................(b) DarylByrne 8 51
(Patrick Morris) *led: rdn and hdd over 2f out: outpcd whn n.m.r ins fnl f* **12/1**

0001 **8** 2 1/4 **Abernethy (IRE)**[7] 4143 3-8-12 **51** 6ex.............................. ShaneBKelly 6 38
(Linda Perratt) *hld up: rdn 3f out: wknd over 1f out* **10/3**[2]

1m 43.44s (-0.36) **Going Correction** -0.175s/f (Firm)
WFA 3 from 4yo+ 8lb **8** Ran SP% **110.5**
Speed ratings (Par 101): **94,93,92,91,91 90,88,86**
Tote Super 7: Win: £10,500 Place: £147.50 CSF £16.66 CT £343.47 TOTE £7.10: £2.00, £1.40, £4.80; EX 21.60 Trifecta £399.90 Part won. Pool of £540.42 - 0.84 winning units..
Owner Play Fair Partnership **Bred** Southill Stud **Trained** Newmill-On-Slitrig, Borders
■ Stewards' Enquiry : Garry Whillans three-day ban: careless riding (Aug 8-10)

FOCUS
A moderate apprentice handicap and not form to dwell on. The pace was uneven and it was a bit of a messy race.
T/Plt: £887.30 to a £1 stake. Pool of £61,746.43 - 50.80 winning tickets. T/Qpdt: £37.90 to a £1 stake. Pool of £5,613.28 - 109.40 winning tickets. RY

[4153]WINDSOR (R-H)

Monday, July 25

OFFICIAL GOING: Good (good to firm in places)

Wind: Light, behind Weather: Fine, warm

4384 BRITISH STALLION STUDS E B F SPORTINGBET.COM MAIDEN STKS 6f

6:10 (6:11) (Class 5) 2-Y-O **£3,234** (£962; £481; £240) **Stalls** Low

Form RPR

62 **1** **Otto The Great**[70] 2143 2-9-3 0 ShaneKelly 4 85+
(Walter Swinburn) *mde all: drew clr over 2f out: pushed out: comf* **13/2**

62 **2** *4* **Not Bad For A Boy (IRE)**[9] 4080 2-9-3 0 RichardHughes 1 72
(Richard Hannon) *chsd wnr 2f: pushed along 1/2-way: wnt 2nd again 2f out: no imp* **5/2**[1]

3 *3/4* **Duke Of Firenze** 2-9-3 0 RyanMoore 2 70+
(Sir Michael Stoute) *awkward s: chsd ldrs: shkn up to go 3rd wl over 1f out: kpt on same pce* **10/3**[2]

4 *7* **Marah Music** 2-9-3 0 FergusSweeney 7 47+
(Peter Makin) *prom: chsd wnr after 2f to 2f out: wknd* **8/1**

5 *nse* **Sugarformyhoney (IRE)** 2-8-12 0 DaneO'Neill 12 42+
(Richard Hannon) *dwlt: rchd 8th after 2f but wl off the pce: pushed along over 2f out on outer: rn green but styd on: nt disgracd* **16/1**

6 *2 3/4* **Rainbow Chorus** 2-9-3 0 JimmyFortune 13 38+
(Paul Cole) *chsd ldrs in 5th but firmly pushed along over 4f out: outpcd fr 1/2-way: no ch after* **16/1**

6 **7** *1* **Spunky**[14] 3917 2-9-3 0 KierenFallon 5 35+
(Luca Cumani) *settled in 7th: outpcd and nudged along 1/2-way: reminder over 1f out: no prog: do bttr in time* **9/2**[3]

8 *2* **Ashes Star** 2-9-3 0 RichardKingscote 6 29
(Jonathan Portman) *dwlt: chsd ldrs in 6th but nt on terms: wl outpcd fr 1/2-way* **66/1**

9 *nk* **George Tilehurst** 2-8-12 0 RyanPowell(5) 10 28
(J S Moore) *s.i.s: rn green in last trio: a wl off the pce* **80/1**

10 *3* **Trisha's Boy (IRE)** 2-9-3 0 MartinDwyer 8 18
(Simon Dow) *sn pushed along: outpcd and a wl in rr* **66/1**

11 *9* **Silver Native (IRE)** 2-9-3 0 TonyCulhane 3 —
(Mike Murphy) *s.s: a bhd in last trio: t.o* **25/1**

12 *3 3/4* **Doctor Dalek (IRE)** 2-9-3 0 EddieCreighton 9 —
(Edward Creighton) *dwlt: rn v green: sn drvn and wl detached in last: t.o* **66/1**

1m 12.44s (-0.56) **Going Correction** -0.20s/f (Firm) **12** Ran SP% **115.6**
Speed ratings (Par 94): **95,89,88,79,79 75,74,71,71,67 55,50**
toteswingers:1&2:£4.10, 1&3:£4.10, 2&3:£2.10 CSF £22.04 TOTE £7.50: £2.30, £1.50, £1.50; EX 21.10 Trifecta £86.50 Pool: £5,532.06 - 47.31 winning units..
Owner Mrs Doreen M Swinburn **Bred** Genesis Green Stud **Trained** Aldbury, Herts

FOCUS

Stands rail dolled out 12yds at 6f and 6yds at winning post. Top bend out 3yds from normal configuration adding 17yds to races of 1m and over. There were two going changes during a dry day, and just before racing the official description was switched to good, good to firm in places. An above average maiden. The winner scored in decent style in a good time from the two market leaders, who were clear of a heavily backed newcomer.

NOTEBOOK

Otto The Great improved on his debut run when just over 2l second of eight in a 6f Bath maiden in May. He had a bit to find but made all to readily hold off the favourite on return from two months off. He is powerful type who is related to plenty of useful winners at 6f-1m6f and should continue to progress. (op 11-2 tchd 5-1)

Not Bad For A Boy(IRE) set the standard on his narrow defeat at 20-1 in 7f Haydock maiden on good to soft nine days earlier. Well positioned for most of the way dropped back to 6f, he tried to launch a challenge 2f out but couldn't pose a serious threat to a dominant rival. (op 11-4 tchd 9-4)

Duke Of Firenze, a Pivotal first foal of top-class miler Nannina, who won the Fillies' Mile/Coronation Stakes, was prominent in the market and shaped with plenty of promise behind two experienced rivals on debut. He could improve significantly next time. (op 11-4 tchd 7-2)

Marah Music, a 20,000gns Royal Applause half-brother to 1m4f winner Remaal, and 7f winner Mouseen, was the subject of a massive on-course gamble and looked fairly streetwise near the pace for a long way but he faded in the final quarter of the race. (op 33-1 tchd 7-1)

Sugarformyhoney(IRE), the stable second-string on jockey bookings, ran green before doing a bit of late work on debut. She has a speedy pedigree, being a Dutch Art first foal of a 5f winning half-sister to a sprint juvenile winner in US, and should improve for the experience.

Spunky, a half-brother to smart 7f-1m4f winners Magic Instinct and Cabinet, seemed to get caught out when the pace increased and was never involved in his attempt to build on his 6l sixth in a C&D maiden on debut. Official explanation: jockey said colt ran too free (op 5-1 tchd 11-2)

4385 SEVENTH HEAVEN EVENTS H'CAP 1m 2f 7y

6:40 (6:41) (Class 5) (0-75,74) 3-Y-O+ **£2,264** (£673; £336; £168) **Stalls** Centre

Form RPR

301 **1** **Colinca's Lad (IRE)**[7] 4165 9-8-5 **56** RosieJessop(5) 2 66
(Peter Charalambous) *led after 2f: drew clr bef 1/2-way: drvn over 2f out: hld on to dwindling advantage fnl f* **5/1**[2]

36-5 **2** *1/2* **Jamhoori**[10] 4060 3-8-12 **68** PhilipRobinson 10 77
(Clive Brittain) *wl in tch: prog to chse wnr over 3f out: sn rdn: grad clsd fr 2f out: nvr quite got there* **6/1**

2-03 **3** *1* **Green Wadi**[7] 4154 6-9-6 **66** GeorgeBaker 3 73
(Gary Moore) *hld up bhd ldrs: stdy prog 3f out looking dangerous: rdn to dispute 2nd 2f out: nt qckn after* **11/2**[3]

6104 **4** *1* **Effigy**[18] 3760 7-9-9 **74** AmyScott(5) 5 79
(Henry Candy) *hld up in last and wl off the pce: pushed along and prog fr 4f out: rchd 4th 1f out and briefly looked threatening: one pce after* **14/1**

2-34 **5** *3 3/4* **Loyaliste (FR)**[77] 1950 4-9-11 **71** PatDobbs 9 69
(Richard Hannon) *hld up in last trio: shkn up and effrt 4f out: sme prog over 2f out: one pce after* **16/1**

-026 **6** *hd* **Hurakan (IRE)**[16] 3844 5-9-13 **73** (t) TonyCulhane 1 70
(George Baker) *sn prom: chsd wnr 6f out to over 3f out: sn rdn: grad fdd* **12/1**

1-5 **7** *7* **The Holyman (IRE)**[98] 1446 3-9-3 **73** DaneO'Neill 4 56
(Jo Crowley) *in tch in midfield: rdn wl over 3f out: no real prog* **9/2**[1]

3642 **8** *1 1/2* **Clarion Call**[21] 3676 3-9-0 **70** CathyGannon 12 50
(Eve Johnson Houghton) *wl in tch in midfield: drvn over 3f out: sn outpcd: struggling and n.d fr 2f out* **12/1**

-53 **9** *5* **New River (IRE)**[38] 3135 3-9-4 **74** RichardHughes 11 44
(Richard Hannon) *prom: pushed along and steadily lost pl fr 4f out: wl in rr fnl 2f* **7/1**

6052 **10** *1* **Cloudy Bay (USA)**[20] 3716 4-9-5 **68** (p) KierenFox(3) 7 36
(John Flint) *led 2f: lost pl 6f out: rdn towards rr and no prog over 2f out* **14/1**

-235 **11** *13* **Daddyow**[20] 3717 3-9-1 **71** DavidProbert 6 13
(Bryn Palling) *settled wl in rr: taken to wd outside and rdn over 3f out: sn btn: t.o* **33/1**

600/ **12** *43* **Yellow Ridge (IRE)**[643] 6917 8-8-9 **55** oh10 ShaneKelly 8 —
(Luke Comer, Ire) *a in last pair: wknd 4f out: wl t.o* **66/1**

2m 5.75s (-2.95) **Going Correction** -0.20s/f (Firm)
WFA 3 from 4yo+ 10lb **12** Ran SP% **116.1**
Speed ratings (Par 103): **103,102,101,101,98 97,92,91,87,86 75,41**
toteswingers:1&2:£8.90, 1&3:£7.90, 2&3:£9.50 CSF £34.30 CT £171.34 TOTE £5.60: £2.40, £4.10, £2.30; EX 52.40 Trifecta £417.30 Pool: £3,666.20 - 6.50 winning units..
Owner P Charalambous **Bred** Peter Charles **Trained** Newmarket, Suffolk
■ Stewards' Enquiry : Philip Robinson one-day ban: used whip with excessive frequency (Aug 8)

FOCUS

A fair handicap. The pace was decent and a well treated veteran made most to cash in on a good chance for a double. He pretty much matched his latest form.

New River(IRE) Official explanation: jockey said filly was unsuited by the good (good to firm places) ground

4386 SPORTINGBET.COM MAIDEN FILLIES' STKS 5f 10y

7:10 (7:11) (Class 5) 2-Y-O **£2,264** (£673; £336; £168) **Stalls** Low

Form RPR

1 **Artistic Jewel (IRE)** 2-9-0 0 GrahamGibbons 3 88+
(Ed McMahon) *chsd ldng pair: prog to go 2nd over 1f out: rdn to ld ent fnl f: sn clr: quite impressive* **5/1**[2]

042 **2** *2 3/4* **Royal Red**[28] 3463 2-9-0 0 JimCrowley 5 76
(Ralph Beckett) *mde most: beat off chalr 2f out: sn rdn: hdd and outpcd ent fnl f* **5/6**[1]

5 **3** *5* **Mae Rose Cottage (IRE)**[19] 3722 2-9-0 0 NickyMackay 4 58+
(Hughie Morrison) *chsd ldrs in 5th: pushed along on wd outside 1/2-way: sn lft bhd: kpt on to take 3rd nr fin* **12/1**

4335 **4** *3/4* **Maltease Ah**[20] 3700 2-9-0 0 DarryllHolland 7 55
(Andrew Reid) *w ldr to 1/2-way: lost 2nd and wknd over 1f out* **8/1**

0 **5** *hd* **Emerald Smile (IRE)**[42] 2997 2-8-9 0 RyanPowell(5) 8 55
(J S Moore) *chsd ldng pair: rdn and edgd lft 2f out: sn lft wl bhd* **20/1**

6 *2 1/4* **Little China** 2-9-0 0 MartinDwyer 6 46+
(William Muir) *dwlt: last of main gp: pushed along over 2f out: no real prog* **33/1**

0 **7** *1* **Periwinkle Way**[10] 4052 2-9-0 0 JamesDoyle 1 43+
(Sylvester Kirk) *slowly away and then hmpd: virtually t.o in last after 1f: lost no further grnd: pushed along and kpt on fnl f* **22/1**

8 *5* **Teth** 2-8-7 0 AntiocoMurgia(7) 2 25
(Mahmood Al Zarooni) *wnt rt s: rn green: tried to rcvr after 1f: no prog 1/2-way: wknd wl over 1f out* **13/2**[3]

59.31 secs (-0.99) **Going Correction** -0.20s/f (Firm) **8** Ran SP% **115.4**
Speed ratings (Par 91): **99,94,86,85,85 81,79,71**
toteswingers:1&2:£2.40, 1&3:£9.20, 2&3:£3.20 CSF £9.44 TOTE £6.50: £1.60, £1.10, £2.70; EX 13.30 Trifecta £103.70 Pool: £7,150.36 - 51.00 winning units..
Owner R L Bedding **Bred** Jim McDonald **Trained** Lichfield, Staffs

FOCUS

A newcomer powered clear of the hot favourite in this fillies' maiden in which they finished well strung out. The time was decent and the runner-up set a good standard.

NOTEBOOK

Artistic Jewel(IRE) was never far away and produced a storming run out wide to win in good style on this debut. There was probably not much strength in depth and the runner-up is starting to look exposed, but this was still a striking performance by a 30,000gns Excellent Art filly who is out of a French winning miler who's bred successful sprinters, including 5f-7f (Listed) winner Ponty Rossa. Trainer Ed McMahon reported that the winner may be targeted at the Cornwallis Stakes. (tchd 11-2)

Royal Red set a clear standard on her narrow defeat by a progressive Richard Hannon-trained subsequent winner in a C&D maiden last month. Ridden positively against the stands' rail again, things seemed to be going well for a long way but she had no answer to surging run of the winner on her fourth start. (op Evens tchd 4-5)

Mae Rose Cottage(IRE) has shaped with a bit of promise in both of her 5f maiden starts. A Dylan Thomas half-sister to useful Irish 7f-1m2f winner Drumbeat, she should continue to get better with time and distance. (tchd 14-1)

Maltease Ah, a front-running fourth off a mark of 68 from a wide draw in a Pontefract nursery on her final run for Richard Fahey, couldn't stay near the firing line back in a maiden, but she looks a possible marker for the form. (tchd 10-1)

Teth, a first foal of a useful 5f winning half-sister to top-class French 2-y-o/Arc winner Bago, looked very inexperienced and was never involved on debut. (op 6-1 tchd 7-1)

4387 SPORTINGBET.COM FILLIES' H'CAP 6f

7:40 (7:40) (Class 4) (0-80,79) 3-Y-O+ **£3,557** (£1,058; £529; £264) **Stalls** Low

Form RPR

2465 **1** **Bianca De Medici**[33] 3278 4-9-2 **69** RyanMoore 13 79
(Hughie Morrison) *settled bhd ldrs: prog on outer fr 2f out: rdn to ld jst ins fnl f: styd on wl* **5/1**[1]

6440 **2** *3/4* **Admirable Spirit**[17] 3819 3-9-7 **79** RichardHughes 5 86+
(Richard Hannon) *hld up bhd ldrs gng strly: produced to chal jst over 1f out: r.o but jst outpcd* **7/1**

5544 **3** *1 1/2* **Chevise (IRE)**[12] 3985 3-9-0 **77** HarryBentley(5) 14 79
(Steve Woodman) *settled wl in rr: prog on outer fr over 2f out: rdn over 1f out: styd on: nvr able to chal* **14/1**

0521 **4** *nk* **Millyluvstobouggie**[23] 3630 3-8-11 **76** LucyKBarry(7) 10 77
(Clive Cox) *hld up and sn last: stdy prog on wd outside fr over 2f out: shkn up and styd on: nvr able to chal* **15/2**

1600 **5** *2 1/4* **Flashbang**[40] 3048 3-8-11 **74** RyanPowell(5) 12 68
(Paul Cole) *hld up wl in rr: urged along and prog fr 2f out: kpt on fnl f: nvr threatened* **18/1**

0-40 **6** *hd* **Caledonia Princess**[11] 3996 5-9-4 **74** RossAtkinson(3) 4 68+
(Jo Hughes) *taken down early: pressed ldrs: led 2f out: hdd & wknd jst ins fnl f* **12/1**

0161 **7** *1 3/4* **Polar Annie**[17] 3801 6-9-8 **75** DaneO'Neill 2 63
(Malcolm Saunders) *led: drvn over 2f out: sn hdd and fdd* **13/2**[3]

3033 **8** *nk* **Commandingpresence (USA)**[9] 4086 5-8-4 **60** oh3 KierenFox(3) 6 47
(John Bridger) *in tch in midfield: rdn and no imp on ldrs fr 2f out* **14/1**

-320 **9** *nk* **Our Piccadilly (IRE)**[10] 4057 6-9-0 **70** LouisBeuzelin(3) 3 56
(Stuart Kittow) *taken down early: trckd ldrs: cl enough wl over 1f out: wknd fnl f* **12/1**

250- **10** *1* **Carcinetto (IRE)**[344] 5114 9-9-0 **70** SophieDoyle(3) 1 53
(David Evans) *prom 2f: sn lost pl and struggling on inner: no prog over 1f out* **20/1**

0606 **11** *nk* **Bathwick Xaara**[35] 3217 4-8-9 **62** CathyGannon 9 44
(Jonathan Portman) *pressed ldrs to 1/2-way: sn lost pl and btn* **22/1**

-015 **12** *3 1/2* **Guided Missile (IRE)**[9] 4101 3-9-6 **78** (v) JimmyFortune 11 48
(Andrew Balding) *stdd s: a wl in rr: shkn up and no prog over 2f out: eased whn no ch last 100yds* **11/2**[2]

320 **13** *2 1/2* **Basle**[10] 4064 4-9-5 **72** DavidProbert 7 35
(Gay Kelleway) *w ldrs over 3f: wknd rapidly wl over 1f out: eased* **16/1**

-000 **14** *15* **Pose (IRE)**[14] 3914 4-8-3 **63** ow1 MatthewLawson(7) 8 —
(Roger Ingram) *w ldrs to 1/2-way: wknd rapidly: t.o and eased* **80/1**

1m 12.51s (-0.49) **Going Correction** -0.20s/f (Firm)
WFA 3 from 4yo+ 5lb 14 Ran SP% **119.9**
Speed ratings (Par 102): **95,94,92,91,88 88,86,85,85,83 83,78,75,55**
toteswingers:1&2:£13.20, 1&3:£15.40, 2&3:£44.00 CSF £38.15 CT £478.36 TOTE £6.40: £2.00, £2.70, £4.20; EX 46.30 Trifecta £1606.10 Part won. Pool: £2,170.52 - 0.10 winning units..
Owner Lady Bland **Bred** Lady Bland **Trained** East Ilsley, Berks

FOCUS
A competitive sprint handicap for fillies'. It was run at a strong pace and the form is rated around the first two.
Commandingpresence(USA) Official explanation: jockey said mare was denied a clear run

4388 SPORTINGBET.COM MAIDEN STKS 1m 67y
8:10 (8:11) (Class 5) 3-4-Y-O **£2,264** (£673; £336; £168) **Stalls** Low

Form RPR

6- **1** **Dumbarton (IRE)**[328] 5629 3-9-3 0 RyanMoore 2 87+
(Sir Michael Stoute) *trckd ldng pair: wnt 2nd 2f out: shkn up to ld over 1f out: sn clr: comf* **9/4**[1]

5 **2** *4 1/2* **Ffajir (IRE)**[32] 3324 3-8-12 0 PhilipRobinson 3 68+
(Clive Brittain) *led: rdn and hdd over 1f out: styd on but no match for wnr* **13/2**

3 *3* **Kalamkas (USA)** 3-8-12 0 RichardHughes 13 61+
(Jeremy Noseda) *chsd ldr to 2f out: pushed along and outpcd after* **3/1**[2]

04- **4** *1/2* **Tarjeyh (IRE)**[409] 2932 3-9-3 0 PatDobbs 6 65+
(Marcus Tregoning) *trckd ldrs: pushed along over 2f out: outpcd fnl 2f* **4/1**[3]

5 *1 1/4* **Counterparty** 3-8-12 0 FergusSweeney 8 57+
(Alan King) *trckd ldrs: shkn up over 2f out: kpt on but readily outpcd* **18/1**

0 **6** *3/4* **Outpost (IRE)**[24] 3594 3-9-3 0 CathyGannon 10 60
(Alan Bailey) *sn in midfield: pushed along over 3f out: kpt on one pce fnl 2f: no ch* **12/1**

7 *1/2* **Monsieur Broughton** 3-9-3 0 StevieDonohoe 12 59
(Willie Musson) *dwlt: wl bhd early: ct up in rr after 3f: shkn up over 2f out: kpt on fnl f* **20/1**

8 *nk* **The Right Time** 3-8-12 0 DavidProbert 5 53
(Tony Carroll) *s.i.s: in tch in rr: plugged on fnl 2f: nvr on terms* **33/1**

0 **9** *2* **Miracle Play (IRE)**[11] 4023 3-8-12 0 JamesDoyle 1 48
(David Evans) *in tch in rr: pushed along and no prog over 2f out: n.d after* **80/1**

10 *5* **Mulberry Brite** 3-8-12 0 DarryllHolland 11 36
(Karen George) *prom tl wknd qckly jst over 2f out* **66/1**

11 *10* **Adaero Star** 3-8-9 0 KierenFox(3) 7 —
(Karen George) *dwlt: wl bhd early: rapid prog rnd outside to join ldrs 4f out: wknd as rapidly 3f out* **80/1**

12 *17* **Melanistic** 4-9-6 0 JimCrowley 9 —
(Ian Williams) *s.s: sn wl t.o* **25/1**

P **Kasla (USA)** 3-8-12 0 KierenFallon 4 —
(Clive Brittain) *s.i.s: lost action and p.u after 1f* **16/1**

1m 44.6s (-0.10) **Going Correction** -0.20s/f (Firm)
WFA 3 from 4yo 8lb 13 Ran SP% **123.5**
Speed ratings (Par 103): **92,87,84,84,82 82,81,81,79,74 64,47,—**
toteswingers:1&2:£13.20, 1&3:£15.40, 2&3:£44.00 CSF £17.26 TOTE £2.80: £1.30, £2.00, £1.80; EX 14.30 Trifecta £46.70 Pool: £741.34 - 11.74 winning units..
Owner Ballymacoll Stud **Bred** Ballymacoll Stud Farm Ltd **Trained** Newmarket, Suffolk

FOCUS
An interesting maiden. It was steadily run and the bare form is probably limited, but the winner was impressive and the four market leaders filled the first four places. The winner is potentially smart.
Outpost(IRE) Official explanation: jockey said colt hung left and made a noise

4389 CHEVRON MALTA HOLIDAYS H'CAP 1m 3f 135y
8:40 (8:41) (Class 5) (0-70,70) 3-Y-O+ **£2,264** (£673; £336; £168) **Stalls** Centre

Form RPR

1356 **1** **Little Jazz**[32] 3325 3-8-11 **65** CathyGannon 5 73
(Paul D'Arcy) *settled in last pair: shkn up and prog fr 3f out: rdn to cl over 1f out: led last 150yds: styd on* **9/1**

504 **2** *1/2* **Waahej**[6] 4177 5-8-10 **59** LucyKBarry(7) 8 66
(Peter Hiatt) *hld up towards rr: prog 4f out: chsd ldr and edgd rt over 2f out: rdn to ld briefly 1f out: styd on but jst outpcd last 100yds* **20/1**

-214 **3** *2 1/4* **Nutshell**[26] 3518 3-8-7 **61** JimmyQuinn 3 64
(Harry Dunlop) *hld up in rr: prog on inner fr 4f out: rdn to cl on ldrs over 1f out: nt qckn fnl f: kpt on to take 3rd last strides* **8/1**[3]

4256 **4** *hd* **Swaninstockwell (IRE)**[12] 3979 3-8-2 **61** JemmaMarshall(5) 10 64
(Pat Phelan) *t.k.h: led: edgd lft fr 2f out: hdd and nt qckn 1f out: lost 3rd last strides* **15/2**[2]

0060 **5** *hd* **Bahkov (IRE)**[13] 3945 5-8-7 **52** oh7 (b) KierenFox(3) 1 54?
(Eric Wheeler) *prom: shkn up 4f out: looked in trble 3f out: effrt u.p 2f out: one pce fr over 1f out* **50/1**

3-36 **6** *8* **Norman The Great**[39] 3095 7-9-11 **67** FergusSweeney 11 56
(Alan King) *towards rr: pushed along 4f out: effrt on wd outside 3f out: no imp over 1f out: wknd* **10/1**

3042 **7** *3 3/4* **Kishanda**[7] 4154 3-8-7 **61** NickyMackay 12 44
(Hughie Morrison) *trckd ldrs: shkn up over 3f out: losing pl whn hmpd over 2f out: sn btn: eased* **13/8**[1]

0010 **8** *1/2* **Gower Rules (IRE)**[14] 3919 3-8-6 **65** HarryBentley(5) 7 47
(John Bridger) *trckd ldrs: shkn up over 3f out: wknd wl over 1f out* **11/1**

2405 **9** *3/4* **Where's Susie**[29] 3434 6-9-11 **67** GeorgeBaker 2 47
(Michael Madgwick) *trckd ldrs: shkn up wl over 3f out: wknd wl over 1f out* **14/1**

3526 **10** *nk* **Layla's Dancer**[29] 2359 4-10-0 **70** DavidProbert 6 50
(Tony Carroll) *awkward s and rousted along early: sn in tch in rr: rdn over 3f out: no prog 2f out: wknd* **12/1**

1400 **11** *nse* **Mons Calpe (IRE)**[25] 3533 5-10-0 **70** (tp) JimCrowley 9 50
(Paul Cole) *trckd ldrs: rdn 3f out: no prog 2f out: sn wknd* **12/1**

-105 **12** *3/4* **Mr Plod**[20] 3715 6-9-0 **56** (v) DarryllHolland 4 35
(Andrew Reid) *t.k.h: pressed ldr to wl over 2f out: sn wknd* **14/1**

2m 27.98s (-1.52) **Going Correction** -0.20s/f (Firm)
WFA 3 from 4yo+ 12lb 12 Ran SP% **123.8**
Speed ratings (Par 103): **97,96,95,95,94 89,87,86,86,86 86,85**
toteswingers:1&2:£27.60, 1&3:£17.40, 2&3:£23.70 CSF £182.69 CT £1518.89 TOTE £10.50: £3.40, £4.90, £3.00; EX 276.90 TRIFECTA Not won..
Owner K Snell **Bred** K Snell **Trained** Newmarket, Suffolk

FOCUS
There was tight finish to this middle-distance handicap. The first five finished a long way clear and the heavily backed favourite was disappointing. The form looks sound amongst the first five.
Kishanda Official explanation: jockey said filly suffered interference
Where's Susie Official explanation: jockey said mare suffered interference
T/Jkpt: £71,445.60 to a £1 stake. Pool:£352,197.09 - 3.50 winning tickets T/Plt: £81.90 to a £1 stake. Pool:£110,057.21 - 980.80 winning tickets T/Qpdt: £31.40 to a £1 stake. Pool:£7,195.00 - 169.46 winning tickets JN

4184 YARMOUTH (L-H)
Monday, July 25

OFFICIAL GOING: Good (good to firm in places; 7.4)
Wind: Fresh behind Weather: Overcast

4390 GREAT YARMOUTH TOURIST AUTHORITY MAIDEN AUCTION STKS 7f 3y
2:15 (2:16) (Class 6) 2-Y-O **£1,617** (£481; £240; £120) **Stalls** High

Form RPR

0 **1** **Hamble**[68] 2194 2-8-12 0 LiamJones 1 81
(William Haggas) *chsd ldrs: rdn to ld over 1f out: edgd rt: styd on* **14/1**

0 **2** *1/2* **Ocean Tempest**[30] 3401 2-8-9 0 KirstyMilczarek 8 76
(John Ryan) *chsd ldrs: led over 2f out: rdn and hdd over 1f out: edgd lft ins fnl f: styd on* **10/1**[3]

5 **3** *2 1/4* **Swing Alone (IRE)**[37] 3152 2-9-1 0 NeilCallan 9 78+
(Gay Kelleway) *s.i.s: hdwy 1/2-way: rdn and swtchd rt over 2f out: styd on to go 3rd wl ins fnl f: nvr nrr* **8/13**[1]

0 **4** *1* **Gold Coin**[17] 3812 2-8-7 0 MartinLane 12 66
(J W Hills) *hld up in tch: rdn over 1f out: no ex and lost 3rd wl ins fnl f* **9/1**[2]

00 **5** *7* **Island Melody (IRE)**[37] 3152 2-8-9 0 LiamKeniry 7 49
(J S Moore) *chsd ldrs: pushed along 1/2-way: rdn and wknd over 1f out* **12/1**

4440 **6** *1* **Indian Lizzy**[42] 2998 2-8-4 0 (p) HayleyTurner 5 41
(Paul Cole) *led over 4f: rdn and wknd over 1f out* **33/1**

445 **7** *2* **Bojangle (IRE)**[70] 2160 2-8-7 0 JimmyQuinn 3 39
(Dominic Ffrench Davis) *racd keenly: prom: pushed along 1/2-way: sn lost pl* **50/1**

0 **8** *hd* **Always A Sinner (USA)**[12] 3986 2-9-1 0 TomQueally 4 46
(William Knight) *s.i.s: sn pushed along in rr: rdn and hung lft over 2f out: nvr on terms* **50/1**

64 **9** *3/4* **Karma Chameleon**[6] 4171 2-8-6 0 MartinHarley(3) 11 38
(Richard Guest) *hld up: pushed along 1/2-way: a in rr* **25/1**

2 **10** *3 1/2* **Lady Tycoon**[20] 3718 2-8-1 0 KieranO'Neill(3) 2 24
(Mark Brisbourne) *chsd ldrs: rdn 1/2-way: wknd over 2f out* **10/1**[3]

11 *34* **Cheviot Quest (IRE)** 2-8-12 0 J-PGuillambert 10 —
(William Jarvis) *s.i.s: outpcd: eased fnl 2f: t.o* **33/1**

1m 24.74s (-1.86) **Going Correction** -0.35s/f (Firm) 11 Ran SP% **118.1**
Speed ratings (Par 92): **96,95,92,91,83 82,80,80,79,75 36**
toteswingers:1&2:£17.40, 2&3:£3.50, 1&3:£5.80 CSF £138.41 TOTE £16.20: £4.20, £2.80, £1.02; EX 168.80.
Owner Mrs Charles Cyzer **Bred** C A Cyzer **Trained** Newmarket, Suffolk

FOCUS
A non-bonus maiden auction and the form looks ordinary, although towards the top end of the race averages. The first four were clear. They raced up the middle of the track.

NOTEBOOK
Hamble was well beaten over 6f on Polytrack on his debut (behind Indian Lizzy), but he had been given over two months off since and returned with a much-improved performance, the longer trip clearly in his favour. He should start off in nurseries at a workable level. (op 12-1)
Ocean Tempest, reported to have run green and hung left on his debut at Newmarket, shaped a lot better this time, finishing clear of the others. There might be more to come. (op 40-1)
Swing Alone(IRE) did not match the form he showed when fifth on his debut in the Chesham, a race that with the exception of the winner, Maybe, is not working out at all. He never travelled with fluency. (op 4-6 tchd 4-5)
Gold Coin showed a bit more than on her debut at Newbury, faring best of the fillies, and gave the impression she'll come on again for this. (op 8-1 tchd 15-2)
Lady Tycoon Official explanation: trainer said filly lost a shoe

4391 GREAT YARMOUTH MARITIME FESTIVAL SEPTEMBER (S) STKS 6f 3y
2:45 (2:46) (Class 6) 2-Y-O **£1,617** (£481; £240; £120) **Stalls** High

Form RPR

1 **Speedi Mouse** 2-8-6 0 MartinLane 4 59
(Philip McBride) *s.i.s: sn pushed along in rr: hdwy over 1f out: rdn: edgd lft and r.o to ld post* **11/2**[3]

00 **2** *nse* **Masters Club**[38] 3132 2-8-11 0 KirstyMilczarek 7 63
(John Ryan) *hld up: hdwy over 3f out: rdn to ld over 1f out: hdd post* **40/1**

6344 **3** *2* **Red Hearts (IRE)**[24] 3595 2-8-8 0 AdamBeschizza(3) 2 57
(Julia Feilden) *chsd ldrs: rdn to ld briefly over 1f out: edgd lft and no ex ins fnl f* **7/4**[1]

0 **4** *1 3/4* **King Kenobi (IRE)**[17] 3816 2-8-11 0 LiamKeniry 6 51
(J S Moore) *hld up: pushed along 1/2-way: r.o ins fnl f: nrst fin* **16/1**

4 **5** *hd* **Little Ted**[56] 2556 2-8-11 0 NeilCallan 5 51
(David Evans) *chsd ldrs: led over 2 out: rdn and hdd over 1f out: no ex ins fnl f* **10/1**

0515 **6** *3 3/4* **Very First Blade**[11] 4021 2-8-13 0 KieranO'Neill(3) 3 44
(Mark Brisbourne) *sn pushed along in rr: styd on ins fnl f: nvr on terms* **20/1**

66 **7** *nk* **Concordia Notte (IRE)**[53] 2644 2-8-6 0 LiamJones 9 33
(Paul D'Arcy) *led: hdd over 4f out: rdn over 2f out: wknd ins fnl f* **5/2**[2]

532 **8** *5* **Miss Medici (IRE)**[6] 4178 2-8-6 0 HayleyTurner 1 17
(Des Donovan) *chsd ldrs: led over 4f out: rdn and hdd over 2f out: edgd lft and wknd over 1f out* **8/1**

1m 12.87s (-1.53) **Going Correction** -0.35s/f (Firm) 8 Ran SP% **113.6**
Speed ratings (Par 92): **96,95,93,90,90 85,85,78**
toteswingers:1&2:£17.20, 2&3:£15.10, 1&3:£2.50 CSF £171.91 TOTE £5.90: £1.90, £7.20, £1.10; EX 228.10.The winner was bought in for 3,400gns. Concordia Notte was claimed by S Arnold for £5000.
Owner P J McBride **Bred** Langham Hall Stud **Trained** Newmarket, Suffolk

FOCUS
A moderate-looking race, even by selling standards. The form is rated around the third's more recent efforts. Again they raced up the middle of the track.
NOTEBOOK
Speedi Mouse, a 10,000gns purchase who is bred to stay further, overcame greenness to make a successful introduction. She missed the break, and then having recovered to travel okay, she looked in trouble when off the bridle by halfway. However, she got the idea as her stamina kicked in late on. There should be more to come with the benefit of this experience and when upped in trip, but things are likely to be a lot tougher outside of this grade. (op 12-1)
Masters Club had shown little on his first two starts, but this was an improved performance. (op 33-1)
Red Hearts(IRE) was the clear form pick on this drop in class, even though she hadn't been at her best the last twice, but she ran disappointingly. She's going the wrong way. (op 2-1 tchd 9-4)
King Kenobi(IRE) was well beaten in a better seller than this on his debut and was again comfortably held.
Little Ted ◆ caught the eye (relative to selling company) on his debut over 5f at Goodwood, but he'd been absent for 56 days since then. This longer trip was expected to help him, but he's a horse with a significant knee action and this ground blatantly failed to suit. He can confirm his initial promise on soft going. (op 8-1)
Concordia Notte(IRE) had been off for 53 days and was disappointing on this drop in class and step back up in trip. (op 2-1 tchd 11-4)

4392 MARTIN FOULGER MEMORIAL H'CAP — 6f 3y
3:15 (3:15) (Class 4) (0-85,83) 3-Y-O+ — £4,075 (£1,212; £606; £303) Stalls High

Form — RPR
1520 **1** **Victorian Bounty**[16] 3850 6-9-10 **82** .... PatCosgrave 6 — 89
(Stef Higgins) *racd alone on stands' side: prom: rdn over 1f out: led overall ins fnl f: jst hld on* **13/2**
26 **2** *nse* **Ursula (IRE)**[37] 3162 5-9-7 **79** .... AndrewElliott 3 — 86
(Mrs K Burke) *hld up: racd centre: hdwy over 1f out: sn rdn: led that gp wl ins fnl f: r.o: 1st of 5 in gp* **3/1**[2]
2110 **3** *1 3/4* **Miss Polly Plum**[18] 3759 4-9-0 **72** ....(p) AndreaAtzeni 1 — 73
(Chris Dwyer) *overall ldr in centre: rdn and hung rt over 1f out: hdd and no ex ins fnl f* **10/1**
600- **4** *1/2* **Ceremonial Jade (UAE)**[241] 7574 8-9-5 **82** ....(t) TobyAtkinson(5) 2 — 82
(Marco Botti) *racd centre: hld up: rdn over 2f out: hdwy over 1f out: r.o: 3rd of 5 in gp* **8/1**
25 **5** *nk* **Seek The Fair Land**[18] 3765 5-9-4 **79** ....(b) MatthewDavies(3) 5 — 78
(Jim Boyle) *racd centre: chsd ldrs: rdn over 1f out: styd on same pce ins fnl f: 4th of 5 in gp* **7/2**[3]
0003 **6** *17* **Greyfriarschorista**[11] 4013 4-9-0 **72** .... J-PGuillambert 4 — 16
(Mark Johnston) *racd centre: chsd ldrs: sn pushed along: rdn and wknd over 2f out* **5/2**[1]

1m 11.52s (-2.88) **Going Correction** -0.35s/f (Firm) — **6** Ran SP% **109.3**
WFA 3 from 4yo+ 5lb
Speed ratings (Par 105): **105,104,102,101,101 78**
toteswingers:1&2:£3.60, 2&3:£4.60, 1&3:£4.70 CSF £24.74 TOTE £6.60: £2.80, £2.60; EX 21.80.
Owner David Gilbert **Bred** Mrs P D Gray And H Farr **Trained** Lambourn, Berks
FOCUS
An ordinary handicap. The main action unfolded towards the near-side rail, but Victorian Bounty was the only runner who raced against the fence from the off - the others were more towards the centre early on. The winner sets the standard.

4393 SHIRLEY GILL MEMORIAL H'CAP — 7f 3y
3:45 (3:45) (Class 4) (0-80,78) 3-Y-O+ — £4,075 (£1,212; £606; £303) Stalls High

Form — RPR
0465 **1** **Amoya (GER)**[10] 4066 4-9-5 **71** ....(t) AdamBeschizza(3) 3 — 78
(Philip McBride) *mde all: set stdy pce: clr 4f out: qcknd 2f out: drvn out* **4/1**[3]
311- **2** *1 1/4* **Sir Mozart (IRE)**[348] 4968 8-9-9 **72** .... TomQueally 4 — 76
(Barney Curley) *hld up: hdwy over 1f out: sn rdn: r.o to go 2nd post: nt rch wnr* **5/2**[1]
1030 **3** *nse* **Batgirl**[17] 3825 4-9-11 **74** .... PatCosgrave 2 — 77
(John Berry) *chsd wnr: rdn and ev ch ins fnl f: styd on same pce: lost 2nd post* **11/4**[2]
0011 **4** *2* **Rough Rock (IRE)**[7] 4160 6-10-1 **78** 6ex .... HayleyTurner 1 — 76
(Chris Dwyer) *plld hrd and prom: rdn over 1f out: styd on same pce fnl f* **11/4**[2]
5503 **5** *2 1/2* **Mottley Crewe**[28] 3471 4-8-11 **63** .... RobertLButler(3) 5 — 54
(Richard Guest) *hld up: racd keenly: rdn over 1f out: nt trble ldrs* **14/1**

1m 25.57s (-1.03) **Going Correction** -0.35s/f (Firm) — **5** Ran SP% **108.6**
Speed ratings (Par 105): **91,89,89,87,84**
CSF £13.85 TOTE £6.00: £2.60, £1.50; EX 20.20.
Owner Black Star Racing **Bred** Gestut Ebbesloh **Trained** Newmarket, Suffolk
FOCUS
Form to treat with caution as Amoya was allowed an incredibly easy lead, racing about 3l clear without having to overexert herself, and she recorded a time 0.83 seconds slower than the earlier weak juvenile maiden. She's rated up 6lb on her British form. They raced towards the middle of the track.
Mottley Crewe Official explanation: jockey said gelding hung right

4394 HAPPY BIRTHDAY PAUL MASON H'CAP — 1m 3y
4:15 (4:15) (Class 5) (0-70,69) 3-Y-O+ — £2,264 (£673; £336; £168) Stalls High

Form — RPR
3111 **1** **Camberley Two**[27] 3481 3-8-11 **67** .... KieranO'Neill(3) 3 — 86+
(Roger Charlton) *a.p: pushed along 1/2-way: led over 1f out: sn hung rt: clr fnl f: readily* **5/4**[1]
0422 **2** *3 3/4* **Madame Excelerate**[6] 4185 4-9-6 **65** .... SebSanders 5 — 71
(Mark Brisbourne) *a.p: chsd ldr 1/2-way: led 2f out: rdn and hdd over 1f out: no ex fnl f* **3/1**[2]
0600 **3** *4* **Hill Tribe**[61] 2399 4-8-12 **60** .... MartinHarley(3) 2 — 57
(Richard Guest) *chsd ldr tl rdn 1/2-way: outpcd over 2f out: styd on u.p to go 3rd wl ins fnl f* **25/1**
0000 **4** *1* **Darcey**[10] 4066 5-9-4 **63** .... HayleyTurner 8 — 58
(Amy Weaver) *led over 5f: sn rdn: wknd ins fnl f* **16/1**
4640 **5** *3/4* **Dervisher (IRE)**[25] 3557 3-9-1 **68** ....(b) TomQueally 4 — 59
(Sir Henry Cecil) *s.i.s: hld up: rdn over 2f out: n.d* **7/1**[3]
3261 **6** *1 1/2* **Fault**[23] 3636 5-9-10 **69** ....(t) PatCosgrave 6 — 59
(Stef Higgins) *hld up: rdn over 2f out: nvr on terms* **7/1**[3]
605 **7** *20* **Isdaal**[32] 3320 4-9-3 **62** .... NeilCallan 9 — —
(Kevin Morgan) *chsd ldrs tl rdn and wknd over 2f out: eased fnl f: t.o* **8/1**

1m 37.9s (-2.70) **Going Correction** -0.35s/f (Firm)
WFA 3 from 4yo+ 8lb — **7** Ran SP% **115.3**
Speed ratings (Par 103): **99,95,91,90,89 88,68**
toteswingers:1&2:£1.80, 2&3:£8.30, 1&3:£7.10 CSF £5.22 CT £57.17 TOTE £2.30: £1.60, £1.80; EX 5.30.
Owner H R H Sultan Ahmad Shah **Bred** Barry Walters Farms **Trained** Beckhampton, Wilts
FOCUS
A modest handicap but a really well-handicapped winner in the shape of Camberley Two, who completed a four-timer. He is still well ahead of his mark.
Isdaal Official explanation: trainer said filly scoped dirty

4395 DIGIBET.COM H'CAP — 5f 43y
4:45 (4:48) (Class 6) (0-65,65) 3-Y-O+ — £1,617 (£481; £240; £120) Stalls High

Form — RPR
0612 **1** **Liberty Ship**[6] 4189 6-9-7 **60** ....(t) RoystonFfrench 7 — 71
(Mark Buckley) *racd centre: a.p: chsd ldr over 2f out: rdn to ld ins fnl f: edgd rt: all out* **9/2**[2]
3354 **2** *hd* **Clear Ice (IRE)**[10] 4041 4-9-11 **64** ....(b) NeilCallan 8 — 74
(Gay Kelleway) *racd stands' side: led that trio: rdn over 1f out: r.o: edgd lft nr fin: 1st of 3 in gp* **4/1**[1]
563 **3** *1 1/2* **Athwaab**[10] 4046 4-9-12 **65** .... TomQueally 6 — 70
(Noel Quinlan) *overall ldr in centre: rdn over 1f out: hdd and unable qck ins fnl f: 2nd of 6 in gp* **8/1**
4563 **4** *1 1/4* **Shakespeares Excel**[6] 4189 4-8-7 **46** .... JimmyQuinn 4 — 46
(Derek Shaw) *racd centre: chsd ldrs: rdn over 2f out: styd on: 3rd of 6 in gp* **5/1**[3]
3664 **5** *2 1/2* **Caramelita**[82] 1816 4-9-10 **63** .... AdrianMcCarthy 10 — 54
(J R Jenkins) *racd stands' side: chsd ldr: rdn and edgd lft over 2f out: styd on same pce fr over 1f out: 2nd of 3 in gp* **12/1**
4206 **6** *nk* **Ace Of Spies (IRE)**[9] 4086 6-9-10 **63** ....(b) HayleyTurner 9 — 53
(Conor Dore) *racd stands' side: prom: rdn 1/2-way: styd on same pce appr fnl f: last of 3 in gp* **10/1**
0340 **7** *2 3/4* **Elhamri**[9] 4086 7-9-9 **62** ....(b[1]) PatCosgrave 5 — 42
(Conor Dore) *racd centre: chsd ldr to 1/2-way: sn rdn: wknd over 1f out: 4th of 6 in gp* **16/1**
253 **8** *2* **These Dreams**[6] 4172 3-8-5 **51** ....(v[1]) MartinHarley(3) 3 — 24
(Richard Guest) *s.i.s: racd centre: hld up: a in rr: rdn and wknd over 1f out: 5th of 6 in gp* **7/1**
0050 **9** *5* **Wreningham**[6] 4182 6-9-0 **53** .... WilliamCarson 2 — —
(Stuart Williams) *racd centre: s.i.s: hld up: a in rr: rdn 1/2-way: wknd wl over 1f out: last of 6 in gp* **14/1**

61.72 secs (-0.98) **Going Correction** -0.35s/f (Firm)
WFA 3 from 4yo+ 4lb — **9** Ran SP% **107.8**
Speed ratings (Par 101): **93,92,90,88,84 83,79,76,68**
toteswingers:1&2:£3.20, 2&3:£6.20, 1&3:£5.10 CSF £20.15 CT £118.41 TOTE £3.70: £1.40, £1.70, £2.80; EX 19.70.
Owner David Lockwood & Fred Lockwood **Bred** Mrs R D Peacock **Trained** Castle Bytham, Stanford
FOCUS
The field split, with the majority racing up the centre and three runners sticking towards the near rail, but just like when there was a difference of opinion earlier on the card, the track seemed fair. This is moderate form, with the winner rated back to last year's best.

4396 TIDE & TIME MUSEUM H'CAP — 2m
5:15 (5:16) (Class 6) (0-65,65) 4-Y-O+ — £1,617 (£481; £240; £120) Stalls High

Form — RPR
0234 **1** **Dr Finley (IRE)**[20] 3712 4-8-13 **60** .... SimonPearce(3) 8 — 69
(Lydia Pearce) *chsd ldrs: led over 2f out: rdn over 1f out: styd on* **9/2**[2]
360- **2** *2* **Go Amwell**[33] 7805 8-8-2 **46** oh1 ....(v) AdrianMcCarthy 5 — 53
(J R Jenkins) *s.i.s: pushed along early in rr: swtchd rt and hdwy over 2f out: sn chsng wnr: no ex ins fnl f* **7/1**
5-64 **3** *9* **Rosie Raymond**[52] 2669 6-8-5 **49** .... KirstyMilczarek 4 — 45
(Charles Smith) *hld up: hdwy over 4f out: rdn over 2f out: wknd over 1f out* **20/1**
0-05 **4** *nk* **Sulliman**[28] 3469 4-8-8 **52** .... MartinLane 12 — 47
(George Margarson) *hld up in tch: rdn over 3f out: wknd over 1f out* **14/1**
4402 **5** *4* **Marcus Antonius**[12] 3978 4-9-2 **60** ....(v[1]) PatCosgrave 6 — 51
(Jim Boyle) *trckd ldrs: wnt 2nd 4f out: rdn over 2f out: wknd over 1f out* **4/1**[1]
3040 **6** *2* **Jackson (BRZ)**[5] 4198 9-8-5 **49** ....(v) JimmyQuinn 10 — 37
(Richard Guest) *hld up: rdn over 3f out: hung lft over 1f out: nvr on terms* **12/1**
50 0 **7** *nk* **Judgethemoment (USA)**[185] 244 6-9-0 **65** .... LauraSimpson(7) 9 — 53
(Jane Chapple-Hyam) *sn chsng ldr: led 4f out: hdd over 2f out: wknd over 1f out* **14/1**
6/00 **8** *8* **Alltheclews**[8] 4129 6-8-0 **47** ....(p) KieranO'Neill(3) 7 — 25
(Lucinda Featherstone) *prom: rdn over 4f out: wknd over 2f out* **16/1**
5305 **9** *11* **Stormy Morning**[19] 3725 5-9-4 **62** .... LiamKeniry 11 — 27
(J S Moore) *hld up: bhd fnl 4f: t.o* **8/1**
-500 **10** *42* **Pyjoma**[20] 3712 4-8-3 **47** ow1 ....(p) HayleyTurner 1 — —
(Julia Feilden) *led 12f: wknd over 2f out: t.o* **10/1**
5110 **11** *10* **Camera Shy (IRE)**[40] 3054 7-9-3 **61** .... TomQueally 2 — —
(Kevin Morgan) *hld up in tch: rdn and wknd over 3f out: t.o* **6/1**[3]

3m 31.52s (-0.88) **Going Correction** -0.35s/f (Firm) — **11** Ran SP% **116.8**
Speed ratings (Par 101): **88,87,82,82,80 79,79,75,69,48 43**
toteswingers:1&2:£5.90, 2&3:£11.90, 1&3:£16.10 CSF £35.88 CT £573.99 TOTE £5.30: £1.60, £2.50, £4.80; EX 38.70.
Owner Killarney Glen **Bred** Darley **Trained** Newmarket, Suffolk
FOCUS
A really moderate staying handicap and they didn't seem to go that quick early on, resulting in a time over seven seconds above standard. The first two were clear and the form is rated around them.
Camera Shy(IRE) Official explanation: jockey said gelding stopped quickly
T/Plt: £48.90 to a £1 stake. Pool of £62,538.40 - 933.59 winning tickets. T/Qpdt: £19.90 to a £1 stake. Pool of £4,609.14 - 170.70 winning tickets. CR

4397a, 4399 - 4401a - (Foreign Racing) - See Raceform Interactive

GALWAY (R-H)
Monday, July 25
OFFICIAL GOING: Good (good to yielding in places)

4398a CARLTON.IE/GALWAYCITY (QR) H'CAP — 2m
6:45 (6:46) (70-100,99) 4-Y-O+
£38,793 (£12,284; £5,818; £1,939; £1,293; £646)

RPR
1 **Fosters Cross (IRE)**[29] 3443 9-10-1 **77** .... MrCMotherway(5) 4 — 83
(Thomas Mullins, Ire) *led fr early: stl travelling wl and clr over 2f out: styd on wl u.p fnl f* **10/1**[3]

2 *4* **Cry For The Moon (USA)**[30] 3420 5-10-6 82............. MrJTCarroll(5) 11 84
(J H Culloty, Ire) *mid-div: hdwy over 2f out: sn no imp u.p: mod 2nd and kpt on fnl f* **12/1**

3 *hd* **Table Mountain (IRE)**[37] 3196 4-11-6 96.....................(p) MrBO'Neill(5) 2 98
(Robert Alan Hennessy, Ire) *chsd ldrs: mod 4th over 2f out: sn no imp u.p: mod 3rd and kpt on fnl f* **20/1**

4 *3 1/2* **Eagle's Pass (IRE)**[13] 2974 9-10-8 86............................ MrJARyan(7) 8 84
(T J O'Mara, Ire) *hld up: t.k.h: 10th after 1/2-way: kpt on wout threatening u.p fr over 2f out* **16/1**

5 *1 1/2* **Bremen**[35] 5432 8-11-2 90......................................(t) MrATDuff(3) 14 86
(Paul W Flynn, Ire) *hld up: rdn to chse ldrs over 2f out: sn no imp: kpt on* **33/1**

6 *4 1/2* **Kalann (IRE)**[15] 3896 4-10-6 80............................... MrJPMcKeown(3) 16 71
(Sabrina J Harty, Ire) *towards rr: rdn and hdwy over 2f out: sn no imp: kpt on* **10/1**[3]

7 *3/4* **Natural High (IRE)**[38] 3150 6-11-3 88........................ MrRPMcNamara 1 79
(D K Weld, Ire) *led early: sn chsd ldr: no imp u.p and kpt on same pce fr over 2f out* **9/2**[1]

8 *3/4* **Much Acclaimed (IRE)**[6] 1780 4-9-13 77.................... MrNMKelly(7) 17 67
(J Morrison, Ire) *sn mid-div: t.k.h: kpt on same pce u.p fr over 2f out* **20/1**

9 *nk* **Blue Ridge Lane (IRE)**[7] 1381 5-9-13 77...............(bt) MsLisaO'Neill(7) 6 66
(John C McConnell, Ire) *chsd ldrs: 9th under 4f out: kpt on same pce u.p fr over 2f out* **50/1**

10 *3/4* **End Of The Affair (IRE)**[13] 3963 7-11-7 99...................... BHayes(7) 19 88
(V C Ward, Ire) *chsd ldrs: 8th under 4f out: kpt on same pce u.p fr over 2f out* **16/1**

11 *3* **Oneeightofamile (IRE)**[17] 3420 6-10-5 83...................... MrDKiely(7) 12 68
(John E Kiely, Ire) *towards rr: hdwy on outer 3f out: no imp u.p and kpt on same pce fr over 2f out* **9/2**[1]

12 *1 1/2* **Rattan (USA)**[29] 3443 6-11-0 85.. MsKWalsh 15 69
(W P Mullins, Ire) *t.k.h: sn chsd ldrs: 6th under 4f out: kpt on same pce u.p fr 2f out* **11/1**

13 *5* **Prospectorous (IRE)**[36] 7263 7-11-5 90......................(tp) MrJJCodd 10 68
(J P Dempsey, Ire) *chsd ldrs: 6th after 1/2-way: kpt on same pce u.p fr 2f out* **16/1**

14 *5* **Zaralabad (IRE)**[24] 3605 7-11-0 85...........................(t) MissNCarberry 20 58
(C F Swan, Ire) *nvr bttr than mid-div* **16/1**

15 *1 1/2* **Praxiteles (IRE)**[14] 3911 7-11-1 86......................(tp) MrDerekO'Connor 7 57
(Rebecca Curtis) *prom: no ex fr 2f out* **8/1**[2]

16 *nk* **Admiral Barry (IRE)**[30] 3418 6-11-10 98.................. MrMPFogarty(3) 13 69
(Eoin Griffin, Ire) *mid-div: 13th early: 10th under 4f out: no ex fr 2f out* **20/1**

17 *1 3/4* **Silk Hall (UAE)**[30] 3420 6-10-12 86....................... MrMMO'Connor(3) 18 55
(J J Lambe, Ire) *towards rr for most: nvr a factor* **14/1**

18 *23* **Baron De'L (IRE)**[8] 4134 8-10-9 87................................(b) MrPHarty(7) 9 30
(Edward P Harty, Ire) *mid-div best: struggling fr early* **33/1**

19 *dist* **Fantasy King**[24] 3605 5-10-7 85..............................(t) MrPJMcMahon(7) 5 —
(Charles O'Brien, Ire) *sn mid-div: 11th after 1/2-way: no ex 2f out: t.o* **16/1**

20 *dist* **Gretzky**[15] 3896 4-10-3 77..(bt[1]) MrPRoche(3) 3 —
(Robert Alan Hennessy, Ire) *chsd ldrs: wknd 4f out: completely t.o* **33/1**

3m 45.02s (0.22) **20** Ran SP% **142.8**
CSF £132.47 CT £2444.67 TOTE £12.60: £2.40, £2.80, £7.20, £4.10; DF 159.50.
Owner Patrick J O'Donovan **Bred** Harry Boyle **Trained** Goresbridge, Co Kilkenny

FOCUS
The form is rated around the runner-up.

NOTEBOOK
Fosters Cross(IRE) will aim for a big-race double in Thursday's Galway Hurdle after a commanding victory in the opening-night feature. A former Grade 3 novice chase winner at the venue, he had gained his most recent win in a conditions hurdle at Downpatrick in March, and had run twice in 1m4f handicaps at the Curragh in recent months. Appreciating a return to the trip over which he won a maiden at Navan, he made the running from an early stage and maintained his effort well for his very capable 5lb-claiming rider. (op 12/1)
Cry For The Moon(USA), a former British-trained gelding who has been performing consistently for Jim Culloty this season, got into contention from 2f down and kept on gamely. (op 14/1)
Table Mountain(IRE) started off for Robbie Hennessy with a win at Roscommon before a disappointing effort in the Ulster Derby. He bounced back from that with a solid display here on his first attempt in a thorough test of stamina.
Eagle's Pass(IRE) responded well to the challenge offered by this venue. Two of the best runs of his career were when placed in the Galway Hurdle and, having ended a barren spell by winning on his handicap chase debut at Killarney, he seems to be in fine shape at the moment. He should be worth looking out for when he goes back over fences. (op 16/1 tchd 18/1)
Bremen did not appear to be one of the stronger contenders, and ran a fine race in the circumstances. The impression that he is badly treated in Flat handicaps may have to be revised.
Kalann(IRE), quite well fancied after winning a 1m4f Fairyhouse event, came from a long way back without posing a serious threat. (op 11/1)
Natural High(IRE) failed to make the impact that might have been expected after a good Limerick win. (op 9/2 tchd 11/2)
Oneeightofamile(IRE) spent much of the race in rear. Official explanation: vet said gelding was found to be coughing post-race (op 7/1)
Praxiteles(IRE) faded after running prominently for a long way. (op 7/1)
Gretzky Official explanation: jockey said gelding suffered interference, was unable to hold his position and dropped back before the turn into the straight; he added it lost its action and was eased in the latter stages

4147 BEVERLEY (R-H)

Tuesday, July 26

OFFICIAL GOING: Good to firm (good in places; 8.2)
Wind: Moderate across Weather: Overcast and chilly wind

4402 EBF HOLDERNESS PONY CLUB MAIDEN STKS — 7f 100y

2:10 (2:13) (Class 5) 2-Y-O — **£3,169** (£943; £471; £235) **Stalls** Low

Form — RPR

2 **1** **Croquembouche (IRE)**[14] 3954 2-9-3 0.............................. WilliamBuick 9 74+
(Sir Michael Stoute) *mde all: pushed along over 2f out: rdn over 1f out: green and edgd lft ins fnl f: kpt on* **4/11**[1]

2 *1/2* **Ghalaa (IRE)** 2-8-12 0.. TadhgO'Shea 4 66+
(Mark Johnston) *trckd ldrs: hdwy to trck wnr 1/2-way: chal 2f out: rdn and green over 1f out: kpt on ins fnl f* **7/2**[2]

0 **3** *3 1/2* **Dr Irv**[68] 2214 2-9-0 0... MichaelO'Connell(3) 6 62
(Kate Walton) *in tch: hdwy over 2f out: rdn wl over 1f out: kpt on to take 3rd ins fnl f* **100/1**

4 *1* **Landown Littlerock** 2-9-0 0.. PaulPickard(3) 7 59
(Reg Hollinshead) *trckd ldr on inner: pushed along to chse ldng pair 1/2-way: rdn along wl over 2f out: sn one pce* **50/1**

65 **5** *3 3/4* **Bitaphon (IRE)**[40] 3082 2-9-3 0..................................... FrederikTylicki 3 50
(Deborah Sanderson) *t.k.h early: chsd ldrs: pushed along 1/2-way: sn rdn and outpcd* **8/1**[3]

6 *1/2* **Astonished Harry (GER)** 2-9-3 0.................................. RussKennemore 5 49
(Reg Hollinshead) *dwlt and in rr: sme hdwy 2f out: n.d* **20/1**

7 *4 1/2* **Up Ten Down Two (IRE)** 2-9-3 0...............................(t) JamesSullivan 1 38
(Michael Easterby) *a in rr* **12/1**

8 *5* **Phoenix Order** 2-8-10 0... NoraLooby(7) 8 25
(Alan McCabe) *chsd ldrs: rdn along over 3f out: sn wknd* **25/1**

1m 37.15s (3.35) **Going Correction** -0.325s/f (Firm) **8** Ran SP% **125.9**
Speed ratings (Par 94): **67,66,62,61,57 56,51,45**
Tote Swingers: 1&2 £1.60, 1&3 £15.50, 2&3 £12.10 CSF £2.37 TOTE £1.40: £1.10, £1.50, £15.80; EX 2.60.
Owner Ballymacoll Stud **Bred** Ballymacoll Stud Farm Ltd **Trained** Newmarket, Suffolk

FOCUS
Bottom bend moved out to provide fresh ground but impact on distances not advised. What turned out to be a two-horse race was run at a very steady early gallop, with the long odds-on favourite forced to dig deep. Dubious form, rated around the winner to his debut effort.

NOTEBOOK
Croquembouche(IRE), Sir Michael Stoute's first runner at the Westwood this year, is by Acclamation, an influence for speed, from the dam-line of Group 1 1m4f winner Gamut. No-one else wanted to lead, so William Buick set just a steady pace. Hotly challenged halfway up the home straight, he had to really knuckle down to hold the filly at bay. He looks a stayer and will no doubt step up to 1m now. He looks a fair prospect. (op 2-5 tchd 4-9 in places)
Ghalaa(IRE), by Nayef from the family of the 1,000 Guineas winner Harayir, moved upsides 3f from home, seemingly travelling the stronger. After a good set to she came off just second best. She looks a certain future winner. (op 10-3)
Dr Irv, a 10,000gns purchase, had finished tailed off last on his debut in May. This was much more encouraging and there should be even better to come.
Landown Littlerock, from a yard without a first-time-out juvenile winner since 2008, is bred to make a middle-distance performer at three.
Bitaphon(IRE), who never got into the race, is now qualified for a nursery mark.
Astonished Harry(GER), another Reg Hollinshead-trained newcomer, likewise may need plenty more time.

4403 PEPPA PIG IS HERE TODAY (S) H'CAP — 1m 4f 16y

2:45 (2:45) (Class 6) (0-65,58) 3-Y-O — **£1,617** (£481; £240; £120) **Stalls** Low

Form — RPR

0660 **1** **Barnum (USA)**[10] 4112 3-8-13 **50**.............................. NeilCallan 5 59
(Mark Johnston) *trckd ldrs on inner: hdwy 3f out: led 2f out: rdn and hung lft over 1f out: drvn and hung bdly rt to rails ins fnl f: drvn clr* **7/1**

4546 **2** *3 1/4* **Dark Spirit (IRE)**[27] 3518 3-9-7 **58**.............................. WilliamBuick 8 65+
(Tim Pitt) *hld up: stdy hdwy over 3f out: chsd ldrs 2f out: rdn and ev ch whn bdly hmpd ins fnl f: kpt on towards fin* **4/1**[1]

5425 **3** *3/4* **Goodmanyourself**[28] 3496 3-8-9 **46**.............................. MickyFenton 11 49
(Paul Midgley) *hld up in rr: hdwy 3f out: rdn to chse ldrs over 1f out: drvn and kpt on ins fnl f: nrst fin* **4/1**[1]

-060 **4** *1 1/4* **Fimias (IRE)**[13] 3976 3-9-4 **55**.............................. DanielTudhope 9 56
(Geoffrey Harker) *chsd ldrs: rdn along over 2f out: drvn over 1f out: kpt on same pce* **9/2**[2]

3534 **5** *1 3/4* **Commander Veejay**[8] 4151 3-8-8 **45**.....................(p) AndrewHeffernan 6 43
(Brian Rothwell) *bmpd s and in rr: swtchd wd and hdwy wl over 2f out: rdn to chse ldrs over 1f out: sn drvn and no imp* **5/1**[3]

3030 **6** *2 1/4* **Mayan Flight (IRE)**[11] 4077 3-8-12 **49**.....................(b[1]) TonyHamilton 1 44
(Richard Whitaker) *cl up: led after 1 1/2f: rdn along 3f out: hdd 2f out and sn drvn: hld whn hmpd ins fnl f* **10/1**

6061 **7** *3 3/4* **Smart Violetta (IRE)**[12] 4018 3-8-8 **48**..........................(t) LeeTopliss(3) 7 37
(Ann Duffield) *midfield: effrt to chse ldrs over 3f out: rdn over 2f out: sn drvn and wknd* **9/1**

0000 **8** *2 3/4* **Go**[10] 2786 3-8-1 **45**.. ShaneBKelly(7) 2 29
(Micky Hammond) *chsd ldrs: rdn along on inner 3f out: grad wknd* **33/1**

00-0 **9** *1 1/4* **Diamond City (IRE)**[109] 1211 3-9-2 **53**..................(p) FrederikTylicki 3 35
(Deborah Sanderson) *led tl rn wd bnd after 1f: chsd ldr: rdn along 3f out and sn wknd* **20/1**

660 **10** *9* **Tuscany Red**[21] 3710 3-8-8 **45**..................................(e) RobbieFitzpatrick 4 13
(Richard Guest) *a in rr* **33/1**

2m 38.17s (-1.63) **Going Correction** -0.325s/f (Firm) **10** Ran SP% **117.1**
Speed ratings (Par 98): **92,89,89,88,87 85,83,81,80,74**
Tote Swingers: 1&2 £6.20, 1&3 £6.70, 2&3 £3.30 CSF £34.57 CT £127.34 TOTE £9.90: £3.50, £1.10, £1.80; EX 32.70.Winner bought by David Easterby for 4,000gns.
Owner Dr Marwan Koukash **Bred** Darley **Trained** Middleham Moor, N Yorks
■ Stewards' Enquiry : Neil Callan four-day ban: careless riding (Aug 9-12)

FOCUS
A rock bottom 3-y-os selling handicap which run at a sound pace. Limited form, with the third setting the level.

4404 WILFORD WATTS MEMORIAL H'CAP — 1m 100y

3:20 (3:20) (Class 4) (0-85,84) 3-Y-O+ — **£4,204** (£1,251; £625; £312) **Stalls** Low

Form — RPR

6430 **1** **Jonny Lesters Hair (IRE)**[10] 4109 6-9-3 **74**.............................. DavidAllan 8 86
(Tim Easterby) *cl up: led after 2f: rdn along 2f out: drvn appr fnl f and kpt on strly* **6/1**[3]

0000 **2** *2 1/2* **Hacienda (IRE)**[18] 3797 4-9-10 **81**.............................. NeilCallan 5 87
(Mark Johnston) *led 2f: trckd ldng pair tl effrt to chse wnr over 3f out: rdn wl over 1f out: drvn appr fnl f and sn no imp* **6/1**[3]

-000 **3** *1 1/4* **Ginger Jack**[49] 2783 4-9-13 **84**.............................. WilliamBuick 11 87+
(Geoffrey Harker) *hld up towards rr: hdwy over 3f out: rdn to chse ldrs 2f out: drvn and styd on ins fnl f: nrst fin* **4/1**[2]

32-1 **4** *3/4* **Mujrayaat (IRE)**[26] 3543 3-9-4 **83**.............................. TadhgO'Shea 4 83
(Roger Varian) *trckd ldrs: hdwy 3f out: rdn over 2f out: sn drvn and one pce appr fnl f* **2/1**[1]

1034 **5** *1 3/4* **Bolodenka (IRE)**[14] 3934 9-9-0 **71**.............................. TonyHamilton 6 69
(Richard Fahey) *chsd ldrs: rdn along wl over 2f out: drvn over 1f out and kpt on same pce* **20/1**

-101 **6** *3/4* **Toto Skyllachy**[14] 3934 6-9-13 **84**.............................. FrederikTylicki 2 80
(Ollie Pears) *hld up towards rr: effrt over 2f out and sn rdn: drvn wl over 1f out: kpt on same pce* **8/1**

0326 **7** *2 1/2* **Ginger Grey (IRE)**[11] 4051 4-9-2 **73**..........................(b) DanielTudhope 1 63
(David O'Meara) *in tch on inner: effrt 3f out: sn rdn along and grad wknd* **16/1**

0000 **8** *6* **Follow The Flag (IRE)**[12] 4004 7-9-8 **79**.................(v) RobertWinston 10 55
(Alan McCabe) *a in rr* **33/1**

6042 **9** *4 1/2* **Ours (IRE)**[8] 4150 8-9-3 **74**..(p) BarryMcHugh 7 40
(John Harris) *dwlt and towards rr: sme hdwy over 2f out: sn rdn and nvr a factor* **12/1**

100 **10** *11* **Ivory Jazz**[11] 4070 4-9-6 **77**.. RobbieFitzpatrick 9 18
(Richard Guest) *prom: cl up 1/2-way: rdn along 3f out and sn wknd* **66/1**

1m 43.27s (-4.33) **Going Correction** -0.325s/f (Firm)
WFA 3 from 4yo+ 8lb **10** Ran SP% **115.8**
Speed ratings (Par 105): **108,105,104,103,101 101,98,92,88,77**
Tote Swingers: 1&2 £4.20, 1&3 £5.60, 2&3 £4.10 CSF £40.77 CT £164.78 TOTE £8.00: £2.40, £2.00, £2.10; EX 33.80.
Owner Reality Partnerships II **Bred** Gary O'Reilly **Trained** Great Habton, N Yorks

FOCUS
A 71-84 handicap run at a very strong pace. Solid form, the winner back to his best.
Jonny Lesters Hair(IRE) Official explanation: trainer's rep said, regarding apparent improvement in form, that the gelding settled better in front and was suited by a return to the track, course and distance winner twice.

4405 THEOLDGRAVELPITLODGES.CO.UK H'CAP 5f
3:55 (3:55) (Class 5) (0-75,74) 3-Y-O+ **£2,264** (£673; £336; £168) **Stalls** Low

Form RPR

4022 **1** **Caranbola**[4] 4288 5-9-8 **70**.. RobertWinston 12 80
(Mel Brittain) *sn trcking ldr: cl up 2f out: rdn to ld appr fnl f: drvn out* **13/8**[1]

0661 **2** *1 ¾* **Red Roar (IRE)**[8] 4152 4-9-4 **66** 6ex............................ RoystonFfrench 7 70
(Alan Berry) *trckd ldng pair: effrt 2f out: rdn to chse wnr ent fnl f: sn drvn and no imp towards fin* **6/1**[2]

6540 **3** *nse* **Captain Scooby**[3] 4327 5-9-2 **67**...................................(p) AmyRyan(3) 9 71
(Richard Whitaker) *towards rr: hdwy 2f out: sn rdn and styd on wl fnl f: nrst fin* **10/1**

4031 **4** *1 ¼* **Media Jury**[14] 3937 4-9-0 **62** ow2......................................(v) DavidNolan 8 61
(John Wainwright) *led: rdn along and jnd 2f out: drvn and hdd appr fnl f: kpt on same pce* **16/1**

4-40 **5** *nk* **Alis Aquilae (IRE)**[25] 3582 5-9-9 **71**................................. WilliamBuick 6 69
(Tim Etherington) *chsd ldrs and edgd rt after 1f: rdn along over 2f out: drvn over 1f out and sn one pce* **6/1**[2]

0344 **6** *¾* **Dispol Kylie (IRE)**[9] 4126 5-9-5 **70**...................... MichaelO'Connell(3) 2 66
(Kate Walton) *chsd ldrs: effrt on inner 1/2-way: rdn along wl over 2f out: sn one pce* **9/1**[3]

345 **7** *¾* **Select Committee**[45] 2938 6-9-5 **74**..........................(b) ShaneBKelly(7) 4 67
(John Quinn) *in tch: sltly hmpd after 1f and towards rr: effrt over 2f out: sn rdn and n.m.r wl over 1f out: sn drvn and n.d* **6/1**[2]

2060 **8** *1 ½* **Ryedane (IRE)**[8] 4152 9-8-12 **65**...............................(b) LanceBetts(5) 10 52
(Tim Easterby) *chsd ldrs on wd outside: rdn along over 2f out: wknd wl over 1f out* **16/1**

-000 **9** *15* **Commanche Raider (IRE)**[8] 4152 4-9-10 **72**..........(b[1]) FrederikTylicki 1 —
(Michael Dods) *cl up on inner whn n.m.r and hmpd after 1f: dropped to rr and sn bhd: eased fr 1/2-way* **20/1**

61.40 secs (-2.10) **Going Correction** -0.325s/f (Firm) **9** Ran SP% **116.6**
Speed ratings (Par 103): **103,100,100,98,97 96,95,92,68**
Tote Swingers: 1&2 £2.10, 1&3 £5.70, 2&3 £10.80 CSF £11.66 CT £75.30 TOTE £1.80: £1.10, £2.50, £3.40; EX 10.70.
Owner Mel Brittain **Bred** T E Pocock **Trained** Warthill, N Yorks

FOCUS
A 62-74 sprint handicap and a convincing winner. The time was good and the form looks solid.
Commanche Raider(IRE) Official explanation: jockey said gelding suffered interference in running

4406 RON BRAY MEMORIAL MAIDEN AUCTION FILLIES' STKS 5f
4:30 (4:31) (Class 5) 2-Y-O **£2,264** (£673; £336; £168) **Stalls** Low

Form RPR

50 **1** **Winter Hill**[54] 2630 2-8-4 0.. AndrewElliott 10 71+
(Tom Dascombe) *wnt lft s: in tch on wd outside: hdwy over 2f out: rdn to ld jst over 1f out: drvn out* **11/4**[1]

4222 **2** *1 ½* **First Fast Now (IRE)**[14] 3932 2-8-4 0........................ DeclanCannon(3) 9 67
(Nigel Tinkler) *hld up towards rr: hdwy 2f out: rdn to chse wnr ins fnl f: kpt on* **9/2**[3]

4063 **3** *1 ¼* **Phoenix Clubs (IRE)**[24] 3639 2-8-4 0............................. JimmyQuinn 3 61
(Paul Midgley) *wnt rt and bmpd s: hld up in tch hdwy whn nt clr run 2f out and again over 1f out: rdn and styd on wl fnl f* **9/1**

4 *nk* **Cried For You (IRE)** 2-8-6 0 ow2....................................... DavidAllan 6 60+
(Tim Easterby) *hld up towards rr: hdwy 2f out: n.m.r over 1f out: rdn and styd on ins fnl f: nrst fin* **14/1**

5 *2 ¼* **Vitalicious** 2-8-7 0.. MartinLane 2 53+
(Ed McMahon) *wnt lft and bmpd s: green and sn pushed along in rr: rdn 1/2-way: swtchd wd and hdwy over 1f out: styd on wl fnl f: nrst fin* **7/2**[2]

6 *nk* **Crimson Sea (IRE)** 2-8-4 0.. JamesSullivan 4 49
(Ben Haslam) *chsd ldrs on inner: effrt and n.m.r 2f out and again over 1f out: kpt on ins fnl f* **33/1**

0336 **7** *shd* **Angel Of Hope (IRE)**[14] 3932 2-8-11 0......................... RoystonFfrench 5 56
(Bryan Smart) *cl up: rdn 2f out: sn drvn and grad wknd* **16/1**

425 **8** *2* **Mantuana (IRE)**[14] 3932 2-8-4 0...................................... TadhgO'Shea 8 42
(David O'Meara) *prom: effrt over 2f out: sn rdn: edgd lft and wknd* **8/1**

6 **9** *½* **Lady Hello (IRE)**[10] 4106 2-8-4 0.................................. AndrewHeffernan 7 40
(Mick Channon) *prom: rdn along 2f out: sn wandered and wknd* **8/1**

5060 **10** *1 ¼* **Economic Crisis (IRE)**[4] 4283 2-8-4 0........................... AndrewMullen 1 35
(Alan Berry) *led: rdn along 2f out: drvn and hdd over 1f out: wknd qckly* **25/1**

62.94 secs (-0.56) **Going Correction** -0.325s/f (Firm) **10** Ran SP% **118.6**
Speed ratings (Par 91): **91,88,86,86,82 82,81,78,77,75**
Tote Swingers: 1&2 £3.20, 1&3 £8.10, 2&3 £5.40 CSF £15.48 TOTE £4.90: £1.70, £1.90, £3.70; EX 17.70.
Owner The MHS 4x10 Partnership **Bred** Burns Farm Stud **Trained** Malpas, Cheshire

FOCUS
A modest maiden auction fillies' race and the first two home made their efforts widest of all. The time was slow but the winner looks a shade better than the bare form.

NOTEBOOK
Winter Hill, a creditable fifth on her debut at Newbury, ran poorly when turned out two weeks later at Hamilton. Given a 54-day break, she still looked inexperienced, but was in command at the line. She looks ideal nursery material. (op 4-1)
First Fast Now(IRE), beaten two heads and a neck when runner-up on her three most recent starts, again had to settle for the silver medal. Her turn must come. (op 7-2)
Phoenix Clubs(IRE), awkward exiting the stalls, was left short of room at a crucial stage. She may not be entirely straightforward but has the ability to make her mark. (op 17-2 tchd 8-1)
Cried For You(IRE), a cheap purchase, made eyecatching late headway and will be a lot sharper next time. (op 16-1)
Vitalicious, speedily-bred and a half-sister to three juvenile winners, soon found herself in a poor position. Sticking on at the finish, this should have taught her plenty. (op 4-1)
Crimson Sea(IRE), another bred for speed, looked fairly clueless but was picking up in her own time late on. She will have learnt plenty. (tchd 28-1)
Angel Of Hope(IRE) was up against it trying to give weight away all round. (op 12-1)
Lady Hello(IRE) didn't improve on her debut effort at Ripon. (op 17-2)

4407 BEVERLEY MIDDLE DISTANCE SERIES H'CAP 1m 4f 16y
5:05 (5:05) (Class 5) (0-75,75) 3-Y-O+ **£2,587** (£770; £384; £192) **Stalls** Low

Form RPR

6026 **1** **Grey Command (USA)**[2] 4366 6-8-10 **57** oh5............. RobertWinston 3 63
(Mel Brittain) *trckd ldng pair: effrt on inner over 2f out: rdn over 1f out: led appr fnl f: drvn out* **10/1**

5411 **2** *1* **Lemon Drop Red (USA)**[21] 3715 3-8-13 **72**.................... WilliamBuick 1 76
(Ed Dunlop) *trckd ldrs: hdwy on outer 3f out: effrt 2f out: rdn to chal whn hung bdly rt ent fnl f: drvn and one pce after* **11/4**[2]

4-42 **3** *2 ¼* **Alfouzy**[20] 3739 3-9-2 **75**.. NeilCallan 7 78+
(Roger Varian) *trckd ldr: hdwy and cl up 4f out: rdn to chal 2f out: drvn and ev ch whn hmpd ent fnl f: one pce after* **9/4**[1]

-140 **4** *¾* **Red Fama**[18] 3828 7-9-11 **72**.. AndrewElliott 6 72
(Neville Bycroft) *trckd ldrs on inner: effrt 3f out: rdn along 2f out: drvn over 1f out: kpt on same pce* **4/1**[3]

0006 **5** *nk* **Kingsdale Orion (IRE)**[14] 3938 7-9-0 **61**......................... JimmyQuinn 5 60+
(Brian Ellison) *hld up in rr: hdwy wl over 2f out: rdn wl over 1f out: sn drvn and one pce* **9/2**

1506 **6** *nk* **Kingaroo (IRE)**[12] 4024 5-8-8 **58**... BillyCray(3) 4 57
(Garry Woodward) *led: rdn along wl over 2f out: drvn over 1f out: hdd jst over 1f out: cl up whn hmpd ent fnl f: wknd after* **33/1**

4000 **7** *2 ½* **Record Breaker (IRE)**[15] 3911 7-9-7 **73**.......................(b) DarylByrne(5) 2 68
(Mark Johnston) *a in rr: rdn along 4f out: nvr a factor* **16/1**

2m 41.12s (1.32) **Going Correction** -0.325s/f (Firm)
WFA 3 from 5yo+ 12lb **7** Ran SP% **113.5**
Speed ratings (Par 103): **82,81,79,79,79 78,77**
Tote Swingers: 1&2 £2.30, 1&3 £2.90, 2&3 £1.70 CSF £37.13 TOTE £19.30: £3.80, £2.70; EX 40.70.
Owner Mel Brittain **Bred** Darley **Trained** Warthill, N Yorks
■ Stewards' Enquiry : William Buick two-day ban: careless riding (Aug 9-10)

FOCUS
A modest 57-73 handicap and the pace was very steady until the foot of the final hill. The form is a bit dubious, with the winner 5lb wrong.
Kingaroo(IRE) Official explanation: jockey said, regarding riding, appearing to ease, that as he was only four strides from the line, he had not lost momentum and therefore would not have achieved a better position.

4408 LADY JANE BETHELL MEMORIAL LADY RIDERS' H'CAP (FOR LADY AMATEUR RIDERS) (DIV I) 1m 1f 207y
5:35 (5:36) (Class 6) (0-65,65) 3-Y-O+ **£1,317** (£405; £202) **Stalls** Low

Form RPR

4043 **1** **Lucayan Dancer**[6] 4198 11-9-1 **52**............................. MissJWalker(7) 9 61
(David Nicholls) *in rr: effrt over 2f out and sn rdn: hdwy over 1f out: str run ent fnl f: styd on wl to ld last 50yds* **15/2**

5224 **2** *1 ¼* **Kyle Of Bute**[14] 3938 5-10-4 **62**................................. MissSBrotherton 5 68
(Brian Baugh) *trckd ldrs: hdwy over 3f out and sn chsng ldr: led 1 1/2f out: sn rdn clr: drvn ins fnl f: hdd and no ex last 50yds* **4/1**[1]

2655 **3** *1 ½* **Rub Of The Relic (IRE)**[14] 3938 6-9-0 **51**...............(v) MissHDukes(7) 11 54
(Paul Midgley) *led to 1/2-way: cl up: effrt over 2f out: sn ev ch: rdn wl over 1f out and kpt on same pce* **15/2**

6000 **4** *1 ¼* **Tropical Duke (IRE)**[14] 3938 5-9-1 **50** ow1..................(p) MissVBarr(5) 2 51
(Ron Barr) *hld up towards rr: hdwy wl over 2f out: swtchd lft and rdn to chse ldrs over 1f out: kpt on same pce* **15/2**

0535 **5** *1 ¼* **Grethel (IRE)**[8] 4142 7-9-2 **46** oh1..................................... MrsCBartley 3 44
(Alan Berry) *midfield: hdwy over 3f out: chsd ldrs over 2f out: sn rdn and one pce* **7/1**[3]

00/0 **6** *2* **Freddie Bolt**[56] 2591 5-8-9 **46** oh1.......................... MissVictoriaCasey(7) 7 40
(Frederick Watson) *towards rr: rdn along over 3f out: kpt on u.p fnl 2f: nrst fin* **66/1**

-000 **7** *1 ½* **Hurricane Thomas (IRE)**[14] 3938 7-9-5 **54**.......... MissPhillipaTutty(5) 6 45
(Karen Tutty) *hld up: hdwy over 4f out: effrt to chse ldrs over 2f out: sn rdn and no imp* **14/1**

6665 **8** *shd* **Twisted**[10] 4112 5-9-13 **57**..(b) MissJCoward 13 48
(Michael Easterby) *dwlt: sn in tch: hdwy to trck ldrs 7f out: effrt over 3f out: sn rdn and wknd 2f out* **10/1**

00-0 **9** *2 ¼* [illegible][43] [illegible] 6-9-11 [illegible].. [illegible](7) 14 10
(Micky Hammond) *a bhd* **12/1**

2050 **10** *3 ½* **Verluga (IRE)**[90] 1615 4-9-2 **53**.. MissJGillam(7) 4 32
(Tim Easterby) *cl up: pushed along 1/2-way: sn wknd* **14/1**

1600 **11** *3* **Visions Of Johanna (USA)**[6] 4198 6-10-7 **65**........(bt[1]) MissZoeLilly 12 38
(Richard Guest) *cl up: led 1/2-way: rdn over 2f out: hdd and drvn 1 1/2f out: sn wknd* **16/1**

000- **12** *15* **Feuergott (GER)**[294] 6662 5-9-2 **46** oh1........................... MissEJJones 1 —
(Ian Williams) *a towards rr* **6/1**[2]

00-0 **13** *1* **Govenor Eliott (IRE)**[25] 3569 6-9-2 **46** oh1...............(v[1]) MissADeniel 10 —
(Alan Lockwood) *chsd ldrs: rdn along 4f out: sn wknd* **50/1**

-000 **14** *10* **Fitzwarren**[130] 895 10-8-9 **46** oh1..............................(tp) MissMKeegan(7) 8 —
(Alan Brown) *dwlt: a bhd* **40/1**

2m 5.37s (-1.63) **Going Correction** -0.325s/f (Firm) **14** Ran SP% **124.0**
Speed ratings (Par 101): **93,92,90,89,88 87,86,85,84,81 78,66,66,58**
Tote Swingers: 1&2 £4.80, 1&3 £9.70, 2&3 £8.90 CSF £38.40 CT £242.95 TOTE £9.20: £2.80, £1.90, £2.20.
Owner D Nicholls **Bred** The National Stud Owner Breeders Club Ltd **Trained** Sessay, N Yorks
■ Jenny Walker's first winner.
■ Stewards' Enquiry : Miss Phillipa Tutty four-day ban: careless riding (Aug 11-13,17)

FOCUS
Part one of a low-grade lady amateur riders' handicap and the pace as usual in this type of event was very sound. it was the faster of the two divisions. Sound form.
Fitzwarren Official explanation: jockey said gelding lost near-fore shoe

4409 LADY JANE BETHELL MEMORIAL LADY RIDERS' H'CAP (FOR LADY AMATEUR RIDERS) (DIV II) 1m 1f 207y
6:05 (6:07) (Class 6) (0-65,65) 3-Y-O+ **£1,317** (£405; £202) **Stalls** Low

Form RPR

-522 **1** **Obara D'Avril (FR)**[6] 4198 9-8-11 **45**.....................(p) MissCarlyFrater(7) 2 54
(Simon West) *in tch: hdwy on inner to trck ldrs after 3f: effrt over 2f out: rdn to chal wl over 1f out: kpt on ins fnl f to ld nr line* **5/1**[1]

0206 **2** *hd* **Silly Gilly (IRE)**[9] 4127 7-9-13 **59**....................................... MissVBarr(5) 5 67
(Ron Barr) *led: rdn 2f out: kpt on gamely fnl f: hdd and no ex nr line* **11/1**

4040 **3** *1 ¼* **Kheskianto (IRE)**[14] 3938 5-9-4 **45**.......................(bt) MissSBrotherton 11 51
(Michael Chapman) *hld up towards rr: gd hdwy on inner to trck ldrs halfwfy: effrt to chse ldng pair 2f out: effrt and nt clr run over 1f out: swtchd rt and rdn ins fnl f: kpt on* **7/1**[3]

0003 **4** *nk* **Politbureau**[10] 4111 4-9-5 **51**............ MissJoannaMason(5) 7 56
(Michael Easterby) *hld up and bhd: hdwy on inner 3f out: chsd ldrs over 1f out: sn rdn and hung lft ins fnl f: kpt on wl towards fin* **13/2**[2]

6402 **5** *2 3/4* **Rowan Lodge (IRE)**[14] 3938 9-10-2 **62**............(b) MissHBethell(5) 10 62
(Ollie Pears) *hld up: hdwy on outer over 4f out: chsd ldrs over 2f out: sn rdn and hung lft over 1f out: one pce* **13/2**[2]

-550 **6** *1* **Royal Composer (IRE)**[14] 3938 8-8-13 **45**......... MissRRichardson(5) 3 43
(Tim Easterby) *chsd ldrs: rdn along on outer over 2f out: sn hung lft and one pce* **17/2**

0220 **7** *nse* **Baby Driver**[28] 3495 3-9-7 **65**............ MissALMurphy(7) 9 62
(Tom Dascombe) *dwlt and plld hrd in rr: sme hdwy 2f out: kpt on fnl f: n.d* **10/1**

6-06 **8** *nk* **Rising Kheleyf (IRE)**[11] 4076 5-10-0 **60**............(p) MissCBoxall(5) 4 57
(John Harris) *t.k.h early: a in rr* **25/1**

-650 **9** *1 3/4* **Harare**[14] 3938 10-9-6 **52**............(v) MissPhillipaTutty(5) 13 45
(Karen Tutty) *chsd ldrs: pushed along over 4f out: sn wknd* **16/1**

0000 **10** *4 1/2* **Bold Indian (IRE)**[9] 4123 7-9-6 **47**............ MissEJJones 12 31
(Mike Sowersby) *in tch: hdwy to chse ldrs 7f out: cl up over 3f out: rdn over 2f out and sn wknd* **40/1**

2224 **11** *7* **Jay Jays Joy**[40] 3077 3-9-8 **62**............ MissWGibson(3) 6 32
(Paul Midgley) *prom: rdn along and lost pl bef 1/2-way: bhd after* **18/1**

2m 7.08s (0.08) **Going Correction** -0.325s/f (Firm)
WFA 3 from 4yo+ 10lb **11** Ran SP% **101.2**
Speed ratings (Par 101): **86,85,84,84,82 81,81,81,79,76 70**
Tote Swingers: 1&2 £12.10, 1&3 £6.50, 2&3 £6.40. Tote Super 7: Win: Not won Place: £324.10
CSF £41.92 CT £204.22 TOTE £5.20: £1.50, £3.20, £2.00; EX 54.30.
Owner S G West **Bred** Eurl Guittet **Trained** Middleham Moor, N Yorks
■ Carly Frater's first winner. Back To Paris (4/1F) was withdrawn after proving unruly at the start. Deduct 20p in the £ under R4.

FOCUS
The gallop was less even than the first division of the race and the time was over a second slower. Few got involved. The winner is rated to her recent best.
T/Plt: £46.90 to a £1 stake. Pool of £51,621.63 - 802.56 winning tickets. T/Qpdt: £32.40 to a £1 stake. Pool of £3,603.15 - 443.28 winning tickets. JR

3117 GOODWOOD (R-H)
Tuesday, July 26

OFFICIAL GOING: Good (8.4)
Wind: virtually nil Weather: overcast, brighter spells

4410 BET365.COM STKS (H'CAP) 1m 1f 192y
2:00 (2:01) (Class 2) 4-Y-0+
£28,012 (£8,388; £4,194; £2,097; £1,048; £526) **Stalls** Low

Form RPR

4130 **1** **Arlequin**[57] 2573 4-8-5 **91**............ GrahamGibbons 9 101
(James Bethell) *t.k.h: chsd ldrs: rdn and effrt over 1f out: led ins fnl f: hld on gamely cl home* **20/1**

-102 **2** *nk* **Modun (IRE)**[17] 3876 4-9-1 **101**............ RyanMoore 7 110+
(Sir Michael Stoute) *hld up in midfield: lost pl and dropped towards rr over 4f out: rdn hands and heels over 2f out: str run jst over 1f out: drvn and chsd wnr ins fnl f: r.o: nt quite rch wnr* **10/3**[1]

0032 **3** *1* **Our Joe Mac (IRE)**[37] 3203 4-8-5 **91**............(p) PaulHanagan 11 98
(Richard Fahey) *broke v fast: t.k.h: led for 1f: stdd and hld up wl in tch: rdn and effrt jst over 2f out: ev ch ent fnl f: drvn and kpt on same pce fnl 150yds* **10/1**[3]

0100 **4** *1 1/4* **Jutland**[17] 3876 4-8-13 **99**............ SilvestreDeSousa 4 104
(Mark Johnston) *lw: t.k.h: chsd ldr tl led over 6f out: rdn jst over 2f out: hrd pressed and battled on gamely tl hdd ins fnl f: no ex* **28/1**

-112 **5** *3/4* **Prince Of Johanne (IRE)**[57] 2573 5-8-3 **92**............(p) JohnFahy(3) 5 95
(Tom Tate) *swtg: hld up in tch: effrt and rdn to chse ldrs wl over 2f out: drvn and styd on same pce fr over 1f out* **20/1**

3006 **6** *1 3/4* **Bikini Babe (IRE)**[11] 4058 4-7-13 **85**............ LukeMorris 1 85
(Mark Johnston) *lw: chsd ldrs: rdn 3f out: unable qck u.p 2f out: styd on same pce after* **33/1**

-210 **7** *nk* **Kings Gambit (SAF)**[38] 3153 7-9-11 **111**............ JamieSpencer 8 110
(Tom Tate) *chsd ldrs tl led after 1f: hdd over 6f out: chsd ldr tl over 1f out: drvn and btn ent fnl f: styd on same pce after* **11/1**

6350 **8** *1/2* **Forte Dei Marmi**[25] 3591 5-9-8 **108**............ KierenFallon 16 106+
(Luca Cumani) *lw: hld up in rr: hdwy and nt clr run ent fnl 2f: swtchd rt and hdwy over 1f out: r.o wl fnl f: nvr able to chal* **11/1**

-006 **9** *1 1/4* **Circumvent**[10] 4100 4-8-13 **99**............(p) RichardHughes 13 94+
(Paul Cole) *hld up towards rr: rdn and effrt over 2f out: hdwy on outer over 1f out: styd on fnl f: nvr able to chal* **12/1**

5005 **10** *hd* **Fareer**[17] 3843 5-9-7 **107**............ RichardHills 6 102
(Ed Dunlop) *lw: hld up in midfield: pushed along over 6f out: rdn and unable qck 3f out: styd on same pce and no threat to ldrs fnl 2f* **16/1**

4451 **11** *1 1/4* **Halicarnassus (IRE)**[24] 3625 7-9-3 **103**............ HughBowman 10 96
(Mick Channon) *racd in midfield: rdn over 3f out: styng on same pce and wl hld whn nt clr run and hmpd ent fnl f* **20/1**

6221 **12** *nse* **All Action (USA)**[17] 3844 4-8-12 **98**............ TomQueally 2 90
(Sir Henry Cecil) *dwlt: sn rcvrd and in midfield: rdn and unable qck over 2f out: no prog and no threat to ldrs fr over 1f out* **13/2**[2]

-100 **13** *nk* **Spanish Duke (IRE)**[39] 3107 4-9-3 **103**............ TedDurcan 15 95
(John Dunlop) *hld up in rr: hdwy and nt clr run 3f out: swtchd lft and sme hdwy 2f out: no imp ent fnl f* **25/1**

1500 **14** *1 1/4* **Mirrored**[17] 3877 5-8-3 **89**............ DuranFentiman 17 78
(Tim Easterby) *taken down early: hld up in rr: effrt and rdn on outer ent fnl 2f: no imp* **16/1**

2010 **15** *hd* **Resurge (IRE)**[39] 3107 6-9-2 **102**............ FergusSweeney 18 91
(Stuart Kittow) *hld up towards rr: rdn and effrt on outer over 2f out: no imp* **25/1**

0000 **16** *nse* **Gunner Lindley (IRE)**[25] 3592 4-8-2 **88**............ WilliamCarson 14 77
(B W Hills) *lw: a towards rr: rdn wl over 3f out: no imp* **25/1**

-210 **17** *4 1/2* **Constant Contact**[17] 3876 4-8-10 **96**............(p) JimmyFortune 3 84
(Andrew Balding) *chsd ldrs: rdn and wknd 2f out: bhd and eased fnl f* **12/1**

06 **18** *1 1/4* **Absolute Heretic (AUS)**[158] 603 5-8-12 **98**............ FrannyNorton 12 75
(Tom Tate) *hld up towards rr: nt clr run and swtchd rt wl over 2f out: no prog: wl bhd fnl f* **66/1**

2m 5.93s (-2.07) **Going Correction** +0.025s/f (Good) **18** Ran SP% **123.0**
Speed ratings (Par 109): **109,108,107,106,106 104,104,104,103,103 102,102,101,100,100 100,97,96**
Tote Swingers: 1&2 £19.40, 1&3 £47.90, 2&3 £5.20 CSF £76.19 CT £742.13 TOTE £30.00: £4.80, £1.40, £2.50, £7.30; EX 145.20 Trifecta £535.10 Pool: £3,398.78 - 4.70 winning units..
Owner J Carrick **Bred** Dr A J F Gillespie **Trained** Middleham Moor, N Yorks

FOCUS
Running rail from 6f on lower bend to winning post dolled out 5yds increasing distances by 12yds. Top bend dolled out 3yds adding 5yds to distances on that course. This was a red-hot handicap, which has not been a great race for favourites over the years. The early pace was ordinary and didn't pick up until Jutland quickened things up from the home bend. The race was dominated by those that raced handily. Solid form with a 3lb step up from the winner.

NOTEBOOK
Arlequin had a question mark against him following his modest effort in the Zetland Gold Cup, but his previous runs this year gave him every chance, especially his third off 1lb higher in a hot handicap at York. Running in this having missed the cut for the John Smith's Cup, he was always close to the pace and presented with a dream gap against the inside rail around half a furlong from home. He made full use of it and, once in front, kept finding just enough to hold off the runner-up, who was finishing well. His trainer immediately nominated a Group race in Germany at the end of August. (tchd 25-1 in a place)

Modun(IRE) was put up 2lb for his fine effort to finish runner-up in the John Smith's Cup. Held up in midfield, he was off the bridle passing the 2f pole and took a while to respond with his effort down the wide outside. He finished well, but the winner proved very game and he just failed to reel him in. His defeat extended the wretched run of favourites in this contest, but this effort can still be marked up as he was the only one of the first seven to come from off the pace and this lightly raced gelding looks sure to relish the return to 1m4f. (op 7-2 tchd 3-1 and 4-1 in places)

Our Joe Mac(IRE), 2lb higher than when unlucky at Pontefract last month, was another to race up with the pace from the start and kept battling all the way to the line. This was a fine effort, especially as he would probably have preferred easier ground.

Jutland quickened things up rounding the home bend, soon establishing a significant advantage. To his credit, he kept on really well and wasn't swamped by the front three until well inside the last furlong. Unfortunately, he isn't very consistent and, although he'd won twice at Chester this year, his other efforts apart from this have been very modest.

Prince Of Johanne(IRE) was bidding for a four-timer when runner-up in the Zetland Gold Cup last time and had been raised 3lb for that effort. Always close to the pace, he had every chance but the handicapper may have a grip of him now. (op 25-1)

Bikini Babe(IRE) has been disappointing so far this season, despite a plummeting mark, and this was better, but she is still without a win since her second start at two.

Kings Gambit(SAF) was having his first start in a handicap since beaten a whisker off 6lb lower in last season's John Smith's Cup, having plied his trade with aplomb in conditions/Pattern-company in the meantime. Another to race handily, he hung in there until coming to the last furlong and is probably at his best when able to dictate. (op 12-1)

Forte Dei Marmi ◆ has found life tough in Pattern-company this term and was 6lb higher than when winning an ultra-valuable handicap at Newbury on his final start of last season. Held up right out the back, he tried for an optimistic run through the field once in line for home, but was never getting there and probably had no chance in view of the bias towards the pace-setters. He is worth another chance. (op 9-1 tchd 12-1)

Fareer was having his first try beyond 1m and travelled well to a point, but ran like a non-stayer. (op 20-1)

All Action(USA) was still travelling well enough passing the 3f pole, but then found little for pressure and his whopping 10lb rise for his easy Ascot success may have proved too much. (op 7-1)

Spanish Duke(IRE) ◆ had failed to beat a rival in two starts since winning the City And Suburban off 8lb lower on his reappearance, but ran better than it might have looked here as he was stopped in his run on a few occasions when trying to get closer between the 2f and 1f poles. His rider reported that he was denied a clear run. Official explanation: jockey said gelding was denied a clear run (op 22-1 tchd 33-1 in a place)

4411 BET365 GORDON STKS (GROUP 3) 1m 4f
2:35 (2:36) (Class 1) 3-Y-O
£28,355 (£10,750; £5,380; £2,680; £1,345; £675) **Stalls** High

Form RPR

2431 **1** **Namibian (IRE)**[39] 3108 3-9-3 103............ SilvestreDeSousa 10 115
(Mark Johnston) *lw: t.k.h: hld up wl in tch: rdn and effrt over 2f out: drvn to ld over 1f out: clr w rival 1f out: battled on v gamely* **7/1**[3]

512 **2** *nk* **Fiorente (IRE)**[39] 3105 3-9-0 106............ RyanMoore 2 111+
(Sir Michael Stoute) *chsd ldrs: rdn and effrt over 2f out: hdwy to chal over 1f out: drvn and clr w wnr 1f out: kpt on wl u.p tl no ex towards fin* **11/10**[1]

-101 **3** *1 1/4* **Hunter's Light (IRE)**[12] 4015 3-9-0 101............ TedDurcan 5 109
(Saeed Bin Suroor) *hld up in tch in last trio: rdn and effrt jst over 2f out: hdwy u.p to chse clr ldng pair jent fnl f: kpt on but nvr gng to rch ldrs* **8/1**

1-36 **4** *1* **Yaseer (IRE)**[75] 2030 3-9-0 104............(v[1]) RichardHills 7 108
(Marcus Tregoning) *s.i.s: hld up in rr: rdn wl over 1f out: hdwy u.p 1f out: styd on wl past btn horses ins fnl f: nt rch ldrs* **20/1**

311 **5** *2* **Highland Castle**[24] 3623 3-9-0 93............ DaneO'Neill 8 104
(David Elsworth) *t.k.h: hld up in tch in midfield: rdn and effrt on outer jst over 2f out: hung rt wl over 1f out: kpt on ins fnl f but no threat to ldrs* **16/1**

2004 **6** *nk* **Hurricane Higgins (IRE)**[19] 3772 3-9-0 102............ DarryllHolland 9 104
(Mark Johnston) *chsd ldr: ev ch and pushed along 4f out: drvn and stl ev ch 2f out: unable qck and outpcd over 1f out: plugged on same pce fnl f* **33/1**

-133 **7** *1 1/2* **Slumber**[40] 3068 3-9-0 101............ MichaelHills 11 102
(B W Hills) *lw: chsd ldrs: hdwy to press ldrs over 3f out: pushed into ld over 2f out: rdn and hdd over 1f out: sn btn: wknd fnl f* **4/1**[2]

-320 **8** *1 3/4* **Moriarty (IRE)**[40] 3068 3-9-0 105............ RichardHughes 6 99
(Richard Hannon) *t.k.h: hld up in tch in midfield: rdn and effrt over 2f out: no imp over 1f out: wknd fnl f* **20/1**

2230 **9** *1 1/4* **Measuring Time**[31] 3405 3-9-0 102............(b[1]) JimmyFortune 1 97
(Richard Hannon) *hld up in last trio: rdn and no real imp over 2f out: drvn and wknd over 1f out* **33/1**

6135 **10** *1/2* **Well Sharp**[19] 3774 3-9-0 91............ PhillipMakin 3 96
(Michael Dods) *led: rdn 3f out: hdd over 2f out: drvn and stl ev ch tl over 1f out: sn wknd* **33/1**

2m 39.55s (1.15) **Going Correction** +0.025s/f (Good) **10** Ran SP% **115.5**
Speed ratings (Par 110): **97,96,95,95,93 93,92,91,90,90**
Tote Swingers: 1&2 £2.70, 1&3 £3.80, 2&3 £3.10 CSF £14.04 TOTE £8.40: £2.00, £1.10, £1.90; EX 18.00 Trifecta £111.70 Pool: £8,712.46 - 57.70 winning units..
Owner Sheikh Hamdan Bin Mohammed Al Maktoum **Bred** Hascombe And Valiant Studs **Trained** Middleham Moor, N Yorks

FOCUS
A race usually contested by at least one highly promising colt. Arctic Cosmos was third last year ahead of his triumph in the final classic of the season. Visually the pace looked ordinary (time slow, over five seconds above standard), but it's impossible to tell for sure without sectional timing and the fact neither Mark Johnston runner went to the front suggests they weren't going that slowly. Indeed, winning rider Silvestre de Sousa confirmed afterwards he thought the tempo was good. Fiorente set the standard and namibian is a typical Johnston improver. The form makes a fair bit of sense.

NOTEBOOK

Namibian(IRE) could become yet another Gordon Stakes winner to follow up in the St Leger. This was surely an improvement on his Queen's Vase success, the colt showing new-found tactical speed and proving fully effective on quicker ground, and he is deserving of extra credit considering he became the first horse to defy a 3lb penalty since the same trainer's Bandari (defeated only three rivals) in 2002. All things considered, not least this race's rich history, the 10-1 available for Doncaster is fair. (op 8-1 tchd 10-1)

Fiorente(IRE) was bidding to emulate Sir Michael Stoute's Conduit, who was runner-up in the same Royal Ascot race en-route to Goodwood, but the well-backed favourite came up just short, and it's a defeat that goes some way to summing up his trainer's season to date, this being yet another high-profile reverse. It's quite possible Fiorente is not as good as was believed, but this is a run that should bring him on plenty. He was well enough placed by Ryan Moore, but could never get away from Namibian and eventually found that far more battle-hardened rival too strong. This lightly raced sort was in effect having his first proper race considering he didn't face a duel when runner-up last time (tactics that saw him race away from majority of rivals for some of the way backfired), and plus time may show he bumped into a very smart colt, albeit he was getting 3lb. His trainer didn't rule out the St Leger, although the impression is his connections don't see the horse as a stayer, and anyway Stoute has Sea Moon for Doncaster. It's likely Group 1s will come too soon for Fiorente this year, but he is not one to give up on. (tchd 10-11 and 6-5)

Hunter's Light(IRE), the subject of a late jockey change with Frankie Dettori not making it to the course in time, found this tougher than the 1m3f Hamilton Listed race he won last time and was simply beaten by two better colts. (op 17-2 tchd 9-1)

Yaseer(IRE), fitted with a visor on his first start since flopping in the Dante, was set a hopeless task, the colt still being last 3f out. He didn't pick up when first asked, initially hanging right, but was straightened up and was running on at the line. (op 16-1)

Highland Castle was up significantly in class after winning a maiden and a handicap off 86, and he lacked the pace of some of these. A horse with scope, he should get further, as well as appreciate more cut in the ground, and he rates a nice long-term staying prospect.

Hurricane Higgins(IRE) is a disappointing sort who needs his sights lowered.

Slumber was travelling too well entering the straight and found little for pressure, looking a non-stayer. He also failed to see his race out when third in a red-hot edition of the Chester Vase (1m4f), and then most recently in the Tercentenary (1m2f) he was one-paced after being short of room at a crucial stage. It seems 1m2f is the absolute limit of his stamina. (op 9-2 tchd 5-1)

Moriarty(IRE) was denied a clear run. Official explanation: jockey said colt was denied a clear run (tchd 22-1)

4412 BET365 LENNOX STKS (GROUP 2) — 7f

3:10 (3:10) (Class 1) 3-Y-O+

£79,394 (£30,100; £15,064; £7,504; £3,766; £1,890) **Stalls** Low

Form				RPR
-613	**1**		**Strong Suit (USA)**[23] [3670] 3-8-9 116 .... RichardHughes 5 (Richard Hannon) *lw: t.k.h: chsd ldrs: wnt 2nd 4f out: upsides ldrs and travelling wl over 1f out: rdn and qcknd ahd ins fnl f: sn in command: comf* **5/2**[1]	119+
-354	**2**	*1 ½*	**Red Jazz (USA)**[17] [3843] 4-9-2 115 .... MichaelHills 2 (B W Hills) *lw: sn bustled along to chse ldr: led after 1f: rdn wl over 1f out: hdd and nt pce of wnr ins fnl f: hld on for 2nd cl home* **7/1**	115
1533	**3**	*hd*	**Beacon Lodge (IRE)**[31] [3404] 6-9-2 109 .... AdamKirby 6 (Clive Cox) *taken down early: hld up in tch in rr: rdn and effrt 2f out: swtchd lft to outer ent fnl f: r.o wl and pressing for 2nd cl home: no threat to wnr* **16/1**	114+
4314	**4**	*¾*	**Libranno**[17] [3863] 3-8-9 112 .... RyanMoore 4 (Richard Hannon) *led for 1f: chsd ldr after tl 4f out: styd on same pce u.p fr over 1f out* **5/1**[3]	109
0324	**5**	*½*	**Doncaster Rover (USA)**[17] [3852] 5-9-2 106 .... SilvestreDeSousa 9 (David Brown) *in tch towards rr on outer: rdn 3f out: no imp u.p tl styd on ins fnl f: no threat to wnr* **25/1**	111
-600	**6**	*1 ¼*	**Dalghar (FR)**[17] [3863] 5-9-2 110 .... DavidProbert 3 (Andrew Balding) *taken down early: t.k.h: hld up wl in tch in midfield: rdn and effrt 2f out: hanging rt and styd on same pce fnl f* **8/1**	107
1501	**7**	*1*	**Majestic Myles (IRE)**[17] [3852] 3-8-9 102 .... PaulHanagan 7 (Richard Fahey) *t.k.h: chsd ldrs: rdn and effrt over 2f out: unable qck u.p over 1f out: wknd ins fnl f* **16/1**	102
10-0	**8**	*2*	**Balthazaar's Gift (IRE)**[73] [2101] 8-9-2 111 .... PhilipRobinson 1 (Clive Cox) *s.i.s: hld bhd: effrt on inner bhd a wall of horses wl over 1f out: no imp over 1f out: n.d* **28/1**	99
0-15	**9**	*2*	**Delegator**[17] [3863] 5-9-6 112 .... FrankieDettori 8 (Saeed Bin Suroor) *t.k.h: hld up in tch in rr: swtchd lft and rdn wl over 1f out: no hdwy [illegible]* **[illegible]**	98

1m 25.65s (-1.25) **Going Correction** +0.025s/f (Good)

WFA 3 from 4yo+ 7lb **9** Ran SP% **110.1**

Speed ratings (Par 115): **108,106,106,105,104 103,102,99,97**

Tote Swingers: 1&2 £4.00, 1&3 £6.90, 2&3 £11.30 CSF £18.85 TOTE £3.60: £1.80, £3.10, £4.10; EX 18.50 Trifecta £144.30 Pool: £10,919.68 - 55.97 winning units..

Owner Mrs J Wood **Bred** Mcdowell Farm, Gainsborough Farm Et Al **Trained** East Everleigh, Wilts

FOCUS

The 12th running of a race which was promoted to Group 2 status in 2003. The different generations had enjoyed almost equal success with older horses taking it six times and the classic generation five. This year's line-up looked well up to scratch, with seven of the nine runners previously successful in Group company, whilst the other pair had won at Listed level. The pace was solid enough and again those that raced handily were at an advantage. Strong Suit is rated value for another length but still only to form.

NOTEBOOK

Strong Suit(USA) has thrived since having a breathing operation, judging by his success in the Jersey, and his narrow defeat over 1m in the Group 1 Prix Jean Prat, where his rider was adamant the colt wasn't at his best. He was slightly over-racing in the first half of this contest, but then settled and travelled like a dream. He was still on the bridle when asked to pick up the leader well inside the last furlong and quickened up in impressive style. Richard Hannon Jnr immediately nominated races like the Hungerford and Prix de la Foret for the colt, but believes he will be suited by 1m in time. (tchd 11-4 in places)

Red Jazz(USA) hadn't quite been at his best in three starts over 1m this year, but was successful in his last try over this trip when winning the Challenge Stakes on his final outing of last season. His rider was keen to grab the initiative as early as possible, set a solid pace, and wasn't worn down by the winner until over half a furlong from home, though he was totally outclassed by his rival. This confirms that this is indeed his best trip and there should be another Group race in him over it, provided he can avoid Strong Suit. (tchd 13-2 and 15-2)

Beacon Lodge(IRE) finished just over 1l behind Libranno in the Criterion at Newmarket last time and managed to turn that form around. Indeed this was a fine performance as he was attempting the impossible in trying to come from the back of the field as things turned out, but finished with a rare rattle when switched to the wide outside over 1f from home and nearly got up for second. There are more good prizes to be won with him. (tchd 18-1 in a place)

Libranno was favoured by the draw when winning the Criterion at Newmarket last month and when a fine fourth in the July Cup. He was in front early, but soon had the advantage taken from him by Red Jazz and had to be content with a stalking role. It appeared that he might be stuck in a pocket for much of the home straight with Red Jazz immediately in front of him and his stable companion (the winner) on his outside, but he never seemed to be that inconvenienced and just failed to quicken sufficiently once under pressure. (tchd 11-2 in a place)

Doncaster Rover(USA), without a win in almost a year, didn't run at all badly as he was always seeing a lot of daylight on the wide outside. He looks well up to winning another Listed event. (op 22-1)

Dalghar(FR), 3l behind Delegator in the Duke Of York on his seasonal return and debut for the yard, hasn't had much luck in two tries at the top level since (drawn on the wrong side in the Golden Jubilee and pulled too hard in the July Cup), but he had some decent form last year for Alain De Royer-Dupre, including when beaten less than a length into third in this race. Not for the first time, he was a bit of a lad beforehand, having to be walked to post, and took a strong hold once under way. He never managed to land a blow and, although talented, looks to be his own worst enemy. (tchd 9-1 and 10-1 in a place)

Majestic Myles(IRE) won well at Chester last time, but had a mountain to climb in order to reverse previous Jersey Stakes form with Strong Suit and he dropped away after racing keenly early. (op 20-1)

Balthazaar's Gift(IRE), runner-up in this race in 2009 and fifth last year, ran poorly in the Lockinge in his only previous start this year, having pulled a muscle, but again he failed to get involved with no apparent excuse. (op 20-1)

Delegator was beaten by the draw in the July Cup, but still finished a very creditable fifth. At least as good over this trip and beyond, his Duke Of York success landed him with a 4lb penalty, but the extra burden wasn't the reason for this tame performance as he never made any impression at all from off the pace. Frankie Dettori reported that the horse was unsuited by the good ground, but the vet subsequently reported that, during routine testing, he found that Delegator had been struck into on his left hind. Official explanation: jockey said horse was unsuited by the good ground; vet said horse had been struck into on left-hind (tchd 4-1 in a place)

4413 BET365 MOLECOMB STKS (GROUP 3) — 5f

3:45 (3:49) (Class 1) 2-Y-O

£22,684 (£8,600; £4,304; £2,144; £1,076; £540) **Stalls** High

Form				RPR
51	**1**		**Requinto (IRE)**[17] [3884] 2-9-0 0 .... WMLordan 14 (David Wachman, Ire) *w'like: in tch: outpcd and sltly hmpd 1/2-way: hdwy and switching rt over 1f out: r.o wl u.p to ld ins fnl f: in command towards fin* **6/1**[2]	106+
2142	**2**	*1 ¼*	**Burwaaz**[19] [3776] 2-9-0 0 .... RichardHills 11 (Ed Dunlop) *pressed ldrs: rdn and ev ch ent fnl f: no ex and styd on same pce fnl 100yds* **7/1**[3]	101
6101	**3**	*nk*	**Charles The Great (IRE)**[10] [4094] 2-9-0 0 .... JimmyFortune 4 (Andrew Balding) *swtg: racd in centre trio: midfield overall: rdn and effrt 2f out: styd on u.p to press ldrs ins fnl f: nt pce of wnr fnl 100yds* **8/1**	100
13	**4**	*nk*	**Crown Dependency (IRE)**[40] [3064] 2-9-0 0 .... RichardHughes 8 (Richard Hannon) *s.i.s and hmpd sn after s: bhd and outpcd: hdwy 2f out: styd on u.p and swtchd lft ins fnl f: gng on fin: nt rch ldrs* **10/3**[1]	99
1300	**5**	*nk*	**On The Dark Side (IRE)**[10] [4094] 2-8-11 0 .... PhillipMakin 1 (Kevin Ryan) *racd in centre trio: bhd: hdwy jst over 2f out: styd on u.p and swtchd lft ins fnl f: no imp towards fin* **33/1**	95
2201	**6**	*hd*	**Vocational (USA)**[18] [3808] 2-8-11 0 .... SilvestreDeSousa 6 (Mark Johnston) *swtg: led and set fast gallop: rdn over 1f out: hdd ins fnl f: no ex and lost 4 pls towards fin* **14/1**	94
2121	**7**	*shd*	**Stonefield Flyer**[12] [4001] 2-9-0 0 .... TomEaves 5 (Keith Dalgleish) *taken down early: chsd ldrs: rdn 2f out: swtchd rt 2f out: kpt on u.p ins fnl f* **7/1**[3]	97
3	**8**	*3*	**Boris Grigoriev (IRE)**[9] [4131] 2-9-0 0 .... (v[1]) RyanMoore 3 (A P O'Brien, Ire) *str: sn outpcd and wl bhd: hdwy 1f out: styd on u.p ins fnl f: nvr trbld ldrs* **15/2**	86
1110	**9**	*hd*	**Miss Work Of Art**[18] [3821] 2-8-11 0 .... PaulHanagan 10 (Richard Fahey) *lw: sn outpcd in rr: rdn 1/2-way: styd on ins fnl f: nvr gng pce to threaten ldrs* **10/1**	82
10	**10**	*hd*	**Church Music (IRE)**[19] [3773] 2-9-0 0 .... RichardMullen 9 (Kevin Ryan) *racd off the pce in midfield: rdn and clsd 1/2-way: chsd ldrs over 1f out: wknd ins fnl f* **33/1**	85
1030	**11**	*1 ½*	**Pyman's Theory (IRE)**[10] [4094] 2-8-11 0 .... RichardKingscote 2 (Tom Dascombe) *lw: racd in centre trio: midfield overall: rdn and effrt jst over 2f out: hung rt and no imp over 1f out* **16/1**	76
5612	**12**	*3 ¾*	**Powerful Wind (IRE)**[5] [4228] 2-9-0 0 .... LukeMorris 7 (Ronald Harris) *pressed ldrs tl jst over 2f out: wknd over 1f out: fdd ins fnl f* **100/1**	66
551	**13**	*10*	**Chunky Diamond (IRE)**[15] [3915] 2-9-0 0 .... JackMitchell 13 (Peter Chapple-Hyam) *chsd ldrs early: hung rt thrght: struggling 1/2-way: wknd 2f out* **33/1**	30

57.51 secs (-0.89) **Going Correction** +0.025s/f (Good) 2y crse rec **13** Ran SP% **116.7**

Speed ratings (Par 104): **108,106,105,105,104 104,104,99,98,98 96,90,74**

Tote Swingers: 1&2 £9.60, 1&3 £10.60, 2&3 £11.00 CSF £45.34 TOTE £8.80: £2.50, £2.40, £2.30; EX 59.10 Trifecta £430.10 Pool: £6,517.62 - 11.21 winning units..

Owner M Tabor, D Smith & Mrs John Magnier **Bred** Liberty Bloodstock **Trained** Goolds Cross, Co Tipperary

FOCUS

The majority of these raced stands' side, while three runners (Charles The Great, On The Dark Side and Pyman's Theory) started off up the middle, and by halfway those near side looked well clear, but there wasn't much in it at the line, the two groups merging. This looked an up-to-scratch running, typically competitive, and the juvenile course record, dating back to Poets Cove's victory in the 1990 running, was lowered by 0.02 seconds. The time was also 0.06 seconds faster than the later older-horse Class 3 handicap.

NOTEBOOK

Requinto(IRE) was suited by the drop back to 5f when winning a Tipperary Listed race on his previous start (too keen on his two runs over 6f) and followed up to take his record over the minimum trip to 3-3. He's similarly speedy to his dam Damson, who won the 2004 Queen Mary and followed up in the Phoenix Stakes. Requinto is himself in the Phoenix (his only big-race entry in Britain and Ireland), but he looks all speed and will have to settle better if going back up in trip. (op 9-2)

Burwaaz, a well-beaten runner-up to Richmond Stakes hopeful Harbour Watch in a 6f conditions race at the July course last time, was suited by the drop in trip but couldn't fend off the winner after chasing the strong gallop. This looks about as good as he is for now, but he has the scope to progress. (op 10-1)

Charles The Great(IRE) showed good speed up the centre, and considering the proximity of On The Dark Side (plenty to find at this level), who followed him up the middle, it's hard to argue he was at a disadvantage. (op 7-1)

Crown Dependency(IRE) was third in the Norfolk over this trip last time, but his debut maiden win at this track was gained over 6f and he lacked the speed for this fast 5f. He would probably get away with this trip on a stiff track, but he ideally needs another furlong. (op 4-1 tchd 9-2 in places)

On The Dark Side(IRE) ran well after coming up the middle of the course. (op 40-1)

Vocational(USA) went off too fast. Her natural pace can see her pick up black type if ridden more sensibly. (op 10-1)

Stonefield Flyer didn't run up the form of his Windsor Castle second. He had been out since Royal Ascot, winning a minor event, and his recent exertions seemed to tell. (tchd 8-1)

Boris Grigoriev(IRE) looked interesting on this drop in trip with a visor on for the first time, but he was never going. He had to be re-shod at the start, which can't have helped. (op 8-1 tchd 7-1)

4414 CASINO AT BET365 EBF "ASSERTIVE" MAIDEN STKS (C&G) 6f

4:20 (4:21) (Class 2) 2-Y-O **£9,703** (£2,887; £1,443; £721) **Stalls** High

Form RPR

24 **1** **Moustache (IRE)**27 3511 2-9-0 0 RichardHughes 7 87+
(Richard Hannon) *t.k.h: hld up in midfield: hdwy gng wl jst over 2f out: swtchd lft and rdn to chal ins fnl f: wnt clr w ldr fnl 100yds: led on post* **6/1**3

2 *nse* **Llanarmon Lad (IRE)** 2-9-0 0 DarryllHolland 2 86+
(B W Hills) *str: s.i.s: bhd and niggled along early: clsd and in tch 1/2-way: hdwy and rdn to chal ins fnl f: led fnl 100yds and drew clr w wnr: hdd on post* **33/1**

43 **3** *2* **Tidy Affair (IRE)**22 3686 2-9-0 0 RyanMoore 10 79+
(Richard Hannon) *w ldrs: hmpd sn after s: rdn and ev ch wl over 1f out: outpcd and btn ins fnl f: plugged on same pce fnl 100yds* **17/2**

4 **4** *1* **Sequoia**18 3793 2-9-0 0 MichaelHills 8 76
(B W Hills) *lw: w ldrs: hmpd sn after s: led 2f out: sn rdn: hdd ins fnl f: wknd fnl 75yds* **7/2**2

640 **5** *2 3/4* **Drummoyne (USA)**6 4192 2-9-0 0 SilvestreDeSousa 5 67
(Mark Johnston) *lw: in tch: rdn and effrt 2f out: drvn and unable qck over 1f out: wknd ins fnl f* **33/1**

6 *1/2* **Muarrab** 2-9-0 0 RichardHills 4 66+
(Ed Dunlop) *unf: scope: bit bkwd: dwlt: sn in tch: chsd ldrs and rdn 2f out: unable qck and drvn over 1f out: wknd ins fnl f* **8/1**

7 *3/4* **Blue Surf** 2-9-0 0 PatDobbs 12 63
(Amanda Perrett) *lengthy: leggy: in tch: rdn and unable qck 2f out: n.m.r and swtchd rt over 1f out: wknd ent fnl f* **40/1**

0 **8** *1/2* **Menelik (IRE)**18 3823 2-9-0 0 RichardKingscote 6 62
(Tom Dascombe) *w ldrs: hmpd sn after s: led 4f out tl 2f out: sn drvn and unable qck: wknd jst over 1f out* **14/1**

23 **9** *1 1/4* **Wolf Spirit (IRE)**25 3583 2-9-0 0 PhillipMakin 1 58
(Kevin Ryan) *in tch in rr: shkn up and effrt 2f out: swtchd rt and drvn over 1f out: sn wknd* **16/1**

10 *hd* **Larwood (IRE)** 2-9-0 0 DaneO'Neill 9 57
(Henry Candy) *leggy: bit bkwd: t.k.h: chsd ldrs: hmpd sn after s: pressing ldrs and rdn over 2f out: struggling and btn over 1f out: wknd fnl f* **33/1**

11 *1* **Warcrown (IRE)** 2-9-0 0 PaulHanagan 11 54+
(Richard Fahey) *lengthy: lw: restless in stalls: rrd and slowly away: sn rcvrd and hmpd sn after s: rdn and unable qck 2f out: wknd ent fnl f* **2/1**1

12 *3 1/4* **Kinglami** 2-9-0 0 FrannyNorton 13 43
(Brian Gubby) *w'like: bit bkwd: rn green and hung rt thrght: led: wnt violently rt sn after s: hdd 4f out: wknd and continued to hang 2f out: bhd fnl f* **100/1**

1m 12.52s (0.32) **Going Correction** +0.025s/f (Good) **12** Ran SP% **116.3**
Speed ratings (Par 100): **98,97,95,93,90 89,88,87,86,86 84,80**
Tote Swingers: 1&2 £29.20, 1&3 £3.90, 2&3 £24.90 CSF £194.58 TOTE £6.10: £2.10, £10.30, £2.80; EX 293.00 Trifecta £1774.90 Part won. Pool: £2,398.62 - 0.82 winning units..
Owner Raymond Tooth **Bred** John Cullinan **Trained** East Everleigh, Wilts

FOCUS

There are no stars among the list of recent winners of this event, but it's always a decent maiden. The action unfolded towards the stands' rail, but there was no obvious bias. The level of the form is set around the third to the fifth.

NOTEBOOK

Moustache(IRE) ◆ did well to win considering he was keen for most of the way, and then had to wait for a gap until around 1f out, although he had the help of Richard Hughes, who rides Goodwood just about better than anyone and produced his mount to lead on the line. The winner was confirming the promise of his debut second at Newbury, having had an excuse at Chepstow on his next outing, and can do even better if relaxing in future. He could get a workable opening mark for nurseries.

Llanarmon Lad(IRE), a 25,000euros half-brother to, among others, 1m winner Aciano, out of a 1m2f scorer, almost overcame greenness on his racecourse debut. He was behind for much of the way and made his move wide, but just failed. Clear of the others, he could be quite useful if improving off this. (op 40-1 tchd 50-1 in places)

Tidy Affair(IRE) ◆ is still learning. He's now qualified to run in nurseries and should progress. (op 9-1 tchd 8-1)

Sequoia, who is in the Gimcrack and Champagne Stakes, was a bit short of room early on, but that didn't cost him. He failed to improve on his Ascot debut. (tchd 10-3 and 4-1)

Drummoyne(USA) found this company a bit hot but ran okay. (tchd 40-1 in a place)

Muarrab ◆, a 280,000gns purchase, is out of a mare whose six earlier off-spring have won at least once, including some decent types, the pick of them being smart sprint Group Therapy, although interestingly none of them went in first-time out. This Royal Lodge entrant should come on plenty. (tchd 9-1)

Blue Surf showed ability and ought to improve. (tchd 50-1 in places)

Menelik(IRE), who's in the Gimcrack, didn't step up as expected on his July course introduction. (op 12-1)

Warcrown(IRE), a 42,000euros half-brother to a few winners, most notably very useful 7f performer Silk Fan, has been entered in the Champagne Stakes and Royal Lodge and was extremely well backed. However, having started awkwardly, he was soon short of room and despite appearing to recover to a point, he dropped away tamely. Surely he's better than this. (op 9-4 tchd 11-4 in a place and 5-2 in places)

Kinglami's jockey reported that his horse hung right handed. Official explanation: jockey said colt hung right-handed (op 125-1)

4415 POKER AT BET365 STKS (H'CAP) 1m

4:50 (4:53) (Class 3) (0-90,90) 3-Y-O+ **£9,703** (£2,887; £1,443; £721) **Stalls** Low

Form RPR

2220 **1** **Red Gulch**17 3862 4-9-8 **89** J-PGuillambert 10 101
(Ed Walker) *lw: hld up in tch: trcking ldrs gng wl over 1f out: swtchd lft and hdwy 1f out: qcknd to ld fnl 150yds: sn in command: r.o wl* **16/1**

2525 **2** *1 3/4* **Guest Book (IRE)**90 1603 4-9-6 **87** SilvestreDeSousa 11 95
(Mark Johnston) *chsd ldrs: rdn over 2f out: challenged wl over 1f out: led ent fnl f: hdd and nt pce of wnr fnl 150yds: hld on for 2nd cl home* **7/1**2

0-01 **3** *nk* **Truism**46 2876 5-9-8 **89** RyanMoore 1 96
(Amanda Perrett) *lw: in tch in midfield: swtchd lft and effrt wl over 1f out: drvn and hdwy over 1f out: chsd ldrs ins fnl f: kpt on and pressing for 2nd cl home: no ch w wnr* **7/1**2

6-33 **4** *1* **Don't Call Me (IRE)**3 4310 4-9-7 **88** AdrianNicholls 3 95+
(David Nicholls) *hld up in midfield: effrt towards inner 2f out: nt clr run and switching lft ent fnl 100yds: styd on wl ins fnl f: no threat to wnr* **13/2**1

0420 **5** *1* **Viva Vettori**18 3825 7-9-3 **84** NickyMackay 12 89+
(David Elsworth) *stdd and dropped in bhd after s: hld up towards rr: effrt and hdwy over 1f out: nt clr run 1f out: swtchd lft and r.o wl ins fnl f: nvr able to chal* **11/1**

0152 **5** *dht* **Duster**18 3802 4-9-8 **89** DaneO'Neill 18 92
(Hughie Morrison) *chsd ldrs: rdn and unable qckn over 2f out: rallied u.p over 1f out: kpt on same pce ins fnl f* **14/1**

-000 **7** *3/4* **Rulesn'regulations**60 2470 5-9-9 **90** (b[1]) GeorgeBaker 2 91
(Matthew Salaman) *swtg: led: rdn jst over 2f out: drvn and hdd ent fnl f: wknd ins fnl f* **20/1**

-060 **8** *1/2* **Chapter And Verse (IRE)**41 3032 5-9-4 **85** TonyCulhane 17 85
(Mike Murphy) *stdd and dropped in bhd after s: swtchd to outer and effrt jst over 2f out: styd on ins fnl f: nt rch ldrs* **16/1**

3621 **9** *shd* **Charlie Cool**18 3831 8-9-5 **86** (b) PJMcDonald 16 86
(Ruth Carr) *hld up in rr: sme hdwy over 1f out: nt clr run and swtchd lft 1f out: r.o wl fnl 100yds: nvr able to chal* **16/1**

0034 **10** *1 1/4* **Chilli Green**26 3536 4-9-0 **81** DavidProbert 9 78
(John Akehurst) *chsd ldr: ev ch and rdn ent fnl 2f: wknd 1f out* **33/1**

3140 **11** *hd* **Veroon (IRE)**18 3825 5-9-2 **83** (p) TomQueally 5 79
(James Given) *chsd ldrs: rdn over 2f out: unable qck u.p over 1f out: wknd 1f out* **25/1**

3101 **12** *1/2* **Munsarim (IRE)**23 3659 4-9-0 **81** PhillipMakin 13 76
(Keith Dalgleish) *in tch on outer: rdn and effrt 2f out: styd on same pce fr over 1f out* **12/1**

2205 **13** *3/4* **Lord Aeryn (IRE)**17 3877 4-9-7 **88** (b[1]) PaulHanagan 15 81
(Richard Fahey) *t.k.h: hld up in midfield: rdn and no imp wl over 1f out: styng on same pce and n.d whn hmpd jst ins fnl f* **18/1**

0330 **14** *1 1/2* **Marajaa (IRE)**18 3825 9-9-2 **83** KierenFallon 7 83+
(Willie Musson) *hld up in rr: effrt towards inner 2f out: keeping on but stl plenty to do whn nt clr run 1f out: n.d after and eased ins fnl f* **8/1**3

0-00 **15** *1* **Desert Creek (IRE)**74 2075 5-9-6 **87** CathyGannon 14 75
(David Nicholls) *t.k.h: hld up towards rr: rdn and effrt 2f out: sn drvn and no hdwy over 1f out: n.d* **33/1**

0003 **16** *nse* **Suited And Booted (IRE)**13 3982 4-9-7 **88** LukeMorris 19 76
(Jane Chapple-Hyam) *lw: hld up towards rr: rdn and no hdwy 2f out: no prog and wl hld whn swtchd rt over 1f out* **25/1**

3000 **17** *1 1/2* **Breakheart (IRE)**11 4058 4-9-5 **86** (v) TomEaves 20 70
(Michael Dods) *swtg: hld up in rr: rdn and no hdwy 2f out: n.d* **28/1**

-030 **18** *7* **Kajima**10 4100 4-9-9 **90** RichardHughes 6 65+
(Richard Hannon) *lw: in tch in midfield: rdn and effrt 2f out: no prog and btn 1f out: eased fnl 150yds* **16/1**

5252 **R** **Stefanki (IRE)**49 2789 4-8-12 **82** MatthewDavies(3) 4 —
(George Baker) *ref to r* **33/1**

1m 38.09s (-1.81) **Going Correction** +0.025s/f (Good) **19** Ran SP% **125.7**
Speed ratings (Par 107): **110,108,107,106,105 105,105,104,104,103 103,102,101,100,99 99,97,90,—**
Tote Swingers: 1&2 £24.70, 1&3 £15.90, 2&3 £5.20 CSF £115.23 CT £892.72 TOTE £23.10: £4.50, £1.80, £2.00, £1.80; EX 182.90 Trifecta £1450.90 Pool: £2,548.98 - 1.30 winning units..
Owner S Al Ansari **Bred** Cheveley Park Stud Ltd **Trained** Newmarket, Suffolk

FOCUS

A fiercely competitive handicap, but surprisingly a good race for favourites, with the market leader successful four times in the previous ten years and in the frame on four other occasions. The field was reduced by two with Master Mylo being withdrawn after getting upset in the stalls and Stefanki returning to his bad old ways by refusing to come out of them. It was the pick of the round course times and the form is solid.

NOTEBOOK

Red Gulch was trying 1m proper for the first time and it was easy to put a line through his Bunbury Cup effort as, apart from that being an unsatisfactory race, it transpired that he wasn't right. He was always in a good position just behind the leaders and quickened up nicely to lead inside the last furlong. There are no specific plans for him, with his trainer waiting to see what the handicapper does, but he was of the opinion that he appreciated the slight cut in the ground, so he could be in for a good autumn. (tchd 18-1)

Guest Book(IRE), returning from three months off and awash with sweat, held a handy position throughout, had every chance and never gave up. He is yet to win a handicap, but showed that he had the ability to win a nice one when things go his way. (op 15-2)

Truism's 9lb rise for last month's win over 7f here left him off a career-high mark, but he finished well to record another fine effort on a track he thrives at. (op 6-1)

Don't Call Me(IRE) ◆ had twice run well since his belated return last month and this was another decent effort as he got caught in traffic for much of the home straight and wasn't extricated until it was too late. He looks a winner waiting to happen. (op 7-1 tchd 6-1 and 15-2 in places)

Viva Vettori was given plenty to do and didn't enjoy the clearest of passages, including when hampered well inside the last furlong, so he did well to finish so close. However, his record of 0-22 on turf is obviously off-putting. (op 12-1 tchd 10-1 in places)

Duster, up 1lb to a new career-high mark, was never too far off the pace and this was another decent effort from his wide draw. (op 12-1 tchd 10-1 in places)

Rulesn'regulations had shown little since winning over 7f at this meeting last year, but he was backed at big prices to run better back at this venue and duly did so. Soon in front, it looked as though he was travelling better than his nearest pursuers for much of the home straight, but eventually capitulated entering the last furlong and dropped right out of the placings. (op 18-1)

Chapter And Verse(IRE) had been running well, though unplaced, in hotter handicaps than this recently and he got the strong pace he needs, but his wide draw meant he had to be switched off and tucked in out the back. He was also forced to switch very wide to make his effort and his final position was as close as he got. (op 20-1 tchd 33-1 in a place)

Charlie Cool was back in a handicap after winning a York claimer, but he was another done few favours by the draw and being forced to make his effort from well off the pace. He stayed on late, but never had a prayer of making the frame. (op 20-1)

Veroon(IRE) Official explanation: jockey said gelding was denied a clear run

4416 MOBILE AT BET365 STKS (H'CAP) 5f

5:25 (5:25) (Class 3) (0-90,89) 4-Y-O+ **£9,703** (£2,887; £1,443; £721) **Stalls** High

Form RPR

0040 **1** **Secret Asset (IRE)**11 4075 6-9-7 **89** GeorgeBaker 13 99
(Jane Chapple-Hyam) *hld up in midfield: pushed along and hdwy over 1f out: led ins fnl f: sn in command: pushed out* **14/1**

-035 **2** *1* **La Fortunata**19 3778 4-8-13 **81** TonyCulhane 1 87
(Mike Murphy) *racd solo in centre: a.p: ev ch 1f out: styd on same pce ins fnl f* **12/1**

0504 **3** *nk* **Fathom Five (IRE)**10 4104 7-9-5 **87** AdrianNicholls 11 92
(David Nicholls) *w ldr: led 1/2-way: rdn over 1f out: hdd and nt pce of wnr ins fnl f: kpt on same pce fnl 100yds* **10/1**3

4002 **4** *nk* **Estonia**6 4207 4-8-2 **70** oh8 CathyGannon 15 74
(Michael Squance) *taken down early: bhd: swtchd lft and hdwy u.p 1f out: r.o wl ins fnl f: nt rch ldrs* **50/1**

322 **5** *hd* **Boogie Waltzer**5 4239 4-8-0 **73** (t) HarryBentley(5) 4 76
(Stuart Williams) *taken down early: rdr struggling to remove blind leaving stalls: midfield: drvn 2f out: styd on wl u.p fnl f* **10/1**3

6-33 **6** *shd* **Sutton Veny (IRE)**44 2959 5-9-2 **84** RyanMoore 18 87
(Jeremy Gask) *racd off the pce towards rr: rdn and hdwy over 1f out: r.o wl ins fnl f: nt rch ldrs* **9/1**2

-360 **7** *1/2* **Invincible Lad (IRE)**[53] 2694 7-8-9 **77** .... PaulHanagan 16 78
(David Nicholls) *in tch: rdn jsut over 2f out: drvn and edgd rt 1f out: kpt on ins fnl f* **12/1**

2232 **8** *1/2* **Noodles Blue Boy**[11] 4075 5-9-3 **85** .... FrannyNorton 2 84
(Ollie Pears) *in tch in midfield: effrt and edging rt over 1f out: styd on same pce ins fnl f* **8/1**[1]

-140 **9** *1 3/4* **Soap Wars**[18] 3796 6-8-12 **87** .... LucyKBarry(7) 8 80
(Hugo Palmer) *hld up in midfield: wnt rt 1/2-way: rdn and hdwy over 1f out: kpt on ins fnl f: nvr gng pce to rch ldrs* **14/1**

2233 **10** *shd* **Verinco**[32] 3357 5-9-2 **84** ....(v) TomEaves 10 77
(Bryan Smart) *in tch: drvn and chsd ldrs over 1f out: styd on same pce and no imp fnl f* **16/1**

0003 **11** *1 1/4* **Arganil (USA)**[6] 4195 6-9-0 **82** ....(p) PhillipMakin 19 70
(Kevin Ryan) *s.i.s: outpcd in rr: r.o wl past btn horses ins fnl f: nvr trbld ldrs* **12/1**

3651 **12** *3/4* **Maze (IRE)**[30] 3427 6-8-11 **79** .... DavidProbert 14 64
(Tony Carroll) *taken down early: towards rr: effrt and rdn 2f out: drvn and no imp over 1f out: wknd ins fnl f* **8/1**[1]

0302 **13** *1/2* **Brynfa Boy**[7] 3869 5-8-4 **75** ....(t) JohnFahy(3) 7 59
(Paul D'Arcy) *taken down early: s.i.s: bhd: hdwy into midfield and pushed rt 1/2-way: no imp over 1f out* **12/1**

212 **14** *shd* **Admirable Duchess**[17] 3847 4-9-0 **82** .... JamesDoyle 6 65
(Dominic Ffrench Davis) *led tl 1/2-way: rdn and edgd rt over 1f out: wknd ins fnl f* **14/1**

4434 **15** *1 1/2* **Judge 'n Jury**[2] 4357 7-9-5 **87** .... LukeMorris 9 65
(Ronald Harris) *t.k.h: chsd ldrs: rdn 2f out: hung rt u.p over 1f out: wknd ins fnl f* **12/1**

0-05 **16** *5* **High Spice (USA)**[17] 3847 4-8-8 **76** ....(v[1]) JimCrowley 17 36
(Robert Cowell) *s.i.s: a outpcd in rr: n.d* **25/1**

0030 **17** *nk* **Curtains**[17] 3845 4-9-0 **82** .... KierenFallon 3 41
(Simon Dow) *rrd as stalls opened and v.s.a: bhd: rdn and modest hdwy jst over 2f out: no imp 1f out: sn eased* **16/1**

57.57 secs (-0.83) **Going Correction** +0.025s/f (Good) **17** Ran SP% **126.4**
Speed ratings (Par 107): **107,105,104,104,104 103,103,102,99,99 97,96,95,95,92 84,84**
Tote Swingers: 1&2 £31.50, 1&3 £18.80, 2&3 £21.10 CSF £177.46 CT £1840.67 TOTE £17.00: £3.80, £3.20, £2.20, £14.60; EX 290.90 Trifecta £1815.30 Part won. Pool: £2,453.15 - 0.96 winning units..
Owner Simon & Jeanette Pierpoint & Paul Salisbury **Bred** Mrs C Hartery **Trained** Dalham, Suffolk

FOCUS
The action unfolded up the middle of the track and there was no obvious bias. A competitive handicap run at a predictably strong pace, although the time was fractionally slower than the earlier Molecomb (juvenile track record). Solid-looking form.

NOTEBOOK
Secret Asset(IRE) is a strong traveller who needs the leaders to come back, and this race perhaps unsurprisingly set up well for him. The return of George Baker, the last jockey who managed to win on the horse in December 2010, was also a positive. The winner couldn't be fancied to follow up. He's in the Stewards' Cup, but seeing as he was weighted for that race off his old mark of 92, and has picked up a penalty, he would be fully 9lb higher. (tchd 16-1)
La Fortunata raced alone for much of the way, towards the far side but away from the rail, and this was a fine effort in defeat. (tchd 16-1 in a place)
Fathom Five(IRE) has dropped to an attractive mark and ran an encouraging race. (op 9-1)
Estonia, like the winner, is at her best chasing a strong gallop, so the race set up well for her and she ran a good race from out of the handicap.
Boogie Waltzer has won over this C&D and posted a solid effort in defeat. (tchd 11-1 in a place)
Sutton Veny(IRE) took a while to get going, yet didn't finish as well as some. All of her wins have been gained over 6f. (op 17-2)
Noodles Blue Boy, who had Secret Asset well behind last time, didn't look particularly well handicapped and so it proved. (op 9-1)
Maze(IRE) won last time in a race confined to horses aged six and above, and this was a lot tougher off 3lb higher, especially with a professional taking over from useful 7lb claimer Lucy Barry. (op 14-1)
Curtains reared as the stalls opened. Official explanation: jockey said filly reared as stalls opened (op 20-1)
T/Jkpt: Not won. T/Plt: £52.00 to a £1 stake. Pool of £265,548.27 - 3,727.47 winning tickets. T/Qpdt: £20.50 to a £1 stake. Pool of £12,297.85 - 443.28 winning tickets. SP

4417a, 4419 - 4422a - (Foreign Racing) - See Raceform Interactive

4397 GALWAY (R-H)
Tuesday, July 26

OFFICIAL GOING: Good

4418a TOPAZ MILE EUROPEAN BREEDERS FUND H'CAP (PREMIER HANDICAP) 1m 100y
6:45 (6:51) 3-Y-0+

£59,482 (£18,836; £8,922; £2,974; £1,982; £991)

RPR

1 **Stunning View (IRE)**[41] 3032 4-9-5 98 .... PJSmullen 4 104+
(D K Weld, Ire) *mid-div: 7th 1/2-way: hdwy into 3rd and rdn ent st: styd on wl to ld cl home* **7/1**[1]

2 *2* **Royal Blue Star (IRE)**[40] 3100 3-8-8 95 .... ShaneFoley 6 95
(Mrs John Harrington, Ire) *attempted to make all: rdn clr ent st: strly pressed fnl f: hdd and no ex cl home* **15/2**[2]

3 *1 1/4* **Defining Year (IRE)**[86] 1735 3-8-11 98 .... GFCarroll 1 95
(M Halford, Ire) *trckd ldrs: 3rd 3f out: sn rdn: kpt on same pce in 3rd st* **8/1**[3]

4 *1* **Mid Mon Lady (IRE)**[32] 3371 6-8-13 99 ....(b) DJBenson(7) 3 96
(H Rogers, Ire) *dwlt: sn mid-div: rdn in 7th 2 1/2f out: kpt on wout threatening st* **20/1**

5 *4* **Pires**[12] 2748 7-8-11 90 .... KLatham 5 78
(A J Martin, Ire) *in rr of mid-div: bmpd sltly and prog fr 3f out: rdn in 6th ent st: no ex* **12/1**

6 *3* **Bay Knight (IRE)**[6] 4220 5-8-10 96 .... RossCoakley(7) 11 78
(K J Condon, Ire) *trckd ldrs: 2nd 3f out: sn rdn: no imp st* **25/1**

7 *hd* **Hujaylea (IRE)**[10] 4116 8-9-5 105 ....(p) CPHoban(7) 13 86
(M Halford, Ire) *s.i.s and in rr: kpt on wout threatening fr 3f out* **20/1**

8 *1 1/2* **Separate Ways (IRE)**[23] 1930 6-9-1 99 ....(b) SHJames(5) 14 77
(David Marnane, Ire) *trckd ldrs: 3f out: rdn and no imp fr 3f out* **14/1**

9 *nk* **New Magic (IRE)**[31] 3419 4-8-13 92 ....(t) NGMcCullagh 10 69
(Dermot Anthony McLoughlin, Ire) *trckd ldrs: rdn and no imp fr 3f out* **11/1**

10 *nk* **Lightening Stricks (IRE)**[41] 3057 4-9-0 93 ....(tp) FMBerry 8 70
(Richard Brabazon, Ire) *trckd ldrs: rdn in 4th 3f out: sn no imp* **8/1**[3]

11 *1 1/4* **Waydownsouth (IRE)**[28] 3500 4-9-3 101 .... LFRoche(5) 12 75
(Patrick J Flynn, Ire) *mid-div: rdn 4f out: sn no imp* **12/1**

12 *1/2* **Toraidhe (IRE)**[12] 4034 5-8-13 92 ....(bt) KJManning 15 65
(J S Bolger, Ire) *dwlt and in rr on outer: no imp fr 3f out* **20/1**

13 *nk* **Moran Gra (USA)**[30] 3445 4-9-3 103 ....(p) RPWhelan(7) 17 75
(Ms Joanna Morgan, Ire) *trckd ldrs: rdn in 6th on outer ent st: no imp* **14/1**

14 *3/4* **Ask Jack (USA)**[30] 3444 7-9-11 104 ....(p) CDHayes 9 74
(Joseph G Murphy, Ire) *mid-div: wknd fr 3f out* **7/1**[1]

15 *1 3/4* **Elusive Ridge (IRE)**[16] 3894 5-8-9 88 ....(p) CO'Donoghue 18 55
(H Rogers, Ire) *in rr of mid-div on outer: rdn and wknd fr 4f out* **20/1**

16 *1 1/4* **Kyllachy Star**[24] 3645 5-9-3 96 .... DPMcDonogh 16 60
(Richard Fahey) *mid-div on outer: rdn and no imp fr 3f out: eased fnl f* **14/1**

17 *nk* **Drombeg Dawn (IRE)**[31] 3419 5-8-8 87 .... BACurtis 7 50
(A J McNamara, Ire) *slowly away and sn struggling in rr: no imp on outer st* **12/1**

1m 46.08s (-4.12)
WFA 3 from 4yo+ 8lb **17** Ran SP% **133.3**
CSF £57.49 CT £336.72 TOTE £5.30: £1.50, £2.80, £2.40, £5.50; DF 77.90.
Owner Dr R Lambe **Bred** Irish National Stud **Trained** The Curragh, Co Kildare

FOCUS
A finish dominated by horses drawn low. The recent history of the race has been dominated by older horses, although 3yos won seven of the runnings between Timarida's win in 1995 and Palace Star in 2004. This year there were only two of the younger generation in the line-up. It has been rated around the second and fourth.

NOTEBOOK
Stunning View(IRE), a course winner as a juvenile, asserted in the closing stages to master the front-running Royal Blue Star. Winning trainer Dermot Weld said "It's always a hard race to win, but after running in the Royal Hunt Cup I thought he could go well in what is a very competitive event. He has earned a shot at a Listed race now." Official explanation: trainer said, regarding the apparent improvement in form shown, that colt ran quite well last time despite meeting with slight interference in running; he added that today's slightly easier ground had helped the animal. (op 8/1)
Royal Blue Star(IRE) ran her heart out in search for a third win of the season. (op 10/1)
Defining Year(IRE), never far from the pace from his number one draw, emerged with credit in taking the placings behind a winner who is to be given a chance in Listed company. (op 8/1 tchd 9/1)
Mid Mon Lady(IRE) has done plenty of racing since second in this event last year, produced another grand display. Group 3-placed behind the talented Banimpire earlier in the season, she deserves to pick up another race, but is not the easiest to place.
Pires suffered a little from being involved in some close riding at a stage which was possibly crucial.
Bay Knight(IRE) did not run at all badly over this stiff trip.
Ask Jack(USA) failed to run to expectations and finished with only three behind him. (op 8/1)

4410 GOODWOOD (R-H)
Wednesday, July 27

OFFICIAL GOING: Good (8.2)
Wind: light, half behind Weather: partly cloudy, bright spells

4423 GOODWOOD STKS (H'CAP) 2m 5f
2:00 (2:01) (Class 2) (0-95,89) 3-Y-0+

£18,675 (£5,592; £2,796; £1,398; £699; £351)

Form RPR

-020 **1** **Hollins**[38] 3205 7-8-10 **75** .... PaulHanagan 20 85
(Micky Hammond) *got a flyer and led for 1f: stdd and chsd ldrs: pushed along and hdwy to press ldrs 4f out: rdn to ld over 2f out: hrd drvn and edgd lft ins fnl f: forged ahd and asserted fnl 75yds* **20/1**

1142 **2** *3/4* **Seaside Sizzler**[28] 3522 4-9-3 **82** ....(vt[1]) JimCrowley 5 91
(Ralph Beckett) *hld up in midfield: rdn and effrt whn edgd rt wl over 2f out: hdwy to chse ldrs over 1f out: hrd drvn and ev ch 1f out: no ex and btn fnl 75yds* **14/1**

1630 **3** *5* **Exemplary**[88] 1679 4-9-9 **88** .... SilvestreDeSousa 19 92
(Mark Johnston) *chsd ldrs: rdn 4f out: drvn and chsd wnr 2f out: pressing wnr over 1f out tl no ex and struggling jst over 1f out: 3rd and styd on same pce fnl f* **16/1**

002 **4** *1 1/2* **Bow To No One (IRE)**[19] 3828 5-8-12 **80** .... HarryBentley(3) 7 83
(Alan Jarvis) *hld up towards rr: effrt and hung rt over 2f out: sn swtchd lft: hdwy 2f out: styd on to chse ldng trio 1f out: no imp after* **12/1**

5106 **5** *hd* **Cosimo de Medici**[11] 4097 4-9-0 **79** ....(t) RichardHughes 4 81
(Hughie Morrison) *hld up in last quartet: effrt and nt clr run over 3f out: rdn and hdwy over 2f out: kpt on steadily fr over 1f out: nvr trbld ldrs* **9/1**[2]

4463 **6** *2* **Bowdler's Magic**[25] 3625 4-9-8 **87** .... NeilCallan 9 87
(Mark Johnston) *chsd ldrs: short of room and sltly hmpd over 3f out: sn rdn: swtchd lft u.p 2f out: no ex and btn over 1f out* **12/1**

300/ **7** *1/2* **Liberate**[35] 2994 8-9-5 **84** .... JamieSpencer 17 84
(Philip Hobbs) *in tch: rdn and unable qck whn bmpd over 2f out: sn swtchd lft: wknd wl over 1f out* **6/1**[1]

0-53 **8** *1/2* **Royal Diamond (IRE)**[11] 4097 5-9-3 **82** .... GeorgeBaker 6 81
(Jonjo O'Neill) *racd keenly: chsd ldrs tl led after 2f: sn clr: rdn and hdd over 2f out: wknd over 1f out* **12/1**

3420 **9** *3 1/4* **Dazinski**[19] 3794 5-9-9 **88** .... KierenFallon 15 84
(Mark H Tompkins) *hld up in rr: effrt and nt clr run over 3f out: swtchd ins and sme hdwy over 2f out: drvn 2f out: plugged on but nvr any threat to ldrs* **16/1**

6-50 **10** *2 1/4* **L Frank Baum (IRE)**[5] 4266 4-9-8 **87** ....(b[1]) JimmyFortune 18 81
(Gay Kelleway) *chsd ldrs: rdn and effrt on inner 3f out: sn struggling and nt qckning: wknd 2f out* **25/1**

330 **11** *hd* **Trovare (USA)**[31] 3428 4-9-6 **85** .... PatDobbs 2 79
(Amanda Perrett) *t.k.h: hld up towards rr: rdn and effrt over 3f out: no real prog: no ch fr wl over 1f out* **16/1**

0010 **12** *3 3/4* **My Arch**[32] 3396 9-9-10 **89** .... TomQueally 1 79
(Ollie Pears) *t.k.h: hld up in midfield: rdn over 3f out: sn struggling and btn: no ch fnl 2f* **10/1**[3]

-215 **13** *1* **Addwaitya**[11] 4097 6-8-12 **77** .... IanMongan 14 66
(Laura Mongan) *hld up in last quartet: short-lived effrt and nt clr run over 3f out: wl bhd fr over 2f out* **20/1**

4113 **14** *4* **John Forbes**[15] 3935 9-8-8 **73** .... TomEaves 13 58
(Brian Ellison) *hld up in rr: rdn and short-lived effrt over 3f out: sn btn and no ch fnl 2f* **20/1**

2/04 **15** *1 3/4* **Souter Point (USA)**[7] 4216 5-9-1 **80** .... DavidProbert 16 63
(Tony Carroll) *hld up in midfield: rdn and pushed lft over 3f out: sn struggling: wknd 3f out* **50/1**

0006 **16** *4 1/2* **Herostatus**[19] 3794 4-8-11 **76** .... RichardHills 10 55
(Mark Johnston) *hld up towards rr: rdn 4f out: wknd ent fnl 3f: no ch whn hung rt over 1f out* **28/1**

30/0 **17** *10* **Raslan**[11] 4097 8-8-9 **77**....................(vt) AdamBeschizza(3) 3 46
(David Pipe) *towards rr and pushed along early: hdwy into midfield after 4f out: drvn and struggling 4f out: wknd over 3f out: t.o* **33/1**

116/ **18** *1* **Spirit Of Adjisa (IRE)**[82] 7151 7-9-5 **84**....................RyanMoore 8 52
(Tim Vaughan) *t.k.h: chsd ldr tl led after 1f tl after 2f: chsd ldr after tl over 3f out: wknd over 2f out: wl bhd and eased ins fnl f: t.o* **6/1**[1]

40/6 **19** *70* **Font**[11] 3157 8-9-5 **84**....................(t) RichardKingscote 12 —
(Lawney Hill) *hld up towards rr: rdn 6f out: wknd and lost tch over 3f out: virtually p.u fnl 2f: t.o* **25/1**

4m 29.3s (-1.70) **Going Correction** 0.0s/f (Good) **19** Ran SP% **125.4**
Speed ratings (Par 109): **103,102,100,100,100 99,99,99,97,96 96,95,95,93,92 91,87,86,60**
toteswingers:1&2: £101.10, 2&3: £59.00, 1&3: £65.70 CSF £256.91 CT £4566.52 TOTE £26.60: £4.60, £2.40, £5.00, £4.30; EX 444.90 Trifecta £2111.00 Part won. Pool of £2852.77 - 0.94 winning units..

Owner R D Bickenson **Bred** Bricklow Ltd And Hyperion Stud Ltd **Trained** Middleham Moor, N Yorks

FOCUS
The running rail from the 6f marker on the lower bend to the winning post on the inside was dolled out by approximately 5yds, increasing distances by 12yds, while the top bend was also dolled out 3yds, increasing race distances on that course by 5yds. A big field for this marathon handicap, but strictly speaking the race was flattered to carry class 2 status, as the top-weight was rated 6lb below the ceiling. There were no stalls, and it was an uneven start. The form looks pretty sound for a race of its type.

NOTEBOOK
Hollins, in poaching an early advantage, got a bit of a jump on his rivals. Never too far of the pace, he was in the prime position entering the straight and, once he kicked for home, was always just holding his nearest rival in the closing stages. Sixth, beaten nine lengths, in this last year, he got to race off a 10lb lower mark this time around, so was fully entitled to respect, although his disappointing effort at Pontefract last time explains his SP. Apparently the plan was to send him novice chasing, but he'll be entered for the Cesarewitch now. Official explanation: trainer said, regarding apparent improvement in form, that the previous race may have come too soon for the gelding.
Seaside Sizzler, wearing a visor instead of the usual blinkers, was stepping up from 2m and racing off a career-high mark, but he posted another career-best, improving for the greater test of stamina. Having come to have his chance, though, he was outbattled in the finish, and perhaps he's not the heartiest of battlers. (op 16-1)
Exemplary, returning from a three-month break, had every chance 2f out but didn't quite see out the trip as well as the first two. He's got little in hand of the handicapper off his current mark.
Bow To No One(IRE), up 3lb for her good effort at York last time, confirmed that she's back in form, finishing well down the outside to take fourth. (op 16-1)
Cosimo de Medici was another keeping on at the finish after not getting the clearest of runs. (op 14-1)
Bowdler's Magic was prominent throughout and had every chance, but his stamina ran out.
Liberate came here on the back of a win over fences, but wasn't handicapped far off his best Flat form. (tchd 11-2)
Royal Diamond(IRE), up there most of the way, was a bit keen early and didn't get home over this extended trip. He has dropped to a fair mark, though, his third to Keys last time out is very solid form, and he'll be of interest back over 1m6f-2m.
Dazinski, second over 2m2f at Pontefract last month, proved disappointing. He has always been an in-and-out sort. (tchd 18-1 in a place)
My Arch, a winner over 2m2f at Pontefract last month, disappointed. The ground possibly wasn't soft enough for him, and he was also keen. (op 11-1)
Spirit Of Adjisa(IRE) came here on the back of success in a Grade 1 hurdle at Punchestown, but had plenty to prove on the stamina front, and didn't help himself by racing keenly. (op 9-2)

4424 VEUVE CLICQUOT VINTAGE STKS (GROUP 2) 7f
2:35 (2:36) (Class 1) 2-Y-O
£34,026 (£12,900; £6,456; £3,216; £1,614; £810) **Stalls** Low

Form RPR
102 **1** **Chandlery (IRE)**[18] 3861 2-9-0 0....................RichardHughes 6 107
(Richard Hannon) *mde all: rdn hands and heels and fnd ex over 1f out: rdn and r.o wl ins fnl f* **5/2**[1]

1 **2** *1* **Rockinante (FR)**[32] 3401 2-9-0 0....................RyanMoore 2 104
(Richard Hannon) *t.k.h early: chsd ldrs: rdn and effrt ent fnl 2f: drvn to chse wnr ins fnl f: kpt on wl but no threat to wnr* **5/1**

311 **3** *1 3/4* **Red Duke (USA)**[18] 3861 2-9-3 0....................KierenFallon 3 107+
(John Quinn) *stdd s: t.k.h: hld up wl in tch: hemmed in and nt clr run fr over 2f out tl swtchd rt jst ins fnl f: r.o wl to snatch 3rd last stride: nvr able to chal* **11/4**[2]

224 **4** *shd* **Lethal Force (IRE)**[43] 3012 2-9-0 0....................AdamKirby 7 99
(Clive Cox) *t.k.h early: hld up in last pair: rdn and effrt on outer over 2f out: hdwy and edgd rt 2f out: chsd ldrs jst ins fnl f: kpt on same pce fnl 150yds* **3/1**[3]

431 **5** *1 1/4* **Elkhart (IRE)**[25] 3609 2-9-0 0....................SilvestreDeSousa 4 96
(Mark Johnston) *t.k.h: chsd wnr: rdn over 2f out: drvn and unable qck over 1f out: wknd jst ins fnl f: wl hld whn n.m.r and eased nr fin* **14/1**

3231 **6** *1/2* **Minal**[11] 4087 2-9-0 0....................DaneO'Neill 1 95
(Richard Hannon) *hld up in last: pushed along over 3f out: rdn and no prog 2f out: wl hld and styd on same pce fr over 1f out* **25/1**

11 **7** *1 3/4* **Red Seventy**[19] 3795 2-9-0 0....................PatDobbs 5 90
(Richard Hannon) *in tch in midfield: rdn and effrt whn edging rt 2f out: btn ent fnl f: wknd ins fnl f* **16/1**

1m 27.0s (0.10) **Going Correction** 0.0s/f (Good) **7** Ran SP% **113.3**
Speed ratings (Par 106): **99,97,95,95,94 93,91**
totesswingers:1&2: £3.50, 2&3: £3.20, 1&3: £2.00 CSF £15.15 TOTE £3.70: £1.80, £2.70; EX 18.80.

Owner Mrs J Wood **Bred** Owenstown Stud **Trained** East Everleigh, Wilts

FOCUS
This Group 2 race featured a rematch between the Superlative Stakes one-two. It was rather messy and the winner made all at a steady pace. The form is rated around the winner to the bottom end of the race averages.

NOTEBOOK
Chandlery(IRE) reversed Newmarket form with Red Duke on 3lb better terms, but the result had much more to do with the way tactics played out than any difference in the weights carried. Richard Hannon held a strong hand in the race and, with Chandlery, who is an uncomplicated ride, being sent out in front, his other runners were able to slot in behind where they could play both the stalking and team game. Allowed to dictate things to suit himself, Hughes kept plenty in reserve and only had to go for Chandlery seriously heading into the final furlong. In the circumstances he achieved no more than he should have given the way the race panned out, and on the face of it he'll struggle when upped to Group 1 company. (tchd 10-3 and 7-2 in places)
Rockinante(FR), the least experienced runner in the line-up, tracked the leader on the rail and remained in that position throughout. In what was a tactical race he couldn't pick up his stablemate but showed he's well up to competing at Group level, and it could be that the Solario fits into his schedule. (tchd 9-2)
Red Duke(USA), who beat Chandlery in the Superlative Stakes and was therefore saddled with a 3lb penalty here, was given a surprisingly naïve ride by Fallon, who, while understandably needing to get cover for his mount, allowed himself to get boxed in, with Hannon runners in front of him and to his left, meaning that when it came to the closing stages he was reliant on getting help from Pat Dobbs aboard the winner's stablemate Red Seventy, to his left, in letting him out, which was never going to happen. Denied a clear run from 2f out to well inside the last while clearly still having plenty to give, he eventually managed to grab third, but with an untroubled passage he would surely have run the winner close. He gives the impression that the faster the early gallop the better he will look. (op 3-1 tchd 5-2)
Lethal Force(IRE), who appeared to excel himself when fourth in the Coventry Stakes last time out, had his chance down the outside if good enough, but he hung right under pressure and was comfortably held. The race wasn't run to suit him, but he got the trip alright and he might be able to find a Listed race somewhere. (op 9-2)
Elkhart(IRE), whose trainer has a decent record in this race, was beaten 4l by Rockinante in a Newmarket maiden two starts back. He finished closer to that rival this time and can't have too many excuses given where he raced (nearest the leader) almost throughout. (op 11-1 tchd 9-1 amd 16-1 in a place)
Minal, the most exposed runner in the line-up, had it to do in this company and, held up in last place, wasn't ideally placed in what was a tactical affair. (tchd 28-1in places and 33-1 in a place)
Red Seventy, two from two, was stepping up in class. While not good enough as it turned out, Dobbs ensured he held his position to the second-favourite's outer for long enough to ensure his stablemate Chandlery wasn't threatened by his Newmarket conqueror. (op 11-1 tchd 18-1 in a place)

4425 QIPCO SUSSEX STKS (BRITISH CHAMPIONS' SERIES) (GROUP 1) 1m
3:10 (3:12) (Class 1) 3-Y-O+ **£170,130** (£64,500; £32,280; £16,080) **Stalls** Low

Form RPR
-111 **1** **Frankel**[43] 3011 3-8-13 130....................TomQueally 3 137+
(Sir Henry Cecil) *t.k.h but a under control: mde all: shkn up and readily qcknd clr over 1f out: r.o strly in n.d fnl f: impressive* **8/13**[1]

1-11 **2** *5* **Canford Cliffs (IRE)**[43] 3009 4-9-7 127....................RichardHughes 2 125
(Richard Hannon) *trckd wnr: rdn over 1f out: immediately outpcd by wnr and btn whn hung bdly lft fr 1f out* **7/4**[2]

1-34 **3** *2 1/2* **Rio De La Plata (USA)**[43] 3009 6-9-7 120....................FrankieDettori 1 119
(Saeed Bin Suroor) *a same pl: hld up in tch: rdn wl over 1f out: sn outpcd and wl btn 1f out* **22/1**[3]

6013 **4** *2 1/2* **Rajsaman (FR)**[66] 2343 4-9-7 117....................(b) ThierryJarnet 4 114
(F Head, France) *hld up in last: rdn 2f out: outpcd and wl hld over 1f out* **22/1**[3]

1m 37.47s (-2.43) **Going Correction** 0.0s/f (Good)
WFA 3 from 4yo+ 8lb **4** Ran SP% **107.0**
Speed ratings (Par 117): **112,107,104,102**
CSF £1.88 TOTE £1.90; EX 2.10.

Owner K Abdulla **Bred** Juddmonte Farms Ltd **Trained** Newmarket, Suffolk

FOCUS
This was the smallest Sussex Stakes field since Sallust beat two rivals in 1972, but few Flat races in recent years have been as keenly anticipated as this one with a pair of outstanding milers squaring up, and the race did not disappoint. Dream Ahead in the July Cup and Nathaniel in the King George have beaten the older horses in recent Group 1s, and Frankel is the ninth of his age in the last 13 years to win the Sussex, in which three-year-olds receive an 8lb weight-for-age allowance from their elders. There is no question, though, that he was a deserving winner. The pace was soon solid and the time was a thoroughly respectable 0.87sec outside the standard. Frankel is rated among the top 3yos since RPRs began, although Canford Cliffs was below his best. Rio De La Plata is a good guide.

NOTEBOOK
Frankel gave a stunning display. The tactics Tom Queally would use were the subject of much speculation in the build-up, the colt having blasted off ahead in the Guineas then made a mid-race burst to the front in the St James's Palace Stakes. Apparently the plan here was to settle him in behind if possible, but Queally found he had no option but to make the running. It briefly appeared as if we were in for a falsely run race, but after a furlong or so he let his mount stride on, the colt racing a shade keenly as usual but always comfortably within himself. The pace thereafter was honest. Only shaken up approaching the furlong pole, Frankel quickened immediately, soon leaving Canford Cliffs in his wake, and ran on strongly to the line for a tremendously impressive win. The margin of superiority was perhaps exaggerated as the runner-up drifted left, but that does not hide the fact that this was a brilliant victory. Frankel had been clinging on at the end at Ascot, looking to most observers to be tiring, although Queally and Sir Henry Cecil were adamant that the colt was merely idling in the closing stages. This time, though, he was not stopping at the line - indeed he took a deal of pulling up - and provided that he can settle properly at the slightly slower gallop he has strong claims of getting further. He is likely to be given a break now until British Champions day at Ascot in October, when his prefered option would be the Queen Elizabeth II Stakes over a mile. Longer term he is very likely to stay in training at four. He is surely one of the all-time greats and we should enjoy him while we can. (op 4-6 tchd 8-11 in places)
Canford Cliffs(IRE)' rider had suggested that he would be prepared to make the running should the need arise, but was no doubt happy to accept a lead from Frankel. Sitting perhaps a length and a half down, and soon giving the impression he was being taken along a stride quicker than was desirable, Hughes got after his mount a fraction before Queally made his move, but could not prevent the winner from skating clear. The colt was held in second when he hung over to his left inside the final furlong. He had done the same when he was beaten by stablemate Dick Turpin in last season's Greenham Stakes, and hung to his right when third behind Makfi and Dick Turpin in the Guineas. Richard Hannon was inclined to believe that the Goodwood track does not really suit his colt, despite last year's Sussex Stakes win, and he and Hughes were convinced that the colt was not at his best. It's true that Rio De La Plata finished closer to him than he had in the Queen Anne at Ascot, and his move to the left accentuated the margin of defeat. This ends a magnificent run of five successive Group 1 wins, and the search for a dual Sussex Stakes winner goes on. The Queen Elizabeth II Stakes at Ascot in October, switched to Ascot's straight mile this year, is the obvious race for him and connections would not run scared of taking on Frankel again. Before then, the Prix du Moulin at Longchamp may come under consideration. (op 13-8 tchd 6-4)
Rio De La Plata(USA), who won the Vintage Stakes on this card as a juvenile four years ago, is a proven performer in the highest grade with three Group 1 wins to his name, all abroad. He ran perfectly creditably, never out of third place, and his consistency means he is a good guide to this form. (op 33-1)
Rajsaman(FR), Freddy Head's first runner at Goodwood, has never won a Group 1 but was third to stablemate Goldikova at this level in the Prix d'Ispahan last time out. Held up again, he was always bringing up the rear but there seems no reason to think he didn't run his race. Bigstone in 1993 was the last French-trained Sussex Stakes winner. (op 25-1 tchd 28-1)

4426 UBS STKS (H'CAP) 1m 4f
3:45 (3:49) (Class 2) (0-105,100) 3-Y-O
£24,900 (£7,456; £3,728; £1,864; £932; £468) **Stalls** High

Form RPR
-201 **1** **Whiplash Willie**[35] 3291 3-8-12 **91**....................(v) DavidProbert 5 103
(Andrew Balding) *t.k.h: hld up in last trio: rdn 4f out: nt clr run over 2f out: hdwy u.p 2f out: drvn to ld ent fnl f: hld on wl towards fin: all out* **7/1**

013 **2** *hd* **Arch Fire (USA)**[18] [3844] 3-8-9 **88**....................................(v) RyanMoore 2 99
(Sir Michael Stoute) *hld up towards rr: rdn 3f out: swtchd lft arnd 4 horses over 1f out: str run u.p 1f out: pressing wnr fnl 50yds:r.o: nt quite get up* **9/2**[1]

15-0 **3** *1 ¼* **Pivotman**[35] [3291] 3-8-6 **85**... MartinDwyer 11 94
(Amanda Perrett) *chsd ldr tl 1/2-way: in tch after: rdn and lost pl 3f out: rallied u.p on outer and hung rt over 1f out: kpt edging rt to hdwy to chse ldrs ins fnl f: no imp fnl 100yds* **25/1**

-125 **4** *1 ½* **Four Nations (USA)**[27] [3551] 3-7-9 **77**........................... KieranO'Neill(3) 1 84
(Amanda Perrett) *t.k.h: hld up in midfield: rdn and effrt towards inner 3f out: hdwy and edging out lft jst over 1f out: kpt on u.p: nt gng pce to rch ldrs* **9/2**[1]

2141 **5** *hd* **Tanfeeth**[18] [3867] 3-9-2 **95**.. RichardHills 4 101
(Ed Dunlop) *t.k.h: in tch: hdwy to join ldr over 3f out: pushed ahd over 2f out: sn rdn: drvn and hdd over 1f out: edgd rt and wknd ins fnl f* **11/2**[2]

6301 **6** *2* **Bridle Belle**[11] [4108] 3-8-11 **90**... PaulHanagan 10 93
(Richard Fahey) *hld up in tch towards rr: pushed along and hdwy 4f out: chsd ldrs and drvn over 1f out: unable qck: wknd ins fnl f* **12/1**

-115 **7** *5* **Halifax (IRE)**[40] [3108] 3-9-0 **93**.. KierenFallon 7 88
(Mark Johnston) *dwlt: sn t.k.h and rcvrd to r in midfield: hdwy to chse ldrs over 5f out: rdn and unable qck over 3f out: styng on same pce and btn whn bmpd and pushed rt over 1f out: n.d fnl f* **15/2**

-104 **8** *½* **Sadler's Risk (IRE)**[83] [1822] 3-9-7 **100**................................. NeilCallan 8 94
(Mark Johnston) *led: stdd gallop after 2f: rdn and hdd over 2f out: wknd u.p jst over 1f out: fdd ins fnl f* **13/2**[3]

2100 **9** *¾* **The Bells O Peover**[11] [4108] 3-8-4 **83**........................... JimmyQuinn 12 76
(Mark Johnston) *chsd ldrs: wnt 2nd 1/2-way tl 3f out: sn drvn and unable qck: wkng and towards rr whn pushed rt and hmpd over 1f out: no ch ins fnl f* **33/1**

0451 **10** *16* **Watercourse (IRE)**[26] [3585] 3-8-7 **86**................................ AndreaAtzeni 6 53
(Nigel Tinkler) *chsd ldrs: rdn and dropped to rr wl over 2f out: wknd and lost tch over 1f out* **16/1**

1004 **11** *3 ¼* **Greyfriars Drummer**[19] [3829] 3-8-5 **84**..................... SilvestreDeSousa 9 46
(Mark Johnston) *s.i.s: bhd: pushed along and sme hdwy 6f out: rdn and toiling over 3f out: lost tch wl over 2f out* **14/1**

2m 36.37s (-2.03) **Going Correction** 0.0s/f (Good) **11** Ran SP% **116.4**
Speed ratings (Par 106): **106,105,105,104,103 102,99,98,98,87 85**
toteswingers:1&2: £7.10, 2&3: £24.70, 1&3: £32.80 CSF £38.10 CT £749.60 TOTE £9.60: £2.40, £1.80, £7.10; EX 43.70 Trifecta £1349.30 Pool: £3482.75 - 1.91 winning units..
Owner J C & S R Hitchins **Bred** J C & S R Hitchins **Trained** Kingsclere, Hants
■ Stewards' Enquiry : David Probert two-day ban: careless riding (Aug 10-11); two-day ban: used whip with excessive frequency (Aug 12-13)

FOCUS
A competitive handicap in which the first two came from well behind, and this is form that should work out. The race is rated on the positive side.

NOTEBOOK
Whiplash Willie had been raised 12lb for his Salisbury stroll, but he holds a St Leger entry and is steadily heading towards being a pattern-class performer. Having been held up at the back of the field, he threaded a way between horses and saw his race out really well. Both his style of running and pedigree suggest he'll have no trouble with another 2f, and it'll be interesting to see where he goes next - the Melrose was mentioned. (op 8-1)
Arch Fire(USA) had looked in need of this trip when flashing home at Ascot over 1m2f last time, and indeed he improved for it, staying on strongly to press the winner close home. He was being held in the final few yards but he's a progressive sort and he's probably up to defying a higher mark. (op 11-2)
Pivotman's trainer has a great record in this race and both her entries ran well in defeat. This one ran badly on his reappearance behind Whiplash Willie, but as a 2-y-o he beat Carlton House by 4l on his debut. After getting outpaced early in the straight, he kept on again for pressure and this unexposed son of Pivotal has further improvement in him, probably back on easier ground. (op 20-1 tchd 33-1)
Four Nations(USA), who won here on his reappearance, kept on for pressure but this was a better race than he's been competing in of late and he wasn't quite good enough. He's probably a good marker for the form, though. (op 6-1)
Tanfeeth, a little keen early, hit the front going well but was eventually swamped by rivals who had been ridden with more patience. He can probably still win off this mark given a different pace scenario. (tchd 13-2 in places)
Bridle Belle, up 8lb for her Ripon win, was one paced under pressure and looked beaten on merit. (op 11-1 tchd 10-1)
Halifax(IRE), down in class and grade, weakened out of contention in the closing stages having had plenty of use made of him. (op 6-1)
Sadler's Risk(IRE) weakened out of contention in the closing stages having had plenty of use made of him. (op 8-1)

4427 MARKEL INTERNATIONAL MAIDEN FILLIES' STKS 6f

4:20 (4:21) (Class 2) 2-Y-O **£9,703** (£2,887; £1,443; £721) **Stalls** High

Form RPR

1 **Rakasa** 2-9-0 0.. FrankieDettori 1 84+
(Mahmood Al Zarooni) *stdd s: towards rr: stdy hdwy 1/2-way: rdn over 2f out: chsd ldr ent fnl f: drvn and ev ch ins fnl f: r.o wl to ld towards fin* **11/2**[3]

0 **2** *hd* **Lulla**[47] [2880] 2-9-0 0...(t) HayleyTurner 2 83
(Marcus Tregoning) *chsd ldrs tl led and crossed to r on stands' rail over 4f out: rdn over 1f out: kpt on wl tl hdd and no ex towards fin* **33/1**

5 **3** *¾* **My Queenie (IRE)**[12] [4061] 2-9-0 0......................... RichardHughes 8 81+
(Richard Hannon) *stdd s: bhd: stl plenty to and rdn over 1f out: hdwy ent fnl f: kpt on wl u.p ins fnl f: wnt 3rd wl ins fnl f: nt rch ldrs* **8/1**

4 *1* **Sunday Times** 2-9-0 0.. JackMitchell 7 77+
(Peter Chapple-Hyam) *wnt rt s and s.i.s: bhd: rdn and hdwy wl over 2f out: chsd ldrs u.p 1f out: no ex fnl 100yds* **9/2**[2]

044 **5** *2 ½* **Miss Astragal (IRE)**[19] [3813] 2-9-0 0................................... RyanMoore 6 69
(Richard Hannon) *racd in midfield: pushed along and outpcd 4f out: rdn and effrt 2f out: styd on ins fnl f: nvr gng pce to threaten ldrs* **12/1**

434 **6** *¾* **Sunrise Dance**[18] [3878] 2-9-0 0.. KierenFallon 4 67
(Alan Jarvis) *wnt rt and flashed tail leaving stalls: sn racd keenly and dashed up to chse ldr over 4f out: rdn and unable qck over 1f out: drvn and wknd 1f out* **13/2**

23 **7** *shd* **Scrooby Doo**[15] [3947] 2-9-0 0.. AdrianNicholls 11 67
(David Nicholls) *broke fast and w ldr early: stdd and in tch in midfield after 2f: rdn and edging rt but no prog wl over 1f out: no threat to ldrs but plugged on ins fnl f* **20/1**

8 *2 ¾* **Deduction (IRE)** 2-9-0 0.. MichaelHills 10 58+
(B W Hills) *s.i.s: bhd: hung bdly rt 4f out: in tch but stl hanging whn urged along over 1f out: keeping on same pce whn eased fnl 100yds* **12/1**

6 **9** *¾* **Ishiamiracle**[18] [3868] 2-9-0 0... DavidProbert 3 55
(Andrew Balding) *dwlt and hmpd sn after s: sn in tch in midfield: rdn and rn green over 2f out: no imp over 1f out: wknd ins fnl f* **50/1**

2 **10** *1 ¾* **Diamond Finesse (IRE)**[72] [2153] 2-9-0 0...................... JimmyFortune 5 57
(Ed Dunlop) *chsd ldrs: pushed along and unable qck 2f out: rdn and btn over 1f out: wknd fnl f* **11/4**[1]

30 **11** *2 ¾* **Quiet Appeal (IRE)**[12] [4073] 2-9-0 0......................... SilvestreDeSousa 9 41
(Mark Johnston) *led tl over 4f out: steadily lost pl: rdn and wknd 2f out* **33/1**

6 **12** *3 ¾* **Ice Missile**[12] [4052] 2-9-0 0... LiamKeniry 13 29
(Sylvester Kirk) *rn green in midfield: rdn and lost pl over 2f out: wknd and wl bhd whn hung rt over 1f out* **16/1**

1m 11.81s (-0.39) **Going Correction** 0.0s/f (Good) **12** Ran SP% **118.5**
Speed ratings (Par 97): **102,101,100,99,96 95,94,91,90,87 84,79**
toteswingers:1&2: £20.70, 2&3: £21.90, 1&3: £5.20 CSF £182.38 TOTE £6.80: £2.20, £6.20, £2.50; EX 182.30 TRIFECTA Not won..
Owner Godolphin **Bred** Darley **Trained** Newmarket, Suffolk

FOCUS
It's hard to know the value of this maiden form, but it does seem to underline the strength of the Godolphin stable in the juvenile fillies' division this season. The form is rated towards the top of the race averages.

NOTEBOOK
Rakasa, the first foal of an unraced half-sister to French 1000 Guineas winner Valentine Waltz, knew her job on her debut and finished well to collar and then hold the front-running runner-up close home. While the bare result looks nothing special, she's entitled to come on for the outing and be given a chance in Listed/Group company, although on the face of it her stable boasts stronger contenders for the top prizes. (op 13-2)
Lulla who had a tongue tie on this time, stepped up hugely on her debut effort, showing plenty of pace alongside the stands' rail. Her dam was a speedy front-runner as well and she shouldn't have any trouble with dropping back to the minimum. (op 25-1)
My Queenie(IRE) picked up well from off the pace to flash home for third and, as her pedigree suggests, a return to 7f will do her no harm. (op 15-2 tchd 13-2 and 9-1 in a place)
Sunday Times, along with the winner, challenged down the outside. She came in for plenty of support so had clearly been showing something at home, and on this evidence she shouldn't be too long in winning her maiden. (op 6-1)
Miss Astragal(IRE) may be the best guide to the level of the form, having already posted a couple of fair efforts in defeat prior to this. (op 14-1)
Sunrise Dance used up a lot of energy early in not settling so it wasn't the greatest surprise to see her fail to see her race out. (op 15-2)
Deduction(IRE), who was far too green to do herself justice, hung right into the middle of the track and wasn't subjected to a hard ride, indeed she was eased some way from home. She has more ability than her finishing position suggests and is entitled to come on a great deal for this debut effort. Official explanation: jockey said filly hung right-handed (op 10-1)
Diamond Finesse(IRE) was the disappointment of the race. Runner-up on her debut, she was expected to put up a bold show with that experience behind her, but having chased the leaders she dropped out tamely from 1f out. (op 3-1 tchd 10-3 in a place)

4428 HARWOODS E B F "HELLVELYN" CLASSIFIED STKS 7f

4:55 (4:56) (Class 2) 3-Y-O+

£12,450 (£3,728; £1,864; £932; £466; £234) **Stalls** Low

Form RPR

-622 **1** **Webbow (IRE)**[26] [3578] 9-9-4 93....................................... KierenFallon 11 100
(Mark Campion) *mde all: pushed along and asserted 2f out: kpt on wl u.p ins fnl f* **9/1**

2110 **2** *¾* **Common Touch (IRE)**[41] [3067] 3-8-11 95...................... PaulHanagan 2 95
(Richard Fahey) *in tch in midfield: rdn 3f out: hdwy u.p towards inner over 1f out: styd on wl to chse wnr fnl 50yds: kpt on* **10/3**[1]

0100 **3** *hd* **Smarty Socks (IRE)**[18] [3876] 7-9-4 93..................... SilvestreDeSousa 6 97
(David O'Meara) *v.s.a: hld up in rr: swtchd lft and effrt on outer wl over 1f out: r.o strly u.p ins fnl f: nt rch ldrs* **15/2**[3]

0000 **4** *shd* **Golden Desert (IRE)**[39] [3155] 7-9-4 92.......................... JamieSpencer 4 97+
(Robert Mills) *hld up in rr: stl plenty to do but stl travelling wl whn swtchd sharply lft over 1f out: r.o strly fnl f: nt rch ldrs* **25/1**

1440 **5** *nk* **Decent Fella (IRE)**[25] [3645] 5-9-4 92...............................(v) LiamKeniry 5 96
(Andrew Balding) *t.k.h: trckd ldrs: rdn and effrt jst over 1f out: styd on same pce ins fnl f* **13/2**[2]

2031 **6** *1 ¾* **Shavansky**[19] [3802] 7-9-4 94.. JamesMillman 7 92
(Rod Millman) *in tch in midfield: pushed along ent fnl 2f: rdn and styd on same pce fr over 1f out* **10/1**

0000 **7** *shd* **Rulesn'regulations**[1] [4415] 5-9-4 90............................(b) GeorgeBaker 15 91
(Matthew Salaman) *chsd ldrs: rdn and effrt over 1f out: unable qck ent fnl f: styd on same pce after* **20/1**

0601 **8** *1* **Space Station**[27] [3536] 5-9-4 88.....................................(b) SebSanders 13 69
(Simon Dow) *hld up towards rr on outer: rdn and effrt 2f out: styd on same pce and no imp fnl f* **20/1**

4622 **9** *½* **Lutine Bell**[18] [3841] 4-9-4 94..(b) HughBowman 8 87
(Mike Murphy) *t.k.h: hld up towards rr: rdn and effrt over 2f out: hdwy wl over 1f out: kpt on fnl f: nvr gng pce to threaten ldrs* **8/1**

P000 **10** *¾* **Capital Attraction (USA)**[18] [3877] 4-9-4 87..................(b) TomQueally 3 85
(Sir Henry Cecil) *s.i.s and bustled along early: hdwy into midfield whn nt clr and shuffled bk towards rr 5f out: swtchd lft and drvn 2f out: kpt on fnl f: nvr trbld ldrs* **25/1**

-104 **11** *1 ¾* **Enderby Spirit (GR)**[12] [4042] 5-9-4 92.............................. TomEaves 14 81
(Bryan Smart) *w wnr: pushed along over 2f out: rdn and unable qck w wnr wl over 1f out: wknd fnl f* **25/1**

0003 **12** *2 ¾* **Shamandar (FR)**[12] [4049] 4-9-1 93...............................(b[1]) RyanMoore 1 70
(William Haggas) *t.k.h: hld up in midfield: rdn and hung rt ent fnl 2f: wknd and stl hanging over 1f out* **8/1**

21-6 **13** *3* **Zenella**[18] [3852] 3-8-8 93.. FrannyNorton 12 59
(Ann Duffield) *in tch: rdn: hung lft and lost pl wl over 2f out: bhd and no ch over 1f out* **16/1**

-000 **14** *6* **Prince Shaun (IRE)**[136] 6-9-4 93...................................... PatDobbs 9 49
(Richard Guest) *awkward s: hld up in rr: rdn and no hdwy jst over 2f out: sn bhd* **66/1**

1m 25.98s (-0.92) **Going Correction** 0.0s/f (Good)
WFA 3 from 4yo+ 7lb **14** Ran SP% **117.9**
Speed ratings (Par 109): **105,104,103,103,103 101,101,100,99,98 96,93,90,83**
toteswingers:1&2: £6.70, 2&3: £5.20, 1&3: £10.60 CSF £34.54 TOTE £10.30: £2.90, £1.90, £2.30; EX 44.90 Trifecta £291.40 Pool: £3138.72 - 7.97 winning units..
Owner Wentdale Limited **Bred** Joe O'Callaghan **Trained** Norton, N Yorks

FOCUS
Just a few pounds separated the bulk of the field in this valuable classified stakes, which has gone to some smart sorts in the past decade. The pace was respectable and the form seems sound enough for Goodwood, with a mix of prominent racers and hold-up horses involved in the finish. The winner is probably the bset guide.

NOTEBOOK
Webbow(IRE) got across to lead and made just about all the running, holding on well after opening up a decisive margin heading down to the furlong pole. He had been running well since joining the Campion outfit and this was his first win on turf since 2007. He has run plenty of solid races in defeat since then, making the frame in the last two Totesport Miles at this fixture. (op 8-1)

Common Touch(IRE) cut no ice in the Britannia, but had won a pair of handicaps over this trip at York previously. He bounced back here on this first venture against older horses, taking time to wind up but running on strongly against the rail in the latter stages, and will not mind a return to a mile. (op 5-1)
Smarty Socks(IRE), a narrow winner from Webbow at Doncaster last month, is often slowly away and he stumbled leaving the stalls. Still at the back with a quarter of a mile left, he then picked up before flying home down the outer in tandem with the fourth. The pair of them were fast catching the first two at the line. (op 8-1 tchd 13-2 and 9-1 in a place)
Golden Desert(IRE) ◆ travelled well under a hold-up ride and finished strongly once switched out for a clear run and let down. This was a return to form after a sequence of 'duck eggs' this year and he clearly likes this track, having won twice and been second twice in four previous visits. He should be kept in mind if he returns to Goodwood. (op 22-1)
Decent Fella(IRE) was never far from the pace, but could not quite get to the winner and he was run out of the frame late on. He was back at his ideal trip. (op 7-1)
Shavansky was never far from the action over the shortest distance he's ever run over, and this was a sound enough effort. (tchd 11-1)
Rulesn'regulations, last year's winner, who ran creditably in first-time blinkers here on Tuesday, ran another fair race from the widest draw on this quick reappearance. (op 25-1)
Space Station had work to do at these weights and a wide draw didn't help either. (op 16-1)
Lutine Bell had been in good heart over 6f of late, but raced keenly back up in trip and was slightly impeded when trying to pick up from mid-field. (op 13-2)
Enderby Spirit(GR), another drawn wide, raced prominently for a long way but his stamina for this longer trip was definitely ebbing away late on. (tchd 28-1)
Shamandar(FR), drawn on the inside, was keen in the first-time blinkers and weakened disappointingly. Official explanation: jockey said filly hung left-handed (tchd 15-2)
Zenella Official explanation: jockey said filly hung left-handed

4429 E B F NAYEF FILLIES' AND MARES' STKS (H'CAP) 1m 1f

5:30 (5:31) (Class 3) (0-95,91) 3-Y-O+

£9,337 (£2,796; £1,398; £699; £349; £175) **Stalls** Low

Form | | | | RPR
005 **1** **Askaud (IRE)**[4] 4325 3-8-9 **81** .....(p) TomQueally 7 90
(David Nicholls) *in tch in midfield: effrt jst over 2f out: rdn to chal over 1f out: led narrowly jst over 1f out: hung rt u.p 1f out: drvn and forged ahd fnl 50yds* **14/1**
3331 **2** *½* **Totheendoftheearth (IRE)**[16] 3918 3-8-3 **75** ..... SilvestreDeSousa 8 83
(Sylvester Kirk) *in tch: pushed along 4f out: rdn and effrt over 2f out: drvn and ev ch over 1f out: no ex towards fin* **7/1**[3]
325 **3** *1 ¼* **Imaginary World (IRE)**[5] 4265 3-8-1 **73** .....(be) DavidProbert 13 78
(Alan McCabe) *stdd s: hld up in rr: swtchd lft and hdwy over 2f out: drvn to chse ldrs 1f out: kpt on u.p ins fnl f* **22/1**
4212 **4** *shd* **Valencha**[18] 3845 4-9-1 **78** ..... SteveDrowne 2 84
(Hughie Morrison) *in tch in midfield: pushed along 5f out: hmpd sn after: rdn and hdwy jst over 2f out: chsd ldrs and drvn over 1f out: kpt on u.p ins fnl f* **15/2**
0-64 **5** *½* **Desert Kiss**[12] 4058 6-9-13 **90** ..... AdamKirby 6 95
(Walter Swinburn) *chsd ldrs: rdn over 2f out: drvn to ld narrowly over 1f out: sn hdd: stl ev ch tl no ex and btn ins fnl f: lost 2 pls towards fin* **25/1**
-640 **6** *1 ¾* **Musharakaat (IRE)**[41] 3065 3-9-5 **91** ..... RichardHills 11 91
(Ed Dunlop) *in midfield early: lost pl and towards rr over 4f out: rdn over 2f out: hdwy over 1f out: styd on steadily ins fnl f: nvr gng pce to rch ldrs* **20/1**
231 **7** *½* **Miss Aix**[53] 2735 3-8-10 **82** ..... HayleyTurner 3 81
(Michael Bell) *in tch: rdn and unable qck 3f out: outpcd 2f out: rallied and kpt on u.p 1f out: swtchd lft and styd on ins fnl f* **9/1**
5-10 **8** *¾* **Sweet Child O'Mine**[113] 1154 4-9-6 **83** ..... PatDobbs 18 81
(Richard Guest) *in tch in midfield: swtchd lft and effrt u.p ent fnl 2f: drvn and no imp over 1f out: one pce fnl f* **33/1**
4-52 **9** *½* **Fanny May**[13] 4022 3-9-1 **87** ..... JamieSpencer 10 83
(Denis Coakley) *midfield tl lost pl and dropped to rr over 7f out: effrt on outer whn pushed rt and hmpd over 2f out: rallied and edgd rt over 1f out: styd on ins fnl f: nvr able to chal* **12/1**
0030 **10** *hd* **Totally Ours**[26] 3592 4-9-8 **85** ..... GeorgeBaker 16 82
(William Muir) *hld up in rr: rdn and effrt over 2f out: hdwy over 1f out: kpt on fnl f: nvr gng pce to rch ldrs* **40/1**
2-01 **11** *nk* **Miss Diagnosis (IRE)**[36] 3260 3-9-2 **88** ..... JimCrowley 9 83
(Ralph Beckett) *hld up in rr: stl plenty to do and rdn over 2f out: sme hdwy ent fnl f: styd on ins fnl f but nvr any threat to ldrs* **9/2**[1]
3-12 **12** *nk* **Ken's Girl**[25] 3632 7-9-5 **82** ..... IanMongan 17 77
(Stuart Kittow) *stmbld leaving stalls: led: rdn over 2f out: hdd over 1f out: btn 1f out: wknd ins fnl f* **16/1**
0-61 **13** *3 ½* **Blessed Biata (USA)**[23] 3689 3-9-2 **88** ..... RyanMoore 5 75
(William Haggas) *taken down early: t.k.h: chsd ldrs: rdn over 2f out: wkng whn short of room and hmpd over 1f out: no ch ins fnl f* **13/2**[2]
0440 **14** *hd* **Bahati (IRE)**[11] 4093 4-9-7 **84** ..... LiamKeniry 4 71
(Jonathan Portman) *a towards rr: rdn and effrt over 2f out: drvn and no hdwy over 1f out: nvr trbld ldrs* **50/1**
0621 **15** *hd* **Hip Hip Hooray**[30] 3468 5-8-2 **72** oh6 ..... LukeRowe(7) 1 59
(Luke Dace) *stdd s: hld up in rr: c wd over 3f out: rdn and no hdwy whn sltly hmpd over 2f out: plugged on but n.d* **40/1**
2101 **16** *1* **Abdicate (IRE)**[12] 4045 3-8-7 **79** ..... PaulHanagan 14 62
(Richard Fahey) *chsd ldr tl over 2f out: sn struggling: wkng and edgd lft u.p over 1f out: fdd ins fnl f* **20/1**
1611 **17** *46* **Apache Glory (USA)**[25] 3632 3-8-12 **84** ..... RichardHughes 15 —
(Richard Hannon) *in tch: rdn and effrt whn wnt lft over 2f out: rdr looking down and sn nt pushed: virtually p.u fr over 1f out: t.o* **8/1**

1m 54.36s (-1.94) **Going Correction** 0.0s/f (Good)
WFA 3 from 4yo+ 9lb **17** Ran SP% **124.6**
Speed ratings (Par 104): **108,107,106,106,105 104,103,103,102,102 102,102,98,98,98 97,56**
toteswingers:1&2: £101.10, 2&3: £59.00, 1&3: £65.70 CSF £99.85 CT £2186.18 TOTE £17.10: £3.80, £2.30, £4.30, £2.60; EX 153.60 Trifecta £2073.30 Pool: £2801.80 - 1.00 winning units..
Owner Paul J Dixon **Bred** John P Jones **Trained** Sessay, N Yorks

FOCUS
An open fillies' handicap, and a good race of its type containing a number of progressive contestants. Three-year-olds have won nine of the last eleven renewals now. Sound form.

NOTEBOOK
Askaud(IRE) ran a decent race at Newcastle over the weekend and she had a good effort to her name at this track earlier this season. She hung a little when brought with her challenge, but found plenty to hold off her pursuers. The step back up in trip helped, as did the first-time cheekpieces. (op 12-1)
Totheendoftheearth(IRE) lacked the experience of most of these but ran a solid race off a 3lb higher mark than when winning at Windsor. The winner carried her slightly to the right, but it did not affect the outcome. (op 13-2 tchd 6-1)
Imaginary World(IRE) was found wanting in a recent Listed race but made the frame once again back in handicap company. She is pretty reliable but her win ratio is not good. (op 28-1)
Valencha, successful in a four-runner race here before finding a stablemate too good last time, was 2lb ahead of the handicapper. She was hampered on the inside going into the final bend and did well to finish as close as she did, but the incident did not cost her victory. (op 8-1)
Desert Kiss ran another creditable race, only fading out of the places late on, and is nicely handicapped off just a pound above her last winning mark.
Musharakaat(IRE), who ran in the Ribblesdale last time, was keeping on at the end on this handicap debut and will be suited by returning to a little further. She is due to be dropped a pound now. (tchd 25-1 in a place)
Miss Aix, another handicap debutante, shaped as if this trip was a bit on the short side for her. (op 10-1 tchd 17-2 and 12-1 in a place)
Miss Diagnosis(IRE)'s Newbury win has been working out well and a 9lb rise looked fair, but she could never get into it. She was staying on at the end and should be afforded another chance. (tchd 5-1)
Ken's Girl stumbled badly exiting the stalls and did well to make the running until over a furlong out. She is currently on a career-high mark. Official explanation: jockey said mare stumbled leaving stalls (op 14-1, tchd 20-1 in a place)
Blessed Biata(USA) only scrambled home when long odds-on for a maiden last time and she disappointed on this return to handicaps. Official explanation: jockey said filly suffered interference in running (op 15-2, tchd 8-1 in places)
Apache Glory(USA), bidding for a fifth win in her last six starts, was close enough when suddenly veering right, and her jockey soon eased her off. Official explanation: jockey said filly hung badly left-handed
T/Jkpt: Not won. T/Plt: £504.10 to £1 stake. Pool of £251,698.02 - 364.49 winning tickets. T/Qpdt: £44.40 to a £1 stake. Pool of £15,605.08 - 260.07 winning tickets. SP

4199 LEICESTER (R-H)

Wednesday, July 27

OFFICIAL GOING: Good to firm (8.1)
Wind: Light behind Weather: Overcast

4430 BRITISH STALLION STUDS SUPPORTING BRITISH RACING E B F MEDIAN AUCTION MAIDEN FILLIES' STKS 5f 218y

6:10 (6:10) (Class 5) 2-Y-O **£3,234** (£962; £481; £240) **Stalls** High

Form | | | | RPR
1 **Jessie's Spirit (IRE)** 2-9-0 0 ..... DavidNolan 7 73+
(Ann Duffield) *a.p: swtchd rt over 1f out: rdn to ld ins fnl f: r.o* **12/1**
0 **2** *1 ¾* **Lollina Paulina**[25] 3610 2-9-0 0 ..... CathyGannon 8 67
(Kevin Ryan) *w ldr: rdn and ev ch ins fnl f: styd on same pce* **6/1**[2]
0 **3** *nk* **Heartsong (IRE)**[9] 4155 2-9-0 0 ..... MartinLane 9 66
(John Gallagher) *led: rdn over 1f out: edgd lft and hdd ins fnl f: styd on same pce* **12/1**
3 **4** *1 ¼* **By Invitation (USA)**[21] 3736 2-9-0 0 ..... RichardKingscote 3 63+
(Ralph Beckett) *hld up: hdwy over 2f out: effrt and nt clr run ins fnl f: swtchd rt: r.o: nvr able to chal* **4/6**[1]
3633 **5** *9* **Reina Sofia**[29] 3491 2-9-0 0 ..... LiamJones 6 34
(Tony Carroll) *w ldrs tl rdn over 2f out: wknd over 1f out* **8/1**[3]
04 **6** *nse* **Lilygloves**[105] 1301 2-9-0 0 ..... SamHitchcott 5 33
(Mick Channon) *hld up: rdn over 2f out: wknd over 1f out* **20/1**
0 **7** *¾* **Music Girl**[51] 2767 2-9-0 0 ..... FrankieMcDonald 2 31
(Michael Blanshard) *sn outpcd* **33/1**
03 **8** *3 ½* **Picura**[23] 3673 2-9-0 0 ..... RichardMullen 1 20
(William Muir) *prom: rdn over 2f out: wknd wl over 1f out* **20/1**

1m 12.35s (-0.65) **Going Correction** -0.125s/f (Firm) **8** Ran SP% **113.2**
Speed ratings (Par 91): **99,96,96,94,82 82,81,76**
toteswingers:1&2: £10.00, 2&3: £6.80, 1&3: £14.00 CSF £77.86 TOTE £12.50: £4.60, £1.30, £3.40; EX 77.80.
Owner David & Carole McMahon **Bred** Mountarmstrong Stud **Trained** Constable Burton, N Yorks

FOCUS
No more than a modest fillies' median auction maiden and one run at a slightly muddling pace too with the early gallop steady and the favourite denied a clear run. The form is rated around the race averages with the winner to her debut form.

NOTEBOOK
Jessie's Spirit(IRE) might be out of a mare that won at 1m4f but several of her foals have won at up to 6f and she emulated Cut The Cackle among those who also made a winning start. There was little fluke about it, either, as she was well on top at the line having had to wait for a run and she's sure to improve with a step up to 7f likely to suit before long. (tchd 14-1)
Lollina Paulina hadn't shown much on her recent debut when very green but she'd clearly learnt from that, always in the firing line. A maiden win is likely to elude her before she goes into nurseries, but she did enough to suggest she can win a claimer if dropped in grade. (op 7-1 tchd 8-1)
Heartsong(IRE) had beaten only a couple home at Windsor on her debut when 100-1, so her proximity also gives the form a weakish look and she'll need to curb some slightly wayward tendencies late on if she's to progress. (op 22-1)
By Invitation(USA), bidding to give her stable their third win in this race in the last four years, looked a shade unfortunate not to have finished second, although whether she'd have beaten the winner is a moot point. She ended up poorly placed after being restrained just at the point the early pace increased and then found the gap she was going for on the rail closed by the third. Her debut form has worked out well and she's worth another chance, but she won't find many easier maidens than this. (op 4-7)
Reina Sofia stayed with the second and third to 2f out, but is exposed as modest having been held in a Fibresand claimer last time. (op 7-1)
Lilygloves never threatened on her first run since finishing fourth in a seller at Catterick in April. (op 16-1)

4431 SHANGTON (S) STKS 7f 9y

6:40 (6:40) (Class 6) 3-Y-O **£1,617** (£481; £240; £120) **Stalls** High

Form | | | | RPR
1210 **1** **Cootehill Lass (IRE)**[38] 3207 3-8-12 70 .....(p) RobertWinston 8 73
(Geoffrey Harker) *s.i.s: racd centre: hld up: hdwy over 2f out: led over 1f out: drvn out* **5/2**[2]
3232 **2** *3 ¼* **Bilko Pak (IRE)**[14] 3972 3-8-12 70 .....(p) DavidNolan 3 64
(Ann Duffield) *racd centre: hld up in tch: rdn over 1f out: styd on same pce ins fnl f* **2/1**[1]
0464 **3** *¾* **Prince Of Passion (CAN)**[9] 4149 3-8-12 62 ..... TedDurcan 7 62
(Michael Dods) *racd centre: led that gp: overall ldr over 2f out: rdn and hdd over 1f out: edgd lft and no ex ins fnl f* **8/1**[3]
3262 **4** *1 ½* **Tony Hollis**[114] 1132 3-8-9 59 ..... LouisBeuzelin(3) 5 58
(Rod Millman) *racd centre: chsd ldrs: rdn and ev ch over 1f out: styng on same pce whn nt clr run and swtchd rt ins fnl f* **10/1**
-056 **5** *5* **Piccarello**[26] 3571 3-8-12 64 .....(b1) PhilipRobinson 1 45
(Mark H Tompkins) *racd centre: chsd ldr: rdn over 2f out: wknd over 1f out* **12/1**

The Form Book, Raceform Ltd, Compton, RG20 6NL

3340 **6** *1 3/4* **Captain Dimitrios**[7] 4199 3-8-12 66.........................(v) StevieDonohoe 11 40
(David Evans) *racd stands' side: chsd ldr: rdn to ld that gp over 2f out: hung rt and wknd over 1f out* **14/1**

005 **7** *3 1/2* **Ossie Ardiles (IRE)**[22] 3716 3-8-12 55............................ NeilChalmers 6 30
(Michael Appleby) *racd centre: hld up: rdn 1/2-way: wknd over 2f out* **33/1**

-050 **8** *nk* **Nettis**[15] 3958 3-8-9 50... CagriMetin(3) 12 30
(George Prodromou) *overall ldr on stands' side tl rdn and hdd over 2f out: sn hung rt and wknd* **33/1**

3314 **9** *1 1/4* **Granny Anne (IRE)**[166] 510 3-8-12 61........................ CathyGannon 10 26
(Alan Bailey) *racd stands' side: sn pushed along in rr: wknd over 2f out* **12/1**

0500 **10** *1 1/2* **Avon Light**[161] 558 3-8-12 52.................................... RichardKingscote 9 22
(Milton Bradley) *racd stands' side: prom: rdn and hung rt 1/2-way: wknd over 2f out: eased over 1f out* **40/1**

1m 25.23s (-0.97) **Going Correction** -0.125s/f (Firm) **10** Ran SP% **112.5**
Speed ratings (Par 98): **100,96,95,93,88 86,82,81,80,78**
toteswingers:1&2: £2.10, 2&3: £4.60, 1&3: £3.70 CSF £7.39 TOTE £3.90: £1.50, £1.10, £3.80; EX 8.90.The winner was bought by D Evans for 8,000gns. Bilko Pak was claimed by D Shaw for £7000.
Owner An Englishman, Irishman & Scotsman **Bred** Speers Bloodstock Ltd **Trained** Thirkleby, N Yorks

FOCUS
An ordinary seller in which the runners split into two groups with the four that kept nearest the stands' rail all finishing well held. The form pair finished 1-2.
Avon Light Official explanation: jockey said gelding lost its action

4432 WILLIS ANNIVERSARY H'CAP 1m 1f 218y
7:15 (7:15) (Class 4) (0-80,80) 3-Y-O+ **£3,881** (£1,155; £577; £288) **Stalls** Low

Form RPR

0131 **1** **Judicious**[26] 3572 4-9-9 75... RobertWinston 6 84
(Geoffrey Harker) *hld up: hdwy over 3f out: rdn to ld and edgd rt over 1f out: styd on* **4/1**[1]

1310 **2** *nk* **Destiny Of A Diva**[33] 3338 4-10-0 80................................... ChrisCatlin 4 88
(Reg Hollinshead) *prom: rdn over 1f out: styd on* **9/2**[2]

3000 **3** *2 3/4* **Kidlat**[18] 3844 6-10-0 80... CathyGannon 5 83
(Alan Bailey) *led: rdn and hdd over 2f out: styd on same pce ins fnl f* **16/1**

-205 **4** *1/2* **Wiggy Smith**[33] 3366 12-9-6 77.. AmyScott(5) 2 79
(Henry Candy) *hld up and bhd: hdwy over 1f out: sn rdn and edgd rt: nt rch ldrs* **5/1**[3]

100- **5** *1 1/4* **Eastern Paramour (IRE)**[293] 6691 6-9-9 78............. LouisBeuzelin(3) 8 77
(Rod Millman) *chsd ldr tl led over 2f out: rdn: hung rt and hdd over 1f out: no ex ins fnl f* **16/1**

44-0 **6** *nk* **Lyric Poet (USA)**[15] 3959 4-9-7 73..............................(t) WilliamCarson 1 71
(Giles Bravery) *hld up: hdwy u.p over 2f out: styd on same pce fnl f* **12/1**

5655 **7** *nse* **Franco Is My Name**[19] 3815 5-9-5 74............................ KierenFox(3) 11 72
(Peter Hedger) *mid-div: hdwy over 2f out: sn rdn: no ex fnl f* **6/1**

-050 **8** *nk* **Cloudy Start**[14] 3982 5-9-10 79.................................... SophieDoyle(3) 9 77
(Jamie Osborne) *s.i.s: hld up: r.o ins fnl f: nvr nrr* **7/1**

2300 **9** *2 1/2* **Black Coffee**[18] 3848 6-9-5 71..(b) ShaneKelly 3 64
(Mark Brisbourne) *s.i.s: sn mid-div: rdn over 3f out: hdwy over 2f out: styd on same pce fr over 1f out: eased ins fnl f* **14/1**

400 **10** *7* **Oasis Storm**[11] 4109 3-9-0 76...(b1) TedDurcan 12 67
(Michael Dods) *trckd ldrs: plld hrd: rdn and hung rt over 1f out: sn wknd and eased* **10/1**

2m 6.28s (-1.62) **Going Correction** -0.125s/f (Firm)
WFA 3 from 4yo+ 10lb **10** Ran SP% **116.8**
Speed ratings (Par 105): **101,100,98,98,97 96,96,96,94,89**
CSF £21.88 CT £260.62 TOTE £2.60: £1.10, £2.60, £4.40; EX 14.80.
Owner The Unique Partnership **Bred** Cheveley Park Stud Ltd **Trained** Thirkleby, N Yorks

FOCUS
A fair handicap run at what looked a decent pace with the field well strung out by the home turn. The winner is generally progressive and the second built on last month's C&D win.
Oasis Storm Official explanation: jockey said colt hung right

4433 BRITISH STALLION STUDS SUPPORTING BRITISH RACING E B F MAIDEN STKS 5f 218y
7:45 (7:45) (Class 4) 2-Y-O **£4,001** [illegible] **Stalls** High

Form RPR

1 **Gold City (IRE)** 2-9-3 0... TedDurcan 5 87+
(Saeed Bin Suroor) *hld up: swtchd lft and hdwy over 2f out: chsd ldr over 1f out: shkn up to ld ins fnl f: edgd rt: r.o* **5/4**[1]

0 **2** *2 3/4* **Forest Edge (IRE)**[7] 4201 2-9-3 0 ow3..................... RichardEvans(3) 6 79+
(David Evans) *led: rdn and edgd rt over 1f out: hdd and unable qck ins fnl f* **28/1**[3]

3 *9* **Towbee** 2-9-3 0.. JamesSullivan 1 47
(Michael Easterby) *chsd ldrs: shkn up and edgd lft over 1f out: wknd ins fnl f* **12/1**[2]

00 **4** *1 3/4* **Rocco Breeze (IRE)**[40] 3132 2-9-3 0............................ RichardMullen 2 41
(Philip McBride) *chsd ldrs: rdn over 2f out: wknd over 1f out* **12/1**[2]

5 *3/4* **Ghost Train (IRE)** 2-9-3 0.. RobertWinston 3 39+
(Mark Johnston) *dwlt: hdwy over 4f out: rdn over 2f out: wknd over 1f out* **5/4**[1]

05 **6** *1 1/2* **Valley Of Stars (IRE)**[33] 3349 2-9-3 0......................... EddieCreighton 4 34
(Edward Creighton) *chsd ldr: rdn and hung rt over 2f out: sn wknd* **28/1**[3]

1m 12.24s (-0.76) **Going Correction** -0.125s/f (Firm) **6** Ran SP% **111.2**
Speed ratings (Par 96): **100,96,84,82,81 79**
CSF £37.42 TOTE £1.70: £1.10, £19.00; EX 31.50.
Owner Godolphin **Bred** Darley **Trained** Newmarket, Suffolk

FOCUS
Not easy to know what the form of this maiden is worth with one of the two that dominated the betting running disappointingly and the eventual second having been tailed off on its only run to date. The time was relatively quick and the form is rated around the race averages.

NOTEBOOK
Gold City(IRE) is very well bred being by Pivotal out of a daughter of the top-class miler Crimplene. He ran out a comfortable winner but it wasn't achieved without some concern, running very green as he was produced from off the pace with the penny taking a long while to drop. He seems sure to improve quite a bit from this, not least at 7f, without for the time being looking anything special. (op 6-4 after 13-8 in places)
Forest Edge(IRE) hadn't shown anything on his debut just a week ago but was more clued up here, deserving some credit for beating the rest readily enough, but it's doubtful whether he'll be up to winning a maiden before he goes into nurseries. (op 16-1 tchd 33-1)
Towbee wasn't given a hard time once third place was the best he could do and, like most youngsters from this yard, this colt by Doyen, out of a 2yo 5f winner, can be expected to improve with experience. (tchd 11-1)
Rocco Breeze(IRE) found himself tapped for toe as the race developed in earnest but he's at least qualified for nurseries now. That said, given his pedigree, he'll only make some appeal in them once he's upped to 1m. (op 14-1)
Ghost Train(IRE), a half-brother by Holy Roman Emperor to the 2yo 1m winner La Teranga, was clearly expected to run well judging by the market, but instead found the occasion all too much as youngsters from this yard sometimes can first time up. Out of a mare by the stamina influence Monsun, he'll do better in time over further. Official explanation: jockey said colt hung left from halfway (tchd 11-10)

4434 PAULL'S VEHICLE RENTAL H'CAP 5f 218y
8:20 (8:20) (Class 5) (0-70,70) 3-Y-O+ **£2,264** (£673; £336; £168) **Stalls** High

Form RPR

3602 **1** **Mata Hari Blue**[13] 4025 5-9-6 **64**....................................(t) AndreaAtzeni 6 76
(John Holt) *racd stands' side: chsd ldr tl led overall over 1f out: sn rdn: edgd rt ins fnl f: r.o* **7/2**[2]

1624 **2** *3/4* **Emiratesdotcom**[28] 3512 5-9-7 **65**............................ RichardKingscote 9 75
(Milton Bradley) *racd stands' side: prom: rdn to chse wnr over 1f out: r.o: 2nd of 3 in gp* **3/1**[1]

006 **3** *3 1/2* **Earlsmedic**[33] 3351 6-9-11 **69**.......................................(v) WilliamCarson 1 68
(Stuart Williams) *racd centre: chsd ldr tl led that gp over 2f out: rdn and ev ch over 1f out: edgd lft: no ex ins fnl f: 1st of 6 in gp* **9/1**

2411 **4** *2 1/4* **Bermondsey Bob (IRE)**[15] 3940 5-9-9 **70**........................ KierenFox(3) 2 62
(John Spearing) *racd centre: led overall to 1/2-way: hdd that gp over 2f out: sn rdn and hung lft: no ex fnl f: 2nd of 6 in gp* **8/1**

5404 **5** *nk* **Seamus Shindig**[47] 2879 9-9-4 **67**.................................... AmyScott(5) 5 58
(Henry Candy) *racd centre: bhd: hdwy over 1f out: no ex ins fnl f: 3rd of 6 in gp* **17/2**

2210 **6** *3* **Volito**[25] 3617 5-9-10 **68**.. TedDurcan 3 49
(Anabel K Murphy) *racd centre: sn outpcd: 4th of 6 in gp* **8/1**

000 **7** *hd* **Alpha Tauri (USA)**[37] 3222 5-9-8 **66**........................(t) RobbieFitzpatrick 8 46
(Richard Guest) *led stands' side: overall ldr 1/2-way: rdn and hdd over 1f out: wknd fnl f: last of 3 in gp* **33/1**

6023 **8** *1 1/2* **Chinese Democracy (USA)**[5] 4270 4-8-9 **53**............(v) CathyGannon 4 29
(David Evans) *racd centre: chsd ldrs tl rdn and wknd over 2f out: 5th of 6 in gp* **7/1**[3]

0020 **9** *1/2* **Errigal Lad**[13] 4025 6-8-9 **53**... RobertWinston 7 27
(Garry Woodward) *racd centre: s.i.s: sme hdwy over 1f out: sn wknd: last of 6 in gp* **8/1**

1m 11.74s (-1.26) **Going Correction** -0.125s/f (Firm) **9** Ran SP% **116.5**
Speed ratings (Par 103): **103,102,97,94,93 89,89,87,87**
toteswingers:1&2: £4.00, 2&3: £11.50, 1&3: £12.70 CSF £14.60 CT £87.19 TOTE £5.30: £1.50, £1.60, £2.50; EX 16.30.
Owner M J Golding **Bred** R T And Mrs Watson **Trained** Peckleton, Leics

FOCUS
A run-of-the-mill sprint handicap in which the field split into two groups, with first and second both coming from among the stands' side trio. the first two are both progressing.

4435 GREASE NIGHTS H'CAP 1m 60y
8:50 (8:51) (Class 6) (0-65,65) 3-Y-O **£1,617** (£481; £240; £120) **Stalls** Low

Form RPR

0110 **1** **Alluring Star**[18] 3854 3-9-5 **64**.. JamesSullivan 8 73
(Michael Easterby) *mde all: rdn over 1f out: styd on* **6/1**[2]

145- **2** *3/4* **Ebony Song (USA)**[279] 7035 3-9-6 **65**........................... RichardMullen 5 72
(Jo Crowley) *hld up in tch: rdn to chse wnr over 1f out: r.o* **6/1**[2]

560 **3** *3 1/4* **Full Pelt (USA)**[71] 2174 3-9-2 **61**..........................(v1) RichardKingscote 2 61
(Tom Dascombe) *chsd ldrs: rdn over 2f out: styd on same pce fnl f* **10/1**

0424 **4** *1 3/4* **Crown Ridge (IRE)**[7] 4200 3-9-3 **62**............................ SamHitchcott 13 58
(Mick Channon) *prom: rdn over 2f out: styd on same pce fr over 1f out* **11/1**

6-00 **5** *shd* **Spartan King (IRE)**[11] 4081 3-8-12 **60**............................... RyanClark(3) 3 55
(Ian Williams) *hld up: plld hrd: hdwy over 1f out: nt rch ldrs* **7/1**[3]

0035 **6** *1/2* **Marie Rose**[11] 4081 3-9-6 **65**..(p) ShaneKelly 10 59
(Brian Meehan) *hmpd s: hld up: hdwy over 2f out: sn rdn: hung rt fr over 1f out: one pce* **7/2**[1]

0553 **7** *1 1/4* **Joyful Sound (IRE)**[16] 3913 3-9-4 **63**.......................... StevieDonohoe 11 54
(Andrew Haynes) *prom: rdn over 2f out: wknd fnl f* **6/1**[2]

56-4 **8** *shd* **Phoenix Flame**[25] 3633 3-8-13 **61**.............................. MartinHarley(3) 12 54
(Alan McCabe) *hld up: rdn over 2f out: nvr on terms* **7/1**[3]

[illegible] **9** [illegible] **Thank You Joy**[illegible] [illegible] 3-9-[illegible] 54.. LiamJones 9 19
(J R Jenkins) *hld up: plld hrd: rdn over 3f out: n.d* **25/1**

4100 **10** *11* **Bountiful Guest**[11] 4081 3-9-4 **63**.........................(vt1) RobertWinston 6 21
(Brian Baugh) *chsd wnr: rdn over 2f out: wknd over 1f out* **20/1**

1m 45.07s (-0.03) **Going Correction** -0.125s/f (Firm) **10** Ran SP% **116.1**
Speed ratings (Par 98): **95,94,91,89,89 88,87,87,84,73**
toteswingers:1&2: £4.00, 2&3: £11.50, 1&3: £12.70 CSF £41.70 CT £355.87 TOTE £6.50: £2.90, £3.80, £3.10; EX 52.80.
Owner Jeff Hamer & Bernard Bargh **Bred** B Bargh **Trained** Sheriff Hutton, N Yorks

FOCUS
A modest finale run at an uneven gallop that favoured those ridden handily. The winner is rated up 6lb.
Spartan King(IRE) Official explanation: jockey said gelding ran too free
T/Plt: £445.40 to a £1 stake. Pool of £59957.39 - 98.25 winning units. T/Qpdt: £33.40 to a £1 stake. Pool of £8704.17 - 192.60 winning units. CR

4122 REDCAR (L-H)
Wednesday, July 27

OFFICIAL GOING: Good to firm (8.5)
Wind: moderate 1/2 against Weather: fine

4436 BRITISH STALLION STUDS SUPPORTING BRITISH RACING E B F MAIDEN STKS 6f
1:40 (1:40) (Class 5) 2-Y-O **£3,135** (£925; £463) **Stalls** Centre

Form RPR

530 **1** **Singalat**[39] 3152 2-9-3 0... FrederikTylicki 10 77
(James Given) *w ldrs: led over 1f out: drvn out* **3/1**[1]

0 **2** *1 1/2* **Premier Choice**[41] 3082 2-9-3 0.. DavidAllan 3 72
(Tim Easterby) *led tl over 1f out: kpt on same pce last 150yds* **13/2**

35 **3** *1* **The Rising (IRE)**[16] 3915 2-9-3 0..............................(v1) GrahamGibbons 6 69
(Ed McMahon) *w ldrs: kpt on same pce ins fnl f* **6/1**

05 **4** *1 3/4* **Laffan (IRE)**[32] 3398 2-9-3 0.. PhillipMakin 1 63
(Kevin Ryan) *w ldrs: kpt on same pce over 1f out* **5/1**[3]

5 **5** *1 1/4* **Lowtherwood**[30] 3452 2-9-3 0.. RoystonFfrench 2 59
(Bryan Smart) *chsd ldrs: one pce fnl 2f* **20/1**

6 shd **Sabhan (IRE)** 2-9-3 0 .... DanielTudhope 12 59+
(Geoffrey Harker) *mid-div: outpcd 3f out: edgd rt 2f out: kpt on ins fnl f* **33/1**

4 7 3 ½ **Elusive Island (USA)**[13] 4012 2-9-3 0 .... DavidNolan 4 47
(Ann Duffield) *wnt rt s and slipped s: sn drvn along: sme hdwy 3f out: wknd over 1f out* **13/2**

8 1 ¼ **Loukas (IRE)** 2-9-3 0 .... PJMcDonald 8 43+
(Alan Swinbank) *dwlt: outpcd and in rr: reminders after 2f: sme hdwy over 1f out: nvr on terms* **9/2**[2]

0 9 3 ½ **Dream Walker (FR)**[15] 3932 2-9-3 0 .... PatrickMathers 9 32
(Ian McInnes) *chsd ldrs: edgd rt and wknd over 1f out* **100/1**

05 10 hd **Docs Legacy (IRE)**[12] 4047 2-9-3 0 .... TonyHamilton 5 32
(Richard Fahey) *hmpd s: sn outpcd and in rr* **25/1**

11 hd **Goodfellows Quest (IRE)** 2-9-3 0 .... DuranFentiman 11 31
(Ann Duffield) *sn outpcd and in rr* **66/1**

12 4 ½ **Findhornbay** 2-8-12 0 .... RobertWinston 7 12
(Mark Johnston) *s.s: sn chsng ldrs: lost pl over 2f out* **20/1**

1m 11.71s (-0.09) **Going Correction** -0.10s/f (Good) **12** Ran SP% **119.6**
Speed ratings (Par 94): **96,94,92,90,88 88,83,82,77,77 77,71**
toteswingers:1&2:£5.40, 2&3: £8.50, 1&3: £4.30 CSF £21.31 TOTE £4.20: £1.80, £2.80, £2.40; EX 26.10.

Owner Danethorpe Racing Partnership **Bred** Mrs S Clifford **Trained** Willoughton, Lincs

■ Stewards' Enquiry : David Nolan two-day ban: careless riding (Aug 10-11)

FOCUS
An ordinary juvenile maiden. The winner stood out on his Leicester form and rates a small personal best.

NOTEBOOK
Singalat, well beaten in the Chesham on his debut for connections, was made plenty of use of on this drop to 6f and always looked to be holding the runner-up. He'll need further in time and nurseries seem the obvious route now, although he is in a valuable Doncaster sales race. (op 11-4 tchd 5-2)
Premier Choice, gambled on before disappointing on debut, showed that running to be all wrong on this faster ground. He's got some scope and should have no trouble winning a maiden. (op 7-1 tchd 8-1)
The Rising(IRE), up to 6f, ran well in first-time visor and looks one for nurseries. (tchd 5-1)
Laffan(IRE) showed his last running to be wrong and should be able to win once handicapping. (op 9-1)
Lowtherwood improved on his initial effort and will be suited by further.
Sabhan(IRE), whose dam is a half-sister to Regal Parade, shaped with promise and should improve. (tchd 25-1)
Elusive Island(USA) failed to build on his debut effort. Official explanation: jockey said colt slipped leaving stalls (op 7-1 tchd 11-2)
Loukas(IRE) was very green. (tchd 4-1)

4437 CARIBBEAN CARNIVAL DAY SATURDAY 6TH AUGUST RATING RELATED MAIDEN STKS 7f
2:10 (2:11) (Class 5) 3-Y-0+ **£2,102** (£625; £312; £156) **Stalls** Centre

Form RPR

-264 1 **Fenella Fudge**[26] 3586 3-8-12 70 .... (b[1]) FrederikTylicki 4 71
(James Given) *mde all: rdn: edgd rt and rdn clr over 1f out: unchal* **11/8**[1]

5054 2 8 **Wandering Lad**[15] 3933 3-9-1 58 .... MickyFenton 2 52
(Paul Midgley) *hld up in rr: effrt 3f out: chsd clr ldr 1f out: kpt on same pce* **9/1**

2005 3 ¾ **Chardonnay Star (IRE)**[18] 3857 4-9-5 46 .... (v) AndrewMullen 3 50
(Colin Teague) *chsd ldrs: reminders after 2f: lost pl over 2f out: hung rt and kpt on ins fnl f* **33/1**

032- 4 shd **Daffydowndilly**[252] 7485 3-8-12 69 .... NickyMackay 6 47
(Hughie Morrison) *sn trcking ldrs: effrt and edgd lft over 2f out: wknd ins fnl f* **6/4**[2]

0-06 5 6 **Valentine's Gift**[20] 3756 3-9-1 65 .... DanielTudhope 1 34
(Neville Bycroft) *led to s: wnt rt s: pushed along in rr: bhd fnl 2f: eased towards fin* **15/2**[3]

0040 6 8 **Toffee Nose**[5] 4286 4-9-1 46 .... ShaneBKelly[(7)] 5 15
(Ron Barr) *trckd ldrs: t.k.h: lost pl over 2f out: bhd whn eased fnl f* **100/1**

1m 24.54s (0.04) **Going Correction** -0.10s/f (Good)
WFA 3 from 4yo 7lb **6** Ran SP% **107.8**
Speed ratings (Par 103): **95,85,85,84,78 68**
toteswingers:1&2:£2.70, 2&3:£8.10, 1&3:£5.40 CSF £12.95 TOTE £2.40: £1.70, £2.40; EX 11.90.

Owner Danethorpe Racing Partnership **Bred** Onslow, Given, Stratton & Cashin **Trained** Willoughton, Lincs

■ Stewards' Enquiry : Frederik Tylicki caution: used whip when clearly winning.

FOCUS
A really weak maiden. The winner may not have had to improve on this year's modest form.

4438 FOLLOW REDCARRACING ON FACEBOOK & TWITTER (S) STKS 1m 2f
2:45 (2:46) (Class 6) 3-Y-0+ **£1,704** (£503; £251) **Stalls** Low

Form RPR

0600 1 **Yorksters Prince (IRE)**[10] 4125 4-8-13 39 .... (b[1]) ShaneBKelly[(7)] 6 52
(Tony Coyle) *s.s: hdwy to ld after 1f: hdd 6f out: led over 2f out: edgd lft over 1f out: hld on wl* **20/1**

2012 2 1 ½ **White Deer (USA)**[36] 3243 7-9-11 65 .... (p) DanielTudhope 3 54
(Geoffrey Harker) *hld up: hdwy over 3f out: n.m.r and swtchd rt over 1f out: hung lft: tk 2nd nr fin* **5/2**[2]

0300 3 nk **Magic Millie (IRE)**[8] 4173 4-9-1 56 .... GrahamGibbons 2 43
(David O'Meara) *reluctant ldr: hdd after 1f: led 6f out tl over 2f out: kpt on same pce appr fnl f* **15/8**[1]

4006 4 shd **So Bazaar (IRE)**[12] 4045 4-9-6 59 .... PJMcDonald 4 48
(Alan Swinbank) *trckd ldrs: chal over 3f out: kpt on one pce over 1f out* **5/2**[2]

5603 5 2 ½ **Crocodile Bay (IRE)**[10] 4123 8-9-3 50 .... (b) RobertLButler[(3)] 7 43
(Richard Guest) *t.k.h in last: sddle slipped 5f out: hdwy on ins 4f out: nvr trbld ldrs* **8/1**[3]

0000 5 dht **Charity Fair**[14] 3974 4-8-8 36 .... (v) GarryWhillans[(7)] 1 38
(Ron Barr) *trckd ldrs: effrt 3f out: one pce* **66/1**

2m 10.4s (3.30) **Going Correction** -0.10s/f (Good) **6** Ran SP% **109.3**
Speed ratings (Par 101): **82,80,80,80,78 78**
toteswingers:1&2: £3.80, 2&3: £1.60, 1&3: £3.90 CSF £65.96 TOTE £23.60: £6.00, £1.30; EX 54.20.There was no bid for the winner.

Owner Tony Coyle **Bred** Lady Legard & Sir Tatton Sykes **Trained** Norton, N Yorks

FOCUS
The early pace was a steady one for this seller. Weak, muddling form, and a shock winner.
Yorksters Prince(IRE) Official explanation: trainer said, regarding apparent improvement in form, that the gelding appreciated the better ground and first-time blinkers
Crocodile Bay(IRE) Official explanation: jockey said saddle slipped

4439 JOHN SMITH'S REDCAR STRAIGHT-MILE CHAMPIONSHIP (QUALIFIER) (H'CAP) 1m
3:20 (3:20) (Class 4) (0-85,83) 3-Y-O **£2,587** (£770; £384; £192) **Stalls** Centre

Form RPR

502- 1 **Mullins Way (USA)**[379] 3985 3-9-7 83 .... TonyCulhane 1 90
(Jo Hughes) *hld up: hdwy over 3f out: 2nd over 2f out: crowded over 1f out: hrd rdn: led post* **4/1**[3]

5-2 2 nse **File And Paint (IRE)**[10] 4127 3-8-7 74 .... LanceBetts[(5)] 4 81
(Lawrence Mullaney) *w ldr: led over 3f out: edgd lft over 1f out: hdd post* **5/2**[1]

5322 3 5 **Abidhabidubai**[15] 3933 3-8-5 74 .... ShaneBKelly[(7)] 5 70
(John Quinn) *sn trcking ldrs: effrt over 3f out: wknd over 1f out* **3/1**[2]

1-00 4 9 **Stansonnit**[11] 4108 3-9-1 77 .... PJMcDonald 2 52
(Alan Swinbank) *hld up: hdwy after 3f: drvn over 3f out: sn wknd* **11/2**

-215 5 ¾ **Royal Hush**[26] 3586 3-8-13 75 .... PhillipMakin 3 48
(Kevin Ryan) *drvn to ld: hdd over 3f out: sn btn* **4/1**[3]

1m 37.14s (-0.86) **Going Correction** -0.10s/f (Good) **5** Ran SP% **109.0**
Speed ratings (Par 102): **100,99,94,85,85**
CSF £13.96 TOTE £4.80: £4.00, £1.10; EX 13.20.

Owner B Allen, H Downs & J Hughes **Bred** Loft Hall Stud **Trained** Lambourn, Berks

FOCUS
An ordinary handicap and weak form for the grade, rated around the runner-up.
Royal Hush Official explanation: trainer had no explanation for the poor form shown

4440 MARKET CROSS JEWELLERS H'CAP 1m 2f
3:55 (4:11) (Class 5) (0-75,80) 3-Y-O+ **£2,102** (£625; £312; £156) **Stalls** Low

Form RPR

0243 1 **Christmas Light**[10] 4127 4-9-8 68 .... DanielTudhope 3 76
(David O'Meara) *hld up in rr: nt clr run on inner over 2f out: swtchd rt over 1f out: r.o wl to ld last 100yds* **6/1**

6000 2 1 ¼ **Gold Rules**[22] 3701 4-9-4 71 .... DavidSimmonson[(7)] 9 76
(Michael Easterby) *hld up in rr: effrt over 3f out: hdwy on outside over 1f out: styd on wl to take 2nd post* **9/1**

3311 3 shd **Persian Peril**[8] 4173 7-9-13 80 12ex .... GarryWhillans[(7)] 4 85
(Alan Swinbank) *trckd ldrs: t.k.h: effrt 3f out: led over 1f out: hdd and no ex ins fnl f* **9/2**[2]

1005 4 ½ **Tapis Libre**[13] 4005 3-8-10 66 .... GrahamGibbons 6 70
(Michael Easterby) *trckd ldr: led 6f out tl over 3f out: upsides over 1f out: one pce ins fnl f* **15/2**

3024 5 shd **Hidden Glory**[12] 4045 4-10-0 74 .... FrederikTylicki 2 78
(James Given) *s.i.s: sn mid-div: effrt 3f out: w ldrs 1f out: kpt on same pce* **4/1**[1]

1133 6 3 ¼ **Miss Blink**[21] 3726 4-9-5 65 .... LeeNewman 7 62
(Robin Bastiman) *trckd ldrs: drvn over 3f out: sn outpcd: kpt on ins fnl f* **5/1**[3]

-054 7 1 **Torun City**[14] 3976 3-8-8 64 ow1 .... TonyHamilton 5 59
(Richard Fahey) *trckd ldrs: outpcd over 2f out: one pce* **16/1**

1113 8 2 **I Confess**[15] 3934 6-9-11 71 .... (p) DuranFentiman 11 62
(Geoffrey Harker) *led tl 6f out: wknd over 1f out* **16/1**

1536 9 2 ¼ **Sinatramania**[10] 4128 4-8-11 60 .... PaulPickard[(3)] 10 47
(Tracy Waggott) *mid-div: hdwy to trck ldrs 6f out: led over 3f out: hdd & wknd qckly over 1f out* **9/1**

2m 5.26s (-1.84) **Going Correction** -0.10s/f (Good)
WFA 3 from 4yo+ 10lb **9** Ran SP% **112.7**
Speed ratings (Par 103): **103,102,101,101,101 98,98,96,94**
toteswingers:1&2: £11.30, 2&3: £8.10, 1&3: £5.90 CSF £56.84 CT £263.47 TOTE £5.60: £1.60, £3.40, £1.90; EX 53.70.

Owner Mrs Lynne Lumley **Bred** Rabbah Bloodstock Limited **Trained** Nawton, N Yorks

■ Stewards' Enquiry : Garry Whillans caution: used whip with excessive frequency.

FOCUS
A low-grade handicap, but it was certainly competitive and it was sound run. The form makes sense.

4441 RACING UK ON CHANNEL 432 H'CAP (DIV I) 1m
4:30 (4:34) (Class 6) (0-65,65) 3-Y-O+ **£1,293** (£385; £192; £96) **Stalls** Centre

Form RPR

4015 1 **Broctune Papa Gio**[10] 4123 4-8-12 52 .... DeclanCannon[(3)] 6 72
(Keith Reveley) *mid-div: effrt over 2f out: led appr fnl f: forged clr* **4/1**[2]

3001 2 6 **Master Leon**[12] 4039 4-9-1 59 .... (p) JustinNewman[(7)] 2 65
(Bryan Smart) *w ldr: led over 3f out: hdd over 2f out: led briefly over 1f out: kpt on same pce* **3/1**[1]

0305 3 3 ½ **Oldmeldrum (IRE)**[11] 4084 3-8-2 50 .... BillyCray[(3)] 1 46
(Peter Salmon) *chsd ldrs: drvn 4f out: sn outpcd: styd on appr fnl f: tk modest 3rd last 50yds* **20/1**

3445 4 1 ¼ **Intiqaal (IRE)**[29] 3477 4-10-0 65 .... PhillipMakin 7 60
(Keith Dalgleish) *s.i.s: hdwy over 3f out: edgd lft over 1f out: wknd last 150yds* **3/1**[1]

0442 5 ¾ **Lady Excel (IRE)**[10] 4128 5-9-0 51 .... (p) FrederikTylicki 8 45
(Brian Rothwell) *trckd ldrs: led over 2f out: hdd over 1f out: wknd last 150yds* **5/1**[3]

0040 6 ½ **Pictures (IRE)**[10] 4123 4-8-2 46 oh1 .... (p) ShaneBKelly[(7)] 9 38
(Ron Barr) *s.i.s: sn detached and reminders: styd on fnl 2f: nvr a factor* **16/1**

6005 7 4 **El Dececy (USA)**[12] 4076 7-9-12 63 .... TonyCulhane 5 46
(Richard Guest) *led: hdd over 3f out: lost pl over 2f out* **13/2**

0-00 8 1 ¼ **Catawollow**[5] 3496 4-8-10 47 .... (e) AndrewMullen 4 27
(Richard Guest) *hld up in rr: drvn over 3f out: sn bhd* **28/1**

05/ 9 19 **Evelith Regent (IRE)**[297] 2264 8-9-4 55 .... PaddyAspell 11 —
(John Davies) *chsd ldrs: drvn 4f out: sn lost pl and bhd: t.o* **40/1**

1m 35.9s (-2.10) **Going Correction** -0.10s/f (Good)
WFA 3 from 4yo+ 8lb **9** Ran SP% **116.5**
Speed ratings (Par 101): **106,100,96,95,94 94,90,88,69**
toteswingers:1&2: £3.70, 2&3: £8.00, 1&3: £7.10 CSF £16.24 CT £215.20 TOTE £5.60: £1.10, £1.80, £6.10; EX 19.70.

Owner Broctune Partners I **Bred** Lesley Winn And Reveley Farms **Trained** Lingdale, Redcar & Cleveland

FOCUS
The first division of a moderate handicap but a fast time for the grade. Sound form.

Intiqaal(IRE) Official explanation: jockey said gelding had a breathing problem

4442 RACING UK ON CHANNEL 432 H'CAP (DIV II) 1m

5:05 (5:06) (Class 6) (0-65,64) 3-Y-0+ **£1,293** (£385; £192; £96) **Stalls** Centre

Form RPR

-003 **1** **Talent Scout (IRE)**[22] 3719 5-9-5 **55**.......................(p) GrahamGibbons 7 69
(Tim Walford) *wnt rt s: sn trcking ldrs: led and wnt lft over 1f out: hung lft and drew clr ins fnl f* **9/2**[3]

3510 **2** *2 ¼* **Wiseman's Diamond (USA)**[12] 4076 6-9-8 **58**...........(b) MickyFenton 2 67
(Paul Midgley) *trckd ldrs: edgd rt 2f out: chsd wnr fnl f: no imp* **10/3**[1]

4000 **3** *1* **Desert Vision**[22] 3701 7-10-0 **64**.......................(vt) PhillipMakin 5 71
(Michael Easterby) *led: hdd and hmpd over 1f out: kpt on same pce* **7/2**[2]

6000 **4** *2 ½* **Mr Emirati (USA)**[10] 4128 4-8-10 **46**.......................(p) RoystonFfrench 4 47
(Bryan Smart) *trckd ldrs: drvn 4f out: sn outpcd: edgd lft and one pce fnl 2f* **8/1**

00- **5** *3 ¼* **Demo Jo**[320] 5931 5-8-9 **45**.......................... DuranFentiman 8 38
(Geoffrey Harker) *dwlt: in rr: effrt 3f out: nvr nr ldrs* **9/1**

5564 **6** *2 ¾* **Fairy Mist (IRE)**[11] 4112 4-9-6 **56**.......................... PaddyAspell 3 43
(Brian Rothwell) *trckd ldrs: drvn over 3f out: wknd 2f out* **9/2**[3]

006 **7** *4 ½* **Littlepromisedland (IRE)**[25] 3619 3-8-1 **45**............... AndrewMullen 10 20
(Richard Guest) *reluctant to go bhd stalls: dwlt: in rr: lost pl over 3f out: sn bhd* **33/1**

-R00 **8** *14* **Erfaan (USA)**[22] 3719 4-8-11 **47**.......................... BarryMcHugh 1 —
(Julie Camacho) *mid-div: effrt 3f out: sn wknd: bhd whn eased ins fnl f* **16/1**

050- **9** *26* **Applaude**[308] 6298 6-9-5 **58**.......................... BillyCray(3) 9 —
(Jason Ward) *chsd ldrs: lost pl over 3f out: sn wl bhd: t.o whn eased 2f out* **18/1**

1m 36.89s (-1.11) **Going Correction** -0.10s/f (Good)
WFA 3 from 4yo+ 8lb **9** Ran SP% **116.9**
Speed ratings (Par 101): **101,98,97,95,92 89,84,70,44**
toteswingers:1&2: £3.40, 2&3: £3.10, 1&3: £4.40 CSF £20.18 CT £59.01 TOTE £4.20: £1.30, £1.10, £1.90; EX 14.10.
Owner John Stacey **Bred** Johnston King **Trained** Sheriff Hutton, N Yorks

FOCUS
This second division of the weak 1m handicap proved a lively betting heat. It was run at a solid pace but there was something of a slow-motion finish and the time was slower than division I. Straightforward form.

4443 WIN A VIP DAY OUT AT REDCARRACING.CO.UK H'CAP 6f

5:40 (5:40) (Class 6) (0-65,65) 3-Y-0+ **£1,617** (£481; £240; £120) **Stalls** Centre

Form RPR

-000 **1** **Song Of Parkes**[33] 3341 4-9-7 **60**.......................... DavidAllan 9 71
(Eric Alston) *trckd ldrs: led jst ins fnl f: edgd lft: drvn out* **5/1**[2]

4533 **2** *¾* **Sea Salt**[6] 4233 8-8-13 **59**.......................... ShaneBKelly(7) 12 68
(Ron Barr) *w ldrs: no ex fnl 75yds* **5/1**[2]

0005 **3** *¾* **Pearly Wey**[12] 4078 8-8-12 **54**.......................... PaulPickard(3) 4 60+
(Ian McInnes) *slowly away: bhd: hdwy over 2f out: chsng ldrs 1f out: n.m.r and one pce last 75yds* **10/1**

0-40 **4** *½* **Greek Secret**[15] 3931 8-9-3 **56**.......................(b) FrederikTylicki 3 61
(Deborah Sanderson) *in tch: hdwy over 2f out: kpt on ins fnl f* **16/1**

0-05 **5** *½* **Red River Boy**[14] 3972 6-8-11 **50**.......................... KellyHarrison 8 53
(Chris Fairhurst) *chsd ldrs: kpt on same pce ins fnl f* **14/1**

1004 **6** *½* **Rio's Girl**[43] 3027 4-9-4 **57**.......................(p) PhillipMakin 6 58
(Kevin Ryan) *w ldrs: led after 1f: hdd jst ins fnl f: wknd towards fin* **9/1**

354 **7** *¾* **Electioneer (USA)**[9] 4152 4-9-11 **64**.......................... GrahamGibbons 10 63
(Michael Easterby) *mid-div: drvn over 3f out: styd on wl ins fnl f* **9/2**[1]

6000 **8** *¾* **Micky Mac (IRE)**[16] 3901 7-8-11 **50**.......................... MickyFenton 2 47+
(Colin Teague) *chsd ldrs on outer: one pce appr fnl f* **20/1**

0060 **9** *5* **Moon Lightning (IRE)**[21] 3733 5-8-7 **46** oh1.......... AndrewHeffernan 16 27
(Tina Jackson) *racd alone stands' side: bhd fnl 3f* **33/1**

5000 **10** *½* **Mujahope**[14] 3972 6-8-7 **46** oh1.......................(v) AndrewMullen 13 25
(Colin Teague) *reminders after s and a towards rr* **40/1**

5002 **11** *1 ¾* **Bahamian Jazz (IRE)**[11] 4110 4-9-2 **55**.......................... LeeNewman 1 28
(Robin Bastiman) *w ldrs on outside: hung rt and wknd over 1f out: eased towards fin* **6/1**[3]

3050 **12** *½* **Roman Ruler (IRE)**[24] 3661 3-8-10 **54**.......................... TonyHamilton 14 25
(Chris Fairhurst) *led 1f: lost pl over 3f out* **22/1**

[illegible]010 **13** *hd* **[illegible] (IRE)**[12] [illegible].......................... [illegible] 11 [illegible]
(John Harris) *chsd ldrs: rdn and lost pl over 2f out* **10/1**

0045 **14** *3* **Craicattack (IRE)**[16] 3903 4-8-7 **46** oh1.......................... PJMcDonald 15 —
(Sharon Watt) *a in rr* **25/1**

-000 **15** *7* **Annalika**[14] 3977 3-8-2 **46** oh1.......................... DuranFentiman 5 —
(Colin Teague) *chsd ldrs: sn drvn along lost pl over 2f out: sn bhd* **100/1**

1m 11.37s (-0.43) **Going Correction** -0.10s/f (Good)
WFA 3 from 4yo+ 5lb **15** Ran SP% **125.9**
Speed ratings (Par 101): **98,97,96,95,94 94,93,92,85,84 82,81,81,77,68**
toteswingers:1&2: £6.50, 2&3: £14.50, 1&3: £19.80. CSF £29.13 CT £258.22 TOTE £6.50: £2.30, £2.60, £4.30; EX 28.80.
Owner Joseph Heler **Bred** Joseph Heler **Trained** Longton, Lancs

FOCUS
A wide-open sprint handicap in which it paid to race handily. Ordinary form.
Bahamian Jazz(IRE) Official explanation: jockey said gelding hung right throughout
T/Plt: £150.90 to a £1 stake. Pool of £38,513.30 - 186.22 winning tickets. T/Qpdt: £35.40 to a £1 stake. Pool of £2,442.79 - 50.95 winning tickets. WG

4250 SANDOWN (R-H)

Wednesday, July 27

OFFICIAL GOING: Good (good to firm in places; 8.0)
Wind: Light, against Weather: Fine but cloudy

4444 THAMES DITTON APPRENTICE H'CAP 1m 14y

5:50 (5:53) (Class 5) (0-70,70) 4-Y-0+ **£2,264** (£673; £336; £168) **Stalls** Low

Form RPR

4222 **1** **Madame Excelerate**[2] 4394 4-9-2 **65**.......................... RyanClark(3) 7 73
(Mark Brisbourne) *taken down early: mde all: kicked on over 2f out: drvn and flashed tail over 1f out: edgd rt but styd on* **9/2**[1]

0-23 **2** *1 ¾* **Daneside (IRE)**[28] 3515 4-8-2 **53** ow2.................. MatthewLawson(5) 14 57
(Gary Harrison) *taken steadily to post: racd wd: hld up early: prog after 3f: more hdwy over 2f out: drvn and kpt on to take 2nd ins fnl f: unable to chal* **14/1**

0201 **3** *¾* **Come On Safari (IRE)**[11] 4089 4-9-3 **68**...............(b) CharlesBishop(5) 3 70
(Joseph Tuite) *t.k.h: trckd ldng pair: wnt 2nd over 3f out: rdn 2f out: hung rt and nt qckn over 1f out: lost 2nd ins fnl f* **14/1**

0643 **4** *1 ½* **Belle Park**[16] 3926 4-8-6 **52**.......................... JohnFahy 9 51
(Karen George) *hld up in 8th: sme prog 2f out but outpcd by ldrs: kpt on: n.d* **16/1**

1660 **5** *nk* **Byrd In Hand (IRE)**[9] 4154 4-8-12 **58**.......................... KieranO'Neill 5 56
(John Bridger) *chsd ldrs in 5th: rdn and nt qckn 2f out: one pce and no imp after* **6/1**[2]

006 **6** *½* **El Libertador (USA)**[22] 3720 5-8-7 **56**.......................(b) RyanPowell(3) 8 53+
(Eric Wheeler) *hld up in last trio: effrt and nowhere to go over 2f out: tried again and n.m.r over 1f out: kpt on: no ch to rch ldrs* **25/1**

2245 **7** *1 ½* **Ivory Lace**[23] 3674 10-9-3 **66**.......................... HarryBentley(3) 13 60
(Steve Woodman) *trckd ldng trio: rdn over 2f out: steadily fdd fr over 1f out* **12/1**

0050 **8** *hd* **Gazboolou**[22] 3719 7-8-6 **55**.......................... JamesRogers(3) 12 48
(David Pinder) *a in midfield: urged along and no prog over 2f out* **22/1**

60-0 **9** *1 ¼* **Red Flash (IRE)**[41] 3096 4-8-5 **51** oh3.......................... RossAtkinson 15 41
(Gary Harrison) *chsd wnr to over 3f out: lost pl u.p over 2f out: btn after* **66/1**

0056 **10** *hd* **Ancient Greece**[13] 4006 4-9-3 **68**.......................(t) DavidKenny(5) 2 58
(George Baker) *nt that wl away: settled in last pair: shkn up and no prog over 2f out: nt clrest of runs after: plugged on* **22/1**

3341 **11** *nse* **Olney Lass**[15] 3942 4-8-5 **51** oh1.......................... SimonPearce 4 41
(Lydia Pearce) *hld up in last: pushed along and no prog 3f out: no ch after* **6/1**[2]

3532 **12** *nk* **Bold Cross (IRE)**[12] 4051 8-9-4 **67**.......................... MatthewCosham(3) 10 56
(Edward Bevan) *taken down early: hld up in rr: tried to make prog on outer 3f out: no hdwy and btn 2f out* **10/1**

4005 **13** *shd* **Prince Of Thebes (IRE)**[23] 3677 10-8-8 **54**.............. MatthewDavies 11 43
(Michael Attwater) *settled in rr: no prog and struggling over 2f out: no threat after* **25/1**

1220 **14** *2* **Strike Force**[30] 3456 7-9-10 **70**.......................(t) AdamBeschizza 1 54
(Clifford Lines) *settled in rr: tried to make prog over 2f out: n.m.r wl over 1f out: sn wknd* **8/1**[3]

2313 **15** *5* **Phluke**[23] 3677 10-9-5 **65**.......................(v) PatrickHills 6 38
(Eve Johnson Houghton) *nvr bttr than midfield: rdn and no prog whn short of room on inner over 1f out: wknd* **12/1**

1m 43.41s (0.11) **Going Correction** +0.10s/f (Good) **15** Ran SP% **119.4**
Speed ratings (Par 103): **103,101,100,99,98 98,96,96,95,95 95,94,94,92,87**
toteswingers:1&2: £12.70, 2&3: £34.70, 1&3: £12.10 CSF £62.89 CT £845.86 TOTE £5.40: £2.00, £5.10, £4.10; EX 77.40.
Owner Equiform Nutrition Limited **Bred** Brown Moss Stud **Trained** Great Ness, Shropshire

FOCUS
Rail out 3yds from 9f to start of bend, 6yds around bend and 4yds up home straight adding about 8yds to race distances. This looked a really competitive race of its type and there was a sound pace on, but few got seriously involved. Modest form, but it makes sense.
Bold Cross(IRE) Official explanation: jockey said gelding suffered interference shortly after start

4445 BNY MELLON CLAIMING STKS 1m 14y

6:20 (6:20) (Class 5) 4-Y-0+ **£2,264** (£673; £336; £168) **Stalls** Low

Form RPR

0410 **1** **Miami Gator (IRE)**[18] 3877 4-9-7 85.......................(v) AndrewElliott 7 88
(Mrs K Burke) *mde all: rdn over 2f out: hrd pressed fnl f: jst hld on* **6/4**[1]

1/-0 **2** *shd* **Doctor Crane (USA)**[116] 1094 5-9-7 93.......................[1] RobertHavlin 4 88
(John Gosden) *t.k.h: trckd wnr after 3f: rdn over 2f out: nt qckn and no imp over 1f out: styd on to grad cl the gap fnl f: jst failed* **6/1**[3]

2022 **3** *2 ½* **Avon River**[20] 3764 4-8-13 85.......................(b) KieranO'Neill(3) 1 77
(Richard Hannon) *chsd wnr 3f: urged along over 3f out: stl cl enough wl over 1f out: one pce* **13/8**[2]

2233 **4** *¾* **Dr Wintringham (IRE)**[19] 3801 5-8-7 72.......................... JohnFahy(3) 6 69
(Karen George) *slowly away: hld up last: prog on outer over 3f out: rdn to dispute 2nd 2f out: nt qckn and fdd ins fnl f* **7/1**

0455 **5** *6* **Durgan**[20] 3768 5-8-8 51.......................(p) RyanPowell(5) 2 58
(Linda Jewell) *in tch: rdn and struggling wl over 2f out: sn lft bhd* **66/1**

2445 **6** *2* **Musashi (IRE)**[51] 2759 6-9-0 58.......................(b) FergusSweeney 3 55
(Laura Mongan) *hld up bhd ldrs: rdn and fnd nil over 2f out: wl btn after* **22/1**

0 **7** *22* **Polly Adler**[23] 3224 4-8-6 0.......................... JimmyQuinn 5 —
(Stuart Howe) *dwlt: a in last pair: wknd 3f out: t.o* **100/1**

1m 43.70s (0.40) **Going Correction** +0.10s/f (Good) **7** Ran SP% **111.7**
Speed ratings (Par 103): **101,100,98,97,91 89,67**
toteswingers:1&2: £1.90, 2&3: £2.30, 1&3: £1.30 CSF £10.45 TOTE £1.90: £1.10, £3.20; EX 11.40.
Owner Aricabeau Racing Limited **Bred** Newlands House Stud **Trained** Middleham Moor, North Yorks
■ Stewards' Enquiry : Robert Havlin four-day ban: used whip with excessive frequency (Aug 10-13)

FOCUS
A good little claimer and it saw another winner from the front. The form is rated around the second and tird and it was the slowest of the three C&D times.

4446 BRITISH STALLION STUDS SUPPORTING BRITISH RACING E B F MAIDEN STKS 7f 16y

6:55 (6:56) (Class 5) 2-Y-0 **£3,881** (£1,155; £577; £288) **Stalls** Low

Form RPR

1 **Archbishop (USA)** 2-9-3 0.......................... MartinDwyer 3 86+
(Brian Meehan) *trckd ldr in slowly run r: led 3f out: pushed along firmly over 1f out: rn green but hld on* **8/1**

2 *hd* **Farraaj (IRE)** 2-9-3 0.......................... NeilCallan 8 86+
(Roger Varian) *green in preliminaries: settled towards rr: prog 2f out: chsd wnr ins fnl f: urged along but wout whip and clsd nr fin: jst hld* **3/1**[2]

2 **3** *1 ½* **Surfer (USA)**[19] 3826 2-9-3 0.......................... AhmedAjtebi 6 81+
(Mahmood Al Zarooni) *t.k.h: hld up in midfield: prog over 2f out: rdn to chse ldng pair over 1f out: nt qckn and hld ins fnl f* **2/1**[1]

02 **4** *2 ¼* **Freddy Q (IRE)**[11] 4087 2-9-3 0.......................... DaneO'Neill 2 75
(Richard Hannon) *led: set modest pce early: hdd 3f out: nt qckn 2f out: wknd ins fnl f* **5/1**[3]

5 *1 ¾* **Silver Lime (USA)** 2-9-3 0.......................... RobertHavlin 10 70+
(Roger Charlton) *green in preliminaries: dwlt: hld up in last pair: pushed along over 2f out: kpt on steadily fr over 1f out: nt disgracd* **14/1**

6 *1 ½* **Black Minstrel (IRE)** 2-9-0 0.......................... HarryBentley(3) 5 66
(Amanda Perrett) *cl up: pushed along over 2f out: steadily wknd over 1f out* **8/1**

7 *2* **Chocolat Chaud (IRE)** 2-8-12 0.......................... SebSanders 9 56
(J W Hills) *s.s: hld up in last pair: shkn up and no prog 3f out: nvr on terms* **33/1**

8 *nk* **Dandy (GER)** 2-9-3 0.......................... JimmyFortune 1 60
(Andrew Balding) *dwlt: sn cl up: pushed along and wknd over 2f out* **16/1**

00 **9** *nse* **Inniscastle Boy**[16] 3917 2-9-3 0 .... LukeMorris 4 60
(William Muir) *chsd ldng pair: rdn 3f out: steadily wknd 2f out* **100/1**

00 **10** *5* **Scouting For Girls**[13] 4007 2-9-3 0 .... StephenCraine 7 46
(Jim Boyle) *in tch: wknd over 2f out* **50/1**

1m 32.94s (3.44) **Going Correction** +0.10s/f (Good) **10** Ran SP% **115.7**
Speed ratings (Par 94): **84,83,82,79,77 75,73,73,73,67**
toteswingers:1&2: £6.70, 2&3: £1.90, 1&3: £3.30 CSF £31.81 TOTE £10.80: £3.30, £1.80, £1.10; EX 32.20.
Owner Catesby W Clay **Bred** Runnymede Farm, J Clay II & M O'Dowd **Trained** Manton, Wilts

FOCUS
This looked an interesting juvenile maiden and the first pair both look potentially smart. It was steadily run though and the bare form might not be the most solid. It has been rated around the third.

NOTEBOOK
Archbishop(USA) ◆ is a sizeable individual and he made a winning debut under a good ride from Martin Dwyer. He knew his job and was never far away from his good draw which, considering the usual bias on quick ground around here, proved the place to be. He wasn't fully extended to hold off the runner-up and, while he wouldn't be at all certain to confirm form in the future with that rival, the market suggested he would need this initial outing. His Group entries indicate he's held in high regard by Brian Meehan and when a 2yo from this yard wins first time out, they nearly always tend to have a touch of class. Considering his US pedigree and ownership, it wouldn't be at all surprising were connections eyeing a possible trip to the Breeders' Cup later on. (op 12-1)
Farraaj(IRE) ◆ was unlucky. He was restrained from his modest draw, which was not the place to be, and had to wait to get out for his challenge in the home straight. His rider looked confident of reeling in the winner when he picked up, but he took a little time to hit top gear and that bird had already flown. This half-brother to the top-class Ifraaj looks sure to improve and is a certain winner of a maiden in the coming weeks. (op 7-2)
Surfer(USA) probably should have made a winning start under today's rider at York 19 days earlier and he understandably headed the betting. However, he got very warm beforehand here and ran free to post. He was unsurprisingly keen in the race and he too got further back than ideal. It wasn't enough to cost him the race and he bumped into two decent sorts here, but he is capable of a little better. (op 6-4)
Freddy Q(IRE) finished a close second to a winning stablemate at Lingfield 11 days earlier and he helps to set the level here. Nurseries are now an option. (op 6-1)
Silver Lime(USA) ◆, who met support at long odds, proved too green to do himself justice but showed promise. His yard's juveniles most often improve for an outing and he can step up on this next time. (op 25-1)
Black Minstrel(IRE) needed this debut outing and should prove sharper for the experience. (op 15-2)

4447 BCL BURTON COPELAND H'CAP — 1m 14y
7:30 (7:30) (Class 4) (0-80,80) 3-Y-O — **£5,822** (£1,732; £865; £432) **Stalls** Low

Form — RPR

21 **1** **Electra Star**[31] 3437 3-9-1 **77** .... AdamBeschizza(3) 6 88
(William Haggas) *s.i.s: settled in last quartet: rdn over 2f out: gd prog to chse ldr 1f out: styd on wl u.p to ld nr fin* **5/1**[2]

3352 **2** *¾* **Little Black Book (IRE)**[4] 4335 3-9-0 **76** .... (t) HarryBentley(3) 8 85
(Gerard Butler) *trckd ldng trio: rdn over 2f out: prog to ld over 1f out and looked decisive move: stvd on fnl f: worn down nr fin* **2/1**[1]

-460 **3** *2 ¾* **John Biscuit (IRE)**[19] 3825 3-9-7 **80** .... JimmyFortune 9 83
(Andrew Balding) *hld up in 9th: plenty to do and rdn over 2f out: styd on fr over 1f out: tk 3rd nr fin* **8/1**[3]

-351 **4** *nk* **Oetzi**[20] 3783 3-8-8 **67** .... SilvestreDeSousa 11 69
(Alan Jarvis) *chsd ldrs in 6th: rdn over 2f out: styd on u.p fr over 1f out: pressed for 3rd nr fin* **8/1**[3]

1030 **5** *1 ¼* **Yojimbo (IRE)**[5] 4290 3-9-4 **77** .... HughBowman 7 76
(Mick Channon) *trckd ldr: rdn to chal 2f out: nt qckn and hld whn sltly checked over 1f out: fdd* **17/2**

4521 **6** *1 ¾* **Icebuster**[25] 3633 3-8-11 **70** .... JamesMillman 10 65
(Rod Millman) *hld up in last quartet: shkn up over 2f out: limited prog fr over 1f out: no threat* **17/2**

0514 **7** *nk* **Uncle Dermot (IRE)**[13] 4011 3-8-10 **69** .... KierenFallon 1 63
(Brendan Powell) *led: shkn up over 2f out: hdd & wknd over 1f out* **14/1**

0013 **8** *3* **Dunhoy (IRE)**[19] 3797 3-9-7 **80** .... JimmyQuinn 4 67
(Stef Higgins) *trckd ldrs in 5th: rdn over 2f out: sn lost pl and wknd* **8/1**[3]

551- **9** *1 ¼* **Charles Fosterkane**[261] 7379 3-9-4 **77** .... LukeMorris 5 62
(John Best) *t.k.h: trckd ldng pair: rdn wl over 2f out: sn wknd* **20/1**

2004 **10** *2 ¾* **My Vindication (USA)**[11] 4081 3-8-11 **73** .... KieranO'Neill(3) 3 51
(Richard Hannon) *sn last: struggling over 3f out: nvr a factor* **20/1**

1m 43.7s (0.40) **Going Correction** +0.10s/f (Good) **10** Ran SP% **120.6**
Speed ratings (Par 102): **102,101,98,98,96 95,94,91,90,87**
toteswingers:1&2: £2.00, 2&3: £5.40, 1&3: £6.90 CSF £15.95 CT £78.80 TOTE £7.00: £2.00, £1.80, £2.00; EX 17.00.
Owner Mohamed Obaida **Bred** Rabbah Bloodstock Limited **Trained** Newmarket, Suffolk

FOCUS
A competitive 3yo handicap, run at a fair pace. The form looks fairly solid, rated around the runner-up.
Uncle Dermot(IRE) Official explanation: jockey said colt lost its action

4448 XL INSURANCE FILLIES' H'CAP — 1m 1f
8:05 (8:07) (Class 5) (0-75,76) 3-Y-O+ — **£2,587** (£770; £384; £192) **Stalls** Low

Form — RPR

1 **Hunter Forward (AUS)**[292] 5-9-2 **61** .... KierenFallon 8 75+
(Luca Cumani) *t.k.h: trckd ldr: led jst over 2f out: shkn up over 1f out: styd on wl and in command ins fnl f* **13/8**[1]

-400 **2** *1 ½* **Heatherbird**[56] 2615 3-8-13 **70** .... HarryBentley(3) 7 77
(William Jarvis) *taken down early: hld up in 9th: prog on outer 3f out: shkn up and hd quite high 2f out: chsd wnr over 1f out: styd on but nvr able to chal* **16/1**

4-36 **3** *2 ¾* **Indian Valley (USA)**[33] 3366 4-10-0 **73** .... NeilCallan 12 75
(Hugo Palmer) *hld up in 7th: shkn up over 2f out: kpt on fr over 1f out to take 3rd last strides* **13/2**[3]

331 **4** *hd* **Bella Noir**[10] 4127 4-10-3 **76** 6ex .... (v) AndrewElliott 11 78
(Mrs K Burke) *led: drvn and hdd jst over 2f out: lost 2nd over 1f out: grad fdd* **15/2**

505- **5** *½* **History Repeating**[231] 7758 3-8-0 **54** oh1 .... DavidProbert 5 53
(Mark Usher) *reluctant to enter stalls: trckd ldrs in 5th: rdn to go 3rd 2f out: no imp over 1f out: one pce* **40/1**

4-00 **6** *2 ¼* **Present Story**[9] 4154 4-8-9 **57** .... MarkLawson(3) 1 52
(Gary Harrison) *plld hrd in 4th: hrd rdn over 2f out: sn lost pl and btn* **33/1**

-121 **7** *shd* **Lady Gabrielle (IRE)**[16] 3919 3-9-5 **73** .... DaneO'Neill 9 67
(David Elsworth) *trckd ldng pair: rdn and nt qckn over 2f out: sn lost pl and struggling* **11/4**[2]

-065 **8** *nk* **Poyle Judy**[20] 3782 3-8-13 **67** .... JimCrowley 10 61
(Ralph Beckett) *hld up in 8th: pushed along and no prog over 2f out: reminders over 1f out: wl btn after* **18/1**

1000 **9** *½* **Miss Chicane**[16] 3919 3-9-1 **72** .... JohnFahy(3) 2 64
(Walter Swinburn) *dwlt: early reminder and swished tail in last: rdn wl over 2f out: no prog* **20/1**

5350 **10** *7* **Beauchamp Xiara**[37] 3228 5-8-10 **62** .... LucyKBarry(7) 4 40
(Hans Adielsson) *hld up in 6th: rdn wl over 2f out: sn wknd and bhd* **16/1**

1m 55.94s (0.24) **Going Correction** +0.10s/f (Good)
WFA 3 from 4yo+ 9lb **10** Ran SP% **117.0**
Speed ratings (Par 100): **102,100,98,98,97 95,95,95,94,88**
toteswingers:1&2: £7.30, 2&3: £18.00, 1&3: £3.00 CSF £30.44 CT £144.99 TOTE £2.50: £1.10, £4.40, £2.50; EX 34.10.
Owner O T I Racing **Bred** Alwyn Park **Trained** Newmarket, Suffolk

FOCUS
A decent fillies' handicap for the class, run at a solid pace. The form should prove sound and the winner was value for a bit extra.

4449 BROTHERS PEAR CIDER H'CAP — 1m 6f
8:35 (8:35) (Class 4) (0-80,79) 3-Y-O — **£4,075** (£1,212; £606; £303) **Stalls** Low

Form — RPR

3213 **1** **Cunning Act**[33] 3364 3-9-5 **77** .... StephenCraine 3 93
(Jonathan Portman) *chsd ldrs: rdn and prog to go 2nd 2f out: clsd to ld 1f out: styd on wl* **7/2**[2]

0-03 **2** *2 ¼* **Blazing Field**[16] 3907 3-8-7 **68** .... JohnFahy(3) 8 81
(Clive Cox) *trckd ldr: led over 3f out and kicked on: hdd and edgd lft 1f out: styd on but no ch w wnr* **16/1**

4411 **3** *6* **Memory Lane**[14] 3976 3-9-6 **78** .... SebSanders 6 83
(Sir Mark Prescott Bt) *led at decent pce: breather 1/2-way: rdn and hdd over 3f out: lost 2nd and wl btn 2f out: clung on for 3rd* **5/1**[3]

-510 **4** *½* **Schism**[27] 3551 3-9-2 **74** .... DaneO'Neill 9 78
(Henry Candy) *s.i.s and urged along to go prom: rdn and effrt over 2f out: sn lft bhd* **8/1**

544 **5** *3 ½* **Handles For Forks (IRE)**[16] 3907 3-8-3 **68** .... CharlesBishop(7) 10 67
(Mick Channon) *hld up in last: lost tch over 5f out: wl bhd over 3f out: modest late hdwy: nvr a factor* **16/1**

5-31 **6** *½* **Mungo Park**[13] 4014 3-9-7 **79** .... SilvestreDeSousa 4 77
(Mark Johnston) *chsd ldrs: pushed along over 6f out: lost tch and struggling over 4f out: wl btn after* **5/2**[1]

1553 **7** *nse* **Dubai Glory**[18] 3872 3-9-3 **75** .... JamesDoyle 2 73
(Sheena West) *chsd ldng pair: rdn and wknd 2f out* **11/2**

-003 **8** *¾* **Strength And Stay (IRE)**[14] 3989 3-8-2 **60** oh1 .... LukeMorris 7 57
(Eve Johnson Houghton) *hld up in 7th: urged along sn after 1/2-way: lost tch over 5f out: wl bhd 3f out* **10/1**

6064 **9** *18* **Grecian Goddess (IRE)**[8] 4190 3-7-13 **60** oh3 .... SimonPearce(3) 5 32
(John Ryan) *hld up in last pair: lost tch over 5f out: wl bhd after: wknd over 2f out: t.o* **33/1**

3m 5.15s (0.65) **Going Correction** +0.10s/f (Good) **9** Ran SP% **117.8**
Speed ratings (Par 102): **102,100,97,97,95 94,94,94,83**
toteswingers:1&2: £22.40, 2&3: £13.60, 1&3: £2.00 CSF £58.53 CT £283.21 TOTE £4.90: £1.50, £5.00, £2.10; EX 70.70.
Owner M J Vandenberghe **Bred** The Hon Mrs R Pease **Trained** Compton, Berks

FOCUS
A fair staying handicap for 3yos, run at a searching early pace and few landed a serious blow. The winner continues on the upgrade.
Schism Official explanation: jockey said filly suffered interference in running
Strength And Stay(IRE) Official explanation: jockey said gelding hung right
T/Plt: £43.30 to a £1 stake. Pool of £59,615.09 - 1005.01 winning units. T/Qpdt: £6.40 to a £1 stake. Pool of £6,456.25 - 736.70 winning units. JN

4450 - 4453a (Foreign Racing) - See Raceform Interactive

4238 EPSOM (L-H)
Thursday, July 28

OFFICIAL GOING: Good (good to firm in places; stands' side 8.6 far side 8.1)
Wind: Light, across Weather: Fine, warm

4454 BROTHERS PEAR CIDER APPRENTICE H'CAP — 1m 2f 18y
6:00 (6:01) (Class 5) (0-70,65) 4-Y-O+ — **£2,264** (£673; £336; £168) **Stalls** Low

Form — RPR

10-0 **1** **Count Ceprano (IRE)**[47] 2923 7-9-10 **65** .... SimonPearce 6 72
(Lydia Pearce) *trckd ldng pair: effrt to dispute ld 2f out: narrowly hdd ins fnl f: rallied to ld last strides* **8/1**

0035 **2** *shd* **Ermyntrude**[12] 4090 4-8-10 **56** .... LucyKBarry(5) 8 63
(Pat Phelan) *dwlt but sn chsd ldr: effrt to dspute ld 2f out w wnr: rdn to ld narrowly fnl f: hdd last strides* **9/4**[2]

0-50 **3** *4* **Hotfoot**[50] 2828 4-8-7 **55** .... HannahNunn(7) 4 54
(John Berry) *sn hld up in 4th: rdn over 2f out: steadily lft bhd: tk modest 3rd nr fin* **9/1**

0525 **4** *½* **Rodrigo De Freitas (IRE)**[7] 4242 4-9-1 **63** .... (v) DanielCremin(7) 7 61
(Jim Boyle) *dwlt but sn led: racd wd: rdn and hdd 2f out: steadily fdd: lost 3rd nr fin* **4/1**[3]

4633 **5** *hd* **Miss Bounty**[7] 4242 6-9-2 **62** .... (v) NathanAlison(5) 2 60
(Jim Boyle) *hld up in last: rdn over 2f out: ill at ease on crse and nt qckn: n.d after* **13/8**[1]

2m 12.01s (2.31) **Going Correction** -0.15s/f (Firm) **5** Ran SP% **110.0**
Speed ratings (Par 103): **84,83,80,80,80**
CSF £26.07 TOTE £6.30: £3.30, £1.60; EX 24.90 Trifecta £91.10 Pool: £12126.15 - 98.49 winning units..
Owner Mrs Louise Marsh **Bred** Pendley Farm **Trained** Newmarket, Suffolk

FOCUS
The rail was on the innermost (Derby) configuration and all distances were as advertised. After a dry night and day the ground was altered slightly to "good, good to firm in places". Exposed performers in an uncompetitive event in which the market leader disappointed. The gallop was a steady one to 3f out but the first two pulled clear in the closing stages. The winner's best form for two years.
Miss Bounty Official explanation: jockey said mare lost its action

4455 SPARKS CHARITY "RACING FOR RESEARCH" E B F MAIDEN STKS — 7f
6:35 (6:36) (Class 5) 2-Y-O — **£3,881** (£1,155; £577; £288) **Stalls** Low

Form — RPR

6 **1** **Producer**[13] 4053 2-9-3 0 .... JimmyFortune 1 78+
(Richard Hannon) *mde all: pushed along to assert 2f out: in n.d after: styd on wl* **15/8**[2]

5 **2** *4* **Courtesy Call (IRE)**[9] 4171 2-9-3 0 .... GeorgeBaker 2 67+
(Mark Johnston) *hld up in 4th: effrt over 2f out: rdn to chse wnr wl over 1f out: kpt on but no imp* **11/2**[3]

3 **3** *3 1/4* **Takeitfromalady (IRE)**[14] 3997 2-9-3 0............................ JimCrowley 3 58
(Ralph Beckett) *hld up in last but cl up: rdn over 2f out: sn outpcd: kpt on to take 3rd ins fnl f* **25/1**

64 **4** *7* **Lucky Money**[11] 4122 2-9-3 0............................ SebSanders 5 42
(Sir Mark Prescott Bt) *racd wd: pressed ldng pair: hanging bnd over 3f out: nt qckn over 2f out: wl btn over 1f out: wknd* **11/10**[1]

5 **5** *6* **Atlantis Crossing (IRE)**[33] 3408 2-9-3 0...................... StephenCraine 4 23
(Jim Boyle) *pressed wnr to jst over 2f out: wknd rapidly* **12/1**

1m 23.78s (0.48) **Going Correction** -0.15s/f (Firm) **5** Ran SP% **109.3**
Speed ratings (Par 94): **91,86,82,74,67**
CSF £11.90 TOTE £2.90: £1.20, £2.40; EX 8.60.

Owner J Palmer-Brown **Bred** Cheveley Park Stud Ltd **Trained** East Everleigh, Wilts

FOCUS
A couple of fair sorts on show but a race that took less winning than seemed likely with the market leader disappointing. The winner showed big improvement. An ordinary gallop increased around the 2f pole and the winning rider described the ground as "good to firm".

NOTEBOOK
Producer ◆, who made a pleasing debut, had the run of the race but showed both a good attitude and improved form when asked for an effort. He's the type physically to make further progress, he should have no problems with 1m and will be one to bear in mind when switched to nursery company. (tchd 2-1 and 7-4 in a place)

Courtesy Call(IRE) ◆ seemed much more professional in the race than on his debut at Musselburgh and he duly showed much-improved form. He has plenty to recommend him on looks, he is in good hands and is sure to win a race in the short term. (op 5-1)

Takeitfromalady(IRE) achieved little when third of four on his debut at Bath but he stepped up on that level in this muddling event. He's likely to remain vulnerable against the better types in this grade but will be of more interest once qualified for a nursery mark granted a better gallop. (op 16-1)

Lucky Money didn't look happy on this track (pulled hard and hung left) and failed by a long way to reproduce his improved Redcar effort. However he's now qualified for a mark and should do better in nursery company at a more conventional course. Official explanation: trainer had no explanation for the poor form shown (op 11-8 tchd 6-4 in a place)

Atlantis Crossing(IRE) again had his limitations firmly exposed and, while the step into ordinary company will suit in due course, he'll have to show a fair bit more before he is a solid betting proposition. (op 10-1)

4456 TRY TOTEQUICKPICK IF YOU'RE FEELING LUCKY CONDITIONS STKS — 1m 2f 18y
7:10 (7:10) (Class 3) 3-Y-O+ **£6,411** (£1,919; £959; £479) **Stalls** Low

Form RPR

2-60 **1** **Prince Siegfried (FR)**[27] 3591 5-9-0 108......................... KierenFallon 2 98+
(Saeed Bin Suroor) *trckd ldng pair: led over 3f out and c centre: shkn up and drew clr 2f out: in n.d after* **10/11**[1]

6-52 **2** *9* **Jamhoori**[3] 4385 3-8-4 68.. KirstyMilczarek 3 80
(Clive Brittain) *chsd ldr to over 3f out: chsd wnr in centre over 2f out: lft bhd wl over 1f out* **16/1**

3220 **3** *7* **Enak (ARG)**[12] 4095 5-9-0 111...(t) TedDurcan 4 70
(Saeed Bin Suroor) *hld up in last: styd alone on inner st: nvr on terms and sn btn: eased whn no ch last 100yds* **7/2**[3]

0-03 **4** *12* **Lord Zenith**[14] 4003 4-9-0 105... JimmyFortune 1 58
(Andrew Balding) *taken down early: led: c centre st: sn hdd & wknd: no ch fnl 2f: virtually p.u nr fin* **5/2**[2]

2m 5.95s (-3.75) **Going Correction** -0.15s/f (Firm)
WFA 3 from 4yo+ 10lb **4** Ran SP% **109.1**
Speed ratings (Par 107): **109,101,96,86**
CSF £13.30 TOTE £2.40; EX 15.80.

Owner Godolphin **Bred** Haras Saint Pair Du Mont **Trained** Newmarket, Suffolk

FOCUS
Three smart performers but, given two of them failed to give their running and the fact the runner-up was rated only 68 confirms this race took very little winning. Muddling conditions form. Although the gallop to the straight was a steady one, the winner's time dipped fractionally below Racing Post Standard.

NOTEBOOK
Prince Siegfried(FR), minus the headgear this time, faced a straightforward task with his two main market rivals disappointing and he didn't have to be anywhere near his best to beat a 68-rated rival with plenty in hand. He has won both his starts over course-and-distance but would not be an obvious one to follow up returned to Listed or Group company. (op Evens tchd 6-4 and 11-10 in a place)

Jamhoori, who has shown steadily progressive form in maidens and handicaps, ran well in the face of a stiff task but owes his finishing position to the below-par efforts of the second and third favourites. It remains to be seen what the handicapper makes of this but he'll be seen to much better effect back in that grade and back on a flatter track if the assessor doesn't go overboard. (op 18-1)

Enak(ARG), a Grade 1 turf winner in Argentina who had shown smart form at the Dubai Carnival earlier in the year, raced with the choke out and was again a long way below the pick of his smart form after staying by himself on the far side turning for home. He has plenty to prove at present. (op 5-2 tchd 9-4)

Lord Zenith developed into a smart sort last year up to this trip but he didn't look happy on the track and he proved a big disappointment returned to this longer trip. The return to a flatter track will suit but he will have to show a good deal more before he is a solid betting proposition. Official explanation: jockey said gelding hung right (op 7-2)

4457 BROTHERS STRAWBERRY CIDER H'CAP — 1m 114y
7:40 (7:42) (Class 4) (0-80,77) 3-Y-O+ **£4,075** (£1,212; £606; £303) **Stalls** Low

Form RPR

3315 **1** **You've Been Mowed**[16] 3952 5-9-4 77.................. MatthewLawson(7) 1 87
(Richard Price) *mde all: shkn up whn pressed 3f out: rdn to assert fr 2f out: styd on wl* **8/1**

5304 **2** *2* **Super Duplex**[24] 3685 4-9-0 66.. IanMongan 4 71
(Pat Phelan) *wnt rt s: chsd ldng pair: drvn over 2f out: wnt 2nd over 1f out: one pce after and readily hld* **5/2**[1]

5041 **3** *1 1/2* **Battle Of Britain**[49] 2853 3-9-1 76...................................(t) KierenFallon 2 80+
(Giles Bravery) *chsd ldrs in 4th: drvn wl over 2f out: trying to cl but no ch whn hmpd jst ins fnl f: kpt on: fin 4th: plcd 3rd* **6/1**

3-01 **4** *shd* **Cross Culture (IRE)**[14] 4011 3-9-2 77............................ DavidProbert 3 77
(Andrew Balding) *taken down early: chsd wnr: chal 3f out: nt qckn 2f out: lost 2nd and hung lft over 1f out: fin 3rd, 2l, shd: disq: plcd 4th* **7/2**[2]

0-34 **5** *3/4* **With Hindsight (IRE)**[89] 1682 3-9-2 77......................... PhilipRobinson 5 76
(Clive Cox) *nudged by rival s: hld up in 5th: pushed along and off the pce over 2f out: no prog tl styd on ins fnl f: no ch* **5/1**

1116 **6** *9* **Song To The Moon (IRE)**[21] 3763 4-9-4 73........(b) MatthewDavies(3) 7 52
(Jim Boyle) *s.i.s and stdd: hld up last: shkn up and wl bhd in st: no prog* **9/2**[3]

1m 43.51s (-2.59) **Going Correction** -0.15s/f (Firm)
WFA 3 from 4yo+ 9lb **6** Ran SP% **111.0**
Speed ratings (Par 105): **105,103,101,103,101 93**
CSF £27.63 CT £124.22 TOTE £6.50: £2.10, £1.60; EX 25.60 Trifecta £285.20 Pool: £3168.47 - 8.22 winning units..

Owner Mrs K Oseman **Bred** T E Pocock **Trained** Ullingswick, H'fords

■ Stewards' Enquiry : David Probert one-day ban: careless riding (Aug 14)

FOCUS
A fair handicap but, although the gallop seemed reasonable, those held up were at a disadvantage. The winner is better than ever.

4458 TOTEPOOL A BETTER WAY TO BET FILLIES' H'CAP — 7f
8:10 (8:11) (Class 5) (0-75,73) 3-Y-O+ **£2,587** (£770; £384; £192) **Stalls** Low

Form RPR

2512 **1** **Caelis**[20] 3818 3-9-6 72..(v) JimCrowley 2 83
(Ralph Beckett) *trckd ldr: pushed along 3f out: rdn and clsd to ld over 1f out: styd on wl and clr ins fnl f* **11/4**[2]

0023 **2** *2* **Cat Hunter**[8] 4210 4-9-7 66.. KirstyMilczarek 3 74
(Ronald Harris) *t.k.h: trckd ldng pair: rdn 2f out: styd on fnl f to take 2nd last 75yds: no ch to threaten wnr* **6/1**

00 **3** *1 1/4* **Leadenhall Lass (IRE)**[14] 4010 5-9-7 66........................... IanMongan 1 71
(Pat Phelan) *led at decent pce: drvn and hdd over 1f out: one pce and lost 2nd last 75yds* **8/1**

3-01 **4** *3* **Push Me (IRE)**[7] 4255 4-9-2 64 6ex........................ MichaelO'Connell(3) 5 61
(Jamie Poulton) *a in same pl: rdn and outpcd 2f out: no imp on ldng trio after* **11/2**[3]

40-1 **5** *1 1/2* **Treasure Way**[87] 1766 4-9-9 68.. GeorgeBaker 8 61
(Patrick Chamings) *a abt same pl: outpcd and shkn up over 2f out: rdn and no prog over 1f out* **9/4**[1]

4650 **6** *2 1/4* **Silvee**[14] 4010 4-8-9 54 oh2... NeilChalmers 6 41
(John Bridger) *a abt same pl: rdn and outpcd over 2f out: no ch after* **20/1**

540 **7** *4* **Countess Ellen (IRE)**[14] 4011 3-8-7 62.......................... HarryBentley(3) 7 35
(Gerard Butler) *s.i.s: a in last: no prog and hanging lft fr 2f out* **10/1**

1m 22.46s (-0.84) **Going Correction** -0.15s/f (Firm)
WFA 3 from 4yo+ 7lb **7** Ran SP% **112.1**
Speed ratings (Par 100): **98,95,94,90,89 86,82**
toteswingers:1&2:£2.60, 2&3:£4.30, 1&3:£3.40 CSF £18.65 CT £114.21 TOTE £3.50: £1.90, £2.40; EX 8.80 Trifecta £50.30 Pool: £423.51 - 6.22 winning units..

Owner Belmore Lane Stud Racing Partnership **Bred** S J And Mrs Pembroke **Trained** Kimpton, Hants

FOCUS
An ordinary handicap but one run over a second quicker than the maiden earlier on the card. The early gallop was less than frenetic and those held up were again at a disadvantage. The winner has improved since the visor was fitted.
Treasure Way Official explanation: jockey said filly hung left under pressure

4459 SIR GEOFF HURST AND SPARKS CHARITY H'CAP — 6f
8:40 (8:40) (Class 4) (0-80,79) 3-Y-O **£4,075** (£1,212; £606; £303) **Stalls** High

Form RPR

1111 **1** **Roodee Queen**[7] 4231 3-9-5 77 6ex......................... RichardKingscote 3 83
(Milton Bradley) *trckd ldr: clsd 2f out: reminder sn after: edgd rt but pushed into ld 1f out: a in control after* **3/1**[2]

1452 **2** *1/2* **Perfect Pastime**[21] 3765 3-9-6 78..................................... KierenFallon 6 82
(Walter Swinburn) *settled in 5th: prog over 2f out: sn rdn: styd on u.p fnl f to take 2nd last strides* **11/4**[1]

3031 **3** *nk* **Welsh Inlet (IRE)**[30] 3482 3-8-11 69................................ NeilChalmers 1 72
(John Bridger) *led: drvn 2f out: hung rt after: hdd 1f out: kpt on but lost 2nd last strides* **11/1**

1420 **4** *3 3/4* **Dream Catcher (FR)**[22] 3737 3-9-7 79.......................... JimmyFortune 5 70
(David Pinder) *chsd ldng pair: rdn and nt qckn 2f out: stl cl enough 1f out: fdd* **12/1**

0352 **5** *9* **Cocohatchee**[7] 4238 3-9-1 73..(v1) IanMongan 4 35
(Pat Phelan) *chsd ldng trio: racd awkwardly downhill: dropped to last pair and struggling over 2f out: no ch after* **7/2**[3]

-035 **6** *49* **Regal Approval**[52] 2770 3-9-4 76.................................... GeorgeBaker 2 —
(Hughie Morrison) *v restless in stalls: dwlt: a in last: wknd over 2f out: virtually p.u ins fnl f* **7/2**

69.18 secs (-0.22) **Going Correction** -0.15s/f (Firm) **6** Ran SP% **112.1**
Speed ratings (Par 102): **95,94,93,88,76 11**
totesswingers:1&2:£1.90, 2&3:£7.40, 1&3:£3.50 CSF £11.64 TOTE £4.20: £2.30, £1.90; EX 9.30.

Owner T A Godbert **Bred** Tom & Evelyn Yates **Trained** Sedbury, Gloucs

FOCUS
A fair handicap but, although the pace was sound, this was yet another race on the card that favoured those right up with the pace. The winner pretty much matched her Bath mark, with the runner-up close to his best.
Welsh Inlet(IRE) Official explanation: jockey said filly hung right
Regal Approval Official explanation: jockey said gelding was upset in the stalls and lost its action
T/Plt: £114.40 to a £1 stake. Pool of £59,063.14 - 376.85 winning tickets. T/Qpdt: £8.90 to a £1 stake. Pool of £5,809.55 - 483.00 winning tickets. JN

3907 FFOS LAS (L-H)
Thursday, July 28

OFFICIAL GOING: Good to firm (8.5)
Wind: light behind Weather: overcast

4460 GRAVELLS NURSERY — 5f
5:50 (5:51) (Class 5) 2-Y-O **£2,393** (£712; £355; £177) **Stalls** High

Form RPR

6120 **1** **Powerful Wind (IRE)**[2] 4413 2-9-4 80.......................... KieranO'Neill(3) 6 83
(Ronald Harris) *mde all: rdn and kicked clr 1f out: strly chal ins fnl f: jst hld on: all out* **5/2**[1]

0431 **2** *shd* **Molly Jones**[12] 4085 2-8-11 70...................................... FergusSweeney 5 73
(Derek Haydn Jones) *prom: rdn to chse ldr 2f out: briefly outpcd over 1f out: styd on strly ins fnl f: jst failed* **11/4**[2]

3510 **3** *hd* **Courtland King (IRE)**[5] 4343 2-9-1 77 ow2............(t) RichardEvans(3) 7 79
(David Evans) *midfield: rdn and hdwy and swtchd rt 2f out: chsd ldrs 1f out: styd on wl ins fnl f: fin wl* **11/1**

5456 **4** *2 1/4* **Sweet Ovation**[14] 4019 2-8-0 59 oh6 ow2................... FrankieMcDonald 4 53
(Mark Usher) *s.i.s: rdn and outpcd 2f out: kpt on ins fnl f: no imp on ldrs* **28/1**

2240 **5** *1 ½* **Night Angel (IRE)**[19] 3842 2-8-12 **71**............................ JamesMillman 3 60
(Rod Millman) *midfield: rdn 3f out: hung lft 2f out: wknd wl over 1f out* **11/2**[3]

005 **6** *1* **Russian Bullet**[17] 3921 2-7-10 **60**.................................... RyanPowell(5) 2 45
(Jamie Osborne) *chsd ldr tl rdn 2f out: wknd 1f out* **6/1**

5145 **7** *6* **Faraway**[13] 4069 2-8-8 **67**.. CathyGannon 1 30
(David Evans) *bustled along thrght: midfield: dropped last 2f out: eased and btn ins fnl f* **11/2**[3]

58.39 secs (0.09) **Going Correction** +0.05s/f (Good) 7 Ran SP% **112.1**
Speed ratings (Par 94): **94,93,93,89,87 85,76**
toteswingers:1&2:£3.00, 2&3:£7.70, 1&3:£3.40 CSF £9.22 TOTE £3.30: £1.60, £2.80; EX 6.00.
Owner Anthony Cooke **Bred** Miss Ciara Doyle **Trained** Earlswood, Monmouths

FOCUS
An ordinary nursery but not a bad time. The form has been given a chance through the winner and fourth.

NOTEBOOK
Powerful Wind(IRE) had finished down the field in the Molecomb Stakes earlier in the week but this was much more realistic despite conceding weight all round and, having bounced out to bag the stands rail, he made all. He was hanging on for dear life in the closing stages though as his stamina began to give way and he looks all about speed, so a sharp track will play to his strengths, and he clearly takes his racing well. (op 11-4 tchd 3-1)
Molly Jones won a 6f nursery last time and the way she finished her race, closing on the winner with every stride, suggests she probably needs that trip, or a stiffer test at 5f. Given she was up 5lb here, this was a solid effort and she is definitely still going the right way. (tchd 3-1)
Courtland King(IRE) doesn't look particularly well handicapped so this was a good effort to get so close to the winner. His only success in ten races has come in a seller but on this evidence he's got an ordinary nursery in him off this sort of mark. (op 10-1 tchd 9-1)
Sweet Ovation shaped as though she can do better over 6f.

4461 GRAVELLS MAIDEN STKS — 5f

6:20 (6:21) (Class 5) 3-Y-O+ **£2,393** (£712; £355; £177) **Stalls** High

Form RPR

50-0 **1** **Sulis Minerva (IRE)**[21] 3756 4-8-13 65......................(t) KieranO'Neill(3) 4 73
(Jeremy Gask) *stdd s: t.k.h: chsd ldng pair: swtchd rt and rdn 2f out: drvn to ld 1f out: sn drew rt away* **11/4**[2]

0226 **2** *3 ¾* **Whitecrest**[14] 3994 3-8-12 68... CathyGannon 7 59
(John Spearing) *led: rdn and shifted lft 2f out: hdd 1f out: kpt on: nt pce of wnr* **5/4**[1]

5000 **3** *2 ¾* **Too Many Questions (IRE)**[7] 4230 3-9-3 65............ FergusSweeney 5 54
(David Evans) *chsd ldr: rdn 2f out: drvn and ev ch 1f out: hung lft and wknd ins fnl f* **11/4**[2]

5 **4** *6* **London Avenue (IRE)**[8] 4203 3-9-3 0.............................. MartinLane 2 32
(Dominic Ffrench Davis) *4th and last of those in tch early: rdn to chal 2f out: wknd over 1f out: lost tch w ldng trio fnl f* **22/1**

-500 **5** *10* **Autocracy**[14] 4017 4-9-2 51...(b) RyanPowell(5) 3 —
(Eric Alston) *rdr removed blindfold late: nvr on terms: rdn and no hdwy 3f out* **12/1**[3]

6 *1 ¼* **Coalburn** 3-8-10 0... JohnLawson(7) 1 —
(Gary Harrison) *dwlt: sn rdn and lost tch and hanging lft: t.o 1/2-way* **50/1**

- **7** *2 ¾* **Backstreet Fighter (IRE)** 3-9-0 0............................ MarkLawson(3) 6 —
(Gary Harrison) *wnt lft s: s.i.s: sn lost tch and clueless: t.o 1/2-way* **50/1**

57.42 secs (-0.88) **Going Correction** +0.05s/f (Good)
WFA 3 from 4yo 4lb 7 Ran SP% **113.7**
Speed ratings (Par 103): **101,95,90,81,65 63,58**
toteswingers:1&2:£1.80, 2&3:£1.40, 1&3:£2.50 CSF £6.50 TOTE £3.60: £2.60, £1.70; EX 7.30.
Owner Richard L Page **Bred** Kevin Blake **Trained** Sutton Veny, Wilts

FOCUS
No depth to this maiden and they were well strung out from the off, but the winner managed to dip under standard. The favourite disappointed and this is weak form.
Autocracy Official explanation: jockey said, regarding running and riding, that on trying to remove gelding's blinds they got caught on blinkers causing it to be slowly away.
Backstreet Fighter(IRE) Official explanation: jockey said gelding hung left

4462 E B F "STIMULATION" MAIDEN STKS — 6f

6:50 (6:51) (Class 4) 2-Y-O **£4,528** (£1,347; £673; £336) **Stalls** High

Form RPR

00 **1** **Lunar Deity**[15] 3986 2-9-0 0.. JohnFahy(3) 1 87+
(Eve Johnson Houghton) *cl up on outer: hdwy to press ldrs and gng wl 2f out: pushed ahd over 1f out: sn wl clr: easy* **20/1**

45 **2** *5* **Continuity (IRE)**[15] 3981 2-8-12 0...................................... MartinLane 6 65
(Ralph Beckett) *dwlt: rdn ins fnl 4f: drifted lft and hdwy over 2f out: kpt on ins fnl f: tk 2nd cl home: no ch w wnr* **7/1**[3]

04 **3** *nk* **Red Senor (IRE)**[24] 3686 2-9-0 0................................. KieranO'Neill(3) 4 69
(B W Hills) *t.k.h in midfield: rdn to chse ldr over 2f out: drvn and outpcd by wnr 1f out: lost 2nd cl home* **10/11**[1]

2306 **4** *1 ¾* **Meloneras**[10] 4155 2-8-12 0.. JamesMillman 7 58
(Rod Millman) *led: rdn 2f out: wandered u.p and hdd over 1f out: lost 2 pls ins fnl f* **6/1**[2]

02 **5** *3 ½* **Monty Fay (IRE)**[17] 3921 2-9-3 0.................................. FergusSweeney 5 52
(Derek Haydn Jones) *midfield: rdn and outpcd over 2f out: no imp ins fnl f* **9/1**

0042 **6** *2 ¾* **Bajan Hero**[51] 2788 2-9-3 0... CathyGannon 3 43
(David Evans) *hung lft thrght: chsd ldr tl rdn 3f out: wknd ins fnl 2f* **8/1**

7 *3 ½* **Alexandra Palace (IRE)** 2-8-12 0................................ MartinDwyer 9 27
(Mark Johnston) *sn outpcd: lost tch 4f out* **11/1**

8 *3 ¼* **Shining Grace** 2-8-7 0... RyanPowell(5) 8 17
(Bryn Palling) *rn green thrght: midfield: rdn 3f out: wknd 2f out* **50/1**

69.93 secs (-0.07) **Going Correction** +0.05s/f (Good) 2y crse rec 8 Ran SP% **115.3**
Speed ratings (Par 96): **100,93,92,90,85 82,77,73**
toteswingers:1&2:£20.30, 2&3:£1.50, 1&3:£5.60 CSF £152.44 TOTE £33.80: £9.60, £2.70, £1.10; EX 222.90.
Owner Eden Racing (III) & P A Deal **Bred** Hermes Services Ltd **Trained** Blewbury, Oxon

FOCUS
This looked ordinary fare on paper but it was lit up by quite a performance from Lunar Deity, who left her two previous runs miles behind and absolutely bolted up, lowering the two-year-old course record in the process. It was no fluke as the form makes sense.

NOTEBOOK
Lunar Deity hadn't shown a great deal in two 7f maidens but, despite not shaping like the drop back in trip would bring about improvement, he improved beyond recognition, travelling powerfully throughout and forging clear in the final furlong to prove different class to his rivals. Given the distance and manner of victory, the handicapper will ask a serious question now in terms of his mark for nurseries, but on this evidence connections could hardly be blamed if they set their sights on something a bit loftier. (op 22-1 tchd 33-1)
Continuity(IRE) had shown much more promise in previous starts than the winner but, whereas the drop back to 6f clearly suited that rival, this filly shaped like she'll improve again when upped to 7f. She is now eligible for a mark, and she'll be an interesting proposition if upped in trip for handicap debut. There is more to come from her. (op 8-1 tchd 13-2)
Red Senor(IRE) looked the one to beat on his latest Windsor fourth but he couldn't really build on that. (op 6-5, tchd 5-4 after early 11-8)
Meloneras confirmed the impression of her previous runs in that she doesn't really want to go further than 5f at present. She showed good speed before weakening away but has a race of this nature in her back over the minimum trip. (tchd 13-2)
Bajan Hero Official explanation: jockey said gelding hung left

4463 PORSCHE CARDIFF H'CAP — 2m (R)

7:25 (7:25) (Class 4) (0-80,75) 4-Y-O+ **£4,140** (£1,232; £615; £307) **Stalls** Low

Form RPR

600/ **1** **West With The Wind**[135] 6218 6-8-3 **60**........................ KieranO'Neill(3) 4 69
(Evan Williams) *mde all: qckd tempo 5f out: drvn along 2f out: strly pressed ins fnl f but kpt finding generously for press: hld on wl: gd ride* **7/2**[3]

1151 **2** *½* **Money Money Money**[15] 3978 5-9-7 **75**...................... JamesMillman 3 83
(Rod Millman) *w.w on inner: swtchd to outer over 4f out: rdn and hdwy 3f out: chsd wnr 2f out: chal for ld thrght fnl f: unable to get by game rival* **3/1**[2]

043 **3** *4* **Boa**[14] 4024 6-8-11 **65**.. CathyGannon 1 68
(Reg Hollinshead) *t.k.h: chsd ldng pair: rdn 3f out: drvn and ev ch 2f out: one pce fnl 1f* **6/1**

0-30 **4** *5* **Callisto Moon**[12] 4097 7-9-2 **73**...............................(p) RossAtkinson(3) 2 70
(Jo Hughes) *chsd ldr: rdn 3f out: outpcd and lost 2 pls 2f out: sn lost tch w ldng trio* **18/1**

1-52 **5** *2 ¼* **Salontyre (GER)**[48] 2873 5-8-13 **67**................................(p) MartinLane 7 62
(Bernard Llewellyn) *v awkward leaving stalls: in rr: rdn over 4f out: btn and no imp fnl 3f* **11/4**[1]

5-53 **6** *6* **Hawridge King**[49] 2846 9-9-4 **72**.................................... FergusSweeney 5 59
(Stuart Kittow) *w.w: rdn 4f out: lost tch and btn 3f out: nt hrd pushed after* **15/2**

0-02 **7** *49* **Markington**[2] 3935 8-9-5 **73**...(b) MartinDwyer 6 —
(Peter Bowen) *midfield: reminders ins fnl m: sn gave up and dropped last 6f out: t.o 4f out* **14/1**

3m 30.19s (0.19) **Going Correction** +0.15s/f (Good) 7 Ran SP% **111.9**
Speed ratings (Par 105): **105,104,102,100,99 96,71**
toteswingers:1&2:£3.60, 2&3:£1.70, 1&3:£17.40 CSF £13.76 TOTE £4.70: £3.10, £1.10; EX 14.80.
Owner Mrs Janet Davies **Bred** Newsells Park Stud **Trained** Llancarfan, Vale Of Glamorgan

FOCUS
A competitive little staying race. The winner was very well in on his old Flat form and can do a bit better still in this sphere.

4464 THREE RIVERS H'CAP — 1m 4f (R)

7:55 (7:55) (Class 3) (0-90,86) 3-Y-O+ **£6,792** (£2,021; £1,010; £505) **Stalls** Low

Form RPR

1156 **1** **Saint Helena (IRE)**[51] 2791 3-8-6 **79**.............................. JohnFahy(3) 8 85
(Harry Dunlop) *in tch: hdwy on inner 4f out: rdn to ld over 2f out: kpt on wl u.p: all out* **11/1**

5101 **2** *½* **Plattsburgh (USA)**[7] 4237 3-8-8 **78** 6ex.............................. LiamJones 3 83
(Mark Johnston) *taken to post v early: in tch: urged along 5f out: hdwy on outer over 3f out sn hanging lft and looking ungainly u.p: styd on strly ins fnl f: wnt 2nd cl home* **3/1**[2]

12-4 **3** *¾* **Alazan (IRE)**[33] 3406 5-9-11 **86**.................................... KieranO'Neill(3) 5 90
(Philip Hobbs) *trckd ldr: rdn along 4f out: drvn to press ldr and ev ch 2f out: one pce ins fnl f* **2/1**[1]

5210 **4** *1* **Yes Chef**[27] 3585 4-9-7 **79**.. JamesMillman 6 81
(Rod Millman) *taken to post early: led: rdn 3f out: drvn and hdd over 2f out and sn lost 2 pls: wknd and lost 3rd ins fnl f* **8/1**[3]

4103 **5** *11* **Porgy**[19] 3867 6-10-0 **86**.. MartinLane 2 71
(David Simcock) *v awkward leaving stalls: in last pair: hdwy 4f out: brief effrt over 3f out: no imp fnl 2f: sn eased* **3/1**[2]

2542 **6** *14* **Pelham Crescent (IRE)**[17] 3911 8-9-8 **80**................. CathyGannon 4 42
(Bryn Palling) *slowly away: nvr on terms: rdn over 4f out: no imp after: eased whn btn: t.o* **11/1**

3003 **7** *23* **Parhelion**[17] 3911 4-9-6 **78**.. FergusSweeney 7 —
(Derek Haydn Jones) *chsd ldr: rdn and wknd rapidly 4f out: t.o* **20/1**

2m 36.28s (-1.12) **Going Correction** +0.15s/f (Good)
WFA 3 from 4yo+ 12lb 7 Ran SP% **115.9**
Speed ratings (Par 107): **107,106,106,105,98 88,73**
toteswingers:1&2:£5.00, 2&3:£2.80, 1&3:£4.90 CSF £45.15 CT £95.18 TOTE £16.60: £7.10, £1.10; EX 65.00.
Owner W R B Racing 47 **Bred** Frank O'Malley **Trained** Lambourn, Berks

FOCUS
A competitive handicap which was run at an ordinary gallop. The winner showed her Lingfield Oaks Trial fifth doesn't flatter.

NOTEBOOK
Saint Helena(IRE) had dropped back down 5lb from the 12lb she was raised for her fifth in the Lingfield Oaks Trial in May and she left behind that latest Salisbury effort over 1m2f to score in dogged style. The assessor can't go overboard given her margin of victory and she is relatively unexposed over this trip so further progress can't be ruled out.
Plattsburgh(USA) is also unexposed over this trip and he went close to defying a penalty for his Doncaster success but his progress in the straight was hindered by his propensity to lug in behind Alazan. He eventually edged past that rival but had too much to do to reel in the winner and although he's a handicapper going forward, he's got his quirks. Official explanation: jockey said colt hung left (op 11-4)
Alazan(IRE) threw down a big challenge in the straight but the burden of 10st proved too much and he couldn't get to grips with the winner in the closing stages. On this evidence he doesn't have anything in hand of the assessor in this sphere. (op 9-4 tchd 5-2)
Yes Chef kept on well enough to suggest this trip is no problem for him and he bounced back from a disappointing run last time. (op 9-1)
Porgy lost his race at the start. (op 7-2)

4465 WALTERS UK H'CAP — 1m 4f (R)

8:30 (8:30) (Class 5) (0-75,74) 4-Y-O+ **£2,328** (£693; £346; £173) **Stalls** Low

Form RPR

2524 **1** **Shabak Hom (IRE)**[34] 3354 4-9-7 **74**.............................. MartinLane 2 80
(David Simcock) *unruly and mounted outside paddock: stl last over 5f out: smooth hdwy on outer 4f out: led ins fnl 2f: drvn along and a doing enough ins fnl f* **11/4**[2]

2221 **2** *nk* **On The Feather**[19] 3872 5-9-3 **70**................................ JamesMillman 3 76
(Rod Millman) *hld up: hdwy and gng wl 3f out: short of room and angling for run over 2f out: swtchd rt and rdn 1f out: styd on wl: nt rch wnr* **2/1**[1]

225S **3** *1 ½* **Aviso (GER)**[22] 3726 7-8-7 **63**.. JohnFahy(3) 7 66
(David Evans) *taken down early: led: rdn 3f out: hdd ins fnl 2f: wknd cl home and lost 2nd* **8/1**

0304 **4** *3* **Green Lightning (IRE)**[21] 3758 4-9-3 **70**.........................(b) LiamJones 4 68
(Mark Johnston) *in tch: rn in snatches early: rdn to chse ldr 4f out: carried hd high u.p: ev ch tl wknd ins fnl 2f* **7/2**[3]
1423 **5** *1 ¾* **Penang Cinta**[30] 3479 8-8-8 **61**... CathyGannon 6 56
(David Evans) *in tch: rdn and hdwy 4f out: drvn and one pce fnl 2f* **9/1**
50 **6** *51* **Charmeur (USA)**[17] 3911 4-9-2 **72**...........................(bt) KieranO'Neill(3) 5 —
(Philip Hobbs) *chsd ldr: rdn 5f out: sn gave up and wknd rapidly 4f out: sn tailed himself off* **12/1**

2m 36.71s (-0.69) **Going Correction** +0.15s/f (Good) **6** Ran SP% **111.0**
Speed ratings (Par 103): **106,105,104,102,101 67**
toteswingers:1&2:£8.00, 2&3:£5.60, 1&3:£12.00 CSF £8.48 TOTE £4.70: £2.40, £1.10; EX 11.40.
Owner Tick Tock Partnership **Bred** Rabbah Bloodstock Limited **Trained** Newmarket, Suffolk

FOCUS
They went a reasonable gallop and the time compared quitwe well to the previous race. The third sets the standard.

4466 QUANTUM GB GEOTECHNICAL & CIVIL ENGINEERING H'CAP 6f
9:00 (9:01) (Class 6) (0-60,60) 3-Y-O **£1,681** (£500; £250; £125) **Stalls** High

Form RPR
1 **1** **Miss Elegance**[17] 3909 3-9-7 **60**..(t) LiamJones 8 69+
(Brian Meehan) *mde all: pushed along 2f out: rdn to assert 1f out: a doing enough* **5/4**[1]
0300 **2** *¾* **Atia**[16] 3956 3-8-13 **55**...(p) JohnFahy(3) 9 62
(Jonathan Portman) *mounted outside paddock: rdn and hdwy 2f out: pressed ldr and ev ch 1f: kpt on wl ins fnl f* **12/1**
604 **3** *2 ¼* **Nafa (IRE)**[17] 3909 3-8-7 **53**... JosephYoung(7) 5 53
(Michael Mullineaux) *cl up: rdn and hung lft over 1f out: outpcd and lost tch w ldng pair ins fnl f: jst hld on for 3rd* **20/1**
05-2 **4** *hd* **Dixie Gwalia**[10] 4162 3-8-2 **46** oh1.................................... LauraPike(5) 7 45
(David Simcock) *hld up: hdwy on outer over 2f out: pressing ldrs and ev ch 1f out: wknd ins fnl f* **2/1**[2]
006 **5** *3 ¾* **Decadence**[8] 4199 3-8-4 **48**... RyanPowell(5) 1 35
(Eric Alston) *prom: rdn over 3f out: wknd fnl 2f* **16/1**
0043 **6** *4 ½* **Lady Excellentia (IRE)**[7] 4224 3-8-4 **46** oh1................... KieranO'Neill(3) 3 19
(Ronald Harris) *t.k.h: chsd ldr tl rdn and wknd over 2f out* **7/1**[3]
-600 **7** *1 ½* **Burst Of Stardust**[20] 3803 3-8-13 **52**.............................. CathyGannon 2 20
(Bryn Palling) *prom: rdn and lost pl after 2f: dropped last of main gp 3f out: sn btn* **12/1**
0053 **8** *¾* **Local Diktator**[22] 3724 3-9-1 **54**.. MartinDwyer 6 20
(Ronald Harris) *in rr: sn hanging lft: unrideable fnl 4f* **20/1**

1m 10.69s (0.69) **Going Correction** +0.15s/f (Good) **8** Ran SP% **121.1**
Speed ratings (Par 98): **99,98,95,94,89 83,81,80**
toteswingers:1&2:£8.00, 2&3:£5.60, 1&3:£12.00 CSF £19.87 CT £210.79 TOTE £2.60: £1.10, £4.20, £6.50; EX 26.20.
Owner Mr T G & Mrs M E Holdcroft **Bred** Bearstone Stud **Trained** Manton, Wilts

FOCUS
A weak sprint handicap. The winner might be capable of bettering this bare form.
Local Diktator Official explanation: jockey said colt hung left
T/Plt: £18.90 to a £1 stake.Pool of £61,460.76 - 2370.59 winning units. T/Qpdt: £12.80 to a £1 stake. Pool of £5,733.29 - 330.70 winning units. CS

4423 GOODWOOD (R-H)
Thursday, July 28

OFFICIAL GOING: Good changing to good to firm (good in places) after race 1 (2:15)
Wind: light, across Weather: bright, sunny spells, light cloud

4467 BETFRED THE BONUS KING STKS (H'CAP) 1m 1f 192y
2:15 (2:22) (Class 2) 3-Y-O **£[illegible]** ([illegible]; [illegible]; £2,097; £1,048; £526) **Stalls** Low

Form RPR
-423 **1** **Labarinto**[21] 3774 3-9-0 **93**... RyanMoore 6 104+
(Sir Michael Stoute) *lw: hld up in midfield: rdn and hdwy 2f out: chse ldrs u.p 1f out: drvn to ld ins fnl f: r.o wl* **4/1**[1]
-102 **2** *¾* **Chain Lightning**[27] 3592 3-9-2 **95**................................ RichardHughes 4 104
(Richard Hannon) *hld up in midfield: rdn and hdwy 2f out: drvn and ev ch ins fnl f: no ex fnl 75yds* **8/1**
4420 **3** *hd* **Swift Alhaarth (IRE)**[21] 3774 3-8-6 **85**........................... FrannyNorton 2 94
(Mark Johnston) *led: clr 6f out: hrd pressed and rdn over 2f out: kpt on wl: edgd lft u.p 1f out: hdd ins fnl f: styd on same pce after* **28/1**
1215 **4** *¾* **Las Verglas Star (IRE)**[19] 3864 3-8-8 **87**........................ PaulHanagan 3 94
(Richard Fahey) *chsd ldr: clsd and pressed ldr over 2f out: edgd lft u.p and unable qck 1f out: no ex fnl 150yds* **25/1**
0351 **5** *1 ½* **Fulgur**[21] 3774 3-9-6 **99**.. KierenFallon 5 103
(Luca Cumani) *racd in midfield: rdn and effrt towards inner over 2f out: kpt on fr over 1f out: swtchd lft ins fnl f: no imp fnl 150yds* **13/2**[2]
1-13 **6** *¾* **Boogie Shoes**[54] 2711 3-9-0 **93**... NeilCallan 1 96
(Roger Varian) *chsd ldrs: rdn to press ldrs and wandered u.p 2f out: unable qck over 1f out: one pce and btn 1f out* **8/1**
5320 **7** *nse* **Tinkertown (IRE)**[42] 3067 3-9-5 **98**............................... JamieSpencer 9 101
(Roger Varian) *hld up towards rr: effrt and swtchd ins over 2f out: hdwy over 1f out: swtchd lft and styd on ins fnl f: nt rch ldrs* **12/1**
-143 **8** *¾* **Belgian Bill**[20] 3802 3-9-7 **100**.......................................(t) FrankieDettori 12 101
(George Baker) *hld up in midfield: rdn and effrt on outer over 2f out: unable qck 2f out: styd on same pce and no imp fr over 1f out* **14/1**
0221 **9** *½* **Calaf**[20] 3809 3-8-0 **79**.. LukeMorris 10 79
(Richard Fahey) *in tch: swtchd lft and rdn over 2f out: unable qck and carried lft 2f out: one pce and no imp fr over 1f out* **33/1**
5112 **10** *1 ¼* **Oceanway (USA)**[6] 4267 3-8-12 **91**........................... SilvestreDeSousa 15 89
(Mark Johnston) *stmbld leaving stalls: towards rr: pushed along and effrt over 2f out: no real prog tl styd on ins fnl f: nvr trbld ldrs* **10/1**
-404 **11** *1 ½* **Specific Gravity (FR)**[42] 3068 3-9-7 **100**.......................... TomQueally 8 95
(Sir Henry Cecil) *chsd ldrs: rdn and edgd lft ent fnl 2f: drvn and unable qck over 1f out: wknd ent fnl f* **25/1**
4505 **12** *1 ¼* **Ashva (USA)**[20] 3830 3-8-3 **82**..(p) JimmyQuinn 7 74
(Michael Dods) *lw: hld up in midfield: pushed along and nt qckn over 1f out: rdn and wknd ins fnl f* **33/1**
6130 **13** *1 ¼* **Barney Rebel (IRE)**[20] 3825 3-8-9 **88** ow1........................ MichaelHills 13 78
(B W Hills) *swtg: rrd as stalls opened: hld up in rr: stl travelling wl over 2f out: rdn and fnd little wl over 1f out: sn wknd* **20/1**
2204 **14** *nk* **Tropical Beat**[19] 3864 3-8-7 **86**.......................................(v) WilliamBuick 16 75
(John Gosden) *lw: hld up in rr: rdn and effrt over 2f out: racd awkwardly u.p and no hdwy 2f out: sn wknd* **7/1**[3]
1351 **15** *hd* **Cool Macavity (IRE)**[26] 3650 3-7-12 **84**.............. MatthewLawson(7) 11 73
(B W Hills) *swtg: hld up in rr: rdn and effrt on outer over 2f out: no prog: n.d* **33/1**

2m 4.60s (-3.40) **Going Correction** -0.10s/f (Good) **15** Ran SP% **116.2**
Speed ratings (Par 106): **109,108,108,107,106 105,105,105,104,103 102,101,100,100,100**
toteswingers:1&2:£6.20, 1&3:£24.70, 2&3:£43.00 CSF £29.93 CT £771.88 TOTE £4.70: £2.00, £2.90, £9.80; EX 30.10 Trifecta £631.20 Pool: £4,291.00 - 5.03 winning units..
Owner K Abdulla **Bred** Juddmonte Farms Ltd **Trained** Newmarket, Suffolk

FOCUS
Lower bend out 5yds increasing distances by 6yds. Top bend out 3yds adding 5yds to distances on that course. A good-quality 3-y-o handicap, although it wasn't as competitive as the field-size suggested and, despite the pace appearing to be a generous one, few actually got into the race. Good handicap form, and pretty solid, with a 3lb personal best from Labarinto.

NOTEBOOK
Labarinto was a bit worse than midfield and under pressure with 3f to run, so deserves credit for this. He'd twice run better than the bare facts suggested in valuable handicaps at Newbury and Newmarket of late, being denied a clear run behind Fulgur last time, and it was no surprise to see him reverse form on 9lb better terms. Clearly progressive, this looks his trip, and he ought to be up to winning at pattern level in the autumn. (op 9-2)

Chain Lightning, 2lb well in after his recent Sandown second, settled better this time and readily picked up to challenge, but the favourite was always getting the better of him. He remains progressive and appeals as a likely type for the Cambridgeshire, assuming his rating doesn't climb much further. (tchd 15-2, 9-1 in a place)

Swift Alhaarth(IRE), last of 18 in the Newmarket race contested by the winner last time (probably found race coming too soon), was actually 3lb higher, but showed that to be all wrong with a cracking effort under an aggressive ride. He was rallying close home, despite drifting away from the rail in the straight, but will be nudged up again by the handicapper. (op 25-1)

Las Verglas Star(IRE), 8lb above his last winning mark and going beyond 1m for the first time, took a nice tow from the third and was produced with a winning chance, but his stamina wasn't quite up to it. He'll get home better in a less competitive heat. (op 33-1)

Fulgur was dropping in grade, having taken on Nathaniel at Royal Ascot, when winning a similar race to this at Newmarket last time, but he'd gone up 10lb and wasn't as well suited to this course, keeping on late having been under pressure running down hill. Both breeding and run-style suggest he'll be suited by a return to 1m4f on a more conventional track. (op 5-1)

Boogie Shoes had an ideal sit and things opened up perfectly for him when the third edged away from the rail. However, he was unable to respond immediately and, despite keeping on, simply wasn't up to it off a mark of 93. (tchd 15-2)

Tinkertown(IRE), making his debut for Roger Varian, has been shaping as though a return to this trip would suit (third in the Dee Stakes one previous try), and he stayed on from well back, but placing him shall remain difficult off his current rating. (op 16-1 tchd 11-1)

Belgian Bill, trying 1m2f for the first time, was going on at the finish, but always seemed likely to come up short off a mark of 100. (op 12-1 tchd 11-1)

Oceanway(USA), denied a hat-trick off this mark at Ascot six days earlier, could never get into it having stumbled leaving the gate. She's due to race off 4lb higher in future. (op 9-1 tchd 8-1)

Barney Rebel(IRE) is probably worth another chance as, having reared at the start, he was forced to make ground wide, which he did comfortably, but then had little left for the finish. (op 16-1)

Tropical Beat has solid course form to his name, but not for the first time, didn't look straightforward under pressure. (op 10-1)

4468 AUDI KING GEORGE STKS (GROUP 2) 5f
2:45 (2:52) (Class 1) 3-Y-O+
£48,203 (£18,275; £9,146; £4,556; £2,286; £1,147) **Stalls** High

Form RPR
3101 **1** **Masamah (IRE)**[19] 3874 5-9-0 **107**.................................. JamieSpencer 8 117
(Kevin Ryan) *taken down early: mde all: grad crossed to r against stands' rail: rdn: fnd ex and stormed clr ins fnl f: eased cl home* **4/1**[2]
00-2 **2** *1 ¾* **Amour Propre**[19] 3874 5-9-0 **106**.................................. DaneO'Neill 11 111
(Henry Candy) *chsd ldrs: rdn and nt clr run over 1f out: swtchd rt and hdwy 1f out: chsd wnr jst ins fnl f: r.o u.p but no imp fnl 100yds* **6/1**[3]
0505 **3** *½* **Group Therapy**[19] 3874 6-9-0 **105**.................................. JimCrowley 12 112+
(David Barron) *taken down early: t.k.h: hld up in tch: sltly hmpd and swtchd rt after [illegible] and looking to switch rt jst over 1f out: swtchd bk lft ins fnl f: r.o wl fnl 100yds: no ch w wnr* **16/1**
-642 **4** *1* **Beyond Desire**[26] 3644 4-8-11 **103**...................................... NeilCallan 7 102
(Roger Varian) *wnt lft s: sn rcvrd and chsd wnr tl 1/2-way: chsd ldrs after: drvn and hdwy over 1f out: styd on same pce fnl 150yds* **9/1**
0153 **5** *2* **Humidor (IRE)**[26] 3644 4-9-0 **104**.............................(t) MatthewDavies 10 98
(George Baker) *taken down early: racd in midfield: pushed along and hdwy 1/2-way: drvn to chse ldrs over 1f out: no ex 1f out: wknd ins fnl f* **14/1**
1000 **6** *½* **Breathless Kiss (USA)**[85] 1809 4-8-11 **100**..................(b) PhillipMakin 9 93
(Kevin Ryan) *dwlt: sn bustled along and outpcd in rr: hdwy and edging rt jst over 1f out: kpt on ins fnl f: nvr trbld ldrs* **40/1**
2606 **7** *¾* **Kingsgate Native (IRE)**[26] 3644 6-9-0 **113**........................ RyanMoore 1 94
(Sir Michael Stoute) *midfield: hdwy 1/2-way: rdn and effrt over 1f out: fnd little and no imp 1f out: rdn and wknd ins fnl f* **4/1**[2]
2000 **8** *½* **Rain Delayed (IRE)**[19] 3874 5-9-0 **103**........................ RichardHughes 3 92
(Michael Dods) *stdd s: wl bhd: edging rt and sme hdwy 1f out: kpt on fnl f: n.d* **22/1**
-121 **9** *1* **Noble Storm (USA)**[62] 2456 5-9-0 **110**........................ GrahamGibbons 4 88
(Ed McMahon) *chsd ldrs tl wnt 2nd 1/2-way: rdn and unable qck over 1f out: lost 2nd jst ins fnl f: sn wknd* **7/2**[1]
-100 **10** *½* **Stone Of Folca**[44] 3010 3-8-10 **104**....................................[1] LukeMorris 2 85
(John Best) *outpcd towards rr and sltly hmpd wl over 3f out: drvn and edgd rt over 1f out: kpt on but nvr gng pce to threaten ldrs* **22/1**
0-04 **11** *4* **Golden Destiny (IRE)**[19] 3874 5-8-11 **102**...................(b) WilliamBuick 5 69
(Peter Makin) *dwlt and hmpd sn after s: a struggling in rr* **16/1**

56.67 secs (-1.73) **Going Correction** -0.10s/f (Good)
WFA 3 from 4yo+ 4lb **11** Ran SP% **116.1**
Speed ratings (Par 115): **109,106,105,103,100 99,98,97,96,95 89**
toteswingers:1&2:£4.80, 1&3:£13.80, 2&3:£12.80 CSF £27.18 TOTE £4.80: £1.80, £2.40, £5.10; EX 26.10 Trifecta £290.00 Pool: £8,070.84 - 20.59 winning units..
Owner Dr Marwan Koukash **Bred** Stanley Estate & Stud Co & Mount Coote Stud **Trained** Hambleton, N Yorks

FOCUS
This looked up to scratch and the pace was predictably quick, backed up by a fast time. The rails proved the best place to be. Masamah's form in this has been bettered only by Kingsgate Native in the past ten years.

NOTEBOOK

Masamah(IRE) won a Listed race at York last time from Amour Propre (Golden Destiny, Group Therapy and Rain Delayed further behind), and made the leap up to Group level quite comfortably. Showing his usual speed from the stalls, he bagged the stands' rail and fought off all challengers, winning a shade comfortably. Considering his early pace it makes sense for Masamah to head for the Nunthorpe, although the stable will also presumably have exciting juvenile Bapak Chinta representing them off a feather weight. (op 9-2 tchd 5-1 in places)

Amour Propre, who was a little disappointing in this last year, ran really well on his first outing for 345 days behind Masamah and at least ran to that level again after having every chance. He is relatively fresh for the remainder of the campaign, so it wouldn't be a surprise to see him collect at this level before the season is out. (op 5-1 tchd 7-1)

Group Therapy, runner up to Borderlescott here in 2010 for Jeremy Noseda, raced a little keenly early on while sitting in the slipstream of the leaders before then being forced to check in his run just over 1f. He was going as well as Amour Propre at the time and looks best rated alongside the runner-up. (op 10-1)

Beyond Desire, who won here on her racecourse debut, finished in front of both Humidor and Kingsgate Native at Sandown last time and easily saw off those rivals again. Always close up, she ran well but never looked like winning. (op 11-1 tchd 8-1 in places)

Humidor(IRE), who was walked to the start, held an unbeaten record at this course and must have run as well as connections would have hoped for in this company. (op 12-1 tchd 10-1)

Breathless Kiss(USA), absent since the start of May, was back in Group company after a modest effort in a Chester handicap. A horse who has gone well fresh in the past, she stayed on towards the rail but never threatened.

Kingsgate Native(IRE), the 2009 winner of this contest, has become disappointing and weakened quickly once under strong pressure. Connections have been trying him in headgear this season, so presumably they think he needs something to spark him into life. (op 11-2)

Noble Storm(USA), who'd won over C&D on his only other previous start here, had held his form this season after reportedly suffering from a virus in 2010 but was really disappointing here, dropping out rapidly once the winner stretched on. Presumably something was amiss and he should be given another chance. (op 9-2)

4469 ARTEMIS GOODWOOD CUP (GROUP 2) 2m

3:15 (3:20) (Class 1) 3-Y-O+

£56,710 (£21,500; £10,760; £5,360; £2,690; £1,350) **Stalls** Low

Form RPR

2342 **1** **Opinion Poll (IRE)**[42] 3066 5-9-7 116 .... FrankieDettori 16 114+
(Mahmood Al Zarooni) *hld up off the pce in midfield: clsd 7f out: outpcd whn ldr qcknd 5f out: swtchd lft and effrt over 2f out: chsd ldr and edgd rt over 1f out: led 1f out: hrd drvn ins fnl f: all out* **9/2**[1]

0223 **2** *hd* **Lost In The Moment (IRE)**[19] 3876 4-9-7 105 ....(p) WilliamBuick 3 115+
(Saeed Bin Suroor) *hld up wl off the pce in last quartet: hdwy on inner over 7f out: outpcd whn ldr qcknd 5f out: rdn and hdwy over 2f out: styng on whn nt clr run and swtchd lft 1f out: str run fnl f: nt quite get up* **11/1**

6210 **3** *nk* **Blue Bajan (IRE)**[42] 3066 9-9-10 111 .... DanielTudhope 10 116
(David O'Meara) *swtg: racd off the pce in midfield: clsd 7f out: outpcd whn ldr qcknd and lost pl over 4f out: swtchd lft and effrt 3f out: hdwy over 1f out: chsd wnr ins fnl f: styd on wl: lost 2nd nr fin* **20/1**

4112 **4** *nse* **Fox Hunt (IRE)**[19] 3875 4-9-7 110 ....(v) SilvestreDeSousa 9 113+
(Mark Johnston) *racd off the pce in midfield: clsd and in tch 7f out: outpcd whn ldr qcknd and lost pl wl over 4f out: drvn 3f out: hdwy u.p ent fnl f: r.o strly ins fnl f: nt quite rch ldrs* **5/1**[2]

0-02 **5** *1 ¾* **Bergo (GER)**[140] 826 8-9-7 109 .... RyanMoore 4 111
(Gary Moore) *prom in chsng gp: clsd on ldr 7f out: outpcd whn ldr qcknd 5f out: rdn to chse clr ldr 3f out tl over 1f out: styd on same pce ins fnl f* **22/1**

5402 **6** *½* **Aaim To Prosper (IRE)**[26] 3647 7-9-7 107 .... LouisBeuzelin 11 110
(Brian Meehan) *prom in chsng gp: clsd and in tch 7f out: outpcd whn ldr qcknd 5f out: drvn over 3f out: kpt on wl on u.p and chsng ldrs 1f out: one pce fnl f* **28/1**

0-16 **7** *½* **Overturn (IRE)**[33] 3396 7-9-7 106 .... RichardHughes 2 110
(Donald McCain) *led and sn clr: stdd gallop and c bk to field 7f out: rdn and qcknd clr bnd 5f out: drvn and c bk to field over 1f out: hdd 1f out: kpt on gamely but no ex ins fnl f* **8/1**

3-34 **8** *1 ¼* **Manighar (FR)**[42] 3066 5-9-7 112 .... KierenFallon 8 108
(Luca Cumani) *wl bhd in last quartet: clsd and in tch 7f out: outpcd and wl bhd again whn ldr qcknd 5f out: rdn wl over 2f out: styng on but stl plenty to do whn sltly hmpd over 1f out: kpt on fnl f: n.d* **7/1**[3]

0411 **9** *2 ¼* **Chiberta King**[26] 3647 5-9-7 108 .... JimmyFortune 6 106
(Andrew Balding) *prom in main gp: clsd and in tch 7f out: outpcd whn ldr qcknd 5f out: rdn and squeezed through on rail over 2f out: drvn and chsd ldrs over 1f out: no imp ins fnl f: eased wl ins fnl f* **12/1**

0141 **10** *13* **Red Cadeaux**[33] 3418 5-9-7 110 .... TomMcLaughlin 13 95+
(Ed Dunlop) *racd oiff the pce in midfield: clsd and in tch 7f out: outpcd whn ldr qcknd 5f out: sn rdn: hdwy u.p 3f out: no hdwy and btn over 1f out: eased ins fnl f* **10/1**

-061 **11** *2 ¾* **Swingkeel (IRE)**[40] 3157 6-9-7 104 ....(p) TedDurcan 14 87
(John Dunlop) *hld up wl off the pce in last quartet: clsd and in tch 7f out: outpcd whn ldr qcknd 5f out: rdn and no hdwy over 3f out: no ch after* **40/1**

0322 **12** *2 ¾* **Montaff**[33] 3396 5-9-7 106 .... HughBowman 1 83
(Mick Channon) *hld up wl off the pce in last quartet: clsd 7f out: outpcd whn ldr qcknd 5f out: sn rdn and no hdwy: wl bhd fnl 2f* **16/1**

0-03 **13** *nk* **Electrolyser (IRE)**[26] 3647 6-9-7 109 ....(p) AdamKirby 15 83
(Clive Cox) *swtg: prom in main gp: clsd and in tch 7f out: outpcd whn ldr qcknd 5f out: rdn and rallied over 3f out: wknd 2f out: eased ins fnl f* **20/1**

1-2P **14** *4* **Tastahil (IRE)**[42] 3066 7-9-7 115 .... RichardHills 12 78
(B W Hills) *chsd ldr: clsd up 7f out: outpcd whn ldr qcknd 5f out: lost 2nd 3f out and sn wknd: eased fnl f* **12/1**

33/P **15** *55* **Geordieland (FR)**[42] 3066 10-9-7 109 .... JimCrowley 7 —
(Jamie Osborne) *hld up wl off the pce in last: clsd and in tch 7f out: outpcd whn ldr qcknd 5f out: lost tch over 3f out: wl t.o and virtually p.u fnl 2f* **33/1**

3m 23.85s (-5.15) **Going Correction** -0.10s/f (Good) **15** Ran SP% **119.9**
Speed ratings (Par 115): **108,107,107,107,106 106,106,105,104,98 96,95,95,93,65**
toteswingers:1&2:£10.40, 1&3:£23.20, 2&3:£36.50 CSF £47.62 TOTE £3.30: £1.40, £4.10, £6.60; EX 51.30 Trifecta £729.60 Pool: £6,239.65 - 6.32 winning units..
Owner Godolphin **Bred** Darley **Trained** Newmarket, Suffolk

■ Stewards' Enquiry : Frankie Dettori two-day ban: used whip with excessive frequency (Aug 11-12)

FOCUS

One of the more open runnings of recent times. The continued weakness of the staying division was highlighted by the fact both the second and fourth were stepping up from handicap-company, albeit they are both progressive.

NOTEBOOK

Opinion Poll(IRE) went in pursuit of the leaders at precisely the right time and held on for the biggest victory of his career to date. The only horse to get near Fame And Glory in the Ascot Gold Cup, he wouldn't have wanted the ground any quicker and, whilst undoubtedly fortunate to hold on from the unlucky runner-up, it was hard to begrudge him the win. The Group 3 Long Distance Cup (Jockey Club Cup) on British Champions Day is the long-term aim. (op 5-1)

Lost In The Moment(IRE) had never previously raced beyond 1m3f and looked far from a certain stayer on breeding, but he's from a yard that's had its fair share of success in this division over the years, and would almost certainly have won had he not been stopped in his tracks when making a move at the same time as the winner. He rattled home once switched, being in front a stride after the line, and is sure to be considered for 1m6f-2m Group races later in the year, but first has the option of the Ebor, which connections may find hard to resist as he's sure to be a few pounds well in. (op 14-1 tchd 10-1)

Blue Bajan(IRE) ran a blinder considering he was carrying a penalty for his Group 2 Henry II Stakes victory in the spring. Having been outpaced, he did well to reach the position he did and, in theory, it was his penalty that cost him victory. He remains a dangerous stayer at the right level on his day.

Fox Hunt(IRE) has hardly put a foot wrong this season, improving since being fitted with a visor and, despite being a touch keen early and then badly outpaced having lost his position, really came strong in the final 2f, losing out narrowly. He's another in the Ebor, currently off a big weight, and it would be no surprise to see him turn up there. (op 6-1 tchd 7-1 in a place)

Bergo(GER), one place ahead of the winner on his final start in Dubai earlier in the year, is the most dour of stayers and probably ran up to his best. (op 18-1 tchd 25-1, 33-1 in a place)

Aaim To Prosper(IRE) continues to perform creditably at Group/Listed level. (op 25-1)

Overturn(IRE) set a reasonable gallop and increased it significantly when kicked into the top bend and getting the entire field on the stretch running down the hill. However, the fact this resolute galloper couldn't press home his advantage suggests he was committed too soon, ultimately fading into seventh. (op 10-1)

Manighar(FR) ended up with an awful lot to do and was interfered with when trying to keep on late. He's a smart stayer, but hasn't won since 2009. (op 6-1)

Chiberta King was unable to confirm last-time-out Sandown form with Aaim To Prosper on this first try at Group level. (tchd 14-1)

Red Cadeaux found this tougher than the Curragh Group 3 he ran away with on soft ground last month. (op 12-1)

Tastahil(IRE), pulled up in the Gold Cup, was unable to bounce back to his best. (tchd 14-1 in a place)

Geordieland(FR) reportedly finished lame, and has been retired. Official explanation: trainer said horse finished lame (tchd 40-1)

4470 I-SHARES FILLIES' STKS (REGISTERED AS THE LILLIE LANGTRY STAKES) (GROUP 3) (F&M) 1m 6f

3:45 (3:51) (Class 1) 3-Y-O+

£28,355 (£10,750; £5,380; £2,680; £1,345; £675) **Stalls** Low

Form RPR

0-32 **1** **Meeznah (USA)**[12] 4099 4-9-6 109 .... FrankieDettori 5 115
(David Lanigan) *hld up in midfield: rdn and effrt over 2f out: led and edgd rt over 1f out: drvn and wnt clr 1f out: in command and kpt on wl fnl f: eased nr fin* **6/1**[3]

3 **2** *2 ½* **Shankardeh (IRE)**[32] 3447 3-8-6 107 .... Christophe-PatriceLemaire 7 112
(M Delzangles, France) *leggy: hld up wl off the pce in last pair: clsd and in tch over 3f out: rdn wl over 1f out: chsd clr wnr ins fnl f: kpt on but no threat to wnr* **6/1**[3]

32-0 **3** *2 ¼* **Motrice**[42] 3066 4-9-6 106 .... SebSanders 4 108
(Sir Mark Prescott Bt) *chsd ldrs: rdn to chse ldr 2f out: chsd wnr over 1f out: outpcd by wnr and btn 1f out: lost 2nd ins fnl f* **9/1**

2245 **4** *1* **Polly's Mark (IRE)**[26] 3624 5-9-6 106 .... RichardHughes 3 107
(Clive Cox) *chsd ldrs tl wnt 2nd over 3f out: rdn to ld and edgd rt over 2f out: drvn and hdd over 1f out: sn outpcd: 4th and wl hld fnl f* **14/1**

211 **5** *hd* **Wild Coco (GER)**[12] 4099 3-8-6 113 .... TomQueally 9 107
(Sir Henry Cecil) *hld up off the pce in last quartet: hdwy and in tch 4f out: rdn and effrt on outer wl over 2f out: edgd rt and btn jst over 1f out: wknd fnl f* **13/8**[1]

6-44 **6** *½* **Roxy Flyer (IRE)**[68] 2292 4-9-6 100 .... JimmyQuinn 6 106
(Amanda Perrett) *towards rr: hdwy 4f out: drvn to chse ldrs 2f out: wknd u.p over 1f out* **40/1**

0606 **7** *10* **Gallic Star (IRE)**[41] 3107 4-9-6 96 .... HughBowman 1 92
(Mick Channon) *hld up in midfield: rdn and unable qck over 2f out: wknd u.p 2f out: wl btn and eased ins fnl f* **66/1**

6-35 **8** *6* **Bramalea**[39] 3204 6-9-6 85 .... SteveDrowne 8 84
(Hughie Morrison) *lw: led at fast gallop: wnt clr 12f out: rdn and hdd over 2f out: sn btn and wknd 2f out: wl btn and eased ins fnl f* **100/1**

-122 **9** *57* **Field Of Miracles (IRE)**[42] 3065 3-8-6 110 .... WilliamBuick 10 —
(John Gosden) *lw: pressed ldr tl allowed ldr to go clr 12f out: chsd ldr after and rdn along at times: lost 2nd and dropped out qckly over 3f out: t.o and virtually p.u fnl 2f* **7/2**[2]

2-44 **10** *shd* **Ship's Biscuit**[26] 3647 4-9-6 99 .... RyanMoore 2 —
(Sir Michael Stoute) *swtg: nvr gng wl in rr: detached and toiling 6f out: lost tch 4f out: t.o and virtually p.u fnl 2f* **20/1**

2m 57.61s (-5.99) **Going Correction** -0.10s/f (Good) course record
WFA 3 from 4yo+ 14lb **10** Ran SP% **115.2**
Speed ratings (Par 110): **113,111,110,109,109 109,103,100,67,67**
toteswingers:1&2:£5.80, 1&3:£8.30, 2&3:£9.00 CSF £40.18 TOTE £6.10: £1.70, £1.40, £3.10; EX 34.80 Trifecta £302.10 Pool: £10,322.35 - 25.27 winning units..
Owner Saif Ali & Saeed H Altayer **Bred** Swettenham Stud **Trained** Newmarket, Suffolk

FOCUS

Considering some of these have run well at a higher level, this looked a strong contest for a Group 3. The pace was good thanks to Bramalea, who had no obvious chance on official figures, and the course record, set by Eastern Aria in this race last season, was lowered. Sound form even if the favourite was a bit disappointing.

NOTEBOOK

Meeznah(USA), ridden by Frankie Dettori for the first time, had a bit to find with the favourite on their meeting recently at Newmarket, but the ground was much more in her favour this time and it can't be considered too much of a surprise that the form was reversed. A really talented filly at her best, she will surely be tried at a higher level again after this confidence-boosting victory. The Park Hill Stakes at Doncaster looks the next logical race for her. (op 8-1)

Shankardeh(IRE) ◆ ran in a Group 2 at Saint-Cloud on her previous start and that form had already been boosted by the German-trained Danedream, who bolted up in a Group 1 recently. The early signs weren't good early as she needed to be niggled towards the rear, but her jockey held her together and was able to produce his mount with a winning chance. She wasn't able to get past the classy winner but was far from disgraced on a style of track she had not encountered before. (op 9-2 tchd 13-2)

Motrice ran okay in the Gold Cup on her seasonal debut, and this drop in distance looked sure to suit. Her jockey was keen to roust her up early and, although she never appeared to have a winning chance, she stuck on well to gain some more valuable black type. (op 12-1)

Polly's Mark(IRE) finished a place behind Motrice last season and put up her usual game effort, this time without headgear, and will no doubt continue to run well in similar contests.

Wild Coco(GER) ◆ on the face of it was a bit disappointing, especially as she beat Meeznah last time, and was 4lb better off with that rival for winning, but her final position doesn't tell the whole story. She travelled strongly in rear, in the manner of a good horse, but wandering a bit while making her bid down the home straight and didn't appear to get home. The ground was not in her favour either, but this scopey sort can easily be given another chance. (op 6-4 tchd 7-4, 15-8 in places and 11-8 in places)
Roxy Flyer(IRE), a dual course winner, remains in good heart this season and is holding her form well.
Field Of Miracles(IRE), who looked warm down her neck, ran a brave race in the Ribblesdale last time (winner finished second in the Irish Oaks on her next start), but she dropped out quickly this time after tracking Bramalea, suggesting something was not quite right. John Gosden reported afterwards that his filly was unsuited by the good to firm, good in places ground and the track. The Stewards also ordered that she was routine tested. Official explanation: trainer said filly was unsuited by the good to firm (good in places) ground and by the track. (op 9-2)
Ship's Biscuit reportedly got upset in the stalls and was never travelling. Official explanation: jockey said filly got upset in stalls and never travelled (op 16-1)

4471 E B F MEDICEAN NEW HAM MAIDEN FILLIES' STKS — 7f
4:20 (4:22) (Class 2) 2-Y-O — **£11,320** (£3,368; £1,683; £841) **Stalls** Low

Form — RPR
3 **1** **Gifted Girl (IRE)**[20] 3813 2-9-0 0 .... NeilCallan 6 84+
(Paul Cole) *lw: mde all: rdn and qcknd clr 2f out: in n.d but kpt up to work fnl f: rdn out* **4/1**[1]
2 *4* **Amber Silk (IRE)** 2-9-0 0 .... MichaelHills 8 75+
(B W Hills) *w'like: leggy: s.i.s: t.k.h: hld up in midfield: hdwy but nt clr run 2f out tl swtchd lft jst ins fnl f: styd on wl to go 2nd last strides: no ch w wnr* **20/1**
6 **3** *hd* **Perfect Delight**[20] 3812 2-9-0 0 .... LukeMorris 16 72
(Clive Cox) *lw: t.k.h: chsd wnr tl drvn and nt pce of wnr 2f out: no ch w wnr fr over 1f out but kpt on u.p: lost 2nd last strides* **12/1**
4 *hd* **Swingland** 2-9-0 0 .... JimCrowley 7 72+
(Paul Cole) *w'like: scope: rangy: wnt bdly lft s: hld up in midfield on outer: rdn: outpcd and rn green jst over 2f out: hdwy and rdn over 1f out: no ch w wnr but styd on wl ins fnl f: gng on fin* **25/1**
5 *1* **Negin** 2-9-0 0 .... WilliamBuick 19 69+
(Ed Dunlop) *hld up towards rr: rn green over 2f out: hdwy and swtchd to outer over 1f out: styd on wl ins fnl f: no ch w wnr* **33/1**
0 **6** *½* **Viola Da Gamba (IRE)**[20] 3812 2-9-0 0 .... ShaneKelly 2 68
(William Knight) *in tch: rdn and outpcd by wnr whn n.m.r on inner 2f out: kpt on ins fnl f but no ch w wnr* **15/2**[3]
7 *1 ¾* **Distant Love (IRE)** 2-9-0 0 .... DavidProbert 4 63
(Andrew Balding) *lengthy: chsd ldrs: rdn and outpcd by wnr 2f out: no threat to wnr over 1f out but stl battling for placings: wknd ins fnl f* **33/1**
8 *½* **Spirit Na Heireann (IRE)** 2-9-0 0 .... PaulHanagan 5 62+
(Richard Fahey) *leggy: in tch in midfield: rdn and nt pce of wnr 2f out: plugging on same pce and n.d whn hmpd jst ins fnl f* **12/1**
3 **9** *½* **Sunley Valentine**[12] 4087 2-9-0 0 .... SamHitchcott 1 60
(Mick Channon) *chsd ldrs: rdn and outpcd by wnr 2f out: one pce and n.d over 1f out: wknd ins fnl f* **25/1**
10 *nk* **Estedaama (IRE)** 2-9-0 0 .... RichardHills 14 59+
(Marcus Tregoning) *lw: towards rr: pushed along and rn green over 2f out: sn outpcd and no ch w wnr after: nudged along and kpt on ins fnl f* **12/1**
654 **11** *½* **Glad Eye Gladys**[6] 4285 2-9-0 0 .... AdrianNicholls 9 58
(David Nicholls) *towards rr: rdn over 3f out: outpcd and plenty to do 2f out: plugged on fnl f but no ch w wnr* **16/1**
5 **11** *dht* **Rock On Candy**[28] 3547 2-9-0 0 .... JamesDoyle 12 58
(Sylvester Kirk) *t.k.h: chsd ldrs: rdn 3f out: outpcd and struggling 2f out: n.d whn edgd rt jst over 1f out* **10/1**
13 *shd* **Star Of Bombay (FR)** 2-9-0 0 .... RyanMoore 10 58
(Richard Hannon) *w'like: scope: dwlt: sn pushed along in rr: rdn and struggling over 2f out: plugged on but n.d fnl 2f* **12/1**
46 **14** *1* **Musically**[15] 3981 2-9-0 0 .... HughBowman 15 55
(Mick Channon) *in tch in midfield: rdn and unable qck over 2f out: wknd wl over 1f out* **33/1**
15 *4* **Waspy** 2-9-0 0 .... JamieSpencer 13 44
[illegible] *lost tch jst over 2f out* **25/1**
0 **16** *nse* **Cat Queen**[19] 3865 2-9-0 0 .... [illegible] 44
(Gay Kelleway) *v.s.a: a in rr: lost tch 2f out* **25/1**
17 *½* **Santarini (IRE)** 2-9-0 0 .... RichardHughes 17 43
(Richard Hannon) *in tch in midfield: rdn and unable qck over 2f out: wknd over 1f out: eased wl ins fnl f* **9/2**[2]

1m 27.64s (0.74) **Going Correction** -0.10s/f (Good) **17** Ran SP% **124.7**
Speed ratings (Par 97): **91,86,86,85,84 84,82,81,81,80 80,80,80,78,74 74,73**
toteswingers:1&2:£28.60, 1&3:£10.30, 2&3:£59.10 CSF £90.49 TOTE £5.10: £2.00, £8.10, £4.30; EX 120.10 Trifecta £885.20 Pool: £2,272.91 - 1.90 winning units..
Owner A D Spence **Bred** Airlie Stud **Trained** Whatcombe, Oxon
■ Stewards' Enquiry : Michael Hills one-day ban: careless riding (Aug 11)

FOCUS
An interesting fillies' maiden which should provide winners. The winner built on her taking debut.

NOTEBOOK
Gifted Girl(IRE) was clearly best on the day, but had the run of things to boot, which may have exaggerated her authority. A promising third on her debut at Newbury, she's thought a fair bit of by her trainer, who indicated afterwards that she may well take up her Fillies' Mile engagement. (tchd 9-2 in places)
Amber Silk(IRE), whose dam is a half-sister to Oaks third High Heeled, wasn't the best away and then met some trouble in running when trying to close. She pleased with the way she saw her race out and is entitled to win a standard maiden, with 1m likely to suit. (op 16-1)
Perfect Delight finished just under 1l closer to the winner than she had done on debut, keeping on better than expected considering she'd been keen. Her half-sister was speedy, and she may prove more effective over 6f for the time being. (op 14-1)
Swingland, also in the Fillies' Mile, did really well considering she darted left at the start and then ran green. She ran on takingly out wide and normal progress should see her win a maiden, with the step up to 1m set to suit on breeding.
Negin, another to take from the race with the future in mind, is a Selkirk newcomer who had the worst of the draw. Like the horse immediately ahead of her, she put in some good late work, having earlier run green, and a stiffer test will suit on breeding.
Viola Da Gamba(IRE) confirmed the promise of her debut effort and is a likely type for nurseries. (op 9-1 tchd 10-1)
Distant Love(IRE) appeared to know her job well enough and stuck on for pressure. She's entitled to improve.
Spirit Na Heireann(IRE) was given a nice introduction and should have no trouble winning a maiden back up north.
Estedaama(IRE), whose dam is a half-sister to US Grade 2 winner Makderah, got well back and showed distinct signs of greenness. Once it finally clicked what was required of her, though, she finished nicely, not being given a hard time, and she's definitely one to be with next time, with 1m almost certain to suit. (op 11-1)
Star Of Bombay(FR) was never a danger, but can improve.
Cat Queen Official explanation: jockey said filly reared in stalls
Santarini(IRE) holds a couple of Group 1 entries and was beaten too far for this to be her true running. (op 4-1)

4472 TATLER STKS (H'CAP) — 7f
4:55 (4:56) (Class 2) (0-105,103) 3-Y-O
£12,450 (£3,728; £1,864; £932; £466; £234) **Stalls** Low

Form — RPR
4662 **1** **Casual Glimpse**[21] 3777 3-9-3 **99** .... RichardHughes 2 107
(Richard Hannon) *hld up in midfield: travelling wl but n.m.r jst over 2f out: swtchd lft and hdwy over 1f out: drvn to chal ins fnl f: led fnl 50yds: eased nr fin* **16/1**
1562 **2** *nk* **Dimension**[19] 3864 3-8-6 **88** .... KierenFallon 7 95+
(James Fanshawe) *in tch: rdn and effrt over 2f out: led narrowly and drvn over 1f out: kpt on wl u.p tl hdd and no ex fnl 50yds* **9/2**[1]
2041 **3** *nk* **El Viento (FR)**[24] 3682 3-8-10 **92** ....(b) PaulHanagan 1 98
(Richard Fahey) *sn bustled up to chse ldrs: rdn over 2f out: styd on u.p and swtchd lft 1f out: pressing ldrs wl ins fnl f: kpt on* **16/1**
1301 **4** *nk* **Chilworth Lad**[12] 4096 3-9-7 **103** .... HughBowman 11 108
(Mick Channon) *stdd and dropped in bhd after s: rdn and hdwy on outer jst over 1f out: r.o strly ins fnl f: nt quite rch ldrs* **25/1**
3131 **5** *shd* **Bertiewhittle**[33] 3378 3-8-2 **84** .... SilvestreDeSousa 10 89+
(David Barron) *in tch in midfield: rdn 3f out: hdwy on outer over 2f out: drvn and ev ch over 1f out: unable qck fnl 100yds* **9/1**
4501 **6** *2* **Bridgefield (USA)**[21] 3777 3-9-6 **102** .... FrankieDettori 4 104+
(Mahmood Al Zarooni) *lw: hld up towards rr: effrt on inner 2f out: hdwy over 1f out: chsng ldrs u.p and swtchd lft ins fnl f: no imp fnl 100yds: eased towards fin* **5/1**[2]
4202 **7** *1 ¾* **King Of Jazz (IRE)**[12] 4096 3-9-5 **101** .... PatDobbs 13 96
(Richard Hannon) *lw: towards rr: rdn and effrt over 2f out: drvn and styd on same pce fr jst over 1f out* **25/1**
15-4 **8** *¾* **Tuscania**[20] 3819 3-8-8 **90** .... RyanMoore 14 86+
(Sir Michael Stoute) *in tch: rdn over 2f out: drvn and unable qck over 1f out: struggling 1f out and btn jst ins fnl f: eased towards fin* **9/2**[1]
5010 **9** *2* **Norse Blues**[42] 3067 3-8-8 **90** .... JamesDoyle 9 78
(Sylvester Kirk) *in tch in midfield: rdn and lsot pl 3f out: tried to rally u.p over 1f out: kpt on same pce and no imp fnl f* **20/1**
0-36 **10** *1 ¼* **Shropshire (IRE)**[78] 2003 3-8-13 **95** .... MichaelHills 6 79
(B W Hills) *chsd ldr tl pushed into ld 2f out: drvn and hdd over 1f out: wknd fnl f* **20/1**
-215 **11** *3 ¼* **St Augustine (IRE)**[20] 3820 3-8-3 **85** .... LukeMorris 12 60
(John Best) *lw: hld up in midfield on outer: wd on bnd and lost pl over 3f out: sn rdn: no imp fr over 2f out* **8/1**
4121 **12** *½* **Sinfonico (IRE)**[47] 2926 3-8-8 **90** .... DaneO'Neill 8 64
(Richard Hannon) *towards rr: rdn and no imp whn swtchd lft 2f out: bhd over 1f out* **16/1**
1303 **13** *3* **The Tichborne (IRE)**[42] 3067 3-8-8 **90** .... JackMitchell 3 56
(Roger Teal) *led tl over 2f out: wknd u.p over 1f out: fdd fnl f* **7/1**[3]
-320 **14** *1* **Reposer (IRE)**[20] 3796 3-7-11 **86** oh5 ow2 .... GeorgeanBuckell(7) 5 49
(John Best) *chsd ldrs tl over 2f out: sn wknd* **66/1**

1m 25.45s (-1.45) **Going Correction** -0.10s/f (Good) **14** Ran SP% **123.0**
Speed ratings (Par 106): **104,103,103,102,102 100,98,97,95,94 90,89,86,85**
toteswingers:1&2:£17.80, 1&3:£22.40, 2&3:£14.70 CSF £83.00 CT £1240.33 TOTE £13.70: £3.50, £1.90, £4.80; EX 82.80 Trifecta £2425.20 Part won. Pool: £3,277.37 - 0.70 winning units..

Owner M A Al-Attiyah **Bred** Wickfield Farm Partnership **Trained** East Everleigh, Wilts
■ Stewards' Enquiry : Hugh Bowman two-day ban: careless riding (Aug 11-12)
Silvestre De Sousa one-day ban: used whip with excessive frequency down shoulder in the forehand (Aug 11)

FOCUS
A typically tricky handicap in which a lot of these could be considered. The early pace was strong and a few who were patiently ridden early came home strongly. Decent handicap form, but there are one or two doubts.

NOTEBOOK
Casual Glimpse's rider locked his mount away in the middle of the pack and the pair looked in a bit of trouble when the field closed up around them, but the gaps opened at the right time and the pair came home comfortable winners. The horse is obviously good on his day but whether he will be easy to place is open to question.
Dimension ran into what looked a handicap blot at Newmarket last time (subsequently good second at Ascot), continuing his upward curve this season. He raced prominently, had ever chance and ran up to his best. (tchd 5-1 and 11-2 in places)
El Viento(FR), winner over 6f at Ripon last time, was trying 7f for the first time and seemed to get the distance okay, staying on well for strong driving. (tchd 14-1)
Chilworth Lad won a small-field race last time at Newbury (King Of Jazz runner-up) and had been raised 5lb. Given a cool hold-up ride, he stayed on well down the outside of the field, one that looked like taking him to the front before the effort flattened out.
Bertiewhittle has run really well since being moved up to 7f, but didn't appear to get home here after briefly hitting the front. (tchd 12-1 in places)
Bridgefield(USA) followed a similar path to the winner but Casual Glimpse got first run and Bridgefield couldn't get to him. Frankie Dettori wasn't hard on his mount in the final 50 yards after he met a wall of three horses in front of him. (tchd 11-2 in places)
Tuscania, thought good enough to run in the Listed Radley Stakes last year, made a satisfactory return in a Newmarket handicap earlier this month but never figured here. Ryan Moore reported afterwards that the filly ran flat. Official explanation: jockey said filly ran flat (tchd 6-1 and 13-2 in places)
Shropshire(IRE) had the strongest form on offer considering his effort behind both Frankel and Excelebration, but had been absent since flopping on his handicap debut. Returning after an absence for a stable in good heart, he showed a lot of early speed and will surely be better suited by a drop in distance. (op 16-1)
St Augustine(IRE) had run all of his previous races at about 6f and made no impression here after needing to be pushed along shortly after entering the home straight. (tchd 15-2)
The Tichborne(IRE) ran out of his skin in the Britannia last time when going off at 100-1 but weakened steadily from over 1f out here after leading. (op 8-1)

4473 BETFRED.COM STKS (H'CAP) — 1m 3f
5:25 (5:31) (Class 3) (0-90,89) 3-Y-O
£9,337 (£2,796; £1,398; £699; £349; £175) **Stalls** Low

Form — RPR
4-12 **1** **Kinyras (IRE)**[36] 3291 3-9-0 **82** .... RyanMoore 1 92+
(Sir Michael Stoute) *lw: in tch: swtchd ins and chsd ldrs over 3f out: led over 2f out: hrd pressed and drvn ent fnl f: hld on wl: all out* **4/1**[2]

0134 **2** *nse* **Aldwick Bay (IRE)**[7] 4253 3-8-8 **76** .... DaneO'Neill 5 86
(Richard Hannon) *hld up in last trio: hdwy on inner and nt clr run over 2f out: hdwy to chse ldrs wl over 1f out: rdn and ev ch 1f out: kpt on wl u.p: jst hld* **12/1**

5221 **3** *2 ¾* **Amistress**[22] 3744 3-8-5 **73** .... ChrisCatlin 11 78
(Eve Johnson Houghton) *hld up in tch towards rr: hdwy on outer to chse ldrs and hung rt 2f out: 3rd and nt pce of ldng pair fnl f: kpt on* **25/1**

6333 **4** *5* **Orthodox Lad**[14] 4011 3-8-4 **72** .... LukeMorris 8 68+
(John Best) *lw: s.i.s: hld up in rr: rdn and hdwy whn squeezed out and lost pl jst over 2f out: no ch w ldrs but rallied u.p jst over 1f out: wnt 4th nr fin* **16/1**

1150 **5** *½* **Art History (IRE)**[42] 3069 3-9-6 **88** .... SilvestreDeSousa 14 83
(Mark Johnston) *dwlt: in tch in midfield on outer: rdn and hdwy to chse ldrs whn pushed rt 2f out: sn outpcd and no threat to ldng trio over 1f out: lost 4th nr fin* **7/1**[3]

2200 **6** *2* **Mica Mika (IRE)**[21] 3774 3-9-1 **83** .... TomEaves 7 75
(Richard Fahey) *lw: in tch in midfield: rdn and chsng ldrs whn short of room and hmpd 2f out: n.d and plugged on same pce after* **16/1**

-421 **7** *¾* **Parvana (IRE)**[13] 4074 3-8-13 **81** .... JamieSpencer 6 71+
(William Haggas) *swtg: led tl 1 1/2-way: chsd ldrs after rdn and struggling 3f out: wknd wl over 1f out* **8/1**

-316 **8** *10* **Misty Isles**[15] 3988 3-8-9 **77** .... TomQueally 15 49
(Heather Main) *swtg: dwlt: bhd: hdwy into midfield 8f out: chsd ldrs 5f out: rdn 3f out: wknd and wl btn whn hung rt over 1f out: eased ins fnl f* **33/1**

0-20 **9** *6* **Isolate**[37] 3260 3-9-0 **82** .... SteveDrowne 10 43
(Hughie Morrison) *in tch in midfield: lost pl and rdn along 4f out: wknd u.p over 2f out: wl bhd and eased ins fnl f* **16/1**

10 **10** *1 ¼* **Action Front (USA)**[50] 2819 3-9-1 **83** .... PatDobbs 3 42
(Amanda Perrett) *swtg: in tch: rdn and lost pl ent fnl 3f: wl bhd and hung rt over 1f out: eased ins fnl f* **12/1**

20-4 **11** *1* **Goldenveil (IRE)**[116] 1113 3-9-0 **82** .... PaulHanagan 2 39
(Richard Fahey) *hld up in tch: effrt whn nt clr run and hmpd over 2f out: lost any ch: eased fnl f* **10/1**

1203 **12** *3 ¾* **Reflect (IRE)**[26] 3623 3-9-7 **89** .... RichardHughes 12 40
(Richard Hannon) *chsd ldrs: wnt 2nd over 5f out: led jst over 3f out: sn rdn and hdd over 2f out: wknd and wl btn whn eased over 1f out: virtually p.u ins fnl f: t.o* **7/2**[1]

0110 **13** *16* **Good Boy Jackson**[26] 3623 3-9-1 **83** .... PhillipMakin 9 —
(Kevin Ryan) *sn bustled up to chse ldr: led 1/2-way: rdn and hdd over 3f out: dropped out qckly over 2f out: wl bhd and virtually p.u fr over 1f out: t.o* **11/1**

2m 25.62s (-0.88) **Going Correction** -0.10s/f (Good) **13** Ran SP% **123.1**
Speed ratings (Par 104): **99,98,96,93,92 91,90,83,79,78 77,74,63**
toteswingers:1&2:£11.00, 1&3:£12.60, 2&3:£19.40. Tote Super 7: Win: Not won Place: £316.70 CSF £53.56 CT £1091.43 TOTE £4.90: £2.00, £3.40, £4.00; EX 68.60 Trifecta £907.80 Pool: £3,079.36 - 2.51 winning units..
Owner Athos Christodoulou **Bred** A Christodoulou **Trained** Newmarket, Suffolk
■ Stewards' Enquiry : Chris Catlin three-day ban: careless riding (Aug 11-13)

FOCUS
An open handicap in which the early pace was fair. The front three drew a little way on from the remainder, who finished well strung out. There are reasons to be positive about the form.

NOTEBOOK
Kinyras(IRE), no match for the previous day's handicap winner Whiplash Willie at Salisbury on his most recent outing (wore first-time visor), refused to go into the stalls at Ripon earlier this month, but had no trouble on this occasion, and seemed happier without the headgear. He looked vulnerable when the placed runners came to challenge, but found plenty when the runner-up drew level, just shading it in a tight finish. He should remain capable of being competitive in good handicaps after a rise. (op 9-2 tchd 5-1 in a place)
Aldwick Bay(IRE) travelled smoothly into contention, but his forward momentum couldn't carry him past Kinyras, who ultimately nailed him on the line. He's progressing and may prove best at 1m2f. (op 10-1)
Amistress had the run of things when winning at Lingfield, but she showed herself versatile by running a good race under contrasting tactics, making good headway wide and drawing on from the fourth. (op 16-1)
Orthodox Lad, trying this trip for the first time, was unlucky not to finish a good bit closer, losing ground at the start and meeting trouble when trying to close. He remains capable of better. (op 14-1)
Art History(IRE) didn't receive the best of rides, being stuck out wide, and he deserves a chance to show himself better than this bare form. Official explanation: jockey said, regarding riding & dropping hands shortly before line, that if he continued riding he would have caught the heels of Dimension, placed second (op 8-1 tchd 13-2)
Mica Mika(IRE) is a tough sort who's found it tougher going of late. He remains 13lb above his last winning mark.
Parvana(IRE) found this tougher than the fillies' handicap she dominated off 6lb lower at Pontefract last time. (op 6-1 tchd 9-1)
Goldenveil(IRE) was soon beaten having been squeezed up on the rail. (op 14-1)
Reflect(IRE), for the second time in two runs, turned in a shocking effort, dropping right out to finish last. This clearly wasn't his true form. (op 6-1 tchd 7-1 in places)
T/Jkpt: £39,054.40 to a £1 stake. Pool:£55,006.21 - 1.00 winning ticket. T/Plt: £761.40 to a £1 stake. Pool:£291,455.50 - 279.43 winning tickets T/Qpdt: £124.80 to a £1 stake. Pool:£12,328.35 - 73.09 winning tickets SP

4067 NOTTINGHAM (L-H)
Thursday, July 28

OFFICIAL GOING: Good to firm (firm in places on round course; 8.4)
Wind: Virtually nil Weather: Fine and dry

4474 EBF EXCLUSIVE NETWORKS - EXCLUSIVE-NETWORKS.CO.UK MAIDEN FILLIES' STKS 6f 15y
2:35 (2:37) (Class 5) 2-Y-O **£3,234** (£962; £481; £240) **Stalls** Centre

Form RPR

1 **Pussycat Dream** 2-9-0 0 .... RichardMullen 6 78+
(Ed McMahon) *trckd ldrs: hdwy over 2f out: swtchd lft and rdn to chse ldr over 1f out: rdn to chal enterring fnl f: kpt on to ld last 100yds* **11/2**[3]

42 **2** *¾* **Al Mahmeyah**[22] 3736 2-9-0 0 .... PatCosgrave 7 76
(Richard Hannon) *cl up: led over 3f out: rdn wl over 1f out: jnd and drvn ent fnl f: hdd and no ex last 100yds* **8/13**[1]

503 **3** *8* **Ave Sofia**[14] 4021 2-9-0 0 .... StevieDonohoe 8 50
(John Holt) *led: hdd over 3f out: sn rdn along and outpcd over 2f out: kpt on u.p fnl f* **20/1**

0 **4** *1 ¾* **Love Tale**[17] 3915 2-9-0 0 .... PJMcDonald 4 45
(Mark Rimell) *cl up: chsd ldr wl over 2f out: sn rdn and edgd lft wl over 1f out: grad wknd* **66/1**

5 *1 ¾* **Ashbina** 2-9-0 0 .... LiamJones 5 39
(William Haggas) *dwlt: in tch: green and pushed along after 2f: sme hdwy 1/2-way: rdn wl over 2f out and sn no imp* **9/2**[2]

5 **6** *1 ½* **Pitti Sing**[17] 3899 2-9-0 0 .... TonyHamilton 3 34
(Richard Fahey) *towards rr: pushed along and outpcd 1/2-way: kpt on fnl f* **12/1**

7 *13* **Four Poorer (IRE)** 2-8-11 0 .... SophieDoyle(3) 2 —
(Jamie Osborne) *dwlt: a in rr: outpcd and bhd fr 1/2-way* **25/1**

1m 14.21s (-0.69) **Going Correction** 0.0s/f (Good) **7** Ran SP% **113.3**
Speed ratings (Par 91): **104,103,92,90,87 85,68**
toteswingers:1&2:£1.90, 1&3:£6.70, 2&3:£4.20 CSF £9.17 TOTE £5.10: £2.10, £1.30; EX 8.50.
Owner J C Fretwell **Bred** Bloomsbury Stud **Trained** Lichfield, Staffs

FOCUS
All races on Outer course. Stands bend out 2m, bottom bend out 8m adding 27yds to 8f and 10f races and 34yds to 2m race. Watered ground and the going was given as good to firm, firm in places on the round course. Two came clear in this maiden and the winner could be rated up to 8lb higher.

NOTEBOOK
Pussycat Dream put up a decent performance to get the better of the more experienced Al Mahmeyah. Blanketed for stalls entry, she sat in behind the pace and was being pushed along before halfway, but she responded to pressure and stayed on well to take the favourite's measure inside the last. Another furlong looks likely to suit her in time. (op 3-1)
Al Mahmeyah had the benefit of previous experience and set the standard on her second last time out. She may have bumped into a useful newcomer as she finished well clear of the rest. (op 10-11)
Ave Sofia, only third in a seller last time out, showed speed, but she had the rail to help and may have been slightly flattered. (op 14-1)
Love Tale, well held on debut, raced further away from the rail, which may have been a disadvantage, and lost out in the battle for third with Ave Sofia. (op 100-1 tchd 50-1)
Ashbina, a 72,000gns daughter of Royal Applause, was slowly away and ran green. She clearly needed this experience-wise and should come on for it. (op 13-2 tchd 7-1)

4475 TRAFFIC SHAPING - WAN OPTIMISATION BY EXINDA H'CAP 5f 13y
3:05 (3:05) (Class 5) (0-75,75) 3-Y-O+ **£2,264** (£673; £336; £168) **Stalls** Centre

Form RPR

0002 **1** **Go Nani Go**[21] 3759 5-9-9 **72** .... PatCosgrave 1 79
(Ed de Giles) *trckd ldrs: smooth hdwy 2f out: swtchd lft and rdn to ld appr fnl f: kpt on wl* **9/4**[2]

4401 **2** *1* **Grudge**[31] 3471 6-9-5 **68** ....(b) HayleyTurner 6 71
(Conor Dore) *led 1f: cl up tl led again wl over 1f out: rdn and hdd appr fnl f: sn drvn and edgd lft: kpt on* **15/2**

2106 **3** *shd* **Straboe (USA)**[44] 3015 5-8-7 **56** oh3........(v) WilliamCarson 8 59
(Stuart Williams) *trckd ldrs on inner: effrt 2f out: nt clr run over 1f out: rdn and kpt on wl fnl f* **4/1**[3]

-040 **4** *2* **Bertie Southstreet**[10] 4152 8-9-6 **69** ....(v) MickyFenton 5 64
(Paul Midgley) *cl up: rdn along 2f out: drvn and ev ch over 1f out: kpt on same pce* **9/1**

1512 **5** *5* **Baby Queen (IRE)**[14] 3994 5-9-12 **75** .... J-PGuillambert 4 52
(Brian Baugh) *bmpd and awkward s: sn cl up: led after 1 1/2f: rdn along 2f out: sn hdd & wknd over 1f out* **7/4**[1]

040/ **6** *11* **Diademas (USA)**[1009] 6907 6-8-2 **58** oh9 ow2........ DavidKenny(7) 3 —
(Conor Dore) *a in rr: rdn along 1/2-way: sn outpcd* **40/1**

60.58 secs (-0.42) **Going Correction** 0.0s/f (Good) **6** Ran SP% **111.3**
Speed ratings (Par 103): **103,101,101,98,90 72**
toteswingers:1&2:£2.00, 1&3:£2.20, 2&3:£3.00 CSF £18.51 CT £60.67 TOTE £3.00: £1.70, £2.40; EX 23.20.
Owner T Gould **Bred** D J And Mrs Deer **Trained** Ledbury, Herefordshire

FOCUS
An ordinary sprint and once again they came up the stands' side. The winner is only rated in line with this year's form.
Baby Queen(IRE) Official explanation: trainer said, regarding running, that the mare became upset in the preliminaries.

4476 FORTINET - REAL TIME NETWORK PROTECTION H'CAP 2m 9y
3:30 (3:30) (Class 6) (0-65,65) 3-Y-O **£1,681** (£500; £250; £125) **Stalls** Low

Form RPR

615 **1** **Final Liberation (FR)**[29] 3518 3-9-4 **62** .... StevieDonohoe 5 81+
(Sir Mark Prescott Bt) *mde all: qcknd 5f out: rdn and qcknd clr 4f out: styd on strly fnl 2f: unchal* **3/1**[2]

2 *7* **Kie (IRE)**[78] 3-8-2 **46** oh1........(t) AndreaAtzeni 2 55
(Frank Sheridan) *hld up towards rr: hdwy over 5f out: effrt to chse wnr wl over 3f out and sn rdn: drvn 2f out and sn no imp* **12/1**

013 **3** *11* **Tidal Run**[27] 3587 3-9-4 **65** .... MartinHarley(3) 1 60+
(Mick Channon) *hld up and bhd: gd hdwy over 4f out: chsd ldng pair over 3f out and sn rdn: drvn 2f out and no imp* **5/2**[1]

3034 **4** *13* **C P Joe (IRE)**[27] 3587 3-9-3 **61** .... PatCosgrave 9 41
(Paul Green) *midfield: hdwy 5f out: rdn to chse ldrs over 3f out: sn drvn and plugged on same pce* **6/1**[3]

4032 **5** *1 ¾* **Revolutionary**[9] 4181 3-8-10 **57** .... SophieDoyle(3) 7 35
(Jamie Osborne) *cl up: pushed along 5f out: rdn 4f out: sn outpcd* **6/1**[3]

0-63 **6** *19* **If What And Maybe**[9] 4181 3-8-9 **56** ow1........ MichaelO'Connell(3) 8 11
(John Ryan) *midfield: rdn along 5f out: drvn 4f out and sn outpcd* **25/1**

5045 **7** *nk* **Geminus (IRE)**[10] 4151 3-8-12 **56** ....(b[1]) TonyHamilton 6 11
(Jedd O'Keeffe) *chsd ldrs: rdn along over 5f out: sn wknd* **16/1**

2306 **8** *4 ½* **Fleeting Storm**[36] 3268 3-9-0 **58** ....(b) HayleyTurner 4 —
(Hughie Morrison) *chsd ldng pair: rdn along over 6f out: drvn over 4f out: sn outpcd* **8/1**

1500 **9** *34* **Blue Cossack (IRE)**[47] 2904 3-9-2 **60** .... RobertHavlin 3 —
(Mark Usher) *s.i.s: a in rr: bhd 4f out: t.o and eased fnl 3f* **25/1**

3m 32.04s (1.74) **Going Correction** 0.0s/f (Good) **9** Ran SP% **114.5**
Speed ratings (Par 98): **95,91,86,79,78 69,68,66,49**
toteswingers:1&2:£8.50, 1&3:£2.50, 2&3:£8.40 CSF £38.30 CT £100.08 TOTE £3.10: £1.40, £3.60, £1.60; EX 45.70.
Owner P Bamford **Bred** R & E Bamford Limited **Trained** Newmarket, Suffolk

FOCUS
A modest staying event on paper, but it produced an empathic winner. He made all, like two of the other three winners on the round course. It's hard to know exactly what he achieved, but he rates a clear personal best.

4477 COMPLETE DATA SECURITY FROM IMPERVA H'CAP 1m 2f 50y
4:05 (4:05) (Class 4) (0-85,85) 3-Y-O+ **£4,075** (£1,212; £606; £303) **Stalls** Low

Form RPR

-311 **1** **Set To Music (IRE)**[26] 3642 3-9-4 **85** .... HayleyTurner 5 96+
(Michael Bell) *trckd ldr: effrt over 2f out and sn pushed along: rdn wl over 1f out: styd on to chal ins fnl f: led last 75yds* **13/8**[1]

6102 **2** *1 1/2* **Destiny Blue (IRE)**[16] 3959 4-9-9 **80**................................ PatCosgrave 4 88
(Jamie Osborne) *sn led: qcknd clr 3f out: rdn wl over 1f out: drvn ent fnl f: hdd and no ex last 75yds* **11/2**[3]

-000 **3** *4* **Chilly Filly (IRE)**[19] 3867 5-9-10 **81**................................ FrederikTylicki 7 81
(James Given) *trckd ldng pair: effrt 3f out: rdn over 2f out: drvn and no imp fr wl over 1f out* **8/1**

1551 **4** *3* **Gala Casino Star (IRE)**[40] 3170 6-9-2 **76**...................... LeeTopliss(3) 1 70
(Richard Fahey) *trckd ldrs on inner: hdwy 4f out: rdn to chse ldng pair 3f out: drvn over 2f out and kpt on same pce* **7/1**

-006 **5** *8* **Jo'Burg (USA)**[14] 4004 7-9-11 **82**................................ TonyHamilton 2 60
(Ollie Pears) *v.s.a: towards rr: effrt 4f out: rdn along over 3f out: swtchd rt over 2f out: n.d* **11/1**

6522 **6** *nk* **Standpoint**[14] 4004 5-9-4 **78**................................ PaulPickard(3) 8 55
(Reg Hollinshead) *hld up: hdwy 1/2-way: effrt to chse ldrs 3f out: rdn over 2f out: sn drvn and btn* **4/1**[2]

-612 **7** *4* **Burns Night**[35] 3319 5-9-5 **76**................................ DuranFentiman 9 45
(Geoffrey Harker) *hld up and bhd: pushed along over 3f out: nvr a factor* **12/1**

3000 **8** *5* **Sharakti (IRE)**[12] 4109 4-8-11 **71**................................ DeclanCannon(3) 6 30
(Alan McCabe) *chsd ldrs: pushed along 1/2-way: rdn 4f out: drvn wl over 2f out and sn wknd* **25/1**

2m 10.82s (-0.88) **Going Correction** 0.0s/f (Good)
WFA 3 from 4yo+ 10lb **8** Ran SP% **117.0**
Speed ratings (Par 105): **103,101,98,96,89 89,86,82**
toteswingers:1&2:£3.40, 1&3:£3.80, 2&3:£7.80 CSF £11.24 CT £56.19 TOTE £2.50: £1.30, £1.20, £2.60; EX 9.50.
Owner The Queen **Bred** His Highness The Aga Khan's Studs S C **Trained** Newmarket, Suffolk

FOCUS
Few got into this fair handicap and the first pair were always 1-2. The winner more than confirmed her latest wide-margin win.
Standpoint Official explanation: trainer had no explanation for the poor form shown
Burns Night Official explanation: jockey said gelding never travelled

4478 SAFENET - LEADERS IN ENTERPRISE DATA PROTECTION MEDIAN AUCTION MAIDEN STKS 1m 75y
4:40 (4:41) (Class 6) 3-4-Y-O **£1,681** (£500; £250; £125) **Stalls** Centre

Form RPR
6-F **1** **Mrs Dee Bee (IRE)**[38] 3232 3-8-12 0................................ WilliamCarson 4 76
(B W Hills) *mde all: rdn along 2f out: styd on strly fnl f* **5/1**[3]

6220 **2** *1 3/4* **Ferruccio (IRE)**[16] 3959 3-9-3 70................................ HayleyTurner 9 77
(James Fanshawe) *trckd ldng pair: hdwy and cl up 3f out: rdn to chse wnr 2f out: drvn ent fnl f: no imp towards fin* **4/1**[2]

3 *5* **Double Trouble** 3-8-12 0................................ AndreaAtzeni 2 61
(Marco Botti) *midfield: hdwy 3f out: rdn over 2f out: kpt on same pce u.p fr wl over 1f out* **10/1**

0625 **4** *1 1/2* **Brick Dust (IRE)**[21] 3781 3-9-3 75................................ J-PGuillambert 3 62
(Luca Cumani) *t.k.h: trckd ldrs on inner: pushed along over 2f out: rdn wl over 1f out: swtchd rt and drvn appr fnl f: one pce* **4/1**[2]

6 **5** *nk* **Anrheg**[27] 3594 3-8-12 0................................ FrederikTylicki 5 56
(David Brown) *chsd wnr: rdn along 2f out: sn drvn and grad wknd* **25/1**

40 **6** *4 1/2* **Knowe Head (NZ)**[14] 4023 4-9-11 0................................ PatCosgrave 8 53+
(James Unett) *hld up in rr: hdwy 3f out: rdn to chse ldrs 2f out: sn no imp* **100/1**

5202 **7** *5* **Beechcraft Baron (IRE)**[15] 3977 3-9-0 65................. GilmarPereira(3) 7 40
(William Haggas) *t.k.h: chsd ldrs: rdn along wl over 2f out: drvn wl over 1f out and sn wknd* **11/1**

06 **8** *15* **Tigerbill**[38] 3236 3-9-3 0................................ RussKennemore 6 —
(Nicky Vaughan) *dwlt: a in rr* **100/1**

5 **9** *1 1/4* **Maloof**[28] 3543 3-9-3 0................................ TadhgO'Shea 1 —
(Roger Varian) *dwlt and towards rr: effrt and sme hdwy wl over 3f out: sn rdn and nvr a factor* **13/8**[1]

6 **10** *1 1/2* **Nubian Gem (IRE)**[179] 360 3-8-9 0...................... AdamBeschizza(3) 10 —
(John Best) *dwlt and towards rr: effrt 4f out: rdn 3f out: sn hung lft and bhd* **66/1**

1m 47.98s (2.38) **Going Correction** 0.0s/f (Good)
WFA 3 from 4yo 8lb **10** Ran SP% **119.5**
Speed ratings (Par [illegible]): [illegible]
toteswingers:1&2:£4.60, 1&3:£7.30, 2&3:£7.80 CSF £25.78 TOTE £6.50: £1.90, £2.00, £3.10, EX 26.90.
Owner South Bank Thoroughbred Racing **Bred** M Fahy **Trained** Lambourn, Berks

FOCUS
A modest maiden with the favourite disappointing. The early gallop was ordinary and once again it paid to be up with the pace.
Maloof Official explanation: jockey said colt never travelled

4479 VALUE DISTRIBUTION FROM EXCLUSIVE NETWORKS H'CAP 1m 75y
5:15 (5:15) (Class 5) (0-75,75) 3-Y-0+ **£2,264** (£673; £336; £168) **Stalls** Centre

Form RPR
0230 **1** **Labore**[28] 3557 3-9-0 **71**................................(b[1]) AndreaAtzeni 5 79
(Marco Botti) *mde all: pushed along 3f out: rdn clr 2f out: kpt on fnl f* **9/2**[2]

-305 **2** *3/4* **Gallant Eagle (IRE)**[34] 3354 4-9-5 **71**................................ MartinHarley(3) 2 78
(Ed de Giles) *trckd ldrs: hdwy 3f out: rdn over 2f out: drvn to chse wnr ins fnl f: kpt on wl u.p towards fin* **9/2**[2]

6202 **3** *1* **Satwa Dream (IRE)**[17] 3925 4-9-12 **75**...................... RoystonFfrench 8 80
(Ed Dunlop) *prom: trckd wnr after 2f: rdn along over 2f out: drvn and one pce appr fnl f* **11/2**[3]

1600 **4** *3 3/4* **She Ain't A Saint**[20] 3825 3-9-4 **75**................................ PatCosgrave 3 69+
(Jane Chapple-Hyam) *hld up towards rr: hdwy on inner wl over 2f out: sn rdn and kpt on u.p appr fnl f* **13/2**

6146 **5** *3* **Sergeant Troy (IRE)**[20] 3815 3-9-1 **72**......................(v[1]) RichardMullen 1 59
(Roger Charlton) *hld up in tch: hdwy 4f out: chsd ldrs 3f out: sn rdn: edgd lft and btn* **9/4**[1]

5000 **6** *7* **Tuxedo**[7] 4255 6-9-7 **70**................................ MickyFenton 7 43
(Peter Hiatt) *a in rr* **33/1**

6225 **7** *8* **Symphonic Dancer (USA)**[122] 1017 4-9-7 **70**................................ J-PGuillambert 6 25
(Brian Baugh) *in tch: effrt over 3f out: sn rdn along and wknd wl over 2f out* **10/1**

2336 **8** *3/4* **Cape Melody**[114] 1147 5-9-11 **74**................................ HayleyTurner 4 27
(George Baker) *chsd ldrs: rdn along 3f out: wknd over 2f out* **16/1**

1m 47.84s (2.24) **Going Correction** 0.0s/f (Good)
WFA 3 from 4yo+ 8lb **8** Ran SP% **113.8**
Speed ratings (Par 103): **88,87,86,82,79 72,64,63**
CSF £24.75 CT £113.14 TOTE £4.80: £1.30, £1.80, £1.70; EX 26.30.
Owner Lok Ho Ting **Bred** Brook Stud Bloodstock Ltd **Trained** Newmarket, Suffolk

FOCUS
Yet another winner who made every yard. He's rated back to his May Redcar form.

T/Plt: £60.20 to a £1 stake. Pool:£44,452.60 - 538.96 winning tickets T/Qpdt: £14.50 to a £1 stake. Pool:£2,191.39 - 111.70 winning tickets JR

4480 - 4482a & 4484a (Foreign Racing) - See Raceform Interactive

OVREVOLL (R-H)
Thursday, July 28

OFFICIAL GOING: Turf: good

4483a POLAR CUP (GROUP 3) (3YO+) (TURF) 6f 187y
7:20 (12:00) 3-Y-0+ **£33,039** (£11,013; £5,506; £3,303; £2,202)

RPR
1 **Giant Sandman (IRE)**[76] 4-9-4 0................................ RafaelSchistl 6 —
(Rune Haugen, Norway) *hld up in midfield: rdn and hdwy 2f out: r.o wl to ld 150yds out: comf* **99/10**

2 *1* **Exhibition (IRE)**[58] 6-9-4 0................................ ManuelMartinez 1 —
(Francisco Castro, Sweden) *led: clr 1/2-way: hrd rdn 2f out: hdd 150yds out: no ex fnl 100yds* **26/1**

3 *hd* **Silverside (USA)**[39] 5-9-4 0................................ JulienGrosjean 3 —
(F Sanchez, France) *chsd ldrs in 3rd: ev ch 2f out: kpt on wl* **7/1**[2]

4 *2 1/2* **Entangle**[42] 5-9-1 0................................ JacobJohansen 5 —
(Arnfinn Lund, Norway) *hld up in midfield: c wd fnl bnd: sn hrd rdn: unable qck* **1/2**[1]

5 *2 1/2* **Elusive Time (IRE)**[42] 3-8-11 0................................ ElioneChaves 8 —
(Francisco Castro, Sweden) *chsd ldr: effrt 3f out: u.p fr 2f out and no imp: no ex ins fnl f* **204/10**

6 *1* **Hansinger (IRE)**[35] 6-9-4 0................................ EspenSki 7 —
(Cathrine Erichsen, Norway) *settled towards rr: rdn 2f out: nt qckn: fdd fnl f* **92/10**

7 *1/2* **Emil (DEN)**[40] 7-9-4 0................................(b) MarcStott 2 —
(Ole Larsen, Sweden) *a bhd: nvr in contention* **31/1**

8 *6* **Heureux (USA)**[21] 8-9-4 0................................ FernandoDiaz 9 —
(Jens Erik Lindstol, Norway) *hld up towards rr: swtchd outside 2f out: no imp u.p: wknd and eased fnl f* **114/10**

9 *1/2* **Alyshakeys (DEN)**[35] 4-9-5 0................................ CarlosLopez 10 —
(Wido Neuroth, Norway) *racd in midfield: sme hdwy 3f out: sn rdn and nt qckn: wknd fnl 1 1/2f* **81/10**[3]

1m 20.6s (80.60)
WFA 3 from 4yo+ 7lb **9** Ran SP% **128.7**
PARI-MUTUEL (all including 1krone stakes): WIN 10.90; PLACE 3.55, 8.01, 3.91; DF 237.36.
Owner Sandman Stables **Bred** Barronstown Stud **Trained** Norway

4224 BATH (L-H)
Friday, July 29

OFFICIAL GOING: Good to firm
Wind: Nil

4485 GAYMERS MAIDEN AUCTION STKS 5f 161y
5:05 (5:05) (Class 5) 2-Y-0 **£2,587** (£770; £384; £192) **Stalls** Centre

Form RPR
2U **1** **Uncle Roger (IRE)**[8] 4229 2-8-9 0................................ CathyGannon 6 67+
(Eve Johnson Houghton) *trckd ldr: slt advantage appr fnl f but hrd pressed and u.p: hld on all out* **10/11**[1]

4 **2** *nse* **Key Addition (IRE)**[8] 4250 2-8-11 0................................ SebSanders 1 69
(William Muir) *chsd ldrs: str chal appr fnl f and styd upsides tl jst hld last stride* **8/1**[3]

50 **3** *2* **Our Cool Cat (IRE)**[21] 3816 2-8-9 0.........................(b) FergusSweeney 5 60
(Gary Moore) *bmpd s and s.i.s: sn rcvrd to chse ldrs: rdn to chal on outer over 1f out: one pce ins fnl f* **25/1**

05 **4** *2* **Emerald Smile (IRE)**[4] 4386 2-8-6 0................................ RyanPowell(5) 2 56
(J S Moore) *led tl hdd over 1f out: wknd ins fnl f* **8/1**[3]

050 **5** *6* **Gadreel (IRE)**[9] 4201 2-8-9 0................................ DaneO'Neill 3 34
[illegible] **4/1**[2]

6 *1 3/4* **Trending (IRE)** 2-9-2 0................................ MartinLane 4 [illegible]
(Jeremy Gask) *wnt rt s: s.i.s: and green: pushed along 3f out and in tch: wknd ins fnl 2f* **8/1**[3]

1m 10.8s (-0.40) **Going Correction** -0.25s/f (Firm) **6** Ran SP% **109.6**
Speed ratings (Par 94): **92,91,89,86,78 76**
toteswingers:1&2:£1.70, 2&3:£8.40, 1&3:£4.40 CSF £8.44 TOTE £1.40: £1.10, £3.10; EX 5.50.
Owner Mrs J E O'Halloran **Bred** Mrs J O'Halloran **Trained** Blewbury, Oxon

FOCUS
After a dry day the going was changed to good to firm. The odds-on favourite just held on in this maiden auction. The time was modest and the form is rated slightly negatively.

NOTEBOOK
Uncle Roger(IRE) was well on the way to fulfilling his Brighton debut promise when jinking and unseating his rider in the final furlong over this C&D last week. He stayed focussed this time but had to work really hard to prevail in the dying strides. The form looks ordinary, but he has made a decent start to his career, particularly as he was retained for just 800 euros as a yearling. (tchd 5-6 tchd evens in a place)
Key Addition(IRE) was too green to do himself justice when fourth of five on Sandown debut last week, but he looked more clued up this time and was just denied in an exciting finish. Closely related to 7f-1m1f winner Retirement, he should continue to get better with time and distance. (op 15-2)
Our Cool Cat(IRE) was well beaten at 25-1 in a seller last time on his second run. He did a lot better dropped in trip and switched to fast ground but his proximity casts a shadow over the form.
Emerald Smile(IRE) set the pace before being overhauled turning in. She has found only marginal improvement in three starts but could do better when aimed at nurseries. (op 17-2 tchd 9-1)
Gadreel(IRE) looked a non-stayer over 7f last week but he could out quickly again dropped back in trip. (op 9-2)

4486 ADDLESTONES H'CAP 5f 161y
5:35 (5:35) (Class 5) (0-75,75) 3-Y-0 **£2,587** (£770; £384; £192) **Stalls** Centre

Form RPR
5311 **1** **Dreams Of Glory**[8] 4227 3-8-2 **59** 6ex.......................... SimonPearce(3) 4 66
(Ron Hodges) *trckd ldr: led over 2f out: rdn fnl f: styd on wl fnl 100yds* **7/2**[2]

0551 **2** *3/4* **Delira (IRE)**[28] 3597 3-8-12 **66**................................ StephenCraine 6 71
(Jonathan Portman) *in rr: rdn along 3f out: hdwy over 1f out: styd on to chse wnr ins fnl f but no imp fnl 100yds* **16/1**

2212 **3** *hd* **Sarangoo**[8] 4227 3-8-8 **62** ow2................................ DaneO'Neill 10 66
(Malcolm Saunders) *in rr and racd on outside: hdwy over 2f out: styd on u.p fnl f to cl on 2nd nr fin but no imp on wnr* **15/8**[1]

3416 **4** *1* **Indian Shuffle (IRE)**[15] 3995 3-9-4 **72**.............................. SebSanders 8 73
(Jonathan Portman) *in tch: drvn to chal over 1f out: chsd wnr ins fnl f but no imp: one pce into 4th clsng stages* **10/1**

-005 **5** *2* **Forty Proof (IRE)**[16] 3975 3-9-7 **75**..................................(p) MartinLane 3 69
(William Knight) *chsd ldrs: drvn to chal 2f out: wknd ins fnl f* **12/1**

0-65 **6** *1* **Simpulse**[18] 3909 3-8-2 **56** oh6.................................. FrankieMcDonald 9 47
(Norma Twomey) *in rr: hdwy on outside over 2f out: nvr gng pce to rch ldrs: mod prog clsng stages* **40/1**

6625 **7** *1 ¼* **Mister Ben Vereen**[22] 3783 3-8-7 **61**..........................(p) CathyGannon 2 48
(Eve Johnson Houghton) *chsd ldrs: rdn over 2f out: wknd over 1f out* **7/1**

3124 **8** *2 ¾* **Juarla (IRE)**[8] 4227 3-8-13 **67**...................................... TomMcLaughlin 5 45
(Ronald Harris) *chsd ldrs: ev ch 2f out: wknd u.p sn after* **14/1**

1632 **9** *shd* **Shes Rosie**[27] 3630 3-9-3 **71**...................................... RussKennemore 1 48
(John O'Shea) *led on rail tl hdd over 2f out: sn btn* **6/1**[3]

1m 10.23s (-0.97) **Going Correction** -0.25s/f (Firm) 9 Ran SP% **115.6**
Speed ratings (Par 100): **96,95,94,93,90 89,87,84,83**
toteswingers:1&2:£18.60, 2&3:£9.20, 1&3:£1.50 CSF £57.31 CT £135.11 TOTE £4.60: £1.10, £5.40, £1.60; EX 44.80.
Owner P E Axon **Bred** P E Axon **Trained** Charlton Mackrell, Somerset
■ Stewards' Enquiry : Dane O'Neill one-day ban: used whip with excessive frequency (12 Aug)

FOCUS
A competitive handicap in which an improving front-runner made it three wins in a row. Straightforward form.

4487 IMPERIAL WINDOWS H'CAP 5f 11y
6:10 (6:10) (Class 6) (0-60,60) 4-Y-O+ **£2,587** (£770; £384; £192) **Stalls** Centre

Form RPR

0216 **1** **My Meteor**[8] 4230 4-9-0 **53**... DaneO'Neill 9 65
(Tony Newcombe) *in rr: hdwy on outside fr 2f out: drvn and qcknd fnl f to ld fnl 120yds: readily* **3/1**[1]

3300 **2** *1* **Spic 'n Span**[10] 4182 6-8-11 **50**..............................(b) CathyGannon 8 58
(Ronald Harris) *trckd ldrs: led over 3f out: travelling wl 2f out: rdn over 1f out: hdd and outpcd fnl 120yds* **8/1**[3]

0-00 **3** *½* **Charlie Delta**[61] 1828 8-9-2 **55**...............................(b) RussKennemore 4 61
(John O'Shea) *s.i.s: in rr: hdwy over 1f out: styd on u.p fnl f to take 3rd clsng stages but no imp on ldng duo* **33/1**

6502 **4** *nk* **The Name Is Frank**[8] 4224 6-9-7 **60**.........................(t) FergusSweeney 6 65
(Mark Gillard) *chsd ldrs: rdn 1/2-way: styd on to dispute 3rd ins fnl f: one pce into 4th clsng stages* **3/1**[1]

4422 **5** *2 ¼* **Miss Firefly**[8] 4230 6-8-13 **55**..................................(p) SimonPearce(3) 3 52
(Ron Hodges) *in rr but in tch: hdwy fr 2f out: rdn and no imp on ldrs over 1f out: wknd ins fnl f* **10/3**[2]

0000 **6** *4 ½* **Best One**[7] 4272 7-8-10 **49**......................................(b) TomMcLaughlin 7 30
(Ronald Harris) *chsd ldrs: rdn 1/2-way wknd wl over 1f out* **20/1**

530 **7** *1* **Lithaam (IRE)**[23] 3721 7-8-7 **46**......................................(tp) ChrisCatlin 2 23
(Milton Bradley) *in tch tl rdn and btn over 2f out* **18/1**

3400 **8** *1 ¾* **Charlietoo**[24] 3714 5-8-7 **49**...(p) KierenFox(3) 10 20
(Edward Bevan) *a outpcd* **8/1**[3]

0340 **9** *3 ¾* **What Katie Did (IRE)**[8] 4230 6-8-7 **46**............................(p) MartinLane 5 —
(Milton Bradley) *drvn to ld: hdd over 3f out: wknd u.p over 2f out* **10/1**

61.10 secs (-1.40) **Going Correction** -0.25s/f (Firm) 9 Ran SP% **117.4**
Speed ratings (Par 101): **101,99,98,98,94 87,85,82,76**
toteswingers:1&2:£5.40, 2&3:£26.80, 1&3:£20.90 CSF £28.24 CT £668.86 TOTE £4.10: £1.70, £2.70, £7.80; EX 32.20.
Owner A G Newcombe **Bred** M P B Bloodstock Ltd **Trained** Yarnscombe, Devon

FOCUS
A minor handicap run at a decent pace. The first five were clear of the rest. A reworking of a couple of similar races here, with a length personal best from the winner.

4488 BLACKBERRY BOLT H'CAP 2m 1f 34y
6:45 (6:45) (Class 5) (0-70,70) 4-Y-O+ **£2,587** (£770; £384; £192) **Stalls** Centre

Form RPR

20-1 **1** **Lastroseofsummer (IRE)**[28] 3599 5-9-7 **70**....................... MartinLane 2 79+
(Rae Guest) *mde all: rdn and qcknd over 3f out: styd on strly u.p fr over 2f out: in command fr over 1f out: unchal* **1/1**[1]

00 **2** *3 ¼* **Epsom Salts**[43] 3095 6-9-4 **67**...................................... FergusSweeney 1 72
(Pat Phelan) *trckd ldrs in 3rd: drvn to chse wnr 3f out: no imp u.p fnl 2f: wl hld fnl f* **6/1**[3]

1264 **3** *8* **Rosewood Lad**[30] 3522 4-9-5 **68**..................................(b) CathyGannon 4 63
(J S Moore) *chsd wnr: rdn 4f out: dropped to 3rd 3f out and sn no ch* **5/2**[2]

0-34 **4** *4* **Gremlin**[21] 3799 7-9-1 **67**.. KierenFox(3) 3 58
(Bernard Llewellyn) *plld hrd: chsd ldrs in cl 4th tl rdn and wknd over 3f out* **7/1**

54-5 **5** *7* **Poppy Gregg**[19] 3281 6-7-13 **51** oh6.............................(v) AmyBaker(3) 5 33
(Dr Jeremy Naylor) *a in last pl but in tch tl wknd qckly over 3f out* **20/1**

3m 51.32s (-0.58) **Going Correction** -0.20s/f (Firm) 5 Ran SP% **110.1**
Speed ratings (Par 103): **93,91,87,85,82**
CSF £7.55 TOTE £2.00: £1.20, £2.20; EX 9.10.
Owner E P Duggan **Bred** Mount Coote Stud **Trained** Newmarket, Suffolk

FOCUS
A small-field staying handicap. Most of the runners had something to prove but the favourite put in a strong galloping display to deliver in decent style. This was a career best.

4489 ASSET PROPERTY BROKERS H'CAP 1m 2f 46y
7:20 (7:21) (Class 4) (0-80,78) 3-Y-O **£4,851** (£1,443; £721; £360) **Stalls** Low

Form RPR

1255 **1** **Area Fifty One**[27] 3650 3-8-10 **72**.............................. JamesRogers(5) 8 84
(William Muir) *led: styd wd down bk st: hdd over 4f out: styd trcking ldr: led again appr fnl 2f: rdn over 1f out: styd on strly to go clr ins fnl f* **2/1**[1]

0424 **2** *4* **Mr Perceptive (IRE)**[16] 3988 3-9-3 **77**............................ SeanLevey(3) 6 81
(Richard Hannon) *in rr: hdwy on outside 3f out: chsd wnr fr 2f out and sn rdn: no imp over 1f out and readily outpcd fnl f* **7/2**[2]

0500 **3** *2 ¼* **Stentorian (IRE)**[13] 4103 3-9-7 **78**.............................. SilvestreDeSousa 1 78
(Mark Johnston) *sn chsng ldr: dropped bk to cl 3rd over 4f out: styd chsng ldrs and rdn over 3f out: styd on same pce for one pce 3rd fnl 2f* **6/1**

5160 **4** *3 ¾* **Malice Or Mischief (IRE)**[35] 3363 3-9-7 **78**.................... LiamJones 5 70
(Tony Carroll) *unruly stalls: in tch: rdn and sme hdwy 3f out: nvr rchd ldrs and no ch fnl 2f* **25/1**

51-0 **5** *7* **For What (USA)**[27] 3650 3-9-7 **78**..................................... ChrisCatlin 2 56
(David Lanigan) *t.k.h: chsd ldrs: rdn in 3rd 3f out: no imp and wknd over 2f out* **16/1**

5020 **6** *¾* **Circus Star (USA)**[18] 3919 3-8-13 **70**.............................. TadhgO'Shea 4 47
(Brian Meehan) *chsd ldrs: wnt 2nd 6f out: led over 4f out: drvn over 3f out: hdd over 2f out: sn wknd* **11/2**[3]

0550 **7** *7* **Montegonian (USA)**[51] 2819 3-9-3 **74**............................... MartinLane 7 37
(Marcus Tregoning) *plld hrd: in tch: rdn over 3f out: sn btn* **8/1**

5110 **8** *11* **Gud Day (IRE)**[11] 4154 3-8-11 **68**.............................. TomMcLaughlin 3 —
(Ronald Harris) *in rr: rdn over 3f out and sn lost tch* **12/1**

2m 8.34s (-2.66) **Going Correction** -0.20s/f (Firm) 8 Ran SP% **113.8**
Speed ratings (Par 102): **102,98,97,94,88 87,82,73**
toteswingers:1&2:£2.20, 2&3:£6.40, 1&3:£3.70 CSF £8.86 CT £34.18 TOTE £3.70: £1.70, £1.10, £3.00; EX 12.00.
Owner Martin P Graham **Bred** Carmel Stud **Trained** Lambourn, Berks

FOCUS
A fair handicap. The early pace was steady but it increased at halfway. The winner turned round Sandown form with the runner-up.

4490 BRITISH STALLION STUDS E.B.F./BLACKTHORN FILLIES' H'CAP 1m 2f 46y
7:55 (7:59) (Class 4) (0-80,77) 3-Y-O+ **£4,851** (£1,443; £721; £360) **Stalls** Low

Form RPR

4501 **1** **Tenby Lady (USA)**[6] 4344 3-9-10 **77** 6ex........................... SebSanders 3 91+
(Sir Mark Prescott Bt) *t.k.h: hld up in rr: hdwy 3f out: drvn to ld jst ins fnl 2f: pushed clr fnl f* **4/7**[1]

3215 **2** *3 ¼* **Golden Waters**[27] 3641 4-9-13 **70**................................... CathyGannon 4 75
(Eve Johnson Houghton) *chsd ldrs: rdn 3f out: styd on u.p and flashed tail fnl f: tk wl hld 2nd fnl cl home* **8/1**[3]

1534 **3** *1 ¾* **Wishformore (IRE)**[18] 3918 4-9-2 **64**............................ RyanPowell(5) 1 66
(J S Moore) *chsd ldr: t.k.h: rdn 3f out: styd disputing one pce 2nd fr 2f out: dropped to 3rd cl home* **18/1**

1023 **4** *4 ½* **Flying Phoenix**[18] 3918 3-9-0 **67**..........................(p) SilvestreDeSousa 6 60
(Gay Kelleway) *plld hrd and led: 6 l clr over 5f out: hdd 2f out: sn btn* **7/2**[2]

1210 **5** *12* **Cane Cat (IRE)**[39] 3228 4-8-13 **56**...................................(t) LiamJones 5 32
(Tony Carroll) *t.k.h early and stdd in rr: rdn 3f out: sn dropped away* **11/1**

2m 12.07s (1.07) **Going Correction** -0.20s/f (Firm)
WFA 3 from 4yo 10lb 5 Ran SP% **110.6**
Speed ratings (Par 102): **87,84,83,79,69**
CSF £5.97 TOTE £1.60: £1.30, £3.90; EX 8.20.
Owner David F O'Rourke **Bred** O'Rourke's Silver Springs Stud Farm Llc **Trained** Newmarket, Suffolk

FOCUS
A progressive Sir Mark Prescott-trained runner completed a double with plenty in hand in this fillies' handicap which was run at a stop-start gallop. The level of the form is set around the runner-up.

4491 JAMES HAY PARTNERSHIP H'CAP 1m 3f 144y
8:25 (8:26) (Class 6) (0-60,62) 3-Y-O **£1,940** (£577; £288; £144) **Stalls** Low

Form RPR

4521 **1** **Peachez**[8] 4248 3-9-5 **62** 6ex...(p) AmyScott(5) 5 74+
(Alastair Lidderdale) *hld up in rr: hdwy 3f out: str run and hung lft over 2f out: led 1f out: sn edgd lft: pushed out: comf* **11/2**[3]

5552 **2** *3* **Madison Square (USA)**[5] 4364 3-9-6 **58**............... SilvestreDeSousa 2 64
(Mark Johnston) *trckd ldr tl led over 6f out: rdn 2f out: hdd 1f out: hld whn hmpd sn after: kpt on for one pce 2nd* **7/4**[1]

0432 **3** *1* **Arctic Reach**[13] 3220 3-8-2 **47**.................................(p) BrendanPowell(7) 3 50
(Brendan Powell) *chsd ldrs: rdn and hung rt 2f out and one pce: kpt on again fnl f to take one pce 3rd cl home* **7/1**

-063 **4** *hd* **Hawridge Knight**[18] 3910 3-8-11 **49** ow2....................... JamesMillman 4 52
(Rod Millman) *chsd ldrs: rdn and bmpd over 2f out: styd on u.p fnl f to press for one pce 3rd but nvr any threat to wnr: dropped to 4th cl home* **5/1**[2]

4405 **5** *5* **Disturbia (IRE)**[18] 3910 3-8-8 **46**...................................... JimmyQuinn 8 41
(J W Hills) *in rr but in tch: rdn 3f out: styng on one pce whn hmpd over 2f out: no ch after* **10/1**

0633 **6** *hd* **Sum Satisfaction**[18] 3922 3-9-7 **59**..............................(t) TadhgO'Shea 7 53
(Dominic Ffrench Davis) *led tl hdd over 6f out: rdn 3f out: wknd and hung lft over 2f out* **9/1**

0-25 **7** *2 ¼* **Sea The Flames (IRE)**[16] 3989 3-8-10 **55**.................... KatiaScallan(7) 1 45
(Marcus Tregoning) *a in rr* **7/1**

3054 **8** *6* **Sir Randolf (IRE)**[16] 3979 3-9-3 **55**................................(t) JamesDoyle 6 35
(Sylvester Kirk) *chsd ldrs: rdn and wkng whn hmpd over 2f out* **18/1**

2m 29.69s (-0.91) **Going Correction** -0.20s/f (Firm) 8 Ran SP% **117.8**
Speed ratings (Par 98): **95,93,92,92,88 88,87,83**
toteswingers:1&2:£1.00, 2&3:£5.00, 1&3:£4.80 CSF £16.08 CT £69.68 TOTE £5.60: £1.80, £1.70, £2.90; EX 9.70.
Owner The P And P Partnership **Bred** Mrs Sally Doyle **Trained** Eastbury, Berks

FOCUS
A low-grade middle-distance handicap run at a good pace. The winner was impressive under a patient ride and recorded a clear personal best.
T/Plt: £31.80 to a £1 stake. Pool:£35,131.88 - 806.41 winning tickets T/Qpdt: £18.60 to a £1 stake. Pool:£3,886.46 - 154.34 winning tickets ST

4467 GOODWOOD (R-H)
Friday, July 29

OFFICIAL GOING: Good to firm (good in places; selective watering)
Wind: nil Weather: overcast

4492 COUTTS GLORIOUS STKS (GROUP 3) 1m 4f
2:00 (2:00) (Class 1) 4-Y-O+
£28,355 (£10,750; £5,380; £2,680; £1,345; £675) **Stalls** High

Form RPR

4613 **1** **Drunken Sailor (IRE)**[41] 3153 6-9-0 **114**.........................(b) KierenFallon 7 116
(Luca Cumani) *stdd and dropped in bhd after s: hld up in tch in rr: nt clr run 3f out: hdwy on inner 2f out: rdn to chse ldrs over 1f out: chal ins fnl f: r.o wl to ld nr fin* **9/2**[2]

1-32 **2** *hd* **Harris Tweed**[41] 3153 4-9-0 **116**.. LiamJones 3 116
(William Haggas) *lw: led: rdn and qcknd over 2f out: hrd pressed and battled on v gamely u.p tl hdd and no ex nr fin* **9/2**[2]

04-1 **3** *nk* **Jukebox Jury (IRE)**[34] 3403 5-9-0 **116**............................... NeilCallan 1 115
(Mark Johnston) *chsd ldng pair: hemmed in on rail 3f out: swtchd lft and rdn to chse ldr jst over 2f out: drvn and ev ch 1f out: kpt on wl u.p* **11/2**[3]

2-22 **4** *2 ¼* **Redwood**[22] 3775 5-9-0 **116**... MichaelHills 4 112
(B W Hills) *swtg: hld up in tch in midfield: nt clr run 3f out tl over 2f out: rdn to chse ldrs wl over 1f out: drvn and styd on same pce fr over 1f out* **9/4**[1]

4510 **5** *2 ¼* **Halicarnassus (IRE)**[3] 4410 7-9-0 **103**.......................... HughBowman 2 108
(Mick Channon) *on toes: wl in tch: rdn: unable qck and lost pl 3f out: nt clr run and swtchd rt wl over 1f out: no threat to ldrs but kpt on ins fnl f* **40/1**

43-0 **6** *nse* **Rasmy**[28] 3591 4-9-0 104........................ RichardHills 9 108
(Marcus Tregoning) *lw: stdd s: hld up in tch in last trio: rdn 3f out: hdwy u.p on outer over 1f out: kpt on ins fnl f: no threat to ldrs* **33/1**

-201 **7** *2 1/2* **Distant Memories (IRE)**[40] 3204 5-9-0 111................. JamieSpencer 5 104
(Tom Tate) *chsd ldrs tl jst over 2f out: wknd u.p over 1f out: wl btn and eased wl ins fnl f* **12/1**

0-46 **8** *3 1/2* **Nouriya**[78] 2029 4-8-11 104........................ RyanMoore 6 95
(Sir Michael Stoute) *lw: hld up wl in tch in last trio: nt clr run 3f out: rdn and unable qck over 2f out: wknd wl over 1f out* **22/1**

1355 **9** *5* **Indian Days**[33] 3448 6-9-3 114........................ TomQueally 10 93
(James Given) *chsd ldrs on outer: rdn and unable qck 3f out: drvn and wknd over 2f out: wl btn over 1f out* **20/1**

4255 **10** *1* **Campanologist (USA)**[22] 3775 6-9-0 115..................... FrankieDettori 8 89
(Saeed Bin Suroor) *lw: hld up wl in tch: rdn and effrt on outer wl over 2f out: wknd wl over 1f out and bhd whn hung rt over 1f out* **9/1**

2m 34.79s (-3.61) **Going Correction** -0.075s/f (Good) **10** Ran SP% **114.7**
Speed ratings (Par 113): **109,108,108,107,105 105,103,101,98,97**
toteswingers:1&2:£5.70, 2&3:£5.00, 1&3:£4.30 CSF £23.40 TOTE £6.30: £2.20, £1.80, £2.90; EX 23.90 Trifecta £93.70 Pool: £6203.04 - 48.94 winning units..
Owner Samanda Racing & Tony Bloom **Bred** Cyril Kiernan **Trained** Newmarket, Suffolk

FOCUS
Top bend dolled out 3yds increasing distances on that course by 5yds. Clerk of the course Seamus Buckley decided to selectively water the previous evening and applied 4mm to the straight and other areas. The lower rail was also moved back to its original position, which opened up some fresh ground. This opening Group 3 contest was a decent race for the grade and as expected it was run at a solid pace, resulting in a creditable winning time. The principals came clear in a fantastic finish and the form looks good for the grade and sound.

NOTEBOOK
Drunken Sailor(IRE) reversed Royal Ascot form with Harris Tweed under a brave ride from Kieren Fallon at a track he clearly enjoys, as his form figures here of 311 now indicate. He was well held by the runner-up in the Hardwicke, but still ran a decent race that day on ground softer than he wants and he relished the way this event unfolded. He got the split on the inside at just the right time, but didn't appear to be helping Fallon that much when asked to win the race. He always just looked like getting there, though, and rates value for a bit better than the bare margin. This gave his trainer Luca Cumani a third success in the race in the past decade and his last winner in 2007, Purple Moon, went on to follow up in the Ebor before a creditable sixth in the Melbourne Cup. It was also the 6-y-o's first Group success and a return to Flemington in November is firmly on his agenda. He was just 11th there last year, but returned with a bloodstained near-fore hoof that day and Fallon reported after this that he cannot remember riding a horse that has improved so much in such a short space of time. He can be backed at 25-1 for that and Cumani also added afterwards he believes his horse has a better chance this time around. (op 11-2)
Harris Tweed had pretty much his own way out in front and very nearly resumed winning ways, but found his old rival that bit too speedy for him. He ideally wants a stiffer test and, now placed on his three outings since resuming, really deserves to go one better again. (op 4-1 tchd 5-1 in a place)
Jukebox Jury(IRE), a Group 1 winner without a penalty, gamely resumed winning ways on his seasonal debut at Newmarket last month when able to dictate. He couldn't lead here, but was still nicely placed when the tempo began to lift 4f out. He was tightened up passing the 3f marker, which didn't help, but he still held every chance when in the clear and went down fighting. He's clearly in top form. (op 5-1 tchd 9-2)
Redwood, last year's winner, was thrashed by Crystal Cappella on his domestic return at Newmarket 22 days earlier. Connections believed he needed it that day, however, and he was well backed to resume winning ways. He was visibly sweating through the race and, despite being a little tight for room around 3f out, his finishing effort proved laboured. This leaves him with a bit to prove. (op 5-2 tchd 11-4)
Halicarnassus(IRE) struggled in a handicap here on the opening day, but showed his true colours again with a sound effort. (tchd 50-1 in places)
Rasmy was ridden to get this longer trip and came wide with his effort in the home straight. He posted a much better effort than his reappearance effort at Sandown 28 days earlier, but probably needs dropping back in trip/class if he's to get his head back in front. (op 40-1 tchd 50-1 in a place)
Distant Memories(IRE) won his first race over this trip at Pontefract last time out, but he scraped home that day and his stamina was found out in this better race on a stiffer track. (op 14-1)
Nouriya had stamina to prove and didn't look to fully stay the trip, for all that she was faced with a stiff task. She's entitled to come on for the run. (tchd 25-1)
Indian Days was beaten a long way out under his Group 1 penalty. (op 16-1)
Campanologist(USA) remains out of form. (op 10-1)

4493 RSA THOROUGHBRED STKS (LISTED RACE) 1m
2:35 (2:35) (Class 1) 3-Y-O

£17,013 (£6,450; £3,228; £1,608; £807; £405) **Stalls** Low

Form RPR

1346 **1** **Neebras (IRE)**[26] 3670 3-9-0 117........................ FrankieDettori 3 106
(Mahmood Al Zarooni) *b: taken down early: t.k.h: chsd ldng pair: swtchd lft and effrt over 1f out: drvn to chal ins fnl f: r.o wl to ld towards fin* **4/1[2]**

-614 **2** *1/2* **Chef**[34] 3405 3-9-0 101........................ JimmyFortune 2 105
(Andrew Balding) *lw: sn led: rdn and qcknd over 2f out: drvn and kpt on gamely fr over 1f out: narrowly hdd ins fnl f: kpt on and wnt 2nd again last strides* **9/1**

1-13 **3** *hd* **Western Aristocrat (USA)**[44] 3029 3-9-0 108.................. RyanMoore 4 104
(Jeremy Noseda) *lw: t.k.h early: led briefly: chsd ldr after: pushed along to chal over 2f out: drvn over 1f out: led narrowly ins fnl f: hdd and no ex towards fin: lost 2nd last strides* **11/8[1]**

-115 **4** *1/2* **Tazahum (USA)**[43] 3068 3-9-4 107........................ RichardHills 7 107
(Sir Michael Stoute) *stdd and dropped in bhd sn after s: hld up in last pair: plld out and effrt 2f out: hdwy u.p over 1f out: kpt on wl ins fnl f: nt rch ldrs* **4/1[2]**

4040 **5** *1/2* **Vanguard Dream**[43] 3067 3-9-0 93........................ RichardHughes 8 102
(Richard Hannon) *stdd after s: hld up in tch in rr: rdn and effrt 2f out: no imp: swtchd lft jst ins fnl f: r.o wl fnl 100yds: nt rch ldrs* **40/1**

145P **6** *1* **Trade Storm**[27] 3645 3-9-0 99........................ TomQueally 1 99
(John Gallagher) *dwlt and bustled along early: in tch in midfield: rdn and effrt jst over 2f out: drvn and sltly outpcd over 1f out: kpt on ins fnl f* **33/1**

-353 **7** *3/4* **Questioning (IRE)**[34] 3405 3-9-0 101........................ WilliamBuick 6 97
(John Gosden) *swtg: hld up in tch in last trio: rdn and hdwy to chse ldrs wl over 1f out: drvn over 1f out: no imp 1f out: wknd and edgd rt ins fnl f* **6/1[3]**

4004 **8** *2* **Slim Shadey**[22] 3777 3-9-0 96........................(b) KierenFallon 5 92
(J S Moore) *on toes: restless in stalls: in tch in midfield: rdn: unable qck and lost pl over 2f out: plugged on same pce and n.d fr over 1f out* **22/1**

1m 38.08s (-1.82) **Going Correction** -0.075s/f (Good) **8** Ran SP% **116.1**
Speed ratings (Par 108): **106,105,105,104,104 103,102,100**
toteswingers:1&2:£5.80, 2&3:£4.10, 1&3:£2.00 CSF £38.49 TOTE £5.10: £1.70, £2.20, £1.10; EX 46.30 Trifecta £128.90 Pool: £3618.67 - 20.76 winning units..
Owner Godolphin **Bred** Michael E Wates **Trained** Newmarket, Suffolk

FOCUS
Previously run on the Saturday of the meeting, this was won by star milers Where Or When and Court Masterpiece in 2002-3, but the seven winners since have managed to win just two further races between them, one of them the Celebration Mile which Zacinto got on a disqualification. This year's running looked a fair Listed race on paper, but the pace was pretty steady and there was a bunch finish with under two lengths covering the first five. The first three were always to the fore and the form is best rated around the runner-up and fourth.

NOTEBOOK
Neebras(IRE) was 9lb clear on BHA figures, his fourth behind Frankel in the St James' Palace Stakes the best previous form on offer, but he disappointed kept to Group 1 company in the Prix Jean Prat last time out. Taking a marked drop back in grade, he broke on terms this time and was ridden more prominently than usual. He lost a little ground on the first two when needing to be switched, but then picked up well to get up near the line. He is a smart performer on his day who should be up to winning a Group 3. He is in the Celebration Mile back here in a month's time. (op 9-2)
Chef made much of the running and although he could not resist the winner's late charge, he battled on against the rail to retake second almost on the line. The only gelding in the field, he is well at home over the mile but would not mind a return to 1m2f on this evidence. (tchd 10-1)
Western Aristocrat(USA)'s third in the Jersey Stakes last time was given a big boost here on Tuesday when the Ascot winner Strong Suit hacked up in the Lennox Stakes, and the Noseda colt looked sure to improve for this extra furlong. Keen early on, he found Chef a tough horse to pass in the straight but eventually went a head or more up, only for the winner to swoop past the pair of them. Pipped for second in the last couple of strides, there was nothing wrong with his application but perhaps a return to 7f will be to his benefit. (tchd 5-4 and 13-8 in a place)
Tazahum(USA) had Neebras back in third when landing Sandown's Heron Stakes by a nose in May, a Listed win that earned him a 4lb penalty here. Back in trip after failing to see out 1m2f in easy ground last time, he stayed on well from the rear of the field without quite reaching the leaders. The race was not run to suit, and this was a decent effort. (tchd 9-2 in places)
Vanguard Dream, another who was doing his best work down the outer when it was just too late, is proving hard to place successfully in his second season, he had the least chance of these on official figures and may have been flattered to finish as close as he did. (op 33-1)
Trade Storm stuck on along the inside but lacked the required pace. He remains relatively unexposed at this trip. Official explanation: jockey said that the colt hung right handed
Questioning(IRE) was a head in front of Chef in a Newmarket sales race last time, but the drop back to a mile didn't see him to best effect in this steadily run race. (op 8-1 tchd 9-1 in places)
Slim Shadey needs a fast-run mile to be seen to best effect, which he didn't get here. He has not built on his well beaten Guineas fourth. (tchd 20-1)

4494 TOTESPORT MILE (HERITAGE H'CAP) 1m
3:10 (3:12) (Class 2) 3-Y-O+

£77,812 (£23,300; £11,650; £5,825; £2,912; £1,462) **Stalls** Low

Form RPR

1115 **1** **Boom And Bust (IRE)**[34] 3409 4-8-10 **94**........................ HayleyTurner 1 103
(Marcus Tregoning) *mde all: rdn along wl over 1f out: drvn ins fnl f: hld on v gamely cl home* **22/1**

-420 **2** *nk* **Proponent (IRE)**[44] 3032 7-8-13 **97**........................ TedDurcan 6 105
(Roger Charlton) *b: lw: in tch: rdn and effrt 2f out: n.m.r ent fnl f: sn drvn and hdwy to chse ldrs: styd on wl u.p fnl 150yds: snatched 2nd last stride* **14/1**

2400 **3** *shd* **Pintura**[20] 3876 4-8-11 **95**........................ NeilCallan 3 103
(David Simcock) *lw: chsd ldrs: rdn to chse wnr over 1f out: drvn and ev ch ins fnl f: kpt on wl u.p: lost 2nd last stride* **18/1**

2031 **4** *1 1/4* **Sooraah**[7] 4265 4-8-8 **95** 3ex........................ JohnFahy(3) 12 100+
(William Haggas) *on toes: hld up in last quartet: hdwy jst over 2f out: swtchd rt jst over 1f out: nt clr run and hmpd 1f out: kpt on wl u.p ins fnl f: snatched 4th last stride* **14/1**

0312 **5** *shd* **Dance And Dance (IRE)**[44] 3032 5-9-10 **108**............ JamieSpencer 15 116+
(Edward Vaughan) *swtchd rt after s: hld up towards rr: hdwy on inner over 2f out: rdn to chse ldrs 1f out: kpt on u.p: pressing ldrs but styng on same pce whn squeezed out and eased towards fin* **14/1**

2-06 **6** *1* **Man Of Action (USA)**[27] 3645 4-8-11 **95**..................(v) FrankieDettori 20 97+
(Saeed Bin Suroor) *stdd and swtchd rt after s: hld up towards rr: hdwy on inner 2f out: nt clr run and swtchd lft ent fnl f: styd on wl ins fnl f: nvr able to chal* **25/1**

[illegible] **7** *1 1/4* **Cai Shen (IRE)**[22] 3777 3-8-13 **105**........................ RichardHughes 9 104
(Richard Hannon) *pushed along after s and sn in tch in midfield: rdn and effrt 2f out: swtchd lft over 1f out: kpt on ins fnl f: nvr able to rch ldrs* **12/1[3]**

5321 **8** *nk* **Highland Knight (IRE)**[27] 3645 4-8-12 **96**..................(t) DavidProbert 13 95
(Andrew Balding) *chsd ldrs: rdn over 2f out: drvn and unable qck whn hung lft ent fnl f: one pce ins fnl f* **16/1**

4420 **9** *3/4* **Vainglory (USA)**[29] 3542 7-8-3 **92**........................ LauraPike(5) 8 89
(David Simcock) *hld up towards rr: rdn and effrt 2f out: hdwy ent fnl f: styd on ins fnl f: nt rch ldrs* **33/1**

4000 **10** *1 1/4* **Advanced**[6] 4314 8-8-7 **91**........................ SilvestreDeSousa 14 85
(Kevin Ryan) *swtg: in tch in midfield: rdn and effrt over 2f out: styng on but no real imp whn pushed lft over 1f out: kpt on same pce fnl f* **66/1**

-061 **11** *3 1/2* **Namecheck (GER)**[13] 4100 4-9-0 **98** 3ex........................ AhmedAjtebi 11 84
(Mahmood Al Zarooni) *stdd s: hld up towards rr: nt clr run over 2f out: edgd rt and no imp wl over 1f out: kpt on past btn horses fnl f: n.d* **28/1**

1-00 **12** *1/2* **Riggins (IRE)**[42] 3107 7-9-6 **104**........................[1] WilliamBuick 7 89
(Ed Walker) *hld up in midfield: rdn and effrt jst over 2f out: edgd rt u.p and wkng whn hmpd over 1f out* **16/1**

4-15 **13** *hd* **Confront**[27] 3646 6-9-9 **107**........................ RyanMoore 22 92
(Sir Michael Stoute) *lw: chsd wnr: rdn over 2f out: drvn and lost 2nd over 1f out: wkng and btn 1f out: eased fnl 100yds* **28/1**

0010 **14** *1 1/2* **Pleasant Day (IRE)**[20] 3876 4-8-8 **92**........................(b) PaulHanagan 19 73
(Richard Fahey) *chsd ldrs on outer: rdn over 2f out: styng on same pce and looked hld whn pushed lft and hmpd over 1f out: nt rcvr and n.d fnl f* **100/1**

-200 **15** *1* **Mont Agel**[20] 3862 4-8-13 **97**........................(v[1]) OlivierPeslier 17 76
(Michael Bell) *stdd s: hld up in rr: rdn and effrt jst over 2f out: no real hdwy: betean whn edgd rt over 1f out* **40/1**

-101 **16** *nk* **Green Destiny (IRE)**[20] 3876 4-9-0 **101** 3ex........... AdamBeschizza(3) 2 79+
(William Haggas) *lw: in tch: rdn over 2f out: drvn and keeping on same pce over 1f out: nt clr run and hmpd ent fnl f: no ch and eased fnl 100yds* **15/8[1]**

-211 **17** *1/2* **Sagramor**[43] 3067 3-8-7 **99**........................ NickyMackay 4 76+
(Hughie Morrison) *lw: restless in stalls: t.k.h: hld up in tch in midfield: rdn and unable qck 3f out: wknd over 1f out: fin lame* **11/2[2]**

0-04 **18** *1 1/2* **Mr David (USA)**[20] 3862 4-8-11 **95**........................ KierenFallon 10 69
(Jamie Osborne) *hld up towards rr: rdn and no prog on outer ent fnl 2f: n.d* **25/1**

5050 **19** *35* **Lovelace**[20] 3862 7-9-4 **102**.. AdrianNicholls 16 —
(David Nicholls) *s.i.s: sn swtchd rt and a last: lost tch 2f out: hung rt over 1f out and virtually p.u ins fnl f: t.o* **40/1**

1m 37.01s (-2.89) **Going Correction** -0.075s/f (Good)
WFA 3 from 4yo+ 8lb **19** Ran SP% **124.1**
Speed ratings (Par 109): **111,110,110,109,109 108,107,106,105,104 101,100,100,99,98 97,97,95,60**
toteswingers:1&2:£87.40, 2&3:£42.90, 1&3:£59.70 CSF £283.37 CT £2999.46 TOTE £29.20: £4.60, £3.40, £4.20, £4.40; EX 215.60 Trifecta £5206.70 Part won. Pool of £7036.19 - 0.80 winning units..
Owner Jas Singh **Bred** Duncan A McGregor **Trained** Lambourn, Berks
■ The Rectifier (22/1) was withdrawn after proving unruly at the stalls.

FOCUS
One of the most famous draw races of the entire season with those berthed on the inside at a big advantage and this time stall position played a massive part in proceedings again, with the first three home drawn 1, 6 and 3 respectively. It was run at a searching pace and there were the usual amount of hard-luck stories in behind. The first five came clear and the form is rated around the reliable runner-up, third and fourth, with the fifth rated as runner-up.

NOTEBOOK
Boom And Bust(IRE) was housed in stall one and made most for an ultra-game success, his fourth from five outings since resuming this year as a 4-y-o. He flopped in his quest for a four-timer at Windsor in Listed company last time, but a return to aggressive tactics with Hayley Turner back aboard, who was previously 2-2 on him, made the difference again. This was another clear personal-best from this rapidly improving performer and, while his inside draw no doubt proved a massive advantage, he looks up to success in Pattern company. (op 20-1 tchd 25-1 in places)
Proponent(IRE) finished fourth in this last year from a poor draw, but fared much better on that front and ran a massive race in defeat. He was doing his best work at the finish and his optimum distance appears to be 1m1f. He holds no secrets from the handicapper and only wins in his turn, but no-one would begrudge him a big-race success. Hopefully he will find one this term and another crack at the Cambridgeshire at Newmarket in October looks his most viable target.
Pintura had a lovely draw in stall three and got the run of the race just off the pace. He held every chance and threw down a strong challenge, but was always just being held. This was much better again back down in trip and he's evidently up to defying this sort of mark. (op 20-1)
Sooraah ◆, a stablemate of Green Destiny, was 4lb well in under her penalty for winning a Listed event against her own sex at Ascot a week earlier and came in for support. She got well back and met trouble around 1f out, so has to rate as somewhat unfortunate as she also had a double-figure draw. The way she finished indicates she is still on the up and she looks well worth a go in Group company back against females. Official explanation: jockey said that the filly wasdenied a clear run (op 16-1 tchd 12-1)
Dance And Dance(IRE) ◆ was the really unlucky horse and was up 6lb for another unlucky run in the Hunt Cup at Royal Ascot on his previous outing. Under a cracking ride, he somehow made his way to the inside rail from stall 15 and really caught the eye nearing the final furlong. He had to snatch up as things got tight in the closing stages and that no doubt cost him a place. He helps to set a solid standard and richly deserves to find another opening. With an official mark of 108, he's probably better off trying his luck up in class now, though.
Man Of Action(USA) had a horrible draw and he emerges with plenty of credit. He's a tricky sort, but should be well up to winning off this mark when things go his way. (tchd 33-1 in place)
Cai Shen(IRE) fared best of the two 3-y-os. He has developed into a very consistent handicapper and looks fully capable of landing a big-field handicap before the year is out. Perhaps the Cambridgeshire is the race for him.
Highland Knight(IRE) bolted up at Sandown last time and was 7lb higher here. He had his chance from a modest draw, but was unable to confirm last-time-out form with Man Of Action, who was 8lb better off. (op 14-1)
Vainglory(USA), stablemate of Pintura, didn't get a good passage and was noted doing some decent work late in the day. He needs everything to fall right, however. (op 40-1 tchd 50-1 in a place)
Advanced, drawn in 14, stayed on late and caught the eye. He gets this trip nowadays and his turn could be nearing again.
Riggins(IRE), a C&D winner, sported a first-time hood and was surprisingly a market drifter. He flattened right out from the 2f marker and wasn't on a going day. Official explanation: jockey said that the gelding suffered interference in running
Green Destiny(IRE), the easy John Smith's Cup winner, was officially 8lb ahead of the handicapper under his penalty and had a great draw. The worry was the drop back in trip on quick ground, however, and he never looked happy after being ridden just off the pace as he could not relax into a rhythm. His chance was apparent from 2f out and, while this will disappoint many, he shouldn't be fully judged on the back of it. Jockey Adam Beschizza later reported he was never travelling. Official explanation: jockey said that the gelding was never travelling (op 9-4 tchd 5-2 in places)
Sagramor sneaked into the race as first reserve and was bidding to emulate 2007 winner Third Set, who had also won the Britannia at Royal Ascot on his previous outing. He was 6lb higher and faced with quicker ground, but had a decent draw. He ultimately ran no sort of race after getting very upset in the stalls, however, and was later found to be lame on both his hind legs. Official explanation: vet said the colt was lame on both hind legs (tchd 6-1 in places)

4495 TANQUERAY RICHMOND STKS (GROUP 2) (C&G) 6f
3:45 (3:48) (Class 1) 2-Y-O
£34,026 (£12,900; £6,456; £3,216; £1,614; £810) **Stalls** High

Form RPR

11 **1** **Harbour Watch (IRE)**[22] 3776 2-9-0 0........................ RichardHughes 2 117+
(Richard Hannon) *unf: scope: lw: chsd ldrs: rdn and effrt ent fnl 2f: carried bdly rt over 1f out: drvn to chse ldr 1f out: led ins fnl f: drew clr fnl 100yds: wl in command towards fin* **1/1**[1]

1263 **2** *2 ¼* **Bannock (IRE)**[22] 3773 2-9-0 0................................ SilvestreDeSousa 4 108
(Mark Johnston) *led: rdn 2f out: hung bdly rt 1f out: hdd ins fnl f: sn btn: hung on for 2nd cl home* **13/2**[2]

2432 **3** *½* **Caspar Netscher**[14] 4055 2-9-0 0.............................. RobertWinston 10 107
(Alan McCabe) *hld up towards rr: hmpd after 2f: nt clr run 1/2-way: effrt and rdn 2f out: styd on u.p ins fnl f: pressing for 2nd cl home: no threat to wnr* **20/1**

1023 **4** *1 ½* **Silverheels (IRE)**[20] 3861 2-9-0 0................................... OlivierPeslier 8 102
(Paul Cole) *in rr of main gp: swtchd rt 4f out: rdn and effrt over 2f out: outpcd and drvn over 1f out: no threat to wnr but plugged on ins fnl f* **16/1**

11 **5** *hd* **Saigon**[14] 4055 2-9-0 0.. KirstyMilczarek 3 102
(James Toller) *hld up in tch in midfield: rdn and effrt over 2f out: drvn and outpcd over 1f out: no threat to wnr but kpt on ins fnl f* **8/1**[3]

115 **6** *½* **Eureka (IRE)**[13] 4094 2-9-0 0.. RyanMoore 9 100
(Richard Hannon) *swtg: on toes: chsd ldrs: rdn and unable qck ent fnl 2f: drvn and outpcd wl over 1f out: styd on same pce and no threat to ldrs after* **8/1**[3]

1 **7** *2 ¼* **Bogart**[65] 2395 2-9-0 0.. PhillipMakin 1 93+
(Kevin Ryan) *str: lengthy: chsd ldr: rdn and hung bdly rt fr 2f out: lost 2nd 1f out: fdd ins fnl f* **12/1**

321 **8** *½* **Right To Dream (IRE)**[34] 3408 2-9-0 0........................... MartinDwyer 5 92
(Brian Meehan) *leggy: athletic: hmpd s: in tch towards rr: rdn over 2f out: struggling and drvn ent fnl 2f: wknd wl over 1f out* **20/1**

113 **9** *¾* **Factory Time (IRE)**[14] 4055 2-9-0 0.............................. HughBowman 7 90
(Mick Channon) *in tch in midfield: rdn and unable qck ent fnl 2f: wknd over 1f out* **22/1**

11 **10** *2 ½* **Parc De Launay**[36] 3313 2-9-0 0.................................... JamieSpencer 6 82
(Tom Tate) *athletic: attr: restless in stalls: wnt rt s: a bhd* **28/1**

1m 10.23s (-1.97) **Going Correction** -0.075s/f (Good) **10** Ran SP% **116.5**
Speed ratings (Par 106): **110,107,106,104,104 103,100,99,98,95**
CSF £6.99 TOTE £1.90: £1.10, £2.10, £5.30; EX 7.10 Trifecta £85.30 Pool: £17009.84 - 147.50 winning units..
Owner H Robin Heffer **Bred** T Molan **Trained** East Everleigh, Wilts

FOCUS
This historic juvenile event has now been won for the last four years by Richard Hannon, with Dick Turpin, successful for him in 2009, the best recent winner of the race. This was a strong renewal. The winner was impressive and the form looks straightforward and solid, with the runner-up rated to his July Stakes form.

NOTEBOOK
Harbour Watch(IRE) ◆ looks a potentially top colt. Two from two arriving here, his clear-cut Newmarket defeat of Burwaaz was given a boost when that horse was runner-up in the Molecomb here on Tuesday. Chasing the pace, he was carried to his right by the hanging Bogart just at the wrong time, but once clear of that horse's attentions he ran on strongly to the line for a comfortable success, the margin of victory underplaying his superiority. Undoubtedly a smart juvenile, he will be kept to 6f this season with races like the Mill Reef and Middle Park Stakes sure to enter calculations, and he is going to take a good bit of beating. He is now favourite in some lists for next season's 2000 Guineas, but while he is highly regarded by connections, who say he works as well at home as any of their recent juveniles bar Canford Cliffs, it might pay not to get too carried away at this stage. He is by Acclamation, whose best progeny have been sprinters, and although his dam is a half-sister to smart 1m2f colt Kabool, he still has his stamina to prove. History is against him as far as Classic glory is concerned, as no Richmond Stakes winner has won the Newmarket Guineas since Palestine in 1949-50, although the 1999 Richmond winner Bachir did win the French and Irish Guineas the following year. (op 4-5)
Bannock(IRE) showed smart form when third to Frederick Engels in the July Stakes on his latest start, and was top on adjusted official figures here. He showed fine pace, but edged to his right in the latter stages and was readily put in his place by the winner. He has kept his form well and the Gimcrack might be a suitable target. (op 7-1)
Caspar Netscher was another to have finished third behind Frederick Engels this year, in his case in the Windsor Castle Stakes at the Royal meeting. Racing closest to the fence, he was hampered early on but stuck to his task and stayed on for third. He turned around recent Newbury form with Saigon. (op 25-1)
Silverheels(IRE), who after taking a bump leaving the stalls, was switched from the inside to avoid trouble and ran on for fourth without threatening the principals. Third in Newmarket's Superlative Stakes behind Red Duke and Chandlery, who did not let the form down here on Wednesday, he probably found this a bit sharp and will not mind a return to 7f. (op 25-1 tchd 28-1)
Saigon forfeited his unbeaten status and could not confirm his Rose Bowl superiority over Caspar Netscher, but was keeping on quite nicely at the end and could be open to improvement at 7f. (tchd 9-1)
Eureka(IRE), back up in trip and deserted by Richard Hughes, played up in the paddock and required a blanket for stalls entry, but did not repeat his Newbury antics down at the start. He tracked the pace but was unable to quicken up. (op 12-1)
Bogart has been given a break since his winning debut at Ayr in May, form which has worked out well. The colt raced up with the pace and seemed set to be involved in the finish, only to drift badly to his right when the pressure was on, taking the winner with him. Finishing up well held, something may well have been amiss and he is worth giving the benefit of the doubt. Official explanation: jockey said that the colt hung right (op 14-1 tchd 16-1 in a place)
Right To Dream(IRE) was found wanting in this much better grade. (tchd 25-1 in a place)
Factory Time(IRE) travelled well to a point but was beaten further by Caspar Netscher and Saigon than he had been at Newbury. (tchd 25-1)
Parc De Launay, unbeaten in two races, became restless in the stalls and did not break well. He was always at the back, and the ground might have been faster than he'd have cared for. (tchd 33-1)

4496 ROTHSCHILD WADDESDON WINES STKS (NURSERY H'CAP) 7f
4:20 (4:21) (Class 2) 2-Y-O **£9,703** (£2,887; £1,443; £721) **Stalls** Low

Form RPR

502 **1** **Goldoni (IRE)**[15] 4007 2-8-5 **78**.................................. DavidProbert 1 84+
(Andrew Balding) *in tch in midfield: rdn and effrt towards inner 2f out: drvn and ev ch 1f out: kpt on wl u.p to ld last stride* **11/2**[2]

21 **2** *shd* **West Leake Hare (IRE)**[36] 3308 2-8-2 **75**................ SilvestreDeSousa 8 81+
(B W Hills) *chsd ldr tl led 5f out tl 4f out: w ldr after tl rdn to ld again wl over 1f out: hrd pressed and battled on gamely u.p fnl f tl hdd last stride* **4/1**[1]

212 **3** *shd* **Lord Ofthe Shadows (IRE)**[67] 2367 2-9-7 **94**............ RichardHughes 5 101+
(Richard Hannon) *hld up towards rr: swtchd rt and effrt on inner 3f out: chsd ldrs and swtchd lft ent fnl f: drvn and ev ch fnl 100yds: kpt on wl* **10/1**

433 **4** *½* **Bronze Angel (IRE)**[33] 3424 2-8-8 **81**............................ HayleyTurner 7 85+
(Marcus Tregoning) *lw: s.i.s: in rr: effrt on inner and nt clr run 3f out: hdwy and n.m.r over 1f out: rdn to chse ldrs 1f out: kpt on but unable qck towards fin* **7/1**[3]

2401 **5** *1* **Pride And Joy (IRE)**[25] 3673 2-8-4 **77**........................... MartinDwyer 14 79
(Jamie Osborne) *v.s.a: bhd: effrt and nt clr run 2f out: hdwy over 1f out: chsd ldrs and drvn jst ins fnl f: kpt on: no imp fnl 100yds* **16/1**

313 **6** *hd* **Poetic Dancer**[21] 3795 2-8-3 **79**...................................... JohnFahy(3) 12 80
(Clive Cox) *lw: hld up in midfield: n.m.r ent fnl 2f: swtchd lft and hdwy jst over 1f out: kpt on wl u.p ins fnl f: nt rch ldrs* **25/1**

01 **7** *1 ½* **Captain Cardington (IRE)**[29] 3534 2-8-2 **75**.................... LukeMorris 9 73
(Mick Channon) *edgy: on toes: s.i.s: sn pushed along in last trio: rdn over 3f out: hdwy u.p over 1f out: styd on u.p ins fnl f: nvr trbld ldrs* **33/1**

043 **8** *1 ½* **Mr Knightley (IRE)**[20] 3868 2-7-11 **73**........................ KieranO'Neill(3) 3 67
(Richard Hannon) *lw: led for 2f: chsd ldrs after: rdn and unable qck jst over 2f out: styd on same pce u.p fr over 1f out* **12/1**

646 **9** *hd* **Whinging Willie (IRE)**[20] 3878 2-8-5 **78**....................... SamHitchcott 10 72
(Gary Moore) *green: noisy in paddock: bustled along early: in midfield: lost pl: bhd and u.p 2f out: nt clr run over 1f out: hdwy 1f out: styd on ins fnl f: no threat to ldrs* **20/1**

21 **10** *1 ¼* **Glee**[72] 2187 2-8-6 **79** ow1.. WilliamBuick 2 71
(Richard Hannon) *in tch: rdn and effrt over 2f out: pressing ldrs and drvn over 1f out: wkng whn hmpd jst ins fnl f: btn and eased sn after* **7/1**[3]

120 **11** *1 ¼* **Sir Glanton (IRE)**[20] 3861 2-9-3 **90**.................................. JimCrowley 4 77
(Amanda Perrett) *hld up in midfield: rdn and effrt over 2f out: drvn and no imp over 1f out: nvr trbld ldrs* **14/1**

5431 **12** *¾* **Commanche**[10] 4171 2-8-3 **82** 6ex.............................. PaulHanagan 15 61
(Bryan Smart) *a towards rr: rdn and no imp 3f out: no threat to ldrs fnl 2f: plugged on ins fnl f* **20/1**

21 **13** *3 ¾* **Royal Blush**[77] 2063 2-7-12 **74**.................................... HarryBentley(3) 13 50+
(Paul Cole) *sddle slipped leaving stalls: racd wd for 3f: chsd ldrs tl jnd ldr over 4f out: sn led: rdn and hung lft 2f out: sn hdd: wknd over 1f out* **16/1**

141 **14** *2 ¾* **Mabroor (USA)**[37] 3284 2-9-4 **91**.................................... RichardHills 11 60
(Mark Johnston) *in tch: rdn and unable qck over 2f out: wknd u.p over 1f out* **18/1**

440 **15** *5* **Bounty Seeker (USA)**[41] 3152 2-8-8 **81**.............................. NeilCallan 6 37
(Mark Johnston) *lw: awkward s but sn rcvrd and chsng ldrs: rdn over 2f out: wknd u.p over 1f out* **12/1**

1m 26.18s (-0.72) **Going Correction** -0.075s/f (Good) **15** Ran SP% **124.9**
Speed ratings (Par 100): **101,100,100,100,99 98,97,95,95,93 92,91,87,84,78**
toteswingers:1&2:£6.60, 2&3:£5.80, 1&3:£12.20 CSF £27.06 CT £229.23 TOTE £6.80: £2.20, £2.30, £3.10; EX 36.80 Trifecta £199.80 Pool: £3933.09 - 14.56 winning units..
Owner Mick and Janice Mariscotti **Bred** Marston Stud **Trained** Kingsclere, Hants
■ Stewards' Enquiry : Silvestre De Sousa two-day ban: used whip in the incorrect place (12-13 Aug)

FOCUS
A warm nursery contested by a number of horses who have been given Group-race entries. The pace was solid, but it was a slightly messy race with a very tight finish. The form looks strong for the grade and should work out.

NOTEBOOK
Goldoni(IRE) ◆, drawn right on the inside, tracked the pace before running on bravely to poke his head in front. By Dylan Thomas, he has further improvement in him as he steps up in trip and looks the type to make a good handicapper. His half-brother Gunner Lindley was runner-up in this race two years ago. (op 8-1)
West Leake Hare(IRE) was on his toes in the paddock and took a keen hold on the way to the start. Always up with the pace, he established a narrow lead and battled on, but was just pipped. A Middle Park Stakes entry, he won't be up to that level but he should win more races. He was due for a 2lb rise before this. (op 11-2)
Lord Ofthe Shadows(IRE) ◆ had been off since a useful effort at Windsor in May. Stepping up 2f in trip, this Mill Reef entry met trouble on the fence and had to be switched, which might have cost him victory. The Hannon team had won two of the last three runnings of this event. (op 11-2)
Bronze Angel(IRE) was another short of racing room on the rail at a crucial stage, but stayed on once in the clear. This looks his trip for now. (op 8-1)
Pride And Joy(IRE), for whom things did not work out, was dropped in from his wide draw and failed to handle the bend. He met trouble when trying to improve too and did well to reach fifth. (op 20-1 tchd 25-1)
Poetic Dancer was not best drawn and ran respectably, seeing out the slightly longer trip well.
Captain Cardington(IRE), who was edgy in the paddock, was held up at the back as he had been when winning at Epsom, but this time the leaders did not come back to him. This was still a respectable showing.
Glee, not seen since winning over 6f here in May, was the shortest-priced of the Hannon trio. She was already on the retreat when she was hampered late on. (op 6-1 tchd 15-2 in a place)
Royal Blush, another off since a maiden win in May, showed up well for a long way from her wide draw. Her rider later reported that the saddle had slipped. She may be worth another chance on a more conventional track Official explanation: jockey said that the saddle slipped coming out of the stalls (tchd 14-1)

4497 OAK TREE STKS (GROUP 3) (F&M) 7f
4:50 (4:52) (Class 1) 3-Y-O+

£28,355 (£10,750; £5,380; £2,680; £1,345; £675) **Stalls** Low

Form RPR

-312 **1** **Chachamaidee (IRE)**[44] 3030 4-9-2 109.......................... TomQueally 2 115
(Sir Henry Cecil) *lw: hld up in tch: hdwy to trck ldrs gng wl over 1f out: swtchd lft and effrt between horses 1f out: qcknd to ld ins fnl f: sn clr: easily* **9/2**[2]

-502 **2** *2 ¾* **Dever Dream**[21] 3827 4-9-2 105.......................... RyanMoore 11 108
(William Haggas) *lw: hld up in tch in midfield: sltly hmpd over 2f out: rdn and hdwy on inner over 1f out: r.o wl ins fnl f to go 2nd nr fin: no ch w wnr* **6/1**[3]

4111 **3** *½* **Law Of The Range**[24] 3703 4-9-2 103...................... SilvestreDeSousa 4 107
(Marco Botti) *led: rdn over 2f out: battled on v gamely tl hdd ins fnl f: sn no ch w wnr: lost 2nd nr fin* **8/1**

2-10 **4** *hd* **Rimth**[75] 2137 3-8-12 107.. OlivierPeslier 15 106+
(Paul Cole) *t.k.h: hld up in tch on outer: rdn and effrt 2f out: chsd ldrs and hung rt over 1f out: kpt on same pce ins fnl f* **18/1**

3300 **5** *2 ¼* **Maqaasid**[21] 3822 3-8-9 110.. RichardHills 3 97
(John Gosden) *hld up in tch: effrt and n.m.r over 2f: swtchd lft wl over 1f [illegible] on same pce ins fnl f* **4/1**[1]

-263 **6** *nse* **Magic Eye (IRE)**[19] 3897 6-9-2 102.............................. [illegible] 100
(Andreas Lowe, Germany) *in tch: rdn and effrt 2f out: stl chsng ldrs and keeping on same pce whn hmpd 1f out: one pce ins fnl f* **66/1**

-250 **7** *shd* **Thai Haku (IRE)**[27] 3654 4-9-2 105.............................. JimmyFortune 6 100
(M Delzangles, France) *t.k.h: chsd ldrs: rdn 2f out: unable qck u.p over 1f out: wknd 1f out* **33/1**

6512 **8** *1* **Rockatella (IRE)**[19] 3897 4-9-2 105.............................. PaulHanagan 9 97
(W Hefter, Germany) *hld up in tch towards rr: rdn over 2f out: drvn and no real imp over 1f out: plugged on ins fnl f* **40/1**

-321 **9** *½* **Khor Sheed**[36] 3323 3-8-9 105.. KierenFallon 14 93+
(Luca Cumani) *lw: chsd ldr: jnd ldr over 3f out: rdn wl over 1f out: unable qck u.p over 1f out: wknd ins fnl f* **10/1**

5121 **10** *hd* **Rhythm Of Light**[44] 3034 3-8-9 103...................... RichardKingscote 17 92+
(Tom Dascombe) *lw: stdd s: hld up in last trio: pushed along and no real imp 2f out: nvr trbld ldrs* **20/1**

-250 **11** *¾* **Sharnberry**[30] 3527 3-8-9 104.. WilliamBuick 12 90+
(Ed Dunlop) *hld up in tch in last trio: effrt and hmpd over 2f out: no imp after* **25/1**

2-65 **12** *hd* **Cochabamba (IRE)**[27] 3648 3-8-9 98.............................. JackMitchell 8 89
(Roger Teal) *hld up in tch towards rr: rdn and unable qck over 2f out: wknd over 1f out* **100/1**

0116 **13** *hd* **Perfect Tribute**[54] 2752 3-8-12 107.............................. LukeMorris 5 92
(Clive Cox) *in tch: rdn over 2f out: wknd u.p over 1f out* **12/1**

-304 **14** *½* **Dawn Eclipse (IRE)**[19] 3892 6-9-2 102.............................. JimCrowley 16 91+
(T G McCourt, Ire) *hld up in tch in last trio: hmpd and swtchd lft over 2f out: rdn and no hdwy 2f out: n.d after* **100/1**

1-44 **15** *¾* **Tropical Paradise (IRE)**[60] 2558 5-9-2 105.................... IanMongan 13 89
(Peter Winkworth) *rrd as stalls opened: t.k.h and in midfield after 2f: rdn and unable qck over 2f out: wknd u.p over 1f out* **16/1**

-000 **R** **Memory (IRE)**[21] 3822 3-8-9 111.............................. RichardHughes 10 —
(Richard Hannon) *lw: ref to r* **8/1**

3-30 **P** **Pyrrha**[55] 2744 5-9-2 105.. TedDurcan 1 —
(Chris Wall) *chsd ldr tl ent fnl 3f: sn dropped out qckly over 2f out: lost actionand eventually p.u and dismntd over 1f out* **20/1**

1m 25.1s (-1.80) **Going Correction** -0.075s/f (Good)
WFA 3 from 4yo+ 7lb **17** Ran SP% **124.8**
Speed ratings (Par 113): **107,103,103,103,100 100,100,99,98,98 97,97,97,96,95 —,—**
toteswingers:1&2:£6.40, 2&3:£9.60, 1&3:£6.70 CSF £29.73 TOTE £5.50: £1.90, £3.20, £3.80; EX 33.90 Trifecta £191.20 Pool: £5901.77 - 22.83 winning units..
Owner R A H Evans **Bred** Cheval Court Stud **Trained** Newmarket, Suffolk

FOCUS
A solid Group 3 for fillies', run at a good pace. Things unsurprisingly got tight in the home straight, but the form makes sense rated around the third and fourth.

NOTEBOOK
Chachamaidee(IRE) ◆ posted a personal-best effort when runner-up in the Windsor Forest at Royal Ascot on her previous outing and readily went one better again on this drop back down in trip. She travelled sweetly into contention, but had to wait for her challenge at the furlong marker. However, once the gap came half a furlong out she quickened and put the race to bed decisively. She's had a cracking season and was just too classy for this lot. On this showing, returning to 1m could well bring out even further improvement and her master trainer believes she could be Group 1 class down the line. Perhaps the Sun Chariot at Newmarket would be her best opportunity of glory at the top level, remembering she was placed on her comeback at that undulating track over 1m1f back in May. (op 4-1 tchd 5-1 in places)
Dever Dream ◆ was just caught in this class over 6f at York 21 days earlier when bouncing back to form. She was more patiently ridden back up in trip and found herself well back in the home straight. She motored home against the rail inside the final furlong and looks very likely to end her losing run in the coming weeks. (op 15-2)
Law Of The Range was back down a furlong in her quest for a four-timer, but very well drawn for a front-runner and set out to make all. She only gave way nearing the finish and this does rate another career-best in defeat. (op 17-2 tchd 9-1)
Rimth ◆, back from a 75-day break, ran a big race from her poor draw and returned near the form that saw her land the Fred Darling at Newbury on her comeback in April. This proved her French Guineas run to be wrong and she ought to come on plenty, so there's every chance she'll get her head back in front next time out. (op 20-1 tchd 16-1)
Maqaasid just grabbed fifth. She had to bounce back from a woeful display at Newmarket last time, but the pick of her previous form this year entitled her to start favourite here. She was lit up early and didn't get a great passage, but did prove laboured on this drop back a furlong. She has become frustrating, but is better than she showed here. (op 9-2 tchd 5-1 in places)
Magic Eye(IRE) ran a sound race and reversed her last-time-out Group 3 form with Rockatella, another German-trained filly. They both add substance to this form.
Khor Sheed was bang there nearing the final furlong, but her refusal to settle through the early stages saw her empty when it mattered. (op 9-1 tchd 8-1)
Rhythm Of Light took the Listed Sandringham Handicap at Royal Ascot last month and was faced with her toughest race to date. She was never going to get involved as things panned out from her outside stall back down a furlong and, finishing with promise, could still be improving. (op 18-1 tchd 16-1)
Memory(IRE) once again disgraced herself by refusing to jump out and was subsequently retired by connections. (op 9-1 tchd 10-1)
Pyrrha looked to break down on the inside around 3f out and was taken to the racecourse veterinary centre. The mare injured her pelvis and has gone for x-rays. Her trainer later said it was "touch and go" but she was better in the stables than on the course. (op 22-1)

4498 TURF CLUB STKS (H'CAP) 5f
5:25 (5:26) (Class 3) (0-95,95) 3-Y-O

£9,337 (£2,796; £1,398; £699; £349; £175) **Stalls** High

Form RPR

5146 **1** **Catfish (IRE)**[21] 3807 3-8-8 **82**.............................. WilliamBuick 4 92
(Brian Meehan) *taken down early: led centre trio and midfield overall: clsd on ldrs 1/2-way: led over 1f out: rdn clr and hanging lft 1f out: kpt on wl* **8/1**

114 **2** *1 ½* **Albany Rose (IRE)**[14] 4075 3-8-12 **86**.............................. TedDurcan 5 91
(Rae Guest) *dwlt: sn wl outpcd and pushed along in rr: hdwy 2f out: kpt on wl to chse wnr fnl 100yds: nvr able to chal* **13/2**[3]

-320 **3** *¾* **The Thrill Is Gone**[48] 2928 3-9-6 **94**.............................. HughBowman 1 96
(Mick Channon) *racd in centre trio: towards rr overall: hdwy 3f out: rdn and chsd wnr over 1f out: kpt on same pce ins fnl f* **16/1**

5020 **4** *shd* **Bathwick Bear (IRE)**[6] 4333 3-9-4 **95**.................(v[1]) RichardEvans(3) 10 97
(David Evans) *sn rdn and struggling to go pce in midfield: clsd and in tch wl over 2f out: drvn and styd on same pce fr over 1f out* **25/1**

0040 **5** *½* **Jamesway (IRE)**[22] 3778 3-8-13 **87**.............................. PaulHanagan 3 87
(Richard Fahey) *taken down early: racd in centre trio: hld up wl in rr: rdn and hdwy over 1f out: styd on ins fnl f: no threat to wnr* **5/1**[2]

1611 **6** *8* **Redvers (IRE)**[16] 3983 3-8-11 **85**.............................. JimCrowley 6 56
(Ralph Beckett) *sn wl outpcd and rdn in rr: sme hdwy 1/2-way: drvn over 1f out: wknd ins fnl f* **7/1**

3200 **7** *½* **Ballista (IRE)**[21] 3820 3-9-2 **90**.............................(v[1]) RichardKingscote 8 60+
[illegible] *rdn 1/2-way: wknd over 1f out: fdd ins fnl f* [illegible]

2265 **8** *nk* **Bold Bidder**[21] 3807 3-8-12 **86**.............................(b[1]) PhillipMakin 13 55+
(Kevin Ryan) *led at fast gallop: hdd over 1f out: wknd ent fnl f: fdd ins fnl f* **12/1**

6301 **9** *¾* **Cadeaux Pearl**[16] 3975 3-9-1 **89**.............................(b) AdrianNicholls 9 55
(David Nicholls) *outpcd in midfield: hdwy 1/2-way: wknd u.p over 1f out: fdd ins fnl f* **13/2**[3]

4160 **10** *1 ½* **Even Stevens**[7] 4295 3-8-8 **85**.............................(p) BillyCray(3) 12 45+
(David Nicholls) *w ldrs tl 2f out: sn wknd* **20/1**

2114 **11** *6* **Quality Art (USA)**[41] 3181 3-9-2 **90**.............................. RyanMoore 11 51+
(Gary Moore) *w ldrs tl 2f out: sn fdd: wl bhd and eased ins fnl f* **4/1**[1]

57.38 secs (-1.02) **Going Correction** -0.075s/f (Good) **11** Ran SP% **118.2**
Speed ratings (Par 104): **105,102,101,101,100 87,86,86,85,82 73**
toteswingers:1&2:£9.10, 2&3:£24.50, 1&3:£17.40 CSF £59.59 CT £597.38 TOTE £8.00: £2.50, £2.40, £4.50; EX 81.70 Trifecta £1799.40 Pool: £3915.10 - 1.61 winning units..
Owner Raymond Tooth **Bred** Castellane Partnership **Trained** Manton, Wilts

FOCUS
A competitive sprint handicap run at a very strong pace, with a line of four blasting off near the stands' side. They cut each other's throats and all dropped away to finish well beaten. A group of three raced some way apart from the rest down the centre and they ended up first, third and fifth. The third and fourth set the standard.

NOTEBOOK
Catfish(IRE) soon travelled strongly, and as the leaders near the rail fell away she found herself in a clear lead overall heading to the furlong pole. She ran on well to win decisively, edging towards the stands' side when in command, but it remains to be seen what the form is worth. There is no doubt she is a speedy filly, and connections will try to find a fillies' Listed race for her. She gets 6f too. (op 12-1)
Albany Rose(IRE) did best of those to race among the stands' side eight, albeit always being positioned some way off the fence. She ran on well from the rear of the field without threatening the winner and has run two decent races now from this mark, which is 15lb higher than the last leg of her quickfire hat-trick. (op 7-1)
The Thrill Is Gone ran well on her handicap debut, but as the race turned out it could be that she was flattered as one of the trio to race down the middle. (tchd 20-1)
Bathwick Bear(IRE) ran creditably in the first-time visor and would have been third in another stride. This is his trip and he is due to be dropped a pound now.
Jamesway(IRE) was always last of the three in the centre and, while this was a respectable effort on the face of it, there have to be doubts given the way the race was run. (op 13-2)
Redvers(IRE), to whom there was a yawning gap, was 5lb higher on this hat-trick bid. He had never run over the bare 5f before and found it all too sharp for him. (op 13-2 tchd 6-1)

Ballista(IRE) probably did too much in the first-time visor, but still beat the other three trailblazers. (tchd 8-1)
Quality Art(USA) helped make the running but was eased markedly when beaten by Ryan Moore, who was previously three from three on him. Official explanation: trainer said, regarding the poor performance shown, that the gelding was not suited by being unable to dominate in this race (tchd 7-2 and 9-2 in places)
T/Jkpt: Not won. T/Plt: £120.70 to a £1 stake. Pool of £282,661.34 - 1,708.71 winning tickets. T/Qpdt: £54.60 to a £1 stake. Pool of £13,440.25 182.00 winning tickets. SP

4170 MUSSELBURGH (R-H)

Friday, July 29

OFFICIAL GOING: Good to firm (good in places)
Wind: Almost nil Weather: Sunny

4499 BLACKROCK AMATEUR RIDERS' H'CAP (A QUALIFIER FOR BETFAIR BONUS SCOTTISH RACING STAYERS FINAL) 1m 5f

6:00 (6:00) (Class 5) (0-70,72) 4-Y-0+ **£4,055** (£1,257; £628; £314) **Stalls** Low

Form RPR
0141 **1** **Jewelled Dagger (IRE)**[4] 4382 7-11-6 **72** 6ex.................... MrSWalker 8 81
(Keith Dalgleish) *trckd ldrs: rdn to ld over 2f out: hld on wl u.p fnl f* **2/1**[1]
050- **2** *1 ¾* **Toshi (USA)**[29] 7176 9-9-9 **47**.. MrsCBartley 9 53
(Jim Goldie) *hld up towards rr: hdwy to chse wnr over 2f out: kpt on fnl f* **11/2**[3]
4150 **3** *nk* **Dimashq**[30] 3509 9-9-7 **48**.. MissWGibson(3) 1 54
(Paul Midgley) *dwlt: hld up: hdwy to dispute 2nd pl 2f out: kpt on ins fnl f* **18/1**
60 **4** *7* **Morning Time (IRE)**[20] 3858 5-10-6 **65**..........................(p) MrCNichol(7) 7 61
(Lucinda Russell) *hld up in midfield: rdn and edgd rt over 2f out: kpt on fnl f: no imp* **20/1**
4421 **5** *4 ½* **Amir Pasha (UAE)**[9] 4198 6-10-2 **59**..........................(p) MissRSmith(5) 3 48
(Micky Hammond) *hld up: effrt and swtchd lft 2f out: nvr able to chal* **9/2**[2]
0100 **6** *8* **Oddsmaker (IRE)**[42] 3129 10-10-6 **63**.............(t) MissAngelaBarnes(5) 4 40
(Maurice Barnes) *in tch: effrt on outside and cl up 1/2-way: rdn and wknd 2f out* **22/1**
4050 **7** *3 ¼* **Birkside**[10] 4173 8-9-12 **53**.. LucyAlexander(3) 11 25
(Linda Perratt) *dwlt: hld up: shortlived effrt over 2f out: nvr able to chal* **16/1**
0000 **8** *13* **Hurricane Thomas (IRE)**[3] 4408 7-9-11 **54**......... MissPhillipaTutty(5) 5 —
(Karen Tutty) *hld up in midfield: effrt over 2f out: sn wknd* **18/1**
-650 **9** *11* **Fantastic Storm**[27] 3622 4-9-4 **47** oh2.........................(v) MrSBushby(5) 2 —
(Robin Bastiman) *led to over 2f out: sn wknd and eased: lost action* **50/1**
5221 **10** *1* **Obara D'Avril (FR)**[3] 4409 9-9-6 **51** 6ex..............(p) MissCarlyFrater(7) 10 —
(Simon West) *t.k.h: prom: hdwy and cl up 1/2-way: wknd over 2f out* **7/1**
0600 **11** *35* **Wicked Daze (IRE)**[4] 4382 8-10-7 **66**............................ MrSFeeney(7) 6 —
(Linda Perratt) *chsd ldrs: hdwy 1/2-way: rdn and wknd fr 3f out: t.o* **11/1**

2m 48.2s (-3.80) **Going Correction** -0.275s/f (Firm) course record **11** Ran SP% **115.2**
Speed ratings (Par 103): **100,98,98,94,91 86,84,76,69,69 47**
toteswingers:1&2:£4.40, 2&3:£15.50, 1&3:£6.90 CSF £11.99 CT £151.90 TOTE £2.60: £2.00, £2.20, £5.00; EX 11.50.
Owner A R M Galbraith **Bred** Ballyhane Stud **Trained** Carluke, South Lanarkshire

FOCUS
Bottom bend moved in 3m from previous meeting. After a lovely summer's day the ground continued to dry out and was pretty quick. An amateur riders' handicap and as usual in this type of event the gallop was unrelenting. The winner is rated to last year's best with the third setting the standard.

4500 EASTERN ELECTRIC (SCOTLAND) LTD NURSERY 5f

6:30 (6:30) (Class 6) 2-Y-0 **£1,940** (£577; £288; £144) **Stalls** High

Form RPR
2135 **1** **Amadeus Denton (IRE)**[13] 4079 2-9-2 **76**...................... JulieBurke(5) 4 85+
(Michael Dods) *w ldr: led 1/2-way: sn edgd lft: kpt on strly fnl f* **15/8**[2]
0006 **2** *3 ½* **Stans Deelyte**[15] 3993 2-7-12 **56** oh11.......................... JamesSullivan 1 49
(Lisa Williamson) *chsd ldrs: effrt and wnt 2nd 2f out: sn rdn: kpt on same pce fnl f* **25/1**
5225 **3** *1 ½* **Superplex**[30] 3505 2-8-10 **72**.. ShaneBKelly(7) 2 64
(John Quinn) *in tch: sn pushed along: effrt u.p over 1f out: kpt on: no imp* **7/4**[1]
055 **4** *½* **Just Dixie**[71] 2234 2-7-7 **56** oh11.. NeilFarley(5) 5 42
(John Weymes) *dwlt: sn drvn bhd ldng gp: effrt on outside over 1f out: sn no imp* **22/1**
6601 **5** *2 ½* **Lady Caprice**[23] 3728 2-8-5 **60**...............................(b) RoystonFfrench 6 40
(Ann Duffield) *slt ld: hdd whn hmpd 2f out: sn btn* **11/4**[3]

59.58 secs (-0.82) **Going Correction** -0.275s/f (Firm) **5** Ran SP% **106.0**
Speed ratings (Par 92): **95,89,87,86,82**
CSF £31.85 TOTE £3.00: £1.90, £11.00; EX 20.10.
Owner Denton Hall Racing Ltd **Bred** Shane Moroney **Trained** Denton, Co Durham
■ Stewards' Enquiry : Julie Burke two-day ban: careless riding (12-13 Aug)

FOCUS
A nursery with little strength in depth but an easy winner.

NOTEBOOK
Amadeus Denton(IRE), a winner second time out at Doncaster, had finished third behind two useful types at Thirsk. Unsuited by the easy ground on his nursery bow at Haydock, he was surprisingly dropped 6lb as a result. He always looked in command from the front here and came right away in the final furlong. It probably took little winning but he could hardly have done it in better fashion. (op 2-1)
Stans Deelyte, 11lb out of the handicap, had finished second last on his first try in nursery company two weeks earlier. This was a much improved effort but exactly what he achieved remains to be seen. (op 16-1)
Superplex, runner-up three times before a below-par effort over 6f at Catterick, was never going the pace. A really sharp five like this didn't suit him but he is looking fully exposed already. (op 15-8 tchd 2-1)
Just Dixie, 11lb out of the weights, gave away three lengths at the start. His proximity puts another question mark over the overall value of the form. (tchd 20-1)
Lady Caprice, who took a claimer in first-time blinkers at Catterick, attempted to match strides with the winner and was already feeling the strain when hampered soon after halfway. (tchd 9-4)

4501 WILKINSON & ASSOCIATES (S) STKS 1m 1f

7:05 (7:05) (Class 6) 3-Y-0+ **£1,940** (£577; £288; £144) **Stalls** Low

Form RPR
11-2 **1** **Belle Noverre (IRE)**[51] 2807 7-9-0 **75**............................ FrederikTylicki 5 67+
(Shaun Harley, Ire) *prom: smooth hdwy to ld over 2f out: edgd rt over 1f out: drew clr fnl f* **15/8**[1]
206 **2** *5* **Georgebernardshaw (IRE)**[13] 4107 6-9-3 **76**.........(p) ShaneBKelly(7) 6 66
(John Quinn) *led to over 2f out: sn rdn: no ex fr over 1f out* **2/1**[2]
0003 **3** *5* **Cold Quest (USA)**[4] 4383 7-9-0 **47**.................................. JulieBurke(5) 2 50
(Linda Perratt) *in tch: effrt over 2f out: sn no imp* **20/1**
6000 **4** *3 ½* **Tukitinyasok (IRE)**[6] 4349 4-9-5 **77**.............................. JamesSullivan 1 42
(Clive Mulhall) *hld up in tch: rdn over 2f out: sn btn* **12/1**
1135 **5** *1 ¾* **Fremen (USA)**[21] 3831 11-9-3 **75**............................ ShirleyTeasdale(7) 3 43
(David Nicholls) *cl up tl rdn and wknd over 1f out* **11/4**[3]

1m 51.1s (-2.80) **Going Correction** -0.275s/f (Firm)
WFA 3 from 4yo+ 9lb **5** Ran SP% **107.2**
Speed ratings (Par 101): **101,96,92,89,87**
CSF £5.61 TOTE £3.60: £2.00, £2.50; EX 6.50.The winner was bought in for £10,500
Owner Lough Derg Syndicate **Bred** Rozelle Bloodstock **Trained** Letterkenny, Co Donegal

FOCUS
A run-of-the-mill seller and a straightforward task for the horse top on official ratings. The form is limited by the proximity of the third.

4502 BLACKROCK E.B.F. CONDITIONS STKS 5f

7:40 (7:40) (Class 3) 2-Y-0 **£7,762** (£2,310; £1,154; £577) **Stalls** High

Form RPR
4221 **1** **Excelette (IRE)**[20] 3849 2-8-8 0.............................. RoystonFfrench 2 78
(Bryan Smart) *mde all: rdn over 1f out: kpt on wl fnl f* **5/2**[2]
6204 **2** *1 ¼* **Cravat**[21] 3810 2-8-13 0.. FrederikTylicki 3 79
(Mark Johnston) *chsd ldrs: n.m.r briefly over 2f out: sn rdn: kpt on to chse wnr ins fnl f: r.o* **11/4**[3]
321 **3** *shd* **Verbeeck**[49] 2880 2-9-2 0.. RichardMullen 1 81
(Ed McMahon) *trckd ldr to over 1f out: sn rdn: edgd rt and disp 2nd wl ins fnl f: r.o* **9/4**[1]
1 **4** *1 ¼* **Al Shaqab (IRE)**[24] 3707 2-8-11 0.............................. JulieBurke(5) 4 77
(Kevin Ryan) *dwlt: sn trcking ldrs: effrt and pressed wnr over 1f out to ins fnl f: r.o same pce* **4/1**
1 **5** *1* **Class Monitor**[11] 4147 2-8-8 0.................................. AndrewElliott 5 67+
(Mrs K Burke) *dwlt: in tch: effrt whn n.m.r over 1f out: sn no imp* **14/1**

59.06 secs (-1.34) **Going Correction** -0.275s/f (Firm) **5** Ran SP% **112.7**
Speed ratings (Par 98): **99,97,96,94,93**
CSF £9.98 TOTE £4.10: £2.80, £1.50; EX 8.80.
Owner Crossfields Racing **Bred** David John Brown **Trained** Hambleton, N Yorks

FOCUS
Quite a valuable Class 3 event contested by five previous winners. The runner-up is the best guide to the level.

NOTEBOOK
Excelette(IRE), who did well to get up on the line at Chester on her fourth start after being forced wide, hit the traps running. She came off the rail but, showing a very willing attitude, was always doing more than enough. She is progressing nicely. (tchd 11-4 in a place)
Cravat, a winner first time, was having his sixth start. Fourth in a Chester 6f nursery, that trip may suit him slightly better. (tchd 3-1)
Verbeeck, a Sandown easy-ground winner, was very warm at the start. He hung violently and looked anything but a straightforward ride. (tchd 2-1 and 11-4)
Al Shaqab(IRE), a Southwell all-weather maiden race winner, looked to have plenty to find, so this marked a big step-up. It will not have done his nursery mark any good however. (op 15-2 tchd 8-1)
Class Monitor, who landed a touch in a Beverley claimer, had a lot more on her plate. She was far from disgraced and would have finished a fraction closer with a better run. However, this effort will have blown a possible lenient nursery mark out of the water. (op 11-1)

4503 WILKINSON & ASSOCIATES H'CAP (A QUALIFIER FOR BETFAIR BONUS SCOTTISH RACING MILE FINAL) 7f 30y

8:15 (8:18) (Class 5) (0-75,74) 4-Y-0+ **£4,204** (£1,251; £625; £312) **Stalls** Low

Form RPR
5050 **1** **Al Muheer (IRE)**[6] 4314 6-9-7 **74**................................(b) JamesSullivan 1 86
(Ruth Carr) *trckd ldrs: swtchd lft and led over 1f out: edgd lft: drvn and kpt on fnl f* **4/1**[2]
5235 **2** *2* **Berbice (IRE)**[5] 4362 6-8-9 **67**.. JulieBurke(5) 4 74
(Linda Perratt) *s.i.s: hld up: hdwy over 2f out: ev ch ins fnl f: no ex last 50yds* **10/1**
0526 **3** *2 ¾* **Nufoudh (IRE)**[21] 3806 7-8-12 **68**................................ PaulPickard(3) 2 68
(Colin Teague) *sn led: rdn over 2f out: hdd over 1f out: kpt on same pce fnl f* **15/2**
4213 **4** *¾* **Tamasou (IRE)**[18] 3924 6-9-7 **74**.................................... RichardMullen 6 72
(Ed McMahon) *hld up towards rr: rdn over 3f out: hdwy over 2f out: no imp fnl f* **7/2**[1]
4412 **5** *1 ½* **Gemma's Delight (IRE)**[21] 3806 4-8-10 **63**.............(p) PatrickMathers 7 57
(James Unett) *walked to s: dwlt: hld up: effrt on outside over 2f out: sn no imp* **13/2**
1336 **6** *1 ¼* **Hinton Admiral**[15] 4013 7-9-4 **71**.................................. DanielTudhope 5 61
(Keith Dalgleish) *in tch: rdn over 2f out: btn over 1f out* **7/1**
0-60 **7** *4 ½* **Angaric (IRE)**[20] 3856 8-8-5 **58**................................ RoystonFfrench 3 36
(Bryan Smart) *plld hrd: cl up tl rdn and wknd fr 2f out* **20/1**
5050 **8** *1 ¼* **Ghost (IRE)**[6] 4349 4-8-13 **73**.................................. ShirleyTeasdale(7) 8 48
(David Nicholls) *early ldr: cl up tl rdn and wknd 2f out* **20/1**
2041 **9** *3* **Frequency**[26] 3657 4-9-6 **73**..(b) FrederikTylicki 9 40
(Keith Dalgleish) *hld up: effrt on outside over 2f out: wknd over 1f out* **5/1**[3]

1m 26.94s (-2.06) **Going Correction** -0.275s/f (Firm) **9** Ran SP% **115.1**
Speed ratings (Par 103): **100,97,94,93,92 90,85,84,80**
toteswingers:1&2:£9.10, 2&3:£10.80, 1&3:£6.80 CSF £43.25 CT £283.99 TOTE £5.60: £1.10, £2.60, £1.70; EX 50.50.
Owner Sprint King Racing (Antigua Cavaliers) **Bred** Foursome Thoroughbreds **Trained** Huby, N Yorks

FOCUS
A modest 58-74 handicap run at a furious pace and half-a-dozen almost in a line over a furlong out. The runner-up is probably the best guide.

4504 BLACKROCK H'CAP (A QUALIFIER FOR BETFAIR BONUS SCOTTISH RACING SPRINT FINAL) 5f

8:45 (8:46) (Class 5) (0-70,69) 3-Y-0+ **£4,204** (£1,251; £625; £312) **Stalls** High

Form RPR
1540 **1** **Midnight Dynamo**[15] 4013 4-9-8 **65**............................ DanielTudhope 11 77
(Jim Goldie) *in tch: rdn and hdwy over 1f out: led ins fnl f: comf* **7/1**
0004 **2** *1 ¼* **Blown It (USA)**[11] 4144 5-8-7 **50** oh1............................ JamesSullivan 9 58
(Keith Dalgleish) *slt ld to ins fnl f: kpt on towards fin* **10/1**
3021 **3** *½* **Arriva La Diva**[18] 3901 5-9-1 **63**...................................... JulieBurke(5) 6 69
(Linda Perratt) *disp ld to ins fnl f: kpt on same pce towards fin* **13/2**[3]
0000 **4** *1* **Ya Boy Sir (IRE)**[14] 4041 4-8-7 **50** oh5......................(b) DuranFentiman 2 52
(Ian Semple) *s.i.s: sn wl bhd: gd hdwy fnl f: nrst fin* **50/1**
0002 **5** *¾* **Argentine (IRE)**[15] 4017 7-8-13 **56**................................(b) LeeNewman 4 56
(George Foster) *prom: bmpd after 1f: effrt 2f out: kpt on same pce fnl f* **8/1**

5244 **6** *½* **Lees Anthem**[18] [3901] 4-8-12 **58**........ PaulPickard(3) 5 56+
(Colin Teague) *dwlt: bhd and pushed along: hdwy on outside 1/2-way: effrt and edgd lft over 1f out: one pce fnl f* **6/1**[2]

651 **7** *¾* **Hypnosis**[28] [3579] 8-9-7 **69**........ NeilFarley(5) 8 64+
(Noel Wilson) *dwlt: bhd and pushed along: effrt on outside 1/2-way: no imp fnl f* **6/1**[2]

6032 **8** *shd* **Dower Glen**[18] [3901] 4-8-13 **56**........(v) RichardMullen 10 51
(Keith Dalgleish) *in tch: rdn 1/2-way: no ex over 1f out* **12/1**

3233 **9** *½* **Ingleby Star (IRE)**[11] [4152] 6-9-9 **69**........(p) GaryBartley(3) 3 62+
(Ian McInnes) *prom: rdn over 2f out: checked over 1f out: sn btn* **3/1**[1]

0-00 **10** *4½* **Cayman Fox**[6] [4327] 6-9-11 **68**........ TonyHamilton 1 45
(Linda Perratt) *cl up tl rdn and wknd fr 2f out* **20/1**

58.91 secs (-1.49) **Going Correction** -0.275s/f (Firm) **10** Ran SP% **114.0**
Speed ratings (Par 103): **100,98,97,95,94 93,92,92,91,84**
toteswingers:1&2:£5.10, 2&3:£7.70, 1&3:£9.20 CSF £73.04 CT £475.47 TOTE £9.50: £2.40, £4.00, £1.40; EX 118.00.
Owner Lorimer Racing **Bred** E W Hyslop **Trained** Uplawmoor, E Renfrews
■ Stewards' Enquiry : Lee Newman three-day ban: careless riding (12-14 Aug)

FOCUS
A very modest sprint handicap run at a breakneck pace. The form looks sound though, rated around the third and several of those unplaced.
Midnight Dynamo Official explanation: trainer said, regarding the apparent improvement of form, that the filly appreciated the drop back to five furlongs

4505 EVEN ODDER H'CAP (A QUALIFIER FOR BETFAIR BONUS SCOTTISH RACING MILE FINAL) 1m
9:15 (9:16) (Class 6) (0-65,64) 3-Y-O **£2,587** (£770; £384; £96; £96) **Stalls** Low

Form RPR
601 **1** **Last Destination (IRE)**[11] [4149] 3-9-6 **64** 6ex........ ShaneBKelly(7) 1 71
(Nigel Tinkler) *hld up: hdwy over 2f out: rdn over 1f out: edgd rt and led ins fnl f: r.o* **9/4**[1]

0020 **2** *1* **Cannon Bolt (IRE)**[23] [3724] 3-8-13 **50**........(b) LeeNewman 7 54
(Robin Bastiman) *led at str pce and clr w one other: rdn over 2f out: hdd ins fnl f: kpt on u.p* **12/1**

-603 **3** *nk* **Syncopated Lady (IRE)**[7] [4284] 3-8-13 **50**........(e) DanielTudhope 9 53
(David O'Meara) *stmbld sn after s: towards rr: rdn along 3f out: gd hdwy over 1f out: styd on wl fnl f* **7/2**[2]

0032 **4** *1¼* **Hardrock Diamond**[11] [4146] 3-8-10 **47**........ DuranFentiman 3 47
(Ian Semple) *hld up: rdn and hdwy over 2f out: kpt on same pce ins fnl f* **6/1**

300 **4** *dht* **Diamond Sunrise (IRE)**[32] [3455] 3-8-7 **49**........ NeilFarley(5) 8 49
(Noel Wilson) *in tch: effrt over 2f out: edgd rt: kpt on same pce ins fnl f* **40/1**

6006 **6** *8* **Langtoon Lass**[11] [4149] 3-8-8 **52**........ ShirleyTeasdale(7) 11 34
(David Nicholls) *chsd clr ldng pair: rdn and hung lft over 2f out: sn wknd* **40/1**

0502 **7** *1¾* **Deep Applause**[7] [4284] 3-9-2 **53**........(p) TonyHamilton 6 31
(Michael Dods) *s.i.s: hld up: effrt and hdwy over 1f out: nvr able to chal* **11/2**[3]

0-30 **8** *8* **Chillianwallah**[80] [1984] 3-8-11 **48**........ PatrickMathers 2 —
(James Unett) *s.i.s: bhd: rdn along over 3f out: nvr on terms* **33/1**

6004 **9** *1¼* **Smart Step**[15] [4018] 3-8-11 **48**........(b[1]) AndrewElliott 4 —
(Mark Johnston) *pressed ldr and clr of rest: rdn over 2f out: hung rt and wknd wl over 1f out* **7/1**

0306 **10** *7* **Crabbies Bay**[18] [3913] 3-8-13 **50**........ FrederikTylicki 5 —
(Lisa Williamson) *midfield: drvn and outpcd over 3f out: btn fnl 2f* **25/1**

-604 **11** *3¼* **Sheedal (IRE)**[4] [4383] 3-8-8 **45**........ JamesSullivan 10 —
(Linda Perratt) *hld up on outside: struggling over 3f out: sn btn* **20/1**

1m 40.09s (-1.11) **Going Correction** -0.275s/f (Firm) **11** Ran SP% **119.3**
Speed ratings (Par 98): **94,93,92,91,91 83,81,73,72,65 62**
toteswingers:1&2:£4.00, 2&3:£11.20, 1&3:£3.10 CSF £29.76 CT £95.40 TOTE £2.90: £2.00, £4.50, £2.10; EX 45.20.
Owner A Killoran **Bred** Pier House Stud **Trained** Langton, N Yorks

FOCUS
The home turn was sanded before this low-grade 45-64 handicap in which the two leaders went off very fast.
[illegible] Pool£29,904.60 - 88.45 winning tickets T/Qpdt: £65.70 to a £1 stake. Pool:£4,213.96 - 47.40 winning tickets [illegible]

[4330] NEWMARKET (R-H)
Friday, July 29

OFFICIAL GOING: Good to firm
Wind: Light across Weather: Overcast

4506 GRANTS WHISKY H'CAP 1m
5:50 (5:50) (Class 4) (0-80,80) 3-Y-O+ **£4,528** (£1,347; £673; £336) **Stalls** High

Form RPR
/0-0 **1** **Stevie Thunder**[15] [4004] 6-9-9 **78**........ RyanClark(3) 3 93
(Ian Williams) *trckd ldrs: led over 2f out: rdn and hung lft over 1f out: sn clr: easily* **7/1**

0165 **2** *4½* **Aciano (IRE)**[20] [3840] 3-9-6 **80**........ ShaneKelly 4 83
(Brian Meehan) *chsd ldr: rdn and ev ch 2f out: no ex fnl f* **7/4**[1]

5050 **3** *¾* **Inpursuitoffreedom**[42] [3130] 4-9-2 **68**........ PatCosgrave 1 71
(Philip McBride) *hld up in tch: rdn over 2f out: sn ev ch: hung lft and no ex fnl f* **8/1**

6033 **4** *nk* **Joe Strummer (IRE)**[7] [4281] 3-8-0 **63**........(v) LouisBeuzelin(3) 6 63
(Michael Bell) *hld up: hdwy over 2f out: rdn over 1f out: styd on same pce* **7/2**[2]

-140 **5** *7* **Two Certainties**[7] [4278] 4-8-12 **64**........ WilliamCarson 5 50
(Stuart Williams) *prom: rdn over 2f out: wknd over 1f out* **11/2**[3]

0026 **6** *14* **Old English (IRE)**[10] [4176] 3-8-10 **70**........ DarryllHolland 2 22
(Mark Johnston) *sn led: rdn and hdd over 2f out: wknd over 1f out: eased* **15/2**

1m 39.23s (-0.77) **Going Correction** +0.10s/f (Good)
WFA 3 from 4yo+ 8lb **6** Ran SP% **109.3**
Speed ratings (Par 105): **107,102,101,101,94 80**
toteswingers:1&2:£2.90, 2&3:£3.20, 1&3:£8.90 CSF £18.73 TOTE £12.00: £7.30, £1.02; EX 22.10.
Owner Steve Gray **Bred** Sir Eric Parker **Trained** Portway, Worcs

FOCUS
Stands side track used with stalls on far side except 1m4f, centre. A one-sided handicap. The winner was well in and is rated back to his old level.
Stevie Thunder Official explanation: trainer's representative said, regarding the apparent improvement of form, that the gelding had been dropped in trip

4507 RUSSIAN STANDARD VODKA EBF MYBOYCHARLIE MAIDEN STKS 6f
6:20 (6:24) (Class 4) 2-Y-O **£4,528** (£1,347; £673; £336) **Stalls** High

Form RPR
32 **1** **Justineo**[29] [3553] 2-9-3 0........ JamieSpencer 2 85+
(William Haggas) *hld up: hdwy to ld over 2f out: sn hung lft: rdn out* **1/1**[1]

2 *2½* **Go Dutch (IRE)** 2-9-3 0........ NeilCallan 9 75+
(Roger Varian) *a.p: swtchd rt over 1f out: shkn up and styd on to go 2nd wl ins fnl f: nt trble wnr* **6/1**[3]

0 **3** *1¼* **Philipstown**[9] [4201] 2-9-3 0........ PatDobbs 8 71
(Richard Hannon) *led: rdn and hdd over 2f out: no ex and lost 2nd pl wl ins fnl f* **8/1**

2 **4** *1½* **Grizzle**[13] [4098] 2-9-3 0........ FrankieDettori 6 66
(Mahmood Al Zarooni) *hld up: hdwy over 3f out: ev ch over 2f out: nt clr run sn after: no ex fnl f* **9/4**[2]

00 **5** *hd* **Voodoo Rhythm (USA)**[15] [4007] 2-9-0 0........ LouisBeuzelin(3) 5 66
(Brian Meehan) *w ldrs: rdn and ev ch over 2f out: styd on same pce fr over 1f out* **66/1**

54 **6** *8* **Storm Belt (USA)**[37] [3282] 2-9-3 0........ AhmedAjtebi 1 42
(Mahmood Al Zarooni) *prom: rdn and ev ch over 2f out: wknd over 1f out* **25/1**

0 **7** *2½* **Queens Sandridge (IRE)**[18] [3915] 2-9-3 0........ AdamKirby 3 34
(Alan Bailey) *w ldrs: rdn and ev ch over 2f out: wknd over 1f out* **33/1**

1m 13.47s (0.97) **Going Correction** +0.10s/f (Good) **7** Ran SP% **114.4**
Speed ratings (Par 96): **97,93,92,90,89 79,75**
toteswingers:1&2:£1.80, 2&3:£6.00, 1&3:£3.70 CSF £7.58 TOTE £1.90: £1.50, £1.80; EX 8.50.
Owner Saleh Al Homaizi & Imad Al Sagar **Bred** Saleh Al Homaizi & Imad Al Sagar **Trained** Newmarket, Suffolk

FOCUS
Not the strongest maiden by the track's standards, but the winner repeated the good level he'd shown at Yarmouth.

NOTEBOOK
Justineo, who was just touched off by a subsequent Listed winner at Yarmouth last time, and made no mistake this time, travelling strongly and leaving the impression he was doing no more than required in front. He'll have to improve a fair bit to justify his Pattern entries, but he's certainly going the right way. (op 11-10 tchd 5-4)
Go Dutch(IRE), a son of Dutch Art, is in top hands and made a promising start, tapped for speed at halfway but keeping on well in the closing stages. His dam had form up to 1m2f so it's reasonable to assume he'll stay a bit further. (op 15-2 tchd 8-1)
Philipstown duly improved on his debut. There's speed in his pedigree and the drop back to 6f suited if anything, cutting out the running. He could be the sort to progress with racing. (op 20-1)
Grizzle had shaped with promise in second on his debut over C&D a couple of weeks ago so this was a shade disappointing, particularly given the form of the yard in general. It's still early days, though. (op 15-8 tchd 7-4)
Voodoo Rhythm(USA) achieved a bit more than previously and it would be no surprise if there's more to come now he's eligible for nurseries, shaping as if a return to 7f might suit if anything.
Storm Belt(USA), who got rid of his rider at one stage down at the start, looks one of the yard's lesser lights at this stage, though this does at least open up the nursery route for him. (op 28-1 tchd 33-1)

4508 RUSSIAN STANDARD "VODKA AS IT SHOULD BE" NOVICE STKS 7f
6:55 (6:55) (Class 4) 2-Y-O **£3,881** (£1,155; £577; £288) **Stalls** High

Form RPR
1 **1** **Crius (IRE)**[22] [3780] 2-9-2 0........ PatDobbs 1 88+
(Richard Hannon) *chsd ldr: rdn to ld ins fnl f: r.o* **4/1**[2]

01 **2** *¾* **Jubilance (IRE)**[9] [4201] 2-8-13 0........ JohnFahy(3) 3 86
(Jeremy Noseda) *hld up in tch: led over 1f out: rdn and hdd ins fnl f: kpt on* **6/4**[1]

01 **3** *1½* **Mister Music**[16] [3986] 2-9-2 0........ KierenFallon 4 82+
(Richard Hannon) *trckd ldrs: racd keenly: nt clr run over 1f out: swtchd rt: rdn and hung lft ins fnl f: nvr able to chal* **6/4**[1]

1 **4** *3* **Broxbourne (IRE)**[38] [3242] 2-8-11 0........ DarryllHolland 2 69
(Mark Johnston) *led: rdn over 2f out: hdd over 1f out: no ex ins fnl f* **14/1**[3]

1m [illegible] **Going Correction** [illegible] **4** Ran SP% **106.7**
Speed ratings (Par 96): **94,93,91,88**
CSF £10.17 TOTE £6.40; EX 12.30.
Owner Titan Assets **Bred** Oak Lodge Bloodstock **Trained** East Everleigh, Wilts

FOCUS
A useful conditions event, with all four previous winners. Predictably, the pace wasn't strong, the race not beginning in earnest until the final 3f. The form is rated at face value but could be worth a bit more.

NOTEBOOK
Crius(IRE) made it 2-2 in determined fashion. His lack of Pattern entries suggests he perhaps doesn't figure that high up his top yard's juvenile pecking order but his likeable attitude should continue to hold him in good stead. (op 11-2)
Jubilance(IRE) confirmed he has a useful level of ability without having any obvious excuses. He's only had the three starts, though, so it's not unreasonable to expect further progress. (op 13-8 tchd 5-4)
Mister Music couldn't really be described as unlucky, though the race didn't pan out ideally for him either, searching for a run just as the race things were hotting up, which left him with a bit to do. His tendency to lug left near the finish was a sign that he's still not the finished article and he's worth another chance. (op 5-4)
Broxbourne(IRE)'s debut form isn't that strong and she was fairly readily brushed aside after dictating the pace for a long way. (op 8-1)

4509 ENJOY RUSSIAN STANDARD VODKA RESPONSIBLY H'CAP 7f
7:30 (7:31) (Class 4) (0-85,85) 4-Y-O+ **£4,528** (£1,347; £673; £336) **Stalls** High

Form RPR
63-6 **1** **Dominium (USA)**[23] [3737] 4-8-10 **74**........ SteveDrowne 1 82
(Jeremy Gask) *racd centre: chsd ldr of that gp tl rdn to ld ins fnl f: jst hld on* **12/1**

21-0 **2** *shd* **Avon Lady**[93] [1610] 4-8-13 **77**........ PatCosgrave 11 85
(James Fanshawe) *racd far side: chsd ldrs: rdn over 1f out: led that gp wl ins fnl f: r.o u.p: jst failed* **15/2**[3]

0002 **3** *nk* **Big Noise**[15] [4020] 7-9-4 **82**........(v[1]) TedDurcan 7 89+
(Dr Jon Scargill) *racd far side: hld up: swtchd rt over 2f out: rdn and r.o wl ins fnl f* **8/1**

0002 **4** *nk* **Hacienda (IRE)**[3] [4404] 4-9-3 **81**........ DarryllHolland 3 87
(Mark Johnston) *overall ldr in centre: rdn over 1f out: edgd lft: hdd ins fnl f: styd on* **10/3**[1]

11-2 **5** *nk* **Sir Mozart (IRE)**[4] [4393] 8-8-8 **72**........ TomQueally 9 77
(Barney Curley) *racd far side: hld up: rdn over 1f out: r.o: nt rch ldrs* **5/1**[2]

-000 6 ½ **Saint Pierre (USA)**[28] 3578 4-9-6 **84** J-PGuillambert 4 88
(Luca Cumani) *racd far side: trckd ldr: racd keenly: rdn to ld that gp over 1f out tl hdd and unable qck wl ins fnl f* **10/1**

2-20 7 2 **Hot Spark**[37] 3290 4-9-6 **84** (t) NeilCallan 10 83
(John Akehurst) *led far side tl rdn and hdd over 1f out: no ex ins fnl f* **10/1**

-210 8 1¼ **Tariq Too**[42] 3134 4-8-13 **80** AdamBeschizza(3) 5 75
(David Simcock) *racd centre: hld up: hdwy over 2f out: sn rdn and edgd lft: no ex ins fnl f* **10/3**[1]

3-00 9 nk **Plume**[29] 3536 4-8-11 **78** JohnFahy(3) 12 72
(Roger Teal) *racd far side: prom: rdn over 1f out: styd on same pce* **28/1**

1023 10 8 **Frognal (IRE)**[15] 4006 5-9-1 **79** (b) HayleyTurner 13 52
(Conor Dore) *racd far side: prom: rdn and wknd over 1f out* **20/1**

1m 26.35s (0.65) **Going Correction** +0.10s/f (Good) **10** Ran SP% **119.8**
Speed ratings (Par 105): **100,99,99,99,98 98,96,94,94,85**
toteswingers:1&2:£20.00, 2&3:£12.20, 1&3:£21.30 CSF £101.55 CT £794.59 TOTE £22.60: £5.00, £2.90, £2.80; EX 119.10.

Owner Richard L Page **Bred** Corbett Farm **Trained** Sutton Veny, Wilts

FOCUS
A messy affair, with a group of three, including the winner, racing wide of the main body of runners on the far rail, and they finished in a bit of a heap, but quite a few of the principals are relatively unexposed, so it might pay to view the form fairly positively for now. The winner rates a 5lb personal best.

4510 PIPER-HEIDSIECK CHAMPAGNE H'CAP 1m 4f
8:05 (8:07) (Class 5) (0-70,70) 3-Y-O **£2,587** (£770; £384; £192) **Stalls** Centre

Form RPR

-006 1 **Apparel (IRE)**[71] 2225 3-8-12 **61** JamieSpencer 6 71
(Ed Dunlop) *hld up: hdwy over 5f out: chsd ldr over 1f out: shkn up to ld ins fnl f: styd on* **4/1**[3]

-230 2 2¼ **Maher (USA)**[20] 3872 3-9-4 **70** AdamBeschizza(3) 7 76
(David Simcock) *hld up: hdwy over 3f out: led over 2f out: rdn over 1f out: hdd and unable qck ins fnl f* **5/1**

000 3 8 **Bright Abbey**[33] 3430 3-8-13 **62** KierenFallon 9 55
(Walter Swinburn) *prom: chsd ldr over 8f out: rdn over 2f out: wknd fnl f* **7/2**[2]

5044 4 ¾ **Band Of Thunder**[7] 4274 3-8-5 **54** (v) HayleyTurner 2 46
(Andrew Balding) *chsd ldr over 3f: remained handy: rdn over 4f out: wknd over 1f out* **10/3**[1]

1615 5 nk **Jeu De Vivre (IRE)**[20] 3858 3-9-6 **69** DarryllHolland 8 61
(Mark Johnston) *chsd ldrs: led 3f out: rdn and hdd over 2f out: wknd over 1f out* **4/1**[3]

0640 6 37 **Grecian Goddess (IRE)**[2] 4449 3-8-8 **57** AhmedAjtebi 1 —
(John Ryan) *led: hdd 3f out: sn wknd: t.o* **14/1**

4000 7 7 **Varlak**[14] 4060 3-8-2 **51** oh5 (p) JamieMackay 4 —
(K F Clutterbuck) *hld up: hdwy 6f out: wknd over 3f out: t.o* **40/1**

2m 34.04s (1.14) **Going Correction** +0.10s/f (Good) **7** Ran SP% **111.1**
Speed ratings (Par 100): **100,98,93,92,92 67,63**
toteswingers:1&2:£4.00, 2&3:£3.70, 1&3:£2.50 CSF £22.64 CT £72.31 TOTE £5.30: £2.00, £2.70; EX 26.10.

Owner Cliveden Stud **Bred** Cliveden Stud Ltd **Trained** Newmarket, Suffolk

FOCUS
Hard to believe this was a strong handicap but the first two have to be given a bit of credit for pulling so far clear, particularly the winner who appeals as the type to go on from this. She rates a 10lb personal best.

4511 PIPER-HEIDSIECK ROSE SAUVAGE H'CAP 6f
8:35 (8:35) (Class 5) (0-70,70) 3-Y-O **£2,587** (£770; £384; £192) **Stalls** High

Form RPR

0003 1 **Brave Dream**[14] 4067 3-8-12 **61** NeilCallan 7 69
(Kevin Ryan) *racd centre: led that gp: overall ldr over 1f out: rdn out* **9/2**[2]

2 1¼ **Showboating (IRE)**[29] 3564 3-8-13 **65** (p) MartinHarley(3) 9 69
(Alan McCabe) *racd far side: chsd ldr tl led overall 2f out: rdn and hdd over 1f out: styd on: 1st of 2 in gp* **12/1**

0221 3 ¾ **Golden Compass**[11] 4162 3-8-7 **56** 6ex WilliamCarson 3 58
(Giles Bravery) *racd centre: chsd wnr: rdn over 1f out: hung lft ins fnl f: r.o: 2nd of 7 in gp* **9/2**[2]

5554 4 1 **Whipphound**[14] 4048 3-9-7 **70** ShaneKelly 5 68
(Mark Brisbourne) *racd centre: prom: rdn over 1f out: r.o: 3rd of 7 in gp* **9/2**[2]

0200 5 hd **Rafaaf (IRE)**[30] 3523 3-9-7 **70** DarryllHolland 1 68
(Robert Eddery) *racd centre: hld up in tch: rdn over 2f out: r.o: nt trble ldrs: 4th of 7 in gp* **7/1**[3]

4605 6 hd **Chillie Peppar**[11] 4162 3-8-0 **52** oh2 ow1 CagriMetin(3) 2 49
(George Prodromou) *racd centre: hld up: rdn over 1f out: r.o ins fnl f: nrst fin: 5th of 7 in gp* **25/1**

2325 7 nk **Roman Strait**[14] 4062 3-9-5 **68** TedDurcan 6 64
(Michael Blanshard) *racd centre: hld up in tch: rdn and edgd lft over 2f out: styd on same pce ins fnl f: 6th of 7 in gp* **4/1**[1]

-055 8 4½ **Magic Stella**[14] 4067 3-9-5 **68** KierenFallon 10 50
(Alan Jarvis) *overall ldr far side over 3f: sn rdn: wknd and eased fnl f: last of 2 in gp* **8/1**

0404 9 15 **Reginald Claude**[9] 4199 3-9-0 **68** (v) LeeNewnes(5) 4 —
(Mark Usher) *racd centre: hld up: rdn over 2f out: wknd over 1f out: last of 7 in gp* **16/1**

1m 13.1s (0.60) **Going Correction** +0.10s/f (Good) **9** Ran SP% **115.6**
Speed ratings (Par 100): **100,98,97,96,95 95,95,89,69**
toteswingers:1&2:£21.70, 2&3:£8.00, 1&3:£2.70 CSF £56.78 CT £258.65 TOTE £2.90: £2.50, £4.20, £1.90; EX 75.40.

Owner Hokey Cokey Partnership **Bred** Emma Thorman & Trickledown Stud **Trained** Hambleton, N Yorks

FOCUS
Just an ordinary sprint which not many got into. Two, including the runner-up, stuck to the far rail, the main group, headed by the winner, coming up the centre. Modest form.

T/Plt: £1,857.80 to a £1 stake. Pool:£49,245.51 - 19.35 winning tickets T/Qpdt: £452.30 to a 31 stake. Pool:£4,340.33 - 7.10 winning tickets CR

4282 THIRSK (L-H)
Friday, July 29

OFFICIAL GOING: Good (8.7)
Wind: Virtually nil Weather: Cloudy

4512 HAMBLETON INN CLAIMING STKS 7f
2:20 (2:21) (Class 4) 2-Y-O **£3,881** (£1,155; £577; £288) **Stalls** Low

Form RPR

54 1 **Lolita Lebron (IRE)**[21] 3816 2-8-7 0 ow1 GrahamGibbons 1 66
(Tim Pitt) *mde all: rdn along and hung rt 2f out: drvn ins fnl f: kpt on strly* **4/1**[1]

011 2 1¾ **Lady Jourdain (IRE)**[9] 4193 2-8-9 0 AndrewElliott 8 64
(Mrs K Burke) *hld up in midfield: stdy hdwy 3f out: swtchd lft 2f out and sn chsng wnr: rdn over 1f out: drvn ins fnl f: no imp towards fin* **4/1**[1]

3300 3 2¾ **Yammos (IRE)**[20] 3866 2-8-11 0 (v[1]) MartinHarley(3) 12 62
(Mick Channon) *hld up: hdwy on outer 3f out: chsd ldrs 2f out and sn rdn: drvn over 1f out: no imp ins fnl f* **5/1**[2]

6260 4 hd **Jimmy The Lollipop (IRE)**[13] 4094 2-9-2 0 AmyRyan(3) 6 67
(Kevin Ryan) *in tch: hdwy on inner 3f out: rdn to chse ldrs wl over 1f out: sn drvn and kpt on same pce* **8/1**[3]

6562 5 nk **Koalition (IRE)**[16] 3973 2-9-0 0 TomEaves 10 61
(Deborah Sanderson) *wnt rt s: sn chsng ldrs: rdn over 2f out: drvn wl over 1f out: kpt on same pce* **12/1**

4662 6 1¾ **Jaci Uzzi (IRE)**[9] 4193 2-8-4 0 AndrewMullen 3 47
(David Evans) *towards rr: hdwy on outer over 2f out: sn rdn along and kpt on fnl f: nrst fin* **33/1**

4245 7 ½ **Latte**[26] 3656 2-8-12 0 TonyHamilton 5 53
(Linda Stubbs) *chsd ldrs: rdn along wl over 2f out: drvn wl over 1f out: sn wknd* **17/2**

0 8 6 **Bea Persuasive**[13] 4105 2-7-13 0 DanielleMcCreery(5) 9 30
(Shaun Harris) *a in rr* **100/1**

4150 9 ½ **Choice Of Remark (IRE)**[21] 3816 2-8-12 0 StevieDonohoe 2 37
(David Evans) *prom: rdn along wl over 2f out: sn drvn and grad wknd* **4/1**[1]

130 10 3¾ **Beaumaris (IRE)**[9] 4194 2-8-13 0 FrannyNorton 4 29
(Ann Duffield) *a towards rr* **10/1**

11 1¼ **Loving Emma** 2-8-4 0 ChrisDCogan(5) 13 22
(John Weymes) *dwlt and swtchd lft s: green and sn outpcd in rr: t.o 1/2-way: sme late hdwy* **80/1**

00 12 13 **Lady Advocate (IRE)**[25] 3680 2-8-7 0 (b) DuranFentiman 14 —
(Tim Easterby) *wnt rt s: t.k.h and sn chsng wnr: hung rt bnd after 2f: rdn along 3f out: sn wknd* **50/1**

1m 28.78s (1.58) **Going Correction** +0.175s/f (Good) **12** Ran SP% **122.2**
Speed ratings (Par 96): **97,95,91,91,91 89,88,81,81,77 75,60**
.Lolita Lebron was claimed by L. A. Mullaney for £7000.\n\x\x

Owner S E Sangster **Bred** Epona Bloodstock Ltd **Trained** Newmarket, Suffolk

FOCUS
An ordinary juvenile claimer in which few were ever seriously competitive. Straightforward form.

NOTEBOOK
Lolita Lebron(IRE) ◆ failed to confirm the promise she showed over 6f at Goodwood on her debut when only fourth in a Newbury seller last time, but she took this in the manner of a filly better than claiming class. Having her first start since leaving Richard Hannon, the slight step up in trip suited and she won with something in hand, carrying 1lb overweight. There should be more to come and she looks a shrewd claim at £7,000. (op 17-2)
Lady Jourdain(IRE) had won back-to-back sellers on softish ground, but she was no match at all for the winner this time. She won't mind a return to easier conditions and sellers and claimers are her level. (op 3-1 tchd 11-4)
Yammos(IRE) ran a bit better than of late dropped in grade and visored for the first time, but he was still short of his best early season form. (op 11-2 tchd 9-2)
Jimmy The Lollipop(IRE) had never previously raced beyond 5f and had no easy task under top weight. (op 17-2)
Choice Of Remark(IRE) was disappointing when behind today's winner in a Newbury seller last time and this was another performance that fell well short of his best form. Official explanation: jockey said that the colt lost action in the final half furlong (op 9-2 tchd 5-1)
Beaumaris(IRE) Official explanation: jockey said the filly was never travelling

4513 NORTHALLERTON SHOOTING & COUNTRY WEAR H'CAP (DIV I) 7f
2:55 (3:01) (Class 5) (0-70,70) 3-Y-O+ **£2,587** (£770; £384; £192) **Stalls** Low

Form RPR

3205 1 **Muftarres (IRE)**[27] 3636 6-9-8 **64** (p) TonyCulhane 7 74
(Paul Midgley) *in tch: hdwy 3f out: rdn to ld over 1f out: drvn and edgd lft ins fnl f: kpt on towards fin* **8/1**[3]

5-45 2 1 **Dialogue**[42] 3142 5-9-8 **67** MichaelO'Connell(3) 2 74
(Ollie Pears) *hld up in rr: hdwy on outer over 2f out: rdn to chse wnr ins fnl f: edgd lft and no imp towards fin* **5/2**[1]

1205 3 1¼ **Hayek**[11] 4141 4-9-9 **65** (b) DuranFentiman 1 69
(Tim Easterby) *chsd ldrs: hdwy 3f out: rdn 2f out and ev ch tl drvn and one pce ent fnl f* **8/1**[3]

0006 4 ¾ **Emeralds Spirit (IRE)**[4] 4383 4-9-2 **58** PJMcDonald 8 60
(John Weymes) *chsd ldrs: hdwy 3f out: swtchd lft to inner over 2f out and sn led: rdn and hdd over 1f out: drvn and one pce ins fnl f* **12/1**

0220 5 6 **Sairaam (IRE)**[34] 3387 5-9-5 **68** MatthewLawson(7) 3 53
(Charles Smith) *towards rr: hdwy 3f out: rdn along 2f out: drvn and no imp fr over 1f out* **9/1**

-405 6 nk **Wigram's Turn (USA)**[155] 674 6-9-0 **56** (t) GrahamGibbons 11 41
(Michael Easterby) *hld up towards rr: sme hdwy 2f out: n.d* **8/1**[3]

325 7 1¼ **Mark Anthony (IRE)**[67] 2356 4-9-10 **69** PaulPickard(3) 9 50
(Shaun Harris) *led: rdn along 3f out: hdd over 2f out and sn wknd* **33/1**

3-01 8 shd **Carragold**[14] 4076 5-8-11 **53** FrannyNorton 10 34
(Mel Brittain) *a towards rr* **7/2**[2]

6000 9 1 **Ellies Image**[43] 3093 4-8-10 **52** PatrickMathers 6 30
(Brian Baugh) *prom: hdwy and cl up 3f out: sn rdn and wknd wl over 1f out* **40/1**

5100 10 5 **J R Hartley**[13] 4107 3-9-7 **70** (p) TomEaves 4 32
(Bryan Smart) *chsd ldr: rdn along 1/2-way: sn wknd* **16/1**

1m 27.6s (0.40) **Going Correction** +0.175s/f (Good)
WFA 3 from 4yo+ 7lb **10** Ran SP% **113.1**
Speed ratings (Par 103): **104,102,101,100,93 93,91,91,90,84**
CSF £27.37 CT £169.23 TOTE £9.30: £2.70, £1.20, £2.20; EX 35.80.

Owner 21st Century Racing & T W Midgley **Bred** Shadwell Estate Company Limited **Trained** Westow, N Yorks

FOCUS
The pace was overly strong, the race setting up well for those held up, and this is weak form. The winner's best effort since late 2009.
Carragold Official explanation: jockey said that the gelding was denied a clear run

4514 STANLAND LAUNDRY MAIDEN STKS 1m
3:30 (3:32) (Class 4) 3-Y-O+ £4,528 (£1,347; £673; £336) Stalls Low

Form RPR

032 **1** **Federation**[14] 4065 3-8-12 78 GrahamGibbons 11 86+
(Roger Charlton) *mde all: qcknd clr wl over 2f out: kpt on strly* **6/4**[1]

2 *4* **Paramour** 4-9-11 0 DanielTudhope 9 79+
(David O'Meara) *hld up towards rr: hdwy on outer 3f out: rdn wl over 1f out: kpt on ins fnl f: nrst fin* **8/1**

3232 **3** *1* **Burj Hatta (USA)**[16] 3980 3-9-3 78 (p) FrannyNorton 6 74
(Saeed Bin Suroor) *hld up in tch: hdwy wl over 2f out: sn chsng wnr: rdn wl over 1f out: kpt on same pce* **7/4**[2]

42- **4** *4 1/2* **Dean Swift**[273] 7202 3-9-3 0 EddieCreighton 3 64
(Brian Meehan) *chsd ldrs: rdn along wl over 2f out: sn one pce* **5/1**[3]

5 *1 1/2* **Hills Of Dakota** 3-9-3 0 LeeNewman 2 60
(David Barron) *prom: rdn along on inner wl over 2f out: drvn wl over 1f out and kpt on same pce* **33/1**

5 **6** *3 3/4* **Isheforreal (IRE)**[7] 4282 4-9-8 0 PaulPickard(3) 8 53
(Brian Ellison) *nvr bttr than in midfield* **80/1**

7 *3/4* **Painted Tail (IRE)**[172] 4-9-6 0 PJMcDonald 1 46
(Alan Swinbank) *s.i.s and bhd: sme late hdwy* **50/1**

-00 **8** *1 1/2* **Srimenanti**[14] 4072 3-8-12 0 PaddyAspell 10 41
(Brian Rothwell) *chsd ldrs: rdn along over 3f out: sn wknd* **200/1**

00 **9** *12* **Ellemental**[77] 2045 3-8-9 0 MartinHarley(3) 4 12
(Mrs K Burke) *chsd wnr: rdn along 3f out and sn wknd* **100/1**

10 *13* **Gulf Of Naples (IRE)** 3-8-12 0 DarylByrne(5) 7 —
(Mark Johnston) *s.i.s: green and sn rdn along: a bhd* **16/1**

0 **11** *1 1/4* **Miss Kessie**[10] 4180 5-9-6 0 TonyCulhane 5 —
(Paul Midgley) *a in rr* **200/1**

1m 40.36s (0.26) **Going Correction** +0.175s/f (Good)
WFA 3 from 4yo+ 8lb **11** Ran SP% **118.1**
Speed ratings (Par 105): **105,101,100,95,94 90,89,88,76,63 61**
toteswingers:1&2:£3.20, 2&3:£4.30, 1&3:£1.20 CSF £14.64 TOTE £2.70: £1.10, £2.40, £1.20; EX 16.00.
Owner Duke Of Roxburghe **Bred** Floors Farming **Trained** Beckhampton, Wilts

FOCUS
An uncompetitive maiden in which Federation was helped by the combination of an uncontested lead and her two main rivals according to the market underperforming. The winner is rated value for 6l.
Miss Kessie Official explanation: jockey said that the mare hung right throughout

4515 THIRSK CASTLE FILLIES' H'CAP 1m 4f
4:05 (4:06) (Class 5) (0-70,70) 3-Y-O £2,911 (£866; £432; £216) Stalls Low

Form RPR

1042 **1** **Miss Topsy Turvy (IRE)**[14] 4074 3-9-5 68 FrannyNorton 3 75+
(John Dunlop) *chsd clr ldr: hdwy over 3f out: rdn along 2f out: drvn and hung rt 1f out: flashed tail ins fnl f but styd on to ld nr fin* **9/4**[2]

20 **2** *3/4* **Celani**[15] 4005 3-9-4 67 (p) GrahamGibbons 1 72
(Tim Walford) *led and sn clr: pushed along and qcknd 3f out: rdn 2f out: drvn over 1f out: hdd and no ex nr fin* **10/1**

-331 **3** *5* **Sangar**[15] 4005 3-8-12 61 TomEaves 6 58
(Ollie Pears) *hld up in rr: hdwy 4f out: rdn to chse ldng pair over 2f out: drvn wl over 1f out and kpt on same pce* **2/1**[1]

0045 **4** *3/4* **Bollin Mandy**[16] 3976 3-9-0 63 DanielTudhope 5 59
(Tim Easterby) *towards rr: hdwy over 3f out: rdn along over 2f out: drvn and kpt on same pce fr over 1f out* **17/2**

1222 **5** *8* **Pretty Diamond (IRE)**[40] 3210 3-9-2 70 DarylByrne(5) 7 53
(Mark Johnston) *in tch: hdwy to chse ldng pair over 3f out: rdn along wl over 2f out: sn drvn and wknd* **10/3**[3]

4606 **6** *15* **May Burnett (IRE)**[7] 4284 3-7-9 51 oh6 (t) NoelGarbutt(7) 2 10
(Brian Rothwell) *in tch: rdn along 4f out: sn wknd* **80/1**

2m 39.05s (2.85) **Going Correction** +0.175s/f (Good) **6** Ran SP% **108.0**
Speed ratings (Par 97): **97,96,93,92,87 77**
CSF £21.70 TOTE £2.70: £1.10, £5.30; EX 21.80.
Owner Windflower Overseas Holdings Inc **Bred** Windflower Overseas **Trained** Arundel, W Sussex

FOCUS
A modest fillies' handicap run at a reasonable pace.

4516 PETER BELL MEMORIAL H'CAP 6f
4:40 (4:45) (Class 4) (0-85,85) 3-Y-O+ £4,528 (£1,347; £673; £336) Stalls High

Form RPR

0262 **1** **Hotham**[7] 4291 8-9-4 77 BarryMcHugh 6 86
(Noel Wilson) *trckd ldrs: effrt and nt clr run over 1f out: sn swtchd lft and rdn to ld ent fnl f: drvn and edgd rt ins fnl f: hld on gamely* **15/2**

0030 **2** *nk* **Arganil (USA)**[3] 4416 6-9-6 82 (p) AmyRyan(3) 4 90+
(Kevin Ryan) *hld up in rr: hdwy 2f out: nt clr run over 1f out and again ent fnl f: squeezed through and rdn to chal wl ins fnl f: nt qckn towards fin* **7/1**

2061 **3** *nk* **Jarrow (IRE)**[15] 4013 4-9-3 79 MichaelO'Connell(3) 2 86+
(David Nicholls) *dwlt and swtchd rt to stands' rails after s: hld up in rr: hdwy 2f out: effrt and nt clr run over 1f out: rdn and qcknd to chal ins fnl f: ev ch whn edgd lft and nt qckn nr fin* **7/2**[1]

6525 **4** *2* **Cornus**[5] 4369 9-8-13 75 (be) MartinHarley(3) 7 76+
(Alan McCabe) *in rr: hdwy and n.m.r over 1f out: rdn ent fnl f: fin strly* **12/1**

0506 **5** *nk* **The Nifty Fox**[9] 4195 7-9-10 83 (v) GrahamGibbons 3 83
(Tim Easterby) *t.k.h early: trckd ldrs: effrt 2f out: rdn and n.m.r over 1f out: kpt on* **20/1**

5520 **6** *nse* **Magical Macey (USA)**[14] 4075 4-9-8 81 LeeNewman 11 80
(David Barron) *led: rdn along wl over 1f out: drvn: edgd lft and hdd ent fnl f: sn edgd rt and one pce* **7/1**

4442 **7** *hd* **Feel The Heat**[12] 4126 4-8-12 71 (v) TomEaves 10 70
(Bryan Smart) *trckd ldrs: hdwy 2f out: sn rdn and ev ch tl edgd rt and wknd ins fnl f* **5/1**[3]

-000 **8** *2* **Tallahasse (IRE)**[13] 4101 3-9-7 85 PJMcDonald 13 77
(Alan Swinbank) *trckd ldrs: hdwy on stands' rail 2f out: sn rdn and wknd appr fnl f* **20/1**

1625 **9** *3 1/2* **Bedloe's Island (IRE)**[6] 4327 6-9-4 77 FrannyNorton 8 58+
(Neville Bycroft) *hld up in rr: hdwy 2f out: sn rdn and nt clr run wl over 1f out: n.d* **12/1**

0221 **10** *3/4* **Caranbola**[3] 4405 5-8-10 76 6ex JohnCavanagh(7) 5 55
(Mel Brittain) *cl up: ev ch 2f out: sn rdn and wknd over 1f out* **9/2**[2]

0000 **11** *1 3/4* **Bahamian Lad**[20] 3850 6-8-9 68 (p) KellyHarrison 9 41
(Reg Hollinshead) *cl up: rdn along 2f out: sn wknd* **33/1**

101- **12** *7* **La Zamora**[313] 6221 5-9-7 85 LMcNiff(5) 1 36
(David Barron) *dwlt: hdwy and in tch on outer 1/2-way: sn rdn and wknd* **28/1**

1m 12.97s (0.27) **Going Correction** +0.05s/f (Good)
WFA 3 from 4yo+ 5lb **12** Ran SP% **125.1**
Speed ratings (Par 105): **100,99,99,96,96 96,95,93,88,87 85,75**
toteswingers:1&2:£8.20, 2&3:£5.90, 1&3:£8.10 CSF £59.65 CT £223.28 TOTE £8.90: £3.50, £2.70, £2.40; EX 57.50.
Owner Far 2 Many Sues **Bred** Capt J H Wilson **Trained** Sandhutton, N Yorks

FOCUS
A competitive handicap, and with the field tightly bunched towards the near rail, plenty found trouble. The winner is rated up slightly on his recent starts.
Bedloe's Island(IRE) Official explanation: jockey said that the gelding was denied a clear run

4517 NORTHALLERTON SHOOTING & COUNTRY WEAR H'CAP (DIV II) 7f
5:15 (5:16) (Class 5) (0-70,69) 3-Y-O+ £2,587 (£770; £384; £192) Stalls Low

Form RPR

4021 **1** **Dhhamaan (IRE)**[4] 4379 6-9-9 64 6ex (b) PJMcDonald 5 75
(Ruth Carr) *mde all: rdn wl over 1f out: drvn and kpt on wl ins fnl f* **11/4**[1]

6-34 **2** *2 1/4* **He's A Humbug (IRE)**[8] 4233 7-9-4 59 TonyCulhane 10 63
(Paul Midgley) *sn chsng wnr: effrt over 2f out: sn rdn and ev ch tl drvn and no imp ins fnl f* **14/1**

2546 **3** *1/2* **Piccolo Express**[39] 3241 5-9-2 57 GrahamGibbons 4 60
(Brian Baugh) *trckd ldrs: hdwy to chse ldng pair 2f out: drvn over 1f out: kpt on ins fnl f* **12/1**

0236 **4** *nk* **No Quarter (IRE)**[5] 4362 4-9-8 63 FrannyNorton 9 65
(Tracy Waggott) *hld up: hdwy over 3f out: rdn to chse ldrs 2f out: drvn over 1f out: kpt on same pce* **10/1**

1462 **5** *1* **Lindoro**[45] 3025 6-9-9 64 AndrewHeffernan 6 63
(Kevin M Prendergast) *in tch: hdwy on outer wl over 2f out: rdn wl over 1f out: kpt on same pce* **5/1**[3]

6043 **6** *1/2* **Ishetoo**[21] 3806 7-10-0 69 TomEaves 2 67
(Ollie Pears) *midfield: hdwy over 2f out: rdn and n.m.r over 1f out: sn swtchd lft and drvn: no imp* **8/1**

/066 **7** *1 1/4* **Big Slick (IRE)**[45] 3024 6-8-3 51 oh2 ow1 JohnCavanagh(7) 3 45
(Mel Brittain) *chsd ldrs: rdn along wl over 2f out: sn drvn and grad wknd* **16/1**

006 **8** *1 1/2* **Blue Noodles**[14] 4041 5-9-0 55 (p) PaddyAspell 11 45
(John Wainwright) *a towards rr* **33/1**

6110 **9** *1* **Flying Applause**[27] 3643 6-9-12 67 MarcHalford 1 55
(Roy Bowring) *chsd ldng pair on inner: rdn along wl over 2f out: grad wknd* **9/1**

31-2 **10** *13* **Opus Dei**[20] 3856 4-9-11 69 (v[1]) MichaelO'Connell(3) 8 22
(David Nicholls) *s.i.s: a in rr* **4/1**[2]

1m 28.38s (1.18) **Going Correction** +0.175s/f (Good) **10** Ran SP% **116.7**
Speed ratings (Par 103): **100,97,96,96,95 94,93,91,90,75**
toteswingers:1&2:£9.00, 2&3:£17.10, 1&3:£8.00 CSF £43.78 CT £414.21 TOTE £3.80: £1.80, £3.80, £4.00; EX 37.90.
Owner S B Clark **Bred** D Veitch And Musagd Abo Salim **Trained** Huby, N Yorks

FOCUS
The time was 0.78 seconds slower than the first division, although the ground would have deteriorated a touch. The 1-2 were always the front pair, and this was the winner's best run since he was a 3yo.
Opus Dei Official explanation: jockey said that the gelding missed the break

4518 HELMSLEY APPRENTICE H'CAP 6f
5:45 (5:46) (Class 5) (0-70,69) 3-Y-O+ £2,911 (£866; £432; £216) Stalls High

Form RPR

6600 **1** **Downhill Skier (IRE)**[21] 3806 7-9-8 60 JackDuern 8 72
(Mark Brisbourne) *hld up in rr: stdy hdwy on stands' rail 2f out: rdn to chal ins fnl f: kpt on to ld nr line* **20/1**

5011 **2** *nk* **Spinatrix**[11] 4146 3-9-12 69 6ex LukeRowe 13 79
(Michael Dods) *led: rdn wl over 1f out: drvn and edgd lft ins fnl f: hdd and no ex nr line* **6/4**[1]

0200 **3** *6* **Uddy Mac**[59] 2588 4-8-4 50 TerenceFury(8) 10 42
(Neville Bycroft) *in tch: hdwy to chse ldrs 2f out: swtchd lft and rdn over 1f out: kpt on same pce fnl f* **28/1**

0600 **4** *2* **Ryedane (IRE)**[3] 4405 9-9-13 65 (b) LauraBarry 7 50
(Tim Easterby) *in tch: hdwy to chse ldrs over 2f out: sn rdn and one pce: sddle slipped* **16/1**

5535 **5** *2 3/4* **Mawjoodah**[34] 3390 3-9-5 65 JacobButterfield(3) 3 41
(Brian Ellison) *dwlt and rr tl styd on fnl 2f: n.d* **13/2**[2]

0561 **6** *2 1/2* **Mazovian (USA)**[9] 4199 3-9-11 68 6ex NoelGarbutt 9 36
(Michael Chapman) *towards rr and rdn along 1/2-way: nvr a factor* **17/2**[3]

5020 **7** *1 1/4* **Divertimenti (IRE)**[20] 3880 7-9-9 66 (b) TimClark(5) 6 31+
(Roy Bowring) *awkward s and rdr lost iron in 1st f: prom: rdn along 2f out: sn wknd* **9/1**

0003 **8** *hd* **Grand Stitch (USA)**[11] 4144 5-9-2 62 (v) JasonHart(8) 11 26
(Declan Carroll) *cl up: rdn along over 2f out: grad wknd* **16/1**

00-6 **9** *shd* **Fulford**[101] 1463 6-8-13 51 LukeStrong 4 15
(Mel Brittain) *in tch: rdn along 1/2-way: sn wknd* **20/1**

-055 **10** *1 1/4* **Red River Boy**[2] 4443 6-8-12 50 NicolaJackson 5 10+
(Chris Fairhurst) *hld up in rr hdwy on stands' rail whn hmpd over 1f out: nt rcvr* **16/1**

-234 **11** *2 1/4* **I Got You Babe (IRE)**[28] 3571 3-9-5 62 (p) KevinLundie 12 13
(Richard Guest) *cl up: rdn along 2f out: wkng and edgd rt over 1f out* **13/2**[2]

2015 **12** *4 1/2* **Almaty Express**[15] 4000 9-9-3 55 (b) DavidSimmonson 1 —
(John Weymes) *racd wd: prom: rdn along over 2f out: sn wknd* **33/1**

1m 12.52s (-0.18) **Going Correction** +0.05s/f (Good)
WFA 3 from 4yo+ 5lb **12** Ran SP% **120.8**
Speed ratings (Par 103): **103,102,94,91,88 84,83,83,82,81 78,72**
toteswingers:1&2:£13.50, 2&3:£14.00, 1&3:£71.00. Tote Super 7: Win: Not won. Place: Not won. CSF £49.25 CT £928.12 TOTE £32.60: £6.70, £1.20, £8.30; EX 80.70.
Owner Miss P D Insull **Bred** Swettenham Stud **Trained** Great Ness, Shropshire
■ Stewards' Enquiry : Kevin Lundie two-day ban: careless riding (12-13 Aug)

FOCUS
It's hard to be sure of the exact merit of the form, but despite hat-trick-seeking Spinatrix failing to take advantage of being 11lb well in, she probably wasn't too far off her recent level and could yet do better. The winner is rated back to his old turf best (this race in 2009).
Divertimenti(IRE) Official explanation: jockey said that he lost his irons
T/Plt: £34.30 to a £1 stake. Pool of £46,111.85 - 980.04 winning tickets. T/Qpdt: £13.40 to a £1 stake. Pool of £2,964.68 - 163.20 winning tickets. JR

4519 - 4523a (Foreign Racing) - See Raceform Interactive

^{3889}DEAUVILLE (R-H)

Friday, July 29

OFFICIAL GOING: Turf: good to soft; fibresand: standard

4524a PRIX DU CARROUSEL (LISTED RACE) (4YO+) (TURF) 1m 7f

2:25 (12:00) 4-Y-O+ **£22,413** (£8,965; £6,724; £4,482; £2,241)

Pos	Dist	Horse	Jockey	RPR
1		**Terre Du Vent (FR)**^{44} [3063] 5-8-11 0 (Y De Nicolay, France) **29/1**	Pierre-CharlesBoudot 11	101
2	*snk*	**Lacateno**^{28} 4-9-1 0 (W Hickst, Germany) **53/10**^{3}	JohanVictoire 4	105
3	*1 ½*	**Flamingo Fantasy (GER)**^{33} [3446] 6-9-1 0 (S Smrczek, Germany) **12/1**	DominiqueBoeuf 1	103
4	*nk*	**Blek (FR)**^{44} [3063] 6-8-11 0 (E Lellouche, France) **7/1**	AnthonyCrastus 7	99
5	*nk*	**Flying Cross (IRE)**^{278} [7110] 4-8-11 0 (John Gosden) *led: stl in front 2 1/2f out: rdn: r.o wl: hdd 1f out: no ex fnl 50yds and lost 3rd cl home* **13/2**	RobertHavlin 8	98
6	*snk*	**Dawn Twister (GER)**^{44} [3063] 4-9-1 0 (J Hirschberger, Germany) **11/1**	MCadeddu 9	102
7	*snk*	**Distingue Lovers (IRE)**^{68} 4-8-11 0 (G Collet, France) **22/1**	ThierryThulliez 5	98
8	*½*	**Angolaner (GER)**^{33} 4-8-11 0 (F Head, France) **33/10**^{1}	ThierryJarnet 10	98
9	*nk*	**Green Tango (FR)**^{67} 8-8-11 0 (P Van De Poele, France) **83/10**	RonanThomas 3	97
10	*4*	**Oranais (IRE)**^{89} 4-8-11 0 (E Lellouche, France) **5/1**^{2}	(b) ChristopheSoumillon 12	92

3m 18.21s (-0.89) **10** Ran SP% **116.1**
WIN (incl. 1 euro stake): 29.90. PLACES: 6.70, 2.50, 4.10. DF 92.20. SF 229.70..
Owner Claude Lambert **Bred** Claude Lambert **Trained** France

NOTEBOOK
Flying Cross(IRE), who had a sound chance on his third in the Irish St Leger when with Aidan O'Brien, ran quite well from the front on this reappearance, only fading in the last furlong. This should bring him on with an autumn campaign in mind.

^{4232}DONCASTER (L-H)

Saturday, July 30

OFFICIAL GOING: Good to firm (7.4)
Wind: Virtually nil Weather: Cloudy with sunny periods, warm

4525 UNISON FOR PUBLIC SERVICES RACEDAY MAIDEN AUCTION STKS 7f

2:10 (2:11) (Class 5) 2-Y-O **£2,911** (£866; £432; £216) **Stalls** High

Form	Pos	Dist	Horse	Jockey	RPR
	1		**Dance The Rain** 2-8-6 0 (Bryan Smart) *hld up in rr: sltly hmpd after 1f: stdy hdwy 1/2-way: effrt to chse ldrs over 1f out: sn rdn and styd on strly ins fnl f to ld nr line* **14/1**	RoystonFfrench 5	73+
	2	*hd*	**Ghost Protocol (IRE)** 2-8-13 0 (David Simcock) *dwlt and in rr: smooth hdwy on outer wl over 2f out: led 1 1/2f out: sn rdn and hung lft ins fnl f: hdd and no ex nr fin* **13/2**^{3}	RobertHavlin 8	79+
	3	*1 ¾*	**Livia's Dream (IRE)** 2-8-11 0 (Ed Walker) *dwlt: towards rr whn sltly hmpd after 1f: hdwy into midfield 1/2-way: chsd ldrs wl over 1f out: n.m.r appr fnl f: kpt on* **9/1**	J-PGuillambert 4	73+
023	4	*2*	**Siouxperhero (IRE)**^{10} [4201] 2-8-12 72 ow1 (William Muir) *cl up: rdn to ld briefly over 2f out: hdd and drvn 1 1/2f out: n.m.r and one pce appr fnl f* **7/2**^{1}	SebSanders 3	69
004	5	*2*	**Spoken Words**^{32} [3483] 2-8-4 56 (Hugh McWilliams) *led: rdn along 3f out: hdd over 2f out: grad wknd and n.m.r appr fnl f* **33/1**	JamesSullivan 1	56
0	6	*2 ½*	**Ashkan**^{8} [4276] 2-8-13 0 (William Haggas) *chsd ldrs: rdn along wl over 2f out: sn one pce* **16/1**	KellyHarrison 2	59
0	7	*3*	**La Confession**^{22} [3813] 2-8-8 0 (J W Hills) *prom: rdn along 3f out: grad wknd* **9/1**	DarryllHolland 10	46
	8	*½*	**Big Time Charlie (IRE)** 2-8-10 0 (Richard Hannon) *trckd ldrs: effrt 3f out: sn rdn along and wknd 2f out* **7/2**^{1}	SeanLevey$^{(3)}$ 9	50
0	9	*9*	**Mexican Wave**^{10} [4201] 2-8-13 0 (Michael Bell) *t.k.h: hung lft after 1f: in tch: rdn along 3f out: sn outpcd* **20/1**	MickyFenton 7	28
	10	*shd*	**Mister Bob (GER)** 2-8-11 0 (James Bethell) *s.i.s: hdwy and in tch 1/2-way: sn rdn along and wknd* **4/1**^{2}	PhilipRobinson 11	25+

1m 26.83s (0.53) **Going Correction** -0.175s/f (Firm) **10** Ran SP% **118.0**
Speed ratings (Par 94): **89,88,86,84,82 79,75,75,65,64**
toteswingers: 1&2 £16.70, 1&3 £33.60, 2&3 £9.00. CSF £103.34 TOTE £14.30: £3.40, £2.60, £3.10; EX 81.00.
Owner Ceffyl Racing **Bred** Lordship Stud **Trained** Hambleton, N Yorks

FOCUS
Inside rail on Round course dolled out 6yds adding circa 57yds to 1m2f races and 72yds to 1m4f race. Dry overnight and the going was given as good to firm (GoingStick 7.4). While the early pace of this maiden was average, the lead was contested from some way out and the first two came from behind. The fourth and fifth are the best guide to the level.

NOTEBOOK
Dance The Rain was outpaced early on and was in last place, but as the leaders stopped in front she found her stamina kicking in and she finished well to see off the favourite close home. Out of a mare who won at up to 1m but is from the family of Shirley Heights, she was weak in the market and presumably expected to need this, so there should be better to come. (op 12-1)
Ghost Protocol(IRE) ◆, who is closely related to 6-7f 2yo winner Sohcahtoa, is the one to take from the race as he looked all over the winner when quickening up past almost the entire field heading to the 2f pole, but in hindsight he was probably asked for his effort too soon as he ran a bit green and idled once in front, and was caught close to the line. Winning a similar race should be a formality, and with the turn of foot he possesses he can surely be held on to for much longer in future. (op 8-1)
Livia's Dream(IRE), a half-sister to a 1m2f winner, was one of the first to be niggled along but she too benefited from those in front beginning to race from too far out, and she stayed on for a promising third. (op 6-1)
Siouxperhero(IRE), whose rider put up 1lb overweight, showed early pace but was taken on in front by the keen-going Spoken Words and La Confession and together they ended up setting the race up for the closers. (tchd 3-1)
Spoken Words helped set a good gallop and eventually paid the price. (op 25-1 tchd 40-1)
Big Time Charlie(IRE) travelled well enough behind the leaders but found little under pressure. (op 4-1 tchd 9-2 in places)
Mister Bob(GER), who is a big, rangy sort, was coltish in the preliminaries. Awkward from the stalls, he was far too green on his debut and will do better in time. (op 5-1)

4526 UNISON THE TRADE UNION AND THOMPSONS SOLICITORS CONDITIONS STKS 6f

2:45 (2:45) (Class 3) 3-Y-O+
£8,092 (£2,423; £1,211; £605; £302; £152) **Stalls** High

Form	Pos	Dist	Horse	Jockey	RPR
0005	1		**Prime Defender**^{28} [3626] 7-9-4 97 (B W Hills) *mde all: rdn 2f out: drvn clr ent fnl f: kpt on strly* **5/1**^{3}	SebSanders 3	113
100-	2	*2 ¾*	**Al Aasifh (IRE)**^{302} [6531] 3-8-8 105 (Saeed Bin Suroor) *chsd wnr: hdwy to chal 2f out: sn rdn and ev ch tl drvn and nt qckn ent fnl f* **9/2**^{2}	(p) DarryllHolland 5	98
-060	3	*1 ¼*	**New Planet (IRE)**^{22} [3820] 3-8-11 102 (John Quinn) *chsd ldng pair: rdn 2f out: drvn over 1f out and kpt on same pce* **11/4**^{1}	JamesSullivan 1	97
400	4	*1 ½*	**Palace Moon**^{35} [3404] 6-8-13 103 (William Knight) *chsd ldrs: pushed along and sltly outpcd 1/2-way: rdn 2f out and kpt on same pce* **9/1**	(t) J-PGuillambert 2	90
3300	5	*½*	**Angel's Pursuit (IRE)**^{14} [4092] 4-8-10 100 (Richard Hannon) *trckd ldrs: hdwy 3f out: rdn along 2f out: sn drvn and no imp* **9/2**^{2}	(b) SeanLevey$^{(3)}$ 6	89
0/60	6	*¾*	**Winker Watson**^{21} [3863] 6-8-13 103 (Mick Channon) *rrd s: in tch: effrt over 2f out: sn rdn along and no imp* **9/2**^{2}	SamHitchcott 4	86
0060	7	*3 ¼*	**Mister Hughie (IRE)**^{7} [4346] 4-9-2 98 (Tim Easterby) *sn rdn along and outpcd in rr: nvr a factor* **20/1**	(p) DuranFentiman 8	79

1m 11.13s (-2.47) **Going Correction** -0.175s/f (Firm)
WFA 3 from 4yo+ 5lb **7** Ran SP% **112.6**
Speed ratings (Par 107): **109,105,103,101,101 100,95**
toteswingers: 1&2 £4.70, 1&3 £6.40, 2&3 £2.30. CSF £26.66 TOTE £6.90: £3.20, £2.80; EX 33.80.
Owner S Falle, M Franklin, J Sumsion **Bred** Christopher J Mason **Trained** Lambourn, Berks

FOCUS
This looked a competitive conditions race on paper although there was a distinct lack of good recent form on offer. The winner is rated back towards his best.

NOTEBOOK
Prime Defender once plied his trade in top sprinting company but he's struggled somewhat this season, including in handicaps. A 5lb penalty for his Group 2 win last season left him worst in at the weights here, but he bounced back to winning form in fine style, disputing the early lead before stretching clear of his nearest pursuer in the closing stages. He clearly retains plenty of ability and has earned a return to better company. Apparently the Hungerford Stakes is on the agenda. (op 15-2)
Al Aasifh(IRE), who was making a belated seasonal reappearance, kept the winner company in front until being seen off heading to the last furlong. Perhaps the lack of a recent outing just found him out, but this was a promising return. (op 4-1 tchd 7-2)
New Planet(IRE) couldn't match the winner's turn of foot in the closing stages but kept on well enough to hold third. Like many in this field he's a difficult horse to place off his current mark. (op 7-2)
Palace Moon appreciated the return to better ground and ran a sound enough race. (op 8-1)
Angel's Pursuit(IRE) was a little disappointing, failing to pick up once the race got serious. (tchd 5-1)
Winker Watson didn't help his cause by again rearing as the stalls opened and made little progress once pressure was applied. (tchd 5-1)

4527 UNISON AND LV-FRIZZELL CAR INSURANCE H'CAP 5f

3:20 (3:20) (Class 5) (0-70,65) 3-Y-O **£3,234** (£962; £481; £240) **Stalls** High

Form	Pos	Dist	Horse	Jockey	RPR
1034	1		**Swendab (IRE)**^{24} [3723] 3-9-7 **65** (John O'Shea) *qckly away: mde all: qcknd clr wl over 1f out: rdn out* **7/2**^{2}	(v^{1}) DarryllHolland 3	77+
0306	2	*1 ¼*	**My Love Fajer (IRE)**^{10} [4207] 3-8-0 **51** (Alan McCabe) *wnt lft s: in tch: hdwy over 2f out: sn rdn: chsd wnr ins fnl f: kpt on* **10/1**	NoraLooby$^{(7)}$ 1	56
-420	3	*1 ¾*	**Pitkin**^{72} [2216] 3-9-7 **65** (Michael Easterby) *chsd wnr: rdn along 1/2-way: drvn wl over 1f out and sn one pce* **7/4**^{1}	(t) JamesSullivan 6	64
5000	4	*3 ¼*	**Il Battista**^{9} [4234] 3-9-7 **65** (Alan McCabe) *s.i.s and bhd: rdn along and sme hdwy fnl 2f: nvr a factor* **5/1**	(p) SebSanders 4	52
2145	5	*1 ½*	**Beautiful Day**^{56} [2736] 3-9-5 **63** (Kevin Ryan) *dwlt: sn chsng ldrs: rdn along over 2f out: sn drvn and btn* **4/1**^{3}	DavidNolan 8	45
2400	6	*6*	**Mini Bon Bon**^{36} [3360] 3-8-10 **54** (David O'Meara) *chsd ldrs: rdn along bef 1/2-way: sn wknd* **14/1**	DuranFentiman 7	14

59.94 secs (-0.56) **Going Correction** -0.175s/f (Firm) **6** Ran SP% **111.0**
Speed ratings (Par 100): **97,95,92,87,84 75**
toteswingers: 1&2 £4.60, 1&3 £1.40, 2&3 £4.50. CSF £34.61 CT £76.10 TOTE £4.60: £1.50, £5.50; EX 50.80.
Owner The Cross Racing Club & Patrick Brady **Bred** P Brady **Trained** Elton, Gloucs

FOCUS
Just a modest sprint handicap, with the top-weight weighing in 5lb below the ceiling for the race. A clear personal best from the winner.

4528 UNISON "SPEAKING UP FOR PUBLIC SERVICES" H'CAP 1m 2f 60y

3:55 (3:56) (Class 2) (0-100,99) 3-Y-O+
£12,450 (£3,728; £1,864; £932; £466; £234) **Stalls** Low

Form	Pos	Dist	Horse	Jockey	RPR
0513	1		**Barren Brook**^{21} [3877] 4-9-1 **86** (Michael Easterby) *hld up towards rr: hdwy over 4f out: str run on outer over 2f out: led over 1f out: rdn ent fnl f and kpt on strly* **6/1**^{2}	JamesSullivan 10	94+
0540	2	*¾*	**Dhaular Dhar (IRE)**^{22} [3825] 9-8-10 **84** (Jim Goldie) *hld up in rr: hdwy on outer 3f out: rdn wl over 1f out: styd on strly ins fnl f: nrst fin* **18/1**	GaryBartley$^{(3)}$ 13	91+
0506	3	*shd*	**Licence To Till (USA)**^{9} [4253] 4-8-10 **81** (Mark Johnston) *trckd ldrs: hdwy over 3f out: rdn to ld over 2f out: hdd and drvn over 1f out: kpt on u.p fnl f: lost 2nd on line* **10/1**	DarryllHolland 7	88
1410	4	*nk*	**Eltheeb**^{8} [4280] 4-8-9 **80** (George Moore) *trckd ldrs on inner: hdwy 3f out: rdn over 2f out: drvn wl over 1f out: kpt on u.p fnl f* **14/1**	AndrewMullen 2	86
1306	5	*¾*	**Kay Gee Be (IRE)**^{21} [3876] 7-9-7 **92** (Richard Fahey) *trckd ldrs: hdwy over 3f out: rdn to dispute ld wl over 2f out: ev ch whn drvn wl over 1f out: kpt on* **13/2**^{3}	DavidNolan 5	97

5000 **6** *½* **Mirrored**[4] 4410 5-9-4 **89** .... DuranFentiman 1 93
(Tim Easterby) *hld up in rr: hdwy over 3f out: rdn wl over 1f out: kpt on appr fnl f: nrst fin* **8/1**

4102 **7** *½* **Bourne**[28] 3625 5-9-5 **90** .... J-PGuillambert 11 93
(Luca Cumani) *hld up towards rr: stdy hdwy over 4f out: chsd ldrs over 2f out: sn rdn and no imp appr fnl f* **11/4**[1]

5400 **8** *2 ¼* **Snow Dancer (IRE)**[25] 3703 7-9-1 **86** .... RoystonFfrench 8 84
(Hugh McWilliams) *hld up towards rr: hdwy 3f out: rdn to chse ldrs over 2f out: drvn wl over 1f out and no imp* **28/1**

0130 **9** *nse* **Bay Willow (IRE)**[28] 3625 4-10-0 **99** .... PhilipRobinson 3 97
(Saeed Bin Suroor) *prom: rdn along over 3f out: drvn 2f out and grad wknd* **9/1**

-010 **10** *1 ¼* **Pass Muster**[41] 3203 4-9-2 **87** .... WilliamCarson 12 82
(Ollie Pears) *hld up towards rr: sme hdwy on inner over 3f out: n.m.r and swtchd rt wl over 2f out: effrt and nt clr run 2f out: nvr a factor* **25/1**

0560 **11** *½* **Space War**[21] 3877 4-8-10 **88** .... DavidSimmonson(7) 4 82
(Michael Easterby) *midfield: effrt 4f out: sn rdn along and wknd wl over 2f out* **20/1**

1030 **12** *¾* **Desert Romance (IRE)**[14] 4100 5-9-7 **92** .... SebSanders 6 85
(David O'Meara) *led: rdn along 4f out: drvn 3f out: sn hdd & wknd* **14/1**

043- **13** *3 ½* **Braveheart Move (IRE)**[329] 5743 5-9-10 **95** .... MickyFenton 9 81
(Geoffrey Harker) *chsd ldr: rdn along 4f out: sn wknd* **20/1**

2m 8.69s (-0.71) **Going Correction** -0.075s/f (Good) **13** Ran SP% **119.9**
Speed ratings (Par 109): **99,98,98,98,97 97,96,94,94,93 93,92,90**
toteswingers: 1&2 £31.00, 1&3 £7.60, 2&3 £41.50. CSF £102.57 CT £1073.30 TOTE £7.30: £2.10, £5.30, £2.10; EX 122.10.
Owner D Scott, Mrs E Wright & J Clark **Bred** David Allan **Trained** Sheriff Hutton, N Yorks

FOCUS
A decent, competitive handicap, and probably solid enough form for the grade. There could be more to come from the winner.

NOTEBOOK
Barren Brook, held up at the back of the field, quickened up well down the outside heading to the 2f pole and then idled a little once he hit the front. He got the longer trip well, is worth rating better than the bare form and will be interesting when he returns to York for the Ebor meeting. (op 13-2)
Dhaular Dhar(IRE), who has dropped to an attractive mark, was racing off a mark 1lb lower than when last successful. He posted a sound effort in defeat, running on late to take second. (op 20-1 tchd 16-1)
Licence To Till(USA) is another who has slipped to a winnable mark. He went to the front going nicely enough 2f out but was almost immediately tackled by the winner and, try as he might, he had no answer. He's getting closer, though. (op 11-1)
Eltheeb's record suggests he may be better going the other way round, although this was a sound effort off what looked a stiff mark.
Kay Gee Be(IRE) isn't quite as good over this trip as he is over 1m. (op 8-1)
Mirrored didn't run too badly considering he didn't get the clearest of runs. (op 9-1)
Bourne was a little disappointing given the way the race was set up for those coming from off the pace. A return to 1m4f might be in his favour. (tchd 5-2)

4529 UNISON AND UIA HOME INSURANCE MAIDEN STKS — 1m 2f 60y
4:25 (4:28) (Class 5) 3-4-Y-O — **£2,911** (£866; £432; £216) **Stalls** Low

Form — RPR

1 **Look Left** 3-9-0 0 .... RobertHavlin 7 80+
(John Gosden) *dwlt: hld up in rr: hdwy over 3f out: trckd ldrs on bridle 2f out: shkn up to chal over 1f out: drvn ins fnl f: edgd lft and kpt on wl to ld last 100yds* **9/4**[1]

-306 **2** *1* **Muqtarrib (IRE)**[28] 3623 3-9-0 82 .... EddieCreighton 5 78
(Brian Meehan) *trckd ldrs: hdwy 3f out: rdn to chal wl over 1f out: drvn to ld jst ins fional f: hdd and no ex last 100yds* **3/1**[2]

5 **3** *2 ¼* **Lifetime (IRE)**[11] 4186 3-9-0 0 .... DarryllHolland 10 76+
(Mark Johnston) *set stdy pce: qcknd 4f out: rdn and qcknd over 2f out: drvn over 1f out: hdd jst ins fnl f: no ex last 100yds* **14/1**

40 **4** *½* **Spanish Plume**[19] 3925 3-8-7 0 .... JackDuern(7) 1 73
(Reg Hollinshead) *hld up: hdwy on inner 1/2-way: cl up over 3f out: rdn over 2f out and ev ch tl drvn appr fnl f and grad wknd* **40/1**

00 **5** *½* **Sit Tight**[61] 2551 3-9-0 0 .... SebSanders 4 72
(Chris Wall) *hld up in rr: hdwy 4f out: rdn to chse ldrs over 2f out: drvn wl over 1f out and sn one pce* **20/1**

2 **6** *3 ½* **Tiny Temper (IRE)**[25] 3705 3-8-9 0 .... JamesSullivan 11 60
(Richard Fahey) *prom: rdn along over 3f out: drvn and wknd wl over 2f out* **3/1**[2]

00- **7** *15* **Makyaal (IRE)**[297] 6676 3-9-0 0 .... PhilipRobinson 2 35
(John Dunlop) *t.k.h: trckd ldr: effrt and cl up 3f out: rdn 2f out: drvn and wknd wl over 1f out* **16/1**

0 **8** *12* **Line of Sight (USA)**[22] 3824 3-9-0 0 .... RoystonFfrench 8 —
(Mahmood Al Zarooni) *t.k.h: trckd ldrs on outer: hdwy to chse ldng pair 1/2-way: rdn along over 3f out: wknd over 2f out: sn bhd and eased* **11/1**[3]

9 *92* **Balandra** 3-8-9 0 .... J-PGuillambert 6 —
(Luca Cumani) *dwlt and virtually ref to r: a wl t.o* **11/1**[3]

2m 12.06s (2.66) **Going Correction** -0.075s/f (Good) **9** Ran SP% **117.2**
Speed ratings (Par 103): **86,85,83,83,82 79,67,58,—**
toteswingers: 1&2 £2.40, 1&3 £7.40, 2&3 £8.40. CSF £9.22 TOTE £3.90: £1.30, £1.50, £2.90; EX 12.00.
Owner K Abdulla **Bred** Juddmonte Farms Ltd **Trained** Newmarket, Suffolk

FOCUS
No more than an ordinary maiden, and the early gallop was pretty steady. It turned into something of a sprint. The form is rated on the negative side around the runner-up.
Line of Sight(USA) Official explanation: jockey said that the colt ran too free and lost its action

4530 UNISON "YOUR FRIEND AT WORK" H'CAP — 1m 4f
5:05 (5:07) (Class 4) (0-85,85) 3-Y-O — **£4,528** (£1,347; £673; £336) **Stalls** Low

Form — RPR

0330 **1** **Qushchi**[43] 3108 3-9-7 **85** .... DarryllHolland 3 94
(William Jarvis) *led: rdn along and hdd marginally over 2f out: rallied to ld again over 1f out: drvn and edgd rt ins fnl f: styd on gamely* **3/1**[2]

1110 **2** *½* **Anton Dolin (IRE)**[30] 3551 3-9-1 **79** .... J-PGuillambert 6 87
(John Dunlop) *trckd ldrs: hdwy 3f out: rdn to chse wnr ent fnl f: ev ch tl drvn and no ex fnl 75yds* **7/2**[3]

0030 **3** *2 ½* **Waltz Darling (IRE)**[23] 3774 3-9-5 **83** .... DavidNolan 4 87
(Richard Fahey) *trckd ldng pair: effrt over 3f out: rdn along and sltly outpcd over 2f out: swtchd rt and drvn ent fnl f: kpt on* **10/1**

4114 **4** *4 ½* **Pintrada**[28] 3623 3-8-12 **76** .... PhilipRobinson 5 73
(James Bethell) *hld up in rr: effrt on outer and hdwy over 3f out: rdn along 2f out: sn drvn and btn over 1f out* **7/4**[1]

132 **5** *2 ¼* **Libritish**[14] 4090 3-8-12 **76** .... (b) SebSanders 2 69
(Marco Botti) *trckd wnr: cl up 3f out: rdn to take narrow advantage over 2f out: drvn and hdd over 1f out: wknd ent fnl f* **4/1**

2m 33.31s (-1.59) **Going Correction** -0.075s/f (Good) **5** Ran SP% **112.7**
Speed ratings (Par 102): **102,101,100,97,95**
toteswinger: 1&2 £7.10. CSF £13.93 TOTE £3.70: £1.90, £2.60; EX 16.00.
Owner Gillian, Lady Howard De Walden **Bred** Avington Manor Stud **Trained** Newmarket, Suffolk

FOCUS
They didn't go a great gallop early here and the winner made all. A slightly positive view has been taken of the form.
T/Plt: £862.50 to a £1 stake. Pool of £73,785.35 - 62.45 winning tickets. T/Qpdt: £44.80 to a £1 stake. Pool of £5,200.29 - 85.75 winning tickets. JR

4492 GOODWOOD (R-H)
Saturday, July 30

OFFICIAL GOING: Good to firm (good in places; overall 8.7, round course 8.8, straight course 8.4, centre 8.5, far side 8.7)
Wind: fairly light, against Weather: light cloud, brighter spells

4531 BLUESQUARE.COM STEWARDS' SPRINT STKS (H'CAP) — 6f
2:05 (2:05) (Class 2) 3-Y-O+
£18,675 (£5,592; £2,796; £1,398; £699; £351) **Stalls** High

Form — RPR

1056 **1** **Son Of The Cat (USA)**[68] 2370 5-9-9 **91** .... (t) FrannyNorton 3 106
(Brian Gubby) *racd far side: hld up in tch in midfield: hdwy 2f out: rdn to ld over 1f out: clr and drvn 1f out: r.o strly* **18/1**

2030 **2** *1 ¾* **Confessional**[13] 4135 4-9-10 **92** .... (e) SilvestreDeSousa 16 101
(Tim Easterby) *on toes: racd far side: in tch: rdn and effrt 2f out: chsd wnr over 1f out: kpt on u.p but no imp ins fnl f: 2nd of 19 in gp* **14/1**

00-3 **3** *1 ½* **Valery Borzov (IRE)**[38] 3279 7-9-3 **85** .... (v) PaulHanagan 17 89
(Richard Fahey) *lw: racd far side: in tch but sn pushed along: rdn over 2f out: drvn to chse ldng pair: kpt on but no imp ins fnl f: 3rd of 19 in gp* **20/1**

1050 **4** *1 ½* **Joseph Henry**[7] 4314 9-9-6 **91** .... MichaelO'Connell(3) 23 90+
(David Nicholls) *on toes: racd stands' side: w gp ldr but only in tch in midfield overall: rdn 2f out: kpt on u.p fnl f: no threat to ldrs: 1st of 6 in gp* **20/1**

5311 **5** *½* **Saucy Brown (IRE)**[21] 3880 5-9-0 **82** 3ex .... AdrianNicholls 7 80
(David Nicholls) *on toes: racd far side: in tch: rdn and swtchd lft 2f out: kpt on ins fnl f: 4th of 19 in gp* **11/1**[3]

6540 **6** *1* **Racy**[7] 4346 4-9-8 **90** .... PhillipMakin 22 85+
(Kevin Ryan) *lw: taken down early: led stands' side gp but only in tch in midfield overall: rdn and kpt on fr over 1f out but no threat to ldrs: 2nd of 6 in gp* **16/1**

1420 **7** *nk* **Klynch**[6] 4369 5-9-3 **85** .... (b) TomEaves 8 79
(Ruth Carr) *racd far side: chsd ldrs: rdn 2f out: stl pressing ldrs whn squeezed for room and hmpd over 1f out: styd on same pce and no threat to ldrs fnl f: 5th of 19 in gp* **33/1**

0302 **8** *¾* **Five Star Junior (USA)**[15] 4063 5-9-8 **90** .... DaneO'Neill 19 81+
(Linda Stubbs) *racd far side: bhd: swtchd lft and effrt 2f out: styd on wl fnl f: nvr trbld ldrs: 6th of 19 in gp* **20/1**

255 **9** *½* **Seek The Fair Land**[5] 4392 5-8-7 **80** .... (b) NathanAlison(5) 12 70
(Jim Boyle) *racd far side: chsd ldrs tl led 1/2-way: rdn 2f out: hung rt and hdd over 1f out: wknd ins fnl f: 7th of 19 in gp* **33/1**

5041 **10** *½* **Mac Gille Eoin**[30] 3535 7-9-5 **87** .... TomQueally 1 75
(John Gallagher) *swtg: racd far side: chsd ldrs: rdn and unable qck whn squeezed for room and hmpd over 1f out: nt rcvr and no threat to ldrs after: 8th of 19 in gp* **16/1**

2400 **11** *½* **Oldjoesaid**[6] 4369 7-9-1 **83** .... ChrisCatlin 5 69+
(Kevin Ryan) *taken down early: racd far side: wl outpcd in rr: sme hdwy and nt clr run over 1f out: styd on past btn horses fnl f: nvr trbld ldrs: 9th of 19 in gp* **66/1**

0030 **12** *nse* **Secret Witness**[21] 3841 5-9-10 **92** .... (b) TomMcLaughlin 4 78+
(Ronald Harris) *racd far side: racd in midfield: swtchd rt and hdwy in far rail 2f out: chsng ldrs whn nt clr run and bdly hmpd over 1f out: nt rcvr and no ch after: eased fnl 100yds: 10th of 19 in gp* **22/1**

520 **13** *nk* **Dubai Media (CAN)**[22] 3827 4-9-9 **91** .... JamieSpencer 18 76+
(Ed Dunlop) *racd far side: hld up in rr: hdwy travelling wl and edging rt over 2f out: in tch whn nt clr run and hmpd over 1f out: lost any ch: swtchd lft 1f out and kpt on fnl f: 11th of 19 in gp* **12/1**

6020 **14** *shd* **Everymanforhimself (IRE)**[15] 4042 7-9-6 **88** .... (b) PatCosgrave 15 73
(Kevin Ryan) *lw: racd far side: towards rr: rdn and effrt whn n.m.r ent fnl 2f: no threat to ldrs after: plugged on fnl f: 12th of 19 in gp* **40/1**

0500 **15** *1 ¼* **Noverre To Go (IRE)**[28] 3627 5-9-7 **89** .... (t) RichardKingscote 11 70
(Tom Dascombe) *swtg: racd far side: bhd: rdn and effrt over 2f out: n.m.r wl over 1f out: no threat to ldrs after: plugged on fnl f: 13th of 19 in gp* **14/1**

5400 **16** *nk* **Yer Woman (IRE)**[22] 3796 4-9-2 **87** .... KieranO'Neill(3) 6 67+
(Richard Hannon) *racd far side: towards rr: sme hdwy whn carried rt over 2f out: stl plenty to do whn nt clr run and swtchd lft jst over 1f out: kpt on fnl f: nvr trbld ldrs: 14th of 19 in gp* **33/1**

6311 **17** *shd* **Mymumsaysimthebest**[31] 3517 6-9-7 **89** .... RyanMoore 2 69+
(Gary Moore) *racd far side: bhd: sme hdwy on far rail but stl plenty to do whn nt clr run and bdly hmpd over 1f out: lost any ch and wl hld after: 15th of 19 in gp* **8/1**[1]

-010 **18** *½* **Novellen Lad (IRE)**[28] 3627 6-9-8 **90** .... KierenFallon 21 68
(Willie Musson) *racd stands' side: sn pushed along in rr: rdn over 2f out: nvr trbld ldrs: 3rd of 6 in gp* **12/1**

4011 **19** *shd* **Thunderball**[25] 3704 5-9-1 **90** 3ex .... (b) LeonnaMayor(7) 26 68
(David Nicholls) *b: racd stands' side: hld up towards rr: effrt and hung rt fr over 2f out: nvr trbld ldrs: 4th of 6 in gp* **10/1**[2]

5025 **20** *2 ¼* **Baby Strange**[7] 4346 7-9-7 **89** .... RobbieFitzpatrick 24 60
(Derek Shaw) *racd stands' side: towards rr: rdn 1/2-way: carried rt and no imp over 2f out: n.d: 5th of 6 in gp* **20/1**

0004 **21** *¾* **Golden Desert (IRE)**[3] 4428 7-9-10 **92** .... JimCrowley 25 60
(Robert Mills) *racd stands' side: a bhd: rdn and no hdwy 1/2-way: n.d: 6th of 6 in gp* **11/1**[3]

436 **22** *1 ½* **Kingsgate Choice (IRE)**[22] 3796 4-9-1 **83** .... (b) SteveDrowne 10 46
(John Best) *lw: swtchd rt s and racd far side: chsd overall ldr tl over 3f out: wkng whn short of room over 1f out: fdd fnl f: 16th of 19 in gp* **28/1**

1156 **23** *5* **We Have A Dream**[15] 4042 6-9-6 **88** .... MartinDwyer 14 35
(William Muir) *racd far side: in tch: rdn and struggling 1/2-way: wkng whn short of room and hmpd over 1f out: wl bhd fnl f: 17th of 19 in gp* **33/1**

0542 **24** *nk* **Quasi Congaree (GER)**[15] 4064 5-8-7 **75**............(t) GrahamGibbons 20 21
(Ian Wood) *racd far side: a bhd: no ch whn hmpd over 1f out: n.d: 18th of 19 in gp* **33/1**

0060 **25** *13* **Courageous (IRE)**[21] 3841 5-9-7 **89**............................ JimmyFortune 13 —
(Kevin Ryan) *taken down early: racd far side: overall ldr tl 1/2-way: wknd ent fnl 2f: dropping to rr whn hmpd over 1f out: virtually p.u ins fnl f: t.o: 19th of 19 in gp* **25/1**

1m 10.32s (-1.88) **Going Correction** -0.10s/f (Good) **25** Ran SP% **131.9**
Speed ratings (Par 109): **108,105,103,101,101 99,99,98,97,96 96,96,95,95,94 93,93,92,92,89 88,86,80,79,62**
Tote Swingers: 1&2 £281.40, 1&3 £43.80, 2&3 £337.70 CSF £212.36 CT £5119.29 TOTE £29.00: £6.10, £4.70, £7.10, £4.70; EX 926.60 TRIFECTA Not won..
Owner Brian Gubby **Bred** Andover Stable Llc **Trained** Bagshot, Surrey
■ Stewards' Enquiry : Nathan Alison six -day ban: careless riding (13, 14, 15 Aug)

FOCUS
Rail at normal configuration and distances as advertised. A consolation race for those who failed to make the cut for the Stewards' Cup, and run for the first time on the same day as the main event. It was predictably competitive, but lacked unexposed improvers and lots found trouble. The majority raced towards the far side, and tight against the rail looked to provide an advantage, but otherwise there wasn't much in it. The runner-up and third were drawn 16 and 17 respectively, well away from the rail, and the fourth-placed finisher fared best of just six runner who stayed stands' side. A time 0.41 seconds slower than Hoof It's top-class performance in the Stewards' Cup was highly respectable.

NOTEBOOK
Son Of The Cat(USA), reported to have run too free when a bit outclassed in Listed company on his previous start over two months previously, went without the blinkers on his return and recorded a second C&D success, confirming his suitability for Goodwood. The draw probably helped as it enabled him to get on the far rail with over a furlong to run, and clearly plenty went his way. He's smart on his day, though, and is only five, so there may be more to come. (tchd 20-1)
Confessional ◆put up a fine effort, and one that might even want upgrading a touch. He was crossed by a rival when waiting for a run around 2f out, but then picked up well to get within striking distance of the winner, who may have been on the best ground. He's one to follow. (op 20-1)
Valery Borzov(IRE) was stuck widest of all in the far-side group for much of the way but kept on. This was only his second run of the season so he could step forward again.
Joseph Henry was 7lb higher (1lb wrong) than when winning this last year and ran well, faring best of the six runners who raced near side.
Saucy Brown(IRE), only 26th in this last year, came into the race searching for a hat-trick but came up short. He was a bit tight for room in the closing stages, but wasn't unlucky. (op 12-1 tchd 9-1)
Racy, 1lb wrong, showed good speed in the smaller near-side group, but was inclined to race at a bit of an angle, hanging right, and gradually faded.
Klynch didn't have a great deal of room in the closing stages, but it didn't cost him.
Five Star Junior(USA), sixth in this last year, was 4lb well in but he was more inconvenienced by his high draw than some and never got seriously involved.
Seek The Fair Land's rider reported the gelding hung right. Official explanation: jockey that the gelding hung right handed (op 40-1)
Mac Gille Eoin's rider reported that the gelding suffered interference in running. Official explanation: jockey said the horse suffered interference in running
Dubai Media(CAN) looked to have something to offer when badly squeezed for room over a furlong out. That cost her any chance, though she didn't pick up that well when in the clear. Official explanation: jockey said that the filly suffered interference in running (op 14-1 tchd 20-1 in a place)
Everymanforhimself(IRE) would have finished a bit closer with a better trip.
Noverre To Go(IRE) was fifth in the Stewards' Cup off 8lb higher last year, but other than a promising fifth at Chester's May meeting, he's not been in the same form this time. He was short of room late on, but that was no excuse. (op 16-1)
Yer Woman(IRE) was forced to switch several times and is better than she showed. (op 40-1)
Mymumsaysimthebest, whose jockey never looked that happy when it mattered, not getting really serious with his mount, albeit the gelding didn't have much room. The horse has won over C&D on quick ground, but his recent improvement has been on Polytrack (won last two starts) and perhaps he didn't let himself down back on a lively surface. Ryan Moore reported the gelding suffered interference in running. Official explanation: jockey said that the gelding suffered interference in running (op 10-1)
Thunderball was searching for a hat-trick but could fare no better than fourth on the stands' side. (tchd 9-1)
Quasi Congaree(GER)'s rider reported the geldingp suffered interference in running. Official explanation: jockey said that the gelding suffered interference in running
Courageous(IRE), debuting for this yard, showed speed but weakened quite quickly and was also short of room when on the retreat. He was reported to have run too free. Official explanation: jockey said that the gelding ran too free

4532 TOYO TIRES SUMMER STKS (H'CAP) 1m 6f
2:35 (2:35) (Class 2) (0-105,105) 3-Y-0+

£24,900 (£7,456; £3,728; £1,864; £932; £468) **Stalls** High

Form RPR

0-44 **1** **Petara Bay (IRE)**[35] 3396 7-9-9 **103**................................ JimCrowley 10 111
(Robert Mills) *hld up towards rr: hdwy on outer fr over 4f out: rdn to chse ldrs over 2f out: drifted rt ins fnl f: styd on u.str driving to ld nr fin* **12/1**

0006 **2** *nk* **Icon Dream (IRE)**[21] 3875 4-9-1 **95**.......................... SilvestreDeSousa 8 103
(David Simcock) *trckd ldr: lft in front over 4f out: rdn 3f out: kpt on v gamely u.p: hdd nring fin* **8/1**

3/10 **3** *1 3/4* **Investissement**[35] 3396 5-9-5 **99**..................................... NickyMackay 5 105
(John Gosden) *trckd ldrs: rdn to chal 3f out: styd on but no ex fnl f* **14/1**

0010 **4** *3/4* **Sirvino**[28] 3625 6-9-4 **98**..................................... GrahamGibbons 12 103
(David Barron) *b: in tch: hdwy over 3f out: rdn to chal over 2f out: styd on: no ex towards fin* **25/1**

4-30 **5** *1* **Mystery Star (IRE)**[35] 3396 6-9-3 **97**............................ PaulHanagan 13 100
(Mark H Tompkins) *lw: hld up towards rr: pushed along over 3f out: rdn and hdwy to chse ldrs over 2f out: styd on same pce* **25/1**

-210 **6** *shd* **Harlestone Times (IRE)**[35] 3396 4-9-7 **101**....................... TedDurcan 4 104+
(John Dunlop) *hld up towards rr: beginning to cl whn short of room over 4f out: sn rdn: no imp tl styd on ins fnl f: nrst fin* **5/1**[1]

-010 **7** *1 1/4* **Classic Vintage (USA)**[28] 3625 5-9-0 **94**......................... TomQueally 1 95
(Amanda Perrett) *trckd ldr: rdn over 3f out: styd on same pce fnl 2f* **16/1**

6-06 **8** *nk* **Sentry Duty (FR)**[28] 3647 9-9-5 **99**.................................. KierenFallon 9 100
(Nicky Henderson) *lw: mid-div: hmpd over 4f out: sn rdn: styd on fnl f: nvr threatened* **20/1**

01-0 **9** *2 1/4* **Woolfall Treasure**[21] 3875 6-9-4 **98**..........................(v) GeorgeBaker 11 96
(Gary Moore) *stmbld leaving stalls: hld up towards rr: forced wd over 4f out: sn rdn: nt pce to get on terms* **40/1**

2550 **10** *2 1/4* **Sabotage (UAE)**[21] 3875 5-9-11 **105**........................... FrankieDettori 7 99
(Saeed Bin Suroor) *trckd ldrs: hmpd by long time ldr over 4f out: rdn 3f out: wknd ent fnl f* **14/1**

-200 **11** *18* **Sharaayeen**[28] 3625 4-9-2 **96**..................................... RichardHills 2 65+
(B W Hills) *mid-div: clsng whn bdly hmpd and lost pl over 4f out: nt travelling after: eased fnl f* **13/2**[2]

1-10 **B** **Activate**[35] 3396 4-9-2 **96**.. JamieSpencer 14 —
(Michael Bell) *edgy: on toes: swtchd rt sn after s: hld up bhd: b.d heavily over 4f out* **13/2**[2]

-534 **B** **Verdant**[35] 3403 4-9-11 **105**..(v[1]) RyanMoore 3 —
(Sir Michael Stoute) *lw: mid-div whn b.d heavily over 4f out* **7/1**[3]

5511 **P** **Captain John Nixon**[31] 3522 4-9-3 **97**................................ ChrisCatlin 6 —
(Pat Eddery) *led tl lost action over 4f out: immediately eased and p.u: fatally injured* **8/1**

3m 1.55s (-2.05) **Going Correction** -0.10s/f (Good) **14** Ran SP% **119.9**
Speed ratings (Par 109): **101,100,99,99,98 98,98,97,96,95 85,—,—,—**
Tote Swingers: 1&2 £88.10, 1&3 £5.70, 2&3 £39.50 CSF £99.76 CT £1375.72 TOTE £16.60: £4.20, £2.70, £4.70; EX 128.60 Trifecta £1649.20 Part won. Pool: £ 2,228.75 - 0.91 winning units..
Owner B Ecclestone **Bred** Swettenham Stud **Trained** Headley, Surrey
■ Ryan Moore broke a shoulder in this fall and may be out for the rest of the season.

FOCUS
A high-class staying handicap featuring a number of runners that had finished well beaten in the Northumberland Plate on their previous start. The race was marred when the front-running Captain John Nixon went badly wrong running down the hill and, as he dropped back quickly through the field, several horses were badly hampered and Verdant, who had nowhere to go as the field bunched up, fell bringing down Activate. The complexion of the race therefore changed and the finish was mainly fought out by those that raced near the pace and missed the trouble. Four were in line 2f out and the form is best rated at face value.

NOTEBOOK
Petara Bay(IRE) had not won since 2007 but had been comparatively lightly raced and ran well on both previous starts this season, including when beating several of today's opponents in the Northumberland Plate. He had also run well on both previous starts over C&D and clearly likes the track, as he made his ground to challenge around 2f out and wore down the leader near the finish. The Cesarewitch is on the agenda now. (op 11-1)
Icon Dream(IRE) ran reasonably well to finish seventh in the Northumberland Plate but had not won since his racecourse debut in Ireland debut back in 2009. He was always in the first two and was left clear when the leader broke a leg. He fought off several challenges in the last 2f but could not quite hold off the winner. (op 14-1)
Investissement had Petara Bay behind when scoring over C&D in April on his first start for this yard but had finished well behind in the Northumberland Plate next time. He was never far away and had every chance, but weakened in the last furlong. (tchd 12-1 and 16-1)
Sirvino ended a two-year losing run when scoring at Windsor in June, but was 9lb higher here and trying his longest trip to-date. He was another who had his chance and did not quite get home. (op 22-1)
Mystery Star(IRE) won here on his last visit back in 2009 but had since stepped up successfully to staying trips, finishing third in the Chester Cup. He was held up out the back before running on steadily in the closing stages, as if another quarter-mile would have suited.
Harlestone Times(IRE) had won both his starts here over shorter trips but did not appear to get home in the Northumberland Plate last time. He was another held up out the back and, although not appearing to get significantly hampered, was given a fair amount to do before keeping on in the closing stages. (op 11-2 tchd 6-1 in places)
Classic Vintage(USA), a winner over 1m4f here in 2009, had returned to winning form over shorter at Haydock this season but was another who appeared to find the trip beyond him.
Sentry Duty(FR), who finished third in this race last season, was another who suffered interference and, although recovering quite well to chase the leaders 2f out, could not sustain the effort. (tchd 16-1)
Woolfall Treasure won over C&D before finishing fourth in this race last season, but, even with the visor back on here, failed to figure having been held up out the back. (op 33-1)
Sabotage(UAE), who was closely matched with Verdant on Newmarket June form, made a mid-race move to join the leaders. He suffered interference running down the hill but still had a chance 2f out before fading, which was surprising considering he stays further. (tchd 12-1)
Sharaayeen lost all chance when badly hampered in the melee running down the hill and was eased. This run can be ignored. Official explanation: jockey said that the gelding was hampered in running (op 7-1)

4533 MARKEL INSURANCE NASSAU STKS BRITISH CHAMPIONS' SERIES (GROUP 1) (F&M) 1m 1f 192y
3:10 (3:13) (Class 1) 3-Y-0+

£104,913 (£39,775; £19,906; £9,916; £4,976; £2,497) **Stalls** Low

Form RPR

-122 **1** **Midday**[35] 3417 5-9-6 **119**.. TomQueally 6 121+
(Sir Henry Cecil) *lw: chsd ldrs: jnd ldrs gng best ent fnl 2f: led 2f out: rdn and qcknd clr over 1f out: edgd lft 1f out: styd on strly under hands and heels fnl 100yds: readily* **6/4**[1]

11-4 **2** *2* **Snow Fairy (IRE)**[28] 3646 4-9-6 **120**................................ FrankieDettori 7 117
(Ed Dunlop) *lw: hld up in tch: rdn and effrt to press ldrs ent fnl 2f: outpcd by wnr over 1f out: swtchd rt 1f out: chsd wnr ins fnl f: r.o but no imp* **5/2**[2]

0-31 **3** *1 1/4* **Principal Role (USA)**[36] 3356 4-9-6 **106**........................ RichardHughes 5 114
(Sir Henry Cecil) *stdd and short of room s: hld up in last pair: rdn over 2f out: styd on u.p ins fnl f: wnt 3rd towards fin: no ch w wnr* **12/1**

0-41 **4** *nk* **Crystal Capella**[23] 3775 6-9-6 **120**................................ JimmyFortune 3 113
(Sir Michael Stoute) *t.k.h: hld up in tch: rdn and effrt to r on far rail and join ldrs over 3f out: 2nd and nt pce of wnr wl over 1f out: lost 2nd and no ex ins fnl f* **4/1**[3]

1523 **5** *1 3/4* **Barefoot Lady (IRE)**[43] 3106 3-8-10 **108**........................ PaulHanagan 1 110
(Richard Fahey) *lw: led and set stdy gallop: jnd and jostled over 3f out: hdd and rdn 2f out: drvn and wknd ent fnl f* **10/1**

-406 **6** *3/4* **Field Day (IRE)**[45] 3030 4-9-6 **105**..................................(t) KierenFallon 2 108
(Brian Meehan) *t.k.h: chsd ldr: upsides ldr and bmpd over 3f out: rdn and unable qck wl over 1f out: drvn and wknd ent fnl f* **25/1**

2m 7.72s (-0.28) **Going Correction** -0.10s/f (Good)
WFA 3 from 4yo+ 10lb **6** Ran SP% **109.2**
Speed ratings (Par 117): **97,95,94,94,92 92**
Tote Swingers: 1&2 £88.10, 1&3 £5.70, 2&3 £39.50 CSF £5.09 TOTE £2.00: £1.10, £1.90; EX 4.10.
Owner K Abdulla **Bred** Juddmonte Farms Ltd **Trained** Newmarket, Suffolk
■ Midday became the first filly to win the Nassau Stakes three times, the race having been opened up to older fillies in 1975.

FOCUS
The smallest field since Favourable Terms defeated five rivals in 2004, and the absence of Misty For Me because of the quick ground was a shame. Aidan O'Brien's filly slammed Midday in the Pretty Polly at the Curragh in June and this race could have gone a long way to deciphering the reliability of that form. The pace seemed steady for much of the way, Paul Hanagan riding a waiting race in front on the only remaining 3-y-o. The form is muddling and limited by the the proximity of the fifth and sixth.

NOTEBOOK

Midday was gaining her tenth consecutive top two finish and hasn't finished outside the top three since 2008. She was disappointing when 6l behind Misty For Me last time, although we will have to wait to learn just good Aidan O'Brien's runner really is, and in any case this mare's two previous victories in the Nassau had been preceded by a defeat. It would be wrong to get carried away considering the runner-up still seemed short of her peak, the third is exposed as short of this class, and the fourth had an excuse, but Midday is a hard filly to knock. Her continued positive attitude towards racing is a credit to her connections and her record suggests she's unlikely to be out of the action any time soon, especially if kept to racing against her own sex. (op 11-8)

Snow Fairy(IRE) was well short of her best when belatedly reappearing after a setback in the Eclipse, but she blew for 45 minutes afterwards according to Ed Dunlop, who also reported the filly had since worked fantastically. This was much more like it, a run that suggests all her ability most likely remains, and one that she can improve again from. No match for the winner, she edged right inside the final furlong, changed her legs and her stride noticeably shortened. A rematch with Midday would be interesting. (tchd 11-4)

Principal Role(USA) had plenty to find judged on her recent victory in a weak Listed race (form not worked out) at Newcastle, although she had the scope for further improvement. She was never seen with a winning chance, being held up in a slowly run race, although such tactics allowed her to run on past beaten horses to grab some Group 1-placed black type, an outcome her connections will no doubt be delighted with. (op 10-1)

Crystal Capella really impressed when winning the Group 2 Princess of Wales's Stakes at Newmarket's July meeting, but that was 1m4f on good ground, and in contrast this steadily run 1m2f on a fast surface was no use to her. She was a bit keen and then couldn't muster the pace when not always having that much room against the rail. When conditions are more suitable she can certainly be given another chance. (tchd 7-2, 9-2 and 5-1 in a place)

Barefoot Lady(IRE)dictated the gallop but struggled, however, readily being done for pace in the straight. She ran well to be fifth in the 1000 Guineas and third in the Coronation Stakes, but was outclassed against her elders, perhaps finding the ground too quick. (op 14-1)

Field Day(IRE) was a bit keen and became short of room early in the straight, but was essentially disappointing. Strictly on the figures this was something of a revival, but the steady pace compressed the distances and there remains no solid evidence she's trained on from three to four. (tchd 28-1)

4534 BLUE SQUARE STEWARDS' CUP (HERITAGE H'CAP) 6f

3:45 (3:48) (Class 2) 3-Y-0+

£62,250 (£18,640; £9,320; £4,660; £2,330; £1,170) **Stalls** High

Form / RPR

101 **1** **Hoof It**[7] 4346 4-10-0 **111** 6ex.......... KierenFallon 18 124
(Michael Easterby) *lw: wl in tch and travelling strly in centre gp: allowed to drift to far side rail and led wl over 1f out: rdn clr: r.o strly: readily* **13/2**[1]

0410 **2** *2 ½* **Tax Free (IRE)**[21] 3874 9-8-11 **94**.......... MartinDwyer 13 99
(David Nicholls) *chsd ldrs in centre gp: ev ch 2f out: sn outpcd by wnr: kpt on fnl f* **33/1**

-203 **3** *hd* **Mac's Power (IRE)**[21] 3841 5-9-3 **100**..........(t) PatCosgrave 1 104+
(James Fanshawe) *taken down early: towards rr of far side gp: rdn over 2f out: hdwy ent fnl f: edgd lft: r.o wl: nrst fin* **13/2**[1]

1300 **4** *shd* **Nasri**[21] 3862 5-8-11 **97**.......... MichaelO'Connell(3) 27 101+
(David Nicholls) *lw: led stands' side gp of 4 but overall chsd ldrs: rdn and hung rt across to main gp but ch wl over 1f out: kpt on ins fnl f* **20/1**

-021 **5** *1* **Kanaf (IRE)**[22] 3796 4-8-12 **95** 6ex.......... RichardHills 20 98+
(Ed Dunlop) *taken down early: s.i.s: towards rr of centre gp: nt clr run over 1f out: picked up wl whn gap opened ent fnl f: running on strly whn nt clr run again nring fin* **25/1**

1305 **6** *nse* **Pastoral Player**[14] 4092 4-9-6 **103**.......... SteveDrowne 24 104+
(Hughie Morrison) *taken down early: sn swtchd to centre gp: hld up bhd: hdwy over 1f out: r.o wl fnl f: nrst fin* **20/1**

0401 **7** *½* **Secret Asset (IRE)**[4] 4416 6-9-1 **98** 6ex.......... GeorgeBaker 5 97
(Jane Chapple-Hyam) *mid-div on far side: hdwy 2f out: sn rdn to dispute 2nd: no ex ins fnl f* **25/1**

1031 **8** *nse* **Ancient Cross**[36] 3357 7-9-4 **101**..........(t) GrahamGibbons 23 100
(Michael Easterby) *mid-div of centre gp: chsd ldrs over 1f out: kpt on same pce fnl f* **33/1**

0265 **9** *nk* **Atlantic Sport (USA)**[7] 4314 6-9-3 **100**.......... HughBowman 9 98
(Mick Channon) *hld up towards rr on far side: rdn over 2f out: r.o ins fnl f: nvr nrr* **25/1**

2052 **10** *½* **Tajneed (IRE)**[7] 4346 8-9-5 **102**.......... FrannyNorton 17 98
[illegible] **25/1**

-301 **11** *hd* **Edinburgh Knight (IRE)**[35] 3395 4-8-12 **95**.......... JimCrowley 10 91
(Paul D'Arcy) *edgy: on toes: kpt on fnl f but nvr bttr than mid-div in centre gp* **16/1**

0003 **12** *hd* **Jimmy Styles**[14] 4092 7-9-10 **107**..........(p) AdamKirby 12 102
(Clive Cox) *kpt on fnl f but a mid-div of centre gp* **25/1**

-611 **13** *½* **Quest For Success (IRE)**[15] 4042 6-9-3 **103** 6ex.......... LeeTopliss(3) 11 96
(Richard Fahey) *lw: led far side gp but overall chsd ldrs: one pce fr over 1f out* **28/1**

200 **14** *½* **Global City (IRE)**[35] 3410 5-8-11 **94**..........(t) FrankieDettori 4 86
(Saeed Bin Suroor) *taken down early: prom on far side: wkng whn bmpd ent fnl f* **33/1**

0000 **15** *nk* **Evens And Odds (IRE)**[15] 4042 7-8-12 **102**.......... MatthewLawson(7) 14 93
(David Nicholls) *swtg: racd centre: overall ldr tl wl over 1f out: wknd fnl f* **28/1**

2-40 **16** *½* **Victoire De Lyphar (IRE)**[42] 3155 4-9-4 **101**.......... AdrianNicholls 15 90
(David Nicholls) *b: b.hind: taken down early: chsd ldrs in centre gp: rdn over 3f out: wknd ent fnl f* **16/1**

3456 **17** *nk* **Docofthebay (IRE)**[21] 3862 7-9-0 **97**..........(b) TomQueally 25 85
(David Nicholls) *chsd ldr on stands' side rail tl hung rt over 1f out* **20/1**

6034 **18** *hd* **Fathsta (IRE)**[7] 4346 6-8-11 **94**.......... SilvestreDeSousa 7 87+
(David Simcock) *taken down early: towards rr on far side: hdwy in tch 2f out: hld whn squeezed up and eased jst ins fnl f* **8/1**[2]

20F2 **19** *1 ¾* **Mon Cadeaux**[21] 3852 4-8-12 **95**.......... LiamKeniry 3 77+
(Andrew Balding) *lw: mid-div on far side: btn whn squeezed up on rails over 1f out* **18/1**

0130 **20** *nk* **Fitz Flyer (IRE)**[21] 3874 5-8-12 **95**..........(b1) TomEaves 16 76
(Bryan Smart) *chsd ldr in centre gp tl wknd over 1f out* **66/1**

0105 **21** *½* **Crown Choice**[21] 3862 6-9-0 **97**.......... JimmyFortune 6 77
(Walter Swinburn) *taken down early: chsd ldrs on far side: rdn over 2f out: wknd over 1f out* **16/1**

0002 **22** *shd* **Colonel Mak**[15] 4042 4-8-11 **94**.......... JamieSpencer 21 73
(David Barron) *a towards rr of centre gp* **12/1**[3]

3000 **23** *½* **Brave Prospector**[15] 4042 6-9-3 **100**.......... PaulHanagan 8 78
(Richard Fahey) *racd far side: a towards rr* **22/1**

0320 **24** *¾* **Tiddliwinks**[48] 2967 5-9-9 **106**.......... PhillipMakin 26 81
(Kevin Ryan) *chsd ldr in group of 4 on stands' sides rail but nvr on terms w main bunch: wknd wl over 1f out* **16/1**

4050 **25** *shd* **Lui Rei (ITY)**[21] 3846 5-8-11 **97**.......... AdamBeschizza(3) 22 72
(Robert Cowell) *lw: s.i.s: a towards rr of centre gp* **40/1**

3200 **26** *nk* **Cape To Rio (IRE)**[14] 4092 3-8-11 **99**.......... RichardHughes 19 73
(Richard Hannon) *a towards rr of centre gp* **66/1**

6201 **27** *½* **High Standing (USA)**[28] 3626 6-9-6 **103**.......... ChrisCatlin 28 75
(William Haggas) *taken down early: s.i.s: a bhd on stands' side* **28/1**

69.91 secs (-2.29) **Going Correction** -0.10s/f (Good)

WFA 3 from 4yo+ 5lb **27** Ran SP% **136.7**

Speed ratings (Par 109): **111,107,107,107,105 105,105,105,104,104 103,103,102,102,101 101,100,100,98,97 97,96,96,95,95**

Tote Swingers: 1&2 £88.10, 1&3 £5.70, 2&3 £39.50 CSF £223.31 CT £1514.94 TOTE £6.30: £2.50, £9.90, £2.10, £6.30; EX 619.90 Trifecta £5614.60 Pool: £49,791.40 - 6.56 winning units..

Owner A Chandler & L Westwood **Bred** Bond Thoroughbred Corporation **Trained** Sheriff Hutton, N Yorks

■ No horse had previously carried more than 9-10 to victory in the Stewards' Cup.

FOCUS

Arguably the hottest sprint handicap of the season and a race from which a number of recent winners have gone on to score at Group level, most notably the Group 1 winning pair Patavellian and Borderlescott. This looked a strong renewal with half of the field officially rated 100 or more and, after the way the consolation race was run earlier in the afternoon, all but four of the runners raced centre to far side of the track. The time was 0.41secs faster than the opening contest and, although it did not prove easy to come from behind, the form should prove reliable.

NOTEBOOK

Hoof It ◆ turned this usually competitive handicap into something of a procession, much as he had done at York the weekend before. Always going well tracking the leaders, he went across to the far rail as he made his move soon after halfway. He struck the front around 2f from home and it was clear entering the final furlong the race was his. He took this off a mark of 111, which when compared with those future Group 1 winners, who scored off 95 and 102 respectively, suggests he is already a long way down the road to featuring in the top sprints. His trainer was considering supplementing him for the Nunthorpe, but otherwise The Betfred Sprint Cup at Haydock looks an obvious target. (tchd 7-1 in places)

Tax Free(IRE), a multiple Group winner in his prime when ideally suited by 5f, did win over C&D back in 2006 and had not been beaten far in two other starts at the track. Well handicapped on his old form and still capable of winning races, as he showed at Beverley in June, he raced just behind the leaders up the centre and stayed on in the closing stages, despite having no chance against the winner. (tchd 40-1 in a place)

Mac's Power(IRE) progressed last backend and had run well in some decent handicaps this time around. Despite being 10lb above his last winning mark, he was well drawn and finished strongly, having been hampered when going for a gap near the rail. (op 7-1)

Nasri ◆ had been running run well in good handicaps for his current trainer and was unlucky, as he had to race on the stands' side for most of the way. Despite drifting across the track in the closing stages, he kept galloping and was not beaten far. He deserves to win a decent race after this, and is as effective at 7f as he is at six. (op 25-1)

Kanaf(IRE) ◆ has been in good form in mainly lesser company and, although 6lb higher for his recent Ascot success, ran well, having to be eased off the heels of the placed horses near the finish. He looks progressive and could have a good handicap in him on this evidence. (tchd 28-1 in a place)

Pastoral Player ◆ finished third to Deacon Blues in the Wokingham but had been well beaten in the Stewards' Sprint last year on his only his previous visit here. His rider originally intended to go stands' side from his draw but soon changed his mind and ended up at the back of the main group. However, his mount found his stride in the latter stages and finished as well as any, and is one to keep in mind for a decent sprint handicap.

Secret Asset(IRE) benefited from a drop in the weights to win over 5f at this track earlier in the week but had to race off his old mark plus a penalty, so was 9lb higher here. However, he finished sixth in this last year off 1lb lower and again ran creditably, showing up behind the leaders for much of the trip.

Ancient Cross, a stablemate of the winner and an improved performer this season, ran pretty well considering his high draw and the fact he had to race up the centre of the track. A return to 5f at the Ebor meeting could see him back to winning ways.

Atlantic Sport(USA) recorded his best placing since returning from Dubai when second to High Standing at Newbury, but arguably bettered that when fifth in a valuable 7f Ascot handicap the previous weekend and was noted staying on well in the closing stages. He should have his turn back over another furlong. (op 33-1 tchd 50-1 in a place)

Tajneed(IRE), something of a Ripon specialist, was 3lb better off with Hoof It for a 3/4l defeat last time. Although never looking likely to reverse that form, he stayed on steadily and the Great St Wilfrid will no doubt be the target now.

Edinburgh Knight(IRE), who had gained most of his wins on Polytrack, scored his first turf success last time on easy ground. He probably found these conditions faster than ideal and can be given another chance.

Jimmy Styles won the Ayr Gold Cup in 2009 and a third to Deacon Blues in a Group 3 last time showed he was in form. He ran creditably and presumably connections will be targeting the Western meeting feature once again.

Quest For Success(IRE), came into this in form and showed up for a fair way. (op 33-1 tchd 25-1)

Global City(IRE) did not ran badly from his good draw.

Evens And Odds(IRE), last year's winner of this and second in 2009 on his only two previous visits to the track, was 4lb above last year's winning mark but had a bit to find with several of these on recent form and faded after making the running.

Victoire De Lyphar(IRE) was being pushed along to hold his place from an early stage. (op 14-1 tchd 12-1)

Docofthebay(IRE) raced mostly on the stands' side from his high draw but followed the fourth over towards the main group in the closing stages. (op 28-1)

Fathsta(IRE), who was well-backed, was short of room in the closing stages, which was confirmed by Silvestre De Sousa. Official explanation: jockey said that the gelding suffered interference in running (op 16-1 tchd 33-1 in a place)

Mon Cadeaux did not get the best of runs and was eased late on. (op 16-1 tchd 20-1)

Fitz Flyer(IRE) has run well in several good handicaps and had blinkers on for the first time instead of a visor. He showed good early pace before fading. (op 50-1)

Crown Choice got over to race close to the rail but failed to make any impression before being allowed to coast home.

Colonel Mak races up the centre, never landed a blow and was noticeably eased in the final furlong. He was subsequently reported to have hit his head on the stalls and lost several teeth, so clearly had excuses. (op 11-1)

Tiddliwinks raced on the stands' side along with the fourth, Docofthebay and High Standing, but it was clear over a furlong out they were all struggling. (tchd 18-1 in places)

4535 OVERTONES EBF "SCHIAPARELLI" MAIDEN STKS 7f

4:20 (4:22) (Class 2) 2-Y-0 **£11,320** (£3,368; £1,683; £841) **Stalls** Low

Form / RPR

3 **1** **Nawwaar (USA)**[22] 3793 2-9-0 0.......... RichardHills 4 85+
(John Dunlop) *cmpt: lw: in tch in midfield: hmpd bnd over 4f out: nt clr run over 2f out: swtchd lft and over 1f out and again jst over 1f out: gd hdwy u.p 1f out: chal fnl 100yds: sn led and r.o wl* **7/2**[2]

2 *hd* **Grandeur (IRE)** 2-9-0 0.......... ChrisCatlin 13 82+
(Jeremy Noseda) *unf: scope: in rr of main gp and nudged along early: stl plenty to do and pushed lft over 2f out: gd hdwy and edging rt over 1f out: led fnl 100yds: sn hdd: r.o wl and drew clr w wnr after: jst hld* **25/1**

54 **3** *2* **Opera Buff**[15] 4054 2-9-0 0........ LiamKeniry 16 77
(Sylvester Kirk) *lw: in tch: rdn over 2f out: drvn and hdwy 1f out: pressed ldrs ins fnl f: outpcd by ldng pair fnl 75yds: kpt on* **50/1**

0 **4** *1 1/2* **Amazing Storm (IRE)**[21] 3870 2-9-0 0........ RichardHughes 15 73+
(Richard Hannon) *str: tall: swtg: t.k.h: chsd ldrs on outer: trckd ldr 3f out: rdn and unable qck over 1f out: stl ev ch tl wknd fnl 100yds* **25/1**

2 **5** *hd* **Sports Section**[22] 3823 2-9-0 0........ FrankieDettori 7 72
(Mahmood Al Zarooni) *lw: led: rdn wl over 1f out: drvn and hdd fnl 100yds: wknd towards fin* **5/2**[1]

0 **6** *1 1/2* **Blank Czech (IRE)**[86] 1835 2-9-0 0........ AdamKirby 5 69+
(Amanda Perrett) *dwlt: sn rcvrd and in tch in midfield: n.m.r over 2f out: effrt and edging rt 2f out: swtchd lft 1f out: nt clr run and swtchd lft again ins fnl f: kpt on* **40/1**

5 **7** *1 1/4* **Expense Claim (IRE)**[14] 4091 2-9-0 0........ JimmyFortune 1 65+
(Andrew Balding) *chsd ldrs: hmpd bnd over 4f out: rdn 2f out: wknd ent fnl f* **20/1**

8 *hd* **Foster's Road** 2-9-0 0........ HughBowman 10 65+
(Mick Channon) *w'like: bit bkwd: stdd and dropped in bhd after s: hdwy on inner over 2f out: n.m.r wl over 1f out: swtchd lft and kpt on ins fnl f* **66/1**

0 **9** *1* **Hyperlink (IRE)**[74] 2181 2-9-0 0........ SilvestreDeSousa 6 62+
(Mark Johnston) *lengthy: dwlt: sn in tch in midfield: hmpd and pushed wd bnd over 4f out: swtchd lft 3f out: drvn and no imp over 1f out: edgd rt ins fnl f* **33/1**

10 *4 1/2* **Eurystheus (IRE)** 2-9-0 0........ DaneO'Neill 11 51+
(Richard Hannon) *rn green and sn pushed along in rr of main gp: struggling 3f out: rdn over 1f out: plugged on past btn horses fnl f: n.d* **25/1**

3 **11** *4* **Mickdaam (IRE)**[22] 3823 2-9-0 0........ PaulHanagan 3 41
(Richard Fahey) *lw: chsd ldrs: rdn and struggling jst over 2f out: wknd qckly over 1f out* **11/2**[3]

2 **12** *5* **Niceofyoutotellme**[23] 3780 2-9-0 0........ JimCrowley 2 29+
(Ralph Beckett) *mostly chsd ldr tl 3f out: sn struggling: wknd qckly wl over 1f out: eased ins fnl f* **7/2**[2]

13 *4 1/2* **Le Cagnard** 2-9-0 0........ MartinDwyer 8 17
(Michael Bell) *w'like: in rr of main gp: pushed along and wknd qckly 2f out: wl btn and eased fnl f* **40/1**

14 *5* **Scarlet Prince** 2-9-1 0 ow1........ GeorgeBaker 14 6
(Gary Moore) *leggy: attr: rn green: sn wl detached in last pair: nvr on terms: t.o* **50/1**

15 *1 1/4* **True Prince (USA)** 2-9-0 0........ TomQueally 9 —
(Amanda Perrett) *w'like: scope: bit bkwd: rn v green: sn wl detached in last and rdn along: nvr on terms: t.o* **66/1**

02 **16** *5* **Daddy Warbucks (IRE)**[11] 4171 2-9-0 0........ AdrianNicholls 12 —
(David Nicholls) *w'like: trsn: chsd ldrs: wkng qckly whn sltly hmpd over 2f out: wl bhd and eased fnl f: t.o* **20/1**

1m 27.43s (0.53) **Going Correction** -0.10s/f (Good) **16** Ran SP% **124.2**
Speed ratings (Par 100): **92,91,89,87,87 85,84,84,83,77 73,67,62,56,55 49**
Tote Swingers: 1&2 £21.30, 1&3 £39.60, 2&3 £104.40 CSF £94.45 TOTE £5.40: £1.90, £6.50, £12.50; EX 136.00 Trifecta £2175.20 Part won. Pool: £2,939.47 - 0.60 winning units..
Owner Hamdan Al Maktoum **Bred** Shadwell Farm LLC **Trained** Arundel, W Sussex

FOCUS
This is often a good maiden and three of the last six winners were all subsequently successful in Pattern company, namely Opera Cape, Jukebox Jury and most recently Pausanias. The complexion of the race changed in the last furlong, suggesting the pace was plenty fast enough, and a few of these also found trouble, so the form could be a bit misleading. Whatever, though, it's a race that seems sure to produce some nice winners and the winner should go on to rate higher.

NOTEBOOK
Nawwaar(USA) ◆ overcame a troubled trip to confirm the promise he showed when third over 6f on his debut at Ascot. He was squeezed for room on the bend at around halfway, and then had to switch wide after being denied a clear run in the straight, but he still picked up in taking fashion. Entered in a number of Group races, his connections will doubtless now step him up in grade and he's a smart prospect. (op 11-2)
Grandeur(IRE), an 85,000euros half-brother to 1m4f winner Sixty Eight Guns, out of a 1m4f scorer, showed a deal of ability on debut. He didn't get the clearest of runs, having to be switched, but finished well and was just held by a rival with the benefit of previous experience. Although he doesn't hold any big-race entries in Britain or Ireland, this was promising. (op 16-1)
Opera Buff ran a nice race, confirming the improvement he showed on his second start. The type to keep progressing, he can win an ordinary maiden and also now has the option of nurseries. (op 66-1)
Amazing Storm(IRE) ◆ showed a lot of ability, improving on his debut effort with a performance that's even better than the result suggests. He was caught wide throughout from an unfavourable draw and, having been keen, he found himself bang on the pace much sooner than ideal. It's interesting he was the stable's first string in a race the Hannon team had won three times in the last four years and there's a lot better to come when he settles. (op 16-1)
Sports Section couldn't confirm the promise of his debut second at the July meeting, fading in a manner that suggests he went off plenty fast enough. (tchd 2-1)
Blank Czech(IRE) ◆ was far too green to do himself justice on his debut over 6f here back in May, but this was a lot better and he would have been closer with a cleaner trip. He's looks quite a nice long-term prospect. (op 33-1)
Expense Claim(IRE), like the winner, was a bit short of room on the bend at around halfway. He can yet do better. (op 16-1)
Foster's Road didn't get the best of runs and can improve.
Hyperlink(IRE), reported to have run green on his debut 74 days earlier, still looked badly in need of the experience.
Eurystheus(IRE) ◆, an £80,000 purchase, is from a family the stable know well. He's a half-brother to Sweepstake, a 5f juvenile Listed winner for the Hannon's, as well as Luxuria, who won over 6f for the yard. He was passed over by Richard Hughes and was badly in need of the experience, but there should be much better to come.
Mickdaam(IRE) was sporting famous colours and is a half-brother to May Hill and Prix de l'Opera winner Kinnaird, but he was disappointing. He was one place behind Sports Section (finished fifth here) on his debut and that form has obviously taken a severe knock. (tchd 5-1)
Niceofyoutotellme, for whom there was a lot of money around, is in the Royal Lodge, but he couldn't confirm the ability he showed when runner-up on his debut at Warwick. (op 4-1 tchd 5-1)
Scarlet Prince's rider George Baker reported the colt ran green. Official explanation: jockey said that the colt ran green (op 80-1 tchd 40-1)
Daddy Warbucks(IRE)'s rider Adrian Nicholls reported the gelding lost its action. Official explanation: jockey said that the gelding lost its action (op 16-1)

4536 BEST WESTERN HORSES HELP HEROES NURSERY STKS (H'CAP) 6f
4:55 (5:10) (Class 2) 2-Y-O **£9,703** (£2,887; £1,443; £721) **Stalls** High

Form RPR

2301 **1** **Bayleyf (IRE)**[23] 3761 2-9-2 **87**........ GeorgeBaker 11 94
(John Best) *led main gp nr stand-side rail: mde all: kpt on wl whn chal fr 2f out: asserted towards fin: rdn out* **10/1**

1205 **2** *2* **Es Que Love (IRE)**[21] 3866 2-9-0 **85**........ SilvestreDeSousa 7 86
(Mark Johnston) *lw: chsd wnr: chal over 2f out: ev ch ent fnl f: no ex fnl 75yds* **5/1**[1]

441 **3** *1/2* **Safari Storm (USA)**[17] 3984 2-8-6 **77**........(t) MartinDwyer 5 77
(Brian Meehan) *mid-div: hdwy over 2f out: rdn whn swtchd lft over 1f out: running on whn swtchd rt ins fnl f: kpt on* **9/1**

5211 **4** *2* **Amis Reunis**[9] 4228 2-8-6 **77**........ AdrianNicholls 3 71
(Richard Hannon) *mid-div: hdwy in centre whn rdn and hung rt over 2f out: kpt on same pce fnl f* **9/1**

2230 **5** *nk* **Tell Dad**[44] 3064 2-9-0 **85**........ RichardHughes 9 78
(Richard Hannon) *on toes: hld up: sme hdwy 2f out: sn rdn: kpt on same pce fnl f: nvr threatened ldrs* **7/1**[3]

454 **6** *1 1/4* **Tina's Spirit (IRE)**[15] 4052 2-8-1 **75**........ KieranO'Neill(3) 14 64
(Richard Hannon) *lw: chsd ldrs tl outpcd 2f out: nvr bk on terms* **16/1**

0520 **7** *1 3/4* **Signifer (IRE)**[14] 4094 2-9-2 **87**........ HughBowman 2 71
(Mick Channon) *racd alone in centre: disp ld after 2f tl rdn over 2f out: wknd fnl f* **25/1**

621 **8** *nk* **Avon Pearl**[31] 3511 2-8-8 **79**........ DaneO'Neill 16 62
(Henry Candy) *mid-div: rdn over 2f out: nvr gng pce to get involved* **10/1**

5012 **9** *hd* **Indepub**[25] 3700 2-8-7 **78**........ PaulHanagan 8 60
(Kevin Ryan) *awkwardly away: sn struggling in rr: sme late prog: nvr a factor* **12/1**

310 **10** *2 1/4* **Airborne Again (IRE)**[14] 4094 2-9-1 **86**........ JimmyFortune 13 61
(Richard Hannon) *lw: chsd wnr tl over 2f out: wknd over 1f out* **10/1**

214 **11** *1/2* **Travis County (IRE)**[34] 3429 2-8-6 **77**........ TomEaves 6 51
(Brian Ellison) *s.i.s: a towards rr* **9/1**

0221 **12** *1/2* **Apostle (IRE)**[30] 3552 2-9-2 **87**........(v[1]) FrankieDettori 15 59
(Michael Bell) *lw: s.i.s: a towards rr* **6/1**[2]

1m 12.22s (0.02) **Going Correction** -0.10s/f (Good) **12** Ran SP% **118.1**
Speed ratings (Par 100): **95,92,91,89,88 86,84,84,83,80 80,79**
Tote Swingers: 1&2 £10.60, 1&3 £21.80, 2&3 £12.50 CSF £59.16 CT £482.47 TOTE £12.30: £3.80, £2.00, £3.10; EX 75.70 Trifecta £1114.40 Pool: £2,786.16 - 1.85 winning units..
Owner Graham Jones & Partners **Bred** Marchwood Aggregates **Trained** Hucking, Kent

FOCUS
A good nursery rated around the placed horses to previous form. They all avoided both rails for much of the way, but the main action ended up unfolding towards the near side.

NOTEBOOK
Bayleyf(IRE) showed loads of speed and kept on well to decisively follow up his Epsom maiden success. This was a really useful performance off a mark of 87 and it's not out of the question he could be Pattern class before the year's out. (op 12-1 tchd 9-1)
Es Que Love(IRE), entered in the National Stakes, Dewhurst and Middle Park, was dropped in trip after showing speed over 7f last time and ran his race. (op 15-2)
Safari Storm(USA), off the mark over 5f at Sandown, didn't get the best of trips and was going on at the finish. There's more to come. (op 8-1)
Amis Reunis was on a hat-trick after wins at 5f, but she didn't prove quite as effective over this longer trip in better company. This was still a good run in defeat, though. (op 7-1)
Tell Dad ran okay but doesn't look particularly well handicapped. (op 8-1 tchd 9-1 in places)
Signifer(IRE) might be a bit better than he showed as he raced away from the others, towards the far side, for much of the way.
Avon Pearl didn't build on his Chepstow success. (op 15-2 tchd 7-1)
Apostle(IRE), who had a visor on for the first time dispite winning at Yarmouth on his previous outing, was never going after a slow start. (tchd 7-1 in places)

4537 TELEGRAPH APPRENTICE STKS (H'CAP) 1m 1f
5:35 (5:38) (Class 3) (0-90,89) 4-Y-O+ **£9,703** (£2,887; £1,443; £721) **Stalls** Low

Form RPR

061 **1** **Albaqaa**[22] 3825 6-9-8 **87**........ KieranO'Neill 16 99
(P J O'Gorman) *stdd after s: hld up in last quartet: c wd and smooth hdwy 3f out: hung rt fr 2f out: led over 1f out: styd on wl to go clr ins fnl f* **10/1**

3001 **2** *2* **Night Lily (IRE)**[15] 4070 5-9-1 **80**........ PatrickHills 17 88
(Paul D'Arcy) *hld up towards rr: swtchd lft and effrt on outer 3f out: edging rt and chal over 1f out: wnt clr w wnr 1f out: no ex and btn ins fnl f* **14/1**

-013 **3** *nk* **Truism**[4] 4415 5-9-10 **89**........ AdamBeschizza 8 96
(Amanda Perrett) *lw: hld up in midfield: rdn and effrt over 2f out: drvn and chsd ldrs over 1f out: kpt on ins fnl f: pressing for 2nd cl home* **5/1**[2]

0024 **4** *3/4* **Moynahan (USA)**[22] 3802 6-9-0 **84**........(p) MatthewLawson(5) 5 90
(Paul Cole) *s.i.s: bhd: swtchd lft and effrt wl over 2f out: drvn and edging rt over 1f out: kpt on ins fnl f* **9/1**

5252 **5** *1 1/2* **Guest Book (IRE)**[4] 4415 4-9-3 **87**........ DarylByrne(5) 9 89
(Mark Johnston) *lw: dwlt: sn niggled along in midfield: rdn and effrt wl over 2f out: edgd rt u.p and kpt on same pce fr over 1f out* **9/2**[1]

0000 **6** *3* **South Cape**[22] 3797 8-9-1 **80**........ HarryBentley 12 76
(Gary Moore) *hld up in midfield: rdn and effrt over 2f out: styd on same pce and no imp fr over 1f out* **25/1**

-036 **6** *dht* **Diescentric (USA)**[29] 3592 4-9-0 **84**........ CharlesEddery(5) 6 80
(Sir Henry Cecil) *lw: chsd ldr: rdn over 2f out: ev ch over 1f out: btn 1f out: wknd ins fnl f* **8/1**[3]

203 **8** *1 3/4* **Audemar (IRE)**[34] 3436 5-9-6 **85**........ MatthewDavies 11 77
(Edward Vaughan) *hld up in last quartet: rdn and effrt over 2f out: edgd rt and no imp over 1f out* **14/1**

1063 **9** *7* **My Gacho (IRE)**[31] 3506 9-8-12 **77**........(b) MichaelO'Connell 13 54+
(David Nicholls) *led: wntr clr 4f out: rdn 2f out: drvn and hdd over 1f out: sn wknd: eased ins fnl f* **33/1**

6020 **10** *1* **Edgewater (IRE)**[21] 3844 4-8-13 **78**........ KierenFox 4 52
(John Akehurst) *chsd ldrs: rdn and ent fnl 3f: wknd over 2f out* **20/1**

-260 **11** *3/4* **Changing The Guard**[86] 1824 5-9-1 **83**........ LeeTopliss(3) 15 56
(Richard Fahey) *hld up in midfield: rdn and struggling over 3f out: no ch fnl 2f* **20/1**

3204 **12** *3 1/4* **Ethics Girl (IRE)**[17] 3987 5-8-12 **84**........(t) HannahNunn(7) 2 50
(John Berry) *hld up in last quartet: n.m.r on inner 3f out: sn lost tch and no ch fnl 2f* **25/1**

0425 **13** *2 1/4* **Kathleen Frances**[22] 3829 4-9-4 **83**........ SimonPearce 14 44
(Mark H Tompkins) *stmbld s: in tch in midfield: rdn and struggling over 3f out: wknd over 2f out* **12/1**

1025 **14** *5* **Osgood**[14] 4109 4-8-8 **78**........ CharlesBishop(5) 10 28
(Mick Channon) *chsd ldrs: rdn over 3f out: sn struggling and wknd 3f out: wl btn fnl 2f* **20/1**

0646 **15** *3 1/4* **Champagne Style (USA)**[14] 3659 4-8-5 **73**........(p) RyanPowell(3) 18 15
(Richard Guest) *racd wd tl 1/2-way: in tch: rdn and wknd 3f out: wl bhd and eased ins fnl f* **33/1**

-062 **16** *30* **Fastnet Storm (IRE)**[14] 4109 5-9-7 **86**.......................... AlanCreighton 1 —
(David Barron) *chsd ldrs: struggling u.p 4f out: sn wknd: t.o fnl 2f* **8/1**[3]

1m 53.69s (-2.61) **Going Correction** -0.10s/f (Good) **16** Ran SP% **125.0**
Speed ratings (Par 107): **107,105,104,104,102 100,100,98,92,91 90,88,86,81,78 52**
Tote Swingers: 1&2 £20.10, 1&3 £32.80, 2&3 £13.10 CSF £131.85 CT £826.07 TOTE £14.60: £3.40, £2.90, £1.60, £2.40; EX 258.40 Trifecta £1654.40 Part won. Pool: £2,235.76 - 0.20 winning units..
Owner Racing To The Max **Bred** C Eddington And Partners **Trained** Newmarket, Suffolk

FOCUS
A good, competitive handicap in which the strong early gallop played a big part, as it enabled those drawn on the outside to come from off the pace and dominate the finish. The winner remains on a good mark, while the runner-up and fourth set the standard.

NOTEBOOK
Albaqaa, raised 5lb for his shock success at the Newmarket July meeting, was drawn out wide but settled at the back of the field before moving up smoothly on the outside early in the straight. He found plenty when asked and is clearly at the top of his game right now. (op 12-1)
Night Lily(IRE), well suited by 1m, a turning track and fast ground and in decent form; was another who travelled well off the pace before coming through to lead. Although unable to hold off the winner, she at least proved she stays this far. (op 12-1)
Truism, a regular visitor here who had only twice failed to be placed in ten starts at the track, including two wins, was being urged along to make ground early in the straight. He was close enough to the winner 2f out but, although he did stay on, could not match the extra gears that rival produced to settle the race. (tchd 11-2)
Moynahan(USA) has a good record on this track and is effective at the trip. He came here in reasonably good form, was 3lb below his last winning mark, and had cheekpieces back on instead of blinkers. He was held up at the back and followed the winner through but could not pull out extra under pressure. Matthew Lawson later reported that the gelding missed the break. Official explanation: jockey said that the gelding missed the break (op 15-2)
Guest Book(IRE) finished ahead of Truism when behind Red Gulch here earlier in the week and they met here on the same terms. He was never travelling fluently though and, although he kept on without threatening to win, clearly did not run up to that mark with his old rival this time. (op 5-1 tchd 11-2 in places)
South Cape was held up before staying on but could not find the pace to get involved. (op 11-1 tchd 12-1 in places)
Diescentric(USA), a lightly raced, fast-ground winner who stays 1m2f, helped with the pacemaking and, although faring best of the front-running trio, paid for his efforts in the last quarter-mile. (op 11-1 tchd 12-1 in places)
My Gacho(IRE) set the strong early gallop but has never won beyond 7f and did not last home. (op 28-1)
Kathleen Frances's rider reported that the filly stumbled leaving the stalls. Official explanation: jockey said that the filly stumbled leaving the stalls (tchd 14-1 in a place)
Fastnet Storm(IRE) was one of those that helped set the strong early gallop, along with My Gacho and Diescentric, and they paid for their efforts in the last 2f. Alan Creighton, the rider later reported that the gelding was unsuited by the going. Official explanation: jockey said that the gelding was unsuited by the good to firm (good in places) going (op 10-1)
T/Jkpt: Not won. T/Plt: £3,221.40 to a £1 stake. Pool of £295,183.26 - 66.89 winning units. T/Qpdt: £68.10 to a £1 stake. Pool of £18,334.93 - 98.25 winning units. SP

4039 HAMILTON (R-H)
Saturday, July 30

OFFICIAL GOING: Good (8.0)
GOOD (8.0)
Wind: Almost nil Weather: Sunny

4538 AVIA SIGNS NURSERY 6f 5y
6:40 (6:40) (Class 6) 2-Y-O **£2,264** (£673; £336; £168) **Stalls** High

Form RPR
601 **1** **Bop It**[38] 3274 2-8-10 **73**.......................... JustinNewman(7) 5 87+
(Bryan Smart) *t.k.h early: prom: smooth hdwy over 2f out: led over 1f out: pushed clr fnl f* **2/1**[1]
323 **2** *3 ¼* **Tortoni (IRE)**[57] 2672 2-9-2 **77**.......................... JulieBurke(5) 6 79
(Kevin Ryan) *led to over 1f out: rdn and kpt on same pce fnl f* **3/1**[2]
034 **3** *1 ¾* **Fast On (IRE)**[19] 3921 2-8-3 **66**..........................(v1) ShaneBKelly(7) 4 63
(Ed McMahon) *dwlt and bmpd s: chsd ldng gp on outside: effrt over 1f* [illegible] **4/1**
100 **4** *½* **Chevanah (IRE)**[illegible] [illegible] 2-8-9 [illegible].......................... [illegible] 1 [illegible]
(Ann Duffield) *in tch on outside: effrt over 2f out: kpt on same pce fnl f* **25/1**
0306 **5** *2* **Always Ends Well (IRE)**[15] 4069 2-8-7 **63**.......................... AndrewElliott 9 53
(Mark Johnston) *chsd ldrs: drvn and outpcd 2f out: kpt on fnl f: no imp* **22/1**
3310 **6** *6* **Pen Bal Crag (IRE)**[14] 4094 2-9-4 **74**.......................... TonyHamilton 2 46
(Richard Fahey) *cl up: lost pl over 2f out: n.d after* **7/2**[3]
004 **7** *shd* **Lady Gadfly**[31] 3505 2-7-7 **54** oh2.......................... DanielleMcCreery(5) 3 25
(Micky Hammond) *cl up tl rdn and wknd over 1f out* **28/1**
3404 **8** *3 ½* **Fortune Star (IRE)**[10] 4193 2-8-0 **56** oh4 ow2.......................... KellyHarrison 8 17
(Linda Perratt) *t.k.h: chsd ldrs tl rdn and wknd fr 2f out* **50/1**

1m 11.59s (-0.61) **Going Correction** -0.15s/f (Firm) **8** Ran SP% **114.2**
Speed ratings (Par 92): **98,93,91,90,88 80,79,75**
toteswingers: 1&2 £2.00, 1&3 £2.30, 2&3 £2.00. CSF £7.84 CT £20.77 TOTE £2.90: £1.50, £1.40, £1.10; EX 9.20.
Owner A Turton, J Blackburn & R Bond **Bred** Bond Thoroughbred Corporation **Trained** Hambleton, N Yorks

FOCUS
Races on round course run over 8yds further than advertised. An ordinary nursery lacking strength in depth judged by the market (22-1 bar four) but the winner won well and can continue to progress. The form makes sense. The stalls were stand side and the pace only really picked up passing halfway.

NOTEBOOK
Bop It had finished seven lengths behind Tortoni in a decent York maiden on their respective debuts in May but has clearly progressed the better of the pair since and could be named the winner 2f out as he loomed up travelling well. Like his close relative Hoof It, who won the Stewards' Cup earlier in the day, he looks a grand sort who'll improve with racing and, well on top passing the line, probably has more improvement in him than the hike in the weights he'll receive for this. He's one to keep on the right side in 6f nurseries. (op 5-2)
Tortoni(IRE) ran his best race since his debut and while he's going to remain vulnerable to more progressive sorts in nurseries, did enough to suggest he might just pinch a modest race off this sort of mark, always looking clear second best once headed by the winner. (tchd 10-3)
Fast On(IRE) wasn't done any favours by being squeezed at the start and probably ran as well in a first-time visor as he has before, while once again giving the impression a stiffer test of stamina will suit him better. (op 9-2)
Chevanah(IRE) hasn't really gone on since making a winning debut but this was a step back in the right direction, albeit readily outpaced once the race began in earnest. (op 20-1)
Always Ends Well(IRE) matched strides with the runner-up to halfway but was soon left in his wake and is struggling to rediscover her early-season form. (op 18-1)
Pen Bal Crag(IRE), who was on edge beforehand and needed two handlers to calm him down, was taking a drop in grade having contested the Super Sprint last time but his yard can't buy a winner at the moment and he never threatened. His opening nursery mark of 74 didn't look excessive on the evidence of his Carlisle win last month. Official explanation: trainer's representative was unable to offer any explanation for the poor performance shown

4539 MACGREGOR FLOORING H'CAP (QUALIFIER FOR THE BETFAIR BONUS SCOTTISH RACING SPRINT FINAL) 5f 4y
7:10 (7:13) (Class 5) (0-75,73) 3-Y-O+ **£4,204** (£1,251; £625; £312) **Stalls** Centre

Form RPR
03 **1** **Dancing Freddy (IRE)**[8] 4272 4-9-3 **67**..........................(tp) RobertLButler(3) 7 76
(Richard Guest) *t.k.h: trckd ldrs: smooth hdwy 2f out: led ins fnl f: r.o wl* **9/1**
2444 **2** *¾* **Bosun Breese**[23] 3759 6-9-7 **73**.......................... LMcNiff(5) 3 79
(David Barron) *disp ld to ins fnl f: kpt on towards fin* **5/1**[3]
6056 **3** *½* **Mandarin Spirit (IRE)**[16] 4017 11-8-8 **55** ow1..........(b) TonyHamilton 5 59
(Linda Perratt) *mde most tl rdn and hdd ins fnl f: kpt on same pce* **28/1**
0025 **4** *½* **Argentine (IRE)**[1] 4504 7-8-6 **56**..........................(b) PatrickDonaghy(3) 6 58
(George Foster) *prom: effrt over 2f out: rallied appr fnl f: one pce ins fnl f* **8/1**
0604 **5** *shd* **Sandwith**[11] 4174 8-8-11 **58**..........................(v) AndrewElliott 8 60
(George Foster) *hld up in tch: rdn over 2f out: kpt on fnl f: nrst fin* **33/1**
2330 **6** *nk* **Ingleby Star (IRE)**[1] 4504 6-9-4 **70**..........................(p) JulieBurke(5) 11 71+
(Ian McInnes) *racd alone stands' side: in tch: rdn 2f out: kpt on fnl f* **4/1**[2]
2352 **7** *2 ½* **Berbice (IRE)**[1] 4503 6-9-6 **67**..........................(b) KellyHarrison 10 59
(Linda Perratt) *missed break: hld up: shkn up and sme late hdwy: nvr on terms* **6/1**
-065 **8** *1* **Avertuoso**[8] 4289 7-8-12 **66**..........................(v) JustinNewman(7) 4 54
(Bryan Smart) *dwlt and wnt rt s: chsd ldng gp: rdn and hung rt over 1f out: kpt on same pce fnl f* **25/1**
2431 **9** *nk* **Senate Majority**[42] 3166 4-9-10 **71**..........................(b) DavidAllan 1 58
(Tim Easterby) *trckd ldrs: drvn over 2f out: wknd appr fnl f* **10/3**[1]
300- **10** *10* **Monte Mayor One**[273] 7225 4-8-4 **58**.......................... ShaneBKelly(7) 9 —
(Jim Goldie) *sn bhd: struggling over 2f out: sn btn* **9/1**
400/ **11** *7* **Blue Tomato**[680] 6051 10-9-8 **69**..........................(p) PatrickMathers 2 —
(Donal Nolan) *chsd ldrs: rdn and outpcd 1/2-way: sn wknd* **50/1**

58.82 secs (-1.18) **Going Correction** -0.15s/f (Firm) **11** Ran SP% **117.3**
Speed ratings (Par 103): **103,101,101,100,100 99,95,93,93,77 66**
toteswingers: 1&2 £10.30, 1&3 £68.30, 2&3 £56.40. CSF £51.69 CT £1223.41 TOTE £8.40: £2.90, £2.20, £6.00; EX 74.80.
Owner Rakebackmypoker.com **Bred** Vincent Duignan **Trained** Stainforth, S Yorks
■ Stewards' Enquiry : Patrick Donaghy one-day ban: careless riding (13 Aug) caution: use of whip

FOCUS
Just a fair sprint handicap contested in the main by exposed veterans. The stalls were in the centre and those ridden prominently held sway. Straightforward form.
Senate Majority Official explanation: trainer's representative was unable to offer any explanation for the poor performance shown

4540 KANE GANG H'CAP (QUALIFIER FOR THE BETFAIR BONUS SCOTTISH RACING STAYERS FINAL) 1m 3f 16y
7:40 (7:41) (Class 5) (0-75,75) 3-Y-O+ **£4,204** (£1,251; £625; £312) **Stalls** Low

Form RPR
-005 **1** **Lucky Windmill**[14] 4107 4-10-0 **75**.......................... PJMcDonald 8 83
(Alan Swinbank) *hld up in tch: hdwy 3f out: rdn to ld over 1f out: kpt on wl fnl f* **9/1**
3362 **2** *¾* **Sharp Sovereign (USA)**[6] 4366 5-9-0 **66**.......................... LMcNiff(5) 9 73
(David Barron) *led: clr over 3f out: sn rdn: hdd over 1f out: rallied: kpt on same pce wl ins fnl f* **3/1**[2]
3151 **3** *¾* **Countrywide Flame**[14] 2635 3-8-7 **72**.......................... ShaneBKelly(7) 4 78
(John Quinn) *chsd ldr: effrt and rdn over 2f out: kpt on same pce ins fnl f* **11/4**[1]
-003 **4** *1* **Hawdyerwheesht**[8] 4287 3-8-13 **71**.......................... AndrewElliott 5 75
(Mark Johnston) *prom: rdn over 2f out: kpt on same pce ins fnl f* **14/1**
4000 **5** *1 ¾* **The Galloping Shoe**[5] 4380 6-9-7 **75**.......................... GarryWhillans(7) 7 76
(Ian Semple) *hld up: hdwy over 2f out: kpt on fnl f: no imp* **16/1**
[illegible] **6** [illegible] [illegible][5] [illegible] [illegible] **75**.......................... PatrickDonaghy(3) 2 71
(Linda Perratt) *hld up: hdwy over 2f out: wknd ins fnl f* [illegible]
123 **7** *hd* **Petomic (IRE)**[11] 4170 6-9-3 **67**.......................... RobertLButler(3) 1 63
(Richard Guest) *hld up: rdn over 2f out: nvr able to chal* **12/1**
4051 **8** *1 ¼* **Key Breeze**[18] 3938 4-8-13 **65**..........................(t) JulieBurke(5) 3 59
(Kevin Ryan) *hld up: hdwy to trck ldrs over 2f out: wknd ins fnl f* **6/1**[3]
-103 **9** *7* **Pandoro De Lago (IRE)**[32] 3486 3-9-2 **74**.......................... TonyHamilton 6 55
(Richard Fahey) *prom: outpcd over 3f out: btn fnl 2f* **20/1**

2m 23.23s (-2.37) **Going Correction** -0.15s/f (Firm)
WFA 3 from 4yo+ 11lb **9** Ran SP% **115.2**
Speed ratings (Par 103): **102,101,100,100,98 97,96,96,90**
toteswingers: 1&2 £4.70, 1&3 £3.90, 2&3 £1.30. CSF £36.14 CT £95.36 TOTE £12.40: £4.10, £1.10, £1.80; EX 54.80.
Owner Porter, Watson, Valentine **Bred** R V Young **Trained** Melsonby, N Yorks

FOCUS
An ordinary handicap but plenty of in-form runners and quite solid form for the grade, rated around the second and third. It was run at a decent pace as expected with several confirmed front runners in the field.
Key Breeze Official explanation: jockey said that the gelding ran too free

4541 BRITISH STALLION STUDS SUPPORTING BRITISH RACING E B F FILLIES' H'CAP 5f 4y
8:10 (8:11) (Class 4) (0-85,81) 3-Y-O+ **£5,498** (£1,636; £817; £408) **Stalls** Centre

Form RPR
2511 **1** **Wicked Wilma (IRE)**[12] 4144 7-8-5 **65**.......................... JulieBurke(5) 4 73
(Alan Berry) *mde all: rdn 2f out: kpt on wl fnl f* **5/1**[3]
-052 **2** *¾* **Ballinargh Girl (IRE)**[21] 3853 3-8-7 **73**.......................... ShaneBKelly(7) 2 77
(Robert Wylie) *t.k.h early: cl up: rdn 2f out: kpt on ins fnl f* **7/2**[1]
4401 **3** *shd* **Berberana (IRE)**[8] 4295 3-9-8 **81**.......................... DavidAllan 6 85
(Tim Easterby) *w wnr: rdn 2f out: kpt on same pce ins fnl f* **4/1**[2]
4602 **4** *nk* **Mango Music**[19] 3900 8-9-6 **75**.......................... TonyHamilton 5 79
(Richard Fahey) *chsd ldng gp: rdn over 2f out: r.o fnl f: nrst fin* **15/2**
0622 **5** *nk* **Saxonette**[6] 4359 3-8-9 **68**.......................... PBBeggy 3 70
(Linda Perratt) *prom: effrt u.p 2f out: kpt on ins fnl f* **12/1**
5401 **6** *nk* **Midnight Dynamo**[1] 4504 4-9-2 **65** 6ex.......................... DanielTudhope 8 73
(Jim Goldie) *bhd: rdn 1/2-way: styd on fnl f: nrst fin* **6/1**
6131 **7** *¾* **Bouncy Bouncy (IRE)**[11] 4189 4-8-10 **65**..........................(t) PJMcDonald 9 64
(Michael Bell) *sn bhd: hdwy 2f out: rdn over 1f out: no imp fnl f* **4/1**[2]

-000 8 6 **Cayman Fox**[1] 4504 6-8-10 65 KellyHarrison 1 42
(Linda Perratt) *chsd ldrs tl rdn and wknd fr 2f out* **22/1**

59.00 secs (-1.00) **Going Correction** -0.15s/f (Firm)
WFA 3 from 4yo+ 4lb **8 Ran SP% 117.0**
Speed ratings (Par 102): **102,100,100,100,99 99,98,88**
toteswingers: 1&2 £3.10, 1&3 £3.80, 2&3 £2.90. CSF £23.46 CT £77.79 TOTE £7.30: £2.50, £1.70, £2.00; EX 25.50.
Owner Mrs Thelma White **Bred** Gerry O'Sullivan **Trained** Cockerham, Lancs

FOCUS
The feature race of the night for which the stalls were once again in the middle of the track. All but one of the runners had in the first two last time out and so despite the tight finish it looks reliable form, for all it wasn't a strong race for the grade with only two of the runners officially rated 75 or more. The first three were always to the fore.
Bouncy Bouncy(IRE) Official explanation: jockey said that the filly was unsuited by the good ground

4542 FAKE BAKE MAIDEN STKS 6f 5y
8:40 (8:42) (Class 5) 3-Y-0+ **£2,975** (£885; £442; £221) **Stalls** High

Form RPR
6 1 **Chookie Royale**[17] 3977 3-9-3 0 DavidAllan 8 79
(Keith Dalgleish) *prom: checked sn after s: hdwy over 2f out: effrt over 1f out: styd on to ld towards fin* **8/1**[3]
-222 2 *nk* **Vizean (IRE)**[23] 3756 3-8-12 74 TonyHamilton 3 73
(Ed McMahon) *taken early to post: led 1f: cl up: led over 2f out: rdn over 1f out: kpt on fnl f: hdd nr fin* **2/5**[1]
0 3 6 **So Wise (USA)**[47] 3001 3-9-3 0 PBBeggy 6 59
(Keith Dalgleish) *in tch: checked sn after s: rdn and effrt over 2f out: no imp over 1f out* **20/1**
4 3 ¾ **Naafetha (IRE)** 3-8-12 0 DanielTudhope 7 42
(George Foster) *missed break: bhd and outpcd tl sme late hdwy: nvr rchd ldrs* **33/1**
0003 5 1 ½ **King Bertolini (IRE)**[21] 3857 4-9-3 47 JulieBurke(5) 1 43
(Alan Berry) *bhd and outpcd: nvr rchd ldrs* **28/1**
5 6 ½ **Needwood Park**[23] 3756 3-8-12 0 LMcNiff(5) 2 40
(David Barron) *sn outpcd and drvn along: no ch fr 1/2-way* **6/1**[2]
05 7 4 **Missile Attack (IRE)**[28] 3616 3-9-0 0 (b[1]) PatrickDonaghy(3) 5 28
(Ian Semple) *dwlt: plld hrd and swtchd to stands' rail sn after s: led after 1f to over 2f out: wknd over 1f out* **12/1**

1m 11.1s (-1.10) **Going Correction** -0.15s/f (Firm)
WFA 3 from 4yo 5lb **7 Ran SP% 115.7**
Speed ratings (Par 103): **101,100,92,87,85 84,79**
toteswingers: 1&2 £1.70, 1&3 £6.00, 2&3 £3.00. CSF £11.87 TOTE £10.00: £3.80, £1.10; EX 17.20.
Owner Raeburn Brick Limited **Bred** D And J Raeburn **Trained** Carluke, South Lanarkshire

FOCUS
Little strength in depth to this maiden, for which the stalls were placed near the stand rail. The pace was only fair, with the runaway leader ignored. The form is taken at face value.
Missile Attack(IRE) Official explanation: jockey said the gelding ran too free

4543 RACING UK H'CAP (QUALIFIER FOR THE BETFAIR BONUS SCOTTISH RACING MILE FINAL) 1m 65y
9:10 (9:11) (Class 5) (0-75,70) 3-Y-0+ **£4,204** (£1,251; £625; £312) **Stalls** Low

Form RPR
4503 1 **I'm Super Too (IRE)**[6] 4361 4-9-10 66 PJMcDonald 10 75
(Alan Swinbank) *hld up: hdwy over 2f out: rdn to ld over 1f out: kpt on wl fnl f* **3/1**[1]
2125 2 ¾ **Retreat Content (IRE)**[6] 4364 3-8-12 67 JulieBurke(5) 5 72
(Linda Perratt) *trckd ldrs: effrt over 2f out: chsd wnr ins fnl f: r.o* **4/1**[3]
6003 3 ¾ **Hill Tribe**[5] 4394 4-9-4 60 AndrewElliott 8 65
(Richard Guest) *wnt lft s: cl up: led after 2f: rdn and hdd over 1f out: kpt on same pce ins fnl f* **17/2**
6231 4 2 **Seldom (IRE)**[12] 4150 5-8-13 62 JohnCavanagh(7) 3 63+
(Mel Brittain) *hld up: pushed along over 3f out: hdwy 2f out: styd on fnl f: nrst fin* **10/3**[2]
6303 5 4 ½ **Royal Straight**[5] 4380 6-9-8 64 KellyHarrison 2 54
(Linda Perratt) *hld up: outpcd over 3f out: sme hdwy over 1f out: nvr able to chal* **11/2**
0401 6 1 **Mangham (IRE)**[11] 4170 6-9-9 65 (p) TonyHamilton 4 53
(George Foster) *t.k.h: hld up: pushed along over 3f out: sme hdwy 2f out: sn no imp* **17/2**
00 7 3 ½ **Honest And True (IRE)**[12] 4143 4-8-9 54 (p) PatrickDonaghy(3) 7 34
(Ian Semple) *trckd ldrs tl hung rt and wknd over 2f out* **25/1**
51 8 2 **On The Cusp (IRE)**[11] 4179 4-9-7 66 (p) RobertLButler(3) 6 41
(Richard Guest) *led 2f: cl up: ev ch and rdn over 2f out: wknd over 1f out* **9/1**

1m 48.19s (-0.21) **Going Correction** -0.15s/f (Firm)
WFA 3 from 4yo+ 8lb **8 Ran SP% 118.4**
Speed ratings (Par 103): **95,94,93,91,87 86,82,80**
toteswingers: 1&2 £3.10, 1&3 £6.80, 2&3 £3.30. CSF £15.93 CT £93.49 TOTE £3.80: £1.50, £1.80, £2.80; EX 17.80.
Owner David C Young **Bred** Norelands Bloodstock, J Hanly & H Lascelles **Trained** Melsonby, N Yorks
■ Stewards' Enquiry : Julie Burke caution: use of whip

FOCUS
Three last-time-out winners made for an interesting finale. It was run at a reasonable pace and there weren't any hard-luck stories. The winner is rated similar to his latest claimer form.
T/Plt: £35.90 to a £1 stake. Pool of £62,166.72 - 1,262.58 winning tickets. T/Qpdt: £5.80 to a £1 stake. Pool of £5,729.39 - 727.47 winning tickets. RY

4317 LINGFIELD (L-H)
Saturday, July 30

OFFICIAL GOING: Turf - good to firm (goingstick 7.9); all-weather - standard
Turf - GOOD TO FIRM (GoingStick 7.9); All-Weather - STANDARD
Wind: Almost nil Weather: Sunny, warm

4544 MAYBE GAGA HERE 13TH AUGUST APPRENTICE H'CAP (TURF) 7f 140y
5:55 (5:59) (Class 6) (0-65,67) 3-Y-0+ **£2,181** (£644; £322) **Stalls** Centre

Form RPR
430 1 **Lutine Charlie (IRE)**[31] 3512 4-9-11 62 LeonnaMayor 11 70
(Ronald Harris) *hld up bhd ldrs against nr side rail: prog to ld over 2f out: sn rdn: kpt on wl* **9/1**
2534 2 ½ **Unlimited**[25] 3716 9-9-13 64 GeorgeDowning 8 71+
(Tony Carroll) *trckd ldrs: effrt to chal on outer over 2f out: chsd wnr to over 1f out: kpt on to take 2nd again ins fnl f: clsng at fin* **13/2**[3]
6660 3 1 **Kathleen Kennet**[14] 4090 11-8-8 47 KatiaScallan(2) 16 52
(Jonathan Geake) *sn last: wl off the pce 1/2-way: gd prog fr 2f out: styd on wl fnl f to take 3rd nr fin* **15/2**
6050 4 1 **Inquisitress**[12] 4154 7-9-0 51 (v) RachaelKneller 15 53
(John Bridger) *hld up in tch: stdy prog nr side 3f out: rdn to chse wnr over 1f out: fnd nil: wknd ins fnl f* **8/1**
0053 5 *nse* **Batchworth Blaise**[67] 2386 8-8-7 48 (b) BrendanPowell(4) 6 50
(Eric Wheeler) *dwlt: hld up in tch: gng wl 3f out: prog over 2f out: rdn and nt qckn wl over 1f out: kpt on ins fnl f* **14/1**
6061 6 4 ½ **All Honesty**[9] 4244 3-9-6 67 LukeRowe(2) 3 56+
(William Knight) *dwlt: hld up wl in rr and racd wdst of all: prog 1/2-way: rdn over 2f out: no imp over 1f out: wknd* **11/4**[1]
4065 7 1 ½ **Dichoh**[44] 3096 8-9-3 54 JakePayne 2 41
(Michael Madgwick) *racd wd: hld up towards rr: prog 3f out: cl up but rdn jst over 2f out: fdd* **16/1**
3044 8 10 **Dies Solis**[25] 3714 4-9-2 57 ShirleyTeasdale(4) 7 19
(Jeremy Gask) *prom: rdn to chal over 2f out: wknd rapidly over 1f out* **11/2**[2]
2000 9 *nse* **Avalon Bay**[23] 3783 3-8-13 62 (p) JacobButterfield(4) 10 22
(Pat Eddery) *racd against rail: led 2f: chsd ldr to 3f out: sn wknd* **14/1**
-000 10 5 **Swing Door (IRE)**[11] 4179 3-8-6 55 TimClark(4) 12 —
(Robert Eddery) *racd on outer: u.p fr 1/2-way: sn struggling* **14/1**
000 11 9 **Phlorian**[25] 3716 5-8-8 49 (bt[1]) LukeStrong(4) 4 —
(Ian Patrick Browne, Ire) *led after 2f: swtchd to nr side rail and sn clr: wknd rapidly and hdd over 2f out: t.o* **66/1**
5500 12 15 **Sonny G (IRE)**[7] 4322 4-8-10 51 GeorgeanBuckell(4) 5 —
(John Best) *w ldr 2f: prom to 1/2-way: wknd rapidly under heavy press: wl t.o* **14/1**

1m 33.57s (1.27) **Going Correction** +0.125s/f (Good)
WFA 3 from 4yo+ 8lb **12 Ran SP% 122.3**
Speed ratings (Par 101): **98,97,96,95,95 90,89,79,79,74 65,50**
toteswingers: 1&2 £6.80, 1&3 £31.20, 2&3 £15.20. CSF £68.66 CT £479.05 TOTE £10.90: £3.70, £2.50, £4.20; EX 77.70.
Owner Jason Tucker **Bred** Patrice O'Connell **Trained** Earlswood, Monmouths

FOCUS
A moderate handicap, confined to apprentice riders. The winner is rated to last year's form, backed up by the placed horses.
Kathleen Kennet Official explanation: vet said the mare lost a left fore shoe

4545 MARSH GREEN MEDIAN AUCTION MAIDEN STKS (TURF) 7f 140y
6:25 (6:26) (Class 6) 2-Y-O **£2,181** (£644; £322) **Stalls** Centre

Form RPR
3 1 **Long Lost Love**[10] 4205 2-8-12 0 FrannyNorton 12 70+
(Mark Johnston) *mde all and racd against rail: gng easily over 2f out: shkn up over 1f out: styd on and nvr seriously threatened* **8/11**[1]
50 2 1 ¼ **Accustomed**[22] 3812 2-8-12 0 JamesDoyle 5 67+
(Sylvester Kirk) *s.i.s: pushed along in rr early: prog fr 3f out: rdn 2f out: styd on to take 2nd nr fin* **16/1**
0 3 ¾ **City Dazzler (IRE)**[15] 4052 2-8-12 0 SteveDrowne 9 65
(Richard Hannon) *chsd wnr to over 2f out: sn pushed along: styd on again fnl f* **15/2**[3]
0 4 2 ½ **Hearts And Minds (IRE)**[10] 4205 2-9-3 0 FergusSweeney 2 64
(Jamie Osborne) *prom: chsd wnr over 2f out: sn rdn and no imp: wknd ins fnl f* **33/1**
5 2 ¾ **Obliterfeight (IRE)** 2-9-3 0 JimCrowley 8 58+
(William Knight) *pushed along in rr early and rn green: prog to chse clr ldng trio 1/2-way: tried to cl 2f out: wknd fnl f* **9/1**
0 6 1 ½ **Emma Jean Boy**[10] 4201 2-9-3 0 LiamKeniry 1 54
(J S Moore) *chsd ldrs: outpcd 1/2-way: pushed along 3f out: tried to cl 2f out: wknd over 1f out* **66/1**
7 5 **Fantasy Hero** 2-9-3 0 TomMcLaughlin 10 43
(Ronald Harris) *sn pushed along in last: nvr a factor: wl btn over 2f out* **33/1**
06 8 *shd* **Vergrigio (IRE)**[15] 4054 2-9-3 0 PatCosgrave 3 42
(Brian Meehan) *pushed along after 2f to stay in tch: shkn up and effrt 3f out: wknd wl over 1f out* **7/1**[2]
9 *shd* **Cato Minor** 2-9-3 0 AdamKirby 7 42
(Amanda Perrett) *rn green in rr and sn pushed along: reminder 5f out: no prog over 2f out: wl btn after* **7/1**[2]
0 10 17 **The Boomingbittern**[30] 3547 2-8-12 0 FrankieMcDonald 6 —
(Edward Creighton) *chsd ldrs 3f: sn lost pl: t.o* **100/1**

1m 34.62s (2.32) **Going Correction** +0.125s/f (Good) **10 Ran SP% 118.9**
Speed ratings (Par 92): **93,91,91,88,85 84,79,79,79,62**
CSF £15.48 TOTE £1.70: £1.10, £4.40, £1.80; EX 14.90.
Owner Miss K Rausing **Bred** Miss K Rausing **Trained** Middleham Moor, N Yorks

FOCUS
A modest juvenile maiden in which the level of the form is fluid.

NOTEBOOK
Long Lost Love had finished a promising second on the Polytrack here on her debut and was a popular choice to open her account. She had the ideal draw and her rider set sensible fractions at the head of affairs, gradually winding up the pace and fending off her rivals in workmanlike manner. She is no world-beater, but should pay her way. (tchd evens, 10-11 and 4-5 in places)
Accustomed ◆ was easy to back, having failed to build on the promise of her debut at Kempton when well beaten in a better event at Newbury last time. She was still a little green but stayed on in taking fashion and was never nearer than at the line. She is capable of picking up a race or two before too long. Official explanation: jockey said the filly had hung right handed (op 14-1)
City Dazzler(IRE) tracked the winner through up the rail and battled gamely. This was only her second start (she was unfancied on her debut) and this was a major improvement. She is progressive and will be interesting in handicaps later on. (op 10-1)
Hearts And Minds(IRE) didn't show a great deal on his AW debut ten days previously when slowly away, yet he bounced out and travelled well here on his turf debut, putting it up to the winner until he tired late on. This was a major improvement and he looks progressive.
Obliterfeight(IRE) did the best of the newcomers. A powerful-looking colt, he was relaxed in the preliminaries. Slowly away, the penny didn't drop until late but he stayed on in good style and would have learned plenty, coming past tiring rivals. He has a future on this evidence.

4546 VAL & DON MEREDITH DIAMOND WEDDING H'CAP (TURF) 7f
6:55 (6:57) (Class 5) (0-75,74) 3-Y-0+ **£3,067** (£905; £453) **Stalls** High

Form RPR
5441 1 **Starwatch**[7] 4322 4-9-4 67 SeanLevey(3) 5 74+
(John Bridger) *trckd ldng pair: lost pl over 2f out and sn rdn in last pair: rallied jst over 1f out: styd on strly to ld post* **7/2**[2]

4062 **2** *nse* **Hawk Moth (IRE)**[32] 3481 3-8-12 **65**.................................. ChrisCatlin 3 69
(John Spearing) *dwlt: in tch on outer: prog to ld over 2f out and swtchd to rail: drvn over 1f out: kpt on: hdd post* **6/1**

-660 **3** *1* **My Learned Friend (IRE)**[15] 4066 7-9-5 **72**........... SophieSilvester(7) 4 76
(Andrew Balding) *hld up on outer: prog to go 2nd jst over 2f out: sn chalng: upsides and nudged along 1f out: nt qckn* **16/1**

0052 **4** *½* **Cativo Cavallino**[12] 4160 8-9-3 **66**........................ NataliaGemelova(3) 6 69
(John E Long) *hld up in last pair: taken to outer and rdn over 2f out: styd on fr over 1f out: nvr rchd ldrs* **11/2**

-330 **5** *1 ½* **Eager To Bow (IRE)**[59] 2605 5-9-5 **65**.............................. LiamKeniry 2 64
(Patrick Chamings) *hld up in tch: effrt over 2f out: cl enough and rdn over 1f out: fdd* **5/1**[3]

2550 **6** *1* **Red Yarn**[19] 3918 4-9-11 **71**..(b) GeorgeBaker 7 67
(Gary Moore) *led against rail: hdd over 2f out: sn lost pl and btn* **3/1**[1]

4551 **7** *¾* **Italian Tom (IRE)**[21] 3869 4-10-0 **74**.................................. LukeMorris 1 68
(Ronald Harris) *pressed ldr to over 2f out: sn lost pl u.p and btn* **11/2**

1m 25.26s (1.96) **Going Correction** +0.125s/f (Good)
WFA 3 from 4yo+ 7lb 7 Ran SP% **114.8**
Speed ratings (Par 103): **93,92,91,91,89 88,87**
toteswingers: 1&2 £4.60, 1&3 £12.30, 2&3 £18.80. CSF £24.70 TOTE £3.90: £1.40, £3.70; EX 28.00.
Owner J J Bridger **Bred** Mrs J A Chapman **Trained** Liphook, Hants

FOCUS
A competitive handicap for the paucity of runners but the pace was very sluggish early on. The form looks muddling, with the runner-up the best guide.
Eager To Bow(IRE) Official explanation: vet said gelding had been struck into

4547 BURRIDGE GOLF & RACING TROPHIES H'CAP (TURF) 6f
7:25 (7:28) (Class 6) (0-65,62) 3-Y-0+ **£1,704** (£503; £251) **Stalls** High

Form RPR

6606 **1** **Simple Rhythm**[16] 4000 5-9-0 **50**...................................(p) AdamKirby 12 62
(John Ryan) *trckd ldrs: prog gng easily over 2f out: led over 1f out: hrd rdn whn pressed ins fnl f: hld on wl* **5/1**[2]

0330 **2** *½* **Commandingpresence (USA)**[5] 4387 5-9-4 **57**......... SeanLevey(3) 13 68
(John Bridger) *settled in rr: prog over 2f out: hrd rdn to chal ins fnl f: nt qckn nr fin* **9/2**[1]

0651 **3** *2 ¼* **Flaxen Lake**[9] 4230 4-9-0 **50**... LukeMorris 9 54+
(Milton Bradley) *towards rr and pushed along bef 1/2-way: prog on outer 2f out: styd on fnl f to take 3rd nr fin* **10/1**

6020 **4** *½* **Commander Wish**[6] 4371 8-9-6 **56**..................................(p) DaneO'Neill 1 58
(Lucinda Featherstone) *settled in rr: taken to outer and prog over 2f out: drvn to take 2nd briefly 1f out: one pce* **40/1**

/44- **5** *3 ½* **Gooseberry Bush**[332] 5668 4-9-11 **61**............................ SteveDrowne 8 52
(Peter Makin) *trckd ldr after 1f: shkn up to ld jst over 2f out to over 1f out: wknd* **10/1**

456 **6** *1 ¼* **Briannsta (IRE)**[115] 1180 9-9-0 **50**.........................(b) RichardThomas 16 37
(John E Long) *hld up against rail: dropped to rr over 2f out: nt clr run and pushed along after: sme prog fnl f* **33/1**

0506 **7** *½* **Riflessione**[9] 4224 5-9-12 **62**...................................(p) TomMcLaughlin 15 47
(Ronald Harris) *led against rail 1f: lost pl over 3f out: drvn over 2f out: steadily wknd* **6/1**[3]

0401 **8** *1 ¾* **Karate (IRE)**[19] 3924 3-9-5 **60**.. JamesDoyle 14 40
(Hans Adielsson) *lost pl after 1f and sn in midfield: taken to outer over 2f out and drvn: no real prog* **13/2**

2600 **9** *½* **Rio Royale (IRE)**[46] 3020 5-9-10 **60**.............................(p) JimCrowley 10 38
(Amanda Perrett) *pressed ldrs: rdn over 2f out: wknd wl over 1f out* **7/1**

066 **10** *½* **Zee Zee Dan (IRE)**[19] 3909 3-9-5 **60**......................... RobbieFitzpatrick 7 36
(Noel Quinlan) *pushed along in last quartet after 2f: nvr a factor* **22/1**

040- **11** *hd* **Sabot D'Or**[355] 4902 3-8-10 **58**.................................. HarryPoulton(7) 5 34
(Roger Ingram) *pressed ldrs tl wknd 2f out* **33/1**

2265 **12** *2 ¾* **Talamahana**[9] 4231 6-9-5 **55**...(v) ChrisCatlin 4 22
(Andrew Haynes) *s.v.s: a in last quartet and bhd* **20/1**

504 **13** *¾* **Kokojo (IRE)**[19] 3908 3-9-3 **58**..................................(p) FergusSweeney 6 23
([illegible]) *[illegible] in last quartet: brief effrt 3f out: no prog and wl btn 2f out* [illegible]

5256 **14** *nk* **Porthgwidden Beach (USA)**[19] 3914 3-8-12 **53**............. LiamKeniry 2 17
(Anthony Middleton) *spd fr low draw to cross over and ld: hdd jst over 2f out: wknd qckly and eased* **14/1**

00-0 **15** *3 ¾* **Bella Nemica**[67] 2384 3-8-4 **45**........................... FrankieMcDonald 11 —
(Edward Creighton) *v slowly and awkwardly away: a struggling in last pair* **100/1**

1m 11.66s (0.46) **Going Correction** +0.125s/f (Good)
WFA 3 from 4yo+ 5lb 15 Ran SP% **122.1**
Speed ratings (Par 101): **101,100,97,96,92 90,89,87,86,86 85,82,81,80,75**
toteswingers: 1&2 £5.70, 1&3 £8.60, 2&3 £10.50. CSF £25.79 CT £223.78 TOTE £6.20: £2.00, £2.10, £2.60; EX 35.70.
Owner J Ryan **Bred** P Quinlan **Trained** Newmarket, Suffolk

FOCUS
A run-of-the-mill handicap for horses raced 0-65 and the pace was sensible, with the two market leaders fighting out the finish. They drew a little way clear of the remainder, suggesting the form, rated around the first two, might be viable.
Gooseberry Bush Official explanation: jockey said that the filly ran too freely
Talamahana Official explanation: jockey said that the mare reared at the start

4548 LADBROKES.COM BRITISH STALLION STUDS EBF MAIDEN STKS 5f (P)
7:55 (7:55) (Class 5) 2-Y-0 **£3,169** (£943; £471; £235) **Stalls** High

Form RPR

3263 **1** **Sea Odyssey (IRE)**[14] 4079 2-9-3 71.............................. MichaelHills 1 79+
(B W Hills) *trckd ldrs: prog to ld over 1f out: shkn up and sn clr: comf* **4/5**[1]

0 **2** *3 ½* **Zain Point (IRE)**[19] 3917 2-9-3 0...(t) TedDurcan 5 66
(Gerard Butler) *s.i.s: in tch in 6th: rdn wl over 1f out: styd on w hd quite high to take 2nd last 100yds: no ch w wnr* **5/1**[3]

4224 **3** *1 ¼* **Gin Twist**[10] 4212 2-8-9 69... HarryBentley(3) 4 57
(Tom Dascombe) *chsd ldrs: rdn 2f out: plugged on to take 3rd wl ins fnl f* **7/2**[2]

2304 **4** *1 ¼* **Copper Falls**[26] 3673 2-8-12 61.................................... FergusSweeney 3 52
(Brendan Powell) *led to over 1f out: wknd fnl f* **20/1**

03 **5** *2 ½* **Princess Alessia**[35] 3388 2-8-12 0.. DaneO'Neill 6 43
(Terry Clement) *mostly chsd ldr to wl over 1f out: sn wknd* **7/1**

0 **6** *¾* **Compton Target (IRE)**[15] 4054 2-9-3 0........................... JamesDoyle 2 46
(Hans Adielsson) *prom to 1/2-way: rdn and wknd 2f out* **66/1**

00 **7** *3* **Compton Bird**[15] 4052 2-8-12 0... ChrisCatlin 7 30
(Hans Adielsson) *dwlt: racd wd and bdly outpcd: sn t.o: plugged on nr fin* **66/1**

60.28 secs (1.48) **Going Correction** +0.20s/f (Slow) 7 Ran SP% **114.7**
Speed ratings (Par 94): **96,90,88,86,82 81,76**
toteswingers: 1&2 £1.80, 1&3 £1.10, 2&3 £2.90. CSF £5.38 TOTE £1.80: £1.40, £1.70; EX 6.90.
Owner H R Mould **Bred** Mrs C Regalado-Gonzalez **Trained** Lambourn, Berks

FOCUS
A fairly good AW sprint maiden for the money and they went a strong gallop from the start. The winner scored with plenty in hand while the runner-up, sixth and seventh help set the level.

NOTEBOOK
Sea Odyssey(IRE) sweated up beforehand but settled well and travelled nicely, delivering his challenge four wide off the final bend. He quickly asserted his authority under the minimum of persuasion to register a decisive success. He is progressive, shows a willing attitude and now has plenty of options, particularly in nurseries. (op 11-10 tchd 6-4 in a place)
Zain Point(IRE) had shown plenty of zip on his 6f Windsor debut before fading. Fitted with a tongue-tie here, he'd clearly learned from that first experience and, although he carried his head high, he showed a good turn of foot off the final bend to finish with a flourish. He looks progressive and is worth trying again over this trip. (op 7-1)
Gin Twist was the most experienced in the line-up, having had six previous outings. She'd found the ground too soft when flopping in a 5f nursery at Sandown last time and was more at home on the Polytrack. She ran a fine race, travelling sweetly, but she was not vigorously ridden once the winner had flown. There's more to come from this filly and she won't be long in getting off the mark. (op 5-2)
Copper Falls was weak in the market and reluctant to go out on to the track. She made most of the running but while she stuck gamely to the task, she was outclassed. This was a much better effort than on her last run at Brighton, the drop back in trip seemed to help her here. (op 16-1)
Princess Alessia tracked the leader but was found wanting for pace. This was only her third run and she will be interesting in nurseries. (op 11-2 tchd 15-2)
Compton Bird Official explanation: jockey said, regarding the running and riding that stated that he had received no specific instructions from the trainer. He said that the filly jumped out awkwardly, was flat out in the early stages and went wide to avoid the bad kickback. He added that he did not ask for an effort until the home straight because he did not want to get the filly disorganised. He then rode the filly hands and heels to the line. Trainer said that the filly had been disappointing in her previous runs and he therefore did not wish to tie the jockey down with specific orders. He added that in his opinion that she ran better in this race despite being slowly away

4549 LADBROKES MOBILE H'CAP 1m 2f (P)
8:25 (8:26) (Class 6) (0-55,55) 3-Y-0+ **£1,567** (£462; £231) **Stalls** Low

Form RPR

1004 **1** **Fastinthestraight (IRE)**[42] 3176 4-9-9 **55**..................(v1) DaneO'Neill 11 68+
(Jim Boyle) *slowest away: grad worked way into midfield: shkn up and prog to take 4th over 2f out: drvn and clsd to ld jst over 1f out: sn clr* **9/4**[1]

0400 **2** *2 ¼* **Laconicos (IRE)**[15] 4060 9-9-4 **55**..................................(t) LauraPike(5) 9 62
(William Stone) *w.w in midfield: rdn and effrt over 2f out: styd on fr over 1f out to take 2nd last 50yds: no ch w wnr* **8/1**[3]

4056 **3** *1* **Olimamu (IRE)**[12] 4164 4-9-3 **52**..............................(t) SimonPearce(3) 10 57
(Lydia Pearce) *prom in chsng gp: smooth prog to take 2nd over 2f out: rdn to ld wl over 1f out: hdd and outpcd jst over 1f out: lost 2nd last 50yds* **12/1**

00-0 **4** *3 ½* **Lunar Limelight**[52] 2820 6-9-7 **53**................................ SteveDrowne 7 51
(Peter Makin) *w.w in midfield: rdn and effrt over 2f out: kpt on one pce u.p after* **20/1**

0200 **5** *2* **Herecomethegirls**[7] 4317 5-8-12 **51**.................(b) HarryPoulton(7) 12 45+
(Olivia Maylam) *stdd s: t.k.h: hld up last: stl in last pair and pushed along over 2f out: prog over 1f out: styd on: no ch* **25/1**

3P06 **6** *1* **Moonlight Fantasy (IRE)**[13] 4123 8-8-12 **47**.................... JohnFahy(3) 3 39
(Lucinda Featherstone) *led at gd pce: hdd & wknd wl over 1f out* **10/1**

1226 **7** *½* **Mr Maximas**[95] 1582 4-9-9 **55**..............................(tp) RichardKingscote 13 46
(Bryn Palling) *chsd ldr and clr of rest: lost 2nd over 2f out: wknd over 1f out* **7/2**[2]

5060 **8** *½* **Queenie's Star (IRE)**[7] 4317 4-9-0 **49**......................... KierenFox(3) 14 39
(Michael Attwater) *hld up in last pair: effrt on outer over 3f out: rchd midfield u.p over 2f out: no hdwy over 1f out: fdd* **18/1**

203- **9** *1 ¼* **Qaraqum (USA)**[337] 5469 4-9-9 **55**.............................. TadhgO'Shea 1 43
(Denis Coakley) *dwlt: hld up wl in rr: pushed along 3f out: no real prog and no ch over 1f out* **12/1**

1004 **10** *6* **Kenswick**[8] 4270 4-9-4 **50**...(v) ChrisCatlin 8 26
([illegible]) *[illegible] towards rr: [illegible] over 2f out: wknd* **10/1**

0602 **11** *2 ¾* **Bell's Ocean (USA)**[14] 4089 4-9-8 **54**.................................. AdamKirby 4 24
(John Ryan) *wl plcd bhd clr ldrs tl wknd wl over 2f out* **8/1**[3]

500- **12** *2* **Under Fire (IRE)**[352] 4992 8-9-0 **53**......................... GeorgeDowning(7) 6 19
(Tony Carroll) *rdn in midfield bef 1/2-way: struggling and no prog 3f out* **25/1**

00-0 **13** *1* **Annacaboe (IRE)**[26] 3690 4-9-3 **49**..................................... GeorgeBaker 5 13
(Martin Bosley) *chsd clr ldng pair to 3f out: wknd qckly* **33/1**

2m 9.08s (2.48) **Going Correction** +0.20s/f (Slow) 13 Ran SP% **129.4**
Speed ratings (Par 101): **98,96,95,92,91 90,89,89,88,83 81,79,79**
toteswingers: 1&2 £7.30, 1&3 £6.80, 2&3 £22.50. CSF £21.91 CT £195.92 TOTE £2.70: £1.50, £3.20, £5.10; EX 32.20.
Owner John Hopkins (t/a South Hatch Racing) **Bred** Patrick J Ryan **Trained** Epsom, Surrey

FOCUS
A very modest AW handicap with few in-form horses and plenty of exposed types. The pace was solid for the class and the form looks sound.
T/Plt: £98.30 to a £1 stake. Pool of £70,282.39 - 6,521.44 winning tickets. T/Qpdt: £21.40 to a £1 stake. Pool of £6,710.55 - 231.60 winning tickets. JN

4506 NEWMARKET (R-H)
Saturday, July 30
OFFICIAL GOING: Good to firm (8.1)
Wind: Light across Weather: Cloudy

4550 ADNAMS BROADSIDE H'CAP 7f
2:20 (2:22) (Class 3) (0-90,90) 3-Y-0 **£9,703** (£2,887; £1,443; £721) **Stalls** Low

Form RPR

-152 **1** **Fityaan**[22] 3830 3-8-10 **79**.. TadhgO'Shea 1 94+
(B W Hills) *racd stands' side hld up: hdwy over 2f out: rdn over 1f out: edgd lft and r.o to ld nr fin: 1st of 3 in gp* **12/1**

5-1 **2** *nk* **Lay Time**[14] 4102 3-8-11 **80**.. DavidProbert 11 94+
(Andrew Balding) *racd centre: chsd ldrs: led over 1f out: rdn and edgd lft ins fnl f: hdd nr fin: 1st of 13 in gp* **9/4**[1]

1601 **3** *2 1/2* **Flynn's Boy**[7] 4342 3-8-8 **77** NeilCallan 12 84
(Rae Guest) *racd centre: a.p: rdn and ev ch over 1f out: styd on same pce ins fnl f: 2nd of 13 in gp* **7/1**[2]
1052 **4** *1* **Sluggsy Morant**[12] 4156 3-8-9 **78** FergusSweeney 5 82
(Henry Candy) *s.i.s: racd centre: hld up: swtchd lft and hdwy over 1f out: styd on: nt rch ldrs: 3rd of 13 in gp* **20/1**
2361 **5** *nk* **Sacrosanctus**[15] 4062 3-8-13 **82** IanMongan 6 85
(David Nicholls) *racd centre: chsd ldr tl led overall over 4f out: rdn and hdd over 1f out: styd on same pce ins fnl f: 4th of 13 in gp* **12/1**
0200 **6** *2 3/4* **Mubtadi**[21] 3864 3-9-0 **83** MartinLane 17 79
(David Simcock) *racd centre: hld up: swtchd lft and hdwy over 2f out: rdn over 1f out: wknd ins fnl f: 5th of 13 in gp* **10/1**
4-21 **7** *1 1/4* **Easy Over (IRE)**[29] 3575 3-8-9 **78** StevieDonohoe 3 71
(Ed McMahon) *s.i.s: racd stands' side tl swtchd centre over 4f out: bhd: rdn 1/2-way: r.o ins fnl f: nrst fin: 6th of 13 in gp* **14/1**
12-5 **8** *shd* **Try The Chance**[28] 3649 3-9-1 **87** MartinHarley(3) 15 79
(Mick Channon) *racd centre: mid-div: hdwy over 2 out: rdn over 1f out: one pce fnl f: 7th of 13 in gp* **16/1**
6110 **9** *1 1/4* **Bajan Bear**[10] 4214 3-8-6 **75** LukeMorris 10 64
(Michael Blanshard) *racd centre: dwlt: hld up: hdwy over 2f out: sn rdn: wknd fnl f: 8th of 13 in gp* **20/1**
1401 **10** *2 1/4* **Exchange**[7] 4338 3-8-6 **75** HayleyTurner 7 58
(Andrew Haynes) *racd centre: hld up: rdn over 2f out: wknd over 1f out: 9th of 13 in gp* **28/1**
2300 **11** *nk* **Azrael**[23] 3774 3-9-4 **90** JohnFahy(3) 8 72
(Alan McCabe) *racd centre: chsd ldrs tl rdn and wknd over 1f out: 10th of 13 in gp* **40/1**
1306 **12** *nk* **Amwell Pinot**[7] 4335 3-9-2 **85** (b) CathyGannon 14 66
(Alan Bailey) *racd centre: led: hdd over 4f out: rdn and wknd over 1f out: 11th of 13 in gp* **20/1**
2442 **13** *hd* **Majestic Dream (IRE)**[22] 3798 3-9-2 **85** ShaneKelly 16 66
(Walter Swinburn) *racd centre: mid-div: hdwy 1/2-way: rdn and wknd over 1f out: 12th of 13 in gp* **8/1**[3]
-010 **14** *2 1/2* **Spes Nostra**[12] 4141 3-8-6 **75** LeeNewman 9 49
(David Barron) *racd centre: prom: rdn 1/2-way: wknd over 1f out: last of 13 in gp* **40/1**
-143 **15** *nk* **Choral**[37] 3310 3-8-6 **75** FrankieMcDonald 4 48
(Richard Hannon) *racd stands' side: chsd ldr that side but off the pce of the centre gp: hdwy over 2f out: wknd over 1f out: 2nd of 3 in gp* **33/1**
3103 **16** *9* **Watneya**[14] 4093 3-8-12 **81** WilliamBuick 2 30
(William Haggas) *led stands' side but off the pce of the centre gp: hdwy over 2f out: wknd over 1f out: last of 3 in gp* **9/1**

1m 24.01s (-1.69) **Going Correction** -0.025s/f (Good) **16** Ran SP% **127.0**
Speed ratings (Par 104): **108,107,104,103,103 100,98,98,97,94 94,93,93,90,90 80**
toteswingers: 1&2 £9.60, 1&3 £26.00, 2&3 £9.40. CSF £37.27 CT £226.22 TOTE £16.90: £3.30, £1.60, £2.40, £3.90; EX 68.70 Trifecta £710.30 Pool: £1,055.95 - 1.10 winning units..
Owner Hamdan Al Maktoum **Bred** Usk Valley Stud **Trained** Lambourn, Berks

FOCUS
Stands' side track used with stalls on stands' side except 1m2f and 1m4f, centre. There was a significant dew overnight but clerk of the course Michael Prosser felt the ground was a little bit quicker than it had been for the previous evening's card. The stalls position was switched to the stands' side. On paper this looked a very competitive event with several last-time-out winners, including a couple who were taking their handicap bow. The form looks sound rated around the fourth and fifth.

NOTEBOOK
Fityaan ◆ came to nail a second career success in a time that was 1.11s outside standard. A Warwick maiden winner earlier in the season, he may not have been suited by the track at Epsom last month where he was a well-beaten fifth. They probably went too quick up front here which played into Fityaan's hands as he was delivered with a well-timed hold-up ride by Tadhg O'Shea. While this was his seventh race, he gave the impression that he is very much still improving and looks capable of progressing again. (op 14-1 tchd 16-1 in places)
Lay Time ◆, who is entered in the Group 1 Sun Chariot Stakes, was given an introductory mark of 80 for her C&D victory on easy ground a fortnight earlier. Perhaps the surface here was a little quicker than she'd have liked but this was another encouraging performance by a lightly raced filly, who looks sure to go on and gain swift compensation for this reverse. (op 11-4 tchd 3-1 in places)
Flynn's Boy is a very progressive gelding, who has won three times in 2011 and was up 2lb in the weights for this after a last-time-out success at Salisbury a week ago. If it wasn't for the fact that he was bumping into two very progressive types, he would have made the winner's enclosure again. Clearly in good form, he should continue to pay his way. (op 12-1)
Sluggsy Morant was trying 7f for the first time after appearing a little outpaced early on in his last start at Windsor where he finished second. He was slowly away here but the strong early gallop allowed him to prove that he stays this distance, keeping on well enough. This performance opens up options for him and he should be capable of making his mark at this trip. (op 14-1)
Sacrosanctus was raised 6lb for a C&D success a fortnight ago earlier. He was unable to overcome that added burden here, but still ran a fair race, just finding himself unable to sustain his front-running effort in the closing furlong. (op 10-1)
Mubtadi has been running in some very hot handicaps this season and was cut some slack by the handicapper after being well beaten in a hot 1m handicap at the July festival. Back in trip here, he probably wasn't favourably drawn widest of all. He may just need a slice or two of good fortune to help him get his head back in front because he travelled well here without being able to go on when the front two drew away. (op 14-1)
Easy Over(IRE) ◆ was a comfortable 7f maiden winner three weeks earlier and was starting off in handicaps off a mark of 78. He was slowly away towards the near side and was plum last as the race began to develop in earnest. However, he managed to stay on in dogged fashion and this lightly raced type is one to keep on the right side, perhaps in slightly less competitive company. (op 17-2)
Watneya Official explanation: jockey said that the filly was unsuited by the good to firm ground.

4551 ADNAMS SPINDRIFT FILLIES' NURSERY 6f
2:50 (2:51) (Class 2) 2-Y-O **£25,876** (£7,700; £3,848; £1,924) **Stalls** Low

Form RPR
011 **1** **Roger Sez (IRE)**[14] 4079 2-9-6 **81** NeilCallan 11 84
(Tim Easterby) *hld up: bhd and drvn along over 3f out: hdwy over 2f out: rdn to ld ins fnl f: hmpd sn after: r.o* **5/1**[3]
5261 **2** *1/2* **Nearly A Gift (IRE)**[41] 3200 2-9-7 **82** TadhgO'Shea 10 84
(Tim Easterby) *chsd ldrs: led over 2f out: rdn and hung rt over 1f out: hung lft and hdd ins fnl f: r.o* **12/1**
6133 **3** *1/2* **My Lucky Liz (IRE)**[21] 3842 2-8-13 **74** MartinLane 9 74
(David Simcock) *chsd ldrs: rdn over 1f out: r.o* **11/2**
431 **4** *shd* **Imelda Mayhem**[26] 3680 2-8-13 **74** LukeMorris 4 74
(J S Moore) *prom: outpcd over 2f out: r.o ins fnl f* **10/1**
410 **5** *1 1/4* **Mention (IRE)**[14] 4094 2-9-5 **80** ShaneKelly 5 76
(Brian Meehan) *chsd ldrs: rdn over 1f out: styd on* **4/1**[2]
511 **6** *nk* **Piranha (IRE)**[24] 3745 2-9-7 **82** WilliamBuick 8 77
(Ed Dunlop) *trckd ldrs: rdn over 1f out: hung lft and styd on same pce ins fnl f* **7/2**[1]
002 **7** *hd* **Correct**[17] 3981 2-8-9 **70** HayleyTurner 3 64
(Michael Bell) *dwlt: sn chsng ldrs: led over 3f out: hdd over 2f out: styd on same pce fnl f* **11/1**
103 **8** *1 3/4* **Judas Jo (FR)**[17] 3973 2-8-12 **73** DavidProbert 1 62
(Gay Kelleway) *hld up: rdn over 1f out: nt trble ldrs* **14/1**
2303 **9** *2 1/4* **Redair (IRE)**[22] 3808 2-9-3 **78** CathyGannon 6 66
(David Evans) *plld hrd and prom: rdn over 2f out: wknd ins fnl f* **22/1**
313 **10** *nk* **Ballyea (IRE)**[22] 3800 2-9-4 **79** PatDobbs 7 61
(Richard Hannon) *plld hrd: led tl over 3f out: rdn and hung lft over 1f out: sn wknd* **12/1**
2520 **11** *6* **Princess Banu**[14] 4094 2-8-12 **76** MartinHarley(3) 2 40
(Mick Channon) *prom: rdn over 2f out: wknd fnl f* **33/1**

1m 13.26s (0.76) **Going Correction** -0.025s/f (Good) **11** Ran SP% **121.0**
Speed ratings (Par 97): **93,92,91,91,89 89,89,86,83,83 75**
toteswingers: 1&2 £6.30, 1&3 £6.80, 2&3 £16.00. CSF £65.74 CT £283.72 TOTE £5.50: £2.00, £4.40, £1.90; EX 39.10 Trifecta £228.60 Pool: £840.46 - 2.72 winning units..
Owner R Sidebottom **Bred** B Kennedy **Trained** Great Habton, N Yorks

FOCUS
This looked a tight-knit nursery with a couple carrying fancy entries. In reality, it was only run at an unsatisfactory modest gallop - reflected in the the time, which was over 3seconds outside of standard - and 1l covered the first four home. The form looks straightforward rated around the principals.

NOTEBOOK
Roger Sez(IRE) is proving a real moneyspinner for connections and completed a hat-trick here. Bought for £13,000, she is proven on easy and quick ground and defied a 6lb rise in the weights, leaving the impression that she won a shade cosier than the bare margin suggests. She would probably have preferred a stronger gallop and wasn't helped either as the runner-up edged into her ground, giving her a bump inside the final furlong. (tchd 11-2 in places)
Nearly A Gift(IRE) was an easy winner of Pontefract maiden last time and went into nursery company off an introductory mark of 82. According to the betting, she was the lesser fancied of the stable's two runners, but she ran a good race until possibly finding the track not to her liking. She drifted right in the dip and then hung left upon meeting the rising ground. Certainly, she maintained her effort until the line, so it was probably inexperience that contributed to her wayward path in the closing stages. (op 10-1 tchd 14-1)
My Lucky Liz(IRE) has been kept busy and has responded by running consistently well over sprint trips. This was her sixth race of the season and she has not finished out of the frame in the last four. She was only beaten a length, so it's unlikely that the handicapper will ease up on her, but her game attitude suggests she can add to a sole maiden victory before the season is out. (op 13-2)
Imelda Mayhem ◆ was the eyecatcher. A Ripon maiden winner last time out, she was not suited by the lack of a true tempo in the early part of the race and was initially outpaced when push came to shove. A Lowther Stakes entry may be aiming too high, but she really picked up in the closing stages and flashed home to suggest she'll relish a further furlong. (op 8-1)
Mention(IRE) ran a respectable enough race when mid-division in the Super Sprint at Newbury a fortnight earlier. Back up to a more suitable 6f - she won her maiden over the trip at Newbury - she didn't threaten to get a blow in, but is another who may not have been suited by the way the race was run. (op 6-1)
Piranha(IRE) was also looking to complete a three-timer but was unable to demonstrate a sufficient turn of foot when it turned into a real dash late on. She, too, is probably worth giving another chance. (op 4-1)
Ballyea(IRE) Official explanation: jockey said that the filly hung left

4552 ADNAMS BITTER EBF MAIDEN FILLIES' STKS 7f
3:25 (3:26) (Class 4) 2-Y-O **£4,528** (£1,347; £673; £336) **Stalls** Low

Form RPR
1 **Fallen For You** 2-9-0 0 WilliamBuick 3 82+
(John Gosden) *s.i.s: hld up: hdwy over 1f out: shkn up to ld and edgd rt ins fnl f: r.o: readily* **5/2**[1]
2 *2* **Rythmic** 2-8-7 0 AntiocoMurgia(7) 10 74+
(Mahmood Al Zarooni) *mid-div: hdwy over 2f out: led 1f out: sn hdd: styd on same pce* **16/1**
3 *nk* **Buzkashi (IRE)** 2-9-0 0 NeilCallan 4 73+
(Roger Varian) *hld up in tch: shkn up over 1f out: sn ev ch: styd on* **11/2**[3]
0 **4** *hd* **Farleaze**[22] 3813 2-9-0 0 ShaneKelly 5 73
(Brian Meehan) *chsd ldrs: led over 1f out: sn rdn and hdd: styd on* **66/1**
5 *1 1/2* **Specific (IRE)** 2-9-0 0 AhmedAjtebi 2 69+
(Mahmood Al Zarooni) *dwlt: hld up: hdwy over 2f out: rdn: hung lft and outpcd over 1f out: r.o ins fnl f* **10/1**
6 *shd* **Defy The Odds** 2-9-0 0 IanMongan 1 69+
(Sir Henry Cecil) *hld up in tch: shkn up over 1f out: styd on same pce ins fnl f* **10/3**[2]
7 *nk* **Aniseed (IRE)** 2-9-0 0 MichaelHills 7 68
(William Haggas) *w ldr tl led over 4f out: hdd over 1f out: no ex ins fnl f* **22/1**
8 *1* **Really Lovely (IRE)** 2-8-11 0 JohnFahy(3) 13 65
(Jeremy Noseda) *trckd ldrs: racd keenly: stdd and lost pl 5f out: n.d after* **15/2**
00 **9** *hd* **Shannon Spree**[15] 4052 2-9-0 0 PatDobbs 12 65
(Richard Hannon) *prom: rdn over 2f out: edgd lft over 1f out: no ex ins fnl f* **28/1**
60 **10** *1/2* **Madame St Clair (IRE)**[15] 4061 2-8-11 0 LouisBeuzelin(3) 11 63
(Brian Meehan) *led: hdd over 4f out: rdn and ev ch over 1f out: no ex ins fnl f* **25/1**
11 *1/2* **Eastern Destiny** 2-9-0 0 BarryMcHugh 6 62+
(Richard Fahey) *prom: racd keenly: rdn over 1f out: no ex fnl f* **20/1**
0 **12** *1/2* **Joyful Spirit (IRE)**[22] 3812 2-9-0 0 MartinLane 14 61
(John Dunlop) *hld up: pushed along 1/2-way: styng on whn nt clr run ins fnl f: nvr trbld ldrs* **66/1**
13 *1/2* **Malekat Jamal (IRE)** 2-9-0 0 JackMitchell 15 59
(David Simcock) *s.i.s: a in rr* **66/1**
6 **14** *12* **Alupka (IRE)**[33] 3463 2-9-0 0 HayleyTurner 8 28
(Richard Hannon) *hld up: a in rr: wknd over 2f out* **25/1**

1m 26.69s (0.99) **Going Correction** -0.025s/f (Good) **14** Ran SP% **118.5**
Speed ratings (Par 93): **93,90,90,90,88 88,87,86,86,86 85,84,84,70**
toteswingers: 1&2 £13.00, 1&3 £4.10, 2&3 £20.80. CSF £39.87 TOTE £3.20: £1.40, £4.60, £2.20; EX 54.50.
Owner Normandie Stud Ltd **Bred** Normandie Stud Ltd **Trained** Newmarket, Suffolk

FOCUS
Always likely to be an informative maiden, it was won by Theyskens' Theory last year. It looked all about the newcomers, with the five that that had racecourse experience not having shown a great deal. Indeed, debutantes filled the first three places. The race should produce winners but cannot be rated much higher for now, with the field quite well bunched at the finish.

NOTEBOOK

Fallen For You ◆ created a very favourable impression to score for the yard that won it with Sense Of Joy four seasons ago. The time was considerably slower than the opening 3-y-o handicap and was well outside standard, but the manner in which Fallen For You won suggested bigger stages await this filly, who hails from a classy family. She is a half-sister to Fallen Idol who was a Listed winner at 1m, while her mother also won in that company over the same distance. She looks sure to improve a ton on what was a useful debut effort, having been slowly into stride. With the pace merely adequate, it looked like she had plenty to do with those on the front end appearing to be favoured. However, she was switched left and took off with a low skimming action that indicated her appreciation for the quick surface. Ultimately, she won as she pleased and could head next to the May Hill Stakes at Doncaster with the Fillies' Mile also on the agenda. (op 15-8 tchd 11-4)

Rythmic ◆ offered plenty of encouragement with her effort. The first foal of an unraced mare who hails from a very good family, she is likely to take the beating in whichever maiden she tackles next. (op 25-1)

Buzkashi(IRE) ◆, who cost 175,000gns as a yearling, was another to shape with lots of promise. She is out of a dam who herself won over this trip at two, and subsequently went on to produce plenty of winners. She won't take long before she enhances the family name and her pedigree suggests 1m-plus will eventually see in an even more favourable light. (op 6-1 tchd 7-1)

Farleaze can be judged to have improved significantly on her debut in which she only beat one home. The penny has clearly dropped with her now, and the way in which she was doing some strong work late on hints that going further will hold no fears for her.

Specific(IRE) ◆ didn't enjoy the smoothest of passages and was given a bump by Defy The Odds. That and overall inexperience probably contributed to her hanging left through the closing stages, but there was no mistaking the way she ran on again as the line loomed. Her dam is an influence for stamina and she is another who is likely to appreciate going at least 1m. It will take a smart one to beat her next time. (op 12-1 tchd 8-1)

Defy The Odds possesses a significantly above-average pedigree, being related to several winners, and her breeding strongly suggests she will improve over longer distances and with time, particularly with another winter behind her. (op 9-2)

Aniseed(IRE) cost 60,000gns and showed up well for much of this. (op 16-1)

Really Lovely(IRE) made a satisfactory debut. The first foal of two-time Group 1 winner Simply Perfect, also trained by Jeremy Noseda, she showed that she was getting the hang of things late on and 1m-plus will be within her range as her career develops. (op 8-1 tchd 7-1)

4553 ADNAMS TALLY HO H'CAP 1m 2f

4:05 (4:06) (Class 3) (0-90,89) 3-Y-0+ **£9,703** (£2,887; £1,443; £721) **Stalls** Centre

Form				RPR
-220	**1**		**Haylaman (IRE)**[35] 3376 3-9-0 **85** ... WilliamBuick 3 (Ed Dunlop) *chsd ldrs: rdn to ld ins fnl f: r.o* **11/2**[2]	93
0015	**2**	*½*	**Ellemujie**[21] 3844 6-9-9 **84** ... (p) LukeMorris 9 (Dean Ivory) *a.p: rdn and ev ch ins fnl f: r.o* **14/1**	91
3001	**3**	*½*	**Bahamian Music (IRE)**[42] 3164 4-9-6 **81** ... BarryMcHugh 8 (Richard Fahey) *a.p: rdn over 1f out: r.o* **16/1**	87
0441	**4**	*¾*	**El Muqbil (IRE)**[17] 3980 3-8-12 **83** ... (t) TadhgO'Shea 10 (Brian Meehan) *chsd ldrs: led over 2f out: sn rdn and hung rt: hdd and unable qck ins fnl f* **11/2**[2]	88
1311	**5**	*shd*	**Art Scholar (IRE)**[16] 4004 4-9-3 **78** ... NeilChalmers 4 (Michael Appleby) *hld up: hdwy over 1f out: sn rdn: styd on* **12/1**	82
2125	**6**	*hd*	**Trojan Nights (USA)**[14] 4103 3-9-4 **89** ... ShaneKelly 12 (William Haggas) *hld up: hdwy 4f out: rdn over 1f out: styd on* **7/2**[1]	93
005	**7**	*½*	**Nice Style (IRE)**[35] 3411 6-9-13 **88** ... (t) NeilCallan 2 (Jeremy Gask) *hld up: nt clr run over 1f out: r.o: nvr able to chal* **8/1**	91
2-06	**8**	*18*	**Emerald Wilderness (IRE)**[17] 3982 7-9-10 **88** ... (p) JohnFahy(3) 1 (Robert Cowell) *sn led: rdn and hdd over 2f out: wknd over 1f out* **16/1**	55
1231	**9**	*¾*	**King Kurt (IRE)**[25] 3701 3-8-12 **83** ... StevieDonohoe 11 (Kevin Ryan) *hld up: hdwy 1/2-way: rdn over 3f out: wknd over 1f out* **6/1**[3]	48
10	**10**	*6*	**Lord Theo**[36] 3366 7-8-10 **71** ... MichaelHills 7 (Nick Littmoden) *chsd ldrs: rdn over 2f out: wknd over 1f out* **40/1**	24

2m 4.88s (-0.62) **Going Correction** -0.025s/f (Good)
WFA 3 from 4yo+ 10lb **10** Ran SP% **107.0**
Speed ratings (Par 107): **101,100,100,99,99 99,98,84,83,79**
toteswingers: 1&2 £12.60, 1&3 £15.40, 2&3 £49.50. CSF £65.72 CT £843.86 TOTE £6.40: £2.10, £3.90, £5.80; EX 73.90.
Owner Ahmad Al Shaikh **Bred** M Morrin **Trained** Newmarket, Suffolk

FOCUS

An interesting combination of some battle hardened campaigners up against some potential improvers. There was a nice even gallop and the time was 2.98s beyond standard. Overall, the form (rated around the placed horses) has a solid look without being anything out of the ordinary, as only two lengths covered the first six home.

NOTEBOOK

Haylaman(IRE) looked an interesting prospect when second over this trip in May but didn't appear to see out 1m4f at Chester where maybe the soft ground was also against him last time. It was no surprise that connections brought him back in distance to 1m2f here and he regained his progressive profile with a professional display. He probably didn't win with a ton in hand and it's likely that his immediate future depends on how the handicapper assesses this. (op 7-1)

Ellemujie was a C&D winner off a 5lb lower mark just over a month ago and again ran with a lot of credit. Now six, he is potentially vulnerable to a lightly raced improver such as Haylaman but is a reliable type, who will more often than not give a good account of himself. (op 12-1)

Bahamian Music(IRE) was successful in the soft at Ayr over the distance in June. Racing off a 3lb higher mark here, she proved her versatility as to ground by serving up a sustained challenge late on to make the frame. (tchd 20-1)

El Muqbil(IRE) was going a furlong further than he'd ever done in the past and left the impression that the stiff finish probably found him out. The positives were that he again travelled well and, at a less taxing track, may be capable of scoring over this distance. He is unlikely to go up in the weights for this and remains of interest. (op 13-2)

Art Scholar(IRE) is a four-time winner already this year and has gone up no less than 29lb since June. Judging by his strong finish here, it is debatable whether the handicapper has fully got him in his grasp yet. (op 9-1)

Trojan Nights(USA) was perhaps a touch disappointing. On a surface that was expected to suit him, he didn't find as much as might have been anticipated after moving smoothly into contention approaching the closing stages. Rated 89, it may be that the handicapper has his number. (tchd 10-3)

Nice Style(IRE) Official explanation: vet said gelding had a small cut on its' left foreleg

King Kurt(IRE) Official explanation: jockey said that the gelding was never travelling

4554 ADNAMS COPPER HOUSE EBF HERNANDO CONDITIONS STKS 1m

4:40 (4:40) (Class 2) 4-Y-0+

£12,450 (£3,728; £1,864; £932; £466; £234) **Stalls** Low

Form				RPR
-004	**1**		**Balducci**[35] 3409 4-8-9 **100** ... DavidProbert 3 (Andrew Balding) *chsd ldr: rdn over 1f out: led ins fnl f: r.o* **2/1**[2]	105
0032	**2**	*1*	**Invisible Man**[16] 4003 5-8-9 **107** ... (b) WilliamBuick 5 (Saeed Bin Suroor) *chsd ldrs: rdn and hung rt over 1f out: r.o to go 2nd wl ins fnl f: nt rch wnr* **11/10**[1]	103
4005	**3**	*1 ¼*	**Colonial (IRE)**[16] 4003 4-9-0 **105** ... NeilCallan 4 (Saeed Bin Suroor) *led: rdn over 1f out: hung rt and hdd ins fnl f: styd on same pce* **20/1**	105
0040	**4**	*2*	**King Of Dixie (USA)**[21] 3862 7-8-9 **97** ... ShaneKelly 6 (William Knight) *hld up: rdn over 1f out: styd on: nvr able to chal* **16/1**	95
5-00	**5**	*3 ½*	**Al Khaleej (IRE)**[21] 3862 7-8-9 **98** ... MartinLane 2 (David Simcock) *s.s: hld up: plld hrd: rdn over 1f out: n.d* **11/2**[3]	87
120/	**6**	*24*	**Dark Islander (IRE)**[460] 8-8-9 **95** ... LukeMorris 1 (J S Moore) *plld hrd and prom: rdn over 2f out: hung rt and wknd over 1f out* **25/1**	32

1m 38.96s (-1.04) **Going Correction** -0.025s/f (Good) **6** Ran SP% **110.8**
Speed ratings (Par 109): **104,103,101,99,96 72**
toteswingers: 1&2 £1.30, 1&3 £2.90, 2&3 £2.40. CSF £4.42 TOTE £3.10: £2.10, £1.10; EX 5.30.
Owner McMahon/Gorell/Pausewang/Russell **Bred** G Russell **Trained** Kingsclere, Hants

FOCUS

A good conditions race but the form is muddling, with the winner the best guide.

NOTEBOOK

Balducci was 7lb wrong at the weights with Invisible Man, but he made a mockery of the figures, taking advantage of being well placed to launch his challenge through the closing 2f. Jockey David Probert had the winner ideally placed throughout, travelling in the slipstream of the pace-setting Colonial early on. His mount was always entitled to be very competitive in this, coming into it off a decent piece of form at Windsor last month when he was beaten less than 2l into fourth in a Listed contest. He is very useful, verging on smart, and is more than entitled to return to Listed company. (op 5-2)

Invisible Man was the highest-rated on official figures and favoured at the weights. Thus, it looked the ideal opportunity for him to get his head back in front for the first time since his 2010 Royal Hunt Cup victory. However, he was given plenty to do and, while he finished with a flourish, the winner had already got the race in safe-keeping. His form in successive Hunt Cups indicates that he is well suited by a big field and a strong gallop - neither of which he had here. (op 5-4 tchd 11-8 in places)

Colonial(IRE) set a decent enough pace. He was well beaten at Doncaster in a similar race at Doncaster two weeks earlier, but was entitled to need that after almost six months off. He showed up better here, although was ultimately well held. (op 16-1 tchd 22-1)

King Of Dixie(USA) has rather lost his way this season. This was better but it is hard to make a strong case for him returning to winning ways soon. (op 14-1)

Al Khaleej(IRE) is possibly not an easy horse to place. He was a never-nearer ninth in the Bunbury Cup three weeks earlier and once again didn't look like entering the picture, stepped back up to 1m. (op 5-1 tchd 6-1)

Dark Islander(IRE) was returning to action after well over a year off. Back in Britain after being trained in America for a couple of years, he was perhaps too fresh, which in the circumstances wasn't entirely surprising. (op 16-1)

4555 ADNAMS MAY DAY H'CAP 1m 4f

5:15 (5:15) (Class 4) (0-85,84) 4-Y-0+ **£5,175** (£1,540; £769; £384) **Stalls** Centre

Form				RPR
0523	**1**		**Full Speed (GER)**[6] 4360 6-8-13 **76** ... WilliamBuick 8 (Alan Swinbank) *a.p: rdn to ld ins fnl f: edgd rt: styd on* **9/4**[1]	86
5/36	**2**	*½*	**Nobunaga**[14] 4083 6-8-9 **72** ... DavidProbert 2 (Venetia Williams) *trckd ldrs: racd keenly: led over 3f out: hdd over 2f out: led again over 1f out: rdn and hdd ins fnl f: styd on* **5/1**[3]	81
0556	**3**	*2 ¾*	**Mister Angry (IRE)**[23] 3762 4-9-0 **77** ... MichaelHills 1 (Mark Johnston) *hld up: rdn over 2f out: r.o ins fnl f: wnt 3rd post: nt rch ldrs* **12/1**	82
3-12	**4**	*shd*	**Peintre D'Argent (IRE)**[71] 2262 5-8-13 **79** ... JohnFahy(3) 4 (William Knight) *hld up: hdwy 2f out: rdn over 1f out: no ex ins fnl f* **5/1**[3]	83
2252	**5**	*3*	**Incendo**[29] 3580 5-9-7 **84** ... (t) HayleyTurner 9 (James Fanshawe) *hld up: hdwy over 1f out: sn rdn: no ex fnl f* **4/1**[2]	84
0234	**6**	*4 ½*	**Crocus Rose**[19] 3911 5-9-5 **82** ... CathyGannon 7 (Harry Dunlop) *chsd ldrs: rdn over 2f out: wknd over 1f out* **8/1**	74
120-	**7**	*1 ½*	**Isobar (GER)**[292] 6808 5-9-3 **80** ... KirstyMilczarek 5 (Luca Cumani) *prom: led over 2f out: rdn and hdd over 1f out: wknd fnl f* **14/1**	70+
-000	**8**	*54*	**Epic (IRE)**[16] 4008 4-9-0 **77** ... NeilCallan 3 (Mark Johnston) *led: rdn and hdd over 3f out: wknd 2f out: t.o* **22/1**	—

2m 33.72s (0.82) **Going Correction** -0.025s/f (Good) **8** Ran SP% **113.9**
Speed ratings (Par 105): **96,95,93,93,91 88,87,51**
toteswingers: 1&2 £3.80, 1&3 £3.90, 2&3 £12.40. CSF £13.58 CT £107.95 TOTE £3.00: £1.40, £2.50, £2.40; EX 20.40.
Owner Ryan P Hadfield & Panther Racing **Bred** Dr K Schulte **Trained** Melsonby, N Yorks

FOCUS

This appeared a wide-open handicap but a slowly run race went the way of the favourite. The winner is rated to the best of his old form with a persoanl-best from the second.

4556 ROBERT PALMER MEMORIAL H'CAP 6f

5:50 (5:54) (Class 3) (0-90,90) 3-Y-0+ **£9,703** (£2,887; £1,443; £721) **Stalls** Low

Form				RPR
0042	**1**		**Zero Money (IRE)**[6] 4369 5-9-10 **88** ... (b) WilliamBuick 18 (Roger Charlton) *mde all: clr over 1f out: rdn and edgd rt ins fnl f: styd on* **2/1**[1]	102
5023	**2**	*2 ¼*	**Whozthecat (IRE)**[15] 4075 4-9-9 **87** ... (v) StevieDonohoe 14 (Declan Carroll) *a.p: chsd wnr over 3f out: rdn over 1f out: styd on* **12/1**	94
140	**3**	*1*	**Hezmah**[22] 3819 3-9-2 **85** ... TadhgO'Shea 7 (John Gosden) *dwlt: hld up: hdwy over 1f out: sn rdn and hung lft: styd on: nt rch ldrs* **11/2**[2]	88
6610	**4**	*2*	**New Leyf (IRE)**[22] 3796 5-9-9 **87** ... (b) DavidProbert 9 (Jeremy Gask) *hld up: rdn over 1f out: r.o ins fnl f: nvr nrr* **14/1**	84
0300	**5**	*1 ½*	**Fireback**[21] 3862 4-9-5 **90** ... ThomasBrown(7) 16 (Andrew Balding) *got loose on the way to post: mid-div: rdn and swtchd rt over 1f out: r.o: nt trble ldrs* **9/1**[3]	83
0023	**6**	*hd*	**Lujeanie**[23] 3778 5-9-5 **83** ... (p) ShaneKelly 3 (Dean Ivory) *hld up: hdwy over 2f out: rdn over 1f out: hung lft ins fnl f: styd on same pce* **11/1**	75
0046	**7**	*nk*	**Beat The Bell**[28] 3627 6-9-10 **88** ... LeeNewman 4 (David Barron) *mid-div: rdn over 2f out: nvr trbld ldrs* **18/1**	79
0030	**8**	*hd*	**Corporal Maddox**[7] 4346 4-9-11 **89** ... HayleyTurner 12 (Jamie Osborne) *hld up: hdwy over 1f out: no imp fnl f* **16/1**	79
-200	**9**	*2 ¼*	**Tagula Night (IRE)**[22] 3796 5-9-11 **89** ... (vt) PatDobbs 2 (Walter Swinburn) *hld up: hdwy over 3f out: rdn over 1f out: wknd fnl f* **25/1**	72
0045	**10**	*½*	**Jack My Boy (IRE)**[11] 4188 4-9-4 **82** ... (v) CathyGannon 6 (David Evans) *prom: rdn over 2f out: wknd over 1f out* **22/1**	64
0050	**11**	*nk*	**Befortyfour**[7] 4346 6-9-6 **84** ... TonyCulhane 13 (Richard Guest) *hld up: swtchd rt over 1f out: nvr on terms* **25/1**	65
0610	**12**	*2 ¼*	**Below Zero (IRE)**[7] 4314 4-9-7 **85** ... NeilCallan 17 (Mark Johnston) *chsd ldrs: rdn over 2f out: wknd fnl f* **12/1**	65

-203 **13** ½ **Cloud's End**[14] 4101 4-8-11 **78** .... JohnFahy(3) 11 50
(Robert Cowell) *mid-div: rdn over 2f out: wknd over 1f out* **33/1**

0002 **14** 1 ¾ **Bravo Echo**[22] 3796 5-9-6 **84** .... JackMitchell 8 50
(Michael Attwater) *prom: sn drvn along: lost pl 4f out: n.d after* **9/1**[3]

00-0 **15** 48 **Arteus**[64] 2470 5-9-10 **88** ....(b) MartinLane 15 —
(George Margarson) *chsd ldr tl rdn over 3f out: wknd 2f out: t.o* **66/1**

1m 11.3s (-1.20) **Going Correction** -0.025s/f (Good)
WFA 3 from 4yo+ 5lb **15** Ran SP% **126.7**
Speed ratings (Par 107): **107,104,102,100,98 97,97,97,94,93 93,90,89,87,23**
toteswingers: 1&2 £4.90, 1&3 £4.70, 2&3 £11.50. CSF £27.30 CT £128.53 TOTE £2.50: £1.40, £3.80, £2.40; EX 34.20.
Owner Ms Gillian Khosla **Bred** Carrigbeg Stud **Trained** Beckhampton, Wilts

FOCUS
A decent handicap run at a sound gallop with the winner probably improving slightly on recent form.

NOTEBOOK
Zero Money(IRE) ◆ poured it on from the front, never giving any of his rivals a sniff. The time wasn't bad, being 1.1secs beyond standard, and he won as he pleased after finishing second at Pontefract over 6f the previous Sunday off the same mark. He would be of considerable interest if turned out under a penalty as he is clearly in great heart. (op 11-4 tchd 7-4)
Whozthecat(IRE) has been placed on each of his three starts this month. Back up to 6f here, it is worth noting that he has still yet to win at the trip. (op 10-1)
Hezmah ◆ is the one to take from the race. Racing for the first time at 6f, she just about lost her chance by breaking slowly. Nevertheless, she cruised up, passing many rivals with ease and it was possibly inexperience that resulted in her markedly hanging left across the track. (op 7-1)
New Leyf(IRE) failed to fire at Ascot earlier in the month after winning at Doncaster but he bounced back to something like his best here. He ran on from the off the pace but could never trouble the principals. (tchd 16-1)
Fireback didn't help himself by getting loose beforehand. Dropped in trip after running mid-division in the Bunbury Cup three weeks earlier, it was no surprise to see him staying on past weakening rivals in the closing stages. (op 8-1 tchd 10-1)
Lujeanie, a C&D winner off 5lb lower mark a year ago, was third in a 5f handicap earlier in the month. He ran a solid race again but might just be in the grip of the handicapper. (op 9-1 tchd 12-1)
Corporal Maddox Official explanation: jockey said that the gelding hung right
Bravo Echo was one of the first beaten and this wasn't his running after an encouraging second at Ascot in a similar race earlier this month. (op 11-1 tchd 12-1)
T/Plt: £165.50 to a £1 stake. Pool of £96,703.54 - 426.53 winning tickets. T/Qpdt: £25.20 to a £1 stake. Pool of £4,029.43 - 117.94 winning tickets. CR

4512 THIRSK (L-H)

Saturday, July 30

OFFICIAL GOING: Good (good to firm in places; 8.9)
Wind: light 1/2 behind Weather: fine

4557 EBF "MILLKOM" MAIDEN STKS 5f
1:55 (1:57) (Class 4) 2-Y-O **£4,528** (£1,347; £673; £336) **Stalls** High

Form RPR

6 **1** **Full Support (IRE)**[19] 3915 2-9-3 0 .... RichardMullen 9 77
(David Brown) *chsd ldrs: sn drvn along: swtchd stands' side over 1f out: r.o to ld last 75yds* **10/1**

602 **2** 1 ¼ **I'll Be Good**[8] 4283 2-9-0 68 .... GaryBartley(3) 1 72
(Robert Johnson) *dwlt: mid-division whn swvd rt 2f out: edgd rt over 1f out: styd on wl stands' side fnl f* **40/1**

40 **3** ½ **Kune Kune**[21] 3865 2-8-12 0 .... AndreaAtzeni 4 65
(Marco Botti) *w ldrs: upsides jst ins fnl f: no ex* **3/1**[2]

52 **4** 1 **Tahnee Mara (IRE)**[21] 3849 2-8-12 0 .... StephenCraine 11 62
(Kevin Ryan) *led: hdd ins fnl f: fdd* **9/4**[1]

0445 **5** ½ **Busy Bimbo (IRE)**[14] 4106 2-8-12 56 .... RobertWinston 12 60
(Alan Berry) *chsd ldrs: hung lft and wknd jst ins fnl f* **40/1**

46 **6** 2 ¼ **Magic Bounty**[23] 3755 2-8-12 0 .... AdamCarter(5) 7 57
(Tim Easterby) *sn outpcd and in rr: hdwy in centre 2f out: kpt on fnl f* **7/1**

3432 **7** hd **Rougini (IRE)**[28] 3639 2-8-12 68 .... AndrewElliott 8 51
(Mrs K Burke) *chsd ldrs: wknd fnl f* **14/1**

5230 **8** 1 **Dream Whisperer**[44] 3092 2-8-12 74 .... FrederikTylicki 3 48
(Dominic Ffrench Davis) *w ldrs: wknd fnl 150yds* **20/1**

60 **9** 1 ¼ **Bang Tidy (IRE)**[7] 4347 2-9-0 0 .... PaulPickard(3) 10 48
(Brian Ellison) *sn outpcd and drvn along: hdwy over 2f out: wknd fnl f* **5/1**[3]

2352 **10** 2 ½ **Blue Shoes (IRE)**[10] 4192 2-8-12 66 .... DavidAllan 2 34
(Tim Easterby) *sn outpcd and in rr* **10/1**

11 1 ¾ **Jack Barker** 2-9-3 0 .... DanielTudhope 6 33
(Robin Bastiman) *dwlt: sn outpcd and wl bhd* **66/1**

00 **12** 1 **Samasana (IRE)**[34] 3424 2-8-7 49 ....(v) RosieJessop(5) 5 24
(Ian Wood) *sn in rr: edgd rt 2f out: sn bhd* **100/1**

59.74 secs (0.14) **Going Correction** -0.05s/f (Good) **12** Ran SP% **121.9**
Speed ratings (Par 96): **96,94,93,91,90 87,86,85,83,79 76,74**
Tote Swingers: 1&2 £13.30, 1&3 £12.40, 2&3 £27.00 CSF £366.98 TOTE £15.80: £3.90, £10.10, £1.70; EX 632.00.
Owner J C Fretwell **Bred** Mount Coote New England Barton & Myriad **Trained** Averham Park, Notts

FOCUS
A modest maiden in which there was plenty of pace on. The form looks straightforward with the third and fourth a bit below their marks and the fifth fitting in in a straightforward race to rate.

NOTEBOOK
Full Support(IRE) was supported in the market and stayed on best once switched on to the favoured stands' rail. Green and outpaced on debut, he was without the tongue-tie this time and has clearly improved a lot. He should prove just as effective at 6f and can make his mark in nurseries. (op 18-1 tchd 20-1)
I'll Be Good, much-improved when second at 100-1 over C&D last time, showed that was no fluke with another big-price placing. 5f on a sound surface seems to suit him well and he shouldn't be long in going one better.
Kune Kune faced competition for the lead, which didn't help her chance, but she still bounced back from a below-par effort last time. Nurseries are now an option. (tchd 7-2)
Tahnee Mara(IRE) was below form, being pressed hard for the lead and possibly doing too much in the early stages. She can win a small race when getting her own way. (op 5-2 tchd 2-1)
Busy Bimbo(IRE) had the favoured rail to race against and performed above expectations. (op 50-1)
Magic Bounty was keeping on and will be of interest switched to handicaps over further. (op 14-1)
Bang Tidy(IRE), although disappointing, is evidently thought capable of better. (op 4-1)

4558 CONSTANT SECURITY NURSERY 5f
2:30 (2:30) (Class 3) 2-Y-O **£7,439** (£2,213; £1,106; £553) **Stalls** High

Form RPR

3164 **1** **Guru Girl**[34] 3435 2-8-7 **70** .... AndrewElliott 10 74
(Mrs K Burke) *led: narrowly hdd last 100yds: kpt on to ld fnl strides* **4/1**[2]

10 **2** hd **Mitie Mouse**[46] 3014 2-8-11 **74** .... TonyCulhane 7 77
(Mike Murphy) *stdd s: t.k.h: sn trcking ldrs: tk narrow advantage ins fnl f: hdd post* **8/1**

2122 **3** 1 ½ **Kool Henry (IRE)**[7] 4343 2-9-7 **84** .... DanielTudhope 3 82+
(David O'Meara) *w ldrs: ev ch tl fdd last 50yds* **9/4**[1]

614 **4** nk **Ocean Myth**[15] 4069 2-8-8 **71** .... LiamJones 9 68
(William Haggas) *trckd ldrs: edgd lft 1f out: styd on towards fin* **5/1**[3]

2410 **5** 2 **Almond Branches**[7] 4343 2-9-0 **77** .... PJMcDonald 6 67
(George Moore) *outpcd and towards rr: hdwy over 1f out: nvr nr ldrs* **6/1**

0361 **6** 1 **See Clearly**[14] 4106 2-8-11 **74** .... DavidAllan 5 60
(Tim Easterby) *sn outpcd and pushed along in rr: hdwy over 1f out: nvr nr ldrs* **15/2**

0222 **7** ½ **Beechey's Beauty**[12] 4147 2-8-2 **65** ....(p) AndrewHeffernan 8 49
(Ann Duffield) *w ldrs: edgd lft and wknd appr fnl f* **11/1**

2020 **8** ½ **Red Shadow**[14] 4106 2-8-0 **63** oh2 ow2 .... JimmyQuinn 2 45
(Alan Brown) *chsd ldrs: wknd over 1f out* **40/1**

1650 **9** 10 **Van Go Go**[14] 4079 2-8-2 **68** ....(p) BillyCray(3) 1 23
(David Nicholls) *led rdrless to post: rrd s: lost pl over 2f out: eased whn bhd ins fnl f* **25/1**

59.32 secs (-0.28) **Going Correction** -0.05s/f (Good) **9** Ran SP% **119.2**
Speed ratings (Par 98): **100,99,97,96,93 92,91,90,74**
Tote Swingers: 1&2 £3.90, 1&3 £3.40, 2&3 £2.80 CSF £37.24 CT £90.39 TOTE £5.80: £1.40, £2.70, £1.50; EX 39.50.
Owner D Redvers & Mrs E Burke **Bred** Redmyre Bs & Trinity Gate Bs **Trained** Middleham Moor, North Yorks

FOCUS
An ordinary nursery run at a fair gallop and the form looks straightforward, rated around the placed horses. It again appeared an advantage to race near the stands' rail.

NOTEBOOK
Guru Girl had faced some stiff opposition since winning her Ascot maiden, but she was ideally berthed for a front-runner, and with the assistance of the rail, she was able to rally back past the runner-up. She shouldn't go up much and is worth another try at 6f. (op 5-1)
Mitie Mouse, poorly drawn and outclassed at Royal Ascot, found this more his level, travelling well and looking the likely winner, only to give in close home. He has a ton of speed and can win something similar.
Kool Henry(IRE) got warm, was taken on for the lead, and raced away from the stands' rail. All things considering, he didn't run badly. (op 15-8)
Ocean Myth lacked the pace and probably needs a stiffer 5f, or 6f. (op 8-1)

4559 BUCK INN MAUNBY MAIDEN FILLIES' STKS 7f
3:05 (3:06) (Class 5) 3-Y-O+ **£3,881** (£1,155; £577; £288) **Stalls** Low

Form RPR

-024 **1** **Al Mayasah (IRE)**[14] 4093 3-9-0 78 .... RichardMullen 3 81+
(David Simcock) *trckd ldrs: wnt 2nd 3f out: shkn up to ld over 2f out: pushed clr over 1f out: eased towards fin* **4/6**[1]

-002 **2** 2 ¾ **Map Of Heaven**[15] 4067 3-9-0 67 ....(b) LiamJones 8 69
(William Haggas) *led tl over 4f out: wnt 2nd appr fnl f: no ch w wnr* **10/3**[2]

3 7 **Lady By Red (IRE)** 3-9-0 0 .... FrederikTylicki 9 50+
(Michael Dods) *w ldrs: hung rt and led over 4f out: hdd over 2f out: wknd appr fnl f* **9/1**[3]

00 **4** 3 ½ **Tootie Flutie**[68] 2361 3-9-0 0 .... RobertWinston 1 41
(Richard Whitaker) *dwlt: sn mid-div: outpcd over 3f out: kpt on fnl 2f: nvr a factor* **66/1**

-200 **5** ½ **Dream Dream Dream (IRE)**[8] 4288 4-9-7 51 ......(p) AndrewHeffernan 6 42
(Kevin M Prendergast) *chsd ldrs: outpcd 3f out: grad wknd* **20/1**

0 **6** 1 ½ **Marina Ballerina**[62] 2529 3-9-0 0 .... PaulQuinn 2 35
(Roy Bowring) *s.i.s: in rr: nvr on terms* **33/1**

0 **7** 1 **Cranworth Quest (IRE)**[29] 3577 3-9-0 0 .... JimmyQuinn 10 33
(Tim Etherington) *mid-div: outpcd over 3f out: kpt on fnl 2f: nvr on terms* **16/1**

8 4 **Tiger Royale** 3-8-7 0 .... JosephYoung(7) 5 22
(Michael Mullineaux) *s.i.s: in rr and drvn over 3f out: sn bhd* **25/1**

0- **9** 3 ½ **She Deals**[230] 7843 3-9-0 0 .... RussKennemore 7 12
(Paul Midgley) *s.i.s: t.k.h: hung lft and lost pl over 2f out: eased towards fin* **66/1**

1m 27.7s (0.50) **Going Correction** +0.125s/f (Good)
WFA 3 from 4yo 7lb **9** Ran SP% **113.5**
Speed ratings (Par 100): **102,98,90,86,86 84,83,78,74**
Tote Swingers: 1&2 £1.02, 2&3 £3.40 CSF £2.61 TOTE £1.50: £1.02, £1.30, £2.70; EX 2.40.
Owner Ahmad Al Shaikh **Bred** Grangecon Stud **Trained** Newmarket, Suffolk

FOCUS
A weak maiden rated around the principals, who finished clear.
She Deals Official explanation: jockey said that the filly hung left throughout

4560 SHIRLEY ANNE FAILL MEMORIAL H'CAP 1m
3:40 (3:40) (Class 5) (0-70,70) 3-Y-O **£2,911** (£866; £432; £216) **Stalls** Low

Form RPR

1024 **1** **Goal (IRE)**[16] 4005 3-9-2 **68** ....(t) RyanClark(3) 13 79
(Richard Guest) *in rr: gd hdwy on outer over 2f out: hung lft and led 1f out: drvn out* **18/1**

032 **2** 2 ¼ **Icy Blue**[37] 3318 3-9-4 **67** .... RobertWinston 14 72
(Richard Whitaker) *mid-div: hdwy over 2f out: nt clr run tl over 1f out: styd on to take 2nd nr fin* **14/1**

3630 **3** nk **To The Spring**[28] 3633 3-9-5 **68** ....(b[1]) LiamJones 7 73
(William Haggas) *stmbld sttart: sn mid-div: effrt over 2f out: swtchd rt over 1f out: kpt on: tk 3rd nr fin* **10/1**

0011 **4** hd **Ryedale Dancer (IRE)**[8] 4284 3-9-3 **66** .... DavidAllan 15 70
(Tim Easterby) *w ldr: led over 2f out: hdd 1f out: kpt on same pce: lost 2 pls nr fin* **7/1**[2]

1220 **5** shd **Save The Bees**[8] 4290 3-9-2 **70** .... NeilFarley(5) 2 74
(Declan Carroll) *chsd ldrs: kpt on same pce fnl f* **4/1**[1]

2360 **6** 1 ¾ **Hernando Torres**[11] 4177 3-8-13 **62** .... PaddyAspell 4 62
(Michael Easterby) *in rr: hdwy on ins over 2f out: kpt on fnl f: nt rch ldrs* **17/2**[3]

3356 **7** ¾ **Lady Gar Gar**[28] 3614 3-9-6 **69** .... RussKennemore 3 67
(Geoffrey Oldroyd) *chsd ldrs: one pce over 1f out* **16/1**

442 **8** 1 ¾ **Dr Red Eye**[14] 4081 3-9-3 **69** .... BillyCray(3) 10 67
(David Nicholls) *led tl 2f out: wknd fnl f: eased nr fin* **7/1**[2]

5641 **9** *nse* **Ventura Sands (IRE)**[14] 4081 3-9-7 **70**.......................... FrederikTylicki 6 64+
(Richard Fahey) *dwlt: hld up in rr: sme hdwy and nt clr run over 1f out: swtchd rt: styd on wl towards fin* **7/1**[2]

0003 **10** *1* **Subramaniam**[9] 4236 3-8-6 **55**.......................................(b) PJMcDonald 12 47
(James Given) *towards rr: nvr a factor* **12/1**

-233 **11** *shd* **Izzet**[28] 3619 3-8-8 **60**.................................... PaulPickard(3) 8 52
(Ron Barr) *towards rr: effrt and swtchd outside over 2f out: wknd over 1f out* **22/1**

2054 **12** *5* **Rapturous Applause**[8] 4284 3-8-8 **57**........................(p) RichardMullen 5 37
(Micky Hammond) *mid-div: effrt over 2f out: sn wknd* **25/1**

-602 **13** *1 ¼* **Cottam Stella**[12] 4149 3-8-2 **51**.. JimmyQuinn 1 28
(Mel Brittain) *mid-div: sme hdwy on ins over 2f out: sn wknd* **25/1**

1536 **14** *7* **Foxley (IRE)**[33] 3468 3-9-2 **65**....................................... DanielTudhope 11 26
(Robin Bastiman) *chsd ldrs: wknd over 2f out: bhd whn eased clsng stages* **18/1**

2-00 **15** *12* **Bigalo's Laura B (IRE)**[81] 1967 3-8-0 **52** ow1.......(e) DeclanCannon(3) 9 —
(G P Kelly) *chsd ldrs: lost pl over 2f out: heavily eased whn wl bhd clsng stages* **66/1**

1m 40.54s (0.44) **Going Correction** +0.125s/f (Good) **15** Ran SP% **121.4**
Speed ratings (Par 100): **102,99,99,99,99 97,96,94,94,93 93,88,87,80,68**
Tote Swingers: 1&2 £54.00, 1&3 £46.90, 2&3 £32.70 CSF £241.51 CT £2723.20 TOTE £17.00: £6.20, £4.70, £4.20; EX 361.20.
Owner Willie McKay **Bred** A M F Persse **Trained** Stainforth, S Yorks

FOCUS
Those closing from off the pace came to the fore in what was a modest handicap. The form looks fair for the grade, rated around the third, fourth and fifth.
To The Spring Official explanation: jockey said that the filly stumbled on leaving the stalls
Ventura Sands(IRE) Official explanation: jockey said that the gelding was denied a clear run

4561 EKOSGEN H'CAP 1m
4:10 (4:12) (Class 3) (0-90,90) 3-Y-O+ **£9,703** (£2,887; £1,443; £721) **Stalls** Low

Form RPR

0000 **1** **Osteopathic Remedy (IRE)**[35] 3397 7-10-0 **90**.......... RobertWinston 7 100
(Michael Dods) *trckd ldrs: led jst ins fnl f: styd on* **20/1**

0000 **2** *1 ¼* **Mujaadel (USA)**[21] 3877 6-9-1 **77**...............................(p) JamieGoldstein 13 84
(David Nicholls) *mid-div: hdwy over 2f out: led 1f out: sn hdd: kpt on same pce* **20/1**

2224 **3** *hd* **Dolphin Rock**[29] 3585 4-9-8 **84**.. PJMcDonald 11 91
(David Barron) *w ldr: led over 1f out: sn hdd: kpt on same pce* **8/1**[3]

1410 **4** *¾* **Fazza**[28] 3620 4-8-13 **75**... AndrewHeffernan 1 80
(Edwin Tuer) *dwlt: drvn along to sn chse ldrs: kpt on same pce fnl f* **20/1**

2112 **5** *hd* **Powerful Presence (IRE)**[7] 4349 5-9-4 **80**............... DanielTudhope 12 84
(David O'Meara) *prom: effrt over 2f out: n.m.r and swtchd lft: kpt on ins fnl f* **5/2**[1]

2063 **6** *nk* **Marjury Daw (IRE)**[15] 4070 5-9-0 **76**.............................. FrederikTylicki 8 80
(James Given) *mid-div: hdwy over 1f out: styd on towards fin* **16/1**

2560 **7** *hd* **Staff Sergeant**[22] 3829 4-9-0 **79**............................ PaulPickard(3) 9 82+
(Jim Goldie) *in rr: styd on fnl 2f: nt rch ldrs* **14/1**

5-00 **8** *1* **Piceno (IRE)**[7] 4325 3-8-1 **74**.. BillyCray(3) 2 73
(David Nicholls) *led: hdd 2f out: hung rt and wknd appr fnl f* **33/1**

2212 **9** *1 ½* **Just Bond (IRE)**[53] 2783 9-9-11 **87**............................ RussKennemore 14 84
(Geoffrey Oldroyd) *s.i.s: hdwy over 2f out: kpt on fnl f* **11/1**

3500 **10** *½* **Iceblast**[7] 4349 3-8-5 **78**... DeclanCannon(3) 10 72
(Michael Easterby) *s.i.s: hdwy on outside over 2f out: kpt on fnl f* **14/1**

2100 **11** *½* **Vito Volterra (IRE)**[7] 4325 4-9-6 **82**............................ StephenCraine 16 77
(Michael Smith) *trckd ldrs: wknd over 1f out* **18/1**

0150 **12** *3 ¼* **Blue Moon**[132] 925 4-9-1 **80**....................................... AmyRyan(3) 17 68
(Kevin Ryan) *chsd ldrs: hung lft and wknd over 1f out* **20/1**

0344 **13** *hd* **Arabian Spirit**[14] 4100 6-9-13 **89**...(b[1]) PBBeggy 5 76
(Richard Fahey) *s.i.s: nvr on terms* **15/2**[2]

0054 **14** *½* **Oriental Scot**[15] 4070 4-9-7 **83**................................ RichardMullen 15 69
(William Jarvis) *hld up towards rr: hdwy on outer over 2f out: wknd over 1f out: eased towards fin* **9/1**

3100 **15** *1 ¼* **Amethyst Dawn (IRE)**[7] 4344 5-9-5 **86**........................... LanceBetts(5) 6 69
(Tim Easterby) *a towards rr* **14/1**

[illegible] **16** *7* **[illegible] (USA)**[281] 7076 [illegible] **81** MattieBatchelor 4 48
(Mrs K Burke) *trckd ldrs: t.k.h: wknd 2f out* **[illegible]/1**

104 **17** *2* **Majuro (IRE)**[48] 2955 7-9-5 **84**...(t) RyanClark(3) 3 46
(Richard Guest) *mid-div: lost pl over 3f out: sn bhd* **12/1**

1m 39.62s (-0.48) **Going Correction** +0.125s/f (Good)
WFA 3 from 4yo+ 8lb **17** Ran SP% **135.4**
Speed ratings (Par 107): **107,105,105,104,104 104,104,103,101,101 100,97,97,96,95 88,86**
Tote Swingers: 1&2 £0.00, 1&3 £20.80, 2&3 £47.80 CSF £378.05 CT £3488.72 TOTE £28.90: £5.40, £7.80, £2.20, £4.00; EX 979.20.
Owner Kevin Kirkup **Bred** Airlie Stud **Trained** Denton, Co Durham

FOCUS
A decent handicap, which was obviously open given the field size, but not that many got into it from off the pace. The form is rated around the third and fourth.

NOTEBOOK
Osteopathic Remedy(IRE) had slipped 2lb below his last winning mark and, having always been well positioned, stayed on strongly once in front for his third C&D victory. Consistency isn't his strong point, so it would be a surprise were he to follow up off a higher mark. Official explanation: trainer said, regarding the apparent improvement of form, that the gelding appeared to be better suited by its return to Thirsk where it had run well in the past (op 25-1)
Mujaadel(USA) was another bidding to capitalise on a slipping mark. He's never won over 1m, but this wasn't far off his best form.
Dolphin Rock bounced back from a lesser effort at Haydock, but remains above his last winning mark. (op 9-1)
Fazza disappointed from this mark last time, but this effort suggests he's up to winning off it. (op 25-1)
Powerful Presence(IRE) has been on a cracking run of form but had gone up another 4lb and, well though he ran, he wouldn't have won even if he'd avoided interference late on. (op 4-1)
Marjury Daw(IRE) got going late and is weighted to win returned to 1m2f.
Piceno(IRE) Official explanation: jockey said that the gelding hung right
Arabian Spirit Official explanation: jockey said that the trainer was unable to offer any explanation for the poor performance shown

4562 GLENRIDDING H'CAP 2m
4:45 (4:46) (Class 5) (0-75,73) 4-Y-O+ **£2,911** (£866; £432; £216) **Stalls** Low

Form RPR

4644 **1** **Beat The Shower**[21] 3851 5-8-13 **65**........................... RobertWinston 11 74
(Peter Niven) *hld up: hdwy 7f out: led 2f out: hld on towards fin* **9/1**[3]

0/15 **2** *½* **Riptide**[18] 3935 5-9-1 **67**..(v) JamieGoldstein 2 75
(Michael Scudamore) *sn trck ldrs: upsides over 1f out: kpt on towards fin* **14/1**

3133 **3** *¾* **Golden Future**[13] 4129 8-8-7 **62**.................................. DeclanCannon(3) 6 69
(Peter Niven) *trckd ldrs: chal over 1f out: kpt on same pce last 75yds* **12/1**

0303 **4** *2 ¾* **Simple Jim (FR)**[6] 4366 7-8-2 **54**.............................. JimmyQuinn 7 58
(David O'Meara) *hld up: hdwy over 4f out: drvn over 2f out: kpt on one pce appr fnl f* **6/5**[1]

5436 **5** *shd* **Puy D'Arnac (FR)**[24] 3730 8-8-13 **65**........................ FrederikTylicki 9 69
(George Moore) *hld up towards rr: hdwy 3f out: kpt on one pce over 1f out* **22/1**

00/- **6** *4* **Bulwark (IRE)**[623] 7402 9-9-1 **70**................................. RyanClark(3) 4 69
(Ian Williams) *s.i.s: rn in snatches: dropped to rr over 4f out: kpt on fnl 2f* **9/1**[3]

6512 **7** *1 ½* **Los Nadis (GER)**[24] 3730 7-9-7 **73**.............................. DanielTudhope 3 70
(Jim Goldie) *trckd ldrs: effrt on ins 3f out: wknd over 1f out* **6/1**[2]

0533 **8** *6* **Capable Guest (IRE)**[31] 3507 9-8-5 **62**............................ NeilFarley(5) 1 52
(George Moore) *in rr: bhd fnl 2f* **12/1**

0500 **9** *8* **Boston Blue**[24] 3738 4-9-6 **72**..............................(b[1]) MattieBatchelor 8 52
(Tim Etherington) *led: reminders over 4f out: hdd 2f out: sn wknd and heavily eased* **20/1**

1-30 **10** *3 ½* **Andorn (GER)**[13] 4129 7-9-2 **68**................................ RussKennemore 10 44
(Philip Kirby) *chsd ldrs: pushed along over 4f out: hung lft and lost pl 2f out* **11/1**

26-0 **11** *5* **Into The Light**[50] 2060 6-8-5 **60**...................................(p) PaulPickard(3) 5 30
(Philip Kirby) *trckd ldrs: lost pl over 2f out* **50/1**

3m 29.79s (1.49) **Going Correction** +0.125s/f (Good) **11** Ran SP% **121.2**
Speed ratings (Par 103): **101,100,100,99,98 96,96,93,89,87 84**
Tote Swingers: 1&2 £12.40, 1&3 £23.00, 2&3 £27.40 CSF £128.06 CT £1531.62 TOTE £10.30: £2.70, £4.40, £2.90; EX 165.00.
Owner Mrs Kate Young **Bred** C P E Brooks **Trained** Barton-le-Street, N Yorks

FOCUS
A relatively low-grade staying handicap but the form looks fairly sound.
Bulwark(IRE) Official explanation: jockey said that the gelding missed the break and was never travelling thereafter
Andorn(GER) Official explanation: jockey said that the horse ran flat

4563 WHITE ROSE SADDLERY LADY AMATEUR RIDERS' H'CAP (DIV I) 6f
5:20 (5:25) (Class 6) (0-55,55) 3-Y-O+ **£2,183** (£677; £338; £169) **Stalls** High

Form RPR

4642 **1** **Avoncreek**[18] 3943 7-9-12 **46**....................................(v) MissSBrotherton 10 54
(Brian Baugh) *w ldrs: hung lft and kpt on to ld last 100yds: hld on towards fin* **7/2**[1]

-060 **2** *nk* **Just Sam (IRE)**[21] 3856 6-10-2 **55**............................ MissVBarr(5) 11 62
(Ron Barr) *w ldrs: led 3f out: edgd lft and hdd last 100yds: no ex towards fin* **9/1**[3]

6365 **3** *½* **Itsthursdayalready**[11] 4187 4-10-0 **53**........... MissBeckyBrisbourne(5) 6 58
(Mark Brisbourne) *mid-div: hdwy over 2f out: chsng ldrs whn swtchd lft ins fnl f: kpt on* **7/1**[2]

0046 **4** *1 ½* **Lady Lube Rye (IRE)**[7] 4328 4-9-7 **46** oh1................. MissKBannon(5) 3 46+
(Noel Wilson) *in tch: hdwy on outside over 2f out: chsng ldrs 1f out: kpt on same pce* **10/1**

0-00 **5** *nk* **Danzig Fox**[36] 3341 6-9-9 **46** oh1........................(be) MissMMullineaux(3) 9 45
(Michael Mullineaux) *in rr: hdwy over 2f out: kpt on fnl f* **33/1**

6040 **6** *¾* **Ubenkor (IRE)**[18] 3953 6-10-1 **52**...........................(p) LucyAlexander(3) 8 49
(Michael Herrington) *mid-div: effrt over 2f out: sn outpcd: kpt on fnl f* **7/1**[2]

3234 **7** *1* **Cool In The Shade**[8] 4288 3-9-12 **54**.......................... MissWGibson(3) 7 48
(Paul Midgley) *w ldrs: hung lft and wknd jst ins fnl f* **7/2**[1]

1600 **8** *nk* **Fathey (IRE)**[16] 4025 5-10-0 **48**.. MissADeniel 4 41
(Charles Smith) *chsd ldrs: outpcd and lost pl over 3f out: kpt on fnl f* **14/1**

5-00 **9** *¾* **Adam De Beaulieu (USA)**[32] 3489 4-10-6 **54**...............(t) MrsCBartley 5 44
(Ben Haslam) *dwlt: hdwy on outside over 2f out: hung lft: one pce appr fnl f* **11/1**

6460 **10** *1* **Exceedingly Good (IRE)**[18] 3937 5-10-3 **51**.................. MissZoeLilly 2 38
(Roy Bowring) *w ldrs on outside: wknd fnl f* **10/1**

000- **11** *2 ½* **High Window (IRE)**[298] 6644 11-9-7 **46** oh1....... MissRRichardson(5) 1 25
(G P Kelly) *sn outpcd and in rr: bhd fnl 3f* **100/1**

1m 14.03s (1.33) **Going Correction** -0.05s/f (Good)
WFA 3 from 4yo+ 5lb **11** Ran SP% **116.6**
Speed ratings (Par 101): **[illegible]**
Tote Swingers: 1&2 £7.70, 1&3 £6.60, 2&3 £19.00 CSF £[illegible] CT £[illegible] TOTE [illegible], £3.00, £2.60; EX 42.90.
Owner Messrs Chrimes, Winn & Wilson **Bred** J H Chrimes **Trained** Audley, Staffs

FOCUS
The draw played its part in the first division of this lady amateurs' handicap. The form looks reasonable, rated around the first two, close to their best, and the fourth.
Adam De Beaulieu(USA) Official explanation: jockey said that the gelding hung left throughout

4564 WHITE ROSE SADDLERY LADY AMATEUR RIDERS' H'CAP (DIV II) 6f
5:45 (5:56) (Class 6) (0-55,54) 3-Y-O+ **£2,183** (£677; £338; £169) **Stalls** High

Form RPR

0300 **1** **Andrasta**[7] 4328 6-9-13 **46**.. MrsCBartley 11 55
(Alan Berry) *reluctant to go to s: stmbld s: mid-div: hdwy on stands' side rail 2f out: led 1f out: kpt on wl* **11/1**

4500 **2** *2 ¾* **Isle Of Ellis (IRE)**[24] 3733 4-9-7 **45**................................(v) MissVBarr(5) 1 45+
(Ron Barr) *in rr: hdwy and edgd lft 2f out: styd on to chse wnr towards fin* **28/1**

0060 **3** *½* **Classlin**[5] 4379 4-9-9 **45**.. LucyAlexander(3) 5 44
(Jim Goldie) *s.s: hdwy over 1f out: edgd lft: kpt on ins fnl f* **16/1**

0053 **4** *shd* **Pearly Wey**[3] 4443 8-10-2 **54**... MissHBethell(5) 10 52
(Ian McInnes) *taken down early and gave problems: s.s: in rr: hdwy over 1f out: kpt on same pce ins fnl f* **3/1**[1]

0405 **5** *½* **Francis Albert**[19] 3908 5-10-3 **53**..................(be) MissMMullineaux(3) 12 50
(Michael Mullineaux) *led: hung lft and hdd 1f out: one pce* **16/1**

0-00 **6** *nk* **Royal Premium**[27] 3662 5-9-5 **45**..............................(v) MissNStead(7) 4 42
(Bruce Hellier) *s.s: edgd rt after s: in rr: hdwy over 1f out: disputing 2nd whn rdr tk hands off reign and celebrated 100yds out: eased* **100/1**

4403 **7** *¾* **Winning Draw (IRE)**[27] 3661 3-9-11 **52**...................(v) MissWGibson(3) 8 45
(Paul Midgley) *w ldrs: one pce over 1f out* **11/2**[3]

3356 **8** *2* **Hootys Agogo**[13] 4124 3-9-9 **52**...................................... MissFCumani(5) 9 39
(Declan Carroll) *w ldrs: wknd fnl f* **11/2**[3]

2406 **9** *½* **Fleurie Lover (IRE)**[36] 3347 3-10-2 **54**................. MrsAdeleMulrennan 3 39
(Richard Guest) *chsd ldrs: edgd lft over 2f out: wkng whn hmpd jst ins fnl f* **9/1**

0401 **10** *3 ¾* **Boga (IRE)**[24] 3732 4-9-13 **51**.................................. MissPhillipaTutty(5) 6 24
(Karen Tutty) *chsd ldrs: edgd lft and n.m.r 2f out: sn wknd* **8/1**

5-00 **11** *hd* **Bon Appetit**[42] 3192 3-9-11 **54**....................................... MissRSmith(5) 2 27
(Micky Hammond) *dwlt: sn chsng ldrs on outer: lost pl over 2f out* **28/1**

125 12 *nk* **Avonlini**[9] 4230 5-10-7 54 .... MissSBrotherton 7 26
(Brian Baugh) *chsd ldrs: wknd appr fnl f: eased towards fin* **5/1**[2]

1m 13.82s (1.12) **Going Correction** -0.05s/f (Good)
WFA 3 from 4yo+ 5lb **12** Ran SP% **121.5**
Speed ratings (Par 101): **90,86,85,85,84 84,83,80,80,75 74,74**
Tote Swingers: 1&2 £7.70, 1&3 £6.60, 2&3 £19.60 CSF £289.73 CT £4922.05 TOTE £13.10: £3.90, £8.80, £5.40; EX 572.90.
Owner Alan Berry **Bred** Peter Barclay **Trained** Cockerham, Lancs

FOCUS
The second division of this lady amateurs' handicap and run fractionally faster than the first leg. The form looks limited, with the winner rated back to her 2009 form.
Avonlini Official explanation: jockey said that the mare lost her action
T/Plt: £1,552.60 to a £1 stake. Pool of £56,681.21 - 26.65 winning units. T/Qpdt: £74.20 to a £1 stake. Pool of £3,721.61 - 37.09 winning units. WG

4565 - (Foreign Racing) - See Raceform Interactive

4519 GALWAY (R-H)
Saturday, July 30

OFFICIAL GOING: Good

4566a LADBROKES "BIGGEST NAMES BEST PRICES" H'CAP (PREMIER HANDICAP) 7f
4:00 (4:01) 3-Y-0+
£36,206 (£11,465; £5,431; £1,810; £1,206; £603)

RPR
1 **Rock Critic (IRE)**[2] 4480 6-8-13 92 5ex .... PJSmullen 2 100+
(D K Weld, Ire) *cl up: disp ld after 3f: rdn to be definte ldr fr over 1f out: styd on wl: all out at the fin* **10/11**[1]
2 *nk* **Jamesie (IRE)**[20] 3893 3-8-7 93 ow1 .... CO'Donoghue 15 97
(David Marnane, Ire) *trckd ldrs: 3rd 2f out: styd on wl u.p fnl f: jst failed* **7/1**[2]
3 *shd* **Sean Og Coulston (IRE)**[21] 3883 7-8-10 89 .... NGMcCullagh 10 96
(John J Coleman, Ire) *sn chsd ldrs: 5th 2f out: rdn to cl and styd on wl fnl f: nt quite get to 1st 2* **14/1**
4 *1 ½* **Northern Rocked (IRE)**[18] 3969 5-9-0 98 ....(b) LFRoche(5) 1 101
(D K Weld, Ire) *sn mid-div: tight for room on inner appr st: rdn into 7th 1f out: styd on wl wout threatening fnl f* **12/1**
5 *hd* **Jembatt (IRE)**[18] 3964 4-8-6 85 .... WJSupple 6 87
(Michael Mulvany, Ire) *led: jnd after 3f: hdd fr early st: kpt on same pce ins fnl f* **20/1**
6 *½* **Back Burner (IRE)**[34] 3445 3-8-4 90 .... ShaneFoley 7 88
(Mrs John Harrington, Ire) *mid-div: rdn to chse ldrs into st: kpt on same pce ins fnl f* **14/1**
7 *shd* **Elusive Award (USA)**[16] 4034 4-8-7 86 ....(b) CDHayes 8 87
(Andrew Oliver, Ire) *towards rr: kpt on wout threatening u.p fr 2f out* **14/1**
8 *¾* **Bay Knight (IRE)**[4] 4418 5-8-10 96 .... RossCoakley(7) 9 94
(K J Condon, Ire) *sn prom: struggling fr 2f out: kpt on same pce fnl f* **20/1**
9 *¾* **Castle Bar Sling (USA)**[16] 4034 6-8-11 90 .... FMBerry 12 86
(T J O'Mara, Ire) *towards rr: kpt on wout threatening u.p fr 2f out* **16/1**
10 *1* **Collingwood (IRE)**[13] 4135 9-8-11 90 ....(bt) WMLordan 5 84
(T M Walsh, Ire) *sn prom: struggling fr 2f out: kpt on same pce* **10/1**[3]
11 *hd* **Snaefell (IRE)**[14] 4116 7-8-12 98 ....(bt) CPHoban(7) 4 91
(M Halford, Ire) *dwlt: towards rr for most: kpt on same pce fr over 2f out* **20/1**
12 *¾* **Ask Jack (USA)**[4] 4418 7-9-4 104 ....(p) RPWhelan(7) 3 95
(Joseph G Murphy, Ire) *towards rr for most: nvr a factor* **10/1**[3]
13 *¾* **Obama Rule (IRE)**[13] 4132 4-9-6 99 .... DPMcDonogh 11 88
(Ms Joanna Morgan, Ire) *dwlt: towards rr for most: nvr a factor* **20/1**
14 *1 ¼* **Drombeg Dawn (IRE)**[4] 4418 5-8-8 87 .... BACurtis 13 73
(A J McNamara, Ire) *trckd ldrs: wknd st: eased whn btn* **20/1**
15 *5* **He's Got Rhythm (IRE)**[31] 3526 6-7-11 83 .... SAGray(7) 16 55
(David Marnane, Ire) *dwlt: a towards rr* **25/1**
16 *2 ½* **Douze Points (IRE)**[24] 3740 5-8-6 85 ....(b) RPCleary 14 51
(Ed de Giles) *towards rr for most: nvr a factor* **16/1**

1m 25.41s (-6.19)
WFA 3 from 4yo+ 7lb **16** Ran SP% **150.2**
CSF £8.85 CT £87.39 TOTE £2.00: £1.02, £1.60, £4.60, £2.30; DF 9.90.
Owner Moyglare Stud Farm **Bred** Moyglare Stud Farm Ltd **Trained** The Curragh, Co Kildare

FOCUS
A typically competitive handicap for Galway. The fifth and sixth help set the level.

NOTEBOOK
Rock Critic(IRE) literally scrambled home here in this typically competitive handicap, which was run at a sensible pace. He looked to have around a stone to spare after winning here midweek and his draw to a large degree negated the negative of the trip being a little on the short side. Pat Smullen had him soon handy and he got a perfect run along the rail throughout. Smullen rides Galway better than anyone and he made use of the horse's stamina, hitting the front early enough. He was flat out at the finish and obviously needs further. (op 1/1)
Jamesie(IRE) ran a blinder having to come from gate 15. He had to bide his time and was gaining fast at the finish. His trainer excels with these tough handicappers and he is progressive. (op 8/1)
Sean Og Coulston(IRE) is another horse who still seems to be improving and ran a similar race to the runner-up from stall ten. He stays further than this and probably wants a mile ideally. The hustle and bustle seemed to bring out the best in him. (op 14/1 tchd 16/1)
Northern Rocked(IRE) might have finished much closer but for having to come from the rear, despite his excellent draw. He was also tight for room at a crucial stage and is well treated on this evidence.
Jembatt(IRE) shaped better on his first start for this yard, though he had the run of the race.

4524 DEAUVILLE (R-H)
Saturday, July 30

OFFICIAL GOING: Turf: good to soft; fibresand: standard

4569a PRIX SIX PERFECTIONS (LISTED RACE) (2YO FILLIES) (TURF) 7f
4:30 (12:00) 2-Y-0 **£23,706** (£9,482; £7,112; £4,741; £2,370)

RPR
1 **Elusive Kate (USA)**[45] 3046 2-9-0 0 .... OlivierPeslier 3 100+
(John Gosden) *broke wl: settled in 6th: dropped to last bef st: rdn 2 1/2f out: swtchd to outside: qcknd wl u.p over 1f out: fin strly to ld 50yds out: comf* **71/10**[3]
2 *1 ½* **Pestagua (IRE)**[39] 2-9-0 0 .... ThierryJarnet 2 97
(X Thomas-Demeaulte, France) **15/1**
3 *hd* **Dear Lavinia (USA)**[30] 2-9-0 0 .... ChristopheSoumillon 5 96
(J-C Rouget, France) **2/1**[2]
4 *1* **Restiadargent (FR)**[66] 2-9-0 0 .... MickaelBarzalona 8 94
(H-A Pantall, France) **18/1**
5 *2 ½* **Sylvan Song (USA)**[39] 2-9-0 0 .... MaximeGuyon 1 87
(A Fabre, France) **1/1**[1]
6 *¾* **L'Espagna (FR)** 2-9-0 0 .... IoritzMendizabal 6 85
(T Trapenard, France) **29/1**
7 *snk* **Tibaldi (FR)**[36] 2-9-0 0 .... JohanVictoire 4 85
(Mme C Head-Maarek, France) **12/1**
8 *4* **Miabeach (FR)**[11] 4191 2-9-0 0 ....(b) StephanePasquier 7 75
(C Boutin, France) **21/1**

1m 25.5s (-2.80) **8** Ran SP% **122.8**
WIN (incl. 1 euro stake): 8.10. PLACES: 2.00, 2.60, 1.60. DF: 43.40. SF: 96.90.
Owner Magnolia Racing LLC & Ms Rachel Hood **Bred** Clovelly Farms **Trained** Newmarket, Suffolk

NOTEBOOK
Elusive Kate(USA), who beat two subsequent winners when winning her maiden on Polytrack, produced a good turn of foot to take this Listed race going away. She is likely to come back here for the Group 3 Prix du Calvados over C&D, although her rider thinks she needs a mile.

4570a PRIX DE PSYCHE (GROUP 3) (3YO FILLIES) (TURF) 1m 2f
5:30 (12:00) 3-Y-0 **£34,482** (£13,793; £10,344; £6,896; £3,448)

RPR
1 **Dalarua (IRE)**[27] 3671 3-8-11 0 .... StephanePasquier 2 107
(S Wattel, France) *racd in 4th: cl up bhd ldrs: short of room whn rdn 1f out: fnd split 50yds out: fin strly to ld fnl strides* **167/10**
2 *nse* **Dream Peace (IRE)**[27] 3671 3-8-11 0 .... ThomasHuet 9 107
(Robert Collet, France) *settled towards rr: gd prog 1 1/2f out on outer: r.o strly fnl 50yds: hdd fnl strides* **18/1**
3 *hd* **Dorcas Lane**[28] 3624 3-8-11 0 .... IoritzMendizabal 5 107
(Lucy Wadham) *racd cl up bhd ldrs fr s: rdn 1 1/2f out: r.o wl fnl f: led briefly 25yds out: narrowly failed to hold on* **9/1**
4 *¾* **La Pernelle (IRE)**[69] 2342 3-8-11 0 .... Christophe-PatriceLemaire 6 105
(Y De Nicolay, France) *settled in 2nd: r.o wl in st: ev ch fnl 100yds: no ex cl home* **11/1**
5 *½* **Camelia Rose (FR)**[69] 2342 3-8-11 0 .... MickaelBarzalona 4 104
(J-C Rouget, France) *settled towards rr: rdn and qcknd wl in st: r.o wl fnl 100yds wout threatening ldrs* **13/1**
6 *snk* **Malicia (USA)**[27] 3671 3-8-11 0 .... Roberto-CarlosMontenegro 7 104
(X Thomas-Demeaulte, France) *towards rr tl st: suffered interference 1f out whn making move: fin wl fnl 100yds whn in the clr: wout threatening ldrs* **46/1**
7 *nk* **Beatrice Aurore (IRE)**[27] 3671 3-9-2 0 .... OlivierPeslier 11 108
(John Dunlop) *settled towards rr: prog early in st on outside: unable qck fnl f* **63/10**[2]
8 *hd* **Haya Landa (FR)**[48] 2977 3-8-11 0 .... JohannBensimon 1 103
(Mme L Audon, France) *racd 3rd on rail fr s: following ldr: short of room in st and nvr figured fnl f* **8/1**[3]
9 *snk* **Glorious Sight (IRE)**[27] 3670 3-8-11 0 .... GeraldMosse 3 103
(Robert Collet, France) *sent st to ld: r.o wl in st: hdd 1f out: failed to qckn: fdd* **6/4**[1]
10 *2 ½* **Siete Vidas (IRE)**[20] 3-8-11 0 .... GregoryBenoist 10 98
(M Delzangles, France) *amongst bkmarkers: rdn but no ex in st* **23/1**
0 **Margravine (USA)**[27] 3671 3-8-11 0 .... MaximeGuyon 12 —
(A Fabre, France) *towards rr tl rdn bef st: mde prog on outer 2f out but sn fdd* **17/1**
0 **Angalia (IRE)**[25] 3-8-11 0 .... ChristopheSoumillon 8 —
(E Lellouche, France) *one of the bkmakers fr s: rdn but no ex in st: eased fnl f* **13/1**

2m 6.20s (-4.00) **12** Ran SP% **120.2**
WIN (incl. 1 euro stake): 17.70. PLACES: 5.20, 5.70, 3.60. DF: 107.30. SF: 288.20.
Owner Haras De La Perelle **Bred** Haras De La Perelle **Trained** France

NOTEBOOK
Dalarua(IRE), who had picked up an infection after being supplemented for the Prix Saint-Alary, showed the benefit of her return behind Beatrice Aurore last time by coming through late to record her first Group success. She looks progressive but there are no immediate plans for her.
Dream Peace(IRE), who finished third, a length ahead of today's winner, in the Prix Chloe, got a clearer run than the winner but just lost out. Her turn at this level is not far away.
Dorcas Lane, placed in both the Ribblesdale and Lancashire Oaks since winning the Pretty Polly, appreciated the drop back in distance and only lost out narrowly, having hit the front well inside the last. She might return to France for the Prix de la Nonette and the E.P Taylor could be on the agenda in the autumn.
Beatrice Aurore(IRE), who finished ahead of todays first two when taking the Prix Chloe, was forced to race wide throughout this time and could not pick up. Her rider also thought the ease in the ground did not suit her.

3848 CHESTER (L-H)
Sunday, July 31

OFFICIAL GOING: Good to firm (8.2)
Wind: Light, across Weather: Overcast

4571 M&S MONEY PREMIUM CLUB E B F MAIDEN STKS 7f 2y
2:20 (2:23) (Class 4) 2-Y-O **£4,851** (£1,443; £721; £360) **Stalls** Low

Form RPR
632 1 **Stellar Express (IRE)**[30] 3584 2-8-12 58 .... RobbieFitzpatrick 4 75
(Michael Appleby) *mde all: rdn over 1f out: r.o and a in command ins fnl f* **25/1**
2 2 *2 ¼* **Arley Hall**[17] 4002 2-8-12 0 .... PaulHanagan 9 69
(Richard Fahey) *w wnr tl rdn and nt qckn over 1f out: kpt on u.p but no imp ins fnl f* **3/1**[2]
42 3 *½* **Storming Bernard (USA)**[8] 4330 2-9-3 0 .... SamHitchcott 1 73
(Alan Bailey) *racd keenly: chsd ldrs: rdn and nt qckn over 1f out: kpt on same pce ins fnl f* **1/1**[1]
00 4 *1* **Hamis Al Bin (IRE)**[50] 2936 2-9-3 0 .... SilvestreDeSousa 11 70
(Mark Johnston) *chsd ldrs: n.m.r 3f out: lost pl over 2f out: sn outpcd: swtchd lft over 1f out: kpt on ins fnl f but no imp* **16/1**
5 *1* **Cool Hand Luke (IRE)** 2-9-3 0 .... RichardKingscote 3 68+
(Tom Dascombe) *dwlt: rn green in rr: outpcd 2f out: kpt on ins fnl f: unable to trble ldrs* **13/2**[3]
05 6 *½* **Amoure Medici**[9] 4292 2-9-3 0 .... PJMcDonald 5 66
(Noel Quinlan) *sweating: s.i.s: hld up: hdwy over 3f out: effrt on outer wl over 1f out: wknd fnl 100yds* **22/1**

7 *13* **Skyeron** 2-8-12 0.. GrahamGibbons 2 28
(Mark Brisbourne) *hld up: niggled along over 3f out: lft bhd over 1f out*
33/1

1m 29.09s (2.59) **Going Correction** +0.175s/f (Good) **7** Ran SP% **105.4**
Speed ratings (Par 96): **92,89,88,87,86 86,71**
Tote Swingers:1&2:£2.80, 2&3:£1.10, 1&3:£4.00 CSF £82.43 TOTE £15.80: £3.80, £1.90; EX 70.40 Trifecta £131.60 Pool £494.68 - 2.78 winning units..
Owner Mr & Mrs James Sumsion **Bred** Adrian Purvis **Trained** Danethorpe, Notts

FOCUS
Rail out the maximum 9yds from 6f to top of home straight (1.5f) with a drop in. Races of 6f, 7f and 7.5f increased by 38yds, 1m2f by 40yds and 1m4f by 59yds. On paper the first two in the betting looked to have this between them, but there was a shock result. Big improvement from the winner, with the fourth and sixth the best guides.

NOTEBOOK
Stellar Express(IRE), debuting for a new stable having been beaten in a seller on her third start for Barry Hills last time out, was quickly away, grabbed the rail and made every yard. On the face of it this was a huge step up on her previous efforts and she can expect a big rise in the ratings now, but on this evidence she's improved for the change of yard and step up to 7f, so she might be up to dealing with it in nurseries. (op 20-1)
Arley Hall, a fine second on her debut, had a wide draw to overcome. Rushed up to dispute to the winner's outer early on, she had to work to maintain her position and eventually paid for that effort. She can do better back on a more conventional track. (op 9-4)
Storming Bernard(USA), who was led to post, had the box draw but he rather missed the break and had to settle in behind the leader. Keener than ideal, he was one-paced in the finish as a result, and he should do a lot better off a stronger all-round gallop in nurseries. (op 5-4)
Hamis Al Bin(IRE), drawn widest of all, tracked the runner-up one off the rail and ran his best race to date. Nurseries are now open to him and he should do better in that sphere. (op 18-1 tchd 20-1)
Cool Hand Luke(IRE) was very slowly away, green and trailed the field in the early stages, but he was making some late headway in the straight and shaped with some promise. He'll know more next time. (op 8-1 tchd 6-1)
Amoure Medici challenged wide around the turn into the straight and ran a bit better than his finishing position might suggest. He's another now eligible to race in nurseries. (op 25-1)

4572 HAYLEY KELLY 40TH CELEBRATIONS NURSERY 6f 18y
2:55 (2:55) (Class 4) 2-Y-O **£4,851** (£1,443; £721; £360) **Stalls** Low

Form RPR
1200 **1** **Bling King**[16] 4055 2-9-9 **92**.. PhillipMakin 4 94
(Eve Johnson Houghton) *in tch: effrt over 1f out: r.o ins fnl f to ld post*
10/3[1]
5300 **2** *nse* **Middleton Flyer (IRE)**[23] 3810 2-8-1 **70**.................. SilvestreDeSousa 2 72
(David Evans) *led: rdn over 1f out: hrd pressed ins fnl f: hdd post* **7/1**
2160 **3** *½* **Musical Valley**[16] 4069 2-8-4 **73**..............................(t) RichardKingscote 3 73
(Tom Dascombe) *sn trckd ldrs: wnt 2nd 3f out: chalng fr 2 out: rdn ins fnl f: hld towards fin* **8/1**
044 **4** *1 ¼* **Our Boy Jack (IRE)**[15] 4106 2-7-12 **67** oh4...................... JimmyQuinn 5 63
(Richard Fahey) *hld up: rdn over 1f out: styd on ins fnl f: nt pce to get to ldrs* **7/2**[2]
3261 **5** *4* **Silvas Romana (IRE)**[23] 3810 2-7-12 **67** oh1....................... PaulQuinn 1 51
(Mark Brisbourne) *chsd ldr to 3f out: remained handy: pushed along over 1f out: outpcd fnl f* **7/2**[2]
6502 **6** *nk* **He's So Cool (IRE)**[15] 4085 2-9-1 **87**........................ KierenFox(3) 6 70
(Bill Turner) *hld up in rr: pushed along over 2f out: nvr able to get on terms w ldrs* **4/1**[3]
0035 **7** *26* **Come To Mind**[22] 3855 2-7-5 **67** oh18........................... NoelGarbutt(7) 7 —
(Alan Berry) *hld up in tch on outer: hdwy to chse ldrs over 3f out: wknd wl over 1f out* **50/1**

1m 16.06s (2.26) **Going Correction** +0.175s/f (Good) **7** Ran SP% **113.1**
Speed ratings (Par 96): **91,90,90,88,83 82,48**
Tote Swingers:1&2:£4.10, 2&3:£5.50, 1&3:£6.20 CSF £26.07 CT £170.12 TOTE £3.20: £1.90, £3.00; EX 24.80 Trifecta £110.60 Pool £451.42 - 3.02 winning units..
Owner P Deal & C Brown **Bred** Whitsbury Manor Stud And Mrs M E Slade **Trained** Blewbury, Oxon

FOCUS
A competitive nursery and best efforts from the first two.

NOTEBOOK
Bling King, who was taking a drop in class having contested Listed races in his previous two starts, travelled well in midfield and came home strongly to just edge ahead on the line. He shapes like this is the minimum trip for him now, and a return to 7f should suit. (op 9-2)
Middleton Flyer(IRE) broke well and won the battle for the early lead. She kept finding for pressure and was only caught on the line, proving she does get this trip after all. (op 8-1 tchd 9-1)
Musical Valley was not best away but settled in behind the pace and came there travelling strongly on the home turn, but once pressure was applied he couldn't see off the leader and he came off worst in a three-way photo. His style of running suggests a return to 5f won't inconvenience him. (op 11-2)
Our Boy Jack(IRE), who was 4lb out of the handicap, still looks rather green and continues to give the impression that there's better to come from him. (tchd 3-1)
Silvas Romana(IRE), a C&D winner last time out, was 1lb wrong at the weights but had the best draw. Having had a nice run through the race on the rail though, she found little for pressure and this has to go down as a disappointing effort.
He's So Cool(IRE) keeps coming back here but he's not once looked happy on the track, and he was never seen with a chance. (op 9-2)

4573 COLIN KERSLEY QUEENSFERRY STKS (LISTED RACE) 6f 18y
3:30 (3:31) (Class 1) 3-Y-O+
£17,013 (£6,450; £3,228; £1,608; £807; £405) **Stalls** Low

Form RPR
5004 **1** **Rock Jock (IRE)**[21] 3892 4-9-0 104.................................... PShanahan 3 104
(Tracey Collins, Ire) *dwlt: sn in midfield: nt clr run over 2f out: hdwy over 1f out: r.o to ld ins fnl f: in command towards fin* **9/2**[3]
0603 **2** *1 ¼* **Rose Blossom**[23] 3827 4-8-9 104.................................... PaulHanagan 8 95+
(Richard Fahey) *displayed gd spd to ld: rdn over 1f out: hdd ins fnl f: kpt on but wl hld by wnr towards fin* **9/2**[3]
4626 **3** *½* **Star Rover (IRE)**[8] 4346 4-9-0 87...........................(v) SilvestreDeSousa 2 98
(David Evans) *chsd ldrs: rdn over 1f out: styd on and tried to chal ins fnl f: nt quite pce of ldrs* **7/1**
1012 **4** *½* **Lexi's Hero (IRE)**[23] 3820 3-8-9 103...............................(b) PhillipMakin 9 96+
(Kevin Ryan) *a.p: tk 2nd wl over 2f out: rdn over 1f out: lost 2nd ins fnl f: nt qckn: kpt on same pce towards fin* **3/1**[1]
0146 **5** *1 ¾* **Anne Of Kiev (IRE)**[23] 3827 6-8-13 101........................(t) PatCosgrave 6 90
(Jeremy Gask) *hld up: rdn over 1f out: kpt on but nt pce to trble ldrs fnl f* **4/1**[2]
0200 **6** *nk* **Silaah**[8] 4346 7-9-0 91...(p) AdrianNicholls 5 90
(David Nicholls) *racd keenly: hld up: effrt on outer 2f out: carried hd awkwardly: no imp on ldrs: one pce fnl f* **20/1**
0006 **7** *2 ¾* **Blue Jack**[29] 3626 6-9-0 97......................................(v) RichardKingscote 7 81
(Tom Dascombe) *midfield: hdwy over 3f out: nt clr run over 2f out: effrt over 1f out: no imp on ldrs: outpcd and wl btn fnl f* **20/1**
00-4 **8** *14* **Tropical Treat**[45] 3073 4-8-9 100...................................... JimCrowley 10 31
(Ralph Beckett) *s.i.s: hld up in rr: outpcd over 1f out: nvr on terms: eased whn wl btn ins fnl f* **20/1**
0360 **9** *11* **Button Moon (IRE)**[15] 4101 3-8-4 90.............................(b[1]) MartinLane 4 —
(Ian Wood) *chsd ldr after 1f tl wl over 2f out: sn wknd: eased whn wl btn ins fnl f* **11/1**

1m 13.49s (-0.31) **Going Correction** +0.175s/f (Good)
WFA 3 from 4yo+ 5lb **9** Ran SP% **116.5**
Speed ratings (Par 111): **109,107,106,106,103 103,99,80,66**
Tote Swingers:1&2:£4.50, 2&3:£5.90, 1&3:£5.50 CSF £24.42 TOTE £6.00: £2.00, £2.10, £2.10; EX 27.10 Trifecta £138.70 Pool £716.13 - 3.82 winning units..
Owner Thistle Bloodstock Ltd **Bred** Mrs C L Weld **Trained** The Curragh, Co Kildare

FOCUS
Not the highest quality of Listed race, but pretty competitive, and it was run at a good pace. The form is ordinary for the grade and limited by the proximity of the third.

NOTEBOOK
Rock Jock(IRE)'s only win in 24 previous starts came back in September 2009 but he'd been as good as ever in defeat in his last two starts, and he came out third-best on adjusted figures here. Held up on the rail, he had the race run to suit with the leader setting a good gallop, and the gaps came at the right time for him to be delivered with a winning challenge in the straight. He's a reliable sort in this sort of company. (op 5-1 tchd 11-2 in places)
Rose Blossom showed blistering early pace to cross over from stall eight and make the running on the rail, and turning in it still looked as though she had things under control, but she got a little tired inside the final furlong and the winner stayed on too strongly for her. The early speed she shows suggests 5f is her trip, and she'll be hard to catch if returning here over that distance. (op 5-1 tchd 6-1)
Star Rover(IRE) was drawn well, had a nice run on the rail and repeated last year's third-place finish in this race. He had no excuses. (op 8-1)
Lexi's Hero(IRE), one of two 3-y-os in the race, showed good speed from his wide draw to race to secure a prominent early pitch and had every chance. He came up a little short, but it was a fair effort at the weights. (op 10-3 tchd 7-2)
Anne Of Kiev(IRE) struggled to get into it from behind. (op 9-2 tchd 5-1 in places)
Silaah, who faced a stiff task at the weights, raced wider than ideal at times.
Blue Jack continues to disappoint. (op 12-1)

4574 HALLIWELL JONES BMW MILE (H'CAP) 7f 122y
4:05 (4:06) (Class 3) (0-95,95) 3-Y-O+ **£7,762** (£2,310; £1,154; £577) **Stalls** Low

Form RPR
4010 **1** **Kingscroft (IRE)**[8] 4314 3-8-13 **88**.............................. SilvestreDeSousa 2 96
(Mark Johnston) *chsd ldrs: wnt 2nd 2f out: led 1f out: r.o wl: in command fnl 100yds* **5/1**[1]
5420 **2** *1 ¼* **One Scoop Or Two**[22] 3848 5-8-11 **78**..................(p) GrahamGibbons 12 85
(Reg Hollinshead) *chsd ldrs: rdn over 1f out: styd on to take 2nd ins fnl f: no imp on wnr* **15/2**
0410 **3** *hd* **Viva Ronaldo (IRE)**[15] 4100 5-9-6 **87**.............................. PaulHanagan 3 93
(Richard Fahey) *midfield: pushed along wl over 2f out: hdwy over 1f out: styd on and edgd lft ins fnl f: clsd towards fin* **13/2**[3]
0451 **4** *1* **Captain Ramius (IRE)**[8] 4310 5-9-9 **95**.................... BrianToomey(5) 11 99+
(Kevin Ryan) *hld up in rr: nt clr run wl over 1f out: hdwy sn after: r.o and clsd ins fnl f: nt quite get to ldrs* **9/1**
6046 **5** *nk* **Glenridding**[10] 4243 7-8-9 **76** oh1.................................. FrederikTylicki 5 79
(James Given) *led: rdn over 1f out: sn hdd and outpcd by wnr: no ex fnl 50yds* **20/1**
6622 **6** *½* **Sunrise Safari (IRE)**[17] 4013 8-8-13 **80**.....................(v) TonyHamilton 4 82
(Richard Fahey) *hld up: rdn and hdwy over 1f out: styd on ins fnl f: nt pce to chal ldrs* **12/1**
3220 **7** *2 ½* **Suffolk Punch (IRE)**[8] 4310 4-8-12 **79**.........................(v) DavidProbert 8 74
(Andrew Balding) *midfield: effrt over 1f out: nvr able to chal: one pce fnl f* **13/2**[3]
0-00 **8** *1 ¾* **Ishiadancer**[8] 4349 6-8-9 **76** oh1.................................. RobertWinston 1 67
(Eric Alston) *chsd ldr tl pushed along 2f out: wknd over 1f out: eased whn wl btn ins fnl f* **14/1**
6160 **9** *¾* **Fred Willetts (IRE)**[8] 4333 3-8-11 **91**.................(v) MatthewCosham(5) 7 78
(David Evans) *hld up: rdn over 1f out: swtchd rt ins fnl f: nvr able to chal* **6/1**[2]
4003 **10** *½* **My Kingdom (IRE)**[20] 3704 5-9-5 **80**.............................(t) FrannyNorton 0 71
(David Nicholls) *hld up: pushed along over 1f out: nvr on terms: eased whn n.d ins fnl f* **7/1**
4203 **11** *2 ½* **Major Conquest (IRE)**[11] 4214 3-8-6 **81**............................ MartinLane 6 61
(J W Hills) *midfield: rdn 2f out: struggling to hold pl whn n.m.r over 1f out: bhd fnl f* **12/1**

1m 33.23s (-0.57) **Going Correction** +0.175s/f (Good)
WFA 3 from 4yo+ 8lb **11** Ran SP% **118.7**
Speed ratings (Par 107): **109,107,107,106,106 105,103,101,100,100 97**
Tote Swingers:1&2:£5.80, 2&3:£9.50, 1&3:£4.40 CSF £42.54 CT £253.74 TOTE £6.00: £2.10, £2.60, £2.50; EX 43.10 Trifecta £653.20 Part won. Pool £882.74 - 0.30 winning units..
Owner Dr Marwan Koukash **Bred** J Beckett **Trained** Middleham Moor, N Yorks
■ Stewards' Enquiry : Frederik Tylicki two-day ban: careless riding (14-15 Aug)

FOCUS
A fair handicap, run at a decent pace and the third sets the level. Once again it paid to save ground on the rail. The third to previous course form is the best guide to the level.

NOTEBOOK
Kingscroft(IRE), who was drawn in stall two, enjoyed the run of things in behind the leader Glenridding. With that rival beginning to tire, the end of the false rail couldn't come soon enough for Kingscroft and, as soon as he had the opportunity, he darted to the inside in the straight and stayed on strongly for a comfortable success. Winning off a career-high mark, he may yet have more to offer, but it should not be forgotten that he very much had things go perfectly for him here. He could be back here for a similar race later this month. (op 11-2 tchd 9-2)
One Scoop Or Two may have been drawn out in stall 12 but he didn't have to work too hard to cross over and take a prominent early position and, although wider than ideal through the first half of the race, he saved ground by heading to the inside on the turn into the straight. This was a good effort considering easier ground suits him best. (op 10-1)
Viva Ronaldo(IRE), drawn in stall three, wasn't best away but he secured a position tracking the winner on the rail and stayed on well for third. His form figures round here now read 214213 so he should always be considered when returning to this track. (op 6-1 tchd 7-1 in places)
Captain Ramius(IRE), dropped in on the rail in last place from his wide draw, never threatened to get seriously involved but he stayed on up the rail in the closing stages to be nearest at the finish. He remains in good form and is another better suited by easier ground. (op 10-1 tchd 11-1)
Glenridding, who has dropped to an attractive mark, had the box draw and made the most of it, taking them along most of the way, but he couldn't hold them off in the straight. (op 14-1)
Sunrise Safari(IRE) had to wait and wait to make his challenge, having been held up a fair way back on the rail and denied much of a run until well into the straight. (op 8-1)

Major Conquest(IRE) Official explanation: jockey said that the gelding hung right off the bend

4575 PICCOLO E B F CONDITIONS STKS (C&G) 6f 18y
4:40 (4:41) (Class 2) 2-Y-O **£9,451** (£2,829; £1,414; £708; £352) **Stalls** Low

Form RPR
5310 1 **Alejandro (IRE)**[15] 4094 2-9-4 88 PaulHanagan 4 93
(Richard Fahey) *mde all: qcknd to go over 2 l clr over 1f out: sn rdn: hrd pressed towards fin: all out to jst hold on* **15/2**

6211 2 *hd* **Red Art (IRE)**[36] 3375 2-9-4 91 RobertWinston 3 92+
(B W Hills) *hld up: rdn and hdwy 2f out: wnt 2nd over 1f out: r.o ins fnl f: pressed wnr towards fin: jst failed* **7/2**[2]

1 3 *2 ½* **Big Note (IRE)**[50] 2907 2-9-1 0 DavidProbert 5 82
(Andrew Balding) *racd keenly: chsd wnr tl rdn over 1f out: nt qckn: one pce fnl 100yds* **13/8**[1]

0503 4 *2 ½* **Jack Who's He (IRE)**[8] 4311 2-9-3 88 SilvestreDeSousa 2 76
(David Evans) *chsd ldrs: rdn over 1f out: outpcd fnl f* **4/1**[3]

5 *6* **I'm A Doughnut** 2-8-9 0 RichardKingscote 8 50
(Tom Dascombe) *slowly away: in rr: outpcd 2f out: nvr a danger* **22/1**

2360 6 *1 ¾* **Hamza (IRE)**[15] 4094 2-9-1 89 PhillipMakin 6 51
(Kevin Ryan) *in tch on outer: pushed along over 2f out: sn wknd* **5/1**

1m 15.57s (1.77) **Going Correction** +0.175s/f (Good) **6** Ran SP% **113.1**
Speed ratings (Par 100): **95,94,91,88,80 77**
Tote Swingers:1&2:£2.60, 2&3:£1.80, 1&3:£2.80 CSF £33.93 TOTE £8.50: £3.10, £2.30; EX 31.20 Trifecta £34.20 Pool £717.88 - 15.51 winning units..
Owner F L F S Ltd **Bred** Yeomanstown Stud **Trained** Musley Bank, N Yorks

FOCUS
A good conditions event. The winner got quite a soft lead but showed improved form in any case.

NOTEBOOK
Alejandro(IRE) got away from the stalls best of all and was soon in front dictating matters. Paul Hanagan slowed things down a touch, leading to some of his rivals racing keenly, before kicking on the turn into the straight, gaining a decisive advantage over the rest that he was just about able to maintain to the line. The sixth furlong proved a plus. (op 13-2)
Red Art(IRE), a winner over 5f here last time out, was reined back as they went to the first turn and settled better than some in the chasing pack. He had to be taken wide to challenge off the bend, though, and in the end came up just a little short. He clearly got the longer trip perfectly well. (op 5-2)
Big Note(IRE) was inconvenienced by the leader slowing the pace down and pulled for his head. As a result his finishing effort was tame, but he remains capable of better off a stronger gallop. (op 9-4)
Jack Who's He(IRE) wasn't quick enough away from the stalls to get to the front and, like Big Note, ended up racing too keenly in behind the leader. (op 9-2)
I'm A Doughnut faced a stiff task on his debut and, having missed the break, was never seen with a chance. He's by Piccolo out of a winning sprinter though, so is bred for this sort of trip, and he can do better with this experience behind him. (op 14-1)
Hamza(IRE) raced three wide the whole way and was beaten some way out. He's better than this. Official explanation: trainer's representative said that the colt was never travelling (op 15-2)

4576 CHESTER THE HOME OF M&S MONEY H'CAP 1m 2f 75y
5:10 (5:12) (Class 5) (0-75,73) 3-Y-O **£4,043** (£1,203; £601; £300) **Stalls** High

Form RPR
1153 1 **Unknown Rebel (IRE)**[22] 3858 3-9-5 71 PhillipMakin 1 78
(Kevin Ryan) *mde all: rdn over 1f out: pressed ins fnl f: fnd ex for press towards fin* **11/8**[1]

-454 2 *¾* **Cadore (IRE)**[37] 3340 3-9-7 73 SilvestreDeSousa 5 78
(Peter Chapple-Hyam) *chsd ldrs: stdd over 7f out: effrt 2f out: wnt 2nd on inner over 1f out: chal wnr ins fnl f: hld towards fin* **2/1**[2]

4536 3 *nk* **Glyn Ceiriog**[34] 3467 3-9-0 66 TonyCulhane 2 70
(George Baker) *hld up bhd ldrs: wnt 2nd over 2f out: lost 2nd whn rdn and unable qck over 1f out: kpt on u.p ins fnl f: a hld* **7/2**[3]

00-6 4 *15* **Lord Of The Storm**[11] 4209 3-8-11 66 (p) KierenFox(3) 4 40
(Bill Turner) *in rr: pushed along over 7f out: outpcd over 1f out: wl bhd after: lost tch* **14/1**

05-6 5 *3 ¼* **Jossy Johnston (IRE)**[15] 4084 3-8-5 57 DuranFentiman 3 25
(Eric Alston) *racd keenly: chsd wnr tl over 2f out: sn wknd: lost tch fnl f* **18/1**

2m 12.84s (1.64) **Going Correction** +0.175s/f (Good) **5** Ran SP% **109.6**
Speed ratings (Par 100): **100,99,99,87,84**
CSF £4.35 TOTE £2.30: £1.30, £1.50; EX 3.60.
Owner D Reilly & Mrs C Reilly **Bred** Kilfrush Stud **Trained** Hambleton, N Yorks

FOCUS
A modest handicap and, not for the first time on the card, the winner made every yard. The placed horses set the standard.

4577 M&S TRAVEL MONEY H'CAP 1m 4f 66y
5:45 (5:45) (Class 4) (0-85,84) 3-Y-O+ **£4,851** (£1,443; £721; £360) **Stalls** Low

Form RPR
0216 1 **Shernando**[11] 4216 4-9-10 80 SilvestreDeSousa 10 87
(Mark Johnston) *hld up in tch: hdwy and swtchd lft over 1f out: r.o to ld ins fnl f: gamely kpt finding more towards fin* **3/1**[1]

-123 2 *shd* **Amazing King (IRE)**[16] 4059 7-9-8 78 RussKennemore 7 84
(Philip Kirby) *hld up: rdn and hdwy over 1f out: swtchd rt ins fnl f: r.o and clsd towards fin* **8/1**

0000 3 *nk* **Montparnasse (IRE)**[37] 3344 4-9-10 80 FrannyNorton 4 86
(Mark Johnston) *ponied to s: in tch: wnt 2nd over 2f out: led briefly ins fnl f: r.o for press but hld towards fin* **4/1**[2]

5105 4 *1 ½* **Danderek**[22] 3848 5-9-8 78 PaulHanagan 9 82
(Richard Fahey) *led: increased pce over 3f out: hdd ins fnl f: no ex fnl 50yds* **6/1**[3]

4013 5 *4* **Granny McPhee**[22] 3848 5-9-10 80 SamHitchcott 8 77
(Alan Bailey) *missed break: in rr: effrt over 1f out: chsd ldrs ins fnl f: one pce and no imp fnl 100yds* **6/1**[3]

2165 6 *2 ¾* **Oriental Cavalier**[17] 4004 5-9-7 77 RoystonFfrench 3 70
(Mark Buckley) *chsd ldrs: pushed along over 3f out: rdn over 1f out: wknd ins fnl f* **4/1**[2]

04F6 7 *15* **Embsay Crag**[15] 4109 5-9-7 77 (p) RobertWinston 12 46
(Kate Walton) *racd keenly: sn chsd ldr: pushed along 3f out: lost 2nd over 2f out: wknd wl over 1f out: sn eased* **9/1**

2m 40.14s (1.64) **Going Correction** +0.175s/f (Good)
WFA 3 from 4yo+ 12lb **7** Ran SP% **114.7**
Speed ratings (Par 105): **101,100,100,99,97 95,85**
Tote Swingers:1&2:£3.70, 2&3:£5.90, 1&3:£2.70; Tote Super 7: Win: Not won. Place: £811.30. CSF £27.48 CT £96.41 TOTE £3.90: £1.90, £3.50; EX 27.70 Trifecta £101.40 Pool £777.16 - 5.67 winning units..
Owner The Originals **Bred** Miss K Rausing **Trained** Middleham Moor, N Yorks

FOCUS
With five of the original 12 declared not running this wasn't as competitive as had been expected, but it was still a tight handicap and there was a close finish. The form is muddling but best rated around the first two.
Granny McPhee Official explanation: jockey said that the mare did not stay the one and a half mile trip
Embsay Crag Official explanation: jockey said that the gelding ran too freely
T/Plt: £307.60 to a £1 stake. Pool £101,577.04. 241.04 winning tickets T/Qpdt: £14.20 to a £1 stake. Pool £7,168.95. 371.58 winning tickets DO

4091 NEWBURY (L-H)
Sunday, July 31

OFFICIAL GOING: Good (good to firm in places; 7.0)
Wind: Virtually nil Weather: Sunny

4578 QUEENSLAND HOUSE AMATEUR RIDERS' H'CAP (DIV I) 1m 2f 6y
2:10 (2:10) (Class 5) (0-70,69) 3-Y-O+ **£2,183** (£677; £338; £84; £84) **Stalls** Low

Form RPR
-3 1 **Rajnagan (IRE)**[15] 1750 7-10-4 59 (t) MrDHannig(7) 10 70+
(Paul Webber) *trckd ldrs: drvn to ld 2f out: pushed along and styd on wl fnl f* **5/4**[1]

-550 2 *½* **Swift Blade (IRE)**[71] 2293 3-10-8 66 MrSWalker 2 74
(Lady Herries) *hld up in rr: hdwy over 2f out and swtchd rt: drvn to chse wnr appr fnl f: hung lft u.p fnl 120yds: no imp* **3/1**[2]

6300 3 *4* **Aflaam (IRE)**[13] 4158 6-10-10 63 (p) MissHDavies(5) 3 63
(Ronald Harris) *chsd ldr tl led appr fnl 3f: rdn and hdd 2f out: styd on same pce ins fnl f* **28/1**

-030 4 *hd* **Formidable Guest**[9] 4275 7-10-2 55 MrFMitchell(5) 6 55
(Jamie Poulton) *in rr but in tch: hdwy over 2f out: styd on fnl f: nvr gng pce to rch ldrs* **10/1**

000/ 4 *dht* **The Ducking Stool**[651] 6874 4-9-13 50 oh5 MrRBirkett(3) 1 50
(Julia Feilden) *in rr: hdwy to chse ldrs 3f out: pushed along and styd on same pce fr over 1f out* **50/1**

0323 6 *1 ¼* **Advertise**[8] 4337 5-10-5 58 MrARawlinson(5) 8 55
(Joseph Tuite) *t.k.h: trckd ldrs: rdn and outpcd over 2f out: styd on again clsng stages* **7/1**[3]

0130 7 *10* **Buddy Holly**[22] 3867 6-11-0 69 MrJEddery(7) 7 51
(Robert Eddery) *led tl hdd appr fnl 3f: wknd qckly appr fnl f* **12/1**

0450 8 *4 ½* **Love In The Park**[50] 2900 6-9-13 50 MrCMartin(3) 4 18
(Roy Brotherton) *racd towards outside fr over 4f out: bhd most of way* **16/1**

5404 9 *7* **Chez Vrony**[157] 675 5-10-0 53 MrBMMorris(5) 9 —
(Dave Morris) *racd wd into st over 4f out: bhd most of way* **16/1**

2m 11.79s (2.99) **Going Correction** -0.20s/f (Firm)
WFA 3 from 4yo+ 10lb **9** Ran SP% **115.9**
Speed ratings (Par 103): **80,79,76,76,76 75,67,63,58**
Tote Swingers:1&2:£1.80, 2&3:£16.20, 1&3:£11.90 CSF £4.92 CT £64.49 TOTE £2.00: £1.10, £1.30, £9.00; EX 5.70.
Owner Mrs W Morrell **Bred** His Highness The Aga Khan's Studs S C **Trained** Mollington, Oxon

FOCUS
Rail realignment increased advertised distances on round course by about 20m. The first division of a moderate amateur riders' handicap and slower than the second leg, although the winner is well treated compared with his best form and could do better.

4579 QUEENSLAND HOUSE AMATEUR RIDERS' H'CAP (DIV II) 1m 2f 6y
2:45 (2:45) (Class 5) (0-70,66) 3-Y-O+ **£2,183** (£677; £338; £169) **Stalls** Low

Form RPR
005 1 **Rather Cool**[20] 3916 3-9-7 51 ow3 MrRBirkett(3) 5 61
(John Bridger) *hld up in rr: hdwy fr 3f out: chsd ldr appr fnl f: drvn to ld fnl 100yds: r.o strly* **16/1**

1236 2 *1 ½* **Mrs Neat (IRE)**[16] 4056 3-10-4 64 (p) MissCBoxall(5) 10 71
(Sylvester Kirk) *in rr: hdwy over 3f out: led 2f out: hrd rdn and hung lft fnl f: hdd fnl 100yds: no ex* **7/2**[1]

0120 3 *2 ½* **Mustajed**[24] 3754 10-10-9 59 (b) MrPMillman(5) 6 61
(Rod Millman) *slowly away: wnt lft s: drvn along 3f out: stl plenty to do whn r.o appr fnl f: rdn and styd on to take 3rd fnl 75yds: nt rch ldng duo* **9/2**[2]

5130 4 *1 ¼* **Entrance**[9] 4275 3-9-13 61 MissSBirkett(7) 2 61
(Julia Feilden) *led but sn jnd: hdd appr 7f out: styd chalng and led again over 4f out: hung rt sn after: hdd 2f out: wknd fnl f* **7/2**[1]

240- 5 *5* **Larkrise Star**[235] 7765 4-10-7 59 MissECrossman(7) 4 49
(Dean Ivory) *chsd ldrs: hmpd 4f out: drvn to chal over 2f out: wknd wl over 1f out* **6/1**

0225 6 *1* **Bentley**[29] 3643 7-10-11 56 MissSBrotherton 3 44
(Brian Baugh) *t.k.h: chsd ldrs: rdn and ev ch over 3f out: wknd 2f out* **5/1**[3]

6030 7 *2 ½* **Corlough Mountain**[19] 3946 7-9-11 47 oh2 MissMBryant(5) 1 30
(Paddy Butler) *t.k.h: chsd ldrs: rdn and wknd 2f out* **40/1**

00/0 8 *nk* **Serious Choice (IRE)**[10] 4253 6-11-4 66 (b) MrJABest(3) 7 48
(Philip Hobbs) *chsd ldrs: hmpd 4f out: ev ch over 3f out: sn wknd* **9/1**

-600 9 *8* **Cragganmore Creek**[61] 2600 8-9-11 47 oh2 (v) MrBMMorris(5) 9 13
(Dave Morris) *w ldr tl slt ld over 7f out: hdd over 4f out: hmpd and wknd sn after* **50/1**

2m 10.07s (1.27) **Going Correction** -0.20s/f (Firm)
WFA 3 from 4yo+ 10lb **9** Ran SP% **113.9**
Speed ratings (Par 103): **86,84,82,81,77 77,75,74,68**
Tote Swingers:1&2:£10.60, 2&3:£2.80, 1&3:£8.10 CSF £70.48 CT £300.22 TOTE £18.60: £4.20, £1.50, £1.90; EX 89.00.
Owner W Wood **Bred** R J Barber And T E Pocock **Trained** Liphook, Hants
■ Stewards' Enquiry : Miss C Boxall four-day ban: used whip in the incorrect place (22, 27 Aug and 20, 29 Sep)

FOCUS
The faster of the two legs and the 3-y-os came to the fore in this second division. The winner built on a better recent effort while the second is rated to the best of her previous efforts.

4580 IRISH STALLION FARMS E B F MAIDEN STKS 6f 8y
3:20 (3:21) (Class 4) 2-Y-O **£4,463** (£1,328; £663; £331) **Stalls** Centre

Form RPR
0 1 **Balty Boys (IRE)**[23] 3823 2-9-3 0 MichaelHills 1 93+
(B W Hills) *mde all: shkn up and c readily clr fnl f: easily* **7/4**[1]

4 2 *4 ½* **Firestarter**[15] 4098 2-9-3 0 KierenFallon 7 79+
(David Elsworth) *in rr but in tch: pushed along 3f out: hdwy over 1f out: styd on wl fnl f to take 2nd clsng stages but nvr any ch w easy wnr* **9/1**

34U **3** *1/2* **Lady Jameela**[10] 4225 2-8-12 0 .... HughBowman 4 72
(Mick Channon) *chsd wnr: rdn and no imp fr ins fnl 2f: one pce and lost 2nd clsng stages* **8/1**

03 **4** *2 1/2* **Gold Sceptre (FR)**[16] 4054 2-9-3 0 .... RichardHughes 9 70
(Richard Hannon) *chsd ldrs: pushed along and nt qckn fr 2f out: styd on same pce ins fnl f* **6/1**[3]

026 **5** *nk* **Orders From Rome (IRE)**[15] 4094 2-9-3 92 .... FergusSweeney 5 69
(Eve Johnson Houghton) *chsd ldrs: rdn over 2f out: wknd ins fnl f* **2/1**[2]

6 *1/2* **Usain Colt** 2-9-3 0 .... PatDobbs 3 67
(Richard Hannon) *wnt lft s: sn in tch: hdwy to chse ldrs over 2f out: wknd fnl f* **20/1**

7 *4 1/2* **Sandfrankskipsgo** 2-9-3 0 .... IanMongan 2 54
(Brett Johnson) *pushed lft s: sn rcvrd and in tch: pushed along and hdwy 2f out: nvr rchd ldrs and sn wknd* **66/1**

8 *3/4* **Mince** 2-8-12 0 .... SteveDrowne 8 46
(Roger Charlton) *s.i.s: rn green and bhd: rdn 1/2-way: sme prog ins fnl f* **28/1**

0 **9** *7* **Doc Hill**[54] 2788 2-9-3 0 .... ChrisCatlin 6 30
(Michael Blanshard) *in tch tl wknd 2f out* **100/1**

1m 12.21s (-0.79) **Going Correction** -0.125s/f (Firm) **9** Ran SP% **115.8**
Speed ratings (Par 96): **100,94,93,90,89 88,82,81,72**
Tote Swingers:1&2:£4.10, 2&3:£6.40, 1&3:£4.60 CSF £17.84 TOTE £2.40: £1.20, £2.60, £2.40; EX 21.10.
Owner Sir A Ferguson,Cavendish InvLtd,J Hanson **Bred** Lynn Lodge Stud **Trained** Lambourn, Berks

FOCUS
Probably a decent maiden, with nice performances from the front two. The winner looks useful.

NOTEBOOK
Balty Boys(IRE) didn't get home having over-raced on his debut at Newmarket (7f), so the drop to this trip was likely to suit, and having been allowed an easy lead, he pulled right away inside the final furlong for a rather impressive victory. Evidently thought a bit of, hence his Group 1 Middle Park and Dewhurst entries, he's also in the Champagne, and it'll be interesting to see where he goes next. (op 2-1)
Firestarter wasn't the best away and still looked inexperience but came strong inside the final furlong and shaped like a certain future winner once faced with an extra furlong. (op 8-1)
Lady Jameela, who unseated leaving the stalls when a red-hot 1-5 favourite last time, ran well in a stronger race and can get off the mark back against her own sex. (tchd 7-1)
Gold Sceptre(FR) is now qualified for nurseries and should fare better returned to 7f. (tchd 13-2)
Orders From Rome(IRE) was disappointing. Back up to 6f, he was beaten before stamina came into it, fading late on, and clearly failed to give his running. Perhaps this came too soon. (op 5-2)
Usain Colt, half-brother to a triple 5f winner, showed some promise and ought to improve. (op 18-1)

4581 GRUNDON RECYCLE NURSERY 7f (S)
3:55 (3:56) (Class 4) 2-Y-O £**3,881** (£1,155; £577; £288) **Stalls** Centre

Form RPR

253 **1** **Dare To Dream**[23] 3812 2-8-10 **75** .... RichardHughes 7 79+
(Richard Hannon) *trckd ldr: rdn over 1f out: led fnl 150yds: hld on wl clsng stages* **15/8**[1]

1012 **2** *nk* **Wolfgang (IRE)**[22] 3866 2-9-7 **86** .... JimmyFortune 1 89+
(Richard Hannon) *hld up in rr: drvn and hdwy over 1f out: styd on u.p ins fnl f: fin wl but nt quite rch wnr* **4/1**[2]

3513 **3** *3/4* **Xinbama (IRE)**[17] 4019 2-8-4 **69** .... MartinDwyer 9 70
(J W Hills) *t.k.h: chsd ldrs: rdn to go 3rd over 1f out but no imp tl styd on wl clsng stages* **9/1**

4602 **4** *1 1/4* **Karuga**[9] 4277 2-7-10 **64** .... KieranO'Neill(3) 5 62
(Richard Hannon) *led: rdn and jnd over 1f out: hdd fnl 150yds: wknd clsng stages* **14/1**

01 **5** *3 1/2* **Meanwhile (IRE)**[26] 3718 2-7-12 **66** .... HarryBentley(3) 6 55
(William Knight) *chsd ldrs: rdn 3f out: outpcd 2f out: styd on again clsng stages* **9/1**

003 **6** *hd* **Melting Pot**[13] 4159 2-8-1 **66** ....[1] NickyMackay 3 54
(Hugo Palmer) *in rr tl hdwy fr 3f out to chse ldrs over 2f out: no imp: wknd fnl f* **25/1**

223 **7** *5* **Costa Del Fortune (IRE)**[32] 3520 2-8-8 **73** .... PatDobbs 2 48
(Richard Hannon) *t.k.h: chsd ldrs: rdn over 2f out: wknd sn after* **8/1**[3]

[illegible] [illegible] [illegible] [illegible] (IRE)[10] [illegible] [illegible] .... (t) CathyGannon 4 38
(David Evans) *hld up in rr: rdn and sme prog over 2f out:* [illegible] *and wknd sn after* **16/1**

032 **9** *1 3/4* **Dickens Rules (IRE)**[11] 4205 2-8-6 **71** .... ChrisCatlin 10 41
(Sylvester Kirk) *chsd ldrs tl wknd qckly over 2f out* **8/1**[3]

1m 26.78s (1.08) **Going Correction** -0.125s/f (Firm) **9** Ran SP% **113.4**
Speed ratings (Par 96): **88,87,86,85,81 81,75,75,73**
Tote Swingers:1&2:£2.10, 2&3:£6.60, 1&3:£5.80 CSF £8.85 CT £51.71 TOTE £2.40: £1.10, £1.80, £3.60; EX 6.00.
Owner Carmel Stud **Bred** Carmel Stud **Trained** East Everleigh, Wilts

FOCUS
They went a steady gallop in this fair 7f nursery. The form looks solid and should work out.

NOTEBOOK
Dare To Dream showed improved form for the switch to nurseries and just holding on from top weight Wolfgang. She should not go up much and can continue to give a good account, with her likely to prove as effective back at 6f. (tchd 5-2 in a place)
Wolfgang(IRE), runner-up in a Newmarket nursery latest and conceding 11lb or more, was held up in a steadily run race and there is little doubt he would have won had he been placed more handily through the early stages, flashing home to just miss out. He is still progressing. (tchd 9-2 in a place)
Xinbama(IRE) ran up to his best and gives the form a solid look, but he is likely to remain vulnerable to more progressive types.
Karuga had the run of things but has done enough in two nurseries to suggest she can win one, with 6f likely to suit better. (op 12-1 tchd 16-1)
Meanwhile(IRE) ran on without threatening and will find easier opportunities. (tchd 8-1)
Costa Del Fortune(IRE) did not settle and stopped quickly. (tchd 10-1 in a place)
Dickens Rules(IRE) ran below the level shown when second at Lingfield last time. (op 15-2)

4582 EUROPEAN BREEDERS' FUND "PACO BOY" CHALICE STKS (LISTED RACE) (F&M) 1m 4f 5y
4:30 (4:30) (Class 1) 3-Y-O+
£**17,013** (£6,450; £3,228; £1,608; £807; £405) **Stalls** Low

Form RPR

-242 **1** **Sea Of Heartbreak (IRE)**[48] 2994 4-9-3 103 .... SteveDrowne 4 106
(Roger Charlton) *in rr but in tch: gd hdwy fr 3f out: qcknd between horses 2f out: led wl over 1f out and sn edgd rt: rdn and styd on strly fnl f: wl in command clsng stages* **5/2**[2]

2-54 **2** *1 1/4* **Mirror Lake**[48] 2994 4-9-3 102 .... PatDobbs 7 104
(Amanda Perrett) *in rr: hdwy 3f out: styd on u.p fnl f to take 2nd fnl 50yds but no imp on wnr* **13/2**

215- **3** *3/4* **Cill Rialaig**[379] 4143 6-9-3 99 .... JimmyFortune 5 103
(Hughie Morrison) *hld up in rr: hdwy and nt clr run 2f out: hdwy to chse ldrs over 1f out and wnt 2nd ins fnl f: no imp on wnr and one pce: lost 2nd fnl 50yds* **11/1**

3-1 **4** *1 1/2* **Polygon (USA)**[52] 2840 3-8-6 93 ow1 .... WilliamBuick 3 102
(John Gosden) *trckd ldrs: rdn to chal over 2f out: stl wl there whn n.m.r over 1f out: kpt on same pce* **9/4**[1]

0-00 **5** *3/4* **Shimmering Surf (IRE)**[29] 3647 4-9-3 94 .... (p) IanMongan 1 99
(Peter Winkworth) *led: rdn over 2f out: hdd wl over 1f out: wknd fnl 120yds* **25/1**

533 **6** *2 1/2* **Western Pearl**[22] 3875 4-9-3 93 .... ShaneKelly 6 95
(William Knight) *sn chsng ldr: rdn 3f out: wknd appr fnl 2f* **14/1**

1053 **7** *2 1/4* **Zain Al Boldan**[24] 3772 3-8-9 103 ow1 .... RichardHughes 2 96
(Mick Channon) *chsd ldrs: rdn 3f out: sn btn* **9/2**[3]

5020 **8** *1 1/2* **Fontley**[14] 4132 4-9-3 99 .... FergusSweeney 8 89
(Eve Johnson Houghton) *in rr: sme prog on outside 3f out: nvr rchd ldrs and no ch fnl 2f* **25/1**

2m 33.22s (-2.28) **Going Correction** -0.20s/f (Firm)
WFA 3 from 4yo+ 12lb **8** Ran SP% **113.5**
Speed ratings (Par 111): **99,98,97,96,96 94,93,92**
Tote Swingers:1&2:£3.90, 2&3:£8.10, 1&3:£7.00 CSF £18.90 TOTE £4.20: £1.60, £1.60, £2.90; EX 21.40.
Owner D G Hardisty Bloodstock **Bred** D G Hardisty Bloodstock **Trained** Beckhampton, Wilts

FOCUS
No more than an ordinary gallop for this Listed prize. The form is muddling an is best rated around the sixth to her latest handicap form.

NOTEBOOK
Sea Of Heartbreak(IRE) was able to travel strongly into contention and picked up well between rivals to take a winning advantage. A tough and consistent filly, she certainly deserved this first success at Pattern level and should be up to winning a minor Group 3 against her own sex. (op 11-4)
Mirror Lake, behind the winner at Warwick last time, saw this new trip out well, just lacking the acceleration of the winner. She remains steadily progressive and can win a race at this level. (op 11-2 tchd 7-1)
Cill Rialaig, returning from 379 days off, was tough and progressive in handicaps last year and it was no surprise to see her run a big race. She was presumably pretty straight for this, though, so it remains to be seen how much she improves. (tchd 10-1)
Polygon(USA) created a very favourable impression when sweeping through to win a 1m2f course maiden which has worked out well last month, just being ridden out hands and heels, and had missed an intended Listed engagement at Longchamp earlier in the month. Things worked out differently this time, though, racing keen early and seeing plenty of daylight, and despite a spirited effort, she just lacked the knowhow of her rivals. She should leave this form behind in time and still rates a smart prospect. (op 15-8 tchd 7-4)
Shimmering Surf(IRE), unlucky in the race last year, hasn't been as good this time round and she just teed it up for the others. (op 18-1)
Zain Al Boldan dropped out disappointingly, failing to match the form of her last-time-out Group 3 third at Newmarket. (op 13-2)

4583 ASSET LAND INC H'CAP 5f 34y
5:00 (5:01) (Class 4) (0-85,85) 3-Y-O+ £**4,528** (£1,347; £673; £336) **Stalls** Centre

Form RPR

4341 **1** **Tyfos**[16] 4064 6-9-7 **80** .... J-PGuillambert 7 89
(Brian Baugh) *mde all: drvn along over 2f out: kpt finding u.p ins fnl f: in command clsng stages* **4/1**[2]

054 **2** *3/4* **Fantasy Explorer**[22] 3847 8-9-1 **74** .... (p) JimmyFortune 4 81
(John Quinn) *hld up trcking ldrs: rdn and qcknd to chse wnr ins fnl f: kpt on but no imp clsng stages* **13/2**

3516 **3** *1 1/4* **Ebraam (USA)**[7] 4357 8-9-3 **76** .... AndreaAtzeni 5 78
(Ronald Harris) *hld up in rr: drvn and hdwy appr fnl f: r.o to take 3rd clsng stages but no imp on ldng duo* **11/2**[3]

613 **4** *1 1/2* **Your Gifted (IRE)**[14] 4135 4-9-9 **85** .... KieranO'Neill(3) 1 81
(Patrick Morris) *chsd wnr: rdn 2f out: no imp fnl f: sn lost 2nd and wknd into 4th clsng stages* **3/1**[1]

3346 **5** *3 1/2* **Osiris Way**[27] 3687 9-9-10 **83** .... GeorgeBaker 6 67
(Patrick Chamings) *in rr: pushed along and hdwy over 1f out: styd on fnl f but nvr gng pce to rch ldrs* **10/1**

[illegible] **6** *7* **Sharpened Edge**[50] 2929 5-9-5 **78** .... FergusSweeney 8 37
[illegible] *sn btn* [illegible]

1235 **7** *5* **Speightowns Kid (USA)**[36] 3389 3-8-9 **72** .... WilliamBuick 3 13
(Matthew Salaman) *chsd ldrs: rdn 2f out: sn btn: eased whn no ch ins fnl f* **6/1**

60.09 secs (-1.31) **Going Correction** -0.125s/f (Firm)
WFA 3 from 4yo+ 4lb **7** Ran SP% **109.6**
Speed ratings (Par 105): **105,103,101,99,93 82,74**
Tote Swingers:1&2:£5.70, 2&3:£4.80, 1&3:£3.20 CSF £27.08 CT £129.86 TOTE £4.90: £2.30, £3.00; EX 33.10.
Owner J Tomlinson/G Williams **Bred** J Tomlinson And G Williams **Trained** Audley, Staffs

FOCUS
A fair sprint handicap but the form is ordianry, rated around the first two.

4584 AJC PREMIER FILLIES' H'CAP 1m 2f 6y
5:30 (5:30) (Class 5) (0-75,73) 3-Y-O £**2,264** (£673; £336; £168) **Stalls** Low

Form RPR

5043 **1** **Silken Thoughts**[18] 3988 3-8-12 **64** .... CathyGannon 2 78
(John Berry) *in rr: hdwy 3f out: drvn to chal 1f out: sn led: pushed out cl home* **9/1**[2]

13 **2** *1* **Lady Chloe**[29] 3641 3-9-6 **72** .... KierenFallon 7 84
(Philip Kirby) *trckd ldr: led 3f out: drvn over 2f out: jnd 1f out and sn hdd: kpt on but a hld by wnr* **4/1**[1]

013 **3** *3/4* **Chatterer (IRE)**[24] 3771 3-9-1 **67** .... (t) GeorgeBaker 11 78
(Marcus Tregoning) *in rr: hdwy on outside fr 3f out: r.o wl fr 2f out to take 3rd jst ins fnl f: kpt on clsng stages but nt rch ldng duo* **10/1**[3]

4331 **4** *4 1/2* **Ice Nelly (IRE)**[20] 3912 3-9-0 **66** .... SteveDrowne 9 68
(Hughie Morrison) *in tch: rdn over 2f out: styd on u.p to take wl hld 4th ins fnl f* **4/1**[1]

-032 **5** *1/2* **Miss Exhibitionist**[26] 3717 3-9-6 **72** .... WilliamBuick 5 73
(James Eustace) *in rr: swtchd to outside and rdn over 2f out: hung lft u.p wl over 1f out: mod prog fnl 120yds* **12/1**

0605 **6** *1 1/2* **Kalahaag (IRE)**[40] 3260 3-9-7 **73** .... (b) RichardHughes 4 71
(Richard Hannon) *led tl narrowly hdd 3f out: styd chsng ldr tl over 2f out: wknd wl over 1f out* **10/1**[3]

6563 **7** *1 3/4* **Trend Line (IRE)**[15] 4090 3-9-7 **73** .... JimmyFortune 8 67
(Peter Chapple-Hyam) *chsd ldrs: wknd wl over 1f out* **16/1**

25-0 **8** *4* **Ninfea (IRE)**[16] 4056 3-9-5 **71** .... (p) JamesDoyle 10 57
(Sylvester Kirk) *chsd ldrs: rdn 3f out: sn btn* **14/1**

211 **9** *nk* **Mystic Edge**[17] 4009 3-9-7 73.. HayleyTurner 1 58
(Michael Bell) *chsd ldrs: rdn 3f out: sn btn* **4/1**[1]

-434 **10** *6* **Zing Wing**[11] 4202 3-9-7 73.. ChrisCatlin 3 46
(Paul Cole) *in rr: sme hdwy 4f out: sn rdn and btn* **14/1**

5-00 **11** *5* **Renoir's Lady**[35] 3437 3-8-8 60.. MartinDwyer 6 23
(Simon Dow) *a in rr* **33/1**

2m 6.68s (-2.12) **Going Correction** -0.20s/f (Firm) 11 Ran SP% **118.0**
Speed ratings (Par 97): **100,99,98,95,94 93,92,88,88,83 79**
Tote Swingers:1&2:£16.70, 2&3:£9.80, 1&3:£24.10 CSF £45.08 CT £374.90 TOTE £12.90: £3.20, £2.10, £2.20; EX 61.60.
Owner The Renewal Partnership **Bred** Burton Agnes Stud Co Ltd **Trained** Newmarket, Suffolk

FOCUS
They went a good gallop early for what was a modest fillies' handicap. The winner is rated in line with her latest Sandown form and the runner-up recorded a personal-best.
T/Jkpt: £23,562.10 to a £1 stake. Pool £66,372.30. 2.00 winning tickets T/Plt: £62.10 to a £1 stake. Pool £85,138.70. 999.63 winning tickets T/Qpdt: £18.10 to a £1 stake. Pool £5,166.29. 210.50 winning tickets ST

4585 - 4588a (Foreign Racing) - See Raceform Interactive

2965 CORK (R-H)
Sunday, July 31

OFFICIAL GOING: Good to firm (good in places)

4589a IRISH STALLION FARMS EUROPEAN BREEDERS FUND GIVE THANKS STKS (GROUP 3) (F&M) 1m 4f
4:10 (4:11) 3-Y-0+ **£43,426** (£12,693; £6,012; £2,004)

RPR

1 **Pink Symphony**[48] 2994 4-9-9 100.. JPO'Brien 6 104+
(David Wachman, Ire) *settled in rr of mid-div: wnt mod 5th on outer 2f out: clsr 1f out: styd on wl u.p to ld fnl 100yds* **8/1**

2 *1 1/4* **Haziyna (IRE)**[27] 3695 3-8-11 102.. NGMcCullagh 4 102
(John M Oxx, Ire) *mid-div: 8th 1/2-way: hdwy into 4th early st: rdn to chal over 1f out: kpt on u.p: hdd and nt match wnr fnl 100yds* **11/4**[2]

3 *shd* **Amazing Beauty (IRE)**[14] 4133 3-8-11 100.. CO'Donoghue 5 102
(A P O'Brien, Ire) *hld up towards rr: mod 6th 2f out: rdn and styd on wl ins fnl f* **16/1**

4 *1 1/2* **Negotiate**[20] 3930 3-8-11 95.. KJManning 2 99
(Andrew Oliver, Ire) *trckd ldrs on inner: 6th 1/2-way: wnt 2nd early st: led 2f out: kpt on wl u.p: edgd rt and hdd 100yds out: no ex* **12/1**

5 *1/2* **Unity (IRE)**[27] 3695 4-9-9 98..(p) WMLordan 3 99
(David Wachman, Ire) *led: hdd bef 1/2-way: led again appr st: strly pressed and hdd 2f out: rallied u.p on inner 1f out: no ex wl ins fnl f* **12/1**

6 *1 3/4* **Vivacious Vivienne (IRE)**[63] 2534 5-9-9 102.. CDHayes 8 96
(Donal Kinsella, Ire) *mid-div: 7th 1/2-way: rdn and no imp 2f out: kpt on same pce wout threatening* **8/1**

7 *3* **Spin (IRE)**[81] 2012 3-8-11 101.. SeamieHeffernan 1 91
(A P O'Brien, Ire) *stmbld leaving stalls: sn trckd ldrs in 3rd: pushed along in 4th 2f out: swtchd rt and keeping on u.p whn bdly hmpd 100yds out: nt rcvr* **5/2**[1]

8 *3* **Zarebiya (IRE)**[346] 5249 4-9-9 103.. BACurtis 7 86
(John M Oxx, Ire) *towards rr: nvr a factor: kpt on one pce in st* **12/1**

9 *nk* **Why (IRE)**[17] 4035 3-8-11 98..(p) DavidMcCabe 10 86
(A P O'Brien, Ire) *chsd ldrs: 5th 1/2-way: rdn and no imp early st: no ex* **16/1**

10 *13* **Siren's Song (IRE)**[36] 3405 3-8-11 101.. ShaneFoley 12 65
(Mrs John Harrington, Ire) *trckd ldrs in 4th: rdn appr st: sn no ex: wknd* **7/1**[3]

11 *2 1/2* **Make My Heart Sing (IRE)**[45] 3065 3-8-11 90.. WJLee 11 61
(A P O'Brien, Ire) *prom: led bef 1/2-way: rdn and hdd appr st: sn wknd* **25/1**

2m 33.83s (-14.07)
WFA 3 from 4yo+ 12lb 11 Ran SP% **128.6**
CSF £33.24 TOTE £7.10: £1.40, £1.50, £4.40; DF 62.30.
Owner Mrs Fitri Hay **Bred** Ronchalon Racing Uk Ltd **Trained** Goolds Cross, Co Tipperary
■ Stewards' Enquiry : K J Manning two-day ban: careless riding (Aug 14-15)

FOCUS
The fifth looks a good marker and the winner was close to her 3yo best.

NOTEBOOK
Pink Symphony stayed on better than anything to score. Held up in mid-division, she just appeared to be possibly feeling the ground a little as she came widest of all in the straight, but she hung a little bit left when pressure was applied. When her rider managed to straighten her up inside the last she stayed on strongly. She'll be at least as effective over an extra couple of furlongs and is certainly a nice import. Winning trainer David Wachman said "She didn't really have to improve on her form with Paul Cole to win this. She'll step up in grade now over 1m 4f to 1m6f."
Haziyna(IRE) hasn't enjoyed a great deal of luck recently in this sort of contest. Also held up in mid-division, she appeared to have been brought with a very well-timed challenge inside the last furlong but the momentum which the winner built up was something she couldn't cope with. She does deserve a change of fortune. (op 10/3 tchd 7/2)
Amazing Beauty(IRE) is a filly who belongs in this sort of grade on her best form. She was never really close enough to lay down an effective challenge here but came home well and could be one to consider for a race like the Park Hill Stakes. (op 20/1)
Negotiate justified the decision to run her in this company. Held up just behind the pace, she quickened quite well to deliver her challenge a furlong out but she tended to drift to her right when coming under pressure inside the last. Her effort flattened out and in this sort of company she might just need to come with the one run.
Unity(IRE) helped to set the pace and appeared to be travelling well when kicking into the lead before the straight. She couldn't last it out. (op 10/1)
Spin(IRE) might have been a bit disappointing but all of her bad luck seemed to strike in this race. She almost came down coming out of the stalls and was then badly squeezed up inside the last furlong although she was struggling to make an impression at the time. (op 7/2)

4590 - 4595a & 4598a (Foreign Racing) - See Raceform Interactive

4569 DEAUVILLE (R-H)
Sunday, July 31

OFFICIAL GOING: Turf: good; fibresand: standard

4596a PRIX DE CABOURG - JOCKEY CLUB DE TURQUIE (GROUP 3) (2YO) (TURF) 6f
1:30 (12:00) 2-Y-0 **£34,482** (£13,793; £10,344; £6,896; £3,448)

RPR

1 **Dabirsim (FR)**[26] 2-8-11 0.. PhilippeSogorb 7 110
(C Ferland, France) *towards rr fr s: rdn 2 1/2f out: picked up wl u.p: r.o strly fnl f: tk ld 50yds out: comf* **9/2**[2]

2 *1* **B Fifty Two (IRE)**[16] 4055 2-8-11 0.. SebSanders 6 107
(J W Hills) *broke wl to r in 2nd: tk ld 2 1/2f out: swtchd to rail: r.o wl fnl f: hdd 50yds out: no ex cl home* **14/1**

3 *2 1/2* **Chica Loca (FR)**[64] 2-8-8 0.. MaximeGuyon 2 97
(M Figge, Germany) *towards rr: u.str.p 2f out: picked up 1f out: r.o wl to go 3rd cl home* **12/1**

4 *snk* **Ponte Vespucci (FR)**[25] 2-8-9 0 ow1.. ChristopheSoumillon 3 98
(Y De Nicolay, France) *racd in 3rd: rdn 2f out: nt qckn fnl f: styd on: lost 3rd cl home* **5/2**[1]

5 *1 1/2* **Ruby's Day**[46] 3033 2-8-8 0.. IoritzMendizabal 8 92
(E J O'Neill, France) *broke slowly: in rr on outside: hrd rdn 2f out: r.o fnl f: clst at fin* **5/1**[3]

6 *nk* **Hi Molly (FR)**[31] 3567 2-8-11 0.. ThierryJarnet 5 94
(D Guillemin, France) *broke wl to ld: set gd pce: hdd 2 1/2f out: rdn but nt qckn: fdd* **11/2**

7 *shd* **Bear Behind (IRE)**[7] 4375 2-8-11 0.. DavyBonilla 4 94
(Tom Dascombe) *racd in 4th on rail: rdn 2 1/2f out: no ex fnl 1 1/2f* **12/1**

69.12 secs (-1.88) **Going Correction** -0.45s/f (Firm) 7 Ran SP% **100.9**
Speed ratings: **94,92,89,89,87 86,86**
WIN (incl. 1 euro stake): 2.70. PLACES: 1.70, 4.80, 3.60. DF: 21.30. SF: 37.60.
Owner Simon Springer **Bred** Mme L Monfort **Trained** France

NOTEBOOK
Dabirsim(FR), stepping up in grade, was settled towards the back before picking up in good style and scored with a bit in hand. This was his trainer's first Group winner and his colt will return here for the Prix Morny later in the month.
B Fifty Two(IRE) looked to have a bit to do in this Group 3 after being held in the Coventry and a Listed race, took the lead soon after halfway and made the best of his way home. He stuck on well but the winner proved too strong.
Bear Behind(IRE) finished fourth in the Robert Papin but finished well held here and needs a drop in grade.

4597a PRIX ROTHSCHILD (GROUP 1) (F&M) (TURF) 1m (R)
2:40 (12:00) 3-Y-0+ **£147,775** (£59,120; £29,560; £14,767; £7,396)

RPR

1 **Goldikova (IRE)**[47] 3009 6-9-2 0.. OlivierPeslier 8 122+
(F Head, France) *settled in 2nd bhd pcemaker: shkn up to ld 1 1/2f out: qcknd clr 1f out: eased cl home: comf* **4/9**[1]

2 *snk* **Sahpresa (USA)**[23] 3822 6-9-2 0.. Christophe-PatriceLemaire 6 120+
(Rod Collet, France) *settled towards rr: shkn up 2f out: qcknd to go 2nd 1f out: r.o strly fnl f: threatened ldr fnl 50yds: a being hld* **5/1**[2]

3 *2* **Timepiece**[23] 3822 4-9-2 0.. TomQueally 1 115
(Sir Henry Cecil) *settled in 3rd: shkn up 1 1/2f out: wnt 2nd 1f out: r.o wl: lost 2nd 100yds out: styd on wl* **13/2**[3]

4 *4* **First City**[23] 3822 5-9-2 0.. ChristopheSoumillon 3 106
(David Simcock) *settled in midfield: rdn 2f out: nt qckn to go w ldrs: styd on wl fnl f* **28/1**

5 *nk* **One Clever Cat (IRE)**[15] 4120 5-9-2 0.. FlavienPrat 2 106
(T Clout, France) *settled in midfield: rdn 2f out: nt qckn to go w ldrs: styd on fnl f* **66/1**

6 *1 1/2* **Vanjura (GER)**[21] 3897 4-9-2 0.. APietsch 7 102
(R Dzubasz, Germany) *racd in 5th on outer: rdn 2f out: no ex: styd on fnl f* **20/1**

7 *1 1/2* **Nova Hawk**[44] 3106 3-8-8 0.. StephanePasquier 4 99
(Rod Collet, France) *a towards rr: no ex fr 2f out* **12/1**

8 *4* **Flash Dance (IRE)**[47] 3009 5-9-2 0.. MickaelBarzalona 5 89
(F Head, France) *wnt st to ld: stl in front over 2f out: rdn but no ex: hdd 1 1/2f out: grad fdd* **100/1**

1m 34.3s (-6.50) **Going Correction** -0.45s/f (Firm)
WFA 3 from 4yo+ 8lb 8 Ran SP% **117.6**
Speed ratings: **114,113,111,107,107 106,104,100**
WIN (incl. 1 euro stake): 1.40 (Goldikova couple with Flash Dance). PLACES: 1.10, 1.10, 1.10. DF: 2.80. SF: 3.60.
Owner Wertheimer & Frere **Bred** Wertheimer Et Frere **Trained** France

NOTEBOOK
Goldikova(IRE) was bidding for her fourth successive win in the race and her 14th Group 1 success in total. She did not disappoint, tracking her pacemaker Flash Dance, who ensured a sensible gallop, and then producing too much pace for her rivals. The margin of victory was no reflection of her superiority, as Olivier Peslier took things rather easy in the last 50 metres, allowing the runner-up to close her down. The four successive wins in the same Group1 race is a record in France since the European Pattern was introduced in 1971, equalling the feat achieved by Yeats in the Ascot Gold Cup and Vinnie Roe in the Irish St Leger. Suggestions that her powers were waning seem to be premature after this, although she is likely to face a tougher task if returning here in a fortnight for the Prix Jacques Le Marois, when she will be taking on the colts.
Sahpresa(USA), who looked unsuited by the way the race was run when second to today's third in the Falmouth Stakes, appreciated the better gallop and was held up for a late run as usual. She was produced towards the stands' side as the winner made her effort towards the centre, but could make no impression, despite pulling away from the rest, until Peslier took his foot off the gas in the closing strides. She is sure to win more Group 1s if avoiding the great mare, and presumably her main target will be to win a third successive Sun Chariot in the autumn.
Timepiece, who was given a good tactical ride when beating today's runner-up in the Falmouth, was again ridden close to the pace, keeping the winner company behind the pacemaker. However, she could not go with Goldikova when that one made her effort and, despite keeping on, was outclassed by the principals.
First City has improved this season and achieved a personal best when third in the Falmouth. However, that still gave her a bit to do and she did not help herself by being keen early. She kept on for fourth, which is probably as much as could have been expected.
One Clever Cat(IRE) has been progressive and stays further than this, but was up against the best fillies around on her first try at this level and failed to make an impression.

Vanjura(GER) is a decent German-trained filly whose best effort was when touched off by Rio De La Plata in Italy last autumn. That form still gave her a lot to find with the winner, and she would have probably needed more testing ground to produce her best.
Nova Hawk\n\x\x , the only 3yo in the line-up, has put up her best efforts when the going was softer than this, and she was always at the rear here.

2345 MUNICH (L-H)

Sunday, July 31

OFFICIAL GOING: Turf: soft

4599a GROSSER DALLMAYR-PREIS - BAYERISCHES ZUCHTRENNEN (GROUP 1) (3YO+) (TURF) 1m 2f

4:05 (12:00) 3-Y-O+ **£78,448** (£31,034; £15,517; £8,620)

RPR

1 **Durban Thunder (GER)**[35] 3446 5-9-6 0 THellier 4 119
(T Mundry, Germany) *broke wl: sent to ld: set gd pce: led into st: r.o wl u.p: nvr seriously threatened* **99/10**

2 *1 ½* **Famous Name**[10] 4259 6-9-6 0 PJSmullen 1 118+
(D K Weld, Ire) *settled in 5th: patiently rdn: proged arnd fnl turn and sn rdn to chal but nvr threatened wnr* **4/5**[1]

3 *½* **Elle Shadow (IRE)**[38] 3334 4-9-3 0 AStarke 6 112+
(P Schiergen, Germany) *settled as bkmarker following Famous Name: r.o wl in st but no threat to first two* **11/5**[2]

4 *9* **Russian Tango (GER)**[35] 3446 4-9-6 0 EPedroza 2 97
(A Wohler, Germany) *broke wl: racd freely bhd ldr: r.o wl into st but no real threat to ldrs* **5/1**[3]

5 *5* **Impostor (GER)**[70] 2345 3-8-10 0 FilipMinarik 3 87
(W Figge, Germany) *racd in midfield: styd on in st but no real threat to ldrs* **105/10**

6 *2* **Innovator (GER)**[21] 4-9-6 0 ZSmida 5 83
(Zuzana Kubovicova, Salvador) *settled in midfield fr s then moved forward to r bhd ldr: sn spent force in st* **181/10**

2m 6.39s (-2.58)
WFA 3 from 4yo+ 10lb **6** Ran SP% **126.6**
WIN (incl. 10 euro stake): 109. PLACES: 24, 12. SF: 279.
Owner Stall Tinsdal **Bred** Frau M Sohl **Trained** Germany

4358 CARLISLE (R-H)

Monday, August 1

OFFICIAL GOING: Good to firm (firm in places; 8.5) changing to good after race 1 (6.25)

Wind: Almost nil Weather: Overcast, drizzling

4600 CFM RADIO H'CAP (PRO-AM LADY RIDERS' RACE) 5f 193y

6:25 (6:26) (Class 6) (0-60,60) 4-Y-O+ **£1,704** (£503; £251) **Stalls** Low

Form RPR

5303 **1** **Newbury Street**[21] 3902 4-9-13 **57** MrsFreyaBrewer(5) 3 69
(Patrick Holmes) *in tch: hdwy against far rail to ld over 1f out: drew clr fnl f* **14/1**

0046 **2** *3* **Rio's Girl**[5] 4443 4-10-4 **57** (p) JulieBurke 17 59
(Kevin Ryan) *chsd ldrs: effrt and ev ch over 1f out: kpt on fnl f: nt pce of wnr* **17/2**

6061 **3** *hd* **Simple Rhythm**[2] 4547 5-10-3 **56** 6ex KirstyMilczarek 1 50
(John Ryan) *in tch: rdn over 2f out: ev ch over 1f out: kpt on same pce ins fnl f* **9/2**[1]

050 **4** *½* **Red Scintilla**[21] 3903 4-10-4 **57** CathyGannon 5 57
(Nigel Tinkler) *stall opened fractionally early: led 1f: cl up: effrt and rdn over 2f out: kpt on fnl f* **7/1**[3]

0133 **5** *2 ½* **Weetentherty**[7] 4378 4-9-11 **50** (p) KellyHarrison 2 42
(Linda Perratt) *midfield: pushed along over 2f out: kpt on fnl f: no imp* **9/2**[1]

6320 **6** *hd* **Two Turtle Doves (IRE)**[29] 3662 5-10-7 **60** MissMMullineaux 8 52
(Michael Mullineaux) *prom: effrt and pushed along over 2f out: kpt on same pce over 1f out* **16/1**

0-60 **7** *shd* **Brisbane (IRE)**[80] 2047 4-9-3 **47** MissRobynGray(5) 4 38
(Dianne Sayer) *led after 1f: hung lft and hdd over 1f out: sn wknd* **20/1**

0-34 **8** *¾* **Ivestar (IRE)**[54] 2803 6-10-2 **60** (vt) MissCharlotteHolmes(5) 13 49
(Ben Haslam) *s.i.s: bhd tl hdwy over 1f out: kpt on fnl f: nvr able to chal* **20/1**

5332 **9** *½* **Sea Salt**[5] 4443 8-10-1 **59** MissVBarr(5) 9 46
(Ron Barr) *racd wd: w ldr: edgd lft over 2f out: wknd fnl f* **11/2**[2]

0035 **10** *1 ¾* **King Bertolini (IRE)**[2] 4542 4-9-8 **47** MrsCBartley 10 29
(Alan Berry) *bhd and sn pushed along: sme late hdwy: nvr on terms* **16/1**

06 **11** *hd* **Welcome Approach**[18] 3999 8-10-1 **54** SophieDoyle 12 35
(John Weymes) *towards rr: pushed along 1/2-way: sme late hdwy: nvr able to chal* **20/1**

0006 **12** *½* **Bahamian Kid**[59] 2670 6-9-9 **48** (v) AmyScott 7 27
(George Foster) *towards rr: pushed along on outside over 2f out: nvr able to chal* **25/1**

4010 **13** *1 ½* **Boga (IRE)**[2] 4564 4-9-7 **51** MissPhillipaTutty(5) 16 26
(Karen Tutty) *midfield: pushed along over 2f out: outpcd over 1f out* **25/1**

0053 **14** *shd* **Chardonnay Star (IRE)**[5] 4437 4-9-7 **46** (v) LucyAlexander 15 20
(Colin Teague) *midfield: drvn over 3f out: wknd fnl 2f* **25/1**

0450 **15** *1 ¾* **Craicattack (IRE)**[5] 4443 4-9-7 **46** oh1 MissLHorner 11 15
(Sharon Watt) *bhd: rdn on outside over 2f out: nvr on terms* **50/1**

-006 **16** *7* **Royal Premium**[2] 4564 5-9-2 **46** oh1 (v) MissNStead(5) 14 —
(Bruce Hellier) *racd wd in rr: no ch fr 1/2-way* **40/1**

1m 14.28s (0.58) **Going Correction** +0.10s/f (Good) **16** Ran SP% **123.4**
Speed ratings (Par 101): **100,96,95,95,91 91,91,90,89,87 87,86,84,84,81 72**
toteswingers: 1&2 £41.10, 1&3 £14.50, 2&3 £9.80. CSF £115.14 CT £660.60 TOTE £16.90: £3.40, £2.40, £1.50, £2.20; EX 177.30.
Owner Di Midwinter Foulrice Park Racing Ltd **Bred** R A Fahey **Trained** Brandsby, N. Yorks

FOCUS
Rail out 6m from home bend into home straight adding 12yds to races of 7f and beyond. The world's first lady riders only meeting with a wide range of ability and experience in the saddle. The track had dried right out and the going was on the quick side despite the light pre-race drizzle. It was changed to good after the first race. This was a low-grade opener and the runners fanned out right across the whole width of the track. The third looks the best guide to the level.

4601 BEADLE & HILL CLAIMING STKS (PRO-AM LADY RIDERS' RACE) 1m 1f 61y

6:55 (6:56) (Class 6) 3-Y-O+ **£1,704** (£503; £251) **Stalls** Low

Form RPR

0135 **1** **Opus Maximus (IRE)**[8] 4361 6-10-1 70 (p) SophieDoyle 9 64
(Jennie Candlish) *t.k.h: hld up and bhd: effrt whn hmpd 3f out: gd hdwy over 1f out: styd on to ld wl ins fnl f: kpt on* **3/1**[2]

3000 **2** *1 ¼* **Camerooney**[37] 3397 8-10-2 85 MissHBethell(5) 6 67
(Brian Ellison) *led: hrd rdn fr 2f out: hdd wl ins fnl f: one pce* **9/4**[1]

6553 **3** *shd* **Rub Of The Relic (IRE)**[6] 4408 6-9-10 51 (v) MissHDukes(5) 5 61
(Paul Midgley) *in tch: effrt and pushed along over 2f out: kpt on fnl f: no ex nr fin* **11/1**

0-05 **4** *¾* **Island Chief**[17] 4051 5-9-8 63 (p) MissJoannaMason(5) 12 57
(Michael Easterby) *trckd ldrs: effrt and ev ch over 1f out: kpt on same pce ins fnl f* **40/1**

6020 **5** *2 ½* **Bell's Ocean (USA)**[2] 4549 4-9-8 50 KirstyMilczarek 2 47
(John Ryan) *hld up towards rr: hdwy 2f out: no ex last 75yds* **8/1**

0431 **6** *3 ½* **Lucayan Dancer**[6] 4408 11-9-8 51 MissJWalker(5) 15 44
(David Nicholls) *bhd tl hdwy over 1f out: kpt on fnl f: nvr able to chal* **11/2**[3]

606 **7** *2* **Lord Lansing (IRE)**[15] 4125 4-10-5 62 KellyHarrison 10 46
(Mrs K Burke) *hld up: hdwy over 2f out: no imp over 1f out* **14/1**

-002 **8** *3* **Saloon (USA)**[14] 4165 7-9-12 58 (p) MissAZetterholm(5) 8 37
(Jane Chapple-Hyam) *midfield: effrt over 2f out: sn hung lft: no ex fnl f* **16/1**

-406 **9** *4 ½* **Second Reef**[17] 4039 9-9-8 47 (p) MissHCuthbert(5) 3 23
(Thomas Cuthbert) *bhd tl hdwy over 1f out: nvr able to chal* **100/1**

0005 **10** *3 ½* **Charity Fair**[5] 4438 4-9-6 36 (v) MissVBarr(5) 13 14
(Ron Barr) *midfield: effrt 3f out: wknd fr 2f out* **100/1**

040- **11** *nk* **Penton Hook**[65] 5624 5-10-1 67 LucyAlexander 4 17
(Barry Murtagh) *w ldr: rdn over 3f out: wknd fr 2f out* **50/1**

0035 **12** *¾* **Spread Boy (IRE)**[7] 4383 4-10-2 46 CathyGannon 7 16
(Alan Berry) *in tch: rdn and wknd over 2f out: sddle slipped* **20/1**

/0-0 **13** *7* **Worth A King'S**[8] 4360 5-10-7 80 (b) MissECSayer 11 6
(Dianne Sayer) *bhd: pushed along after 4f: no ch fnl 4f* **25/1**

-05P **14** *22* **Weetfromthechaff**[39] 3317 6-9-10 47 (t) MissAngelaBarnes(5) 14 —
(Maurice Barnes) *in tch: bmpd after 2f: rdn over 4f out: wknd over 3f out* **33/1**

2m 0.28s (2.68) **Going Correction** +0.10s/f (Good) **14** Ran SP% **121.1**
Speed ratings (Par 101): **92,90,90,90,87 84,83,80,76,73 72,72,66,46**
toteswingers: 1&2 £2.90, 1&3 £7.30, 2&3 £6.80. CSF £9.60 TOTE £5.40: £2.00, £1.10, £2.70; EX 16.50.
Owner Alan Baxter **Bred** Mrs Anne Marie Burns **Trained** Basford Green, Staffs

■ Stewards' Enquiry : Miss H Bethell one-day ban: used whip with excessive frequency (Aug 22)
Miss Joanna Mason four-day ban: used whip with excessive frequency without giving gelding time to respond (Aug 22,29,Sep 20,29)

FOCUS
Plenty of dead wood in this claimer run at a sound pace. The third sets the level but also limits the form.

Spread Boy(IRE) Official explanation: jockey said saddle slipped

4602 LLOYD MINI H'CAP (PRO-AM LADY RIDERS' RACE) 2m 1f 52y

7:25 (7:25) (Class 6) (0-65,62) 4-Y-O+ **£1,617** (£481; £240; £120) **Stalls** Low

Form RPR

0-2 **1** **Soprano (GER)**[6] 3450 9-9-8 **49** MrsCBartley 6 62
(Jim Goldie) *hld up in midfield: stdy hdwy and prom after 6f: hdwy to ld over 2f out: clr over 1f out: styd on strly* **4/1**[1]

2544 **2** *7* **Bandanaman (IRE)**[30] 3622 5-10-3 **58** LucyAlexander 14 63
(Alan Swinbank) *t.k.h: hld up: hdwy and in tch after 6f: effrt and chsd wnr appr fnl f: r.o: no imp* **9/2**

1345 **3** *2 ½* **Spruzzo**[46] 3072 5-10-3 **58** KellyHarrison 17 60
(Chris Fairhurst) *pressed ldr: led over 3f out tl hdd over 2f out: kpt on same pce appr fnl f* **15/2**

1032 **4** *3 ½* **Heart Of Dubai (USA)**[18] 3754 6-9-11 **57** (p) MissRSmith(5) 5 55
(Micky Hammond) *t.k.h: prom: effrt and rdn over 2f out: edgd rt wl over 1f out: one pce* **6/1**[3]

0-31 **5** *shd* **Sendali (FR)**[25] 3754 7-10-7 **62** MissLHorner 3 60
(Chris Grant) *hld up: stdy hdwy after 7f: effrt over 2f out: edgd rt: kpt on same pce fnl f* **9/2**[2]

6/04 **6** *2 ¼* **Sergeant Pink (IRE)**[39] 3300 5-10-1 **61** MissNSayer(5) 15 56
(Dianne Sayer) *bhd tl rdn and hdwy fnl 2f: nvr rchd ldrs* **12/1**

3040 **7** *nk* **Rare Coincidence**[35] 3450 10-9-9 **50** CathyGannon 12 45
(Alan Berry) *led to over 3f out: rdn and outpcd fr 2f out* **9/1**

000/ **8** *5* **Knight Valliant**[89] 2752 8-9-2 **48** MissEButterworth(5) 13 37
(Barry Murtagh) *hld up on outside: hdwy 4f out: drifted lft and wknd fnl 2f* **20/1**

6/0- **9** *¾* **Clueless**[86] 4648 9-9-5 **51** MissElrving(5) 8 39
(Keith Dalgleish) *midfield: outpcd over 6f out: sme late hdwy: nvr on terms* **20/1**

010/ **10** *8* **Hoar Frost**[22] 7010 6-9-13 **59** MissGTutty(5) 11 37
(Karen Tutty) *midfield: outpcd over 4f out: sn btn* **33/1**

/0-0 **11** *3 ½* **Samizdat (FR)**[12] 3300 8-8-13 **45** MissRobynGray(5) 4 19
(Dianne Sayer) *t.k.h: trckd ldrs tl rdn and wknd fr 3f out* **66/1**

0/0- **12** *31* **Sharp And Chic**[36] 7413 4-9-4 **45** MissPernillaHermansson 9 —
(Richard Ford) *bhd: struggling 1/2-way: nvr on terms: t.o* **66/1**

0400 **U** **Valdan (IRE)**[24] 3828 7-10-3 **58** (tp) KirstyMilczarek 7 —
(Maurice Barnes) *stmbld: jinked lft and uns rdr s* **16/1**

3m 54.2s (1.20) **Going Correction** +0.10s/f (Good) **13** Ran SP% **121.4**
Speed ratings (Par 101): **101,97,96,94,94 93,93,91,90,87 85,70,—**
toteswingers: 1&2 £5.80, 1&3 £12.60, 2&3 £10.30. CSF £20.89 CT £132.71 TOTE £4.90: £1.70, £2.40, £2.70; EX 17.50.
Owner Johnnie Delta Racing **Bred** Gestut Hof Vesterberg **Trained** Uplawmoor, E Renfrews

■ Stewards' Enquiry : Miss Robyn Gray two-day ban: careless riding (Aug 22,27)

FOCUS
A low-grade stayers' handicap and the gallop was unrelenting. The form is rated around the placed horses.

Sendali(FR) Official explanation: jockey said gelding hung right-handed

4603 EDINBURGH WOOLLEN MILL STKS (PRO-AM LADY RIDERS' H'CAP) 7f 200y

7:55 (7:55) (Class 4) (0-85,85) 4-Y-0+ **£5,822** (£1,732; £865; £432) **Stalls** Low

Form RPR

0011 **1** **Hot Rod Mamma (IRE)**[16] 4111 4-9-2 **66** oh2 .... MissECSayer 8 81
(Dianne Sayer) *t.k.h: hld up: smooth hdwy over 2f out: effrt and swtchd lft over 1f out: qcknd to ld ins fnl f: readily* **5/1**[3]

1100 **2** 3 3/4 **Moody Tunes**[23] 3848 8-9-5 **74** .... MissALMurphy(5) 2 81
(Tom Dascombe) *chsd ldrs: effrt over 2f out: chsd wnr ins fnl f: r.o: no imp* **14/1**

3-10 **3** 3/4 **Fujin Dancer (FR)**[8] 4360 6-9-8 **77** .... MissHBethell(5) 1 82
(Brian Ellison) *hld up in midfield: stdy hdwy over 2f out: rdn over 1f out: kpt on same pce fnl f* **9/2**[2]

2042 **4** 1 1/2 **Sunnyside Tom (IRE)**[8] 4361 7-9-10 **79** .... LauraBarry(5) 4 81
(Richard Fahey) *led: rdn over 2f out: hdd over 1f out: kpt on same pce fnl f* **4/1**[1]

0000 **5** 1/2 **Tartan Gigha (IRE)**[39] 3315 6-10-5 **83** .... CathyGannon 11 83
(Mark Johnston) *in tch: rdn and outpcd 3f out: rallied over 1f out: kpt on fnl f: no imp* **7/1**

1143 **6** shd **Botham (USA)**[17] 4045 7-9-2 **66** oh3 .... MrsCBartley 7 66
(Jim Goldie) *hld up: hdwy on ins over 2f out: rdn and no imp over 1f out* **20/1**

0315 **7** 3 3/4 **Moheebb (IRE)**[19] 3987 7-10-7 **85** .... (b) KellyHarrison 9 77
(Ruth Carr) *sn pushed along in rr: no imp tl sme late hdwy: nvr on terms* **6/1**

1464 **8** 5 **Ra Junior (USA)**[13] 4170 5-9-2 **66** oh1 .... (p) MissWGibson 12 46
(Paul Midgley) *hld up towards rr: pushed along over 3f out: nvr on terms* **16/1**

232 **9** 1 **Just Five (IRE)**[34] 3486 5-9-8 **72** .... JulieBurke 10 50
(John Weymes) *hld up: rdn over 3f out: btn fnl 2f* **12/1**

00-2 **10** 1 1/2 **Motafarred (IRE)**[17] 4076 9-9-2 **66** oh1 .... AmyRyan 5 40
(Micky Hammond) *in tch: rdn over 3f out: wknd fr 2f out* **7/1**

4010 **11** 5 **Guilded Warrior**[9] 4310 8-9-11 **80** .... MissMBryant(5) 6 43
(Paddy Butler) *chsd ldrs on outside tl rdn and wknd fr 2f out* **25/1**

1m 41.84s (1.84) **Going Correction** +0.10s/f (Good) **11** Ran SP% **123.0**
Speed ratings (Par 105): **94,90,89,88,87 87,83,78,77,76 71**
toteswingers: 1&2 £14.30, 1&3 £6.20, 2&3 £9.30. CSF £76.54 CT £351.24 TOTE £5.20: £2.10, £5.80, £2.30; EX 121.20.
Owner A Slack **Bred** Philip Hore Jnr **Trained** Hackthorpe, Cumbria

FOCUS
A decent 66-85 handicap and the pace was strong. The form is best rated around the placed horses.

4604 ALEXANDRA BURKE LIVE TONIGHT H'CAP (PRO-AM LADY RIDERS' RACE) 6f 192y

8:25 (8:26) (Class 5) (0-70,70) 4-Y-0+ **£4,158** (£1,227; £614) **Stalls** Low

Form RPR

5113 **1** **Boy The Bell**[29] 3662 4-10-1 **67** .... MissHBethell(5) 6 76
(Brian Ellison) *chsd clr ldrs: rdn over 3f out: hdwy to ld ins fnl f: hld on wl* **6/1**[2]

0101 **2** 3/4 **Fortunate Bid (IRE)**[27] 3719 5-9-6 **58** .... (p) MissSLWatson(5) 2 65
(Linda Stubbs) *hld up in midfield: stdy hdwy to ld over 1f out: hdd ins fnl f: kpt on* **14/1**

2062 **3** hd **Silly Gilly (IRE)**[6] 4409 7-9-5 **57** .... MissVBarr(5) 8 63
(Ron Barr) *in tch: effrt over 2f out: kpt on ins fnl f* **6/1**[2]

601 **4** nk **Schoolboy Champ**[8] 4362 4-9-12 **59** 6ex .... (v) KirstyMilczarek 10 65
(Patrick Morris) *trckd ldrs: rdn over 2f out: kpt on: no ex wl ins fnl f* **7/1**[3]

2053 **5** nk **Hayek**[3] 4513 4-9-12 **64** .... (p) MissRRichardson(5) 12 69
(Tim Easterby) *hld up and bhd: hdwy on outside wl over 1f out: kpt on fnl f: no ex nr fin* **7/1**[3]

2051 **6** 3/4 **Muftarres (IRE)**[3] 4513 6-10-9 **70** 6ex .... (p) MissWGibson 11 73
(Paul Midgley) *hld up: rdn over 3f out: hdwy over 1f out: r.o fnl f* **15/2**

2013 **7** 1 1/4 **Come On Safari (IRE)**[5] 4444 4-10-7 **68** .... (b) CathyGannon 3 67
(Joseph Tuite) *hld up and bhd: rdn over 2f out: hdwy over 1f out: kpt on fnl f* **9/2**[1]

4000 **8** 1/2 **Bajan Pride**[13] 4183 7-8-12 **50** .... MissHDukes(5) 5 48
(Paul Midgley) *hld up in tch: effrt over 2f out: no imp over 1f out* **50/1**

0-05 **9** 3 1/4 **Paradise Spectre**[100] 1520 4-9-12 **59** .... KellyHarrison 9 48
(Mrs K Burke) *t.k.h: slt ld to over 1f out: wknd ins fnl f* **14/1**

0500 **10** hd **Verluga (IRE)**[6] 4408 4-9-1 **53** .... MissJGillam(5) 7 42
(Tim Easterby) *hld up: pushed along over 2f out: no imp fnl f* **16/1**

0020 **11** nk **Cawdor (IRE)**[23] 3856 5-10-4 **65** .... KristinStubbs 13 53
(Linda Stubbs) *hld up: rdn over 3f out: sme late hdwy: nvr on terms* **40/1**

6010 **12** 1 **Meydan Style (USA)**[27] 3720 5-8-13 **51** .... MissNStead(5) 1 36
(Bruce Hellier) *bhd: pushed along over 3f out: nvr on terms* **40/1**

2000 **13** 1 3/4 **Call Of Duty (IRE)**[16] 4109 6-10-6 **67** .... MissECSayer 4 48
(Dianne Sayer) *disp ld: rdn over 2f out: wknd over 1f out* **7/1**[3]

1m 30.41s (3.31) **Going Correction** +0.10s/f (Good) **13** Ran SP% **122.1**
Speed ratings (Par 103): **85,84,83,83,83 82,80,80,76,76 76,74,72**
toteswingers: 1&2 £22.50, 1&3 £6.70, 2&3 £23.80. CSF £88.33 CT £554.06 TOTE £9.60: £3.70, £3.90, £1.80; EX 114.10.
Owner L S Keys **Bred** D J P Turner **Trained** Norton, N Yorks

FOCUS
A modest 50-70 7f handicap and again they took no prisoners, the two clear pacesetters dropping right out in the end. The third is the best guide to the level.

4605 NEWS & STAR H'CAP (PRO-AM LADY RIDERS' RACE) 1m 3f 107y

8:55 (8:55) (Class 6) (0-60,60) 4-Y-0+ **£1,704** (£503; £251) **Stalls** High

Form RPR

5-00 **1** **Daytime Dreamer (IRE)**[12] 4198 7-10-1 **54** .... LucyAlexander 14 63
(Martin Todhunter) *hld up: c to stands' side over 3f out: effrt over 2f out: styd on wl u.p fnl f: led last stride* **25/1**

4345 **2** hd **Beneath**[24] 3811 4-10-5 **58** .... (b) AmyRyan 12 69+
(Kevin Ryan) *hld up in tch: c stands' side over 4f out: led over 2f out: drvn along fnl f: rdr tk things easy cl home: hdd post* **7/2**[2]

3033 **3** 3 3/4 **Talk Of Saafend (IRE)**[18] 3300 6-10-1 **54** .... MissECSayer 9 57
(Dianne Sayer) *missed break: t.k.h: hld up: hdwy in centre of crse over 2f out: chsd wnr over 1f out to ins fnl f: sn outpcd* **9/1**

5355 **4** 2 **Grethel (IRE)**[6] 4408 7-9-11 **50** .... CathyGannon 7 50
(Alan Berry) *bhd: rdn and c stands' side over 3f out: styd on fnl 2f: nrst fin* **13/2**[3]

-000 **5** 1 3/4 **Edas**[17] 4045 9-10-2 **60** .... MissHCuthbert(5) 6 57
(Thomas Cuthbert) *hld up: hdwy far side over 3f out: edgd rt and no ex over 1f out* **12/1**

5612 **6** 1 1/4 **Dane Cottage**[13] 4173 4-9-10 **54** .... MissHBethell(5) 1 49
(Brian Ellison) *prom: effrt far side over 2f out: one pce over 1f out* **5/2**[1]

000- **7** 1 3/4 **Shy Glance (USA)**[255] 7055 9-10-0 **53** .... (p) JulieBurke 3 45
(Iain Jardine) *hld up in midfield: hdwy stands' side over 3f out: rdn and no imp fnl 2f* **20/1**

0004 **8** 2 1/2 **Tropical Duke (IRE)**[6] 4408 5-9-5 **49** .... (p) MissVBarr(5) 2 37
(Ron Barr) *pressed ldr tl edgd lft and wknd over 1f out* **8/1**

260- **9** 1/2 **Winged Farasi**[49] 6114 7-9-5 **49** .... MissJFoster(5) 10 36
(Joanne Foster) *bhd: pushed along over 3f out: nvr rchd ldrs* **14/1**

6500 **10** 2 1/2 **Harare**[6] 4409 10-9-8 **52** .... (v) MissGTutty(5) 8 35
(Karen Tutty) *midfield: effrt over 4f out: outpcd over 2f out* **40/1**

0-60 **11** 1/2 **Cool Baranca (GER)**[18] 3129 5-10-0 **58** .... MissNSayer(5) 11 41
(Dianne Sayer) *dwlt: t.k.h and sn prom: effrt far side 3f out: wknd 2f out* **12/1**

0600 **12** 21 **Pilgrim Dancer (IRE)**[7] 4383 4-10-3 **56** .... (v) KirstyMilczarek 5 —
(Patrick Morris) *led to over 2f out: wknd over 1f out* **25/1**

000- **13** 11 **Lyrical Intent**[22] 6668 5-9-9 **53** .... (t) MissAngelaBarnes(5) 15 —
(Maurice Barnes) *bhd: rdn over 4f out: nvr on terms* **50/1**

646- **14** 3 3/4 **Middlemarch (IRE)**[396] 2761 11-10-3 **56** .... (p) MrsCBartley 13 —
(Jim Goldie) *midfield on outside: slipped bnd over 5f out: sn btn* **16/1**

2m 30.66s (7.56) **Going Correction** +0.10s/f (Good) **14** Ran SP% **130.0**
Speed ratings (Par 101): **76,75,73,71,70 69,68,66,66,64 63,48,40,37**
toteswingers: 1&2 £22.00, 1&3 £13.30, 2&3 £3.90. CSF £114.58 CT £903.91 TOTE £15.30: £3.50, £2.10, £3.40; EX 197.60.
Owner James Callow **Bred** Genesis Green Stud Ltd **Trained** Orton, Cumbria
■ Stewards' Enquiry : Amy Ryan 28-day ban: failed to ride out for first (Aug 15-Sep 11)

FOCUS
A low-grade extended 1m3f handicap. The rain had arrived and as in the previous five races on this unique evening the pace was very strong early in the fading light. The first four came to the stands' side and there was a controversial finish. The form is moderate.
Daytime Dreamer(IRE) Official explanation: trainer said, regarding apparent improvement in form, that the gelding was suited by the change in tactics of being held up.
Middlemarch(IRE) Official explanation: jockey said gelding slipped on bend turning out of back straight and never travelled thereafter
T/Plt: £171.20 to a £1 stake. Pool: £77,643.18. 331.04 winning tickets. T/Qpdt: £43.50 to a £1 stake. Pool: £4,997.47. 84.90 winning tickets. RY

4105 RIPON (R-H)

Monday, August 1

OFFICIAL GOING: Good (8.3)
Wind: Virtually nil Weather: Cloudy and warm

4606 E B F CHILDREN'S DAY MAIDEN STKS 6f

2:15 (2:16) (Class 5) 2-Y-O **£3,557** (£1,058; £529; £264) **Stalls** High

Form RPR

322 **1** **Mehdi (IRE)**[10] 4264 2-9-3 87 .... ShaneKelly 4 87+
(Brian Meehan) *qckly away: mde all: clr 1/2-way: unchal* **1/5**[1]

3 **2** 9 **Bapak Pintar**[21] 3899 2-9-3 0 .... PhillipMakin 6 60+
(Kevin Ryan) *chsd wnr: effrt over 2f out: sn rdn along and one pce* **11/2**[2]

4U6 **3** 1 1/4 **Margo Channing**[15] 4122 2-8-12 0 .... PJMcDonald 3 48
(Micky Hammond) *chsd ldng pair: pushed along 1/2-way: rdn over 2f out: kpt on same pce* **50/1**

4 1/2 **Indyend** 2-8-12 0 .... DuranFentiman 2 47
(Tim Easterby) *trckd ldrs: effrt 1/2-way: sn rdn along: green and one pce* **25/1**

5 12 **Alfred George** 2-9-3 0 .... RobertWinston 5 16
(Richard Whitaker) *sn rdn along in rr and v green: outpcd and bhd after 2f* **14/1**[3]

1m 12.56s (-0.44) **Going Correction** -0.275s/f (Firm) **5** Ran SP% **111.2**
Speed ratings (Par 94): **91,79,77,76,60**
toteswingers: 1&2 £2.20. CSF £1.86 TOTE £1.20: £1.10, £1.50.
Owner Iraj Parvizi **Bred** Douglas Taylor **Trained** Manton, Wilts

FOCUS
Rail on bend from back straight to home straight moved out 3m adding circa 7yds to distances on Round course. Despite a dry week the official going remained good, helped by 2mm of watering overnight. The jockeys reported the ground was on the fast side. A small field for this maiden. The winner hacked up but didn't need to improve much.

NOTEBOOK
Mehdi(IRE) set a good standard and was long odds-on. He jumped out and made the running and, clear 2f out, scored easily. This should serve as a good confidence-booster. (tchd 1-4 in a place)
Bapak Pintar, third at Ayr on his debut, chased the winner early but was a little keen and could not respond when his rival started to draw away. He did not appear that comfortable on the track and still looks immature, but can pick up a small maiden before long. (op 5-1)
Margo Channing, a moderate sort dropping in trip, ran her race and is probably the best guide to the level. (op 66-1)
Indyend showed a bit of ability on this debut despite looking as if the experience was needed. (op 33-1)
Alfred George, a half-brother to Cosmic Art, ran green and was always out the back. The rider reported that the bit slipped through the colt's mouth. Official explanation: jockey said bit slipped through colt's mouth (op 16-1 tchd 18-1)

4607 FOLLOW @RIPONRACES ON TWITTER (S) H'CAP 5f

2:45 (2:46) (Class 6) (0-65,54) 3-Y-O **£2,045** (£603; £302) **Stalls** High

Form RPR

0064 **1** **Melodize**[15] 4124 3-9-7 54 .... SilvestreDeSousa 2 62
(David O'Meara) *chsd ldrs: hdwy 2f out: sn rdn and edgd lft over 1f out: drvn to ld ins fnl f: kpt on* **9/4**[1]

2542 **2** 2 **Tancred Spirit**[13] 4172 3-9-0 47 .... (v) TonyHamilton 9 48
(Paul Midgley) *sn led: rdn along wl over 1f out: jnd and drvn ent fnl f: sn hdd and one pce* **4/1**[2]

060 **3** 2 1/4 **Brian Sprout**[14] 4146 3-9-3 53 .... DeclanCannon(3) 1 46
(John Weymes) *towards rr and pushed along 1/2-way: rdn and hdwy whn edgd lft over 1f out: drvn and styd on ins fnl f: tk 3rd on line* **9/1**

6244 **4** nse **Majestic Millie (IRE)**[13] 4172 3-8-7 45 .... ShaneBKelly(5) 7 38
(David O'Meara) *wnt rt s: chsd ldrs: rdn along 2f out: sn drvn and one pce: lost 3rd on line* **11/2**

6063 **5** 1 1/2 **Vintage Grape (IRE)**[18] 4017 3-9-0 47 .... (b) AndrewMullen 10 34
(Eric Alston) *cl up on inner: rdn along over 2f out: sn drvn and grad wknd* **5/1**[3]

6000 **6** 3 **Bellemere**[10] 4288 3-9-5 52 .... GrahamGibbons 8 29
(Michael Easterby) *chsd ldrs: rdn along over 2f out: drvn wl over 1f out and wknd* **9/1**

4060 **7** *11* **Hereselle (IRE)**[41] 3247 3-8-12 52................................ NoelGarbutt(7) 4 —
(Michael Chapman) *midfield: rdn and edgd rt 1/2-way: sn outpcd and bhd* **28/1**

00-0 **8** *10* **Key Impeller**[9] 4320 3-8-9 49.. JakePayne(7) 6 —
(Bill Turner) *sn rdn along in rr: outpcd and bhd fr 1/2-way* **50/1**

0060 **9** *10* **Ivy And Gold**[8] 4359 3-8-12 45...................................(b) StevieDonohoe 5 —
(Alan Berry) *s.i.s and sltly hmpd s: a in rr: t.o fr 1/2-way* **25/1**

59.02 secs (-1.68) **Going Correction** -0.275s/f (Firm) **9** Ran SP% **112.1**
Speed ratings (Par 98): **102,98,95,95,92 87,70,54,38**
toteswingers: 1&2 £2.50, 1&3 £4.70, 2&3 £5.90. CSF £10.51 CT £64.73 TOTE £3.30: £1.10, £1.70, £3.20; EX 12.60 Trifecta £148.00 Pool: £458.08 - 2.29 winning units..There was no bid for the winner.
Owner Mrs Lynne Lumley **Bred** Foursome Thoroughbreds **Trained** Nawton, N Yorks

FOCUS
A moderate but quite competitive selling handicap. They went off at a rate of knots and finished well strung out. The form is relatively weak and best rated around the first two.

4608 DESTINATION HARROGATE H'CAP — 1m 1f 170y
3:15 (3:15) (Class 4) (0-85,83) 3-Y-O+ **£4,095** (£1,225; £612; £306; £152) **Stalls** Low

Form RPR

2300 **1** **San Cassiano (IRE)**[10] 4267[2] 4-9-9 78................................ PhillipMakin 1 90
(Ruth Carr) *mde all: rdn along over 2f out: drvn ent fnl f and kpt on wl* **7/2**[1]

4106 **2** *2* **Kensei (IRE)**[31] 3585 4-9-9 78..................................... SilvestreDeSousa 3 86
(David O'Meara) *t.k.h early: trckd ldrs: hdwy to chse wnr 2f out: sn rdn and edgd rt: drvn ent fnl f: sn edgd rt and kpt on same pce* **4/1**[2]

0213 **3** *2* **Rio's Rosanna (IRE)**[51] 2906 4-9-7 76....................... RussKennemore 6 80
(Richard Whitaker) *hld up in rr: hdwy on outer 3f out: rdn to chal wl over 1f out: sn drvn and edgd rt ent fnl f: one pce* **4/1**[2]

4301 **4** *5* **Jonny Lesters Hair (IRE)**[6] 4404 6-9-11 80 6ex.............. DavidNolan 2 74
(Tim Easterby) *trckd ldrs: chsd wnr after 2f: rdn along over 3f out: drvn over 2f out and sn wknd* **7/2**[1]

-200 **5** *11* **Oneofapear (IRE)**[54] 2814 5-10-0 83............................... PJMcDonald 5 54
(Alan Swinbank) *trckd ldrs on inner: effrt over 3f out: sn rdn along and wknd wl over 2f out* **9/2**[3]

-303 **6** *1* **Next Edition (IRE)**[21] 3904 3-9-0 78.................................... TomEaves 4 47
(Howard Johnson) *prom on outer: pushed along 1/2-way: rdn 4f out and sn wknd* **12/1**

2m 2.01s (-3.39) **Going Correction** -0.20s/f (Firm)
WFA 3 from 4yo+ 9lb **6** Ran SP% **110.3**
Speed ratings (Par 105): **105,103,101,97,89 88**
toteswingers: 1&2 £3.00, 1&3 £3.30, 2&3 £2.60. CSF £16.96 TOTE £5.00: £2.30, £2.80; EX 19.60.
Owner The Bottom Liners & Mrs R Carr **Bred** Peter Savill **Trained** Huby, N Yorks

FOCUS
A competitive handicap despite the size of the field but an all-the-way winner. The form looks straightforward rated around the principals.

4609 ARMSTRONG MEMORIAL H'CAP — 6f
3:45 (3:46) (Class 3) (0-95,95) 3-Y-O+ **£6,616** (£1,980; £990; £495; £246) **Stalls** High

Form RPR

1001 **1** **Pepper Lane**[15] 4126 4-9-5 88................................. SilvestreDeSousa 7 102+
(David O'Meara) *dwlt: sn in tch far side: hdwy 1/2-way: rdn to ld overall wl over 1f out: clr ins fnl f: edgd rt and kpt on: 1st of 8 in gp* **15/2**[3]

0000 **2** *2 1/4* **Gap Princess (IRE)**[37] 3383 7-8-11 80......................... GrahamGibbons 4 87
(Geoffrey Harker) *trckd ldrs far side: swtchd lft and effrt 2f out: rdn over 1f out: styd on to chse wnr ins fnl f: no imp towards fin: 2nd of 8 in gp* **25/1**

0560 **3** *1/2* **Midnight Martini**[9] 4346 4-9-5 88...................................(t) TomEaves 8 93
(Tim Easterby) *cl up far side: effrt and overall ldr over 2f out: sn rdn and hdd wl over 1f out: drvn and one pce fnl f: 3rd of 8 in gp* **12/1**

6024 **4** *3/4* **Mango Music**[2] 4541 8-8-7 79 oh1 ow3........................... LeeTopliss(3) 10 82
(Richard Fahey) *trckd ldrs stands' side: hdwy 2f out: rdn wl over 1f out: sn edgd rt: styd on wl fnl f: nrst fin: 1st of 8 in gp* **18/1**

6600 **5** *1/2* **Damika (IRE)**[9] 4325 8-9-5 88...................................... RobertWinston 5 89
(Richard Whitaker) *trckd ldrs far side: effrt over 2f out: sn rdn and ch tl drvn and one pce ent fnl f: 4th of 8 in gp* **8/1**

100 **6** *1* **Flowing Cape (IRE)**[27] [illegible] 85.................. PaulPickard(3) 11 83
(Reg Hollinshead) *led stands' side gp: rdn and ev ch over 2f out: drvn and edgd rt wl over 1f out: sn one pce: 2nd of 8 in gp* **25/1**

0010 **7** *nse* **Baldemar**[23] 3880 6-9-0 83... BarryMcHugh 12 81
(Richard Fahey) *cl up stands' side: effrt over 2f out: sn rdn and ev ch tl edgd rt and one pce appr fnl f: 3rd of 8 in gp* **14/1**

33-0 **8** *3/4* **Celtic Sultan (IRE)**[114] 1240 7-9-7 90............................. MickyFenton 6 85
(Tom Tate) *overall ldr far side: rdn along and hdd over 2f out: wknd over 1f out: 5th of 8 in gp* **50/1**

1503 **9** *3/4* **King Of Eden (IRE)**[24] 3796 5-9-4 87............................. TomQueally 13 80
(Eric Alston) *prom on stands' rail: rdn along over 2f out: grad wknd: 4th of 8 in gp* **9/1**

0200 **10** *1/2* **Everymanforhimself (IRE)**[2] 4531 7-9-5 88.................(b) PhillipMakin 2 79
(Kevin Ryan) *trckd ldrs far side: rdn along over 2f out: grad wknd: 6th of 8 in gp* **16/1**

0441 **11** *3/4* **Red Cape (FR)**[9] 4327 8-8-11 80.. PJMcDonald 3 69
(Ruth Carr) *dwlt: a towards rr far side: 7th of 8 in gp* **12/1**

5-02 **12** *nk* **Clockmaker (IRE)**[9] 4325 5-9-7 90................................ DuranFentiman 9 78
(Tim Easterby) *towards rr stands' side: effrt over 2f out: sn rdn and nvr a factor: 5th of 8 in gp* **11/1**

-044 **13** *3 1/4* **Oil Strike**[24] 3796 4-9-3 86.. PBBeggy 1 63
(Peter Winkworth) *towards rr far side: effrt and sme hdwy over 2f out: sn rdn and wknd: last of 8 in gp* **4/1**[1]

600- **14** *2* **Gallagher**[290] 6888 5-9-12 95.. AdrianNicholls 15 66
(David Nicholls) *dwlt: hdwy to trck ldrs stands' side 1/2-way: effrt and cl up 2f out: sn rdn and wknd qckly over 1f out: 6th of 8 in gp* **7/1**[2]

/00- **15** *9* **Whistledownwind**[436] 2311 6-9-1 87.................. MichaelO'Connell(3) 14 29
(David Nicholls) *a towards rr stands' side: 7th of 8 in gp* **50/1**

-500 **16** *nk* **Tamagin (USA)**[17] 4063 8-9-12 95............................(p) StevieDonohoe 16 36
(Lydia Pearce) *cl up stands' side: rdn along over 2f out: sn wknd: last of 8 in gp* **33/1**

1m 10.88s (-2.12) **Going Correction** -0.275s/f (Firm) **16** Ran SP% **121.5**
Speed ratings (Par 107): **103,100,99,98,97 96,96,95,94,93 92,92,87,85,73 72**
toteswingers: 1&2 £22.50, 1&3 £16.50, 2&3 £55.30. CSF £193.89 CT £2227.66 TOTE £5.40: £1.60, £4.20, £3.40, £4.10; EX 162.00 TRIFECTA Not won..
Owner Mrs Lynne Lumley & K Nicholson **Bred** Conor J C Parsons & Brian M Parsons **Trained** Nawton, N Yorks

FOCUS
A good, competitive sprint handicap where the draw played its part. The field split into two groups and those that raced on the far side filled the first three places. The form could rate a little higher with the winner improving on her Redcar success.

NOTEBOOK
Pepper Lane, who bolted up over C&D after a fast start on her seasonal return, had disappointed twice before bouncing back to form at Redcar. She was restless in the stalls this time though and missed the break, but was soon close to the pace on the far side and found plenty under pressure, drawing away in the closing stages. Connections might be looking at the Great St Wilfrid back here later in the month, but she will have to go up in the weights to make the cut. (op 6-1)
Gap Princess(IRE) won this race last season but had not scored since and was 2lb lower. She came through to chase the winner but was making no impression in the latter stages. (tchd 28-1)
Midnight Martini showed plenty of pace on the far side but could not maintain her effort, although she did keep on quite well. She has not won since her juvenile days but her consistency means she has only just started to be given leeway by the handicapper. (tchd 10-1)
Mango Music ◆ ran a great race from 1lb out of the handicap, especially as she raced in the stands'-side group until drifting across the track late on. She also completed a clean sweep for the four females in the race. (op 14-1)
Damika(IRE) won the Great St Wilfrid last season and showed his best form for a while on a surface faster than ideal. This should put him spot on for his attempt to complete the double next week, when easier ground will be an advantage. (op 9-1)
Flowing Cape(IRE) put up a creditable effort, leading up the stands' side before drifting and fading under pressure.
Baldemar has a good record on this track and ran well, especially as he raced more up the centre of the course than most. He is another who will appreciate some give in the ground. (op 12-1)
Oil Strike was always struggling to go the pace on the far side and eventually finished last of those to race there. His rider reported that the gelding was unsuited by the track. Official explanation: trainer's rep said, regarding running, that the gelding was unsuited by the track. (op 9-2 tchd 5-1)
Gallagher was well backed on this first start of the season for new connections but raced stands' side and faded in the last 2f. (op 12-1)

4610 AT THE RACES SKY 415 H'CAP — 5f
4:15 (4:15) (Class 4) (0-85,81) 3-Y-O **£4,204** (£1,251; £625; £312) **Stalls** High

Form RPR

0521 **1** **Lady Royale**[27] 3702 3-9-7 81.................................(b) SilvestreDeSousa 7 88
(Geoffrey Oldroyd) *trckd ldrs: hdwy 2f out and sn rdn: drvn to ld ins fnl f: kpt on* **9/2**[3]

3433 **2** *1* **Crimson Knot (IRE)**[10] 4295 3-8-13 76.......................... LeeTopliss(3) 5 79
(Alan Berry) *trckd ldrs: effrt wl over 1f out: rdn and n.m.r ent fnl f: kpt on* **7/2**[2]

0220 **3** *3/4* **Bay Of Fires (IRE)**[17] 4048 3-9-0 74............................. DanielTudhope 2 74
(David O'Meara) *cl up: chal 2f out: rdn to ld 1 1/2f out: drvn and edgd lft ent fnl f: sn hdd and one pce* **8/1**

225 **4** *nk* **Restless Bay (IRE)**[11] 4234 3-9-4 78...............................(v) ChrisCatlin 6 77
(Reg Hollinshead) *sn rdn along and outpcd in rr: bhd 1/2-way: hdwy wl over 1f out: styd on strly fnl f: nrst fin* **8/1**

0306 **5** *1 1/2* **Captain Kolo (IRE)**[10] 4295 3-8-10 70.......................... DuranFentiman 4 64
(Tim Easterby) *led: rdn along over 2f out: drvn and hdd 1 1/2f out: grad wknd* **8/1**

4122 **6** *3/4* **Eland Ally**[30] 3628 3-9-7 81... TomQueally 3 72
(Tom Tate) *trckd ldrs: effrt over 2f out: sn rdn and btn wl over 1f out* **13/8**[1]

58.98 secs (-1.72) **Going Correction** -0.275s/f (Firm) **6** Ran SP% **111.8**
Speed ratings (Par 102): **102,100,99,98,96 95**
toteswingers: 1&2 £2.70, 1&3 £4.20, 2&3 £5.00. CSF £20.23 TOTE £5.00: £2.70, £1.70; EX 17.20.
Owner R C Bond **Bred** Bond Thoroughbred Corporation **Trained** Brawby, N Yorks

FOCUS
A closely matched field in this 3-y-o sprint handicap and the early pace was good, but the pace collapsed and the time was only slightly faster than the juvenile seller. The form is rated around the placed horses.
Eland Ally Official explanation: jockey said gelding was unsuited by the track

4611 TOTEEXACTA MAIDEN STKS — 1m 4f 10y
4:45 (4:46) (Class 5) 3-Y-O+ **£2,264** (£673; £336; £168) **Stalls** Low

Form RPR

03 **1** **Cape Rising (IRE)**[18] 4014 4-9-9 0.................................... PJMcDonald 6 79
(Alan Swinbank) *mde all: rdn 3f out: drvn clr appr fnl f: styd on strly* **7/2**[3]

6 **2** *5* **Viva Diva**[17] 4072 3-8-12 0... ChrisCatlin 1 71
(David Lanigan) *trckd ldrs on inner: hdwy 3f out: swtchd lft and rdn to chse wnr over 1f out: sn drvn and one pce* **9/4**[1]

66 **3** *3 1/4* **Tourtiere**[17] [illegible] 3-9-3 0.......................... [illegible] 2 71
(George Moore) *hld up in tch: hdwy to trck ldrs 1/2-way: effrt wl over 2f out: rdn wl over 1f out: kpt on same pce fnl f* **20/1**

0-5 **4** *1 1/4* **Elfaaten (USA)**[74] 2231 3-9-3 0.................................... TadhgO'Shea 10 69
(Marcus Tregoning) *sn trcking wnr: rdn along over 3f out: drvn over 2f out: sn one pce* **11/2**

0 **5** *1 3/4* **Jacob McCandles**[27] 3705 4-9-9 0.................................. LMcNiff(5) 7 66
(David Barron) *s.i.s and in rr: hdwy on outer 3f out: sn rdn and kpt on fnl 2f: nvr nr ldrs* **50/1**

6 *3/4* **Millennium Star (IRE)** 3-8-12 0......................................[1] TomQueally 4 60+
(Sir Henry Cecil) *trckd ldrs: hdwy and cl up over 3f out: rdn along over 2f out: sn btn* **5/2**[2]

7 *19* **Colliers Castle (IRE)**[82] 5-9-6 0................................ RobertLButler(3) 8 29
(Lisa Williamson) *in tch on outer: effrt over 4f out: sn rdn along and wknd* **100/1**

0 **8** *1 3/4* **Afrikaans (IRE)**[27] 3705 3-9-3 0............................... SilvestreDeSousa 5 45
(Mark Johnston) *chsd ldrs: rdn along over 3f out: sn wknd* **11/1**

50 **9** *3/4* **Manager Mick (IRE)**[15] 4125 3-9-3 0.............................(v) PaddyAspell 9 30
(John Norton) *a towards rr* **200/1**

60 **10** *12* **Snare**[8] 4363 4-9-9 0... DavidNolan 3 —
(Ann Duffield) *midfield: rdn along bef 1/2-way: sn lost pl and bhd* **200/1**

2m 35.75s (-0.95) **Going Correction** -0.20s/f (Firm)
WFA 3 from 4yo+ 11lb **10** Ran SP% **114.0**
Speed ratings (Par 103): **95,91,89,88,87 87,74,73,72,64**
toteswingers: 1&2 £2.80, 1&3 £11.70, 2&3 £9.10. CSF £11.35 TOTE £4.70: £1.50, £1.50, £4.20; EX 11.80 Trifecta £184.80 Pool: £746.87 - 2.99 winning units..
Owner John Wills **Bred** J R Wills **Trained** Melsonby, N Yorks

FOCUS
A relatively inexperienced bunch in this older-horse maiden and mixed levels of ability on what they had shown to date. The form is rated at face value around the first two.
Afrikaans(IRE) Official explanation: jockey said colt had no more to give

4612 SIS LIVE H'CAP — 1m 4f 10y
5:15 (5:15) (Class 5) (0-70,68) 3-Y-O+ **£2,264** (£673; £336; £168) **Stalls** Low

Form RPR

1115 **1** **Fossgate**[13] 4173 10-9-9 66.. AmyRyan(3) 1 81
(James Bethell) *hld up towards rr: gd hdwy on outer wl over 3f out: led 2f out: rdn clr and edgd rt over 1f out: kpt on strly* **11/2**[1]

0454 **2** *6* **Hurlingham**[13] 4173 7-8-13 **53**................................(b) GrahamGibbons 13 58
(Michael Easterby) *trckd ldrs on inner: hdwy 3f out: rdn to chse wnr over 1f out: sn drvn and no imp* **11/2**[1]

-662 **3** *3/4* **Royal Bonsai**[16] 4111 3-8-7 **58**................................ PBBeggy 16 61
(John Quinn) *midfield: hdwy and in tch 1/2-way: rdn to chse ldrs 3f out: drvn 2f out: styd on same pce appr fnl f* **9/1**

0261 **4** *shd* **Grey Command (USA)**[6] 4407 6-9-4 **58** 6ex.............. RobertWinston 15 61
(Mel Brittain) *hld up towards rr: hdwy on inner 3f out: n.m.r 2f out: swtchd lft and rdn wl over 1f out: styd on ins fnl f: nrst fin* **7/1**[3]

4603 **5** *2 3/4* **Hathaway (IRE)**[16] 4112 4-8-8 **51**................................ RyanClark(3) 5 49
(Mark Brisbourne) *in tch: effrt and rdn along over 3f out: styd on fnl 2f: nrst fin* **14/1**

5253 **6** *shd* **King's Counsel (IRE)**[24] 3811 5-10-0 **68**..................(b) DanielTudhope 7 66
(David O'Meara) *led: rdn clr over 3f out: drvn and hdd 2f out: grad wknd* **6/1**[2]

0-64 **7** *3 1/4* **Agapanthus (GER)**[19] 2170 6-9-10 **64**.............................. TomQueally 6 57
(Barney Curley) *hld up and bhd: hdwy whn hung rt over 2f out: kpt on: nvr nr ldrs* **33/1**

5053 **8** *8* **Come And Go (UAE)**[14] 4148 5-9-0 **57**........................ PaulPickard(3) 3 37
(Ian McInnes) *nvr bttr than midfield* **20/1**

5505 **9** *1* **Pinsplitter (USA)**[20] 3951 4-8-9 **49**........................(p) SilvestreDeSousa 4 27
(Alan McCabe) *trckd ldrs: hdwy to chse ldrs 4f out: rdn along over 3f out: sn drvn and wknd* **16/1**

4466 **10** *4* **Rosbay (IRE)**[13] 4173 7-9-13 **67**..................................(p) PhillipMakin 11 39
(Tim Easterby) *midfield: hdwy and wd st: sn rdn along and wknd* **9/1**

0064 **11** *6* **So Bazaar (IRE)**[5] 4438 4-9-5 **59**...................................... PJMcDonald 8 21
(Alan Swinbank) *chsd ldrs: rdn along over 3f out: sn wknd* **16/1**

-060 **12** *8* **Cabal**[31] 3581 4-9-10 **64**.. DuranFentiman 14 14
(Andrew Crook) *a in rr* **100/1**

5640 **13** *1/2* **Quaestor (IRE)**[12] 4198 4-8-9 **49** oh4..............................(p) ChrisCatlin 10 —
(Andrew Crook) *chsd ldr: rdn along over 4f out: wknd over 3f out* **100/1**

2601 **14** *3/4* **Downtown Boy (IRE)**[17] 4044 3-8-2 **53**............................ AndrewMullen 2 —
(Tom Tate) *prom: rdn along 4f out: drvn 3f out and sn wknd* **8/1**

2m 34.47s (-2.23) **Going Correction** -0.20s/f (Firm)
WFA 3 from 4yo+ 11lb **14** Ran SP% **116.8**
Speed ratings (Par 103): **99,95,94,94,92 92,90,85,84,81 77,72,72,71**
toteswingers: 1&2 £7.50, 1&3 £11.70, 2&3 £13.80. CSF £32.83 CT £268.74 TOTE £5.70: £2.30, £3.30, £3.50; EX 45.00 Trifecta £393.90 Part won. Pool: £532.30 - 0.20 winning units..
Owner Mrs James Bethell **Bred** Mrs P A Clark **Trained** Middleham Moor, N Yorks

FOCUS
A big field for this modest handicap but the pace was good throughout, and the time was 1.28secs faster than the preceding maiden. The form is rated around those in the frame behind the winner and looks sound.
Rosbay(IRE) Official explanation: jockey said gelding had no more to give
T/Plt: £87.10 to a £1 stake. Pool: £70,564.11. 591.15 winning tickets. T/Qpdt: £50.20 to a £1 stake. Pool: £4,266.44. 62.80 winning tickets. JR

4384 WINDSOR (R-H)
Monday, August 1

OFFICIAL GOING: Good to firm (good in places; 8.0)
Wind: Light, across Weather: Sunny, very warm

4613 ROYAL BERKSHIRE ODDFELLOWS AMATEUR RIDERS' H'CAP 1m 3f 135y
6:10 (6:10) (Class 5) (0-75,72) 3-Y-0+ **£2,183** (£677; £338; £169) **Stalls** Centre

Form RPR

0530 **1** **On Khee**[24] 3815 4-10-5 **70**..................................(b[1]) MissNDumelow(7) 11 81
(Hughie Morrison) *dwlt: rcvrd to ld and racd freely: clr over 3f out: nudged along and unchal after* **3/1**[2]

4124 **2** *4 1/2* **Choral Festival**[25] 3771 5-10-6 **64**.............................. MissSBrotherton 9 68
(John Bridger) *hld up in midfield: prog over 3f out: chsd wnr over 2f out: rdn and no imp over 1f out* **11/4**[1]

2400 **3** *1 3/4* **Maslak (IRE)**[8] 4366 7-10-8 **66**..................................(b[1]) MrPCollington 7 67
(Peter Hiatt) *prom: chsd wnr 4f out to over 2f out: one pce u.p* **6/1**[3]

0656 **4** *nk* **Squad**[49] 3003 5-10-1 **64**..(v) MrJCoffill-Brown(5) 1 65
(Simon Dow) *s.s: hld up in last pair: lft bhd 4f out: prog 3f out: rdn to dispute 3rd over 1f out: one pce after* **16/1**

1-00 **5** *3 1/4* **Sula Two**[92] 1729 4-10-9 **72**.. MrPPrince(5) 8 67
(Ron Hodges) *hld up last: lft bhd 4f out: pushed along and effrt on wd outside 3f out: one pce fnl 2f* **12/1**

0610 **6** *1* **Bavarica**[51] 2932 9-10-10 **71**.. MrRBirkett(3) 10 65
(Julia Feilden) *s.s: hld up in tch: rdn over 3f out: sn outpcd and btn* **8/1**

610- **7** *4* **Ebony Boom (IRE)**[366] 4573 4-10-9 **72**............... MissHayleyMoore(5) 4 59
(Gary Moore) *prom: shkn up 4f out: wknd over 2f out* **8/1**

0000 **8** *1/2* **Golden Hinde**[37] 3399 3-9-11 **71**.................................. MrFMitchell(5) 3 58
(Ronald Harris) *in tch: lft bhd 4f out: rdn and no prog 3f out: no ch whn hung lft 1f out* **12/1**

55-0 **9** *12* **Sand Repeal (IRE)**[25] 3754 9-9-2 **53** oh4....................... MissSBirkett(7) 2 20
(Julia Feilden) *chsd wnr to 4f out: hung lft and wknd 3f out: t.o* **40/1**

2m 29.14s (-0.36) **Going Correction** -0.05s/f (Good)
WFA 3 from 4yo+ 11lb **9** Ran SP% **111.9**
Speed ratings (Par 103): **99,96,94,94,92 91,89,88,80**
toteswingers: 1&2 £2.10, 1&3 £5.40, 2&3 £2.70. CSF £11.14 CT £43.74 TOTE £4.30: £2.00, £1.10, £2.10; EX 12.50 Trifecta £54.10 Pool: £4,957.23 - 67.71 winning units..
Owner Mr & Mrs R Sweet & G Balding **Bred** Miss B Swire **Trained** East Ilsley, Berks

FOCUS
The stands' rail was dolled out 12yds at 6f and 6yds at the winning post. The top bend was dolled out 7yds, adding 29yds to races over 1m and more. The early pace was a steady one for this amateur riders' handicap and the runner-up sets the standard.

4614 BRITISH STALLION STUDS SUPPORTING BRITISH RACING E B F MAIDEN FILLIES' STKS 6f
6:40 (6:41) (Class 5) 2-Y-0 **£3,557** (£1,058; £529; £264) **Stalls** Low

Form RPR

3 **1** **Salford Art (IRE)**[14] 4155 2-9-0 0.................................. DaneO'Neill 2 78+
(David Elsworth) *chsd ldng pair: wnt 2nd jst over 2f out: sn rdn: styd on wl fnl f to ld last 50yds* **9/4**[1]

0 **2** *1/2* **Flamborough Breeze**[23] 3865 2-9-0 0.............................. JackMitchell 1 76
(Edward Vaughan) *led: hung lft fr over 2f out: kpt on u.p: hdd last 50yds* **16/1**

26 **3** *1/2* **Show Flower**[11] 4252 2-9-0 0.. HughBowman 13 74
(Mick Channon) *sweating: in tch in midfield: prog 2f out: rdn and cl enough on outer jst over 1f out: styd on: a hld* **15/2**

0 **4** *1/2* **Silke Top**[23] 3865 2-9-0 0.. SteveDrowne 10 73
(William Jarvis) *in tch in midfield: shuffled along over 2f out: prog over 1f out: reminders and styd on fnl f: nrst fin* **100/1**

5 *shd* **Perfect Step (IRE)** 2-9-0 0... NeilCallan 3 72
(Roger Varian) *s.i.s: rcvrd to chse ldrs disputing 5th: pushed along over 2f out: rn green but kpt on fr over 1f out* **7/1**[3]

6 *2 1/4* **Princess Of Orange** 2-9-0 0... TedDurcan 12 65+
(Rae Guest) *swtchd fr wd draw to nr side: settled in rr: pushed along over 2f out: kpt on steadily fr over 1f out: bttr for r* **7/1**[3]

7 *shd* **Chapellerie (IRE)** 2-9-0 0.. MartinDwyer 5 65
(Brian Meehan) *chsd ldr to jst over 2f out: steadily fdd over 1f out* **14/1**

05 **8** *3/4* **Jumeirah Palm Star**[18] 4002 2-8-11 0.......................... SeanLevey(3) 15 63+
(Richard Hannon) *settled in rr: shkn up over 2f out: kpt on fr over 1f out: nt disgracd* **28/1**

3 **9** *2 1/4* **Ligurian Sea**[32] 3547 2-9-0 0.. ShaneKelly 4 56
(Walter Swinburn) *prom: shkn up over 2f out in 4th: fdd over 1f out* **4/1**[2]

0 **10** *3/4* **Tea Cup**[109] 1337 2-9-0 0... RichardHughes 8 54
(Richard Hannon) *wl in tch: shkn up over 2f out: no prog over 1f out: wknd* **10/1**

11 *3/4* **Authora (IRE)** 2-8-11 0.. KieranO'Neill(3) 11 52
(Richard Hannon) *mostly in last trio: shkn up and no prog over 2f out* **100/1**

12 *2 1/4* **Silent Laughter** 2-9-0 0... JimCrowley 9 45
(Jonathan Portman) *hld up in last trio: effrt on wd outside 1/2-way: no prog 2f out: fdd* **100/1**

0 **13** *3 3/4* **Valiant Runner**[10] 4276 2-9-0 0.................................... HayleyTurner 14 34
(Jeremy Noseda) *dwlt and stdd s: rn green and hld up in last trio: nvr a factor* **20/1**

00 **14** *7* **Make Up**[33] 3520 2-9-0 0... PatDobbs 6 13
(Richard Hannon) *reminder in midfield after 1f: struggling on inner fr 1/2-way: t.o* **66/1**

1m 12.82s (-0.18) **Going Correction** -0.05s/f (Good) **14** Ran SP% **121.8**
Speed ratings (Par 91): **99,98,97,97,96 93,93,92,89,88 87,84,79,70**
toteswingers: 1&2 £15.40, 1&3 £2.90, 2&3 £28.80. CSF £42.01 TOTE £3.50: £1.70, £3.70, £2.50; EX 64.00 Trifecta £630.50 Pool: £1,883.22 - 2.21 winning units..
Owner A J Thompson & Matthew Green **Bred** Eimear Mulhern **Trained** Newmarket, Suffolk

FOCUS
Few got into what looked an ordinary juvenile maiden, with the front two being up there throughout. It's hard to get excited about the bare form, but the winner can rate higher.

NOTEBOOK
Salford Art(IRE) had made a pleasing debut at the course two weeks earlier and improved enough on that to take this in workmanlike fashion, getting up late. The way she races suggests further will suit and it's probable there's more to come, although whether she's up to fulfilling her Group 1 entries remains to be seen. Nurseries are a more appealing option. (op 11-4 tchd 10-3)
Flamborough Breeze was afforded a soft lead and duly stepped up markedly on her debut effort. She may have won had she not run green under pressure early in the straight, hanging left, and she can come on again. (op 20-1)
Show Flower ran well considering she got warm, and a return to 7f/switch to nurseries ought to see her winning a small race. (op 9-1 tchd 7-1)
Silke Top, who had finished one place behind the runner-up on debut, stayed on nicely and looks a ready-made winner once upped to 7f. (op 66-1)
Perfect Step(IRE) ◆ is probably the one to take from the race. Her inexperience was evident on this racecourse debut, edging left under minimal pressure, and the way she saw it out, without being given anything like a hard time, was most encouraging. It'll be disappointing if she's not going close next time. (op 6-1 tchd 15-2)
Princess Of Orange, sold for 48,000gns as a 2-y-o, kept on late against the stands' rail and should improve. (op 8-1)
Chapellerie(IRE), a half-sister to the previous week's Goodwood winner Catfish, is entered in the Group1 Cheveley Park and showed some ability before fading. (op 16-1 tchd 12-1)

4615 WILL YOU MARRY ME EILEEN SPORTINGBET.COM H'CAP 5f 10y
7:10 (7:11) (Class 5) (0-70,70) 3-Y-0+ **£2,264** (£673; £336; £168) **Stalls** Low

Form RPR

2341 **1** **Rebecca Romero**[17] 4057 4-9-1 **61**.............................. RichardHughes 4 71+
(Denis Coakley) *w.w in 5th: effrt and squeezed though 1f out: rdn to ld last 75yds: hld on* **2/1**[1]

0461 **2** *hd* **Imaginary Diva**[20] 3939 5-8-3 **54**................................ RyanPowell(5) 3 61
(George Margarson) *hld up in 6th: plld off rail and prog 1f out: rdn to chal last 50yds: jst hld* **11/1**

0313 **3** *3/4* **Welsh Inlet (IRE)**[4] 4459 3-9-6 **69**.............................. NeilChalmers 2 72
(John Bridger) *chsd ldr: rdn to ld 1f out: hdd and outpcd last 75yds* **11/2**[2]

6022 **4** *1/2* **Even Bolder**[17] 4057 8-9-7 **70**...................................... KierenFox(3) 7 73
(Eric Wheeler) *chsd ldng pair: effrt over 1f out: rdn to chal jst ins fnl f: edgd lft and nt qckn* **15/2**

0014 **5** *nk* **Triple Dream**[10] 4272 6-9-10 **70**..................................(tp) LiamKeniry 1 71
(Milton Bradley) *chsd ldng pair: shkn up and nt qckn over 1f out: kpt on fnl f: nvr able to chal* **6/1**[3]

2564 **6** *2* **Catalinas Diamond (IRE)**[17] 4057 3-9-0 **63**................... RobertHavlin 5 56
(Pat Murphy) *hld up in 7th: effrt on outer over 1f out: no imp on ldrs fnl f* **12/1**

0255 **7** *nse* **Crew Cut (IRE)**[14] 4156 3-9-7 **70**................................ SteveDrowne 6 63
(Jeremy Gask) *hld up in last pair: reminder over 1f out: pushed along and kpt on fnl f: nvr nr ldrs* **8/1**

6000 **8** *1 3/4* **Cape Royal**[23] 3847 11-9-8 **68**....................................(bt) DaneO'Neill 8 56
(Milton Bradley) *led to over 1f out: wknd fnl f* **25/1**

6405 **9** *shd* **Brandywell Boy (IRE)**[36] 3427 8-9-0 **67**........................ LucyKBarry(7) 9 54
(Dominic Ffrench Davis) *a in last pair: rdn and no prog 2f out* **16/1**

59.57 secs (-0.73) **Going Correction** -0.05s/f (Good)
WFA 3 from 4yo+ 3lb **9** Ran SP% **111.6**
Speed ratings (Par 103): **103,102,101,100,100 97,96,94,93**
toteswingers: 1&2 £4.50, 1&3 £1.20, 2&3 £8.50. CSF £24.30 CT £101.83 TOTE £2.40: £1.10, £2.90, £1.90; EX 12.60 Trifecta £55.00 Pool: £5,546.68 - 74.51 winning units..
Owner Keepers Racing Ii **Bred** D W Armstrong **Trained** West Ilsley, Berks

FOCUS
A modest sprint handicap. There was plenty of pace on early, thanks to veteran Cape Royal, and the race suited those coming from behind. The form is modest rated around the placed horses.

4616 SPORTINGBET.COM H'CAP 1m 67y
7:40 (7:40) (Class 4) (0-85,85) 3-Y-0+ **£3,557** (£1,058; £529; £264) **Stalls** Low

Form RPR

2006 **1** **Uncle Fred**[19] 3987 6-9-1 **77**.. JimCrowley 2 84
(Patrick Chamings) *hld up in 5th: rdn and effrt 2f out: clsd fnl f: drvn ahd last 75yds* **7/1**

0-15 **2** *3/4* **Pat's Legacy (USA)**[24] 3802 5-8-9 **78**........................ JoshBaudains(7) 5 83
(Jo Hughes) *plld hrd early: chsd ldr 3f: styd prom: rdn to chal over 1f out: led briefly ins fnl f: nt qckn nr fin* **5/1**[3]

0000 **3** ¾ **Elna Bright**[24] 3796 6-9-6 **82**.................................... KierenFallon 8 86
(Brett Johnson) *led: drvn 2f out: hdd ins fnl f: one pce* **9/2**[2]
3121 **4** *nse* **Jewelled**[36] 3436 5-9-0 **76**.................................... SebSanders 4 82+
(Lady Herries) *hld up last: pushed along and stl there 2f out: slng to run on whn nt clr run ins fnl f: styd on: nrst fin* **15/8**[1]
5-00 **5** *hd* **Mahadee (IRE)**[24] 3802 6-9-9 **85**..................................(b) PatCosgrave 9 88
(Ed de Giles) *prom: rdn on wd outside over 2f out: chal over 1f out: nt qckn ins fnl f* **25/1**
3-05 **6** *1* **Spectait**[17] 4070 9-9-7 **83**.................................... GeorgeBaker 7 84
(Jonjo O'Neill) *blindfold late off and missed break: in tch: pushed along over 3f out: no imp on ldrs fnl 2f but kpt on* **12/1**
4000 **7** *shd* **Santefisio**[49] 2995 5-9-4 **80**.................................... SteveDrowne 1 80
(Peter Makin) *hld up in last trio: pushed along 2f out: no ch whn reminder ins fnl f: styd on* **11/2**
5-05 **8** *1* **Hurricane Spirit (IRE)**[19] 3982 7-9-6 **82**.......................... DaneO'Neill 3 80
(Terry Clement) *sn prom: wnt 2nd 5f out: rdn over 2f out: hd high and nt qckn over 1f out: sn lost pl and btn* **20/1**
1m 45.16s (0.46) **Going Correction** -0.05s/f (Good) **8** Ran SP% **113.8**
Speed ratings (Par 105): **95,94,93,93,93 92,92,91**
toteswingers: 1&2 £7.20, 1&3 £8.30, 2&3 £4.10. CSF £41.31 CT £176.85 TOTE £7.90: £1.70, £1.80, £1.90; EX 45.70 Trifecta £385.90 Part won. Pool: £521.51 - 0.40 winning units..
Owner Inhurst Players **Bred** Netherfield House Stud **Trained** Baughurst, Hants

FOCUS
Just a fair handicap and the form is a bit muddling, so a cautious approach has been taken, with the runner-up to his Chepstow form.

4617 DJB CLEANING LTD MAIDEN STKS 1m 2f 7y
8:10 (8:10) (Class 5) 3-4-Y-0 **£2,264** (£673; £336; £168) **Stalls** Centre

Form RPR
322 **1** **Polperro (USA)**[18] 4023 3-9-3 83..............................(p) SaleemGolam 2 91
(John Gosden) *sn led and set decent pce: breather 1/2-way: kicked on again over 3f out: in command over 1f out: rdn out* **2/1**[2]
64 **2** 2 ¼ **Ashiri (IRE)**[14] 4157 3-9-0 0.................................... LouisBeuzelin(3) 3 86
(Sir Michael Stoute) *prom: chsd wnr 1/2-way: rdn and trying to chal whn rdr dropped whip 2f out: styd on but readily hld after* **13/2**[3]
3 *9* **Haman (CAN)** 3-9-3 0.................................... AhmedAjtebi 4 68+
(Mahmood Al Zarooni) *dwlt: hld up in last trio: taken to outer and pushed along over 3f out: styd on to take modest 3rd fnl f* **12/1**
0 **4** *3* **Palazzo Bianco**[10] 4279 3-9-3 0.................................... RobertHavlin 9 62+
(John Gosden) *hld up last: no prog over 3f out and wl off the pce: stl only 8th jst over 1f out: styd on in taking style fnl f* **33/1**
00 **5** *hd* **Miracle Play (IRE)**[7] 4388 3-8-12 0.................................... JamesDoyle 10 57
(David Evans) *in tch towards rr: shkn up over 3f out: sn lft bhd: plugged on fnl 2f* **100/1**
5-20 **6** 1 ½ **General Synod**[79] 2100 3-9-3 83.................................... RichardHughes 6 59
(Richard Hannon) *prom: chsd wnr after 3f to 1/2-way: shkn up and nt qckn in 3rd over 3f out: wl btn sn after: lost pls fnl f* **5/4**[1]
40 **7** *1* **Fairling**[14] 4157 3-8-12 0.................................... SteveDrowne 8 52
(Hughie Morrison) *hld up in midfield: rdn over 3f out: sn lft bhd and btn* **100/1**
6- **8** *6* **Queen's Silk**[374] 4317 3-8-12 0.................................... KierenFallon 1 40
(Brett Johnson) *t.k.h: trckd wnr 3f: wknd jst over 2f out: eased* **14/1**
9 *4* **Broken Eagle (USA)** 3-9-3 0..................................(b[1]) GeorgeBaker 5 37
(Mikael Magnusson) *chsd ldrs in 5th: wknd qckly wl over 2f out* **20/1**
00- **10** *3* **Tiger's Pride**[293] 6831 3-9-3 0.................................... JamesMillman 11 31
(Rod Millman) *a in rr: wknd over 3f out* **66/1**
2m 6.38s (-2.32) **Going Correction** -0.05s/f (Good) **10** Ran SP% **116.6**
Speed ratings (Par 103): **107,105,98,95,95 94,93,88,85,83**
toteswingers: 1&2 £2.80, 1&3 £5.30, 2&3 £7.90. CSF £14.94 TOTE £2.80: £1.40, £1.50, £3.00; EX 16.30 Trifecta £73.40 Pool: £523.03 - 5.27 winning units..
Owner H R H Princess Haya Of Jordan **Bred** Colts Neck Stables Llc **Trained** Newmarket, Suffolk

FOCUS
An uncompetitive maiden, but one that should provide its share of winners. The winner is the best guide and the form appears sound.
Miracle Play(IRE) Official explanation: trainer's rep said filly had a breathing problem
General Synod Official explanation: jockey said colt had no more to give

4618 PREMIER LEAGUE 20 SEASONS H'CAP 6f
8:40 (8:42) (Class 5) (0-75,75) 3-Y-O+ **£2,264** (£673; £336; £168) **Stalls** Low

Form RPR
2161 **1** **Efistorm**[11] 4246 10-9-7 **70**.................................... HayleyTurner 1 76+
(Conor Dore) *sn hld up in last trio: effrt and nt clr run on inner over 1f out: gap appeared fnl f: r.o wl last 150yds to ld fnl strides* **3/1**[2]
1504 **2** *nk* **Silver Turn**[26] 3731 3-9-2 **69**.................................... TonyCulhane 7 73
(Jeremy Gask) *stdd s: hld up in last trio: prog 2f out: chal fnl f: jst led 50yds out: hdd fnl strides* **20/1**
3000 **3** *nse* **Memphis Man**[13] 4187 8-8-3 **57**.................................... MatthewCosham(5) 2 62
(David Evans) *settled in rr: effrt on wd outside over 1f out: r.o ins fnl f: jst hld* **12/1**
0400 **4** ½ **Silver Wind**[9] 4349 6-9-10 **73**..................................(b) ShaneKelly 5 76
(Alan McCabe) *chsd ldr 2f: styd prom: drvn over 1f out: styd on to chal last 100yds: outpcd* **8/1**
2344 **5** *nk* **Scarlet Rocks (IRE)**[11] 4231 3-9-6 **73**.................................... JamesDoyle 9 74
(David Evans) *chsd ldr after 2f: rdn to ld over 1f out: swamped last 50yds* **14/1**
0662 **6** 1 ¾ **Silenzio**[11] 4243 3-9-2 **69**.................................... RichardHughes 4 72+
(Richard Hannon) *trckd ldrs: nt clr run more than once over 1f out: trying again but no ch whn nowhere to go last 75yds* **5/2**[1]
1004 **7** *nk* **Kyllachy Storm**[18] 3995 7-9-3 **66**.................................... GeorgeBaker 3 62
(Ron Hodges) *sn hld up in rr: effrt on outer 2f out: no prog 1f out: fdd* **9/1**
0030 **8** ½ **Sermons Mount (USA)**[48] 3020 5-9-4 **67**.................................... DaneO'Neill 8 61
(Peter Hedger) *trckd ldrs: rdn over 1f out: cl enough ent fnl f: fdd* **12/1**
155/ **9** *5* **Miss Chamanda (IRE)**[688] 5856 5-9-9 **75**.............. RichardEvans(3) 10 53
(David Evans) *led to over 1f out: wknd qckly fnl f* **13/2**[3]
1m 12.61s (-0.39) **Going Correction** -0.05s/f (Good)
WFA 3 from 4yo+ 4lb **9** Ran SP% **114.8**
Speed ratings (Par 103): **100,99,99,98,98 96,95,95,88**
toteswingers: 1&2 £13.70, 1&3 £10.20, 2&3 £66.90. CSF £59.71 CT £635.54 TOTE £3.20: £1.60, £9.10, £3.10; EX 63.00 Trifecta £209.10 Pool: £907.29 - 3.21 winning units..
Owner Sean J Murphy **Bred** E Duggan And D Churchman **Trained** Cowbit, Lincs

FOCUS
A competitive sprint handicap but the level of the form is a bit fluid.
Silenzio Official explanation: jockey said colt was denied a clear run
T/Jkpt: £3,550.00 to a £1 stake. Pool: £10,000.00. 2.00 winning tickets. T/Plt: £65.30 to a £1 stake. Pool: £107,507.94. 1,200.67 winning tickets. T/Qpdt: £28.60 to a £1 stake. Pool: £7,679.97. 198.30 winning tickets. JN

4619 - 4623a (Foreign Racing) - See Raceform Interactive

CLAIREFONTAINE (R-H)
Monday, August 1

OFFICIAL GOING: Turf: very soft

4624a PRIX DEAUVILLE AIME LE CHEVAL (PRIX MATAHAWK) (MAIDEN) (2YO COLTS & GELDINGS) (TURF) 7f
1:50 (12:00) 2-Y-O **£10,344** (£4,137; £3,103; £2,068; £1,034)

RPR
1 **Camarade (FR)**[20] 2-9-2 0.................................... ChristopheSoumillon 8 83
(J-C Rouget, France) **6/5**[1]
2 *shd* **Sysmo (FR)** 2-9-2 0.................................... OlivierPeslier 2 83
(J-M Beguigne, France) **68/10**
3 1 ½ **Kelkene (FR)** 2-9-2 0.................................... MaximeGuyon 10 79
(C Diard, France) **17/1**
4 *2* **Louvigny (FR)** 2-9-2 0.................................... Christophe-PatriceLemaire 6 74
(C Lerner, France) **4/1**[2]
5 *nse* **Daliance (IRE)** 2-9-2 0.................................... RichardKingscote 7 74
(Tom Dascombe) *racd in midfield: u.p 2f out as field swung over to stands' rail: short of room ent fnl f: styd on* **13/1**
6 *1* **Sisyphe (FR)** 2-9-2 0.................................... ThierryThulliez 1 72
(P Demercastel, France) **22/1**
7 *3* **Around The Moon (IRE)**[21] 2-8-10 0.................................... EddyHardouin(6) 4 64
(Robert Collet, France) **6/1**[3]
8 *5* **Catchword (FR)** 2-9-2 0.................................... YannickLetondeur 3 52
(M Mace, France) **97/1**
9 *3* **Majestic Art**[17] 2-9-2 0.................................... SylvainRuis 5 44
(F Sanchez, France) **50/1**
10 *2* **Category Five (IRE)** 2-9-2 0.................................... MickaelBarzalona 9 39
(A Klimscha Jr, Hungary) **20/1**
1m 29.5s (89.50) **10** Ran SP% **117.4**
WIN (incl. 1 euro stake): 2.20. places: 1.30, 1.90, 3.00. DF: 6.50. SF: 12.30.
Owner Haras D'Etreham **Bred** Haras D'Etreham **Trained** Pau, France

NOTEBOOK
Daliance(IRE), who cost 120,000euros, is a half-brother to Samsa, a triple 7f-1m winner at 2-3 in France, Lasting Applause, a 1m4f winner at 3 and dual 1m2f winner Honorable Love. He showed promise on this debut despite not getting a clear run in the closing stages.

4485 BATH (L-H)
Tuesday, August 2

OFFICIAL GOING: Firm (9.1)
Wind: Virtually nil Weather: Sunny spells

4625 GET MOBILE AT BET365.COM APPRENTICE H'CAP 1m 3f 144y
2:15 (2:15) (Class 5) (0-75,79) 3-Y-O **£2,264** (£673; £336) **Stalls** Low

Form RPR
0002 **1** **Tegan (IRE)**[27] 3726 3-8-5 **55** oh4.................................... CharlesBishop 2 68
(Richard Hannon) *racd in 3rd tl hdwy on ins to trck ldr over 5f out: chal 4f out: slt ld 3f out: rdn over 2f out: styd on strly fr over 1f out and sn in command* **8/1**[3]
-061 **2** 2 ¾ **Mariners Lodge (USA)**[8] 4380 3-10-1 **79** 6ex.............. AntiocoMurgia 4 87
(Mark Johnston) *led: jnd 4f out: narrowly hdd 3f out: rdn over 2f out: hung bdly lft u.p wl over 1f out and no imp on wnr: eased whn wl-hld clsng stages* **2/5**[1]
[illegible] **3** [illegible] **[illegible]**[22] 3010 [illegible] **74** .... LucyKBarry 3 76
(Clive Cox) *[illegible] wd into st over 3f out: sn rdn: btn over 2f out* **3/1**[2]
2m 29.06s (-1.54) **Going Correction** -0.125s/f (Firm) **3** Ran SP% **107.5**
Speed ratings (Par 100): **100,98,95**
CSF £12.32 TOTE £4.90; EX 10.60.
Owner Derek And Jean Clee **Bred** D D & Mrs J P Clee **Trained** East Everleigh, Wilts

FOCUS
A moderate apprentice handicap and although the early gallop was modest, the winning time was creditable, demonstrating just how quick the ground was. The form looks relatively weak despite a personal best from the winner.

4626 BET365.COM FILLIES' H'CAP 1m 5f 22y
2:45 (2:45) (Class 5) (0-70,70) 4-Y-O+ **£2,264** (£673; £336; £168) **Stalls** High

Form RPR
120P **1** **Gems**[21] 3946 4-8-7 **63**.................................... LucyKBarry(7) 2 69+
(Peter Hiatt) *trckd ldr: pushed along to ld 2f out: styd on wl thrght fnl f: readily* **8/1**[3]
1412 **2** ¾ **Dancing Primo**[15] 4164 5-8-7 **59**.................................... KieranO'Neill(3) 1 64
(Mark Brisbourne) *in rr but in tch: hdwy 4f out: rdn to take 3rd ins fnl 3f: styng on whn hung lft over 1f out: kpt on u.p fnl f to take 2nd cl home but no imp on wnr* **5/2**[1]
433 **3** ½ **Boa**[5] 4463 6-9-2 **65**.................................... ChrisCatlin 3 69
(Reg Hollinshead) *drvn to ld fr stalls and t.k.h: wd and awkward bnd ins fnl 5f: hdd 2f out: styd chsng wnr and hrd drvn fnl f: sn one pce: lost 2nd cl home* **7/2**[2]
6264 **4** ¾ **Now What**[10] 4341 4-8-13 **65**.................................... HarryBentley(3) 4 68
(Jonathan Portman) *in rr but in tch: hdwy on ins 3f out: rdn and outpcd 2f out: styd on again ins fnl f but nvr gng pce to rch wnr* **7/2**[2]
1043 **5** *7* **Laverre (IRE)**[18] 4074 4-9-7 **70**.................................... GeorgeBaker 6 62
(Lucy Wadham) *in rr but in tch: hdwy over 3f out: rdn and btn over 2f out* **7/2**[2]
330- **6** *44* **Joan D'Arc (IRE)**[246] 7626 4-8-13 **62**.................................... PatDobbs 5 —
(Noel Quinlan) *chsd ldrs in 3rd tl rdn over 4f out: wknd appr fnl 3f: eased whn no ch* **16/1**
2m 49.08s (-2.92) **Going Correction** -0.125s/f (Firm) **6** Ran SP% **112.2**
Speed ratings (Par 100): **103,102,102,101,97 70**
toteswingers:1&2:£4.70, 1&3:£9.80, 2&3:£2.70 CSF £28.24 TOTE £10.40: £4.30, £1.70; EX 29.40.
Owner R Robinson **Bred** Bishop Wilton Stud **Trained** Hook Norton, Oxon

FOCUS
An ordinary fillies' handicap in which the early pace was sound enough. The race is rated around the placed horses to form.

4627 BET365.COM H'CAP — 1m 2f 46y
3:15 (3:15) (Class 5) (0-70,69) 3-Y-O — £2,264 (£673; £336; £168) Stalls Low

Form — RPR

2423 1 **Watered Silk**[10] 4336 3-9-6 68 (b[1]) PatDobbs 2 — 84+
(Marcus Tregoning) *mde all: c clr fr 2f out: nvr off the bridle* **5/4**[1]

0611 2 11 **Highlife Dancer**[10] 4317 3-9-3 68 MartinHarley(3) 1 — 62
(Mick Channon) *disp 2nd tl dropped to 3rd over 6f out: rdn over 3f out and tk wl hld 2nd over 1f out* **15/8**[2]

0-20 3 2 ¼ **Frederick William**[15] 4154 3-9-7 69 (b[1]) FergusSweeney 3 — 59
(Peter Makin) *disp 2nd tl chsd wnr over 6f out: awkward bnd ins fnl 5f: drvn 3f out and no ch w wnr whn hung lft 2f out: hd high and hanging again whn lost mod 2nd over 1f out* **6/1**

6410 4 11 **Princess Gail**[11] 4284 3-8-2 53 KieranO'Neill(3) 4 — 21
(Mark Brisbourne) *awkward stalls: a in last: v awkward and wd bnd ins fnl 5f: sn lost tch fr 3f out* **11/2**[3]

2m 8.33s (-2.67) **Going Correction** -0.125s/f (Firm) — 4 Ran SP% **108.9**
Speed ratings (Par 100): **105,96,94,85**
CSF £3.90 TOTE £2.00; EX 3.90.
Owner Mr And Mrs A E Pakenham **Bred** Mr & Mrs A E Pakenham **Trained** Lambourn, Berks

FOCUS
A modest small-field handicap and form to treat with caution.

4628 BET365.COM /BRITISH STALLION STUDS EBF FILLIES' H'CAP — 5f 11y
3:45 (3:45) (Class 5) (0-75,73) 3-Y-O+ — £3,169 (£943; £471; £235) Stalls Centre

Form — RPR

-142 1 **Beauty Pageant (IRE)**[32] 3579 4-9-7 73 SeanLevey(3) 5 — 84
(Ed McMahon) *mde virtually all: rdn to assert over 1f out: styd on strly ins fnl f: readily* **1/1**[1]

4042 2 1 ¼ **Adventure Story**[32] 3597 4-9-2 65 FergusSweeney 3 — 71
(Peter Makin) *hld up in rr: hdwy on outside over 2f out: styng on whn hung lft ins fnl f: sn tk 2nd but continued to hang and no ch w wnr fnl 120yds* **13/2**

2552 3 3 ½ **Kinigi (IRE)**[12] 4231 5-9-2 68 (b) KieranO'Neill(3) 2 — 61
(Ronald Harris) *in rr tl hdwy to chse ldrs 1/2-way: chsd wnr ins fnl 2f but sn no imp: lost 2nd ins fnl f: wknd fnl 100yds* **11/2**[3]

035 4 4 **Festival Dance**[19] 3998 3-8-10 65 (t) MatthewDavies(3) 1 — 44
(Ron Hodges) *chsd ldrs: rdn 1/2-way and nvr gng pce to rch wnr: wknd fnl f* **33/1**

164 5 1 **The Jailer**[36] 3464 8-8-10 64 RyanPowell(5) 6 — 39
(John O'Shea) *broke wl: sn pushed along: chsd ldrs and rdn 2f out: wknd wl over 1f out* **11/1**

001 6 6 **Atlantic Cycle (IRE)**[14] 4174 4-9-7 70 LiamKeniry 7 — 24
(Milton Bradley) *sn chsng wnr: rdn 1/2-way: wknd qckly ins fnl 2f* **9/2**[2]

61.57 secs (-0.93) **Going Correction** -0.125s/f (Firm)
WFA 3 from 4yo+ 3lb — 6 Ran SP% **108.2**
Speed ratings (Par 100): **102,100,94,88,86 76**
toteswingers:1&2:£1.70, 1&3:£1.40, 2&3:£3.00 CSF £7.35 TOTE £1.80: £1.50, £2.70; EX 6.80.
Owner J C Fretwell **Bred** Mesnil, Mount Coote, New England Stud **Trained** Lichfield, Staffs

FOCUS
An ordinary fillies' sprint handicap, run at a solid pace. The form is rated around the placed horses to recent marks.
Atlantic Cycle(IRE) Official explanation: jockey said filly was unsuited by the firm ground

4629 BET365 MAIDEN AUCTION FILLIES' STKS — 5f 161y
4:15 (4:15) (Class 6) 2-Y-O — £1,681 (£500; £250; £125) Stalls Centre

Form — RPR

65 1 **Colourful Event (IRE)**[20] 3984 2-8-8 0 FrankieMcDonald 2 — 59+
(David Arbuthnot) *racd in 4th tl hdwy 3f out: chsd ldr ins fnl f: drvn to ld fnl 120yds: pushed out: comf* **13/8**[2]

4053 2 ½ **Nude (IRE)**[19] 3993 2-8-5 55 KieranO'Neill(3) 3 — 56
(Sylvester Kirk) *led tl hdd ins fnl 2f: sn hrd drvn: led again jst ins fnl f: hdd fnl 120yds: sn one pce* **6/4**[1]

6 3 ¾ **Lady Heartbeat**[11] 4269 2-8-1 0 RyanPowell(5) 1 — 54+
(Michael Blanshard) *trckd ldrs 1/2-way and nt clr run bhd horses ins fnl 2f: swtchd rt fnl 120yds and styd on cl home but nt rch ldrs* **3/1**[3]

50 4 5 **Lady Cresta (IRE)**[35] 3491 2-8-8 0 KirstyMilczarek 5 — 37
(Ronald Harris) *chsd ldrs: chal over 2f out: slt ld sn after: hdd jst ins fnl f: wknd fnl 120yds* **25/1**

1m 13.02s (1.82) **Going Correction** -0.125s/f (Firm) — 4 Ran SP% **106.9**
Speed ratings (Par 89): **82,81,80,73**
CSF £4.35 TOTE £3.10; EX 4.10.
Owner Eventmasters Racing **Bred** Tally-Ho Stud **Trained** Compton, Berks

FOCUS
A weak maiden and not a race to dwell on. Selling form in all but name.

NOTEBOOK
Colourful Event(IRE) showed ability in her first two starts despite looking green both times and, although she stayed on to take this modest race inside the last furlong, she gave the impression she was still learning the game. Having just beaten a 55-rated rival here suggests she should get a modest nursery mark, but she will probably need to step up again from this to be competitive at that level. (tchd 6-4)
Nude(IRE) set the standard with her third of seven behind a subsequent winner off 53 in a nursery over slightly shorter here last month, but that form was far from bombproof. She tried to make all the running, but may have been softened up by the close attentions of Lady Cresta for much of the way and couldn't match the winner in the run to the line. She looks exposed now. (op 13-8 tchd 7-4 and 11-8)
Lady Heartbeat was far too green to do herself justice on her Chepstow debut 11 days earlier and although she didn't see a lot of daylight here, she didn't find as much as had looked likely once in the clear. Her rider reported that the filly was denied a clear run. Official explanation: jockey said filly was denied a clear run (tchd 7-2)

4630 CASINO AT BET365 H'CAP — 2m 1f 34y
4:45 (4:45) (Class 6) (0-60,60) 4-Y-O+ — £2,264 (£673; £336; £168) Stalls Centre

Form — RPR

4515 1 **Lucky Diva**[19] 4024 4-8-4 50 (p) JakePayne(7) 2 — 57
(Bill Turner) *hld up in rr but in tch: hdwy 1/2-way: wnt 3rd over 6f out: drvn on ins to take slt ld over 2f out: styd on wl fnl f: r.o wl* **7/1**

3-45 2 ¾ **Viviani (IRE)**[20] 3978 4-9-7 60 PatDobbs 10 — 66
(Amanda Perrett) *drvn fr stalls: in rr but in tch: hdwy to chse ldr 10f out: drvn to chal ins fnl 3f: chsd wnr fnl 2f but no imp thrght fnl f* **15/8**[1]

0/23 3 3 ½ **Orbital Orchid**[16] 2873 6-9-3 56 ChrisCatlin 8 — 58
(Nick Williams) *chsd ldrs early: dropped in rr 7f out: rdn fr 4f out: styd on u.p fnl 2f to take wl hld 3rd fnl 30yds* **5/2**[2]

5-50 4 shd **The Composer**[32] 3599 9-8-7 46 oh1 LiamKeniry 6 — 48
(Michael Blanshard) *chsd ldrs: pushed along and dropped in rr 5f out: hdwy on outside 3f out and ev ch u.p 2f out: outpcd fnl f and lost wl hld 3rd fnl 30yds* **9/1**

1310 5 1 ½ **Annelko**[21] 3960 4-9-7 60 MartinLane 4 — 60
(Andrew Haynes) *led: t.k.h: early: hdd u.p over 2f out: wknd appr fnl f* **3/1**[3]

3m 49.14s (-2.76) **Going Correction** -0.125s/f (Firm) — 5 Ran SP% **110.9**
Speed ratings (Par 101): **101,100,99,98,98**
CSF £20.69 TOTE £6.70: £2.70, £1.90; EX 23.20.
Owner Darren Coombes **Bred** Gracelands Stud **Trained** Sigwells, Somerset

FOCUS
This race was decimated by non-runners with only half of those declared at the 48-hour stage going to post. The pace wasn't strong, so not the test of stamina it might have been. The form makes sense at face value, rated around the placed horses.

4631 POKER AT BET365 H'CAP — 5f 11y
5:15 (5:17) (Class 6) (0-65,71) 3-Y-O+ — £1,617 (£481; £240; £120) Stalls Centre

Form — RPR

3002 1 **Spic 'n Span**[4] 4487 6-8-9 50 (v[1]) KirstyMilczarek 1 — 58
(Ronald Harris) *mde all: drvn to assert over 1f out: styd on wl thrght fnl f: unchal* **15/8**[1]

4216 2 1 ½ **The Tatling (IRE)**[21] 3940 14-9-10 65 LiamKeniry 2 — 68
(Milton Bradley) *chsd ldrs: swtchd rt over 2f out: styd on fnl f to take 2nd fnl 100yds but no ch w wnr* **9/2**[3]

3030 3 1 **Bateleur**[12] 4224 7-9-0 58 MartinHarley(3) 6 — 57
(Mick Channon) *chsd wnr: rdn and no imp fr ins fnl 2f: one pce and lost 2nd fnl 100yds* **5/2**[2]

0030 4 hd **Ridgeway Sapphire**[12] 4224 4-8-0 46 oh1 (v) RyanPowell(5) 3 — 45
(Mark Usher) *s.i.s: in rr: hdwy on outside wl over 1f out: styd on ins fnl f to cl on 3rd but nvr any ch w wnr* **6/1**

0436 5 nk **Lady Excellentia (IRE)**[5] 4466 3-8-3 46 oh1 ow1 ChrisCatlin 4 — 44
(Ronald Harris) *in rr: hdwy 3f out: chsd ldrs 2f out: outpcd: styd on again clsng stages but nvr any threat* **15/2**

62.21 secs (-0.29) **Going Correction** -0.125s/f (Firm)
WFA 3 from 4yo+ 3lb — 5 Ran SP% **107.6**
Speed ratings (Par 101): **97,94,93,92,92**
Tote Super 7: Win: Not won. Place: £327.60 CSF £9.95 TOTE £3.10: £2.10, £2.30; EX 7.30.
Owner P Nurcombe **Bred** C A Cyzer **Trained** Earlswood, Monmouths

FOCUS
A weak sprint handicap with the winner rated to his turf best and the second to recent form.
Ridgeway Sapphire Official explanation: jockey said filly hung left-handed
T/Plt: £616.90 to a £1 stake. Pool:£69,009.46 - 81.65 winning tickets T/Qpdt: £25.40 to a £1 stake. Pool:£5,295.79 - 153.74 winning tickets ST

4192 CATTERICK (L-H)
Tuesday, August 2

OFFICIAL GOING: Good to firm (good in places) changing to good after race 3 (3:00)
Wind: fresh across Weather: overcast with showers

4632 BRITISH STALLION STUDS SUPPORTING BRITISH RACING EBF MAIDEN STKS — 7f
2:00 (2:00) (Class 5) 2-Y-O — £3,040 (£904; £452; £226) Stalls Low

Form — RPR

05 1 **Eraada**[15] 4140 2-8-12 0 SilvestreDeSousa 8 — 74+
(Mark Johnston) *w ldr: rdn over 2f out: led appr fnl f: kpt on* **5/1**[3]

2422 2 1 ¼ **Flambard House (IRE)**[22] 3899 2-9-0 74 DaleSwift(3) 6 — 74
(Howard Johnson) *trckd ldng pair: rdn over 2f out: kpt on: wnt 2nd fnl 75yds* **15/2**

3 3 1 ¼ **Code Cracker**[12] 4245 2-8-12 0 SebSanders 3 — 66
(Sir Mark Prescott Bt) *led narrowly: rdn whn hdd appr fnl f: no ex: lost 2nd fnl 75yds* **1/1**[1]

4 4 5 **Dorry K (IRE)**[32] 3583 2-8-12 0 LeeNewman 5 — 53
(David Barron) *in tch: rdn and outpcd over 3f out: kpt on fnl f: no threat ldng trio* **12/1**

00 5 11 **Catchy Tune (IRE)**[22] 3917 2-9-3 0 RichardMullen 2 — 29
(David Brown) *dwlt: sn outpcd in rr: n.d* **50/1**

56 6 1 ½ **Villa Reigns**[14] 4171 2-9-3 0 PhillipMakin 4 — 25
(John Weymes) *trckd ldng pair: rdn over 2f out: sn wknd* **125/1**

2222 7 ¾ **Joshua The First**[15] 4140 2-9-3 72 (v) PaulHanagan 7 — 23
(Keith Dalgleish) *sn pushed along towards rr: a bhd* **3/1**[2]

0 8 4 ½ **Landaho**[71] 2346 2-8-12 0 TomEaves 1 — 7
(Hugh McWilliams) *dwlt: a towards rr* **250/1**

1m 27.35s (0.35) **Going Correction** +0.075s/f (Good) — 8 Ran SP% **114.3**
Speed ratings (Par 94): **101,99,98,92,79 78,77,72**
toteswingers:1&2:£3.00, 1&3:£2.20, 2&3:£2.70 CSF £41.07 TOTE £6.20: £1.50, £1.20, £1.10; EX 36.10 Trifecta £65.40 Pool: £737.59 - 8.34 winning units..
Owner Hamdan Al Maktoum **Bred** Shadwell Estate Company Limited **Trained** Middleham Moor, N Yorks

FOCUS
They went a good pace in what was just a fair maiden. the winner did it in good style.

NOTEBOOK
Eraada ◆ didn't progress as expected from her debut when quite well backed at Ayr last time, finishing behind Joshua The First, but she was the subject of a positive jockey change on this occasion and trying a fast surface for the first time. Always going well in a handy position, she stayed on strongly to win with something to spare. This was an important success for her long-term future as a broodmare, being a close relative of Dubai World Cup winner Almutawakel and 1000 Guineas runner-up Muwakleh, but she has more to offer on the racecourse and the aim will presumably be to try and secure black type at some stage. (op 13-2 tchd 9-2)
Flambard House(IRE) was up in trip but still lacked the required speed. He ran on reasonably well in the closing stages and should be suited by a more demanding track. (tchd 8-1)
Code Cracker was strongly supported to build on her debut third at Folkestone, but she failed to see her race out. She set quite a quick pace, being pressured by the winner, but was in trouble early in the straight. It seems she needs a bit more time. (op 10-11 tchd 11-10 and 5-4 in places)
Dorry K(IRE), who showed ability over 6f on her debut, couldn't go the pace but kept on gradually. (op 16-1)
Catchy Tune(IRE) ◆ hadn't shown much on his first two starts, but he really impressed respected paddock watchers and shaped with promise. Having missed the break, he struggled for most of the way, but made some late progress to hint at ability. He still has a lot of learning to do, but can progress in nurseries/handicaps. (tchd 40-1)

Joshua The First came here following five consecutive second-place finishes and looked thoroughly awkward. Never going, he hung left in the straight and did not run on. He's one to avoid. Official explanation: jockey said colt never travelled (tchd 11-4)

4633 YORKSHIRE-OUTDOORS.CO.UK (S) STKS 1m 7f 177y
2:30 (2:30) (Class 6) 3-5-Y-O £1,704 (£503; £251) Stalls Low

Form RPR

5462 **1** **Dark Spirit (IRE)**[7] 4403 3-8-2 58 .... SilvestreDeSousa 5 72+
(Tim Pitt) *midfield: hdwy to go 2nd over 4f out: led on bit 2f out: sn clr: heavily eased fnl f* **5/4**[1]

51-3 **2** *12* **Rhyton (IRE)**[28] 3712 4-9-8 62 .... (b) PaulHanagan 6 64
(Donald McCain) *led: rdn whn hdd 2f out: sn no ch w wnr* **4/1**[2]

0024 **3** *12* **Drop The Hammer**[2] 3507 5-9-3 56 .... (b) DanielTudhope 4 46
(David O'Meara) *trckd ldr: rdn over 5f out: sn outpcd: poor 3rd fr over 3f out* **4/1**[2]

4010 **4** *5* **Valantino Oyster (IRE)**[30] 2804 4-9-11 64 .... (v) PatrickDonaghy(3) 7 47
(Ben Haslam) *hld up: pushed along and early reminders: plugged on into poor 4th over 1f out* **12/1**

0604 **5** *2 3/4* **Fimias (IRE)**[7] 4403 3-8-7 55 .... (p) RobertWinston 1 37
(Geoffrey Harker) *dwlt: hld up in tch: reminders over 6f out: sn struggling* **7/1**[3]

6254 **6** *5* **Frameit (IRE)**[7] 3281 4-10-0 59 .... (v) FrederikTylicki 2 37
(James Given) *trckd ldr: rdn over 5f out: sn wknd* **20/1**

0-00 **7** *34* **Diamond City (IRE)**[7] 4403 3-8-2 53 .... (bt[1]) NeilFarley(5) 3 —
(Deborah Sanderson) *hld up: pushed along over 7f out: sn wknd: eased* **100/1**

3m 33.31s (1.31) **Going Correction** +0.075s/f (Good)
WFA 3 from 4yo+ 15lb **7** Ran SP% **110.4**
Speed ratings (Par 101): **99,93,87,84,83 80,63**
toteswingers:1&2:£2.20, 1&3:£1.90, 2&3:£2.60 CSF £5.94 TOTE £2.30: £1.50, £1.90; EX 7.30.The winner was sold to Alison Thorpe for 12,500gns.

Owner Recycled Products Limited **Bred** Thomas G N Burrage **Trained** Newmarket, Suffolk

■ Stewards' Enquiry : Patrick Donaghy two-day ban: used whip with excessive frequency without giving gelding time to respond (Aug 16,20)

FOCUS
An uncompetitive seller and they finished strung out behind Dark Spirit, who showed herself better than this level. The runner-up looks the best guide to the level.

Fimias(IRE) Official explanation: jockey said gelding hung left throughout

Diamond City(IRE) Official explanation: jockey said gelding ran too free in first-time blinkers

4634 12TH AUGUST IS LADIES EVENING H'CAP 5f 212y
3:00 (3:01) (Class 5) (0-75,75) 3-Y-O+ £2,070 (£616; £307; £153) Stalls Low

Form RPR

200 **1** **Night Trade (IRE)**[11] 4291 4-9-5 **73** .... NeilFarley(5) 8 83
(Deborah Sanderson) *hld: rdn and hdwy on outer over 2f out: led over 1f out: kpt on* **5/1**[3]

5245 **2** *1 1/4* **North Central (USA)**[8] 4378 4-9-3 **66** .... (p) DanielTudhope 9 72
(Jim Goldie) *hld up: pushed along 3f out: hdwy on outer 2f out: chsd wnr over 1f out: sn edgd lft: kpt on* **7/2**[1]

060 **3** *2 1/2* **Welcome Approach**[1] 4600 8-8-7 **56** oh2 .... PJMcDonald 3 54
(John Weymes) *midfield: rdn over 2f out: hdwy over 1f out: wnt 3rd ins fnl f: kpt on* **33/1**

4056 **4** *nk* **Wigram's Turn (USA)**[4] 4513 6-8-7 **56** .... (t) GrahamGibbons 7 55
(Michael Easterby) *s.i.s: hld up: short of room over 1f out: swtchd rt 1f out: kpt on: wnt 4th towards fin* **6/1**

0300 **5** *1/2* **Indieslad**[48] 3052 3-9-8 **75** .... PaulHanagan 6 69
(Ann Duffield) *midfield: hdwy over 2f out: rdn and ev ch over 1f out: wknd ins fnl f* **7/1**

4062 **6** *2 3/4* **Tombellini (IRE)**[13] 4196 4-8-8 **57** .... AndrewMullen 1 44
(David Nicholls) *led: rdn whn hdd over 1f out: sn wknd* **5/1**[3]

[illegible] **7** *2 [illegible]* **Born To Be Achamp (BRZ)**[31] 3620 5-9-7 **70** .... SilvestreDeSousa 5 48
(Geoffrey Harker) *prom on outer: rdn over 2f out: sn wknd* **[illegible]/1**

5235 **8** *1 1/2* **Galpin Junior (USA)**[15] 4152 5-8-7 **56** .... JamesSullivan 2 29
(Ruth Carr) *w ldr: rdn over 2f out: wknd over 1f out* **4/1**[2]

1m 13.54s (-0.06) **Going Correction** +0.075s/f (Good)
WFA 3 from 4yo+ 4lb **8** Ran SP% **113.0**
Speed ratings (Par 103): **103,101,98,97,96 93,89,87**
toteswingers:1&2:£3.00, 1&3:£19.30, 2&3:£14.10 CSF £22.27 CT £515.25 TOTE £8.90: £3.00, £1.10, £8.60; EX 23.30 Trifecta £572.70 Part won. Pool: £773.95 - 0.50 winning units..

Owner R J Budge **Bred** John Foley **Trained** Sturton le Steeple, Notts

FOCUS
The pace was overly strong with Tombellini being harassed by Born To Be Achamp and Galpin Junior. That trio had little chance, the race being set up for those ridden patiently. The rwinner is rated close to last season's winning mark with the runner-up helping to set the standard.

Wigram's Turn(USA) ◆ Official explanation: jockey said gelding was denied a clear run

4635 EAT SLEEP DRINK AT NAGS HEAD PICKHILL H'CAP 1m 5f 175y
3:30 (3:30) (Class 4) (0-85,76) 3-Y-O+ £4,204 (£1,251; £625; £312) Stalls Low

Form RPR

0030 **1** **Union Island (IRE)**[9] 4360 5-9-5 **76** .... DaleSwift(3) 2 84
(Brian Ellison) *trckd ldr: rdn to ld wl over 1f out: strly pressed ins fnl f: kpt on: hld on wl towards fin* **11/4**[3]

5100 **2** *1/2* **Dark Ranger**[34] 3522 5-8-10 **69** .... JulieBurke(5) 3 76
(Tim Pitt) *hld up in tch: rdn over 2f out: hdwy to chal over 1f out: upsides ins fnl f: kpt on: hld nr fin* **17/2**

4353 **3** *6* **Descaro (USA)**[24] 3851 5-9-5 **73** .... DanielTudhope 1 72
(David O'Meara) *hld up: rdn and outpcd over 3f out: kpt on fr over 1f out: wnt 3rd towards fin* **5/2**[2]

2200 **4** *1/2* **Dubara Reef (IRE)**[24] 3851 4-9-0 **68** .... RobertWinston 4 66
(Paul Green) *trckd ldr: pushed along and reminders over 4f out: drvn to ld over 2f out: hdd wl over 1f out: sn wknd: lost 3rd towards fin* **12/1**

6032 **5** *8* **Cat O' Nine Tails**[8] 4382 4-9-5 **73** .... SilvestreDeSousa 5 60
(Mark Johnston) *led: rdn whn hdd over 2f out: sn wknd* **13/8**[1]

3m 3.30s (-0.30) **Going Correction** +0.075s/f (Good) **5** Ran SP% **111.6**
Speed ratings (Par 105): **103,102,99,99,94**
CSF £23.72 TOTE £2.70: £2.40, £2.50; EX 21.50.

Owner Union Of Friends **Bred** Barouche Stud Ireland Ltd **Trained** Norton, N Yorks

■ Stewards' Enquiry : Julie Burke one-day ban: used whip with excessive frequency (Aug 16)

FOCUS
The top weight was rated 9lb below the race ceiling of 85, and only two of these gave their true running, finishing well clear. The winner is rated to last year's best but the second limits the form to some extent.

4636 BOOK NOW FOR SATURDAY 17TH SEPTEMBER H'CAP 5f
4:00 (4:02) (Class 6) (0-60,66) 3-Y-O+ £1,704 (£503; £251) Stalls Low

Form RPR

0042 **1** **Blown It (USA)**[4] 4504 5-8-9 **48** .... PaulHanagan 7 58
(Keith Dalgleish) *bmpd s: hld up: hdwy on outer over 2f out: chsd ldr appr fnl f: kpt on: led post* **6/4**[1]

6121 **2** *hd* **Liberty Ship**[8] 4395 6-9-13 **66** 6ex .... (t) RoystonFfrench 2 75
(Mark Buckley) *in tch: rdn and hdwy over 2f out: led appr fnl f: kpt on: hdd post* **7/2**[2]

0035 **3** *3 1/4* **Kalahari Desert (IRE)**[21] 3937 4-8-7 **46** oh1 .... (v) PaulQuinn 6 44
(Richard Whitaker) *wnt rt s: chsd ldrs: rdn and ev ch over 1f out: no ex ins fnl f* **16/1**

4000 **4** *3/4* **Piste**[10] 4328 5-8-7 **46** oh1 .... AndrewHeffernan 1 41
(Tina Jackson) *trckd ldrs: rdn over 2f out: kpt on one pce* **20/1**

0305 **5** *3/4* **Spirit Of Coniston**[36] 3451 8-9-2 **55** .... MickyFenton 5 47
(Paul Midgley) *w ldr: led 2f out: hung lft whn hdd appr fnl f: sn wknd* **12/1**

3001 **6** *1 1/2* **Andrasta**[3] 4564 6-8-8 **52** 6ex .... JulieBurke(5) 4 39
(Alan Berry) *outpcd in rr tl kpt on fnl f: n.d* **4/1**[3]

0000 **7** *5* **Future Gem**[20] 3972 5-8-7 **46** oh1 .... (p) FrederikTylicki 8 15
(David Thompson) *squeezed out s: sn pushed along in rr: nvr threatened* **80/1**

0000 **8** *1 1/4* **Hold On Tiger (IRE)**[35] 3489 4-8-0 **46** oh1 .... ShirleyTeasdale(7) 9 10
(Nicky Richards) *chsd ldrs: wknd over 2f out* **28/1**

6601 **9** *13* **Inde Country**[22] 3920 3-8-10 **52** .... (t) LeeNewman 3 —
(Nicky Vaughan) *led narrowly: hdd 2f out: sn wknd* **10/1**

59.31 secs (-0.49) **Going Correction** -0.05s/f (Good)
WFA 3 from 4yo+ 3lb **9** Ran SP% **114.3**
Speed ratings (Par 101): **101,100,95,94,93 90,82,80,59**
toteswingers:1&2:£1.60, 1&3:£5.60, 2&3:£6.80 CSF £6.46 CT £56.97 TOTE £2.40: £1.10, £1.20, £3.40; EX 8.40 Trifecta £51.90 Pool: £948.62 - 13.52 winning units..

Owner D G Savala **Bred** H & W Thoroughbreds & Adrian Regan **Trained** Carluke, South Lanarkshire

FOCUS
Not a bad race for the class. There was a speed duel, Spirit Of Coniston taking on Inde Country, and those two were unsurprisingly picked off by the closers. The third and fourth limit the form, despite running close to their recent best.

Spirit Of Coniston Official explanation: jockey said, regarding riding, that the gelding hung badly left final furlong

4637 RACINGUK.COM CLASSIFIED CLAIMING STKS 1m 3f 214y
4:30 (4:30) (Class 6) 3-Y-O+ £1,704 (£503; £251) Stalls Low

Form RPR

0121 **1** **Eijaaz (IRE)**[20] 3974 10-9-1 60 .... (p) RobertWinston 2 65
(Geoffrey Harker) *hld up in rr: pushed along briefly over 4f out: sn gd hdwy: trckd ldr over 2f out: rdn to ld fnl 100yds: drvn out* **2/1**[2]

1532 **2** *1/2* **Hel's Angel (IRE)**[20] 3974 5-9-4 67 .... PaulHanagan 4 67
(Ann Duffield) *led: hdd 7f out: led again 3f out: sn rdn: hdd fnl 100yds: no ex* **1/1**[1]

6000 **3** *2 3/4* **Lakeman (IRE)**[21] 3938 5-8-12 59 .... DaleSwift(3) 5 60
(Brian Ellison) *hld up in tch: pushed along over 3f out: hdwy over 2f out: wnt 3rd over 1f out: kpt on one pce* **20/1**

-506 **4** *13* **Harsh But Fair**[31] 3622 5-8-13 42 .... (b[1]) JamesSullivan 3 37
(Michael Easterby) *trckd ldrs: pushed along over 4f out: wknd over 1f out* **20/1**

105 **5** *11* **Unex Goya (IRE)**[16] 4125 3-8-8 57 .... (b) TomEaves 6 25
(Michael Smith) *midfield: rdn over 3f out: sn wknd* **14/1**

1300 **6** *nk* **Relative Strength (IRE)**[20] 3974 6-9-1 64 .... (bt) StephenCraine 7 21
(Jennie Candlish) *trckd ldr: led 7f out: rdn whn hdd 3f out: sn wknd* **10/1**[3]

00/- **7** *24* **Royal Jet**[766] 3382 9-8-8 67 .... LanceBetts(5) 1 —
(Colin Teague) *in tch: pushed along and reminders over 4f out: sn lost pl and wknd* **33/1**

2m 38.88s (-0.02) **Going Correction** +0.075s/f (Good)
WFA 3 from 5yo+ 11lb **7** Ran SP% **111.6**
Speed ratings (Par 101): **103,102,100,92,84 84,68**
toteswingers:1&2:£1.50, 1&3:£5.80, 2&3:£4.70 CSF £4.05 TOTE £3.10: £1.80, £1.10; EX 4.00 Trifecta £27.20 Pool: £923.76 - 25.04 winning units..

Owner A S Ward **Bred** Shadwell Estate Company Limited **Trained** Thirkleby, N Yorks

FOCUS
A weak claimer run at a fair pace, and the front three finished a long way clear. The winner is probably the best guide, with the third and fourth not far off their marks if taken at face value.

4638 GO RACING IN YORKSHIRE H'CAP 7f
5:00 (5:01) (Class 6) (0-65,65) 3-Y-O £2,726 (£805; £402) Stalls Low

Form RPR

5356 **1** **One Of Twins**[55] 2809 3-8-3 **47** .... JamesSullivan 3 60
(Michael Easterby) *in tch: pushed along over 3f out: rdn and hdwy over 1f out: chal strly fnl f: led post* **5/1**[2]

0264 **2** *shd* **Catallout (IRE)**[30] 3661 3-8-13 **57** .... DanielTudhope 13 70
(Declan Carroll) *in tch: rdn over 2f out: hdwy over 1f out: led narrowly 1f out: strly pressed thrght fnl f: hdd post* **9/1**

4063 **3** *5* **Meandmyshadow**[21] 3931 3-9-2 **60** .... (p) RobertWinston 14 59
(Alan Brown) *sn pushed along towards rr: gd hdwy over 1f out: wnt 3rd ins fnl f: kpt on: no threat ldng pair* **22/1**

4510 **4** *1 1/4* **Dotty Darroch**[24] 3860 3-8-13 **57** .... LeeNewman 2 53
(Robin Bastiman) *trckd ldrs: rdn to ld 2f out: hdd 1f out: wknd* **14/1**

4004 **5** *3/4* **Love For Love**[36] 3455 3-7-13 **48** .... NeilFarley(5) 7 42
(David O'Meara) *midfield: effrt on outer over 1f out: kpt on one pce* **12/1**

5523 **6** *1* **Alensgrove (IRE)**[32] 3571 3-9-2 **60** .... (p) MickyFenton 11 51
(Paul Midgley) *dwlt: sn pushed along in rr: hdwy over 1f out: one pce fnl f: n.d* **12/1**

2664 **7** *3/4* **Stilettoesinthemud (IRE)**[20] 3977 3-9-0 **58** .... FrederikTylicki 5 47
(James Given) *hld up in midfield: rdn over 2f out: no imp* **7/1**[3]

-004 **8** *1* **Deliberation (IRE)**[24] 3857 3-9-2 **60** .... PhillipMakin 9 46
(Kevin Ryan) *prom: led gng wl over 2f out: rdn whn hdd 2f out: wknd over 1f out* **15/2**

0606 **9** *nse* **Sleights Boy (IRE)**[15] 4162 3-8-3 **47** .... (p) PatrickMathers 10 33
(Ian McInnes) *prom on outer: rdn over 2f out: wknd over 1f out* **66/1**

0013 **10** *3 1/2* **Twennyshortkid**[15] 4149 3-8-7 **51** .... (v) PaulHanagan 4 28
(Paul Midgley) *dwlt: midfield: rdn over 2f out: sn no imp* **4/1**[1]

5205 **11** *1 1/2* **Brave Battle**[18] 4041 3-8-13 **60** .... DaleSwift(3) 15 33
(Ron Barr) *s.i.s: hld up: a in rr* **25/1**

0600 **12** *2 ½* **Poppy's Rocket (IRE)**[13] 4196 3-8-3 **47**...................(p) DuranFentiman 1 —
(Marjorie Fife) *in tch on inner: rdn over 2f out: sn wknd* **33/1**

3340 **13** *5* **Guinea Seeker**[15] 4146 3-9-1 **59**.. DavidAllan 6 —
(Tim Easterby) *led: rdn whn hdd over 2f out: sn wknd* **15/2**

1m 27.06s (0.06) **Going Correction** +0.075s/f (Good) **13** Ran SP% **117.4**
Speed ratings (Par 98): **102,101,96,94,93 92,91,90,90,86 84,82,76**
toteswingers:1&2:£11.60, 1&3:£17.70, 2&3:£21.40 CSF £46.72 CT £941.93 TOTE £7.60: £2.40, £4.30, £5.80; EX 63.40 TRIFECTA Not won..
Owner Clark Industrial Services Partnership **Bred** Clark Industrial Services Partnership **Trained** Sheriff Hutton, N Yorks

FOCUS
Not for the first time on this card, the lead was contested and those ridden with a touch of patience were favoured. The third is the best guide, rated just below his 5f form.
Alensgrove(IRE) Official explanation: jockey said filly was slowly away and never travelled
Guinea Seeker Official explanation: jockey said gelding stopped quickly
T/Jkpt: £2,366.60 to a £1 stake. Pool:£10,000.00 - 3.00 winning tickets T/Plt: £28.70 to a £1 stake. Pool:£70,492.67 - 1,787.32 winning tickets T/Qpdt: £13.30 to a £1 stake. Pool:£4,516.45 - 249.90 winning tickets AS

4460 FFOS LAS (L-H)
Tuesday, August 2

OFFICIAL GOING: Good to firm (good in places; watered; 8.1)
Wind: moderate against Weather: fine

4639 UC BETTER MAIDEN STKS 6f
5:30 (5:31) (Class 5) 2-Y-O **£2,264** (£673; £336; £168) **Stalls** High

Form RPR

3 **1** **Gabrial The King (USA)**[9] 4365 2-9-3 0........................ JamieSpencer 4 90+
(Michael Bell) *mde all: nudged along over 1f out: sn coasted clr: v easily* **1/4**[1]

56 **2** *5* **Tweet Lady**[28] 3718 2-8-12 0.. JamesMillman 5 64
(Rod Millman) *trckd ldrs: pushed along over 3f out: drvn 2f out: hmpd wl over 1f out: styd on to go 2nd fnl 100yds: no ch w easy wnr* **12/1**[3]

3 *2 ½* **Knocker Knowles (IRE)** 2-9-3 0................................ CathyGannon 1 62
(David Evans) *veered lft leaving stalls: qckly in tch racing keenly: trckd wnr after 1f: drvn 2f out: sn hung rt: edgd lft appr fnl f: lost 2nd fnl 100yds* **6/1**[2]

0 **4** *1* **Welsh Royale**[18] 4068 2-9-3 0... LukeMorris 3 59
(William Muir) *racd in 4th virtually thrght: pushed along over 3f out: swtchd lft 2f out: sn no imp* **18/1**

5 *123* **Tenbridge** 2-8-12 0.. DaneO'Neill 2 —
(Derek Haydn Jones) *rrd over in paddock and mounted on trck: wnt bdly lft s: rel to r and flashed tail wildly: immediately t.o: fin in own time* **33/1**

1m 11.81s (1.81) **Going Correction** +0.225s/f (Good) **5** Ran SP% **110.2**
Speed ratings (Par 94): **95,88,85,83,—**
CSF £4.41 TOTE £1.30: £1.10, £3.00; EX 3.40.
Owner Dr Marwan Koukash **Bred** St George Farm LLC **Trained** Newmarket, Suffolk

FOCUS
A modest maiden. The winner hacked up and could be quite good.

NOTEBOOK
Gabrial The King(USA) ♦ made all against the stands' rail and opened his account with the minimum amount of fuss. He was a strong fancy on his debut when finishing third just nine days earlier at Pontefract and unsurprisingly proved all the rage here over the extra furlong against weaker opposition. However, he compromised his chance by getting very worked up when being saddled and had to be taken down quietly to post. With that in mind, despite the fact this was a moderate maiden, he clearly has a good deal of talent and is in the right hands to fulfil his potential. It will be fascinating to see what mark he is now given by the handicapper. This was Jamie Spencer's first-ever ride at the course. (op 1-3 tchd 2-5 in places)
Tweet Lady, down in trip, returned to something more like her debut form at Kempton in June and now has the option of nurseries. (tchd 14-1)
Knocker Knowles(IRE) shot violently out to his left from the gates and lost two lengths or so. He then proved keen after being rushed up to recover and that blunted his finishing effort. He wouldn't have got that much closer to the winner at the finish had he raced more professionally, but would have finished second. This debut experience won't be lost on him. Perhaps a drop to the minimum would suit in the short term. (op 9-2)

4640 LINCWEAR H'CAP 6f
6:00 (6:01) (Class 6) (0-65,65) 3-Y-O+ **£1,772** (£523; £261) **Stalls** High

Form RPR

6242 **1** **Emiratesdotcom**[6] 4434 5-9-12 **65**.................................... CathyGannon 1 72+
(Milton Bradley) *hld up bhd ldrs: rdn 3f out: r.o to ld 1f out: edgd sltly rt ins fnl f: drvn out* **6/4**[1]

0632 **2** *½* **George Thisby**[10] 4337 5-9-9 **62**.................................... JamesMillman 3 69+
(Rod Millman) *chsd ldrs: pushed along 1/2-way: n.m.r 2f out: sn swtchd off rail: r.o u.p ins fnl f: wnt 2nd nr fin* **3/1**[2]

6103 **3** *½* **Athaakeel (IRE)**[13] 4206 5-9-5 **58**.....................................(b) LukeMorris 5 62
(Ronald Harris) *sltly hmpd s: towards rr and sn pushed along: drvn over 2f out: sn swtchd lft: hdwy and continued to edge lft: r.o ins fnl f* **8/1**

0053 **4** *¾* **Justbookie Dot Com (IRE)**[22] 3920 3-9-2 **59**.............(v[1]) KierenFallon 6 60
(David Evans) *a.p: pushed along 3f out: drvn over 1f out: kpt on same pce* **13/2**

6-53 **5** *1* **Zalano**[20] 3983 3-9-8 **65**.. DaneO'Neill 2 62
(Derek Haydn Jones) *trckd ldr tl led after 2f: drvn wl over 1f out: hdd 1f out: grad wknd fnl 150yds* **6/1**[3]

05-0 **6** *nk* **Mystica (IRE)**[11] 4270 3-8-8 **54**...................................... JohnFahy[(3)] 7 50
(Dominic Ffrench Davis) *led 2f: chsd ldrs: drvn 2f out: kpt on same pce* **20/1**

0600 **7** *14* **Ellielusive (IRE)**[47] 3090 4-8-8 **50**................................. RyanClark[(3)] 4 —
(Mark Brisbourne) *squeezed out s: in rr: rdn over 2f out: wknd appr fnl f: t.o* **22/1**

1m 11.57s (1.57) **Going Correction** +0.225s/f (Good)
WFA 3 from 4yo+ 4lb **7** Ran SP% **112.8**
Speed ratings (Par 101): **97,96,95,94,93 92,74**
toteswingers:1&2:£1.30, 1&3:£2.10, 2&3:£3.90 CSF £5.91 TOTE £2.90: £2.90, £1.10; EX 6.70.
Owner Ms S Howell **Bred** Newsells Park Stud **Trained** Sedbury, Gloucs

FOCUS
A moderate sprint handicap that was run at a brisk pace, but the time was only marginally quicker than the opening juvenile maiden. The third looks the best guide, rated to his turf form.

4641 DESIGN OFFICE MAIDEN STKS 1m 4f (R)
6:30 (6:30) (Class 5) 3-4-Y-O **£2,264** (£673; £336; £168) **Stalls** Low

Form RPR

53 **1** **Qahriman**[19] 4023 3-9-3 0... KierenFallon 1 83+
(Luca Cumani) *s.i.s: hld up in 4th: shkn up and hdwy to ld 3f out: sn rdn along: drvn over 1f out: styd on wl to draw clr fnl f* **8/15**[1]

5 **2** *3 ¾* **Shaqira**[18] 4072 3-8-12 0.. TadhgO'Shea 3 69
(Marcus Tregoning) *trckd ldng pair tl wnt 2nd after 2f: rdn and dropped to 3rd 3f out: sn n.m.r and swtchd rt: chsd wnr over 1f out: a being hld but kpt on for 2nd* **5/2**[2]

0- **3** *1 ¼* **Mount Crystal (IRE)**[265] 7385 3-8-12 0............................. SteveDrowne 5 67
(B W Hills) *led: hdd 3f out: sn rdn: lost 2nd over 1f out: kpt on one pce* **10/1**[3]

5 **4** *3* **Madam Tessa (IRE)**[43] 3218 3-8-12 0............................. DavidProbert 4 62?
(Bryn Palling) *s.s: in rr but in tch: drvn and hung rt over 2f out: one pce and no imp on ldrs fr over 1f out* **20/1**

0-06 **5** *11* **Unbeatable**[46] 3119 3-8-5 0.. LukeRowe[(7)] 2 44
(William Knight) *trckd ldr 2f: racd in 3rd tl dropped in rr 3f out: sn rdn: steadily wknd fnl 2f* **80/1**

2m 39.16s (1.76) **Going Correction** +0.225s/f (Good) **5** Ran SP% **108.9**
Speed ratings (Par 103): **101,98,97,95,88**
CSF £2.03 TOTE £1.60: £1.10, £1.10; EX 1.60.
Owner Sheikh Mohammed Obaid Al Maktoum **Bred** Darley **Trained** Newmarket, Suffolk

FOCUS
Not a bad little maiden and potentially a very useful winner. The runner-up is rated to her debut form.

4642 TOPPERS WALES LTD H'CAP 1m 6f (R)
7:05 (7:06) (Class 6) (0-65,66) 3-Y-O+ **£1,681** (£500; £250; £125) **Stalls** Low

Form RPR

5445 **1** **Corr Point (IRE)**[21] 3960 4-10-0 **65**..................................(t) KierenFallon 2 73
(Jamie Osborne) *racd in 3rd: pushed along to chse clr ldr over 3f out: sn rdn: chal 2f out: carried rt over 1f out: led ins fnl f: wl on top fnl 50yds* **7/2**[2]

5050 **2** *1 ¼* **Oculist**[22] 3922 3-8-8 **61**... SophieDoyle[(3)] 4 67
(Jamie Osborne) *chsd ldr tl relegated to 3rd over 3f out: sn rdn: styd on u.p ins fnl f: wnt 2nd cl home* **16/1**

00/1 **3** *nk* **West With The Wind**[5] 4463 6-10-1 **66** 6ex.................... JamieSpencer 1 72
(Evan Williams) *led: grad drew clr fr 1/2-way: stl 5 l clr over 3f out: drvn over 2f out: sn jnd: edgd rt u.p over 1f out: hdd ins fnl f: no ex nr fin* **8/15**[1]

/000 **4** *14* **Rock Peak (IRE)**[11] 4274 6-8-11 **48** oh1.......................(b) SteveDrowne 3 34
(Bernard Llewellyn) *in rr: rdn along 5f out: lost tch 3f out: wnt mod 4th ins fnl f* **28/1**

6420 **5** *8* **Captain Sharpe**[11] 4273 3-9-0 **64**..................................... DavidProbert 6 39
(Bernard Llewellyn) *hld up in 4th: rdn 4f out: sn wknd: lost mod 4th ins fnl f: t.o* **7/1**[3]

3m 7.01s (3.21) **Going Correction** +0.225s/f (Good)
WFA 3 from 4yo+ 13lb **5** Ran SP% **109.3**
Speed ratings (Par 101): **99,98,98,90,85**
CSF £43.56 TOTE £4.70: £2.70, £11.50; EX 22.00.
Owner John Duddy **Bred** T J Pabst And Newtown Stud **Trained** Upper Lambourn, Berks

FOCUS
A modest staying handicap, which was a proper test. The winner is rated pretty much to his turf best, but the runner-up is a surprising improver and the form could prove unreliable.

4643 ROYAL BRITISH LEGION POPPY H'CAP 6f
7:40 (7:42) (Class 4) (0-85,85) 3-Y-O **£4,140** (£1,232; £615; £307) **Stalls** High

Form RPR

-231 **1** **Cape Classic (IRE)**[10] 4340 3-8-11 **75**............................ LiamJones 4 80+
(William Haggas) *trckd ldrs: rdn 2f out: led appr fnl f: r.o wl u.p* **5/4**[1]

011 **2** *¾* **Cruise Tothelimit (IRE)**[13] 4195 3-8-9 **73**.................... JamieSpencer 3 76
(Patrick Morris) *led: rdn and hdd appr fnl f: kpt on* **11/2**

3404 **3** *hd* **Remotelinx (IRE)**[9] 4353 3-9-7 **85**.................................... DaneO'Neill 6 87
(J W Hills) *hld up: nt clr run on rail 3f out to 2f out: sn drvn: r.o ins fnl f* **11/4**[2]

5544 **4** *1 ¼* **Whipphound**[4] 4511 3-8-3 **70**... JohnFahy[(3)] 5 68
(Mark Brisbourne) *hld up: stdy hdwy on outer fr 3f out: shkn up and nt qckn over 1f out: drvn and one pce ins fnl f* **9/2**[3]

-506 **5** *10* **Belle Bayardo (IRE)**[18] 4063 3-9-5 **83**.............................. LukeMorris 1 49
(Ronald Harris) *chsd ldr: rdn wl over 2f out: wknd over 1f out* **33/1**

4000 **6** *9* **Penny's Pearl (IRE)**[15] 4156 3-8-11 **75**..........................(t) KierenFallon 2 12
(David Evans) *s.i.s: sn trcking ldrs: rdn over 3f out: wknd and eased over 1f out: t.o* **16/1**

1m 10.49s (0.49) **Going Correction** +0.225s/f (Good) **6** Ran SP% **113.5**
Speed ratings (Par 102): **104,103,102,101,87 75**
toteswingers:1&2:£2.10, 1&3:£1.20, 2&3:£1..50 CSF £8.98 TOTE £3.30: £2.60, £5.40; EX 6.20.
Owner Bernard Kantor **Bred** Wentworth Racing **Trained** Newmarket, Suffolk

FOCUS
A decent little 3-y-o sprint handicap rated around the placed horses.

4644 DIGIBET.COM H'CAP 5f
8:15 (8:17) (Class 3) (0-95,94) 3-Y-O+ **£6,792** (£2,021; £1,010; £505) **Stalls** High

Form RPR

6263 **1** **Star Rover (IRE)**[2] 4573 4-9-3 **87**.................................(v) DavidProbert 3 94
(David Evans) *chsd ldrs: drvn over 1f out: r.o between horses to ld fnl 50yds* **7/4**[1]

6-06 **2** *½* **Above Limits (IRE)**[88] 1848 4-9-8 **92**.......................... JamieSpencer 4 97
(David Simcock) *led tl appr fnl f: rdn and kpt on* **9/1**

600 **3** *shd* **Secret Millionaire (IRE)**[24] 3847 4-8-10 **83**................. SeanLevey[(3)] 7 88
(Patrick Morris) *t.k.h early: trckd ldr: rdn to ld appr fnl f: hdd and no ex fnl 50yds* **9/2**[3]

0001 **4** *nk* **Drawnfromthepast (IRE)**[19] 3996 6-9-3 **90**................ SophieDoyle[(3)] 5 94
(Ed Walker) *hld up bhd ldrs: nt clr run over 1f out: sn swtchd rt: r.o u.p ins fnl f* **9/2**[3]

0204 **5** *hd* **Bathwick Bear (IRE)**[4] 4498 3-9-7 **94**............................ KierenFallon 2 96
(David Evans) *in rr but in cl tch: pushed along fr 1/2-way: ev ch 1f out: kpt on same pce u.p ins fnl f* **7/2**[2]

5246 **6** *2 3/4* **Steelcut**[24] 3869 7-8-5 **75** oh1...(p) CathyGannon 1 68
(David Evans) *racd keenly: hld up in tch: rdn 2f out: outpcd by ldrs appr fnl f* **14/1**

58.34 secs (0.04) **Going Correction** +0.225s/f (Good)
WFA 3 from 4yo+ 3lb **6** Ran SP% **111.6**
Speed ratings (Par 107): **107,106,106,105,105 100**
toteswingers:1&2:£4.90, 1&3:£2.60, 2&3:£6.10 CSF £17.95 TOTE £2.50: £1.10, £4.70; EX 17.20.
Owner Christy Leo **Bred** Yeomanstown Stud **Trained** Pandy, Monmouths

FOCUS
Another decent little sprint handicap. There wasn't that strong an early pace on and it resulted in a blanket finish. Interestingly the field went away from the stands' rail and ended up more towards the far side. The winner sets the standard backed up by the third and fifth.

NOTEBOOK
Star Rover(IRE) gamely got his head back in front under strong handling from David Probert. He was put under maximum pressure at the furlong marker and, briefly tightened up shortly after, really dug deep where it mattered. This ultra-tough little 4-y-o had run gallant races in defeat on his three previous outings in strong company, including in Listed class over 6f at Chester just two days earlier, and so it was a much-deserved end to a losing run that dated back to this month last year. (tchd 15-8)
Above Limits(IRE) ◆ did the donkey work on her return from an 88-day break and made a bold bid. She has just a maiden win back in 2009 to her name, but is now on a more workable mark and her turn isn't looking far off again. (op 7-1 tchd 6-1)
Secret Millionaire(IRE) would have very likely come out on top had this been more of a test. He is proving hard to win with, but can land one of these when things go his way. (op 6-1)
Drawnfromthepast(IRE) still looked potentially well handicapped up just 1lb for resuming winning ways at Bath last month. He was forced to wait for his challenge, and having to switch late on cost him any chance of following up. It could well be that he wins again next time. (op 7-2)
Bathwick Bear(IRE), a stablemate of the winner, was 1lb lower than when finishing a decent fourth at Goodwood last week. He had to make his effort closest to the far side and wasn't beaten at all far, but it wouldn't be surprising to see headgear back on next time. (op 9-2 tchd 5-1)

4645 IWEC INTERNATIONAL H'CAP 1m 2f (R)
8:45 (8:45) (Class 6) (0-60,58) 3-Y-O+ **£1,681** (£500; £250; £125) **Stalls** Low

Form RPR
-055 **1** **Only You Maggie (IRE)**[15] 4158 4-9-5 **58**..........(v) MatthewLawson(7) 5 66
(Gary Harrison) *hld up in rr: hdwy over 4f out: rdn 3f out: led appr fnl f: r.o wl* **10/1**

-006 **2** *1 3/4* **Present Story**[6] 4448 4-9-4 **53**...................................... MarkLawson(3) 7 57
(Gary Harrison) *in tch: rdn over 2f out: ev ch over 1f out: one pce ins fnl f* **5/1**[3]

4056 **3** *nse* **Chik's Dream**[22] 3912 4-9-6 **52**... DaneO'Neill 2 56
(Derek Haydn Jones) *set modest gallop: qckınd pce 4f out: drvn 2f out: hdd appr fnl f: one pce* **5/1**[3]

3604 **4** *4 1/2* **Dream Of Fortune (IRE)**[17] 4088 7-9-8 **57**...........(bt) RichardEvans(3) 1 52
(David Evans) *trckd ldrs: rdn over 2f out: nt qckn and sn no ch w ldrs: kpt on same pce* **10/1**

/0-3 **5** *2* **Sweet World**[11] 4273 7-9-11 **57**.. DavidProbert 6 48
(Bernard Llewellyn) *midfield: rdn over 2f out: sn outpcd by ldrs: styd on towards fin* **2/1**[1]

0353 **6** *1* **Market Puzzle (IRE)**[15] 4165 4-8-10 **45**........................ RyanClark(3) 4 34
(Mark Brisbourne) *trckd ldr: drvn over 2f out: wknd over 1f out* **9/4**[2]

5550 **7** *19* **Farmer's Wife**[131] 951 3-8-8 **52**.. JohnFahy(3) 3 —
(Bernard Llewellyn) *towards rr: rdn 3f out: wknd over 1f out: t.o* **16/1**

2m 14.15s (4.75) **Going Correction** +0.225s/f (Good)
WFA 3 from 4yo+ 9lb **7** Ran SP% **121.5**
Speed ratings (Par 101): **86,84,84,80,79 78,63**
toteswingers:1&2:£6.90, 1&3:£5.80, 2&3:£4.50 CSF £62.84 TOTE £8.60: £9.50, £2.00; EX 33.40.
Owner Gary Harrison **Bred** Thomas And Linda Heffernan **Trained** Llandeilo, Carmarthens

FOCUS
A weak handicap, run at an ordinary early pace. The form looks dubious, despite being rated around the first two.
T/Plt: £47.30 to a £1 stake. Pool:£66,652.58 - 1,027.48 winning tickets T/Qpdt: £11.20 to a £1 stake. Pool:£8,227.49 - 542.06 winning tickets RL

4177 SOUTHWELL (L-H)
Tuesday, August 2

OFFICIAL GOING: Standard
Wind: Virtually nil Weather: Cloudy with sunny periods and warm

4646 BRITISH STALLION STUDS SUPPORTING BRITISH RACING EBF MAIDEN STKS 1m (F)
5:50 (5:51) (Class 5) 2-Y-O **£3,234** (£962; £481; £240) **Stalls** Low

Form RPR
0 **1** **Position**[41] 3282 2-9-3 0.. SebSanders 5 79+
(Sir Mark Prescott Bt) *trckd ldr: led over 4f out: rdn clr over 2f out: green and edgd lft over 1f out: unchal* **6/4**[1]

50 **2** *10* **Alborz (IRE)**[15] 4159 2-9-3 0....................................... SilvestreDeSousa 6 56
(Mark Johnston) *led: pushed along and hdd over 4f out: rdn over 3f out: drvn and one pce fnl 2f* **7/2**[3]

2 **3** *7* **Behlul (IRE)**[21] 3947 2-9-3 0.. TedDurcan 2 40
(Gerard Butler) *t.k.h: trckd ldrs: effrt to chse ldng pair 1/2-way: rdn 3f out and sn outpcd* **2/1**[2]

4 *18* **Canning Vale** 2-8-12 0.. JimmyQuinn 3 —
(Julia Feilden) *s.i.s and green in rr: nvr on terms* **50/1**

324 **5** *3 3/4* **Dougie Boy**[84] 1988 2-9-0 65.. KierenFox(3) 4 —
(Bill Turner) *t.k.h: chsd ldrs: rdn along 1/2-way: outpcd and bhd fr over 3f out* **9/1**

0 **6** *14* **Phoenix Order**[7] 4402 2-8-10 0.. NoraLooby(7) 1 —
(Alan McCabe) *sn rdn along: a in rr: outpcd and bhd fr over 3f out* **66/1**

1m 43.65s (-0.05) **Going Correction** -0.15s/f (Stan) **6** Ran SP% **109.0**
Speed ratings (Par 94): **94,84,77,59,55 41**
toteswingers:1&2:£1.20, 1&3:£1.50, 2&3:£1.90 CSF £6.71 TOTE £2.30: £1.30, £1.80; EX 7.40.
Owner Cheveley Park Stud **Bred** Cheveley Park Stud Ltd **Trained** Newmarket, Suffolk

FOCUS
14mm of water was applied to the track in the previous two days, but the time suggested the ground was just on the slow side. The first running of this race went to last month's Group 2 Prix Eugene Adam winner Pisco Sour but, although this race didn't take much winning given the second favourite underperformed, the winner looks the type to hold his own at a higher level. The gallop was reasonable and the winner came down the centre in the straight. The front three were all eased off slightly in the last 100yds.

NOTEBOOK
Position ◆, tailed off after running green on his debut at Kempton, was very well supported and duly left that form a long way behind with a convincing display. He has plenty of size and scope, should stay 1m2f and is in good hands. Although this bare form is nothing out of the ordinary, he looks the sort to hold his own in stronger company. (op 7-4 tchd 2-1)
Alborz(IRE) had achieved little in his first two starts on turf but travelled strongly and bettered that form by some way on all-weather debut over this longer trip. He is likely to remain vulnerable against better sorts in this grade, but should be able to pick up a small event at some point. (op 4-1 tchd 3-1)
Behlul(IRE), who showed ability at a moderate level at this course on his debut, was fairly easy in the market and failed to build on that form over this longer trip after racing with the choke out early on. He should do better in ordinary nurseries. (op 7-4 tchd 6-4 and 9-4)
Canning Vale, out of an unraced half-sister to Dewhurst and St James's Palace winner Grand Lodge, should be better for this debut run but didn't show enough against the boys to suggest she would be of much short-term interest. (op 33-1)
Dougie Boy, the only one of these with an official rating, had been gelded since his last run in May but was well beaten after taking a good grip on this first run beyond sprint distances. He is another with something to prove. (tchd 8-1 and 12-1)

4647 32REDBET.COM (S) STKS 6f (F)
6:20 (6:23) (Class 6) 3-Y-O **£1,704** (£503; £251) **Stalls** Low

Form RPR
0300 **1** **Suddenly Susan (IRE)**[35] 3489 3-8-0 60................(b) LeonnaMayor(7) 1 63
(David Nicholls) *mde all: rdn 2f out: styd on wl fnl f* **4/1**[3]

005 **2** *3* **Brio**[31] 3633 3-8-12 61...(p) JamesDoyle 12 58
(Alan McCabe) *qckly away: chsd wnr: rdn to chal over 2f out: drvn and ev ch over 1f out: one pce ent fnl f* **8/1**

0 **3** *1 3/4* **Salik Tag (USA)**[11] 4286 3-8-9 0..........................(t) MichaelO'Connell(3) 6 53+
(David Nicholls) *dwlt and bhd: pushed along and hdwy 1/2-way: rdn wl over 2f out: styd on wl appr fnl f: tk 3rd nr line* **7/1**

0- **4** *nk* **Beachwood Bay**[441] 2210 3-8-5 0.............................. JoshBaudains(7) 4 52
(Jo Hughes) *prom: rdn along over 2f out: drvn wl over 1f out: sn one pce: lost 3rd nr line* **40/1**

3034 **5** *4 1/2* **Lady Platinum Club**[17] 4110 3-8-7 60...................(p) SilvestreDeSousa 7 32
(Geoffrey Oldroyd) *in tch: hdwy 1/2-way: rdn to chse ldng pair over 2f out: sn drvn and wknd wl over 1f out* **10/3**[2]

-101 **6** *3 3/4* **Paper Dreams (IRE)**[20] 3972 3-8-9 65...........................(p) AmyRyan(3) 9 25
(Kevin Ryan) *chsd ldrs: wd st: rdn over 2f out: sn no imp* **5/2**[1]

4-30 **7** *1* **Be A Good Lady**[13] 4196 3-8-7 46.................................. BarryMcHugh 3 17
(Tony Coyle) *midfield: on inner: rdn along 1/2-way: nvr a factor* **18/1**

0-00 **8** *8* **Look For Love**[63] 2581 3-8-12 45.............................. RussKennemore 10 —
(Reg Hollinshead) *s.i.s: a in rr* **100/1**

0- **9** *1 1/4* **Musical Leap**[233] 7843 3-8-7 0.............................. DanielleMcCreery(5) 2 —
(Shaun Harris) *a towards rr* **100/1**

5300 **10** *6* **Three Scoops**[85] 1952 3-8-7 47...(t) HayleyTurner 5 —
(Dominic Ffrench Davis) *a towards rr* **25/1**

0306 **11** *4* **Stravsambition**[18] 4067 3-8-7 56.............................. GrahamGibbons 13 —
(Reg Hollinshead) *chsd ldrs on outer: rdn along 1/2-way: sn wknd* **16/1**

60 **12** *nk* **Styleyf**[47] 3075 3-8-7 0.. RichardMullen 11 —
(David Brown) *chsd ldrs: rdn along bef 1/2-way and sn wknd* **14/1**

00 **13** *14* **Partly Pickled**[32] 3594 3-8-9 0...(b[1]) BillyCray(3) 8 —
(David Nicholls) *a in rr: bhd fr 1/2-way* **66/1**

1m 15.79s (-0.71) **Going Correction** -0.15s/f (Stan) **13** Ran SP% **122.8**
Speed ratings (Par 98): **98,94,91,91,85 80,78,68,66,58 53,52,34**
toteswingers:1&2:£7.00, 1&3:£10.10, 2&3:£8.90 CSF £36.47 TOTE £6.80: £1.60, £1.20, £3.00; EX 44.30.There was no bid for winner.
Owner Paul J Dixon **Bred** L Mulryan **Trained** Sessay, N Yorks

FOCUS
No more than a modest seller. The gallop was sound but very few figured. The winner came down the centre in the straight and sets the level rated to previous C&D form.
Paper Dreams(IRE) Official explanation: jockey said, regarding running, that the filly never travelled
Look For Love Official explanation: jockey said gelding stumbled leaving stalls

4648 32RED MOBILE CASINO MAIDEN AUCTION STKS 5f (F)
6:55 (7:04) (Class 6) 2-Y-O **£1,704** (£503; £251) **Stalls** High

Form RPR
00 **1** **Laura's Bairn**[43] 3229 2-8-9 0...(v[1]) FrannyNorton 3 60
(J R Jenkins) *cl up: rdn to ld 1 1/2f out: drvn clr ins fnl f: kpt on* **4/1**[3]

660 **2** *2 3/4* **Concordia Notte (IRE)**[8] 4391 2-8-1 0..................... DeclanCannon(3) 4 50
(Richard Guest) *prom: rdn along and sltly outpcd 2f out: sn drvn and kpt on* **13/2**

60 **3** *hd* **Tuibama (IRE)**[21] 3932 2-8-9 0.. PJMcDonald 5 54
(Ben Haslam) *led 1f: cl up: effrt 2f out: sn rdn and ev ch tl drvn and wknd ent fnl f* **10/3**[2]

4 *nse* **Bogey Hole (IRE)** 2-8-6 0...(v[1]) SilvestreDeSousa 1 51+
(Tom Dascombe) *wnt lft s: green and sn rdn along in rr: styd on appr fnl f: nrst fin* **9/4**[1]

0056 **5** *2* **Russian Bullet**[5] 4460 2-8-9 60.......................................(b[1]) JamesDoyle 7 47
(Jamie Osborne) *led after 1f: rdn along over 2f out: hdd 1 1/2f out and sn wknd* **5/1**

04 **6** *3* **Clodhopper (IRE)**[12] 4225 2-8-4 0.................................... HayleyTurner 6 31
(Jamie Osborne) *towards rr: rdn along over 2f out: n.d* **8/1**

62.04 secs (2.34) **Going Correction** +0.25s/f (Slow) **6** Ran SP% **115.0**
Speed ratings (Par 92): **91,86,86,86,83 78**
toteswingers:1&2:£5.90, 1&3:£3.80, 2&3:£4.30 CSF £29.82 TOTE £6.00: £3.80, £2.10; EX 45.50.
Owner Mark Goldstein **Bred** Greg Parsons **Trained** Royston, Herts

FOCUS
A modest and uncompetitive maiden. The gallop was sound and the winner raced towards the centre throughout. He improved for the switch in surface.

NOTEBOOK
Laura's Bairn attracted support and showed much-improved form back in trip in the first-time visor on this all-weather debut. This wasn't much of a race but he may do better on this surface. (new market new market op 7-1)
Concordia Notte(IRE) was easy to back on this first run for her new yard but was far from disgraced on her all-weather debut. Low-grade nurseries returned to 6f will be the way forward with her. (new market new market op 4-1)
Tuibama(IRE) wasn't disgraced on all-weather debut but is going to have to show a fair bit more before he's a solid betting proposition in this grade. (new market new market op 7-2 tchd 3-1)
Bogey Hole(IRE), who has several winners over a variety of distances in her pedigree, showed her inexperience on this racecourse debut but showed a modicum of ability. The step up to 6f should suit and, while she lacks much in the way of physical scope, she is entitled to improve. (new market new market op 4-1)

Russian Bullet again had limitations exposed on this Fibresand debut and is likely to remain vulnerable in this type of event. Official explanation: jockey said colt hung right (new market new market op 4-1 tchd 6-1)

4649 32RED CASINO H'CAP — 1m 4f (F)
7:30 (7:32) (Class 5) (0-70,69) 4-Y-0+ **£2,264** (£673; £336; £168) **Stalls** Low

Form RPR
0500 **1** **Daaweitza**[17] 4083 8-9-7 **69**....................(be) SilvestreDeSousa 2 82
(Brian Ellison) *hld up in tch on inner: hdwy over 4f out: chsd ldng pair 3f out: rdn to ld over 1f out: drvn out* **9/2**[3]
0061 **2** 3 ¼ **Think Its All Over (USA)**[14] 4177 4-9-0 **62**.................. MickyFenton 11 70
(Julie Camacho) *a.p: cl up 4f out: chal 3f out and ev ch tl drvn and one pce fr over 1f out* **2/1**[1]
-042 **3** *shd* **Mighty Mambo**[14] 4177 4-9-3 **65**.................... SebSanders 3 73
(George Margarson) *trckd ldrs on inner: hdwy over 4f out: led 3f out: sn rdn: drvn and hdd over 1f out: kpt on same pce* **7/2**[2]
2254 **4** *10* **Mediterranean Sea (IRE)**[77] 2176 5-9-3 **65**................ StephenCraine 8 57
(J R Jenkins) *hld up in tch: smooth hdwy to trck ldrs 4f out: shkn up 3f out: sn rdn and no imp* **10/1**
4526 **5** *2* **Straversjoy**[25] 3811 4-9-5 **67**.................... PJMcDonald 5 55
(Reg Hollinshead) *trckd ldrs: hdwy 6f out: rdn along over 3f out: drvn wl over 2f out and sn outpcd* **16/1**
211- **6** *12* **Resplendent Ace (IRE)**[106] 6744 7-9-2 **64**.................. BarryMcHugh 9 33
(Karen Tutty) *bhd tl sme late hdwy* **20/1**
2320 **7** *12* **Carnac (IRE)**[14] 4177 5-8-2 **57**....................(p) NoraLooby[(7)] 1 7
(Alan McCabe) *midfield whn n.m.r bnd after 2f: in rr after* **25/1**
0040 **8** *hd* **Scarab (IRE)**[17] 4111 6-9-6 **68**....................(p) GrahamGibbons 7 18
(Tim Walford) *led: rdn along over 4f out: hdd over 3f out and wknd qckly* **25/1**
1060 **9** 2 ½ **Sail Home**[17] 4090 4-8-11 **62**.................... AdamBeschizza[(3)] 6 8
(Julia Feilden) *chsd ldrs: rdn along 5f out: sn wknd* **14/1**
2250 **10** *13* **Dunaskin (IRE)**[9] 4366 11-8-7 **55**....................(b) JamesSullivan 12 —
(Richard Guest) *sn rdn along and cl up tl lost pl 1/2-way: bhd and eased fnl 2f* **50/1**
0-00 **11** *6* **Street Devil (USA)**[27] 2413 6-9-0 **62**.................... RobbieFitzpatrick 4 —
(Jo Hughes) *a in rr: bhd and eased fnl 3f* **80/1**
6300 **12** *35* **Camps Bay (USA)**[14] 4177 7-8-12 **60**.................... HayleyTurner 10 —
(Conor Dore) *a in rr: bhd and eased fnl 3f* **20/1**

2m 39.1s (-1.90) **Going Correction** -0.15s/f (Stan) **12** Ran SP% **115.8**
Speed ratings (Par 103): **100,97,97,91,89 81,73,73,71,63 59,35**
toteswingers:1&2:£3.20, 1&3:£5.00, 2&3:£2.30 CSF £12.31 CT £34.74 TOTE £3.50: £1.20, £1.10, £2.00; EX 19.10.
Owner Mrs Andrea M Mallinson **Bred** C Mallinson **Trained** Norton, N Yorks
■ Stewards' Enquiry : Seb Sanders two-day ban: careless riding (Aug 16,20)

FOCUS
A modest handicap run at a reasonable gallop. The winner came down the centre and the first three pulled a long way clear. The form is straightforward and sound.
Scarab(IRE) Official explanation: jockey said gelding moved poorly throughout

4650 £32 FREE AT 32RED.COM H'CAP — 5f (F)
8:05 (8:08) (Class 6) (0-55,55) 3-Y-0+ **£1,704** (£503; £251) **Stalls** High

Form RPR
0005 **1** **No Mean Trick (USA)**[14] 4182 5-9-2 **55**.................... MickyFenton 9 67
(Paul Midgley) *cl up: led over 3f out: rdn clr appr fnl f: kpt on* **11/2**[3]
5313 **2** *2* **Novalist**[9] 4359 3-8-12 **54**....................(b) LeeNewman 2 58
(Robin Bastiman) *cl up: ev ch 2f out: sn rdn and one pce ent fnl f* **11/4**[2]
5634 **3** *nk* **Shakespeares Excel**[8] 4395 4-8-9 **48**.................... JimmyQuinn 5 52
(Derek Shaw) *trckd ldrs: effrt and n.m.r over 2f out: sn rdn and no imp appr fnl f* **5/2**[1]
6601 **4** *5* **Duke Of Rainford**[10] 4328 4-8-13 **52**.................... TomEaves 4 38
(Michael Herrington) *chsd ldrs: effrt 2f out: sn rdn and wknd over 1f out* **13/2**
6000 **5** *hd* **Egyptian Lord**[35] 3493 8-8-7 **46** oh1....................(b) RobbieFitzpatrick 8 31
(Peter Grayson) *chsd ldrs: rdn along over 2f out: sn drvn and n.d* **50/1**
/006 **6** 4 ½ **Mrs Medley**[14] 4189 5-8-7 **46** oh1.................... KellyHarrison 1 15
(Garry Woodward) *chsd ldrs on wd outside: rdn along 1/2-way: grad wknd* **40/1**
0003 **7** 2 ¾ **Pickled Pumpkin**[21] 3950 3-8-10 **52**.................... SilvestreDeSousa 6 —
(Olivia Maylam) *s.i.s and rel to r: sn drvn along and a bhd* **13/2**
40/6 **8** *nk* **Diademas (USA)**[5] 4475 6-8-8 **47**.................... HayleyTurner 3 —
(Conor Dore) *led: hdd over 3f out and sn pushed along: rdn 1/2-way: sn wknd* **14/1**
60-0 **9** *13* **Bombay Mist**[175] 453 4-8-7 **46** oh1....................(e) JamesSullivan 7 —
(Richard Guest) *towards rr: outpcd 1/2-way and sn bhd* **33/1**

60.81 secs (1.11) **Going Correction** +0.25s/f (Slow)
WFA 3 from 4yo+ 3lb **9** Ran SP% **111.3**
Speed ratings (Par 101): **101,97,97,89,89 81,77,76,56**
toteswingers:1&2:£3.60, 1&3:£3.40, 2&3:£1.70 CSF £19.81 CT £45.27 TOTE £9.30: £1.70, £1.50, £1.50; EX 25.20.
Owner John Allan Milburn **Bred** Larry Byer **Trained** Westow, N Yorks

FOCUS
A moderate handicap run at a decent gallop and raced around the placed horses to recent marks. The winner raced towards the stands' rail throughout and the first three pulled clear.

4651 32REDPOKER.COM H'CAP — 7f (F)
8:35 (8:39) (Class 6) (0-60,60) 4-Y-0+ **£1,704** (£503; £251) **Stalls** Low

Form RPR
0-23 **1** **Clever Omneya (USA)**[14] 4183 5-9-4 **57**.................... FrannyNorton 12 70
(J R Jenkins) *qckly away and cl up: rdn to ld over 2f out: drvn over 1f out: kpt on gamely fnl f* **9/2**[2]
5522 **2** 1 ¼ **Elusive Warrior (USA)**[14] 4183 8-9-2 **55**....................(p) JamesDoyle 1 65
(Alan McCabe) *slt ld: rdn along and hdd over 2f out: drvn and ev ch tl no ex ins fnl f* **6/1**[3]
5322 **3** *7* **Amtired**[14] 4179 5-9-3 **56**....................(be) SilvestreDeSousa 5 47
(Brian Ellison) *in tch: effrt on inner and n.m.r 1/2-way: hdwy 3f out: rdn to chse ldng pair 2f out: sn swtchd rt and drvn: no imp fr over 1f out* **7/4**[1]
6000 **4** 3 ½ **Minortransgression (USA)**[13] 4210 4-9-3 **59**...... AdamBeschizza[(3)] 11 41
(H Edward Haynes) *in tch: hdwy wl over 2f out: sn rdn: kpt on appr fnl f: nvr rchd ldrs* **33/1**
2540 **5** ½ **St Ignatius**[21] 3942 4-8-12 **51**....................(p) NeilChalmers 2 31
(Michael Appleby) *chsd ldrs: rdn along 1/2-way: drvn wl over 2f out and plugged on same pce* **16/1**
0501 **6** *2* **Norcroft**[14] 4183 9-8-3 **49**....................(p) DanielHarris[(7)] 13 24
(Christine Dunnett) *dwlt and towards rr: hdwy 1/2-way: rdn over 2f out: nvr nr ldrs* **20/1**
0000 **7** *10* **Prices Lane**[15] 4150 4-9-0 **53**.................... JamesSullivan 6 —
(Michael Easterby) *a towards rr* **33/1**
0203 **8** *shd* **Caldermud (IRE)**[14] 4187 4-9-7 **60**....................(t) HayleyTurner 14 —
(Olivia Maylam) *dwlt and a towards rr* **12/1**
0010 **9** ½ **Tenancy (IRE)**[10] 4328 7-8-9 **53**.................... DanielleMcCreery[(5)] 4 —
(Shaun Harris) *cl up: rdn along 3f out: drvn over 2f out and grad wknd* **25/1**
0000 **10** 1 ¼ **Bishopbriggs (USA)**[14] 4183 6-9-1 **54**.................... JamieMackay 7 —
(K F Clutterbuck) *sn rdn along and wl bhd 1/2-way: sme hdwy fr over 2f out: nvr a factor* **80/1**
6035 **11** *2* **Crocodile Bay (IRE)**[6] 4438 8-8-10 **49**....................(b) RobbieFitzpatrick 9 —
(Richard Guest) *in tch: rdn along 1/2-way: sn wknd* **22/1**
6556 **12** *2* **Vogarth**[39] 3089 7-8-2 **46**....................(v) JamesRogers[(5)] 10 —
(Michael Chapman) *s.i.s: a bhd* **50/1**
-060 **13** 1 ¾ **Gracie's Gift (IRE)**[49] 3024 9-9-4 **60**....................(e[1]) RobertLButler[(3)] 3 —
(Richard Guest) *chsd ldrs: rdn along bef 1/2-way: sn wknd* **10/1**
0-60 **14** *87* **Scruffy Skip (IRE)**[187] 317 6-8-13 **52**....................(p) SebSanders 8 —
(Christine Dunnett) *towards rr whn eased 3f out: virtually p.u fnl 2f* **8/1**

1m 29.55s (-0.75) **Going Correction** -0.15s/f (Stan) **14** Ran SP% **124.6**
Speed ratings (Par 101): **98,96,88,84,84 81,70,70,69,68 65,63,61,—**
toteswingers:1&2:£5.90, 1&3:£2.90, 2&3:£3.10 CSF £30.55 CT £68.28 TOTE £7.00: £1.90, £2.20, £1.10; EX 36.40.
Owner Fhad Al Harthi **Bred** Lantern Hill Farm Llc **Trained** Royston, Herts

FOCUS
A moderate handicap but, although the pace was sound, this was another race on the card where those held up were at a disadvantage. The first two, who raced down the centre, pulled clear in the straight and the runner-up is rated in line with this year's best handicap mark.
Bishopbriggs(USA) Official explanation: jockey said, regarding running and riding, that his orders were to ride the race as he found it and ride the gelding to the line, having dwelt, it would not face the kickback and only made moderate headway in the home straight.
Vogarth Official explanation: jockey said gelding missed the break
Scruffy Skip(IRE) Official explanation: jockey said saddle slipped
T/Plt: £47.30 to a £1 stake. Pool:£66,652.58 - 1,027.48 winning tickets T/Qpdt: £11.20 to a £1 stake. Pool:£8,227.49 - 542.06 winning tickets JR

[4595] DEAUVILLE (R-H)
Tuesday, August 2

OFFICIAL GOING: Turf: good; fibresand: standard

4652a PRIX DE TANCARVILLE (MAIDEN) (UNRACED 2YO COLTS & GELDINGS) (TURF) — 6f
1:20 (12:00) 2-Y-0 **£10,344** (£4,137; £3,103; £2,068; £1,034)

RPR
1 **Sofast (FR)** 2-9-2 0.................... OlivierPeslier 5 85
(F Head, France) **5/2**[2]
2 ¾ **Abtaal (USA)** 2-9-2 0.................... ChristopheSoumillon 3 83
(J-C Rouget, France) **9/10**[1]
3 *4* **Anaconda (FR)** 2-9-2 0.................... RichardKingscote 2 71
(Tom Dascombe) *broke smartly: settled in 2nd on rail: shkn up 2 1/2f out: nt qckn: styd on fnl f* **58/10**
4 *1* **Break Free (FR)** 2-9-2 0.................... Christophe-PatriceLemaire 1 68
(Y De Nicolay, France) **48/10**[3]
5 *1* **Chief Hawkeye (IRE)** 2-9-2 0.................... AllanBonnefoy 4 65
(J-V Toux, France) **18/1**

1m 14.02s (3.02) **5** Ran SP% **118.4**
WIN (incl. 1 euro stake): 3.50. PLACES: 1.60, 1.20. SF: 7.70.
Owner Wertheimer & Frere **Bred** Wertheimer Et Frere **Trained** France

4653a - See RI

[3939] BRIGHTON (L-H)
Wednesday, August 3

OFFICIAL GOING: Good to firm (7.8)
Wind: almost nil Weather: very hot and sunny

4654 TOBY STRICKLAND (S) H'CAP — 1m 3f 196y
2:30 (2:32) (Class 6) (0-55,55) 3-Y-0+ **£1,940** (£577; £288; £144) **Stalls** High

Form RPR
0064 **1** **What About Now**[16] 4153 3-8-8 **53** ow1....................(b[1]) PatrickHills[(3)] 3 65
(J W Hills) *settled in midfield: effrt to ld over 2f out: sn rdn clr: eased fnl 100yds* **7/1**
6326 **2** *6* **Barbirolli**[22] 3946 9-8-13 **47**.................... AdamBeschizza[(3)] 11 49
(William Stone) *towards rr and hld up: effrt and drvn over 2f out: wnt 2nd fnl 100yds: one pce and no ch w wnr* **9/1**
-536 **3** *nk* **Easydoesit (IRE)**[55] 2858 3-8-4 **46**....................(p) SilvestreDeSousa 7 48
(Jane Chapple-Hyam) *t.k.h early and cl up: pushed along 6f out: rdn to ld 4f out: edgd lft: hdd over 2f out: plodded on and no ch w wnr ins fnl f* **7/4**[1]
-000 **4** *3* **Alhaque (USA)**[20] 4024 5-9-9 **54**....................(b) TonyCulhane 1 51
(Paul Midgley) *midfield: rdn and racd awkwardly fr 1/2-way: nvr keen after: plugged on reluctantly fnl 2f* **4/1**[2]
-000 **5** *7* **Le Corvee (IRE)**[17] 2905 9-8-12 **50**.................... LucyKBarry[(7)] 4 36
(Tony Carroll) *racd keenly and prom: rdn wl over 3f out: btn over 2f out* **6/1**[3]
5555 **6** *shd* **Senor Tibor (USA)**[60] 2721 3-8-4 **46** oh1..........(bt) FrankieMcDonald 9 31
(Edward Creighton) *drvn to get gng and reluctant in rr: str reminders and no rspnse 1/2-way: no ch after* **100/1**
0-04 **7** *10* **Special Endeavour (IRE)**[22] 3945 3-8-8 **50**................(p) MartinDwyer 5 19
(William Muir) *pressed ldr: upsides 4f out: rdn and lost pl 3f out: eased 1f out: t.o* **12/1**
6000 **8** *4* **Richo**[11] 4329 5-9-1 **46**.................... RobbieFitzpatrick 2 9
(Shaun Harris) *s.s: in last pair: rdn 4f out: no rspnse: btn over 3f out: eased 1f out: t.o* **25/1**
0535 **9** *4* **Bobby Dazzler (IRE)**[17] 2722 3-8-13 **55**.................... PaulDoe 6 12
(Jim Best) *led and plld hrd: hdd 4f out: sn gave up: last and eased 1f out: t.o* **16/1**

2m 32.7s **Going Correction** 0.0s/f (Good)
WFA 3 from 5yo+ 11lb **9** Ran SP% **111.6**
Speed ratings (Par 101): **100,96,95,93,89 89,82,79,77**
toteswingers:1&2:£3.90, 2&3:£3.60, 1&3:£3.00 CSF £62.28 CT £137.60 TOTE £8.30: £2.80, £2.50, £1.40; EX 58.90 Trifecta £304.10 Pool: £550.66 - 1.34 winning units..The winner was bought in for 6,600gns.

Owner Gary And Linnet Woodward **Bred** Highclere Stud And Quarry Bloodstock **Trained** Upper Lambourn, Berks

FOCUS

Rail dolled out from 6f to 2.5f adding about 10yds to advertised distances. This is really moderate form, as you'd expect for the race type. They all stayed far side and the form is rated around the second.

4655 E B F FLYING SCOTSMAN MAIDEN STKS 6f 209y

3:00 (3:03) (Class 5) 2-Y-O **£3,234** (£962; £481; £240) **Stalls** Centre

Form RPR

1 **Counterglow (IRE)** 2-8-10 0 .... AntiocoMurgia(7) 5 83+
(Mahmood Al Zarooni) *trckd ldng pair: effrt gng wl to ld 1f out: sn pushed clr: comf* **13/2[3]**

05 **2** *4* **Royal Academician (USA)**[20] 4007 2-9-3 0 .... GeorgeBaker 2 73
(Gary Moore) *t.k.h in 2nd: jnd ldr 2f out: rdn and sn hung lft in ld: hdd 1f out: wl outpcd after* **1/1[1]**

220 **3** *2 1/4* **Marcus Augustus (IRE)**[48] 3064 2-9-3 75 .... PatDobbs 4 68
(Richard Hannon) *led: jnd 2f out: ev ch over 1f out: squeezed for room: sn btn* **9/4[2]**

6 **4** *7* **Grand Rapids (USA)**[22] 3954 2-9-3 0 .... AhmedAjtebi 1 49
(Mahmood Al Zarooni) *in last pair: drvn 1/2-way: wknd over 1f out: eased whn btn* **13/2[3]**

1m 23.93s (0.83) **Going Correction** 0.0s/f (Good) **4 Ran SP% 107.4**
Speed ratings (Par 94): **95,90,87,79**
CSF £13.58 TOTE £9.00; EX 15.90.

Owner Godolphin **Bred** Colin Kennedy **Trained** Newmarket, Suffolk

FOCUS

They raced far side. Just the four runners and this is ordinary form, but at least it went to the only newcomer, who was quite impressive.

NOTEBOOK

Counterglow(IRE), a 15,500gns foal, is a half-brother to a few winners, including multiple sprint scorer Who's Winning (successful here), and the course wasn't a problem. He travelled well and didn't have to be seriously asked to draw clear, but it's questionable what he achieved. Still, he has the scope to progress and could start off in nurseries at a reasonable level. (op 8-1 tchd 10-1)

Royal Academician(USA) failed to build on the improvement he showed on his second start at Epsom. He travelled okay, but didn't handle the track under pressure, hanging left. It may also be worth nothing his trainer had gone 41 runners without a winner prior to this. (op 6-5 tchd 10-11)

Marcus Augustus(IRE), totally outclassed in the Norfolk last time, was disappointing on this return to maiden company, failing to confirm earlier promise. (tchd 2-1)

Grand Rapids(USA) didn't exhibit the signs of greenness he had when well beaten on his debut. He just looked short of ability and looks expensive at $325,000. (op 4-1 tchd 7-1)

4656 JOHN SMITH'S BRIGHTON MILE CHALLENGE TROPHY (H'CAP) 7f 214y

3:30 (3:31) (Class 4) (0-80,80) 3-Y-O+

£9,337 (£2,796; £1,398; £699; £349; £175) **Stalls** Centre

Form RPR

-500 **1** **Conciliatory**[38] 3436 4-9-7 80 .... (p) AdamBeschizza(3) 13 91
(Rae Guest) *trckd ldrs: rdn 3f out: chal over 1f out: urged ahd fnl 100yds: r.o gamely* **10/1**

0015 **2** *1 1/4* **Green Earth (IRE)**[11] 4317 4-8-7 63 .... FergusSweeney 10 71
(Pat Phelan) *cl up: t.k.h: rdn to ld over 2f out: hdd 100yds out: nt qckn after* **16/1**

4000 **3** *1 1/4* **Eastern Gift**[40] 3361 6-8-5 64 .... HarryBentley(3) 1 69
(Gay Kelleway) *towards rr: prog 2f out: n.m.r over 1f out: swtchd rt: kpt on ins fnl f: nt rch ldrs* **22/1**

2646 **4** *shd* **First Cat**[11] 4310 4-9-10 80 .... PatDobbs 7 85
(Richard Hannon) *blind off eye: detached in last tl 1/2-way: c w run fr over 2 out but n.m.r and all over the pl u.p: styd on cl home but nvr gng to win* **15/2[3]**

0012 **5** *1/2* **Night Lily (IRE)**[4] 4537 5-9-7 80 .... PatrickHills(3) 2 84+
(Paul D'Arcy) *hdwy over 2f out: rdn wl over 1f out: n.m.r sn after: no imp fnl f* **9/4[1]**

3331 **6** *2 3/4* **Rondeau (GR)**[26] 4010 6-9-10 80 .... GeorgeBaker 8 78
(Patrick Chamings) *prom: drvn over 2f out: nt qckn over 1f out* **14/1**

2344 **7** *1 1/2* **Signora Frasi (IRE)**[23] 3926 6-8-3 59 .... SilvestreDeSousa 3 53
(Tony Newcombe) *towards rr: hrd drvn and effrt over 3f out: unable to chal* **14/1**

6066 **8** *2 1/4* **Mujood**[26] 3801 8-9-10 80 .... (b) LiamKeniry 9 69
(Eve Johnson Houghton) *drvn along and prom: led 1/2-way: hdd over 2f out: steadily lost pl* **50/1**

0-00 **9** *3/4* **Rock Anthem (IRE)**[14] 4215 7-9-5 75 .... MartinDwyer 12 62
(Mike Murphy) *midfield: rdn and btn 2f out* **28/1**

6046 **10** *1 1/4* **Diddums**[11] 4322 5-7-8 57 .... KatiaScallan(7) 5 41
(Alastair Lidderdale) *bhd: n.d fnl 3f* **40/1**

0033 **11** *1* **Catalyze**[13] 4243 3-9-3 80 .... (t) DavidProbert 14 61
(Andrew Balding) *chsd ldrs tl rdn and wknd over 2f out* **6/1[2]**

1410 **12** *3/4* **Bold Marc (IRE)**[12] 4278 9-9-6 79 .... SeanLevey(3) 16 59
(Mrs K Burke) *led tl 1/2-way: rdn and wknd over 2f out* **14/1**

0251 **13** *12* **Dazeen**[18] 4107 4-9-9 79 .... TonyCulhane 15 32
(Paul Midgley) *chsd ldrs: rdn and wknd over 2f out: eased and t.o* **8/1**

1426 **14** *1* **Hail Promenader (IRE)**[32] 3634 5-9-10 80 .... TomQueally 4 30
(Andrew Haynes) *lost pl over 3f out: hung lft: eased fnl f: t.o* **25/1**

00 **15** *13* **Captain Macarry (IRE)**[32] 3620 6-9-0 70 .... (v) WilliamCarson 6 —
(Stuart Williams) *taken down early: effrt on outside over 3f out: sn hrd drvn and btn: eased fnl f: wl t.o* **33/1**

1m 34.82s (-1.18) **Going Correction** 0.0s/f (Good)
WFA 3 from 4yo+ 7lb **15 Ran SP% 121.9**
Speed ratings (Par 105): **105,103,102,102,101 99,97,95,94,93 92,91,79,78,65**
toteswingers:1&2:£54.60, 2&3:£104.60, 1&3:£50.00 CSF £148.84 CT £3493.87 TOTE £11.80: £3.80, £5.30, £5.50; EX 225.40 TRIFECTA Not won..

Owner Miss K Rausing **Bred** Miss K Rausing **Trained** Newmarket, Suffolk

FOCUS

A valuable race for the grade, but while it was predictably competitive, the form looks ordinary. The winner was close to her Goodwood level. The action unfolded towards the far rail and room was at a premium in the closing stages.

Eastern Gift Official explanation: jockey said gelding was denied a clear run

First Cat Official explanation: jockey said gelding was denied a clear run

Night Lily(IRE) Official explanation: jockey said mare was denied a clear run

Catalyze Official explanation: vet said colt lost left-fore shoe

Hail Promenader(IRE) Official explanation: jockey said gelding hung left

4657 DRINK IN BRIGHTON H'CAP 5f 213y

4:00 (4:00) (Class 6) (0-55,55) 3-Y-O **£1,940** (£577; £288; £144) **Stalls** Centre

Form RPR

6604 **1** **Silca Conegliano (IRE)**[20] 3998 3-8-5 47 .... (v) MartinHarley(3) 5 53
(Mick Channon) *chsd ldrs: n.m.r and swtchd lft wl over 2f out: effrt to chal over 1f out: led fnl 75yds: jst hung on* **9/2[1]**

00-0 **2** *hd* **Deslaya (IRE)**[40] 3343 3-8-13 52 .... NickyMackay 4 57
(Chris Wall) *prom: led over 2f out: drvn and hdd 75yds out: kpt on wl cl home* **9/2[1]**

3-40 **3** *2* **Brave Tiger (IRE)**[79] 2155 3-8-4 50 .... (t) CharlesBishop(7) 7 49
(Hugo Palmer) *midfield: effrt on outside wl over 1f out: rdn and no imp ins fnl f* **5/1[2]**

00-0 **4** *hd* **Disco Doll**[28] 3747 3-9-2 55 .... LiamKeniry 9 53
(Patrick Chamings) *last away: plld hrd in rr: effrt over 1f out: hld by ldng pair fnl f* **16/1**

6000 **5** *1/2* **Microlight**[16] 4162 3-8-8 47 .... (b) RichardThomas 3 44
(John E Long) *nvr bttr than midfield: rdn over 2f out: btn over 1f out* **16/1**

-100 **6** *3 1/2* **Henrys Air**[23] 3913 3-9-1 54 .... RobbieFitzpatrick 11 40
(David Bridgwater) *drvn in rr 1/2-way: n.d* **14/1**

00-0 **7** *3 1/2* **Arakova (IRE)**[28] 3724 3-8-11 50 .... J-PGuillambert 2 24
(Matthew Salaman) *chsd ldr: drvn over 2f out: sn btn* **8/1**

2560 **8** *nk* **Porthgwidden Beach (USA)**[4] 4547 3-9-0 53 .... JackMitchell 1 26
(Anthony Middleton) *led: rdn and hdd over 2f out: rapidly lost pl* **6/1[3]**

0-00 **9** *shd* **Zartina (IRE)**[28] 3724 3-8-11 50 .... SilvestreDeSousa 10 33
(Sylvester Kirk) *bhd: rdn and btn 2f out* **8/1**

-656 **10** *2* **Mi Sun Donk**[168] 558 3-8-12 51 .... IanMongan 8 18
(Brett Johnson) *midfield: drvn 1/2-way: last and racing awkwardly fr over 1f out* **6/1[3]**

1m 11.0s (0.80) **Going Correction** 0.0s/f (Good) **10 Ran SP% 122.3**
Speed ratings (Par 98): **94,93,91,90,90 85,80,80,80,77**
toteswingers:1&2:£5.10, 2&3:£6.90, 1&3:£5.20 CSF £25.93 CT £108.51 TOTE £5.40: £1.80, £2.40, £2.50; EX 33.20 Trifecta £654.00 Part won. Pool of £883.89 - 0.50 winning units..

Owner Mrs T Burns **Bred** J Costello **Trained** West Ilsley, Berks

FOCUS

A moderate 3-y-o handicap. They raced middle to far side. The form is rated around the winner's efforts this year.

Zartina(IRE) Official explanation: jockey said filly was denied a clear run

4658 MANOR HOTEL NURSERY 5f 59y

4:30 (4:30) (Class 5) (0-75,77) 2-Y-O **£2,587** (£770; £384; £192) **Stalls** Low

Form RPR

2631 **1** **Sea Odyssey (IRE)**[4] 4548 2-9-4 77 6ex .... MatthewLawson(7) 3 82+
(B W Hills) *enthusiatic and mde all: pushed along over 1f out: kpt on wl and a in command* **8/15[1]**

5533 **2** *1 1/2* **Leenavesta (USA)**[18] 4085 2-9-4 70 .... PatDobbs 6 68
(Richard Hannon) *pressed wnr: rdn over 2f out: a 2nd best ins fnl f* **11/4[2]**

5303 **3** *6* **Clarkson (IRE)**[13] 4226 2-8-8 60 .... (b[1]) FergusSweeney 4 36
(Jamie Osborne) *plld v hrd in 3rd: rdn over 2f out: floundering over 1f out* **17/2[3]**

0104 **4** *1 1/2* **Selinda**[13] 4226 2-7-12 57 .... CharlesBishop(7) 5 28
(Mick Channon) *a in last: rdn and tried to cl wd of others after 1/2-way: wl btn over 1f out* **16/1**

63.66 secs (1.36) **Going Correction** 0.0s/f (Good) **4 Ran SP% 108.3**
Speed ratings (Par 94): **89,86,77,74**
CSF £2.26 TOTE £1.70; EX 2.10.

Owner H R Mould **Bred** Mrs C Regalado-Gonzalez **Trained** Lambourn, Berks

FOCUS

An uncompetitive nursery and they finished in the order in which they raced. They stayed far side in the straight. Weak form but the winner has got his act together.

NOTEBOOK

Sea Odyssey(IRE) was 2lb well in under his penalty for a Polytrack maiden success four days earlier, and also had the advantage of his rider being able to claim 7lb despite having ridden his 20th winner the evening before (claim due to be reduced to 5lb). This was straightforward - he travelled well in the lead and was never in danger, and he's now fulfilling his potential. He could reappear quickly. (tchd 8-13 and 4-6 in a place)

Leenavesta(USA), back in trip, was no match for the well-handicapped winner. (op 7-2)

Clarkson(IRE) didn't improve for first-time blinkers, racing keenly under restraint. (op 9-1 tchd 8-1)

Selinda has gained both her wins in 6f sellers at Yarmouth. (op 9-1)

4659 ALICE RYAN MEMORIAL H'CAP 5f 59y

5:00 (5:00) (Class 5) (0-75,74) 4-Y-O+ **£2,587** (£770; £384; £192) **Stalls** Low

Form RPR

3542 **1** **Clear Ice (IRE)**[9] 4395 4-8-11 64 .... (b) DavidProbert 4 72
(Gay Kelleway) *mde all: rdn over 1f out: kpt finding enough through fnl f* **13/8[1]**

4501 **2** *1/2* **Highland Harvest**[14] 4206 7-8-9 62 .... RobertHavlin 5 68
(Jamie Poulton) *pressed wnr: racd w awkward hd carriage: edgd lft and drvn over 1f out and upsides after: hld fnl 75yds* **15/2**

50-0 **3** *1 1/4* **Safari Mischief**[28] 3737 8-9-2 72 .... HarryBentley(3) 2 74
(Peter Winkworth) *chsd ldrs: drvn in 3rd on rails over 1f out: sn swtchd rt: no imp after* **2/1[2]**

4-46 **4** *3/4* **Luisa Tetrazzini (IRE)**[11] 4340 5-8-4 57 oh2 ow2 .... RichardThomas 1 56
(Michael Attwater) *in last mostly: rdn wl over 2f out: no imp after* **14/1**

1304 **5** *1/2* **Magical Speedfit (IRE)**[23] 3914 6-9-7 74 .... TomQueally 3 71
(George Margarson) *pressed ldng pair: drvn over 2f out: btn over 1f out* **7/2[3]**

62.70 secs (0.40) **Going Correction** 0.0s/f (Good) **5 Ran SP% 112.1**
Speed ratings (Par 103): **96,95,93,92,91**
CSF £14.00 TOTE £2.10: £1.10, £3.80; EX 10.30.

Owner Whispering Winds **Bred** Mrs Noelle Walsh **Trained** Exning, Suffolk

FOCUS

Like in the preceding nursery, it proved difficult to make up ground and for most of the way the front three raced in the order they finished. It wasn't strong run and the form raises a bit of doubt.

Safari Mischief Official explanation: jockey said gelding was denied a clear run

T/Plt: £902.30 to a £1 stake. Pool of £76,130.63 - 61.59 winning tickets. T/Qpdt: £56.80 to a £1 stake. Pool of £5,875.28 - 76.45 winning tickets. IM

[3735]KEMPTON (A.W) (R-H)

Wednesday, August 3

OFFICIAL GOING: Standard

Wind: Moderate, half behind Weather: Sunny, hot

4660 FREE ENTRY FOR BETDAQ MEMBERS APPRENTICE H'CAP 1m 3f (P)

6:00 (6:02) (Class 4) (0-85,85) 4-Y-0+ **£4,075** (£1,212; £606; £303) **Stalls** Low

Form RPR

-140 **1** **Milnagavie**[52] 2958 4-9-7 **82** ... RyanPowell 1 92
(Richard Hannon) *trckd ldr: led over 2f out: sn rdn: kpt on wl u.p fr over 1f out* **10/1**

5003 **2** *1 1/4* **Elmfield Giant (USA)**[28] 3739 4-8-3 **67** ow1 ... AntiocoMurgia(3) 8 75
(Richard Fahey) *sn restrained towards rr fr wd draw: prog over 4f out: rdn over 2f out: chsd wnr over 1f out: tried to chal last 150yds: a hld* **4/1**[1]

0066 **3** *3 1/4* **Bikini Babe (IRE)**[8] 4410 4-9-7 **85** ... DarylByrne(3) 3 87
(Mark Johnston) *trckd ldng pair: effrt gng strly on inner to press wnr jst over 2f out: nt qckn over 1f out and sn lost 2nd: wknd ins fnl f* **4/1**[1]

5402 **4** *1 1/4* **Potentiale (IRE)**[27] 3760 7-8-12 **73** ... AmyScott 6 73
(J W Hills) *hld up last: effrt 3f out: kpt on one pce to take 4th over 1f out: no imp after* **5/1**[2]

2346 **5** *2* **Beat Route**[16] 4148 4-8-7 **68** ... MatthewCosham 7 64
(Michael Attwater) *settled midfield: effrt 4f out: rdn and no imp on ldrs over 2f out* **5/1**[2]

0003 **6** *3 1/4* **Kidlat**[7] 4432 6-9-0 **82** ... MissAlexOwen(7) 9 72
(Alan Bailey) *sn led at decent pce: rdn and hdd over 2f out: steadily wknd* **17/2**

0364 **7** *2 1/4* **Rosco Flyer (IRE)**[19] 4059 5-8-11 **72** ... TobyAtkinson 5 58
(Roger Teal) *rn in snatches: drvn in midfield 7f out: effrt u.p over 2f out but nt look keen: sn btn* **8/1**[3]

1-64 **8** *26* **Querido (GER)**[161] 341 7-8-3 **67** ... NathanAlison(3) 2 —
(Paddy Butler) *chsd ldrs tl wknd rapidly wl over 3f out: t.o* **20/1**

2020 **9** *4* **Lisahane Bog**[36] 2051 4-8-8 **72** ...(b) LucyKBarry(3) 4 —
(Peter Hedger) *uns rdr on way to post: s.s: nvr gng wl in rr: wknd over 3f out: t.o* **20/1**

2m 19.96s (-1.94) **Going Correction** 0.0s/f (Stan) **9** Ran SP% **113.6**

Speed ratings (Par 105): **107,106,103,102,101 99,97,78,75**

toteswingers:1&2:£7.60, 2&3:£3.10, 1&3:£5.70 CSF £48.97 CT £186.94 TOTE £12.10: £3.60, £1.30, £2.40; EX 62.20.

Owner Mrs R Ablett **Bred** Darley **Trained** East Everleigh, Wilts

FOCUS

Some decent types taking part in this apprentices' handicap but only three really figured in the last quarter mile. The time was not far outside the standard. The form loos sound enough.

Potentiale(IRE) Official explanation: jockey said gelding lost an off-fore shoe

4661 BETDAQ.COM EXCHANGE PRICE MULTIPLES NURSERY 6f (P)

6:30 (6:30) (Class 4) (0-85,85) 2-Y-0 **£3,428** (£1,020; £509; £254) **Stalls** Low

Form RPR

334 **1** **Shere Khan**[53] 2907 2-8-10 **74** ... PatDobbs 4 79
(Richard Hannon) *hld up in 5th: taken to outer and shkn up 2f out: prog over 1f out: r.o to ld last 150yds: sn clr: pushed out* **16/1**

016 **2** *2 1/4* **Democretes**[25] 3866 2-8-12 **76** ... RichardHughes 6 74
(Richard Hannon) *led: rdn over 2f out: kpt on u.p: hdd and outpcd last 150yds* **15/8**[2]

1121 **3** *1 1/4* **Pint Size**[15] 4178 2-8-13 **84** ... AntiocoMurgia(7) 1 79
(Gay Kelleway) *trckd ldng pair: shkn up 2f out: wanting to hang lft over 1f out whn cl enough: nt qckn* **8/1**

01 **4** *3/4* **Mahkama (USA)**[28] 3736 2-9-7 **85** ... TedDurcan 3 77
(Saeed Bin Suroor) *dwlt: t.k.h: hld up in 4th: rdn and effrt 2f out: clsd to chal 1f out: wknd last 150yds* **5/4**[1]

0525 **5** *1/2* **Brimstone Hill (IRE)**[25] 3842 2-8-11 **75** ... MichaelHills 5 67
(B W Hills) *trckd ldr: rdn over 2f out: lost 2nd jst over 1f out: hld whn squeezed for room sn after: fdd* **7/1**[3]

040 **6** *5* **Illustrious Lad (IRE)**[23] 3917 2-8-6 **70** ... NickyMackay 2 46
(Jim Boyle) *a in last: no prog on inner fnl 2f* **40/1**

1m 13.53s (0.43) **Going Correction** 0.0s/f (Stan) **6** Ran SP% **111.2**

Speed ratings (Par 96): **97,94,92,91,90 84**

toteswingers:1&2:£5.60, 2&3:£2.50, 1&3:£5.00 CSF £45.61 TOTE £11.20: £3.70, £1.20; EX 44.90.

Owner G Howard-Spink & D Weatherstone **Bred** West Lodge Stud **Trained** East Everleigh, Wilts

FOCUS

Richard Hannon won this in 2009 and was doubly represented. They finished first and second, but not in the order the market suggested. The pace was strng and the winner did it well.

NOTEBOOK

Shere Khan had run to a reasonable level in 5f maidens and was making his handicap and AW debut having been gelded since his previous start. He was settled off the pace but picked up well in the closing stages and swept past his rivals to win with a little in hand. He could be open to further progress on this surface. (op 14-1 tchd 18-1)

Democretes won over this trip in May but had failed to get home over 7f next time, following a break. His rider was keen to make the running and his mount responded well to hold off several challenges before his stablemate swept by. This is clearly his trip. (op 11-4)

Pint Size has been a consistent performer on turf and Fibresand but his wins had all come in claimers. Trying this surface for the first time, he travelled well on it and stuck on well for pressure. He could win a similar contest on sand. (op 15-2 tchd 9-1)

Mahkama(USA), who won in good style over C&D when making all, missed the break slightly and was again keen. She came through to have every chance around a furlong out but paid for not settling thereafter. She might be better off in front. (op Evens)

Brimstone Hill(IRE) had run reasonably on a sound surface on turf and had his chance on this AW debut. However, he was feeling the pinch when short of room inside the last furlong. (tchd 6-1 and 15-2)

4662 LONDON IRISH EBF MAIDEN FILLIES' STKS 7f (P)

7:00 (7:00) (Class 5) 2-Y-0 **£3,299** (£981; £490; £245) **Stalls** Low

Form RPR

2 **1** **Way Too Hot**[43] 3258 2-9-0 0 ... AdamKirby 6 83+
(Clive Cox) *wl plcd bhd ldrs: effrt over 2f out: drvn to ld over 1f out: sn hung rt: clr whn hung bdly lft and swished tail ins fnl f* **2/1**[2]

2 **2** *2 1/2* **Na Zdorovie**[26] 3812 2-9-0 ... MichaelHills 7 75
(B W Hills) *slowly away: rcvrd to rch 3rd after 3f: rdn over 2f out: outpcd by wnr over 1f out: kpt on* **5/4**[1]

4 **3** *1 1/2* **Parisian Princess (IRE)**[18] 4087 2-9-0 0 ... JimmyFortune 1 71+
(George Baker) *sn towards rr: outpcd over 2f out and pushed along: prog over 1f out: r.o to take 3rd nr fin* **33/1**

60 **4** *3/4* **Iced Opal**[19] 4052 2-9-0 0 ... LiamKeniry 8 69
(Michael Blanshard) *trckd ldr: pushed into ld over 2f out: rdn and hdd over 1f out: one pce* **66/1**

5 *1 3/4* **Dust On The Ground** 2-9-0 0 ... AndreaAtzeni 4 64
(Marco Botti) *sn in last trio: sme prog fr 2f out: pushed along firmly and styd on to take 5th nr fin* **12/1**

6 *shd* **Arch Of Colours** 2-9-0 0 ... AhmedAjtebi 10 64
(Mahmood Al Zarooni) *wl in tch: rdn and outpcd by ldng quartet 2f out: no imp after* **14/1**

2 **7** *4 1/2* **Roman Province (IRE)**[13] 4245 2-9-0 0 ... DaneO'Neill 3 52
(Roger Teal) *led: rdn and hdd over 2f out: wknd qckly over 1f out* **8/1**[3]

0 **8** *2 3/4* **Idols Eye**[19] 4052 2-9-0 0 ... RichardHughes 5 45
(Richard Hannon) *in tch: rn green and reminders 3f out: sn lft bhd: no ch fnl 2f* **16/1**

3354 **9** *1 3/4* **Maltease Ah**[9] 4386 2-9-0 70 ... DarryllHolland 9 40
(Andrew Reid) *a towards rr on outer: no prog over 2f out: wl btn after* **50/1**

0 **10** *3* **Fox's Ambers (FR)**[20] 4007 2-9-0 0 ... PatDobbs 12 33
(Richard Hannon) *mostly last: struggling sn after 1/2-way* **80/1**

53 **11** *2 1/2* **Bit A Craic**[29] 3718 2-9-0 0 ... KierenFallon 2 26
(John Ryan) *prom: pushed along after 3f: wknd over 2f out: eased fnl f* **25/1**

1m 27.32s (1.32) **Going Correction** 0.0s/f (Stan) **11** Ran SP% **120.6**

Speed ratings (Par 91): **92,89,87,86,84 84,79,76,74,70 67**

toteswingers:1&2:£1.70, 2&3:£9.60, 1&3:£10.30 CSF £4.82 TOTE £2.30: £1.10, £1.40, £7.80; EX 6.20.

Owner Mr And Mrs P Hargreaves & A D Spence **Bred** Mr & Mrs P Hargreaves & A D Spence **Trained** Lambourn, Berks

FOCUS

A decent-looking fillies' maiden with several promising types on show plus a couple of newcomers, and an appropriate winner on a stifling evening. The winner can rate higher if going the right way.

NOTEBOOK

Way Too Hot was sent off favourite when runner-up on her debut at Newbury in June, a race from which the third has since won. Obviously well regarded, she produced a good turn of foot to settle the issue in a matter of strides entering the final furlong. She looks potentially classy but also displayed several quirks. She needed to be loaded with a blanket, swished her tail when hit and swerved about once in front. Much depends on how she handles this mentally as to whether she progresses. (op 3-1)

Na Zdorovie is related to several winners at varying trips. She was sent off favourite, having made a promising debut over this trip at Newbury, a race from which the third had won since. She slightly missed the break but had her chance and is flattered by her proximity to the winner. (op 11-10 tchd Evens)

Parisian Princess(IRE) ◆ ran with promise on her debut in a Lingfield turf maiden, but was 5l behind the first three and they had all been beaten since. Held up but quite keen, she was noted keeping on in good style and is clearly going the right way.

Iced Opal, who was long prices when well beaten in two 6f maidens, ran much better on this AW debut. Now qualified for nurseries, she could well be competitive in handicaps after this.

Dust On The Ground, a sharply bred half-sister to a juvenile winner at 6f, made a promising debut, staying on late. Both of her siblings handled Polytrack, and she clearly does too, so is likely to be much sharper if returning here. (tchd 14-1)

Arch Of Colours is a half-sister to 7f and 1m winners at three but her dam stayed 1m4f and her sire is an influence for stamina. She gives the impression she already needs a bit further. (op 12-1)

4663 LAY BACK AND WIN AT BETDAQ.COM MAIDEN STKS 1m (P)

7:30 (7:35) (Class 5) 3-Y-0+ **£2,264** (£673; £336; £168) **Stalls** Low

Form RPR

45- **1** **Port Hollow**[277] 7232 3-8-12 0 ... MichaelHills 5 83+
(B W Hills) *mde all and sn 4 l clr: maintained advantage thrght: rdn over 1f out: styd on wl* **3/1**[1]

0 **2** *4 1/2* **Phoenix City (USA)**[100] 1568 3-8-12 0 ... JimmyFortune 11 72
(Michael Bell) *chsd clr wnr: drvn over 2f out: no imp over 1f out: styd on* **40/1**

44 **3** *3* **John Louis**[16] 4163 3-9-3 0 ... RichardHughes 3 70
(Philip McBride) *chsd clr ldng pair to 4f out: rdn to go 3rd again over 2f out: no imp: pushed out fnl f* **13/2**

0 **4** *1* **Isometric (USA)**[19] 4065 3-9-3 0 ... AhmedAjtebi 8 68+
(Mahmood Al Zarooni) *towards rr: pushed along in 8th 1/2-way and wl off the pce: styd on fnl 2f: nrst fin* **12/1**

64 **5** *1 3/4* **Tamara Bay**[19] 4065 3-8-9 0 ... GilmarPereira(3) 14 58+
(William Haggas) *sn settled in last and wl off the pce: pushed along and styd on steadily fr over 2f out: nrst fin: do bttr* **25/1**

6 *1 1/2* **Ganas (IRE)** 3-9-3 0 ... AdamKirby 4 60+
(Clive Cox) *chsd ldrs but nt on terms rdn to dispute 6th over 3f out: no imp after* **9/1**

0-4 **7** *1 1/2* **Encore Un Fois**[18] 4102 3-9-3 0 ... KierenFallon 13 56+
(Luca Cumani) *prom: chsd ldng pair 4f out to over 2f out: wknd* **9/2**[3]

8 *2* **Akarana (IRE)** 4-9-10 0 ... TonyCulhane 10 51
(Willie Musson) *sn restrained in last pair and wl off the pce: pushed along fr 3f out: nvr a factor but kpt on showing hint of promise* **40/1**

9 *1* **Violet's Gift (IRE)** 3-8-12 0 ... JackMitchell 7 44
(James Fanshawe) *chsd ldrs: rdn in 5th 1/2-way: wknd wl over 2f out* **20/1**

10 *12* **Princess Icicle** 3-8-12 0 ... DaneO'Neill 12 15
(Jo Crowley) *dwlt and rousted along to rcvr: rdn in 6th sn after 1/2-way: wknd 3f out: t.o* **40/1**

5- **11** *25* **Feather Falls (USA)**[417] 2958 3-8-12 0 ... SilvestreDeSousa 2 —
(Mark Johnston) *dwlt: t.k.h early: rdn in 9th 1/2-way: sn wknd and wl t.o* **7/2**[2]

12 *7* **Lucky Dime** 3-8-12 0 ... LiamKeniry 6 —
(Noel Quinlan) *s.s: a wl bhd: wl t.o* **66/1**

1m 39.77s (-0.03) **Going Correction** 0.0s/f (Stan)

WFA 3 from 4yo+ 7lb **12** Ran SP% **113.8**

Speed ratings (Par 103): **100,95,92,91,89 88,86,84,83,71 46,39**

toteswingers:1&2:£38.20, 2&3:£51.20, 1&3:£2.60 CSF £137.58 TOTE £4.20: £1.30, £11.40, £1.30; EX 162.50.

Owner K Abdulla **Bred** Juddmonte Farms Ltd **Trained** Lambourn, Berks

FOCUS

A fair-looking older-horse maiden which was won by the subsequent Group 3 winner Fanunalter in 2009. However, with several returning from long absences and others making their debuts there was every chance one of these would be better than those with recent modest form at best, and so it proved. The form makes some sense.

The Form Book, Raceform Ltd, Compton, RG20 6NL

Akarana(IRE) Official explanation: vet said gelding lost left-fore shoe

4664 BETDAQ MOBILE APPS H'CAP 1m 3f (P)
8:00 (8:03) (Class 5) (0-75,74) 3-Y-O **£2,264** (£673; £336; £168) **Stalls** Low

Form RPR

5 **1** **Planetoid (IRE)**[68] 2469 3-9-7 **74** .... TedDurcan 5 86+
(David Lanigan) *early reminders to r properly: sn gng bttr and trckd ldrs in 6th: drvn and prog over 2f out: clsd u.p to ld 1f out: forged clr* **1/1**[1]

21-4 **2** *2 ½* **Reem Star**[83] 2022 3-9-5 **72** .... GeorgeBaker 9 79
(Ed Dunlop) *trckd ldng trio: moved up to chal 2f out: led wl over 1f out to 1f out: styd on but outpcd* **7/2**[2]

033 **3** *2 ¼* **Princesse Gaelle**[23] 3925 3-9-2 **69** .... AndreaAtzeni 6 72
(Marco Botti) *chsd ldr: rdn to ld jst over 2f out: hdd and one pce wl over 1f out* **20/1**

0401 **4** *hd* **Ugo (USA)**[41] 3325 3-9-5 **72** .... KierenFallon 7 75
(Heather Main) *trckd ldng pair to over 2f out: sn shkn up and nt qckn: kpt on one pce u.p fnl f* **11/2**[3]

-254 **5** *4* **See The Smile (USA)**[47] 3131 3-9-5 **72** .... JimmyFortune 10 67
(Jim Boyle) *led: rdn and hdd jst over 2f out: steadily fdd u.p* **20/1**

1305 **6** *7* **Diplomasi**[12] 4268 3-9-1 **68** ....(p) PhilipRobinson 8 51
(Clive Brittain) *dwlt: sn tk fierce hold in last trio: rdn 3f out: hanging and nt keen over 2f out: wl btn after* **10/1**

5106 **7** *hd* **Classic Voice (IRE)**[20] 4009 3-9-2 **69** ....(p) WilliamCarson 4 51
(Roy Brotherton) *settled in last trio: rdn and no prog over 2f out: no ch after: fin lame* **28/1**

3506 **8** *7* **Woop Woop (IRE)**[27] 3771 3-8-12 **65** ow1 .... AdamKirby 3 35
(Stef Higgins) *chsd ldrs in 5th: rdn and wknd 3f out* **12/1**

1-00 **9** *86* **Irons On Fire (USA)**[28] 3740 3-9-6 **73** .... TonyCulhane 2 —
(George Baker) *settled in last trio: shkn up and wknd 4f out: eased 3f out: wl t.o* **40/1**

2m 21.23s (-0.67) **Going Correction** 0.0s/f (Stan) **9** Ran SP% **119.8**
Speed ratings (Par 100): **102,100,98,98,95 90,90,85,22**
toteswingers:1&2:£2.60, 2&3:£5.00, 1&3:£6.10 CSF £4.51 CT £43.73 TOTE £1.60: £1.10, £2.40, £4.40; EX 7.60.
Owner B E Nielsen **Bred** Bjorn Nielsen **Trained** Newmarket, Suffolk

FOCUS
The form looks sound enough. The time was 1.27secs slower than the opening apprentice handicap.
Diplomasi Official explanation: jockey said gelding ran too free
Classic Voice(IRE) Official explanation: jockey said gelding finished lame left-fore

4665 TULLAMORE DEW H'CAP (LONDON MILE QUALIFIER) 1m (P)
8:30 (8:31) (Class 4) (0-85,83) 3-Y-O **£4,075** (£1,212; £606; £303) **Stalls** Low

Form RPR

4141 **1** **Queen Of Cash (IRE)**[27] 3782 3-9-6 **82** .... DarryllHolland 9 89
(Hughie Morrison) *trckd ldr after 3f: pushed into ld over 2f out: drvn and edgd lft over 1f out: jnd ins fnl f: hld on: all out* **9/1**

-026 **2** *hd* **Switchback**[16] 4161 3-8-8 **70** .... RichardMullen 8 76
(Sir Michael Stoute) *wl in tch: rdn and prog over 2f out: chsd wnr over 1f out: drvn and upsides ins fnl f: no ex last strides* **25/1**

-12 **3** *nse* **Galiando**[21] 3987 3-9-7 **83** .... JimmyFortune 5 89+
(Jeremy Noseda) *settled in last trio: plenty to do whn plld out and drvn 2f out: prog u.p over 1f out: clsd on ldrs fnl f: jst hld* **5/2**[1]

0464 **4** *1* **Kingarrick**[13] 4255 3-8-11 **73** .... SilvestreDeSousa 1 77
(Eve Johnson Houghton) *towards rr: rdn and prog on inner over 2f out: tried to chal fnl f: no ex last 50yds* **16/1**

0322 **5** *6* **Focail Maith**[16] 4142 3-8-9 **71** .... KierenFallon 10 61
(John Ryan) *towards rr: prog on wd outside bnd 4f out to 3f out: lost pl and rdn over 2f out: sn outpcd: plugged on* **13/2**[3]

5-40 **6** *1 ½* **Tick Tock Lover**[13] 4253 3-9-4 **80** .... FergusSweeney 4 67
(Jo Crowley) *chsd ldr 3f: styd handy: rdn over 2f out: wknd over 1f out* **9/2**[2]

2210 **7** *1* **Whistle On By**[26] 3825 3-9-4 **80** .... MichaelHills 2 64
(R W Hills) *prom: rdn over 2f out: wknd wl over 1f out* **7/1**

10 **8** *3* **Diamond Vision (IRE)**[84] 2052 3-8-13 **78** .... SeanLevey(3) 6 60
(Robert Mills) *led: drvn and hdd over 2f out: wknd over 1f out* **9/1**

21-1 **9** *16* **Golden Creek (USA)**[29] 3710 3-8-11 **73** .... JimCrowley 7 14
(Mrs K Burke) *a in rr: wknd 1/2-way: t.o* **15/2**

1m 39.64s (-0.16) **Going Correction** 0.0s/f (Stan) **9** Ran SP% **114.1**
Speed ratings (Par 102): **100,99,99,98,92 91,90,87,71**
CSF £198.86 CT £727.56 TOTE £8.20: £2.70, £6.60, £1.60; EX 201.40.
Owner Hugh Scott-Barrett And Partners **Bred** Grangemore Stud **Trained** East Ilsley, Berks

FOCUS
Another competitive 3yo handicap and the time was fractionally slower than the earlier maiden over the trip. The form is rated around the fourth.

4666 OLLY MURS 12.08.11 H'CAP 1m (P)
9:00 (9:01) (Class 6) (0-65,65) 3-Y-O+ **£1,617** (£481; £240; £120) **Stalls** Low

Form RPR

0040 **1** **Rio Tinto**[13] 4249 4-9-12 **63** .... WilliamCarson 1 74+
(Giles Bravery) *mde all: kicked clr 3f out: drvn 2f out: a holding on ins fnl f* **4/1**[1]

625 **2** *¾* **Tilsworth Glenboy**[67] 2490 4-9-10 **61** .... AdamKirby 9 70
(J R Jenkins) *hld up: last over 3f out: gd prog on inner over 2f out: drvn to go 2nd ins fnl f: clsd on wnr but nvr gng to get there* **6/1**

0600 **3** *2 ½* **Desert Chieftain**[18] 4081 3-8-11 **55** ....(b[1]) KierenFallon 2 57
(Luca Cumani) *s.i.s: rousted along to take prom pl: outpcd over 2f out: kpt on same pce: tk 3rd nr fin* **5/1**[2]

1612 **4** *1 ½* **Kielty's Folly**[11] 4322 7-9-6 **62** .... JamesRogers(5) 8 62
(Brian Baugh) *chsd wnr: clr of rest but no imp over 2f out: lost 2nd ins fnl f* **11/2**[3]

000 **5** *nk* **Heart Of Dixie (IRE)**[19] 4072 3-8-11 **55** .... SilvestreDeSousa 13 53+
(Paul Cole) *towards rr: prog on outer over 3f out to chse ldrs: outpcd over 2f out: one pce after* **7/1**

0046 **6** *2 ½* **Woolston Ferry (IRE)**[14] 4210 5-9-12 **63** .... FergusSweeney 5 56
(David Pinder) *hld up in rr: nt clr run briefly over 2f out: shkn up and sme prog over 1f out: kpt on fnl f: no ch* **11/1**

06B0 **7** *2 ½* **Leitzu (IRE)**[13] 4249 4-9-6 **60** .... MartinHarley(3) 6 48
(Mick Channon) *a in midfield: outpcd fr 3f out: no ch after* **15/2**

00-0 **8** *3 ¾* **Welsh Dancer**[12] 4281 3-8-13 **57** ....(v[1]) PatDobbs 3 35
(Marcus Tregoning) *chsd ldrs: rdn over 3f out: wknd 2f out* **12/1**

6600 **9** *3 ¾* **Gallantry**[34] 3558 9-9-9 **60** .... JimmyQuinn 10 30
(Michael Squance) *a in rr and nvr gng wl: struggling sn after 1/2-way* **16/1**

3400 **10** *1 ½* **Rainsborough**[30] 3677 4-9-1 **52** ....(e) DaneO'Neill 11 19
(Peter Hedger) *dwlt: hld up in rr: sme prog over 3f out: no hdwy and wl outpcd over 2f out* **20/1**

0050 **11** *1 ¾* **Ossie Ardiles (IRE)**[7] 4431 3-8-11 **55** .... NeilChalmers 14 17
(Michael Appleby) *racd wd: nvr beyond midfield: wl in rr and no ch over 2f out* **66/1**

424 **12** *11* **Dubai Gem**[29] 3709 5-8-11 **48** .... NickyMackay 7 —
(Olivia Maylam) *a in rr: no ch over 2f out: t.o* **18/1**

-360 **13** *7* **Heavenly Music (IRE)**[18] 4090 3-8-13 **57** .... LiamKeniry 12 —
(Sylvester Kirk) *prom: wnt 3rd over 3f out: wknd rapidly over 2f out: t.o* **25/1**

1m 39.84s (0.04) **Going Correction** 0.0s/f (Stan)
WFA 3 from 4yo+ 7lb **13** Ran SP% **127.9**
Speed ratings (Par 101): **99,98,95,94,93 91,88,85,81,79 78,67,60**
toteswingers:1&2:£8.00, 2&3:£10.50, 1&3:£9.30 CSF £29.21 CT £133.67 TOTE £5.10: £1.70, £1.80, £2.40; EX 40.70.
Owner Miss K McManus **Bred** Skymarc Farm **Trained** Cowlinge, Suffolk

FOCUS
A modest handicap and a lively betting market, but the time was the slowest of the three races over the trip on the night. The winner was back to his early maiden form for Godolphin.
Dubai Gem Official explanation: jockey said mare would not face the kickback
T/Jkpt: Not won. T/Plt: £19.90 to a £1 stake. Pool of £66,157.41 2423.41 winning units. T/Qpdt: £3.50 to a £1 stake. Pool of £6,907.09 - 1456.76 winning units. JN

4323 NEWCASTLE (L-H)
Wednesday, August 3

OFFICIAL GOING: Good (7.2)
Wind: breezy, half behind Weather: Overcast

4667 IGNITION FESTIVAL NURSERY 7f
2:20 (2:21) (Class 4) (0-85,77) 2-Y-O **£3,234** (£721; £721; £240) **Stalls** Centre

Form RPR

0425 **1** **Flurry Of Hands (IRE)**[14] 4194 2-8-2 **58** ....(p) AndrewHeffernan 1 59
(Ann Duffield) *mde all at stdy gallop: qcknd over 2f out: hld on wl ins fnl f* **7/1**[2]

300 **2** *¾* **Priestley's Reward (IRE)**[46] 3186 2-8-10 **66** .... AndrewElliott 4 65
(Mrs K Burke) *prom: drvn along 1/2-way: hdwy wl over 1f out: kpt on ins fnl f* **7/1**[2]

141 **2** *dht* **Act Your Shoe Size**[14] 4194 2-9-7 **77** .... DavidAllan 2 76
(Keith Dalgleish) *cl up: pushed along and chsd wnr 1/2-way: effrt 2f out: kpt on ins fnl f* **4/9**[1]

0510 **4** *5* **Schmooze (IRE)**[14] 4194 2-8-2 **63** ....(b) JulieBurke(5) 3 49
(Linda Perratt) *t.k.h: chsd wnr to 1/2-way: outpcd over 2f out: n.d after* **8/1**[3]

1m 27.45s (-0.35) **Going Correction** -0.375s/f (Firm) **4** Ran SP% **105.4**
Speed ratings (Par 96): **92,91,91,85**
EX: Flurry Of Hands/Act Your Shoe Size £4.90; FH/Priestley's Reward £23.80 CSF: FH/AS £5.25 FH/PR £20.18 TOTE £5.80.
Owner Bobby Donworth **Bred** Round Hill Stud **Trained** Constable Burton, N Yorks
■ Stewards' Enquiry : Andrew Heffernan one-day ban: failed to ride to draw (Aug 20)

FOCUS
A moderate nursery. The raced stands' side and there was a tight three-way finish. Straightforward form.

NOTEBOOK
Flurry Of Hands(IRE) made all on the near rail for a somewhat surprising career-first success. She had finished well behind Act Your Shoe Size a fortnight earlier at Catterick, but looked to have her work cut out reversing form with that rival even allowing for a 6lb pull in the weights. This quicker ground proved much more in her favour, however, and the application of first-time cheekpieces clearly helped her cause. She doesn't appeal as one to follow up. (op 9-2)
Priestley's Reward(IRE) ◆ was off the bridle along way out and, despite this being her third outing, still ran distinctly green. She picked up as the race progressed, though, and was doing some decent late work. She looks to be crying out for an even stiffer test and has begun life in nurseries on a workable mark. (op 13-2 tchd 8-1)
Act Your Shoe Size was up 9lb for making it 2-3 on soft ground at Catterick a fortnight previously and proved all the rage to follow up. However, it was clear from halfway she was in trouble and, although she was not beaten far, clearly didn't act so well on this sounder surface. (op 13-2 tchd 8-1)
Schmooze(IRE) was again well beaten and a return to plating company looks on the cards. (tchd 7-1 and 9-1)

4668 LA TAXIS MEDIAN AUCTION MAIDEN STKS 6f
2:50 (2:53) (Class 6) 2-Y-O **£1,617** (£481; £240; £120) **Stalls** Centre

Form RPR

3 **1** **Ruby Night (IRE)**[12] 4276 2-9-3 0 .... JamieSpencer 3 79+
(Michael Bell) *hld up: hdwy on outside to ld over 1f out: sn hrd pressed: pushed out ins fnl f* **1/4**[1]

2 *hd* **Passionada** 2-8-9 0 .... MichaelO'Connell(3) 6 73+
(Ollie Pears) *green in paddock and bef s: chsd ldrs: chal over 1f out to ins fnl f: kpt on: jst hld* **5/1**[2]

0026 **3** *8* **Roy's Legacy**[22] 3948 2-8-12 52 ....(t) DanielleMcCreery(5) 10 53
(Shaun Harris) *trckd ldrs: effrt over 2f out: outpcd by first two ins fnl f* **66/1**

0 **4** *1 ¼* **After Timer (IRE)**[19] 4073 2-8-9 0 .... DaleSwift(3) 9 45
(Julie Camacho) *hld up in tch: rdn over 2f out: no imp over 1f out* **20/1**

0 **5** *¾* **Heidi's Delight (IRE)**[18] 4106 2-8-12 0 .... RoystonFfrench 1 42
(Ann Duffield) *led to over 1f out: rdn and wknd ins fnl f* **50/1**

000 **6** *5* **Nadia's Place**[13] 4232 2-8-9 42 ....(v[1]) LouisBeuzelin(3) 7 27
(Nigel Tinkler) *towards rr: rdn and hung lft over 2f out: btn over 1f out* **66/1**

7 *3 ½* **Valiant Arthur** 2-9-3 0 .... FrederikTylicki 5 22
(Michael Dods) *s.i.s: bhd and sn pushed along: nvr on terms* **20/1**

5 **8** *5* **True Bond**[32] 3611 2-8-12 0 .... RussKennemore 2 —
(Geoffrey Oldroyd) *chsd ldrs tl rdn and wknd over 1f out* **9/1**[3]

00 **9** *9* **Hatsumomo (IRE)**[13] 4232 2-8-12 0 .... DavidAllan 4 —+
(Tim Easterby) *trckd ldrs: rdn over 2f out: sn wknd* **66/1**

1m 14.23s (-0.37) **Going Correction** -0.375s/f (Firm) **9** Ran SP% **122.6**
Speed ratings (Par 92): **87,86,76,74,73 66,62,55,43**
toteswingers:1&2:£1.40, 2&3:£14.20, 1&3:£6.60 CSF £2.05 TOTE £1.30: £1.02, £1.30, £8.70; EX 3.10.
Owner Timeform Betfair Racing Club Ltd **Bred** Century Bloodstock **Trained** Newmarket, Suffolk

FOCUS
A modest maiden, rated around the exposed third. The first pair pulled clear and both are likely to do better.

NOTEBOOK
Ruby Night(IRE) was confidently expected to step up on his debut third at Newmarket 12 days earlier by taking this. Things looked good for any supporters as he quickened to lead more towards the far side 2f out, but the runner-up went with him and it seemed at one stage as though he would lose out. It was probably a case of Spencer trying to give his mount as easy a race as possible, though, as he found that bit extra when it mattered. This son of Red Clubs' future looks to lie with the handicapper. (op 2-9)
Passionada ◆ was backed into clear second favourite and was clearly expected to go well on this racecourse debut. She took an age to load up and proved free through the early parts, but caught the eye travelling sweetly at halfway. She quickened to throw down a strong challenge, finishing well clear of the remainder, and looks a sure-fire maiden winner in the coming weeks. (tchd 4-1 and 11-2)
Roy's Legacy, having his sixth outing, showed up well under a positive ride and this was much better again back on turf but his proximity does little for the form. (op 50-1)
After Timer(IRE) was given something of an educational ride and was noted staying on encouragingly inside the final furlong. He's going the right way and qualifies for nurseries after his next assignment.
Heidi's Delight(IRE) broke a lot better than was the case on her debut 18 days earlier and posted a much more encouraging effort on the quicker ground. She too needs another run before entering nurseries. (op 66-1)

4669 TRADERS BETTING EXCHANGE H'CAP 5f
3:20 (3:20) (Class 5) (0-75,74) 3-Y-0 **£2,264** (£673; £336; £168) **Stalls** Centre

Form RPR
1040 **1** **Lady Kildare (IRE)**[17] 4124 3-8-5 **59**........................ PatrickDonaghy(3) 2 66
(Jedd O'Keeffe) *trckd ldrs: effrt 2f out: styd on fnl f: led cl home* **12/1**
-364 **2** *hd* **Ice Trooper**[32] 3628 3-9-7 **72**........................ DuranFentiman 3 78
(Linda Stubbs) *led: rdn and edgd lft over 1f out: kpt on fnl f: hdd cl home* **10/1**
11 **3** *1 ½* **Little Jimmy Odsox (IRE)**[17] 4124 3-9-7 **72**........................ DavidAllan 6 73
(Tim Easterby) *trckd ldrs: rdn along 2f out: kpt on same pce fnl f* **1/1**[1]
0221 **4** *nk* **Rylee Mooch**[10] 4359 3-9-9 **74** 6ex........................(e) JamieSpencer 5 74
(Richard Guest) *dwlt: sn cl up: rdn 2f out: no ex ins fnl f* **5/2**[2]
6225 **5** *shd* **Saxonette**[4] 4541 3-9-0 **68**........................ DaleSwift(3) 1 67
(Linda Perratt) *in tch: outpcd 1/2-way: kpt on fnl f: nvr able to chal* **5/1**[3]

59.36 secs (-1.74) **Going Correction** -0.375s/f (Firm) **5** Ran SP% **112.0**
Speed ratings (Par 100): **98,97,95,94,94**
CSF £104.37 TOTE £20.30: £4.40, £4.40; EX 72.80.
Owner The Fatalists **Bred** Glending Bloodstock **Trained** Middleham Moor, N Yorks

FOCUS
A moderate little 3-y-o sprint handicap. It was run at a sound pace down the centre of the track, but there was still something of a blanket finish. The two outsiders finished 1-2 and the winner is rated back to something like her best.

4670 SWARLANDSELFSTORAGE.CO.UK H'CAP 7f
3:50 (3:50) (Class 5) (0-75,75) 3-Y-O+ **£2,264** (£673; £336; £168) **Stalls** Centre

Form RPR
0212 **1** **Istiqdaam**[15] 4176 6-9-0 **63**........................(b) PaddyAspell 13 78
(Michael Easterby) *in tch: pushed along over 2f out: hdwy over 1f out: led ins fnl f: edgd lft: kpt on wl* **6/1**[2]
1- **2** *¾* **Present Danger**[317] 6240 3-9-3 **72**........................ RichardKingscote 14 83+
(Tom Dascombe) *hld up: rdn over 2f out: gd hdwy over 1f out: kpt on ins fnl f* **2/1**[1]
045 **3** *1 ¾* **Northern Flyer (GER)**[25] 3859 5-8-2 **56**........................(p) ShaneBKelly(5) 4 64
(John Quinn) *chsd ldrs: drvn along fr over 2f out: kpt on ins fnl f* **11/1**
0-00 **4** *nse* **Flameoftheforest (IRE)**[20] 4020 4-9-10 **73**........................ JamieSpencer 1 81
(Ed de Giles) *hld up: hdwy over 2f out: chsd ldrs ins fnl f: kpt on same pce* **14/1**
0053 **5** *1* **Our Boy Barrington (IRE)**[15] 4176 4-9-2 **68**...(v) MichaelO'Connell(3) 10 73
(David Nicholls) *led: rdn over 2f out: hdd ins fnl f: sn outpcd* **11/1**
0035 **6** *1* **Illustrious Prince (IRE)**[11] 4349 4-9-5 **75**........................(v) JasonHart(7) 6 78
(Declan Carroll) *t.k.h: prom: rdn over 2f out: edgd lft over 1f out: one pce* **10/1**
3564 **7** *½* **Dubai Celebration**[10] 4362 3-9-0 **72**........................(p) PatrickDonaghy(3) 7 71
(Jedd O'Keeffe) *in tch: effrt over 2f out: no imp appr fnl f* **20/1**
0150 **8** *1 ¾* **Striker Torres (IRE)**[22] 3936 5-9-8 **71**........................ DavidAllan 9 68
(Geoffrey Oldroyd) *chsd ldrs: rdn over 2f out: wknd ent fnl f* **20/1**
0023 **9** *½* **Bandstand**[10] 4362 5-9-3 **73**........................ JustinNewman(7) 5 68
(Bryan Smart) *trckd ldrs: rdn over 2f out: wknd ins fnl f* **8/1**[3]
5440 **10** *1 ¾* **Let's Face Facts**[31] 3658 4-8-7 **56** oh2........................ AndrewMullen 3 47
(Jim Goldie) *sn pushed along towards rr: drvn 1/2-way: nvr able to chal* **50/1**
3520 **11** *2 ¾* **Just The Tonic**[16] 4141 4-9-0 **63**........................ LeeNewman 8 46
(Marjorie Fife) *trckd ldrs tl rdn and wknd fr 2f out* **16/1**
-600 **12** *¾* **Social Rhythm**[16] 4141 7-9-0 **63**........................ TonyHamilton 12 44
(Alistair Whillans) *missed break: bhd and pushed along: nvr on terms* **66/1**
0-04 **13** *½* **Touch Tone**[16] 4141 4-9-10 **73**........................ FrederikTylicki 2 53
(Michael Dods) *hld up in midfield: rdn over 2f out: edgd lft and sn btn* **14/1**
0000 **14** *¾* **Without Prejudice (USA)**[32] 3617 6-8-12 **68**.... DavidSimmonson(7) 11 46
(Michael Easterby) *dwlt: bhd and pushed along 1/2-way: nvr on terms* **40/1**

1m 25.52s (-2.28) **Going Correction** -0.375s/f (Firm)
WFA 3 from 4yo+ 6lb **14** Ran SP% **119.1**
Speed ratings (Par 103): **103,102,100,100,98 97,97,95,94,92 89,88,88,87**
toteswingers:1&2:£4.20, 2&3:£7.10, 1&3:£7.40 CSF £17.06 CT £136.19 TOTE £5.50: £2.20, £1.40, £3.70; EX 24.70.
Owner Two Old Pals **Bred** Cheveley Park Stud Ltd **Trained** Sheriff Hutton, N Yorks
■ Stewards' Enquiry : Paddy Aspell caution: careless riding

FOCUS
A competitive handicap for the class and fair form for the grade, rated on the positive side.

4671 GOSFORTH DECORATING & BUILDING SERVICES H'CAP 1m 6f 97y
4:20 (4:20) (Class 5) (0-70,68) 3-Y-O+ **£2,264** (£673; £336; £168) **Stalls** Low

Form RPR
4206 **1** **Mason Hindmarsh**[9] 4382 4-9-12 **66**........................ FrederikTylicki 1 72
(Karen McLintock) *led at stdy gallop: rdn and hdd over 2f out: rallied: regained ld ins fnl f: hld on wl* **7/1**
-202 **2** *nk* **Finellas Fortune**[32] 3622 6-8-13 **53**........................ AndrewMullen 6 59
(George Moore) *in tch: stdy hdwy 1/2-way: effrt over 2f out: kpt on u.p fnl f: tk* **14/1**
2522 **3** *nk* **Falcun**[11] 4326 4-9-4 **58**........................(p) JamieSpencer 2 63
(Micky Hammond) *hld up in tch: hdwy and cl up 1/2-way: rdn to ld over 2f out: edgd lft and hdd ins fnl f: hld cl home* **5/2**[1]
6-36 **4** *1 ½* **Mohawk Ridge**[52] 2952 5-9-11 **68**........................ LeeTopliss(3) 3 71
(Michael Dods) *t.k.h: trckd ldrs: effrt over 2f out: kpt on same pce fnl f* **7/2**[3]
0100 **5** *nk* **Dechiper (IRE)**[20] 3450 9-8-11 **51** oh3........................ TonyHamilton 4 54
(Robert Johnson) *hld up: rdn 3f out: sn outpcd: styd on fnl f: nrst fin* **50/1**
-014 **6** *shd* **Tillietudlem (FR)**[11] 4326 5-9-10 **64**........................ LeeNewman 5 67
(Jim Goldie) *trckd ldrs: rdn and outpcd over 2f out: kpt on fnl f: no imp* **5/1**
5542 **7** *5* **Body Language (IRE)**[16] 4151 3-8-12 **65**........................ RoystonFfrench 7 62
(Ann Duffield) *hld up on outside: rdn and outpcd over 4f out: btn fnl 2f* **10/3**[2]

3m 10.87s (-0.43) **Going Correction** -0.125s/f (Firm)
WFA 3 from 4yo+ 13lb **7** Ran SP% **111.7**
Speed ratings (Par 103): **96,95,95,94,94 94,91**
toteswingers:1&2:£8.30, 2&3:£3.10, 1&3:£3.20 CSF £88.56 TOTE £10.20: £5.50, £6.40; EX 86.00.
Owner I R Clements **Bred** Newsells Park Stud **Trained** Ingoe, Northumberland
■ Stewards' Enquiry : Andrew Mullen caution: used whip with excessive frequency.

FOCUS
An ordinary staying handicap that was run at an uneven pace and there was a tight finish as a result. The form is rated a bit negatively and should be treated with a degree of caution.
Body Language(IRE) Official explanation: jockey said filly never travelled and hung right-handed throughout

4672 PARKLANDS GOLF COURSE H'CAP 6f
4:50 (4:51) (Class 6) (0-65,63) 3-Y-O+ **£1,617** (£481; £240; £120) **Stalls** Centre

Form RPR
-064 **1** **Cross Of Lorraine (IRE)**[11] 4328 8-9-4 **55**........................(b) TonyHamilton 6 63
(Chris Grant) *mde all: rdn over 1f out: edgd rt: kpt on wl ins fnl f* **9/1**
1335 **2** *½* **Weetentherty**[2] 4600 4-8-8 **50**........................(p) JulieBurke(5) 2 56
(Linda Perratt) *hld up in tch: hdwy over 1f out: rdn and disp 2nd pl ins fnl f: kpt on* **3/1**[1]
4060 **3** *nse* **Fleurie Lover (IRE)**[4] 4564 3-8-13 **54**........................ AndrewMullen 7 59
(Richard Guest) *hld up in tch: rdn and hdwy over 1f out: disp 2nd ins fnl f: kpt on fin* **16/1**
0602 **4** *¾* **Just Sam (IRE)**[4] 4563 6-8-11 **55**........................ GarryWhillans(7) 4 59
(Ron Barr) *pressed wnr: rdn over 2f out: lost 2nd and no ex ins fnl f* **11/2**[3]
00/4 **5** *¾* **Here Now And Why (IRE)**[20] 4017 4-8-12 **49**........................ FrederikTylicki 9 50
(Ian Semple) *t.k.h: trckd ldrs: effrt 2f out: kpt on same pce fnl f* **3/1**[1]
504 **6** *1* **Red Scintilla**[2] 4600 4-9-3 **57**........................ LouisBeuzelin(3) 1 55
(Nigel Tinkler) *prom: rdn over 2f out: kpt on same pce appr fnl f* **4/1**[2]
5650 **7** *4* **Noels Princess**[11] 4328 4-8-3 **45**........................ ShaneBKelly(5) 8 30
(David O'Meara) *dwlt: hld up: rdn and hung lft 2f out: nvr on terms* **20/1**
53-0 **8** *44* **Bint Mazyouna**[42] 3278 3-9-8 **63**........................ JamieSpencer 3 —
(Richard Guest) *hld up: rdn and struggling over 2f out: eased whn no ch fnl f* **12/1**

1m 13.52s (-1.08) **Going Correction** -0.375s/f (Firm)
WFA 3 from 4yo+ 4lb **8** Ran SP% **113.7**
Speed ratings (Par 101): **92,91,91,90,89 87,82,23**
toteswingers:1&2:£6.10, 2&3:£8.30, 1&3:£10.80 CSF £35.82 CT £431.57 TOTE £8.00: £2.90, £2.50, £6.50; EX 31.10.
Owner Nigel E M Jones **Bred** Kildaragh Stud **Trained** Newton Bewley, Co Durham

FOCUS
A weak sprint handicap, run at a solid pace and again they raced down the centre. The winner's best form since this time last year.
Bint Mazyouna Official explanation: jockey said filly hung right-handed throughout

4673 BORDER MINSTREL PUB APPRENTICE H'CAP 1m 2f 32y
5:20 (5:20) (Class 6) (0-60,60) 3-Y-O+ **£1,617** (£481; £240; £120) **Stalls** Low

Form RPR
050- **1** **La Bacouetteuse (FR)**[265] 7407 6-8-13 **48**........(p) GeorgeChaloner(3) 7 60
(Iain Jardine) *hld up: pushed along over 2f out: hdwy over 1f out: led ins fnl f: kpt on wl* **14/1**
/60- **2** *2 ½* **Piper's Song (IRE)**[12] 2952 8-8-10 **47**........................ RossSmith(5) 3 54
(Linda Perratt) *midfield: rdn 3f out: hdwy to ld over 1f out: hdd ins fnl f: r.o same pce* **6/1**[2]
0610 **3** *¾* **Pattern Mark**[17] 4128 5-9-11 **57**........................ LMcNiff 8 63
(Ollie Pears) *hld up: hdwy on outside over 2f out: kpt on ins fnl f* **13/2**[3]
0-00 **4** *2 ½* **Captain Peachey**[14] 4198 5-9-0 **46** oh1........................ GarryWhillans 4 53+
(Alistair Whillans) *in tch: effrt whn nt clr run and lost pl over 2f out: styd on fnl f: nt rch ldrs* **33/1**
0504 **5** *1 ¼* **Media Stars**[11] 4329 6-9-7 **58**........................ LauraBarry(5) 11 56
(Robert Johnson) *hld up in midfield: smooth hdwy over 2f out: effrt and ev ch over 1f out: sn one pce* **11/1**
6001 **6** *1* **Yorksters Prince (IRE)**[7] 4438 4-9-5 **51** 6ex........................(b) ShaneBKelly 5 47
(Tony Coyle) *prom: effrt over 2f out: sn rdn: one pce over 1f out* **7/1**
0060 **7** *2 ½* **Royal Deal**[22] 3936 4-9-9 **60**........................ DavidSimmonson(5) 10 51
(Michael Easterby) *hld up: outpcd over 4f out: styd on fnl f: nvr rchd ldrs* **20/1**
0406 **8** *½* **Pictures (IRE)**[7] 4441 4-8-9 **46** oh1........................ JackDuern(5) 12 36
(Ron Barr) *hld up: effrt on outside over 2f out: no ex over 1f out* **20/1**
060 **9** *nk* **Littlepromisedland (IRE)**[7] 4442 3-8-5 **46** oh1.......... CharlesEddery 13 35
(Richard Guest) *s.i.s: bhd: rdn over 2f out: no imp whn hmpd ins fnl f* **66/1**
0060 **10** *½* **Bunacurry**[31] 3658 6-8-11 **46**........................ JustinNewman(3) 9 34
(Barry Murtagh) *trckd ldrs: effrt over 3f out: wknd wl over 1f out* **25/1**
040 **11** *4 ½* **Morning Air (IRE)**[19] 4072 3-8-9 **55**........................ ShirleyTeasdale(5) 1 34
(Ann Duffield) *prom tl rdn and wknd 2f out* **25/1**
2521 **12** *1* **Border Abby**[11] 4329 3-8-12 **58**........................ NoelGarbutt(5) 2 35
(Rae Guest) *led: qcknd 3f out: hdd over 1f out: sn btn* **7/4**[1]
400 **13** *1 ¼* **Maharanee (USA)**[19] 4072 3-9-0 **60**........................ JacobButterfield(5) 6 35
(Ann Duffield) *t.k.h: trckd ldrs tl wknd fr 2f out* **16/1**

2m 10.26s (-1.64) **Going Correction** -0.125s/f (Firm)
WFA 3 from 4yo+ 9lb **13** Ran SP% **119.0**
Speed ratings (Par 101): **101,99,98,96,95 94,92,92,91,91 87,87,86**
toteswingers:1&2:£16.60, 2&3:£7.10, 1&3:£15.40. Tote Super 7: Win: Not won. Place: Not won. CSF £87.24 CT £610.93 TOTE £16.20: £5.60, £1.30, £3.10; EX 138.00.
Owner Corsby Racing **Bred** Sarl Classic Breeding & Maria R Mendes **Trained** Hawick, Borders
■ Iain Jardine's first winner as a trainer.

FOCUS
A moderate handicap, confined to apprentice riders. The race was set up for the closers and the winner is rated back to his best.
T/Plt: £2,511.60 to a £1 stake. Pool of £55,738.90 - 16.20 winning tickets T/Qpdt: £828.00 to a £1 stake. Pool of £4,476.09 - 4.00 winning tickets. RY

[4365]PONTEFRACT (L-H)

Wednesday, August 3

OFFICIAL GOING: Good to firm (good in places; 7.5)

Wind: Virtually nil Weather: Warm and dry

4674 PONTEFRACT GENTLEMEN'S H'CAP (FOR GENTLEMAN AMATEUR RIDERS) 1m 2f 6y

2:10 (2:10) (Class 5) (0-75,75) 3-Y-0+ **£2,183** (£677; £338; £169) **Stalls** Low

Form RPR

-564 **1** **James Pollard (IRE)**[12] [4273] 6-10-3 **62**..................(t) MrRJWilliams(5) 2 70
(Bernard Llewellyn) *trckd ldng pair on inner: hdwy over 2f out: swtchd rt and rdn to chal over 1f out: led ent fnl f: kpt on* **10/1**

0040 **2** *1/2* **Artisan**[18] [4089] 3-9-7 **63**................................ MrJohnWilley(7) 7 70+
(Brian Ellison) *dwlt and hld up in rr: swtchd wd home turn and hdwy over 1f out: rdn and styd on strly fnl f* **8/1**[3]

3310 **3** *1 1/4* **Amazing Blue Sky**[10] [4360] 5-11-0 **75**........................ MrBHowe(7) 1 79
(Ruth Carr) *led: rdn along 2f out: drvn and hdd ent fnl f: one pce* **9/4**[2]

0016 **4** *6* **Resplendent Light**[19] [4059] 6-10-11 **70**....................(t) MrPMillman(5) 5 62
(Bernard Llewellyn) *dwlt: hdwy 1/2-way: chsd ldrs 3f out: rdn 2f out: sn one pce* **16/1**

3215 **5** *2 1/4* **Emperor Of Rome (IRE)**[19] [4050] 3-10-9 **72**.................... MrSWalker 8 60
(Michael Dods) *sn trcking ldr: cl up 3f out: rdn 2f out: drvn: edgd lft and wknd over 1f out* **15/8**[1]

3244 **6** *2 1/4* **Desert Hunter (IRE)**[17] [4123] 8-10-0 **57**.......................... MrJHamer(3) 4 40
(Micky Hammond) *trckd ldrs: effrt 3f out: sn rdn and wknd 2f out* **8/1**[3]

6050 **7** *5* **Herrera (IRE)**[10] [4366] 6-10-0 **61**................................. MrJHamilton(7) 6 34
(Richard Fahey) *hld up in tch: hdwy on wd outside to chse ldrs over 3f out: sn rdn and wknd over 2f out* **12/1**

2m 13.7s **Going Correction** -0.225s/f (Firm) **7** Ran SP% **110.4**
WFA 3 from 5yo+ 9lb
Speed ratings (Par 103): **91,90,89,84,83 81,77**
CSF £78.62 CT £231.15 TOTE £11.60: £3.00, £4.80; EX 94.90.
Owner Granville Reynolds **Bred** Gainsborough Stud Management Ltd **Trained** Fochriw, Caerphilly

FOCUS
A modest amateur riders' event. A 4lb personal best from the winner.

4675 BRITISH STALLION STUDS E.B.F./HATFIELDS JAGUAR MAIDEN STKS 6f

2:40 (2:41) (Class 4) 2-Y-0 **£4,398** (£1,309; £654; £327) **Stalls** Low

Form RPR

3 **1** **Heeraat (IRE)**[18] [4098] 2-9-3 0.. RichardHills 4 92+
(William Haggas) *mde all: pushed clr over 2f out: kpt on strly: unchal* **8/15**[1]

0 **2** *11* **Champagne Valley**[20] [4002] 2-8-12 0.............................. PJMcDonald 5 53
(Sharon Watt) *chsd wnr: rdn along over 2f out: drvn wl over 1f out: kpt on same pce* **25/1**

3 *3/4* **Zakreet** 2-9-3 0... PhillipMakin 1 62+
(Kevin Ryan) *dwlt: green and sn pushed along in rr: rdn along over 2f out: green and n.m.r in rr over 1f out: swtchd rt and styd on ins fnl f* **4/1**[2]

4 *1 1/4* **Sabore** 2-8-12 0... PaulHanagan 6 47
(Richard Fahey) *trckd ldrs: effrt over 2f out: sn rdn and kpt on same pce* **6/1**[3]

0 **5** *4* **Dark Celt (IRE)**[39] [3382] 2-9-3 0..................................... EddieAhern 2 40
(Tim Pitt) *chsd ldng pair: rdn along over 2f out: sn drvn and wknd* **18/1**

1m 16.5s (-0.40) **Going Correction** -0.225s/f (Firm) **5** Ran SP% **108.6**
Speed ratings (Par 96): **93,78,77,75,70**
CSF £14.81 TOTE £1.50: £1.30, £2.60; EX 11.40.
Owner Hamdan Al Maktoum **Bred** John McEnery **Trained** Newmarket, Suffolk
■ Stewards' Enquiry : Paul Hanagan caution: careless riding.

FOCUS
An extremely one-sided maiden and an impressive winner, but the form has been rated conservatively.

NOTEBOOK
Heeraat(IRE) ♠ had shown plenty of promise when third of five on his Newmarket debut and could hardly have been more impressive. Soon in front, he pulled clear of his rivals just after halfway without much of an effort and, although he probably hasn't beaten much, this 140,000gns colt remains an interesting prospect. He isn't bred to get much further than this. (op 8-13 tchd 4-6 and 4-5 in places early)
Champagne Valley was always closest to the winner, but was left choking on his dust and may not have achieved much in finishing ahead of the other three. (tchd 20-1)
Zakreet, a £19,000 2-y-o, proved very green on this debut and should improve. The dam's side of his pedigree suggests he will appreciate middle-distances. (tchd 9-2)
Sabore, bred for speed, looks to need more time. (op 11-2 tchd 5-1)

4676 BOOK YOUR FAMILY TICKETS FOR 14TH AUGUST H'CAP 1m 4y

3:10 (3:11) (Class 5) (0-75,75) 3-Y-0 **£2,264** (£673; £336; £168) **Stalls** Low

Form RPR

1111 **1** **Camberley Two**[9] [4394] 3-9-2 **73** 6ex........................... KieranO'Neill(3) 2 90+
(Roger Charlton) *mde all: rdn and qcknd clr 2f out: drvn out* **4/6**[1]

2055 **2** *3* **Jade**[13] [4235] 3-9-7 **75**.. PaulHanagan 3 83
(Ollie Pears) *chsd wnr: effrt over 2f out and sn rdn along: drvn over 1f out: no imp ins fnl f* **7/2**[2]

2414 **3** *10* **Byron Bear (IRE)**[17] [4128] 3-8-2 **56**............................ PaulQuinn 6 44
(Paul Midgley) *t.k.h early: hld up in rr: hdwy over 2f out: sn rdn and one pce* **8/1**

1502 **4** *10* **Youhavecontrol (IRE)**[10] [4362] 3-9-5 **73**........................ TomEaves 4 42
(Michael Dods) *chsd ldng pair: hdwy 3f out: rdn 2f out: sn wknd* **13/2**[3]

1m 43.65s (-2.25) **Going Correction** -0.225s/f (Firm) **4** Ran SP% **106.7**
Speed ratings (Par 100): **102,99,89,79**
CSF £3.15 TOTE £1.50; EX 3.00.
Owner H R H Sultan Ahmad Shah **Bred** Barry Walters Farms **Trained** Beckhampton, Wilts

FOCUS
The order hardly changed during the course of this modest four-runner handicap. The winner is rated in line with his recent win and there may be more to come still.

4677 TOTEPOOL A BETTER WAY TO BET H'CAP 1m 4f 8y

3:40 (3:40) (Class 3) (0-95,90) 3-Y-0- **£7,781** (£2,330; £1,165; £582; £291) **Stalls** Low

Form RPR

-624 **1** **Berling (IRE)**[39] [3411] 4-10-0 **90**... EddieAhern 1 99
(John Dunlop) *trckd ldng pair: hdwy on inner over 2f out: n.m.r over 1f out: swiitched rt ent fnl f: rdn and styd on wl to ld last 75yds* **2/1**[1]

1240 **2** *nk* **Hong Kong Island (IRE)**[12] [4280] 4-9-7 **83**.................... PaulHanagan 5 91
(Micky Hammond) *trckd ldng pair: hdwy 3f out: cl up wl over 1f out: sn rdn: drvn to ld briefly last 100yds: sn hdd and no ex* **5/2**[2]

5422 **3** *1* **The Caped Crusader (IRE)**[18] [4082] 4-9-1 **77**............. BarryMcHugh 4 84
(Ollie Pears) *led: rdn along 2f out and sn jnd: drvn over 1f out: hdd and no ex last 100yds* **9/2**[3]

310 **4** *1 1/2* **Gogeo (IRE)**[76] [2220] 4-9-7 **83**...................................... PJMcDonald 6 87+
(Alan Swinbank) *hld up in rr: stdy hdwy over 2f out: chsd ldrs over 1f out: keeping on whn nt clr run on inner wl ins fnl f* **8/1**

631 **5** *7* **Cluain Dara (IRE)**[15] [4180] 3-8-5 **78**.............................. FrannyNorton 3 74
(Mark Johnston) *chsd ldr: effrt 3f out: rdn along 2f out: hld whn sltly hmpd appr fnl f* **9/2**[3]

2m 38.68s (-2.12) **Going Correction** -0.225s/f (Firm)
WFA 3 from 4yo 11lb **5** Ran SP% **109.4**
Speed ratings (Par 107): **98,97,97,96,91**
CSF £7.16 TOTE £2.70: £1.40, £1.30; EX 6.50.
Owner Benny Andersson **Bred** Ballylinch Stud **Trained** Arundel, W Sussex
■ Stewards' Enquiry : Eddie Ahern one-day ban: careless riding (Aug 20)

FOCUS
A small field, but a decent handicap and an interesting race. The pace seemed solid enough. Straightforward form.

NOTEBOOK
Berling(IRE) is very talented, but is also a renowned hard ride. Having travelled smoothly off the pace, he looked to be stuck in a pocket starting up the home straight, but that probably helped him as he couldn't be committed until the last minute and, when switched to make his effort between the two leaders, found a decisive turn of foot. Things won't always pan out so well for him. (tchd 11-4)
Hong Kong Island(IRE) came into this 2-2 here and had every chance when produced with his effort on the outside after turning in, but the winner cut him down late. He remains 12lb above his last winning mark and won't get much respite after this. (op 7-2)
The Caped Crusader(IRE) tried to make his stamina count under a positive ride and wasn't overwhelmed until well inside the last furlong. He probably prefers a bit more cut. (op 4-1 tchd 7-2)
Gogeo(IRE) had been given a short break since his disappointing effort at Haydock in May and proved the main eyecatcher here. Held up last, he came briefly off the bridle on a couple of occasions, but was soon back on it. He would have gone even closer had he seen more daylight inside the last furlong and he passed the line still on the bridle with apparently a lot more left in the tank. With this being only his fourth start on the Flat, he remains a horse of potential and it will be very interesting to see how he is campaigned in the coming weeks. His rider reported that the gelding hung left in the straight. Official explanation: jockey said gelding hung left in straight (op 6-1 tchd 5-1)
Cluain Dara(IRE) become outpaced when the race began in earnest and probably needs a slower surface than this. (op 4-1)

4678 CHAPLINS CLUB H'CAP 5f

4:10 (4:10) (Class 5) (0-75,74) 3-Y-0+ **£2,264** (£673; £336; £168) **Stalls** Low

Form RPR

6223 **1** **Comptonspirit**[13] [4231] 7-9-3 **72**................................ JamesRogers(5) 6 81
(Brian Baugh) *towards rr: pushed along 1/2-way: rdn wl over 1f out: str run ent fnl f to ld nr line* **6/1**

0050 **2** *nk* **Chosen One (IRE)**[16] [4144] 6-8-13 **63**.......................... JamesSullivan 2 71+
(Ruth Carr) *cl up: led 2f out: rdn over 1f out: drvn ins fnl f: hdd and no ex nr line* **9/1**

2033 **3** *1/2* **Desert Strike**[10] [4371] 5-9-2 **66**.................................(p) RobertWinston 8 72
(Alan McCabe) *in rr: hdwy on inner wl over 1f out: sn rdn and styd on strly ins fnl f: no ex towards fin* **4/1**[2]

0000 **4** *1 1/4* **Commanche Raider (IRE)**[8] [4405] 4-9-4 **68**................(b) PhillipMakin 1 70
(Michael Dods) *trckd ldrs on inner: effrt and hdwy wl over 1f out: sn swtchd rt and drvn ins fnl f: kpt on same pce* **20/1**

0300 **5** *2 1/2* **Silvanus (IRE)**[10] [4371] 6-9-1 **65**.................................(p) PaulHanagan 9 58
(Paul Midgley) *chsd ldrs: effrt on outer 2f out: sn rdn and no imp* **12/1**

4062 **6** *2* **Mr Wolf**[10] [4371] 10-9-5 **69**..(p) TomEaves 7 54
(John Quinn) *prom: rdn along 2f out: drvn wl over 1f out and grad wknd* **7/2**[1]

600- **7** *4* **Igoyougo**[383] [4090] 5-9-10 **74**.. DanielTudhope 3 45
(Noel Wilson) *led: rdn along 2f out: sn hdd & wknd over 1f out* **9/2**[3]

211 **F** **Port Ronan (USA)**[10] [4371] 5-8-0 59 [illegible]..................(p) [illegible] 3 —
(John Wainwright) *s.i.s and wl bhd: rdn along and t.o whn staggered, uns rdr and fell 2f out: fatally injured* **5/1**

63.61 secs (0.31) **Going Correction** -0.125s/f (Firm) **8** Ran SP% **113.8**
Speed ratings (Par 103): **92,91,90,88,84 81,75,—**
toteswingers:1&2:£11.10, 2&3:£6.40, 1&3:£4.20 CSF £57.28 CT £242.48 TOTE £8.10: £1.80, £3.10, £1.80; EX 81.50.
Owner G B Hignett **Bred** Mrs F Wilson **Trained** Audley, Staffs

FOCUS
This sprint handicap was run in pouring rain but that did not stop the leaders going off at a rate of knots early. The form is rated around the third.
Port Ronan(USA) Official explanation: jockey said blindfold became caught in bridle and horse was slowly away; jockey said he jumped off when horse felt out of control

4679 MATTY BOWN VETERANS H'CAP 1m 4y

4:40 (4:45) (Class 4) (0-80,80) 6-Y-0+ **£4,075** (£1,212; £606; £303) **Stalls** Low

Form RPR

5010 **1** **Willow Dancer (IRE)**[35] [3521] 7-9-7 **80**.........................(p) EddieAhern 12 88
(Walter Swinburn) *sn led: rdn 1 1/2f out: drvn ins fnl f: kpt on wl* **15/2**

5606 **2** *1 1/4* **Sir George (IRE)**[19] [4070] 6-9-4 **77**................................ BarryMcHugh 3 82
(Ollie Pears) *trckd ldrs on inner: hdwy over 2f out: swtchd rt and rdn to chse wnr over 1f out: drvn to chal ent fnl f and ev ch tl no ex last 100yds* **5/1**[3]

6353 **3** *nk* **Elijah Pepper (USA)**[39] [3386] 6-9-2 **75**.......................... GrahamGibbons 4 79
(David Barron) *hld up towards rr: hdwy 2f out: swtchd rt and rdn wl over 1f out: styd on ins fnl f: nrst fin* **7/2**[2]

0-20 **4** *1/2* **Motafarred (IRE)**[2] [4603] 9-8-6 **65**................................... PaulHanagan 2 68
(Micky Hammond) *prom on inner: effrt over 2f out: rdn wl over 1f out: drvn ent fnl f and sn one pce* **3/1**[1]

1540 **5** *2* **The Which Doctor**[88] [1908] 6-8-12 **74**.........................(e) RobertLButler(3) 1 73
(Richard Guest) *hld up and bhd: hdwy on inner wl over 1f out: n.m.r and swtchd rt ins fnl f: kpt on* **14/1**

1130 **6** *nk* **I Confess**[7] [4440] 6-8-12 **71**..(b) RobertWinston 11 69
(Geoffrey Harker) *prom: cl up 1/2-way: effrt over 2f out and sn rdn: drvn wl over 1f out and grad wknd* **14/1**

3034 **7** *3 1/4* **Violent Velocity (IRE)**[22] [3936] 8-8-8 **70**...................... DeclanCannon(3) 6 61
(John Quinn) *towards rr: effrt and sme hdwy 1/2-way: rdn 3f out: wd st and sn btn* **8/1**

0000 **8** *12* **Follow The Flag (IRE)**[8] [4404] 7-8-13 **79**.................(p) DavidKenny(7) 10 42
(Alan McCabe) *a towards rr* **33/1**

404 **9** *3* **Ahlawy (IRE)**[72] 2359 8-9-2 **75**........................(bt) JamesDoyle 9 31
(Frank Sheridan) *towards rr: hdwy on outer to chse ldrs after 2f: rdn along 3f out: wd st and sn wknd* **25/1**

0003 **10** *3¼* **Aussie Blue (IRE)**[19] 4076 7-8-2 **61** oh2........................ PaulQuinn 5 10
(Richard Whitaker) *in tch: pushed along 1/2-way: rdn over 3f out and sn wknd* **12/1**

4066 **11** *¾* **Dabbers Ridge (IRE)**[16] 4150 9-8-8 **67**........................ PatrickMathers 7 14
(Ian McInnes) *chsd ldrs: rdn along 3f out: wknd 2f out* **22/1**

1m 46.34s (0.44) **Going Correction** -0.025s/f (Good) **11** Ran SP% **118.9**
Speed ratings: **96,94,94,93,91 91,88,76,73,70 69**
toteswingers:1&2:£8.00, 2&3:£4.90, 1&3:£7.10 CSF £44.38 CT £159.66 TOTE £9.90: £3.40, £2.30, £1.80; EX 47.60.
Owner The Weeping Willows **Bred** Exors Of The Late R E Sangster **Trained** Aldbury, Herts

FOCUS
A competitive veterans' handicap but the earlier rain must have had an effect, as the time was 2.69 secs slower than the earlier race over the trip, although a steady early pace also contributed. A personal best from the winner.
The Which Doctor Official explanation: jockey said, regarding running and riding, that his orders were to take his time, drop the gelding in and try to get a run up the inside rail in the straight so that it could be produced as late as possible on the line, it hung left preventing it from a clear run and had to switch right.

4680 KEITH HAMMILL MEMORIAL H'CAP 6f
5:10 (5:10) (Class 5) (0-75,75) 3-Y-O **£2,264** (£673; £336; £168) **Stalls** Low

Form RPR

6-03 **1** **Lady Paris (IRE)**[11] 4324 3-9-5 **73**........................ TomEaves 3 93
(Bryan Smart) *cl up on inner: led over 2f out: rdn clr wl over 1f out: kpt on wl* **5/1**[3]

-420 **2** *6* **Arrivaderci**[18] 4110 3-8-8 **65**........................(p) AmyRyan(3) 1 66
(Richard Whitaker) *in tch: hdwy on inner 2f out: rdn to chse ldrs wl over 1f out: drvn and kpt on ins fnl f: no ch w wnr* **10/1**

1110 **3** *½* **Sound Amigo (IRE)**[53] 2926 3-9-6 **74**........................ BarryMcHugh 9 73+
(Ollie Pears) *trckd ldrs: hdwy 2f out: rdn to chse wnr wl over 1f out: drvn ent fnl f and kpt on same pce* **11/4**[1]

0031 **4** *8* **Brave Dream**[5] 4511 3-8-13 **67** 6ex........................ PhillipMakin 6 41
(Kevin Ryan) *led: rdn along and hdd over 2f out: sn drvn and wknd wl over 1f out* **5/1**[3]

6060 **5** *1¼* **Sleights Boy (IRE)**[1] 4638 3-8-0 **57** oh9 ow1........... DeclanCannon(3) 7 27
(Ian McInnes) *towards rr: sme hdwy wl over 1f out: sn rdn and nvr nr ldrs* **50/1**

5450 **6** *¾* **Morermaloke**[17] 4124 3-8-13 **67**........................ PJMcDonald 2 34
(Ian McInnes) *hld up: a towards rr* **33/1**

-363 **7** *11* **Spartic**[137] 907 3-8-6 **67**........................ DavidKenny(7) 4 —
(Alan McCabe) *chsd ldrs: rdn along 1/2-way: wknd over 2f out* **20/1**

03-1 **8** *12* **Lizzie (IRE)**[12] 4288 3-9-2 **70**........................(b) GrahamGibbons 10 —
(Tim Easterby) *chsd ldrs on outer: rdn along over 2f out: sn drvn and wknd* **5/1**[3]

2 **9** *2¾* **Showboating (IRE)**[5] 4511 3-8-11 **65**........................(p) RobertWinston 5 —
(Alan McCabe) *cl up: rdn along 1/2-way: wknd over 2f out* **9/2**[2]

1m 17.58s (0.68) **Going Correction** +0.075s/f (Good) **9** Ran SP% **113.6**
Speed ratings (Par 100): **98,90,89,78,77 76,61,45,41**
toteswingers:1&2:£5.80, 2&3:£7.10, 1&3:£4.10 CSF £51.15 CT £164.24 TOTE £6.40: £1.90, £2.60, £1.30; EX 41.10.
Owner R C Bond **Bred** D Cantillon **Trained** Hambleton, N Yorks

FOCUS
A modest 3yo sprint handicap that was run over a second slower than the earlier juvenile maiden, indicating that the rain had got into the ground, even if that earlier winner is a potentially useful type. The field tended to race six abreast until beyond halfway. The winner could rate higher at face value.
Lizzie(IRE) Official explanation: jockey said filly hung right
Showboating(IRE) Official explanation: jockey said gelding ran flat
T/Plt: £180.50 to a £1 stake. Pool of £56,639.46 - 229.02 winning tickets. T/Qpdt: £16.80 to a £1 stake. Pool of £4,041.79 - 177.62 winning tickets JR

4390 YARMOUTH (L-H)
Wednesday, August 3

OFFICIAL GOING: Good to firm (7.7)
Wind: light across Weather: dy and warm turning wet

4681 GEORGE DARLING MEMORIAL APPRENTICE H'CAP 7f 3y
5:40 (5:41) (Class 5) (0-70,70) 4-Y-O+ **£2,264** (£673; £336; £168) **Stalls** High

Form RPR

0544 **1** **Aleqa**[34] 3555 4-9-7 **70**........................ LukeRowe(3) 3 79+
(Chris Wall) *trckd ldrs: rdn and chalng whn short of room and swtchd rt over 1f out: rallied to ld fnl 100yds: styd on wl: pushed out* **11/8**[1]

-564 **2** *1½* **Ela Gonda Mou**[12] 4265 4-9-9 **69**........................ LeonnaMayor 1 74
(Peter Charalambous) *led tl jst over 2f out: ev ch and carried lft by ldr fr over 1f out: led ins fnl f: sn hdd and one pce* **5/2**[2]

2205 **3** *1¾* **Sairaam (IRE)**[5] 4513 5-9-8 **68**........................ JakePayne 5 68
(Charles Smith) *w ldr tl led jst over 2f out: rdn and hung lft fr over 1f out: hdd ins fnl f: wknd fnl 100yds* **5/1**[3]

0660 **4** *2* **Yakama (IRE)**[15] 4179 6-8-0 **51** oh4........................(v) DanielHarris(5) 4 46
(Christine Dunnett) *s.i.s: sn pushed along and rcvrd to chse ldrs after 2f: rdn and pressing ldrs whn carried lft over 1f out: wknd ins fnl f* **16/1**

0000 **5** *8* **Gambatte**[18] 4110 4-8-5 **51**........................ GeorgeDowning 6 24
(Tony Carroll) *stdd s: hld up in rr: shkn up over 3f out: rdn and lost tch ent fnl 2f* **28/1**

-644 **6** *½* **Rigid**[173] 517 4-8-4 **53** oh5 ow2........................ ThomasBrown(3) 2 25
(Tony Carroll) *t.k.h: chsd ldrs tl lost pl over 2f out: wknd 2f out* **11/1**

1m 26.88s (0.28) **Going Correction** -0.025s/f (Good) **6** Ran SP% **105.0**
Speed ratings (Par 103): **97,95,93,91,81 81**
toteswingers:1&2:£1.50, 2&3:£1.90, 1&3:£1.90 CSF £4.20 TOTE £1.90: £1.20, £1.90; EX 3.10.
Owner Ms Aida Fustoq **Bred** Deerfield Farm **Trained** Newmarket, Suffolk
■ Stewards' Enquiry : Jake Payne caution: careless riding.

FOCUS
Back straight and bottom bend dolled out 3m ending at 4.5f increasing distances by 15yds on round course. It is hard to escape the conclusion this was anything other than a weak handicap. The winner rates a weak personal best.

4682 SPIFFING CRABBIE'S ALCOHOLIC GINGER BEER MAIDEN AUCTION STKS 7f 3y
6:10 (6:10) (Class 6) 2-Y-O **£1,617** (£481; £240; £120) **Stalls** High

Form RPR

452 **1** **My Sharona**[15] 4184 2-8-6 70........................ ChrisCatlin 5 69
(Sylvester Kirk) *t.k.h: hld up wl in tch: effrt to ld wl over 2f out: drvn over 1f out: kpt on u.p: in command whn edgd rt towards fin* **5/2**[2]

4043 **2** *¾* **Tidal's Baby**[15] 4184 2-8-12 73........................ NeilCallan 1 73
(Noel Quinlan) *stdd s: t.k.h: hld up in tch: chsd ldng pair wl over 2f out: drvn whn swtchd rt over 1f out: edging lft u.p and chsd wnr ins fnl f: keeping on same pce whn carried rt towards fin* **4/1**[3]

232 **3** *1½* **Alice Rose (IRE)**[13] 4232 2-8-7 74........................ MartinLane 2 64
(Rae Guest) *t.k.h: pressed ldrs and flashing tail at times: w wnr and rdn jst over 2f out: ev ch after tl flashed tail u.p and btn fnl 75yds* **10/11**[1]

0 **4** *6* **Cheviot Quest (IRE)**[9] 4390 2-8-12 0........................ LukeMorris 3 54
(William Jarvis) *t.k.h: w ldr tl led over 3f out: hdd wl over 2f out: and sn struggling u.p: wknd wl over 1f out* **25/1**

00 **5** *47* **Red Hot Penny (IRE)**[26] 3816 2-8-11 0........................ ShaneKelly 4 —
(Brian Meehan) *rn green: sn bustled along and mde most tl jst over 3f out: sn struggling: wl btn and virtually p.u fr over 1f out: t.o* **40/1**

1m 27.45s (0.85) **Going Correction** -0.025s/f (Good) **5** Ran SP% **107.2**
Speed ratings (Par 92): **94,93,91,84,30**
CSF £11.84 TOTE £4.30: £1.70, £2.30; EX 9.60.
Owner Verano Quartet **Bred** Seaton Partnership **Trained** Upper Lambourn, Berks
■ Stewards' Enquiry : Chris Catlin one-day ban: careless riding (Aug 20)

FOCUS
A weak maiden but straightforward form.

NOTEBOOK
My Sharona is progressing steadily and got off the mark upped to 7f for the first time. The way she wandered about a bit once hitting the front suggested she probably had a bit in the locker if needed. A first juvenile winner of the campaign for her trainer, she seems pretty versatile regards ground (second on soft last time) and appeals as the type to make her mark in nurseries. (op 15-8)
Tidal's Baby was 4l behind My Sharona here last time so has clearly improved a bit for the step up in trip, that perhaps being no surprise given his dam was a 1m4f winner. This form isn't anything out of the ordinary but he could well improve a little as his stamina is drawn out more. (op 7-2)
Alice Rose(IRE)'s Doncaster second last time just about the standard so it was perhaps a little disappointing she didn't put up more of a fight in the final furlong. It's early days to be questioning her temperament, but she has given a flick of her tail in the closing stages on her last two starts now. (op 11-8)
Cheviot Quest(IRE) fared a little better than his debut but doesn't look like being of any interest until he's qualified for nurseries. (op 28-1 tchd 33-1)
Red Hot Penny(IRE), who was well beaten in a seller last time, looks very much one of his yard's lesser lights at this stage. (op 66-1)

4683 MOULTON NURSERIES H'CAP 6f 3y
6:40 (6:40) (Class 5) (0-70,67) 3-Y-O+ **£2,264** (£673; £336; £168) **Stalls** High

Form RPR

6-05 **1** **South African Gold (USA)**[161] 654 4-9-5 **60**........................(p) LukeMorris 3 68
(James Eustace) *mde all: rdn over 1f out: hld on wl u.p towards fin* **8/1**

1660 **2** *hd* **Watch Chain (IRE)**[34] 3555 4-9-8 **63**........................(p) NeilCallan 4 70
(Alan McCabe) *hld up in tch: rdn and effrt 1f out: pressed wnr fnl 75yds: r.o: jst hld* **6/1**[3]

6550 **3** *¾* **Yahafedh Alaih**[11] 4321 3-9-5 **64**........................ ChrisCatlin 6 68
(Clive Brittain) *w ldr: ev ch and rdn wl over 1f out: drvn and styd on same pce fnl f* **6/1**[3]

-000 **4** *2* **Angel Of Fashion (IRE)**[16] 4160 4-8-7 **53**........................ LauraPike(5) 1 52
(Peter Charalambous) *chsd ldrs: rdn and effrt 2f out: drvn and unable qck ent fnl f: no ex and btn fnl 150yds* **16/1**

0423 **5** *1¼* **Desert Icon (IRE)**[25] 3869 5-9-10 **65**........................(b[1]) MartinLane 2 60
(David Simcock) *taken down early: stdd s: t.k.h: hld up in last pair: hdwy on outer over 2f out: rdn and nt qckn 2f out: wknd 1f out* **2/1**[1]

0001 **6** *3* **Danzoe (IRE)**[22] 3957 4-9-12 **67**........................ SebSanders 8 52
(Christine Dunnett) *stdd after s: t.k.h: hld up in last pair: rdn and effrt ent fnl 2f: hrd drvn and unable qck over 1f out: wknd 1f out* **4/1**[2]

5-50 **7** *3½* **Clerical (USA)**[22] 3956 5-8-9 **53**........................(p) JohnFahy(3) 7 27
(Robert Cowell) *hld up wl in tch: rdn and unable qck ent fnl 2f: wknd over 1f out* **15/2**

1m 13.7s (-0.70) **Going Correction** -0.025s/f (Good)
WFA 3 from 4yo+ 4lb **7** Ran SP% **110.7**
Speed ratings (Par 103): **103,102,101,99,97 93,88**
toteswingers:1&2:£4.20, 2&3:£3.30, 1&3:£3.00 CSF £50.70 CT £294.55 TOTE £9.40: £3.30, £3.30; EX 58.50.
Owner William Mocatta **Bred** Douglas S Arnold **Trained** Newmarket, Suffolk

FOCUS
A run-of-the-mill sprint. The winner and third were in front rank throughout and very few threatened a serious blow. Modest form.

4684 SJT MEDIA H'CAP 5f 43y
7:10 (7:11) (Class 6) (0-60,55) 3-Y-O **£1,617** (£481; £240; £120) **Stalls** High

Form RPR

0240 **1** **Dangerous Illusion (IRE)**[47] 3136 3-8-11 **45**........................ PatCosgrave 4 49
(Michael Quinn) *led for over 1f: w ldr after: shkn up 3f out: led again ent fnl 2f: drvn over 1f out: hdd wl ins fnl f: battled on to ld again on post* **7/1**

3- **2** *nse* **Till Dawn (IRE)**[250] 7577 3-9-7 **55**........................ LukeMorris 1 59
(Tony Carroll) *stdd and dropped in bhd after s: hdwy on outer jst over 2f out: drvn to press ldrs 1f out: drvn to ld wl ins fnl f: hdd on post* **13/8**[1]

6040 **3** *¾* **See Vermont**[17] 4124 3-9-5 **53**........................ NeilCallan 5 54
(Robin Bastiman) *trckd ldrs: nt clr run wl over 1f out tl gap opened and rdn to chal 1f out: no ex and btn fnl 50yds* **9/4**[2]

-655 **4** *3½* **Cliffords Reprieve**[13] 4224 3-9-4 **52**........................ EddieCreighton 2 41
(Eric Wheeler) *in tch: pushed along 1/2-way: rdn 2f out: wknd ent fnl f* **9/2**[3]

-050 **5** *3½* **Instructress**[47] 3136 3-9-4 **55**........................ JohnFahy(3) 3 31
(Robert Cowell) *t.k.h: w ldr tl led after 1f: hdd ent fnl 2f: hld hd high u.p over 1f out: wknd qckly 1f out* **12/1**

62.58 secs (-0.12) **Going Correction** -0.025s/f (Good) **5** Ran SP% **107.2**
Speed ratings (Par 98): **99,98,97,92,86**
CSF £17.93 TOTE £6.60: £2.60, £2.40; EX 10.20.
Owner M Quinn **Bred** Miss Niamh Hackett **Trained** Newmarket, Suffolk

FOCUS
It is hard to escape the conclusion this was anything other than a very weak handicap. However, the time was not bad.

Cliffords Reprieve Official explanation: trainer's rep said gelding was unsuited by the good to firm ground

4685 CUSTOM KITCHENS CLAIMING STKS — 1m 2f 21y

7:40 (7:41) (Class 6) 3-Y-O — **£1,617** (£481; £240; £120) **Stalls** Low

Form — RPR

1604 **1** — **Malice Or Mischief (IRE)**[5] 4489 3-9-3 78 .... NeilCallan 1 — 80
(Tony Carroll) *v.s.a: bhd: swtchd rt and hdwy jst over 2f out: led over 1f out: edging lft after: r.o wl and drew clr fnl 100yds: pushed out* **9/4**[1]

4005 **2** *2* — **Conducting**[28] 3739 3-8-13 73 .... ShaneKelly 2 — 72
(Brian Meehan) *stdd s: hld up in tch: effrt and pushed along to chal wl over 1f out: stl pressing wnr but looking hld whn short of room and swtchd rt ins fnl f: one pce after* **9/4**[1]

0115 **3** *2 ½* — **Dew Reward (IRE)**[16] 4153 3-8-6 65 .... KierenFox(3) 4 — 63
(Bill Turner) *sn bustled along: chsd ldrs tl led 4f out: sn rdn: hdd over 1f out: styng on same pce and looked btn whn squeezed for room and hmpd 1f out: one pce and wl hld after* **16/1**[3]

-231 **4** *2 ¾* — **Janet's Pearl (IRE)**[18] 3679 3-8-6 70 .... (p) ChrisCatlin 3 — 55
(Ann Duffield) *t.k.h: chsd ldr: upsides ldrr 4f out: rdn and fnd little jst over 2f out: wknd u.p 1f out* **9/4**[1]

0206 **5** *12* — **Zaheeb**[20] 4005 3-8-13 55 .... LukeMorris 5 — 38
(Dave Morris) *hld up in tch: rdn and little rspnse over 2f out: drvn and wknd over 1f out* **14/1**[2]

03 **6** *3 ¾* — **Refusal**[94] 1728 3-9-2 0 .... SophieDoyle(3) 6 — 36
(Andrew Reid) *racd freely: led tl 4f out: wknd and bhd over 2f out: sn lost tch* **50/1**

2m 8.99s (-1.51) **Going Correction** -0.025s/f (Good) — **6** Ran SP% **106.8**
Speed ratings (Par 98): **105,103,101,99,89 86**
toteswingers:1&2:£2.10, 2&3:£5.90, 1&3:£2.40 CSF £6.63 TOTE £2.60: £1.20, £1.10; EX 8.00.

Owner Bill Adams **Bred** Kilnamoragh Stud **Trained** Cropthorne, Worcs

FOCUS
This was by no means a bad race of its type, a few of these well capable at this level.

4686 COOPERNORWICHBMW.CO.UK H'CAP — 1m 3f 101y

8:10 (8:10) (Class 6) (0-65,63) 3-Y-O — **£1,617** (£481; £240; £120) **Stalls** Low

Form — RPR

004 **1** — **Peira**[34] 3558 3-9-3 59 .... LukeMorris 1 — 68
(Jane Chapple-Hyam) *chsd ldng pair: swtchd rt over 3f out: led over 2f out: rdn and wnt clr over 1f out: in n.d fnl f: eased towards fin* **7/2**[1]

4305 **2** *3 ½* — **Lady Barastar (IRE)**[27] 3771 3-9-2 61 .... JohnFahy(3) 5 — 64
(Walter Swinburn) *stdd s: t.k.h: hld up in last trio: hdwy on inner 3f out: rdn and nt qckn 2f out: no ch w wnr 1f out: wnt 2nd fnl 75yds* **9/2**[3]

440 **3** *1* — **Hygrove Welshlady (IRE)**[42] 3267 3-9-6 62 .... SebSanders 6 — 63
(J W Hills) *stdd s: t.k.h: hld up in last trio: hdwy over 3f out: rdn to chse wnr 2f out: outpcd and btn over 1f out: lost 2nd fnl 75yds* **7/1**

5530 **4** *1 ½* — **Joyful Sound (IRE)**[7] 4435 3-9-7 63 .... StevieDonohoe 7 — 62
(Andrew Haynes) *stdd s: hld up in rr: effrt on outer 3f out: no ch w wnr and plugged on same pce fr over 1f out* **11/2**

0-00 **5** *8* — **Black Iceman**[44] 3227 3-8-5 50 .... SimonPearce(3) 2 — 41
(Lydia Pearce) *in tch: rdn over 3f out: losing pl and rr whn stmbld bdly over 2f out: no ch after* **33/1**

4-50 **6** *2 ¾* — **Rosa Midnight (USA)**[84] 1997 3-9-4 60 .... HayleyTurner 3 — 41
(Michael Bell) *led tl over 2f out: sn rdn and lost pl qckly 2f out: wl btn over 1f out* **4/1**[2]

0053 **7** *1 ½* — **Rowan Ridge**[13] 4248 3-9-2 58 .... (p) PatCosgrave 8 — 36
(Jim Boyle) *chsd ldr tl over 3f out: sn drvn and fnd little: wknd 2f out* **9/2**[3]

2m 28.68s (-0.02) **Going Correction** -0.025s/f (Good) — **7** Ran SP% **109.4**
Speed ratings (Par 98): **99,96,95,94,88 86,85**
toteswingers:1&2:£4.90, 2&3:£3.10, 1&3:£3.80 CSF £17.65 CT £92.75 TOTE £5.70: £2.50, £3.10; EX 24.60.

Owner Wood Hall Stud Limited **Bred** Whatton Manor Stud **Trained** Dalham, Suffolk

FOCUS
By no means a strong 3yo handicap, but the pace was decent. The form makes sense.

Black Iceman Official explanation: jockey said gelding stumbled in home straight

4687 BANHAM POULTRY H'CAP — 1m 6f 17y

8:40 (8:40) (Class 5) (0-75,74) 3-Y-O+ — **£2,264** (£673; £336; £168) **Stalls** High

Form — RPR

151 **1** — **Final Liberation (FR)**[6] 4476 3-8-9 68 6ex .... SebSanders 4 — 78+
(Sir Mark Prescott Bt) *mde all: rdn clr wl over 2f out: styd on* **4/9**[1]

-316 **2** *4* — **Ghufa (IRE)**[38] 3434 7-9-6 69 .... SimonPearce(3) 5 — 75
(Lydia Pearce) *hld up: hdwy to chse clr wnr over 2f out: no imp* **14/1**

P-65 **3** *1 ¾* — **Ugalla**[11] 4341 4-9-10 70 .... LukeMorris 6 — 72
(Jane Chapple-Hyam) *chsd ldr to 8f out: rdn and struggling 4f out: no ch fnl 2f: snatched 3rd post* **9/1**[3]

2133 **4** *nse* — **Sancho Panza**[52] 2952 4-9-5 68 .... AdamBeschizza(3) 1 — 70
(Julia Feilden) *chsd ldrs: lost pl 6f out: hdwy to go 3rd wl over 2f out: no imp* **5/1**[2]

1420 **5** *7* — **Treacle Tart**[46] 3184 6-9-3 68 .... LauraPike(5) 3 — 60
(Peter Charalambous) *t.k.h: hld up: hdwy to press ldr 8f out to over 3f out: wknd 2f out* **28/1**

1-06 **6** *23* — **Dalhaan (USA)**[174] 486 6-10-0 74 .... ShaneKelly 2 — 42
(Luke Dace) *chsd ldrs: wnt 2nd over 3f out to wl over 2f out: sn wknd: t.o* **40/1**

3m 6.35s (-1.25) **Going Correction** -0.025s/f (Good)
WFA 3 from 4yo+ 13lb — **6** Ran SP% **108.5**
Speed ratings (Par 103): **102,99,98,98,94 81**
toteswingers:1&2:£1.30, 2&3:£4.00, 1&3:£2.00 CSF £7.42 TOTE £1.50: £1.30, £2.50; EX 7.60.

Owner P Bamford **Bred** R & E Bamford Limited **Trained** Newmarket, Suffolk

FOCUS
A staying handicap which went the way of the one obviously progressive type in the line-up. The form seems sound enough.

T/Plt: £110.20 to a £1 stake. Pool of £49,458.69 - 327.35 winning tickets. T/Qpdt: £41.20 to a £1 stake. Pool of £4,932.38 - 88.50 winning tickets. SP

4688 - 4694a (Foreign Racing) - See Raceform Interactive

4654 BRIGHTON (L-H)

Thursday, August 4

OFFICIAL GOING: Soft (good to soft in places)

Wind: Very changeable. Weather: foggy (100yds visibility at 13.15) visibility fine after race 3

4695 PLAY MECCA BINGO ON YOUR IPHONE H'CAP — 5f 213y

2:30 (2:30) (Class 5) (0-75,75) 3-Y-O — **£2,587** (£770; £384; £192) **Stalls** Centre

Form — RPR

3134 **1** — **Cheylesmore (IRE)**[14] 4244 3-8-9 63 .... (v) WilliamCarson 2 — 69+
(Stuart Williams) *mounted outside paddock and taken down early: rdn to ld: 3 l clr and drvn 100yds out: heavily eased nr fin* **6/4**[1]

6200 **2** *2 ¾* — **Roman Dancer (IRE)**[17] 4156 3-9-2 70 .... (v[1]) MartinLane 5 — 67
(John Gallagher) *pushed along to leave stalls: chsng wnr vainly 100yds out* **8/1**

2544 **3** *2* — **Paradise Place**[14] 4238 3-8-8 62 .... EddieAhern 1 — 53
(Robert Cowell) *wl hld 3rd 100yds out* **4/1**[3]

4443 **4** *1* — **Tiberius Claudius (IRE)**[17] 4160 3-9-7 75 .... TomQueally 4 — 63
(George Margarson) *last after 2f and stl there and btn 100yds out* **7/4**[2]

1m 15.22s (5.02) **Going Correction** +0.625s/f (Yiel) — **4** Ran SP% **107.5**
Speed ratings (Par 100): **91,87,84,83**
CSF £11.76 TOTE £2.60; EX 8.80.

Owner Keith & Meta Pryce **Bred** John Cullinan **Trained** Newmarket, Suffolk

FOCUS
Rail dolled out from 6f to 2.5f adding about 10yds to advertised distances. A sea fret had set in, meaning visibility was poor, and the course had to pass an inspection. Heavy rain (at least 20mm) led to a dramatic change in going, with it being soft, good to soft, from an original good to firm. Predictably they came stands' side in the straight for this opening sprint handicap. Weak form.

Paradise Place Official explanation: vet said filly moved poorly

4696 SOUTH'S PREMIUM USED CAR SUPERMARKET/E.B.F. FILLIES' H'CAP — 6f 209y

3:00 (3:30) (Class 5) (0-70,67) 3-Y-O+ — **£3,234** (£962; £481; £240) **Stalls** Centre

Form — RPR

6500 **1** — **Lady Florence**[14] 4233 6-9-3 58 .... JamesDoyle 4 — 69
(David C Griffiths) *mde all for normal game Brton effrt* **7/2**[3]

5606 **2** *1 ¾* — **Leelu**[24] 3924 5-9-2 57 .... LiamKeniry 5 — 63
(David Arbuthnot) *appeared to chse wnr thrght* **10/3**[2]

5261 **3** *2 ¼* — **Bold Ring**[23] 3943 5-9-2 57 .... TomQueally 7 — 57
(Edward Creighton) *btn 100yds out* **5/2**[1]

2450 **4** *¾* — **Ivory Lace**[8] 4444 10-9-11 66 .... JackMitchell 8 — 64
(Steve Woodman) *wl btn 100yds out* **5/1**

0360 **5** *1 ¾* — **Makheelah**[16] 4185 3-9-1 62 .... KirstyMilczarek 6 — 54
(Clive Brittain) *last away: a bhd* **7/1**

0530 **6** *shd* — **Wotatomboy**[34] 3573 5-8-7 48 oh2 .... ChrisCatlin 2 — 39
(Richard Whitaker) *wl btn 100yds out* **12/1**

1m 26.63s (3.53) **Going Correction** +0.625s/f (Yiel)
WFA 3 from 5yo+ 6lb — **6** Ran SP% **110.7**
Speed ratings (Par 100): **104,102,99,98,96 96**
toteswingers:1&2:£3.30, 2&3:£2.60, 1&3:£1.50 CSF £15.02 CT £31.15 TOTE £4.20: £2.50, £1.50; EX 14.60 Trifecta £56.30.

Owner David Greenwood **Bred** The National Stud **Trained** Bawtry, S Yorks

FOCUS
A further inspection had to be passed after the opener and, as a consequence, racing was put back 30 minutes. A low-grade fillies' handicap. The front pair raced 1-2. The winner has a good record here.

Makheelah Official explanation: jockey said filly was outpaced

4697 DYNAMIC NEW CORSA NOW AT FROSTS CHALLENGE CUP (H'CAP) — 1m 3f 196y

3:30 (4:00) (Class 4) (0-80,79) 3-Y-O+

£9,337 (£2,796; £1,398; £699; £349; £175) **Stalls** High

Form — RPR

3262 **1** — **Romeo Montague**[14] 4237 3-8-9 75 .... (v) ChrisCatlin 10 — 84
(Ed Dunlop) *hld up: last 4f out: in ld over 1f out: kpt on fnl f but needed plenty of coaxing to stay in front and nt looking v resolute* **9/2**[2]

4362 **2** *¾* — **Vertueux (FR)**[12] 4318 6-7-11 55 .... HarryBentley(3) 6 — 63
(Tony Carroll) *hld up: chsng wnr and rdn over 1f out: kpt on steadily but ears flat and nvr looked like overtaking* **8/1**[3]

5011 **3** *2* — **Hawaana (IRE)**[28] 3760 6-9-10 79 .... RobertWinston 3 — 84
(Gay Kelleway) *disputing 3rd and drvn and btn over 1f out* **11/4**[1]

132 **4** *hd* — **My Valley (IRE)**[41] 3352 9-9-3 72 .... IanMongan 4 — 76
(Pat Phelan) *5th and drvn and btn over 1f out* **8/1**[3]

6036 **5** *2* — **Bedouin Bay**[26] 3867 4-9-3 75 .... (v) KieranO'Neill(3) 2 — 76
(Alan McCabe) *disputing 3rd in centre of crse but drvn and wkng over 1f out* **8/1**[3]

1012 **6** *23* — **Plattsburgh (USA)**[7] 4464 3-8-13 79 .... DarryllHolland 1 — 43
(Mark Johnston) *taken down early: 2nd 4f out: t.o and drvn over 1f out: nt keen* **11/4**[1]

0503 **7** *2 ¼* — **Cornish Beau (IRE)**[15] 4204 4-8-9 64 .... TomQueally 9 — 25
(Mark H Tompkins) *in ld but drvn 4f out: drvn and t.o and nt looking keen over 1f out* **11/1**

2m 39.14s (6.44) **Going Correction** +0.625s/f (Yiel)
WFA 3 from 4yo+ 11lb — **7** Ran SP% **113.2**
Speed ratings (Par 105): **103,102,101,101,99 84,82**
toteswingers:1&2:£12.00, 2&3:£4.90, 1&3:£3.30 CSF £38.30 CT £115.44 TOTE £5.70: £3.00, £3.30; EX 54.60 TRIFECTA Not won..

Owner Mrs G A Rupert **Bred** Issa Syndicate **Trained** Newmarket, Suffolk

FOCUS
The runners came into view over 1f out for this 1m4f handicap. The quirky winner got the stands' rail and recorded a small personal best.

Plattsburgh(USA) Official explanation: trainer had no explanation for the poor form shown

4698 SEAT ECOMOTIVE. LESS EMISSIONS, MORE EMOTIONS MAIDEN AUCTION STKS — 7f 214y

4:00 (4:30) (Class 5) 2-Y-O — **£2,328** (£693; £346; £173) **Stalls** Centre

Form — RPR

6 **1** — **Tingo In The Tale (IRE)**[28] 3780 2-8-11 0 .... JamesDoyle 3 — 73
(David Arbuthnot) *hld up in rr: effrt wl over 1f out: drvn to ld ins fnl f: styd on gamely: readily* **7/2**[3]

5220 **2** 1 ¾ **Sheila's Buddy**[26] 3866 2-8-10 72.. LiamKeniry 1 68
(J S Moore) *led and t.k.h: swtchd fr outside to stands' rails 1/2-way: drvn over 1f out: hdd ins fnl f: nt qckn* **5/2**[2]

60 **3** 5 **Single Girl (IRE)**[58] 2788 2-8-3 0.................................. HarryBentley(3) 7 53
(Jonathan Portman) *w ldr 2f: remained prom: outpcd by ldng pair over 1f out: rdr fumbling w whip ins fnl f* **12/1**

5 **4** 1 ¾ **Piers Gaveston (IRE)**[26] 3870 2-8-12 0.................. MatthewDavies(3) 8 58
(George Baker) *midfield: rdn 1/2-way: nvr gng wl enough after: btn over 1f out* **15/8**[1]

0 **5** 1 **Mount St Mistress**[26] 3870 2-8-10 0.............................. CathyGannon 5 51
(George Baker) *racd keenly: chsd ldrs tl rdn and fdd over 1f out* **25/1**

0 **6** ½ **Welsh Nayber**[20] 4053 2-9-1 0... EddieAhern 2 55
(Amanda Perrett) *awkward leaving stalls: drvn to go prom in centre over 3f out: wknd wl over 1f out* **9/1**

0 **7** 3 ½ **Singspiel Spirit**[65] 2594 2-9-1 0.. ChrisCatlin 4 47
(Clive Brittain) *pushed along after 2f: bhd: hrd rdn and hanging lft fr 3f out: nvr travelling after* **14/1**

1m 41.52s (5.52) **Going Correction** +0.625s/f (Yiel) 7 Ran SP% **113.8**
Speed ratings (Par 94): **97,95,90,88,87 87,83**
toteswingers:1&2:£1.70, 2&3:£4.30, 1&3:£9.20 CSF £12.57 TOTE £4.00: £1.60, £1.80; EX 15.80 Trifecta £56.60 Pool: £451.63 - 5.90 winning units..
Owner George S Thompson **Bred** Brian Williamson **Trained** Compton, Berks

FOCUS
The sea fret had cleared by the time of this race. A modest juvenile maiden with the runner-up the bset guide.

NOTEBOOK
Tingo In The Tale(IRE) had run well in a decent race on his debut and really knuckled down under pressure here, drawing away close home. He cleared handled the ground and there could be more to come in nurseries. (op 9-2)
Sheila's Buddy, although exposed, gives the form a solid look and deserves to find a small race. (op 11-4)
Single Girl(IRE) left her previous efforts behind and can come on again switched to handicaps. (op 16-1)
Piers Gaveston(IRE) failed to improve on his initial effort and possibly found the soft ground against him. He deserves another chance. (op 2-1 tchd 7-4)
Welsh Nayber Official explanation: jockey said colt hung left

4699 2012 JAGUAR RANGE AT FROSTS H'CAP 7f 214y
4:30 (4:55) (Class 6) (0-60,60) 3-Y-0+ **£1,940** (£577; £288; £144) **Stalls** Centre

Form RPR

5504 **1** **Ocean Countess (IRE)**[23] 3944 5-9-3 **54**.........(v) MichaelO'Connell(3) 9 63
(Tony Carroll) *dropped out last: effrt 1/2-way: swtchd to bag stands' rails and ld 3f out: rdn and kpt on wl in her normal game Brton fashion ins fnl f: comf* **7/2**[2]

4466 **2** 1 ¾ **Adelina Patti**[14] 4244 3-9-5 **60**.. EddieAhern 3 64
(Walter Swinburn) *plld hrd: prom: led after 3f tl hdd 3f out: drvn in 2nd after: no ch w wnr ins fnl f* **7/2**[2]

0504 **3** 2 ¾ **Inquisitress**[5] 4544 7-9-3 **51**... CathyGannon 10 50
(John Bridger) *chsd ldrs: hrd drvn 2f out: nt qckn over 1f out and wl hld but kpt trying* **7/2**[2]

3023 **4** 1 **Indian Violet (IRE)**[12] 4322 5-9-12 **60**........................... JamieGoldstein 1 56
(Ralph Smith) *chsd ldrs tl rdn over 2f out: rdr fumbling w rein over 1f out: fading ins fnl f* **5/2**[1]

050 **5** 10 **Storm Runner (IRE)**[14] 4244 3-9-4 **59**...........................(v[1]) TomQueally 8 31
(George Margarson) *led and t.k.h: hdd after 3f: sn unbalanced and racing awkwardly: struggling 1/2-way: t.o over 1f out* **7/1**[3]

00-0 **6** 1 ¼ **Ain't Talkin'**[161] 662 5-8-9 **46** oh1................................(p) HarryBentley(3) 2 16
(Michael Attwater) *taken down early: keen in rr early: drvn and lost pl over 3f out: t.o fnl 2f and carried hd high* **16/1**

1m 40.73s (4.73) **Going Correction** +0.625s/f (Yiel)
WFA 3 from 4yo+ 7lb 6 Ran SP% **113.6**
Speed ratings (Par 101): **101,99,96,95,85 84**
toteswingers:1&2:£2.70, 2&3:£2.60, 1&3:£3.20 CSF £16.36 CT £44.62 TOTE £5.30: £1.90, £2.20; EX 24.90 Trifecta £60.50 Pool: £306.89 - 3.75 winning units..
Owner W McLuskey **Bred** Don Commins **Trained** Cropthorne, Worcs

FOCUS
A well run handicap but modest form.

4700 SPIFFING CRABBIE'S ALCOHOLIC GINGER BEER LADY AMATEUR RIDERS' H'CAP 1m 1f 209y
5:00 (5:16) (Class 5) (0-70,70) 3-Y-0+ **£2,495** (£774; £386) **Stalls** High

Form RPR

2105 **1** **Megalala (IRE)**[20] 4059 10-10-5 **65**............................. MissSBrotherton 8 79
(John Bridger) *mde all: wisely brought to r up stands' rail in st: clr over 1f out: game but racing idly and kpt up to work for 6th Brton win* **5/4**[1]

0423 **2** 15 **Mighty Mambo**[2] 4649 4-9-12 **65**............................ MissKMargarson(7) 6 55
(George Margarson) *chsd wnr: rdn and outpcd wl over 1f out: fading ins fnl f* **13/8**[2]

0300 **3** 1 **Corlough Mountain**[4] 4579 7-9-7 **53** oh6 ow2..............(p) MissZoeLilly 5 41
(Paddy Butler) *a in last: rdn 3f out: ev ch of 2nd over 1f out: plodded on: fading ins fnl f* **16/1**[3]

2m 9.65s (6.05) **Going Correction** +0.625s/f (Yiel)
WFA 3 from 4yo+ 9lb 3 Ran SP% **88.4**
Speed ratings (Par 103): **100,88,87**
CSF £2.29 TOTE £2.00; EX 2.40 TRIFECTA Cancelled..
Owner Tommy Ware **Bred** Joseph Gallagher **Trained** Liphook, Hants
■ Polly Holder was withdrawn (4/1, spread plate going to s). Deduct 20p in the £ under R4.

T/Jkpt: Part won. £8,771.30 to a £1 stake. Pool of £12353.96 - 0.50 winning units. T/Plt: £311.80 to a £1 stake. Pool of £78,303.99 - 183.32 winning tickets. T/Qpdt: £43.40 to a £1 stake. Pool of £4,697.64 - 80.00 winning tickets. IM

4269 CHEPSTOW (L-H)
Thursday, August 4

OFFICIAL GOING: Good to soft
Wind: mild against Weather: cloudy with sunny periods

4701 HEREFORD LAND ROVER H'CAP (FOR LADY AMATEUR RIDERS) 1m 14y
5:20 (5:20) (Class 5) (0-70,70) 3-Y-0+ **£2,183** (£677; £338; £169) **Stalls** Centre

Form RPR

3050 **1** **Mr Udagawa**[12] 4337 5-9-7 **59**.................................(p) MissSallyRandell(5) 5 69
(Bernard Llewellyn) *a.p: led 2f out: clr ent fnl f: drifted lft: kpt on wl: pushed out* **7/1**

2040 **2** 3 **Tuscan King**[9] 1730 4-9-1 **53** ow1..............................(bt) MissCBoxall(5) 7 56
(Bernard Llewellyn) *outpcd in rr: rdn and hdwy over 2f out: chsd wnr over 1f out: kpt on but a being readily hld* **14/1**

1050 **3** 2 ½ **Bidable**[17] 4158 7-10-9 **70**... MissEJJones 6 67
(Bryn Palling) *mid-div: pushed along 4f out: rdn and stdy prog fr over 2f out: styd on: wnt 3rd ins fnl f: nvr trbld ldrs* **5/1**[3]

2140 **4** 1 ¼ **Hits Only Jude (IRE)**[17] 4142 8-9-11 **63**............(v) MissAZetterholm(5) 3 57
(Declan Carroll) *dwlt bdly: chsd ldrs after 1f: rdn over 2f out: styd on same pce fnl f* **4/1**[1]

0600 **5** 1 ¾ **Sweet Possession (USA)**[29] 3741 5-8-13 **51**.......(tp) MissAWallace(5) 1 41
(Pat Eddery) *awkward leaving stalls: racd keenly: sn led: rdn and hdd 2f out: fdd fnl f* **13/2**

00-0 **6** 2 ¼ **Chicamia**[32] 3657 7-9-1 **51** oh2.............................. MissMMullineaux(3) 11 36
(Michael Mullineaux) *outpcd in rr: styd on fr over 1f out: nvr a danger* **16/1**

2500 **7** 1 **Needwood Ridge**[72] 2378 4-9-11 **63**......................(bt[1]) MissCHJones(5) 10 46
(Frank Sheridan) *mid-div: rdn over 2f out: sn btn* **10/1**

1130 **8** nse **Qeethaara (USA)**[18] 4127 7-10-3 **69**.............. MissBeckyBrisbourne(5) 9 52
(Mark Brisbourne) *mid-div: smooth hdwy 3f out: rdn 2f out: sn hung lft: wknd fnl f* **9/2**[2]

-060 **9** 1 ½ **Safari Guide**[14] 4224 5-9-1 **51** oh2............................ MissRachelKing(3) 8 30
(Dai Burchell) *chsd ldrs tl wknd over 2f out* **11/1**

000/ **10** 24 **Hohrod**[594] 7797 5-8-11 **51** oh6... MissKClark(7) 2 —
(Ron Hodges) *mid-div for over 3f: sn bhd: t.o fr over 2f out* **50/1**

1m 37.91s (1.71) **Going Correction** +0.05s/f (Good) 10 Ran SP% **112.6**
Speed ratings (Par 103): **93,90,87,86,84 82,81,81,79,55**
toteswingers:1&2:£8.20, 1&3:£7.20, 2&3:£7.90 CSF £96.27 CT £530.06 TOTE £5.30: £1.20, £3.70, £1.30; EX 47.30.
Owner B J Llewellyn **Bred** Richard C J Manning **Trained** Fochriw, Caerphilly

FOCUS
A typically open race of its type, run at a sound enough pace, and they finished fairly strung out. Not form to be taking too literally, with the winner the best guide.
Mr Udagawa Official explanation: trainer's rep said, regarding apparent improvement in form, that the gelding was better suited by the track.

4702 RHOMCO CONSULTING LTD MEDIAN AUCTION MAIDEN FILLIES' STKS 5f 16y
5:50 (5:50) (Class 5) 2-Y-0 **£2,264** (£673; £336; £168) **Stalls** Centre

Form RPR

353 **1** **Miss Lahar**[12] 4312 2-8-11 95.. MartinHarley(3) 3 96+
(Mick Channon) *mde all: pushed clr over 1f out: r.o wl: comf* **1/3**[1]

3064 **2** 8 **Meloneras**[7] 4462 2-9-0 71... TomMcLaughlin 2 66
(Rod Millman) *chsd wnr thrght: rdn over 2f out: sn hung to far rail: no ex ent fnl f* **4/1**[2]

0 **3** 8 **Brilliant Crystal**[13] 4283 2-8-11 0.................................... SeanLevey(3) 6 37
(Mrs K Burke) *chsd ldrs: rdn over 2f out: edgd lft: wknd over 1f out* **14/1**

043 **4** 2 ¼ **Empressive**[14] 4225 2-8-9 56... JamesRogers(5) 4 29
(William Muir) *taken down early: chsd ldrs: rdn over 2f out: wknd over 1f out* **12/1**[3]

5 4 **Brown Eyed Lass** 2-8-7 0... DavidKenny(7) 1 15+
(Laura Young) *cantered loose after unseating rdr leaving paddock: dwlt: sn outpcd: nvr on terms* **33/1**

064 **6** 4 ½ **Imperial Weapon (IRE)**[54] 2919 2-9-0 42........................ SaleemGolam 5 —
(John Spearing) *taken down early: chsd ldrs: rdn over 2f out: sn hung to far rail: wknd over 1f out* **50/1**

59.86 secs (0.56) **Going Correction** +0.05s/f (Good) 6 Ran SP% **114.3**
Speed ratings (Par 91): **97,84,71,67,61 54**
toteswingers:1&2:£1.10, 1&3:£1.80, 2&3:£2.40 CSF £2.16 TOTE £1.40: £1.10, £1.20; EX 1.90.
Owner Barry Walters Catering **Bred** Barry Walters **Trained** West Ilsley, Berks

FOCUS
An uncompetitive fillies' maiden, rated around the runner-up. The winner confirmed her Ascot improvement.

NOTEBOOK
Miss Lahar duly opened her account by thrashing her rivals. She stepped up massively when third in the Group 3 Princess Margaret Stakes at Ascot 12 days earlier on her fourth outing and she proved that no fluke with a taking effort here, winning under a no-nonsense ride. Some cut in the ground is clearly right up her street and, while she may not be the easiest to place from here on, she ought to be full of confidence now. A return to Group company in the Mill Reef at Newbury next month could figure in her plans. (op 2-5, tchd 4-9 in places)
Meloneras was the chief danger to the winner and proved the only one to give her any sort of race, but was very much put in her place from the halfway stage. She can find a nursery back on quicker ground over an easy 6f. (op 9-2)
Brilliant Crystal shaped more encouragingly and showed the benefit of her debut 13 days earlier, but didn't look that happy on the ground when asked for everything. She needs one more run before entering nurseries. (op 12-1 tchd 11-1)
Empressive lacked the required early pace back over this trip and on the softer surface. She's rated 56 and still probably ran close to that mark, though (op 14-1)

4703 FIREWORK SPOOKTACULAR HERE 29TH OCTOBER H'CAP 1m 4f 23y
6:20 (6:21) (Class 6) (0-60,58) 3-Y-0+ **£1,617** (£481; £240; £120) **Stalls** Low

Form RPR

0046 **1** **Soundbyte**[29] 3738 6-9-8 **58**.. JohnFahy(3) 8 74
(John Gallagher) *s.i.s: sn mid-div: reminders after 2f: hdwy to trck ldr over 6f out: rdn over 4f out: led over 3f out: drvn clr over 1f out: styd on strly* **10/1**

0/4- **2** 9 **Spice Bar**[29] 7157 7-9-1 **48**.. SaleemGolam 10 50
(Declan Carroll) *trckd ldrs tl outpcd u.p wl over 2f out: styd on again fr over 1f out: wnt 2nd fnl f: no ch w wnr* **5/1**[3]

263- **3** 1 ½ **Red Current**[14] 4991 7-8-5 **45**... DavidKenny(7) 11 44
(Michael Scudamore) *trckd ldrs: rdn over 4f out: styd on same pce fnl 3f: wnt 3rd fnl f* **25/1**

004 **4** 1 **Milton Hill**[29] 3743 4-9-0 **50**... SeanLevey(3) 4 48
(Dominic Ffrench Davis) *in tch: rdn over 4f out: styd on same pce: wnt 4th fnl f* **40/1**

506- **5** ½ **Cruise Control**[137] 7958 5-8-5 **45**.......................... MatthewLawson(7) 12 42
(Richard Price) *hld up towards rr: hdwy over 4f out: sn hung lft: chsd wnr whn rdn over 2f out: on far rail whn wknd fnl f* **25/1**

4503 **6** ½ **Tiger Tess**[17] 4153 3-8-13 **57**... NeilChalmers 6 57+
(Jonathan Portman) *taken down early and unruly at s: hld up towards rr: rdn and hdwy 3f out: styng on whn nt clr run on rails over 1f out: hld but kpt on after* **8/1**

0605 **7** shd **Bahkov (IRE)**[10] 4389 5-8-12 **45**.................................(b) WilliamCarson 7 41
(Eric Wheeler) *hld up in rr of mid-div: rdn 5f out: styd on steadily fr 3f out: no ex fnl f* **12/1**

5030 **8** 4 ½ **Boogie Dancer**[44] 3256 7-8-12 **45**.................................(t) TomMcLaughlin 5 34
(Stuart Howe) *towards rr: sme hdwy u.p 4f out: no further imp and eased whn hld ent fnl f* **33/1**

5522 **9** 2 1/2 **Madison Square (USA)**[6] 4491 3-8-9 **58**........................ DarylByrne(5) 2 43
(Mark Johnston) *trckd ldr tl over 6f out: cl up: rdn 4f out: wknd 2f out* **9/4**[1]
6224 **10** 2 3/4 **Oak Leaves**[24] 3910 4-9-4 **51**.. LiamJones 9 31
(Nikki Evans) *led tl rdn over 3f out: wknd ent fnl f* **4/1**[2]
001/ **11** 3 **Windpfeil (IRE)**[294] 6742 5-9-7 **54**.............................. FrankieMcDonald 1 29
(Brendan Powell) *s.i.s: sn in tch: rdn over 4f out: wknd over 2f out* **20/1**
00-0 **12** 1 1/4 **Feuergott (GER)**[9] 4408 5-8-7 **45**................................ RyanPowell(5) 3 18
(Ian Williams) *a towards rr: wl btn 4f out* **20/1**

2m 39.16s (0.16) **Going Correction** +0.05s/f (Good)
WFA 3 from 4yo+ 11lb **12** Ran SP% **117.9**
Speed ratings (Par 101): **101,95,94,93,93 92,92,89,87,86 84,83**
toteswingers:1&2:£12.00, 1&3:£27.30, 2&3:£24.20 CSF £53.48 CT £1231.07 TOTE £10.50: £3.10, £2.30, £3.30; EX 42.70.
Owner Oliver Parsons **Bred** Mrs R J Gallagher **Trained** Chastleton, Oxon

FOCUS
This moderate handicap was run at a fair pace and it produced a most decisive winner. He showed his best turf form for nearly two years, but this is not form to take too literally.
Boogie Dancer Official explanation: jockey said mare hung left-handed

4704 CHEPSTOW STAMPEDE HERE 13TH NOVEMBER NURSERY 6f 16y
6:55 (6:55) (Class 5) (0-70,69) 2-Y-O **£2,264** (£673; £336; £168) **Stalls** Centre

Form RPR
2615 **1** **Silvas Romana (IRE)**[4] 4572 2-9-4 **66**........................ TomMcLaughlin 5 73+
(Mark Brisbourne) *trckd ldrs: rdn wl over 2f out: sn chsng ldr: kpt on wl ent fnl f: led fnl 75yds: rdn out* **13/2**
3304 **2** 3/4 **Worth**[21] 4019 2-8-13 **64**..(b[1]) LouisBeuzelin(3) 8 69
(Brian Meehan) *led: 2 l clr over 2f out: rdn over 1f out: no ex whn hdd fnl 75yds* **9/2**[2]
2452 **3** 6 **Emma Jean (IRE)**[14] 4225 2-8-5 **58**................................ RyanPowell(5) 2 45
(J S Moore) *hld up: hdwy 3f out: sn rdn: styd on to go 3rd fnl f: nvr gng pce to get on terms* **11/2**
443 **4** 3/4 **King's Ciel**[14] 4229 2-9-0 **69**.. DavidKenny(7) 6 54
(George Baker) *trckd wnr: rdn over 2f out: kpt on same pce* **5/1**[3]
000 **5** 1/2 **High Five Prince (IRE)**[15] 4201 2-8-0 **51**................(p) SimonPearce(3) 4 34
(Mark Usher) *taken down early: in tch: rdn 3f out: nt pce to chal: fdd ins fnl f* **7/1**
4435 **6** 3 3/4 **Balm**[21] 3993 2-9-2 **67**.. SeanLevey(3) 3 39
(Richard Hannon) *hld up: rdn and hdwy into 4th over 2f out: wknd ent fnl f* **6/1**
464 **7** 1 1/2 **J Cunningham**[21] 4021 2-8-1 **49**..............................(p) FrankieMcDonald 1 17
(Mark Usher) *awkward leaving stalls: sn outpcd: nvr on terms* **28/1**
446 **8** 3 1/4 **Armiger**[36] 3505 2-9-0 **67**.. JamesRogers(5) 7 25
(William Muir) *trckd ldrs: rdn 3f out: sn hld: wknd 1f out: eased* **4/1**[1]

1m 12.49s (0.49) **Going Correction** +0.05s/f (Good) **8** Ran SP% **113.8**
Speed ratings (Par 94): **98,97,89,88,87 82,80,76**
CSF £35.38 CT £172.24 TOTE £7.20: £2.30, £1.10, £3.00; EX 34.40.
Owner The Bourne Connection **Bred** Limetree Stud **Trained** Great Ness, Shropshire

FOCUS
An ordinary nursery. It was run at a brisk pace and few got involved from out the back as the first pair dominated late on. The form is rated around the second.

NOTEBOOK
Silvas Romana(IRE) got back to winning ways by getting up near the finish and showed real guts to do so. She had got off the mark at Chester on her penultimate outing, but was disappointing back there off a 1lb higher mark just four days earlier. She showed that effort to be wrong, though, and it rates a career-best effort. (op 5-1)
Worth was lit up by the first-time blinkers and streaked into a clear lead. She looked the most likely winner half a furlong out, but her stride shortened thereafter and she was mugged near the finish. She did plenty early on, but probably wasn't helping her rider when it mattered most and looks one to tread carefully with. (tchd 5-1)
Emma Jean(IRE) got behind early but came through the fare best of those racing from off the pace. This was a respectable effort on her nursery debut and she looks well worth trying over a stiffer test. (op 13-2 tchd 5-1)
King's Ciel lacked the pace to land a serious blow on this switch to a nursery and probably wants quicker ground. (tchd 6-1)
Armiger dropped out disappointingly and his stable's runners continue to perform indifferently this term. (op 7-2)

4705 FESTIVAL RACING H'CAP 7f 16y
7:30 (7:31) (Class 6) (0-60,59) 3-Y-O+ **£1,617** (£481; £240; £120) **Stalls** Centre

Form RPR
-654 **1** **Sopran Nad (ITY)**[16] 4179 7-8-4 **45**........................(b[1]) SimonPearce(3) 13 57
(Frank Sheridan) *trckd ldrs: clsd smoothly over 3f out: led wl over 1f out: sn rdn: styd on strly* **7/1**[2]
0040 **2** 2 3/4 **Kenswick**[5] 4549 4-9-1 **56**..(v) SeanLevey(3) 3 61
(Pat Eddery) *s.i.s: sn chsng ldr: rdn over 3f out: led over 2f out: hdd wl over 1f out: sn hld: kpt on same pce* **7/1**[2]
5341 **3** nk **Dancing Welcome**[13] 4270 5-9-2 **54**........................(b) TomMcLaughlin 14 58
(Milton Bradley) *mid-div: rdn 3f out: hdwy 2f out: styd on fnl f* **11/2**[1]
003 **4** 2 1/4 **Tourist**[23] 3942 6-8-9 **52**.. RyanPowell(5) 7 50
(Ian Williams) *in tch: rdn over 3f out: nvr gng pce to get on terms: styd on fnl f* **15/2**[3]
2000 **5** 1/2 **Cwmni**[13] 4270 5-8-11 **56**.. ThomasBrown(7) 2 53+
(Bryn Palling) *taken down early: s.i.s: bhd: rdn 3f out: styd on fr over 1f out: nvr any danger* **9/1**
000- **6** nk **She's Untouchable**[331] 5839 4-8-5 **50**.................... MatthewLawson(7) 8 46
(Gary Harrison) *taken down early: mid-div: rdn over 3f out: no impression tl styd on fnl f* **50/1**
0604 **7** nse **Trade Centre**[14] 4224 6-8-12 **50**................................. RussKennemore 11 46
(Milton Bradley) *mid-div: rdn over 3f out: no imp on ldrs tl styd on fnl f* **12/1**
5-00 **8** nk **Gee Major**[89] 1905 4-9-1 **53**.. SaleemGolam 1 48
(Nicky Vaughan) *nvr bttr than mid-div* **16/1**
3203 **9** 1 3/4 **Valley Tiger**[14] 4244 3-8-10 **59**..................................... JamesRogers(5) 9 47
(William Muir) *s.i.s: bhd: stdy prog u.p fr over 2f out: styd on but nvr threatened ldrs* **11/2**[1]
0-00 **10** 8 **Rich Harvest (USA)**[149] 793 6-8-6 **47** ow2................. MartinHarley(3) 5 16
(Ray Peacock) *led tl rdn over 2f out: wknd over 1f out* **66/1**
-000 **11** hd **Iztaccihuatl**[13] 4270 3-8-3 **50** ow1.................................... JohnFahy(3) 15 16
(Michael Scudamore) *taken down early: sn struggling: a towards rr* **33/1**
0-00 **12** 2 3/4 **Fair Breeze**[27] 3804 4-8-9 **50**......................................(p) LouisBeuzelin(3) 10 11
(Richard Phillips) *s.i.s: sn mid-div: rdn 4f out: sn lost pl* **33/1**
005 **13** nk **Aaranyow (IRE)**[22] 3980 3-8-9 **58**................................... DarylByrne(5) 17 16
(Bryn Palling) *mid-div: rdn over 3f out: wknd 2f out* **40/1**
005 **14** nk **Habsburg**[31] 3675 3-9-0 **58**.......................................(p) FrankieMcDonald 16 15
(Paul Fitzsimons) *mid-div: rdn 4f out: nvr any imp: wknd over 2f out* **40/1**
00-6 **15** 5 **Cool Water Oasis**[23] 3956 3-9-0 **58**...................................... LiamJones 6 —
(Rae Guest) *chsd ldrs: rdn over 3f out: wknd over 2f out* **12/1**
2135 **16** 62 **Pie Poudre**[24] 3926 4-9-6 **58**.......................................(v) WilliamCarson 12 —
(Roy Brotherton) *jockey slow removing hood: v.s.a: nvr any ch: a detached* **10/1**

1m 24.51s (1.31) **Going Correction** +0.05s/f (Good)
WFA 3 from 4yo+ 6lb **16** Ran SP% **122.1**
Speed ratings (Par 101): **94,90,90,87,87 87,86,86,84,75 75,72,71,71,65 —**
toteswingers:1&2:£10.70, 1&3:£9.30, 2&3:£8.30 CSF £52.96 CT £307.92 TOTE £9.40: £1.90, £2.00, £1.60, £1.90; EX 72.30.
Owner Frank Sheridan **Bred** Leonardo Ciampoli **Trained** Wolverhampton, W Midlands

FOCUS
An ordinary handicap. Once more it was a race where it proved hard to make up ground from off the pace as the early tempo was hot. The second and third set the level.
Pie Poudre Official explanation: jockey said gelding ducked away as stalls opened and snatched blindfold from his hands.

4706 HEREFORD LAND ROVER MAIDEN STKS 7f 16y
8:05 (8:07) (Class 5) 3-Y-O+ **£2,264** (£673; £336; £168) **Stalls** Centre

Form RPR
0423 **1** **Lady Bayside**[13] 4271 3-8-12 68.................................. TomMcLaughlin 5 69
(Malcolm Saunders) *trckd ldrs: swtchd rt whn pushed along 2f out: led over 1f out: drifted lft: r.o: rdn out* **13/8**[2]
0 **2** 1 **Orpen'Arry (IRE)**[12] 4340 3-9-3 0.. JamesDoyle 8 71+
(Andrew Haynes) *chsd ldrs tl outpcd 4f out: stl plenty to do in 5th over 1f out: styd on wl fnl f: wnt 2nd towards fin* **28/1**
3426 **3** 3/4 **Red Marling (IRE)**[13] 4271 3-8-10 68.................... MatthewLawson(7) 4 69
(B W Hills) *prom: rdn and ev ch 2f out: hung lft and no ex fnl f* **7/2**[3]
42 **4** 1 1/4 **Dreams Of Dawn**[24] 3909 3-9-0 0.................................. MartinHarley(3) 7 66
(Mick Channon) *awkward away: sn led: rdn whn hrd pressed 2f out: hdd over 1f out: sn edgd lft and hld: no ex whn lost 2nd towards fin* **6/4**[1]
00 **5** 5 **Greyemkay**[28] 3781 3-9-3 0.. WilliamCarson 6 52
(Richard Price) *little slowly away: sn chsng ldrs: rdn over 2f out: wknd ent fnl f* **100/1**
00 **6** nk **Poyle Todream**[82] 2103 3-9-0 0... JohnFahy(3) 2 52
(Ralph Beckett) *trckd ldrs: rdn and ev ch 2f out: wknd jst over 1f out* **16/1**
00/ **7** 4 1/2 **Bawdsey Bank**[645] 7126 5-9-6 0..................................... SimonPearce(3) 3 41
(Ron Hodges) *hld up: rdn over 3f out: wknd over 1f out* **100/1**
8 1/2 **Fleetwood Daughter**[367] 9-8-11 0..................................... ThomasBrown(7) 1 35
(Bernard Llewellyn) *in tch: rdn over 3f out: sn btn* **66/1**
9 7 **Millers Dhustone**[18] 5-9-1 0... SeanLevey(3) 9 —
(Pam Ford) *a last: lost tch 4f out* **100/1**

1m 25.06s (1.86) **Going Correction** +0.05s/f (Good)
WFA 3 from 5yo+ 6lb **9** Ran SP% **114.1**
Speed ratings (Par 103): **91,89,89,87,81 81,76,75,67**
toteswingers:1&2:£7.70, 1&3:£1.50, 2&3:£12.70 CSF £46.09 TOTE £2.80: £1.20, £5.50, £1.10; EX 50.40.
Owner Tim Bostwick **Bred** M Saunders & T Bostwick **Trained** Green Ore, Somerset

FOCUS
An ordinary maiden, run at a strong pace. The favourite disappointed and the time was slow.
Bawdsey Bank Official explanation: jockey said gelding lost an off-fore shoe

4707 DIGIBET.COM FILLIES' H'CAP 1m 14y
8:35 (8:35) (Class 5) (0-75,75) 3-Y-O+ **£2,264** (£673; £336; £168) **Stalls** Centre

Form RPR
1610 **1** **Polar Annie**[10] 4387 6-9-11 **75**.. SeanLevey(3) 10 84
(Malcolm Saunders) *mde all: rdn over 2f out: kpt on gamely: jst hld on: all out* **5/2**[1]
0551 **2** hd **Only You Maggie (IRE)**[2] 4645 4-9-0 **64** 6ex...........(v) MarkLawson(3) 7 73+
(Gary Harrison) *chsd ldrs: rdn 3f out: chsd wnr over 1f out: styd on ins fnl f: drifted rt towards fin: jst hld off* **6/1**
-605 **3** 6 **Folly Drove**[13] 4270 3-8-10 **64**.. JamesDoyle 2 58
(Jonathan Portman) *in tch: rdn whn outpcd 3f out: styd on fr over 1f out: wnt 3rd sn after: no ch w ldng pair* **5/1**[3]
-524 **4** 2 1/4 **Tap Dance Way (IRE)**[62] 2663 4-9-9 **70**............................ LiamKeniry 5 60
(Patrick Chamings) *chsd ldrs: rdn over 3f out: fdd ins fnl f* **9/2**[2]
1606 **5** hd **Silent Oasis**[54] 2915 5-8-13 **67**.................................... BrendanPowell(7) 8 57
(Brendan Powell) *hld up: rdn 3f out: hung lft but styd on fr over 1f out: nvr threatened ldrs* **10/1**
1405 **6** 2 1/4 **National Hope (IRE)**[24] 3918 3-8-10 **67**..................(t) MatthewDavies(3) 9 50
(George Baker) *in tch: rdn over 3f out: wknd ent fnl f* **12/1**
2-00 **7** 1 1/2 **Crazy Chris**[17] 4158 6-9-11 **72**.................................... RussKennemore 3 53
(John Flint) *chsd wnr: rdn over 3f out: sn edgd to far side rail: lost 2nd over 1f out: wknd ent fnl f* **13/2**
23-0 **8** 18 **Superior Edge**[54] 2903 4-9-9 **75**.................................... RyanPowell(5) 4 15
(Christopher Mason) *rrd leaving stalls: towards rr: wknd over 2f out: t.o* **16/1**

1m 36.3s (0.10) **Going Correction** +0.05s/f (Good)
WFA 3 from 4yo+ 7lb **8** Ran SP% **113.7**
Speed ratings (Par 100): **101,100,94,92,92 90,88,70**
toteswingers:1&2:£2.00, 1&3:£3.60, 2&3:£5.90 CSF £17.57 CT £69.14 TOTE £2.70: £1.10, £1.70, £2.10; EX 15.20.
Owner Lockstone Business Services Ltd **Bred** Cobhall Court Stud **Trained** Green Ore, Somerset

FOCUS
A moderate fillies' handicap which was another race where nothing landed a blow from off the strong pace. The first two were clear with the winner rated back to her best.
T/Plt: £65.50 to a £1 stake. Pool:£40,192.80 - 447.94 winning tickets T/Qpdt: £29.90 to a £1 stake. Pool:£5,352.36 - 132.30 winning tickets TM

4244 FOLKESTONE (R-H)
Thursday, August 4

OFFICIAL GOING: Good to soft (good in places)
Wind: Moderate, half-behind. Weather: Overcast becoming fine

4708 EVA LONG MEDIAN AUCTION MAIDEN STKS 7f (S)
5:30 (5:31) (Class 6) 2-Y-O **£1,567** (£462; £231) **Stalls** High

Form RPR
1 **Brickfielder (IRE)** 2-9-3 0... DaneO'Neill 5 75+
(Roger Charlton) *s.v.s: rcvrd to trck ldng trio: shkn up and squeezed through against rail to ld 1f out: rdn to assert fnl 100yds* **1/2**[1]
063 **2** 3/4 **Monessa (IRE)**[28] 3767 2-8-12 63.................................... TonyCulhane 6 65
(Edward Creighton) *led against rail: rdn 2f out: hdd 1f out: kpt on wl but readily hld* **16/1**

00 **3** *8* **Ice Loch**[21] 4007 2-9-3 0 LukeMorris 3 50
(Michael Blanshard) *racd wd: pressed ldr: rdn over 2f out: wknd over 1f out* **14/1**

4 *1 3/4* **Final Delivery** 2-8-12 0 TobyAtkinson(5) 1 46
(Marco Botti) *s.v.s: wl off the pce in last: pushed along and sme prog 2f out: wknd over 1f out* **7/1**[2]

340 **5** *11* **Fairy Moss (IRE)**[40] 3388 2-8-12 52 J-PGuillambert 2 13
(Richard Hannon) *dwlt: pushed along in 5th: no prog over 2f out: wknd qckly over 1f out* **8/1**[3]

0 **6** *3* **Classy Strike (IRE)**[40] 3408 2-9-3 0 StevieDonohoe 4 11
(Richard Hannon) *dwlt: pushed up to press ldr: rdn 1/2-way: wknd qckly over 2f out* **8/1**[3]

1m 30.43s (3.13) **Going Correction** +0.35s/f (Good) 6 Ran SP% **113.9**
Speed ratings (Par 92): **96,95,86,84,71 68**
Tote Swingers:1&2:£2.80, 2&3:£11.20, 1&3:£2.90 CSF £10.85 TOTE £1.50: £1.60, £2.20; EX 8.50.
Owner R A Pegum **Bred** Michael Downey & Roalso Ltd **Trained** Beckhampton, Wilts

FOCUS
Little strength in depth to a median auction maiden run at a fair pace. The winner could step up a lot on the bare form.

NOTEBOOK
Brickfielder(IRE), a half-brother to the useful 2010 2yo Forjatt, was well supported in the betting (probably as a consequence of the limitations of the opposition as much as anything else) to make a winning debut and did so without looking much out of the ordinary. That said, he showed clear signs of inexperience as well as a roundish action and is sure to improve, not least given that it is rare for his yard to have their youngsters fully wound up first time out. (op Evens)
Monessa(IRE)seems to be going the right way and looked more effective at this trip than 5f hitherto, allowed to dictate and keeping the winner up to his work as they came clear. She would be up to winning a claimer.
Ice Loch is now qualified for nurseries but can only get a lowly mark and doesn't appeal as a winner waiting to happen after getting readily outpaced once the race began in earnest. (op 20-1 tchd 12-1)
Final Delivery is by a first-season stallion, Three Valleys, who has hardly set the world alight and he showed only limited promise on his debut after looking inexperienced early and ill at ease on the track. He is entitled to improve. (op 7-2)
Fairy Moss(IRE) went backwards for the longer distance and looks ready for a drop into sellers. (op 7-1 tchd 13-2)
Classy Strike(IRE) once again showed next to nothing. (op 6-1)

4709 LADBROKES.COM H'CAP 7f (S)
6:00 (6:01) (Class 5) (0-70,68) 3-Y-0+ **£2,385** (£704; £352) **Stalls** High

Form RPR
6460 **1** **Kipchak (IRE)**[12] 4322 6-8-8 61 (b) LucyKBarry(7) 1 69
(Conor Dore) *mde all and sn clr: c bk to field over 1f out and looked vulnerable: styd on wl fnl f* **7/2**[2]

0344 **2** *2 1/4* **Custom House (IRE)**[12] 4321 3-9-2 68 DaneO'Neill 4 68
(John E Long) *hld up in 4th: prog to chse wnr wl over 1f out and sn clsd: drvn and no imp fnl f* **4/1**[3]

3655 **3** *5* **Proper Charlie**[35] 3536 3-9-1 67 J-PGuillambert 2 53
(William Knight) *chsd wnr: rdn and no imp over 2f out: lost 2nd wl over 1f out: fdd* **9/2**

5302 **4** *9* **Diamond Johnny G (USA)**[16] 4182 4-9-4 64 (t) TonyCulhane 3 28
(Edward Creighton) *chsd ldng pair to 3f out: wknd 2f out* **6/1**

6542 **5** *49* **Delaware Dancer (IRE)**[13] 4270 4-9-0 60 (t) LukeMorris 5 —
(Jeremy Gask) *ref to r properly after leaving stalls: sn t.o* **7/4**[1]

1m 29.17s (1.87) **Going Correction** +0.35s/f (Good)
WFA 3 from 4yo+ 6lb 5 Ran SP% **111.1**
Speed ratings (Par 103): **103,100,94,84,28**
CSF £17.37 TOTE £7.40: £3.30, £2.60; EX 17.50.
Owner Liam Breslin **Bred** Miss Mary Davidson & Mrs Steffi Von Schilcher **Trained** Cowbit, Lincs

FOCUS
A weak handicap, rendered even less competitive when the favourite virtually pulled up after leaving the stalls. The winner dictated his own pace. There is a bit of doubt over the form.
Diamond Johnny G(USA) Official explanation: vet said gelding lost an off-fore shoe

4710 BRITISH STALLION STUDS SUPPORTING BRITISH RACING E B F MAIDEN STKS 6f
6:35 (6:35) (Class 5) 2-Y-0 **£3,234** (£962; £481; £240) **Stalls** High

Form RPR
42 **1** **Ewell Place (IRE)**[91] 1835 2-9-3 0 StevieDonohoe 5 77
(Robert Mills) *pressed ldr: pushed into narrow ld over 1f out: rdn fnl f: a jst holding the edge* **10/11**[1]

33 **2** *hd* **School Fees**[24] 3915 2-8-12 0 DaneO'Neill 3 71
(Henry Candy) *led against rail: rdn and narrowly hdd over 1f out: battled on wl but a hld* **2/1**[2]

3 *3 1/2* **Shamahan** 2-9-3 0 LukeMorris 2 66+
(Gary Moore) *chsd ldng pair: shkn up wl over 1f out: one pce and no imp* **17/2**

50 **4** *6* **Mr Hendrix**[21] 4007 2-9-3 0 TravisBlock 6 48
(Brett Johnson) *t.k.h: trckd ldng pair: rdn over 2f out: wknd over 1f out* **50/1**

60 **5** *2 1/4* **Spunky**[10] 4384 2-9-3 0 KirstyMilczarek 1 41
(Luca Cumani) *hld up in last: shuffled along and no prog 2f out: eased fnl f* **13/2**[3]

1m 14.48s (1.78) **Going Correction** +0.35s/f (Good) 5 Ran SP% **111.5**
Speed ratings (Par 94): **102,101,97,89,86**
CSF £3.03 TOTE £2.00: £1.40, £1.10; EX 2.90.
Owner Brendan Kerr, Exors Of the Late T G Mills **Bred** Peter & Hugh McCutcheon **Trained** Headley, Surrey

FOCUS
Hard work for the favourite in what wasn't anything more than an ordinary maiden. The pace looked reasonable considering the small field. Straightforward form, rated around the winner.

NOTEBOOK
Ewell Place(IRE) had nothing of the calibre of Norfolk third Crown Dependency to face on this occasion but the test of stamina this race turned into on the back of a three-month absence nearly caught him out, looking to be travelling comfortably at halfway but only getting on top very late as the runner-up proved willing. The handicapper isn't going to let him off lightly for his last run and he might find things tough in nurseries from now on. (op Evens tchd 5-6)
School Fees had looked in both her runs to date as if she was in urgent need of a step up to 6f and she nearly pulled off an upset under a sensibly aggressive ride, keeping on strongly. She'll prove just as good at 7f, so might yet have more to offer in nurseries. (tchd 5-2)
Shamahan, a colt by Shamardal and the first foal of a mare that won at around 1m4f, was quite a costly yearling and made a satisfactory debut, outpaced by the first two late on. His yard doesn't get many first-time-out 2yo winners, so this was a promising effort with the likelihood of better to come once he's stepped up to 7f. (op 8-1 tchd 15-2 and 9-1)
Mr Hendrix showed more than he had on his debut without ever looking a serious threat.
Spunky once again didn't run up to his debut form albeit not given a hard race in rear with the switchback course possibly against him. His dam stayed 1m4f and he might well prove a different proposition given longer trips in nurseries. (tchd 6-1 and 7-1)

4711 GDS RECRUITMENT, KENT RECRUITMENT SOLUTION FILLIES' H'CAP 6f
7:10 (7:11) (Class 5) (0-70,66) 3-Y-0+ **£2,385** (£704; £352) **Stalls** High

Form RPR
2162 **1** **Anjomarba (IRE)**[14] 4246 4-9-12 66 HayleyTurner 2 75
(Conor Dore) *taken down early: mde all: grabbed nr side rail after 2f: shkn up to assert 1f out: readily* **6/5**[1]

4224 **2** *1 3/4* **Suzy Alexander**[34] 3597 4-9-4 58 MartinLane 4 61
(David Simcock) *hld up last: prog 1/2-way: chsd wnr 2f out: chal over 1f out: nt qckn and wl hld fnl f* **2/1**[2]

1055 **3** *4 1/2* **Dualagi**[21] 3995 7-9-8 62 DaneO'Neill 1 51
(Martin Bosley) *cl up: chsd wnr 1/2-way to 2f out: sn wknd* **11/2**[3]

5300 **4** *hd* **Timpanist (USA)**[64] 2605 4-9-5 59 LukeMorris 3 47
(Simon Dow) *hld up in 4th: rdn over 2f out: no prog and wl btn over 1f out* **13/2**

0060 **5** *4 1/2* **Gessabelle**[21] 4006 4-8-7 47 oh2 (t) KirstyMilczarek 5 21
(Phil McEntee) *reluctant to go to post: chsd wnr to 1/2-way: sn wknd* **33/1**

1m 14.4s (1.70) **Going Correction** +0.35s/f (Good) 5 Ran SP% **110.4**
Speed ratings (Par 100): **102,99,93,93,87**
CSF £3.87 TOTE £2.10: £1.10, £2.20; EX 4.30.
Owner Liam Breslin **Bred** Tally-Ho Stud **Trained** Cowbit, Lincs

FOCUS
Little of interest going forward behind the first two in a very modest handicap. The form is rated around the front two.

4712 LADBROKESPOKER.COM H'CAP 1m 7f 92y
7:45 (7:45) (Class 5) (0-70,70) 3-Y-0+ **£1,908** (£563; £281) **Stalls** High

Form RPR
-221 **1** **Fire Fighter (IRE)**[28] 3770 3-9-0 70 StevieDonohoe 1 88+
(Sir Mark Prescott Bt) *led at stdy pce: hung lft bnd 10f out: hung lft bnd 7f out then hmpd rival: sn pushed clr: 8 l up over 2f out: idled and edgd lft 1f out: jnd 100yds out: picked up again to assert* **2/9**[1]

0321 **2** *1* **Kadouchski (FR)**[28] 3769 7-9-0 63 HannahNunn(7) 3 67
(John Berry) *trckd wnr: outpcd over 5f out but nt asked any questions: 8 l down over 2f out: shkn up and clsd qckly over 1f out: upsides last 100yds: nt qckn* **4/1**[2]

-055 **3** *28* **Whitcombe Spirit**[12] 4318 6-8-12 54 oh9 (b) LukeMorris 2 22
(Jamie Poulton) *cl up: tried to nip through on inner bnd 7f out but bdly hmpd and hit rail: sn rdn: wknd 3f out: t.o* **20/1**[3]

3m 35.74s (6.04) **Going Correction** +0.35s/f (Good)
WFA 3 from 6yo+ 14lb 3 Ran SP% **106.6**
Speed ratings (Par 103): **97,96,81**
CSF £1.43 TOTE £1.20; EX 1.30.
Owner J Fishpool - Osborne House **Bred** Airlie Stud And Sir Thomas Pilkington **Trained** Newmarket, Suffolk
■ Stewards' Enquiry : Stevie Donohoe three-day ban: careless riding (Aug 20-22)

FOCUS
Just the three runners but an eventful affair with the long odds-on favourite making very hard work of things despite seemingly winning with a fair bit in hand. He continues to improve. The pace was steady.

4713 LADBROKESBINGO.COM FILLIES' H'CAP 1m 1f 149y
8:15 (8:15) (Class 5) (0-70,69) 3-Y-0+ **£2,385** (£704; £352) **Stalls** Centre

Form RPR
-332 **1** **Destiny Of Dreams**[27] 3803 3-9-3 67 DaneO'Neill 2 74
(Jo Crowley) *smartly away: mde all: rdn and pressed over 1f out: jst hld on* **2/1**[1]

5210 **2** *nse* **Full Bloom**[13] 4275 3-9-5 69 (b1) LukeMorris 6 76
(Gerard Butler) *hld up in tch: shkn up and prog on outer over 2f out: pressed wnr wl over 1f out: persistent chal fnl f: jst failed* **4/1**[3]

0006 **3** *4 1/2* **Satwa Sunrise (FR)**[41] 3353 4-9-4 59 HayleyTurner 1 57
(Ed Dunlop) *cl up in 3rd: pushed along on inner 2f out: nt qckn and steadily outpcd after* **3/1**[2]

445 **4** *2 1/2* **Miss Excel**[37] 3478 4-9-0 55 MartinLane 3 47
(Edward Creighton) *trckd wnr to wl over 1f out: hanging and nt qckn: sn btn* **16/1**

0234 **5** *2 3/4* **Flying Phoenix**[6] 4490 3-9-3 67 (b) StevieDonohoe 4 54
(Gay Kelleway) *t.k.h: hld up in tch: shkn up over 2f out: wknd over 1f out* **3/1**[2]

150- **6** *8* **Baoli**[287] 7038 4-9-4 64 LauraPike(5) 5 34
(Tim McCarthy) *dwlt: a last: rdn 3f out: wknd 2f out* **20/1**

2m 8.28s (3.38) **Going Correction** +0.35s/f (Good)
WFA 3 from 4yo 9lb 6 Ran SP% **114.0**
Speed ratings (Par 100): **100,99,96,94,92 85**
Tote Swingers:1&2:£2.30, 2&3:£2.80, 1&3:£1.10 CSF £10.68 TOTE £3.90: £2.30, £2.20; EX 11.20.
Owner Kilstone Limited **Bred** Black Horse Farm **Trained** Whitcombe, Dorset

FOCUS
An open finale in which several had something to prove, so probably not strong form despite the first two pulling clear. The pace was just fair. A small personal best from the winner.
T/Plt: £25.00 to a £1 stake. Pool of £33,584.43 . 979.80 winning tickets T/Qpdt: £2.60 to a £1 stake. Pool of £3,603.69. 998.06 winning tickets JN

4079 HAYDOCK (L-H)
Thursday, August 4

OFFICIAL GOING: Good (good to soft in places) changing to good to soft after race 1 (2.10)
Wind: light 1/2 against Weather: 6 hours rain from 7am to 1pm, fine race 3 onwards

4714 SMOOTH RADIO MAIDEN STKS 1m
2:10 (2:11) (Class 5) 2-Y-0 **£2,264** (£673; £336; £168) **Stalls** Low

Form RPR
1 **Attenborough (USA)** 2-9-3 0 GeorgeBaker 1 79+
(Jeremy Noseda) *hld up wl in tch: smooth hdwy to chal over 2f out: shkn up to ld over 1f out: rdn and hung rt ins fnl f: hld on towards fin* **7/4**[2]

442 **2** *1/2* **Badea**[33] 3609 2-9-3 78 PaulHanagan 4 76
(Richard Fahey) *chsd ldrs: drvn 4f out: kpt on fnl f: tk 2nd nr fin* **13/2**[3]

3 **3** *hd* **Beyond Conceit (IRE)**[18] 4122 2-9-3 0.......................... JamieSpencer 7 76
(Tom Tate) *chsd ldrs: led over 6f out: hdd over 3f out: kpt on ins fnl f* **6/4**[1]
403 **4** *2 1/4* **Flying Trader (USA)**[22] 3986 2-9-3 69.................................. NeilCallan 9 71
(Jane Chapple-Hyam) *chsd ldrs: led over 3f out: hdd over 1f out: wknd towards fin* **10/1**
5 *8* **Chelsea Mick** 2-9-3 0.. GrahamGibbons 6 53
(Ed McMahon) *led over 1f: sn hmpd bnd: hung lft and wknd over 1f out* **40/1**
4 **6** *1 1/2* **Sygnature**[17] 4140 2-9-3 0.. PJMcDonald 8 50
(Alan Swinbank) *trckd ldrs: t.k.h: wknd over 1f out* **8/1**
0 **7** *15* **Goodfellows Quest (IRE)**[8] 4436 2-9-3 0..................... FrannyNorton 2 17
(Ann Duffield) *s.i.s: bhd fnl 3f* **100/1**
8 *3/4* **Goon Piper** 2-9-3 0.. RichardKingscote 5 15
(Tom Dascombe) *s.s: bhd fnl 3f* **40/1**

1m 46.03s (3.13) **Going Correction** +0.175s/f (Good) **8** Ran SP% **115.8**
Speed ratings (Par 94): **91,90,90,88,80 78,63,62**
toteswingers:1&2:£2.70, 2&3:£2.60, 1&3:£1.70 CSF £13.79 TOTE £2.10: £1.10, £1.80, £1.30; EX 17.10.
Owner The Honorable Earle I Mack **Bred** J M Herbener Jr & Dr & Mrs P J Ford **Trained** Newmarket, Suffolk
■ Stewards' Enquiry : Jamie Spencer two-day ban: careless riding (Aug 20-21)

FOCUS
Sprints run on inner home straight. All other races finish on stands' side home straight and rail realignment increased distances on round course by 43yds. Probably nothing more than a fair maiden, in which a couple of these had good enough form in the book to take this. The form looks solid and the winner's effort could rate higher.

NOTEBOOK
Attenborough(USA) ◆, a Royal Lodge entrant, is a March foal by Medaglia D´Oro, so the going change didn't look to suit. Green early, he took time to get going but threaded his way to the front once on an even keel and cruised into the lead. Once there, he didn't streak away but the future does look bright for him, as his action strongly suggested he will be better on faster ground. (op 5-2)
Badea has enough ability to win a race of this nature considering previous efforts but was always going to be susceptible to something unexposed. He kept on well after hitting a flat spot but the winner was clearly better. (op 7-1)
Beyond Conceit(IRE) made a highly satisfactory start to his career last time at Redcar but didn't appear to have a lot of pace in this after being joined in front. A huge horse, one couldn't fault his attitude, however, and he was another to run all the way to the line. (op 6-5)
Flying Trader(USA), up to 1m, appeared to be going best at one point down the home straight and may have gained an advantage over 3f out but he didn't get home. (op 14-1)
Chelsea Mick, a 6,000gns first foal of a sister to a Listed 1m juvenile winner. He wasn't completely disgraced on debut after getting squeezed for room on the bend. (op 50-1)

4715 DAVE LEACH HAD STYLE H'CAP 6f
2:40 (2:42) (Class 5) (0-70,70) 3-Y-O **£2,264** (£673; £336; £168) **Stalls** Centre

Form RPR
0000 **1** **Rowan Spirit (IRE)**[13] 4271 3-8-13 **62**.............................. KierenFallon 1 73
(Mark Brisbourne) *trckd ldrs: upsides last 100yds: led post* **3/1**[2]
60 **2** *shd* **Celtic Sixpence (IRE)**[30] 3702 3-9-7 **70**....................... JamieSpencer 2 81
(Noel Quinlan) *led: jnd last 100yds: hdd post* **3/1**[2]
0025 **3** *2* **Rutterkin (USA)**[17] 4146 3-8-7 **56**.. PaulHanagan 6 61
(Alan Berry) *hld up: effrt over 2f out: kpt on to take 3rd fnl strides* **6/1**[3]
13 **4** *hd* **Diamond Blue**[47] 3189 3-9-6 **69**... MichaelHills 5 73
(Richard Whitaker) *bmpd s: hld up: hdwy over 3f out: chsng ldrs over 1f out: kpt on same pce* **5/2**[1]
500 **5** *9* **Misshollygolightly**[49] 3091 3-8-2 **51** oh6....................... JamesSullivan 3 26
(Brian Baugh) *trckd ldr: effrt over 2f out: wknd over 1f out* **40/1**
000- **6** *19* **Ime Not Bitter**[300] 6712 3-8-0 **56**............................ MatthewMcGhee(7) 7 —
(Bill Moore) *stdd s: outpcd and edgd lft over 3f out: wknd over 2f out: sn bhd* **100/1**
0244 **7** *13* **Pippa's Gift**[22] 3983 3-9-2 **65**.. NeilCallan 4 —
(William Muir) *stmbld s: sn trcking ldrs: lost pl over 2f out: bhd whn eased ins fnl f* **6/1**[3]

1m 15.83s (2.03) **Going Correction** +0.175s/f (Good) **7** Ran SP% **110.6**
Speed ratings (Par 100): **91,90,88,87,75 50,33**
toteswingers:1&2:£2.50, 2&3:£3.10, 1&3:£3.40 CSF £11.56 TOTE £4.20: £1.60, £2.10; EX 15.60.
Owner Deva Racing Captain Rio Partnership **Bred** Secret Justice Syndicate **Trained** Great Ness, Shropshire

FOCUS
A modest handicap, rated around the third.
Pippa's Gift Official explanation: trainer said colt was unsuited by the good to soft ground

4716 BLUE PRISM OPERATIONAL AGILITY H'CAP 1m 2f 95y
3:10 (3:11) (Class 5) (0-70,70) 3-Y-O+ **£2,264** (£673; £336; £168) **Stalls** Centre

Form RPR
1 **1** **Hunter Forward (AUS)**[8] 4448 5-9-11 **67** 6ex................. KierenFallon 9 81+
(Luca Cumani) *ponied to s: trckd ldrs early: sn settled in rr: effrt over 3f out: led over 1f out: drvn out* **4/6**[1]
2033 **2** *1 1/2* **Pivot Bridge**[33] 3614 3-8-13 **64**.. MichaelHills 10 74
(B W Hills) *hld up in rr: hdwy stands' side over 2f out: styd on to take 2nd nr fin* **6/1**[2]
2300 **3** *1/2* **Brouhaha**[90] 1855 7-10-0 **70**...................................... RichardKingscote 5 79
(Tom Dascombe) *s.i.s: hdwy over 3f out: chsng wnr over 1f out: kpt on same pce* **25/1**
1-02 **4** *3 3/4* **Rockweiller**[17] 4148 4-9-7 **63**...................................(v) JamieSpencer 8 65
(Steve Gollings) *w ldrs: led over 2f out: hdd over 1f out: sn wknd* **8/1**[3]
2242 **5** *4* **Kyle Of Bute**[9] 4408 5-9-6 **62**.. PaulHanagan 6 56
(Brian Baugh) *hld up in rr: effrt over 3f out: sn chsng ldrs: wknd appr fnl f* **10/1**
0006 **6** *hd* **Strong Knight**[20] 4077 4-8-12 **54**.................................(p) GrahamGibbons 2 51
(Tim Walford) *overall ldr: styd far side in st and racd alone: hdwy over 2f out: wknd and heavily eased last 100yds* **50/1**
5001 **7** *1 1/2* **Escape Artist**[18] 4123 4-8-11 **53**.................................(p) DavidAllan 4 44
(Tim Easterby) *hld up in rr: drvn over 3f out: wknd 2f out* **14/1**
334- **8** *1 3/4* **Forks**[358] 4951 4-9-9 **65**.. GeorgeBaker 7 53
(Jane Chapple-Hyam) *trckd ldrs: t.k.h: chal over 2f out: wknd over 1f out: eased clsng stages* **25/1**
5001 **9** *8* **Reset To Fit**[20] 4077 4-9-2 **58**... DuranFentiman 3 31
(Eric Alston) *trckd ldrs: wknd over 2f out: eased ins fnl f* **20/1**

2m 16.29s (0.29) **Going Correction** +0.175s/f (Good)
WFA 3 from 4yo+ 9lb **9** Ran SP% **115.6**
Speed ratings (Par 103): **105,103,103,100,97 97,95,94,88**
toteswingers:1&2:£2.40, 2&3:£12.40, 1&3:£7.80 CSF £4.61 CT £52.10 TOTE £1.50: £1.10, £1.70, £4.60; EX 5.60.
Owner O T I Racing **Bred** Alwyn Park **Trained** Newmarket, Suffolk

FOCUS
A competitive-looking contest for the level. The winner is clearly on a favourable mark and could stil be ahead of the handicapper after this.
Brouhaha Official explanation: jockey said blindfold got stuck in bridle and gelding was slowly away

4717 BRITISH STALLION STUDS E B F ST HELENS NOVICE STKS 7f
3:40 (3:40) (Class 4) 2-Y-O **£5,822** (£1,732; £865) **Stalls** Low

Form RPR
1424 **1** **Basantee**[11] 4372 2-8-13 78...................................... RichardKingscote 1 81
(Tom Dascombe) *led: qcknd over 3f out: sn hrd drvn: hld on gamely* **9/2**[3]
01 **2** *1 3/4* **Clare Island Boy (IRE)**[15] 4213 2-9-4 0................................ PatDobbs 2 82
(Richard Hannon) *trckd wnr: drvn over 3f out: sn outpcd: kpt on to chse wnr appr fnl f: styd on same pce ins fnl f* **15/8**[2]
210 **3** *3 1/2* **Brocklebank (IRE)**[51] 3012 2-9-4 90.................................. PhillipMakin 3 73
(Kevin Ryan) *trckd wnr: chal over 2f out: sn rdn: wknd over 1f out* **10/11**[1]

1m 32.86s (1.96) **Going Correction** +0.175s/f (Good) **3** Ran SP% **105.3**
Speed ratings (Par 96): **95,93,89**
CSF £11.51 TOTE £4.70; EX 6.90.
Owner The MHS 8X8 Partnership **Bred** R Phillips And Tweenhills Farm And Stud **Trained** Malpas, Cheshire

FOCUS
There wasn't a lot between this lot on RPRs, so tactics were always going to play a big part in this contest. A step up from the winner, and the form could be rated higher.

NOTEBOOK
Basantee, fourth in a German Listed race when last seen, made every yard and responded well to pressure to win comfortably. This isn't a result to take too seriously for future reference but does at least prove she is up for a battle. (op 10-3)
Clare Island Boy(IRE) won a fair-looking maiden last time after racing from the front, but wasn't able to dominate this time and was under strong riding early in the home straight. He stuck on well for pressure but the winning line came too soon. (op 9-4)
Brocklebank(IRE), absent since finishing third last in the Coventry Stakes, ranged up to look a likely winner about 2f out but found nothing for pressure. The Stewards considered his running, and having received a report that the trainer was unable to offer any explanation. Official explanation: trainer had no explanation for the poor form shown (op Evens tchd 5-6)

4718 TURFTV.CO.UK H'CAP 1m
4:10 (4:11) (Class 3) (0-95,92) 3-Y-O **£6,663** (£1,982; £990; £495) **Stalls** Low

Form RPR
5-12 **1** **Maraheb**[26] 3871 3-9-5 **90**...(t) RichardHills 7 105
(John Dunlop) *dwlt: hdwy to ld after 1f: styd on strly to draw clr ins fnl f* **9/2**[3]
0131 **2** *5* **Ingleby Exceed (IRE)**[13] 4290 3-8-5 **76**........................ PaulHanagan 5 79
(David O'Meara) *led 1f: chsd ldrs: effrt over 2f out: edgd rt over 1f out: styd on same pce* **5/1**
-504 **3** *nk* **Seattle Drive (IRE)**[12] 4313 3-9-4 **89**........................... JamieSpencer 9 91
(David Elsworth) *stdd and swtchd lft after s: hld up: hdwy over 2f out: sn chsng ldrs: n.m.r over 1f out: kpt on same pce* **7/2**[2]
01-6 **4** *hd* **Roman Eagle (IRE)**[26] 3864 3-9-7 **92**................................ NeilCallan 3 94
(Roger Varian) *sn chsng ldrs: effrt over 3f out: kpt on same pce over 1f out* **11/4**[1]
4222 **5** *nk* **No Poppy (IRE)**[14] 4235 3-8-11 **82**..................................... DavidAllan 1 83
(Tim Easterby) *hld up in rr: effrt on ins over 3f out: one pce fnl 2f* **14/1**
104 **6** *nk* **Midsummer Fair (USA)**[61] 2707 3-9-0 **92**.............. AntiocoMurgia(7) 2 92
(Mahmood Al Zarooni) *hld up in mid-div: effrt over 3f out: sn chsng ldrs: one pce appr fnl f: fdd nr fin* **9/1**
-512 **7** *15* **Early Applause**[56] 2847 3-8-10 **81**................................ MichaelHills 8 63
(B W Hills) *trckd ldrs: effrt on outside over 3f out: wknd 2f out: eased ins fnl f* **15/2**

1m 43.41s (0.51) **Going Correction** +0.175s/f (Good) **7** Ran SP% **112.2**
Speed ratings (Par 104): **104,99,98,98,98 97,82**
toteswingers:1&2:£4.20, 2&3:£2.30, 1&3:£3.50 CSF £25.89 CT £85.75 TOTE £6.00: £3.30, £2.90; EX 28.70.
Owner Hamdan Al Maktoum **Bred** Shadwell Estate Company Limited **Trained** Arundel, W Sussex

FOCUS
A cracking little contest on paper, weakened slightly by the defection of Baptist. However, there must be a slight suspicion that this isn't reliable form. It does make some sense, though, and the winner produced a smart effort.

NOTEBOOK
Maraheb ◆, up 5lb despite finishing only second on his previous outing, and with a tongue-tie on for the first time (reported afterwards to have made a huge difference), was pushed into the lead early and appeared to steal this race under a canny front-running ride by Richard Hills. There is no denying this big sort is potentially up to Listed company after this effort, but one would imagine he won't enjoy such an easy time of it in front too often. (op 5-1)
Ingleby Exceed(IRE), now 12lb higher than for the first of her two fairly recent successes, gave a good account off a low weight after racing a little keenly, but wasn't in the same league as the winner. (op 4-1)
Seattle Drive(IRE) had run well since taking part in the Newmarket race a couple of these had contested, and looked a bit unlucky in the sense that he didn't always have a clear passage down the home straight. (op 5-1)
Roman Eagle(IRE) finished in front of Seattle Drive last time, his first outing of the season, and looked sure to improve for that run. It's debatable whether he did, though, as he seemed to have every chance but couldn't get on terms. He already had form in easy ground, albeit in a match, so one can only presume the handicapper has him about right. (tchd 3-1)
No Poppy(IRE), trying 1m for the first time, was held up to presumably conserve her stamina but she wasn't able to get on terms. (op 11-1)
Midsummer Fair(USA), back down in trip, ran in a small conditions race last time (first and third in that race were placed in Group company next time) but was found out off this mark in handicaps. He may not be the easiest to place. (tchd 10-1)
Early Applause, given a short break since his last run, dropped out quickly as though something was amiss. The Stewards considered his running and, having received a report that the trainer was unable to offer any explanation. Official explanation: trainer had no explanation for the poor form shown (op 8-1 tchd 9-1)

4719 REAL RADIO H'CAP 1m 6f
4:40 (4:40) (Class 4) (0-80,79) 4-Y-O+ **£4,204** (£1,251; £625; £312) **Stalls** Low

Form RPR
436 **1** **Pittodrie Star (IRE)**[26] 3851 4-9-3 **75**............................ DavidProbert 1 83
(Andrew Balding) *trckd ldrs: effrt over 3f out: edgd lft over 1f out: hrd rdn and styd on to ld nr fin* **5/1**[3]
1512 **2** *hd* **Money Money Money**[7] 4463 5-9-3 **75**..................... JamesMillman 10 82
(Rod Millman) *hld up in rr: hdwy over 3f out: edgd lft and led over 1f out: hdd nr fin* **3/1**[1]
1033 **3** *1* **Bollin Greta**[27] 3828 6-9-6 **78**..(t) DavidAllan 8 84+
(Tim Easterby) *hld up in rr: nt clr run and swtchd stands' side rail over 1f out: styd on strly: fin wl* **4/1**[2]

0/00 **4** ¾ **Double Handful (GER)**[34] 3593 5-8-13 **71** .... PaulHanagan 9 76
(Venetia Williams) *chsd ldrs: kpt on same pce ins fnl f* **14/1**
5021 **5** 1½ **Gunslinger (FR)**[32] 2846 6-9-5 **77** .... JamieSpencer 6 80
(Michael Scudamore) *reluactnt ldr: styd far side in home st: hdd over 1f out: wknd last 75yds* **9/1**
0263 **6** 2¼ **Madamlily (IRE)**[16] 4173 5-8-10 **68** .... PBBeggy 4 69
(John Quinn) *dwlt: hld up towards rr: drvn and hdwy towards far side 4f out: wknd over 1f out* **7/1**
1635 **7** nk **Arab League (IRE)**[24] 3911 6-9-7 **79** .... ShaneKelly 7 79
(Richard Price) *trckd ldrs: effrt over 3f out: edgd lft 2f out: wknd appr fnl f* **9/1**
1203 **8** 2½ **Rare Ruby (IRE)**[19] 4082 7-9-5 **77** .... StephenCraine 11 74
(Jennie Candlish) *hld up in rr: hdwy to chse ldrs over 4f out: edgd lft and wknd over 1f out* **14/1**
1020 **9** 38 **Accumulate**[55] 2888 8-9-2 **74** .... NeilCallan 2 —
(Bill Moore) *chsd ldrs: styd far side in the home st: lost pl over 2f out: bhd whn eased over 1f out: t.o* **12/1**
3m 6.75s (5.55) **Going Correction** +0.175s/f (Good) **9 Ran SP% 115.2**
Speed ratings (Par 105): **91,90,90,89,89 87,87,86,64**
toteswingers:1&2:£4.30, 2&3:£3.70, 1&3:£5.10 CSF £20.33 CT £65.50 TOTE £5.10: £1.90, £2.00, £1.40; EX 23.00.
Owner Evan M Sutherland **Bred** Gary O'Reilly **Trained** Kingsclere, Hants
■ Stewards' Enquiry : David Probert one-day ban: used whip with excessive frequency (Aug 20)

FOCUS
The early gallop looked far from strong and most of these had a chance of sorts down the home straight as they fanned out across the course. The first two finished on the far side but the unlucky looking third was closer to the stands' side, so there didn't seem any obvious bias. It's hard to rate the form too positively.
T/Plt: £80.20 to a £1 stake. Pool of £58,094.24 - 528.76 winning tickets T/Qpdt: £18.10 to a £1 stake. Pool of £3,169.40 - 129.32 winning tickets. WG

4444 SANDOWN (R-H)
Thursday, August 4

OFFICIAL GOING: Good to soft (7.5)
GOOD TO SOFT (7.5)
Wind: Brisk, ahead Weather: Sunny periods.

4720 BRITISH STALLION STUDS SUPPORTING BRITISH RACING E B F MAIDEN FILLIES' STKS 5f 6y
5:40 (5:41) (Class 5) 2-Y-O **£3,234** (£962; £481; £240) **Stalls** Low

Form RPR
1 **Kyanight (IRE)** 2-9-0 0 .... AdamKirby 5 83+
(Clive Cox) *trckd ldrs: swtchd lft to take narrow ld 2f out: drvn out: rdn: rn green and hung rt jst ins fnl f: sn rcvrd and r.o strly* **7/2**[2]
2 1½ **Gallery** 2-9-0 0 .... KierenFallon 2 77+
(William Haggas) *s.i.s: in rr: swtchd lft to outside and hdwy fr 2f out: chsd wnr and edgd rt fnl 150yds: kpt on encouragingly but no imp* **4/1**[3]
3 2¾ **Esprit Danseur** 2-9-0 0 .... JimmyFortune 8 67
(Jim Boyle) *s.i.s: in rr: drvn and rn green 2f out: hdwy to chse ldrs fnl f and edgd rt sn after: no imp on ldng duo fnl 120yds* **28/1**
65 **4** 1½ **Guava**[17] 4155 2-9-0 0 .... RichardHughes 6 64
(Richard Hannon) *sn led: hdd 2f out: fading whn hmpd jst ins fnl f* **9/2**
20 **5** 2½ **Blanc De Chine (IRE)**[19] 4094 2-9-0 0 .... SteveDrowne 1 55
(Peter Makin) *t.k.h: trckd ldrs on rail: swtchd lft and drvn to chal 2f out: wknd 1f out* **2/1**[1]
6 2¾ **Magik Maggie** 2-9-0 0 .... JackMitchell 4 43
(Chris Wall) *trckd ldrs: drvn 1/2-way: wknd ins fnl 2f* **16/1**
04 **7** ¾ **Arabian Flight**[12] 4319 2-9-0 0 .... WilliamBuick 7 40
(Ed Dunlop) *t.k.h: chsd ldrs: rdn 1/2-way: wknd ins fnl 2f* **16/1**
8 3 **Romany Spirit (IRE)** 2-9-0 0 .... MartinDwyer 3 30
(Jim Boyle) *slowly away: rn green and sn rdn: a in rr* **20/1**
64.94 secs (3.34) **Going Correction** +0.70s/f (Yiel) **8 Ran SP% 113.7**
Speed ratings (Par 91): **101,98,94,91,87 83,82,77**
Tote Swingers:1&2:£5.50, 2&3:£22.40, 1&3:£6.80 CSF £17.71 TOTE £4.20: £1.80, £1.60, £5.40; EX 17.40.
Owner H E Sheikh Sultan Bin Khalifa Al Nahyan **Bred** Tally-Ho Stud **Trained** Lambourn, Berks

FOCUS
There was consistent rain throughout the day and the going was changed to good to soft. The round course was dolled out up to 6yds from 1m1f to the home straight and the bend was at the outermost configuration, adding approximately 8yds to race distances on the round course.The experienced favourite didn't find a great deal after travelling well in this fillies' maiden in which newcomers filled the first three places. Nice starts from the first pair.

NOTEBOOK
Kyanight(IRE), a 75,000gns half-sister to high-class 2-y-o/sprinter Monsieur Chevalier and other 2-y-o 5f winners, looked quite streetwise near the pace before finding a surging run to score with something in hand on debut. She may have benefited from racing against a faster strip of ground near the far rail but this was an impressive start by a Kodiac filly who holds a stack of entries in valuable sales races and looks a decent prospect. (op 4-1)
Gallery showed signs of inexperience marooned out wide before staying on well on an eye-catching debut. She was unsold at 20,000gns last autumn, but she was prominent in the betting for this first run and holds numerous entries in valuable races later on, so is clearly well regarded. Her first-season sire has made a promising start and her fair 1m2f 3-y-o winning dam should add some stamina into the mix. (op 9-2)
Esprit Danseur, a £46,000 breeze-up buy who is by a sprinter out of a lightly raced maiden half-sister to dual 1m2f French Listed winner Otaiti, shaped with promise, staying on steadily at a big price from a tough draw on debut. She should have learned a lot and should improve next time. (op 16-1)
Guava had not lasted home in 6f maidens and it was a bit disappointing that she was comfortably overhauled back at 5f after adopting a prominent position against the far rail. (op 4-1 tchd 7-2)
Blanc De Chine(IRE) chased home an odds-on winner in a Bath maiden on debut and showed good pace before fading in the hotly contested Super Sprint at Newbury. She had strong form claims from a rail draw back in a maiden and travelled smoothly into contention but her effort petered out. This was a setback and she will have a bit to prove next time, but there is a lot to like about her high cruising speed and the slow ground may have dulled her powers. Official explanation: jockey said filly ran too freely (op 9-4 tchd 5-2)

4721 REWARDS4RACING AND RACING LOTTERY H'CAP 5f 6y
6:10 (6:11) (Class 4) (0-80,77) 3-Y-O **£4,075** (£1,212; £606) **Stalls** Low

Form RPR
2213 **1** **Volcanic Dust (IRE)**[14] 4238 3-9-3 **76** .... RyanClark(3) 1 82
(Milton Bradley) *led after 1f: pushed clr fnl f: easily* **5/4**[1]
0222 **2** 4 **Grandmas Dream**[40] 3389 3-9-4 **74** ....(b) PaulDoe 4 64
(Jim Best) *led 1f: styd chsng wnr but rdn and no imp 2f out: easily outpcd and wl btn fnl f* **5/2**[3]
31 **3** 1 **Upper Lambourn (IRE)**[23] 3950 3-9-7 **77** .... FergusSweeney 5 63
(Jamie Osborne) *a in 3rd: sn drvn along in rr and struggling to go pce: styd on fnl f but nvr any ch* **15/8**[2]
65.65 secs (4.05) **Going Correction** +0.70s/f (Yiel) **3 Ran SP% 107.8**
Speed ratings (Par 102): **95,88,87**
CSF £4.39 TOTE £2.20; EX 3.00.
Owner Miss Diane Hill **Bred** Top Of The Form Syndicate **Trained** Sedbury, Gloucs

FOCUS
Just three runners lined up for this sprint handicap for 3-y-os and there was a dominant display by the well backed favourite. Weak form, with the winner probably scoring by default.

4722 BRITISH STALLION STUDS SUPPORTING BRITISH RACING E B F MAIDEN STKS 1m 14y
6:45 (6:46) (Class 5) 2-Y-O **£3,234** (£962; £481; £240) **Stalls** Low

Form RPR
5 **1** **Martin Chuzzlewit (IRE)**[20] 4053 2-9-3 0 .... TomQueally 3 83+
(Sir Michael Stoute) *trckd ldr tl drvn and outpcd into 3rd 3f out: styd on again fnl 2f to chal appr fnl f: sn led: rdn clr fnl 150yds: won gng away* **6/4**[1]
33 **2** 3¼ **Cavaleiro (IRE)**[13] 4264 2-9-3 0 .... SebSanders 6 76
(Marcus Tregoning) *led: rdn over 2f out: jnd 1f out: hdd sn after and no ch w wnr but kpt on wl for 2nd* **9/4**[2]
53 **3** 1 **Swing Alone (IRE)**[10] 4390 2-9-3 0 .... RobertWinston 2 74
(Gay Kelleway) *chsd ldrs: wnt 2nd 3f out: sn rdn: one pce 1f out: jst hld on for 3rd last strides* **6/1**[3]
4 nse **Amoralist** 2-9-3 0 .... KierenFallon 5 74+
(Ed Dunlop) *s.i.s: in rr: pushed along and hdwy towards outside fr 2f out: styd on on strly ins fnl f to press for 3rd cl home but no ch w wnr* **25/1**
5 ¾ **Hefner (IRE)** 2-9-3 0 .... JimmyFortune 7 72+
(Richard Hannon) *s.i.s: in rr tl hdwy over 1f out: styd on wl fnl f: nt rch ldrs but gng on cl home* **33/1**
6 **6** 1¼ **Spanish Wedding**[22] 3986 2-9-3 0 .... AdamKirby 8 69
(Marco Botti) *in tch: rdn 3f out: styd on same pce fnl 2f* **13/2**
63 **7** 1¾ **Poetic Lord**[35] 3534 2-9-3 0 .... RichardHughes 9 67
(Richard Hannon) *trckd ldrs: pushed along and outpcd fr 3f out: sme hdwy fr 2f out: no imp fnl f and fdd clsng stages* **14/1**
8 6 **Paloma's Prince (IRE)** 2-9-3 0 .... JackMitchell 11 52
(Jim Boyle) *outpcd most of way* **66/1**
0 **9** 39 **Cold Blow Den**[19] 4087 2-9-3 0 ....(b[1]) MartinDwyer 1 —
(Jim Boyle) *v.s.a: v green: sn rdn and a wl bhd* **100/1**
1m 47.49s (4.19) **Going Correction** +0.475s/f (Yiel) **9 Ran SP% 114.3**
Speed ratings (Par 94): **98,94,93,93,92 91,89,83,44**
Tote Swingers:1&2:£1.90, 2&3:£2.90, 1&3:£2.30 CSF £4.78 TOTE £2.70: £1.10, £1.30, £1.90; EX 6.30.
Owner Sir Robert Ogden **Bred** M V Magnier & Lynch-Bages Ltd **Trained** Newmarket, Suffolk

FOCUS
A useful maiden. The three market leaders were always in the first three places and they eventually finished in the order the market suggested they would. The winner built on his initial effort but the next two were below their best.

NOTEBOOK
Martin Chuzzlewit(IRE) ran as though the experience was needed when a staying-on fifth in a decent 7f Newbury maiden on debut. He had a bit to find on form and there were some warning signs when pressure was applied but he knuckled well before powering to an impressive win on his second attempt. An imposing 420,000euros Galileo colt who is out of an unraced half-sister to French 10.5f Group 3/French Oaks second Abbatiale, he holds a Derby entry and could have a bright future over middle-distances. (op 7-4 tchd 2-1)
Cavaleiro(IRE) shaped like a step up to 1m would suit when third in a pair of 7f maidens at Salisbury and Ascot. Ridden positively, he gave it a decent shot but had no answer to the late burst from the winner. He probably ran into a very useful rival and this well-connected 78,000gns colt should not have too much trouble winning an average maiden. (op 11-4)
Swing Alone(IRE) set the standard on his highly creditable 40-1 fifth in the Chesham Stakes on debut. An odds-on defeat at Yarmouth last time added a complication to his chance but he bounced back with a decent enough effort stepped up to 1m. It is concern that his form seems to have stalled at this early stage but he has quite a bit of ability for a £15,000 purchase and the early signs suggest he may need give underfoot to show his best form. (op 9-2)
Amoralist ran green before staying-on late on an encouraging debut. His sales price leapt to £45,000 at the breeze-ups and he is a first foal of a placed half-sister to winners at a variety of distances, the best of them sprinter Espartero who was later a 1m winner in US. (op 20-1)
Hefner(IRE), a relatively cheap buy as a foal, did well to work his way into fifth after missing the break on debut.
Spanish Wedding got outpaced when the leader cranked it up before rallying. This probably represents a step forward on his debut form and this brother to a moderate 2m winner shapes like stamina will be his forte. (op 7-1 tchd 6-1)
Poetic Lord ran respectably in a race where he had plenty to find on form. He showed a slightly awkward head carriage but that may have been because he was uncomfortable on the ground and he looks the type who should find a stronger competitive edge when targeted at nurseries. (op 11-1)

4723 CHELSEA F.C. FOUNDATION H'CAP 1m 2f 7y
7:20 (7:21) (Class 3) (0-90,90) 3-Y-O **£6,663** (£1,982; £990; £495) **Stalls** Low

Form RPR
5011 **1** **Tenby Lady (USA)**[6] 4490 3-9-1 **84** 6ex .... SebSanders 3 96+
(Sir Mark Prescott Bt) *sn led: styd alone far side and drvn along fr 3f out and kpt overall ld: rdr dropped whip but in command fnl f: unchal* **4/1**[2]
1260 **2** 1¾ **Fadhaa (IRE)**[28] 3774 3-8-12 **81** .... TadhgO'Shea 7 89
(B W Hills) *in rr: c stands' side and hdwy over 2f out: drvn and styd on to ld that gp fnl 150yds but no imp on wnr racing alone far side* **9/1**
4-21 **3** ¾ **Caraboss**[70] 2432 3-9-7 **90** .... JimmyFortune 2 97
(Sir Michael Stoute) *chsd ldrs: c stands' side: rdn and one pce over 2f out: styd on again fnl f to take 2nd that gp cl home but no imp on wnr racing alone far side* **10/1**
2241 **4** shd **Sacred Shield**[20] 4056 3-8-10 **79** .... TomQueally 8 85
(Sir Henry Cecil) *in tch: c stands' side and led that gp 3f out but nvr quite on terms w wnr racing alone far side: hdd & wknd fnl 150yds* **6/1**[3]
2-15 **5** 1½ **Blue Destination**[69] 2471 3-8-12 **81** .... WilliamBuick 1 84
(Philip McBride) *in tch c to r stands' side over 3f out and sn rdn and outpcd: styd on again fnl f but nvr in contention* **6/1**[3]
2-16 **6** ¾ **Tahaamah**[19] 4103 3-9-0 **83** ....(t) KierenFallon 4 85
(Saeed Bin Suroor) *in rr: c stands' side and hdwy 3f out: rdn 2f out: styd on same pce fr over 1f out* **8/1**
0462 **7** 1 **Cruiser**[26] 3840 3-9-3 **86** .... MartinDwyer 5 86
(William Muir) *in tch: c stands' side: hrd drvn to press ldrs over 2f out but nvr on terms w wnr racing alone far side: wknd fnl f* **10/1**

3036 **8** *1* **Star Surprise**[28] 3774 3-9-6 **89** .... AdamKirby 6 87
(Michael Bell) *racd in 2nd tl lft in ld on stands' side whn wnr styd alone far side wl over 3f out: hdd 3f out: wknd ins fnl 2f* **7/2**[1]

2m 12.89s (2.39) **Going Correction** +0.475s/f (Yiel) **8** Ran SP% **110.1**
Speed ratings (Par 104): **109,107,107,106,105 105,104,103**
Tote Swingers:1&2:£8.40, 2&3:£6.30, 1&3:£9.00 CSF £36.21 CT £310.59 TOTE £4.20: £1.50, £2.90, £2.20; EX 49.80.
Owner David F O'Rourke **Bred** O'Rourke's Silver Springs Stud Farm Llc **Trained** Newmarket, Suffolk

FOCUS
A decent handicap involving three last-time-out winners and several unexposed types. Most of the runners converged to the stands' rail in the straight but the progressive front-running winner stayed on the far side. Not the easiest race to assess, but the form is taken at face value for now.

NOTEBOOK
Tenby Lady(USA) completed a double in good style when powering clear from off a stop-start gallop at Bath last week. She looked well treated under a penalty and delivered under an attacking ride after racing solo for most of the straight. Her form stuttered a bit after a maiden win but it has really taken off in the last few weeks and she could take some stopping in a bid for a four-timer. (op 3-1)
Fadhaa(IRE) was an AW maiden winner in April and a good second to Brown Panther on his handicap debut the following month. He hadn't seen his races out in his last two starts but he stayed on well switched to more patient tactics and came out on top on the near side. (op 10-1)
Caraboss improved on each of her three starts in maidens, culminating in a 6l win at odds-on over 1m2f at Newcastle in May. She had a lot more to do off a mark of 90 on handicap debut but ran a good race on return from over two months off. Closely related to connections' smart and relentlessly progressive My Kingdom Of Fife, she still has plenty of scope for further progress. (op 8-1)
Sacred Shield gained her first handicap win when staying on well to strike over a similar trip at Newbury last month. She found a 4lb rise too much to overcome in a stronger race but she did travel well for a long way and showed some fighting qualities. Another jolt of improvement will be needed to get back in the groove but she is not fully exposed and is from a classy family that her trainer has had plenty of success with. (tchd 11-2)
Blue Destination ran away with a 1m2f Yarmouth maiden in May but was well held on handicap debut at Newmarket and couldn't threaten from off the pace back from a break and gelding operation. However, this unexposed type should be sharper for the run and his style and the dam's side of his pedigree suggests a step up to 1m4f could work in his favour. (op 10-1)
Tahaamah looked one to follow when landing a Chester handicap on his seasonal run but that was followed by a heavy defeat as favourite at Newmarket. The application of a tongue-tie hinted at a possible reason for that blowout but he couldn't sustain his effort as well as some others here. (op 13-2)
Star Surprise arrived with a record of 51133 at this track and attracted plenty of support, but he put in a tame effort on his second try at 1m2f. (tchd 10-3)

4724 VARIETY CLUB DAY ON AUGUST 20TH H'CAP — 1m 2f 7y
7:55 (7:55) (Class 4) (0-80,80) 3-Y-0+ **£4,075** (£1,212; £606; £303) **Stalls** Low

Form RPR
4005 **1** **Silver Grey (IRE)**[14] 4253 4-9-12 **78** ....(p) JackMitchell 9 90
(Roger Ingram) *trckd ldrs: led appr fnl 2f: pushed clr fnl f: comf* **8/1**
6224 **2** *2 1/4* **Ramona Chase**[21] 4008 6-9-9 **80** ....(t) MarkCoumbe(5) 1 87
(Michael Attwater) *in rr but in tch: drvn along and no prog over 3f out: stl plenty to do whn styd on u.p fnl f to take 2nd last stride but no ch w wnr* **12/1**
1102 **3** *shd* **Dysios (IRE)**[33] 3629 3-9-1 **76** .... KierenFallon 7 83+
(Luca Cumani) *stdd towards rr: pushed along and hdwy fr 3f out: chsd wnr appr fnl f but no imp: edgd rt and fdd clsng stages: lost 2nd last strides* **4/1**[1]
1061 **4** *3* **Rock The Stars (IRE)**[15] 4211 4-9-11 **77** .... SebSanders 10 78
(J W Hills) *in tch: drvn along fr over 3f out: styd on to take one pce 4th clsng stages* **5/1**[3]
1022 **5** *1/2* **Destiny Blue (IRE)**[7] 4477 4-10-0 **80** .... JimCrowley 11 80
(Jamie Osborne) *pressed ldr tl led 7f out: narrowly hdd 6f out but styd upsides: led again over 3f out: hdd appr fnl 2f: wknd fr 1f out* **9/2**[2]
0663 **6** *1 1/2* **Mattoral**[15] 4215 3-8-11 **72** ....(b) SteveDrowne 5 69
(Peter Makin) *in tch: rdn over 3f out and sn struggling: mod prog clsng stages* **4/1**[1]
1044 **7** *2 3/4* **Effigy**[10] 4385 7-9-3 **74** .... AmyScott(5) 3 65
(Henry Candy) *in rr: pushed along over 3f out: nvr gng pce to get into contention* **10/1**
20 **8** *1 1/4* **Rowan Tiger**[43] 3277 5-9-11 **77** .... NickyMackay 4 66
(Jim Boyle) *trckd ldrs: slt ld 6f out tl hdd over 3f out: wknd wl over 2f out* **16/1**
0465 **9** *9* **Silverglas (IRE)**[28] 3762 5-9-2 **68** ....(v[1]) WilliamBuick 2 39
(William Knight) *slowly away: rdn and little rspnse 3f out: a in rr* **12/1**
0-40 **10** *50* **Safari Team (IRE)**[50] 3044 3-9-3 **78** .... FergusSweeney 12 —
(Peter Winkworth) *led tl hdd 7f out: rdn 4f out: wknd qckly over 3f out: t.o* **40/1**

2m 13.95s (3.45) **Going Correction** +0.475s/f (Yiel)
WFA 3 from 4yo+ 9lb **10** Ran SP% **117.4**
Speed ratings (Par 105): **105,103,103,100,100 99,96,95,88,48**
Tote Swingers:1&2:£12.10, 2&3:£11.80, 1&3:£11.00 CSF £100.00 CT £443.98 TOTE £8.10: £2.40, £3.50, £2.40; EX 129.20.
Owner Ellangowan Racing Partners 1 **Bred** Tally-Ho Stud **Trained** Epsom, Surrey
■ Stewards' Enquiry : Mark Coumbe caution: used whip with excessive frequency.

FOCUS
A fair handicap. They were tightly grouped off a steady pace in the early stages and they all stayed on the far side in the straight. The winner will still be well treated after this on her best form.

4725 ESHER RUGBY CLUB H'CAP — 1m 14y
8:25 (8:27) (Class 5) (0-75,75) 3-Y-0+ **£2,264** (£673; £336; £168) **Stalls** Low

Form RPR
5300 **1** **Spa's Dancer (IRE)**[12] 4331 4-10-0 **75** .... SebSanders 4 87
(J W Hills) *chsd ldrs: wnt to r alone stands' side over 3f out: def overall ldr 2f out: in n.d fr far side gp fnl f: r.o strly* **7/2**[2]
-003 **2** *4 1/2* **Bloodsweatandtears**[21] 4009 3-9-7 **75** ....(b) WilliamBuick 9 76
(William Knight) *in tch: styd w main gp far side and hdwy to chal 2f out: led gp wl over 1f out: hung rt u.p ins fnl f and no ch w wnr on stands' side* **7/2**[2]
0061 **3** *1 1/2* **Cultural Desert**[12] 4337 3-9-7 **75** .... JimCrowley 8 72
(Ralph Beckett) *in rr and styd w main gp far side: hdwy u.p fr 2f out: styd on u.p fnl f to take narrow one pce 2nd that gp but nvr any ch w wnr stands' side* **3/1**[1]
6210 **4** *1/2* **Hip Hip Hooray**[8] 4429 5-9-5 **66** .... FergusSweeney 7 63
(Luke Dace) *in rr and styd w main gp far side: hdwy u.p 2f out: one pce fnl f and no ch w lone wnr stands' side: wknd nr fin* **7/1**[3]
0113 **5** *5* **Salient**[17] 4150 7-9-13 **74** .... J-PGuillambert 10 60
(Michael Attwater) *chsd ldr: styd far side and led that gp 3f out: hdd by wnr on stands' side 2f out: and hdd in far side gp wl over 1f out: sn wknd* **15/2**
0605 **6** *3/4* **Kavachi (IRE)**[13] 4278 8-9-5 **66** .... TomQueally 1 50
(Gary Moore) *in tch: styd w main gp far side: wknd ins fnl 2f* **8/1**
0210 **7** *35* **Paphos**[20] 4066 4-8-6 **56** oh1 ....(v) RyanClark(3) 3 —
(Stuart Williams) *led: styd w main gp far side: hdd 3f out: sn wknd* **12/1**

1m 48.07s (4.77) **Going Correction** +0.475s/f (Yiel)
WFA 3 from 4yo+ 7lb **7** Ran SP% **112.5**
Speed ratings (Par 103): **95,90,89,88,83 82,47**
Tote Swingers:1&2:£1.90, 2&3:£3.20, 1&3:£3.80 CSF £15.60 CT £39.32 TOTE £5.30: £2.10, £3.00; EX 16.20.
Owner The Seventh Pheasant Inn Partnership **Bred** Giacinto Gugliemi **Trained** Upper Lambourn, Berks

FOCUS
They went a steady pace in this tight handicap. Seb Sanders had scored on a runner who raced solo on the far side in 7:20 race but this time he was successful with a heavily backed runner who race alone against the near rail. The form is hard to assess but has been rated around the winner to his turf best.
T/Plt: £134.50 to a £1 stake. Pool of £49,422.87. 268.05 winning tickets T/Qpdt: £22.10 to a £1 stake. Pool of £5,839.99. 195.10 winning tickets ST

4681 YARMOUTH (L-H)
Thursday, August 4

OFFICIAL GOING: Good changing to good to soft after race 2 (2.50)
Wind: fairly light, across Weather: rain

4726 BRITISH STALLION STUDS SUPPORTING BRITISH RACING E B F MAIDEN STKS — 6f 3y
2:20 (2:20) (Class 5) 2-Y-0 **£2,911** (£866; £432; £216) **Stalls** High

Form RPR
1 **Daraa (IRE)** 2-8-12 0 .... PhilipRobinson 1 73+
(Clive Brittain) *hld up in tch: effrt to chal over 1f out: rdn to ld 1f out: kpt on wl ins fnl f: hrd pressed cl home: jst hld on* **6/1**[3]
2 *nse* **My Body Is A Cage (IRE)** 2-8-12 0 .... RichardMullen 3 73+
(Peter Chapple-Hyam) *led: rdn and rn green over 1f out: hdd 1f out and sltly outpcd jst ins fnl f: rallied and kpt on fnl 75yds: clsng on wnr cl home: jst failed* **8/1**
3 *1/2* **Khaleejiya (IRE)** 2-8-12 0 .... RobertHavlin 4 71+
(James Toller) *chsd ldng pair: rdn and effrt over 1f out: pressed wnr jst ins fnl f tl fnl 75yds: kpt on same pce* **15/8**[2]
4 *4* **Fa'Iz (IRE)** 2-9-3 0 .... TedDurcan 2 64
(Saeed Bin Suroor) *chsd ldr: rdn and unable qck ent fnl 2f: drvn and outpcd over 1f out: btn whn rn green and hung lft ins fnl f* **11/10**[1]

1m 17.29s (2.89) **Going Correction** +0.20s/f (Good) **4** Ran SP% **107.8**
Speed ratings (Par 94): **88,87,87,81**
CSF £38.83 TOTE £7.00; EX 20.10.
Owner Saeed Manana **Bred** Rabbah Bloodstock Limited **Trained** Newmarket, Suffolk

FOCUS
Back straight and bottom bend dolled out 3m ending at 4.5f increasing distances by 15yds on round course. All four runners were making their debuts in this maiden and they decided to race down the centre of the track. The winning jockey felt that the ground was on the soft side of good. Probably fair form, with promise from the first three.

NOTEBOOK
Daraa(IRE), a 28,000gns filly out of a winning half-sister to the high-class Laaheb, was slowest to break but she quickened up nicely towards the far side of the quartet to lead inside the last furlong. She only just managed to hold on at the line and the form is hard to evaluate, but she is likely to improve as she steps up in trip. (op 15-2 tchd 8-1 and 11-2)
My Body Is A Cage(IRE), an 18,000euros half-sister to two winners at up to 7f, proved very weak in the market and her trainer had suggested he wasn't expecting her to win, so connections must have been pleased with the way she battled back after losing the lead and she would have won in another stride. (op 9-2 tchd 9-1)
Khaleejiya(IRE), a 50,000gns half-sister to two winners at up to 1m2f and in the same ownership as the winner, had every chance in the final furlong and wasn't beaten far. She holds a Cheveley Park entry, but on this evidence she may need a bit further. (op 2-1 tchd 9-4)
Fa'Iz(IRE), a Derby entry out of a winning half-sister to some smart performers including the Irish Oaks winner Moonstone, was a huge disappointment. He was the first to come under pressure over 2f from home and then started to hang badly. This was too bad to be true. (op 5-4 tchd Evens)

4727 SEALIFE CENTRE FILLIES' H'CAP — 1m 3y
2:50 (2:51) (Class 5) (0-75,74) 3-Y-0 **£2,264** (£673; £336; £168) **Stalls** High

Form RPR
0225 **1** **Empress Charlotte**[21] 4011 3-8-12 **65** .... HayleyTurner 6 72+
(Michael Bell) *hld up in tch: smooth hdwy to join ldrs wl over 1f out: pushed into narrow ld 1f out: kpt on under hands and heels riding: edgd wl ins fnl f* **10/3**[2]
2344 **2** *shd* **Swift Bird (IRE)**[28] 3766 3-9-3 **70** ....(b[1]) RichardMullen 1 76
(Noel Quinlan) *w ldrs tl led 3f out: jnd and drvn over 1f out: hdd narrowly 1f out: edgd rt u.p ins fnl f: kpt on: jst hld* **16/1**
-421 **3** *3 1/4* **Starbound (IRE)**[31] 3675 3-9-0 **70** .... AdamBeschizza(3) 4 69
(William Haggas) *stdd and short of room s: t.k.h: hld up in tch: effrt and rdn 2f out: outpcd by ldng pair ent fnl f: plugged on to go 3rd fnl 75yds* **10/3**[2]
-535 **4** *1 1/2* **Lucy Limelites**[20] 4056 3-9-6 **73** ....(b) TedDurcan 5 69
(Roger Charlton) *w ldrs: rdn jst over 2f out: drvn: hld hd high and fnd little over 1f out: btn 1f out: wknd ins fnl f* **15/8**[1]
5-40 **5** *1 1/2* **Beyeh (IRE)**[58] 2791 3-9-4 **71** .... PhilipRobinson 3 63
(Clive Brittain) *hld up in tch: rdn and effrt over 2f out: drvn and wknd over 1f out* **11/1**
3-61 **6** *12* **Celestyna**[28] 3766 3-9-0 **74** .... CharlesEddery(7) 2 46
(Sir Henry Cecil) *taken down early and walked to s: plld hrd: led tl 3f out: sn rdn: wknd wl over 1f out: wl bhd and eased wl ins fnl f* **13/2**[3]

1m 42.65s (2.05) **Going Correction** +0.20s/f (Good) **6** Ran SP% **108.5**
Speed ratings (Par 97): **97,96,93,92,90 78**
toteswingers:1&2:£6.70, 2&3:£4.70, 1&3:£1.90 CSF £44.96 TOTE £4.30: £2.60, £5.50; EX 44.40.
Owner Lord Derby **Bred** Stanley House Stud **Trained** Newmarket, Suffolk

FOCUS
An ordinary fillies' handicap, rated around the second. They split into two groups early with two racing out in the centre of the course and the other four nearer to the stands' rail, but the two groups had merged by halfway.

Starbound(IRE) Official explanation: trainer's rep said filly was unsuited by the good to soft ground

4728 GOLDEN MILE GREAT YARMOUTH (S) STKS 1m 3y
3:20 (3:20) (Class 6) 3-Y-O £1,617 (£481; £240; £120) Stalls High

Form RPR
2242 1 **Chilledtothebone**[15] 4200 3-9-3 62 ....(tp) TomEaves 6 62
(Linda Stubbs) *trckd ldrs: hdwy to join ldr jst over 1f out: drvn ahd fnl 75yds: fnd enough u.p: drvn out* 11/4[1]
2314 2 *nk* **Janet's Pearl (IRE)**[1] 4685 3-9-3 70 ....(p) SamHitchcott 7 62
(Ann Duffield) *led: rdn wl over 1f out: drvn ent fnl f: hdd and no ex fnl 75yds* 3/1[2]
4244 3 *1 ½* **Crown Ridge (IRE)**[8] 4435 3-9-3 62 .... TedDurcan 4 58
(Mick Channon) *stdd s: hld up in last pair: hdwy to chse ldng pair ent fnl f: pressed ldrs and drvn ins fnl f: fnd little and wknd fnl 100yds* 3/1[2]
0006 4 *2 ¼* **Ippi N Tombi (IRE)**[47] 3175 3-8-9 40 .... AdamBeschizza(3) 8 48
(Phil McEntee) *chsd ldr: rdn jst over 2f out: drvn and unable qck over 1f out: one pce and wl hld ins fnl f* 33/1
5000 5 *hd* **Imperial Fong**[30] 3709 3-8-12 47 .... AndreaAtzeni 2 48
(Chris Dwyer) *t.k.h: hld up in tch: shkn up and effrt over 1f out: drvn and fnd nil ent fnl f: wl hld after* 18/1[3]
6 *3 ½* **Maz** 3-8-5 0 .... CharlesBishop(7) 1 39
(Alan Bailey) *hld up in tch in rr: rdn and unable qck 2f out: rn green and struggling whn hung lft over 1f out: n.d after* 11/4[1]

1m 43.52s (2.92) **Going Correction** +0.20s/f (Good) 6 Ran SP% 111.5
Speed ratings (Par 98): **93,92,91,88,88 85**
toteswingers:1&2:£1.30, 2&3:£2.00, 1&3:£2.20 CSF £11.19 TOTE £3.60: £2.20, £1.20; EX 9.10.There was no bid for the winner. Janet's Pearl was claimed by P. T. Midgley for £4500.
Owner G & T Bloodstock **Bred** Broughton Bloodstock **Trained** Norton, N Yorks

FOCUS
A weak seller with the fourth and fifth limiting. The winner did not need to match his recent best.

4729 GREAT YARMOUTH TOURIST AUTHORITY MAIDEN H'CAP 6f 3y
3:50 (3:51) (Class 6) (0-65,62) 3-Y-O+ £1,617 (£481; £240; £120) Stalls High

Form RPR
-250 1 **Oh So Spicy**[56] 2845 4-9-8 58 .... TedDurcan 1 72
(Chris Wall) *in tch: rdn and effrt to ld over 1f out: edgd rt u.p 1f out: clr and in command but kpt up to work ins fnl f: rdn out* 11/4[2]
2340 2 *4 ½* **I Got You Babe (IRE)**[6] 4518 3-9-8 62 .... RichardMullen 5 61
(Richard Guest) *hld up in tch: rdn and effrt to chse wnr jst over 1f out: no imp* 4/1[3]
0034 3 *2* **Avec Moi**[21] 4025 4-8-3 46 ....(v[1]) DanielHarris(7) 4 39
(Christine Dunnett) *s.i.s: sn rcvrd and dashed up to ld: rdn over 2f out: drvn and hdd over 1f out: drvn and hdd over 1f out: sn outpcd by wnr:3rd and kpt on same pce fnl f:* 5/1
0243 4 *hd* **Cathcart Castle**[14] 4247 3-8-8 55 ....(v) CharlesBishop(7) 6 47
(Mick Channon) *taken down early: in tch: rdn and fnd little ent fnl 2f: one pce and no ch w wnr fr over 1f out* 5/2[1]
3603 5 *½* **His Grace (IRE)**[37] 3481 3-9-8 62 .... RobertHavlin 2 52
(Andrew Haynes) *rrd as stalls opened and slowly away: sn rcvrd to chse ldr after 1f tl over 1f ouit: sn wknd* 6/1
/64- R **Flotate (USA)**[482] 1209 4-8-6 45 ....(b[1]) AdamBeschizza(3) 7 —
(Gay Kelleway) *mounted on crse; ref to r* 20/1

1m 16.63s (2.23) **Going Correction** +0.40s/f (Good)
WFA 3 from 4yo 4lb 6 Ran SP% 111.0
Speed ratings (Par 101): **101,95,92,92,91** —
toteswingers:1&2:£2.80, 2&3:£3.10, 1&3:£3.00 CSF £13.69 TOTE £2.40: £1.10, £2.70; EX 15.70.
Owner The Eight Of Diamonds **Bred** Mrs C J Walker **Trained** Newmarket, Suffolk

FOCUS
A moderate maiden handicap and these 3-y-os appeared to find this hard work. The early pace was moderate for a sprint with the pair who fluffed the start soon holding the first two positions. Not form to be confident about.
His Grace(IRE) Official explanation: jockey said gelding reared as stalls opened

4730 TIME & TIDE MUSEUM H'CAP 1m 1f
4:20 (4:21) (Class 6) (0-65,65) 3-Y-O+ £1,617 (£481; £240; £120) Stalls Low

Form RPR
-330 1 **Diverting**[38] 3467 3-8-12 57 .... LeeNewman 4 69
(William Jarvis) *chsd ldrs: pushed along wl over 4f out: rdn and chsd ldr jst over 2f out: clr w ldr jst over 1f out: drvn ahd fnl 50yds: kpt on wl* 15/2[3]
53-6 2 *1 ½* **Smirfy's Silver**[48] 3139 7-10-0 65 .... TomEaves 6 74
(Deborah Sanderson) *led: rdn 2f out: drvn and clr w wnr jst over 1f out: hdd and no ex fnl 50yds* 14/1
0-40 3 *2 ¼* **Toballa**[19] 4090 6-8-6 46 oh1 ....(t[1]) AdamBeschizza(3) 12 51
(Clifford Lines) *t.k.h: hld up towards rr: rdn and hung lft 3f out: swtchd rt and hdwy 2f out: styd on to go 3rd ins fnl f: plugged on but no threat to ldrs* 22/1
32/2 4 *2 ¾* **Flame Of Hestia (IRE)**[35] 3558 5-10-0 65 .... PatCosgrave 2 64
(James Fanshawe) *chsd ldr: rdn over 2f out: struggling and lost pl 2f out: 4th and wl hld over 1f out* 9/4[1]
4556 5 *2* **Midnight Trader (IRE)**[14] 4249 3-9-1 63 ....(t) PatrickHills(3) 9 58
(Paul D'Arcy) *t.k.h: hld up in midfield: rdn and hdwy over 2f out: chsd ldng pair 2f out: no prog and btn over 1f out: wknd ins fnl f* 8/1
5263 6 *nk* **Negotiation (IRE)**[23] 3959 5-10-0 65 .... RichardMullen 8 59
(Michael Quinn) *v.s.a and early reminders: clsd and in tch in rr after 2f: rdn and sme hdwy 3f out: no prog 2f out: wl hld whn hung lft 1f out* 7/2[2]
0510 7 *4 ½* **Patriotic (IRE)**[13] 4281 3-9-1 60 .... AndreaAtzeni 1 45
(Chris Dwyer) *in tch in midfield: rdn and struggling over 3f out: wknd 2f out* 8/1
55-0 8 *11* **Alioonagh (USA)**[38] 3457 4-9-12 63 ....(b[1]) RobertHavlin 7 26
(Peter Chapple-Hyam) *t.k.h: chsd ldrs: rdn and struggling wl over 2f out: wknd 2f out* 14/1
6000 9 *1* **Folio (IRE)**[31] 3690 11-8-9 46 oh1 .... TedDurcan 3 —
(Willie Musson) *hld up in tch in last trio: hdwy on inner over 3f out: wknd 2f out: wl btn and eased ins fnl f* 12/1
000- 10 *28* **Topaze Star**[328] 5902 4-9-9 60 .... AdrianMcCarthy 10 —
(George Margarson) *in tch in midfield: lost pl and dropped to rr over 3f out: sn lost tch: t.o* 66/1

1m 57.19s (1.39) **Going Correction** +0.20s/f (Good)
WFA 3 from 4yo+ 8lb 10 Ran SP% 113.8
Speed ratings (Par 101): **101,99,97,95,93 93,89,79,78,53**
toteswingers:1&2:£15.00, 2&3:£28.90, 1&3:£27.80 CSF £104.00 CT £2225.66 TOTE £9.80: £2.20, £3.50, £7.80; EX 144.00.
Owner A Reed **Bred** Anthony Reed **Trained** Newmarket, Suffolk

FOCUS
The biggest field of the day, but a moderate race and they finished well spread out. It appeared well run and the form is basically sound.
Negotiation(IRE) Official explanation: vet said gelding lost a left-hind shoe
Folio(IRE) Official explanation: jockey said gelding had no more to give

4731 BRITISH HEART FOUNDATION H'CAP 5f 43y
4:50 (4:51) (Class 4) (0-80,75) 3-Y-O+ £4,075 (£1,212; £606; £303) Stalls High

Form RPR
-243 1 **Midnight Rider (IRE)**[28] 3785 3-9-5 73 ....(p) TedDurcan 3 79
(Chris Wall) *stdd s: wl off the pce in last: clsd 2f out: rdn to chal jst ins fnl f: led fnl 50yds: r.o wl* 9/4[2]
0120 2 *½* **Whiskey Junction**[14] 4233 7-9-1 69 .... AdamBeschizza(3) 5 74
(Michael Quinn) *racd alone on stands' rail: outpcd in 4th: rdn 1/2-way: styd on strly ins fnl f: snatched 2nd on post* 8/1
-333 3 *nse* **Star Twilight**[15] 4207 4-8-11 62 ....(p) TomEaves 1 67
(Derek Shaw) *chsd ldng pair: effrt and rdn to ld jst over 1f out: drvn ins fnl f: hdd and no ex fnl 50yds: lost 2nd on post* 7/1
1103 4 *4 ½* **Miss Polly Plum**[10] 4392 4-9-7 72 ....(p) AndreaAtzeni 2 61
(Chris Dwyer) *t.k.h: pushed lft sn after s: w ldr: ev ch and rdn over 1f out: sn struggling: wknd 1f out* 7/2[3]
215 5 *2* **Equuleus Pictor**[24] 3914 7-9-10 75 ....(p) PhilipRobinson 4 56
(John Spearing) *led: swtchd lft sn after s: rdn 2f out: hdd over 1f out: wknd 1f out* 2/1[1]

64.64 secs (1.94) **Going Correction** +0.40s/f (Good)
WFA 3 from 4yo+ 3lb 5 Ran SP% 109.9
Speed ratings (Par 105): **100,99,99,91,88**
CSF £18.65 TOTE £2.50: £1.10, £4.10; EX 17.30.
Owner The Leap Year Partnership **Bred** M Smith & Grennanstown Stud **Trained** Newmarket, Suffolk

FOCUS
The leaders probably went off too fast in the conditions and paid for it late on, whilst the first two horses home came from well off the pace. There was a difference of opinion as to where the best ground was with the runner-up being taken to race alone against the stands' rail. it's hard to be positive about the form.

4732 AVENUE PUB H'CAP 1m 6f 17y
5:25 (5:25) (Class 6) (0-58,58) 3-Y-O+ £1,617 (£481; £240; £120) Stalls High

Form RPR
6051 1 **Mina's Boy**[17] 4151 3-8-12 57 .... RoystonFfrench 5 63+
(Ed Dunlop) *in tch in midfield: rdn over 3f out: drvn and hdwy to press ldrs 2f out: ev ch over 1f out: drvn ahd wl ins fnl f: styd on* 6/4[1]
6326 2 *1* **Miss Whippy**[23] 3960 4-9-1 50 .... AdamBeschizza(3) 7 55
(Michael Squance) *flashed tail thrght: led: sn clr: hrd pressed and rdn wl over 1f out: drvn and much tail flashing fr 1f out: hdd and no ex wl ins fnl f: eased last strides* 10/1
5505 3 *nse* **Can Can Dancer**[16] 4177 6-9-0 46 oh1 .... RobbieFitzpatrick 4 51
(Charles Smith) *in tch: rdn and effrt 4f out: hdwy u.p to chse ldng pair wl over 1f out: kpt on same pce ins fnl f* 25/1
5026 4 *5* **Newby Lodge (IRE)**[23] 3958 3-8-7 52 ow2 .... SamHitchcott 8 50
(Alan Bailey) *t.k.h: chsd ldng pair: jnd ldr gng wl 3f out: rdn and fnd nil 2f out: wknd over 1f out* 7/1
0510 5 *8* **Royal Premier (IRE)**[11] 4366 8-9-12 58 ....(b) TedDurcan 1 45
(Tom Keddy) *hld up in last: rdn 5f out: no prog and wl btn fnl 2f* 11/2[3]
0-52 6 *3 ½* **Astrovenus**[28] 3769 4-9-4 50 .... PhilipRobinson 2 32
(Mark H Tompkins) *t.k.h: hld up in last trio: rdn and no hdwy over 3f out: wknd 2f out* 4/1[2]
-054 7 *14* **Sulliman**[10] 4396 4-9-6 52 .... PatCosgrave 3 14
(George Margarson) *chsd ldr: drvn 3f out: lost pl qckly ent fnl 2f: wl bhd and eased ins fnl f* 8/1

3m 14.19s (6.59) **Going Correction** +0.40s/f (Good)
WFA 3 from 4yo+ 13lb 7 Ran SP% 111.9
Speed ratings (Par 101): **97,96,96,93,88 86,78**
toteswingers:1&2:£5.40, 2&3:£18.90, 1&3:£10.50. Tote Super 7: Win: Not won. Place: Not won. CSF £17.05 CT £257.31 TOTE £2.70: £1.30, £3.70, £22.20; EX 147.05 Trifecta £22.20.
Owner P A Deal, G Lowe & M J Silver **Bred** Hermes Services Ltd **Trained** Newmarket, Suffolk

FOCUS
A very moderate staying handicap, though the pace was solid enough in the conditions. The winner progressed from his Beverley win.
Astrovenus Official explanation: jockey said filly was unsuited by the good to soft ground
T/Plt: £3,012.70 to a £1 stake. Pool of £49,524.34 - 12.00 winning tickets. T/Qpdt: £133.20 to a £1 stake. Pool of £4,476.18 - 24.85 winning tickets. SP

4733 - 4736a (Foreign Racing) - See Raceform Interactive

4256 LEOPARDSTOWN (L-H)
Thursday, August 4

OFFICIAL GOING: Good

4737a BALLYROAN STKS (GROUP 3) 1m 4f
8:00 (8:00) 3-Y-O+ £32,219 (£9,418; £4,461; £1,487)

RPR
1 **Sense Of Purpose (IRE)**[21] 4035 4-9-6 102 .... PJSmullen 6 108
(D K Weld, Ire) *mde all: drvn along fr early st: kpt on wl u.p ins fnl f: hld on* 6/1
2 *½* **Marksmanship (IRE)**[21] 4038 3-8-12 106 .... SeamieHeffernan 3 110+
(A P O'Brien, Ire) *trckd ldrs mainly 4th: rdn in 3rd early st: kpt on wl u.p ins fnl f: nt rch wnr* 7/4[1]
3 *shd* **Bob Le Beau (IRE)**[21] 4035 4-9-9 110 .... FMBerry 4 110
(Mrs John Harrington, Ire) *trckd ldr in 2nd: drvn along ent st: kpt on wl u.p ins fnl f: nt rch wnr* 11/4[3]
4 *3* **Mount Athos (IRE)**[33] 3625 4-9-9 .... JamieSpencer 1 105+
(David Wachman, Ire) *trckd ldrs mainly 3rd: rdn and dropped to 4th early st: no ex u.p fnl f* 9/4[2]
5 *7* **Leceile (USA)**[6] 4520 5-9-6 91 ....(b) JMurtagh 5 91+
(Noel Meade, Ire) *hld up in rr: stl in tch ent st: no ex fr under 2f out* 33/1

2m 36.39s (1.09) **Going Correction** +0.10s/f (Good)
WFA 3 from 4yo+ 11lb 5 Ran SP% 111.0
Speed ratings: **100,99,99,97,92**
CSF £17.13 TOTE £5.40: £2.10, £1.40; DF 15.30.
Owner Moyglare Stud Farm **Bred** Moyglare Stud Farm Ltd **Trained** The Curragh, Co Kildare

FOCUS
The third sets the standard.

NOTEBOOK
Sense Of Purpose(IRE) dictated proceedings at the head of affairs and turning in the challengers were queuing up in behind, but the Galileo filly answered every call from the saddle and kept finding more. As her trainer said afterwards, she's a joy to train and never quits, and that was underlined here with this most courageous display. The Betfred Ebor was ruled out with next month's Park Hill Stakes at Doncaster put forward as her next likely target, although the Irish St Leger might also enter calculations. (op 5/1)
Marksmanship(IRE) had finished sixth in the Group 1 Grand Prix De Paris on his latest start and had his sights lowered having his first run in Ireland since winning his maiden in good style at the Curragh in soft ground last April. He closed to mount his challenge passing the 2f pole but, despite plenty of encouragement from the saddle, couldn't reel in the leader. (op 6/4)
Bob Le Beau(IRE) was meeting the winner on 3lb better terms since his narrow Challenge Stakes defeat over 2f longer at this venue last month but couldn't reverse form. (op 10/3)
Mount Athos(IRE) bypassed the Goodwood Cup last month and was fancied to play a prominent role since his fourth in the Old Newton Cup Handicap at Haydock over this trip. He raced keenly in third and when the race developed in the straight he had no more to offer. (op 5/2)
Leceile(USA) still appeared to be travelling rounding the home turn but the 89-rated mare was soon found wanting when they straightened for home. (op 25/1)

4738 - (Foreign Racing) - See Raceform Interactive

4652 DEAUVILLE (R-H)
Thursday, August 4

OFFICIAL GOING: Turf: good; fibresand: standard

4739a PRIX DU CERCLE (LISTED RACE) (3YO+) (TURF) 5f
2:20 (12:00) 3-Y-O+ **£22,413** (£8,965; £6,724; £4,482; £2,241)

RPR
1 **Lisselan Diva (IRE)**[41] 3374 5-8-11 0 .... WilliamsSaraiva 6 107
(Mme J Bidgood, France) **24/1**
2 *snk* **Mar Adentro (FR)**[11] 5-9-1 0 ....(p) ChristopheSoumillon 17 110
(R Chotard, France) **3/1**[1]
3 *nk* **Bluster (FR)**[41] 3374 5-9-1 0 .... Christophe-PatriceLemaire 18 109
(Robert Collet, France) **32/1**
4 *1 1/2* **Le Valentin (FR)**[25] 5-9-1 0 .... AnthonyCrastus 4 104
(Y De Nicolay, France) **13/1**
5 *nse* **Piccadilly Filly (IRE)**[20] 4063 4-8-11 0 ....(b) EddieCreighton 3 100
(Edward Creighton) *broke wl on stands' side: hrd rdn fr 1/2-way: styd on wl fnl f to claim 5th on line* **20/1**
6 *shd* **Chinese Wall (IRE)**[98] 1646 3-8-8 0 .... ThierryJarnet 15 98
(D Guillemin, France) **10/1**
7 *3/4* **Swiss Franc**[11] 4357 6-9-1 0 .... GeraldMosse 2 101
(David Elsworth) *broke wl: racd bhd ldrs in centre of trck: rdn 1/2-way: no ex: styd on fnl f* **15/1**
8 *snk* **Swiss Dream**[12] 4333 3-8-8 0 .... IoritzMendizabal 8 95
(David Elsworth) *broke wl towards stands' rail: u.p 1/2-way: grad drifted towards centre of trck: styd on fnl f* **78/10**[3]
9 *1 1/2* **Broox (IRE)**[33] 3644 3-8-11 0 .... OlivierPeslier 10 93
(E J O'Neill, France) **10/1**
10 *1* **Stone Of Folca**[7] 4468 3-8-11 0 .... StephanePasquier 9 89
(John Best) *prom fr s: rdn 1/2-way: no ex: wknd fnl f* **51/1**
0 **Nuit De Glace (FR)**[25] 7-8-11 0 .... SebastienMaillot 16 —
(Mlle Valerie Boussin, France) **26/1**
0 **Rappel**[25] 5-8-11 0 .... ThierryThulliez 14 —
(J E Hammond, France) **24/1**
0 **Green Dandy (IRE)**[19] 4121 4-8-11 0 .... ThomasHuet 13 —
(E J O'Neill, France) **72/1**
0 **Prinzde Glas (IRE)**[41] 3374 4-9-1 0 ....(b) MaximeGuyon 5 —
(E Danel, France) **53/10**[2]
0 **Its You Again**[41] 3374 3-8-11 0 ....(b) SylvainRuis 11 —
(Braem Horse Racing Sprl, Belgium) **13/1**
0 **Kagura (USA)**[25] 3898 3-8-13 0 .... MickaelBarzalona 7 —
(G Henrot, France) **40/1**
0 **Star Dust Melody (FR)**[11] 3-8-8 0 .... GaetanMasure 12 —
(N Caullery, France) **62/1**

57.50 secs
WFA 3 from 4yo+ 3lb **17 Ran SP% 117.0**
WIN (incl. 1 euro stake): 25.50. places: 6.70, 2.10, 7.00. DF: 50.00. SF: 143.30.
Owner Haras de Bouquetot Sarl **Bred** Colman O'Flynn **Trained** France

NOTEBOOK
Lisselan Diva(IRE) made virtually all the running and may now be given a rest before being brought back for an ambitious tilit at the Abbaye.

4695 BRIGHTON (L-H)
Friday, August 5

OFFICIAL GOING: Good (good to soft in places) changing to good after race 1 (2.30)
Wind: light, across Weather: bright and sunny

4740 IINSURE365.CO.UK LANDLORD BUILDINGS INSURANCE H'CAP 5f 59y
2:30 (2:30) (Class 6) (0-60,58) 3-Y-O+ **£1,811** (£539; £269; £134) **Stalls** Low

Form RPR
5306 1 **Wotatomboy**[1] 4696 5-8-9 **46** ....(v) ChrisCatlin 7 53
(Richard Whitaker) *mde virtually all: rdn ent fnl 2f: drvn over 1f out: led 1f out: kpt on u.p: eased nr fin* **9/1**
6222 2 *3/4* **Do More Business (IRE)**[24] 3939 4-9-1 **52** .... IanMongan 4 56
(Pat Phelan) *w wnr: rdn 2f out: drvn and stl ev ch over 1f out: styd on same pce ins fnl f* **2/1**[1]
0-30 3 *2* **Pocket's Pick (IRE)**[17] 4189 5-9-7 **58** ....(bt) PaulDoe 1 55
(Jim Best) *stdd after s: hld up in last: swtchd rt and effrt over 2f out: drvn over 1f out: kpt on same pce fnl f* **13/2**
1305 4 *1 1/4* **Stonecrabstomorrow (IRE)**[24] 3940 8-9-2 **58** ......(v) MarkCoumbe(5) 5 51
(Michael Attwater) *nudged along in 4th: drvn wl over 1f out: kpt on same pce and no imp fnl f* **3/1**[3]
5434 5 *3* **Bookiesindex Boy**[17] 4182 7-9-0 **51** ....(bt) NeilChalmers 3 33
(J R Jenkins) *chsd ldng pair tl over 1f out: sn rdn and fnd nil: wknd fnl f* **5/2**[2]

63.57 secs (1.27) **Going Correction** +0.20s/f (Good) **5 Ran SP% 110.2**
Speed ratings (Par 101): **97,95,92,90,85**
CSF £27.33 TOTE £12.40: £3.50, £1.60; EX 30.90.
Owner Mrs Jill Willows **Bred** Hellwood Stud Farm **Trained** Scarcroft, W Yorks

FOCUS
Following a dry night the ground had dried out to good, good to soft in places (GoingStick 6.9). All the races were run on the inner, giving at least 4yds of fresh ground from 6f-2f. Rail at normal configuration and distances as advertised. A moderate sprint handicap run in a slow time. The form is rated negatively.
Wotatomboy Official explanation: trainer said, rwegarding apparent improvement in form, that the mare was better suited by the faster ground and reapplication of headgear.

4741 IINSURE365.CO.UK COMMERCIAL PROPERTY INSURANCE (S) STKS 5f 213y
3:00 (3:00) (Class 6) 3-Y-O+ **£1,811** (£539; £269; £134) **Stalls** Low

Form RPR
0104 1 **Deerslayer (USA)**[42] 3351 5-9-7 72 ....(p) PaulDoe 2 74
(Jim Best) *bustled along early and sn led: mde rest: c towards stands' rail 3f out: hrd drvn over 1f out: edgd rt 1f out: kpt on u.str.p and a holding rival* **9/4**[2]
3400 2 *nk* **Hand Painted**[31] 3713 5-8-13 62 .... JohnFahy(3) 1 68
(Anthony Middleton) *s.i.s: sn pushed along: clsd and in tch after 2f: chsd wnr and c towards stands' side 3f out: ev ch and drvn over 1f out: hrd drvn and unable qck ins fnl f* **5/2**[3]
3200 3 *8* **Basle**[11] 4387 4-8-11 72 .... ChrisCatlin 3 37
(Gay Kelleway) *t.k.h: broke wl: sn stdd and chsd wnr tl 3f out: carried rt wl over 2f out: swtchd lft bk to far rail and outpcd by ldrs over 2f out: btn over 1f out: wknd ins fnl f* **7/4**[1]
-660 4 *3 3/4* **Desert Falls**[90] 1906 5-9-2 57 .... CathyGannon 4 30
(Richard Whitaker) *t.k.h: hld up in tch: carried rt 3f out: swtchd lft bk towards far rail over 2f out: sn outpcd by ldng pair and rdn: btn over 1f out: wknd fnl f* **7/1**

1m 11.1s (0.90) **Going Correction** +0.20s/f (Good) **4 Ran SP% 108.2**
Speed ratings (Par 101): **102,101,90,85**
CSF £8.01 TOTE £2.30; EX 8.50.The winner was sold to Richard Guest for 2,900gns.
Owner M&R Refurbishments Ltd **Bred** Bjorn Nielsen **Trained** Lewes, E Sussex
■ Stewards' Enquiry : Paul Doe caution: used whip with excessive frequency.
John Fahy two-day ban: used whip with excessive frequency (Aug 20-21)

FOCUS
The going was changed to good prior to this race. Not the worst seller in the world despite only four runners. The form is rated around the runner-up. The first two came up the centre of the track, while the other two stayed near the far-side rail.

4742 HARRY BLOOM MEMORIAL H'CAP 5f 213y
3:30 (3:30) (Class 4) (0-80,79) 3-Y-O-**£7,246** (£2,168; £1,084; £542; £270) **Stalls** Low

Form RPR
5421 1 **Clear Ice (IRE)**[2] 4659 4-9-3 **70** 6ex ....(b) ChrisCatlin 1 78
(Gay Kelleway) *mde all: styd far side 3f out: drvn over 1f out: hld on wl u.p fnl f* **13/2**[3]
5013 2 *hd* **Aye Aye Digby (IRE)**[29] 3765 6-9-11 **78** .... FergusSweeney 11 85
(Patrick Chamings) *in tch in midfield: c stands' side 3f out: hdwy over 2f out: rdn over 1f out: drvn and chsd wnr ins fnl f: kpt on wl: jst hld: 1st of 7 in gp* **7/1**
-210 3 *3/4* **Titus Gent**[21] 4064 6-8-12 **72** ....(p) RaulDaSilva(7) 4 77
(Jeremy Gask) *chsd wnr: c stands' side 3f out: stl pressing wnr and rdn ent fnl 2f: no ex and btn fnl 100yds: 2nd of 7 in gp* **7/1**
4311 4 *1/2* **Ajjaadd (USA)**[27] 3847 5-9-12 **79** .... RichardMullen 12 82+
(Ted Powell) *stdd s: hld up towards rr: hdwy and c stands' side 3f out: chsd ldrs and rdn ent fnl f: drvn and styd on fnl 100yds: nt rch ldrs: 3rd of 7 in gp* **5/1**[1]
2003 5 *2* **Katmai River (IRE)**[15] 4230 4-8-9 **62** ....(v) DavidProbert 3 59
(Mark Usher) *sn rdn along in last trio: c stands' side 3f out: styd on u.p ins fnl f: nvr trbld ldrs: 4th of 7 in gp* **10/1**
3263 6 *nk* **Yurituni**[22] 3996 4-9-10 **77** ....(v) CathyGannon 9 73
(Eve Johnson Houghton) *in tch in midfield: styd far side 3f out: rdn ent fnl 2f: drvn and kpt on same pce fr over 1f out: 2nd of 3 in gp* **10/1**
5254 7 *1 1/2* **Cornus**[7] 4516 9-9-5 **75** ....(be) KieranO'Neill(3) 2 66
(Alan McCabe) *stdd s: hld up in rr: styd far side 3f out: rdn: effrt and hung rt 2f out: kpt on ins fnl f: nvr able to chal: 3rd of 3 in gp* **6/1**[2]
5001 8 *5* **Lady Florence**[1] 4696 6-8-11 **64** 6ex .... AdrianMcCarthy 8 46
(David C Griffiths) *chsd ldrs: pushed along over 4f out: c stands' side and rdn 3f out: wknd 2f out: wl btn and eased ins fnl f: 5th of 7 in gp* **16/1**
0014 9 *nse* **Altresco**[40] 3427 7-9-8 **75** ....(b) KieranFallon 14 57
(John Best) *in tch in midfield: rdn and c stands' side 3f out: wknd wl over 1f out: wl bhd and eased ins fnl f: 6th of 7 in gp* **15/2**
0-04 10 *1* **Spanish Acclaim**[15] 4239 4-9-3 **70** ....(b) NeilChalmers 13 41
(Andrew Balding) *chsd ldrs: losing pl and c stands' side 3f out: bhd and rdn over 2f out: wl btn 2f out: eased ins fnl f: 7th of 7 in gp* **8/1**

1m 11.43s (1.23) **Going Correction** +0.20s/f (Good)
WFA 3 from 4yo+ 4lb **10 Ran SP% 116.2**
Speed ratings (Par 105): **99,98,97,97,94 94,92,85,85,83**
Tote Swingers: 1&2 £8.60, 1&3 £6.30, 2&3 £8.30 CSF £51.28 CT £336.60 TOTE £8.70: £2.40, £3.20, £2.70; EX 52.00 TRIFECTA Not won..
Owner Whispering Winds **Bred** Mrs Noelle Walsh **Trained** Exning, Suffolk

FOCUS
A very open handicap and close finish between two horses on either side of the track. The time was slower than the previous seller and it's hard to rate the form too positively.

4743 IINSURE365.CO.UK 01273 827090 MAIDEN H'CAP 6f 209y
4:00 (4:00) (Class 6) (0-65,65) 3-Y-O+ **£1,811** (£539; £269; £134) **Stalls** Low

Form RPR
0006 1 **Songsmith**[14] 4281 3-9-3 **62** ....(p) IanMongan 5 67
(Lucy Wadham) *chsd ldrs on outer: upsides ldr fr over 2f out: drvn over 1f out: led fnl 75yds: forged ahd towards fin* **2/1**[1]
6250 2 *3/4* **Mister Ben Vereen**[7] 4486 3-9-2 **61** ....(b) CathyGannon 1 64
(Eve Johnson Houghton) *sn led: rdn and hung rt over 2f out: drvn over 1f out: hdd fnl 75yds: no ex* **9/2**[2]
-304 3 *1 3/4* **Valeo Si Vales (IRE)**[25] 3913 3-9-2 **61** ....(b[1]) FergusSweeney 7 59
(Jamie Osborne) *t.k.h: hld up wl in tch: rdn and effrt 2f out: chsd ldng pair ent fnl f: hung lft and one pce ins fnl f* **6/1**[3]
0602 4 *6* **Fluctuation (IRE)**[31] 3710 3-9-0 **59** .... KierenFallon 2 41
(Ian Williams) *t.k.h: chsd ldr: rdn and unable qck whn n.m.r over 2f out: drvn: hung lft and wknd ent fnl f* **2/1**[1]
4-04 5 *6* **Dualite (IRE)**[54] 2963 3-9-6 **65** .... ChrisCatlin 4 31
(John Dunlop) *stdd after s: t.k.h: hld up in tch: rdn and effrt on inner over 2f out: wknd over 1f out* **8/1**

1m 24.75s (1.65) **Going Correction** +0.20s/f (Good) **5 Ran SP% 110.2**
Speed ratings (Par 101): **98,97,95,88,81**
CSF £11.29 TOTE £3.60: £2.10, £2.70; EX 12.30 Trifecta £35.60 Pool: £437.05 - 9.08 winning units..
Owner Team Supreme **Bred** Providence Stud **Trained** Newmarket, Suffolk

FOCUS
Hard to be enthusiastic about the value of this form. The runner-up sets the moderate stabndard.

4744 IINSURE365.CO.UK BUY-TO-LET SPECIALISTS H'CAP 7f 214y
4:30 (4:30) (Class 5) (0-70,74) 3-Y-O **£2,522** (£750; £375; £187) **Stalls** Low

Form RPR
2132 **1** **Whitby Jet (IRE)**[23] 3979 3-9-5 **66** KierenFallon 5 76
(Edward Vaughan) *t.k.h: rdn to ld over 2f out: edgd lft u.p and forged clr ins fnl f: eased towards fin* **5/2**[1]
0241 **2** *2 ¾* **Goal (IRE)**[6] 4560 3-9-6 **74** 6ex (t) MatthewLawson(7) 6 78
(Richard Guest) *stdd s: hld up in tch in rr: effrt on outer over 2f out: chsd wnr over 1f out: edgd lft u.p and no ex jst ins fnl f: plugged on to hold 2nd* **7/2**
1060 **3** *1 ½* **Tagansky**[53] 3002 3-9-1 **62** JackMitchell 4 62
(Simon Dow) *stdd after s: t.k.h: hld up in tch in last pair: effrt and swtchd rt over 2f out: sme hdwy and barging match w rival wl over 1f out: no threat to wnr but kpt on u.p ins fnl f* **14/1**
-420 **4** *1 ¼* **Salvationist**[24] 3944 3-8-11 **58** ChrisCatlin 2 55
(John Dunlop) *t.k.h: hld up in tch: effrt and rdn on inner over 2f out: drvn and no ex ent fnl f: wknd fnl 150yds* **11/4**[2]
0034 **5** *1 ¾* **Prophet In A Dream**[15] 4247 3-8-13 **63** RobertLButler(3) 3 56
(Paddy Butler) *led at stdy gallop: hdd and rdn over 2f out: wknd over 1f out* **25/1**
1254 **6** *1 ¾* **Elvira Delight (IRE)**[32] 3688 3-9-5 **66** JimmyFortune 7 55
(Jeremy Noseda) *t.k.h: chsd ldrs: rdn and unable qck whn edgd lft wl over 1f out: sn wknd* **3/1**[3]

1m 37.58s (1.58) **Going Correction** +0.20s/f (Good) **6** Ran SP% **113.0**
Speed ratings (Par 100): **100,97,95,94,92 91**
Tote Swingers: 1&2 £4.10, 1&3 £2.10, 2&3 £4.20 CSF £11.78 TOTE £3.30: £2.00, £2.30; EX 10.70.
Owner A M Pickering **Bred** Rathasker Stud **Trained** Newmarket, Suffolk
FOCUS
Not a bad handicap but they didn't go that fast early. A 5lb personal best from the winner.

4745 IINSURE365 FREEHOLD INSURANCE H'CAP 1m 1f 209y
5:00 (5:02) (Class 6) (0-60,59) 3-Y-O **£1,811** (£539; £269; £134) **Stalls** High

Form RPR
255 **1** **Out Of The Storm**[24] 3945 3-9-3 **55** KierenFallon 6 64
(Simon Dow) *mde all and dictated gallop: travelling best wl over 2f out: drvn and c clr ent fnl f: in command after: eased towards fin* **5/1**
3-30 **2** *4* **Avon Supreme**[15] 4244 3-9-1 **53** JackMitchell 3 54
(Gay Kelleway) *stdd s: hld up in tch in rr: rdn and effrt over 2f out: chsd wnr and edgd lft over 1f out: plugged on but no threat to wnr fnl f* **16/1**
-213 **3** *3 ¾* **Ishikawa (IRE)**[13] 4317 3-9-4 **56** FergusSweeney 7 50
(Alan King) *t.k.h: hld up in tch: rdn wl over 2f out: drvn and unable qck wl over 1f out: wknd jst over 1f out* **85/40**[1]
-326 **4** *nk* **Snowy Peak**[140] 898 3-9-7 **59** (t) JimmyFortune 5 52
(Jeremy Noseda) *chsd ldr: rdn 3f out: drvn and unable qck ent fnl 2f: wknd jst over 1f out* **3/1**[3]
2353 **5** *9* **Drumadoon (IRE)**[29] 3770 3-9-3 **55** (b[1]) ChrisCatlin 8 30
(John Dunlop) *stdd s: plld hrd and hdwy to chse wnr over 8f out tl over 4f out: rdn and struggling 3f out: wknd over 2f out: wl bhd over 1f out* **11/4**[2]
0-00 **6** *15* **Notify**[30] 3742 3-8-7 **45** JimmyQuinn 4 —
(Patrick Chamings) *t.k.h: hld up wl in tch: rdn and struggling 3f out: sn wknd: wl bhd fnl 2f: eased ins fnl f* **33/1**

2m 6.56s (2.96) **Going Correction** +0.20s/f (Good) **6** Ran SP% **109.2**
Speed ratings (Par 98): **96,92,89,89,82 70**
Tote Swingers: 1&2 £6.40, 1&3 £2.30, 2&3 £2.70 CSF £66.11 CT £198.27 TOTE £6.00: £3.10, £4.20; EX 55.90 Trifecta £255.30 Pool: £576.23 - 1.67 winning units..
Owner R E Anderson **Bred** R E Anderson **Trained** Epsom, Surrey
FOCUS
They went steady early on here and Fallon dictated throughout. Modest form, the winner rated back to her best.

4746 IINSURE365 SECURE YOUR INVESTMENT H'CAP 1m 3f 196y
5:30 (5:30) (Class 6) (0-65,69) 3-Y-O+ **£1,811** (£539; £269) **Stalls** High

Form RPR
3620 **1** **Lauberhorn**[22] 4024 4-9-8 **59** (b) CathyGannon 2 68
(Eve Johnson Houghton) *mde all: rdn wl over 2f out: drvn and forged ahd ent fnl f: clr ins fnl f: styd on wl* **15/8**[2]
0031 **2** *2 ¼* **Come On The Irons (USA)**[24] 3945 3-9-0 **62** (t) JamieGoldstein 1 67
(Ralph Smith) *stdd s: hld up in tch: rdn and swtchd rt over 2f out: drvn and plugged on same pce fr over 1f out: chsd wnr and no imp ins fnl f* **5/6**[1]
0020 **3** *6* **Professor John (IRE)**[15] 4242 4-9-6 **57** (v) JackMitchell 5 54
(Ian Wood) *chsd wnr: upsides and rdn 3f out: drvn and u.p over 1f out: btn ent fnl f: wknd fnl 150yds: eased wl ins fnl f* **9/2**[3]

2m 34.53s (1.83) **Going Correction** +0.20s/f (Good)
WFA 3 from 4yo+ 11lb **3** Ran SP% **107.5**
Speed ratings (Par 101): **101,99,95**
CSF £3.87 TOTE £2.60; EX 4.10.
Owner R F Johnson Houghton **Bred** Grasshopper 2000 Ltd **Trained** Blewbury, Oxon
FOCUS
There was a predictably steady early gallop to this three-runner affair. The winner is given a bit of credit, posting just about his best figure since last summer.
T/Plt: £539.20 to a £1 stake. Pool of £66,708.19 - 90.30 winning tickets. T/Qpdt: £54.60 to a £1 stake. Pool of £5,806.88 - 78.65 winning tickets. SP

4714 HAYDOCK (L-H)
Friday, August 5

OFFICIAL GOING: Good to soft (good in places; straight course 7.6, round course 7.1)
Wind: light 1/.2 against Weather: fine and sunny

4747 BETDAQ THE BETTING EXCHANGE HAYDOCK PARK APPRENTICE TRAINING SERIES H'CAP (EXCELLENCE INITIATIVE) 1m 3f 200y
6:00 (6:00) (Class 5) (0-75,73) 4-Y-O+ **£2,587** (£770; £384; £192) **Stalls** High

Form RPR
4122 **1** **Dancing Primo**[3] 4626 5-8-7 **59** LucyKBarry(3) 7 71
(Mark Brisbourne) *trckd ldrs: t.k.h: qcknd to ld 3f out: drvn clr fnl f* **5/2**[1]
4215 **2** *5* **Amir Pasha (UAE)**[7] 4499 6-8-13 **65** (p) ShaneBKelly(3) 1 69
(Micky Hammond) *trckd ldrs: t.k.h: effrt 4f out: chsd wnr 2f out: no imp* **7/2**[3]
-200 **3** *½* **Indochina**[42] 3352 4-9-4 **67** RyanClark 6 70
(Ian Williams) *led: qcknd 4f out: hdd 3f out: one pce whn edgd lft over 1f out* **13/2**
5000 **4** *3 ½* **Kames Park (IRE)**[45] 3243 9-8-6 **60** LukeRowe(5) 4 58
(Richard Guest) *s.s: hdwy on inner over 3f out: chsng ldrs 1f out: fdd* **12/1**
-415 **5** *1 ½* **Muwalla**[12] 4366 4-9-3 **66** LeeTopliss 8 61
(Chris Grant) *trckd ldrs: one pce whn hmpd over 1f out: sn wknd* **10/3**[2]
4000 **6** *1 ¾* **Indefinite Hope (ITY)**[108] 1473 4-8-2 **56** oh4 ow2 (t) JakePayne(5) 2 48
(Frank Sheridan) *trckd ldrs: wknd over 1f out* **20/1**
016 **7** *2 ½* **Amana (USA)**[29] 3760 7-9-5 **73** RachealKneller(5) 3 61
(Mark Brisbourne) *s.i.s: hld up in rr: hdwy over 6f out: lost pl over 1f out* **8/1**

2m 33.77s (-0.23) **Going Correction** +0.075s/f (Good) **7** Ran SP% **110.8**
Speed ratings (Par 103): **103,99,99,97,96 94,93**
Tote Swingers: 1&2 £2.20, 1&3 £2.20, 2&3 £6.30 CSF £10.64 CT £45.91 TOTE £2.90: £2.10, £2.00; EX 8.50.
Owner L R Owen **Bred** L R Owen **Trained** Great Ness, Shropshire
■ Stewards' Enquiry : Ryan Clark two-day ban: careless riding (Aug 20-21)
FOCUS
Sprints run on inner home straight. All other races finish on stands' side home straight and rail realignment increased distances on round course by 43yds. This was an uncompetitive apprentices' handicap, but they went a fair pace. The winner made her move up the centre of the track and most of these avoided the far rail. Straightforward form with the winner resuming her progess.

4748 E.B.F./"KIKI" BY KIRSTY DOYLE MAIDEN STKS 6f
6:35 (6:36) (Class 5) 2-Y-O **£3,234** (£962; £481; £240) **Stalls** Centre

Form RPR
3 **1** **Gusto**[13] 4339 2-9-3 0 PatDobbs 7 85+
(Richard Hannon) *trckd ldrs: shkn up to ld over 1f out: drvn clr: v readily* **11/2**[2]
2 **2** *4* **Glen Moss (IRE)**[12] 4352 2-9-3 0 MichaelHills 5 73
(B W Hills) *led: hdd appr fnl f: styd on same pce* **8/13**[1]
2 **3** *1 ¼* **Magic Destiny**[21] 4047 2-8-12 0 AndrewElliott 6 64
(Mrs K Burke) *trckd ldrs: effrt over 2f out: kpt on same pce over 1f out* **11/1**
4 *hd* **Brubeck (IRE)** 2-9-3 0 RichardKingscote 8 69+
(Tom Dascombe) *s.i.s: drvn and hdwy 3f out: chsng ldrs over 1f out: kpt on same pce* **25/1**
23 **5** *2* **Pea Shooter**[97] 1699 2-9-3 0 PhillipMakin 4 63
(Kevin Ryan) *stdd s: hld up in mid-div: effrt over 1f out: kpt on same pce* **7/1**[3]
40 **6** *1* **Darling Lexi (IRE)**[15] 4232 2-8-12 0 PaulHanagan 10 55
(Richard Fahey) *trckd ldrs: hung lft and nt clr run over 1f out: sn wknd* **40/1**
00 **7** *½* **Astraios (IRE)**[16] 4201 2-9-3 0 EddieCreighton 3 58+
(Brian Meehan) *sn outpcd and in rr: kpt on fnl f: nvr a factor* **66/1**
05 **8** *½* **Duke Of Aricabeau (IRE)**[14] 4283 2-9-3 0 GrahamGibbons 2 57
(Michael Easterby) *chsd ldrs: lost pl over 2f out* **50/1**
9 *4 ½* **Chalk And Cheese (USA)** 2-9-3 0 WilliamBuick 1 43
(John Gosden) *dwlt: j. path after 100yds: sme hdwy over 2f out: lost pl over 1f out: eased towards fin* **12/1**
0 **10** *1* **My New Angel (IRE)**[14] 4283 2-8-12 0 JamesSullivan 9 35
(Paul Green) *s.s: a bhd* **100/1**

1m 14.37s (0.57) **Going Correction** +0.075s/f (Good) **10** Ran SP% **116.6**
Speed ratings (Par 94): **97,91,90,89,87 85,85,84,78,77**
Tote Swingers: 1&2 £2.80, 2&3 £5.30 CSF £9.08 TOTE £7.70: £2.00, £1.10, £3.00; EX 12.50.
Owner Highclere Thoroughbred Racing-Rock Sand **Bred** New England, Mount Coote & P Barrett **Trained** East Everleigh, Wilts
FOCUS
This looked a good juvenile maiden - the front two both recorded RPRs in the 80s on their respective debuts - and the winner was impressive. The time seems to confirm this is a decent form, being 0.99 seconds faster than the following Class 4 nursery. They raced up the centre of the track.
NOTEBOOK
Gusto ◆, a promising third on his introduction over this trip at Salisbury two weeks earlier, travelled well just in behind the pace before bounding clear when asked. While the runner-up blatantly hasn't progressed from his debut, the winner still looks to have run to a very useful level and there should be more to come. It looks a case of the stronger the pace the better he'll travel, which bodes well for when he inevitably goes up in class, and he is probably pattern-race material. He doesn't hold any Group entries in Britain or Ireland, though. (op 6-1 tchd 13-2)
Glen Moss(IRE) had got slightly warm and looked to over race a touch in front, being hassled by Darling Lexi (hung left under pressure), and he was no match for the smart-looking winner. This doesn't represent progression from his encouraging debut second at Ascot 12 days earlier, and it was disappointing considering he holds a number of Group-race entries, but he did keep on to fare best of the rest. (op 8-11, tchd 4-5 in places)
Magic Destiny, runner-up in a weaker race over C&D on her debut, was off the bridle sooner than some but kept on. She might want an extra furlong but will have learnt more. (op 10-1)
Brubeck(IRE) ◆, one of only two newcomers, reportedly joined Tom Dascombe in May, and he ran green but showed plenty of ability. Weak in the market, he went in snatches but there was much to like about how he readily made ground to briefly look a threat 2f out. This 27,000gns purchase is related to a number of winners and ought to progress. (op 20-1)
Pea Shooter, up in trip, carried his head a bit high throughout and was one-paced when in the clear after being a bit tight for room when first looking to make a bid. Nurseries are now an option, but he's not progressing. (op 15-2)
Duke Of Aricabeau(IRE) ◆, just as on his first two starts, hinted at ability without being given a hard time. He is one to keep in mind for nurseries/handicaps.
Chalk And Cheese(USA), related to some winners abroad (dam won eight times in Argentina, including in Group company), has already been gelded and never recovered after jumping the path early on. (op 10-1)

4749 COUNTRYWIDE FREIGHT NURSERY 6f
7:10 (7:11) (Class 4) (0-80,78) 2-Y-O **£3,881** (£1,155; £577; £288) **Stalls** Centre

Form RPR
0041 **1** **Mister Musicmaster**[16] 4212 2-9-5 **76** JamesMillman 1 84
(Rod Millman) *mde all: drvn over 2f out: styd on to forge clr ins fnl f* **12/1**
021 **2** *2 ¼* **The Blue Banana (IRE)**[14] 4269 2-9-4 **75** EddieCreighton 7 76
(Brian Meehan) *dwlt: outpcd and drvn in rr: hdwy over 2f out: edgd lft and chsng wnr over 1f out: kpt on same pce* **5/2**[1]
61 **3** *1 ½* **Bomber Jet**[25] 3899 2-9-7 **78** PaulHanagan 2 75
(Nigel Tinkler) *s.i.s: hld up: effrt over 2f out: chsng ldrs over 1f out: kpt on same pce* **10/3**[2]
5000 **4** *1 ¼* **La Taniere**[21] 4047 2-8-2 **59** JamesSullivan 4 52
(Michael Easterby) *in rr: drvn and outpcd over 2f out: styd on fnl f* **25/1**
4100 **5** *4* **Pink Sapphire (IRE)**[15] 4252 2-9-7 **78** PatDobbs 3 59
(Richard Hannon) *trckd ldrs: wknd fnl f* **6/1**

3232 **6** 2 ½ **Tortoni (IRE)**^{6} [4538] 2-9-6 **77**.. PhillipMakin 6 51
(Kevin Ryan) *hld up: smooth hdwy to trck ldrs 3f out: rdn and hung lft over 1f out: sn wknd* **7/2**^{3}

030 **7** 12 **Storm Fairy**^{17} [4171] 2-7-9 **55** oh2.................................. HarryBentley$^{(3)}$ 5 —
(Mrs K Burke) *trckd ldrs: t.k.h: wknd 2f out: bhd whn eased clsng stages* **7/1**

1m 15.36s (1.56) **Going Correction** +0.075s/f (Good) **7** Ran SP% **112.2**
Speed ratings (Par 96): **90,87,85,83,78 74,58**
Tote Swingers: 1&2 £6.60, 1&3 £5.20, 2&3 £2.90 CSF £40.63 TOTE £11.30: £5.10, £2.40; EX 61.20.
Owner Mrs Jan Fuller **Bred** Mrs J Fuller And S Dutfield **Trained** Kentisbeare, Devon
■ Stewards' Enquiry : Eddie Creighton caution: careless riding.

FOCUS
A fair nursery, although they didn't seem to go that fast for a sprint and the time was 0.99 seconds slower than the earlier maiden won by a smart prospect. Again they raced up the centre of the track. The winner built on his Sandown win.

NOTEBOOK
Mister Musicmaster travelled just about best of all, showing good speed in a decent rhythm, and found plenty when asked. This was a significant improvement on the form he showed when off the mark in a soft-ground nursery over 5f last time. He should continue to progress. (op 8-1)
The Blue Banana(IRE), winner of a Chepstow maiden over this trip last time, didn't travel that well, showing signs he was possibly still a bit green, but he kept on, albeit he was always held. (op 3-1, tchd 7-2 in places)
Bomber Jet raced keenly and found this tougher than the Ayr maiden he won last time. (op 3-1 tchd 7-2)
La Taniere hung slightly left under pressure and made no impression. He might want his sights lowered a touch in the short term. (op 20-1)
Pink Sapphire(IRE) was dropped significantly in grade but didn't find much after racing keenly. She is not progressing and looks one to swerve. (op 13-2 tchd 11-2)
Tortoni(IRE) was 2lb well in following his recent second to a useful prospect in a Hamilton nursery, but he raced with his head to one side and gave the impression something was bothering him. Kevin Ryan reported that the colt became upset in the preliminaries. Official explanation: trainer said colt became upset in the preliminaries (op 4-1, tchd 9-2 in places)

4750 CHRIS FAYLE MEMORIAL H'CAP 1m
7:40 (7:40) (Class 4) (0-80,79) 3-Y-O **£4,528** (£1,347; £673; £336) **Stalls** Low

Form RPR
1111 **1** **Camberley Two**^{2} [4676] 3-9-1 **79** 12ex........................ CharlesBishop$^{(7)}$ 2 87
(Roger Charlton) *trckd ldr: t.k.h: chal 3f out: led narrowly 2f out: rdn and edgd rt: kpt on to gain upper hand nr fin* **4/5**^{1}

03 **2** ½ **Buzz Law (IRE)**^{14} [4290] 3-9-3 **74**........................ AndrewElliott 1 81
(Mrs K Burke) *trckd ldr: t.k.h: chal 3f out: no ex clsng stages* **4/1**^{3}

5324 **3** 3 **Scoglio**^{116} [1277] 3-8-5 **62**..(tp) PaulHanagan 6 62
(Frank Sheridan) *hld up: hdwy over 2f out: kpt on one pce to take 3rd nr fin* **20/1**

1522 **4** hd **Maggie Mey (IRE)**^{14} [4290] 3-9-4 **75**............................. DanielTudhope 5 75
(David O'Meara) *led tl 2f out: fdd and lost 3rd nr fin* **7/2**^{2}

6-50 **5** 2 **Squires Gate (IRE)**^{30} [3737] 3-9-4 **75**............................. MichaelHills 7 70
(B W Hills) *hld up: rdn over 2f out: nvr a threat: eased last 50yds* **12/1**

1m 44.22s (1.32) **Going Correction** +0.075s/f (Good) **5** Ran SP% **110.2**
Speed ratings (Par 102): **96,95,92,92,90**
CSF £4.37 TOTE £1.70: £1.40, £1.80; EX 4.30.
Owner H R H Sultan Ahmad Shah **Bred** Barry Walters Farms **Trained** Beckhampton, Wilts

FOCUS
A fair handicap. The form seems sound enough and the winner didn't need to match his Pontefract effort recently.

4751 BUCKLEY FAMILY CELEBRATING REBECCA BELLARD'S 21ST H'CAP 1m 2f 95y
8:10 (8:10) (Class 5) (0-75,78) 3-Y-O **£2,587** (£770; £384; £192) **Stalls** Centre

Form RPR
011 **1** **Dubawi Dancer**^{15} [4236] 3-9-0 **66**.................................... PaulHanagan 2 84+
(William Haggas) *hld up: effrt over 3f out: drvn to ld over 1f out: styd on wl* **1/1**^{1}

2551 **2** 2 ¾ **Area Fifty One**^{7} [4489] 3-9-7 **78** 6ex............................ JamesRogers$^{(5)}$ 1 87
(William Muir) *on trcking ldr: led narrowly over 3f out: hdd over 1f out: kpt on same pce* **6/1**^{2}

-434 **3** 1 ¼ **Alshazah**^{18} [4158] 3-9-4 **70**... JamesMillman 6 77
(Rod Millman) *hld up detached in last: hdwy over 4f out: effrt 3f out: edgd rt: wnt 3rd 1f out: one pce* **15/2**^{3}

150 **4** 4 ½ **Protractor (IRE)**^{30} [3740] 3-9-6 **72**.................................... MichaelHills 3 70
(B W Hills) *led: qcknd 4f out: hdd over 2f out: wknd over 1f out* **8/1**

6601 **5** 7 **Barnum (USA)**^{10} [4403] 3-8-4 **56** 6ex............................. JamesSullivan 7 40
(Michael Easterby) *t.k.h: trckd ldr: drvn 4f out: hung lft and wknd over 1f out* **16/1**

2m 15.95s (-0.05) **Going Correction** +0.075s/f (Good) **5** Ran SP% **109.5**
Speed ratings (Par 100): **103,100,99,96,90**
CSF £3.41 TOTE £1.80: £1.30, £1.80; EX 3.20.
Owner F W Golding, E Kirtland & N A Callaghan **Bred** Allan Munnis & Laurance Walwin **Trained** Newmarket, Suffolk

FOCUS
Only five runners but the pace seemed fair and that suited the winner. They raced towards the stands' side, but not against the rail. The form seems sound and the winner was value for further.

4752 ANDREW & SUZANNE ARE GETTING MARRIED H'CAP 1m 3f 200y
8:40 (8:41) (Class 5) (0-75,75) 3-Y-O **£2,587** (£770; £384; £192) **Stalls** High

Form RPR
60-3 **1** **Lordofthehouse (IRE)**^{22} [4005] 3-8-6 **60**........................ PaulHanagan 4 70+
(William Haggas) *dwlt: led after 1f: qcknd over 3f out: narrowly hdd over 1f out: styd on to ld last 100yds: edgd lft and kpt on wl* **13/8**^{2}

502 **2** 1 **Man Of God (IRE)**^{15} [4236] 3-9-6 **74**............................ WilliamBuick 3 82
(John Gosden) *trckd ldr: drvn over 3f out: narrow ld over 1f out: edgd rt: hdd and no ex last 100yds* **11/8**^{1}

521- **3** 4 **Mazagee (FR)**^{309} [6512] 3-9-7 **75**................................ DarryllHolland 5 77
(David Lanigan) *hld up in last: effrt over 4f out: outpcd over 3f out: rallied over 1f out: sn wknd* **15/2**

5002 **4** 3 **Singzak**^{12} [4367] 3-8-7 **61**.. JamesSullivan 1 58
(Michael Easterby) *led 1f: trckd ldrs: drvn over 4f out: wknd over 1f out* **9/2**^{3}

2m 34.75s (0.75) **Going Correction** +0.075s/f (Good) **4** Ran SP% **110.1**
Speed ratings (Par 100): **100,99,96,94**
CSF £4.34 TOTE £2.90; EX 3.50.
Owner Lael Stable **Bred** Lael Stables **Trained** Newmarket, Suffolk
■ Stewards' Enquiry : William Buick caution: used whip down shoulder in the forehand.

FOCUS
The action unfolded stands' side in the straight. There wasn't much pace on early but the time didn't compare unfavourably with the opening older-horse Class 5 handicap. The winner is getting his act together.
T/Plt: £16.60 to a £1 stake. Pool of £56,202.00 - 2,469.87 winning tickets. T/Qpdt: £11.50 to a £1 stake. Pool of £4,795.00 - 307.95 winning tickets. WG

4544 LINGFIELD (L-H)
Friday, August 5

OFFICIAL GOING: Turf course - good to soft (7.6); all-weather - standard
Wind: Light, behind Weather: Fine, warm

4753 SPORTS 360 KINGS OF FOOTBALL MAIDEN STKS (TURF) 1m 6f
2:10 (2:10) (Class 5) 3-Y-O+ **£2,658** (£785; £392) **Stalls** High

Form RPR
4064 **1** **Wayward Glance**^{13} [4336] 3-9-0 **80**.................................. JamieSpencer 1 78+
(Michael Bell) *mde all: kicked on over 3f out: drvn over 2f out: maintained gallop and in n.d over 1f out* **15/8**^{1}

6-0 **2** 8 **Rien Ne Vas Plus (IRE)**^{103} [1549] 3-8-6 0.................. LouisBeuzelin$^{(3)}$ 8 66+
(Sir Michael Stoute) *hld up in 5th: prog over 3f out: drvn to chse wnr wl over 2f out: no imp over 1f out: eased whn no ch last 100yds* **13/2**

0-0 **3** 1 ¼ **Mancunian (IRE)**^{77} [2257] 3-9-0 0............................ WilliamCarson 7 61
(John Best) *hld up in 6th: rdn and prog over 3f out: chsd ldng pair 2f out: no real imp after* **66/1**

00 **4** shd **Himalayan Moon**^{16} [4208] 4-9-8 0...................................... JackMitchell 6 56?
(Ian Wood) *hld up last: lot to do whn sed to make prog over 3f out: kpt on to chal for 3rd fnl f: no ch* **100/1**

5 9 **Scotsbrook Cloud**^{10} 6-9-10 0.................................... RichardEvans$^{(3)}$ 2 48
(David Evans) *hld up in last trio: outpcd and shkn up over 3f out: nvr on terms after: plugged on* **33/1**

5-2 **6** 13 **Jamr**^{16} [4208] 3-9-0 0...(v) TedDurcan 5 30
(Saeed Bin Suroor) *dwlt: trckd ldng pair: chsd wnr over 3f out to wl over 2f out: wknd qckly* **2/1**^{2}

2544 **7** 1 **High Samana**^{23} [3978] 3-9-0 **73**......................................(v^{1}) JimCrowley 10 29
(Ralph Beckett) *chsd wnr: reminders 5f out: lost 2nd and wknd over 3f out* **8/1**

62 **8** 10 **Fairy Pose**^{25} [3907] 3-8-9 0.. EddieAhern 3 10
(Amanda Perrett) *trckd ldng trio: rdn over 4f out: sn wknd: t.o* **6/1**^{3}

0 **9** 2 ½ **Veradis**^{64} [2639] 3-8-9 0.. LukeMorris 9 —
(Clive Cox) *dwlt: a in last trio: pushed along 1/2-way: wknd over 3f out: t.o* **66/1**

3m 13.3s (3.30) **Going Correction** +0.425s/f (Yiel)
WFA 3 from 4yo+ 13lb **9** Ran SP% **113.8**
Speed ratings (Par 103): **107,102,101,101,96 89,88,82,81**
Tote Swingers: 1&2 £3.40, 1&3 £19.40, 2&3 £52.80 CSF £14.27 TOTE £3.90: £1.10, £2.40, £8.50; EX 18.30.
Owner The Queen **Bred** The Queen **Trained** Newmarket, Suffolk

FOCUS
With a couple of the market leaders disappointing, the form of this maiden is hard to gauge behind the easy winner. It's doubtful if he needed to improve.
Jamr Official explanation: jockey said gelding was unsuited by the good to soft ground
Fairy Pose Official explanation: jockey said filly was unsuited by the good to soft ground

4754 KH ELECTRICAL SERVICES H'CAP (TURF) 1m 2f
2:40 (2:40) (Class 6) (0-65,65) 3-Y-O+ **£1,908** (£563; £281) **Stalls** Low

Form RPR
0-01 **1** **Count Ceprano (IRE)**^{8} [4454] 7-9-11 **65**...................... SimonPearce$^{(3)}$ 9 74
(Lydia Pearce) *hld up last: stdy prog fr 3f out: chsd ldr over 1f out: clsd to ld last 150yds: pushed out* **10/3**^{2}

-400 **2** 1 **Rosy Dawn**^{177} [466] 6-8-10 **47**...................................... WilliamCarson 3 54
(Mark Hoad) *led: kicked at least 5 l clr over 4f out: hrd rdn over 2f out: hdd last 150yds: kpt on gamely* **11/1**

-065 **3** 1 ¾ **Jodawes (USA)**^{15} [4249] 4-9-12 **63**.................................... JimCrowley 8 67
(John Best) *hld up in last trio: rdn 3f out: prog on outer over 2f out: hanging and hung rt over 1f out: kpt on* **7/1**^{3}

25S3 **4** 3 **Aviso (GER)**^{8} [4465] 7-9-9 **63**...................................... RichardEvans$^{(3)}$ 5 61
(David Evans) *trckd ldr after 3f: rdn and nt qckn wl over 2f out: lost 2nd over 1f out: fdd* **3/1**^{1}

5002 **5** 4 ½ **Trecase**^{13} [4317] 4-9-0 **51**..(t) EddieAhern 4 40
(Tony Carroll) *chsd ldr 3f: drvn 3f out: nt qckn and lost pl over 2f out: wknd over 1f out* **3/1**^{1}

0050 **6** 14 **Prince Of Thebes (IRE)**^{9} [4444] 10-9-3 **54**...................... J-PGuillambert 6 15
(Michael Attwater) *dwlt and rousted along early: a in last trio: wknd over 2f out: eased: t.o* **16/1**

2m 14.44s (3.94) **Going Correction** +0.425s/f (Yiel)
WFA 3 from 4yo+ 9lb **6** Ran SP% **109.5**
Speed ratings (Par 101): **101,100,98,96,92 81**
Tote Swingers: 1&2 £4.80, 1&3 £2.80, 2&3 £4.50 CSF £34.59 CT £123.10 TOTE £4.10: £2.10, £3.40; EX 33.50.
Owner Mrs Louise Marsh **Bred** Pendley Farm **Trained** Newmarket, Suffolk

FOCUS
A weak handicap. it was sound run thanks to the runer-up, who sets the standard.
Aviso(GER) Official explanation: jockey said gelding was unsuited by the good to soft ground
Trecase Official explanation: jockey said gelding was unsuited by the good to soft ground

4755 SPORTS 360 SPECIALISE IN GAMING INDUSTRY H'CAP (TURF) 1m 3f 106y
3:10 (3:10) (Class 5) (0-70,70) 3-Y-O+ **£2,658** (£785; £392) **Stalls** High

Form RPR
0-00 **1** **Distant Waters**^{13} [4322] 4-8-9 **51** oh1.................................. JimCrowley 5 61
(Alan Jarvis) *trckd ldrs: prog to go 2nd over 2f out: sn rdn: led wl over 1f out: styd on* **12/1**

1-05 **2** 1 ¼ **Flying Power**^{12} [4367] 3-9-4 **70**...................................... TedDurcan 1 76
(David Lanigan) *awkward s: settled in rr: shkn up 3f out: prog 2f out but in ungainly style: wnt 2nd 1f out: no imp on wnr after* **4/1**^{2}

2302 **3** 2 **Maher (USA)**^{7} [4510] 3-9-1 **70**.................................... AdamBeschizza$^{(3)}$ 7 73
(David Simcock) *hld up in last: pushed along 4f out and stl there: prog u.p 2f out: kpt on to go 3rd ins fnl f: nvr able to threaten* **15/8**^{1}

45 **4** 2 ¼ **Supa Seeker (USA)**^{18} [4154] 5-9-5 **61**...................................... JamesDoyle 3 60
(Tony Carroll) *trckd ldr: led 5f out and upped the pce: hdd wl over 1f out: steadily fdd* **4/1**^{2}

2556 **5** 7 **Novel Dancer**^{13} [4338] 3-9-0 **69**...................................... SeanLevey$^{(3)}$ 6 56
(Richard Hannon) *trckd ldng pair: wnt 2nd 4f out to over 2f out: sn btn u.p* **11/2**^{3}

0424 **6** *40* **Dare To Bare (IRE)**[29] 3770 3-9-3 **69**................................ EddieAhern 2 —
(Amanda Perrett) *led to 5f out: wknd qckly over 3f out: t.o* **8/1**

2m 36.18s (4.68) **Going Correction** +0.425s/f (Yiel)
WFA 3 from 4yo+ 10lb **6** Ran SP% **109.0**
Speed ratings (Par 103): **99,98,96,95,89 60**
Tote Swingers: 1&2 £5.70, 1&3 £3.90, 2&3 £2.30 CSF £54.88 TOTE £14.00: £3.80, £1.90; EX 62.60.
Owner G E Dudfield **Bred** Natton House Thoroughbreds **Trained** Twyford, Bucks

FOCUS
An ordinary handicap and the early pace didn't seem that strong. Weak, dubious form which has been rated negatively.
Dare To Bare(IRE) Official explanation: jockey said gelding was unsuited by the good to soft ground

4756 MAYBE GAGA PERFORMS HERE 13TH AUGUST FILLIES' (S) STKS 6f (P)
3:40 (3:41) (Class 6) 2-Y-O **£1,533** (£452; £226) **Stalls** Low

Form RPR

00 **1** **Miserere Mei (IRE)**[47] 3200 2-8-9 0..........................(p) MartinHarley(3) 4 61
(Alan McCabe) *trckd ldrs: prog on outer fr 2f out to chse ldr jst over 1f out: styd on u.p to ld last 75yds* **33/1**

2035 **2** *½* **Aquasulis (IRE)**[20] 4085 2-9-0 68.................................. SeanLevey(3) 8 64
(David Evans) *wl away fr wd draw: led: rdn 2f out: edgd rt u.p fnl f: worn down last 75yds* **10/3**[2]

002 **3** *2* **Flirty Gerty (IRE)**[22] 4021 2-8-9 60..........................(p) RossAtkinson(3) 2 53
(Tom Dascombe) *trckd ldrs: effrt on inner 2f out: disp 2nd over 1f out: nt qckn and edgd rt fnl f* **10/1**

6353 **4** *4* **River Nova**[34] 3631 2-8-12 49..(v[1]) JimCrowley 5 41
(Alan Jarvis) *pressed ldng pair: shkn up to chal 2f out: nt qckn wl over 1f out: tamely outpcd* **9/1**

4523 **5** *2* **Emma Jean (IRE)**[1] 4704 2-8-12 58................................. PatCosgrave 6 35
(J S Moore) *chsd ldrs but sn pushed along: struggling over 2f out: no imp after* **9/2**[3]

6335 **6** *¾* **Reina Sofia**[9] 4430 2-8-12 63..(t) LukeMorris 9 33
(Tony Carroll) *s.s: nvr looked keen and sn drvn in last pair: modest late prog* **9/2**[3]

046 **7** *2* **Lilygloves**[9] 4430 2-8-9 0.. MatthewDavies(3) 1 27
(Mick Channon) *dwlt: mostly in last trio: u.p by 1/2-way: nvr figured* **20/1**

00 **8** *1 ¾* **Waterloo Girl**[15] 4232 2-8-12 0.................................. FrankieMcDonald 3 22
(Michael Blanshard) *dwlt: a in last trio and struggling after 2f* **66/1**

3443 **9** *hd* **Red Hearts (IRE)**[11] 4391 2-9-0 73......................... AdamBeschizza(3) 7 26
(Julia Feilden) *pressed ldr: drvn to chal jst over 2f out: wknd rapidly over 1f out* **3/1**[1]

1m 13.95s (2.05) **Going Correction** +0.125s/f (Slow) **9** Ran SP% **112.7**
Speed ratings (Par 89): **91,90,87,82,79 78,76,73,73**
Tote Swingers: 1&2 £16.50, 1&3 £26.40, 2&3 £5.30 CSF £135.74 TOTE £43.10: £7.60, £1.20, £2.50; EX 234.80.The winner was bought in for 9,100gns.
Owner Mrs Z Wentworth **Bred** Rathbarry Stud **Trained** Averham Park, Notts
■ Stewards' Enquiry : Adam Beschizza Fine: £80, failed to weigh-in.

FOCUS
A fair seller for fillies. The form looks pretty solid.

NOTEBOOK
Miserere Mei(IRE) had been beaten a long way in two turf maidens, though she had a valid excuse second time. She was always travelling well behind the leaders and showed a good attitude to get on top of the leader close to the line. The form is ordinary, but after being bought in for 9,100gns at the auction she could be the type for a winter campaign on Polytrack.
Aquasulis(IRE) showed herself to be effective at this level on turf and Polytrack earlier in the summer and made a bold bid to make every yard. She lacks the scope of the winner. (op 11-4)
Flirty Gerty(IRE) improved for the fitting of cheekpieces when runner-up in a Leicester seller last month and ran well in them again, but she may not have been helped by making her effort tight against the inside rail. (op 7-1 tchd 13-2)
River Nova, third in a couple of sellers, was tried in a visor and had every chance but didn't improve for the headgear. (op 10-1 tchd 11-1 and 17-2)
Emma Jean(IRE), making a quick reappearance after finishing a remote third in a Chepstow nursery the previous evening, never looked that happy. (op 7-1)
Reina Sofia, making her debut in a seller in a first-time tongue-tie, completely missed the break. (op 6-1)
Red Hearts(IRE) was best in at the weights, but has become disappointing on turf and ran another tame race on this Polytrack debut. (tchd 11-4)

4757 SPORTS360.CO.UK NOVICE STKS 5f (P)
4:10 (4:10) (Class 5) 2-Y-O **£2,658** (£785; £392) **Stalls** High

Form RPR

12 **1** **Quite A Thing**[35] 3570 2-8-11 0... SebSanders 4 86+
(Sir Mark Prescott Bt) *trckd ldr: pushed along 2f out: shkn up to ld jst over 1f out: r.o wl: readily* **1/1**[1]

413 **2** *2* **Mr Majeika (IRE)**[44] 3284 2-9-2 82................................ SeanLevey(3) 3 85
(Richard Hannon) *led: urged along jst over 2f out: hdd jst over 1f out: kpt on wl but no match for wnr* **12/1**

201 **3** *2 ¼* **Hidden Passion (USA)**[30] 3722 2-8-11 84..............(t) LouisBeuzelin(3) 1 73
(Brian Meehan) *trckd ldng pair: rdn 2f out: nt qckn and no imp over 1f out: one pce* **9/4**[2]

1 **4** *1 ¾* **Waseem Faris (IRE)**[22] 3997 2-9-2 0......................... MartinHarley(3) 5 71
(Mick Channon) *stdd s: t.k.h: hld up last: effrt 2f out: sn outpcd: wknd fnl f* **7/2**[3]

59.71 secs (0.91) **Going Correction** +0.125s/f (Slow) **4** Ran SP% **110.7**
Speed ratings (Par 94): **97,93,90,87**
CSF £11.93 TOTE £2.10; EX 7.60.
Owner Lady Fairhaven & The Hon C & H Broughton **Bred** Whitsbury Manor Stud & Pigeon House Stud **Trained** Newmarket, Suffolk

FOCUS
A fascinating little novice event with all four runners previous winners. Only the front pair's positions changed during the contest. The winner was back to form and could make an impact at Listed level.

NOTEBOOK
Quite A Thing ◆, who was very impressive on her turf debut here, had excuses for her subsequent defeat at odds of 1-4 in a three-runner event at Beverley (gave away plenty of ground at the start) and the winner has gone in again since. Loaded with a blanket for stalls entry here, she broke on terms this time and although she was being pushed along on the home bend, she still picked up the leader in nice style and won going away. There is lot more to come from this filly. (op 6-4 tchd 13-8 in a place)
Mr Majeika(IRE), who reportedly finished lame when third of four at Kempton last time, tried to make all and kept on well, but was up against a nice filly. He probably needs a stiffer test now. (tchd 11-1 and 14-1)
Hidden Passion(USA) had no problem landing long odds-on in a Bath maiden last month, though that form was let down by the runner-up at Sandown the previous evening. She could never get on terms with the front pair and this looks about as good as she is. (op 2-1 tchd 15-8)
Waseem Faris(IRE), a very easy winner over three rivals on his Bath debut, raced keenly in last place but never managed to land a blow. This track may not have been ideal for this big colt and he is worth another chance. (op 5-2)

4758 SPORTS 360 LEADERS IN SPORTS ADVERTISING H'CAP 7f (P)
4:40 (4:40) (Class 6) (0-60,60) 3-Y-O **£1,533** (£452; £226) **Stalls** Low

Form RPR

-060 **1** **Diamond Run**[13] 4340 3-8-13 **52**... SebSanders 3 65+
(J W Hills) *pressed ldrs: led jst over 2f out: drvn clr over 1f out: styd on wl* **14/1**

0045 **2** *3* **Putin (IRE)**[17] 4179 3-8-13 **52**.. AndreaAtzeni 4 57
(Derek Haydn Jones) *led to over 4f out: lost pl over 3f out: drvn in 4th over 2f out: rallied over 1f out: styd on to take 2nd last strides* **16/1**

0534 **3** *nk* **Justbookie Dot Com (IRE)**[3] 4640 3-9-3 **59**............. RichardEvans(3) 8 63
(David Evans) *trckd ldng trio: rdn to chal over 2f out: nt qckn wl over 1f out: wl hld by wnr after: lost 2nd last strides* **6/1**[2]

0000 **4** *¾* **Paperetto**[46] 3230 3-9-4 **60**... SeanLevey(3) 12 62+
(Robert Mills) *hld up towards rr disputing 9th: effrt over 2f out: rdn and styd on fr over 1f out: nrst fin* **10/1**

-040 **5** *½* **Pearl Opera**[30] 3742 3-9-1 **54**.. ShaneKelly 13 55+
(Denis Coakley) *s.i.s: hld up in last trio and wl off the pce: trapped bhd rivals on inner fr over 2f out to jst over 1f out: shkn up and styd on wl: no ch* **12/1**

-322 **6** *1 ¼* **Love Nest**[32] 3677 3-9-0 **53**.. EddieAhern 9 50+
(John Dunlop) *hld up towards rr disputing 9th: nt clr run 2f out: shkn up over 1f out: kpt on but nvr qckly enough to threaten* **11/4**[1]

050 **7** *2* **Lightning Spirit**[13] 4320 3-9-1 **57**................................ MartinHarley(3) 1 49
(Gary Moore) *hld up in midfield on inner: n.m.r over 2f out: sme prog over 1f out: fdd ins fnl f* **6/1**[2]

5-00 **8** *2 ½* **Dusty Bluebells (IRE)**[59] 2790 3-9-7 **60**........................... LukeMorris 6 45
(J S Moore) *in tch in midfield but pushed along after 2f: stl same pl over 2f out: sn btn* **12/1**

000 **9** *¾* **Gay Gallivanter**[17] 4185 3-9-2 **55**................................ PatCosgrave 11 38
(Michael Quinn) *s.i.s: rdn in last trio over 4f out and wl off the pce: nvr a factor* **33/1**

0501 **10** *2 ¼* **Litotes**[46] 3226 3-8-10 **54**..(p) MarkCoumbe(5) 14 31
(Michael Attwater) *w ldrs: led over 4f out to jst over 2f out: sn btn: wknd qckly fnl f* **12/1**

-255 **11** *4* **Trojan Rocket (IRE)**[24] 3956 3-9-5 **58**......................... J-PGuillambert 2 24
(George Prodromou) *hld up in midfield: nt a lot of room over 2f out: sn rdn and wknd qckly* **9/1**[3]

0000 **12** *1 ½* **Hertford Street**[30] 3724 3-8-12 **51**................................ JimCrowley 10 13
(Peter Makin) *struggling bdly in last after 2f: a wl bhd* **25/1**

1006 **13** *½* **Henrys Air**[2] 4657 3-9-1 **54**.. RobbieFitzpatrick 5 15
(David Bridgwater) *chsd ldrs sn pushed along: wknd rapidly u.p over 2f out* **33/1**

1m 26.02s (1.22) **Going Correction** +0.125s/f (Slow) **13** Ran SP% **119.7**
Speed ratings (Par 98): **98,94,94,93,92 91,89,86,85,82 78,76,75**
Tote Swingers: 1&2 £29.40, 1&3 £17.60, 2&3 £14.10 CSF £216.38 CT £1492.07 TOTE £21.70: £6.00, £4.00, £2.70; EX 250.00.
Owner Hills' Angels **Bred** T W Bloodstock Ltd **Trained** Upper Lambourn, Berks

FOCUS
A moderate handicap. The first three were always prominent and the form seems sound enough amongst the principals.
Diamond Run ◆ Official explanation: trainer's rep said, regarding apparent improvement in form, that the filly had benefited from the change of tactics by being allowed to make the running.

4759 HOOPER NAYLOR FRIEND H'CAP 6f (P)
5:10 (5:10) (Class 6) (0-60,60) 3-Y-O+ **£1,533** (£452; £226) **Stalls** Low

Form RPR

0000 **1** **Valmina**[13] 4322 4-9-6 **56**...(t) LukeMorris 1 68
(Tony Carroll) *in tch in midfield: prog over 2f out: chsd ldr wl over 1f out: cajoled along to ld last 150yds: sn clr* **4/1**[1]

6251 **2** *3 ¼* **Jimmy Ryan (IRE)**[16] 4207 10-9-10 **60**.......................(t) J-PGuillambert 4 62
(Tim McCarthy) *chsd ldr: clsng whn lft in ld sn after 2f out: drvn over 1f out: hdd and one pce last 150yds* **5/1**[3]

0400 **3** *nk* **One Cool Chick**[20] 4086 3-8-7 **50** ow2............................... SeanLevey(3) 3 50
(John Bridger) *chsd ldrs early: lost pl and in rr over 3f out: rdn over 2f out: styd on again over 1f out: clsng on runner-up fin* **11/1**

0406 **4** *1 ¼* **Loose Quality (USA)**[17] 4183 3-8-8 **55**..............(v[1]) BrendanPowell(7) 11 51
(Chris Gordon) *s.i.s: hld up in last trio: effrt 2f out: rdn and nt qckn over 1f out: styd on fnl f* **5/1**[3]

-632 **5** *2* **Louphole**[128] 1045 9-9-9 **59**.. EddieAhern 12 50
(J R Jenkins) *s.i.s: hld up in last trio: prog to chse ldng pair over 1f out: fnd nil: wknd ins fnl f* **6/1**

0035 **6** *4* **Doctor Hilary**[24] 3939 9-9-5 **55**..................................(v) WilliamCarson 9 33
(Mark Hoad) *trckd ldrs on outer: shkn up whn rn wd bnd 2f out: wl btn after* **9/2**[2]

-640 **7** *3 ½* **Heavenly Pursuit**[18] 4162 3-8-10 **53**......................... MatthewDavies(3) 5 19
(Jim Boyle) *chsd ldr: drvn over 2f out: sn lost pl and wknd* **8/1**

-000 **8** *6* **Private Olley**[20] 4086 4-9-10 **60**...............................(bt) SebSanders 8 —
(Harry Dunlop) *t.k.h: led and clr: hung bdly rt bnd 2f out: sn hdd and gave up: t.o* **16/1**

1m 13.47s (1.57) **Going Correction** +0.125s/f (Slow)
WFA 3 from 4yo+ 4lb **8** Ran SP% **111.1**
Speed ratings (Par 101): **94,89,89,87,84 79,74,66**
Tote Swingers: 1&2 £4.00, 1&3 £9.60, 2&3 £7.60 CSF £22.61 CT £168.19 TOTE £4.70: £1.90, £1.50, £4.20; EX 23.90.
Owner Mayden Stud **Bred** Mayden Stud, J A And D S Dewhurst **Trained** Cropthorne, Worcs

FOCUS
Another moderate handicap and the clues were in the market. the winner is rated back to his C&D form of this time last year.
Private Olley Official explanation: jockey said colt was unsteerable

T/Plt: £1,643.60 to a £1 stake. Pool of £60,679.66 - 26.95 winning tickets. T/Qpdt: £85.50 to a £1 stake. Pool of £4,685.72 - 40.40 winning tickets. JN

[4550] NEWMARKET (R-H)

Friday, August 5

OFFICIAL GOING: Good (7.8)

Wind: Light across Weather: Cloudy with sunny spells

4760 DOWNLOAD THE BLUE SQUARE BET APP NURSERY — 7f

5:50 (5:50) (Class 4) (0-85,85) 2-Y-O — **£3,881** (£1,155; £577; £288) **Stalls** High

Form				RPR
603	**1**		**Maroosh**[37] 3511 2-8-10 **74** .... MartinDwyer 2 (Brian Meehan) *chsd ldr tl led over 1f out: sn rdn: edgd rt ins fnl f: styd on u.p* **10/1**	76
0433	**2**	*nk*	**Roedean (IRE)**[14] 4277 2-8-13 **77** .... RichardHughes 5 (Richard Hannon) *led at stdy pce tl qcknd over 2f out: hdd over 1f out: rallied and edgd rt ins fnl f: styd on* **10/1**	78
14	**3**	*2*	**Citizen's Charter (USA)**[29] 3776 2-9-2 **80** .... FrankieDettori 6 (Mahmood Al Zarooni) *chsd ldrs: nt clr run over 2f out: swtchd rt over 1f out: sn rdn: styd on* **4/1**[3]	76
401	**4**	*2*	**Fresa**[18] 4140 2-8-8 **72** .... StevieDonohoe 7 (Sir Mark Prescott Bt) *dwlt: hld up: rdn and swtchd rt over 1f out: edgd lft ins fnl f: r.o: nt rch ldrs* **5/2**[2]	62+
402	**5**	*3 ¼*	**Casa Bex**[18] 4159 2-8-5 **69** .... MartinLane 1 (Philip McBride) *prom: rdn over 2f out: edgd lft over 1f out: sn wknd* **16/1**	51
41	**6**	*3 ½*	**Shamaal Nibras (USA)**[46] 3237 2-9-7 **85** .... JamieSpencer 3 (Ed Dunlop) *hld up in tch: rdn over 2f out: wknd fnl f* **13/8**[1]	57

1m 28.42s (2.72) **Going Correction** +0.20s/f (Good) — **6** Ran SP% **110.7**

Speed ratings (Par 96): **92,91,89,87,83 79**

Tote Swingers: 1&2 £3.70, 1&3 £2.90, 2&3 £2.70 CSF £93.03 TOTE £11.80: £3.50, £2.80; EX 58.90.

Owner Trelawny II **Bred** Brightwalton Stud **Trained** Manton, Wilts

■ Stewards' Enquiry : Jamie Spencer caution: careless riding.

FOCUS

Stands' side track used with stalls on far side except 1m2f: centre. They only went a modest pace upfront and the first two virtually had it between themselves when the tempo belatedly lifted. The form is probably best treated with some caution, bearing in mind the way the race unfolded. The time, well outside standard, reflected the steady early gallop.

NOTEBOOK

Maroosh coped well with the step up in trip on his nursery bow. He showed a genuine attitude in a close-fought finish. He is likely to progress again with this experience under his belt, but he will need to, once the handicapper has had his say. (op 8-1 tchd 11-1)

Roedean(IRE) has yet to open her own account after five starts. That said, there was little wrong with her effort here and she has shown enough ability to more than indicate a race will fall her way at some point. (op 15-2)

Citizen's Charter(USA) impressed on paddock inspection and travelled well in the race, probably being the last off the bridle. But the sedate early pace, added to the fact he had to be switched for a run after being short of room, prevented him from taking closer order in the finish. He deserves another chance and should build on his debut success at Newcastle. (op 7-2)

Fresa, who won an Ayr maiden over this trip, was most unfavoured by the manner in which the race was run. Held up off a slow pace, she'd have much preferred a true test and never threatened to get involved. (op 3-1)

Casa Bex travelled on the outside and may have benefited from some cover to help. He would probably be more competitive at a lesser track, having shaped with some encouragement at Yarmouth previously. (op 12-1)

Shamaal Nibras(USA), on the face of it, appears to have been given a high enough mark for running away with a 6f Wolverhampton maiden in June. (op 2-1)

4761 MECCA BINGO IPHONE APP (S) STKS — 7f

6:20 (6:20) (Class 5) 2-Y-O — **£3,234** (£962; £481; £240) **Stalls** High

Form				RPR
4	**1**		**Tweedle Dee**[18] 4159 2-8-9 0 ow1 .... TomQueally 8 (Noel Quinlan) *hld up: hdwy over 2f out: led over 1f out: rdn ins fnl f: r.o* **4/1**[2]	61+
1	**2**	*1 ¾*	**Speedi Mouse**[11] 4391 2-8-13 0 .... MartinLane 5 (Philip McBride) *dwlt: sn chsng ldrs: rdn over 1f out: styd on same pce ins fnl f* **11/4**[1]	60
04	**3**	*½*	**King Kenobi (IRE)**[11] 4391 2-8-13 0 .... JamesDoyle 4 (J S Moore) *chsd ldr: led wl over 1f out: sn rdn and hdd: styd on same pce ins fnl f* **6/1**[3]	59
3003	**4**	*3 ¼*	**Yammos (IRE)**[7] 4512 2-8-13 74 .... (v) SamHitchcott 10 (Mick Channon) *hld up: hdwy u.p over 2f out: nt clr run and swtchd rt over 1f out: styd on same pce ins fnl f* **4/1**[2]	51
2333	**5**	*2 ¼*	**Queen Of The Hop**[24] 3955 2-8-8 57 .... (p) LiamKeniry 6 (J S Moore) *led: rdn and hdd over 2f out: wknd fnl f* **12/1**	40
000	**6**	*hd*	**Make Up**[4] 4614 2-8-8 0 .... RichardHughes 3 (Richard Hannon) *chsd ldrs: reminders 1/2-way: led over 2f out: rdn and hdd wl over 1f out: wknd fnl f* **12/1**	39
0	**7**	*7*	**George Tilehurst**[11] 4384 2-8-10 0 .... RossAtkinson(3) 9 (J S Moore) *s.i.s: rdn over 2f out: wkng whn hung lft over 1f out* **50/1**	26
5	**8**	*8*	**River Valley**[15] 4250 2-8-13 0 .... NeilCallan 2 (Gary Moore) *s.i.s: hld up: hdwy over 4f out: wknd 2f out* **14/1**	5
002	**9**	*1 ½*	**Masters Club**[11] 4391 2-8-13 0 .... KirstyMilczarek 7 (John Ryan) *chsd ldrs: rdn over 2f out: wknd over 1f out* **8/1**	1

1m 28.33s (2.63) **Going Correction** +0.20s/f (Good) — **9** Ran SP% **116.1**

Speed ratings (Par 94): **92,90,89,85,83 82,74,65,64**

Tote Swingers: 1&2 £3.10, 1&3 £6.70, 2&3 £5.40 CSF £15.52 TOTE £4.50: £2.00, £1.40, £1.70; EX 19.80.There was no bid for the winner.

Owner G Wilding **Bred** G Wilding **Trained** Newmarket, Suffolk

FOCUS

A rare seller at the track, the time was marginally quicker than the preceding nursery and won in creditable style by the unexposed winner. She is rated up 10lb from her debut.

NOTEBOOK

Tweedle Dee knew sufficient to grind her way between two rivals and score convincingly in the end. There was no bid for her and she's likely to continue to be well placed by her shrewd connections, so remains of interest. (op 5-1 tchd 7-2)

Speedi Mouse was very well backed to make a winning debut at Yarmouth in a Class 6 seller in which she just obliged. Bought back for 3,400gns, she was marginally stepping up in trip here, which her pedigree suggested would be in her favour. She ran her race again but just bumped into an improver and there is no reason why she shouldn't continue to pay her way competing at this level. (op 3-1 tchd 10-3 and 7-2 in places)

King Kenobi(IRE) got closer to Speedi Mouse here than he did at Yarmouth last time, but was favoured by re-opposing on 5lb better terms with that rival. (op 12-1)

Yammos(IRE), the highest rated of the trio that had an offical handicap mark, is still without a win after six starts and is not progressing.

Masters Club Official explanation: trainer said colt was unsuited by the track

4762 BET AT BLUESQ.COM MAIDEN STKS — 7f

6:55 (6:56) (Class 5) 2-Y-O — **£3,234** (£962; £481; £240) **Stalls** High

Form				RPR
	1		**Kinglet (USA)** 2-9-3 0 .... FrankieDettori 10 (Mahmood Al Zarooni) *s.s and wnt lft: hld up: hdwy and hung lft fr over 1f out: r.o to ld post* **3/1**[2]	86+
	2	*shd*	**Most Improved (IRE)** 2-9-3 0 .... MartinDwyer 8 (Brian Meehan) *hld up in tch: led 1f out: sn edgd rt: hdd post* **9/4**[1]	86+
	3	*2 ½*	**Big Johnny D (IRE)** 2-9-3 0 .... TedDurcan 3 (John Dunlop) *hld up: hdwy 2f out: swtchd lft over 1f out: styd on same pce ins fnl f* **20/1**	78
	4	*1*	**Cryptic Choice (IRE)** 2-9-3 0 .... RobertWinston 1 (B W Hills) *dwlt: hld up: hdwy over 2f out: rdn to ld and edgd lft over 1f out: sn hdd: no ex ins fnl f* **25/1**	75
	5	*½*	**Haymarket** 2-8-10 0 .... AntiocoMurgia(7) 2 (Mahmood Al Zarooni) *chsd ldrs: led 2f out: rdn and hdd over 1f out: no ex ins fnl f* **12/1**	74
	6	*3 ½*	**Juvenal (IRE)** 2-9-3 0 .... DaneO'Neill 5 (Richard Hannon) *hld up: hdwy over 2f out: sn rdn: styd on same pce fr over 1f out* **40/1**	65+
	7	*1*	**Wrotham Heath** 2-9-3 0 .... TomQueally 12 (Sir Henry Cecil) *hld up: hdwy over 2f out: shkn up over 1f out: wknd ins fnl f* **7/2**[3]	62+
	8	*½*	**Wayne Manor (IRE)** 2-9-3 0 .... StevieDonohoe 13 (Ralph Beckett) *chsd ldrs: rdn over 2f out: wknd ins fnl f* **25/1**	61
	9	*3 ¼*	**Quixote** 2-9-3 0 .... HayleyTurner 9 (Clive Brittain) *hld up: rdn over 2f out: nvr on terms* **50/1**	52
	10	*1 ¾*	**Metalmark (IRE)** 2-9-3 0 .... AhmedAjtebi 6 (Mahmood Al Zarooni) *hld up: rdn over 2f out: a in rr* **14/1**	48
	11	*½*	**Regal Gold** 2-9-3 0 .... RichardHughes 7 (Richard Hannon) *prom tl wknd over 1f out* **20/1**	46
	12	*½*	**Alshmemi (USA)** 2-9-3 0 .... RichardHills 11 (John Gosden) *chsd ldr: pushed along over 2f out: wknd over 1f out* **12/1**	45
	13	*3 ¾*	**California English (IRE)** 2-9-3 0 .... AdamKirby 4 (Marco Botti) *s.i.s: sn rcvrd to ld: hdd 2f out: sn wknd* **33/1**	35

1m 27.24s (1.54) **Going Correction** +0.20s/f (Good) — **13** Ran SP% **124.6**

Speed ratings (Par 94): **99,98,96,94,94 90,89,88,84,82 82,81,77**

Tote Swingers: 1&2 £3.20, 1&3 £11.80, 2&3 £14.20 CSF £9.69 TOTE £4.50: £1.40, £1.20, £5.00; EX 13.20.

Owner Godolphin **Bred** Darley **Trained** Newmarket, Suffolk

■ Stewards' Enquiry : Frankie Dettori caution: careless riding.

FOCUS

Confined to unraced juveniles. Paddock inspection revealed a cluster of good-looking individuals. The front pair appeal as likely improvers with plenty of other promising types on show.

NOTEBOOK

Kinglet(USA) ◆ impressed as one of the fitter runners for this newcomers-only event. The winner is the first foal out of a Group 3 scorer, who herself hailed from a classy family. A neat-looking February foal, he was one of the last away and came from out the back to pip the favourite Most Improved on the line. He clearly possesses plenty of talent and it would be no surprise to see him stepped up in grade next time. (op 5-1)

Most Improved(IRE) ◆ cost 65,000euros and is the half-sister to a 10-11f winner. A May foal, this was a very promising debut and a Royal Lodge entry is not misplaced. With this experience behind him, he'll take the beating wherever he lines up next and is also a nice prospect. (op 5-2 tchd 15-8)

Big Johnny D(IRE) shaped with definite potential. He was green enough in his race, edging left but made up significant ground in the closing stages. His pedigree suggests he'll improve for going further and he, too, has a bright future (op 18-1 tchd 16-1)

Cryptic Choice(IRE), the first foal out of a three-time winner in the US, broke slowly but travelled sweetly into the business end of the race before being hampered late on. He'll know a lot more for next time and won't be long in opening his account. (op 28-1)

Haymarket is the fourth foal out of a mare whose other progeny have all won and on this evidence he won't be letting the side down. (op 20-1)

Juvenal(IRE) looked the stable second-string on jockey bookings but made a satisfactory debut. With plenty of stamina on the dam side, he may well improve for going further in time.

Wrotham Heath had been noted doing some pleasing homework ahead of this. An imposing type, this May foal will benefit for another winter behind him. (op 10-0 tchd 4-1)

Wayne Manor(IRE) will want a test of stamina further down the line. (op 22-1)

Alshmemi(USA) cost $550,000 and is a big model who fills the eye. He could probably have done with some cover here and, early on, wanted to do just a little bit too much on the front end. (op 9-1)

4763 GET £50 FREE PLAY AT MECCABINGO.COM H'CAP — 1m 2f

7:30 (7:30) (Class 5) (0-75,75) 3-Y-O+ — **£2,587** (£770; £384; £192) **Stalls** Centre

Form				RPR
-531	**1**		**Proud Chieftain**[21] 4060 3-9-5 **75** .... JamesDoyle 10 (Clifford Lines) *a.p: rdn to ld and edgd rt wl ins fnl f* **2/1**[1]	88
5-4	**2**	*nk*	**Figaro**[36] 3543 3-9-4 **74** .... JamieSpencer 1 (William Haggas) *led: pushed along over 3f out: hrd rdn fr over 1f out: hdd wl ins fnl f* **7/2**[2]	86
2206	**3**	*3 ½*	**Chain Of Events**[14] 4280 4-10-0 **75** .... HayleyTurner 6 (Neil King) *chsd ldr: rdn over 1f out: styd on same pce ins fnl f* **8/1**	80
0405	**4**	*1 ¼*	**Classically (IRE)**[51] 3042 5-9-5 **66** .... NeilCallan 9 (Peter Hedger) *hld up: hdwy over 2f out: rdn over 1f out: no ex ins fnl f* **33/1**	69
0645	**5**	*1 ½*	**No Larking (IRE)**[15] 4244 3-8-8 **64** .... DaneO'Neill 11 (Henry Candy) *hld up: plld hrd: rdn and edgd lft over 1f out: nvr trbld ldrs* **16/1**	64
2310	**6**	*½*	**Trumpington Street (IRE)**[14] 4290 3-9-5 **75** .... NickyMackay 2 (John Gosden) *prom: rdn over 1f out: wknd fnl f* **7/1**	74
30-5	**7**	*nk*	**Ryton Runner (IRE)**[125] 1096 3-9-4 **74** .... RobertHavlin 4 (John Gosden) *s.i.s: hld up: hdwy over 2f out: wknd over 1f out* **4/1**[3]	72
-530	**8**	*1*	**New River (IRE)**[11] 4385 3-9-4 **74** .... RichardHughes 5 (Richard Hannon) *chsd ldrs: rdn over 2f out: wknd fnl f* **16/1**	70
-330	**9**	*1*	**Cry Alot Boy**[21] 4060 8-8-11 **58** .... PatCosgrave 8 (Kevin Morgan) *dwlt: hld up: plld hrd: rdn: hung lft and wknd over 1f out* **25/1**	52

2m 7.10s (1.60) **Going Correction** +0.20s/f (Good)

WFA 3 from 4yo+ 9lb — **9** Ran SP% **117.7**

Speed ratings (Par 103): **101,100,97,96,95 95,95,94,93**

Tote Swingers: 1&2 £2.10, 2&3 £4.70 CSF £9.16 CT £45.99 TOTE £3.20: £1.20, £1.10, £2.20; EX 12.30.

Owner Prima Racing Partnership **Bred** John James **Trained** Exning, Suffolk

■ Stewards' Enquiry : Jamie Spencer caution: used whip with excessive frequency.

FOCUS
There wasn't a great deal of early pace in this race and the time was 5.2secs outside standard. However there are grounds for thinking the first two are ahead of their marks. The third has a pretty solid record here.

4764 PLAY RAINBOW RICHES AT BLUESQ.COM CONDITIONS STKS 1m 2f
8:00 (8:01) (Class 3) 3-Y-O £7,158 (£2,143; £1,071; £535; £267) Stalls Centre

Form RPR
1425 1 **Barbican**69 2507 3-9-0 96 TomQueally 1 106
(Alan Bailey) *a.p: chsd ldr over 1f out: rdn to ld ins fnl f: r.o* 9/2[3]
-111 2 1 **Halfsin (IRE)**20 4103 3-9-0 98 AdamKirby 6 104
(Marco Botti) *chsd ldrs: led over 3f out: rdn and hung lft fr over 2f out: hdd ins fnl f: kpt on* 11/8[1]
3200 3 1 3/4 **Moriarty (IRE)**10 4411 3-9-0 105 RichardHughes 5 101
(Richard Hannon) *led after 1f: rdn and hdd over 3f out: styng on same pce whn nt clr run ins fnl f* 5/2[2]
41-0 4 1 **Roayh (USA)**183 411 3-9-0 101 FrankieDettori 4 98
(Saeed Bin Suroor) *hld up: hdwy 2f out: styd on same pce ins fnl f* 5/1
0040 5 10 **Slim Shadey**7 4493 3-9-0 96 LiamKeniry 3 78
(J S Moore) *led 1f: chsd ldr tl 4f out: rdn and wknd over 1f out* 16/1
2m 5.25s (-0.25) **Going Correction** +0.20s/f (Good) 5 Ran SP% **111.4**
Speed ratings (Par 104): **109,108,106,106,98**
Tote Swingers: 1&2 £6.50 CSF £11.37 TOTE £5.70: £2.20, £1.60; EX 11.40.
Owner John Stocker **Bred** Hascombe And Valiant Studs **Trained** Newmarket, Suffolk

FOCUS
The race was run at a proper pace and produced a worthy winner in Barbican, who posted a clear personal best.

NOTEBOOK
Barbican was not favoured at the weights in terms of how the race was framed, but scored anyway. He was kept busy in the spring before being given a break. Returning after 69 days off, he won in a time that was almost two seconds quicker than the preceding handicap over the same distance. He has run in Listed races before and is well worth another crack in such company and should stay further. (op 4-1 tchd 7-2)
Halfsin(IRE) has been in great form so far this season, running up a hat-trick, sealed with a C& D triumph three weeks earlier. He probably put up a career-best effort in defeat here and maintained his progressive profile. (op 9-4)
Moriarty(IRE) was second in a a Group 3 in the spring. Tried over 1m4f in the Gordon Stakes the previous week, his sights were lowered here. He set a nice even gallop, but didn't have anything in reserve to repel the first two home. (tchd 9-4 and 11-4)
Roayh(USA) was a winner at 6f and 7f as a 2yo but was a beaten favourite on his one start at the Dubai International Racing Carnival. Returning after 183 days and stepped up considerably in trip, he did briefly threaten to lay down a challenge before flattening out. This was perhaps understandable given the length of time he has been on the sidelines. With this run under his belt, he may strip sharper next time, so it would be wrong, on this evidence alone, to dismiss him as a non-stayer at this distance. (op 4-1 tchd 11-2)
Slim Shadey may be better suited at 1m, the trip over which he was not beaten that far in a Listed race a week earlier at Glorious Goodwood. (op 12-1)

4765 PLAY MECCA BINGO ON YOUR MOBILE H'CAP 6f
8:30 (8:30) (Class 4) (0-85,85) 3-Y-0+ £4,528 (£1,347; £673; £336) Stalls High

Form RPR
5420 1 **Quasi Congaree (GER)**6 4531 5-9-4 77 (t) RichardHughes 12 95+
(Ian Wood) *awkward leaving stalls: hld up in tch: led ins fnl f: shkn up and r.o wl: readily* 8/1[3]
0333 2 2 3/4 **Desert Strike**2 4678 5-8-0 66 (p) RyanTate(7) 11 72
(Alan McCabe) *trckd ldrs: racd keenly: rdn over 1f out: styd on to go 2nd wl ins fnl f* 11/1
10/0 3 nk **Fabreze**29 3784 6-9-7 80 TomQueally 6 85
(Peter Makin) *trckd ldrs: plld hrd: rdn over 1f out: styd on* 16/1
430 4 1/2 **Merchant Of Medici**28 3825 4-9-7 80 MartinDwyer 5 83+
(William Muir) *s.i.s: hld up: rdn over 1f out: edgd lft and r.o ins fnl f: nvr nrr* 13/2[2]
-414 5 hd **Macdillon**35 3588 5-9-6 79 LiamKeniry 3 82
(Stuart Kittow) *led: rdn: hung lft and hdd over 1f out: styd on same pce ins fnl f* 11/1
2-14 6 nk **Long Awaited (IRE)**27 3850 3-9-6 83 NeilCallan 8 85
(Roger Varian) *trckd ldrs: led over 1f out: sn hung lft: hdd and no ex ins fnl f* 5/4[1]
6114 7 1/2 **Rough Rock (IRE)**11 4393 6-9-5 78 FrankieDettori 2 78
(Chris Dwyer) *hld up: rdn over 1f out: hung lft ins fnl f: nvr trbld ldrs* 10/1
2005 8 3 1/4 **Rafaaf (IRE)**7 4511 3-8-7 70 (b1) AndreaAtzeni 7 60
(Robert Eddery) *w ldr: rdn and ev ch over 1f out: wknd ins fnl f* 20/1
3045 9 2 **Clear Praise (USA)**15 4239 4-9-4 77 HayleyTurner 1 60
(Simon Dow) *s.i.s: hld up: rdn and wknd over 1f out* 14/1
0430 10 2 **Rocket Rob (IRE)**56 2890 5-9-12 85 StevieDonohoe 9 62
(Willie Musson) *hld up: wknd over 1f out* 9/1
1m 12.89s (0.39) **Going Correction** +0.20s/f (Good)
WFA 3 from 4yo+ 4lb 10 Ran SP% **122.0**
Speed ratings (Par 105): **105,101,100,100,100 99,98,94,91,89**
Tote Swingers: 1&2 £17.30, 1&3 £25.70, 2&3 £6.80 CSF £96.54 CT £1418.04 TOTE £10.70: £3.10, £3.00, £5.10; EX 94.30.
Owner M Forbes & C R Lamborne **Bred** Graf And Grafin Von Stauffenberg **Trained** Upper Lambourn, Berks

FOCUS
A useful-looking sprint won with authority by Quasi Congaree, who posted a clear personal best. The pace was sound enough.
T/Jkpt: Not won. T/Plt: £329.00 to a £1 stake. Pool of £60,936.00 - 135.19 winning tickets. T/Qpdt: £17.00 to £1. Pool of £7,715.00 - 335.37 w. tckts CR 4766a - Raceform Interactive

3881 TIPPERARY (L-H)
Friday, August 5
OFFICIAL GOING: Good to firm (watered)

4767a DAN DOOLEY FORD CENTRE H'CAP 5f
5:45 (5:47) (60-100,95) 3-Y-0+ £11,487 (£3,357; £1,590; £530)

RPR
1 **Roicead (USA)**40 3440 4-9-5 86 (t) WJSupple 12 99+
(Brendan W Duke, Ire) *a.p on stands' side: led 2f out: asserted ins fnl f and kpt on wl clsng stages* 9/2[2]
2 2 **The Reaper (IRE)**13 4333 3-9-11 95 (b) KLatham 8 100
(G M Lyons, Ire) *chsd ldrs on stands' side: rdn in 5th 1f out: kpt on u.p wout threatening wnr* 4/1[1]
3 nk **Your Gifted (IRE)**5 4583 4-9-2 86 ow1 JPO'Brien(3) 11 90
(Patrick Morris) *trckd ldrs on stands' side: 5th 1/2-way: kpt on same pce fr over 1f out* 7/1[3]
4 1 3/4 **Secret Millionaire (IRE)**3 4644 4-8-11 83 SHJames(5) 7 82
(Patrick Morris) *trckd ldrs in centre: 3rd 1/2-way: chal over 1f out: no ex ins fnl f* 7/1[3]
5 1 **Blue Dahlia (IRE)**16 4219 4-9-7 95 SAGray(7) 4 90
(T Stack, Ire) *mid-div on far side: hdwy 2f out: 3rd early fnl f: no ex clsng stages* 12/1
6 hd **Ability N Delivery**5 4587 6-8-4 71 oh3 (p) ShaneFoley 10 65
(Michael J Browne, Ire) *in rr of mid-div: wnt 6th 1f out: no imp ins fnl f* 20/1
7 hd **Patrickswell (IRE)**19 4135 7-8-12 84 (p) LFRoche(5) 13 78
(Marcus Callaghan, Ire) *led on stands' side: hdd after 1/2-way: no ex fr 1f out* 33/1
8 nk **Geraldines Lass (IRE)**19 4137 3-8-10 80 WMLordan 9 72
(W McCreery, Ire) *chsd ldrs on stands' side: no threat fr over 1f out* 10/1
9 nk **Partner (IRE)**26 3892 5-9-9 93 (b) EJMcNamara(3) 6 85
(David Marnane, Ire) *towards rr: kpt on fr 2f out wout threatening* 7/1[3]
10 shd **Tsar Paul (IRE)**24 3961 6-8-10 77 (t) CO'Donoghue 3 68
(J A Nash, Ire) *towards rr on far side: kpt on ins fnl f wout threatening* 11/1
11 1 1/4 **Liberty Island (IRE)**5 4587 6-7-13 73 RossCoakley(7) 2 60
(K J Condon, Ire) *prom early on far side: 7th 2f out: sn no ex* 16/1
12 4 **Airspace (IRE)**19 4135 5-8-12 86 (p) CPHoban(7) 1 58
(M Halford, Ire) *prom on far side: no imp fr wl over 1f out* 14/1
13 7 **Moonlit Garden (IRE)**16 4219 3-9-6 90 (b) PJSmullen 5 36
(D K Weld, Ire) *nvr a factor: towards rr in centre of crse fr under 2f out* 16/1
57.18 secs (-1.82)
WFA 3 from 4yo+ 3lb 13 Ran SP% **126.9**
CSF £24.43 CT £131.72 TOTE £5.70: £2.20, £2.20, £1.50; DF 21.80.
Owner Michael Gerard Daly **Bred** Michael Daly **Trained** Pollardstowm, Co Kildare

FOCUS
The runner-up and third have been rated to their marks.

NOTEBOOK
Roicead(USA) continued his steady progression with his most impressive victory yet in this competitive handicap. Soon in a good position on the stands' side, he travelled powerfully and had things well under control over a furlong out. He leaned a little towards the centre of the track but Willie Supple did not need to get too serious with him. Brendan Duke is talking about the Portland at Doncaster and that is understandable. If trained for that race - and his trainer is keen to be careful with the horse - he would have to be respected, given his rate of progression. (op 5/1)
The Reaper(IRE) ran a cracker considering he probably wants a stiffer test. He was predictably strong at the finish and is one to be of interest in next time. He is thriving with racing. (op 5/1)
Your Gifted(IRE) travelled nicely for a long way and ran another good race. She is in foal and her opportunities will now be limited. (op 8/1 tchd 6/1)
Secret Millionaire(IRE) came there to challenge but was soon brushed aside by the winner. He seems to be back to something like his best. (op 13/2 tchd 6/1)
Blue Dahlia(IRE) could never really get involved over this trip but kept on when the race was over. (op 10/1)
Moonlit Garden(IRE) was soon floundering and has become really disappointing.

4768a ABERGWAUN STKS (LISTED RACE) 5f
6:15 (6:15) 3-Y-0+ £22,413 (£6,551; £3,103; £1,034)

RPR
1 **Inxile (IRE)**40 3441 6-9-9 (p) AdrianNicholls 1 118+
(David Nicholls) *mde all on far side: kpt on wl fr over 1f out* 4/1[2]
2 2 **Move In Time**40 3441 3-9-1 TomEaves 3 103
(Bryan Smart) *trckd ldr in 2nd on far side: rdn and no imp in 3rd over 1f out: kpt on same pce u.p fnl f: no ch w wnr* 14/1
3 hd **Invincible Ash (IRE)**16 4219 6-9-6 109 (tp) GFCarroll 4 105
(M Halford, Ire) *chsd ldrs on far side: drvn along in 4th under 2f out: kpt on one pce u.p* 11/1
4 nk **Group Therapy**8 4468 6-9-4 KLatham 2 102
(David Barron) *chsd ldrs on far side: 2nd over 1f out: no imp on wnr: no ex and dropped to 4th clsng stages* 9/2[3]
5 1/2 **Sole Power**52 3010 4-9-11 117 WMLordan 7 107
(Edward Lynam, Ire) *dwlt: chsd ldrs in centre: no imp fr 1f out: kpt on one pce* 2/1[1]
6 1 **Celerina (IRE)**48 3158 4-9-1 100 WJLee 6 94
(T Stack, Ire) *prom in centre: no ex fr wl over 1f out* 11/2
7 3 **Santo Padre (IRE)**26 3892 7-9-4 102 CO'Donoghue 8 86
(David Marnane, Ire) *a towards rr: nvr a factor* 7/1
56.86 secs (-2.14)
WFA 3 from 4yo+ 3lb 7 Ran SP% **114.4**
CSF £54.85 TOTE £5.10: £3.60, £5.80; DF 61.50.
Owner D Nicholls & Mrs J Love **Bred** Denis And Mrs Teresa Bergin **Trained** Sessay, N Yorks

FOCUS
The winner and runner-up have been rated to their marks.

NOTEBOOK
Inxile(IRE) made every yard while the rest were struggling to get there. He was pretty relaxed after the race and his trainer admitted he would have run him on Sunday if he had been entered at The Curragh. Though not entirely straightforward, the Nicholls clan have the key to the horse at this stage. He will probably struggle in the Nunthorpe, with a far bigger and better field there, but that is an obvious plan and the Prix de l'Abbaye is on the agenda later on. (op 4/1 tchd 10/3)
Move In Time ran a cracker and should have plenty of these Irish sprints on his agenda over the next few years, given the paucity of good sprinters in Ireland. He was no threat to the winner but did nothing wrong and is improving with racing. (op 10/1)
Invincible Ash(IRE), a huge market drifter, ran another sound race. She is probably a bit shy of the class of Inxile but continues to give her all and this is her trip. (op 8/1)
Group Therapy had no more to give in the closing stages and had no obvious excuses. This is as good as he is. (op 4/1 tchd 5/1)
Sole Power was again really disappointing, as he was in this last year, but small fields just seem totally against him. That said, he has now broken tardily twice in succession and that is a worry ahead of his bid to win the Nunthorpe again. He can be expected to run much better there. (op 9/4)
Celerina(IRE) led them on the stands' side before giving best. She is a bit shy of this class of race. (op 7/1)

4769 - 4773a - (Foreign Racing) - See Raceform Interactive

4352 ASCOT (R-H)

Saturday, August 6

OFFICIAL GOING: Good to soft (good in places; straight 8.9, round 8.2)
Wind: Virtually nil. Weather: Overcast

4774 LES AMBASSADEURS CASINO SHERGAR CUP MILE (H'CAP) 1m (R)

12:50 (12:55) (Class 2) (0-100,98)
4-Y-0+

£14,754 (£5,166; £2,361; £1,842; £1,623; £1,182) **Stalls** Low

Form RPR

6020 **1** **Sarrsar**[28] 3876 4-9-4 **96**........(v) PaulHanagan 6 109
(Saeed Bin Suroor) *trckd ldrs: drvn to chal between horses 2f out: led wl over 1f out: sn edgd rt: drvn out fnl f* **6/1**[3]

0060 **2** *3 1/2* **Circumvent**[11] 4410 4-9-4 **96**........(p) DouglasWhyte 10 101
(Paul Cole) *chsd ldrs: rdn 2f out: chsd wnr fnl f but no imp* **15/2**

2530 **3** *1/2* **Dubai Dynamo**[14] 4314 6-9-3 **95**........ RichardHughes 3 99+
(Ruth Carr) *in rr: hdwy ins fnl 2f: styd on wl fnl f to take 3rd clsng stages and gaining on 2nd but no ch w wnr* **11/2**[2]

1000 **4** *nk* **Wannabe King**[21] 4100 5-9-5 **97**........(b) MircoDemuro 2 100
(David Lanigan) *chsd ldrs: rdn and styd on fnl 2f: tk 3rd fnl f but no imp and one pce into 4th cl home* **16/1**

025- **5** *1* **Swift Gift**[315] 6349 6-9-6 **98**........ HughBowman 1 99
(Ed Dunlop) *hld up in rr: hdwy and swtchd lft to outer fr 2f out: styd on wl fnl f: gng on cl home: nt rch ldrs* **4/1**[1]

/00- **6** *1/2* **Master Of Arts (USA)**[533] 629 6-9-3 **95**........ YutakaTake 7 95
(Mark Johnston) *bmpd s and stmbld: in rr: pushed along and hdwy appr fnl f: r.o wl clsng stages but nvr a threat* **16/1**

/-02 **7** *3/4* **Doctor Crane (USA)**[10] 4445 5-9-1 **93**........ OlivierPeslier 8 91
(John Gosden) *in tch: styng on whn bmpd 2f out: kpt on again clsng stages: nvr any threat* **10/1**

3325 **8** *2 1/4* **Snow Bay**[21] 4100 5-9-4 **96**........ JimCrowley 11 89
(David Nicholls) *chsd ldr: rdn and ev ch 2f out: wknd rapidly fnl f* **6/1**[3]

-410 **9** *2 3/4* **Dunn'o (IRE)**[35] 3645 6-9-6 **98**........ FMBerry 12 84
(Clive Cox) *led tl hdd wl over 1f out: wknd rapidly* **7/1**

300- **10** *1 1/4* **Autumn Blades (IRE)**[245] 7689 6-9-3 **95**........(v) HayleyTurner 9 79
(Alan Bailey) *a in rr* **25/1**

1m 41.84s (1.14) **Going Correction** +0.30s/f (Good) **10** Ran SP% **112.9**
Speed ratings (Par 109): **106,102,102,101,100 100,99,97,94,93**
Tote Swingers:1&2:£10.60, 2&3:£8.60, 1&3:£3.90 CSF £48.75 CT £265.09 TOTE £7.60: £2.50, £2.90, £1.70; EX 42.90 Trifecta £182.60 Pool £873.61 - 3.54 winning units..
Owner Godolphin **Bred** Darley **Trained** Newmarket, Suffolk

FOCUS
Rail on Round course placed 4yds in for whole circuit adding 6yds to Old (Round) mile, 16yds to 1m4f and 20yds to 2m. A competitive handicap but it wasn't strong run. The winner belatedly picked up his progress from last year.

NOTEBOOK
Sarrsar burst to the lead over 1f out and drew clear. He isn't the most consistent, but appreciated the return to 1m and his rider reported that challenging between horses seem to spur him on. Official explanation: trainer's rep said, regarding apparent improvement in form, that the gelding was inconsistent and was better suited by the drop back in trip. (op 5-1)
Circumvent was well weighted on the pick of his efforts and held every chance, but unsurprisingly found one too speedy over a trip short of his best. (op 7-1 tchd 8-1)
Dubai Dynamo is still 10lb above his last winning mark, but that didn't stop him running a big race, appreciating the return to 1m and finishing best of all. (tchd 5-1 and 6-1 in places)
Wannabe King took a step back in the right direction and is only just above his last winning mark.
Swift Gift, making his debut for Ed Dunlop, goes well here, but took a while to pick up and never looked like winning. He should be sharper next time. (op 5-1)
Master Of Arts(USA) got too far back having been slowly into stride and stumbled. But for that he'd have gone close to placing, looking at how he finished. (op 18-1 tchd 20-1)
Snow Bay has lost his form looks best left alone at present. (op 11-2)

4775 DUBAI DUTY FREE SHERGAR CUP STAYERS H'CAP 2m

1:25 (1:25) (Class 2) (0-100,95) 4-Y-0+

£14,754 (£5,166; £2,361; £1,842; £1,623; £1,182) **Stalls** Low

Form RPR

4/6 **1** **Ile De Re (FR)**[49] 3156 5-9-5 **91**........ YutakaTake 9 99
(Ian Williams) *t.k.h: hld up in tch: pushed along 2f out: led jst ins fnl f: pushed out* **9/2**[3]

1-00 **2** *1* **Woolfall Treasure**[7] 4532 6-9-9 **95**........(v) PaulHanagan 2 101
(Gary Moore) *in tch: drvn 3f out: swtchd lft to outer fr 2f out: styd on u.p fnl f to take 2nd clsng stages but no imp on wnr* **12/1**

0000 **3** *nk* **La Vecchia Scuola (IRE)**[28] 3875 7-9-5 **91**........ HughBowman 6 97
(Jim Goldie) *chsd ldrs: rdn and one pce over 2f out: styd on u.p fnl f over 1f out to take 3rd last strides but no imp on wnr* **6/1**

1-22 **4** *shd* **Ermyn Lodge**[53] 3013 5-9-4 **90**........(v) HayleyTurner 12 96
(Pat Phelan) *disp 2nd: rdn 3f out: chal 2f out: led over 1f out: hdd jst ins fnl f: lost 2 pls clsng stages* **7/2**[1]

4636 **5** *1 1/2* **Bowdler's Magic**[10] 4423 4-9-0 **86**........ JimCrowley 4 90
(Mark Johnston) *disp 2nd: rdn over 3f out: slt ld u.p over 2f out: hdd over 1f out: wknd nr fin* **10/1**

0030 **6** *nse* **Phoenix Flight (IRE)**[38] 3522 6-9-3 **89**........ FMBerry 10 93
(James Evans) *in rr: rdn over 3f out: styd on u.p fnl f: kpt on clsng stages but nt rch ldrs* **18/1**

123 **7** *6* **Hawk Mountain (UAE)**[14] 4348 6-9-4 **90**........ OlivierPeslier 11 86
(John Quinn) *hld up in rr: pushed along over 5f out: drvn over 2f out and no imp: no ch after* **4/1**[2]

0-50 **8** *2 1/2* **Chink Of Light**[49] 3157 4-9-4 **90**........(v) MircoDemuro 1 83
(Andrew Balding) *in rr but in tch: rdn over 3f out: little rspnse and no ch after* **16/1**

1 **9** *6* **Balajo (FR)**[54] 5-9-4 **90**........ Christophe-PatriceLemaire 8 76
(Alison Batchelor) *a towards rr* **22/1**

6303 **10** *1/2* **Exemplary**[10] 4423 4-9-2 **88**........ CO'Donoghue 5 74
(Mark Johnston) *led tl hdd over 2f out: sn wknd* **9/1**

3m 32.67s (3.67) **Going Correction** +0.30s/f (Good) **10** Ran SP% **117.0**
Speed ratings (Par 109): **102,101,101,101,100 100,97,96,93,93**
Tote Swingers:1&2:£12.70, 2&3:£10.80, 1&3:£6.50 CSF £57.50 CT £328.78 TOTE £6.00: £2.30, £3.40, £2.20; EX 71.10 Trifecta £599.60 Part won. Pool £810.34 - 0.20 winning units..
Owner Michael H Watt **Bred** R Moser & Haras De S A Aga Khan Scea **Trained** Portway, Worcs

FOCUS
The pace increased from halfway in this staying handicap. Ordinary form for the grade, and not a strong run race.

NOTEBOOK
Ile De Re(FR), a keeping-on sixth in the Duke Of Edinburgh over 1m4f at the royal meeting, had finished runner-up over this trip last year and he saw it out well under an effective ride from Yutaka Take. He has scope to progress further as a stayer and could develop into a Cesarewitch contender, although it's worth noting he also has an Ebor entry. (op 11-2)
Woolfall Treasure, last year's runner-up, bounced back from a couple of moderate efforts to fill the same position, staying on well having been outpaced. (op 14-1)
La Vecchia Scuola(IRE) wouldn't have found this enough of a test, but still ran well and ought to be up to winning from this sort of mark. (tchd 11-2)
Ermyn Lodge loves it here and ran another cracker when second in the Ascot Stakes over 2m4f last time. He again ran well, considering he couldn't lead, but is now 11lb higher than when last winning. (tchd 10-3 tchd 4-1 on places)
Bowdler's Magic's losing run continues. He had a perfect tow into the race, so it was disappointing he could manage no better than fifth. (op 9-1)
Phoenix Flight(IRE) got going all too late, but pretty much ran to Royal Ascot form with Ermyn Lodge. (op 16-1)
Hawk Mountain(UAE), who has been in good form this year, failed to run his race on ground that was perhaps softer than ideal. (tchd 9-2)
Exemplary stopped quickly after making the running. (op 10-1)

4776 BARCLAYS SHERGAR CUP DASH (H'CAP) 5f

2:00 (2:00) (Class 2) (0-105,106) 3-Y-0+

£14,754 (£5,166; £2,361; £1,842; £1,623; £1,182) **Stalls** High

Form RPR

0610 **1** **Dungannon**[28] 3841 4-9-4 **95**........ HughBowman 2 103+
(Andrew Balding) *s.i.s: hld up in rr: swtchd lft over 1f out: drvn to ld ins fnl f: rdn out* **7/2**[2]

3211 **2** *nk* **Medicean Man**[13] 4357 5-10-1 **106**........(p) Christophe-PatriceLemaire 8 113+
(Jeremy Gask) *hld up in rr: hdwy and hmpd over 1f out: swtchd rt and rapid hdwy ins fnl f: chsd wnr clsng stages but a hld* **10/3**[1]

0112 **3** *1/2* **Duchess Dora (IRE)**[13] 4357 4-9-10 **101**........ FMBerry 4 106
(John Quinn) *chsd ldr: rdn and ev ch fr 2f out tl nt qckn w ldng duo fnl 100yds* **6/1**

1501 **4** *1/2* **Shoshoni Wind**[29] 3807 3-9-2 **96**........ MircoDemuro 11 98
(Kevin Ryan) *led tl narrowly hdd 2f out: styd chalng tl outpcd fnl 120yds* **12/1**

4145 **5** *nk* **Addictive Dream (IRE)**[28] 3846 4-9-7 **98**........(p) PaulHanagan 12 100+
(Walter Swinburn) *s.i.s: sn rcvrd and in tch: hdwy on ins whn nt clr run over 1f out: fnlly got daylight ins fnl f and styd on wl clsng stages to take 5th but nt rch ldrs* **9/2**[3]

1020 **6** *1/2* **Sohraab**[13] 4357 7-9-0 **91**........ RichardHughes 7 91
(Hughie Morrison) *in tch: rdn to take slt advantage over 1f out: hdd ins fnl f: wknd clsng stages* **15/2**

250- **7** *3/4* **Reverence**[342] 5569 10-9-9 **100**........ DouglasWhyte 9 98
(Eric Alston) *chsd ldrs: n.m.r over 2f out and again jst ins fnl f: styd on but nvr gng pce to rch ldrs* **20/1**

1240 **8** *1 1/4* **Doctor Parkes**[28] 3874 5-9-6 **97**........ HayleyTurner 3 90
(Eric Alston) *chsd ldrs: rdn 1/2-way: wknd ins fnl f* **16/1**

6050 **9** *1 3/4* **Mister Manannan (IRE)**[28] 3846 4-9-4 **95**........(p) OlivierPeslier 6 82
(David Nicholls) *t.k.h early: chsd ldrs: slt ld 2f out: hdd over 1f out: sn wknd* **16/1**

1000 **10** *17* **Burning Thread (IRE)**[28] 3874 4-9-6 **97**........ CO'Donoghue 5 23
(Tim Etherington) *chsd ldrs 3f: wknd qckly ins fnl 2f: heavily eased whn no ch fnl f* **28/1**

61.13 secs (-0.07) **Going Correction** +0.225s/f (Good)
WFA 3 from 4yo+ 3lb **10** Ran SP% **117.2**
Speed ratings (Par 109): **109,108,107,106,106 105,104,102,99,72**
Tote Swingers:1&2:£3.60, 2&3:£3.00, 1&3:£5.40 CSF £15.71 CT £69.23 TOTE £4.30: £1.80, £1.60, £1.70; EX 18.70 Trifecta £30.90 Pool £1,241.70 - 29.64 winning units..
Owner I G Burbidge **Bred** J A E Hobby **Trained** Kingsclere, Hants
■ Stewards' Enquiry : Mirco Demuro caution: careless riding.

FOCUS
A really good sprint handicap. The right horses came to the fore, although there's little doubt that the runner-up would have won had he not twice been stopped inside the final 2f. The time was ordinary and the form is rated around the winner and third.

NOTEBOOK
Dungannon has long been a sprinter of potential and, although below par here over 6f last time, he picked up well from the rear and found the gaps opening at the perfect time. Seemingly well suited by a bit of give, this was only his 12th start and there should be more to come, with his primary aim being the Portland, over a trip that could prove ideal. (op 9-2)
Medicean Man up a total of 10lb for last month's two C&D victories, was again ridden confidently, but didn't get the breaks, having to be switched sharply right after getting impeded and finding the line coming too soon. A fine effort from a mark of 106, he's a similar sort to last year's winner Prohibit, who won this season's King's Stand, and he too may make his mark at Group level before long. The Prix de L'Abbaye looks a reasonable long-term target. (op 7-2)
Duchess Dora(IRE), another at the top of her game, ran right up to form with the runner-up and shouldn't be far off winning at Listed level on this evidence. (tchd 11-2)
Shoshoni Wind, 4lb higher than when winning at Chester last time, grabbed the early lead against the rail and ran well on this step up in grade. She's clearly progressing. (op 14-1)
Addictive Dream(IRE), wearing first-time cheekpieces, had nowhere to go when cruising under Hanagan and, despite staying on once in the clear, lacked the speed to recover the lost momentum. (op 6-1)
Reverence made a satisfactory comeback, but won't be easy to place off this mark. (op 14-1)

4777 TITANIC BELFAST SHERGAR CUP CLASSIC (H'CAP) 1m 4f

2:30 (2:31) (Class 3) (0-95,92) 3-Y-0

£14,754 (£5,166; £2,361; £1,842; £1,623; £1,182) **Stalls** Low

Form RPR

1344 **1** **Parlour Games**[14] 4316 3-9-3 **86**........ CO'Donoghue 8 97+
(Mahmood Al Zarooni) *mid-div: hdwy fr 3f out: str run on outside to take slt ld 1f out: drvn out* **15/2**

611 **2** *3/4* **Ithoughtitwasover (IRE)**[15] 4280 3-9-5 **88**........ RichardHughes 9 97+
(Mark Johnston) *in tch: nt clr run 2f out: swtchd lft and hdwy over 1f out: styd on u.p to take 2nd cl home but nt rch wnr* **4/1**[1]

4203 **3** *hd* **Swift Alhaarth (IRE)**[9] 4467 3-9-3 **86**........ DouglasWhyte 2 95
(Mark Johnston) *led tl narrowly hdd 1f out: styd on u.p but nt pce of wnr: ct for 2nd cl home* **13/2**[3]

-221 **4** *shd* **Thubiaan (USA)**[32] 3705 3-9-2 **85**........ Christophe-PatriceLemaire 12 94
(William Haggas) *chsd ldrs: rdn 3f out: styd on wl fr over 1f out but nvr quite gng pce to get upsides: one pce fnl 120yds* **6/1**[2]

2130 **5** *1 1/4* **Seelo (USA)**[30] 3774 3-9-9 **92**........ JimCrowley 3 99+
(John Gosden) *mid-div: hdwy on ins whn nt clr run over 2f out: swtchd lft and hdwy sn after: kpt on u.p but nvr gng pce to rch ldrs* **6/1**[2]

1150 **6** *10* **Halifax (IRE)**[10] 4426 3-9-8 **91** .... OlivierPeslier 6 82
(Mark Johnston) *s.i.s: in rr: pushed along over 3f out: nvr gng pce to get into contention and no ch fr over 2f out* **13/2**[3]

1505 **7** *1* **Art History (IRE)**[9] 4473 3-9-4 **87** .... YutakaTake 5 76
(Mark Johnston) *a towards rr* **14/1**

-140 **8** *½* **Jehanbux (USA)**[51] 3069 3-9-8 **91** .... FMBerry 4 79
(Richard Hannon) *a towards rr* **20/1**

0640 **9** *1 ½* **State Opera**[29] 3828 3-9-2 **85** .... HughBowman 1 71
(Mark Johnston) *chsd ldrs: rdn 3f out: wknd ins fnl 2f* **20/1**

5-03 **10** *shd* **Pivotman**[10] 4426 3-9-4 **87** .... HayleyTurner 11 73
(Amanda Perrett) *chsd ldr: rdn 3f out: wknd appr fnl 2f* **6/1**[2]

2m 33.98s (1.48) **Going Correction** +0.30s/f (Good) **10** Ran SP% **117.5**
Speed ratings (Par 104): **107,106,106,106,105 98,98,97,96,96**
Tote Swingers:1&2:£6.70, 2&3:£2.40, 1&3:£10.00 CSF £37.90 CT £204.89 TOTE £9.80: £2.90, £1.50, £2.30; EX 55.60 Trifecta £471.90 Pool £1,095.65 - 1.71 winning units..
Owner Godolphin **Bred** Darley **Trained** Newmarket, Suffolk

FOCUS
The most open race on the card and predictably there were any number in with a chance rounding the final bend. The winning time was almost identical to the following handicap for older horses. The first five were clear and this looks good form. Improvement from the first two.

NOTEBOOK
Parlour Games didn't receive the best of rides when fourth over C&D last time, but Colm O'Donoghue had him ideally placed to strike off the final bend and, having hit the front, he proved too streetwise for the runner-up. He's strong stayer at the trip and it would be no surprise to see him go for the Melrose Handicap at York in a couple of weeks. (op 8-1)
Ithoughtitwasover(IRE), better than the bare form when winning narrowly off 4lb lower at Newmarket last time, still looks to be learning and he may have come out on top were he a bit more battle-hardened. That will come with experience, though, and he remains a horse to keep on side. (op 9-2)
Swift Alhaarth(IRE) ran a storming race at Goodwood last time and had his own way up front here. The return to this longer trip raised a question, though, and despite giving his all, couldn't see it out as strongly as some. (op 5-1)
Thubiaan(USA), winner of a minor Pontefract maiden last time, ran well on this handicap debut and is another likely to learn as he gains further experience. (tchd 13-2)
Seelo(USA) hasn't progressed in the manner expected, but there's little doubt he should have been a good bit closer here, keeping on late having been stuck on the inside with nowhere to go for the best part of a furlong. He's a one-paced galloper who may appreciate a return to front-running. (op 8-1)
Halifax(IRE) isn't the quickest and appeals as the type to do better as a jumper. (op 15-2)
Art History(IRE) was never involved. (op 16-1 tchd 12-1)
Pivotman failed to build on his Goodwood third, although looking at how far he was beaten, it's probable there was something amiss. (tchd 11-2 and 7-1)

4778 MICHAEL PAGE INTERNATIONAL SHERGAR CUP CHALLENGE (H'CAP) 1m 4f

3:00 (3:00) (Class 3) (0-95,95) 4-Y-O+

£14,754 (£5,166; £2,361; £1,842; £1,623; £1,182) **Stalls** Low

Form RPR

-623 **1** **Averroes (IRE)**[49] 3156 4-9-4 **94** .... MircoDemuro 5 105
(Clive Cox) *t.k.h: in tch: hdwy 3f out: drvn to ld over 1f out: pushed out* **11/2**[2]

-434 **2** *2 ½* **Zuider Zee (GER)**[50] 3120 4-9-2 **92** .... JimCrowley 4 99
(John Gosden) *in rr: hdwy on outer fr 3f out: hrd drvn fr 2f out: styd on fnl f to take 2nd fnl 100yds but no ch w wnr* **7/1**

3403 **3** *1 ¼* **Life And Soul (IRE)**[42] 3411 4-9-1 **91** .... HayleyTurner 1 96+
(Amanda Perrett) *chsd ldrs: rdn over 2f out: chsd wnr over 1f out but no imp: lost 2nd fnl 100yds* **6/1**[3]

/2-2 **4** *½* **Waldvogel (IRE)**[29] 3829 7-9-5 **95** .... OlivierPeslier 7 100+
(Nicky Richards) *stdd in rr: hdwy fr 3f out and styng on whn nt clr run 2f out: swtchd lft to outside and hdwy over 1f out: kpt on clsng stages but nt rch ldrs* **11/1**

-003 **5** *1 ½* **Chock A Block (IRE)**[13] 4354 5-9-5 **95** .... RichardHughes 8 97
(Saeed Bin Suroor) *in rr early: hdwy 7f out: rdn to chse ldrs fr 3f out: wknd appr fnl f* **9/1**

0100 **6** *nk* **Classic Vintage (USA)**[7] 4532 5-9-3 **93** .... DouglasWhyte 2 94
(Amanda Perrett) *chsd ldrs: hmpd on rails after 4f: hdwy 4f out: chsd ldr 3f out: led u.p 2f out: hdd over 1f out: wknd ins fnl f* **20/1**

3140 **7** *½* **Rock A Doodle Doo (IRE)**[28] 3875 4-9-5 **95** .... YutakaTake 6 96
(William Jarvis) *hld up in rr: stl plenty to do over 2f out: rdn over 1f out and sme late prog* **10/3**[1]

1006 **8** *1* **English Summer**[13] 4354 4-9-1 **91** .... PaulHanagan 3 90
(Mark Johnston) *chsd ldrs: drvn along 6f out: stl pressing ldrs 2f out: wknd over 1f out* **18/1**

-604 **9** *4* **Pipette**[15] 4267 4-9-4 **94** ....(t) CO'Donoghue 12 87
(Andrew Balding) *in rr: hdwy on ins and n.m.r 3f out: in tch but stl nt much daylight 2f out: wknd qckly fnl f* **6/1**[3]

50-0 **10** *6* **Australia Day (IRE)**[53] 3013 8-9-2 **92** .... Christophe-PatriceLemaire 11 75
(Paul Webber) *led: sn clr: 10 l ahd 5f out: pushed along 3f out: hdd & wknd 2f out* **12/1**

2m 33.96s (1.46) **Going Correction** +0.30s/f (Good) **10** Ran SP% **115.6**
Speed ratings (Par 107): **107,105,104,104,103 102,102,101,99,95**
Tote Swingers:1&2:£4.60, 2&3:£7.90, 1&3:£7.10 CSF £43.37 CT £239.21 TOTE £6.50: £2.20, £2.50, £2.10; EX 40.10 Trifecta £364.30 Pool £1,296.56 - 2.63 winning units..
Owner H E Sheikh Sultan Bin Khalifa Al Nahyan **Bred** G Stimola **Trained** Lambourn, Berks

FOCUS
Largely exposed handicappers contested this and this is ordinary form for the grade. There was a strong gallopand the winning time was almost identical to the earlier handicap for 3-y-os. Those coming from just off the pace were favoured.

NOTEBOOK
Averroes(IRE) has previously been frustrating, but was suited by the strong gallop and finally got his head in front for the first time since his 2-y-o days. It wasn't a total surprise, however, given he'd been running well and was placed at the royal meeting. He may go to Dubai now. (op 6-1)
Zuider Zee(GER) bounced back from a modest effort over 1m6f in soft ground last time, but the way he stayed on here having hit a flat spot suggests he does in fact need that longer trip. His progressed has levelled out this year and he would no doubt appeal to jumps buyers. (op 15-2)
Life And Soul(IRE) didn't get the best of runs, but then couldn't quicken once in the clear anyway, looking fortunate to hold on for third. (op 7-1)
Waldvogel(IRE) met trouble when trying to stay on down the straight. He may have a decent race in him returned to hurdles this jumps season. (op 8-1)
Chock A Block(IRE) didn't run badly considering he needs quicker ground. (op 11-1)
Classic Vintage(USA), hampered with around 1m to run, did well to work his way to the front, but was then swamped inside the final furlong. (op 14-1)
Rock A Doodle Doo(IRE) was never given a chance to get into the race, keeping on late and shaping better than the bare form. He's in the Ebor, but the concern is he ran poorly over that C&D last time. Wherever he heads next, there's a race in him off this sort of mark. (op 7-2 tchd 3-1)
Pipette, although well beaten, never got much of a run and can be given another chance. (op 7-1)
Australia Day(IRE) raced into a clear lead down the far side, setting a good gallop. (tchd 11-1)

4779 DUBAI DUTY FREE SHERGAR CUP SPRINT (H'CAP) 6f

3:35 (3:36) (Class 2) (0-100,99) 3-Y-O

£14,754 (£5,166; £2,361; £1,842; £1,623; £1,182) **Stalls** High

Form RPR

12-0 **1** **Morache Music**[35] 3649 3-9-6 **91** .... FMBerry 3 108
(Peter Makin) *in rr: rdn over 2f out: hdwy u.p over 1f out: chsd ldr ins fnl f: led fnl 120yds: drvn out* **6/1**[3]

-204 **2** *1 ¾* **Desert Law (IRE)**[29] 3820 3-9-12 **97** .... CO'Donoghue 12 109
(Andrew Balding) *chsd ldrs: led appr fnl f: hdd fnl 120yds: no ex* **3/1**[2]

2311 **3** *1 ½* **Firebeam**[29] 3830 3-10-0 **99** .... PaulHanagan 7 106
(William Haggas) *trckd ldr: led over 2f out: rdn and hdd appr fnl f: styd on same pce fnl 120yds* **6/4**[1]

1301 **4** *nk* **Azzurra Du Caprio (IRE)**[42] 3384 3-9-2 **87** Christophe-PatriceLemaire 9 93
(Ben Haslam) *in tch: rdn 1/2-way: styd on to chse ldrs 2f out: one pce insde fnl f* **16/1**

11-0 **5** *3 ½* **Loki's Revenge**[14] 4333 3-9-0 **85** .... RichardHughes 2 80
(William Jarvis) *wnt rt s: in rr: rdn over 2f out: styd on fnl f: nvr gng pce to rch ldrs* **12/1**

0060 **6** *4 ½* **Avonmore Star**[14] 4333 3-9-3 **88** .... JimCrowley 10 68
(Richard Hannon) *chsd ldrs: rdn 3f out: wknd wl over 1f out* **25/1**

21-0 **7** *1* **Googlette (IRE)**[49] 3158 3-9-2 **87** ....(v[1]) YutakaTake 5 64
(Edward Vaughan) *led tl hdd over 2f out: sn btn* **25/1**

0101 **8** *½* **Kingscroft (IRE)**[6] 4574 3-9-6 **91** 3ex .... DouglasWhyte 6 67
(Mark Johnston) *s.i.s: stdd in rr: pushed along 1/2-way and nvr gng pce to get into contention* **11/1**

0064 **9** *10* **Glas Burn**[21] 4101 3-9-4 **89** .... MircoDemuro 8 33
(Jonathan Portman) *outpcd most of way* **33/1**

0002 **10** *¾* **Julius Geezer (IRE)**[33] 3682 3-9-2 **87** .... HughBowman 11 28
(Tom Dascombe) *in tch early: rdn and bhd fr 1/2-way* **10/1**

1m 14.37s (-0.03) **Going Correction** +0.225s/f (Good) **10** Ran SP% **120.9**
Speed ratings (Par 106): **109,106,104,104,99 93,92,91,78,77**
Tote Swingers:1&2:£6.10, 2&3:£1.80, 1&3:£4.20 CSF £24.84 CT £42.82 TOTE £8.40: £2.40, £1.50, £1.40; EX 34.80 Trifecta £30.50 Pool £1,770.99 - 42.86 winning units..
Owner R P Marchant,D Ahier,Mrs E Lee **Bred** Michael E Broughton **Trained** Ogbourne Maisey, Wilts

FOCUS
A decent 3-y-o sprint handicap. The form looks good and has been rated positively. A clear best from the winner.

NOTEBOOK
Morache Music, who appeared not to stay 7f on his reappearance, won three times as a juvenile and, with the ground coming in his favour, it was no surprise to see him backed. He came with a strong run from over 1f out, clicking into another gear once switched to race against the rail, and was well on top at the line. He looks a sprinter of potential and it's hoped he goes on. (op 9-1)
Desert Law(IRE) tracked the favourite through and readily went past, but found himself unable to fend off the winner, to whom he was conceding 6lb. Although largely running well, one gets the impression he hasn't quite lived up to his trainers expectations this season. (op 7-2 tchd 4-1)
Firebeam, up 14lb for romping home in a 7f handicap at York last time (form worked out well), was potentially vulnerable down in trip and he couldn't lead this time. He was readily beaten off and not quite up to it off this mark. (op 9-4 tchd 11-8)
Azzurra Du Caprio(IRE) found this tougher than the Doncaster handicap she won last time, but still ran well, finishing nicely to just miss third. (op 11-1)
Loki's Revenge was keeping on late and may soon be on a mark he can win off. (op 14-1)
Kingscroft(IRE) has been kept busy (17th run this year) and continued his run of inconsistent form. (op 15-2)
T/Jkpt: Not won. T/Plt: £39.90 to a £1 stake. Pool £128,299.33. 2,343.77 winning tickets. T/Qpdt: £4.10 to a £1 stake. Pool £10,760.38. 1,902.75 winning tickets. ST

4377 AYR (L-H)
Saturday, August 6

OFFICIAL GOING: Good (good to firm in places; 9.1) changing to good after race 3 (6.40)
Wind: Almost nil Weather: Overcast, dull

4780 JOCKEYJAN.CO.UK JAN WILSON MEMORIAL APPRENTICE H'CAP 6f

5:40 (5:40) (Class 5) (0-75,71) 3-Y-O+ **£2,328** (£693; £346; £173) **Stalls** Low

Form RPR

4411 **1** **Blues Jazz**[28] 3856 5-9-4 **64** .... GeorgeChaloner(3) 4 81
(Ian Semple) *in tch: effrt over 1f out: styd on to ld nr fin* **11/2**[3]

0421 **2** *¾* **Blown It (USA)**[4] 4636 5-9-0 **57** 6ex .... ShaneBKelly 5 72
(Keith Dalgleish) *chsd ldrs: effrt and led appr fnl f: kpt on fnl f: hdd nr fin* **11/4**[1]

0000 **3** *2 ¼* **Haadeeth**[19] 4141 4-9-5 **67** .... LauraBarry(5) 7 75
(Richard Fahey) *trckd ldrs: rdn over 2f out: effrt over 1f out: kpt on same pce ins fnl f* **8/1**

2121 **4** *3 ½* **Royal Blade (IRE)**[12] 4378 4-8-12 **62** .... DanielleMooney(7) 1 59
(Alan Berry) *cl up: led over 2f out to appr fnl f: wknd ins fnl f* **7/2**[2]

2340 **5** *2 ¾* **Absa Lutte (IRE)**[14] 4310 8-9-9 **71** .... JosephYoung(5) 10 59
(Michael Mullineaux) *t.k.h: hld up: hdwy 1/2-way: rdn over 1f out: sn no imp* **17/2**

3352 **6** *¾* **Weetentherty**[3] 4672 4-8-8 **56** ....(p) RossSmith(5) 11 41
(Linda Perratt) *hld up on outside: rdn over 2f out: nvr able to chal* **8/1**

3006 **7** *hd* **Distant Sun (USA)**[12] 4378 7-8-9 **52** .... MatthewLawson 6 37
(Linda Perratt) *hld up: rdn along over 2f out: nvr on terms* **40/1**

00-0 **8** *3 ¾* **Monte Mayor One**[7] 4539 4-8-13 **56** .... LMcNiff 8 29
(Jim Goldie) *dwlt: hld up: rdn whn hmpd over 2f out: sn btn* **22/1**

0 **9** *19* **Atyaab**[60] 2781 4-9-5 **62** .... GarryWhillans 3 —
(Alan Swinbank) *led to over 2f out: sn wknd: t.o* **10/1**

1m 12.14s (-0.26) **Going Correction** -0.15s/f (Firm) **9** Ran SP% **112.9**
Speed ratings (Par 103): **103,102,99,94,90 89,89,84,59**
Tote Swingers:1&2:£3.90, 2&3:£9.50, 1&3:£7.30 CSF £20.47 CT £118.86 TOTE £5.30: £2.10, £1.30, £2.40; EX 20.80.
Owner Robert Reid **Bred** David Sugars And Bob Parker **Trained** Carluke, S Lanarks
■ Stewards' Enquiry : Shane B Kelly two-day ban: careless riding (Aug 20-21)

FOCUS
Back straight dolled out 6m, home bend out 8m, home straight out 14m from innermost line, adding circa 24yds to races between 7f and 1m2f and 48yds to 1m3f race. Just a modest event overall, but the front two came here in top form and the field were quite well strung out behind them in the end. Sound form for the grade.

4781 CHAMPAGNE G. H. MUMM DE CRAMANT/EBF MAIDEN STKS 7f 50y
6:10 (6:10) (Class 5) 2-Y-O £3,299 (£981; £490; £245) Stalls High

Form RPR
0 **1** **Loukas (IRE)**[10] 4436 2-8-10 0.................................... GarryWhillans(7) 3 77
(Alan Swinbank) *t.k.h early: trckd ldrs: hdwy to ld appr fnl f: rdn and r.o wl* **11/2**
5 **2** *3/4* **Trail Blaze (IRE)**[21] 4080 2-9-0 0.................................... DaleSwift(3) 4 75
(Kevin Ryan) *t.k.h early: led: rdn and hdd appr fnl f: rallied: no ex last 75ds* **11/4**[3]
33 **3** *4 1/2* **Rasputin (IRE)**[19] 4140 2-9-3 0.................................... FrederikTylicki 2 64
(Michael Dods) *trckd ldrs: drvn along over 2f out: outpcd by first two ins fnl f* **13/5**[2]
60 **4** *3 1/4* **Nayef Flyer**[19] 4140 2-8-10 0.................................... GeorgeChaloner(7) 1 56
(Richard Fahey) *hld up bhd ldng gp: effrt over 2f out: wknd fnl f* **25/1**
52 **5** *9* **Courtesy Call (IRE)**[9] 4455 2-9-3 0.................................... RobertWinston 6 33
(Mark Johnston) *trckd ldrs: hdwy over 4f out: rdn and ev ch over 2f out: wknd appr fnl f* **12/5**[1]
6 *3 1/2* **Madam Bonny (IRE)** 2-8-12 0.................................... DanielTudhope 5 20
(Jim Goldie) *t.k.h: stdd in rr: rdn over 2f out: sn wknd* **12/1**

1m 34.1s (0.70) **Going Correction** -0.025s/f (Good) **6** Ran SP% **110.8**
Speed ratings (Par 94): **95,94,89,85,75 71**
Tote Swingers:1&2:£3.10, 2&3:£2.30, 1&3:£2.80 CSF £20.34 TOTE £5.70: £1.90, £2.20; EX 26.80.
Owner Mrs J Porter **Bred** Keatly Overseas Ltd **Trained** Melsonby, N Yorks

FOCUS
A small-field maiden, but some decent yards were represented and the front two deserve credit for pulling clear. The winner looks an improver and the third and fourth set the level.

NOTEBOOK
Loukas(IRE) had been quite well backed on his debut, so it was no big surprise to see him improve a good deal second time up, the step up to 7f definitely suiting this son of a 1m2f winner, and he got on top inside the last despite still showing signs of greenness under pressure. There's more to come from him. (tchd 9-2)
Trail Blaze(IRE) was much sharper with his debut behind him and should be adding to his yard's juvenile tally before long. He was unable to fend off the winner inside the last but pulled nicely clear of the rest. (op 7-2)
Rasputin(IRE) has now filled the same spot over this C&D on all three starts and does not appear to be progressing at this stage, but this does at least open up the nursery route for him. (op 9-4 tchd 11-4 and 3-1 in a place)
Nayef Flyer offered a bit more than previously and appeals as the type to keep on improving, with nurseries presumably on his agenda next. (op 18-1 tchd 16-1)
Courtesy Call(IRE)'s Epsom second looked to give him sound claims and he clearly can't have been right, weakening pretty tamely in the end. He wouldn't be the first from the yard to bounce straight back from a poor effort. (op 9-4)
Madam Bonny(IRE) didn't offer any immediate promise. (op 25-1)

4782 UNISON'S AYRSHIRE & ARRAN HEALTH BRANCH H'CAP 7f 50y
6:40 (6:40) (Class 5) (0-70,70) 3-Y-O+ £2,328 (£693; £346; £173) Stalls High

Form RPR
5-05 **1** **Benny The Bear**[12] 4379 4-8-4 53.................................... ShaneBKelly(5) 1 65
(Linda Perratt) *t.k.h: mde all: sn clr: rdn 2f out: kpt on wl: unchal* **11/2**
4265 **2** *3* **Music Festival (USA)**[12] 4380 4-9-9 67.................................... DanielTudhope 9 71
(Jim Goldie) *chsd wnr thrght: rdn over 2f out: effrt over 1f out: kpt on fnl f: nt rch wnr* **11/4**[2]
050 **3** *1 1/4* **Paradise Spectre**[5] 4604 4-8-10 59.................................... MatthewLawson(5) 3 60
(Mrs K Burke) *chsd ldrs: effrt over 2f out: kpt on same pce fnl f* **7/1**
440- **4** *1/2* **Chookie Avon**[113] 7705 4-9-0 58....................................(p) FrederikTylicki 6 57
(Keith Dalgleish) *t.k.h: hld up: rdn over 2f out: sn btn* **9/2**[3]
0462 **5** *4 1/2* **Burnwynd Boy**[12] 4379 6-8-9 60.................................... GarryWhillans(7) 5 47
(Ian Semple) *hld up in tch: rdn over 2f out: sn no imp* **5/2**[1]
0000 **6** *9* **Cheyenne Red (IRE)**[36] 3573 5-8-9 53 ow2....................(b) RobertWinston 4 16
(Michael Dods) *dwlt: hld up: rdn over 2f out: sn btn* **18/1**
5620 **7** *1 1/4* **Desert Auction (IRE)**[60] 2789 4-9-9 67 PatrickMathers 2 36
(Ian Semple) *hld up: rdn along over 2f out: sn wknd* **12/1**

1m 33.54s (0.14) **Going Correction** -0.025s/f (Good)
WFA 3 from 4yo+ 6lb **7** Ran SP% **114.3**
Speed ratings (Par 103): **98,94,93,92,87 77,75**
Tote Swingers:1&2:£3.30, 2&3:£4.30, 1&3:£6.40 CSF £20.97 CT £106.61 TOTE £4.80: £1.30, £2.70; EX 20.00.
Owner R R Whitton **Bred** R R Whitton **Trained** East Kilbride, S Lanarks
■ Stewards' Enquiry : Shane B Kelly one-day ban: used whip in incorrect place (Aug 22)

FOCUS
Not the easiest race to assess, the order barely changing throughout. It has been rated around the winner to a small personal best.

4783 GAS SURE & JAMES FREW 100 YEAR H'CAP 1m
7:10 (7:10) (Class 6) (0-65,65) 3-Y-O+ £1,704 (£503; £251) Stalls Low

Form RPR
/014 **1** **Invincible Hero (IRE)**[25] 3952 4-9-11 62....................(t) DanielTudhope 10 79+
(Declan Carroll) *chsd ldr: led over 2f out: kpt on strly fnl f* **7/2**[1]
4016 **2** *3 3/4* **Mangham (IRE)**[7] 4543 6-9-9 65....................(p) LMcNiff(5) 1 73
(George Foster) *in tch: effrt over 2f out: chsd wnr appr fnl f: r.o: no imp* **9/1**
4562 **3** *3* **Jaldarshaan (IRE)**[12] 4383 4-9-8 59.................................... RobertWinston 3 60
(Alan Swinbank) *hld up: effrt over 2f out: kpt on fnl f: no imp* **7/2**[1]
3460 **4** *1* **Machir Bay**[12] 4379 4-8-9 46 oh1....................(p) FrederikTylicki 11 45
(Keith Dalgleish) *led: rdn and hdd over 2f out: rdn and outpcd appr fnl f* **12/1**
041 **5** *2 1/4* **Military Call**[12] 4383 4-9-2 60....................(p) GarryWhillans(7) 13 54
(Alistair Whillans) *hld up: rdn and hdwy on outside 2f out: no imp fnl f* **5/1**[2]
0010 **6** *1/2* **Abernethy (IRE)**[12] 4383 3-8-3 52 ow1.................... MatthewLawson(5) 5 44
(Linda Perratt) *s.i.s: hld up: rdn and hdwy over 1f out: nvr able to chal* **16/1**
3030 **7** *2* **Shunkawakhan (IRE)**[19] 4143 8-9-1 52....................(p) SaleemGolam 4 40
(Linda Perratt) *t.k.h: trckd ldrs tl rdn and wknd over 1f out* **20/1**
0033 **8** *2 1/2* **Hill Tribe**[7] 4543 4-9-5 59.................................... RobertLButler(3) 12 41
(Richard Guest) *in tch: pushed along over 3f out: wknd 2f out* **7/1**[3]
0033 **9** *2* **Cold Quest (USA)**[8] 4501 7-8-7 49.................................... ShaneBKelly(5) 6 27
(Linda Perratt) *dwlt: bhd: hdwy on ins 3f out: wknd wl over 1f out* **14/1**
/00- **10** *hd* **Bubber (IRE)**[437] 2438 4-8-10 50.................................... DaleSwift(3) 8 27
(Ollie Pears) *midfield: rdn whn checked over 2f out: sn btn* **14/1**
6040 **11** *16* **Sheedal (IRE)**[8] 4505 3-8-2 46 oh1.................................... PatrickMathers 9 —
(Linda Perratt) *trckd ldrs tl wknd qckly over 2f out* **50/1**
0000 **12** *9* **Flyjack (USA)**[20] 4128 4-8-5 47 oh1 ow1....................(v) DarylByrne(5) 14 —
(Lisa Williamson) *missed break: bhd: struggling 3f out: sn btn* **50/1**

1m 43.32s (-0.48) **Going Correction** -0.025s/f (Good)
WFA 3 from 4yo+ 7lb **12** Ran SP% **119.2**
Speed ratings (Par 101): **101,97,94,93,91 90,88,86,84,83 67,58**
Tote Swingers:1&2:£7.30, 2&3:£5.60, 1&3:£2.50 CSF £35.55 CT £120.53 TOTE £5.60: £2.00, £3.60, £1.10; EX 36.10.
Owner Mrs Sarah Bryan **Bred** Fortbarrington Stud **Trained** Sledmere, E Yorks
■ Stewards' Enquiry : Robert Winston caution: careless riding.

FOCUS
A one-sided handicap in which not many ever threatened a serious blow. The winner can rate higher while the runner-up ran his best race of the year so far.
Flyjack(USA) Official explanation: jockey said gelding was slowly away

4784 CHAMPAGNE G.H. MUMM ROSE H'CAP 1m 2f
7:40 (7:40) (Class 5) (0-75,75) 3-Y-O+ £2,328 (£693; £346; £173) Stalls Low

Form RPR
/-46 **1** **All For You (IRE)**[12] 4380 5-8-13 63.................................... GaryBartley(3) 6 72+
(Jim Goldie) *s.i.s: hld up: smooth hdwy over 2f out: rdn to ld ins fnl f: kpt on wl* **8/1**
010 **2** *1/2* **Sartingo (IRE)**[13] 4367 4-9-6 67.................................... RobertWinston 5 75
(Alan Swinbank) *cl up: rdn and ev ch over 1f out to ins fnl f: kpt on fin* **5/1**[3]
0304 **3** *nk* **Sirgarfieldsobers (IRE)**[21] 4109 5-10-0 75.................... DanielTudhope 4 82
(Declan Carroll) *led: rdn over 2f out: hdd ins fnl f: kpt on: hld nr fin* **4/1**[2]
0060 **4** *5* **Raleigh Quay (IRE)**[28] 3859 4-9-2 63.................................... FrederikTylicki 8 60
(Micky Hammond) *hld up in tch: rdn and outpcd over 3f out: rallied over 1f out: kpt on fnl f* **20/1**
1140 **5** *2 3/4* **Frontline Phantom (IRE)**[23] 4004 4-9-5 71.......... MatthewLawson(5) 1 63
(Mrs K Burke) *trckd ldrs: effrt and swtchd rt over 2f out: wknd over 1f out* **4/1**[2]
3650 **6** *1 3/4* **Cosmic Moon**[13] 4367 3-8-13 69.................................... PatrickMathers 2 57
(Richard Fahey) *prom: effrt and rdn over 2f out: edgd rt: wknd over 1f out* **9/1**
230 **7** *2* **Petomic (IRE)**[7] 4540 6-9-2 66.................................... RobertLButler(3) 3 50
(Richard Guest) *t.k.h: hld up: rdn over 2f out: btn over 1f out* **14/1**
1252 **8** *1/2* **Retreat Content (IRE)**[7] 4543 3-8-3 67.................................... DaleSwift(3) 9 50
(Linda Perratt) *hld up in tch: rdn over 4f out: struggling fnl 3f* **3/1**[1]

2m 12.36s (0.36) **Going Correction** -0.025s/f (Good)
WFA 3 from 4yo+ 9lb **8** Ran SP% **114.2**
Speed ratings (Par 103): **97,96,96,92,90 88,87,86**
Tote Swingers:1&2:£7.80, 2&3:£4.80, 1&3:£6.00 CSF £47.37 CT £184.34 TOTE £7.00: £2.60, £2.40, £1.90; EX 47.70.
Owner Jim Goldie Racing Club **Bred** Whitewood Stables **Trained** Uplawmoor, E Renfrews
■ Stewards' Enquiry : Robert Winston one-day ban: used whip with excessive frequency (Aug 20)

FOCUS
A fair handicap in which the front three came clear. The form looks sound rated around the placed horses.

4785 MCKENZIE HAIR STUDIO 10TH ANNIVERSARY H'CAP 1m 7f
8:10 (8:10) (Class 6) (0-65,63) 4-Y-O+ £1,704 (£503; £251) Stalls Low

Form RPR
056/ **1** **Circus Clown (IRE)**[86] 6156 6-8-1 48 ow1.................... ShaneBKelly(5) 7 56+
(Jim Goldie) *hld up in tch: niggled after 4f: pushed along 1/2-way: effrt and squeezed through against far rail to chse clr ldng pair over 2f out: led ins fnl f: styd on wl* **1/1**[1]
/0-0 **2** *3/4* **Clueless**[5] 4602 9-8-7 52 ow1.................................... DaleSwift(3) 4 60
(Keith Dalgleish) *mde most tl rdn and hdd ins fnl f: kpt on towards fin* **13/2**
604 **3** *5* **Morning Time (IRE)**[8] 4499 5-8-13 62....................(p) GarryWhillans(7) 2 63
(Lucinda Russell) *t.k.h: trckd ldrs: effrt and disp ld over 3f out to over 1f out: outpcd ins fnl f* **11/2**[3]
-004 **4** *4 1/2* **Ballade De La Mer**[73] 2400 5-8-3 45....................(v) PatrickMathers 3 40
(George Foster) *t.k.h: trckd ldrs: rdn and outpcd over 3f out: n.d after* **11/1**
5412 **5** *7* **Terenzium (IRE)**[26] 3906 9-8-13 55 (p) FrederikTylicki 8 41
(Micky Hammond) *cl up: chal 1/2-way to over 3f out: wknd fnl 2f* **4/1**[2]
0500 **6** *23* **Birkside**[8] 4499 8-8-7 49.................................... SaleemGolam 5 —
(Linda Perratt) *hld up in tch: rdn fr 3f out: wknd 2f out* **25/1**

3m 30.9s (10.50) **Going Correction** -0.025s/f (Good) **6** Ran SP% **110.9**
Speed ratings (Par 101): **71,70,67,65,61 49**
Tote Swingers:1&2:£1.10, 2&3:£1.90, 1&3:£2.40 CSF £7.90 CT £22.29 TOTE £2.10: £1.20, £2.60; EX 4.80.
Owner David McKenzie **Bred** Floors Farming & The Duke Of Devonshire **Trained** Uplawmoor, E Renfrews
■ Stewards' Enquiry : Dale Swift one-day ban: used whip with excessive frequency down shoulder in the forehand (Aug 20)
Shane B Kelly caution: used whip with excessive frequency.

FOCUS
An ordinary staying event overall, with the third setting the standard.

4786 CHAMPAGNE G.H. MUMM CORDON ROUGE H'CAP 5f
8:40 (8:43) (Class 6) (0-65,61) 3-Y-O £1,704 (£503; £251) Stalls Low

Form RPR
6043 **1** **Nafa (IRE)**[9] 4466 3-8-13 53.................................... DanielTudhope 5 58
(Michael Mullineaux) *mde virtually all: rdn 2f out: hld on wl fnl f* **13/2**
5-04 **2** *nse* **Myjestic Melody (IRE)**[19] 4146 3-8-11 51.................................... RobertWinston 8 56
(Noel Wilson) *swtchd to r alone stands' side sn after s: rdn over 2f out: kpt on wl fnl f: jst failed* **15/2**
0324 **3** *nk* **Hardrock Diamond**[8] 4505 3-8-2 47.................................... ShaneBKelly(5) 4 51
(Ian Semple) *hld up in tch: effrt and swtchd lft 2f out: kpt on fnl f: hld towards fin* **5/2**[1]
3560 **4** *1 1/4* **Hootys Agogo**[7] 4564 3-8-3 50.................................... JasonHart(7) 1 49
(Declan Carroll) *w ldrs: rdn over 2f out: drifted rt and one pce ins fnl f* **5/1**
1455 **5** *2 1/2* **Beautiful Day**[7] 4527 3-9-4 61....................(b) DaleSwift(3) 6 51
(Kevin Ryan) *t.k.h: w ldrs: rdn 2f out: no ex appr fnl f* **4/1**[2]
463 **6** *nk* **Chester Deelyte (IRE)**[20] 4124 3-8-12 52....................(v) FrederikTylicki 7 41
(Lisa Williamson) *in tch: rdn over 2f out: no ex over 1f out* **9/2**[3]
-503 **7** *1 1/4* **Tinzo (IRE)**[19] 4146 3-8-6 46.................................... SaleemGolam 2 31
(Alan Berry) *prom tl rdn and wknd over 1f out* **25/1**

60.18 secs (0.78) **Going Correction** -0.15s/f (Firm) **7** Ran SP% **112.4**
Speed ratings (Par 98): **93,92,92,90,86 85,83**
Tote Swingers:1&2:£12.70, 2&3:£1.20, 1&3:£3.70 CSF £50.99 CT £152.66 TOTE £8.30: £3.90, £2.20; EX 61.50.

Owner Michael Mullineaux **Bred** Basil Brindley **Trained** Alpraham, Cheshire

FOCUS

A low-grade sprint to conclude proceedings. It has been rated around the winner to the best view of her previous form.

T/Plt: £150.10 to a £1 stake. Pool £51,814.82 - 251.87 winning tickets. T/Qpdt: £16.60 to a £1 stake. Pool £5,352.37 - 238.44 winning tickets. RY

4747 HAYDOCK (L-H)

Saturday, August 6

OFFICIAL GOING: Good (straight 8.2, round 7.6)

Wind: Light, half-against. Weather: overcast becoming fine and sunny

4787 REWARDS4RACING.COM NURSERY — 5f

1:45 (1:46) (Class 3) (0-95,87) 2-Y-O — **£7,439** (£2,213; £1,106; £553) **Stalls** Centre

Form			Horse	Jockey	RPR
1033	**1**		**Rent Free**[14] 4343 2-8-9 **75** (Nigel Tinkler) *led centre gp over 1f out: chsd ldrs: edgd lft and styd on to ld towards fin* **16/1**	TomEaves 5	78
1641	**2**	*nk*	**Guru Girl**[7] 4558 2-8-9 **75** (Mrs K Burke) *racd stands' side: overall ldr over 3f out: hdd and no ex towards fin* **7/1**[3]	AndrewElliott 7	77
51	**3**	*nk*	**O'Gorman**[15] 4283 2-9-3 **83** (Kevin Ryan) *trckd ldrs: t.k.h: drvn 2f out: no ex last 75yds* **10/11**[1]	PhillipMakin 4	84
5200	**4**	*1 ¾*	**Signifer (IRE)**[7] 4536 2-9-4 **84** (Mick Channon) *hld up: swtchd stands' side over 2f out: sn chsng ldrs: styd on same pce fnl 100yds* **7/1**[3]	KierenFallon 3	79
3234	**5**	*1 ¾*	**Beau Mistral (IRE)**[42] 3375 2-8-3 **69** (Paul Green) *chsd ldr stands' side: rdn 2f out: no imp* **33/1**	FrannyNorton 6	57
3111	**6**	*8*	**Last Bid**[14] 4343 2-9-7 **87** (Tim Easterby) *chsd ldrs on outside: drvn over 2f out: lost pl over 1f out: heavily eased fnl 100yds* **10/3**[2]	DavidAllan 2	60

61.44 secs (0.64) **Going Correction** +0.05s/f (Good) **6** Ran SP% **109.3**

Speed ratings (Par 98): **98,97,97,94,91 78**

Tote Swingers:1&2:£2.60, 2&3:£3.50, 1&3:£6.60 CSF £109.90 TOTE £14.40: £3.10, £2.30; EX 74.00.

Owner Maze Rattan Limited **Bred** L T Roberts **Trained** Langton, N Yorks

FOCUS

Sprint races run on the inner home straight. Races over 1m and further finished on the stands' side home straight. Races advertised as 1m run over 1m 51yds, races advertised as 1m2f 95yds run over 1m2f 145yds. Drying ground, described as good all round. A decent nursery run at a sound clip. A couple of the leading condenders were below par so the form may not prove that solid. Two raced on the stands' rail through the early parts with the other four further out on the track. The winner is rated back towards his Ayr form.

NOTEBOOK

Rent Free, one of the four to race out towards the centre, lost his pitch with two to run but rallied under pressure to get up late on. Third to Last Bid in York nurseries on his last two starts, he enjoyed a 9lb pull with that filly, who was clearly below her best here. (op 14-1)

Guru Girl showed bright pace and claimed the rail, only succumbing to the winner's late charge. This was a sound effort from a 5lb higher mark than when winning at Thirsk. (op 9-1)

O'Gorman looked to have got in lightly on this nursery debut off a mark of 83. After racing keenly he came to have every chance, but was unable to quicken up and this has to go down as a disappointing run from a well regarded colt with Group-race entries. Quicker ground may suit. (op 5-6 tchd 8-11 and evens in places)

Signifer(IRE), down in trip, was close enough at the furlong pole before his challenge fizzled out. (op 15-2)

Beau Mistral(IRE) was unable to get to the front, instead tracking the runner-up on the stands' rail. She is a consistent filly and probably gave her running again. (op 28-1 tchd 40-1)

Last Bid was attempting a four-timer, but was unable to cement her York superiority over Rent Free. Racing out widest, she was the first under pressure and failed to pick up. This was not her true running, and David Allan reported that she was never travelling. Official explanation: jockey said filly never travelled (op 7-2 tchd 3-1)

4788 WATCH RACES LIVE AT RACINGUK.COM H'CAP — 1m 2f 95y

2:15 (2:20) (Class 2) (0-105,104) 3-Y-O+ **£12,938** (£3,850; £1,924; £962) **Stalls** Centre

Form			Horse	Jockey	RPR
-340	**1**		**Dhaamer (IRE)**[15] 4267 4-8-10 **86** (v[1]) (John Gosden) *mid-div: hdwy over 3f out: led over 2f out: edgd rt: forged clr fnl f* **9/1**[3]	TadhgO'Shea 8	102+
4061	**2**	*4*	**Auld Burns**[23] 4022 3-9-3 **102** (Richard Hannon) *trckd ldrs: styd on to chse wnr ins fnl f: no imp* **7/1**[2]	PatDobbs 7	109
3014	**3**	*¾*	**The Only Key**[36] 3592 5-8-9 **85** (Jane Chapple-Hyam) *trckd ldrs: chal over 3f out: kpt on same pce appr fnl f* **11/1**	LukeMorris 13	91
1004	**4**	*2 ¾*	**Jutland**[11] 4410 4-9-9 **99** (Mark Johnston) *mid-div: outpcd over 3f out: edgd lft and styd on appr fnl f* **14/1**	DarryllHolland 10	100
0006	**5**	*1*	**Mirrored**[7] 4528 5-8-11 **87** (Tim Easterby) *hld up in rr: hdwy over 2f out: kpt on fnl f: nt rch ldrs* **14/1**	DuranFentiman 9	86+
0100	**6**	*½*	**Resurge (IRE)**[11] 4410 6-9-11 **101** (Stuart Kittow) *edgd lft after s: in rr: outpcd and lost pl over 3f out: edgd rt and hdwy over 1f out: kpt on* **20/1**	WilliamBuick 16	99
0013	**7**	*3 ¼*	**Tinshu (IRE)**[15] 4267 5-8-10 **86** (Derek Haydn Jones) *mid-div: effrt over 3f out: wknd over 1f out* **14/1**	DaneO'Neill 2	77
-106	**8**	*¾*	**Sam Sharp (USA)**[15] 4267 5-8-9 **88** (Ian Williams) *dwlt: swtchd lft after s: gd hdwy over 3f out: sn chsng ldrs: wknd over 1f out* **9/1**[3]	RyanClark(3) 17	78
0100	**9**	*1 ¼*	**Pleasant Day (IRE)**[8] 4494 4-8-11 **90** (b) (Richard Fahey) *mid-div: drvn over 3f out: nvr nr ldrs* **20/1**	LeeTopliss(3) 15	77
/54-	**10**	*½*	**Bauer (IRE)**[323] 6148 8-9-7 **104** (Luca Cumani) *hld up in rr: swtchd ins and sme hdwy over 3f out: wknd over 1f out* **25/1**	SAJackson(7) 4	91+
5402	**11**	*nk*	**Dhaular Dhar (IRE)**[7] 4528 9-8-9 **85** (Jim Goldie) *mid-div: drvn over 3f out: nvr a factor* **14/1**	TomEaves 3	71
1/10	**12**	*1*	**Burj Nahar**[13] 4354 4-9-11 **101** (Saeed Bin Suroor) *hld up in rr: effrt over 3f out: nvr on terms* **9/2**[1]	MickaelBarzalona 11	85+
0-05	**13**	*5*	**Never Forget (FR)**[21] 4099 4-9-9 **99** (Luca Cumani) *trckd ldrs: slipped bnd 5f out: led over 3f out: sn hdd: lost pl over 1f out* **20/1**	KirstyMilczarek 14	73
U-0	**14**	*47*	**All Annalena (IRE)**[14] 4331 5-8-11 **87** (t) (Lucy Wadham) *led 1f: chsd ldr: led 4f out: sn hdd: lost pl and heavily eased over 2f out: virtually p.u: t.o* **33/1**	StevieDonohoe 12	—
1300	**15**	*7*	**Wrekin Sunset**[15] 4293 3-8-2 **87** ow1 (Mrs K Burke) *dwlt: hdwy to ld after 1f: hdd 4f out: sn lost pl and heavily eased: virtually p.u: t.o* **40/1**	FrannyNorton 1	—

2m 11.82s (-4.18) **Going Correction** -0.175s/f (Firm)

WFA 3 from 4yo+ 9lb **15** Ran SP% **108.3**

Speed ratings (Par 109): **109,105,105,103,102 101,99,98,97,97 96,96,92,54,48**

Tote Swingers:1&2:£17.80, 2&3:£23.10, 1&3:£22.80 CSF £48.34 CT £446.96 TOTE £8.40: £2.80, £2.20, £3.50; EX 64.60 Trifecta £1296.70 Pool £29,650.53 - 16.92 winning units..

Owner Hamdan Al Maktoum **Bred** Shadwell Estate Company Limited **Trained** Newmarket, Suffolk

■ Naqshabban was withdrawn (5/1, unruly and ref to ent stalls). Deduct 15p in the £ under R4.

FOCUS

A good handicap, but a race which has lost its heritage handicap designation and the prize money was down considerably as a result. The early gallop was strong and the field tacked over to the stands' side in the straight. The pacesetters dropped out to finish at the back. It looked a competitive race beforehand, but that was not how it turned out. Solid form amongst the principals.

NOTEBOOK

Dhaamer(IRE) ran out a very comfortable winner. The first-time visor clearly made a big difference to the gelding, who travelled up well and had his race won heading to the final furlong. He had run a couple of creditable placed races earlier in the season before a lesser effort at Ascot, where the easy ground may not have suited and where he finished behind Tinshu and Sam Sharp. In this mood he could win again, but he will be up in the weights and there is no guarantee that the headgear will work as well again. (op 10-1)

Auld Burns was never far from the pace but was no threat to the winner once that one kicked. He was one of only two 3yos in the field and this was a pleasing handicap debut. (op 10-1)

The Only Key had every chance and this was another solid run. The drying ground was perhaps not to her advantage and she is capable of winning off this mark. (op 14-1)

Jutland stayed on from the rear despite hanging to his left. He is not that consistent but has put together two consecutive good runs now, following his fourth at Goodwood.

Mirrored, who went to post early, was short of room as the field stacked up approaching the home turn, but for which he might have finished closer. (tchd 12-1)

Resurge(IRE), an Epsom specialist, was last into the straight before running on. (op 22-1)

Tinshu(IRE) ran her race again and confirmed her Ascot superiority over Sam Sharp. (op 11-1)

Sam Sharp(USA) improved after a slow start before his effort flattened out. (op 8-1)

Bauer(IRE), injured out in Australia when being trained for another crack at the Melbourne Cup, made a satisfactory comeback under an apprentice having his first ride in public.

Burj Nahar found himself caught wide in the straight and never figured. The ground was going against him but he has something to prove now. (op 5-1)

Never Forget(FR) Official explanation: jockey said filly slipped on bend

All Annalena(IRE) Official explanation: jockey said mare lost its action

Wrekin Sunset Official explanation: jockey said filly lost its action

4789 BETFRED ROSE OF LANCASTER STKS (GROUP 3) — 1m 2f 95y

2:45 (2:47) (Class 1) 3-Y-O+

£28,355 (£10,750; £5,380; £2,680; £1,345; £675) **Stalls** Centre

Form			Horse	Jockey	RPR
-214	**1**		**Class Is Class (IRE)**[14] 4345 5-9-3 114 (v) (Sir Michael Stoute) *trckd ldrs: led stands' side 3f out: edgd lft and drvn clr appr fnl f: eased towards fin* **3/1**[1]	KierenFallon 7	118
-365	**2**	*3 ½*	**Elusive Pimpernel (USA)**[21] 4095 4-9-3 113 (John Dunlop) *mid-div: outpcd over 3f out: styd on fnl 2f: tk 2nd nr fin* **12/1**	EddieAhern 4	111
46-2	**3**	*¾*	**Hot Prospect**[21] 4095 4-9-3 110 (Roger Varian) *hld up in mid-div: hdwy to trck ldrs 6f out: drvn over 3f out: chsd wnr over 1f out: kpt on same pce* **9/2**[2]	NeilCallan 8	110
0-34	**4**	*2 ¼*	**Critical Moment (USA)**[93] 1821 4-9-3 107 (B W Hills) *set stdy pce: qcknd over 3f out: sn hdd: kpt on same pce fnl 2f* **22/1**	MichaelHills 6	105
54-5	**5**	*1 ¾*	**Fallen Idol**[36] 3591 4-9-3 105 (John Gosden) *hld up in rr: checked over 4f out: outpcd over 3f out: kpt on fnl 2f* **15/2**	WilliamBuick 3	102
-002	**6**	*4 ½*	**Myplacelater**[15] 4293 4-9-0 108 (David Elsworth) *hld up in rr: lost pl over 4f out: no ch after* **16/1**	TomEaves 2	90
-241	**7**	*½*	**Sajjhaa**[15] 4293 4-9-0 112 (Saeed Bin Suroor) *sn trcking ldrs: wknd over 1f out: eased towards fin* **3/1**[1]	TedDurcan 1	94
1-10	**U**		**Simon De Montfort (IRE)**[156] 757 4-9-3 113 (Mahmood Al Zarooni) *t.k.h towards rr: bmpd and uns rdr over 4f out* **7/1**[3]	MickaelBarzalona 5	—

2m 15.4s (-0.60) **Going Correction** -0.175s/f (Firm) **8** Ran SP% **110.4**

Speed ratings (Par 113): **95,92,91,89,88 84,84,—**

Tote Swingers:1&2:£8.20, 2&3:£11.80, 1&3:£2.00 CSF £37.44 TOTE £3.50: £1.30, £3.50, £1.60; EX 34.80 Trifecta £289.30 Pool £1,266.90 - 3.24 winning units..

Owner R Ahamad & P Scott **Bred** P And C Scott & Exors Of The Late N Ahamad **Trained** Newmarket, Suffolk

FOCUS

An ordinary edition of this Group 3 event and a tight race on adjusted official figures. Six of the last nine runnings went to 3yos, but there were none from that generation in the line-up here. The pace was pretty steady initially and the runners again headed for the stands' side in the straight. The time was well over three seconds slower than the previous Class 2 handicap. The winner is the ebst guide to the form.

NOTEBOOK

Class Is Class(IRE) took it up early in the home straight and, winding up the pace, ran on strongly for an emphatic win, his first victory at this level. Runner-up to Poet in this race last year, he settled better than he had last time at York, where he reportedly became upset before the start. This likeable gelding should find further success at this level. (op 7-2 tchd 4-1 in places)

Elusive Pimpernel(USA) had been below his best this season but this was more like his old self. He was only fifth going to the furlong pole, but stayed on well from there if much too late to trouble the winner. A race over this trip should be found for him.

Hot Prospect, winner of the valuable handicap on this card a year ago, was caught for second inside the last by Elusive Pimpernel, whom he had beaten at Newbury. He could have done with softer ground, but ought to get his ideal conditions at some point during the autumn. (op 4-1 tchd 7-2 in places)

Critical Moment(USA), off the track since Chester's May meeting, made a lot of the running but could only keep on at the one pace once headed. He gets this trip but may be happier back at a mile. (op 16-1 tchd 25-1)

Fallen Idol, fourth in this event 12 months ago and running for just the second time since, was outpaced in the straight and was never a factor. He ran close to his Sandown Listed form with Class Is Class. (op 9-1)

Myplacelater was carried badly wide by the faller on the home turn and was never a factor after, but she did keep on to catch Sajjhaa, to whom she had finished runner-up in a Listed fillies' race at York. (op 14-1 tchd 12-1)

Sajjhaa top rated on official figures following her York win, had her chance but faded badly inside the last. This was disappointing, and a routine test was ordered. Official explanation: trainer had no explanation for the poor form shown (tchd 10-3 in places)

Simon De Montfort(IRE), off the track since the Dubai Carnival in March, raced keenly towards the rear until appearing to clip heels and unseating his jockey as the field turned in. Horse and rider appeared none the worse. (op 6-1)

4790 EBF "KAYF TARA" DICK HERN FILLIES' STKS (LISTED RACE) 1m
3:20 (3:22) (Class 1) 3-Y-O+

£17,013 (£6,450; £3,228; £1,608; £807; £405) **Stalls** Low

Form RPR

0640 **1** **Crystal Gal (IRE)**[28] 3876 4-9-0 94 .... DaneO'Neill 6 103
(Lucy Wadham) *chsd ldrs: n.m.r 3f out: edgd lft and styd on to ld towards fin* **11/1**

3533 **2** *hd* **Off Chance**[13] 4368 5-9-0 99 .... DuranFentiman 5 103
(Tim Easterby) *ponied to s: hld up in mid-div: effrt over 3f out: nt clr run over 2f out: swtchd stands' side and styd on strly fnl f: jst failed* **11/2**[3]

4-21 **3** *nk* **Heavenly Dawn**[21] 4093 4-9-0 95 .... WilliamBuick 7 102
(Sir Michael Stoute) *led 1f: trckd ldrs: edgd rt 3f out: led 2f out: edgd lft fnl f: hdd and no ex clsng stages* **11/8**[1]

5-3R **4** *2 ¾* **Jacqueline Quest (IRE)**[52] 3030 4-9-0 111 .... EddieAhern 9 96
(Ian Williams) *chsd ldrs early: sn hld up towards rr: smooth hdwy over 3f out: sn n.m.r: chal over 1f out: wknd last 150yds* **10/1**

6120 **5** *2* **Sylvestris (IRE)**[28] 3873 3-8-7 93 .... StevieDonohoe 11 90
(Ralph Beckett) *led after 1f: hdd 2f out: wknd fnl f* **33/1**

0012 **6** *1 ½* **Golden Delicious**[14] 4332 3-8-8 83 ow1 .... DarryllHolland 12 87
(Hughie Morrison) *hld up detached in last: hdwy and swtchd centre 2f out: one pce* **16/1**

-411 **7** *½* **Submission**[30] 3757 3-8-7 90 .... KierenFallon 1 85
(Luca Cumani) *trckd ldrs: effrt 3f out: wknd over 1f out* **7/2**[2]

3205 **8** *hd* **Blaise Chorus (IRE)**[17] 4208 3-8-8 94 ow1 .... MichaelHills 2 86
(B W Hills) *chsd ldrs: upsides over 2f out: wknd over 1f out* **20/1**

6225 **9** *12* **Belle Royale (IRE)**[21] 4093 3-8-7 90 .... FrannyNorton 10 57
(Mark Brisbourne) *s.i.s: in rr: slipped bnd 5f out: outpcd over 3f out: sn bhd* **25/1**

2-6 **10** *nk* **Madonna Dell'Orto**[42] 3413 4-9-0 73 .... AdamKirby 4 58
(Walter Swinburn) *hld up in rr: drvn over 3f out: sn bhd* **50/1**

1m 43.66s (0.76) **Going Correction** +0.35s/f (Good)
WFA 3 from 4yo+ 7lb **10 Ran SP% 116.5**
Speed ratings (Par 108): **110,109,109,106,104 103,102,102,90,90**
Tote Swingers:1&2:£10.60, 2&3:£3.20, 1&3:£5.40 CSF £67.39 TOTE £11.90: £3.30, £2.20, £1.30; EX 62.40.
Owner Mr And Mrs A E Pakenham **Bred** Castlemartin Stud And Skymarc Farm **Trained** Newmarket, Suffolk
■ Stewards' Enquiry : William Buick three-day ban: careless riding (Aug 20-22)

FOCUS
A decent renewal of this Listed event, which was formerly run at Bath. The runner-up is a solid guide to the form. They went a good pace and once more came over on the home turn. There were a number holding chances heading down to the furlong pole.

NOTEBOOK
Crystal Gal(IRE) was hard at work over a furlong out, but she ran on well to assert despite edging to her left. She had not been easy to place this term and ran down the field in the John Smith's Cup, but this slightly easier ground was a help. Her one previous win came on her racecourse debut for Kevin Prendergast in deep ground. (op 16-1)
Off Chance was second top on BHA ratings and she ran another thoroughly creditable race, staying on well in the final furlong and keeping straight, in contrast to the winner and third. This consistent mare has contested Listed races on each of her last eight starts and has missed the frame only once. (op 6-1)
Heavenly Dawn ◆ looked well worth a try at this level and she ran well, securing black type, but just lacked a change of pace and was drifting to her left late on. She remains one to keep on the right side and a return to 1m2f should see her off the mark in Listed company. (op 6-4)
Jacqueline Quest(IRE) has been transferred by her owner from Sir Henry Cecil to Ian Williams since she declined to come out of the stalls at Royal Ascot. There must have been a doubt over her consenting to run - Sariska and Memory are recent examples of high-profile fillies who developed a taste for refusing to race - but she gave no problems this time. Coming with her run nearest the stands' rail, she looked to be travelling best heading to the furlong pole, but she did not find as much as she had promised once let down. She might benefit from a return to 7f. (tchd 9-1)
Sylvestris(IRE), who stayed away from the rail in the straight, stuck on once headed for a creditable fifth. She is high enough in the weights these days and it makes sense to persevere at this level.
Golden Delicious kept on from the rear once switched to the outer of the bunch and saw out the mile well enough. This was a respectable effort at the weights. (op 14-1)
Submission was worth a try in this grade after handicap wins at Nottingham and Doncaster, but those successes came on fast ground and she was not quite as effective on this slightly easier surface. She had her chance, but dropped away entering the final furlong. (tchd 4-1)
Blaise Chorus(IRE) has not gone on from her Cheshire Oaks second to Wonder Of Wonders and her best trip remains a puzzle. (tchd 25-1)
Belle Royale(IRE) Official explanation: jockey said filly slipped on bend

4791 WATCH RACING UK ON SKY432 H'CAP (DIV I) 6f
3:55 (3:55) (Class 4) (0-85,86) 3-Y-O+ **£5,175** (£1,540; £769; £384) **Stalls** Centre

Form RPR

2002 **1** **Strike Up The Band**[18] 4174 8-9-12 85 .... AdrianNicholls 10 94
(David Nicholls) *mde all stands' side: kpt on fnl f: all out* **10/1**

1216 **2** *nk* **Rothesay Chancer**[28] 3853 3-8-10 76 .... GaryBartley(3) 11 83
(Jim Goldie) *hld up in mid-div: hdwy 2f out: str run fnl f: jst hld* **13/2**

6056 **3** *hd* **Mappin Time (IRE)**[14] 4324 3-9-1 78 .... DavidAllan 8 84
(Tim Easterby) *in rr: hdwy over 2f out: edgd lft over 1f out: chsd ldrs ins fnl f: styd on* **11/1**

01-0 **4** *½* **La Zamora**[8] 4516 5-9-10 83 .... GrahamGibbons 9 89+
(David Barron) *hood removed v late and rrd s: hld up towards rr: nt clr run stands' side over 2f out tl edgd rt 100yds out: fin wl* **14/1**

262 **5** *nk* **Ursula (IRE)**[12] 4392 5-9-7 80 .... AndrewElliott 1 85
(Mrs K Burke) *racd alone towards centre: chsd ldrs: outpcd over 2f out: kpt on fnl f* **4/1**[1]

0-15 **6** *½* **Lucky Dan (IRE)**[179] 455 5-9-2 75 .... FrannyNorton 12 78
(Paul Green) *hld up towards rr: t.k.h: hdwy to trck ldrs after 2f: one pce fnl f* **8/1**

4000 **7** *1 ¼* **Oldjoesaid**[7] 4531 7-9-9 82 .... PhillipMakin 5 81
(Kevin Ryan) *trckd ldrs: wknd fnl f* **9/2**[2]

1-05 **8** *nk* **Above The Stars**[22] 4048 3-9-0 80 .... LeeTopliss(3) 6 77
(Richard Fahey) *mid-div: hdwy over 2f out: chsd ldrs over 1f out: hung lft: fdd fnl 150yds* **8/1**

0500 **9** *1 ¼* **Befortyfour**[7] 4556 6-9-8 81 .... RobbieFitzpatrick 2 75
(Richard Guest) *outpcd in rr and drvn along: sme hdwy over 1f out: nvr a factor* **16/1**

0044 **10** *1 ¾* **Green Park (IRE)**[15] 4291 8-9-4 77 .... (b) StevieDonohoe 4 66
(Declan Carroll) *chsd ldrs: t.k.h: lost pl over 1f out* **6/1**[3]

1m 15.07s (1.27) **Going Correction** +0.275s/f (Good)
WFA 3 from 5yo+ 4lb **10 Ran SP% 118.0**
Speed ratings (Par 105): **100,99,99,98,98 97,95,95,93,91**
Tote Swingers:1&2:£7.40, 2&3:£14.50, 1&3:£18.30 CSF £74.44 CT £737.70 TOTE £12.20: £3.10, £1.80, £4.70; EX 69.30.
Owner Barker Moser Nicholls Short **Bred** Miss A J Rawding & P M Crane **Trained** Sessay, N Yorks

FOCUS
Division one of this fair sprint handicap and a race weakened by the non-participation of the two paper favourites. The time was slow and those drawn high came out on top. The winner is rated to his best in the past year.
Above The Stars Official explanation: jockey said filly hung left-handed final furlong
Green Park(IRE) Official explanation: jockey said gelding ran too free

4792 WATCH RACING UK ON SKY432 H'CAP (DIV II) 6f
4:30 (4:30) (Class 4) (0-85,85) 3-Y-O+ **£5,175** (£1,540; £769; £384) **Stalls** Centre

Form RPR

00 **1** **Mirza**[14] 4314 4-9-9 82 .... AdamKirby 8 99+
(Rae Guest) *bmpd s: in rr: pushed along over 4f out: hdwy and nt clr run over 2f out: gd hdwy and swtchd lft over 1f out: str run to ld last 50yds: eased nr fin* **9/2**[2]

0124 **2** *1 ½* **Pelmanism**[14] 4349 4-9-1 74 .... PhillipMakin 1 86
(Brian Ellison) *rrd s: hld up on outer: hdwy over 2f out: edgd rt over 1f out: led last 150yds: sn hdd and no ex* **5/1**[3]

2306 **3** *3* **Rio Cobolo (IRE)**[43] 3339 5-9-2 75 .... AdrianNicholls 3 78
(David Nicholls) *w ldrs on outer: led over 2f out: edgd rt over 1f out: hdd and no ex ins fnl f* **14/1**

3103 **4** *3* **Ryan Style (IRE)**[16] 4239 5-9-8 81 .... TomEaves 2 74
(Lisa Williamson) *mid-div: outpcd over 2f out: kpt on same pce fnl f* **14/1**

5043 **5** *hd* **Mayoman (IRE)**[20] 4126 6-9-4 77 .... StevieDonohoe 9 69
(Declan Carroll) *in rr: sme hdwy whn nt clr run and hmpd 1f out: styd on towards fin* **10/1**

0522 **6** *nk* **Ballinargh Girl (IRE)**[7] 4541 3-8-10 73 .... KierenFallon 7 64+
(Robert Wylie) *hld up in midfield: nt clr run over 2f out and over 1f out: edgd lft: kpt on ins fnl f* **4/1**[1]

0000 **7** *¾* **Tombi (USA)**[42] 3395 7-9-9 85 .... MichaelO'Connell(3) 12 74
(Ollie Pears) *chsd ldrs stands' side: wknd over 1f out* **8/1**

0102 **8** *1 ¼* **All Right Now**[26] 3924 4-9-2 75 .... DaneO'Neill 10 60
(Derek Haydn Jones) *dwlt: sn trcking ldrs: wknd appr fnl f* **14/1**

0022 **9** *1 ¼* **Pavershooz**[14] 4327 6-9-11 84 .... DuranFentiman 6 65
(Noel Wilson) *led tl over 2f out: wknd over 1f out* **9/1**

0036 **10** *1* **Greyfriarschorista**[12] 4392 4-8-12 71 .... DarryllHolland 11 49
(Mark Johnston) *in rr: drvn 3f out: nvr on terms: eased nr fin* **10/1**

0205 **11** *10* **Legal Eagle (IRE)**[64] 2668 6-9-5 78 .... (p) EddieAhern 5 24+
(Paul Green) *half rrd s: sn chsng ldrs on outer: wkng whn hmpd over 1f out: sn heavily eased* **12/1**

1m 14.37s (0.57) **Going Correction** +0.275s/f (Good)
WFA 3 from 4yo+ 4lb **11 Ran SP% 121.8**
Speed ratings (Par 105): **105,103,99,95,94 94,93,91,90,88 75**
Tote Swingers:1&2:£5.30, 2&3:£25.30, 1&3:£15.80 CSF £28.45 CT £306.32 TOTE £5.60: £2.10, £1.90, £4.70; EX 33.00.
Owner C J Mills **Bred** C J Mills **Trained** Newmarket, Suffolk

FOCUS
The quicker of the two divisions by over half a second. The winner is rated back to his 3yo best.

4793 DUKE OF LANCASTER'S OWN YEOMANRY H'CAP 6f
5:00 (5:01) (Class 5) (0-70,70) 3-Y-O+ **£3,234** (£962; £481; £240) **Stalls** Centre

Form RPR

0001 **1** **Kings 'n Dreams**[16] 4233 4-9-11 69 .... (b) KierenFallon 14 79
(Dean Ivory) *hld up: hdwy stands' side over 2f out: str run fnl f: led last strides* **4/1**[1]

0056 **2** *hd* **Piddie's Power**[23] 4020 4-9-12 70 .... GrahamGibbons 4 79
(Ed McMahon) *dwlt: sn w ldrs: led over 1f out: hdd nr fin* **9/1**

6001 **3** *1 ¼* **Downhill Skier (IRE)**[8] 4518 7-9-8 66 .... EddieAhern 8 71
(Mark Brisbourne) *dwlt: in rr: hdwy and edgd rt over 1f out: styd on ins fnl f* **6/1**[3]

100 **4** *nse* **Gracie's Games**[15] 4270 5-8-13 60 .... SophieDoyle(3) 1 65
(Richard Price) *awkward s: sn chsng ldrs on outer: sn drvn along: kpt on same pce fnl f* **12/1**

5004 **5** *1* **Bond Fastrac**[19] 4145 4-9-8 66 .... (v) DaneO'Neill 6 68
(Geoffrey Oldroyd) *dwlt: sn chsng ldrs: kpt on same pce appr fnl f* **6/1**[3]

0-05 **6** *1 ¼* **Belinsky (IRE)**[15] 4291 4-9-3 61 .... FrannyNorton 11 59
(Mark Campion) *mid-div: sn drvn along: one pce fnl 2f: eased nr fin* **14/1**

0550 **7** *2 ¾* **Red River Boy**[8] 4518 6-8-7 51 oh2 .... AdrianNicholls 12 40
(Chris Fairhurst) *towards rr: sme hdwy over 1f out: nvr a factor* **33/1**

0050 **8** *hd* **El Dececy (USA)**[10] 4441 7-9-2 60 .... (t) RobbieFitzpatrick 5 49
(Richard Guest) *edgd rt s and led over 2f: chsd ldrs stands' side: lost pl and hmpd over 1f out* **16/1**

01 **9** *1 ¼* **Northern Bolt**[17] 4196 6-9-7 68 .... LeeTopliss(3) 13 53
(Ian McInnes) *a towards rr* **15/2**

4642 **10** *nk* **Mount Hollow**[16] 4233 6-9-0 58 .... (v) MickaelBarzalona 3 42
(Reg Hollinshead) *racd w ldrs: led over 3f out: rdn and carried hd high: hdd over 1f out: sn wknd: eased nr fin* **9/2**[2]

0200 **11** *½* **Divertimenti (IRE)**[8] 4518 7-9-7 65 .... (b) RussKennemore 7 47
(Roy Bowring) *dwlt: sn trcking ldrs: wknd over 2f out* **25/1**

1100 **12** *3* **Flying Applause**[8] 4517 6-9-8 66 .... (bt) MarcHalford 2 38
(Roy Bowring) *towards rr on outer: bhd fnl 2f* **25/1**

1m 15.23s (1.43) **Going Correction** +0.275s/f (Good) **12 Ran SP% 119.4**
Speed ratings (Par 103): **99,98,97,97,95 94,90,90,88,88 87,83**
Tote Swingers:1&2:£7.20, 2&3:£10.20, 1&3:£4.30 CSF £39.69 CT £220.87 TOTE £4.60: £2.30, £1.80, £2.00; EX 38.80.
Owner Ian Gethin & Richard Gethin **Bred** P A Blows **Trained** Radlett, Herts
■ Stewards' Enquiry : Eddie Ahern two-day ban: careless riding (Aug 21-22)

FOCUS
A modest sprint handicap and the slowest of the three C&D times. The form looks sound.

4794 TURFTV.CO.UK H'CAP 1m
5:35 (5:35) (Class 3) (0-95,91) 3-Y-O+ **£8,409** (£2,502; £1,250; £625) **Stalls** Low

Form RPR

0-43 **1** **Markazzi**[29] 3825 4-9-4 86 .... TadhgO'Shea 5 98+
(Sir Michael Stoute) *hld up in mid-div: hdwy on outer over 2f out: edgd lft over 1f out: styd on to ld last 100yds: drvn out* **10/3**[1]

-030 **2** *1 ¼* **Venutius**[29] 3825 4-9-3 85 .... GrahamGibbons 2 94
(Ed McMahon) *led: hdd ins fnl f: no ex* **16/1**

-334 **3** *shd* **Don't Call Me (IRE)**[11] 4415 4-9-6 **88** .... AdrianNicholls 10 97+
(David Nicholls) *stdd s: in rr: hdwy over 3f out: edgd rt over 1f out: 8th 1f out: swtchd lft and styd on strly towards fin* **9/2**[2]

2243 **4** *1 ¾* **Dolphin Rock**[7] 4561 4-9-2 **84** .... EddieAhern 11 89
(David Barron) *chsd ldrs: one pce whn sltly hmpd last 50yds* **10/1**

6321 **5** *1* **First Post (IRE)**[15] 4268 4-9-0 **82** .... DaneO'Neill 15 84
(Derek Haydn Jones) *trckd ldrs: upsides over 1f out: one pce* **16/1**

3231 **6** *½* **Karaka Jack**[14] 4349 4-9-0 **85** .... MichaelO'Connell(3) 8 86
(David Nicholls) *mid-div: hdwy over 2f out: edgd rt: chsng ldrs over 1f out: kpt on same pce* **10/1**

5556 **7** *1 ¼* **Mr Rainbow**[14] 4325 5-9-4 **86** .... AndrewElliott 1 84
(Alan Swinbank) *trckd ldr: t.k.h: hung rt over 1f out: fdd ins fnl f* **16/1**

6210 **8** *¾* **Charlie Cool**[11] 4415 8-9-3 **85** .... (b) PhillipMakin 3 82
(Ruth Carr) *trckd ldrs: effrt whn hmpd 2f out: one pce over 1f out* **10/1**

6225 **9** *2* **She's A Character**[30] 3763 4-8-11 **82** .... LeeTopliss(3) 16 74
(Richard Fahey) *t.k.h in rr: kpt on fnl 2f: nvr a factor* **25/1**

2120 **10** *1* **Just Bond (IRE)**[7] 4561 9-9-5 **87** .... AdamKirby 14 77
(Geoffrey Oldroyd) *mid-div: outpcd over 3f out: no threat after* **25/1**

0506 **11** *1 ¼* **Kiwi Bay**[28] 3877 6-9-5 **87** .... TomEaves 13 74
(Michael Dods) *t.k.h in rr: effrt over 3f out: sme hdwy 2f out: nvr a factor* **20/1**

0151 **12** *5* **Norman Orpen (IRE)**[28] 3877 4-9-9 **91** .... WilliamBuick 6 66
(Jane Chapple-Hyam) *hld up towards rr: sme hdwy over 3f out: wknd over 1f out: eased ins fnl f* **7/1**[3]

040 **13** *2 ¼* **Majuro (IRE)**[7] 4561 7-9-0 **82** .... (t) RobbieFitzpatrick 4 52
(Richard Guest) *t.k.h: trckd ldrs: drvn over 3f out: lost pl 2f out* **50/1**

-310 **14** *8* **Dream Achieved**[51] 3067 3-9-1 **90** .... MichaelHills 17 42
(B W Hills) *t.k.h in rr: sme hdwy on outer over 3f out: bhd and eased ins fnl f* **12/1**

6-00 **15** *3* **Oratory (IRE)**[42] 3397 5-9-5 **87** .... FrannyNorton 12 32
(Geoffrey Harker) *swtchd lft after s: a in rr* **40/1**

1m 44.25s (1.35) **Going Correction** +0.35s/f (Good)
WFA 3 from 4yo+ 7lb **15** Ran SP% **123.2**
Speed ratings (Par 107): **107,105,105,103,102 102,101,100,98,97 96,91,88,80,77**
Tote Swingers:1&2:£10.90, 2&3:£16.20, 1&3:£3.20 CSF £56.65 CT £257.27 TOTE £3.90: £1.60, £3.90, £2.80; EX 63.70.
Owner Hamdan Al Maktoum **Bred** Miss R J Dobson **Trained** Newmarket, Suffolk

FOCUS
An open handicap, but not a particularly strong race for the grade. The second and fourth set a solid standard. The pace was solid and, as with all the races on the round course, they headed over to the stands' side in the straight.

NOTEBOOK
Markazzi had plenty on his plate with three furlongs left, but he stayed on well down the outside and was nicely on top at the finish. Also effective at 1m2f, he had been threatening this and remains relatively lightly raced. (tchd 7-2)
Venutius tried to make all and claimed the rail moving easily, but could not hold off the winner, who had finished in front of him at Newmarket. Well suited by front-running tactics, he gained his last win over C&D in June last year.
Don't Call Me(IRE) came home well from off the pace once switched and would have been second in another stride. This is his trip and his luck could change soon. (op 5-1)
Dolphin Rock was never far from the pace but was already held when he was slightly hampered late on and his jockey stopped pushing. He has a good record at this track but is a bit too consistent for his own good. (op 11-1)
First Post(IRE), only 2lb higher than when winning at Ascot, ran another sound race. He did not swerve to his left this time, but gave the impression he would have done had there not been horses that side of him.
Karaka Jack ran creditably off this 6lb higher mark. He stays this trip but all his victories have come at 7f.
Just Bond(IRE) Official explanation: jockey said gelding had no more to give
Norman Orpen(IRE) Official explanation: jockey said gelding never travelled
T/Plt: £2,032.90 to a £1 stake. Pool £101,367.88. 36.40 winning tickets. T/Qpdt: £24.90 to a £1 stake. Pool £6,863.72. 203.24 winning tickets. WG

4753 LINGFIELD (L-H)
Saturday, August 6

OFFICIAL GOING: Turf course - good (7.8); all-weather - standard
Wind: Moderate, behind Weather: Fine but cloudy

4795 BLACKBERRY LANE H'CAP (TURF) 6f
5:50 (5:50) (Class 5) (0-75,70) 3-Y-O+ **£2,045** (£603; £302)

Form RPR

6506 **1** **Silvee**[9] 4458 4-8-8 **52** .... NeilChalmers 3 62
(John Bridger) *cl up: trckd ldr 1/2-way: led 2f out: rdn and steadily drew clr* **5/1**

4114 **2** *4* **Bermondsey Bob (IRE)**[10] 4434 5-9-9 **70** .... KierenFox(3) 2 67
(John Spearing) *led and sn crossed to nr side rail: drvn over 2f out: sn hdd: one pce* **5/2**[1]

5305 **3** *1* **Little Perisher**[21] 4086 4-8-4 **51** oh2 .... (b) HarryBentley(3) 4 45
(Karen George) *racd wd: sn rdn to stay in tch: outpcd over 2f out: plugged on to take 3rd nr fin* **8/1**

0040 **4** *nk* **Kyllachy Storm**[5] 4618 7-9-8 **66** .... GeorgeBaker 1 59
(Ron Hodges) *chsd ldr to 1/2-way: nt qckn over 2f out: fdd* **9/2**[3]

4340 **5** *2* **Make My Dream**[15] 4272 8-9-9 **67** .... LiamKeniry 7 54
(John Gallagher) *chsd ldrs: rdn fr 1/2-way: fdd fr 2f out* **11/2**

-420 **6** *9* **C'Mon You Irons (IRE)**[42] 3412 6-9-6 **64** .... (b) AndreaAtzeni 6 22
(Mark Hoad) *chsd ldrs: rdn 1/2-way: wknd 2f out: eased fnl f* **7/2**[2]

1m 11.2s **Going Correction** -0.10s/f (Good)
WFA 3 from 4yo+ 4lb **6** Ran SP% **112.1**
Speed ratings (Par 103): **96,90,89,88,86 74**
Tote Swingers:1&2:£3.90, 2&3:£7.00, 1&3:£11.10 CSF £17.84 CT £95.97 TOTE £9.10: £3.60, £1.50; EX 32.50.
Owner Mr & Mrs K Finch **Bred** Mr And Mrs K Finch **Trained** Liphook, Hants

FOCUS
With only two stall handlers present after some major traffic problems holding up the remainder, this ordinary sprint handicap was flip started. Weak form, rated around the winner.

4796 MAYBE GAGA PERFORMING HERE 13TH AUGUST MAIDEN STKS (TURF) 6f
6:20 (6:21) (Class 5) 3-Y-O+ **£3,067** (£905; £453)

Form RPR

3 **1** **Awjila**[21] 4102 3-8-12 0 .... JimCrowley 5 61
(Ralph Beckett) *smartly away: mde all and racd against rail: drvn over 1f out: styd on wl* **2/5**[1]

0005 **2** *2 ¼* **Control Chief**[21] 4088 3-9-3 52 .... GeorgeBaker 2 59
(Ralph Beckett) *chsd wnr: pushed along 2f out: shkn up and no imp over 1f out: styd on* **25/1**

02 **3** *3 ¾* **Mucky Molly**[17] 4203 3-8-12 0 .... LiamKeniry 6 42
(Olivia Maylam) *chsd ldrs against rail: wnt 3rd over 2f out: pushed along and outpcd wl over 1f out: reminder fnl f: kpt on* **20/1**

-632 **4** *3* **Dictionary**[35] 3616 3-9-3 64 .... (t) LiamJones 7 37
(William Haggas) *s.i.s: rdn in last pair after 2f: effrt u.p 2f out: no hdwy over 1f out* **5/1**[2]

04 **5** *nk* **Saktoon (USA)**[30] 3756 3-8-12 0 .... LukeMorris 3 31
(Clive Brittain) *sn rdn in last pair: a struggling and nvr a factor* **15/2**[3]

4 **6** *2 ¼* **Royal Selection (IRE)**[14] 4340 3-8-12 0 .... TomMcLaughlin 4 24
(Karen George) *s.i.s: chsd ldrs: rdn over 2f out: sn wknd* **16/1**

5060 **7** *10* **Fairy Tales**[16] 4247 3-8-12 47 .... NeilChalmers 1 —
(John Bridger) *led in s and slowly away: rcvrd to chse ldng pair on outer to over 2f out: wknd rapidly* **66/1**

1m 11.8s (0.60) **Going Correction** -0.10s/f (Good) **7** Ran SP% **115.8**
Speed ratings (Par 103): **92,89,84,80,79 76,63**
Tote Swingers:1&2:£3.40, 2&3:£16.30, 1&3:£2.40 CSF £17.44 TOTE £1.50: £1.10, £11.40; EX 13.30.
Owner Jeremy Gompertz **Bred** Ptarmigan Bloodstock Ltd **Trained** Kimpton, Hants

FOCUS
Another flip start for a maiden that lacked any strength. The winner didn't need to match her debut form.
Royal Selection(IRE) Official explanation: jockey said filly hung left

4797 ASHURSTWOOD H'CAP (TURF) 6f
6:50 (6:50) (Class 4) (0-85,83) 3-Y-O **£4,528** (£1,347; £673; £336)

Form RPR

-114 **1** **Farlow (IRE)**[22] 4078 3-9-1 **77** .... JimCrowley 6 94
(Ralph Beckett) *racd against rail: mde all: rdn clr over 1f out: r.o wl* **5/2**[2]

-316 **2** *5* **Midnight Feast**[19] 4156 3-9-5 **81** .... LukeMorris 3 82
(Peter Winkworth) *chsd ldng pair: rdn 1/2-way: kpt on u.p to take 2nd over 1f out: no ch w wnr* **10/3**[3]

-U41 **3** *¾* **Numeral (IRE)**[17] 4203 3-8-13 **75** .... PatCosgrave 1 74
(Richard Hannon) *rousted along to press wnr: drvn over 2f out: sn outpcd: lost 2nd over 1f out: one pce* **12/1**

2410 **4** *½* **Psychic's Dream**[29] 3819 3-9-2 **78** .... AndreaAtzeni 7 75
(Marco Botti) *hld up in 4th: rdn and effrt 2f out: disp 2nd over 1f out: one pce after* **11/2**

4043 **5** *3 ½* **Remotelinx (IRE)**[4] 4643 3-9-4 **83** .... PatrickHills(3) 8 69+
(J W Hills) *stdd s and allowed ldrs several l advantage: hld up last: taken to outer 4f out: rdn over 2f out: no prog and wl btn over 1f out: eased ins fnl f* **15/8**[1]

1m 10.2s (-1.00) **Going Correction** -0.10s/f (Good) **5** Ran SP% **109.5**
Speed ratings (Par 102): **102,95,94,93,89**
CSF £10.92 TOTE £4.00: £2.00, £2.20; EX 13.00.
Owner Lawrence, Deal & Carolyn Thornton **Bred** Patrick J Monahan **Trained** Kimpton, Hants

FOCUS
Flip start. A small field with three defections but a tight little contest where tactics played quite an integral part. The winner has been rated an improver, with the runner-up to his turf best and the third to his 2yo best.
Remotelinx(IRE) Official explanation: jockey said gelding missed the break and hung right

4798 BRITISH STALLION STUDS SUPPORTING BRITISH RACING EBF MAIDEN STKS 1m (P)
7:20 (7:21) (Class 5) 2-Y-O **£3,340** (£986; £493)

Form RPR

1 **Tamarrud** 2-9-3 0 .... TedDurcan 7 78+
(Saeed Bin Suroor) *trckd ldrs gng wl: prog 2f out: shkn up to take 2nd 1f out: rdn to ld narrowly but decisively last 100yds* **3/1**[1]

2 *nk* **Gassin Golf** 2-9-3 0 .... SebSanders 9 77+
(Sir Mark Prescott Bt) *prom: trckd ldr over 4f out: rdn to ld over 1f out: hdd and hld last 100yds* **6/1**

63 **3** *5* **Art Law (IRE)**[21] 4080 2-9-3 0 .... ShaneKelly 6 66+
(Brian Meehan) *hld up in rr: prog on wd outside over 3f out: rdn over 2f out: styd on u.p to take 3rd last 75yds* **5/1**[3]

0 **4** *1 ¾* **Lionrock (FR)**[17] 4213 2-8-12 0 .... AntiocoMurgia(5) 1 62
(Mahmood Al Zarooni) *mde most to over 1f out: wknd ins fnl f* **15/2**

0 **5** *1* **Northern Territory (IRE)**[21] 4087 2-9-3 0 .... PatCosgrave 2 59
(Jim Boyle) *pressed ldr to over 4f out: rdn over 2f out: steadily wknd* **100/1**

5 **6** *nk* **Perfect Gratitude (USA)**[25] 3954 2-9-3 0 .... GeorgeBaker 4 59
(Ed Dunlop) *hld up in midfield: rdn in 6th over 2f out: no prog after* **9/2**[2]

0 **7** *1* **Methaen (USA)**[30] 3755 2-9-3 0 .... ChrisCatlin 11 56
(Ed Dunlop) *settled in rr: pushed along over 2f out: steadily fdd on inner* **25/1**

0 **8** *3 ¾* **Saint Irene**[29] 3812 2-8-12 0 .... FrankieMcDonald 8 43
(Michael Blanshard) *in tch in rr: effrt over 3f out: no prog over 2f out: sn wknd* **20/1**

9 *8* **Romantic (IRE)** 2-9-3 0 .... IanMongan 3 29+
(Sir Henry Cecil) *lost many l in shambolic s: ct up at bk of field after 3f: wknd 3f out* **7/1**

0 **10** *1 ¼* **Cato Minor**[7] 4545 2-9-3 0 .... JimCrowley 5 27
(Amanda Perrett) *prom: rdn and lost pl over 3f out: bhd fnl 2f* **50/1**

U05 **L** **Thecornishcockney**[17] 4205 2-9-3 0 .... TomMcLaughlin 10 —
(John Ryan) *uns rdr and rn off bef r: restless bef s: facing wrong way whn field set off* **14/1**

1m 39.4s (1.20) **Going Correction** +0.05s/f (Slow) **11** Ran SP% **116.6**
Speed ratings (Par 94): **96,95,90,88,87 87,86,82,74,73 —**
Tote Swingers:1&2:£6.50, 2&3:£9.30, 1&3:£1.80 CSF £20.21 TOTE £2.80: £2.00, £2.30, £1.70; EX 29.30.
Owner Godolphin **Bred** Darley **Trained** Newmarket, Suffolk

FOCUS
An unsatisfactory flip start to this maiden which saw Thecornishcockney go the wrong way and Romantic completely missing the break, but it did feature some very interesting horses making their debuts. A fair pace but the front two pulled clear of the remainder and looked to be ones to keep an eye on for the future. Time will tell the true worth of the form.

NOTEBOOK
Tamarrud, a 50,000gns yearling from a family including St Leger winner Rule Of Law, opened his account in decent fashion. He travelled well just behind the leaders and when making his challenge found plenty to repel the runner-up in the closing stages, showing a very willing attitude. He's a very nice prospect who holds an entry in the Derby and as he was rather green beforehand he can only improve with experience. (op 2-1)

Gassin Golf is related to a couple of useful sorts including Listed winner Hotel Du Cap and looked the part in the paddock. He came there to win his race approaching the final furlong and picked up well when challenged inside the final furlong. He lost little in defeat here and looks certain to open his account before long. As with the winner he holds a Derby entry. (op 9-1)

Art Law(IRE) has been progressing with experience and this was another step in the right direction. He stayed on well enough from the rear and is up to winning races. (op 4-1)

Lionrock(FR), an expensive purchase, had to step up on his debut but he did look in need of the experience and ran respectably. He cut out the running at just a fair pace and had little more to offer when headed over a furlong out. Nonetheless this was more encouraging. (op 10-1 tchd 7-1)

Northern Territory(IRE) built upon his debut effort but could only stay on at the same pace after sitting prominently.

Perfect Gratitude(USA) shaped with promise on his debut and again did so here but could never get involved with the principals and will do better when eligible for nurseries. (op 15-2)

4799 LADBROKES MOBILE H'CAP — 7f (P)

7:50 (7:50) (Class 5) (0-75,75) 3-Y-O — **£2,045** (£603; £302) **Stalls** Low

Form — RPR

0613 **1** — **The Guru Of Gloom (IRE)**[23] [4020] 3-9-6 **74** .... GeorgeBaker 3 — 77+
(William Muir) *hld up in 6th: prog over 1f out towards inner: drvn to ld last 100yds: styd on wl* **11/4**[1]

0-50 **2** 1 **Greek Islands (IRE)**[15] [4281] 3-9-2 **70** .... PatCosgrave 4 — 70
(Ed de Giles) *chsd ldrs in 5th: drvn over 2f out: styd on u.p fnl f to take 2nd post* **12/1**

21-5 **3** hd **Mon Visage**[17] [4202] 3-9-5 **73** .... TedDurcan 1 — 73
(Chris Wall) *trckd ldng pair: effrt on inner over 1f out: upsides ins fnl f: one pce last 75yds* **9/2**[3]

0-00 **4** shd **Rafella (IRE)**[74] [2383] 3-8-13 **67** .... LukeMorris 7 — 66
(Simon Dow) *trckd ldr: rdn to chal 2f out: upsides ins fnl f: nt qckn last 100yds* **40/1**

4000 **5** 1/2 **Silly Billy (IRE)**[24] [3983] 3-8-8 **67** .... JemmaMarshall(5) 2 — 65
(Sylvester Kirk) *mde most: rdn and jnd 2f out: hdd and fdd last 100yds* **33/1**

6005 **6** nk **Flashbang**[12] [4387] 3-9-4 **72** .... ShaneKelly 9 — 69+
(Paul Cole) *dwlt: hld up in last: stl there 2f out: pushed along and sme prog over 1f out: rdn last 100yds and styd on: nvr nr to chal* **10/1**

0622 **7** nk **Hawk Moth (IRE)**[7] [4546] 3-8-13 **67** .... ChrisCatlin 5 — 63
(John Spearing) *hld up in last trio: rdn 2f out: styd on fnl f: nvr rchd ldrs* **11/2**

3253 **8** nk **Dark Isle**[59] [2802] 3-9-7 **75** .... SebSanders 6 — 71+
(J W Hills) *hld up in last trio and racd wd: rdn 2f out: kpt on u.p fnl f: nvr rchd ldrs* **4/1**[2]

3250 **9** 1 1/4 **Roman Strait**[8] [4511] 3-8-12 **66** .... LiamKeniry 8 — 58
(Michael Blanshard) *chsd ldng pair: rdn over 2f out: nt qckn over 1f out: wknd fnl f* **11/2**

1m 27.08s (2.28) **Going Correction** +0.05s/f (Slow) — 9 Ran SP% **117.8**
Speed ratings (Par 100): **88,86,86,86,85 85,85,84,83**
Tote Swingers:1&2:£13.00, 2&3:£32.10, 1&3:£3.90 CSF £38.71 CT £146.84 TOTE £4.50: £1.20, £2.10, £2.00; EX 62.10.
Owner R Haim **Bred** Oak Lodge Bloodstock **Trained** Lambourn, Berks

FOCUS
The stall handlers had finally arrived following their long trek stuck in traffic so the stalls were now in place for this competitive 7f handicap. It was slowly run and the form is a bit dubious.

4800 PLAY ROULETTE AT LADBROKES.COM MEDIAN AUCTION MAIDEN STKS — 1m 2f (P)

8:20 (8:22) (Class 6) 3-4-Y-O — **£2,181** (£644; £322) **Stalls** Low

Form — RPR

03 **1** — **O Ma Lad (IRE)**[67] [2591] 3-9-3 75 .... JamesDoyle 7 — 84
(Sylvester Kirk) *trckd ldrs: rdn to go 3rd over 2f out: clsd u.p 1f out: styd on to ld last 50yds* **3/1**[2]

-423 **2** 1/2 **Sally Friday (IRE)**[22] [4056] 3-8-12 72 .... LukeMorris 5 — 78
(Peter Winkworth) *prom: chsd ldr over 3f out: rdn to chal over 2f out: narrow ld over 1f out but hanging and idling: hrd rdn fnl f: hdd last 50yds* **4/5**[1]

0- **3** 1 **Beat Of The Blues**[287] [7034] 3-9-3 0 .... LiamKeniry 12 — 81
(Andrew Balding) *prog to ld after 2f: drvn and jnd over 2f out: hdd over 1f out: kpt on but lost 2nd ins fnl f* **11/2**[3]

-00 **4** 3/4 **Height Of Summer (IRE)**[54] [3001] 3-8-12 0 .... TedDurcan 10 — 74
(Chris Wall) *hld up in midfield: prog over 2f out: drvn to chse ldrs wl over 1f out: kpt on same pce* **66/1**

5 1 1/2 **Grand Theft Equine** 3-9-0 0 .... MatthewDavies(3) 8 — 76
(Jim Boyle) *dwlt: v green and reminder sn after s: prog fr rr on outer over 3f out: chsd ldrs and rdn over 2f out: one pce after* **40/1**

50 **6** 1 **The Calling Curlew**[19] [4157] 3-9-3 0 .... FrankieMcDonald 4 — 74+
(Henry Candy) *led 2f: chsd ldr to over 3f out: sn rdn: fdd over 1f out* **22/1**

-636 **7** 12 **If What And Maybe**[9] [4476] 3-9-3 50 .... TomMcLaughlin 2 — 50
(John Ryan) *prom: rdn over 3f out: wknd over 2f out* **33/1**

8 1 **In The Long Grass (IRE)** 3-9-3 0 .... GeorgeBaker 6 — 48
(Jim Boyle) *dwlt: a in rr: lost tch 3f out: bhd after* **16/1**

0 **9** 1 1/4 **Sister Andrea**[32] [3717] 3-8-12 0 .... PatCosgrave 3 — 41
(James Fanshawe) *in tch in midfield: rdn and wknd 3f out* **12/1**

0 **10** 1 1/2 **Raynell**[15] [4279] 3-9-3 0 .... ShaneKelly 9 — 43
(Noel Quinlan) *s.s and stdd: hld up in last trio: lost tch over 3f out: bhd after* **40/1**

11 2 1/2 **Treasure Act** 3-8-12 0 .... JimCrowley 1 — 33
(Patrick Chamings) *dwlt: a in last trio: lost tch 3f out: bhd after* **18/1**

0 **12** 9 **Cinematique (IRE)**[24] [3980] 3-9-3 0 .... IanMongan 11 — 20
(Laura Mongan) *chsd ldrs on outer: rdn 4f out: sn wknd rapidly and bhd* **66/1**

2m 6.80s (0.20) **Going Correction** +0.05s/f (Slow) — 12 Ran SP% **129.9**
Speed ratings (Par 101): **101,100,99,99,98 97,87,86,85,84 82,75**
Tote Swingers:1&2:£1.50, 2&3:£2.10, 1&3:£3.60 CSF £6.09 TOTE £3.90: £1.80, £1.10, £1.30; EX 7.00.
Owner John Duddy **Bred** Mrs Brid Cosgrove **Trained** Upper Lambourn, Berks

FOCUS
A weak maiden which wasn't strongly run. The level is set around the fourth to sixth.

T/Plt: £18.90 to £1 stake. Pool £61,550.86 - 2,368.90 winning tickets. T/Qpdt: £7.50 to a £1 stake. Pool £6,309.57 - 618.70 winning tickets. JN

4760 NEWMARKET (R-H)

Saturday, August 6

OFFICIAL GOING: Good (8.0)
Wind: Light, across. Weather: Cloudy with sunny spells

4801 HOPPEGARTEN.COM H'CAP — 1m 2f

2:05 (2:06) (Class 2) (0-100,97) 3-Y-O+ — **£12,938** (£3,850; £1,924; £962) **Stalls** Centre

Form — RPR

-054 **1** — **Classic Punch (IRE)**[14] [4331] 8-9-11 **94** .... JamieSpencer 5 — 105
(David Elsworth) *mde all: clr 8f out: shkn up over 1f out: styd on wl: eased nr fin* **8/1**

5063 **2** 1 3/4 **Licence To Till (USA)**[7] [4528] 4-8-12 **81** .... JimmyFortune 8 — 87
(Mark Johnston) *a.p: chsd wnr over 3f out: rdn over 1f out: styd on* **8/1**

5400 **3** 1/2 **World Heritage**[21] [4100] 5-9-12 **95** .... AndreaAtzeni 7 — 100
(Robert Eddery) *chsd ldrs: rdn over 2f out: styd on* **25/1**

4-03 **4** 1 1/2 **Demolition**[14] [4331] 7-9-10 **93** .... TonyHamilton 3 — 95
(Richard Fahey) *chsd wnr over 6f out: rdn over 1f out: styd on same pce* **12/1**

-012 **5** 1 **Kirthill (IRE)**[21] [4103] 3-9-2 **94** .... J-PGuillambert 11 — 94
(Luca Cumani) *mid-div: hdwy u.p 3f out: styd on: nt rch ldrs* **7/2**[2]

1-10 **6** 3/4 **Pekan Star**[28] [3876] 4-9-12 **95** .... FrankieDettori 9 — 94
(Roger Varian) *hld up: hdwy over 3f out: sn rdn: styd on: nt trble ldrs* **5/2**[1]

005 **7** 3 1/2 **Taqleed (IRE)**[14] [4331] 4-9-8 **91** ....(v[1]) RichardHills 1 — 83
(John Gosden) *hld up: rdn over 2f out: nvr on terms* **5/1**[3]

0052 **8** 3 1/4 **Tiger Reigns**[14] [4331] 5-10-0 **97** .... TomQueally 10 — 82
(Michael Dods) *hld up: rdn over 2f out: n.d* **14/1**

00-5 **9** 15 **Sour Mash (IRE)**[70] [2509] 4-9-4 **87** .... GeorgeBaker 6 — 42
(Ed Dunlop) *prom tl wknd over 3f out* **25/1**

06-0 **10** 3 **Starkat**[43] [3356] 5-8-12 **81** .... SebSanders 2 — 30
(George Margarson) *hld up: wknd over 3f out* **40/1**

2m 2.68s (-2.82) **Going Correction** -0.05s/f (Good)
WFA 3 from 4yo+ 9lb — 10 Ran SP% **114.2**
Speed ratings (Par 109): **109,107,107,106,105 104,101,99,87,84**
toteswingers:1&2:£11.00, 2&3:£38.20, 1&3:£41.70 CSF £67.21 CT £1520.78 TOTE £11.00: £2.60, £2.60, £7.40; EX 57.90 Trifecta £668.50 Part won. Pool £903.43 - 0.30 winning units..
Owner The Classic Bunch **Bred** Granham Farm **Trained** Newmarket, Suffolk

FOCUS
Stands' side track used with stalls on stands' side except 1m2f, 1m4f & 2m: Centre. Following a dry night the ground was given as good (GoingStick 8.0). A decent handicap run at a sound gallop. The front four were always prominent. The winner's best form for a year.

NOTEBOOK

Classic Punch(IRE) didn't have to battle for the lead like last time and he was able to dominate at his own pace throughout. Although they came to challenge, he had plenty in reserve and cosily recorded his fourth win at the course from 11 starts. He was fully entitled to go close having dropped to the mark off which he dotted up here last July. (op 15-2)

Licence To Till(USA), running off the same mark as when a close third at Doncaster last time, ran another solid race in an event dominated from the front by the winner. He will remain interesting even off a slightly higher rating. (op 17-2 tchd 15-2)

World Heritage is now rated 13lb lower than at the beginning of the season and this performance gave some indication that he might now be on a mark he can be competitive off.

Demolition was never too far off the pace, but he couldn't confirm recent course form with Classic Punch as that one had much more of the run of the race this time. (op 10-1 tchd 8-1)

Kirthill(IRE) didn't get cover on the outside of the field and was under pressure some way out. This was a somewhat disappointing, but he had gone up 8lb for getting beaten last time. (tchd 4-1)

Pekan Star settled better this time with cover but this was not a race where one wanted to be held up in rear, and he struggled to get competitive. (tchd 11-4)

Taqleed(IRE) has been a real disappointment this year and the application of a first-time visor did nothing to change his fortunes. (op 15-2)

4802 BADEN-RACING.COM H'CAP — 7f

2:40 (2:40) (Class 2) (0-105,105) 3-Y-O+
£12,450 (£3,728; £1,864; £932; £466; £234) **Stalls** Low

Form — RPR

4514 **1** — **Captain Ramius (IRE)**[10] [4574] 5-9-0 **95** .... FrankieDettori 4 — 107
(Kevin Ryan) *mde all in centre: rdn over 1f out: edgd rt: r.o* **5/1**[1]

-400 **2** 1 1/2 **Axiom**[50] [3109] 7-9-1 **96** .... J-PGuillambert 14 — 104
(Ed Walker) *racd centre: hld up: hdwy over 1f out: r.o to go 2nd wl ins fnl f: nt rch wnr* **25/1**

-040 **3** 1 **Mr David (USA)**[8] [4494] 4-8-13 **94** .... JamieSpencer 5 — 99+
(Jamie Osborne) *racd stands' side: hmpd s: hld up in tch: shkn up and hung lft over 2f out: rdn ins fnl f: styd on* **8/1**[3]

0500 **4** nk **Lowther**[22] [4042] 6-9-3 **98** .... JimmyFortune 11 — 102
(Alan Bailey) *racd centre: a.p: rdn over 1f out: styd on* **16/1**

1050 **5** hd **Imperial Guest**[14] [4314] 5-9-2 **97** .... SebSanders 7 — 101
(George Margarson) *racd stands' side: prom: rdn over 1f out: r.o* **8/1**[3]

4363 **6** 1/2 **Internationaldebut (IRE)**[13] [4369] 6-8-7 **88** .... MickyFenton 16 — 91
(Paul Midgley) *racd centre: chsd ldrs: rdn over 1f out: edgd rt and styd on same pce ins fnl f* **14/1**

-304 **7** 1 1/4 **Primaeval**[29] [3797] 5-8-5 **86** ....(v) DavidProbert 8 — 85
(James Fanshawe) *racd centre: hld up: hdwy 2f out: rdn over 1f out: styd on same pce* **11/1**

2210 **8** 1/2 **Reem (AUS)**[133] [998] 4-9-10 **105** .... PatCosgrave 3 — 103
(M F De Kock, South Africa) *led stands' side: rdn and hung lft fr over 2f out: no ex ins fnl f* **16/1**

2100 **9** 1/2 **Bawaardi (IRE)**[42] [3397] 5-8-9 **90** .... TonyHamilton 13 — 87
(Richard Fahey) *racd centre: hld up: swtchd lft and hdwy over 1f out: sn rdn: no ex wl ins fnl f* **25/1**

2100 **10** hd **Manassas (IRE)**[14] [4314] 6-9-5 **100** .... MartinDwyer 1 — 96
(Brian Meehan) *racd stands' side: chsd ldrs: rdn over 2f out: sn outpcd: styd on ins fnl f* **8/1**[3]

0-00 **11** nk **Citrus Star (USA)**[64] [2679] 4-9-5 **100** .... GeorgeBaker 10 — 98
(Chris Wall) *racd centre: chsd ldr: rdn and n.m.r over 1f out: styng on same pce whn hmpd ins fnl f* **7/1**[2]

-000 **12** 1 1/4 **Kellys Eye (IRE)**[50] [3134] 4-8-6 **87** .... RichardMullen 12 — 79
(George Foster) *racd centre: hld up: rdn over 1f out: hung lft ins fnl f: n.d* **28/1**

1001 **13** 1 1/4 **Masked Dance (IRE)**[14] [4325] 4-8-11 **92** ....(p) TomQueally 15 — 80
(Kevin Ryan) *racd centre: chsd ldrs: rdn over 2f out: wknd ins fnl f* **14/1**

1050 **14** 1 **Imperial Djay (IRE)**[14] [4314] 6-8-12 **93** .... MartinLane 4 — 79
(Ruth Carr) *wnt lft s: racd stands' side: rdn over 2f out: wknd over 1f out* **20/1**

22-U **15** *10* **Unex El Greco**[119] 1234 3-8-0 **90**................ LouisBeuzelin(3) 6 49
(John Gosden) *s.i.s: and hmpd s: racd stands' side: hld up: hdwy over 2f out: sn rdn and hung lft: wknd and eased ins fnl f* **8/1**[3]

1m 24.76s (-0.94) **Going Correction** -0.05s/f (Good)
WFA 3 from 4yo+ 6lb **15** Ran SP% **122.9**
Speed ratings (Par 109): **103,101,100,99,99 99,97,97,96,96 95,94,93,91,80**
CSF £142.73 CT £1029.56 TOTE £4.70: £1.80, £8.20, £3.30; EX 190.20 Trifecta £551.70 Pool £745.65 - 1 winning unit..
Owner Mrs Clodagh McStay **Bred** P G Lyons **Trained** Hambleton, N Yorks
■ Stewards' Enquiry : J-P Guillambert two-day ban: careless riding (Aug 26-27)

FOCUS
They split into two groups here before merging once again around 2f out. No side appeared to have an advantage. The form is taken at face value.

NOTEBOOK
Captain Ramius(IRE) ◆ had no chance from a bad draw at Chester last time but still showed enough to suggest he was on a winning mark. He was given a far more prominent ride this time, taking them along in the centre group and finding plenty once hitting the rising ground. This is clearly his best trip, and one of those valuable 7f heritage handicaps at Ascot will surely be a suitable target for him. (tchd 4-1 and 6-1 in places)
Axiom had dropped to a mark 1lb lower than when last successful and so was entitled to go close. He bumped into a progressive rival here but showed he's going to be interesting in similar races in the coming weeks.
Mr David(USA), who could easily be excused his Goodwood run, had finished fourth in the Bunbury Cup on his previous start and this was a return to that level of form. He was first home from the group that raced on the stands' side. (op 11-1)
Lowther returned to form back over a more suitable trip, but he remains a shade high in the weights.
Imperial Guest, third in this race last year, was 4lb higher this time around and probably ran to a similar level.
Internationaldebut(IRE) ran well enough, but he's become a hard horse to win with.
Primaeval has shown a higher level of form on Polytrack. (op 12-1)
Citrus Star(USA) travelled well for some way but didn't get home and might be more effective on a sharper track and quicker ground. (tchd 13-2)
Unex El Greco Official explanation: trainer's rep said colt made a noise

4803 GERMAN-THOROUGHBRED.COM SWEET SOLERA STKS (GROUP 3) (FILLIES) 7f
3:15 (3:18) (Class 1) 2-Y-O
£25,519 (£9,675; £4,842; £2,412; £1,210; £607) **Stalls** Low

Form RPR
1 **1** **Discourse (USA)**[43] 3362 2-8-12 0................ FrankieDettori 5 112+
(Mahmood Al Zarooni) *trckd ldrs: led over 1f out: shkn up and edgd rt ins fnl f: r.o wl: impressive* **5/2**[1]
3512 **2** *4 ½* **Lily's Angel (IRE)**[21] 4094 2-8-12 96................ TonyHamilton 7 100
(Richard Fahey) *hld up: hdwy over 1f out: sn rdn and hung lft: edgd rt and styd on same pce ins fnl f* **7/1**
211 **3** *1 ¼* **Kinetica**[16] 4252 2-8-12 98................ SebSanders 8 97
(Sir Mark Prescott Bt) *led and sn crossed over to stands' side rail: rdn and hdd over 1f out: no ex ins fnl f* **4/1**[2]
1 **4** *4* **Desert Gazelle (USA)**[28] 3865 2-8-12 0................ JamieSpencer 2 87
(Saeed Bin Suroor) *hld up: hdwy over 1f out: sn edgd rt: wknd ins fnl f* **4/1**[2]
4 **5** *5* **Wahylah (IRE)**[15] 4263 2-8-12 0................ PhilipRobinson 9 74
(Clive Brittain) *mid-div: hdwy 1/2-way: rdn over 1f out: wknd ins fnl f* **66/1**
153 **6** *2 ¾* **Hawfinch**[16] 4252 2-8-12 88................ RobertHavlin 11 68
(John Gosden) *hld up: effrt 2f out: sn edgd rt and wknd* **25/1**
1 **7** *3* **Zingana**[29] 3813 2-8-12 0................ FergusSweeney 1 60
(Eve Johnson Houghton) *hld up: rdn: hung lft and wknd over 1f out* **33/1**
136 **8** *2 ¾* **Illaunglass (IRE)**[29] 3821 2-8-12 99................ JimmyFortune 4 53
(Jeremy Noseda) *chsd ldr tl rdn over 2f out: wknd and eased over 1f out* **5/1**[3]
01 **9** *10* **Golden Valley**[16] 4232 2-8-12 76................ JamesMillman 3 28
(Rod Millman) *chsd ldrs: rdn over 2f out: sn wknd* **66/1**

1m 23.96s (-1.74) **Going Correction** -0.05s/f (Good) 2y crse rec **9** Ran SP% **107.5**
Speed ratings (Par 101): **107,101,100,95,90 87,83,80,69**
toteswingers:1&2:£4.10, 2&3:£5.00, 1&3:£2.40 CSF £17.68 TOTE £3.20: £1.50, £1.80, £1.30; EX 16.90 Trifecta £65.90 Pool £1,772.50 - 19.89 winning units..
Owner Godolphin **Bred** Darley **Trained** Newmarket, Suffolk

FOCUS
This race has produced several high-class winners in recent years, including Soviet Song, Rainbow View and White Moonstone. The likes of Maids Causeway and Nasheej also went on to be placed in the 1,000 Guineas, and it wouldn't be at all surprising if this year's winner was another to go on and prove herself one of the best of her generation. She looks a smart prospect, although there wasn't a great deal of depth to the race.

NOTEBOOK
Discourse(USA) ◆, whose debut defeat of her stablemate Gamilati was given a healthy boost when that one took the Cherry Hinton next time out, looks the better prospect of the two. She was weak in the betting beforehand and a little keen early, but came through to challenge the winner going strongly and, once Dettori asked her to lengthen, she quickened up like a really good filly and drew clear to win impressively, eased down in a juvenile course record time that was 0.80sec quicker than the 95-rated 5yo Captain Ramius recorded in the preceding class 2 handicap. If Discourse follows the same path as White Moonstone it'll be the May Hill and Fillies' Mile (this year run over the same C&D as next year's Guineas) for her next, and it'll take a good one to beat her in those races. A mile shouldn't cause her any bother on pedigree and odds as big as 12-1 for the Guineas look on the generous side. It's understandable that potential backers might be reluctant to step in and support a Godolphin horse for the Classics in view of being burnt several times in recent years, but Mahmood Al Zarooni hit the ground running this spring (25% strike-rate in April and May combined), and did win the 1,000 Guineas (albeit with a filly who due to a setback spent the winter in Newmarket) and there's probably less to be concerned about on that front than in past seasons. (op 15-8 tchd 11-4)
Lily's Angel(IRE) tracked the winner through, but couldn't stay with her in the closing stages. The most experienced runner in the line-up, she looks to have run a career-best on this step up to 7f. This opens up some new opportunities for her. (op 8-1)
Kinetica made all to win a Listed race at Sandown last time and Seb Sanders attempted to repeat the tactics again. Allowed to dominate, she wasn't good enough to take advantage, but she came up against a smart filly here and is probably well up to winning at this level. (op 9-2)
Desert Gazelle(USA) was an impressive winner here on her debut, but Dettori had ditched her in favour of Discourse this time. Held up at the back of the field, she kept on quite nicely for fourth, but this competition just proved a bit tough for her at this stage of her career. She'll get further and there's better to come. (op 9-2 tchd 7-2)
Wahylah(IRE) stepped up quite a bit on her debut effort at Ascot in this much more competitive race, although still beaten a long way.
Hawfinch, almost 5l behind Kinetica at Sandown last time when taking a different route up the straight, finished well behind her again but under different circumstances. (tchd 33-1)
Zingana, a shock winner at Newbury on her debut, hung under pressure and didn't run to that level on this rise in class. (tchd 40-1 in places)

Illaunglass(IRE), third in the Cherry Hinton, chased the leader through the first half of the race but came under pressure heading to the 2f pole and dropped out quickly. Eased down, this was not her true form. Official explanation: jockey said filly ran flat (op 15-2)

4804 WATCH GERMAN RACES LIVE AT GERMAN-TOTE.COM MAIDEN FILLIES' STKS 7f
3:45 (3:50) (Class 4) 2-Y-O **£4,528** (£1,347; £673; £336) **Stalls** Low

Form RPR
1 **Minidress** 2-9-0 0................ AhmedAjtebi 2 85+
(Mahmood Al Zarooni) *hld up: hdwy over 2f out: rdn to ld 1f out: r.o wl* **15/2**[3]
2 *4* **Everlong** 2-9-0 0................ JackMitchell 8 75
(Peter Chapple-Hyam) *chsd ldrs: rdn over 2f out: styd on same pce ins fnl f: wnt 2nd post* **11/2**[1]
3 *nse* **Mugazala (IRE)** 2-9-0 0................ RichardHills 10 75
(Ed Dunlop) *chsd ldrs: led wl over 1f out: sn rdn: hdd 1f out: no ex ins fnl f* **6/1**[2]
4 *½* **Candycakes (IRE)** 2-9-0 0................ JamieSpencer 6 74
(Michael Bell) *s.i.s: sn pushed along to chse ldrs: led 1/2-way: hdd wl over 1f out: no ex ins fnl f* **11/2**[1]
5 *1* **Fashion's Flight (USA)** 2-9-0 0................ MartinDwyer 5 71+
(Brian Meehan) *hld up: hdwy and shkn up over 1f out: no imp ins fnl f* **16/1**
6 *1 ¾* **Ironically (IRE)** 2-9-0 0................ RichardMullen 3 67+
(David Lanigan) *s.i.s: hld up: rdn over 2f out: r.o ins fnl f: nrst fin* **33/1**
7 *¾* **Saratoga Slew (IRE)** 2-9-0 0................ WilliamCarson 4 65
(B W Hills) *chsd ldrs: rdn and ev ch over 1f out: hung rt and wknd ins fnl f* **6/1**[2]
8 *1 ½* **Symphony Star (IRE)** 2-8-11 0................ JohnFahy(3) 9 61
(Paul D'Arcy) *led to 1/2-way: rdn over 1f out: wknd fnl f* **25/1**
9 *1 ¾* **Marhoona (USA)** 2-9-0 0................ PhilipRobinson 14 57
(John Dunlop) *prom: rdn over 2f out: hung rt and wknd over 1f out* **16/1**
10 *1 ¼* **Maria Letizia** 2-9-0 0................ RobertHavlin 7 54
(John Gosden) *chsd ldrs tl wknd wl over 1f out* **11/2**[1]
11 *3 ¾* **Melodrama (IRE)** 2-9-0 0................ ChrisCatlin 11 44
(David Lanigan) *hld up: a in rr: wknd over 2f out* **40/1**
12 *4* **Singmeasong** 2-9-0 0................ SebSanders 15 34
(J W Hills) *mid-div: rdn 1/2-way: wknd over 2f out* **25/1**
13 *3 ¼* **Loved By All (IRE)** 2-9-0 0................ ShaneKelly 1 26
(Brian Meehan) *s.i.s: in rr: wknd 1/2-way* **28/1**
14 *2 ½* **Lady Ocarina** 2-9-0 0................ TomQueally 12 20
(John Dunlop) *s.i.s: sn outpcd* **25/1**

1m 27.63s (1.93) **Going Correction** -0.05s/f (Good) **14** Ran SP% **118.6**
Speed ratings (Par 93): **86,81,81,80,79 77,76,75,73,71 67,62,59,56**
toteswingers:1&2:£10.00, 2&3:£8.00, 1&3:£7.30 CSF £43.70 TOTE £8.80: £3.20, £2.50, £2.20; EX 57.10 Trifecta £370.20 Pool £910.55 - 1.82 winning units..
Owner Godolphin **Bred** Darley **Trained** Newmarket, Suffolk

FOCUS
A field of newcomers and another success for the Godolphin stable, once again underlining the wealth of talent in the stable when it comes to the juvenile fillies' division. The early pace was steady, though, and that goes some way to explaining a final time which was 3.67sec slower than that recorded by Discourse in the Sweet Solera. The form is rated around the race averages.

NOTEBOOK
Minidress ◆ did well in the circumstances to come from off the pace with a sustained challenge up the stands' side and win going away. By Street Cry out of a Musidora winner, she's bred to be more of a middle-distance filly next year, and a stronger pace/step up to 1m is likely to suit her next time out. (op 11-2 tchd 8-1)
Everlong ◆, who holds a Fillies' Mile entry, can do a lot better as she didn't settle off the steady early gallop and it's to her credit that she was still capable of keeping on for second. She should soon go one better. (op 5-1 tchd 6-1)
Mugazala(IRE) was always well placed in a race that lacked pace. That said, she hails from a stable whose 2yos generally improve for an outing so she should be capable of better again. (tchd 5-1)
Candycakes(IRE), a half-sister to multiple 6f-1m winner Cheyenne Star, was also in the front rank from the start, which was an advantage given the way the race played out. (op 8-1)
Fashion's Flight(USA), who cost $390,000, is also from a stable whose 2yos are rarely buzzed up to win first time. She ran a pleasing race and should improve plenty for this. (op 11-1)
Ironically(IRE) was unfancied in the market but put in some nice work at the finish and clearly has ability. She's the type that will do much better next year.
Saratoga Slew(IRE), another who was quite keen, also showed enough to suggest she'll be up to winning a maiden. (op 12-1)

4805 ROYAL BRITISH LEGION MAIDEN STKS 1m 4f
4:20 (4:22) (Class 5) 3-Y-O+ **£3,881** (£1,155; £577; £288) **Stalls** Centre

Form RPR
2 **1** **Cops And Robbers**[15] 4279 3-9-1 0................ RichardMullen 6 83+
(Sir Michael Stoute) *chsd ldrs: led 2f out: rdn and edgd rt over 1f out: styd on* **8/11**[1]
2 *shd* **Asaid** 3-9-1 0................ FrankieDettori 5 83
(Saeed Bin Suroor) *s.i.s: rcvrd to chse ldr after 1f: rdn over 2f out: sn hung lft: ev ch ins fnl f: styd on* **12/1**
-344 **3** *3* **Monopolize**[43] 3364 3-9-1 78................ TomQueally 3 78
(Sir Henry Cecil) *a.p: racd keenly: rdn over 2f out: styd on same pce ins fnl f* **4/1**[2]
25 **4** *¾* **Light Blow (USA)**[65] 2639 3-8-11 0 ow1................ IanMongan 9 73
(Sir Henry Cecil) *hld up: hdwy over 2f out: shkn up over 1f out: no ex ins fnl f* **16/1**
5 *4 ½* **Rysbrack (USA)**[38] 5-9-12 0................ SebSanders 4 70
(Paul Webber) *s.i.s: hdwy 10f out: led over 3f out: rdn and hdd 2f out: wknd ins fnl f* **14/1**
6 *½* **Old Navy** 3-9-1 0................ RobertHavlin 8 69+
(John Gosden) *dwlt: hld up: hdwy over 4f out: rdn over 1f out: wknd ins fnl f* **11/2**[3]
05 **7** *10* **Rose Of Sarratt (IRE)**[23] 4014 3-8-10 0................ MartinLane 10 48
(Rae Guest) *s.i.s: hld up: rdn over 3f out: sn wknd* **66/1**
00 **8** *1 ½* **Meshfi**[13] 4370 3-9-1 0................ ChrisCatlin 2 51
(Clive Brittain) *led over 8f: sn rdn: wknd wl over 1f out* **100/1**
64 **9** *7* **Pride Of Mine**[165] 643 8-9-7 0................ AdrianMcCarthy 7 35
(J R Jenkins) *hld up: pushed along 1/2-way: rdn and wknd over 3f out* **125/1**
00 **10** *39* **Ulla**[15] 4279 3-8-10 0................ JackMitchell 1 —
(Chris Wall) *broke wl: racd keenly: sn stdd and lost pl: rdn and wknd over 3f out: t.o* **80/1**

2m 33.29s (0.39) **Going Correction** -0.05s/f (Good)
WFA 3 from 5yo+ 11lb **10** Ran SP% **118.0**
Speed ratings (Par 103): **96,95,93,93,90 90,83,82,77,51**

CSF £12.03 TOTE £1.80: £1.10, £2.30, £1.30; EX 11.10 Trifecta £23.60 Pool £2,449.81 - 76.81 winning units..

Owner Philip Newton **Bred** Philip Newton **Trained** Newmarket, Suffolk

FOCUS

There was a steady early pace here, but this is decent maiden form with the field well strung out.

4806 RED LION FOODS H'CAP 2m 24y

4:50 (4:54) (Class 3) (0-90,89) 3-Y-0+ **£9,056** (£2,695; £1,346; £673) **Stalls** Centre

Form RPR

1132 **1** **Danvilla**[21] 4097 4-9-3 **78**.. WilliamCarson 3 87
(Paul Webber) *led after 1f: rdn over 1f out: hung lft ins fnl f: styd on gamely* **4/1**[1]

315- **2** *2 3/4* **Ambrose Princess (IRE)**[45] 4467 6-8-9 **70**.............(p) JamieGoldstein 1 76
(Michael Scudamore) *wnt lft s: led 1f: chsd wnr: rdn over 3f out: hung lft over 2f out: edgd rt ins fnl f: styd on same pce* **12/1**

300 **3** *1 1/2* **Trovare (USA)**[10] 4423 4-9-7 **82**....................................... MartinDwyer 5 86
(Amanda Perrett) *a.p: rdn and hung lft fr over 2f out: no ex ins fnl f* **9/2**[2]

10/0 **4** *1 1/2* **Downhiller (IRE)**[15] 4266 6-10-0 **89**................................ TomQueally 2 91
(John Dunlop) *hmpd s: sn chsng ldrs: rdn over 2f out: hung lft over 1f out: no ex ins fnl f* **15/2**

6441 **5** *17* **Baltimore Clipper (USA)**[14] 4341 4-9-7 **82**................. JimmyFortune 8 64
(Paul Cole) *hld up: hdwy 11f out: rdn over 2f out: wknd over 1f out* **13/2**

0005 **6** *15* **Very Good Day (FR)**[15] 4266 4-9-12 **87**........................ JamieSpencer 7 51
(Mick Channon) *hld up: hdwy over 2f out: rdn and wknd over 1f out: t.o* **4/1**[1]

1-14 **7** *11* **Roberto Pegasus (USA)**[29] 3794 5-9-3 **78**....................... IanMongan 4 29
(Pat Phelan) *hld up: swtchd lft 6f out: rdn over 3f out: wknd and eased wl over 1f out: t.o* **6/1**[3]

2 **8** *6* **Zakatal**[21] 1367 5-9-8 **83**...(bt) SebSanders 9 26
(Philip Hobbs) *hld up: pushed along 1/2-way: hdwy 5f out: rdn over 3f out: sn wknd: t.o* **9/1**

3m 28.4s (1.40) **Going Correction** -0.05s/f (Good) **8** Ran SP% **115.3**
Speed ratings (Par 107): **94,92,91,91,82 75,69,66**
toteswingers:1&2:£8.80, 2&3:£10.00, 1&3:£5.00 CSF £51.90 CT £224.30 TOTE £4.30: £1.60, £3.50, £2.50; EX 44.10 Trifecta £218.20 Pool £1,233.05 - 4.18 winning units..

Owner Shully Liebermann **Bred** Minster Stud **Trained** Mollington, Oxon

FOCUS

This wasn't a proper test of stamina as they dawdled along early. The progressive winner dictated.

NOTEBOOK

Danvilla was always in the ideal position in front and on the rail and she won fairly comfortably in the end. She was fully entitled to go close on her second to the very well-handicapped Keys last time, but the tactical advantage she was handed only made things easier for her. (op 7-2 tchd 9-2 in places)

Ambrose Princess(IRE), a faller over fences when last seen in June, was running off a mark 10lb higher than when last successful on the Flat. She ran well, although she did occupy second place almost throughout in a race that was dictated by the winner from the front. (op 25-1 tchd 11-1)

Trovare(USA) hung left all the way over to the far-side rail in the straight and didn't look the most straightforward. His stamina for this trip in a truly-run race remains in question. Official explanation: jockey said gelding hung left (op 11-2)

Downhiller(IRE) was entitled to have needed his reappearance from a long layoff at Ascot last time, was interesting off an attractive mark and the money came for him. Things didn't go his way in the race itself, though, as he got a bump at the start and raced keenly off the steady early gallop. Outpaced as the sprint for home began, he kept on fairly well, but a stronger all-round gallop would have surely seen him in a better light. (op 11-1 tchd 12-1 in places)

Baltimore Clipper(USA), who was competing off a career-high mark and had his stamina to prove, carried his head high under his pressure and didn't get home. (op 11-2 tchd 7-1 and 15-2 in places)

Very Good Day(FR) was disappointing, although he was held up out the back and failed to get competitive in what was a tactical race. (op 9-2 tchd 5-1 in places)

Roberto Pegasus(USA) was another who didn't threaten from off the pace. (op 11-2 tchd 13-2 in places)

4807 EUROPEAN BREEDERS FUND "VIRTUAL" FILLIES' H'CAP 1m

5:20 (5:21) (Class 4) (0-80,79) 3-Y-0+ **£5,175** (£1,540; £769; £384) **Stalls** Low

Form RPR

0010 **1** **Pinch Of Posh (IRE)**[35] 3630 3-8-8 **66**...................... FergusSweeney 10 74+
(Paul Cole) *hld up: hdwy over 1f out: rdn to ld ins fnl f: r.o* **40/1**

0112 **2** *hd* **Hurricane Lady (IRE)**[26] 3918 3-9-5 **77**........................ JamieSpencer 9 85
(Walter Swinburn) *chsd ldrs: rdn and hung rt 2f out: led and wandered over 1f out: hdd ins fnl f: r.o u.p* **3/1**[2]

314 **3** *1* **Bella Noir**[10] 4448 4-9-10 **75**...(v) NeilCallan 5 81
(Mrs K Burke) *chsd ldr tl led 3f out: rdn and hdd over 1f out: styd on* **8/1**

002- **4** *2 1/4* **Vita Lika**[280] 7231 3-9-5 **77**... MartinDwyer 1 77
(Brian Meehan) *hld up in tch: shkn up over 1f out: styd on same pce ins fnl f* **14/1**

1412 **5** *1* **Bakoura**[17] 4202 3-9-4 **76**.. RichardHills 8 74
(John Dunlop) *hld up: hdwy u.p over 1f out: swtchd lft and r.o ins fnl f: nt rch ldrs* **9/2**[3]

-610 **6** *1 1/2* **Loving Thought**[17] 4202 3-8-10 **68**................................ TomQueally 11 62
(Sir Henry Cecil) *hld up: hdwy 2f out: rdn over 1f out: no ex ins fnl f* **16/1**

4651 **7** *2 3/4* **Amoya (GER)**[12] 4393 4-9-6 **74**...........................(t) AdamBeschizza(3) 6 63
(Philip McBride) *led 5f: rdn and wknd over 1f out* **10/1**

6-61 **8** *1/2* **Complexion**[18] 4185 3-9-7 **79**.. RichardMullen 2 66
(Sir Michael Stoute) *hld up: rdn over 3f out: hung lft over 2f out: n.d* **9/4**[1]

-230 **9** *17* **Sahafh (USA)**[57] 2883 3-8-13 **71**..................................(p) FrankieDettori 4 19
(Saeed Bin Suroor) *s.i.s: hld up: hdwy u.p over 2f out: wknd over 1f out* **16/1**

1m 39.47s (-0.53) **Going Correction** -0.05s/f (Good)
WFA 3 from 4yo 7lb **9** Ran SP% **115.0**
Speed ratings (Par 102): **100,99,98,96,95 94,91,90,73**
toteswingers:1&2:£26.00, 2&3:£3.70, 1&3:£23.60 CSF £157.14 CT £1101.89 TOTE £30.00: £5.50, £1.50, £2.00; EX 195.40 Trifecta £658.10 Pool £1,085.09 - 1.22 winning units..

Owner Mrs Melba Bryce **Bred** Swordlestown Stud **Trained** Whatcombe, Oxon

FOCUS

A shock result to this fillies' handicap but no fluke, and ordinary form for the grade.

Complexion Official explanation: jockey said filly never travelled

T/Plt: £204.80 to a £1 stake. Pool £91,252.26 - 325.18 winning tickets. T/Qpdt: £9.50 to a £1 stake. Pool £5,362.26 - 416.11 winning tickets. CR

4436 REDCAR (L-H)

Saturday, August 6

OFFICIAL GOING: Good changing to good to soft after race 5 (4.05)

Wind: Virtually nil Weather: Obvercast and showers

4808 DEREK & EILEEN BROWN WEDDING ANNIVERSARY (S) STKS 6f

1:55 (1:55) (Class 6) 2-Y-O **£1,704** (£503; £251) **Stalls** Centre

Form RPR

2402 **1** **Artists Corner**[35] 3631 2-8-6 63.................................... BarryMcHugh 10 60
(Richard Fahey) *in tch and pushed along 1/2-way: hdwy over 2f out: swtchd lft and rdn to chse ldrs wl over 1f out: styd on to chal ins fnl f: sltly hmpd and led nr fin* **1/1**[1]

4050 **2** *hd* **Tyre Giant Dot Com**[21] 4105 2-8-11 64............................ JimmyQuinn 2 64
(Geoffrey Oldroyd) *prom: cl up 1/2-way: rdn along 2f out: styd on to ld ent fnl f: sn drvn: edgd lft last 100yds: hdd and no ex nr fin* **7/2**[2]

000 **3** *1* **Emley Moor**[23] 4002 2-8-6 44.. KellyHarrison 7 56
(Chris Fairhurst) *in tch: pushed along over 2f out: rdn wl over 1f out: kpt on ins fnl f: nrst fin* **20/1**

6015 **4** *3 1/4* **Lady Caprice**[8] 4500 2-8-12 63...(p) DavidNolan 4 53
(Ann Duffield) *led: rdn along 2f out: drvn and hdd ent fnl f: wknd* **11/2**[3]

0350 **5** *5* **Come To Mind**[6] 4572 2-8-6 49... JulieBurke(5) 6 37
(Alan Berry) *chsd ldrs: rdn along 1/2-way: sn outpcd* **50/1**

6 **6** *1/2* **Needwood Rose**[21] 4105 2-8-6 0.................................... AndrewMullen 3 30
(David Nicholls) *dwlt: in tch: rdn along 1/2-way: sn one pce* **28/1**

004 **7** *1 1/4* **Bertie Dancing (IRE)**[21] 4105 2-8-8 45.................(p) DeclanCannon(3) 5 31
(Nigel Tinkler) *cl up: rdn along 1/2-way: wknd 2f out* **20/1**

6043 **8** *hd* **Spring Daisy (IRE)**[18] 4178 2-8-6 49....................... RichardKingscote 9 26
(Tom Dascombe) *a towards rr* **10/1**

0 **9** *1* **Loving Emma**[8] 4512 2-8-1 0.. ChrisDCogan(5) 8 23
(John Weymes) *s.i.s: hung lft thrght: sme hdwy on wd outside 1/2-way: rdn and hung bdly lft to far rails: sn bhd* **40/1**

1m 14.15s (2.35) **Going Correction** +0.25s/f (Good) **9** Ran SP% **114.1**
Speed ratings (Par 92): **94,93,92,88,81 80,79,78,77**
toteswingers:1&2:£1.40, 2&3:£16.70, 1&3:£9.50 CSF £4.04 TOTE £1.90: £1.10, £1.10, £6.20; EX 6.50.The winner was bought in for £4,200.

Owner Derwent Arms Racing Club Malton **Bred** Berry Racing **Trained** Musley Bank, N Yorks

■ Stewards' Enquiry : Jimmy Quinn caution: used whip with excessive frequency.

FOCUS

A weak contest, but the pace looked strong and the winner's time was better than the nursery later on the card. The form makes sense.

NOTEBOOK

Artists Corner had finished runner-up twice, once in this grade, but finally got on the scoresheet with a narrow success. This looks about her level, using the runner-up as a marker, although she'd have to come under some consideration off a low weight in a nursery. (op 6-4 tchd 13-8)

Tyre Giant Dot Com, without the blinkers he wore last time when well beaten in this grade for the first time, showed good pace and just failed to hang on after getting to the front inside the final furlong. (tchd 3-1)

Emley Moor showed nothing in maidens, so this was much better. Another 6f race at this level is within her grasp. (op 25-1 tchd 18-1)

Lady Caprice, wearing cheekpieces for the first time, had not run over this trip for a while but showed good pace until not appearing to get home. (op 9-2 tchd 4-1)

4809 GOODSWENS SOLICITORS NURSERY 6f

2:25 (2:26) (Class 4) (0-85,73) 2-Y-O **£3,234** (£962; £481; £240) **Stalls** Centre

Form RPR

0444 **1** **Our Boy Jack (IRE)**[6] 4572 2-8-11 **63**.............................. JimmyQuinn 4 66+
(Richard Fahey) *trckd ldrs: hdwy 2f out: rdn to chal over 1f out: drvn to ld jst ins fnl f: kpt on wl* **5/2**[1]

3105 **2** *3/4* **Fayr Fall (IRE)**[14] 4343 2-9-1 **67**...................................... BarryMcHugh 8 68
(Tim Easterby) *prom on wd outside: hdwy 2f out and sn edgd lft: rdn to chal over 1f out: sn hdd: hung lft jst ins fnl f: drvn and styd on wl towards fin* **3/1**[2]

630 **3** *nk* **Just Like Heaven (IRE)**[54] 2983 2-8-12 **69**.................. LanceBetts(5) 2 69
(Tim Easterby) *led: rdn along 2f out: sn edgd lft: drvn and hung lft ent fnl f: sn hdd: kpt on* **12/1**

1603 **4** *2 1/4* **Musical Valley**[6] 4572 2-9-7 **73**..............................(t) RichardKingscote 3 66
(Tom Dascombe) *trckd ldrs: hdwy on wd outside 1/2-way: rdn to chal 2f out: sn drvn and wknd* **6/1**

0045 **5** *1/2* **Spoken Words**[7] 4525 2-8-6 **58**.. JamesSullivan 1 50
(Hugh McWilliams) *prom: rdn along and outpcd wl over 2f out: kpt on u.p ins fnl f* **14/1**

266 **6** *2 1/2* **Ingleby Angel (IRE)**[45] 3274 2-8-7 **59**............................ LeeNewman 7 43
(David O'Meara) *prom: rdn along wl over 2f out and sn wknd* **4/1**[3]

2220 **7** *hd* **Beechey's Beauty**[7] 4558 2-8-12 **64** ow1.........................(p) DavidNolan 5 48
(Ann Duffield) *t.k.h: hld up: a in rr* **11/2**

1m 14.44s (2.64) **Going Correction** +0.25s/f (Good) **7** Ran SP% **117.6**
Speed ratings (Par 96): **92,91,90,87,86 83,83**
toteswingers:1&2:£2.70, 2&3:£5.10, 1&3:£10.40 CSF £10.75 CT £75.00 TOTE £3.40: £2.20, £2.00; EX 12.60.

Owner Middleham Park Racing XXXVI **Bred** Mrs Ian Fox **Trained** Musley Bank, N Yorks

FOCUS

A modest nursery. The winner continued his steady improvement.

NOTEBOOK

Our Boy Jack(IRE) finished behind Musical Valley the previous Sunday at Chester but readily reversed that form despite racing a bit keenly just in behind. He showed a good attitude once making his challenge and saw the trip out well, so is capable of winning again this season. (op 7-4)

Fayr Fall(IRE) looked sure to be suited by this step back up in distance and did keep on well but compromised his chance by hanging across the course once under pressure. (op 5-1)

Just Like Heaven(IRE) ◆, off since mid-June, showed a hint of ability in maidens and was a bit unlucky not to get a place here after showing good pace from the stalls. He was another to hang a bit once off the bridle, which obviously did not help. (op 9-1 tchd 14-1)

Musical Valley finished a place in front of the winner when they last met but never looked like doing the same again. (op 5-1 tchd 9-2)

Spoken Words, dropping in trip, raced freely early and did not get home as strongly as some others. (op 10-1)

Ingleby Angel(IRE) did not look easy to fancy on the balance of his form but still attracted some support. However, after racing towards the head of affairs, he weakened quickly and dropped out. (op 6-1)

4810 CLAIRE & JESSICA H'CAP 7f
2:55 (2:57) (Class 4) (0-85,80) 3-Y-0+ **£2,587** (£770; £384; £192) **Stalls** Centre

Form RPR
1614 **1** **Roninski (IRE)**[15] 4290 3-8-8 **77** JustinNewman(7) 4 87+
(Bryan Smart) *trckd ldrs: hdwy 3f out: led over 2f out: jnd and rdn over 1f out: drvn ins fnl f and kpt on wl* **15/8**[1]

-006 **2** *½* **Robert The Painter (IRE)**[29] 3830 3-9-4 **80** DavidNolan 6 87
(Richard Fahey) *hld up in rr: hdwy 2f out: swtchd rt and rdn over 1f out: styd on wl ins fnl f* **7/1**

044 **3** *nk* **Layla's Hero (IRE)**[43] 3339 4-9-10 **80** PBBeggy 5 88
(John Quinn) *hld up in rr: hdwy on outer 3f out: rdn to chal wl over 1f out: drvn ent fnl f and kpt on same pce* **5/1**[3]

6200 **4** *2* **George Benjamin**[14] 4349 4-9-6 **76** PaulQuinn 3 79
(David Nicholls) *led: pushed along and hdd 3f out: sn rdn and kpt on same pce fnl 2f* **8/1**

0500 **5** *2 ¾* **Ghost (IRE)**[8] 4503 4-9-0 **70** AndrewMullen 1 65
(David Nicholls) *t.k.h: chsd ldrs: rdn along 3f out: grad wknd* **16/1**

0501 **6** *8* **Al Muheer (IRE)**[8] 4503 6-9-8 **78**(b) JamesSullivan 7 52
(Ruth Carr) *cl up: led 1/2-way: rdn and hdd over 2f out: sn wknd* **11/4**[2]

1000 **7** *13* **Thrust Control (IRE)**[32] 3704 4-9-3 **78** AdamCarter(5) 8 16
(Tracy Waggott) *prom: rdn along 1/2-way: sn wknd* **25/1**

1m 25.87s (1.37) **Going Correction** +0.25s/f (Good)
WFA 3 from 4yo+ 6lb **7 Ran SP% 111.5**
Speed ratings (Par 105): **102,101,101,98,95 86,71**
toteswingers:1&2:£5.60, 2&3:£7.00, 1&3:£2.00 CSF £14.81 CT £53.86 TOTE £3.10: £2.40, £1.20; EX 13.00.

Owner Ron Hull **Bred** Peter Hodgson And Star Pointe Limited **Trained** Hambleton, N Yorks

FOCUS
Again the pace looked sound for the conditions and the result ought to prove reliable as a guide. The first three came well clear.

Layla's Hero(IRE) Official explanation: caution: used whip with excessive frequency.
Al Muheer(IRE) Official explanation: jockey said gelding ran too free

4811 JOHN SMITH'S REDCAR STRAIGHT-MILE CHAMPIONSHIP H'CAP (QUALIFIER) 1m
3:30 (3:30) (Class 4) (0-85,81) 3-Y-0+ **£3,234** (£962; £481; £240) **Stalls** Centre

Form RPR
2-50 **1** **Silvery Moon (IRE)**[23] 4004 4-9-0 **69** DavidNolan 6 86+
(Tim Easterby) *prom: cl up 3f out: rdn to ld 2f out and sn edgd lft: clr ins fnl f: kpt on strly* **7/2**[1]

3605 **2** *5* **Law To Himself (IRE)**[18] 4170 4-8-11 **66** KellyHarrison 1 71
(Alan Swinbank) *hld up in tch: hdwy 3f out: rdn to chse ldng pair over 1f out: drvn and kpt on ins fnl f: no ch w wnr* **7/1**

0224 **3** *½* **Cono Zur (FR)**[15] 4268 4-9-6 **75**(b) JamesSullivan 2 79
(Ruth Carr) *prom: effrt to chal over 2f out: sn rdn and ev ch tl drvn and one pce ent fnl f* **4/1**[2]

431 **4** *1* **Thatcherite (IRE)**[15] 4286 3-8-2 **69** ow1(t) JulieBurke(5) 5 70+
(Tony Coyle) *blind removed late and s.i.s: bhd and rdn along 1/2-way: hdwy wl over 1f out: styd on ins fnl f: nrst fin* **7/2**[1]

3140 **5** *nk* **Elusive Sue (USA)**[14] 4349 4-9-3 **72** BarryMcHugh 3 73
(Richard Fahey) *trckd ldrs: hdwy wl over 2f out: rdn wl over 1f out and sn one pce* **5/1**[3]

0400 **6** *hd* **Cara's Request (AUS)**[60] 2783 6-9-12 **81** AndrewMullen 7 81
(David Nicholls) *led: rdn along 3f out: hdd 2f out: grad wknd* **11/1**

2326 **7** *½* **The Osteopath (IRE)**[13] 4361 8-9-9 **78** RoystonFfrench 4 77
(Michael Dods) *trckd ldrs: rdn along over 3f out: drvn 2f out: sn wknd* **7/1**

1m 38.83s (0.83) **Going Correction** +0.25s/f (Good)
WFA 3 from 4yo+ 7lb **7 Ran SP% 114.4**
Speed ratings (Par 105): **105,100,99,98,98 98,97**
CSF £28.08 TOTE £5.10: £3.10, £3.90; EX 34.00.

Owner R J Swinbourne **Bred** Colin Kennedy **Trained** Great Habton, N Yorks

FOCUS
A solid looking handicap. Improvement from the winner, who clocked a decent time.

Thatcherite(IRE) Official explanation: jockey said gelding was slowly away as blindfold became caught on the bridle.

4812 MARKET CROSS JEWELLERS CLAIMING STKS 1m
4:05 (4:05) (Class 6) 3-Y-O **£1,704** (£503; £251) **Stalls** Centre

Form RPR
3223 **1** **Abidhabidubai**[10] 4439 3-9-0 72 PBBeggy 6 74
(John Quinn) *cl up: slt ld over 2f out and sn rdn: drvn over 1f out: kpt on wl towards fin* **9/4**[2]

0266 **2** *1* **Old English (IRE)**[8] 4506 3-8-7 68 RoystonFfrench 2 65
(Mark Johnston) *led: rdn along and hdd over 2f out: cl up and drvn over 1f out: ev ch tl no ex last 50yds* **11/2**[3]

1612 **3** *3 ½* **Urban Kode (IRE)**[19] 4153 3-8-7 65(v) BarryMcHugh 1 57
(Ollie Pears) *cl up: rdn along over 2f out: drvn over 1f out and ev ch tl edgd lft and wknd last 100yds* **2/1**[1]

0356 **4** *6* **Inca Blue**[21] 4111 3-9-1 52 DavidNolan 5 51
(Tim Easterby) *trckd ldrs: effrt 3f out: rdn along over 2f out: sn one pce* **11/1**

5603 **5** *5* **Full Pelt (USA)**[10] 4435 3-9-1 60(v) RichardKingscote 4 39
(Tom Dascombe) *trckd ldrs: rdn along over 3f out: sn outpcd* **13/2**

1300 **6** *34* **Aquilifer (IRE)**[74] 2383 3-9-9 73 PatrickDonaghy(3) 3 —
(Mrs K Burke) *t.k.h: trckd ldrs: rdn along over 3f out: sn outpcd and bhd: eased ins fnl f* **7/1**

1m 41.74s (3.74) **Going Correction** +0.50s/f (Yiel) **6 Ran SP% 113.7**
Speed ratings (Par 98): **101,100,96,90,85 51**
CSF £15.14 TOTE £3.70: £2.40, £2.50; EX 14.70.Old English was claimed by Miss L. A. Perratt for £6000. Urban Kode was claimed by Lucinda V. Russell for £6000.

Owner Nigel S Cooper **Bred** Brightwalton Stud **Trained** Settrington, N Yorks
■ Padraig Beggy's first winner in Britain.

FOCUS
A fair-looking claimer on paper in which three came well clear of the remainder. The winenr is probably the best guide.

4813 KEITH AND THE LADS DAY OUT MEDIAN AUCTION MAIDEN STKS 7f
4:40 (4:41) (Class 5) 3-4-Y-O **£1,940** (£577; £288; £144) **Stalls** Centre

Form RPR
322 **1** **Icy Blue**[7] 4560 3-9-0 67 AmyRyan(3) 5 65
(Richard Whitaker) *trckd ldrs: hdwy wl over 2f out: rdn to chal over 1f out: led ent fnl f: sn edgd rt: styd on* **4/6**[1]

64 **2** *2* **Andiamo Via**[15] 4282 4-9-9 0 BarryMcHugh 4 62
(Michael Smith) *trckd ldrs: smooth hdwy 1/2-way: led 2f out: jnd and rdn over 1f out: hdd ent fnl f: cl up whn green and hit in face by opponents whip: swtchd lft and no ex last 100yds* **8/1**

56 **3** *6* **Needwood Park**[7] 4542 3-9-3 0 LeeNewman 10 44
(David Barron) *chsd ldrs: hdwy 3f out: cl up 2f out: sn rdn and ev ch tl drvn and wknd appr fnl f* **6/1**[2]

4 *2* **Think**[57] 4-9-9 0 PaddyAspell 11 38
(Clive Mulhall) *towards rr and pushed along 1/2-way: rdn and hdwy over 2f out: styd on appr fnl f: nrst fin* **22/1**

5002 **5** *½* **Isle Of Ellis (IRE)**[7] 4564 4-9-2 45(v) JustinNewman(7) 6 39
(Ron Barr) *prom: rdn along over 2f out: sn drvn and grad wknd* **20/1**

-500 **6** *14* **Indigo Sands (IRE)**[25] 3949 3-8-12 45 JulieBurke(5) 9 —
(Alan Berry) *led: rdn along 3f out: drvn and hdd 2f out: sn wknd* **80/1**

4060 **7** *6* **Colamandis**[26] 3905 4-9-4 43(p) JamesSullivan 8 —
(Hugh McWilliams) *chsd ldrs: effrt and cl up 1/2-way: rdn along 3f out and sn wknd* **28/1**

8 *2 ¼* **Sendarose (IRE)** 3-8-12 0 LanceBetts(5) 7 —
(Tim Easterby) *s.i.s: a in rr* **7/1**[3]

9 *¾* **Secret Lodge** 3-8-12 0 RoystonFfrench 3 —
(Garry Woodward) *a in rr* **20/1**

0 **10** *37* **Shoulder Arms**[15] 4286 3-8-12 0 ChrisDCogan(5) 1 —
(John Weymes) *chsd ldr: rdn along over 4f out: sn lost pl and bhd: eased fnl 2f* **100/1**

1m 29.42s (4.92) **Going Correction** +0.75s/f (Yiel)
WFA 3 from 4yo 6lb **10 Ran SP% 117.4**
Speed ratings (Par 103): **101,98,91,89,89 73,66,63,62,20**
toteswingers:1&2:£1.80, 2&3:£4.40, 1&3:£1.90 CSF £5.89 TOTE £1.60: £1.10, £2.70, £2.00; EX 7.80.

Owner Country Lane Partnership **Bred** Cheveley Park Stud Ltd **Trained** Scarcroft, W Yorks

FOCUS
When a horse wins a maiden at the 14th attempt it is not difficult to suggest the race was far from strong. The winning time was considerably slower than the earlier handicap. The form is rated around the first two.

4814 LADIES' & GENTS' EVENING 27TH AUGUST H'CAP 1m 6f 19y
5:10 (5:11) (Class 6) (0-60,58) 3-Y-0+ **£1,617** (£481; £240; £120) **Stalls** Low

Form RPR
6150 **1** **Zefooha (FR)**[20] 4129 7-10-0 **58**(b) PaddyAspell 4 67
(Tim Walford) *led to 1/2-way: chsd ldrs: rdn along over 2f out: styd on to chal wl over 1f out: drvn to ld jst ins fnl f: kpt on strly* **10/1**

6-30 **2** *4* **Haka Dancer (USA)**[23] 3599 8-9-1 **45**(p) JimmyQuinn 6 48
(Philip Kirby) *hld up: stdy hdwy over 4f out: chsd ldrs 3f out: led over 2f out: rdn wl over 1f out: hdd jst ins fnl f and sn one pce* **14/1**

6160 **3** *1 ¼* **Denison Flyer**[20] 4129 4-9-0 **49**(p) LanceBetts(5) 11 51
(Lawrence Mullaney) *cl up: led 1/2-way: hdd over 5f out and sn rdn along: cl up 3f out: drvn and ev ch 2f out: kpt on same pce appr fnl f* **10/1**

2404 **4** *¾* **Spahi (FR)**[6] 4129 5-9-5 **53**(t) LeeNewman 14 54
(David O'Meara) *hld up towards rr: hdwy on inner 4f out: effrt 2f out: sn swtchd rt and rdn to chse ldrs: drvn and one pce ins fnl f* **9/2**[2]

-660 **5** *2 ¾* **Maxi Moo (IRE)**[44] 3317 4-9-1 **45** DavidNolan 5 42
(Ollie Pears) *trckd ldrs: effrt over 4f out: rdn along over 3f out: drvn 2f out and sn no imp* **5/1**[3]

3345 **6** *¾* **Strikemaster (IRE)**[14] 4326 5-9-1 **50**(t) DanielleMcCreery(5) 15 46
(Lee James) *dwlt and in rr: hdwy 10f out: cl up 7f out: led over 5f out: rdn along and hdd wl over 2f out: sn drvn and one pce* **13/2**

0353 **7** *9* **Tasman Tiger**[26] 3906 4-9-4 **48** RoystonFfrench 10 31
(Kate Walton) *nvr bttr than midfield* **16/1**

0-64 **8** *4* **Tigerino (IRE)**[68] 2571 3-7-13 **45** DeclanCannon(3) 8 23
(Chris Fairhurst) *nvr bttr than midfield* **3/1**[1]

4552 **9** *3* **Magic Haze**[25] 3951 5-9-12 **56**(p) RichardKingscote 7 29
(Sally Hall) *trckd ldrs: effrt over 4f out: rdn along over 3f out: sn wknd* **7/1**

5-00 **10** *9* **Lisbon Lion (IRE)**[11] 4329 6-8-11 **46** JulieBurke(5) 2 —
(Martin Todhunter) *a towards rr: bhd fnl 3f* **16/1**

3m 14.54s (9.84) **Going Correction** +0.75s/f (Yiel)
WFA 3 from 4yo+ 13lb **10 Ran SP% 122.3**
Speed ratings (Par 101): **101,98,98,97,96 95,90,88,86,81**
toteswingers:1&2:£9.70, 2&3:£33.20, 1&3:£25.00 CSF £146.89 CT £1453.24 TOTE £12.60: £3.70, £3.00, £5.50; EX 126.40.

Owner Shaun Conway **Bred** Darley Stud Management Co Ltd **Trained** Sheriff Hutton, N Yorks

FOCUS
The early gallop was really slow in the easy ground and a few of these had a chance of sorts. Weak form, but the winner was back to her best.

Tigerino(IRE) Official explanation: trainer said gelding was unsuited by the good to soft ground
T/Plt: £27.00 to a £1 stake. Pool of £47,210.19 - 1,274.16 winning tickets. T/Qpdt: £23.20 to a £1 stake. Pool of £2,275.76 - 72.40 winning tickets. JR

4430 LEICESTER (R-H)
Sunday, August 7

OFFICIAL GOING: Good to firm (good in places; 7.8)
Wind: Fresh, behind Weather: Cloudy with sunny spells

4815 BRITISH STALLION STUDS SUPPORTING BRITISH RACING EBF MAIDEN STKS 7f 9y
2:15 (2:16) (Class 5) 2-Y-O **£3,557** (£1,058; £529; £264) **Stalls** High

Form RPR
1 **Stipulate** 2-9-3 0 TomQueally 9 79+
(Sir Henry Cecil) *trckd ldrs: shkn up over 2f out: led 1f out: rdn and edgd rt: r.o: jst hld on* **4/1**[3]

34 **2** *nse* **Devdas (IRE)**[29] 3870 2-9-3 0 AdamKirby 10 76+
(Clive Cox) *hld up in tch: rdn over 2f out: ev ch ins fnl f: edgd lft: r.o: jst failed* **7/1**

00 **3** *3 ¼* **Il Pazzo**[18] [4201] 2-9-3 0 .... MickyFenton 6 68
(Mike Murphy) *chsd ldrs: rdn and ev ch 1f out: hung lft ins fnl f: styd on same pce* **150/1**

0 **4** *nk* **Abhaath (USA)**[22] [4087] 2-9-3 0 .... FrankieDettori 2 67
(Saeed Bin Suroor) *chsd ldrs: rdn and ev ch over 1f out: styd on same pce ins fnl f* **11/2**

02 **5** *shd* **Flavius Victor (IRE)**[48] [3237] 2-9-3 0 .... RobertWinston 5 67
(Richard Hannon) *plld hrd: sn led: rdn and hdd 1f out: no ex ins fnl f* **20/1**

6 **6** *½* **Gabrial's Gift (IRE)**[20] [4159] 2-9-3 0 .... ChrisCatlin 3 65
(David Simcock) *hld up: racd keenly: hdwy over 1f out: styd on* **50/1**

5 **7** *1 ½* **Strada Facendo (USA)**[30] [3823] 2-9-3 0 .... J-PGuillambert 8 61
(Luca Cumani) *s.i.s: hld up: hdwy 1/2-way: rdn over 1f out: nt trble ldrs* **85/40**[1]

6 **8** *1* **Orwellian**[45] [3308] 2-9-3 0 .... MartinDwyer 7 59
(Brian Meehan) *hld up: rdn over 1f out: nvr on terms* **33/1**

2 **9** *nk* **Snooky**[29] [3870] 2-9-3 0 .... FergusSweeney 11 58
(Henry Candy) *chsd ldrs tl wknd over 1f out* **7/2**[2]

10 *nk* **Wyndham Wave** 2-9-3 0 .... JamesMillman 1 57
(Rod Millman) *mid-div: hdwy over 1f out: edgd lft sn after: wknd ins fnl f* **100/1**

0 **11** *18* **Big Time Charlie (IRE)**[8] [4525] 2-9-3 0 .... DarryllHolland 4 10
(Richard Hannon) *mid-div: rdn 1/2-way: sn bhd* **33/1**

1m 24.58s (-1.62) **Going Correction** -0.30s/f (Firm) **11** Ran SP% **116.4**
Speed ratings (Par 94): **97,96,93,92,92 92,90,89,89,88 68**
toteswingers: 1&2 £5.90, 1&3 £74.10, 2&3 £21.10 CSF £29.76 TOTE £7.80: £3.40, £4.00, £32.20; EX 39.70.
Owner K Abdulla **Bred** Juddmonte Farms Ltd **Trained** Newmarket, Suffolk

FOCUS
The ground was riding much as advertised. Several leading stables were represented in this maiden, but it was probably just an ordinary race with the third home appearing to hold down the form.

NOTEBOOK
Stipulate was one of only two newcomers in the field. A grandson of Oaks runner-up All At Sea, he moved well through the race and found enough for pressure to shade the photo. His Royal Lodge and Dewhurst entries are perhaps over-ambitious on this evidence, but he is entitled to come on for the experience and will improve on what he showed here. (op 3-1)
Devdas(IRE) came in for backing and he just failed to repay the support. He reverted to more patient tactics and went down by the minimum margin after hanging slightly left under pressure. (op 14-1)
Il Pazzo ◆ showed little on his first two starts, but outran his price here and had every chance at the furlong pole. His rider was by no means hard on him from that point and the front pair pulled away, but he held on for third. This was a big improvement, but his proximity clouds the form. (op 125-1)
Abhaath(USA), an expensive flop on his debut at Lingfield, was Frankie Dettori's only ride of the meeting. The colt travelled nicely but found less than expected once let down and, while this was a better effort, he is not living up to his price tag. (op 9-2)
Flavius Victor(IRE), runner-up at Wolverhampton, did not really build on that, racing rather keenly, but now qualifies for nurseries. (op 14-1)
Gabrial's Gift(IRE) was buzzed up in the paddock but ran respectably and is getting the hang of things. (op 40-1)
Strada Facendo(USA) ran a promising race on his debut at the Newmarket July festival but that race is not really working out. He came under pressure to hold his pitch with over 2f to run and faded inside the last. (op 9-4 tchd 2-1)
Orwellian ◆ was struggling in rear with 2f left but came home quite nicely once his rider put the stick down. He is one to keep an eye on.
Snooky finished ahead of Devdas when runner-up at Salisbury and was well supported here, but could not confirm that form. (op 6-1)

4816 RUTLAND (S) STKS — 7f 9y

2:45 (2:46) (Class 6) 3-4-Y-O **£1,811** (£539; £269; £67; £67) **Stalls** High

Form RPR

001 **1** **Night Trade (IRE)**[5] [4634] 4-8-11 73 .... NeilFarley(5) 5 72
(Deborah Sanderson) *chsd ldrs: rdn to ld over 1f out: r.o* **8/11**[1]

6560 **2** *hd* **Saharia (IRE)**[26] [3936] 4-9-2 72 .... (p) TomQueally 7 71
(Ollie Pears) *hld up: hdwy over 2f out: rdn to chse wnr over 1f out: r.o u.p* **9/4**[2]

0406 **3** *8* **Whats For Pudding (IRE)**[20] [4146] 3-8-5 46 .... JamesSullivan 3 42
(Declan Carroll) *chsd ldrs: rdn over 2f out: wknd fnl f* **40/1**

6660 **4** *shd* **Sophie's Beau (USA)**[68] [2588] 4-8-13 44 .... HarryBentley(3) 1 49
(Michael Chapman) *plld hrd and prom: led 5f out: rdn and hdd over 1f out: wknd ins fnl f* **66/1**

P-00 **4** *dht* **Into The Wind**[22] [4086] 4-8-13 55 ow2 .... JamesMillman 2 46
(Rod Millman) *hld up: rdn over 2f out: kpt on ins fnl f: nvr trbld ldrs* **14/1**[3]

1306 **6** *1 ¾* **Eternal Youth (IRE)**[27] [3920] 3-9-1 63 .... (v[1]) TomMcLaughlin 4 47
(Ronald Harris) *sn led: hdd 5f out: rdn and wknd over 1f out* **25/1**

56 **7** *nk* **Isheforreal (IRE)**[9] [4514] 4-8-13 0 .... DaleSwift(3) 6 43
(Brian Ellison) *hld up: plld hrd: rdn over 2f out: sn wknd* **16/1**

1m 23.56s (-2.64) **Going Correction** -0.30s/f (Firm)
WFA 3 from 4yo 6lb **7** Ran SP% **109.0**
Speed ratings (Par 101): **103,102,93,93,93 91,91**
toteswingers: 1&2 £1.10, 1&3 £4.20, 2&3 £8.30 CSF £2.16 TOTE £1.40: £1.10, £1.30; EX 2.80.The winner was sold to Ron Harris for for 7,200gns. Saharia was claimed by M J Attwater for 6,000.
Owner R J Budge **Bred** John Foley **Trained** Sturton le Steeple, Notts

FOCUS
A weak seller that looked a two-horse race according to the official adjusted ratings and so it turned out. The pace was steady but the time was slightly quicker than the 2yo maiden.

4817 LEICESTER MERCURY FAMILY FUN DAY H'CAP — 5f 218y

3:15 (3:16) (Class 3) (0-90,88) 3-Y-O **£6,490** (£1,942; £971; £486; £242) **Stalls** High

Form RPR

-333 **1** **Levitate**[38] [3557] 3-8-9 76 .... (p) RobertWinston 3 87
(Alan McCabe) *sn led: hdd over 4f out: chsd ldrs: rdn to ld over 1f out: r.o wl* **7/1**

3311 **2** *2 ¼* **Fast Shot**[17] [4234] 3-8-10 77 .... DavidAllan 7 80
(Tim Easterby) *hld up: hdwy 1/2-way: rdn and ev ch over 1f out: styd on same pce ins fnl f* **5/2**[1]

2130 **3** *¾* **Close To The Edge (IRE)**[20] [4156] 3-8-10 77 .... DavidProbert 8 78
(Alan McCabe) *unruly in stalls: s.i.s: hld up: hdwy and swtchd rt over 1f out: sn rdn: styd on same pce ins fnl f* **11/1**

1111 **4** *hd* **Roodee Queen**[10] [4459] 3-8-11 81 .... HarryBentley(3) 1 81
(Milton Bradley) *chsd ldrs: rdn and ev ch over 1f out: no ex ins fnl f* **9/2**[3]

001 **5** *¾* **Highland Colori (IRE)**[26] [3949] 3-8-8 75 .... RichardKingscote 10 73
(Tom Dascombe) *hld up: hdwy over 1f out: edgd rt and no imp ins fnl f* **7/2**[2]

2023 **6** *13* **Indian Ballad (IRE)**[34] [3682] 3-9-0 86 .... ShaneBKelly(5) 5 42
(Ed McMahon) *chsd ldrs tl wknd wl over 1f out* **5/1**

5065 **7** *1* **Belle Bayardo (IRE)**[5] [4643] 3-9-2 83 .... (v[1]) TomMcLaughlin 4 36
(Ronald Harris) *s.i.s: sn prom: led over 4f out: hdd & wknd over 1f out* **50/1**

254 **U** **Restless Bay (IRE)**[6] [4610] 3-8-4 78 .... (v) JackDuern(7) 2 —
(Reg Hollinshead) *reluctant to s: wl bhd whn wnt rt and uns rdr leaving stalls* **14/1**

69.92 secs (-3.08) **Going Correction** -0.30s/f (Firm) **8** Ran SP% **115.1**
Speed ratings (Par 104): **108,105,104,103,102 85,84,—**
toteswingers: 1&2 £2.50, 1&3 £10.40, 2&3 £5.40 CSF £25.08 CT £193.49 TOTE £10.30: £2.70, £2.20, £4.70; EX 23.80.
Owner Charles Wentworth **Bred** Cheveley Park Stud Ltd **Trained** Averham Park, Notts

FOCUS
A fair sprint handicap, run in a time inside the standard. Improvement from the winner with the form rated at face value.

NOTEBOOK
Levitate ◆, sold out of Sir Michael Stoute's yard for 38,000gns, made a winning debut for Alan McCabe. With cheekpieces replacing a visor, he ran on strongly against the rail in the latter stages, scoring with something to spare. The drop in trip suited him and he looks a sprinter to follow. (op 6-1)
Fast Shot, on a hat-trick after victories at Catterick and Doncaster, has gone up 12lb in that time. He ran a solid race but was no match for the winner in the final furlong. (tchd 3-1)
Close To The Edge(IRE), racing for the same connections as the winner, stayed on for third after being switched to the outside. For by no means the first time she had reared in the stalls, but the trait obviously does not preclude a decent performance. (op 14-1)
Roodee Queen's fine run of victories came to an end, but she did nothing much wrong. The first of her four handicap wins, gained at the end of June, came off an 18lb lower mark. (tchd 4-1)
Highland Colori(IRE), winner of a 5f Fibresand maiden last time, disappointed on this handicap debut back up in trip. He still has to prove his effectiveness on turf. (op 5-1)
Indian Ballad(IRE) came here in decent heart but was below par. (tchd 4-1)
Belle Bayardo(IRE) may have done too much on this quick reappearance in first-time headgear.

4818 HAPPY 70TH BIRTHDAY JACK PALEY H'CAP — 1m 1f 218y

3:45 (3:49) (Class 4) (0-85,85) 4-Y-O+ **£4,528** (£1,347; £673; £336) **Stalls** Low

Form RPR

3001 **1** **San Cassiano (IRE)**[6] [4608] 4-9-6 84 6ex .... JamesSullivan 7 93
(Ruth Carr) *mde all: set stdy pce tl qcknd over 2f out: rdn over 1f out: r.o wl* **7/2**[1]

0046 **2** *2 ¼* **Resentful Angel**[15] [4344] 6-9-7 85 .... ChrisCatlin 8 90
(Pat Eddery) *chsd wnr: rdn and hung rt fr over 2f out: nt run on* **7/1**[3]

6043 **3** *2* **Scamperdale**[24] [4004] 9-8-12 81 .... JamesRogers(5) 2 82+
(Brian Baugh) *hld up: hdwy 2f out: nt clr run over 1f out: rdn and no ex ins fnl f* **11/2**[2]

0000 **4** *1 ½* **Follow The Flag (IRE)**[4] [4679] 7-8-10 74 .... (p) RobertWinston 4 72
(Alan McCabe) *chsd ldrs: rdn over 2f out: styd on same pce fr over 1f out* **25/1**

3115 **5** *½* **Art Scholar (IRE)**[8] [4553] 4-9-0 78 .... TomQueally 6 75
(Michael Appleby) *hld up: rdn and edgd rt fr over 1f out: styd on: nt trble ldrs* **7/2**[1]

354 **6** *7* **Minsky Mine (IRE)**[23] [4077] 4-8-3 67 .... DavidProbert 1 50
(Michael Appleby) *hld up: hdwy over 3f out: sn rdn: edgd rt and wknd over 1f out* **16/1**

4660 **7** *¾* **Tartan Gunna**[36] [3620] 5-9-2 80 .... (p) DarryllHolland 5 61
(Mark Johnston) *dwlt: hdwy 8f out: rdn over 3f out: wknd over 1f out* **8/1**

2m 6.21s (-1.69) **Going Correction** -0.025s/f (Good) **7** Ran SP% **93.2**
Speed ratings (Par 105): **105,103,101,100,100 94,93**
toteswingers: 1&2 £4.90, 1&3 £3.00, 2&3 £4.00 CSF £18.00 CT £64.84 TOTE £3.30: £1.40, £4.30; EX 24.80.
Owner The Bottom Liners & Mrs R Carr **Bred** Peter Savill **Trained** Huby, N Yorks

FOCUS
An ordinary handicap run at a false pace. The first two always occupied the same positions and this is not form to take too seriously. The winner rates back to his best.

4819 LEICESTER MERCURY WEEKEND EDITION H'CAP — 5f 218y

4:15 (4:15) (Class 5) (0-70,70) 3-Y-O **£2,522** (£750; £375; £187) **Stalls** High

Form RPR

20 **1** **Showboating (IRE)**[4] [4680] 3-8-11 67 .... (tp) NoraLooby(7) 2 73
(Alan McCabe) *chsd ldrs: led over 3f out: rdn and hung rt fr over 1f out: styd on* **15/2**

0605 **2** *¾* **Diamond Vine (IRE)**[16] [4271] 3-9-4 67 .... (p) TomMcLaughlin 6 71
(Ronald Harris) *sn outpcd: hdwy u.p over 2f out: styd on* **6/1**[3]

5451 **3** *4 ½* **Rambo Will**[17] [4247] 3-9-7 70 .... DavidProbert 3 60
(J R Jenkins) *chsd ldrs: rdn over 2f out: styd on same pce appr fnl f* **5/2**[1]

6106 **4** *½* **Cadmium Loch**[31] [3783] 3-8-12 61 .... (p) RussKennemore 5 49
(Reg Hollinshead) *prom: rdn over 2f out: edgd rt and wknd ins fnl f* **10/3**[2]

5616 **5** *nse* **Mazovian (USA)**[9] [4518] 3-9-2 68 .... HarryBentley(3) 4 56
(Michael Chapman) *led 1f: chsd ldrs: outpcd over 2f out: rdn and hung rt over 1f out: n.d after* **10/3**[2]

5005 **6** *3* **Misshollygolightly**[3] [4715] 3-8-2 51 oh6 .... KellyHarrison 7 29
(Brian Baugh) *sn outpcd: rdn over 2f out: nvr on terms* **40/1**

0660 **7** *2 ¾* **Zee Zee Dan (IRE)**[8] [4547] 3-8-11 60 .... (p) TomQueally 1 29
(Noel Quinlan) *led 5f out: hdd over 3f out: wknd over 2f out* **12/1**

1m 11.46s (-1.54) **Going Correction** -0.30s/f (Firm) **7** Ran SP% **110.9**
Speed ratings (Par 100): **98,97,91,90,90 86,82**
toteswingers: 1&2 £6.00, 1&3 £4.40, 2&3 £2.60 CSF £47.83 TOTE £14.00: £7.80, £5.40; EX 67.10.
Owner Mr & Mrs L Cooke A Pierce A McCabe **Bred** Crone Stud Farms Ltd **Trained** Averham Park, Notts

■ Stewards' Enquiry : Tom McLaughlin caution: used whip with excessive frequency.

FOCUS
A modest handicap, run a second and a half slower than the earlier Class 3 race. The first pair pulled clear. The winenr is rated to his 2yo best.

4820 EDMONDS AND SLATTER 25TH ANNIVERSARY H'CAP — 5f 2y

4:45 (4:45) (Class 6) (0-65,65) 3-Y-O+ **£1,940** (£577; £288; £144) **Stalls** High

Form RPR

4250 **1** **We'll Deal Again**[37] [3573] 4-9-9 64 .... (b) GrahamGibbons 7 77
(Michael Easterby) *mde all: shkn up over 1f out: clr fnl f: easily* **7/2**[2]

2066 **2** *4 ½* **Ace Of Spies (IRE)**[13] [4395] 6-9-2 60 .... (b) HarryBentley(3) 9 59
(Conor Dore) *chsd ldrs: rdn over 2f out: styd on same pce fr over 1f out: wnt 2nd wl ins fnl f* **16/1**

U201 **3** *1 ¼* **Pinball (IRE)**[16] [4272] 5-9-0 55 .... (p) TomEaves 5 50
(Lisa Williamson) *hood removed sltly late and s.i.s: sn prom: rdn over 2f out: chsd wnr over 1f out: no ex and lost 2nd wl ins fnl f* **11/1**

2162 **4** *1 ¼* **The Tatling (IRE)**[5] 4631 14-9-10 **65**........................ RichardKingscote 4 56+
(Milton Bradley) *s.i.s: outpcd: styd on fr over 1f out: nvr nrr* **9/1**

6602 **5** *hd* **Watch Chain (IRE)**[4] 4683 4-9-8 **63**........................(p) RobertWinston 2 53+
(Alan McCabe) *stdd s: hld up: hung rt and hdwy fr over 1f out: nvr on terms* **10/3**[1]

4406 **6** *4 ½* **King Of Swords (IRE)**[14] 4371 7-8-3 **47**................(p) LouisBeuzelin(3) 8 23
(Nigel Tinkler) *prom: rdn 1/2-way: wknd over 1f out* **15/2**

0030 **7** *½* **Grand Stitch (USA)**[9] 4518 5-9-0 **60**............................(v) NeilFarley(5) 6 34
(Declan Carroll) *w wnr tl rdn 1/2-way: wknd over 1f out* **12/1**

3062 **8** *hd* **My Love Fajer (IRE)**[8] 4527 3-8-0 **51**............................ NoraLooby(7) 1 25
(Alan McCabe) *wnt rt s: sn outpcd* **15/2**

0314 **9** *3 ¼* **Media Jury**[12] 4405 4-9-4 **59**..(v) DavidNolan 3 22
(John Wainwright) *sn outpcd* **7/1**[3]

58.55 secs (-1.45) **Going Correction** -0.30s/f (Firm)
WFA 3 from 4yo+ 3lb **9** Ran SP% **113.2**
Speed ratings (Par 101): **99,91,89,87,87 80,79,79,73**
toteswingers: 1&2 £10.60, 1&3 £6.90, 2&3 £14.40 CSF £56.02 CT £556.00 TOTE £3.50: £1.50, £6.00, £3.80; EX 61.80.
Owner K Wreglesworth **Bred** K Wreglesworth **Trained** Sheriff Hutton, N Yorks

FOCUS
A low-grade sprint handicap and again prominent racers did best. The winner's effort was rather out of line with his profile.
My Love Fajer(IRE) Official explanation: jockey said gelding was slowly away

4821 ROTHERBY H'CAP — 1m 60y
5:15 (5:15) (Class 5) (0-75,74) 3-Y-0+ **£2,522** (£750; £375; £187) **Stalls** Low

Form RPR

0405 **1** **West End Lad**[26] 3934 8-9-10 **70**..............................(b) RussKennemore 7 78
(Roy Bowring) *plld hrd: led over 6f out: rdn over 1f out: styd on* **10/1**

0561 **2** *1 ¼* **Solar Spirit (IRE)**[14] 4361 6-9-9 **74**.............................. ShaneBKelly(5) 3 79
(Tracy Waggott) *sed slowy: hld up: nt clr run over 2f out: hdwy over 1f out: r.o to go 2nd wl ins fnl f: nt rch wnr* **4/1**[2]

5320 **3** *¾* **Bold Cross (IRE)**[11] 4444 8-9-6 **66**...................................... TomEaves 6 69
(Edward Bevan) *awkward leaving stalls: hdwy over 6f out: rdn to chse wnr over 1f out: sn hung rt: styd on same pce and lost 2nd wl ins fnl f* **9/2**[3]

0656 **4** *3* **Ajdaad (USA)**[36] 3643 4-8-13 **66**...................................... RyanTate(7) 5 62
(Alan McCabe) *hld up: r.o ins fnl f: nvr nrr* **5/1**

2553 **5** *¾* **Barista (IRE)**[15] 4338 3-9-5 **72**..(v[1]) ChrisCatlin 2 65
(Mick Channon) *led: hdd and hmpd over 6f out: chsd wnr tl rdn over 1f out: wknd ins fnl f* **3/1**[1]

2256 **6** *4 ½* **Bentley**[7] 4579 7-8-5 **56**..(p) JamesRogers(5) 1 40
(Brian Baugh) *chsd ldrs: rdn over 3f out: wknd over 1f out* **6/1**

5230 **7** *6* **Lord Of The Dance (IRE)**[57] 2910 5-9-12 **72**........... TomMcLaughlin 4 42
(Mark Brisbourne) *prom: rdn over 2f out: wknd over 1f out* **8/1**

1m 45.0s (-0.10) **Going Correction** -0.025s/f (Good)
WFA 3 from 4yo+ 7lb **7** Ran SP% **114.3**
Speed ratings (Par 103): **99,97,97,94,93 88,82**
toteswingers: 1&2 £6.30, 1&3 £8.00, 2&3 £3.70 CSF £49.34 TOTE £13.50: £5.00, £2.10; EX 58.90.
Owner K Nicholls **Bred** Keith Nicholls **Trained** Edwinstowe, Notts

FOCUS
A weak, uncompetitive handicap, in which the winner set a moderate pace. His best form this year.
T/Plt: £454.20 to a £1 stake. Pool: £78,440.46. 126.05 winning tickets. T/Qpdt: £125.20 to a £1 stake. Pool: £6,521.66. 38.54 winning tickets. CR

4613 WINDSOR (R-H)
Sunday, August 7

OFFICIAL GOING: Good to firm (9.2)
Wind: Fresh, across Weather: Sunny spells and blustery showers; heavy downpour race 6

4822 READING POST H'CAP (DIV I) — 1m 67y
2:00 (2:00) (Class 6) (0-65,65) 3-Y-0+ **£1,567** (£462; £231) **Stalls** Low

Form RPR

-232 **1** **Daneside (IRE)**[11] 4444 4-9-0 **54**................................ MarkLawson(3) 11 69
(Gary Harrison) *trckd ldrs: hdd to far side rail over 3f out: overall ldr over 2f out: drvn clr over 1f out: in n.d after* **5/2**[1]

2613 **2** *4 ½* **Bold Ring**[3] 4696 5-9-4 **58**.. AlanCreighton(3) 5 63
(Edward Creighton) *hld up in midfield: prog on far side over 2f out: chsd wnr over 1f out: no imp* **9/1**[3]

3003 **3** *1* **Aflaam (IRE)**[7] 4578 6-9-12 **63**..............................(p) KirstyMilczarek 9 66
(Ronald Harris) *disp ld: styd nr side in st: hdd by far side wnr over 2f out: drifted across over 1f out and disp 2nd: one pce* **14/1**

4354 **4** *1 ¾* **Recalcitrant**[17] 4249 8-10-0 **65**.. EddieAhern 3 64
(Simon Dow) *chsd ldng pair: rdn and no imp on wnr wl over 1f out: one pce after* **9/2**[2]

4602 **5** *½* **Links Drive Lady**[17] 4244 3-9-2 **65**.......................... TobyAtkinson(5) 7 62
(Mark Rimmer) *hld up in rr: rdn over 3f out: sme prog 2f out: nt pce to threaten* **9/1**[3]

200- **6** *1* **Curlew (IRE)**[153] 7307 5-9-11 **65**.............................. RobertLButler(3) 2 60
(Chris Down) *hld up towards rr: styd nr side and no real prog over 2f out: drifted to far side over 1f out: kpt on* **66/1**

0550 **7** *1* **Talkative Guest (IRE)**[17] 4248 3-8-8 **57**...................(p) RyanPowell(5) 1 49
(George Margarson) *hld up in midfield: wnt across to centre fr 3f out: no prog over 2f out: fdd* **20/1**

0404 **8** *4* **Galloping Queen (IRE)**[25] 3980 3-9-4 **65**.................. MartinHarley(3) 6 48
(Mick Channon) *hld up in last pair: struggling at rr of far side gp over 2f out: no great prog* **20/1**

0500 **9** *8* **Gazboolou**[11] 4444 7-9-2 **53**.. NeilChalmers 12 18
(David Pinder) *disp ld to 3f out: sn wknd in centre* **12/1**

660 **10** *5* **Charlie Fable (IRE)**[20] 4157 3-9-4 **62**............................ JimCrowley 8 15
(Hughie Morrison) *s.i.s: sn rcvrd into midfield: effrt in 5th over 3f out: rdn and wknd rapidly over 2f out* **9/2**[2]

3260 **11** *11* **Angelena Ballerina (IRE)**[15] 4337 4-10-0 **65**..............(v) SebSanders 4 —
(Karen George) *t.k.h: hld up in last pair: rdn 4f out: styd nr side and wl bhd fnl 2f: t.o* **14/1**

0000 **12** *2 ¼* **Scintillating (IRE)**[19] 4183 4-8-9 **46** oh1.......................(v) JimmyQuinn 10 —
(Ray Peacock) *w ldrs 2f: restrained: wknd qckly over 3f out and styd nr side: t.o* **125/1**

1m 44.34s (-0.36) **Going Correction** 0.0s/f (Good)
WFA 3 from 4yo+ 7lb **12** Ran SP% **117.8**
Speed ratings (Par 101): **101,96,95,93,93 92,91,87,79,74 63,61**
toteswingers: 1&2 £5.80, 1&3 £7.50, 2&3 £21.00 CSF £24.89 CT £270.96 TOTE £3.80: £1.40, £2.80, £4.40; EX 27.70 Trifecta £244.40 Part won. Pool: £330.33 - 0.17 winning units..
Owner Gary Harrison **Bred** Iona Equine **Trained** Llandeilo, Carmarthens

FOCUS
Stands rail dolled out 18yds at 6f and 7yds at winning post, top bend dolled out 7yds from normal configuration adding 32yds to races of 1m and over. It was dry overnight and the going was changed to good to firm an hour before racing, although a shower soon afterwards may have softened the ground a touch and the runners headed for the far side soft-ground style in the first. A pretty ordinary contest to kick things off. The time was relatively good and the winner showed improved form.

4823 WINDSOR VEHICLE LEASING MAIDEN AUCTION STKS — 6f
2:30 (2:30) (Class 5) 2-Y-O **£2,658** (£785; £392) **Stalls** Low

Form RPR

3 **1** **I'm So Glad**[16] 4263 2-8-7 0... MartinHarley(3) 1 77
(Mick Channon) *trckd ldrs: wnt 2nd over 2f out: rdn to ld narrowly 1f out and flashed tail: edgd lft and drvn out* **3/1**[1]

05 **2** *½* **Gifted Dancer**[23] 4052 2-8-0 0.. AmyScott(5) 10 71
(Henry Candy) *chsd ldrs and in tch: prog on outer over 2f out: rdn to chal 1f out: styd on: a jst hld* **7/2**[2]

04 **3** *½* **Poker Hospital**[41] 3463 2-8-9 0.. TonyCulhane 3 73
(George Baker) *led: drvn and hdd 1f out: hanging lft but styd on fnl f* **7/2**[2]

4 *3* **Theresnoneedfordat (IRE)** 2-8-12 0 ow1.......................... SebSanders 2 67
(Lydia Pearce) *trckd ldrs: shkn up over 2f out: wanting to hang lft over 1f out and nvr quite on terms: kpt on* **12/1**

44 **5** *3 ¾* **Ashpan Sam**[31] 3779 2-8-9 0... LiamJones 4 53
(John Spearing) *t.k.h: trckd ldrs: outpcd fr 2f out and wl btn in 5th over 1f out* **15/2**[3]

6 *3 ¾* **Haafhd Handsome** 2-8-11 0.. PatDobbs 9 44
(Richard Hannon) *sn off the pce in last quartet: pushed along over 2f out: sme prog and reminder over 1f out: kpt on* **8/1**

7 *1* **Yarra Valley** 2-8-5 0... JamieMackay 5 35
(Willie Musson) *dwlt: wl bhd in last pair: virtually t.o 1/2-way: pushed along and styd on fr over 1f out* **80/1**

00 **8** *nk* **Ventus D'Or**[15] 4339 2-8-13 0.. EddieAhern 8 42
(Walter Swinburn) *chsd ldrs and jst abt in tch to over 2f out: wknd* **33/1**

064 **9** *2 ¼* **The Name Is Don (IRE)**[29] 3868 2-8-6 67............... SimonPearce(3) 13 31
(Mark Gillard) *dwlt: wl off the pce in last quartet: pushed along and no real prog fnl 2f* **25/1**

60 **10** *5* **Chater Garden (IRE)**[70] 2523 2-8-8 0.................. MatthewDavies(3) 12 18
(Alan Jarvis) *chsd ldr to over 2f out: wknd rapidly* **40/1**

11 *2 ¼* **Conowen** 2-8-12 0.. JimCrowley 7 12+
(William Jarvis) *pressed ldrs: taken to far side fr 1/2-way: sn lost pl and struggling* **25/1**

12 *28* **Fallible** 2-9-0 0.. NeilCallan 11 —
(Tony Carroll) *dwlt and veered lft s: a wl bhd: one of pair to go far side fr 1/2-way: t.o* **33/1**

1m 11.85s (-1.15) **Going Correction** -0.20s/f (Firm) **12** Ran SP% **117.3**
Speed ratings (Par 94): **99,98,97,93,88 83,82,81,78,72 69,31**
toteswingers: 1&2 £3.50, 1&3 £3.30, 2&3 £4.60 CSF £12.36 TOTE £2.90: £1.10, £2.20, £1.90; EX 11.70 Trifecta £108.40 Pool: £392.65 - 2.68 winning units..
Owner Chris Wright & The Hon Mrs J M Corbett **Bred** Stratford Place Stud **Trained** West Ilsley, Berks

FOCUS
They stayed stands' side in the straight this time and the betting got it right, with the three market leaders fighting it out inside the last.

NOTEBOOK
I'm So Glad, third in an Ascot maiden on her debut, saw that form given a little boost when the fourth finished a respectable fifth in Group 3 company on Saturday. Always well placed tracking the leader, she found plenty for pressure despite flashing her tail and gained a hard-fought success. She shouldn't be overburdened with nurseries in mind. (op 4-1)
Gifted Dancer is improving with racing and still looked a shade green. The winner appeared to want it more this time but she's going the right way and nurseries are now an option for her. (op 5-2)
Poker Hospital, green on the way to post, didn't settle as well as she might have in front and then hung under pressure. Once again she carried her head a touch high and gave the impression she's not be the easiest ride in the world. (op 4-1 tchd 3-1)
Theresnoneedfordat(IRE), whose rider put up 1lb overweight, was representing a stable that has been in among the winners recently. He did best of the newcomers despite wanting to hang left in the straight and should come on for this. (op 20-1)
Ashpan Sam ◆ broke well from the stalls but didn't settle early and predictably dropped away in the closing stages. He once again showed ability, though, and will be interesting when switched to handicaps. (op 11-2)
Haafhd Handsome, niggled along before the turn in, is bred to want a good deal further in time. (op 11-1 tchd 12-1)
Yarra Valley, who passed a few late on without being given a hard race, is one who will do better once eligible for handicaps. (op 66-1)

4824 OSSIE & HUTCH MEMORIAL FILLIES' AUCTION NURSERY — 6f
3:00 (3:02) (Class 5) 2-Y-O **£2,658** (£785; £392) **Stalls** Low

Form RPR

2200 **1** **Toffee Tart**[51] 3104 2-9-1 **70**.. SebSanders 6 73
(J W Hills) *s.i.s: wl in tch in rr: prog over 2f out: rdn to chse ldr over 1f out: styd on strly fnl f: led last strides* **7/2**[1]

3016 **2** *½* **Marygold**[29] 3842 2-9-6 **75**.. HayleyTurner 3 77
(John Akehurst) *led after 2f: drvn more than a l clr over 1f out: styd on: hdd fnl strides* **7/1**[2]

032 **3** *2 ¼* **Lady Gibraltar**[47] 3257 2-9-4 **76**................................ MatthewDavies(3) 1 71
(Alan Jarvis) *cl up: rdn to chse ldr briefly wl over 1f out: hanging bdly lft and nt qckn after: kpt on* **7/2**[1]

006 **4** *1 ¼* **Raspberry Fizz**[67] 2602 2-8-1 **56**....................................(p) JimmyQuinn 4 47
(Eve Johnson Houghton) *in tch: rdn in last wl over 2f out and struggling: hanging and plenty of tail swishing but styd on wl fnl f* **25/1**

046 **5** *¾* **Zuzu Angel (IRE)**[30] 3813 2-9-0 **69**.................................... ShaneKelly 11 58
(William Knight) *led 2f: w ldr to over 2f out: fdd over 1f out* **8/1**

15 **6** *hd* **Bellechance**[30] 3795 2-8-2 **60**.. DeclanCannon(3) 8 48
(Nigel Tinkler) *cl up: rdn over 2f out: racd awkwardly and nt qckn wl over 1f out: one pce after* **15/2**[3]

51 **7** *11* **Chandigarh (IRE)**[17] 4229 2-8-8 **70**................................ DavidKenny(7) 9 25
(Paul Fitzsimons) *chsd ldrs: rdn and wknd qckly fr 2f out* **14/1**

041 **P** **Especially Red (IRE)**[17] 4250 2-9-2 **71**................................ MartinLane 2 —
(Lisa Williamson) *chsd ldrs: hanging and wknd rapidly wl over 1f out: p.u and dismntd nr fin* **8/1**

1m 13.05s (0.05) **Going Correction** -0.20s/f (Firm) **8** Ran SP% **101.4**
Speed ratings (Par 91): **91,90,87,85,84 84,69,—**
toteswingers: 1&2 £4.80, 1&3 £3.00, 2&3 £3.50 CSF £21.78 CT £63.24 TOTE £4.70: £1.80, £2.20, £1.60; EX 21.60 Trifecta £59.90 Pool: £339.57 - 4.19 winning units..
Owner Gary And Linnet Woodward **Bred** Gary Woodward **Trained** Upper Lambourn, Berks

FOCUS
A fairly competitive nursery and this time the whole field crossed over to race on the far side in the straight.

NOTEBOOK
Toffee Tart boasts a Cheveley Park entry and, while that is pie in the sky, she battled on really well here to grab the runner-up close home and defy a mark of 70. Out of her depth at Royal Ascot last time, she was much more at home at this level and there's probably more to come from her as she won't mind another furlong, and a return to quicker ground will help, too. (op 4-1 tchd 9-2 in places)
Marygold, hampered in a better race than this at Ascot last time, looked to have things under control heading into the final furlong, only to be caught in the final strides. She did little wrong but is likely to remain vulnerable to less exposed rivals in this sphere. (op 8-1)
Lady Gibraltar didn't help her rider by hanging badly left under pressure, but this was a solid enough effort off top weight. Official explanation: jockey said filly hung left (op 4-1)
Raspberry Fizz flashed her tail every time she was hit with the whip and hung left into the far rail. She didn't look an easy ride but was staying on at the finish and another furlong will be to her advantage. (op 22-1)
Zuzu Angel(IRE) was given a positive ride dropped back a furlong on her handicap debut but the tactics didn't work and she was readily seen off. (op 9-1 tchd 15-2)
Bellechance still looked green, wandering about under pressure and perhaps the rain-softened ground didn't suit her. (op 8-1 tchd 7-1)
Especially Red(IRE) Official explanation: vet said pulled up lame right-fore

4825 AW CREATIVE H'CAP — 1m 2f 7y
3:30 (3:30) (Class 5) (0-75,75) 3-Y-O+ — **£2,385** (£704; £352) **Stalls** Centre

Form / RPR

1242 **1** **Choral Festival**[6] 4613 5-9-3 **64** .... NeilChalmers 8 — 71
(John Bridger) *hld up disputing 5th: effrt over 2f out: chsd ldr over 1f out: cajoled along and readily clsd to ld last 100yds* **5/1**[3]

1500 **2** *½* **Understory (USA)**[57] 2915 4-9-12 **73** .... NeilCallan 1 — 79
(Tim McCarthy) *led at stdy pce but untrbld: kicked on over 3f out: styd on fnl 2f: hdd and outpcd last 100yds* **16/1**

2411 **3** *4½* **One Hit Wonder**[20] 4154 4-9-8 **69** .... LiamKeniry 4 — 66
(Jonathan Portman) *mostly chsd ldr after 3f: nt qckn over 2f out: lost 2nd over 1f out: fdd* **5/2**[1]

3635 **4** *shd* **Lang Shining (IRE)**[18] 4211 7-9-8 **72** .... (b[1]) SophieDoyle(3) 10 — 69
(Jamie Osborne) *prom: disp 2nd briefly over 3f out: nt qckn over 2f out: kpt on* **18/1**

4424 **5** *½* **Edgeworth (IRE)**[38] 3546 5-9-4 **72** .... JoshBaudains(7) 5 — 68
(David Bridgwater) *hld up in 7th: effrt on outer gng wl enough over 2f out: edgd lft and fnd nil over 1f out: wl btn after* **9/1**

-026 **6** *1½* **Sweet Secret**[16] 4275 4-9-0 **68** .... RaulDaSilva(7) 3 — 61
(Jeremy Gask) *hld up disputing 5th: effrt on outer over 2f out: nt qckn wl over 1f out: fdd* **8/1**

565 **7** *1* **Wordiness**[20] 4157 3-9-0 **70** .... FrankieMcDonald 6 — 61
(Barry Brennan) *t.k.h: hld up in last trio in steadily run contest: effrt 3f out: no prog and btn 2f out* **14/1**

12 **8** *½* **Mauritino (GER)**[66] 2649 7-10-0 **75** .... JimCrowley 9 — 65
(Jonjo O'Neill) *hld up last in steadily run contest: lot to do whn pce lifted over 3f out: rdn over 1f out: nvr nr ldrs* **4/1**[2]

3000 **9** *hd* **Black Coffee**[11] 4432 6-9-6 **67** .... (b) ShaneKelly 7 — 56
(Mark Brisbourne) *hld up in last trio in steadily run contest: rdn over 2f out: no prog* **20/1**

0040 **10** *2¼* **My Vindication (USA)**[11] 4447 3-9-0 **70** .... PatDobbs 2 — 55
(Richard Hannon) *chsd ldr 3f: styd prom tl wknd qckly 2f out* **10/1**

2m 10.32s (1.62) **Going Correction** 0.0s/f (Good)
WFA 3 from 4yo+ 9lb — **10** Ran SP% **118.0**
Speed ratings (Par 103): **93,92,89,88,88 87,86,86,85,84**
toteswingers: 1&2 £28.10, 1&3 £2.90, 2&3 £7.80 CSF £82.33 CT £247.80 TOTE £7.30: £1.70, £5.70, £1.30; EX 158.00 TRIFECTA Not won..
Owner Mrs Liz Gardner **Bred** Cheveley Park Stud Ltd **Trained** Liphook, Hants

FOCUS
They didn't go a great pace early in this modest handicap. The first pair were clear but the bare form is limited.

4826 BRITISH STALLION STUDS SUPPORTING BRITISH RACING E B F MAIDEN FILLIES' STKS — 1m 2f 7y
4:00 (4:02) (Class 5) 3-Y-O+ — [illegible] **Stalls** Centre

Form / RPR

23 **1** **Word Power**[20] 4157 3-8-11 0 .... IanMongan 10 — 79
(Sir Henry Cecil) *in tch: pushed along bef 1/2-way: rdn and hdwy 4f out: wnt 2nd over 1f out: clsd to ld last 150yds: styd on but mde heavy weather of it* **8/13**[1]

0 **2** *½* **Lily In Pink**[20] 4157 3-8-11 0 .... EddieAhern 5 — 78
(Jonathan Portman) *chsd ldr 4f and again 4f out: led over 3f out: drvn and flashed tail fr 2f out: hdd last 150yds: styd on* **25/1**

50 **3** *4½* **Indian Mist (IRE)**[14] 4356 3-8-11 0 .... NeilCallan 1 — 69
(Roger Varian) *prom: chsd ldr after 4f to 4f out: nt qckn over 2f out: one pce after* **10/3**[2]

4 *7* **Mazij**[83] 3-8-11 0 .... WilliamCarson 9 — 55
(Peter Hiatt) *wl in rr: pushed along over 4f out: sme prog to take v modest 4th wl over 1f out: no imp* **20/1**

6 **5** *1* **Avon Blaise**[25] 3980 4-9-3 0 .... JohnFahy(3) 7 — 53?
(Peter Hedger) *hld up in last pair: pushed along 1/2-way: sn wl off the pce: sme prog over 2f out: no threat* **66/1**

6 *nse* **Agadir Summer** 3-8-11 0 .... MartinLane 8 — 53
(David Simcock) *dwlt: hld up in last pair: shkn up 4f out: modest prog 3f out: no hdwy and wl btn after* **6/1**[3]

00 **7** *8* **Haafhd Decent (IRE)**[27] 3925 3-8-12 0 ow1 .... SebSanders 2 — 38
(Karen George) *led: clr after 4f to 4f out: hdd over 3f out: wknd qckly* **40/1**

64 **8** *nse* **Beckfield Dancer**[17] 4241 3-8-8 0 .... RyanClark(3) 4 — 37
(Stuart Williams) *in tch in midfield: rdn and outpcd in 4th over 3f out: sn wknd* **50/1**

0 **9** *8* **Lechlade Lass**[39] 3513 3-8-8 0 .... SophieDoyle(3) 11 — 21
(Adrian Chamberlain) *chsd ldrs: pushed along 1/2-way: sn outpcd: wknd 3f out* **50/1**

10 *2* **Brunston Keys** 3-8-11 0 .... JamesDoyle 3 — 17
(Tony Carroll) *difficult to load into stalls: s.s: a in rr: shkn up sn after 1/2-way: wknd 3f out* **20/1**

2m 8.17s (-0.53) **Going Correction** 0.0s/f (Good)
WFA 3 from 4yo 9lb — **10** Ran SP% **120.5**
Speed ratings (Par 100): **102,101,98,92,91 91,85,85,78,77**
toteswingers: 1&2 £5.00, 1&3 £1.20, 2&3 £8.10 CSF £27.02 TOTE £1.70: £1.02, £5.20, £1.60; EX 17.70 Trifecta £38.40 Pool: £714.12 - 13.74 winning units..
Owner K Abdulla **Bred** Juddmonte Farms Ltd **Trained** Newmarket, Suffolk

FOCUS
An ordinary fillies' maiden where three were clear. The winner should improve on the bare form.

4827 THAMES VALLEY AND CHILTERN AIR AMBULANCE H'CAP — 1m 2f 7y
4:30 (4:32) (Class 6) (0-55,55) 3-Y-O — **£1,908** (£563; £281) **Stalls** Centre

Form / RPR

0021 **1** **Tegan (IRE)**[5] 4625 3-8-12 **51** .... PatDobbs 2 — 61
(Richard Hannon) *chsd ldrs in 6th: pushed along firmly 4f out: clsd over 2f out: drvn and hung lft jst over 1f out: styd on to ld last 75yds* **7/2**[1]

0034 **2** *1¼* **Scarborough Lily**[26] 3958 3-8-12 **51** .... JimCrowley 15 — 58
(Edward Vaughan) *trckd ldrs in 5th: clsd fr 3f out: rdn to ld over 1f out: hdd and outpcd last 75yds* **5/1**[3]

0005 **3** *4* **Heart Of Dixie (IRE)**[4] 4666 3-9-2 **55** .... NeilCallan 16 — 54
(Paul Cole) *chsd ldr: rdn 3f out: clsd to ld briefly wl over 1f out: fdd fnl f* **8/1**

-000 **4** *½* **Fastada (IRE)**[34] 3690 3-8-10 **49** ow1 .... (v) EddieAhern 13 — 49+
(Jonathan Portman) *chsd ldng trio: effrt 3f out: keeping on against far rail whn hmpd jst ins fnl f: nt rcvr* **8/1**

3000 **5** *2* **Indian Wish (USA)**[26] 3945 3-8-4 **48** .... LauraPike(5) 10 — 42
(Tim McCarthy) *led: clr over 4f out: hdd and n.m.r wl over 1f out: steadily wknd* **33/1**

1000 **6** *1½* **Appyjack**[37] 3596 3-8-9 **51** .... MichaelO'Connell(3) 9 — 42
(Tony Carroll) *settled in midfield: tried to cl on ldrs fr 3f out: no imp wl over 1f out* **25/1**

0051 **7** *½* **Rather Cool**[7] 4579 3-9-1 **54** 6ex .... NeilChalmers 3 — 44+
(John Bridger) *dwlt: hld up in last pair: lost tch w ldng gp 4f out: prog 3f out: styd on fnl 2f: too much to do* **11/2**

6000 **8** *5* **Salesiano**[69] 2549 3-9-1 **54** .... TravisBlock 4 — 34
(Peter Makin) *settled wl in rr: lost tch w ldng gp 4f out: sme modest prog over 2f out: nvr a factor* **20/1**

5000 **9** *5* **Warbond**[42] 3432 3-8-13 **52** .... FrankieMcDonald 11 — 22
(Michael Madgwick) *dwlt hld up in rr: lost tch w ldng gp 4f out: nvr on terms after* **80/1**

00-4 **10** *4½* **My Mate Les (IRE)**[34] 3675 3-8-10 **52** .... KierenFox(3) 1 — 13
(John Best) *chsd ldng pair to 3f out: sn wknd qckly u.p* **10/1**

00-0 **11** *1¾* **First Pressing**[64] 2710 3-8-9 **55** .... HannahNunn(7) 8 — 13
(John Berry) *in tch in midfield early: dropped to rr bef 1/2-way: struggling in last over 4f out: bhd after* **28/1**

0060 **12** *9* **Ollywood**[16] 4284 3-8-9 **48** .... LiamJones 6 — —
(Tony Carroll) *in tch in midfield: rdn 4f out: wknd qckly fr 3f out* **40/1**

6000 **13** *1¼* **Burst Of Stardust**[10] 4466 3-8-11 **50** .... LiamKeniry 7 — —
(Bryn Palling) *a wl in rr: lost tch fr 4f out: wl bhd after* **33/1**

0040 **R** **Arctic Maiden**[22] 4111 3-8-12 **54** .... AdamBeschizza(3) 14 — —
(Willie Musson) *ref to r: tk no part* **9/2**[2]

2m 9.67s (0.97) **Going Correction** 0.0s/f (Good) — **14** Ran SP% **125.4**
Speed ratings (Par 98): **96,95,91,91,89 88,88,84,80,76 75,68,67,—**
toteswingers: 1&2 £4.60, 1&3 £4.50, 2&3 £9.80 CSF £20.11 CT £137.85 TOTE £4.60: £1.80, £1.10, £3.10; EX 20.00 Trifecta £45.40 Pool: £742.91 - 12.10 winning units..
Owner Derek And Jean Clee **Bred** D D & Mrs J P Clee **Trained** East Everleigh, Wilts
■ Stewards' Enquiry : Pat Dobbs four-day ban: careless riding (Aug 21-24)

FOCUS
A plating-class standard of handicap for three-year-olds. Modest but sound form, and the principals raced prominently.

4828 TICKETS FOR TROOPS H'CAP — 6f
5:00 (5:01) (Class 6) (0-65,65) 3-Y-O+ — **£1,908** (£563; £281) **Stalls** Low

Form / RPR

0-34 **1** **Minety Lass**[31] 3783 3-9-1 **65** .... LucyKBarry(7) 11 — 76+
(Adrian Chamberlain) *mde all: rdn and def advantage fr 2f out: kpt on: all out* **11/1**

0000 **2** *¾* **Pose (IRE)**[13] 4387 4-9-0 **58** .... (t) MatthewLawson(5) 1 — 65
(Roger Ingram) *prom: chsd wnr over 2f out: kpt on u.p but nvr able to chal* **25/1**

00-6 **3** *1* **Whitstable Native**[17] 4247 3-8-8 **58** .... GeorgeanBuckell(7) 13 — 61
(John Best) *prom: urged along fr 2f out: kpt on fr over 1f out but nvr able to chal* **25/1**

0002 **4** *¾* **Comadoir (IRE)**[26] 3940 5-9-11 **64** .... (p) IanMongan 7 — 66
(Jo Crowley) *chsd ldrs: u.p fr 1/2-way: no imp tl styd on fnl f: nrst fin* **7/1**

0613 **5** *nse* **Simple Rhythm**[6] 4600 5-9-0 **58** .... RyanPowell(5) 2 — 59
(John Ryan) *cl up: rdn and effrt on outer over 2f out: pressed for 2nd over 1f out: nt qckn after* **7/2**[1]

3302 **6** *nk* **Commandingpresence (USA)**[8] 4547 5-9-10 **63** .... NeilChalmers 8 — 63
(John Bridger) *trckd ldrs: rdn and nt qckn 2f out: styd on ins fnl f: n.d* **6/1**[2]

5024 **7** *1½* **The Name Is Frank**[9] 4487 6-9-6 **62** .... (t) SimonPearce(3) 3 — 58
(Mark Gillard) *in rr of tighly-packed field: rdn over 2f out: kpt on one pce fr over 1f out* **13/2**[3]

0304 **8** *hd* **Ridgeway Sapphire**[5] 4631 4-8-7 **46** oh1 .... (v) HayleyTurner 14 — 41
(Mark Usher) *cl up: no imp on ldrs wl over 1f out: fdd fnl f* **16/1**

4000 **9** *hd* **Sumbe (USA)**[23] 4066 5-9-7 **60** .... AndreaAtzeni 5 — 57+
(Michael Wigham) *sn last: pushed along 2f out: stl in last pair over 1f out and nt clr run: styd on fnl f* **15/2**

5060 **10** *4½* **Riflessione**[8] 4547 5-9-7 **60** .... (p) JamesDoyle 4 — 40
(Ronald Harris) *pressed ldrs to over 2f out: sn btn* **15/2**

3024 **11** *3½* **Diamond Johnny G (USA)**[3] 4709 4-9-8 **64** .... (t) AlanCreighton(3) 10 — 33
(Edward Creighton) *blindfold off as stalls opened and s.i.s: rcvrd to chse ldrs: rdn 1/2-way: wknd over 2f out* **10/1**

656 **12** *2½* **Simpulse**[9] 4486 3-8-7 **50** .... FrankieMcDonald 12 — 10
(Norma Twomey) *prom to 1/2-way: wknd rapidly over 1f out* **33/1**

1m 15.01s (2.01) **Going Correction** +0.375s/f (Good)
WFA 3 from 4yo+ 4lb — **12** Ran SP% **119.8**
Speed ratings (Par 101): **101,100,98,97,97 97,95,94,94,88 84,80**
toteswingers: 1&2 £70.10, 1&3 £30.10, 2&3 £46.60 CSF £262.76 CT £6646.60 TOTE £13.10: £4.20, £10.70, £6.30; EX 348.50 TRIFECTA Not won..
Owner Colin Rogers **Bred** Longdon Stud Ltd **Trained** Ashton Keynes, Wilts

FOCUS
Another moderate contest, and there are doubts over the form. The race was not all that strong run.
The Name Is Frank Official explanation: jockey said gelding stumbled leaving stalls
Sumbe(USA) Official explanation: jockey said gelding was denied a clear run

4829 READING POST H'CAP (DIV II) — 1m 67y
5:30 (5:32) (Class 6) (0-65,65) 3-Y-O+ — **£1,567** (£462; £231) **Stalls** Low

Form / RPR

31-0 **1** **Yensi**[22] 4090 4-9-10 **64** .... MatthewDavies(3) 7 — 80
(George Baker) *mde all: kicked clr over 2f out: in n.d over 1f out: styd on wl* **9/2**[2]

0500 **2** 6 **Rojo Boy**16 4281 3-9-7 65......(b) TedDurcan 3 68
(David Elsworth) *hld up in rr: prog 3f out: hrd rdn 2f out: wnt 2nd 1f out: styd on but no ch w wnr: eased last 75yds* **4/1**1

6446 **3** 6 **Rigid**4 4681 4-8-8 48 ow2...... MichaelO'Connell(3) 12 36
(Tony Carroll) *chsd wnr: rdn and outpcd over 2f out: fdd and lost 2nd 1f out* **33/1**

3236 **4** ½ **Advertise**7 4578 5-9-7 58...... TadhgO'Shea 2 45
(Joseph Tuite) *prog to chse ldrs after 3f: rdn 3f out: wl outpcd fr 2f out: fdd* **4/1**1

0535 **5** 2 **Regal Rave (USA)**41 3468 4-9-6 57...... LiamKeniry 6 40
(Peter Hedger) *chsd ldrs: rdn over 3f out: lft bhd fr over 2f out: wknd* **9/1**

0030 **6** 2 **Invent**19 4183 3-8-7 51...... AndreaAtzeni 5 28
(Robert Eddery) *wl in rr: rousted along over 5f out: struggling fnl 3f* **11/1**

0056 **7** 4½ **Night Witch (IRE)**26 3953 3-9-0 58...... EddieCreighton 4 25
(Edward Creighton) *chsd ldng pair: rdn over 3f out: wknd 2f out* **10/1**

0066 **8** 1¾ **El Libertador (USA)**11 4444 5-9-1 55......(b) KierenFox(3) 1 19
(Eric Wheeler) *in tch: rdn sn after 1/2-way: struggling in rr fr 3f out* **5/1**3

300 **9** 2 **Notabadlad**18 4208 4-10-0 65...... HayleyTurner 10 24
(Simon Dow) *s.s and rousted along early: mostly in last: rdn and struggling over 3f out* **20/1**

0505 **10** shd **Storm Runner (IRE)**3 4699 3-9-1 59......(v) EddieAhern 8 —
(George Margarson) *nvr bttr than midfield: struggling in rr 3f out: no ch after* **18/1**

1m 47.86s (3.16) **Going Correction** +0.425s/f (Yiel)
WFA 3 from 4yo+ 7lb 10 Ran SP% **115.2**
Speed ratings (Par 101): **101,95,89,88,86 84,80,78,76,76**
toteswingers: 1&2 £4.30, 1&3 £14.70, 2&3 £17.90. totesuper7: Win: Not won; Place: Not won. CSF £22.57 CT £536.73 TOTE £6.30: £2.00, £1.80, £5.90; EX 25.50 TRIFECTA Not won..
Owner Wayne Hennessey **Bred** Michael Ng **Trained** Whitsbury, Hants

FOCUS
This was run in a time 3.52sec slower than the first division, but that was the first race on the card and the ground had eased since then and this race was run at a noticeably steady early pace. A clear personal best from the winner, worth more at face value.
T/Jkpt: £1,024.70 to a £1 stake. Pool: £35,895.44. 24.87 winning tickets. T/Plt: £9.60 to a £1 stake. Pool: £97,656.44. 7,370.42 winning tickets. T/Qpdt: £4.00 to a £1 stake. Pool: £6,266.78. 1,142.08 winning tickets. JN

4130 CURRAGH (R-H)

Sunday, August 7

OFFICIAL GOING: Straight course - good to yielding; round course - good

4831a KEENELAND ROYAL WHIP STKS (GROUP 2) 1m 2f
2:35 (2:35) 3-Y-0+

£49,267 (£15,560; £7,370; £2,456; £1,508; £818)

RPR

1 **Banimpire (IRE)**21 4133 3-9-1 114...... KJManning 5 114+
(J S Bolger, Ire) *hld up in rr: niggled along ent st: hdwy on outer to ld under 2f out: sn edgd rt: drvn out and kpt on wl fnl f* **4/5**1

2 ¾ **Dunboyne Express (IRE)**17 4259 3-9-1 111...... DPMcDonogh 6 112
(Kevin Prendergast, Ire) *broke wl and sn settled in 4th: hdwy to dispute briefly 2f out: sn hdd and edgd rt: kpt on u.p wout matching wnr* **4/1**2

3 3 **Mutahadee (IRE)**18 4220 3-9-1 108...... WMLordan 4 106
(T Stack, Ire) *settled on inner mainly 5th: nt clr run early st: kpt on same pce fnl f wout threatening first 2* **13/2**3

4 ½ **Aoife Alainn (IRE)**43 3417 4-9-10 111...... PJSmullen 3 105
(Tracey Collins, Ire) *trckd ldrs in 3rd: rdn and no imp fr over 1f out: kpt on one pce* **16/1**

5 1 **Cocozza (USA)**18 4220 3-9-1 ...... JMurtagh 1 103
(John M Oxx, Ire) *sn led: jnd 1/2-way: drvn along and hdd under 2f out: 3rd whn checked over 1f out: swtchd lft and kpt on one pce fnl f* **7/1**

6 7 **Gemstone (IRE)**21 4133 3-8-12 106......(b) CO'Donoghue 2 86
(A P O'Brien, Ire) *trckd ldr in 2nd: hdwy to dispute ld fr 1/2-way: rdn and hdd whn sltly checked under 2f out: sn no ex* **20/1**

2m 10.43s (-3.87) **Going Correction** 0.0s/f (Good)
WFA 3 from 4yo 9lb 6 Ran SP% **112.0**
Speed ratings: **115,114,112,111,110 105**
CSF £4.27 TOTE £1.60: £1.02, £1.70; DF 2.80.
Owner Mrs J S Bolger **Bred** Kilcarn Stud **Trained** Coolcullen, Co Carlow

FOCUS
The winner and runner-up have been rated to their previous best, with the third improving as expected.

NOTEBOOK
Banimpire(IRE) gained her fifth Group race success of the season and her second at Group 2 level. After being pushed along at the back of the field turning for home, she made her bid on the outside 2f out and was in front soon afterwards. She would have preferred a stronger pace and although she edged right a couple of times after taking the lead, she kept on well. She may step back up in trip in search of a Group 1 success in the Yorkshire Oaks. (op 9/10 tchd 1/1)
Dunboyne Express(IRE), fifth in both the Irish 2,000 Guineas and the Irish Derby, had been easily outpointed by Famous Name when second to that multiple winner in a Group 3 event over 1m1f at Leopardstown on his previous start. He improved into third turning for home and had every chance from 2f out. He edged right after the winner went towards him over 1f out and kept on under pressure. (op 4/1 tchd 7/2)
Mutahadee(IRE) was having his first run in a Pattern race on only his third ever start. Successful over 1m at Dundalk late last year, he had run third over 1m at Naas last month. He handled the step up in class quite well and, after running into a spot of bother early in the straight, he stayed on from over 1f out without troubling the first two. (op 7/1)
Aoife Alainn(IRE), a Group 1 winner on soft ground in Italy in October, had made little impact behind Misty For Me in the Pretty Polly Stakes over this course and trip in June. She performed creditably here and was always close up although unable to raise her effort sufficiently from over 1f out. (op 14/1 tchd 12/1)
Cocozza(USA), another with limited experience and taking a big step up on only his second start of the season, was tackling the trip for the first time. Soon in front, he led and disputed until under 2f out and appeared beaten in third when he was tightened for room over 1f out. (op 13/2)

4833a KEENELAND DEBUTANTE STKS (GROUP 2) (FILLIES) 7f
3:35 (3:35) 2-Y-0 **£53,232** (£15,560; £7,370; £2,456)

RPR

1 **Maybe (IRE)**24 4031 2-9-0 107...... JPO'Brien 9 112+
(A P O'Brien, Ire) *trckd ldr in 2nd: hdwy to ld 2f out: sn asserted and kpt on wl fnl f: comf* **5/4**1

2 2½ **Yellow Rosebud (IRE)**59 2859 2-9-0 ...... PJSmullen 6 105
(D K Weld, Ire) *towards rr: pushed along on outer and sme hdwy into 4th 1f out: kpt on u.p to go 2nd cl home: no ch w wnr* **7/1**3

3 hd **Lightening Pearl (IRE)**34 3691 2-9-0 ...... KLatham 1 104
(G M Lyons, Ire) *trckd ldrs on far rail in 3rd: rdn in 2nd 2f out and sn no imp on wnr: kpt on same pce u.p fnl f* **16/1**

4 1½ **Rubina (IRE)**52 3097 2-9-0 ...... JMurtagh 8 100
(John M Oxx, Ire) *trckd ldrs: 4th 1/2-way: rdn in 3rd 2f out and sn no imp on wnr: kpt on one pce fnl f* **8/1**

5 ½ **Remember Alexander**17 4257 2-9-0 106...... RichardHughes 2 99
(Mrs John Harrington, Ire) *trckd ldrs on far rail: 7th 1/2-way: drvn along in 8th under 3f out: kpt on u.p fr over 1f out* **4/1**2

6 nk **Soon (IRE)**12 4419 2-9-0 ...... SeamieHeffernan 4 98
(A P O'Brien, Ire) *trckd ldrs: 6th 1/2-way: no imp fr 2f out: kpt on one pce* **12/1**

7 1¼ **Redoutable (IRE)**12 4419 2-9-0 ...... DPMcDonogh 7 95
(Kevin Prendergast, Ire) *chsd ldrs: 5th 1/2-way: rdn and no imp under 2f out* **33/1**

8 1¾ **Chieftess (IRE)**32 3749 2-9-0 ...... CO'Donoghue 10 91
(A P O'Brien, Ire) *led: hdd 2f out: sn no ex and wknd* **66/1**

9 nk **Teolane (IRE)**51 3104 2-9-0 105...... KJManning 5 90
(J S Bolger, Ire) *a towards rr: rdn and no imp 2f out* **7/1**3

1m 27.43s (-3.37) **Going Correction** -0.575s/f (Hard) 9 Ran SP% **118.6**
Speed ratings: **96,93,92,91,90 90,88,86,86**
CSF £11.18 TOTE £2.00: £1.02, £2.70, £3.70; DF 12.40.
Owner Michael Tabor **Bred** Epona Bloodstock Ltd **Trained** Ballydoyle, Co Tipperary

FOCUS
The winner is probably value for more than the bare margin, but it's hard to be confident about the level considering the performances of the second, third and fourth, while the eighth finished a little close for comfort.

NOTEBOOK
Maybe(IRE) continues to go from strength to strength and she made it four wins from four starts here with a comfortably achieved victory following on from her Chesham Stakes win and her success in a Group 3 event at Leopardstown last month. Close up behind her front-running stablemate Chieftess, she went to the front 2f out and soon asserted to have the race wrapped up entering the final furlong. She will return to the Curragh to put her unbeaten record on the line in the Group 1 Moyglare Stud Stakes on August 28. (op 6/4)
Yellow Rosebud(IRE), winner of a maiden over the trip at Leopardstown in June on her only previous start, showed that she has progressed with a decent effort. She ran on steadily over the last 2f and got up close home to take second spot. She may renew rivalry with the winner in the Moyglare. (op 13/2)
Lightening Pearl(IRE) was another to emerge from the race with her reputation enhanced. Winner of a maiden over the trip at Roscommon on her previous start, she tracked the leaders and, although unable to match the winner from a furlong and a half out, she kept on and only lost second place close home. (op 20/1)
Rubina(IRE), successful on her debut over 6f at Leopardstown in June, ran a solid race although was unable to make much impression from over 1f out.
Remember Alexander, a four-length winner of a Group 3 event over the trip at Leopardstown last month, was held up. Ridden along at the back of the field 2f out, she only began to respond entering the final furlong and was doing her best work late on. (op 7/2)
Teolane(IRE), twice a winner early in the season, had disappointed at Royal Ascot where she lost ground at the start of the Albany Stakes and reportedly failed to handle the easy going. She never counted at any stage here and whether her display could be put down entirely to the ground is debatable. Official explanation: jockey said filly was slowly away, ran free early and found little (op 6/1)

4834a KEENELAND PHOENIX STKS (GROUP 1) (ENTIRE COLTS & FILLIES) 6f
4:05 (4:05) 2-Y-0

£95,000 (£31,120; £14,741; £4,913; £3,275; £1,637)

RPR

1 **La Collina (IRE)**24 4031 2-8-12 ...... DPMcDonogh 9 114+
(Kevin Prendergast, Ire) *towards rr: swtchd rt under 2f out: hdwy into 4th 1f out: styd on wl u.p to ld cl home* **33/1**

2 nk **Power**54 3012 2-9-1 112...... SeamieHeffernan 4 116
(A P O'Brien, Ire) *a.p: disp ld bef 1/2-way: led under 2f out: sn rdn and kpt on wl ins fnl f: hdd cl home* **7/4**1

3 1¾ **Tough As Nails (IRE)**42 3439 2-9-1 111...... GFCarroll 2 111
(Michael Mulvany, Ire) *trckd ldrs: 5th 1/2-way: 3rd over 1f out: sn no imp u.p: kpt on same pce* **12/1**

4 ½ **Lilbourne Lad (IRE)**42 3439 2-9-1 112...... RichardHughes 6 109
(Richard Hannon) *led and disp ld: hdd under 2f out: sn rdn and no ex ins fnl f* **8/1**

5 1¾ **Reply (IRE)**77 2329 2-9-1 ...... JPO'Brien 7 104
(A P O'Brien, Ire) *prom: trckd ldrs in 4th 1/2-way: no imp in 5th fr over 1f out* **7/1**

6 hd **Frederick Engels**31 3773 2-9-1 ...... JMurtagh 8 105
(David Brown) *hld up towards rr: sme hdwy on stands' side rail whn bdly hmpd 2f out: nt rcvr: kpt on ins fnl f* **10/3**2

7 ½ **Gatepost (IRE)**54 3012 2-9-1 ...... JamieSpencer 1 102
(Mick Channon) *chsd ldrs: 6th on outer 2f out: no impresion fr over 1f out* **5/1**3

8 ¾ **Parish Hall (IRE)**17 4257 2-9-1 ...... KJManning 5 100
(J S Bolger, Ire) *prom: disp ld bef 1/2-way: hdd over 2f out: sn edgd lft: no ex fr over 1f out* **14/1**

9 nk **After (IRE)**21 4131 2-8-12 97...... CO'Donoghue 3 96
(A P O'Brien, Ire) *a towards rr: in tch 2f out: no ex fr over 1f out* **50/1**

1m 13.3s (-1.70) **Going Correction** -0.40s/f (Firm) 9 Ran SP% **119.0**
Speed ratings: **95,94,92,91,89 89,88,87,86**
CSF £94.00 TOTE £22.00: £4.20, £1.10, £2.10; DF 212.20.
Owner Joerg Vasicek **Bred** Manister House Stud **Trained** Friarstown, Co Kildare
■ Stewards' Enquiry : K J Manning 750euro fine; three-day ban: careless riding (Aug 22-24)
D P McDonogh caution: used whip with excessive frequency
J Murtagh caution: careless riding

FOCUS
A shock winner but decent, solid form rated around the second, third and fourth.

NOTEBOOK
La Collina(IRE) was sent off a 33-1 chance despite her claims having been boosted by the success of her Leopardstown conqueror, Maybe, in the previous race. A neck had separted the pair in the Group 3 Silver Flash Stakes and La Collina justified her trainer's decision to take on the colts rather than renew rivalry with Maybe. At the back of the field in a race run at a good pace, she was still in rear entering the last 2f and had to be switched a couple of times before swooping to lead near the finish. She will renew rivalry with Maybe in the Moyglare Stud Stakes.
Power, the Coventry winner, went into the race at the head of the 2,000 Guineas market. Always in the front rank, he went on under 2f out and kept on well only to give best late on. A step up to 7f is on the cards and it would be unwise to knock his Guineas claims because of this defeat, which ended his unbeaten run. (op 9/4 tchd 13/8)

Tough As Nails(IRE) is well named but he isn't short on ability either, having been touched off by Power in the 5f Marble Hill Stakes here in June and subsequently run second to Lilbourne Lad in the Railway Stakes here last month. He raced prominently towards the centre of the track here and stuck to his task despite fighting a losing battle over the final furlong.
Lilbourne Lad(IRE) ran fast and was disputing the lead until Power went on passing the 2f marker. He could raise no extra and might have found the ground a bit on the slow side.
Reply(IRE), a four-length winner of a maiden over the course and trip in May, showed speed but was unable to make any impression from well over 1f out. (op 8/1)
Frederick Engels, the Windsor Castle and July Stakes winner, was about to begin his run from the back when he was badly hampered under 2f out. He had to be snatched up and lost all chance before making late headway. With a clear run it would be reasonable to suggest that he would have gone close. (op 11/4 tchd 7/2)

4836a PATRICK P. O'LEARY MEMORIAL PHOENIX SPRINT STKS (GROUP 3) 6f

5:05 (5:11) 3-Y-0+ **£35,021** (£10,237; £4,849; £1,616)

RPR

1 **Deacon Blues**[22] 4092 4-9-8 .... JMurtagh 8 125
(James Fanshawe) *hld up: smooth hdwy to chal 2f out: sn led and stretched clr fnl f: impressive* **4/11**[1]

2 *7* **Empowering (IRE)**[18] 4219 3-9-1 103........ JPO'Brien 6 99
(A P O'Brien, Ire) *a.p: 3rd 1/2-way: pushed along in 4th 2f out: kpt on u.p fnl f: no ch w easy wnr* **5/1**[2]

3 *1* **Arctic (IRE)**[42] 3441 4-9-5 106........(p) PJSmullen 4 96
(Tracey Collins, Ire) *reluctant to enter stalls: sn led: strly pressed 2f out: sn hdd and no ch w wnr fnl f: kpt on one pce* **12/1**[3]

4 *2 1/2* **Norville (IRE)**[23] 4049 4-9-5 .... CathyGannon 7 88
(David Evans) *towards rr: 8th 2f out: kpt on ins fnl f wout threatening* **20/1**

5 *1 1/4* **Winker Watson**[8] 4526 6-9-5 .... HughBowman 5 84
(Mick Channon) *chsd ldrs: 5th 2f out: sn no imp u.p* **14/1**

6 *2 1/2* **Radharcnafarraige (IRE)**[18] 4219 3-9-1 100........ KJManning 9 75
(J S Bolger, Ire) *towards rr: nvr a factor: kpt on one pce fnl f* **25/1**

7 *hd* **Six Of Hearts**[22] 4116 7-9-5 109........(b) SHJames 3 76
(Cecil Ross, Ire) *chsd ldrs: 4th 1/2-way: no ex fom under 2f out* **12/1**[3]

8 *3 1/2* **Oor Jock (IRE)**[29] 3852 3-9-1 95........ PShanahan 2 64
(Tracey Collins, Ire) *prom: 2nd 1/2-way: no ex fr wl over 1f out: wknd* **33/1**

1m 10.6s (-4.40) **Going Correction** -0.40s/f (Firm)
WFA 3 from 4yo+ 4lb **8** Ran SP% **123.6**
Speed ratings: **113,103,102,99,97 94,93,89**
CSF £3.02 TOTE £1.20: £1.02, £1.60, £3.00; DF 3.20.
Owner Jan & Peter Hopper & Michelle Morris **Bred** Mr & Mrs K W Grundy, Mr & Mrs P Hopper **Trained** Newmarket, Suffolk

FOCUS
Bar the winner everything else has been rated off their best.

NOTEBOOK
Deacon Blues trounced his rivals. He was completing a hat-trick following his wins in the Wokingham at Royal Ascot and the Group 3 Shadwell Stakes at Newbury, and the easy ground was a plus for him here. Held up, he moved through smoothly to lead under 2f out and quickly went clear to win very easily. (op 2/5)
Empowering(IRE), a Group 3 winner over 7f at Leopardstown in March, had lost out narrowly when dropped to this trip at Naas on her previous start. She emerged as second best albeit seven lengths adrift of the winner. (op 6/1)
Arctic(IRE), tried in cheekpieces, was reluctant to load, but he had the ease in the ground that he relishes and he led and disputed until the winner arrived and put the race as a contest to bed 2f out. (op 10/1)
Norville(IRE), a six-time winner, had plenty to prove at this level and was never in serious contention, although he did make some late headway.
Winker Watson, a smart two-year-old in 2007 when his wins included the July Stakes, has not won since and returned to the track in June having been sent to stud. He had run reasonably well in the July Cup last month before losing his chance at the start at Doncaster on his previous outing. The ground was far from ideal for him, but he isn't the force he was.

4830a, 4832a, 4835a & 4837a - (Foreign Racing) - See Raceform Interactive

4739 DEAUVILLE (R-H)

Sunday, August 7

OFFICIAL GOING: Turf: soft; fibresand: standard

4838a PRIX MAURICE DE GHEEST - GOLDIKOVA (GROUP 1) (3YO+) (TURF) 6f 110y(S)

2:45 (12:00) 3-Y-0+ **£123,146** (£49,267; £24,633; £12,306; £6,163)

RPR

1 **Moonlight Cloud**[36] 3654 3-8-8 0........ ThierryJarnet 12 122+
(F Head, France) *settled in rr: grad tk clsr order on outside fr 3f out: in tch and poised on outside 1 1/2f out: qcknd to ld ent fnl f: clr fnl 100yds* **9/1**

2 *4* **Society Rock (IRE)**[50] 3154 4-9-2 0........ PatCosgrave 5 115
(James Fanshawe) *dwlt and swtchd rt to r in centre of trck: settled midfield on heels of ldng gp: in share of 5th trcking Wootton Bassett 2f out: rdn appr fnl 1 1/2f and r.o to go 2nd ent fnl f: r.o u.p* **7/1**[3]

3 *nk* **Marchand D'Or (FR)**[36] 3654 8-9-2 0........ DavyBonilla 4 114
(M Delzangles, France) *hld up towards rr: last and pushed along ins fnl 2f: hdwy u.p and swtchd to r alone on stands' rail appr fnl f: r.o strly u.p to take 3rd cl home* **33/1**

4 *nse* **Genki (IRE)**[29] 3863 7-9-2 0........(b) GeorgeBaker 11 114
(Roger Charlton) *settled towards rr: rdn and hdwy over 1 1/2f out: wnt 3rd abt 75yds out: kpt on wl but lost 3rd on line* **25/1**

5 *1 1/2* **Wootton Bassett**[54] 3011 3-8-11 0........ PaulHanagan 6 109
(Richard Fahey) *w ldrs (middle of three): led over 2f out: rdn 1 1/2f out: hdd ent fnl f: no ex fnl 100yds and lost two pls ins fnl 75yds* **14/1**

6 *nk* **Evaporation (FR)**[36] 3654 4-8-13 0........ OlivierPeslier 2 106
(C Laffon-Parias, France) *settled in midfield towards ins: in tch travelling wl 2 1/2f out: rdn 1 1/2f out: kpt on at one pce u.p: nt pce to chal* **33/1**

7 *1* **Dream Ahead (USA)**[29] 3863 3-8-11 0........ WilliamBuick 7 105
(David Simcock) *dwlt: settled midfield: rdn and effrt appr 2f out: disputing 6th ent fnl f: no imp* **1/1**[1]

8 *1* **Smooth Operator (GER)**[22] 4121 5-9-2 0........(b) MaximeGuyon 9 103
(Mario Hofer, Germany) *a.p bhd ldng trio: disputing 3rd but hrd rdn 1 1/2f out: grad wknd* **40/1**

9 *1/2* **Split Trois (FR)**[22] 4121 3-8-8 0........ Pierre-CharlesBoudot 10 97
(Y De Nicolay, France) *w.w towards rr: rdn and sme prog on outside 1 1/2f out: no imp fnl f* **80/1**

10 *nk* **Markab**[22] 4092 8-9-2 0........ DaneO'Neill 1 101
(Henry Candy) *broke wl and led: jnd after 1 1/2f: rdn and wknd appr fnl f* **22/1**

11 *1* **Libranno**[12] 4412 3-8-11 0........ JimmyFortune 8 97
(Richard Hannon) *broke wl: disp ld after 1 1/2f: rdn 1 1/2f out: nt qckn: wknd fnl f* **22/1**

12 *1/2* **Zoffany (IRE)**[35] 3670 3-8-11 0........ ChristopheSoumillon 13 95
(A P O'Brien, Ire) *sn prom on outside: settled midfield: tk clsr order fr 3f out: disputing 2nd but strly rdn 1 1/2f out: wknd fnl f: eased fnl 100yds* **5/1**[2]

13 *hd* **Havane Smoker**[53] 3029 3-8-11 0........ Christophe-PatriceLemaire 3 95
(J-C Rouget, France) *chsd ldrs: 6th and rdn ins fnl 2f: wknd fnl 1 1/2f* **12/1**

1m 16.4s (-0.80) **Going Correction** +0.325s/f (Good)
WFA 3 from 4yo+ 4lb **13** Ran SP% **125.6**
Speed ratings: **117,112,112,112,110 109,108,107,107,106 105,105,104**
WIN (incl. 1 euro stake): 9.30. PLACES: 2.90, 4.70, 3.80. DF: 46.20. SF: 92.60.
Owner George Strawbridge **Bred** George Strawbridge **Trained** France

FOCUS
This looked one of the better renewals of this contest when considering the classy horses representing the Classic generation, many of which held serious Guineas aspirations at one stage of their careers. The older contingent were all battle-hardened performers, mainly capable of holding their own at the highest level, but it wasn't a big surprise to see one of the 3yos dominate the final stages. The form reads sound enough.

NOTEBOOK
Moonlight Cloud, even allowing for the fact that she got all the allowances, put up a stunning performance. Always highly regarded by Freddy Head, who knows how to handle a good filly (he also looked after Marchand D'Or when he won this three times), she was smart as a juvenile and only disappointed once this season when unsuited by conditions in the 1,000 Guineas. Two good runs followed over 7f in Group 3s afterwards, one when second to Sahpresa (subsequently runner-up to Goldikova), and another when winning what's traditionally a hot race last time. This contest was always the winner's mid-summer plan according to connections and the drop to sprinting proved ideal, as after travelling with real menace in behind, it just looked a matter of whether she'd produce what looked likely. The acceleration she showed when Thierry Jarnet asked her to quicken was instant and she came well away from the horses that stayed towards the middle. This sort of distance looks absolutely ideal for Moonlight Cloud, although she clearly gets 7f, but the trainer wasn't sure afterwards where she'd head next, although he conceded that the Prix de la Foret was an option, a race won last year by Goldikova. She isn't short of entries, however, ranging from the Matron Stakes (Group 1) to the British Champions Sprint Stakes (Group 2).
Society Rock(IRE), this season's Golden Jubilee winner, had reportedly got over the problem with his foot that had been keeping him on the sidelines and ran a blinder here giving weight away. This effort, if anyone needed more evidence, proved he is a Group 1 performer at this trip when at his best and, considering he is relatively lightly raced for his age, should have a bit more to come. He's the type who could be good for travelling, with races like the Nearctic Stakes at Woodbine (now a Group 1) and the Hong Kong Sprint at Sha Tin towards the end of the year coming into play. However, the most immediate plan will surely be the Sprint Cup at Haydock.
Marchand D'Or(FR), who won this three years in a row between 2006 and 2008, finished behind Moonlight Cloud last time and never looked like reversing that form as the filly strode clear. However, he stuck to his task well after drifting to the stands' rail and is probably still capable of winning at Group level when everything falls right.
Genki(IRE) was unlucky not to finish a length or so closer when sixth in the July Cup, and had blinkers (won last time they were fitted) replacing a usual visor. Settled towards the rear, this tough and experienced campaigner stayed on admirably to the line but was ultimately beaten by at least two better horses on the day. He looks another that will head towards the Sprint Cup next.
Wootton Bassett finished his juvenile campaign unbeaten in five races, culminating in a Group 1 success over 7f in the Prix Jean-Luc Lagardere (Moonlight Cloud not given hard time in fourth that day), but it's fair to say he's struggled this term after going too fast from a wide draw in Poule d'Essai des Poulains before being beaten a long way in the St James's Palace. The drop in trip looked to his advantage here but, after showing tons of pace early under restraint, he kept on at only the one pace. He is probably worth a try at 5f considering how much natural speed he appears to have, but he holds a couple of Group 2 entries over 7f and will presumably run in one of them unless connections take up the Sprint Cup entry.
Evaporation(FR) is obviously talented but isn't up to winning at this level.
Dream Ahead(USA) took the July Cup in the manner of a top-class sprinter in the making but the form of that contest hadn't been boosted by subsequent events. He wasn't quickest away here but wasn't hampered by it and was able to race in midfield comfortably, although possibly a bit free. It was soon clear that, for whatever reason, he wasn't going to repeat his Newmarket heroics and his trainer was mystified by the performance. David Simcock reported afterwards that the Sprint Cup remained his target.
Zoffany(IRE) was probably flattered to get so close to Frankel in the St James's Palace and then didn't appear straightforward when narrowly beaten in the Jean Part (hung right), though arguably he would have won had he been galvanised sooner. Winner of the Group 1 Phoenix Stakes over 6f as a 2yo, he had a chance if improving for the drop in trip, but that wasn't the case and he won't be easy to place now.

4138 DUSSELDORF (R-H)

Sunday, August 7

OFFICIAL GOING: Turf: soft

4839a HENKEL-PREIS DER DIANA - DEUTSCHES STUTEN-DERBY (GROUP 1) (3YO FILLIES) (TURF) 1m 3f

4:00 (12:00) 3-Y-0 **£198,275** (£77,586; £38,793; £21,551; £8,620)

RPR

1 **Dancing Rain (IRE)**[21] 4133 3-9-2 0........ KierenFallon 12 114+
(William Haggas) **8/5**[1]

2 *3* **Djumama (IRE)**[21] 3-9-2 0........ AHelfenbein 10 107
(Andreas Lowe, Germany) **48/10**[3]

3 *2 1/2* **Aigrette Garzette (IRE)**[36] 3651 3-9-2 0........ MircoDemuro 8 103
(P Schiergen, Germany) **42/1**

4 *shd* **Navarra Queen**[42] 3449 3-9-2 0........ AStarke 11 102
(P Schiergen, Germany) **4/1**[2]

5 *1* **Night Of Dubai (IRE)**[56] 2981 3-9-2 0........ THellier 4 101
(Mario Hofer, Germany) *a.p in 2nd: trcking the ldr: r.o wl in st but wknd fnl f* **208/10**

6 *3* **Kapitale (GER)**[21] 3-9-2 0........ EPedroza 16 95
(A Wohler, Germany) **245/10**

7 *nk* **Alkhana (IRE)**[36] 3651 3-9-2 0........ MrDennisSchiergen 14 95
(P Schiergen, Germany) **42/1**

8 *1 1/4* **Dalarna (GER)**[56] 2981 3-9-2 0........ ASuborics 13 92
(W Hickst, Germany) **27/1**

9 *hd* **Leopardin (GER)**[21] 3-9-2 0........ WPanov 3 92
(H J Groschel, Germany) **139/10**

10 *hd* **Heaven's Gift (GER)**[21] 3-9-2 0........ JBojko 6 92
(S Smrczek, Germany) **65/1**

11 *1/2* **Karsabruni (FR)**[36] 3651 3-9-2 0........ FabriceVeron 9 91
(H-A Pantall, France) **147/10**

12 1 ¼ **Next Holy (IRE)**[21] 3-9-2 0 .... FilipMinarik 2 88
(P Schiergen, Germany) **32/1**
13 1 ½ **Achinora**[29] 3-9-2 0 .... APietsch 1 86
(M G Mintchev, Germany) **66/1**
14 ½ **Breezy Hawk (GER)**[21] 3-9-2 0 .... DPorcu 5 85
(S Smrczek, Germany) **53/1**
15 2 **Labrice**[36] 3651 3-9-2 0 .... AnthonyCrastus 15 81
(T Mundry, Germany) **227/10**
16 1 ½ **Selkis (GER)**[56] 2981 3-9-2 0 .... ADeVries 7 79
(J Hirschberger, Germany) *broke wl: settled 5th: rdn on bk st: fnd no ex in st and sn wknd to rr* **53/10**

2m 20.32s (140.32) **16** Ran SP% **133.5**
WIN (incl. 10 euro stake): 26. PLACES: 21, 20, 93. SF: 113.
Owner M J & L A Taylor **Bred** Swettenham Stud **Trained** Newmarket, Suffolk
■ Dancing Rain was the first British-trained winner of this race, which was first opened to foreign opposition in 1992.

NOTEBOOK
Dancing Rain(IRE) dictated from the front, setting reasonably slow fractions, and cleared away from her rivals on turning in. This was a fine piece of placing by William Haggas, who wanted his filly to avoid another slog against the best of her sex in the Yorkshire Oaks, and an intelligent ride by Fallon. The long-term plan is to go for the Queen Elizabeth II Cup in Japan, a race won by Snow Fairy last year, and the idea is to keep her in training next year.
Djumama(IRE) was the best of the German fillies on paper, and proved it by easily holding her compatriots off for second. She beat Danedream as a 2-y-o, who has won a quality all-aged Group 1 this year, so set a respectable standard.
Aigrette Garzette(IRE) has often been fancied in the betting but disappointed most times. She was the owner's second string on jockey bookings, but Mirco Demuro is a hugely talented rider and he may well have got that little bit extra from his mount.
Navarra Queen had looked one-paced in the past and did so again.

KLAMPENBORG
Sunday, August 7
OFFICIAL GOING: Turf: good

4840a RIDER CUP SPRINT (CONDITIONS) (3YO+) (TURF) 6f 110y
1:15 (1:15) 3-Y-O+ **£2,880** (£1,440; £720; £432)

RPR
1 **Piccoluck**[17] 4247 3-8-9 0 ....(b) ElioneChaves 2 66
(Amy Weaver) *mde virtually all: clr ins fnl f: comf* **22/6**[3]
2 2 **Artful Dawkins** 3-9-0 0 ....(b) FDiaz 1 59
(Bent Olsen, Denmark) *fin 3rd: plcd 2nd* **41/5**
3 3 **Kaldera (IRE)**[371] 3-8-11 0 .... DinaDanekilde 5 48
(Bodil Hallencreutz, Sweden) *fin 4th: plcd 3rd* **63/10**
4 2 **Silver Shine (IRE)**[300] 6809 3-9-2 0 .... JacobJohansen 3 47
(Bent Olsen, Denmark) *fin 5th: plcd 4th* **18/5**[2]
D 2 **Malgoof (IRE)**[306] 6647 3-8-11 0 .... EmiliaHvitved(7) 4 69
(Torben Christensen, Denmark) *fin 2nd: disqualified* **7/10**[1]

1m 22.3s (82.30) **5** Ran SP% **126.6**
PARI-MUTUEL (all including 1krone stakes): WIN 4.66; PLACE 3.51, 4.06; DF 26.24.
Owner Random Stalkers **Bred** Sarah Watkins And Dawn Carey **Trained** Newmarket, Suffolk

NOTEBOOK
Piccoluck, a modest maiden coming into this, found this race relatively easy pickings, making every yard.

4841a DANSK HESTEFORSIKRING 2-ARS MAIDENSERIEN (MAIDEN) (2YO) (TURF) 7f
1:45 (1:45) 2-Y-O **£2,880** (£1,152; £576; £345; £230)

RPR
1 **Khan (DEN)** 2-8-11 0 .... OliverWilson(6) 7 —
(Soren Jensen, Denmark) **44/5**
2 shd **Madame Jane (IRE)** 2-9-0 0 .... DinaDanekilde 4 —
(Ole Larsen, Sweden) **12/5**[2]
3 ½ **Angel Cake (IRE)**[16] 4276 2-9-0 0 .... ElioneChaves 8 —
(Amy Weaver) *a.p: ev ch fnl f: no ex cl home* **6/4**[1]
4 shd **Florence Craye** 2-9-0 0 .... JacobJohansen 1 —
(Bent Olsen, Denmark) **36/5**
5 2 **Jersey Girl (DEN)** 2-9-0 0 .... EspenSki 5 —
(Lennart Reuterskiold Jr, Sweden) **103/10**
6 1 **Road To Glory** 2-9-3 0 .... NikolajStott 9 —
(Hanne Bechmann, Denmark) **4/1**[3]
7 5 **Majestic Dowsing (IRE)** 2-9-3 0 .... FDiaz 6 —
(Bent Olsen, Denmark) **151/10**

1m 29.2s (89.20) **7** Ran SP% **126.9**
PARI-MUTUEL (all including 1krone stakes): WIN 9.82; PLACE 1.90, 1.34, 1.50; DF 34.72.
Owner Stald Ras **Bred** Jupiter Farms **Trained** Denmark

NOTEBOOK
Angel Cake(IRE), sent off at big prices in each of her previous three starts in maidens, ran a much better race on this visit to Denmark.

4842a LANWADES STUD SCANDINAVIAN OPEN CHAMPIONSHIP (GROUP 3) (3YO+) (TURF) 1m 4f
3:05 (3:05) 3-Y-O+ **£34,562** (£8,640; £3,456; £2,304)

RPR
1 **Ovambo Queen (GER)**[45] 3334 4-9-1 0 .... GaetanMasure 12 99
(Dr A Bolte, Germany) *hld up towards rr: hdwy to chal ldrs 2f out: sn disputing ld: led 1f out: kpt on wl u.p fnl f* **11/5**[1]
2 1 ½ **Peas And Carrots (DEN)**[42] 8-9-2 0 .... FJohansson 4 98
(Lennart Reuterskiold Jr, Sweden) *hld up: mde grnd 3f out: disputing ld early in the st: hdd 1f out: no ex clsng stages: jnd for 2nd on line* **11/2**[3]
2 dht **Bank Of Burden (USA)**[31] 4-9-4 0 ....(b) Per-AndersGraberg 7 100
(Niels Petersen, Norway) *hld up in mid-div: traffic problems midway in st: fin strly fnl f: got up to share 2nd on line* **27/10**[2]
4 2 **Django (SWE)**[28] 8-9-4 0 .... EspenSki 9 96
(Jessica Long, Sweden) *settled in tch in mid-div: effrt 2f out: ev ch appr fnl f: nt qckn* **69/10**
5 1 ½ **Boxing Day**[42] 4-9-2 0 .... JacobJohansen 1 92
(Bent Olsen, Denmark) *hld up in rr of mid-div: hdwy in st: styd on wl: nt pce to chal* **171/10**
6 6 **Condor (DEN)**[42] 6-9-2 0 .... RafaelSchistl 8 82
(Soren Jensen, Denmark) *racd in midfield: racd against ins rail and effrt 2f out: kpt on at one pce and nt trble ldrs* **243/10**
7 ¾ **Master Kid (DEN)**[31] 6-9-2 0 .... FDiaz 13 81
(Bent Olsen, Denmark) *hld up in last: pushed along over 2 1/2f out: sn no ex: wknd* **57/1**
8 ½ **Sir Henry (DEN)**[406] 4-9-2 0 .... ElioneChaves 2 80
(Soren Jensen, Denmark) *chsd ldrs: pushed along in st: sn wknd* **41/1**
9 hd **Mulan (GER)**[31] 4-9-2 0 .... ManuelSantos 5 80
(Elisabeth Gautier, Sweden) *disp ld w Mariyca: qckly wknd u.p ins fnl 2f* **66/10**
10 3 **Mariyca (IRE)**[701] 5687 5-8-13 0 .... DinaDanekilde 6 72
(Ole Larsen, Sweden) *sn disputing ld: tk str hold: hdd over 2f out: sn wknd* **176/10**
11 5 **Alnitak (USA)**[31] 10-9-2 0 ....(b) Jan-ErikNeuroth 3 67
(Bent Olsen, Denmark) *towards rr: nvr threatened* **68/1**
12 dist **Alpacco (IRE)**[42] 9-9-2 0Always prom: wknd qckly 3f out: virtually p.u fnl f ManuelMartinez 11 —
(Sandie Kjaer Nortoft, Denmark) *Always prom: wknd qckly 3f out: virtually p.u fnl f* **171/10**

2m 31.3s (151.30) **12** Ran SP% **125.4**
PARI-MUTUEL (all including 1krone stakes): WIN 3.18; PLACE 1.45, 1.82 (Peas And Carrots), 1.60 (Bank Of Burden); DF 7.01 (Peas And Carrots), 12.65 (Bank Of Burden)..
Owner Dr H H Leimbach **Bred** Gestut Rietberg **Trained** Germany

3335 LA TESTE DE BUCH (R-H)
Thursday, August 4
OFFICIAL GOING: Turf: good

4843a CRITERIUM DU BEQUET - VENTES OSARUS (LISTED RACE) (2YO) (TURF) 6f
5:20 (12:00) 2-Y-O **£23,706** (£9,482; £7,112; £4,741; £2,370)

RPR
1 **Vladimir (IRE)**[11] 2-9-2 0 .... BFayosMartin 9 101
(M Delcher-Sanchez, Spain) **12/1**
2 1 ½ **Luv U Forever**[12] 4312 2-8-13 0 .... PhilippeSogorb 7 93
(Jo Hughes) *broke fast: rdn to ld: stl in front ent st: r.o wl: hdd over 1f out: styd on wl* **10/1**
3 ½ **Ruby's Day**[4] 4596 2-8-13 0 .... Francois-XavierBertras 11 92
(E J O'Neill, France) **78/10**[3]
4 2 ½ **Star Seed (FR)** 2-8-13 0 .... JohanVictoire 10 84
(J-C Rouget, France) **17/2**
5 hd **Kendam (FR)**[16] 4191 2-8-13 0 .... FabriceVeron 2 83
(H-A Pantall, France) **22/1**
6 2 ½ **Bay Shore (IRE)**[32] 3669 2-8-13 0 .... Jean-BernardEyquem 1 76
(J-C Rouget, France) **6/4**[1]
7 2 ½ **La Bauloise (FR)**[30] 2-8-13 0 .... Pierre-CharlesBoudot 3 68
(T Lemer, France) **21/1**
8 6 **Lady Orpen (FR)**[21] 4036 2-8-13 0 ....(p) RaphaelMarchelli 5 50
(Y Durepaire, Spain) **14/1**
9 ¾ **Skadar Lake**[30] 2-8-13 0 .... Jean-BaptisteHamel 8 48
(D Guillemin, France) **9/2**[2]
10 ¾ **Albret (IRE)**[11] 2-9-2 0 .... Roberto-CarlosMontenegro 4 49
(G Arizkorreta Elosegui, Spain) **24/1**
11 **Chacha Heels (FR)** 2-8-13 0 .... SebastienCastellier 6 46
(H-A Pantall, France) **28/1**

1m 12.73s (72.73) **11** Ran SP% **119.9**
WIN (incl. 1 euro stake): 13.20. PLACES: 4.20, 3.50, 3.30. DF: 54.40. SF: 91.70.
Owner Sunday Horses Club S.L. **Bred** D Noonan & Loughphilip Bloodstock **Trained** Spain

FOCUS
Straightforward form, the winner average for the grade.
NOTEBOOK
Luv U Forever showed good pace again and picked up black type.

4795 LINGFIELD (L-H)
Monday, August 8
OFFICIAL GOING: Turf course - soft (7.6); all-weather - standard
Wind: fresh, half against Weather: bright spells, showers

4844 FIZZTIVAL AT LINGFIELD PARK 13TH AUGUST H'CAP (TURF) 2m
2:00 (2:00) (Class 5) (0-75,75) 4-Y-O+ **£2,385** (£704; £352) Stalls Low

Form RPR
002 1 **Morar**[19] 4216 5-9-7 **75** .... IanMongan 4 81
(Laura Mongan) *stdd s: hld up in tch in last: rdn and qcknd to ld over 2f out: kpt edging lft u.p: styd on wl fnl f: rdn out* **10/3**[2]
1231 2 1 ¼ **Mohanad (IRE)**[16] 4318 5-9-4 **75** .... HarryBentley(3) 5 82+
(Sheena West) *in tch: chsd wnr over 2f out: wnt to switch rt and then swtchd bk lft to inner over 1f out: pressing wnr but n.m.r after tl squeezed out and swtchd rt fnl 100yds: nt rcvr and styd on same pce after* **6/4**[1]
245- 3 14 **Sinbad The Sailor**[67] 7781 6-9-1 **72** ....(v) MatthewDavies(3) 3 60
(George Baker) *chsd ldrs: swtchd rt and rdn 3f out: fnd little and sn btn: 3rd and no ch w ldrs fnl 2f* **11/2**
0000 4 15 **Tobernea (IRE)**[16] 4326 4-8-8 **62** .... NeilCallan 2 32
(Mark Johnston) *led for 2f: chsd ldr after tl rdn to ld over 3f out: hdd over 2f out: sn wl btn: eased ins fnl f* **5/1**[3]
0660 5 15 **Albeed**[16] 4341 4-8-13 **67** ....(b[1]) EddieAhern 6 19
(John Dunlop) *t.k.h: chsd ldr tl led after 2f: hdd over 3f out: immediately dropped out and t.o over 2f out* **6/1**

3m 41.61s (6.81) **Going Correction** +0.40s/f (Good) **5** Ran SP% **109.4**
Speed ratings (Par 103): **98,97,90,82,75**
CSF £8.68 TOTE £4.10: £1.80, £1.20; EX 6.40.
Owner Mrs P J Sheen **Bred** St Clare Hall Stud **Trained** Epsom, Surrey
■ Stewards' Enquiry : Ian Mongan 1st caution: careless riding; 2nd two-day ban: careless riding (Aug 22-23)

FOCUS
A moderate staying contest run at a fair pace. The winner is rated to her british best with the second a narrow winner.

Albeed Official explanation: jockey said filly ran too free

4845 HARE LANE H'CAP (TURF) 1m 1f
2:30 (2:30) (Class 5) (0-75,75) 3-Y-O+ **£2,385** (£704; £352) **Stalls** Low

Form RPR

6112 **1** **Highlife Dancer**[6] 4627 3-8-10 **68** .... MartinHarley(3) 5 77
(Mick Channon) *chsd ldrs: rdn to ld 2f out: clr and in command whn edgd lft 1f out: kpt on wl* **4/1**[3]

-345 **2** *2 1/4* **With Hindsight (IRE)**[11] 4457 3-9-6 **75** .... PhilipRobinson 3 79
(Clive Cox) *led for 1f: chsd ldr after: rdn and ev ch over 2f out: outpcd by wnr over 1f out: plugged on same pce fnl f* **11/4**[1]

6420 **3** *1/2* **Clarion Call**[14] 4385 3-9-1 **70** .... EddieAhern 6 73
(Eve Johnson Houghton) *hld up in tch in last: rdn and effrt 3f out: no threat to wnr but hdwy u.p 1f out: wnt 3rd ins fnl f: no threat to wnr* **14/1**

2636 **4** *1* **Negotiation (IRE)**[4] 4730 5-9-4 **65** .... PatCosgrave 2 66
(Michael Quinn) *rdn along leaving stalls: led after 1f: drvn over 2f out: hdd 2f out: sn hrd drvn and nt qckn: plugged on same pce fnl f* **4/1**[3]

50-6 **5** *6* **Fluvial (IRE)**[67] 2643 3-9-3 **72** .... NeilCallan 4 60
(Mark Johnston) *hld up in tch: rdn and effrt wl over 2f out: unable qck and struggling ent fnl 2f: wknd over 1f out* **11/2**

-033 **6** *2 3/4* **Green Wadi**[14] 4385 6-9-7 **68** .... GeorgeBaker 1 50
(Gary Moore) *t.k.h early: trckd ldrs: rdn and fnd little over 2f out: wknd 2f out: wl btn and eased wl ins fnl f* **7/2**[2]

1m 59.42s (2.82) **Going Correction** +0.40s/f (Good)
WFA 3 from 5yo+ 8lb **6** Ran SP% **110.9**
Speed ratings (Par 103): **103,101,100,99,94 91**
toteswingers:1&2:£2.80, 1&3:£7.70, 2&3:£8.40 CSF £14.99 TOTE £4.60: £2.00, £2.62; EX 17.50.
Owner The Highlife Racing Club **Bred** Imperial & Mike Channon Bloodstock Ltd **Trained** West Ilsley, Berks

FOCUS
A moderate contest but run at a good pace and the form looks sound despite the small field.

4846 LINGFIELDPARK.CO.UK (S) STKS (TURF) 1m 2f
3:00 (3:00) (Class 6) 3-Y-O+ **£1,704** (£503; £251) **Stalls** Low

Form RPR

6100 **1** **Catching Zeds**[31] 3814 4-9-1 57 ....(v[1]) MichaelO'Connell(3) 5 58
(Ian Williams) *chsd ldr: rdn and hdwy to chal 2f out: led over 1f out: styd on wl and drew clr ins fnl f: rdn out* **13/2**[2]

-040 **2** *3 1/4* **Special Endeavour (IRE)**[5] 4654 3-8-9 50 ....(p) MartinDwyer 1 51
(William Muir) *in tch: rdn and effrt to press ldrs 2f out: unable qck over 1f out: outpcd by wnr ins fnl f: plugged on to go 2nd wl ins fnl f* **11/1**[3]

3113 **3** *3/4* **Carlton Scroop (FR)**[23] 4088 8-9-9 70 .... PaulDoe 4 55
(Jim Best) *led: jnd and rdn 2f out: hdd over 1f out: w wnr tl outpcd and btn ins fnl f: lost 2nd wl ins fnl f* **7/2**[1]

4 *7* **Paragraph** 4-9-4 0 .... FrankieMcDonald 2 36
(Paul Fitzsimons) *rn green: t.k.h early: hld up in tch: reminders 7f out: sme hdwy 6f out: rdn: rn green and outpcd 3f out: no ch fnl 2f* **33/1**

2m 17.07s (6.57) **Going Correction** +0.40s/f (Good)
WFA 3 from 4yo+ 9lb **4** Ran SP% **46.8**
Speed ratings (Par 101): **89,86,85,80**
CSF £9.97 TOTE £4.10; EX 8.30.There was no bid for the winner.
Owner The Ferandlin Peaches **Bred** White Horse Bloodstock Ltd **Trained** Portway, Worcs

FOCUS
This seller was severely weakened by the late withdrawal of Country Road on vet's advice. The form is weak rated around the first two.

4847 DORMANS PARK H'CAP (TURF) 1m 3f 106y
3:30 (3:30) (Class 6) (0-60,60) 3-Y-O+ **£1,704** (£503; £251) **Stalls** High

Form RPR

4360 **1** **Prince Blue**[54] 3047 4-9-4 **50** .... SamHitchcott 8 57
(John E Long) *dwlt: hdwy to press ldr after 2f: pushed ahd 2f out: drvn and hdd jst over 1f out: kpt on wl to ld again towards fin* **16/1**

-004 **2** *hd* **Jovial (IRE)**[49] 3225 4-10-0 **60** .... EddieAhern 2 67
(Denis Coakley) *chsd ldrs: swtchd rt and rdn wl over 2f out: ev ch wl over 1f out: led jst over 1f out: hdd and no ex towards fin* **3/1**[1]

1000 **3** *1 1/4* **Disturbia (IRE)**[10] 1181 3-8-3 47 ow1 .... MartinDwyer 6 51
(J W Hills) *stdd s: hld up in tch in rr: hdwy on inner wl over 2f out: drvn and chsd ldrs over 1f out: kpt on same pce ins fnl f* **7/2**[2]

0135 **4** *1 3/4* **Royal Defence (IRE)**[21] 4165 5-9-12 **58** .... PatCosgrave 1 59
(Michael Quinn) *led: rdn 3f out: hrd drvn and hdd 2f out: wknd ins fnl f* **6/1**

6050 **5** *5* **Art Thief**[21] 4162 3-8-11 **53** .... JamesDoyle 10 46
(Sylvester Kirk) *hld up in tch: hdwy into midfield 5f out: rdn and nt qckn 3f out: one pce and no threat to ldrs fnl 2f* **15/2**

03-3 **6** *1 3/4* **Zelos Diktator**[151] 277 5-9-10 **56** ....(p) GeorgeBaker 4 46
(Gary Moore) *in tch: rdn and fnd nil wl over 2f out: one pce and no threat to ldrs fnl 2f* **5/1**[3]

0066 **7** *nk* **Swords**[31] 3799 9-8-11 **46** oh1 ....(v) MartinHarley(3) 7 35
(Ray Peacock) *t.k.h: hld up in tch: rdn and nt qckn 3f out: plugging on same pce and wl hld whn edgd lft over 1f out* **40/1**

004 **8** *dist* **Robby Bobby**[18] 4242 6-10-0 **60** .... IanMongan 5 —
(Laura Mongan) *in tch tl dropped to rr 4f out: lost tch 3f out: virtually p.u fr over 2f out* **11/2**

2m 38.8s (7.30) **Going Correction** +0.40s/f (Good)
WFA 3 from 4yo+ 10lb **8** Ran SP% **113.6**
Speed ratings (Par 101): **89,88,87,86,82 81,81,—**
toteswingers:1&2:£11.50, 1&3:£14.10, 2&3:£3.30 CSF £63.04 CT £211.18 TOTE £23.20: £5.60, £1.30, £1.10; EX 99.40 TRIFECTA Not won..
Owner Downlands Racing **Bred** Downlands Racing **Trained** Caterham, Surrey
■ Stewards' Enquiry : Sam Hitchcott two-day ban: used whip with excessive frequency (Aug 22-23)

FOCUS
A moderate contest and little solid about the form.
Prince Blue Official explanation: trainer said, regarding apparent improvement in form, that the gelding was suited by the shorter trip and easier ground.
Robby Bobby Official explanation: vet said gelding returned distresed

4848 LINGFIELD PARK EUROPRO PGA GOLF TOURNAMENT MEDIAN AUCTION MAIDEN STKS 5f (P)
4:00 (4:01) (Class 5) 2-Y-O **£1,704** (£503; £251) **Stalls** High

Form RPR

64 **1** **Royal Award**[28] 3915 2-8-12 0 .... NeilCallan 10 75+
(Ian Wood) *w ldr: led 2f out: rdn and drew wl clr over 1f out: r.o wl: easily* **3/1**[3]

4 **2** *6* **Citybell (IRE)**[17] 4283 2-8-12 0 .... BarryMcHugh 7 55+
(Richard Fahey) *hld up in rr of main gp: effrt and hung rt on bnd 2f out: rdn and hdwy ent fnl f: kpt on to go 2nd towards fin: no ch w wnr* **9/4**[1]

06 **3** *1/2* **Bookiesindexdotnet**[43] 3435 2-8-12 0 .... JackMitchell 6 52
(J R Jenkins) *led: hdd and rdn 2f out: outpcd and btn over 1f out: tired ins fnl f and lost 2nd towards fin* **8/1**

05 **4** *1 1/2* **Get The Trip**[35] 3673 2-8-12 0 .... KirstyMilczarek 3 46
(James Toller) *chsd ldrs: rdn and struggling over 2f out: 3rd and wl btn ent fnl f* **20/1**

42 **5** *1 1/2* **Key Addition (IRE)**[10] 4485 2-9-3 0 .... MartinDwyer 8 46
(William Muir) *sn pushed along in midfield: rdn and outpcd over 2f out: no ch over 1f out* **5/2**[2]

00 **6** *shd* **Sudden Wish (IRE)**[32] 3780 2-8-12 0 .... PaulDoe 2 40
(Jim Best) *towards rr of main gp: short of room jst over 2f out: rdn and effrt on inner wl over 1f out: no prog* **40/1**

7 *1 1/2* **Arctic Stryker** 2-9-3 0 .... JimCrowley 4 40
(John Best) *s.i.s: sn wl outpcd in last pair: sme late hdwy: nvr on terms* **11/1**

30 **8** *12* **Joe M**[56] 2997 2-9-3 0 .... EddieAhern 5 —
(Simon Dow) *sn outpcd and wl bhd: t.o fr 1/2-way* **40/1**

59.34 secs (0.54) **Going Correction** +0.175s/f (Slow) **8** Ran SP% **113.4**
Speed ratings (Par 94): **102,92,91,89,86 86,84,65**
toteswingers:1&2:£2.20, 1&3:£3.80, 2&3:£3.80 CSF £9.90 TOTE £4.10: £1.20, £1.20, £2.90; EX 12.40 Trifecta £58.50 Pool: £561.65 - 7.10 winning units..
Owner Miss Jacqueline Goodearl **Bred** Miss Jacqueline Goodearl **Trained** Upper Lambourn, Berks

FOCUS
This didn't look a strong race, but Royal Award overcame being drawn widest of all to win in impressive fashion. The winner improved but the form looks limited.

NOTEBOOK
Royal Award showed loads of speed, yet wasn't able to dominate, almost getting involved in a speed duel with Bookiesindexdotnet, so she deserves extra credit for keeping on so strongly. Out of a fair multiple sprint winner for this yard (including on turf), she looks quite useful and deserves her chance in something better. (op 4-1)
Citybell(IRE) showed ability on her debut at Thirsk, although she seemed quite well educated that day and didn't improve much this time. That said, she could have handled the bend into the straight better, and a more galloping track may help. (op 3-1 tchd 2-1)
Bookiesindexdotnet showed a lot of speed and should be competitive in modest nurseries. (tchd 15-2 and 17-2)
Get The Trip was comfortably held, but she can now switch to nurseries. (op 28-1)
Key Addition(IRE), runner-up over just shy of 6f last time, was unsuited by this particularly quick 5f. He now has the option of nurseries and can do better over further. (op 2-1)
Arctic Stryker, a £5,000 purchase, ran green but showed ability. (op 12-1 tchd 14-1)

4849 LADBROKES MOBILE MAIDEN STKS 7f (P)
4:30 (4:30) (Class 5) 3-Y-O **£2,385** (£704; £352) **Stalls** Low

Form RPR

22 **1** **Kawssaj**[46] 3320 3-9-3 0 .... NeilCallan 9 86+
(Roger Varian) *styd wd: w ldr tl crossed towards inner and led over 4f out: mde rest: pushed clr 2f out: in command after: v easily* **2/5**[1]

05 **2** *5* **Jumeira Field (USA)**[69] 2596 3-9-3 0 .... PatDobbs 5 73
(Robert Cowell) *chsd ldrs: chsd wnr over 3f out: rdn and outpcd 2f out: no ch w wnr but kpt on to hold 2nd fnl f* **20/1**

42 **3** *1* **Cahala Dancer (IRE)**[16] 4320 3-8-12 0 .... EddieAhern 1 65
(Roger Teal) *in tch: shuffled bk and lost pl over 3f out: swtchd rt and hdwy to chse ldng pair jst over 2f out: sn outpcd and no ch w wnr: plugged on* **8/1**

4 *1* **Cookieshake** 3-9-3 0 .... KirstyMilczarek 4 67+
(Luca Cumani) *dwlt: in tch towards rr: hdwy over 3f out: rdn and outpcd 2f out: plugging on same pce and wl hld whn edgd lft 1f out* **12/1**

520 **5** *2 1/4* **Brinmore**[21] 4163 3-8-12 0 .... JimCrowley 2 56
(William Knight) *stdd s: hld up in tch in rr: rdn 2f out: midfield and no ch w wnr whn short of room 1f out: n.d* **11/2**[2]

024 **6** *1 1/4* **Noverton**[20] 4186 3-8-12 75 .... JackMitchell 8 53
(James Eustace) *s.i.s: hld up in rr: rdn and effrt on outer bnd 2f: rn green and no imp wl over 1f out: n.d* **6/1**[3]

60 **7** *2 1/4* **Nubian Gem (IRE)**[11] 4478 3-8-5 0 .... GeorgeanBuckell(7) 6 47
(John Best) *in tch towards rr: pushed along and struggling over 2f out: wl bhd over 1f out* **100/1**

00 **8** *2 1/2* **Pastoral Jet**[38] 3594 3-8-10 0 .... LukeRowe(7) 7 45
(Richard Rowe) *led tl over 4f out: lost pl jst over 3f out: wl bhd over 1f out* **100/1**

1m 26.27s (1.47) **Going Correction** +0.175s/f (Slow) **8** Ran SP% **126.6**
Speed ratings (Par 100): **98,92,91,90,87 86,83,80**
toteswingers:1&2:£4.50, 1&3:£2.20, 2&3:£7.40 CSF £16.19 TOTE £1.40: £1.02, £4.60, £1.70; EX 14.20 Trifecta £44.50 Pool: £728.31 - 12.11 winning units..
Owner Sheikh Ahmed Al Maktoum **Bred** Darley **Trained** Newmarket, Suffolk

FOCUS
A straightforward success for the smartly bred Kawssaj and the form is initially rated through the third.
Noverton Official explanation: jockey said filly hit its head on gate and missed the break; trainer said filly did not face the kickback

4850 PLAY ROULETTE AT LADBROKES.COM H'CAP 6f (P)
5:00 (5:01) (Class 5) (0-70,70) 3-Y-O+ **£2,045** (£603; £302) **Stalls** Low

Form RPR

5012 **1** **Highland Harvest**[5] 4659 7-9-11 **69** .... RobertHavlin 3 80
(Jamie Poulton) *racd off the pce in midfield: swtchd rt and effrt 2f out: clsd on ldr and edgd lft over 1f out: continued to hang lft but styd on to ld ins fnl f: kpt on* **8/1**

0001 **2** *1 3/4* **Valmina**[3] 4759 4-9-4 **62** 6ex ....(t) NeilCallan 7 67
(Tony Carroll) *short of room s: hld up towards rr: short of room again after 1f out: hdwy on inner and rdn over 1f out: r.o to go 2nd last strides* **5/2**[1]

505 **3** *hd* **Towy Boy (IRE)**[19] 4207 6-9-6 **64** ....(bt) MartinLane 11 68
(Ian Wood) *chsd clr ldr: clsd u.p over 1f out: led ins fnl f: sn hdd and kpt on same pce: lost 2nd last strides* **25/1**

0505 **4** *1/2* **Defector (IRE)**[19] 4206 5-9-12 **70** .... FrankieMcDonald 8 73
(Seamus Durack) *racd off the pce in midfield: swtchd rt and effrt jst over 2f out: styng on whn hung lft and swtchd rt jst ins fnl f: r.o fnl 75yds* **6/1**[2]

2145 **5** *1 1/4* **Interchoice Star**[111] 1463 6-9-6 **64** ....(p) WilliamCarson 12 63
(Ray Peacock) *led and sn clr: drvn and coming bk to field over 1f out: hdd ins fnl f: wknd fnl 100yds* **16/1**

6000 **6** *3/4* **Rio Royale (IRE)**[9] 4547 5-9-5 **63** ....(p) PatDobbs 4 59
(Amanda Perrett) *chsd ldrs: rdn jst over 2f out: styd on same pce fr over 1f out* **15/2**[3]

2440 **7** *1* **Pippa's Gift**[4] 4715 3-9-8 **70** .... GeorgeBaker 5 63
(William Muir) *a in last trio: n.d* **8/1**

6164 **8** 7 **Speak The Truth (IRE)**[104] 1581 5-9-1 **62**............(p) MatthewDavies(3) 6 33
(Jim Boyle) *rrd as stalls opened: a last trio: wknd over 1f out* **15/2**[3]
6645 **9** 3 1/4 **Caramelita**[14] 4395 4-9-3 **61**.. JackMitchell 10 21
(J R Jenkins) *a last trio: rdn wl over 3f out: struggling over 2f out: wl btn fnl 2f* **16/1**

1m 12.37s (0.47) **Going Correction** +0.175s/f (Slow)
WFA 3 from 4yo+ 4lb **9** Ran SP% **104.2**
Speed ratings (Par 103): **103,100,100,99,98 97,95,86,82**
toteswingers:1&2:£2.50, 1&3:£12.00, 2&3:£7.00 CSF £21.44 CT £262.45 TOTE £5.50: £1.90, £1.30, £4.90; EX 14.80 Trifecta £73.50 Pool: £438.41 - 4.41 winning units..
Owner J Wotherspoon **Bred** John Wotherspoon **Trained** Telscombe, E Sussex
FOCUS
A modest but competitive sprint handicap run at a good pace. The runner-up is rated to his latest C&D win and looks the best guide.
Defector(IRE) Official explanation: jockey said gelding hung left under pressure
T/Plt: £238.30 to a £1 stake. Pool:£58,436.12 - 179.00 winning tickets T/Qpdt: £33.20 to a £1 stake. Pool:£4,418.72 - 98.30 winning tickets

4557 THIRSK (L-H)

Monday, August 8

OFFICIAL GOING: Good to soft (good in places; 8.1)
Wind: fresh 1/2 behind Weather: changeable

4851 BRITISH STALLION STUDS SUPPORTING BRITISH RACING E B F MAIDEN STKS 5f

6:00 (6:01) (Class 4) 2-Y-O **£4,398** (£1,309; £654; £327) **Stalls** High

Form RPR
004 **1** **Dutch Heritage**[16] 4347 2-9-3 73.................................... PaulHanagan 10 72
(Richard Fahey) *mde all stands' side: drvn out* **5/4**[1]
3 **2** 1 1/2 **Towbee**[12] 4433 2-9-3 0.. JamesSullivan 8 67+
(Michael Easterby) *chsd ldrs: hung lft over 1f out: kpt on towards fin* **6/1**[3]
00 **3** 1 **Dazzlin Bluebell (IRE)**[37] 3609 2-8-12 0...................... RobertWinston 1 58
(Tim Easterby) *w wnr: hung rt 1f: kpt on same pce* **16/1**
00 **4** 1/2 **Doyouknowwhoiam**[16] 4347 2-9-3 0............................ TomEaves 7 61+
(Bryan Smart) *hld up towards rr: hdwy over 2f out: styng on whn swtchd lft last 75yds* **25/1**
5 hd **Majestic Breeze (IRE)** 2-8-9 0.............................. PaulPickard(3) 6 55+
(Brian Ellison) *in rr: hdwy wd outside over 2f out: kpt on same pce fnl f: nvr trbld ldrs* **16/1**
66 **6** 2 1/2 **Uncle Timmy**[21] 4147 2-9-3 0.. PBBeggy 4 51
(John Quinn) *s.i.s: sn chsng ldrs: wknd over 1f out* **66/1**
00 **7** 3/4 **Divine Success (IRE)**[15] 4365 2-9-3 0.......................... TonyHamilton 5 49
(Richard Fahey) *mid-div: outpcd over 2f out: kpt on ins fnl f* **12/1**
0 **8** nk **Time To Excel**[24] 4047 2-9-3 0...................................... PhillipMakin 2 48
(Michael Dods) *dwlt: detached in last: kpt on ins fnl f* **7/1**
454 **9** 5 **Whisky Bravo**[62] 2780 2-9-3 67....................................... JamieSpencer 9 39
(David Brown) *upset in stalls: sn chsng ldrs: drvn over 2f out: hung lft and lost pl over 1f out: sn eased* **9/2**[2]

60.76 secs (1.16) **Going Correction** -0.05s/f (Good) **9** Ran SP% **114.2**
Speed ratings (Par 96): **88,85,84,83,82 78,77,77,69**
toteswingers:1&2:£2.10, 1&3:£9.20, 2&3:£56.90 CSF £8.93 TOTE £2.20: £1.20, £1.40, £6.30; EX 10.30.
Owner P Timmins & A Rhodes Haulage **Bred** Red House Stud **Trained** Musley Bank, N Yorks
FOCUS
A relatively weak maiden and the form is limited, with the winner the best guide.
NOTEBOOK
Dutch Heritage, dropping to 5f for the first time, was made plenty of use of from the rails' draw and never looked in danger from 1f out. He should prove as effective back at 6f and can make his mark in nurseries. (op 13-8 tchd 6-5)
Towbee was being niggled from an early stage and still looked green, but did keep on right the way to the line to improve on his debut effort. He should have no trouble winning, with a return to 6f in his favour. (op 17-2 tchd 9-1)
Dazzlin Bluebell(IRE) did well to get across from stall one and dispute it with the winner. She was unable to race on from 1f out, but held third and looks an obvious nursery type. (op 20-1 tchd 22-1)
Doyouknowwhoiam had to wait for a run, but was going on better than anything inside the final furlong and will be of interest switched to nurseries. (op 22-1)
Majestic Breeze(IRE) is bred to be fast and she showed plenty despite looking inexperienced. (op 10-1)
Uncle Timmy is one to watch out for once contesting nurseries.
Time To Excel is another who can do better once contesting nurseries. (tchd 13-2)
Whisky Bravo's jockey reported that the gelding became upset in the stalls. Official explanation: jockey said gelding became upset in stalls (op 4-1 tchd 7-2)

4852 ADMIRALS COURT (S) H'CAP 1m

6:30 (6:30) (Class 6) (0-65,63) 3-Y-O+ **£2,587** (£770; £384; £192) **Stalls** Low

Form RPR
0010 **1** **Escape Artist**[4] 4716 4-9-4 **53**...................................(p) GrahamGibbons 1 63
(Tim Easterby) *s.i.s: hdwy over 4f out: swtchd lft to ins 2f out: styd on to ld last 100yds* **11/2**[1]
405 **2** 1 **Goninodaethat**[25] 4016 3-8-8 **50**...................................... LeeNewman 18 56
(Jim Goldie) *racd v wd for 1st 3f: led: hdd and no ex ins fnl f* **40/1**
6230 **3** 1 1/2 **Jupiter Fidius**[37] 3612 4-9-8 **62**...................................(p) JulieBurke(5) 17 66
(Kate Walton) *towards rr: gd hdwy on outside over 2f out: kpt on same pce last 75yds* **15/2**
060 **4** 1/2 **Blue Noodles**[10] 4517 5-9-4 **53**....................................(p) PaddyAspell 15 56
(John Wainwright) *chsd ldrs: kpt on same pce ins fnl f* **28/1**
0205 **5** 1 1/4 **Bell's Ocean (USA)**[7] 4601 4-9-0 **49**.............................. PaulHanagan 13 49
(John Ryan) *in rr: hdwy on outer over 2f out: kpt on: nvr rchd ldrs* **7/1**[3]
-600 **6** hd **Brisbane (IRE)**[7] 4600 4-8-7 **47**.................................. ShaneBKelly(5) 7 49+
(Dianne Sayer) *wnt rt s: bhd: hdwy on ins whn hmpd wl over 1f out: kpt on ins fnl f: nvr a factor* **9/1**
-204 **7** 5 **Lujano**[24] 4076 6-9-5 **54**.. TomEaves 11 42
(Ollie Pears) *chsd ldr: edgd rt over 1f out: sn wknd* **9/1**
0540 **8** 3/4 **Rapturous Applause**[9] 4560 3-8-13 **55**.......................... FrederikTylicki 9 40
(Micky Hammond) *mid-div: effrt over 2f out: nvr a factor* **12/1**
0640 **9** 1 **So Bazaar (IRE)**[7] 4612 4-9-6 **55**................................ RobertWinston 4 39
(Alan Swinbank) *chsd ldrs: wknd over 1f out* **8/1**
1404 **10** 2 1/4 **Hits Only Jude (IRE)**[4] 4701 8-9-9 **63**............................(v) NeilFarley(5) 12 42
(Declan Carroll) *s.i.s: a in rr* **6/1**[2]
2144 **11** nk **Classic Descent**[21] 4143 6-9-10 **59**...........................(bt) JamesSullivan 6 37
(Ruth Carr) *chsd ldrs: lost pl over 1f out: eased towards fin* **8/1**
0406 **12** 3 **Ubenkor (IRE)**[9] 4563 6-9-1 **50**...................................... TonyHamilton 3 21
(Michael Herrington) *in rr: sme hdwy on ins over 2f out: sn wknd* **14/1**
4500 **13** 6 **Craicattack (IRE)**[7] 4600 4-8-10 **45**..................................(p) KellyHarrison 8 —
(Sharon Watt) *mid-div: lost pl over 2f out* **40/1**

1m 41.59s (1.49) **Going Correction** +0.15s/f (Good)
WFA 3 from 4yo+ 7lb **13** Ran SP% **118.8**
Speed ratings (Par 101): **98,97,95,95,93 93,88,87,86,84 84,81,75**
toteswingers:1&2:£17.50, 2&3:£61.90, 1&3:£10.40 CSF £228.01 CT £1702.11 TOTE £7.00: £2.50, £9.70, £3.60; EX 265.10.There was no bid for the winner.
Owner Habtons Baggie Rams **Bred** Sarah J Leigh And Robin S Leigh **Trained** Great Habton, N Yorks
FOCUS
A typically competitive selling handicap with the third and fourth setting the level.

4853 TURFTV.CO.UK MAIDEN AUCTION STKS 7f

7:00 (7:02) (Class 5) 2-Y-O **£2,911** (£866; £432; £216) **Stalls** Low

Form RPR
2 **1** **Bountiful Girl**[17] 4285 2-8-7 0.. PaulHanagan 11 76
(Richard Fahey) *w ldrs: led over 1f out: hld on gamely* **11/4**[1]
20 **2** 1/2 **Rockme Cockney**[50] 3201 2-8-7 0................................ RoystonFfrench 2 75
(Jeremy Gask) *chsd ldrs: chal 1f out: no ex towards fin* **16/1**
02 **3** 2 1/2 **Benzanno (IRE)**[19] 4201 2-8-12 0................................... DavidProbert 13 74
(Andrew Balding) *t.k.h: trckd ldrs: chal over 1f out: kpt on same pce* **7/2**[3]
4 **4** 3/4 **Landown Littlerock**[13] 4402 2-8-6 0.............................. PaulPickard(3) 5 69
(Reg Hollinshead) *mid-div: effrt over 2f out: styd on ins fnl f* **28/1**
65 **5** 1/2 **Thirkleby (IRE)**[31] 3826 2-8-12 0................................... GrahamGibbons 8 71
(David Barron) *chsd ldrs: drvn over 4f out: fdd appr fnl f* **3/1**[2]
0 **6** 2 1/4 **Farzan (IRE)**[16] 4347 2-8-9 0... RobertWinston 7 62
(Tim Easterby) *s.i.s: hdwy on inner over 2f out: sn chsng ldrs: fdd ins fnl f* **50/1**
0 **7** 1 1/4 **Martha's Way**[17] 4285 2-8-4 0....................................... JamesSullivan 6 54
(Michael Easterby) *hld up in rr: hdwy to chse ldrs over 2f out: wknd over 1f out* **50/1**
8 1 3/4 **Reine Du Froid (IRE)** 2-8-4 0.. AndrewMullen 1 50
(Ben Haslam) *s.s: hdwy to chse ldrs over 2f out: wknd over 1f out* **100/1**
45 **9** 1 **Fine Kingdom**[22] 4122 2-8-12 0..................................... FrederikTylicki 10 55
(Michael Dods) *mid-div: effrt over 2f out: nvr nr ldrs* **14/1**
0 **10** 1/2 **Up Ten Down Two (IRE)**[13] 4402 2-8-9 0.......................(t) PaddyAspell 4 51
(Michael Easterby) *s.i.s: hdwy on inner over 2f out: wknd over 1f out* **100/1**
4 **11** 1 3/4 **Symphony Time (IRE)**[18] 4232 2-8-8 0 ow1.................. JamieSpencer 3 45
(Brian Meehan) *w ldr: led over 4f out: hdd over 1f out: sn wknd* **4/1**
0 **12** 15 **Only A Round (IRE)**[24] 4073 2-8-9 0............................. KellyHarrison 9 9
(Micky Hammond) *in rr: wl bhd fnl 2f* **150/1**
03 **13** 15 **Dr Irv**[13] 4402 2-8-12 0.. TonyHamilton 14 —
(Kate Walton) *racd wd: led tl over 4f out: lost pl over 2f out: bhd whn eased: virtually p.u* **33/1**

1m 29.3s (2.10) **Going Correction** +0.15s/f (Good) **13** Ran SP% **119.4**
Speed ratings (Par 94): **94,93,90,89,89 86,85,83,82,81 79,62,45**
toteswingers:1&2:£5.80, 2&3:£29.80, 1&3:£1.90 CSF £47.17 TOTE £4.70: £1.80, £4.40, £1.10; EX 39.30.
Owner D W Barker **Bred** E J Harper & Whitsbury Manor Stud **Trained** Musley Bank, N Yorks
FOCUS
Just an ordinary maiden but straightforward form rated around the placed horses.
NOTEBOOK
Bountiful Girl, a promising second over C&D on debut, was more streetwise this time and, under a positive ride, was good enough to go one better, Hanagan being seen at his strongest. She ought to stay 1m and can make her mark in nurseries. (tchd 5-2 and 3-1)
Rockme Cockney bounced back from a disappointing effort at Pontefract, appreciating the step up to 7f and returning to the sort of form shown on debut. (op 12-1)
Benzanno(IRE) was a touch keen early and proved one-paced. He was a bit below his last-time-out second, but has got it in him to win a small race. (op 11-4 tchd 4-1)
Landown Littlerock improved a touch on his debut effort and will be suited by 1m. (op 40-1)
Thirkleby(IRE) is now qualified for a mark and should fare better in nurseries. (op 4-1)
Symphony Time(IRE) failed to improve on her initial effort, stopping quickly once headed and clearly did not run up to expectations. (op 6-1)

4854 LADIES DAY ON SATURDAY 3RD SEPTEMBER H'CAP 1m

7:30 (7:32) (Class 5) (0-75,75) 3-Y-O **£2,911** (£866; £432; £216) **Stalls** Low

Form RPR
4132 **1** **Uptown Guy (USA)**[17] 4281 3-9-5 **73**...........................(b) PaulHanagan 3 86
(William Haggas) *s.i.s: hdwy over 3f out: swtchd rt 2f out: led 1f out: edgd rt: rdn out* **11/4**[1]
200 **2** 2 3/4 **Diablo Dancer**[55] 3025 3-8-11 **65**................................ GrahamGibbons 6 72
(Tim Walford) *dwlt: sn trcking ldrs: led over 1f out: sn hdd and no ex* **28/1**
3466 **3** 1/2 **My Single Malt (IRE)**[38] 3578 3-9-7 **75**.......................... JamieSpencer 5 81+
(Tom Tate) *hld up towards rr: t.k.h: hdwy and swtchd rt over 2f out: edgd lft and styd on strly ins fnl f* **5/1**[2]
0-36 **4** 1 3/4 **Scottish Lake**[17] 4290 3-8-10 **67**.............................. PatrickDonaghy(3) 4 69
(Jedd O'Keeffe) *sn chsng ldrs: led over 3f out: hdd over 1f out: one pce* **14/1**
2412 **5** 1 1/2 **Goal (IRE)**[3] 4744 3-9-3 **74**...(t) RyanClark(3) 10 72
(Richard Guest) *hld up in mid-div: effrt over 2f out: one pce ins fnl f* **6/1**[3]
0642 **6** 3/4 **First Class Favour (IRE)**[23] 4107 3-9-2 **75**..................... LanceBetts(5) 1 72
(Tim Easterby) *trckd ldrs: kpt on same pce ins fnl f* **8/1**
4-36 **7** 3/4 **St Oswald**[82] 2197 3-8-9 **63**.. RobertWinston 2 58
(David O'Meara) *prom: drvn 3f out: one pce* **5/1**[2]
003 **8** 6 **Totally Trusted**[17] 4282 3-7-13 **60**............................. LeonnaMayor(7) 9 41
(David Nicholls) *hld up towards rr: hdwy on ins 3f out: wknd over 1f out* **40/1**
1101 **9** 1/2 **Alluring Star**[12] 4435 3-9-3 **71**...................................... JamesSullivan 7 51
(Michael Easterby) *led after 1f: hdd over 3f out: wknd over 1f out* **12/1**
0400 **10** 1 1/4 **Watts Up Son**[23] 4081 3-8-13 **67**................................(t) DanielTudhope 8 44
(Declan Carroll) *w ldrs: wknd over 1f out* **22/1**
1400 **11** 2 **My Mate Jake (IRE)**[45] 3340 3-8-11 **65**........................ FrederikTylicki 14 38
(James Given) *in rr: bhd fnl 3f* **18/1**
3005 **12** hd **Stamp Duty (IRE)**[19] 4199 3-8-10 **64**................................. TomEaves 13 36
(Ollie Pears) *towards rr: bhd fnl 2f* **33/1**
6430 **P** **Chokidar (IRE)**[15] 4370 3-9-5 **73**................................... AdrianNicholls 12 —
(David Nicholls) *led 1f: chsd ldrs: lost pl over 4f out: sn t.o: p.u 3f out* **25/1**

1m 41.17s (1.07) **Going Correction** +0.15s/f (Good) **13** Ran SP% **122.0**
Speed ratings (Par 100): **100,97,96,95,93 92,92,86,85,84 82,82,—**
toteswingers:1&2:£34.10, 2&3:£53.20, 1&3:£2.70 CSF £98.97 CT £383.54 TOTE £4.00: £1.70, £9.10, £2.00; EX 71.40.
Owner Andrew Tinkler **Bred** Tom Clark & Nancy Clark **Trained** Newmarket, Suffolk
FOCUS
The winning time for this 3-y-o event was 0.42secs quicker than the earlier selling handicap. The form looks sound enough rated around the placed horses.

Chokidar(IRE) Official explanation: jockey said gelding lost its action

4855 THIRSK RACECOURSE & CONFERENCE CENTRE H'CAP — 5f

8:00 (8:01) (Class 4) (0-85,83) 3-Y-O **£4,075** (£1,212; £606; £303) **Stalls** High

Form RPR

2122 **1** **York Glory (USA)**[18] 4234 3-9-7 **83**..............................(b) PhillipMakin 2 95+
(Kevin Ryan) *hld up: hdwy over 3f out: styd on wl ins fnl f: led last 50yds* **15/8**[1]

3132 **2** *nk* **Thirteen Shivers**[17] 4295 3-9-7 **83**.............................. GrahamGibbons 7 94
(Michael Easterby) *wnt lft s: trckd ldr: led 1f out: hung lft and hdd clsng stages* **5/2**[3]

1340 **3** *3* **Royal Bajan (USA)**[18] 4234 3-8-9 **71**.............................. FrederikTylicki 3 72
(James Given) *led: hdd 1f out: wknd fnl 75yds* **20/1**

2016 **4** *3 3/4* **Gottcher**[26] 3975 3-9-3 **79**.............................. LeeNewman 5 66
(David Barron) *hmpd s: chsd ldrs: outpcd over 2f out: wknd ins fnl f* **14/1**

2-13 **5** *4* **Jamaican Bolt (IRE)**[31] 3832 3-9-0 **76**.............................. TomEaves 4 49
(Bryan Smart) *sltly hmpd s: chsd ldrs on outer: edgd lft 2f out: wknd fnl f* **9/4**[2]

1600 **6** *13* **Even Stevens**[10] 4498 3-9-4 **80**.............................. AdrianNicholls 1 —
(David Nicholls) *gave problems in stalls: racd wd: chsd ldrs: wknd 2f out* **22/1**

3006 **7** *7* **Boundaries**[58] 2911 3-9-4 **80**..............................(v) DavidAllan 6 —
(Tim Easterby) *hmpd s: in rr: bhd and eased 2f out: sn wl bhd: virtually p.u* **12/1**

59.09 secs (-0.51) **Going Correction** -0.05s/f (Good) 7 Ran SP% **117.6**
Speed ratings (Par 102): **102,101,96,90,84 63,52**
toteswingers:1&2:£1.10, 2&3:£13.10, 1&3:£9.50 CSF £7.25 CT £68.62 TOTE £2.60: £1.10, £2.50; EX 7.90.
Owner Salman Rashed **Bred** Paget Bloodstock & Horse France **Trained** Hambleton, N Yorks

FOCUS
A decent 3-y-o sprint handicap. The finish was fought out by two in-form runners, and the runner-up looks the best guide to the level.
Boundaries Official explanation: jockey said gelding never travelled

4856 RACING AGAIN NEXT MONDAY - 15TH AUGUST H'CAP — 2m

8:30 (8:30) (Class 6) (0-65,65) 4-Y-O+ **£2,587** (£770; £384; £192) **Stalls** Low

Form RPR

0-21 **1** **Soprano (GER)**[7] 4602 9-8-11 **55** 6ex.............................. DanielTudhope 2 66+
(Jim Goldie) *trckd ldrs: drvn over 3f out: led over 2f out: styd on strly: readily* **15/8**[1]

3034 **2** *2 3/4* **Simple Jim (FR)**[9] 4562 7-8-10 **54**.............................. JamieSpencer 18 61
(David O'Meara) *swtchd lft after s: hld up in rr: hdwy on outer over 2f out: tk 2nd 1f out: styd on same pce* **10/3**[2]

-144 **3** *1 1/4* **Short Supply (USA)**[111] 1466 5-8-11 **55**.............................. GrahamGibbons 1 60
(Tim Walford) *led 2f: chsd ldrs: drvn over 3f out: outpcd over 2f out: rallied fnl f: tk 3rd nr fin* **20/1**

45-6 **4** *hd* **Bijou Dan**[40] 3510 10-9-3 **61**.............................. AndrewMullen 7 66
(George Moore) *in rr: drvn 6f out: hdwy over 3f out: wnt 3rd 1f out: kpt on same pce* **33/1**

-001 **5** *1/2* **Neptune Equester**[37] 3622 8-9-3 **61**.............................. TomEaves 16 65
(Brian Ellison) *led after 2f: hdd 7f out: kpt on same pce fnl 2f* **4/1**[3]

-533 **6** *1 1/4* **Folk Tune (IRE)**[12] 3510 8-9-4 **62**..............................(v) PBBeggy 17 65
(John Quinn) *mid-div: effrt over 3f out: styd on fnl 2f: nt rch ldrs* **20/1**

-620 **7** *2 1/2* **Word Of Warning**[37] 3622 7-8-8 **55**.............................. LeeTopliss(3) 20 55
(Martin Todhunter) *swtchd lft after s: towards rr: hdwy 9f out: effrt over 3f out: one pce fnl 2f* **20/1**

-006 **8** *3* **Follow The Sun (IRE)**[16] 4326 7-8-0 **47** oh1 ow1... DeclanCannon(3) 11 43
(Peter Niven) *hld up in rr: sme hdwy on outside over 2f out: nvr a factor* **40/1**

3200 **9** *2* **They All Laughed**[51] 3185 8-8-4 **48**..............................(p) AndrewHeffernan 13 42
(Marjorie Fife) *in rr: effrt on wd outside over 2f out: kpt on fnl f: nvr on terms* **33/1**

5000 **10** *1/2* **Hi Dancer**[16] 4326 8-8-3 **52**.............................. ShaneBKelly(5) 3 45
(Ben Haslam) *trckd ldrs: effrt on inner 3f out: wknd over 1f out* **22/1**

5064 **11** *1 1/4* **Harsh But Fair**[6] 4637 5-8-2 **46** oh1..............................(b) JamesSullivan 8 38
(Michael Easterby) *mid-div: sme hdwy 3f out: lost pl over 1f out* **28/1**

4044 **12** *nse* **Spahi (FR)**[2] 4814 5-8-6 **53**.............................. NataliaGemelova(3) 19 45
(David O'Meara) *w ldrs: led 7f out tl over 2f out: wknd over 1f out* **12/1**

2010 **13** *6* **Trojan Gift (USA)**[16] 4326 4-9-10 **57**..............................(p) TonyHamilton 10 10
(Julie Camacho) *sn trcking ldrs: drvn over 3f out: wknd over 1f out* **28/1**

4003 **14** *2* **Silent Lucidity (IRE)**[16] 4326 7-8-6 **50**..............................(p) PaulHanagan 4 32
(Peter Niven) *a towards rr: nvr a factor* **8/1**

4-65 **15** *17* **Park's Prodigy**[14] 3754 7-9-2 **60**..............................(t) PhillipMakin 5 22
(David Thompson) *mid-div: hdwy 6f out: lost pl over 2f out: eased clsng stages* **80/1**

6204 **16** *12* **Ritsi**[19] 4198 8-8-5 **49**.............................. LeeNewman 10 —
(Marjorie Fife) *mid-div: effrt 3f out: lost pl over 1f out: heavily eased: virtually p.u* **33/1**

3m 32.41s (4.11) **Going Correction** +0.15s/f (Good) 16 Ran SP% **134.7**
Speed ratings (Par 101): **95,93,93,92,92 92,90,89,88,88 87,87,84,83,74 68**
toteswingers:1&2:£2.20, 2&3:£11.90, 1&3:£12.70 CSF £7.46 CT £110.65 TOTE £4.00: £1.40, £1.50, £3.70, £5.40; EX 11.70.
Owner Johnnie Delta Racing **Bred** Gestut Hof Vesterberg **Trained** Uplawmoor, E Renfrews

FOCUS
A moderate staying handicap best rated around those in the frame behind the winner.
T/Plt: £14.40 to a £1 stake. Pool of £63,643.30 - 3,214.69 winning tickets. T/Qpdt: £3.80 to a £1 stake. Pool of £5,602.60 - 1,078.65 winning tickets. WG

[4822] WINDSOR (R-H)

Monday, August 8

OFFICIAL GOING: Good changing to good to soft after race 1 (5.40)
Wind: Fresh, behind Weather: Fine but cloudy

4857 E B F MICHAEL SCALLY MEMORIAL MAIDEN STKS — 6f

5:40 (5:42) (Class 5) 2-Y-O **£3,363** (£1,001; £500; £250) **Stalls** Low

Form RPR

04 **1** **Amazing Storm (IRE)**[9] 4535 2-9-3 0.............................. RichardHughes 10 86+
(Richard Hannon) *trckd ldrs: swtchd rt and prog 2f out: clsd to ld jst ins fnl f: sn in command: eased nr fin* **2/1**[1]

4 **2** *1 1/2* **Sir Fredlot (IRE)**[16] 4339 2-9-3 0.............................. LukeMorris 2 79
(Peter Winkworth) *prom: chsd ldr 2f out: rdn to ld jst over 1f out: hdd jst ins fnl f: styd on* **10/3**[2]

45 **3** *3 1/2* **Backtrade (IRE)**[59] 2880 2-9-3 0.............................. JimmyFortune 8 68
(Andrew Balding) *led: rdn against far rail 2f out: hdd and one pce jst over 1f out* **10/1**

03 **4** *3/4* **Elegant Flight**[26] 3984 2-8-9 0.............................. HarryBentley(3) 3 61
(Alan Jarvis) *wl in tch bhd ldrs: shkn up 2f out: edgd lft over 1f out: outpcd but kpt on* **50/1**

00 **5** *3/4* **Laurel Lad (IRE)**[49] 3237 2-9-3 0.............................. MichaelHills 9 64
(B W Hills) *settled in last quartet: pushed along fr 2f out: styd on steadily after: nrst fin* **66/1**

5 **6** *1* **Red Quartet (IRE)**[17] 4276 2-9-3 0.............................. AndreaAtzeni 12 61
(Robert Eddery) *pressed ldrs: rdn 2f out: steadily fdd over 1f out* **20/1**

7 *nk* **Derfenna Art (IRE)** 2-9-3 0.............................. MickyFenton 1 60
(Seamus Durack) *dwlt: sn in midfield: drvn on outer 2f out: no real prog over 1f out* **100/1**

02 **8** *3/4* **Elusive Flame**[21] 4155 2-8-12 0.............................. KierenFallon 7 52
(David Elsworth) *racd freely: prom: chsd ldr after 2f to 2f out: steadily wknd* **4/1**[3]

0 **9** *1/2* **Next Cry (USA)**[24] 4054 2-9-3 0.............................. DaneO'Neill 4 56
(Richard Hannon) *s.s: wl off the pce in last pair: pushed along 2f out: kpt on quite steadily ins fnl f* **66/1**

0U2 **10** *1/2* **Berlusca (IRE)**[24] 4068 2-9-3 0.............................. LiamJones 6 54
(William Jarvis) *chsd ldr 2f: prom tl wknd 2f out* **33/1**

60 **11** *nk* **Finley Connolly (IRE)**[61] 2817 2-9-3 0.............................. ShaneKelly 14 53
(Brian Meehan) *dwlt: nvr beyond midfield: struggling 2f out: fdd* **50/1**

305 **12** *1/2* **Come On Blue Chip (IRE)**[57] 2953 2-9-3 **71**.............................. TonyCulhane 16 52
(Paul D'Arcy) *dwlt: sn rcvrd into midfield: pushed along 2f out: steadily fdd* **25/1**

13 *1/2* **Look At Me Now** 2-9-3 0.............................. PatCosgrave 5 50
(Jim Boyle) *settled in midfield: shkn up over 2f out: fdd over 1f out* **100/1**

6 **14** *1/2* **Rainbow Chorus**[14] 4384 2-9-3 0.............................. TomQueally 13 49
(Paul Cole) *reminder in last after 2f: nvr on terms* **66/1**

15 *1* **Jinker Noble** 2-9-3 0.............................. AdamKirby 11 46
(Clive Cox) *s.s: rn green in last quartet: reminder over 3f out: no prog* **11/2**

1m 12.28s (-0.72) **Going Correction** -0.25s/f (Firm) 15 Ran SP% **122.8**
Speed ratings (Par 94): **94,92,87,86,85 84,83,82,81,81 80,80,79,78,77**
toteswingers:1&2:£2.70, 1&3:£6.20, 2&3:£8.70 CSF £8.04 TOTE £3.50: £1.50, £1.90, £2.70; EX 18.40 Trifecta £78.10 Pool: £2159.30 - 20.44 winning units..
Owner W P Drew **Bred** Nore Lee Syndicate **Trained** East Everleigh, Wilts

FOCUS
Stands' rail dolled out 18yds at 6f and 7yds at winning post. Top bend out 7yds from normal configuration adding 32yds to races of 1m and over. Not a bad juvenile maiden and the form looks sound enough. The main action unsurprisingly developed more towards the far side in the home straight. It was a respectable winning time but there was a strong tailwind. The form looks decent rated around those in the frame behind the winner.

NOTEBOOK
Amazing Storm(IRE) left the impression a maiden such as this was within his compass when fourth at Goodwood last time and he readily made it third time lucky. He took time to get fully organised, but this was his first outing over shorter than 7f and he was nicely on top near the finish. His future now looks to lie with the handicapper, but the best of him has still to be seen. (op 7-2)
Sir Fredlot(IRE) ◆ finished strongly on his debut at Salisbury and, showing the benefit of that experience, raced a lot more professionally this time. He held every chance and posted an improved effort, but had his rider delivered him earlier the result may well have been different as he finished with what appeared to be a fair bit left in the tank. He shouldn't be long in going one better and a stiffer track should suit. (op 4-1 tchd 9-2)
Backtrade(IRE) raced from the front and turned in his most encouraging effort to date. Nurseries are now an option. (op 15-2)
Elegant Flight, stepped up from 5f, was doing her best work late and is going the right way. She now qualifies for nurseries.
Laurel Lad(IRE) had shown next to nothing in two previous outings, but this was a lot more like it on his return from a 49-day break and he stayed on stoutly. He is another for whom nurseries are now an option. (op 50-1)
Red Quartet(IRE) Official explanation: jockey said colt lost its action
Elusive Flame was not beaten far over C&D on her second start and set the standard on that effort, but she was a late market drifter. She was done with at the furlong-marker after having her chance and perhaps the ground was against her. She's not one to write off now that she can enter nurseries. Official explanation: jockey said filly was unsuited by the good ground (op 11-4)
Jinker Noble met support for his debut, but ran incredibly green. (op 13-2 tchd 5-1)

4858 HAPPY BIRTHDAY JEAN MACIVER SPORTINGBET.COM CONDITIONS STKS — 6f

6:10 (6:14) (Class 3) 2-Y-O **£5,822** (£1,732; £865; £432) **Stalls** Low

Form RPR

10 **1** **Rebellious Guest**[55] 3012 2-8-10 **90**.............................. TomQueally 3 99+
(George Margarson) *hld up in last: quick move over 2f out to ld wl over 1f out: sn clr: shkn up and in n.d fnl f: decisively* **7/2**[3]

1 **2** *3 1/4* **Compton**[28] 3917 2-8-12 0.............................. JimCrowley 1 89
(Ralph Beckett) *mde most: rdn and hdd wl over 1f out: wl outpcd by wnr* **11/4**[1]

3221 **3** *3/4* **Mehdi (IRE)**[7] 4606 2-8-12 **87**.............................. ShaneKelly 2 87
(Brian Meehan) *mostly chsd ldr to jst over 2f out: rdn and one pce* **11/4**[1]

1044 **4** *3* **North Star Boy (IRE)**[24] 4055 2-8-12 **98**.............................. RichardHughes 4 78
(Richard Hannon) *trckd ldrs: effrt to chal on outer 2f out: sn outpcd: pushed along and wknd ins fnl f* **3/1**[2]

2001 **5** *1* **Bling King**[8] 4572 2-8-12 **92**.............................. MickyFenton 5 75
(Eve Johnson Houghton) *hld up in last pair: cl enough 2f out: sn shkn up and wl outpcd: wknd fnl f* **9/1**

01 **6** *1* **Gung Ho Jack**[17] 4276 2-8-10 0.............................. LukeMorris 6 70
(John Best) *trckd ldrs: rdn over 2f out: sn lost pl: wl btn over 1f out* **20/1**

1m 11.7s (-1.30) **Going Correction** -0.25s/f (Firm) 6 Ran SP% **115.3**
Speed ratings (Par 98): **98,93,92,88,87 86**
toteswingers:1&2:£2.20, 1&3:£2.60, 2&3:£2.40 CSF £14.05 TOTE £5.50: £2.60, £2.40; EX 21.00.
Owner John Guest Racing **Bred** Equity Bloodstock Partnership **Trained** Newmarket, Suffolk

FOCUS
The ground was changed to good to soft prior to this decent conditions event. Solid form with the third the best guide.

NOTEBOOK
Rebellious Guest ◆ could have been called the winner a fair way out and slammed his rivals. Talked up by his trainer after scoring on his debut over C&D in June, he wasn't disgraced when 12th in the Coventry turned out quickly for his next assignment. Given a break since, he had clearly done well for it, as he couldn't have been much more impressive. Easy ground clearly suits and this progressive colt looks well up to making his mark in Pattern company. He holds plenty of fancy entries, but his trainer revealed the Mill Reef at Newbury is most likely. (op 9-2)

Compton ◆ won readily on his debut over C&D, but it was a little surprising he was having another outing over this trip as he had appeared sure to want another furlong. After coming in for solid support he tried to make it a test from the front, but he was a sitting duck for the winner. He still finished a clear second-best and stayed on well once headed, so is likely to resume winning ways when faced with a suitably stiffer test. (op 4-1)
Mehdi(IRE) hacked up from the front when dropped to this trip on his fourth outing at Ripon and proved popular to go in again. He couldn't dominate in this much better company and proved one-paced, but still turned in a respectable effort. (tchd 3-1 and 10-3 in places)
North Star Boy(IRE) was the one to beat on official figures down markedly in class. He did look more exposed than most, however, and turned in a laboured effort on this slower surface. He's not going to prove simple to place now. (tchd 7-2)
Bling King had scraped home on his nursery debut at Chester eight days earlier, but that did come off a mark of 92. Keen to post this time, he was beaten a long way out and probably found the easier ground against him (op 15-2 tchd 10-1)

4859 VESTRA WEALTH MANAGEMENT H'CAP — 6f
6:40 (6:41) (Class 3) (0-95,94) 3-Y-0+ **£6,663** (£1,982; £990; £495) **Stalls** Low

Form				RPR
-000	**1**		**Joe Packet**[93] 1888 4-9-7 **91** ... JimCrowley 1	102
			(Jonathan Portman) *prom: effrt on outer to ld wl over 1f out: drvn and styd on wl* **14/1**
1560	**2**	1 1/4	**We Have A Dream**[9] 4531 6-9-3 **87** ... MartinDwyer 2	94
			(William Muir) *led: rdn and hdd wl over 1f out: one pce and readily hld by wnr* **14/1**
0100	**3**	*nk*	**Novellen Lad (IRE)**[9] 4531 6-9-5 **89** ... KierenFallon 3	95
			(Willie Musson) *in tch in midfield: rdn on outer 2f out: prog over 1f out: r.o ins fnl f: nrst fin* **11/2**[1]
5400	**4**	*nk*	**Face The Problem (IRE)**[31] 3820 3-8-10 **89** ... MatthewLawson(5) 11	93+
			(B W Hills) *n.m.r at s: mostly in last pair: rdn and prog on outer over 1f out: styd on wl ins fnl f: nrst fin* **12/1**
5201	**5**	1/2	**Victorian Bounty**[14] 4392 6-9-0 **84** ... PatCosgrave 14	87
			(Stef Higgins) *pressed ldr to 2f out: one pce against far rail fr over 1f out* **11/1**
0300	**6**	*nse*	**Secret Witness**[9] 4531 5-9-6 **90** ...(v) TomMcLaughlin 8	93
			(Ronald Harris) *hld up rt bhd ldrs: shkn up and nt qckn over 1f out: kpt on same pce after* **6/1**[2]
0050	**7**	1	**Swilly Ferry (USA)**[16] 4346 4-9-7 **91** ... MichaelHills 15	91
			(B W Hills) *wl in tch in midfield: rdn and nt qckn against far rail wl over 1f out: one pce after* **11/1**
6104	**8**	1 1/2	**New Leyf (IRE)**[9] 4556 5-9-2 **86** ...(b) LukeMorris 16	81
			(Jeremy Gask) *taken down early: pushed along and no prog 1/2-way: n.d over 1f out* **12/1**
4000	**9**	*nk*	**Yer Woman (IRE)**[9] 4531 4-9-1 **85** ... RichardHughes 6	79
			(Richard Hannon) *nvr beyond midfield: rdn and no prog 2f out* **10/1**
-605	**10**	1/2	**Dorback**[31] 3796 4-9-2 **86** ... DaneO'Neill 13	79
			(Henry Candy) *in tch in rr: rdn and no prog 2f out* **6/1**[2]
0410	**11**	1/2	**Mac Gille Eoin**[9] 4531 7-9-2 **86** ... TadhgO'Shea 10	81
			(John Gallagher) *t.k.h: pressed ldng pair: losing pl whn short of room jst over 1f out: eased* **9/1**[3]
2000	**12**	*nse*	**Tagula Night (IRE)**[9] 4556 5-9-3 **87** ...(tp) AdamKirby 12	80
			(Walter Swinburn) *towards rr: pushed along bef 1/2-way: no prog and no ch whn nt clr run 1f out* **9/1**[3]

1m 11.67s (-1.33) **Going Correction** -0.025s/f (Good)
WFA 3 from 4yo+ 4lb **12** Ran SP% **118.4**
Speed ratings (Par 107): **107,105,104,104,103 103,102,100,100,99 98,98**
toteswingers:1&2: £25.20, 2&3: £16.40, 1&3: £17.60 CSF £195.72 CT £859.91 TOTE £21.60: £5.10, £3.50, £2.60; EX 207.30 Trifecta £325.60 Pool: £1412.43 - 3.21 winning units..
Owner Stuart McPhee & Paul Moulton **Bred** Stuart McPhee Bloodstock Ltd **Trained** Compton, Berks

FOCUS
A good sprint handicap which, despite the non-runners, was highly competitive. There was a sound pace on and the riders were desperate to get over to the far side after straightening for home. The form looks straightforward rated through the runner-up.

NOTEBOOK
Joe Packet was asked for everything at the furlong marker and gamely kept on to land his first win of the season. He'd run well below his mark, albeit in decent company, on his previous three runs this term, but he was returning from a 93-day break here with his yard in fine form. He coped fine with the ground and is firmly back on track, but it remains to be seen whether he will follow this up off a higher mark. (op 16-1)
We Have A Dream bounced back from a lacklustre effort at Goodwood nine days earlier and threw down a strong challenge. He just looks held by the handicapper.
Novellen Lad(IRE) wasn't best placed from his low draw but was given a strong ride and kept on gamely inside the final furlong. His turn may be nearing again, especially if reverting to a sounder surface. (op 5-1, tchd 6-1 in places)
Face The Problem(IRE) ◆ motored home late in the day and clearly gets the trip. This was his most encouraging display since the spring and he's evidently now dropped to a good mark. (op 16-1)
Victorian Bounty had his chance against the far rail and posted a solid effort off his 2lb higher mark for winning narrowly at Carlisle a fortnight earlier. He helps to set the standard. (op 9-1)
Secret Witness had finished runner-up on both his previous outings here and acts with cut, so it wasn't surprising to see him backed. He ran an improved race, but he looks in the handicapper's grip. (tchd 13-2)
Yer Woman(IRE) Official explanation: vet said filly finished distressed
Mac Gille Eoin Official explanation: jockey said horse hung badly left

4860 VESTRA WEALTH PRIVATE CLIENT H'CAP — 1m 67y
7:10 (7:10) (Class 4) (0-85,85) 3-Y-0+ **£3,557** (£1,058; £529; £264) **Stalls** Low

Form				RPR
4411	**1**		**Starwatch**[9] 4546 4-8-13 **70** ... NeilChalmers 9	79
			(John Bridger) *sn trckd ldr: rdn 2f out: clsd to chal over 1f out: disp ld jst ins fnl f: edgd lft but asserted last 100yds* **6/1**
1626	**2**	1/2	**Ree's Rascal (IRE)**[25] 4010 3-8-13 **77** ... PatCosgrave 7	84
			(Jim Boyle) *hld up in 4th: prog 2f out: rdn to chal over 1f out: upsides jst ins fnl f: nt qckn last 100yds* **7/2**[2]
-110	**3**	2 1/2	**Rustic Deacon**[23] 4107 4-9-5 **76** ... RichardHughes 5	78
			(Willie Musson) *led at mod pce: stl gng easily over 2f out: rdn over 1f out: hdd and nt qckn jst ins fnl f* **5/1**[3]
-050	**4**	1 1/4	**Hurricane Spirit (IRE)**[7] 4616 7-9-11 **82** ... DaneO'Neill 8	81
			(Terry Clement) *hld up in last trio: rdn wl over 1f out: kpt on ins fnl f: nvr a threat to ldrs* **20/1**
5405	**5**	*nk*	**Orientalist**[26] 3988 3-8-9 **73** ... TomQueally 1	71
			(Eve Johnson Houghton) *hld up in last trio: shoved along over 3f out: no prog tl kpt on fnl f: n.d* **9/4**[1]
0350	**6**	1 1/2	**Ocean Legend (IRE)**[16] 4310 6-9-4 **75** ... AdamKirby 2	70
			(Tony Carroll) *mostly chsd ldng pair: nt qckn 2f out: wknd ins fnl f* **16/1**
4503	**7**	2 1/4	**Mr Hichens**[17] 4268 6-9-12 **83** ... TadhgO'Shea 6	73
			(Karen George) *stdd s: hld up in last: taken to outer and rdn over 2f out: no prog* **7/1**
-005	**8**	1	**Mahadee (IRE)**[7] 4616 6-9-11 **85** ...(b) JohnFahy(3) 4	73
			(Ed de Giles) *trckd ldrs in 5th: rdn and no prog 2f out: wknd ins fnl f* **12/1**

1m 45.3s (0.60) **Going Correction** +0.15s/f (Good)
WFA 3 from 4yo+ 7lb **8** Ran SP% **114.8**
Speed ratings (Par 105): **103,102,100,98,98 96,94,93**
toteswingers:1&2:£5.30, 2&3:£5.30, 1&3:£2.10 CSF £27.41 CT £113.64 TOTE £6.60: £2.00, £1.20, £1.70; EX 32.40 Trifecta £101.60 Pool: £2177.00 - 15.85 winning units..
Owner J J Bridger **Bred** Mrs J A Chapman **Trained** Liphook, Hants
■ Stewards' Enquiry : Neil Chalmers one-day ban: careless riding (Aug 22)

FOCUS
This fair handicap was blown wide open by the defection of the heavily backed Viva Vettori. It was run at an uneven pace and it paid to race handily, so not form to rate too positively.

4861 SPORTINGBET.COM MAIDEN STKS — 1m 67y
7:40 (7:40) (Class 5) 3-Y-0+ **£2,264** (£673; £336; £168) **Stalls** Low

Form				RPR
0422	**1**		**Lucky Legs (IRE)**[15] 4363 3-8-12 72 ... MichaelHills 9	81
			(B W Hills) *mde all: set decent pce: rdn and hung lft over 1f out: sn hrd pressed: hld on wl ins fnl f* **7/2**[2]
-233	**2**	*nk*	**Aerial Acclaim (IRE)**[16] 4313 3-9-3 80 ... AdamKirby 13	85
			(Clive Cox) *hld up in 6th: prog on outer over 3f out: chsd wnr 2f out: sn rdn: chal over 1f out: nt qckn nr fin* **4/7**[1]
52	**3**	12	**Ffajir (IRE)**[14] 4388 3-8-12 0 ... PhilipRobinson 14	53
			(Clive Brittain) *chsd wnr: awkward bnd over 5f out: lost 2nd 2f out: sn lft bhd* **11/2**[3]
0	**4**	1/2	**The Right Time**[14] 4388 3-8-12 0 ... LukeMorris 6	52
			(Tony Carroll) *chsd ldrs in 5th: rdn over 3f out: wl outpcd fnl 2f out* **33/1**
5	**5**	1 1/4	**Nuba (IRE)**[18] 4254 3-8-12 0 ... ShaneKelly 5	49
			(Luke Dace) *settled in midfield: nt on terms w ldrs in 8th over 3f out: shuffled along and no ch fnl 2f: nt disgracd* **66/1**
00	**6**	*nk*	**Tawseef (IRE)**[21] 4157 3-9-3 0 ... WilliamCarson 10	53
			(Roy Brotherton) *dwlt: rchd midfield and 7th 1/2-way: rdn over 3f out: no hdwy after* **100/1**
0-5	**7**	*nse*	**Grandad Mac**[23] 4102 3-9-3 0 ... RichardHughes 3	53
			(Jane Chapple-Hyam) *chsd ldng pair: rdn over 3f out: wknd 2f out* **12/1**
00	**8**	6	**Beggers Belief**[51] 3173 3-9-3 0 ... EddieCreighton 1	39
			(Eric Wheeler) *dwlt and rousted along s: a wl in rr: bhd in last quartet 1/2-way* **66/1**
9	1/2	**Teutonic Knight (IRE)**[41] 4-9-10 0 ... LiamJones 12	38
			(Ian Williams) *taken down early: chsd ldng trio: rdn 1/2-way: wknd 3f out* **25/1**
0	**10**	2	**Adaero Star**[14] 4388 3-8-12 0 ... TomMcLaughlin 4	28
			(Karen George) *a wl in rr: wl bhd in last 1/2-way* **100/1**
00	**11**	13	**Lady Valtas**[24] 4065 3-8-12 0 ... AndreaAtzeni 2	—
			(Robert Eddery) *in tch in midfield early: wknd 1/2-way: t.o* **100/1**
12	1/2	**Femme D'Espere**[94] 5-9-5 0 ... NeilChalmers 11	—
			(Christopher Kellett) *a wl in rr: wl bhd fr 1/2-way: t.o* **100/1**

1m 44.81s (0.11) **Going Correction** +0.15s/f (Good)
WFA 3 from 4yo+ 7lb **12** Ran SP% **122.7**
Speed ratings (Par 103): **105,104,92,92,90 90,90,84,84,82 69,68**
toteswingers:1&2:£1.10, 2&3:£1.40, 1&3:£2.40 CSF £5.95 TOTE £4.40: £1.30, £1.02, £1.90; EX 8.20 Trifecta £18.50 Pool: £2503.76 - 100.05 winning units..
Owner J Acheson **Bred** Lynch Bages Ltd **Trained** Lambourn, Berks

FOCUS
A fair maiden in which the first pair came well clear and the form is rated around them.
Grandad Mac Official explanation: jockey said colt hung right

4862 VESTRAWEALTH.COM H'CAP — 1m 3f 135y
8:10 (8:10) (Class 5) (0-75,72) 3-Y-0+ **£2,264** (£673; £336; £168) **Stalls** Centre

Form				RPR
3300	**1**		**Urban Space**[43] 3434 5-9-7 **65** ... JimCrowley 4	77
			(John Flint) *trckd ldrs: gng strly over 3f out: effrt to ld 2f out: drifted lft ins fnl f: styd on wl* **7/1**
-601	**2**	1 3/4	**Snow Hill**[20] 4190 3-9-3 **72** ... JackMitchell 8	81
			(Chris Wall) *trckd ldrs: rdn to chal 2f out: pressed wnr tl anging lft and nt qckn ins fnl f* **5/2**[1]
5042	**3**	3 3/4	**Waahej**[14] 4389 5-8-13 **62** ... LucyKBarry(5) 7	65
			(Peter Hiatt) *led at decent pce but pressed: narrowly hdd 4f out: stl upsides over 2f out: sn one pce* **15/2**
5-06	**4**	1/2	**One Lucky Lady**[28] 3919 3-8-12 **72** ... MatthewLawson(5) 1	74
			(B W Hills) *settled in last pair: urged along wl over 3f out: sn struggling: kpt on ins fnl f* **6/1**[3]
43-1	**5**	1/2	**Pullyourfingerout (IRE)**[19] 4204 4-9-11 **69** ...(t) KierenFallon 3	70
			(Brendan Powell) *pressed ldr at decent pce: narrow ld 4f out to 2f out: wknd* **11/4**[2]
0100	**6**	3 1/2	**Gower Rules (IRE)**[14] 4389 3-8-8 **63** ... NeilChalmers 6	58
			(John Bridger) *unable to ld: chsd ldrs: lost pl and struggling over 4f out: nt on terms after* **16/1**
-345	**7**	15	**Loyaliste (FR)**[14] 4385 4-9-12 **70** ... RichardHughes 2	52
			(Richard Hannon) *a in last trio: rdn and struggling 3f out: wknd 2f out: eased* **6/1**[3]

2m 30.24s (0.74) **Going Correction** +0.15s/f (Good)
WFA 3 from 4yo+ 11lb **7** Ran SP% **114.0**
Speed ratings (Par 103): **103,101,99,99,98 96,86**
toteswingers:1&2:£5.20, 2&3:£5.50, 1&3:£9.90 CSF £24.70 CT £135.47 TOTE £11.00: £4.10, £2.10; EX 29.00 Trifecta £133.00 Pool: £749.54 - 4.17 winning units..
Owner Andrew Page **Bred** Winterbeck Manor Stud **Trained** Kenfig Hill, Bridgend
■ Stewards' Enquiry : Jim Crowley one-day ban: careless riding (Aug 22)

FOCUS
A modest handicap run at a fair pace with the winner improving on recent marks back with this yard.

T/Jkpt: Not won. T/Plt: £27.40 to a £1 stake. Pool of £102,145.22 - 2,711.89 winning tickets. T/Qpdt: £7.30 to a £1 stake. Pool of £7,896.31 - 793.82 winning tickets. JN

3920 WOLVERHAMPTON (A.W) (L-H)

Monday, August 8

OFFICIAL GOING: Standard

Wind: Fresh behind Weather: Overcast

4863 DINE IN THE HORIZONS RESTAURANT MAIDEN STKS 5f 20y(P)

2:15 (2:15) (Class 5) 3-4-Y-0 **£2,385** (£704; £352) **Stalls** Low

Form RPR

22-2 **1** **Supercharged (IRE)**[27] [3949] 3-8-12 75 .... TedDurcan 6 70
(Chris Wall) *chsd ldr: rdn over 1f out: r.o to ld post* **4/7**[1]

2 **2** *hd* **Sannibel**[53] [3091] 3-8-12 0 .... ShaneKelly 2 69
(Kevin Morgan) *led: rdn over 1f out: hdd post* **7/2**[2]

05- **3** *6* **Cheeky Wee Red**[350] [5352] 3-8-9 0 .... LeeTopliss(3) 3 47
(Richard Fahey) *chsd ldrs: rdn 1/2-way: outpcd fr over 1f out* **14/1**

4 **4** *5* **Howyadoingnotsobad (IRE)**[84] [2141] 3-9-3 0 .... DarryllHolland 9 34
(Karen George) *chsd ldrs: rdn 1/2-way: wknd over 1f out* **6/1**[3]

4 **5** *1 1/4* **Boucher Garcon (IRE)**[27] [3949] 3-9-3 0 .... StevieDonohoe 7 30
(Declan Carroll) *hld up: rdn 1/2-way: nvr on terms* **22/1**

060 **6** *1* **Renesmee (IRE)**[104] [1589] 3-8-12 42 .... RobbieFitzpatrick 1 21
(Peter Grayson) *chsd ldrs: rdn over 3f out: wknd 2f out* **100/1**

-00 **7** *nk* **Ivory Trilogy (IRE)**[53] [3075] 3-9-3 0 ....(b[1]) GregFairley 5 25
(Tim Etherington) *s.i.s: a in rr* **33/1**

5-0 **8** *1 3/4* **By Implication**[15] [4363] 3-9-3 0 .... StephenCraine 4 19
(Patrick Morris) *prom tl rdn 1/2-way:* **66/1**

9 *10* **Avon Rising** 4-9-3 0 .... DaleSwift(3) 8 —
(Derek Shaw) *dwlt: outpcd* **25/1**

61.75 secs (-0.55) **Going Correction** +0.025s/f (Slow)
WFA 3 from 4yo 3lb **9** Ran SP% **120.4**
Speed ratings (Par 103): **105,104,95,87,85 83,83,80,64**
toteswingers:1&2:£1.50, 1&3:£3.00, 2&3:£5.50 CSF £2.86 TOTE £1.70: £1.02, £1.20, £4.20; EX 3.00.
Owner Des Thurlby **Bred** D J Maher **Trained** Newmarket, Suffolk

FOCUS
The first meeting to take place here since the surface was rewaxed. A weak maiden, lacking strength in depth, and the front pair pulled well clear. The third to her juvenile form looks the best guide.

4864 BRITISH STALLION STUDS SUPPORTING BRITISH RACING E B F MAIDEN STKS 5f 216y(P)

2:45 (2:47) (Class 5) 2-Y-0 **£3,234** (£962; £481; £240) **Stalls** Low

Form RPR

00 **1** **Queens Sandridge (IRE)**[10] [4507] 2-9-0 0 .... AmyBaker(3) 4 79
(Alan Bailey) *chsd ldr tl led over 3f out: rdn over 1f out: jst hld on* **100/1**

2 *nk* **Gaul Wood (IRE)** 2-9-3 0 .... RichardKingscote 5 78+
(Tom Dascombe) *a.p: rdn to chse wnr over 1f out: r.o* **6/1**[3]

24 **3** *3* **Pickled Pelican (IRE)**[73] [2448] 2-9-3 0 .... ShaneKelly 11 69
(William Haggas) *prom: rdn over 1f out: styd on* **2/1**[1]

36 **4** *2 1/4* **Billyrayvalentine (CAN)**[35] [3686] 2-9-3 0 ....(t) TonyCulhane 12 62
(George Baker) *prom: chsd wnr over 2f out tl rdn over 1f out: no ex ins fnl f* **7/2**[2]

5 *2* **Amadeus Wolfe Tone (IRE)** 2-9-3 0 .... FergusSweeney 7 56+
(Jamie Osborne) *hld up: hdwy over 1f out: styd on: nt rch ldrs* **25/1**

44 **6** *hd* **Summer Lane (IRE)**[15] [4358] 2-8-9 0 .... LeeTopliss(3) 13 50
(Richard Fahey) *hld up in tch: rdn over 2f out: styd on same pce appr fnl f* **20/1**

0 **7** *hd* **Small Steps (IRE)**[25] [4002] 2-8-12 0 .... RichardMullen 6 52
(Ed McMahon) *chsd ldrs: rdn over 2f out: wknd over 1f out* **13/2**

0 **8** *4* **Songbird Blues**[19] [4213] 2-8-12 0 .... LiamKeniry 2 37
(Mark Usher) *s.i.s: hld out: nt clr run over 2f out: r.o ins fnl f: nvr trbld ldrs* **50/1**

00 **9** *1 3/4* **Spirit Of The Law (IRE)**[24] [4068] 2-9-3 0 .... ChrisCatlin 3 37
(Ed Dunlop) *sn pushed along in rr: nvr nrr* **40/1**

00 **10** *3/4* **Outlaw Torn (IRE)**[107] [1522] 2-9-3 0 .... SebSanders 1 40+
(Alan McCabe) [illegible] **40/1**

00 **11** *1 1/4* **Hawkino (IRE)**[17] [4276] 2-9-3 0 .... RobbieFitzpatrick 10 30
(Derek Shaw) *sn outpcd* **100/1**

2 **12** *nk* **Miss Purity Pinker (IRE)**[17] [4269] 2-8-12 0 .... StevieDonohoe 8 24
(David Evans) *led: hdd over 3f out: rdn and wknd over 1f out* **7/1**

5 **13** *8* **Al's Memory (IRE)**[30] [3849] 2-9-3 0 .... StephenCraine 9 —
(David Evans) *chsd ldrs tl rdn and wknd 1/2-way* **20/1**

1m 14.94s (-0.06) **Going Correction** +0.025s/f (Slow) **13** Ran SP% **117.9**
Speed ratings (Par 94): **101,100,96,93,90 90,90,85,82,81 80,79,69**
CSF £594.49 TOTE £127.90: £19.00, £2.40, £1.40; EX 676.20.
Owner John Stocker **Bred** David Eiffe **Trained** Newmarket, Suffolk

FOCUS
An ordinary maiden and a major shock. The form looks fine if a little fluid.

NOTEBOOK
Queens Sandridge(IRE) hadn't beaten a rival in a couple of turf maidens, but he cost 50,000gns at the breeze-ups so must have shown plenty there. Always handy, he took over in front well before halfway and responded well to his rider's urgings to hold on with little to spare. The change of surface obviously had a dramatic effect and a winter campaign on the Polytrack seems likely.
Gaul Wood(IRE), a £29,000 half-brother to four winners including Damika, was one of just two newcomers in the field and put in a strong finish, just failing to get up. A similar maiden should come his way. (op 9-2 tchd 13-2)
Pickled Pelican(IRE), gelded since disappointing at odds of 4-7 at Brighton on his second start, plugged on over the last 2f to take third, but even though he might have just needed it he doesn't look anything special. (op 9-4 tchd 11-4)
Billyrayvalentine(CAN), tongue-tied for the first time after showing promise in a couple of Windsor maidens, raced handily from his wide stall and had every chance. He may do better in nurseries. Official explanation: jockey said colt hung left (op 4-1)
Amadeus Wolfe Tone(IRE), a 48,000euros half-brother to Census, was the only one to make any impression from well off the pace and may benefit from a step up in trip. (tchd 28-1)
Small Steps(IRE) didn't seem to get home over 7f on her Doncaster debut and met trouble when still in with a chance turning for home here. She wouldn't have won, but would have been closer. (op 12-1)

4865 BOOK NOW FOR CHRISTMAS H'CAP (DIV I) 7f 32y(P)

3:15 (3:15) (Class 5) (0-70,70) 3-Y-0+ **£2,045** (£603; £302) **Stalls** High

Form RPR

0465 **1** **Glenridding**[8] [4574] 7-9-3 64 .... DaleSwift(3) 7 76
(James Given) *mde all: rdn clr over 1f out: styd on* **13/8**[1]

1250 **2** *1 1/2* **Polemica (IRE)**[77] [2356] 5-9-2 63 ....(bt) SimonPearce(3) 5 71
(Frank Sheridan) *hld up in tch: racd keenly: chsd wnr fnl f: styng on same pce whn rdr dropped reins wl ins fnl f* **14/1**

2250 **3** *1 3/4* **Symphonic Dancer (USA)**[11] [4479] 4-9-9 67 .... J-PGuillambert 8 70
(Brian Baugh) *s.i.s: sn pushed along in rr: hdwy u.p over 1f out: r.o to go 3rd post: nt rch ldrs* **12/1**

4052 **4** *hd* **Army Of Stars (IRE)**[49] [3241] 5-9-1 62 ....(b) RyanClark(3) 2 65
(Michael Blake) *chsd ldrs: rdn over 2f out: styd on same pce fnl f: lost 3rd post* **13/2**[3]

50-0 **5** *1 1/2* **Carcinetto (IRE)**[14] [4387] 9-9-6 67 .... RichardEvans(3) 9 66
(David Evans) *prom: rdn over 2f out: styd on same pce appr fnl f* **14/1**

3110 **6** *1 3/4* **Forward Feline (IRE)**[76] [2376] 5-9-7 68 .... DeclanCannon(3) 4 62
(Bryn Palling) *chsd ldrs: rdn over 2f out: styd on same pce fr over 1f out* **8/1**

0600 **7** *1 1/4* **Buxton**[19] [4210] 7-9-8 66 ....(t) SebSanders 1 57
(Roger Ingram) *mid-div: lost pl 4f out: n.d after* **6/1**[2]

301 **8** *8* **Lutine Charlie (IRE)**[9] [4544] 4-9-7 68 .... SophieDoyle(3) 12 37
(Ronald Harris) *chsd wnr: rdn over 2f out: wknd over 1f out* **10/1**

402- **9** *18* **Green Agenda**[405] [3538] 5-8-13 57 .... RobbieFitzpatrick 3 —
(Derek Shaw) *s.i.s: sn pushed along in rr: bhd fnl 3f: t.o* **33/1**

0000 **10** *12* **Diplomatic (IRE)**[19] [4210] 6-9-0 58 ....(p) DarryllHolland 10 —
(Michael Squance) *sn pushed along in rr: bhd fnl 3f: t.o* **20/1**

1m 30.13s (0.53) **Going Correction** +0.025s/f (Slow)
WFA 3 from 4yo+ 6lb **10** Ran SP% **114.6**
Speed ratings (Par 103): **97,95,93,93,91 89,87,78,58,44**
toteswingers:1&2:£9.10, 1&3:£6.90, 2&3:£18.80 CSF £26.56 CT £208.20 TOTE £2.40: £1.80, £4.10, £3.90; EX 39.50.
Owner Tremousser Partnership **Bred** Bolton Grange **Trained** Willoughton, Lincs

FOCUS
A modest handicap but sound enough rated around the first three.
Diplomatic(IRE) Official explanation: jockey said gelding never travelled

4866 BOOK NOW FOR CHRISTMAS H'CAP (DIV II) 7f 32y(P)

3:45 (3:45) (Class 5) (0-70,70) 3-Y-0+ **£2,045** (£603; £302) **Stalls** High

Form RPR

5000 **1** **Needwood Ridge**[4] [4701] 4-9-5 66 ....(bt) SimonPearce(3) 2 75
(Frank Sheridan) *hld up in tch: rdn over 1f out: r.o to ld 1f out: r.o* **14/1**

4304 **2** *nk* **Khajaaly (IRE)**[35] [3674] 4-9-7 68 .... AdamBeschizza(3) 3 76
(Julia Feilden) *hld up: hdwy over 1f out: rdn and ev ch ins fnl f: r.o* **9/2**[1]

0000 **3** *2* **Bahamian Lad**[10] [4516] 6-9-7 65 ....(p) RussKennemore 9 68
(Reg Hollinshead) *chsd ldrs: led wl over 1f out: rdn and hdd 1f out: styd on same pce ins fnl f* **28/1**

0-10 **4** *2 1/4* **Saturn Way (GR)**[53] [3093] 5-9-9 67 .... FergusSweeney 4 64
(Patrick Chamings) *chsd ldrs: rdn over 1f out: styd on same pce fnl f* **10/1**

-000 **5** *shd* **Silver Alliance**[35] [3674] 3-9-3 70 ....(v[1]) JohnFahy(3) 10 64+
(Walter Swinburn) *hld up: rdn over 1f out: r.o ins fnl f: nrst fin* **6/1**[2]

3015 **6** *1/2* **Euroquip Boy (IRE)**[34] [3714] 4-8-10 61 .... DavidKenny(7) 6 56+
(Michael Scudamore) *s.s: bhd: hdwy over 1f out: r.o: nt rch ldrs* **11/1**

0433 **7** *3/4* **Abriachan**[33] [3735] 4-9-9 67 .... RichardMullen 8 60
(Noel Quinlan) *hld up: hdwy over 2f out: rdn and edgd lft over 1f out: no ex fnl f* **7/1**[3]

50 **8** *2 3/4* **Master Of Dance (IRE)**[37] [3612] 4-8-11 62 ....(b) HannahNunn(7) 11 47
(Peter Salmon) *prom: chsd ldr over 5f out tl rdn over 2f out: wknd fnl f* **33/1**

6014 **9** *1/2* **Schoolboy Champ**[7] [4604] 4-9-2 60 ....(v) DarryllHolland 1 44
(Patrick Morris) *chsd ldrs: rdn over 2f out: wknd over 1f out* **9/2**[1]

2101 **10** *nk* **Fleetwoodsands (IRE)**[42] [3473] 4-9-11 69 ....(t) LiamKeniry 7 52
(Milton Bradley) *led: rdn over 2f out: hdd wl over 1f out: wknd ins fnl f* **6/1**[2]

2200 **11** *5* **Baby Driver**[13] [4409] 3-8-10 60 .... RichardKingscote 12 28
(Tom Dascombe) *prom tl rdn and wknd over 2f out* **14/1**

-006 **12** *7* **Gumnd (IRE)**[20] [4170] 4-9-0 58 .... ChrisCatlin 5 —
(Chris Grant) *sn pushed along in rr: bhd fnl 4f* **33/1**

1m 29.4s (-0.20) **Going Correction** +0.025s/f (Slow)
WFA 3 from 4yo+ 6lb **12** Ran SP% **117.5**
Speed ratings (Par 103): **102,101,99,96,96 96,95,92,91,91 85,77**
toteswingers:1&2:£16.90, 1&3:£44.60, 2&3:£31.30 CSF £74.12 CT £1774.00 TOTE £21.20: £6.50, £2.50, £0.10; EX 117.00.
Owner Frank Sheridan **Bred** Mrs Joy Maund-Powell **Trained** Wolverhampton, W Midlands

FOCUS
The winning time was 0.73 seconds faster than the first division. The first two are the best guides to the level.
Schoolboy Champ Official explanation: jockey said gelding had no more to give

4867 WOLVERHAMPTON-RACECOURSE.CO.UK NURSERY 7f 32y(P)

4:15 (4:15) (Class 4) (0-80,78) 2-Y-0 **£2,911** (£866; £432; £216) **Stalls** High

Form RPR

4015 **1** **Pride And Joy (IRE)**[10] [4496] 2-9-6 77 .... FergusSweeney 6 82+
(Jamie Osborne) *dwlt: hld up: hdwy on outer over 2f out: rdn and hung lft ins fnl f: r.o to ld nr fin* **2/1**[1]

644 **2** *1/2* **Lucky Money**[11] [4455] 2-9-1 72 .... SebSanders 1 76
(Sir Mark Prescott Bt) *hld up: hdwy on inner over 2f out: led over 1f out: sn rdn: hdd nr fin* **9/4**[2]

513 **3** *2 1/2* **Ladykin (IRE)**[30] [3866] 2-9-4 78 .... LeeTopliss(3) 2 76
(Richard Fahey) *led 1f: chsd ldrs: wnt 2nd over 2f out: rdn and ev ch over 1f out: styd on same pce ins fnl f* **6/1**[3]

6321 **4** *1 3/4* **Stellar Express (IRE)**[8] [4571] 2-8-7 64 6ex .... RobbieFitzpatrick 4 57
(Michael Appleby) *led 6f out: rdn and hdd over 1f out: no ex ins fnl f* **6/1**[3]

6241 **5** *13* **Alabanda (IRE)**[17] [4285] 2-9-6 77 .... DavidAllan 5 39
(Tim Easterby) *prom: rdn over 2f out: wknd over 1f out* **6/1**[3]

0640 **6** *32* **Ernest Speak (IRE)**[19] [4194] 2-8-0 57 ....(p) JimmyQuinn 3 —
(Bill Turner) *prom: chsd ldr 6f out tl rdn and wknd over 2f out: t.o* **66/1**

1m 29.63s (0.03) **Going Correction** +0.025s/f (Slow) **6** Ran SP% **108.5**
Speed ratings (Par 96): **100,99,96,94,79 43**
toteswingers:1&2:£2.00, 1&3:£3.00, 2&3:£2.90 CSF £6.27 TOTE £3.10: £2.30, £2.00; EX 7.80.
Owner Miss J Kask **Bred** R P Ryan **Trained** Upper Lambourn, Berks

FOCUS
The surface was an unknown for all bar the rank outsider in this nursery. The early gallop looked pretty strong though and the first two were the last pair 3f from home. The form is rated around the placed horses.

NOTEBOOK
Pride And Joy(IRE), who did not have things work out for him on his nursery debut at Goodwood, was held up at the back and had to come around the field in the straight. However, he found plenty for pressure to run down the runner-up and score more cosily than the official margin suggests. (op 5-2)

Lucky Money, making his handicap and AW debut, was backed against the favourite. He settled out the back and got a dream passage around the inside turning in, getting first run on his market rival. He came away from the rest but could not respond to the winner's surge. (op 11-4 tchd 3-1)
Ladykin(IRE), who had run well in a Newmarket nursery since her soft-ground maiden win, was always in the first three and did best of those that helped set the early pace, especially as she had top weight. (op 7-2)
Stellar Express(IRE), penalised for her recent Chester success on her debut for this yard, won the early battle for the lead but the effort left her vulnerable in the straight. This was no disgrace as this was a decent contest of its type for the track. (tchd 4-1)

4868 GREAT OFFERS AT WOLVERHAMPTON-RACECOURSE.CO.UK (S) STKS — 1m 4f 50y(P)

4:45 (4:45) (Class 6) 3-Y-O+ — **£1,533** (£452; £226) **Stalls** Low

Form	Pos	Dist	Horse / details	RPR
1511	**1**		**Stand Guard**[23] 4088 7-9-12 73 ... StevieDonohoe 6 (Noel Quinlan) *hld up: hdwy to chse ldr over 3f out: rdn to ld over 1f out: hung rt: styd on* **1/2**[1]	66+
0351	**2**	*nk*	**Colonel Sherman (USA)**[28] 3923 6-9-12 60 ... (t) SebSanders 3 (Philip Kirby) *chsd ldr tl led over 4f out: rdn and hdd over 1f out: edgd rt ins fnl f: styd on* **7/2**[2]	65
0	**3**	*4 1/2*	**Fair Dinkum (IRE)**[20] 4180 3-8-10 0 ... FergusSweeney 4 (Jamie Osborne) *hld up: hdwy over 2f out: sn rdn: styd on same pce fnl f* **33/1**	53
1153	**4**	*9*	**Dew Reward (IRE)**[5] 4685 3-8-12 65 ... KierenFox(3) 5 (Bill Turner) *chsd ldrs: rdn 5f out: wknd over 2f out* **5/1**[3]	43
5-06	**5**	*10*	**All Guns Firing (IRE)**[27] 3951 5-9-7 49 ... (p) RussKennemore 2 (Barry Leavy) *sn pushed along to ld: rdn over 7f out: hdd over 4f out: wknd over 2f out* **40/1**	22
00-0	**6**	*19*	**Lyrical Intent**[7] 4605 5-9-7 53 ... (t) JimmyQuinn 1 (Maurice Barnes) *chsd ldrs: rdn over 3f out: wknd over 2f out: t.o* **66/1**	—

2m 40.15s (-0.95) **Going Correction** +0.025s/f (Slow)
WFA 3 from 5yo+ 11lb — **6** Ran SP% **112.4**
Speed ratings (Par 101): **104,103,100,94,88 75**
toteswingers:1&2:£1.10, 1&3:£3.20, 2&3:£5.40 CSF £2.59 TOTE £1.60: £1.10, £1.90; EX 3.60.There was no bid for the winner.
Owner C Owen **Bred** Juddmonte Farms Ltd **Trained** Newmarket, Suffolk

FOCUS
A moderate seller in which only half the field counted according to the market. The form is muddling and rated around - and limited by - the runner-up.

4869 HOTEL & CONFERENCING AT WOLVERHAMPTON H'CAP — 1m 1f 103y(P)

5:15 (5:16) (Class 6) (0-60,59) 4-Y-O+ — **£1,704** (£503; £251) **Stalls** Low

Form	Pos	Dist	Horse / details	RPR
105	**1**		**Cane Cat (IRE)**[10] 4490 4-9-3 55 ... (t) RussKennemore 12 (Tony Carroll) *s.i.s: hld up: rdn over 3f out: hdwy over 1f out: r.o to ld wl ins fnl f* **14/1**	64+
6606	**2**	*nk*	**Final Tune (IRE)**[28] 3926 8-9-0 52 ... JimmyQuinn 1 (Mandy Rowland) *hld up in tch: led over 1f out: sn rdn: hdd wl ins fnl f* **14/1**	60
6044	**3**	*2 1/4*	**Dream Of Fortune (IRE)**[6] 4645 7-9-5 57 ... (bt) StevieDonohoe 4 (David Evans) *mid-div: hdwy over 2f out: rdn and ev ch over 1f out: hung rt ins fnl f: styd on same pce* **8/1**	61
566	**4**	*nk*	**Marino Prince (FR)**[16] 4329 6-8-9 54 ... DavidSimmonson(7) 8 (Paul Midgley) *hld up: hdwy u.p over 1f out: r.o: nt rch ldrs* **14/1**	57
0563	**5**	*1/2*	**Olimamu (IRE)**[9] 4549 4-8-10 51 ... (t) SimonPearce(3) 5 (Lydia Pearce) *hld up: hdwy over 1f out: r.o: nrst fin* **9/2**[1]	53+
4610	**6**	*2 3/4*	**Sunset Boulevard (IRE)**[41] 3480 8-9-4 59 ... (b) RobertLButler(3) 7 (Jim Best) *hld up: rdn over 1f out: r.o ins fnl f: nvr nrr* **28/1**	55+
0002	**7**	*3/4*	**Spinning Ridge (IRE)**[28] 3926 6-9-6 58 ... (b) ChrisCatlin 3 (Ronald Harris) *s.s: hld up: hdwy over 1f out: nt trble ldrs* **7/1**[2]	53
360	**8**	*3/4*	**Madame Boot (FR)**[40] 3516 4-9-6 58 ... SebSanders 11 (Peter Makin) *chsd ldrs: reminders 5f out: rdn and ev ch over 1f out: wknd ins fnl f* **15/2**[3]	51
0006	**9**	*3*	**Indefinite Hope (ITY)**[3] 4747 4-8-5 50 ... (t) DavidKenny(7) 13 (Frank Sheridan) *w ldr: led after 1f: hdd over 3f out: rdn and wknd over 1f out* **16/1**	37
1/00	**10**	*1/2*	**Half A Crown (IRE)**[40] 3512 6-9-0 52 ... GregFairley 2 (Peter Salmon) *led 1f: chsd ldr tl led again over 3f out: rdn and hdd over 1f out: wknd ins fnl f* **40/1**	38
4-50	**11**	*2*	**Beat Up**[79] 2308 5-9-6 58 ... LiamKeniry 6 (Patrick Chamings) *chsd ldrs: rdn over 2f out: wknd fnl f* **9/2**[1]	39
6000	**12**	*2*	**Pilgrim Dancer (IRE)**[7] 4605 4-9-1 53 ... (v) StephenCraine 9 (Patrick Morris) *hld up: rdn over 2f out: n.d* **33/1**	30
0046	**13**	*40*	**Meglio Ancora**[21] 4153 4-8-12 55 ... AmyScott(5) 10 (Alastair Lidderdale) *chsd ldrs: rdn over 4f out: wknd 3f out: t.o* **9/1**	—

2m 2.11s (0.41) **Going Correction** +0.025s/f (Slow) — **13** Ran SP% **116.5**
Speed ratings (Par 101): **99,98,96,96,96 93,92,92,89,89 87,85,50**
toteswingers:1&2:£27.80, 1&3:£23.70, 2&3:£25.20 CSF £188.42 CT £1677.44 TOTE £17.60: £4.30, £5.50, £2.90; EX 178.30.
Owner John W Egan **Bred** Mrs G P Booth And J Porteous **Trained** Cropthorne, Worcs

FOCUS
A moderate handicap in which the leaders may have gone off too quick and set it up for the closers. The winner could do better while the fourth is rated to his best C&D form.
Spinning Ridge(IRE) Official explanation: jockey said gelding missed the break

4870 STAY AT THE WOLVERHAMPTON HOLIDAY INN APPRENTICE H'CAP — 2m 119y(P)

5:45 (5:45) (Class 6) (0-65,71) 4-Y-O+ — **£1,704** (£503; £251) **Stalls** Low

Form	Pos	Dist	Horse / details	RPR
6000	**1**		**Quinsman**[31] 3799 5-9-10 65 ... RachealKneller 7 (J S Moore) *a.p: led over 1f out: rdn out* **6/1**	71
4451	**2**	*1 1/4*	**Corr Point (IRE)**[6] 4642 4-9-9 71 6ex ... (t) JohnLawson(7) 5 (Jamie Osborne) *s.i.s: hld up: hdwy over 7f out: outpcd over 3f out: hdwy over 2f out: styd on to go 2nd wl ins fnl f: nt rch wnr* **9/4**[1]	75+
-344	**3**	*1*	**Gremlin**[10] 4488 7-9-5 63 ... ThomasBrown(3) 4 (Bernard Llewellyn) *s.i.s: hld up: hdwy to chse ldr 3f out: rdn over 1f out: styd on same pce ins fnl f* **9/2**[2]	66
1355	**4**	*3 1/2*	**Delorain (IRE)**[137] 955 8-8-7 53 ... (v) BrendanPowell(5) 3 (William Stone) *chsd ldrs: outpcd over 2f out: styd on ins fnl f* **7/1**	52
6/00	**5**	*1 3/4*	**Katies Tuitor**[17] 4273 8-9-3 58 ... (p) JakePayne 6 (J S Moore) *led over 4f: chsd ldr: led again and qcknd over 4f out: rdn and hdd over 1f out: wknd ins fnl f* **12/1**	55
3200	**6**	*9*	**Carnac (IRE)**[6] 4649 5-9-2 57 ... (p) NoraLooby 2 (Alan McCabe) *chsd ldrs tl wknd over 2f out* **7/1**	43
5060	**7**	*9*	**Why So Serious**[31] 3828 5-8-9 50 ... GeorgeChaloner 8 (Peter Salmon) *hld up in tch: wknd over 3f out* **11/2**[3]	25

3m 45.08s (3.28) **Going Correction** +0.025s/f (Slow) — **7** Ran SP% **111.3**
Speed ratings (Par 101): **93,92,91,90,89 85,81**
toteswingers:1&2:£4.40, 1&3:£6.20, 2&3:£1.30. Totesuper7: Win: Not won; Place: £471.80 CSF £18.84 CT £63.73 TOTE £6.20: £3.40, £1.50; EX 20.70.
Owner The Moore The Merrier **Bred** Mr & Mrs G Middlebrook **Trained** Upper Lambourn, Berks

FOCUS
They went a dawdle in this apprentice staying handicap and the tempo didn't increase until around 5f from home. The form looks muddling and is rated negatively with the third the best guide.
T/Plt: £18.80 to a £1 stake. Pool:£69,090.61 - 2,672.13 winning tickets T/Qpdt: £13.40 to a £1 stake Pool:£4,269.04 - 234.80 w. tckts CR

4871 - 4873a - See Raceform Interactive

LYSA NAD LABEM

Saturday, August 6

OFFICIAL GOING: Turf: soft

4874a ROVINA III CENA SPOLECNOSTI CONSEQ (CONDITIONS) (3YO+) (TURF) — 1m 4f

1:00 (12:00) 3-Y-O+ — **£775** (£356; £232; £108; £77)

Pos	Dist	Horse / details	RPR
1		**Stromboli (CZE)** 3-8-10 0 ... TomasVraj 9 (Cestmir Olehla, Czech Republic) **5/1**[2]	—
2	*1 1/4*	**Rocky Rainbow (ITY)** 3-9-1 0 ... JiriChaloupka 6 (Vaclav Luka II, Czech Republic) **3/5**[1]	—
3	*4*	**Galantery (FR)** 3-8-9 0 ... PetrForet 11 (Helena Blazkova, Czech Republic) **5/1**[2]	—
4	*3 1/2*	**River Speed (GER)**[1805] 7-9-6 0 ... RadekKoplik 8 (V Chaloupka, Czech Republic) **19/1**	—
5	*shd*	**Saracenian** 4-9-6 0 ... JanRaja 4 (Jiri Janda, Czech Republic) **24/1**	—
6	*5*	**New Jape (POL)** 6-9-6 0 ... MilanZatloukal 2 (Pavlina Bastova, Czech Republic) **6/1**[3]	—
7	*7*	**Gardes (IRE)**[1390] 6252 6-9-6 0 ... DusanAndres 3 (Zdena Havlickova, Czech Republic) **5/1**[2]	—
8	*shd*	**Rek (POL)** 5-9-6 0 ... JaromirSafar 10 (Lenka Horakova, Czech Republic) **11/1**	—
9	*3*	**Flying Eagle (POL)** 4-9-0 0 ... PavlinaFilipova 5 (Katerina Berthier, Czech Republic) **9/1**	—
10	*6*	**Apartman (CZE)**[67] 6-8-13 0 ... MartinLaube 12 (George Charlton) **11/1**	—

2m 41.4s (161.40)
WFA 3 from 4yo+ 11lb — **10** Ran SP% **162.5**

Owner WRBNA Racing **Bred** Wrbna Racing a.s **Trained** Czech Republic

NOTEBOOK
Apartman(CZE) was settled in midfield, ridden some way out and soon eased in the home straight.

4780 AYR (L-H)

Tuesday, August 9

OFFICIAL GOING: Good to soft (good in places; 8.7)
Wind: Breezy, half-against. Weather: Cloudy, bright

4875 E.B.F./COURVOISIER MAIDEN FILLIES' STKS — 7f 50y

2:00 (2:03) (Class 4) 2-Y-O — **£4,722** (£1,405; £702; £351) **Stalls** High

Form	Pos	Dist	Horse / details	RPR
3	**1**		**Lady Layla**[18] 4285 2-9-0 0 ... TomEaves 4 (Bryan Smart) *dwlt: sn led at stdy gallop: qcknd clr 2f out: kpt on wl fnl f* **11/10**[1]	77+
	2	*3 3/4*	**Cosmic Halo** 2-9-0 0 ... PaulHanagan 2 (Richard Fahey) *missed break: hld up in tch: effrt over 2f out: edgd lft and chsd clr wnr over 1f out: kpt on fnl f: no imp* **7/2**[2]	66+
U	**3**	*2 1/4*	**Mistress Of Rome**[25] 4073 2-9-0 0 ... PJMcDonald 6 (Michael Dods) *s.i.s: rn green in rr: hdwy on ins wl over 1f out: kpt on fnl f: no imp* **18/1**	60
	4	*1*	**Sally Pepper (USA)** 2-9-0 0 ... FrederikTylicki 1 (James Given) *early ldr: trckd ldrs: effrt and wnt 2nd over 2f out to over 1f out: sn outpcd* **15/2**[3]	58
6	**5**	*2 1/4*	**New Romantic**[25] 4047 2-9-0 0 ... TonyHamilton 5 (Julie Camacho) *t.k.h early: prom: effrt on outside over 2f out: wknd over 1f out* **11/1**	52
00	**6**	*28*	**Reemeya (USA)**[41] 3520 2-9-0 0 ... DarryllHolland 7 (Mark Johnston) *cl up: rdn over 3f out: wknd over 2f out: t.o* **66/1**	—

1m 36.39s (2.99) **Going Correction** +0.20s/f (Good) — **6** Ran SP% **96.7**
Speed ratings (Par 93): **90,85,83,82,79 47**
Tote Swingers:1&2:£1.10, 2&3:£5.90, 1&3:£3.10 CSF £3.49 TOTE £1.50: £1.10, £2.10; EX 3.80.
Owner Dr Marwan Koukash **Bred** H Q Spooner **Trained** Hambleton, N Yorks

FOCUS
Back straight out 6m home bend, out 8m home straight and out 14m from innermost line, adding 24yds to races between 7f and 1m2f and 48yds to 1m5f race. Nothing more than an ordinary maiden and the form is fluid although the winner was quite impressive.

NOTEBOOK
Lady Layla, whose debut second received a boost when the runner-up won the previous evening, was soon dictating from the front and readily drew clear in the straight. She's a bright prospect and it'll be interesting to see what mark she's given by the handicapper. (op 6-4 tchd 13-8)
Cosmic Halo, related to a couple of winners for this yard, was green early but kept on nicely inside the final 2f and should improve for the step up to 1m. She can win a maiden. (op 4-1)
Mistress Of Rome got rid of her rider leaving the stalls on debut, but came out okay this time and fared well considering it was effectively her first run. She too can improve. (op 40-1)
Sally Pepper(USA), half-sister to a 6f winner in the US, appeared to know her job and showed some early promise before steadily fading. (op 7-1 tchd 9-1)
New Romantic is more of a nursery type. (op 9-1)

Reemeya(USA) was tailed off for the third straight run and looks devoid of ability.

4876 WHYTE & MACKAY H'CAP 7f 50y
2:30 (2:31) (Class 6) (0-65,64) 3-Y-0+ **£1,704** (£503; £251) **Stalls** High

Form RPR

4111 **1** **Blues Jazz**[3] 4780 5-9-12 **64** .... TomEaves 12 75+
(Ian Semple) *hld up: hdwy on outside over 2f out: hdwy over 1f out: edgd lft and led ins fnl f: r.o* **11/4**[1]

0064 **2** *3/4* **Emeralds Spirit (IRE)**[11] 4513 4-9-4 **56** .... PJMcDonald 4 65
(John Weymes) *t.k.h: led after 2f: rdn over 1f out: hdd ins fnl f: kpt on* **11/2**[3]

4052 **3** *1 1/4* **Goninodaethat**[1] 4852 3-8-6 **50** .... BarryMcHugh 5 54
(Jim Goldie) *prom: effrt over 2f out: edgd lft over 1f out: kpt on same pce ins fnl f* **14/1**

-051 **4** *1/2* **Benny The Bear**[3] 4782 4-9-2 **59** 6ex .... ShaneBKelly(5) 1 65+
(Linda Perratt) *dwlt: plld hrd and sn prom: effrt over 2f out: kpt on same pce ins fnl f* **3/1**[2]

2514 **5** *1/2* **Tahitian Princess (IRE)**[20] 4196 3-8-11 **55** ....(p) PaulHanagan 8 57+
(Ann Duffield) *in tch: rdn along 3f out: hdwy over 1f out: no imp whn n.m.r ins fnl f: one pce* **8/1**

0660 **6** *3/4* **Big Slick (IRE)**[11] 4517 6-8-10 **48** .... AndrewElliott 10 52+
(Mel Brittain) *in tch: rdn over 2f out: no imp over 1f out* **16/1**

6056 **7** *3/4* **Broughtons Silk**[15] 4379 6-8-8 **46** ow1 .... TonyHamilton 9 45
(Alistair Whillans) *hld up: stdy hdwy over 2f out: rdn wl over 1f out: sn no imp* **20/1**

0503 **8** *3/4* **Monsieur Pontaven**[15] 4379 4-8-13 **51** ....(b) LeeNewman 6 48
(Robin Bastiman) *towards rr: rdn over 3f out: hdwy over 1f out: btn ins fnl f* **17/2**

005 **9** *24* **Hard Rok (IRE)**[47] 3304 3-8-2 **46** ow1 .... FrannyNorton 3 —
(Richard Whitaker) *led 2f: cl up: rdn over 2f out: wknd over 1f out: t.o* **12/1**

1m 34.56s (1.16) **Going Correction** +0.20s/f (Good)
WFA 3 from 4yo+ 6lb **9** Ran SP% **113.7**
Speed ratings (Par 101): **101,100,98,98,97 96,95,95,67**
Tote Swingers:1&2:£5.10, 2&3:£10.90, 1&3:£6.30 CSF £17.89 CT £177.08 TOTE £3.90: £1.30, £1.40, £4.40; EX 22.40 Trifecta £187.10 Pool £447.71 - 1.77 winning units..
Owner Robert Reid **Bred** David Sugars And Bob Parker **Trained** Carluke, S Lanarks
■ Stewards' Enquiry : Tom Eaves caution: careless riding.

FOCUS
A moderate handicap, but one that featured two in-form horses. The form is rated around those in the frame behind the winner.

4877 PIMM'S H'CAP (QUALIFIER FOR BETFAIR BONUS SCOTTISH RACING MILE FINAL) 1m
3:00 (3:01) (Class 5) (0-75,75) 3-Y-0+ **£4,204** (£1,251; £625; £312) **Stalls** Low

Form RPR

2001 **1** **Swiftly Done (IRE)**[18] 4278 4-9-10 **71** ....(b) PaulHanagan 5 86
(Declan Carroll) *hld up: smooth hdwy and swtchd rt over 2f out: led ent fnl f: shkn up: edgd lft and sn clr* **6/1**[3]

2652 **2** *3 3/4* **Music Festival (USA)**[3] 4782 4-9-6 **67** .... DanielTudhope 4 73
(Jim Goldie) *hld up towards rr: pushed along over 2f out: hdwy whn n.m.r briefly over 1f out: chsd wnr ins fnl f: r.o* **7/2**[2]

5031 **3** *1/2* **I'm Super Too (IRE)**[10] 4543 4-9-9 **70** .... PJMcDonald 7 75
(Alan Swinbank) *trckd ldrs: rdn and ev ch over 2f out to over 1f out: kpt on same pce ins fnl f* **7/2**[2]

0636 **4** *4* **Marjury Daw (IRE)**[10] 4561 5-10-0 **75** .... FrederikTylicki 8 71
(James Given) *prom: hdwy on outside to ld over 2f out: hdd ent fnl f: sn outpcd* **3/1**[1]

6145 **5** *1* **Spavento (IRE)**[23] 4127 5-9-4 **65** .... DavidAllan 3 58
(Eric Alston) *trckd ldrs: effrt and ev ch over 2f out: wknd fnl f* **7/1**

2-66 **6** *2 3/4* **Sam Nombulist**[81] 2256 3-9-4 **72** .... MichaelStainton 6 59
(Richard Whitaker) *t.k.h: led 2f: cl up: led over 3f out to over 2f out: wknd over 1f out* **12/1**

4614 **7** *nk* **Casino Night**[42] 3486 6-9-6 **70** .... DaleSwift(3) 1 56
(Barry Murtagh) *dwlt: sn rdn and cl up: led after 2f to over 3f out: wknd over 1f out* **11/1**

4400 **8** *6* **Let's Face Facts**[6] 4670 4-8-4 **56** oh2 .... ShaneBKelly(5) 2 29
(Jim Goldie) *hld up: rdn along 3f out: struggling fr 2f out* **25/1**

1m 43.62s (-0.18) **Going Correction** +0.20s/f (Good)
WFA 3 from 4yo+ 7lb **8** Ran SP% **116.1**
Speed ratings (Par 103): **108,104,103,99,98 96,95,89**
Tote Swingers:1&2:£4.70, 2&3:£2.70, 1&3:£3.90 CSF £27.76 CT £85.20 TOTE £8.30: £2.10, £1.90, £1.10; EX 21.60 Trifecta £57.20 Pool £670.55 - 8.67 winning units..
Owner D Watts, Miss C King, J Syme & M Syme **Bred** Joe Fogarty **Trained** Sledmere, E Yorks

FOCUS
This was quite a competitive handicap on paper, but it didn't work out that way. The winner impressed again and the placed horses set the level.

4878 TENNENT'S LAGER H'CAP (QUALIFIER FOR BETFAIR BONUS SCOTTISH RACING MILE FINAL) 1m 2f
3:30 (3:30) (Class 6) (0-65,64) 3-Y-0 **£2,587** (£770; £384; £192) **Stalls** Low

Form RPR

2335 **1** **She's Got The Luck (IRE)**[16] 4363 3-9-7 **64** .... PaulHanagan 1 72
(Richard Fahey) *trckd ldrs: rdn over 2f out: led and edgd lft ins fnl f: drvn and hld on wl* **7/2**[2]

0610 **2** *nk* **Smart Violetta (IRE)**[14] 4403 3-8-4 **47** ....(t) FrannyNorton 4 56+
(Ann Duffield) *dwlt: hld up in tch: hdwy over 2f out: nt clr run over 1f out and ins fnl f: swtchd rt last 100yds: kpt on wl: jst hld* **16/1**

0364 **3** *2 1/2* **Henrys Gift (IRE)**[15] 4381 3-9-0 **57** .... TomEaves 2 59
(Michael Dods) *led: rdn over 2f out: hdd ins fnl f: kpt on same pce* **10/1**

53 **4** *2 3/4* **Arctic Cat (IRE)**[47] 3325 3-9-2 **59** .... RobertWinston 6 56
(Mrs K Burke) *prom: effrt on outside over 2f out: edgd lft: outpcd over 1f out* **2/1**[1]

4542 **5** *3 1/4* **Purkab**[15] 4381 3-8-12 **55** ....(p) DanielTudhope 5 45
(Jim Goldie) *hld up in tch: nt clr run over 2f out: swtchd lft and sn rdn: wknd over 1f out* **4/1**[3]

003 **6** *1* **Sistine**[16] 4363 3-9-4 **61** .... FrederikTylicki 7 49
(James Given) *cl up: rdn 3f out: wknd wl over 1f out* **7/2**[2]

2m 14.0s (2.00) **Going Correction** +0.20s/f (Good) **6** Ran SP% **112.8**
Speed ratings (Par 98): **100,99,97,95,92 92**
Tote Swingers:1&2:£5.90, 2&3:£6.80, 1&3:£3.20 CSF £50.68 TOTE £3.00: £1.90, £9.70; EX 32.30.
Owner Mrs Phillipa Davies **Bred** Lynch Bages Ltd & Samac Ltd **Trained** Musley Bank, N Yorks

FOCUS
A weak handicap that should probably have gone to the runner-up. The third to his C&D form sets the standard.

4879 CARLING H'CAP (QUALIFIER FOR BETFAIR BONUS SCOTTISH RACING STAYERS FINAL) 1m 5f 13y
4:00 (4:00) (Class 5) (0-75,75) 3-Y-0+ **£4,204** (£1,251; £625; £312) **Stalls** Low

Form RPR

/4-6 **1** **Grandad Bill (IRE)**[43] 3453 8-8-12 **59** .... DanielTudhope 15 65
(Jim Goldie) *chsd ldr: led and rdn over 2f out: hrd pressed fnl f: hld on gamely* **25/1**

460 **2** *shd* **Jonny Delta**[66] 2735 4-9-1 **65** .... GaryBartley(3) 14 71+
(Jim Goldie) *hld up and bhd: hdwy over 2f out: n.m.r briefly over 1f out and ins fnl f: kpt on strly towards fin: jst hld* **7/2**[1]

6155 **3** *shd* **Jeu De Vivre (IRE)**[11] 4510 3-8-9 **68** .... FrannyNorton 9 74
(Mark Johnston) *trckd ldrs: rdn over 2f out: edgd lft over 1f out: ev ch and edgd rt ins fnl f: kpt on: jst hld* **16/1**

6-35 **4** *nk* **Boss's Destination**[15] 4382 4-9-11 **72** .... PJMcDonald 5 78
(Alan Swinbank) *prom: drvn and outpcd over 2f out: rallied over 1f out: kpt on wl fnl f* **8/1**

-000 **5** *nk* **Stags Leap (IRE)**[22] 4142 4-9-3 **64** ....(v) BarryMcHugh 12 69
(Alistair Whillans) *t.k.h: hld up in midfield: effrt over 2f out: kpt on wl fnl f: nrst fin* **50/1**

6154 **6** *shd* **Simonside**[17] 4348 8-9-11 **75** .... DaleSwift(3) 13 80
(Brian Ellison) *prom: drvn along over 3f out: rallied: kpt on ins fnl f* **6/1**

0065 **7** *3 1/2* **Kingsdale Orion (IRE)**[14] 4407 7-8-8 **60** .... JulieBurke(5) 3 60
(Brian Ellison) *hld up: hdwy on outside over 2f out: kpt on fnl f: no imp* **5/1**[3]

5010 **8** *1/2* **Spirit Of A Nation (IRE)**[17] 4348 6-9-9 **75** .... ShaneBKelly(5) 6 74
(James Moffatt) *hld up: rdn over 3f out: no imp fr 2f out* **14/1**

3606 **9** *1/2* **Chookie Hamilton**[53] 3115 7-9-11 **72** .... TomEaves 2 70
(Keith Dalgleish) *hld up: rdn along 3f out: nvr able to chal* **16/1**

0034 **10** *1/2* **Hawdyerwheesht**[10] 4540 3-8-11 **70** ....(p) DarryllHolland 8 67
(Mark Johnston) *led: rdn and hdd over 2f out: wknd ent fnl f* **11/1**

0005 **11** *3 1/2* **Ejteyaaz**[17] 4348 4-9-9 **70** .... PaulHanagan 10 62
(Richard Fahey) *in tch: rdn over 3f out: wknd fr 2f out* **9/2**[2]

3224 **12** *16* **Stadium Of Light (IRE)**[144] 894 4-9-10 **71** .... FrederikTylicki 4 39
(James Given) *hld up: struggling 3f out: sn btn: t.o* **33/1**

2m 58.82s (4.82) **Going Correction** +0.20s/f (Good)
WFA 3 from 4yo+ 12lb **12** Ran SP% **118.0**
Speed ratings (Par 103): **93,92,92,92,92 92,90,89,89,89 87,77**
Tote Swingers:1&2:£18.10, 2&3:£16.00, 1&3:£26.20 CSF £109.18 CT £1489.40 TOTE £23.70: £7.30, £2.50, £6.20; EX 87.30 Trifecta £418.20 Part won. Pool £565.15 - 0.50 winning units..
Owner Connor & Dunne **Bred** M Hosokawa **Trained** Uplawmoor, E Renfrews

FOCUS
A really tricky handicap in which the front six were separated by around half a length. Jim Goldie trained the first two home, but not in the order the market suggested. The form is rated around the winner, thuird and sixth.
Ejteyaaz Official explanation: trainer's rep had no explanation for the poor form shown

4880 APPLETISER H'CAP (QUALIFIER FOR BETFAIR BONUS SCOTTISH RACING SPRINT FINAL) 6f
4:30 (4:30) (Class 5) (0-75,75) 3-Y-0 **£4,204** (£1,251; £625; £312) **Stalls** High

Form RPR

5502 **1** **Another Citizen (IRE)**[17] 4324 3-9-5 **73** ....(p) DavidAllan 6 88
(Tim Easterby) *mde all against stands' rail: rdn and qcknd over 1f out: kpt on strly* **2/1**[1]

0112 **2** *3 1/4* **Spinatrix**[11] 4518 3-9-7 **75** .... FrederikTylicki 5 79
(Michael Dods) *pressed wnr: rdn over 2f out: kpt on same pce fnl f* **11/4**[2]

4350 **3** *1 1/2* **Magic Rhythm**[24] 4081 3-8-8 **62** ....(p) AndrewElliott 7 61
(Mrs K Burke) *in tch: drvn over 2f out: styd on fnl f: nt rch first two* **10/1**

0110 **4** *2* **Monel**[22] 4145 3-8-8 **62** .... LeeNewman 3 55
(Jim Goldie) *in tch: drvn along 1/2-way: no imp fr over 1f out* **5/1**[3]

112 **5** *3 1/4* **Cruise Tothelimit (IRE)**[7] 4643 3-9-0 **73** .... JulieBurke(5) 4 56
(Patrick Morris) *trckd ldrs tl rdn and wknd over 1f out* **5/1**[3]

2255 **6** *2* **Saxonette**[6] 4669 3-9-1 **69** .... PJMcDonald 2 45
(Linda Perratt) *in tch: pushed along over 2f out: sn outpcd* **25/1**

4046 **7** *7* **Normandy Maid**[38] 3613 3-8-12 **66** .... PaulHanagan 1 20
(Richard Fahey) *bhd on outside: struggling 1/2-way: sn btn* **16/1**

1m 11.98s (-0.42) **Going Correction** +0.05s/f (Good) **7** Ran SP% **112.2**
Speed ratings (Par 100): **104,99,97,95,90 88,78**
Tote Swingers:1&2:£2.00, 2&3:£7.50, 1&3:£5.70 CSF £7.33 TOTE £2.80: £1.80, £2.10; EX 9.20.
Owner Middleham Park Racing V & Partners **Bred** Sandro Garavelli **Trained** Great Habton, N Yorks

FOCUS
A fair sprint handicap, but few got into it. The winner is rated to the positive reading of his Newcastle form, backed up by the runner-up to previous C&D form.
Normandy Maid Official explanation: jockey said filly hung left throughout

4881 KOPPARBERG H'CAP (QUALIFIER FOR BETFAIR BONUS SCOTTISH RACING SPRINT FINAL) 5f
5:00 (5:00) (Class 6) (0-65,65) 3-Y-0+ **£2,587** (£770; £384; £192) **Stalls** High

Form RPR

4212 **1** **Blown It (USA)**[3] 4780 5-9-2 **57** 6ex .... PaulHanagan 14 68+
(Keith Dalgleish) *hld up in tch stands' side gp: hdwy over 1f out: shkn up fnl f: led towards fin: comf: 1st of 7 in gp* **15/8**[1]

1214 **2** *3/4* **Royal Blade (IRE)**[3] 4780 4-9-2 **62** .... JulieBurke(5) 13 71
(Alan Berry) *cl up stands' side gp: led 1f out: kpt on fnl f: hdd and no ex towards fin: 2nd of 7 in gp* **4/1**[2]

-004 **3** *1 1/2* **Tongalooma**[20] 4197 5-9-0 **55** .... PJMcDonald 12 59
(James Moffatt) *led stands' side gp to 1f out: kpt on same pce last 150yds: 3rd of 7 in gp* **28/1**

006 **4** *1 1/4* **Sharp Shoes**[20] 4197 4-9-10 **65** ....(p) DarryllHolland 11 68+
(Ann Duffield) *cl up stands' side gp: effrt and ev ch over 1f out: kpt on same pce fnl f: 4th of 7 in gp* **25/1**

35-0 **5** *1/2* **Embra (IRE)**[22] 4144 6-9-1 **56** .... GregFairley 15 55
(Tim Etherington) *dwlt: sn pushed along bhd ldng gp stands' side: styd on fnl f: no imp: 5th of 7 in gp* **18/1**

0254 **6** *hd* **Argentine (IRE)**[10] 4539 7-9-0 **55** ....(b) LeeNewman 7 53
(George Foster) *chsd ldrs on outside of stands' side gp: rdn over 2f out: kpt on same pce fnl f: 6th of 7 in gp* **11/1**

3130 **7** *1/2* **Eternal Instinct**[22] 4145 4-9-7 **65** .... GaryBartley(3) 10 64+
(Jim Goldie) *stdd in rr of stands' side gp: rdn 2f out: hdwy appr fnl f: nvr able to chal: last of 7 in gp* **15/2**

0353 **8** *2 1/4* **Kalahari Desert (IRE)**[7] 4636 4-8-5 **46** oh1 ....(v) FrannyNorton 3 35
(Richard Whitaker) *cl up far side: rdn over 2f out: led that gp ins fnl f: no ch w stands' side gp: 1st of 6 in gp* **20/1**

0000 **9** ¾ **Cayman Fox**[10] 4541 6-9-5 **60** FrederikTylicki 9 47
(Linda Perratt) *taken early to post: cl up far side gp: effrt and ev ch over 1f out: kpt on same pce ins fnl f: 2nd of 6 in gp* **28/1**

4302 **10** *nk* **Ballarina**[22] 4144 5-9-7 **62** DavidAllan 5 48
(Eric Alston) *t.k.h: led far side gp to ins fnl f: nt qckn: 3rd of 6 in gp* **13/2**[3]

0320 **11** 1½ **Dower Glen**[11] 4504 4-9-0 **55** (v) TomEaves 6 36
(Keith Dalgleish) *taken early to post: in tch far side gp: drvn over 2f out: no imp fnl f: 4th of 6 in gp* **25/1**

0004 **12** *nk* **Ya Boy Sir (IRE)**[11] 4504 4-8-6 **47** (b) DuranFentiman 8 27
(Ian Semple) *missed break: bhd far side: hdwy 2f out: no imp fnl f: 5th of 6 in gp* **28/1**

0603 **13** 2¾ **Classlin**[10] 4564 4-8-1 **47** oh1 ow1 ShaneBKelly(5) 1 18
(Jim Goldie) *bhd and sn pushed along in far side gp: nvr on terms: last of 6 in gp* **33/1**

60.01 secs (0.61) **Going Correction** +0.05s/f (Good) **13** Ran SP% **119.2**
Speed ratings (Par 101): **97,95,93,91,90 90,89,85,84,84 81,81,76**
Tote Swingers:1&2:£3.10, 2&3:£21.70, 1&3:£16.00 CSF £7.67 CT £156.79 TOTE £3.10: £1.70, £1.70, £10.50; EX 11.10 Trifecta £240.20 Pool £633.21 - 1.95 winning units..
Owner D G Savala **Bred** H & W Thoroughbreds & Adrian Regan **Trained** Carluke, South Lanarkshire
■ Stewards' Enquiry : Julie Burke two-day ban: careless riding (Aug 23-24)

FOCUS
The stands' side runners were favoured and two in-form sprinters came to the fore. The third sets the level for the form.
Eternal Instinct Official explanation: jockey said filly was denied a clear run
Ya Boy Sir(IRE) Official explanation: jockey said gelding was slowly away
T/Plt: £89.00 to a £1 stake. Pool £63,858.57. 523.25 winning tickets T/Qpdt: £40.10 to a £1 stake. Pool £3,913.95. 72.22 winning tickets RY

4639 FFOS LAS (L-H)
Tuesday, August 9

OFFICIAL GOING: Good to firm (good in places; 8.4)
Wind: Light, half-against. Weather: Fine

4882 SABRINA OWEN H'CAP 5f
5:30 (5:31) (Class 6) (0-65,64) 3-Y-0+ **£1,681** (£500; £250; £125) **Stalls** High

Form RPR

44-5 **1** **Gooseberry Bush**[10] 4547 4-9-6 **60** SteveDrowne 3 69
(Peter Makin) *hld up in midfield: hdwy 3f out: led over 1f out: r.o ins fnl f: a doing enough whn pressed cl home* **9/2**[2]

0-15 **2** *nk* **Just For Mary**[9] 4587 7-9-9 **63** (e) AndreaAtzeni 4 71
(Daniel Mark Loughnane, Ire) *wnt wout declared blinkers: s.i.s: in rr: swtchd lft and hdwy over 1f out: r.o to take 2nd fnl 100yds: clsd on wnr cl home* **7/2**[1]

0004 **3** 1¼ **Madam Isshe**[34] 3721 4-8-12 **52** TomMcLaughlin 1 56
(Malcolm Saunders) *a.p: effrt to chal 2f out: nt qckn over 1f out: kpt on ins fnl f: nt quite pce of front two* **10/1**

0303 **4** ½ **Bateleur**[7] 4631 7-8-11 **58** CharlesBishop(7) 9 60
(Mick Channon) *dwlt: in rr: hdwy over 1f out: prog through narrow gap ins fnl 100yds: styd on but nt quite pce to chal* **6/1**[3]

0021 **5** 1¼ **Spic 'n Span**[7] 4631 6-9-3 **57** 6ex (v) KirstyMilczarek 5 54
(Ronald Harris) *prom: led after 1f: rdn and hdd over 1f out: stl in contention tl no ex fnl 75yds* **6/1**[3]

0006 **6** ¾ **Best One**[11] 4487 7-8-7 **47** (v) LukeMorris 8 42
(Ronald Harris) *midfield: pushed along over 2f out: rdn and wanted to lugg lft over 1f out: nvr able to chal* **20/1**

1645 **7** 3 **The Jailer**[7] 4628 8-9-5 **64** (p) RyanPowell(5) 10 48
(John O'Shea) *led for 1f: remained prom: rdn over 1f out: wknd ins fnl f* **11/1**

-003 **8** ½ **Charlie Delta**[11] 4487 8-9-1 **55** (b) RussKennemore 2 37
(John O'Shea) *midfield: rdn and outpcd 2f out: n.d after* **14/1**

9 *nk* **See You Smile (IRE)**[24] 4118 4-9-6 **63** MartinHarley(3) 6 44
(Liam McAteer, Ire) *prom: pushed along 3f out: rdn 2f out: sn wknd* **9/2**[2]

58.82 secs (0.52) **Going Correction** +0.15s/f (Good) **9** Ran SP% **116.0**
Speed ratings (Par 101): **101,100,98,97,95 94,89,88,88**
Tote Swingers:1&2:£3.60, 2&3:£3.50, 1&3:£8.90 CSF £20.76 CT £149.55 TOTE £4.70: £2.20, £1.90, £4.50; EX 23.00.
Owner Mrs P J Makin **Bred** Mrs D O Joly & Catridge Farm Stud Ltd **Trained** Ogbourne Maisey, Wilts

FOCUS
Ground on the quick side of good and they went off fast in this sprint. The form is modest but the first two are rated slight improvers on recent marks.

4883 BRITISH STALLION STUDS SUPPORTING BRITISH RACING E B F MAIDEN FILLIES' STKS 6f
6:00 (6:01) (Class 4) 2-Y-0 **£4,528** (£1,347; £673; £336) **Stalls** High

Form RPR

1 **Miss Azeza** 2-9-0 0 JamieSpencer 5 79+
(David Simcock) *dwlt: in rr and rn green: hdwy to chse ldrs over 2f out: swtchd lft to chal over 1f out: r.o to ld fnl 120yds: wl on top at fin* **7/1**[3]

263 **2** 1½ **Show Flower**[8] 4614 2-8-11 0 MartinHarley(3) 2 74
(Mick Channon) *led and sn racd against stands' side rail: rdn over 1f out: edgd lft ins fnl f: hdd fnl 120yds: hld by wnr after* **9/2**[2]

530 **3** ½ **Caledonia Lady**[32] 3821 2-9-0 103 LukeMorris 3 73
(Jo Hughes) *racd keenly: handy: w ldrs on outer over 4f out: effrt to chal 2f out: nt qckn ent fnl f: kpt on but a hld after* **1/3**[1]

4 1½ **Villeneuve** 2-9-0 0 MartinDwyer 7 70+
(William Muir) *hld up and rn green: got unbalanced over 3f out: drifted lft over 2f out: kpt on fnl f but no imp on ldng trio: should improve* **25/1**

00 **5** 4½ **Ionwy**[27] 3981 2-9-0 0 AndreaAtzeni 1 55
(Derek Haydn Jones) *w ldr tl rdn under 3f out: wknd wl over 1f out* **66/1**

0 **6** 11 **Skyeron**[9] 4571 2-9-0 0 TomMcLaughlin 6 22
(Mark Brisbourne) *prom: pushed along over 3f out: sn lost pl and struggling: bhd fr over 2f out* **100/1**

1m 11.65s (1.65) **Going Correction** +0.15s/f (Good) **6** Ran SP% **112.0**
Speed ratings (Par 93): **93,91,90,88,82 67**
Tote Swingers:1&2:£1.90, 2&3:£1.10, 1&3:£1.70 CSF £36.02 TOTE £7.30: £3.40, £1.80; EX 27.20.
Owner Saif Ali **Bred** Hugh M Hurst **Trained** Newmarket, Suffolk
■ Stewards' Enquiry : Jamie Spencer caution: careless riding.

FOCUS
A fair contest with the runner-up the best guide to the form.

NOTEBOOK
Miss Azeza looked a potentially smart filly. Despite a slow break from the stalls, she flew home once switched out to the middle of the track to win going away. The way in which she picked up to see off two more experienced rivals who have already shown very useful form suggests she is above average and, at this stage, she could be anything. (tchd 8-1)
Show Flower ran perfectly well but is becoming quite exposed now and, while she again shaped like a maiden success was within reach, is vulnerable to anything with potential. (op 11-2 tchd 6-1)
Caledonia Lady, the Queen Mary runner-up, was long odds-on but fluffed her lines with no real excuses apart from being a little free out wide. She has questions to answer now but is surely better than this. Official explanation: jockey said filly ran too freely (tchd 3-10 and 4-11)
Villeneuve has a middle-distance pedigree but showed plenty of promise on this debut, and wasn't knocked about although she kept on well behind the front three. She has obviously been showing connections plenty at home given her Group 1 entries and, while they may be a touch optimistic at this stage, she looks sure to do much better with this under her belt.

4884 CELTIC ENERGY MEDIAN AUCTION MAIDEN STKS 1m (R)
6:30 (6:32) (Class 5) 2-Y-O **£2,264** (£673; £336; £168) **Stalls** Low

Form RPR

1 **Montaser (IRE)** 2-9-0 0 JamieSpencer 6 79+
(David Simcock) *dwlt: hld up in rr: hdwy gng wl over 2f out: shkn up to go cl 2nd over 1f out: r.o to ld narrowly ins fnl f: leant sltly on runner-up towards fin whn a doing enough* **6/4**[2]

4234 **2** *nk* **Tidal Way (IRE)**[26] 4007 2-8-11 74 MartinHarley(3) 4 74
(Mick Channon) *chsd ldr: led over 2f out: rdn over 1f out: hdd narrowly ins fnl f: a jst hld after* **11/10**[1]

04 **3** 9 **Hearts And Minds (IRE)**[10] 4545 2-9-0 0 FergusSweeney 1 53
(Jamie Osborne) *led: rdn and hdd over 2f out: outpcd by front pair ins fnl f: sn no ch* **7/1**[3]

00 **4** 4 **Music Girl**[13] 4430 2-8-9 0 FrankieMcDonald 2 39
(Michael Blanshard) *chsd ldrs: rdn and lost pl over 3f out: outpcd whn hung lft 2f out: swtchd rt over 1f out: impr past btn horses to take 4th towards fin: no ch w ldrs* **66/1**

20 **5** 1½ **Lady Tycoon**[15] 4390 2-8-6 0 SeanLevey(3) 3 36
(Mark Brisbourne) *in tch: rdn over 3f out: outpcd over 1f out: wknd fnl f* **20/1**

0366 **6** 3¼ **Umph (IRE)**[56] 3021 2-9-0 63 JamesDoyle 7 33
(David Evans) *chsd ldrs: pushed along 4f out: rdn 3f out: outpcd over 1f out: wknd fnl f* **33/1**

06 **7** 7 **Emma Jean Boy**[10] 4545 2-9-0 0 LukeMorris 5 22
(J S Moore) *handy early: lost pl after 2f: sn towards rr: u.p whn swtchd rt under 3f out: sn hung lft and n.d: eased whn wl btn ins fnl f* **33/1**

1m 43.16s (2.16) **Going Correction** +0.275s/f (Good) **7** Ran SP% **112.3**
Speed ratings (Par 94): **97,96,87,83,82 78,71**
Tote Swingers:1&2:£1.30, 2&3:£1.90, 1&3:£2.10 CSF £3.30 TOTE £3.90: £2.50, £1.10; EX 3.90.
Owner Dr Marwan Koukash **Bred** Airlie Stud **Trained** Newmarket, Suffolk

FOCUS
All bar one of these had seen a racecourse at least once before but the winner was the sole newcomer. The runner-up sets the level in a race lacking in depth.

NOTEBOOK
Montaser(IRE) ◆ has the potential to be a nice horse and he made a winning debut by edging out Tidal Way with the pair coming a long way clear. A son of Arc winner Rail Link, he travelled smoothly in the main despite his inexperience and, although it took him some time to master the runner-up, he was nicely on top at the finish despite still looking, very green and he looks a serious colt for next year. (op 15-8 tchd 2-1)
Tidal Way(IRE), stepping up to 1m for the first time, went down fighting and will not be long in going one better if he maintains this level of form. (op Evens tchd 10-11 and 6-5)
Hearts And Minds(IRE) was in the hunt for a long way before dropping off the front two. He isn't finishing his races at the moment so a drop back to 7f may be on the cards.
Music Girl shaped with a little more promise than on her first two starts and is eligible for a handicap mark now. (tchd 80-1)
Lady Tycoon looks one for further down the line in handicaps. (op 18-1)
Emma Jean Boy Official explanation: jockey said bit slipped through colt's mouth

4885 RSS GROUP H'CAP 6f
7:00 (7:01) (Class 5) (0-75,75) 3-Y-O **£2,328** (£693; £346; £173) **Stalls** High

Form RPR

154- **1** **Yellow Dandy (IRE)**[9] 4586 3-9-0 **71** MartinHarley(3) 5 83
(Liam McAteer, Ire) *hld up in last pl: swtchd lft and hdwy 2f out: led jst over 1f out: stretched clr ins fnl f: pushed out* **15/8**[1]

6052 **2** 4½ **Diamond Vine (IRE)**[2] 4819 3-8-13 **67** (p) TomMcLaughlin 1 65
(Ronald Harris) *a.p on outer: led jst over 2f out: rdn and hdd jst over 1f out: no ch w wnr ins fnl f* **2/1**[2]

3406 **3** 1¾ **Captain Dimitrios**[13] 4431 3-8-8 **62** ow2 JamesDoyle 3 54
(David Evans) *led: hdd jst over 2f out: rdn and edgd lft over 1f out: one pce and btn fnl f* **7/1**

-535 **4** 8 **Zalano**[7] 4640 3-8-11 **65** AndreaAtzeni 2 31
(Derek Haydn Jones) *prom: pushed along whn carried lft 2f out: outpcd and n.d after* **11/4**[3]

1m 11.55s (1.55) **Going Correction** +0.275s/f (Good) **4** Ran SP% **107.3**
Speed ratings (Par 100): **94,88,85,75**
CSF £5.84 TOTE £3.90; EX 4.90.
Owner Frank Cosgrove **Bred** Mrs Brid Cosgrove **Trained** Navan, Co Meath

FOCUS
Only four runners, but three of them were involved in setting a strong gallop. The winner is rated to her Irish form but overall not a solid race.

4886 ECO TECHNOLOGY LTD WASTE MANAGEMENT SOLUTIONS H'CAP 5f
7:30 (7:30) (Class 4) (0-85,85) 3-Y-0+ **£4,075** (£1,212; £606; £303) **Stalls** High

Form RPR

0-0U **1** **Thats A Fret (IRE)**[9] 4587 5-8-8 **72** (b) MartinHarley(3) 3 80
(Liam McAteer, Ire) *prom: wnt 2nd 2f out: rdn and str chal ins fnl f: r.o to ld post* **3/1**[2]

0156 **2** *nse* **Bronze Beau**[19] 4239 4-9-6 **81** (t) JamesSullivan 4 89
(Linda Stubbs) *led: edgd lft whn pressed ins fnl f: r.o: hdd post* **14/1**

0450 **3** 3 **Jack My Boy (IRE)**[10] 4556 4-9-4 **79** JamesDoyle 2 76
(David Evans) *in rr: pushed along 3f out: rdn over 1f out: hdwy ins fnl f: tk 3rd fnl 100yds: styd on but no imp on front pair* **13/2**

0333 **4** 1 **Wooden King (IRE)**[26] 3995 6-9-1 **76** TomMcLaughlin 6 70
(Malcolm Saunders) *prom: rdn over 2f out: outpcd over 1f out: kpt on same pce ins fnl f* **9/2**

4340 **5** 3¼ **Judge 'n Jury**[14] 4416 7-9-10 **85** (t) LukeMorris 5 67
(Ronald Harris) *prom: rdn 2f out: wknd ins fnl f* **5/2**[1]

0-01 **6** 1 1/4 **Sulis Minerva (IRE)**[12] 4461 4-8-4 **72**.........................(t) RaulDaSilva[(7)] 1 49
(Jeremy Gask) *hld up: swtchd lft over 2f out: effrt on outer to chse ldrs over 1f out: no imp on ldrs: dropped away ins fnl f* **7/2**[3]

58.26 secs (-0.04) **Going Correction** +0.275s/f (Good) **6** Ran SP% **114.0**
Speed ratings (Par 105): **105,104,100,98,93 91**
Tote Swingers:1&2:£10.70, 2&3:£11.10, 1&3:£6.50 CSF £40.51 TOTE £3.80: £2.30, £1.70; EX 21.60.
Owner Mrs Marie Cusack **Bred** Mrs M Cusack **Trained** Navan, Co Meath

FOCUS
A competitive handicap in which there was no hiding place. The placed horses look the best guides to the form.
Sulis Minerva(IRE) Official explanation: trainer's rep said filly lost off-fore shoe

4887 FINNING UK H'CAP 1m 4f (R)
8:00 (8:00) (Class 4) (0-80,79) 3-Y-O+ **£4,075** (£1,212; £606; £303) **Stalls** Low

Form RPR
05-0 **1** **Dr Livingstone (IRE)**[60] 1325 6-10-0 **79**.......................... SteveDrowne 8 89
(Charles Egerton) *hld up in tch: effrt over 2f out: rdn to chse ldr whn wanted to hang lft over 1f out: styd on for press to ld towards fin* **40/1**
4621 **2** 3/4 **Dark Spirit (IRE)**[7] 4633 3-8-5 **67** 6ex ow1...................... MartinDwyer 5 76
(Alison Thorpe) *chsd ldr: led over 2f out: sn edgd rt and pushed along: abt 2 l clr ent fnl f: rdn and worn down towards fin* **7/2**[2]
2104 **3** 7 **Yes Chef**[12] 4464 4-9-13 **78**..(p) JamesMillman 4 76
(Rod Millman) *led: rdn and hdd over 2f out: lost 2nd over 1f out: outpcd by front pair ins fnl f: no ch last 150yds* **6/1**[3]
0500 **4** 1/2 **Cloudy Start**[13] 4432 5-9-8 **76**..............................(p) SophieDoyle[(3)] 6 73
(Jamie Osborne) *stdd s: hld up: rdn and hdwy over 1f out: kpt on ins fnl f: nt pce to chal* **12/1**
5426 **5** 3 3/4 **Pelham Crescent (IRE)**[12] 4464 8-9-13 **78**.................... DavidProbert 7 69
(Bryn Palling) *hld up in tch: rdn over 2f out: one pce and no imp over 1f out: fin wl btn* **20/1**
301 **6** 2 3/4 **Lady of Burgundy**[29] 3907 5-9-5 **75**.............................. LeeNewnes[(5)] 1 61
(Mark Usher) *s.i.s: hld up in rr: effrt on outer over 2f out: no imp* **10/1**
1221 **7** 7 **Dancing Primo**[4] 4747 5-8-9 **60** oh1............................. JamieSpencer 3 40
(Mark Brisbourne) *chsd ldrs: rdn over 2f out and failed to pick up: wknd over 1f out: eased whn wl btn ins fnl f* **10/11**[1]

2m 38.54s (1.14) **Going Correction** +0.275s/f (Good)
WFA 3 from 4yo+ 11lb **7** Ran SP% **112.9**
Speed ratings (Par 105): **105,104,99,99,97 95,90**
Tote Swingers:1&2:£40.90, 2&3:£2.40, 1&3:£32.30 CSF £169.74 CT £983.92 TOTE £48.30: £12.80, £2.10; EX 149.20.
Owner Longmoor Holdings Ltd **Bred** Stone Ridge Farm **Trained** Chaddleworth, Berks

FOCUS
Hard to know what to make of this form and so it is rated lower than it might have been.
Dancing Primo Official explanation: jockey said mare never travelled

4888 DIGIBET.COM H'CAP 1m 2f (R)
8:30 (8:30) (Class 6) (0-65,65) 3-Y-O **£1,681** (£500; £250; £125) **Stalls** Low

Form RPR
4-00 **1** **Navigation Track**[62] 2813 3-8-13 **57**.............................. JamieSpencer 5 67+
(David Simcock) *hld up: nt clr run and pushed lft over 2f out: swtchd rt and hdwy over 1f out: r.o ins fnl f: led post* **6/4**[1]
6 **2** nse **Yourinthewill (USA)**[18] 4273 3-9-1 **59**........................... AndreaAtzeni 10 66
(Daniel Mark Loughnane, Ire) *hld up: hdwy 2f out: rdn to ld over 1f out: sn edgd lft: hrd pressed ins fnl 100yds: hdd post* **20/1**
0463 **3** 3 3/4 **Like A Boy**[35] 3709 3-8-13 **57**... SteveDrowne 11 56
(Peter Makin) *led: rdn over 2f out: hdd over 1f out: nt qckn ins fnl f: styd on to take 3rd fnl stride: nt pce of front two* **4/1**[2]
0006 **4** hd **Crabbies Gold (IRE)**[24] 4081 3-8-9 **53**......................... JamesSullivan 6 52
(Lisa Williamson) *trckd ldrs: rdn to chal over 1f out: nt qckn ins fnl f: kpt on same pce towards fin* **10/1**
000 **5** 1 1/2 **Dansette**[44] 3437 3-8-9 **53**... FergusSweeney 7 49
(Jim Boyle) *chsd ldrs: wnt 2nd 4f out: rdn to chal over 1f out: no ex fnl 100yds* **16/1**
3460 **6** 3/4 **Beach Babe**[44] 3432 3-8-12 **61**.................................. LucyKBarry[(5)] 9 55
(Jonathan Portman) *in tch: effrt 2f out: kpt on same pce and edgd lft ins fnl f* **5/1**[3]
0300 **7** 8 **Anna Fontenail**[90] 1997 3-9-1 **59**.................................(t) JamesMillman 8 37
(Rod Millman) *plld hrd: hld up: rdn over 2f out: nvr on terms: wl btn fnl f* **16/1**
0-65 **8** 3 **Khaki (IRE)**[155] 791 3-9-0 **58**... JamesDoyle 2 30
(David Evans) *chsd ldr to 4f out: sn rdn: wknd 2f out* **10/1**

2m 11.68s (2.28) **Going Correction** +0.275s/f (Good) **8** Ran SP% **113.2**
Speed ratings (Par 98): **97,96,93,93,92 92,85,83**
Tote Swingers:1&2:£3.50, 2&3:£4.70, 1&3:£2.70 CSF £35.22 CT £102.58 TOTE £2.90: £1.70, £3.60, £1.40; EX 25.00.
Owner Abdullah Saeed Belhab **Bred** Rabbah Bloodstock Limited **Trained** Newmarket, Suffolk

FOCUS
A weak race best rated around the third and fourth.
T/Plt: £306.30 to a £1 stake. Pool £50,917.66. 121.35 winning tickets T/Qpdt: £46.20 to a £1 stake. Pool £5,731.59. 91.70 winning tickets DO

4474 NOTTINGHAM (L-H)
Tuesday, August 9

OFFICIAL GOING: Good to firm (firm in places; 7.6)
Wind: Breezy, half-against. Weather: fine

4889 SIMPLY CARTONS COMMERCIAL APPRENTICE H'CAP 1m 2f 50y
5:15 (5:15) (Class 6) (0-65,62) 4-Y-O+ **£1,681** (£500; £250; £125) **Stalls** Low

Form RPR
-050 **1** **Maybe I Wont**[40] 3533 6-9-2 **62**..................................(p) NoelGarbutt[(5)] 7 70
(Lucinda Featherstone) *sn trcking ldrs: upsides over 5f out: led over 3f out: kpt on wl fnl f* **10/3**[1]
3536 **2** 1 1/4 **Market Puzzle (IRE)**[7] 4645 4-8-1 **45**....................(p) RachealKneller[(5)] 6 50
(Mark Brisbourne) *trckd ldrs: wnt 2nd over 2f out: chal 1f out: no ex last 75yds* **4/1**[3]
0244 **3** 1 1/2 **Mr Chocolate Drop (IRE)**[38] 3643 7-9-3 **58**................(t) NathanAlison 2 60
(Mandy Rowland) *dwlt: t.k.h: hdwy over 4f out: drvn over 2f out: kpt on same pce* **7/2**[2]
-104 **4** 1 **Command Marshal (FR)**[28] 3946 8-9-7 **62**............. MatthewLawson 8 62
(Ed de Giles) *mde most: hdd over 3f out: one pce fnl 2f* **11/2**
5066 **5** 3 1/4 **Kingaroo (IRE)**[14] 4407 5-8-12 **56**........................... JustinNewman[(3)] 4 50
(Garry Woodward) *sn w ldr: drvn 4f out: lost pl over 1f out* **4/1**[3]
005- **6** 9 **Drivemode**[241] 7834 4-8-4 **45**... AntiocoMurgia 3 21
(Dr Jon Scargill) *hld up in last: drvn and hung lft 4f out: nvr a factor: eased fnl 100yds* **11/1**
00-0 **7** 6 **Topaze Star**[5] 4730 4-9-2 **60**..(b[1]) JakePayne[(3)] 1 24
(George Margarson) *trckd ldrs: drvn 4f out: sn outpcd: wknd 2f out: eased fnl f* **40/1**

2m 11.5s (-0.20) **Going Correction** -0.275s/f (Firm) **7** Ran SP% **111.5**
Speed ratings (Par 101): **89,88,86,86,83 76,71**
Tote Swingers:1&2:£4.10, 2&3:£3.90, 1&3:£2.50 CSF £16.04 CT £46.74 TOTE £3.80: £2.30, £3.40; EX 16.60.
Owner J Roundtree **Bred** Wheelersland Stud **Trained** Atlow, Derbyshire

FOCUS
All races were on the outer course, the rails were at the innermost position and distances were as advertised. The early pace was disputed yet the tempo can't have been particularly strong considering Maybe I Wont stalked the leaders before taking over at the top of straight, a good half a mile out. This is moderate form best rated around the first two.
Mr Chocolate Drop(IRE) Official explanation: jockey said gelding hung right-handed

4890 SIMPLY RACING LTD H'CAP 1m 6f 15y
5:45 (5:45) (Class 3) (0-90,90) 3-Y-O+ **£6,663** (£1,982; £990; £495) **Stalls** Low

Form RPR
1150 **1** **Bollin Judith**[17] 4348 5-9-4 **80**...................................(t) GrahamGibbons 4 88
(Tim Easterby) *dwlt: towards rr: hdwy 4f out: swtchd rt and wnt 2nd 1f out: styd on to ld last 50yds* **14/1**
-001 **2** 1 3/4 **Kazbow (IRE)**[46] 3344 5-10-0 **90**.................................... KierenFallon 5 96
(Luca Cumani) *led 1f: trckd ldr: led over 3f out: hdd and no ex clsng stages* **7/2**[1]
0253 **3** 1 1/2 **Regal Park (IRE)**[18] 4280 4-9-10 **86**................................ AdamKirby 10 90
(Marco Botti) *hld up in rr: shkn up after 4f: sme hdwy over 3f out: swtchd rt and styd on over 1f out: edgd lft and tk 3rd nr fin* **6/1**[3]
-403 **4** nk **Rajeh (IRE)**[18] 4280 8-9-7 **83**.. LiamJones 8 86
(John Spearing) *led after 1f: hdd over 3f out: one pce* **20/1**
-223 **5** 3/4 **Plato (JPN)**[32] 3794 4-9-13 **89**... TomQueally 3 91
(Sir Henry Cecil) *mid-div: drvn 7f out: outpcd and lost pl over 3f out: edgd rt and kpt on fnl f* **9/2**[2]
16-2 **6** 3/4 **Jivry**[44] 3434 4-9-7 **83**.. DaneO'Neill 9 84
(Henry Candy) *trckd ldrs: wnt 2nd over 2f out: fdd fnl f* **9/2**[2]
0410 **7** 3 1/4 **Korabushka**[19] 4251 3-8-3 **81**......................................(tp) JohnFahy[(3)] 1 78+
(Jeremy Noseda) *hld up towards rr: hdwy 4f out: sn chsng ldrs: wkng whn hmpd over 1f out* **7/1**
5524 **8** 7 **Comedy Act**[18] 4294 4-9-9 **85**... HayleyTurner 7 72
(Mark Johnston) *trckd ldrs: effrt over 3f out: wknd over 1f out* **18/1**
-014 **9** 17 **Royal Trooper (IRE)**[25] 4043 5-9-8 **84**........................... PhillipMakin 6 47
(James Given) *dwlt: hld up in rr: sme hdwy 4f out: sn wknd: eased whn bhd over 1f out* **16/1**
5200 **10** 3 **Nave (USA)**[32] 3829 4-9-12 **88**.................................(b[1]) J-PGuillambert 2 47
(Mark Johnston) *trckd ldrs: drvn over 5f out: lost pl 3f out: sn bhd: eased over 1f out* **12/1**

3m 0.93s (-6.37) **Going Correction** -0.275s/f (Firm)
WFA 3 from 4yo+ 13lb **10** Ran SP% **115.6**
Speed ratings (Par 107): **107,106,105,104,104 104,102,98,88,86**
Tote Swingers:1&2:£11.00, 2&3:£6.80, 1&3:£14.70 CSF £62.15 CT £333.62 TOTE £23.00: £6.00, £1.50, £2.80; EX 101.80.
Owner Sir Neil Westbrook **Bred** Sir Neil & Exors Of Late Lady Westbrook **Trained** Great Habton, N Yorks
■ Stewards' Enquiry : Adam Kirby one-day ban: careless riding (Aug 23)

FOCUS
A good staying handicap with the fourth and fifth close to recent marks. The pace seemed fair with Rajeh racing in a clear lead for much of the way and sticking on reasonably well for fourth.

NOTEBOOK
Bollin Judith was hard to fancy on recent form, but she travelled well for a long way and found plenty when getting in the clear halfway up the straight. Indeed, she would have been an unlucky loser had she not got in the open soon enough. The good pace helped bring her stamina into play. (tchd 12-1)
Kazbow(IRE) was committed early in the straight after leading the chasing pack and was picked off by a rival who raced further back, but considering the early leader kept plugging on, it's hard to argue Luca Cumani's runner is much better than he showed. This was still a useful performance off 6lb higher than when winning at Doncaster last time. (tchd 9-2 in places)
Regal Park(IRE) isn't an easy ride as he looks a horse best covered up yet needs plenty of stoking and Adam Kirby probably did well to get him so close, especially as he really needs 2m. (op 13-2)
Rajeh(IRE)'s clearly now back in reasonable form, this following on from a respectable effort at the July course. (op 18-1 tchd 25-1)
Plato(JPN) struggled for most of the straight but was going on at the finish. The way he's been racing lately and a 1-13 record suggests he's become lazy and some headgear might help, as will a return to 2m. (op 4-1 tchd 7-2)
Jivry went wide into the straight and gradually faded, looking a non-stayer on this step up from 1m4f. (op 11-2 tchd 6-1)
Korabushka travelled okay but found disappointingly little for pressure with the first-time tongue-tie clearly not the answer. (op 12-1)

4891 E B F SIMPLY CARTONS SALES NOVICE STKS 6f 15y
6:15 (6:15) (Class 5) 2-Y-O **£3,234** (£962; £481) **Stalls** Centre

Form RPR
1 **1** **Gold City (IRE)**[13] 4433 2-9-5 0...................................... FrankieDettori 3 94+
(Saeed Bin Suroor) *mde all: pushed along over 2f out: drew clr 1f out: v readily* **2/5**[1]
1200 **2** 3 3/4 **Evervescent (IRE)**[25] 4055 2-9-2 87.................................. LiamKeniry 1 78
(J S Moore) *trckd ldng pair: drvn 3f out: sn outpcd: styd on appr fnl f: tk 2nd towards fin* **10/1**[3]
1 **3** 3/4 **Chooseday (IRE)**[25] 4047 2-9-5 0.................................... PhillipMakin 5 79
(Kevin Ryan) *trckd wnr: chal over 2f out: rdn over 1f out: no imp* **3/1**[2]

1m 14.03s (-0.87) **Going Correction** -0.125s/f (Firm) **3** Ran SP% **105.5**
Speed ratings (Par 94): **100,95,94**
CSF £4.22 TOTE £1.20; EX 4.20.
Owner Godolphin **Bred** Darley **Trained** Newmarket, Suffolk

FOCUS
A confusing race to assess and cautiously rated - it could be much higher.

NOTEBOOK
Gold City(IRE) recorded a time 2.15 seconds faster than the 55-rated Dansili Dutch, carrying 15lb less, managed in the following nursery. However, in this race the action unfolded middle to far side, whereas in the nursery they raced more towards the stands' side, so maybe that comparison shouldn't be taken too literally. However, the time also compared well with the later Class 6 handicap for older horses, being almost identical, and in that race the principals raced up a similar strip to this trio. There's substance to this form as well with the runner-up, who was getting 3lb, officially rated 87, so it seems the winner has run to a decent level. However, to further cloud the issue, Frankie Dettori was quick to play down the colt's future prospects and the horse doesn't hold any Group race entries in Britain or Ireland. (op 8-15)

Evervescent(IRE) was ridden to finish his race well, sitting in behind the front two in the market, and the tactics were rewarded with a second-place finish. However, while strictly speaking he seemed to run to a useful level, he never threatened to win and only passed a beaten rival. (tchd 12-1)
Chooseday(IRE) only recorded an RPR in the 70s when winning on his debut under similar conditions at Haydock and he struggled in this better company. (op 9-4)

4892 SIMPLY CARTONS PRODUCTION NURSERY 6f 15y

6:45 (6:45) (Class 5) (0-75,72) 2-Y-O **£2,264** (£673; £336; £168) **Stalls** Centre

Form RPR

656 **1** **Dansili Dutch (IRE)**[37] 3656 2-8-4 **55**.......... WilliamCarson 1 62+
(David Barron) *swtchd rt after s: hld up: hdwy and c stands' side over 2f out: led last 100yds: styd on* **10/1**

441 **2** *1* **Dixie's Dream (IRE)**[28] 3941 2-9-7 **72**.......... PatDobbs 7 76
(Richard Hannon) *dwlt: hdwy 3f out: chal over 1f out: sn led: hdd and kpt on same pce last 100yds* **4/1**[3]

6135 **3** *3 ½* **First Bid**[24] 4105 2-9-2 **70**.......... AmyRyan(3) 2 64
(Kevin Ryan) *w ldr: led 3f out: edgd rt over 1f out: hdd 1f out: no ex* **9/1**

600 **4** *nk* **Arrowroot**[48] 3274 2-8-3 **54**.......... KellyHarrison 4 47
(Tim Easterby) *sn outpcd and drvn along: hdwy over 1f out: kpt on same pce* **33/1**

2405 **5** *½* **Night Angel (IRE)**[12] 4460 2-9-2 **67**.......... GrahamGibbons 5 58
(Rod Millman) *led 3f: one pce over 1f out* **16/1**

640 **6** *1 ¼* **Inya House**[47] 3314 2-8-3 **57**.......... DeclanCannon(3) 8 44
(Nigel Tinkler) *sn outpcd and drvn along: kpt on fnl f: nvr a factor* **7/2**[2]

31 **7** *14* **Long Lost Love**[10] 4545 2-9-5 **70**.......... KierenFallon 6 15
(Mark Johnston) *trckd ldrs: drvn over 2f out: hung lft: lost pl over 1f out: eased* **5/4**[1]

0413 **8** *6* **Lady Nickandy (IRE)**[26] 4001 2-8-5 **59**..........(p) KieranO'Neill(3) 9 —
(Alan McCabe) *t.k.h: sn trcking ldrs: rdn and edgd lft 2f out: sn lost pl: eased* **12/1**

1m 16.18s (1.28) **Going Correction** -0.125s/f (Firm) **8** Ran SP% **122.3**
Speed ratings (Par 94): **86,84,80,79,78 77,58,50**
Tote Swingers:1&2:£14.60, 2&3:£3.20, 1&3:£27.90 CSF £53.25 CT £391.36 TOTE £21.70: £5.50, £1.50, £2.80; EX 77.50.
Owner Raymond Miquel **Bred** Castlefarm Stud **Trained** Maunby, N Yorks
■ Stewards' Enquiry : Amy Ryan caution: careless riding.

FOCUS
A modest nursery and the time was much slower than the other two 6f races on the card. The form looks sound with the first pair clear.

NOTEBOOK
Dansili Dutch(IRE) was suited by the drop back in trip on her nursery debut, and she was the only runner with a rail to help late on. At the right end of the handicap, she could defy a rise. Official explanation: trainer's rep had no explanation regarding apparent improvement in form (tchd 12-1)
Dixie's Dream(IRE), successful in a Brighton maiden last time, travelled okay and found enough to pull clear of the others, but the winner was too strong. (op 9-2 tchd 7-2)
First Bid was suited by the return to quick ground, but he looks too high in the weights. (op 8-1 tchd 7-1)
Arrowroot might be better for this first run in 48 days.
Inya House never looked like justifying a market move, lacking the required pace, but he had been off for 47 days. He was eased late on and might be capable of a bit better. (op 7-1 tchd 15-2)
Long Lost Love had much go her way when winning a maiden over an extended 7f last time and she struggled badly on this occasion with the drop in trip and a more competitive field finding her out. Official explanation: trainer's rep said, regarding running, that the filly was possibly outpaced (tchd 13-8 in places)

4893 SIMPLY "NEW V" H'CAP 6f 15y

7:15 (7:15) (Class 6) (0-60,60) 3-Y-O+ **£1,940** (£577; £288; £144) **Stalls** Centre

Form RPR

4050 **1** **Rainy Night**[35] 3713 5-9-3 **60**..........(v) JackDuern(7) 3 73
(Reg Hollinshead) *w ldr: led over 2f out: pushed clr 1f out: styd on wl* **12/1**

3400 **2** *5* **Elhamri**[15] 4395 7-9-10 **60**.......... HayleyTurner 4 57
(Conor Dore) *led tl over 2f out: kpt on to take 2nd towards fin* **12/1**

0204 **3** *1* **Commander Wish**[10] 4547 8-9-6 **56**..........(p) DaneO'Neill 2 50
(Lucinda Featherstone) *chsd ldrs: wnt 2nd over 1f out: kpt on same pce* **10/1**

6513 **4** *5* **Flaxen Lake**[10] 4547 4-9-0 **50**.......... LiamKeniry 1 28+
(Milton Bradley) *in rr: swtchd rt after s: sn bhd: edgd rt over 2f out: kpt on to take modest 4th nr fin* **6/1**[3]

-005 **5** *1 ¼* **Danzig Fox**[10] 4563 6-8-3 **46** oh1..........(be) JosephYoung(7) 5 20
(Michael Mullineaux) *chsd ldrs: lost pl over 2f out: kpt on ins fnl f* **33/1**

-342 **6** *2 ½* **He's A Humbug (IRE)**[11] 4517 7-9-9 **59**.......... MickyFenton 10 25
(Paul Midgley) *hld up: hdwy over 2f out: wknd over 1f out* **7/2**[2]

-603 **7** *nk* **Wong Again**[34] 3747 3-8-12 **55**.......... PatrickHills(3) 6 20
(J W Hills) *trckd ldrs: effrt over 2f out: wknd over 1f out* **8/1**

0000 **8** *13* **Takajan (IRE)**[21] 4189 4-8-8 **49**.......... JamesRogers(5) 7 —
(Mark Brisbourne) *chsd ldrs: lost pl over 2f out* **40/1**

5000 **9** *16* **Secret City (IRE)**[31] 3856 5-9-2 **52**..........(b) KierenFallon 9 —
(Robin Bastiman) *dwlt: sn drvn along: sme hdwy over 3f out: sn wknd: bhd whn eased over 1f out* **2/1**[1]

2000 **10** *5* **Charles Parnell (IRE)**[20] 4196 8-9-5 **55**..........(b) AdrianNicholls 11 —
(Simon Griffiths) *s.s: racd stands' side: in rr: bhd and eased over 1f out* **25/1**

1m 14.06s (-0.84) **Going Correction** -0.125s/f (Firm)
WFA 3 from 4yo+ 4lb **10** Ran SP% **114.7**
Speed ratings (Par 101): **100,93,92,85,83 80,79,62,41,34**
Tote Swingers:1&2:£24.70, 2&3:£9.30, 1&3:£19.30 CSF £140.61 CT £1014.62 TOTE £26.20: £5.70, £3.70, £4.10; EX 137.20.
Owner N Chapman **Bred** Broughton Bloodstock **Trained** Upper Longdon, Staffs

FOCUS
A bizarre race, the field finishing remarkably strung out behind a runner who had previously looked well exposed. The time of the earlier novice event (runners raced towards the far side) was significantly quicker than the nursery (raced towards stands' side), and that, combined with the low numbers totally dominating here, suggests there may have been a bias. Although not exactly borne out in the 5f races, it's entirely possible it was exclusive to this distance. The winner is rated to last year's AW form.
Secret City(IRE) Official explanation: trainer said, regarding running, that the gelding boiled over in the preliminaries

4894 SIMPLY CARTONS LTD CONDITIONS STKS 5f 13y

7:45 (7:45) (Class 3) 3-Y-O+ **£6,663** (£1,982; £990; £495) **Stalls** Centre

Form RPR

3200 **1** **Tiddliwinks**[10] 4534 5-8-11 **104**.......... PhillipMakin 1 108
(Kevin Ryan) *trckd ldrs: smooth hdwy to ld over 1f out: pushed clr: easily* **8/11**[1]

1300 **2** *1 ¾* **Fitz Flyer (IRE)**[10] 4534 5-8-11 **95**..........(b) RoystonFfrench 2 101
(Bryan Smart) *led: hdd over 1f out: kpt on: no ch w wnr* **10/1**

0150 **3** *1 ½* **Poppy Seed**[16] 4357 4-8-3 **91**.......... KieranO'Neill(3) 5 91
(Richard Hannon) *wnt lft s: t.k.h: w ldr: chal over 2f out: kpt on same pce over 1f out* **9/1**[3]

2631 **4** *2* **Star Rover (IRE)**[7] 4644 4-9-0 **87**..........(v) GrahamGibbons 4 91
(David Evans) *dwlt: in rr and pushed along: edgd lft and kpt on fnl f: tk 4th nr fin* **10/1**

3020 **5** *nse* **Five Star Junior (USA)**[10] 4531 5-8-11 **94**.......... KierenFallon 3 88
(Linda Stubbs) *fly-jmpd s: hdwy to chse ldrs over 2f out: wknd fnl f* **5/1**[2]

0660 **6** *1 ½* **Masta Plasta (IRE)**[66] 2714 8-9-0 **93**.......... AdrianNicholls 6 86
(David Nicholls) *w ldrs: drvn over 2f out: wknd appr fnl f* **11/1**

59.18 secs (-1.82) **Going Correction** -0.125s/f (Firm) **6** Ran SP% **111.1**
Speed ratings (Par 107): **109,106,103,100,100 98**
Tote Swingers:1&2:£1.40, 2&3:£11.50, 1&3:£5.70 CSF £8.78 TOTE £1.80: £1.60, £4.00; EX 7.90.
Owner Guy Reed **Bred** Guy Reed **Trained** Hambleton, N Yorks
■ Stewards' Enquiry : Royston Ffrench one-day ban: used whip with excessive force (Aug 23)

FOCUS
The only runner in the line-up with a three-figure official rating, Tiddliwinks was much too good for this lot. The runner-up sets the standard.

NOTEBOOK
Tiddliwinks cruised along throughout and didn't require a hard ride. It's fair to say he was entitled to win like this considering he would have been 9lb worse off with Fitz Flyer in a handicap, but this should serve as a timely confidence-booster. He's now set to take his chance in the Nunthorpe, a race in which his trainer is well represented, and it will be no surprise if he runs a big race at a price. (tchd evens in a place)
Fitz Flyer(IRE) ran with real credit in defeat, showing loads of speed and keeping on well when headed by the classy winner. (op 8-1)
Poppy Seed has gained her three wins to date over 6f. (op 14-1)
Star Rover(IRE), like last year, filled fourth and was a bit outclassed. (tchd 11-1)
Five Star Junior(USA) couldn't repeat his performance of 12 months earlier when he was runner-up in this. (tchd 6-1)
Masta Plasta(IRE) won this last year, but he had been off for 66 days and has yet to find his best form in 2011. (op 8-1)

4895 SIMPLY CARTONS OPERATIONS H'CAP 5f 13y

8:15 (8:15) (Class 5) (0-70,70) 3-Y-O+ **£4,204** (£1,251; £625; £312) **Stalls** Centre

Form RPR

4055 **1** **Francis Albert**[10] 4564 5-8-6 **52**.......... JimmyQuinn 9 61
(Michael Mullineaux) *mid-div: hdwy over 2f out: styd on wl fnl f: led post* **28/1**

0145 **2** *shd* **Triple Dream**[8] 4615 6-9-10 **70**..........(tp) LiamKeniry 12 78
(Milton Bradley) *chsd ldrs: led over 1f out: hung rt: hdd post* **6/1**[3]

3332 **3** *1* **Desert Strike**[4] 4765 5-9-3 **70**..........(p) RyanTate(7) 5 74
(Alan McCabe) *dwlt: in rr: hdwy over 1f out: kpt on same pce fnl 100yds* **5/1**[2]

1400 **4** *1 ¼* **Bilash**[38] 3640 4-9-4 **67**.......... PaulPickard(3) 13 67
(Reg Hollinshead) *hld up in rr: hdwy 2f out: kpt on last 150yds* **16/1**

6005 **5** *3* **Look Who's Kool**[20] 4197 3-9-6 **69**..........(b) GrahamGibbons 6 58
(Ed McMahon) *led tl over 1f out: wknd ins fnl f* **14/1**

633 **6** *¾* **Athwaab**[15] 4395 4-9-0 **65**.......... LauraPike(5) 4 51
(Tim McCarthy) *chsd ldrs: wknd jst ins fnl f* **7/1**

4506 **7** *1 ¾* **Morermaloke**[6] 4680 3-9-1 **67**..........(p) LeeTopliss(3) 7 47
(Ian McInnes) *mid-div: sme hdwy over 2f out: one pce whn stirrup leather c loose and rdr lost irons wl ins fnl f* **40/1**

4050 **8** *2* **Brandywell Boy (IRE)**[8] 4615 8-9-7 **67**.......... KierenFallon 10 40
(Dominic Ffrench Davis) *mid-div: drvn over 2f out: sn outpcd* **7/1**

0000 **9** *6* **Cape Royal**[8] 4615 11-9-5 **68**..........(bt) RyanClark(3) 1 19
(Milton Bradley) *chsd ldrs: wknd over 1f out* **16/1**

4310 **10** *¾* **Senate Majority**[10] 4539 4-9-10 **70**..........(b) DavidNolan 14 19
(Tim Easterby) *racd alone towards stands' side: edgd lft over 2f out: sn bhd* **4/1**[1]

1063 **11** *2 ¼* **Straboe (USA)**[12] 4475 5-8-10 **56**..........(v) WilliamCarson 8 —
(Stuart Williams) *dwlt: swtchd rt s to r alone stands' side: sn bhd* **8/1**

0404 **12** *30* **Bertie Southstreet**[12] 4475 8-9-7 **67**..........(v) MickyFenton 2 —
(Paul Midgley) *banged hd on stalls: dwlt: bhd whn virtually p.u 2f out* **12/1**

59.91 secs (-1.09) **Going Correction** -0.125s/f (Firm)
WFA 3 from 4yo+ 3lb **12** Ran SP% **119.1**
Speed ratings (Par 103): **103,102,101,99,94 93,90,87,77,76 72,24**
Tote Swingers:1&2:£46.40, 2&3:£11.60, 1&3:£28.20 CSF £189.48 CT £1013.18 TOTE £28.70: £8.70, £2.50, £1.60; EX 343.40.
Owner Michael Mullineaux **Bred** R S And Mrs S H Kitching **Trained** Alpraham, Cheshire

FOCUS
The time was a highly respectable 0.72 seconds slower than the earlier conditions race. The action unfolded around the middle of the track. The form is not that solid but is best rated through the third to his recent best.
Morermaloke Official explanation: jockey said buckle became undone and his foot came out of the near-side stirrup
Senate Majority Official explanation: jockey said gelding never travelled
Bertie Southstreet Official explanation: jockey said gelding hit its head on the gate and cut its nose

T/Plt: £218.80 to a £1 stke. Pool £41,694.07. 139.07 winning tickets T/Qpdt: £68.00 to a £1 stake. Pool £4,158.18. 45.20 winning tickets WG

4838 DEAUVILLE (R-H)

Tuesday, August 9

OFFICIAL GOING: Turf: soft; fibresand: standard

4896a PRIX BEACHCOMBER HOTELS "LE SHANDRANI" (PRIX DE LEAUPARTIE) (CONDITIONS) (3YO) (TURF) 6f 110y(S)

3:25 (12:00) 3-Y-O **£12,500** (£5,000; £3,750; £2,500; £1,250)

RPR

1 **Realisatrice (FR)**[14] 4422 3-9-1 0.......... IoritzMendizabal 7 91
(Robert Collet, France) **7/2**[2]

2 *¾* **Millet (FR)**[112] 3-9-4 0.......... StephanePasquier 8 92
(G Botti, Italy) **17/2**

3 *¾* **Vauville (IRE)**[24] 3-9-1 0..........(p) Christophe-PatriceLemaire 4 87
(Y De Nicolay, France) **16/1**

4 *hd* **Western Choice (USA)**[7] 3-9-1 0.......... MaximeGuyon 1 86
(A Fabre, France) **13/10**[1]

5 *2 ½* **Trebetherick (IRE)**[130] 3-9-1 0.......... TheoBachelot(3) 6 82
(J E Hammond, France) **63/10**[3]

6 1 1/2 **Wolf Slayer**[27] 3983 3-8-8 0... DavyBonilla 9 68
(Tom Dascombe) *broke fast: racd in front rnk in centre of trck: rdn 2f out: r.o u.p but no ex fnl f* **25/1**
7 4 **Venetien (FR)**[151] 3-9-1 0... GregoryBenoist 5 63
(M Delzangles, France) **20/1**
8 3 **Luna Negra (GER)**[14] 3-9-1 0............................. ChristopheSoumillon 2 55
(C Boutin, France) **44/5**
9 nse **Baileys Etoile**[121] 3-8-8 0... JohanVictoire 3 47
(M Figge, Germany) **47/1**

1m 19.8s (2.60) **9** Ran SP% **116.7**
WIN (incl. 1 euro stake): 4.50. PLACES: 1.60, 2.50, 3.60. DF: 16.90. SF: 25.20.
Owner Fabrice Zouari **Bred** Haras Du Quesnay **Trained** Chantilly, France

4402 BEVERLEY (R-H)

Wednesday, August 10

OFFICIAL GOING: Soft (6.3)
Wind: Breezy half against Weather: Overcast andheavy showers

4897 JOURNAL CLASSIFIED CLAIMING STKS 7f 100y
2:10 (2:10) (Class 6) 3-Y-O+ **£1,811** (£539; £269; £134) **Stalls** Low

Form RPR
0345 **1** **Bolodenka (IRE)**[15] 4404 9-9-0 69.................................. PaulHanagan 3 78
(Richard Fahey) *chsd clr ldr: gd hdwy to ld 2f out and sn clr: rdn out* **9/4**[1]
0633 **2** 8 **Meandmyshadow**[8] 4638 3-8-8 60.........................(p) GrahamGibbons 2 56
(Alan Brown) *chsd ldrs: hdwy 3f out: rdn to chse wnr wl over 1f out: sn drvn and no imp* **16/1**
3260 **3** 1 1/4 **Ginger Grey (IRE)**[15] 4404 4-9-2 71......................(b) SilvestreDeSousa 7 57
(David O'Meara) *in tch: hdwy on inner over 2f out: rdn wl over 1f out: kpt on same pce* **3/1**[2]
5443 **4** nk **Bonnie Prince Blue**[29] 3953 8-8-11 68.............................. DaleSwift(3) 6 54
(Ian McInnes) *chsd ldrs: effrt wl over 2f out: sn rdn and one pce* **14/1**
1351 **5** 1 **Opus Maximus (IRE)**[9] 4601 6-9-2 67.....................(p) StephenCraine 11 54
(Jennie Candlish) *hld up in rr: hdwy on outer over 2f out: rdn along wl over 1f out: kpt on ins fnl f: n.d* **4/1**[3]
2616 **6** 1 1/4 **Fault**[16] 4394 5-9-6 68..(t) MickyFenton 10 55
(Stef Higgins) *in tch: rdn along 3f out: sn drvn and n.d* **10/1**
020/ **7** 5 **Monthly Medal**[387] 4218 8-8-5 75...(t) JulieBurke(5) 5 32
(Wilf Storey) *hld up: a in rr* **6/1**
250 **8** nse **Mark Anthony (IRE)**[12] 4513 4-9-1 67..............(b) DanielleMcCreery(5) 8 42
(Shaun Harris) *sn led and clr: rdn over 2f out: sn hdd & wknd qckly* **28/1**
-000 **9** 80 **Bigalo's Laura B (IRE)**[11] 4560 3-8-5 46........(e) DavidSimmonson(7) 14 —
(G P Kelly) *wnt lft s: a in rr: rdn along bef 1/2-way: sn bhd and t.o whn hung bdly lft 2f out* **100/1**

1m 36.72s (2.92) **Going Correction** +0.525s/f (Yiel)
WFA 3 from 4yo+ 6lb **9** Ran SP% **116.1**
Speed ratings (Par 101): **104,94,93,93,91 90,84,84,—**
toteswingers:1&2:£7.50, 2&3:£7.20, 1&3:£2.20 CSF £41.20 TOTE £3.20: £1.50, £3.00, £1.50; EX 49.60.Meandmyshadow was subject to a friendly claim.
Owner Aidan J Ryan **Bred** Kildaragh Stud **Trained** Musley Bank, N Yorks

FOCUS
Rail on inside of 5f course moved in but distances as advertised. Ladies' day at Beverley and a very wet and breezy day. After over 34mm rain in the previous 24 hours the ground was very soft and getting softer all the time. A claimer run at a strong pace and the winner came wide and raced towards the stands' side. The winner is rated to this year's form, although the race could be rated higher if taken at face value.
Bigalo's Laura B(IRE) Official explanation: trainer said filly was found to have a virus following the race

4898 EBF MOTORS.CO.UK MAIDEN STKS 7f 100y
2:40 (2:40) (Class 5) 2-Y-O **£3,428** (£1,020; £509; £254) **Stalls** Low

Form RPR
0 **1** **Swift Encounter (IRE)**[24] 4122 2-9-3 0.......................... TonyHamilton 3 70
(Ann Duffield) *awkward s and towards rr: pushed along 1/2-way: rdn over 2f out: hdwy over 1f out: swtchd rt ent fnl f: styd on strly to ld nr fin* **25/1**
46 **2** 1/2 **Ventura Spirit**[33] 3826 2-9-3 0.. PaulHanagan 9 69
(Richard Fahey) *led: wd st: jnd and rdn 2f out: drvn ent fnl f: sn hung rt and hdd last 50yds* **11/4**[3]
40 **3** 4 **Curtain Patch (USA)**[24] 4122 2-8-12 0.............................. TomEaves 6 55
(Bryan Smart) *in tch: hdwy 1/2-way: rdn to chse ldrs 2f out: drvn over 1f out: kpt on ins fnl f* **20/1**
00 **4** 2 **Forster Street (IRE)**[40] 3583 2-9-3 0.............................. DavidAllan 8 55+
(Tim Easterby) *chsd ldng pair: rdn along wl over 2f out: drvn over 1f out: kpt on same pce* **33/1**
2 **5** 2 1/2 **Ghalaa (IRE)**[15] 4402 2-8-12 0.. RichardHills 1 44
(Mark Johnston) *trckd wnr: hdwy to chal over 2f out: sn rdn and ev ch tl drvn and wknd ent fnl f* **5/4**[1]
0 **6** 1 1/2 **Sweet Fairnando**[27] 4002 2-8-12 0.............................. DuranFentiman 5 41
(Tim Easterby) *a towards rr* **50/1**
0 **7** 7 **Zavier (FR)**[19] 4264 2-9-3 0.. SilvestreDeSousa 2 29
(Mahmood Al Zarooni) *chsd ldrs on inner: rdn along wl over 2f out: drvn over 1f out and sn wknd* **9/4**[2]
8 14 **Eastern Seel** 2-8-12 0.. AdamCarter(5) 4 —
(Tim Easterby) *s.i.s: a in rr: bhd fr 1/2-way: eased over 1f out* **25/1**

1m 39.74s (5.94) **Going Correction** +0.525s/f (Yiel) **8** Ran SP% **119.2**
Speed ratings (Par 94): **87,86,81,79,76 75,67,51**
toteswingers:1&2:£5.70, 2&3:£5.20, 1&3:£11.70 CSF £92.27 TOTE £26.20: £3.30, £1.20, £3.10; EX 108.20.
Owner Middleham Park Racing Vii **Bred** C McEvoy **Trained** Constable Burton, N Yorks

FOCUS
The rain continued to fall and this extended 7f was a real test of stamina for these juveniles. It was almost certainly an ordinary event and the form must be treated with caution, although it appears relatively sound.

NOTEBOOK
Swift Encounter(IRE), who had shown little on his quick ground debut at Redcar, had it all to do straightening up but he stuck to his task in willing fashion and grabbed the spoils near the line. He looks a backward type and, a half-brother to a chase winner, he should make a decent handicapper over middle distances at three.
Ventura Spirit ◆, having his third run after two reasonable efforts at York, set out as if stamina was not a worry. He shook off the favourite but edged right and was nabbed near the line. He can certainly find a race. (op 3-1 tchd 5-2)
Curtain Patch(USA), half-a-dozen lengths behind Swift Encounter when having his second start at Redcar, seemed to show vast improvement and is now qualified for a nursery mark. (op 16-1)
Forster Street(IRE), who gave an anxious moment or two at the start, had shown little in two previous runs and is another who now has the option of the nursery route. (op 28-1)
Ghalaa(IRE), narrowly beaten by an odds-on shot in a slowly run fast-ground affair over this C&D, moved upsides the runner-up once in line for home but jinked left and stopped to nothing a furlong out. Her powerful stable is struggling for winners at present but the heavy ground was presumably to blame. (op 5-6)
Sweet Fairnando, well beaten on her debut, stuck on in her own time to finish on the heels of the first five. She looks to have stamina in abundance.
Zavier(FR), who cost 110,000 euros at the breeze-up sales, lacks size and was struggling to keep up once in line for home. His rider brought him across the track from the far side rail to the stands' side, presumably checking out the state of the ground for his subsequent mounts. (op 4-1)

4899 HULL DAILY MAIL MAIDEN AUCTION STKS 5f
3:15 (3:17) (Class 5) 2-Y-O **£2,264** (£673; £336; £168) **Stalls** Low

Form RPR
2 **1** **Key Ambition**[17] 4358 2-8-13 0.. TomEaves 11 80+
(Bryan Smart) *cl up: led 1/2-way: rdn and qcknd wl ent fnl f: kpt on strly* **10/3**[2]
2222 **2** 3 3/4 **First Fast Now (IRE)**[15] 4406 2-8-8 69.................... SilvestreDeSousa 7 62
(Nigel Tinkler) *in tch: hdwy over 2f out and sn pushed along: rdn over 1f out: drvn to chse wnr ins fnl f: no imp* **4/1**[3]
0200 **3** 1/2 **Red Shadow**[11] 4558 2-8-4 57.. AndrewMullen 1 56
(Alan Brown) *cl up: rdn along 2f out and ev ch tl drvn and one pce ent fnl f* **14/1**
000 **4** 3 **Elusive Bonus (IRE)**[39] 3610 2-8-4 55.......................... JamesSullivan 6 45
(David O'Meara) *towards rr: hdwy wl over 1f out: sn rdn and styd on ins fnl f: nrst fin* **16/1**
544 **5** 1 3/4 **Baltic Bomber (IRE)**[17] 4365 2-8-11 69.............................. PBBeggy 3 46
(John Quinn) *cl up: effrt 1/2-way: sn rdn and ev ch tl drvn and wknd over 1f out* **5/2**[1]
0 **6** nse **Hareem Dancer**[19] 4283 2-8-3 0....................................(e[1]) NeilFarley(5) 9 42
(David Nicholls) *in rr tl sme late hdwy* **20/1**
5 **7** 1/2 **No More Games**[23] 4147 2-8-13 0.............................. PhillipMakin 12 46
(Kevin Ryan) *wnt lft s: chsd ldrs: cl up 1/2-way: rdn along 2f out and grad wknd* **14/1**
8 3/4 **Sir Windsorlot (IRE)** 2-8-11 0.. BarryMcHugh 5 41+
(John Quinn) *dwlt and in rr: hdwy 2f out: swtchd rt and rdn wl over 1f out: sn no imp* **10/1**
00 **9** 1 1/2 **Dream Walker (FR)**[14] 4436 2-8-11 0.......................... PatrickMathers 2 36
(Ian McInnes) *cl up: rdn along 1/2-way: drvn wl over 1f out and grad wknd* **40/1**
4 **10** 3 1/4 **Indyend**[9] 4606 2-8-4 0.. DuranFentiman 4 17+
(Tim Easterby) *wnt lft s: chsd ldrs: rdn along over 2f out: sn wknd* **12/1**
6 **11** 5 **Crimson Sea (IRE)**[15] 4406 2-8-7 0 ow1.......................... PJMcDonald 8 —
(Ben Haslam) *led: rdn along and hdd 1/2-way: wknd wl over 1f out* **9/1**

65.46 secs (1.96) **Going Correction** +0.325s/f (Good) **11** Ran SP% **124.8**
Speed ratings (Par 94): **97,91,90,85,82 82,81,80,78,72 64**
toteswingers:1&2:£2.80, 2&3:£9.60, 1&3:£9.50 CSF £18.41 TOTE £3.20: £1.30, £1.50, £5.20; EX 11.80.
Owner Ron Hull **Bred** Giles W Pritchard-Gordon (farming) Ltd **Trained** Hambleton, N Yorks

FOCUS
A modest maiden auction race with the vast majority of the field in a line across the track at the halfway stage but in the end a most decisive winner of some potential. The form looks straigfhtforward, although the winner is potentially better, but is limited by the placed horses.

NOTEBOOK
Key Ambition, a likeable-type, had finished runner-up behind a clear-cut winner first time at Carlisle. Making light of the conditions and racing towards the stands' side rail, he travelled strongly and came clear in the end. He should be competitive in nurseries from a mark in the low-80s. (op 3-1 tchd 7-2)
First Fast Now(IRE) finished runner-up for the fifth time in a succession. She does nothing wrong but her nursery mark of 69 looks on the high side. (op 3-1)
Red Shadow, having her eighth start and rated just 57, had run below-par on her two most recent outings. (op 16-1)
Elusive Bonus(IRE), rated 55 after three starts, seemed to show much-improved form, clearly being suited by the rain-soaked ground. (op 14-1 tchd 12-1)
Baltic Bomber(IRE), progressive in three previous starts and rated 69, was another who seemed to find the testing conditions against him. (op 7-2)
Hareem Dancer, withdrawn after injuring her rider at the start on her second intended outing, wore an eyeshield. Walked to post, she put in some steady late work and hopefully is learning to settle down and finding out what the game is about. (tchd 25-1)

4900 RAWFIELD AND PARAGON DATA H'CAP 5f
3:45 (3:45) (Class 5) (0-75,75) 3-Y-O+ **£3,234** (£962; £481; £240) **Stalls** Low

Form RPR
2210 **1** **Caranbola**[12] 4516 5-9-8 **73**.. RobertWinston 8 85
(Mel Brittain) *towards rr and swtchd lft after s: hdwy to chse ldrs over 2f out and sn rdn: drvn to chal ins fnl f: kpt on wl to ld last 40yds* **5/1**[2]
0004 **2** 1/2 **Haajes**[18] 4327 7-9-10 **75**.. MickyFenton 13 86
(Paul Midgley) *cl up: rdn and slt ld over 1f out: drvn ins fnl f: hdd and nt qckn last 40yds* **5/1**[2]
4314 **3** 1 **Sleepy Blue Ocean**[17] 4371 5-9-3 **68**....................(p) SilvestreDeSousa 7 75
(John Balding) *in tch: hdwy wl over 1f out: rdn ent fnl f and ev ch tl no ex last 75yds* **9/2**[1]
3123 **4** 1 1/2 **Sands Of Dee (USA)**[21] 4197 4-9-6 **71**.......................... AdrianNicholls 11 73
(David Nicholls) *towards rr: hdwy on stands' rail 2f out: sn rdn and styd on strly ins fnl f: nrst fin* **8/1**
3306 **5** shd **Ingleby Star (IRE)**[11] 4539 6-9-1 **69**..............................(p) PaulPickard(3) 9 70
(Ian McInnes) *qckly away: led: rdn 2f out: drvn and hdd over 1f out: kpt on same pce ins fnl f* **16/1**
450 **6** 2 1/2 **Select Committee**[15] 4405 6-9-2 **72**..............................(v) ShaneBKelly(5) 5 64+
(John Quinn) *in tch: hdwy to chse ldrs 2f out: sn rdn and one pce appr fnl f* **12/1**
1531 **7** 1 **Eastern Hills**[22] 4182 6-9-1 **71**.......................................(p) NeilFarley(5) 6 60
(Alan McCabe) *chsd ldrs: rdn along bef 1/2-way: sn one pce* **6/1**[3]
031 **7** dht **Dancing Freddy (IRE)**[11] 4539 4-9-2 **70**.............(tp) RobertLButler(3) 10 59
(Richard Guest) *cl up: effrt 2f out and ev ch tl rdn and wknd over 1f out* **12/1**
0502 **9** 3 3/4 **Chosen One (IRE)**[7] 4678 6-8-12 **63**.............................. JamesSullivan 3 38
(Ruth Carr) *cl up: rdn along over 2f out: sn wknd* **6/1**[3]
3140 **10** 2 3/4 **Media Jury**[3] 4820 4-8-8 **59**..(v) BarryMcHugh 1 24
(John Wainwright) *a in rr* **14/1**

64.71 secs (1.21) **Going Correction** +0.325s/f (Good)
WFA 3 from 4yo+ 3lb **10** Ran SP% **119.1**
Speed ratings (Par 103): **103,102,100,98,98 94,92,92,86,82**
toteswingers:1&2:£8.20, 2&3:£5.60, 1&3:£5.90 CSF £30.99 CT £125.73 TOTE £6.50: £2.40, £1.90, £1.80; EX 34.50.
Owner Mel Brittain **Bred** T E Pocock **Trained** Warthill, N Yorks

FOCUS
The rain had stopped ahead of this tight sprint handicap with the main action towards the stands' side rail. The runner-up was showing his best form this year.

4901 WOLD CONSTRUCTION BRIAN AUCHTERLOUNIE MEMORIAL H'CAP — 1m 1f 207y
4:20 (4:20) (Class 4) (0-85,82) 3-Y-0+ **£4,528** (£1,347; £673; £336) **Stalls** Low

Form RPR

5620 **1** **Ailsa Craig (IRE)**[49] 3275 5-9-7 **75** .... TonyHamilton 1 83
(Edwin Tuer) *trckd ldng pair: hdwy to chse ldr 2f out: rdn to chal over 1f out: sn drvn and styd on gamely to ld last 50yds* **14/1**

0632 **2** ½ **Licence To Till (USA)**[4] 4801 4-9-13 **81** .... SilvestreDeSousa 5 88
(Mark Johnston) *led: wd on home turn to stands' rail: rdn over 2f out: drvn over 1f out: hdd and no ex last 50yds* **15/8**[1]

3113 **3** 6 **Quanah Parker (IRE)**[25] 4109 5-9-12 **80** .... RobertWinston 10 75
(Neil King) *trckd ldrs: hdwy to chse wnr 3f out: n.m.r and swtchd rt wl over 1f out: sn drvn and one pce* **11/4**[2]

1151 **4** 1¾ **Fossgate**[9] 4612 10-9-1 **72** 6ex .... AmyRyan(3) 6 64
(James Bethell) *hld up in rr: hdwy wl over 2f out: rdn wl over 1f out: nvr nr ldrs* **9/1**

4354 **5** 6 **Count Bertoni (IRE)**[27] 4004 4-9-10 **78** .... DanielTudhope 9 58
(David O'Meara) *chsd ldrs: pushed along 3f out: rdn over 2f out and sn one pce* **11/1**

0-00 **6** 4 **Gritstone**[46] 3406 4-9-11 **79** .... PaulHanagan 2 51
(Richard Fahey) *in tch: pushed along and sme hdwy 3f out: rdn over 2f out and sn btn* **7/1**

3103 **7** 1¼ **Amazing Blue Sky**[7] 4674 5-9-7 **75** .... JamesSullivan 7 44
(Ruth Carr) *chsd ldr: rdn along and n.m.r 3f out: sn drvn and wknd* **11/2**[3]

2300 **8** 5 **Petomic (IRE)**[4] 4784 6-8-9 **66** .... RobertLButler(3) 3 25
(Richard Guest) *dwlt: a in rr* **33/1**

2m 11.0s (4.00) **Going Correction** +0.525s/f (Yiel) **8** Ran SP% **117.3**
Speed ratings (Par 105): **105,104,99,98,93 90,89,85**
toteswingers:1&2:£7.30, 2&3:£2.50, 1&3:£9.90 CSF £41.83 CT £98.59 TOTE £19.40: £4.10, £1.10, £1.10; EX 70.00.
Owner Ontoawinner **Bred** P J B O'Callaghan **Trained** Great Smeaton, N Yorks
■ Stewards' Enquiry : Tony Hamilton caution; careless riding
FOCUS
A strong pace and the first two pulled clear in the end. They set the standard.
Amazing Blue Sky Official explanation: jockey said gelding hung right

4902 DOVE HOUSE, LOVE YOU 2 H'CAP — 1m 1f 207y
4:50 (4:50) (Class 5) (0-70,70) 3-Y-0+ **£2,264** (£673; £336; £168) **Stalls** Low

Form RPR

-010 **1** **Carragold**[12] 4513 5-8-11 **53** .... RobertWinston 11 63
(Mel Brittain) *trckd ldrs: hdwy and wd st: rdn to chal 2f out: drvn to ld ent fnl f: sn edgd lft and kpt on wl* **9/1**

2533 **2** 2 **Philharmonic Hall**[17] 4364 3-8-11 **62** .... (p) BarryMcHugh 8 68
(Richard Fahey) *hld up: hdwy and wd st to stands' rail: rdn to ld over 2f out: drvn and hdd ent fnl f: sn n.m.r and swtchd rt: kpt on towards fin* **12/1**

4542 **3** nk **Hurlingham**[9] 4612 7-8-11 **53** .... (be) PhillipMakin 15 58
(Michael Easterby) *in tch on outer: hdwy 3f out: swtchd rt 2f out: rdn to chal over 1f out and ev ch tl drvn and one pce ins fnl f* **4/1**[1]

-106 **4** 1¾ **Bouggatti**[68] 2677 3-9-1 **66** .... PaulHanagan 13 71+
(William Jarvis) *dwlt and in rr: hdwy on outer and wd to stands' rail 3f out: rdn to chse ldrs over 1f out: drvn and edgd rt ins fnl f: one pce* **9/2**[2]

-434 **5** 1¾ **Bright Applause**[23] 4150 3-8-8 **62** .... PaulPickard(3) 7 60
(Tracy Waggott) *trckd ldrs: hdwy over 2f out: rdn to chse ldrs over 1f out: drvn and wknd ent fnl f* **7/1**[3]

2200 **6** 4½ **Nolecce**[17] 4367 4-9-3 **62** .... (p) RobertLButler(3) 5 51
(Richard Guest) *midfield: hdwy to chse ldrs over 2f out: rdn wl over 1f out and no imp* **16/1**

404 **7** 5 **Spanish Plume**[11] 4529 3-9-5 **70** .... GrahamGibbons 10 49
(Reg Hollinshead) *chsd ldrs: rdn along over 4f out: sn wknd* **16/1**

3563 **8** 10 **Star Addition**[24] 4128 5-8-9 **51** oh3 .... DavidAllan 2 10
(Eric Alston) *nvr nr ldrs* **16/1**

3003 **9** 1 **Magic Millie (IRE)**[14] 4438 4-8-10 **52** .... DanielTudhope 9 —
(David O'Meara) *led: rdn along and hdd 3f out: sn wknd* **11/1**

3604 **10** 1¼ **Highland Love**[17] 4367 6-8-10 **52** .... TonyHamilton 1 —
(Jedd O'Keeffe) *cl up on inner: led 3f out: sn rdn and hdd over 2f out: wknd wl over 1f out* **17/2**

0002 **11** 1 **Celtic Step**[25] 4112 7-8-8 **53** .... LeeTopliss(3) 4 —
(Peter Niven) *a towards rr* **10/1**

6020 **12** 7 **Cottam Stella**[11] 4560 3-7-9 **51** .... NeilFarley(5) 14 —
(Mel Brittain) *a in rr: bhd fnl 3f* **16/1**

000 **13** 20 **Mainland (USA)**[25] 4109 5-9-4 **60** .... FrederikTylicki 12 —
(Tracy Waggott) *a in rr: bhd fnl 3f* **33/1**

2m 11.52s (4.52) **Going Correction** +0.525s/f (Yiel)
WFA 3 from 4yo+ 9lb **13** Ran SP% **122.8**
Speed ratings (Par 103): **102,100,100,98,97 93,89,81,80,79 79,73,57**
toteswingers:1&2:£21.80, 2&3:£12.70, 1&3:£11.30 CSF £115.76 CT £509.93 TOTE £11.70: £3.20, £4.70, £2.20; EX 109.90.
Owner Mel Brittain **Bred** Darley **Trained** Warthill, N Yorks
FOCUS
The top-weight was 8lb below the race ceiling. Modest fare but a sound pace and significantly the first four home steered a wide course in the back straight. The third is probably the best guide.

4903 FINDAPROPERTY H'CAP (DIV I) (PART OF THE BEVERLEY MIDDLE DISTANCE SERIES) — 1m 4f 16y
5:20 (5:20) (Class 6) (0-65,63) 3-Y-0+ **£2,264** (£673; £336; £168) **Stalls** Low

Form RPR

-646 **1** **Ferney Boy**[24] 4129 5-8-13 **48** .... RobertWinston 9 57
(Chris Fairhurst) *towards rr: racd wd bk st and hdwy to trck ldrs over 4f out: effrt and wd st to stands' rail over 2f out: sn rdn and chal over 1f out: drvn ent fnl f: styd on strly to ld last 75yds* **11/2**[2]

0-04 **2** ¾ **Maybeme**[24] 4125 5-8-10 **52** .... TerenceFury(7) 8 59
(Neville Bycroft) *in tch: hdwy to trck ldrs 3f out: effrt and n.m.r wl over 1f out: swtchd rt and rdn appr fnl f: styd on to chal and ev ch whn hung rt and no ex last 50yds* **18/1**

1160 **3** nk **Light The City (IRE)**[17] 4366 4-9-6 **55** .... JamesSullivan 3 62
(Ruth Carr) *hld up: hdwy 2f out: rdn to ld briefly ins fnl f: drvn: edgd rt and hdd last 75yds* **11/2**[2]

4003 **4** ½ **Maslak (IRE)**[9] 4613 7-10-0 **63** .... MickyFenton 7 69
(Peter Hiatt) *towards rr: hdwy wl over 2f out: sn rdn and styd on wl ins fnl f: nrst fin* **6/1**[3]

0301 **5** 2¾ **Kian's Delight**[17] 4366 3-8-11 **57** .... DuranFentiman 4 59
(Jedd O'Keeffe) *led: rdn along 3f out: drvn wl over 1f out: hdd & wknd jst ins fnl f* **9/4**[1]

-066 **6** 1 **Deferto Delphi**[40] 3574 4-8-9 **49** .... ShaneBKelly(5) 10 49
(Barry Murtagh) *hld up: hdwy to chse ldrs over 4f out: wd to stands' rail and n.m.r over 2f out: sn rdn and kpt on same pce* **10/1**

5646 **7** 2¼ **Fairy Mist (IRE)**[14] 4442 4-9-4 **53** .... (t) FrederikTylicki 11 49
(Brian Rothwell) *cl up: rdn along over 2f out: drvn over 1f out: wknd appr fnl f* **10/1**

14-0 **8** 2¼ **Master Nimbus**[17] 4366 11-9-10 **59** .... PBBeggy 2 52
(John Quinn) *trckd ldrs: effrt on inner 3f out: rdn along 2f out: drvn and wknd over 1f out* **10/1**

5506 **9** 4 **Royal Composer (IRE)**[15] 4409 8-8-10 **45** .... DavidAllan 6 31
(Tim Easterby) *prom: rdn along 5f out: sn wknd* **10/1**

2m 48.8s (9.00) **Going Correction** +0.525s/f (Yiel)
WFA 3 from 4yo+ 11lb **9** Ran SP% **117.5**
Speed ratings (Par 101): **91,90,90,89,88 87,85,84,81**
toteswingers:1&2:£14.30, 2&3:£13.40, 1&3:£6.90 CSF £98.46 CT £573.62 TOTE £6.60: £2.10, £4.00, £2.40; EX 98.70.
Owner Mrs P J Taylor-Garthwaite **Bred** K And P J Garthwaite **Trained** Middleham Moor, N Yorks
FOCUS
A low-grade handicap and the pace was sound in the deteriorating conditions. The time was slow compared with division II and the winner is rated to his early maiden form.

4904 FINDAPROPERTY H'CAP (DIV II) (PART OF THE BEVERLEY MIDDLE DISTANCE SERIES) — 1m 4f 16y
5:50 (5:51) (Class 6) (0-65,65) 3-Y-0+ **£2,264** (£673; £336; £168) **Stalls** Low

Form RPR

2614 **1** **Grey Command (USA)**[9] 4612 6-9-10 **61** .... RobertWinston 6 73
(Mel Brittain) *trckd ldrs: hdwy on outer 4f out: wd st and rdn to take slt ld 2f out: drvn clr appr fnl f: styd on strly* **5/1**[3]

0034 **2** 6 **Politbureau**[15] 4409 4-9-0 **51** .... JamesSullivan 9 53
(Michael Easterby) *hld up towards rr: hdwy over 4f out: wd st to stands' rail and sn chsng ldrs: rdn wl over 1f out: drvn and kpt on ins fnl f: tk 2nd nr line* **11/2**

0-42 **3** nk **Kodicil (IRE)**[92] 1972 3-8-8 **56** .... GrahamGibbons 4 58
(Tim Walford) *cl up: effrt 3f out: sn rdn and ev ch tl drvn and one pce appr fnl f: lost 2nd nr line* **5/2**[1]

4623 **4** 8 **Market Maker (IRE)**[23] 4151 3-8-6 **54** ow1 .... (b) DavidAllan 10 43
(Tim Easterby) *hld up: hdwy 4f out: rdn to chse ldrs wl over 2f out: sn drvn and no imp fnl 2f* **7/2**[2]

1603 **5** 3¼ **Denison Flyer**[4] 4814 4-8-7 **49** .... (p) LanceBetts(5) 5 33
(Lawrence Mullaney) *trckd ldrs on inner: pushed along 5f out: rdn over 3f out: drvn and wknd fnl 2f* **7/1**

-543 **6** 6 **Operateur (IRE)**[58] 2571 3-8-12 **63** .... PatrickDonaghy(3) 11 37
(Ben Haslam) *led: rdn along 4f out: hdd 3f out and sn wknd* **13/2**

0/06 **7** 46 **Freddie Bolt**[15] 4408 5-8-9 **46** oh1 .... PJMcDonald 3 —
(Frederick Watson) *a in rr: bhd fnl 3f* **28/1**

000- **8** 1½ **French Applause (IRE)**[285] 7214 5-8-13 **50** .... PatrickMathers 2 —
(Mike Sowersby) *chsd ldrs: rdn along 1/2-way: sn lost pl and bhd fnl 3f* **28/1**

2m 46.7s (6.90) **Going Correction** +0.525s/f (Yiel)
WFA 3 from 4yo+ 11lb **8** Ran SP% **115.6**
Speed ratings (Par 101): **98,94,93,88,86 82,51,50**
toteswingers:1&2:£7.50, 2&3:£3.70, 1&3:£4.20. Tote Super 7: Win: Not won. Place: £385.70. CSF £32.87 CT £82.97 TOTE £5.00: £2.00, £2.30, £1.10; EX 36.50.
Owner Mel Brittain **Bred** Darley **Trained** Warthill, N Yorks
■ Stewards' Enquiry : Robert Winston one day ban; careless riding
FOCUS
More of the same and again the pace was sound. The quicker division and the winner is rated back to his best.
Freddie Bolt Official explanation: jockey said horse was unsuited by soft ground
T/Jkpt: Not won. T/Plt: £93.00 to a £1 stake. Pool of £67,929.34 - 532.89 winning tickets. T/Qpdt: £11.40 to a £1 stake. Pool of £4,941.09 - 318.92 winning tickets. JR

4660 KEMPTON (A.W) (R-H)
Wednesday, August 10

OFFICIAL GOING: Standard
Wind: Brisk across Weather: Sunny spells early

4905 FREE ENTRY FOR BETDAQ MEMBERS APPRENTICE H'CAP — 1m 3f (P)
6:00 (6:00) (Class 4) (0-80,80) 3-Y-O **£4,075** (£1,212; £606; £303) **Stalls** Low

Form RPR

0044 **1** **Twice Bitten**[26] 4060 3-9-7 **77** .... MatthewCosham 7 86
(James Toller) *trckd ldr: chal fr 4f out tl slt advantage over 2f out: pushed out fnl f* **7/2**[2]

2025 **2** 1 **Swindy**[17] 4355 3-9-10 **80** .... RyanPowell 1 87
(Paul Cole) *chsd ldrs: rdn and styd on over 2f out to chse wnr 1f out: kpt on but a hld* **7/2**[2]

1006 **3** 3½ **Gower Rules (IRE)**[2] 4862 3-8-7 **63** .... RosieJessop 2 64
(John Bridger) *led: rdn and jnd fr 4f out: hdd over 2f out: sn drvn: one pce and lost 2nd 1f out* **16/1**

1-42 **4** 4½ **Reem Star**[7] 4664 3-8-13 **72** .... CharlesBishop(3) 4 65
(Ed Dunlop) *mid-div: rdn 3f out and sn no imp on ldrs: wl hld fnl 2f* **7/4**[1]

1325 **5** 5 **Libritish**[11] 4530 3-9-6 **76** .... (b) TobyAtkinson 6 60
(Marco Botti) *in rr: sn rdn: rn in snatches after: drvn over 3f out: and no imp on ldrs: wl btn fnl 2f* **15/2**[3]

4025 **6** 4½ **Persian Herald**[33] 3809 3-9-3 **73** .... JamesRogers 8 49
(William Muir) *s.i.s: rdn 4f out: a in rr* **14/1**

4014 **7** 2¼ **Ugo (USA)**[7] 4664 3-8-11 **72** .... JakePayne(5) 5 44
(Heather Main) *chsd ldrs: rdn over 3f out: btn sn after* **11/1**

2m 19.5s (-2.40) **Going Correction** -0.05s/f (Stan) **7** Ran SP% **113.5**
Speed ratings (Par 102): **106,105,102,99,95 92,90**
toteswingers: 1&2 £3.20, 1&3 £12.80, 2&3 £12.20. CSF £15.89 CT £168.29 TOTE £5.20: £2.90, £1.70; EX 22.30 Trifecta £689.90 Pool: £8,400.52 - 9.01 winning units..
Owner The Cobra Partnership **Bred** M E Wates **Trained** Newmarket, Suffolk
FOCUS
This was a modest 3yo handicap, confined to apprentice riders. It was run at a decent early pace but few landed a serious blow and the first pair dominated from the furlong pole. There are doubts over the form but the winner rates a personal best.

Reem Star Official explanation: one-day ban; careless riding (24th Aug)

4906 BETDAQ.COM EXCHANGE PRICE MULTIPLES MEDIAN AUCTION MAIDEN STKS — 7f (P)

6:30 (6:31) (Class 5) 2-Y-O — **£2,264** (£673; £336; £168) **Stalls** Low

Form — RPR

02 **1** **Charitable Act (FR)**[18] 4339 2-9-3 0 DarryllHolland 8 — 76
(William Muir) *s.i.s: t.k.h: hdwy on outside fr 4f out to chse ldr over 3f out: str chal fr 2f out: led appr fnl f: drvn out* **2/1**[2]

5 **2** 1 ¾ **Obliteright (IRE)**[11] 4545 2-9-3 0 JimCrowley 11 — 71
(William Knight) *sn led: rdn along 3f out: jnd 2f out: hdd appr fnl f: kpt on but nt pce of wnr fnl 120yds* **14/1**

42 **3** nk **Firestarter**[10] 4580 2-9-3 0 KierenFallon 10 — 76+
(David Elsworth) *chsd ldr tl rdn along and dropped to 3rd over 3f out: styng on again whn veered bdly lft over 2f out and wnt to r alone stands' rail: styd on again fnl f to take 3rd clsng stages: gng on cl home but nt rcvr* **6/5**[1]

00 **4** 2 **Onebytheknows**[18] 4339 2-9-3 0 PatDobbs 6 — 67+
(Richard Hannon) *in rr: drvn and hdwy fr 3f out: styng on whn hmpd over 2f out: kpt on again fnl f but nt trble ldrs* **50/1**

6 **5** 1 **Viscount Vert (IRE)**[64] 2787 2-9-3 0 LiamKeniry 3 — 65+
(Andrew Balding) *s.i.s: in rr: pushed along and hdwy over 2f out: kpt on fnl f: nt rch ldrs* **13/2**[3]

00 **6** ½ **Always A Sinner (USA)**[16] 4390 2-9-3 0 ShaneKelly 13 — 62
(William Knight) *s.i.s: in rr: pushed along over 2f out: styd on fnl f: nt rch ldrs* **100/1**

7 ½ **Swift Cat** 2-9-0 0 KierenFox(3) 4 — 60
(John Best) *in tch: rdn and outpcd over 3f out: styd on again u.p fr over 2f out: nt trble ldrs* **25/1**

0 **8** ¾ **Dont Take Me Alive**[28] 3986 2-9-0 0 JohnFahy(3) 1 — 58
(Clive Cox) *t.k.h: chsd ldrs: rdn 3f out: wknd fr 2f out* **33/1**

9 shd **Compton Air (USA)** 2-9-3 0 (t) JamesDoyle 7 — 58
(Hans Adielsson) *s.i.s: in rr: sme hdwy on ins over 2f out: no imp on ldrs and wknd over 1f out* **40/1**

0 **10** 5 **Waspy**[13] 4471 2-8-12 0 RoystonFfrench 2 — 40
(Ed Dunlop) *chsd ldrs: rdn over 2f out: wknd wl over 1f out* **33/1**

0 **11** 9 **Pinseeker (IRE)**[21] 4205 2-9-3 0 (b[1]) IanMongan 5 — 22
(Peter Winkworth) *sn drvn to chse ldrs but t.k.h: rdn and btn 3f out* **33/1**

1m 27.82s (1.82) **Going Correction** -0.05s/f (Stan) — **11** Ran SP% **116.8**
Speed ratings (Par 94): **87,85,84,82,81 80,80,79,79,73 63**
toteswingers: 1&2 £6.50, 1&3 £1.10, 2&3 £6.00. CSF £27.11 TOTE £3.70: £1.30, £2.50, £1.40; EX 42.50 Trifecta £129.60 Pool: £1,973.53 - 11.26 winning units..
Owner Muir Racing Partnership - Chester **Bred** Aleyrion Bloodstock Ltd **Trained** Lambourn, Berks

FOCUS
A fair juvenile maiden run at an average pace. The third threw it away and can be rated as having finished upsides the winner.

NOTEBOOK
Charitable Act(FR) finished second in a maiden that is working out nicely at Salisbury 18 days earlier and, relishing this extra furlong, went one better with a professional display. He was always doing enough from the furlong marker and should be open to further improvement now his best short-term trip has been established. A mark of around 80 can be expected for nurseries. (tchd 7-4)
Obliteight(IRE) stepped up nicely on his debut effort at Lingfield 11 days earlier and will not mind returning to another furlong. He can be found a race before that long. (op 12-1)
Firestarter\n\x\x seemed sure to enjoy stepping up a furlong for this AW debut. However, he proved reluctant to load into the gates and then refused to settle after being rushed up from his poor draw. He was still in there with every chance 2f out but went violently left over to the stands' rail, nearly causing Fallon to come off, and lost all chance. The fact he kept on thereafter to bag third proves his engine, but he evidently has a lot of maturing to do and now plenty to prove. Official explanation: jockey said colt veered left in the straight (op 11-8)
Onebytheknows ◆, who came into this AW debut with two duck eggs next to his name. He was hampered by the third in the home straight and would have finished closer but for that, so the extra furlong obviously helped him. Nurseries are now an option. Official explanation: jockey said colt suffered interference in the straight (op 40-1)
Viscount Vert(IRE) was another who seemed sure to enjoy stepping up a furlong. He raced lazily early on but managed to find all sorts of trouble from the home turn and finished with purpose once getting organised. He's well worth another chance over this distance. Official explanation: jockey said colt was hampered turning in (op 7-1 tchd 8-1)
Compton Air(USA) Official explanation: jockey said gelding missed the break
Pinseeker(IRE) Official explanation: jockey said gelding ran green

4907 LAY BACK AND WIN AT BETDAQ.COM NURSERY — 7f (P)

7:00 (7:01) (Class 6) (0-65,65) 2-Y-O — **£1,617** (£481; £240; £120) **Stalls** Low

Form — RPR

420 **1** **Royal Majestic**[21] 4201 2-9-4 65 MartinHarley(3) 6 — 70
(Mick Channon) *chsd ldrs: rdn along over 2f out: styd on go 2nd jst ins fnl f: led fnl 120yds: styd on strly* **7/1**[3]

0001 **2** ¾ **Nifty Shiftin**[19] 4277 2-9-6 64 (b) NickyMackay 1 — 67
(David Elsworth) *chsd ldrs on ins: rdn 2f out: led appr fnl f: hdd and nt qckn fnl 120yds* **8/1**

050 **3** 2 ¼ **Clean Bowled (IRE)**[34] 3780 2-9-1 59 (bt) MartinDwyer 3 — 56
(Brian Meehan) *chsd ldrs: rdn and outpcd over 2f out: styd on again fr over 1f out: kpt on fnl f to take 3rd last strides but no imp on ldng duo* **9/1**

546 **4** nse **Storm Belt (USA)**[12] 4507 2-8-11 60 AntiocoMurgia(5) 10 — 57
(Mahmood Al Zarooni) *chsd ldrs: chal fr 4f out tl slt ld over 2f out: sn rdn: hdd appr fnl f: sn one pce: lost 3rd last strides* **9/1**

605 **5** 3 **Artistic Thread (IRE)**[23] 4159 2-9-2 60 SebSanders 7 — 49+
(Sir Mark Prescott Bt) *sn rdn to chse ldrs: drvn again 4f out: rdn over 2f out and no imp whn behnd horses wl over 1f out: styd on same pce* **3/1**[1]

5554 **6** nse **Purple Affair (IRE)**[25] 4085 2-9-5 63 (p) JamesDoyle 11 — 52
(J S Moore) *s.i.s: in rr: drvn and styd on fnl 2f: nvr rchd ldrs* **10/1**

000 **7** ¾ **Carolingian (IRE)**[21] 4205 2-9-1 59 ShaneKelly 4 — 46
(William Knight) *led: jnd 3f out: hdd over 2f out: wknd appr fnl f* **10/1**

3335 **8** 3 ½ **Queen Of The Hop**[5] 4761 2-8-13 57 LiamKeniry 9 — 35
(J S Moore) *chsd ldrs: rdn 3f out: wknd 2f out* **25/1**

503 **9** 6 **Electrickery**[27] 4012 2-9-4 62 KierenFallon 2 — 24
(Mark Johnston) *t.k.h: chsd ldrs: rdn over 2f out: sn btn* **10/3**[2]

0460 **10** ½ **Lilygloves**[5] 4756 2-7-12 45 HarryBentley(3) 13 — —
(Mick Channon) *s.i.s: swtchd sharply rt after 1f: rdn 3f out: sn no prog and wl btn fnl 2f* **40/1**

0461 **11** 3 ¾ **Abercandy (IRE)**[29] 3955 2-8-5 49 TadhgO'Shea 5 — —
(David Evans) *bhd most of way* **20/1**

0352 **12** 96 **Aljosan**[29] 3955 2-8-3 50 SophieDoyle(3) 8 — —
(David Evans) *t.k.h and hmpd sn after s: lost tch fr 4f out: eased fnl 2f: t.o* **33/1**

1m 27.23s (1.23) **Going Correction** -0.05s/f (Stan) — **12** Ran SP% **123.9**
Speed ratings (Par 92): **90,89,86,86,83 83,82,78,71,70 66,—**
toteswingers: 1&2 £15.00, 1&3 £14.50, 2&3 £17.70. CSF £62.25 CT £529.84 TOTE £9.90: £2.90, £2.30, £4.10; EX 59.70 Trifecta £1268.70 Part won. Pool: £1,714.45 - 0.10 winning units..
Owner Jaber Abdullah **Bred** Mrs B Skinner **Trained** West Ilsley, Berks

FOCUS
This modest nursery proved a messy race and it paid to race handily. The winner is rated back to his debut form.

NOTEBOOK
Royal Majestic bounced back to the sort of form that saw him finish second at Warwick on his penultimate outing and gamely defied top weight on this nursery debut. He obviously stays well and it will be interesting to see if he takes up his forthcoming entry at Newmarket. (op 11-1)
Nifty Shiftin, who was well-drawn, was only just held and showed his success from 7lb out of the handicap at Newmarket last month to be no fluke. The application of blinkers has obviously helped his cause and he rates a sound benchmark. (op 13-2)
Clean Bowled(IRE) had a decent draw and showed by far his best form to date on this switch to a nursery. He wouldn't be certain to build on this, but has found his level now. (op 12-1)
Storm Belt(USA) was another to register a career-best effort on this nursery debut and looked to need all of the trip. (op 12-1)
Artistic Thread(IRE) was unsurprisingly popular on this first run outside of maiden company, but he didn't show anything like his true colours. He proved lazy from the gates and forfeited a handy position. He also got a little messed about in the home straight and, looking at the way he kept on late, should be winning races when racing more professionally from the start. (tchd 4-1)
Purple Affair(IRE) was equipped with first-time cheekpieces and kept on at the same pace under pressure. He helps to set the level. (tchd 12-1)
Electrickery was well drawn for her nursery debut and got well backed stepping up a furlong. She found nothing when put under pressure, though, and something may have gone amiss. (op 7-2)
Aljosan Official explanation: jockey said filly was hampered in the in the early stages

4908 BETDAQ MOBILE APPS H'CAP (LONDON MILE QUALIFIER) — 1m (P)

7:30 (7:30) (Class 5) (0-70,70) 3-Y-O — **£2,264** (£673; £336; £168) **Stalls** Low

Form — RPR

005 **1** **Point Du Jour (FR)**[19] 4281 3-9-3 66 JamesDoyle 5 — 74
(Ian Wood) *t.k.h and led 1f: stdd trcking ldrs in 3rd: wnt 2nd 2f out: qckd to ld wl over 1f out: drvn ins fnl f: r.o wl* **8/1**

0302 **2** 1 ½ **Whodathought (IRE)**[18] 4338 3-9-3 69 (t) KieranO'Neill(3) 10 — 74
(Richard Hannon) *led after 1f: rdn ins fnl 3f: hdd wl over 1f out: sn outpcd by wnr: styd on same pce fnl 120yds and jst hld on for 2nd* **9/1**

063 **3** shd **Ibiza Sunset (IRE)**[18] 4320 3-9-5 68 IanMongan 9 — 73+
(Peter Winkworth) *in rr but in tch: rdn and hdwy fr 2f out: styd on to take 3rd ins fnl f: clsng on 2nd last strides* **16/1**

4350 **4** 1 ¼ **Beautiful Lando (FR)**[53] 3172 3-8-12 61 (b) EddieAhern 4 — 63
(Heather Main) *in rr: rdn and hdwy on ins over 2f out: chsd ldng duo 1f out but no imp: sn one pce into 4th fnl f* **10/1**

0456 **5** ¾ **Glass Mountain (IRE)**[23] 4160 3-9-5 68 [1] PatCosgrave 7 — 68
(James Fanshawe) *chsd ldrs: rdn over 2f out: outpcd fnl f* **5/1**[3]

2334 **6** nk **Sammy Alexander**[23] 4160 3-9-7 70 MartinLane 8 — 69+
(David Simcock) *in rr: pushed along over 2f out: styd on fnl f: nt rch ldrs* **4/1**[2]

-230 **7** 2 ¼ **Matavia Bay (IRE)**[73] 2527 3-9-1 64 KierenFallon 3 — 58
(Alan Jarvis) *t.k.h: in tch: rdn over 2f out: wknd ins fnl 2f* **7/2**[1]

011 **8** 5 **Last Destination (IRE)**[12] 4505 3-9-2 68 MartinHarley(3) 2 — 51
(Nigel Tinkler) *in tch: rdn and hdwy to chse ldrs 2f out: wknd over 1f out* **13/2**

5010 **9** 1 ¼ **Litotes**[5] 4758 3-8-5 54 (p) LukeMorris 6 — 34
(Michael Attwater) *chsd ldr after 1f tl 2f out: sn wknd* **20/1**

-506 **10** 88 **Rockerfellow**[20] 4254 3-9-5 68 SebSanders 1 — —
(J W Hills) *a in rr: lost tch fnl 3f and virtually p.u fnl 3f* **20/1**

1m 39.6s (-0.20) **Going Correction** -0.05s/f (Stan) — **10** Ran SP% **117.8**
Speed ratings (Par 100): **99,97,97,96,95 95,92,87,86,—**
toteswingers: 1&2 £14.40, 1&3 £15.40, 2&3 £19.40. CSF £78.60 CT £1138.54 TOTE £11.60: £2.90, £3.00, £2.70; EX 99.30 TRIFECTA Not won..
Owner Paddy Barrett **Bred** Frederic & Christine Ehlinger **Trained** Upper Lambourn, Berks

FOCUS
A modest 3-y-o handicap, run at a fair enough pace but those held up struggled to make a big impact. The runner-up sets the standard.
Rockerfellow Official explanation: jockey said colt was never travelling. trainer said had a breathing problem post race

4909 OLLY MURS LIVE HERE ON FRIDAY H'CAP — 6f (P)

8:00 (8:00) (Class 4) (0-85,85) 3-Y-O+ — **£4,075** (£1,212; £606; £303) **Stalls** Low

Form — RPR

/0-2 **1** **Capone (IRE)**[22] 4188 6-9-12 85 HayleyTurner 8 — 101+
(David Nicholls) *trckd ldrs: hdwy 2f out: rdn to ld appr fnl f: drvn out* **6/1**[3]

6120 **2** 2 ½ **Another Try (IRE)**[32] 3880 6-9-6 82 HarryBentley(3) 2 — 88
(Alan Jarvis) *trckd ldr: drvn to chal 2f out: led over 1f out: hdd appr fnl f: styd on same pce* **8/1**

066 **3** ¾ **Tislaam (IRE)**[21] 4206 4-8-5 67 (p) MartinHarley(3) 10 — 71
(Alan McCabe) *t.k.h: chsd ldrs: rdn and styd on to go 3rd fnl f: styd on same pce fnl 120yds* **11/1**

1001 **4** 2 ¾ **Great Acclaim**[35] 3737 3-9-3 80 EddieAhern 3 — 74+
(James Fanshawe) *in rr: rdn and styd on over 1f out: tk one pce 4th ins fnl f* **11/4**[1]

0004 **5** ¾ **Diriculous**[26] 4064 7-9-7 83 SeanLevey(3) 7 — 75
(Robert Mills) *in rr: rdn over 2f out: styd on fnl f but no imp on ldrs* **25/1**

0-15 **6** nse **Munaaseb**[84] 2199 3-9-5 82 TadhgO'Shea 5 — 73
(Ed Dunlop) *in rr: rdn and hdwy 2f out: nvr rchd ldrs and one pce fnl f* **7/2**[2]

-030 **7** 6 **Zip Lock (IRE)**[19] 4291 5-9-5 78 KierenFallon 4 — 51
(David Elsworth) *chsd ldrs: rdn over 2f out: wknd appr fnl f* **12/1**

5216 **8** 6 **Chaussini**[47] 3367 4-9-4 77 RoystonFfrench 1 — 31
(James Toller) *chsd ldrs: rdn and wknd over 2f out* **25/1**

0/63 **9** ½ **Quaroma**[100] 1762 6-9-6 79 LiamKeniry 11 — 31
(Peter Hedger) *r on outside: a in rr* **50/1**

1502 **10** 1 ½ **Best Trip (IRE)**[51] 3222 4-9-8 81 PatCosgrave 9 — 28+
(Richard Guest) *broke smartly to sn ld: rdn over 2f out: hdd & wknd rapidly over 1f out* **7/1**

1m 11.58s (-1.52) **Going Correction** -0.05s/f (Stan)
WFA 3 from 4yo+ 4lb — **10** Ran SP% **112.5**
Speed ratings (Par 105): **108,104,103,100,99 98,90,82,82,80**
toteswingers: 1&2 £9.90, 1&3 £10.40, 2&3 £10.70. CSF £50.04 CT £522.58 TOTE £8.80: £2.40, £3.20, £4.00; EX 56.80 TRIFECTA Not won..
Owner Brooklands Racing **Bred** S J Macdonald **Trained** Sessay, N Yorks

FOCUS
This looked a fair sprint handicap. It was run at a sound pace, but once again those waited with proved at a disadvantage. The form looks reasonable, rated around the placed horses.

Zip Lock(IRE) Official explanation: jockey said gelding stopped quickly

4910 LADIES DAY AT KEMPTON 03.09.11 H'CAP — 7f (P)
8:30 (8:32) (Class 5) (0-75,75) 3-Y-0+ — **£2,264** (£673; £336; £168) **Stalls** Low

Form — RPR

0206 **1** **Qenaa**[19] 4268 3-9-2 **74** .... TadhgO'Shea 5 — 81
(Mark Johnston) *in rr: sn pushed along: drvn and qcknd to ld 1f out: pushed out* — **11/1**

0-40 **2** ½ **Be A Devil**[19] 4278 4-9-4 **70** .... MartinDwyer 9 — 80+
(William Muir) *in rr: hdwy on ins whn nt clr run over 1f out: drvn and qcknd ins fnl f: styd on wl to take 2nd cl home but nt rch wnr* — **9/2**[1]

6060 **3** ½ **Mishrif (USA)**[42] 3514 5-9-3 **69** .... (b) EddieAhern 6 — 75
(J R Jenkins) *hld up in tch: hdwy fr 2f out to take slt ld appr fnl f: sn hdd: styd on same pce and lost 2nd cl home* — **10/1**

3553 **4** 1 **Hereford Boy**[18] 4349 7-9-3 **69** .... (b) ShaneKelly 1 — 74+
(Dean Ivory) *s.i.s: in rr: hdwy and nt clr run ins fnl 2f: swtchd rt and hdwy appr fnl f: styd on to take one pce 4th fnl 150yds* — **7/1**[3]

2100 **5** shd **Paphos**[6] 4725 4-8-11 **66** .... (v) RyanClark(3) 3 — 69
(Stuart Williams) *chsd ldrs: drvn to chal over 1f out: wknd ins fnl f* — **10/1**

2010 **6** 7 **April Fool**[18] 4310 7-9-9 **75** .... (b) LukeMorris 4 — 59
(Ronald Harris) *rrd in stalls: led after 1f: pushed along 2f out: hdd over 1f out: sn wknd* — **9/2**[1]

003 **7** 1 **Llewellyn**[22] 4186 3-9-2 **74** .... PatCosgrave 8 — 53
(James Fanshawe) *in rr: rdn and hung rt wl over 2f out: mod prog fnl f* — **5/1**[2]

6030 **8** 1 ¼ **Dvinsky (USA)**[21] 4206 10-9-2 **68** .... (b) IanMongan 11 — 46
(Michael Squance) *chsd ldrs tl lost pl and eased fnl f* — **28/1**

0000 **9** 3 **Beauchamp Yorker**[19] 4268 4-9-4 **70** .... (t) JamesDoyle 7 — 40
(Hans Adielsson) *chsd ldrs: rdn over 2f out: sn btn* — **33/1**

2600 **10** ½ **Fivefold (USA)**[21] 4210 4-9-1 **67** .... (p) HayleyTurner 2 — 36
(John Akehurst) *led 1f: chsd ldrs: rdn 2f out: wknd sn after* — **16/1**

0620 **11** 1 ¼ **Tubby Isaacs**[26] 4066 7-9-3 **69** .... (p) KierenFallon 10 — 34
(Dean Ivory) *s.i.s: in rr: sme hdwy on outside fr 3f out: wknd over 2f out* — **7/1**[3]

1m 25.28s (-0.72) **Going Correction** -0.05s/f (Stan)
WFA 3 from 4yo+ 6lb — **11** Ran SP% **116.8**
Speed ratings (Par 103): **102,101,100,99,99 91,90,89,85,85 83**
toteswingers: 1&2 £4.60, 1&3 £19.00, 2&3 £9.20. CSF £59.56 CT £520.08 TOTE £10.80: £4.30, £3.00, £4.10; EX 91.50 Trifecta £551.80 Part won. Pool: £745.67 - 0.61 winning units..

Owner Hamdan Al Maktoum **Bred** Mrs M Campbell-Andenaes **Trained** Middleham Moor, N Yorks

FOCUS
A wide-open handicap, run at a decent pace. The third sets the standard, based on his winter form.

Dvinsky(USA) Official explanation: jockey said gelding hung right

Beauchamp Yorker Official explanation: jockey said gelding stopped quickly

4911 DINE IN STYLE AT THE PANORAMIC H'CAP — 7f (P)
9:00 (9:00) (Class 6) (0-65,63) 3-Y-O — **£1,617** (£481; £240; £120) **Stalls** Low

Form — RPR

5614 **1** **Russian Ice**[43] 3481 3-9-4 **60** .... (b) ShaneKelly 7 — 70
(Dean Ivory) *s.i.s: in rr: hdwy over 2f out: drvn and styd on to ld fnl 120yds: r.o strly* — **12/1**

4010 **2** 2 ½ **Karate (IRE)**[11] 4547 3-9-3 **59** .... JamesDoyle 6 — 62
(Hans Adielsson) *towards rr: hdwy over 2f out: drvn and styd on wl fnl f to take 2nd cl home but no imp on wnr* — **12/1**

0601 **3** 1 **Diamond Run**[5] 4758 3-9-2 **58** 6ex .... SebSanders 4 — 59+
(J W Hills) *sn led: hdd 4f out: styd chalng tl led again ins fnl 2f: styd on tl hdd fnl 120yds and lost 2nd cl home* — **11/4**[1]

544 **4** ½ **West Side (IRE)**[47] 3343 3-9-4 **60** .... (vt[1]) DarryllHolland 8 — 59
(Jeremy Noseda) *s.i.s: in rr: rdn and hdwy over 2f out: styd on u.p fnl f: nt rch ldrs* — **7/2**[2]

-006 **5** ½ **Elegant Muse**[19] 4270 3-9-7 **63** .... EddieAhern 9 — 61
(Walter Swinburn) *in rr: rn wd into st and hdwy fr 2f out: kpt on fnl f: nt rch ldrs* — **10/1**

030 **6** 1 ¾ **Lady Mango (IRE)**[35] 3742 3-8-13 **55** .... LukeMorris 1 — 48
(Ronald Harris) *in rr: rdn and hdwy over 2f out: nvr quite gng pce to rch ldrs and wknd fnl f* — **33/1**

0000 **7** 3 ¾ **Avalon Bay**[11] 4544 3-9-1 **60** .... (p) SeanLevey(3) 11 — 43
(Pat Eddery) *chsd ldr: led 4f out: hdd ins fnl 2f: wknd qckly ins fnl f* — **16/1**

0000 **8** ¾ **Serial Sinner (IRE)**[20] 4244 3-9-1 **57** .... (tp) ChrisCatlin 3 — 38
(Paul Cole) *t.k.h: hld up towards rr: rdn and hdwy on ins over 2f out: nvr gng pce to chal and wknd over 1f out* — **22/1**

2502 **9** 3 ¾ **Mister Ben Vereen**[5] 4743 3-9-3 **59** .... (b) LiamKeniry 2 — 30
(Eve Johnson Houghton) *chsd ldrs tl wknd 2f out* — **8/1**

-500 **10** 6 **I Hate To Lose (USA)**[62] 2853 3-9-7 **63** .... (t) KierenFallon 10 — 18
(Philip McBride) *in tch: racd towards outside and rdn ins fnl 3f: wknd 2f out* — **11/2**[3]

60-0 **11** 19 **Marmaduke**[18] 4321 3-8-0 **45** .... KieranO'Neill(3) 5 — —
(John Bridger) *chsd ldrs tl wknd 3f out: eased whn no ch* — **66/1**

1m 25.8s (-0.20) **Going Correction** -0.05s/f (Stan) — **11** Ran SP% **114.5**
Speed ratings (Par 98): **99,96,95,94,93 91,87,86,82,75 53**
toteswingers: 1&2 £16.90, 1&3 £5.10, 2&3 £6.90. CSF £140.84 CT £510.82 TOTE £19.70: £2.40, £4.40, £1.90; EX 118.70 Trifecta £436.10 Part won. Pool: £589.39 - 0.20 winning units..

Owner Roger Beadle & Ben Bennett **Bred** Kingwood Bloodstock & Mrs M Gutkin **Trained** Radlett, Herts

FOCUS
This moderate 3-y-o handicap was run at a suicidal early pace which set it up for the closers. The runner-up sets the standard.

West Side(IRE) Official explanation: jockey said gelding was slowly away

T/Plt: £820.80 to a £1 stake. Pool of £61,643.19 - 54.82 winning tickets. T/Qpdt: £232.20 to a £1 stake. Pool of £4,802.16 - 15.30 winning tickets. ST

4337 SALISBURY (R-H)
Wednesday, August 10

OFFICIAL GOING: Good to firm
Wind: Moderate against Weather: sunny

4912 BRITISH STALLION STUDS EBF MOLSON COORS MAIDEN STKS — 6f
2:30 (2:31) (Class 4) 2-Y-O — **£4,237** (£1,260; £630; £315) **Stalls** Low

Form — RPR

0 **1** **Jacob Cats**[89] 2049 2-9-3 0 .... RichardHughes 5 — 83+
(Richard Hannon) *mde all: kpt on wl whn chal fr 2f out: on top at fin: rdn out* — **15/8**[1]

2 ½ **Top Cop** 2-9-3 0 .... JimmyFortune 9 — 82+
(Andrew Balding) *trckd ldr: rdn to chal 2f out: ev ch thrght fnl f: no ex nring fin* — **2/1**[2]

3 nk **Performing Pocket (USA)** 2-9-3 0 .... FrankieDettori 8 — 81+
(George Baker) *hld up: hdwy 3f out: sn rdn: wnt 3rd ent fnl f: kpt on but nvr quite getting there* — **13/2**

0 **4** 3 ¾ **Dishy Guru**[85] 2181 2-9-3 0 .... LukeMorris 11 — 69
(Michael Blanshard) *in tch: rdn to chse ldng pair 2f out tl ent fnl f: no ex* — **33/1**

04 **5** 2 ¾ **Bewilder**[29] 3954 2-9-3 0 .... NickyMackay 1 — 61
(John Gosden) *trckd ldrs: rdn over 2f out: nt gng pce to chal: fdd ins fnl f* — **5/1**[3]

6 nk **Blackburn** 2-9-3 0 .... AdamKirby 4 — 60+
(Clive Cox) *s.i.s: racd green in tch: sn pushed along: nt gng pce to get on terms: fdd ins fnl f* — **10/1**

00 **7** 5 **Showmepower (IRE)**[18] 4339 2-9-3 0 .... EddieAhern 7 — 45
(John Dunlop) *prom tl rdn over 2f out: wknd ins fnl f* — **50/1**

6 **8** 7 **Peg Peg**[18] 4339 2-8-13 0 ow1 .... JamesMillman 6 — 20
(Nerys Dutfield) *in tch: rdn over 2f out: wknd over 1f out* — **33/1**

9 1 **The Ploughman** 2-9-3 0 .... NeilChalmers 2 — 21
(John Bridger) *hld up: rdn 3f out: wknd 2f out* — **66/1**

1m 15.19s (0.39) **Going Correction** +0.025s/f (Good) — **9** Ran SP% **116.5**
Speed ratings (Par 96): **98,97,96,91,88 87,81,71,70**
toteswingers:1&2:£1.50, 2&3:£3.00, 1&3:£2.50 CSF £5.83 TOTE £2.70: £1.10, £1.80, £2.40; EX 7.40 Trifecta £22.70 Pool: £473.90 - 15.43 winning units..

Owner Michael Pescod & Justin Dowley **Bred** Highclere Stud **Trained** East Everleigh, Wilts

FOCUS
Rail erected up to 16ft off permanent far-side rail from 6.5f to finish. This looked a good maiden, although the form is fluid at this stage.

NOTEBOOK
Jacob Cats ◆ appeared the stable second string when declared with Pat Dobbs aboard, but Richard Hughes took over after Daunt was pulled out, and a significant market move suggests plenty of people knew full well a big run was likely. The winner had been absent since showing plenty of ability in a hot Newbury maiden on his debut (eased fair way out) in May and readily confirmed that promise. It's fair to say he was given a canny ride by Hughes, who saved plenty, but he does look useful. (op 7-2)
Top Cop ◆ is from a good sprinting family, being a half-brother to 6f scorer Desert Law, out of a triple 5f winner who herself was out of disqualified Nunthorpe winner Blue Siren. He was well fancied, although his trainer expressed concerns beforehand the ground might be quicker than ideal. As it turned out, the winner's edge on experience made the difference, but Andrew Balding's runner travelled like an above-average colt. (op 15-8 tchd 9-4)
Performing Pocket(USA) ◆ was the subject of an eyecatching jockey booking, not least because the rider came into this 2-3 for George Baker. This 60,000gns purchase, who is out of a multiple winner (including a minor stakes race on dirt at a sprint trip), raced further back than the first two finishers, but gradually got the idea. He could be quite decent. (op 6-1 tchd 7-1)
Dishy Guru missed the break after being unruly in the stalls when showing little on his debut, but this was a lot better. (op 50-1)
Bewilder found disappointingly little after tracking the pace. (op 7-2 tchd 11-2)
Blackburn, who has already been gelded, struggled for much of the way and required pressure a long way out, but he should have learnt plenty. (op 9-1 tchd 8-1)

4913 STEVENS GARNIER LTD NURSERY — 6f 212y
3:00 (3:03) (Class 5) (0-75,75) 2-Y-O — **£2,587** (£770; £384; £192) **Stalls** Centre

Form — RPR

01 **1** **Bu Naaji (IRE)**[21] 4205 2-9-5 **73** .... FrankieDettori 2 — 77+
(Roger Varian) *racd keenly: trckd ldrs: swtchd lft over 2f out: sn pushed upsides: led ent fnl f: kpt on: rdn out* — **11/4**[1]

51 **2** nk **Fire Ship**[53] 3171 2-9-0 **68** .... LukeMorris 10 — 71+
(Peter Winkworth) *mid-div: rdn over 2f out: no imp tl r.o wl fnl 140yds: wnt 2nd fnl strides* — **7/1**

0304 **3** nk **Hi There (IRE)**[19] 4277 2-8-11 **65** .... SebSanders 8 — 67
(J W Hills) *mid-div: rdn 3f out: hdwy 2f out: wnt 3rd ins fnl f: kpt on* — **12/1**

002 **4** shd **Dark Ambition (IRE)**[20] 4240 2-8-12 **66** .... KierenFallon 3 — 68
(William Haggas) *led: rdn whn chal over 2f out: hdd ent fnl f: kpt on but no ex* — **13/2**[3]

460 **5** 1 **Musically**[13] 4471 2-8-11 **68** .... MartinHarley(3) 1 — 68
(Mick Channon) *in tch: rdn 3f out: kpt on same pce* — **20/1**

0443 **6** ¾ **Tudor Empire (IRE)**[19] 4292 2-9-6 **74** .... NickyMackay 5 — 72
(John Gosden) *trckd ldrs: rdn over 2f out: 6th and hld whn sltly hmpd ins fnl f* — **13/2**[3]

4450 **7** 1 **Bojangle (IRE)**[16] 4390 2-7-8 **53** oh2 ow1 .... RyanPowell(5) 4 — 48
(Dominic Ffrench Davis) *trckd ldr: rdn over 2f out: sn ev ch: kpt on same pce ins fnl f* — **50/1**

6410 **8** nk **My Solitaire (IRE)**[32] 3842 2-9-5 **73** .... AdamKirby 11 — 67
(Clive Cox) *mid-div: rdn 3f out: nt gng pce to get on terms* — **20/1**

2412 **9** nk **That's Dangerous**[27] 4019 2-9-4 **75** .... KieranO'Neill(3) 7 — 68
(Roger Charlton) *wnt rt and bmpd s: sn pushed along towards rr: sme hdwy over 1f out: no further imp ins fnl f* — **5/1**[2]

6236 **10** ½ **Ivor's Princess**[19] 4263 2-9-7 **75** .... JamesMillman 12 — 67
(Rod Millman) *s.i.s: hld up bhd fr wd draw: rdn over 2f out: nvr any imp* — **22/1**

350 **11** 2 ¾ **Verse Of Love**[60] 2936 2-9-4 **72** .... JimmyFortune 6 — 57
(David Evans) *bmpd leaving stalls: mid-div: rdn over 2f out: wknd fnl f* — **22/1**

0430 **12** ½ **Mr Knightley (IRE)**[12] 4496 2-9-5 **73** .... RichardHughes 9 — 57
(Richard Hannon) *towards rr: rdn over 3f out: no imp: wknd ins fnl f* — **11/1**

1m 29.28s (0.68) **Going Correction** +0.025s/f (Good) — **12** Ran SP% **118.7**
Speed ratings (Par 94): **97,96,96,96,95 94,93,92,92,91 88,88**
toteswingers:1&2:£6.60, 2&3:£19.30, 1&3:£10.40 CSF £20.07 CT £205.30 TOTE £3.10: £1.10, £3.00, £4.80; EX 31.30 Trifecta £119.00 Pool: £804.25 - 5.00 winning units..

Owner Sheikh Ahmed Al Maktoum **Bred** Darley **Trained** Newmarket, Suffolk

FOCUS
A competitive nursery run at what looked just an ordinary pace and the form looks limited.

NOTEBOOK
Bu Naaji(IRE), as when winning a maiden on the Lingfield Polytrack over this trip last time, was a bit keen, and though he did enough, he had little left, not galloping out strongly. He'll need to learn to settle better to progress, although a less-demanding track might help. (op 2-1 tchd 15-8)
Fire Ship had been absent for 53 days since winning a maiden over this trip on soft ground. He took an age to get going but was over a length clear shortly after the line. A return to an easier surface might help, while he's entitled to be sharper for the run. (op 10-1)
Hi There(IRE) didn't get the clearest of runs before finishing well, but he didn't look unlucky. He can win a similar race. (tchd 14-1)
Dark Ambition(IRE), up in trip on his nursery debut, was allowed a relatively soft lead against the far rail, but he raced with his mouth open, looking awkward, and that can't have aided his chance. (op 6-1 tchd 5-1)
Musically didn't show herself particularly well handicapped. (op 33-1 tchd 40-1)
That's Dangerous, who was 2lb well in, was never competitive after a slow start and being short of room. (op 6-1)

4914 GOLDRING SECURITY SERVICES PEMBROKE CUP (H'CAP) 1m
3:35 (3:35) (Class 4) (0-85,85) 3-Y-0 **£4,204** (£1,251; £625; £312) **Stalls** Low

Form RPR
21- **1** **Terdaad (IRE)**[294] 7020 3-9-3 **81**........(p) FrankieDettori 11 97+
(Saeed Bin Suroor) *immediately swtchd rt fr wdst draw: hld up last: gd hdwy on outer fr 3f out: led 2f out: sn rdn: kpt on gamely whn pressed fnl f: all out* **2/1**[1]
211 **2** *nk* **Electra Star**[14] 4447 3-9-5 **83**........KierenFallon 3 98
(William Haggas) *mid-div: nt clr run and lost pl jst under 3f out: swtchd lft and hdwy 2f out: chal u.p ent fnl f: ev ch whn edgd lft briefly fnl 10yds: kpt on* **5/2**[2]
5216 **3** *hd* **Icebuster**[14] 4447 3-8-6 **70**........LukeMorris 6 85
(Rod Millman) *slowly away: towards rr: pushed along and hdwy fr 3f out: swtchd lft to chal 2f out: sn rdn: ev ch ins fnl f: kpt on* **16/1**
2233 **4** *2 3/4* **Uppercut**[18] 4342 3-9-0 **78**........SebSanders 5 87
(Stuart Kittow) *hld up towards rr: nt clr run 4f out: swtchd lft 3f out: rdn and hdwy sn after: chsd ldng trio fr over 1f out: styd on same pce* **20/1**
-260 **5** *2 3/4* **Discovery Bay**[18] 4310 3-8-13 **77**........SteveDrowne 8 79
(Roger Charlton) *trckd ldr tl rdn over 2f out: one pce after* **9/1**[3]
1652 **6** *4* **Aciano (IRE)**[12] 4506 3-9-2 **80**........MartinDwyer 9 73
(Brian Meehan) *mid-div: pushed along whn squeezed out and snatched up 2f out: sn rdn but wl hld after* **9/1**[3]
2-50 **7** *2* **Try The Chance**[11] 4550 3-9-4 **85**........MartinHarley(3) 1 74
(Mick Channon) *trckd ldrs: rdn over 2f out: wknd ent fnl f* **16/1**
3-53 **8** *8* **Perfect Cracker**[34] 3766 3-8-13 **77**........AdamKirby 7 47
(Clive Cox) *led tl rdn 2f out: sn wknd* **20/1**
6110 **9** *17* **Apache Glory (USA)**[14] 4429 3-9-6 **84**........RichardHughes 2 —
(Richard Hannon) *trckd ldrs: rdn 3f out: wknd over 1f out* **12/1**
01 **10** *5* **Silver Bullitt**[62] 2848 3-9-4 **82**........EddieAhern 10 —
(Walter Swinburn) *trckd ldrs: rdn 3f out: sn eased* **28/1**

1m 41.07s (-2.43) **Going Correction** -0.25s/f (Firm) **10** Ran SP% **114.3**
Speed ratings (Par 102): **102,101,101,98,96 92,90,82,65,60**
toteswingers:1&2:£1.30, 2&3:£11.60, 1&3:£4.90 CSF £6.52 CT £59.08 TOTE £2.20: £1.10, £1.80, £5.60; EX 7.30 Trifecta £73.80 Pool: £831.75 - 8.33 winning units..
Owner Godolphin **Bred** Darley **Trained** Newmarket, Suffolk

FOCUS
Judging by the early positions of those who fought out the finish, it seems the leaders went too fast. This was a decent handicap and the winner should do better.
Apache Glory(USA) Official explanation: jockey said filly hung left
Silver Bullitt Official explanation: trainer said filly was lame behind

4915 EBF "EXCEED AND EXCEL" UPAVON FILLIES' STKS (LISTED RACE) (F&M) 1m 1f 198y
4:05 (4:05) (Class 1) 3-Y-O+
£21,266 (£8,062; £4,035; £2,010; £1,008; £506) **Stalls** Low

Form RPR
4422 **1** **Primevere (IRE)**[19] 4265 3-8-5 98........HayleyTurner 3 107
(Roger Charlton) *trckd ldr: pushed along over 2f out: sn swtchd lft to chal: rdn to ld jst over 1f out: drifted lft: r.o wl* **13/2**[3]
2353 **2** *1 3/4* **Opera Gal (IRE)**[25] 4099 4-9-0 95........JimmyFortune 6 103
(Andrew Balding) *taken down early: led: rdn over 2f out: kpt on gamely: hdd jst over 1f out: sn hld by wnr: jst hld on for 2nd* **10/1**
0-10 **3** *hd* **Seta**[56] 3030 4-9-4 109........KierenFallon 12 107
(Luca Cumani) *mid-div: hdwy over 2f out: sn rdn and hung rt: disp 3rd ent fnl f: kpt on* **9/4**[1]
4153 **4** *2* **Piano**[47] 3356 4-9-0 99........RichardHughes 2 99
(John Gosden) *mid-div: hdwy over 3f out: sn rdn: ev ch 2f out: hld ent fnl f: no ex* **13/2**[3]
1324 **5** *2 3/4* **Imperial Pippin (USA)**[25] 4099 3-8-5 93........NickyMackay 4 93
(John Gosden) *mid-div: hdwy over 3f out: rdn over 2f out: ch wl over 1f out: fdd ins fnl f* **16/1**
0-20 **6** *1 1/2* **Anna Salai (USA)**[56] 3030 4-9-0 105........FrankieDettori 10 90
(Mahmood Al Zarooni) *hld up towards rr on outer: hdwy over 3f out: sn rdn: one pce fnl 2f* **4/1**[2]
6-30 **7** *1 1/2* **Clinical**[54] 3106 3-8-5 100........ChrisCatlin 9 90
(Sir Mark Prescott Bt) *trckd ldr tl rdn over 2f out: hld whn squeezed out wl over 1f out: wknd* **17/2**
1-26 **8** *2* **Charleston Lady**[25] 4099 3-8-5 96........RoystonFfrench 7 83
(Ralph Beckett) *mid-div: rdn over 4f out: nt pce to get involved: wknd ent fnl f* **20/1**
4156 **9** *1* **Bea Remembered**[19] 4293 4-9-0 98........MartinDwyer 8 81
(Brian Meehan) *a towards rr* **16/1**
0051 **10** *2* **Silver Grey (IRE)**[6] 4724 4-9-0 78........(p) SteveDrowne 5 77
(Roger Ingram) *in tch tl lost pl 4f out: sn rdn and bk in tch: wknd over 1f out* **33/1**
4204 **11** *15* **Fanditha (IRE)**[19] 4293 5-9-0 100........EddieAhern 11 47
(Mick Channon) *s.i.s: a towards rr: virtually p.u ins fnl f* **25/1**

2m 4.81s (-5.09) **Going Correction** -0.25s/f (Firm) course record
WFA 3 from 4yo+ 9lb **11** Ran SP% **120.4**
Speed ratings (Par 108): **110,108,108,106,104 103,102,100,99,98 86**
toteswingers:1&2:£11.50, 2&3:£7.70, 1&3:£5.60 CSF £69.70 TOTE £9.70: £2.70, £4.10, £1.40; EX 41.00 Trifecta £426.30 Pool: £921.84 - 1.60 winning units..
Owner A E Oppenheimer **Bred** Hascombe And Valiant Studs **Trained** Beckhampton, Wilts

FOCUS
A fair contest for the level and the track record, dating back to Zante's success in the 1998 running, was lowered by 0.18 seconds. The time was also exactly four seconds faster than the following Class 5 maiden handicap. The pace looked fast early, Opera Gal racing in a clear lead early on, but she came back to the field as Jimmy Fortune shrewdly got a lengthy breather in, and despite the fast time those ridden prominently were favoured. The fourth and fifth are rated 3lb off recent marks.

NOTEBOOK
Primevere(IRE) was well placed throughout by Hayley Turner, chasing the clear leader. She was a beaten favourite on her only previous start at this trip, in Newmarket's Pretty Polly in May, but that was only her second outing and she got the trip well this time. Plenty went her way, so this isn't form to get carried away with, but she's only had six races and there could be more to come. (op 15-2)
Opera Gal(IRE) might be a bit flattered, but she was picking up black type for the second time, and being by Galileo she's a valuable broodmare prospect. (op 12-1)
Seta ran creditably in defeat considering she was conceding upwards of 4lb all round and fared best of those who raced off the pace. Stepped up from 1m for the first time, she made plenty of ground on the front two to briefly look a threat, but gradually got tired as her exertions told, and also wandered a bit suggesting conditions were faster than ideal. She might get the trip better off a more even gallop, but 1m seems to suit best. (tchd 11-4, 2-1 in places)
Piano might have preferred a stronger-run race, but essentially wasn't good enough. (op 6-1 tchd 11-2)
Imperial Pippin(USA) tends to travel well before not seeing her race out, and it was the same story again. The suspicion is she's more talented than she's showing (looked fine prospect when winning her maiden, Dancing Rain won the other division), and she strikes as the type who could fulfil her potential if joining Juddmonte's US wing. Her dam also started off with John Gosden before switching to the States and landing a Grade 2. (tchd 14-1)
Anna Salai(USA) wasn't best placed considering how the race unfolded, but she didn't look to be striding out that well in the straight. She has been disappointing to varying degrees on each of her three starts this season. Official explanation: jockey said filly hung left handed (op 6-1)
Fanditha(IRE) Official explanation: jockey said mare was never travelling

4916 CHAMPAGNE JOSEPH PERRIER H'CAP 1m 1f 198y
4:40 (4:40) (Class 5) (0-70,69) 3-Y-O+ **£2,425** (£721; £360; £180) **Stalls** Low

Form RPR
4032 **1** **Sciampin**[27] 4005 3-8-11 **66**........AntiocoMurgia(5) 11 76
(Marco Botti) *trckd ldr: rdn to ld over 2f out: drifted lft over 1f out: kpt on: rdn out* **9/4**[1]
600- **2** *1 1/4* **Bolanderi (USA)**[337] 5840 6-9-8 **63**........RichardHughes 4 70
(Andy Turnell) *in tch: sltly outpcd over 3f out: hdwy over 2f out: styd on to go 2nd ins fnl f: kpt on wl* **11/1**
0205 **3** *2 1/2* **Royal Opera**[18] 4338 3-9-4 **68**........JamesMillman 10 70
(Rod Millman) *led: rdn and hdd over 2f out: ev ch briefly jst ins fnl f: no ex and lost 2nd sn after* **8/1**
0356 **4** *2 1/4* **Marie Rose**[14] 4435 3-9-0 **64**........(p) MartinDwyer 8 62
(Brian Meehan) *trckd ldrs: rdn 3f out: styd on same pce fnl 2f* **15/2**
00-0 **5** *1* **Makyaal (IRE)**[11] 4529 3-8-2 **52**........TadhgO'Shea 7 48
(John Dunlop) *short of room and snatched up after 1f: in last pair: hdwy 3f out: sn rdn and hung rt: wnt cl 3rd 2f out: fdd ins fnl f* **7/1**
0062 **6** *2 3/4* **Present Story**[8] 4645 4-8-8 **52**........MarkLawson(3) 13 42
(Gary Harrison) *trckd ldrs: rdn 3f out: nt pce to chal: wknd ins fnl f* **13/2**[3]
5624 **7** *3 1/4* **Oriental Girl**[23] 4154 6-10-0 **69**........(p) SteveDrowne 9 57
(Jonathan Geake) *in tch: pushed along fr over 2f out: nt pce to get involved: wknd ins fnl f: eased* **5/1**[2]
3005 **8** *1* **Prime Mover**[23] 4148 3-9-4 **68**........(e1) ChrisCatlin 12 50
(Ed Dunlop) *struggling 4f out: a towards rr* **9/1**

2m 8.81s (-1.09) **Going Correction** -0.25s/f (Firm)
WFA 3 from 4yo+ 9lb **8** Ran SP% **114.5**
Speed ratings (Par 103): **94,93,91,89,88 86,83,82**
toteswingers:1&2:£6.40, 2&3:£7.70, 1&3:£5.90 CSF £28.70 CT £168.90 TOTE £2.00: £1.10, £3.60, £3.50; EX 37.60 Trifecta £378.30 Part won. Pool: £511.28 - 0.81 winning units..
Owner Scuderia Rencati Srl **Bred** Franconson Partners **Trained** Newmarket, Suffolk

FOCUS
A typical maiden handicap, and they didn't go that strong a pace. The time was exactly four seconds slower than the earlier Listed race, which was run in a new track record. A personal best from the winner with the second to last year's best.
Oriental Girl Official explanation: jockey said mare was unsuited by good to firm ground

4917 AXMINSTER CARPETS RACING EXCELLENCE APPRENTICE H'CAP (WHIPS SHALL BE CARRIED BUT NOT USED) 6f 212y
5:10 (5:10) (Class 5) (0-70,67) 3-Y-O+ **£2,425** (£721; £360; £180) **Stalls** Low

Form RPR
6322 **1** **George Thisby**[8] 4640 5-9-4 **62**........LukeRowe(5) 6 70
(Rod Millman) *trckd ldrs: pushed along over 2f out: led wl over 1f out: strly chal thrght fnl f: hld on* **6/4**[1]
0335 **2** *shd* **Annes Rocket (IRE)**[18] 4337 6-9-1 **59**........(p) ThomasBrown(5) 3 67
(Jimmy Fox) *little slowly away: sn in tch: pushed along and hdwy 2f out: str chal thrght fnl f: jst hld* **5/1**[3]
4504 **3** *2* **Ivory Lace**[6] 4696 10-9-9 **65**........LeonnaMayor(3) 5 68
(Steve Woodman) *hld up: swtchd lft 2f out: hdwy over 1f out: styd on wout threatening ldrs* **7/1**
0-00 **4** *2 3/4* **Red Flash (IRE)**[14] 4444 4-8-4 **48** oh1........JohnLawson(5) 1 43
(Gary Harrison) *led tl wl over 1f out: one pce after* **12/1**
5622 **5** *4* **Arctic Mirage**[19] 4271 3-9-8 **67**........DavidKenny 4 51
(Michael Blanshard) *trckd ldrs: short of room to make chal over 2f out tl wl over 1f out: wknd ins fnl f* **7/2**[2]
0230 **6** *2 1/2* **Chinese Democracy (USA)**[14] 4434 4-8-9 **53**........(v) KevinLundie(5) 7 31
(David Evans) *hld up: hdwy over 3f out to chse ldrs: wknd 1f out* **12/1**
3000 **7** *hd* **Three Scoops**[8] 4647 3-7-12 **48** oh1........(t) KatiaScallan(5) 2 25
(Dominic Ffrench Davis) *prom tl squeezed up 2f out: wknd 1f out* **25/1**

1m 28.23s (-0.37) **Going Correction** +0.025s/f (Good)
WFA 3 from 4yo+ 6lb **7** Ran SP% **110.6**
Speed ratings (Par 103): **103,102,100,97,92 90,89**
toteswingers:1&2:£1.90, 2&3:£4.50, 1&3:£2.70 CSF £8.63 TOTE £1.90: £1.10, £3.70; EX 9.30.
Owner Robert Thisby **Bred** Meon Valley Stud **Trained** Kentisbeare, Devon

■ Stewards' Enquiry : John Lawson seven-day ban; improper riding (26th Aug-2nd Sept)

FOCUS
A modest handicap and these apprentices were not allowed to use their whips. The pace was solid and the form looks sound, rated around the first three.

T/Plt: £8.30 to a £1 stake. Pool of £57,918.59 - 5,067.35 winning tickets. T/Qpdt: £4.50 to a £1 stake. Pool of £2,993.03 - 483.44 winning tickets. TM

4863 **WOLVERHAMPTON (A.W)** (L-H)

Wednesday, August 10

OFFICIAL GOING: Standard

Wind: Fresh behind Weather: Overcast

4918 SPONSOR A RACE BY CALLING 01902 390000 H'CAP 7f 32y(P)

6:20 (6:21) (Class 6) (0-60,60) 3-Y-O+ £1,704 (£503; £251) Stalls High

Form RPR

013 1 **Royal Box**42 3512 4-9-0 55 ....(p) KellyHarrison 12 65
(Dai Burchell) *chsd ldr tl led wl over 2f out: rdn over 1f out: r.o* 16/1

1012 2 nk **Fortunate Bid (IRE)**9 4604 5-9-3 58 ....(p) TomQueally 3 67
(Linda Stubbs) *hld up: hdwy over 2f out: trckd wnr on bit 1f out: rdn ins fnl f: nt go by* 11/4[1]

4631 3 ½ **Katy's Secret**22 4187 4-9-5 60 .... SilvestreDeSousa 7 68
(William Jarvis) *s.i.s: hld up: hdwy u.p over 1f out: r.o* 11/2

0564 4 ¾ **Wigram's Turn (USA)**8 4634 6-9-2 57 ....(t) PaddyAspell 8 63
(Michael Easterby) *s.i.s: hld up: hdwy over 1f out: r.o: nt rch ldrs* 5/1[3]

3653 5 ½ **Itsthursdayalready**11 4563 4-9-4 59 .... TomMcLaughlin 1 64
(Mark Brisbourne) *chsd ldrs: rdn over 1f out: r.o* 14/1

5463 6 1¾ **Piccolo Express**12 4517 5-9-2 57 .... J-PGuillambert 2 57
(Brian Baugh) *prom: chsd wnr 2f out: sn rdn: no ex ins fnl f* 4/1[2]

620- 7 ¾ **Monashee Rock (IRE)**316 6439 6-9-0 55 .... StevieDonohoe 6 53
(Matthew Salaman) *hld up: hdwy over 2f out: rdn and edgd lft over 1f out: styd on same pce* 20/1

000- 8 7 **Cut The Cackle (IRE)**225 7991 5-9-0 60 ....(e[1]) LMcNiff(5) 5 39
(Richard Guest) *led: hdd wl over 2f out: wknd fnl f* 20/1

02-0 9 11 **Green Agenda**2 4865 5-9-2 57 .... RobbieFitzpatrick 9 —
(Derek Shaw) *s.i.s: a in rr: wknd 3f out* 40/1

0005 10 hd **Cwmni**6 4705 5-8-12 56 .... DeclanCannon(3) 11 —
(Bryn Palling) *chsd ldrs tl rdn and wknd over 2f out* 8/1

1m 29.55s (-0.05) **Going Correction** -0.025s/f (Stan) 10 Ran SP% 114.3

Speed ratings (Par 101): **99,98,98,97,96 94,93,85,73,73**

toteswingers: 1&2 £5.80, 1&3 £8.40, 2&3 £2.10. CSF £57.47 CT £287.14 TOTE £20.80: £4.50, £1.70, £1.40; EX 80.70.

Owner T R Pearson **Bred** The Queen **Trained** Briery Hill, Blaenau Gwent

FOCUS

Largely exposed sorts in a moderate handicap and one in which the gallop was reasonable. The winner raced centre to far side in the straight. Modest form.

4919 BETTER WIN PRICES EVERY AT CORAL.CO.UK MAIDEN STKS 7f 32y(P)

6:50 (6:51) (Class 5) 2-Y-O £2,328 (£693; £346; £173) Stalls High

Form RPR

400 1 **Bounty Seeker (USA)**12 4496 2-9-3 78 .... SilvestreDeSousa 3 75
(Mark Johnston) *mde all: rdn over 1f out: styd on* 4/1[3]

5 2 ½ **Cool Hand Luke (IRE)**10 4571 2-9-3 0 .... RichardKingscote 2 74
(Tom Dascombe) *chsd ldrs: rdn over 1f out: r.o* 3/1[2]

6 3 ½ **Harrier Hill (USA)**25 4087 2-9-3 0 .... AhmedAjtebi 7 73
(Mahmood Al Zarooni) *chsd wnr: rdn over 1f out: styd on* 9/1

05 4 2½ **Ex Oriente (IRE)**40 3590 2-9-3 0 .... TomQueally 1 66
(John Gosden) *sn pushed along and prom: rdn over 1f out: no ex ins fnl f* 5/6[1]

6 5 7 **Astonished Harry (GER)**15 4402 2-9-3 0 .... J-PGuillambert 6 49
(Reg Hollinshead) *hld up: rdn 1/2-way: nvr on terms* 33/1

6 hd **Aglaja** 2-8-7 0 .... LucyKBarry(5) 9 44
(Frank Sheridan) *dwlt: hld up: hdwy over 1f out: wknd fnl f* 33/1

7 2½ **Recway Striker** 2-9-3 0 .... AndreaAtzeni 4 43
(Des Donovan) *prom tl rdn and wknd over 2f out* 66/1

1m 31.92s (2.32) **Going Correction** -0.025s/f (Stan) 7 Ran SP% 116.9

Speed ratings (Par 94): **85,84,83,81,73 72,69**

toteswingers: 1&2 £3.10, 1&3 £1.70, 2&3 £4.20. CSF £16.83 TOTE £3.70: £1.60, £2.30; EX 14.70.

Owner A D Spence **Bred** Arindel **Trained** Middleham Moor, N Yorks

FOCUS

A couple of interesting runners in a fair maiden. The gallop was moderate to the 3f marker and the winner raced just off the inside rail in the straight. He enjoyed an easy lead but can probably better the bare form.

NOTEBOOK

Bounty Seeker(USA) ◆, had been well beaten over this trip on turf on his last two starts but this represented a much easier task and he returned to his best on this all-weather debut after being allowed an easy lead. He will be equally effective over 1m, has plenty of physical scope and is the sort to win more races. (op 7-2)

Cool Hand Luke(IRE) showed promise on his debut at Chester and bettered that effort over this longer trip on this Polytrack debut. He too should be as effective over 1m and should be able to pick up an ordinary event in this grade before going into handicaps. (tchd 7-2)

Harrier Hill(USA) had been well beaten after running green on his debut but, despite getting upset in the stalls, fared much better after being well positioned throughout on this all-weather debut. He's capable of picking up a run-of-the-mill event. (op 8-1 tchd 15-2)

Ex Oriente(IRE) failed to build on his latest form on this all-weather debut. Admittedly, things didn't go entirely his way after a tardy start and after running wide into the straight and he should be able to pick up an ordinary handicap at some point. (op 5-4)

Astonished Harry(GER) again had his limitations exposed in this grade and will be of more interest once qualified for a handicap mark.

4920 HOTEL & CONFERENCING (S) STKS 1m 141y(P)

7:20 (7:20) (Class 6) 3-Y-O+ £1,636 (£483; £241) Stalls Low

Form RPR

4405 1 **Empress Leizu (IRE)**16 2401 4-9-2 52 .... AndreaAtzeni 5 60
(Tony Carroll) *mde all: rdn over 1f out: edgd lft ins fnl f: r.o* 22/1

4046 2 1½ **Nicholas Pocock (IRE)**12 4233 5-9-7 60 .... SilvestreDeSousa 3 62
(Brian Ellison) *a.p: rdn to chse wnr over 1f out: edgd lft: nt clr run and swtchd rt ins fnl f: r.o* 3/1[3]

3140 3 ½ **Granny Anne (IRE)**14 4431 3-9-0 61 ....(p) LiamJones 8 62
(Alan Bailey) *s.i.s: hld up: rdn over 3f out: hdwy over 1f out: r.o: nt rch ldrs* 14/1

0500 4 1½ **Ossie Ardiles (IRE)**7 4666 3-8-13 53 ....(p) RobbieFitzpatrick 6 57
(Michael Appleby) *chsd wnr tl rdn over 1f out: styd on same pce ins fnl f* 50/1

6041 5 ¾ **Whispering Spirit (IRE)**36 3716 5-9-8 72 ....(v) FrannyNorton 7 57
(Ann Duffield) *prom: pushed along 3f out: rdn and swtchd lft over 1f out: nt clr run and swtchd rt ins fnl f: no ex* 6/4[1]

4353 6 1¼ **Cobo Bay**36 3716 6-9-13 72 ....(b) TomQueally 1 59
(Conor Dore) *s.i.s: sn pushed along in rr: r.o ins fnl f: nvr nrr* 9/4[2]

7 9 **Ellephil (IRE)** 3-8-5 0 .... DeclanCannon(3) 4 27
(Bryn Palling) *s.s: a in rr: rdn over 3f out: sn lost tch* 33/1

1000 8 24 **Bountiful Guest**14 4435 3-9-5 67 .... J-PGuillambert 9 —
(Brian Baugh) *rdn to chse ldrs: wknd over 2f out: t.o* 14/1

1m 50.13s (-0.37) **Going Correction** -0.025s/f (Stan)

WFA 3 from 4yo+ 8lb 8 Ran SP% 118.4

Speed ratings (Par 101): **100,98,98,96,96 95,87,65**

toteswingers: 1&2 £15.00, 1&3 £14.50, 2&3 £6.10. CSF £89.20 TOTE £26.70: £2.80, £1.20, £4.30; EX 129.20.There was no bid for the winner. Cobo Bay was claimed by Mrs Linda Stubbs for £6,000.

Owner Dark Horse Racing Partnership Five **Bred** Lynn Lodge Stud **Trained** Cropthorne, Worcs

FOCUS

A mixed bag but a race that didn't take as much winning as seemed likely with the two market leaders disappointing to varying degrees. The form is rated on the negative side. The gallop was an ordinary one and the winner raced just off the inside rail in the straight.

Cobo Bay Official explanation: jockey said gelding missed break

4921 ENHANCED WIN ODDS FROM NOON AT CORAL.CO.UK H'CAP 7f 32y(P)

7:50 (7:50) (Class 4) (0-80,80) 3-Y-O+ £3,234 (£962; £481; £240) Stalls High

Form RPR

5342 1 **Unlimited**11 4544 9-9-7 75 .... TomQueally 9 86
(Tony Carroll) *s.i.s and hmpd s: hld up: hdwy over 2f out: r.o to ld wl ins fnl f* 8/1[3]

1020 2 1 **All Right Now**4 4792 4-9-7 75 .... AndreaAtzeni 2 83
(Derek Haydn Jones) *chsd ldr tl led over out: rdn and hdd wl ins fnl f* 13/2[2]

1-00 3 6 **Tedsmore Dame**32 3854 3-9-0 74 ....(t) RichardKingscote 3 64
(James Unett) *s.i.s: sn prom: rdn over 1f out: hung lft and wknd ins fnl f* 33/1

5204 4 1 **Invincible Force (IRE)**26 4046 7-9-9 77 ....(b) SilvestreDeSousa 1 66
(Paul Green) *led: rdn and hdd over 2f out: wknd ins fnl f* 10/1

5354 5 hd **Huzzah (IRE)**21 4215 6-9-4 77 .... MatthewLawson(5) 10 66
(B W Hills) *hld up: r.o ins fnl f: nvr nrr* 11/4[1]

5405 6 shd **The Which Doctor**7 4679 6-9-3 74 ....(e) RobertLButler(3) 4 62
(Richard Guest) *dwlt: hld up: hdwy over 1f out: nvr on terms* 14/1

2101 7 2 **Orpenindeed (IRE)**81 2286 8-9-7 80 ....(t) LucyKBarry(5) 6 63
(Frank Sheridan) *chsd ldrs: rdn over 2f out: wknd over 1f out* 17/2

3200 8 hd **Sir Bruno (FR)**39 3634 4-9-5 75 ....(p) DeclanCannon(3) 7 58
(Bryn Palling) *prom: rdn over 2f out: wkng whn hung lft fnl f* 12/1

4-10 9 7 **Tax Break**72 2545 4-9-7 80 .... LMcNiff(5) 8 43
(David Barron) *hld up: rdn and wknd over 2f out* 11/4[1]

1m 27.9s (-1.70) **Going Correction** -0.025s/f (Stan)

WFA 3 from 4yo+ 6lb 9 Ran SP% 114.7

Speed ratings (Par 105): **108,106,100,98,98 98,96,96,88**

toteswingers: 1&2 £5.50, 1&3 £24.70, 2&3 £44.70. CSF £58.54 CT £1627.00 TOTE £10.30: £1.60, £1.10, £8.00; EX 35.90.

Owner M B Clarke **Bred** J Wise **Trained** Cropthorne, Worcs

FOCUS

A fair handicap run at a reasonable gallop and in a fair time but, although a couple of the market leaders disappointed, the first two did well to pull clear. The winner raced just off the inside rail throughout and posted a personal best.

Tax Break Official explanation: jockey said gelding was unsuited by going right handed.

4922 RINGSIDE CONFERENCE SUITE NURSERY 5f 216y(P)

8:20 (8:21) (Class 6) (0-65,65) 2-Y-O £1,704 (£503; £251) Stalls Low

Form RPR

660 1 **Selbaar**19 4276 2-8-11 55 ....(p) AndreaAtzeni 4 60+
(Chris Dwyer) *hld up: hdwy over 2f out: rdn to ld ins fnl f: r.o* 8/1[3]

030 2 ¾ **Vociferous (USA)**19 4285 2-9-2 60 .... SilvestreDeSousa 9 63
(Mark Johnston) *chsd ldrs: pushed along over 2f out: rdn and ev ch 1f out: styd on* 15/8[1]

5156 3 ½ **Very First Blade**16 4391 2-8-11 55 .... FrannyNorton 1 57
(Mark Brisbourne) *w ldr tl led over 1f out: sn rdn: hdd and unable qck ins fnl f* 9/1

3046 4 5 **Thorpe Bay**25 4085 2-9-2 60 ....(be) MarcHalford 8 47
(Mark Rimmer) *sn led: rdn and hdd over 1f out: wknd ins fnl f* 12/1

5033 5 1 **Ave Sofia**13 4474 2-8-12 56 .... StevieDonohoe 3 40
(John Holt) *sn pushed along in rr: styd on fr over 1f out: nvr on terms* 10/1

500 6 ¾ **Maria Medecis (IRE)**18 4343 2-9-3 61 ....(v[1]) TomEaves 6 42
(Ann Duffield) *chsd ldrs: rdn over 1f out: wknd fnl f* 16/1

3650 7 1¼ **Adranian (IRE)**21 4194 2-8-13 57 .... TomMcLaughlin 7 35
(David Evans) *in rr and sn pushed along: bhd 1/2-way: nvr nrr* 25/1

0532 8 1¼ **Nude (IRE)**8 4629 2-8-11 55 ....(p) FrankieMcDonald 2 29
(Sylvester Kirk) *prom: rdn over 3f out: nt clr run over 2f out: sn wknd* 12/1

663 9 2¼ **Littlecote Lady**20 4250 2-8-13 57 .... TomQueally 13 24
(Mark Usher) *hld up: n.d* 16/1

6602 10 6 **Concordia Notte (IRE)**8 4648 2-8-10 57 ow3 .... RobertLButler(3) 10 6
(Richard Guest) *prom tl wknd over 2f out* 14/1

455 11 8 **Gypsy Rider**42 3511 2-9-0 61 .... DeclanCannon(3) 5 —
(Bryn Palling) *sn pushed along and a in rr: lost tch over 2f out* 9/2[2]

1m 16.11s (1.11) **Going Correction** -0.025s/f (Stan) 11 Ran SP% 120.8

Speed ratings (Par 92): **91,90,89,82,81 80,78,77,74,66 55**

toteswingers: 1&2 £6.20, 1&3 £24.50, 2&3 £5.60. CSF £23.94 CT £147.91 TOTE £9.40: £2.80, £1.40, £3.30; EX 31.30.

Owner Masaood Ahmed Al Masaood **Bred** Mohammed Masaood Al Masaood **Trained** Burrough Green, Cambs

FOCUS

A modest nursery in which the gallop was reasonable. The first three pulled clear in the last furlong and the winner raced just off the inside rail in the straight. Sound form.

NOTEBOOK

Selbaar, who had hinted at ability at big prices in maidens at Yarmouth and Newmarket, attracted plenty of support and duly turned in an improved effort on this all-weather and nursery debut in the first-time cheekpieces. He should prove equally effective over 7f and may be capable of further progress. Official explanation: trainer said regarding apparent improvement in form that the first time cheekpieces and drop in class appeared to suit. (op 16-1)

Vociferous(USA) ◆ took a bit of stoking up but turned in his best effort on this nursery and Polytrack debut. He too should appreciate the return to 7f and should be able to pick up a similar event either on sand or on turf. (tchd 6-4)

Very First Blade, a selling 5f winner on Fibresand, ran as well as he ever has done on this nursery debut returned to Polytrack for the first time since his debut. He pulled clear of the rest and his trainer should be able to place him to best advantage.

Thorpe Bay, better than his previous run suggested (saddle slipped), raced with the choke out and consequently didn't get home on this all-weather and nursery debut. He'll have to show a bit more before he is a solid betting proposition. (op 10-1)

Ave Sofia failed to land a blow on this nursery and all-weather debut but she once again left the impression that a stiffer overall test of stamina would have been more to her liking. (op 9-1)

Gypsy Rider was soundly beaten after a tardy start (eased when clearly held) on this nursery and all-weather debut. (op 7-1)

4923 HOTEL & CONFERENCING AT WOLVERHAMPTON MAIDEN STKS 5f 216y(P)
8:50 (8:51) (Class 5) 3-Y-O+ **£2,264** (£673; £336; £168) **Stalls Low**

Form | | | | RPR
5355 **1** **Mawjoodah**[12] 4518 3-8-12 67 SilvestreDeSousa 8 73+
(Brian Ellison) *a.p: chsd ldr over 2f out: led on bit ins fnl f: r.o wl: readily* **11/10**[1]
-555 **2** 1 1/2 **Eshoog (IRE)**[44] 3461 3-8-5 69 (bt[1]) LeonnaMayor(7) 9 63
(Phil McEntee) *sn led: rdn over 1f out: hdd and unable qck ins fnl f* **14/1**
3 1 1/2 **Strong Man** 3-9-3 0 PaddyAspell 4 63
(Michael Easterby) *s.i.s: hdwy over 4f out: shkn up over 1f out: styd on* **18/1**
0 **4** 1/2 **Galloping Minister (IRE)**[118] 1338 3-9-3 0 RichardKingscote 10 62
(Tom Dascombe) *chsd ldr over 3f: sn rdn: no ex ins fnl f* **7/2**[3]
5 7 **Goldstorm** 3-8-12 0 TomMcLaughlin 2 34
(Brian Baugh) *s.s: outpcd: nvr nrr* **14/1**
0-0 **6** 1 3/4 **Illandrane (IRE)**[97] 1836 3-8-12 70 TomQueally 7 29
(Ed Dunlop) *prom over 3f* **3/1**[2]
0 **7** 10 **Avon Rising**[2] 4863 4-9-4 0 DaleSwift(3) 1 —
(Derek Shaw) *sn pushed along in rr: bhd fr 1/2-way* **66/1**

1m 14.85s (-0.15) **Going Correction** -0.025s/f (Stan)
WFA 3 from 4yo 4lb **7 Ran SP% 114.9**
Speed ratings (Par 103): **100,98,96,95,86 83,70**
CSF £19.58 TOTE £2.70: £2.20, £5.30; EX 13.10.
Owner Dan Gilbert **Bred** St Clare Hall Stud **Trained** Norton, N Yorks

FOCUS
A modest and uncompetitive maiden in which the gallop was only fair. The first four finished clear and the winner raced centre to far side in the closing stages. The winner is the best guide to the form.

4924 THE BLACK COUNTRY'S ONLY RACETRACK H'CAP 5f 20y(P)
9:20 (9:20) (Class 6) (0-60,60) 3-Y-O **£1,704** (£503; £251) **Stalls Low**

Form | | | | RPR
0620 **1** **My Love Fajer (IRE)**[3] 4820 3-9-2 55 TomQueally 8 63
(Alan McCabe) *stdd s: hld up: hdwy 1/2-way: edgd rt over 1f out: rdn and r.o to ld nr fin* **6/1**
050 **2** 3/4 **Missile Attack (IRE)**[11] 4542 3-9-2 55 TomEaves 1 60
(Ian Semple) *sn led: rdn over 1f out: hdd nr fin* **8/1**
2 **3** nk **Till Dawn (IRE)**[7] 4684 3-9-2 55 LiamJones 2 59
(Tony Carroll) *a.p: chsd wnr over 1f out: sn rdn: r.o* **7/4**[1]
3424 **4** 3 **Ginzan**[51] 3216 3-9-5 58 TomMcLaughlin 7 51
(Malcolm Saunders) *prom: outpcd over 3f out: r.o ins fnl f* **7/2**[3]
0003 **5** 3 **Too Many Questions (IRE)**[13] 4461 3-9-7 60 SilvestreDeSousa 3 42
(David Evans) *chsd ldr tl rdn over 1f out: wknd fnl f* **11/4**[2]
3600 **6** shd **Consistant**[26] 4067 3-9-7 60 J-PGuillambert 4 42
(Brian Baugh) *chsd ldrs: rdn 1/2-way: wknd over 1f out* **11/1**

61.89 secs (-0.41) **Going Correction** -0.025s/f (Stan) **6 Ran SP% 119.0**
Speed ratings (Par 98): **102,100,100,95,90 90**
toteswingers: 1&2 £9.40, 1&3 £6.40, 2&3 £4.60. CSF £52.88 CT £119.87 TOTE £8.70: £4.90, £5.20; EX 41.10.
Owner Fahed Al Dabbous **Bred** James Waldron **Trained** Averham Park, Notts

FOCUS
Mainly exposed types in a moderate handicap. The gallop was sound and the winner came down the centre. The winner rates back to his latter 2yo form.
T/Plt: £246.80 to a £1 stake. Pool of £77,310.50 - 228.61 winning tickets. T/Qpdt: £71.30 to a £1 stake. Pool of £5,952.34 - 61.70 winning tickets. CR

4726 YARMOUTH (L-H)
Wednesday, August 10

OFFICIAL GOING: Good (good to soft in places; 7.0)
Wind: fresh, half against Weather: breezy, overcast with showers threatening

4925 BRITISH STALLION STUDS SUPPORTING BRITISH RACING E B F MAIDEN FILLIES' STKS 6f 3y
2:20 (2:20) (Class 5) 3-Y-O **£2,587** (£770; £384; £192) **Stalls High**

Form | | | | RPR
5202 **1** **Mrs Greeley**[18] 4340 3-9-0 67 WilliamCarson 6 70
(Eve Johnson Houghton) *racd against stands' rail: led: rdn and wanting to hang lft over 1f out: hdd ins fnl f: kpt on to ld again towards fin* **11/8**[2]
2222 **2** nk **Vizean (IRE)**[11] 4542 3-9-0 71 RichardMullen 1 69
(Ed McMahon) *taken down early: racd in centre quartet: w wnr: ev ch whn rdn and hung rt over 1f out: led narrowly ins fnl f: hdd and no ex towards fin* **10/11**[1]
6 **3** 3 3/4 **Maz**[6] 4728 3-9-0 0 JamieSpencer 2 57
(Alan Bailey) *racd in centre quartet: dwlt: in tch: rdn and effrt 2f out: chsd ldng pair over 1f out: no imp and wl hld fnl f* **25/1**
4 4 1/2 **Dolly Bay** 3-8-11 0 AdamBeschizza(3) 5 43
(Julia Feilden) *dwlt: chsd wnr on stands' rail: rdn and edgd 2f out: sn outpcd and wl btn ent fnl f* **33/1**
4 **5** 3 1/4 **A'Faal**[123] 1236 3-9-0 0 TedDurcan 3 32
(Clive Brittain) *racd in centre quartet: in tch: rdn over 2f out: wknd qckly wl over 1f out* **14/1**[3]
50 **6** 19 **Femme Royale**[18] 4320 3-9-0 0 JackMitchell 4 —
(Robert Cowell) *racd in centre quartet: in tch: rdn and struggling 1/2-way: wl bhd over 1f out: t.o* **100/1**

1m 15.22s (0.82) **Going Correction** +0.25s/f (Good) **6 Ran SP% 108.9**
Speed ratings (Par 97): **104,103,98,92,88 62**
toteswingers:1&2:£1.10, 2&3:£2.60, 1&3:£4.50 CSF £2.71 TOTE £3.10: £1.10, £1.10; EX 2.90.
Owner Mrs Romilla Arber **Bred** Minster Stud **Trained** Blewbury, Oxon

FOCUS
Back straight and bottom bend dolled out 3m ending at 4.5f increasing distances by 15yds on round course. This was a match according to the market and so it proved, though the pair took very different routes and that may have had an effect on the result. The winner looks the best guide to the form.

4926 ODDSCHECKER.COM H'CAP 7f 3y
2:50 (2:50) (Class 5) (0-75,75) 3-Y-O+ **£2,264** (£673; £336; £168) **Stalls High**

Form | | | | RPR
1134 **1** **Dashwood**[26] 4066 4-9-11 74 (t) WilliamCarson 5 80
(Giles Bravery) *awkward leaving stalls: sn led and racd against stands' rail: rdn wl over 1f out: hung lft after but a holding rivals ins fnl f: rdn out* **9/4**[2]
0004 **2** 1/2 **Satwa Laird**[33] 3815 5-9-12 75 JamieSpencer 6 80
(Ed Dunlop) *w ldr: swtchd lft to r in centre over 5f out: rdn wl over 1f out: drvn over 1f out: kpt on same pce and a hld ins fnl f* **13/8**[1]
4-00 **3** 1/2 **Cornish Quest**[19] 4281 3-8-5 60 (b[1]) JimmyQuinn 1 62
(Mark H Tompkins) *racd on stands' rail: hld up in tch in rr: rdn and effrt wl over 1f out: hdwy u.p ins fnl f: styd on wl: nt rch ldrs* **8/1**
5503 **4** 3 3/4 **Yahafedh Alaih**[7] 4683 3-8-9 64 KirstyMilczarek 4 56
(Clive Brittain) *t.k.h: hld up in tch: swtchd to racd in centre trio over 5f out: rdn over 1f out: wknd qckly jst ins fnl f* **6/1**[3]
-140 **5** 1 3/4 **Here To Eternity (USA)**[49] 3292 3-9-0 69 JackMitchell 2 56
(Peter Chapple-Hyam) *hld up in tch: swtchd lft to r in centre trio over 5f out: rdn over 2f out: wknd ent fnl f* **7/1**

1m 29.68s (3.08) **Going Correction** +0.25s/f (Good)
WFA 3 from 4yo+ 6lb **5 Ran SP% 106.8**
Speed ratings (Par 103): **92,91,90,86,84**
CSF £5.89 TOTE £3.90: £1.30, £1.20; EX 5.10.
Owner Macattack, William Lea Screed & Form IT **Bred** Darley **Trained** Cowlinge, Suffolk

FOCUS
An ordinary handicap. The quintet raced against the stands' rail early, but then divided with two staying on the rail, whilst the other three made for the centre. As in the opener, it was one of those that stayed stands' side who came out on top. A small personal best from the winner.

4927 ODDSCHECKER.MOBI H'CAP (DIV I) 1m 3y
3:25 (3:25) (Class 6) (0-60,60) 3-Y-O+ **£1,617** (£481; £240; £120) **Stalls High**

Form | | | | RPR
0/10 **1** **Dannios**[44] 3475 5-9-0 55 (t) MichaelJMurphy(7) 2 71+
(Ed Walker) *awkward leaving stalls and slowly away: bhd: rdn over 2f out: gd hdwy 2f out: led over 1f out: in command 1f out: r.o wl: comf* **11/1**
0342 **2** 5 **Scarborough Lily**[3] 4827 3-8-10 51 (b) JamieSpencer 1 54
(Edward Vaughan) *in tch: hdwy to join ldrs travelling wl over 2f out: chsd ldr 2f out: sn rdn and outpcd by wnr jst over 1f out: no ch w wnr but plugged on u.p to hold 2nd fnl f* **6/4**[1]
-460 **3** 3/4 **Strike A Deal (IRE)**[29] 3952 4-9-12 60 JackMitchell 11 62
(Chris Wall) *racd solo against stands' rail: overall ldr: rdn over 2f out: hdd over 1f out: nt gng pce of wnr and btn ent fnl f: plugged on same pce after* **5/1**[2]
0000 **4** shd **Warden Bond**[25] 4111 3-8-2 48 ow2 (p) LauraPike(5) 3 49
(William Stone) *in tch in midfield: rdn 1/2-way: sme hdwy u.p to chse ldrs 2f out: sn outpcd and no threat to wnr 1f out: plugged on fnl f* **40/1**
0363 **5** 1 1/4 **Exopuntia**[19] 4278 5-9-6 57 (t) AdamBeschizza(3) 9 56
(Julia Feilden) *dwlt: sn bustled along and qckly rcvrd and chsd ldrs: rdn and nt qckn over 2f out: outpcd and btn over 1f out: one pce and wl hld ins fnl f* **5/1**[2]
0-00 **6** 1 3/4 **Wodian (IRE)**[51] 3223 3-8-12 53 (t) TedDurcan 4 47
(David Lanigan) *in tch in midfield: rdn and fnd little jst over 2f out: plugged on same pce and n.d fr over 1f out* **16/1**
4040 **7** 1 3/4 **Chez Vrony**[10] 4578 5-9-5 53 MartinLane 7 44
(Dave Morris) *in tch in midfield: effrt u.p jst over 2f out: sn struggling: wl btn over 1f out* **33/1**
-005 **8** 3 1/4 **Spartan King (IRE)**[14] 4435 3-9-0 58 RyanClark(3) 6 40
(Ian Williams) *s.i.s: hld up in last pair: rdn and no hdwy over 2f out: sn wknd* **13/2**[3]
0006 **9** 2 **Carlcol Girl**[41] 3559 4-8-12 46 oh1 (v) AdrianMcCarthy 8 25
(Christine Dunnett) *chsd ldr tl jst over 2f out: sn dropped out u.p: wl btn over 1f out* **100/1**
-330 **10** 20 **Miss Firefox**[82] 2243 3-9-1 56 (t) RichardMullen 10 —
(Nicky Vaughan) *t.k.h: hld up in tch: rdn and wknd over 2f out: wl bhd and eased fr over 1f out: t.o* **16/1**

1m 42.34s (1.74) **Going Correction** +0.25s/f (Good)
WFA 3 from 4yo+ 7lb **10 Ran SP% 113.1**
Speed ratings (Par 101): **101,96,95,95,93 92,90,87,85,65**
toteswingers:1&2:£3.50, 2&3:£2.50, 1&3:£11.20 CSF £26.87 CT £97.52 TOTE £18.80: £3.50, £1.50, £1.20; EX 36.60.
Owner Mrs T Walker **Bred** Roseland Thoroughbreds Ltd **Trained** Newmarket, Suffolk
■ Stewards' Enquiry : Michael J Murphy caution; used whip down shoulder

FOCUS
A modest handicap and, despite the evidence of the earlier races, all bar one of the field raced down the centre. The winner is rated back to his early form.
Dannios Official explanation: trainer said regarding apparent improvement in form. Gelding was very slowly away on last start and lost ground.

4928 ODDSCHECKER.MOBI H'CAP (DIV II) 1m 3y
3:55 (3:55) (Class 6) (0-60,57) 3-Y-O+ **£1,617** (£481; £240; £120) **Stalls High**

Form | | | | RPR
5003 **1** **Tinkerbell Will**[50] 3253 4-9-0 45 RichardThomas 9 54
(John E Long) *chsd ldr: rdn ent fnl 2f: led over 1f out: edging lft but forged ahd ins fnl f: kpt on wl: rdn out* **8/1**
303 **2** 1 3/4 **Viking Rose (IRE)**[22] 4185 3-9-5 57 LeeNewman 7 61
(James Eustace) *led: rdn jst over 2f out: hdd over 1f out: styd on same pce u.p ins fnl f* **4/1**[3]
5066 **3** nk **King Columbo (IRE)**[22] 4179 6-9-1 49 (p) AdamBeschizza(3) 10 53
(Julia Feilden) *in tch: rdn over 2f out: drvn and chsd ldrs over 1f out: no imp tl kpt on u.p fnl 75yds* **12/1**
000 **4** hd **Hierarch (IRE)**[162] 719 4-9-12 57 MartinLane 3 61
(David Simcock) *in tch towards rr: hdwy over 2f out: rdn to chse ldrs wl over 1f out: edgd rt and kpt on u.p fnl 100yds* **11/4**[1]
0-00 **5** 7 **Hilltop Artistry**[63] 2828 5-9-0 45 JackMitchell 8 33
(J R Jenkins) *taken down early: hld up in tch in last pair: effrt and rdn ent fnl 2f: no prog over 1f out: wknd ins fnl f* **40/1**
5-40 **6** hd **My Jeanie (IRE)**[39] 3636 7-9-0 45 TedDurcan 4 32
(Jimmy Fox) *hld up in tch: rdn and unable qck jst over 2f out: wknd over 1f out* **16/1**
000 **7** 4 1/2 **Satwa Ballerina**[51] 3224 3-8-12 50 JamieSpencer 2 26
(Ed Dunlop) *in tch in midfield: rdn 3f out: sn struggling and btn: no ch fnl 2f* **9/2**
4526 **8** 1 **Crinan Classic**[100] 1756 4-9-11 56 TonyCulhane(3) 1 34
(George Baker) *t.k.h: chsd ldrs: rdn and unable qck over 2f out: wknd wl over 1f out* **7/2**[2]
50/0 **9** 9 **Millers Crossing**[22] 4177 5-9-7 52 WilliamCarson 6 —
(Michael Squance) *taken down early: hld up bhd: hdwy 1/2-way: rdn and racd awkwardly over 2f out: wknd 2f out* **33/1**

1m 43.62s (3.02) **Going Correction** +0.25s/f (Good)
WFA 3 from 4yo+ 7lb **9 Ran SP% 117.1**
Speed ratings (Par 101): **94,92,91,91,84 84,80,79,70**
CSF £40.64 CT £388.28 TOTE £14.90: £3.70, £1.60, £6.40; EX 20.60.
Owner T H Bambridge **Bred** The Willow Stud **Trained** Caterham, Surrey

FOCUS
A race dominated by those that raced handily from the start as the result of a modest early pace. The winning time was 1.28 seconds slower than the first division. A weak race, rated around the runner-up.

4929 BEST ODDS AT ODDSCHECKER.COM H'CAP — 7f 3y

4:30 (4:31) (Class 6) (0-55,55) 3-Y-O — **£1,617** (£481; £240; £120) **Stalls** High

Form — RPR

2065 **1** **Zaheeb**^{7} [4685] 3-8-13 **55**......(p) AdamBeschizza$^{(3)}$ 2 — 63
(Dave Morris) *chsd ldrs: wnt 2nd over 4f out: rdn to ld wl over 1f out: idled 1f out: drvn and ins fnl f: fnd ex and hld on fnl 75yds* **15/2**^{3}

0-06 **2** 3/4 **All In A Paddy**^{21} [4200] 3-8-11 **50**......(b) RichardMullen 15 — 56
(Ed McMahon) *towards rr: rdn wl over 2f out: hdwy u.p and swtchd lft over 1f out: styd on to press wnr fnl 100yds: no ex and hld fnl 50yds* **25/1**

0553 **3** 1 1/2 **Trust Me Boy**^{23} [4162] 3-8-7 **46** oh1......(v) KirstyMilczarek 16 — 48
(John E Long) *towards rr: rdn 3f out: hdwy u.p over 1f out: chsd ldng pair ins fnl f: no imp fnl 75yds* **15/2**^{3}

0600 **4** 1 1/2 **Daliana**^{29} [3958] 3-8-6 **52**...... IanBurns$^{(7)}$ 9 — 50
(Michael Bell) *chsd ldrs: rdn over 1f out: unable qck ent fnl f: styd on same pce fnl f* **16/1**

060- **5** 3/4 **Wealth Whispers (IRE)**^{231} [7962] 3-8-10 **49**...... TedDurcan 11 — 45
(Paul D'Arcy) *t.k.h early: hld up in midfield: pushed along and effrt wl over 1f out: nt clr run and swtchd lft over 1f out: rdn and plugged on fnl 75yds: nvr threatened ldrs* **13/2**^{2}

0202 **6** 1/2 **Cannon Bolt (IRE)**^{12} [4505] 3-8-13 **52**......(b) LeeNewman 1 — 47
(Robin Bastiman) *led: rdn 2f out: hdd wl over 1f out: outpcd and btn 1f out: plugged on same pce ins fnl f* **7/2**^{1}

0040 **7** 1 3/4 **Blazing Apostle (IRE)**^{45} [3431] 3-8-0 **46** oh1...... DanielHarris$^{(7)}$ 13 — 36
(Christine Dunnett) *taken down early: towards rr and niggled along: swtchd rt and rdn 2f out: sme hdwy over 1f out: one pce and no imp ins fnl f* **28/1**

-050 **8** 1 3/4 **Rural Pursuits**^{71} [2599] 3-8-7 **46** oh1......(p) AdrianMcCarthy 3 — 31
(Christine Dunnett) *taken down early: towards rr: rdn over 4f out: sme hdwy over 1f out: nt clr run and swtchd lft ins fnl f: nvr trbld ldrs* **80/1**

5224 **9** shd **See The Storm**^{17} [4364] 3-8-13 **52**...... JamieSpencer 10 — 40
(Patrick Morris) *in tch: rdn and fnd little jst over 2f out: wknd over 1f out* **7/2**^{1}

000 **10** 1/2 **Astroverdi**^{34} [3781] 3-8-7 **46** oh1...... JimmyQuinn 12 — 29
(Mark H Tompkins) *a towards rr: rdn over 3f out: kpt on and sme hdwy u.p over 1f out: n.d* **33/1**

6056 **11** 4 1/2 **Chillie Peppar**^{12} [4511] 3-8-7 **49**...... CagriMetin$^{(3)}$ 8 — 20
(George Prodromou) *chsd ldr tl over 4f out: wknd wl over 1f out* **18/1**

603 **12** nk **Fleurie Lover (IRE)**^{7} [4672] 3-8-10 **52**...... SimonPearce$^{(3)}$ 7 — 35
(Richard Guest) *stdd s: hld up in tch: hdwy 1/2-way: chsd wnr wl over 1f out: rdn and unable qck w wnr over 1f out: lost action 1f out and sn eased: virtually p.u ins fnl f: dismntd after fin* **10/1**

5-00 **13** 6 **Cat Island**^{43} [3485] 3-9-0 **53**......(b^{1}) PhilipRobinson 14 — —
(Mark H Tompkins) *s.i.s: a bhd: toiling u.p 1/2-way: wl bhd fnl 3f* **22/1**

1m 29.99s (3.39) **Going Correction** +0.25s/f (Good) — **13** Ran SP% **117.4**
Speed ratings (Par 98): **90,89,87,85,84 84,82,80,80,79 74,74,67**
toteswingers:1&2:£31.00, 2&3:£46.70, 1&3:£10.00 CSF £188.04 CT £1508.86 TOTE £10.30: £3.50, £8.80, £2.10; EX 212.20.
Owner Stuart Wood **Bred** Theakston Stud **Trained** Baxter's Green, Suffolk

FOCUS
A poor handicap with only one previous winner in the field. The form is not that solid and the winner is rated back to his May form here.

4930 AVENUE PUB H'CAP — 5f 43y

5:00 (5:01) (Class 6) (0-55,55) 3-Y-O+ — **£1,617** (£481; £240; £120) **Stalls** High

Form — RPR

4612 **1** **Imaginary Diva**^{9} [4615] 5-9-3 **54**...... JamieSpencer 1 — 66
(George Margarson) *stdd s: hld up wl bhd: clsng qckly and weaving through field over 1f out: swtchd lft ent fnl f: rdn to ld fnl 100yds: sn in command* **9/4**^{1}

0500 **2** 1 1/2 **Wreningham**^{16} [4395] 6-8-13 **50**...... WilliamCarson 11 — 57
(Stuart Williams) *led: rdn over 1f out: hdd and drvn fnl 100yds: no ex* **15/2**^{2}

0062 **3** hd **Colourbearer (IRE)**^{19} [4272] 4-9-4 **55**......(t) TedDurcan 8 — 64+
(Milton Bradley) *stdd after s: hld up towards rr: hdwy and rdn over 1f out: keeping on whn nt clr run and swtchd rt ins fnl f: r.o to press for 2nd cl home* **9/4**^{1}

300 **4** 1 3/4 **Lithaam (IRE)**^{12} [4487] 7-8-9 **46**......(tp) RussKennemore 2 — 46
(Milton Bradley) *w ldr: rdn 2f out: drvn and unable qck jst over 1f out: wknd fnl 100yds* **22/1**

-650 **5** 1/2 **Kwik Time**^{23} [4162] 3-8-8 **48**......(b^{1}) LeeNewman 7 — 46
(Robin Bastiman) *chsd ldrs: rdn and unable qck 2f out: plugged on same pce u.p ins fnl f* **9/1**

4345 **6** 1 1/2 **Bookiesindex Boy**^{5} [4740] 7-9-0 **51**...... JackMitchell 4 — 44
(J R Jenkins) *hld up in rr: hdwy 1/2-way: chsd ldrs and rdn jst over 1f out: fnd little and sn btn: wknd ins fnl f* **8/1**^{3}

0005 **7** 1 1/2 **Microlight**^{7} [4657] 3-8-7 **47**......(b) RichardThomas 5 — 34
(John E Long) *sn bustled along and outpcd in rr: sme late hdwy: n.d* **14/1**

6010 **8** 9 **Inde Country**^{8} [4636] 3-8-12 **52**......(bt^{1}) RichardMullen 3 — —
(Nicky Vaughan) *in tch: rdn 2f out: wkng whn pushed lft ent fnl f: fdd ins fnl f* **22/1**

0/60 **9** 3 **Diademas (USA)**^{8} [4650] 6-8-9 **46**......(b) KirstyMilczarek 9 — —
(Conor Dore) *chsd ldrs tl lost pl qckly ent fnl 2f: wl bhd fnl f* **33/1**

64.16 secs (1.46) **Going Correction** +0.25s/f (Good)
WFA 3 from 4yo+ 3lb — **9** Ran SP% **112.7**
Speed ratings (Par 101): **98,95,95,92,91 89,86,72,67**
toteswingers: 1&2 £5.30, 1&3 £1.60, 2&3 £3.70. CSF £19.19 CT £40.83 TOTE £2.70: £1.40, £2.50, £1.20; EX 19.70.
Owner Graham Lodge Partnership **Bred** Norcroft Park Stud **Trained** Newmarket, Suffolk
■ Stewards' Enquiry : Jamie Spencer caution; careless riding

FOCUS
Two horses dominated the market in this moderate sprint handicap and they eventually finished first and third. The winner is rated back to her old best.

4931 BETTERBET IN NORWICH CITY CENTRE FILLIES' H'CAP — 1m 1f

5:30 (5:31) (Class 4) (0-80,77) 3-Y-O+ — **£4,075** (£1,212; £606; £303) **Stalls** High

Form — RPR

01 **1** **Jiwen (CAN)**^{26} [4072] 3-9-6 **77**...... JackMitchell 4 — 89
(Roger Varian) *mde all: flashed tail at times: jnd and rdn whn stmbld over 2f out: drew clr 2f out and in command fafter: pushed out: comf* **2/1**^{2}

214 **2** 3 **Jewelled**^{9} [4616] 5-9-10 **76**...... AdamBeschizza$^{(3)}$ 7 — 81
(Lady Herries) *stdd s: hld up in last: rdn and effrt over 3f out: hdwy u.p to chse clr wnr over 1f out: no imp* **10/3**^{3}

043 **3** 9 **Golden Slipper**^{58} [3001] 3-9-5 **76**...... JamieSpencer 3 — 70
(Ed Dunlop) *chsd ldr: jnd ldr 3f out: sn rdn: unable qck and struggling 2f out: sn btn: 3rd and no ch whn eased ins fnl f* **7/4**^{1}

01-2 **4** 5 **Midas Moment**^{103} [1659] 3-9-1 **72**...... RichardMullen 8 — 46
(William Muir) *t.k.h: hld up in 3rd: rdn and dropped to last over 2f out: wknd 2f out* **6/1**

2m 0.26s (4.46) **Going Correction** +0.25s/f (Good)
WFA 3 from 4yo+ 8lb — **4** Ran SP% **107.1**
Speed ratings (Par 102): **90,87,79,74**
toteswinger: 1&2 £8.50. CSF £8.45 TOTE £3.70; EX 7.10.
Owner Hamdan Al Maktoum **Bred** Adena Springs **Trained** Newmarket, Suffolk

FOCUS
This race was hit hard with half the declared field non-runners. The early pace was only steady and didn't increase until around 3f from home. The form is taken at something like face value.

4932 DIGIBET.COM H'CAP — 1m 3f 101y

6:05 (6:05) (Class 5) (0-70,74) 3-Y-O — **£2,264** (£673; £336; £168) **Stalls** Low

Form — RPR

4231 **1** **Watered Silk**^{8} [4627] 3-9-13 **74** 6ex......(b) RichardMullen 3 — 84
(Marcus Tregoning) *mde all: shkn up whn pressed over 1f out: rdn 1f out and sn readily asserted: comf* **1/2**^{1}

0041 **2** 2 1/2 **Peira**^{7} [4686] 3-9-1 **65** 6ex...... AdamBeschizza$^{(3)}$ 1 — 71
(Jane Chapple-Hyam) *chsd ldng pair: rdn and swtchd rt 2f out: drvn to press wnr over 1f out: easily brushed aside jst ins fnl f: kpt on* **5/2**^{2}

4265 **3** 3 **Battery Power**^{18} [4336] 3-9-7 **68**...... PhilipRobinson 5 — 69
(Mark H Tompkins) *hld up in tch in last: rdn and effrt over 2f out: 3rd and no imp u.p over 1f out* **6/1**^{3}

060 **4** 15 **Rasteau (IRE)**^{30} [3922] 3-8-2 **49** oh4......(p) JimmyQuinn 4 — 29
(Tom Keddy) *chsd wnr: drvn 3f out: wknd and dropped to last wl over 1f out: wl btn and eased ins fnl f* **40/1**

2m 34.56s (5.86) **Going Correction** +0.25s/f (Good) — **4** Ran SP% **112.0**
Speed ratings (Par 100): **88,86,84,73**
CSF £2.19 TOTE £1.50; EX 2.10.
Owner Mr And Mrs A E Pakenham **Bred** Mr & Mrs A E Pakenham **Trained** Lambourn, Berks

FOCUS
Another tactical affair and another all-the-way winner in this uncompetitive handicap. The form's rated around the second and third.
T/Plt: £28.30 to a £1 stake. Pool of £57,880.40 - 1,492.06 winning tickets. T/Qpdt: £15.10 to a £1 stake. Pool of £3,644.62 - 177.50 winning tickets. SP

4933 - 4939a (Foreign Racing) - See Raceform Interactive

4897 BEVERLEY (R-H)

Thursday, August 11

OFFICIAL GOING: Soft (heavy in places)
Wind: Light against Weather: Overcast and showers

4940 E B F BEVERLEY ANNUAL BADGEHOLDERS MAIDEN FILLIES' STKS — 5f

2:10 (2:10) (Class 5) 2-Y-O — **£3,428** (£1,020; £509; £254) **Stalls** Low

Form — RPR

50 **1** **True Bond**^{8} [4668] 2-8-11 0...... DaleSwift$^{(3)}$ 6 — 64
(Geoffrey Oldroyd) *pushed along and towards rr after 1f: hdwy wl over 1f out: rdn to chal ins fnl f: kpt on to ld last 75yds* **16/1**

2 hd **First Phase** 2-9-0 0...... DavidAllan 7 — 63
(Mel Brittain) *pushed along and outpcd in rr: hdwy wl over 1f out: rdn ent fnl f and sn ev ch tl no ex nr fin* **20/1**

4 **3** 1/2 **Thewinningmachine**^{20} [4276] 2-9-0 0...... TonyHamilton 4 — 62
(Richard Fahey) *cl up: led 1/2-way: rdn over 1f out: drvn ins fnl f: hdd and no ex last 75yds* **4/9**^{1}

3600 **4** 6 **Rhianna Brianna (IRE)**^{24} [4147] 2-9-0 55......(t) PaddyAspell 2 — 40
(Michael Easterby) *cl up: rdn along over 2f out: drvn wl over 1f out and grad wknd* **33/1**

5 4 1/2 **Kara's Vision** 2-9-0 0...... GrahamGibbons 1 — 24
(Robert Cowell) *cl up: rdn 2f out ev ch tl drvn and wknd ent fnl f* **17/2**^{3}

4250 **6** 1 1/4 **Mantuana (IRE)**^{16} [4406] 2-9-0 60...... SilvestreDeSousa 8 — 19
(David O'Meara) *slt ld: rdn along 1/2-way: sn hdd & wknd* **4/1**^{2}

67.10 secs (3.60) **Going Correction** +0.45s/f (Yiel) — **6** Ran SP% **113.4**
Speed ratings (Par 91): **89,88,87,78,71 69**
Tote Swingers: 1&2 £13.20, 1&3 £3.60, 2&3 £1.10 CSF £241.60 TOTE £25.60: £4.50, £3.70; EX 214.30.
Owner Only Tyres & Horses **Bred** Bond Thoroughbred Corporation **Trained** Brawby, N Yorks

FOCUS
Rail on inside of 5f course moved in but distances as advertised. Not the easiest race to assess, those with previous experience faced with much more testing conditions than previously. The runners came towards the stands' side.

NOTEBOOK
True Bond had hinted at ability on her two previous starts but this still represents a marked improvement, seemingly suited by the stiff test at the trip, off the bridle before most but responding to lead late on. Nurseries will presumably be next up and it's doubtful the assessor will go overboard. (op 14-1)
First Phase's yard had a treble here the day before and this daughter of First Trump made a promising start, particularly as she was clearly green, keeping on well as she grasped what was required. It's doubtful this was a strong maiden but she's entitled to improve. (op 12-1 tchd 8-1)
Thewinningmachine, a short-priced favourite, failed to reproduce the form she showed on her debut at Newmarket. She is probably best given the benefit of the doubt for now, conditions much softer than when she made her debut, while it's possible she went hard enough in front (fellow pacesetters all well beaten). (op 1-2 tchd 8-11)
Rhianna Brianna(IRE) is starting to look exposed as poor, a first-time tongue tie not making any difference.
Kara's Vision, a daughter of Kyllachy, was better than the bare result on her debut, recovering from a slow start to travel comfortably up with the pace for a long way and not knocked about as she faded inside the last. She's likely to achieve a good bit more next time. (op 10-1 tchd 8-1)
Mantuana(IRE)'s Southwell second is a bit of a stand out, and she dropped away tamely here. (op 5-1 tchd 7-2)

4941 BEVERLEY-RACECOURSE.CO.UK H'CAP — 2m 35y

2:40 (2:40) (Class 4) (0-85,79) 3-Y-O+ — **£4,075** (£1,212; £606; £303) **Stalls** Low

Form — RPR

6441 **1** **Beat The Shower**^{12} [4562] 5-9-4 **69**...... RobertWinston 5 — 83
(Peter Niven) *hld up in rr: smooth hdwy over 3f out: wd st and chal on bit 2f out: led over 1f out and sn rdn: drvn ins fnl f and kpt on wl* **6/1**

0015 **2** ½ **Neptune Equester**[3] [4856] 8-8-7 **61**.................................. DaleSwift(3) 1 74
(Brian Ellison) *cl up: led over 3f out: wd to stands' rail: jnd 2f out and sn rdn: hdd over 1f out: drvn and rallied ins fnl f: ev ch tl no ex nr fin* **9/4**[1]

3533 **3** *15* **Descaro (USA)**[9] [4635] 5-9-8 **73**.................................... DanielTudhope 7 68
(David O'Meara) *trckd ldrs: hdwy 4f out: rdn to chse ldng pair over 2f out: drvn wl over 1f out and plugged on same pce* **12/1**

-525 **4** *hd* **Salontyre (GER)**[14] [4463] 5-9-2 **67**..................................(p) JimmyQuinn 9 62
(Bernard Llewellyn) *hld up in tch: hdwy 6f out: chsd ldrs over 3f out: rdn over 2f out: drvn wl over 1f out and plugged on same pce* **20/1**

2201 **5** 2 ¼ **Shifting Gold (IRE)**[30] [3951] 5-9-0 **68**.............................(b) AmyRyan(3) 6 60
(Kevin Ryan) *towards rr: pushed along and outpcd 6f out: rdn and sme hdwy over 2f out: plugged on: nvr a factor* **16/1**

4543 **6** *38* **Argocat (IRE)**[27] [4050] 3-8-12 **78**.................................. GrahamGibbons 2 25
(Tom Tate) *in tch: hdwy on inner to chse ldrs over 5f out: prom and rdn 3f out: sn drvn and wknd* **8/1**

6131 **7** *31* **Mojolika**[30] [3935] 3-8-9 **75**...(e) DavidAllan 4 —
(Tim Easterby) *led: rdn along 5f out: drvn and hdd over 3f out: sn wknd and eased whn bhd fnl 2f* **9/2**[3]

-316 **8** *39* **Mungo Park**[15] [4449] 3-8-13 **79**.................................. SilvestreDeSousa 3 —
(Mark Johnston) *trckd ldng pair: pushed along 7f out: rdn 6f out: sn lost pl and bhd: t.o and eased fnl 3f* **4/1**[2]

3m 50.47s (10.67) **Going Correction** +0.80s/f (Soft)
WFA 3 from 4yo+ 15lb **8** Ran SP% **112.7**
Speed ratings (Par 105): **105,104,97,97,96 77,61,42**
Tote Swingers: 1&2 £3.40, 1&3 £8.50, 2&3 £7.10 CSF £19.32 CT £154.92 TOTE £8.60: £2.50, £1.60, £3.80; EX 28.20.
Owner Mrs Kate Young **Bred** C P E Brooks **Trained** Barton-le-Street, N Yorks

FOCUS
This unsurprisingly developed into a real stamina test, the field well strung out behind the leading pair. Few showed their form in the conditions.
Shifting Gold(IRE) Official explanation: jockey said gelding had a breathing problem
Mojolika Official explanation: jockey said gelding was unsuited by ground soft, heavy in places.

4942 BULLET DAY IS ON 27 AUGUST FILLIES' H'CAP 5f
3:15 (3:15) (Class 5) (0-70,70) 3-Y-0+ **£2,264** (£673; £336; £168) **Stalls** Low

Form RPR
6612 **1** **Red Roar (IRE)**[16] [4405] 4-8-13 **64**.................................... JulieBurke(5) 1 75
(Alan Berry) *hld up and swtchd lft after 1f: towards rr: hdwy wl over 1f out: sn rdn: drvn ins fnl f: kpt on wl to ld last 50yds* **6/4**[1]

2340 **2** *1* **Cool In The Shade**[12] [4563] 3-8-5 **54**...............................(b[1]) PaulQuinn 8 60
(Paul Midgley) *wnt lft s: cl up: led 1/2-way: rdn clr over 1f out: drvn ins fnl f: wknd and hdd last 50yds* **8/1**

2204 **3** *5* **Rhal (IRE)**[37] [3702] 3-9-0 **70**.. JustinNewman(7) 2 58
(Bryan Smart) *trckd ldrs: hdwy 2f out: rdn over 1f out: drvn ent fnl f and sn no imp* **5/1**[2]

6606 **4** *hd* **Foreign Rhythm (IRE)**[20] [4288] 6-8-13 **64**................... ShaneBKelly(5) 3 52
(Ron Barr) *in rr: rdn along wl over 1f out: styd on ins fnl f: nrst fin* **6/1**[3]

-006 **5** 1 ½ **Kinlochrannoch**[45] [3461] 3-9-7 **70**.................................... PhillipMakin 7 52
(Ben Haslam) *led: rdn along and hdd 1/2-way: drvn wl over 1f out and grad wknd* **25/1**

2003 **6** ¾ **Basle**[6] [4741] 4-9-10 **70**..(b) RobertWinston 5 50
(Gay Kelleway) *in tch: effrt 2f out: sn rdn and n.d* **9/1**

0-06 **7** 2 ¾ **Milton Of Campsie**[35] [3759] 6-9-8 **68**......................... GrahamGibbons 6 38
(John Balding) *chsd ldrs: rdn along 2f out: sn drvn and wknd* **8/1**

4006 **8** *8* **Mini Bon Bon**[12] [4527] 3-8-3 **52**................................ SilvestreDeSousa 4 —
(David O'Meara) *chsd ldrs: rdn along over 2f out: sn drvn and wknd* **16/1**

65.37 secs (1.87) **Going Correction** +0.45s/f (Yiel)
WFA 3 from 4yo+ 3lb **8** Ran SP% **112.9**
Speed ratings (Par 100): **103,101,93,93,90 89,85,72**
Tote Swingers: 1&2 £4.80, 1&3 £1.90, 2&3 £4.00 CSF £13.88 CT £48.05 TOTE £2.40: £1.10, £3.00, £1.10; EX 13.80.
Owner Sporting Kings **Bred** Tally-Ho Stud **Trained** Cockerham, Lancs
■ Stewards' Enquiry : Justin Newman caution: used whip down the shoulder in the forehand position

FOCUS
Not a strong race overall but the leading pair deserve some credit for coming so far clear. Modest form but a personal best from the winner.

4943 RACING UK ON SKY 432 NURSERY 7f 100y
3:50 (3:51) (Class 5) (0-75,72) 2-Y-0 **£2,264** (£673; £336; £168) **Stalls** Low

Form RPR
4130 **1** **Loyal Master (IRE)**[33] [3866] 2-9-7 **72**............................ LeeNewman 2 77
(George Foster) *cl up: wd st: led over 2f out and sn rdn on stands' rail: jnd and drvn ent fnl f: styd on gamely* **9/1**

0310 **2** 1 ½ **Nameitwhatyoulike**[37] [3700] 2-9-7 **72**.........................(b) JamesSullivan 8 73
(Michael Easterby) *trckd ldrs: hdwy over 2f out: chal wl over 1f out: rdn and ev ch ent fnl f: drvn and edgd rt last 100yds: no ex* **20/1**

050 **3** *nse* **Docs Legacy (IRE)**[15] [4436] 2-8-8 **59**............................ FrederikTylicki 4 59+
(Richard Fahey) *towards rr: hdwy 2f out: rdn and nt clr run ent fnl f: styd on strly towards fin* **8/1**

0000 **4** ½ **Peters Pursuit (IRE)**[20] [4277] 2-8-7 **58**........................ BarryMcHugh 11 57+
(Richard Fahey) *hmpd s and sn in rr: hdwy 1/2-way: rdn to chse ldrs 2f out: styd on to chse ldng pair ins fnl f: hld whn n.m.r and rdr dropped whip nr fin* **7/1**[3]

300 **5** 3 ¾ **Bedlam**[28] [4002] 2-9-5 **70**.. DavidAllan 3 58+
(Tim Easterby) *in rr: hdwy 2f out: sn rdn and styd on ins fnl f: nrst fin* **5/1**[2]

336 **6** *hd* **Sunny Side Up (IRE)**[19] [4347] 2-8-10 **61**........................ TonyHamilton 6 48+
(Richard Fahey) *t.k.h early: hld up in rr: hdwy on inner over 2f out: rdn to chse ldrs wl over 1f out: drvn and one pce ent fnl f* **5/1**[2]

14 **7** *1* **Broxbourne (IRE)**[13] [4508] 2-9-5 **70**......................... SilvestreDeSousa 7 54
(Mark Johnston) *in tch: effrt to chse ldrs over 2f out: sn rdn: edgd rt and wknd over 1f out* **7/2**[1]

446 **8** ¾ **Pearl Catcher (IRE)**[19] [4323] 2-8-8 **59** ow1................ GrahamGibbons 9 41
(Tim Easterby) *chsd ldng pair: rdn along over 2f out: wknd wl over 1f out* **25/1**

303 **9** 1 ¼ **Rosie's Lady (IRE)**[23] [4171] 2-8-5 **56**......................... DuranFentiman 12 34
(David O'Meara) *chsd ldrs: rdn along over 2f out: sn wknd* **22/1**

005 **10** 1 ½ **Dylan's Dream (IRE)**[38] [3680] 2-7-13 **50** oh2 ow1........... JimmyQuinn 1 24
(Tim Easterby) *chsd ldrs on inner: rdn along over 2f out: sn wknd* **20/1**

2604 **11** *4* **Jimmy The Lollipop (IRE)**[13] [4512] 2-9-5 **70**..............(p) PhillipMakin 5 32
(Kevin Ryan) *led: rdn along 3f out: wd to stands' rail: hdd over 2f out and sn wknd* **10/1**

506 **12** 2 ¼ **In A Jiffy (IRE)**[28] [4012] 2-7-7 **49** oh1.............................. NeilFarley(5) 13 4
(David Barron) *a in rr* **16/1**

1m 41.32s (7.52) **Going Correction** +0.80s/f (Soft) **12** Ran SP% **121.9**
Speed ratings (Par 94): **89,87,87,86,82 82,81,80,78,77 72,69**
Tote Swingers: 1&2 £16.20, 1&3 £11.00, 2&3 £30.40 CSF £182.66 CT £1536.75 TOTE £10.10: £2.90, £4.80, £2.40; EX 263.10.
Owner Ron Hull **Bred** Castleton Lyons & Kilboy Estate **Trained** Haddington, East Lothian
■ Stewards' Enquiry : Phillip Makin caution: careless riding

FOCUS
A fair nursery which conditions ensured was a stamina test for juveniles.

NOTEBOOK
Loyal Master(IRE) hadn't cut any ice in a strong nursery at Newmarket last time but found this easier, adding to his maiden success over the C&D. Stamina is clearly very much his forte, seeing it out well after being up there throughout.
Nameitwhatyoulike confirmed his York improvement at the second time of asking and will remain one to bear in mind, particularly back over slightly shorter as he travelled noticeably strongly for a long way. (op 16-1)
Docs Legacy(IRE) made a promising nursery debut and is one to bear in mind for a similar event next time. As expected, he was well suited by the step up in trip, rattling home having been outpaced at halfway. (op 15-2)
Peters Pursuit(IRE) stepped up on his nursery debut with conditions here more testing than he'd faced previously. He stuck to his task having been off the bridle a fair way out. (op 8-1 tchd 13-2)
Bedlam has yet to confirm the promise of his York debut third, off the bridle in rear a long way out here and merely passing tiring rivals in the straight. (op 8-1)
Sunny Side Up(IRE), a stablemate of the third and fourth, was better than the bare result, taking a bit of time to settle and unable to sustain what briefly looked a promising run. This was simply too much of a test at this stage of her career and she's likely to make more impact from this mark next time. (op 7-1)
Broxbourne(IRE) was sent off favourite back at the scene of her debut success but never looked like justifying it, perhaps not suited by the more testing conditions. The form of her debut win is nothing special, however. (op 10-3 tchd 3-1)
Jimmy The Lollipop(IRE) didn't stay the trip but doesn't look one of his yard's progressive juveniles anyway. (tchd 9-1)

4944 HOLD YOUR CHRISTMAS PARTY HERE (S) H'CAP 1m 4f 16y
4:25 (4:25) (Class 6) (0-60,60) 3-Y-0+ **£1,617** (£481; £240; £120) **Stalls** Low

Form RPR
1 **Ocean Bluff (IRE)**[20] [4301] 3-8-3 **46** oh1...................... JamesSullivan 11 56
(Mike Sowersby) *hld up in rr: stdy hdwy over 4f out: chsd ldrs over 2f out: sn chal: rdn to ld over 1f out: clr ins fnl f: kpt on strly* **9/1**

0003 **2** *6* **Lakeman (IRE)**[9] [4637] 5-9-10 **59**.. DaleSwift(3) 5 60
(Brian Ellison) *hld up in rr: bhd 1/2-way: hdwy 4f out: rdn over 2f out: drvn wl over 1f out: styd on appr fnl f: tk 2nd nr line* **5/2**[1]

2000 **3** *nk* **They All Laughed**[3] [4856] 8-9-2 **48**.................................. PhillipMakin 6 49
(Marjorie Fife) *racd wd: in tch: hdwy over 4f out: rdn to chse ldr 3f out: n.m.r and swtchd rt wl over 1f out: kpt on u.p appr fnl f* **6/1**[3]

0600 **4** 2 ¾ **Royal Deal**[8] [4673] 4-10-0 **60**.. GrahamGibbons 2 56
(Michael Easterby) *prom: rdn along and outpcd over 3f out: drvn over 2f out: plugged on appr fnl f* **8/1**

0016 **5** ½ **Yorksters Prince (IRE)**[8] [4673] 4-9-2 **53**.................(b) ShaneBKelly(5) 12 49
(Tony Coyle) *led 2f: cl up tl led again 5f out: wd st to stands' rail: jnd and rdn 2f out: drvn and hdd appr fnl f: sn wknd* **7/1**

5664 **6** 2 ¼ **Marino Prince (FR)**[3] [4869] 6-9-1 **54**..................... DavidSimmonson(7) 9 46
(Paul Midgley) *towards rr: rdn along 4f out: n.d* **3/1**[2]

00 **7** *51* **Doberdan (USA)**[40] [3622] 6-8-9 **46** oh1.....................(b) ChrisDCogan(5) 4 —
(Patrick Holmes) *chsd ldrs: led after 2f: rdn along and hdd 5f out: sn wknd and bhd* **33/1**

6230 **8** *7* **Yossi (IRE)**[18] [4367] 7-9-1 **50**......................................(b) RobertLButler(3) 3 —
(Richard Guest) *trckd ldrs: effrt over 4f out: sn rdn along and wknd 3f out: sn bhd and eased* **8/1**

2m 49.4s (9.60) **Going Correction** +0.80s/f (Soft)
WFA 3 from 4yo+ 11lb **8** Ran SP% **115.5**
Speed ratings (Par 101): **100,96,95,93,93 92,58,53**
Tote Swingers: 1&2 £6.10, 1&3 £10.60, 2&3 £5.50 CSF £32.22 CT £149.00 TOTE £8.80: £2.60, £1.40, £2.60; EX 41.40.There was no bid for the winner.
Owner M E Sowersby **Bred** Gerry Flannery Developments **Trained** Goodmanham, E Yorks

FOCUS
A weak seller, though a clear cut winner in Ocean Bluff who recorded a 6lb personal best. The form's rated around the runner-up.
Ocean Bluff(IRE) Official explanation: trainer said, regading the apparent improvement in form shown, filly was having it's first run for him and appeared suited by the softer ground

4945 WHITE ROSE SADDLERY CHRIS HOGGARD MEMORIAL H'CAP (DIV I) (FOR AMATEUR RIDERS) 1m 100y
5:00 (5:01) (Class 6) (0-65,64) 4-Y-0+ **£1,559** (£483; £241; £121) **Stalls** Low

Form RPR
0005 **1** **Edas**[10] [4605] 9-10-5 **60**.. MissHCuthbert(5) 4 66
(Thomas Cuthbert) *towards rr: gd hdwy over 3f out: chsd ldrs over 2f out: sn swtchd rt and rdn to ld 1 1/2f out: hung rt to far rail ent fnl f: kpt on wl* **15/2**

055 **2** *1* **Carlitos Spirit (IRE)**[24] [4150] 7-10-5 **55**............................ MrsCBartley 2 58
(Ian McInnes) *chsd ldng pair on inner: styd far rail in home st: rdn over 2f out: chsd wnr ent fnl f: kpt on* **5/1**[2]

5000 **3** ½ **Harare**[10] [4605] 10-9-7 **50**...(v) MissGTutty(7) 13 52
(Karen Tutty) *towards rr: hdwy over 2f out: rdn wl over 1f out: styd on ins fnl f: nrst fin* **33/1**

4-0 **4** ½ **Xpres Maite**[51] [3245] 8-10-7 **60**..(b) MrCMartin(3) 6 61
(Roy Bowring) *cl up: led 1/2-way: rdn wl over 2f out: hdd 1 1/2f out: sn drvn and one pce* **7/1**[3]

330 **5** 3 ½ **Hill Tribe**[5] [4783] 4-10-9 **59**... MrSWalker 7 52
(Richard Guest) *midfield: hdwy to chse ldrs and wd st to stands' rail: rdn over 2f out and ev ch: drvn wl over 1f out and sn one pce* **7/1**[3]

000- **6** 1 ¾ **Convitezza**[368] [4866] 5-9-4 **45**...............................(t) MrsFreyaBrewer(5) 10 34
(Mike Sowersby) *in rr: hdwy and wd st to stands' rail: rdn over 2f out: kpt on: nvr nr ldrs* **100/1**

0535 **7** 1 ¼ **Hayek**[10] [4604] 4-10-9 **64**..(p) MissRRichardson(5) 8 50
(Tim Easterby) *in tch: hdwy on wd outside to chse ldrs over 3f out: wd to stands' rails and rdn over 2f out: sn wknd* **9/2**[1]

-060 **8** *2* **Business Bay (USA)**[24] [4164] 4-9-2 **45**................. MissABlakemore(7) 3 26
(Patrick Clinton) *nvr bttr than midfield* **40/1**

0403 **9** 3 ¾ **Kheskianto (IRE)**[16] [4409] 5-9-9 **45**...................(bt) MissSBrotherton 11 18
(Michael Chapman) *hld up: hdwy and in tch over 3f out: wd st to stands' rails: rdn wl over 2f out and sn btn* **7/1**[3]

-054 **10** 2 ¾ **Island Chief**[10] [4601] 5-10-13 **63**.................................(p) MissJCoward 12 30
(Michael Easterby) *led to 1/2-way: cl up: rdn along wl over 2f out: sn wknd* **7/1**[3]

2005 **11** 2 ½ **Herecomethegirls**[12] 4549 5-9-4 **47**..........................(b) MissCEwart(7) 5 8
(Olivia Maylam) *a towards rr* **20/1**
4060 **12** 3 ¼ **Pictures (IRE)**[8] 4673 4-9-4 **45**.. MissVBarr(5) 1 —
(Ron Barr) *a bhd* **10/1**
0-00 **13** 18 **Smarty Sam (USA)**[25] 4125 4-10-9 **62**....................(p) MissWGibson(3) 9 —
(Paul Midgley) *a in rr* **28/1**
1m 55.76s (8.16) **Going Correction** +0.80s/f (Soft) **13** Ran SP% **120.3**
Speed ratings (Par 101): **91,90,89,89,85 83,82,80,76,74 71,68,50**
Tote Swingers: 1&2 £9.00, 1&3 £86.10, 2&3 £23.80 CSF £43.07 CT £1231.24 TOTE £11.60: £2.90, £1.50, £13.90; EX 77.00.
Owner Mrs Joyce Cuthbert **Bred** Stilvi Compania Financiera Sa **Trained** Little Corby, Cumbria

FOCUS
A very ordinary contest, though it was at least soundly run. In common with most races during the afternoon, the majority edged over towards the stands' side in the straight but it was a couple who stayed far side who came out on top. The winner is rated towards his form of this time last year.

4946 WHITE ROSE SADDLERY CHRIS HOGGARD MEMORIAL H'CAP (DIV II) (FOR AMATEUR RIDERS) 1m 100y
5:30 (5:35) (Class 6) (0-65,63) 4-Y-O+ £1,559 (£483; £241; £121) Stalls Low

Form RPR
0/6- **1** **Freda's Rose (IRE)**[427] 2902 7-9-3 **45**.................. MissBAndrews(7) 10 53
(Owen Brennan) *in tch: hdwy to join ldrs over 4f out: pushed along to chse ldng pair 3f out: rdn to chse ldr appr fnl f: styd on to ld nr line* **33/1**
2006 **2** hd **Nolecce**[1] 4902 4-10-13 **62**..(p) MissSBrotherton 11 70
(Richard Guest) *cl up: led over 3f out: styd far rail in home st and rdn wl over 1f out: drvn ins fnl f: hdd and no ex nr line* **9/2**[2]
4060 **3** 3 **Second Reef**[10] 4601 9-9-7 **47**..............................(p) MissHCuthbert(5) 13 48
(Thomas Cuthbert) *hld up in tch: hdwy to chse ldrs over 2f out: sn rdn and hung lft: kpt on fnl f* **40/1**
5533 **4** ½ **Rub Of The Relic (IRE)**[10] 4601 6-9-8 **50**.................(v) MissHDukes(7) 6 49
(Paul Midgley) *in rr: bhd 1/2-way: sme hdwy wl over 2f out: sn rdn and kpt on appr fnl f: nrst fin* **3/1**[1]
4040 **5** 2 ¼ **Hits Only Jude (IRE)**[3] 4852 8-10-9 **63**.............(v) MissAZetterholm(5) 9 57
(Declan Carroll) *trckd ldrs: hdwy 3f out: rdn to chse ldr 2f out: wknd appr fnl f* **15/2**
50-0 **6** 6 **Applaude**[15] 4442 6-10-3 **57**....................................(p) MissCarlyFrater(5) 3 38
(Jason Ward) *in rr: sme hdwy over 2f out: sn rdn and nvr a factor* **33/1**
1440 **7** 5 **Classic Descent**[3] 4852 6-10-3 **59**.............................(bt) MrBHowe(7) 2 28
(Ruth Carr) *s.i.s and sn detached in rr: rapid hdwy to chse ldrs 5f out: rdn along wl over 2f out and sn wknd* **5/1**[3]
0623 **8** 3 **Silly Gilly (IRE)**[10] 4604 7-10-6 **60**.................................... MissVBarr(5) 7 22
(Ron Barr) *led: rdn along and hdd over 3f out: sn wknd* **9/2**[2]
4025 **9** ¾ **Rowan Lodge (IRE)**[16] 4409 9-10-13 **62**.........................(b) MrSWalker 8 22
(Ollie Pears) *trckd ldrs: effrt and wd st to stands' rail: sn rdn and btn whn eased wl over 1f out* **5/1**[3]
1m 56.96s (9.36) **Going Correction** +0.80s/f (Soft) **9** Ran SP% **114.8**
Speed ratings (Par 101): **85,84,81,81,79 73,68,65,64**
Tote Swingers: 1&2 £9.30, 1&3 £18.70, 2&3 £18.50. Tote Super 7: Win: Not won. Place: Not won. CSF £173.00 CT £4029.12 TOTE £30.50: £4.60, £1.90, £6.70; EX 227.90.
Owner Mrs Violet J Hannigan **Bred** E A Bourke M R C V S **Trained** Worksop, Notts
■ Owen Brennan's first winner since coming out of retirement, and Bridget Andrews' first ever under rules.
■ Stewards' Enquiry : Miss A Zetterholm four-day ban: used whip with excessive frequency (tbn)
Miss H Dukes nine-day ban: used whip with excessive frequency (tbn)

FOCUS
A similar standard to the first division. Given the way that panned out it was no surprise most stayed centre to far side in the straight, the pace once again a sound one. The form is rated through the runner-up.
Classic Descent Official explanation: jockey said he lost his irons on leaving the stalls
T/Plt: £9,305.40 to a £1 stake. Pool of £54,175.00 - 4.25 winning tickets. T/Qpdt: £61.50 to a £1 stake. Pool of £4,697.00 - 56.45 winning tickets. JR

4701 CHEPSTOW (L-H)
Thursday, August 11

OFFICIAL GOING: Good (6.9)
Wind: Moderate, across Weather: white cloud

4947 E B F "PASSING GLANCE" MAIDEN STKS 5f 16y
5:15 (5:15) (Class 5) 2-Y-O £3,234 (£962; £481; £240) Stalls Centre

Form RPR
04 **1** **Subtle Embrace (IRE)**[20] 4269 2-8-9 0............................ JohnFahy(3) 2 65
(Harry Dunlop) *chsd ldrs: chal fr 2f out: hrd drvn fnl f to take slt ld fnl 120yds: hld on wl* **11/2**[3]
06 **2** nk **Compton Target (IRE)**[12] 4548 2-9-0 0..................... SimonPearce(3) 9 69
(Hans Adielsson) *trckd ldr tl slt ld appr fnl 2f: sn jnd and hrd pressed fnl f: hdd and nt qckn fnl 120yds* **16/1**
60 **3** 2 ¼ **Rock Of Monet**[20] 4276 2-9-3 0.................................(b[1]) EddieCreighton 5 61
(David Simcock) *towards rr but in tch: rdn and hdwy over 1f out: styd on fnl f to take 3rd clsng stages but no imp on ldng duo* **10/3**[2]
654 **4** hd **Guava**[7] 4720 2-8-9 0... KieranO'Neill(3) 1 55
(Richard Hannon) *chsd ldrs: rdn and effrt over 1f out: nvr on terms and hung lft ins fnl f: one pce* **6/4**[1]
54 **5** nk **Courtland Avenue (IRE)**[21] 4229 2-9-3 0..................... StephenCraine 7 59
(Jonathan Portman) *chsd ldrs: pushed along ins fnl 2f: kpt on same pce fnl f* **13/2**
00 **6** 5 **Compton Monarch**[33] 3870 2-9-3 0........................ FrankieMcDonald 3 41
(Hans Adielsson) *led tl hdd appr fnl 2f: sn wknd* **12/1**
5 **7** 6 **Brown Eyed Lass**[7] 4702 2-8-5 0.............................. DavidKenny(7) 10 15
(Laura Young) *slowly away and wnt rt s: hung lft to far rail and green sn after: a bhd* **22/1**
656 **U** **Early Ambition**[94] 1954 2-8-12 30................................... MartinLane 8 —
(Andrew Haynes) *rrd s and uns rdr* **66/1**
61.60 secs (2.30) **Going Correction** +0.075s/f (Good) **8** Ran SP% **111.2**
Speed ratings (Par 94): **84,83,79,79,79 71,61,—**
toteswingers: 1&2 £16.90, 1&3 £3.40, 2&3 £15.50 CSF £80.93 TOTE £11.60: £1.80, £4.90, £1.40; EX 122.90.
Owner Dean Woodley & Partners **Bred** Liam Cashman And M Fahy **Trained** Lambourn, Berks

NOTEBOOK
Subtle Embrace(IRE), fourth over 6f here on her second run, made it third-time lucky. Always close to the pace, she grabbed the lead at around halfway and battled on gamely under pressure. Low grade nurseries at this trip will surely be on her agenda from now on. (op 6-1 tchd 5-1)
Compton Target(IRE), sixth of seven on Lingfield's Polytrack last time out, showed his best form so far. Another near the front from the outset, he tried hard, but could not quite match the winner's finishing drive. (op 20-1)
Rock Of Monet, prominent in the betting when only 11th of 13 at Newmarket three weeks previously, was again rather disappointing, despite the addition of blinkers. He was in midfield early on and made only limited late progress. (op 4-1 tchd 3-1)
Guava, fourth in a Sandown maiden last time out, did not match that standard here. She tended to hang in the closing stages and, on this evidence, an official rating of 67 flatters her. (op 5-4)
Courtland Avenue(IRE) was dropped in distance for this third outing but still seemed to struggle to get home. Fourth early, he tired late on. (op 5-1)

4948 BLUE CHIP FEED H'CAP 1m 14y
5:50 (5:51) (Class 6) (0-55,60) 3-Y-O+ £1,617 (£481; £240; £120) Stalls Centre

Form RPR
6626 **1** **Tanforan**[30] 3944 9-9-6 **54**.. KellyHarrison 1 63
(Brian Baugh) *in rr: gd hdwy fr 2f out: rdn and r.o wl fnl f to ld fnl 30yds* **14/1**
2321 **2** nk **Daneside (IRE)**[4] 4822 4-9-9 **60** 6ex.............................. MarkLawson(3) 5 68
(Gary Harrison) *chsd ldrs: wnt 2nd 3f out: led ins fnl 2f: kpt on u.p tl hdd and nt qckn fnl 30yds* **6/4**[1]
2235 **3** ½ **Fitz**[19] 4322 5-9-1 **54**... LeeNewnes(5) 6 61
(Matthew Salaman) *towards rr: swtchd rt and hdwy fr 2f out: styd on wl fnl f to take 3rd fnl 75yds: nt rch ldng duo* **10/1**[3]
6541 **4** 2 **Sopran Nad (ITY)**[7] 4705 7-9-0 **51** 6ex.....................(b) SimonPearce(3) 7 53
(Frank Sheridan) *chsd ldrs: rdn to chse ldng duo ins fnl 2f: one pce fnl f and lost 3rd fnl 75yds* **6/1**[2]
034 **5** ½ **Tourist**[7] 4705 6-9-1 **52**.. RyanClark(3) 15 53
(Ian Williams) *sn led: rdn 3f out: hdd ins fnl 2f: wknd ins fnl f* **14/1**
3413 **6** ½ **Dancing Welcome**[7] 4705 5-9-6 **54**......................(b) RussKennemore 12 54
(Milton Bradley) *chsd ldrs: rdn over 2f out: outpcd ins fnl f* **10/1**[3]
0402 **7** 2 **Tuscan King**[7] 4701 4-9-4 **52**...(bt) MartinLane 8 48
(Bernard Llewellyn) *in rr: rdn over 2f out: hdwy over 1f out: nvr rchd ldrs and one pce ins fnl f* **18/1**
5041 **8** ¾ **Ocean Countess (IRE)**[7] 4699 5-9-5 **60** 6ex.............(v) DavidKenny(7) 3 54
(Tony Carroll) *s.i.s: in rr: hdwy 2f out: kpt on fnl f but nvr gng pce to rch ldrs* **16/1**
3050 **9** 2 ¼ **Prohibition (IRE)**[22] 4215 5-9-0 **55**........................... KatiaScallan(7) 16 44
(Alastair Lidderdale) *in rr: sme hdwy over 2f out: nvr gng pce to rch ldrs* **14/1**
3-00 **10** 3 ¼ **Croeso Mawr**[20] 4270 5-9-2 **50**.................................... StephenCraine 14 31
(John Spearing) *s.i.s: nvr bttr than mid-div* **40/1**
-000 **11** 5 **Gee Major**[7] 4705 4-9-0 **53**...................................... MatthewLawson(5) 9 23
(Nicky Vaughan) *chsd ldrs 5f* **28/1**
0-00 **12** 1 **Bold Argument (IRE)**[21] 4230 8-9-2 **50**................... FrankieMcDonald 4 17
(Nerys Dutfield) *chsd ldrs 5f* **100/1**
2260 **13** ½ **Mr Maximas**[12] 4549 4-9-3 **54**.................................(tp) DeclanCannon(3) 17 20
(Bryn Palling) *chsd ldrs to 1/2-way* **16/1**
000- **14** hd **Floating Angel (USA)**[453] 2121 4-8-11 **48**.................. KieranO'Neill(3) 2 14
(John Best) *chsd ldrs: rdn and wknd qckly over 3f out* **33/1**
0-00 **15** 3 **Sir Ike (IRE)**[27] 4076 6-9-4 **55**...................................(bt[1]) JohnFahy(3) 11 14
(Michael Appleby) *in tch: sme hdwy 3f out: sn btn* **28/1**
00-6 **16** 4 **Teazel**[19] 4320 3-9-0 **55**.. RoystonFfrench 10 —
(Dominic Ffrench Davis) *early spd: sn bhd* **18/1**
1m 37.42s (1.22) **Going Correction** +0.075s/f (Good)
WFA 3 from 4yo+ 7lb **16** Ran SP% **128.0**
Speed ratings (Par 101): **96,95,95,93,92 92,90,89,87,83 78,77,77,77,74 70**
toteswingers: 1&2 £10.80, 1&3 £25.90, 2&3 £3.40 CSF £35.55 CT £237.52 TOTE £21.10: £2.60, £1.20, £2.10, £1.40; EX 60.50.
Owner Miss S M Potts **Bred** Bearstone Stud **Trained** Audley, Staffs
■ Stewards' Enquiry : Mark Lawson one-day ban: used whip with excessive frequency (Aug 25)

FOCUS
A low-grade handicap in which the joint top-weights were rated just 60. Straightforward form, the winner's best figure since last summer.
Mr Maximas Official explanation: jockey said gelding was unsuited by the good ground

4949 BLUECHIPFEED.COM FILLIES' H'CAP 1m 14y
6:20 (6:22) (Class 5) (0-75,72) 3-Y-O+ £2,264 (£673; £336; £168) Stalls Centre

Form RPR
0650 **1** **Poyle Judy**[15] 4448 3-8-13 **64**.. MartinLane 2 73
(Ralph Beckett) *chsd ldrs tl rdn and outpcd fr 3f out: rallied and styd on u.p fnl f to ld last strides* **16/1**
-600 **2** hd **Ashkalara**[40] 3632 4-8-11 **55**....................................... RoystonFfrench 11 65
(Stuart Howe) *in rr: rdn and hdwy over 2f out: styd on strly fnl f to take slt ld nr fin: hdd last strides* **33/1**
2130 **3** nk **Miss Bootylishes**[21] 4255 6-9-7 **72**............................. DavidKenny(7) 14 81
(Paul Burgoyne) *trckd ldrs tl led over 3f out: rdn and edgd lft ins fnl f: hdd and no ex nr fin* **14/1**
3120 **4** 2 ½ **Mini's Destination**[27] 4060 3-8-10 **66**........................ LucyKBarry(5) 1 69
(John Holt) *in rr: hdwy over 2f out: chsd ldrs fnl f but nvr gng pce to chal* **6/1**[2]
0503 **5** 4 ½ **Bidable**[7] 4701 7-9-9 **70**.. DeclanCannon(3) 7 63
(Bryn Palling) *chsd ldrs: rdn over 2f out: wknd over 1f out* **20/1**
0232 **6** nse **Cat Hunter**[14] 4458 4-9-8 **66**.. KirstyMilczarek 13 59
(Ronald Harris) *s.i.s: in rr: hdwy 3f out: rdn over 2f out: btn whn hung lft fnl f* **9/1**[3]
-363 **7** ½ **Indian Valley (USA)**[15] 4448 4-9-11 **72**........................... RyanClark(3) 12 64
(Hugo Palmer) *chsd ldrs: rdn 3f out: wknd fr 2f out* **5/1**[1]
-304 **8** 6 **My Sister**[19] 4322 4-8-3 **54**.. RachealKneller(7) 8 32
(Mark Usher) *chsd ldrs: rdn 3f out: sn wknd* **9/1**[3]
4-60 **9** 5 **Cotswold Village (AUS)**[28] 4020 5-9-7 **65**............. RussKennemore 10 32
(Adrian Chamberlain) *mid-div: rdn and sme hdwy 1/2-way: wknd fr 3f out* **20/1**
1/0- **10** 2 ¾ **Halling Gal**[38] 239 5-9-11 **72**....................................... KieranO'Neill(3) 6 32
(Evan Williams) *broke wl: bhd fr 1/2-way* **66/1**
6-00 **11** 11 **July Days (IRE)**[34] 3805 5-9-12 **70**................................. KellyHarrison 5 —
(Brian Baugh) *led tl hdd over 3f out: wknd qckly* **33/1**
1m 36.67s (0.47) **Going Correction** +0.075s/f (Good)
WFA 3 from 4yo+ 7lb **11** Ran SP% **80.4**
Speed ratings (Par 100): **100,99,99,97,92 92,91,85,80,78 67**
toteswingers: 1&2 £12.40, 1&3 £7.70, 2&3 £36.60 CSF £214.52 CT £2135.75 TOTE £14.20: £4.20, £7.00, £2.70; EX 152.20.
Owner Cecil And Miss Alison Wiggins **Bred** Cecil And Miss Alison Wiggins **Trained** Kimpton, Hants
■ Stewards' Enquiry : Royston Ffrench caution: used whip with excessive frequency

FOCUS
Just a run-of-the-mill fillies' handicap, with the top-weight rated 72, and weakened by the late withdrawal of the 13/8 market leader Yensi (ref to ent stalls, deduct 35p in the £). The bare form is modest.

4950 TSG TIME SECURITY GROUP MAIDEN H'CAP — 6f 16y
6:50 (6:51) (Class 6) (0-65,65) 3-Y-O — **£1,617** (£481; £240; £120) **Stalls** Centre

Form — RPR

0336 **1** — **Full Shilling (IRE)**[19] 4321 3-8-7 **51** ... JamesDoyle 8 — 58
(John Spearing) *in tch: swtchd rt towards stands' side and hdwy fr 2f out: led jst ins fnl f: rdn and edgd lft: readily* **11/4**[1]

6035 **2** 2 3/4 **His Grace (IRE)**[7] 4729 3-9-4 **62** ... MartinLane 11 — 60
(Andrew Haynes) *t.k.h: chsd ldrs: led over 2f out: sn drvn: hdd jst ins fnl f: kpt on but nt pce of wnr* **10/1**

5000 **3** 2 1/4 **Avon Light**[15] 4431 3-8-5 **49** ... (p) RoystonFfrench 1 — 40
(Milton Bradley) *chsd ldrs: led 4f out: rdn and hdd over 2f out: styd chsng ldrs tl wknd ins fnl f* **33/1**

5-24 **4** 1/2 **Dixie Gwalia**[14] 4466 3-8-3 **52** ... LauraPike(5) 4 — 41
(David Simcock) *in tch: drvn to chse ldrs 2f out but nvr on terms: styd on one pce* **7/2**[2]

0-00 **5** 2 1/4 **Bella Nemica**[12] 4547 3-8-2 **46** oh1 ... AdrianMcCarthy 13 — 28
(Edward Creighton) *sn led: hdd 4f out: wknd over 1f out* **80/1**

040 **6** 3/4 **Kokojo (IRE)**[12] 4547 3-8-11 **55** ... (p) FrankieMcDonald 12 — 35
(Brendan Powell) *in rr: sn drvn along: mod prog fnl f* **12/1**

6-0 **7** 2 **Future Impact (IRE)**[116] 1429 3-9-3 **61** ... PatCosgrave 7 — 34
(Ed de Giles) *pressed ldrs tl wknd wl over 1f out* **4/1**[3]

5300 **8** 5 **Frosty Reception**[122] 1270 3-8-8 **55** ... JohnFahy(3) 3 — 12
(Michael Appleby) *rrd stalls: a towards rr* **16/1**

040 **9** 2 **Dark Pegasus**[19] 4320 3-8-4 **51** ... KierenFox(3) 9 — —
(Karen George) *bhd fr 1/2-way* **9/1**

000- **10** 1/2 **Sister June (IRE)**[356] 5268 3-7-13 **46** oh1 ... AmyBaker(3) 10 — —
(Edward Creighton) *a wl bhd* **100/1**

4025 **11** nk **Adaeze (IRE)**[21] 4227 3-8-11 **55** ... StephenCraine 2 — —
(Jonathan Portman) *chsd ldrs over 3f* **7/1**

1m 13.16s (1.16) **Going Correction** +0.075s/f (Good) — **11** Ran SP% **119.2**
Speed ratings (Par 98): **95,91,88,87,84 83,81,74,71,71 70**
toteswingers: 1&2 £5.50, 1&3 £8.70, 2&3 £11.20 CSF £32.09 CT £777.08 TOTE £4.10: £1.80, £3.20, £5.80; EX 48.40.
Owner Not The Full Shilling Syndicate **Bred** Michael Dalton **Trained** Kinnersley, Worcs

FOCUS
A weak event with the top-weight rated 65. The form is rated around the runner-up.
Adaeze(IRE) Official explanation: trainer said filly was unsuited by the ground, which in his opinion was softer than the official description of good

4951 ONSHORE MARINE MEDICAL SERVICES BRISTOL MAIDEN STKS (H'CAP) — 2m 2f
7:25 (7:29) (Class 6) (0-65,62) 3-Y-O+ — **£1,617** (£481; £240; £120) **Stalls** Low

Form — RPR

0004 **1** — **Rock Peak (IRE)**[9] 4642 6-9-0 **48** oh1 ... (b) MartinLane 6 — 58
(Bernard Llewellyn) *trckd ldrs: led over 2f out: pushed clr over 1f out: comf* **28/1**

0-33 **2** 2 1/2 **Captain Oats (IRE)**[20] 4274 8-8-9 **50** ... RachealKneller(7) 10 — 57
(Pam Ford) *hld up in rr: stdy hdwy on outside fr 4f out: kpt on to chse wnr over 1f out but nvr any ch* **10/1**

-452 **3** 4 1/2 **Viviani (IRE)**[9] 4630 4-9-12 **60** ... PatCosgrave 4 — 62
(Amanda Perrett) *chsd ldrs: rdn to take slt ld ins fnl 3f: hdd over 2f out and sn no ch w wnr: one pce into 3rd over 1f out* **9/2**[2]

23-2 **4** hd **Haldibari (IRE)**[6] 1297 7-9-5 **53** ... RussKennemore 1 — 55
(Shaun Lycett) *led: rdn over 4f out: hdd ins fnl 3f: styd on same pce u.p fnl 2f* **5/2**[1]

6-20 **5** 9 **Ned Ludd (IRE)**[98] 1839 8-9-8 **56** ... (p) StephenCraine 8 — 48
(Jonathan Portman) *hld up in mid-div: hdwy on ins 4f out: rdn 3f out: wknd qckly over 2f out* **9/1**

0/-3 **6** 2 3/4 **Rawaaj**[23] 3622 5-9-9 **62** ... HenryBrooke(5) 7 — 51
(Donald McCain) *chsd ldrs tl rdn and wknd qckly over 3f out* **17/2**[3]

4-55 **7** 2 **Poppy Gregg**[13] 4488 6-8-11 **48** oh3 ... (v) AmyBaker(3) 2 — 35
(Dr Jeremy Naylor) *in tch 1/2-way: rdn and wknd 5f out* **33/1**

0-5 **8** 7 **Ancient Times (USA)**[77] 4100 4-9-2 **60** ... JamesDoyle 9 — 29
(Philip Kirby) *in tch: rdn and effrt over 4f out: wknd qckly over 3f out* **10/1**

440 **9** 14 **Orpen Bid (IRE)**[31] 3910 6-8-7 **48** oh2 ... JosephYoung(7) 11 — 12
(Michael Mullineaux) *a in rr: lost tch 6f out* **33/1**

4m 5.52s (1.92) **Going Correction** +0.075s/f (Good)
WFA 3 from 4yo+ 18lb — **9** Ran SP% **94.8**
Speed ratings (Par 101): **98,96,94,94,90 89,88,85,79**
toteswingers: 1&2 £16.10, 1&3 £9.10, 2&3 £4.90 CSF £183.58 CT £801.39 TOTE £30.40: £5.10, £3.00, £2.10; EX 155.00.
Owner B J Llewellyn **Bred** G Callanan **Trained** Fochriw, Caerphilly
■ Band Of Thunder (7/2) was withdrawn due to broken tack. Deduct 20p in the £ under R4.

FOCUS
A very modest long-distance handicap seemingly lacking depth. The winner's best form since February 2009.
Ancient Times(USA) Official explanation: jockey said gelding hung left

4952 PIERCEFIELD OUB CHEPSTOW H'CAP — 1m 4f 23y
8:00 (8:00) (Class 6) (0-60,60) 3-Y-O+ — **£1,617** (£481; £240; £120) **Stalls** Low

Form — RPR

4300 **1** — **Shy**[20] 4273 6-9-11 **57** ... (b[1]) CathyGannon 11 — 71+
(Rod Millman) *trckd ldr: led over 2f out: sn drvn clr: readily* **13/2**[3]

0-35 **2** 4 **Sweet World**[9] 4645 7-9-11 **57** ... MartinLane 7 — 64
(Bernard Llewellyn) *chsd ldrs towards outer: hdwy and rdn fr 3f out: chsd wnr over 1f out but nvr any ch* **16/1**

3263 **3** 3 1/2 **Outland (IRE)**[24] 4164 5-9-13 **59** ... StephenCraine 8 — 60
(J R Jenkins) *in tch: hdwy fr 3f out: rdn to take one pce 3rd fnl 120yds* **8/1**

021 **4** 1/2 **Thundering Home**[24] 4164 4-9-7 **56** ... (t) MatthewDavies(3) 1 — 57
(George Baker) *in rr: stl plenty to do whn pushed along over 2f out: r.o to take 4th fnl 120yds and clsng on 3rd but nvr any ch w ldng duo* **3/1**[1]

0062 **5** 2 **Crazy Bold (GER)**[14] 4273 8-9-1 **47** ... RussKennemore 4 — 44
(Tony Carroll) *in rr: rdn and hdwy fr 3f out: styd on same pce fnl 2f and nvr any threat* **8/1**

6/6- **6** 1 1/2 **Dantari (IRE)**[110] 621 6-9-8 **57** ... KieranO'Neill(3) 9 — 52
(Evan Williams) *chsd ldrs: rdn and one pce fnl 3f* **7/2**[2]

56/0 **7** nk **Son Of Sophie**[41] 3600 9-8-7 **46** oh1 ... RachealKneller(7) 3 — 41
(Christopher Kellett) *in rr and stl wl bhd over 2f out: r.o fnl f and gng on clsng stages* **40/1**

2240 **8** 1 1/2 **Oak Leaves**[7] 4703 4-9-5 **51** ... PatCosgrave 6 — 43
(Nikki Evans) *led tl hdd over 2f out: sn btn* **8/1**

040- **9** 1 1/4 **Feeling (IRE)**[10] 7397 7-9-0 **46** oh1 ... (p) KellyHarrison 5 — 36
(Dai Burchell) *chsd ldrs: rdn 3f out: wknd qckly 2f out* **20/1**

-450 **10** shd **Taste The Wine (IRE)**[112] 1107 5-9-7 **58** ... LauraPike(5) 12 — 48
(Bernard Llewellyn) *t.k.h: hdwy on outside fr 6f out to chse ldrs over 3f out: wknd over 2f out* **10/1**

0400 **11** 1 3/4 **Bussell Along (IRE)**[20] 4270 5-8-11 **46** oh1 ... AmyBaker(3) 2 — 33
(Pam Ford) *s.i.s: in rr: hdwy 6f out: wknd fr 3f out* **50/1**

2m 40.43s (1.43) **Going Correction** +0.075s/f (Good)
WFA 3 from 4yo+ 11lb — **11** Ran SP% **118.0**
Speed ratings (Par 101): **98,95,93,92,91 90,90,89,88,88 87**
toteswingers: 1&2 £12.80, 1&3 £7.50, 2&3 £13.60 CSF £102.98 CT £848.97 TOTE £8.90: £4.00, £5.00, £2.20; EX 101.30.
Owner Mrs Jenny Willment **Bred** Mrs Jenny Willment **Trained** Kentisbeare, Devon

FOCUS
A very weak event with the top-weight's official rating being a mere 60. It was sound run and the form looks fair for the grade.

4953 LINDLEY CATERING H'CAP — 1m 2f 36y
8:30 (8:31) (Class 6) (0-55,55) 3-Y-O+ — **£1,617** (£481; £240; £120) **Stalls** Low

Form — RPR

0305 **1** — **Miskin Diamond (IRE)**[52] 3214 3-8-3 **46** oh1 ... CathyGannon 15 — 51
(Bryn Palling) *chsd ldrs: rdn to ld over 2f out: hrd rdn fnl f: all out* **16/1**

000- **2** hd **Hint Of Honey**[460] 1919 5-8-6 **47** ... DavidKenny(7) 6 — 51
(Tony Newcombe) *chsd ldrs: rdn and one pce 2f out: rallied and styd on again thrght fnl f to chse wnr clsng stages: nt quite get up* **16/1**

0004 **3** 1/2 **Fastada (IRE)**[4] 4827 3-8-2 **48** ... (v) JohnFahy(3) 8 — 51
(Jonathan Portman) *chsd ldrs: rdn over 2f out: styd on u.p to chse wnr fnl f: no imp and lost 2nd clsng stages* **9/4**[1]

4454 **4** 3/4 **Miss Excel**[7] 4713 4-9-7 **55** ... EddieCreighton 13 — 56
(Edward Creighton) *in rr: rdn 3f out: hdwy fr 2f out: kpt on ins fnl f but nt rch ldng trio* **18/1**

0060 **5** 1/2 **Indefinite Hope (ITY)**[3] 4869 4-8-13 **50** ... (tp) SimonPearce(3) 11 — 50
(Frank Sheridan) *in rr tl hdwy towards outside fr 3f out: pushed along and kpt on fr over 1f out: gng on clsng stages but nt rch ldrs* **12/1**[3]

06-5 **6** 3/4 **Cruise Control**[7] 4703 5-8-7 **46** oh1 ... MatthewLawson(5) 7 — 45
(Richard Price) *towards rr: hdwy on ins fr 3f out: sn rdn: chsd ldrs 2f out: wknd ins fnl f* **7/1**[2]

0-00 **7** 1 1/4 **Feuergott (GER)**[7] 4703 5-8-9 **46** oh1 ... (b[1]) RyanClark(3) 1 — 42
(Ian Williams) *sn led: hdd over 2f out: wknd fnl f* **12/1**[3]

4500 **8** 4 1/2 **Love In The Park**[11] 4578 6-9-2 **50** ... PatCosgrave 10 — 37
(Roy Brotherton) *in rr tl rdn and hdwy 3f out: nvr rchd ldrs* **16/1**

0040 **9** 3 3/4 **It's Dubai Dolly**[45] 3467 5-9-4 **52** ... (b) JamesDoyle 16 — 32
(Alastair Lidderdale) *plld hrd and trckd ldrs: stl t.k.h 5f out: rdn and effrt over 3f out: sn btn* **7/1**[2]

00-6 **10** 2 3/4 **She's Untouchable**[7] 4705 4-8-13 **50** ... MarkLawson(3) 2 — 24
(Gary Harrison) *t.k.h: towards rr and plenty to do over 2f out: styd on fnl f but nvr any ch* **12/1**[3]

00-0 **11** nk **Under Fire (IRE)**[12] 4549 8-9-3 **51** ... MartinLane 4 — 24
(Tony Carroll) *chsd ldrs: rdn and wknd 3f out* **16/1**

506 **12** 1 3/4 **Lunar River (FR)**[42] 3546 8-9-2 **55** ... (t) JamesRogers(5) 9 — 25
(David Pinder) *s.i.s: bhd most of way* **12/1**[3]

0266 **13** 1 1/2 **Excellent Vision**[30] 3945 4-9-1 **49** ... (t) RussKennemore 14 — 16
(Milton Bradley) *in tch: rdn 3f out: sn wknd* **12/1**[3]

5500 **14** nk **Farmer's Wife**[9] 4645 3-8-4 **52** ... LauraPike(5) 12 — 18
(Bernard Llewellyn) *s.i.s: nvr bttr than mid-div: bhd fnl 4f* **33/1**

2m 12.49s (1.89) **Going Correction** +0.075s/f (Good)
WFA 3 from 4yo+ 9lb — **14** Ran SP% **126.0**
Speed ratings (Par 101): **95,94,94,93,93 92,91,88,85,83 82,81,80,79**
toteswingers: 1&2 £88.70, 1&3 £6.60, 2&3 £17.70 CSF £261.80 CT £809.02 TOTE £22.00: £4.90, £9.60, £1.40; EX 389.80.
Owner Maywood Racing **Bred** Castlefarm Stud **Trained** Tredodridge, Vale Of Glamorgan

FOCUS
A poor finale, rated slightly negatively.
She's Untouchable Official explanation: jockey said filly ran too free
Excellent Vision Official explanation: jockey said gelding ran too free
T/Plt: £2,421.40 to a £1 stake. Pool: £43,950.76. 13.25 winning tickets. T/Qpdt: £169.40 to a £1 stake. Pool: £5,494.14. 24.00 winning tickets. ST

4531 GOODWOOD (R-H)
Thursday, August 11

OFFICIAL GOING: Good (good to firm in places; 8.2)
Wind: Fresh, half against Weather: Cloudy

4954 LADIES NIGHT MAIDEN AUCTION STKS — 6f
4:55 (4:56) (Class 4) 2-Y-O — **£3,557** (£1,058; £529; £264) **Stalls** High

Form — RPR

4 **1** — **Sunday Times**[15] 4427 2-8-6 0 ... WilliamBuick 2 — 83+
(Peter Chapple-Hyam) *trckd ldrs: led over 2f out: drew clr over 1f out: easily* **4/11**[1]

023 **2** 3 1/4 **King Of Wing (IRE)**[20] 4269 2-8-6 67 ... SeanLevey(3) 9 — 72+
(Richard Hannon) *trckd ldrs: chal over 2f out: easily outpcd by wnr over 1f out: styd on* **6/1**[2]

52 **3** 8 **Shout For Joy (IRE)**[19] 4319 2-8-1 0 ... RyanPowell(5) 3 — 45
(Richard Hannon) *prom on outer: chal over 2f out: sn outpcd: fdd over 1f out but hld on for 3rd* **7/1**[3]

4 1 1/4 **Morning Muse (IRE)** 2-8-8 0 ... LiamKeniry 4 — 43+
(Peter Winkworth) *dwlt: outpcd in last: in tch 1/2-way: sn outpcd again: shkn up and kpt on fnl f* **12/1**

00 **5** 1 1/4 **Merv (IRE)**[46] 3424 2-8-13 0 ... DarryllHolland 1 — 45
(Henry Candy) *trckd ldrs: outpcd and jst pushed along 2f out: sn no ch* **9/1**

46 **6** 3 1/4 **Moment In The Sun**[21] 4232 2-8-4 0 ... MartinDwyer 5 — 26
(William Muir) *t.k.h: disp ld to over 2f out: wknd* **20/1**

7 1/2 **Kaylee** 2-8-4 0 ... JamieMackay 8 — 24
(Gary Moore) *dwlt: rn green and t.k.h: in tch in rr tl wknd 2f out* **33/1**

0 **8** 3 3/4 **Four Poorer (IRE)**[14] 4474 2-8-3 0 ... SophieDoyle(3) 6 — 15
(Jamie Osborne) *racd against rail: disp ld to over 2f out: wknd qckly* **50/1**

1m 12.96s (0.76) **Going Correction** +0.025s/f (Good) — **8** Ran SP% **127.5**
Speed ratings (Par 96): **95,90,80,78,76 72,71,66**
toteswingers: 1&2 £1.10, 1&3 £2.50, 2&3 £2.60 CSF £4.01 TOTE £1.30: £1.02, £1.70, £1.70; EX 4.00.
Owner Allan Belshaw **Bred** Times Of Wigan Ltd **Trained** Newmarket, Suffolk

FOCUS

The lower bend was dolled out 8yds, increasing distances by approximately 10yds on the 1m course. A dry night and day and the ground remained good, with good to firm places. The second running of a race won last year by the very useful Winter's Night and, although this race was rendered uncompetitive when Dance Party was withdrawn earlier in the day, this year's winner looks the sort to hold her own in stronger company. The gallop was fair and the first two pulled clear.

NOTEBOOK

Sunday Times ◆, who shaped promisingly over C&D on her debut, was much more professional this time and made short work of some ordinary opposition. There was plenty to like about the way she strode clear and this Lowther/Cheveley Park entry appeals as the sort to hold her own in stronger company. (op 2-5)

King Of Wing(IRE), who had shown ability at a modest level in his previous two starts, seemed to give it his best shot again and he looks a good guide to the worth of this form. He's likely to remain vulnerable in this type of event and will be of more interest in ordinary nursery company.

Shout For Joy(IRE) failed to build on her previous turf run over a trip that she is bred to appreciate. She is another that may do better in run-of-the-mill nurseries. (op 6-1)

Morning Muse(IRE), a £16,500 half-sister to smart (up to 1m2f) Polytrack winner Questioning, was noticeably green on this racecourse debut but did hint at ability over a trip that looked very much on the sharp side. She will be much better suited by 7f and beyond and should be able to leave this bare form behind in due course.

Merv(IRE) again had his limitations exposed dropping back in trip but he should do better granted a much stiffer test (half-brother to multiple 1m3f-2m winner Isa'af) in low-grade nurseries. Official explanation: jockey said colt hung left (op 10-1)

4955 KENNELS STKS (NURSERY H'CAP) 5f

5:30 (5:32) (Class 5) (0-70,70) 2-Y-O **£2,587** (£770; £384; £192) **Stalls** High

Form RPR

6255 **1** **Stepper Point**[22] 4212 2-9-5 **68** MartinDwyer 5 75+
(William Muir) *trckd ldrs: led over 1f out gng strly: pushed along and wl in command fnl f* **4/1**[2]

6144 **2** 1 ½ **Ocean Myth**[12] 4558 2-9-7 **70** ShaneKelly 2 70
(William Haggas) *hld up in tch: effrt on outer 1/2-way: rdn to chse wnr jst over 1f out: no imp* **3/1**[1]

5332 **3** *hd* **Leenavesta (USA)**[8] 4658 2-9-4 **70** SeanLevey(3) 3 69
(Richard Hannon) *pressed ldrs: rdn fr 1/2-way: nt qckn wl over 1f out: kpt on fnl f to press for 2nd* **9/2**[3]

4564 **4** 1 ½ **Sweet Ovation**[14] 4460 2-8-4 **53** HayleyTurner 6 47
(Mark Usher) *sltly awkward s: pushed along in last early: effrt 2f out: kpt on to take 4th ins fnl f* **15/2**

0424 **5** 1 ¼ **Dressed In Lace**[33] 3849 2-9-2 **65** LiamKeniry 4 54
(Andrew Balding) *led to over 1f out: wknd* **4/1**[2]

0565 **6** 8 **Russian Bullet**[9] 4648 2-8-7 **59** (b) SophieDoyle(3) 7 20
(Jamie Osborne) *t.k.h: racd against rail: pressed ldr to jst over 2f out: wknd rapidly* **20/1**

59.87 secs (1.47) **Going Correction** +0.025s/f (Good) **6 Ran SP% 99.7**
Speed ratings (Par 94): **89,86,86,83,81 69**
toteswingers: 1&2 £2.40, 1&3 £2.70, 2&3 £2.80 CSF £12.73 TOTE £5.90: £2.40, £1.90; EX 14.90.

Owner C L A Edginton **Bred** Whitsbury Manor Stud **Trained** Lambourn, Berks

■ Sister Guru (6/1) was withdrawn after becoming unruly in the stalls. Deduct 10p in the £ under R4.

FOCUS

A modest nursery run at a reasonable gallop.

NOTEBOOK

Stepper Point ◆, who reportedly scoped dirty when disappointing in soft ground on his nursery debut, attracted support and showed that to be all wrong back on a sound surface, despite racing with the choke out. He'll be up in the weights for this, but the way he travelled through the race suggested there should be a bit more to come. (op 7-1)

Ocean Myth doesn't seem to have much in hand of her mark at present but she ran creditably and looks a good guide to the worth of this form. She will be worth another try over 6f and should be able to pick up another race away from progressive types. (tchd 10-3)

Leenavesta(USA) turned in another creditable effort, in the process shaping as though the return to 6f would be more to her liking. She has yet to win but should continue to give a good account.

Sweet Ovation was again found out through lack of pace over this trip on a sound surface. Her form has a patchy look to it but she will be suited by the step up to 6f and isn't one to write off just yet. (op 8-1 tchd 13-2)

Dressed In Lace had shown ability at a modest level in maidens but had her limitations exposed from this mark on this nursery debut. She lacks much in the way of physical scope and will have to improve to win a race of this nature. (tchd 7-2 and 9-2 in places)

4956 CHICHESTER CITY MAIDEN STKS 1m 1f 192y

6:00 (6:01) (Class 5) 3-Y-O+ **£2,587** (£770; £384; £192) **Stalls** Low

Form RPR

42-4 **1** **Dean Swift**[13] 4514 3-9-3 75 MartinDwyer 3 83
(Brian Meehan) *mde all: set modest pce to 1/2-way: had rest in trble over 2f out: shkn up and drew clr over 1f out: r.o wl* **5/1**[3]

3 **2** 4 **Fruehling (IRE)**[27] 4065 3-9-3 0 WilliamBuick 7 75
(Sir Michael Stoute) *trckd wnr: rdn 3f out: nt qckn over 2f out: wl hld after* **3/1**[2]

0-4 **3** 1 ¼ **Midnight Moon**[20] 4279 3-9-3 0 (v) TedDurcan 6 73
(Saeed Bin Suroor) *trckd ldrs in 4th: rdn wl over 2f out: wandering and nt qckn: tk wl hld 3rd jst over 1f out* **9/1**

0-23 **4** 3 ¾ **Hayaku (USA)**[40] 3632 3-8-12 74 JimCrowley 1 60
(Ralph Beckett) *trckd ldng pair: shkn up and nt qckn over 2f out: wl btn and lost 3rd jst over 1f out: wknd* **1/1**[1]

0-3 **5** 6 **Knightly Escapade**[94] 1950 3-9-3 0 IanMongan 5 53
(John Dunlop) *dwlt: hld up in last pair: rdn 3f out: effrt on outer 2f out: sn wknd* **10/1**

0-0 **6** 15 **Pani Ash**[29] 3980 3-8-7 0 (t) JemmaMarshall(5) 2 18
(Pat Phelan) *in tch in last pair tl wknd qckly 2f out: t.o* **125/1**

2m 11.17s (3.17) **Going Correction** -0.075s/f (Good) **6 Ran SP% 111.6**
Speed ratings (Par 103): **84,80,79,76,72 60**
toteswingers: 1&2 £2.20, 1&3 £2.60, 2&3 £3.60 CSF £19.98 TOTE £4.90: £2.20, £2.10; EX 16.20.

Owner Lady Rothschild **Bred** Kincorth Investments Inc **Trained** Manton, Wilts

FOCUS

A couple of fair sorts but a steady pace resulted in a time nearly seven seconds above Racing Post Standard and this bare form doesn't look reliable. The form is rated around the winner.

Hayaku(USA) Official explanation: trainer said filly was unsuited by the track

4957 SOUTHERN DAILY ECHO STKS (H'CAP) 1m 4f

6:30 (6:33) (Class 4) (0-85,81) 3-Y-O+ **£4,204** (£1,251; £625; £312) **Stalls** High

Form RPR

4021 **1** **Rastaban**[20] 4287 3-9-0 **80** WilliamBuick 2 90+
(William Haggas) *racd in 2nd and put it up to ldr on several occasions: rdn to chal again 3f out: drvn to ld narrowly 1f out: styd on and hld on* **5/4**[1]

6630 **2** *nk* **Trip The Light**[18] 4360 6-9-7 **79** (v) LeeTopliss(3) 3 88
(Richard Fahey) *led at decent pce but harried: rdn 3f out: hdd narrowly 1f out: fought on wl but jst hld* **14/1**

0015 **3** 6 **Kings Bayonet**[22] 4216 4-9-8 **77** HayleyTurner 1 77
(Alan King) *t.k.h: hld up in last pair: prog to go 3rd over 2f out: sn rdn and nt qckn: fdd over 1f out* **10/1**

1-45 **4** 2 ½ **Foxhaven**[28] 4008 9-9-10 **79** (v) JimCrowley 4 75
(Patrick Chamings) *trckd ldng pair: rdn 3f out: grad wknd over 2f out* **8/1**

0030 **5** ½ **Dynamic Drive (IRE)**[26] 4097 4-9-8 **77** EddieAhern 6 72
(Walter Swinburn) *trckd ldng trio: rdn and effrt 3f out: no prog over 2f out: sn wknd* **15/2**[3]

1342 **6** 23 **Aldwick Bay (IRE)**[14] 4473 3-9-1 **81** RichardHughes 5 39
(Richard Hannon) *hld up in last pair: rdn over 3f out: wknd over 2f out: t.o: fin lame* **5/2**[2]

2m 35.95s (-2.45) **Going Correction** -0.075s/f (Good)
WFA 3 from 4yo+ 11lb **6 Ran SP% 111.6**
Speed ratings (Par 105): **105,104,100,99,98 83**
toteswingers: 1&2 £3.60, 1&3 £3.80, 2&3 £6.60 CSF £19.56 TOTE £2.00: £1.10, £6.00; EX 20.70.

Owner Abdulla Al Khalifa **Bred** Sheikh Abdullah Bin Isa Al-Khalifa **Trained** Newmarket, Suffolk

FOCUS

A fair handicap but one that didn't take as much winning as seemed likely given the below-par run of the second favourite. An ordinary gallop steadied around halfway and the first two were at the head of affairs throughout. The winner is progressive and can rate higher.

Aldwick Bay(IRE) Official explanation: vet said colt finished lame on the right fore

4958 WESTERTON STKS (H'CAP) 1m

7:05 (7:05) (Class 4) (0-85,85) 3-Y-O+ **£4,204** (£1,251; £625; £312) **Stalls** Low

Form RPR

-123 **1** **Take It To The Max**[50] 3276 4-9-5 **79** LeeTopliss(3) 7 90
(Richard Fahey) *trckd ldng pair: wnt 2nd over 3f out: rdn to ld 2f out: pressed fr over 1f out: styd on wl* **9/2**[2]

3312 **2** ¾ **Romantic Wish**[27] 4062 3-9-4 **85** SeanLevey(3) 9 93
(Robert Mills) *hld up in midfield and off the pce: prog on outer over 2f out: rdn to press wnr over 1f out: styd on but a jst hld* **11/2**[3]

0000 **3** *hd* **Santefisio**[10] 4616 5-9-9 **80** WilliamBuick 8 89
(Peter Makin) *hld up in midfield and off the pce: prog on outer over 2f out: rdn in cl 3rd over 1f out: kpt on same pce* **13/2**

3105 **4** 1 ¾ **Galatian**[34] 3801 4-9-11 **82** JamesMillman 10 87
(Rod Millman) *led at str pce: drvn and hdd 2f out: steadily outpcd* **20/1**

6464 **5** *nk* **First Cat**[8] 4656 4-9-9 **80** RichardHughes 4 84
(Richard Hannon) *stdd s: hld up in last pair and wl off the pce: cajoled along and no real prog over 2f out: r.o over 1f out: nvr a threat* **4/1**[1]

0610 **6** 2 ½ **Shamir**[33] 3840 4-9-9 **80** IanMongan 5 78
(Jo Crowley) *hld up in midfield and off the pce: shkn up 3f out: no imp on ldrs 2f out: fdd* **10/1**

0006 **7** 2 ¾ **South Cape**[12] 4537 8-9-7 **78** TadhgO'Shea 1 70
(Gary Moore) *hld up in last quartet and wl off the pce: shkn up and nt qckn over 2f out: nvr on terms* **12/1**

610- **8** ½ **Avertis**[338] 5834 6-9-5 **79** (tp) HarryBentley(3) 2 70
(Alastair Lidderdale) *pressed ldrs: rdn over 2f out: sn lost pl and wknd* **40/1**

1135 **9** 1 ¼ **Salient**[7] 4725 7-9-3 **74** J-PGuillambert 6 62
(Michael Attwater) *pressed ldr to over 3f out: sn lost pl and btn: eased whn no ch ins fnl f* **20/1**

0244 **10** *nk* **Moynahan (USA)**[12] 4537 6-9-13 **84** (p) JimmyFortune 11 71
(Paul Cole) *hld up in last quartet and wl off the pce: awkward bnd 5f out: no prog over 2f out: eased whn no ch ins fnl f* **9/2**[2]

6460 **11** 11 **Champagne Style (USA)**[12] 4537 4-9-0 **71** (p) TedDurcan 3 33
(Richard Guest) *s.s: a last: t.o* **28/1**

1m 39.66s (-0.24) **Going Correction** -0.075s/f (Good)
WFA 3 from 4yo+ 7lb **11 Ran SP% 117.3**
Speed ratings (Par 105): **98,97,97,95,95 92,89,89,88,87 76**
toteswingers: 1&2 £5.40, 1&3 £8.20, 2&3 £9.70 CSF £27.85 CT £161.62 TOTE £5.40: £1.70, £2.30, £2.70; EX 38.50.

Owner Mrs Phillipa Davies **Bred** Whatton Manor Stud **Trained** Musley Bank, N Yorks

FOCUS

Not many progressive sorts but still a fairly good handicap. The gallop was a reasonable one but those attempting to come from off the pace weren't seen to best advantage. The winner is rated back to his 3yo best.

4959 GOLF AT GOODWOOD STKS (H'CAP) 1m 1f 192y

7:40 (7:40) (Class 3) (0-95,88) 3-Y-O+ **£6,792** (£2,021; £1,010; £505) **Stalls** Low

Form RPR

0-15 **1** **Cry Fury**[82] 2295 3-9-5 **88** SteveDrowne 4 101+
(Roger Charlton) *hld up in last pair: prog on outer over 2f out: led over 1f out and qckly assumed command: r.o wl: readily* **11/4**[2]

0032 **2** 3 ½ **Absinthe (IRE)**[21] 4253 5-10-0 **88** AdamKirby 1 95
(Walter Swinburn) *trckd ldng pair: trying to chal whn n.m.r and swtchd lft 2f out: styd on wl to take 2nd ins fnl f: no ch w wnr* **9/4**[1]

1561 **3** 2 ½ **Arabian Star (IRE)**[42] 3557 3-8-11 **80** HayleyTurner 2 81
(Andrew Balding) *trckd ldr: led over 2f out to over 1f out: one pce and lost 2nd ins fnl f* **9/2**

-100 **4** 2 ¼ **Sweet Child O'Mine**[15] 4429 4-9-7 **81** TedDurcan 5 78
(Richard Guest) *hld up in last pair: nt qckn over 2f out: one pce and no ch w ldrs after* **16/1**

2600 **5** *shd* **Changing The Guard**[12] 4537 5-9-4 **81** LeeTopliss(3) 6 77
(Richard Fahey) *trckd ldng pair: effrt on outer over 2f out: wl outpcd over 1f out: fdd* **9/1**

-106 **6** 1 ½ **Audacious**[19] 4316 3-8-13 **82** WilliamBuick 3 75
(Sir Michael Stoute) *led: shkn up and hdd over 2f out: qckly gave up tamely* **7/2**[3]

2m 7.69s (-0.31) **Going Correction** -0.075s/f (Good)
WFA 3 from 4yo+ 9lb **6 Ran SP% 113.7**
Speed ratings (Par 107): **98,95,93,91,91 90**
toteswingers: 1&2 £1.10, 1&3 £3.40, 2&3 £3.40 CSF £9.60 TOTE £3.40: £2.40, £1.50; EX 7.40.

Owner K Abdulla **Bred** Juddmonte Farms Ltd **Trained** Beckhampton, Wilts

■ Stewards' Enquiry : Hayley Turner two-day ban: careless riding (Aug 25-26)

FOCUS
A useful handicap in which an ordinary gallop steadied after a couple of furlongs. The unexposed winner clearly improved again.

NOTEBOOK
Cry Fury ◆, absent since running a creditable fifth to Brown Panther in a race that worked out tremendously well at Haydock in May, showed a fine turn of foot to win a useful handicap in decisive manner after racing with the choke out early on. He'll be even better in a more truly run race and this progressive sort appeals strongly as the sort to win again. (op 3-1)
Absinthe(IRE), fresh from a career-best effort from a 4lb lower mark at Sandown, was chopped for room at a vital stage but it's unlikely he'd have beaten the more progressive winner even with a clear run. He'll be 1lb higher in future but should be able to pick up another race away from the more progressive sorts. (op 2-1 tchd 15-8)
Arabian Star(IRE) had the run of the race and ran creditably from this 2lb higher mark. He's capable of winning away from the better handicapped or more progressive sorts for his new stable. (op 5-1)
Sweet Child O'Mine failed to improve for the return to this trip in a muddling race and was again below her best. She's high enough in the weights but it is worth remembering that her four wins have been either on Fibresand or in heavy ground. (op 12-1)
Changing The Guard has run well at this course in the past but was below his best here for the second run in succession. He hasn't won for over two years and he'll have to show a fair bit more before he's a solid betting proposition. (op 10-1)
Audacious, back in trip after failing to get home over 1m4f at Ascot, had the run of the race but looked less than straightforward under pressure and was a long way below his best. He'll be worth a try in some form of headgear after this display. (op 9-2)

4960 GOODWOOD H'CAP STKS 6f
8:10 (8:10) (Class 5) (0-75,73) 3-Y-O+ **£2,587** (£770; £384; £192) **Stalls** High

Form RPR
0300 **1** **Sermons Mount (USA)**[10] 4618 5-9-6 **67** .... LiamKeniry 5 78
(Peter Hedger) *trckd ldr: clsd gng wl to ld over 2f out: shkn up over 1f out: hrd pressed nr fin: jst hld on* **16/1**
4045 **2** *nse* **Seamus Shindig**[15] 4434 9-8-13 **65** .... AmyScott(5) 7 76
(Henry Candy) *sn in 7th but in tch: prog 2f out: chsd wnr 1f out: clsd fnl f: jst failed* **8/1**
3054 **3** *2 ¼* **Stonecrabstomorrow (IRE)**[6] 4740 8-8-6 **58** .... MarkCoumbe(5) 1 62
(Michael Attwater) *dwlt: outpcd and detached in last to 1/2-way: prog 2f out: styd on to take 3rd ins fnl f: nt pce to chal* **20/1**
6021 **4** *1 ¼* **Mata Hari Blue**[15] 4434 5-9-8 **69** .... AndreaAtzeni 2 69
(John Holt) *trckd ldrs on outer: wnt 2nd 2f out: nt qckn over 1f out: one pce after* **2/1**[1]
3026 **5** *1* **Commandingpresence (USA)**[4] 4828 5-8-13 **63** .... SeanLevey(3) 3 60
(John Bridger) *wl in tch: prog on outer over 2f out: nt qckn over 1f out: one pce after* **13/2**
0-03 **6** *4* **Safari Mischief**[8] 4659 8-9-11 **72** .... JimCrowley 6 56
(Peter Winkworth) *trckd ldrs: shkn up and nt qckn over 2f out: wl btn over 1f out: fdd* **9/2**[2]
1142 **7** *nk* **Bermondsey Bob (IRE)**[5] 4795 5-9-9 **70** .... SteveDrowne 10 53
(John Spearing) *dwlt: detached in last pair: nvr on terms w ldrs: no real prog fnl 2f* **5/1**[3]
0055 **8** *3 ¼* **Forty Proof (IRE)**[13] 4486 3-9-7 **72** ....(p) ShaneKelly 9 45
(William Knight) *wl in tch: nt qckn over 2f out: wknd over 1f out* **12/1**
-040 **9** *3 ¾* **Spanish Acclaim**[6] 4742 4-9-9 **70** ....(b) NeilChalmers 8 31
(Andrew Balding) *led against rail and sn clr: hdd over 2f out and dropped out rapidly* **12/1**

1m 11.87s (-0.33) **Going Correction** +0.025s/f (Good)
WFA 3 from 4yo+ 4lb **9** Ran SP% **118.7**
Speed ratings (Par 103): **103,102,99,98,96 91,91,86,81**
toteswingers: 1&2 £12.20, 1&3 £14.90, 2&3 £14.30 CSF £140.59 CT £2596.39 TOTE £12.70: £3.60, £2.80, £4.20; EX 114.50.
Owner Fairley Risky **Bred** Sherman Family Tbs Llc **Trained** Dogmersfield, Hampshire

FOCUS
Exposed performers in an ordinary handicap. The gallop was sound, the first five finished clear and this form should prove reliable. Slight improvement from the winner.
Stonecrabstomorrow(IRE) Official explanation: jockey said gelding stumbled leaving the stalls
Bermondsey Bob(IRE) Official explanation: jockey said gelding was slowly away
T/Plt: £17.80 to a £1 stake. Pool: £32,633.77. 1,332.67 winning tickets. T/Qpdt: £8.20 to a £1 stake. Pool: £2,818.19. 253.55 winning tickets. JN

4801 NEWMARKET (R-H)
Thursday, August 11
OFFICIAL GOING: Good to firm changing to good after race 5 (4.35)
Wind: fresh, half behind Weather: showers

4961 FENNERS CHAMBERS MEDIAN AUCTION MAIDEN FILLIES' STKS 6f
2:20 (2:22) (Class 5) 2-Y-O **£3,234** (£962; £481; £240) **Stalls** Low

Form RPR
52 **1** **Besito (IRE)**[20] 4263 2-9-0 0 .... KierenFallon 1 85
(William Jarvis) *mde all: clr after 2f: rdn ent fnl f: styd on wl: comf* **4/1**[2]
2 *3 ½* **Alhira** 2-9-0 0 .... DaneO'Neill 9 75+
(David Simcock) *rn green: dwlt: towards rr: hdwy into midfield 1/2-way: wnt modest 5th and edging rt 2f out: rdn and rn green over 1f out: r.o wl ins fnl f: snatched 2nd last strides: no threat to wnr* **40/1**
3 **3** *nk* **Appointee (IRE)**[48] 3362 2-9-0 0 .... WilliamBuick 6 74
(John Gosden) *sn chsng wnr: rdn and clsd on wnr over 1f out: drvn and tried to chal ent fnl f: sn btn: wknd fnl 100yds and lost 2nd last strides* **4/5**[1]
34U3 **4** *2* **Lady Jameela**[11] 4580 2-9-0 0 .... TonyCulhane 4 68
(Mick Channon) *hld up in midfield: hdwy to chse ldng pair ent fnl 2f: sn rdn and no imp fr over 1f out* **12/1**[3]
3 **5** *1 ½* **Lady Loch**[19] 4347 2-9-0 0 .... PaulHanagan 11 64+
(Richard Fahey) *racd off the pce in midfield: pushed along after 2f: outpcd and dropped towards rr 1/2-way: rallied and styd on ins fnl f: nvr trbld ldrs* **4/1**[2]
6 *hd* **Soho Rocks** 2-9-0 0 .... KirstyMilczarek 3 63
(James Toller) *chsd ldrs: rdn 1/2-way: struggling and lost pl jst over 2f out: n.d fr over 1f out* **25/1**
7 *5* **Willow Beauty** 2-9-0 0 .... FrannyNorton 7 48
(J R Jenkins) *chsd ldrs early: steadily lost pl: towards rr and rdn 3f out: n.d after* **100/1**
0 **8** *hd* **Country Wolf**[29] 3981 2-9-0 0 .... AndreaAtzeni 2 47+
(Michael Wigham) *hld up off the pce in midfield: rdn and edgd lft 2f out: no imp and n.d after* **100/1**
9 *2 ¾* **Al Jabreiah** 2-9-0 0 .... LiamJones 5 39+
(William Haggas) *sn pushed along in last trio: lost tch 1/2-way* **40/1**
00 **10** *2* **Cat Queen**[14] 4471 2-9-0 0 .... TomQueally 8 33
(Gay Kelleway) *awkward leaving stalls: t.k.h: chsd ldrs: rdn and struggling 1/2-way: sn wknd* **40/1**
5 **11** *2 ¾* **Bridgets Call**[63] 2854 2-8-11 0 .... AdamBeschizza(3) 12 25
(Des Donovan) *a in rr: rdn and struggling 1/2-way: sn lost tch* **150/1**
12 *1 ¾* **Norfolk Sky** 2-9-0 0 .... JackMitchell 10 20
(Chris Wall) *v.s.a: a bhd: lost tch bef 1/2-way* **100/1**

1m 13.44s (0.94) **Going Correction** +0.125s/f (Good) **12** Ran SP% **118.0**
Speed ratings (Par 91): **98,93,92,90,88 88,81,81,77,74 71,68**
Tote Swingers: 1&2 £23.10, 1&3 £1.60, 2&3 £13.20 CSF £149.95 TOTE £5.60: £1.50, £7.10, £1.20; EX 154.90 Trifecta £458.50 Pool: £867.60 - 1.40 winning units..
Owner Anthony Foster **Bred** Roger O'Callaghan **Trained** Newmarket, Suffolk

FOCUS
Far side track used with stalls on stands' side except 1m2f &1m4f: centre. Rail realignment on bend into straight added 16m to races of 1m2f & 1m4f. Despite the track receiving 5mm of water the previous day and 1.5mm of rain leading up to the meeting, the ground officially remained good to firm, though the rider of the beaten favourite in the opener described it as good.

NOTEBOOK
Besito(IRE) had hung right when runner-up at Ascot on her second start, but being drawn against the stands' rail here removed the chances of a repeat. Soon in front, she kept on answering for Fallon and was always keeping the favourite at bay. Things very much went her way here, but she is undoubtedly progressing. (tchd 9-2)
Alhira ◆ was the main eyecatcher. He was held up in the early stages but stayed on nicely from over a furlong out and snatched second place close to the line without being by any means knocked about. Out of a half-sister to three winners at up to 1m, this was a hugely promising debut and she looks a sure-fire future winner. (op 50-1)
Appointee(IRE), a well-beaten third behind the subsequent Sweet Solera winner Discourse and Cherry Hinton winner Gamilati on her debut over C&D in June, appeared to have been found a decent opportunity to go two better here but, after racing handily and holding every chance, made heavy weather of trying to get on terms with the winner and finished weakly. She has a bit to prove now. (op 5-6 tchd 8-11)
Lady Jameela was the most experienced in the field with an official mark of 73 and she ran her race, but she is vulnerable to improvers and this looks about as good as she is. She may do better in nurseries. (op 11-1 tchd 9-1)
Lady Loch, a promising third of 11 on her York debut last month, was always struggling to go the pace and didn't get into gear until it was too late. A step up to 7f may be in order. (op 5-1)
Soho Rocks, a 110,000gns filly out of a winning sprinter from the family of Milligram, looked to need the experience but she did show ability. (op 16-1)
Country Wolf's rider reported that the filly was never travelling. Official explanation: jockey said filly was never travelling (op 80-1)

4962 HOLDENS STUD H'CAP 1m 2f
2:50 (2:52) (Class 4) (0-85,85) 3-Y-O+ **£4,204** (£1,251; £625; £312) **Stalls** Centre

Form RPR
5543 **1** **Sonoran Sands (IRE)**[26] 4103 3-9-4 **84** .... MichaelHills 8 92
(Peter Chapple-Hyam) *chsd ldr tl pushed ahd 2f out: drvn over 1f out: kpt on wl fnl f* **6/1**[3]
1331 **2** *½* **Broughtons Paradis (IRE)**[20] 4275 5-9-0 **71** .... StevieDonohoe 2 78
(Willie Musson) *hld up in tch in midfield: nt clr run over 2f out: swtchd lft and hdwy ent fnl f: drvn and pressed wnr ins fnl f: hld towards fin* **15/2**
0113 **3** *½* **Hawaana (IRE)**[7] 4697 6-9-8 **79** .... PaulHanagan 5 86+
(Gay Kelleway) *chsd ldrs: shuffled bk and bhd a wall of horses ent fnl 2f: swtchd lft to outer and hdwy u.p ins fnl f: r.o wl: nt rch ldrs* **5/1**[2]
156 **4** *1 ¼* **George Adamson (IRE)**[19] 4331 5-9-5 **76** .... PJMcDonald 9 80
(Alan Swinbank) *chsd ldrs: rdn and effrt over 2f out: edgd rt and chsd wnr over 1f out tl jst ins fnl f: one pce fnl 150yds* **13/2**
30 **5** *½* **Love Over Gold (FR)**[19] 4344 4-9-10 **81** .... KierenFallon 1 84
(Ralph Beckett) *led: hdd and rdn 2f out: unable qck over 1f out: styd on one pce and hld fnl f* **13/2**
3/20 **6** *¾* **Vimiero (USA)**[33] 3844 4-9-9 **80** .... TomQueally 4 81
(Walter Swinburn) *travelled wl: chsd ldrs: swtchd lft and effrt ent fnl 2f: wanting to hang and fnd little whn rdn wl over 1f out: one pce and no threat to ldrs fnl f* **11/4**[1]
0006 **7** *7* **Signor Verdi**[60] 2955 4-9-9 **80** .... WilliamBuick 7 67
(Brian Meehan) *chsd ldrs: hdwy and pressing ldrs over 2f out: rdn 2f out: nt qckning whn hit by rivals whip wl over 1f out: wknd 1f out* **9/1**
-600 **8** *18* **Mr Willis**[50] 2068 5-9-13 **84** .... PatDobbs 3 35
(Terry Clement) *stdd s: hld up in last pair: rdn and struggling over 3f out: wl bhd fnl 2f* **40/1**
6/ **9** *dist* **Lastofthemohicans (FR)**[321] 6343 4-9-13 **84** .... TonyCulhane 10 —
(Paul Webber) *stdd s: hld up in last pair: stmbld and rdr looking down over 4f out: eased and virtually p.u fr over 3f out: wl t.o* **20/1**

2m 6.19s (0.69) **Going Correction** +0.125s/f (Good)
WFA 3 from 4yo+ 9lb **9** Ran SP% **113.3**
Speed ratings (Par 105): **102,101,101,100,99 99,93,79,—**
Tote Swingers: 1&2 £5.20, 1&3 £7.70, 2&3 £3.10 CSF £49.19 CT £240.00 TOTE £7.30: £2.60, £1.60, £2.00; EX 61.20 Trifecta £410.30 Part won. Pool: £554.56 - 0.40 winning units..
Owner Tony Elliott **Bred** Lynn Lodge Stud **Trained** Newmarket, Suffolk

FOCUS
The rain started to come down again before this race. This was a rough contest, run at an ordinary pace, and there wasn't much covering the front six at the line. The winner rates back to his 2yo best.
Lastofthemohicans(FR) Official explanation: jockey said, regarding running and riding, his instructions were to see how he jumped, settle the horse and finish in the best possible position. He stated the gelding had lost it's action on a couple of occasions and eased the horse, as he felt the gelding may have injured himself. He later reported the gelding had lost it's action at scale. The trainer confirmed these instructions; vet confirmed gelding appeared to be intermittently lame on both front legs.

4963 HISCOX PROPERTY MAIDEN FILLIES' STKS 7f
3:25 (3:25) (Class 5) 3-Y-O+ **£3,234** (£962; £481; £240) **Stalls** Low

Form RPR
02 **1** **Phoenix City (USA)**[8] 4663 3-8-12 0 .... TomQueally 2 86
(Michael Bell) *mde all and racd against stands' rail: rdn over 1f out: edgd lft u.p 1f out: styd on wl and drew wl clr fnl 150yds* **9/1**[3]
4 **2** *4* **Interaction**[18] 4356 3-8-12 0 .... WilliamBuick 4 75
(John Gosden) *racd in centre trio: chsd ldrs: rdn jst over 2f out: drvn and btn over 1f out: no ch w wnr but plugged on to go 2nd towards fin* **7/4**[2]
5-33 **3** *1 ¼* **Regal Heiress**[18] 4356 3-8-12 79 .... KierenFallon 6 72
(Sir Michael Stoute) *racd in centre: chsd wnr: rdn and effrt 2f out: drvn and tried to chal ent fnl f: sn btn: wknd fnl 150yds* **10/11**[1]
0 **4** *5* **Bashama**[41] 3577 3-8-12 0 .... PhilipRobinson 1 58
(Clive Brittain) *racd against stands' rail: a in rr: rdn and btn jst over 2f out: no ch fr over 1f out* **16/1**

-04 **5** 3½ **Amazing Win (IRE)**[50] 3289 3-8-12 0 .... TonyCulhane 3 49
(Mick Channon) *racd towards stands' side: t.k.h: chsd ldrs tl rdn and wknd 2f out* **16/1**

0 **6** 33 **Shikra**[161] 751 3-8-12 0 .... (e[1]) WilliamCarson 5 —
(Eugene Stanford) *racd in centre: stdd s: t.k.h: hld up in rr: rdn and struggling 1/2-way: hung lft and lost tch wl over 2f out: t.o* **100/1**

1m 25.55s (-0.15) **Going Correction** +0.125s/f (Good) 6 Ran SP% **111.5**
Speed ratings (Par 100): **105,100,99,93,89 51**
Tote Swingers: 1&2 £2.20, 1&3 £1.50, 2&3 £1.30 CSF £24.96 TOTE £9.10: £3.30, £1.20; EX 27.60.
Owner Ali Saeed **Bred** M D Hall, K N Blazer & Adena Springs **Trained** Newmarket, Suffolk

FOCUS
A modest race by Newmarket standards but still fair fillies' form despite the favourite disappointing. The field split into two groups of three early and once again the stands' rail was the place to be.

4964 SAGECARE NURSING AND CARE CONDITIONS STKS 7f
4:00 (4:00) (Class 2) 2-Y-O £7,762 (£2,310; £1,154; £577) Stalls Low

Form RPR

3102 **1** **Trumpet Major (IRE)**[19] 4311 2-9-1 101 .... PatDobbs 4 106+
(Richard Hannon) *chsd ldr tl led on bit jst over 1f out: shkn up and r.o strly fnl f: easily* **8/11**[1]

4315 **2** 6 **Elkhart (IRE)**[15] 4424 2-8-13 95 .... KierenFallon 1 86
(Mark Johnston) *led: rdn wl over 1f out: hdd jst over 1f out: outpcd by wnr and wl btn fnl f* **5/2**[2]

1 **3** 3¾ **Dance The Rain**[12] 4525 2-8-8 0 .... TomEaves 3 72
(Bryan Smart) *chsd ldrs: rdn wl over 2f out: drvn and ev ch over 1f out: sn outpcd: wknd fnl f* **12/1**

3106 **4** 2½ **Commissar**[33] 3861 2-9-1 90 .... TomQueally 2 72
(Mahmood Al Zarooni) *a same pl: rdn and effrt 2f: wknd over 1f out* **13/2**[3]

1m 25.49s (-0.21) **Going Correction** +0.125s/f (Good) 4 Ran SP% **107.5**
Speed ratings (Par 100): **106,99,94,92**
CSF £2.74 TOTE £1.60; EX 2.80.
Owner John Manley **Bred** John Cullinan **Trained** East Everleigh, Wilts

FOCUS
An interesting little conditions event, but with just the four runners the perceived stands'-rail bias wasn't really a factor. The winning time was fractionally faster than the older fillies in the preceding maiden.

NOTEBOOK
Trumpet Major(IRE) put his modest Coventry Stakes effort behind him when narrowly beaten in an Ascot Listed event over this trip last time and only had to run to that form to go one better here, but he impressed with the way he travelled and also with the way he left his three rivals for dead inside the last furlong. He looks ready for a step back up in class. (op 5-6 tchd 10-11 in places)
Elkhart(IRE) was found out when stepped up to Group 2 company in the Vintage Stakes at Goodwood and tried to make all here, racing near the stands' rail if not tight against it. He was overwhelmed by the winner's turn of foot from over a furlong out, however, and he may not be the easiest to place from now on. (op 11-4)
Dance The Rain was an unknown quantity after narrowly winning a Doncaster maiden on her debut last month. Weak in the market, she had a chance tight against the stands' rail over a furlong out, but was then firmly put in her place by the front pair. She isn't up to this level, but still has a bit of scope and can win more races in the right company. (op 17-2)
Commissar had disappointed in both the Coventry and the Superlative for his current yard after leaving Paul Cole, but again failed to sparkle despite the big drop in grade. (op 6-1 tchd 15-2)

4965 SOLID WALL INSULATION H'CAP 7f
4:35 (4:35) (Class 2) (0-100,99) 3-Y-O £10,350 (£3,080; £1,539; £769) Stalls Low

Form RPR

22-1 **1** **White Frost (IRE)**[20] 4282 3-8-2 80 .... WilliamCarson 6 90
(B W Hills) *chsd ldr: ev ch and hanging lft wl over 1f out: rdn to ld over 1f out: stl hanging but kpt on wl fnl f* **4/1**[1]

-400 **2** 1 **Forjatt (IRE)**[34] 3820 3-9-1 98 .... AntiocoMurgia[(5)] 7 105
(Roger Varian) *hld up in tch in last trio: hdwy on outer over 2f out: rdn to chse ldrs ent fnl f: kpt on: wnt 2nd and swtchd lft towards fin* **9/2**[2]

5-21 **3** nse **Sea Soldier (IRE)**[49] 3320 3-8-2 80 .... FrannyNorton 2 87
(Andrew Balding) *racd keenly: led: rdn 2f out: hdd over 1f out: kpt on same pce u.p ins fnl f: lost 2nd towards fin* **9/2**[2]

0505 **4** 2½ **Ahlaain (USA)**[19] 4313 3-9-1 93 .... TomEaves 4 93
(David Simcock) *stdd s: hld up in last pair: hdwy 2f out: drvn jst over 1f out: styd on same pce and no imp ins fnl f* **12/1**[3]

0413 **5** shd **El Viento (FR)**[14] 4472 3-9-1 93 .... (b) PaulHanagan 1 93
(Richard Fahey) *chsd ldrs: rdn over 2f out: unable qck and outpcd over 1f out: kpt on same pce u.p fnl f* **9/2**[2]

45P6 **6** 1¼ **Trade Storm**[13] 4493 3-9-7 99 .... TomQueally 3 95
(John Gallagher) *in tch: hdwy to chse ldrs after 2f: rdn and unable qck over 1f out: sn outpcd and btn 1f out: styd on same pce u.p fnl f* **14/1**

0060 **7** 2 **Sonning Rose (IRE)**[19] 4332 3-7-13 80 .... LouisBeuzelin[(3)] 8 71
(Mick Channon) *stdd s: hld up in last: swtchd rt and rdn over 2f out: no imp: nvr trbld ldrs* **25/1**

1100 **8** nk **Seal Rock**[19] 4333 3-9-3 95 .... DaneO'Neill 5 85
(Henry Candy) *chsd ldrs: rdn jst over 2f out: wknd ent fnl f* **4/1**[1]

1m 25.39s (-0.31) **Going Correction** +0.125s/f (Good) 8 Ran SP% **112.8**
Speed ratings (Par 106): **106,104,104,101,101 100,98,97**
Tote Swingers: 1&2 £4.90, 1&3 £3.30, 2&3 £4.80 CSF £21.47 CT £82.89 TOTE £4.70: £2.00, £1.40, £1.70; EX 16.40 Trifecta £102.20 Pool: £1,074.81 - 7.78 winning units..
Owner Mr And Mrs J D Cotton **Bred** M Henochsberg & Mme D Hazan-Ades **Trained** Lambourn, Berks

FOCUS
Another heavy shower hit the track before this race. A decent handicap and a wide-open one according to the market, but the pace wasn't strong and those who raced prominently were at an advantage. The form is taken at face value.

NOTEBOOK
White Frost(IRE) ◆ was making his handicap debut following a successful return from 294 days off in a Thirsk maiden last month and had shown as a juvenile that he could handle testing conditions, so the rain wasn't a problem. Always handy, he took over coming to the last furlong and despite hanging away to his left in the latter stages (something he did here last season) had done enough by then. He gives the impression there is still more improvement in him. (op 9-2)
Forjatt(IRE) had enjoyed no luck at all in his three previous starts this term and was trying this trip for the first time. The easing ground wasn't necessarily an advantage, but he ran a corker and did well to get so close considering that, unlike the other principals, he came from off the pace. He deserves a change in his fortunes. (tchd 4-1)
Sea Soldier(IRE) was making his handicap debut and the form of his Warwick maiden success last time was boosted by the second and third horses winning since. Allowed to dominate from the start, he battled back well when headed and can still make the grade back on a quicker surface. (op 4-1)
Ahlaain(USA) had suggested he would be suited by the drop back to this trip and kept on well despite never looking like winning. (tchd 10-1, 16-1 in a place)
El Viento(FR) appeared to prove his stamina for the trip when beaten under a length into third at Goodwood last time, but that was on fast ground and this may have been too severe a test, despite having the advantage of the stands' rail. (tchd 11-2)
Trade Storm, back in a handicap for the first time since finishing fifth in the Britannia off 1lb lower, had every chance but didn't get home and lacks the scope of a few of these. (op 11-1 tchd 16-1)
Sonning Rose(IRE), who has found life tough despite dropping in class and being 18lb lower than at this time last year, never threatened at any stage here. (op 20-1)
Seal Rock ran another tame race and seems to have gone the wrong way after looking so promising at the start of the season. The Stewards ordered him to be routine tested. Official explanation: jockey said gelding had no more to give (op 9-2)

4966 TURFTV H'CAP 1m 4f
5:10 (5:11) (Class 4) (0-80,80) 3-Y-O £4,204 (£1,251; £625; £312) Stalls Centre

Form RPR

51 **1** **Planetoid (IRE)**[8] 4664 3-9-7 80 6ex .... TomQueally 4 92
(David Lanigan) *led for 2f: chsd ldr after tl led again gng wl 3f out: rdn over 1f out: drvn whn pressed ins fnl f: wandered u.p but fnd ex fnl 75yds: r.o* **6/4**[2]

5-21 **2** ½ **A Boy Named Suzi**[45] 3469 3-9-3 76 .... JackMitchell 1 87
(James Eustace) *hld up in tch: rdn and effrt jst over 2f out: edgd lft u.p and chsd wnr over 1f out: pressed wnr ins fnl f: keeping on same pce and hld whn rdr dropped whip towards fin* **9/2**[3]

5411 **3** 3 **Franciscan**[26] 4084 3-9-4 77 .... KierenFallon 6 83
(Luca Cumani) *chsd ldr tl led after 2f: hdd 3f out: sn rdn: drvn and lost 2nd over 1f out: one pce fnl f* **11/8**[1]

3561 **4** 13 **Little Jazz**[17] 4389 3-8-11 70 .... PhilipRobinson 3 55
(Paul D'Arcy) *stdd s: chsd ldrs after 2f: rdn over 3f out: wknd over 1f out* **10/1**

2m 36.76s (3.86) **Going Correction** +0.125s/f (Good) 4 Ran SP% **109.4**
Speed ratings (Par 102): **92,91,89,81**
CSF £8.14 TOTE £2.50; EX 9.60.
Owner B E Nielsen **Bred** Bjorn Nielsen **Trained** Newmarket, Suffolk

FOCUS
The ground was changed to good before this race. Just the four runners and they went no pace early. They also raced well away from the stands' rail once into the home straight. The form is rated around the third and the winner can do better.

4967 JULY COURSE H'CAP 5f
5:45 (5:46) (Class 4) (0-80,86) 3-Y-O+ £4,204 (£1,251; £625; £312) Stalls Low

Form RPR

3-60 **1** **Picabo (IRE)**[49] 3322 3-8-12 71 .... PaulHanagan 8 82+
(Lucy Wadham) *stdd s: hld up in tch: hdwy over 1f out: rdn to ld fnl 75yds: r.o wl* **5/2**[2]

3411 **2** ¾ **Tyfos**[11] 4583 6-9-11 86 6ex .... BrianToomey[(5)] 4 94
(Brian Baugh) *led: rdn jst over 1f out: drvn ins fnl f: hdd and no ex fnl 75yds* **15/8**[1]

1202 **3** 1¼ **Whiskey Junction**[7] 4731 7-8-10 69 .... AdamBeschizza[(3)] 9 73
(Michael Quinn) *chsd ldrs: rdn over 1f out: styd on same pce u.p ins fnl f* **9/1**

4216 **4** 2¼ **Bobby's Doll**[30] 3957 4-8-9 65 ow1 .... StevieDonohoe 1 60
(Terry Clement) *chsd ldr: rdn and unable qck over 1f out: wknd jst ins fnl f* **14/1**

3333 **5** 1 **Star Twilight**[7] 4731 4-8-6 62 .... (p) TomEaves 3 54
(Derek Shaw) *hld up in tch: effrt and n.m.r jst over 1f out: rdn and no imp jst ins fnl f: wknd fnl 75yds* **10/1**

0566 **6** 1¾ **Shifting Star (IRE)**[18] 4369 6-9-8 78 .... (v) TomQueally 7 64
(Walter Swinburn) *dwlt: hld up in last: rdn 2f out: no prog and wl hld whn swtchd lft ins fnl f* **7/2**[3]

59.13 secs (0.03) **Going Correction** +0.125s/f (Good)
WFA 3 from 4yo+ 3lb 6 Ran SP% **111.3**
Speed ratings (Par 105): **104,102,100,97,95 92**
Tote Swingers: 1&2 £2.00, 1&3 £2.20, 2&3 £1.80 CSF £7.48 CT £31.66 TOTE £3.10: £2.50, £2.00; EX 6.00 Trifecta £21.30 Pool: £210.73 - 7.29 winning units..
Owner Tom Ford **Bred** A B Mulholland **Trained** Newmarket, Suffolk

FOCUS
A fair sprint handicap, but a race hit by four non-runners. They raced down the centre and the form is rated around the third.
T/Plt: £62.90 to a £1 stake. Pool of £56,361.00 - 653.75 winning tickets. T/Qpdt: £129.50 to a £1 stake. Pool of £2,583.00 - 129.50 winning tickets. SP

4912 SALISBURY (R-H)
Thursday, August 11

OFFICIAL GOING: Good to firm (8.7)
Wind: quite strong against Weather: overcast with rain

4968 RSM TENON MAIDEN AUCTION STKS (DIV I) 6f 212y
2:00 (2:01) (Class 5) 2-Y-O £2,587 (£770; £384; £192) Stalls Centre

Form RPR

0 **1** **Goodwood Atlantis (IRE)**[22] 4213 2-9-2 0 .... TedDurcan 11 80+
(John Dunlop) *str: coltish: mid-div: hdwy 3f out: pushed along whn nt clrest of runs 2f out: styd on to ld ins fnl f: hld on: all out* **12/1**

2 shd **Presburg (IRE)** 2-8-9 0 .... EddieCreighton 13 73+
(Joseph Tuite) *unf: s.i.s: sn pushed along racing green in rr: rdn and stdy prog fr over 2f out: 6th 1f out: styd on strly to draw upsides fnl 75yds: jst hld* **100/1**

3 2½ **Poisson D'Or** 2-8-8 0 .... SteveDrowne 1 65
(Rae Guest) *athletic: lw: trckd ldrs: rdn to chal 2f out: led jst ins fnl f: sn hdd: no ex* **14/1**

33 **4** nk **Takeitfromalady (IRE)**[14] 4455 2-8-11 0 .... JimCrowley 14 67
(Ralph Beckett) *lw: mid-div: reminder over 3f out: hdwy sn after: rdn over 2f out: styd on same pce fnl f* **14/1**

0 **5** shd **Beau Duke (IRE)**[27] 4053 2-8-11 0 .... JimmyFortune 5 67
(Andrew Balding) *in tch: rdn to chse ldrs over 2f out: kpt on same pce* **11/4**[2]

022 **6** ¾ **Maccabees**[29] 3986 2-8-10 71 ow1 .... JamesMillman 2 64
(Rod Millman) *trckd ldr: led wl over 2f out: sn riddn and hung rt: hdd jst ins fnl f: no ex* **7/4**[1]

7 1 **Lone Foot Laddie (IRE)** 2-8-11 0 .... LiamKeniry 12 63+
(Sylvester Kirk) *tall: unf: scope: hld up towards rr: pushed along fr over 3f out: stdy prog fr over 1f out: styd on: nrst fin* **66/1**

06 **8** hd **Welsh Nayber**[7] 4698 2-8-13 0 .... EddieAhern 10 64+
(Amanda Perrett) *mid-div: pushed along fr over 3f out: nvr any imp* **50/1**

9 2 ¼ **Dalacara** 2-8-8 0 .... LukeMorris 8 53+
(Clive Cox) *w'like: trckd ldrs: u.p whn squeezed up 2f out: wknd fnl f* **10/1**[3]

10 1 ½ **Caledonian Lad** 2-8-9 0 .... HayleyTurner 7 50+
(Hughie Morrison) *w'like: leggy: lw: s.i.s: racd green: sme late prog but mainly towards rr* **16/1**

0 11 10 **Scarlet Prince**[12] 4535 2-8-9 0 .... FergusSweeney 3 24
(Gary Moore) *s.i.s: sn nudged along in mid-div: wknd 2f out* **100/1**

12 3 ½ **Clianthus** 2-9-2 0 .... GeorgeBaker 4 22
(Paul Cole) *tall: green: edgy: led tl wl over 2f out: sn rdn: wknd wl over 1f out* **16/1**

0 13 6 **Shark In The Sea**[22] 4201 2-9-2 0 .... PatCosgrave 9 7
(Brian Meehan) *in tch: rdn over 2f out: sn wknd* **25/1**

14 1 ¼ **Glitter (IRE)** 2-8-13 0 .... RichardHughes 6 —
(Richard Hannon) *w'like: bit bkwd: stdd s: t.k.h: a towards rr* **10/1**[3]

1m 28.98s (0.38) **Going Correction** +0.025s/f (Good) **14** Ran SP% **123.3**
Speed ratings (Par 94): **98,97,95,94,94 93,92,92,89,88 76,72,65,64**
Tote Swingers: 1&2 £130.90, 1&3 £37.10, 2&3 £116.10 CSF £920.72 TOTE £17.00: £3.70, £13.90, £5.50; EX 1350.10.
Owner Goodwood Racehorse Owners Group (18)Ltd **Bred** John O'Connor **Trained** Arundel, W Sussex

FOCUS
A fair maiden auction, though the standard set by the market leader was not high and it wasn't a surprise to see something unexposed come through and win the race. The pace was good and the principals largely came from off it.

NOTEBOOK
Goodwood Atlantis(IRE) hadn't fared too badly in a better race at Sandown on his debut and showed the benefit of that experience with a much-improved performance, rallying gamely after he'd been headed. He still looked clueless for much of the race, so can be expected to improve further and promises to be an interesting nursery prospect in the autumn over further. (op 14-1 tchd 11-1)
Presburg(IRE), who's a half-brother to several winners, ran a cracker on his debut. Slowly away and bringing up the rear for much of way, he put in a sustained run from halfway that took him to the front briefly inside the last. He's clearly more ability than his starting price suggests.
Poisson D'Or ◆ looks the one to take from the race. Out of a Park Hill second and a half-sister to several middle-distance winners, she fared best of those up with the pace throughout, despite hailing from a yard that rarely have first-time-out 2yo winners. She'll surely improve and win a similar event, with the promise of even more progress upped to 1m. (tchd 16-1)
Takeitfromalady(IRE) looks to have improved again and will presumably head for nurseries now. He looks a strong-galloping type who'll be better suited by 1m in due course. Official explanation: jockey said gelding hung right (op 12-1 tchd 10-1)
Beau Duke(IRE) was well backed to give his yard their fourth winner in this race since 2006, but didn't build as expected on his debut Newbury form which has already started to work out well. He didn't look to have any excuses. (op 7-1)
Maccabees was the clear form pick but didn't find as much as looked likely. It could be that he went too hard for home too soon. (op 6-4 tchd 15-8 and 2-1 in a place)
Lone Foot Laddie(IRE), a half-brother by Red Clubs to 7f winner Ghost, shaped well under a considerate ride and seems sure to be all the better for the race.
Welsh Nayber showed more than previously but might have blown his cover as a nursery mark is concerned. (op 40-1)
Dalacara is bred much more for longer trips next year but shaped as if she had ability until seeming to find lack of race-fitness catching her out. (op 20-1)
Glitter(IRE) was backed beforehand but didn't promise much with her slow start not an inconvenience as the race panned out. (op 7-1)

4969 RSM TENON MAIDEN AUCTION STKS (DIV II) 6f 212y
2:30 (2:32) (Class 5) 2-Y-O **£2,587** (£770; £384; £192) **Stalls** Centre

Form RPR

3 1 **Frog Hollow**[27] 4068 2-8-13 0 .... JimCrowley 3 86+
(Ralph Beckett) *str: nudged along towards rr: hdwy over 3f out: rdn over 2f out: wnt 2nd ent fnl f: led fnl 85yds: styd on wl* **3/1**[1]

53 2 1 ½ **My Queenie (IRE)**[15] 4427 2-8-11 0 .... PatCosgrave 4 80
(Richard Hannon) *lw: led: rdn 2f out: kpt on gamely tl hdd and no ex fnl 85yds* **4/1**[2]

0 3 2 ¼ **Blue Surf**[16] 4414 2-9-2 0 .... EddieAhern 1 80+
(Amanda Perrett) *lw: trckd ldrs tl rdn over 2f out: styng on but looking hld whn short of room ent fnl f* **12/1**

2322 4 ½ **Tight Lipped (IRE)**[22] 4104 2-9-12 81 .... RichardMullen 9 75
(David Brown) *prom: rdn to chse ldr 2f out: kpt on same pce fnl f: lost 3rd nr fin* **4/1**[2]

6 5 3 **Zamarelle**[22] 4205 2-8-8 0 .... SteveDrowne 13 62
(Roger Charlton) *w'like: lw: sn mid-div: hdwy over 3f out: sn rdn: wknd fnl f* **7/1**

3 6 1 ¼ **Titus Star (IRE)**[34] 3816 2-8-9 0 .... LukeMorris 6 60+
(J S Moore) *mid-div: effrt 2f out: sn one pce* **20/1**

622 7 1 ½ **Not Bad For A Boy (IRE)**[17] 4384 2-9-2 71 .... RichardHughes 11 63
(Richard Hannon) *hld up: rdn and hdwy fr 2f out: wknd ins fnl f* **9/2**[3]

00 8 10 **Doc Hill**[11] 4580 2-8-9 0 .... LiamKeniry 2 30
(Michael Blanshard) *trckd ldrs: rdn over 2f out: sn wknd* **100/1**

0 9 1 **Garrarufa (IRE)**[129] 1136 2-8-11 0 .... JamesMillman 8 29
(Rod Millman) *cmpt: chunky: little slowly away: a towards rr: wknd 2f out* **100/1**

44 10 64 **Daring Damsel (IRE)**[22] 4201 2-8-11 0 .... JimmyFortune 5 —
(Paul Cole) *hld up towards rr: eased fr 3f out: virtually p.u* **20/1**

1m 28.67s (0.07) **Going Correction** +0.025s/f (Good) **10** Ran SP% **114.9**
Speed ratings (Par 94): **100,98,95,95,91 90,88,77,76,2**
Tote Swingers: 1&2 £4.50, 1&3 £7.70, 2&3 £11.50 CSF £14.27 TOTE £4.10: £1.30, £1.90, £4.40; EX 21.00.
Owner R A Pegum **Bred** Reid & Shriver **Trained** Kimpton, Hants

FOCUS
More strength in depth and proven form on show than in the first division and a race run in a faster time too, despite the time taken to get to the path over 3f out being almost 0.9 secs slower. The winner deserves plenty of credit in the circumstances.

NOTEBOOK
Frog Hollow ◆ had finished third in a Newbury maiden on his debut that is turning out to be very muddling form, but he'd clearly improved as the market hinted he had, and ultimately ran out a cosy winner. That looked unlikely at halfway after a slow start, but the further he went the better he got as he ran down rivals who had got a start on him and he's sure to improve again, with a step up to 1m set to suit. He's more than likely got a nursery at least in him. (op 9-2)
My Queenie(IRE) seemed well suited by the return to 7f, for all she was able to dictate matters, and she's shown more than enough once again to think she can win a maiden, possibly back among her own sex. (tchd 7-2 and 9-2)
Blue Surf typically improved from his first run to his second like so many from his yard without impressing as much out of the ordinary, but even this trip looked to be too sharp for this Derby entry and he'll progress again over further. (op 10-1 tchd 14-1)
Tight Lipped(IRE) had every chance as the race developed but his merit is fairly well established now and he's going to be better off back in nurseries. (tchd 7-2)

Zamarelle, loaded into the stalls early, didn't improve perhaps quite as much as looked likely on her recent AW debut. (tchd 13-2 and 8-1)
Titus Star(IRE) showed enough despite still looking very green to think he can win a seller if risked again back down in grade. (op 25-1)
Not Bad For A Boy(IRE) had stayed this trip at Haydock on his second start but didn't seem to get home here, running well below form. Maybe 6f is his trip. (op 4-1 tchd 7-2)

4970 MARY WORT MEMORIAL MAIDEN STKS 6f 212y
3:05 (3:08) (Class 5) 3-4-Y-O **£2,911** (£866; £432; £216) **Stalls** Centre

Form RPR

02 1 **Orpen'Arry (IRE)**[7] 4706 3-9-3 0 .... RichardHughes 8 78+
(Andrew Haynes) *trckd ldr: rdn to ld 2f out: r.o strly to assert fnl f: readily* **13/2**

3004 2 2 ½ **Obiter Dicta**[34] 3803 3-8-12 65 .... FergusSweeney 14 66
(Henry Candy) *mid-div: hdwy 3f out: sn rdn: chsd wnr wl over 1f out: outpcd fnl f* **9/1**

002 3 3 **Semmsu (IRE)**[35] 3766 3-9-3 77 .... J-PGuillambert 2 63
(Luca Cumani) *lw: trckd ldrs: rdn over 2f out: styd on same pce* **10/3**[2]

-0 4 1 ¾ **Backstreet Fighter (IRE)**[14] 4461 3-8-12 0 .... JamesRogers(5) 5 58
(Gary Harrison) *trckd ldrs: rdn over 2f out: styd on same pce* **150/1**

0 5 2 **Fleetwoodmaxi (USA)**[19] 4340 4-9-9 0 .... EddieAhern 1 59
(Peter Makin) *mid-div: rdn 3f out: nvr any imp on ldrs* **33/1**

26 6 ¾ **Rohlindi**[41] 3577 3-8-8 0 ow1 .... LucyKBarry(5) 6 47
(Clive Cox) *mid-div: hdwy 3f out: sn rdn to chse ldrs: fdd fnl f* **8/1**

34-0 7 hd **Latansaa**[43] 3521 4-9-9 80 .... TadhgO'Shea 11 52
(Marcus Tregoning) *trckd ldrs: rdn over 2f out: wknd jst over 1f out* **11/4**[1]

8 nk **Gaelic Wizard (IRE)** 3-9-3 0 .... HayleyTurner 4 50
(Dominic Ffrench Davis) *led tl rdn 2f out: wknd jst over 1f out* **50/1**

9 1 ¾ **The Flying Cholita (IRE)** 3-8-12 0 .... CathyGannon 7 40
(Eve Johnson Houghton) *leggy: a towards rr* **40/1**

0 10 ½ **Prana (USA)**[26] 4102 3-8-12 0 .... SteveDrowne 3 39
(Jeremy Gask) *unf: a towards rr* **28/1**

04-4 11 hd **Tarjeyh (IRE)**[17] 4388 3-9-3 68 .... (v[1]) SebSanders 12 43
(Marcus Tregoning) *mid-div: rdn wl over 2f out: wknd over 1f out* **5/1**[3]

12 4 ½ **Bunkered Again** 4-9-4 0 .... AdamKirby 13 28
(Jeremy Gask) *w'like: uns rdr gng to s but sn ct: a towards rr* **25/1**

6000 13 5 **A B Celebration**[29] 3979 3-8-12 46 .... NeilChalmers 10 12
(John Bridger) *mid-div for 2f: sn towards rr: nvr a danger* **150/1**

1m 28.74s (0.14) **Going Correction** +0.025s/f (Good)
WFA 3 from 4yo 6lb **13** Ran SP% **116.8**
Speed ratings (Par 103): **100,97,93,91,89 88,88,88,86,85 85,80,74**
Tote Swingers: 1&2 £4.10, 1&3 £7.90, 2&3 £7.20 CSF £59.26 TOTE £6.30: £2.00, £3.20, £1.60; EX 45.90.
Owner Mrs Barbara Fuller **Bred** Thomas Kelly **Trained** Limpley Stoke, Bath

FOCUS
A modest maiden run at a steady pace to past halfway, and with the field well bunched it turned into something of a sprint. The form looks weak behind the runner-up but the winner should do better still.
Fleetwoodmaxi(USA) Official explanation: jockey said gelding was denied a clear run

4971 E B F "TOBOUGG" FILLIES' H'CAP 1m 4f
3:40 (3:40) (Class 4) (0-80,78) 3-Y-0+ **£5,175** (£1,540; £769; £384) **Stalls** Low

Form RPR

5530 1 **Dubai Glory**[15] 4449 3-8-13 74 .... JamesDoyle 12 84
(Sheena West) *trckd ldrs: led over 2f out: sn rdn clr: styd on strly* **12/1**

-002 2 2 **Sugar Hiccup (IRE)**[27] 4056 3-8-4 65 .... LukeMorris 4 72
(Clive Cox) *in tch: pushed along over 4f out: rdn over 3f out: styd on steadily: wnt 2nd ins fnl f: no ch w wnr* **16/1**

0202 3 2 ½ **Sunday Bess (JPN)**[28] 4014 3-9-1 76 .... RichardKingscote 7 79
(Tom Dascombe) *lw: mid-div: rdn and stdy prog fr over 2f out: chsd wnr over 1f out tl no ex ins fnl f* **12/1**

1210 4 ½ **Lady Gabrielle (IRE)**[15] 4448 3-8-12 73 .... NickyMackay 5 75+
(David Elsworth) *hld up towards rr: pushed along over 4f out: rdn over 3f out: hdwy over 1f out: styd on wl fnl f* **14/1**

4111 5 nk **Twin Soul (IRE)**[148] 866 3-8-11 72 .... RichardHughes 10 74
(Andrew Balding) *hld up towards rr: nt clrest of runs over 2f out: sn rdn and weaved path through: styd on but nvr getting there* **8/1**

2213 6 ¾ **Amistress**[14] 4473 3-8-12 73 .... CathyGannon 6 75+
(Eve Johnson Houghton) *hld up towards rr: rdn 4f out: no imp tl styng on w 4th plcd horse whn squeezed out over 1f out: kpt on but no ch after* **7/2**[1]

3122 7 1 ¼ **Undulant Way**[19] 4341 3-9-2 77 .... SebSanders 8 76
(Amanda Perrett) *lw: hld up: hdwy fr 4f out: rdn to chse wnr over 2f out tl over 1f out: fdd ins fnl f* **4/1**[2]

2212 8 7 **On The Feather**[14] 4465 5-9-7 71 .... JamesMillman 1 58
(Rod Millman) *mid-div: rdn 3f out: wknd over 1f out: eased ins fnl f* **7/1**[3]

5301 9 12 **On Khee**[10] 4613 4-9-12 76 6ex .... (b) JimmyFortune 2 44
(Hughie Morrison) *lw: led tl rdn over 2f out: grad fdd: eased ins fnl f* **15/2**

3051 10 3 ¼ **Goldtrek (USA)**[42] 3533 4-10-0 78 .... (p) SteveDrowne 9 41
(Roger Charlton) *cl up: ldr tl 3f out: sn rdn: wknd 2f out: eased fnl f* **11/1**

6445 11 2 ¼ **Goodlukin Lucy**[22] 4204 4-9-3 67 .... (p) JimCrowley 11 26
(Pat Eddery) *chsd ldrs tl wknd over 2f out: eased fnl f* **28/1**

2m 35.46s (-2.54) **Going Correction** -0.075s/f (Good)
WFA 3 from 4yo+ 11lb **11** Ran SP% **117.3**
Speed ratings (Par 102): **105,103,102,101,101 100,100,95,87,85 83**
Tote Swingers: 1&2 £32.70, 1&3 £28.20, 2&3 £22.70 CSF £188.05 CT £2347.21 TOTE £14.40: £4.00, £3.80, £4.50; EX 199.60.
Owner The Affordable (2) Partnership **Bred** Hascombe And Valiant Studs **Trained** Falmer, E Sussex

FOCUS
A wide-open handicap contested by plenty of in-form horses, and a fair fillies' race for the grade. The gallop looked a decent one and most of the principals came from off the pace, the winner the exception.

4972 TOTEPOOL SOVEREIGN STKS (GROUP 3) (C&G) 1m
4:15 (4:16) (Class 1) 3-Y-0+
£28,355 (£10,750; £5,380; £2,680; £1,345; £675) **Stalls** Low

Form RPR

3113 1 **Side Glance**[33] 3843 4-9-0 115 .... JimmyFortune 4 115+
(Andrew Balding) *led early: trckd ldr: chal 2f out: sn rdn: disp ent fnl f: picked up wl to assert whn runner-up chal nring fin* **2/1**[1]

3125 2 nk **Dance And Dance (IRE)**[13] 4494 5-9-0 108 .... RichardHughes 8 114+
(Edward Vaughan) *lw: hld up: pushed along and gd hdwy over 1f out: rdn and str run ins fnl f: fin wl* **5/1**[2]

6422 **3** *1* **The Rectifier (USA)**[47] 3409 4-9-0 104.......................... MickyFenton 10 112
(Jim Boyle) *sn led: rdn and hrd pressed fr 2f out: battled on v gamely tl no ex whn hdd towards fin* **28/1**

4-10 **4** *¾* **Secrecy**[18] 4373 5-9-0 110.................................. RichardMullen 2 110
(Saeed Bin Suroor) *mid-div: hdwy 3f out: sn rdn: swtchd lft ent fnl f: styd on but nt pce to chal* **14/1**

2312 **5** *shd* **Fanunalter**[33] 3843 5-9-3 116.................................. AdamKirby 3 113+
(Marco Botti) *lw: hld up: travelling wl but nt clr run fr wl over 1f out tl ins fnl f: r.o: nvr any ch* **13/2**

-430 **6** *¾* **Premio Loco (USA)**[68] 2713 7-9-0 117.......................... GeorgeBaker 6 108+
(Chris Wall) *mid-div: rdn over 2f out: no imp tl r.o ins fnl f* **13/2**

-421 **7** *nse* **Emerald Commander (IRE)**[18] 4368 4-9-0 113..............(t) TedDurcan 1 108
(Saeed Bin Suroor) *trckd ldrs: rdn over 2f out: one pce fnl f* **6/1**[3]

-331 **8** *1 ¾* **Julienas (IRE)**[57] 3032 4-9-0 100.............................. EddieAhern 12 104
(Walter Swinburn) *racd keenly: trckd ldrs: rdn over 2f out: wknd fnl f* **10/1**

6005 **9** *3* **Mac Love**[68] 2713 10-9-0 102.................................. PatCosgrave 7 97
(Stef Higgins) *hld up: rdn over 2f out: nvr any imp* **33/1**

-240 **10** *nse* **Field Of Dream**[47] 3404 4-9-0 105...........................(b) J-PGuillambert 11 97
(Luca Cumani) *hld up: pushed along over 3f out: in tch whn rdn over 2f out: wknd ent fnl f* **50/1**

-000 **11** *3* **Frozen Power (IRE)**[182] 503 4-9-0 104.......................... AhmedAjtebi 9 90
(Mahmood Al Zarooni) *in tch: rdn over 2f out: wknd ent fnl f* **50/1**

1m 41.01s (-2.49) **Going Correction** +0.025s/f (Good) **11 Ran SP% 117.0**
Speed ratings: **113,112,111,110,110 110,110,108,105,105 102**
Tote Swingers: 1&2 £4.40, 1&3 £10.40, 2&3 £19.90 CSF £11.27 TOTE £3.20: £1.50, £2.30, £6.80; EX 16.90.

Owner Pearl Bloodstock Ltd **Bred** Kingsclere Stud **Trained** Kingsclere, Hants

FOCUS
A competitive Group 3 on paper but not as things turned out with the two highest-rated horses on official figures either finding trouble or having too much to do, and those handily ridden in a messy and steadily run affair favoured. This said the form is up to scratch for the grade, although the winner did not need to match his early-season wins.

NOTEBOOK
Side Glance has been much improved this season but whether he needed to be at his best to edge out two horses officially rated much lower than he is, having been well placed throughout as the race developed, is open to question. His yard aren't afraid to travel with their best horses and his prospects of success at a higher level might well be abroad. Given its value, presumably his connections have their eye on the Topkapi Trophy in Turkey at the start of September. (op 11-4)

Dance And Dance(IRE) had been making great strides recently in handicaps and did enough here in recording a personal best to suggest he has it in him to win a Group race too, always having too much to do to catch the winner as the race panned out but nearly managing it. He handles soft ground well, so should continue his progress into the autumn. (op 11-2 tchd 6-1)

The Rectifier(USA) was allowed to get on with his usual front-running role unhassled and for a long way looked to have every chance of pulling off an upset. Whether this really represents improved form remains has to be questionable, as Side Glance had beaten him by 4l at Windsor back in May in a race run at a stronger gallop. (op 22-1)

Secrecy was third in this last year but never looked like emulating that feat here, let alone improving on it, and he's still to win anything better than a minor event. (tchd 16-1)

Fanunalter ◆ looked unlucky. He'd finished over 2l ahead of Side Glance in the Summer Mile last time but found being waited with here backfiring as he twice ended up finding his path blocked only to flash home when in the clear. He looked the moral winner on the day Official explanation: jockey said gelding was denied a clear run (op 11-2 tchd 7-1)

Premio Loco(USA) was another who passed the post with plenty of running left in him after also enduring a fraught passage, though arguably not as unlucky as Fanunalter. (op 5-1 tchd 4-1)

Emerald Commander(IRE) found this race more of a demand than his win in a three-runner race Listed race at Pontefract last time and came up short despite being well placed throughout. (op 13-2 tchd 11-2)

4973 BILL GARNETT MEMORIAL FILLIES' H'CAP — 6f

4:50 (4:53) (Class 5) (0-70,70) 3-Y-O+ **£2,425** (£721; £360; £180) **Stalls** Low

Form RPR

5262 **1** **Aristeia**[22] 4199 3-9-5 **69**.................................. JimmyFortune 14 83+
(Richard Hannon) *patiently rdn in last pair: making smooth hdwy whn swtchd lft 2f out: hrd rdn and str run fnl f: led towards fin* **8/1**

3131 **2** *1 ½* **Interakt**[21] 4224 4-9-0 **63**.................................. HarryBentley(3) 12 72
(Joseph Tuite) *mid-div: rdn and hdwy fr over 2f out: led over 1f out: kpt on but no ex whn hdd towards fin* **9/2**[2]

0562 **3** *¾* **Piddie's Power**[5] 4793 4-9-10 **70**.......................... RichardMullen 9 77
(Ed McMahon) *taken down early: trckd ldrs: chal over 2f out: led briefly over 1f out: kpt on same pce* **4/1**[1]

3360 **4** *¾* **Diapason (IRE)**[73] 2566 5-9-8 **68**...........................(t) RichardKingscote 7 75+
(Tom Dascombe) *mid-div: nt clr run over 2f out: sn rdn: r.o fnl f: wnt 4th fnl stride* **20/1**

0553 **5** *hd* **Dualagi**[7] 4711 7-9-2 **62**.................................. GeorgeBaker 3 66
(Martin Bosley) *chsd ldrs: rdn over 2f out: nt pce to chal: kpt on* **25/1**

5110 **6** *½* **Dead Cool**[34] 3818 3-9-6 **70**.................................. SteveDrowne 5 71
(Hughie Morrison) *wnt lft s: mid-div: rdn to chse ldrs over 2f out: one pce fnl f* **11/2**[3]

2650 **7** *¾* **Talamahana**[12] 4547 6-8-8 **54**...........................(v) FergusSweeney 6 54
(Andrew Haynes) *towards rr: rdn 3f out: styd on fnl f: nvr trbld ldrs* **50/1**

5061 **8** *2 ½* **Silvee**[5] 4795 4-8-12 **58** 6ex.................................. NeilChalmers 2 50
(John Bridger) *chsd ldr: led over 2f out: sn rdn: hdd over 1f out: fdd fnl f* **7/1**

2123 **9** *¾* **Sarangoo**[13] 4486 3-9-2 **66**.................................. TomMcLaughlin 10 57
(Malcolm Saunders) *mid-div: rdn over 2f out: wknd fnl f* **15/2**

1033 **10** *2 ½* **Athaakeel (IRE)**[9] 4640 5-8-12 **58**...........................(b) CathyGannon 11 39
(Ronald Harris) *s.i.s: a towards rr* **16/1**

400 **11** *1 ¾* **Miss Dutee**[34] 3818 3-8-3 **60**.................................. CharlesBishop(7) 4 35
(Richard Hannon) *in tch: rdn over 3f out: wknd 2f out* **16/1**

1000 **12** *2 ½* **Fettuccine (IRE)**[34] 3818 3-9-1 **65**.......................... TadhgO'Shea 1 32
(John Gallagher) *led tl rdn over 2f out: wknd over 1f out* **28/1**

0 **13** *4* **Style Margi (IRE)**[40] 3630 3-9-2 **66**.......................... PatCosgrave 8 20
(Ed de Giles) *rdn wl over 2f out: a towards rr* **20/1**

1m 15.23s (0.43) **Going Correction** +0.025s/f (Good)
WFA 3 from 4yo+ 4lb **13 Ran SP% 119.5**
Speed ratings (Par 100): **98,96,95,94,93 93,92,88,87,84 82,78,73**
Tote Swingers: 1&2 £8.60, 1&3 £8.20, 2&3 £4.70 CSF £40.81 CT £151.94 TOTE £9.80: £3.10, £2.20, £1.70; EX 55.50.

Owner K N Dhunjibhoy, V B Shirke, B M Desai **Bred** Poulton Farm Stud **Trained** East Everleigh, Wilts

FOCUS
Plenty came here near the top of their game and it looked a fair race, although a bit of bunching led to a slightly false result. Ordinary fillies' form.

4974 PAT BOAKES MEMORIAL H'CAP — 1m 6f 21y

5:20 (5:20) (Class 5) (0-70,69) 3-Y-O+ **£2,425** (£721; £360; £180)

Form RPR

0222 **1** **May Contain Nuts**[29] 3989 3-8-12 **66**.......................... FergusSweeney 5 74
(Brendan Powell) *led for 4f: trckd ldr: led 3f out: sn rdn: styd on dourly: rdn out* **6/1**[2]

5236 **2** *3* **Dr Darcey**[21] 4242 3-8-7 **61**...........................(b) CathyGannon 8 65
(Richard Hannon) *trckd ldr: led after 4f out tl 3f out: sn rdn: kpt chsng wnr but a being hld: jst hung on for 2nd* **7/1**[3]

0004 **3** *hd* **Jinto**[19] 4317 4-8-13 **54**.................................. NickyMackay 13 58
(David Elsworth) *mid-div: rdn over 4f out: styd on steadily: wnt 3rd ins fnl f: nrst fin: jst failed to snatch 2nd* **8/1**

6050 **4** *hd* **Bahkov (IRE)**[7] 4703 5-8-11 **52**...........................(b) MickyFenton 2 55
(Eric Wheeler) *trckd ldrs: rdn over 4f out: nt pce to get on terms: styd on ins fnl f* **25/1**

0064 **5** *3 ¼* **Green Future (USA)**[30] 3960 3-8-6 **60**.......................... LukeMorris 4 59
(Amanda Perrett) *mid-div: rdn over 3f out: styd on same pce fnl 2f* **10/1**

2520 **6** *2 ¼* **Sunny Future (IRE)**[19] 4341 5-10-0 **69**.......................... TomMcLaughlin 12 65
(Malcolm Saunders) *hld up bhd: stdy prog fr over 5f out: wnt 3rd whn rdn 3f out: fdd fr over 1f out* **7/1**[3]

3566 **7** *2* **Prince Charlemagne (IRE)**[87] 2140 8-8-9 **55**...(p) MatthewCosham(5) 6 48
(Dr Jeremy Naylor) *hld up towards rr: struggling over 3f out: sme late prog: nvr a danger* **40/1**

320/ **8** *¾* **Bathwick Man**[10] 5885 6-8-11 **52** oh3.......................... RichardMullen 10 44
(David Pipe) *trckd ldrs: struggling wl over 3f out: nvr threatened: wknd over 1f out* **3/1**[1]

0/53 **9** *nk* **Dream Catcher (SWE)**[19] 4318 8-9-3 **58**...................(p) GeorgeBaker 3 49
(Jonjo O'Neill) *t.k.h: trckd ldrs: rdn over 3f out: wknd over 1f out* **16/1**

0001 **10** *1 ½* **Quinsman**[3] 4870 5-9-7 **65**.................................. RossAtkinson(3) 7 54
(J S Moore) *mid-div: rdn 3f out: wknd over 1f out* **7/1**[3]

0556 **11** *35* **Raktiman (IRE)**[22] 4204 4-9-12 **67**...................(v[1]) RichardKingscote 11 —
(Tom Dascombe) *hld up towards rr: plld hrd whn swtchd wd after 4f: wknd 3f out: virtually p.u* **16/1**

0055 **12** *1 ¾* **Talbot Green**[23] 4190 3-8-3 **62**.................................. JamesRogers(5) 9 —
(William Muir) *chsd ldrs tl lost pl after 4f: midfield: rdn over 4f out: wknd 3f out: virtually p.u* **33/1**

3m 6.13s (-1.27) **Going Correction** -0.075s/f (Good)
WFA 3 from 4yo+ 13lb **12 Ran SP% 118.0**
Speed ratings (Par 103): **100,98,98,98,96 94,93,93,93,92 72,71**
Tote Swingers: 1&2 £4.60, 1&3 £13.10, 2&3 £10.60 CSF £46.61 CT £341.93 TOTE £6.20: £1.40, £3.20, £2.50; EX 63.40.

Owner I S Smith **Bred** S A Douch **Trained** Upper Lambourn, Berks

FOCUS
A run-of-the-mill staying handicap to end proceedings and something of a tactical affair with those ridden handily favoured. The winner continued his gradual improvement.
Raktiman(IRE) Official explanation: jockey said gelding hung left throughout
Talbot Green Official explanation: jockey said colt hung left
T/Jkpt: Not won. T/Plt: £6,223.30 to a £1 stake. Pool of £75,874.00 - 8.90 winning tickets. T/Qpdt: £59.30 to a £1 stake. Pool of £5,753.00 - 71.70 winning tickets. TM

4975 - 4977a (Foreign Racing) - See Raceform Interactive

4733 LEOPARDSTOWN (L-H)

Thursday, August 11

OFFICIAL GOING: Good (good to yielding in places)

4978a DESMOND STKS (GROUP 3) — 1m

7:05 (7:05) 3-Y-O+ **£32,219** (£9,418; £4,461; £1,487)

RPR

1 **Future Generation (IRE)**[26] 4116 3-8-12 102.......................... KLatham 5 108
(G M Lyons, Ire) *sn led and mde virtually all: strly pressed early st: swished tail but kpt on gamely u.p fr over 1f out* **3/1**[2]

2 *¾* **Emiyna (USA)**[81] 2334 3-9-1 106.................................. JMurtagh 4 109+
(John M Oxx, Ire) *trckd ldrs: 3rd ent st: rdn to cl 1f out: kpt on u.p fnl f: nt rch wnr* **1/1**[1]

3 *1 ¾* **Moran Gra (USA)**[16] 4418 4-9-8 103...........................(p) KJManning 3 106
(Ms Joanna Morgan, Ire) *a.p: trckd ldr in 2nd: rdn to chal early st: no imp u.p ins fnl f* **8/1**

4 *2 ½* **Hujaylea (IRE)**[11] 4588 8-9-8 105...........................(p) CPHoban 1 100
(M Halford, Ire) *towards rr: 5th on inner 1/2-way: niggled along ent st: kpt on one pce wout threatening* **13/2**[3]

5 *¾* **Duff (IRE)**[22] 4220 8-9-8 102.................................. DPMcDonogh 6 99
(Edward Lynam, Ire) *dwlt: towards rr: sme hdwy on outer early st: no imp in 4th wl over 1f out: no ex fnl f* **15/2**

6 *5 ½* **Croisultan (IRE)**[46] 3440 5-9-8 102.......................... NGMcCullagh 2 86
(Liam McAteer, Ire) *trckd ldrs on inner in 3rd: rdn along ent st and sn no ex: wknd over 1f out* **20/1**

1m 39.91s (-1.29) **Going Correction** +0.175s/f (Good)
WFA 3 from 4yo+ 7lb **6 Ran SP% 116.0**
Speed ratings: **113,112,110,108,107 101**
CSF £6.71 TOTE £4.30: £1.80, £1.40; DF 9.60.

Owner Viking Syndicate **Bred** Ennistown Stud **Trained** Dunsany, Co. Meath

FOCUS
The gradually progressive winner rates a personal best, with the standard set around the second and third.

NOTEBOOK
Future Generation(IRE) is an improving filly and this was her fourth win and her first at Pattern level in a race in which the two three-year-olds, both of them fillies, in the line-up ran first and second. The winner had finished second in a similar type 7f event at the Curragh on her previous start and she delivered a game effort here, going to the front over 6f out and making the rest to win driven out. The ease in the ground helped her. (op 7/2 tchd 4/1)

Emiyna(USA) had won the Group 3 Athasi Stakes on fast ground in May prior to running well below expectations in the Irish 1000 Guineas. This was her first run since and she arrived with her challenge 1f out and kept on without finding enough to get to the winner. In view of her long break it would be reasonable to expect improvement. She went into this race rated 4lb above the winner to whom she was conceding 3lb, so the form looks reliable enough. (op 9/10 tchd 11/10)

Moran Gra(USA), the winner of two handicaps over the trip, had been well beaten in the Topaz Mile at Galway on his previous start. He produced a much better effort here, disputing the early lead and remaining prominent throughout. He just couldn't raise his game sufficiently over the final furlong. (op 10/1)

Hujaylea(IRE), a seven-time winner, mostly in handicaps, was seeking a first win of the season. Held up, he was pushed along into the straight and kept on without posing a real threat. (op 7/1 tchd 6/1)

Duff(IRE) has several Listed race wins plus a Group 2 and two Group 3's on his CV although he hasn't won a race for close on two years. Only touched off on his previous start, he was held up after missing the break and began his effort soon after turning in before failing to make much impression from 1f out. At his best, 7f is the trip that seems to suit him best. (op 8/1)

4979 - 4981a (Foreign Racing) - See Raceform Interactive

4632 CATTERICK (L-H)

Friday, August 12

OFFICIAL GOING: Good to soft (soft in places; 7.0)

Wind: moderate 1/2 behind Weather: overcast, light rain

4982 PIN POINT RECRUITMENT AMATEUR RIDERS' H'CAP 1m 3f 214y

5:50 (5:51) (Class 5) (0-75,75) 3-Y-O+ £1,996 (£619; £309; £154) Stalls Low

Form RPR

4155 **1** **Patavium (IRE)**[19] 4360 8-11-0 72 MissSBrotherton 9 81
(Edwin Tuer) *in rr: hdwy over 5f out: wnt 3rd 2f out: styd on to ld last 100yds* **5/2**[1]

0640 **2** *2 1/4* **Danceintothelight**[19] 4366 4-9-12 61 MissRSmith(5) 10 66
(Micky Hammond) *trckd ldr: kpt on to take 2nd last 100yds* **6/1**[2]

1006 **3** *1 1/4* **Oddsmaker (IRE)**[14] 4499 10-9-11 60 (t) MissAngelaBarnes(5) 5 63
(Maurice Barnes) *led: clr 7f out: hdd and no ex ins fnl f* **20/1**

-043 **4** *5* **Tropical Bachelor (IRE)**[20] 4341 5-10-6 67 MissPernillaHermansson(3) 6 62
(Richard Ford) *sn detached in last: hdwy over 4f out: edgd lft and kpt on fnl 2f: nvr nr to chal* **8/1**

0333 **5** *nse* **Talk Of Saafend (IRE)**[11] 4605 6-9-7 54 (p) MissECSayer(3) 8 49
(Dianne Sayer) *hld up in mid-div: effrt 3f out: sn outpcd: kpt on fnl f* **8/1**

5334 **6** *3 3/4* **Rub Of The Relic (IRE)**[1] 4946 6-9-2 53 oh3 (v) MissHDukes(7) 3 42
(Paul Midgley) *chsd ldrs: drvn 5f out: outpcd and lost pl over 2f out* **13/2**[3]

503 **7** *3* **Dimashq**[14] 4499 9-9-6 53 oh5 MissWGibson(3) 2 37
(Paul Midgley) *rr-div: pushed along over 6f out: nvr a factor* **17/2**

0164 **8** *2 1/2* **Resplendent Light**[9] 4674 6-10-7 70 (t) MrRJWilliams(5) 7 50
(Bernard Llewellyn) *mid-div: effrt and 4th over 2f out: sn wknd* **12/1**

5001 **9** *nk* **Daaweitza**[10] 4649 8-10-12 75 6ex (be) MissHBethell(5) 11 55
(Brian Ellison) *trckd ldrs: swtchd rt to r alone stands' side over 2f out: sn lost pl* **13/2**[3]

2m 43.19s (4.29) **Going Correction** +0.35s/f (Good) **9** Ran SP% **114.7**

Speed ratings (Par 103): **99,97,96,93,93 90,88,87,86**

toteswingers:1&2:£3.80, 2&3:£25.60, 1&3:£11.10 CSF £17.19 CT £241.84 TOTE £3.20: £1.60, £2.30, £6.80; EX 20.20.

Owner J A Nixon **Bred** M Channon **Trained** Great Smeaton, N Yorks

■ Stewards' Enquiry : Miss R Smith two-day ban: careless riding (tbn)

FOCUS

An uncompetitive opener with several out of form as well as a couple out of the weights. The pace seemed uneven and very few were ever seen with a chance. The advantage was with those ridden handily. A small personal best from the winner.

4983 DECLAN CAMPBELL MEMORIAL (S) STKS 7f

6:20 (6:20) (Class 6) 2-Y-O £1,704 (£503; £251) Stalls Low

Form RPR

0 **1** **Annie Walker (IRE)**[21] 4285 2-8-6 0 PaulQuinn 9 67
(David Nicholls) *w ldr: t.k.h: chal over 2f out: hung lft and led over 1f out: drew clr fnl 100yds: eased nr fin* **7/1**

5625 **2** *6* **Koalition (IRE)**[14] 4512 2-8-8 65 PaulPickard(3) 1 58
(Deborah Sanderson) *mde most: hdd over 1f out: wknd last 100yds* **4/6**[1]

0040 **3** *3* **Lady Gadfly**[13] 4538 2-8-7 52 ow1 FrederikTylicki 5 46
(Micky Hammond) *in rr: hdwy to chse ldrs 4f out: one pce and 3rd over 1f out* **6/1**[3]

030 **4** *7* **Angel Kiss (IRE)**[29] 4002 2-8-6 56 BarryMcHugh 2 27
(David O'Meara) *dwlt: in rr: bhd over 4f out: nvr on terms* **9/2**[2]

53 **5** *7* **Brackendale**[23] 4193 2-8-11 0 (v1) PJMcDonald 6 15
(John Weymes) *in rr: drvn and lost pl over 4f out* **20/1**

6626 **6** *shd* **Sophar**[45] 3491 2-8-11 45 FrannyNorton 7 11
(Jason Ward) *chsd ldrs: wknd over 1f out* **50/1**

00 **7** *2 1/4* **Bea Persuasive**[14] 4512 2-8-1 0 (b1) DanielleMcCreery(5) 8 4
(Shaun Harris) *drvn to chse ldrs on outside 3f out: wknd 3f out: sn bhd* **80/1**

1m 30.56s (3.56) **Going Correction** +0.35s/f (Good) **7** Ran SP% **112.9**

Speed ratings (Par 92): **93,86,82,74,66 66,64**

toteswingers:1&2:£2.10, 2&3:£2.20, 1&3:£3.60 CSF £11.93 TOTE £4.90: £4.30, £1.30; EX 32.70.There was no bid for the winner.

Owner D Nicholls **Bred** Round Hill Stud **Trained** Sessay, N Yorks

■ Stewards' Enquiry : Paul Quinn six-day ban: used whip with excessive frequency down shoulder in the forehand (Aug 26-31)

FOCUS

A modest seller that involved only the front two from the home turn. Once again the runners kept to the far side. The winner scored in good style and the form makes sense.

NOTEBOOK

Annie Walker(IRE) had never got involved on her debut in a Thirsk maiden but took this readily after looking green and ill at ease on the track. A substantial sort, she attracted no bid but will improve again and wouldn't be one to underestimate in a nursery, with 1m easily within her grasp this season. (op 8-1 tchd 13-2)

Koalition(IRE) was a strong favourite taking a drop in grade but fifth place in a Thirsk claimer last time had hinted at his limitations and he had no excuse under a front-running ride, bumped inside the last by the winner but fighting a losing battle at the time. He is going to be hard to win with. (op 5-6 tchd 10-11)

Lady Gadfly plugged on for third and has now run her two best races here, but this effort suggests her previous fourth over 6f at the track flatters her. (op 11-2)

Angel Kiss(IRE) clearly has a modicum of ability but it was a bit disconcerting to see her get so far behind dropping in grade before making some late headway. She might not have handled the track but probably needs further anyway. (op 4-1 tchd 7-2)

Sophar Official explanation: jockey said colt had no more to give

Bea Persuasive ran too freely. Official explanation: trainer said filly was found to be suffering from an infection (tchd 100-1)

4984 ALPHA DENTAL EXCELLENCE IN NHS DENTISTRY NURSERY 5f 212y

6:55 (6:55) (Class 4) (0-85,84) 2-Y-O £3,946 (£1,174; £586; £293) Stalls Low

Form RPR

3616 **1** **See Clearly**[13] 4558 2-8-11 74 RobertWinston 4 75
(Tim Easterby) *w ldrs on outer: rdn over 2f out: upsides and edgd rt over 1f out: styd on to ld post* **11/1**

2042 **2** *shd* **Cravat**[14] 4502 2-9-7 84 FrannyNorton 5 85
(Mark Johnston) *chsd ldrs on outer: edgd lft over 1f out: styd on to ld nr fin: hdd post* **8/1**

223 **3** *1/2* **Half A Billion (IRE)**[19] 4358 2-8-10 73 PJMcDonald 7 72
(Michael Dods) *carried rt s: in rr: hmpd bnd over 4f out: hdwy over 2f out: led jst ins fnl f: hdd and no ex clsng stages* **8/1**

14 **4** *3* **Al Shaqab (IRE)**[14] 4502 2-9-5 82 PhillipMakin 8 73
(Kevin Ryan) *hmpd s: hdwy to chse ldrs whn n.m.r and lost pl over 4f out: hung lft and kpt on fnl f* **7/1**

401 **5** *2* **Balti's Sister (IRE)**[32] 3921 2-8-1 64 JamesSullivan 1 48
(Michael Easterby) *gave problems in stalls: trckd ldrs on ins: chal over 1f out: wknd jst ins fnl f* **11/2**[3]

31 **6** *3/4* **Stormy Whatever (FR)**[23] 4192 2-9-0 77 FrederikTylicki 3 59
(James Given) *led: hdd jst ins fnl f: sn wknd* **9/4**[1]

654 **7** *nk* **Valley Of Hope**[23] 4192 2-8-3 66 PaulHanagan 6 47
(Richard Fahey) *wnt rt s: t.k.h on outer 1st 2f: sn trcking ldrs: wandered over 1f out: sn wknd* **11/4**[2]

1m 16.22s (2.62) **Going Correction** +0.35s/f (Good) **7** Ran SP% **115.9**

Speed ratings (Par 96): **96,95,95,91,88 87,87**

toteswingers:1&2:£8.90, 2&3:£14.30, 1&3:£13.20 CSF £94.62 CT £748.33 TOTE £13.10: £5.10, £3.30; EX 78.80.

Owner Ryedale Partners No 4 **Bred** Rabbah Bloodstock Limited **Trained** Great Habton, N Yorks

FOCUS

A fair nursery and competitive despite the small field, with plenty coming here in good heart, so the form is probably reliable despite the bunch finish. The runners again stayed far side.

NOTEBOOK

See Clearly was much better suited by the longer trip here than the fast 5f at Thirsk last time and showed plenty of spirit to fend off a couple of strong challenges inside the last. She is taking her racing well and clearly very much at home on softish ground. (op 9-1)

Cravat has had excuses in his two runs since being thrown in at the deep end at Royal Ascot and might well have had another here too, looking unbalanced for much of the way on this tricky track and possibly not really relishing the underfoot conditions either. Faster ground and a more galloping track should see him in a better light. (op 7-1 tchd 13-2)

Half A Billion(IRE) ran well on his first start in a nursery and rates a bit better than the result in that he made his ground very quickly from the rear and might even have showed ahead briefly late on. That said, he has already been turned over at long odds-on, so perhaps isn't one to make too many excuses for. (op 7-1)

Al Shaqab(IRE) had finished behind Cravat at Musselburgh last time and did so again without ever threatening to reverse the form after a bump at the start, never going through the race with any fluency. (op 17-2 tchd 9-1)

Balti's Sister(IRE) didn't get home so well as when ridden more patiently at Wolverhampton last time. (op 15-2 tchd 5-1)

Stormy Whatever(FR) had looked promising under similar underfoot conditions here last time but couldn't dominate in the same fashion and dropped away tamely. (op 5-2 tchd 11-4)

Valley Of Hope, who had caught the eye behind Stormy Whatever last time, was inclined to pull too hard for his own good. Official explanation: jockey said gelding ran too free (op 3-1 tchd 5-2 and 100-30 in a place)

4985 TRY TOTEQUICKPICK IF YOU'RE FEELING LUCKY MAIDEN STKS 1m 3f 214y

7:25 (7:25) (Class 5) 3-Y-O+ £2,522 (£750; £375; £187) Stalls Low

Form RPR

0 **1** **Gulf Of Naples (IRE)**[14] 4514 3-9-2 0 FrannyNorton 8 82+
(Mark Johnston) *sn chsng ldrs: sn drvn along: reminders 7f out: lost pl over 4f out: wnt modest 4th 2f out: edgd rt: styd on strly to ld last 50yds* **28/1**

5 **2** *1 1/2* **My Heart's On Fire (IRE)**[74] 2551 3-8-11 0 RobertWinston 9 74
(Tom Dascombe) *sn trcking ldrs: 2nd over 5f out: led over 2f out: hdd and no ex towards fin* **15/2**[3]

26 **3** *1 1/2* **Tiny Temper (IRE)**[13] 4529 3-8-11 0 TonyHamilton 2 72
(Richard Fahey) *sn chsng ldrs: handy 3rd 4f out: upsides 1f out: kpt on same pce* **15/2**[3]

32 **4** *3/4* **Floral Beauty**[64] 2836 3-8-11 0 PaulHanagan 4 71
(Sir Michael Stoute) *led: hdd over 2f out: hung lft and upsides 1f out: wknd towards fin* **4/9**[1]

05 **5** *8* **Jacob McCandles**[11] 4611 4-9-8 0 LMcNiff(5) 6 63
(David Barron) *hld up in rr: bhd 4f out: kpt on fnl 2f: nvr on terms* **28/1**

6-2 **6** *shd* **Raajih**[126] 1211 3-9-2 0 DavidAllan 7 63
(Keith Dalgleish) *hld up in mid-div: drvn over 5f out: lost pl over 4f out* **9/2**[2]

46 **7** *3 3/4* **River Dragon (IRE)**[126] 1211 6-9-8 0 BrianToomey(5) 1 57
(Tony Coyle) *chsd ldrs: lost pl over 3f out* **50/1**

660 **8** *27* **Good Faith**[27] 4112 3-9-2 43 PJMcDonald 5 14
(George Moore) *hld up in rr: reminders over 6f out: sn wl bhd: t.o* **100/1**

00 **9** *8* **Nha Trang (IRE)**[126] 1212 4-9-8 0 LanceBetts(5) 3 —
(Deborah Sanderson) *mid-div: lost pl over 4f out: sn bhd: t.o* **100/1**

2m 42.74s (3.84) **Going Correction** +0.35s/f (Good)

WFA 3 from 4yo+ 11lb **9** Ran SP% **121.8**

Speed ratings (Par 103): **101,100,99,98,93 93,90,72,67**

toteswingers:1&2:£8.90, 2&3:£5.80, 1&3:£8.30 CSF £224.23 TOTE £24.50: £4.90, £2.80, £2.00; EX 268.50.

Owner Sheikh Hamdan Bin Mohammed Al Maktoum **Bred** Stone Ridge Farm **Trained** Middleham Moor, N Yorks

FOCUS

No more than a fair maiden and something of a shock result, one that looked unlikely for much of the way, but the winner promises to rate higher. The pace was sound and again the stands' rail was ignored.

Floral Beauty Official explanation: trainer's rep said filly was unsuited by the good to soft (soft in places) ground

4986 TRY TOTEQUICKPICK ON ALL TOTEPOOL BETS H'CAP 5f

8:00 (8:01) (Class 6) (0-65,65) 3-Y-O+ £1,704 (£503; £251) Stalls Low

Form RPR

0043 **1** **Tongalooma**[3] 4881 5-9-0 55 PJMcDonald 8 67
(James Moffatt) *w ldrs centre: led over 2f out: edgd lft fnl f: kpt on* **10/1**

2121 **2** *1* **Blown It (USA)**[3] 4881 5-9-8 63 12ex PaulHanagan 11 71+
(Keith Dalgleish) *bmpd s: towards rr stands' side: gd hdwy and edgd rt over 1f out: styd on to chse wnr last 75yds* **2/1**[1]

4453 **3** *1 1/4* **Sharp Bullet (IRE)**[20] 4328 5-9-3 58 (p) FrederikTylicki 6 62
(Bruce Hellier) *led centre tl over 2f out: kpt on same pce fnl f* **10/1**

1012 **4** *3/4* **Dispol Grand (IRE)**[20] 4328 5-9-5 60 MickyFenton 10 61
(Paul Midgley) *wnt rt s: sn in rr stands' side: effrt over 2f out: kpt on wl fnl f* **9/1**[3]

6045 **5** *shd* **Sandwith**[13] 4539 8-8-11 57 (v) LMcNiff(5) 12 58
(George Foster) *bmpd s: w ldrs stands' side: hung lft over 1f out: kpt on same pce* **16/1**

1212 **6** 3/4 **Liberty Ship**[10] 4636 6-9-7 **65**....(t) DaleSwift(3) 1 63+
(Mark Buckley) *w ldrs far side: chsd wnr over 1f out: kpt on same pce* **5/2**[2]

3530 **7** *nk* **Kalahari Desert (IRE)**[3] 4881 4-8-5 **46** oh1....(v) PaulQuinn 5 43
(Richard Whitaker) *hld up: hdwy 2f out: sn chsng ldrs: one pce over 1f out* **12/1**

000 **8** 1 3/4 **Ingenti**[21] 4282 3-8-2 **46** oh1.... JamesSullivan 9 36
(Christopher Wilson) *chsd ldrs: wknd 1f out* **40/1**

0-00 **9** 2 1/2 **Speedy Senorita (IRE)**[59] 3027 6-9-2 **57**.... PhillipMakin 3 39
(James Moffatt) *trckd ldrs towards far side: effrt over 1f out: grad wknd* **20/1**

0004 **10** 1 1/2 **Piste**[10] 4636 5-8-5 **46** oh1.... PatrickMathers 4 22
(Tina Jackson) *led towards far side: hdd over 2f out: wknd over 1f out* **28/1**

0300 **11** 1/2 **Grand Stitch (USA)**[5] 4820 5-9-0 **60**....(v) NeilFarley(5) 7 35
(Declan Carroll) *chsd ldrs: drvn over 2f out: sn wknd* **20/1**

0000 **12** 12 **Future Gem**[10] 4636 5-8-5 **46** oh1....(p) DuranFentiman 2 —
(David Thompson) *sn chsng ldrs towards far side: lost pl over 2f out: sn bhd: eased* **66/1**

60.79 secs (0.99) **Going Correction** +0.225s/f (Good)
WFA 3 from 4yo+ 3lb **12 Ran SP% 120.6**
Speed ratings (Par 101): **101,99,97,96,96 94,94,91,87,85 84,65**
toteswingers:1&2:£6.30, 2&3:£5.50, 1&3:£9.30 CSF £29.17 CT £219.92 TOTE £17.80: £3.60, £1.20, £3.20; EX 53.50.
Owner Mrs Jennie Moffatt **Bred** Mrs J A Moffatt And Brian T Clark **Trained** Cartmel, Cumbria

FOCUS
A two-horse contest according to the betting but that was not the way things turned out. The runners kept to the centre of the track. Modest form, with a personal best from the winner.
Sandwith Official explanation: jockey said gelding hung left throughout

4987 JIMMY GEORGE CURLY ANTHONY H'CAP 7f
8:30 (8:30) (Class 6) (0-60,59) 3-Y-0+ **£1,704** (£503; £251) **Stalls** Low

Form RPR

4063 **1** **Whats For Pudding (IRE)**[5] 4816 3-8-0 **46**.... NeilFarley(5) 10 59
(Declan Carroll) *prom: c stands' side and led over 2f out: hld on towards fin* **18/1**

2642 **2** *nk* **Catallout (IRE)**[10] 4638 3-9-2 **57**.... DanielTudhope 8 69
(Declan Carroll) *chsd ldrs: effrt and edgd rt over 2f out: chsd wnr last 100yds: no ex nr fin* **9/4**[1]

0642 **3** 2 1/4 **Emeralds Spirit (IRE)**[3] 4876 4-9-7 **56**.... PhillipMakin 12 64
(John Weymes) *w ldrs: t.k.h: kpt on same pce fnl f* **7/2**[2]

20-0 **4** 2 1/4 **My Name Is Bert**[38] 3719 5-8-13 **55**.... NoelGarbutt(7) 4 57
(Lucinda Featherstone) *hmpd s: sn mid-div: hdwy to join ldrs over 2f out: one pce fnl f* **16/1**

40-4 **5** *hd* **Chookie Avon**[6] 4782 4-9-9 **58**....(p) PaulHanagan 9 59
(Keith Dalgleish) *blindfold removed v late: s.i.s: in rr: effrt over 2f out: styd on fnl f* **7/2**[2]

0100 **6** 3/4 **Boga (IRE)**[11] 4600 4-9-2 **51**.... BarryMcHugh 1 50
(Karen Tutty) *dwlt: hdwy over 2f out: kpt on one pce appr fnl f* **16/1**

0626 **7** 3/4 **Tombellini (IRE)**[10] 4634 4-9-8 **57**.... AndrewMullen 2 54
(David Nicholls) *led to post: led: hdd over 2f out: wknd fnl f* **8/1**[3]

6003 **8** 5 **Fair Bunny**[23] 4196 4-8-12 **47**....(b) AndrewElliott 6 31
(Alan Brown) *wnt lft s: chsd ldrs: hung rt and wknd over 1f out* **16/1**

0000 **9** 3/4 **Prices Lane**[10] 4651 4-9-4 **53**.... JamesSullivan 11 35
(Michael Easterby) *s.i.s: in rr: swtchd stands' side over 2f out: nvr rchd ldrs* **28/1**

0530 **10** 4 **Chardonnay Star (IRE)**[11] 4600 4-9-1 **50**....(v) DavidAllan 5 21
(Colin Teague) *in rr: sme hdwy 3f out: sn wknd* **33/1**

0003 **11** 3/4 **Spin A Wish**[31] 3933 3-8-6 **50**.... AmyRyan(3) 14 17
(Richard Whitaker) *chsd ldrs: lost pl 2f out* **28/1**

1m 30.62s (3.62) **Going Correction** +0.35s/f (Good)
WFA 3 from 4yo+ 6lb **11 Ran SP% 119.1**
Speed ratings (Par 101): **93,92,90,87,87 86,85,79,79,74 73**
toteswingers:1&2:£6.50, 2&3:£2.40, 1&3:£17.70 CSF £58.41 CT £185.12 TOTE £29.50: £7.40, £1.10, £2.50; EX 82.00.
Owner R J Ball **Bred** Kenneth Greer **Trained** Sledmere, E Yorks

FOCUS
Very modest fare to end proceedings and something of a muddling affair with several pulling hard early. The field tended to edge towards the stands' side and the winner had the rail from 2f out. A 1-2 for Decaln Carroll, the form rated around the second.
Chookie Avon ◆ Official explanation: jockey said blindfold became caught in bridle
T/Plt: £1,008.20 to a £1 stake. Pool £41,366.52 - 29.95 winning tickets. T/Qpdt: £189.30 to a £1 stake. Pool £3,812.57 - 14.90 winning tickets. WG

4905 KEMPTON (A.W) (R-H)
Friday, August 12

OFFICIAL GOING: Standard
Wind: Light, half behind Weather: Cloudy

4988 RACING AT SKYSPORTS.COM H'CAP 5f (P)
6:10 (6:10) (Class 5) (0-75,75) 3-Y-0+ **£2,522** (£750; £375; £187) **Stalls** Low

Form RPR

2213 **1** **Fair Passion**[100] 1816 4-9-7 **72**.... AdamKirby 1 83
(Derek Shaw) *trckd ldng pair: shkn up and clsd over 1f out: led jst ins fnl f: styd on wl* **9/2**[1]

2350 **2** 1 1/2 **Speightowns Kid (USA)**[12] 4583 3-9-4 **72**.... LiamKeniry 4 77
(Matthew Salaman) *chsd ldng pair: rdn and nt qckn over 1f out: styd on again to take 2nd ins fnl f* **9/2**[1]

2054 **3** 1 1/4 **Crimson Cloud**[21] 4295 3-9-2 **73**.... LeeTopliss(3) 6 73
(Richard Fahey) *led: drvn and hdd jst ins fnl f: wkng towards fin* **5/1**[2]

-406 **4** *hd* **Caledonia Princess**[18] 4387 5-9-4 **72**.... RossAtkinson(3) 7 72+
(Jo Hughes) *dwlt: settled in last: stl there over 1f out: rdn and gd prog fnl f: styng on wl fin* **7/1**

2222 **5** *hd* **Grandmas Dream**[8] 4721 3-9-3 **74**....(p) MartinHarley(3) 3 73
(Richard Guest) *dwlt and crossed by rival s: towards rr: rdn bef 1/2-way: no prog tl styd on fnl f* **13/2**[3]

4662 **6** *nk* **Patch Patch**[23] 4197 4-8-9 **63**....(p) SophieDoyle(3) 2 62
(Derek Shaw) *pressed ldr to over 1f out: fdd fnl f* **14/1**

0556 **7** 2 1/4 **Ignatieff (IRE)**[70] 2667 4-9-2 **67**.... DarryllHolland 8 57
(Linda Stubbs) *racd wd: chsd ldng pair: rdn 2f out: sn lost pl and btn* **15/2**

4002 **8** *nse* **Elhamri**[3] 4893 7-9-0 **68**.... JohnFahy(3) 9 58
(Conor Dore) *racd wd towards rr: hd to one side whn rdn wl over 1f out: no prog* **7/1**

1200 **9** 5 **Punching**[127] 1197 7-9-3 **75**.... SophieSilvester(7) 5 47
(Conor Dore) *a towards rr: wknd over 1f out: t.o* **20/1**

60.08 secs (-0.42) **Going Correction** -0.025s/f (Stan)
WFA 3 from 4yo+ 3lb **9 Ran SP% 114.6**
Speed ratings (Par 103): **102,99,97,97,96 96,92,92,84**
toteswingers:1&2:£3.80, 2&3:£5.30, 1&3:£6.60 CSF £24.40 CT £104.83 TOTE £6.50: £1.80, £1.30, £2.40; EX 26.90.
Owner The Whiteman Partnership **Bred** D R Tucker **Trained** Sproxton, Leics

FOCUS
A fairly competitive sprint handicap, five of the runners had finished in the frame on their previous start. The pace was just fair and the first three were always well positioned. Straightforward form.

4989 TOTEPOOL A BETTER WAY TO BET MAIDEN STKS 1m 2f (P)
6:45 (6:46) (Class 4) 3-Y-0 **£4,528** (£1,347; £673; £336) **Stalls** Low

Form RPR

3 **1** **Gobooll**[55] 3183 3-9-3 0.... LiamJones 6 88+
(William Haggas) *trckd ldng pair: pushed along wl over 2f out: clsd over 1f out: led jst ins fnl f: drvn out* **15/8**[2]

02 **2** 1/2 **Deraasa (USA)**[22] 4241 3-8-12 0.... TedDurcan 8 82
(Saeed Bin Suroor) *trckd ldr: pushed along wl over 2f out: clsd to ld over 1f out: hdd jst ins fnl f: kpt on wl but a hld* **6/1**[3]

5-2 **3** 3 1/2 **Raahin (IRE)**[56] 3135 3-9-3 0.... TadhgO'Shea 1 80
(Sir Michael Stoute) *led at decent pce: pushed along wl over 2f out: rdn and hdd over 1f out: one pce* **5/4**[1]

04 **4** 1 **Palazzo Bianco**[11] 4617 3-9-3 0.... NickyMackay 3 78+
(John Gosden) *hld up in 5th and off the pce: pushed along to go 4th 3f out: shkn up wl over 1f out: kpt on fnl f: likely improver* **8/1**

0 **5** 27 **In The Long Grass (IRE)**[6] 4800 3-9-0 0.... MatthewDavies(3) 7 24
(Jim Boyle) *towards rr: pushed along 6f out: lost tch 4f out: t.o but won battle for remote 5th* **25/1**

00 **6** *nk* **Farmers Hill**[36] 3781 3-9-3 0.... FergusSweeney 5 23
(Mark Hoad) *towards rr: lost tch 4f out: t.o* **66/1**

00- **7** 3 1/4 **Jibouti (IRE)**[415] 3326 3-9-3 0.... KirstyMilczarek 4 17
(Clive Brittain) *chsd ldng pair: pushed along 1/2-way: wknd rapidly 3f out: t.o* **40/1**

0 **8** 4 **She Wolf**[109] 1568 3-8-12 0.... AdamKirby 10 —
(Michael Bell) *rousted along in rr after 3f: lost tch 4f out: t.o* **16/1**

9 29 **Empyrean (USA)** 3-8-12 0.... SebSanders 9 —
(Sir Mark Prescott Bt) *s.s: immediately rdn and v green in last: lost tch 4f out: wl t.o* **12/1**

2m 5.46s (-2.54) **Going Correction** -0.025s/f (Stan) **9 Ran SP% 126.0**
Speed ratings (Par 102): **109,108,105,105,83 83,80,77,54**
toteswingers:1&2:£2.30, 2&3:£2.50, 1&3:£1.60 CSF £15.26 TOTE £3.80: £1.60, £1.20, £1.10; EX 14.80.
Owner Sheikh Ahmed Al Maktoum **Bred** London Thoroughbred Services Ltd **Trained** Newmarket, Suffolk

FOCUS
A decent maiden for the track and time of year. It was run at a fair pace and the four market leaders finished a long way clear of the rest. There is more to come from the winner.

4990 BETFRED "TEXT FRED TO 89660" CLASSIFIED CLAIMING STKS 6f (P)
7:15 (7:15) (Class 6) 3-5-Y-0 **£1,811** (£539; £269; £134) **Stalls** Low

Form RPR

0300 **1** **Dark Lane**[21] 4291 5-8-8 70 ow1.... LeeTopliss(3) 8 80
(Richard Fahey) *chsd ldr: drvn over 2f out: grad clsd fnl f: led last stride* **15/2**

1041 **2** *nse* **Deerslayer (USA)**[7] 4741 5-8-7 72....(p) MartinHarley(3) 7 79
(Richard Guest) *fast away: led: drvn over 2f out: edgd rt 1f out but looked like holding on: hdd last stride* **4/1**[3]

3020 **3** 3 **Brynfa Boy**[17] 4416 5-8-11 74....(t) MatthewDavies(3) 2 73
(Paul D'Arcy) *chsd ldrs: rdn and nt qckn over 2f out: kpt on fr over 1f out: snatched 3rd last strides* **3/1**[2]

0300 **4** *shd* **Co Dependent (USA)**[24] 4182 5-8-8 67.... FergusSweeney 5 67+
(Jamie Osborne) *stdd s: hld up last: promising hdwy on wd outside over 2f out: chsd ldng pair 1f out: effrt petered out and lost 3rd last strides* **12/1**

1520 **5** 1 1/4 **Jordaura**[20] 4310 5-9-0 74.... AdamKirby 1 69
(Tony Carroll) *chsd ldng pair: drvn over 2f out: no imp: lost 3rd 1f out and fdd* **11/4**[1]

0000 **6** 2 3/4 **Olynard (IRE)**[19] 4369 5-9-2 70....(v) JimmyFortune 6 62
(Dr Richard Newland) *t.k.h: prog on outer to chse ldng pair over 3f out: gng bttr than most over 2f out: shkn up and fnd nil wl over 1f out: fdd* **10/1**

2246 **7** 1/2 **Lastkingofscotland (IRE)**[27] 4089 5-9-0 73....(b) KirstyMilczarek 3 59
(Conor Dore) *in tch in rr: drvn and struggling over 2f out: no prog* **15/2**

1m 12.3s (-0.80) **Going Correction** -0.025s/f (Stan) **7 Ran SP% 112.0**
Speed ratings (Par 101): **104,103,99,99,98 94,93**
toteswingers:1&2:£4.20, 2&3:£2.90, 1&3:£4.40 CSF £35.72 TOTE £9.30: £3.70, £2.00; EX 53.40.Dark Lane was claimed by A. W. Carroll for £6,000.
Owner Wildcard Racing Syndicate **Bred** David Jamison Bloodstock **Trained** Musley Bank, N Yorks
■ Stewards' Enquiry : Martin Harley one-day ban: used whip with arm above shoulder (Aug 26)

FOCUS
A tight claimer, six of the runners holding official marks between 70 and 74. The pace was not very strong and there was an exciting finish between a pair who pulled clear. Ordinary form.

4991 BETFRED BINGO MEDIAN AUCTION MAIDEN STKS 7f (P)
7:50 (7:56) (Class 6) 3-5-Y-0 **£1,811** (£539; £269; £134) **Stalls** Low

Form RPR

20 **1** **Blink Of An Eye**[131] 1108 3-9-3 0.... AdamKirby 1 77
(Michael Bell) *most reluctant to enter stalls: mde all: drew clr over 2f out: in n.d but hrd drvn over 1f out* **4/1**[2]

300- **2** 5 **Poppy**[288] 7185 3-8-12 60.... EddieAhern 3 59
(Richard Hannon) *chsd ldng pair: wnt 2nd wl over 2f out: sn lft bhd by wnr: kpt on* **11/2**

0 **3** 2 1/2 **Princess Willow**[20] 4320 3-8-12 0.... RichardThomas 6 52
(John E Long) *fractious bef ent stalls: chsd ldrs but racd awkwardly: rdn over 2f out: kpt on to take 3rd jst over 1f out: n.d* **25/1**

325- **4** 1 **Sinchiroka (FR)**[387] 4261 5-9-5 68.... JamieGoldstein 8 54
(Ralph Smith) *chsd wnr to wl over 2f out: racd awkwardly and steadily outpcd* **6/1**

5 3/4 **En Hiver** 3-8-12 0.... StevieDonohoe 5 47+
(Ralph Beckett) *dwlt: rcvrd on outer to press ldrs 4f out: racd wd after: rdn and outpcd over 2f out: plugged on* **11/4**[1]

6 3/4 **George Guru** 4-9-4 0.... MarkCoumbe(5) 7 52+
(Michael Attwater) *sed slowest of all: pushed along in last and rn green: sme prog over 2f out: no hdwy and wl btn over 1f out* **25/1**

The Form Book, Raceform Ltd, Compton, RG20 6NL

7 *5* **Jumeirah Liberty** 3-9-3 0 .... TadhgO'Shea 9 37+
(William Haggas) *dwlt: racd wd towards rr: no prog over 2f out: wknd* **13/2**

8 *1 ½* **Collaborate (IRE)** 3-9-3 0 .... JimmyFortune 10 32+
(Andrew Balding) *unruly in stalls: taken out and put in again: dwlt: a wl in rr: bhd fnl 2f* **9/2**[3]

9 *½* **Our Princess Ellie (USA)** 3-8-12 0 .... NickyMackay 2 26
(Derek Shaw) *mounted on crse: dwlt: a towards rr: wknd over 2f out* **18/1**

10 *13* **Main Opinion (IRE)** 3-8-9 0 .... MartinHarley(3) 4 —
(Mick Channon) *dwlt: in tch towards rr tl wknd over 2f out: t.o* **12/1**

1m 25.63s (-0.37) **Going Correction** -0.025s/f (Stan)
WFA 3 from 4yo+ 6lb **10** Ran SP% **128.5**
Speed ratings (Par 101): **101,95,92,91,90 89,83,82,81,66**
toteswingers:1&2:£2.30, 2&3:£30.70, 1&3:£16.60 CSF £29.49 TOTE £4.60: £1.60, £2.10, £7.70; EX 18.50.
Owner Billy Maguire **Bred** Whatton Manor Stud **Trained** Newmarket, Suffolk

FOCUS
An ordinary maiden but the leading form contender was an emphatic front-running winner. he improved, but there are some doubts over the form.

4992 TOTEPOOL EBF MAIDEN FILLIES' STKS 7f (P)
8:20 (8:24) (Class 4) 2-Y-O **£4,398** (£1,309; £654; £327) **Stalls** Low

Form RPR

1 **Ittasal** 2-9-0 0 .... TedDurcan 1 77+
(Saeed Bin Suroor) *slowest away: hld up in last trio: taken to outer and prog over 2f out: rdn to ld jst over 1f out: pushed out and in command last 100yds* **9/4**[1]

0 2 *¾* **Emmuska**[25] 4155 2-9-0 0 .... EddieAhern 10 73+
(Richard Hannon) *restless stalls: dwlt: sn in midfield: rdn on wd outside and prog 2f out: chsd wnr fnl f: styd on but a readily hld* **12/1**

U4 3 *½* **Equity Card (FR)**[22] 4245 2-8-9 0 .... AntiocoMurgia(5) 2 72
(Mahmood Al Zarooni) *dwlt: hld up in midfield: urged along and prog wl over 1f out: chsd ldng pair ins fnl f: styd on but nvr able to chal* **8/1**

42 4 *2 ¼* **Naseem Alyasmeen (IRE)**[78] 2430 2-8-11 0 .... MartinHarley(3) 9 66
(Mick Channon) *prom: shkn up and nt qckn over 2f out: kpt on again over 1f out: n.d* **17/2**

33 5 *2 ¾* **Code Cracker**[10] 4632 2-9-0 0 .... SebSanders 6 59
(Sir Mark Prescott Bt) *trckd ldrs: prog to go 2nd jst over 2f out: rdn to ld briefly over 1f out: wknd fnl f* **9/2**[3]

000 6 *2 ¾* **Compton Bird**[13] 4548 2-8-11 0 .... SophieDoyle(3) 5 52
(Hans Adielsson) *led to jst over 1f out: wknd* **50/1**

6 7 *¾* **Perfect Paradise**[29] 4002 2-9-0 0 .... NickyMackay 11 50
(John Gosden) *dwlt: chsd ldr after 1f to jst over 2f out: wknd* **4/1**[2]

8 *1 ¼* **Chatterati (USA)** 2-9-0 0 .... JimmyFortune 4 47
(Mahmood Al Zarooni) *dwlt: a wl in rr on outer: no prog over 2f out* **9/1**

0 9 *1 ¾* **Aliante**[35] 3826 2-9-0 0 .... DarryllHolland 3 42
(Mark Johnston) *prom on inner tl wknd qckly 2f out* **12/1**

0 10 *1 ¾* **Compton Shuttle (IRE)**[95] 1957 2-9-0 0 .... AdamKirby 7 38
(Hans Adielsson) *t.k.h: restrained to last sn after s: no prog* **80/1**

1m 26.78s (0.78) **Going Correction** -0.025s/f (Stan) **10** Ran SP% **119.2**
Speed ratings (Par 93): **94,93,92,90,86 83,82,81,79,77**
toteswingers:1&2:£7.20, 2&3:£20.20, 1&3:£6.60 CSF £32.80 TOTE £3.50: £1.80, £2.80, £2.50; EX 46.00.
Owner Godolphin **Bred** Darley **Trained** Newmarket, Suffolk

FOCUS
A competitive fillies' maiden. Four of the runners were closely matched on form but there was a stylish debut win from a well backed Godolphin performer.

NOTEBOOK
Ittasal had quite a lot of work to do after a slow start but she travelled smoothly into contention and showed a good turn of foot to seize the initiative and score on debut. This was a quite impressive start by a scopey half-sister to useful 6f 2yo winner La Presse, useful French 1m winner Emirates Girl and smart 7f-1m handicapper Paper Talk. (tchd 2-1 and 5-2)
Emmuska, an 8l seventh of 14 behind a stablemate in a fair 6f Windsor maiden on debut, stayed on well out wide to give the favourite a scare stepped up to 7f. She has plenty of winners at 6f-1m4f on her dam's side and should continue to progress. (tchd 14-1)
Equity Card(FR) shaped with plenty of promise, staying on well against the far rail. A first foal of an unplaced dam who is closely related to Derby/King George/Arc hero Lammtarra, she is going the right way after three runs and should appreciate a stiffer test. (op 12-1)
Naseem Alyasmeen(IRE) had fair form claims on her second in a 6f Newcastle fillies' maiden in May. A market springer, she ran a respectable race from a tough draw on return from a break. (op 16-1)
Code Cracker is out of connections' French Oaks and Guineas runner-up Confidential Lady, but she was overhauled by two rivals when a well backed favourite at Catterick last time and her effort petered out in the closing stages in this stronger race on AW. (op 4-1)
Perfect Paradise was a promising sixth of 13 in decent 7f Doncaster fillies' maiden on debut but she found a limited response in an unsuccessful attempt to build on that. (op 7-2)

4993 BETFRED "THE BONUS KING" H'CAP (LONDON MILE QUALIFIER) 1m (P)
8:50 (8:51) (Class 3) (0-95,95) 3-Y-O+
£7,158 (£2,143; £1,071; £535; £267; £134) **Stalls** Low

Form RPR

3040 1 **Primaeval**[6] 4802 5-9-4 91 .... (v) StevieDonohoe 2 105
(James Fanshawe) *trckd ldrs in 5th: followed runner-up through on inner to go 2nd wl over 1f out: drvn and clsd to ld last 100yds: shot clr* **11/2**[3]

2201 2 *2 ¼* **Red Gulch**[17] 4415 4-9-8 95 .... J-PGuillambert 1 104
(Ed Walker) *prom: dashed through on inner to ld jst over 2f out: rdn over 1f out: hdd and outpcd last 100yds* **7/2**[1]

0300 3 *1 ¼* **Kajima**[17] 4415 4-9-7 94 .... JimmyFortune 11 100
(Richard Hannon) *prom bhd ldrs: rdn and outpcd jst over 2f out: styd on again over 1f out to take 3rd fnl f* **10/1**

0030 4 *hd* **Suited And Booted (IRE)**[17] 4415 4-9-1 88 .... TedDurcan 7 94
(Jane Chapple-Hyam) *wl in tch in midfield: rdn and outpcd over 2f out: styd on again fr over 1f out* **12/1**

1002 5 *¾* **Benandonner (USA)**[27] 4100 8-9-3 93 .... MartinHarley(3) 4 97
(Mike Murphy) *led to jst over 2f out: outpcd u.p after* **8/1**

0051 6 *½* **Layline (IRE)**[30] 3982 4-9-6 93 .... AdamKirby 5 96+
(Gay Kelleway) *hld up towards rr: gng wl but stl in rr over 2f out: swtchd lft wl over 1f out: rdn and r.o: nvr nr ldrs* **11/1**

0125 7 *1 ¾* **Night Lily (IRE)**[9] 4656 5-9-8 95 .... LiamJones 3 94+
(Paul D'Arcy) *settled in midfield: rdn over 2f out: disp wl btn 4th briefly over 1f out: fdd* **10/1**

000 8 *½* **Freeforaday (USA)**[56] 3109 4-9-6 93 .... SteveDrowne 13 90+
(John Best) *hld up in last quartet: urged along and no prog over 2f out: nvr on terms* **16/1**

3060 9 *½* **Amwell Pinot**[13] 4550 3-9-0 94 .... (b) SamHitchcott 8 90
(Alan Bailey) *chsd ldr to wl over 2f out: sn lost pl u.p and btn* **18/1**

0600 10 *1 ½* **Chapter And Verse (IRE)**[17] 4415 5-9-6 93 .... TonyCulhane 9 86+
(Mike Murphy) *snatched up sn after s: hld up last: stl there 2f out: jst pushed along and kpt on steadily: nvr nr ldrs* **5/1**[2]

5005 11 *3 ¾* **Gouray Girl (IRE)**[56] 3134 4-9-5 92 .... EddieAhern 10 76
(Walter Swinburn) *hld up in last quartet: jst pushed along fr over 2f out: nvr nr ldrs: eased ins fnl f* **9/1**

200- 12 *1* **Councellor (FR)**[480] 1430 9-8-11 87 .... (t) JohnFahy(3) 14 69
(Stef Higgins) *racd wd in midfield: drvn and wknd over 2f out* **50/1**

00-0 13 *3 ¾* **Autumn Blades (IRE)**[6] 4774 6-9-1 95 .... (p) MissAlexOwen(7) 6 68
(Alan Bailey) *snatched up sn after s: wl in rr: effrt on inner over 2f out: sn wknd* **16/1**

1m 38.32s (-1.48) **Going Correction** -0.025s/f (Stan)
WFA 3 from 4yo+ 7lb **13** Ran SP% **128.6**
Speed ratings (Par 107): **106,103,102,102,101 101,99,98,98,96 93,92,88**
toteswingers:1&2:£5.30, 2&3:£13.00, 1&3:£18.00 CSF £27.07 CT £205.56 TOTE £6.50: £2.10, £2.50, £4.20; EX 36.10.
Owner The Foncey Syndicate **Bred** Stowell Park Stud **Trained** Newmarket, Suffolk

FOCUS
A useful handicap. The pace was fairly steady and the hold-up runners struggled to get involved. The form is rated around the third and fourth.

NOTEBOOK
Primaeval had not made a big impact in four turf runs this season but the switch back to AW worked as he found a surging run to score with plenty in hand. His progressive Polytrack profile includes a record of 15211 at this track and he should be able to win more races. (op 5-1 tchd 6-1)
Red Gulch hit a personal best stepped back up to 1m when scoring in good style from off the pace in 19-runner handicap at Goodwood last month. He looked on his way to defying a 6lb rise when kicking clear from just off the pace but he had no answer to the rampaging burst of the winner. However, this was a good effort from a likeable type who has scope for further improvement at this trip. (tchd 4-1 in places)
Kajima ran as if something was amiss when 19l behind Red Gulch at Goodwood last time but he bounced back with a solid run to get a lot closer to that rival. (op 12-1)
Suited And Booted(IRE) emerges with credit for doing best of the runners who came from some way off the pace. He has a very up and down profile this year but is well weighted on his best efforts during a profitable campaign for Richard Hannon last year. (tchd 14-1)
Benandonner(USA) showed there is still plenty of life left in him when winning at Newmarket in May and finishing second at the same track last time, but he couldn't fight off the closers back on Polytrack, despite having the run of the race from a good draw.
Layline(IRE) appreciated a switch back to Polytrack when scoring in a 0-90 classified last time. He couldn't threaten off 3lb higher back in a handicap but he was a bit keen and things didn't really go his way in a steadily run race. (op 10-1 tchd 12-1)
Chapter And Verse(IRE) was never anywhere near the leaders after getting hampered at the start. Official explanation: jockey said gelding was hampered at start (op 9-1)

4994 BETFRED H'CAP 7f (P)
9:20 (9:21) (Class 4) (0-80,80) 3-Y-O **£4,528** (£1,347; £673; £336) **Stalls** Low

Form RPR

3200 1 **Reposer (IRE)**[15] 4472 3-9-5 78 .... LiamJones 9 87
(John Best) *racd freely: mde all: drvn and hrd pressed over 1f out: styd on wl u.p* **20/1**

5631 2 *1 ¼* **Saskia's Dream**[20] 4321 3-9-2 75 .... (p) AdamKirby 5 80
(Jane Chapple-Hyam) *chsd ldrs: rdn over 2f out: styd on to take 2nd ins fnl f: no imp on wnr* **9/2**[2]

5443 3 *2 ¼* **Chevise (IRE)**[18] 4387 3-9-3 79 .... MatthewDavies(3) 10 78
(Steve Woodman) *chsd wnr: rdn over 2f out: stl chsng 1f out but no imp: one pce fnl f* **12/1**

221 4 *nk* **Escape To Glory (USA)**[23] 4210 3-9-7 80 .... LiamKeniry 4 79
(Mikael Magnusson) *t.k.h: trckd ldng pair: effrt on inner 2f out: tried to chal over 1f out: nt qckn* **11/10**[1]

51-0 5 *nk* **Charles Fosterkane**[16] 4447 3-9-4 77 .... SteveDrowne 6 75
(John Best) *plld hrd early: hld up in rr: reminders wl over 1f out: styd on: nvr nr ldrs* **10/1**

4522 6 *1 ¾* **Perfect Pastime**[15] 4459 3-9-6 79 .... EddieAhern 2 72
(Walter Swinburn) *hld up towards rr: shkn up and effrt over 2f out: no prog over 1f out* **7/1**[3]

4643 7 *¾* **Prince Of Passion (CAN)**[16] 4431 3-8-2 61 oh1 .... NickyMackay 3 52
(Derek Shaw) *hld up in rr: shkn up and brief effrt on inner 2f out: sn no prog* **33/1**

0-20 8 *2 ½* **Song Of The Siren**[34] 3845 3-9-4 77 .... JimmyFortune 7 61
(Andrew Balding) *racd wd: in tch and keen after 2f: wknd over 2f out* **10/1**

14-0 9 *1 ½* **Gentleman Is Back (USA)**[28] 4062 3-9-1 77 .... JohnFahy(3) 8 57
(Ed de Giles) *sweating: s.i.s: hld up last: fnd nil whn rdn over 2f out* **12/1**

1m 26.24s (0.24) **Going Correction** -0.025s/f (Stan) **9** Ran SP% **119.6**
Speed ratings (Par 102): **97,95,93,92,92 90,89,86,84**
toteswingers:1&2:£18.70, 2&3:£15.40, 1&3:£11.70 CSF £111.42 CT £1165.31 TOTE £13.90: £5.00, £2.00, £2.60; EX 144.10.
Owner John Foulger & Simon Malcolm **Bred** Keene Bloodstock Ltd **Trained** Hucking, Kent

FOCUS
A fair handicap in which there was a dominant display by an outsider in a steadily run race. The form is taken at something like face value.
T/Plt: £66.70 to £1 stake. Pool:£55,635.65 - 608.22 winning tickets T/Qpdt: £28.70 to a £1 stake. Pool:£3,882.26 - 100.00 winning tickets. JN

4578 NEWBURY (L-H)
Friday, August 12

OFFICIAL GOING: Good (7.2)
Wind: Virtually nil Weather: Cloudy

4995 DON DEADMAN MEMORIAL EUROPEAN BREEDERS' FUND MAIDEN STKS (DIV I) 7f (S)
1:30 (1:33) (Class 4) 2-Y-O **£4,140** (£1,232; £615; £307) **Stalls** Centre

Form RPR

1 **Tales Of Grimm (USA)** 2-9-3 0 .... KierenFallon 6 88+
(Sir Michael Stoute) *trckd ldrs: led appr fnl 2f: drvn and styd on wl fnl f: jst hld on* **11/1**

2 *hd* **Firdaws (USA)** 2-8-12 0 .... RichardHills 9 82+
(Roger Varian) *s.i.s: sn rcvrd into mid-div: nt clr run and bmpd appr fnl 2f: rapid hdwy 1f out to chse wnr fnl 120yds: fin wl: nt quite get up* **11/10**[1]

3 *1 ¼* **The Nile** 2-9-3 0 .... WilliamBuick 5 84+
(John Gosden) *in tch: hdwy 2f out: chsd wnr appr fnl f: drvn and kpt on wl but outpcd for 2nd fnl 120yds* **9/2**[2]

4 4 *5* **Humungosaur**[19] 4352 2-9-3 0 .... JimmyFortune 10 71
(Paul Cole) *sn led: rdn along and hdd appr fnl 2f: readily outpcd by ldng trio fnl f* **8/1**[3]

43 **5** *1* **Nant Saeson (IRE)**[23] 4213 2-9-3 0........................ RichardHughes 11 69
(Richard Hannon) *chsd ldrs: pushed along and styd on same pce fnl 2f* **8/1**[3]

6 *nse* **Chil The Kite** 2-9-3 0........................ SteveDrowne 14 69+
(Hughie Morrison) *s.i.s: in rr: hdwy fr 2f out: kpt on fnl f: nvr gng pce to rch ldrs* **40/1**

7 *½* **Kings Decree** 2-9-3 0........................ JamesMillman 8 67
(Rod Millman) *s.i.s: in rr: pushed along and hdwy fr 2f out: kpt on wl clsng stages* **100/1**

8 *1* **Never Satisfied** 2-9-3 0........................ MichaelHills 7 65
(B W Hills) *in rr: pushed along 2f out: hdwy fnl f: kpt on cl home* **28/1**

43 **9** *shd* **Thirsty Bear**[18] 4397 2-9-3 0........................ AdamKirby 3 64
(Rebecca Curtis) *pressed ldrs 3f: styd front rnk tl rdn 2f out: wknd 1f out: edgd lft clsng stages* **28/1**

10 *1 ½* **Byron Blue (IRE)** 2-9-3 0........................ JimCrowley 4 60
(Jamie Osborne) *s.i.s: in rr: pushed along 2f out: styd on fnl f* **50/1**

6 **11** *1 ¼* **Johnno**[21] 4264 2-9-3 0........................ SebSanders 12 57
(J W Hills) *in tch: pushed along and fdd 2f out* **16/1**

0 **12** *6* **True Prince (USA)**[13] 4535 2-9-3 0........................ EddieAhern 15 42
(Amanda Perrett) *chsd ldrs tl wknd appr fnl 2f* **100/1**

13 *8* **Sammie Fallon (IRE)** 2-8-12 0........................ CathyGannon 2 16
(Andrew Haynes) *chsd ldrs over 4f* **100/1**

14 *nk* **Hint Of Mint** 2-9-3 0........................ LiamKeniry 1 20
(Andrew Balding) *sn outpcd* **66/1**

000 **15** *6* **Clone Devil (IRE)**[28] 4068 2-8-12 20........................(b[1]) AmyScott[(5)] 13 —
(Alastair Lidderdale) *sn bhd* **150/1**

1m 26.83s (1.13) **Going Correction** +0.05s/f (Good) **15** Ran SP% **118.7**
Speed ratings (Par 96): **95,94,93,87,86 86,85,84,84,82 81,74,65,65,58**
toteswingers:1&2:£5.90, 1&3:£8.30, 2&3:£2.80 CSF £22.26 TOTE £11.50: £2.70, £1.10, £2.00; EX 35.90 Trifecta £101.60 Pool: £608.54 - 4.43 winning units..
Owner Sir Robert Ogden **Bred** Winsong Farms **Trained** Newmarket, Suffolk

FOCUS
Rail moved in to the measured distance on the round course on to fresh ground. The ground seemed to be riding as advertised. The time was the best part of four seconds outside the standard but was slightly quicker than the second division. Divisions of this maiden have been won in the last couple of seasons by Champagne Stakes scorer Saamidd and Pounced, who later took the Breeders' Cup Juvenile Turf, and this was an interesting race, contested by some nice prospects. The first three finished clear, showing useful form.

NOTEBOOK
Tales Of Grimm(USA), whose dam won at up to 1m2f, including a US Grade 3, cost no less than 320,000gns at the breeze-ups in the spring. Racing a shade keenly behind the leaders before taking over, he showed a robust attitude to hold off the challengers. There are no fancy entries for him yet, but he is a decent prospect who will have no problem with a mile. (op 12-1 tchd 10-1)
Firdaws(USA) ◆ has been backed recently for both of next year's fillies' Classics and was the subject of a strong word for this. A daughter of 2005 Oaks winner Eswarah, herself out of a dual Classic winner in Midway Lady, she took a bit of time to roll and had to be switched for a run, but she came home in good style. There should be improvement in her fitness-wise and she should be hard to beat next time. (op 5-4 tchd 11-8)
The Nile is a half-brother to three juvenile winners, most notably the useful Flood Plain. Subject of good reports, he showed abundant promise but lacked the pace of the first two close home. He was clear of the rest and his maiden status should not last for long. (op 3-1)
Humungosaur, a big colt, had been fourth of seven on his debut last month. He was well held by the first three in the end over this extra furlong and probably performed close to his debut form. (op 11-1 tchd 15-2)
Nant Saeson(IRE), in the frame in a pair of Sandown maidens, ran his race again. He gets 7f, but may be worth dropping back in trip, and a nursery should come his way. (op 10-1)
Chil The Kite has five winning half-siblings, best of them the Morrison yard's smart sprinter Pastoral Player. He made late progress after a slow start and has improvement in him.
Kings Decree, a cheap yearling whose dam won at 1m4f, made late ground after a slow start and should improve.
Never Satisfied shaped satisfactorily on this debut. (op 33-1)
Thirsty Bear, happier back on a straight track, faded after showing pace. (tchd 25-1)
Byron Blue(IRE) hinted at better to come in time. (tchd 40-1)
Johnno could not improve on his debut showing. (op 28-1)

4996 DON DEADMAN MEMORIAL EUROPEAN BREEDERS' FUND MAIDEN STKS (DIV II) 7f (S)
2:00 (2:05) (Class 4) 2-Y-O **£4,140** (£1,232; £615; £307) **Stalls** Centre

Form RPR

1 **Top Offer** 2-9-3 0........................ SteveDrowne 3 94+
(Roger Charlton) *s.i.s: t.k.h and stdd towards rr: shkn up and rapid hdwy over 2f out to ld wl over 1f out: pushed clr fnl f: impressive* **6/4**[1]

2 *3 ½* **Pulverize (USA)** 2-9-3 0........................ RichardHills 1 85+
(Sir Michael Stoute) *trckd ldrs: pushed along and qcknd to chse wnr appr fnl f: nvr any ch but kpt on wl for clr 2nd* **6/1**[3]

06 **3** *3 ½* **Blank Czech (IRE)**[13] 4535 2-9-3 0........................ AdamKirby 8 74
(Amanda Perrett) *chsd ldr: rdn over 2f out: one pce into 3rd appr fnl f* **14/1**

4 *1* **Unex Michelangelo (IRE)** 2-9-3 0........................ WilliamBuick 4 71+
(John Gosden) *hld up towards rr: pushed along and hdwy over 2f out: styd on to take 4th fnl f to cl on 3rd but no ch w ldng duo* **8/1**

5 *1 ½* **Gloriam (USA)** 2-9-3 0........................ TedDurcan 10 68+
(David Simcock) *in tch whn edgd rt and looking for room ins fnl 3f: pushed along and styd on fr 2f out: kpt on fnl f but nvr a threat* **7/1**

6 *2* **Charley's Mount (IRE)** 2-9-3 0........................ TadhgO'Shea 5 62
(Brian Meehan) *sn led: hdd wl over 1f out: wknd ins fnl f* **22/1**

0 **7** *2 ¼* **April Ciel**[20] 4339 2-9-3 0........................ FergusSweeney 2 56
(Andrew Haynes) *pressed ldrs: rdn over 2f out: wknd wl over 1f out* **100/1**

8 *1* **I'm Harry** 2-9-3 0........................ MichaelHills 9 54
(B W Hills) *towards rr: pushed along over 2f out: styd on fnl f* **20/1**

9 *nk* **Cape Samba** 2-9-3 0........................ JimmyFortune 7 53
(Peter Chapple-Hyam) *chsd ldrs: shkn up over 2f out: wknd fnl f* **33/1**

433 **10** *2 ¼* **Tidy Affair (IRE)**[17] 4414 2-9-3 79........................ RichardHughes 14 47+
(Richard Hannon) *chsd ldrs: pushed along over 2f out: wknd wl over 1f out* **11/2**[2]

0 **11** *2* **Darrow (IRE)**[20] 4330 2-9-3 0........................ JimCrowley 15 42
(William Knight) *in rr tl sme prog over 1f out* **100/1**

12 *nse* **Season Spirit** 2-9-3 0........................ PhillipMakin 11 42
(James Given) *s.i.s: outpcd* **66/1**

13 *nk* **Navajo Charm** 2-8-9 0........................ MatthewDavies[(3)] 6 36
(Alan Jarvis) *t.k.h: chsd ldrs tl wknd over 2f out* **100/1**

14 *¾* **Rock Song** 2-9-3 0........................ EddieAhern 13 39
(Amanda Perrett) *in tch whn pushed rt ins fnl 3f: sn btn* **28/1**

15 *½* **Seemples (IRE)** 2-9-3 0........................ FrankieMcDonald 12 38
(Richard Hannon) *in tch whn pushed along and pushed rt ins fnl 3f: sn wknd* **66/1**

1m 27.0s (1.30) **Going Correction** +0.05s/f (Good) **15** Ran SP% **119.5**
Speed ratings (Par 96): **94,90,86,84,83 80,78,77,76,74 71,71,71,70,70**
toteswingers:1&2:£4.10, 1&3:£7.20, 2&3:£11.70 CSF £9.44 TOTE £2.70: £1.60, £1.90, £3.80; EX 12.10 Trifecta £66.30 Pool: £695.24 - 7.75 winning units..
Owner K Abdulla **Bred** Juddmonte Farms Ltd **Trained** Beckhampton, Wilts

FOCUS
Marginally the slower of the two divisions. The principals raced on the far side of the group.

NOTEBOOK
Top Offer ◆ produced a taking debut performance, quickening up nicely to lead before stretching clear. From a good Juddmonte family, he is highly regarded by his trainer and holds a string of pattern-race entries, including the Dewhurst and the Racing Post Trophy this autumn. Perhaps he will take the Saamidd route and go for the Champagne Stakes at Doncaster next. He should get 1m this year if so desired and looks an intriguing prospect. (op 13-8 tchd 15-8)
Pulverize(USA) has a smart American pedigree, being out of a dual Grade 1 winner over 1m1f. He could not race on with the favourite, but himself finished clear of the remainder. A maiden should soon be found. (op 13-2 tchd 9-2)
Blank Czech(IRE), always towards the fore, was held together when the first two drew clear of him. He is progressing nicely and looks a decent handicap prospect. (op 11-1)
Unex Michelangelo(IRE), whose dam is a sister to High Chaparral, has a Derby entry and comes from a stable successful in divisions of this race both last year and in 2009. Another to race on the far side of the group, he ran on from the rear but was never going to threaten the first two. (tchd 13-2, 9-1 in a place)
Gloriam(USA), who came in for support, caught the eye in the paddock and represented a yard whose juveniles are running well. There was nothing wrong with this debut effort and he should be winning before too long. (op 10-1 tchd 12-1)
Charley's Mount(IRE) made a lot of the running on this debut and should find a maiden.
April Ciel showed more than on his debut over 6f but did appear to be racing on the favoured part of the track.
I'm Harry, taken out of the Washington Singer Stakes here at the final declaration stage, came home quite well and there should be races for him further down the line. (op 16-1)
Tidy Affair(IRE), in the frame on each of his first three starts, set a fairly useful standard, but he ran below par. The extra furlong was probably less to blame than the fact that he was racing on the stands' side of the group, where the ground appeared to be slower. The other runners to race there also finished well beaten and he can be afforded another chance. (op 5-1 tchd 9-2)

4997 CHRISTOPHER SMITH ASSOCIATES 30TH ANNIVERSARY CLAIMING STKS 7f (S)
2:35 (2:36) (Class 5) 3-Y-O+ **£2,587** (£770; £384; £192) **Stalls** Centre

Form RPR

0-42 **1** **Woodcote Place**[29] 4006 8-9-12 86........................ JimCrowley 9 93
(Patrick Chamings) *in tch: nt clr run fr over 2f out tl drvn and qcknd over 1f out: led ins fnl f: pushed clr* **9/2**[3]

6100 **2** *4* **Ezdeyaad (USA)**[30] 3982 7-9-3 87........................ MichaelJMurphy[(7)] 10 80
(Ed Walker) *trckd ldrs: c towards stands' side and drvn to take narrow ld appr fnl 2f: sn rdn: hdd and outpcd ins fnl f* **13/2**

2610 **3** *½* **Grand Piano (IRE)**[46] 3473 4-8-7 68........................ SophieSilvester[(7)] 3 69
(Andrew Balding) *unruly stalls: s.i.s: in rr: swtchd lft 2f out and hdwy sn after styd on fnl f: clsng on 2nd but no ch w wnr* **25/1**

5-60 **4** *2 ¾* **Wisecraic**[47] 3436 4-9-4 72........................ LiamKeniry 7 66
(J S Moore) *chsd ldrs: hrd drvn over 2f out: styd on same pce fnl f* **33/1**

5011 **5** *hd* **Zomerlust**[29] 4016 9-9-11 85........................(v) PhillipMakin 2 72
(John Quinn) *slt ld: rdn whn narrowly hdd appr 2f out: wknd u.p ins fnl f* **11/2**

5024 **6** *½* **Nezami (IRE)**[29] 4006 6-9-0 72........................(b) AdamKirby 8 60
(John Akehurst) *chsd ldrs: rdn and ev ch over 2f out: wknd appr fnl f* **10/1**

0300 **7** *2 ¼* **Corporal Maddox**[13] 4556 4-9-10 88........................ KierenFallon 6 64
(Jamie Osborne) *in tch: swtchd rt to r towards stands' side over 3f out: drvn to chal over 2f out: wknd appr fnl f* **7/2**[1]

2-00 **8** *2 ¾* **Seneschal**[21] 4268 10-9-9 76........................ LucyKBarry[(5)] 4 60
(Adrian Chamberlain) *pressed ldrs: chal towards centre crse over 2f out tl wknd over 1f out* **80/1**

0660 **9** *2 ¾* **Mujood**[9] 4656 8-9-4 80........................(v) CathyGannon 5 43
(Eve Johnson Houghton) *s.i.s: swtchd rt to r towards stands' side after 3f: sn rdn and btn* **16/1**

0223 **10** *15* **Avon River**[16] 4445 4-9-8 84........................(b) RichardHughes 11 —
(Richard Hannon) *racd alone on stands' rail 4f and upsides w ldr of main gp: wknd qckly fr 2f out: eased whn no ch fnl f* **4/1**[2]

1m 26.71s (1.01) **Going Correction** +0.05s/f (Good) **10** Ran SP% **112.1**
Speed ratings (Par 103): **96,91,90,87,87 86,84,81,78,60**
toteswingers:1&2:£6.70, 1&3:£23.80, 2&3:£17.10 CSF £31.87 TOTE £5.60: £1.90, £2.00, £6.50; EX 39.40 Trifecta £276.40 Pool: £736.01 - 1.97 winning units..
Owner The Foxford House Partnership **Bred** Mrs Ann Jenkins **Trained** Baughurst, Hants

FOCUS
A good claimer, with six of the ten runners officially rated 80 or above. It's doubtful how literally the form can be taken.
Corporal Maddox Official explanation: jockey said gelding hung right

4998 PUNTER SOUTHALL TRANSACTION SERVICES H'CAP 1m 5f 61y
3:10 (3:10) (Class 3) (0-90,84) 3-Y-O+ **£4,851** (£1,443; £721; £360) **Stalls** Low

Form RPR

-163 **1** **Rockfella**[35] 3817 5-9-4 **74**........................ EddieAhern 2 83
(Denis Coakley) *mde virtually all: rdn fr over 2f out: kpt finding u.p thrght fnl f: hld on gamely* **11/1**

2001 **2** *1 ¼* **Spice Fair**[23] 4216 4-9-6 **76**........................ RichardHughes 9 83
(Mark Usher) *hld up in rr off pce: stdy hdwy fr 3f out drvn and styd on u.p to chse wnr fnl 120yds but a hld* **15/2**

4365 **3** *hd* **Time To Work (IRE)**[20] 4316 3-9-1 **83**........................(v) LiamKeniry 3 90
(Andrew Balding) *in tch: stdy hdwy to trck ldrs 3f out: chsd wnr over 2f out: sn rdn: no imp: one pce and lost 2nd fnl 120yds* **5/1**[2]

3104 **4** *5* **Gogeo (IRE)**[9] 4677 4-9-13 **83**........................ WilliamBuick 5 82
(Alan Swinbank) *trckd ldrs: drvn and no imp 3f out: wknd ins fnl 2f* **7/2**[1]

44-1 **5** *6* **Samsons Son**[47] 3434 7-9-13 **83**........................ JimmyFortune 8 73
(Alan King) *hld up in rr off pce: stdy hdwy fr 4f out: drvn to chse ldrs ins fnl 3f: wknd ins fnl 2f* **8/1**

0/0- **6** *1 ½* **Secret Tune**[264] 4817 7-9-12 **82**........................(t) RussKennemore 1 70
(Shaun Lycett) *chsd ldrs: reminder 9f out: rdn over 4f out: wknd ins fnl 3f* **40/1**

4210 **7** *1 ¾* **Galivant (IRE)**[29] 4036 3-8-13 **81**........................ SebSanders 6 66
(J W Hills) *in rr but in tch: rdn and hdwy 5f out: wknd fr 3f out* **7/1**

00-1 **8** *16* **Bullet Man (USA)**[105] 1651 6-9-8 **78**........................(t) DarryllHolland 7 39
(Paul Webber) *sn chsng wnr: rdn 4f out: wknd 3f out* **6/1**[3]

Gold Tobougg Official explanation: trainer's rep had no explanation for the poor form shown

5008 NORTHUMBRIAN WATER H'CAP (DIV I) 6f
4:30 (4:30) (Class 6) (0-65,63) 3-Y-0+ **£2,458** (£731; £365; £182) **Stalls** Centre

Form RPR

3320 **1** **Sea Salt**[11] 4600 8-9-5 **61** ShaneBKelly(5) 3 74
(Ron Barr) *cl up towards far rail (jst away fr main gp): led over 2f out: pushed clr fnl f* **7/2**[2]

0006 **2** *6* **Cheyenne Red (IRE)**[6] 4782 5-9-0 **51** FrederikTylicki 4 46
(Michael Dods) *led to over 2f out: lost 2nd over 1f out: rallied to take 2nd towards fin: no ch w wnr* **10/1**

3550 **3** *3/4* **Hellbender (IRE)**[40] 3657 5-9-2 **58** LMcNiff(5) 10 51
(George Foster) *t.k.h: cl up: rdn and hdwy to chse wnr over 1f out: no ex and lost 2nd nr fin* **5/1**

5046 **4** *2 1/2* **Red Scintilla**[9] 4672 4-9-6 **57** PaulHanagan 8 42
(Nigel Tinkler) *trckd ldrs: rdn over 2f out: wknd over 1f out* **11/4**[1]

0016 **5** *2* **Andrasta**[10] 4636 6-9-2 **53** TonyHamilton 7 32
(Alan Berry) *hld up bhd ldng gp: effrt over 2f out: sn no imp* **16/1**

6-00 **6** *7* **Elegant Dancer (IRE)**[74] 2546 4-8-8 **45** JamesSullivan 2 —
(Paul Green) *bhd: drvn along 1/2-way: edgd lft: nvr on terms* **16/1**

-000 **7** *5* **Ruler's Honour (IRE)**[20] 4328 4-8-13 **50** (b) GregFairley 9 —
(Tim Etherington) *s.v.s: a wl bhd* **40/1**

0006 **8** *6* **Dream Express (IRE)**[37] 3732 6-8-3 **45** NeilFarley(5) 6 —
(David Thompson) *in tch: struggling over 3f out: sn btn* **25/1**

6606 **9** *8* **Big Slick (IRE)**[3] 4876 6-8-11 **48** RobertWinston 5 15
(Mel Brittain) *chsd ldrs: rdn over 3f out: wknd over 2f out: eased whn no ch appr fnl f* **4/1**[3]

1m 17.8s (3.20) **Going Correction** +0.325s/f (Good) **9** Ran SP% **112.7**
Speed ratings (Par 101): **91,83,82,78,76 66,60,52,41**
toteswingers:1&2:£5.20, 1&3:£4.60, 2&3:£6.90 CSF £37.08 CT £172.95 TOTE £4.30: £1.20, £2.80, £2.70; EX 21.40.
Owner R E Barr **Bred** D R Tucker **Trained** Seamer, N Yorks

FOCUS
A weak sprint handicap and only the winner showed their form on the testing ground. Not a race to take too literally.
Big Slick(IRE) Official explanation: jockey said horse lost its action

5009 NORTHUMBRIAN WATER H'CAP (DIV II) 6f
5:05 (5:06) (Class 6) (0-65,64) 3-Y-0+ **£2,458** (£731; £365; £182) **Stalls** Centre

Form RPR

0641 **1** **Cross Of Lorraine (IRE)**[9] 4672 8-9-9 **61** 6ex (b) TonyHamilton 10 72
(Chris Grant) *t.k.h: cl up centre: led 1/2-way: drvn out fnl f* **11/2**[3]

3402 **2** *2* **I Got You Babe (IRE)**[8] 4729 3-9-5 **61** PaulHanagan 4 65
(Richard Guest) *prom centre: effrt over 2f out: chsd wnr ins fnl f: r.o* **4/1**[2]

6030 **3** *3 1/2* **Classlin**[3] 4881 4-8-2 **45** ShaneBKelly(5) 6 40
(Jim Goldie) *dwlt: hld up centre: hdwy to chse wnr over 1f out to ins fnl f: sn btn* **12/1**

4203 **4** *4 1/2* **Pitkin**[13] 4527 3-9-8 **64** (t) PaddyAspell 3 44
(Michael Easterby) *hld up in tch on outside of centre gp: drvn and outpcd over 2f out: edgd lft and rallied over 1f out: no imp* **5/2**[1]

0464 **5** *1 1/2* **Lady Lube Rye (IRE)**[13] 4563 4-8-7 **45** AdrianNicholls 9 22
(Noel Wilson) *led to 1/2-way in centre: edgd lft and wknd over 1f out* **11/2**[3]

4666 **6** *1 1/2* **Running Water**[19] 4359 3-7-13 **48** ow2 VictorSantos(7) 7 19
(Hugh McWilliams) *hld up: hdwy in centre over 2f out: rdn and wknd over 1f out* **33/1**

-060 **7** *1/2* **Russian Brigadier**[78] 2415 4-9-0 **52** RobertWinston 1 23
(Mel Brittain) *swtchd to far rail after 1f: prom: drvn 1/2-way: wknd 2f out* **12/1**

0-60 **8** *1 1/4* **Fulford**[14] 4518 6-8-3 **48** LukeStrong(7) 2 15
(Mel Brittain) *sn swtchd to far rail: cl up tl wknd over 2f out* **12/1**

3055 **9** *1 3/4* **Spirit Of Coniston**[10] 4636 8-9-0 **55** DeclanCannon(3) 8 17
(Paul Midgley) *trckd ldrs centre tl rdn and wknd over 2f out* **10/1**

1m 18.19s (3.59) **Going Correction** +0.325s/f (Good)
WFA 3 from 4yo+ 4lb **9** Ran SP% **114.4**
Speed ratings (Par 101): **89,86,81,75,73 71,71,69,67**
toteswingers:1&2:£4.40, 1&3:£11.30, 2&3:£8.20 CSF £27.51 CT £253.65 TOTE £6.10: £2.40, £2.10, £4.20; EX 19.90.
Owner Nigel E M Jones **Bred** Kildaragh Stud **Trained** Newton Bewley, Co Durham

FOCUS
The second division of the weak sprint handicap. Those held up were once again at a big disadvantage and the principals dominated inside the final furlong. Again few showed their form on the ground.
Lady Lube Rye(IRE) Official explanation: jockey said filly hung left and lost its action

5010 WATERAID H'CAP 5f
5:40 (5:40) (Class 5) (0-70,70) 3-Y-0 **£2,522** (£750; £375; £187) **Stalls** Centre

Form RPR

0206 **1** **Ever Roses**[31] 3950 3-8-1 **53** (v) DeclanCannon(3) 5 63
(Paul Midgley) *prom: hdwy to chse ld over 2f out: led ins fnl f: carried hd high: r.o* **11/1**

3402 **2** *1 3/4* **Cool In The Shade**[1] 4942 3-8-5 **54** (b) KellyHarrison 6 58
(Paul Midgley) *cl up: led after 1f: rdn and hdd ins fnl f: kpt on same pce towards fin* **7/4**[2]

-042 **3** *9* **Myjestic Melody (IRE)**[6] 4786 3-8-2 **51** DuranFentiman 1 24
(Noel Wilson) *t.k.h: cl up: rdn over 2f out: outpcd by first two wl over 1f out* **4/1**[3]

0006 **4** *1 1/4* **Bygones For Coins (IRE)**[24] 4172 3-7-11 **51** oh6 NeilFarley(5) 2 19
(Alan Berry) *t.k.h early: in tch: outpcd over 2f out: drifted lft and sn n.d* **25/1**

3065 **5** *8* **Captain Kolo (IRE)**[11] 4610 3-9-7 **70** DavidAllan 3 10
(Tim Easterby) *led 1f: cl up tl rdn and wknd qckly over 1f out* **13/8**[1]

62.64 secs (1.54) **Going Correction** +0.325s/f (Good) **5** Ran SP% **106.6**
Speed ratings (Par 100): **100,97,82,80,68**
CSF £28.84 TOTE £10.40: £3.70, £1.90; EX 28.10.
Owner K L Man **Bred** I M Emes **Trained** Westow, N Yorks

FOCUS
Another weak sprint handicap, this time for 3-y-os. The first pair pulled well clear to give trainer Paul Midgley a 1-2. The form's rated around the second's Beverley run the previous day.
Captain Kolo(IRE) Official explanation: trainer had no explanation for the poor form shown
T/Plt: £161.90 to a £1 stake. Pool:£49,633.83 - 223.79 winning tickets T/Qpdt: £10.70 to a £1 stake. Pool:£5,089.07 - 349.10 winning tickets RY

4961 NEWMARKET (R-H)
Friday, August 12

OFFICIAL GOING: Good (7.8)
Wind: virtually nil Weather: cloudy, dry

5011 TALK NIGHT CLUB MEDIAN AUCTION MAIDEN STKS 7f
5:30 (5:31) (Class 5) 2-Y-0 **£3,234** (£962; £481; £240) **Stalls** High

Form RPR

2 **1** **Farhaan (USA)**[28] 4054 2-9-3 0 RichardHills 3 87+
(John Dunlop) *lw: in tch and a travelling wl: hdwy to ld 2f out: edgd lft but qcknd clr ent fnl f: r.o strly: comf* **5/4**[1]

2 *4* **Revered Citizen (USA)** 2-9-0 0 LouisBeuzelin(3) 7 77+
(Sir Michael Stoute) *w'like: tall: scope: in tch in midfield: rdn and outpcd ent fnl 2f: swtchd rt over 1f out: rallied and r.o wl ins fnl f: wnt 2nd fnl 50yds: no ch w wnr* **16/1**

3 *3/4* **Validus** 2-9-3 0 KierenFallon 18 75+
(Luca Cumani) *athletic: attr: lw: in tch: rdn and effrt 2f out: chsd clr wnr ent fnl f: kpt on same pce and no imp: lost 2nd fnl 50yds* **14/1**

4 *1 1/2* **Initiator** 2-9-3 0 JMurtagh 17 72+
(Jeremy Noseda) *athletic: narrow: s.i.s: sn rcvrd and in tch in rr: hdwy on far side and rdn to chse ldrs over 1f out: outpcd and btn ent fnl f: nt given hrd time whn btn ins fnl f* **3/1**[2]

0 **5** *1* **Travelling**[28] 4061 2-8-12 0 MichaelHills 12 64
(J W Hills) *chsd ldrs: rdn and chsd wnr 2f out: outpcd and lost 2nd ent fnl f: styd on same pce and no ch w wnr fnl f* **12/1**

03 **6** *2* **Vinnie Jones**[43] 3553 2-9-3 0 WilliamBuick 11 64
(John Gosden) *str: lw: t.k.h: w ldrs: rdn and unable qck ent fnl 2f: outpcd and btn over 1f out: plugged on* **7/1**[3]

7 *hd* **Free House** 2-9-3 0 ShaneKelly 13 64
(Brian Meehan) *w'like: str: bit bkwd: s.i.s: sn rcvrd and in tch: pushed along and outpcd ent fnl 2f: rdn and kpt on steadily fnl f: no threat to wnr* **22/1**

8 *3/4* **Tallevu (IRE)** 2-9-3 0 StephenCraine 10 62
(Tom Dascombe) *str: bit bkwd: t.k.h: chsd ldrs tl rdn and btn over 1f out: wknd fnl f* **50/1**

9 *1* **Andalieb** 2-9-3 0 MartinLane 1 59
(David Simcock) *unf: swtg: edgy: s.i.s: sn in tch in rr: rdn: rn green and struggling over 2f out: n.d but kpt on past btn horses ins fnl f: n.d* **22/1**

10 *nk* **Rogue Reporter (IRE)** 2-8-10 0 HayleyBurton(7) 8 58+
(Luca Cumani) *w'like: led and set stdy gallop: hdd 2f out: sn outpcd and wl btn ent fnl f* **66/1**

11 *2 3/4* **Harry Buckle** 2-9-0 0 AdamBeschizza(3) 5 52
(Philip McBride) *lengthy: rn green: in tch in rr: rdn and struggling 3f out: sn outpcd and no ch fr wl over 1f out* **66/1**

00 **12** *3/4* **Highly Likely (IRE)**[20] 4330 2-9-3 0 IanMongan 16 50+
(John Dunlop) *t.k.h: hld up wl in tch in midfield: rdn ent fnl 2f: sn btn and hung lft over 1f out: wknd fnl f* **80/1**

0 **13** *shd* **Flugelhorn (IRE)**[42] 3583 2-9-3 0 RichardMullen 14 49
(Ed McMahon) *lengthy: rn green: sn bustled along in rr: rdn and struggling 3f out: wl btn fnl 2f* **20/1**

14 *1 1/2* **Widow Flower (IRE)** 2-8-12 0 LukeMorris 4 41
(Michael Bell) *hld up in tch towards rr: hdwy into midfield 1/2-way: rdn and unable qck over 2f out: wknd u.p over 1f out* **40/1**

15 *8* **Shek O Lad** 2-9-3 0 GeorgeBaker 2 26
(Alan Jarvis) *a towards rr: rdn and wknd jst over 2f out: wl bhd and eased wl ins fnl f* **66/1**

16 *4 1/2* **Buckley Boy** 2-9-3 0 JamieMackay 9 14
(K F Clutterbuck) *w'like: a in rr and rn green: rdn and wknd over 2f out: wl bhd and eased ins fnl f* **150/1**

17 [illegible] [illegible] AndreaAtzeni 6 8
(Chris Dwyer) *w'like: tall: t.k.h: w ldrs tl lost pl qckly jst over 2f out: wl bhd 1f out: eased ins fnl f: t.o* **80/1**

1m 27.16s (1.46) **Going Correction** +0.15s/f (Good) **17** Ran SP% **127.7**
Speed ratings (Par 94): **97,92,91,89,88 86,86,85,84,83 80,79,79,78,68 63,60**
toteswingers:1&2:£8.00, 2&3:£19.00, 1&3:£7.00 CSF £24.75 TOTE £2.50: £1.40, £3.50, £3.70; EX 34.20.
Owner Hamdan Al Maktoum **Bred** Shadwell Farm LLC **Trained** Arundel, W Sussex

FOCUS
Far side track used with stalls on far side except 1m2f: centre. Repositioning of bend into home straight added 16m to races of 1m2f and 1m4f. There was a lack of early pace in this maiden.

NOTEBOOK
Farhaan(USA) ◆ was well backed to build on the promise of his debut second at Newbury four weeks earlier. He had clearly benefitted from that experience and was very professional in running out a convincing winner. Always in the right place, he quickened up the tempo in decisive fashion to lead with two furlongs left to run. He was still going strong when he hit the line and should get a little further this year. He holds several Group entries and it might not be too long before he takes up one, based on this impressive display. He demonstrated an athletic action and long stride, moving with real class through the closing stages. (op 9-4)

Revered Citizen(USA) looks well bought at $20,000 and made a most promising debut. For a few strides either inexperience or lack of tactical pace allowed the winner to get away from him, but he was making up ground in eyecatching fashion late on and a further furlong will be within his range. (op 12-1 tchd 11-1)

Validus, the second foal out of a dam who won on her 3yo at debut at 1m, was another to offer encouragement first time out. From a yard whose horses can progress for experience and time, he knew enough to lie handy and wasn't weakening at the business end of the race. This should bring him on and a maiden can be found for him in the near future. (op 9-1)

Initiator was a 50,000gns purchase and is a half-brother to a triple 6f-1m winner. He was slowly away before making up some ground on the opposite side to the winner. Another, who will benefit both mentally and physically for a run, he is likely to be there or thereabouts next time. (op 7-2 tchd 4-1)

Travelling performed respectably when finishing seventh over C&D on her debut four weeks earlier and this was another fair effort, without suggesting she is good enough to win a maiden at a course like Newmarket. (op 14-1 tchd 11-1)

Vinnie Jones, stepping up to 7f here, is now qualified for nurseries where he may be seen in a better light. (op 5-1)

Free House is related to winners and should know more for next time after this debut effort in which he was slowly into stride. (op 33-1 tchd 20-1)

Andalieb, a half-brother to a winner over this trip at three, was green when the stalls opened. (op 20-1)

5012 MONTE CARLO AMUSEMENTS, SOUTHEND H'CAP — 6f

6:00 (6:00) (Class 4) (0-85,85) 3-Y-0+ **£4,528** (£1,347; £673; £336) **Stalls** High

Form / RPR

3615 **1** **Sacrosanctus**[13] 4550 3-9-5 **82** .... IanMongan 1 — 91
(David Nicholls) *s.i.s: sn rcvrd and led after 1f: mde rest: rdn wl over 1f out: edgd lft u.p ins fnl f: kpt on wl* **9/1**

4201 **2** *nk* **Quasi Congaree (GER)**[7] 4765 5-9-10 **83** 6ex........(t) JamesDoyle 4 — 92+
(Ian Wood) *hld up in last pair: swtchd rt and effrt wl over 1f out: str run u.p fnl f: pressed wnr and gng on cl home: nvr quite getting to wnr* **7/1[3]**

21-5 **3** *½* **Gentle Lord**[119] 1361 3-9-4 **81**........(t) KierenFallon 7 — 88
(Tom Dascombe) *stdd s: t.k.h and sn chsng ldrs: rdn and chsd wnr wl over 1f out: sn rdn: kpt on u.p fnl 100yds: lost 2nd cl home* **6/1[2]**

-153 **4** *1 ½* **Arctic Lynx (IRE)**[140] 961 4-9-6 **79**........ GeorgeBaker 13 — 82
(John Best) *swtg: hld up in tch in midfield: rdn and effrt whn edgd rt over 1f out: kpt on u.p ins fnl f: nt pce to rch ldrs* **14/1**

1403 **5** *½* **Hezmah**[13] 4556 3-9-8 **85**........ RichardHills 10 — 88+
(John Gosden) *lw: awkward leaving stalls: hld up in tch: hdwy and rdn to chse ldng pair over 1f out: drvn and unable qck ent fnl f: sn short of room and hmpd: wknd fnl 100yds* **7/2[1]**

1-05 **6** *hd* **Loki's Revenge**[6] 4779 3-9-5 **85**........ HarryBentley(3) 8 — 85
(William Jarvis) *hld up in tch towards rr: effrt whn nt clr run briefly and swtchd lft over 1f out: styd on u.p ins fnl f: nt pce to rch ldrs* **11/1**

4004 **7** *nk* **Silver Wind**[11] 4618 6-9-0 **73**........(b) ShaneKelly 2 — 73
(Alan McCabe) *b: s.i.s: sn rcvrd and chsd wnr after 1f tl wl over 1f out: sn drvn and unable qck over 1f out: styd on same pce fnl f* **25/1**

304 **8** *nse* **Merchant Of Medici**[7] 4765 4-9-7 **80**........ LukeMorris 14 — 80
(William Muir) *lw: taken down early: hld up in tch in midfield: rdn and effrt wl over 1f out: styd on same pce and no imp fnl f* **9/1**

0002 **9** *1 ½* **Gap Princess (IRE)**[11] 4609 7-9-7 **80**........ WilliamBuick 6 — 75
(Geoffrey Harker) *in tch in midfield: rdn and effrt ent fnl 2f: no imp and no threat to ldrs fnl f* **9/1**

550 **10** *2* **Seek The Fair Land**[13] 4531 5-9-5 **78**........ JMurtagh 5 — 66
(Jim Boyle) *swtg: chsd ldrs: rdn and unable qck 2f out: outpcd and btn over 1f out: eased wl ins fnl f* **11/1**

1300 **11** *nse* **Bassett Road (IRE)**[43] 3536 3-9-5 **82**........ JamieMackay 12 — 69
(Willie Musson) *s.i.s: a bhd: rdn and struggling jst over 2f out: sme modest hdwy ins fnl f: n.d* **25/1**

0540 **12** *1 ¼* **Oriental Scot**[13] 4561 4-9-8 **81**........ RichardMullen 3 — 65
(William Jarvis) *in tch in midfield but sn niggled along: rdn and struggling 1/2-way: wknd wl over 1f out* **14/1**

1214 **13** *nk* **Jack Rackham**[48] 3383 7-9-5 **78**........(v) TomEaves 11 — 61
(Bryan Smart) *swtg; led for 1f: sn stdd and hld up in tch: rdn and unable qck 2f out: wknd u.p over 1f out* **18/1**

1m 12.54s (0.04) **Going Correction** +0.15s/f (Good)
WFA 3 from 4yo+ 4lb — **13** Ran SP% **122.0**
Speed ratings (Par 105): **105,104,103,101,101 101,100,100,98,95 95,94,93**
toteswingers:1&2:£12.80, 2&3:£9.20, 1&3:£14.00 CSF £72.26 CT £427.72 TOTE £12.70: £3.70, £2.50, £2.60; EX 97.50.
Owner Paul J Dixon **Bred** Worksop Manor Stud **Trained** Sessay, N Yorks
■ Stewards' Enquiry : Ian Mongan one-day ban: careless riding (Aug 26)

FOCUS
This was run a a modest early gallop. The form looks respectable for the grade with a 5lb personal best from the winner.

5013 SUNSPOT AMUSEMENTS, SOUTHEND EBF MAIDEN STKS — 1m

6:35 (6:35) (Class 4) 2-Y-0 **£4,528** (£1,347; £673; £336) **Stalls** High

Form / RPR

2 **1** **Harvard N Yale (USA)**[28] 4053 2-9-3 0........ JMurtagh 13 — 89+
(Jeremy Noseda) *lw: mde all: rdn 2f out: drvn jst over 1f out: asserted and forged ahd ins fnl f: styd on wl and gng away at fin* **8/15[1]**

0 **2** *1 ½* **Endowing (IRE)**[20] 4330 2-9-3 0........ PatCosgrave 1 — 86
(Richard Hannon) *s.i.s: rn green: in tch in last trio: edging lft and hdwy over 2f out: rdn and chsd wnr ent fnl f: no ex and btn ins fnl f: one pce fnl 100yds* **50/1**

3 *1* **Gospel Choir** 2-9-3 0........ KierenFallon 4 — 83+
(Sir Michael Stoute) *w'like: str: scope: bit bkwd: b.off hind: in tch towards rr: pushed along and outpcd over 3f out: rallied ent fnl f: r.o wl to go 3rd fnl 75yds: gng on fin: nvr trbld ldrs* **7/1[2]**

5 **4** *1 ¾* **Greek War (IRE)**[23] 4213 2-9-3 0........ AhmedAjtebi 3 — 79
(Mahmood Al Zarooni) *lw: hld up in tch in midfield: rdn and effrt over 2f out: drvn to chse ldng pair ent fnl f: no ex and btn fnl 150yds: lost 3rd and wknd fnl 75yds* **7/1[2]**

0 **5** *½* **Mubaraza (IRE)**[20] 4330 2-9-3 0........ RichardHills 5 — 78+
(John Dunlop) *str: lw: stdd s: hld up in tch towards rr: hdwy over 3f out: chsd ldrs and unable qck wl over 1f out: plugged on same pce fnl f* **10/1[3]**

6 *2* **Dynamic Duo (IRE)** 2-9-0 0........ SeanLevey(3) 7 — 73
(Richard Hannon) *w'like: bit bkwd: chsd ldrs: rdn and ev ch 2f out: btn ent fnl f: wknd ins fnl f* **33/1**

7 *1 ½* **Daneking** 2-9-3 0........ WilliamBuick 8 — 70+
(John Gosden) *str: bit bkwd: in tch in midfield: pushed along and rn green over 2f out: outpcd 2f out: rallied and hdwy jst over 1f out: styd on steadily fnl f but no threat to wnr* **20/1**

0 **8** *nk* **Holiday Reading (USA)**[23] 4213 2-9-3 0........ ShaneKelly 14 — 69
(Brian Meehan) *chsd wnr: rdn and ev ch 2f out: drvn and lost 2nd ent fnl f: wknd qckly ins fnl f* **20/1**

4034 **9** *2 ¾* **Flying Trader (USA)**[8] 4714 2-9-3 69........ LukeMorris 11 — 63
(Jane Chapple-Hyam) *in tch: rdn and unable qck over 2f out: wknd and btn 2f out: plugged on same pce but no threat to ldrs fr over 1f out* **25/1**

0 **10** *¾* **Topanga Canyon**[21] 4264 2-9-0 0........ SimonPearce(3) 2 — 61+
(Andrew Balding) *lengthy: scope: lw: in tch: rdn and unable qck over 2f out: wknd qckly over 1f out* **33/1**

11 *2 ¼* **Aldgate (USA)** 2-9-3 0........ RichardMullen 9 — 56
(Mahmood Al Zarooni) *w'like: tall: scope: s.i.s: in tch in rr: rdn and struggling 3f out: outpcd and btn 2f out: no ch after* **20/1**

12 *16* **Verona Bay (FR)** 2-9-0 0........ AdamBeschizza(3) 12 — 19
(Julia Feilden) *w'like: in tch in midfield: rdn and struggling 3f out: wknd 2f out: wl bhd and eased ins fnl f: t.o* **100/1**

13 *1 ¾* **Men Don't Cry (IRE)** 2-9-3 0........ GeorgeBaker 6 — 15
(Ed Dunlop) *athletic: attr: b.bkwd: rn green: a in rr: lost tch over 2f out: wl bhd fnl f: t.o* **25/1**

14 *2 ¼* **Bank On Me** 2-9-3 0........ MartinLane 10 — 10
(Philip McBride) *w'like: attr: a towards rr: rdn and struggling 3f out: wknd 2f out: wl bhd and eased ins fnl f: t.o* **25/1**

1m 40.17s (0.17) **Going Correction** +0.15s/f (Good) — **14** Ran SP% **134.0**
Speed ratings (Par 96): **105,103,102,100,100 98,96,96,93,92 90,74,72,70**
toteswingers:1&2:£16.30, 2&3:£42.40, 1&3:£1.60 CSF £63.68 TOTE £1.50: £1.10, £18.80, £1.90; EX 120.60.
Owner The Honorable Earle I Mack **Bred** Earle I Mack **Trained** Newmarket, Suffolk

FOCUS
This maiden has earned a lofty reputation, having been won by the likes of Motivator, Centennial and, famously, Frankel from Nathaniel last year. This renewal might not be up to the heady heights of a year ago but plenty of winners are likely to emerge from it.

NOTEBOOK
Harvard N Yale(USA) was stepped up to 1m here and that looks the bare minimum for him. He made every yard and was well in command in the closing strides after momentarily appearing under pressure approaching the furlong-marker. He holds some smart entries but wasn't being committed to any of them by his trainer Jeremy Noseda after this win. (tchd 4-7 in places)
Endowing(IRE) ◆ was slowly away and showed other signs of inexperience as he hung from one side of the course to the other. Considering how green he was, he did very well to get himself into contention. He will have learnt plenty from this and should tighten up all round for his next appearance when he is likely to be the one to beat. (tchd 66-1)
Gospel Choir ◆, the fourth foal out of the top-class Chorist, was one of the first off the bridle, outpaced for a few strides, but once he got going he made up considerable ground and was the eyecatcher. The experience gained will stand him in good stead for any maiden he contests next time. (tchd 13-2)
Greek War(IRE) was a beaten favourite on his debut at Sandown. Stepped up to 1m here for his second start, he weakened late on after an effort from 2f out. He should be up to winning a maiden but perhaps at a smaller track. (tchd 6-1)
Mubaraza(IRE) was upped in trip to 1m after a respectable debut effort over 7f at the same course. He should be up to winning a routine maiden. (op 9-1)
Dynamic Duo(IRE), a half-brother to the smart Cai Shen, is entitled to progress with this run under his belt. (op 40-1)
Daneking looks open to plenty of improvement, having been green when coming under pressure.
Flying Trader(USA) Official explanation: trainer's rep said colt finished distressed
Men Don't Cry(IRE) was arguably the greenest of all. (op 20-1)

5014 GL EVENTS H'CAP — 1m

7:05 (7:05) (Class 5) (0-75,75) 3-Y-0+ **£2,587** (£770; £384; £192) **Stalls** High

Form / RPR

4330 **1** **Abriachan**[4] 4866 4-9-2 **63**........ JackMitchell 2 — 72
(Noel Quinlan) *hld up in rr: hdwy 2f out: chsng ldrs whn nt clr run 1f out: rdn and r.o wl ins fnl f to ld towards fin* **20/1**

0503 **2** *¾* **Inpursuitoffreedom**[14] 4506 4-9-3 **67**........ AdamBeschizza(3) 9 — 74
(Philip McBride) *swtg: on toes: hld up in tch in midfield: rdn and effrt 2f out: drvn to chal 1f out: led ins fnl f: hdd and no ex towards fin* **10/1[3]**

1100 **3** *nk* **Iron Step**[21] 4281 3-9-6 **74**........(t) JamesDoyle 3 — 79+
(Nicky Vaughan) *t.k.h: hld up in tch in midfield: effrt u.p over 1f out: led 1f out tl hdd ins fnl f: kpt on same pce towards fin* **20/1**

2343 **4** *1 ¼* **So Is She (IRE)**[38] 3710 3-8-3 **60**........(b) AmyBaker(3) 13 — 62
(Alan Bailey) *swtg: chsd ldrs: rdn and sltly outpcd over 1f out: rallied ins fnl f: kpt on wl fnl 100yds* **50/1**

-506 **5** *shd* **Oh So Saucy**[21] 4278 7-9-13 **74**........ GeorgeBaker 4 — 77
(Chris Wall) *hld up in rr: hdwy over 1f out: drvn and styd on ins fnl f: nvr gng pce to rch ldrs* **8/1[2]**

0004 **6** *nse* **Skyfire**[21] 4278 4-9-10 **71**........ PatCosgrave 12 — 74
(Ed de Giles) *w ldr ev ch and rdn 2f out: stl ev ch tl no ex and btn ins fnl f: styd on same pce fnl 100yds* **8/1[2]**

1321 **7** *2 ½* **Whitby Jet (IRE)**[7] 4744 3-9-4 **72** 6ex........ KierenFallon 15 — 68
(Edward Vaughan) *chsd ldrs: hdwy to join ldrs 3f out: rdn and ev ch 2f out: struggling u.p ent fnl f: wknd fnl 150yds* **3/1[1]**

-223 **8** *3* **Zafeen's Pearl**[147] 889 4-9-1 **62**........ IanMongan 14 — 52
(Dean Ivory) *racd keenly: led: rdn 2f out: hdd 1f out: sn wknd* **8/1[2]**

040 **9** *½* **Red Somerset (USA)**[47] 3426 8-9-2 **63**........(b) MartinLane 16 — 52
(Mike Murphy) *swtg; chsd ldrs: rdn ent fnl 2f: unable qck u.p over 1f out: wknd 1f out* **14/1**

1403 **10** *2 ¾* **Granny Anne (IRE)**[2] 4920 3-8-3 **57**........ CathyGannon 11 — 39
(Alan Bailey) *in tch: rdn and effrt jst over 2f out: wknd u.p ent fnl f* **20/1**

5-35 **11** *5* **Another For Joe**[49] 3340 3-9-4 **72**........ TomEaves 10 — 42
(Ian Williams) *t.k.h: hld up in tch towards rr: rdn and unable qck jst over 2f out: wknd over 1f out* **8/1[2]**

4623 **12** *2 ¼* **Loyal N Trusted**[165] 714 3-8-11 **65**........ AndreaAtzeni 5 — 30
(Michael Wigham) *swtg: t.k.h: hld up in tch towards rr: rdn and struggling over 2f out: wknd and hung lft wl over 1f out: sn lost tch* **20/1**

0206 **13** *14* **Circus Star (USA)**[14] 4489 3-9-0 **68**........ ShaneKelly 7 — —
(Brian Meehan) *lw: chsd ldrs tl lost pl qckly 2f out: wl bhd and eased ins fnl f: t.o* **12/1**

2023 **14** *1 ¾* **Satwa Dream (IRE)**[15] 4479 4-9-11 **75**........(p) HarryBentley(3) 1 — —
(Ed Dunlop) *hld up in rr: rdn and lost tch over 2f out: wl bhd and eased ins fnl f: t.o* **8/1[2]**

006 **15** *1* **Big Bay (USA)**[44] 3521 5-9-4 **65**........ LukeMorris 8 — —
(Jane Chapple-Hyam) *lw: a towards rr: rdn and struggling over 2f out: wknd 2f out: wl bhd and eased ins fnl f: t.o* **25/1**

3635 **16** *17* **Exopuntia**[2] 4927 5-8-10 **57**........(t) SaleemGolam 6 — —
(Julia Feilden) *swtg: rrd over in stalls: s.i.s: nvr travelling wl in rr: lost tch over 2f out: t.o and virtually p.u ins fnl f* **20/1**

1m 40.67s (0.67) **Going Correction** +0.15s/f (Good)
WFA 3 from 4yo+ 7lb — **16** Ran SP% **133.6**
Speed ratings (Par 103): **102,101,100,99,99 99,97,94,93,90 85,83,69,67,66 49**
toteswingers::1&2:£69.00, 2&3:£59.80, 1&3:£103.70 CSF £209.01 CT £4242.31 TOTE £31.00: £7.50, £2.70, £6.60, £11.70; EX 719.40.
Owner Thomas Mann **Bred** Plantation Stud **Trained** Newmarket, Suffolk

FOCUS
This was a competitive race of its type that was half a second slower than the preceding juvenile maiden. The form seems pretty sound overall, rated around the second.

5015 NGK SPARK PLUGS H'CAP — 1m 2f

7:40 (7:44) (Class 5) (0-70,70) 3-Y-0+ **£2,587** (£770; £384; £192) **Stalls** Centre

Form / RPR

200- **1** **Cheddar George**[233] 7966 5-9-6 **62**........ GeorgeBaker 7 — 73
(Peter Chapple-Hyam) *stdd s: hld up wl in rr: stdy hdwy 4f out: rdn to chal and drew clr w runner-up 1f out: led ins fnl f: hld on u.p towards fin* **22/1**

2611 **2** *shd* **Eagle Nebula**[25] 4153 7-9-9 **65**........ IanMongan 3 — 76
(Brett Johnson) *hld up in rr: hdwy 3f out: rdn to ld over 1f out: drew clr w wnr 1f out: drvn and hdd ins fnl f: kpt on wl but a jst hld* **14/1**

4002 **3** *2 ½* **Laconicos (IRE)**[13] 4549 9-8-13 **60**................................(t) LauraPike(5) 6 66
(William Stone) *taken down early: t.k.h: hld up in midfield: drvn and effrt over 1f out: styd on to go 3rd ins fnl f: kpt on u.p but no threat to ldng pair* **16/1**

-011 **4** *1* **Broughtons Swinger**[46] 3466 4-9-8 **67**.................. AdamBeschizza(3) 8 73+
(Willie Musson) *hld up in midfield: shuffled bk towards rr 3f out: nt clr run over 2f out: hdwy u.p wl over 1f out: r.o fnl f but unable to chal* **8/1**

-610 **5** *1 ¼* **Hot Spice**[19] 4367 3-9-2 **67**.. JMurtagh 9 69+
(John Dunlop) *lw: t.k.h: hld up in tch: shuffled bk towards rr 3f out: rdn and hdwy over 1f out: kpt on ins fnl f: no threat to ldrs* **3/1**[2]

-000 **6** *3 ½* **Silent Applause**[29] 4024 8-8-8 **53**.................................. SeanLevey(3) 16 48
(Dr Jon Scargill) *hld up in rr: pushed along 5f out: hdwy and rdn to press ldrs 3f out: drvn and wknd over 1f out* **25/1**

-31 **7** *3 ½* **Rajnagan (IRE)**[12] 4578 7-9-9 **65** 6ex...........................(t) KierenFallon 14 53
(Paul Webber) *b.hind: stdd s: hld up towards rr: hdwy to chse ldrs 7f out: led wl over 2f out and sn rdn: hdd over 1f out: wknd 1f out: wl btn and eased ins fnl f* **5/2**[1]

5-06 **8** *1 ¼* **Myboyalfie (USA)**[37] 3739 4-9-11 **67**.......................... StephenCraine 10 52
(J R Jenkins) *swtg: hld up in tch in midfield: rdn and unable qck over 2f out: wknd over 1f out* **25/1**

3035 **9** *1 ¼* **Royal Straight**[13] 4543 6-9-7 **63**... TomEaves 12 46
(Linda Perratt) *hld up in tch towards rr: hdwy over 3f out: rdn and unable qck over 2f out: wknd wl over 1f out* **20/1**

0306 **10** *2 ½* **Invent**[5] 4829 3-8-0 **51**..(p) AndreaAtzeni 13 29
(Robert Eddery) *chsd ldrs tl rdn and wknd over 2f out: wl btn over 1f out* **40/1**

2060 **11** *10* **Burning Stone (USA)**[20] 4310 4-9-7 **66**...................... HarryBentley(3) 2 24
(Gay Kelleway) *hld up in tch: drvn and no rspnse over 2f out: sn wknd* **8/1**

5224 **12** *8* **Wily Fox**[77] 2473 4-9-13 **69**.. LukeMorris 11 11
(James Eustace) *t.k.h: chsd ldr tl over 3f out: sn wknd: wl bhd over and eased ins fnl f: t.o* **7/1**[3]

50-6 **13** *13* **Baoli**[8] 4713 4-9-8 **64**... JamesDoyle 5 —
(Tim McCarthy) *led tl wl over 2f out: sn dropped out: t.o and eased ins fnl f* **40/1**

2m 8.29s (2.79) **Going Correction** +0.15s/f (Good)
WFA 3 from 4yo+ 9lb **13** Ran SP% **122.5**
Speed ratings (Par 103): **94,93,91,91,90 87,84,83,82,80 72,66,55**
toteswingers:1&2:£33.50, 2&3:£23.50, 1&3:£24.00 CSF £285.78 CT £5001.68 TOTE £20.50: £3.90, £4.20, £6.60; EX 711.60.
Owner The Comic Strip Heroes **Bred** Cheveley Park Stud Ltd **Trained** Newmarket, Suffolk
■ Stewards' Enquiry : Laura Pike caution: careless riding.

FOCUS
A modest handicap which was well run, and the first two came from the rear. The form is rated around the next two.
Rajnagan(IRE) Official explanation: jockey said saddle slipped
Wily Fox Official explanation: jockey said gelding had no to give

5016 KELLY SHEA FILLIES' H'CAP 7f
8:10 (8:12) (Class 3) (0-95,90) 3-Y-0+ **£7,439** (£2,213; £1,106; £553) **Stalls** High

Form RPR

510/ **1** **Theladyinquestion**[686] 6241 4-8-11 **75**........................... WilliamBuick 5 86+
(Andrew Balding) *hld up in tch in last: swtchd rt and effrt ent fnl f: rdn and qcknd to ld fnl 75yds: r.o wl* **10/1**

2-30 **2** *1* **Wake Up Call**[20] 4332 5-9-12 **90**................................ GeorgeBaker 2 98
(Chris Wall) *t.k.h: hld up in tch in last trio: rdn and effrt jst over 1f out: edgd lft u.p and chal ins f: styd on same pce fnl 75yds* **4/1**[2]

5-40 **3** *1* **Tuscania**[15] 4472 3-9-6 **90**.. TomQueally 7 96+
(Sir Michael Stoute) *lw: hld up in tch in last trio: nt clr run and swtchd rt over 1f out: n.m.r and pushed lft ins fnl f: swtchd rt and r.o cl home: unable to chal* **4/1**[2]

5112 **4** *hd* **Chokurei (IRE)**[35] 3819 3-8-12 **82**...................................... LukeMorris 8 85
(Clive Cox) *led at stdy gallop: rdn and qcknd over 1f out: drvn ins fnl f: hdd and outpcd fnl 75yds* **10/3**[1]

1252 **5** *1 ¾* **Russian Rave**[27] 4101 5-9-5 **83**................................ StephenCraine 6 85+
(Jonathan Portman) *lw: t.k.h: hld up trcking ldrs: nt clr run and hmpd over 1f out: rdn and wnt between horses to chse ldrs 1f out: keeping on same pce and btn whn squeezed for room and [illegible]* [illegible]

[illegible] **6** *3 ¾* **Avon Lady**[14] 4509 4-9-1 **79**.. PatCosgrave 9 69
(James Fanshawe) *lw: chsd ldrs: rdn and effrt over 1f out: drvn and unable qck ins fnl f: wknd qckly ins fnl f* **4/1**[2]

23 **7** *1* **Primo Lady**[22] 4235 3-8-9 **82**...............................(b) HarryBentley(3) 1 67
(Gay Kelleway) *chsd ldrs: rdn and edgd lft u.p over 1f out: wkng whn short of room ins fnl f* **10/1**

-201 **8** *nk* **Our Gal**[24] 4186 3-8-3 **76**.. KieranO'Neill(3) 3 60
(Noel Quinlan) *chsd ldr tl over 1f out: unable qck u.p and losing pl whn hmpd over 1f out: wknd and bhd 1f out* **14/1**

1m 27.32s (1.62) **Going Correction** +0.15s/f (Good)
WFA 3 from 4yo+ 6lb **8** Ran SP% **117.9**
Speed ratings (Par 104): **96,94,93,93,91 87,86,85**
toteswingers:1&2:£9.80, 2&3:£6.10, 1&3:£5.50 CSF £51.32 CT £192.06 TOTE £11.80: £2.70, £1.70, £1.90; EX 54.10.
Owner D H Caslon & Mildmay Racing **Bred** Middle Park Stud Ltd **Trained** Kingsclere, Hants

FOCUS
There was an unsatisfactory feel to this race. Chokurei set just a modest gallop and consequently two or three were keen in behind. More tellingly, the closing stages saw two situations occur that resulted in horses being tightened up. The winner still did it well and the second sets the standard.

NOTEBOOK
Theladyinquestion was reported to have suffered a suspensory injury in a valuable sales race at Ascot as a two-year-old and returned to action here after a 686-day lay-off. That she has been kept in training hinted connections always felt she was a filly of above-average ability as she duly demonstrated, despite looking a little dull in her coat beforehand. She avoided all the trouble by coming with a decisive challenge around the outside and there should be more to come as she is entitled to tighten up physically for the run. (op 12-1)
Wake Up Call put up a fine performance off top weight, carrying 6lb more than the next in the handicap. (tchd 7-2 and 9-2)
Tuscania didn't get the gaps when needed and would probably have finished closer with a smoother passage. (op 9-2)
Chokurei(IRE) can have no excuses, having had the run of the race. (op 4-1 tchd 9-2)
Russian Rave was hampered by Primo Lady over 1f out and was again short of room as Wake Up Call drifted in the same direction late on. That said, her challenge had flattened out and her final position is probably a fair reflection. (tchd 8-1)
Avon Lady was on that far rail in the vicinity of where a shortage of space became an issue, but she didn't appear to be greatly affected by it. (tchd 7-2 and 9-2)
Primo Lady edged left over 1f out, hampering Russian Rave. (op 9-1 tchd 12-1)
T/Jkpt: Not won. T/Plt: £2,032.60 to a £1 stake. Pool £84,507.67 - 30.35 winning tickets. T/Qpdt: £275.90 to a £1 stake. Pool £4,527.30 - 12.14 winning tickets. SP

[4889] NOTTINGHAM (L-H)
Friday, August 12
OFFICIAL GOING: Good to firm (7.1)
Wind: Virtually nil Weather: Cloudy with brighter periods

5017 E B F "SAMRAAN" MAIDEN STKS 6f 15y
2:20 (2:21) (Class 5) 2-Y-O **£3,234** (£962; £481; £240) **Stalls** Centre

Form RPR

2 **1** **Rex Imperator**[32] 3917 2-9-3 0.. GeorgeBaker 3 94+
(Roger Charlton) *trckd ldrs: smooth hdwy 1/2-way: led over 1f out: sn qcknd clr: unchal* **2/5**[1]

03 **2** *7* **Heartsong (IRE)**[16] 4430 2-8-12 0...................................... DaneO'Neill 2 65
(John Gallagher) *cl up: led 1/2-way: rdn 2f out: drvn and hdd over 1f out: kpt on: no ch w wnr* **14/1**[3]

0 **3** *11* **Stepturn**[39] 3686 2-9-3 0.. TomQueally 1 36
(Sir Michael Stoute) *dwlt and awkward s: sn trcking ldrs: effrt and cl up 1/2-way: rdn over 2f out: green and kpt on same pce* **10/3**[2]

55 **4** *¾* **Lowtherwood**[16] 4436 2-9-3 0.. TomEaves 5 34
(Bryan Smart) *cl up: rdn along 1/2-way: drvn over 2f out and one pce* **22/1**

06 **5** *26* **Sonsie Lass**[18] 4377 2-8-12 0... AndrewElliott 4 —
(Mark Johnston) *led: rdn along and hdd 1/2-way: sn wknd* **66/1**

1m 13.65s (-1.25) **Going Correction** -0.325s/f (Firm) **5** Ran SP% **107.0**
Speed ratings (Par 94): **95,85,71,70,35**
toteswingers:1&2:£3.60, 1&3:£2.30, 2&3:£4.50 CSF £6.79 TOTE £1.40: £1.02, £3.10; EX 3.50.
Owner Michael Pescod **Bred** Christopher J Mason **Trained** Beckhampton, Wilts

FOCUS
All races were to be run on the outer course, the rails were at the innermost position and distances were as advertised. The track hadn't seen much rain in recent days - it was just damp and drizzly in the morning - but plenty of water had been added. Conditions were described as good to firm, but runners were kicking the top off. They raced up the middle of the track. The time was 1.02 seconds slower than following older-horse Class 4 handicap. A poor numerical turnout for this maiden, despite the race being £1,100 over the tariff set by The Horsemen's Group.

NOTEBOOK
Rex Imperator, who was the clear form choice after finishing second on his debut at Windsor, had the field extremely well strung out, winning with a lot in hand. It's hard to know exactly what he achieved, but the runner-up had shown ability (RPR in the 60s last time) and he looks decent. He certainly looks the part physically and is probably an out-and-out sprinter. (op 4-9 tchd 1-2)
Heartsong(IRE), who showed improved form when third at Leicester on his second start, didn't progress enough to give the winner a race, but she was a long way clear of the others. Nurseries are now an option. (op 9-1)
Stepturn didn't show much on his debut at Windsor and this was even worse. He'll only become interesting if persevered with by these connections in the relative long term. (op 4-1 tchd 3-1)
Lowtherwood couldn't match the form he showed second-time out and didn't offer much, even with nurseries now an option. (op 16-1 tchd 14-1)
Sonsie Lass's rider reported the filly went too freely to post. Official explanation: jockey said filly went too freely to post (op 33-1)

5018 1STSECURITYSOLUTIONS.CO.UK FILLIES' H'CAP 6f 15y
2:55 (2:55) (Class 4) (0-80,80) 3-Y-0+ **£4,528** (£1,347; £673; £336) **Stalls** Centre

Form RPR

-031 **1** **Lady Paris (IRE)**[9] 4680 3-9-3 **79** 6ex................................... TomEaves 5 95+
(Bryan Smart) *cl up: led over 3f out: rdn and qcknd clr over 1f out: comf* **10/11**[1]

4104 **2** *2 ¾* **Psychic's Dream**[6] 4797 3-9-2 **78**...................................... JimmyQuinn 7 83
(Marco Botti) *wnt rt s: hld up in rr: hdwy 1/2-way: rdn to chse wnr ent fnl f: sn drvn and no imp* **9/2**[2]

2636 **3** *2* **Yurituni**[7] 4742 4-9-5 **77**...(v) TomQueally 4 77
(Eve Johnson Houghton) *trckd ldrs: hdwy to chse wnr 2f out: sn rdn and one pce* **8/1**

1621 **4** *2 ¼* **Anjomarba (IRE)**[8] 4711 4-9-0 **72** 6ex............................... JamesDoyle 2 64
(Conor Dore) *cl up: rdn along wl over 2f out: drvn wl over 1f out and sn one pce* [illegible]

[illegible] **5** [illegible] [illegible] 3-9-8 [illegible].. PatDobbs 3 64
(J R Jenkins) *trckd ldrs: effrt wl over 2f out: sn rdn and btn wl over 1f out* **9/1**

0000 **6** *10* **Breedj (IRE)**[20] 4332 3-9-4 **80**..................................... PhilipRobinson 6 31
(Clive Brittain) *slt ld: rdn along over 3f out: sn hdd & wknd over 2f out* **16/1**

1m 12.63s (-2.27) **Going Correction** -0.325s/f (Firm)
WFA 3 from 4yo+ 4lb **6** Ran SP% **110.1**
Speed ratings (Par 102): **102,98,95,92,89 75**
toteswingers:1&2:£1.10, 1&3:£3.70, 2&3:£6.80 CSF £5.01 TOTE £1.70: £1.20, £2.00; EX 5.20.
Owner R C Bond **Bred** D Cantillon **Trained** Hambleton, N Yorks

FOCUS
Again the action unfolded up the middle. Another disappointing turnout numerically for a race that met the tariff, and the form is ordinary behind the rapidly improving winner. The form is rated around the first two.

5019 1ST SECURITY SOLUTIONS H'CAP 5f 13y
3:30 (3:30) (Class 6) (0-55,61) 3-Y-0+ **£1,940** (£577; £288; £144) **Stalls** Centre

Form RPR

4004 **1** **Crimson Queen**[22] 4230 4-9-0 **51**...................................... JamesDoyle 1 63
(Roy Brotherton) *cl up: led after 2f: rdn and qcknd clr wl over 1f out: styd on* **5/1**

6014 **2** *2 ½* **Duke Of Rainford**[10] 4650 4-9-0 **51**.. PatDobbs 8 54
(Michael Herrington) *wnt rt s: sn trcking ldrs: hdwy to chse wnr appr fnl f: sn rdn and no imp* **8/1**

0064 **3** *¾* **Tyrannosaurus Rex (IRE)**[74] 2546 7-8-2 **46** oh1... GeorgeChaloner(7) 2 46
(David O'Meara) *sn led: pushed along and hdd after 2f: sn rdn and chsd wnr tl drvn and one pce ent fnl f* **3/1**[2]

0-02 **4** *shd* **Deslaya (IRE)**[9] 4657 3-8-12 **52**................................... JackMitchell 4 51
(Chris Wall) *prom: effrt over 2f out: sn rdn and kpt on same pce appr fnl f* **11/4**[1]

6201 **5** *13* **My Love Fajer (IRE)**[2] 4924 3-9-3 **57** 6ex.......................... TomQueally 7 9
(Alan McCabe) *t.k.h: trckd ldrs: shkn up 1/2-way: sn rdn and outpcd* **9/2**[3]

0051 **6** *¾* **No Mean Trick (USA)**[10] 4650 5-9-10 **61** 6ex.................. MickyFenton 5 11
(Paul Midgley) *cl up: rdn along 1/2-way: sn wknd* **13/2**

60.54 secs (-0.46) **Going Correction** -0.325s/f (Firm)
WFA 3 from 4yo+ 3lb **6** Ran SP% **111.0**
Speed ratings (Par 101): **90,86,84,84,63 62**
toteswingers:1&2:£39.00, 1&3:£9.80, 2&3:£10.20 CSF £40.82 CT £133.75 TOTE £8.30: £4.20, £3.40; EX 43.60.
Owner Arthur Clayton **Bred** Cheveley Park Stud Ltd **Trained** Elmley Castle, Worcs

FOCUS
A moderate handicap in which few were ever involved. The winner is rated to her AW best with the second to his mark.

5020 MITIE FILLIES' H'CAP — 1m 2f 50y
4:05 (4:05) (Class 4) (0-85,85) 3-Y-O — £4,528 (£1,347; £673; £336) Stalls Low

Form — RPR

4234 1 **El Torbellino (IRE)**[27] 4103 3-8-12 **76**.......... DanielTudhope 4 91
(David O'Meara) *mde all: rdn over 2f out: drvn and clr ent fnl f: styd on strly* 7/1

011 2 5 **Street Secret (USA)**[43] 3538 3-9-3 **81**.......... JackMitchell 1 86
(Roger Varian) *trckd ldrs on inner: hdwy 3f out: swtchd rt over 2f out and sn chsng wnr: rdn wl over 1f out: drvn ins fnl f and no imp* 5/1[2]

2310 3 1 3/4 **Miss Aix**[16] 4429 3-9-3 **81**.......... PatDobbs 6 83
(Michael Bell) *trckd ldrs: effrt over 3f out: rdn over 2f out: drvn and kpt on same pce appr fnl f* 13/2[3]

21 4 hd **Neumark (GER)**[22] 4241 3-9-3 **81**.......... TomQueally 7 82
(Sir Henry Cecil) *t.k.h: chsd ldng pair: effrt over 3f out: rdn and hung lft over 2f out: sn btn* 9/4[1]

2125 5 1 **Baqaat (USA)**[20] 4344 3-8-13 **77**.......... DaneO'Neill 9 76
(Ed Dunlop) *hld up: hdwy 3f out: rdn over 2f out: kpt on fnl f: nrst fin* 17/2

1-45 6 hd **Umseyat (USA)**[20] 4335 3-9-4 **82**..........(p) SaleemGolam 10 81
(John Gosden) *dwlt and in rr: hdwy on outer 3f out: rdn 2f out: kpt on fnl f* 13/2[3]

45 7 1 1/4 **Regal Kiss**[42] 3572 3-8-9 **73**.......... AndrewElliott 3 69
(Mark Johnston) *in tch: effrt over 3f out: sn rdn along and wknd* 20/1

-405 8 6 **Beyeh (IRE)**[8] 4727 3-8-7 **71**.......... IvaMilickova 14 55
(Clive Brittain) *a in rr* 40/1

41 9 3/4 **Sleek Gold**[41] 3615 3-8-7 **71**.......... EddieCreighton 2 54
(Brian Meehan) *trckd wnr: pushed along 4f out: rdn 3f out and sn wknd* 9/1

2m 11.1s (-0.60) **Going Correction** -0.075s/f (Good) **9** Ran SP% **114.3**
Speed ratings (Par 99): **99,95,93,93,92 92,91,86,86**
toteswingers:1&2:£7.90, 1&3:£10.60, 2&3:£4.30 CSF £41.42 CT £238.64 TOTE £11.00: £3.70, £2.60, £2.20; EX 55.20.
Owner Crowther, Fell & Everitt **Bred** Tally-Ho Stud **Trained** Nawton, N Yorks

FOCUS
A good fillies' handicap despite the non-runners, but the winner was allowed an uncontested lead. The race is rated at something like face value, with the third to her best maiden form.

5021 FAMILY FUN DAY 17TH AUGUST MAIDEN STKS — 1m 75y
4:40 (4:40) (Class 5) 3-Y-O — £2,522 (£750; £375; £187) Stalls Centre

Form — RPR

23 1 **Garud (IRE)**[22] 4254 3-9-3 0.......... TomQueally 4 86
(Marco Botti) *mde all: rdn and qcknd 2f out: clr appr fnl f and kpt on wl* 3/1[2]

54 2 2 **Eclipseoftheheart**[22] 4254 3-8-12 0.......... JackMitchell 2 76
(James Fanshawe) *trckd ldrs on inner: hdwy 3f out: swtchd rt and rdn to chse wnr 2f out: drvn appr fnl f: no imp* 10/1

6- 3 2 1/2 **Looking On**[287] 7202 3-9-3 0.......... DaneO'Neill 8 75
(Henry Candy) *trckd wnr: pushed along 4f out: rdn 3f out: drvn 2f out and kpt on same pce* 6/1[3]

3220 4 nk **Maali (IRE)**[57] 3068 3-9-3 95.......... PhilipRobinson 10 74
(Clive Brittain) *trckd ldrs on outer: hdwy and cl up over 3f out: rdn wl over 2f out: sn drvn and btn* 1/2[1]

06 5 17 **Marina Ballerina**[13] 4559 3-8-12 0.......... JimmyQuinn 9 30
(Roy Bowring) *a towards rr* 66/1

504 6 3/4 **Sally Anne**[28] 4071 3-8-12 0.......... AndrewElliott 5 28
(John Harris) *dwlt and a in rr* 100/1

7 17 **Peace Seeker** 3-9-3 0.......... WilliamCarson 1 —
(Giles Bravery) *v.s.a: a bhd* 25/1

0-0 P **Musical Leap**[10] 4647 3-8-10 0.......... GeorgeChaloner(7) 6 —
(Shaun Harris) *chsd ldrs: sddle slipped after 2f: in rr and p.u 5f out* 100/1

1m 45.65s (0.05) **Going Correction** -0.075s/f (Good) **8** Ran SP% **122.4**
Speed ratings (Par 100): **96,94,91,91,74 73,56,—**
toteswingers:1&2:£3.10, 1&3:£2.10, 2&3:£4.00 CSF £32.91 TOTE £3.20: £1.20, £2.80, £2.40; EX 24.80.
Owner A Rosati-Colarieti **Bred** Azienda Agricola Rosati Colarieti **Trained** Newmarket, Suffolk

FOCUS
Just a fair maiden and, like in the previous race, the meeting's first event on the round course, the winner made all. The first two are rated close to their Sandown form.
Marina Ballerina Official explanation: jockey said filly was difficult to steer around bend

5022 MITIE H'CAP — 1m 6f 15y
5:15 (5:17) (Class 6) (0-60,60) 3-Y-O — £1,940 (£577; £288; £144) Stalls Low

Form — RPR

000 1 **Sharp Relief (IRE)**[23] 4208 3-9-6 **59**.......... TomQueally 2 70+
(Hughie Morrison) *trckd ldrs: pushed along and sltly outpcd 4f out: hdwy on inner to ld 2f out: sn rdn clr: kpt on wl* 5/1[3]

-250 2 1 1/4 **Sea The Flames (IRE)**[14] 4491 3-9-0 **53**.......... DaneO'Neill 3 60
(Marcus Tregoning) *hld up and bhd: hdwy on wd outside over 3f out: rdn 2f out: str run fr over 1f out: nt rch wnr* 7/1

0004 3 1 1/4 **Mountain Myst**[32] 3922 3-8-5 **49**.......... JamesRogers(5) 8 54
(William Muir) *led: hdd over 6f out: styd prom: effrt 3f out: ev ch whn rdn and hung rt 2f out: sn drvn and kpt on same pce* 10/1

-604 4 2 1/4 **Xenophon**[14] 3175 3-8-1 **47** oh1 ow1..........(tp) BrendanPowell(7) 7 49
(Brendan Powell) *prom: led over 6f out: rdn along over 3f out: drvn and hdd 2f out: grad wknd fr over 1f out* 6/1

000 5 1 3/4 **Dhampas**[39] 3690 3-8-7 **46** oh1..........(b[1]) SamHitchcott 10 46
(Jim Boyle) *in rr: hdwy over 3f out: swtchd lft and rdn over 2f out: drvn and kpt on appr fnl f: nrst fin* 25/1

00-5 6 7 **Romantic Girl (IRE)**[42] 3596 3-8-7 **46** oh1.......... AndrewElliott 11 36
(Alan Juckes) *hld up and bhd: sme late hdwy* 28/1

0321 7 3/4 **Hal Of A Lover**[24] 4175 3-9-7 **60**.......... DanielTudhope 6 49
(David O'Meara) *trckd ldrs: hdwy 4f out: rdn along 3f out: sn drvn over 2f out and sn wknd* 9/2[2]

2 8 9 **Kie (IRE)**[15] 4476 3-8-10 **49**..........(t) JimmyQuinn 4 25
(Frank Sheridan) *in tch: effrt on outer 4f out: rdn along over 3f out: drvn over 2f out and sn wknd* 3/1[1]

-030 9 18 **Tommy Tiger**[51] 3268 3-8-13 **52**.......... WilliamCarson 5 —
(Stuart Williams) *trckd ldrs: cl up 1/2-way: chal 4f out: rdn along over 3f out: sn drvn and wknd* 8/1

3m 9.44s (2.14) **Going Correction** -0.075s/f (Good) **9** Ran SP% **114.1**
Speed ratings (Par 98): **90,89,88,87,86 82,81,76,66**
toteswingers:1&2:£4.30, 1&3:£9.20, 2&3:£8.10 CSF £39.26 CT £335.24 TOTE £5.40: £1.40, £3.30, £3.20; EX 35.40.
Owner The Hon W H Smith & Partners **Bred** Declan Gardiner **Trained** East Ilsley, Berks

FOCUS
A moderate staying handicap rated slightly positively around the third and fourth.
Sharp Relief(IRE) Official explanation: trainer's rep said, regarding apparent improvement in form, that the filly was better suited by the step up in trip and drop in class.
T/Plt: £490.10 a £1 stake. Pool:£43,978.43 - 65.50 winning tickets T/Qpdt: £104.30 a £1 stake. Pool:£ 2,622.72 - 18.60 winning tickets JR

5023 - 5026a (Foreign Racing) - See Raceform Interactive

4896 DEAUVILLE (R-H)
Friday, August 12

OFFICIAL GOING: Turf: good; fibresand: standard

5027a PRIX MINERVE (GROUP 3) (3YO FILLIES) (TURF) — 1m 4f 110y
2:20 (12:00) 3-Y-O — £34,482 (£13,793; £10,344; £6,896; £3,448)

RPR

1 **Shareta (IRE)**[29] 4036 3-8-9 0.......... Christophe-PatriceLemaire 7 109+
(A De Royer-Dupre, France) *dwlt and shkn up to r promly: wnt on after 1 1/2f: mde rest: pressed fr 2 1/2f out: shkn up and qcknd clr appr 1 1/2f out: 4 l clr whn eased ins fnl 50yds: easily* 6/4[1]

2 3 **Pacifique (IRE)**[26] 4139 3-8-9 0.......... GeraldMosse 5 104
(A De Royer-Dupre, France) *slowly away and sltly stmbld leaving stalls: hld up in rr: shkn up appr 2f out: rdn and prog 1 1/2f out: styd on u.p fnl f to grab 2nd cl home: no ch w wnr* 3/1[2]

3 hd **Polygon (USA)**[12] 4582 3-8-9 0.......... ThierryJarnet 3 104
(John Gosden) *a.p: cl up 4th on outside much of the way: wnt 3rd on outside of three 3f out: hrd rdn ins fnl 2 1/2f and outpcd 2f out: styd on again fnl f: tk 3rd cl home* 13/1

4 nse **Sanrivale (FR)**[26] 4139 3-8-9 0.......... IoritzMendizabal 9 104
(D Rabhi, France) *reluctant ldr and plld hrd: hdd after 1 1/2f and settled in 3rd on rail: 4th and travelling wl enough 2 1/2f out: kpt on u.p to go 2nd ins fnl f: lost two pls cl home* 32/1

5 3/4 **Semester**[26] 4139 3-8-9 0.......... Pierre-CharlesBoudot 2 102
(A Fabre, France) *w ldrs racing keenly: sn settled in midfield: 7th on rail 2 1/2f out: swtchd outside and rdn 2f out: sme hdwy but nt pce to chal ldrs* 31/1

6 1 1/2 **La Pomme D'Amour**[29] 4036 3-8-9 0.......... MaximeGuyon 1 100
(A Fabre, France) *w.w in rr: rdn and sme hdwy on outside 2 1/2f out: no imp down middle of trck fr 1 1/2f out* 8/1

7 1 **Mourasana**[29] 4036 3-8-9 0.......... JohanVictoire 8 98
(C Lerner, France) *sn trcking Shareta (whn latter wnt on after 1 1/2f): pressed ldr fr 2 1/2f out: 2nd and ev ch 2f out: sn rdn: wknd u.p fnl f* 16/1

8 6 **Campanillas (IRE)**[47] 3447 3-8-9 0.......... OlivierPeslier 6 89
(C Laffon-Parias, France) *prom under heavy restraint as failed to settle: so keen jinked rt and hmpd Venise Jelois after 1f: continued to r keenly on outside towards rr: prog to be cl 5th on ins fnl 2 1/2f: sn rdn and wknd fnl 1 1/2f* 19/5[3]

9 3/4 **Venise Jelois (FR)**[97] 1922 3-8-9 0.......... SebastienMaillot 4 88
(Robert Collet, France) *midfield: hmpd by Campanillas and stmbld after 1f: racd in 5th: rdn and nt qckn 2 1/2f out: wknd fnl 1 1/2f* 52/1

2m 41.73s (-4.67) **9** Ran SP% **118.0**
WIN (incl. 1 euro stake): 2.50. PLACES: 1.30, 1.50, 2.80. DF: 4.70. SF: 7.50.
Owner H H Aga Khan **Bred** His Highness The Aga Khan's Studs S C **Trained** Chantilly, France

NOTEBOOK
Shareta(IRE) was rushed into a prominent position from her wide draw by Lemaire, who was keen not to get trapped wide around four turns. He managed to slow the pace from in front, and when he asked the daughter of Sinndar for her effort at the two furlong pole, she picked up and quickly put daylight between herself and her pursuers. She'll head for the Prix Vermeille next.
Pacifique(IRE), the winner's stablemate, came out of the pursuing pack to snatch second.
Polygon(USA), upped in grade and having only her fourth start, stayed on well having tracked the leader for most of the way. She should get further.

5028a PRIX DE LIEUREY (GROUP 3) (3YO FILLIES) (TURF) — 1m (R)
3:25 (12:00) 3-Y-O — £34,482 (£13,793; £10,344; £6,896; £3,448)

RPR

1 **Sandy's Charm (FR)**[66] 2796 3-8-11 0.......... Francois-XavierBertras 12 113+
(F Rohaut, France) *broke wl and sn led and swtchd to ins to r on rail after 2f: mde rest: shkn up appr 1 1/2f out: qcknd 3 l clr ent fnl f: r.o strly under hands and heels: eased cl home* 7/2[1]

2 5 **Mixed Intention (IRE)**[33] 3898 3-9-2 0.......... Christophe-PatriceLemaire 8 106
(F Vermeulen, France) *settled towards rr: 10th and three off rail 2 1/2f out (abt 7 l off ldr): sn pushed along: hdwy on outside over 1 1/2f out: styd on u.p fnl f: tk 2nd 75yds out: no ch w wnr* 63/10

3 1/2 **Rhythm Of Light**[14] 4497 3-8-11 0.......... RichardKingscote 2 100
(Tom Dascombe) *hld up on rail: 7th and travelling wl 1/2-way: effrt on rail over 2f out: swtchd outside but nowhere to go 1 1/2f out: disputing 5th and gng wl whn clipped heels of horse in front and stmbld appr fnl f: fin wl* 15/1

4 snk **Warm Hands**[33] 3898 3-8-11 0.......... MaximeGuyon 7 100
(A Fabre, France) *hld up: last 2 1/2f out: sn pushed along: sme hdwy on outside 1 1/2f out: styd on wl fnl 110yds: tk 4th cl home: nvr nrr* 12/1

5 nk **Miss Liberty (FR)**[17] 4422 3-8-11 0.......... GregoryBenoist 13 99
(Mme Pia Brandt, France) *racd keenly and sn trcking ldr: rdn over 1 1/2f out: lost 2nd 1f out: kpt on wout qckning: lost two pls cl home* 53/10[3]

6 nse **Espirita (FR)**[33] 3898 3-8-11 0.......... ChristopheSoumillon 9 99
(E Lellouche, France) *settled on heels of ldrs: 4th over 3f out: 3rd and shkn up 2f out: wnt 2nd ent fnl f: fdd u.p fnl 100yds* 5/1[2]

7 3/4 **Procrastination**[34] 3-8-11 0.......... Pierre-CharlesBoudot 4 97
(A Fabre, France) *chsd ldng gp racing keenly: settled in share of 5th: rdn and no imp fnl 1 1/f* 11/1

8 snk **Salona (GER)**[54] 3209 3-8-11 0.......... JohanVictoire 3 97
(J-P Carvalho, Germany) *w.w towards rr: 9th towards ins 3f out: hrd rdn 2f out: no imp* 35/1

9 nse **Realisatrice (FR)**[3] 4896 3-8-11 0.......... IoritzMendizabal 1 97
(Robert Collet, France) *trckd ldr on rail: a.p: 4th and shkn up to hold pl 2f out: stl 4th but hrd rdn appr fnl 110yds: no ex* 12/1

10 1/2 **Nova Step**[33] 3898 3-8-11 0.......... StephanePasquier 11 95
(F Rohaut, France) *midfield: settled on outside: tk clsr order on outside fr 2 1/2f out: 4th and rdn over 2f out: wknd ins fnl f* 17/1

0 **Futurista (USA)**[26] 4139 3-8-11 0.......... OlivierPeslier 5 —
(F Head, France) *a bhd: nvr in contention* 10/1

0 **Sunday Nectar (IRE)**[50] 3335 3-8-11 0..... Roberto-CarlosMontenegro 6 —
(X Thomas-Demeaulte, France) *racd in midfield: 8th ins fnl 3f: rdn and wknd fnl 1 1/2f* **40/1**

1m 41.47s (0.67) **12** Ran SP% **118.3**
WIN (incl. 1 euro stake): 4.50. PLACES: 1.90, 2.20, 4.70. DF: 14.90. SF: 20.60.
Owner Mme Magalen Bryant **Bred** J P H Dubois **Trained** Sauvagnon, France

NOTEBOOK
Sandy's Charm(FR) drew right away from her field having led from the gate. Clearly improving, she'll stay at this trip and may go for a race in the US.
Mixed Intention(IRE) stayed on for second but was well held by the all-the-way winner.
Rhythm Of Light looked unlucky, finishing, full of running in third after being denied a run at least twice in the straight. Her target is the Group 2 Topkapi Trophy in Istanbul on September 4.

4525 DONCASTER (L-H)
Saturday, August 13

OFFICIAL GOING: Good (good to firm in places on round course; 7,3)
Wind: Virtually nil Weather: Cloudy

5029 EBF ROBINSONSOFBAWTRY.COM DESIGNER CLOTHES BOUTIQUE MAIDEN FILLIES' STKS 1m (S)
2:05 (2:07) (Class 5) 2-Y-O **£3,234** (£962; £481; £240) **Stalls** High

Form RPR
2 **1** **Rythmic**[14] 4552 2-9-0 0..... AhmedAjtebi 1 80+
(Mahmood Al Zarooni) *hld up towards rr: smooth hdwy on outer over 2f out: cl up 2f out: rdn to ld over 1f out: sn qcknd clr* **4/1**[2]
63 **2** *3 ¾* **Perfect Delight**[16] 4471 2-8-11 0..... JohnFahy(3) 12 69
(Clive Cox) *cl up: led 3f out: rdn 2f out: drvn and hdd over 1f out: one pce ins fnl f* **6/1**[3]
6540 **3** *1 ½* **Glad Eye Gladys**[16] 4471 2-8-9 65..... NeilFarley(5) 10 66
(David Nicholls) *chsd ldrs: hdwy 3f out: cl up over 2f out: sn rdn and ev ch tl one pce appr fnl f* **20/1**
0 **4** *hd* **Maliha (IRE)**[55] 3201 2-9-0 0..... BarryMcHugh 13 66+
(Kevin Ryan) *in tch: pushed along and sltly outpcd over 3f out: hdwy over 2f out: sn rdn and kpt on ins fnl f* **100/1**
4 **5** *½* **Scarlet Whispers**[30] 4002 2-9-0 0..... MickyFenton 3 66+
(Pam Sly) *towards rr: hdwy wl over 2f out: rdn wl over 1f out: styd on ins fnl f: nrst fin* **11/1**
0 **6** *½* **Zaahya (IRE)**[44] 3547 2-9-0 0..... TadhgO'Shea 8 63
(John Dunlop) *midfield: hdwy to trck ldrs 3f out: effrt over 2f out: sn rdn and edgd lft wl over 1f out: sn btn* **10/3**[1]
22 **7** *hd* **Arley Hall**[13] 4571 2-9-0 0..... TonyHamilton 2 63
(Richard Fahey) *trckd ldrs: hdwy and cl up 1/2-way: rdn along over 2f out: sn one pce* **6/1**[3]
0 **8** *1 ¾* **Chocolat Chaud (IRE)**[17] 4446 2-9-0 0..... StevieDonohoe 6 59
(J W Hills) *in rr tl sme late hdwy* **66/1**
9 *½* **Astronomy Domine** 2-9-0 0..... NickyMackay 4 58
(John Gosden) *dwlt and towards rr: stdy hdwy on outer to chse ldrs over 3f out: sn rdn and wknd over 2f out* **15/2**
10 *8* **Absolute Fun (IRE)** 2-9-0 0..... DuranFentiman 11 39
(Tim Easterby) *dwlt: a towards rr* **50/1**
11 *¾* **Finity Run (GER)** 2-9-0 0..... RoystonFfrench 9 37
(Mark Johnston) *led: pushed along 1/2-way: hdd 3f out and sn wknd* **33/1**
0 **12** *20* **Phoenician Blaze**[22] 4285 2-9-0 0..... GregFairley 7 —
(Tim Etherington) *prom: cl up 1/2-way: rdn along over 3f out: sn wknd and bhd* **200/1**

1m 41.69s (2.39) **Going Correction** +0.10s/f (Good) **12** Ran SP% **104.4**
Speed ratings (Par 91): **92,88,86,86,86 85,85,83,83,75 74,54**
toteswingers:1&2:£3.10, 2&3:£14.50, 1&3:£19.00 CSF £21.21 TOTE £4.40: £1.80, £2.00, £4.80; EX 20.10.
Owner Godolphin **Bred** Darley **Trained** Newmarket, Suffolk
■ Ajaweed (17/2) was withdrawn on vet's advice. Deduct 10p in the £ under R4.

FOCUS
Inside rail on round course dolled out 6yds adding 37yds to 1m2f race and 72yds to 1m6f race. An interesting maiden fillies' event to start the card, with a couple of these holding some fancy entries, but the early pace was by no means strong and they didn't quicken until around 3f from home. The proximity of the 65-rated third may hold the form down a bit. This race was won by the dual Classic-winner Blue Bunting last year and the same owner/trainer/jockey combination collected this time. The winner was value for extra and the third and sixth help with the form, which could rate higher.

NOTEBOOK
Rythmic, a very promising runner-up on her Newmarket debut, she had obviously learned from that and quickened away nicely after leading over 1f from home. She should be up to winning something better. (op 7-2)
Perfect Delight had already shown ability in a couple of fair maidens and this was another step forward, as she was always on the pace and kept on to fare much the best of the rest. She could be interesting in a nursery.
Glad Eye Gladys, rated 65 having shown some ability in four maidens, appeared to run above herself and it may be that she was just a bit more streetwise than a few of those behind her. Even so, she could also be interesting in a nursery off this mark. (tchd 18-1)
Maliha(IRE), beaten a long way on her Pontefract debut, ran a lot better here, especially as she was off the bridle a long way out. She may well improve again.
Scarlet Whispers, around 3l behind Arley Hall on her debut here last month, turned that form around and looks the type for nurseries after one more run (op 10-1 tchd 12-1)
Zaahya(IRE), green when seventh on her Newbury debut over 6f, is bred to be much better suited by this longer trip but finished weakly, having looked a threat coming to the last 2f. Perhaps she needs a bit more time. (op 7-2 tchd 3-1)
Arley Hall had every chance but didn't seem to see out the longer trip. (op 15-2)
Astronomy Domine made a brief effort 3f from home having been held up last early, but was soon on the retreat again. This 280,000euros half-sister to three smart winners over middle distances, two of them at Listed level, is surely better than this. (op 8-1 tchd 17-2)

5030 CROWNHOTEL-BAWTRY.COM MAIDEN STKS 6f
2:40 (2:43) (Class 5) 3-4-Y-O **£2,911** (£866; £432; £216) **Stalls** High

Form RPR
6 **1** **Ganas (IRE)**[10] 4663 3-9-0 0..... JohnFahy(3) 7 86
(Clive Cox) *trckd ldrs: hdwy over 2f out: rdn to ld wl over 1f out: edgd rt ent fnl f: sn clr: kpt on strly* **7/2**[2]
430P **2** *6* **Chokidar (IRE)**[5] 4854 3-8-12 73..... (p) NeilFarley(5) 4 67
(David Nicholls) *cl up: led over 3f out: rdn 2f out: drvn and hdd appr fnl f: one pce* **7/2**[2]
3 **3** *2 ½* **Fabulouslyspirited**[21] 4340 3-8-12 0..... StevieDonohoe 2 54
(Ralph Beckett) *trckd ldrs: effrt wl over 2f out: sn rdn and outpcd: kpt on u.p ins fnl f* **13/8**[1]
4 *1* **Libys Dream (IRE)** 3-8-12 0..... MickyFenton 1 51
(Michael Mullineaux) *prom: effrt wl over 2f out: sn rdn and ev ch tl drvn wl over 1f out and grad wknd* **20/1**
03 **5** *2* **So Wise (USA)**[14] 4542 3-9-3 0..... PBBeggy 3 49
(Keith Dalgleish) *dwlt and sn rdn along in rr: hdwy 4f out: in tch 1/2-way: rdn over 2f out and sn no imp* **10/1**
3 **6** *14* **Lady By Red (IRE)**[14] 4559 3-8-12 0..... TonyHamilton 6 —
(Michael Dods) *led: hdd over 3f out: cl up tl rdn wl over 2f out and sn wknd* **8/1**[3]
7 *1 ¾* **Diamond Fay (IRE)** 3-8-12 0..... RobbieFitzpatrick 10 —
(Richard Guest) *s.i.s: sn outpcd and a bhd* **40/1**
00 **8** *3 ½* **Donnywardsbird**[42] 3616 3-9-3 0..... AndrewMullen 8 —
(Eric Alston) *towards rr: rdn along 1/2-way: sn edgd lft and wknd* **100/1**
9 *shd* **Queen's Princess** 3-8-9 0..... DeclanCannon(3) 9 —
(John Wainwright) *s.i.s: green and a outpcd in rr* **66/1**

1m 13.64s (0.04) **Going Correction** +0.10s/f (Good) **9** Ran SP% **112.4**
Speed ratings (Par 103): **103,95,91,90,87 69,66,62,61**
toteswingers:1&2:£3.30, 2&3:£1.30, 1&3:£2.20 CSF £15.29 TOTE £4.50: £1.40, £1.50, £1.20; EX 14.90.
Owner H E Sheikh Sultan Bin Khalifa Al Nahyan **Bred** Sheikh Sultan Bin Khalifa Al Nayhan **Trained** Lambourn, Berks

FOCUS
This wasn't a great maiden apart from the winner, with the favourite disappointing. The form's rated around the first two.

5031 PC EXCAVATIONS LTD H'CAP (DIV I) 7f
3:10 (3:12) (Class 5) (0-70,69) 3-Y-0+ **£2,587** (£770; £384; £192) **Stalls** High

Form RPR
-012 **1** **Ted's Brother (IRE)**[42] 3621 3-9-1 **64**..... TadhgO'Shea 11 74+
(Richard Guest) *stdd s and hld up in rr: sn swtchd lft and smooth hdwy on outer 3f out: led 1 1/2f out: rdn and edgd rt ent fnl f: sn drvn and jst hld on* **11/4**[1]
53 **2** *shd* **Northern Flyer (GER)**[10] 4670 5-8-5 **56**..... (p) ShaneBKelly(5) 4 68
(John Quinn) *trckd ldrs: hdwy to chal 2f out: sn rdn and ev ch ins fnl f: kpt on wl towards fin: hld* **5/1**[2]
6025 **3** *2* **Watch Chain (IRE)**[6] 4820 4-9-4 **64**..... (p) JohnFahy(3) 1 71
(Alan McCabe) *dwlt and hld up in rr: stdy hdwy 4f out: cl up 3f out: effrt and ev ch 2f out: sn rdn and n.m.r ent fnl f: one pce* **8/1**
0516 **4** *4 ½* **Muftarres (IRE)**[12] 4604 6-9-12 **69**..... (p) MickyFenton 9 63
(Paul Midgley) *towards rr: hdwy over 2f out: rdn wl over 1f out: styd on ins fnl f: nrst fin* **6/1**[3]
0500 **5** *¾* **El Dececy (USA)**[7] 4793 7-9-0 **57**..... RobbieFitzpatrick 2 49
(Richard Guest) *led: pushed along 1/2-way: hdd 3f out: drvn over 2f out and grad wknd* **14/1**
6004 **6** *shd* **Ryedane (IRE)**[15] 4518 9-9-0 **62**..... (b) AdamCarter(5) 3 54
(Tim Easterby) *sn cl up: slt ld 3f out: rdn over 2f out: sn hdd & wknd over 1f out* **16/1**
0436 **7** *6* **Ishetoo**[15] 4517 7-9-11 **68**..... FrannyNorton 8 44
(Ollie Pears) *trckd ldrs: pushed along 3f out: rdn wl over 2f out: sn btn* **7/1**
065 **8** *7* **Kool Shuffle (GER)**[40] 3684 3-8-7 **56**..... AndrewMullen 5 11
(Tom Tate) *prom: rdn along over 3f out: sn wknd* **11/1**
2053 **9** *1 ¼* **Sairaam (IRE)**[10] 4681 5-9-10 **67**..... KirstyMilczarek 12 21
(Charles Smith) *racd alone towards stands' rail: in tch: rdn along 3f out: sn wknd* **9/1**
2005 **10** *23* **Dream Dream Dream (IRE)**[14] 4559 4-8-7 **50** oh2(p) AndrewHeffernan 6 —
(Kevin M Prendergast) *a in rr: outpcd and bhd fr wl over 2f out* **28/1**

1m 26.35s (0.05) **Going Correction** +0.10s/f (Good)
WFA 3 from 4yo+ 6lb **10** Ran SP% **115.6**
Speed ratings (Par 103): **103,102,100,95,94 94,87,79,78,51**
toteswingers:1&2:£2.40, 2&3:£14.40, 1&3:£6.00 CSF £15.82 CT £99.18 TOTE £3.10: £1.50, £2.30, £3.30; EX 9.30.
Owner Maze Rattan Limited **Bred** T Counihan **Trained** Stainforth, S Yorks

FOCUS
A modest handicap, with recent winning form thin on the ground, but the time was good compared to division II and the form is rated on the positive side. Most of the field came down the centre.

5032 ONE CALL INSURANCE H'CAP 7f
3:45 (3:58) (Class 2) (0-105,105) 4-Y-0+ **£12,938** (£3,850; £1,924; £962) **Stalls** High

Form RPR
1251 **1** **Grissom (IRE)**[20] 4369 5-8-4 **88**..... DuranFentiman 11 97
(Tim Easterby) *in tch: hdwy to chse ldrs over 2f out: swtchd lft and rdn over 1f out: styd on to ld ins fnl f: drvn out* **12/1**[3]
0000 **2** *¾* **Irish Heartbeat (IRE)**[21] 4346 6-8-4 **88**..... (p) BarryMcHugh 14 95+
(Richard Fahey) *in tch: hdwy to trck ldrs over 2f out: effrt over 1f out: n.m.r ent fnl f: sn rdn and styd on* **8/1**[2]
4560 **3** *½* **Docofthebay (IRE)**[14] 4534 7-8-11 **95**..... (p) StevieDonohoe 20 100
(David Nicholls) *towards rr: hdwy on outer over 2f out: rdn wl over 1f out: styd on strly ins fnl f: nrst fin* **6/1**[1]
0053 **4** *shd* **Colonial (IRE)**[14] 4554 4-9-7 **105**..... FrannyNorton 8 110
(Saeed Bin Suroor) *trckd ldrs: smooth hdwy over 2f out and sn cl up: rdn to ld over 1f out: edgd rt and hdd ins fnl f: sn no ex* **22/1**
0404 **5** *½* **King Of Dixie (USA)**[14] 4554 7-8-13 **97**..... TadhgO'Shea 7 100
(William Knight) *trckd ldrs: hdwy 3f out: led wl over 1f out: rdn and hdd appr fnl f: one pce* **33/1**
6044 **6** *1 ½* **Jeannie Galloway (IRE)**[23] 4235 4-7-13 **86** oh4..... SophieDoyle(3) 3 85
(Richard Fahey) *in tch on wd outside: hdwy to chse ldrs 2f out: rdn wl over 1f out: kpt on same pce appr fnl f* **25/1**
0110 **7** *2* **Orpsie Boy (IRE)**[20] 4369 8-8-1 **88**..... DeclanCannon(3) 18 80
(Ruth Carr) *chsd ldrs: rdn along over 2f out: sn drvn and kpt on same pce* **33/1**
3636 **8** *shd* **Internationaldebut (IRE)**[7] 4802 6-8-4 **88**..... (b[1]) PaulQuinn 17 80
(Paul Midgley) *hld up in rr: smooth hdwy 3f out: chsd ldrs 2f out: rdn whn n.m.r over 1f out: sn one pce* **12/1**[3]
-000 **9** *nk* **Mass Rally (IRE)**[49] 3397 4-8-6 **90**..... (v) RoystonFfrench 9 81
(Michael Dods) *hld up in rr: sme hdwy 2f out: sn rdn and no imp fnl f* **40/1**
1000 **10** *2* **Manassas (IRE)**[7] 4802 6-9-1 **99**..... NickyMackay 13 84+
(Brian Meehan) *hld up in rr: sme hdwy 2f out: n.d* **8/1**[2]
46-2 **11** *shd* **Mia's Boy**[44] 3548 7-9-2 **100**..... AndreaAtzeni 4 84
(Chris Dwyer) *nvr bttr than midfield* **8/1**[2]
1000 **12** *shd* **Bawaardi (IRE)**[7] 4802 5-8-5 **89**..... PatrickMathers 5 73
(Richard Fahey) *a towards rr* **28/1**
0-25 **13** *1* **Swop (IRE)**[170] 682 8-9-2 **100**..... KirstyMilczarek 12 81
(Luca Cumani) *a towards rr* **18/1**
0010 **14** *¾* **Reignier**[21] 4314 4-9-2 **100**..... AndrewElliott 10 78
(Mrs K Burke) *midfield: rdn along wl over 2f out: n.d* **20/1**

0110 **15** ¾ **Thunderball**[14] 4531 5-8-2 **93**....(b) LeonnaMayor(7) 15 69+
(David Nicholls) *prom: led 3f out: sn rdn and hdd 2f out: sn wknd* **16/1**

1050 **16** ½ **Crown Choice**[14] 4534 6-8-12 **96**.... MickyFenton 1 70
(Walter Swinburn) *a towards rr* **14/1**

4200 **17** 1 ½ **Klynch**[14] 4531 5-8-2 **86**....(b) JamesSullivan 6 56
(Ruth Carr) *prom: disp ld 3f out: rdn over 2f out: sn wknd* **33/1**

3-00 **18** 1 ½ **Celtic Sultan (IRE)**[12] 4609 7-8-4 **88**.... AndrewMullen 16 53
(Tom Tate) *led: rdn along 1/2-way: sn hdd & wknd* **40/1**

1m 25.69s (-0.61) **Going Correction** +0.10s/f (Good) **18** Ran SP% **110.9**
Speed ratings (Par 109): **107,106,105,105,104 103,100,100,100,98 98,97,96,95,95 94,92,91**
toteswingers:1&2:£14.00, 2&3:£5.50, 1&3:£17.40 CSF £73.52 CT £487.66 TOTE £10.20: £2.50, £2.20, £1.60, £3.70; EX 97.80.

Owner Jim & Helen Bowers **Bred** Michael McGlynn **Trained** Great Habton, N Yorks

FOCUS

A red-hot handicap and wide open according to the market, but there was a delay after Captain Ramius went down and got stuck under the stalls (withdrawn, 7/1, deduct 10p in the £ under R4. The field raced as one down the centre and the pace was good, with those helping to dispute it fading and setting it up for the closers. The time was ordinary, which tempers enthusiasm for the form.

NOTEBOOK

Grissom(IRE), raised 6lb for his Pontefract win, was up to this trip for the first time since November 2009, but he is in such good form just now that it made no difference. Moving into contention over 2f from home, the gap came at just the right time and, once through it, he quickened up well to lead inside the last and got first run on the runner-up.

Irish Heartbeat(IRE), 3lb below his last winning mark, came into this 2-3 here and may have been a bit unlucky not to improve that statistic. Having moved closer coming to the last 2f, he didn't see a lot of daylight inside the last furlong and, once the gap appeared, his late charge fell short. He still may not have won otherwise, but it would have been close. (tchd 9-1)

Docofthebay(IRE), still 5lb higher than for his last win at Newmarket in October, had the cheekpieces back on and ran another fine race in a hot handicap. He isn't the easiest to win with these days, but has the ability to nail a decent prize when the race goes his way. (op 7-1)

Colonial(IRE), making his handicap debut in Britain, travelled well and was in front over 1f out before getting run out of it. He did best of those to race handily and has the ability but isn't going to be the easiest to place. (op 20-1)

King Of Dixie(USA) ◆ has been disappointing since beating Cityscape on his reappearance last season, but this was much better. He is worth watching out for as long as the ground remains on the quick side.

Jeannie Galloway(IRE) ◆ ran a blinder towards the far side of the field considering she was 4lb wrong and would be interesting if turning out off her proper mark in the near future.

Orpsie Boy(IRE) was disappointing in his hat-trick bid at Pontefract last time when a long way behind Grissom. This was better, without suggesting he can defy this sort of mark these days.

Internationaldebut(IRE) had blinkers on for the first time and was travelling better than anything coming to the last 2f, but he didn't find a lot off the bridle and is now on a losing run of 31. (op 14-1)

Manassas(IRE) was reportedly never travelling. Official explanation: jockey said gelding never travelled (op 11-1)

Mia's Boy was reportedly unsuited by the good ground. Official explanation: trainer said gelding was unsuited by the good ground (op 15-2 tchd 7-1)

5033 ARICABEAURACING.COM H'CAP 5f

4:20 (4:29) (Class 3) (0-95,94) 3-Y-O+

£8,092 (£2,423; £1,211; £605; £302; £152) **Stalls** High

Form RPR

3006 **1** **Secret Witness**[5] 4859 5-9-6 **90**....(b) TomMcLaughlin 17 99
(Ronald Harris) *chsd ldr on stands' rail: hdwy wl over 1f out: sn rdn and styd on ins fnl f to ld last 50yds* **9/1**[3]

5062 **2** ½ **Hazelrigg (IRE)**[42] 3613 6-9-3 **87**....(be) BarryMcHugh 19 94
(Tim Easterby) *led and sn clr on stands' rail: rdn over 1f out: hdd and nt run on last 50yds* **7/1**[2]

0010 **3** hd **Master Rooney (IRE)**[29] 4075 5-9-0 **84**.... RoystonFfrench 15 90
(Bryan Smart) *chsd ldrs: hdwy 1/2-way: rdn over 1f out: drvn and kpt on wl ins fnl f* **20/1**

035- **4** nk **Crimea (IRE)**[379] 4536 5-9-2 **86**.... PaulQuinn 9 91
(David Nicholls) *a.p: rdn wl over 1f out: drvn and kpt on wl ins fnl f* **16/1**

343 **5** nse **Your Gifted (IRE)**[8] 4767 4-8-8 **85**.... DavidKenny(7) 11 90
(Patrick Morris) *midfield: hdwy 2f out: rdn to chse ldrs over 1f out: kpt on ins fnl f* **25/1**

0600 **6** ½ **Courageous (IRE)**[14] 4531 5-9-3 **87**.... PJMcDonald 12 90+
(Kevin Ryan) *prom: pushed along over 2f out: rdn and n.m.r over 1f out: swtchd rt and kpt on ins fnl f* **22/1**

1603 **7** 1 **Ginger Ted (IRE)**[21] 4346 4-9-6 **90**....(p) RobbieFitzpatrick 4 89+
(Richard Guest) *hld up in rr: hdwy 2f out: sn rdn and styd on ins fnl f: nrst fin* **9/1**[3]

4300 **8** nk **Rocket Rob (IRE)**[8] 4765 5-8-13 **83**.... StevieDonohoe 6 81+
(Willie Musson) *towards rr: hdwy wl over 1f out: sn rdn and styd on ins fnl f* **16/1**

00-3 **9** ½ **Rasaman (IRE)**[21] 4327 7-8-12 **85**.... PaulPickard(3) 5 81
(Jim Goldie) *bhd: hdwy wl over 1f out: sn rdn and kpt on ins fnl f* **20/1**

3130 **10** hd **Lost In Paris (IRE)**[20] 4357 5-9-2 **86**....(p) TadhgO'Shea 14 82
(Tim Easterby) *towards rr: hdwy wl over 1f out: sn rdn and kpt on ins fnl f* **16/1**

5043 **11** nk **Fathom Five (IRE)**[18] 4416 7-9-4 **88**.... AndrewMullen 13 83
(David Nicholls) *prom: rdn along over 2f out: sn wknd* **16/1**

0232 **12** 1 ½ **Whozthecat (IRE)**[14] 4556 4-9-3 **87**....(v) SaleemGolam 10 76
(Declan Carroll) *chsd ldrs: rdn along over 2f out: sn n.m.r and wknd* **13/2**[1]

0205 **13** ½ **Five Star Junior (USA)**[4] 4894 5-9-10 **94**.... JamesSullivan 20 81
(Linda Stubbs) *a towards rr* **20/1**

0014 **14** hd **Drawnfromthepast (IRE)**[11] 4644 6-9-3 **90**.... SophieDoyle(3) 8 77
(Ed Walker) *chsd ldrs: rdn along over 2f out: sn wknd* **20/1**

24-0 **15** ½ **Lenny Bee**[129] 1166 5-9-2 **89**....(t) DaleSwift(3) 3 74
(George Foster) *prom: rdn along over 2f out: sn wknd* **40/1**

0025 **16** hd **Foxy Music**[24] 4195 7-9-1 **85**.... TonyHamilton 16 69
(Eric Alston) *a towards rr* **28/1**

1000 **17** ¾ **Discanti (IRE)**[42] 3627 6-9-2 **86**....(t) DuranFentiman 7 68
(Tim Easterby) *a towards rr* **40/1**

2320 **18** ¾ **Noodles Blue Boy**[18] 4416 5-9-0 **84**.... FrannyNorton 2 63
(Ollie Pears) *prom: rdn along 2f out: sn wknd* **11/1**

0460 **19** 2 **Beat The Bell**[14] 4556 6-9-2 **86**.... MickyFenton 18 58+
(David Barron) *v.s.a and a bhd* **14/1**

3010 **20** ¾ **Cadeaux Pearl**[15] 4498 3-8-10 **88**....(b) NeilFarley(5) 1 57
(David Nicholls) *prom on wd outside: rdn along 1/2-way: sn wknd* **16/1**

59.47 secs (-1.03) **Going Correction** +0.10s/f (Good)
WFA 3 from 4yo+ 3lb **20** Ran SP% **125.8**
Speed ratings (Par 107): **112,111,110,110,110 109,107,107,106,106 105,103,102,102,101 101,100,98,95,94**
CSF £60.14 CT £819.27 TOTE £11.70: £3.40, £2.80, £5.10, £5.80; EX 72.70.

Owner Paul Moulton **Bred** Cheveley Park Stud Ltd **Trained** Earlswood, Monmouths

FOCUS

With so many front-runners in opposition in this decent sprint handicap, there was never going to be much hanging around. The field utilised the full with of the track but those drawn towards the far side never had a prayer and the pair who raced closest to the stands' rail dominated. The form makes sense.

NOTEBOOK

Secret Witness came into this on a losing run of 20 and still looked handicapped to the hilt, but the drop to the minimum trip for the first time in a year and racing towards what appeared the favoured stands' rail did the trick. He was always close to the pace and kept on well to catch the fading pacemaker in the final 50 yards. (op 12-1)

Hazelrigg(IRE), up 3lb for his narrow Beverley defeat by Master Rooney last month, blazed a trail against the stands' rail and it looked for a long way as though he wouldn't be caught, but he started to tire inside the last furlong and was just run out of it. This may have been an opportunity missed and the handicapper is likely to put him up for it. (tchd 8-1)

Master Rooney(IRE) was always handy out in the centre of the track and fared best of that group, though he couldn't quite confirm Beverley form with Hazelrigg on 1lb worse terms. (op 22-1)

Crimea(IRE) was another to show decent pace up the centre of the track and did well to hang in there, considering he was returning from an absence of 379 days. Provided he comes out of this fit and well, he is worth watching out for while the ground remains fast. (op 18-1)

Your Gifted(IRE) had every chance in the centre group and ran with a lot of credit, but is still 6lb above her last winning mark.

Courageous(IRE) ran a decent race, never being far away in the centre of the track, but has now been beaten 23 times since a successful racecourse debut. (op 25-1)

Ginger Ted(IRE), whose third behind Hoof It and Tajneed at York last month looks very good form now, needs a strongly run race over this trip, which he got, but he became outpaced at halfway and by the time he found his stride again, it was much too late. (op 8-1 tchd 10-1)

Rocket Rob(IRE) ◆ hasn't won on turf for two years but but up a remarkable effort here as he was behind and outpaced from the start but made up a lot of late ground. He is well enough handicapped now if he can build on it.

Whozthecat(IRE) has been running well in defeat recently, but his supporters knew their fate from a long way out here and he is without a win on turf since his reappearance last season. His trainer reported that the gelding was unsuited by the good ground. Official explanation: trainer said gelding was unsuited by the good ground (op 8-1)

Beat The Bell Official explanation: jockey said blindfold became stuck and gelding was slowly away

5034 PC EXCAVATIONS LTD H'CAP (DIV II) 7f

4:55 (4:57) (Class 5) (0-70,69) 3-Y-O+ **£2,587** (£770; £384; £192) **Stalls** High

Form RPR

000 **1** **Ellies Image**[15] 4513 4-8-7 **50** oh1.... DuranFentiman 4 65
(Brian Baugh) *towards rr: hdwy over 2f out: rdn to chse ldr wl over 1f out: styd on to ld jst ins fnl f: kpt on strly* **12/1**

0211 **2** 3 **Dhhamaan (IRE)**[15] 4517 6-9-12 **69**....(b) PJMcDonald 7 76
(Ruth Carr) *led: clr over 2f out: sn rdn along: drvn and hdd jst ins fnl f: one pce* **13/8**[1]

1000 **3** 3 ½ **Flying Applause**[7] 4793 6-9-8 **65**....(bt) RussKennemore 5 62
(Roy Bowring) *chsd ldng pair: hdwy to chse ldr 2f out: sn rdn and one pce* **11/2**[3]

5236 **4** 2 ½ **Alensgrove (IRE)**[11] 4638 3-8-9 **58**....(p) MickyFenton 11 49
(Paul Midgley) *chsd ldrs: rdn along wl over 2f out: sn drvn and no imp* **4/1**[2]

0200 **5** 5 **Cawdor (IRE)**[12] 4604 5-8-13 **63**.... KristinStubbs(7) 12 40
(Linda Stubbs) *a towards rr* **11/1**

500 **6** hd **Mark Anthony (IRE)**[3] 4897 4-9-10 **67**....(e[1]) FrannyNorton 8 44
(Shaun Harris) *trckd ldr: rdn along 3f out: sn wknd* **12/1**

0600 **7** ¾ **Gracie's Gift (IRE)**[11] 4651 9-9-0 **57**.... KirstyMilczarek 2 32
(Richard Guest) *in tch: rdn along over 3f out: sn outpcd* **12/1**

05-0 **8** 9 **Freedom Trail**[150] 868 3-8-8 **57**....(p) BarryMcHugh 1 —
(Tim Fitzgerald) *a in rr: bhd fnl 2f* **25/1**

000 **9** 9 **Alpha Tauri (USA)**[17] 4434 5-9-3 **60**....(t) RobbieFitzpatrick 10 —
(Richard Guest) *racd alone stands' rail: in tch to 1/2-way: sn outpcd and bhd* **25/1**

1m 26.94s (0.64) **Going Correction** +0.10s/f (Good)
WFA 3 from 4yo+ 6lb **9** Ran SP% **112.6**
Speed ratings (Par 103): **100,96,92,89,84 83,82,72,62**
toteswingers:1&2:£5.30, 2&3:£2.60, 1&3:£11.70 CSF £30.99 CT £122.09 TOTE £19.50: £3.10, £1.20, £1.80; EX 61.60.

Owner F Gillespie **Bred** Miss S M Potts **Trained** Audley, Staffs

FOCUS

The winning time was 0.59 seconds slower than the first division and few came into this in any sort of form. The main bulk of the field raced up the centre. Pretty ordinary form.

Ellies Image Official explanation: trainer said, regarding apparent improvement in form, that the yard is in better form.

Gracie's Gift(IRE) Official explanation: jockey said gelding lost a shoe

5035 UNIVERSAL RECYCLING COMPANY H'CAP 1m 6f 132y

5:30 (5:31) (Class 4) (0-85,85) 3-Y-O+ **£5,175** (£1,540; £769; £384) **Stalls** Low

Form RPR

1524 **1** **Manifestation**[23] 4251 3-9-0 **85**.... NickyMackay 11 96
(John Gosden) *hld up in tch: hdwy 4f out: led wl over 2f out: rdn and edgd lft over 1f out: drvn ins fnl f and hld on gamely* **11/1**

1254 **2** ½ **Four Nations (USA)**[17] 4426 3-8-6 **77**.... FrannyNorton 9 89+
(Amanda Perrett) *hld up: hdwy on inner 3f out: rdn to chse ldrs over 1f out: drvn and edgd rt ins fnl f: ev ch tl no ex nr fin* **3/1**[1]

0333 **3** ½ **Bollin Greta**[9] 4719 6-9-9 **80**....(t) BarryMcHugh 12 89
(Tim Easterby) *hld up in rr: hdwy on outer 4f out: chsd wnr 2f out: rdn to chal over 1f out: drvn and ev ch ins fnl f: no ex last 100yds* **12/1**

-200 **4** 1 ¾ **Kitty Wells**[43] 3593 4-9-11 **82**.... KirstyMilczarek 14 89
(Luca Cumani) *midfield: hdwy 4f out: chsd ldrs 3f out: rdn and hung lft over 1f out: drvn ins fnl f and kpt on wl towards fin* **14/1**

4/46 **5** 4 ½ **Spiekeroog**[21] 4348 5-8-12 **72**.... DeclanCannon(3) 6 73
(David O'Meara) *hld up in rr: hdwy 4f out: chsd ldrs over 2f out: sn rdn and one pce appr fnl f* **11/1**

6350 **6** 1 ½ **Dazzling Light (UAE)**[21] 4344 6-9-3 **77**.... PaulPickard(3) 3 76
(Jim Goldie) *hld up in rr: hdwy on outer over 3f out: rdn to chse ldrs wl over 1f out: sn drvn and no imp* **16/1**

6041 **7** 4 **Elrasheed**[21] 4336 3-8-4 **75**.... TadhgO'Shea 2 69
(John Dunlop) *prom: effrt 3f out: sn disputing ld and rdn 2f out: drvn and hld whn n.m.r over 1f out: wknd* **4/1**[2]

214 **8** 2 ½ **Lady Amakhala**[28] 4108 3-8-7 **78**.... PJMcDonald 1 69
(George Moore) *in rr and pushed along 1/2-way: rdn along over 4f out: nvr a factor* **9/1**[3]

-032 **9** nk **Blazing Field**[17] 4449 3-8-1 **72** ow3.... JohnFahy(3) 13 65
(Clive Cox) *prom: chsd ldr 1/2-way: rdn along 3f out: drvn 2f out and wkng whn n.m.r over 1f out* **10/1**

0620 **10** *2 ¼* **Thin Red Line (IRE)**[20] 4360 5-9-8 **79**........................ TonyHamilton 8 66
(Michael Dods) *hld up: a towards rr* **25/1**

6442 **11** *¾* **Penangdouble O One**[38] 3738 4-8-11 **68**..............(tp) StevieDonohoe 7 54
(Ralph Beckett) *trckd ldrs: rdn along 4f out: drvn over 3f out and sn wknd* **12/1**

1411 **12** *8* **Jewelled Dagger (IRE)**[15] 4499 7-9-2 **76**.................... DaleSwift(3) 10 52
(Keith Dalgleish) *led: rdn along 4f out: drvn 3f out: sn hdd & wknd* **14/1**

0022 **13** *9* **Rubi Dia**[45] 3509 4-8-9 **66** oh1..............................(v) AndrewHeffernan 4 30
(Kevin M Prendergast) *trckd ldrs on inner: effrt 4f out: rdn along 3f out: sn wknd* **25/1**

3m 8.02s (0.62) **Going Correction** +0.10s/f (Good)
WFA 3 from 4yo+ 14lb **13** Ran SP% **123.1**
Speed ratings (Par 105): **102,101,101,100,98 97,95,93,93,92 92,87,83**
toteswingers:1&2:£11.60, 2&3:£3.50, 1&3:£28.20 CSF £45.20 CT £417.40 TOTE £10.70: £2.50, £1.60, £3.60; EX 61.30.
Owner H R H Princess Haya Of Jordan **Bred** Mrs S L Brimble **Trained** Newmarket, Suffolk

FOCUS
A decent staying handicap, but run at an ordinary pace. The field came up the centre of the track on reaching the straight. The winner resumed his progress but the second was arguably unlucky.

5036 ANTHONY ESTRIN'S 60TH BIRTHDAY BASH APPRENTICE H'CAP 1m 2f 60y
6:00 (6:01) (Class 5) (0-75,76) 4-Y-0+ **£2,911** (£866; £432; £216) **Stalls** Low

Form RPR

4060 **1** **Hail Bold Chief (USA)**[20] 4366 4-8-8 **62**.................... GarryWhillans(3) 4 76
(Alan Swinbank) *in tch: hdwy to trck ldrs 4f out: led 2f out: sn rdn and edgd rt ent fnl f: drvn out* **14/1**

0004 **2** *2 ½* **Veiled Applause**[23] 4237 8-9-3 **71**.............................. ShaneBKelly(3) 5 80
(John Quinn) *hld up: hdwy over 3f out: chsd ldrs over 2f out: swtchd rt and rdn to chal over 1f out: drvn ins fnl f and ev ch tl one pce last 100yds* **9/4**[1]

6564 **3** *2 ¾* **Ajdaad (USA)**[6] 4821 4-8-10 **66**.................................. RyanTate(5) 13 70
(Alan McCabe) *hld up in midfield: hdwy to chse ldrs 3f out: effrt over 2f out: rdn wl over 1f out: kpt on same pce appr fnl f* **16/1**

6126 **4** *1 ¾* **Dane Cottage**[12] 4605 4-8-5 **56** oh2.................................. AmyScott 2 56
(Brian Ellison) *s.i.s and bhd: hdwy over 4f out: rdn along 2f out: kpt on: nt rch ldrs* **8/1**

1405 **5** *5* **Frontline Phantom (IRE)**[7] 4784 4-9-1 **69**...................... LMcNiff(3) 9 60
(Mrs K Burke) *in tch: hdwy on outer to chse ldrs 4f out: rdn along wl over 2f out: drvn wl over 1f out and sn one pce* **6/1**[3]

6060 **6** *nk* **Lord Lansing (IRE)**[12] 4601 4-8-4 **60**......................... NoraLooby(5) 11 50
(Mrs K Burke) *midfield: hdwy to trck ldrs 4f out: rdn to chse ldr 3f out: drvn 2f out and sn one pce* **20/1**

3450 **7** *¾* **The Oil Magnate**[35] 3858 6-8-13 **69**........................ JustinNewman(5) 6 58
(Michael Dods) *cl up: led over 3f out: rdn along over 2f out: sn hdd and grad wknd* **14/1**

0000 **8** *9* **Black Coffee**[6] 4825 6-9-2 **67**.................................(b) JamesRogers 10 39
(Mark Brisbourne) *s.i.s: a bhd* **25/1**

2005 **9** *3* **Hydrant**[22] 4294 5-9-1 **71**.. GeorgeChaloner(5) 8 37
(Peter Salmon) *trckd ldrs: hdwy on inner 4f out: rdn along 3f out: drvn over 2f out and sn wknd* **10/1**

2420 **10** *hd* **Thunderstruck**[133] 1098 6-9-5 **75**............................(p) LeonnaMayor(5) 1 41
(David Nicholls) *prom: rdn along over 3f out: drvn wl over 2f out and sn wknd* **16/1**

3043 **11** *19* **Sirgarfieldsobers (IRE)**[7] 4784 5-9-11 **76**......................... NeilFarley 7 —
(Declan Carroll) *led: rdn along 4f out: hdd over 3f out and sn wknd* **9/2**[2]

2m 10.67s (1.27) **Going Correction** +0.10s/f (Good) **11** Ran SP% **117.1**
Speed ratings (Par 103): **98,96,93,92,88 88,87,80,77,77 62**
toteswingers:1&2:£10.80, 2&3:£11.00, 1&3:£19.80 CSF £45.42 CT £530.77 TOTE £18.00: £4.80, £1.60, £3.90; EX 66.20.
Owner Solway Stayers **Bred** Tracy Farmer **Trained** Melsonby, N Yorks

FOCUS
A moderate apprentices' handicap in which the leaders may have gone off too quick and paid for it late on. The majority of the field came up the middle on reaching the straight. The winner is rated back to last year's best.
Hail Bold Chief(USA) ◆ Official explanation: trainer said, regarding apparent improvement in form, that the gelding appreciated the drop in trip and the stable appears to be back in form.
Lord Lansing(IRE) Official explanation: jockey said gelding hung right handed in straight
Sirgarfieldsobers(IRE) Official explanation: jockey said gelding ran too free
T/Plt: £31.50 to a £1 stake. Pool of £72,852.64 - 1,688.22 winning tickets. T/Qpdt: £11.80 to a £1 stake. Pool of £4,016.89 - 251.00 winning tickets. JR

4844 LINGFIELD (L-H)
Saturday, August 13

OFFICIAL GOING: Turf course - good (good to firm in places); all-weather - standard
Wind: fairly modest, across Weather: overcast, dry

5037 BETFAIR RACING EXCELLENCE APPRENTICE JOCKEYS TRAINING SERIES H'CAP (TURF) 6f
5:40 (5:40) (Class 5) (0-70,66) 4-Y-0+ **£3,067** (£905; £453) **Stalls** High

Form RPR

4235 **1** **Desert Icon (IRE)**[10] 4683 5-9-2 **63**.............................. AliceHaynes(5) 6 73
(David Simcock) *racd in last pair: urged along and clsd over 1f out: edgd lft and chal 1f out: led ins fnl f: sn in command and r.o wl* **11/4**[2]

5245 **2** *1 ¾* **Jonnie Skull (IRE)**[29] 4064 5-9-1 **57**............................(vt) LucyKBarry 2 61
(Phil McEntee) *led and crossed to r against stands' rail: rdn over 2f out: edging lft u.p fr over 1f out: hdd ins fnl f: nt gng pce of wnr fnl 100yds* **7/2**[3]

02-0 **3** *¾* **River Bounty**[121] 1336 6-8-4 **51**.................................. JordanUys(5) 4 53
(Alan Jarvis) *chsd ldr: jnd ldr gng wl 2f out: urged along over 1f out: edgd lft and nt gng pce of wnr fnl 100yds* **12/1**

4002 **4** *1 ¼* **Hand Painted**[8] 4741 5-9-5 **66**...................................(p) LukeRowe(5) 1 64
(Anthony Middleton) *stdd and dropped in bhd after s: clsd and chsng ldrs whn nt clr run ent fnl f: styd on same pce and no imp fnl 150yds* **11/2**

0610 **5** *1* **Silvee**[2] 4973 4-9-3 **59**.. CharlesBishop 3 53
(John Bridger) *chsd ldrs: rdn over 2f out: ev ch over 1f out tl wknd fnl 150yds* **2/1**[1]

69.86 secs (-1.34) **Going Correction** -0.30s/f (Firm) **5** Ran SP% **105.3**
Speed ratings (Par 103): **96,93,92,91,89**
CSF £11.34 TOTE £3.60: £1.40, £1.70; EX 12.50.
Owner Tick Tock Partnership **Bred** Lynch Bages Ltd & Samac Ltd **Trained** Newmarket, Suffolk

FOCUS
This ordinary sprint handicap, confined to apprentice riders, was run at a sound tempo and once again the stands' rail proved the place to be late on. The runner-up has been rated to her turf best.

5038 FIZZTIVAL AT LINGFIELD SPARKLING (S) STKS (TURF) 6f
6:10 (6:14) (Class 6) 3-Y-0+ **£1,533** (£452; £226) **Stalls** High

Form RPR

-342 **1** **Nine Before Ten (IRE)**[81] 2391 3-8-7 76.....................(t) EddieCreighton 3 75
(Deborah Sanderson) *taken down early: mde all: sn crossed to r against stands' rail and clr thrght: eased wl ins fnl f: unchal* **8/11**[1]

4225 **2** *5* **Miss Firefly**[15] 4487 6-8-8 57..(p) SimonPearce(3) 1 60
(Ron Hodges) *led rdrless to s: racd in midfield: rdn to chse clr wnr ent fnl 2f: no imp* **9/1**

0356 **3** *5* **Doctor Hilary**[8] 4759 9-8-13 53... KierenFox(3) 2 49
(Mark Hoad) *a struggling to go pce in rr: 5th and no ch whn hung lft over 1f out: plugged on to go modest 3rd ins fnl f* **16/1**

0-03 **4** *3 ¾* **For Life (IRE)**[23] 4246 9-8-13 68............................ NataliaGemelova(3) 4 37
(John E Long) *taken down early: chsd wnr but nvr on terms: rdn and no imp over 2f out: wknd 2f out* **5/1**[3]

0000 **5** *6* **Scintillating (IRE)**[6] 4822 4-8-11 35.....................................(v) NeilChalmers 6 13
(Ray Peacock) *sn outpcd towards rr: rdn and lost tch 1/2-way* **80/1**

0352 **6** *1 ¼* **His Grace (IRE)**[2] 4950 3-8-12 60.. MartinLane 7 24
(Andrew Haynes) *rrd s and s.i.s: hdwy into midfield and rdn after 2f: toiling 1/2-way and sn wl btn: wl bhd and eased ins fnl f* **4/1**[2]

69.17 secs (-2.03) **Going Correction** -0.30s/f (Firm)
WFA 3 from 4yo+ 4lb **6** Ran SP% **111.7**
Speed ratings (Par 101): **101,94,87,82,74 73**
CSF £8.31 TOTE £1.70: £1.10, £3.80; EX 6.60.The winner was sold to W McKay for 9,000gns.
Owner R J Budge **Bred** Deerpark Stud **Trained** Sturton le Steeple, Notts

FOCUS
Straightforward selling form, with the winner not needing to match her Ripon form to win.

5039 ENGLAND'S VINEYARD BRITISH STALLION STUDS EBF NOVICE STKS (TURF) 7f
6:40 (6:40) (Class 5) 2-Y-0 **£3,234** (£962; £481; £240) **Stalls** High

Form RPR

31 **1** **Emirates Art**[25] 4184 2-8-11 79.. MartinLane 8 81
(David Simcock) *trckd ldrs: rdn to chse ldr 2f out: edgd lft over 1f out: drvn and chal ins fnl f: r.o to ld towards fin* **15/2**

31 **2** *hd* **Vital Gold**[29] 4073 2-9-5 0... LiamJones 5 88
(William Haggas) *led and crossed to r against stands' rail: pushed along and qcknd clr 2f out: jnd and rdn ins fnl f: kpt on same pce and hdd towards fin* **7/2**[2]

5301 **3** *5* **Singalat**[17] 4436 2-9-5 81.. GeorgeBaker 1 75
(James Given) *chsd ldr tl 2f out: sn rdn and outpcd by ldng pair: in 3rd and wl hld 1f out* **16/1**

61 **4** *½* **Graphic (IRE)**[48] 3424 2-9-5 89.. PatDobbs 3 74
(Richard Hannon) *in tch in last pair: rdn and little rspnse jst over 2f out: plugged on same pce and no ch w ldng pair over 1f out* **4/1**[3]

61 **5** *1 ½* **Elbe**[30] 4002 2-9-0 0.. TomQueally 2 65
(Sir Henry Cecil) *stdd s: plld hrd: hld up in last pair: rdn and effrt 2f out: fnd little and sn btn: wknd jst over 1f out* **10/11**[1]

1m 22.45s (-0.85) **Going Correction** -0.30s/f (Firm) **5** Ran SP% **112.3**
Speed ratings (Par 94): **92,91,86,85,83**
CSF £33.23 TOTE £8.10: £3.10, £2.00; EX 30.50.
Owner M M Racing **Bred** David Elsworth & Matthew Green **Trained** Newmarket, Suffolk

FOCUS
This was weakened by the non-runners. There was a sound pace on but it's probably not form to trust, with the fifth too free and the fourth poorly positioned on a pace-favouring track.

NOTEBOOK
Emirates Art responded strongly once asked for his effort at the furlong marker and got on top near the finish to win with more in hand than the bare margin suggests, giving her yard a double on the card. She had only scraped home when winning her maiden at Yarmouth last time, but this extra furlong saw her in a much better light and a little cut underfoot is clearly to her liking. Stepping up another furlong before the year is out ought to be within her compass and it will be interesting to see where she heads next. (op 8-1 tchd 7-1)
Vital Gold, off the mark at Pontefract last month, did his best to make all against the rail but was a sitting duck for the winner. This confirms his limitations, but he still only just went down and is in the right hands to land a nursery at least. (op 4-1)
Singalat, off the mark at the fourth attempt 17 days earlier, wasn't disgraced and looks up to this sort of mark. (tchd 20-1)
Graphic(IRE) got off the mark when last seen at Salisbury in June, but he proved ring-rusty on this return to action and perhaps the easier ground was against him. (tchd 7-2)
Elbe proved popular to follow up her Doncaster maiden win, but she lost out here by running far too keen under restraint. A more positive ride may have helped, but her Group 1 entry looks fanciful at this stage. (op Evens tchd 11-10)

5040 BRAVO SOCIAL ENTERPRISE H'CAP (TURF) 7f 140y
7:10 (7:13) (Class 6) (0-65,66) 3-Y-0+ **£2,181** (£644; £322) **Stalls** Centre

Form RPR

4244 **1** **Ellie In The Pink (IRE)**[37] 3782 3-9-2 **63**..................... HarryBentley(3) 6 70
(Alan Jarvis) *mde all: grad crossed to r against stands' rail: set stdy gallop: rdn and qcknd over 1f out: pushed out hands and heels and a doing enough ins fnl f* **9/2**[1]

6132 **2** *½* **Bold Ring**[6] 4822 5-9-3 **57**...................................... AlanCreighton(3) 7 64
(Edward Creighton) *hld up wl in tch: swtchd rt and effrt on stands' rail 1f out: chsd wnr fnl 75yds: r.o wl* **8/1**

0061 **3** *¾* **Songsmith**[8] 4743 3-9-8 **66**...(p) NeilCallan 2 70
(Lucy Wadham) *chsd wnr and grad crossed to r nr stands' rail: rdn and unable qck over 1f out: drvn and styd on same pce ins fnl f* **5/1**[2]

2030 **4** *1* **Caldermud (IRE)**[11] 4651 4-9-2 **60**.............................(t) HarryPoulton(7) 9 62+
(Olivia Maylam) *taken down early: t.k.h: hld up in tch in rr: hdwy and swtchd arnd wkng rival jst over 1f out: r.o wl ins fnl f: nt rch wnr* **20/1**

6025 **5** *shd* **Links Drive Lady**[6] 4822 3-9-7 **65**..............................(b[1]) TomQueally 14 68+
(Mark Rimmer) *in tch: shkn up and nt qckning whn n.m.r over 1f out: drvn ins fnl f: styd on fnl 100yds: no threat to wnr* **6/1**[3]

0004 **6** *nk* **Paperetto**[8] 4758 3-8-12 **59**... SeanLevey(3) 5 59
(Robert Mills) *t.k.h: chsd ldrs: drvn and unable qck over 1f out: styd on same pce ins fnl f: lost 2 pls last strides* **8/1**

1350 **7** *1 ¾* **Pie Poudre**[9] 4705 4-9-7 **58**......................................(v) WilliamCarson 13 54
(Roy Brotherton) *dwlt: sn rdn along and nvr travelling in rr: sme hdwy u.p and swtchd lft wl over 1f out: styd on fnl f: nvr trbld ldrs* **16/1**

6605 **8** *1 ½* **Byrd In Hand (IRE)**[17] 4444 4-9-6 **57**............................ NeilChalmers 10 49
(John Bridger) *in tch: shuffled bk towards rr jst over 2f out: styd on same pce and no imp fr over 1f out* **13/2**

406 9 ½ **Knowe Head (NZ)**[16] 4478 4-9-9 **60**.....(t) LiamJones 1 51
(James Unett) *chsd ldrs: rdn and unable qck ent fnl 2f: drvn over 1f out: wknd jst ins fnl f* **25/1**

4604 10 ¾ **Diddums**[1] 5002 5-8-11 **55**..... KatiaScallan(7) 15 44
(Alastair Lidderdale) *a in rr: swtchd lft after 2f: rdn and effrt towards centre over 1f out: kpt on but n.d* **10/1**

352 11 1 ¾ **Lilli Palmer (IRE)**[52] 3280 4-9-5 **56**..... MartinLane 8 40
(Mike Murphy) *s.i.s: a in rr: effrt in centre and drvn over 2f out: no imp and wl hld ent fnl f* **10/1**

60-0 12 13 **So Choosy**[21] 4340 3-8-11 **55**..... EddieCreighton 4 —
(Jeremy Gask) *stdd s: t.k.h: hld up in midfield: rdn and lost pl over 2f out: wl bhd over 1f out* **40/1**

1m 30.9s (-1.40) **Going Correction** -0.30s/f (Firm)
WFA 3 from 4yo+ 7lb **12** Ran SP% **119.8**
Speed ratings (Par 101): **95,94,93,92,92 92,90,89,88,87 86,73**
CSF £39.95 CT £190.19 TOTE £5.50: £2.40, £2.40, £2.10; EX 26.20.
Owner Jakellie **Bred** J Jamgotchian **Trained** Twyford, Bucks

FOCUS

Predictably the stands' rail proved the place to be in this moderate handicap. Very few got involved and the runner-up has been rated to her best, with the third rated up a length on her Brighton win.
Links Drive Lady Official explanation: jockey said filly was denied a clear run
So Choosy Official explanation: trainer said filly had a breathing problem and pulled up lame

5041 MEET GATQWICK CLAIMING STKS 1m (P)

7:40 (7:40) (Class 6) 3-Y-O **£1,533** (£452; £226) **Stalls** High

Form RPR

0020 1 **Sky Diamond (IRE)**[22] 4284 3-8-9 62.....(b) TomQueally 3 66
(James Given) *chsd ldrs and t.k.h after 2f: wnt 2nd over 3f out: led over 2f out: styd on wl u.p ins fnl f* **9/2**[3]

0405 2 1 ¾ **Pearl Opera**[8] 4758 3-8-6 53..... EddieCreighton 7 59
(Denis Coakley) *hld up in tch in last: rdn and effrt bnd 2f out: chsd ldrs and drvn jst over 1f out: chsd wnr ins fnl f: no imp* **4/1**[2]

4010 3 1 ¾ **Exchange**[14] 4550 3-9-7 75..... GeorgeBaker 6 70
(Andrew Haynes) *broke wl: sn stdd and hld up in tch: hdwy to chse wnr 2f out: rdn and hung lft over 1f out: continued to edge lft fnd little: no imp and lost 2nd ins fnl f* **6/5**[1]

5043 4 1 ¾ **Jackie Love (IRE)**[28] 4089 3-7-13 50.....(b) KieranO'Neill(3) 5 47
(Olivia Maylam) *in tch: t.k.h after 2f: rdn and effrt to chse ldrs over 1f out: drvn 1f out: wknd ins fnl f* **9/1**

0565 5 6 **Piccarello**[17] 4431 3-8-13 60.....(b) NeilCallan 4 44
(Mark H Tompkins) *led for 2f: chsd ldr after tl over 3f out: wknd qckly wl over 1f out* **14/1**

4360 6 5 **Danceyourselfdizzy (IRE)**[24] 4200 3-8-9 63.....(v1) WilliamCarson 1 29
(Phil McEntee) *sn bustled along and chsd ldr for over 1f: stdd and in midfield after: rdn and lost pl over 2f out: wl btn over 1f out* **14/1**

6-5 7 5 **Smart Performance**[109] 1578 3-8-6 0..... HarryBentley(3) 2 17
(Alan Jarvis) *chsd ldrs tl led after 2f and stdd gallop: hdd over 2f out: sn dropped out: wl btn fnl 2f* **28/1**

1m 39.74s (1.54) **Going Correction** +0.125s/f (Slow) **7** Ran SP% **110.4**
Speed ratings (Par 98): **97,95,93,91,85 80,75**
toteswingers:1&2:£2.30, 2&3:£1.80, 1&3:£1.30 CSF £21.10 TOTE £6.40: £2.40, £3.10; EX 19.90.
Owner Danethorpe Racing Partnership **Bred** David Bourke **Trained** Willoughton, Lincs

FOCUS

This claimer was run at a stop-start pace and the form is somewhat suspect.
Piccarello Official explanation: jockey said gelding hung right

5042 CHOIROKE CONCERT H'CAP 1m 2f (P)

8:10 (8:10) (Class 6) (0-62,62) 3-Y-O+ **£2,181** (£644; £322) **Stalls** Low

Form RPR

-000 1 **Librettela**[74] 2599 3-8-2 **48**..... HarryBentley(3) 4 57
(Alan Jarvis) *rn green: pushed along early: chsd ldr: rdn and hung rt fr over 1f out: pushed along and kpt on ins fnl f to ld nr fin* **40/1**

6360 2 ½ **If What And Maybe**[7] 4800 3-8-5 **51**.....(b1) KieranO'Neill(3) 3 59
(John Ryan) *led: rdn wl over 2f out: clr w wnr over 1f out: kpt on u.p tl hdd and no ex nr fin* **14/1**

5604 3 8 **Black Pond (USA)**[22] 4287 3-9-5 **62**..... NeilCallan 8 54
(Mark Johnston) *t.k.h: chsd ldrs: rdn and outpcd whn hung lft bnd 2f out: 3rd and wl btn over 1f out* **4/1**[2]

0506 4 ¾ **Prince Of Thebes (IRE)**[8] 4754 10-9-10 **58**..... TomQueally 7 49
(Michael Attwater) *dwlt: racd in last trio: rdn and effrt but plenty to do bnd 2f out: no ch w ldrs over 1f out: kpt on u.p to go 4th wl ins fnl f* **25/1**

6106 5 ¾ **Sunset Boulevard (IRE)**[5] 4869 8-9-8 **59**.....(b) RobertLButler(3) 2 48
(Jim Best) *hld up in midfield: rdn and struggling whn lft modest 4th and sltly hmpd wl over 1f out: no prog and wl btn after* **7/1**[3]

0041 6 5 **Fastinthestraight (IRE)**[14] 4549 4-10-0 **62**.....(v) DaneO'Neill 10 41
(Jim Boyle) *dwlt: racd in last trio: rdn and no prog over 2f out: wl btn whn sltly hmpd wl over 1f out* **11/8**[1]

1560 7 ¾ **Adoyen Spice**[38] 3739 4-9-13 **61**.....(b1) MartinLane 6 39
(Mike Murphy) *s.i.s and pushed along early: rdn and no prog whn hmpd wl over 1f out: no ch after* **10/1**

0020 8 4 ½ **Spinning Ridge (IRE)**[5] 4869 6-9-10 **58**.....(b) TomMcLaughlin 11 27
(Ronald Harris) *s.i.s: bhd: clsd and in tch 7f out: rdn and effrt over 2f out: lft modest 5th and sltly hmpd wl over 1f out: sn wknd* **7/1**[3]

0-00 9 9 **Last Act (IRE)**[48] 3432 3-8-5 **48**..... WilliamCarson 9 —
(Mark Hoad) *t.k.h: hld up in midfield: lost pl and dropped in rr 5f out: wknd u.p over 3f out: t.o* **33/1**

0-66 B **Misefi**[30] 4023 3-8-2 **48**..... SimonPearce(3) 5 —
(Martin Bosley) *taken down early: chsd ldrs: 4th and outpcd by ldrs whn short of room: clipped heels and b.d wl over 1f out* **25/1**

2m 7.38s (0.78) **Going Correction** +0.125s/f (Slow)
WFA 3 from 4yo+ 9lb **10** Ran SP% **115.9**
Speed ratings (Par 101): **101,100,94,93,93 89,88,84,77,—**
toteswingers:1&2:£85.60, 2&3:£13.60, 1&3:£28.80 CSF £493.36 CT £2740.87 TOTE £63.60: £12.30, £5.40, £1.50; EX 1227.70.
Owner Jarvis Associates **Bred** L Dettori **Trained** Twyford, Bucks

FOCUS

A weak handicap that was run at a moderate pace and the first pair were gifted the race. The form cannot be taken at face value. The race was marred by the fall of Misefi on the home turn, who was hampered by Black Pond, but luckily the filly emerged unscathed.
Librettela Official explanation: trainer said, regarding apparent improvement in form, that the gelding was better suited by the trip and had matured since its last run two months ago.
T/Plt: £296.80 to a £1 stake. Pool of £55,325.37 - 136.05 winning tickets. T/Qpdt: £136.20 to a £1 stake. Pool of £4,435.85 - 24.10 winning tickets. SP

4995 NEWBURY (L-H)

Saturday, August 13

OFFICIAL GOING: Good (7.5)
Wind: Moderate ahead Weather: Overcast

5043 CGA LADIES DAY H'CAP 7f (S)

2:00 (2:01) (Class 3) (0-95,93) 3-Y-O+
£6,225 (£1,864; £932; £466; £233; £117) **Stalls** Centre

Form RPR

0561 1 **Directorship**[35] 3840 5-9-5 **86**..... FergusSweeney 14 97
(Patrick Chamings) *hld up in rr: str run on stands' side over 1f out to ld fnl 120yds: r.o strly and edgd lft cl home* **9/1**

0030 2 2 **My Kingdom (IRE)**[13] 4574 5-9-2 **83**.....(t) RichardHughes 1 89
(Patrick Morris) *stdd s: in rr: hdwy fr 2f out drvn and styd on to chal fnl 120yds: sn outpcd by wnr but kpt on wl for 2nd* **14/1**

6010 3 nk **Space Station**[17] 4428 5-9-7 **88**.....(b) NeilCallan 10 93
(Simon Dow) *chsd ldrs: rdn to ld over 1f out: kpt slt advantage tl hdd fnl 120yds: no ex clsng stages* **12/1**

0060 4 1 ¾ **Moretta Blanche**[35] 3845 4-8-10 **77**..... RichardKingscote 9 77
(Ralph Beckett) *t.k.h and hld up in rr: drvn and hdwy over 1f out: kpt on ins fnl f but nt gng pce to rch ldrs* **20/1**

1-00 5 1 ¼ **Kuanyao (IRE)**[42] 3627 5-9-10 **91**..... WilliamBuick 4 88
(Peter Makin) *led: narrowly hdd over 1f out: styd pressing ldr and ev ch fnl 120yds: sn wknd* **16/1**

3-61 6 nk **Dominium (USA)**[15] 4509 4-8-10 **77**..... PatCosgrave 3 73
(Jeremy Gask) *chsd ldrs: rdn fr 3f out: styd on fnl f: nt gng pce of ldrs* **8/1**[2]

0040 7 1 ¼ **Golden Desert (IRE)**[14] 4531 7-9-12 **93**..... EddieAhern 15 86
(Robert Mills) *in rr: rdn and hdwy 2f out: styd on same pce ins fnl f* **10/1**

3300 8 ¾ **Marajaa (IRE)**[18] 4415 9-9-0 **81**..... PhilipRobinson 16 72
(Willie Musson) *stdd s: in rr: pushed along 2f out: styd on fnl f but nvr a threat* **11/1**

0006 9 nse **Saint Pierre (USA)**[15] 4509 4-9-2 **83**..... J-PGuillambert 6 74
(Luca Cumani) *in tch: rdn and hdwy fr 2f out: no imp on ldrs ins fnl f* **10/1**

-200 10 3 ¼ **Hot Spark**[15] 4509 4-9-2 **83**.....(t) LukeMorris 2 65
(John Akehurst) *in tch: rdn along 3f out: styd on ins fnl f: nt rch ldrs* **20/1**

0003 11 ½ **Elna Bright**[12] 4616 6-9-1 **82**..... JMurtagh 8 62
(Brett Johnson) *pressed ldr: chal ins fnl 2f tl wknd ins fnl f* **7/1**[1]

32 12 2 ½ **Rigolleto (IRE)**[24] 4214 3-8-12 **88**..... MartinHarley(3) 5 62
(Mick Channon) *chsd ldrs: rdn over 2f out: wknd wl over 1f out* **7/1**[1]

0020 13 1 ¼ **Bravo Echo**[14] 4556 5-9-2 **83**..... TomQueally 11 53
(Michael Attwater) *chsd ldrs over 4f* **16/1**

5023 14 nse **Dukes Art**[31] 3987 5-9-1 **82**..... JimmyFortune 13 52
(James Toller) *in rr: sme prog ins fnl 2f: nvr in contention* **17/2**[3]

0000 15 8 **Rulesn'regulations**[17] 4428 5-9-8 **89**.....(b) GeorgeBaker 7 38
(Matthew Salaman) *chsd ldrs over 4f* **10/1**

1m 26.95s (1.25) **Going Correction** +0.175s/f (Good)
WFA 3 from 4yo+ 6lb **15** Ran SP% **122.1**
Speed ratings (Par 107): **99,96,96,94,92 92,91,90,90,86 85,83,81,81,72**
toteswingers:1&2:£33.60, 2&3:£46.40, 1&3:£25.10 CSF £130.07 CT £1549.95 TOTE £11.10: £3.30, £4.50, £5.20; EX 203.90 TRIFECTA Not won..
Owner Mrs R Lyon,Mrs P Hayton,P R Chamings **Bred** Mrs D O Joly **Trained** Baughurst, Hants

FOCUS

Rail at normal configuration and distances as advertised. The ground remained officially good despite 2.5mm of rain overnight. The jockeys had mixed opinions on how the ground was riding, varying between 'good' and 'dead'. A good, competitive handicap in which 3-y-os have the best recent record, but there was only one from that age group this time. Ordinary form for the grade, with a length personal best from the winner.

NOTEBOOK

Directorship ◆, raised 2lb for a narrow success over 1m at Ascot, was taking a drop in trip, having never run over shorter than 1m. Appreciating what looked a sound gallop, he produced a fine turn of foot to come from the rear and won this going away. Clearly on a roll, the hat-trick looks a distinct possibility providing the handicapper does not over-react. (op 11-1 tchd 12-1)
My Kingdom(IRE) had gained all his wins on sharp tracks for Hughie Morrison but did run some decent races for David Nicholls. Switched to Patrick Morris and 3lb below his last winning mark, he was delivered at the right time but the winner proved too strong.
Space Station, another who had gained all his wins on sharp, and/or turning tracks, ran a decent race on this straight course, only fading inside the last having had every chance. (op 14-1)
Moretta Blanche, a dual 7f winner, including over C&D on her debut, had dropped 1lb below her last winning mark and ran much better. She is reasonably treated if able to build on this.
Kuanyao(IRE) won six successive races between October 2009 and September 2010 but had struggled off higher marks this season and was still 7lb above his last winning rating. However, the yard had hit form recently though and he ran a decent race from the front, albeit unable to sustain his effort. (op 14-1)
Dominium(USA), who scored last time on his turf debut over 7f on fast ground, was 3lb higher and ran creditably in this higher grade. He remains relatively unexposed.
Golden Desert(IRE), a close second in this race two years ago on only previous visit here, has been showing mixed form this season but this suggested the ability is still there.
Marajaa(IRE) is well suited by a big field and fast gallop but had disappointed the last twice after decent efforts in the late spring. He stayed on having run into a pocket when making headway and will appreciate the return to 1m. (op 10-1)
Saint Pierre(USA), a lightly raced dual Polytrack winner at this trip, was being pushed along a fair way from home but kept responding. A return to the AW may well see him in a more favourable light.
Rigolleto(IRE) had performed well on his only visit here, over C&D in April, and was sent off favourite. He appeared to have his chance but dropped away in the last quarter-mile. (op 15-2 tchd 8-1)
Rulesn'regulations's rider reported that the gelding ran flat. Official explanation: jockey said gelding ran flat (op 12-1)

5044 DENFORD STUD STKS (REGISTERED AS THE WASHINGTON SINGER STAKES) (LISTED RACE) 7f (S)

2:30 (2:33) (Class 1) 2-Y-O
£12,192 (£4,622; £2,313; £1,152; £578; £290) **Stalls** Centre

Form RPR

3 1 **Fencing (USA)**[21] 4330 2-9-0 0..... WilliamBuick 1 103+
(John Gosden) *trckd ldrs: led over 2f out: shkn up and stl green: drvn and qcknd ins fnl f: won gng away: readily* **5/4**[1]

5165 2 2 ½ **Telwaar**[29] 4055 2-9-0 96..... JimmyFortune 3 97
(Peter Chapple-Hyam) *hld up in rr but in tch: gd hdwy over 2f out to chse wnr over 1f out: drvn and str effrt ins fnl f but nvr quite upsides: outpcd fnl 120yds* **12/1**

12 **3** 2 1/2 **Leqqaa (USA)**[28] 4091 2-9-0 0 RichardHills 5 91
(Mark Johnston) *led tl hdd over 2f out: sn drvn: lost 2nd over 1f out: one pce fnl f* **13/2**[3]

013 **4** 1 1/2 **Mister Music**[15] 4508 2-9-0 80 JMurtagh 7 87
(Richard Hannon) *chsd ldrs: rdn over 2f out: sn hanging lft and no ch w ldng trio* **8/1**

1 **5** 6 **Rougemont (IRE)**[36] 3823 2-9-0 0 RichardHughes 2 72
(Richard Hannon) *chsd ldrs: rdn over 2f out: sn btn* **5/2**[2]

0 **6** 10 **Foster's Road**[14] 4535 2-9-0 0 EddieAhern 4 47
(Mick Channon) *a in rr: rdn 3f out: sn lost tch* **25/1**

7 1/2 **Shivsingh** 2-8-11 0 MartinHarley 6 43
(Mick Channon) *in tch: rdn and green 3f out: sn btn* **33/1**

1m 26.44s (0.74) **Going Correction** +0.175s/f (Good) 7 Ran SP% **111.9**
Speed ratings (Par 102): **102,99,96,94,87 76,75**
toteswingers:1&2:£3.90, 2&3:£4.80, 1&3:£1.70 CSF £17.17 TOTE £2.20: £1.40, £5.00; EX 14.90.
Owner George Strawbridge **Bred** George Strawbridge Jr **Trained** Newmarket, Suffolk

FOCUS
An interesting juvenile Listed race, the best recent winner of which was the subsequent 2000 Guineas and Champion Stakes winner Haafhd. Big improvement from the winner, with the second and fourth the best guides.

NOTEBOOK
Fencing(USA) ◆, the first foal of a French Oaks winner who was a half-sister to the French Derby winner Lawman, had made a promising debut over 7f at Newmarket. Although the second in that race had been beaten since, he was heavily backed here and fully justified the support. He travelled well, if a little keenly, just off the pace but, once he ranged upsides the leader, was always going to win. The time was just over half a second quicker than the preceding handicap and he looks a good prospect. Although quoted at around 16-1 for next year's 2,000 Guineas after this, with his pedigree he appeals more for something like the Prix du Jockey Club rather than the Newmarket Classic. (op 5-2)
Telwaar, a winner on his second start but held in Listed races since, came into this rated 96 and ran pretty well, coming to challenge the winner before that rival found extra. He probably represents the guide to the level of this form. (op 10-1)
Leqqaa(USA), a $310,000 Derby entered half-brother to Zaham, had been narrowly beaten over C&D last month by Coupe De Ville. He made the running here and stayed on again once headed, looking as if longer trips will suit him in future. (op 7-2)
Mister Music, a winner over 7f on his second start before being beaten by a stablemate in a novice stakes next time, ran creditably but might have spoilt his handicap mark by finishing as close as he did. Johnny Murtagh reported that the colt hung left. Official explanation: jockey said colt hung left (op 9-1)
Rougemont(IRE) was easy in the market and folded pretty tamely after coming under pressure over 2f out. The form of his maiden win has not worked out but this was still disappointing. (op 2-1)

5045 CGA GEOFFREY FREER STKS (GROUP 3) 1m 5f 61y
3:05 (3:06) (Class 1) 3-Y-O+
£28,355 (£10,750; £5,380; £2,680; £1,345; £675) **Stalls** Low

Form RPR

-122 **1** **Census (IRE)**[37] 3772 3-8-6 105 RichardHughes 2 118
(Richard Hannon) *broke slowly: sn pushed along to chse ldrs: qcknd to ld appr fnl 3f: hrd drvn ins fnl f: styd on strly* **4/1**[3]

1115 **2** 1 1/4 **Brown Panther**[41] 3672 3-8-6 109 RichardKingscote 3 116
(Tom Dascombe) *hld up in rr: stdy hdwy fr 3f out: chsd wnr ins fnl 2f: sn drvn along: hung lft fnl f and kpt on clsng stages but no imp* **7/2**[2]

4112 **3** 4 1/2 **Times Up**[30] 4037 5-9-4 109 EddieAhern 1 110
(John Dunlop) *towards rr tl hdwy 3f out: disp 2nd over 2f out: one pce fr over 1f out* **6/1**

1233 **4** 3 **Buthelezi (USA)**[37] 3775 3-8-6 104 WilliamBuick 10 105
(John Gosden) *chsd ldrs: drvn along 4f out: hmpd and lost pl 3f out: rdn: hung lft and rallied over 1f out: styd on to take wl hld 4th ins fnl f* **9/1**

0-50 **5** 2 3/4 **Mores Wells**[30] 4037 7-9-4 113 (bt) GregoryBenoist 6 101
(M Delzangles, France) *in rr tl stdy hdwy to chse ldrs 3f out: chsd wnr briefly over 2f out: wknd over 1f out and lost wl hld 4th ins fnl f* **33/1**

40-0 **6** 3 1/4 **Alwaary (USA)**[49] 3403 5-9-4 99 MichaelHills 7 96
(John Gosden) *s.i.s: in rr: sme hdwy on ins over 3f out: sn n.m.r: no ch after but mod prog fnl f* **50/1**

-321 **7** 32 **Meeznah (USA)**[16] 4470 4-9-3 113 FrankieDettori 5 47
(David Lanigan) *chsd ldrs: hrd drvn over 3f out: sn btn: eased: t.o* **10/3**[1]

-364 **8** 4 **Yaseer (IRE)**[18] 4411 3-8-7 104 ow1 (b1) RichardHills 11 43
(Marcus Tregoning) *t.k.h: chsd ldr after 5f: rdn to chal over 3f out: n.m.r sn after and wknd qckly: eased t.o* **14/1**

0510 **9** 24 **Claremont (IRE)**[156] 826 5-9-4 110 (v) JMurtagh 9 —
(Mahmood Al Zarooni) *sn led: hdd appr 3f out: sn n.m.r on rails and wknd qckly: eased: t.o* **14/1**

56/4 **10** 16 **All The Aces (IRE)**[43] 3591 6-9-4 107 NeilCallan 8 —
(Roger Varian) *in tch: rdn 4f out: wknd 3f out: heavily eased 2f out* **14/1**

2m 48.46s (-3.54) **Going Correction** +0.075s/f (Good)
WFA 3 from 4yo+ 12lb 10 Ran SP% **114.5**
Speed ratings (Par 113): **113,112,109,107,105 103,84,81,67,57**
toteswingers:1&2:£4.10, 2&3:£6.00, 1&3:£6.20 CSF £18.03 TOTE £6.30: £2.30, £2.10, £1.90; EX 21.60 Trifecta £107.30 Pool: £6,389.58 - 44.05 winning units..
Owner Highclere Thoroughbred Racing (Beeswing) **Bred** Brian Williamson **Trained** East Everleigh, Wilts

FOCUS
This long-established Group 3 has been attracting bigger fields in recent years following a spell when four or five runners was the norm. Some classy types have taken this, not least last year's winner Sans Frontieres, the subsequent Irish St Leger victor. The time was decent, suggesting the ground was pretty good on the round course. A pair of unexposed 3yos pulled clear and the form looks solid.

NOTEBOOK
Census(IRE) ◆, a progressive sort who has won here and was touched off in a Group 3 last time, had a lot to find with the runner-up on Royal Ascot form. However, after missing the break slightly and being ridden to track the early pace, he came to challenge going well and ground it out in the style of a horse who will relish the test the St Leger trip sets. He was quoted at between 5-1 and 8-1 for that race. (tchd 9-2)
Brown Panther, another progressive colt, had won in good style at Royal Ascot before failing to make all on heavy ground in the Deutsches Derby. Stepping up in trip, he came to have every chance but appeared to be outstayed by the winner as he tended to drift in behind his rival in the last furlong. (op 4-1 tchd 3-1)
Times Up, a progressive stayer who was touched off in a 1m6f Group 2 in France last time, travelled well into contention but could not respond when the principals joined issue. He looks the best guide to the level. (op 5-1 tchd 9-2)
Buthelezi(USA) looked a useful handicapper in the spring at 1m2f but had been well beaten over 1m4f last time, his first try in Group company. He was up in trip again but did stay on steadily, without ever looking likely to trouble the first three. (op 16-1)
Mores Wells had won on his debut for this yard at Lyon in June but had finished behind today's third next time. Fitted with a tongue-tie and blinkers combination for the first time, he travelled well into the race but did not appear to get home. (op 22-1)
Alwaary(USA) promised a lot in 2009 but was off for over a year before returning in October 2010 and had been lightly raced since. Over the longest trip he had tried so far, he was noted staying on at the finish and all is not lost with him. (op 40-1)
Meeznah(USA), the disqualified 2010 Oaks runner-up, had rediscovered her form of late, winning 1m6f Group 3 last time. Taking on colts and geldings for the first time, she came under pressure fully half a mile from home, and was soon beaten. This was clearly not her running and Frankie Dettori reported that the filly ran flat. The stewards ordered the filly to be routine tested. Official explanation: jockey said filly ran flat (op 4-1)
Yaseer(IRE), in first-time blinkers, raced close to the pace before dropping away tamely around 3f out. Richard Hills reported that the colt ran too free and hung left. Official explanation: jockey said colt ran too free and hung left (op 11-1)
Claremont(IRE), having his first start since racing in Meydan early in the year, made the running but dropped out quickly once headed over 3f from home. Johnny Murtagh reported that the horse ran too free. Official explanation: jockey said horse ran too free (tchd 16-1)
All The Aces(IRE), having his second run back after a long absence, was under pressure and beaten soon after turning for home. (op 10-1)

5046 CGA HUNGERFORD STKS (GROUP 2) 7f (S)
3:40 (3:42) (Class 1) 3-Y-O+
£45,368 (£17,200; £8,608; £4,288; £2,152; £1,080) **Stalls** Centre

Form RPR

-213 **1** **Excelebration (IRE)**[60] 3011 3-8-13 117 AdamKirby 3 127+
(Marco Botti) *trckd ldr: led over 2f out: rdn 1f out: hung rt u.p ins fnl f but styd on to go clr fnl 100yds: readily* **5/4**[1]

5333 **2** 6 **Beacon Lodge (IRE)**[18] 4412 6-9-3 112 GeorgeBaker 7 111
(Clive Cox) *stdd s: in rr: hdwy 2f out: rdn and styd on wl fnl f to chse wnr fnl 75yds but nvr any ch* **8/1**[3]

2203 **3** 1/2 **Musir (AUS)**[110] 1576 5-9-3 118 PatCosgrave 11 110
(M F De Kock, South Africa) *pressed ldr: rdn and chsd wnr fr over 2f out: no imp fr over 1f out: one pce and lost 2nd fnl 75yds* **10/1**

1226 **4** 3/4 **Dubawi Gold**[60] 3011 3-8-11 117 JMurtagh 4 106+
(Richard Hannon) *t.k.h: stdd in tch: hdwy and nt clr run appr fnl 2f: swtchd lft wl over 1f out and styd on fnl f to cl on plcd horses but nvr any ch w wnr* **5/2**[2]

3245 **5** nk **Doncaster Rover (USA)**[18] 4412 5-9-3 109 EddieAhern 12 107
(David Brown) *in tch: rdn over 2f out: styd on ins fnl f but nvr any threat* **20/1**

2144 **6** hd **The Cheka (IRE)**[28] 4116 5-9-3 109 TomQueally 6 106
(Eve Johnson Houghton) *chsd ldrs: rdn over 2f out: nt qckn and styd on same pce fr over 1f out* **12/1**

0-00 **7** 5 **Balthazaar's Gift (IRE)**[18] 4412 8-9-3 109 PhilipRobinson 10 93
(Clive Cox) *s.i.s: in rr: rdn and little rspnse over 2f out* **33/1**

1160 **8** 8 **Perfect Tribute**[15] 4497 3-8-8 106 LukeMorris 8 66
(Clive Cox) *unruly in stalls: s.i.s: t.k.h and in tch 4f out* **16/1**

00-4 **9** 12 **Ceremonial Jade (UAE)**[19] 4392 8-9-3 81 WilliamBuick 5 39
(Marco Botti) *led: rdn along 3f out: hdd and btn over 2f out: eased whn no ch* **100/1**

1m 24.72s (-0.98) **Going Correction** +0.175s/f (Good)
WFA 3 from 4yo+ 6lb 9 Ran SP% **115.5**
Speed ratings (Par 115): **112,105,104,103,103 103,97,88,74**
CSF £12.15 TOTE £2.60: £1.10, £1.80, £2.10; EX 13.80 Trifecta £33.40 Pool: £9,778.39 - 216.47 winning units..
Owner Giuliano Manfredini **Bred** Owenstown Stud **Trained** Newmarket, Suffolk

FOCUS
A strong renewal of this Group 2 whose best recent winner was subsequent triple Group 1 scorer Paco Boy. Excelebration could be rated higher but are doubts over which of his rivals were at their best.

NOTEBOOK
Excelebration(IRE) ◆ ran away with the German 2000 Guineas in between taking on Frankel in the Greenham and the St James's Palace, and was a well-backed favourite. Given a good lead by Ceremonial Jade, it was clear when he hit the front at around the quarter-mile pole that all of his rivals were in trouble. He found plenty for pressure, scooting away to win by a wide margin, paying yet another compliment to Frankel. The time was 1.72 secs faster than the quicker of the earlier races over the trip. Excelebration has been one of the few horses to give Frankel any sort of race this season and he is clearly a high-class performer in his own right. His trainer jokingly suggested he might take that colt on again at Ascot, but he also has the option of going to France, with the Prix du Moulin or the Foret very feasible targets. (op 7-4)
Beacon Lodge(IRE) is a very consistent performer at this sort of level and ran his race again without ever looking like troubling the winner. He is a sound guide to the level of the form and deserves to pick up another group race before long. (op 7-1)
Musir(AUS) was having his first run since finishing a close third in a Group 1 in Sha Tin in April. He ran pretty well, although no match for the winner, and this should set him up for an autumn/winter campaign. (op 6-1)
Dubawi Gold, another who has had to chase Frankel's tail a couple of times this season, had a bit to find with today's winner on Royal Ascot form, and like that colt, was having his first start since. He was held up but ran into traffic problems when trying to get through and could make no headway in the last furlong. He is better than this effort indicates. (op 3-1)
Doncaster Rover(USA) is a reliable sort and he ran almost to the pound with today's runner-up compared with their Goodwood running. He can win again at a slightly lower level. (op 16-1)
The Cheka(IRE) has not really built on his decisive Haydock win in May. (tchd 10-1 and 14-1 in a place)
Balthazaar's Gift(IRE), who took this race in 2009, but he has not yet hit form this season and failed to figure. (op 20-1)
Perfect Tribute missed the break and then got involved in the scrimmaging with Dubawi Gold. She was probably out of her depth at this level in any case. (op 20-1)

5047 BATHWICK TYRES EUROPEAN BREEDERS' FUND MAIDEN FILLIES' STKS (DIV I) 6f 8y
4:15 (4:15) (Class 4) 2-Y-O **£4,075** (£1,212; £606; £303) **Stalls** Centre

Form RPR

1 **Dreamwriter (USA)** 2-9-0 0 JimmyFortune 10 90+
(Richard Hannon) *s.i.s: in rr: stl last 2f out swtchd lft and rapid hdwy over 1f out: led jst ins fnl f: edgd rt: sn clr: easily* **14/1**

0 **2** 6 **Chapellerie (IRE)**[12] 4614 2-9-0 0 JMurtagh 2 72
(Brian Meehan) *trckd ldrs tl lost position over 2f out: swtchd sharply lft wl over 1f out: styd on ins fnl f to take 2nd fnl 120yds but nvr nr easy wnr* **6/1**[3]

3 1/2 **Serene Oasis (IRE)** 2-8-11 0 MartinHarley(3) 1 71
(Mick Channon) *pressed ldrs: led ins fnl 2f: narrowly hdd 1f out: styd chsng wnr sn after: one pce into 3rd fnl 120yds* **20/1**

02 **4** 2 **Lulla**[17] 4427 2-9-0 0 (t) FrankieDettori 6 65
(Marcus Tregoning) *led tl hdd over 3f out: styd pressing ldrs and led again briefly 1f out: sn hdd: wknd fnl 120yds* **5/4**[1]

6 **5** *1 ¾* **Roman Seal (IRE)**[50] 4342 2-9-0 0 .... RichardKingscote 8 59
(Tom Dascombe) *in rr but in tch: hdwy whn hmpd wl over 1f out: styd on ins fnl f but nvr any ch* **16/1**

6 *½* **Whimsical (IRE)** 2-9-0 0 .... RichardHughes 5 58+
(Richard Hannon) *slowly away: in rr: hdwy and in tch 1/2-way: chsd ldrs and pushed along over 1f out: wknd ins fnl f* **3/1**[2]

0 **7** *1 ½* **Deduction (IRE)**[17] 4427 2-8-9 0 .... MatthewLawson(5) 4 53
(B W Hills) *chsd ldrs: led over 3f out: hdd ins fnl 2f: wknd ins fnl f* **8/1**

00 **8** *7* **Periwinkle Way**[19] 4386 2-9-0 0 .... NeilCallan 7 32
(Sylvester Kirk) *spd over 3f* **40/1**

06 **9** *5* **Camrock Star (IRE)**[23] 4245 2-9-0 0 .... WilliamBuick 3 17
(William Knight) *unruly in stalls: in rr: lost tch fnl 2f* **22/1**

1m 14.18s (1.18) **Going Correction** +0.175s/f (Good) 9 Ran SP% **118.9**
Speed ratings (Par 93): **99,91,90,87,85 84,82,73,66**

CSF £95.52 TOTE £9.60: £2.30, £1.60, £3.60; EX 97.70 TRIFECTA Not won..

Owner Axom XXIX **Bred** Coffee Pot Stable **Trained** East Everleigh, Wilts

FOCUS
The first division of this fillies' maiden in which 2009 scorer and subsequent Listed winner Queen's Grace apart, most of the recent winners had failed to build on victory here. Unlike earlier in the day, the field came to race up the stands' rail and the time was 0.39 secs faster than the second division. The winner was very impressive and could be smart.

NOTEBOOK
Dreamwriter(USA) ◆, a $50,000 half-sister to three winners including Doncaster Rover, who had run well in the earlier Group 2, put up a visually stunning performance. The stable's second string on jockey bookings, she was a market drifter and missed the break. She was still last of all with 2f to go, but then cut her way through the field so quickly that she was in front just inside the final furlong and shot away to score with her rider barely having to move a muscle. There was a feeling that the leaders may have gone too fast, but two of them finished in the frame, so it remains to be seen how good this performance was. (op 9-1)

Chapellerie(IRE), a half-sister to the Goodwood winner Catfish, is entered in the Group1 Cheveley Park. She built on her fair effort in a Windsor maiden at the beginning of the month, having her chance and keeping on well for pressure. Although that Group 1 entry looks optimistic, she should win races. (tchd 11-2 and 13-2)

Serene Oasis(IRE), an 18,000gns half-sister to a 7f juvenile winner, made an encouraging debut, coming through to challenge around 2f out and sticking to her task to the line. She should improve for the experience. (op 12-1)

Lulla, whose dam won the King's Stand, had improved on her debut when runner-up over 6f at Goodwood. She made the early running up the rail but was taken on for the lead by Deduction. She still seemed to be going well 2f out but could not pick up off the bridle. She might be worth dropping back to 5f. (op 11-8 tchd 11-10 and 6-4 in places)

Roman Seal(IRE), a 65,000 euros half-sister to a 6f soft-ground winner, had been outpaced on her debut but the easier ground here was expected to suit. She ran better and can make her mark in handicaps after one more outing. (op 20-1)

Whimsical(IRE), a 76,000euros first foal of a 5f winner, was the stable first string on this debut and was backed against the favourite. However, she missed the break and, despite making headway after halfway, ended up more towards the centre of the track and faded in the last furlong. She should improve for the experience. (op 5-1 tchd 11-2)

Camrock Star(IRE)'s rider reported that the filly reared in the stalls. Official explanation: jockey said filly reared in stalls (op 14-1)

5048 BATHWICK TYRES EUROPEAN BREEDERS' FUND MAIDEN FILLIES' STKS (DIV II) 6f 8y

4:50 (4:51) (Class 4) 2-Y-O **£4,075** (£1,212; £606; £303) **Stalls** Centre

Form RPR

1 **Gray Pearl** 2-9-0 0 .... MichaelHills 10 84+
(B W Hills) *s.i.s: in rr tl stdy hdwy fr 2f out to ld over 1f out: pushed along fnl 120yds: comf* **2/1**[1]

2 *2* **Ziefhd** 2-9-0 0 .... NeilCallan 4 78+
(Paul Cole) *in tch: pushed along and styd on wl ins fnl f to take 2nd last strides but no ch w comfortable wnr* **7/1**

3 *nk* **She Spirit Di Su (IRE)** 2-9-0 0 .... JimmyFortune 7 77
(Peter Chapple-Hyam) *led tl hdd 3f out: styd front rnk and rallied to chse wnr fnl 120yds: nvr any ch and ct for 2nd last strides* **7/1**

4 *3* **Little Rainbow** 2-9-0 0 .... AdamKirby 8 68
(Clive Cox) *chsd ldr: led 3f out: hdd over 1f out: sn outpcd and dropped 2 pls fnl 120yds* **14/1**

3 **5** *3 ½* **Dance Company**[29] 4052 2-9-0 0 .... WilliamBuick 2 58
(William Knight) *s.i.s: in rr tl hdwy to press ldrs over 2f out: sn rdn and btn* **11/4**[2]

6 *10* **Sugar Loaf** 2-9-0 0 .... LukeMorris 9 28
(William Muir) *chsd ldrs 3f: sn dropped away* **16/1**

7 *1 ¾* **Princess Of Rock** 2-9-0 0 .... RichardHughes 1 22
(Richard Hannon) *s.i.s: sn in tch: wknd qckly over 2f out* **9/2**[3]

1m 14.59s (1.59) **Going Correction** +0.175s/f (Good) 35 Ran SP% **115.7**
Speed ratings (Par 93): **96,93,92,88,84 70,68**
toteswingers:1&2:£4.90, 2&3:£7.70, 1&3:£3.30 CSF £17.17 TOTE £3.60: £2.10, £5.20; EX 26.70 Trifecta £129.50 Pool: £1,203.08 - 6.87 winning units..

Owner H R Mould **Bred** T E Pocock **Trained** Lambourn, Berks

FOCUS
The second leg of this fillies' maiden was run 0.39secs slower than the first. There was little form to go on, but the form is rated quite positively.

NOTEBOOK
Gray Pearl ◆, a 95,000gns half-sister to three winners, was a well-backed favourite on this debut and scored in comfortable fashion. Held up early travelling well, she moved up smoothly to join issue and lengthened nicely to hold the late finishers. She looks to have a fair bit of size about her and can be expected to progress from this debut. She is entered in a valuable sales race at the Doncaster St Leger meeting, and that could fit in nicely as her next target. (op 3-1)

Ziefhd ◆, a half-sister to a 7f juvenile winner out of a 6f-1m winner who scored at Listed level, stayed on late on this debut. She should benefit from the experience and longer trips will be in her favour in future. (op 15-2 tchd 8-1)

She Spirit Di Su(IRE), a 46,000euros yearling who was retained for 80,000gns at the breeze-ups, is related to several decent winners in Italy. She showed good early pace and then rallied well under pressure. She should have races in her on this evidence. (op 11-2)

Little Rainbow, the first foal of 7f-1m winner, was another to show good speed until fading in the last furlong. She is another who can win races if building on this. (op 10-1)

Dance Company had made a promising debut over C&D behind a well-regarded sort, but the form of those behind had not worked out. The market signals were not good and then she rather played up in the stalls before missing the break. She seemed to travel well enough to about halfway but, when her rider asked for an effort, there was little response. This was disappointing and she now has questions to answer. (op 10-3 tchd 7-2)

5049 COLLINGWOOD FIRST ERVICE LTD H'CAP 1m 2f 6y

5:20 (5:20) (Class 4) (0-85,84) 3-Y-O **£5,175** (£1,154; £1,154; £384) **Stalls** Low

Form RPR

021 **1** **Anatolian**[26] 4157 3-9-5 **82** .... FrankieDettori 5 103+
(Mahmood Al Zarooni) *trckd ldrs: led over 2f out: pushed clr ins fnl f: easily* **9/2**[3]

0431 **2** *3 ½* **Silken Thoughts**[13] 4584 3-8-6 **69** .... FergusSweeney 2 81
(John Berry) *in rr but in tch: hdwy 3f out: chsd wnr 1f out but nvr any ch: one pce and jnd for 2nd last stride* **10/1**

-241 **2** *dht* **Mountain Range (IRE)**[23] 4253 3-9-5 **82** .... RichardHughes 1 94+
(John Dunlop) *in tch: pushed along fr 4f out: swtchd rt and styd on ins fnl f to dead hd for 2nd last stride: nvr any ch w wnr* **4/1**[2]

4414 **4** *8* **El Muqbil (IRE)**[14] 4553 3-9-6 **83** .... (t) RichardHills 6 79
(Brian Meehan) *led: rdn and hdd over 2f out: wknd rapidly 1f out* **7/1**

-406 **5** *¾* **Levantera (IRE)**[54] 3233 3-7-13 **67** .... RyanPowell(5) 8 62
(Clive Cox) *chsd ldr to 3f out: wknd appr fnl 2f* **25/1**

-310 **6** *½* **Aldedash (USA)**[92] 2076 3-8-13 **76** .... EddieAhern 11 70
(Sir Henry Cecil) *in rr: rdn and stl wl bhd fr 3f out: mod prog ins fnl f* **20/1**

035 **7** *shd* **Little Cottonsocks**[20] 4356 3-8-10 **73** .... (t) LukeMorris 9 66
(Clive Cox) *rdn over 3f out whn rr: mod prog fnl f* **25/1**

1341 **8** *5* **Shamdarley (IRE)**[33] 3904 3-9-3 **80** .... JMurtagh 7 63
(Michael Dods) *t.k.h towards rr: sme hdwy 4f out: sn rdn and btn* **8/1**

5663 **9** *3* **Muntasib (USA)**[20] 4355 3-9-5 **82** .... WilliamBuick 10 59
(Marcus Tregoning) *trckd ldrs on outside: rdn and hung rt 3f out: fnd nthing and sn btn* **7/1**

6-1 **10** *10* **Dumbarton (IRE)**[19] 4388 3-9-7 **84** .... JimmyFortune 4 58
(Sir Michael Stoute) *plld hrd: chsd ldrs tl wknd fr 4f out: eased whn no ch* **7/2**[1]

2m 8.84s (0.04) **Going Correction** +0.075s/f (Good) 10 Ran SP% **118.1**
Speed ratings (Par 102): **102,99,99,92,92 91,91,87,85,77**PL: Mountain Range £1.70, Silken Thoughts £3.60 EX: Anatolian/MR £11.28 A/ST £23.95 TRI: A/MR/ST £84.61 A/ST/MR £96.74. toteswingers: 1&MR £2.70, 1&ST £5.80, MR&ST £7.50 Trifecta: 5,6,10 £108.10 5,10,6 £112.70 CSF £23.95 CT £96.74 TOTE £5.90: £2.00; EX 34.50 27.

FOCUS
A fair but quite competitive 3-y-o handicap which often falls to an improving type. They did not appear to go that quick, and that was backed up by the time, but they still finished fairly well strung out. The first three finished clear and the form is rated around Silken Thoughts.
Shamdarley(IRE) Official explanation: jockey said gelding felt wrong behind
Dumbarton(IRE) Official explanation: jockey said colt ran too free

5050 UK HYGIENE LADIES DERBY H'CAP (FOR LADY AMATEUR RIDERS) 1m 4f 5y

5:55 (5:55) (Class 4) (0-80,79) 3-Y-O+ **£3,743** (£1,161; £580; £290) **Stalls** Low

Form RPR

2143 **1** **Covert Decree**[11] 4625 3-9-3 **73** .... MissRachelKing(3) 5 86
(Clive Cox) *trckd clr ldr: led appr fnl 3f: pushed out fnl f: readily* **7/1**

1060 **2** *3* **High On A Hill (IRE)**[36] 3794 4-10-2 **77** .... MissCBoxall(5) 6 85
(Sylvester Kirk) *chsd ldrs in 3rd: chsd wnr 2f out: kpt on but no imp fnl f* **7/1**

2362 **3** *3 ½* **Mrs Neat (IRE)**[13] 4579 3-8-13 **66** .... (p) MissSBrotherton 7 68
(Sylvester Kirk) *in rr but in tch bhd clr ldrs: hdwy 3f out: styd on to take one pce 3rd over 1f out* **7/2**[1]

-005 **4** *6* **Sula Two**[12] 4613 4-9-10 **71** .... MissBeckyBrisbourne(5) 1 64
(Ron Hodges) *in rr: pushed along and hdwy over 3f out: styd on to take one pce 4th 1f out* **7/1**

00-5 **5** *9* **Eastern Paramour (IRE)**[17] 4432 6-10-2 **77** .... MissJennyCarr(5) 8 55
(Rod Millman) *led: sn clr: hdd appr fnl 3f: wknd 2f out* **9/2**[2]

0052 **6** *4 ½* **Overrule (USA)**[22] 4294 7-10-4 **79** .... MissHBethell(5) 3 50
(Brian Ellison) *in rr: sme prog 4f out but nvr nr clr ldrs: no ch fnl 3f and hung rt fnl f* **9/2**[2]

1533 **7** *nk* **New Code**[30] 4008 4-10-4 **79** .... MissHayleyMoore(5) 4 50
(Gary Moore) *a wl bhd: no ch whn hung rt fnl f* **11/2**[3]

10-0 **8** *28* **Venir Rouge**[44] 3546 7-9-6 **67** .... MissJessicaLodge(5) 2 —
(Matthew Salaman) *a bhd: lost tch 4f out: t.o* **20/1**

2m 36.09s (0.59) **Going Correction** +0.075s/f (Good)
WFA 3 from 4yo+ 11lb 8 Ran SP% **116.2**
Speed ratings (Par 105): **101,99,96,92,86 83,83,64**
toteswingers:1&2:£12.80, 2&3:£3.70, 1&3:£5.60 CSF £55.57 CT £201.60 TOTE £8.30: £2.30, £3.00, £1.30; EX 71.70 TRIFECTA Not won..
Owner Lakes Bathrooms Ltd **Bred** A M Tombs **Trained** Lambourn, Berks

FOCUS
An ordinary handicap for lady amateur riders and, although the pace appeared nothing special and the time was modest, the field was well strung out early. The runner-up sets the standard.
T/Plt: £547.80 to a £1 stake. Pool of £141,090.00 - 188.00 winning tickets. T/Qpdt: £42.90 to a £1 stake. Pool of £7,038.32 - 121.35 winning tickets. ST

5011 NEWMARKET (R-H)

Saturday, August 13

OFFICIAL GOING: Good (7.8)
Wind: Light half-behind Weather: Overcast

5051 EBF COCKNEY REBEL MAIDEN STKS 6f

1:40 (1:40) (Class 4) 2-Y-O **£5,175** (£1,540; £769; £384) **Stalls** High

Form RPR

1 **Tidentime (USA)** 2-9-3 0 .... TedDurcan 2 80
(Mick Channon) *chsd ldrs: rdn over 1f out: r.o to ld nr fin* **16/1**

0 **2** *nk* **Out Do**[21] 4347 2-9-3 0 .... KierenFallon 4 79
(Luca Cumani) *led: edgd rt 1/2-way: rdn over 1f out: hung lft ins fnl f: hdd nr fin* **10/3**[2]

2 **3** *1 ¼* **Go Dutch (IRE)**[15] 4507 2-9-3 0 .... JackMitchell 5 75
(Roger Varian) *w ldr: edgd rt 1/2-way: rdn and ev ch over 1f out: styd on same pce ins fnl f* **6/4**[1]

4 *½* **Rawaafed (IRE)** 2-9-3 0 .... MartinDwyer 7 74+
(Brian Meehan) *chsd ldrs: pushed along 1/2-way: n.m.r ins fnl f: styd on* **4/1**[3]

5 *7* **Nelson's Bay** 2-9-3 0 .... ShaneKelly 3 53+
(Brian Meehan) *s.i.s: hld up: pushed along 1/2-way: wknd over 1f out* **40/1**

6 *1* **Ruscello (IRE)** 2-9-3 0 .... PatDobbs 1 50+
(Sir Michael Stoute) *s.i.s: sn prom: pushed along 1/2-way: wknd over 1f out* **17/2**

7 *8* **Alnoomaas (IRE)** 2-9-3 0 .... JimCrowley 6 26
(Roger Varian) *hld up: wknd 2f out* **7/1**

1m 13.73s (1.23) **Going Correction** +0.05s/f (Good) **7** Ran SP% **114.4**
Speed ratings (Par 96): **93,92,90,90,80 79,68**
Tote Swingers: 1&2 £4.80, 1&3 £5.20, 2&3 £1.60 CSF £68.56 TOTE £15.30: £5.20, £2.20; EX 67.20.
Owner Jon and Julia Aisbitt **Bred** Big C Farms **Trained** West Ilsley, Berks

FOCUS
Repositioning of bend from Beacon Course to far-side course increased distance of 1m2f and 1m4f races by 16m. Far side track used with stalls on far side except 1m2f and 1m4f centre. The ground was described as good but the winning jockey in the opener thought it was a bit loose on top. There was not much previous form to go on, but in all likelihood this was just an ordinary race of its type for the track. The first four finished clear and the time was around three and a half seconds outside the standard.

NOTEBOOK
Tidentime(USA) came with a sustained challenge down the outside and stuck his head in front close home to make a winning debut. A 75,000gns buy, and half-brother to a couple of winners in the USA, he should get at least another furlong. He holds engagements in all the big sales races later in the season. (op 12-1 tchd 11-1)
Out Do disappointed on his debut at York but knew much more here. After seeing off the favourite he hung a little to his left inside the last and could not repel the winner. (op 5-1)
Go Dutch(IRE) set a useful standard on his debut second over C&D last month. Matching strides with the runner-up, he was being niggled along with over two to run and could not quicken up when required. The loose ground might not have suited him. (op 5-4 tchd 13-8 in places)
Rawaafed(IRE) ◆ was keeping on near the finish without being subjected to a hard time and should be much more polished with this experience behind him. A first British runner for Dubai World Cup winner Invasor, he cost a tidy $300,000 as a yearling and has been entered in the Champagne Stakes and Racing Post Trophy. (op 5-1 tchd 11-2)
Nelson's Bay was never a factor but should be able to step up on the bare form. (op 25-1)
Ruscello(IRE) was a little green, and coltish beforehand, but he's from a decent family and should be capable of better over further in the future. (op 8-1 tchd 9-1)
Alnoomaas(IRE), the favourite's stablemate, offered little. (op 8-1)

5052 LIVE IN-PLAY FOOTBALL ON SKYBET MOBILE FILLIES' NURSERY 7f

2:15 (2:15) (Class 2) 2-Y-O **£10,350** (£3,080; £1,539; £769) **Stalls** High

Form RPR

12 **1** **Pimpernel (IRE)**[30] 4001 2-9-7 **90** .... KierenFallon 9 97
(Mahmood Al Zarooni) *hld up: racd keenly: hdwy over 2f out: led over 1f out: rdn out* **8/1**

31 **2** *3/4* **Salford Art (IRE)**[12] 4614 2-8-11 **80** .... DaneO'Neill 2 85
(David Elsworth) *hld up: rdn over 3f out: hdwy over 1f out: hung lft ins fnl f: r.o u.p: wnt 2nd post: nt rch wnr* **11/4**[1]

51 **3** *hd* **Nimiety**[79] 2430 2-8-2 **71** .... JimmyQuinn 10 76
(Mark Johnston) *led: rdn and hdd over 1f out: styd on: lost 2nd post* **15/2**[3]

210 **4** *4* **Glee**[15] 4496 2-8-9 **78** .... PatDobbs 5 73
(Richard Hannon) *w ldr tl pushed along over 2f out: rdn over 1f out: hung lft and wknd ins fnl f* **8/1**

501 **5** *3/4* **Winter Hill**[18] 4406 2-7-11 **69** .... HarryBentley(3) 7 62
(Tom Dascombe) *trckd ldrs: plld hrd: rdn over 3f out: wknd ins fnl f* **9/1**

4105 **6** *2 3/4* **Mention (IRE)**[14] 4551 2-8-9 **78** .... ShaneKelly 4 64
(Brian Meehan) *prom: rdn over 2f out: wkng whn hung lft ins fnl f* **7/1**[2]

210 **7** *2 1/2* **Royal Blush**[15] 4496 2-8-5 **74** .... MartinDwyer 6 54
(Paul Cole) *mid-div: hdwy 1/2-way: rdn and wknd over 1f out* **10/1**

035 **8** *1 3/4* **Emperors Pearl (IRE)**[28] 4087 2-8-1 **70** .... WilliamCarson 8 45
(B W Hills) *chsd ldrs tl rdn over 2f out: wknd over 1f out* **9/1**

4314 **9** *1 3/4* **Imelda Mayhem**[14] 4551 2-8-6 **75** .... LiamKeniry 3 46
(J S Moore) *hld up: rdn over 2f out: a in rr* **8/1**

0146 **10** *3* **Lady Victory (IRE)**[22] 4277 2-8-1 **70** .... CathyGannon 1 33
(Mick Channon) *wnt rt s: hld up: rdn over 2f out: sn wknd* **25/1**

1m 25.67s (-0.03) **Going Correction** +0.05s/f (Good) **10** Ran SP% **117.2**
Speed ratings (Par 97): **102,101,100,96,95 92,89,87,85,82**
Tote Swingers: 1&2 £1.00, 1&3 £4.70, 2&3 £2.00 CSF £30.43 CT £179.61 TOTE £6.10: £2.10, £1.50, £2.30; EX 17.60 Trifecta £38.90 Pool: £399.98 - 7.60 winning units..
Owner Godolphin **Bred** Peter Harris **Trained** Newmarket, Suffolk

FOCUS
A decent nursery confined to fillies and all but one of the runners had won races. The pace was only modest. The first three finished clear and showed useful form.

NOTEBOOK
Pimpernel(IRE) was conceding at least 10lb to her rivals. Held up and taking quite a tug, she was pulled off the rail to challenge and found enough once showing ahead. Out of a mare who won at 1m2f and is a half-sister to Derby runner-up Eagle Mountain, she saw out the longer trip well. (op 6-1)
Salford Art(IRE) ◆, a well regarded filly, was being niggled along by halfway and appeared held soon afterwards, but she found her stride in the final furlong and came home in good style. The extra furlong was to her liking and she can gain compensation. (op 10-3 tchd 7-2)
Nimiety had not run since winning her maiden in May. She showed plenty of pace near the rail but stuck on when headed, suggesting that the longer trip suited this relatively stoutly bred filly. (op 6-1)
Glee raced more prominently than she had at Goodwood and disputed the overall lead down the centre of the track. She could only stick on at the one pace when let down. (op 10-1)
Winter Hill, a Beverley maiden winner, was another who was outpaced by the principals in the latter stages. (tchd 10-1)
Mention(IRE) ought to have been suited by the longer trip, but she was on the retreat in the final furlong. (op 11-1)
Royal Blush, who did not find much when let down, finished a similar distance behind Glee than she had at Goodwood, where her saddle had slipped early. (op 9-1)
Imelda Mayhem was reported to have been in season. Official explanation: trainer said filly was in season

5053 SKY BET GREY HORSE H'CAP (FOR GREY HORSES ONLY) 6f

2:45 (2:45) (Class 4) (0-85,85) 3-Y-O+ **£12,450** (£3,728; £1,864; £932; £466; £234) **Stalls** High

Form RPR

2001 **1** **Time Medicean**[43] 3573 5-8-2 **70** .... RaulDaSilva(7) 7 81
(Tony Carroll) *hld up: swtchd rt over 1f out: sn rdn: r.o wl ins fnl f: hung lft and led towards fin* **11/1**

5000 **2** *1* **Tadalavil**[26] 4145 6-8-1 **62** .... MartinLane 11 70
(Linda Perratt) *chsd ldrs: led over 2f out: rdn over 1f out: edgd lft: hdd towards fin* **40/1**

000- **3** *1 1/2* **Quarrel (USA)**[287] 7238 4-8-8 **72** ....[1] AdamBeschizza(3) 1 75
(Julia Feilden) *hld up: hdwy over 1f out: sn rdn: hung lft ins fnl f: r.o* **12/1**

3004 **4** *nse* **Silver Rime (FR)**[21] 4325 6-9-10 **85** .... TedDurcan 16 88
(Linda Perratt) *s.i.s: hld up: hdwy over 1f out: sn rdn: r.o* **11/1**

2214 **5** *1/2* **Rylee Mooch**[10] 4669 3-8-1 **73** ....(e) CharlesEddery(7) 4 74
(Richard Guest) *led over 3f: rdn over 1f out: styd on same pce* **20/1**

3301 **6** *nk* **Witchry**[28] 4086 9-8-5 **66** .... MartinDwyer 13 66
(Tony Newcombe) *hld up: rdn and r.o ins fnl f: nt rch ldrs* **8/1**[2]

3520 **7** *nk* **Berbice (IRE)**[14] 4539 6-8-6 **67** .... KellyHarrison 2 66
(Linda Perratt) *s.i.s: hld up: hdwy over 1f out: r.o: nt rch ldrs* **33/1**

663 **8** *nk* **Tislaam (IRE)**[3] 4909 4-8-0 **64** ....(p) KieranO'Neill(3) 5 62
(Alan McCabe) *mid-div: hdwy 2f out: sn rdn: styng on same pce whn n.m.r towards fin* **10/1**

-336 **9** *1* **Sutton Veny (IRE)**[18] 4416 5-9-9 **84** .... DaneO'Neill 10 79
(Jeremy Gask) *hld up: hdwy over 1f out: sn rdn: styng on same pce whn hmpd towards fin* **13/2**[1]

0010 **10** *hd* **Lady Florence**[8] 4742 6-8-1 **62** ....(p) JimmyQuinn 19 57
(David C Griffiths) *chsd ldrs: rdn over 2f out: no ex ins fnl f* **50/1**

2604 **11** *hd* **Den's Gift (IRE)**[21] 4310 7-9-0 **80** ....(b) LucyKBarry(5) 20 74
(Clive Cox) *chsd ldrs: rdn over 1f out: no ex ins fnl f* **9/1**[3]

0006 **12** *3/4* **Zowington**[60] 3020 9-7-11 **61** ....(v) HarryBentley(3) 6 52
(Stuart Williams) *hld up: nt clr run over 1f out: nvr nrr* **20/1**

50-0 **13** *1/2* **Whitechapel**[23] 4255 4-8-9 **70** .... LiamKeniry 14 60
(Andrew Balding) *s.i.s: hdwy over 4f out: rdn and nt clr run over 1f out: no ex ins fnl f* **25/1**

5523 **14** *nk* **Kinigi (IRE)**[11] 4628 5-8-5 **66** ....(b) CathyGannon 9 55
(Ronald Harris) *hld up in tch: rdn and edgd lft over 1f out: wknd ins fnl f* **33/1**

0644 **15** *3 1/2* **Sunshine Always (IRE)**[23] 4243 5-8-8 **69** .... ShaneKelly 3 47
(Michael Attwater) *prom: rdn over 2f out: wknd over 1f out* **16/1**

-006 **16** *1 1/2* **Sarah's Art (IRE)**[63] 2903 8-8-10 **71** ....(t) JimCrowley 17 44
(Stef Higgins) *hld up: rdn over 2f out: a in rr* **11/1**

5056 **17** *nse* **Emma's Gift (IRE)**[22] 4265 3-9-1 **85** .... TobyAtkinson(5) 8 58
(Julia Feilden) *sn pushed along and a in rr* **16/1**

4211 **18** *1 3/4* **Clear Ice (IRE)**[8] 4742 4-8-12 **73** ....(b) KierenFallon 15 40
(Gay Kelleway) *chsd ldrs: rdn whn hmpd over 1f out: sn wknd* **13/2**[1]

120 **19** *1/2* **Admirable Duchess**[18] 4416 4-9-7 **82** .... JamesDoyle 18 48
(Dominic Ffrench Davis) *prom: rdn over 2f out: wknd over 1f out* **18/1**

1m 11.96s (-0.54) **Going Correction** +0.05s/f (Good)
WFA 3 from 4yo+ 4lb **19** Ran SP% **130.2**
Speed ratings (Par 105): **105,103,101,101,100 100,100,99,98,98 97,96,96,95,91 89,89,86,86**
Tote Swingers: 1&2 £0.00, 1&3 £96.90, 2&3 £80.80 CSF £419.31 CT £5446.14 TOTE £15.30: £3.90, £14.30, £4.30, £3.30; EX 2371.90 TRIFECTA Not won..
Owner A W Carroll **Bred** C A Cyzer **Trained** Cropthorne, Worcs

FOCUS
The ninth running of this popular novelty event and the biggest field so far. It was something of a messy race with a number finding trouble in running and they finished in a bit of a heap, although the result was unaffected. The winner built on his Beverley win.
Sunshine Always(IRE) Official explanation: jockey said gelding was unsuited by the good ground
Clear Ice(IRE) Official explanation: jockey said gelding ran too free

5054 PREMIER LEAGUE KICK OFF ON SKYBET MOBILE STKS (H'CAP) 6f

3:20 (3:20) (Class 2) (0-105,104) 3-Y-O **£24,900** (£7,456; £3,728; £1,864; £932; £468) **Stalls** High

Form RPR

1315 **1** **Bertiewhittle**[16] 4472 3-7-12 **84** .... HarryBentley(3) 8 98
(David Barron) *hld up: hdwy and nt clr run over 1f out: rdn to ld wl ins fnl f: r.o* **8/1**[2]

1006 **2** *1* **Elusive Prince**[21] 4333 3-8-0 **83** ....(v[1]) CathyGannon 1 94
(David Barron) *chsd ldrs: rdn to ld 1f out: hdd wl ins fnl f* **16/1**

4111 **3** *nk* **Louis The Pious**[21] 4324 3-8-5 **88** .... JimmyQuinn 2 98
(Kevin Ryan) *hld up: rdn over 1f out: r.o wl ins fnl f: nt rch ldrs* **8/1**[2]

2224 **4** *hd* **Elusivity (IRE)**[29] 4062 3-7-12 **84** .... LouisBeuzelin(3) 17 93
(Brian Meehan) *hld up: hdwy over 2f out: rdn and ev ch ins fnl f: unable qck towards fin* **10/1**[3]

1104 **5** *shd* **Barnet Fair**[21] 4333 3-8-6 **89** .... LiamKeniry 16 98
(Richard Guest) *hld up: hdwy over 2f out: rdn and ev ch whn edgd rt ins fnl f: styd on same pce* **14/1**

0124 **6** *1 1/2* **Lexi's Hero (IRE)**[13] 4573 3-9-6 **103** .... DarryllHolland 13 107
(Kevin Ryan) *led: rdn and edgd rt over 1f out: sn hdd: styd on same pce ins fnl f* **11/1**

3331 **7** *1 1/4* **Levitate**[6] 4817 3-7-10 **82** 6ex ....(p) KieranO'Neill(3) 6 82
(Alan McCabe) *chsd ldrs: rdn 1/2-way: outpcd over 2f out: r.o ins fnl f* **8/1**[2]

2162 **8** *1/2* **Rothesay Chancer**[7] 4791 3-7-5 **81** oh4 .... NoelGarbutt(7) 10 79
(Jim Goldie) *hld up: hdwy over 1f out: rdn whn n.m.r ins fnl f: styd on same pce* **33/1**

6013 **9** *shd* **Flynn's Boy**[14] 4550 3-7-12 **81** oh2 .... JamieMackay 3 79
(Rae Guest) *hld up: hdwy over 1f out: sn rdn: no ex ins fnl f* **16/1**

-312 **10** *1/2* **Bless You**[31] 3985 3-8-1 **84** .... FrankieMcDonald 18 80
(Henry Candy) *prom: rdn over 1f out: no ex ins fnl f* **12/1**

5100 **11** *1* **Mr Optimistic**[21] 4333 3-8-1 **84** .... MartinLane 15 77
(Richard Fahey) *hld up: rdn over 2f out: nvr on terms* **33/1**

3251 **12** *1/2* **Blanche Dubawi (IRE)**[20] 4353 3-8-5 **88** .... LiamJones 9 80
(Noel Quinlan) *trckd ldrs: plld hrd: hmpd over 1f out: wknd ins fnl f* **13/2**[1]

2020 **13** *2 1/2* **King Of Jazz (IRE)**[16] 4472 3-9-4 **101** .... PatDobbs 11 85
(Richard Hannon) *trckd ldrs: rdn over 1f out: wknd ins fnl f* **20/1**

1144 **14** *3/4* **Namwahjobo (IRE)**[21] 4324 3-7-11 **83** .... SimonPearce(3) 4 64
(Jim Goldie) *s.i.s: a in rr* **20/1**

-602 **15** *4* **Pabusar**[21] 4333 3-9-7 **104** .... JimCrowley 7 72
(Ralph Beckett) *hld up: hdwy whn hmpd over 1f out: nt rcvr* **10/1**[3]

0500 **16** *4* **Arctic Feeling (IRE)**[21] 4333 3-8-12 **95** .... JackMitchell 14 70
(Richard Fahey) *chsd ldrs: rdn over 2f out: looked btn whn hmpd and eased ins fnl f* **40/1**

5152 **17** *13* **King Ferdinand**[20] 4353 3-8-7 **90** .... MartinDwyer 5 —
(Andrew Balding) *prom: rdn whn hmpd and wknd over 1f out: eased* **10/1**[3]

1m 11.15s (-1.35) **Going Correction** +0.05s/f (Good) **17** Ran SP% **126.2**
Speed ratings (Par 106): **111,109,109,109,108 106,105,104,104,103 102,101,98,97,92 86,69**
Tote Swingers: 1&2 £36.00, 1&3 £22.20, 2&3 £47.10 CSF £125.17 CT £1116.20 TOTE £9.50: £3.10, £5.20, £2.60, £2.80; EX 191.60 TRIFECTA Not won..
Owner Norton Common Farm Racing **Bred** E Dafydd **Trained** Maunby, N Yorks
■ Stewards' Enquiry : Harry Bentley two-day ban: careless riding (Aug 27-28)

FOCUS
A valuable sprint handicap which went to the subsequent Prix Maurice de Gheest winner King's Apostle in 2007. Last year the placed horses were Deacon Blues and Bated Breath, who have both made an impact in Group sprints this season. The forecast favourite Dimension was an absentee, but this was still a competitive event. The principals came from all sides of the track and the form seems sound. It has been rated on the positive side.

NOTEBOOK

Bertiewhittle had run four solid races over 7f, but the drop back to this trip proved no barrier to success and he asserted readily once the gap had appeared for him. He is versatile and consistent. (op 9-1 tchd 15-2)

Elusive Prince raced a short distance apart from the rest of the field, on the stands' side of the pack, and was up with the pace throughout. The first-time visor clearly sharpened him up. (op 20-1)

Louis The Pious had won four of his last five starts, albeit lucky at Newcastle last time, and he ran a big race again off this 5lb higher mark. Like the runner-up, he raced on the near side of the field. (op 9-1)

Elusivity(IRE) was positioned on the far side from his high draw. Back over a sprint trip for the first time this season, he has now made the frame on his last seven starts without getting his head in front. (op 14-1)

Barnet Fair, another drawn high and taken early to post, had every chance and battled on but was just run out of the frame. He is 9lb higher than when last winning on turf. (op 12-1)

Lexi's Hero(IRE), without the blinkers this time, led down the centre before edging right under pressure. He is 8lb higher than when taking the valuable Bond Tyres Trophy at York in June and will no doubt be back in Listed company before long. (op 9-1)

Levitate, penalised for his recent Leicester win, ran a strange race, dropping back to the rear of the field under pressure before running on again when it was all over. He is perhaps not straightforward but has more to offer. (op 12-1)

Rothesay Chancer was 4lb 'wrong' and would have been slightly closer had he not needed to check inside the last.

Flynn's Boy performed creditably down in trip from 2lb out of the weights.

Bless You is lightly raced and it's probably worth forgiving her this. (op 11-1)

Blanche Dubawi(IRE) was a little disappointing off this 6lb higher mark, not finding a great deal after taking a hold. (op 7-1)

5055 WT'S SNOOKER AND SPORTING CLUB CONDITIONS STKS 1m 2f

3:55 (3:55) (Class 2) 3-Y-O+ **£12,450** (£3,728; £1,864; £932; £466) **Stalls** Centre

Form RPR

15- **1** **French Navy**[286] 7265 3-8-9 110 .... KierenFallon 5 113+
(Mahmood Al Zarooni) *hld up in tch: plld hrd: swtchd to centre 4f out: led and edgd rt over 2f out: hung rt over 1f out: r.o: comf* **1/1**[1]

510- **2** *2 ¼* **Joshua Tree (IRE)**[114] 4-9-11 114 .... SebSanders 2 115
(Marco Botti) *hld up: hdwy over 2f out: chsd wnr and nt clr run over 1f out: rdr dropped reins sn after: styd on same pce ins fnl f* **3/1**[2]

2123 **3** *½* **Mahbooba (AUS)**[140] 998 4-9-5 110 ....(b[1]) ShaneKelly 4 108
(M F De Kock, South Africa) *trckd ldr: plld hrd: wnt centre to r alone over 6f out: led over 5f out: sn clr: rdn: hung lft and hdd over 2f out: hung rt over 1f out: styd on same pce ins fnl f* **4/1**[3]

-330 **4** *7* **Age Of Reason (UAE)**[156] 826 6-9-1 108 .... TedDurcan 6 90
(Saeed Bin Suroor) *led over 4f: chsd ldr: rdn over 2f out: wknd over 1f out* **17/2**

3506 **5** *2 ¾* **Caymans (AUS)**[49] 3409 6-9-1 105 .... DaneO'Neill 3 85
(Saeed Bin Suroor) *chsd ldrs: rdn over 3f out: wknd over 1f out* **20/1**

2m 6.74s (1.24) **Going Correction** +0.05s/f (Good)
WFA 3 from 4yo+ 9lb **5** Ran SP% **110.3**
Speed ratings (Par 109): **97,95,94,89,87**
CSF £4.26 TOTE £1.80: £1.30, £1.70; EX 3.00.
Owner Godolphin **Bred** Darley **Trained** Newmarket, Suffolk

FOCUS

A real international flavour to this decent conditions race and it was tight on the official figures with only 4lb between the five runners. It was a bit of a muddling race but the form is taken at face value.

NOTEBOOK

French Navy was a smart juvenile for Andre Fabre last term, but lost his unbeaten record behind Roderic O'Connor in the Group 1 Criterium International at Saint-Cloud on his final start when the heavy ground was against him. He was making a belated debut for Mahmood Al Zarooni here having picked up a stress fracture last year. Racing a little keenly, the winner showed in front a quarter of a mile out and was always in command from that point, winning with something in hand. This was a nice start to his Godolphin career and he should enjoy a fruitful autumn. He is in the St Leger as well as the Champion Stakes at both Leopardstown and Ascot, but is likely to be kept at a lower level for his next start at any rate. (op 11-10 tchd 10-11, 6-5 and 5-4 in places)

Joshua Tree(IRE), a Grade 1 winner in Canada for Aidan O'Brien before a spell racing in Qatar, ran a pleasing debut for Marco Botti on this first start since the spring, chasing the winner through without really troubling him. This trip is on the short side. (op 4-1)

Mahbooba(AUS), successful at the top level on turf for this trainer in South Africa, won the UAE 1,000 Guineas at Meydan earlier this year. Racing keenly in the first-time blinkers, she was taken to race alone down the centre of the track and hung both ways when the pressure was on. She is talented but highly strung and may not prove easy to place. (tchd 5-1)

Age Of Reason(UAE) was well beaten on this first run since the Dubai Carnival but is entitled to do better over further with this run behind him. (op 7-1)

Caymans(AUS), a one-time smart performer in Australia, has now shown little in two starts in this country. (op 11-1)

5056 MICKEY FLYNN'S AMERICAN POOL HALL H'CAP 1m

4:30 (4:32) (Class 4) (0-85,85) 3-Y-O **£5,175** (£1,540; £769; £384) **Stalls** High

Form RPR

2-1 **1** **Nordic Sky (USA)**[20] 4370 3-9-7 85 .... KierenFallon 14 92+
(William Haggas) *chsd ldrs: rdn to ld 1f out: styd on* **5/2**[1]

2060 **2** *¾* **Mutajare (IRE)**[21] 4335 3-9-1 79 .... DarryllHolland 6 84
(Mark Johnston) *w ldr tl led over 6f out: rdn and edgd lft over 1f out: sn hdd: styd on u.p* **28/1**

253 **3** *nk* **Imaginary World (IRE)**[17] 4429 3-8-9 76 ....(be) KieranO'Neill[(3)] 9 80
(Alan McCabe) *hld up: plld hrd: rdn over 1f out: r.o wl ins fnl f: nt rch ldrs* **14/1**

030 **4** *nk* **Change The Subject (USA)**[85] 2258 3-8-10 74 ow1.(b[1]) IanMongan 15 78
(Sir Henry Cecil) *hld up: rdn over 3f out: hdwy over 1f out: styd on* **17/2**

5310 **5** *½* **My Son Max**[36] 3798 3-8-13 80 .... SeanLevey[(3)] 1 82
(Richard Hannon) *wnt rt s: hld up: hdwy over 2f out: rdn and hung lft over 1f out: styd on* **16/1**

525 **6** *1* **Roy The Boy (USA)**[29] 4065 3-9-0 78 .... ShaneKelly 2 78
(Jane Chapple-Hyam) *hld up: hdwy over 2f out: rdn and hung lft over 1f out: styd on same pce ins fnl f* **20/1**

6526 **7** *¾* **Aciano (IRE)**[3] 4914 3-9-2 80 .... MartinDwyer 7 78
(Brian Meehan) *led: hdd over 6f out: chsd ldr: rdn over 1f out: styd on same pce* **13/2**[3]

522 **8** *4 ½* **Little Black Book (IRE)**[17] 4447 3-9-1 79 ....(t) DaneO'Neill 11 67
(Gerard Butler) *hld up: hdwy 1/2-way: rdn and wknd over 1f out* **4/1**[2]

0130 **9** *hd* **Dunhoy (IRE)**[17] 4447 3-9-2 80 .... JimmyQuinn 5 68
(Stef Higgins) *hld up: rdn over 2f out: nvr on terms* **12/1**

0305 **10** *shd* **Yojimbo (IRE)**[17] 4447 3-8-11 75 .... TedDurcan 13 62
(Mick Channon) *hld up: hdwy over 2f out: rdn over 1f out: sn wknd* **16/1**

-120 **11** *25* **Taqaat (USA)**[45] 3521 3-9-3 81 .... JackMitchell 8 11
(Tim McCarthy) *prom tl rdn and wknd over 2f out: t.o* **40/1**

3000 **12** *2 ¼* **Adaria**[24] 4202 3-8-12 76 .... JimCrowley 4 —
(David C Griffiths) *s.i.s: hld up: a in rr: rdn and wknd over 2f out: t.o* **33/1**

664 **13** *3 ¼* **Come Here Yew (IRE)**[20] 4370 3-8-11 75 ow1 .... SebSanders 12 —
(Declan Carroll) *hld up in tch: plld hrd: rdn and wknd over 2f out: t.o* **10/1**

1m 39.81s (-0.19) **Going Correction** +0.05s/f (Good) **13** Ran SP% **121.2**
Speed ratings (Par 102): **102,101,100,100,100 99,98,93,93,93 68,66,63**
Tote Swingers: 1&2 £28.40, 1&3 £11.20, 2&3 £86.20 CSF £89.26 CT £878.71 TOTE £3.30: £1.60, £9.20, £4.30; EX 91.80.
Owner Paddy Twomey **Bred** Hawthorn Villa Stud **Trained** Newmarket, Suffolk

FOCUS

A fair handicap but not many became involved. The winner is a likely improver with the next two setting the standard.

5057 NEWMARKETRACECOURSES.CO.UK H'CAP 1m 4f

5:05 (5:05) (Class 4) (0-85,85) 3-Y-O+ **£5,175** (£1,540; £769; £384) **Stalls** Centre

Form RPR

0510 **1** **Midnight Oil**[28] 4108 3-9-3 85 .... KierenFallon 3 96+
(Luca Cumani) *hld up in tch: racd keenly: rdn to ld and hung lft fr over 1f out: r.o: readily* **10/3**[1]

0215 **2** *1* **Crassula**[35] 3867 3-9-0 82 .... DaneO'Neill 11 89
(Terry Clement) *a.p: swtchd to chse ldr in centre over 6f out: rdn over 1f out: styd on* **9/2**[2]

262- **3** *¾* **Protaras (USA)**[284] 7282 4-9-7 78 .... IanMongan 7 84
(Sir Henry Cecil) *hld up: hdwy and nt clr run over 1f out: r.o* **9/2**[2]

/362 **4** *½* **Nobunaga**[14] 4555 6-9-4 75 .... SebSanders 1 80
(Venetia Williams) *chsd ldr tl led over 2f out: rdn and hdd over 1f out: styd on same pce ins fnl f* **6/1**

25-4 **5** *2* **Iron Condor**[189] 209 4-8-9 66 .... JackMitchell 10 68
(James Eustace) *hld up: hdwy over 1f out: sn rdn: styd on same pce fnl f* **25/1**

0000 **6** *1 ¼* **Becausewecan (USA)**[21] 4348 5-10-0 85 .... DarryllHolland 9 85
(Mark Johnston) *overall ldr tl rdn and hdd over 2f out: styd on same pce fr over 1f out* **8/1**

-414 **7** *5* **Star In Flight**[20] 4354 4-9-12 83 .... MartinDwyer 6 75
(Brian Meehan) *trckd ldrs: racd keenly: wnt centre and led that pair over 6f out: rdn and hung lft fr over 2f out: wknd over 1f out* **11/2**[3]

2040 **8** *1 ½* **Ethics Girl (IRE)**[14] 4537 5-9-5 83 .... HannahNunn[(7)] 8 73
(John Berry) *hld up: racd keenly: hdwy over 6f out: rdn and wknd over 1f out* **25/1**

03-0 **9** *12* **Gomrath (IRE)**[140] 994 4-9-5 76 .... TedDurcan 2 46
(Mick Channon) *hld up: wknd 2f out: eased* **20/1**

2m 33.39s (0.49) **Going Correction** +0.05s/f (Good)
WFA 3 from 4yo+ 11lb **9** Ran SP% **112.7**
Speed ratings (Par 105): **100,99,98,98,97 96,93,92,84**
Tote Swingers: 1&2 £6.70, 1&3 £4.70, 2&3 £4.60 CSF £17.21 CT £65.72 TOTE £4.40: £1.70, £1.80, £1.20; EX 19.80.
Owner Castle Down Racing **Bred** Meon Valley Stud **Trained** Newmarket, Suffolk

FOCUS

Fairly ordinary handicap form, but the winner is capable of better still The field raced down the centre in the home straight, apart from two who raced further out on the track.

Star In Flight Official explanation: jockey said gelding hung left

T/Jkpt: Not won. T/Plt: £640.40 to a £1 stake. Pool:£113,562.00 - 129.45 winning tickets T/Qpdt: £81.60 to a £1 stake. Pool:£6,669.00 - 60.44 winning tickets CR

4606 RIPON (R-H)

Saturday, August 13

OFFICIAL GOING: Good to soft (7.8)

Wind: fresh half behind Weather: cloudy

5058 BRENNANDS ARE YORKSHIRE POST WINNERS MAIDEN AUCTION STKS 6f

2:20 (2:21) (Class 5) 2-Y-O **£3,234** (£962; £481; £240) **Stalls** High

Form RPR

3520 **1** **Blue Shoes (IRE)**[14] 4557 2-8-4 64 .... PaulHanagan 10 65
(Tim Easterby) *mde all stands' side: rdn over 1f out: kpt on* **6/1**[3]

6303 **2** *½* **Just Like Heaven (IRE)**[7] 4809 2-8-9 70 .... DavidAllan 4 69
(Tim Easterby) *led far side: rdn over 1f out: kpt on: jst hld by stands' side wnr: 1st of 6 in gp* **13/2**

0005 **3** *hd* **On The Hoof**[21] 4347 2-9-3 72 .... PaddyAspell 5 76
(Michael Easterby) *trckd ldr far side: rdn over 1f out: kpt on fnl f: 2nd of 6 in gp* **11/1**

33 **4** *1 ½* **Oddysey (IRE)**[23] 4232 2-8-6 0 .... TomEaves 2 60
(Michael Dods) *trckd ldr far side: rdn over 1f out: kpt on: 3rd of 6 in gp* **5/2**[1]

0 **5** *3 ¾* **Celestial Dawn**[102] 1797 2-8-1 0 .... AmyBaker[(3)] 12 47
(John Weymes) *chsd ldr stands' side: rdn 2f out: wknd ins fnl f: 2nd of 6 in gp* **50/1**

3 **6** *½* **Zakreet**[10] 4675 2-8-13 0 .... PhillipMakin 3 55
(Kevin Ryan) *trckd ldrs far side: rdn over 2f out: wknd over 1f out: 4th of 6 in gp* **5/1**[2]

5 **7** *½* **Vitalicious**[18] 4406 2-8-6 0 .... RichardMullen 9 46
(Ed McMahon) *w ldr stands' side: rdn 2f out: sn wknd: 3rd of 6 in gp* **13/2**

46 **8** *2* **Sygnature**[9] 4714 2-8-13 0 .... PJMcDonald 1 51
(Alan Swinbank) *hld up far side: nvr threatened: 5th of 6 in gp* **9/1**

0645 **9** *6* **Never In (IRE)**[20] 4358 2-7-13 54 .... DanielleMcCreery[(5)] 6 20
(Alan Berry) *trckd ldrs stands' side: rdn over 2f out: wknd over 1f out: 4th of 6 in gp* **66/1**

04 **10** *¾* **After Timer (IRE)**[10] 4668 2-7-13 0 .... AmyScott[(5)] 7 18
(Julie Camacho) *s.i.s: a in rr far side: last of 6 in gp* **50/1**

06 **11** *1* **Simpson Millar**[20] 4358 2-8-11 0 .... StephenCraine 8 22
(Noel Wilson) *dwlt: sn pushed along in midfield stands' side: wknd over 1f out: 5th of 6 in gp* **100/1**

0 **12** *21* **Majestic Manannan (IRE)**[49] 3398 2-9-1 0 .... AdrianNicholls 11 —
(David Nicholls) *dwlt: sn in tch stands' side: rdn 2f out: sn wknd: last of 6 in gp* **18/1**

1m 15.45s (2.45) **Going Correction** +0.15s/f (Good) **12** Ran SP% **116.2**
Speed ratings (Par 94): **89,88,88,86,81 80,79,77,69,68 66,38**
Tote Swingers: 1&2 £3.10, 1&3 £7.70, 2&3 £8.10 CSF £43.47 TOTE £6.40: £2.00, £2.00, £3.10; EX 21.10.
Owner C H Stevens **Bred** Mountarmstrong Stud **Trained** Great Habton, N Yorks

FOCUS

Rail at innermost configuration and distances as advertised. An ordinary looking affair in which the field split into two groups - there appeared little bias. The first three home were Easterby-trained, the first two by Tim. It is probably best to presume this is modest form, but it seems solid enough.

The Form Book, Raceform Ltd, Compton, RG20 6NL

NOTEBOOK

Blue Shoes(IRE) was back up to 6f, had a mark of 64 after six previous tries. One couldn't fault her attitude, as she was alone for the final stages of the race down the stands' side, but it would be surprising if she had much more to come. (op 13-2 tchd 5-1)

Just Like Heaven(IRE), officially rated 6lb superior to his stablemate, finished third in a nursery on his previous outing, showing a degree of promise returning from a break, and duly built on that after racing prominently again. He clearly has the ability to get his head in front. (op 11-2)

On The Hoof, the highest-rated of those with an official mark, maintained his upward progression with another solid keeping-on effort. (op 15-2)

Oddysey(IRE), dropping in distance, had shown more than enough ability to go close in a race of this nature but, after racing prominently, didn't get home as well as the two in front of her down that side. She'll be interesting up in trip again. (op 3-1 tchd 10-3)

Celestial Dawn improved significantly for her debut effort and kept on well after showing pace. (op 100-1)

Zakreet looked green and lost his position before keeping on. (op 15-2)

Vitalicious gave the impression she needs a bit more time. (op 7-1)

After Timer(IRE) reportedly failed to handle the track. Official explanation: trainer's rep said filly failed to handle the track (op 66-1)

5059 VW VAN CENTRE WEST YORKSHIRE H'CAP — 1m

2:55 (2:56) (Class 3) (0-90,90) 3-Y-O £8,821 (£2,640; £1,320; £660; £329) **Stalls** Low

Form — RPR

0366 **1** **Diescentric (USA)**[14] 4537 4-9-7 **83**........ PaulHanagan 2 — 97+
(Sir Henry Cecil) *midfield: pushed along 4f out: swtchd lft wl over 2f out: sn gd hdwy: led over 1f out: kpt on wl* **4/1**[1]

3236 **2** *1 ¾* **Amazing Star (IRE)**[38] 3740 6-9-1 **77**........ RichardMullen 7 — 85
(Declan Carroll) *midfield: rdn over 2f out: hdwy over 1f out: chsd wnr ins fnl f: kpt on* **20/1**

3343 **3** *¾* **Don't Call Me (IRE)**[7] 4794 4-10-0 **90**........ AdrianNicholls 13 — 96+
(David Nicholls) *hld up: rdn over 3f out: hdwy towards outer over 2f out: kpt on: nrst fin* **11/2**[2]

0300 **4** *1* **Desert Romance (IRE)**[14] 4528 5-10-0 **90**........ DanielTudhope 5 — 94
(David O'Meara) *trckd ldrs: rdn over 2f out: kpt on same pce* **25/1**

1213 **5** *1 ¼* **Koo And The Gang (IRE)**[35] 3840 4-8-12 **77**........ DaleSwift(3) 6 — 78
(Brian Ellison) *chsd ldrs: rdn over 2f out: kpt on same pce* **11/1**

6423 **6** *nk* **Extraterrestrial**[21] 4325 7-9-10 **89**........ LeeTopliss(3) 4 — 89
(Richard Fahey) *midfield: rdn and hdwy over 1f out: kpt on fnl f* **9/1**[3]

3150 **7** *1 ¼* **Moheebb (IRE)**[12] 4603 7-9-9 **85**........(b) PJMcDonald 1 — 83
(Ruth Carr) *hld up in midfield on inner: rdn over 3f out: kpt on ins fnl f: n.d* **18/1**

4104 **8** *½* **Fazza**[14] 4561 4-8-13 **75**........ TomEaves 12 — 71
(Edwin Tuer) *hld up: rdn over 3f out: hdwy over 1f out: kpt on fnl f: n.d* **16/1**

1400 **9** *1 ½* **Veroon (IRE)**[18] 4415 5-9-5 **81**........(p) FrederikTylicki 10 — 74
(James Given) *midfield: rdn over 2f out: n.d* **22/1**

1000 **10** *1 ¼* **Amethyst Dawn (IRE)**[14] 4561 5-9-9 **85**........ DavidAllan 11 — 75
(Tim Easterby) *hld up in midfield: rdn over 2f out: no imp* **25/1**

3231 **11** *2 ¾* **Polish World (USA)**[32] 3936 7-9-4 **80**........ PhillipMakin 14 — 64
(Paul Midgley) *chsd ldr: rdn over 2f out: wknd over 1f out* **20/1**

4006 **12** *7* **Cara's Request (AUS)**[7] 4811 6-9-1 **80**........ MichaelO'Connell(3) 3 — 48
(David Nicholls) *sn led: clr over 5f out tl 3f out: hdd over 1f out: sn wknd* **22/1**

250 **13** *½* **Osgood**[14] 4537 4-9-1 **77**........ SamHitchcott 18 — 43
(Mick Channon) *trckd ldrs: rdn over 2f out: wknd over 1f out* **33/1**

5000 **14** *1 ¾* **Christmas Carnival**[21] 4349 4-8-13 **75**........(b) GrahamGibbons 17 — 37
(Michael Easterby) *hld up in midfield: rdn over 3f out: wknd over 1f out* **50/1**

2110 **15** *2* **Daring Dream (GER)**[21] 4325 6-9-2 **81**........ GaryBartley(3) 8 — 39
(Jim Goldie) *hld up: a towards rr* **22/1**

0002 **16** *26* **Mujaadel (USA)**[14] 4561 6-9-1 **77**........(p) JamieGoldstein 19 — —
(David Nicholls) *rrd and hood removed late: v.s.a: a towards rr* **25/1**

042 **17** *3 ½* **Prince Of Dance**[51] 3315 5-9-9 **85**........ RobertWinston 9 — —
(Tom Tate) *s.i.s: hld up: a towards rr* **11/2**[2]

1m 41.18s (-0.22) **Going Correction** +0.15s/f (Good) **17** Ran SP% **119.8**
Speed ratings (Par 107): **107,105,104,103,102 101,100,100,98,97 94,87,87,85,83 57,53**
Tote Swingers: 1&2 £34.40, 1&3 £7.00, 2&3 £33.20 CSF £80.30 CT £404.07 TOTE £4.80: £1.40, £3.70, £2.10, £6.00; EX 133.20.
Owner Axom (XVIII) **Bred** Morgan's Ford Farm **Trained** Newmarket, Suffolk

FOCUS

A decent handicap and wide-open stuff, with plenty of horses having a chance on pieces of form. Those drawn wide didn't look to have an easy task over this distance, so the third can be marked up. The early gallop was frenetic so it wasn't surprising to see those chasing the pace feature late on.

NOTEBOOK

Diescentric(USA) ◆ still had a bit of scope for improvement considering he hadn't been over-raced for his age, and won this nicely after being given an uncomplicated ride. Even after being reassessed, he'll remain of interest in handicaps. (op 9-2)

Amazing Star(IRE), last seen running on Polytrack, was pulled out from an inside position to make his bid but proved to be one-paced. (op 25-1)

Don't Call Me(IRE) has been in good form this season and did well again after emerging from stall 13, staying on wide the field. (op 5-1)

Desert Romance(IRE), dropping in trip, had run modestly on his last two starts so this was a little better, although he never looked like winning.

Koo And The Gang(IRE) is another who has been running well recently, and he deserves credit for chasing the runaway leader for a respectable distance and keeping on.

Extraterrestrial, although short of room at times, appeared to run up to his current level after travelling smoothly in behind. (op 8-1)

Moheebb(IRE) could be seen making late headway past runners, but he isn't the most trustworthy of horses to repeat form. (op 16-1)

Polish World(USA) reportedly hung right. Official explanation: jockey said gelding hung right (op 18-1)

Mujaadel(USA) Official explanation: jockey said gelding reared as stalls opened causing him to lose his balance and being unable to remove the blindfold.

Prince Of Dance, off since a good effort at Newcastle at the end of June, finished lame. Official explanation: jockey said gelding finished lame (op 6-1)

5060 WILLIAM HILL GREAT ST WILFRID STKS (H'CAP) — 6f

3:30 (3:30) (Class 2) 3-Y-O+

£43,575 (£13,048; £6,524; £3,262; £1,631; £819) **Stalls** High

Form — RPR

0011 **1** **Pepper Lane**[12] 4609 4-8-12 **95**........ DanielTudhope 17 — 107
(David O'Meara) *mde all stands' side: rdn 2f out: kpt on wl* **11/1**

2056 **2** *1 ½* **Our Jonathan**[21] 4314 4-9-5 **102**........ PhillipMakin 20 — 109
(Kevin Ryan) *hld up stands' side: rdn and hdwy over 1f out: chsd wnr ins fnl f: kpt on: 2nd of 8 in gp* **10/1**[3]

126- **3** *2 ¾* **Mayson**[329] 6192 3-8-13 **100**........ DavidNolan 19 — 98
(Richard Fahey) *in tch stands' side: hdwy over 2f out: rdn to chse wnr over 1f out: one pce fnl f: 3rd of 8 in gp* **40/1**

-003 **4** *1* **Parisian Pyramid (IRE)**[84] 2288 5-8-10 **93**........ StephenCraine 6 — 88
(Kevin Ryan) *led far side: rdn clr of gp fnl f: no ch w stands' side ldrs: 1st of 11 in gp* **18/1**

6110 **5** *2 ¾* **Quest For Success (IRE)**[14] 4534 6-9-2 **102**........ LeeTopliss(3) 13 — 88
(Richard Fahey) *w ldr stands' side: rdn over 2f out: wknd ins fnl f: 4th of 8 in gp* **25/1**

0020 **6** *½* **Colonel Mak**[14] 4534 4-8-12 **95**........ GrahamGibbons 4 — 80
(David Barron) *chsd ldrs far side: rdn over 2f out: kpt on to go 2nd in gp towards fin* **11/1**

0000 **7** *hd* **Evens And Odds (IRE)**[14] 4534 7-9-0 **100**........ MichaelO'Connell(3) 1 — 84
(David Nicholls) *midfield far side: rdn over 2f out: kpt on: 3rd of 11 in gp* **16/1**

0520 **8** *1 ½* **Tajneed (IRE)**[14] 4534 8-9-4 **104**........ GaryBartley(3) 3 — 83
(David Nicholls) *sn pushed along in rr far side: kpt on fnl f: nvr threatened: 4th of 11 in gp* **15/2**[1]

0302 **9** *shd* **Confessional**[14] 4531 4-8-12 **95**........(e) FrederikTylicki 8 — 74
(Tim Easterby) *w ldr far side: rdn over 1f out: wknd ins fnl f: 5th of 11 in gp* **14/1**

0300 **10** *nk* **Striking Spirit**[21] 4314 6-8-10 **93**........(p) DavidAllan 14 — 71
(Tim Easterby) *chsd ldrs stands' side: rdn and hung rt over 2f out: no imp: 5th of 8 in gp* **20/1**

0340 **11** *1 ¼* **Fathsta (IRE)**[14] 4534 6-8-10 **93**........ RobertWinston 2 — 67
(David Simcock) *hld up far side: rdn over 1f out: n.d: 6th of 11 in gp* **15/2**[1]

2425 **12** *¾* **Waffle (IRE)**[49] 3394 5-9-5 **107**........ LMcNiff(5) 12 — 78
(David Barron) *hld up in tch stands' side: rdn over 2f out: sn no imp: 6th of 8 in gp* **9/1**[2]

0030 **13** *nk* **Johannes (IRE)**[35] 3841 8-8-9 **92**........ PaulHanagan 7 — 63
(Richard Fahey) *a towards rr far side: 7th of 11 in gp* **16/1**

3010 **14** *½* **Edinburgh Knight (IRE)**[14] 4534 4-8-12 **95**........ TonyCulhane 18 — 64
(Paul D'Arcy) *hld up stands' side: rdn over 2f out: nvr threatened: 7th of 8 in gp* **16/1**

2650 **15** *nk* **Atlantic Sport (USA)**[14] 4534 6-9-3 **100**........ SamHitchcott 10 — 68
(Mick Channon) *hld up far side: rdn over 2f out: nvr threatened: 8th of 11 in gp* **28/1**

4102 **16** *4 ½* **Tax Free (IRE)**[14] 4534 9-8-12 **95**........ AdrianNicholls 15 — 49
(David Nicholls) *chsd ldr stands' side: rdn over 2f out: wknd over 1f out: last of 8 in gp* **12/1**

1455 **17** *3 ¼* **Addictive Dream (IRE)**[7] 4776 4-9-1 **98**........(p) RichardMullen 9 — 41
(Walter Swinburn) *midfield on far side: wknd over 1f out: eased fnl f: 9th of 11 in gp* **11/1**

1040 **18** *¾* **Enderby Spirit (GR)**[17] 4428 5-8-9 **92**........ TomEaves 5 — 33
(Bryan Smart) *dwlt: sn chsd ldrs far side: wknd over 2f out: 10th of 11 in gp* **25/1**

00-0 **19** *nk* **Gallagher**[12] 4609 5-8-9 **92**........ JamieGoldstein 11 — 32
(David Nicholls) *racd far side: sn midfield: rdn over 1f out: wknd qckly: eased: last of 11 in gp* **28/1**

1m 12.34s (-0.66) **Going Correction** +0.15s/f (Good)
WFA 3 from 4yo+ 4lb **19** Ran SP% **126.7**
Speed ratings (Par 109): **110,108,104,103,99 98,98,96,96,95 94,93,92,92,91 85,81,80,80**
Tote Swingers: 1&2 £46.60, 1&3 £129.10, 2&3 £125.80 CSF £108.78 CT £2448.34 TOTE £10.50: £2.60, £2.30, £12.00, £5.20; EX 203.90 Trifecta £11486.00 Pool £37,252.07 - 2.40 winning units..
Owner Mrs Lynne Lumley & K Nicholson **Bred** Conor J C Parsons & Brian M Parsons **Trained** Nawton, N Yorks

FOCUS

One of the big sprint handicaps of the season, where the draw can often be crucial. This year it appeared that being on the stands' side (high draw) was a big advantage, as the first three home raced down that side and were drawn 17, 20 and 19. Despite the bias the form has not been rated too negatively, and the winner improved again.

NOTEBOOK

Pepper Lane ◆ had improved from a starting mark of 74 this season, and had good course form on her side, so it looked merely whether her draw was a hindrance or not. Smartly into stride, she showed speed on the rail and won in the manner of a horse good enough to try her luck in Group company, with something like The Flying Five at the Curragh or Newbury's Dubai Airport World Trophy making appeal considering the pace she shows. However, it appears that the Ayr Gold Cup is firmly on the agenda in the longer-term.

Our Jonathan ◆ took a while to get going back down in distance but kept on really well once hitting top gear. He is a fine horse to have on your side in big-field handicaps. (op 16-1)

Mayson ◆ had a fine record at this course, including a victory in the Horn Blower as a juvenile, and ran a blinder on his first outing of the season. If he can go on from this, more success looks on the cards. (op 50-1)

Parisian Pyramid(IRE) ◆, returning from an 84-day absence, showed terrific pace and comfortably won on his side of the track He had run well at this course on his previous visit, so is one to watch out for next year if sent here again. (op 14-1)

Quest For Success(IRE) repeated his performance in this race last season with a fifth-placed finish, and helped to confirm that stands' side was the place to be. (op 22-1, tchd 20-1 in places)

Colonel Mak was interesting on his best form (had excuse in the Stewards' Cup after losing teeth in the stalls) but was one-paced after being thereabouts on the far side of the course. (op 12-1)

Evens And Odds(IRE) needed switching from his rails position to make a challenge, and was never a factor despite being given every chance to get involved. (op 18-1)

Tajneed(IRE) came under pressure really early in the contest but did keep on. This was a long way below what he is capable of, even allowing for being on the 'wrong' side. His jockey subsequently reported his mount was never travelling. Official explanation: jockey said gelding never travelled (op 7-1)

Striking Spirit was dropped in trip again, but compromised his chance by hanging away from the favoured side under pressure. Official explanation: jockey said gelding hung right-handed throughout (op 25-1 tchd 28-1)

Fathsta(IRE) ran disappointingly and shaped as though he may not have handled the course. (op 10-1)

Waffle(IRE) is a horse that ideally needs cover in amongst horses, and one got the impression that he saw too much daylight here, wide of his bunch early. (op 10-1, tchd 11-1 in a place)

Edinburgh Knight(IRE)'s jockey reported that the gelding was unsuited by the track. Official explanation: trainer said gelding was unsuited by the track (op 14-1)

Tax Free(IRE) is a solid performer and rarely runs a bad race, so this was clearly not his true form.

Addictive Dream(IRE), who finished well in front of the winner over C&D earlier this season, hasn't always looked the most straightforward but was unlucky at Ascot the previous weekend when tried in cheekpieces for the first time. Racing in the far-side group, one got the impression again he wasn't helping his jockey as much as he could under pressure and was eased once their chance had gone. He is, however, the type to pop up one day in a decent handicap. Official explanation: trainer had no explanation for the poor form shown

5061 RIPON HORN BLOWER CONDITIONS STKS — 6f

4:05 (4:06) (Class 3) 2-Y-0 — £7,561 (£2,263; £1,131; £566; £282) Stalls High

Form — RPR

1 **1** Jessie's Spirit (IRE)[17] 4430 2-8-12 0 ... DavidNolan 4 — 82+
(Ann Duffield) *hld up in tch: hdwy over 3f out: sn trckd ldr: rdn to ld over 1f out: kpt on wl* — **11/4**[1]

1 **2** *1 ¼* **Hot Sugar (USA)**[47] 3452 2-9-5 0 ... PhillipMakin 5 — 85+
(Kevin Ryan) *s.i.s: sn pushed along to chse ldr: rdn over 1f out: chsd wnr ins fnl f: a hld* — **4/1**[3]

012 **3** *9* **Son Du Silence (IRE)**[35] 3868 2-9-3 74 ... PaulHanagan 3 — 56
(J S Moore) *led: rdn whn hdd over 1f out: wknd ins fnl f* — **6/1**

11 **4** *¾* **Ralphy Boy (IRE)**[44] 3540 2-9-10 0 ... AdrianNicholls 2 — 61
(David Nicholls) *dwlt: sn w ldr: rdn over 2f out: wknd over 1f out* — **7/2**[2]

3213 **5** *1* **Verbeeck**[15] 4502 2-9-5 86 ... RichardMullen 1 — 53
(Ed McMahon) *chsd ldrs on outer: rdn over 2f out: sn wknd* — **11/4**[1]

1m 14.84s (1.84) **Going Correction** +0.15s/f (Good) — 5 Ran SP% **109.8**
Speed ratings (Par 98): **93,91,79,78,77**
CSF £13.69 TOTE £3.20: £1.80, £3.10; EX 10.90.
Owner David & Carole McMahon **Bred** Mountarmstrong Stud **Trained** Constable Burton, N Yorks

FOCUS
This didn't look a strong contest despite the amount of victories the field had previously managed. The first two came clear of a trio who failed to give their running.

NOTEBOOK
Jessie's Spirit(IRE) beat some modest rivals on her debut at Leicester at 12-1, but looked a fair prospect here up against the colts considering the way she cruised into conetention and then went on. The weight allowance she got may have helped, but she was clearly the best on the day under these conditions. (op 7-2 tchd 5-2)
Hot Sugar(USA) took quite a while to get going and probably learnt more here than he did on his debut, when he made all. He is entitled to respect next time. (op 7-2 tchd 9-2)
Son Du Silence(IRE) has size about him and can can be given another chance, although he should have run better in ground he'd won in before. (op 11-2 tchd 5-1 and 13-2)
Ralphy Boy(IRE), carrying a double penalty, had his chance but offered little off the bridle. (tchd 10-3 and 4-1)
Verbeeck didn't look an easy conveyance in a conditions event at the end of July and was soon struggling after leaving the stalls. The trainer could offer no explanation for the horse's poor performance. Official explanation: trainer had no explanation for the poor form shown (op 3-1)

5062 EBF "BAHRI" FILLIES' H'CAP — 1m 1f 170y

4:40 (4:40) (Class 4) (0-80,80) 3-Y-0+
£5,670 (£1,697; £848; £424; £105; £105) Stalls Low

Form — RPR

1-40 **1** **Tameen**[29] 4056 3-8-12 73 ... PhillipMakin 6 — 85+
(John Dunlop) *hld up: n.m.r over 2f out: sn hdwy: chsd ldr 2f out: led fnl 100yds: kpt on* — **7/2**[2]

3211 **2** *1 ¼* **Kenyan Cat**[35] 3848 4-10-0 80 ... RichardMullen 9 — 87
(Ed McMahon) *t.k.h: midfield on outer: rdn to chse ldr 2f out: kpt on: wnt 2nd post* — **4/1**[3]

512 **3** *nk* **Izzy The Ozzy (IRE)**[33] 3904 3-9-4 79 ... GrahamGibbons 2 — 85+
(David Barron) *midfield on inner: hdwy to trck ldr over 4f out: led over 2f out: rdn over 1f out: edgd lft and hdd fnl 100yds: lost 2nd post* — **3/1**[1]

2431 **4** *7* **Christmas Light**[17] 4440 4-9-6 72 ... DanielTudhope 4 — 64
(David O'Meara) *dwlt: hld up: swtchd lft over 2f out: sn rdn: chsd ldng trio over 1f out: wknd ins fnl f* — **10/1**

5-22 **5** *5* **File And Paint (IRE)**[17] 4439 3-8-11 77 ... LanceBetts(5) 3 — 59
(Lawrence Mullaney) *t.k.h: trckd ldr: rdn over 3f out: wknd over 1f out* — **15/2**

1010 **5** *dht* **Abdicate (IRE)**[17] 4429 3-9-3 78 ... PaulHanagan 8 — 60
(Richard Fahey) *sn led: rdn whn hdd over 2f out: wknd ent fnl f* — **5/1**

0/0 **7** *1 ¼* **Lil Ella (IRE)**[22] 4294 4-9-4 75 ... ChrisDCogan(5) 7 — 54
(Patrick Holmes) *prom: rdn over 3f out: wknd over 1f out* — **33/1**

22-5 **8** *16* **Moonsail**[49] 3385 3-9-0 80 ... AntiocoMurgia(5) 5 — 26
(Mahmood Al Zarooni) *midfield: rdn over 3f out: wknd over 1f out: eased* — **10/1**

2m 7.25s (1.85) **Going Correction** +0.15s/f (Good)
WFA 3 from 4yo 9lb — 8 Ran SP% **116.8**
Speed ratings (Par 102): **98,97,96,91,87 87,86,73**
Tote Swingers: 1&2 £5.00, 1&3 £5.40, 2&3 £1.80 CSF £18.39 CT £46.52 TOTE £4.80: £1.50, £1.90, £1.50; EX 26.50.
Owner Hamdan Al Maktoum **Bred** Shadwell Estate Company Limited **Trained** Arundel, W Sussex
■ Stewards' Enquiry : Antioco Murgia one-day ban: used whip without giving filly time to respond (Aug 27)

FOCUS
An intriguing contest full of in-form or promising types. The early gallop didn't look strong. The first three came clear and the form looks sound.
Moonsail Official explanation: jockey said filly hung right-handed

5063 E-TECH GROUP TOTAL ELECTRICAL SOLUTIONS MAIDEN STKS — 5f

5:15 (5:16) (Class 5) 3-Y-0+ — £3,234 (£962; £481; £240) Stalls High

Form — RPR

5 **1** **Hills Of Dakota**[15] 4514 3-9-3 0 ... GrahamGibbons 4 — 73+
(David Barron) *w ldr: drvn over 2f out: led narrowly over 1f out: kpt on to assert fnl 100yds* — **15/8**[1]

-050 **2** *1 ¾* **Surely This Time (IRE)**[73] 2611 3-9-3 64 ... (p) PhillipMakin 5 — 67
(Kevin Ryan) *led narrowly: rdn whn hdd over 1f out: remained w ev ch tl no ex fnl 100yds* — **10/3**[3]

03 **3** *½* **Salik Tag (USA)**[11] 4647 3-9-3 0 ... (t) AdrianNicholls 6 — 65
(David Nicholls) *dwlt: sn pushed along in rr: hdwy over 2f out: rdn to chse ldng pair over 1f out: kpt on fnl f* — **11/2**

3400 **4** *6* **Guinea Seeker**[11] 4638 3-9-3 57 ... PaulHanagan 3 — 44
(Tim Easterby) *chsd ldrs: rdn over 2f out: sn no imp: wknd ins fnl f* — **3/1**[2]

0064 **5** *¾* **Bygones For Coins (IRE)**[1] 5010 3-8-12 44 ... RobertWinston 1 — 36
(Alan Berry) *prom on outer: rdn over 2f out: wknd over 1f out* — **25/1**

6 *11* **Kwik As Kwik** 3-9-3 0 ... DanielTudhope 2 — —
(Robin Bastiman) *chsd ldrs: pushed along and lost pl 3f out: sn wknd: eased* — **10/1**

60.87 secs (0.17) **Going Correction** +0.15s/f (Good) — 6 Ran SP% **111.2**
Speed ratings (Par 103): **104,101,100,90,89 72**
Tote Swingers: 1&2 £1.10, 1&3 £3.20, 2&3 £5.50 CSF £8.22 TOTE £2.50: £1.50, £2.30; EX 8.80.
Owner J Cringan & D Pryde **Bred** Messinger Stud Ltd **Trained** Maunby, N Yorks

FOCUS
A modest maiden in which the winner built on his Thirsk promise.

5064 SIS LIVE H'CAP — 1m 4f 10y

5:45 (5:45) (Class 5) (0-75,75) 3-Y-0 — £3,234 (£962; £481; £240) Stalls Low

Form — RPR

0314 **1** **Getabuzz**[28] 4084 3-9-6 74 ... TomEaves 10 — 83
(Tim Easterby) *dwlt: midfield: hdwy 4f out: sn trckd ldr: rdn to ld 2f out: kpt on wl* — **15/2**

4221 **2** *1 ¼* **Number Theory**[28] 4083 3-9-7 75 ... PaulHanagan 5 — 82
(John Holt) *hld up in midfield: hdwy 4f out: rdn to chse ldrs over 2f out: wnt 2nd ins fnl f: kpt on* — **9/2**[2]

031 **3** *1* **Korngold**[22] 4273 3-9-1 69 ... PhillipMakin 8 — 79+
(John Dunlop) *hld up: hdwy 4f out: short of room towards inner 3f out tl ins fnl f: swtchd lft fnl 100yds: kpt on: wnt 3rd nr fin: unlucky* — **13/8**[1]

1513 **4** *½* **Countrywide Flame**[14] 4540 3-9-4 72 ... PBBeggy 1 — 77
(John Quinn) *dwlt: pushed along to ld after 2f: rdn over 3f out: hdd 2f out: no ex ins fnl f: lost 3rd nr fin* — **13/2**

3606 **5** *5* **Hernando Torres**[14] 4560 3-8-7 61 ... GrahamGibbons 4 — 58
(Michael Easterby) *midfield: hdwy 4f out: rdn to chse ldrs over 2f out: no ex appr fnl f: eased fnl 100yds* — **10/1**

306 **6** *42* **Mayan Flight (IRE)**[18] 4403 3-8-2 56 oh8 ... PatrickMathers 7 — —
(Richard Whitaker) *hld up: rdn over 4f out: sn btn* — **66/1**

0054 **7** *¾* **Tapis Libre**[17] 4440 3-8-5 66 ... DavidSimmonson(7) 6 — —
(Michael Easterby) *chsd ldrs on outer: w ldr 7f out: rdn over 4f out: sn wknd* — **28/1**

-423 **8** *3 ¾* **Alfouzy**[18] 4407 3-9-2 75 ... AntiocoMurgia(5) 3 — —
(Roger Varian) *midfield: rdn over 3f out: sn wknd* — **6/1**[3]

2155 **9** *44* **Emperor Of Rome (IRE)**[10] 4674 3-9-2 70 ... FrederikTylicki 2 — —
(Michael Dods) *led for 2f: prom: rdn and wknd qckly 4f: t.o* — **14/1**

2m 40.92s (4.22) **Going Correction** +0.15s/f (Good) — 9 Ran SP% **116.4**
Speed ratings (Par 100): **91,90,89,89,85 57,57,54,25**
Tote Swingers: 1&2 £3.70, 1&3 £4.40, 2&3 £2.80 CSF £41.53 CT £81.90 TOTE £9.30: £3.00, £1.10, £1.60; EX 39.20.
Owner Langham Hall Stud Three **Bred** Peter Botham **Trained** Great Habton, N Yorks

FOCUS
An ordinary if controversial handicap. It was strong run and the form is rated around the second and fourth. The third appeared unlucky.
Korngold ◆ Official explanation: jockey said colt was denied a clear run
Alfouzy Official explanation: jockey said filly never travelled
T/Plt: £267.30 to a £1 stake. Pool:£74,500.00 - 203.46 winning tickets T/Qpdt: £30.80 to a £1 stake. Pool:£4,977.00 - 119.30 winning tickets AS

5065 - 5071a (Foreign Racing) - See Raceform Interactive

ARLINGTON PARK (L-H)

Saturday, August 13

OFFICIAL GOING: Turf: yielding

5072a SECRETARIAT STKS (GRADE 1) (3YO) (TURF) — 1m 2f

9:52 (10:18) 3-Y-0
£149,230 (£49,743; £24,871; £12,435; £7,461; £4,974)

RPR

1 **Treasure Beach**[30] 4038 3-8-11 0 ... CO'Donoghue 3 — 119+
(A P O'Brien, Ire) — **6/4**[1]

2 *nk* **Ziyarid (IRE)**[42] 3653 3-8-7 0 ... Christophe-PatriceLemaire 2 — 114
(A De Royer-Dupre, France) — **8/1**

3 *1 ½* **Banned (USA)**[27] 3-8-11 0 ... GKGomez 6 — 115
(Thomas F Proctor, U.S.A) — **33/10**[2]

4 *1 ¾* **Willcox Inn (USA)**[35] 3-8-11 0 ... (b) RAlbarado 8 — 112
(Michael Stidham, U.S.A) — **43/10**[3]

5 *1 ¼* **Casino Host (USA)**[27] 3-8-7 0 ... RADominguez 4 — 105+
(Chad C Brown, U.S.A) — **93/10**

6 *3 ½* **Newsdad (USA)**[27] 3-8-7 0 ... (b[1]) JRosario 1 — 98
(William Mott, U.S.A) — **112/10**

7 *½* **Derby Kitten (USA)**[35] 3-8-11 0 ... (b) JRLeparoux 7 — 101
(Michael J Maker, U.S.A) — **172/10**

8 *3* **Suntracer (USA)**[35] 3-8-7 0 ... SXBridgmohan 5 — 91
(Chris Block, U.S.A) — **25/1**

P **L'Aiglon (USA)**[16] 3-8-7 0 ... (b) FGeroux 9 — —
(Gennadi Dorochenkous, U.S.A) — **65/1**

2m 3.91s (2.27) — 9 Ran SP% **122.0**
PARI-MUTUEL (all including $2 stakes): WIN 5.00; PLACE (1-2) 3.80, 8.20; SHOW (1-2-3) 2.40, 4.40, 2.20; SF 29.00.
Owner D Smith, Mrs J Magnier, M Tabor **Bred** Ashley House Stud **Trained** Ballydoyle, Co Tipperary

FOCUS
The ground was yielding after a brief thunderstorm earlier in the afternoon. It paid to be prominent and the form is rated around the third and fourth.

NOTEBOOK
Treasure Beach, whose trainer had won the race with Ciro in 2000, arrived in Chicago on the back of star billing as the best horse ever to cross the Atlantic for the $400,000 event. The Irish Derby winner did not have it easy and had to battle all the way down the stretch to get the better of a game rival, just getting his head in front inside the final furlong. Colm O'Donoghue suggested Treasure Beach has been idling, making it look harder work than was actually the case. Initial thoughts after the race suggested the winner, who raced on first-time Lasix, is likely to be targeted at the Breeders' Cup Turf at the end of the season.
Ziyarid(IRE), a Group 3 winner last time and in receipt of 4lb from Treasure Beach, set the pace and kept on in determined fashion, just missing out to his fellow European challenger.
Willcox Inn(USA), winner of the Grade 2 American Derby here last time, tried to get involved but his effort proved short-lived.

5073a BEVERLY D. STKS (GRADE 1) (3YO+ FILLIES & MARES) (TURF) — 1m 1f 110y

10:33 (10:46) 3-Y-0+
£274,038 (£91,346; £45,673; £22,836; £13,701; £9,134)

RPR

1 **Stacelita (FR)**[42] 3655 5-8-11 0 ... RADominguez 1 — 120
(Chad C Brown, U.S.A) — **9/5**[1]

2 *1 ¼* **Dubawi Heights**[74] 4-8-11 0 ... JRosario 5 — 117
(Simon Callaghan, U.S.A) — **44/5**

3 *hd* **River Jetez (SAF)**[36] 3822 8-8-11 0 ... ChristopheSoumillon 6 — 117
(M F De Kock, South Africa) — **39/10**[2]

4 *2 ½* **Fantasia**[35] 5-8-11 0 ... RMaragh 3 — 112
(Jonathan Sheppard, U.S.A) — **76/10**

The Form Book, Raceform Ltd, Compton, RG20 6NL

5 nk **Upperline (USA)**49 4-8-11 0......(b) JamesGraham 4 111
(Michael Stidham, U.S.A) **42/1**
6 ½ **Eclair De Lune (GER)**74 5-8-11 0...... JAlvarado 9 110
(Ronald McAnally, U.S.A) **26/1**
7 nse **Never Retreat (USA)**34 6-8-11 0...... SXBridgmohan 11 110
(Chris Block, U.S.A) **115/10**
8 1¾ **Pachattack (USA)**77 5-8-11 0......(b) FGeroux 8 107
(Gerard Butler) **181/10**
9 ¾ **Cheetah**35 4-8-11 0...... GKGomez 7 105
(Christophe Clement, U.S.A) **42/10**3
10 nse **Check The Label (USA)**40 4-8-11 0...... JRLeparoux 2 105
(H Graham Motion, U.S.A) **31/1**
11 4 **Romin Robin (USA)**35 5-8-11 0...... JZSantana 10 97
(David Kassen, U.S.A) **44/1**

1m 57.57s (2.10) **11** Ran SP% **121.8**
PARI-MUTUEL (all including $2 stakes): WIN 5.60; PLACE (1-2) 3.80, 6.80; SHOW (1-2-3) 2.80, 5.20, 3.60; SF 57.40.
Owner Martin S Schwartz **Bred** Jean-Pierre Dubois **Trained** USA

FOCUS
It paid to be on the pace. Stacelita is rated close to her 2010 level.

NOTEBOOK
Stacelita(FR), winner of the Prix de Diane in 2009 for former trainer Jean-Claude Rouget, recorded a decisive victory to land her fifth top-level success. She is likely to go for a Breeders' Cup race. \n\x\x Winner of the Prix de Diane in 2009 for former trainer Jean-Claude Rouget,\n
Dubawi Heights, formerly trained in Britain by Simon Callaghan, continues on the upgrade.
River Jetez(SAF) raced in mid-division and was never able to get anywhere near on terms with the winner, making up ground only once Stacelita had put the race to bed.
Pachattack(USA) never figured.

5074a ARLINGTON MILLION XXIX (GRADE 1) (3YO+) (TURF) 1m 2f

11:15 (11:21) 3-Y-O+
£369,230 (£123,076; £61,538; £30,769; £18,461; £12,307)

RPR
1 **Cape Blanco (IRE)**35 3888 4-9-0 0...... JamieSpencer 7 122
(A P O'Brien, Ire) **21/10**1
2 2½ **Gio Ponti (USA)**35 3888 6-9-0 0...... RADominguez 5 117+
(Christophe Clement, U.S.A) **23/10**2
3 nk **Dean's Kitten (USA)**35 4-9-0 0......(b) JRLeparoux 3 116
(Michael J Maker, U.S.A) **193/10**
4 ½ **Wigmore Hall (IRE)**83 2340 4-9-0 0...... HayleyTurner 9 115+
(Michael Bell) **103/10**
5 ½ **Rahystrada (USA)**55 7-9-0 0...... SheldonRussell 1 114
(Byron G Hughes, U.S.A) **87/10**
6 4 **Tajaaweed (USA)**35 6-9-0 0...... JamesGraham 2 106
(Daniel Peitz, U.S.A) **132/10**
7 hd **Mission Approved (USA)**35 3888 7-9-0 0...... JLEspinoza 8 106
(Naipaul Chatterpaul, U.S.A) **74/10**3
8 1¾ **Proceed Bee (USA)**21 5-9-0 0...... CEmigh 6 103
(Scott Becker, U.S.A) **47/1**
9 ¾ **Zack Hall (FR)**48 3448 4-9-0 0...... ChristopheSoumillon 4 101
(M Delzangles, France) **76/10**
10 1¼ **General Perfect (USA)**13 8-9-0 0......(b) GKGomez 10 99
(Glenn R Thompson, U.S.A) **38/1**

2m 5.39s (3.75) **10** Ran SP% **121.9**
PARI-MUTUEL (all including $2 stakes): WIN 6.20; PLACE (1-2) 3.80, 3.40; SHOW (1-2-3) 3.40, 2.80, 7.20; SF 16.60.
Owner Mrs F Hay,D Smith,Mrs J Magnier,M Tabor **Bred** Jack Ronan And Des Vere Hunt Farm Co **Trained** Ballydoyle, Co Tipperary

FOCUS
The form is rated around the winner, third and fifth.

NOTEBOOK
Cape Blanco(IRE) easily confirmed recent form with dual US turf champ Gio Ponti, who he beat last month in the Man o'War Stakes. An ultra-confident Spencer asked him to enter the fray on the far turn and then asked him to claim the race at least two furlongs out. While this was an early move, it was also the right one and Cape Blanco's opponents were all in trouble as the 4yo powered home for an impressive victory in one of North America's most celebrated races. Aidan O'Brien's second winner of the Million after Powerscourt in 2005, Cape Blanco is being seriously considered for Australasia's number one weight-for-age race, the Cox Plate.
Gio Ponti(USA), the winner in 2009 and runner-up to Debussy last year, is admirably consistent but was no match for his old rival.
Dean's Kitten(USA) just got up for third.
Wigmore Hall(IRE) enjoyed a ground-saving trip but could not accelerate in the closing stages.

5132 CLAIREFONTAINE (R-H)
Saturday, August 13

OFFICIAL GOING: Turf: soft

5075a PRIX 5 ANS RADIO BALANCES (PRIX LUTH ENCHANTEE) (LISTED RACE) (4YO+ FILLIES & MARES) (TURF) 1m 1f

1:00 (12:00) 4-Y-O+ **£22,413** (£8,965; £6,724; £4,482; £2,241)

RPR
1 **Babycakes (IRE)**50 3338 4-8-11 0...... StephanePasquier 5 103
(Michael Bell) *broke wl and settled 5th on outside of rivals: wnt 4th after 2f (abt 2 1/2 f off ldr): rdn ins fnl 2f: grad wore down ldr to get up fnl 30yds* **161/10**
2 1 **Peinted Song (USA)**20 4-8-11 0...... FabienLefebvre 8 101
(A De Royer-Dupre, France) **10/1**
3 nse **Intarsia (GER)**20 4-8-11 0...... MickaelBarzalona 9 101
(A Fabre, France) **49/1**
4 snk **Kartica**20 4-8-11 0......(p) OlivierPeslier 10 101
(P Demercastel, France) **10/1**
5 nk **Fadela Style (FR)**42 4-8-11 0...... FranckBlondel 2 100
(F Rossi, France) **14/5**1
6 snk **Akarlina (FR)**103 1784 5-9-2 0...... ThierryThulliez 3 105
(N Clement, France) **4/1**2
7 ½ **Roche Ambeau (FR)**20 4-8-11 0...... AnthonyCrastus 7 99
(E Lellouche, France) **11/1**
8 2½ **Numerologie (FR)**18 5-8-11 0...... AlexisBadel 12 93
(Mme M Bollack-Badel, France) **63/10**3
9 4 **Guiana (GER)** 4-8-11 0...... ADeVries 1 85
(J Hirschberger, Germany) **63/10**3
10 1 **Convidada (IRE)**244 4-8-11 0...... MaximeGuyon 4 83
(M Delcher-Sanchez, Spain) **15/1**
11 **Fanditha (IRE)**3 4915 5-8-11 0...... DominiqueBoeuf 6 83
(Mick Channon) *hld up towards rr (9th on rail): pushed along over 2f out: no imp u.p fnl 1 1/2f: eased fnl 150yds: nvr in contention* **21/1**

1m 51.7s (111.70) **11** Ran SP% **118.9**
PARI-MUTUEL (all including 1 euro stakes): WIN 17.10; PLACE 5.90, 3.20, 11.40; DF 79.10; SF 203.30.
Owner J Acheson **Bred** Alan Dargan **Trained** Newmarket, Suffolk

NOTEBOOK
Babycakes(IRE), a consistent filly, was successful on her first start in Listed company. The soft ground proved no problem.
Fanditha(IRE) was never a factor.

5076a - (Foreign Racing) - See Raceform Interactive

4674 PONTEFRACT (L-H)
Sunday, August 14

OFFICIAL GOING: Good to firm (good in places; 7.7)
Wind: Light, behind. Weather: Cloudy

5077 BRITISH STALLION STUDS E B F TREVOR WOODS MEMORIAL MAIDEN STKS 5f

2:00 (2:03) (Class 4) 2-Y-O **£4,851** (£1,443; £721; £360) **Stalls** Low

Form RPR
403 1 **Kune Kune**15 4557 2-8-12 68...... SilvestreDeSousa 1 81
(Marco Botti) *trckd ldr: led 3f out: rdn clr over 1f out: kpt on wl* **5/2**1
2220 2 5 **Nayarra (IRE)**50 3402 2-8-12 82...... SamHitchcott 7 63
(Mick Channon) *sn pushed along in tch: rdn and hdwy over 1f out: wnt 2nd appr fnl f: kpt on: no ch w wnr* **9/2**3
6022 3 1¾ **I'll Be Good**15 4557 2-9-0 74...... GaryBartley(3) 3 62
(Robert Johnson) *trckd ldr: rdn over 2f out: kpt on same pce* **7/1**
22 4 ¾ **Kimbali (IRE)**29 4106 2-9-3 0...... PaulHanagan 8 59
(Richard Fahey) *hld up: rdn over 2f out: hdwy over 1f out: kpt on ins fnl f: nvr threatened* **4/1**2
6552 5 3¾ **Reve Du Jour (IRE)**21 4365 2-8-9 66......(p) MartinHarley(3) 4 41
(Alan McCabe) *led: hdd 3f out: sn rdn: wknd appr fnl f* **14/1**
0 6 nk **Larwood (IRE)**19 4414 2-9-3 0...... DaneO'Neill 9 44
(Henry Candy) *hld up: sn pushed along: brief hdwy over 1f out: no imp fnl f* **13/2**
3005 7 3¾ **Sabusa (IRE)**33 3948 2-8-10 68...... NoraLooby(7) 5 31
(Alan McCabe) *hld up: nvr threatened* **66/1**
8 ½ **Miss Ella Jade** 2-8-12 0...... MichaelStainton 10 24
(Richard Whitaker) *wnt rt s: bdly outpcd in rr tl minor late hdwy* **66/1**
020 9 nk **Free Zone**29 4094 2-9-3 77......(v1) TomEaves 6 28
(Bryan Smart) *chsd ldrs on outer: rdn over 2f out: sn wknd: hung bdly rt over 1f out* **8/1**

62.88 secs (-0.42) **Going Correction** -0.10s/f (Good) **9** Ran SP% **113.3**
Speed ratings (Par 96): **99,91,88,87,81 80,74,73,73**
Tote Swingers:1&2:£2.60, 2&3:£6.00, 1&3:£5.00 CSF £13.48 TOTE £3.50: £1.60, £1.60, £2.40; EX 14.90 Trifecta £41.60 Pool £532.14 - 9.45 winning units..
Owner Mrs Anita Nicol **Bred** Miss S E Hall **Trained** Newmarket, Suffolk

FOCUS
Jockeys praised the ground after the first, describing it as 'good' and 'beautiful'. An ordinary juvenile maiden which has been won in the last couple of seasons by the decent Kevin Ryan pair Lexi's Hero and Our Jonathan. It was a sound run race and the winning time was just over a second outside the standard. It's hard to know how literally to take this form but it seems solid as rated.

NOTEBOOK
Kune Kune, drawn in the inside stall, was a bit slow to break but was in front before halfway and she pretty much had things wrapped up entering the final furlong, although her rider kept her up to her work. Things had not gone her way on her first three starts but she is clearly quite speedy and she may be able to add to this. She should have no problem with a sixth furlong. (op 10-3 tchd 7-2)
Nayarra(IRE), minus the headgear this time, chased the winner through without ever looking like pegging her back. Not beaten far in a 6f Listed race on her latest outing in June, and 10lb clear on official figures, she has now found one to beat her on each of her four starts in maidens. It doesn't help that she is not very big. (op 4-1 tchd 7-2)
I'll Be Good was runner-up at Thirsk on his last two starts, half a length in front of Kune Kune on the most recent of them. He ran his race and is a fair guide to the form. (tchd 13-2)
Kimbali(IRE) was a shade slow to break again and did not get an entirely smooth run through in the straight, but he can't be classed as unlucky. He probably needs further now. (op 3-1)
Reve Du Jour(IRE) showed early dash but could not hold off the winner for long. She may not be entirely straightforward. (op 16-1)
Larwood(IRE) came in for a bit of support but he was outpaced early on and was never really in it. (op 7-1)
Free Zone, visored for the first time, hung badly to his right in the straight after chasing the pace. (tchd 10-1)

5078 FAMILY FUNDAY H'CAP 1m 4f 8y

2:30 (2:30) (Class 3) (0-90,88) 3-Y-O+
£7,158 (£2,143; £1,071; £535; £267; £134) **Stalls** Low

Form RPR
1-30 1 **Rain Mac**38 3774 3-9-1 **86**...... WilliamBuick 6 100+
(John Gosden) *hld up: pushed along over 3f out: hdwy over 2f out: kpt on strly fnl f: led towards fin* **2/1**1
2-30 2 ¾ **Northside Prince (IRE)**95 2002 5-9-13 **87**...... PJMcDonald 3 97
(Alan Swinbank) *midfield: rdn and hdwy over 2f out: led appr fnl f: kpt on: hdd towards fin* **20/1**
2402 3 3 **Hong Kong Island (IRE)**11 4677 4-9-6 **83**...... DaleSwift(3) 4 88
(Micky Hammond) *trckd ldr: rdn over 2f out: kpt on* **11/2**3
0100 4 ¾ **Pass Muster**15 4528 4-9-9 **86**...... MichaelO'Connell(3) 1 90
(Ollie Pears) *dwlt: hld up and t.k.h: hdwy over 2f out: rdn over 1f out: kpt on ins fnl f* **18/1**
6302 5 3¾ **Trip The Light**3 4957 6-9-2 **79**......(v) LeeTopliss(3) 5 77
(Richard Fahey) *trckd ldr: rdn over 2f out: one pce* **7/1**
2136 6 ½ **Stagecoach Danman (IRE)**24 4251 3-8-12 **83**..... SilvestreDeSousa 11 80
(Mark Johnston) *led: rdn over 2f out: hdd appr fnl f: no ex* **5/1**2
2120 7 12 **War Poet**43 3625 4-9-9 **83**...... DanielTudhope 8 61
(David O'Meara) *s.i.s: hld up: rdn over 2f out: sn no imp* **7/1**
3255 8 16 **Granston (IRE)**23 4280 10-10-0 **88**...... GrahamGibbons 10 40
(James Bethell) *in tch and t.k.h: rdn over 2f out: wknd over 1f out* **22/1**
4000 9 21 **Snow Dancer (IRE)**15 4528 7-9-9 **83**...... PaulHanagan 13 —
(Hugh McWilliams) *hld up: rdn over 2f out: wknd over 1f out: eased* **25/1**

0000 **10** *21* **Epic (IRE)**[15] 4555 4-8-11 **71**........ NeilCallan 7 —
(Mark Johnston) *midfield: pushed along and lost pl over 3f out: sn wknd: t.o* **50/1**

20-0 **11** *25* **Isobar (GER)**[15] 4555 5-9-5 **79**........ KierenFallon 12 —
(Luca Cumani) *trckd ldrs: rdn over 3f out: wknd qckly: t.o* **12/1**

2m 37.23s (-3.57) **Going Correction** -0.10s/f (Good)
WFA 3 from 4yo+ 11lb **11** Ran SP% **118.3**
Speed ratings (Par 107): **107,106,104,104,101 101,93,82,68,54 37**
Tote Swingers:1&2:£3.40, 2&3:£16.50, 1&3:£3.40 CSF £51.87 CT £199.21 TOTE £3.00: £1.50, £4.70, £1.80; EX 47.00 Trifecta £332.80 Pool £629.63 - 1.40 winning units..
Owner K Abdulla **Bred** Juddmonte Farms Ltd **Trained** Newmarket, Suffolk

FOCUS
A decent handicap and the form looks sound. The winner shaped better than the bare form.

NOTEBOOK
Rain Mac required niggling along at various stages of the race and had half a dozen in front of him entering the fairly short home straight, but he picked up well down the outside and won a shade readily in the end. Tackling older horses for the first time, he appreciated the step up to 1m4f and will be suited by a truer test at this trip. There is further improvement in him. (op 9-4 tchd 15-8)
Northside Prince(IRE) had not had things go his way in two outings in the spring, but he was open to improvement at this longer trip. He came there to win his race but could not repel the progressive youngster. This was a sound effort, but he remains 9lb above his last winning mark. (op 16-1)
Hong Kong Island(IRE) was never far from the forefront and ran another good race at a track which clearly suits him. He is currently 17lb higher than when winning over 1m2f here in April. (op 5-1 tchd 6-1)
Pass Muster made late progress from the rear on this second run for the Ollie Pears yard. He was sticking on at the end and got the longer trip well, but lacks a change of pace. (op 20-1)
Trip The Light, 7lb lower than when runner-up in this last year, ran well for a long way on this quick reappearance. (op 6-1)
Stagecoach Danman(IRE) had ground conditions to suit and got his way in front, but he could not fend off the challengers in the straight. (op 7-1)
War Poet never threatened and is starting to become a little disappointing. The ability is there and he might benefit from some headgear. (op 15-2)
Granston(IRE), who was too free, was soundly beaten. Official explanation: jockey said gelding ran too free (op 20-1)
Isobar(GER) dropped away tamely before the straight and this wasn't his running.

5079 BETFAIR SUPPORTS GO RACING IN YORKSHIRE H'CAP 2m 1f 22y
3:00 (3:00) (Class 5) (0-70,76) 3-Y-0+ **£4,204** (£1,251; £625; £312) **Stalls** Low

Form RPR
1224 **1** **Petella**[52] 3316 5-9-7 **63**........ JimmyFortune 11 74
(George Moore) *hld up: hdwy on outer over 5f out: trckd ldrs 4f out: led wl over 2f out: drvn clr over 1f out: kpt on wl* **12/1**[2]

0342 **2** *3* **Simple Jim (FR)**[6] 4856 7-8-12 **54**........ SilvestreDeSousa 1 61
(David O'Meara) *t.k.h in midfield: rdn and hdwy on outer 3f out: kpt on: wnt 2nd fnl 100yds* **3/1**[1]

5442 **3** *1* **Bandanaman (IRE)**[13] 4602 5-8-11 **60**........ GarryWhillans(7) 17 66
(Alan Swinbank) *midfield on outer: rdn and hdwy 3f out: chsd wnr over 1f out: one pce fnl f: lost 2nd fnl 100yds* **16/1**

2201 **4** *nk* **Jeu De Roseau (IRE)**[22] 4326 7-9-11 **67**........ PJMcDonald 2 72
(Chris Grant) *midfield on inner: rdn over 3f out: hdwy over 1f out: kpt on fnl f* **12/1**[2]

/152 **5** *1* **Riptide**[15] 4562 5-9-7 **70**........(v) DavidKenny(7) 9 74
(Michael Scudamore) *in tch: rdn over 5f out: outpcd over 3f out: styd on again fr over 1f out* **12/1**[2]

2022 **6** *shd* **Finellas Fortune**[11] 4671 6-8-12 **54**........ AndrewMullen 10 58
(George Moore) *prom: rdn 3f out: kpt on one pce* **22/1**

0146 **7** *2 ¾* **Tillietudlem (FR)**[11] 4671 5-9-6 **62**........ DanielTudhope 13 63
(Jim Goldie) *in tch: rdn over 3f out: one pce* **12/1**[2]

2211 **8** *1* **Fire Fighter (IRE)**[10] 4712 3-9-5 **76**........ SebSanders 16 76
(Sir Mark Prescott Bt) *trckd ldr on outer: led 4f out: hdd wl over 2f out: wknd fnl f* **3/1**[1]

3453 **9** *24* **Spruzzo**[13] 4602 5-9-2 **58**........ KellyHarrison 14 29
(Chris Fairhurst) *led: rdn over 5f out: hdd 4f out: wknd over 2f out* **20/1**

015 **10** *10* **No Time For Tears (IRE)**[30] 4074 4-8-8 **53**........(p) KieranO'Neill(3) 6 12
(Lucinda Featherstone) *in tch: rdn over 3f out: wknd over 2f out* **25/1**

60-2 **11** *2* **Go Amwell**[20] 4396 8-8-9 **51** oh2........(v) AdrianMcCarthy 8 —
(J R Jenkins) *hld up: nvr threatened* **33/1**

5-05 **12** *9* **Uncle Keef (IRE)**[23] 4274 5-8-13 **55**........ KierenFallon 7 —
(Brendan Powell) *hld up: rdn over 4f out: sn no imp* **14/1**[3]

0440 **13** *2 ½* **Spahi (FR)**[6] 4856 5-8-10 **52**........ JamieSpencer 3 —
(David O'Meara) *hld up: hdwy 4f out: rdn over 2f out: sn wknd* **12/1**[2]

5-00 **14** *7* **Solis**[19] 4408 5-9-2 **58**........ TomEaves 15 —
(Micky Hammond) *hld up on outer: a towards rr* **66/1**

0/-6 **15** *nk* **Bulwark (IRE)**[15] 4562 9-9-13 **69**........(v) JimCrowley 4 —
(Ian Williams) *hld up: a towards rr* **16/1**

1333 **16** *17* **Golden Future**[15] 4562 8-9-8 **64**........ PaulHanagan 12 —
(Peter Niven) *prom: rdn and lost pl qckly 4f out: sn wknd* **14/1**[3]

3m 45.55s (0.95) **Going Correction** -0.10s/f (Good)
WFA 3 from 4yo+ 15lb **16** Ran SP% **130.9**
Speed ratings (Par 103): **93,91,91,90,90 90,89,88,77,72 71,67,66,63,62 54**
Tote Swingers:1&2:£7.80, 2&3:£17.80, 1&3:£36.00 CSF £48.54 CT £622.54 TOTE £12.30: £2.50, £1.40, £4.40, £3.00; EX 50.10 Trifecta £386.00 Pool £678.22 - 1.30 winning units..
Owner A Crute & Partners **Bred** C And Mrs Wilson **Trained** Middleham Moor, N Yorks

FOCUS
An open staying handicap, but just ordinary form. The pace was strong. A personal best for the winner.

5080 E B F "SHOWCASING" FLYING FILLIES' STKS (LISTED RACE) 6f
3:30 (3:31) (Class 1) 3-Y-0+
£19,848 (£7,525; £3,766; £1,876; £941; £472) **Stalls** Low

Form RPR
6032 **1** **Rose Blossom**[14] 4573 4-9-0 103........ PaulHanagan 1 104
(Richard Fahey) *mde all: rdn clr over 1f out: kpt on* **9/2**[3]

-054 **2** *1 ¼* **Darajaat (USA)**[30] 4063 3-8-10 95........ TadhgO'Shea 2 99
(Marcus Tregoning) *trckd wnr: rdn over 2f out: kpt on: nvr rchd wnr* **40/1**

0221 **3** *nk* **Desert Poppy (IRE)**[29] 4101 4-9-0 95........ KierenFallon 9 99
(Walter Swinburn) *trckd ldrs: rdn over 2f out: edgd lft and kpt on ins fnl f* **7/1**

022 **4** *¾* **Dever Dream**[16] 4497 4-9-0 105........ EddieAhern 11 101+
(William Haggas) *hld up: pushed along over 2f out: gd hdwy over 1f out: short of room appr fnl f: swtchd rt: kpt on* **9/4**[1]

0-34 **5** *2* **Ishbelle**[22] 4332 3-8-10 93........(v[1]) JimCrowley 4 89
(Ralph Beckett) *dwlt: in midfield: rdn 3f out: one pce* **22/1**

5106 **6** *shd* **Sioux Rising (IRE)**[22] 4332 5-9-0 92........ TonyHamilton 6 90
(Richard Fahey) *midfield on outer: rdn over 2f out: kpt on one pce* **33/1**

2500 **7** *3 ¼* **Sharnberry**[16] 4497 3-8-10 103........ WilliamBuick 10 79
(Ed Dunlop) *hld up: rdn 2f out: kpt on fnl f: n.d* **14/1**

4553 **8** *nse* **Capercaillie (USA)**[36] 3852 4-9-0 91........ RoystonFfrench 5 79
(Clive Cox) *trckd ldr: rdn over 2f out: wknd over 1f out* **22/1**

200 **9** *5* **Dubai Media (CAN)**[15] 4531 4-9-0 91........ JamieSpencer 8 63
(Ed Dunlop) *hld up: effrt over 2f out: sn no imp* **16/1**

-104 **10** *1* **Rimth**[16] 4497 3-9-3 107........ TomQueally 7 66
(Paul Cole) *midfield on outer: rdn over 2f out: sn no imp* **4/1**[2]

6165 **11** *3* **Folly Bridge**[22] 4332 4-9-0 99........(v[1]) JimmyFortune 3 51
(Roger Charlton) *s.i.s: sn midfield: rdn over 2f out: wknd over 1f out* **10/1**

1m 14.78s (-2.12) **Going Correction** -0.10s/f (Good)
WFA 3 from 4yo+ 4lb **11** Ran SP% **117.2**
Speed ratings (Par 108): **110,108,107,106,104 104,99,99,93,91 87**
Tote Swingers:1&2:£21.00, 2&3:£32.20, 1&3:£4.50 CSF £180.20 TOTE £4.20: £1.30, £11.60, £2.90; EX 153.50 Trifecta £725.80 Pool £1,206.43 - 1.23 winning units..
Owner Highclere Thoroughbred Racing (Blossom) **Bred** J R Mitchell **Trained** Musley Bank, N Yorks

FOCUS
A decent renewal of this fillies' sprint. Not many got into it with the first two home, from stalls one and two, occupying the same positions throughout. The form is rated around the second to her 2yo best.

NOTEBOOK
Rose Blossom, ideally drawn for one who has to make the running, was out of the stalls like a bullet and, although her stamina for this stiff 6f was put to the test, she proved up to the task and kept going well. She is clearly effective at this trip and is a consistent and likeable filly.
Darajaat(USA) is a pacey type and she chased the winner all the way. She is not the easiest to place but should continue to give it a good shot at this trip or down at five. (op 50-1)
Desert Poppy(IRE) has improved of late and she backed up her Newmarket handicap win with a sound run on this rise in grade, picking up black type on this first attempt at Listed company. (op 8-1 tchd 11-2)
Dever Dream, a non-runner in Saturday's Hungerford Stakes at Newbury, had been running well in Group 3 company lately and won her last two starts in Listed races. This trip is on the short side for her though, and she had plenty of ground to make up turning into the short straight from her high draw. A gap closed on her and she had to switch outside, costing her momentum, but for which she would probably have finished second. She remains in good heart. (op 15-8 tchd 5-2)
Ishbelle, whose trainer won this two years ago with Mullein, was visored for the first time. She was staying on at the end after seeming to find this too sharp. (op 20-1)
Sioux Rising(IRE), the winner's stablemate, was never a factor, but this was still a creditable effort.
Sharnberry was back at a sprint trip for the first time this season and she could never get into the race. (op 16-1 tchd 20-1)
Rimth was forced to race wide when fourth in a Goodwood Group 3 recently, two places behind Dever Dream, and it was a similar story here. Carrying a 7lb penalty for Fred Darling win in April, and 7lb worse off with Dever Dream, she was always caught out wide towards the rear of the field and could never get into the hunt. She had not run over this short since finishing second in the Cheveley Park Stakes in the autumn, and needs another furlong now. She can probably be forgiven this. (tchd 9-2)

5081 JOHN HIRST - 50TH BIRTHDAY H'CAP 1m 4y
4:00 (4:00) (Class 3) (0-95,87) 3-Y-O
£7,158 (£2,143; £1,071; £535; £267; £134) **Stalls** Low

Form RPR
-160 **1** **Polar Kite (IRE)**[59] 3067 3-9-6 **86**........ PaulHanagan 9 95+
(Richard Fahey) *in tch: rdn and hdwy 2f out: chal appr fnl f: kpt on: led fnl 50yds* **9/2**[3]

-120 **2** *nk* **Tullius (IRE)**[38] 3774 3-9-7 **87**........ JimCrowley 2 95
(Peter Winkworth) *trckd ldr: rdn over 2f out: led narrowly jst ins fnl f: kpt on: hdd fnl 50yds* **3/1**[2]

5224 **3** *1 ¾* **Maggie Mey (IRE)**[9] 4750 3-8-9 **75**........ SilvestreDeSousa 7 79
(David O'Meara) *led: rdn over 2f out: hdd jst ins fnl f: no ex* **10/1**

003 **4** *1* **Baptist (USA)**[36] 3864 3-9-7 **87**........ JimmyFortune 4 89
(Andrew Balding) *s.i.s: hld up and t.k.h: rdn over 2f out: no imp tl kpt on fnl f: nt rch ldrs* **5/2**[1]

1130 **5** *nk* **Chosen Character (IRE)**[36] 3864 3-9-2 **82**........(t) RichardKingscote 3 83
(Tom Dascombe) *hld up: rdn over 2f out: kpt on one pce: nvr threatened ldrs* **9/1**

032 **6** *1 ½* **Buzz Law (IRE)**[9] 4750 3-8-12 **78**........ AndrewElliott 10 76
(Mrs K Burke) *trckd ldr: rdn over 2f out: wknd over 1f out* **16/1**

0552 **7** *6* **Jade**[11] 4676 3-8-9 **75**........ KierenFallon 11 59
(Ollie Pears) *in tch: hdwy and ev ch 2f out: wknd appr fnl f* **5/1**

1m 44.08s (-1.82) **Going Correction** -0.10s/f (Good) **7** Ran SP% **113.4**
Speed ratings (Par 104): **105,104,102,101,101 100,94**
Tote Swingers:1&2:£2.20, 2&3:£6.60, 1&3:£13.40 CSF £18.07 CT £125.77 TOTE £5.70: £3.30, £2.60; EX 21.30 Trifecta £117.50 Pool £540.12 - 3.40 winning units..
Owner Mr And Mrs J D Cotton **Bred** Holborn Trust Co **Trained** Musley Bank, N Yorks

FOCUS
A decent handicap, albeit weakened by non-runners. The pace was sound and the winner resumed on the upgrade. The second is progressive too.

NOTEBOOK
Polar Kite(IRE) had been found wanting behind Sagramor in a couple of the hottest 3yo handicaps of the season, latterly the Britannia at Royal Ascot, but was down in grade here after a break. He settled in midfield and delivered a sustained challenge in the straight which was always going to get him there. He is still relatively inexperienced and has more to offer. (op 5-1)
Tullius(IRE) ran better back down at 1m and went down fighting. He is 10lb higher than when winning at Sandown in May and running too well to expect any significant drop. (op 4-1)
Maggie Mey(IRE) stuck to her guns and was only caught entering the final furlong. She is a reliable filly.
Baptist(USA), down in class after a decent effort at Newmarket, was sluggish leaving the stalls before racing keenly in rear. He did pick up in the straight, but too late to get into the mix. This was a little disapppointing (op 2-1)
Chosen Character(IRE), held up this time after a slow start, was never in the hunt but did finish appreciably closer to Baptist than he had at Newmarket. The visor was discarded here. (op 11-1)
Buzz Law(IRE), 4lb higher than when runner-up to the improver Camberley Two at Haydock, was a bit below his recent level and finished behind old rival Maggie Mey this time. (op 14-1)
Jade faded in the final furlong and may need some help from the handicapper. (op 9-2)

5082 S W INSTALLATIONS FOR WINDOWS AND DOORS MAIDEN STKS 1m 4y
4:30 (4:31) (Class 4) 3-Y-O+ **£4,528** (£1,347; £673; £336) **Stalls** Low

Form RPR
2 **1** **Paramour**[16] 4514 4-9-7 0........ DanielTudhope 7 91+
(David O'Meara) *bmpd s: in midfield: gd hdwy over 2f out: rdn to ld appr fnl f: sn clr: eased towards fin* **13/8**[1]

4 **2** *2 ¾* **Cairncross (IRE)**[21] 4363 3-8-9 0........ SilvestreDeSousa 16 76
(Mark Johnston) *flashed tail: sn led: rdn whn hdd appr fnl f: kpt on: no ch w wnr* **7/1**

3 5 **Alfred Hutchinson** 3-8-11 0 .... DaleSwift(3) 3 69
(Geoffrey Oldroyd) *dwlt: in midfield: rdn over 3f out: hdwy over 1f out: kpt on fnl f: wnt 3rd fnl 75yds* **40/1**

6303 4 2 1/2 **To The Spring**[15] 4560 3-8-9 68 .... (b) KierenFallon 10 58
(William Haggas) *wnt lft s: trckd ldrs: chal over 2f out: drvn and one pce over 1f out: lost 3rd fnl 75yds* **4/1**[3]

5 2 **Neutrafa (IRE)** 3-8-9 0 .... GrahamGibbons 15 54+
(John Mackie) *s.i.s: sn in midfield on outer: hdwy 3f out: ev ch 2f out: rdn and one pce fnl f* **33/1**

3 6 3 1/4 **Lady Sledmere (IRE)**[21] 4370 3-8-9 0 .... MickyFenton 2 46+
(Paul Midgley) *racd keenly: in tch on inner: pushed along whn bdly hmpd wl over 2f out: one pce after* **7/2**[2]

0 7 1 1/2 **Painted Tail (IRE)**[16] 4514 4-9-2 0 .... PJMcDonald 11 44
(Alan Swinbank) *hld up: rdn over 2f out: kpt on fnl f: nvr trbld ldrs* **25/1**

8 15 **Ferroviere** 3-9-0 0 .... BarryMcHugh 4 —
(Ollie Pears) *t.k.h: trckd ldrs: losing pl whn sltly hmpd over 2f out: sn wknd: eased fnl f* **66/1**

43 9 10 **Lizzy's Dream**[33] 3949 3-8-9 0 .... ChrisDCogan(5) 8 —
(Robin Bastiman) *bmpd s: sn w ldr: racd keenly: rdn and edgd lft over 2f out: wknd over 1f out* **33/1**

0-65 10 6 **Illawalla**[83] 2350 3-8-7 44 .... VictorSantos(7) 1 —
(Hugh McWilliams) *hld up: a towards rr* **150/1**

4 11 7 **Takhreej (IRE)**[71] 2723 3-9-0 0 .... TomEaves 9 —
(Keith Dalgleish) *hld up: nvr threatened* **16/1**

12 30 **Aqua Lad** 3-9-0 0 .... NeilCallan 12 —
(Mark Johnston) *chsd ldrs on outer: pushed along over 3f out: sn wknd: t.o* **20/1**

13 11 **Bash On (IRE)** 3-9-0 0 .... (t) TomQueally 13 —
(James Bethell) *sn pushed along in rr: a bhd: t.o* **22/1**

1m 44.45s (-1.45) **Going Correction** -0.10s/f (Good)
WFA 3 from 4yo 7lb **13** Ran SP% **122.1**
Speed ratings (Par 105): **103,100,95,92,90 87,86,71,61,55 48,18,7**
Tote Swingers:1&2:£4.90, 2&3:£37.40, 1&3:£15.20 CSF £12.96 TOTE £2.50: £1.60, £2.80, £12.60; EX 16.70 Trifecta £643.40 Part won. Pool £869.56 - 0.60 winning units..
Owner R G Fell **Bred** Cheveley Park Stud Ltd **Trained** Nawton, N Yorks

FOCUS
A weakish maiden with little strength in depth. They finished well strung out and the time was only slighty slower than the Class 3 handicap. The winner was value for a bit extra and the runner-up improved on her debut effort.
Neutrafa(IRE) Official explanation: jockey said filly lost its action

5083 NOVA DISPLAY H'CAP 6f
5:00 (5:00) (Class 5) (0-75,74) 3-Y-0+ **£2,587** (£770; £384; £192) **Stalls** Low

Form RPR

2040 1 **Last Sovereign**[22] 4349 7-9-12 **74** .... (bt1) TomQueally 6 86
(Ollie Pears) *mde most: drvn clr over 1f out: kpt on* **11/1**

2540 2 2 1/4 **Cornus**[9] 4742 9-9-9 **74** .... (be) MartinHarley(3) 13 79+
(Alan McCabe) *chsd ldrs: rdn over 2f out: wnt 2nd 1f out: kpt on: nvr trbld wnr* **10/1**

3502 3 2 **Mingun Bell (USA)**[30] 4066 4-9-12 **74** .... PatCosgrave 4 72
(Ed de Giles) *midfield: rdn over 2f out: hdwy over 1f out: kpt on fnl f: wnt 3rd post* **5/1**[1]

4101 4 shd **Toby Tyler**[23] 4291 5-9-11 **73** .... (v) MickyFenton 5 71
(Paul Midgley) *hld up: rdn and hdwy 2f out: chsd ldrs over 1f out: kpt on* **9/1**[3]

0356 5 1 1/2 **Illustrious Prince (IRE)**[11] 4670 4-9-5 **74** .... JasonHart(7) 11 67
(Declan Carroll) *midfield on outer: rdn over 2f out: kpt on* **16/1**

3005 6 hd **Indieslad**[12] 4634 3-9-7 **73** .... FrannyNorton 2 66
(Ann Duffield) *hld up in midfield: rdn and hdwy over 1f out: kpt on fnl f* **14/1**

4510 7 2 3/4 **Powerful Pierre**[22] 4349 4-9-4 **69** .... (b) DaleSwift(3) 10 53
(Ian McInnes) *dwlt: pushed along early: bhd tl late hdwy: nvr on terms* **16/1**

2043 8 hd **Commander Wish**[5] 4893 8-8-5 **56** .... (p) KieranO'Neill(3) 9 39
(Lucinda Featherstone) *outpcd towards rr tl sme late hdwy: nvr on terms* **25/1**

0003 9 3/4 **Haadeeth**[8] 4780 4-9-4 **66** .... PaulHanagan 12 47
(Richard Fahey) [illegible]

0534 10 3/4 **Pearly Wey**[15] 4564 8-8-5 **56** oh1 ow1 .... PaulPickard(3) 8 34+
(Ian McInnes) *hld up on inner: bdly hmpd over 2f out: nt rcvr* **20/1**

5226 11 3 **Ballinargh Girl (IRE)**[8] 4792 3-9-7 **73** .... BarryMcHugh 14 42
(Robert Wylie) *cl up on outer: rdn and wknd over 1f out* **6/1**[2]

5020 12 3 3/4 **Sonny Red (IRE)**[23] 4291 7-9-5 **74** .... ShirleyTeasdale(7) 1 31
(David Nicholls) *led early: in tch on inner: rdn over 2f out: wknd over 1f out* **16/1**

2000 13 1 1/2 **Divertimenti (IRE)**[8] 4793 7-9-1 **63** .... (b) RussKennemore 3 24
(Roy Bowring) *chsd ldrs: rdn over 2f out: wknd over 1f out: eased* **20/1**

0634 14 4 **Chambers (IRE)**[20] 4378 5-8-7 **55** .... SilvestreDeSousa 7 —
(Eric Alston) *sn pushed along in midfield: wknd over 1f out* **9/1**[3]

1m 16.05s (-0.85) **Going Correction** -0.10s/f (Good)
WFA 3 from 4yo+ 4lb **14** Ran SP% **120.3**
Speed ratings (Par 103): **101,98,95,95,93 92,89,89,88,87 83,78,76,70**
Tote Swingers:1&2:£23.10, 2&3:£15.50, 1&3:£10.70 CSF £113.32 CT £643.65 TOTE £12.40: £3.40, £3.80, £1.80; EX 184.60 TRIFECTA Not won..
Owner Richard Walker **Bred** Gestut Hof Ittlingen & Cheveley Park Stud Ltd **Trained** Norton, N Yorks
■ Stewards' Enquiry : Pat Cosgrave one-day ban: used whip with excessive frequency (Aug 28)

FOCUS
An ordinary handicap which looked wide open beforehand. The time was decent and the winner is rated back to something like his best.
Divertimenti(IRE) Official explanation: jockey said gelding lost its action
T/Jkpt: £21,196.80 to a £1 stake. Pool £59,709.57. 2.00 winning tickets. T/Plt: £197.80 to a £1 stake. Pool £116,489.97. 429.71 winning tickets. T/Qpdt: £52.10 to a £1 stake. Pool £5,535.08. 78.50 winning tickets. AS

5084 - 5085a, 5087 - 5089a (Foreign Racing) - See Raceform Interactive

3961 DUNDALK (A.W) (L-H)
Sunday, August 14

OFFICIAL GOING: Standard

5086a BAR ONE RACING H'CAP (PREMIER HANDICAP) 6f (P)
3:35 (3:36) 3-Y-0+ **£21,012** (£6,142; £2,909; £969)

RPR

1 **Below Zero (IRE)**[15] 4556 4-8-11 85 .... FMBerry 3 101
(Mark Johnston) *mde all: rdn wl over 1f out: kpt on strly ins fnl f* **15/2**

2 4 **The Reaper (IRE)**[9] 4767 3-9-5 97 .... (b) JMurtagh 9 99
(G M Lyons, Ire) *trckd ldr in 2nd: drvn along fr 2f out: no imp on wnr fr 1f out: kpt on same pce u.p* **4/1**[1]

3 2 **Bajan Tryst (USA)**[85] 2317 5-9-12 100 .... PhillipMakin 4 97
(Kevin Ryan) *a.p: trckd ldrs on inner in 3rd 1/2-way: rdn 2f out: no imp fr over 1f out: kpt on one pce* **5/1**[2]

4 1 3/4 **Copper Dock (IRE)**[19] 4420 7-8-6 80 .... BACurtis 5 71
(T G McCourt, Ire) *chsd ldrs on inner: 4th 1/2-way: rdn and no imp fr over 1f out: kpt on one pce* **8/1**

5 2 1/2 **Knock Stars (IRE)**[49] 3440 3-9-3 95 .... PJSmullen 10 77+
(Patrick Martin, Ire) *towards rr: sme hdwy on outer early st: mod 5th 1f out: kpt on one pce* **7/1**

6 hd **Luisant**[49] 3444 8-10-0 105 .... JPO'Brien(3) 13 88+
(J A Nash, Ire) *in rr of mid-div: mod 7th on outer under 2f out: no imp and kpt on one pce* **10/1**

7 2 1/2 **Partner (IRE)**[9] 4767 5-8-13 92 .... (p) LFRoche(5) 14 67+
(David Marnane, Ire) *towards rr: sme hdwy on outer to go mod 8th over 1f out: kpt on one pce* **16/1**

8 3/4 **Maarek**[11] 4690 4-9-1 89 .... WMLordan 7 61+
(David Peter Nagle, Ire) *chsd ldrs: 5th 1/2-way: sn drvn along: no ex fr wl over 1f out* **13/2**[3]

9 1 3/4 **Quinmaster (USA)**[93] 2078 9-9-6 94 .... (p) GFCarroll 11 61+
(M Halford, Ire) *chsd ldrs: 7th 1/2-way: no threat fr 2f out* **33/1**

10 3 **Tell The Wind (IRE)**[7] 4835 3-8-2 85 .... SHJames(5) 8 41+
(Kevin Prendergast, Ire) *chsd ldrs: 6th 1/2-way: sn rdn and no ex fr 1 1/2f out* **20/1**

11 3/4 **Finicius (USA)**[42] 2533 7-9-8 101 .... (t) RPWhelan(5) 2 56+
(Eoin Griffin, Ire) *rrd and s.i.s: a towards rr* **20/1**

12 3/4 **Kargali (IRE)**[287] 7259 6-10-2 104 .... (t) NGMcCullagh 6 56+
(Luke Comer, Ire) *chsd ldrs: 8th 1/2-way: no ex fr 2f out* **33/1**

13 3 1/2 **Fred Archer (IRE)**[33] 3969 3-8-12 90 .... CO'Donoghue 1 30+
(David Marnane, Ire) *chsd ldrs on inner early: no threat fr 1/2-way: eased whn btn ins fnl f* **20/1**

14 9 **So Stylish (USA)**[14] 4588 3-8-12 90 .... SeamieHeffernan 12 —+
(A P O'Brien, Ire) *a towards rr: eased whn btn ins fnl f* **15/2**

1m 11.24s (71.24)
WFA 3 from 4yo+ 4lb **14** Ran SP% **132.3**
CSF £38.66 CT £178.99 TOTE £10.40: £3.20, £1.50, £2.50; DF 62.70.
Owner Sheikh Hamdan Bin Mohammed Al Maktoum **Bred** Darley **Trained** Middleham Moor, N Yorks

NOTEBOOK
Below Zero(IRE) made all the running from his favourable draw to register a fifth career win. Always travelling at the head of affairs, his only serious rival The Reaper had no more to give entering the final furlong and it was a comprehensive victory in the end for the outsider of the two British challengers. Winning trainer Mark Johnston told the stewards that he could find no apparent reason for poor performances at Ascot and Newmarket other than to suspect that his charge is not the most consistent type. They noted the explanation. Official explanation: trainer said, regarding the apparent improvement in form shown, that he could find no apparent reason for the gelding's two previous poor outings but can only suspect that his charge is not the most most consistent type. (op 7/1)
The Reaper(IRE) wasn't disgraced to continue his excellent record at this track. He tacked over to the near side from his unfavourable draw and tracked the winner into the straight, but he soon had no more to offer when more was needed approaching the final furlong, running off a career-high mark. (op 9/2)
Bajan Tryst(USA) was drawn alongside the winner. Kevin Ryan's challenger was 11lb higher this time and it showed in the end when asked for more after travelling well into the straight. That said, this was a more promising display than his seasonal debut effort over a furlong shorter at York in May and he can hopefully build on this when dropped down to the minimum trip. (op 11/2)
Copper Dock(IRE) was another to race in the leading group but never looked like imposing his presence when asked for his effort. (op 9/1)
Knock Stars(IRE) kept on in the straight without threatening.
Luisant, winner of this race in 2009 and runner-up 12 months ago, never got competitive from his unfavourable high draw
Fred Archer(IRE) Official explanation: jockey said colt hung badly in the race

5090a IRISH STALLION FARMS EUROPEAN BREEDERS FUND AUGUST H'CAP (PREMIER HANDICAP) 1m 2f 150y(P)
5:35 (5:38) 3-Y-0+ **£25,215** (£7,370; £3,491; £1,163)

RPR

1 **Jackaroo (IRE)**[58] 3147 3-9-3 102 ow3 .... JPO'Brien(3) 2 106
(A P O'Brien, Ire) *trckd ldrs: 4th 1/2-way: wnt 2nd early st: rdn to chal 1f out: led 100yds out and kpt on wl* **8/1**

2 hd **Northgate (IRE)**[49] 3445 6-9-12 99 .... CDHayes 1 102
(Joseph G Murphy, Ire) *trckd ldrs on inner: 6th 1/2-way: 4th early st: hdwy to chal and led briefly early fnl f: hdd 100yds out and kpt on same pce u.p* **8/1**

3 3 **Pires**[19] 4418 7-9-2 89 .... SeamieHeffernan 10 86
(A J Martin, Ire) *in rr of mid-div on inner: hdwy into 5th 2f out: no imp u.p over 1f out: kpt on one pce* **16/1**

4 3/4 **Elusive Ridge (IRE)**[19] 4418 5-9-1 88 .... (p) CO'Donoghue 14 83
(H Rogers, Ire) *led: rdn 2f out: strly pressed and hdd early fnl f: sn no ex* **20/1**

5 3/4 **Creekside**[24] 4259 3-9-4 100 .... (p) JMurtagh 7 95
(John M Oxx, Ire) *trckd ldrs: 5th 1/2-way: pushed along ent st: no imp wl over 1f out: kpt on one pce* **8/1**

6 1/2 **Back Burner (IRE)**[15] 4566 3-8-8 90 .... DPMcDonogh 8 84
(Mrs John Harrington, Ire) *chsd ldrs on outer: 7th 1/2-way: no imp early st: 7th over 1f out: kpt on one pce* **7/1**[3]

7 hd **Plum Sugar (IRE)**[24] 4260 4-9-0 87 .... BACurtis 6 79
(P J Prendergast, Ire) *towards rr: kpt on fr over 1f out wout rching ldrs* **20/1**

8 2 1/2 **Stephen's Green (USA)**[49] 3443 4-9-7 94 .... FMBerry 5 82
(James M Ryan, Ire) *trckd ldr in 2nd: rdn ent st: no imp u.p in 4th 1f out: no ex* **8/1**

9 3/4 **Printmaker (IRE)**[37] 3837 3-8-5 87 .... NGMcCullagh 3 74
(G M Lyons, Ire) *towards rr: nvr a factor: no imp early st: kpt on one pce* **9/2**[2]

10 1 3/4 **Spirit Of Cuba (IRE)**[11] 4691 3-8-6 93 .... SHJames(5) 13 77
(Kevin Prendergast, Ire) *nvr a factor* **12/1**

11 nk **Honey Of A Kitten (USA)**[16] 4520 3-8-2 89 .... LFRoche(5) 4 72
(D K Weld, Ire) *mid-div: nvr a factor: no threat in st* **16/1**

12 hd **Park Ranger (IRE)**[13] 2326 5-8-13 86 .... (b) WJSupple 11 68
(C Roche, Ire) *a towards rr* **25/1**

13 *1 1/4* **Gentleman Duke (IRE)**[20] 4400 3-8-6 88 .... WMLordan 9 68
(A L T Moore, Ire) *hld up in rr of mid-div on outer: 9th 1/2-way: no threat fr 2f out* **7/1**[3]
14 *17* **Oceanway (USA)**[17] 4467 3-8-12 94 .... PJSmullen 12 41
(Mark Johnston) *trckd ldrs in 3rd: pushed along appr st: sn no ex: wknd fr 2f out: eased ins fnl f (clinically abnormal post-r)* **3/1**[1]

2m 12.25s (132.25)
WFA 3 from 4yo+ 10lb **14** Ran SP% **145.5**
CSF £83.99 CT £1070.74 TOTE £7.60: £3.20, £3.80, £4.80; DF 125.30.
Owner Mrs John Magnier **Bred** Robert Power Bloodstock Ltd **Trained** Ballydoyle, Co Tipperary

NOTEBOOK
Jackaroo(IRE) showed tremendous battling qualities under a powerful ride to get his head in front again. His rider was unable to claim the 3lb, but his drive inside the final furlong was enough to get the Galileo colt up where it mattered. He showed a likeable attitude encountering this surface for the first time and may well be up to winning a stakes race on this evidence at around this trip or perhaps over a little further.
Northgate(IRE) had shown a return to winning form when runner-up at the Curragh over 2f shorter last time. The dual winner ran a cracker in conceding weight all round, and was just denied. (op 14/1)
Pires ran in snatches and kept on under a strong drive for a share of the honours. It would be no surprise to see him head back to Newmarket for the Cambridgeshire, a race he finished third in last year, and this was a more encouraging effort compared with Galway last month. (op 14/1)
Elusive Ridge(IRE) made a bold bid, but had no more to give when the challengers edged ahead in the closing stages. This was a better display, though, from the Bellewstown 1m winner in July.
Creekside was the sole 100-rated runner in the field, and the three-year-old faced a tough task against his older rivals. He ran reasonably well. (op 15/2)
Back Burner(IRE) looked likely to get into the mix, but the Cork maiden winner in June couldn't pick up when asked to go about his business on the outer.
Oceanway(USA) was well enough placed but dropped away soon after turning for home and was found to be clinically abnormal after the race. Official explanation: vet said filly was found to be clinically abnormal post-race (op 7/2)

5091 - (Foreign Racing) - See Raceform Interactive

4372 COLOGNE (R-H)
Sunday, August 14

OFFICIAL GOING: Turf: soft

5092a RHEINLAND-POKAL (GROUP 1) (3YO+) (TURF) 1m 4f
3:45 (3:46) 3-Y-0+ **£86,206** (£25,862; £12,931; £6,034; £2,586)

RPR
1 **Earl Of Tinsdal (GER)**[42] 3672 3-8-9 0 .... EPedroza 5 115
(A Wohler, Germany) *broke wl: led after 100yds: set solid pce: wnt 2 l clr: led into st: shkn up: responded wl and: despite wandering off st line: drew clr easily: comf* **9/10**[1]
2 *4* **Saltas (GER)**[42] 3672 3-8-9 0 .... AStarke 4 109
(P Schiergen, Germany) *settled in 4th: moving wl: mde move early in st on outside: r.o wl u.p but no threat to wnr: but wl clr of others* **27/10**[2]
3 *3 1/2* **Silvaner (GER)**[42] 3672 3-8-9 0 .... FilipMinarik 2 103
(P Schiergen, Germany) *broke fast and led at first bnd but sn settled in 3rd: r.o wl in st u.p: no ex* **145/10**
4 *2* **Dawn Twister (GER)**[16] 4524 4-9-6 0 .... ADeVries 6 100
(J Hirschberger, Germany) *broke wl: racd freely: settled eventually in 5th and then dropped bk to last ent bkstretch: rdn coming out of fnl turn: r.o but no ex in st: wl btn* **5/1**
5 *1 3/4* **Seventh Sky (GER)**[35] 4-9-6 0 .... THellier 1 97
(P Schiergen, Germany) *settled in rr: styd on at one pce in st: nvr figured* **148/10**
6 *2 1/2* **Cavalryman**[21] 4374 5-9-6 0 .... FrankieDettori 3 95
(Saeed Bin Suroor) *broke wl: settled bhd ldr: swtchd towards centre of trck: rdn bef fnl turn: threatened briefly early in st but unable to handle trck conditions and sn wknd: dropped bk to last* **7/2**[3]

2m 35.29s (2.39)
WFA 3 from 4yo+ 11lb **6** Ran SP% **131.3**
WIN (incl. 10 euro stake): 19. PLACES: 11, 13. SF: 36.
Owner Sunrace Stables **Bred** Hannes K Gutschow **Trained** Germany

NOTEBOOK
Earl Of Tinsdal(GER), who was noticably warm, led from the start and easily landed his first Group 1 success. He'll will probably have one more race this season, possibly in the Preis von Europa here in Cologne, before being put away for a 4-y-o campaign.
Cavalryman looks a shadow of the horse he once was and it's not easy to see a way back for him considering this performance. The jockey reported afterwards that the ground was too soft for his mount.

5027 DEAUVILLE (R-H)
Sunday, August 14

OFFICIAL GOING: Turf: heavy; fibresand: standard

5093a PRIX DE POMONE - HARAS D'ETREHAM (GROUP 2) (3YO+ FILLIES & MARES) (TURF) 1m 4f 110y
2:45 (12:00) 3-Y-0+ **£63,879** (£24,655; £11,767; £7,844; £3,922)

RPR
1 **Sarah Lynx (IRE)**[21] 4-9-4 0 ....(b[1]) ChristopheSoumillon 2 107+
(J E Hammond, France) *trckd ldr: moved upsides ldr 2f out: sn led and drifted lft into centre of trck: r.o wl fnl f* **10/1**
2 *1 1/2* **Miss Crissy (IRE)**[31] 4036 3-8-6 0 .... GregoryBenoist 4 105
(M Delzangles, France) *racd in 4th: cl 5th and pushed along on outside appr fnl 2f: hrd rdn 1 1/2f out: styd on u.p to go 2nd 100yds out: unable to chal wnr* **7/1**
3 *3/4* **Shamanova (IRE)**[31] 4037 4-9-4 0 .... Christophe-PatriceLemaire 5 104
(A De Royer-Dupre, France) *dwlt and w.w towards rr: last and moved to outside leaving fnl bnd w over 2f to run: rdn appr 1 1/2f out: styd on fnl f: nt pce to chal* **6/4**[1]
4 *hd* **Toi Et Moi (IRE)**[21] 4-9-4 0 .... ThierryThulliez 10 103
(P Bary, France) *w.w in midfield: 7th 3f out: pushed along towards outside 2f out: rdn 1 1/2f out: styd on fnl f: jst lost fight for 3rd: nt pce to trble first two* **6/1**[3]
5 *1 1/2* **Oekaki (FR)**[21] 4-9-4 0 .... ThierryJarnet 11 101
(Y Barberot, France) *hld up in last: prog over 2f out: disp 3rd ins fnl f: kpt on at one pce* **20/1**
5 *hd* **Rock My Soul (IRE)**[21] 5-9-4 0 .... Pierre-CharlesBoudot 1 101
(A Fabre, France) *trckd ldrs: cl 4th turning for home: jst over 2f out: 3rd and rdn appr 1 1/2f out: no ex* **9/2**[2]
7 *nk* **Santa Biatra (FR)**[51] 5-9-4 0 .... OlivierPeslier 3 100
(A Couetil, France) *settled in midfield: 5th 3f out: 4th and pushed along 2f out: sn rdn and drifted rt: nt qckn* **12/1**
8 *nk* **Myplacelater**[8] 4789 4-9-4 0 .... MartinDwyer 7 100
(David Elsworth) *hld up in rr: pushed along 3f out: 6th and rdn over 2f out: unable qck u.p fnl f* **12/1**
9 *1* **Loonora (FR)**[28] 5-9-4 0 .... FranckBlondel 9 98
(D De Watrigant, France) *led at stdy pce: qcknd up ins fnl 2 1/2f: jnd by eventual wnr 2f out: hdd sn after: rdn and wknd ins fnl 1 1/2f* **20/1**
10 *8* **Lagalp (GER)**[43] 4-9-4 0 .... ASuborics 8 86
(P Schiergen, Germany) *settled in 7th: rdn and no imp over 2f out: wknd ins fnl 1 1/2f: eased fnl f* **16/1**

2m 53.7s (7.30)
WFA 3 from 4yo+ 11lb **10** Ran SP% **124.8**
WIN (incl. 1 euro stake): 7.00. PLACES: 1.70, 2.00, 1.30. DF: 35.30. SF: 83.60.
Owner Mrs Robert G Ehrnrooth **Bred** Grangecon Stud **Trained** France

FOCUS
A very slowly run race.
NOTEBOOK
Sarah Lynx(IRE) didn't have any obvious form credentials to take this (beaten in Listed races and by horses she faced here) but won after getting the best ride. The Prix Vermeille next month could be on the agenda, although the Flower Bowl in New York is also an option.
Miss Crissy(IRE) was one of the least exposed and took her form to another level with a second in this company.
Shamanova(IRE) is a proven stayer but, for some reason, was ridden as though she had a searing turn-of-foot from off the pace. Unsurprisingly, she wasn't able to get anywhere near the winner after hitting the home straight virtually in last place. (op 13-8)
Myplacelater probably wasn't suited by the lack of pace during the early stages of the contest.

5094a PRIX GONTAUT-BIRON - HONG KONG JOCKEY CLUB (GROUP 3) (4YO+) (TURF) 1m 2f
3:20 (12:00) 4-Y-0+ **£34,482** (£13,793; £10,344; £6,896; £3,448)

RPR
1 **Cirrus Des Aigles (FR)**[25] 4223 5-9-4 0 .... FranckBlondel 1 128+
(Mme C Barande-Barbe, France) *settled 3rd abt 6 l off ldr: tk clsr order gng wl 2 1/2f out: moved up smoothly to join ldr ins fnl 1 1/2f: sn led: pushed clr fnl f: easily* **1/1**[1]
2 *8* **Lancelot (FR)**[36] 4-8-9 0 .... OlivierPeslier 2 103
(F Head, France) *racd in 4th in slipstream of eventual wnr: rdn appr fnl 2f: wnt 3rd u.p 1 1/2f out: plugged on in fnl f to go 2nd 50yds out* **16/1**
3 *shd* **Skins Game**[78] 2522 5-9-1 0 .... ChristopheSoumillon 5 109
(J-C Rouget, France) *racd in bk trio: 5th and pushed along 2f out: kpt on u.p fnl f: tk 3rd cl home and jst failed to grab 2nd* **9/1**
4 *3/4* **Poet**[57] 3153 6-8-11 0 .... GeraldMosse 7 104
(Clive Cox) *sn led: 3 to 4 l clr in centre of trck: pushed along 2 1/2f out: hdd under 1 1/2f out: fdd last 100yds: lost two pls cl home* **12/1**
5 *10* **Ransom Note**[22] 4345 4-9-1 0 .... MichaelHills 4 88
(B W Hills) *trckd ldr: shkn up 2 1/2f out: sn hrd rdn and no imp: wknd appr fnl f* **10/1**
6 *6* **Shimraan (FR)**[29] 4095 4-8-9 0 .... Christophe-PatriceLemaire 3 70
(A De Royer-Dupre, France) *racd in bk trio: last and pushed along 2 1/2f out: c v wd into st: no ch fnl 2f* **9/2**[2]
7 *10* **City Leader (IRE)**[85] 2290 6-8-9 0 .... MartinDwyer 6 50
(Brian Meehan) *settled in rr: racd in bk trio: rdn and c wd into st: sn btn* **6/1**[3]

2m 8.60s (-1.60) **7** Ran SP% **115.1**
WIN (incl. 1 euro stake): 1.70. PLACES: 1.20, 4.10. SF: 26.30.
Owner Jean-Claude-Alain Dupouy **Bred** Y Lelimouzin And B Deschamps **Trained** France

FOCUS
They finished strung out on heavy ground, but the winner is going the right way and rates a personal best.
NOTEBOOK
Cirrus Des Aigles(FR), who bypassed the International at York for this, was in a different league to his rivals and fairly bolted up. He is basically a Group 1 performer, so was entitled to win as he did, and the Grand Prix de Deauville at the end of the month is a target. (op 11-10)
Lancelot(FR) improved on his return to France last time with a good runner-up effort. That said, the winner was much too good and some of his rivals disappointed, so this may not be as good as it looked. (op 20-1)
Poet led early but was readily shaken off when challenged. He'll have an autumn campaign and the Prix Dollar could be one objective.
Ransom Note chased Poet early but failed to pick up in ground that was against him. (op 11-1)
City Leader(IRE)'s last race had worked out really well, as he beat four subsequent winners, but this was a terrible effort. The writing was on the wall fairly early, and maybe the ground was too soft for him to handle. (op 7-1)

5095a PRIX DE BEUZEVILLE (CLAIMER) (4YO+) (FIBRESAND) 1m 1f 110y
3:55 (12:00) 4-Y-0+ **£6,465** (£2,586; £1,939; £1,293; £646)

RPR
1 **General Eliott (IRE)**[14] 6780 6-8-10 0 ....(p) ThomasHenderson[(6)] 1 74
(Barry Brennan) *dwlt at s: rdn to take position bhd ldrs: sn wnt 2nd and sent to ld at 1/2-way: rdn to take clr ld ent st: r.o wl: chal ent fnl f but styd on wl: comf* **182/10**
2 *3/4* **Freminius (GER)**[21] 4373 7-9-2 0 .... DominiqueBoeuf 2 72
(W Baltromei, Germany) **3/1**[1]
3 *3/4* **Thsaam (FR)**[235] 4-8-13 0 .... ThierryJarnet 13 67
(Mlle S-V Tarrou, France) **40/1**
4 *hd* **Atila Sher Danon (GER)**[541] 632 5-9-6 0 .... ASuborics 6 74
(W Hickst, Germany) **63/10**[2]
5 *1 1/2* **Russian Davis (IRE)**[9] 4-9-6 0 .... MaximeGuyon 10 71
(P Monfort, France) **8/1**
6 *hd* **Barakanda (IRE)**[31] 4-9-2 0 .... DavyBonilla 5 67
(J Boisnard, France) **44/1**
7 *1 1/2* **Gonetrio (USA)**[31] 4-9-2 0 ....(p) ChristopheSoumillon 8 63
(Rod Collet, France) **13/2**[3]
8 *1 1/2* **Nightdance Victor (GER)** 4-9-6 0 .... MickaelBarzalona 14 64
(P Schiergen, Germany) **9/1**
9 *1 1/2* **Ghaayer**[437] 5-8-11 0 .... GeraldMosse 17 52
(C Von Der Recke, Germany) **26/1**
10 *1 1/2* **Lowenherz (GER)**[39] 7-8-11 0 ....(p) GregoryBenoist 7 49
(J-P Perruchot, France) **22/1**
0 **Menestrol (FR)**[46] 9-9-2 0 ....(p) FranckBlondel 18 —
(D Prod'Homme, France) **10/1**

The Form Book, Raceform Ltd, Compton, RG20 6NL

0 **Auzi (FR)**[39] 8-8-11 0 .... TonyPiccone 12 —
(J Rossi, France) **12/1**
0 **Astarix (FR)**[735] 6-8-10 0 .... AntoineHamelin(6) 3 —
(E Danel, France) **66/1**
0 **Lomirana (FR)**[149] 903 5-8-6 0 .... Georges-AntoineAnselin(5) 9 —
(N Caullery, France) **118/1**
0 **Morning Glory (FR)**[223] 4-8-0 0 .... MathieuTavaresDaSilva(8) 16 —
(A Lyon, France) **17/1**
0 **Quiet Julia (FR)** 4-8-8 0 .... SylvainRuis 11 —
(G Pannier, France) **74/1**
0 **Sublim Star (FR)** 4-8-5 0 .... (p) MatthieuAutier(3) 15 —
(Mlle M Henry, France) **110/1**

2m 0.80s (120.80) **17** Ran SP% **118.0**
WIN (incl. 1 euro stake): 19.20. PLACES: 6.20, 2.10, 9.20. DF: 38.00. SF: 94.00.
Owner F J Brennan **Bred** Maddenstown Equine Enterprise Ltd **Trained** Lambourn, Berks

JAGERSRO (R-H)

Sunday, August 14

OFFICIAL GOING: Dirt: standard

5096a MARGARETA WETTERMARKS MINNESLOPNING (LISTED RACE) (3-5YO FILLIES & MARES) (DIRT) 1m 143y(D)

3:45 (12:00) 3-5-Y-O **£28,735** (£9,578; £4,789; £2,873; £1,915)

RPR

1 **La Zona (IRE)**[75] 5-9-6 0 .... Jan-ErikNeuroth 1 —
(Wido Neuroth, Norway) **363/100[2]**
2 *6* **Tatoosh (IRE)**[24] 5-9-6 0 .... Per-AndersGraberg 7 —
(Niels Petersen, Norway) **26/5**
3 *6* **Match Point (FR)**[24] 5-9-6 0 .... CarlosLopez 3 —
(Niels Petersen, Norway) **19/1**
4 *nse* **Symbol Of Arch (USA)**[24] 4-9-6 0 .... EspenSki 8 —
(Arnfinn Lund, Norway) **13/10[1]**
5 *nk* **Conciliatory**[11] 4656 4-9-6 0 .... (b) FJohansson 4 —
(Rae Guest) *wnt rt leaving stalls fr wd outside draw: sn tacked ins and settled 7th: pushed along ins fnl 3f: sn outpcd: 8th and no imp appr 1 1/2f out: sme prog fnl f: nvr plcd to chal ldrs* **41/10[3]**
6 *2* **Western Memory (USA)**[280] 7374 4-9-6 0 .... JacobJohansen 2 —
(Lennart Reuterskiold Jr, Sweden) **44/5**
7 *nse* **Balsha (USA)**[75] 4-9-6 0 .... ElioneChaves 9 —
(Roy Arne Kvisla, Sweden) **236/10**
8 *5* **Whirly Dancer**[75] 4-9-6 0 .... (b) ManuelMartinez 5 —
(Lennart Reuterskiold Jr, Sweden) **33/1**
9 *5* **Tiger Goddess (IRE)**[75] 5-9-6 0 .... RafaelSchistl 6 —
(Bodil Hallencreutz, Sweden) **32/1**

1m 46.1s (106.10) **9** Ran SP% **126.1**
PARI-MUTUEL (all including 1sek stake): WIN 4.63; PLACE 1.92, 1.77, 3.02; DF 14.17.
Owner Stall Perlen **Bred** Century Farms **Trained** Norway

NOTEBOOK
Conciliatory was caught flat-footed when the pace quickened inside the final three furlongs. She stayed on in the final furlong to grab fifth and a share of the prize money.

4988 KEMPTON (A.W) (R-H)

Monday, August 15

OFFICIAL GOING: Standard
Wind: Virtually nil Weather: Sunny intervals

5097 32RED.COM MEDIAN AUCTION MAIDEN FILLIES' STKS 7f (P)

2:30 (2:30) (Class 6) 2-Y-O **£1,617** (£481; £240; £120) **Stalls** Low

Form RPR

5 1 **Sugarformyhoney (IRE)**[21] 4384 2-9-0 0 .... PatDobbs 10 85+
(Richard Hannon) *trckd ldr: pushed along to ld 2f out: c clr fnl f: easily* **12/1**
2 *3½* **Island Paradise (IRE)** 2-9-0 0 .... LukeMorris 9 75+
(Peter Winkworth) *chsd ldrs: rdn over 2f out: styd on to chse wnr 1f out: nvr any ch but clr of 3rd* **9/2[2]**
04 3 *3½* **Gold Coin**[21] 4390 2-9-0 0 .... SebSanders 1 66
(J W Hills) *led: rdn and hdd 2f out: wknd fdd and lost 2nd 1f out but stl hld on for 3rd* **11/2[3]**
0 4 *1¼* **Malekat Jamal (IRE)**[16] 4552 2-9-0 0 .... JamesDoyle 7 63
(David Simcock) *in rr: pushed along and hdwy over 2f out: styd on same pce and no imp on ldrs over 1f out* **11/2[3]**
5 5 *½* **Dust On The Ground**[12] 4662 2-9-0 0 .... AdamKirby 6 61
(Marco Botti) *in tch: rdn and no imp fr 2f out: styd on same pce* **2/1[1]**
0 6 *1¼* **Elbow Beach**[52] 3362 2-9-0 0 .... StevieDonohoe 5 58
(Dr Jon Scargill) *in rr: pushed along over 2f out: sme prog ins fnl f* **12/1**
7 *½* **Winter Dress** 2-9-0 0 .... MartinDwyer 2 57
(Roger Teal) *in rr: pushed along over 2f out: sme prog fnl f* **25/1**
00 8 *½* **Saint Irene**[9] 4798 2-9-0 0 .... FrankieMcDonald 4 56
(Michael Blanshard) *chsd ldrs: rdn over 2f out: sn btn* **40/1**
0 9 *3¼* **Alexandra Palace (IRE)**[18] 4462 2-9-0 0 .... SilvestreDeSousa 3 47
(Mark Johnston) *in rr: pushed along and sme hdwy over 2f out: nver rchd ldrs and wknd fnl f* **16/1**
10 *2½* **Our Phylli Vera (IRE)** 2-9-0 0 .... KierenFallon 8 41
(Harry Dunlop) *s.i.s: sn in tch on outside: wknd appr fnl 2f* **20/1**

1m 26.08s (0.08) **Going Correction** -0.05s/f (Stan) **10** Ran SP% **114.6**
Speed ratings (Par 89): **97,93,89,87,87 85,85,84,80,77**
toteswingers:1&2:£8.20, 1&3:£2.20, 2&3:£6.10 CSF £62.78 TOTE £12.10: £2.90, £1.30, £1.90; EX 88.50.
Owner Mrs Susan Roy **Bred** Mrs S M Roy **Trained** East Everleigh, Wilts

FOCUS
Probably not the strongest of maidens for the track with none of the seven that had raced before having been placed. The pace held up well and the form might be underestimated slightly.

NOTEBOOK
Sugarformyhoney(IRE) was green when a promising fifth of 12 on her Windsor debut, but isn't bred to have appreciated this extra furlong. That didn't prove to be the case, however, as she pulled right away after leading over a furlong from home and although this wasn't a great race, she is entitled to improve further. (tchd 14-1)
Island Paradise(IRE), a 24,000euros yearling, ran a nice debut, staying on against the inside rail under pressure and, as she is bred to stay on the dam's side of her pedigree, she will appreciate going up in trip. (op 11-2)
Gold Coin had the edge in experience and tried to make it count under a positive ride, but she was readily swept aside by the front pair. She now gets a mark. (op 9-2)
Malekat Jamal(IRE) beat just one home on her Newmarket debut, so at least improved on that, but will need to show more before she becomes a betting proposition. (op 13-2)
Dust On The Ground, a staying-on fifth in a similar event over C&D earlier this month, travelled well in midfield for most of the way, but found disappointingly little when finally off the bridle. (tchd 15-8)

5098 32REDPOKER.COM MEDIAN AUCTION MAIDEN FILLIES' STKS 1m 4f (P)

3:00 (3:00) (Class 6) 3-5-Y-O **£1,617** (£481; £240; £120) **Stalls** Centre

Form RPR

643 1 **Zafarana**[77] 2551 3-8-12 76 .... KierenFallon 4 81
(Ed Dunlop) *trckd ldr: chal fr 7f out tl led 4f out: pushed clr fr 2f out: easily* **3/1[3]**
3222 2 *11* **Oneiric**[37] 3872 3-8-12 73 .... JimCrowley 2 63
(Ralph Beckett) *ld: jnd 7f out: hdd 4f out: sn rdn: no ch w wnr fr over 2f out but stl clr of 3rd* **13/8[1]**
0- 3 *2¾* **Passion Play**[264] 7559 3-8-5 0 .... LukeRowe(7) 5 59
(William Knight) *in rr: rdn and struggling whn pce qcknd 3f out: sn green u.p: styd on fnl 2f to take wl hld 3rd over 1f out* **25/1**
30 4 *3½* **Flaming Nora**[28] 4163 3-8-12 0 .... PatCosgrave 6 56
(James Fanshawe) *in tch tl rdn and struggling whn pce qcknd 3f out: styd on again fnl 2f to take mod 4th over 1f out* **9/1**
3-33 5 *14* **Shuhra (IRE)**[31] 4072 3-8-12 75 .... (b[1]) RichardHills 1 31
(William Haggas) *chsd ldrs: rdn and wknd 3f out: lost poor 3rd over 1f out: eased* **2/1[2]**
45 6 *33* **Frolic Along (IRE)**[27] 4180 4-9-9 0 .... StephenCraine 3 —
(J R Jenkins) *s.i.s: in rr: rdn 7f out: sn lost tch* **100/1**

2m 33.17s (-1.33) **Going Correction** -0.05s/f (Stan)
WFA 3 from 4yo 11lb **6** Ran SP% **111.3**
Speed ratings (Par 98): **102,94,92,90,81 59**
toteswingers:1&2:£1.20, 1&3:£9.00, 2&3:£9.30 CSF £8.15 TOTE £3.70: £1.80, £1.30; EX 10.10.
Owner Mohammed Al Suboosi **Bred** Equine Breeding Ltd **Trained** Newmarket, Suffolk

FOCUS
A particularly weak fillies' maiden in which they finished spread out all over Sunbury. It's hard to know what the winner achieved with the two favourites disappointing.

5099 32 FOR CASINO NURSERY 6f (P)

3:30 (3:30) (Class 5) (0-70,68) 2-Y-O **£2,264** (£673; £336; £168) **Stalls** Low

Form RPR

3042 1 **Worth**[11] 4704 2-9-7 **68** .... (b) MartinDwyer 1 72
(Brian Meehan) *mde all: drvn and qcknd appr fnl 2f: hrd drvn fnl f hld on all out* **5/1**
31 2 *shd* **Miss Rosie**[34] 3932 2-9-6 **67** .... SilvestreDeSousa 2 71
(Mark Johnston) *trckd ldrs: wnt 2nd 3f out: rdn and outpcd whn wnr qcknd over 2f out: styd on u.p thrght fnl f: edgd lft and styd on wl cl home: nt quite get up* **9/4[1]**
534 3 *nk* **Khazium (IRE)**[46] 3534 2-9-7 **68** .... AdamKirby 5 71
(Pat Eddery) *in rr tl hdwy on ins 3f out: styd on u.p fnl f and edgd lft: kpt on wl clsng stages: nt quite get to ldng duo* **7/2[3]**
050 4 *8* **Duke Of Aricabeau (IRE)**[10] 4748 2-9-3 **64** .... KierenFallon 4 46
(Michael Easterby) *t.k.h: stl keen whn n.m.r and lost position 3f out: drvn and styd on fnl 2f but nvr any ch of getting to ldng trio* **11/4[2]**
540 5 *¾* **First Rebellion**[32] 4019 2-8-2 **49** .... LukeMorris 11 26
(Tony Carroll) *sn chsng wnr: rdn and lost 2nd 3f out: outpcd 2f out: wknd over 1f out* **14/1**
0005 6 *6* **High Five Prince (IRE)**[11] 4704 2-7-11 **49** .... (v[1]) RyanPowell(5) 9 8
(Mark Usher) *chsd ldrs on outside: wknd over 2f out* **33/1**
0646 7 *shd* **Imperial Weapon (IRE)**[11] 4702 2-7-12 **45** .... (p) CathyGannon 8 4
(John Spearing) *sddle slipped sn after s: chsd ldrs to 3f out: wknd over 2f out* **66/1**
4640 8 *nk* **J Cunningham**[11] 4704 2-7-9 **45** .... AmyBaker(3) 10 3
(Mark Usher) *s.i.s: a towards rr* **50/1**
3044 9 *5* **Copper Falls**[16] 4548 2-8-13 **60** .... FergusSweeney 7 3
(Brendan Powell) *t.k.h: chsd ldrs: rdn 3f out: sn btn* **16/1**
530 10 *7* **Bit A Craic**[12] 4662 2-8-5 **52** .... KirstyMilczarek 6
(John Ryan) *sn bhd* **16/1**

1m 13.67s (0.57) **Going Correction** -0.05s/f (Stan) **10** Ran SP% **121.2**
Speed ratings (Par 94): **94,93,93,82,81 73,73,73,66,57**
toteswingers:1&2:£2.10, 1&3:£4.10, 2&3:£4.20 CSF £17.26 CT £46.04 TOTE £4.80: £1.10, £1.50, £2.10; EX 8.60.
Owner Miss Penny Zygmant **Bred** Miss P A Zygmant **Trained** Manton, Wilts

FOCUS
An ordinary nursery. Pace held up and the winner made all. The first three were clear and the form has been rated positively.

NOTEBOOK
Worth improved for the fitting of blinkers when narrowly beaten off 4lb lower at Chepstow last time and went one better with the headgear retained. Soon in front, she won the race by taking a length or two out of her rivals running to the intersection, which was just as well as she had nothing to spare at the line. (op 4-1 tchd 7-2)
Miss Rosie, up a furlong for this nursery/Polytrack debut, was close enough from the off, but she just got caught for toe for a few strides passing the 2f pole and when finally gathered together, her late flourish was a stride too late. She should soon be winning again. (op 3-1 tchd 10-3)
Khazium(IRE) was also making his nursery/Polytrack debuts after doing too much early in a first-time visor over 7f at Epsom last time but, minus the headgear and down a furlong here, his strong finishing effort from off the pace fell just short. (op 5-1 tchd 11-2)
Duke Of Aricabeau(IRE), another making his nursery/Polytrack debuts after finishing unplaced in three maidens, though he did show some ability, lost ground when appearing to get into a spot of bother just before halfway and he was then left with an impossible task. Market support earlier in the day suggested better was expected and he remains one to keep an eye on granted a slightly stiffer test. (tchd 5-2)
First Rebellion, making her Polytrack debut, showed up for a long way but has already been well beaten in a seller so probably didn't achieve much here. (op 12-1)
High Five Prince(IRE) Official explanation: jockey said gelding hung left
Imperial Weapon(IRE) Official explanation: jockey said saddle slipped
Bit A Craic Official explanation: jockey said filly was always outpaced

5100 32 FOR POKER FILLIES' H'CAP 7f (P)

4:00 (4:00) (Class 5) (0-75,75) 3-Y-O+ **£2,264** (£673; £336; £168) **Stalls** Low

Form RPR

-214 1 **Elsie's Orphan**[34] 3940 4-9-7 **70** .... LiamKeniry 7 78
(Patrick Chamings) *trckd ldrs: wnt 2nd over 2f out: styd on u.p to ld fnl 120yds: kpt on wl* **14/1**
6062 2 *½* **Leelu**[11] 4696 5-9-1 **64** .... CathyGannon 10 71
(David Arbuthnot) *chsd ldr tl led wl over 2f out: sn rdn: kpt slt ld tl hdd fnl 120yds: kpt on same pce* **10/1**

2-5 **3** *nk* **Junket**[25] 4255 4-9-9 **72** ... TomQueally 1 80+
(Dr Jon Scargill) *in rr: hdwy and n.m.r appr fnl 2f: drvn and styd on wl fnl f: kpt on clsng stages: nt rch ldrs* **7/2**[2]

0-15 **4** *1* **Treasure Way**[18] 4458 4-9-5 **68** ... GeorgeBaker 3 71
(Patrick Chamings) *chsd ldrs: n.m.r on ins over 2f out: drvn and qcknd wl over 1f out: kpt on ins fnl f but nvr gng pce to rch ldrs* **10/1**

1- **5** *3/4* **Swift Breeze**[254] 7686 3-9-2 **71** ... KierenFallon 8 70+
(William Haggas) *s.i.s: hld up in rr: hdwy on outside wl over 2f out: styd on to chse ldrs over 1f out: no imp and styd on same pce* **3/1**[1]

3-05 **6** *1/2* **Requisite**[26] 4210 6-9-11 **74** ... (b) JamesDoyle 9 74
(Ian Wood) *in rr: hdwy on outside 3f out: drvn and kpt on to take 3rd appr fnl f: no imp and wknd fnl 120yds* **10/1**

3360 **7** *3 1/4* **Cape Melody**[18] 4479 5-9-6 **72** ... MatthewDavies(3) 6 63
(George Baker) *s.i.s: in rr: drvn along over 3f out: kpt on but nvr gng pce to get into contention* **33/1**

2422 **8** *3/4* **Finefrenzyrolling (IRE)**[40] 3729 3-8-10 **65** ... (v[1]) LukeMorris 5 52
(Mrs K Burke) *chsd ldrs: hrd drvn 2f out: wknd over 1f out* **7/1**

-435 **9** *1 3/4* **Echo Ridge (IRE)**[53] 3310 3-9-4 **73** ... JimCrowley 2 56
(Ralph Beckett) *towards rr and rdn 3f out: no ch after* **11/2**[3]

-000 **10** *6* **Plume**[17] 4509 4-9-12 **75** ... JackMitchell 4 43
(Roger Teal) *s.i.s: in rr: sme prog into mid-div 3f out: sn rdn and btn* **20/1**

/3-0 **11** *8* **Tomodachi (IRE)**[60] 3091 4-8-11 **65** ... AntiocoMurgia(5) 11 12
(Marco Botti) *led tl hdd wl over 2f out: wknd qckly* **16/1**

1m 26.08s (0.08) **Going Correction** -0.05s/f (Stan)
WFA 3 from 4yo+ 6lb **11** Ran SP% **122.6**
Speed ratings (Par 100): **97,96,96,94,94 93,89,88,86,80 70**
toteswingers:1&2:£19.20, 1&3:£10.20, 2&3:£9.10 CSF £152.70 CT £618.75 TOTE £8.80: £2.70, £2.80, £1.80; EX 73.70.
Owner Mrs J E L Wright **Bred** Wheelers Land Stud **Trained** Baughurst, Hants

FOCUS
A modest fillies' handicap. The winner is generally progressive and the runner-up sets the standard.

5101 32RED.COM H'CAP (LONDON MILE QUALIFIER) 1m (P)
4:30 (4:31) (Class 5) (0-75,75) 3-Y-0+ **£2,264** (£673; £336; £168) **Stalls** Low

Form RPR

204 **1** **Catchanova (IRE)**[23] 4338 4-9-1 **65** ... TomQueally 7 76
(Eve Johnson Houghton) *t.k.h: hld up in rr: stl in last over 2f out: gd hdwy over 1f out: drvn and qcknd between horses ins fnl f: led fnl 120yds: kpt on wl* **9/1**

2202 **2** *1/2* **Ferruccio (IRE)**[18] 4478 3-9-1 **72** ... KierenFallon 5 81
(James Fanshawe) *trckd ldrs: drvn and qcknd to chal over 1f out: styd on ins fnl f to chse wnr fnl 120yds but no imp* **7/2**[1]

-540 **3** *1 1/4* **Cool Hand Jake**[28] 4158 5-9-6 **70** ... FergusSweeney 11 77
(Peter Makin) *chsd ldrs: drvn along over 3f out: chal wl over 1f out and sn slt ld: hdd and no ex fnl 120yds* **14/1**

5430 **4** *1 1/2* **Dunseverick (IRE)**[59] 3133 3-9-2 **73** ... DaneO'Neill 10 76
(David Lanigan) *t.k.h: hld up in tch: hdwy fr 2f out: styd on to chse ldrs fnl f but no imp* **7/2**[1]

5024 **5** *nse* **Lockantanks**[38] 3805 4-9-11 **75** ... SilvestreDeSousa 6 78
(Michael Appleby) *in rr: rdn and hdwy over 2f out: styd on fnl f but nvr gng pce to rch ldrs* **8/1**[3]

-000 **6** *3/4* **Rock Anthem (IRE)**[12] 4656 7-9-1 **65** ... TonyCulhane 8 67
(Mike Murphy) *hmpd after s: in rr: hdwy on outside fr 2f out: kpt on fnl f: nt rch ldrs* **14/1**

3151 **7** *3 3/4* **You've Been Mowed**[18] 4457 5-8-10 **65** ... MatthewLawson(5) 12 58
(Richard Price) *led: rdn over 2f out: hdd wl over 1f out: sn wknd* **7/1**[2]

2426 **8** *2 1/4* **Ssafa**[22] 4356 3-9-1 **72** ... SebSanders 1 59
(J W Hills) *chsd ldr: rdn over 2f out: wknd ins fnl f* **8/1**[3]

252 **9** *2 3/4* **Tilsworth Glenboy**[12] 4666 4-9-0 **64** ... StephenCraine 3 49
(J R Jenkins) *v.s.a: in rr: rdn fr 3f out: hmpd on ins over 2f out: nvr nrr* **12/1**

0006 **10** *hd* **Tuxedo**[18] 4479 6-9-3 **67** ... (b) LukeMorris 4 48
(Peter Hiatt) *in rr: sn rdn along: hdwy on ins 3f out: nvr rchd ldrs and wknd 2f out* **40/1**

3350 **11** *2* **Striding Edge (IRE)**[46] 3546 5-9-1 **65** ... JamesDoyle 2 42
(Hans Adielsson) *chsd ldrs: rdn 3f out: wknd over 2f out* **20/1**

5054 **12** *2 3/4* **Defector (IRE)**[7] 4850 5-9-6 **70** ... FrankieMcDonald 13 40
(Seamus Durack) *chsd ldrs: rdn 3f out: wknd over 2f out* **33/1**

1m 39.28s (-0.52) **Going Correction** -0.05s/f (Stan)
WFA 3 from 4yo+ 7lb **12** Ran SP% **120.3**
Speed ratings (Par 103): **100,99,98,96,96 95,92,89,87,87 85,82**
toteswingers:1&2:£7.70, 1&3:£23.60, 2&3:£10.00 CSF £40.38 CT £459.15 TOTE £7.20: £2.00, £1.80, £5.00; EX 41.00.
Owner Andrew Wyer Darrell Blake Hugh Arthur **Bred** G J King **Trained** Blewbury, Oxon
■ Stewards' Enquiry : Kieren Fallon two-day ban: careless riding (Aug 29-30)

FOCUS
Just a fair handicap, but the early pace was good. Straightforward form, the winner better then ever.

5102 32 FOR BINGO H'CAP 2m (P)
5:00 (5:02) (Class 4) (0-85,84) 4-Y-0+ **£4,075** (£1,212; £606; £303) **Stalls** Low

Form RPR

5563 **1** **Mister Angry (IRE)**[16] 4555 4-8-13 **76** ... SilvestreDeSousa 11 92+
(Mark Johnston) *hld up in rr: nt clr run and plenty to do over 2f out: rdn and rapid hdwy to chse ldr over 1f out but 4 l down: str run ins fnl f to ld fnl 30yds: won gng away* **13/2**[3]

10 **2** *1* **Red Courtier**[23] 4348 4-9-1 **78** ... (p) JimCrowley 4 91
(Paul Cole) *chsd ldrs: chal 4f out: led 3f out: drvn clr fr 2f out and stl 4 l ld over 1f out: styd on tl hdd and outpcd fnl 30yds* **2/1**[1]

4050 **3** *8* **Where's Susie**[21] 4389 6-8-8 **71** ... KirstyMilczarek 5 74
(Michael Madgwick) *in rr: rdn and hdwy over 3f out: styd on fnl 2f to take 3rd over 1f out but nvr any ch w ldng duo* **25/1**

2643 **4** *1 3/4* **Rosewood Lad**[17] 4488 4-8-7 **70** ... CathyGannon 3 71
(J S Moore) *chsd ldrs: rdn fr 4f out: disp 2nd ins fnl 2f: wknd into wl hld 4th fnl f* **16/1**

-653 **5** *5* **Ugalla**[12] 4687 4-8-7 **70** ... LukeMorris 1 65
(Jane Chapple-Hyam) *in tch: rdn and styd on same pce fnl 3f* **14/1**

3640 **6** *5* **Rosco Flyer (IRE)**[12] 4660 5-8-5 **68** ... MartinDwyer 2 57
(Roger Teal) *chsd ldrs: rdn 4f out: wknd ins fnl 2f* **12/1**

5040 **7** *2 1/4* **Storm Hawk (IRE)**[23] 4348 4-8-6 **69** ... (e[1]) ChrisCatlin 6 56
(Pat Eddery) *in rr: rdn along fr 1/2-way: nvr gng pce to get into contention* **12/1**

-500 **8** *1 1/2* **L Frank Baum (IRE)**[19] 4423 4-9-7 **84** ... (b) AdamKirby 9 69
(Gay Kelleway) *sn led: rdn 5f out: jnd 4f out: hdd 3f out: wknd wl over 1f out* **5/1**[2]

4340 **9** *4 1/2* **William's Way**[40] 3738 9-8-1 **67** ... (t) KieranO'Neill(3) 10 46
(Ian Wood) *s.i.s: bhd most of way* **25/1**

221- **10** *1 1/4* **Perception (IRE)**[125] 5722 5-8-10 **73** ... FergusSweeney 12 51
(Alan King) *s.i.s: sn trcking ldrs: rdn and wknd over 3f out* **10/1**

-400 **11** *3 1/2* **Langley**[105] 1775 4-9-3 **80** ... DaneO'Neill 8 54
(Pat Murphy) *mid-div: rdn 5f out: bhd fnl 4f* **33/1**

3m 27.1s (-3.00) **Going Correction** -0.05s/f (Stan) **11** Ran SP% **111.0**
Speed ratings (Par 105): **105,104,100,99,97 94,93,92,90,89 88**
toteswingers:1&2:£3.00, 1&3:£18.00, 2&3:£15.20 CSF £17.49 CT £263.37 TOTE £6.90: £2.60, £1.10, £8.30; EX 13.20.
Owner The Originals **Bred** Darley **Trained** Middleham Moor, N Yorks
■ Broughtons Point (10/1) was withdrawn after refusing to enter the stalls. Deduct 5p in the £ under R4.

FOCUS
Despite a modest early pace in this fair staying handicap, they finished well spread out. There are doubts over the form but it has been taken at face value, with the winner looking back to his best.
Red Courtier Official explanation: jockey said gelding lost both front shoes

5103 £32 FREE AT 32RED.COM H'CAP 1m 3f (P)
5:30 (5:32) (Class 5) (0-75,75) 3-Y-0+ **£2,264** (£673; £336; £168) **Stalls** Low

Form RPR

5220 **1** **Madison Square (USA)**[11] 4703 3-8-3 **60** ... SilvestreDeSousa 9 76+
(Mark Johnston) *trckd ldr: led ins fnl 2f: drvn clr fnl f: comf* **11/2**

3465 **2** *3 1/4* **Beat Route**[12] 4660 4-8-13 **65** ... JemmaMarshall(5) 6 72
(Michael Attwater) *chsd ldrs: drvn and styd on fr 2f out: chsd wnr fnl f but nvr any ch* **16/1**

5050 **3** *2* **Cashpoint**[25] 4253 6-9-11 **75** ... KieranO'Neill(3) 5 78
(Anthony Middleton) *led: rdn 3f out: hdd ins fnl 2f: no ch w wnr appr fnl f and sn lost 2nd* **7/2**[2]

6220 **4** *3 1/4* **Hidden Valley**[31] 4056 3-9-0 **71** ... (p) LiamKeniry 4 69
(Andrew Balding) *in rr: pushed along and no prog u.p fr 4f out: hanging rt 2f out: styd on fr over 1f out: gng on clsng stages but nvr any threat* **8/1**

1-05 **5** *3/4* **For What (USA)**[17] 4489 3-9-4 **75** ... ChrisCatlin 7 71
(David Lanigan) *in rr: hdwy 4f out: sn rdn: no imp on ldrs fr over 2f out: styd on same pce* **25/1**

0032 **6** *1 1/4* **Elmfield Giant (USA)**[12] 4660 4-9-5 **69** ... LeeTopliss(3) 2 63
(Richard Fahey) *chsd ldrs: rdn 3f out: wknd over 2f out* **5/1**[3]

0410 **7** *1 1/4* **Turjuman (USA)**[26] 4216 6-9-1 **62** ... StevieDonohoe 1 54
(Willie Musson) *in rr: pushed along 4f out: nvr gng pce to get into contention* **16/1**

4-32 **8** *1 1/2* **Lion Court (IRE)**[28] 4163 3-8-12 **69** ... SebSanders 8 58
(Sir Mark Prescott Bt) *chsd ldrs: rdn 4f out: wknd ins fnl 3f* **13/8**[1]

-640 **9** *12* **Querido (GER)**[12] 4660 7-9-1 **62** ... IanMongan 3 29
(Paddy Butler) *t.k.h: in rr: rdn and sme hdwy on ins fr 4f out: wknd qckly ins fnl 3f* **50/1**

2m 20.61s (-1.29) **Going Correction** -0.05s/f (Stan)
WFA 3 from 4yo+ 10lb **9** Ran SP% **121.1**
Speed ratings (Par 103): **102,99,98,95,95 94,93,92,83**
toteswingers:1&2:£15.00, 1&3:£5.00, 2&3:£10.80. Tote Super 7: Win: Not won. Place: Not won CSF £91.96 CT £357.30 TOTE £6.20: £1.80, £4.30, £1.70; EX 74.90.
Owner Sheikh Hamdan Bin Mohammed Al Maktoum **Bred** Stoneside Stable **Trained** Middleham Moor, N Yorks

T/Plt: £45.40 to a £1 stake. Pool:£53,008.82 - 851.34 winning tickets T/Qpdt: £15.70 to a £1 stake. Pool:£4,501.33 - 211.86 winning tickets ST

4851 THIRSK (L-H)
Monday, August 15

OFFICIAL GOING: Good to soft (good in places; 7.9)
Wind: Light across Weather: Cloudy with sunny periods

5104 BRITISH STALLION STUDS SUPPORTING BRITISH RACING E B F MAIDEN STKS 6f
2:15 (2:15) (Class 4) 2-Y-0 **£4,463** (£1,328; £663; £331) **Stalls** High

Form RPR

0 **1** **Eastern Destiny**[16] 4552 2-8-12 0 ... PaulHanagan 4 67+
(Richard Fahey) *trckd ldng pair: swtchd lft and hdwy to chal 2f out: shkn up to ld appr fnl f: green and edgd lft ins fnl f: sn rdn and kpt on* **11/4**[2]

2 *1 1/4* **Deepsand (IRE)** 2-9-3 0 ... DavidAllan 5 65+
(Tim Easterby) *trckd ldrs: swtchd wd and hdwy 2f out: rdn to chal appr fnl f: ev ch tl drvn: edgd lft and no ex last 100yds* **18/1**[3]

00 **3** *2 1/4* **Liesl (IRE)**[24] 4285 2-8-12 0 ... PhillipMakin 11 53
(Kevin Ryan) *chsd ldrs: pushed along wl over 2f out: rdn over 1f out: kpt on ins fnl f: tk 3rd nr line* **22/1**

000 **4** *nse* **Man Of My Word**[48] 3490 2-9-0 62 ... BillyCray(3) 10 58
(David Nicholls) *cl up: effrt 2f out and sn ev ch: rdn appr fnl f and kpt on same pce* **66/1**

0 **5** *3 3/4* **Bengaline**[56] 3229 2-9-3 0 ... PaulQuinn 7 47
(David Nicholls) *led: rdn along wl over 2f out: drvn and hdd over 1f out: wknd* **66/1**

6 *6* **Disco Sensation** 2-8-5 0 ... LeonnaMayor(7) 6 24
(David Nicholls) *s.i.s: sn outpcd and bhd* **20/1**

00 **7** *hd* **Martha's Way**[7] 4853 2-8-12 0 ... JamesSullivan 8 23
(Michael Easterby) *a towards rr* **66/1**

8 *12* **Harbour Sands** 2-9-3 0 ... TomEaves 1 —
(James Given) *green and outpcd in rr: sn bhd* **50/1**

6 **U** **Blue Tiger**[22] 4352 2-9-3 0 ... TedDurcan 2 —
(Saeed Bin Suroor) *rrd bdly and ct in stalls: uns rdr s* **11/8**[1]

1m 13.07s (0.37) **Going Correction** +0.075s/f (Good) **9** Ran SP% **89.6**
Speed ratings (Par 96): **100,98,95,95,90 82,82,66,—**
toteswingers:1&2:£3.40, 1&3:£4.30, 2&3:£3.90 CSF £21.55 TOTE £2.80: £1.10, £2.30, £3.60; EX 25.40 Trifecta £105.80 Pool £499.41 - 3.49 winning units..
Owner B H Farr **Bred** Worksop Manor Stud **Trained** Musley Bank, N Yorks

FOCUS
With Passionada (3/1, deduct 25p in the £ under R4) playing up in the stalls and being withdrawn and Blue Tiger rearing violently and eventually unseating his rider in the gate, this became a virtual penalty kick for Eastern Destiny. It's hard to rate his performance any higher given the lack of depth.

NOTEBOOK
Eastern Destiny probably didn't have to improve much on her Newmarket debut run. The way she did it suggests a return to 7f will suit, and it'll be interesting to see what mark she's given with nurseries in mind. (op 4-1)
Deepsand(IRE), a son of Guineas winner Footstepsinthesand, showed plenty of promise on this debut, running green, and should improve enough to win a maiden. (op 20-1)
Liesl(IRE) stayed on into third and looks ready for 7f and handicaps. (tchd 18-1 and 25-1)

Man Of My Word ran an improved race and looks one for low-grade nurseries.
Bengaline ran an improved race and looks one for low-grade nurseries after another run. (tchd 80-1)
Blue Tiger reared violently as the gates opened and eventually got rid of his rider in the stalls. (op 6-4 tchd 13-8)

5105 HAMBLETON CLAIMING STKS 5f
2:45 (2:45) (Class 4) 2-Y-O **£3,881** (£1,155; £577; £288) **Stalls** High

Form RPR
0216 **1** **Sonko (IRE)**[23] 4343 2-8-11 62.................................(p) GrahamGibbons 5 65
(Tim Pitt) *mde all: jnd and rdn wl over 1f out: drvn ins fnl f and kpt on wl* **11/4[2]**
4320 **2** *2* **Rougini (IRE)**[16] 4557 2-8-13 68.................................(v[1]) AndrewElliott 8 60
(Mrs K Burke) *trckd ldng pair: swtchd lft and hdwy 2f out: rdn to chal wl over 1f out and ev ch tl drvn and one pce ins fnl f* **2/1[1]**
0154 **3** *4 ½* **Lady Caprice**[9] 4808 2-8-7 60.................................(p) PaulHanagan 3 38
(Ann Duffield) *cl up: rdn and hung lft 2f out: sn one pce* **10/3[3]**
03 **4** *1* **Wish Again (IRE)**[28] 4147 2-9-7 0................................. AdrianNicholls 7 48
(David Nicholls) *chsd ldrs: rdn along 1/2-way: drvn 2f out and sn one pce* **8/1**
50 **5** *2 ¾* **No More Games**[5] 4899 2-9-2 0.................................(p) PhillipMakin 2 33
(Kevin Ryan) *chsd ldrs: rdn along 1/2-way: sn outpcd* **15/2**
0006 **6** *shd* **Nadia's Place**[12] 4668 2-8-2 40.................................(v) DeclanCannon(3) 6 22
(Nigel Tinkler) *dwlt and towards rr: pushed along bef 1/2-way: sn rdn and n.d* **66/1**
66 **7** *2 ¾* **Needwood Rose**[9] 4808 2-8-7 0................................. PaulQuinn 4 14
(David Nicholls) *s.i.s: sn rdn along and a in rr* **33/1**
00 **8** *10* **Precious Little**[34] 3932 2-8-0 0 ow1................................. LeonnaMayor(7) 1 —
(David Nicholls) *s.i.s: a bhd* **66/1**

60.10 secs (0.50) **Going Correction** +0.075s/f (Good) **8 Ran SP% 111.9**
Speed ratings (Par 96): **99,95,88,87,82 82,78,62**
toteswingers:1&2:£2.10, 1&3:£2.60, 2&3:£2.00 CSF £8.24 TOTE £4.10: £1.40, £1.10, £1.10; EX 8.90 Trifecta £29.50 Pool £709.05 - 17.75 winning units..
Owner Saintly Racing **Bred** Tally-Ho Stud **Trained** Newmarket, Suffolk

FOCUS
Few got into this. The form is rated conservatively around the front pair.

NOTEBOOK
Sonko(IRE) soon bagged the rail and galloped away under a strong ride. She'd been beaten by the third in a similar race earlier in the season, but has improved since, and can win again. (tchd 5-2)
Rougini(IRE) appreciated the drop in grade and showed improved form in the first-time visor. (op 11-4)
Lady Caprice hasn't built on last month's Catterick win when wearing first-time blinkers. (op 3-1 tchd 7-2)
Wish Again(IRE) couldn't quicken and may find it easier off a low mark in nurseries. (op 15-2 tchd 7-1)

5106 BUCK INN, THORNTON WATLASS H'CAP 1m
3:15 (3:15) (Class 5) (0-75,75) 3-Y-O+ **£2,911** (£866; £432; £216) **Stalls** Low

Form RPR
1212 **1** **Thinking**[37] 3859 4-9-4 65................................. DuranFentiman 10 76
(Tim Easterby) *prom: cl up 1/2-way: led over 2f out: rdn clr over 1f out: kpt on strly* **9/2[1]**
2314 **2** *1 ½* **Seldom (IRE)**[16] 4543 5-9-1 62................................. PhillipMakin 8 70
(Mel Brittain) *trckd ldrs: hdwy 3f out: rdn to chse wnr over 1f out: sn drvn and no imp towards fin* **14/1**
0250 **3** *1 ½* **Kerrys Requiem (IRE)**[23] 4349 5-9-9 75.................................(p) JulieBurke(5) 5 79
(Tim Pitt) *hld up: gd hdwy on outer over 2f out: rdn to chse ldrs over 1f out: edgd lft ins fnl f: kpt on same pce* **8/1[2]**
000 **4** *½* **Piceno (IRE)**[16] 4561 3-9-1 72................................. BillyCray(3) 9 74
(David Nicholls) *led: rdn over 3f out: hdd over 2f out: sn drvn: one pce appr fnl f* **8/1[2]**
3533 **5** *nse* **Elijah Pepper (USA)**[12] 4679 6-10-0 75................................. GrahamGibbons 13 78+
(David Barron) *midfield: n.m.r bnd after 3f: hdwy over 2f out: rdn to chse ldrs wl over 1f out: sn drvn and no imp* **8/1[2]**
25-3 **6** *1 ¼* **Glenmuir (IRE)**[45] 3569 8-9-1 67................................. ShaneBKelly(5) 2 67
(John Quinn) *hld up towards rr: hdwy on inner over 2f out: rdn wl over 1f out: kpt on same pce fnl f* **20/1**
3052 **7** *1 ¼* **Gallant Eagle (IRE)**[18] 4479 4-9-9 73................................. MartinHarley(3) 14 70
(Ed de Giles) *in rr: hdwy over 2f out: sn rdn and styd on appr fnl f: nrst fin* **11/1[3]**
4660 **8** *shd* **Rosbay (IRE)**[14] 4612 7-9-5 66.................................(p) TedDurcan 17 63
(Tim Easterby) *towards rr: hdwy over 2f out: rdn wl over 1f out: styng on whn n.m.r appr fnl f: n.d* **16/1**
6006 **9** *½* **Aerodynamic (IRE)**[22] 4367 4-9-2 63................................. PaddyAspell 3 59
(Clive Mulhall) *in rr tl sme late hdwy* **14/1**
00 **10** *1 ½* **Captain Macarry (IRE)**[12] 4656 6-9-4 65.................................(v) WilliamCarson 6 57
(Stuart Williams) *in rr tl sme late hdwy* **50/1**
0010 **11** *1* **Legal Legacy**[23] 4349 5-9-12 73................................. TomEaves 4 63
(Michael Dods) *s.i.s and in rr: hdwy over 3f out: rdn to chse ldrs over 2f out: sn drvn and wknd* **14/1**
2161 **12** *¾* **Postman**[125] 1292 5-9-3 71.................................(p) JustinNewman(7) 7 59
(Bryan Smart) *a towards rr* **16/1**
5623 **13** *¾* **Jaldarshaan (IRE)**[9] 4783 4-8-11 58................................. PJMcDonald 16 45
(Alan Swinbank) *midfield: hdwy on wd outside to chse ldrs 3f out: sn rdn and wknd* **12/1**
2163 **14** *½* **Mighty Clarets (IRE)**[166] 723 4-9-7 75................................. LauraBarry(7) 11 60
(Richard Fahey) *nvr bttr than midfield* **16/1**
0000 **15** *10* **Call Of Duty (IRE)**[14] 4604 6-9-4 65................................. PaulHanagan 1 27
(Dianne Sayer) *trckd ldrs on inner: effrt over 3f out: sn rdn and wknd over 2f out* **18/1**
0066 **16** *5* **Strong Knight**[11] 4716 4-8-9 56 oh7.................................(b[1]) KellyHarrison 12 7
(Tim Walford) *in tch: rdn along wl over 2f out: sn wknd* **40/1**
0004 **17** *shd* **Keys Of Cyprus**[52] 3358 9-10-0 75................................. AdrianNicholls 15 26
(David Nicholls) *chsd ldrs: cl up 1/2-way: rdn over 3f out and sn wknd* **16/1**

1m 41.85s (1.75) **Going Correction** +0.30s/f (Good)
WFA 3 from 4yo+ 7lb **17 Ran SP% 125.5**
Speed ratings (Par 103): **103,101,100,99,99 98,96,96,96,94 93,93,92,91,81 76,76**
toteswingers:1&2:£14.20, 1&3:£13.80, 2&3:£36.60 CSF £68.57 CT £508.05 TOTE £4.10: £1.60, £3.60, £2.50, £1.60; EX 75.30 Trifecta £319.40 Pool £695.04 - 1.61 winning units..
Owner Habton Farms **Bred** L T Roberts **Trained** Great Habton, N Yorks

FOCUS
Just a moderate handicap. Few got involved. The winner rates a personal best with the second back to her old best.
Aerodynamic(IRE) Official explanation: jockey said gelding had a breathing problem
Call Of Duty(IRE) Official explanation: jockey said gelding hung right

5107 WHITE SWAN, AMPLEFORTH FILLIES' H'CAP 1m 4f
3:45 (3:45) (Class 5) (0-70,69) 3-Y-O+ **£2,911** (£866; £432; £216) **Stalls** Low

Form RPR
0324 **1** **Lady Norlela**[22] 4366 5-8-13 54................................. BarryMcHugh 12 65
(Brian Rothwell) *hld up towards rr: hdwy over 4f out: chsd ldrs over 2f out: rdn over 1f out: styd on to ld jst ins fnl f: drvn out* **11/1**
1553 **2** *1 ½* **Jeu De Vivre (IRE)**[6] 4879 3-9-2 68................................. RoystonFfrench 6 77
(Mark Johnston) *trckd ldrs: hdwy over 3f out: chsd ldr over 2f out: rdn to ld briefly jst over 1f out: hdd jst ins fnl f: sn drvn and kpt on same pce* **6/1[3]**
20P1 **3** *2 ¼* **Gems**[13] 4626 4-9-6 66................................. LucyKBarry(5) 7 71
(Peter Hiatt) *led: rdn along 3f out: drvn wl over 1f out: hdd appr fnl f: kpt on same pce* **9/1**
3653 **4** *2 ¼* **Sixty Roses (IRE)**[24] 4275 3-8-11 63.................................(b) PhillipMakin 8 65
(John Dunlop) *hld up towards rr: gd hdwy on outer over 4f out: chsd ldng pair 3f out: rdn over 2f out: sn drvn and one pce appr fnl f* **10/3[2]**
6035 **5** *¾* **Hathaway (IRE)**[14] 4612 4-8-9 50................................. GrahamGibbons 10 51
(Mark Brisbourne) *in tch: hdwy 4f out: chsd ldrs 3f out: rdn 2f out: sn drvn and one pce* **9/1**
0-00 **6** *½* **Kathlatino**[63] 2988 4-8-11 52................................. TomEaves 2 52
(Micky Hammond) *midfield: hdwy 3f out: rdn over 2f out: drvn and no imp fr over 1f out* **50/1**
5-15 **7** *hd* **Dance For Julie (IRE)**[25] 4237 4-9-11 69................................. PatrickDonaghy(3) 4 68
(Ben Haslam) *hld up in rr: hdwy wl over 2f out: kpt on appr fnl f: nvr nr ldrs* **16/1**
4052 **8** *1* **Aegean Destiny**[26] 4204 4-8-12 56................................. DeclanCannon(3) 1 54
(John Mackie) *chsd ldng pair: rdn along over 3f out: grad wknd* **8/1**
-40 **9** *1 ¾* **Miss Ferney**[22] 4367 7-8-9 53................................. PaulPickard(3) 9 48
(Alan Kirtley) *hld up in rr: hdwy on wd outside 3f out: rdn to chse ldrs over 2f out: sn no imp* **50/1**
-600 **10** *1* **Cool Baranca (GER)**[14] 4605 5-9-0 55................................. TonyHamilton 11 48
(Dianne Sayer) *a towards rr* **33/1**
0515 **11** *4 ½* **Playful Girl (IRE)**[21] 4381 3-7-12 50.................................(b) DuranFentiman 5 36
(Tim Easterby) *trckd ldr: effrt over 3f out and sn rdn along: drvn over 2f out and sn wknd* **22/1**
0061 **12** *8* **Apparel (IRE)**[17] 4510 3-9-1 67................................. PaulHanagan 3 40
(Ed Dunlop) *chsd ldrs: rdn along 5f out: sn wknd* **3/1[1]**
0160 **13** *41* **Without Equal**[33] 3974 5-9-1 56................................. PJMcDonald 14 —
(David Thompson) *dwlt: hdwy to chse ldrs after 3f: rdn along over 5f out: sn lost pl and bhd fnl 3f* **33/1**

2m 38.7s (2.50) **Going Correction** +0.30s/f (Good)
WFA 3 from 4yo+ 11lb **13 Ran SP% 121.8**
Speed ratings (Par 100): **103,102,100,99,98 98,98,97,96,95 92,87,59**
toteswingers:1&2:£7.70, 1&3:£12.80, 2&3:£6.40 CSF £73.99 CT £632.38 TOTE £13.20: £3.00, £2.50, £2.90; EX 90.60 Trifecta £609.40 Part won. Pool £823.61 - 0.60 winning units..
Owner Mrs Greta Sparks **Bred** Paul Moorhouse **Trained** Norton, N Yorks

FOCUS
A fair fillies' race for the grade, more competitive than most. The early pace appeared a strong one and that played into the hands of the winner.
Apparel(IRE) Official explanation: trainer's rep had no explanation for the poor form shown

5108 DON'T MISS LADIES DAY - 3RD SEPTEMBER H'CAP 5f
4:15 (4:17) (Class 4) (0-80,80) 4-Y-O+ **£4,075** (£1,212; £606; £303) **Stalls** High

Form RPR
5206 **1** **Magical Macey (USA)**[17] 4516 4-9-7 80.................................(b) LeeNewman 12 91
(David Barron) *cl up: effrt over 1f out: rdn to ld ins fnl f: kpt on strly* **5/1[2]**
0000 **2** *1* **Oldjoesaid**[9] 4791 7-9-7 80.................................(b) PhillipMakin 8 87
(Kevin Ryan) *trckd ldrs: hdwy over 1f out: rdn to chal ins fnl f and ev ch tl drvn and nt qckn last 50yds* **8/1**
225 **3** *1* **Boogie Waltzer**[20] 4416 4-8-11 73.................................(t) RyanClark(3) 14 77
(Stuart Williams) *trckd ldrs on stands' rail: effrt wl over 1f out: rdn ent fnl f: kpt on: nrst fin* **4/1[1]**
0000 **4** *1* **Nadeen (IRE)**[23] 4327 4-9-2 75................................. PaulHanagan 13 75
(Michael Smith) *towards rr: hdwy wl over 1f out: sn rdn and kpt on ins fnl f: nrst fin* **12/1**
0435 **5** *½* **Mayoman (IRE)**[9] 4792 6-9-2 75.................................(v) DavidNolan 10 73
(Declan Carroll) *led: rdn along over 2f out: drvn and hdd jst ins fnl f: wknd* **5/1[2]**
0536 **6** *1 ½* **Go Go Green (IRE)**[48] 3488 5-9-1 74................................. DanielTudhope 7 67
(Jim Goldie) *midfield: hdwy wl over 1f out: rdn to chse ldrs ent fnl f: sn drvn and one pce* **22/1**
5-05 **7** *¾* **Walvis Bay (IRE)**[62] 3028 4-9-6 79................................. FrannyNorton 1 69
(Tom Tate) *cl up: rdn along wl over 1f out: drvn appr fnl f and grad wknd* **8/1**
4410 **8** *1* **Red Cape (FR)**[14] 4609 8-9-6 79................................. PJMcDonald 9 66
(Ruth Carr) *midfield: effrt 2f out: sn rdn and n.d* **11/2[3]**
3600 **9** *½* **Invincible Lad (IRE)**[20] 4416 7-9-3 76................................. AdrianNicholls 6 61
(David Nicholls) *hld up: a towards rr* **16/1**
5-10 **10** *2* **Stratton Banker (IRE)**[93] 2118 4-8-13 72................................. WilliamCarson 4 50
(Stuart Williams) *in tch on outer: hdwy and cl up 2f out: sn rdn and wknd over 1f out* **25/1**
0600 **11** *1 ¾* **Mey Blossom**[45] 3579 6-9-1 74................................. MichaelStainton 5 45
(Richard Whitaker) *a towards rr* **28/1**

59.28 secs (-0.32) **Going Correction** +0.075s/f (Good) **11 Ran SP% 116.2**
Speed ratings (Par 105): **105,103,101,100,99 97,95,94,93,90 87**
toteswingers:1&2:£7.80, 1&3:£3.00, 2&3:£7.00 CSF £42.95 CT £178.90 TOTE £8.00: £2.00, £3.80, £1.90; EX 40.80 Trifecta £226.30 Pool £1,327.72 - 4.34 winning units..
Owner K J Alderson **Bred** Silver Springs Stud Farm Inc & Mrs J Costelloe **Trained** Maunby, N Yorks

FOCUS
The nearer the stands' rail the better in this 5f sprint. The form is sound enough among the principals.
Nadeen(IRE) Official explanation: jockey said gelding hung left
Mayoman(IRE) Official explanation: jockey said he lost an iron on leaving stalls
Invincible Lad(IRE) Official explanation: jockey said gelding was denied a clear run

5109 PINDER DALE H'CAP 7f
4:45 (4:45) (Class 5) (0-75,73) 3-Y-O **£2,911** (£866; £432; £216) **Stalls** Low

Form RPR
3221 **1** **Icy Blue**[9] 4813 3-9-1 67................................. FrannyNorton 5 76
(Richard Whitaker) *in tch: hdwy to chse ldrs 3f out: rdn along 2f out: drvn over 1f out: styd on u.p ins fnl f to ld last 75yds* **3/1[1]**

0001 **2** 3/4 **Rowan Spirit (IRE)**[11] 4715 3-9-0 **66**.................... GrahamGibbons 11 73
(Mark Brisbourne) *trckd ldrs: hdwy 1/2-way: rdn to chal wl over 1f out: sn drvn and ev ch ins fnl f tl no ex towards fin* **9/1**

0114 **3** 3/4 **Ryedale Dancer (IRE)**[16] 4560 3-9-0 **66**.................... DavidAllan 8 71
(Tim Easterby) *trckd ldng pair: hdwy to ld over 2f out: rdn over 1f out: drvn ins fnl f: hdd and no ex last 75yds* **10/3**[2]

2641 **4** 2 1/4 **Fenella Fudge**[19] 4437 3-9-4 **70**....................(b) PaulHanagan 9 69
(James Given) *led: rdn along 3f out: hdd over 2f out: drvn wl over 1f out: kpt on same pce* **5/1**[3]

1016 **5** 1 1/4 **Paper Dreams (IRE)**[13] 4647 3-8-13 **65**.................... PhillipMakin 4 61
(Kevin Ryan) *chsd ldrs: rdn along wl over 2f out: drvn over 1f out and kpt on same pce* **22/1**

4000 **6** 1/2 **Watts Up Son**[7] 4854 3-9-1 **67**....................(t) JamesSullivan 7 61
(Declan Carroll) *in rr: rdn along 1/2-way: styd on u.p fnl 2f: n.d* **16/1**

2241 **7** 3 1/2 **Moral Issue**[33] 3977 3-9-7 **73**.................... TonyHamilton 2 58
(Jedd O'Keeffe) *prom: rdn along 3f out: wknd over 2f out* **8/1**

2203 **8** 2 1/2 **Bay Of Fires (IRE)**[14] 4610 3-9-7 **73**.................... DanielTudhope 6 51
(David O'Meara) *dwlt: a in rr* **8/1**

04 **9** 4 **Dan's Martha**[47] 3508 3-8-10 **65**....................(t) PatrickDonaghy(3) 10 32
(Ben Haslam) *dwlt: a towards rr* **16/1**

1m 28.88s (1.68) **Going Correction** +0.30s/f (Good) **9 Ran SP% 113.1**
Speed ratings (Par 100): **102,101,100,97,96 95,91,88,84**
toteswingers:1&2:£7.80, 1&3:£3.00, 2&3:£7.00 CSF £29.81 CT £93.79 TOTE £4.40: £1.60, £3.20, £2.00; EX 34.60 Trifecta £78.80 Pool £477.35 - 4.48 winning units..
Owner Country Lane Partnership **Bred** Cheveley Park Stud Ltd **Trained** Scarcroft, W Yorks

FOCUS
An ordinary handicap, but the right horses came to the fore and the form looks quite strong for the grade, rated around the second and third.
T/Jkpt: Not won. T/Plt: £55.20 to a £1 stake. Pool:£79,093.36 1,044.70 winning tickets T/Qpdt: £10.90 to a £1 stake. Pool:£6,448.07 434.36 winning tickets JR

4857 WINDSOR (R-H)

Monday, August 15

OFFICIAL GOING: Good to firm (good in places)
Stands' rail dolled out 8yds at 6f and 3yds at winning post. Top bend out 3yds from normal configuration adding 14yds to races of 1m and over.
Wind: Moderate, behind Weather: Cloudy, a little drizzle

5110 SPORTINGBET.COM APPRENTICE H'CAP 1m 2f 7y
5:40 (5:40) (Class 5) (0-75,73) 4-Y-0+ **£2,264** (£673; £336; £168) **Stalls** Centre

Form RPR

011 **1** **Colinca's Lad (IRE)**[21] 4385 9-8-7 **62**.................... RosieJessop(3) 9 72
(Peter Charalambous) *mde all: drew clr 6f out: rdn over 2f out: maintained gallop and nvr seriously threatened* **9/2**[2]

2421 **2** 4 **Choral Festival**[8] 4825 5-9-5 **71** 6ex.................... SeanLevey 4 73
(John Bridger) *hld up in rr: prog fr 1/2-way: rdn to chse wnr over 1f out: no imp* **7/2**[1]

4002 **3** nk **Blue Spartan (IRE)**[25] 4249 6-9-4 **70**.................... LouisBeuzelin 7 71
(Brian Meehan) *chsd wnr: rdn and lost 2nd over 3f out: kpt on one pce fnl 2f* **9/2**[2]

-011 **4** 1 1/4 **Count Ceprano (IRE)**[10] 4754 7-8-12 **69**.................... SophieSilvester(5) 3 68+
(Lydia Pearce) *hld up in rr: dropped to last 1/2-way and detached fr rest: stl last 2f out and no ch: pushed along and styd on after: far too much to do* **11/1**

4245 **5** 1 **Edgeworth (IRE)**[8] 4825 5-8-13 **72**.................... JoshBaudains(7) 8 69
(David Bridgwater) *dwlt: hld up in midfield: no prog 3f out: pushed along 2f out: reminder and kpt on fnl f: no ch* **10/1**[3]

3001 **6** 2 3/4 **Urban Space**[7] 4862 5-9-5 **71** 6ex.................... KierenFox 6 62
(John Flint) *trckd ldng pair: rdn to chse wnr over 3f out: no imp over 2f out: lost 2nd and wknd over 1f out* **7/2**[1]

6354 **7** 1 1/4 **Lang Shining (IRE)**[8] 4825 7-9-6 **72**....................(b) SophieDoyle 2 61
(Jamie Osborne) *t.k.h: trckd ldrs: urged along over 3f out: no rspnse and sn btn* **20/1**

0-10 **8** 1 3/4 **Halyard (IRE)**[46] 3538 4-9-7 **73**....................(v) JohnFahy 1 58
(Walter Swinburn) *s.v.s: hld up last: effrt 4f out: no prog and wl btn 2f out* **11/1**

2m 6.18s (-2.52) **Going Correction** -0.20s/f (Firm) **8 Ran SP% 111.3**
Speed ratings (Par 103): **102,98,98,97,96 94,93,92**
toteswingers:1&2:£1.10, 2&3:£2.80, 1&3:£6.60 CSF £19.48 CT £71.25 TOTE £6.20: £1.70, £1.60, £1.30; EX 14.60.
Owner P Charalambous **Bred** Peter Charles **Trained** Newmarket, Suffolk
■ Stewards' Enquiry : Kieren Fox caution: failed to take all reasonable and permissable measures to obtain best possible placing.

FOCUS
Not a huge field, but a competitive race of its type, with most of them in good form. They went a decent gallop, with the winner dominating, but his rider judged it perfectly. The form may not prove all that solid.

5111 BRITISH STALLION STUDS SUPPORTING BRITISH RACING EBF MAIDEN STKS 6f
6:10 (6:11) (Class 5) 2-Y-0 **£3,299** (£981; £490; £245) **Stalls** Low

Form RPR

3 **1** **Shamahan**[11] 4710 2-9-3.................... GeorgeBaker 9 84+
(Gary Moore) *trckd ldng trio: shkn up and clsd to ld 1f out: rdn clr and styd on wl* **8/1**[3]

2 **2** 2 3/4 **Signor Sassi**[24] 4276 2-9-3.................... NeilCallan 11 76
(Roger Varian) *dwlt: sn rcvrd to trck ldng trio: rdn wl over 1f out: chal and upsides jst over 1f out: sn outpcd* **4/7**[1]

36 **3** 1 **Eightfold**[24] 4276 2-9-3.................... PatDobbs 14 73
(Richard Hannon) *w ldrs: disp ld over 2f out to 1f out: one pce* **9/1**

4 1/2 **La Bocca (USA)** 2-8-12.................... JamesDoyle 13 67
(Roger Charlton) *pressed ldr: led over 3f out: jnd over 2f out: hdd and one pce 1f out* **7/1**[2]

5 1 1/4 **Star Kingdom (IRE)** 2-9-0.................... SeanLevey(3) 6 68
(Robert Mills) *s.i.s: off the pce in 9th: pushed along and sme prog 2f out: styd on ins fnl f* **20/1**

0 **6** 1/2 **Amphora**[31] 4052 2-8-12.................... JimmyFortune 5 61+
(Andrew Balding) *chsd ldng trio: pushed along over 2f out: grad fdd over 1f out* **16/1**

0 **7** 4 1/2 **Kinglami**[20] 4414 2-9-0.................... AdamBeschizza(3) 10 53
(Brian Gubby) *chsd ldrs disputing 7th: rdn and outpcd over 2f out: wl in rr 1f out: kpt on again nr fin* **66/1**

0 **8** hd **Trisha's Boy (IRE)**[21] 4384 2-9-3.................... MartinDwyer 12 52
(Simon Dow) *chsd ldrs disputing 7th: shkn up and no prog 2f out: fdd* **100/1**

0 **9** 3 1/4 **Romany Spirit (IRE)**[11] 4720 2-8-12.................... PatCosgrave 2 37
(Jim Boyle) *led to over 3f out: losing pl whn n.m.r on inner over 2f out* **100/1**

10 3/4 **Notnowstanley** 2-9-3.................... LukeMorris 1 40
(J S Moore) *sn pushed along and rn green: a in last quartet: nvr a factor* **66/1**

11 1 **You Got The Love** 2-8-9.................... KierenFox(3) 8 32
(Jeremy Gask) *dwlt: rn green and a in last quartet: no prog on outer over 2f out* **66/1**

12 nk **Corn Rigs** 2-8-12.................... TomMcLaughlin 3 31
(Ed Dunlop) *dwlt: a in last quartet: pushed along and no prog over 2f out* **28/1**

5 **13** 1/2 **Dana's Present**[80] 2448 2-9-3.................... TonyCulhane 4 35
(George Baker) *hld up in last quartet: shuffled along fnl 2f: no prog and nvr nr ldrs* **25/1**

1m 12.66s (-0.34) **Going Correction** -0.20s/f (Firm) **13 Ran SP% 121.7**
Speed ratings (Par 94): **94,90,89,88,86 86,80,79,75,74 73,72,72**
toteswingers:1&2:£2.80, 2&3:£2.50, 1&3:£9.50 CSF £12.61 TOTE £11.20: £2.40, £1.30, £1.90; EX 22.30.
Owner Heart Of The South Racing **Bred** Frank Brady **Trained** Lower Beeding, W Sussex

FOCUS
A fair maiden with several likely future winners in the line-up. Shamahan impressed and the form looks quite strong.

NOTEBOOK
Shamahan ◆ had shown promise on his debut, but this was a significant improvement on faster ground. Having demonstrated a good cruising speed, he finished the job off in style and looks useful. (op 15-2 tchd 9-1)
Signor Sassi, well backed to go one better than on his debut, was no match for the winner and this has to go down as disappointing. However, there were some fair sorts behind, and he should win a routine maiden. (op 8-15 tchd 4-6 in places)
Eightfold has not yet found his ideal distance but he is effective at both 6f and 7f, on this occasion showing plenty of speed. He is now qualified for nurseries but a maiden should still be within reach. (op 11-1)
La Bocca(USA), related to many smart winners up to 1m1f, made a promising debut. She has plenty of early pace and ought to win a maiden. (op 17-2)
Star Kingdom(IRE), a Marju colt out of a half-sister to the high-class staying filly Summitville, fetched £65,000 at the breeze-ups. He looks sure to improve with racing and 7f should already suit him.
Amphora, a £105,000 Oasis Dream filly out of a well related 7f winner, ran much better than on her debut. More is needed to win a maiden, but she is gradually learning.
You Got The Love Official explanation: jockey said filly ran green

5112 FLORIDITA LONDON (S) STKS 1m 3f 135y
6:40 (6:42) (Class 6) 3-Y-0+ **£1,617** (£481; £240; £120) **Stalls** Centre

Form RPR

1640 **1** **Resplendent Light**[3] 4982 6-9-11 **68**....................(t) NeilCallan 3 64
(Bernard Llewellyn) *hld up: trckd ldrs 4f out: narrow ld against rail jst over 2f out: hrd pressed fnl f: jst hld on* **2/1**[2]

-004 **2** nse **Into The Wind**[8] 4816 4-9-6 **55**.................... JamesMillman 4 59
(Rod Millman) *hld up in last: prog 3f out: rdn 2f out: wnt 2nd jst over 1f out: str chal ins fnl f: jst failed* **15/2**[3]

0443 **3** 4 1/2 **Dream Of Fortune (IRE)**[7] 4869 7-9-11 **55**....................(bt) StevieDonohoe 1 56
(David Evans) *hld up in 6th: prog 1/2-way: chsd ldr wl over 2f out: chal wnr and upsides jst over 2f out to over 1f out: wknd ins fnl f* **8/1**

0020 **4** 4 **Saloon (USA)**[14] 4601 7-9-11 **55**....................(p) SilvestreDeSousa 2 50
(Jane Chapple-Hyam) *t.k.h: trckd ldng pair to 4f out: sn pushed along: outpcd u.p fnl 3f* **15/8**[1]

400- **5** 8 **Dream Spinner**[14] 6290 4-9-11 **65**.................... JimmyFortune 7 36
(Dr Richard Newland) *led 3f: trckd ldr: led again over 4f out to jst over 2f out: wknd and eased* **8/1**

0060 **6** 5 **Henrys Air**[10] 4758 3-8-12 **52**.................... JoshBaudains(7) 6 32
(David Bridgwater) *plld way into ld after 3f: hdd over 4f out: sn btn* **16/1**

0 **7** 9 **Fleetwood Daughter**[11] 4706 9-8-13 **0**.................... ThomasBrown(7) 5 —
(Bernard Llewellyn) *cl up: taken wd and wknd 3f out: eased* **40/1**

2m 30.3s (0.80) **Going Correction** -0.20s/f (Firm)
WFA 3 from 4yo+ 11lb **7 Ran SP% 110.4**
Speed ratings (Par 101): **89,88,85,83,77 74,68**
toteswingers:1&2:£3.20, 2&3:£3.90, 1&3:£3.10 CSF £16.02 TOTE £2.70: £1.60, £3.60; EX 18.00.There was no bid for the winner.
Owner B J Llewellyn **Bred** Usk Valley Stud **Trained** Fochriw, Caerphilly

FOCUS
An uninspiring race even by selling standards, with none of the field in great form.

5113 WINDSOR VEHICLE LEASING FILLIES' H'CAP 1m 67y
7:10 (7:11) (Class 4) (0-85,84) 3-Y-0+ **£4,075** (£1,212; £606; £303) **Stalls** Low

Form RPR

414 **1** **Thistle Bird**[37] 3873 3-9-7 **84**.................... GeorgeBaker 9 101+
(Roger Charlton) *prom: led over 2f out: drew clr over 1f out: shkn up briefly and in n.d after* **11/4**[1]

1240 **2** 3 **Sure Route**[37] 3845 3-9-4 **81**.................... PatDobbs 3 90
(Richard Hannon) *hld up in rr: effrt and nt clr run over 2f out: swtchd outside and prog: wnt 2nd over 1f out: no ch w wnr* **5/1**[2]

1-54 **3** 1 1/2 **Birdolini**[24] 4271 3-8-9 **72**.................... FergusSweeney 8 78
(Alan King) *trckd ldrs: effrt and edgd rt 2f out: rdn to dispute 2nd briefly jst over 1f out: one pce* **15/2**

-550 **4** 1 1/2 **Rosedale**[30] 4093 4-8-13 **69**.................... NeilCallan 6 75+
(James Toller) *trckd ldrs on inner: in tch whn hmpd and bmpd wl over 1f out: nt rcvr and one pce* **12/1**

2045 **5** 2 **Young Dottie**[25] 4243 5-8-10 **66**.................... CathyGannon 2 65
(Pat Phelan) *t.k.h: hld up in 8th: rdn and effrt on outer over 2f out: no imp over 1f out* **12/1**

5642 **6** 2 **Ela Gonda Mou**[12] 4681 4-8-13 **69**.................... KirstyMilczarek 4 67+
(Peter Charalambous) *prom: starting to lose pl whn hmpd and bounced arnd like a pinball off rivals over 1f out* **9/1**

0300 **7** shd **Totally Ours**[19] 4429 4-9-12 **82**....................(b[1]) MartinDwyer 7 76
(William Muir) *racd freely: led: wd bnd after 2f: hdd & wknd over 2f out* **9/1**

-154 **8** 3/4 **Countermarch**[31] 4056 3-8-10 **76**.................... KieranO'Neill(3) 5 67
(Richard Hannon) *hld up in tch: prog on outer 3f out: disp 2nd 2f out: wknd over 1f out* **7/1**[3]

1660 **9** *40* **Cloud Illusions (USA)**[33] 3982 3-9-4 **81**........................ KierenFallon 1 —
(Heather Main) *hld up in last: shkn up 3f out: no rspnse and sn wknd: eased and t.o* **7/1**[3]

1m 41.09s (-3.61) **Going Correction** -0.20s/f (Firm)
WFA 3 from 4yo+ 7lb **9** Ran SP% **115.5**
Speed ratings (Par 102): **110,107,105,104,102 100,99,99,59**
toteswingers:1&2:£6.50, 2&3:£9.90, 1&3:£1.60 CSF £16.18 CT £92.30 TOTE £3.40: £1.80, £1.60, £1.90; EX 23.00.

Owner Lady Rothschild **Bred** The Rt Hon Lord Rothschild **Trained** Beckhampton, Wilts

FOCUS
A combination of experience and potential among the runners, with the first three places filled by less-exposed runners. The gallop was good and so was the time. The winner impressed and posted a big personal best.

Rosedale Official explanation: jockey said filly suffered interference in running

Ela Gonda Mou Official explanation: jockey said filly suffered interference in running

Totally Ours Official explanation: jockey said filly ran too freely

5114 SPORTINGBET.COM MAIDEN STKS — 1m 67y

7:40 (7:41) (Class 5) 3-4-Y-O **£2,264** (£673; £336; £168) **Stalls** Low

Form RPR

042 **1** **Eastern Breeze (IRE)**[22] 4370 3-8-12 78........................ FrankieDettori 5 79+
(Saeed Bin Suroor) *mde all: pushed along 2f out: edgd lft but drew clr over 1f out* **30/100**[1]

0- **2** *5* **Russian Affair**[261] 7595 3-9-3 0........................ NeilCallan 6 73+
(Roger Varian) *chsd wnr: rdn and cl enough wl over 1f out: outpcd after* **7/2**[2]

3 *9* **Tetbury Lass** 3-8-12 0........................ NeilChalmers 2 45
(Adrian Chamberlain) *s.s: wl off the pce in last: plugged on fr 3f out to take modest 3rd over 1f out* **50/1**

0 **4** *2 1/4* **Teutonic Knight (IRE)**[7] 4861 4-9-10 0........................ StevieDonohoe 3 46
(Ian Williams) *mostly in 4th: outpcd bef 1/2-way: n.d after* **33/1**

04- **5** *10* **Ayaarah (IRE)**[329] 6248 3-8-12 0........................ LukeMorris 4 16
(Les Hall) *chsd ldng pair: rdn 1/2-way: sn outpcd: wknd and hanging lft over 1f out* **14/1**[3]

00 **R** **Lechlade Lass**[8] 4826 3-8-7 0........................ JamesRogers(5) 1 —
(Adrian Chamberlain) *veered off onto wrong part of crse shortly after s* **100/1**

1m 42.59s (-2.11) **Going Correction** -0.20s/f (Firm)
WFA 3 from 4yo 7lb **6** Ran SP% **111.7**
Speed ratings (Par 103): **102,97,88,85,75** —
toteswingers:1&2:£1.02, 2&3:£14.50, 1&3:£6.20 CSF £1.64 TOTE £1.20: £1.10, £1.50; EX 1.70.

Owner Godolphin **Bred** Epona Bloodstock Ltd **Trained** Newmarket, Suffolk

FOCUS
Anyone who thought this would turn into an exercise gallop for the winner had an uncomfortable time in the final 3f because it took her longer than expected to see off the runner-up. The race lacked depth and the pace was ordinary. The winner may not have needed to improve.

5115 MR & MRS KLEYNS 30TH WEDDING ANNIVERSARY H'CAP — 5f 10y

8:10 (8:11) (Class 5) (0-75,75) 3-Y-O **£2,264** (£673; £336; £168) **Stalls** Low

Form RPR

0341 **1** **Swendab (IRE)**[16] 4527 3-9-1 **69**........................(v) DarryllHolland 10 78
(John O'Shea) *led or disp thrght and racd in centre: jnd over 1f out: drvn to assert ins fnl f* **11/2**[2]

1033 **2** *3/4* **Best Be Careful (IRE)**[50] 3433 3-8-7 **61**........................ LiamKeniry 11 67
(Mark Usher) *dwlt: sn in tch in midfield on outer: prog to join wnr over 1f out: nt qckn ins fnl f* **16/1**

2262 **3** *hd* **Whitecrest**[18] 4461 3-8-13 **67**........................ CathyGannon 9 72
(John Spearing) *disp ld to 1/2-way: sn rdn: sltly outpcd over 1f out: styd on wl again ins fnl f* **11/1**

3443 **4** *1/4* **Scarlet Rocks (IRE)**[14] 4618 3-9-5 **73**........................ JamesDoyle 1 76
(David Evans) *mostly in midfield: rdn 2f out: styd on ins fnl f: nrst fin* **8/1**[3]

5646 **5** *1/2* **Catalinas Diamond (IRE)**[14] 4615 3-8-4 **61**........................ SophieDoyle(3) 3 62
(Pat Murphy) *hld up in last pair: stl there wl over 1f out: prog after: styd on wl ins fnl f: nrst fin* **14/1**

1000 **6** *hd* **Style And Panache (IRE)**[31] 4048 3-9-7 **75**........................ PatCosgrave 12 75
(David Evans) *pressed ldrs on outer: rdn 2f out: nt qckn over 1f out: one pce after* **20/1**

3642 **7** *1 1/2* **Ice Trooper**[12] 4669 3-9-7 **75**........................ KierenFallon 6 70
(Linda Stubbs) *w ldrs: rdn 2f out: nt qckn over 1f out: fdd ins fnl f* **4/1**[1]

3133 **8** *1/2* **Welsh Inlet (IRE)**[14] 4615 3-9-2 **70**........................ NeilChalmers 7 63
(John Bridger) *a in midfield: in tch over 1f out: no prog whn nt clr run briefly ins fnl f* **8/1**[3]

6356 **9** *nse* **Dubai Affair**[25] 4227 3-8-6 **60**........................ LukeMorris 8 53
(Ronald Harris) *mostly in midfield: cl enough over 1f out: fdd ins fnl f* **33/1**

34 **10** *2 1/2* **Fair Value (IRE)**[91] 2158 3-9-5 **73**........................ NeilCallan 4 57
(Simon Dow) *trckd ldrs nr side: lost pl 2f out: sn btn: wknd ins fnl f* **4/1**[1]

000- **11** *3/4* **Sabys Gem (IRE)**[282] 7346 3-8-5 **59**........................ MartinDwyer 5 40
(Michael Wigham) *stdd s: hld up in last pair: shuffled along over 1f out: no prog: do bttr* **20/1**

40-0 **12** *1/2* **Sabot D'Or**[16] 4547 3-8-2 **56**........................ SilvestreDeSousa 2 35
(Roger Ingram) *reminder in midfield after 1f: sn dropped in rr and struggling* **10/1**

59.46 secs (-0.84) **Going Correction** -0.20s/f (Firm) **12** Ran SP% **120.0**
Speed ratings (Par 100): **98,96,96,95,94 94,91,90,90,86 85,84**
toteswingers:1&2:£16.10, 2&3:£10.30, 1&3:£14.00 CSF £88.53 CT £676.52 TOTE £6.50: £2.20, £3.60, £3.30; EX 134.80.

Owner The Cross Racing Club & Patrick Brady **Bred** P Brady **Trained** Elton, Gloucs

FOCUS
A modest but competitive sprint, with barely 2l covering the first six. Ordinary form, which could rate a little higher.

Ice Trooper Official explanation: jockey said gelding hung left and had no more to give

T/Plt: £27.20 to a £1 stake. Pool £86,169.66 - 2,304.48 winning tickets. T/Qpdt: £10.90 to a £1 stake. Pool of £5,378.72 - 363.70 winning tickets. JN

4925 YARMOUTH (L-H)

Monday, August 15

OFFICIAL GOING: Good to firm (good in places; 7.7) changing to good to firm after race 1 (5.20)

Back straight and bottom bend dolled out 3m, ending at 4.5f adding 15m to races on round course.

Wind: airly modest, across Weather: bright spells and light cloud

5116 BETFAIR RACING EXCELLENCE APPRENTICE TRAINING SERIES H'CAP — 1m 3y

5:20 (5:20) (Class 6) (0-60,61) 3-Y-O+ **£1,617** (£481; £240; £120) **Stalls** High

Form RPR

/101 **1** **Dannios**[5] 4927 5-10-1 **61** 6ex........................(t) MichaelJMurphy(3) 7 76+
(Ed Walker) *s.i.s: bhd: clsd and in tch after 3f: hdwy to chse ldr gng wl jst over 2f out: upsides ldr on bit over 1f out: led ins fnl f: nudged clr towards fin: v easily* **4/6**[1]

5466 **2** *2 1/4* **Derby Desire (IRE)**[116] 1508 7-8-12 **46**........................ RichardOld(5) 3 51
(Des Donovan) *led: jnd and rdn over 1f out: hdd ins fnl f: sn outpcd and btn* **8/1**[3]

0 **3** *3 1/2* **Wings Of Apollo (IRE)**[22] 4370 3-9-2 **52**........................ DavidKenny 5 48
(Mrs K Burke) *hld up in tch: hdwy over 2f out: chsd ldng pair and rdn wl over 1f out: no prog and wl btn 1f out* **7/2**[2]

5016 **4** *2 3/4* **Norcroft**[13] 4651 9-8-13 **47**........................(p) DanielHarris(5) 6 38
(Christine Dunnett) *chsd ldrs: rdn and chsd ldr 1/2-way tl jst over 2f out: sn outpcd and wl btn over 1f out* **10/1**

-300 **5** *18* **Kathindi (IRE)**[48] 3496 4-9-2 **45**........................ CharlesBishop 4 —
(Michael Chapman) *chsd ldrs tl lost pl qckly over 2f out: wl bhd over 1f out* **33/1**

060/ **6** *6* **Finnegans Rainbow**[519] 7817 9-8-13 **45**........................ NoelGarbutt(3) 8 —
(Michael Chapman) *t.k.h: chsd ldr tl 1/2-way: wknd over 3f out: wl bhd fnl 2f: t.o* **66/1**

00 **7** *7* **Littlepromisedland (IRE)**[12] 4673 3-8-9 **45**........................ CharlesEddery 1 —
(Richard Guest) *v.s.a: clsd and in tch after 2f: hdwy to chse ldrs over 4f out: wknd qckly over 2f out: t.o over 1f out* **20/1**

1m 40.65s (0.05) **Going Correction** -0.175s/f (Firm)
WFA 3 from 4yo+ 7lb **7** Ran SP% **111.6**
Speed ratings (Par 101): **92,89,86,83,65 59,52**
toteswingers:1&2:£2.00, 1&3:£1.10, 2&3:£2.90 CSF £6.40 CT £11.21 TOTE £1.60: £1.10, £3.50; EX 4.10.

Owner Mrs T Walker **Bred** Roseland Thoroughbreds Ltd **Trained** Newmarket, Suffolk

FOCUS
This was a desperately weak handicap for apprentice riders in which the main action developed down the middle of the track. The in-form winner is value for further, the form rated around the runner-up.

5117 BRITISH STALLION STUDS SUPPORTING BRITISH RACING E B F MEDIAN AUCTION MAIDEN STKS — 6f 3y

5:50 (5:50) (Class 6) 2-Y-O **£2,264** (£673; £336; £168) **Stalls** High

Form RPR

1 **Alaskan Bullet (IRE)** 2-9-3 0........................ JamieSpencer 1 88+
(Michael Bell) *mde all: rdn and drew clr over 1f out: r.o wl: comf* **5/2**[2]

32 **2** *3 1/2* **Van Der Art**[42] 3680 2-8-9 0........................ HarryBentley(3) 10 70
(Alan Jarvis) *in tch: hdwy jst over 2f out: rdn over 1f out: chsd clr wnr ins fnl f: no imp* **3/1**[3]

3 **3** *2 1/4* **Khaleejiya (IRE)**[11] 4726 2-8-12 0........................ RobertHavlin 7 62
(James Toller) *t.k.h: chsd ldrs tl chsd wnr 1/2-way: rdn and nt pce of wnr over 1f out: btn 1f out: lost 2nd ins fnl f* **15/8**[1]

4 *nk* **Mr Spiggott (IRE)** 2-8-10 0........................ CharlesBishop(7) 3 66
(Mick Channon) *s.i.s: in rr of main gp: rdn jst over 2f out: styd on past btn horses fnl f: no ch w wnr* **25/1**

5 *3/4* **Art Show** 2-8-12 0........................ HayleyTurner 5 59
(Ed Dunlop) *t.k.h: chsd ldrs: rdn and unable qck 2f out: wknd ent fnl f* **13/2**

6 *2 1/4* **Saucy Cat (IRE)** 2-8-12 0........................ ShaneKelly 2 52
(Murty McGrath) *in rr of main gp: rdn and sme hdwy over 1f out: nvr trbld ldrs* **100/1**

7 *1 1/4* **Indian Tinker** 2-9-3 0........................ EddieAhern 9 54
(Robert Cowell) *chsd wnr tl 1/2-way: rdn and struggling 2f out: rn green and wknd over 1f out* **20/1**

8 *8* **Greek Music** 2-8-9 0........................ CagriMetin(3) 6 25
(George Prodromou) *s.i.s: sn detached in rr: nvr on terms* **66/1**

9 *20* **Colori D'Amore** 2-8-12 0........................ RobbieFitzpatrick 4 —
(Derek Shaw) *rn green: chsd ldrs for 2f: lost pl and bhd whn wandering over 3f out: sn lost tch: virtually p.u ins fnl f: t.o* **100/1**

1m 13.43s (-0.97) **Going Correction** -0.175s/f (Firm) **9** Ran SP% **113.8**
Speed ratings (Par 92): **99,94,91,90,89 86,85,74,47**
toteswingers:1&2:£2.30, 2&3:£2.00, 1&3:£1.90 CSF £9.87 TOTE £4.40: £1.20, £1.10, £1.20; EX 13.80.

Owner Partners In Crime **Bred** Pat Heffernan **Trained** Newmarket, Suffolk

FOCUS
A modest maiden and an impressive debut winner. The runner-up is rated to form.

NOTEBOOK
Alaskan Bullet(IRE) ◆ made a winning debut by making all in taking fashion and further enhanced his yard's decent record with 2-y-os at this venue. He arrived at the track with a decent reputation, but surprisingly proved easy to back near the off. However, it was clear as he burst from the gates he was a sharp sort and this is yet another advert of how dangerous jockey Jamie Spencer can be when allowed to dominate the early fractions. He ran a little green once asked for his effort, but had the race shot to pieces at the furlong marker and is potentially very useful. Another furlong won't bother him this year, but there is no reason to step him up just yet. (op 7-4 tchd 11-4)
Van Der Art ◆ came through to run another encouraging race in defeat and rates a solid benchmark. She was never a threat to the winner, but wasn't helped by her draw against the stands' rail and is one to keep on side now she qualifies for nurseries. (op 7-2 tchd 4-1)
Khaleejiya(IRE) wasn't beaten far in third over C&D on her debut 11 days earlier and was expected to improve. However, she never looked that comfortable on this quicker surface and lacked the required gear change. That's not surprising considering she's bred to enjoy further and it's probably unwise to judge her on this effort. Her Group 1 entry looks far too ambitious, though. (op 5-2 tchd 7-4)
Mr Spiggott(IRE) is speedily bred on the dam's side and was doing some encouraging late work on his racecourse debut. He'll get closer next time. (op 18-1)
Art Show, bred to make her mark over this trip at two, showed up nicely early on but displayed her inexperience at halfway. She has an engine and is entitled to get a deal closer next time out. (op 10-1)

Indian Tinker, speedily bred, travelled nicely enough until fitness became an issue and this was a fairly encouraging debut effort. (op 16-1 tchd 14-1)

5118 RACING WELFARE CLAIMING STKS — 1m 2f 21y
6:20 (6:21) (Class 6) 3-4-Y-O — **£1,617** (£481; £240; £120) **Stalls** Low

Form — RPR

6041 **1** — **Malice Or Mischief (IRE)**[12] 4685 3-9-2 78 .... LiamJones 3 — 64
(Tony Carroll) *led for 1f: chsd ldr after tl pushed ahd 3f out: drvn over 2f out: wnt clr over 1f out: in command but idling and kpt up to work ins fnl f: rdn out* — **4/9**[1]

5363 **2** *2* **Easydoesit (IRE)**[12] 4654 3-8-4 46 ....(p) HayleyTurner 2 — 48
(Jane Chapple-Hyam) *in tch in last pair: rdn over 5f out: drvn and outpcd over 4f out: hdwy u.p ent fnl f: wnt 2nd fnl 75yds: no threat to wnr* — **7/2**[2]

0005 **3** *1 1/2* **Imperial Fong**[11] 4728 3-7-13 47 ....[1] AndreaAtzeni 5 — 40
(Chris Dwyer) *hld up in tch in rr: rdn and outpcd 4f out: hdwy u.p over 1f out: chsd clr wnr jst ins fnl f: no imp and lost 2nd fnl 75yds* — **25/1**

-056 **4** *3 1/2* **Colzium**[27] 4177 3-8-8 43 ....(b[1]) JimmyQuinn 1 — 42
(Mark H Tompkins) *t.k.h: chsd ldng pair: drvn and outpcd over 3f out: plugged on same pce u.p and no threat to ldrs fnl 3f* — **28/1**

05 **5** *1 1/2* **Ocean's Dream Day (IRE)**[101] 1872 3-8-4 48 ....(p) MartinLane 4 — 35
(John Ryan) *led after 1f: rdn and qcknd 4f out: hdd and drvn 3f out: pressed wnr tl over 1f out: wknd and lost 2nd jst ins fnl f: fdd* — **12/1**[3]

2m 12.35s (1.85) **Going Correction** +0.125s/f (Good)
WFA 3 from 4yo 9lb — 5 Ran SP% **106.5**
Speed ratings (Par 101): **97,95,94,91,90**
CSF £2.02 TOTE £1.30: £1.10, £1.50; EX 2.30.Easydoesit was claimed by Mr T. R. Pearson for £4,000.
Owner Bill Adams **Bred** Kilnamoragh Stud **Trained** Cropthorne, Worcs
■ Stewards' Enquiry : Andrea Atzeni one-day ban: used whip down the shoulder in the forehand (Aug 29)

FOCUS
An uncompetitive claimer and suspect form due to the muddling pace. The winner did not need to match his best.

5119 ROGERS & NORTON SOLICITORS H'CAP — 7f 3y
6:50 (6:50) (Class 4) (0-80,80) 3-Y-O+ — **£4,075** (£1,212; £606; £303) **Stalls** High

Form — RPR

3203 **1** — **Ongoodform (IRE)**[31] 4064 4-9-5 73 ....(v[1]) EddieAhern 7 — 82
(Paul D'Arcy) *chsd ldr: rdn over 1f out: drvn ent fnl f: kpt on wl u.p to ld on post* — **4/1**[2]

-050 **2** *nse* **Cloud Rock**[44] 3634 3-9-6 80 .... RobertHavlin 5 — 87
(Peter Chapple-Hyam) *led and set stdy gallop: rdn and qcknd over 1f out: drvn ins fnl f: kpt on but grad worn down and hdd on post* — **7/1**

26-5 **3** *2 3/4* **Elspeth's Boy (USA)**[32] 4010 4-9-9 77 .... JamieSpencer 8 — 79
(William Haggas) *t.k.h: hld up wl in tch in midfield: chsd ldng pair 2f out: sn rdn: drvn 1f out: styd on same pce after* — **6/4**[1]

021 **4** *1 3/4* **Bravo King (IRE)**[40] 3747 3-9-1 78 .... RobertLButler[(3)] 1 — 73
(Richard Guest) *t.k.h: chsd ldng pair tl 2f out: sn rdn and unable qck: styd on same pce and no imp fr over 1f out* — **9/1**

1140 **5** *3/4* **Rough Rock (IRE)**[10] 4765 6-9-9 77 .... HayleyTurner 2 — 72
(Chris Dwyer) *stdd and dropped in bhd after s: hld up in rr: rdn and effrt over 2f out: no imp and nvr trbld ldrs* — **9/1**

441 **6** *1 1/2* **Aleqa**[12] 4681 4-9-6 74 .... NickyMackay 4 — 65
(Chris Wall) *hld up in midfield: rdn and effrt ent fnl 2f: drvn and outpcd over 1f out: wl hld ins fnl f* — **5/1**[3]

3210 **7** *2 1/4* **My Own Way Home**[25] 4234 3-8-10 70 .... AndreaAtzeni 3 — 53
(Des Donovan) *stdd s: t.k.h: hld up in last pair: rdn and no hdwy ent fnl 2f: n.d* — **20/1**

1m 27.43s (0.83) **Going Correction** -0.175s/f (Firm)
WFA 3 from 4yo+ 6lb — 7 Ran SP% **113.9**
Speed ratings (Par 105): **88,87,84,82,81 80,77**
toteswingers:1&2:£6.20, 2&3:£3.30, 1&3:£2.60 CSF £31.18 CT £58.92 TOTE £7.60: £2.90, £4.30; EX 25.40.
Owner Dr J S Kinnear **Bred** Stephanie Hanly **Trained** Newmarket, Suffolk

FOCUS
A fair handicap, but it was spoilt by a farcical early pace. This time they kept stands' side and the first pair drew clear from the front. Muddling form.

5120 WT WASTE H'CAP — 7f 3y
7:20 (7:21) (Class 6) (0-60,60) 3-Y-O — **£1,617** (£481; £240; £120) **Stalls** High

Form — RPR

1500 **1** — **Spirit Of Oakdale (IRE)**[39] 3783 3-9-4 57 ....(v) JamieSpencer 1 — 67
(Walter Swinburn) *chsd ldrs: chsd ldr 2f out: drvn to chal 1f out: led ins fnl f: styd on wl: drvn out* — **6/1**[3]

2213 **2** *1 3/4* **Golden Compass**[17] 4511 3-9-3 56 .... SaleemGolam 5 — 61
(Giles Bravery) *led: rdn over 1f out: hdd and drvn ins fnl f: styd on same pce fnl 100yds* — **7/2**[2]

2443 **3** *2 1/4* **Crown Ridge (IRE)**[11] 4728 3-8-13 59 .... CharlesBishop[(7)] 3 — 58
(Mick Channon) *t.k.h: hld up in rr of main gp: rdn and hdwy 2f out: chsd ldng pair jst over 1f out: styd on same pce ins fnl f* — **6/1**[3]

5-00 **4** *2 1/2* **Five Hearts**[28] 4163 3-9-7 60 .... JimmyQuinn 8 — 52
(Mark H Tompkins) *stdd s: t.k.h: hld up in tch in rr of main gp: rdn and outpcd 2f out: rallied and styd on ins fnl f: no threat to ldrs* — **7/1**

0- **5** *nse* **Thunder Gulf**[269] 7509 3-8-5 47 .... HarryBentley[(3)] 2 — 39
(Mrs K Burke) *chsd ldrs: rdn and unable qck 2f out: edgd lft and outpcd over 1f out: plugged on same pce and no threat to ldrs ins fnl f* — **13/8**[1]

4640 **6** *1 3/4* **Slatey Hen (IRE)**[28] 4149 3-9-1 57 .... RobertLButler[(3)] 4 — 44
(Richard Guest) *stdd s: t.k.h: hld up in tch: rdn and unable qck wl over 1f out: wknd ins fnl f* — **33/1**

0560 **7** *1* **Chillie Peppar**[5] 4929 3-8-7 49 .... CagriMetin[(3)] 6 — 34
(George Prodromou) *t.k.h chsd ldr tl 2f out: sn rdn and wknd* — **25/1**

6064 **8** *4* **Ereka (IRE)**[28] 4162 3-8-9 48 ....(v) ShaneKelly 10 — 22
(Murty McGrath) *in tch: pushed along and fnd little ent fnl 2f: wknd qckly over 1f out* — **16/1**

0500 **9** *18* **Rural Pursuits**[5] 4929 3-8-7 46 oh1 ....(p) AdrianMcCarthy 9 — —
(Christine Dunnett) *taken down early: s.i.s: nvr gng wl in last: lost tch 1/2-way: t.o and eased ins fnl f* — **33/1**

1m 26.97s (0.37) **Going Correction** -0.175s/f (Firm) — 9 Ran SP% **117.0**
Speed ratings (Par 98): **90,88,85,82,82 80,79,74,54**
toteswingers:1&2:£2.60, 2&3:£3.30, 1&3:£4.80 CSF £27.20 CT £131.78 TOTE £6.70: £2.30, £1.80, £1.60; EX 27.90.
Owner Tops **Bred** Denis McDonnell **Trained** Aldbury, Herts

FOCUS
A weak handicap, run at a fair pace down the middle of the track. The first pair drew clear inside the final furlong and both are credited with improving.

5121 PFK (UK) LLP MAIDEN H'CAP — 6f 3y
7:50 (7:50) (Class 5) (0-70,66) 3-Y-O+ — **£2,264** (£673; £336; £168) **Stalls** High

Form — RPR

503 **1** — **Paradise Spectre**[9] 4782 4-9-1 58 .... HarryBentley[(3)] 1 — 68
(Mrs K Burke) *in tch: rdn and effrt to chse ldr over 1f out: kpt on wl ins fnl f to ld fnl 50yds* — **4/1**[3]

0-02 **2** *hd* **Comrade Bond**[34] 3942 3-8-13 57 .... JimmyQuinn 4 — 65
(Mark H Tompkins) *led: rdn over 1f out: drvn and kpt on wl ins fnl f tl hdd and no ex fnl 50yds* — **6/1**

6324 **3** *1 1/2* **Dictionary**[9] 4796 3-9-2 60 ....(t) JamieSpencer 7 — 64
(William Haggas) *in tch: rdn 2f out: drvn and chsd ldrs over 1f out: styd on same pce ins fnl f* — **2/1**[1]

4335 **4** *hd* **Climaxfortackle (IRE)**[22] 4359 3-9-5 63 ....(v) RobbieFitzpatrick 2 — 66
(Derek Shaw) *hld up in last: rdn and effrt over 1f out: drvn and kpt on ins fnl f: unable to chal* — **12/1**

3325 **5** *1 1/2* **El Maachi**[23] 4321 3-9-8 66 .... AndrewHeffernan 3 — 65
(Jim Best) *pressed ldr tl rdn and outpcd jst over 2f out: rallied u.p 1f out: styd on same pce and no imp fnl f* — **11/4**[2]

0020 **6** *6* **Bahamian Jazz (IRE)**[19] 4443 4-9-1 55 ....(b[1]) MartinLane 5 — 35
(Robin Bastiman) *fly-jmpd leaving stalls and s.i.s: racd alone on stands' rail: sn rcvrd and w ldrs tl rdn 2f out: wknd qckly u.p jst over 1f out* — **9/1**

1m 12.77s (-1.63) **Going Correction** -0.175s/f (Firm)
WFA 3 from 4yo 4lb — 6 Ran SP% **112.0**
Speed ratings (Par 103): **103,102,100,100,98 90**
toteswingers:1&2:£5.70, 2&3:£1.30, 1&3:£2.70 CSF £27.03 TOTE £5.20: £1.80, £2.30; EX 31.30.
Owner The Paradise Partnership **Bred** Bearstone Stud **Trained** Middleham Moor, North Yorks

FOCUS
A maiden handicap, so it's obviously very ordinary form. Just the one stuck to the stands' rail (well beaten) as the majority kept down the middle. The winner is rated to last year's best.

5122 MS SOCIETY MAIDEN H'CAP — 1m 6f 17y
8:20 (8:20) (Class 5) (0-70,67) 3-Y-O+ — **£2,264** (£673; £336; £168) **Stalls** High

Form — RPR

6002 **1** — **Native Colony**[34] 3960 3-8-13 65 .... AndreaAtzeni 5 — 75+
(Roger Varian) *chsd ldng pair: reminders and hung lft over 3f out: hdwy to chal 2f out: sn led and edgd lft: in command whn idled ins fnl f: rdn and fnd ex fnl 100yds: styd on* — **10/11**[1]

5445 **2** *1 3/4* **Handles For Forks (IRE)**[19] 4449 3-8-8 67 .... CharlesBishop[(7)] 3 — 72
(Mick Channon) *t.k.h: hld up in last pair: hdwy to chse ldr 4f out: led over 2f out: hdd and rdn along over 1f out: rallied briefly ins fnl f: no ex and readily hld fnl 75yds* — **7/2**[3]

2003 **3** *nk* **Indochina**[10] 4747 4-9-13 66 .... JamieSpencer 6 — 71
(Ian Williams) *led: wnt clr 6f out: edgd rt and rdn over 3f out: hdd over 2f out: outpcd over 1f out: swtchd rt and rallied ins fnl f: kpt on* — **11/4**[2]

-650 **4** *3 1/2* **Astromoon**[18] 3622 4-8-12 51 .... JimmyQuinn 2 — 51
(Mark H Tompkins) *t.k.h: hld up in last: rdn and effrt jst over 2f out: wnt 4th jst over 1f out: no imp ins fnl f* — **20/1**

6500 **5** *4 1/2* **Fantastic Storm**[17] 4499 4-8-6 50 oh5 ....(v) ChrisDCogan[(5)] 4 — 44
(Robin Bastiman) *chsd ldr tl 4f out: stl pressing ldrs u.p 2f out: wknd over 1f out* — **50/1**

3m 9.15s (1.55) **Going Correction** +0.125s/f (Good)
WFA 3 from 4yo 13lb — 5 Ran SP% **108.0**
Speed ratings (Par 103): **100,99,98,96,94**
CSF £4.24 TOTE £1.90: £1.10, £1.90; EX 3.30.
Owner Native Colony Partnership **Bred** Mrs B V Chennells **Trained** Newmarket, Suffolk

FOCUS
Another maiden handicap, this time for stayers. It was run at a stop-start pace. The fifth holds down the firm but the winner can rate higher.
Indochina Official explanation: jockey said gelding hung right
T/Plt: £51.70 to a £1 stake. Pool of £50,052.24 - 705.99 winning tickets. T/Qpdt: £29.70 to a £1 stake Pool of £4,064.84 101.00 w. tckts SP

5123 -5127a - See Raceform Interactive

5093 DEAUVILLE (R-H)
Monday, August 15
OFFICIAL GOING: Turf: good to soft; fibresand: standard

5128a PRIX GUILLAUME D'ORNANO (GROUP 2) (3YO) (TURF) — 1m 2f
2:20 (12:00) 3-Y-O — **£196,551** (£75,862; £36,206; £24,137; £12,068)

RPR

1 — **Galikova (FR)**[64] 2977 3-8-13 0 .... OlivierPeslier 8 — 115+
(F Head, France) *settled towards rr (7th) on outside: pushed along and prog on outside 2 1/2f out: running on u.p in 5th 2f out: led appr fnl 110yds: r.o wl* — **9/4**[2]

2 *2* **Slow Pace (USA)**[22] 4376 3-9-2 0 .... MickaelBarzalona 5 — 114
(F Head, France) *led early: hdd after 1f: a.p on wd outside of ldr: shkn up and qcknd to ld 2 1/2f out: hdd appr fnl 110yds: no ex* — **33/1**

3 *1 1/2* **Golden Lilac (IRE)**[64] 2977 3-8-13 0 .... MaximeGuyon 3 — 108
(A Fabre, France) *broke wl and racd keenly in share of 2nd early: sn settled bhd ldr on rail in 5th: 3rd and shkn up on rail 2f out: rdn appr fnl f: nt qckn u.p* — **5/4**[1]

4 *snk* **Colombian (IRE)**[22] 4376 3-9-2 0 .... WilliamBuick 1 — 111
(John Gosden) *led after 1f: set stdy pce on rail: hdd 2 1/2f out: 2nd and rdn 2f out: nt qckn u.p fnl f* — **12/1**

5 *snk* **Glaswegian**[22] 4376 3-9-2 0 .... StephanePasquier 6 — 111
(P Bary, France) *settled last out of stalls on outside: last (abt 6 l off ldr): and pushed along 2 1/2f out: hrd rdn and swtchd to wd outside 2f out: kpt on but nt pce to chal* — **20/1**

6 *1/2* **Waldpark (GER)**[43] 3672 3-9-2 0 .... EPedroza 2 — 110
(A Wohler, Germany) *racd in midfield (cl 4th: 5th or 6th most of way): 5th and scrubbed along 2f out: sn rdn and nt qckn* — **6/1**[3]

7 *3* **Dunboyne Express (IRE)**[8] 4831 3-9-2 0 .... DPMcDonogh 7 — 104
(Kevin Prendergast, Ire) *trckd slow pce on outside in 4th or 5th much of r: tk clsr order to go 3rd 2 1/2f out: hrd rdn 2f out: no imp: wknd u.p fnl f* — **20/1**

8 6 **Red Dubawi (IRE)**21 4401 3-9-2 0 FabienLefebvre 4 92
(A De Royer-Dupre, France) *sn w ldrs pulling hrd: 3rd and racing freely on ldr's quarters: 3rd and settled 4f out: pushed along and nt qckn 2f out: sn btn and eased fnl f* **20/1**

2m 7.60s (-2.60) **Going Correction** +0.05s/f (Good) **8 Ran SP% 114.4**
Speed ratings: **112,110,109,109,108 108,106,101**
WIN (incl. 1 euro stake): 3.40 (Galikova and Slow Pace coupled). PLACES: 1.30, 4.60, 1.10. DF: 67.50. SF: 114.20 CSF: 76.67.
Owner Wertheimer & Frere **Bred** Wertheimer & Frere **Trained** France

FOCUS
The early pace was a steady one for this good Group 2 event. Galikova did it cosily but the winning margin looked less than the official 2l.

NOTEBOOK
Galikova(FR) took revenge for her Diane defeat in June. Felt to be below her best at Chantilly and subsequently found to be in season, she would have preferred a stronger gallop, but produced a sustained run in the straight to win going away. Her run-style very much suggests she'll relish 1m4f, so with considerable improvement anticipated still from this Galileo filly, it's not hard to see her developing into a legitimate Arc contender in the autumn, with the Prix Vermeille set to be used as her prep race. It'll be a surprise if she's beaten there.
Slow Pace(USA), a stablemate of the winner, split the big two and reversed Eugene Adam form with Colombian and Glaswegian.
Golden Lilac(IRE) looked the best 3yo filly around in the first half of the season, albeit she did get first run on Galikova in the Diane, and it would be foolish to judge her on this defeat. She was very free in the early stages of the race and Andre Fabre had admitted he'd have liked more time with her, so it's fairly safe to assume she wasn't fully wound up, and it's to her credit she held on for third. Whilst clearly very effective at this trip, 1m looks to suit her best, and she'll be a front-runner for the Prix Du Moulin next, a race her dam won in 2004.
Waldpark(GER), the German Derby winner, needs a stiffer test than this, so it was a surprise his rider didn't attempt to make more use of him.

5129a PRIX DU HARAS DE FRESNAY-LE-BUFFARD - JACQUES LE MAROIS (GROUP 1) (COLTS, FILLIES & MARES) (TURF) 1m (R)
2:55 (12:00) 3-Y-0+ £295,551 (£118,241; £59,120; £29,534; £14,793)

RPR

1 **Immortal Verse (IRE)**59 3106 3-8-8 0 GeraldMosse 6 123+
(Robert Collet, France) *settled in rr: last 3f out: swtchd towards stands' side and hdwy appr 2f out: smooth prog to ld ins fnl 1 1/2f: r.o u.p and drifted rt 1f out: stened up and r.o wl fnl 110yds: eased cl* **10/1**

2 1 **Goldikova (IRE)**15 4597 6-9-1 0 OlivierPeslier 11 122
(F Head, France) *w.w in midfield: swtchd outside and hdwy appr 2f out: w ldrs 1 1/2f out: 2nd and hrd rdn ent fnl f: r.o u.p: no ex cl home and jst hld 2nd* **11/10**1

3 nse **Sahpresa (USA)**15 4597 6-9-1 0 Christophe-PatriceLemaire 12 121
(Rod Collet, France) *hld up towards rr on outside: gd hdwy 2f out: 6th and rdn appr fnl f: r.o wl fnl 150yds: jst failed to grab 2nd* **12/1**

4 2 **Royal Bench (IRE)**85 2340 4-9-4 0 IoritzMendizabal 5 119
(Robert Collet, France) *settled towards rr: prog towards stands' side fr 2f out: in tch whn rdn appr 1 1/2f out: nt qckn tl styd on ins fnl f to take 4th cl home* **40/1**

5 ½ **Planteur (IRE)**61 3031 4-9-4 0 AnthonyCrastus 9 118
(E Lellouche, France) *racd in 6th thrght: 5th and effrt appr 2f out: w ldng quartet whn hrd rdn 1 1/2f out: nt qckn fnl f* **9/1**3

6 shd **Tin Horse (IRE)**71 2751 3-8-11 0 ThierryJarnet 10 117
(D Guillemin, France) *w.w towards rr: 11th 2 1/2f out: hdwy appr fnl 1 1/2f: short of room nring fnl f: swtchd outside and styd on fnl 150yds* **16/1**

7 ¾ **Dick Turpin (IRE)**37 3843 4-9-4 0 RichardHughes 2 116
(Richard Hannon) *racd in 7th (abt 4 l off ldr): 5th and ev ch ins fnl 2f: rdn 1 1/2f out: nt qckn fnl f* **12/1**

8 2 **Cityscape**62 3009 5-9-4 0 SteveDrowne 1 112
(Roger Charlton) *chsd ldrs in 4th: disputing 2nd 2f out: 3rd and rdn appr fnl f: wknd fnl 150yds* **11/1**

9 6 **Worthadd (IRE)**78 2541 4-9-4 0 MircoDemuro 8 98
(Vittorio Caruso, Italy) *a.p: disputing 2nd 2f out: led appr fnl 1 1/2f out: hdd ins fnl 1 1/2f: sn rdn and wknd: eased fnl 150yds* **12/1**

10 4 **Mutual Trust**43 3670 3-8-11 0 MaximeGuyon 4 88
(A Fabre, France) *racd in 5th early: in midfield appr 1/2-way: pushed along nring 3f out: n.m.r over 2f out: effrt and sightly hmpd ins fnl 1 1/2f: no imp and eased fnl f* **6/1**2

11 15 **Flash Dance (IRE)**15 4597 5-9-1 0 MickaelBarzalona 3 51
(F Head, France) *a.p: led 4f out: hdd appr 1 1/2f out: sn wknd: eased fnl f* **150/1**

12 10 **Polemique (IRE)**44 3-8-8 0 AurelienLemaitre 7 27
(F Head, France) *led: rdn and hdd 4f out: wknd and eased appr 2f out* **200/1**

1m 38.3s (-2.50) **Going Correction** +0.05s/f (Good)
WFA 3 from 4yo+ 7lb **12 Ran SP% 121.9**
Speed ratings: **114,113,112,110,110 110,109,107,101,97 82,72**
WIN (incl. 1 euro stake): 14.20(Immortal Verse coupled with Royal Bench). PLACES: 2.90, 1.10, 2.30. DF: 13.20. SF: 28.80 CSF: 21.92.
Owner R C Strauss **Bred** Kilfrush Stud **Trained** Chantilly, France

FOCUS
A strong renewal of this major European mile race and the finish was dominated by three females. Immortal Verse is on the upgrade and Goldikova is rated to the same level as this race last year.

NOTEBOOK
Immortal Verse(IRE) has not stopped improving since finishing down the field in the Pouliches, and followed up her Coronation Stakes win with a decisive success here. Held up in rear, she cruised up to join issue inside the last quarter-mile and produced a better turn of foot than her rivals. She now has claims to being the best miling filly in Europe and could return to Ascot in October to take on Frankel in the Queen Elizabeth II Stakes, although the Moulin is a reasonable alternative.
Goldikova(IRE) does not get beaten often but was second in this last year having won it in 2009. She was held up further back than usual but made her ground on the outside to deliver her challenge, only to find the younger filly on the other flank too strong. Her pattern in the last two seasons has been to go for the Foret next before attempting an unprecedented fourth success in the Breeders' Cup Mile. (op 6-5)
Sahpresa(USA), who was flattered to finish quite as close as she did to Goldikova last time, repeated the form by coming with a late run to almost snatch second off her old rival. She is likely to go to Longchamp next month before attempting to win a third Sun Chariot.
Royal Bench(IRE) went globetrotting after winning at last year's Arc meeting but had been given a break since May. Held up with his stablemate out the back, he made his ground at the same time as the filly but could not stay with her, although he stuck on well for pressure. He should be better for the outing and can be expected to try to win a second Daniel Wildenstein before going on his travels again.
Planteur(IRE) the Prix Ganay winner, was dropping to this trip for the first time since his juvenile days. He was produced with a late run as usual, but did not quite have the raw speed to cope with these specialist milers.
Tin Horse(IRE), the Poulains winner, was dropping back in trip having run creditably when fifth in the Prix du Jockey Club. He did not get the clearest of passages and did pretty well to finish so close. (op 18-1)
Dick Turpin(IRE) had bounced back from a disappointing effort in the Ispahan to win a Group 2 last time. He looked a threat when moving up around 2f out but did not have the extra gears to get involved from that point. He falls just below the very top level.
Cityscape had finished a good third in the Queen Anne when the ground was possibly too fast but conditions here promised to suit him better. He was never far away and had every chance, but faded out of it in the closing stages. (op 10-1)
Worthadd(IRE), a classy performer in Italy, had made the running when finishing second to Canford Cliffs in the Lockinge. However, with two pacemakers here he could not lead and raced quite keenly close behind. Consequently, when the race began in earnest he had no more to offer and was not given a hard time once his chance had gone.
Mutual Trust, the winner of the Prix Jean Prat, was buried in the centre of the pack but appeared short of room and briefly lost his place around 3f out. He still appeared to be going well entering the last quarter-mile but then got carried back as the front-runners weakened in front of him. He was not persevered with after and can be given another chance.

5130a PRIX FRANCOIS BOUTIN (LISTED RACE) (2YO) (TURF) 7f
3:30 (12:00) 2-Y-0 £23,706 (£9,482; £7,112; £4,741; £2,370)

RPR

1 **Rockinante (FR)**19 4424 2-9-2 0 RichardHughes 7 102
(Richard Hannon) *dwlt: racd keenly in 4th on outside: settled after 2f and disp ld after 3f: shkn up to ld appr 1 1/2f out: 1 l up and rdn appr fnl f: hld on gamely u.p fnl 110yds* **23/10**1

2 nk **Vaniloquio (IRE)**16 2-9-2 0 ThierryThulliez 1 101
(N Clement, France) **44/5**

3 snk **Lidari (FR)**39 2-9-2 0 Christophe-PatriceLemaire 6 101
(J-C Rouget, France) **23/10**1

4 1½ **Private Riviera**8 2-8-13 0 Pierre-CharlesBoudot 3 94
(C Boutin, France) **33/1**

5 nk **Aesop's Fables (USA)**32 4036 2-9-2 0 MaximeGuyon 4 96
(A Fabre, France) **7/2**2

6 2½ **Influence (FR)** 2-8-13 0 OlivierPeslier 5 87
(G Henrot, France) **7/1**3

7 8 **Anaconda (FR)**13 4652 2-9-2 0 RichardKingscote 8 70
(Tom Dascombe) *broke wl on wd outside and racd in 3rd: sn settled 2nd and disp ld after 3f: shkn up appr 2f out: hdd fnl 1 1/2f: fdd fnl f* **32/1**

8 6 **Ideechic (FR)**18 4484 2-8-13 0 AlexandreRoussel 2 52
(D Allard, France) **20/1**

1m 28.0s (-0.30) **Going Correction** +0.05s/f (Good) **8 Ran SP% 116.3**
Speed ratings: **103,102,102,100,100 97,88,81**
WIN (incl. 1 euro stake): 3.30. PLACES: 1.40, 2.10, 1.40. DF: 18.10. SF: 23.60.
Owner Coriolan Links Partnership Iii **Bred** Azienda Agricola Il Tiglio **Trained** East Everleigh, Wilts

NOTEBOOK
Rockinante(FR) was always up with the pace and held off the opposition. The victory qualified him for a bonus as he was purchased at Deauville. He could go for the Prix Jean-Luc Lagardere at Longchamp in the autumn.

5131a PRIX MICHEL HOUYVET (LISTED RACE) (3YO) (TURF) 1m 7f
4:00 (12:00) 3-Y-0 £23,706 (£9,482; £7,112; £4,741; £2,370)

RPR

1 **Gaily Game**79 2521 3-8-11 0 IoritzMendizabal 6 107+
(J-C Rouget, France) **11/10**1

2 3 **Miss Lago (IRE)**30 3-8-8 0 AnthonyCrastus 2 100
(E Lellouche, France) **20/1**

3 1 **Opera Vert (FR)**42 3698 3-8-11 0 FabienLefebvre 3 102
(D Sepulchre, France) **14/1**

4 1½ **Colour Vision (FR)**24 4266 3-8-11 0 GeraldMosse 7 100
(Mark Johnston) *settled sharing 2nd: gng easily: rdn early in st and swtchd to stands' side: chal for ld 1 1/2f out: wandered off st line to hamper wkng rival: rdn but no ex fnl f: styd on for 4th* **7/2**2

5 3 **Manjakani**30 3-8-11 0 MickaelBarzalona 1 97
(A Fabre, France) **13/2**

6 5 **Maxi Chop (FR)**61 3062 3-8-11 0 ThierryJarnet 5 91
(A De Watrigant, France) **14/1**

7 6 **Sheniyan (IRE)**37 3-8-11 0 Christophe-PatriceLemaire 4 84
(A De Royer-Dupre, France) **48/10**3

3m 17.5s (-1.60) **Going Correction** +0.05s/f (Good) **7 Ran SP% 118.5**
Speed ratings: **106,104,103,103,101 98,95**
WIN (incl. 1 euro stake): 2.10. places: 1.60, 4.60. SF: 24.40.
Owner Ecurie I M Fares **Bred** Ecurie I M Fares **Trained** Pau, France

NOTEBOOK
Gaily Game quickened well and won with a bit to spare.
Colour Vision(FR) wandered when the pressure was on but this was still a creditable first try in Listed company.

4624 CLAIREFONTAINE (R-H)
Monday, August 8

OFFICIAL GOING: Turf: heavy

5132a PRIX CLUB MARMARA TROPICANA MONASTIR (PRIX VITIGES) (MAIDEN) (3YO COLTS & GELDINGS) (TURF) 1m 4f
3:25 (12:00) 3-Y-0 £10,344 (£4,137; £3,103; £2,068; £1,034)

RPR

1 **Caroun (IRE)**32 3-9-2 0 Christophe-PatriceLemaire 7 82
(A De Royer-Dupre, France) **16/5**2

2 4 **Val De Saone (FR)**73 3-9-2 0 MaximeGuyon 12 76
(J-C Rouget, France) **5/2**1

3 1½ **Evergreen Forest (IRE)**77 2368 3-9-2 0 MickaelBarzalona 8 73
(Alastair Lidderdale) **73/10**

4 ½ **Zarambar (IRE)**56 3-9-2 0 DavyBonilla 10 72
(R Laplanche, France) **78/10**

5 2½ **Turbotin (FR)** 3-8-6 0 MatthieuAutier(5) 11 63
(J-P Gallorini, France) **46/1**

6 ¾ **Brehat** 3-9-2 0 AnthonyCrastus 13 67
(E Lellouche, France) **29/1**

7 3 **Kapga De Cerisy (FR)**71 3-9-2 0 FlavienPrat 9 62
(Mme L Audon, France) **44/1**

8 8 **Rosebel (FR)** 3-8-11 0 NicolasEven 1 45
(Y Fouin, France) **144/1**

9 2½ **Vollon (IRE)** 3-9-2 0 ChristopheSoumillon 4 46
(M Delzangles, France) 10/1

10 6 **Softsong (FR)**[103] 3-9-2 0 OlivierPeslier 6 36
(C Laffon-Parias, France) 9/2[3]

0 **Nanard De Pail (FR)** 3-9-2 0 VincentVion —
(B Beaunez, France) 83/1

0 **El Zorrito (FR)** 3-9-2 0 (p) FabienLefebvre —
(Mme M-L Oget, France) 50/1

0 **Light Show** 3-8-8 0 (b[1]) RufusVergette(8) —
(A Fabre, France) 30/1

2m 42.0s (4.10) **13** Ran SP% **117.8**
PARI-MUTUEL (all including 1 euro stakes): WIN 4.20; PLACE 1.60, 1.40, 4.60; DF 4.90; SF 9.70.
Owner H H Aga Khan **Bred** Haras De Son Altesse L'Aga Khan Scea **Trained** Chantilly, France

4740 BRIGHTON (L-H)
Tuesday, August 16

OFFICIAL GOING: Good to firm
All races on inner and distances as advertised.
Wind: Fresh, against Weather: Cloudy

5133 BRITISH STALLION STUDS/HARDINGS CATERING EBF MEDIAN AUCTION MAIDEN STKS 6f 209y
2:30 (2:30) (Class 5) 2-Y-O **£3,169** (£943; £471; £235) **Stalls** Low

Form RPR

2 **1** **Grandeur (IRE)**[17] 4535 2-9-3 WilliamBuick 1 85+
(Jeremy Noseda) *prom: wnt 2nd 2f out: drvn to ld fnl 100yds* **8/13[1]**

4334 **2** 1¼ **Bronze Angel (IRE)**[18] 4496 2-9-3 83 HayleyTurner 2 82
(Marcus Tregoning) *disp ld: led and gng wl over 2f out: shkn up over 1f out: hrd rdn and hdd fnl 100yds: nt qckn* **9/4[2]**

3 2 **Spoke To Carlo** 2-9-3 NeilCallan 4 77
(Eve Johnson Houghton) *s.i.s: sn in tch in 5th: rdn to chse ldrs 2f out: kpt on u.p* **12/1**

0 **4** 7 **Venetian View (IRE)**[43] 3686 2-9-3 GeorgeBaker 3 58
(Gary Moore) *towards rr: rdn 3f out: styd on to take modest 4th ins fnl f* **50/1**

000 **5** 2 **Samasana (IRE)**[17] 4557 2-8-12 49 (v) MartinLane 7 48
(Ian Wood) *bhd tl styd on past btn horses fr over 1f out* **100/1**

0234 **6** hd **Siouxperhero (IRE)**[17] 4525 2-9-3 70 MartinDwyer 8 53
(William Muir) *chsd ldrs: pushed along 4f out: wknd over 2f out* **16/1**

03 **7** 2½ **Philipstown**[18] 4507 2-9-3 PatDobbs 9 46
(Richard Hannon) *a bhd* **10/1[3]**

60 **8** 3½ **Rainbow Chorus**[8] 4857 2-9-3 JimCrowley 11 37
(Paul Cole) *hld up in 6th: hrd rdn 3f out: sn wknd* **80/1**

0 **9** 16 **Itsonlymakebelieve (IRE)**[51] 3425 2-8-12 (b[1]) JamesDoyle 10 —
(Ian Wood) *disp ld tl edgd rt over 2f out: sn hrd rdn and wknd* **66/1**

1m 23.42s (0.32) **Going Correction** +0.075s/f (Good) **9** Ran SP% **121.0**
Speed ratings (Par 94): **101,99,97,89,87 86,83,79,61**
toteswingers:1&2:£1.20, 2&3:£4.90, 1&3:£3.40 CSF £2.34 TOTE £1.30: £1.02, £1.10, £2.70; EX 2.60 Trifecta £9.20 Pool of: £1218.41 - 97.95 winning units..
Owner Miss Yvonne Jacques **Bred** Mrs Cherry Faeste **Trained** Newmarket, Suffolk

FOCUS
A well above average maiden for the track. The finish was fought out by two colts who had run really well in defeat at Glorious Goodwood, and they were chased home by a sympathetically handled newcomer who might have won most Brighton maidens.

NOTEBOOK
Grandeur(IRE) had to work harder than expected to get off the mark, but he really grabbed the rising ground on the run to the line, and always looked set to get up. He ought to improve for the step up to 1m, but with the runner-up rated 83, he'll probably be starting handicap life off a mark in the high 80s. (op 4-6)
Bronze Angel(IRE) looked unfortunate not to win a decent 7f nursery at Glorious Goodwood, and he was made plenty of use of on this return to maiden-company. It briefly looked like he was holding the winner, but the final climb to the line proved too much. He should find something similar before long. (op 2-1)
Spoke To Carlo ◆, a 27,000gns son of Halling, was slowly away on this racecourse debut, but made good headway mid-race and was close enough with 2f to run. His inexperience held him back this time, and he was not given too hard a time, but he looks more than capable of winning a similar race granted normal improvement. (op 14-1)
Venetian View(IRE) stepped up on his initial effort and will be of some interest once qualified for nurseries.
Samasana(IRE) ran with a bit more promise, seeming to appreciate the waiting tactics on this return to 7f.
Philipstown is now qualified for a mark and should fare better in nurseries. (op 12-1)

5134 ARGUS NEWS FOR SUSSEX H'CAP 1m 3f 196y
3:00 (3:01) (Class 5) (0-70,62) 3-Y-O **£2,264** (£673; £336; £168) **Stalls** High

Form RPR

0264 **1** **Newby Lodge (IRE)**[12] 4732 3-8-9 50 CathyGannon 1 59
(Alan Bailey) *trckd ldng pair: n.m.r 3f out: led and kicked on 2f out: hrd drvn and tiring fnl f: jst hld on* **11/2**

-356 **2** nk **Dolly Colman (IRE)**[26] 4248 3-8-4 45 LukeMorris 3 53
(Andrew Haynes) *in tch: effrt and nt clr run over 2f out: wnt 2nd jst ins fnl 2f: clsng on wnr fnl 150yds: nt quite get up* **16/1**

641 **3** 6 **What About Now**[13] 4654 3-9-4 62 (b) PatrickHills(3) 5 61
(J W Hills) *chsd ldrs: rdn and nt qckn 2f out: hld whn hung lft ins fnl f* **9/4[1]**

050 **4** 3 **Rose Of Sarratt (IRE)**[10] 4805 3-9-7 62 MartinLane 2 56
(Rae Guest) *s.i.s: hld up in rr: effrt on outer over 2f out: hrd rdn: no imp* **5/2[2]**

0510 **5** 7 **Rather Cool**[9] 4827 3-8-12 56 SeanLevey(3) 4 39
(John Bridger) *chsd ldr: drew level 1/2-way: led 3f out tl wknd qckly 2f out* **8/1**

5304 **6** 31 **Joyful Sound (IRE)**[13] 4686 3-9-6 61 NeilCallan 6 —
(Andrew Haynes) *led: jnd 1/2-way: hdd & wknd qckly 3f out: bhd whn virtually p.u fr over 1f out* **9/2[3]**

2m 34.87s (2.17) **Going Correction** +0.075s/f (Good) **6** Ran SP% **109.9**
Speed ratings (Par 100): **95,94,90,88,84 63**
toteswingers:1&2:£8.80, 2&3:£5.20, 1&3:£2.40 CSF £73.15 TOTE £7.90: £4.20, £7.90; EX 64.00.
Owner A J H **Bred** S McCann **Trained** Newmarket, Suffolk

FOCUS
The front pair drew clear in what was a weak handicap, and clearly improved. It was sound run and the first two look improved..

5135 SPIFFING CRABBIES ALCOHOLIC GINGER BEER H'CAP 1m 1f 209y
3:30 (3:30) (Class 5) (0-70,74) 3-Y-O+ **£2,264** (£673; £336; £168) **Stalls** High

Form RPR

2204 **1** **Celestial Girl**[31] 4090 4-9-13 69 ChrisCatlin 6 77
(Hughie Morrison) *hld up towards rr: gd hdwy on outer to ld ins fnl 2f: qcknd clr and edgd lft: rdn out* **9/2[2]**

0203 **2** 1¼ **Professor John (IRE)**[11] 4746 4-8-13 55 (v) JamesDoyle 8 60
(Ian Wood) *hld up in rr: rdn over 2f out: styd on wl fr over 1f out: wnt 2nd fnl 50yds: nt rch wnr* **11/1**

1121 **3** ½ **Highlife Dancer**[8] 4845 3-9-7 74 6ex MartinHarley(3) 4 78
(Mick Channon) *prom: wnt 2nd 1/2-way: chal 2f out: sn outpcd by wnr: kpt on ins fnl f* **9/2[2]**

0336 **4** nse **Green Wadi**[8] 4845 6-9-12 68 GeorgeBaker 3 72
(Gary Moore) *t.k.h: trckd ldrs: rdn over 2f out: kpt on ins fnl f* **13/2**

551 **5** hd **Out Of The Storm**[11] 4745 3-8-11 61 NeilCallan 2 65
(Simon Dow) *chsd ldr tl 1/2-way: prom after: rdn and kpt on same pce fnl 2f* **13/2**

1000 **6** 1¼ **Beaubrav**[61] 3095 5-9-10 66 (t) JimCrowley 7 67
(Michael Madgwick) *hld up in 5th: hrd rdn over 2f out: no imp* **8/1**

2152 **7** 1 **Golden Waters**[18] 4490 4-10-0 70 CathyGannon 1 69
(Eve Johnson Houghton) *hld up towards rr: rdn 3f out: nt gng pce to chal* **4/1[1]**

233 **8** 2¼ **Timocracy**[16] 3912 6-9-13 69 StevieDonohoe 5 68
(Andrew Haynes) *led tl ins fnl 2f: n.m.r on ins rail and wknd over 1f out* **6/1[3]**

2m 4.32s (0.72) **Going Correction** +0.075s/f (Good)
WFA 3 from 4yo+ 8lb **8** Ran SP% **116.8**
Speed ratings (Par 103): **100,99,98,98,98 97,96,94**
toteswingers:1&2:£7.70, 2&3:£12.60, 1&3:£3.40 CSF £53.09 CT £236.67 TOTE £5.20: £2.00, £3.30, £1.90; EX 35.60 Trifecta £442.30 Pool of £729.28 - 1.22 winning units..
Owner Helena Springfield Ltd **Bred** Meon Valley Stud **Trained** East Ilsley, Berks

FOCUS
Not a bad handicap for Brighton and the form looks sound rated around the runner-up , fourth and fifth.

5136 ABF THE SOLDIERS CHARITY H'CAP 6f 209y
4:00 (4:00) (Class 5) (0-70,69) 3-Y-O+ **£2,264** (£673; £336; £168) **Stalls** Low

Form RPR

332 **1** **Konstantin (IRE)**[24] 4321 3-9-7 69 HayleyTurner 8 79
(Marcus Tregoning) *chsd ldrs: led over 1f out: drvn out* **15/8[1]**

010 **2** 1¾ **Fire King**[35] 3944 5-9-8 65 (p) NeilCallan 1 72
(Andrew Haynes) *towards rr: hrd rdn and hdwy wl over 1f out: styd on to take 2nd fnl 50yds* **8/1**

1341 **3** nk **Cheylesmore (IRE)**[12] 4695 3-9-6 68 (v) WilliamCarson 5 72
(Stuart Williams) *led: hrd rdn and hdd over 1f out: kpt on same pce* **5/1[3]**

5043 **4** 2¼ **Inquisitress**[12] 4699 7-8-4 50 KieranO'Neill(3) 2 50
(John Bridger) *prom: effrt and n.m.r on rail ins fnl 2f: one pce* **16/1**

1223 **5** ½ **Mandhooma**[35] 3940 5-9-9 66 ChrisCatlin 4 65
(Peter Hiatt) *hld up in rr: hrd rdn and hdwy in centre over 1f out: nt rch ldrs* **4/1[2]**

-435 **6** 6 **Thunda**[41] 3723 3-9-5 67 CathyGannon 3 47
(Eve Johnson Houghton) *prom tl wknd 2f out* **7/1**

5043 **7** 1¾ **Ivory Lace**[6] 4917 10-9-8 65 JackMitchell 7 43
(Steve Woodman) *hld up in 5th: rdn over 3f out: n.d fnl 2f* **8/1**

1m 23.0s (-0.10) **Going Correction** +0.075s/f (Good)
WFA 3 from 5yo+ 5lb **7** Ran SP% **112.1**
Speed ratings (Par 103): **103,101,100,98,97 90,88**
toteswingers:1&2:£3.50, 2&3:£5.20, 1&3:£2.60 CSF £16.92 CT £63.20 TOTE £3.30: £1.80, £4.90; EX 19.50 Trifecta £212.30 Pool of £955.52 - 3.33 winning units..
Owner Lady Tennant **Bred** Miss Annmarie Burke **Trained** Lambourn, Berks

FOCUS
An ordinary handicap. It was well run and the form is sound.
Thunda Official explanation: jockey said filly hung left

5137 ODDSCHECKER.COM H'CAP 7f 214y
4:30 (4:30) (Class 6) (0-65,65) 3-Y-O **£1,617** (£481; £240; £120) **Stalls** Low

Form RPR

032 **1** **Viking Rose (IRE)**[6] 4928 3-8-13 57 LukeMorris 3 66
(James Eustace) *trckd ldng pair: led 2f out: hrd rdn and edgd lft over 1f out: hld on gamely* **9/2[3]**

4662 **2** nk **Adelina Patti**[12] 4699 3-9-2 60 AdamKirby 8 68
(Walter Swinburn) *t.k.h: settled in 4th: drvn to press wnr 2f out: sustained chal: r.o* **4/1[2]**

6455 **3** 1 **No Larking (IRE)**[11] 4763 3-9-4 62 DaneO'Neill 1 69+
(Henry Candy) *sn led: rdn and hdd 2f out: n.m.r and checked on ins rail over 1f out: kpt on wl nr fin* **7/2[1]**

5210 **4** ¾ **Border Abby**[13] 4673 3-9-0 58 MartinLane 4 62
(Rae Guest) *in rr: rdn 5f out: hdwy 2f out: drvn to chse ldrs over 1f out: styd on* **6/1**

0603 **5** 4 **Tagansky**[11] 4744 3-9-2 60 NeilCallan 7 55
(Simon Dow) *t.k.h towards rr: rdn over 2f out: nt gng pce to chal* **9/2[3]**

-003 **6** 1¾ **Cornish Quest**[6] 4926 3-9-2 60 (b) JimmyQuinn 5 51
(Mark H Tompkins) *t.k.h: hld up in 6th: effrt on rail over 2f out: wknd over 1f out* **13/2**

000 **7** 12 **Elite Syncopations**[41] 3724 3-8-5 49 CathyGannon 9 —
(Andrew Haynes) *pressed ldr tl wknd over 2f out* **33/1**

0-0 **8** 7 **Lucky Tricks**[36] 3909 3-8-2 46 oh1 NickyMackay 6 —
(Jeremy Gask) *stdd s: sn in tch in 5th: hrd rdn over 2f out: sn wknd* **20/1**

1m 37.14s (1.14) **Going Correction** +0.075s/f (Good) **8** Ran SP% **113.9**
Speed ratings (Par 98): **97,96,95,94,90 89,77,70**
toteswingers:1&2:£3.60, 2&3:£3.80, 1&3:£4.10 CSF £22.65 CT £69.48 TOTE £3.40: £1.10, £2.50, £1.70; EX 28.50 Trifecta £78.20 Pool: £1081.01 - 12.88 winning units..
Owner J C Smith **Bred** Littleton Stud **Trained** Newmarket, Suffolk
■ Stewards' Enquiry : Luke Morris two-day ban: careless riding (Aug 30-31)

FOCUS
An open-looking 3-y-o handicap. It was sound run but the form is very modest.
Cornish Quest Official explanation: jockey said gelding jumped awkwardly

Elite Syncopations Official explanation: jockey said filly hung right and had no more to give

5138 ODDSCHECKER.MOBI H'CAP 5f 213y
5:00 (5:00) (Class 6) (0-60,59) 3-Y-O+ £1,617 (£481; £240; £120) Stalls Low

Form RPR
3040 1 **Ridgeway Sapphire**[9] 4828 4-8-7 **45**............................(v) HayleyTurner 7 54
(Mark Usher) *hld up towards rr: hdwy through narrow gap on rail 2f out: led 1f out: rdn out* **17/2**
6604 2 *2 ¼* **Desert Falls**[11] 4741 5-9-3 **55**............................(v) ChrisCatlin 1 57
(Richard Whitaker) *led: hrd rdn and hdd 1f out: nt qckn* **16/1**
6630 3 *shd* **Boldinor**[33] 4025 8-9-6 **58**............................ GeorgeBaker 5 60
(Martin Bosley) *pressed ldr: hrd rdn over 1f out: one pce ins fnl f* **13/2**
6041 4 *1 ¼* **Silca Conegliano (IRE)**[13] 4657 3-8-8 **52**................(v) MartinHarley(3) 2 49
(Mick Channon) *prom: drvn to chal over 1f out: no ex ins fnl f* **5/1**[3]
0430 5 *hd* **Imjin River (IRE)**[27] 4206 4-9-7 **59**............................(p) JimmyQuinn 8 56
(Mark H Tompkins) *in tch in 5th: effrt 2f out: no imp fnl f* **9/2**[2]
0543 6 *shd* **Stonecrabstomorrow (IRE)**[5] 4960 8-8-13 **56**........ MarkCoumbe(5) 10 57+
(Michael Attwater) *hld up in rr: effrt and swtchd lft over 1f out: n.m.r ins fnl f: nvr able to chal* **4/1**[1]
2222 7 *1 ¼* **Do More Business (IRE)**[11] 4740 4-9-0 **52**...................... IanMongan 9 45
(Pat Phelan) *towards rr: effrt on outer over 2f out: hrd rdn and wknd 1f out* **4/1**[1]
5-06 8 *2 ½* **Mystica (IRE)**[14] 4640 3-8-11 **52**............................(be) JamesDoyle 6 36
(Dominic Ffrench Davis) *chsd ldrs tl wknd wl over 1f out* **11/1**

1m 10.95s (0.75) **Going Correction** +0.075s/f (Good)
WFA 3 from 4yo+ 3lb **8** Ran SP% **112.9**
Speed ratings (Par 101): **98,95,94,93,92 92,91,87**
toteswingers:1&2:£12.40, 2&3:£7.30, 1&3:£10.20 CSF £126.03 CT £940.31 TOTE £11.90: £2.70, £3.80, £3.10; EX 153.80 Trifecta £604.50 Pool: £906.78 - 1.11 winning units..
Owner The Goodracing Partnership **Bred** Ridgeway Bloodstock **Trained** Upper Lambourn, Berks

FOCUS
Few got into this moderate race from off the sound pace, so the performance of the winner, who was held up, could need upgrading although the form looks dubious.
Stonecrabstomorrow(IRE) Official explanation: jockey said gelding was denied a clear run

5139 BEST ODDS @ ODDSCHECKER.COM H'CAP 5f 59y
5:30 (5:30) (Class 6) (0-65,64) 3-Y-O+ £1,617 (£481; £240; £120) Stalls Low

Form RPR
2164 1 **Bobby's Doll**[5] 4967 4-9-7 **64**............................ AdamBeschizza(3) 1 73+
(Terry Clement) *cl up in 3rd: led wl over 1f out: hld on wl ins fnl f* **11/4**[1]
3034 2 *1 ¾* **Bateleur**[7] 4882 7-8-10 **57**............................ CharlesBishop(7) 5 60
(Mick Channon) *hld up in 5th: smooth hdwy through narrow gap to chal over 1f out: nt qckn ins fnl f* **3/1**[2]
464 3 *2 ¼* **Luisa Tetrazzini (IRE)**[13] 4659 5-8-9 **54**................(v[1]) MarkCoumbe(5) 7 49
(Michael Attwater) *s.i.s: in rr: sme hdwy and hrd rdn over 1f out: wnt 3rd ins fnl f: nt trble first 2* **11/1**
3061 4 *¾* **Wotatomboy**[11] 4740 5-8-9 **49**............................(v) ChrisCatlin 6 42
(Richard Whitaker) *chsd ldrs in 4th: effrt in centre 2f out: one pce* **4/1**[3]
0662 5 *2 ¾* **Ace Of Spies (IRE)**[9] 4820 6-9-6 **60**............................(b) HayleyTurner 2 43
(Conor Dore) *chsd ldr tl wknd wl over 1f out* **4/1**[3]
-303 6 *3 ¾* **Pocket's Pick (IRE)**[11] 4740 5-9-3 **57**............................(bt) JimmyQuinn 3 27
(Jim Best) *led tl wknd wl over 1f out* **15/2**

63.74 secs (1.44) **Going Correction** +0.075s/f (Good) **6** Ran SP% **111.8**
Speed ratings (Par 101): **91,88,84,83,79 73**
toteswingers:1&2:£2.20, 2&3:£6.60, 1&3:£4.40. Tote Super 7: Win: Not won. Place: Not won. CSF £11.18 CT £73.22 TOTE £2.40: £1.10, £1.70; EX 11.80 Trifecta £56.20 Pool: £686.80 - 8.96 winning units..
Owner Ms Sarah Jensen **Bred** Peter Balding **Trained** Newmarket, Suffolk

FOCUS
A very modest sprint handicap. It probably didn't take much winning and has been rated around the runner-up.
Pocket's Pick(IRE) Official explanation: jockey said gelding ran too free
T/Plt: £379.70 to a £1 stake. Pool of £74,084.82 - 142.40 winning tickets. T/Qpdt: £69.90 to a £1 stake. Pool of £5,741.75 - 60.78 winning tickets. LM

5097 KEMPTON (A.W) (R-H)
Tuesday, August 16

OFFICIAL GOING: Standard
Wind: Virtually nil Weather: Starting with sunny periods

5140 32RED.COM MEDIAN AUCTION MAIDEN STKS 1m 3f (P)
6:20 (6:21) (Class 6) 3-5-Y-O £1,617 (£481; £240; £120) Stalls Low

Form RPR
2324 1 **Star Commander**[42] 3705 3-9-3 **73**............................ KierenFallon 7 80
(Mark H Tompkins) *hld up in rr: stdy hdwy 3f out: drvn and qcknd to take slt ld appr fnl f: drvn out* **3/1**[2]
-02 2 *hd* **Billy Buttons**[29] 4157 3-9-3 0............................ LiamKeniry 8 79
(Andrew Balding) *t.k.h: trckd ldrs: stmbld and lost pl bnd after 1f: hdwy on outside 1/2-way: drvn and styd on to take slt ld wl over 1f out: edgd rt u.p sn after and hdd: styd chalng: no ex cl home* **8/13**[1]
34-0 3 *6* **Rocky Rebel**[27] 4215 3-9-3 73............................(p) JimCrowley 1 69
(Ralph Beckett) *sn slt ld: hdd over 1m out: styd chsng ldrs: slt ld again ins fnl 3f: hdd wl over 1f out: wknd fnl f* **11/2**[3]
0 4 *2 ½* **Colliers Castle (IRE)**[15] 4611 5-9-7 0............................ ShaneKelly 4 59
(Lisa Williamson) *chsd ldrs: rdn 3f out: wknd 2f out: btn whn swtchd rt over 1f out* **100/1**
0 5 *12* **Full Stretch (USA)**[78] 2568 3-9-3 0............................ TomQueally 5 42
(Pat Eddery) *w ldrs early: sn bhd: rdn: green and no ch fr over 3f out* **18/1**
06 6 *3* **Famagusta**[29] 4163 4-9-2 0............................(v) LauraPike(5) 9 32
(Peter Charalambous) *racd on outside: t.k.h and led over 1f out: hdd ins fnl 3f: sn wknd* **50/1**
7 *26* **Novirak (IRE)** 3-9-3 0............................ PatCosgrave 6 —
(James Fanshawe) *chsd ldrs tl wknd 4f out* **18/1**
0 8 *2 ¼* **Father Martin (IRE)**[29] 4157 4-9-12 0............................(b[1]) RobertHavlin 2 —
(Richard Phillips) *a struggling in rr: t.o* **100/1**
-03 F **Steely**[52] 3392 3-9-3 0............................ PaulDoe 3 61
(Jim Best) *trckd ldrs: rdn and ev ch fr 3f out: stl upsides 2f out: dropping away whn hmpd: clipped heels and fell over 1f out* **16/1**

2m 21.02s (-0.88) **Going Correction** 0.0s/f (Stan)
WFA 3 from 4yo+ 9lb **9** Ran SP% **122.7**
Speed ratings (Par 101): **103,102,98,96,87 85,66,65,—**
toteswingers: 1&2 £1.10, 1&3 £2.40, 2&3 £1.70. CSF £5.53 TOTE £3.30: £1.30, £1.10, £1.50; EX 6.10.
Owner John Brenchley **Bred** Mary-Ann Penfold **Trained** Newmarket, Suffolk
■ Stewards' Enquiry : Liam Keniry five-day ban: careless riding (Aug 30-Sep 3)

FOCUS
This modest maiden proved a very messy race, but the form still makes enough sense, with the first two close to their marks.

5141 32REDPOKER.COM COMPETITION H'CAP 1m 4f (P)
6:50 (6:51) (Class 6) (0-65,65) 3-Y-O+ £1,617 (£481; £240; £120) Stalls Centre

Form RPR
0500 1 **Al Khawaneej**[24] 4336 3-9-4 **65**............................(v[1]) JamieSpencer 5 83+
(Ed Dunlop) *chsd ldrs: led 7f out: rdn clr fr 3f out: in n.d sn after: 10 l clr over 1f out: eased fnl 120yds* **8/1**[3]
2544 2 *7* **Mediterranean Sea (IRE)**[14] 4649 5-9-13 **64**.............. StephenCraine 8 68
(J R Jenkins) *in tch: hdwy 4f out: styd on to take wl hld 2nd 1f out* **12/1**
U603 3 *3* **Holden Eagle**[39] 3799 6-9-5 **56**............................ KierenFallon 7 55
(Tony Newcombe) *in rr: drvn and hdwy on outside fr over 2f out: styd on to take 3rd cl home and gaining on 2nd but nvr any ch w eased wnr* **8/1**[3]
4030 4 *1* **Ministry**[24] 4317 3-8-12 **59**............................ LukeMorris 3 57
(John Best) *chsd ldrs tl rdn and outpcd fr 4f out: mod prog again u.p fr over 1f out* **11/4**[1]
4-23 5 *nk* **Pennfield Pirate**[28] 4177 4-9-11 **62**............................ JimCrowley 6 59
(Hughie Morrison) *sn slt ld: hdd 7f out: styd chsng wnr but nvr any ch fr 3f out: wknd and lost 2nd 1f out* **4/1**[2]
0053 6 *1 ½* **Evergreen Forest (IRE)**[8] 5132 3-9-2 **63**.............. TomQueally 4 58
(Alastair Lidderdale) *w ldr 3f: styd in tch tl dropped to rr fr 5f out: rdn fr 4f out: styd on same pce fnl 2f* **11/4**[1]
0400 7 *1 ½* **Suhailah**[26] 4242 5-9-1 **52**............................ ShaneKelly 1 44
(Michael Attwater) *chsd ldrs: rdn and dropped to rr 5f out: no ch after* **28/1**
0-00 8 *97* **Welsh Dancer**[13] 4666 3-8-6 **53**............................(v) TadhgO'Shea 2 —
(Marcus Tregoning) *sn bhd: t.o* **16/1**

2m 33.08s (-1.42) **Going Correction** 0.0s/f (Stan)
WFA 3 from 4yo+ 10lb **8** Ran SP% **112.6**
Speed ratings (Par 101): **104,99,97,96,96 95,94,29**
toteswingers: 1&2 £10.80, 1&3 £10.70, 2&3 £7.90. CSF £93.60 CT £787.98 TOTE £8.80: £3.40, £3.20, £3.70; EX 51.10.
Owner Ahmad Al Shaikh **Bred** Cliveden Stud Ltd **Trained** Newmarket, Suffolk

FOCUS
This looked trappy. It was run at a sound enough pace and the form is ordinary, with the runner-up rated to his best form on the surface.
Al Khawaneej Official explanation: trainer's rep said, regarding apparent improvement in form, that the colt appeared suited by the first-time visor and first run on the Polytrack.

5142 32 FOR CASINO E B F MAIDEN STKS 1m (P)
7:20 (7:21) (Class 5) 2-Y-O £3,234 (£962; £481; £240) Stalls Low

Form RPR
2 1 **Gassin Golf**[10] 4798 2-9-3 0............................ StevieDonohoe 1 78+
(Sir Mark Prescott Bt) *s.i.s: sn rcvrd and trckd ldrs on ins: drvn and qcknd fr 2f out to take slt ld appr fnl f: styd on strly* **4/7**[1]
6 2 *1 ¾* **Lady Bellatrix**[47] 3534 2-8-12 0............................ KierenFallon 4 66
(Mark H Tompkins) *hld up in tch: hdwy over 2f out: drvn to chal over 1f out: chsd wnr ins fnl f but a readily hld* **25/1**
3 *½* **Cherry Street** 2-9-3 0............................ DavidProbert 2 70
(Andrew Balding) *chsd ldr to 4f out: styd front rnk: chal fr over 1f out: sn one pce but battled bk to take 3rd last strides* **14/1**
056 4 *shd* **Fugitive Motel (IRE)**[27] 4201 2-9-3 67............................ PatDobbs 7 70
(Richard Hannon) *led: rn wd bnd 3f out but stl led tl hdd appr fnl f: styd on one pce and lost 3rd last strides* **8/1**[3]
64 5 *shd* **Stateos (IRE)**[27] 4205 2-9-3 0............................ TomQueally 5 69+
(Sir Henry Cecil) *chsd ldrs: wnt 2nd 4f out: upsides whn pushed bdly wd bnd 3f out: sn rcvrd to chal fr 2f out tl appr fnl f: kpt on same pce* **7/2**[2]
6 *7* **Compton Bell** 2-9-0 0............................ SophieDoyle(3) 6 53
(Hans Adielsson) *s.i.s: pushed along 3f out: a towards rr* **66/1**
0 7 *17* **Fantasy Hero**[17] 4545 2-9-3 0............................ TomMcLaughlin 8 14
(Ronald Harris) *in rr but in tch: pushed along 3f out: hung rt: rn green and wknd sn after* **100/1**

1m 41.45s (1.65) **Going Correction** 0.0s/f (Stan) **7** Ran SP% **110.0**
Speed ratings (Par 94): **91,89,88,88,88 81,64**
toteswingers: 1&2 £3.70, 1&3 £2.40, 2&3 £6.60. CSF £18.13 TOTE £1.60: £1.10, £7.90; EX 15.60.
Owner J L C Pearce **Bred** J L C Pearce **Trained** Newmarket, Suffolk

FOCUS
This was run at a moderate pace and, as a result, the first five were covered by less than a length passing the furlong marker.

NOTEBOOK
Gassin Golf missed the kick, but the early fractions allowed him to recover quickly and he readily went one better than his debut second at Lingfield ten days earlier. He took time to find his full stride once the gap opened on the inside from 2f out, but would have been more impressive in a truly run race and was still easily on top at the finish. He is clearly a useful performer, who ought to relish middle distances next year, and was his in-form trainer's ninth juvenile winner of the season.
Lady Bellatrix showed the clear benefit of her debut experience at Epsom last month and ran a big race in defeat. This more conventional track helped and she can be placed to strike in the coming weeks, but a drop back to 7f might prove ideal in the short term.
Cherry Street kept on nicely near the finish after hitting something of a flat spot when the dash for home developed and this was a pleasing debut effort. He obviously stays very well and shouldn't be too long in winning, considering juveniles from this yard most often improve markedly from their debut outings. (op 16-1)
Fugitive Motel(IRE) ran his most encouraging race on this switch to Polytrack and wasn't given too hard a time late in the day. He still looks green (got excited beforehand) and shaped as though a drop back to 7f in a nursery can see him winning. Official explanation: jockey said colt cocked its jaw and hung left (op 10-1)
Stateos(IRE), up in trip, wasn't helped when the leader went wide into the home turn and would have probably been placed but for that. He looks one of his yard's lesser lights, but now qualifies for nurseries. (op 11-4)

5143 32 FOR POKER H'CAP 7f (P)
7:50 (7:51) (Class 6) (0-60,60) 3-Y-O+ £1,617 (£481; £240; £120) Stalls Low

Form RPR
0452 1 **Putin (IRE)**[11] 4758 3-8-11 **52**............................ AndreaAtzeni 12 59
(Derek Haydn Jones) *chsd ldr 4f out: chal fr over 2f out: styd on u.p fnl f to ld fnl 30yds: drvn out* **9/1**
3352 2 *½* **Annes Rocket (IRE)**[6] 4917 6-9-2 **59**....................(p) ThomasBrown(7) 4 67
(Jimmy Fox) *hld up in rr: hdwy fr 2f out: styd on thrght fnl f to take 2nd last stride: nt rch wnr* **6/1**[3]
3043 3 *shd* **Valeo Si Vales (IRE)**[11] 4743 3-9-5 **60**....................(b) FergusSweeney 5 66
(Jamie Osborne) *chsd ldrs: rdn and styd on to chal ins fnl f: stl ev ch fnl 120yds: no ex last strides* **10/1**

4-60 **4** *shd* **Farmers Dream (IRE)**[195] 382 4-8-5 **46**............ MatthewLawson(5) 11 53
(Richard Price) *in tch: hdwy to chse ldrs 3f out: drvn to take slt ld appr fnl 2f: kpt narrow advantage tl hdd and no ex fnl 30yds* **20/1**

1300 **5** *1 3/4* **Cape Kimberley**[33] 4025 4-9-9 **59**.................................... KierenFallon 10 62
(Tony Newcombe) *chsd ldrs: rdn over 2f out: pressed ldrs over 1f out: wknd ins fnl f* **6/1**[3]

3000 **6** *nk* **Titan Diamond (IRE)**[35] 3942 3-8-5 **53**.................... RachealKneller(7) 8 53
(Mark Usher) *mid-div: pushed along and hdwy on outside fr 2f out: kpt on but nt rch ldrs* **33/1**

0122 **7** *hd* **Fortunate Bid (IRE)**[6] 4918 5-9-10 **60**............................(p) TomQueally 1 61
(Linda Stubbs) *in rr: hdwy on ins fr 2f out: chsd ldrs appr fnl f: sn one pce* **7/2**[1]

0660 **8** *1 3/4* **El Libertador (USA)**[9] 4829 5-9-7 **57**..........................(b) JamieSpencer 2 54
(Eric Wheeler) *in tch: pushed along over 2f out: styd on fnl f: nt rch ldrs* **7/1**

0102 **9** *hd* **Karate (IRE)**[6] 4911 3-9-4 **59**... JamesDoyle 7 53
(Hans Adielsson) *chsd ldrs: rdn over 2f out: styd on one pce fnl f* **5/1**[2]

0000 **10** *3 1/4* **Dingaan (IRE)**[42] 3714 8-8-13 **54**.................................... SladeO'Hara(5) 9 41
(Peter Grayson) *slowly away: in rr: sme prog on outside over 2f out: nvr in contention* **25/1**

2-00 **11** *1/2* **Green Agenda**[6] 4918 5-9-7 **57**...............................(v) RobbieFitzpatrick 3 43
(Derek Shaw) *sn drvn along: a outpcd* **66/1**

60F- **12** *12* **Rabbit Fighter (IRE)**[503] 1072 7-9-0 **53**..................... MarkLawson(3) 13 —
(Jo Hughes) *s.i.s: a towards rr* **25/1**

5260 **13** *6* **Crinan Classic**[6] 4928 4-9-6 **56**...............................(b[1]) TonyCulhane 6 —
(George Baker) *led tl hdd & wknd appr fnl 2f* **16/1**

1m 26.07s (0.07) **Going Correction** 0.0s/f (Stan)
WFA 3 from 4yo+ 5lb 13 Ran SP% **121.8**
Speed ratings (Par 101): **99,98,98,98,96 95,95,93,93,89 89,75,68**
toteswingers: 1&2 £8.70, 1&3 £14.70, 2&3 £15.50. CSF £59.81 CT £581.67 TOTE £8.30: £2.50, £2.40, £5.10; EX 75.20.

Owner Post Haste Partnership **Bred** D Llewelyn & J Runeckles **Trained** Efail Isaf, Rhondda C Taff

FOCUS
There appeared to be a solid pace on in this moderate handicap, but plenty took a keen hold and there was a blanket finish. The form is rated around the placed horses.

Rabbit Fighter(IRE) Official explanation: trainer said gelding finished distressed

5144 32RED.COM NURSERY 7f (P)
8:20 (8:20) (Class 5) (0-70,67) 2-Y-O **£2,264** (£673; £336; £168) **Stalls** Low

Form RPR

562 **1** **Tweet Lady**[14] 4639 2-9-3 **63**.. JamesMillman 4 67
(Rod Millman) *mde all: set mod pce: qcknd over 2f out: rdn over 1f out: styd on wl fnl f and in command clsng stages* **16/1**

452 **2** *1* **Continuity (IRE)**[19] 4462 2-9-4 **64**..................................... JimCrowley 1 65
(Ralph Beckett) *chsd wnr most of way off slow pce: styd on u.p fr over 1f out: ev ch ins fnl f: outpcd clsng stages but hld on wl for 2nd* **7/2**[2]

5635 **3** *hd* **Darnathean**[25] 4277 2-9-6 **66**..(b) LukeMorris 7 66
(Paul D'Arcy) *plld hrd in rr early off mod pce: rdn and hdwy fr 2f out: styd on u.p fnl f to take 3rd fnl 120yds to press for 2nd but no imp on wnr* **12/1**

026 **4** *hd* **Mcvicar**[32] 4073 2-9-5 **65**... JamieSpencer 5 65
(Mick Channon) *plld hrd in rr early off mod pce: hdwy on outside over 1f out: styd on and hung rt u.p ins fnl f: fin wl but nt rch ldrs* **13/2**

0000 **5** *nk* **Clone Devil (IRE)**[4] 4995 2-8-0 **46** ow1.................... FrankieMcDonald 6 45+
(Alastair Lidderdale) *plld hrd and n.m.r early off mod pce: bhd tl hdwy towards outside over 1f out: styng on whn carried rt ins fnl f: kpt on cl home but nt rch ldrs* **66/1**

0302 **6** *hd* **Vociferous (USA)**[6] 4922 2-9-0 **60**.................................. KierenFallon 8 59
(Mark Johnston) *chsd ldrs off modest pce: rdn over 2f out: styd on same pce fnl f* **4/1**[3]

502 **7** *shd* **Accustomed**[17] 4545 2-9-7 **67**.. JamesDoyle 3 65
(Sylvester Kirk) *chsd ldrs off mod pce: rdn 2f out: styd on same pce fnl f* **11/2**

550 **8** *3/4* **Enjoying (IRE)**[25] 4264 2-9-0 **63**...................................... SeanLevey(3) 2 59
(Richard Hannon) *s.i.s: in rr and t.k.h off mod pce: rdn and hdwy on ins to chse ldrs over 1f out: hung rt into far rail fnl f and sn wknd* **3/1**[1]

064 **9** *1 1/4* **Raspberry Fizz**[9] 4824 2-8-10 **56**................................(p) CathyGannon 9 49
(Eve Johnson Houghton) *t.k.h and sn chsng ldrs off mod pce: rdn over 2f out: wknd appr fnl f* **20/1**

1m 28.79s (2.79) **Going Correction** 0.0s/f (Stan) 9 Ran SP% **115.8**
Speed ratings (Par 94): **84,82,82,82,82 81,81,80,79**
toteswingers: 1&2 £6.50, 1&3 £14.30, 2&3 £8.30. CSF £71.66 CT £715.43 TOTE £10.30: £2.70, £2.10, £4.00; EX 50.60.

Owner The People's Horse **Bred** D J And Mrs Deer **Trained** Kentisbeare, Devon

FOCUS
A modest nursery that looked an open heat. There was a very messy early pace on, which resulted in a dash for home and it was another bunched finish.

NOTEBOOK
Tweet Lady made all to shed her maiden tag at the fourth time of asking on this nursery debut. She took time to settle, but was racing in the ideal position out in front and she found plenty when pressed by the runner-up inside the final furlong. This return to 7f worked out nicely and she's begun life in handicaps on a workable mark, but obviously got very much the run of the race. (op 14-1)

Continuity(IRE) has shaped as though this extra furlong may suit ideally and got well backed for this nursery debut. She held every chance after racing handily, but despite this not being a proper test over the distance her stamina was just found out. (op 3-1 tchd 11-4)

Darnathean ◆ once again pulled hard under restraint, but that was due to the farcical early pace and he ran a big race in defeat. He was motoring late on and should be up to this mark when faced with a strong pace. Official explanation: jockey said gelding ran too free

Mcvicar ◆, another nursery debutant, was ridden to get this return to the extra furlong and had to come widest of all with his challenge. He finished with purpose after getting outpaced and is one to be with next time. (op 5-1 tchd 9-2)

Clone Devil(IRE), with the blinkers left off, stepped up greatly on his previous effort and was another finishing fast off the moderate pace. He may be flattered, but the switch to Polytrack looked to suit him and he's worth treating as an improver.

Vociferous(USA) wasn't far from the winner when the tempo lifted in the home straight, so it is somewhat disappointing she didn't fare better. (op 7-2)

Accustomed was undone by the way the race panned out on this slight drop back in trip and is worthy of another chance. (op 6-1 tchd 13-2)

Enjoying(IRE) looked a threat at the furlong marker, but his effort flattened out and he now has a little to prove. (op 13-2)

5145 32 FOR BINGO H'CAP 2m (P)
8:50 (8:51) (Class 5) (0-75,70) 3-Y-O **£2,264** (£673; £336; £168) **Stalls** Low

Form RPR

-013 **1** **Susan Stroman**[28] 4190 3-9-5 **70**.................................... JamieSpencer 4 83+
(Ed Dunlop) *mde all: qcknd pce over 3f out: rdn clr over 2f out: eased clsng stages: unchal* **11/10**[1]

-066 **2** *2* **Secret Edge**[24] 4336 3-9-0 **65**.. FergusSweeney 3 73
(Alan King) *racd in 4th tl hdwy fr 3f out to chse wnr over 2f out but nvr any ch and styd on same pce* **3/1**[3]

-003 **3** *12* **Reillys Daughter**[27] 4209 3-9-3 **68**.................................... LukeMorris 2 62
(J S Moore) *racd in 3rd: reminder 7f out: rdn along fr 5f out: dropped to 4th over 2f out: styd on again past wkng rival to take mod 3rd over 1f out* **9/1**

2101 **4** *6* **Captain Bellamy (USA)**[28] 4181 3-9-0 **65**.................... HayleyTurner 1 52
(Hughie Morrison) *chsd wnr: rdn over 4f out: lost 2nd over 2f out: sn wknd and dropped to 4th over 1f out* **9/4**[2]

3m 29.56s (-0.54) **Going Correction** 0.0s/f (Stan) 4 Ran SP% **113.4**
Speed ratings (Par 100): **101,100,94,91**
CSF £5.02 TOTE £2.00; EX 6.40.

Owner Lord Lloyd-Webber **Bred** Watership Down Stud **Trained** Newmarket, Suffolk

FOCUS
A tight-looking little staying handicap, but Jamie Spencer was able to control matters. The winner is value for a bit more with the runner-up setting the standard on his juvenile form.

5146 £32 FREE AT 32RED.COM H'CAP 6f (P)
9:20 (9:20) (Class 4) (0-85,85) 3-Y-O **£4,075** (£1,212; £606; £303) **Stalls** Low

Form RPR

150 **1** **St Augustine (IRE)**[19] 4472 3-9-7 **85**................................ LukeMorris 3 93+
(John Best) *t.k.h: trckd ldrs: rdn and styd on fr 2f out to ld appr fnl f: drvn out* **11/4**[2]

-200 **2** *1* **Sadafiya**[24] 4333 3-9-5 **83**... TadhgO'Shea 2 87
(Ed Dunlop) *chsd ldr over 4f out: rdn to chal over 2f out and stl upsides over 1f out: styd on to take 2nd fnl 120yds but no imp on wnr* **13/2**[3]

45-1 **3** *hd* **Captain Noble (IRE)**[118] 1483 3-8-8 **72**........................ FergusSweeney 7 75
(Peter Makin) *sn led: rdn and hrd pressed over 2f out: hdd appr fnl f: one pce and lost 2nd fnl 120yds* **8/1**

-611 **4** *1/2* **Manoori (IRE)**[34] 3985 3-9-6 **84**.. TedDurcan 4 86
(Chris Wall) *trckd ldrs: rdn and one pce 2f out: styd on ins fnl f but nvr gng pce to chal* **11/4**[2]

-116 **5** *1 1/2* **Mosaicist (IRE)**[50] 3459 3-9-5 **83**.................................... KierenFallon 1 80
(James Fanshawe) *hld up in tch: pushed along 2f out: rdn: swtchd rt and styd on same pce ins fnl f* **2/1**[1]

1m 13.03s (-0.07) **Going Correction** 0.0s/f (Stan) 5 Ran SP% **111.1**
Speed ratings (Par 102): **100,98,98,97,95**
toteswinger: 1&2 £7.20. CSF £19.54 TOTE £3.80: £1.80, £1.90; EX 11.40.

Owner B Malt, S Malcolm & A Longman **Bred** Paget Bloodstock **Trained** Hucking, Kent

FOCUS
Despite the two non-runners this was still a decent sprint handicap, but it was another race run at an average pace and it once more paid to race handily. The winnner recorded a slight personal best with the runner-up the guide to the level.

T/Plt: £110.00 to a £1 stake. Pool of £56,313.78 - 373.53 winning tickets. T/Qpdt: £28.30 to a £1 stake. Pool of £3,961.68 - 103.50 winning tickets. ST

4499 MUSSELBURGH (R-H)
Tuesday, August 16

OFFICIAL GOING: Round course - good (good to soft in places); straight course - good to soft changing to soft all over after race 3 (3.45)
Wind: Almost nil Weather: Overcast, raining 1-3, cloudy, bright 3-7

5147 SCOTTISH RACING MAIDEN AUCTION STKS 5f
2:15 (2:15) (Class 6) 2-Y-O **£1,617** (£481; £240; £120) **Stalls** High

Form RPR

2222 **1** **First Fast Now (IRE)**[6] 4899 2-8-6 68.......................... SilvestreDeSousa 1 67
(Nigel Tinkler) *cl up: effrt 2f out: led ent fnl f: pushed out* **5/4**[1]

2 *2 3/4* **Verus Delicia (IRE)** 2-8-0 0.. NeilFarley(5) 6 56
(Patrick Morris) *dwlt: sn in tch: effrt over 1f out: edgd lft and chsd (clr) wnr wl ins fnl f: kpt on* **13/2**[3]

2633 **3** *1/2* **Roy's Legacy**[4] 5005 2-8-7 58...(t) BillyCray(3) 5 59
(Shaun Harris) *led tl rdn and hdd ent fnl f: kpt on same pce* **9/1**

3360 **4** *nse* **Angel Of Hope (IRE)**[21] 4406 2-8-8 60..........................(v[1]) TomEaves 3 57
(Bryan Smart) *cl up: rdn and outpcd over 1f out: kpt on ins fnl f: no imp* **8/1**

0600 **5** *1 1/2* **Economic Crisis (IRE)**[21] 4406 2-8-0 55........................ JulieBurke(5) 2 49
(Alan Berry) *cl up: rdn 1/2-way: outpcd over 1f out: n.d after* **22/1**

6 *8* **George Fenton** 2-8-10 0.. RobertLButler(3) 4 28
(Richard Guest) *sn bhd and outpcd: nvr on terms* **9/1**

043 **7** *10* **Koolgreycat (IRE)**[25] 4283 2-8-6 62.................................. AdrianNicholls 7 —
(Noel Wilson) *dwlt: sn drvn along bhd ldng gp: struggling fr 1/2-way* **9/2**[2]

61.78 secs (1.38) **Going Correction** +0.25s/f (Good) 7 Ran SP% **111.4**
Speed ratings (Par 92): **98,93,92,92,90 77,61**
CSF £9.31 TOTE £1.80: £1.20, £3.20; EX 11.90.

Owner Breaking News Partnership **Bred** Holborn Trust Co **Trained** Langton, N Yorks

FOCUS
Rain in the two hours leading up to racing produced ground for the opener just on the easy side of good according to the time, though winning rider Silvestre de Sousa described it as soft. A modest maiden auction event.

NOTEBOOK
First Fast Now(IRE) opened her account at the ninth attempt having finished runner-up on each of her previous five starts. Her backers had a pre-race scare when she got loose briefly in the paddock, but she broke her duck in tidy fashion with her rider never having to use his whip. Rated 68, there is no reason why she should not be competitive in nursery company after a short break. (op Evens tchd 11-8 in places)

Verus Delicia(IRE) did not go without support. A half-sister to two winners, after a tardy start she made her way to the outside. She kept on to snatch second spot near the line and this should have taught her plenty. (op 16-1)

Roy's Legacy, who had a stone to find with the winner on official ratings after already having been beaten in selling company, showed plenty of toe but if the handicapper takes this at face value her nursery mark will increase. (tchd 8-1)

Angel Of Hope(IRE), in a first-time visor, was putting in her best work at the finish. This was her sixth start and she is looking exposed, but a return to 6f will be in her favour. (op 7-1 tchd 13-2)

Economic Crisis(IRE) continues on the decline on her ninth start. (op 33-1 tchd 20-1)

The Form Book, Raceform Ltd, Compton, RG20 6NL

George Fenton missed the break and never figured. A £13,000 purchase, he is surely better than he showed here. (op 16-1)
Koolgreycat(IRE), blanketed for stalls entry, never went a yard and possibly needs quick ground. Official explanation: trainer's rep said filly was unsuited by the good to soft ground (op 7-2)

5148 DAILY RECORD H'CAP (QUALIFIER FOR BETFAIR BONUS SCOTTISH RACING SPRINT FINAL) 5f

2:45 (2:45) (Class 5) (0-75,75) 3-Y-0+ **£4,204** (£1,251; £625; £312) **Stalls** High

Form RPR
0440 **1** **Green Park (IRE)**[10] 4791 8-9-5 **75**.....(b) NeilFarley(5) 13 85
(Declan Carroll) *in tch: effrt over 1f out: swtchd lft and squeezed through against stands' rail to ld wl ins fnl f: r.o* **10/1**
1212 **2** ½ **Blown It (USA)**[4] 4986 5-9-1 **66** 6ex..... PaulHanagan 2 74+
(Keith Dalgleish) *hld up: effrt 2f out: hdwy and ev ch wl ins fnl f: jst hld* **7/2**[1]
310 **3** ½ **Dancing Freddy (IRE)**[6] 4900 4-9-2 **70**.....(tp) RobertLButler(3) 10 76
(Richard Guest) *cl up gng wl: ev ch fr 1/2-way to wl ins fnl f: hld cl home* **11/1**
0431 **4** 1 ½ **Tongalooma**[4] 4986 5-8-10 **61** 6ex..... PJMcDonald 4 62
(James Moffatt) *cl up: led 1/2-way: edgd lft and hdd wl ins fnl f: no ex* **8/1**
5111 **5** ½ **Wicked Wilma (IRE)**[17] 4541 7-8-12 **68**..... JulieBurke(5) 6 70+
(Alan Berry) *trckd ldrs: effrt over 1f out: keeping on same pce whn n.m.r ins fnl f* **11/2**[2]
5000 **6** 1 **Highland Warrior**[39] 3832 12-9-4 **69**..... MickyFenton 8 64
(Paul Midgley) *towards rr and sn pushed along: hdwy over 1f out: no imp ins fnl f* **33/1**
-456 **7** nk **Luscivious**[193] 429 7-9-0 **68**.....(b) MichaelO'Connell(3) 11 62
(David Nicholls) *towards rr: drvn after 2f: hdwy over 1f out: nvr able to chal* **16/1**
4016 **8** ¾ **Midnight Dynamo**[17] 4541 4-9-5 **70**..... DanielTudhope 3 61+
(Jim Goldie) *hld up: shkn up and effrt on outside over 1f out: nvr nr ldrs* **9/1**
1234 **9** ¾ **Sands Of Dee (USA)**[6] 4900 4-9-3 **71**.....(p) BillyCray(3) 12 60
(David Nicholls) *prom: drvn after 2f: rdn and wknd over 1f out* **7/1**[3]
3200 **10** 1 ½ **Dower Glen**[7] 4881 4-8-5 **56** oh1.....(v) JamesSullivan 5 39
(Keith Dalgleish) *bhd and outpcd: sme late hdwy: nvr on terms* **40/1**
1300 **11** 2 **Eternal Instinct**[7] 4881 4-8-12 **66** ow1..... GaryBartley(3) 1 42
(Jim Goldie) *bhd and sn drvn along: nvr on terms* **16/1**
0455 **12** 2 **Sandwith**[4] 4986 8-8-6 **57**.....(v) LeeNewman 7 26
(George Foster) *cl up tl rdn and wknd fr 2f out* **11/1**
00-0 **13** 15 **Igoyougo**[13] 4678 5-9-6 **71**..... AdrianNicholls 9 —
(Noel Wilson) *led to 1/2-way: rdn and wknd over 1f out: eased whn no ch ins fnl f* **22/1**

61.10 secs (0.70) **Going Correction** +0.25s/f (Good) **13** Ran SP% **118.5**
Speed ratings (Par 103): **104,103,102,100,99 97,97,95,94,92 89,85,61**
toteswingers:1&2:£8.80, 2&3:£8.20, 1&3:£23.1 CSF £43.65 CT £415.63 TOTE £14.80: £4.20, £2.00, £4.40; EX 63.60.
Owner G A Fixings Ltd **Bred** James Burns And A Moynan **Trained** Sledmere, E Yorks
■ Stewards' Enquiry : P J McDonald one-day ban: careless riding (Aug 30)

FOCUS
Some familiar faces here in this modest sprint handicap, eight course winners of 17 races here. Solid enough form.
Igoyougo Official explanation: jockey said gelding hung right throughout

5149 WATCH RACING UK ON SKY 432 H'CAP (QUALIFIER FOR BETFAIR BONUS SCOTTISH RACING STAYERS' FINAL) 1m 4f 100y

3:15 (3:15) (Class 5) (0-75,75) 3-Y-0+ **£4,204** (£1,251; £625; £312) **Stalls** Low

Form RPR
6060 **1** **Chookie Hamilton**[7] 4879 7-9-9 **72**..... PaulHanagan 2 83
(Keith Dalgleish) *in tch: hdwy to ld over 1f out: sn hrd pressed: drvn and hld on wl ins fnl f* **12/1**
2304 **2** nk **Meetings Man (IRE)**[23] 4360 4-9-5 **75**..... GarryWhillans(7) 4 85
(Micky Hammond) *t.k.h: hld up: hdwy and hung rt fr over 2f out: ev ch over 1f out: kpt on: hld cl home* **13/2**
0612 **3** 5 **Think Its All Over (USA)**[14] 4649 4-9-0 **63**..... MickyFenton 7 65
(Julie Camacho) *led at modest gallop: qcknd 3f out: hdd over 1f out: kpt on* **15/2**
1130 **4** 3 **John Forbes**[20] 4423 9-9-8 **71**..... TomEaves 1 69
(Brian Ellison) *hld up towards rr: hdwy and c w one other to stands' side over 2f out: no imp w first three fr over 1f out* **9/2**[2]
/60- **5** 8 **Ananda Kanda (USA)**[31] 2033 4-9-8 **71**..... JamesSullivan 5 57
(Brian Ellison) *bhd: pushed along and kpt on fr 2f out: nvr able to chal* **66/1**
2306 **6** 1 ¾ **Grand Diamond (IRE)**[21] 4142 7-9-2 **65**..... DanielTudhope 6 48
(Jim Goldie) *midfield on outside: rdn and outpcd over 2f out: n.d after* **20/1**
3044 **7** ¾ **Green Lightning (IRE)**[19] 4465 4-9-5 **68**.....(b) SilvestreDeSousa 8 50
(Mark Johnston) *hld up: rdn 3f out: sn outpcd: n.d after* **13/2**
512 **8** 14 **Achalas (IRE)**[49] 3479 3-9-1 **74**..... PhillipMakin 10 35
(Heather Main) *cl up: effrt and c to stands' side ent st: wknd fr 2f out* **3/1**[1]
6141 **9** 4 **Grey Command (USA)**[6] 4904 6-9-4 **67** 6ex..... RobertWinston 3 22
(Mel Brittain) *chsd ldrs tl drvn and outpcd over 2f out: sn btn* **6/1**[3]
0000 **10** 37 **Unbreak My Heart (IRE)**[29] 4150 6-8-13 **65**.....(p) RobertLButler(3) 9 —
(Richard Guest) *t.k.h: chsd ldr: rdn and struggling 3f out: lost tch fnl 2f* **66/1**

2m 46.19s (4.19) **Going Correction** +0.25s/f (Good)
WFA 3 from 4yo+ 10lb **10** Ran SP% **111.3**
Speed ratings (Par 103): **96,95,92,90,85 83,83,74,71,46**
CSF £82.61 CT £613.28 TOTE £17.00: £3.80, £2.50, £2.90; EX 91.70.
Owner Raeburn Brick Limited **Bred** D And J Raeburn **Trained** Carluke, South Lanarkshire

FOCUS
The rain had stopped ahead of this modest stayers' handicap. The time suggested the going on the round course was slower than the straight track and there was a divergence of opinion about where to race in the home straight. The winner is rated only to this year's best at face value.
Grey Command(USA) Official explanation: jockey said gelding ran flat

5150 EAST LOTHIAN PIPERS H'CAP (QUALIFIER FOR BETFAIR BONUS SCOTTISH RACING MILE FINAL) 1m 1f

3:45 (3:45) (Class 5) (0-70,68) 3-Y-0+ **£4,204** (£1,251; £625; £312) **Stalls** Low

Form RPR
0101 **1** **Carragold**[6] 4902 5-9-5 **59** 6ex..... RobertWinston 3 73
(Mel Brittain) *in tch: effrt over 2f out: led over 1f out: drvn clr ins fnl f* **3/1**[2]
2303 **2** 3 ¾ **Jupiter Fidius**[8] 4852 4-9-5 **62**.....(p) MichaelO'Connell(3) 9 68
(Kate Walton) *cl up: rdn and led over 2f out: edgd rt and hdd over 1f out: kpt on same pce* **8/1**
2455 **3** 1 ¾ **Nicola's Dream**[25] 4290 3-9-7 **68**..... PaulHanagan 5 70
(Richard Fahey) *chsd ldrs: effrt and drvn over 2f out: edgd rt and one pce over 1f out* **5/2**[1]
6052 **4** 4 ½ **Law To Himself (IRE)**[10] 4811 4-9-12 **66**..... PJMcDonald 6 58
(Alan Swinbank) *hld up in tch: hdwy on outside over 2f out: edgd rt and no imp over 1f out* **9/2**
510 **5** 1 ¾ **On The Cusp (IRE)**[17] 4543 4-9-9 **66**.....(p) RobertLButler(3) 2 54
(Richard Guest) *led: rdn and hdd over 2f out: hung rt: wknd wl over 1f out* **10/1**
0162 **6** 1 **Mangham (IRE)**[10] 4783 6-9-11 **65**.....(p) LeeNewman 7 51
(George Foster) *prom: drvn over 2f out: sn outpcd: n.d after* **4/1**[3]
0106 **7** 2 ½ **Abernethy (IRE)**[10] 4783 3-8-2 **49**..... DuranFentiman 1 30
(Linda Perratt) *hld up: short lived effrt over 2f out: sn rdn and btn over 1f out* **25/1**

1m 55.4s (1.50) **Going Correction** +0.25s/f (Good)
WFA 3 from 4yo+ 7lb **7** Ran SP% **115.8**
Speed ratings (Par 103): **103,99,98,94,92 91,89**
toteswingers:1&2:£4.40, 2&3:£4.70, 1&3:£2.10 CSF £27.41 CT £67.98 TOTE £4.60: £2.80, £3.70; EX 24.90.
Owner Mel Brittain **Bred** Darley **Trained** Warthill, N Yorks

FOCUS
The going was changed to soft all round ahead of this low-grade handicap. Again the pace increased once in line for home. A clear personal best from the winner at face value.

5151 RACING UK CLASSIFIED CLAIMING STKS 1m

4:15 (4:15) (Class 6) 3-Y-0+ **£1,617** (£481; £240; £120) **Stalls** Low

Form RPR
3451 **1** **Bolodenka (IRE)**[6] 4897 9-8-11 69..... PaulHanagan 1 74
(Richard Fahey) *trckd ldrs: effrt over 2f out: edgd rt and led over 1f out: drvn out towards fin* **4/6**[1]
0360 **2** ¾ **Greyfriarschorista**[10] 4792 4-8-13 69..... SilvestreDeSousa 6 74
(Mark Johnston) *cl up: led after 3f: rdn over 2f out: hdd over 1f out: rallied: hld towards fin* **11/2**[3]
420 **3** 2 **Dr Red Eye**[17] 4560 3-8-9 68..... MichaelO'Connell(3) 3 73
(David Nicholls) *led 3f: cl up: rdn 3f out: ev ch over 1f out: swtchd lft ins fnl f: one pce* **9/2**[2]
4640 **4** 2 **Ra Junior (USA)**[15] 4603 5-8-9 64..... FrederikTylicki 9 61
(Paul Midgley) *hld up: hdwy 3f out: sn rdn: kpt on same pce fr 2f out* **7/1**
6200 **5** 23 **Desert Auction (IRE)**[10] 4782 4-9-1 65.....(b[1]) TomEaves 4 14
(Ian Semple) *t.k.h: hld up: rdn over 3f out: sn btn: t.o* **50/1**
3366 **6** 2 ¼ **Hinton Admiral**[18] 4503 7-9-0 70..... PhillipMakin 8 8
(Keith Dalgleish) *in tch tl rdn and wknd fr over 2f out: t.o* **14/1**

1m 42.41s (1.21) **Going Correction** +0.25s/f (Good)
WFA 3 from 4yo+ 6lb **6** Ran SP% **114.7**
Speed ratings (Par 101): **103,102,100,98,75 73**
toteswingers:1&2:£2.00, 2&3:£2.80, 1&3:£1.80 CSF £5.15 TOTE £1.90: £1.60, £2.20; EX 5.10.Bolodenka was subject to a friendly claim. Greyfriarschorista was claimed by B Ellison for £8000.
Owner Aidan J Ryan **Bred** Kildaragh Stud **Trained** Musley Bank, N Yorks
■ Stewards' Enquiry : Silvestre De Sousa one-day ban: used whip with excessive frequency down shoulder in the forehand (Aug 30)

FOCUS
No hanging about in this fair claimer. The usual doubts over the form and the winner did not need to match his Beverley latest.
Hinton Admiral Official explanation: jockey said gelding stopped very quickly having run too free

5152 TURFTV H'CAP 1m 5f

4:45 (4:45) (Class 6) (0-65,60) 3-Y-0 **£1,617** (£481; £240; £120) **Stalls** Low

Form RPR
4232 **1** **Silver Tigress**[28] 4175 3-8-11 **50**..... PJMcDonald 2 61
(George Moore) *t.k.h early: trckd ldrs: smooth hdwy over 2f out: led gng wl over 1f out: shkn up and qcknd clr fnl f: readily* **5/4**[1]
3210 **2** 7 **Hal Of A Lover**[4] 5022 3-9-7 **60**..... SilvestreDeSousa 1 60
(David O'Meara) *hld up in tch: hdwy on outside to ld over 2f out: hdd over 1f out: no ch w wnr* **15/8**[2]
[illegible] **3** ¾ **Caugers Brig**[illegible] [illegible] 3-9-4 [illegible]..... PaulHanagan 4 56
(Keith Dalgleish) *t.k.h early: trckd ldr: rn wd bnd over 3f out: outpcd over 2f out: n.d after* **10/3**[3]
0-02 **4** 1 ¼ **A Southside Boy (GER)**[73] 2730 3-8-1 **45**..... JulieBurke(5) 3 42
(Jim Goldie) *set stdy pce: t.k.h: hung lft bnds after 2f and after 4f: rdn and hdd over 2f out: wknd over 1f out* **16/1**

2m 57.2s (5.20) **Going Correction** +0.25s/f (Good) **4** Ran SP% **108.2**
Speed ratings (Par 98): **94,89,89,88**
CSF £3.88 TOTE £2.50; EX 3.50.
Owner A Crute & Partners **Bred** Mrs J M F Dibben & Mrs Amanda Brudenell **Trained** Middleham Moor, N Yorks

FOCUS
A low-grade 3-y-o stayers' handicap run at a very steady pace. The first pair were closely matched on their C&D form latest.

5153 SCOTTISH RACING YOUR BETTER BET H'CAP 7f 30y

5:15 (5:15) (Class 6) (0-65,62) 3-Y-0+ **£1,617** (£481; £240; £120) **Stalls** Low

Form RPR
0631 **1** **Whats For Pudding (IRE)**[4] 4987 3-8-6 **52** 6ex..... NeilFarley(5) 4 60
(Declan Carroll) *in tch: drvn and sltly outpcd over 2f out: rallied over 1f out: led ins fnl f: styd on wl* **7/2**[1]
4000 **2** 1 **Let's Face Facts**[7] 4877 4-9-4 **54**..... DanielTudhope 1 61
(Jim Goldie) *hld up in tch: effrt 2f out: ev ch ins fnl f: hld towards fin* **12/1**
0560 **3** 1 ¼ **Broughtons Silk**[7] 4876 6-8-9 **45**..... PJMcDonald 2 49
(Alistair Whillans) *trckd ldrs: effrt and led over 1f out to ins fnl f: kpt on same pce* **7/1**
625 **4** 1 ¼ **Eilean Eeve**[28] 4176 5-9-2 **52**.....(p) LeeNewman 6 52
(George Foster) *led: rdn and hdd over 1f out: rallied: no ex wl ins fnl f* **16/1**
0140 **5** 2 ¾ **Schoolboy Champ**[8] 4866 4-9-10 **60**.....(v) SilvestreDeSousa 5 53
(Patrick Morris) *hld up: hdwy on ins over 1f out: kpt on ins fnl f: nvr able to chal* **4/1**[2]
0350 **6** ¾ **King Bertolini (IRE)**[15] 4600 4-8-6 **47**..... JulieBurke(5) 11 38
(Alan Berry) *towards rr: rdn over 2f out: edgd rt and hdwy over 1f out: nvr on terms* **25/1**
0/45 **7** 4 **Here Now And Why (IRE)**[13] 4672 4-8-12 **48**..... TomEaves 8 28
(Ian Semple) *t.k.h: hld up in tch: stdy hdwy over 2f out: sn rdn: wknd over 1f out* **9/2**[3]
0040 **8** 1 **Ya Boy Sir (IRE)**[7] 4881 4-8-11 **47**.....(b) DuranFentiman 3 24
(Ian Semple) *dwlt: bhd and pushed along over 3f out: nvr on terms* **22/1**

-600 **9** 1 ½ **Sensational Love (IRE)**[57] 3230 3-9-7 62 PaulHanagan 10 33
(Keith Dalgleish) *plld hrd: cl up tl wknd fr 2f out* **7/1**
0300 **10** 2 **Shunkawakhan (IRE)**[10] 4783 8-9-0 50 (p) PhillipMakin 7 18
(Linda Perratt) *trckd ldrs: rdn whn n.m.r briefly over 2f out: sn wknd* **11/1**
1m 30.97s (1.97) **Going Correction** +0.25s/f (Good)
WFA 3 from 4yo+ 5lb **10** Ran SP% **115.5**
Speed ratings (Par 98): **98,96,95,94,90 90,85,84,82,80**
toteswingers:1&2:£11.40, 2&3:£12.70, 1&3:£5.60 CSF £45.93 CT £235.51 TOTE £4.40: £1.50, £4.20, £3.40; EX 72.90.
Owner R J Ball **Bred** Kenneth Greer **Trained** Sledmere, E Yorks
■ Stewards' Enquiry : Lee Newman one-day ban: used whip with excessive frequency (Aug 30)
FOCUS
Another low-grade handicap and again the pace was strong. The winner confirmed her Catterick improvement.
Sensational Love(IRE) Official explanation: jockey said filly ran too free
T/Jkpt: Part won. Pool of £11599.33 - 0.50 winning units. T/Plt: £108.50 to a £1 stake. Pool of £66,440.62 - 446.85 winning tickets. T/Qpdt: £26.40 to a £1 stake. Pool of £3,620.08 - 101.10 winning tickets. RY

5154 - 5160a (Foreign Racing) - See Raceform Interactive

4600 CARLISLE (R-H)
Wednesday, August 17

OFFICIAL GOING: Good to soft (soft in places; 6.9)
Wind: Breezy, half against Weather: Cloudy, bright

5161 BRITISH STALLION STUDS/BEDLINGTON STATION EBF MEDIAN AUCTION MAIDEN STKS 5f 193y
2:10 (2:11) (Class 4) 2-Y-O **£4,635** (£1,368; £684) **Stalls** Low

Form RPR
2022 **1** **Tip Top Gorgeous (IRE)**[25] 4347 2-8-12 72 DanielTudhope 5 78+
(David O'Meara) *mde all in far side quartet: rdn over 1f out: drew clr fnl f: 1st of 4 in gp* **13/8**[1]
425 **2** 5 **Key Addition (IRE)**[9] 4848 2-8-12 0 JamesRogers(5) 2 68
(William Muir) *chsd wnr far side: rdn over 2f out: kpt on fnl f: no imp: 2nd of 4 in gp* **9/1**
3 1 ½ **Aleut** 2-8-12 0 JamesSullivan 4 59
(James Given) *in tch far side: sn pushed along: effrt over 2f out: kpt on fnl f: nvr rchd ldrs: 3rd of 4 in gp* **66/1**
2220 **4** 5 **Joshua The First**[15] 4632 2-9-3 71 PJMcDonald 9 58
(Keith Dalgleish) *prom stands' side: effrt and led that gp over 1f out: kpt on fnl f: no ch w far side: 1st of 8 in gp* **6/1**[2]
003 **5** 1 ¼ **Dazzlin Bluebell (IRE)**[9] 4851 2-8-12 0 AndrewElliott 6 49
(Tim Easterby) *cl up stands' side gp: led after 2f to over 1f out: kpt on same pce: 2nd of 8 in gp* **12/1**
6 1 ¼ **Cloud Cuckooland (IRE)** 2-8-12 0 FrederikTylicki 11 45
(James Given) *bhd stands' side gp: hdwy 2f out: kpt on fnl f: nrst fin: 3rd of 8 in gp* **40/1**
4 **7** ½ **My Pearl (IRE)**[23] 4377 2-9-3 0 StephenCraine 12 49
(Kevin Ryan) *trckd ldrs stands' side: rdn over 2f out: hung rt and no ex over 1f out: 4th of 8 in gp* **11/1**
8 4 **Cherchedi (IRE)** 2-8-7 0 JulieBurke(5) 3 23
(Alan Berry) *dwlt: bhd and outpcd far side: nvr rchd ldrs: last of 4 in gp* **150/1**
06 **9** 2 ½ **Farzan (IRE)**[9] 4853 2-9-0 0 LeeTopliss(3) 8 29
(Tim Easterby) *led stands' side gp 2f: cl up tl rdn and wknd over 1f out: 5th of 8 in gp* **28/1**
63 **10** 1 ¾ **Trust Fund Babe (IRE)**[32] 4106 2-8-12 0 DuranFentiman 10 19
(Tim Easterby) *bhd stands' side gp: drvn over 2f out: sn btn: 6th of 8 in gp* **10/1**
004 **11** 2 ¾ **Doyouknowwhoiam**[9] 4851 2-9-3 0 TomEaves 13 18
(Bryan Smart) *hld up: rdn 1/2-way: btn fnl 2f: 7th of 8 in gp* **13/2**[3]
5 **12** 10 **I'm A Doughnut**[17] 4575 2-9-3 0 RobertWinston 7 —
(Tom Dascombe) *sn drvn and cl up stands' side gp: disp ld after 2f to 2f out: sn wknd: last of 8 in gp* **12/1**
1m 15.6s (1.90) **Going Correction** +0.225s/f (Good) **12** Ran SP% **116.6**
Speed ratings (Par 96): **96,89,87,80,79 77,76,71,68,65 62,48**
Tote Swingers: 1&2 £2.90, 1&3 £16.10, 2&3 £58.10 CSF £16.32 TOTE £2.50: £1.30, £3.40, £17.80; EX 19.40.
Owner Mrs Elizabeth Offord **Bred** Tally-Ho Stud **Trained** Nawton, N Yorks
FOCUS
The ground had dried out a bit and was officially described as good to soft, soft in places. Most of the runners shifted over to the stands' rail in this maiden auction but the first three raced on the far side and the 72-rated favourite ran out an emphatic winner.
NOTEBOOK
Tip Top Gorgeous(IRE) had strong claims on he runner-up efforts in maidens at Redcar and York last month. Well backed, she set the pace against the far rail and powered clear for a first win on the sixth attempt. Her profile has not been particularly progressive and this form is hard to weigh up with the runners racing in two separate groups, but there was a lot to like about her resolute galloping style and she handled the slow ground well. (op 9-4)
Key Addition(IRE) seemed to find 5f an insufficient test on Polytrack last time but he had claims on his previous nose defeat at Bath and ran respectably to chase home the winner. (op 10-1)
Aleut, an Iceman half-sister to fair staying handicapper Leyte Gulf, ran green before staying on for third over a trip on the sharp side on debut. (op 50-1)
Joshua The First bounced back with a fair run with a visor removed to win the race on the probably unfavoured stands' side. The balance of his form suggests he is probably worth an official mark of 71 but he does not look entirely straightforward and has been very expensive to follow. (tchd 9-2)
Dazzlin Bluebell(IRE), a 2l third in a slightly weaker 5f Thirsk maiden last week, ran another encouraging race to finish a clear second on the near side. She is a half-sister to a 1m4f-2m winner, but seems to have quite a bit of pace at this early stage. (op 10-1)
Cloud Cuckooland(IRE) looked inexperienced before staying on well from a long way back on debut. (op 33-1)
Doyouknowwhoiam put in an improved effort when fourth in similar conditions at Thirsk last time but he was very laboured here. (op 15-2)

5162 SUNNISIDE WMC CLAIMING STKS 5f 193y
2:40 (2:40) (Class 6) 3-Y-O+ **£1,617** (£481; £240; £120) **Stalls** Low

Form RPR
0520 **1** **Esprit De Midas**[74] 2717 5-9-10 85 AdrianNicholls 6 89
(David Nicholls) *hld up in tch: hdwy on outside to ld 2f out: sn rdn and edgd rt: drvn out fnl f* **3/1**[3]
0000 **2** 2 ¼ **Tombi (USA)**[11] 4792 7-9-10 82 PJMcDonald 3 82
(Ollie Pears) *led to 2f out: sn rdn: hmpd appr fnl f: kpt on same pce* **11/4**[2]
10 **3** 1 ¼ **Northern Bolt**[11] 4793 6-9-2 68 PatrickMathers 5 70
(Ian McInnes) *bhd and sn drvn along: hdwy on outside over 1f out: kpt on ins fnl f* **11/1**
4030 **4** ½ **Winning Draw (IRE)**[18] 4564 3-8-1 50 (v) DeclanCannon(3) 2 59
(Paul Midgley) *chsd ldrs: rdn over 2f out: edgd rt and kpt on same pce fnl f* **33/1**
6226 **5** ¾ **Sunrise Safari (IRE)**[17] 4574 8-9-4 80 (v) LeeTopliss(3) 1 71
(Richard Fahey) *chsd ldrs: drvn 2f out: kpt on same pce fnl f* **13/8**[1]
2003 **6** 7 **Prince Of Vasa (IRE)**[34] 4016 4-9-0 65 (p) TomEaves 4 41
(Michael Smith) *cl up: rdn whn n.m.r briefly 2f out: sn btn* **12/1**
1m 14.85s (1.15) **Going Correction** +0.225s/f (Good)
WFA 3 from 4yo+ 3lb **6** Ran SP% **108.7**
Speed ratings (Par 101): **101,98,96,95,94 85**
Tote Swingers: 1&2 £2.00, 1&3 £3.40, 2&3 £3.80 CSF £10.87 TOTE £3.00: £1.10, £1.70; EX 10.60.
Owner Geoff Copp **Bred** Jeremy Green And Sons **Trained** Sessay, N Yorks
■ Stewards' Enquiry : P J McDonald one-day ban: careless riding (Aug 31)
Adrian Nicholls caution: careless riding.
FOCUS
The first two held official marks in the mid to low 80s in this decent claimer which was run at a fair pace. The fourth surely limits the form.

5163 APPLEBY GOLF CLUB H'CAP 5f
3:15 (3:15) (Class 4) (0-85,85) 3-Y-O+ **£4,075** (£1,212; £606; £303) **Stalls** Low

Form RPR
2330 **1** **Verinco**[22] 4416 5-9-1 83 (v) JustinNewman(7) 3 103
(Bryan Smart) *mde all: rdn clr over 1f out: styd on strly: unchal* **10/3**[1]
0005 **2** 5 **Lucky Numbers (IRE)**[5] 5006 5-9-10 85 JamesSullivan 1 87
(Paul Green) *fly-jmpd s: sn chsng ldrs: effrt and wnt 2nd over 1f out: kpt on fnl f: no ch w wnr* **12/1**
5065 **3** hd **The Nifty Fox**[19] 4516 7-9-6 81 (v) TomEaves 8 82
(Tim Easterby) *hld up: rdn and hdwy over 1f out: kpt on fnl f: nvr able to chal* **12/1**
3115 **4** ½ **Saucy Brown (IRE)**[18] 4531 5-9-8 83 AdrianNicholls 9 82
(David Nicholls) *chsd wnr to over 1f out: rdn and kpt on same pce* **4/1**[2]
0302 **5** 1 ½ **Arganil (USA)**[19] 4516 6-9-5 85 (p) JulieBurke(5) 7 79
(Kevin Ryan) *bhd and sn drvn along: edgd rt 2f out: kpt on fnl f: nvr rchd ldrs* **9/2**[3]
5403 **6** ¾ **Captain Scooby**[22] 4405 5-8-5 66 oh1 DuranFentiman 2 57
(Richard Whitaker) *chsd ldrs: drvn and outpcd over 2f out: edgd rt: no imp over 1f out* **8/1**
1306 **7** ¾ **Doc Hay (USA)**[25] 4327 4-9-9 84 StephenCraine 5 73
(Keith Dalgleish) *hld up: rdn along over 2f out: sn n.d* **11/2**
0000 **8** shd **Rash Judgement**[25] 4327 6-9-3 78 RobertWinston 6 66
(Eric Alston) *prom: drvn over 2f out: edgd rt and wknd over 1f out* **20/1**
-050 **9** 1 ¾ **Above The Stars**[11] 4791 3-8-11 77 LeeTopliss(3) 4 59
(Richard Fahey) *bhd and sn pushed along: shortlived effrt on outside 2f out: sn btn* **12/1**
61.22 secs (0.42) **Going Correction** +0.225s/f (Good)
WFA 3 from 4yo+ 2lb **9** Ran SP% **115.6**
Speed ratings (Par 105): **105,97,96,95,93 92,91,90,88**
Tote Swingers: 1&2 £9.10, 1&3 £10.60, 2&3 £25.50 CSF £44.28 CT £431.27 TOTE £3.80: £1.50, £4.50, £3.00; EX 49.00.
Owner B Smart **Bred** Mrs M Gutkin **Trained** Hambleton, N Yorks
FOCUS
There was a wide-margin front-running winner in this decent sprint handicap. Few got involved and only the winner showed his form.
Above The Stars Official explanation: jockey said filly hung left throughout

5164 BUTCHERS ARMS LYVENNET COMMUNITY PUB FILLIES' H'CAP 6f 192y
3:50 (3:52) (Class 4) (0-80,76) 3-Y-O+ **£4,075** (£1,212; £606; £303) **Stalls** Low

Form RPR
2002 **1** **Diablo Dancer**[9] 4854 3-8-10 65 DanielTudhope 7 77+
(Tim Walford) *prom: smooth hdwy to ld wl over 1f out: drvn out fnl f* **11/2**[2]
1-2 **2** 2 ½ **Present Danger**[14] 4670 3-9-7 76 RobertWinston 5 81
(Tom Dascombe) *t.k.h: hld up in tch: effrt and drvn on outside wl over 2f out: drifted rt over 1f out: rallied and chsd wnr wl ins fnl f: r.o* **6/5**[1]
-000 **3** ½ **Ishiadancer**[17] 4574 6-9-3 72 LMcNiff(5) 3 78
(Eric Alston) *trckd ldr: effrt over 2f out: chsd wnr briefly ins fnl f: kpt on same pce* **20/1**
143 **4** ¾ **Bella Noir**[11] 4807 4-9-12 76 (v) AndrewElliott 9 80
(Mrs K Burke) *in tch on outside: effrt over 2f out: edgd lft over 1f out: kpt on same pce fnl f* **11/2**[2]
1010 **5** 3 ¾ **Alluring Star**[9] 4854 3-9-2 71 JamesSullivan 8 63
(Michael Easterby) *trckd ldrs: effrt and ev ch 2f out: sn rdn: wknd ins fnl f* **10/1**[3]
0363 **6** 1 ¾ **Breezolini**[51] 3461 3-9-5 74 MichaelStainton 2 61
(Richard Whitaker) *hld up: rdn 3f out: hdwy over 1f out: kpt on: nvr able to chal* **10/1**[3]
6426 **7** 3 ¼ **First Class Favour (IRE)**[9] 4854 3-9-6 75 DuranFentiman 4 53
(Tim Easterby) *led tl rdn and hdd wl over 1f out: wknd ent fnl f* **12/1**
6000 **8** 2 **Social Rhythm**[14] 4670 7-8-11 61 PJMcDonald 10 36
(Alistair Whillans) *missed break: bhd: drvn over 3f out: shortlived effrt 2f out: sn btn* **40/1**
13-3 **9** 2 ¼ **Indian Giver**[5] 5006 3-8-12 67 TomEaves 1 34
(Hugh McWilliams) *bhd: struggling over 3f out: btn fnl 2f* **14/1**
1m 28.36s (1.26) **Going Correction** +0.225s/f (Good)
WFA 3 from 4yo+ 5lb **9** Ran SP% **116.0**
Speed ratings (Par 102): **101,98,97,96,92 90,86,84,81**
Tote Swingers: 1&2 £2.70, 1&3 £14.40, 2&3 £8.40 CSF £12.51 CT £123.78 TOTE £5.60: £2.40, £1.10, £5.80; EX 13.20.
Owner GB Walford, A Hulme, M Nield, B Howarth **Bred** Steel's Thoroughbred Breeding **Trained** Sheriff Hutton, N Yorks
FOCUS
The leaders probably went off a bit too hard in this fillies' handicap which was won by a relatively unexposed 3-y-o who attracted support. The form is rated around the fourth.

5165 BLAKELAW AND DISTRICT SOCIAL CLUB H'CAP 7f 200y
4:25 (4:26) (Class 6) (0-60,60) 3-Y-O **£1,617** (£481; £240; £120) **Stalls** Low

Form RPR
5020 **1** **Deep Applause**[19] 4505 3-9-3 56 (p) PJMcDonald 2 59
(Michael Dods) *hld up: hdwy on outside over 2f out: drvn and led wl ins fnl f: r.o* **15/2**
6033 **2** ½ **Syncopated Lady (IRE)**[19] 4505 3-8-13 52 (e) DanielTudhope 3 54
(David O'Meara) *t.k.h: trckd ldrs: effrt and led over 1f out: hung rt: hdd ins fnl f: r.o* **11/4**[1]

066 **3** *hd* **Concrete Jungle (IRE)**[49] 3513 3-9-7 **60**.......................... TomEaves 10 62
(Andrew Haynes) *led: rdn and hdd over 1f out: rallied and regained ld briefly ins fnl f: kpt on: hld cl home* **6/1**[3]

2030 **4** *½* **Valley Tiger**[13] 4705 3-9-0 **58**.............................. JamesRogers(5) 5 58
(William Muir) *s.i.s: hld up: nt clr run and swtchd lft over 2f out: kpt on fnl f: hld whn short of room cl home* **9/2**[2]

2330 **5** *½* **Izzet**[18] 4560 3-9-0 **58**.............................. ShaneBKelly(5) 6 57
(Ron Barr) *prom: hdwy and cl up over 2f out: edgd rt over 1f out: no ex ins fnl f* **13/2**

-065 **6** *1 ¼* **Valentine's Gift**[21] 4437 3-9-5 **58**.............................. StephenCraine 11 54
(Neville Bycroft) *cl up: rdn and ev ch over 2f out: no ex ins fnl f* **25/1**

-000 **7** *6* **Norton Girl**[29] 4183 3-8-13 **52**.............................. JamesSullivan 7 35
(Michael Herrington) *t.k.h: cl up tl rdn and wknd wl over 1f out* **20/1**

2560 **8** *nk* **Phair Winter**[26] 4284 3-8-10 **49**.............................. RobertWinston 9 31
(Alan Brown) *bhd: rdn over 3f out: hdwy 2f out: sn no imp: btn fnl f* **9/1**

000 **9** *20* **Ellemental**[19] 4514 3-8-8 **47**.............................. AndrewElliott 4 —
(Mrs K Burke) *t.k.h: trckd ldrs tl rdn and wknd over 2f out* **14/1**

-650 **10** *2 ¾* **Illawalla**[3] 5082 3-8-7 **46** oh1.............................. DuranFentiman 1 —
(Hugh McWilliams) *t.k.h: in tch tl rdn and wknd over 2f out* **25/1**

1m 44.17s (4.17) **Going Correction** +0.225s/f (Good) **10** Ran SP% **113.4**
Speed ratings (Par 98): **88,87,87,86,86 85,79,78,58,56**
Tote Swingers: 1&2 £5.40, 1&3 £8.60, 2&3 £2.10 CSF £26.83 CT £134.58 TOTE £10.10: £2.80, £1.30, £1.20; EX 26.60.
Owner Appleton - Davison - Spinks **Bred** Lady Fairhaven **Trained** Denton, Co Durham
■ Stewards' Enquiry : P J McDonald caution: used whip with excessive frequency.
Daniel Tudhope two-day ban: careless riding (Aug 31-Sep 1)

FOCUS
All of the runners were maidens in this minor handicap. It was run at a steady pace and there was a tight finish. The first and second were close to their Thirsk form last month.
Deep Applause Official explanation: trainer's rep said, regarding apparent improvement in form, that the gelding was better suited by the slower ground.

5166 CHEVIOT AMATEUR RIDERS' H'CAP (DIV I) 1m 6f 32y
5:00 (5:00) (Class 6) (0-60,60) 4-Y-0+ **£1,646** (£506; £253) **Stalls** Low

Form RPR
00/2 **1** **Bocciani (GER)**[84] 1833 6-10-5 **58**.............................. MrJohnWilley(7) 5 73
(Brian Ellison) *chsd clr ldr: hdwy to ld over 2f out: drifted lft: edgd rt and drvn out fnl f* **11/2**[2]

56/1 **2** *1 ¼* **Circus Clown (IRE)**[11] 4785 6-10-7 **53**.............................. MrsCBartley 2 66
(Jim Goldie) *in tch: sn niggled along: rdn and hdwy over 3f out: ev ch over 1f out: kpt on: hld towards fin* **7/4**[1]

-001 **3** *11* **Daytime Dreamer (IRE)**[16] 4605 7-10-9 **58**.............. LucyAlexander(3) 3 56
(Martin Todhunter) *hld up: shkn up over 3f out: sn outpcd: kpt on fnl 2f: nt pce of first two* **12/1**

0324 **4** *nk* **Heart Of Dubai (USA)**[16] 4602 6-10-5 **56**..................(p) MissRSmith(5) 6 53
(Micky Hammond) *in tch: rdn and outpcd over 3f out: plugged on fnl 2f: no imp* **13/2**[3]

0063 **5** *3 ¼* **Oddsmaker (IRE)**[5] 4982 10-10-9 **60**..............(t) MissAngelaBarnes(5) 10 53
(Maurice Barnes) *led and sn clr: hdd over 2f out: wknd over 1f out* **13/2**[3]

0/ **6** *8* **Bold Apache (IRE)**[10] 3341 7-9-11 **48**.............................. MrGWatters(5) 8 29
(J J Lambe, Ire) *t.k.h: chsd ldrs: drvn and outpcd over 3f out: btn fr 2f out* **25/1**

50 **7** *¾* **Ancient Times (USA)**[6] 4951 4-9-13 **50**..................(p) MissHBethell(5) 9 30
(Philip Kirby) *bhd: struggling over 4f out: nvr on terms* **14/1**

/046 **8** *8* **Sergeant Pink (IRE)**[16] 4602 5-10-11 **60**................(p) MissECSayer(3) 1 29
(Dianne Sayer) *in tch: outpcd 6f out: btn fnl 3f* **10/1**

2040 **9** *5* **Ritsi**[9] 4856 8-9-10 **49**.............................. MissNHayes(7) 7 11
(Marjorie Fife) *bhd: rdn over 4f out: sn struggling: nvr on terms* **12/1**

3m 13.85s (6.35) **Going Correction** +0.225s/f (Good) **9** Ran SP% **113.4**
Speed ratings (Par 101): **90,89,83,82,80 76,75,71,68**
Tote Swingers: 1&2 £3.50, 1&3 £8.50, 2&3 £4.80 CSF £15.19 CT £109.17 TOTE £5.00: £1.80, £1.40, £3.20; EX 10.60.
Owner John Macgregor **Bred** Saturn Stable **Trained** Norton, N Yorks
■ John Willey's first winner.

FOCUS
The two market leaders pulled well clear in this amateur riders' handicap. Modest form with the front pair on good marks compared with their jumps ratings.

5167 CHEVIOT AMATEUR RIDERS' H'CAP (DIV II) 1m 6f 32y
5:30 (5:30) (Class 6) (0-60,60) 4-Y-0+ **£1,646** (£506; £253) **Stalls** Low

Form RPR
0310 **1** **Brasingaman Eric**[24] 4366 4-10-6 **57**.............................. MrMGarnett(5) 8 66
(George Moore) *chsd ldrs: effrt and hdwy over 3f out: led over 1f out: styd on wl* **4/1**[1]

4125 **2** *2* **Terenzium (IRE)**[11] 4785 9-10-3 **54**..........................(p) MissRSmith(5) 6 59
(Micky Hammond) *hld up: stdy hdwy over 4f out: effrt 2f out: chsd (clr) wnr ins fnl f: r.o* **16/1**

066 **3** *1 ¾* **Bavarian Nordic (USA)**[26] 4294 6-10-12 **58**.............................. MissJCoward 5 61
(Richard Whitaker) *in tch: stdy hdwy 1/2-way: led over 4f out to over 1f out: kpt on same pce ins fnl f* **13/2**

0650 **4** *4 ½* **Kingsdale Orion (IRE)**[8] 4879 7-10-9 **60**.................... MissHBethell(5) 9 56+
(Brian Ellison) *bhd: pushed along over 4f out: styd on fnl 2f: nvr able to chal* **9/2**[2]

4400 **5** *3 ¼* **Spahi (FR)**[3] 5079 5-9-13 **52**.............................. MrSMurray(7) 10 44
(David O'Meara) *hld up: stdy hdwy over 3f out: rdn and hung rt over 1f out: sn btn* **5/1**[3]

0-02 **6** *4* **Clueless**[11] 4785 9-10-2 **55**.............................. MissElrving(7) 3 41
(Keith Dalgleish) *cl up: outpcd over 4f out: n.d after* **15/2**

0400 **7** *1 ¼* **Rare Coincidence**[16] 4602 10-10-0 **49**..........................(p) MrCMartin(3) 7 33
(Alan Berry) *led and sn clr: hdd over 4f out: wknd 2f out* **7/1**

8 *nk* **Storm Breaker (IRE)**[18] 4568 9-10-9 **60**..................(tp) MrGWatters(5) 2 44
(J J Lambe, Ire) *rn wout declared tongue-tie: hld up: shkn up over 4f out: nvr on terms* **14/1**

5000 **9** *8* **Verluga (IRE)**[16] 4604 4-9-11 **50**.............................. MrWEasterby(7) 4 23
(Tim Easterby) *in tch: lost pl after 4f: n.d after* **16/1**

0666 **10** *33* **Deferto Delphi**[7] 4903 4-10-0 **49**.............................. LucyAlexander(3) 1 —
(Barry Murtagh) *plld hrd: hld up: rdn over 4f out: sn struggling: t.o* **14/1**

3m 15.55s (8.05) **Going Correction** +0.225s/f (Good) **10** Ran SP% **117.5**
Speed ratings (Par 101): **86,84,83,81,79 77,76,76,71,52**
Tote Swingers: 1&2 £7.10, 1&3 £4.80, 2&3 £19.30. Tote Super 7: Win: Not won. Place: £1,944.00 CSF £69.21 CT £411.88 TOTE £5.20: £1.70, £2.30, £2.90; EX 50.40.
Owner R Morgan **Bred** Mrs Heather Morgan **Trained** Middleham Moor, N Yorks
■ Stewards' Enquiry : Mr S Murray caution: careless riding; three-day ban: used whip with excessive frequency down shoulder in the forehand (Sep 9,13,20)

FOCUS
The second division of a handicap for amateur riders'. The pace was decent, although the time was a bit slower than division I, and the favourite delivered with a bit in hand. The winner continued his gradual progress.
T/Plt: £54.20 to a £1 stake. Pool of £38,295.00 - 515.32 winning tickets. T/Qpdt: £7.70 to a £1 stake. Pool of £2,765.00 - 262.65 winning tickets. RY

4708 FOLKESTONE (R-H)
Wednesday, August 17

OFFICIAL GOING: Good to firm (8.4)
Home bend moved out 3m, bend after winning post moved in 3m.
Wind: light, half against Weather: light cloud, rain later

5168 KMFM ESSENTIAL 90'S VIP PRIZEWINNER AMATEUR RIDERS' H'CAP 1m 4f
5:25 (5:27) (Class 5) (0-70,70) 3-Y-0+ **£2,305** (£709; £354) **Stalls** High

Form RPR
6106 **1** **Bavarica**[16] 4613 9-10-7 **70**.............................. MissSBirkett(7) 5 77
(Julia Feilden) *stdd s: hld up in last: stl last and swtchd rt wl over 1f out: str run ins fnl f to ld wl towards fin* **5/1**[3]

0312 **2** *½* **Come On The Irons (USA)**[12] 4746 3-9-3 **62** ow1(t) MissKMargarson(7) 3 68
(Ralph Smith) *led: rdn and edgd lft wl over 1f out: kpt on wl and ev ch after tl no ex wl ins fnl f* **3/1**[1]

4500 **3** *½* **Taste The Wine (IRE)**[6] 4952 5-9-11 **58**.................... MrRJWilliams(5) 8 63
(Bernard Llewellyn) *hld up: hdwy on inner 3f out: rdn to ld over 1f out: hdd jst ins fnl f: unable qck fnl 100yds* **5/1**[3]

1/ **4** *hd* **King's Road**[30] 4167 6-10-4 **60**..................................(t) MissGAndrews 2 65
(Anabel K Murphy) *hld up in tch: dropped to last pair 5f out: swtchd lft and gd hdwy 2f out: ev ch and carried lft over 1f out: drvn ahd jst ins fnl f: hdd and lost 3 pls towards fin* **7/2**[2]

0-04 **5** *6* **Winning Show**[8] 4318 7-9-2 **51** oh4......................(vt) MissFHickman(7) 1 46
(Chris Gordon) *chsd ldrs: rdn and unable qck whn short of room and swtchd lft 2f out: wknd over 1f out* **25/1**

1133 **6** *5* **Carlton Scroop (FR)**[9] 4846 8-10-9 **70**.............................. MissMBryant(5) 7 57
(Paddy Butler) *pressed ldr tl edgd rt and pushed along 2f out: wknd over 1f out* **12/1**

00/4 **7** *3 ½* **The Ducking Stool**[17] 4578 4-9-9 **51** oh5.............................. MrRBirkett 4 33
(Julia Feilden) *t.k.h: chsd ldrs: lost pl and rdn over 2f out: wknd 2f out* **7/1**

-503 **8** *6* **Hotfoot**[20] 4454 4-9-11 **53**.............................. MissEJJones 6 25
(John Berry) *t.k.h: hld up in tch: rdn and no hdwy over 2f out: wknd wl over 1f out: wl btn whn hung rt ent fnl f* **8/1**

2m 42.84s (1.94) **Going Correction** +0.10s/f (Good)
WFA 3 from 4yo+ 10lb **8** Ran SP% **115.7**
Speed ratings (Par 103): **97,96,96,96,92 88,86,82**
Tote Swingers: 1&2 £3.90, 1&3 £6.10, 2&3 £4.10 CSF £20.68 CT £78.85 TOTE £9.80: £3.20, £1.10, £1.60; EX 23.90 Trifecta £155.00 Pool: £3,905.36 - 18.64 winning units..
Owner Miss J Feilden **Bred** Juddmonte Farms **Trained** Exning, Suffolk
■ The first winner for Shelley Birkett, daughter of the winning trainer.

FOCUS
The principals pulled clear off just a fair pace for this modest amateur riders' handicap. The form is ordinary.
The Ducking Stool Official explanation: jockey said filly was unsuited by the track.

5169 PERSONNEL HEALTH & SAFETY CONSULTANTS MAIDEN STKS 1m 1f 149y
5:55 (5:58) (Class 5) 3-Y-0+ **£2,385** (£704; £352) **Stalls** Centre

Form RPR
040 **1** **Direct Answer (USA)**[[illegible]] 2974 4-9-11 80.............................. PatDobbs 11 82+
(Sir Michael Stoute) *chsd ldrs tl led over 7f out: mde rest: rdn and fnd ex over 1f out: in command and rdn out hands and heels fnl f* **5/2**[1]

2 *2 ¼* **Landaman (IRE)** 3-9-3 0.............................. FrannyNorton 10 77+
(Mark Johnston) *s.i.s: t.k.h: hld up in tch tl dashed up to chse wnr over 6f out: ev ch 3f out: drvn and nt pce of wnr over 1f out: styd on same pce after* **7/1**

00 **3** *¾* **Sister Andrea**[11] 4800 3-8-12 0.............................. JackMitchell 2 71?
(James Fanshawe) *taken down early: broke wl and led: sn hdd: steadily lost pl and rr but stl wl in tch 5f out: swtchd lft and hdwy wl over 2f out: chsd ldng pair over 1f out: styd on same pce fnl f* **100/1**

4 *2 ½* **Yasir (USA)** 3-9-3 0.............................. EddieAhern 9 70+
(Saeed Bin Suroor) *s.i.s: in tch in rr: rdn and effrt wl over 1f out: edgd rt and hdwy over 1f out: styd on steadily fnl f: nvr trbld ldrs* **7/1**

3062 **5** *nk* **Muqtarrib (IRE)**[18] 4529 3-9-3 79.............................. TadhgO'Shea 7 70
(Brian Meehan) *dwlt and pushed along early: hdwy to chse ldrs over 5f out: ev ch and rdn wl over 2f out: drvn and nt qckn 2f out: wknd over 1f out* **7/2**[3]

4002 **6** *1 ½* **Heatherbird**[21] 4448 3-8-12 74.............................. DaneO'Neill 4 62+
(William Jarvis) *taken down early: t.k.h: hld up in tch: hdwy to chse ldng trio 3f out: rdn and unable qck on outer 2f out: sn outpcd and no threat to ldrs after* **11/4**[2]

04 **7** *9* **Isometric (USA)**[14] 4663 3-9-3 0.............................. AhmedAjtebi 3 54
(Mahmood Al Zarooni) *plld hrd: chsd ldrs tl lost pl over 6f out: rdn and no rspnse jst over 2f out: sn wknd and edgd rt: eased ins fnl f* **13/2**

03 **8** *¾* **Lupa Montana (USA)**[35] 3980 3-8-12 0.............................. MartinLane 1 50
(Ralph Beckett) *t.k.h: led sn after s tl hdd over 7f out: chsd ldrs after: losing pl and hit rail bnd 3f out: sn wknd: wl btn and eased ins fnl f* **20/1**

9 *39* **Prince Ayoob** 3-9-3 0.............................. LukeMorris 6 —
(John Best) *chsd ldrs: sn pushed along: grad lost pl and last over 6f out: sn rdn and struggling: lost tch 4f out: t.o* **80/1**

2m 5.16s (0.26) **Going Correction** +0.10s/f (Good)
WFA 3 from 4yo 8lb **9** Ran SP% **122.8**
Speed ratings (Par 103): **102,100,99,97,97 96,88,88,57**
Tote Swingers: 1&2 £2.90, 1&3 £43.30, 2&3 £61.10 CSF £22.15 TOTE £5.60: £1.80, £2.10, £11.90; EX 21.90 Trifecta £920.30 Pool: £2,487.36 - 2.00 winning units..
Owner K Abdulla **Bred** Juddmonte Farms Inc **Trained** Newmarket, Suffolk

FOCUS
Not that strong a pace for this ordinary looking maiden, but hard to take anything away from the performance of the winner. The winner only needed to match his 3-y-o form to score and is rated to that.

Lupa Montana(USA) Official explanation: jockey said filly hung badly right

5170 RSA ENVIRONMENTAL HEALTH MAIDEN AUCTION STKS — 7f (S)
6:30 (6:30) (Class 6) 2-Y-O — **£1,704** (£503; £251) **Stalls** High

Form — RPR

0 **1** **What's Up (IRE)**[57] 3257 2-8-8 0 .... EddieAhern 1 — 71
(Jim Boyle) *racd off the pce in midfield: rdn 1/2-way: sme hdwy and swtchd rt 2f out: chsd clr ldr and hung lft over 1f out: kpt on and clsd u.p ins fnl f: led fnl 50yds* **25/1**

0432 **2** *1 1/4* **Tidal's Baby**[14] 4682 2-8-11 74 .... (p) DaneO'Neill 5 — 71
(Noel Quinlan) *led: rdn and wnt clr wl over 1f out: looked wnr tl tired u.p ins fnl f: hdd fnl 50yds: sn btn* **15/8**[1]

0 **3** *5* **Loved By All (IRE)**[11] 4804 2-8-11 0 .... EddieCreighton 2 — 59+
(Brian Meehan) *sn rdn and wl outpcd towards rr: stl modest 7th and swtchd lft over 2f out: hdwy and swtchd rt over 1f out: kpt on to go 3rd fnl 100yds: nvr trbld ldrs* **16/1**

4 *1/2* **Enery (IRE)** 2-8-11 0 .... AhmedAjtebi 7 — 57+
(Mahmood Al Zarooni) *sn wl outpcd in rr: sme hdwy 3f out: stl only modest 6th over 2f out: styd on to press for 3rd whn edgd rt ins fnl 100yds: no imp after: nvr trbld ldrs* **11/4**[2]

2202 **5** *2* **Sheila's Buddy**[13] 4698 2-8-9 71 .... LiamKeniry 6 — 50
(J S Moore) *chsd ldr tl 3f out: rdn and chsd clr ldr again 2f out: no imp and wl btn over 1f out: wknd and lost 2 pls ins fnl f* **5/1**

0632 **6** *4 1/2* **Monessa (IRE)**[13] 4708 2-8-4 67 .... ChrisCatlin 9 — 34
(Edward Creighton) *sn bustled along to chse ldrs: rdn and struggling 1/2-way: wknd wl over 2f out* **9/2**[3]

7 *8* **Three Tenors** 2-8-4 0 .... RyanPowell(5) 4 — 19
(J S Moore) *s.i.s: a outpcd in rr: wl btn whn nt clr run and swtchd lft over 1f out: n.d* **40/1**

00 **8** *7* **The Boomingbittern**[18] 4545 2-8-4 0 .... FrankieMcDonald 8 — —
(Edward Creighton) *s.i.s: nvr gng pce and a in rr: t.o 1/2-way* **125/1**

9 *2 1/2* **Mount Mayday (IRE)** 2-8-11 0 .... WilliamCarson 3 — —
(Stuart Williams) *s.i.s: sn rcvrd and racd off the pce in midfield: hdwy and rdn to chse ldr 3f out tl 2f out: sn wknd rapidly: wl bhd and eased ins fnl f: t.o* **33/1**

1m 28.27s (0.97) **Going Correction** +0.10s/f (Good) — **9** Ran SP% **112.2**
Speed ratings (Par 92): **98,96,90,90,88 82,73,65,62**
Tote Swingers: 1&2 £7.90, 1&3 £20.10, 2&3 £5.10 CSF £69.35 TOTE £32.80: £5.90, £1.10, £3.80; EX 129.80 Trifecta £527.90 Pool: £3,923.77 - 5.50 winning units..
Owner A & A **Bred** Crone Stud Farms Ltd **Trained** Epsom, Surrey

FOCUS
With the majority of form on offer this will, probably, turn out to be a weak maiden overall. The runner-up is rated to the balance of his better efforts.

NOTEBOOK
What's Up(IRE) showed a very willing attitude and, when the penny finally dropped, finished with a strong run to win with plenty in hand. Clearly she has benefitted from her debut when well beaten at Newbury, even though she remained rather green here for most of this race, but she did pick up well and can go on from this. (op 22-1 tchd 33-1)

Tidal's Baby, with cheekpieces back on (gelded since last worn), looked all over the winner from over a furlong out, after dictating a fair pace, only to get collared in the closing stages, costing in-running punters a princely sum. He looks on a high enough mark in handicaps, but should find a small opening. (op 5-2)

Loved By All(IRE) struggled to make an impact in a good maiden on debut when 28/1 and again struggled to get involved here. Hard to say this was a better effort as it was a much weaker race, but she was staying on past weakening horses in the latter stages. (op 14-1)

Enery(IRE) is a cheap purchase for connections, costing only £10,000 earlier this year after going through the ring as a yearling for 60,000gns. He was struggling to go the early pace and could never land a blow before fading from over a furlong out. (op 2-1 tchd 3-1)

Sheila's Buddy is looking exposed in nurseries and will not get many better opportunities than this when contesting maidens. (tchd 4-1)

5171 INSPECTION SERVICES (UK) H'CAP — 7f (S)
7:00 (7:01) (Class 4) (0-80,80) 3-Y-O — **£2,781** (£2,781; £634) **Stalls** High

Form — RPR

6366 **1** **Apollo D'Negro (IRE)**[24] 4353 3-8-12 71 .... (v[1]) AdamKirby 7 — 79
(Clive Cox) *pressed ldr: rdn to ld narrowly over 1f out: drvn and kpt on wl ins fnl f: jnd on post* **13/2**[3]

0135 **1** *dht* **Silverware (USA)**[28] 4214 3-9-2 75 .... PatDobbs 11 — 83
(Richard Hannon) *led: rdn wl over 1f out: narrowly hdd over 1f out: n.m.r but battled on gamely fnl f: jnd rival on post* **10/1**

4565 **3** *nk* **Yair Hill (IRE)**[46] 3634 3-9-2 75 .... EddieAhern 8 — 82
(John Dunlop) *chsd ldrs: rdn and ev ch over 1f out: drvn and kpt on same pce ins fnl f* **9/2**[2]

0524 **4** *2 1/2* **Sluggsy Morant**[18] 4550 3-9-5 78 .... DaneO'Neill 6 — 78+
(Henry Candy) *hld up towards rr on inner: swtchd rt and effrt 2f out: kpt on ins fnl f: nvr able to chal* **7/2**[1]

3162 **5** *hd* **Midnight Feast**[11] 4797 3-9-7 80 .... LukeMorris 9 — 80
(Peter Winkworth) *t.k.h: rdn and outpcd whn edgd rt 2f out: kpt on same pce u.p fnl f* **15/2**

3060 **6** *6* **Golden Taurus (IRE)**[51] 3461 3-8-10 72 .... PatrickHills(3) 10 — 56
(J W Hills) *s.i.s: hld up in last pair: swtchd rt and effrt wl over 1f out: sn no imp and btn over 1f out: wknd* **28/1**

5146 **7** *nk* **Above Standard (IRE)**[28] 4214 3-8-12 76 .... MatthewLawson(5) 3 — 59
(B W Hills) *hld up in tch towards rr: hdwy to chse ldrs ent fnl 2f: rdn and unable qck wl over 1f out: wknd over 1f out* **9/2**[2]

1-05 **8** *2* **Charles Fosterkane**[5] 4994 3-9-1 74 .... LiamKeniry 5 — 51
(John Best) *t.k.h: hld up in tch towards rr: rdn and racing awkwardly 3f out: wknd over 2f out: sn lost tch* **10/1**

3442 **9** *1/2* **Custom House (IRE)**[13] 4709 3-8-8 67 .... RichardThomas 4 — 43
(John E Long) *wnt rt s: chsd ldrs: rdn over 2f out: wknd u.p wl over 1f out* **20/1**

0134 **10** *1 1/2* **Isingy Red (FR)**[28] 4214 3-8-10 72 .... MatthewDavies(3) 1 — 44
(Jim Boyle) *restless in stalls: stdd and dropped in bhd after s: t.k.h: hld up in last pair: short-lived effrt 2f out: sn wknd* **12/1**

1m 27.5s (0.20) **Going Correction** +0.10s/f (Good) — **10** Ran SP% **117.8**
Speed ratings (Par 102): **102,102,101,98,98 91,91,89,88,86**Win: Silverware £7.90 Apollo D'Negro £4.40 Place: S £4.30 ADN £2.50 Yair Hill £1.90 Ex: S,ADN £21.80 ADN,S £32.30 CSF: S,ADN £37.15 ADN,S £35.18 Tricast: S,ADN,Y £169.28 ADN,S,Y £162.68 Toteswinger: S,ADN £9.60 S,Y £6.10 ADN,Y £6.00., £027, £Owner, £Gwyn Powell and Peter RidgersBred Patrick Cummins Trifecta £Trained Lambourn, Berks.
Owner Mrs J Wood **Bred** Alliand Equine **Trained** East Everleigh, Wilts
■ Stewards' Enquiry : Pat Dobbs two-day ban: used whip down shoulder in the forehand (Aug 31-Sep 1)

FOCUS
Little got into this competitive-looking handicap which produced a cracking finish off a decent pace. A dead-heat was the eventual outcome with the third only a neck behind. The form is rated around the dead-heaters.

5172 TIME AND TIDE WAIT FOR NO HORSE H'CAP — 6f
7:30 (7:30) (Class 6) (0-65,63) 3-Y-O — **£1,704** (£503; £251) **Stalls** High

Form — RPR

6-00 **1** **Jahanara (IRE)**[46] 3633 3-9-7 63 .... PatDobbs 7 — 72+
(Richard Hannon) *w ldrs: sltly hmpd and swtchd rt jst over 2f out: rdn and rallied to chal ins fnl f: led fnl 75yds: eased cl home* **4/1**[2]

0-60 **2** *3/4* **Cool Water Oasis**[13] 4705 3-8-12 54 ow1 .... AdamKirby 8 — 58
(Rae Guest) *dwlt: in tch: hdwy to chse ldrs over 2f out: drvn to chal over 1f out: ev ch ins fnl f: styd on same pce fnl 100yds* **5/2**[1]

6346 **3** *3/4* **Novabridge**[37] 3908 3-9-4 60 .... (b) MartinLane 5 — 62
(Andrew Haynes) *led: edgd lft to stands' rail jst over 2f out: drvn over 1f out: hdd fnl 75yds: sn btn and wknd cl home* **4/1**[2]

0-63 **4** *6* **Whitstable Native**[10] 4828 3-8-9 58 .... GeorgeanBuckell(7) 3 — 41
(John Best) *in tch: rdn and unable qck wl over 1f out: wknd and hung lft over 1f out* **5/2**[1]

-606 **5** *6* **Aurivorous**[75] 2660 3-9-3 59 .... RussKennemore 4 — 23
(Anabel K Murphy) *stdd s: hld up in last pair: rdn and short-lived effrt 2f out: sn wknd: wl btn whn sltly hmpd over 1f out* **25/1**

0345 **6** *2 1/2* **Prophet In A Dream**[12] 4744 3-9-1 60 .... (bt[1]) RobertLButler(3) 6 — 16
(Paddy Butler) *sn bustled along to press ldrs: lost pl and hrd drvn 1/2-way: wl bhd over 1f out* **8/1**[3]

1m 13.9s (1.20) **Going Correction** +0.10s/f (Good) — **6** Ran SP% **112.1**
Speed ratings (Par 98): **96,95,94,86,78 74**
Tote Swingers: 1&2 £2.80, 1&3 £2.20, 2&3 £2.70 CSF £14.36 CT £40.74 TOTE £5.60: £3.10, £3.40; EX 27.20 Trifecta £141.20 Pool: £2,289.96 - 12.00 winning units..
Owner K N Dhunjibhoy, V B Shirke, B M Desai **Bred** Ballyhane Stud **Trained** East Everleigh, Wilts

FOCUS
Light rain had started to fall before this moderate low-grade handicap. The form looks weak with the second rated to her juvenile best backed up by the third.
Jahanara(IRE) Official explanation: trainer's rep said, regarding apparent improvement in form, that the filly benefited from having a ring bit, which helped it settle, and being dropped back in trip having run over 7f and 1m.

5173 LESLEY EVANS 1 OF 60 SENSIBLE THINGS H'CAP — 5f
8:00 (8:00) (Class 5) (0-75,73) 3-Y-O+ — **£2,385** (£704; £352) **Stalls** High

Form — RPR

0630 **1** **Straboe (USA)**[8] 4895 5-8-7 56 .... (v) WilliamCarson 5 — 63
(Stuart Williams) *chsd ldrs: drvn and squeezed through on rail and ev ch over 1f out: led fnl 50yds: styd on wl* **13/2**

4064 **2** *nk* **Caledonia Princess**[5] 4988 5-9-6 72 .... MarkLawson(3) 3 — 78+
(Jo Hughes) *sn pushed along: hdwy 2f out: drvn to ld over 1f out: kpt on u.p tl hdd and no ex fnl 50yds* **5/2**[2]

3045 **3** *shd* **Magical Speedfit (IRE)**[14] 4659 6-9-5 73 .... RyanPowell(5) 4 — 79
(George Margarson) *sn outpcd in last and pushed along: rdn and hdwy over 1f out: styd on ins f: nt quite rch ldrs* **7/1**

2110 **4** *1 1/2* **Clear Ice (IRE)**[4] 5053 4-9-10 73 .... (b) ChrisCatlin 1 — 75
(Gay Kelleway) *chsd ldr tl over 1f out: kpt on same pce u.p after: hld whn nt clr run nr fin* **2/1**[1]

1034 **5** *4 1/2* **Miss Polly Plum**[13] 4731 4-9-5 71 .... (p) MartinHarley(3) 2 — 55
(Chris Dwyer) *taken down early: led at fast gallop: rdn: edgd rt and hdd over 1f out: wknd 1f out* **7/2**[3]

60.74 secs (0.74) **Going Correction** +0.10s/f (Good) — **5** Ran SP% **110.0**
Speed ratings (Par 103): **98,97,97,94,87**
CSF £22.74 TOTE £5.50: £3.90, £2.40; EX 13.60.
Owner Brigid & Damian Hennessy-Bourke **Bred** Darley **Trained** Newmarket, Suffolk

FOCUS
Only five runners, but a fast early pace for a tight little sprint handicap. The third looks the best guide to the level.
T/Plt: £335.80 to a £1 stake. Pool of £51,109.00 - 111.10 winning tickets. T/Qpdt: £72.40 to a £1 stake. Pool of £5,647.00 - 57.70 winning tickets. SP

5017 NOTTINGHAM (L-H)
Wednesday, August 17

OFFICIAL GOING: Good to firm (firm in places in back straight; 7.7)
All races on outer course and rail at normal configuration and distances as advertised.
Wind: Almost nil Weather: Cloudy

5174 BRITISH STALLION STUDS SUPPORTING BRITISH RACING EBF MAIDEN STKS — 5f 13y
1:50 (1:53) (Class 5) 2-Y-O — **£3,234** (£962; £481; £240) **Stalls** Centre

Form — RPR

2345 **1** **Beau Mistral (IRE)**[11] 4787 2-8-12 68 .... CathyGannon 4 — 69
(Paul Green) *sn led: shkn up ins fnl f: r.o* **5/1**[3]

205 **2** *2* **Blanc De Chine (IRE)**[13] 4720 2-8-12 72 .... WilliamBuick 10 — 62
(Peter Makin) *chsd ldrs: rdn and swtchd lft over 1f out: styd on* **2/1**[1]

0 **3** *1 1/2* **Rusty Rocket (IRE)**[26] 4283 2-9-3 0 .... JamesDoyle 5 — 62
(Paul Green) *chsd ldr: rdn and edgd lft over 1f out: no ex ins fnl f* **100/1**

353 **4** *1* **The Rising (IRE)**[21] 4436 2-9-3 71 .... (v) RichardMullen 3 — 58
(Ed McMahon) *s.i.s: sn prom: rdn 1/2-way: no ex fnl f* **5/2**[2]

30 **5** *2 3/4* **Sunley Valentine**[20] 4471 2-8-12 0 .... SamHitchcott 6 — 43
(Mick Channon) *s.i.s: sn pushed along in rr: hdwy over 1f out: nt trble ldrs* **13/2**

0 **6** *5* **Look At Me Now**[9] 4857 2-9-3 0 .... PatCosgrave 8 — 35+
(Jim Boyle) *hld up: pushed along 1/2-way: nvr on terms* **10/1**

05 **7** *1 1/4* **Heidi's Delight (IRE)**[14] 4668 2-8-9 0 .... DaleSwift(3) 2 — 21
(Ann Duffield) *s.i.s: sn pushed along in rr: wknd 1/2-way* **80/1**

8 *4 1/2* **Talya's Storm** 2-8-10 0 .... RaulDaSilva(7) 7 — —
(Jeremy Gask) *s.s: outpcd* **20/1**

504 **9** *3/4* **Lady Cresta (IRE)**[15] 4629 2-8-12 45 .... TomMcLaughlin 9 — —
(Ronald Harris) *prom tl rdn and wknd wl over 1f out* **100/1**

10 *1 1/4* **Oakbrook** 2-9-3 0 .... DavidNolan 11 — —
(Ann Duffield) *sn pushed along in rr: wknd 2f out* **33/1**

61.44 secs (0.44) **Going Correction** +0.025s/f (Good) — **10** Ran SP% **111.9**
Speed ratings (Par 94): **97,93,91,89,85 77,75,68,67,65**
Tote Swingers: 1&2 £1.20, 1&3 £50.80, 2&3 £24.50 CSF £14.37 TOTE £4.80: £1.20, £2.10, £25.30; EX 18.30.
Owner The Winsor Not Group **Bred** John McEnery **Trained** Lydiate, Merseyside

FOCUS
An ordinary-looking race, in which the near-side rail looked the place to be.

NOTEBOOK
Beau Mistral(IRE), the most experienced of these, got across from a low draw to bag the rail and kept going to hold off all challengers. Exposed and officially rated 68, one would imagine she'll do well to hold her own in handicaps off a revised mark, although her bravery will be an asset. (op 9-2)
Blanc De Chine(IRE), the highest-rated of those already with an official mark, is starting to look a little disappointing, as she had every chance in this but wasn't able to trouble the winner deep inside the final furlong. (op 13-8)
Rusty Rocket(IRE) trailed home last at Thirsk on debut, so this was considerably better after showing good pace.
The Rising(IRE), dropping in distance, had some fair form already but didn't look to appreciate this trip. One would imagine he'll be better over further. (op 11-4)
Sunley Valentine had shown ability in two previous starts (both 7f), and didn't look suited by the drop in distance. She'll be of some interest in handicaps over further. (op 9-1)
Talya's Storm, whose dam placed over 7f, was very slowly away on his debut and lost all chance at the start.

5175 REWARDS4RACING.CO.UK H'CAP — 5f 13y
2:20 (2:25) (Class 6) (0-60,58) 4-Y-0+ — **£1,940** (£577; £288; £144) **Stalls** Centre

Form — RPR
0041 **1** — **Crimson Queen**^{5} 5019 4-9-6 **57** 6ex.......... JamesDoyle 7 — 71+
(Roy Brotherton) *chsd ldrs: swtchd lft and led over 1f out: rdn out* **85/40**^{1}
0 **2** *1 1/4* **Avonvalley**^{83} 2424 4-8-8 **45**.......... RobbieFitzpatrick 5 — 53
(Peter Grayson) *sn pushed along in rr: hdwy over 1f out: swtchd lft ins fnl f: r.o* **50/1**
0215 **3** *2 1/4* **Spic 'n Span**^{8} 4882 6-9-4 **55**..........(v) KirstyMilczarek 8 — 54
(Ronald Harris) *led: rdn and hdd over 1f out: no ex ins fnl f* **15/2**
0551 **4** *nk* **Francis Albert**^{8} 4895 5-9-7 **58** 6ex.......... JimmyQuinn 4 — 56
(Michael Mullineaux) *s.i.s: sn prom: rdn over 1f out: styd on same pce ins fnl f* **6/1**
0120 **5** *nk* **Jolly Ranch**^{27} 4224 5-9-7 **58**.......... FergusSweeney 6 — 55
(Tony Newcombe) *chsd ldr tl rdn over 1f out: no ex whn hmpd ins fnl f* **5/1**^{3}
2013 **6** *1 1/4* **Pinball (IRE)**^{10} 4820 5-9-1 **55**..........(p) RobertLButler$^{(3)}$ 3 — 48
(Lisa Williamson) *s.s: bhd and swtchd lft 1/2-way: rdn over 1f out: wknd ins fnl f* **16/1**
-404 **7** *nse* **Greek Secret**^{21} 4443 8-9-0 **56**..........(b) JamesO'Reilly$^{(5)}$ 1 — 49
(Deborah Sanderson) *sn pushed along in rr: rdn 1/2-way: n.d* **17/2**
2446 **8** *1 1/2* **Lees Anthem**^{19} 4504 4-9-3 **57**.......... DaleSwift$^{(3)}$ 2 — 44
(Colin Teague) *sn pushed along and prom: rdn 1/2-way: wknd fnl f* **9/2**^{2}

60.73 secs (-0.27) **Going Correction** +0.025s/f (Good) — **8** Ran SP% **111.3**
Speed ratings (Par 101): **103,101,97,96,96 94,94,91**
Tote Swingers: 1&2 £22.40, 1&3 £3.60, 2&3 £13.80 CSF £103.63 CT £656.05 TOTE £2.90: £1.10, £10.60, £1.20; EX 87.80.
Owner Arthur Clayton **Bred** Cheveley Park Stud Ltd **Trained** Elmley Castle, Worcs
■ Stewards' Enquiry : Robbie Fitzpatrick one-day ban: careless riding (Aug 31)

FOCUS
Plenty of speedy types took their chance in this, so the pace was always going to be strong. The first three raced closest to the rail and the winner was value for a bit extra.

5176 RACING HERE AGAIN 28TH SEPTEMBER MAIDEN STKS — 5f 13y
2:55 (2:57) (Class 5) 3-4-Y-O — **£2,264** (£673; £336; £168) **Stalls** Centre

Form — RPR
2550 **1** — **Crew Cut (IRE)**^{16} 4615 3-8-10 68.......... RaulDaSilva$^{(7)}$ 5 — 71
(Jeremy Gask) *a.p: rdn to chse ldr and hung lft over 1f out: r.o to ld wl ins fnl f* **11/8**^{1}
5552 **2** *3/4* **Eshoog (IRE)**^{7} 4923 3-8-5 69..........(bt) LeonnaMayor$^{(7)}$ 6 — 63
(Phil McEntee) *led: shkn up over 1f out: edgd lft and hdd wl ins fnl f* **7/2**^{3}
4365 **3** *8* **Lady Excellentia (IRE)**^{15} 4631 3-8-12 43.......... TomMcLaughlin 2 — 34
(Ronald Harris) *s.i.s: hld up: hdwy 1/2-way: rdn over 1f out: wknd ins fnl f* **66/1**
0052 **4** *nk* **Control Chief**^{11} 4796 3-9-3 58.......... StevieDonohoe 1 — 38
(Ralph Beckett) *sn pushed along and prom: rdn and outpcd 3f out: n.d after* **3/1**^{2}
54 **5** *4* **Miakora**^{113} 1591 3-8-12 0.......... PatCosgrave 4 — 10
([illegible]) *chsd ldr: rdn 1/2-way: wknd over 1f out* **11/2**
00 **6** *13* **Grayfriars**^{51} 3465 3-9-3 0.......... DavidProbert 3 — —
(J R Jenkins) *hld up: plld hrd: rdn 3f out: sn wknd* **33/1**

60.72 secs (-0.28) **Going Correction** +0.025s/f (Good) — **6** Ran SP% **109.1**
Speed ratings (Par 103): **103,101,89,88,82 61**
Tote Swingers: 1&2 £1.70, 1&3 £3.40, 2&3 £8.80 CSF £6.10 TOTE £2.30: £1.10, £1.30; EX 4.20.
Owner Richard L Page **Bred** Rathbarry Stud **Trained** Sutton Veny, Wilts

FOCUS
An ordinary maiden, in which the first two had the rail. A small personal best from the winner.

5177 NOTTINGHAMRACECOURSE.CO.UK H'CAP — 1m 2f 50y
3:30 (3:30) (Class 3) (0-90,89) 3-Y-O — **£6,663** (£1,982; £990; £495) **Stalls** Low

Form — RPR
01-0 **1** — **Mohedian Lady (IRE)**^{96} 2050 3-9-1 **86**.......... KirstyMilczarek 7 — 98
(Luca Cumani) *hld up: hdwy over 2f out: rdn to ld and hung rt fr over 1f out: styd on* **9/1**
4104 **2** *1/2* **Creme Anglaise**^{25} 4344 3-9-1 **86**.......... HayleyTurner 6 — 97
(Michael Bell) *hld up: hdwy 2f out: sn rdn: carried rt ins fnl f: styd on: hit over hd w rivals whip nr fin* **11/2**^{3}
3221 **3** *6* **Polperro (USA)**^{16} 4617 3-9-1 **86**..........(p) WilliamBuick 8 — 85+
(John Gosden) *chsd ldrs: led over 6f out: rdn over 2f out: hdd over 1f out: edgd rt and no ex fnl f* **6/4**^{1}
0003 **4** *1 1/2* **Sergeant Ablett (IRE)**^{25} 4335 3-9-1 **89**.......... DaleSwift$^{(3)}$ 2 — 85
(James Given) *chsd ldr tl led over 8f out: hdd over 6f out: rdn over 3f out: styd on same pce fnl 2f* **12/1**
5050 **5** *2 1/4* **Art History (IRE)**^{11} 4777 3-8-10 **86**.......... DarylByrne$^{(5)}$ 4 — 78
(Mark Johnston) *sn pushed along to chse ldrs: rdn over 3f out: wknd 2f out* **8/1**
4212 **6** *1/2* **Arabian Heights**^{30} 4161 3-9-0 **85**.......... StevieDonohoe 5 — 76
(Sir Mark Prescott Bt) *hld up: hdwy over 3f out: wknd over 2f out* **5/1**^{2}
1421 **7** *4* **Ivan Vasilevich (IRE)**^{24} 4355 3-9-4 **89**.......... ShaneKelly 3 — 72
(Jane Chapple-Hyam) *led: hdd over 8f out: chsd ldrs: rdn over 3f out: wknd over 1f out* **13/2**
5-10 **8** *18* **Traffic Sister (USA)**^{63} 3034 3-9-0 **85**.......... JamesDoyle 1 — 32
(J S Moore) *sn pushed along and prom: rdn over 4f out: wknd 3f out* **33/1**

2m 10.78s (-0.92) **Going Correction** +0.025s/f (Good) — **8** Ran SP% **117.1**
Speed ratings (Par 104): **104,103,98,97,95 95,92,77**
Tote Swingers: 1&2 £8.70, 1&3 £5.50, 2&3 £2.80 CSF £58.89 CT £116.38 TOTE £13.00: £4.60, £1.80, £1.40; EX 68.70.
Owner Mrs Olivia Hoare **Bred** Kildaragh Stud **Trained** Newmarket, Suffolk
■ Stewards' Enquiry : Kirsty Milczarek two-day ban: careless riding (Aug 31-Sep 1)

FOCUS
This was a strong handicap, with some progressive and interesting types. The form should be sound considering the gallop looked respectable, and the first two came from the back to finish clear.

NOTEBOOK
Mohedian Lady(IRE), off since running in the Fillies' Trial at Newbury in May, a race that contained the subsequent Epsom winner and third, didn't look the most straightforward character in the early stages with her tail held high, but she gradually got into contention before edging towards the middle of the track. She steadily stayed on when in front, grinding out a tough victory, and promises to stay further. (tchd 10-1)
Creme Anglaise came to challenge the winner in good time, despite being carried across the track by her, but couldn't find a way past. She did keep on gamely, however, but appeared held when hit across the face with Kirsty Milczarek's whip in the closing stages. (op 9-2 tchd 4-1)
Polperro(USA), who went down very early, shed his maiden tag on his previous start when cheekpieces/net muzzle were tried for the first time (previous form in similar races looked solid), and was strongly supported in the market to make a winning handicap debut. He moved to the front quite early and stayed on well up the inside rail, but found the two fillies, who stayed down the middle of the course, too good. That said, it's probably wise to give him another chance. (op 7-4)
Sergeant Ablett(IRE), back up in trip, was still seeking his first success since his debut victory and only ran a fair race after racing prominently. (tchd 16-1)
Art History(IRE) has become a bit in-and-out since winning three towards the start of the year, and didn't look an easy ride under pressure. (op 12-1 tchd 14-1)
Arabian Heights, back up in trip, was a bit keen early and made only modest late ground. (op 15-2 tchd 9-1)
Ivan Vasilevich(IRE) has been in great form this season but didn't get home. (op 11-2 tchd 9-2)
Traffic Sister(USA)'s jockey reported that the filly hung right handed. Official explanation: jockey said filly hung right-handed

5178 TURFTV H'CAP — 1m 2f 50y
4:05 (4:06) (Class 6) (0-65,64) 3-Y-0+ — **£1,681** (£500; £250; £125) **Stalls** Low

Form — RPR
040R **1** — **Arctic Maiden**^{10} 4827 3-8-10 **54**.......... StevieDonohoe 1 — 71+
(Willie Musson) *hld up: hdwy over 2f out: led over 1f out: r.o wl: comf* **17/2**
5362 **2** *2 3/4* **Market Puzzle (IRE)**^{8} 4889 4-8-2 **45**..........(p) RachealKneller$^{(7)}$ 7 — 52
(Mark Brisbourne) *a.p: rdn and ev ch over 1f out: styd on same pce ins fnl f* **14/1**
0334 **3** *2 3/4* **Joe Strummer (IRE)**^{19} 4506 3-9-4 **62**..........(v) HayleyTurner 12 — 64
(Michael Bell) *hld up: rdn 3f out: r.o ins fnl f: wnt 3rd nr fin: nvr rchd ldrs* **11/2**^{2}
-500 **4** *hd* **Peaceful Means (IRE)**^{62} 1987 8-9-3 **53**..........(t) RobbieFitzpatrick 3 — 54
(Michael Appleby) *hld up: hdwy over 3f out: rdn over 1f out: styd on: lost 3rd nr fin* **33/1**
0000 **5** *1 1/2* **Hurricane Thomas (IRE)**^{19} 4499 7-9-0 **50**.......... JimmyQuinn 10 — 48
(Karen Tutty) *chsd ldrs: led over 2f out: rdn and hdd over 1f out: no ex fnl f* **40/1**
6003 **6** *2 3/4* **Desert Chieftain**^{14} 4666 3-8-11 **55**..........(b) KirstyMilczarek 8 — 48
(Luca Cumani) *chsd ldrs: rdn and edgd lft over 2f out: wknd ins fnl f* **10/1**
2146 **7** *1* **Corrib (IRE)**^{25} 4317 8-9-5 **55**..........(p) CathyGannon 2 — 46
(Bryn Palling) *prom: rdn over 2f out: wknd ins fnl f* **10/1**
6460 **8** *1 1/4* **Fairy Mist (IRE)**^{7} 4903 4-9-0 **53**..........(t) DaleSwift$^{(3)}$ 13 — 41
(Brian Rothwell) *hld up: rdn over 3f out: hung lft ins fnl f: nvr trbld ldrs* **18/1**
530 **9** *hd* **Come And Go (UAE)**^{16} 4612 5-9-2 **55**.......... PaulPickard$^{(3)}$ 9 — 43
(Ian McInnes) *led: rdn and hdd over 2f out: wknd fnl f* **16/1**
3620 **10** *2* **Chantilly Dancer (IRE)**^{26} 4275 5-8-10 **46** ow1.......... PatCosgrave 14 — 30
(Michael Quinn) *mid-div: rdn over 3f out: wknd 2f out* **25/1**
6020 **11** *2* **Burza**^{26} 4275 5-9-11 **61**.......... DavidProbert 11 — 41
(John Mackie) *hld up: in rr and rdn 6f out: n.d* **7/1**^{3}
-024 **12** *1 3/4* **Rockweiller**^{13} 4716 4-9-12 **62**..........(v) WilliamBuick 15 — 38
(Steve Collings) *[illegible] 3f out: rdn and wknd over 1f out* **9/2**^{1}
4054 **13** *2 1/4* **Classically (IRE)**^{12} 4763 5-10-0 **64**..........(p) FergusSweeney 5 — 36
(Peter Hedger) *prom: rdn and nt clr run over 2f out: wknd over 1f out* **12/1**
0033 **14** *15* **Aflaam (IRE)**^{10} 4822 6-9-11 **61**..........(tp) TomMcLaughlin 6 — 3
(Ronald Harris) *hld up: rdn over 3f out: nvr on terms* **16/1**
00-0 **15** *5* **Shoot The Pot (IRE)**^{147} 944 4-9-5 **55**.......... ShaneKelly 4 — —
(John Mackie) *hld up: bhd fnl 3f* **50/1**

2m 12.88s (1.18) **Going Correction** +0.025s/f (Good)
WFA 3 from 4yo+ 8lb — **15** Ran SP% **117.3**
Speed ratings (Par 101): **96,93,91,91,90 88,87,86,86,84 82,81,79,67,63**
Tote Swingers: 1&2 £24.90, 1&3 £5.40, 2&3 £12.20 CSF £114.47 CT £717.44 TOTE £10.20: £3.20, £2.50, £2.70; EX 164.30.
Owner Saville House Thoroughbreds **Bred** Peter Holmes **Trained** Newmarket, Suffolk

FOCUS
Moderate stuff at best, but it was well run. The winner posted a clear personal best and was value for extra.
Rockweiller Official explanation: trainer said colt was unsuited by the good to firm (firm in places) ground

5179 RACINGUK.COM H'CAP — 1m 75y
4:35 (4:36) (Class 5) (0-70,70) 3-Y-O — **£2,264** (£673; £336; £168) **Stalls** Centre

Form — RPR
0005 **1** — **Adorable Choice (IRE)**^{49} 3508 3-9-2 **65**..........(v) HayleyTurner 2 — 73
(Tom Dascombe) *mde all: shkn up ins fnl f: r.o* **25/1**
002 **2** *1* **The Buska (IRE)**^{26} 4286 3-8-11 **67**.......... JasonHart$^{(7)}$ 4 — 73
(Declan Carroll) *a.p: rdn to chse wnr fnl f: r.o* **14/1**
0436 **3** *1 1/4* **Kalendar Girl (IRE)**^{33} 4060 3-9-0 **63**.......... StevieDonohoe 8 — 66+
(Willie Musson) *hld up: hdwy over 2f out: hung lft over 1f out: r.o* **9/4**^{2}
0621 **4** *1 1/4* **Blue Maisey**^{44} 3688 3-9-5 **68**.......... WilliamBuick 7 — 68
(Peter Makin) *a.p: racd keenly: trckd ldr 6f out: rdn over 2f out: styd on same pce fnl f* **7/4**^{1}
0005 **5** *2 1/4* **Silver Alliance**^{9} 4866 3-9-7 **70**..........(v) FergusSweeney 10 — 65
(Walter Swinburn) *hld up: hdwy over 1f out: nt rch ldrs* **12/1**
5-00 **6** *3 1/2* **Ninfea (IRE)**^{17} 4584 3-9-5 **68**.......... JamesDoyle 5 — 55
(Sylvester Kirk) *hld up: hmpd over 2f out: n.d* **5/1**^{3}
3243 **7** *3 1/4* **Scoglio**^{12} 4750 3-8-13 **62**..........(tp) LiamJones 3 — 41
(Frank Sheridan) *hld up: hdwy over 2f out: rdn and wknd over 1f out* **14/1**
036 **8** *6* **Refusal**^{14} 4685 3-8-5 **57**.......... SophieDoyle$^{(3)}$ 1 — 22
(Andrew Reid) *chsd ldrs: rdn over 2f out: sn wknd* **50/1**

6-40 **9** *shd* **Phoenix Flame**[21] 4435 3-8-10 **59**.. ShaneKelly 6 24
(Alan McCabe) *prom: rdn over 2f out: wknd over 1f out* **25/1**

1m 46.89s (1.29) **Going Correction** +0.025s/f (Good) **9** Ran SP% **114.5**
Speed ratings (Par 100): **94,93,91,90,88 84,81,75,75**
Tote Swingers: 1&2 £14.40, 1&3 £9.10, 2&3 £7.30 CSF £322.06 CT £1115.05 TOTE £30.20: £4.80, £3.70, £1.30; EX 71.30.
Owner John Brown **Bred** John O'Connor **Trained** Malpas, Cheshire

FOCUS
Not many got into this modest handicap. The winner made all and is rated to her 2yo best.
T/Plt: £78.00 to a £1 stake. Pool of £37,969.00 - 355.22 winning tickets. T/Qpdt: £17.40 to a £1 stake. Pool of £2,382.00 - 101.20 winning tickets. CR

[4343]YORK (L-H)

Wednesday, August 17

OFFICIAL GOING: Good to soft (good in places; 6.0)
Rail out 3m from 1m4f to entrance to home straight adding 20yds to races of 1m and beyond.
Wind: almost nil Weather: fine

5180 SYMPHONY GROUP STKS (H'CAP) 5f 89y
2:00 (2:02) (Class 2) (0-105,101) 3-Y-O+**£19,407** (£5,775; £2,886; £1,443) **Stalls** Centre

Form RPR

4010 **1** **Secret Asset (IRE)**[18] 4534 6-9-4 **95**.............................. GeorgeBaker 3 104
(Jane Chapple-Hyam) *chsd ldrs on outer: styd on fnl f: led nr fin* **16/1**

5406 **2** *nk* **Racy**[18] 4531 4-8-12 **89**.. PhillipMakin 1 97
(Kevin Ryan) *clr overall ldrs on outer: hdd towards fin* **10/1**[3]

5350 **3** *shd* **Favourite Girl (IRE)**[25] 4346 5-8-13 **90**.....................(p) JimmyFortune 7 98
(Tim Easterby) *chsd ldrs: kpt on wl fnl f: styd on towards fin* **20/1**

0002 **4** *½* **Irish Heartbeat (IRE)**[4] 5032 6-8-11 **88**.....................(p) PaulHanagan 13 94
(Richard Fahey) *prom: effrt over 2f out: styd on fnl f: kpt on towards fin* **7/1**[1]

0215 **5** *½* **Kanaf (IRE)**[18] 4534 4-9-4 **95**.. RichardHills 14 99+
(Ed Dunlop) *s.i.s: in rr: hmpd twice over 1f out: str run stands' side fnl f: fin wl* **9/1**[2]

0310 **6** *2 ½* **Ancient Cross**[18] 4534 7-9-9 **100**...........................(t) GrahamGibbons 15 96
(Michael Easterby) *in rr: effrt over 2f out: styd on wl fnl f: nt rch ldrs* **9/1**[2]

2006 **7** *½* **Silaah**[17] 4573 7-8-13 **90**..(p) KierenFallon 19 84
(David Nicholls) *chsd ldrs stands' side: kpt on same pce over 1f out* **25/1**

1-10 **8** *hd* **Ritual (IRE)**[39] 3841 4-8-13 **90**.. FrankieDettori 17 83
(Jeremy Noseda) *s.i.s: hld up in rr stands' side: kpt on fnl 2f: nvr nr ldrs* **9/1**[2]

0130 **9** *1 ¼* **Swiss Franc**[13] 4739 6-9-4 **95**.. NeilCallan 4 84
(David Elsworth) *mid-div on outside: kpt on fnl 2f: nvr a factor* **16/1**

5603 **10** *¾* **Midnight Martini**[16] 4609 4-8-11 **88**.................................. DavidAllan 11 74
(Tim Easterby) *chsd ldrs: one pce whn checked 2f out* **12/1**

0200 **11** *nse* **Mon Brav**[39] 3841 4-8-7 **87**.. SeanLevey(3) 10 73
(Brian Ellison) *towards rr: kpt on fnl f: nvr a factor* **20/1**

0300 **12** *nk* **Johannes (IRE)**[4] 5060 8-9-1 **92**.................................... TonyHamilton 18 77
(Richard Fahey) *in rr stands' side: nt clr run over 1f out: nvr a factor* **25/1**

6030 **13** *nk* **Ginger Ted (IRE)**[4] 5033 4-8-13 **90**.........................(p) J-PGuillambert 20 74
(Richard Guest) *in rr stands' side: sn drvn along: kpt on fnl 2f: nvr a factor* **12/1**

0000 **14** *3 ½* **Rain Delayed (IRE)**[20] 4468 5-9-10 **101**.......................(p) TomQueally 16 73
(Michael Dods) *hld up stands' side: effrt over 2f out: wknd over 1f out* **18/1**

4004 **15** *½* **Face The Problem (IRE)**[9] 4859 3-8-10 **89**............ SilvestreDeSousa 6 59
(B W Hills) *s.i.s: sn prom on outer: wknd over 1f out* **12/1**

3002 **16** *¾* **Fitz Flyer (IRE)**[8] 4894 5-9-4 **95**...............................(b) RoystonFfrench 9 63
(Bryan Smart) *hld up in rr: effrt over 2f out: nvr on terms* **40/1**

-360 **17** *2 ¼* **Shropshire (IRE)**[20] 4472 3-8-11 **90**.............................[1] MichaelHills 12 50
(B W Hills) *in rr: hdwy over 3f out: lost pl over 1f out* **14/1**

0021 **18** *2 ½* **Strike Up The Band**[11] 4791 8-8-7 **87**.................. MichaelO'Connell(3) 2 38
(David Nicholls) *chsd ldr: edgd rt and wknd 2f out: eased whn bhd* **33/1**

1620 **19** *5* **Falasteen (IRE)**[74] 2714 4-9-4 **95**...................................... JamieSpencer 8 29
(Kevin Ryan) *chsd ldrs: wknd over 1f out: eased* **16/1**

64.72 secs (0.62) **Going Correction** +0.35s/f (Good)
WFA 3 from 4yo+ 2lb **19** Ran SP% **126.8**
Speed ratings (Par 109): **109,108,108,107,106 102,101,101,99,98 98,97,97,91,91 89,86,82,74**
Tote Swingers: 1&2 £42.40, 1&3 £63.40, 2&3 £41.00 CSF £156.40 CT £1860.24 TOTE £24.30: £4.50, £3.00, £5.50, £2.40; EX 288.40 Trifecta £2675.00 Part won. Pool: £3,614.86 - 0.30 winning units..
Owner Simon & Jeanette Pierpoint & Paul Salisbury **Bred** Mrs C Hartery **Trained** Dalham, Suffolk
■ Stewards' Enquiry : Michael O'Connell three-day ban: careless riding (Aug 31-Sep 2)
Richard Hills one-day ban: careless riding (Aug 31)

FOCUS
Rail moved out 3m from 1m4f to entrance of home straight, adding 20 yards to race distances of 1m and over. A highly competitive edition of this sprint handicap, which was first run two years ago. The time, 1.72sec outside the standard, suggested that the ground was indeed on the soft side of good. The speed in the race was with those drawn low, particularly the runner-up, who led the field down the centre of the track. The pace held up and not many became involved. The winner is rated to his turf best, with a personal best from the second.

NOTEBOOK
Secret Asset(IRE) tracked the speed before putting his head in front close home. The quirky grey, seventh under a penalty in the Stewards' Cup last time, was racing from a mark 6lb higher than when winning a 5f handicap earlier at the Goodwood meeting. (op 18-1)
Racy showed fine speed from stall one and looked sure to hold on even with 100 yards to go, only to be nabbed near the line. The drop back in trip suited and he had run perhaps his best race of the season before this when third to Ancient Cross here in May. (op 14-1)
Favourite Girl(IRE) was towards the fore throughout and in second place inside the last, but could not quite get to the winner. Her yard won 12 months ago with Hamish McGonagall, who had also been runner-up the year before.
Irish Heartbeat(IRE) was running on towards the finish over a trip just on the short side for him. He was 2lb ahead of the handicapper. (op 10-1)
Kanaf(IRE) ◆, the Stewards' Cup fifth, looked unlucky. Finding himself in last place after a slow start, he met trouble when trying to improve and had to switch, but was coming home fast against the stands' rail when in the clear. The Portland Handicap would look an ideal target. (op 10-1)
Ancient Cross, not far behind Kanaf and Secret Asset in the Stewards' Cup won by his stablemate Hoof It, had ground and track to suit. Not best drawn but ending up on the right part of the track, he was motoring home but too late.
Silaah ran well from the wrong side of the course and was still in fourth place a furlong out before ebbing away.
Ritual(IRE) reportedly came home with an infection after finishing down the field at Royal Ascot. Previously progressive, he started slowly here but was staying on quite well in the latter stages. The draw was against him and a return to 6f should be in his favour. (op 8-1 tchd 15-2)
Swiss Franc could not cash in on being drawn where the pace was.
Midnight Martini, a stablemate of the third, ran without the regular tongue strap. Hampered with around 2f to run before fading in the final furlong, she remains winless since taking the big sales race here two years ago. (tchd 14-1 in a place)
Johannes(IRE), down the field in Saturday's Great St Wilfrid at Ripon, was drawn on the wrong side again here but was not noted finishing well. (op 33-1)
Ginger Ted(IRE) had ground conditions in his favour, but the same couldn't be said about the draw. He's set to be dropped a pound now. (op 14-1)
Rain Delayed(IRE), running in a handicap for the first time since the spring and back in headgear, briefly looked like taking a hand when picking up against the stands' fence, but the effort soon flattened out. (op 20-1)
Strike Up The Band showed fine pace alongside Racy but weakened rapidly.

5181 SPORTINGBET.COM ACOMB STKS (GROUP 3) 7f
2:30 (2:30) (Class 1) 2-Y-O **£29,600** (£11,195; £5,595; £2,795) **Stalls** Low

Form RPR

1 **1** **Entifaadha**[25] 4330 2-9-0 0.. RichardHills 2 107
(William Haggas) *hld up in mid-div: hdwy on inner bnd over 4f out: chsng ldrs over 2f out: led over 1f out: kpt on wl towards fin* **7/2**[1]

225 **2** *1 ¼* **Fort Bastion (IRE)**[39] 3861 2-9-0 97............................ RichardHughes 7 104
(Richard Hannon) *trckd ldrs: chal over 2f out: kpt on same pce last 100yds* **15/2**

1 **3** *¾* **Zumbi (IRE)**[24] 4352 2-9-0 0.. KierenFallon 11 102
(Sir Michael Stoute) *hld up: hdwy on outer 3f out: upsides over 1f out: styd on same pce last 100yds* **8/1**

4301 **4** *½* **Caledonian Spring (IRE)**[26] 4264 2-9-0 90...................... TomQueally 1 102+
(Paul D'Arcy) *in rr: hdwy over 2f out: nt clr run: swtchd rt over 1f out: styd on strly fnl f* **25/1**

1 **5** *3 ¼* **Al Khan (IRE)**[41] 3755 2-9-0 0.. JimmyFortune 9 93
(Peter Chapple-Hyam) *hld up: smooth hdwy over 2f out: chsng ldrs over 1f out: wknd jst ins fnl f* **10/1**

1 **6** *2 ¾* **Archbishop (USA)**[21] 4446 2-9-0 0.................................... MartinDwyer 4 86
(Brian Meehan) *led tl over 4f out: led over 3f out tl over 1f out: wknd jst ins fnl f* **7/1**

7 *¾* **Furner's Green (IRE)**[39] 3881 2-9-0 0.................................. JPO'Brien 3 84
(A P O'Brien, Ire) *hld up in rr: hdwy over 3f out: rdn and one pce over 1f out* **5/1**[2]

1 **8** *½* **Moon Pearl (USA)**[40] 3793 2-9-0 0.................................... JimCrowley 8 83
(Ralph Beckett) *hld up towards rr: hdwy over 2f out: nvr nr ldrs* **20/1**

01 **9** *7* **Balty Boys (IRE)**[17] 4580 2-9-0 0.................................... MichaelHills 12 65+
(B W Hills) *swtchd lft after s: in rr: effrt on outer over 2f out: sn wknd* **11/2**[3]

1 **10** *2* **Now My Sun**[32] 4080 2-9-0 0.. NeilCallan 13 60
(Mrs K Burke) *stmbld s: sn chsng ldrs on outer: t.k.h: wknd 2f out* **66/1**

11 *2 ¾* **East Meets West (IRE)**[12] 4770 2-9-0 0.......................... CO'Donoghue 6 53
(A P O'Brien, Ire) *s.i.s: sme hdwy over 3f out: lost pl 2f out: eased whn bhd* **16/1**

21 **12** *2* **Rock Supreme (IRE)**[40] 3826 2-9-0 85............................ PhillipMakin 5 48
(Michael Dods) *prom: effrt over 2f out: sn wknd: eased clsng stages* **33/1**

13 *3 ¼* **Battle Of Saratoga (IRE)**[12] 4770 2-9-0 0............. SeamieHeffernan 10 40
(A P O'Brien, Ire) *led over 4f out: hung rt and hdd over 3f out: sn lost pl: eased whn bhd* **40/1**

1m 26.12s (0.82) **Going Correction** +0.225s/f (Good) **13** Ran SP% **120.1**
Speed ratings (Par 104): **104,102,101,101,97 94,93,92,84,82 79,77,73**
Tote Swingers: 1&2 £6.10, 1&3 £5.30, 2&3 £11.70 CSF £28.34 TOTE £4.10: £1.60, £3.10, £2.50; EX 36.40 Trifecta £146.90 Pool: £2,251.98 - 11.33 winning units..
Owner Hamdan Al Maktoum **Bred** Highclere Stud & Hmh Management **Trained** Newmarket, Suffolk
■ Stewards' Enquiry : Richard Hughes one-day ban: used whip down the shoulder in the forehand (Aug 31)

FOCUS
A race contested by plenty of really decent types over the years, 2003 winner Rule Of Law (won the following season's St Leger) the pick in recent seasons, but this latest running does not look strong form and it will be a surprise if it has a bearing on next year's domestic classics. The pace looked solid, a view supported by winning rider Richard Hills, and the action unfolded up the centre of the track.

NOTEBOOK
Entifaadha's taking debut success over this trip at the July course was hard to assess. He appeared to benefit from a double-figure draw and the runner-up, also drawn high, was beaten next time, but third-placed Fencing, who had a single-figure stall, subsequently won the Listed Washington Singer. This performance, though, confirmed the visual impression that he's a smart colt. He took a little while to pick, but ground it out well. He's bred to be smart, being a half-brother to dual Group 1-winning sprinter Regal Parade, as well as some other decent performers who stay well, and he has done nothing wrong so far. However, he lacks size and scope and is likely to face tougher tasks this season, let alone next term. (op 9-2, tchd 5-1 in a place)
Fort Bastion(IRE) looked better than he showed when negatively ridden in the Superlative Stakes (best of those held up) and so it proved, the colt sticking on tenaciously under a more forward ride. He's still a maiden, so connections have the option of lowering him significantly in grade or continuing at pattern level. (op 9-1)
Zumbi(IRE) won on his debut going 6f at Ascot, and although the form has yet to really work out, he came here representing a trainer who had landed this four times, including with King's Best in 2001. This Dubawi colt could only manage third, but he might be the one to take from the race as he shaped with plenty of promise. Having travelled in the manner of a smart colt, he initially picked up quite well to look one of the likeliest winners, but was found out by his inexperience late on. He's in the Dewhurst and Middle Park and can progress. (tchd 9-1)
Caledonian Spring(IRE) improved for the step up to 7f when winning his maiden at Ascot last time and this represents significant progress, indeed he may have been an unlucky loser. He wasn't able to get a good position from the inside stall, racing out the back (further behind than the front three), and despite looking to have plenty to offer on entering the straight, he was denied a clear run. (op 28-1)
Al Khan(IRE), successful in an ordinary 6f maiden on his debut, was a bit keen early and then didn't see his race out after arriving on the scene appearing to go well. (op 9-1 tchd 11-1)
Archbishop(USA), representing a trainer who had won two of the last three runnings, had looked a nice prospect when winning a good-looking Sandown maiden over this trip on his debut, but he's a sizeable type and appeared to come up weak. He travelled just about as well as anything, but carried his head a bit high when coming under pressure and looked to be climbing. This came too soon in his development. (op 6-1)
Furner's Green(IRE) won well on his debut (Battle Of Saratoga and East Meets West behind), but Aidan O'Brien has not won this since 2000 (two previous winners Saratoga Springs and Hemmingway). The colt, whose rider couldn't claim his usual 3lb, didn't pick up after racing out the back and has not progressed from his first start. (op 11-2 tchd 9-2)
Moon Pearl(USA) won a good 6f maiden on his debut at Ascot (runner-up and third won next time), but he struggled on this rise in class, even though he might have been one place closer had he not been short of room late on.

Balty Boys(IRE), who dropped back to 6f when winning his maiden at Newbury, didn't look good enough on this rise in class. He was soon out the back and never going. (op 8-1)

5182 SPORTINGBET.COM GREAT VOLTIGEUR STKS (GROUP 2) (C&G) 1m 4f
3:05 (3:05) (Class 1) 3-Y-O **£89,871** (£33,990; £16,987; £8,486) **Stalls** Centre

Form				RPR
21-1	**1**		**Sea Moon**[67] [2935] 3-8-12 103 .... RichardHughes 4 (Sir Michael Stoute) *hld up in rr: hdwy over 6f out: chal on bit over 2f out: led over 1f out: drvn clr: eased nr fin: impressive* **11/2**[3]	126+
1-21	**2**	*8*	**Al Kazeem**[95] [2100] 3-8-12 105 .... SteveDrowne 7 (Roger Charlton) *hld up in mid-div: drvn and outpcd over 4f out: hdwy over 2f out: styd on to take 2nd last 100yds* **16/1**	112
2022	**3**	*2 1/4*	**Seville (GER)**[34] [4038] 3-8-12 120 .... SeamieHeffernan 3 (A P O'Brien, Ire) *hld up in mid-div: hdwy to ld over 2f out: hdd over 1f out: kpt on same pce* **5/6**[1]	108
-136	**4**	*3 1/4*	**Genius Beast (USA)**[61] [3105] 3-8-12 110 .... KierenFallon 5 (Mahmood Al Zarooni) *hld up in mid-div: outpcd and drvn over 4f out: kpt on to chse ldrs ocver 2f out: one pce* **12/1**	103
4311	**5**	*3*	**Namibian (IRE)**[22] [4411] 3-8-12 112 .... SilvestreDeSousa 1 (Mark Johnston) *chsd ldrs: drvn over 4f out: wknd 2f out* **9/2**[2]	98
1013	**6**	*3/4*	**Hunter's Light (IRE)**[22] [4411] 3-8-12 106 .... FrankieDettori 8 (Saeed Bin Suroor) *swtchd lft after s: hld up in rr: smooth hdwy to chal over 2f out: wknd fnl f* **10/1**	97
234	**7**	*32*	**Regent Street (IRE)**[61] [3108] 3-8-12 106 ....(v[1]) CO'Donoghue 6 (A P O'Brien, Ire) *led and sn clr: edgd rt and hdd over 3f out: sn lost pl and bhd: eased: t.o* **33/1**	46
-321	**8**	*3 1/2*	**Thimaar (USA)**[26] [4279] 3-8-12 95 .... RichardHills 2 (John Gosden) *sn chsng clr ldrs: led over 3f out: hdd over 2f out: sn lost pl and eased: t.o* **20/1**	40

2m 34.94s (1.74) **Going Correction** +0.375s/f (Good) **8** Ran SP% **118.5**
Speed ratings (Par 112): **109,103,102,100,98 97,76,73**
Tote Swingers: 1&2 £8.60, 1&3 £2.80, 2&3 £3.10 CSF £88.64 TOTE £5.50: £1.70, £3.40, £1.10; EX 57.10 Trifecta £197.50 Pool: £9,990.16 - 37.41 winning units..
Owner K Abdulla **Bred** Juddmonte Farms Ltd **Trained** Newmarket, Suffolk

FOCUS

This is an important race in its own right, in addition to being the principal trial for the St Leger. In the past ten years three colts have completed the double, most recently Lucarno in 2007, while another three St Leger winners were beaten in the York race. The same period also threw up six Leger runners-up, all of whom were beaten in the Voltigeur. The pace was ordinary early on, with the bulk of the field ignoring the favourite's pacemaker Regent Street. Things quickened up at around halfway and they came down the centre of the track in the home straight. Seville and Namibian were both disappointing, but take nothing away from Sea Moon who was highly impressive and already has form superior than most recent Leger winners.

NOTEBOOK

Sea Moon ◆ was a highly impressive winner and is a justifiably short price for the St Leger now. Successful off 92 in a handicap over the extended 1m2f here on his belated reappearance two months ago, he had to find a fair bit of improvement on that bare form but this longer trip was sure to suit him. Travelling up well before changing his legs and quickening clear, he powered away for a wide-margin victory. A half-brother to the 2003 Leger winner Brian Boru, who was runner-up in this race, he hit the line with plenty of running still in him and should have no problem with the extra yardage at Doncaster. With further progress almost assured, as this was only the fourth outing of his life, he is going to be very hard to beat next month. A bit of cut in the ground would be ideal. (op 7-2)

Al Kazeem had been kept off the track by a small setback since winning the London Gold Cup at Newbury in May, a handicap which has worked out very well with the next four home winning since. Up in trip and grade, he was never a threat to the easy winner but stayed on from the rear to take second. This was a fine effort from a colt with more to offer at this sort of trip. He's not entered in the St Leger, with the Cambridgeshire his only big-race entry. The Arc Trial at Newbury next month is a possibility for him. (op 14-1 tchd 12-1 and 18-1 in a place)

Seville(GER) looked the one to beat on form, having finished second in the Dante here at York, the Irish Derby and the Grand Prix de Paris, and was 8lb clear on BHA figures. He came there to show narrowly ahead, but couldn't quicken up for pressure as the winner pulled right away from him and lost second spot too late on. Below par here and deposed as Leger favourite, he is obviously a high-class colt but remains without a win since he scored at Tipperary as a juvenile. It will be interesting to see whether the final Classic remains on his agenda. Aidan O'Brien last won the Voltigeur with Powerscourt in 2003 and has had eight runners placed since. (op 11-10, tchd 5-4 in a place and 6-5 in places)

Genius Beast(USA), from the yard successful in this last year with Rewilding, plugged on from the rear of the field past labouring rivals for a never threatening fourth. He has been held three times in this grade since winning Sandown's Classic Trial in the spring. (op 16-1 tchd 18-1)

Namibian(IRE) came here on a hat-trick following gutsy wins in the Queen's Vase at Ascot and Goodwood's Gordon Stakes. His rider tried to wind things up in the straight but the response from colt was limited, and he was beaten with two to run. The easy ground shouldn't have posed him any problems and perhaps this was just an off-day. (op 5-1)

Hunter's Light(IRE) was a supplementary entry for this. He improved in the straight to have his chance, but weakened away and appeared not to get home in the ground. (op 14-1)

Regent Street(IRE), given another change of headgear, went off rather quickly with his rider looking around in the back straight to see where the rest were. The colt predictably dropped away when tackled.

Thimaar(USA) had a lot on his plate on these terms but it was still disappointing that he dropped out so quickly after leading the main body of the field into the home straight. He had been just a short head behind runner-up Al Kazeem at Newbury in April. (tchd 16-1)

5183 JUDDMONTE INTERNATIONAL STKS (BRITISH CHAMPIONS' SERIES) (GROUP 1) 1m 2f 88y
3:40 (3:40) (Class 1) 3-Y-O+ **£396,970** (£150,500; £75,320; £37,520; £18,830) **Stalls** Low

Form				RPR
0651	**1**		**Twice Over**[25] [4345] 6-9-5 123 .... IanMongan 4 (Sir Henry Cecil) *hld up: effrt over 2f out: wnt 2nd over 1f out: edgd lft and styd on to ld towards fin* **11/2**[3]	126
1221	**2**	*3/4*	**Midday**[18] [4533] 5-9-2 120 .... TomQueally 6 (Sir Henry Cecil) *trckd ldrs: wnt 2nd over 3f out: led over 2f out: hung lft appr fnl f: hdd clsng stages* **5/2**[2]	122
1-11	**3**	*5*	**Await The Dawn (USA)**[60] [3153] 4-9-5 121 .... JPO'Brien 3 (A P O'Brien, Ire) *trckd clr ldr: upsides and rdn 2f out: wknd over 1f out* **8/13**[1]	115
1/0-	**4**	*12*	**Zafisio (IRE)**[339] [6006] 5-9-5 114 .... DarryllHolland 5 (Jo Hughes) *hld up in last: drvn over 2f out: sn wl outpcd* **66/1**	91
0/65	**5**	*17*	**Windsor Palace (IRE)**[87] [2332] 6-9-5 97 .... SeamieHeffernan 2 (A P O'Brien, Ire) *led and sn clr: hdd over 2f out: sn lost pl and bhd: eased ins fnl f: virtually p.u* **100/1**	57

2m 14.7s (2.20) **Going Correction** +0.375s/f (Good)
WFA 3 from 4yo+ 8lb **5** Ran SP% **108.4**
Speed ratings (Par 117): **106,105,101,91,78**
CSF £18.77 TOTE £5.30: £2.20, £1.20; EX 12.40.
Owner K Abdulla **Bred** Juddmonte Farms Ltd **Trained** Newmarket, Suffolk
■ The race sponsor was responsible for the one-two (owner's first win in the race) and also bred the first three.

FOCUS

Only three of the five runners could be given any sort of chance and the strongly supported favourite Await The Dawn, who was priced up according to hype and potential rather than substance of form, ran below general expectations. With Roderic O'Connor taken out there were no 3yos in the field. The race went to Twice Over, and while Henry Cecil's colt is admirably tough, he came into this with a 3-16 Group 1 record. It's hard to consider the form anything other than ordinary for the level, Twice Over rated back to his best. Ballydoyle pacemaker Windsor Palace raced in a clear lead, largely ignored by the others for much of the way. The time was officially 0.86 seconds off the later Class 2 handicap, and rough hand times show the main bunch made it to the straight around 1.10 seconds slower than the leaders in the handicap. They raced up the centre of the track for most of the closing stages.

NOTEBOOK

Twice Over's trainer deserves the utmost praise. This 6yo, who was runner-up in the same race 12 months ago, looked finished as a top-level performer as recently as June when well beaten in the Prince of Wales's Stakes, and he was reportedly distressed afterwards. However, Cecil apparently allowed the horse to stay overnight at the course, rather than travel him back to Newmarket on the same day, and he's clearly greatly benefited from the trainer's attentive nature, this following on from a confidence-boosting success in the Group 2 York Stakes over C&D. Twice Over lacked the acceleration of Midday in the straight, but never allowed his stablemate to get away, helped by the mare hanging left, and wore her down with a sustained challenge, providing Ian Mongan with a first top-level success in the process. The winner is now likely to bid for a third straight Champion Stakes, although it's questionable whether he'll be helped by race's switch from Newmarket to Ascot, where he holds a 0-4 record. It's true he was a slightly unlucky runner-up in the 2010 Prince of Wales's Stakes, but he took a long time to hit full stride here and seems to appreciate a long straight now. (tchd 6-1)

Midday, who ran here instead of the Yorkshire Oaks (won the race last year), may have done enough had she not hung left late on, handing the initiative to her stable companion. She didn't stop trying, though, and this effort is hard to fault. Although now 0-3 against males, finishing second each time, she's clearly seriously competitive with her weight allowance. She may re-oppose Twice Over in the Champion Stakes, although if her owner and trainer want to really try and dominate Ascot's new meeting (connections surely already have the QEII covered with Frankel), perhaps she'll be aimed at the Qipco British Champions Fillies' And Mares' Stakes, even though that means dropping to Group 2 level. The short straight isn't ideal, but the return to 1m4f would negate that somewhat. (op 9-4)

Await The Dawn(USA) came into this ante-post favourite for the Breeders' Cup Classic (said to be long-term aim) with some firms, having had looked a top prospect in lesser company, and his latest victory in the Hardwicke seemed particularly commendable considering it was widely accepted 1m4f on really soft ground represented nothing like his optimum conditions. However, it seems that last race may have left its mark. It's true to argue he had to prove himself in Group 1 company, but clearly he has run well short of his best. He seemed to travel well enough for Joseph O'Brien, who was unable to claim his usual 3lb allowance, but was one paced for pressure. It was reported the following day that he came back with a temperature, and it's worth pointing out of his trainer's other runners on the card underperformed (including Seville in the Great Voltigeur), but he can still only be watched if kept to this level next time. (op 4-6 tchd 8-11)

Zafisio(IRE)'s starting price of 66-1 overestimated his prospects in this line-up after a 339-day break, but it was a shrewd bit of placing, his connections picking up over £37,000 for fourth.

5184 SPORTINGBET.COM STKS (NURSERY) 6f
4:15 (4:17) (Class 2) 2-Y-O **£9,703** (£2,887; £1,443; £721) **Stalls** Centre

Form				RPR
613	**1**		**Bomber Jet**[12] [4749] 2-8-11 77 .... KierenFallon 5 (Nigel Tinkler) *ponied to s: s.i.s: hdwy and nt clr run over 1f out: nt clr run and swtchd lft ins fnl f: styd on to ld nr fin* **20/1**	83
4346	**2**	*nk*	**Sunrise Dance**[21] [4427] 2-8-6 75 .... HarryBentley(3) 3 (Alan Jarvis) *wnt lft s: sn trcking ldrs: led jst ins fnl f: hdd and no ex last 75yds* **25/1**	80
0411	**3**	*hd*	**Mister Musicmaster**[12] [4749] 2-9-4 84 .... JamesMillman 6 (Rod Millman) *in rr on outside: hdwy over 2f out: swtchd lft over 1f out: led last 75yds: hdd nr fin* **12/1**	89
0053	**4**	*1 1/2*	**On The Hoof**[4] [5058] 2-8-6 72 .... GrahamGibbons 13 (Michael Easterby) *towards rr stands' side: hdwy over 2f out: hung lft: kpt on same pce last 150yds* **11/1**	72+
31	**5**	*shd*	**Satanic Beat (IRE)**[25] [4347] 2-9-0 80 .... TomQueally 9 (Jedd O'Keeffe) *mid-div: hdwy over 2f out: nt clr run and hmpd over 1f out: swtchd lft and styd on* **15/2**[3]	80
2013	**6**	*1/2*	**Campanology**[33] [4053] 2-9-5 85 .... RichardHughes 1 (Richard Hannon) *trckd ldr: led over 2f out: wandered over 1f out: hdd and no ex jst ins fnl f* **7/1**[2]	83
4441	**7**	*3 1/2*	**Our Boy Jack (IRE)**[11] [4809] 2-8-2 68 .... PaulHanagan 11 (Richard Fahey) *mid-div: outpcd over 2f out: kpt on fnl f* **10/1**	56+
2630	**8**	*2*	**Dicky Mint**[25] [4343] 2-8-1 67 .... KellyHarrison 2 (Michael Easterby) *bmpd s: led: hdd over 2f out: edgd lft and hmpd over 1f out: one pce* **50/1**	50
2612	**9**	*nk*	**Nearly A Gift (IRE)**[18] [4551] 2-9-4 84 .... DavidAllan 17 (Tim Easterby) *trckd ldrs stands' side: chal over 1f out: wknd last 150yds* **14/1**	65
0120	**10**	*2 1/4*	**Indepub**[18] [4536] 2-8-12 78 .... PhillipMakin 10 (Kevin Ryan) *chsd ldrs: one pce whn hmpd over 1f out* **33/1**	53
2052	**11**	*3*	**Es Que Love (IRE)**[18] [4536] 2-9-7 87 .... SilvestreDeSousa 16 (Mark Johnston) *trckd ldrs stands' side: wkng whn hmpd over 1f out* **8/1**	54
212	**12**	*nk*	**West Leake Hare (IRE)**[19] [4496] 2-8-12 78 .... MichaelHills 15 (B W Hills) *sn trcking ldrs stands' side: wkng whn hmpd 2f out* **9/2**[1]	45
4220	**13**	*nse*	**Midas Medusa (FR)**[39] [3865] 2-8-6 75 .... KieranO'Neill(3) 12 (Richard Hannon) *mid-div: sme hdwy over 2f out: sn lost pl* **66/1**	39
001	**14**	*3 1/2*	**Lunar Deity**[20] [4462] 2-8-13 82 .... JohnFahy(3) 8 (Eve Johnson Houghton) *in rr stands' side: drvn over 2f out: sn bhd* **8/1**	36
0422	**15**	*2 3/4*	**Cravat**[5] [4984] 2-9-4 84 .... NeilCallan 4 (Mark Johnston) *dwlt: sn chsng ldrs on outside: lost pl over 1f out: eased whn bhd* **16/1**	38
01	**16**	*36*	**Sanad (IRE)**[33] [4068] 2-8-13 79 .... RichardHills 7 (Brian Meehan) *chsd ldrs: lost pl over 2f out: sn bhd and heavily eased: virtually p.u: t.o* **12/1**	—

1m 15.05s (3.15) **Going Correction** +0.35s/f (Good) **16** Ran SP% **125.0**
Speed ratings (Par 100): **93,92,92,90,90 89,84,82,81,78 74,74,74,69,66 18**
Tote Swingers: 1&2 £79.20, 1&3 £30.50, 2&3 £74.50 CSF £444.56 CT £3406.06 TOTE £24.70: £4.70, £7.10, £2.90, £3.00; EX 469.00 Trifecta £2007.00 Part won. Pool: £2,712.25 - 0.30 winning units..
Owner Yan Wah Wu **Bred** Whitsbury Manor Stud **Trained** Langton, N Yorks

FOCUS

A warm nursery, the best recent winner of which was subsequent Group 3 scorer Prince Of Light. As in the opening sprint handicap it appeared that those drawn low, and racing in the centre of the track, held the advantage. It was a rough and messy race with any number of these juveniles finding trouble.

NOTEBOOK
Bomber Jet was third to Mister Musicmaster at Haydock recently but enjoyed a 9lb pull with that horse. Ponied to post and again not well away, he came from the rear on the far side and had to weave his way through before thrusting his head in front late on. There's more improvement in him over an extra furlong. His owner is based in Hong Kong and the gelding is likely to end up there this year or next. (op 16-1)
Sunrise Dance took a bump leaving the gates but was soon travelling well. She showed in front inside the last but could not quite hold on, and might be worth a try at 5f. (op 33-1)
Mister Musicmaster was unable to confirm his Haydock superiority over Bomber Jet on 9lb worse terms but still ran a solid race on this hat-trick bid. He was outpaced at halfway but came home well once switched to the outside of the pack. He is 16lb higher than when winning at Sandown last month. (op 14-1)
On The Hoof was 4lb ahead of the handicapper on this quick reappearance and nursery debut. Edging left when beginning his effort, causing trouble for those on his inner, he was keeping on at the line. This was a good run considering he raced on the wrong part of the track, and he should be kept in mind. (op 9-1)
Satanic Beat(IRE), successful in a C&D maiden last time out, was another to encounter trouble before running on quite nicely. (op 10-1)
Campanology raced up with the pace but went left for pressure and was fading inside the last. He's a useful colt but remains without a win to his name, having been disqualified at Haydock. (op 9-1)
Our Boy Jack(IRE) was 5lb higher in this better race but came home in quite taking style. (op 8-1)
Dicky Mint, without the tongue strap this time, he showed plenty of pace from stall two but could not sustain it. (tchd 66-1)
Nearly A Gift(IRE), drawn on the stands' side, just about took it up but she wandered badly, like she had at Newmarket last time, and weakened out of it. She may yet be capable of better. (op 12-1)
Es Que Love(IRE), runner-up in a nursery at Glorious Goodwood, was involved in the trouble caused by On The Hoof but looked held at the time. (op 9-1 tchd 10-1)
West Leake Hare(IRE), touched off in another nursery at the big Goodwood fixture and raised 3lb, was dropping back from 7f and had work to do when he was hampered. He was racing on the wrong flank of the group and can probably be forgiven this. (tchd 5-1 in a place)
Sanad(IRE) Official explanation: jockey said colt lost its action

5185 PATRINGTON HAVEN LEISURE PARK STKS (H'CAP) 1m 2f 88y
4:50 (4:50) (Class 2) (0-105,104) 3-Y-O+ **£12,938** (£3,850; £1,924; £962) **Stalls** Low

Form			Horse	Jockey	RPR
0323	1		**Our Joe Mac (IRE)**[22] 4410 4-9-3 **93** (p)	PaulHanagan 4	105
			(Richard Fahey) *mid-div: hdwy over 2f out: led appr fnl f: all out* **8/1**[3]		
1301	2	hd	**Arlequin**[22] 4410 4-9-6 **96**	PhilipRobinson 15	108
			(James Bethell) *trckd ldrs: effrt on outside and hung lft over 2f out: chal 1f out: no ex nr fin* **20/1**		
1101	3	5	**Club Oceanic**[25] 4331 3-8-13 **97** (p)	FrankieDettori 7	100+
			(Jeremy Noseda) *hld up in rr: hdwy to chse ldrs over 2f out: kpt on one pce over 1f out* **7/1**[2]		
5131	4	1/2	**Barren Brook**[18] 4528 4-8-13 **89**	KierenFallon 9	91+
			(Michael Easterby) *trckd ldrson outer: t.k.h: effrt over 2f out: kpt on fnl f* **7/1**[2]		
1510	5	1	**Norman Orpen (IRE)**[11] 4794 4-9-1 **91**	JamieSpencer 16	91+
			(Jane Chapple-Hyam) *in rr whn swtchd lft after s: swtchd rt over 2f out: kpt on: nt rch ldrs* **33/1**		
1-16	6	nk	**Naqshabban (USA)**[81] 2507 3-9-0 **98**	J-PGuillambert 8	97
			(Luca Cumani) *ponied to s: t.k.h in mid-div: effrt and chsng ldrs over 2f out: kpt on fnl f* **16/1**		
-034	7	1 1/4	**Demolition**[11] 4801 7-8-9 **92**	GeorgeChaloner[(7)] 12	89
			(Richard Fahey) *s.i.s: mid-div: effrt over 2f out: one pce over 1f out* **20/1**		
00-6	8	1 1/2	**Master Of Arts (USA)**[11] 4774 6-9-3 **93**	NeilCallan 3	87
			(Mark Johnston) *trckd ldrs: led on bit over 2f out: hdd appr fnl f: sn wknd* **33/1**		
3065	9	shd	**Kay Gee Be (IRE)**[18] 4528 7-9-1 **91**	TonyHamilton 11	85
			(Richard Fahey) *trckd ldrs: effrt over 2f out: wknd over 1f out* **40/1**		
-000	10	hd	**Riggins (IRE)**[19] 4494 7-9-5 **102**	MichaelJMurphy[(7)] 5	98+
			(Ed Walker) *s.i.s: hdwy and n.m.r 2f out: kpt on: nvr nr ldrs* **33/1**		
0520	11	nk	**Tiger Reigns**[11] 4801 5-9-5 **95**	PhillipMakin 13	88
			(Michael Dods) *chsd ldrs: fdd appr fnl f* **33/1**		
4003	12	1 1/4	**World Heritage**[11] 4801 5-9-4 **94**	AndreaAtzeni 10	84
			(Robert Eddery) *chsd ldrs: wknd over 1f out* **16/1**		
1060	13	1 1/4	**Ingleby Spirit**[79] 2573 4-9-0 **90**	BarryMcHugh 6	78
			(Richard Fahey) *led: hdd over 2f out: wknd over 1f out* **25/1**		
6112	14	1	**Ithoughtitwasover (IRE)**[11] 4777 3-8-5 **89**	SilvestreDeSousa 14	75
			(Mark Johnston) *hld up towards rr: hdwy stands' side over 3f out: wknd 2f out* **7/1**[2]		
1	15	2 1/4	**Eagles Peak**[40] 3824 3-9-0 **98**	RichardHughes 2	80
			(Sir Michael Stoute) *hld up in rr: drvn over 3f out: wknd over 1f out* **5/2**[1]		
5600	16	3 1/2	**Space War**[18] 4528 4-8-10 **86**	PaddyAspell 17	61
			(Michael Easterby) *s.i.s: hdwy 4f out: edgd rt and wknd over 2f out* **50/1**		
0-41	17	1 1/4	**High Twelve (IRE)**[26] 4267 4-9-9 **104**	AntiocoMurgia[(5)] 1	77
			(Mahmood Al Zarooni) *mid-div: hdwy on ins 4f out: wknd over 2f out* **12/1**		

2m 13.84s (1.34) **Going Correction** +0.375s/f (Good)
WFA 3 from 4yo+ 8lb **17 Ran SP% 126.2**
Speed ratings (Par 109): **109,108,104,104,103 103,102,101,101,100 100,99,98,97,96 93,92**
Tote Swingers: 1&2 £17.70, 1&3 £9.50, 2&3 £23.80 CSF £167.21 CT £1198.32 TOTE £9.20: £1.80, £3.70, £2.20, £2.10; EX 122.90 Trifecta £891.00 Pool: £3,672.41 - 3.05 winning units..
Owner A Long **Bred** Castlefarm Stud **Trained** Musley Bank, N Yorks

FOCUS
The pace didn't look that strong, yet the final time was 0.86 quicker than the earlier International Stakes. The action unfolded middle to stands' side. This was a good, competitive handicap. The winner reversed Goodwood form with the second and the form could rate higher at face value.

NOTEBOOK
Our Joe Mac(IRE) was third behind Arlequin at Glorious Goodwood last time but just got the better of a protracted duel with his old rival on 3lb better terms. There was a long gap back to the third and the winner looks a smart type in the making. He's in the Dubai Duty Free Handicap at Newbury and the Cambridgeshire. (op 9-1)
Arlequin just failed to confirm recent Goodwood form with Our Joe Mac, but he did nothing wrong. Much like the winner, he's progressing to a smart level and is also in both the Dubai Duty Free Handicap at Newbury and the Cambridgeshire. (op 16-1)
Club Oceanic, raised 3lb for his latest success, made his move more towards the middle than the front pair and was well held. This lightly raced colt might want better ground and remains progressive. He's another in the Dubai Duty Free Handicap at Newbury and the Cambridgeshire. (op 9-1)
Barren Brook, up 3lb for winning at Doncaster last time, did well to finish so close considering he was keen without cover early. He probably remains on a good mark. (tchd 15-2)
Norman Orpen(IRE), up in trip, was set a lot to do but was going on at the finish.
Naqshabban(USA) had refused to enter the stalls twice since he was last seen in May. He ran alright and is sufficiently lightly raced to believe he can yet improve plenty if going the right way mentally. (op 14-1)
Master Of Arts(USA) ran well for a long way, although ultimately didn't find as much as had looked likely.
Riggins(IRE) was under pressure and seemingly not going anywhere fast when finding trouble in the straight, but when in the clear late on he was finishing better than most without being given a hard time. He had a hood fitted last time, but maybe blinkers will be worth a go. (tchd 40-1 in a place)
Eagles Peak was fancied to follow up his Newmarket debut success, but this was a big ask for one so inexperienced and he was never going that well. He can be given another chance in time, with better ground likely to suit. (op 9-4, tchd 11-4 in places)
T/Jkpt: Not won. T/Plt: £426.40 to a £1 stake. Pool of £263,574.00 - 451.22 winning tickets. T/Qpdt: £46.00 to a £1 stake. Pool of £12,228.00 - 196.53 winning tickets. WG

5186 - 5193a (Foreign Racing) - See Raceform Interactive

5127 DEAUVILLE (R-H)
Wednesday, August 17
OFFICIAL GOING: Turf: good to soft; fibresand: standard

5194a PRIX DE LA VALLEE D'AUGE (LISTED RACE) (2YO) (TURF) 5f
4:50 (12:00) 2-Y-O **£23,706** (£9,482; £7,112; £4,741; £2,370)

		Horse	Jockey	RPR
1		**Calahorra (FR)**[29] 4191 2-8-8 0	MaximeGuyon 3	95
		(C Baillet, France) **9/1**		
2	3/4	**Bear Behind (IRE)**[17] 4596 2-8-11 0	RichardKingscote 6	95
		(Tom Dascombe) *broke fast: sn led on wd outside: rdn 2 1/2f out: r.o wl u.str.p fnl f: ct and hdd in fnl 20yds* **14/1**		
3	3/4	**Sea Trial (FR)**[37] 2-8-11 0	JohanVictoire 1	92
		(Mme C Head-Maarek, France) **68/10**[3]		
4	1/2	**Mac Row (IRE)**[24] 4375 2-8-11 0	IoritzMendizabal 5	91
		(J-C Rouget, France) **5/2**[2]		
5	2 1/2	**Lombatina (FR)**[33] 2-8-8 0	MickaelBarzalona 2	79
		(F Head, France) **4/5**[1]		
6	4	**Vital Spirit (FR)**[19] 2-8-11 0	Francois-XavierBertras 4	67
		(E J O'Neill, France) **28/1**		

59.10 secs (1.60) **6 Ran SP% 117.1**
WIN (incl. 1 euro stake): 10.30. PLACES: 3.80, 4.90. SF: 64.30.
Owner Steeve Berland **Bred** S & C Berland **Trained** France

5195a PRIX DE MARIVEL (CONDITIONS) (4YO+) (LADY RIDERS) (FIBRESAND) 7f 110y
7:20 (12:00) 4-Y-O+ **£9,482** (£3,793; £2,844; £1,896; £948)

		Horse	Jockey	RPR
1		**Kameruka**[22] 5-8-3 0	MlleAmelieFoulon[(5)] 2	84
		(R Pritchard-Gordon, France) **26/5**[2]		
2	hd	**Alanis (BEL)**[99] 6-8-7 0	PamelaBoehm[(6)] 8	89
		(Mme V Botte, Belgium) **68/1**		
3	1 1/2	**Browning Dream (GER)**[10] 4-8-11 0	SabrinaWandt 10	83
		(Frau C Barsig, Germany) **29/1**		
4	1	**Lonsome Drive (FR)**[42] 4-8-3 0	ManonScandella[(5)] 3	77
		(Y De Nicolay, France) **16/1**		
5	nk	**Celebrissime (IRE)**[396] 4166 6-8-11 0	BrigitteRenk 4	80
		(F Head, France) **1/1**[1]		
6	1 1/2	**Jungle Bay**[27] 4255 4-9-2 0	IvaMilickova 5	81
		(Jane Chapple-Hyam) *broke fast: sn hdwy to ld then settled 3rd on rail after 2f: rdn early in st: r.o u.p: stl prom ent fnl f: nt qckn and grad fdd* **9/1**		
7	snk	**Handsome Maestro (IRE)**[654] 7208 5-8-11 0	NadegeOuakli 11	75
		(Robert Collet, France) **15/2**[3]		
8	10	**Attiki Oddo**[132] 4-8-11 0	CelineLaunay 6	50
		(P Monfort, France) **12/1**		
9	1 1/2	**Print (IRE)**[104] 5-8-11 0	CarlaO'Halloran 1	47
		(Mlle M Henry, France) **72/1**		
10	2	**Versaki (IRE)**[252] 5-8-6 0	PaulineDominois[(5)] 9	42
		(J Clais, France) **94/1**		
0		**My Juju (FR)**[300] 4-8-9 0 ow1	MlleNathalieDesoutter 7	—
		(B De Montzey, France) **9/1**		

1m 30.4s (90.40) **11 Ran SP% 118.7**
WIN (incl. 1 euro stake): 6.20. PLACES: 2.20, 9.30, 5.70. DF: 134.60. SF: 182.80.
Owner Giles W Pritchard-Gordon **Bred** Giles W Pritchard-Gordon (farming) Ltd **Trained** France

4454 EPSOM (L-H)
Thursday, August 18
OFFICIAL GOING: Good (7.9) changing to good (good to soft in places) after race 3 (6.15)
Rail dolled out up to 6yds from 1m to 7f and from 6f to winning post adding about 10yds to advertised distances.
Wind: Fresh, across Weather: overcast, chilly wind

5196 CARLING BRITISH STALLION STUDS EBF MEDIAN AUCTION MAIDEN STKS 7f
5:10 (5:10) (Class 5) 2-Y-O **£3,881** (£1,155; £577) **Stalls** Low

Form			Horse	Jockey	RPR
2	1		**Ghost Protocol (IRE)**[19] 4525 2-9-3 0	GeorgeBaker 2	83+
			(David Simcock) *chsd clr ldr: clsd over 2f out: shkn up to ld ent fnl f: edgd rt but in command fnl 100yds* **4/6**[1]		
024	2	1 1/4	**Freddy Q (IRE)**[22] 4446 2-9-0 **78**	SeanLevey[(3)] 4	75+
			(Richard Hannon) *chsd ldng pair: rdn and clsd over 2f out: chsd wnr and edging lft ins fnl f: no imp fnl 100yds* **11/4**[2]		
00	3	1 1/4	**Dollar Bill**[29] 4213 2-9-3 0	DavidProbert 3	72
			(Andrew Balding) *led and sn clr: rdn and qcknd over 3f out: drvn over 2f out: hdd ent fnl f: wknd fnl 100yds* **4/1**[3]		

1m 28.71s (5.41) **Going Correction** +0.225s/f (Good) **3 Ran SP% 106.7**
Speed ratings (Par 94): **78,76,75**
CSF £2.70 TOTE £1.60; EX 2.20.
Owner A & A **Bred** Knockainey Stud **Trained** Newmarket, Suffolk

FOCUS
The course missed most of the rain that was around and the going remained good, on a chilly and windy night. The potentially useful odds-on favourite scored in good style, and was value for more than the winning margin in this small-field maiden auction.

NOTEBOOK

Ghost Protocol(IRE) travelled well for a long way before being just caught close home in a 7f Doncaster maiden auction on debut last month. He set the standard and made smooth headway to range alongside the breakaway leader before quickening well to score with quite a bit in hand on the second attempt. His dam's first three foals have been 6f/7f 2-y-o winners, and this son of Cockney Rebel looks another bright prospect in the family line. (op 4-7 tchd 1-2 in places)

Freddy Q(IRE) stepped up on his debut form when chasing home a better-fancied stablemate at Lingfield before a front-running fourth behind some useful types at Sandown last time. Held-up in last, he was never really a factor and didn't look entirely comfortable on the track, but he showed a good attitude to keep staying on. An Iffraaj colt, he has a fair amount of ability and is out of an unraced half-sister to a Japanese St Leger winner, so should stay further than this in time. (op 3-1 tchd 5-2)

Dollar Bill weakened when beaten 6l+ in a pair of 7f maidens at Newmarket and Sandown. He had plenty to find but was not beaten far after setting a decent pace on his first try on a sound surface. Out of an unraced half-sister to 1m2f Group 3 winner Felicity and high-class 7f-1m performer Sleeping Indian, he is getting the hang of things and will find better opportunities than this. (op 9-2 tchd 5-1)

5197 COORS LIGHT NURSERY — 7f

5:40 (5:41) (Class 5) (0-75,75) 2-Y-O — **£2,587** (£770; £384; £192) **Stalls** Low

Form — RPR

2230 **1** — **Costa Del Fortune (IRE)**[18] 4581 2-9-2 **73**........ KieranO'Neill(3) 9 — 77
(Richard Hannon) *pressed ldr: hung rt and racd awkwardly on downhill run 4f out: drvn to ld over 1f out: kpt on wl fnl f* — **16/1**

505 **2** *½* **Ermyn Flyer**[26] 4319 2-8-1 **55**........ DavidProbert 3 — 58
(Pat Phelan) *in tch: n.m.r and shuffled bk to rr after 2f: swtchd rt and rdn 3f out: hdwy u.p over 1f out: chsd wnr ins fnl f: styd on wl* — **20/1**

0162 **3** *2 ¼* **Marygold**[11] 4824 2-9-7 **75**........ IanMongan 7 — 72
(John Akehurst) *led and crossed to rail: rdn and hdd over 1f out: no ex and btn ins fnl f: wknd towards fin* — **7/1**

6460 **4** *½* **Whinging Willie (IRE)**[20] 4496 2-9-7 **75**........(v[1]) GeorgeBaker 1 — 71
(Gary Moore) *sn bustled along to go handy: rdn and effrt 2f out: nt qckn over 1f out: swtchd rt and kpt on ins fnl f: nvr gng pce to rch ldrs* — **10/3**[1]

435 **5** *2* **Maastricht (IRE)**[62] 3123 2-9-4 **72**........ NeilCallan 4 — 63
(Mark Johnston) *wl in tch in midfield: rdn and edgd lft over 2f out: drvn and unable qck over 1f out: plugged on same pce and no threat to ldrs fnl f* — **13/2**

345 **6** *nk* **Rock Canyon (IRE)**[52] 3472 2-9-3 **74**........ SeanLevey(3) 6 — 64
(Robert Mills) *in tch in last trio: rdn and effrt towards inner 2f out: kpt on ins fnl f: nvr gng pce to rch ldrs* — **5/1**[2]

6151 **7** *1 ¾* **Silvas Romana (IRE)**[14] 4704 2-9-4 **72**........ LiamKeniry 2 — 58
(Mark Brisbourne) *t.k.h: hld up wl in tch in midfield: short of room over 2f out: rdn and unbalanced 2f out: no imp fr over 1f out* — **13/2**

000 **8** *½* **Doctor Banner**[43] 3722 2-8-10 **64**........ SamHitchcott 10 — 48
(Mick Channon) *in tch in last trio: outpcd over 3f out: rdn and effrt on inner 2f out: swtchd rt 1f out: kpt on: nvr trbld ldrs* — **66/1**

610 **9** *5* **Greatest Dancer (IRE)**[40] 3866 2-9-7 **75**........ FergusSweeney 8 — 46
(Jamie Osborne) *in tch in midfield on outer: lost pl and rdn 3f out: bhd and wl btn whn hung lft over 1f out* — **10/1**

5133 **10** *2* **Xinbama (IRE)**[18] 4581 2-9-1 **69**........ DarryllHolland 5 — 35
(J W Hills) *pressed ldrs on outer: hung rt and racd awkwardly on downhill run 4f out: wknd 2f out* — **11/2**[3]

1m 25.54s (2.24) **Going Correction** +0.225s/f (Good) — **10** Ran SP% **115.5**

Speed ratings (Par 94): **96,95,92,92,90 89,87,87,81,79**

Tote Swingers:1&2:£46.70, 2&3:£20.60, 1&3:£8.20 CSF £291.31 CT £2496.01 TOTE £21.00: £6.10, £8.00, £3.00; EX 547.90 TRIFECTA Not won..

Owner L M Power **Bred** Oak Lodge Bloodstock **Trained** East Everleigh, Wilts

FOCUS

They went a steady pace in this nursery and several were keen in a tightly grouped field for a long way.

NOTEBOOK

Costa Del Fortune(IRE) stopped quickly on nursery debut at Newbury and she didn't seem to handle the downhill section very well here, but she managed to maintain a prominent position and stayed on strongly to reconfirm her maiden promise and get off the mark on the fifth attempt. She still needs to learn to settle better but it is very encouraging that she could deliver in this competitive race after not really handling the track, and she has scope for quite a bit of improvement. Official explanation: trainer said, regarding apparent improvement in form, that the filly had settled better. (tchd 18-1)

Ermyn Flyer, well held in three sprint maidens, was supported at biggish prices on this nursery debut and stayed on well out wide to go close stepped up to 7f. By an Arc winner out of a 7f winner, she is open to further progress and could be closing in on a first win. (op 28-1 tchd 33-1)

Marygold is fairly exposed but she was a clear second in a 6f Windsor fillies' nursery last week and gave it a decent shot under usual front-running tactics on this first try at 7f. She could make a bold bid back at 6f next time. (op 6-1)

Whinging Willie(IRE), a big market mover throughout the day, was well positioned but got caught a bit flat footed when the pace increased before staying on again on his first try in a visor. A stronger pace and a more galloping track should play more to his strengths. (op 4-1 tchd 3-1)

Maastricht(IRE) was never really travelling with any fluency but did quite well to keep battling for fifth on nursery debut. A Tiger Hill colt who is out of a very useful mare, he looks a strong galloping type and should be suited chasing a faster pace on a stiffer track. (op 9-1)

Rock Canyon(IRE) didn't really get the breaks against the far rail but shaped with some promise on nursery debut back from a short break. (op 7-1)

Silvas Romana(IRE) made it two wins from three starts in nurseries when swooping late to beat a next-time-out winner at Chepstow last time. A 6lb rise looked fair but she was too keen off the steady pace and couldn't make an impact stepped up in trip. (op 9-2)

Xinbama(IRE), a close third in a similar race at Newbury last month, had every chance but stopped quickly this time. (op 5-1)

5198 MAY FAMILY LADIES' DERBY H'CAP (FOR LADY AMATEUR RIDERS) — 1m 4f 10y

6:15 (6:20) (Class 4) (0-80,80) 4-Y-O+ — **£4,367** (£1,354; £676; £338) **Stalls** Centre

Form — RPR

1051 **1** — **Megalala (IRE)**[14] 4700 10-9-12 **68**........ MissSBrotherton 8 — 79
(John Bridger) *mde all: wnt clr 8f out: in command and pushed along 2f out: kpt on: unchal* — **7/1**[3]

2120 **2** *6* **Zennor**[25] 4360 4-10-2 **77**........ MissALMurphy(5) 10 — 79
(Tom Dascombe) *s.i.s: towards rr: rdn and effrt to go 4th over 2f out: swtchd rt ent fnl f: chsd clr wnr ins fnl f: kpt on but no threat to wnr* **9/2**[1]

4110 **3** *1* **Cotton King**[159] 849 4-10-3 **78**........(vt) MissFCumani(5) 12 — 78
(Tobias B P Coles) *t.k.h: chsd ldrs tl wnt 2nd 9f out: clr of field fr 7f out: rdn and no imp 2f out: lost 2nd ins fnl f: jinked and rdr unbalanced nr fin* — **12/1**

1334 **4** *1 ½* **Sancho Panza**[15] 4687 4-9-7 **68**........ MissSBirkett(5) 4 — 66
(Julia Feilden) *chsd wnr early: grad stdd bk and in rr 8f out: gd hdwy on outer 4f out: no threat to wnr but pressing for placings over 2f out: kpt on same pce after* — **13/2**[2]

2150 **5** *5* **Addwaitya**[22] 4423 6-10-6 **76**........ MissGAndrews 2 — 66
(Laura Mongan) *s.i.s: bhd and nudged along early: rdn and effrt 3f out: 5th and no imp whn hung lft u.p 2f out* — **7/1**[3]

324 **6** *3* **My Valley (IRE)**[14] 4697 9-10-2 **72**........ MissLHorner 6 — 57
(Pat Phelan) *hld up towards rr: rdn and effrt into midfield 3f out: no prog after: nvr trbld ldrs* — **12/1**

6564 **7** *3 ½* **Squad**[17] 4613 5-9-6 **62**........(v) MissEJJones 3 — 41
(Simon Dow) *s.i.s: bhd: rdn and effrt 2f out: no prog: nvr trbld ldrs* — **16/1**

0306 **8** *½* **Solicitor**[25] 4360 4-10-5 **78**........ LucyAlexander(3) 7 — 56
(Mark Johnston) *chsd ldrs: disputing 3rd and wl off the pce whn rdn over 3f out: wknd wl over 2f out* — **13/2**[2]

00 **9** *27* **Lord Theo**[19] 4553 7-9-10 **66**........ MrsEmmaLittmoden 11 — —
(Nick Littmoden) *s.i.s: a in rr: rdn and lost tch 3f out: t.o and eased ins fnl f* — **28/1**

0100 **10** *3 ½* **Guilded Warrior**[17] 4603 8-10-2 **77**........ MissMBryant(5) 5 — —
(Paddy Butler) *chsd wnr after 1f tl 9f out: steadily lost pl: lost tch over 2f out: t.o fnl f* — **40/1**

1235 **11** *10* **Wrecking Crew (IRE)**[50] 3516 7-9-0 **61** oh3........ MrsDBamonte(5) 9 — —
(Rod Millman) *bolted to s: racd in midfield: lost pl qckly over 3f out: sn lost tch: wl t.o over 1f out* — **14/1**

2m 42.02s (3.12) **Going Correction** +0.225s/f (Good) — **11** Ran SP% **103.7**

Speed ratings (Par 105): **98,94,93,92,89 87,84,84,66,64 57**

Tote Swingers:1&2:£4.40, 2&3:£6.90, 1&3:£14.70 CSF £30.83 CT £269.62 TOTE £6.70: £2.20, £1.80, £3.70; EX 34.80 Trifecta £127.50 Pool £1,654.29 - 9.60 winning units..

Owner Tommy Ware **Bred** Joseph Gallagher **Trained** Liphook, Hants

FOCUS

It was raining heavily before this handicap for lady amateur riders. The winner produced a dominant front-running display and hardly any of his rivals got involved. The runner-up is rated 5lb off his best which might overrate the winner, but can be given some sort of chance.

5199 WEATHERBYS BLOODSTOCK INSURANCE H'CAP — 1m 114y

6:45 (6:48) (Class 4) (0-85,82) 3-Y-O — **£6,469** (£1,925; £962; £481) **Stalls** Low

Form — RPR

0310 **1** — **Weapon Of Choice (IRE)**[40] 3864 3-9-4 **82**........ KieranO'Neill(3) 2 — 93+
(David Simcock) *t.k.h: hld up in tch: rdn and effrt to chal over 2f out: led 2f out: kpt on wl fnl f: rdn out* — **8/1**

31 **2** *½* **Shalloon (IRE)**[45] 3684 3-9-2 **77**........ NeilCallan 1 — 87
(Mark Johnston) *chsd ldr: rdn to chal 3f out: drew clr w wnr over 1f out: kpt on wl u.p but a hld* — **7/2**[2]

4603 **3** *2 ¾* **John Biscuit (IRE)**[22] 4447 3-9-5 **80**........ DavidProbert 7 — 84
(Andrew Balding) *s.i.s: t.k.h: hld up in tch: rdn and effrt 3f out: outpcd by ldrs over 1f out: swtchd lft ins fnl f and kpt on to go 3rd towards fin* **4/1**[3]

-031 **4** *½* **Regal Salute**[31] 4158 3-9-6 **81**........ ShaneKelly 3 — 83
(Jeremy Noseda) *led: rdn and hrd pressed 3f out: hdd 2f out: unable qck u.p over 1f out: btn 1f out: lost 3rd towards fin* — **4/1**[3]

1321 **5** *3 ½* **Uptown Guy (USA)**[10] 4854 3-9-1 **79** 6ex........(b) AdamBeschizza(3) 5 — 73+
(William Haggas) *rel to r and v.s.a: sn rdn along: clsd and in tch after 2f: drvn and struggling over 2f out: wknd 2f out* — **10/3**[1]

21 **6** *1 ¼* **Iulus**[25] 4363 3-9-3 **78**........ PBBeggy 4 — 69
(John Quinn) *chsd ldrs: pushed along 5f out: rdn and unable qck over 2f out: wknd wl over 1f out* — **13/2**

1m 47.19s (1.09) **Going Correction** +0.225s/f (Good) — **6** Ran SP% **109.7**

Speed ratings (Par 102): **104,103,101,100,97 96**

Tote Swingers:1&2:£5.10, 2&3:£2.90, 1&3:£6.70 CSF £34.02 TOTE £3.70: £2.20, £3.20; EX 17.70.

Owner Dr Marwan Koukash **Bred** Stone Ridge Farm **Trained** Newmarket, Suffolk

FOCUS

The going was changed to good, good to soft in places. An interesting handicap. They shifted to the near rail in the straight and the most exposed runner in the line-up scored in gritty style. A personal best from the winner with the runner-up a slight improver.

5200 CAPITAL LEISURE H'CAP — 1m 114y

7:20 (7:20) (Class 5) (0-75,76) 4-Y-O+ — **£2,587** (£770; £384; £192) **Stalls** Low

Form — RPR

4111 **1** — **Starwatch**[10] 4860 4-9-5 **76** 6ex........ SeanLevey(3) 4 — 86
(John Bridger) *s.i.s and pushed along early: t.k.h and hld up in tch after 2f: rdn and effrt to chal 3f out: led 2f out and sn edgd rt: r.o wl fnl f: rdn out* — **4/1**[3]

0042 **2** *1* **Veiled Applause**[5] 5036 8-9-0 **71**........ DaleSwift(3) 3 — 79
(John Quinn) *in tch: rdn 4f out: dropped to rr and bhd a wall of horses over 2f out: swtchd lft and hdwy over 1f out: chsd wnr ins fnl f: kpt on* — **11/4**[1]

030 **3** *2 ¼* **Aspectus (IRE)**[27] 4278 8-9-4 **75**........(b) SophieDoyle(3) 1 — 78
(Jamie Osborne) *sn led: stuck in centre and hdd wl over 2f out: drvn and outpcd 2f out: kpt on ins fnl f to go 3rd cl home* — **8/1**

53-6 **4** *½* **Dear Maurice**[43] 3464 7-9-2 **70**........(t) MickyFenton 5 — 72
(Tobias B P Coles) *chsd ldrs: effrt to join ldrs 3f out: led over 2f out: sn hdd: outpcd over 1f out: styd on same pce fnl f* — **14/1**

-360 **5** *shd* **Compton Blue**[26] 4310 5-9-4 **75**........(b) KieranO'Neill(3) 2 — 77
(Richard Hannon) *chsd ldrs: rdn and ev ch over 2f out: chsd wnr over 1f out tl ins fnl f: wknd and lost 2 pls towards fin* — **4/1**[3]

042 **6** *3 ½* **Super Duplex**[21] 4457 4-8-13 **67**........ IanMongan 8 — 61
(Pat Phelan) *t.k.h: hld up in tch: hdwy to join ldrs on outer 4f out: c to stands' rail and led wl over 2f out: sn hdd: wknd over 1f out* — **3/1**[2]

1300 **7** *4 ½* **Qeethaara (USA)**[14] 4701 7-9-0 **68**........ ShaneKelly 9 — 51
(Mark Brisbourne) *s.i.s: hld up in tch in rr: hdwy to press ldrs 3f out: wknd 2f out: wl btn and eased ins fnl f* — **16/1**

1m 47.33s (1.23) **Going Correction** +0.225s/f (Good) — **7** Ran SP% **115.3**

Speed ratings (Par 103): **103,102,100,99,99 96,92**

Tote Swingers:1&2:£2.80, 2&3:£9.20, 1&3:£2.60 CSF £15.72 CT £83.02 TOTE £3.50: £1.50, £2.20; EX 13.00 Trifecta £62.70 Pool £3,932.89 - 46.35 winning units..

Owner J J Bridger **Bred** Mrs J A Chapman **Trained** Liphook, Hants

FOCUS

A competitive handicap with the runner-up close to his latest York mark setting the standard. The runners were tightly bunched off a steady pace in the early stages and they raced centre to near side in the straight.

5201 CAFFREY'S H'CAP — 7f

7:50 (7:50) (Class 5) (0-75,75) 3-Y-O+ — **£2,587** (£770; £384; £192) **Stalls** Low

Form — RPR

0035 **1** — **Katmai River (IRE)**[13] 4742 4-8-12 **61**........(v) DavidProbert 11 — 69
(Mark Usher) *chsd ldrs: rdn over 3f out: drvn to ld over 1f out: kpt on wl u.p ins fnl f* — **7/1**

-004 **2** *hd* **Flameoftheforest (IRE)**[15] 4670 4-9-10 **73**.................... PatCosgrave 10 80+
(Ed de Giles) *awkward leaving stalls and s.i.s: hld up in last quartet: nt clr run over 1f out tl swtchd rt 1f out: str run ins fnl f: pressed wnr cl home: nt quite get up* **7/2**[1]

3004 **3** ½ **Timpanist (USA)**[14] 4711 4-8-5 **57**............................ AdamBeschizza(3) 1 63
(Simon Dow) *in tch in midfield: rdn over 3f out: hdwy u.p to join ldrs 2f out: ev ch over 1f out: no ex towards fin* **25/1**

0246 **4** ¾ **Nezami (IRE)**[6] 4997 6-9-9 **72**... NeilCallan 14 76
(John Akehurst) *led: rdn over 2f out: hdd over 1f out: styd on same pce ins fnl f* **13/2**[3]

3130 **5** ½ **Phluke**[22] 4444 10-8-13 **65**.. LouisBeuzelin(3) 13 68
(Eve Johnson Houghton) *chsd ldr tl over 2f out: kpt on same pce u.p fr over 1f out* **9/1**

0013 **6** *hd* **Downhill Skier (IRE)**[12] 4793 7-9-3 **66**....................... TomMcLaughlin 6 68
(Mark Brisbourne) *in tch in midfield: rdn 4f out: drvn and unable qck over 2f out: styd on same pce u.p fr over 1f out* **13/2**[3]

6440 **7** 1 **Sunshine Always (IRE)**[5] 5053 5-9-6 **69**........................... ShaneKelly 5 68
(Michael Attwater) *hld up in last quartet: stuck bhd a wall of horses over 2f out: swtchd lft and hdwy over 1f out: rdn and no imp ins fnl f* **15/2**

-002 **8** ½ **Scottish Glen**[29] 4210 5-9-4 **67**... LiamKeniry 2 65
(Patrick Chamings) *stdd after s: hld up in last quartet: rdn and effrt over 2f out: swtchd lft and hdwy over 1f out: no imp ins fnl f* **5/1**[2]

6100 **9** 9 **May's Boy**[47] 3649 3-9-7 **75**...................................(p) FergusSweeney 3 47
(Mark Usher) *stdd after s: hld up in rr: shortlived effrt over 2f out: wknd 2f out* **15/2**

1m 25.49s (2.19) **Going Correction** +0.225s/f (Good)
WFA 3 from 4yo+ 5lb **9** Ran SP% **115.4**
Speed ratings (Par 103): **96,95,95,94,93 93,92,91,81**
Tote Swingers:1&2:£6.00, 2&3:£46.70, 1&3:£15.60 CSF £31.72 CT £586.36 TOTE £8.10: £2.50, £1.90, £4.70; EX 43.00 Trifecta £186.70 Pool £328.03 - 1.30 winning units..
Owner M D I Usher **Bred** Mrs S M Roy **Trained** Upper Lambourn, Berks

FOCUS
There was stack of non-runners in this handicap. It was run at a decent pace and there was a tight finish. The form is best rated around the fourth and fifth.
T/Plt: £100.30 to a £1 stake. Pool £40,897.08. 297.55 winning tickets T/Qpdt: £14.60 to a £1 stake. Pool £4,412.74. 223.65 winning tickets SP

4538 HAMILTON (R-H)
Thursday, August 18

OFFICIAL GOING: Good (good to soft in places; 7.2)
Rail realignment increased distances by 8yds on round course and there was fresh ground on far side of home straight.
Wind: Slight, half against Weather: Cloudy

5202 BRITISH STALLION STUDS EBF DEBUTANTS MAIDEN STKS 6f 5y
2:20 (2:21) (Class 5) 2-Y-O **£3,234** (£962; £481; £240) **Stalls** High

Form RPR
1 **Foxtrot Romeo (IRE)** 2-9-3 0.. TomEaves 1 80+
(Bryan Smart) *mde virtually all: rdn and edgd lft ins fnl f: kpt on strly* **5/2**[2]

2 1¾ **Personal Touch** 2-9-0 0.. LeeTopliss(3) 3 75+
(Richard Fahey) *w ldrs: rdn over 1f out: kpt on same pce ins fnl f* **4/1**[3]

3 3½ **Greyhope** 2-9-3 0.. JamieGoldstein 4 64+
(Lucinda Russell) *slowly away and sn wl bhd: gd hdwy over 1f out: kpt on: nt rch first two* **150/1**

4 5 **Glamorous Angel (IRE)** 2-9-3 0.................................... PJMcDonald 7 49
(Alan Swinbank) *cl up: rdn and edgd rt over 2f out: wknd over 1f out* **2/1**[1]

5 7 **Yeeoow (IRE)** 2-9-3 0... AndrewElliott 5 28
(Mrs K Burke) *disp ld to 2f out: sn rdn and wknd* **8/1**

6 4½ **Dubai Rythm** 2-9-3 0.. RobbieFitzpatrick 2 15
(Michael Appleby) *in tch: drvn and outpcd after 2f: nvr on terms: eased whn no ch fnl f* **12/1**

7 2¾ **Bu Samra (IRE)** 2-9-3 0.. StephenCraine 6 —
(Kevin Ryan) *w ldrs to 1/2-way: sn rdn and wknd* **8/1**

1m 15.4s (3.20) **Going Correction** +0.15s/f (Good) **7** Ran SP% **112.5**
Speed ratings (Par 94): **84,81,77,70,61 55,51**
toteswingers:1&2:£2.00, 1&3:£12.20, 2&3:£17.30 CSF £12.50 TOTE £2.90: £1.80, £1.70; EX 11.50.
Owner Andrew Tinkler **Bred** Barronstown Stud **Trained** Hambleton, N Yorks

FOCUS
No previous form to go on in this maiden, but they went a fair pace with five of the seven runners disputing the early advantage in a line across the track.

NOTEBOOK
Foxtrot Romeo(IRE), a 90,000euros brother to the high-class Air Chief Marshal and the smart Misu Bond, was one of those to dispute the lead from the start and saw plenty of daylight on the wide outside, but he kept on going best and saw it out well despite hanging away to his left late on. A Mill Reef entry may be a little optimistic, but he should win more races. (op 9-4 tchd 11-4, 3-1 in a place)
Personal Touch, a 65,000gns half-brother to a winning juvenile sprinter, was another up there from the start and wasn't beaten until half a furlong from home. He should be winning a similar event before long. (tchd 9-2)
Greyhope, a £5,000 gelded half-brother to a couple of modest winners, very much caught the eye as he broke slowly and was soon outpaced, but he made up a lot of late ground. To a certain extent he was running on past beaten horses, but this was still a promising enough debut to suggest he has ability.
Glamorous Angel(IRE), a 105,000gns breeze-up purchase and a half-brother to the high-class Glamorous Spirit, showed early speed against the stands' rail but was beaten passing the 2f pole. He should improve. (op 15-8 tchd 13-8)

5203 TENTS & EVENTS H'CAP 6f 5y
2:55 (2:55) (Class 6) (0-65,58) 3-Y-O **£1,942** (£573; £287) **Stalls** High

Form RPR
0040 **1** **Deliberation (IRE)**[16] 4638 3-9-1 **57**.............................. JulieBurke(5) 3 67
(Kevin Ryan) *mde all: rdn and edgd rt over 1f out: r.o strly fnl f* **85/40**[2]

5145 **2** 2¼ **Tahitian Princess (IRE)**[9] 4876 3-9-4 **55**...................(p) DavidNolan 4 58
(Ann Duffield) *prom: effrt over 2f out: chsd wnr fnl f: r.o* **2/1**[1]

0054 **3** ½ **Babich Bay (IRE)**[30] 4183 3-9-7 **58**.............................(b) FrannyNorton 2 59
(Jo Hughes) *cl up: rdn and edgd rt over 1f out: kpt on same pce fnl f* **7/2**[3]

0605 **4** 11 **Sleights Boy (IRE)**[15] 4680 3-8-8 **45**..........................(b) PatrickMathers 1 11
(Ian McInnes) *cl up: rdn and edgd rt over 2f out: wknd over 1f out* **16/1**

4046 **5** 8 **Kassaab**[40] 3860 3-9-5 **56**.. TomEaves 5 —
(Ian Semple) *prom: drvn over 2f out: sn wknd* **9/1**

5030 **6** 7 **Tinzo (IRE)**[12] 4786 3-8-4 **46**.. ShaneBKelly(5) 6 —
(Alan Berry) *bhd: struggling 1/2-way: nvr on terms* **20/1**

1m 13.31s (1.11) **Going Correction** +0.15s/f (Good) **6** Ran SP% **108.2**
Speed ratings (Par 98): **98,95,94,79,69 59**
toteswingers:1&2:£2.10, 1&3:£1.60, 2&3:£1.80 CSF £6.24 TOTE £2.90: £1.10, £2.20; EX 7.00.
Owner Mrs Angie Bailey **Bred** Berkie Brown **Trained** Hambleton, N Yorks

FOCUS
A weak sprint handicap run at an ordinary pace. The placed horses are rated to their marks.

5204 DENNIS DONNELLY MEMORIAL UNISON GLASGOW HOUSING CLAIMING STKS 5f 4y
3:30 (3:30) (Class 6) 3-Y-O+ **£1,942** (£573; £287) **Stalls** High

Form RPR
103 **1** **Northern Bolt**[1] 5162 6-8-13 68.................................... PatrickMathers 4 76
(Ian McInnes) *in tch: rdn along after 2f: rallied over 1f out: led ins fnl f: rdn out* **4/1**[2]

4561 **2** 3¼ **Fol Hollow (IRE)**[29] 4197 6-9-6 82.................................. AdrianNicholls 2 71
(David Nicholls) *cl up: led over 1f out to ins fnl f: kpt on same pce* **1/2**[1]

6450 **3** 2 **The Jailer**[9] 4882 8-8-2 63 ow2...................................(p) ShaneBKelly(5) 3 51
(John O'Shea) *led to over 1f out: kpt on same pce fnl f* **10/1**[3]

0165 **4** 5 **Andrasta**[6] 5008 6-8-3 52.. JulieBurke(5) 5 34
(Alan Berry) *chsd ldrs: outpcd 1/2-way: n.d after* **10/1**[3]

0030 **5** 1¾ **Charlie Delta**[9] 4882 8-8-8 55 ow1..............................(b) LeeTopliss(3) 1 31
(John O'Shea) *in tch: rdn and hung rt over 2f out: sn btn* **33/1**

60.56 secs (0.56) **Going Correction** +0.15s/f (Good) **5** Ran SP% **107.8**
Speed ratings (Par 101): **101,95,92,84,81**
CSF £6.20 TOTE £4.90: £1.80, £1.10; EX 7.30.
Owner Keith Brown Properties (hull) Ltd **Bred** Mrs C Regalado-Gonzalez **Trained** Catwick, E Yorks

FOCUS
An uncompetitive claimer, but something of a turn-up. The form is rated somewhat cautiously around the winner's non-claiming best.

5205 SCOTTISH TROPHY H'CAP 1m 1f 36y
4:05 (4:06) (Class 4) (0-80,80) 3-Y-O+ **£4,528** (£1,347; £673; £336) **Stalls** Low

Form RPR
313 **1** **I'm Super Too (IRE)**[9] 4877 4-8-11 **70**......................... GarryWhillans(7) 5 85
(Alan Swinbank) *chsd clr ldng pair: smooth hdwy over 2f out: led over 1f out: sn clr: comf* **9/1**[3]

0441 **2** 3 **Muffin McLeay (IRE)**[56] 3304 3-9-7 **80**.......................... LeeNewman 10 88+
(David Barron) *midfield on ins: hdwy over 2f out: chsd (clr) wnr ins fnl f: r.o* **7/1**[2]

3113 **3** 1 **Persian Peril**[22] 4440 7-10-0 **80**...................................... PJMcDonald 11 86+
(Alan Swinbank) *in tch: lost pl over 3f out: effrt wl over 1f out: kpt on ins fnl f* **12/1**

5600 **4** 2¾ **Staff Sergeant**[19] 4561 4-9-12 **78**................................. DanielTudhope 15 78
(Jim Goldie) *midfield: effrt over 2f out: kpt on fnl f: no imp* **5/1**[1]

0510 **5** *nk* **Key Breeze**[19] 4540 4-8-13 **65**.......................................(t) StephenCraine 16 64
(Kevin Ryan) *taken early to post: missed break: hld up: hdwy over 3f out: rdn and edgd rt 2f out: oen pce fnl f* **28/1**

5612 **6** ¾ **Solar Spirit (IRE)**[11] 4821 6-9-3 **74**............................. ShaneBKelly(5) 12 72
(Tracy Waggott) *led and clr w one other: rdn over 2f out: hdd over 1f out: wknd ins fnl f* **25/1**

6526 **7** 1¼ **High Resolution**[19] 4540 4-9-4 **75**..................................... JulieBurke(5) 4 70
(Linda Perratt) *hld up: rdn and hdwy over 2f out: n.m.r briefly ins fnl f: nvr able to chal* **10/1**

2362 **8** 2 **Amazing Star (IRE)**[5] 5059 6-9-6 **77**................................ NeilFarley(5) 7 68
(Declan Carroll) *hld up: rdn and hdwy over 3f out: edgd rt and wknd 1f out* **5/1**[1]

3014 **9** ½ **Jonny Lesters Hair (IRE)**[17] 4608 6-10-0 **80**........... DuranFentiman 14 70
(Tim Easterby) *pressed ldr and clr of rest: rdn and ev ch tl wknd fnl f* **11/1**

425- **10** 5 **Ullswater (IRE)**[318] 6618 3-9-4 **77**................................... AdrianNicholls 1 56
(Mark Johnston) *hld up on ins: drvn and outpcd over 3f out: n.d after* **12/1**

0005 **11** 1¼ **Tartan Gigha (IRE)**[17] 4603 6-10-0 **80**........................... FrannyNorton 9 56
(Mark Johnston) *prom tl rdn and wknd fr 2f out* **14/1**

1436 **12** 6 **Botham (USA)**[17] 4603 7-8-10 **62**.................................. RoystonFfrench 13 25
(Jim Goldie) *hld up: drvn along over 3f out: nvr on terms* **22/1**

0065 **13** 4 **Jo'Burg (USA)**[21] 4477 7-9-11 **80**.................................. LeeTopliss(3) 3 34
(Ollie Pears) *missed break: hld up: hdwy on outside over 3f out: wknd wl over 1f out: eased whn btn ins fnl f* **16/1**

3305 **14** 3½ **Hill Tribe**[7] 4945 4-8-6 **61** oh4.. DeclanCannon(3) 2 —
(Richard Guest) *hld up: rdn and outpcd over 3f out: sn btn* **50/1**

2320 **15** 26 **Just Five (IRE)**[17] 4603 5-8-12 **71**................................ JustinNewman(7) 8 —
(John Weymes) *hld up: drvn along over 4f out: sn struggling: eased whn no ch fnl f* **28/1**

0-10 **16** 50 **First Battalion (IRE)**[97] 2076 3-9-3 **76**............................... TomEaves 6 —
(Keith Dalgleish) *in tch tl wknd over 3f out: lost tch and eased fnl 2f* **20/1**

2m 1.42s (1.72) **Going Correction** +0.325s/f (Good)
WFA 3 from 4yo+ 7lb **16** Ran SP% **123.0**
Speed ratings (Par 105): **105,102,101,99,98 98,96,95,94,90 89,83,80,77,54 9**
toteswingers:1&2:£12.00, 1&3:£12.80, 2&3:£16.00 CSF £65.01 CT £777.86 TOTE £11.40: £3.20, £1.40, £2.50, £1.30; EX 89.30.
Owner David C Young **Bred** Norelands Bloodstock, J Hanly & H Lascelles **Trained** Melsonby, N Yorks

FOCUS
A decent and competitive handicap run at a strong pace. The third is rated close to his best and is the guide.
First Battalion(IRE) Official explanation: trainer said gelding had a breathing problem

5206 PARKS OF HAMILTON MAIDEN STKS 6f 5y
4:40 (4:41) (Class 5) 3-Y-O+ **£2,385** (£704; £352) **Stalls** High

Form RPR
0 **1** **Edgware Road**[124] 1409 3-9-3 0.. TomEaves 5 65+
(Keith Dalgleish) *prom: effrt and swtchd rt over 1f out: led ins fnl f: sn clr* **2/1**[2]

0-4 **2** 3¾ **Beachwood Bay**[16] 4647 3-9-3 0.. FrannyNorton 3 53
(Jo Hughes) *t.k.h: cl up: led over 1f out to ins fnl f: sn one pce* **9/2**[3]

3243 **3** 3¼ **Hardrock Diamond**[12] 4786 3-9-3 49............................ DuranFentiman 1 43
(Ian Semple) *trckd ldrs: effrt and rdn over 1f out: kpt on same pce ins fnl f* **9/2**[3]

04 **4** 4 **Galloping Minister (IRE)**[8] 4923 3-9-3 0...................... StephenCraine 4 30
(Tom Dascombe) *led to over 1f out: sn rdn and wknd* **15/8**[1]

5 2½ **Miss Pronounce** 3-8-12 0... PJMcDonald 6 17
(Linda Perratt) *missed break: hld up in tch: rdn over 2f out: wknd appr fnl f* **14/1**

0600 **6** *6* **Ivy And Gold**[17] 4607 3-8-12 40........................ JulieBurke(5) 2 —
(Alan Berry) *in tch: drvn and hung rt over 2f out: sn btn* **100/1**
1m 14.96s (2.76) **Going Correction** +0.15s/f (Good) **6** Ran SP% **112.1**
Speed ratings (Par 103): **87,82,77,72,69 61**
toteswingers:1&2:£2.10, 1&3:£2.10, 2&3:£1.80 CSF £11.36 TOTE £2.80: £1.20, £1.40; EX 13.90.
Owner Mrs E Johansen-Wooder **Bred** Juddmonte Farms Ltd **Trained** Carluke, South Lanarkshire
FOCUS
A weak maiden and the winning time was 1.65 seconds slower than the earlier 3-y-o handicap. The form looks shaky with the proximity of the third holding things down.

5207 GRIFFITHS & ARMOUR H'CAP 1m 4f 17y
5:15 (5:15) (Class 5) (0-70,70) 3-Y-0+ £2,425 (£721; £360; £180) Stalls Low

Form RPR
5532 **1** **Jeu De Vivre (IRE)**[3] 5107 3-9-2 68.......................... FrannyNorton 1 80+
(Mark Johnston) *t.k.h early: trckd ldr: led over 2f out: edgd rt over 1f out: pushed clr* **6/4**[1]
0005 **2** *2 ¾* **Stags Leap (IRE)**[9] 4879 4-9-1 64...........................(v) GarryWhillans(7) 3 69
(Alistair Whillans) *trckd ldrs: effrt over 2f out: outpcd wl over 1f out: rallied to chse (clr) wnr ins fnl f: no imp* **6/1**[3]
3622 **3** *6* **Sharp Sovereign (USA)**[19] 4540 5-9-6 67.......................... LMcNiff(5) 6 62
(David Barron) *led: rdn and rdr dropped whip over 2f out: sn hdd: no ex fr over 1f out: lost 2nd ins fnl f* **2/1**[2]
50-0 **4** *4* **Regent's Secret (USA)**[23] 3858 11-8-13 55.............(v) DanielTudhope 7 44
(Jim Goldie) *stdd s: hld up: effrt 3f out: no imp fr 2f out* **16/1**
655/ **5** *10* **Acclaben (IRE)**[773] 3684 5-8-9 51 oh1.......................... PJMcDonald 5 24
(Alan Swinbank) *in tch: rdn over 3f out: wknd fr over 2f out* **8/1**
46-0 **6** *9* **Middlemarch (IRE)**[17] 4605 11-8-4 51.......................(p) ShaneBKelly(5) 8 10
(Jim Goldie) *prom: drvn and outpcd over 3f out: sn n.d* **18/1**
2m 43.39s (4.79) **Going Correction** +0.325s/f (Good)
WFA 3 from 4yo+ 10lb **6** Ran SP% **109.9**
Speed ratings (Par 103): **97,95,91,88,81 75**
toteswingers:1&2:£2.80, 1&3:£1.10, 2&3:£2.90 CSF £10.51 CT £15.95 TOTE £2.40: £1.50, £2.80; EX 10.80.
Owner Ms J Bianco **Bred** Rockhart Trading Ltd **Trained** Middleham Moor, N Yorks
FOCUS
An ordinary handicap and the early pace was by no means strong. The runner-up sets the standard.

5208 RACING UK "HANDS AND HEELS" APPRENTICE SERIES H'CAP (ROUND FOUR OF HAMILTON APPRENTICE SERIES) 1m 65y
5:45 (5:49) (Class 6) (0-55,55) 3-Y-0+ £1,942 (£573; £287) Stalls Low

Form RPR
60-2 **1** **Piper's Song (IRE)**[15] 4673 8-8-10 49.......................... RossSmith(5) 9 57+
(Linda Perratt) *s.i.s: hld up: hdwy on outside over 2f out: led wl ins fnl f: r.o* **11/2**[3]
4604 **2** *¾* **Machir Bay**[12] 4783 4-8-7 46 oh1..............................(p) LauraBarry(5) 1 53
(Keith Dalgleish) *led: rdn 2f out: hdd wl ins fnl f: hld cl home* **4/1**[1]
5603 **3** *2 ½* **Broughtons Silk**[2] 5153 6-8-5 46 oh1.......................... JasonHart(7) 6 47
(Alistair Whillans) *trckd ldrs: effrt over 2f out: kpt on same pce ins fnl f* **5/1**[2]
0552 **4** *1* **Carlitos Spirit (IRE)**[7] 4945 7-9-2 55.................. DavidSimmonson(5) 8 54
(Ian McInnes) *cl up: outpcd over 2f out: rallied appr fnl f: kpt on fin* **6/1**
0040 **5** *1 ¼* **Valentino Swing (IRE)**[47] 3617 8-8-9 48......................(p) IanBurns(5) 4 44
(Michael Appleby) *t.k.h: trckd ldrs: effrt over 2f out: no ex ins fnl f* **33/1**
2566 **6** *nse* **Bentley**[11] 4821 7-9-3 54..(b) JustinNewman(3) 3 50
(Brian Baugh) *cl up: rdn over 2f out: no ex ins fnl f* **7/1**
350 **7** *3* **Spread Boy (IRE)**[17] 4601 4-8-5 46 oh1...............(p) JoshBaudains(7) 10 35
(Alan Berry) *hld up: stdy hdwy over 3f out: drifted rt 2f out: sn outpcd* **12/1**
4316 **8** *2 ¼* **Lucayan Dancer**[17] 4601 11-9-2 55....................... ShirleyTeasdale(5) 11 39
(David Nicholls) *hld up: stdy hdwy 4f out: rdn and wknd over 2f out* **10/1**
3600 **9** *2 ¼* **Circuitous**[57] 3272 3-8-12 55.. NoelGarbutt(3) 13 33
(Keith Dalgleish) *dwlt: hld up: effrt on outside over 3f out: wknd fr 2f out* **10/1**
00-0 **10** *hd* **Shy Glance (USA)**[17] 4605 9-9-0 51.............................(p) JakePayne(3) 5 29
(Iain Jardine) *t.k.h: hld up on ins: pushed along and edgd rt over 2f out: sn btn* **8/1**
1m 52.79s (4.39) **Going Correction** +0.325s/f (Good)
WFA 3 from 4yo+ 6lb **10** Ran SP% **118.8**
Speed ratings (Par 101): **91,90,87,86,85 85,82,80,77,77**
toteswingers:1&2:£5.70, 1&3:£6.70, 2&3:£4.00. Totesuper 7: Win: Not won, Place: Not won. CSF £28.36 CT £122.02 TOTE £5.20: £1.50, £1.90, £2.50; EX 23.60.
Owner M Sawers **Bred** Patrick M Ryan **Trained** East Kilbride, S Lanarks
FOCUS
A weak "hands and heels" apprentice handicap. The finish was fought out between two horses given very contrasting rides. The runner-up ran a personal best and the third was rated close to recent marks.
Spread Boy(IRE) Official explanation: jockey said saddle slipped
T/Plt: £27.50 to a £1 stake. Pool: £34,243.27 - 905.99 winning units. T/Qpdt: £13.50 to a £1 stake. Pool: £2,229.56 - 124.40 winning units. RY

4646 SOUTHWELL (L-H)
Thursday, August 18
OFFICIAL GOING: Standard
Wind: Virtually nil Weather: Cloudy - lights showers

5209 SOUTHWELL-RACECOURSE.CO.UK AMATEUR RIDERS' H'CAP 2m (F)
5:00 (5:02) (Class 6) (0-60,56) 3-Y-0+ £1,646 (£506; £253) Stalls Low

Form RPR
6130 **1** **Ivanov (IRE)**[48] 3599 3-9-9 51.......................................(p) JackQuinlan 10 63
(K F Clutterbuck) *midfield: hdwy over 6f out: pushed along to chse ldrs 4f out: rdn to chse ldr 3f out: led 2f out: drvn clr over 1f out: kpt on* **7/2**[2]
130 **2** *4 ½* **Polly Holder (IRE)**[108] 1769 3-9-7 56.......................... MrsRWilson(7) 9 63
(Paul D'Arcy) *in tch: hdwy over 4f out: chsd ldrs over 3f out: kpt on to chse wnr ins fnl f: no imp* **7/1**[3]
-050 **3** *5* **Merrion Tiger (IRE)**[30] 4173 6-9-11 46.......................... MrMAllan(7) 13 47
(George Foster) *trckd ldrs: hdwy over 4f out: led over 3f out: rdn and hdd 2f out: kpt on same pce fr wl over 1f out* **7/1**[3]
3554 **4** *12* **Delorain (IRE)**[10] 4870 8-10-4 53.............................(vt) MissCScott(7) 4 40
(William Stone) *trckd ldrs: hdwy to chse ldr 6f out: rdn along over 3f out: kpt on same pce* **8/1**
332/ **5** *10* **Bring It On Home**[373] 603 7-10-7 56....................(b) MissSKerswell(7) 5 31
(Sophie Leech) *prom: chsd clr ldr 1/2-way: rdn along over 4f out: sn wknd* **22/1**
2500 **6** *2 ¼* **Dunaskin (IRE)**[4] 4649 11-10-7 49..(b) MrSWalker 2 21
(Richard Guest) *led and sn clr: pushed along ovef 6f out: rdn along 4f out: hdd over 3f out and sn wknd* **16/1**
-50 **7** *2* **Revolving World (IRE)**[33] 4112 8-9-10 45.............. MrAaronJames(7) 6 15
(Lee James) *s.i.s and bhd: sme hdwy fnl 3f: nvr a factor* **40/1**
5053 **8** *8* **Can Can Dancer**[14] 4732 6-9-13 46.......................... MissBAndrews(5) 7 —
(Charles Smith) *towards rr: sme hdwy 5f out: rdn along over 3f out: nvr a factor* **8/1**
6/00 **9** *9* **Son Of Sophie**[7] 4952 9-10-3 45.................................... MrPCollington 14 —
(Christopher Kellett) *in tch: rdn along over 6f out: sn lost pl and bhd* **22/1**
0660 **10** *8* **Swords**[10] 4847 9-9-10 45... MissSPeacock(7) 8 —
(Ray Peacock) *a towards rr* **33/1**
004 **11** *16* **Himalayan Moon**[13] 4753 4-10-10 55........................... MrCMartin(3) 11 —
(Ian Wood) *a in rr: bhd fnl 4f* **3/1**[1]
6000 **12** *22* **Cragganmore Creek**[18] 4579 8-9-12 45..................(v) MrBMMorris(5) 12 —
(Dave Morris) *a in rr: rdn along 1/2-way: t.o fnl 4f* **66/1**
020/ **13** *13* **Nounou**[922] 449 10-10-7 52.. MissECSayer(3) 3 —
(Joanne Foster) *chsd clr ldr: rdn along 1/2-way: sn lost pl and bhd: t.o fnl 4f* **33/1**
3m 48.45s (2.95) **Going Correction** +0.10s/f (Slow)
WFA 3 from 4yo+ 14lb **13** Ran SP% **118.8**
Speed ratings (Par 101): **96,93,91,85,80 79,78,74,69,65 57,46,40**
Tote Swingers:1&2:£4.60, 2&3:£10.70, 1&3:£10.90 CSF £25.86 CT £165.63 TOTE £4.60: £1.40, £2.40, £2.30; EX 32.70.
Owner K F Clutterbuck **Bred** Compagnia Generale S R L **Trained** Exning, Suffolk
FOCUS
Several course winners in opposition in a modest opener that went the way of the younger generation, who filled the first two places. The pace was strong and few got competitive and the form looks weak and not that solid.

5210 ATRIUM CAFE BAR H'CAP 1m 4f (F)
5:30 (5:31) (Class 6) (0-60,58) 3-Y-0+ £1,704 (£503; £251) Stalls Low

Form RPR
010 **1** **Sennockian Storm (USA)**[29] 4204 4-9-9 58.................. DarylByrne(5) 3 77
(Mark Johnston) *trckd ldng pair: smooth hdwy to chal over 2f out: led wl over 1f out: sn clr: easily* **15/2**
41-4 **2** *13* **Miereveld**[125] 16 4-9-11 58.. PaulPickard(3) 10 56
(Brian Ellison) *trckd ldrs: hdwy and cl up 4f out: rdn to dispute ld over 2f out and ev ch tl drvn and one pce fr over 1f out* **8/1**
1603 **3** *2 ¾* **Light The City (IRE)**[8] 4903 4-9-11 55.......................... JamesSullivan 4 49
(Ruth Carr) *trckd ldrs: hdwy over 4f out: led 3f out: sn jnd and rdn: hdd wl over 1f out: sn drvn and wknd* **3/1**[1]
5620 **4** *3 ¼* **Bring Sweets (IRE)**[30] 4173 4-9-10 54.......................... TonyHamilton 5 43
(Brian Ellison) *hld up: stdy hdwy 5f out: chsd ldrs 3f out: rdn 2f out: sn drvn and btn* **4/1**[2]
4544 **5** *13* **Miss Excel**[7] 4953 4-9-8 52... EddieCreighton 9 20
(Edward Creighton) *dwlt: a in rr* **10/1**
6605 **6** *¾* **Maxi Moo (IRE)**[12] 4814 4-8-12 45...................(b[1]) MichaelO'Connell(3) 6 12
(Ollie Pears) *led: rdn along 4f out: hdd 3f out: sn drvn and wknd* **6/1**[3]
2300 **7** *31* **Yossi (IRE)**[7] 4944 7-9-6 53......................................(b) RobertLButler(3) 8 —
(Richard Guest) *cl up: rdn along over 4f out: wknd qckly and sn bhd* **28/1**
-530 **8** *4 ½* **Belle Boleyn**[71] 2820 4-9-11 55.. TedDurcan 1 —
(Chris Wall) *midfield: rdn along over 7f out: sn lost pl and bhd* **17/2**
5000 **9** *2 ¾* **Laffraaj (IRE)**[27] 4274 3-8-12 52.......................................(p) ChrisCatlin 7 —
(Pat Eddery) *a in rr: bhd fnl 5f* **8/1**
2m 41.72s (0.72) **Going Correction** +0.10s/f (Slow)
WFA 3 from 4yo+ 10lb **9** Ran SP% **116.3**
Speed ratings (Par 101): **101,92,90,88,79 79,58,55,53**
Tote Swingers:1&2:£12.70, 2&3:£2.40, 1&3:£6.60 CSF £66.26 CT £220.80 TOTE £6.90: £3.10, £1.60, £1.40; EX 60.20.
Owner The Vine Accord **Bred** Overbrook Farm **Trained** Middleham Moor, N Yorks
FOCUS
Low-grade stuff but competitive all the same and an impressive winner, so perhaps not form to underestimate. The pace was solid and the form looks sound
Miss Excel Official explanation: jockey said filly never travelled

5211 ENHANCED WIN ODDS FROM NOON AT CORAL.CO.UK MAIDEN STKS 5f (F)
6:05 (6:06) (Class 5) 2-Y-O £2,587 (£770; £384; £192) Stalls High

Form RPR
4540 **1** **Whisky Bravo**[10] 4851 2-9-3 67.. SteveDrowne 1 69
(David Brown) *prom: effrt on outer 1/2-way: rdn to chal wl over 1f out: led ent fnl f: kpt on* **8/1**
230 **2** *1 ½* **Scrooby Doo**[22] 4427 2-8-9 68.. BillyCray(3) 6 59
(David Nicholls) *led: rdn wl over 1f out: drvn and hdd ent fnl f: kpt on same pce* **2/1**[1]
000 **3** *1 ¾* **Wake Up Sioux (IRE)**[54] 3398 2-8-12 48.......................... TedDurcan 9 53
(David C Griffiths) *cl up: rdn along over 2f out and ev ch tl drvn and one pce appr fnl f* **14/1**
03 **4** *shd* **Rano Pano (USA)**[51] 3490 2-8-9 0.......................... PaulPickard(3) 3 54+
(Brian Ellison) *sn rdn along and outpcd in rr: hdwy over 1f out: styd on strly ins fnl f: nrst fin* **11/4**[2]
5 *2 ½* **Planet I T (IRE)** 2-9-3 0.. RobertHavlin 2 48
(Mark Usher) *s.i.s and bhd: hdwy 2f out: kpt on wl fnl f: nrst fin* **25/1**
5320 **6** *½* **Miss Medici (IRE)**[24] 4391 2-8-9 48.......................... MartinHarley(3) 5 42
(Des Donovan) *cl up: rdn along over 2f out: grad wknd* **25/1**
06 **7** *4* **Hareem Dancer**[8] 4899 2-8-9 0..........................(e) MichaelO'Connell(3) 4 27
(David Nicholls) *chsd ldrs: rdn along over 2f out: sn wknd* **14/1**
0 **8** *2 ½* **Doctor Dalek (IRE)**[24] 4384 2-9-3 0.......................... EddieCreighton 7 23
(Edward Creighton) *s.i.s: a in rr* **80/1**
9 *8* **Great Ability (IRE)**[56] 3327 2-9-3 0.......................... TadhgO'Shea 8 —
(Stephen Michael Cox, Ire) *cl up: rdn along 1/2-way: sn drvn and wknd* **4/1**[3]
61.34 secs (1.64) **Going Correction** +0.20s/f (Slow) **9** Ran SP% **113.4**
Speed ratings (Par 94): **94,91,88,88,84 83,77,73,60**
Tote Swingers:1&2:£3.80, 2&3:£10.00, 1&3:£15.20 CSF £23.60 TOTE £9.70: £2.20, £1.20, £3.00; EX 29.20.
Owner S Bolland & C Watson **Bred** Peter Onslow **Trained** Averham Park, Notts
FOCUS
Modest fare and the fact that the first two home had official ratings of 67 and 68 sums the standard of this maiden up nicely. The fourth might be the most interesting one going forward.

NOTEBOOK

Whisky Bravo had possible excuses for a couple of runs since his debut, but he's probably no better than modest. That said, the switch to Fibresand probably helped him, looking at his action, and he'd almost certainly handle very soft ground too so there is some cause for optimism for autumn nurseries despite an exposed profile. (op 13-2)

Scrooby Doo didn't run badly despite flying too high at Goodwood last time, but if she's to win a race it's going to be at 6f, not 5f as she never looked to be travelling comfortably despite making much of the running. (tchd 9-4)

Wake Up Sioux(IRE) looked to be more of a danger 2f out than she turned out to be, but this still represented an improved effort with the surface almost certainly the explanation. (op 25-1)

Rano Pano(USA) ◆ will be an interesting runner in nurseries. She was further behind Scrooby Doo than when they met over 6f here previously, but found the drop to the minimum all against her and didn't get going until late after losing her place badly at halfway. She's one to keep an eye on back at 6f or maybe even 7f. (tchd 5-2)

Planet I T(IRE) shaped with a glimmer of promise on his debut, keeping on late, and this half-brother to the 6f winner Reach For The Sky is likely to improve. (op 20-1 tchd 18-1)

Miss Medici(IRE) showed up well for a long way, but she's only a plater and was out of her depth. (op 33-1)

Great Ability(IRE) looked an interesting Irish raider but was struggling by halfway. Official explanation: jockey said gelding never travelled (op 9-2)

5212 LADIES DAY 14 AUGUST AT SOUTHWELL MAIDEN STKS — 7f (F)

6:35 (6:36) (Class 5) 3-Y-O+ — **£2,264** (£673; £336; £168) — **Stalls** Low

Form	Pos	Dist	Horse	Jockey	RPR
2020	1		**Beechcraft Baron (IRE)**[21] 4478 3-9-0 65 (William Haggas) *mde all: qcknd clr 3f out: unchal* **7/2**[2]	GilmarPereira(3) 4	78
65	2	8	**Anrheg**[21] 4478 3-8-12 0 (David Brown) *chsd ldrs: hdwy 3f out: rdn to chse wnr fr 2f out: sn drvn and no imp* **6/1**[3]	SteveDrowne 5	51
	3	nk	**Ampleforth** 3-8-12 0 (Mark Johnston) *towards rr and rn green early: sn pushed along: rdn and hdwy 2f out: swtchd rt over 1f out: styd on strly ins fnl f: nrst fin* **3/1**[1]	DarylByrne(5) 10	56+
00-	4	9	**Looney Les (IRE)**[325] 6414 3-9-3 0 (Jo Hughes) *in tch: hdwy 3f out: sn rdn along and plugged on: nvr nr ldrs* **100/1**	MarkLawson 8	31
06	5	1 ½	**Outpost (IRE)**[24] 4388 3-9-3 0 (Alan Bailey) *s.i.s and bhd: hdwy on inner over 2f out: rdn wl over 1f out: kpt on: nrst fin* **8/1**	CathyGannon 1	27+
0	6	1 ¾	**Munaa's Dream**[87] 2361 3-8-12 0 (Mrs K Burke) *prom: rdn along 1/2-way: sn drvn and wknd over 2f out* **20/1**	LukeMorris 2	18
0	7	nk	**Akarana (IRE)**[15] 4663 4-9-8 0 (Willie Musson) *bhd: wd st and sn rdn: sme late hdwy* **16/1**	(e[1]) JamieMackay 6	24
5	8	½	**Swinger**[27] 4286 3-9-0 0 (David Nicholls) *cl up: rdn along 1/2-way: sn drvn and wknd wl over 2f out* **6/1**[3]	MichaelO'Connell(3) 14	20
6	9	½	**Upton Crystal**[27] 4286 3-8-12 0 (Michael Easterby) *a towards rr* **33/1**	JamesSullivan 3	14
00	10	½	**Charmouth Girl**[59] 3218 5-9-3 0 (John Mackie) *midfield: rdn along 1/2-way: n.d* **22/1**	TedDurcan 7	15
-0	11	3	**Blonde Maite**[120] 1496 5-9-8 0 (Roy Bowring) *wnt bdly rt s: a bhd* **100/1**	RussKennemore 11	12
3/	12	21	**Spring Buck (IRE)**[1023] 7074 6-9-8 0 (Paul Cole) *prom: rdn along 1/2-way: wd st and sn wknd* **7/1**	ChrisCatlin 12	—

1m 30.12s (-0.18) **Going Correction** +0.10s/f (Slow)
WFA 3 from 4yo+ 5lb — **12** Ran SP% **119.3**
Speed ratings (Par 103): **105,95,95,85,83 81,81,80,80,79 76,52**
Tote Swingers:1&2:£5.40, 2&3:£4.60, 1&3:£3.70 CSF £23.83 TOTE £3.60: £1.50, £3.10, £1.80; EX 25.90.

Owner D I Scott **Bred** D I Scott **Trained** Newmarket, Suffolk

FOCUS

An uncompetitive maiden that was one-way traffic from the home turn. The winner was impressive and given a chance although the form looks fluid behind.

Outpost(IRE) Official explanation: jockey said colt hung left

Blonde Maite Official explanation: jockey said gelding hung badly right on leaving stalls

5213 BETTER WIN PRICES EVERY AT CORAL.CO.UK H'CAP — 1m (F)

7:10 (7:10) (Class 5) (0-75,74) 3-Y-O — **£2,264** (£673; £336; £168) — **Stalls** Low

Form	Pos	Dist	Horse	Jockey	RPR
004	1		**Piceno (IRE)**[3] 5106 3-9-2 72 (David Nicholls) *mde all: rdn clr wl over 2f out: drvn over 1f out and kpt on wl* **9/2**[3]	(p) BillyCray(3) 5	81
1-10	2	2 ¼	**Golden Creek (USA)**[15] 4665 3-9-4 71 (Mrs K Burke) *trckd ldrs: hdwy to chse wnr 2f out and sn rdn: drvn and kpt on ins fnl f: nt rch wnr* **11/2**	LukeMorris 8	75
4030	3	14	**Granny Anne (IRE)**[6] 5014 3-8-8 61 (Alan Bailey) *towards rr and pushed along 1/2-way: rdn and hdwy on inner over 2f out: drvn and plugged on fr over 1f out: tk modest 3rd ins fnl f* **14/1**	(p) CathyGannon 2	33
6056	4	nk	**Kalahaag (IRE)**[18] 4584 3-9-1 71 (David Nicholls) *chsd ldrs on outer: rdn along 3f out: drvn over 2f out and no hdwy* **8/1**	MichaelO'Connell(3) 7	42
4304	5	½	**Dunseverick (IRE)**[3] 5101 3-9-6 73 (David Lanigan) *trckd ldrs on inner: rdn along 3f out: sn drvn and wknd over 2f out* **11/4**[2]	TedDurcan 1	43
156	6	10	**El Djebena (IRE)**[86] 2383 3-9-7 74 (Sir Mark Prescott Bt) *towards rr and pushed along after 2f: drvn and outpcd over 3f out* **9/4**[1]	StevieDonohoe 6	21
3630	7	10	**Spartic**[15] 4680 3-9-1 68 (Alan McCabe) *trckd wnr: effrt 3f out and sn rdn: drvn over 2f out and sn wknd* **33/1**	JamesDoyle 4	—
0560	8	47	**Night Witch (IRE)**[11] 4829 3-8-11 64 (Edward Creighton) *a in rr: bhd fr over 3f out* **33/1**	EddieCreighton 3	—

1m 43.01s (-0.69) **Going Correction** +0.10s/f (Slow) — **8** Ran SP% **114.7**
Speed ratings (Par 100): **107,104,90,90,89 79,69,22**
Tote Swingers:1&2:£8.30, 2&3:£4.20, 1&3:£12.30 CSF £29.44 CT £316.01 TOTE £5.80: £1.70, £1.50, £2.30; EX 25.00.

Owner Paul J Dixon **Bred** Miss Wendy Fox **Trained** Sessay, N Yorks

FOCUS

Another all-the-way winner in a handicap little else ever looked like winning. The pace looked fair and the runner-up is rated to her best claimer form.

El Djebena(IRE) Official explanation: trainer's rep had no explanation for the poor form shown

Night Witch(IRE) Official explanation: trainer said filly finished lame

5214 TICKETS ON LINE AT SOUTHWELL-RACECOURSE.CO.UK H'CAP — 7f (F)

7:40 (7:41) (Class 6) (0-55,55) 3-Y-O+ — **£1,704** (£503; £251) — **Stalls** Low

Form	Pos	Dist	Horse	Jockey	RPR
5414	1		**Sopran Nad (ITY)**[7] 4948 7-9-1 51 (Frank Sheridan) *mde virtually all: rdn and qcknd clr over 2f out: easily* **7/2**[2]	(b) AndreaAtzeni 3	66+
0005	2	1 ¾	**Spacecraft (IRE)**[30] 4183 4-8-7 46 oh1 (Christopher Kellett) *in rr: swtchd rt and hdwy 1/2-way: rdn to chse ldrs 2f out: swtchd lft and drvn over 1f out: chsd wnr ins fnl f: no imp* **33/1**	PaulPickard(3) 9	51
-322	3	2 ¾	**Master Of Song**[44] 3709 4-9-2 52 (Roy Bowring) *s.i.s and in rr: pushed along 1/2-way: nt clr run and wd st: hdwy on outer 2f out: sn rdn and kpt on u.p fnl f* **11/10**[1]	(p) JimmyQuinn 10	50+
6000	4	1 ½	**Fathey (IRE)**[19] 4563 5-8-11 47 (Charles Smith) *chsd ldrs: rdn along 3f out: drvn over 2f out and kpt on same pce* **50/1**	RobbieFitzpatrick 2	41
060	5	½	**Tigerbill**[21] 4478 3-8-6 47 (Nicky Vaughan) *in tch: hdwy wl over 2f out: sn rdn and no imp fr wl over 1f out* **40/1**	LukeMorris 6	38
0060	6	1 ½	**Prime Circle**[56] 3317 5-9-2 52 (Alan Brown) *cl up: rdn wl over 2f out: drvn wl over 1f out and sn one pce* **14/1**	RobertWinston 11	41
0400	7	1 ¼	**Chez Vrony**[8] 4927 5-9-1 51 (Dave Morris) *in tch: hdwy to chse ldrs wl over 2f out: sn rdn and one pce* **11/1**[3]	(t) MartinLane 14	36
3460	8	nse	**Honest Buck**[38] 3903 4-8-13 52 (Kate Walton) *prom on inner: rdn along to chse wnr 3f out: drvn over 2f out and sn wknd* **12/1**	MichaelO'Connell(3) 1	37
0350	9	2 ¼	**Crocodile Bay (IRE)**[16] 4651 8-8-7 46 (Richard Guest) *in tch: hdwy on outer 3f out: rdn to chse ldrs 2f out: sn drvn and wknd* **25/1**	(be) MartinHarley(3) 5	25
0000	10	11	**Varlak**[20] 4510 3-8-9 50 (K F Clutterbuck) *a in rr* **33/1**	(v) JamieMackay 12	—
06-0	11	shd	**Sister Sioux (IRE)**[146] 966 3-8-0 46 oh1 (Robin Bastiman) *a in rr* **100/1**	ChrisDCogan(5) 13	—
-600	12	1	**Scruffy Skip (IRE)**[16] 4651 6-9-2 52 (Christine Dunnett) *chsd ldrs: rdn along 3f out: sn wknd* **14/1**	(p) JamesDoyle 8	—
-403	13	19	**Brave Tiger (IRE)**[15] 4657 3-8-9 55 (Hugo Palmer) *a in rr: bhd fr 1/2-way* **14/1**	(v[1]) LucyKBarry(5) 7	—

1m 31.03s (0.73) **Going Correction** +0.10s/f (Slow)
WFA 3 from 4yo+ 5lb — **13** Ran SP% **121.0**
Speed ratings (Par 101): **99,97,93,92,91 89,88,88,85,73 73,71,50**
Tote Swingers:1&2:£40.40, 2&3:£15.70, 1&3:£1.40 CSF £128.04 CT £213.47 TOTE £4.10: £1.50, £7.00, £1.10; EX 176.00.

Owner Frank Sheridan **Bred** Leonardo Ciampoli **Trained** Wolverhampton, W Midlands

FOCUS

Bottom-basement stuff but the first three are all of interest here at this level and yet another result that showed the advantage front-runners can have at this track. Once again the pace looked fair and few were seen with a chance. The form looks far from solid.

Master Of Song Official explanation: jockey said gelding was slowly away

Honest Buck Official explanation: jockey said gelding hung right

5215 DINE IN THE PANTRY H'CAP — 5f (F)

8:10 (8:10) (Class 6) (0-60,60) 3-Y-O — **£1,704** (£503; £251) — **Stalls** High

Form	Pos	Dist	Horse	Jockey	RPR
3132	1		**Novalist**[16] 4650 3-9-0 53 (Robin Bastiman) *led: rdn along and hdd wl over 1f out: drvn and rallied to ld ins fnl f: gamely* **4/1**[2]	(b) RobertWinston 3	59
5424	2	¾	**Ladydolly**[80] 2549 3-9-0 53 (Roy Brotherton) *cl up: rdn to ld wl over 1f out: drvn and hdd ins fnl f: no ex towards fin* **9/1**	(b[1]) LukeMorris 1	56
5600	3	shd	**Porthgwidden Beach (USA)**[15] 4657 3-8-12 51 (Anthony Middleton) *chsd ldrs: hdwy 2f out: swtchd rt and rdn over 1f out: styd on u.p fnl f* **18/1**	(t) ChrisCatlin 4	54
0100	4	shd	**Inde Country**[8] 4930 3-8-13 57 (Nicky Vaughan) *racd wd: outpcd and bhd 1/2-way: hdwy 2f out: sn rdn and styd on fnl f: nrst fin* **22/1**	(t) LucyKBarry(5) 2	59
3001	5	¾	**Suddenly Susan (IRE)**[16] 4647 3-9-0 60 (David Nicholls) *hmpd s and towards rr: hdwy on stands' rail to chse ldrs 1/2-way: rdn 2f out: drvn over 1f out: kpt on same pce* **3/1**[1]	(b) LeonnaMayor(7) 7	60+
5422	6	8	**Tancred Spirit**[17] 4607 3-8-8 47 (Paul Midgley) *hmpd s and towards rr: hdwy over 2f out: sn rdn and no imp* **7/1**[3]	(v) TonyHamilton 6	18
-516	7	2 ½	**Princess Dayna**[191] 452 3-9-7 60 (Tom Dascombe) *prom: rdn along over 2f out: sn drvn and wknd* **16/1**	RussKennemore 9	22
052	8	7	**Brio**[16] 4647 3-9-6 59 (Alan McCabe) *hmpd s: sn prom: rdn along over 2f out and sn wknd* **3/1**[1]	(p) JamesDoyle 5	—
530	9	3 ¼	**These Dreams**[24] 4395 3-8-8 50 (Richard Guest) *dwlt and in rr: hdwy and prom after 1f: rdn along 1/2-way: sn wknd* **14/1**	(v) MartinHarley(3) 8	—

60.88 secs (1.18) **Going Correction** +0.20s/f (Slow) — **9** Ran SP% **114.7**
Speed ratings (Par 98): **98,96,96,96,95 82,78,67,62**
Tote Swingers:1&2:£8.80, 2&3:£20.80, 1&3:£20.00 CSF £39.36 CT £577.76 TOTE £3.90: £1.10, £2.30, £3.00; EX 39.00.

Owner Ms M Austerfield **Bred** Whitsbury Manor Stud **Trained** Cowthorpe, N Yorks

FOCUS

Another low-grade handicap but at least not as one-sided as some of the previous races, though the winner was in the van throughout. The form looks pretty straightforward, rated around the placed horses.

T/Plt: £32.10 to a £1 stake. Pool £29,670.82. 674.58 winning tickets T/Qpdt: £8.50 to a £1 stake. Pool £3,519.83. 305.60 winning tickets JR

5180 YORK (L-H)

Thursday, August 18

OFFICIAL GOING: Good to soft (good in places) changing to good (good to soft in places) after race 4 (3.40)

Rail out 3m from 12f to entrance to home straight adding 20yds to races of 1m and beyond.

Wind: light 1/2 against Weather: fine

5216 DBS PREMIER YEARLING STKS 6f

2:00 (2:05) (Class 2) 2-Y-O

£136,867 (£54,769; £20,524; £20,524; £6,846; £6,846) **Stalls** Centre

Form	Pos	Dist	Horse	Jockey	RPR
10	**1**		**Bogart**[20] [4495] 2-8-11 0 / (Kevin Ryan) *trckd ldr: led 2f out: drvn out* **17/2**[3]	PhillipMakin 19	103
1100	**2**	*1 ¾*	**Miss Work Of Art**[23] [4413] 2-8-11 95 / (Richard Fahey) *chsd ldrs: wnt handy 2nd 2f out: styd on same pce last 100yds* **16/1**	PaulHanagan 11	98
21	**3**	*1 ¼*	**Gerfalcon**[26] [4339] 2-8-11 85 / (Brian Meehan) *chsd ldrs on outer: kpt on same pce fnl 150yds* **16/1**	MartinDwyer 2	94
421	**3**	*dht*	**Ewell Place (IRE)**[14] [4710] 2-8-11 79 / (Robert Mills) *chsd ldrs: kpt on same pce fnl 2f* **40/1**	StevieDonohoe 12	94
2112	**5**	*¾*	**Red Art (IRE)**[18] [4575] 2-8-11 93 / (B W Hills) *mid-div: hdwy over 2f out: kpt on wl fnl f* **10/1**	RobertWinston 6	92
3410	**6**	*2 ½*	**Ponty Acclaim (IRE)**[33] [4094] 2-8-6 87 / (Tim Easterby) *chsd ldrs stands' side: kpt on same pce over 1f out* **40/1**	TedDurcan 20	80
2210	**7**	*2 ¾*	**Apostle (IRE)**[19] [4536] 2-8-11 87 / (Michael Bell) *dwlt: in rr and sn drvn along: kpt on fnl 2f stands' side: nvr nr ldrs* **40/1**	HayleyTurner 18	76
3224	**8**	*1 ¼*	**Letsgoroundagain (IRE)**[33] [4091] 2-8-11 85 / (B W Hills) *in rr: kpt on fnl 2f: nt clr run over 1f out: nvr nrr* **40/1**	WilliamCarson 16	73
0111	**9**	*1*	**Roger Sez (IRE)**[19] [4551] 2-8-6 85 / (Tim Easterby) *in rr: styd on stands' side fnl 2f: nvr nr ldrs* **16/1**	DavidAllan 17	65
241	**10**	*¾*	**Moustache (IRE)**[23] [4414] 2-8-11 85 / (Richard Hannon) *hld up in rr: effrt over 2f out: nvr a factor* **20/1**	DaneO'Neill 5	67
1044	**11**	*1 ¼*	**Worthington (IRE)**[28] [4252] 2-8-6 86 / (Richard Fahey) *mid-div: effrt over 2f out: nvr a factor* **33/1**	BarryMcHugh 13	59
330	**12**	*hd*	**Electric Qatar**[33] [4094] 2-8-11 90 / (Tom Dascombe) *in rr-div: sme hdwy on outside over 2f out: nvr a factor* **25/1**	RichardKingscote 1	63
2302	**13**	*½*	**Magic City (IRE)**[26] [4334] 2-8-11 90 / (Richard Hannon) *s.i.s: swtchd lft after s: a towards rr* **14/1**	PatDobbs 15	61
134	**14**	*¾*	**Crown Dependency (IRE)**[23] [4413] 2-8-11 102 / (Richard Hannon) *trckd ldrs: effrt 2f out: wknd appr fnl f* **15/8**[1]	RichardHughes 4	59
110	**15**	*2 ¼*	**Parc De Launay**[20] [4495] 2-8-11 90 / (Tom Tate) *chsd ldrs: lost pl over 2f out* **18/1**	JamieSpencer 8	52
4164	**16**	*nk*	**Ortea**[69] [2868] 2-8-11 79 / (David Evans) *mid-div: hung lft and lost pl 2f out* **100/1**	SilvestreDeSousa 9	52
42	**17**	*¾*	**Byronic Hero**[34] [4073] 2-8-11 0 / (Jedd O'Keeffe) *unruly s: a in rr* **50/1**	TonyHamilton 10	49
11	**18**	*2*	**West Leake Diman (IRE)**[26] [4334] 2-9-0 0 / (B W Hills) *led tl 2f out: sn wknd: eased towards fin* **12/1**	MichaelHills 7	46
	19	*shd*	**Hestian (IRE)**[29] [4217] 2-8-11 0 / (T Stack, Ire) *in tch: effrt over 2f out: sn wknd* **15/2**[2]	WMLordan 14	43
3606	**20**	*5*	**Hamza (IRE)**[18] [4575] 2-8-11 89 / (Kevin Ryan) *in tch: lost pl over 2f out: eased whn bhd* **33/1**	KierenFallon 3	28

1m 12.68s (0.78) **Going Correction** +0.15s/f (Good) **20** Ran SP% **130.6**

Speed ratings (Par 100): **100,97,96,96,95 91,88,86,85,84 82,82,81,80,77 77,76,73,73,66**

Place: Gerfalcon £3.20, Ewell Place £7.60. toteswingers:1&2:£24.00, 2&EP:£69.00, 1&EP:£38.10, 2&GF:£35.20, 1&GF:£19.60 CSF £132.33 TOTE £12.10: £3.50, £4.00; EX 213.40 Trifecta £1315.00 Part won. Pool: £3554.18 - 0.68 winning units..

Owner Mrs Angie Bailey **Bred** Toby Barker **Trained** Hambleton, N Yorks

FOCUS

The rail had been moved out 3 metres from the 1m4f start to the entrance of the home straight, adding 20 yards to the distance of races over 1m and further during the day. After the first race, a couple of jockeys described the going as "on the soft side" and " very loose on top". With six of the runners rated 90 or higher, this was effectively at least a Listed contest in the guise of a sales race. It has produced some really talented horses in the past, recent winners including Acclamation, Somnus, Dark Angel and Wootton Bassett, while Airwave managed only fourth and subsequent 2,000 Guineas winner Cockney Rebel was second. The pace was predictably good, so the form ought to be reliable, with the runner-up the best guide.

NOTEBOOK

Bogart didn't run too badly in the Richmond Stakes at Goodwood despite hanging under pressure (trainer said that he didn't handle the course), his first start after a short break, but showed no signs of being errant this time. The pace he showed strongly suggests this is the right sort of trip for him, as does his pedigree, and although he holds Group entries, one would imagine his other sales race engagements will be taken up considering the money available to connections for his £32,000 purchase, with Doncaster his next likely port of call. (op 10-1 tchd 8-1)

Miss Work Of Art's winning run came to an end when tried in Group company, albeit she hadn't been disgraced, but she reminded everyone with this performance that she is far from done with this season.

Gerfalcon won a race that worked out nicely at Salisbury last time (next two home won subsequently) and deserves a bit of extra credit for his staying on effort as he did the best of those drawn low. (op 25-1 tchd 66-1 in a place)

Ewell Place(IRE) finished second to the favourite in early May (same terms) and ran much the best of that pair with a staying-on performance. He has been getting better with every race and shapes as though he will stay further. (op 25-1 tchd 66-1 in a place)

Red Art(IRE) landed a couple of races in June and attracted market support, but never looked like winning despite staying on. (op 14-1 tchd 8-1)

Ponty Acclaim(IRE) wasn't disgraced in the Super Sprint and again here, but isn't quite up to the level.

Apostle(IRE) (tchd 50-1 in a place)

Crown Dependency(IRE) was the top rated on official figures and looked to have plenty in his favour back up to what looked a more suitable trip. However, he ran nowhere near his best and ran flat. Richard Hughes said afterwards that the colt was unsuited by the good to soft, good places ground. (op 2-1 tchd 9-4 and 5-2 in places)

Byronic Hero Official explanation: jockey said colt was unsuited by the good to soft (good in places) ground

West Leake Diman(IRE) had won both of his previous two outings and showed early speed before capitulating quickly once joined. (op 11-1)

Hestian(IRE) had been an impressive winner on his debut in July and was Ireland's sole representative, but he was always being pushed along in behind and failed to get to competitive at any stage. (op 8-1 tchd 7-1)

5217 JAGUAR CARS LOWTHER STKS (GROUP 2) (FILLIES) 6f

2:30 (2:36) (Class 1) 2-Y-O

£61,380 (£23,270; £11,646; £5,801; £2,911; £1,461) **Stalls** Centre

Form	Pos	Dist	Horse	Jockey	RPR
111	**1**		**Best Terms**[64] [3033] 2-9-1 104 / (Richard Hannon) *mde all: styd on wl fnl f: readily* **11/1**	RichardHughes 10	113+
341	**2**	*2*	**Fire Lily (IRE)**[32] [4131] 2-8-12 0 / (David Wachman, Ire) *trckd ldrs: wnt cl 2nd 2f out: styd on same pce last 150yds* **4/1**[2]	WMLordan 8	104
51	**3**	*3 ¼*	**Hello Glory**[27] [4263] 2-8-12 0 / (David Simcock) *hld up in rr-div: drvn over 2f out: swtchd lft over 1f out: styd on* **16/1**	JamieSpencer 9	94
5303	**4**	*¾*	**Caledonia Lady**[9] [4883] 2-8-12 103 / (Jo Hughes) *dwlt: in rr: swtchd lft and hdwy over 1f out: kpt on same pce* **50/1**	HayleyTurner 5	92
20	**5**	*1 ½*	**After (IRE)**[11] [4834] 2-8-12 0 / (A P O'Brien, Ire) *trckd ldrs stands' side: effrt over 2f out: one pce* **25/1**	CO'Donoghue 11	88
124	**6**	*¾*	**Inetrobil (IRE)**[41] [3821] 2-8-12 103 / (Kevin Ryan) *w wnr: drvn over 2f out: wknd over 1f out* **8/1**	PhillipMakin 4	85
11	**7**	*shd*	**Angels Will Fall (IRE)**[26] [4312] 2-8-12 0 / (B W Hills) *mid-div on outer: t.k.h: effrt 2f out: sn wknd: sixth whn eased nr line* **7/2**[1]	MichaelHills 3	85
41	**7**	*dht*	**Sunday Times**[7] [4954] 2-8-12 0 / (Peter Chapple-Hyam) *hld up in rr: effrt over 2f out: no imp whn carried lft over 1f out: kpt on towards fin* **20/1**	WilliamBuick 6	85
21	**9**	*1 ½*	**Lady Gorgeous**[34] [4052] 2-8-12 85 / (Mick Channon) *trckd ldrs: one pce whn hmpd over 1f out* **20/1**	EddieAhern 1	80
123	**10**	*¾*	**Shumoos (USA)**[41] [3821] 2-8-12 103 / (Brian Meehan) *trckd ldrs: t.k.h: one pce whn hmpd over 1f out: sn lost pl* **9/2**[3]	MartinDwyer 7	78
221	**11**	*hd*	**Gamilati**[41] [3821] 2-9-1 108 / (Mahmood Al Zarooni) *hld up in rr: effrt outside over 2f out: chsng ldrs over 1f out: sn wknd* **5/1**	FrankieDettori 2	81

1m 12.35s (0.45) **Going Correction** +0.15s/f (Good) **11** Ran SP% **117.7**

Speed ratings (Par 103): **103,100,96,95,93 92,91,91,89,88 88**

toteswingers:1&2:£12.20, 1&3:£14.10, 2&3:£17.50 CSF £52.29 TOTE £9.90: £2.10, £2.20, £4.60; EX 62.40 Trifecta £1115.30 Pool: £7,083.85 - 4.70 winning units..

Owner R Barnett **Bred** W And R Barnett Ltd **Trained** East Everleigh, Wilts

■ Stewards' Enquiry : Michael Hills two-day ban: failed to ride out for sixth (Sep 1-2)

FOCUS

One of the major juvenile fillies' races of the season. Although recent winners have had mixed fortunes subsequently, Hooray, Carry On Katie and Queen's Logic all went on to win the Cheveley Park, and Russian Rhythm added to her success in the following year's 1000 Guineas and several other Group 1s. This year's line-up included the first four from the Queen Mary, three of the first four from the Cherry Hinton, and the winner of the Princess Margaret and Anglesey Stakes. Added to that there were a couple of impressive maiden winners stepping up in grade. It looked an intriguing contest and was quite an open betting race, but in the end one filly dominated. The best effort yet from the winner with the second rated to her recent winning mark.

NOTEBOOK

Best Terms ◆, unbeaten in three previous starts, had narrowly beaten Shumoos in the Queen Mary with today's fourth and runner-up the next two home. Carrying a 3lb penalty, she had been off since and was stepping up to 6f for the first time; even so it was surprising she was sent off at double-figure odds. She made the running and, after beating off the challenge of the runner-up, which she just needed one tap of the whip to do, eventually scored comfortably. She is not very big and envokes memories of her erstwhile stable companion Lyric Fantasy - the pocket rocket. She beat most of the top fillies here, and at this stage the Cheveley Park looks hers for the taking. She was quoted as short as 12-1 for next year's 1000 Guineas, which is not that generous as there will be major doubts about her capacity to train on and also whether she will stay the trip. (op 10-1 tchd 12-1)

Fire Lily(IRE) ◆, a strong-finishing fourth in the Queen Mary, had since beaten After in the Anglesey Stakes. Helped by the longer trip, she was the only one able to give the winner a race, although she had no more to offer in the closing stages. She looks likely to appreciate another furlong but the Moyglare Stud Stakes might come too soon. (op 5-1 tchd 6-1 in a place)

Hello Glory ◆ had built on her promising debut when beating two subsequent winners in an easy ground Ascot maiden in July. Stepping up in grade, she ran on from the back to chase the first two home and appears capable of building on this as she still looks immature. (op 12-1 tchd 18-1 and 20-1 in places)

Caledonia Lady was a strong-finishing third in the Queen Mary but had finished further behind the runner-up there since and was beaten in an ordinary maiden last time. Held up at the back, she picked up well when switched but had nothing more to offer in the last furlong.

After(IRE) had won her maiden before finishing second to Fire Lily in the Anglesey, so had a bit to find. She showed up throughout and kept going under pressure, so might also appreciate a little further now. (op 33-1)

Inetrobil(IRE), runner-up in the Albany before finishing fourth in the Cherry Hinton, had a bit to find on that form but was well backed. She showed up early but could not sustain the effort. (op 11-1)

Sunday Times, who had improved on her debut when sluicing up in a Goodwood maiden earlier in the month, was another stepping up in grade. She was out the back early and could not make any impression until running on late, but the experience should not be lost on her and she might have more to offer in future. (tchd 4-1)

Angels Will Fall(IRE) won her maiden before taking the Princess Margaret in taking fashion and was sent off favourite. However, she pulled hard early and saw plenty of daylight, so it was no surprise that she could pick up under pressure. She can be given another chance. (tchd 4-1)

Lady Gorgeous beat an odds-on favourite who previously had finished second to the Cherry Hinton runner-up when winning her maiden. That form put her in the mix here, but she faded after chasing the pace, being done no favours in the scrimmaging amongst the backmarkers over a furlong out. (op 16-1)

Shumoos(USA) looked a world-beater when thrashing subsequent Group 2 winner Frederick Engels at Haydock on her debut, but she then lost out in a close finish with today's winner in the Queen Mary before being too keen behind Gamilati in the Cherry Hinton. Again a little keen under restraint, she could not pick up under pressure and is not progressing. (op 11-2 tchd 4-1)

Gamilati had been narrowly beaten in two good maidens before winning the Cherry Hinton, and her form tied in closely with Angels Will Fall through Regal Realm. She was carrying a 3lb penalty, but her problem was that she was held up and then had to pull to the outside of the field to make her effort. She looked a danger inside the last 2f but faded out of it. Official explanation: jockey said filly was unsuited by the good to soft (good in places) ground (op 4-1)

5218 ADDLESHAW GODDARD STKS (H'CAP) 1m

3:05 (3:08) (Class 2) 3-Y-O+ **£28,463** (£8,470; £4,232; £2,116) **Stalls** Low

Form	Pos	Dist	Horse	Jockey	RPR
2516	**1**		**Navajo Chief**[161] [828] 4-9-3 103 / (Alan Jarvis) *trckd ldrs: effrt stands' side over 2f out: r.o to ld nr fin* **25/1**	HarryBentley(3) 16	113

1003 **2** 3/4 **Smarty Socks (IRE)**[22] 4428 7-8-10 **93**................. SilvestreDeSousa 17 101+
(David O'Meara) *s.i.s: swtchd lft after s: gd hdwy far side over 2f out: led ins fnl f: drifted rt: hdd and no ex clsng stages* **8/1**[3]

4003 **3** *shd* **Pintura**[20] 4494 4-9-0 **97**.. JamieSpencer 1 105
(David Simcock) *led tl over 4f out: led 2f out: hdd and no ex ins fnl f* **6/1**[1]

-300 **4** 1/2 **Prime Exhibit**[124] 1406 6-8-6 **89**.................................. FrederikTylicki 20 96
(Richard Fahey) *w ldr: led 4f out: hdd 2f out: styd on same pce last 50yds* **33/1**

-431 **5** 1/2 **Markazzi**[12] 4794 4-8-9 **92**.. RichardHills 18 98
(Sir Michael Stoute) *hld up in mid-div: effrt stands' side over 2f out: sn chsng ldrs: styd on same pce last 100yds* **15/2**[2]

4200 **6** 3/4 **Vainglory (USA)**[20] 4494 7-8-7 **90**....................................... MartinLane 10 94+
(David Simcock) *hld up in rr: gd hdwy over 2f out: n.m.r appr fnl f: kpt on wl last 100yds* **16/1**

0000 **7** 1/2 **Harrison George (IRE)**[47] 3645 6-9-1 **98**.................. PaulHanagan 12 101
(Richard Fahey) *prom: drvn 3f out: one pce over 1f out* **9/1**

6644 **8** 3 **Pendragon (USA)**[47] 3645 8-8-8 **91**................................. JimmyQuinn 11 87
(Brian Ellison) *in tch: effrt stands' side 3f out: sn outpcd: kpt on fnl f* **9/1**

5303 **9** 1 3/4 **Dubai Dynamo**[12] 4774 6-8-12 **95**................................ HayleyTurner 6 87
(Ruth Carr) *s.i.s: in rr: hdwy far side over 2f out: kpt on fnl f: nvr nr ldrs* **16/1**

4002 **10** *nse* **Axiom**[12] 4802 7-9-2 **99**.. J-PGuillambert 14 91
(Ed Walker) *in rr: effrt stands' side over 3f out: kpt on fnl 2f: nvr nr ldrs* **16/1**

2000 **11** 1 **Mont Agel**[20] 4494 4-8-10 **93**..(v) TomQueally 8 82
(Michael Bell) *hld up towards rr: effrt 3f out: sn rdn and lost pl* **11/1**

106- **12** 2 1/4 **Emirates Dream (USA)**[292] 7233 4-9-1 **98**..................... WilliamBuick 5 82
(Saeed Bin Suroor) *trckd ldrs: effrt far side over 2f out: wknd over 1f out* **18/1**

0050 **13** 1 1/2 **Fareer**[23] 4410 5-9-8 **105**..(b) TadhgO'Shea 7 86
(Ed Dunlop) *in rr: sme hdwy far side 3f out: wknd over 1f out* **16/1**

0130 **14** 1 1/2 **Roker Park (IRE)**[26] 4346 6-8-7 **90**.................................... EddieAhern 2 67
(David O'Meara) *trckd ldrs: wknd over 1f out* **20/1**

0322 **15** 2 1/4 **Invisible Man**[19] 4554 5-9-10 **107**...............................(b) FrankieDettori 4 79
(Saeed Bin Suroor) *dwlt: hld up in mid-div: effrt over 3f out: wknd 2f out* **9/1**

0010 **16** 4 **Masked Dance (IRE)**[12] 4802 4-8-9 **92**.........................(p) PhillipMakin 3 55
(Kevin Ryan) *chsd ldrs: wknd 3f out* **33/1**

0500 **17** 10 **Lovelace**[20] 4494 7-8-9 **95**..................................... MichaelO'Connell[(3)] 13 35
(David Nicholls) *hood removed v late: s.s: sn mid-div: lost pl 3f out: bhd whn eased ins fnl f* **33/1**

/6-5 **18** 30 **Cashelgar (IRE)**[88] 2333 5-9-1 **98**.............................. RichardHughes 15 —
(Jeremy Noseda) *in rr-div: lost pl over 2f out: wl bhd whn heavily eased over 1f out: virtually p.u: t.o* **25/1**

1m 40.36s (1.56) **Going Correction** +0.425s/f (Yiel) **18** Ran SP% **125.6**
Speed ratings (Par 109): **109,108,108,107,107 106,105,102,101,101 100,97,96,94,92 88,78,48**
toteswingers:1&2:£43.40, 1&3:£25.60, 2&3:£9.80 CSF £204.60 CT £1415.94 TOTE £29.60: £5.90, £2.00, £2.30, £7.30; EX 336.10 Trifecta £3718.40 Pool: £5,024.94 - 1.00 winning units..
Owner Geoffrey Bishop **Bred** Eurostrait Ltd **Trained** Twyford, Bucks

FOCUS

Last year's running was won by Ransom Note, who went on to be a Group performer. A race dominated by 3-y-os and 4-y-os over the previous nine years, the pace was good from the start and not many appeared to have hard-luck stories.\n\x\x Earlier races on the day had suggested that positive tactics and coming stands' side was beneficial. The form looks sound with the third the best guide.

NOTEBOOK

Navajo Chief had been off since running in the Group 2 Zabeel Mile at Meydan in March, where he met a couple he faced again today. Confirmed as a prominent racer in the past, and with a good record fresh, he kept responding to pressure to get up near the line after being close-up throughout. Whether there's more to come is debatable, but his courage in a battle cannot be denied. (tchd 33-1)

Smarty Socks(IRE) ◆, an unlucky-looking third at Goodwood last time over 7f, ran a blinder because he came from off the pace (he was sat in last turning in) down what had looked a less-favoured far side of the course. He managed to pass all but one of his rivals under a power-packed finish. (op 9-1)

Pintura is probably fairly handicapped (finished fourth in a Listed race over C&D in May), but was far thrown in on his winning form. A good third in the Totesport Mile last time, Jamie Spencer made full use of his draw with a quick getaway and led for a lot of the race before keeping on nicely. (op 15-2 tchd 8-1)

Prime Exhibit, off since a poor effort in Newbury's Spring Cup, was another to be always up with the leaders before staying on. He's won off a higher mark on the AW so in theory he's handicapped to win if making normal improvement from this.

Markazzi took advantage of an opportunity at Haydock recently, for which he had been raised 6lb, and represented a trainer with a good previous record in this race. The horse moved up going smoothly but found less than expected. (op 8-1)

Vainglory(USA) made late progress despite being crowded over 1f out. That said, he'd been under strong driving for quite a while. (tchd 20-1 in a place)

Harrison George(IRE) has a good record here, and in ground with ease in it, so this was a little disappointing. (op 8-1 tchd 10-1)

Axiom, up in trip, looked awkward under pressure when attempting to come with his effort. The way the race developed wouldn't have suited his style of running, so one can almost forgive this performance.

Mont Agel, down 4lb after a series of disappointing performances, travelled strongly but couldn't get into contention. (op 9-1)

Invisible Man had run well on his last two starts but made no impression here under top weight. (op 10-1 tchd 17-2)

Lovelace Official explanation: jockey said blindfold had been tucked tightly into bridle and was difficult to remove, horse was slowly away.

Cashelgar(IRE), making his debut for this trainer after running for French and Irish trainers previously, was running over 1m and that looked a strange choice given the balance of his form, but that never came into play as he ran poorly. The jockey reported his mount lost its action. Official explanation: jockey said gelding lost its action (op 20-1)

5219 DARLEY YORKSHIRE OAKS (BRITISH CHAMPIONS' SERIES) (GROUP 1) (F&M) 1m 4f

3:40 (3:40) (Class 1) 3-Y-O+

£175,801 (£66,650; £33,356; £16,616; £8,339; £4,185) **Stalls** Centre

Form RPR

-141 **1** **Blue Bunting (USA)**[32] 4133 3-8-11 115......................... FrankieDettori 6 120
(Mahmood Al Zarooni) *hld up in rr: hdwy on ins over 3f out: chal over 2f out: led over 1f out: edgd lft: hld on wl towards fin* **11/4**[1]

-122 **2** 3/4 **Vita Nova (IRE)**[47] 3624 4-9-7 108..................................... TomQueally 9 119
(Sir Henry Cecil) *trckd ldrs: effrt over 3f out: chal over 2f out: styd on same pce last 75yds* **9/2**[3]

-123 **3** 3 3/4 **Wonder Of Wonders (USA)**[32] 4133 3-8-11 113.... SeamieHeffernan 1 113
(A P O'Brien, Ire) *trckd ldr: led over 3f out: hdd over 1f out: faltered jst ins fnl f: kpt on same pce* **8/1**

-414 **4** 2 **Crystal Capella**[19] 4533 6-9-7 120.................................... KierenFallon 2 110
(Sir Michael Stoute) *t.k.h: sn trcking ldrs: drvn 4f out: sn outpcd: kpt on fnl 2f: tk 4th nr line* **3/1**[2]

1121 **5** 3/4 **Banimpire (IRE)**[11] 4831 3-8-11 114.................................... KJManning 7 108
(J S Bolger, Ire) *trckd ldrs: t.k.h: sahekn up over 5f out: hdwy to chse ldrs over 2f out: one pce* **6/1**

50-5 **6** 3 1/4 **Brushing**[98] 2029 5-9-7 102.. PaulHanagan 8 103
(Mark H Tompkins) *dwlt: hld up in last: hdwy over 3f out: one pce fnl 2f* **50/1**

3160 **7** 14 **Rumh (GER)**[32] 4133 3-8-11 103....................................... WilliamBuick 5 91
(Saeed Bin Suroor) *led: qcknd over 4f out: hdd over 3f out: wknd over 1f out: heavily eased last 100yds* **66/1**

-034 **8** 10 **Laughing Lashes (USA)**[32] 4133 3-8-11 113......................... FMBerry 3 78
(Mrs John Harrington, Ire) *hld up in mid-div: drvn 4f out: lost pl over 2f out: eased whn bhd* **7/1**

2m 35.34s (2.14) **Going Correction** +0.425s/f (Yiel)
WFA 3 from 4yo+ 10lb **8** Ran SP% **111.2**
Speed ratings (Par 117): **109,108,106,104,104 102,92,86**
toteswingers:1&2:£3.50, 1&3:£2.90, 2&3:£4.50 CSF £14.56 TOTE £2.90: £1.30, £1.70, £1.90; EX 14.10 Trifecta £63.80 Pool: £11,702.63 - 135.68 winning units..
Owner Godolphin **Bred** B M Kelley **Trained** Newmarket, Suffolk

FOCUS

The roll call of recent winners of this Group 1 reads like a who's who of the top middle-distance fillies and mares, but this year's line-up looked a little below standard, weakened slightly by the withdrawal of the previous year's Oaks winner Snow Fairy. That said, it featured the first four from the Irish Oaks. The winner is rated as having run a personal best with the third close to her mark.

NOTEBOOK

Blue Bunting(USA), a surprise winner of the 1000 Guineas before finishing fourth in the Oaks when the track reportedly did not suit, came late to win the Irish Oaks from three of today's rivals. She came from off the pace set by connections' other runner Rumh to grind out another victory, and deserves extra credit as her rider reported that she was in season. She looks her stable's most likely candidate for the St Leger after this, although she would not have an easy task against the colts there. She also has the option of the Prix Vermeille. (tchd 3-1)

Vita Nova(IRE) ◆ won her first three before losing out in a Listed and a Group 3 at Haydock, having been unlucky as saddle slipped last time. Up in grade, she ran her race and gave the winner a real battle. She has now finished second in her last three races, but there is nothing wrong with her attitude and she should be winning a Group race before the season is out. Something like the Pride Stakes or the Prix Royallieu could be right up her street. (op 4-1 tchd 5-1 in places)

Wonder Of Wonders(USA) finished a close second in the Oaks and a close third in the Irish Oaks, which gave her every chance here. She was ridden close to the pace and hit the front around 3f out going well. However, she could not open up a lead and when challenged rather carried her head awkwardly (not for the first time) and could only stay on at the one pace. The Park Hill Stakes at Doncaster over the St Leger trip might offer her the best chance of Group success.

Crystal Capella, a multiple Group winner who ran away with the Princess Of Wales's Stakes in July, had since finished fourth in the Nassau over a trip on the short side. Although 2-2 on the track coming into this, she had never won at this level and was well held here after never appearing to be going that well. (tchd 11-4 and tchd 10-3 in places)

Banimpire(IRE), a progressive filly who had won six of her nine previous starts this season, including the Ribblesdale and Royal Whip, had been just beaten in the Irish Oaks by today's winner. However, she never appeared to be going that well - her rider was niggling at her rounding the home turn - and although she got into contention around 2f out, her effort petered out thereafter. (op 13-2)

Brushing won the Galtres Stakes at this meeting last year, but was held by a couple of these on more recent form and had not been seen since finishing well beaten in a Group 2 here in May. She moved up from the back to reach the heels of the leaders halfway up the straight, but faded out of things soon after.

Laughing Lashes(USA) had finished third in the Irish 1000 Guineas and fourth in the Irish Oaks this season, but ran nowhere near this form here and finished well beaten. Official explanation: trainer said filly returned home with an elevated temperature (op 8-1 tchd 9-1 in a place)

5220 EBF "SELKIRK" GALTRES STKS (LISTED RACE) 1m 4f

4:15 (4:15) (Class 1) 3-Y-O+ **£23,680** (£8,956; £4,476; £2,236) **Stalls** Centre

Form RPR

3111 **1** **Set To Music (IRE)**[21] 4477 3-8-8 92............................... JamieSpencer 6 107+
(Michael Bell) *hld up in mid-div: smooth hdwy to trck ldrs 3f out: shkn up and wnt 2nd jst ins fnl f: str run to ld last 50yds: readily* **8/1**[3]

2600 **2** 2 1/4 **Cracking Lass (IRE)**[40] 3875 4-9-7 91.......................(b[1]) PaulHanagan 7 102
(Richard Fahey) *hld up in rr: shkn up 7f out: sn outpcd: styd towards far side: hdwy over 2f out: led 1f out: edgd lft: hdd last 50yds* **25/1**

2454 **3** 3 **Polly's Mark (IRE)**[21] 4470 5-9-4 105.......................... RichardHughes 4 94
(Clive Cox) *led: qcknd over 4f out: hdd over 3f out: one pce fnl 2f* **5/1**[2]

0-20 **4** 1 **Spin (IRE)**[18] 4589 3-8-8 101... WMLordan 3 93
(A P O'Brien, Ire) *trckd ldrs: led over 3f out: hdd 1f out: one pce* **16/1**

-542 **5** 10 **Mirror Lake**[18] 4582 4-9-4 100... PatDobbs 1 77
(Amanda Perrett) *trckd ldrs: drvn over 3f out: edgd rt over 1f out: sn wknd* **8/1**[3]

1220 **6** 1 3/4 **Field Of Miracles (IRE)**[21] 4470 3-8-8 112..................... WilliamBuick 5 74
(John Gosden) *chsd ldr: drvn over 4f out: lost pl over 2f out* **5/1**[2]

5303 **7** 1 **Amazing Beauty (IRE)**[18] 4589 3-8-8 101..................... CO'Donoghue 8 72
(A P O'Brien, Ire) *chsd ldrs: drvn over 4f out: wknd 2f out* **16/1**

2115 **8** *hd* **Wild Coco (GER)**[21] 4470 3-9-0 113.................................... TomQually 9 78
(Sir Henry Cecil) *dwlt: hld up on outer: hdwy 7f out: drvn and out;pced 4f out: sme hdwy over 2f out: sn wknd* **11/8**[1]

4143 **9** 10 **Certral**[26] 4344 3-8-8 78.. SilvestreDeSousa 2 56
(Brian Ellison) *in rr: styd far side and racd alone: hdwy over 3f out: lost pl 2f out: sn bhd and eased* **50/1**

2m 35.94s (2.74) **Going Correction** +0.425s/f (Yiel)
WFA 3 from 4yo+ 10lb **9** Ran SP% **115.2**
Speed ratings (Par 111): **107,105,103,102,96 95,94,94,87**
toteswingers:1&2:£14.90, 1&3:£5.60, 2&3:£14.00 CSF £179.85 TOTE £9.00: £2.20, £2.80, £2.20; EX 138.20 Trifecta £1767.90 Pool: £2,723.54 - 1.14 winning units..
Owner The Queen **Bred** His Highness The Aga Khan's Studs S C **Trained** Newmarket, Suffolk

FOCUS

The finish concerned two horses who were among the lowest rated in the line-up, but one of them is progressive and will almost certainly rate higher in due course. However, this is still a result to treat with caution until proven otherwise. The going was changed to good, good to soft in places before the off. The form looks messy with the runner-up the best guide.

NOTEBOOK

Set To Music(IRE) ◆ was stepping out of handicap company in a bid to gain a fourth consecutive victory (also up in distance) and took another leap forward with consummate ease after travelling strongly throughout. Michael Bell had always had a high opinion of his filly, and a tentative entry for the Prix Vermeille had been penned in for her, but the trainer looked genuinely surprised at how comfortably his filly had taken this, so it would appear there is plenty more to come, although there will need to be if she's going to win in Group 1 company. (tchd 7-1)

Cracking Lass(IRE), blinkered for the first time, would have won clearly but for bumping into a progressive sort. It's true to say that she wasn't beaten far in the Musidora last year, but her other efforts at York had been dismal and she hardly looked like collecting when needing to be pushed along early. Things still looked bleak turning in when she was out the back, but she kept staying on when others had given up. Perhaps her proven ability to handle easy ground helped. (op 20-1)
Polly's Mark(IRE), down in trip, is a mainly reliable sort in these types of contests and added some more black type to her profile. She has been a grand sort and is usually a sound benchmark. (tchd 6-1 in a place)
Spin(IRE) finished behind stablemate Amazing Beauty last time at Cork but comfortably reversed that result. In some ways it was improved form, but it was disappointing that she didn't assert when hitting the front.
Mirror Lake didn't seem to get home and has yet to prove conclusively she stays 1m4f. (op 7-1)
Field Of Miracles(IRE) had excuses when running well below her best last time, but her fine effort when well ridden in the Ribblesdale is becoming a distant memory. Official explanation: trainer's rep had no explanation for the poor form shown (op 9-2)
Wild Coco(GER) remained an interesting prospect despite a reversal last time (Polly's Mark finished in front of her that day as well), but one got the feeling things didn't go completely to plan again, although she should have run better. A filly with lots of size, she should be stronger next season if remaining in training and will no doubt prove successful at this level. Official explanation: trainer had no explanation for the poor form shown (tchd 2-1 in places)

5221 EVENTMASTERS.CO.UK STKS (H'CAP) — 2m 88y

4:50 (4:53) (Class 3) (0-95,95) 4-Y-0+ **£9,703** (£2,887; £1,443; £721) **Stalls** Low

Form				RPR
4200	**1**		**Dazinski**[22] 4423 5-8-13 **87** .... PaulHanagan 9	98
			(Mark H Tompkins) *trckd ldrs: led over 1f out: drvn out* **20/1**	
0003	**2**	*¾*	**Chilly Filly (IRE)**[21] 4477 5-8-5 **79** .... JimmyQuinn 5	89
			(Brian Ellison) *mid-div: hdwy to chse ldrs 6f out: edgd rt 2f out: wnt 2nd last 100yds: kpt on* **5/1**[2]	
4434	**3**	*2 ¼*	**Deauville Flyer**[40] 3875 5-9-6 **94** .... KierenFallon 14	101
			(Tim Easterby) *hld up in rr: drvn and hdwy 5f out: chsng ldrs over 1f out: wnt 3rd last 100yds: kpt on same pce* **4/1**[1]	
1230	**4**	*1 ¼*	**Hawk Mountain (UAE)**[12] 4775 6-9-2 **90** .... JamieSpencer 11	96
			(John Quinn) *trckd ldrs: led 8f out: drvn clr over 3f out: hdd over 1f out: one pce* **12/1**	
0031	**5**	*¾*	**Itlaaq**[26] 4348 5-9-6 **94** ....(t) GrahamGibbons 17	99
			(Michael Easterby) *hld up in rr: gd hdwy over 3f out: chsng ldrs over 1f out: kpt on same pce* **8/1**[3]	
0024	**6**	*hd*	**Bow To No One (IRE)**[22] 4423 5-8-3 **80** .... HarryBentley(3) 12	84
			(Alan Jarvis) *hld up in rr: hdwy over 3f out: chsng ldrs over 1f out: kpt on one pce* **14/1**	
0206	**7**	*4 ½*	**Magicalmysterytour (IRE)**[27] 4266 8-8-5 **79** .... AndreaAtzeni 10	78
			(Willie Musson) *in rr: hdwy over 3f out: kpt on fnl 2f: nvr nr ldrs* **20/1**	
2235	**8**	*¾*	**Plato (JPN)**[9] 4890 4-9-1 **89** ....(b[1]) TomQueally 15	87
			(Sir Henry Cecil) *w ldrs: wkng whn hmpd 2f out* **12/1**	
43-0	**9**	*10*	**Braveheart Move (IRE)**[19] 4528 5-9-3 **91** .... RobertWinston 3	77
			(Geoffrey Harker) *t.k.h in midfield: lost pl over 5f out: sn bhd: hung lft and kpt on fnl 3f* **33/1**	
3010	**10**	*¾*	**Denton (NZ)**[40] 3844 8-8-11 **85** ....(t) DaneO'Neill 4	70
			(Jeremy Gask) *led: hdd 8f out: wknd over 1f out* **66/1**	
2-43	**11**	*7*	**Alazan (IRE)**[21] 4464 5-8-12 **86** .... RichardHughes 13	63
			(Philip Hobbs) *hld up in mid-div: hdwy to chse ldrs 6f out: lost pl 2f out* **9/1**	
5240	**12**	*7*	**Comedy Act**[9] 4890 4-8-11 **85** .... WilliamBuick 16	53
			(Mark Johnston) *sn chsng ldrs: drvn over 3f out: lost pl over 1f out (dead-heated 12th)* **28/1**	
132-	**12**	*dht*	**Sea Change (IRE)**[161] 6797 4-8-7 **81** .... BarryMcHugh 7	49
			(Jim Goldie) *trckd ldrs: lost pl over 3f out* **40/1**	
1422	**14**	*½*	**Seaside Sizzler**[22] 4423 4-8-13 **87** ....(vt) JimCrowley 6	55
			(Ralph Beckett) *in rr-div: drvn 5f out: sn bhd* **11/1**	
3030	**15**	*4*	**Exemplary**[12] 4775 4-8-13 **87** .... SilvestreDeSousa 1	50
			(Mark Johnston) *mid-div: drvn over 3f out: sn bhd* **18/1**	
121-	**U**		**Tuscan Gold**[348] 5752 4-8-12 **86** .... StevieDonohoe 2	—
			(Sir Mark Prescott Bt) *stmbld and uns rdr leaving stalls* **8/1**[3]	

3m 39.81s (5.31) **Going Correction** +0.425s/f (Yiel) **16** Ran SP% **124.4**
Speed ratings (Par 107): **103,102,101,100,100 100,98,97,92,92 88,85,85,85,83** —
toteswingers:1&2:£41.50, 1&3:£28.80, 2&3:£8.00 CSF £107.30 CT £438.66 TOTE £25.30: £4.80, £2.30, £1.70, £3.00; EX 450.10 Trifecta £2309.70 Part won. Pool: £3,121.26 - 0.20 winning units..
Owner Mrs Beryl Lockey **Bred** Darley **Trained** Newmarket, Suffolk

FOCUS

Only recently introduced to the Ebor meeting, this strong, competitive staying handicap featured last year's winner, several that have been competing in the major staying handicaps plus a couple who were unexposed at the trip. The early pace was ordinary, not helped by the loose Tuscan Gold, who unseated his rider leaving the starting gate, running about at the head of the field, and three of the first four raced close to the leaders. The form looks straightforward rated around the third and fourth.

NOTEBOOK

Dazinski had lost his way of late after several good efforts in the spring but goes well here and bounced back to form. He is likely to be aimed at the Cesarewitch but was well beaten in both that race and it's trial over the trip last year, so is yet to prove the test is ideal for him. (op 25-1)
Chilly Filly(IRE), a winner at up to 1m6f, had been bought for £20,000 out of James Given's yard and was upped in trip on her first run for her new trainer. She tracked the leaders before making headway up the stands' rail to chase the winner, but swished her tail under pressure and could never reel that rival in. (op 7-1)
Deauville Flyer gained his last win over C&D in June 2010 but was 10lb higher here, having run consistently well this term. He was well backed beforehand but was held up in a race run at an ordinary gallop. He gradually worked his way into the race but could never get close enough to catch the winner. He needs more of a test of stamina than this, and another try at the Cesarewitch might bring out the best in him. (op 7-2)
Hawk Mountain(UAE) won this race last year off 79 but had climbed the weights after good efforts earlier this season and had looked held off this rating the last twice. Given a positive ride, he kicked on early in the straight and tried to make the best of his way home up the stands' rail. He was reeled in by the first three but kept responding to pressure to make the frame. (op 10-1)
Itlaaq, a C&D winner here last month, was 6lb higher but looked progressive. Backed beforehand, as was his stable companion, he was held up before making good headway to join issue, only to have no more to offer in the last furlong. He still looks to be going the right way. (op 11-1)
Bow To No One(IRE), a winner at 2m who stays further, had a bit to find with a couple of these on Goodwood running. However, she had previous form at this track and moved up looking a big threat around 2f out before her effort faltered.
Magicalmysterytour(IRE) had yet to prove he truly gets this trip after two previous tries. Dropped a couple of pounds, he ran on under pressure but never figured and the jury remains out regarding his stamina. (op 33-1)
Plato(JPN), a winner at 1m4f who appeared to stay this trip on his only previous try over it, had bit to find with a couple of these. Blinkered for the first time, he was close enough for a long way but finished up beaten a fair way. (tchd 14-1)

Braveheart Move(IRE)'s rider reported that the gelding hung left. Official explanation: jockey said gelding hung left (op 28-1)
Alazan(IRE), a multiple winning hurdler who has been running well at shorter trips this summer, was up in trip. He had a chance when short of room halfway up the straight but soon came under pressure and dropped away as if either something was amiss or he didn't stay. Richard Hughes reported that the gelding had no more to give. Official explanation: jockey said gelding had no more to give
Seaside Sizzler proved he gets further than this when runner-up in the Goodwood Stakes in a first-time visor but was 5lb higher here. However, he was being urged along leaving the back straight and ran well below his recent form for no obvious reason. (op 10-1)
T/Jkpt: Not won. T/Plt: £841.20 to a £1 stake. Pool: £285,220.02 - 247.50 winning units. T/Qpdt: £46.30 to a £1 stake. Pool: £16,914.78 - 269.84 winning units. WG

5222 - 5227a (Foreign Racing) - See Raceform Interactive

4766 TIPPERARY (L-H)

Thursday, August 18

OFFICIAL GOING: Sprint course - good; round course - good to firm (good in places)

5228a IRISH STALLION FARMS EUROPEAN BREEDERS FUND FAIRY BRIDGE STKS (LISTED RACE) (F&M) — 7f 100y

7:35 (7:37) 3-Y-0+ **£33,620** (£9,827; £4,655; £1,551)

			RPR
1		**Alanza (IRE)**[18] 4588 3-9-1 103 .... JMurtagh 10	111+
		(John M Oxx, Ire) *towards rr: rdn to chse ldrs in 6th 1f out: styd on wl fnl f to ld cl home* **9/2**[3]	
2	*¾*	**Anam Allta (IRE)**[21] 4481 3-8-12 96 .... PJSmullen 1	105
		(D K Weld, Ire) *prom: 4th for much: chal u.p in 3rd 1f out: led briefly clsng stages: hdd cl home* **12/1**	
3	*1 ¼*	**Claiomh Solais (IRE)**[18] 4588 3-8-12 106 .... KJManning 13	102
		(J S Bolger, Ire) *sn led: pressed st: hdd and kpt on same pce wl ins fnl f* **14/1**	
4	*¾*	**Dawn Eclipse (IRE)**[20] 4497 6-9-3 102 .... BACurtis 6	101
		(T G McCourt, Ire) *sn mid-div: 7th appr st: rdn into 5th 1f out: sn no imp and kpt on* **33/1**	
5	*¾*	**Wild Wind (GER)**[18] 4588 3-8-12 103 .... KLatham 4	98
		(A P O'Brien, Ire) *chsd ldrs: 6th appr st: 4th 1f out: sn no imp: kpt on* **14/1**	
6	*½*	**Rose Bonheur**[39] 3892 3-9-1 107 .... DPMcDonogh 3	100
		(Kevin Prendergast, Ire) *trckd ldr: travelling wl into st: no ex ins fnl f* **7/1**	
7	*1 ¾*	**Royal Blue Star (IRE)**[23] 4418 3-8-12 98 .... ShaneFoley 12	93
		(Mrs John Harrington, Ire) *towards rr: wd and effrt st: no imp and kpt on same pce fr over 1f out* **14/1**	
8	*1 ¼*	**Hooray**[61] 3154 3-9-5 .... SebSanders 7	96
		(Sir Mark Prescott Bt) *sn in rr: plld to outer and effrt 2f out: sn no imp and kpt on same pce* **5/2**[1]	
9	*1 ½*	**Lolly For Dolly (IRE)**[64] 3030 4-9-10 112 ....(b) WJLee 5	94
		(T Stack, Ire) *sn racd in 5th: struggling fr 2f out: no imp 1f out* **4/1**[2]	
10	*2*	**Face Reality (USA)**[13] 4773 3-8-12 99 .... GFCarroll 9	81
		(David Marnane, Ire) *mid-div best: wd and effrt st: sn no imp* **20/1**	
11	*2*	**Eirnin (IRE)**[13] 4773 3-8-12 98 .... DavidMcCabe 2	76
		(A P O'Brien, Ire) *sn mid-div: no imp and kpt on same pce fr under 2f out* **40/1**	
12	*nk*	**Look At Me (IRE)**[8] 4936 3-8-12 101 .... WJSupple 8	75
		(A P O'Brien, Ire) [illegible] **16/1**	
13	*2 ½*	**Core Element (IRE)**[11] 4835 4-9-3 79 .... NGMcCullagh 11	70
		(S Buggy, Ire) *prom: no ex fr 2f out* **100/1**	

1m 32.71s (92.71)
WFA 3 from 4yo+ 5lb **13** Ran SP% **124.0**
CSF £58.28 TOTE £5.50: £2.30, £4.00, £3.40; DF 82.10.
Owner H H Aga Khan **Bred** His Highness The Aga Khan's Studs S C **Trained** Currabeg, Co Kildare

FOCUS

With Windsor Forest Stakes heroine Lolly For Dolly joining the likes of last season's Group 1 Cheveley Park winner Hooray this was a quality Listed contest. It has been rated around the third and fourth.

NOTEBOOK

Alanza(IRE) ◆ ran out a smooth winner. Her rider had to snatch her up in the early stages and she found herself at the back. Travelling well, she began to take closer order and picked up in good style to get her head in front close home. She is not among the entries for the Matron Stakes and is unlikely to be supplemented, but the manner of this victory was impressive. She deserves her chance now in Group races. Trainer John Oxx: "She came from a long way back and is a good filly. She was too keen early in her career and her few runs over 6f helped her settle well. I'd say seven and a half furlongs to just over a mile is her trip. She is not in the Matron and we may not supplement her, so I don't know where she'll go next, but fast ground suits." (op 4/1 tchd 7/2)
Anam Allta(IRE) ◆, successful in a fillies' handicap at Galway previously, ran a cracker against higher-rated rivals and is another going the right way.
Claiomh Solais(IRE) broke well and brought them along at a good clip. She had finished further behind Alanza when the pair met in Cork and this was a better effort.
Dawn Eclipse(IRE) stepped up on her Goodwood effort last month and didn't mind the slight ease in the ground judging by this display. (op 25/1)
Wild Wind(GER) Official explanation: jockey said filly was unable to get a clear run in the straight
Rose Bonheur probably wants a quicker surface to be seen at her best. (op 7/1 tchd 8/1)
Hooray was the sole Group 1 winner in the field and she was well-fancied to build on her recent display at Royal Ascot. Sir Mark Prescott's filly had shown plenty of speed before finishing in midfield behind Society Rock in the Group 1 Golden Jubilee and she had a 7lb Group 1 penalty to contend with here. She had been too keen earlier in her career but had landed the Lowther and Sirenia Stakes before bagging the Cheveley Park over 6f last October. Hold-up tactics over this longer journey failed to work. Official explanation: jockey said he tried to restrain filly from the stalls but it ran freely, suffered interference and was checked shortly thereafter (op 4/1)
Lolly For Dolly(IRE) was conceding weight all round because of her penalty for winning the Group 2 Windsor Forest Stakes at Royal Ascot. She was easy to back on course and probably needed this race ahead of her Matron Stakes target next month. (op 10/3)
Eirnin(IRE) Official explanation: trainer's rep said filly stumbled before turn into straight and suffered an overreach

5229 - (Foreign Racing) - See Raceform Interactive

^{2795}LE LION-D'ANGERS (R-H)

Thursday, August 18

OFFICIAL GOING: Turf: soft

5230a GRAND PRIX DU LION D'ANGERS (LISTED RACE) (3YO) (TURF) 1m 2f

6:25 (12:00) 3-Y-O **£23,706** (£9,482; £7,112; £4,741; £2,370)

			RPR
1		**Katmandoune (FR)**^{301} 3-8-8 0 AlexandreRoussel 9 (J Boisnard, France) **24/1**	98
2	*shd*	**Sano Di Pietro**^{26} 4351 3-8-11 0 AnthonyCrastus 7 (A De Royer-Dupre, France) **14/5**^{2}	101
3	*shd*	**Stabilized (FR)**^{34} 3-8-11 0 ThierryThulliez 11 (P Bary, France) **2/1**^{1}	101
4	*3/4*	**Belgian Bill**^{21} 4467 3-8-11 0 TonyCulhane 1 (George Baker) *racd in midfield on rail: hdwy over 2f out: trapped on rail travelling strly fnl 1 1/2f: nvr able to get in clr: unlucky* **42/1**	99
5	*3/4*	**Sant'Alberto (ITY)**^{24} 4401 3-8-11 0 Pierre-CharlesBoudot 10 (F Brogi, Italy) **8/1**	98
6	*nse*	**Divin Leon (FR)**^{24} 4401 3-8-11 0 SebastienMaillot 5 (M Boutin, France) **36/1**	98
7	*3/4*	**Private Eye (FR)**^{140} 1069 3-8-13 0 Jean-BernardEyquem 6 (E Libaud, France) **11/2**^{3}	98
8	*1 1/2*	**Funon (IRE)**^{35} 3-8-11 0 DavyBonilla 3 (F Head, France) **78/10**	93
9	*hd*	**Naromdia (FR)**^{80} 3-8-8 0 MathieuAndrouin 2 (J Boisnard, France) **25/1**	90
10	*3/4*	**Septime Severe (FR)**^{53} 3-8-11 0 ThomasHuet 8 (M Delzangles, France) **20/1**	91

2m 9.22s (129.22) **10** Ran SP% **115.1**

PARI-MUTUEL (all including 1 euro stakes): WIN 25.00; PLACE 4.10, 1.40, 1.50; DF 50.10; SF 117.40.

Owner Ecurie Nepal Sarl **Bred** D Cherdo **Trained** France

^{4968}SALISBURY (R-H)

Friday, August 19

OFFICIAL GOING: Good to soft (soft in places)

Wind: Moderate, against Weather: Sunny

5231 SAVILLS LADY RIDERS' H'CAP (FOR LADY AMATEUR RIDERS) 1m

5:25 (5:25) (Class 5) (0-70,69) 3-Y-O+ **£2,495** (£774; £386; £193) **Stalls** Low

Form				RPR
3022	**1**		**Whodathought (IRE)**^{9} 4908 3-9-10 **69** (b) MissCWalton$^{(5)}$ 9 (Richard Hannon) *mid-div: hdwy 3f out: sddle slipped over 2f out: led and drifted lft to stands' rail over 1f out: kpt on wl* **7/1**^{3}	78
3221	**2**	*1 1/4*	**George Thisby**^{9} 4917 5-9-11 **64** MissJennyCarr$^{(5)}$ 2 (Rod Millman) *trckd ldrs: led 4f out: rdn 2f out: hdd over 1f out: kpt on: hld towards fin* **4/1**^{1}	71
1204	**3**	*3*	**Mini's Destination**^{8} 4949 3-9-5 **66** MissJessicaHolt$^{(7)}$ 7 (John Holt) *mid-div: rdn and hdwy 2f out: styd on same pce fnl f* **9/2**^{2}	65
0663	**4**	*1 3/4*	**King Columbo (IRE)**^{9} 4928 6-8-9 **50** oh1 (p) MissSBirkett$^{(7)}$ 11 (Julia Feilden) *hld up towards rr: rdn and hdwy over 2f out: chsd ldrs over 1f out: kpt on same pce fnl f* **9/1**	46
-014	**5**	*2 1/4*	**Push Me (IRE)**^{22} 4458 4-9-7 **62** MissSiobhanMiller$^{(7)}$ 3 (Jamie Poulton) *led after 3f tl 4f out: rdn over 2f out: wknd fnl f* **8/1**	53
0404	**6**	*1/2*	**Kyllachy Storm**^{13} 4795 7-9-9 **64** MissKClark$^{(7)}$ 6 (Ron Hodges) *stdd s: sme prog into mid-div 3f out: hung lft and no further imp over 1f out* **20/1**	54
2364	**7**	*nse*	**Advertise**^{12} 4829 5-9-10 **58** MissEJJones 1 (Joseph Tuite) *mid-div: rdn 3f out: wknd wl over 1f out* **9/2**^{2}	48
00-6	**8**	*15*	**Curlew (IRE)**^{12} 4822 5-9-10 **65** MissCNosworthy$^{(7)}$ 8 (Chris Down) *prom tl over 3f out* **16/1**	20
0605	**9**	*nk*	**Gessabelle**^{15} 4711 4-8-9 **50** oh5 (tp) MissJSohanta$^{(7)}$ 4 (Phil McEntee) *rrd leaving stalls: sn in mid-div: wknd 2f out* **100/1**	4
603/	**10**	*1 3/4*	**Yellow Printer**^{638} 7456 5-9-10 **63** MissAWallace$^{(5)}$ 5 (Mark Gillard) *led 3f: sn struggling: wknd over 2f out* **20/1**	13
5506	**11**	*4 1/2*	**Red Yarn**^{20} 4546 4-10-2 **69** (b) MissHayleyMoore$^{(5)}$ 13 (Gary Moore) *racd alone in centre: a towards rr* **9/1**	—
000/	**12**	*16*	**General Sam (USA)**^{297} 343 5-8-9 **50** oh4 (b^{1}) MissEMelbourn$^{(7)}$ 12 (Richard Mitchell) *wnt lft s: mid-div tl 4f out: t.o fnl 2f* **100/1**	—

1m 46.43s (2.93) **Going Correction** +0.25s/f (Good)

WFA 3 from 4yo+ 6lb **12** Ran SP% **117.4**

Speed ratings (Par 103): **95,93,90,89,86 86,86,71,70,69 64,48**

toteswingers:1&2:£3.00, 2&3:£4.10, 1&3:£5.40 CSF £33.67 CT £143.27 TOTE £4.90: £2.10, £1.60, £1.80; EX 12.00.

Owner Mrs Philip Snow **Bred** Meadowlands Stud **Trained** East Everleigh, Wilts

■ Stewards' Enquiry : Miss Hayley Moore caution: used whip down shoulder in the forehand

Miss C Walton three-day ban: used whip with excessive frequency (tbn)

FOCUS

An inch and a half of rain (38mm) turned the ground testing on Thursday but, following a dry night and a warm, breezy day, the ground dried out significantly to good to soft, soft in places. The gallop was reasonable and, although the field raced centre-to-far-side for much of the race, the field fanned across the course in the closing stages and there seemed little advantage on any part of the track. The form is rated around the first two.

Red Yarn Official explanation: jockey said filly hung right

5232 BATHWICK TYRES MAIDEN AUCTION STKS 6f

5:55 (5:55) (Class 5) 2-Y-O **£2,911** (£866; £432; £216) **Stalls** Low

Form				RPR
5	**1**		**The Noble Ord**^{28} 4269 2-8-9 0 LiamKeniry 13 (Sylvester Kirk) *s.i.s: towards rr: rdn and hdwy over 2f out: led jst ins fnl f: r.o wl* **7/1**^{3}	71
0	**2**	*1 1/2*	**Essexvale (IRE)**^{79} 2606 2-8-8 0 TedDurcan 1 (Richard Hannon) *s.i.s and hmpd s: towards rr: rdn and nt clr run over 2f out: r.o fr over 1f out* **8/1**	66
	3	*hd*	**Russian Rocker** 2-8-13 0 IanMongan 4 (Stuart Kittow) *s.i.s: towards rr: pushed along and hdwy to chse ldrs whn nt clr run over 1f out: swtchd rt: r.o wl fnl f* **8/1**	72+
	4	*1 1/4*	**Lady Percy (IRE)** 2-8-4 0 DavidProbert 2 (Mark Usher) *wnt rt s: mid-div: rdn over 3f out: hdwy over 2f out: kpt on same pce fnl f* **14/1**	57
20	**5**	*1/2*	**Rafaella**^{59} 3257 2-8-2 0 ow1 JohnFahy$^{(3)}$ 11 (Harry Dunlop) *prom: rdn over 3f out: kpt on same pce fnl f* **11/4**^{1}	57
06	**6**	*2 1/4*	**The Wicked Lord**^{37} 3984 2-8-9 0 FergusSweeney 12 (Stuart Kittow) *led: rdn over 1f out: hdd jst ins fnl f: fdd* **8/1**	54
63	**7**	*1/2*	**Lady Heartbeat**^{17} 4629 2-8-4 0 FrankieMcDonald 5 (Michael Blanshard) *chsd ldrs: rdn over 3f out: wknd over 1f out* **16/1**	48
50	**8**	*nk*	**Rain Dance**^{28} 4263 2-8-11 0 PatDobbs 10 (Richard Hannon) *s.i.s: towards rr: rdn over 2f out: nvr plcd to get on terms* **4/1**^{2}	54+
	9	*11*	**Trusting (IRE)** 2-8-4 0 WilliamCarson 9 (Eve Johnson Houghton) *prom: rdn and ev ch over 1f out: sn wknd* **12/1**	14
00	**10**	*7*	**Distant Voyage**^{30} 4205 2-8-9 0 NeilChalmers 6 (Michael Blanshard) *a towards rr* **50/1**	—

1m 17.34s (2.54) **Going Correction** +0.25s/f (Good) **10** Ran SP% **114.7**

Speed ratings (Par 94): **93,91,90,89,88 85,84,84,69,60**

toteswingers:1&2:£7.20, 2&3:£7.80, 1&3:£10.40 CSF £60.79 TOTE £6.60: £1.80, £2.30, £2.70; EX 95.30.

Owner Verano Quartet **Bred** Speedlith Group **Trained** Upper Lambourn, Berks

FOCUS

A fair gallop but a race lacking anything in the way of strength and this bare form looks no better than modest. Unlike with the lady amateurs in the opener, the field headed straight towards the stands side.

NOTEBOOK

The Noble Ord, just behind a subsequent winner on his debut, attracted support and stepped up a fair way on his debut effort in these easier conditions. He should stay 7f and may be able to build on this in nurseries. (op 8-1 tchd 6-1)

Essexvale(IRE), the lesser-fancied of the yard's runners, stepped up a fair bit on his debut effort on Polytrack. He shaped as though a stiffer overall test of stamina would have suited and should do better over further once qualified for a mark. (op 13-2)

Russian Rocker ◆, a £20,000 half-brother to the yard's triple winner (up to 7f on turf and Polytrack) Russian Rave, showed clear signs of ability, despite not getting the clearest of runs at a crucial stage, on this racecourse debut. He is entitled to improve for this experience. (op 11-1)

Lady Percy(IRE), a £5,000 half-sister to fair 5f-1m1f winner Right Rave, attracted a bit of support at a big price and was far from disgraced on this racecourse debut. She'll have no problems with 7f but is likely to remain vulnerable against the better sorts in this grade. (op 25-1)

Rafaella again failed to match her debut form but she may not have been entirely at home in these conditions and will be worth another chance back on a sound surface in ordinary nursery company. (tchd 3-1)

The Wicked Lord failed to get home having raced with the choke out and may be best on a sound surface in modest nurseries. (op 9-1)

Rain Dance never figured but she wasn't knocked about at any stage and, given she may fare better back on a sound surface and when switched to nurseries, she wouldn't be one to write off yet. (op 3-1)

5233 BATHWICK TYRES NURSERY 1m

6:30 (6:30) (Class 5) (0-75,75) 2-Y-O **£2,911** (£866; £432; £216) **Stalls** Low

Form				RPR
005	**1**		**Plym**^{54} 3425 2-8-8 **62** FrankieMcDonald 9 (Richard Hannon) *mde all: rdn and hrd pressed fr 2f out: kpt on wl to assert ins fnl f: rdn out* **8/1**^{3}	69
512	**2**	*1 1/4*	**Fire Ship**^{9} 4913 2-9-0 **68** IanMongan 3 (Peter Winkworth) *w wnr thrght: rdn over 2f out: ev ch 1f out: kpt on but no ex ins fnl f* **5/2**^{2}	72
4521	**3**	*2*	**My Sharona**^{16} 4682 2-9-3 **71** LiamKeniry 11 (Sylvester Kirk) *broke wl: sn stdd towards rr: hdwy to chse ldrs 2f out: sn rdn: kpt on but nt pce to chal* **14/1**	71
000	**4**	*nk*	**Shannon Spree**^{20} 4552 2-8-11 **65** PatDobbs 7 (Richard Hannon) *hmpd s: towards rr: rdn and hdwy over 2f out: styd on fnl f* **14/1**	65
015	**5**	*2 1/4*	**Meanwhile (IRE)**^{19} 4581 2-8-10 **64** TedDurcan 1 (William Knight) *hld up: rdn over 2f out: hdwy over 1f out: kpt on same pce fnl f* **20/1**	58
600	**6**	*2 1/4*	**Tigers Tale (IRE)**^{27} 4311 2-8-11 **68** JohnFahy$^{(3)}$ 12 (Roger Teal) *hld up: hdwy over 2f out: sn rdn to chse ldrs: fdd fnl f* **8/1**^{3}	56
4300	**7**	*6*	**Mr Knightley (IRE)**^{9} 4913 2-9-5 **73** JimmyFortune 10 (Richard Hannon) *wnt rt leaving stalls: trckd ldrs: rdn over 2f out: wknd over 1f out* **14/1**	48
6442	**8**	*3 3/4*	**Lucky Money**^{11} 4867 2-9-4 **72** DavidProbert 2 (Sir Mark Prescott Bt) *t.k.h trcking ldrs: effrt over 2f out: wknd over 1f out* **9/4**^{1}	38
010	**9**	*1/2*	**Captain Cardington (IRE)**^{21} 4496 2-9-4 **72** SamHitchcott 5 (Mick Channon) *hmpd s: a towards rr* **8/1**^{3}	37+

1m 45.65s (2.15) **Going Correction** +0.25s/f (Good) **9** Ran SP% **117.4**

Speed ratings (Par 94): **99,97,95,95,93 90,84,81,80**

toteswingers:1&2:£5.90, 2&3:£2.60, 1&3:£17.00 CSF £28.85 CT £284.32 TOTE £9.90: £2.60, £1.30, £3.10; EX 28.40.

Owner Mrs James Wigan **Bred** Mrs James Wigan **Trained** East Everleigh, Wilts

FOCUS

A fair handicap but a moderately run race in which those racing prominently held the edge. The field again made for the near-side rail soon after the start.

NOTEBOOK

Plym, who had shown clear signs of ability in maidens, duly appreciated the step into nursery company and the step up to 1m and showed a good attitude and improved form on this first run away from a sound surface. She had the run of the race but may do better. Official explanation: trainer said, regarding apparent improvement in form, that the filly appeared suited by the softer ground and step up in trip.

Fire Ship, up in trip and back on softish ground, ran creditably from the same mark as at this course last week. He will be 2lb higher in future but remains open to improvement and should be able to pick up another small event. (op 3-1)

My Sharona is a steadily progressive sort who was far from disgraced against two rivals who were ridden closer to the steady pace on this nursery debut. A stronger overall test of stamina would have suited and she is capable of better. (op 11-1)

Shannon Spree was another to leave the impression that a much stronger overall stamina test would have suited but she was far from disgraced on this racecourse debut, is in good hands and may do better in due course. (tchd 12-1)

Tigers Tale(IRE) is probably a bit better than he was able to show in this muddling event on his nursery debut. He will be worth another chance when a better gallop looks on the cards. (op 11-1)

Lucky Money raced with the choke out and didn't get home over this longer trip on this first run on softish ground. He will be 3lb higher in future after his improved Polytrack run and hasn't always looked straightforward but will be worth another chance back on a sound surface or on sand returned to 7f. Official explanation: trainer's rep said she had no explanation for the poor form shown (op 3-1)

5234 WEATHERBYS BANK STONEHENGE STKS (LISTED RACE) 1m
7:00 (7:00) (Class 1) 2-Y-O

£12,192 (£4,622; £2,313; £1,152; £578; £290) **Stalls** Low

Form RPR

211 **1** **Coupe De Ville (IRE)**[34] 4091 2-8-13 92 PatDobbs 1 98+
(Richard Hannon) *cl up: jnd ldrs travelling wl over 2f out: led over 1f out: rdn whn chal jst ins fnl f: hld on wl* **15/8**[1]

2123 **2** *nk* **Lord Ofthe Shadows (IRE)**[21] 4496 2-8-13 97 JimmyFortune 4 97+
(Richard Hannon) *hld up but wl in tch: swtchd rt and hdwy 2f out: rdn for str chal jst ins fnl f: kpt on wl: hld nr fin* **5/2**[2]

104 **3** *3 ½* **Sound Advice**[27] 4311 2-8-13 86 RoystonFfrench 3 88
(Keith Dalgleish) *led: rdn 2f out: hdd over 1f out: kpt on same pce* **7/1**

5021 **4** *¾* **Goldoni (IRE)**[21] 4496 2-8-13 82 DavidProbert 6 89+
(Andrew Balding) *trckd ldrs: outpcd 2f out: nt clr run and swtchd rt over 1f out: styd on* **5/1**[3]

05L **5** *1 ½* **Thecornishcockney**[13] 4798 2-8-13 0 (b) StevieDonohoe 7 83
(John Ryan) *slowly away: wnt lft: in last pair but wl in tch: hdwy into 4th ent fnl f: sn rdn: nt pce to get on terms* **50/1**

543 **6** *2 ½* **Opera Buff**[20] 4535 2-8-13 78 LiamKeniry 2 77
(Sylvester Kirk) *trckd ldrs: jnd ldrs 3f out: struggling whn squeezed out 2f out: hld whn edgd lft over 1f out: fdd fnl f* **6/1**

241 **7** *8* **Basantee**[15] 4717 2-8-8 84 RichardKingscote 5 54
(Tom Dascombe) *prom tl rdn over 2f out: sltly squeezed up whn wkng over 1f out* **16/1**

1m 45.4s (1.90) **Going Correction** +0.25s/f (Good) **7** Ran SP% **114.6**
Speed ratings (Par 102): **100,99,96,95,93 91,83**
toteswingers:1&2:£1.70, 2&3:£4.60, 1&3:£2.60 CSF £6.81 TOTE £2.70: £1.60, £2.20; EX 4.00.

Owner Coupe de Ville Partnership **Bred** Flor Ryan **Trained** East Everleigh, Wilts

FOCUS

his wasn't the strongest of Listed races with only the winner and runner-up holding official ratings of above 90 and the race lost some of its interest with the ground-related defection of potentially smart prospect Attenborough. The two highest-rated performers pulled clear of the rest on the back of just an ordinary gallop but the proximity of the fifth holds the form down. The field again tacked to the stands' side at an early stage and Richard Hannon was winning this for the third year in succession.

NOTEBOOK

Coupe De Ville(IRE) ◆ again showed a tendency to race freely but he is a progressive sort who confirmed he is bordering on smart when showing a good attitude to register his third successive win. The way he travelled suggested he will be equally effective back at 7f and remains the type to win more races. (op 7-4)

Lord Ofthe Shadows(IRE), the highest rated of these, ran up to his best on this first run over 1m and away from fast ground. He pulled clear of the remainder and, although he will have to raise his game to win in minor Group company, he is the type to win again.

Sound Advice had his limitations exposed on his last two starts in Listed and Group 2 company and, although he was allowed to do his own thing in front, he was once again brushed aside in the closing stages by a couple bordering on smart. He is useful but will have to improve to win a similar race. (op 9-1)

Goldoni(IRE), who had shown progressive form in maidens and on his nursery debut, had plenty to find at the weights but looks better than the bare facts give him credit for on this debut in Listed company as he was stuck behind horses as the leaders were quickening away. He will be worth another chance back in a nursery. (op 11-2)

Thecornishcockney had previously shown only modest form at best in his two completed races but his proximity owes plenty to the steady pace and he will be seen to much better effort in nursery company if the handicapper doesn't take a literal view of this bare form.

Opera Buff had plenty to find at the weights but was still something of a disappointment given his steadily progressive profile and the fact that he looked sure to be suited by the step up to 1m. He may be ideally suited by a sounder surface and wouldn't be one to write off just yet. (op 7-1 tchd 15-2)

5235 WEATHERBYS BANK H'CAP 1m 4f
7:35 (7:35) (Class 4) (0-85,84) 3-Y-O **£4,528** (£1,347; £673; £336) **Stalls** Low

Form RPR

4015 **1** **Gottany O'S**[29] 4251 3-9-4 81 SamHitchcott 9 87
(Mick Channon) *hld up: hmpd on bnd 5f out: hdwy over 1f out: swtchd rt sn after: styd on strly to ld ins fnl f: drvn out* **7/1**[3]

3642 **2** *¾* **Kleitomachos (IRE)**[34] 4084 3-8-11 74 IanMongan 2 79
(Stuart Kittow) *hld up: prog fr 4f out: rdn over 2f out: chal over 1f out: led briefly ins fnl f: styd on* **5/1**[2]

31-0 **3** *nk* **Encore Une Annee**[107] 1807 3-9-0 77 StevieDonohoe 3 82
(Ralph Beckett) *in tch: lft in ld 5f out: rdn whn hrd pressed fr over 2f out: narrowly hdd jst ins fnl f: styd on* **9/1**

0150 **4** *½* **Gosbeck**[29] 4251 3-9-7 84 FergusSweeney 7 88+
(Henry Candy) *squeezed up s: sn trcking ldrs: in 2nd whn bdly hmpd on bnd 5f out: dropped to last but sn bk in tch: pushed along to cl on ldrs over 1f out: rdn and styd on on fnl f: possibly unlucky nt to have won* **8/1**

6663 **5** *½* **Lunar Phase (IRE)**[34] 4084 3-8-8 74 JohnFahy[(3)] 5 77
(Clive Cox) *in tch: hmpd on bnd 5f out: hdwy over 1f out: sn swtchd rt: styd on* **9/1**

1102 **6** *2* **Anton Dolin (IRE)**[20] 4530 3-9-4 81 TedDurcan 6 81
(John Dunlop) *wnt lft s: sn led: hdd after 3f: trckd ldr: rdn and ev ch fr over 2f out tl ent fnl f: styd on same pce* **9/2**[1]

1 **7** *7* **Look Left**[20] 4529 3-9-6 83 RobertHavlin 4 72
(John Gosden) *in tch: lft trcking ldrs 5f out: short of room on rails over 2f out: sn rdn: wknd over 1f out* **9/2**[1]

0252 **R** **Swindy**[9] 4905 3-9-3 80 JimmyFortune 8 —
(Paul Cole) *led after 3f tl rn out on bnd over 5f out* **9/2**[1]

2m 44.12s (6.12) **Going Correction** +0.10s/f (Good) **8** Ran SP% **114.8**
Speed ratings (Par 102): **83,82,82,81,81 80,75,—**
toteswingers:1&2:£11.70, 2&3:£16.30, 1&3:£11.40 CSF £41.91 CT £318.71 TOTE £9.70: £2.50, £2.00, £2.50; EX 50.50.

Owner Dr Marwan Koukash **Bred** Phil Jen Racing **Trained** West Ilsley, Berks

FOCUS

There were a couple of unexposed sorts in this useful handicap. The gallop was moderate and there was drama as Swindy ran out on the bend into the home straight when in the lead. The field tacked to the near-side rail and the form makes sense, if a little muddling.

5236 WESTOVER GROUP H'CAP 1m 6f 21y
8:05 (8:05) (Class 5) (0-75,75) 3-Y-O+ **£2,587** (£770; £384; £192) **Stalls** Far side

Form RPR

4342 **1** **Slight Advantage (IRE)**[29] 4251 3-8-13 75 JohnFahy[(3)] 1 89+
(Clive Cox) *trckd ldrs: led over 2f out: hung to stands' side rails: rdn clr over 1f out: readily* **13/8**[1]

5104 **2** *4* **Schism**[23] 4449 3-9-0 73 FergusSweeney 7 79
(Henry Candy) *hld up in last pair: nt clr run over 3f out: rdn and hdwy whn short of room over 2f out: chsd wnr ent fnl f but a being hld: jst hld on for 2nd* **11/1**

3 *hd* **Kahsabelle (FR)**[509] 6-9-4 65 DavidProbert 11 71
(Venetia Williams) *trckd ldrs tl lost pl over 5f out: hdwy over 4f out: rdn over 3f out: styd on to weave through btn horses fnl f: nrly snatched 2nd* **20/1**

-536 **4** *2 ¼* **Hawridge King**[22] 4463 9-9-9 70 (v) IanMongan 6 73
(Stuart Kittow) *hld up in last trio: hdwy 4f out: rdn 3f out: styd on same pce fnl 2f* **12/1**

3001 **5** *2* **Shy**[8] 4952 6-9-2 63 6ex (b) JamesMillman 4 63
(Rod Millman) *led: rdn and hdd whn bmpd over 2f out: kpt chsng wnr tl no ex ent fnl f* **7/1**

5022 **6** *1 ¾* **Man Of God (IRE)**[14] 4752 3-9-2 75 JimmyFortune 5 74
(John Gosden) *hld up bhd: pushed along 4f out: rdn over 3f out: nt pce to get on terms* **7/2**[2]

0461 **7** *20* **Soundbyte**[15] 4703 6-9-9 70 ChrisCatlin 8 39
(John Gallagher) *trckd ldrs tl rdn and lost pl 5f out: nvr bk on terms: wknd over 1f out* **20/1**

2362 **8** *1 ¼* **Dr Darcey**[8] 4974 3-8-2 61 (b) FrankieMcDonald 10 29
(Richard Hannon) *prom tl rdn over 4f out: wknd over 1f out* **6/1**[3]

2644 **9** *5* **Now What**[17] 4626 4-9-3 64 RichardKingscote 3 25
(Jonathan Portman) *trckd ldrs: rdn over 3f out: wknd wl over 1f out* **12/1**

3m 7.66s (0.26) **Going Correction** +0.10s/f (Good)
WFA 3 from 4yo+ 12lb **9** Ran SP% **120.3**
Speed ratings (Par 103): **103,100,100,99,98 97,85,85,82**
toteswingers:1&2:£6.50, 2&3:£30.20, 1&3:£25.80 CSF £22.76 CT £265.11 TOTE £2.50: £1.10, £3.80, £7.80; EX 24.50.

Owner The City & Provincial Partnership **Bred** Airlie Stud **Trained** Lambourn, Berks

FOCUS

A fair handicap in which the gallop was ordinary, but there was an improved performance from the progressive winner. The field again came to the stands' side in the straight and the winner is related to his recent Sandown form with a personal best from the runner-up.

Man Of God(IRE) Official explanation: jockey said colt hung left

T/Plt: £102.20 to a £1 stake. Pool £52,316.97 - 373.45 winning tickets T/Qpdt: £23.80 to a £1 stake. Pool:£5,812.26 - 180.60 winning tickets SS

4720 SANDOWN (R-H)

Friday, August 19

OFFICIAL GOING: Good to soft (soft in places; sprint 6.0; round 6.4)

Rail dolled out 3yds from 1m to 2.5f adding about 5yds to races on round course. Sprint track at full width.

Wind: Moderate across Weather: Sunny spells

5237 EPSOM TRAINERS OPEN DAY 28TH AUGUST NURSERY 5f 6y
2:10 (2:11) (Class 4) (0-85,82) 2-Y-O **£3,881** (£1,155; £577; £288) **Stalls** Low

Form RPR

2004 **1** **Signifer (IRE)**[13] 4787 2-9-7 82 JamesDoyle 1 87
(Mick Channon) *trckd ldrs in 3rd: pushed along to go 2nd ins fnl 2f: rdn and kpt on to ld fnl 120yds: edgd rt sn after: r.o wl* **3/1**[3]

463 **2** *3* **Daunt (IRE)**[39] 3917 2-8-12 76 SeanLevey[(3)] 6 70
(Richard Hannon) *chsd ldr after 2f: rdn and dropped to 3rd ins fnl 2f: one pce over 1f out tl styd on again clsng stages to take 2nd last stride: no ch w wnr* **5/1**

1201 **3** *shd* **Powerful Wind (IRE)**[22] 4460 2-9-7 82 TomMcLaughlin 7 76
(Ronald Harris) *broke fast and wnt rt to get far rail: drvn fr 2f out: hdd fnl 120yds: no ch w wnr whn hmpd sn after: lost 2nd last stride* **10/1**

4413 **4** *3 ½* **Safari Storm (USA)**[20] 4536 2-9-3 78 (t) ShaneKelly 5 59
(Brian Meehan) *in tch: pushed along 2f out and no imp: styd on same pce fnl f* **2/1**[1]

10 **5** *19* **Charlotte Rosina**[65] 3033 2-9-1 79 JohnFahy[(3)] 3 —
(Roger Teal) *plld hrd: chsd ldrs 2f: sn wknd: t.o* **11/4**[2]

64.34 secs (2.74) **Going Correction** +0.50s/f (Yiel) **5** Ran SP% **110.8**
Speed ratings (Par 96): **98,93,93,87,57**
CSF £17.52 TOTE £3.60: £2.00, £2.60; EX 18.60.

Owner Insignia Racing (Roundel) **Bred** Maurice Burns **Trained** West Ilsley, Berks

FOCUS

The round course rail was dolled out three yards from 1m to the 2.5f point, adding approximately five yards to race distances. The sprint course was at its full width. An ordinary nursery for the class, the race weakened by three non-runners.

NOTEBOOK

Signifer(IRE) found this easier than the Haydock nursery he contested last time and was doubling his tally, adding to a maiden success he gained on firm ground in May. Although well on top at the line, he wasn't as impressive as the winning margin suggests, taking a long time to get on top. A rise in the weights will probably prevent him from following up in another nursery. (tchd 11-4)

Daunt(IRE) was a bit disappointing on this drop in trip and switch to nursery company, only keeping on at the one pace and posing no threat to the winner. (tchd 9-2 and 6-1)

Powerful Wind(IRE), up 2lb for his Ffos Las win, was allowed an easy lead and might have held on for second had he not been slightly short of room against the rail when weakening late on. (op 6-1)

Safari Storm(USA) wasn't best away and didn't pick up for pressure. He had today's winner behind when third over 6f at Goodwood last time, and prior to that he'd won a C&D maiden, so this was disappointing. His yard could be in better form. Official explanation: trainer's rep said colt was unsuited by the good to soft (soft in places) ground (op 5-2)

Charlotte Rosina won a C&D maiden before finishing down the field in the Queen Mary, and she hadn't been since having reportedly scoped badly. This was not a promising return, finding nothing after racing keenly, and presumably she didn't like the ground. (op 10-3 tchd 7-2)

5238 JIM CAREY MEMORIAL H'CAP 5f 6y
2:40 (2:40) (Class 5) (0-75,76) 3-Y-0+ £2,587 (£770; £384; £192) Stalls Low

Form				RPR
10	1		**Italian Tom (IRE)**[20] 4546 4-9-8 73 .... LukeMorris 3	83
			(Ronald Harris) *trckd ldrs off mod early pce: drvn to chse ldr over 1f out: styd on u.p to ld fnl 150yds: in command cloing stages* 11/4[2]	
1452	2	1 ¼	**Triple Dream**[10] 4895 6-9-4 69 .... (tp) LiamKeniry 7	75
			(Milton Bradley) *sn led and set mod pce on far rail: rdn ins fnl 2f: hdd fnl 150yds: sn one pce* 9/4[1]	
0021	3	6	**Go Nani Go**[22] 4475 5-9-10 75 .... PatCosgrave 2	59
			(Ed de Giles) *t.k.h: hld up in rr but in tch off mod pce: drvn and hdwy to take 3rd over 1f out: styd on but nvr gng pce to rch ldng duo* 11/4[2]	
0016	4	2	**Atlantic Cycle (IRE)**[17] 4628 4-9-5 70 .... RichardKingscote 5	47
			(Milton Bradley) *t.k.h and trckd ldr off mod pce: rdn 2f out: wknd over 1f out* 11/2[3]	
0002	5	2 ¼	**Pose (IRE)**[12] 4828 4-8-3 58 ow1 .... (t) MatthewLawson(5) 4	28
			(Roger Ingram) *a in last pl: off mod pce: rdn 3f out: nvr any ch and wl hld fnl 2f* 11/1	

63.61 secs (2.01) **Going Correction** +0.50s/f (Yiel) 5 Ran SP% **107.8**
Speed ratings (Par 103): **103,101,91,88,84**
CSF £8.90 TOTE £4.30: £2.00, £1.50; EX 9.90.

Owner S & A Mares **Bred** Tom Radley **Trained** Earlswood, Monmouths

FOCUS
A race decimated by six non-runners and this is ordinary form for the level, although it could be rated higher.

5239 BRITISH STALLION STUDS SUPPORTING BRITISH RACING E B F MAIDEN STKS 7f 16y
3:15 (3:15) (Class 5) 2-Y-0 £3,881 (£1,155; £577; £288) Stalls Low

Form				RPR
	1		**Newnton Lodge** 2-9-3 0 .... JamesDoyle 8	83+
			(Roger Charlton) *s.i.s: hld up in rr: stdy hdwy fr 2f out: pushed along and qcknd over 1f out to ld fnl 120yds: comf* 5/1[3]	
	2	1	**Kid Suitor (IRE)** 2-9-0 0 .... SeanLevey(3) 1	78+
			(Richard Hannon) *in rr: hdwy fr 2f out: qcknd to ld 1f out: sn rdn and edgd rt: hdd fnl 120yds: nt pce of wnr but kpt on wl for 2nd* 9/2[2]	
6	3	4 ½	**Juvenal (IRE)**[14] 4762 2-9-3 0 .... EddieAhern 11	67
			(Richard Hannon) *pressed ldrs tl slt advantage 3f out: rdn 2 out and kpt narrow ld tl hdd 1f out: sn lft bhd by ldng duo but hld on wl for 3rd* 7/2[1]	
	4	nk	**Debating Society (IRE)** 2-9-3 0 .... RichardMullen 10	68+
			(Sir Michael Stoute) *trckd ldrs: pushed along: green and outpcd 2f out: kpt on again ins fnl f to press for 3rd cl home but nvr any ch w ldng duo* 12/1	
56	5	¾	**Perfect Gratitude (USA)**[13] 4798 2-9-3 0 .... RoystonFfrench 6	64
			(Ed Dunlop) *pressed ldrs: stl upsides and chalng fr 3f out tl wknd appr fnl f* 20/1	
	6	1 ¼	**Samuel Pickwick (IRE)** 2-9-3 0 .... ShaneKelly 4	61
			(Sir Michael Stoute) *trckd ldrs: pushed along over 2f out: green and wknd ins fnl 2f* 12/1	
	7	½	**Hartside (GER)** 2-9-3 0 .... JimmyFortune 7	60+
			(Sir Michael Stoute) *in tch tl dropped towards rr and then hmpd over 2f out: no ch after but sme prog fnl f* 9/1	
	8	nk	**Watheeq (USA)** 2-9-3 0 .... NeilCallan 5	59+
			(Roger Varian) *in tch tl rdn along 2f out and sn green: wknd wl over 1f out* 7/2[1]	
	9	1	**No Time To Lose** 2-9-3 0 .... FergusSweeney 2	57
			(Jamie Osborne) *s.i.s: pushed along over 3f out: a towards rr* 66/1	
	10	6	**Tectonic (IRE)** 2-9-0 0 .... LouisBeuzelin(3) 3	42
			(Sir Michael Stoute) *slt ld and t.k.h: narrowly hdd 3f out: sn rdn: green and hung rt 2f out: wknd qckly* 15/2	

1m 34.8s (5.30) **Going Correction** +0.50s/f (Yiel) 10 Ran SP% **122.7**
Speed ratings (Par 94): **89,87,82,82,81 80,79,79,78,71**
toteswingers:1&2:£8.50, 1&3:£5.50, 2&3:£3.50 CSF £29.43 TOTE £6.60: £2.00, £2.30, £1.80; EX 24.60.

Owner K Abdulla **Bred** Juddmonte Farms Ltd **Trained** Beckhampton, Wilts

FOCUS
A fascinating maiden with plenty of powerful connections represented, although a distinct lack of juvenile Group-race entries suggests this lot are mainly considered long-term prospects. They raced stands' side in the straight.

NOTEBOOK
Newnton Lodge ◆'s trainer commented beforehand that this newcomer is a big, strong type, but has a tendency to be keen, so he thought the experience might be needed. However, the colt was given a nice, patient ride by James Doyle, and although a touch keen early, he was soon travelling well in a good rhythm. Once in the straight it was clear he was going best, but he still wasn't rushed, being waited with until a narrow gap appeared, and he showed a good attitude when asked. This was just the short of experience the winner should go forward from, and although he doesn't hold any big-race entries in Britain or Ireland, he's bred to be decent considering his dam (unraced) is a half-sister to the likes of Zafonic and Zamindar. A half-brother to a winner over as far as 1m4f, he looks a smart long-term middle-distance prospect. (op 11-1)
Kid Suitor(IRE) ◆, a 40,000euros half-brother to 1m winner Fancy Footsteps, and 7f scorer Tahitian Pearl, was given a similarly nice introduction to winner, travelling well under a hold-up ride from Sean Levey. He wandered a bit under pressure and lacked Newnton Lodge's acceleration, but this was still a promising start. (op 5-1 tchd 10-3)
Juvenal(IRE) had the benefit of experience having shaped well on his debut at the July course, but he couldn't make it count. He did, though, fare best of those that raced handily. (op 15-8 tchd 7-4)
Debating Society(IRE) ◆ fared best of Sir Michael Stoute's four runners and looks a quality long-term prospect. He's from a family the owner and trainer know well, being a half-brother to among others 1m2f Group 2 winner Eleanora Duse. A tall, leggy type, he ran green and looked weak in the straight, but showed plenty of ability and can do a lot better as an older horse. (op 8-1 tchd 14-1)
Perfect Gratitude(USA) found this company a bit hot but can now contest nurseries. (op 33-1)
Samuel Pickwick(IRE) raced furthest away from the stands' side in the straight and can improve plenty. (op 10-1)
Hartside(GER) was short of room early in the straight and then found little when in the clear. (op 10-1)
Watheeq(USA) was the only runner with juvenile Group-race entries in Britain and he was solid in the market, but he found disappointingly little after travelling okay. Maybe he wants better ground. (op 6-1 tchd 7-1)

5240 JIMMY GREEN RACING LEGEND H'CAP 1m 14y
3:50 (3:51) (Class 4) (0-85,85) 3-Y-0+ £4,528 (£1,347; £673; £336) Stalls Low

Form				RPR
3215	1		**First Post (IRE)**[13] 4794 4-9-9 82 .... AndreaAtzeni 8	93
			(Derek Haydn Jones) *chsd ldrs: c to r stands' side and wnt 2nd over 2f out: rdn to take overall ld appr fnl f: drvn out* 9/2[1]	
3001	2	1 ¼	**Top Diktat**[32] 4163 3-8-8 73 .... RichardMullen 6	80
			(Sir Michael Stoute) *in rr: c to r stands' side and rdn over 3f out: styd on strly u.p appr fnl f: fin wl to take 2nd clsng stages but nt rch wnr* 8/1	
3001	3	1	**Spa's Dancer (IRE)**[15] 4725 4-9-8 81 .... EddieAhern 14	87
			(J W Hills) *bmpd s and s.i.s: chsd ldrs 5f out: racd stands' side and led that gp and overall advantage over 3f out: hdd appr fnl f: styd on same pce* 17/2	
-056	4	nk	**Spectait**[18] 4616 9-9-8 81 .... RichardKingscote 5	86
			(Jonjo O'Neill) *sn drvn and in rr and pushed along most of way: styd far side over 3f out and styd on u.p to ld that gp last strides but a hld by main gp on stands' side* 20/1	
0024	5	½	**Hacienda (IRE)**[21] 4509 4-9-8 81 .... FrannyNorton 4	85
			(Mark Johnston) *chsd ldrs: styd far side over 3f out: led that gp u.p over 2f out but no imp on main gp stands' side: lost ld and fin 2nd in gp last strides* 11/2[3]	
4652	6	1	**Fantasy Gladiator**[28] 4268 5-9-7 80 .... (p) JimmyQuinn 15	82
			(Robert Cowell) *towards rr: racd stands' side over 3f out: styd on fnl 2f but nt pce to rch ldrs: fin 4th in gp* 12/1	
260-	7	nk	**King Of Windsor (IRE)**[327] 6391 4-9-11 84 .... JamesDoyle 1	85
			(Ralph Beckett) *chsd ldrs: racd stands' side over 3f out: one pce u.p fnl 2f: fin 5th in gp* 20/1	
1023	8	1	**Dysios (IRE)**[15] 4724 3-8-11 76 .... J-PGuillambert 2	74
			(Luca Cumani) *chsd ldrs and racd stands' side over 3f out: wknd ins fnl 2f: fin 6th in gp* 5/1[2]	
0000	9	3	**L'Hirondelle (IRE)**[58] 3285 7-8-10 69 .... NeilCallan 3	61
			(Michael Attwater) *led and styd to r far side over 3f out but lost overall ld: hdd that gp over 2f out: wknd ins fnl f: fin 3rd in gp* 33/1	
4420	10	1	**Majestic Dream (IRE)**[20] 4550 3-9-6 85 .... (v) AdamKirby 12	73
			(Walter Swinburn) *racd towards rr and styd stands' side over 3f out: wknd over 2f out: fin 7th in gp* 8/1	
0032	11	8	**Bloodsweatandtears**[15] 4725 3-8-10 75 .... (b) ShaneKelly 7	45
			(William Knight) *in tch whn styd to r far side over 3f out: sn wknd: fin 4th in gp* 8/1	
0-05	12	2 ¾	**Tipsy Girl**[41] 3873 3-8-10 75 .... PatCosgrave 9	39
			(Denis Coakley) *racd in rr and c stands' side over 3f out: sn struggling: fin 8th and last in gp* 20/1	
63-0	13	12	**King's Colour**[211] 226 6-8-13 79 .... AccursioRomeo(7) 10	16
			(Brett Johnson) *styd to r far side over 3f out: a bhd: fin 5th and last in gp* 66/1	

1m 46.23s (2.93) **Going Correction** +0.50s/f (Yiel)
WFA 3 from 4yo+ 6lb 13 Ran SP% **120.5**
Speed ratings (Par 105): **105,103,102,102,101 100,100,99,96,95 87,84,72**
toteswingers:1&2:£7.30, 1&3:£5.90, 2&3:£14.00 CSF £37.78 CT £312.50 TOTE £3.60: £1.10, £3.60, £2.70; EX 44.30.

Owner Llewelyn, Runeckles **Bred** D Llewelyn & J Runeckles **Trained** Efail Isaf, Rhondda C Taff
■ Stewards' Enquiry : Andrea Atzeni caution: careless riding.

FOCUS
The majority of these raced stands' side, while only five runners stayed far side, but there wasn't a great deal in it at the line. Clearly this is muddling form but sound enough amongst the stands' side group, with the third setting the standard.

5241 HAAGEN-DAZS MAIDEN FILLIES' STKS 1m 14y
4:25 (4:26) (Class 5) 3-Y-0 £2,587 (£770; £384; £192) Stalls Low

Form				RPR
54	1		**Elraabeya (CAN)**[35] 4072 3-9-0 0 .... RichardMullen 2	70
			(Sir Michael Stoute) *trckd ldr: led ins fnl 2f: rdn and edgd lft 1f out: drvn and asserted fnl 120yds* 10/11[1]	
	2	2 ¼	**Tenavon** 3-9-0 0 .... ShaneKelly 1	65
			(William Knight) *slowly away: sn rcvrd and in tch: drvn and styd on fr 2f out: chsd wnr ins fnl f but no imp and outpcd fnl 120yds* 16/1	
2324	3	1	**Lady Elsie**[43] 3781 3-9-0 72 .... EddieAhern 6	63
			(William Haggas) *led: rdn along fr 3f out: hdd ins fnl 2f: one pce whn crossed by wnr 1f out: no ex and sn dropped to 3rd* 6/4[2]	
	4	6	**Love Your Looks** 3-9-0 0 .... TonyCulhane 5	49
			(Mike Murphy) *slowly away: sn rcvrd and in tch: flashed tail whn rdn and lost tch fnl 3f* 12/1[3]	
0	5	6	**Main Opinion (IRE)**[7] 4991 3-9-0 0 .... FrannyNorton 3	35
			(Mick Channon) *chsd ldrs tl wknd over 2f out* 25/1	

1m 48.56s (5.26) **Going Correction** +0.50s/f (Yiel) 5 Ran SP% **109.8**
Speed ratings (Par 97): **93,90,89,83,77**
CSF £15.45 TOTE £2.00: £1.10, £6.10; EX 10.80.

Owner Hamdan Al Maktoum **Bred** Sam-Son Farm **Trained** Newmarket, Suffolk
■ Stewards' Enquiry : Richard Mullen caution: careless riding.

FOCUS
An uncompetitive fillies' maiden in which they raced stands' side. The form is taken at face value rated around the winner and third.

5242 HAMPTON COURT H'CAP 1m 2f 7y
5:00 (5:01) (Class 4) (0-80,79) 3-Y-0 £4,528 (£1,347; £673; £336) Stalls Low

Form				RPR
5-10	1		**Groomed (IRE)**[26] 4355 3-9-4 79 .... AdamBeschizza(3) 2	89+
			(William Haggas) *chsd ldrs: racd towards centre of crse and tk slt ld ins fnl 2f: drvn and hld on wl thrght fnl f* 10/1	
-155	2	hd	**Blue Destination**[15] 4723 3-9-7 79 .... NeilCallan 10	87
			(Philip McBride) *chsd ldrs: drvn to take slt ld ins fnl 3f: hdd ins fnl 2f and sn outpcd: rallied u.p and styd on strly ins fnl f: gng on cl home: nt quite rch wnr* 7/2[1]	
3334	3	1 ¼	**Orthodox Lad**[22] 4473 3-8-10 71 .... KierenFox(3) 4	76
			(John Best) *chsd ldrs: slt ld 6f out tl narrowly hdd ins fnl 3f: styd pressing ldrs to 2f out: sn one pce: rallied u.p and styd on again clsng stages* 15/2[3]	
-134	4	1 ½	**Great Shot**[84] 2477 3-9-5 77 .... JamesDoyle 3	79
			(Sylvester Kirk) *t.k.h and hld up in rr: racd towards centre of crse and hdwy 3f out to chal 2f out: no ex 1f out and wknd ins fnl f* 14/1	

0-30 **5** 1/2 **Warneford**[28] 4279 3-9-1 **73**.................. ShaneKelly 1 74
(Brian Meehan) *s.i.s: rcvrd to chse ldrs 6f out: outpcd 3f out: drvn and styd on again fr over 1f out: kpt on cl home* **12/1**
055- **6** nk **Spirit Of Gondree (IRE)**[300] 7099 3-8-11 **69**.................. EddieAhern 12 69+
(John Dunlop) *t.k.h chsd ldrs: pushed along and losing position whn n.m.r on ins 2f out: styd on again clsng stages* **15/2**[3]
3452 **7** nk **With Hindsight (IRE)**[11] 4845 3-9-3 **75**.................. PhilipRobinson 9 75
(Clive Cox) *led tl hdd 6f out: styd chalng and ev ch u.p over 2f out: wknd sn after* **7/1**[2]
4242 **8** 3/4 **Mr Perceptive (IRE)**[21] 4489 3-9-3 **78**.................. SeanLevey(3) 5 76
(Richard Hannon) *in rr tl hdwy over 2f out: nvr rchd ldrs and sn btn* **15/2**[3]
040 **9** 1 1/4 **Suzi's A Class Act**[28] 4279 3-9-3 **75**.................. PatCosgrave 6 71
(James Eustace) *in tch: rdn 3f out: sn wknd* **14/1**
3100 **10** 1 3/4 **May Be Some Time**[53] 3466 3-8-8 **69**.................. LouisBeuzelin(3) 7 61
(Stuart Kittow) *in tch: rdn and wknd over 2f out* **25/1**
326 **11** 2 3/4 **Laashak (USA)**[76] 2735 3-9-7 **79**.................. RichardMullen 11 66
(Sir Michael Stoute) *chsd ldrs: rdn 3f out: sn wknd* **8/1**

2m 15.06s (4.56) **Going Correction** +0.50s/f (Yiel) **11** Ran SP% **115.1**
Speed ratings (Par 102): **101,100,99,98,98 98,97,97,96,94 92**
toteswingers:1&2:£37.40, 1&3:£8.10, 2&3:£44.60 CSF £43.94 CT £281.80 TOTE £13.50: £4.20, £1.10, £3.70; EX 60.20.
Owner Scotney,Asplin,Symonds,Ball & Fisher **Bred** Rathbarry Stud **Trained** Newmarket, Suffolk
■ Stewards' Enquiry : Kieren Fox one-day ban: used whip with excessive frequency (Sep 2)

FOCUS
A fair handicap, although something of a slow-motion finish and doubtless a few of these were unsuited by conditions. The action unfolded middle to stands' side. The form looks sound and is rated at face value with the second, fourth, fifth and a couple behind close to their marks.
Groomed(IRE) Official explanation: trainer's rep had no explanation for the apparent improvement in form
Great Shot Official explanation: jockey said gelding hung right
T/Plt: £71.70 to a £1 stake. Pool:£47,338.55 - 481.93 winning tickets T/Qpdt: £12.10 to a £1 stake. Pool:£3,629.71 - 220.85 winning tickets ST

4918 WOLVERHAMPTON (A.W) (L-H)

Friday, August 19

OFFICIAL GOING: Standard
Wind: Fresh behind Weather: Cloudy

5243 TOTEPLACEPOT WIN WITHOUT BACKING A WINNER H'CAP 1m 1f 103y(P)

6:10 (6:10) (Class 6) (0-65,65) 3-Y-O **£1,908** (£563; £281) **Stalls** Low

Form RPR
005 **1** **Miracle Play (IRE)**[18] 4617 3-8-6 **55**.................. MatthewCosham(5) 4 64
(David Evans) *chsd ldrs: led over 1f out: rdn and edgd lft ins fnl f: jst hld on* **8/1**[3]
0264 **2** shd **Ride The Wind**[28] 4275 3-9-2 **60**.................. GeorgeBaker 3 69+
(Chris Wall) *hld up: nt clr run over 2f out: hdwy over 1f out: sn rdn: r.o wl: jst failed* **10/3**[1]
130 **3** 2 **Pinotage**[34] 4112 3-9-0 **58**.................. MichaelStainton 1 63
(Richard Whitaker) *hld up: hdwy over 2f out: rdn over 1f out: hung lft ins fnl f: styd on* **12/1**
1535 **4** 2 3/4 **Crystal Sky (IRE)**[102] 1958 3-9-5 **63**.................. KirstyMilczarek 13 62
(Andrew Haynes) *chsd ldrs: led over 6f out: rdn and hdd over 1f out: no ex ins fnl f* **10/1**
0053 **5** 1 **Heart Of Dixie (IRE)**[12] 4827 3-8-4 **53**.................. RyanPowell(5) 12 50
(Paul Cole) *a.p: chsd ldr 6f out: rdn and ev ch over 1f out: no ex ins fnl f* **7/1**[2]
4040 **6** 2 1/4 **Galloping Queen (IRE)**[12] 4822 3-9-4 **65**.................. MartinHarley(3) 8 57
(Mick Channon) *mid-div: rdn and outpcd over 2f out: styd on ins fnl f* **25/1**
5066 **7** 1/2 **Beauchamp Zest**[55] 3393 3-8-9 **56**..................(t) SophieDoyle(3) 9 47
(Hans Adielsson) *hld up: hdwy over 3f out: rdn and wknd over 1f out* **12/1**
0456 **8** 1 1/4 **Hoofprintinthesnow**[31] 4190 3-9-4 **62**.................. SebSanders 10 51
(Amanda Perrett) *[illegible] and prom: rdn over 3f out: wknd over 1f out* **14/1**
3564 **9** nk **Marie Rose**[9] 4916 3-9-6 **64**..................(b1) JackMitchell 2 52
(Brian Meehan) *hld up: rdn over 2f out: nvr on terms* **8/1**[3]
-000 **10** 3 1/2 **Diamond Bob**[63] 3131 3-9-6 **64**..................(v1) FrederikTylicki 6 45
(Ed Dunlop) *hld up: rdn over 2f out: sn wknd* **9/1**
-000 **11** 10 **Hard Bargain (IRE)**[59] 3259 3-9-6 **64**.................. SaleemGolam 5 24
(Denis Coakley) *hld up: rdn over 2f out: sn wknd* **7/1**[2]
3-00 **12** 11 **Bint Mazyouna**[16] 4672 3-9-3 **61**.................. RobbieFitzpatrick 11 —
(Richard Guest) *sn led: hdd over 6f out: remained handy: rdn and wknd over 2f out: t.o* **50/1**

2m 2.57s (0.87) **Going Correction** +0.001s/f **12** Ran SP% **117.3**
Speed ratings (Par 98): **96,95,94,91,90 88,88,87,86,83 74,65**
toteswingers:1&2:£6.40, 2&3:£9.20, 1&3:£22.40 CSF £34.32 CT £324.73 TOTE £9.20: £3.30, £2.20, £4.60; EX 64.90.
Owner Mrs E Evans **Bred** Rabbah Bloodstock Limited **Trained** Pandy, Monmouths

FOCUS
Only a low-grade handicap, but there were some interestingly bred and likely improvers among the field. The gallop was average and the time was 4.5 seconds above standard. The form is taken at face value through the third.
Miracle Play(IRE) Official explanation: trainer said, regarding apparent improvement in form, that the filly had had a breathing problem and appeared to benefit from the fitting of a cross noseband and being dropped in class.
Marie Rose Official explanation: jockey said filly suffered interference at start
Diamond Bob Official explanation: jockey sasid gelding lost its action

5244 TRY TOTEQUICKPICK ON ALL TOTEPOOL BETS H'CAP 5f 216y(P)

6:45 (6:45) (Class 6) (0-60,66) 3-Y-O+ **£1,908** (£563; £281) **Stalls** Low

Form RPR
0623 **1** **Colourbearer (IRE)**[9] 4930 4-9-1 **55**..................(t) KierenFallon 9 64+
(Milton Bradley) *a.p: pushed along over 2f out: rdn and hung lft fr over 1f out: styd on to ld nr fin* **3/1**[1]
0501 **2** 1/2 **Rainy Night**[10] 4893 5-9-5 **66** 6ex..................(v) JackDuern(7) 1 73
(Reg Hollinshead) *a.p: led wl over 1f out: rdn ins fnl f: hdd nr fin* **11/2**[2]
4022 **3** hd **I Got You Babe (IRE)**[7] 5009 3-9-0 **60**.................. MartinHarley(3) 10 66+
(Richard Guest) *hld up: hdwy over 1f out: sn rdn: r.o wl* **8/1**
0000 **4** nk **Dingaan (IRE)**[3] 5143 8-9-0 **54**.................. RobbieFitzpatrick 4 59
(Peter Grayson) *s.i.s: hdwy over 3f out: rdn over 1f out: styd on* **25/1**
16-4 **5** 3/4 **Mr Skipiton (IRE)**[212] 218 6-9-3 **57**.................. SaleemGolam 2 60
(Brian McMath) *chsd ldrs: rdn over 2f out: styd on* **20/1**
0603 **6** 1/2 **Welcome Approach**[17] 4634 8-9-6 **60**.................. JamesSullivan 7 61
(John Weymes) *hld up: hdwy over 1f out: sn rdn: r.o: nt rch ldrs* **16/1**

0600 **7** nk **Riflessione**[12] 4828 5-9-6 **60**..................(p) JackMitchell 3 60
(Ronald Harris) *chsd ldr tl led 4f out: rdn and hdd wl over 1f out: sn hung rt: styd on same pce ins fnl f* **10/1**
6535 **8** 1 **Itsthursdayalready**[9] 4918 4-9-5 **59**.................. GeorgeBaker 13 56
(Mark Brisbourne) *chsd ldrs: rdn over 2f out: styd on same pce fnl f* **7/1**[3]
0150 **9** 1 **Almaty Express**[21] 4518 9-8-13 **58**..................(b) JulieBurke(5) 5 52
(John Weymes) *hld up: pushed along over 2f out: nvr on terms* **14/1**
2015 **10** nk **My Love Fajer (IRE)**[7] 5019 3-8-11 **61** 6ex.................. NoraLooby(7) 6 54
(Alan McCabe) *hld up: plld hrd: rdn over 1f out: nvr on terms* **25/1**
250 **11** 2 **Avonlini**[20] 4564 5-9-0 **54**.................. KellyHarrison 12 41
(Brian Baugh) *led 2f: chsd ldr tl rdn over 2f out: wknd fnl f* **16/1**
6500 **12** 6 **Talamahana**[8] 4973 6-9-0 **54**..................(b) SebSanders 11 21
(Andrew Haynes) *sn pushed along in rr: rdn 1/2-way: wknd over 2f out* **28/1**
5340 **13** 3 3/4 **Pearly Wey**[5] 5083 8-8-11 **54**.................. PaulPickard(3) 8 9
(Ian McInnes) *s.i.s: a in rr* **14/1**

1m 15.28s (0.28) **Going Correction** +0.001s/f
WFA 3 from 4yo+ 3lb **13** Ran SP% **114.1**
Speed ratings (Par 101): **98,97,97,96,95 95,94,93,91,91 88,80,75**
toteswingers:1&2:£4.90, 2&3:£6.20, 1&3:£3.50 CSF £16.00 CT £121.55 TOTE £2.70: £1.10, £2.60, £2.40; EX 18.60.
Owner E A Hayward **Bred** Corduff Stud & J Corcorcan **Trained** Sedbury, Gloucs

FOCUS
Another low-grade affair, but a race run at a reasonable gallop in which the principals were closely bunched at the finish. The runner-up is rated closest to his recent best and the form looks sound enough.
Riflessione Official explanation: jockey said gelding hung badly right
Pearly Wey Official explanation: jockey said gelding bled from the nose

5245 DEBI ROBERTS 50TH BIRTHDAY CELEBRATION FILLIES' (S) STKS 5f 20y(P)

7:15 (7:16) (Class 6) 2-Y-O **£1,533** (£452; £226) **Stalls** Low

Form RPR
0352 **1** **Aquasulis (IRE)**[14] 4756 2-9-4 68.................. KierenFallon 3 67
(David Evans) *w ldr: pushed along over 1f out: rdn to ld wl ins fnl f: edgd lft: jst hld on* **7/2**[3]
2 hd **Molamento (IRE)** 2-8-9 0.................. MartinHarley(3) 6 60
(Alan McCabe) *trckd ldrs: rdn ins fnl f: r.o* **11/4**[1]
0062 **3** 1 1/2 **Stans Deelyte**[21] 4500 2-8-12 52.................. JamesSullivan 2 55
(Lisa Williamson) *led: shkn up over 1f out: rdn and hdd wl ins fnl f: unable qck* **33/1**
006 **4** 1 3/4 **Maria Medecis (IRE)**[9] 4922 2-8-12 61..................(v) FrederikTylicki 10 49
(Ann Duffield) *chsd ldrs: rdn over 1f out: styd on same pce fnl f* **20/1**
6544 **5** 1 1/4 **Guava**[8] 4947 2-8-12 67.................. SilvestreDeSousa 8 44
(Richard Hannon) *hld up in tch: n.m.r 3f out: rdn 1/2-way: sn outpcd: styd on u.p and hung lft ins fnl f* **3/1**[2]
1543 **6** shd **Lady Caprice**[4] 5105 2-9-4 60..................(b) DavidNolan 7 50
(Ann Duffield) *hld up: hdwy 2f out: rdn over 1f out: no ex ins fnl f* **14/1**
00 **7** 3 **Our Monica (IRE)**[26] 4358 2-8-12 0.................. RussKennemore 9 33
(Ann Duffield) *s.s: hld up: nvr nrr* **100/1**
6 **8** 2 **Magik Maggie**[15] 4720 2-8-12 0.................. JackMitchell 12 26
(Chris Wall) *hld up: pushed along 3f out: rdn and edgd lft fr over 1f out: n.d* **12/1**
0554 **9** 2 3/4 **Just Dixie**[21] 4500 2-8-7 47.................. JulieBurke(5) 1 16
(John Weymes) *chsd ldrs: rdn 1/2-way: wknd over 1f out* **33/1**
054 **10** 1/2 **Emerald Smile (IRE)**[21] 4485 2-8-12 62.................. LukeMorris 13 14
(J S Moore) *chsd ldrs: rdn 3f out: wknd 1/2-way* **9/1**

63.04 secs (0.74) **Going Correction** +0.001s/f **10** Ran SP% **109.9**
Speed ratings (Par 89): **94,93,91,88,86 86,81,78,73,73**
toteswingers:1&2:£3.90, 2&3:£27.60, 1&3:£18.50 CSF £11.72 TOTE £4.70: £1.90, £1.10, £10.00; EX 10.80.There was no bid for the winner. Molamento was caimed by R. A. Green for £6,000.
Owner Bathwick Gold Partnership **Bred** Rathasker Stud **Trained** Pandy, Monmouths

FOCUS
Another race run at a fair gallop and a time just under three seconds slower than standard.

NOTEBOOK
Aquasulis(IRE) has been consistent in this grade since her Windsor win. She was prominent throughout and battled on gamely under a good ride to hold on close home. She is a decent type at this level but another penalty will make life harder for her now. She was retained without a bid. (op 11-4 tchd 4-1)
Molamento(IRE) was the subject of a sustained gamble. She showed a professional attitude throughout and knuckled down well inside the final furlong, and was only just repelled by the far more experienced winner. Connections have shown their hand now but she looks a sure-fire future winner, and will run for a new trainer in future, having been claimed for £6,000. (op 9-1)
Stans Deelyte confirmed her good run from out of the handicap in a Musselburgh nursery was no fluke and was unfortunate to come up against two useful rivals at this level. She is going the right way and can land a similar contest. (op 28-1)
Maria Medecis(IRE) ran her best race and looks to have found her level in this grade. She wasn't competitive in nurseries off a mark in the low-60s. (op 16-1)
Guava eased to this level for the first time, proved a disappointment and never got into a challenging position. She's beginning to look like one to avoid. (op 5-2)
Lady Caprice has struggled under her penalty and the return of blinkers (won in them) after a couple of runs in cheekpieces failed to work the oracle. (op 12-1)

5246 TRY TOTEQUICKPICK IF YOU'RE FEELING LUCKY CLAIMING STKS 7f 32y(P)

7:50 (7:51) (Class 5) 2-Y-O **£2,102** (£625; £312; £156) **Stalls** High

Form RPR
5320 **1** **Snowed In (IRE)**[41] 3866 2-9-0 72.................. LukeMorris 2 70+
(J S Moore) *hld up: rdn 3f out: hdwy u.p over 1f out: edgd lft and r.o to ld post* **6/1**[3]
0112 **2** hd **Lady Jourdain (IRE)**[21] 4512 2-8-7 66.................. AndrewElliott 6 63
(Mrs K Burke) *chsd ldrs: rdn over 1f out: led wl ins fnl f: hdd post* **7/2**[2]
4021 **3** hd **Artists Corner**[13] 4808 2-8-7 63.................. BarryMcHugh 5 62
(Richard Fahey) *hld up: hdwy over 2f out: led over 1f out: rdn and hdd wl ins fnl f* **3/1**[1]
156 **4** 2 1/2 **Bellechance**[12] 4824 2-8-9 60.................. SilvestreDeSousa 9 58
(Nigel Tinkler) *chsd ldr: rdn and ev ch over 1f out: styd on same pce ins fnl f* **10/1**
6626 **5** 1 1/2 **Jaci Uzzi (IRE)**[21] 4512 2-8-1 51..................(v1) SophieDoyle(3) 10 49
(David Evans) *led: rdn and hdd over 1f out: no ex ins fnl f* **25/1**
6 1 1/2 **Ned Causer** 2-8-9 0.................. PaulPickard(3) 1 54
(Reg Hollinshead) *hld up: rdn over 2f out: nvr trbld ldrs* **40/1**
1300 **7** 4 **Beaumaris (IRE)**[21] 4512 2-8-9 72..................(p) FrederikTylicki 8 41
(Ann Duffield) *chsd ldrs: rdn over 2f out: wknd fnl f* **20/1**

6 **8** *1 ¼* **Aglaja**[9] 4919 2-9-1 0 JackMitchell 4 44
(Frank Sheridan) *s.i.s: hld up: rdn over 2f out: sn wknd* **66/1**
1m 30.62s (1.02) **Going Correction** +0.001s/f **8** Ran SP% **83.1**
Speed ratings (Par 94): **94,93,93,90,88 87,82,81**
toteswingers:1&2:£2.80, 2&3:£1.10, 1&3:£2.30 CSF £13.59 TOTE £5.50: £1.70, £1.60, £1.02; EX 19.00.
Owner Norton Common Farm Racing **Bred** T Cahalan & D Cahalan **Trained** Upper Lambourn, Berks
■ Stewards' Enquiry : Barry McHugh caution: careless riding.

FOCUS
A decent contest for the grade and, despite a couple of withdrawn runners at the start; the form choices fought out a tight finish. The early pace was strong.

NOTEBOOK
Snowed In(IRE) was off the bridle with 4f to run but wore down his rivals close home. Nothing went right for him last time at Newmarket and connections were confident this drop in grade would bring dividends. He'll get a mile no problem and his battling attitude will stand him in good stead in the future. (op 11-2 tchd 5-1)

Lady Jourdain(IRE) battled on gamely to get the better of a protracted duel with Artists Corner, only to be collared close home. A thoroughly likeable filly, she can win again. (op 5-2)

Artists Corner, an AW debutante, stepped up on her Redcar selling victory with an improved run in a stronger race and, having proved her effectiveness on the surface, her options are increased. (op 7-2)

Bellechance hadn't progressed since her debut win, so this was a better effort. She looks a little high in the weights for nurseries at the moment. She coped fine with the surface. (op 8-1)

Jaci Uzzi(IRE) in a first-time visor, set a fast gallop but paid for it and faded in the straight. Runner-up to Lady Jourdain earlier in the summer, she is going the wrong way at the moment. (op 28-1)

Ned Causer showed ability on this debut, but more is needed before looking a likely winner.

5247 SUSAN BOX MEMORIAL MEDIAN AUCTION MAIDEN STKS 1m 141y(P)
8:20 (8:21) (Class 6) 3-4-Y-O **£1,908** (£563; £281) **Stalls** Low

Form RPR
204 **1** **Inklet**[60] 3236 3-8-12 75 AdamKirby 3 76
(Marco Botti) *chsd ldrs: rdn over 2f out: r.o u.p to ld ins fnl f* **3/1**[2]
00- **2** *¾* **Zahraan (IRE)**[336] 6149 3-9-3 0 SilvestreDeSousa 9 80
(Marcus Tregoning) *prom: chsd ldr 6f out: rdn over 1f out: edgd lft ins fnl f: r.o* **1/1**[1]
0643 **3** *¾* **Tanmawy (IRE)**[29] 4249 3-9-3 68 TadhgO'Shea 10 78
(Ed Dunlop) *led: rdn over 1f out: hdd and unable qck ins fnl f* **4/1**[3]
005 **4** *8* **Sit Tight**[20] 4529 3-9-3 69 GeorgeBaker 6 60
(Chris Wall) *chsd ldrs: rdn over 2f out: wknd over 1f out* **8/1**
5 *12* **Pacific Reach** 3-9-3 0 KirstyMilczarek 1 32
(Andrew Balding) *s.i.s: sn pushed along in rr: nvr on terms* **12/1**
6 *4 ½* **Just Gillian** 3-8-12 0 LukeMorris 4 17
(Peter Hiatt) *s.i.s: outpcd* **40/1**
0 **7** *shd* **Empyrean (USA)**[7] 4989 3-8-12 0 SebSanders 8 16
(Sir Mark Prescott Bt) *mid-div: sn pushed along: wknd over 2f out* **28/1**
04 **8** *1 ¼* **Teutonic Knight (IRE)**[4] 5114 4-9-7 0 RyanClark(3) 7 19
(Ian Williams) *hld up: a in rr: rdn and wknd over 2f out* **40/1**
0 **9** *nk* **Our Princess Ellie (USA)**[7] 4991 3-8-12 0 RobbieFitzpatrick 2 13
(Derek Shaw) *prom tl rdn and wknd over 2f out* **80/1**
1m 49.43s (-1.07) **Going Correction** +0.001s/f
WFA 3 from 4yo 7lb **9** Ran SP% **123.4**
Speed ratings (Par 101): **104,103,102,95,84 80,80,79,79**
toteswingers:1&2:£1.70, 2&3:£2.00, 1&3:£1.70 CSF £6.77 TOTE £4.00: £1.10, £1.90, £1.40; EX 10.30.
Owner Mrs Anita Nicol **Bred** Baroness Bloodstock **Trained** Newmarket, Suffolk

FOCUS
An interesting maiden in which the gallop was fair and the front trio put plenty of distance between themselves and their rivals in the straight. The winner is rated close to her debut form.

5248 TOTEPOOL A BETTER WAY TO BET APPRENTICE H'CAP 1m 141y(P)
8:50 (8:52) (Class 6) (0-60,61) 3-Y-O+ **£1,908** (£563; £281) **Stalls** Low

Form RPR
500 **1** **Roman Ruler (IRE)**[23] 4443 3-8-6 52 LMcNiff(5) 7 59
(Chris Fairhurst) *mde all: rdn over 1f out: styd on* **8/1**
0030 **2** *1* **Aussie Blue (IRE)**[16] 4679 7-9-7 58 (v) BrianToomey(3) 10 63
(Richard Whitaker) *a.p: chsd ldr 3f out: rdn and ev ch over 1f out: nt qckn towards fin* **9/1**
3561 **3** *nse* **One Of Twins**[17] 4638 3-8-12 53 JamesSullivan 12 58+
(Michael Easterby) *a.p: rdn over 1f out: r.o* **9/4**[1]
2660 **4** *shd* **Excellent Vision**[8] 4953 4-9-0 48 (t) RyanClark 11 53+
(Milton Bradley) *s.i.s: hld up: r.o ins fnl f: nrst fin* **11/1**
051 **5** *½* **Cane Cat (IRE)**[11] 4869 4-9-13 61 6ex (t) MichaelO'Connell 9 65+
(Tony Carroll) *s.i.s: hld up: r.o ins fnl f: nvr nrr* **11/2**[3]
3000 **6** *½* **Petomic (IRE)**[9] 4901 6-9-8 59 TobyAtkinson(3) 4 61
(Richard Guest) *hld up: hdwy over 4f out: rdn over 2f out: styd on* **15/2**
0004 **7** *1 ¼* **Minortransgression (USA)**[17] 4651 4-9-9 57 AdamBeschizza 13 56
(H Edward Haynes) *prom: chsd ldr over 5f out tl pushed along 3f out: rdn over 1f out: styd on same pce fnl f* **25/1**
0003 **8** *¾* **Harare**[8] 4945 10-9-1 49 (v) RossAtkinson 8 47
(Karen Tutty) *hld up: hdwy over 2f out: no ex fnl f* **18/1**
3500 **9** *1* **Beauchamp Xiara**[23] 4448 5-9-5 58 LucyKBarry(5) 5 53
(Hans Adielsson) *hld up: rdn over 2f out: hdwy over 1f out: no ex fnl f* **10/1**
3434 **10** *½* **So Is She (IRE)**[7] 5014 3-9-5 60 (b) AmyBaker 3 54
(Alan Bailey) *hld up: rdn over 3f out: n.d* **9/2**[2]
00-6 **11** *37* **Ime Not Bitter**[15] 4715 3-8-11 52 BillyCray 6 —
(Bill Moore) *chsd ldr 3f: remained handy tl rdn and wknd over 2f out: t.o* **80/1**
1m 51.67s (1.17) **Going Correction** +0.001s/f
WFA 3 from 4yo+ 7lb **11** Ran SP% **125.0**
Speed ratings (Par 101): **94,93,93,92,92 92,90,90,89,88 56**
toteswingers:1&2:£12.60, 2&3:£10.00, 1&3:£6.70 CSF £83.10 CT £224.73 TOTE £13.00: £3.50, £4.10, £2.20; EX 165.00.
Owner S Leggott & S Atkinson **Bred** Gerard Kennedy **Trained** Middleham Moor, N Yorks
■ Stewards' Enquiry : Toby Atkinson three-day ban: used whip with excessive frequency (Sep 2,4,5)
Ryan Clark one-day ban: careless riding (Sep 2)
L McNiff three-day ban: weighed-in 2lb heavy (Sep 2,4,5)

FOCUS
A moderate handicap, and unsurprisingly the time was over two seconds slower than the preceding maiden. The runner-up is rated to his recent turf form with the third to his recent Catterick mark, although the overall form is a little muddling.

5249 BET TOTEPOOL ON ALL UK RACING H'CAP 1m 4f 50y(P)
9:20 (9:20) (Class 5) (0-70,70) 3-Y-O+ **£2,045** (£603; £302) **Stalls** Low

Form RPR
6-11 **1** **Kepler's Law**[79] 2613 3-9-3 69 SebSanders 9 84+
(Sir Mark Prescott Bt) *mde all: shkn up over 1f out: clr fnl f: eased nr fin* **11/10**[1]
4100 **2** *3 ¼* **Zamina (IRE)**[27] 4316 3-9-4 70 JamesDoyle 1 78
(Sylvester Kirk) *chsd wnr 2f: remained handy: chsd wnr again over 2f out: rdn and edgd rt fr over 1f out: styd on same pce fnl f* **6/1**[3]
3512 **3** *2* **Colonel Sherman (USA)**[11] 4868 6-9-4 60 (t) KierenFallon 7 65
(Philip Kirby) *prom: chsd wnr 10f out tl rdn over 2f out: styd on same pce appr fnl f* **7/2**[2]
-363 **4** *2* **Maoi Chinn Tire (IRE)**[21] 3544 4-9-11 67 (p) StephenCraine 2 69
(Jennie Candlish) *hld up: rdn 3f out: styd on ins fnl f: nvr nrr* **10/1**
5265 **5** *hd* **Straversjoy**[17] 4649 4-9-6 65 PaulPickard(3) 3 66
(Reg Hollinshead) *hld up: rdn over 2f out: n.d* **8/1**
5000 **6** *7* **Blue Cossack (IRE)**[22] 4476 3-8-8 60 LukeMorris 4 50
(Mark Usher) *hld up: rdn over 3f out: wknd 2f out* **20/1**
11-6 **7** *3 ¼* **Resplendent Ace (IRE)**[17] 4649 7-9-8 64 BarryMcHugh 8 49
(Karen Tutty) *chsd ldrs tl rdn and wknd 2f out* **33/1**
2m 39.8s (-1.30) **Going Correction** +0.001s/f
WFA 3 from 4yo+ 10lb **7** Ran SP% **112.0**
Speed ratings (Par 103): **104,101,100,99,99 94,92**
toteswingers:1&2:£2.80, 2&3:£4.40, 1&3:£1.50 CSF £7.89 CT £17.02 TOTE £2.00: £1.90, £1.60; EX 9.00.
Owner Rectory Racing **Bred** Chippenham Lodge Stud Ltd **Trained** Newmarket, Suffolk
■ Stewards' Enquiry : Barry McHugh three-day ban: careless riding (Sep 2,4,5)

FOCUS
A modest handicap but the winner is progressive with the placed horses helping to set the level.
T/Plt: £10.50 to a £1 stake. Pool:£68,272.69 - 4,736.70 winning tickets T/Qpdt: £4.80 to a £1 stake. Pool:£7,210.31 - 1,095.15 winning tickets CR

5216 YORK (L-H)
Friday, August 19

OFFICIAL GOING: Good to soft (good in places; overall 6.2; home straight: far side 6.3; centre 6.2; stands' side 6.3)
Rail on traditional racing line and distances as advertised.
Wind: Light across Weather: Fine

5250 RACING UK ON SKY BET MOBILE STKS (H'CAP) 1m 4f
2:00 (2:00) (Class 2) (0-100,97) 3-Y-O+ **£16,172** (£4,812; £2,405; £1,202) **Stalls** Centre

Form RPR
0100 **1** **Crackentorp**[26] 4360 6-9-4 87 DavidAllan 2 98
(Tim Easterby) *in tch on inner: hdwy 3f out: cl up 2f out: sn rdn: drvn ent fnl f: kpt on to ld last 100yds: edgd rt and hld on wl towards fin* **33/1**
1112 **2** *hd* **Kiama Bay (IRE)**[26] 4354 5-9-12 95 JamieSpencer 1 106
(John Quinn) *trckd ldrs: hdwy over 3f out: sn cl up: slt ld 2f out and sn rdn: drvn over 1f out: hdd last 100yds: no ex nr fin* **11/1**
3000 **3** *½* **Prompter**[26] 4354 4-10-0 97 HayleyTurner 4 107
(Michael Bell) *in tch: hdwy 3f out: effrt and n.m.r 2f out: rdn to chse ldng pair ent fnl f: sn hung lft and ev ch tl drvn and no ex last 100yds* **20/1**
1115 **4** *4 ½* **Troopingthecolour**[28] 4267 5-9-6 89 OlivierPeslier 11 92
(Steve Gollings) *prom: led 3f out and sn rdn: hdd and drvn 2f out: grad wknd appr fnl f* **20/1**
2000 **5** *2 ¼* **Sharaayeen**[20] 4532 4-9-11 94 RichardHills 15 93+
(B W Hills) *hld up towards rr: hdwy 3f out: rdn wl over 1f out: kpt on ins fnl f: nt rch ldrs* **11/1**
-001 **6** *hd* **Agent Archie (USA)**[38] 3959 4-9-5 88 RichardHughes 3 87
(William Haggas) *led tl 1 1/2-way: cl up: rdn along over 3f out: drvn 2f out and grad wknd* **13/2**[1]
1352 **7** *2 ¼* **Mcbirney (USA)**[28] 4280 4-9-1 84 TomQueally 20 79
(Paul D'Arcy) *hld up in rr: hdwy 3f out: rdn over 2f out: styd on appr fnl f: nrst fin* **16/1**
2-24 **8** *1* **Waldvogel (IRE)**[13] 4778 7-9-11 94 TomEaves 9 88
(Nicky Richards) *midfield: hdwy wl over 2f out: rdn wl over 1f out: sn no imp* **16/1**
1035 **9** *1 ¼* **Porgy**[22] 4464 6-9-3 86 WilliamBuick 16 78
(David Simcock) *dwlt and towards rr: hdwy wl over 2f out: sn rdn and n.d* **20/1**
4060 **10** *nk* **The Fonz**[28] 4267 5-9-5 88 KierenFallon 14 79+
(Sir Michael Stoute) *hld up: hdwy on outer over 3f out: rdn over 2f out: sn drvn and n.d* **15/2**[2]
4033 **11** *1 ½* **Life And Soul (IRE)**[13] 4778 4-9-7 90 DarryllHolland 6 79+
(Amanda Perrett) *hld up in midfield: hdwy 3f out: swtchd rt towards stands' rail over 2f out: sn rdn and no imp* **16/1**
0201 **12** *3* **Lady Chaparral**[26] 4360 4-9-2 85 SebSanders 10 69
(George Moore) *t.k.h: chsd ldrs: rdn along over 2f out: grad wknd* **10/1**[3]
1006 **13** *1 ½* **Classic Vintage (USA)**[13] 4778 5-9-9 92 JimCrowley 7 74
(Amanda Perrett) *trckd ldrs: pushed along 3f out: rdn wl over 2f out and grad wknd* **20/1**
5215 **14** *1 ¾* **Warlu Way**[26] 4354 4-9-8 91 PhillipMakin 8 70
(John Dunlop) *in tch: rdn along 3f out: wknd over 2f out* **12/1**
6365 **15** *3 ¼* **Bowdler's Magic**[13] 4775 4-9-2 85 SilvestreDeSousa 12 59
(Mark Johnston) *prom: led 1/2-way: rdn along and hdd 3f out: sn wknd* **14/1**
0065 **16** *6* **Mirrored**[13] 4788 5-9-2 85 DuranFentiman 5 49+
(Tim Easterby) *plld hrd: hld up in rr: hdwy on outer 1/2-way: wd st to stands' rail: rdn along 3f out and nvr a factor: sddle slipped* **20/1**
0140 **17** *2* **Royal Trooper (IRE)**[10] 4890 5-9-1 84 FrederikTylicki 13 45
(James Given) *midfield: hdwy on outer 5f and wd st towards stands' rail: rdn along over 3f out and sn wknd* **66/1**
2240 **18** *2 ½* **Right Step**[42] 3829 4-9-11 97 HarryBentley(3) 18 54
(Alan Jarvis) *hld up: wd st and effrt 3f out: rdn over 2f out and nvr a factor* **16/1**
5201 **19** *3 ¼* **Doctor Zhivago**[33] 4125 4-9-0 83 AdrianNicholls 17 35
(Ian McInnes) *a in rr: rdn along over 3f out: sn bhd* **66/1**

1300 **20** ½ **Bay Willow (IRE)**[20] 4528 4-9-12 95 FrankieDettori 19 46
(Saeed Bin Suroor) *in tch on outer: rdn along 4f out: sn wknd* **16/1**

2m 35.14s (1.94) **Going Correction** +0.325s/f (Good) **20** Ran SP% **124.4**
Speed ratings (Par 109): **106,105,105,102,101 100,99,98,97,97 96,94,93,92,90 86,85,83,81,80**
toteswingers:1&2:£39.30, 1&3:£187.60, 2&3:£34.50 CSF £332.28 CT £7299.37 TOTE £53.70: £7.20, £2.20, £4.70, £4.80; EX 459.80 Trifecta £2490.40 Part won. Pool: £3,365.41 - 0.60 winning units..
Owner C H Stevens **Bred** C A Cyzer **Trained** Great Habton, N Yorks

FOCUS
This was a hot handicap run at a decent early pace. The winning time was 5.64 seconds outside standard, suggesting the ground was as advertised. The winner is rated back to his best with the third back to his 3-y-o best.

NOTEBOOK
Crackentorp had twice been well beaten since winning the Queen Mother's Cup for lady amateur riders over C&D in June and was only 13th in this race last year, but he is capable on his day and stays well, so a strongly run race over this trip was no problem. Making his effort from off the pace towards the inside of the track over 3f out, he became involved in a war of attrition with his two nearest rivals after leading over a furlong out, but refused to be denied. His record isn't one of consistency, however, so a repeat can't be guaranteed, especially off a higher mark. Official explanation: trainer said, regarding apparent improvement in form, that the only explanation he could offer was that the gelding runs well on the track.
Kiama Bay(IRE) ran well off this mark when bidding for a four-timer at Ascot last time and this was another cracking effort. He made his effort at about the same time as the winner and had every chance inside the last 2f, but despite giving his all, his rival managed to maintain a narrow advantage over him right to the line. He may well go up in the weights for this. (tchd 10-1)
Prompter is slipping down the weights having been highly tried earlier in his career and travelled particularly smoothly behind the leaders, but he got momentarily stopped in his run when running into the back of the weakening Bowdler's Magic 3f out, and again when going through a narrow gap between Troopingthecolour and Agent Archie a furlong later. It still looked as though he would overhaul the front pair a furlong out, but he then started to hang and couldn't quite go through with it. He is still without a win since his second start at two. (tchd 18-1)
Troopingthecolour wasn't disgraced when bidding for his fifth consecutive Flat victory off 1lb higher at Ascot last time, but this was his first try beyond 1m2f on the level and, having raced up with the pace throughout, he didn't quite get home. This was another solid effort, however. (tchd 22-1 in a place)
Sharaayeen hadn't built on his promising Newmarket reappearance, but looked a threat when moving into contention on the inside coming to the last 2f, He had his chance, but then couldn't find any more under pressure. (tchd 12-1)
Agent Archie(USA) made the perfect start for his new yard when winning at Yarmouth last month, having been gelded, but was hit with an 8lb rise for that and he had not yet proved himself over this longer trip. Nonetheless he was very well supported in the market and was at the sharp end from the start, but it did appear that his stamina gave out over a furlong from home. (op 10-1)
Mcbirney(USA) was another to creep into contention on the inside coming to the last 3f, only to run out of gas before the furlong pole. He only made his racecourse debut back in January, so the best of him may yet to be seen.
Waldvogel(IRE) had run two solid races since returning to the Flat and he looked a danger here when coming under pressure 2f out, but then had no more to offer. He looks a nice dual-purpose type. (tchd 18-1 in a place)
Porgy was given plenty to do and was never getting there quickly enough. He remains 7lb higher than when last successful in a handicap. (op 28-1)
The Fonz, 1lb higher than when winning this last year, made a brief effort coming to the last 2f but it amounted to little and he remains below his best. (tchd 7-1 and 8-1)
Life And Soul(IRE) was reported to have run too free in the early stages. Official explanation: jockey said colt ran too free early
Mirrored was reported to have a slipped saddle. Official explanation: jockey said saddle slipped (op 16-1)

5251 IRISH THOROUGHBRED MARKETING GIMCRACK STKS (GROUP 2) (C&G) 6f
2:30 (2:31) (Class 1) 2-Y-0 **£82,880** (£31,346; £15,666; £7,826) **Stalls** Centre

Form RPR
4323 **1** **Caspar Netscher**[21] 4495 2-8-12 107 RobertWinston 1 114
(Alan McCabe) *hld up: hdwy far side over 2f out: edgd rt and led 1f out: styd on wl* **5/1**[2]
2111 **2** ½ **Lilbourne Lad (IRE)**[12] 4834 2-9-1 0 RichardHughes 4 111
(Richard Hannon) *w ldrs: rdn over 2f out: rallied ins fnl f: tk 2nd nr fin* **10/3**[1]
1422 **3** *hd* **Burwaaz**[24] 4413 2-8-12 104 RichardHills 2 107
(Ed Dunlop) *led: carried rt and hdd 1f out: kpt on: lost 2nd nr fin* **5/1**[2]
321 **4** ¾ **Justineo**[21] 4507 2-8-12 86 JamieSpencer 6 105
(William Haggas) *hld up: effrt over 2f out: kpt on fnl f* **7/1**[3]
1662 **5** ½ **B Fifty Two (IRE)**[19] 4596 2-8-12 105 SebSanders 3 103
(J W Hills) *chsd ldrs: kpt on same pce over 1f out* **8/1**
15 **6** ½ **Reply (IRE)**[12] 4834 2-8-12 0 CO'Donoghue 8 102
(A P O'Brien, Ire) *trckd ldrs: rdn over 2f out: one pce over 1f out* **5/1**[2]
31 **7** 3¾ **Diamondhead (IRE)**[34] 4098 2-8-12 0 MartinDwyer 5 91
(Brian Meehan) *trckd ldrs: drvn over 2f out: lost pl over 1f out* **20/1**
110 **8** *6* **Wise Venture (IRE)**[35] 4055 2-8-12 88 JimCrowley 9 73
(Alan Jarvis) *chsd ldrs: rdn and lost pl over 2f out* **20/1**
1 **9** *4* **Sardanapalus**[36] 4012 2-8-12 0 PhillipMakin 7 61
(Kevin Ryan) *dwlt: outpcd and in rr: bhd fnl 2f* **9/1**

1m 12.74s (0.84) **Going Correction** +0.30s/f (Good) **9** Ran SP% **116.2**
Speed ratings (Par 106): **106,103,102,101,101 100,95,87,82**
toteswingers:1&2:£3.10, 1&3:£5.10, 2&3:£2.80 CSF £22.20 TOTE £9.60: £3.10, £1.10, £1.70; EX 28.50 Trifecta £109.70 Pool: £7,299.64 - 49.24 winning units..
Owner Charles Wentworth **Bred** Meon Valley Stud **Trained** Averham Park, Notts
■ Stewards' Enquiry : Robert Winston two-day ban: careless riding (Sep 2,4)

FOCUS
Just an average Gimcrack. The form makes some sense rated around the placed horses and fifth.

NOTEBOOK
Caspar Netscher deservedly added to his maiden success on his debut back in May and opened his account in Pattern company at the fifth time of asking. Despite just having a maiden win to his name he was still rated highest of those with official marks after his third in the Richmond Stakes at Glorious Goodwood last month. That race is starting to work out very well and his previous experience of this type of race was no doubt a big advantage for him. He enjoyed the way the race was run and quickened into a clear lead nearing the final furlong, but immediately hung right when put under maximum pressure. That hampered the third and didn't do the runner-up many favours, but it didn't affect the overall result. That action may have been down to this different ground, his first run away from a sound surface, but he did also drift the same way when under the cosh at Newbury on his penultimate outing. Future plans seem fluid for the winner, but he shapes as though another furlong is within his compass (stamina on dam's side of pedigree) and perhaps the Champagne Stakes over 7f at Doncaster in September will be next. That will represent a tougher assignment and he would have to carry a penalty, but last year's Gimcrack winner Approve went on to finish runner-up in that on his next outing. One thing is for certain, his cracking attitude will continue to hold him in decent stead wherever he turns up, and his trainer later added he is eyeing a possible tilt at the Breeder's Cup for his final outing this year. (op 13-2)
Lilbourne Lad(IRE) was never far away and turned in a brave effort in defeat, conceding 3lb to his rivals. He would have finished a little closer had the winner not hung right, but it didn't cost him the race. This son of Acclamation rates a solid benchmark and is probably happiest on quicker ground, but is not simple to place now. (op 7-2)
Burwaaz finished second in the Molecomb over 5f at Glorious Goodwood last time out and he travelled best of all here under a positive ride. He was feeling the pinch before being carried right by the winner, but for which he would have gone very close for second place, and such tactics back up in trip looked to find out his stamina. He's proving a touch hard to get right, but a waiting ride over this trip could well see him back to winning ways. (op 13-2)
Justineo ◆ had a lot to find coming into this, but his leading trainer's record in the race entitled him to plenty of respect and the stable had also landed the Group 3 Acomb for 2-y-os at this meeting on the opening day. Having been restrained from the gates, he lacked the tactical speed to land a serious blow but was coming back towards the finish in the manner of a horse that will relish a stiffer test. (op 6-1)
B Fifty Two(IRE) bumped into one on his journey to France 19 days earlier and that form gave him every chance in this, despite it being a higher grade. He had his chance, but proved too one paced to threaten at the business end and probably wants returning to a lower level. (op 10-1)
Reply(IRE) was one place behind Lilbourne Lad in the Group 1 Phoenix Stakes at the Curragh 12 days earlier and was expected to improve for that run. He travelled nicely on the pace until around 2f out, when he became laboured and looked to find this too sharp. This was another disappointment at the meeting for his powerful operation. (op 6-1)
Diamondhead(IRE), another last-time-out maiden winner, had plenty on his plate and was beaten from halfway. The experience will not be lost on him, but he doesn't look up to Group class. (op 16-1 tchd 14-1)
Wise Venture(IRE), winner of his first two outings, was bidding to put his Newbury flop behind him but it was clear from the gates he wasn't going to figure. This leaves him with plenty to prove. (op 22-1)
Sardanapalus defied greenness when winning on his debut at Hamilton last month and was an interesting runner up in class, considering the year his trainer is enjoying with juveniles. He fluffed the start, however, and was never going thereafter. Official explanation: jockey said colt was slowly away (op 7-1)

5252 SKY BET MOBILE STRENSALL STKS (GROUP 3) 1m 208y
3:05 (3:05) (Class 1) 3-Y-0+
£42,532 (£16,125; £8,070; £4,020; £2,017; £1,012) **Stalls** Low

Form RPR
1010 **1** **Green Destiny (IRE)**[21] 4494 4-9-5 109 KierenFallon 2 119+
(William Haggas) *dwlt and hld up towards rr: smooth hdwy 3f out: trckd ldrs 2f out: rdn to ld over 1f out: kpt on wl u.p fnl f* **11/4**[1]
1154 **2** 1¼ **Tazahum (USA)**[21] 4493 3-8-12 107 RichardHills 10 116
(Sir Michael Stoute) *cl up: led after 2f: rdn along 3f out: hdd 2f out: drvn and kpt on wl fnl f* **6/1**[2]
2-31 **3** 2¼ **Dux Scholar**[34] 4095 3-8-12 112 RichardHughes 7 111+
(Sir Michael Stoute) *hld up in rr: hdwy 3f out: effrt 2f out: sn rdn and styd on ins fnl f: nrst fin* **11/4**[1]
0-63 **4** ½ **Anmar (USA)**[34] 4095 5-9-5 109 TadhgO'Shea 8 110
(Ed Dunlop) *hld up: hdwy on outer 4f out: rdn over 2f out: sn chsng ldrs: drvn and one pce ent fnl f* **33/1**
-435 **5** *nk* **Penitent**[54] 3444 5-9-5 108 (v[1]) SilvestreDeSousa 4 109
(William Haggas) *led 2f: cl up on inner: rdn to ld 2f out: drvn and hdd over 1f out: edgd rt and wknd fnl f* **10/1**
0-41 **6** *4* **Nationalism**[55] 3409 4-9-5 105 WilliamBuick 9 101
(John Gosden) *hld up: hdwy over 3f out: rdn along 2f out: sn no imp* **9/1**
-133 **7** *5* **Western Aristocrat (USA)**[21] 4493 3-8-12 108 OlivierPeslier 6 90
(Jeremy Noseda) *a towards rr* **10/1**
2100 **8** *2* **Kings Gambit (SAF)**[24] 4410 7-9-9 109 JamieSpencer 3 89
(Tom Tate) *cl up: rdn along 3f out: drvn over 2f out and sn wknd* **14/1**
-344 **9** 3¼ **Critical Moment (USA)**[13] 4789 4-9-5 106 MichaelHills 1 78
(B W Hills) *trckd ldrs: effrt over 3f out: rdn wl over 2f out and sn wknd* **25/1**
14-2 **10** *23* **Biondetti (USA)**[34] 4120 3-8-12 109 FrankieDettori 5 27
(Mahmood Al Zarooni) *trckd ldrs: effrt 4f out: rdn along 3f out: sn wknd and eased fnl 2f* **15/2**[3]

1m 51.88s (-0.12) **Going Correction** +0.325s/f (Good)
WFA 3 from 4yo+ 7lb **10** Ran SP% **121.0**
Speed ratings (Par 113): **113,111,109,109,109 105,101,99,96,76**
toteswingers:1&2:£4.30, 1&3:£3.20, 2&3:£5.60 CSF £20.41 TOTE £4.00: £1.50, £3.70, £1.40, EX 29.00 Trifecta £149.50 Pool: £7,094.66 - 35.10 winning units..
Owner Saleh Al Homaizi & Imad Al Sagar **Bred** Mubkera Syndicate **Trained** Newmarket, Suffolk

FOCUS
The lessons of the opening contest had been learned, as although the bulk of the field came away from the inside rail after turning in, they didn't come as wide as they often do and one horse, Penitent, stuck tight to the inside. The form looks strong for the grade with a persoanl best from the runner-up and the next two home a few pounds off.

NOTEBOOK
Green Destiny(IRE) disappointed when a hot favourite for the Totesport Mile at Goodwood last time, but the return to that trip had a lot to do with it as he found everything happening too quickly for him. He was much better judged on his previous victory in the John Smith's Cup over the extended 1m2f here and he returned to his very best with Kieren Fallon taking over from Adam Beschizza, who would have been unable to claim. Well backed, he was given a patient ride until moving closer over 3f out and maintained his run to hit the front over a furlong from home. He can win again at this level. (op 9-2)
Tazahum(USA) was entitled to reverse last month's Goodwood form with Western Aristocrat, but there was a slight doubt about him over this trip. His rider didn't seem worried about that, however, as he was given a positive ride and, to his great credit, he never threw in the towel. He certainly stayed the trip well enough and there should be another Listed race in him at least this autumn, with his ability to handle an easy surface not in doubt. (op 8-1 tchd 9-1 in a place)
Dux Scholar returned to winning form in good style at Newbury last month and this ground would have been ideal, but despite plenty of pressure he took far too long in getting into gear and a return to 1m2f looks needed. (op 3-1 tchd 5-2)
Anmar(USA) appeared to be beaten fair and square by Dux Scholar at Newbury last time and this further drop in trip wouldn't necessary have been in his favour, so this wasn't a bad effort at all in the circumstances.
Penitent had the ground in his favour and was tried in a first-time visor. Always up there, sticking to the inside rail didn't seem to harm his chances and he was back in front passing the 2f pole, but he is still to truly convince over further than 1m and the last furlong found him out. His rider reported that the gelding had hung right. Official explanation: jockey said gelding hung right (op 11-1 tchd 12-1)
Nationalism, just ahead of Dux Scholar when narrowly winning a Windsor Listed event last time, tried to come from last place up the straight but his effort was laboured and he never got anywhere near. (op 7-1)
Western Aristocrat(USA), the least-exposed in the field stepping up another furlong in trip, was beaten too far out for stamina to have been the only reason. (op 8-1)
Kings Gambit(SAF), carrying a 4lb penalty for his success in a Sandown Group 3 back in April, can be hard to pass when able to dominate but he never got to the front here and was struggling when coming under pressure over 3f out. (op 16-1)

Critical Moment(USA) has consistently found this level beyond him in six previous attempts and he was never going to win this either. (tchd 28-1)

Biondetti(USA) was keen enough early and eventually dropped out as though something was amiss. His rider reported that the colt was very upset in the preliminaries. Official explanation: jockey said colt was very upset in the preliminaries (op 13-2 tchd 8-1 in a place)

5253 COOLMORE NUNTHORPE STKS (BRITISH CHAMPIONS' SERIES) (GROUP 1) 5f

3:40 (3:40) (Class 1) 2-Y-0+

£156,065 (£59,168; £29,611; £14,750; £7,402; £3,715) **Stalls** Centre

Form				RPR
4114	**1**		**Margot Did (IRE)**[48] 3644 3-9-6 110 ..... HayleyTurner 11 (Michael Bell) *cl up stands' side: led and overall ldr over 1f out: rdn ins fnl f: kpt on strly* **20/1**	118
0423	**2**	*3/4*	**Hamish McGonagall**[41] 3874 6-9-11 106 ..... DavidAllan 15 (Tim Easterby) *overall ldr stands' side: rdn 2f out: hdd over 1f out: sn drvn and kpt on wl fnl f: 2nd of 6 in gp* **28/1**	117
4321	**3**	*1/2*	**Prohibit**[66] 3010 6-9-11 117 ..... (p) JimCrowley 7 (Robert Cowell) *trckd ldrs far side: hdwy 2f out: rdn and hung rt jst ins fnl f: kpt on 1st of 9 in gp* **12/1**	116
6060	**4**	*hd*	**Kingsgate Native (IRE)**[22] 4468 6-9-11 110 ..... RichardHughes 9 (Sir Michael Stoute) *swtchd rt sn after s: trckd ldrs stands' side: hdwy 2f out: rdn over 1f out: kpt on u.p fnl f: nrst fin: 3rd of 6 in gp* **20/1**	115
2-01	**5**	*1/2*	**Wizz Kid (IRE)**[75] 2754 3-9-6 109 ..... IoritzMendizabal 6 (Robert Collet, France) *in tch far side: hdwy 2f out: rdn whn n.m.r over 1f out: styng on whn hmpd and swtchd lft ins fnl f: r.o wl towards fin 2nd of 9 in gp* **14/1**	114+
1011	**6**	*shd*	**Hoof It**[20] 4534 4-9-11 119 ..... KierenFallon 10 (Michael Easterby) *swtchd towards far side sn after s and towards rr: hdwy 2f out: sn rdn: kpt on u.p fnl f: nrst fin: 3rd of 9 in gp* **11/4**[1]	113
6221	**7**	*1 1/4*	**Captain Dunne (IRE)**[76] 2714 6-9-11 108 ..... (p) RobertWinston 16 (Tim Easterby) *cl up: stands' side: effrt 2f out: sn rdn and ev ch tl drvn and wknd ins fnl f 4th of 6 in gp* **33/1**	108
1011	**8**	*nk*	**Masamah (IRE)**[22] 4468 5-9-11 112 ..... JamieSpencer 8 (Kevin Ryan) *qckly away and swtchd to far rail: led fare side gp: cl up: rdn wl over 1f out: grad wknd: 4th of 9 in gp* **8/1**[3]	107
1152	**9**	*1 1/2*	**Bated Breath**[41] 3863 4-9-11 118 ..... SteveDrowne 2 (Roger Charlton) *prom far side: rdn wl over 2f out: sn wknd: 5th of 9 in gp* **5/1**[2]	102
0	**10**	*1/2*	**Swiss Diva**[66] 3010 5-9-8 110 ..... WilliamBuick 17 (David Elsworth) *trckd ldrs stands' side: rdn along 2f out: sn drvn and one pce: 5th of 6 in gp* **20/1**	97
2001	**11**	*1 3/4*	**Tiddliwinks**[10] 4894 5-9-11 104 ..... PhillipMakin 1 (Kevin Ryan) *chsd ldrs far side: rdn along 2f out: sn wknd: 6th of 9 in gp* **25/1**	94
0006	**12**	*nk*	**Breathless Kiss (USA)**[22] 4468 4-9-8 98 ..... (b) PaulHanagan 3 (Kevin Ryan) *prom far side: rdn along over 2f out: sn wknd: 7th of 9 in gp* **80/1**	89
511	**13**	*1 1/4*	**Requinto (IRE)**[24] 4413 2-8-1 0 ..... WMLordan 12 (David Wachman, Ire) *trckd ldrs stands' side: effrt 2f out: sn rdn and btn: last of 6 in gp* **5/1**[2]	80
0535	**14**	*1 3/4*	**Piccadilly Filly (IRE)**[15] 4739 4-9-8 97 ..... (vt) EddieCreighton 4 (Edward Creighton) *racd far side: in rr fr 1/2-way: 8th of 9 in gp* **80/1**	79
3141	**15**	*1 1/2*	**Inxile (IRE)**[14] 4768 6-9-11 112 ..... (p) AdrianNicholls 5 (David Nicholls) *dwlt: sn chsng ldrs towards far side: rdn along over 2f out: sn wknd: 9th of 9 in gp* **16/1**	76

58.66 secs (-0.64) **Going Correction** +0.30s/f (Good) **15** Ran SP% **118.3**

Speed ratings: **117,115,115,114,113 113,111,111,108,108 105,104,102,99,97**

toteswingers:1&2:£55.90, 1&3:£32.00, 2&3:£48.70 CSF £452.34 TOTE £20.50: £6.50, £8.90, £4.20; EX 439.50 Trifecta £6903.40 Part won. Pool: £9,329.00 - 0.33 winning units..

Owner T Redman And P Philipps **Bred** N Hartery **Trained** Newmarket, Suffolk

■ Stewards' Enquiry : Jim Crowley one-day ban: careless riding (Sep 2)

Jamie Spencer three-day ban: careless riding (Sep 2,4,5)

FOCUS

An ordinary Nunthorpe and a messy race with the majority splitting into two groups. The near side was the place to be and the form is muddling, but looks best rated around the third and fourth. The winner recorded a persoanl best and the second is rated to his best handicap mark.

NOTEBOOK

Margot Did(IRE) ran out a ready winner and posted a clear personal-best display on this return to the top level. She was done by the draw when finishing fourth at Sandown in Group 3 company last month, but had returned to her best when winning back-to-back races before that and is a real 5f specialist. All ground seemingly comes alike to her and, while she may have been racing on the best of it, she did travel most powerfully through the race. Indeed she could have been called the winner nearing the final furlong and this was another top-flight success for the massively improved Hayley Turner. She was called a few names thanks to a string of frustrating efforts as a juvenile and her first two runs back this year also marked her down as one to tread carefully with. However, connections have obviously found the key to her this summer and she is now blossoming. Her trainer's horses are also in cracking form at present. The Group 1 Prix de L'Abbaye at Longchamp in October looks the obvious next step for her and that test ought to prove right up her street.

Hamish McGonagall's proximity clouds the water of this form, but he loves this venue and is yet another indication of an in-form sprinter being able to mix it when thrown in at the top level. He posted a career-best when just held over C&D 41 days earlier and this must rate another step up. The ground was in his favour and he was drawn ideally as it turned out. He fully deserves to win a Group race. (tchd 25-1)

Prohibit was laid out for this after making the breakthrough in Group 1 company in the King's Stand at Royal Ascot in June. He proved somewhat free early on, but was noted travelling powerfully 2f out. There is a reason why he sports headgear, though, and he hung markedly right when put under pressure, ending up down the centre having originally kept far side. He still emerged best of those drawn in single figures and helps to give substance to this form. Entitled to come on for the run, another trip to France looks sure to be on his agenda and his previous experience of such travelling dictates he has a fair chance of reversing form with the winner in the Prix de L'Abbaye. (op 10-1)

Kingsgate Native(IRE), the 2007 winner, was having his fourth run in this event and sweated up beforehand. He still travelled sweetly, however, and returned to the sort of form that saw him finish second in the Temple Stakes on his comeback. He too sets the level. (op 18-1 tchd 16-1)

Wizz Kid(IRE) ◆, another 3-y-o filly, beat Prohibit when last seen in a Group 2 at Chantilly in June and she was unlucky not to have confirmed form with that rival. She travelled nicely under restraint on the far side, but got outpaced when things became really serious. She was coming back late on, though, and found trouble when the gap closed near the finish. Her run needs upgrading and she looks sure to strike again when faced with more of a test. (op 12-1)

Hoof It could hardly have been more impressive when carrying ten stone to success in the Stewards' Cup last month and, with his liking for this venue already proven, it wasn't surprising to see him head the betting despite this being an initial crack at the top level. It was his first run back over the minimum this term and that showed as he took time to get into his full stride from off the pace. The plan beforehand was surely to track likely leader Masamah, but it went out of the window when that rival shot over to the far rail and Fallon momentarily looked unsure of which group to tag onto. That resulted in him tracking Inxile more towards the middle and he was always getting there too late inside the final furlong. Things didn't pan out for him this time, but it was still another decent effort and he's not one to abandon, with his trainer later mentioning the Portland Handicap over 5.5f at Doncaster next month as a possible target. (tchd 3-1 in a place)

Captain Dunne(IRE), a stablemate of the runner-up, is a real speedster and won the Epsom Dash on his previous start back in June. He looked a picture beforehand and had his chance racing towards the near side. This level just looks beyond him.

Masamah(IRE) came into this on the back of a career-best win at Glorious Goodwood and was previously 3-3 over C&D. He unsurprisingly shot out to lead, but his unexpected manoeuvre to the far rail (Spencer picked up three-day ban) backfired and he was never going to confirm his previous C&D form with Hamish McGonagall. (op 15-2 tchd 7-1)

Bated Breath confirmed himself a true Group 1 sprinter when second in the July Cup the previous month and was a leading ante-post fancy for this, but reportedly suffered an interrupted preparation. The easier ground was also a concern beforehand, but he still got very well backed near the off. He did his best to get involved racing handily on the far side, but it was apparent 1f out he was in trouble. He's much better than this on a quick surface. (op 15-2 tchd 9-2)

Requinto(IRE) was the only juvenile this year and had been supplemented for the race. Solid in the market with his big weight-for-age allowance, he never got going despite racing in the near-side group and clearly something went amiss. He was later reported to have been unsuited by the going. Official explanation: trainer said colt was unsuited by the good to soft (good places) ground (op 6-1 tchd 9-2)

5254 SKY BET MOBILE CONVIVIAL MAIDEN STKS 7f

4:15 (4:16) (Class 2) 2-Y-O **£16,172** (£4,812; £2,405; £1,202) **Stalls** Low

Form				RPR
5	**1**		**Rugged Cross**[35] 4054 2-9-3 0 ..... DaneO'Neill 6 (Henry Candy) *chsd ldrs: led 1f out: drvn out* **18/1**	93+
423	**2**	*2 1/2*	**Storming Bernard (USA)**[19] 4571 2-9-3 78 ..... SilvestreDeSousa 4 (Alan Bailey) *led: sent 3 l clr over 3f out: hdd 1f out: kpt on same pce* **14/1**	87
2	**3**	*1/2*	**Llanarmon Lad (IRE)**[24] 4414 2-9-3 0 ..... MichaelHills 8 (B W Hills) *chsd ldrs: wnt 3rd 1f out: styd on same pce* **6/1**[2]	86
	4	*3/4*	**Athens (IRE)** 2-9-3 0 ..... SeamieHeffernan 7 (A P O'Brien, Ire) *mid-div: hdwy over 2f out: hrd rdn and styd on fnl f: tk 4th last 50yds* **8/1**[3]	84+
24	**5**	*1 1/2*	**Burano (IRE)**[27] 4330 2-9-3 0 ..... MartinDwyer 11 (Brian Meehan) *in rr: hdwy over 2f out: edgd lft over 1f out: styd on wl fnl f: tk 5th last 50yds* **6/1**[2]	80+
	6	*2 3/4*	**Mizwaaj (IRE)** 2-9-3 0 ..... PaulHanagan 16 (Saeed Bin Suroor) *in rr-div: hdwy on outer over 3f out: sn chsng ldrs: 4th 1f out: wknd ins fnl f* **14/1**	75+
	7	*2 1/4*	**Imperial Order (IRE)** 2-9-3 0 ..... RichardHughes 12 (Richard Hannon) *mid-div: hdwy over 2f out: kpt on fnl f* **16/1**	71+
	8	*1*	**Crusade (USA)** 2-9-3 0 ..... CO'Donoghue 1 (A P O'Brien, Ire) *mid-div: hdwy over 3f out: sn chsng ldrs: wknd fnl 150yds* **33/1**	65+
423	**9**	*1 1/4*	**Firestarter**[9] 4906 2-9-3 0 ..... KierenFallon 9 (David Elsworth) *hld up in mid-div: effrt over 2f out: nvr nr ldrs* **17/2**	62
	10	*1/2*	**Thomas Chippendale (IRE)** 2-9-3 0 ..... TomQueally 15 (Sir Henry Cecil) *chsd ldrs: wkng whn hmpd and eased over 1f out* **9/1**	66+
	11	*1*	**Strictly Silver (IRE)** 2-9-3 0 ..... CathyGannon 14 (Alan Bailey) *in rr: stmbld bnd over 4f out: effrt on outer over 2f out: nvr a factor* **20/1**	63+
6	**12**	*2 3/4*	**Mitch Rapp (USA)**[41] 3870 2-9-3 0 ..... JamieSpencer 2 (Harry Dunlop) *chsd ldrs: wknd over 1f out* **50/1**	51
02	**13**	*6*	**Premier Choice**[23] 4436 2-9-3 0 ..... DavidAllan 10 (Tim Easterby) *chsd ldrs: edgd rt and lost pl over 1f out* **12/1**	36
	14	*1/2*	**Dark Don (IRE)** 2-9-3 0 ..... RobertWinston 5 (B W Hills) *in rr: sme hdwy 3f out: sn wknd* **40/1**	35
3	**15**	*4*	**Shotley Music**[27] 4323 2-9-3 0 ..... AndrewElliott 3 (Neville Bycroft) *s.i.s: detached in last: passed 2 eased horses ins fnl f* **80/1**	25
	16	*5*	**Barberton (USA)** 2-9-3 0 ..... WilliamBuick 13 (Jeremy Noseda) *in rr-div: lost pl over 2f out: eased over 1f out* **12/1**	38+
	17	*9*	**Crying Wolf (USA)** 2-9-3 0 ..... FrankieDettori 17 (Mahmood Al Zarooni) *in rr on outside: effrt over 2f out: bhd and eased over 1f out* **11/2**[1]	—

1m 25.94s (0.64) **Going Correction** +0.05s/f (Good) **17** Ran SP% **128.8**

Speed ratings (Par 100): **98,95,94,93,92 88,86,85,83,83 82,78,72,71,66 61,50**

toteswingers:1&2:£41.70, 1&3:£23.50, 2&3:£13.20 CSF £253.35 TOTE £26.40: £6.00, £4.60, £3.00; EX 273.40 Trifecta £1529.90 Part won. Pool: £2,067.55 - 1.10 winning units..

Owner Thomas Barr **Bred** Rabbah Bloodstock Limited **Trained** Kingston Warren, Oxon

FOCUS

The second running of the most valuable maiden in the calendar since the distance was extended to 7f. A fascinating race, split almost equally between horses that had already shown plenty of promise or ability, and several very interesting newcomers, but experience gained the day with the front three having raced before.

NOTEBOOK

Rugged Cross very much caught the eye when fifth of nine on his Newbury debut last month and confirmed that promise here. Always in a handy position, he quickened up nicely to nail the leader over a furlong out and, although he doesn't hold any big race entries before the end of the season, he should be up to winning something better. (op 20-1 tchd 16-1)

Storming Bernard(USA), officially rated 80, was a disappointing favourite at Chester last time, but had previously split Wednesday's Acomb winner Entifaadha and subsequent Listed winner Fencing (Burano back in fourth) when runner-up in a Newmarket maiden. His rider tried to make his experience tell under a positive ride and he managed to hold off all bar the winner. He deserves to win a race, but lacks the scope for further improvement of several of these.

Llanarmon Lad(IRE) ◆ was only beaten a nose in a 6f Goodwood maiden on his debut last month, though the winner of that race only finished tenth in the big sales race here the previous day. The way he ran here suggested that even this extra furlong was inadequate and he shouldn't be long in breaking his duck. (op 15-2)

Athens(IRE) ◆, a half-brother to four winners including his smart stable-companion Admiralofthefleet, did best of the newcomers and ran on again after getting outpaced at around halfway. He is entered for all the big autumn 2-y-o contests over 7f-1m and will win races. (op 12-1 tchd 15-2)

Burano(IRE) started favourite for that Newmarket maiden in which Storming Bernard finished second, but reportedly lost a shoe when finishing fourth. He ran close to the Newmarket form with the runner-up here, but the way he stayed on late suggests he needs 1m already. (op 7-1)

Mizwaaj(IRE), a half-brother to a winner at up to an extended 1m, ran well on this debut as he was stuck out wide from his wide stall, but he made a promising effort passing the 2f pole before running green and fading. He should improve. (op 12-1)

Imperial Order(IRE), a £75,000 half-brother to a winner over this trip, made some late progress and should improve for the experience. (op 20-1)
Crusade(USA), first foal of a smart US sprinter and the apparent Ballydoyle second string, showed ability on this debut though his pedigree suggests he wouldn't get much further than this.
Firestarter had shown ability in three previous starts and is rated 79, but he looked quirky in his most recent outing. He faced a stiff task against some less-exposed rivals here and may be better off in a nursery. (op 9-1 tchd 10-1)
Thomas Chippendale(IRE), a 375,000gns colt out of the English/Irish Oaks' third All My Loving, showed up early from his wide draw, but was already weakening when hampered over a furlong from home. He looks to need more time. (op 7-1)
Barberton(USA) was reproted to be unsuited by the good to soft, good in places ground. Official explanation: trainer's rep said colt was unsuited by the good to soft (good in places) ground (op 11-1)
Crying Wolf(USA), an $800,000 colt out of an unraced half-sister to One Cool Cat, had the worst of the draw and was forced to race out wide, but he still ran too badly to be true. He seemed to take a knock when Strictly Silver stumbled on the home turn which may have had something to do with it, though the trainer's representative reported that the colt was unsuited by the good to soft, good in places ground. Official explanation: trainer's rep said colt was unsuited by the good to soft (good in places) ground (tchd 6-1)

5255 E B F PAUL MALONE HALF CENTURY STKS (FILLIES' H'CAP) 7f

4:50 (4:50) (Class 2) (0-100,93) 3-Y-O+ **£12,938** (£3,850; £1,924; £962) **Stalls** Low

Form RPR
3413 **1** **Shesastar**[29] 4234 3-8-7 **79** ow1 .... JamieSpencer 8 89+
(David Barron) *hld up towards rr: hdwy wl over 2f out: swtchd rt and rdn to chal over 1f out: led ent fnl f: drvn out* **5/1**[1]
1066 **2** *1 1/2* **Sioux Rising (IRE)**[5] 5080 5-9-4 **92** .... LauraBarry(7) 14 100
(Richard Fahey) *in tch: hdwy on outer over 2f out: rdn to ld 1 1/2f out: sn drvn and edgd lft: hdd ent fnl f: kpt on* **25/1**
0446 **3** *2 1/4* **Jeannie Galloway (IRE)**[6] 5032 4-9-1 **82** .... PaulHanagan 2 91+
(Richard Fahey) *trckd ldrs: effrt and nt clr run 2f out: swtchd rt to outer over 1f out: rdn and styd on wl fnl f: tk 3rd nr line* **7/1**[2]
5121 **4** *nk* **Caelis**[22] 4458 3-8-5 **77** .... (v) MartinLane 10 76
(Ralph Beckett) *in rr and sn pushed along: hdwy over 2f out: rdn wl over 1f out: styd on to chse ldng pair ent fnl f: sn drvn and no imp* **16/1**
533 **5** *2 1/4* **Imaginary World (IRE)**[6] 5056 3-8-4 **76** .... WMLordan 6 72+
(Alan McCabe) *dwlt and in rr: hdwy wl over 2f out: rdn wl over 1f out: styd on ins fnl f: nrst fin* **16/1**
5433 **6** *1 3/4* **Perfect Silence**[27] 4332 6-9-3 **89** .... LucyKBarry(5) 18 79
(Clive Cox) *towards rr: wd st and racd alone stands' rail: hdwy 3f out: rdn to chse ldrs over 2f out: sn drvn and edgd lft fr wl over 1f out: no imp:* **14/1**
0311 **7** *shd* **Lady Paris (IRE)**[7] 5018 3-9-4 **90** 6ex .... TomEaves 17 78
(Bryan Smart) *trckd ldrs: hdwy 1/2-way: rdn to chal over 2f out and ev ch tl drvn and wknd appr fnl f* **10/1**
1-04 **8** *1 3/4* **La Zamora**[13] 4791 5-9-2 **83** .... GrahamGibbons 15 68
(David Barron) *wnt rt and s.i.s: bhd tl styd on fnl 2f: n.d* **14/1**
6301 **9** *hd* **Coolminx (IRE)**[7] 5006 4-8-13 **83** 6ex .... LeeTopliss(3) 4 68
(Richard Fahey) *chsd ldrs: rdn along wl over 2f out: grad wknd* **8/1**[3]
1-60 **10** *1* **Zenella**[23] 4428 3-9-4 **90** .... TomQueally 7 70
(Ann Duffield) *in tch: rdn along 3f out: n.d* **25/1**
106- **11** *1/2* **Madam Macie (IRE)**[421] 3375 4-9-6 **87** .... SilvestreDeSousa 16 68
(David O'Meara) *chsd ldng pair: rdn along wl over 2f out: sn wknd* **10/1**
0-40 **12** *1/2* **Misplaced Fortune**[26] 4369 6-9-0 **84** .... DaleSwift(3) 19 63
(Nigel Tinkler) *stdd and swtchd lft s: a in rr* **16/1**
2225 **13** *1 3/4* **No Poppy (IRE)**[15] 4718 3-8-10 **82** .... DavidAllan 3 55+
(Tim Easterby) *towards rr: hdwy on inner 1/2-way: rdn along whn nt clr run 2f out: sn wknd* **12/1**
-242 **14** *4 1/2* **Clumber Place**[63] 3113 5-8-8 **75** .... MartinDwyer 11 38
(Richard Guest) *cl up: rdn along over 2f out: drvn and wknd wl over 1f out* **22/1**
1411 **15** *3* **Queen Of Cash (IRE)**[16] 4665 3-8-12 **84** .... DarryllHolland 5 36
(Hughie Morrison) *led: rdn along wl over 2f out: drvn wl over 1f out: sn hdd & wknd* **12/1**
4310 **16** *1 1/4* **[illegible]** [illegible] .... MichaelHills 9 36
(B W Hills) *chsd ldrs: rdn along 1/2-way: sn wknd* **16/1**
-225 **17** *6* **File And Paint (IRE)**[6] 5062 3-8-5 **77** .... DuranFentiman 1 —
(Lawrence Mullaney) *in tch on inner: rdn along 1/2-way: sn wknd* **40/1**

1m 24.58s (-0.72) **Going Correction** +0.05s/f (Good)
WFA 3 from 4yo+ 5lb **17** Ran SP% **125.2**
Speed ratings (Par 96): **106,104,101,101,98 96,96,94,94,93 92,92,90,85,81 80,73**
toteswingers:1&2:£37.40, 1&3:£8.10, 2&3:£44.60 CSF £142.31 CT £929.48 TOTE £6.10: £2.10, £5.20, £2.40, £4.30; EX 235.60 Trifecta £906.60 Pool: £2,853.41 - 2.32 winning units..
Owner Star Alliance 4 - Lancs 2 Lincs **Bred** The Welcome Alliance **Trained** Maunby, N Yorks

FOCUS
A strong fillies' handicap. There was a solid pace on and, despite a few hard-luck stories in the home straight, the form is straightforward enough with the third back to her best and the runner-up the best guide to the level.

NOTEBOOK
Shesastar ◆ won her second race from her last three outings with a ready effort. She looked ready for a step up to this trip when placed at Doncaster last month and was reunited with Jamie Spencer back aboard this time, who won on her at that venue two starts back. Everything went perfectly for her and Spencer, who was obviously keen to delay his challenge in the home straight, gave her a typically well-judged ride. Another rise is now forthcoming, but this 3-y-o should have more to offer over the trip and can win again. (op 11-2)
Sioux Rising(IRE) improved as the race went on and made a bold bid passing 2f out. She was reeled in late on, but still finished a clear second-best and was conceding 12lb to the winner, taking into account her rider's claim. This trip does just stretch her stamina.
Jeannie Galloway(IRE) ◆ was the first-string from her yard and she was unlucky not to have gone a lot closer as she was stopped in her run late on. She is now due a rise, but there is very likely another race to be won with her in the coming weeks.
Caelis came through late on to run another solid race off a 7lb higher mark, but she lost third near the finish and this ground looked soft enough for her. (op 14-1)
Imaginary World(IRE) was immediately restrained from her low draw and ridden to get the gaps from out the back. She had plenty on, but was another stopped in her run when winding up for a challenge and she is better than the bare form. It's not the first time she has run an eye-catching race, however and her losing run continues.
Perfect Silence went solo towards the centre after straightening for home, a move that could have been expected to pay off looking at the finish of the Nunthorpe earlier on. However, she was in trouble before things got serious and could only keep on at the same pace. (op 16-1)
Lady Paris(IRE) bolted up at Pontefract a week earlier and looked well treated under a penalty. She had her chance, but was laboured from 2f out and probably the run came that bit too soon. She can be given another chance back at 6f. (op 11-1)
No Poppy(IRE) Official explanation: jockey said filly was denied a clear run
T/Jkpt: Not won. T/Plt: £780.60 to a £1 stake. Pool:£303,023.62 - 283.38 winning tickets T/Qpdt: £117.90 to £1 Pool: £15,265.64 - 95.80 w. tckts JR 5256 & 5261a - Raceform Interactive

4625 BATH (L-H)

Saturday, August 20

OFFICIAL GOING: Good to firm (good in places)
About 12.5yds added to races run around bottom bend.
Wind: Moderate across Weather: Bright spells early

5262 SWINDON DESIGNER OUTLET MAMAS AND PAPAS H'CAP 5f 161y

5:40 (5:40) (Class 4) (0-85,85) 3-Y-O+ **£3,234** (£962; £481; £240) **Stalls** Centre

Form RPR
136 **1** **Barons Spy (IRE)**[42] 3850 10-9-6 **81** .... JamesDoyle 7 90
(Richard Price) *stmbld s: sn picked up and rcvrd: drvn and outpcd 3f out: rdn and hdwy on outside over 1f out: str run u.p fnl f to ld clsng stages* **13/2**
54U **2** *1/2* **Restless Bay (IRE)**[13] 4817 3-8-13 **77** .... (p) FrankieMcDonald 2 84
(Reg Hollinshead) *in tch on ins: rdn along 3f out: stl on inner whn gd prog appr fnl f: str chal clsng stages: nt gng pce of wnr* **12/1**
1400 **3** *nk* **Soap Wars**[25] 4416 6-9-10 **85** .... (v[1]) SebSanders 1 91
(Hugo Palmer) *trckd ldrs: led 2f out: rdn over 1f out: hdd and no ex clsng stages* **9/2**[1]
3334 **4** *1/2* **Wooden King (IRE)**[11] 4886 6-9-0 **75** .... TomMcLaughlin 6 80
(Malcolm Saunders) *in rr tl hdwy to chal fr 2f out: stl ev ch fnl 120yds: one pce clsng stages* **13/2**
2421 **5** *3/4* **Emiratesdotcom**[18] 4640 5-8-7 **68** .... WilliamCarson 9 70
(Milton Bradley) *chsd ldrs: rdn over 2f out: styd on same pce ins fnl f* **11/2**[3]
6510 **6** *3/4* **Maze (IRE)**[25] 4416 6-8-13 **79** .... LucyKBarry(5) 5 79
(Tony Carroll) *chsd ldrs: rdn and ev ch 2f out: wknd ins fnl f* **6/1**
5163 **7** *1 1/2* **Ebraam (USA)**[20] 4583 8-9-1 **76** .... LukeMorris 3 71
(Ronald Harris) *in rr: rdn 1/2-way: styd on fnl f: nvr gng pce to rch ldrs* **15/2**
114 **8** *1 1/2* **Pick A Little**[37] 3996 3-9-0 **81** .... HarryBentley(3) 4 71
(Ron Hodges) *in rr: pushed along on ins over 2f out: outpcd most of way* **5/1**[2]
0400 **9** *1 3/4* **Spanish Acclaim**[9] 4960 4-8-7 **68** .... NeilChalmers 8 52
(Andrew Balding) *broke wl and sn led: hdd 2f out: wknd sn after* **16/1**

1m 10.53s (-0.67) **Going Correction** -0.10s/f (Good)
WFA 3 from 4yo+ 3lb **9** Ran SP% **116.5**
Speed ratings (Par 105): **100,99,98,98,97 96,94,92,89**
toteswingers:1&2:£11.00, 1&3:£3.90, 2&3:£13.10 CSF £81.31 CT £391.13 TOTE £6.20: £1.90, £5.20, £1.60; EX 117.90 Trifecta £1075.40 Pool: £2034.59 - 1.40 winning units..
Owner Barry Veasey **Bred** Tally-Ho Stud **Trained** Ullingswick, H'fords
■ Stewards' Enquiry : James Doyle three-day ban: excessive use of the whip (Sep 4-6)

FOCUS
An open handicap in which claims could be made for most of the field. The pace was good and the complexion of the race changed in the closing stages.

5263 SWINDON DESIGNER OUTLET QUBA & CO/E.B.F. NOVICE STKS 5f 161y

6:10 (6:10) (Class 5) 2-Y-O **£3,234** (£962; £481; £240) **Stalls** Centre

Form RPR
2 **1** **Top Cop**[10] 4912 2-9-0 0 .... JimmyFortune 1 85+
(Andrew Balding) *mde all: pressed fr 3f out to 2f out: chal again fr 1f out and sn drvn: kpt finding and in command fnl 120yds* **7/4**[2]
4 **2** *1/2* **Arnold Lane (IRE)**[84] 2488 2-9-2 85 .... MartinHarley(3) 5 88
(Mick Channon) *trckd ldrs: t.k.h: hdwy to press wnr 1f out: stl ev ch u.p ins fnl f tl outpcd fnl 120yds* **3/1**[3]
121 **3** *2 3/4* **Quite A Thing**[15] 4757 2-9-2 91 .... SebSanders 2 76
(Sir Mark Prescott Bt) *trckd ldrs: drvn along over 1f out: sn no imp on ldng duo and styd on same pce* **6/4**[1]
510 **4** *4* **Chandigarh (IRE)**[13] 4824 2-8-11 69 .... FrankieMcDonald 4 58
(Paul Fitzsimons) *chsd ldr: chal fr 3f out to 2f out: wknd over 1f out* **20/1**
5 *43* **Hatha Zain (IRE)** 2-9-0 0 .... WilliamCarson 3 —
(Milton Bradley) *s.i.s: sn rcvrd and t.k.h: rdn: green and wknd qckly wl over 2f out* **[illegible]**

1m 10.55s (-0.65) **Going Correction** -0.10s/f (Good) **5** Ran SP% **109.1**
Speed ratings (Par 94): **100,99,95,90,33**
CSF £7.21 TOTE £3.10: £1.60, £1.60; EX 7.00.
Owner J C Smith **Bred** Littleton Stud **Trained** Kingsclere, Hants

FOCUS
Quite a useful minor event but though it was run at a muddling pace, the result looked the right one.

NOTEBOOK
Top Cop ◆ significantly took his chance here instead of an ordinary maiden and he confirmed the good impression he'd made at Salisbury with an ultimately decisive success. For all he was at an advantage in being out in front, he left the impression he was the best horse on the day and, a substantial individual with a fair amount of scope who still looked green, is quite probably easily the best long-term prospect too. He'll be suited by a stronger end-to-end gallop back on a flatter track at 6f. (tchd 13-8 and 15-8)
Arnold Lane(IRE), who had been withdrawn four times with either a self certificate or vet's certificate since his last run at Beverley in May, still holds an entry in the Middle Park but he's clearly well short of that level. He travelled well to post halfway but only briefly threatened to run down the winner and was readily held at the line. He's entitled to improve again given his absence.
Quite A Thing has now been a beaten favourite twice from four runs and, though she wasn't helped by conceding the run of the race to the first two, she'd probably have struggled to beat the second anyway. It looks as if a bare 5f might be her trip. (tchd 5-4 tchd 13-8 in places)
Chandigarh(IRE) had won her maiden over C&D but was out of her depth here and will be better off back in low-grade nurseries. (op 18-1 tchd 25-1)
Hatha Zain(IRE), a half-brother to a couple of fair winners by Zafeen, failed to settle and was struggling by halfway. (op 50-1)

5264 SWINDON DESIGNER OUTLET LACOSTE / EBF SOMERSETSHIRE CONDITIONS STKS 5f 161y

6:40 (6:40) (Class 2) 3-Y-O+ **£14,425** (£4,292; £2,145; £1,072) **Stalls** Centre

Form RPR
2042 **1** **Desert Law (IRE)**[14] 4779 3-8-13 98 .... JimmyFortune 9 106+
(Andrew Balding) *s.i.s: in rr tl stdy hdwy on outside fr 2f out to ld wl over 1f out: sn wnt lft to far rail: rdn ins fnl f: sn in n.d and r.o strly: eased clsng stages* **7/4**[1]
0001 **2** *1* **Joe Packet**[12] 4859 4-9-2 96 .... HarryBentley 2 100+
(Jonathan Portman) *stmbld s: sn rcvrd and wl in tch: n.m.r on ins fr over 1f out tl qckrd ins fnl f to chse wnr fnl 75yds: fin wl but a hld* **5/1**[3]
6314 **3** *1 1/2* **Star Rover (IRE)**[11] 4894 4-9-5 90 .... (v) JamesDoyle 7 98
(David Evans) *chsd ldrs: rdn and ev ch 2f out sn one pce but rallied ins fnl f to take 3rd nr fin* **14/1**

3600 **4** 1 **Button Moon (IRE)**[20] 4573 3-8-8 85 ....(p) MartinHarley 1 87
(Ian Wood) *led: rdn and jnd over 2f out but kpt slt ld tl hdd wl over 1f out: dropped to 4th fnl 120yds* **22/1**

0051 **5** nk **Prime Defender**[21] 4526 7-9-5 109 .... SebSanders 5 94
(B W Hills) *chsd ldr: drvn to chal over 2f out tl wl over 1f out: wknd ins fnl f* **7/2**[2]

0061 **6** ½ **Secret Witness**[7] 5033 5-9-2 93 ....(b) TomMcLaughlin 4 89
(Ronald Harris) *s.i.s: rdn and in tch 3f out: styng on same pce and no ch w ldrs whn hmpd and eased fnl 75yds* **11/2**

0000 **7** 1½ **Rulesn'regulations**[7] 5043 5-9-2 87 ....(b) LukeMorris 6 84
(Matthew Salaman) *chsd ldrs: rdn 3f out: sn outpcd: mod prog again fnl 120yds* **18/1**

006 **8** nk **Flowing Cape (IRE)**[19] 4609 6-9-2 84 .... WilliamCarson 3 83
(Reg Hollinshead) *bmpd s: sn pushed along and outpcd: styng on one pce and no ch w ldrs whn nt clr run wl ins fnl f* **20/1**

2045 **9** 5 **Bathwick Bear (IRE)**[18] 4644 3-9-6 94 .... RichardEvans 8 74
(David Evans) *chsd ldrs and rdn 3f out: ev ch 2f out: sn wknd* **33/1**

68.91 secs (-2.29) **Going Correction** -0.10s/f (Good)
WFA 3 from 4yo+ 3lb **9** Ran SP% **114.6**
Speed ratings (Par 109): **111,109,107,106,105 105,103,102,96**
toteswingers:1&2:£1.90, 2&3:£6.70, 1&3:£6.80 CSF £10.29 TOTE £2.80: £1.20, £1.70, £2.40; EX 10.90 Trifecta £56.60 Pool: £2538.46 - 33.17 winning units..
Owner J C Smith **Bred** Littleton Stud **Trained** Kingsclere, Hants
■ Stewards' Enquiry : Harry Bentley two-day ban: careless riding (Sep 4-5)

FOCUS
A welcome change from the usual low-grade sprints run here, though it wasn't particularly competitive all the same with many of the runners having a bit to do at the weights.

NOTEBOOK
Desert Law(IRE) ◆ was very impressive in emulating the victory of his half-brother Top Cop half an hour earlier and looks a sprinter going places. Hampered leaving the stalls, he brought up last place early on but he was ridden with great confidence and it was easy to see why as he quickened to the front to win easing up with far more in hand than the finishing margin suggests. He's in the Ayr Gold Cup and wouldn't be out of place in that line up, with further progress extremely likely. (op 9-4)
Joe Packet had won well at Windsor last time and probably bettered that form despite things not dropping right. It wasn't that he stumbled leaving the stalls that was the problem, but that he never seemed to have much room to get into his stride and by the time he did the winner had gone. He wouldn't have won, but he'd have beaten the third by further and might yet have another handicap in him. Official explanation: vet said gelding had been struck into (op 9-2 tchd 6-1)
Star Rover(IRE) had something to find at the weights and ran as well as could have been expected with no excuses needed. Official explanation: vet said gelding had been struck into (op 16-1)
Button Moon(IRE) had run a shocker in blinkers last time but ran right up to her best here albeit helped by a quick break and being able to dictate on the rail. She might find herself edging back up in the weights after this, so will remain hard to place. (op 20-1)
Prime Defender, who this week last year finished fourth in the Nunthorpe, isn't as good as he was despite what his recent Doncaster (where he goes well) win might suggest and his current mark of 109 almost certainly flatters him. (op 11-4)
Secret Witness never had much room to manoeuvre after a slow start and was squeezed out just as he was beginning to make some late headway, but for which he'd have finished fourth. This was a good run in the circumstances. (op 7-1)
Rulesn'regulations Official explanation: vet said gelding had been struck into
Bathwick Bear(IRE) had been running creditably of late and was a bit disappointing for all he faced a stiff task off top weight. His current official mark still makes him unappealing in handicaps. Official explanation: jockey said gelding hung right (op 25-1)

5265 SWINDON DESIGNER OUTLET KURT GEIGER FILLIES' H'CAP 5f 11y
7:10 (7:10) (Class 4) (0-80,77) 3-Y-O+ **£3,234** (£962; £481; £240) **Stalls** Centre

Form RPR

2231 **1** **Comptonspirit**[17] 4678 7-9-4 76 .... JamesRogers(5) 7 83
(Brian Baugh) *in rr but in tch: hdwy on outside fr 2f out: rdn and str run fnl f to ld fnl 75yds: drvn out* **5/1**[3]

601 **2** ½ **Picabo (IRE)**[9] 4967 3-9-7 76 .... LukeMorris 4 81
(Lucy Wadham) *slowly away: t.k.h and in rr: hdwy 2f out: drvn to chal u.p 1f out: slt ld fnl 120yds: hdd and no ex fnl 75yds* **5/2**[1]

0332 **3** hd **Best Be Careful (IRE)**[5] 5115 3-8-3 61 .... HarryBentley(3) 2 65
(Mark Usher) *chsd ldr: rdn to take slt ld 1f out: hdd and one pce fnl 120yds* **5/2**[1]

3604 **4** 1¼ **Diapason (IRE)**[9] 4973 5-9-1 68 ....(t) SebSanders 1 68
(Tom Dascombe) *t.k.h: sn in tch: rdn over 2f out: r.o u.p ins fnl f but nvr gng pce to get into contention* **9/2**[2]

0006 **5** 1¼ **Penny's Pearl (IRE)**[18] 4643 3-9-3 72 .... JamesDoyle 5 67
(David Evans) *chsd ldrs: rdn and ev ch 2f out: wknd over 1f out* **14/1**

0-60 **6** hd **Avrilo**[47] 3687 5-8-13 66 .... TomMcLaughlin 3 61
(Malcolm Saunders) *sn led: rdn 2f out: hdd 1f out: sn btn* **7/1**

61.67 secs (-0.83) **Going Correction** -0.10s/f (Good)
WFA 3 from 5yo+ 2lb **6** Ran SP% **111.2**
Speed ratings (Par 102): **102,101,100,98,96 96**
toteswingers:1&2:£3.60, 2&3:£1.40, 1&3:£2.50 CSF £17.51 TOTE £5.90: £2.50, £1.20; EX 13.00.
Owner G B Hignett **Bred** Mrs F Wilson **Trained** Audley, Staffs

FOCUS
Just the six runners but four of them came here on the back of winning or promising runs so it's probably not form to underestimate, despite it being a weakish race for the grade and run at a muddling gallop.

5266 SWINDON DESIGNER OUTLET OSPREY LONDON H'CAP 1m 3f 144y
7:40 (7:40) (Class 4) (0-80,80) 3-Y-O+ **£3,234** (£962; £481; £240) **Stalls** Low

Form RPR

-064 **1** **One Lucky Lady**[12] 4862 3-8-8 70 .... WilliamCarson 1 79
(B W Hills) *trckd ldr: chal over 3f out: led over 2f out and sn hrd rdn: styd on gamely ins fnl f* **5/1**[2]

5512 **2** 1 **Area Fifty One**[15] 4751 3-8-13 80 .... JamesRogers(5) 5 87
(William Muir) *led: jnd over 3f out: hdd over 2f out: rallied and styd on wl fr over 1f out but a hld by wnr* **15/8**[1]

-140 **3** nse **Huff And Puff**[70] 2931 4-9-12 78 ....(p) JimmyFortune 8 85
(Amanda Perrett) *chsd ldrs: rdn 3f out: outpcd over 2f out: styd on u.p fnl f to cl on 2nd nr fin but no imp on wnr* **5/1**[2]

3003 **4** ¾ **Brouhaha**[16] 4716 7-9-6 72 .... SebSanders 2 78
(Tom Dascombe) *in rr: pushed along and swtchd rt to outside over 2f out: styd on u.p thrght fnl f but nt rch ldrs* **7/1**

4265 **5** 1½ **Pelham Crescent (IRE)**[11] 4887 8-9-10 76 .... LukeMorris 4 79
(Bryn Palling) *in tch: rdn and hdwy fr 3f out: styd on same pce u.p ins fnl f* **16/1**

3313 **6** 2¾ **Monster Munchie (JPN)**[85] 2463 3-7-13 64 .... HarryBentley(3) 3 63
(William Knight) *t.k.h: chsd ldrs: rdn over 3f out: wknd fr 2f out* **13/2**

3023 **7** hd **Maher (USA)**[15] 4755 3-8-7 72 .... AdamBeschizza(3) 7 71
(David Simcock) *in rr: rdn over 3f out and no prog: no ch fnl 2f* **11/2**[3]

2m 29.36s (-1.24) **Going Correction** -0.10s/f (Good)
WFA 3 from 4yo+ 10lb **7** Ran SP% **115.2**
Speed ratings (Par 105): **100,99,99,98,97 95,95**
toteswingers:1&2:£5.40, 2&3:£2.60, 1&3:£4.40 CSF £15.08 CT £48.99 TOTE £6.70: £3.30, £1.10; EX 18.90 Trifecta £68.90 Pool: £2713.11 - 29.10 winning units..
Owner S W Group Logistics Limited **Bred** Ken Knox **Trained** Lambourn, Berks
■ Barry Hills's last runner as a trainer, and a winner, before he handed the licence over to his son Charlie.

FOCUS
A fair handicap in which those that were ridden handily were favoured, with the third and fourth looking slightly unlucky as things developed.

5267 SWINDON DESIGNER OUTLET JOHN LEWIS HOME OUTLET H'CAP 1m 5f 22y
8:10 (8:10) (Class 6) (0-55,53) 3-Y-O+ **£2,070** (£616; £307; £153) **Stalls** High

Form RPR

63-3 **1** **Red Current**[16] 4703 7-8-9 45 .... DavidKenny(7) 11 55+
(Michael Scudamore) *in tch: hdwy 4f out: drvn to ld appr fnl 2f: rdn clr ins fnl f: readily* **10/1**

0504 **2** 3½ **Bahkov (IRE)**[9] 4974 5-9-9 52 ....(b) SebSanders 12 54
(Eric Wheeler) *chsd ldr: rdn to chal over 2f out: styd chsng wnr fnl 2f but no ch fnl f: hld on all out for 2nd* **4/1**[2]

0/25 **3** nk **Ishismart**[50] 3600 7-9-7 50 .... WilliamCarson 6 52
(Reg Hollinshead) *led: rdn and hdd over 2f out: styd on u.p fnl f to press for 2nd cl home but no ch w wnr* **6/1**[3]

5151 **4** 3¾ **Lucky Diva**[18] 4630 4-9-3 53 ....(p) JakePayne(7) 3 49
(Bill Turner) *chsd ldrs: rdn to chal over 2f out: wknd ins fnl f* **10/3**[1]

6256 **5** shd **Dot's Delight**[83] 1973 7-9-4 47 .... LukeMorris 2 43
(Mark Rimell) *in rr: rdn and hdwy 6f out: outpcd over 3f out: styd on again u.p fr over 1f out: nvr any ch* **9/1**

-000 **6** ½ **Dixie Land Band**[47] 3690 3-8-5 45 .... RichardThomas 4 40
(Bill Turner) *in rr: drvn and hdwy fr 2f out: styd on fnl f but nvr any threat* **50/1**

-065 **7** 5 **Unbeatable**[18] 4641 3-8-3 46 .... HarryBentley(3) 1 34
(William Knight) *chsd ldrs tl wknd over 2f out* **8/1**

400 **8** ½ **Court Princess**[29] 4274 8-9-1 47 .... AdamBeschizza(3) 5 34
(Richard Price) *chsd ldrs tl wknd fr 3f out* **8/1**

200- **9** 1½ **The Bay Bandit**[250] 7863 4-9-10 53 .... JimmyFortune 10 44
(S Donohoe, Ire) *in rr tl hdwy 3f out: sn rdn and no imp on ldrs: wknd ins fnl 2f: eased whn btn fnl f* **13/2**

6600 **10** 2¾ **Swords**[2] 5209 9-8-11 45 ....(p) RyanPowell(5) 7 25
(Ray Peacock) *s.i.s: a towards rr* **40/1**

006- **11** 7 **Lily Eva**[6] 7899 5-8-13 45 .... MartinHarley(3) 8 15
(Des Donovan) *rdn over 3f out: a in rr* **20/1**

2m 53.86s (1.86) **Going Correction** -0.10s/f (Good)
WFA 3 from 4yo+ 11lb **11** Ran SP% **121.2**
Speed ratings (Par 101): **90,87,87,85,85 84,81,81,80,78 74**
toteswingers:1&2:£6.90, 2&3:£3.10, 1&3:£11.00 CSF £50.63 CT £270.33 TOTE £9.30: £2.50, £2.10, £2.70; EX 67.60 Trifecta £247.80 Part won. Pool of £334.96 - 0.60 winning units..
Owner M Scudamore **Bred** Wretham Stud **Trained** Bromsash, Herefordshire

FOCUS
A weak finale in which only a couple of runners came here in good form. The pace was steady and a prominent position was an advantage.
The Bay Bandit Official explanation: jockey said gelding ran too freely
T/Plt: £212.50 to a £1 stake. Pool of £45,789.24 - 157.23 winning units. T/Qpdt: £16.40 to a £1 stake. Pool of £5,257.22 - 237 winning units. ST

4571 CHESTER (L-H)
Saturday, August 20

OFFICIAL GOING: Good to firm (8.1)
Rails on inner line, no drop in and distances as advertised.
Wind: Light, half-behind Weather: Cloudy with light showers

5268 TOTEPLACEPOT H'CAP 5f 110y
2:25 (2:25) (Class 4) (0-85,85) 3-Y-O **£5,822** (£1,732; £865; £432) **Stalls** Low

Form RPR

0563 **1** **Mappin Time (IRE)**[14] 4791 3-9-1 79 ....(p) RobertWinston 1 87
(Tim Easterby) *midfield: hdwy and swtchd rt over 1f out: r.o to ld ent fnl f: a in control after* **7/2**[1]

1530 **2** ¾ **Muffraaj**[28] 4333 3-9-2 80 .... MartinLane 4 86
(David Simcock) *chsd ldrs: rdn over 1f out: ev ch on inner ent fnl f: styd on but nt quite gng pce of wnr* **5/1**[3]

0405 **3** nk **Jamesway (IRE)**[22] 4498 3-9-7 85 .... TonyHamilton 3 90
(Richard Fahey) *in tch: effrt on wd outside 2f out: chsd ldrs over 1f out: styd on ins fnl f: nt quite gng pce of first 2* **4/1**[2]

50 **4** 1 **On The High Tops (IRE)**[29] 4295 3-9-3 81 .... PJMcDonald 6 82
(Ruth Carr) *sn w ldr: rdn over 1f out: nt qckn ins fnl f: styd on same pce towards fin* **14/1**

5035 **5** ¾ **Layla Jamil (IRE)**[28] 4342 3-8-13 77 .... FrannyNorton 9 75+
(Mick Channon) *towards rr: sn pushed along: hdwy on outer wl over 1f out: kpt on ins fnl f: nt quite get to ldrs* **10/1**

4454 **6** 1 **Scarlet Rocks (IRE)**[5] 5115 3-8-9 73 .... CathyGannon 8 68
(David Evans) *towards rr: sn pushed along: rdn over 1f out: swtchd lft ins fnl f: kpt on: nt rch ldrs* **16/1**

3421 **7** ½ **Nine Before Ten (IRE)**[7] 5038 3-8-12 76 ....(t) LiamKeniry 2 69
(Richard Guest) *led: rdn over 1f out: hdd ent fnl f: fdd fnl 120yds* **4/1**[2]

0016 **8** 2¾ **Serena's Pride**[47] 3682 3-8-10 77 .... MatthewDavies(3) 5 60
(Alan Jarvis) *chsd ldrs: pushed along 2f out: wknd 1f out: eased whn btn fnl 100yds* **10/1**

4332 **9** nk **Crimson Knot (IRE)**[19] 4610 3-8-7 76 .... JulieBurke(5) 10 58
(Alan Berry) *outpcd and bhd: nvr able to get on terms* **14/1**

65.28 secs (-0.92) **Going Correction** -0.025s/f (Good) **9** Ran SP% **116.3**
Speed ratings (Par 102): **105,104,103,102,101 99,99,95,95**
CSF £21.32 CT £72.67 TOTE £4.10: £1.80, £1.80, £1.90; EX 26.40.
Owner P Baillie **Bred** J Jamgotchian **Trained** Great Habton, N Yorks

FOCUS
This looked seriously competitive for the class and there was no hanging about from the gates. There were five or so covered by less than a length after straightening for home as the finishers closed up. The form appears sound with the winner back to his best and the third and fourth setting the standard.

Scarlet Rocks(IRE) Official explanation: jockey said filly jumped awkwardly leaving stalls

5269 TOTESWINGER EBF MAIDEN STKS — 7f 2y

3:00 (3:02) (Class 4) 2-Y-O — **£5,336** (£1,588; £793; £396) **Stalls** Low

Form	Pos	Btn	Horse	Jockey	RPR	Comment	SP
22	1		**Na Zdorovie**[17] 4662 2-8-12 0	RobertWinston 2	80+	(B W Hills) *chsd ldrs: effrt under 2f out: rdn to ld 1f out: r.o gamely ins fnl f*	**6/5**[1]
4	2	*1 1/4*	**Fa'lz (IRE)**[16] 4726 2-9-3 0	RobertHavlin 9	82+	(Saeed Bin Suroor) *midfield: hdwy whn nt clr run over 2f out: swtchd rt over 1f out: r.o and hung lft ins fnl f: wnt 2nd towards fin but hld*	**8/1**
02	3	*1 1/4*	**Forest Edge (IRE)**[24] 4433 2-9-3 0	CathyGannon 1	79	(David Evans) *led: rdn and hdd 1f out: no ex towards fin*	**8/1**
	4	*3*	**Sir Trevor (IRE)** 2-9-3 0	RussKennemore 3	71+	(Tom Dascombe) *missed break: hld up: nt clr run over 2f out: hdwy over 1f out: styd on ins fnl f: nt rch ldrs: promising*	**16/1**
6	5	*2 1/4*	**Always Eager**[44] 3779 2-9-3 0	FrannyNorton 7	65	(Mark Johnston) *chsd ldr tl rdn over 1f out: wknd ins fnl f*	**14/1**
5	6	*shd*	**Amadeus Wolfe Tone (IRE)**[12] 4864 2-9-3 0	ShaneKelly 13	65+	(Jamie Osborne) *midfield: pushed along over 2f out: sme prog for press to chse ldrs over 1f out: no imp: one pce whn nt clr run briefly wl ins fnl f*	**33/1**
	7	*1/2*	**Sugarpine (IRE)** 2-8-12 0	TonyHamilton 11	60+	(Richard Fahey) *n.m.r s: sn swited lft: nt clr run and checked over 2f out: hdwy over 1f out: kpt on ins fnl f: no real imp on ldrs*	**33/1**
4	8	*1*	**Rapid Heat Lad (IRE)**[36] 4047 2-9-0 0	PaulPickard(3) 5	61	(Reg Hollinshead) *towards rr: hdwy 2f out: one pce and no imp fnl f*	**33/1**
0	9	*2 3/4*	**Cades Reef (IRE)**[28] 4330 2-9-3 0	LiamKeniry 6	54	(Andrew Balding) *racd keenly in midfield: pushed along and outpcd 2f out: nvr a danger*	**11/2**[2]
53	10	*1 1/4*	**Finbar**[69] 2953 2-9-3 0	FrederikTylicki 8	50	(James Given) *chsd ldrs tl rdn and wknd over 1f out*	**15/2**[3]
	11	*11*	**No Plan B (IRE)** 2-8-12 0	MartinLane 10	17+	(Noel Quinlan) *rrd s: completely missed break: nvr gng wl and a bhd*	**25/1**
50	12	*hd*	**Gabrial's Princess (IRE)**[35] 4080 2-8-12 0	TomEaves 14	16	(Bryan Smart) *midfield on outer: rdn and wknd 2f out*	**33/1**
	13	*9*	**Lord Franklin** 2-9-3 0	AndrewMullen 4	—	(Eric Alston) *chsd ldrs tl pushed along and n.m.r briefly over 2f out: sn wknd*	**66/1**
	14	*4*	**King Of Paradise (IRE)** 2-9-0 0	MichaelO'Connell(3) 12	—	(Eric Alston) *missed break: swtchd lft s: a bhd*	**66/1**

1m 25.63s (-0.87) **Going Correction** -0.025s/f (Good) — **14** Ran SP% **126.0**
Speed ratings (Par 96): **103,101,100,96,94 94,93,92,89,87 75,74,64,60**
CSF £11.29 TOTE £1.90: £1.10, £3.40, £2.30; EX 10.50.
Owner Mrs Mette Campbell-Andenaes **Bred** P M Cunningham **Trained** Lambourn, Berks
■ A winner for trainer Barry Hills with his final runner at one of his favourite tracks.

FOCUS
A fair juvenile maiden, rated around the winner and third.

NOTEBOOK
Na Zdorovie was bidding to enhance her stable's outstanding record in the race, and she duly justified strong support to ensure her departing trainer went out on a high, at one of his favourite racecourses. She had finished runner-up on both her previous outings and had a cracking draw in this bid to go one better, but much depended on her jumping out sufficiently on this tight track as she had blown the start at Kempton 17 days earlier. She wasn't great on that front, but Robert Winston galvanised her to race handily and that ultimately won her the day. She showed a nice attitude in the home straight and is clearly useful, but did have a pretty hard race. Her Group 1 entry looks to be shooting at the stars (op 11-10 tchd 10-11, 5-4 in places)
Fa'lz(IRE) ◆ proved disappointing on his debut at Yarmouth earlier this month, but there was a chance quicker ground would see him in a much better light and he turned in a massively improved effort. He travelled best of all just off the leaders, but proved too green to do himself full justice when asked to pick up the winner. He ought to learn again for the experience and prove very hard to beat on his next assignment. (op 7-1)
Forest Edge(IRE), from the plum draw, set out to make all and only gave way to the winner late on. Such tactics just found out his stamina back up in trip, but he has improved with each of his three outings now and rate the level. Nurseries are also now an option for him.
Sir Trevor(IRE) ◆ was the big eye-catcher. He was well drawn, but considering he got [illegible] after falling out of the gates shows what sort of engine he possesses, and he looks a sure-fire winner in the coming weeks. (op 14-1)
Always Eager Official explanation: jockey said colt hung right
Cades Reef(IRE), well backed, shaped with ability in a good Newmarket maiden and seemed sure to improve for that experience. He looked to find things happening too quickly around here, however, and will most probably leave this behind when getting back on a galloping track. (op 16-1 tchd 20-1)
Finbar was expected to relish this step up a furlong and shaped well through the first half, but ultimately failed to see it out. Perhaps this return from a 69-day break was needed, and his trainer does believe he is better with more cut. He too is now eligible for nurseries. (op 6-1)

5270 TOTEQUADPOT EBF COMBERMERE FILLIES' CONDITIONS STKS — 6f 18y

3:35 (3:39) (Class 2) 2-Y-O — **£11,026** (£3,300; £1,650; £826; £411) **Stalls** Low

Form	Pos	Btn	Horse	Jockey	RPR	Comment	SP
1333	1		**My Lucky Liz (IRE)**[21] 4551 2-9-1 75	MartinLane 2	86	(David Simcock) *towards rr: rdn and hdwy over 1f out: c through gap to chal ins fnl f: r.o to ld towards fin*	**13/2**[3]
1	2	*hd*	**Ladys First**[42] 3878 2-9-3 0	TonyHamilton 4	87+	(Richard Fahey) *midfield: sn pushed along: rdn and hdwy ent fnl f: r.o towards fin: jst hld*	**7/4**[1]
013	3	*1*	**Hidden Passion (USA)**[15] 4757 2-9-1 82	(t) ShaneKelly 8	82	(Brian Meehan) *chsd ldrs: rdn over 1f out: chalng ins fnl f: nt qckn cl home*	**8/1**
6242	4	*hd*	**Luv U Forever**[16] 4843 2-9-1 95	FrannyNorton 9	81	(Jo Hughes) *bustled along to ld: sn edgd over 2 ins rail: rdn over 1f out: hdd and hld towards fin*	**9/4**[2]
3104	5	*1*	**Bubbly Ballerina**[43] 3808 2-8-12 84	RobertWinston 5	75	(Alan Bailey) *snatched up whn n.m.r after 100yds: chsd ldr: rdn over 1f out: chalng ins fnl f: squeezed out fnl 75yds: one pce cl home*	**8/1**
3030	6	*1 1/2*	**Redair (IRE)**[21] 4551 2-9-1 76	CathyGannon 1	76	(David Evans) *restless in stalls: chsd ldrs: rdn over 1f out: chalng ins fnl f: n.m.r and hmpd fnl 100yds: sn lost pl and nt rcvr*	**16/1**
3002	7	*6*	**Middleton Flyer (IRE)**[20] 4572 2-8-12 72	PhillipMakin 7	53	(David Evans) *a bhd: outpcd over 1f out: nvr on terms*	**25/1**
06	8	*3 1/2*	**Skyeron**[11] 4883 2-8-12 0	MickyFenton 6	42	(Mark Brisbourne) *s.i.s: a bhd: lost tch over 1f out*	**100/1**

1m 13.27s (-0.53) **Going Correction** -0.025s/f (Good) — **8** Ran SP% **113.4**
Speed ratings (Par 97): **102,101,100,100,98 96,88,84**
toteswingers:1&2:£4.40, 2&3:£3.50, 1&3:£8.20 CSF £18.00 TOTE £8.00: £1.90, £1.10, £2.50; EX 20.20.
Owner Ahmed Jaber **Bred** Rabbah Bloodstock Limited **Trained** Newmarket, Suffolk
■ Stewards' Enquiry : Franny Norton four-day ban: careless riding (Sep 4-7)

FOCUS
A good juvenile fillies' conditions sprint. It was run at a decent pace and, despite the first six being closely covered inside the final furlong as there was a blanket finish, the best fillies still filled the first two places. The placed horses set the level.

NOTEBOOK
My Lucky Liz(IRE) forged between runners nearing the business end under a peach of a ride and just did enough to score. She travelled sweetly in midfield off the solid early pace from her low draw, but didn't get the breaks until late on and her rider did very well aboard her. It was a clear personal-best and she obviously relished this turning track. (tchd 6-1)
Ladys First ◆ looked a potentially smart filly when winning on her debut at York last month and was unsurprisingly popular here. The worry was whether she would have the trackcraft to win at this course, conceding upwards of 3lb all round, and it was just that which prevented her from following up. She was never on the bridle due to the speed test, but gave her all off the home turn and has to rate unfortunate as she came markedly wider than the winner. She shouldn't be long in finding compensation and remains a decent prospect. (op 9-4 tchd 13-8)
Hidden Passion(USA) wasn't helped by her wide draw, but she got out early and held every chance. This was much better again from her back on turf. (op 6-1)
Luv U Forever was the pick at the weights according to official figures and had finished second on her debut at this venue three runs back. She pinged out to lead from her outside stall, setting strong fractions, and made a bold bid. While she's not simple to place now, she fully deserves another winning turn. (op 11-4 tchd 3-1)
Bubbly Ballerina, who disappointed here on her previous outing, set out to make all but was soon headed by the third. She too showed improved form, holding every chance, and looks handicapped about right on 84. (op 15-2)
Redair(IRE), third in the Lily Agnes back in May, posted a brave effort from the inside draw and only faded out of it near the finish after meeting trouble. However, 6f does look the absolute limit of her stamina. (op 14-1)

5271 TOTEPOOL CHESTER STKS (H'CAP) (LISTED RACE) — 1m 5f 89y

4:10 (4:10) (Class 1) (0-110,104) 3-Y-0+

£19,848 (£7,525; £3,766; £1,876; £941; £472) **Stalls** Low

Form	Pos	Btn	Horse	Jockey	RPR	Comment	SP
6241	1		**Berling (IRE)**[17] 4677 4-8-13 92	PhillipMakin 7	102	(John Dunlop) *midfield: hdwy over 2f out: r.o to ld ins fnl f: pushed out and in command towards fin*	**11/2**[3]
6310	2	*1 1/2*	**Tominator**[42] 3875 4-9-4 97	PaulPickard 13	105	(Reg Hollinshead) *hld up: hdwy on outer 3f out: led over 1f out: hdd ins fnl f: kpt on but hld after*	**7/1**
-620	3	*1 3/4*	**Theology**[42] 3875 4-9-11 104	ShaneKelly 5	109	(Jeremy Noseda) *hld up: nt clr run over 2f out: hdwy over 1f out: styd on to take 3rd wl ins fnl f: nt rch front 2*	**12/1**
4/61	4	*1 1/4*	**Ile De Re (FR)**[14] 4775 5-9-1 94	PJMcDonald 4	97+	(Ian Williams) *in tch: nt clr run 2f out: plld off rail over 1f out: styd on ins fnl f: nt gng pce of ldrs*	**5/1**[2]
5500	5	*1*	**Sabotage (UAE)**[21] 4532 5-9-10 103	RobertWinston 1	107+	(Saeed Bin Suroor) *n.m.r and hmpd after abt 100yds: midfield: swtchd rt u.p over 1f out: one pce ins fnl f*	**12/1**
1040	6	*hd*	**Sadler's Risk (IRE)**[24] 4426 3-8-7 97	FrederikTylicki 10	98	(Mark Johnston) *led: rdn and hdd over 1f out: no ex ins fnl f*	**12/1**
1135	7	*nk*	**Eternal Heart (IRE)**[42] 3875 3-8-5 95	FrannyNorton 6	98+	(Mark Johnston) *trckd ldrs: pushed along over 4f out: outpcd by ldrs over 1f out: keeping on same pce whn n.m.r fnl 75yds: eased*	**3/1**[1]
0200	8	*2 1/2*	**High Office**[42] 3875 5-8-12 91	TonyHamilton 8	88	(Richard Fahey) *trckd ldrs: rdn over 1f out: wknd ins fnl f*	**16/1**
100-	9	*1*	**Precision Break (USA)**[288] 7339 6-9-5 98	MartinLane 3	94	(David Simcock) *n.m.r and hmpd after abt 100yds: in rr: rdn over 1f out: nvr on terms*	**14/1**
-446	10	*10*	**Roxy Flyer (IRE)**[23] 4470 4-9-7 100	JimmyQuinn 12	81	(Amanda Perrett) *in tch: pushed along over 4f out: wknd over 2f out*	**11/2**[3]
3/0-	11	*6*	**Almail (USA)**[307] 6974 5-9-11 104	StephenCraine 2	76	(Jamie Osborne) *a bhd*	**40/1**
060	12	*19*	**Absolute Heretic (AUS)**[25] 4410 5-9-1 94	MickyFenton 14	37	(Tom Tate) *prom: w ldr 6f out: wkng whn n.m.r and hmpd over 2f out*	**50/1**

2m 48.77s (-4.03) **Going Correction** -0.025s/f (Good)
WFA 3 from 4yo+ 11lb — **12** Ran SP% **125.0**
Speed ratings (Par 111): **111,110,109,108,107 107,107,105,105,99 95,83**
toteswingers:1&2:£4.40, 2&3:£3.50, 1&3:£8.20 CSF £46.48 CT £459.55 TOTE £5.40: £2.00, £2.20, £4.00; EX 56.90.
Owner Benny Andersson **Bred** Ballylinch Stud **Trained** Arundel, W Sussex
■ Stewards' Enquiry : Franny Norton four-day ban: careless riding (Sep 8,9,11,12)

FOCUS
A cracking staying handicap and it was run at sound gallop and proved a proper test. The first pair dominated inside the final furlong and the form is solid, with the third and fourth close to their marks.

NOTEBOOK
Berling(IRE) ◆ is finally now delivering on the promise he showed at three, and he won this with something to spare. He has taken time to find his form this year, but warmed up for this with a comfortable success at Pontefract 17 days earlier, which is a track not dissimilar to Chester (in that it has several turns and a short straight). He was upped just 2lb for that due to his narrow winning margin, but he was value for a lot further and so it was surprising he proved so easy to back here. He was sensibly ridden and finding a bit of trouble rounding the home turn was likely in his favour as it ultimately delayed his challenge in the home straight. A tight, turning track is evidently right up his street, and it's a good bet that he has more to offer as a stayer despite a likely rise. Indeed, it wouldn't be at all surprising to see him now aimed at the Chester Cup back here next year. (tchd 7-1 in places)
Tominator ◆ was a strong ante-post fancy for the Ebor at York only to miss the cut, and this would have been Plan B for him. He ran a blinder from his wide draw, over a test sharp enough for him and on ground quick enough for his liking. He will go up again for this, but that will help his chances of making another valuable handicap and he clearly still has a big prize in him this season. (op 13-2 tchd 6-1)
Theology moved well from off the pace and didn't quite get the breaks off the home turn, but it made no difference to the overall result. This was a return to the sort of form that saw him finish runner-up at York two runs back to Berling's talented stablemate Times Up. (op 14-1)
Ile De Re(FR) was up 3lb for winning at Ascot on his second outing for the yard a fortnight earlier and met support to follow up. He is better than the bare form as he met trouble from 2f out, but really this sharper test went against him. (op 11-2 tchd 6-1)
Sabotage(UAE) deserves some credit as he was hampered just after the start and it was a much more encouraging effort in defeat from him. The handicapper does look to have his measure, though. (op 14-1)
Eternal Heart(IRE), who finished in front of the runner-up at York last time out, had a decent draw and raced handily. It was clear from halfway he wasn't enjoying himself, however, and that was probably down the nature of this track. (tchd 7-2 in places)
Roxy Flyer(IRE) was very well backed, but she was beaten a long way out. (op 10-1)

Absolute Heretic(AUS) Official explanation: jockey said gelding had no more to give

5272 TOTEEXACTA H'CAP — 7f 122y

4:45 (4:46) (Class 2) 3-Y-0+

£27,265 (£8,164; £4,082; £2,041; £1,020; £512) **Stalls** Low

Form — RPR

2250 **1** **Belle Royale (IRE)**[14] [4790] 3-8-10 **90**.......................... JamesSullivan 11 — 99
(Mark Brisbourne) *midfield: rdn over 2f out: hdwy over 1f out: r.o to ld wl ins fnl f: wl on top at fin* **40/1**

1001 **2** *1 ¼* **Below Zero (IRE)**[6] [5086] 4-9-3 **91** 6ex.......................... FrederikTylicki 9 — 98
(Mark Johnston) *prom: chalng 2f out: led ins fnl f: sn hdd: hld towards fin* **9/1**

0120 **3** *½* **Crown Counsel (IRE)**[28] [4313] 3-8-13 **93**.................... RobertWinston 3 — 98
(Mark Johnston) *prom: chalng 2f out: led wl over 1f out: hdd ins fnl f: styd on same pce towards fin* **17/2**

0000 **4** *hd* **Advanced**[22] [4494] 8-9-1 **89**..............................(p) PhillipMakin 14 — 94
(Kevin Ryan) *trckd ldrs: effrt on outer over 1f out: styd on ins fnl f: nt quite gng pce to get there* **16/1**

0F20 **5** *½* **Mon Cadeaux**[21] [4534] 4-9-10 **98**.......................... LiamKeniry 4 — 102
(Andrew Balding) *trckd ldrs: effrt whn nt clr run ins fnl f: nt qckn* **6/1**[2]

5004 **6** *nk* **Lowther**[14] [4802] 6-9-10 **98**..............................(be) PhilipRobinson 2 — 101+
(Alan Bailey) *hld up: pushed along 4f out: nt clr run and swtchd rt over 1f out: styd on ins fnl f: no quite get to ldrs* **11/2**[1]

3030 **7** *¾* **Dubai Dynamo**[2] [5218] 6-9-7 **95**.......................... PJMcDonald 16 — 96+
(Ruth Carr) *in rr: rdn and swtchd rt over 1f out: r.o ins fnl f: gng on at fin* **10/1**

0600 **8** *1 ½* **Steed**[8] [5006] 4-8-8 **82**..............................(b) TomEaves 1 — 80
(Richard Guest) *racd keenly in midfield: effrt over 1f out: n.m.r briefly ins fnl f: styd on same pce and no imp on ldrs* **50/1**

24-5 **9** *nse* **Bohemian Melody**[161] [844] 4-9-7 **95**.......................... JimmyQuinn 8 — 93
(Marco Botti) *racd keenly: trckd ldrs: rdn over 1f out: one pce fnl 100yds* **11/1**

4103 **10** *nk* **Viva Ronaldo (IRE)**[20] [4574] 5-8-13 **87**.......................... TonyHamilton 7 — 84
(Richard Fahey) *hld up: rdn over 1f out: kpt on ins fnl f: nvr able to chal* **6/1**[2]

0302 **11** *1 ¼* **My Kingdom (IRE)**[7] [5043] 5-8-7 **84**..............................(t) SeanLevey(3) 15 — 78
(Patrick Morris) *hld up: rdn over 1f out: nvr able to chal* **16/1**

0000 **12** *nk* **Kyllachy Star**[25] [4418] 5-9-4 **95**.......................... LeeTopliss(3) 10 — 88
(Richard Fahey) *hld up: rdn over 1f out: nvr able to get on terms* **16/1**

-000 **13** *nk* **Celtic Sultan (IRE)**[7] [5032] 7-8-11 **85**.......................... MickyFenton 5 — 77
(Tom Tate) *led: rdn and hdd wl over 1f out: wknd ins fnl f* **25/1**

0403 **14** *6* **Mr David (USA)**[14] [4802] 4-9-7 **95**.......................... ShaneKelly 6 — 72
(Jamie Osborne) *in rr: nvr on terms: eased whn wl btn ins fnl f* **8/1**[3]

1010 **15** *29* **Kingscroft (IRE)**[14] [4779] 3-8-12 **92**.......................... FrannyNorton 17 — —
(Mark Johnston) *had hd over side of stall and nt ready: completely missed break: a wl bhd* **16/1**

1m 31.66s (-2.14) **Going Correction** -0.025s/f (Good)
WFA 3 from 4yo+ 6lb — **15** Ran SP% **124.8**
Speed ratings (Par 109): **109,107,107,107,106 106,105,104,103,103 102,102,101,95,66**
toteswingers:1&2:£99.00, 2&3:£19.60, 1&3:£54.60 CSF £376.92 CT £3452.42 TOTE £43.90: £9.00, £3.80, £3.40; EX 635.20.
Owner Peter Mort **Bred** Dxb Bloodstock Ltd **Trained** Great Ness, Shropshire

FOCUS

An ultra-competitive handicap. It was run at a strong pace and unsurprisingly numerous horses got troubled passages. The form is best rated around the placed horses.

NOTEBOOK

Belle Royale(IRE) was under pressure from an early stage, but kept responding and she gamely forged to the front late on. She had looked to be battling with the handicapper of late and wasn't well drawn here, but this was easier than her latest outing in Listed company. It is also her favourite track and she has now won three times at this venue. A rise will probably scupper a follow-up bid, but this 3-y-o will always be entitled to respect around here. (op 33-1)

Below Zero(IRE) was penalised for his ready success on Polytrack at Dundalk six days earlier and he posted a most gutsy effort in defeat. His future mark will make life harder, but his attitude will continue to hold him in decent stead. (op 8-1)

Crown Counsel(IRE) is a stablemate of the runner-up and also helped to force the pace like that rival. He had scored on his only previous outing at this course and it obviously suits him as this was right up there with his best form. (op 11-1 tchd 12-1)

Advanced was an eye-catcher despite being well held in the Totesport Mile at Goodwood last month, and he confirmed himself to be back in decent heart with a sound effort in defeat.

Mon Cadeaux ◆, whose stable has a cracking record in this event, was travelling by far the best turning for home towards the inside. His rider delayed his challenge, though, which saw him meet trouble and thus ended his chance. He should have finished closer. (op 7-1)

Lowther likes this venue, but he got too far back to land a serious blow and was another that met some trouble. (op 9-2)

Bohemian Melody Official explanation: jockey said gelding ran too freely

Mr David(USA) Official explanation: vet said gelding lost a front shoe and was lame

Kingscroft(IRE) ended any chance he may have held when he forfeited around ten lengths or so from the gates and, although things conspired against him, he now has a bit to prove. Official explanation: jockey said gelding had its head over adjacent stall and missed the break

5273 BET TOTEPOOL ON ALL UK RACING H'CAP — 1m 7f 195y

5:15 (5:21) (Class 4) (0-85,83) 3-Y-0+ **£5,822** (£1,732; £865; £432) **Stalls** Low

Form — RPR

5011 **1** **French Hollow**[36] [4043] 6-9-5 **74**.......................... FrederikTylicki 2 — 82
(Tim Fitzgerald) *hld up in tch: effrt over 1f out: led ins fnl f: styd on and won gng away* **9/2**[3]

3422 **2** *1 ¾* **Eshtyaaq**[28] [4348] 4-9-8 **77**.......................... CathyGannon 6 — 83
(David Evans) *trckd ldrs: rdn and chalng ent fnl f: nt qckn fnl 75yds* **11/4**[1]

1210 **3** *1 ¼* **Rosewin (IRE)**[28] [4348] 5-9-9 **83**.......................... JulieBurke(5) 4 — 88
(Ollie Pears) *racd keenly: hld up: pushed along 2f out: nt clr run over 1f out: styd on ins fnl 100yds: nvr able to chal front 2* **4/1**[2]

1232 **4** *nk* **Amazing King (IRE)**[20] [4577] 7-9-10 **79**.......................... RussKennemore 8 — 84+
(Philip Kirby) *trckd ldrs: nt clr run and pushed along over 1f out: nt clr run ins fnl f and swtchd lft: kpt on towards fin but no imp on ldrs* **6/1**

2326 **5** *1* **Hallstatt (IRE)**[43] [3828] 5-9-1 **70**..............................(t) PhillipMakin 10 — 73
(John Mackie) *hld up: rdn over 2f out: one pce and no imp ins fnl f* **11/1**

-304 **6** *½* **Callisto Moon**[23] [4463] 7-9-1 **70**..............................(p) RobertWinston 5 — 72
(Jo Hughes) *led: stmbld over 4f out: rdn over 2f out: hdd ins fnl f: wknd fnl 100yds* **10/1**

2512 **7** *¾* **Dark Dune (IRE)**[36] [4050] 3-8-3 **72**.......................... JamesSullivan 9 — 73
(Tim Easterby) *chsd ldr: rdn 2f out: chalng over 1f out: wknd fnl 100yds* **5/1**

3m 25.39s (-2.61) **Going Correction** -0.025s/f (Good)
WFA 3 from 4yo+ 14lb — **7** Ran SP% **113.2**
Speed ratings (Par 105): **105,104,103,103,102 102,102**
toteswingers:1&2:£3.80, 2&3:£2.90, 1&3:£3.20 CSF £16.93 CT £52.27 TOTE £4.30: £2.40, £2.20; EX 12.70.
Owner T J Fitzgerald **Bred** T J Fitzgerald **Trained** Norton, N Yorks

FOCUS

An open staying handicap. It was run at something of a stop-start pace, but the form still looks sound enough.

5274 TOTEPOOL A BETTER WAY TO BET H'CAP — 5f 110y

5:45 (5:50) (Class 5) (0-70,70) 3-Y-0 **£4,043** (£1,203; £601; £300) **Stalls** Low

Form — RPR

0253 **1** **Rutterkin (USA)**[16] [4715] 3-8-1 **55**.......................... JulieBurke(5) 1 — 66
(Alan Berry) *chsd ldrs: wnt 2nd over 1f out: r.o to ld wl ins fnl f: on top at fin* **9/2**[1]

6500 **2** *¾* **Tamareen (IRE)**[31] [4195] 3-9-7 **70**.......................... TonyHamilton 5 — 78
(Richard Fahey) *led: rdn over 1f out: hdd wl ins fnl f: hld cl home* **13/2**[2]

5343 **3** *2 ½* **Justbookie Dot Com (IRE)**[15] [4758] 3-8-10 **59**........(v) CathyGannon 11 — 58+
(David Evans) *hld up: rdn ent fnl f: r.o wl: tk 3rd cl home: gng on at fin* **10/1**

1064 **4** *1* **Cadmium Loch**[13] [4819] 3-8-8 **60**.......................... PaulPickard(3) 12 — 55
(Reg Hollinshead) *chsd ldrs: ev ch over 2f out: rdn over 1f out: styd on same pce ins fnl f* **10/1**

636 **5** *nk* **Chester Deelyte (IRE)**[14] [4786] 3-8-2 **51**..................(p) JamesSullivan 15 — 45
(Lisa Williamson) *midfield: effrt on outer to chse ldrs over 3f out: edgd lft u.p over 1f out: kpt on same pce ins fnl f* **28/1**

0314 **6** *6* **Boundless Spirit**[27] [4359] 3-9-4 **70**..................(t) MichaelO'Connell(3) 14 — 43
(David Nicholls) *midfield: outpcd over 1f out: no imp after* **8/1**[3]

5060 **7** *2 ¼* **Moremaloke**[11] [4895] 3-8-12 **64**..............................(p) LeeTopliss(3) 2 — 29
(Ian McInnes) *chsd ldrs: rdn over 2f out: wknd wl over 1f out* **14/1**

0431 **8** *2 ¾* **Nafa (IRE)**[14] [4786] 3-8-8 **57**.......................... TomEaves 7 — 12
(Michael Mullineaux) *hld up: outpcd 2f out: no imp after* **9/2**[1]

0035 **9** *nk* **Too Many Questions (IRE)**[10] [4924] 3-8-10 **59**.......................... ShaneKelly 9 — 13
(David Evans) *w ldr to 2f out: rdn and wknd over 1f out* **16/1**

0026 **10** *32* **Wolf Slayer**[11] [4896] 3-9-2 **65**.......................... RussKennemore 8 — —
(Tom Dascombe) *in rr: bdly hmpd jst over 2f out: nt rcvr: t.o* **12/1**

4555 **U** **Beautiful Day**[14] [4786] 3-8-10 **59** ow1..............................(b) PhillipMakin 4 — —
(Kevin Ryan) *racd keenly: n.m.r whn bdly hmpd and uns rdr jst over 2f out* **9/2**[1]

65.91 secs (-0.29) **Going Correction** -0.025s/f (Good) — **11** Ran SP% **120.9**
Speed ratings (Par 100): **100,99,95,94,93 85,82,79,78,36** —
toteswingers:1&2:£6.90, 2&3:£10.60, 1&3:£7.20 CSF £34.39 CT £289.33 TOTE £6.50: £2.20, £2.80, £3.50; EX 44.40.
Owner J W Barrett **Bred** Stonerside Stable **Trained** Cockerham, Lancs

FOCUS

A tight sprint handicap, run at a strong pace. It proved a very rough race, but the first pair came clear and the form makes some sense.

T/Plt: £53.70 to a £1 stake. Pool of £74,078.48 - 1005.53 winning units. T/Qpdt: £20.80 to a £1 stake. Pool of £2,942.37 - 104.24 winning units. DO

5237 SANDOWN (R-H)

Saturday, August 20

OFFICIAL GOING: Good to soft changing to soft after race 1 (2.15)

Round course at innermost configuration and distances as advertised. Sprint track at full width.

Wind: virtually nil Weather: light rain

5275 VARIETY CLUB STKS (H'CAP) — 1m 2f 7y

2:15 (2:15) (Class 2) 3-Y-0+

£27,390 (£8,201; £4,100; £2,050; £1,025; £514) **Stalls** Low

Form — RPR

4-55 **1** **Fallen Idol**[14] [4789] 4-9-7 **103**.......................... MartinDwyer 6 — 113
(John Gosden) *hld up in tch in rr: hdwy wl over 3f out: n.m.r over 2f out: rdn to chse clr ldr wl over 1f out: led jst ins fnl f: edgd rt u.p: kpt on wl* **15/2**

0114 **2** *½* **Beaumont's Party (IRE)**[78] [2681] 4-8-9 **91**.................... JimmyFortune 7 — 100
(Andrew Balding) *t.k.h: hld up in tch in midfield: hdwy and sltly hmpd over 2f out: chsd ldrs and drvn over 1f out: ev ch and carried rt ins fnl f: kpt on but unable qck fnl 100yds* **11/1**

6322 **3** *2* **Licence To Till (USA)**[10] [4901] 4-7-13 **81**................ AdrianMcCarthy 10 — 86
(Mark Johnston) *led for 1f: chsd ldr after: swtchd rt 3f out: led over 2f out: 3 l clr and rdn over 1f out: hdd jst ins fnl f: plugged on same pce after* **14/1**

2242 **4** *½* **Ramona Chase**[16] [4724] 6-7-13 **81** ow1........................(t) AndreaAtzeni 15 — 85
(Michael Attwater) *in tch in midfield: lost pl and dropped to last 4f out: hdwy u.p and swtchd rt over 1f out: wnt 4th 1f out: kpt on steadily but nvr looked like rching ldrs* **25/1**

1022 **5** *6* **Chain Lightning**[23] [4467] 3-8-7 **97**.......................... RichardMullen 4 — 89
(Richard Hannon) *hld up towards rr: swtchd rt and effrt 3f out: drvn and no prog 2f out: wknd over 1f out* **4/1**[2]

0602 **6** *nk* **Circumvent**[14] [4774] 4-9-0 **96**..............................(b[1]) AdamKirby 3 — 87
(Paul Cole) *led after 1f tl hdd and rdn over 2f out: wknd wl over 1f out* **12/1**

0132 **7** *1 ¼* **Arch Fire (USA)**[24] [4426] 3-8-0 **93** ow1.....................(v) LouisBeuzelin(3) 1 — 82
(Sir Michael Stoute) *sn niggled along in midfield: drvn and unable qck wl over 2f out: wknd wl over 1f out* **7/2**[1]

0242 **8** *1* **Malthouse (GER)**[37] [4015] 3-8-9 **99**.......................... NeilCallan 8 — 86
(Mark Johnston) *chsd ldrs: rdn to chse clr ldr briefly 2f out: lost 2nd wl over 1f out and sn wknd* **5/1**[3]

-060 **9** *hd* **Emerald Wilderness (IRE)**[21] [4553] 7-7-11 **82**......(p) KieranO'Neill(3) 14 — 69
(Robert Cowell) *t.k.h: hld up in tch towards rr: rdn and no hdwy over 2f out: sn wknd* **28/1**

0614 **10** *1* **Rock The Stars (IRE)**[16] [4724] 4-7-12 **83** oh3 ow3.... SophieDoyle(3) 11 — 68
(J W Hills) *chsd ldrs tl lost pl qckly jst over 3f out: wknd and n.d fnl 2f* **25/1**

3230 **11** *shd* **Cai Shen (IRE)**[22] [4494] 3-9-0 **104**.......................... PatDobbs 13 — 88
(Richard Hannon) *in tch in midfield: nt clr run and shuffled bk to last over 3f out: n.d after* **17/2**

2m 11.16s (0.66) **Going Correction** +0.30s/f (Good)
WFA 3 from 4yo+ 8lb — **11** Ran SP% **115.0**
Speed ratings (Par 109): **109,108,107,106,101 101,100,99,99,98 98**
CSF £82.78 CT £1127.84 TOTE £8.50: £2.90, £3.10, £3.30; EX 106.20 Trifecta £636.30.
Owner Normandie Stud Ltd **Bred** Normandie Stud Ltd **Trained** Newmarket, Suffolk
■ Stewards' Enquiry : Martin Dwyer 1st incident,caution: careless riding; 2nd, two-day ban: careless riding (Sep 4-5)

FOCUS
Although the ground had dried out during the morning, the rain started an hour before racing and the going was changed to good to soft and there was a raft of non-runners during the afternoon. This was a high-class handicap which was weakened by the withdrawals, including last year's winner Forte Dei Marmi. The pace was sound enough and the field raced stands' side in the straight.

NOTEBOOK
Fallen Idol gained two of his three wins - both his previous turf successes - on this track and took his score here to 3-3. He had been held in Group and Listed company since his last success but was down in grade and, being by Pivotal, handled the soft ground. He came through with the runner-up to collar the leader and the pair had a real battle, which he was always just winning. He had to survive a stewards' inquiry but had done enough to ensure the result would not be changed. (tchd 8-1)
Beaumont's Party(IRE) has progressed again this season and, although all his wins have been on a sound surface, he handles soft and ran well again here. He is, however, 10lb above his last winning mark and handicapper may have him. (op 9-1)
Licence To Till(USA) is a generally consistent performer at around this trip, but he had been below par on both previous starts on this track. Never far away, he went on over 2f out and looked to have opened up a winning lead up the stands' rail. However, he started to tire entering the last furlong and was brushed aside by the principals racing more towards the centre. (op 12-1)
Ramona Chase is an Epsom regular, but he ran well here last time. Stepping up in grade, he was being pushed along in rear at halfway but stayed on past beaten rivals in the straight. (op 28-1 tchd 33-1)
Chain Lightning handles most ground and was 1-2 over C&D. However, he had gone up 6lb for finishing second on previous two starts and was 12lb above last winning mark. He was never going that well and is another who could be in the handicapper's grip.
Circumvent was rated 12lb higher at around this time last year but had dropped in the weights and put up a better effort off this mark last time. With blinkers replacing cheekpieces, he probably ran too free in front and was in trouble well over 2f out.
Arch Fire(USA), a lightly raced 3-y-o whose sole success was over C&D on similar ground, had gone up 5lb for two decent efforts since and was dropping back in trip. He appeared to be close enough if good enough in the straight but faded. (op 5-1)
Malthouse(GER) is ideally suited by faster and he dropped away having been in the firing line early in the straight. (tchd 9-2)
Cai Shen(IRE) was a progressive sort late last summer when his winning run began at the corresponding meeting, and had been running well in similar company of late. However, he raced on the outside of the field and lost a good pitch round the home bend before being short of room near the stands' rail about 3f from home, which ended his chance. (op 8-1 tchd 9-1)

5276 SUNSHINE COACH SOLARIO STKS (GROUP 3) — 7f 16y
2:45 (2:49) (Class 1) 2-Y-O — **£19,848** (£7,525; £3,766; £1,876) **Stalls** Low

Form — RPR
011 **1** — **Talwar (IRE)**[28] [4311] 2-9-0 101 .... JimmyFortune 2 — 107+
(Jeremy Noseda) *mde all: gng best ent fnl 2f: rdn and wnt clr over 1f out: styd on wl: comf* **9/4**[2]
0234 **2** *5* **Silverheels (IRE)**[22] [4495] 2-9-0 103 .... NeilCallan 1 — 94
(Paul Cole) *t.k.h: chsd wnr tl over 4f out: drvn 2f out: chsd clr wnr again jst ins fnl f: no imp and edgd lft after* **9/2**
1 **3** *½* **Eastern Sun (IRE)**[72] [2837] 2-9-0 0 .... MartinDwyer 3 — 93
(John Gosden) *hld up in tch in last: rdn 3f out: outpcd and btn over 1f out: kpt on to go 3rd fnl 100yds: nvr threatened wnr* **4/1**[3]
1021 **4** *3 ¼* **Trumpet Major (IRE)**[9] [4964] 2-9-0 106 .... PatDobbs 4 — 85
(Richard Hannon) *chsd ldrs: wnt 2nd over 4f out: rdn and unable qck ent fnl 2f: btn ent fnl f: wknd and dropped to last fnl 100yds* **6/4**[1]

1m 33.27s (3.77) **Going Correction** +0.55s/f (Yiel) — **4** Ran SP% **109.0**
Speed ratings (Par 104): **100,94,93,90**
CSF £11.57 TOTE £2.90; EX 10.70.
Owner Vimal Khosla **Bred** Philip And Mrs Jane Myerscough **Trained** Newmarket, Suffolk

FOCUS
A well-established juvenile Group 3 whose best recent winner was the subsequent Queen Elizabeth II Stakes and Breeders' Cup Classic hero Raven's Pass. Only a small field for this but three of the four were last-time-out winners and the other came from the Richmond Stakes, a race which is working out well. This was run in heavy rain and they raced on the far side in the straight.

NOTEBOOK
Talwar(IRE) ◆ had bolted up in a maiden over C&D on his second start before getting the better of today's favourite narrowly in a Listed race at Ascot on easy ground. He made the running here and, when his rider asked him around 2f out, stretched clear for another emphatic victory. He has plenty of big-race entries and looks worthy of taking his chance in one or more of them. (op 2-1 tchd 5-2)
Silverheels(IRE) looked a decent yardstick having been in the frame in Group races on his two previous starts. Being by Verglas, he would have been expected to like the softening ground but, after chasing the leader throughout, could not pick up when that rival went for home. (op 5-1)
Eastern Sun(IRE), a half-brother to plenty of winners, including Group 2 scorer Allied Powers, had beaten a subsequent victor on his debut on fast ground. Held up at the back, he never looked happy on the rain-softened ground but kept plugging away to the line. He will be seen to better effect back on a sound surface if this relatively hard race does not have negative consequences. (op 3-1)
Trumpet Major(IRE) had been touched off by today's winner in a Listed race at Ascot but had then bolted up on fast ground in a conditions event. He had his chance in the straight, but faded and clearly was another unsuited by the conditions. (op 2-1)

5277 DE VERE VENUES ATALANTA STKS (LISTED RACE) (F&M) — 1m 14y
3:20 (3:20) (Class 1) 3-Y-O+
£17,013 (£6,450; £3,228; £1,608; £807; £405) **Stalls** Low

Form — RPR
6-10 **1** **Theyskens' Theory (USA)**[64] [3106] 3-8-12 108 .... DavyBonilla 8 — 112
(Brian Meehan) *hld up towards rr: pushed along and hdwy over 3f out: rdn to chse ldr 2f out: chal over 1f out: led jst ins fnl f: edgd rt u.p towards fin: kpt on gamely: all out* **7/1**[3]
/10- **2** *½* **Modeyra**[287] [7349] 4-9-0 108 .... IanMongan 10 — 108
(Saeed Bin Suroor) *chsd ldrs: clsd and led over 2f out: sn rdn: hdd jst ins fnl f: kpt on gamely but a jst hld* **6/1**[1]
411- **3** *½* **Brevity (USA)**[352] [5693] 3-8-8 105 .... MartinDwyer 7 — 106
(Brian Meehan) *hld up in tch: hdwy over 2f out: rdn to chse ldrs over 1f out: styd on wl fnl f: nt quite rch ldng pair* **14/1**
5-12 **4** *½* **Lay Time**[21] [4550] 3-8-9 87 ow1 .... JimmyFortune 6 — 106
(Andrew Balding) *in tch in midfield: swtchd lft and rdn jst over 2f out: swtchd rt 1f out: styd on wl fnl 100yds: nt quite rch ldrs* **6/1**[1]
5332 **5** *1 ½* **Off Chance**[14] [4790] 5-9-0 99 .... DuranFentiman 11 — 102
(Tim Easterby) *taken down early and ponied to s: chsd ldrs: rdn and edgd lft jst over 2f out: styd on same pce ins fnl f* **12/1**
1-15 **6** *2 ¼* **Humdrum**[66] [3034] 3-8-8 90 .... PatDobbs 13 — 96
(Richard Hannon) *hld up in last trio: rdn and effrt jst over 2f out: no real imp fr over 1f out: kpt on but no threat to ldrs fnl f* **16/1**
2-50 **7** *3* **Strawberrydaiquiri**[147] [1000] 5-9-0 113 .... EddieCreighton 17 — 90
(Brian Meehan) *ponied to s: stdd and dropped in bhd after s: rdn and effrt wl over 2f out: no imp over 1f out: plugged on ins fnl f: nvr trbld ldrs* **13/2**[2]
-650 **8** *2* **Cochabamba (IRE)**[22] [4497] 3-8-8 98 .... JackMitchell 9 — 85
(Roger Teal) *led: rdn 3f out: hdd and drvn over 2f out: wknd qckly over 1f out* **33/1**
240- **9** *2* **Ragsah (IRE)**[295] [7204] 3-8-8 100 .... TonyCulhane 15 — 80
(Saeed Bin Suroor) *hld up in rr: stl plenty whn n.m.r wl over 2f out: sme modest late hdwy: n.d* **25/1**
3120 **10** *2* **Raihana (AUS)**[147] [1000] 5-9-0 113 .... PatCosgrave 5 — 76
(M F De Kock, South Africa) *t.k.h: hld up in tch in midfield: rdn wl over 2f out: wknd 2f out* **12/1**
-213 **11** *½* **Heavenly Dawn**[14] [4790] 4-9-0 99 .... RichardMullen 16 — 75
(Sir Michael Stoute) *in tch towards rr: rdn and no prog jst over 2f out: wl btn over 1f out* **7/1**[3]
2636 **12** *7* **Magic Eye (IRE)**[22] [4497] 6-9-0 102 .... AdamKirby 14 — 59
(Marco Botti) *a towards rr: rdn and wknd over 2f out: wl bhd and eased ins fnl f* **15/2**
2100 **13** *13* **Reem (AUS)**[14] [4802] 4-9-4 104 .... J-PGuillambert 12 — 33
(M F De Kock, South Africa) *racd keenly: w ldr tl 3f out: sn struggling and wknd over 2f out: wl bhd and virtually p.u ins fnl f* **20/1**

1m 45.67s (2.37) **Going Correction** +0.55s/f (Yiel)
WFA 3 from 4yo+ 6lb — **13** Ran SP% **118.2**
Speed ratings (Par 111): **110,109,109,108,107 104,101,99,97,95 95,88,75**
toteswingers:1&2:£9.00, 2&3:£24.10, 1&3:£26.60 CSF £46.90 TOTE £8.60: £3.20, £2.50, £5.00; EX 38.50 Trifecta £599.20.
Owner Andrew Rosen **Bred** Ar Enterprises Llc **Trained** Manton, Wilts
■ Stewards' Enquiry : Duran Fentiman one-day ban: careless riding (Sep 4)

FOCUS
A big field and a tricky looking contest for this Listed race.

NOTEBOOK
Theyskens' Theory(USA), a winner in Group and Listed company who handles cut in the ground, had finished well beaten in the Coronation Stakes but this was a more suitable level. Although not the choice of the stable jockey, she was the only ride at the meeting for Davy Bonilla and his trip from France proved worthwhile. She came through to challenge the runner-up inside the last 2f and proved strongest in the closing stages. She could have a successful autumn given ease in the ground. (tchd 15-2)
Modeyra ◆, a lightly raced filly who beat subsequent Group winners Gertrude Bell and Timepiece on her first two starts, had not been seen since November. She stays further than this and was ridden prominently but was a little keen early and ended up going to the front over 2f out. This left her vulnerable to a late challenge and, although she tried hard, could not hold off the winner. She will need time to get over this but has a good race in her. (op 11-2 tchd 13-2)
Brevity(USA) ◆, a useful juvenile at 6f on a sound surface when she was a Listed winner, was having her first start for nearly a year, was up in trip and the soft ground was a question mark. However, she was the stable first string on jockey bookings and she came through to chase the leaders entering the final furlong but could not reel them in. She should come on a fair amount for the outing. (op 12-1)
Lay Time is lightly raced but had won on easy ground and was progressing. Stepping up in trip and grade but with a tough task on official ratings, she made ground to chase the leaders 2f out and stayed on steadily. She should not be long in gaining valuable black type on this evidence. (op 7-1)
Off Chance is a regular performer at this trip in this grade and she ran another honest race having never been far away. She is probably the benchmark for the form. (op 11-1)
Humdrum handles easy ground and had put up a fair effort in the Sandringham Handicap at Royal Ascot. She had a tough task on official ratings in this company but put up a decent effort, if never getting into serious contention. (op 18-1)
Strawberrydaiquiri was trying to repeat her 2009 success on her first start for a new trainer. She stayed on steadily from the back, having been held up, and should be sharper for the outing. However, her two stable companions finished ahead of her in first and third. (tchd 7-1)
Cochabamba(IRE), runner-up in the Rockfel on easy ground and second to today's winner on soft going before that, had struggled this season on a sound surface. She made the early running but, after being headed over 2f out, gradually faded. (op 40-1)

5278 NEWCALLTELECOM.CO.UK H'CAP — 5f 6y
3:55 (3:56) (Class 3) (0-95,95) 3-Y-O+
£8,092 (£2,423; £1,211; [illegible]) **Stalls** Low

Form — RPR
3114 **1** **Ajjaadd (USA)**[15] [4742] 5-8-5 79 .... KieranO'Neill(3) 12 — 89
(Ted Powell) *chsd ldrs: shkn up to ld over 1f out: clr and drvn ins fnl f: coming bk to field cl home but a doing enough* **8/1**
6005 **2** *1* **Damika (IRE)**[19] [4609] 8-9-2 87 .... (p) MichaelStainton 2 — 94+
(Richard Whitaker) *sn bustled along in midfield: rdn and hdwy whn nt clr run and bdly hmpd over 1f out: swtchd rt and rallied 1f out: r.o wl and swtchd lft ins fnl f: wnt 2nd towards fin: unable to rch wnr* **13/2**[3]
0250 **3** *½* **Baby Strange**[21] [4531] 7-9-3 88 .... RobbieFitzpatrick 13 — 93
(Derek Shaw) *stdd s: hld up in rr: rdn along 1/2-way: hdwy whn nt clr run and sltly hmpd over 1f out: swtchd lft ent fnl f: r.o wl fnl 150yds: wnt 3rd towards fin* **14/1**
411 **4** *nk* **Living It Large (FR)**[30] [4239] 4-8-13 87 .... MartinHarley(3) 5 — 91
(Ed de Giles) *chsd ldr tl led over 2f out: hdd and rdn over 1f out: sn outpcd by wnr: kpt on same pce fnl f: lost 2 pls towards fin* **7/1**
0440 **5** *1* **Oil Strike**[19] [4609] 4-9-0 85 .... IanMongan 14 — 85+
(Peter Winkworth) *stdd and dropped in bhd after s: rdn and hdwy 1/2-way: wnt 4th over 1f out: kpt on same pce ins fnl f* **6/1**[2]
0352 **6** *2 ¼* **La Fortunata**[25] [4416] 4-8-12 83 .... TonyCulhane 1 — 75
(Mike Murphy) *taken down early: led tl over 2f out: sn rdn and unable qck: wknd ent fnl f* **5/1**[1]
2164 **7** *5* **Apace (IRE)**[44] [3778] 3-8-13 86 .... RichardMullen 4 — 60
(Sir Michael Stoute) *sn bustled and struggling to go pce towards rr: wknd 2f out* **10/1**
314- **8** *nse* **Drift And Dream**[343] [5967] 4-8-10 81 .... JackMitchell 3 — 55
(Chris Wall) *chsd ldrs: rdn and unable qck jst over 2f out: wknd over 1f out: fdd ins fnl f* **5/1**[1]
2143 **9** *1 ¼* **Alpha Delta Whisky**[38] [3985] 3-7-12 76 .... RyanPowell(5) 11 — 46+
(John Gallagher) *racd on outer: midfield: rdn and struggling 1/2-way: wknd wl over 1f out* **14/1**
1003 **10** *3* **Novellen Lad (IRE)**[12] [4859] 6-9-4 89 .... JamieMackay 6 — 48
(Willie Musson) *awkward leaving stalls: a towards rr: lost tch 1/2-way* **14/1**

63.42 secs (1.82) **Going Correction** +0.55s/f (Yiel)
WFA 3 from 4yo+ 2lb — **10** Ran SP% **113.7**
Speed ratings (Par 107): **107,105,104,104,102 98,90,90,88,84**
toteswingers:1&2:£12.50, 2&3:£15.70, 1&3:£19.40 CSF £57.61 CT £730.73 TOTE £8.70: £2.90, £2.70, £2.90; EX 64.80.
Owner Katy & Lol Pratt **Bred** Darley **Trained** Reigate, Surrey

FOCUS
The big field for this good sprint handicap was decimated by withdrawals. The time indicated the ground on the straight course was fairly soft.
NOTEBOOK
Ajjaadd(USA), a 5f specialist who came into this in pretty good form, had won on his only previous attempt on soft going. The withdrawals helped to offset the disadvantage of a high draw and he was able to track the pace before going to the front over a furlong out and the late finishers were unable to reel him in. His run might not be over yet. (op 10-1)
Damika(IRE) ◆ was the unlucky horse of the race. Having only his second-ever start at 5f and his first since early 2009, he was not surprisingly chased along and a little outpaced early. However, he started to pick up from halfway only to run into trouble on more than one occasion before getting a clear run. When he did get out it was too late to catch the winner. A horse that goes well with cut in the ground, he has been showing signs that he is returning to form and could pick up a decent handicap this autumn by way of compensation. Official explanation: jockey said gelding was denied a clear run (op 11-2 tchd 7-1)
Baby Strange was another who was a little unlucky as he missed the break and had to come from the back of the field. His last two wins have been over 6f at Doncaster and there might be a race at the St Leger meeting for him. (op 12-1)
Living It Large(FR), bidding for a hat-trick, took on the favourite for the lead and won that battle soon after halfway. However, those early efforts left him vulnerable to the late finishers and, after losing the lead to the winner, was run out of the placings late on. (op 15-2)
Oil Strike was dropping to the shortest trip he had run over since his racecourse debut. He was backed beforehand despite being drawn widest of all, but made progress from halfway to chase the leaders only to have no more to offer in the last furlong. (op 9-1 tchd 10-1)
La Fortunata was backed into favouritism after her good effort at Goodwood had been franked by the winner earlier in the week. However, there was a doubt with her about the ground and she was an uneasy favourite. Those concerns proved justified and she was taken on by the fourth early on and was in trouble soon after halfway. She can be given another chance on faster going. (op 4-1 tchd 7-2)
Drift And Dream, another who had gained her wins on a sound surface, has handled soft going in the past. Having her first run for 11 months, she travelled well behind the leaders but found little off the bridle and faded in the final furlong. (tchd 9-2)

5279 CHIEF BARKER'S H'CAP — 5f 6y
4:30 (4:30) (Class 5) (0-75,74) 3-Y-O — **£2,911** (£866; £432; £216) **Stalls** Low

Form				RPR
-313	**1**		**Pearl Blue (IRE)**[31] 4199 3-9-2 **69** .... JackMitchell 6 (Chris Wall) *in tch: hdwy to ld 2f out: sn rdn and qckND wl clr over 1f out: eased fnl 50yds: easily* **5/2**[2]	88
3111	**2**	7	**Dreams Of Glory**[22] 4486 3-8-5 **65** ow1 .... CharlesBishop(7) 2 (Ron Hodges) *led tl hdd and rdn 2f out: outpcd by wnr and wl btn over 1f out: kpt on to hold 2nd fnl f* **5/1**[3]	59
1-33	**3**	½	**Seeking Magic**[8] 5000 3-9-7 **74** .... AdamKirby 7 (Clive Cox) *taken down early: stdd and dropped in bhd after s: t.k.h: rdn and effrt 2f out: sn outpcd and no ch w wnr: 3rd and plugged on same pce fnl f* **15/8**[1]	66
1134	**4**	4	**Dorothy's Dancing (IRE)**[110] 1776 3-8-3 **59** .... KieranO'Neill(3) 1 (Gary Moore) *hld up in tch in last pair: effrt but outpcd whn bdly hmpd wl over 1f out: 4th and wl hld after* **12/1**	37
6233	**5**	3 ¼	**Yasmeena (USA)**[30] 4227 3-9-3 **70** .... DarryllHolland 4 (B W Hills) *taken down early: in tch: hdwy to join ldr after 2f: rdn ent fnl 2f: sn outpcd: btn and hung rt: 5th and wl btn over 1f out* **5/1**[3]	36
4400	**6**	12	**Pippa's Gift**[12] 4850 3-8-10 **63** .... MartinDwyer 3 (William Muir) *w ldr for 2f: sn lost pl and bhd: t.o 1f out* **14/1**	—

63.86 secs (2.26) **Going Correction** +0.55s/f (Yiel) — **6** Ran SP% **111.0**
Speed ratings (Par 100): **103,91,91,84,79 60**
toteswingers:1&2:£2.60, 2&3:£2.40, 1&3:£1.70 CSF £14.82 TOTE £4.40: £2.30, £1.90; EX 13.70.
Owner Archangels 2 **Bred** L Queally **Trained** Newmarket, Suffolk
FOCUS
Just a fair 3-y-o sprint handicap and the time was just 0.44secs slower than the preceding all-aged contest, although they did not appear to go that quickly early.
Yasmeena(USA) Official explanation: trainer said filly was unsuited by the soft ground

5280 FANTASIA CEILING FANS NURSERY — 7f 16y
5:05 (5:05) (Class 4) (0-85,85) 2-Y-O — **£4,528** (£1,347; £673; £336) **Stalls** Low

Form				RPR
0151	**1**		**Pride And Joy (IRE)**[12] 4867 2-9-3 **81** .... PatCosgrave 1 (Jamie Osborne) *stdd s: hld up in tch: hdwy to chse ldrs over 3f out: rdn to ld over 1f out: styd on strly and drew clr fnl 100yds* **10/3**[1]	86
01	**2**	3	**Hamble**[26] 4390 2-9-4 **85** .... AdamBeschizza(3) 12 (William Haggas) *chsd ldr: rdn to chal 2f out: chsd wnr and stl pressing jst ins fnl f: no ex and outpcd fnl 100yds: kpt on to hold 2nd* **9/2**[3]	83
21	**3**	nk	**Croquembouche (IRE)**[25] 4402 2-9-1 **79** .... RichardMullen 4 (Sir Michael Stoute) *chsd ldrs: rdn and pressed ldrs 2f out: kpt on same pce u.p ins fnl f* **5/1**	76
6405	**4**	1 ½	**Drummoyne (USA)**[25] 4414 2-8-6 **70** .... AndrewElliott 10 (Mark Johnston) *chsd ldrs: rdn and effrt 3f out: drvn to ld wl over 1f out: sn hdd: edgd rt and wknd ins fnl f* **20/1**	63
0212	**5**	½	**The Blue Banana (IRE)**[15] 4749 2-8-13 **77** .... MartinDwyer 7 (Brian Meehan) *hld up in tch: effrt and drvn ent fnl 2f: no threat to wnr but plugged on u.p fnl 100yds* **7/2**[2]	69
5255	**6**	nk	**Brimstone Hill (IRE)**[17] 4661 2-8-9 **73** .... DarryllHolland 11 (B W Hills) *racd wd: led and sn clr: rdn jst over 2f out: hdd wl over 1f out: btn ent fnl f: plugged on same pce after* **12/1**	64+
052	**7**	2	**Royal Academician (USA)**[17] 4655 2-8-10 **74** .... NeilCallan 9 (Gary Moore) *hld up in tch: rdn and effrt 2f out: drvn and no prog over 1f out: wl hld ins fnl f* **9/1**	60
102	**8**	8	**Norse Gold**[59] 3284 2-9-4 **82** .... DaneO'Neill 2 (David Elsworth) *stdd s: hld up in rr: rdn and no rspnse over 2f out: sn btn: eased wl ins fnl f* **9/1**	48

1m 34.28s (4.78) **Going Correction** +0.55s/f (Yiel) — **8** Ran SP% **112.6**
Speed ratings (Par 96): **94,90,90,88,87 87,85,76**
toteswingers:1&2:£4.70, 2&3:£4.10, 1&3:£5.90 CSF £17.99 CT £72.63 TOTE £4.00: £1.20, £2.00, £1.90; EX 26.10.
Owner Miss J Kask **Bred** R P Ryan **Trained** Upper Lambourn, Berks
FOCUS
A competitive-looking nursery on paper that became less so after four withdrawals. The time was just over a second slower than the earlier juvenile Group 3, although in this race they came to the stands' side in the straight.
NOTEBOOK
Pride And Joy(IRE) has gradually progressed since winning his maiden and was the only one really able to pick up off the bridle. He tries hard and that attitude will enable him to win more races. (op 7-2)
Hamble won well at Yarmouth last time, but he looked to have a stiff enough mark for this handicap debut. He had every chance, but could only keep on at the one speed and a return to faster will suit. (op 6-1)
Croquembouche(IRE) is bred to stay further than this, but his form so far has been on fast ground and he could not pick up on this surface. A return to further and possibly longer trips will be in his favour. He is related to winners on sand so might be of interest on synthetics. (op 4-1)
Drummoyne(USA) ran reasonably on this step up in trip but again looked less effective when there is cut in the ground. (op 14-1 tchd 12-1)
The Blue Banana(IRE) has handled soft ground in recent runs but was being pushed along on the home turn and was always struggling. This was his first try round a turn but the Veterinary Officer later reported that the gelding lost a right fore shoe. Official explanation: vet said gelding lost a right-fore shoe (op 4-1)
Brimstone Hill(IRE), whose rider went in search of better ground on the outside of the track soon after the start, made the running but was collared around 2f out and had nothing left. The trainer's representative reported that the colt was unsuited by the soft ground. Official explanation: trainer said colt was unsuited by the soft ground (op 9-1)
Royal Academician(USA) was held up and travelled well into the straight, but he did not pick up and probably did not handle the ground. (tchd 11-1)
Norse Gold was held up but probably did not handle the ground, as he finished tailed off. (tchd 11-1)

5281 VARIETY AT WORK H'CAP — 1m 2f 7y
5:35 (5:35) (Class 4) (0-80,82) 3-Y-O+ — **£5,175** (£1,540; £769; £384) **Stalls** Low

Form				RPR
-004	**1**		**Red Inca**[93] 2226 3-8-6 **66** .... MartinDwyer 5 (Brian Meehan) *chsd ldr: styd far side in st: rdn and pressing ldr over 1f out: led ins fnl f: styd on wl and drew clr fnl 100yds* **15/2**	79
2332	**2**	3	**Aerial Acclaim (IRE)**[12] 4861 3-9-8 **82** .... AdamKirby 1 (Clive Cox) *racd in midfield: c to stands' rail in st and chsd ldrs over 2f out: drvn over 1f out: kpt on same pce ins fnl f: wnt 2nd nr fin* **6/4**[1]	89
2063	**3**	nk	**Chain Of Events**[15] 4763 4-9-8 **74** .... DaneO'Neill 9 (Neil King) *led and racd wd: c to stands' rail in st: rdn ent fnl 2f: drvn and hdd ins fnl f: no ex and btn fnl 100yds: lost 2nd nr fin* **5/1**[3]	80
1133	**4**	5	**Hawaana (IRE)**[9] 4962 6-9-10 **79** .... DeclanCannon(3) 7 (Gay Kelleway) *chsd ldrs: styd far side in st: rdn and effrt over 2f out: wknd ent fnl f* **4/1**[2]	75
6-00	**5**	1 ½	**Starkat**[14] 4801 5-9-7 **73** .... AdrianMcCarthy 4 (George Margarson) *hld up in midfield: styd far side in st: rdn and effrt jst over 2f out: wknd over 1f out* **14/1**	66
50-0	**6**	1	**Strategic Mount**[42] 3867 8-9-12 **78** .... NeilCallan 11 (Paul Cole) *hld up in last trio: c to stands' rail in st: rdn and no hdwy over 2f out: sn wknd* **16/1**	69
2104	**7**	21	**Hip Hip Hooray**[16] 4725 5-8-12 **64** .... IanMongan 13 (Luke Dace) *hld up in last pair: styd far side in st: rdn over 2f out: wknd qckly wl over 1f out: eased ins fnl f: t.o* **10/1**	13
6000	**8**	13	**Fonterutoli (IRE)**[28] 4317 4-8-12 **64** .... (t) PatCosgrave 12 (Roger Ingram) *v.s.a: a in rr: c to stands' side in st: rdn and lost tch over 2f out: t.o and eased ins fnl f* **33/1**	—

2m 16.15s (5.65) **Going Correction** +0.55s/f (Yiel)
WFA 3 from 4yo+ 8lb — **8** Ran SP% **113.0**
Speed ratings (Par 105): **99,96,96,92,91 90,73,63**
toteswingers:1&2:£3.40, 2&3:£8.40, 1&3:£2.20 CSF £18.74 CT £61.90 TOTE £9.50: £2.40, £1.20, £1.80; EX 21.30.
Owner Favourites Racing **Bred** Colt Neck Stables, Llc **Trained** Manton, Wilts
■ Stewards' Enquiry : Adam Kirby two-day ban: used whip with excessive frequency (Sep 4,5)
FOCUS
A fair handicap but a depleted field and they split into two equal groups in the straight. The two 3-y-os filled the first two placings.
T/Plt: £635.70 to a £1 stake. Pool of £94,523.62 - 108.54 winning units. T/Qpdt: £44.40 to a £1 stake. Pool of £5,250.78 - 87.37 winning units. SP

5250 YORK (L-H)
Saturday, August 20
OFFICIAL GOING: Good (home straight 6.4; far side 6.4; centre 6.2; stands' side 6.2)
Rail on traditional racing line and distances as advertised.
Wind: moderate, half behind Weather: fine

5282 DEBENHAMS CITY OF YORK STKS (LISTED RACE) — 7f
2:00 (2:01) (Class 1) 3-Y-O+ — **£23,680** (£8,956; £4,476; £2,236) **Stalls** Low

Form				RPR
2455	**1**		**Doncaster Rover (USA)**[7] 5046 5-9-0 108 .... SilvestreDeSousa 8 (David Brown) *midfield: hdwy wl over 2f out: rdn to chse ldrs over 1f out: drvn to chal ins fnl f: led nr fin* **5/1**[1]	112
5010	**2**	hd	**Majestic Myles (IRE)**[25] 4412 3-9-0 104 .... PaulHanagan 6 (Richard Fahey) *trckd ldrs: hdwy and cl up over 2f out: rdn to ld ent fnl f: drvn and edgd rt last 100yds: hdd nr fin* **7/1**	114
0-60	**3**	1 ¼	**Lechevalier Choisi (IRE)**[41] 3892 3-8-9 103 .... (v[1]) EddieAhern 3 (James Bernard McCabe, Ire) *led: rdn along over 2f out: drvn over 1f out: hdd ent fnl f: kpt on* **33/1**	106
110-	**4**	1 ¼	**King Torus (IRE)**[321] 6610 3-8-9 114 .... RichardHughes 1 (Richard Hannon) *chsd ldrs: hdwy over 2f out: rdn over 1f out: drvn and kpt on same pce fnl f* **7/1**	103
132-	**5**	1	**Dafeef**[340] 6063 4-9-0 106 .... RichardHills 12 (William Haggas) *hld up in rr: hdwy wl over 2f out: rdn wl over 1f out: kpt on ins fnl f: nrst fin* **11/2**[2]	102
0201	**6**	1	**Across The Rhine (USA)**[35] 4116 5-9-8 109 .... PShanahan 11 (Tracey Collins, Ire) *prom on outer: wd st: chsd ldrs 3f out: rdn over 2f out: grad wknd* **16/1**	107
2304	**7**	nk	**Regal Parade**[35] 4092 7-9-0 110 .... AdrianNicholls 5 (David Nicholls) *hld up: hdwy over 2f out: rdn wl over 1f out: no imp* **5/1**[1]	99
0-35	**8**	1 ¼	**Dream Eater (IRE)**[107] 1821 6-9-0 116 .... (t) DavidProbert 2 (Andrew Balding) *chsd ldr: rdn along 2f out: ev ch tl drvn and wknd ent fnl f* **13/2**	95
-001	**9**	2 ½	**Yaa Wayl (IRE)**[51] 3548 4-9-0 110 .... (v) FrankieDettori 9 (Saeed Bin Suroor) *in tch: wd st to stands' rail: hdwy over 3f out: rdn over 2f out: sn wknd* **6/1**[3]	88
5-00	**10**	nk	**Rodrigo De Torres**[55] 3440 4-9-0 98 .... JimCrowley 13 (Mrs K Burke) *a towards rr* **66/1**	88
-000	**11**	13	**Himalya (IRE)**[84] 2502 5-9-0 105 .... SteveDrowne 10 (Stef Higgins) *hld up: a in rr* **25/1**	52

1m 23.56s (-1.74) **Going Correction** +0.05s/f (Good)
WFA 3 from 4yo+ 5lb — **11** Ran SP% **115.5**
Speed ratings (Par 111): **111,110,109,107,106 105,105,103,101,100 85**
toteswingers:1&2:£7.40, 1&3:£24.90, 2&3:£30.60 CSF £38.52 TOTE £6.30: £1.90, £2.90, £8.00; EX 41.50 Trifecta £1021.00 Part won. Pool: £1,379.80 - 0.10 winning units..
Owner P Holling I Raeburn S Halsall S Bolland **Bred** Coffeepot Stable **Trained** Averham Park, Notts

FOCUS

A good-quality Listed event and decent form for the grade. The winner looks the best guide to the form.

NOTEBOOK

Doncaster Rover(USA), although winless in the best part of a year coming into the race, he'd twice missed out narrowly at Group 3 level earlier in the season, and also run well in a Group 2 at Goodwood last month, so this hard-earned victory was no surprise, and certainly well deserved. (op 11-2)

Majestic Myles(IRE), behind the winner at Goodwood last time, briefly looked like reversing form when striking for home, but despite a valiant effort, was unable to hold on. He's equally effective at 6f-7f and looks well up to winning again at this level. (op 11-1)

Lechevalier Choisi(IRE) showed improved form when fourth in a 6f Listed race last time (wore first-time blinkers), and he took another step forward here in the first-time visor, showing up well for a long way before being outgunned by two superior horses.

King Torus(IRE) ◆, a dual Group 2 winner as a juvenile, was perhaps the most interesting runner on display and he ran a really encouraging race, travelling well and keeping on without being punished by Richard Hughes. He ought to come on and can make an impact at a similar level when getting his favoured sound surface. (op 11-2)

Dafeef, withdrawn from the Stewards' Cup due to fast ground, made a pleasing start for William Haggas, keeping on from the rear, and he's another who looks capable of scoring at this level. (op 5-1 tchd 6-1)

Across The Rhine(USA), winner of a Group 3 at the Curragh last time, was giving upwards of 8lb to all his rivals and unsurprisingly came up short. (op 20-1)

Regal Parade, who hasn't been at his best of late, was disappointing dropping to Listed level for the first time since winning at Chester in July 2009. (tchd 11-2)

Yaa Wayl(IRE) was kept wide in the straight and found this considerably tougher than the Newbury contest he'd won previously. (op 13-2)

5283 BETFRED MELROSE STKS (H'CAP) 1m 6f

2:30 (2:32) (Class 2) (0-105,102) 3-Y-O **£42,048** (£12,512; £6,253; £3,126) **Stalls** Low

Form RPR

3441 **1** **Parlour Games**[14] 4777 3-8-8 **89** .... FrankieDettori 12 104+
(Mahmood Al Zarooni) *hld up towards rr: hdwy over 4f out: swtchd rt and n.m.r 2f out: switrchd lft to inner and rdn to ld ent fnl f: sn edgd rt: drvn out* **9/1**[3]

2011 **2** 3/4 **Whiplash Willie**[24] 4426 3-9-2 **97** ....(v) DavidProbert 10 110
(Andrew Balding) *midfield: hdwy to trck ldrs 5f out: jnd ldrs 3f out gng wl: led 2f out: hdd and rdn 1 1/2f out: sn led again tl drvn and hdd ent fnl f: kpt on* **10/1**

0 **3** 2 1/4 **Apache (IRE)**[65] 3069 3-9-0 **98** .... JPO'Brien(3) 3 108+
(A P O'Brien, Ire) *hld up: hdwy 4f out: effrt and swtchd lft 2f out: rdn to ld briefly 1 1/2f out: sn hdd and drvn: one pce ins fnl f* **17/2**[2]

-613 **4** 1/2 **Ardlui (IRE)**[59] 3291 3-8-6 **87** .... FergusSweeney 16 96+
(Henry Candy) *hld up: hdwy over 4f out: chsd ldrs over 2f out: sn rdn and n.m.r wl over 1f out: drvn and kpt on fnl f* **10/1**

0641 **5** 5 **Wayward Glance**[15] 4753 3-7-13 **80** .... WMLordan 13 82
(Michael Bell) *led: rdn along over 3f out: hdd 2f out: sn drvn and grad wknd* **20/1**

3-15 **6** shd **Lyric Street (IRE)**[56] 3405 3-9-3 **98** .... KierenFallon 5 100
(Luca Cumani) *towards rr: hdwy 3f out: rdn 2f out: styd on appr fnl f: nrst fin* **17/2**[2]

2621 **7** 1 3/4 **Romeo Montague**[16] 4697 3-8-2 **83** ow3........(v) ChrisCatlin 18 83
(Ed Dunlop) *hld up: hdwy over 3f out: rdn along and n.m.r wl over 1f out: kpt on same pce* **40/1**

2131 **8** 1 1/4 **Cunning Act**[24] 4449 3-7-12 **84** .... NeilFarley(5) 6 82
(Jonathan Portman) *in rr: hdwy 3f out: rdn along 2f out: kpt on appr fnl f: nvr nr ldrs* **16/1**

2214 **9** 2 **Thubiaan (USA)**[14] 4777 3-8-4 **85** .... TadhgO'Shea 4 80
(William Haggas) *chsd ldrs: rdn along over 3f out: drvn and edgd lft over 2f out: grad wknd* **8/1**[1]

141 **10** 13 **Western Prize**[illegible] 3551 3-8-2 **83** .... [illegible] 11 60
(Ralph Beckett) *t.k.h early: prom: rdn along over 4f out: wknd whn n.m.r and hmpd over 2f out* **20/1**

6122 **11** 3 1/4 **Masaraat (FR)**[28] 4316 3-8-7 **88** .... RichardHills 15 60
(John Dunlop) *hld up: a towards rr* **16/1**

0303 **12** 1 1/4 **Waltz Darling (IRE)**[21] 4530 3-8-0 **81** .... PaulHanagan 7 52
(Richard Fahey) *in tch: rdn along over 5f out: sn wknd* **33/1**

-125 **13** 1 1/4 **Motivado**[35] 4108 3-8-7 **88** .... DavidAllan 19 57+
(Sir Mark Prescott Bt) *in rr: rdn along and sme hdwy on inner 3f out: hmpd over 2f out: n.d* **16/1**

-121 **14** 4 1/2 **Kinyras (IRE)**[23] 4473 3-8-7 **88** .... RichardHughes 1 50+
(Sir Michael Stoute) *blind removed late and lost many l s: a bhd* **12/1**

3 **15** nk **Admiral Of The Red (IRE)**[56] 3418 3-9-7 **102**........(p) CO'Donoghue 20 64
(A P O'Brien, Ire) *hdwy to chse ldr after 2f: rdn along over 3f out: wknd qckly wl over 2f* **33/1**

-030 **16** 6 **Pivotman**[14] 4777 3-8-6 **87** .... TedDurcan 2 41
(Amanda Perrett) *midfield on inner: effrt over 4f out: rdn along over 3f out: sn wknd* **28/1**

6214 **17** 1 3/4 **Communicator**[65] 3069 3-8-7 **88** .... HayleyTurner 9 39
(Michael Bell) *chsd ldrs: rdn along over 4f out: sn wknd* **17/2**[2]

1506 **18** 2 3/4 **Halifax (IRE)**[14] 4777 3-8-7 **88** ....(b1) EddieAhern 8 35
(Mark Johnston) *hld up: hdwy on outer 5f out: rdn along over 3f out: sn btn* **16/1**

1000 **19** 8 **The Bells O Peover**[24] 4426 3-7-12 **79** .... SilvestreDeSousa 14 15
(Mark Johnston) *chsd ldrs: rdn along 4f out: sn wknd* **40/1**

2m 59.68s (-0.52) **Going Correction** +0.125s/f (Good) **19** Ran SP% **125.8**

Speed ratings (Par 106): **106,105,104,104,101 101,100,99,98,90 88,88,87,84,84 81,80,78,74**

toteswingers:1&2:£11.00, 1&3:£17.60, 2&3:£8.50 CSF £89.51 CT £808.65 TOTE £10.70: £2.60, £2.00, £2.90; EX 60.60 Trifecta £588.00 Pool: £2,622.57 - 3.30 winning units..

Owner Godolphin **Bred** Darley **Trained** Newmarket, Suffolk

■ Stewards' Enquiry : J P O'Brien two-day ban: careless riding (Sep 4-5)

Tadhg O'Shea two-day ban: careless riding (Sep 4-5)

FOCUS

Traditionally a strong 3yo handicap and the latest running was absolutely no exception, a host of progressive types from well-respected stables lining up. The pace was fair and the time was 1.92sec quicker than the Ebor, although that race was hand timed. They stayed far side in the straight, yet four of the first five finishers were drawn in double figures. The form is rated on the positive side, with the first three all progressing and the fourth to the best view of his maiden win.

NOTEBOOK

Parlour Games initially didn't progress after winning over 1m3f on Polytrack on his reappearance (Brown Panther behind), but he came good in a quick time going 1m4f at the Shergar Cup meeting last time and improved significantly to defy a 3lb higher mark in this stronger contest. Clearly the step up in trip was in his favour and he benefited from more of a ground-saving trip than the runner-up. He looks the type to go on progressing now he's proven stamina is his forte, with even further likely to suit, and it wouldn't surprise if he makes a Cup horse one day - he's certainly bred to be smart considering he's out of triple Group 1 winner Petrushka. The Mallard Handicap at Doncaster's St Leger meeting will presumably be considered, but in the long run he's not sure to take in Meydan's staying series. Mahmood Al Zarooni doubts the horse will suited by the ground in Dubai, although he wasn't ruling out giving it a try. (op 10-1 tchd 8-1)

Whiplash Willie, who was on a hat-trick after wins at Salisbury and Glorious Goodwood, the latter off 6lb lower, produced a smart performance and another career best. It was no surprise he improved for the step up from 1m4f considering he's bred to make a strong stayer, and he deserves extra credit considering he raced wider than the winner, not getting much cover. However, without wishing to knock this likeable type, he's a bit quirky and didn't find as much as had looked likely after being last off the bridle. The suspicion is he was keeping a bit back for himself and there's more improvement in him if connections can maintain his interest - maybe different headgear will be tried. He's still in the St Leger and wouldn't be out of place if the race really cut up, but the Mallard is more realistic, and in the slightly longer term he's of interest for the Cesarewitch. Slightly easier ground should prove more favourable. (tchd 9-1)

Apache(IRE), absent since racing too keenly in King George V Stakes, is bred to stay well and ran a good race despite again refusing to settle, keeping on having moved easier than most. He needs to learn to relax if he's to fulfil his potential, but could be a smart stayer if doing so and he's another with a Cesarewitch entry. (op 11-1 tchd 8-1)

Ardlui(IRE) had been absent since finishing well behind Whiplash Willie and only just behind Kinyras over 1m4f at Salisbury in June, but he's bred for this longer trip. He ran to a decent level, especially as he was caught a bit wider than ideal for a lot of the way (like the runner-up), but he essentially ruined his chance by hanging left in the straight. His trainer was quoted beforehand as saying "the softer the better for him", and it seems this drying ground didn't suit. (tchd 11-1)

Wayward Glance, successful in a weak maiden last time, got a bit warm and gradually faded after making the running, but this was a good performance considering the time, as well as the early positions of the principals, suggests he set a decent pace.

Lyric Street(IRE) came here with strong form at up to 1m2f, but had been absent since June and this was a big ask, going up significantly in trip after his break. He ran a strange race, racing enthusiastically through the first half of the contest, but then coming off the bridle around the final bend and only going on close home. A St Leger entry suggests he's well thought of, however, and this run should sharpen him up. (op 8-1)

Romeo Montague, up 5lb for winning a much lesser race over 1m4f on soft at Brighton, ran well for a long way. He was a good fifth with a furlong to run, but then weakened quite rapidly, losing several lengths and a couple of places. There's little doubt he's capable of better, probably back over shorter. (op 33-1)

Thubiaan(USA) wasn't far behind Parlour Games at Ascot last time, but he was well held over this longer trip having got a bit warm. He didn't get the best of runs, but was not unlucky. (op 17-2 tchd 9-1 in a place)

Kinyras(IRE), up 6lb for winning a Glorious Goodwood handicap (ordinary form for grade) over 1m3f last time, can be excused this as he lost a good 5l or so at the stalls, his rider having difficulty removing the blindfold having not been helped by the horse ducking. Official explanation: jockey said, colt dropped its head as he tried to remove blindfold, lost his balance, and unable to remove it in first attempt and was very slowly away. (tchd 14-1)

Communicator had been absent since finishing fourth in the King George V Handicap and ran as though something was amiss. (op 9-1 tchd 8-1)

5284 WEATHERBYS INSURANCE LONSDALE CUP (BRITISH CHAMPIONS' SERIES) (GROUP 2) 2m 88y

3:05 (3:05) (Class 1) 3-Y-O+

£79,394 (£30,100; £15,064; £7,504; £3,766; £1,890) **Stalls** Low

Form RPR

3421 **1** **Opinion Poll (IRE)**[23] 4469 5-9-4 116........ FrankieDettori 8 120
(Mahmood Al Zarooni) *trckd ldrs: effrt 4f out: chal 2f out: carried rt and bmpd whn taking narrow ld jst ins fnl f: hrd rdn and edgd lft: forged to ld nr line* **3/1**[1]

0-16 **2** 3/4 **Duncan**[65] 3066 6-9-4 116........ EddieAhern 9 119
(John Gosden) *trckd ldrs: effrt over 3f out: ld over 2f out: edgd rt and hdd [illegible] nr fin* **4/1**[3]

-025 **3** 4 **Bergo (GER)**[23] 4469 8-9-1 109........ GeorgeBaker 2 111
(Gary Moore) *chsd ldrs: drvn 4f out: kpt on to take 3rd ins fnl f* **20/1**

-322 **4** 3 3/4 **Harris Tweed**[22] 4492 4-9-1 116........ LiamJones 3 107
(William Haggas) *led: qcknd over 5f out: hdd over 2f out: fdd appr fnl f* **7/2**[2]

2305 **5** 2 **Allied Powers (IRE)**[37] 4037 6-9-1 109........ PaulHanagan 1 104
(Michael Bell) *trckd ldrs: drvn over 3f out: kpt on one pce fnl 2f* **20/1**

20-2 **6** 3 **Elyaadi**[39] 3963 7-8-12 95........ KierenFallon 7 98
(John Queally, Ire) *hld up in last: drvn over 4f out: nvr nr ldrs* **22/1**

2103 **7** 1 **Blue Bajan (IRE)**[23] 4469 9-9-4 113........ DanielTudhope 5 103
(David O'Meara) *in rr-div: effrt 5f out: one pce fnl 2f* **8/1**

3115 **8** 10 **Highland Castle**[25] 4411 3-8-1 101........ NickyMackay 4 88
(David Elsworth) *t.k.h towards rr: effrt 4f out: wknd over 2f out* **12/1**

1140 **9** 5 **Dandino**[27] 4374 4-9-4 113........ TomQueally 10 85
(James Given) *hld up in rr: effrt over 4f out: wknd over 2f out* **9/1**

4110 **10** 2 3/4 **Chiberta King**[23] 4469 5-9-1 108........ RichardHughes 6 78
(Andrew Balding) *trckd ldrs: drvn over 3f out: lost pl over 2f out: eased towards fin* **16/1**

3m 32.48s (-2.02) **Going Correction** +0.125s/f (Good)

WFA 3 from 4yo+ 14lb **10** Ran SP% **115.8**

Speed ratings (Par 115): **110,109,107,105,104 103,102,97,95,93**

toteswingers:1&2:£3.40, 1&3:£10.50, 2&3:£13.70 CSF £14.35 TOTE £2.40: £1.10, £2.20, £6.10; EX 11.20 Trifecta £172.10 Pool: £8,458.34 - 36.36 winning units..

Owner Godolphin **Bred** Darley **Trained** Newmarket, Suffolk

■ Stewards' Enquiry : Frankie Dettori caution: careless riding.

FOCUS

This year's running looked well up to scratch, indeed it was more competitive than when Opion Poll won last season, but he's undoubtedly improved since, highlighted by his Ascot second to Fame And Glory and last-time-out Goodwood Cup success, and it was his superior stamina that saw him through, the bumping that took place between he and the runner-up not directly affecting the result. The winner is rated as having run a small personal best in a decent renewal.

NOTEBOOK

Opinion Poll(IRE) tracked the strong-travelling runner-up into the straight and, having initially taken a while hit top gear, the odds were heavily stacked in his favour once drawing alongside around 1f out. This was a fine effort considering the drying ground wouldn't necessarily have been in his favour, although there's little doubt he's more effective on a sound surface than he used to be. He now has the option of either the Champions Long Distance Cup at Ascot or Doncaster Cup next, a race he was only fourth in last year, before a possible return to Longchamp for the Prix Royal Oak, where he'll hold strong claims of improving on last season's third. (tchd 11-4)

Duncan, who made all in the Yorkshire Cup over 2f shorter here earlier in the season, was too keen and didn't get home in the Ascot Gold Cup, but he goes well fresh and looked all over the winner when cruising up to challenge over 2f out. It wasn't to be, however, this mentally frail sort perhaps lacking the determination of the winner, especially after receiving a bump, and ultimately he couldn't stay on as well. He's a very smart sort up to Group 2 level when things go his way. (op 9-2)

Bergo(GER), just over 2l behind Opinion Poll in the Goodwood Cup on his first start since March, kept grinding away and was rewarded with a place.

Harris Tweed had posted some smart efforts in defeat this season and looked interesting on this first try at 2m. However, having been allowed an uncontested lead and setting his own tempo, he was seen off fairly readily, apparently failing through lack of stamina. There's a suspicion he isn't quite up to Group 2 level. (op 4-1)

Allied Powers(IRE) ran about as well as could have been expected, keeping on without seriously threatening. He was twice a winner in France last year and may pick up another minor Group race sent back on his travels. (op 16-1)

Elyaadi, rated just 95, was runner-up in the Queen Alexandra earlier in the summer but found this much too competitive. (op 18-1)

Blue Bajan(IRE) had very little to find with the front two on separate pieces of form from this season, but was unable to back up his Goodwood Cup second. (op 15-2 tchd 7-1)

Highland Castle was very keen and didn't look up to competing in a race like this at such an early stage of his career. (op 16-1)

Dandino was hugely disappointing and is in danger of losing his way. He was beaten before stamina became an issue and is left with plenty to prove for the moment. (op 10-1)

Chiberta King Official explanation: jockey said gelding had no more to give

5285 BETFRED EBOR (HERITAGE H'CAP) 1m 6f

3:40 (3:42) (Class 2) 3-Y-O+

£130,725 (£39,144; £19,572; £9,786; £4,893; £2,457) **Stalls** Low

Form RPR

2350 **1** **Moyenne Corniche**[42] 3876 6-8-10 **99**............................ DaleSwift(3) 10 110
(Brian Ellison) *hld up in rr: hdwy 3f out: rdn to chse ldrs wl over 1f out: swtchd rt and drvn ent fnl f: styd on strly to ld last 100yds* **25/1**

5-21 **2** *1* **Tactician**[42] 3875 4-9-0 **103**............................ JPO'Brien(3) 20 113
(Michael Bell) *set stdy pce: sddle slipped sltly over 5f out: rdn along 3f out: hdd over 2f out: cl up and ev ch ent fnl f: drvn and kpt on wl towards fin* **9/1**

/103 **3** *½* **Investissement**[21] 4532 5-8-13 **99**............................ NickyMackay 1 108
(John Gosden) *hld up: gd hdwy over 5f out: jnd ldrs over 3f out: led over 2f out and sn rdn: drvn over 1f out: hdd last 100yds: edgd lft and lost 2nd nr fin* **25/1**

1022 **4** *1 ¼* **Modun (IRE)**[25] 4410 4-9-1 **101**............................ RichardHughes 2 108+
(Sir Michael Stoute) *hld up towards rr: stdy hdwy over 5f out: trckd ldrs over 3f out: chal over 2f out: sn rdn and ev ch tl drvn and one pce ins fnl f* **7/1**[2]

-055 **5** *½* **Saptapadi (IRE)**[28] 4345 5-9-5 **105**............................ KierenFallon 22 111
(Brian Ellison) *in tch: pushed along on outer and sltly outpcd over 2f out: rdn to chse ldrs over 1f out: sn drvn and edgd lft: one pce ins fnl f* **15/2**[3]

1124 **6** *nk* **Fox Hunt (IRE)**[23] 4469 4-9-10 **110**............................(v) SilvestreDeSousa 13 118+
(Mark Johnston) *reluctant to go to s: in tch: hdwy to trck ldrs after 4f: pushed along 4f out: rdn and sltly outpcd wl over 2f out: drvn and styng on whn n.m.r and hmpd ent fnl f: kpt on* **12/1**

2232 **7** *¾* **Lost In The Moment (IRE)**[23] 4469 4-9-5 **105**.........(p) FrankieDettori 21 110
(Saeed Bin Suroor) *hld up: hdwy over 4f out: chsd ldrs 2f out and sn rdn: drvn and kpt on same pce appr fnl f* **6/1**[1]

1444 **8** *½* **Mount Athos (IRE)**[16] 4737 4-9-3 **103**............................ WMLordan 18 107
(David Wachman, Ire) *sn chsng ldr: hdwy 3f out: rdn over 2f out and ev ch: one pce and hld whn hmpd ent fnl f* **10/1**

1-22 **9** *nk* **Blissful Moment (USA)**[63] 3156 4-8-12 **98**............................ TomQueally 11 102
(Sir Michael Stoute) *midfield: hdwy and in tch over 5f out: rdn along to chse ldrs over 2f out: sn drvn and one pce* **10/1**

15-3 **10** *1 ¼* **Cill Rialaig**[20] 4582 6-8-13 **99**............................ SteveDrowne 5 101
(Hughie Morrison) *trckd ldrs: hdwy 3f out: cl up and rdn 2f out: ev ch tl drvn and wknd ent fnl f* **18/1**

2106 **11** *nse* **Harlestone Times (IRE)**[21] 4532 4-9-1 **101**............................ TedDurcan 4 103
(John Dunlop) *hld up: hdwy 3f out: rdn along over 2f out: n.d* **20/1**

2/01 **12** *½* **Nehaam**[27] 4354 5-9-3 **103** 4ex............................ RichardHills 9 106+
(John Gosden) *hld up towards rr: hdwy 3f out: rdn along 2f out: n.d* **16/1**

0-30 **13** *nk* **Vulcanite (IRE)**[42] 3875 4-9-3 **103**............................ JimCrowley 16 104
(Ralph Beckett) *hld up and bhd: hdwy 3f out: rdn along 2f out: n.d* **25/1**

5010 **14** *½* **Nanton (USA)**[42] 3876 9-8-11 **104**............................ GarryWhillans(7) 6 104
(Jim Goldie) *hld up towards rr: effrt and sme hdwy 3f out: rdn along over 2f out: sn drvn and n.d* **40/1**

0104 **15** *1 ½* **Sirvino**[21] 4532 6-8-12 **98**............................ GrahamGibbons 15 96
(David Barron) *hld up: wd st: hdwy and in tch on outer over 2f out: sn rdn and wknd* **33/1**

040- **16** *5* **Hillview Boy (IRE)**[367] 5220 7-8-12 **98**............................ DanielTudhope 7 89
(Jim Goldie) *a in rr* **50/1**

0-24 **17** *shd* **Ted Spread**[37] 4037 4-9-8 **108**............................ PaulHanagan 12 99
(Mark H Tompkins) *prom: rdn along wl over 3f out: wknd wl over 2f out* **16/1**

244- **18** *½* **Salute Him (IRE)**[50] 3605 8-9-0 **100**............................ GeorgeBaker 8 90
(A J Martin, Ire) *hld up towards rr: hdwy and wd st: rdn along to chse ldrs wl over 2f out: sn wknd* **33/1**

3220 **19** *21* **Montaff**[23] 4469 5-9-6 **106**............................ EddieAhern 3 67
(Mick Channon) *a towards rr* **33/1**

5105 **20** *36* **Halicarnassus (IRE)**[22] 4492 7-9-3 **103**............................ TadhgO'Shea 19 13
(Mick Channon) *a towards rr: rdn along and lost pl qckly over 3f out: sn bhd and eased* **40/1**

3m 1.60s (1.40) **Going Correction** +0.125s/f (Good) **20** Ran SP% **123.4**
Speed ratings (Par 109): **101,100,100,99,99 98,98,98,98,97 97,97,96,96,95 92,92,92,80,59**
toteswingers:1&2:£9.20, 1&3:£7.10, 2&3:£9.60 CSF £214.47 CT £5641.16 TOTE £31.60: £5.70, £6.10, £2.10; EX 370.50 Trifecta £9446.40 Pool: £85,723.94 - 6.71 winning units..
Owner D Gilbert, M Lawrence, A Bruce **Bred** J L C Pearce **Trained** Norton, N Yorks

■ The richest handicap run on the Flat in Europe this year and for the first time the race was staged on a Saturday.

■ Stewards' Enquiry : Dale Swift one-day ban: careless riding (Sep 4)

FOCUS

A characteristically competitive Ebor, although there was a distinct lack of unexposed runners, the absence of any 3yos for the second consecutive season not helping. They raced up the middle of the track in the closing stages and for the sixth consecutive running the winner was drawn in double figures, but considering the full result it's hard to argue there was a bias. The pace seemed fair, with Tactician taking them along in a clear lead and having enough left to keep on for second, while the winner was well behind early. However, hand times make the race 1.92sec slower than the earlier Melrose Stakes. The form can be taken at face value and, although not outstanding, looks solid enough.

NOTEBOOK

Moyenne Corniche was hard to fancy with confidence considering his only previous win from 24 starts came in a maiden back in 2008, but this was only his eighth run since joining Brian Ellison, evidently a trainer extremely capable at unlocking the potential in an underachieving horse. He's had excuses in recent runs, notably sitting too close to an overly strong pace when finishing behind a few of these in both the Northumberland Plate and the John Smith's Cup. This time, though, he enjoyed a much better trip, travelling well under patient tactics and producing a sustained challenge to lead late on under a fine ride from Dale Swift. He might gain some confidence from this, but he won't be easy to place now.

Tactician, representing a former trainer of the winner, was 6lb higher than when making all in C&D Listed handicap last time (but had 3lb claimer taking over from full jockey). He looked likely to be swamped when strongly challenged on both sides in the straight but kept finding for pressure and deserves extra credit considering his rider's saddle apparently slipped slightly around 5f out, although his connections said it made no difference. He's in the Cesarewitch and certainly shapes as though he'll get further. (op 12-1)

Investissement was given absolutely every chance under a good ride from Nicky Mackay, but he was outstayed, a bit like at Goodwood last time. It's true that earlier in the season he narrowly defeated Moyenne Corniche on 2lb better terms over this trip, but today's winner didn't let himself down fully on that occasion. John Gosden's runner shapes as though worth a try back at 1m4f. (op 22-1)

Modun(IRE) arrived on the scene going as well as any of his rivals, but didn't see his race out and couldn't take advantage of being 4lb well in. There's plenty of stamina in his pedigree, being a half-brother to dual 2m Group 3 winner Patkai, as well as Saptapadi, but there was a suspicion beforehand this trip would stretch him, indeed when asked about the Ebor trip his trainer once said: "I don't think that's his distance." He can do better back at 1m2f-1m4f, but while he looked a definite Pattern performer when bolting up at Newbury on his reappearance, that seems less certain now. (op 13-2 tchd 8-1 in a place)

Saptapadi(IRE), who was 3lb well in, represented the same trainer as the winner and Brian Ellison commented immediately afterwards that he thought this one would have won under more patient tactics. While that's just conjecture, it's certainly hard to argue the horse wouldn't have been quite a bit closer under a different ride. Racing close to the pace wasn't the issue considering the runner-up led, but he was wide without cover for much of the way, and in the circumstances he did well to finish so close. (op 7-1 tchd 8-1)

Fox Hunt(IRE) had to be walked some of the way to the start, but he ran a mighty race considering he was conceding weight all round (9st 4lb or lower traditionally the favoured weight in this race) and had a slightly wider trip than ideal. He might even have been a place or two closer had he not been short of room late on.

Lost In The Moment(IRE) had looked a bit unlucky behind subsequent Group 3 winner Green Destiny (and Modun) in the John Smith's Cup over 1m2f here, and again when behind Opinion Poll (followed up in Lonsdale Cup on this card) when going 2m in the Goodwood Cup, but he ran flat this time, not making the most of being 6lb well-in. He's not one to rely on. (op 13-2 tchd 7-1 in a place)

Mount Athos(IRE) looked a bit unlucky in both the Chester Cup and Old Newton Cup, but he was made to look paceless in a 1m4f Group 3 last time and it was the same story here, despite a forward ride. He has his quirks and probably won't be easy to place.

Blissful Moment(USA) had been absent since finishing runner-up to Fox Hunt off 2lb lower in the Duke of Edinburgh at Royal Ascot, and he never featured. (op 9-1)

Cill Rialaig didn't run badly considering she was having only her second start of the campaign and had stamina to prove. She could win a nice prize back over shorter before the season is out. (op 16-1)

5286 JULIA GRAVES ROSES STKS (LISTED RACE) 5f

4:15 (4:15) (Class 1) 2-Y-O **£14,800** (£5,597; £2,797; £1,397) **Stalls** Centre

Form RPR

010 **1** **My Propeller (IRE)**[43] 3821 2-8-9 95............................ FrankieDettori 10 100+
(Peter Chapple-Hyam) *edgd rt and racd virtually alone on stands' side after 2f out: trckd ldrs: rdn: led ins fnl f: cheekily* **4/1**[2]

1116 **2** *1* **Last Bid**[14] 4787 2-8-9 87............................ DavidAllan 1 96
(Tim Easterby) *w ldrs on outside: led over 1f out: edgd lft and hdd ins fnl f: no ex* **14/1**

2112 **3** *hd* **Excelette (IRE)**[8] 4999 2-8-9 97............................ RoystonFfrench 4 96
(Bryan Smart) *led: hdd over 1f out: kpt on same pce ins fnl f* **6/1**

31 **4** *1 ¾* **Gusto**[15] 4748 2-9-0 0............................ RichardHughes 2 94
(Richard Hannon) *w ldrs: rdn over 1f out: kpt on same pce* **3/1**[1]

2016 **5** *3 ¼* **Vocational (USA)**[25] 4413 2-8-9 98............................ SilvestreDeSousa 11 78
(Mark Johnston) *chsd ldrs towards stands' side: rdn over 2f out: one pce* **9/2**[3]

2015 **6** *1 ½* **Springinmystep (IRE)**[28] 4334 2-9-0 85............................(t) TomQueally 7 77
(Michael Dods) *mid-div: effrt over 2f out: hung lft and wknd fnl f* **25/1**

1130 **7** *nk* **Factory Time (IRE)**[22] 4495 2-9-0 98............................ EddieAhern 9 76
(Mick Channon) *hld up in rr: effrt over 2f out: kpt on ins fnl f* **15/2**

100 **8** *1* **Church Music (IRE)**[25] 4413 2-9-0 93............................ GrahamGibbons 5 73
(Kevin Ryan) *trckd ldrs: effrt over 2f out: wknd jst ins fnl f* **14/1**

1401 **9** *3* **Forevertheoptimist (IRE)**[50] 3589 2-9-3 97............................ KierenFallon 6 65
(Linda Stubbs) *in rr-div: effrt over 2f out: wknd fnl f* **11/1**

42 **10** *2* **Citybell (IRE)**[12] 4848 2-8-9 0............................ PaulHanagan 3 50
(Richard Fahey) *dwlt: sn chsng ldrs: lost pl over 1f out* **40/1**

58.41 secs (-0.89) **Going Correction** -0.10s/f (Good) **10** Ran SP% **117.2**
Speed ratings (Par 102): **103,101,101,98,93 90,90,88,83,80**
toteswingers:1&2:£9.20, 1&3:£7.10, 2&3:£9.60 CSF £58.93 CT £230.80 TOTE £5.20: £1.90, £3.20, £2.70; EX 81.70 Trifecta £230.80 Pool: £1,344.63 - 4.31 winning units..
Owner Joseph Barton **Bred** D J & Mrs Brown **Trained** Newmarket, Suffolk

FOCUS

Probably no more than a fair race for the grade. The stands' rail was explored fully for the first time on the day.

NOTEBOOK

My Propeller(IRE), who had disappointed in the Cherry Hinton last time following her impressive 17l maiden victory, stayed on the strongest against the stands' rail. It's quite probable she enjoyed racing apart from the other runners, and in a race that turned into a decent test at the distance, her assured stamina was a big help. She's been hit-and-miss up to this point and it's hard to be confident she'll build on this next time.

Last Bid, a three-time winner this summer, including twice here, was below par at Haydock last time, but showed her toughness by bouncing back to run a career-best on her first try at Listed level. Considering the winner would have been racing on the better ground, this was a cracking effort. (op 12-1)

Excelette(IRE), another tough and progressive filly, was runner-up in this grade at Newbury last time and she ran another solid race, not for the first time shaping as though 6f may suit. (op 5-1)

Gusto, easy winner of a 6f Haydock maiden, was made favourite on this sharp rise in grade, but lacked the experience of most of these and ultimately the speed also. He still looked a touch inexperienced and can be given another chance to prove himself at this level. (op 7-2 tchd 4-1 in places)

Vocational(USA) looked a player at her best, but comes from a yard going through a quiet spell and she was comfortably held. (tchd 4-1)

Springinmystep(IRE), wearing a first-time tongue-tie, isn't up to this level and doesn't necessarily look to be progressing. (tchd 16-1)

Factory Time(IRE) could never get into it on this drop to 5f, but isn't going to be the easiest to place now. (op 12-1)

Forevertheoptimist(IRE) Official explanation: trainer said gelding was unsuited by the loose ground

5287 BETFRED BONUS KING STKS (NURSERY) 1m

4:50 (4:51) (Class 2) 2-Y-O **£9,703** (£2,887; £1,443; £721) **Stalls** Low

Form RPR

154 **1** **Risky Art**[28] 4343 2-8-8 **75** .... KierenFallon 4 85
(Michael Easterby) *trckd ldrs: hdwy to chse ldr over 2f out: rdn and edgd rt to stands' rail over 1f out: styd on to ld jst ins fnl f: kpt on* **6/1**[2]

11 **2** *nk* **Crius (IRE)**[22] 4508 2-9-5 **86** .... RichardHughes 9 95+
(Richard Hannon) *stdd s and hld up in rr: hdwy wl over 2f out: rdn over 1f out: styd on strly ins fnl f: jst failed* **7/2**[1]

5325 **3** *1 ¾* **Self Centred**[29] 4285 2-8-12 **79** .... MichaelHills 5 84
(B W Hills) *led: qcknd clr over 2f out: rdn over 1f out: drvn and hdd jst ins fnl f: one pce* **8/1**[3]

0122 **4** *3 ¼* **Wolfgang (IRE)**[20] 4581 2-9-7 **88** .... EddieAhern 1 86
(Richard Hannon) *hld up towards rr: hdwy 5f out: chsd ldrs 3f out: rdn along over 2f out: drvn and no imp appr fnl f* **8/1**[3]

462 **5** *3 ¾* **Ventura Spirit**[10] 4898 2-8-4 **71** .... BarryMcHugh 7 61
(Richard Fahey) *hld up towards rr: hdwy 3f out: rdn along over 2f out: styd on appr fnl f: nvr nr ldrs* **10/1**

412 **6** *2* **Act Your Shoe Size**[17] 4667 2-8-10 **77** .... DavidAllan 6 62
(Keith Dalgleish) *chsd ldrs: rdn along 3f out: drvn over 2f out and grad wknd* **16/1**

541 **7** *15* **Lolita Lebron (IRE)**[22] 4512 2-8-2 **69** .... KellyHarrison 8 21
(Lawrence Mullaney) *cl up: rdn along 1/2-way: drvn and wknd over 3f out* **33/1**

241 **8** *¾* **Holy Roman Warrior (IRE)**[29] 4292 2-8-13 **80** .... PaulHanagan 3 31
(Richard Fahey) *in tch: hdwy 1/2-way: rdn along 3f out: wknd 2f out* **7/2**[1]

3005 **9** *1* **Bedlam**[9] 4943 2-8-2 **69** ow2 .... ChrisCatlin 10 17
(Tim Easterby) *hld up: a in rr* **28/1**

5316 **10** *½* **Comical**[28] 4311 2-9-1 **82** .... SilvestreDeSousa 2 29
(Mark Johnston) *chsd ldrs on inner: rdn along 3f out: sn wknd* **9/1**

3224 **11** *1 ½* **Tight Lipped (IRE)**[9] 4969 2-8-13 **80** .... GrahamGibbons 11 24
(David Brown) *a in rr* **14/1**

006 **12** *11* **Angel Warrior (IRE)**[31] 4192 2-7-7 **65** oh4 .... NeilFarley(5) 12 —
(Ben Haslam) *a in rr: bhd fr wl over 2f out* **33/1**

1m 39.38s (0.58) **Going Correction** +0.125s/f (Good) **12** Ran SP% **121.9**
Speed ratings (Par 100): **102,101,99,96,92 90,75,75,74,73 72,61**
toteswingers:1&2:£6.90, 1&3:£9.10, 2&3:£8.30 CSF £27.26 CT £173.56 TOTE £7.40: £2.20, £2.10, £2.70; EX 33.30 Trifecta £179.40 Pool: £1,565.06 - 6.45 winning units..
Owner Sangster Family **Bred** J M Beever **Trained** Sheriff Hutton, N Yorks

FOCUS
An open nursery. The pace appeared to be a fair one.

NOTEBOOK
Risky Art, up from 5f for the first time, saw it out well having steadily been brought across to the stands' rail in the straight, as per her trainer's instructions. Although she pulled a bit in the early stages, Fallon had conserved plenty of energy and she was always holding on. It's doubtful she'd want to go any further than this, but there's every chance she'll win again, with the prospect of more to come. (op 7-1)
Crius(IRE), up to 1m for the first time, had only one behind turning in and had to switch after running into the back of rival. This left him with an awful lot of ground to make up and, despite staying on strongly, was never quite getting there. Richard Hughes will probably be first to admit this wasn't his finest moment, and there's every chance he can win something similar, even if he'll be up in the weights. (op 10-3 tchd 3-1)
Self Centred was given a good ride from the front, bouncing back from a poor effort at Thirsk last time, and she did well to stick on considering she was racing on the most cut-up ground in the final 2f. (tchd 17-2)
Wolfgang(IRE), unlucky not to win off 2lb lower over 7f at Newbury the time before, made good headway from the rear to reach a challenging position, but couldn't see it out as well as the front trio. (op 15-2 tchd 17-2)
Ventura Spirit made some late headway and can win a less competitive race. (op 14-1)
Holy Roman Warrior(IRE) was quickly beaten and plainly failed to run up to expectations. (op 4-1 tchd 9-2)
Comical was again disappointing and has now twice run poorly since winning his maiden. (op 11-1)

5288 TYREGIANT.COM STKS (H'CAP) 5f

5:20 (5:21) (Class 2) (0-100,99) 3-Y-O **£12,938** (£3,850; £1,924; £962) **Stalls** Centre

Form RPR

1221 **1** **York Glory (USA)**[12] 4855 3-8-10 **88** .... (b) KierenFallon 1 106+
(Kevin Ryan) *swtchd rt s: hld up: hdwy and nt clr run 2f out: str run to ld last 75yds: r.o wl* **5/2**[1]

5-10 **2** *2 ¼* **Dickie's Lad (IRE)**[66] 3052 3-8-10 **88** .... (t) ChrisCatlin 13 97
(Kevin Ryan) *led: hdd over 1f out: kpt on to take 2nd last 75yds* **28/1**

5300 **3** *1 ½* **Oor Jock (IRE)**[13] 4836 3-8-9 **94** .... DJBenson(7) 10 98
(Tracey Collins, Ire) *w ldrs: led over 1f out: hdd last 75yds: wknd towards fin* **14/1**

1045 **4** *½* **Barnet Fair**[7] 5054 3-8-12 **90** .... TadhgO'Shea 6 96+
(Richard Guest) *swtchd rt after s: hld up in rr: swtchd lft over 1f out: nt clr run tl styd on last 75yds* **9/1**

5000 **5** *¾* **Arctic Feeling (IRE)**[7] 5054 3-8-7 **92** .... GeorgeChaloner(7) 8 92+
(Richard Fahey) *chsd ldrs: kpt on same pce over 1f out* **25/1**

0003 **6** *nk* **Marine Commando**[43] 3807 3-8-11 **89** .... PaulHanagan 12 87
(Richard Fahey) *chsd ldrs: outpcd whn nt clr run 2f out: kpt on ins fnl f* **11/1**

5211 **7** *2 ¾* **Lady Royale**[19] 4610 3-8-7 **85** .... (b) SilvestreDeSousa 3 74
(Geoffrey Oldroyd) *in rr on outer: hdwy to chse ldrs over 1f out: wknd fnl 150yds* **10/1**

3203 **8** *nk* **The Thrill Is Gone**[22] 4498 3-9-1 **93** .... EddieAhern 5 80
(Mick Channon) *w ldrs: edgd rt and wknd jst ins fnl f* **20/1**

1322 **9** *1 ¼* **Thirteen Shivers**[12] 4855 3-8-9 **87** .... GrahamGibbons 14 70
(Michael Easterby) *sn chsng ldrs stands' side: wknd over 1f out* **9/2**[3]

5226 **10** *1 ¼* **Cocktail Charlie**[43] 3820 3-9-2 **94** .... (p) DavidAllan 4 72
(Tim Easterby) *chsd ldrs: hung rt: wkng whn nt clr run jst ins fnl f* **4/1**[2]

4013 **11** *3 ½* **Berberana (IRE)**[21] 4541 3-8-3 **81** .... KellyHarrison 9 47
(Tim Easterby) *unruly in stalls: chsd ldrs: lost pl over 1f out: eased towards fin* **20/1**

1140 **12** *17* **Quality Art (USA)**[22] 4498 3-8-12 **90** .... RichardHughes 7 —
(Gary Moore) *swtchd rt s to r stands' side rail: bhd fnl 2f: eased ins fnl f* **22/1**

57.98 secs (-1.32) **Going Correction** -0.10s/f (Good) **12** Ran SP% **122.0**
Speed ratings (Par 106): **106,102,100,99,98 97,93,92,90,88 83,55**
toteswingers:1&2:£11.20, 1&3:£10.20, 2&3:£46.70 CSF £90.85 CT £865.68 TOTE £3.30: £1.60, £7.50, £5.20; EX 102.00 TRIFECTA Not won..
Owner Salman Rashed **Bred** Paget Bloodstock & Horse France **Trained** Hambleton, N Yorks

FOCUS
A good 3-y-o sprint handicap, but none of these were a match for the progressive York Glory. They raced stands' side, but the rail was not an advantage. There were a couple of hard-luck stories but the winner stepped up again and the form is rated around the placed horses.

NOTEBOOK
York Glory(USA) had no problem dealing with a 5lb rise for his recent Thirsk win. His only issue was whether or not he'd find a gap when tucked away behind a wall of horses for much of the journey, but he got an opening in good time and sprinted clear. He's looked a quality colt from day one and there should be much more to come. The Ayr Gold Cup is an option, although this looks his best trip for now, even though he's won over as far as 7f. (op 3-1)
Dickie's Lad(IRE) had been absent for 66 days and was trying 5f for the first time. He showed plenty of speed, and although no match for the progressive York Glory, stuck on well. (op 25-1)
Oor Jock(IRE) didn't see his race out after leading over a furlong out. A more patient ride over this trip could see him win a nice race. (op 12-1)
Barnet Fair ◆ failed to find the gaps when they were needed and otherwise might have finished second. Official explanation: jockey said gelding was denied a clear run (op 17-2 tchd 11-1)
Marine Commando did not enjoy the best of trips. He could finally be ready to win again before long. (tchd 12-1)
Thirteen Shivers was disappointing considering he was just behind York Glory last time. Official explanation: jockey said gelding never travelled (op 6-1)
Cocktail Charlie Official explanation: jockey said gelding hung right throughout
Quality Art(USA) Official explanation: jockey said gelding moved poorly throughout
T/Jkpt: Not won T/Plt: £320.40 to a £1 stake. Pool:£272,720.62 - 621.31 winning tickets T/Qpdt: £23.90 to a £1 stake. Pool:£12,335.16 - 380.42 winning tickets JR

5289 - 5290a (Foreign Racing) - See Raceform Interactive

[4830] CURRAGH (R-H)

Saturday, August 20

OFFICIAL GOING: Round course - good; straight course - good to yielding

5291a THE IRISH FIELD ST LEGER TRIAL STKS (LISTED RACE) 1m 6f

3:15 (3:15) 3-Y-O+ **£22,413** (£6,551; £3,103; £1,034)

RPR

1 **Fictional Account (IRE)**[37] 4035 6-9-9 103 .... FMBerry 4 100+
(V C Ward, Ire) *trckd ldr in 2nd: hdwy to ld early st: rdn and edgd rt over 1f out: kpt on u.p fnl f* **14/1**[3]

2 *nk* **Fame And Glory**[65] 3066 5-10-0 122 .... SeamieHeffernan 2 105+
(A P O'Brien, Ire) *trckd ldrs in 4th: hdwy into cl 3rd ent st: pushed along to chal over 1f out: kpt on same pce wout rching wnr* **1/3**[1]

3 *1 ¼* **Saddler's Rock (IRE)**[44] 3790 3-8-11 97 .... (t) JMurtagh 7 99+
(John M Oxx, Ire) *led: strly pressed and hdd early st: no real imp u.p whn hmpd over 1f out: kpt on same pce* **4/1**[2]

4 *1 ¼* **Taameer**[31] 4220 5-9-9 103 .... PJSmullen 5 96+
(D K Weld, Ire) *hld up mainly 5th: 4th early st: rdn and kpt on same pce* **14/1**[3]

5 *shd* **Rising Wind (IRE)**[10] 4935 3-8-8 92 .... DPMcDonogh 6 93
(Kevin Prendergast, Ire) *trckd ldrs in 3rd: rdn ent st and dropped to 5th: kpt on one pce* **33/1**

6 *shd* **Waydownsouth (IRE)**[25] 4418 4-9-9 101 .... DMGrant 1 96+
(Patrick J Flynn, Ire) *hld up mainly 6th: t.k.h: drvn along 2f out: kpt on same pce* **25/1**

7 *5* **Dearest Girl (IRE)**[16] 4738 4-9-6 75 .... NGMcCullagh 3 86?
(Charles O'Brien, Ire) *a towards rr: rdn and no imp fr 2f out: kpt on one pce* **50/1**

(-189.40)
WFA 3 from 4yo+ 12lb **7** Ran SP% **117.1**
CSF £20.13 TOTE £14.20: £3.00, £1.10; DF 30.30.
Owner Cill Choca Syndicate **Bred** Moyglare Stud Farm Ltd **Trained** Kilcock, Co Meath

FOCUS
A minor shock as Fictional Account beat Fame And Glory for the first time having been beaten by him three times previously this season. This was a slowly-run race and it has been rated around the front-running third.

NOTEBOOK
Fictional Account(IRE) was ridden much more handily this time, getting to the front 2f out and, despite edging right and hampering the third-placed horse, she really stayed on strongly and was always holding her more vaunted opponent.
Fame And Glory was disappointing in what was a slowly run race, as it shouldn't have inconvenienced him. He was well positioned to challenge from the 2f pole even when the winner went on. He just didn't pick up in the manner one would expect and clawed the winner back only very gradually. It seems that we're not giving the winner enough credit but there can be no doubt that this horse didn't perform to his best or anything close. (op 2/9)
Saddler's Rock(IRE)'s proximity does reflect the bare form of the race and he would have been closer but for meeting with interference. It should be pointed out though that he is a horse that was open to improvement. (op 6/1)
Taameer was stepping up in trip and may well have benefited from a stronger pace. Having taken his time to pick up in the straight he ended up staying on reasonably effectively.
Rising Wind(IRE) was much more at home at this gentler pace having struggled to go the pace in a handicap at Gowran last time. In the light of that it's hard to take her getting to within less than three lengths of the winner terribly seriously.
Waydownsouth(IRE) ran very well on paper, but mostly due to the lack of pace in the race.
Dearest Girl(IRE) was never out of last place. (op 66/1)

5293a GALILEO EUROPEAN BREEDERS FUND FUTURITY STKS (GROUP 2) 7f

4:25 (4:26) 2-Y-O

£49,267 (£15,560; £7,370; £2,456; £1,508; £818)

RPR

1 **Dragon Pulse (IRE)**[30] 4256 2-9-1 .... FMBerry 7 114
(Mrs John Harrington, Ire) *settled in rr: gd prog on outer 2f out: led early fnl f and kpt on wl* **7/1**

2 *1 ¾* **Parish Hall (IRE)**[13] 4834 2-9-1 105 .... KJManning 3 110
(J S Bolger, Ire) *trckd ldrs in 3rd: rdn 2f out: no imp on wnr ins fnl f: kpt on same pce* **6/1**

3 *¾* **Astrology (IRE)**[9] 4977 2-9-1 .... DavidMcCabe 8 108
(A P O'Brien, Ire) *mid-div: 5th 1/2-way: hdwy to chal 2f out and sn led: hdd u.p early fnl f: sn no imp and edgd lft fnl 100yds* **5/1**[3]

4 *½* **David Livingston (IRE)**[56] 3414 2-9-1 .... SeamieHeffernan 5 107
(A P O'Brien, Ire) *trckd ldr: 2nd 1/2-way: led briefly over 2f out: sn no imp u.p and dropped to 4th: kpt on same pce fnl f* **5/2**[2]

5 *½* **Riviera Poet (IRE)**[26] 4397 2-9-1 .... PJSmullen 1 106
(D K Weld, Ire) *settled towards rr: 8th 1/2-way: pushed along and no imp 2f out: kpt on one pce wout threatening fnl f* **2/1**[1]

6 3/4 **Strait Of Zanzibar (USA)**[15] 4770 2-9-1 97 ShaneFoley 4 104
(K J Condon, Ire) *chsd ldrs mainly 6th: rdn over 2f out: no imp fr over 1f out and kpt on one pce* **20/1**

7 1 1/2 **Vault (IRE)**[21] 4565 2-9-1 101 WJLee 6 100
(A P O'Brien, Ire) *trckd ldrs in 4th: rdn and no ex fr 2f out* **14/1**

8 9 **Cheerful Giver (IRE)**[30] 4257 2-9-1 80 RPCleary 2 78
(J S Bolger, Ire) *led: strly pressed and hdd over 2f out: sn wknd: eased whn btn fnl f* **100/1**

1m 25.5s (-5.30) **Going Correction** -0.60s/f (Hard) 8 Ran SP% **117.8**
Speed ratings: **106,104,103,102,102 101,99,89**
CSF £49.75 TOTE £7.00: £1.70, £1.80, £1.60; DF 35.10.
Owner Tan Kai Chah **Bred** JF Tuthill & Mrs AWF Whitehead **Trained** Moone, Co Kildare
■ Stewards' Enquiry : R P Cleary two-day ban: careless riding (Sep 4-5)

FOCUS
A second consecutive win in this Group 2 event for trainer Jessica Harrington, who sent out Patrhfork to win a year ago before that colt's victory in the Group 1 National Stakes over the same course and trip.

NOTEBOOK
Dragon Pulse(IRE) prevailed having won what looked an ordinary 6f maiden at Leopardstown on his previous start. The step up in trip certainly suited him and he also appreciated the easy conditions here. Held up, he moved up smoothly on the outside 2f out and went to the front entering the final furlong. Kept up to his job, he kept on well to win in good style. He had been supplemented to this race and might be put in the National Stakes next month although he will have alternatives. (op 8/1)
Parish Hall(IRE) had beaten only one home in the Group 1 Phoenix Stakes here 13 days previously. A winner on debut over 6f, he had finished second over this distance on his second start and he acquitted himself well here, tracking the leaders and having every chance from 2f out. He stuck to his task but was no match for the winner in the closing stages. (op 8/1)
Astrology(IRE), a 10-1 shot and his stable's second string when winning over 1m on his debut at Leopardstown, got to the front under 2f out and stayed on when headed by the winner. He will appreciate going back up in trip. (op 5/1 tchd 11/2)
David Livingston(IRE), a three-length winner of a maiden over the course and trip on soft ground in June, raced prominently and touched the front after being slightly hampered over 2f out. Soon headed, he could find no extra for pressure before keeping on. (op 5/2 tchd 9/4)
Riviera Poet(IRE) proved disappointing and, after being held up in rear, he made same progress from 2f out without travelling well enough to mount a serious challenge. It is possible the Galway race, for which he had a rushed preparation, might have taken more out of him than had been thought.

5292 - 5295a (Foreign Racing) - See Raceform Interactive

[5194] DEAUVILLE (R-H)
Saturday, August 20
OFFICIAL GOING: Turf: good; fibresand: standard

5296a PRIX DU CALVADOS - HARAS DES CAPUCINES (GROUP 3) (2YO FILLIES) (TURF) 7f
1:30 (12:00) 2-Y-O **£34,482** (£13,793; £10,344; £6,896; £3,448)

RPR

1 **Elusive Kate (USA)**[21] 4569 2-8-9 0 OlivierPeslier 1 105
(John Gosden) *broke wl: sn led on stands' rail: rdn and qcknd wl 1f out: r.o wl fnl f: comf* **19/10**[1]

2 1 1/2 **Mashoora (IRE)**[18] 2-8-9 0 ChristopheSoumillon 4 102
(J-C Rouget, France) *racd bhd ldrs: pulling hrd: chsd ldr fr 1 1/2f out: r.o wl fnl f wout threatening wnr* **23/10**[2]

3 3/4 **Switcher (IRE)**[64] 3104 2-8-9 0 RichardKingscote 10 100
(Tom Dascombe) *broke fast to be 2nd on outside: r.o wl u.p fr 1 1/2f out: hdd for 2nd 1f out: r.o wl to hold 3rd* **30/1**

4 nk **Ponte Vespucci (FR)**[20] 4596 2-8-9 0 Christophe-PatriceLemaire 6 99
(Y De Nicolay, France) *settled in midfield: gd prog 1 1/2f out: r.o wl fnl f* **11/1**

5 snk **Three Gems (IRE)**[26] 2-8-9 0 IoritzMendizabal 5 99
(E J O'Neill, France) *settled towards rr: following Mashoora: rdn 1 1/2f out: r.o fnl f* **31/1**

6 1 1/2 **Nimohe (FR)**[23] 4484 2-8-9 0 MickaelBarzalona 7 95
(J Heloury, France) *racd bhd ldrs: rdn but no ex fnl 1 1/2f: styd on* **13/1**

7 hd **Sylvan Song (USA)**[21] 4569 2-8-9 0 MaximeGuyon 9 94
(A Fabre, France) *prom fr s: wnt 2nd after 2f: rdn 2 1/2f out: nt qckn: styd on fnl f* **10/1**

8 shd **Pestagua (IRE)**[21] 4569 2-8-9 0 ThierryJarnet 8 94
(X Thomas-Demeaulte, France) *bkmarker fr s: swtchd to outside and rdn 2f out: no ex u.p fnl f* **19/1**

9 1/2 **Gooseberry Fool**[37] 4031 2-8-9 0 Jean-BernardEyquem 3 93
(Sir Mark Prescott Bt) *settled at rr: rdn 2f out: nt qckn: styd on u.p fnl f* **44/5**[3]

10 1/2 **Arsaadi (IRE)**[30] 4252 2-8-9 0 GeraldMosse 2 92
(Ed Dunlop) *settled bhd ldr: rdn but nt qckn fr 1 1/2f out: wknd* **17/1**

1m 25.6s (-2.70) 10 Ran SP% **116.5**
WIN (incl. 1 euro stake): 2.90. PLACES: 1.30, 1.50, 4.90. DF: 3.40. SF: 9.60.
Owner Magnolia Racing LLC & Ms Rachel Hood **Bred** Clovelly Farms **Trained** Newmarket, Suffolk

NOTEBOOK
Elusive Kate(USA), a winner in Listed company over the C&D last time out, was given a more prominent ride on this quicker ground and made just about all the running. for a cosy success. Tactically versatile, it wouldn't be a surprise if she goes for the Boussac next.
Switcher(IRE), fourth in the Albany last time out, was poorly drawn but got a quick start to race up with the pace from the start and kept on well for third. The extra furlong was no problem for her and she's capable of better again, although her trainer is keen not to overrace her at two and intends now to give her the rest of the year off and bring her back for the Fred Darling in the spring.
Arsaadi(IRE) can perhaps be excused her run as she didn't enjoy the best of journeys to the track as the horse box broke down.

[5168] FOLKESTONE (R-H)
Sunday, August 21
OFFICIAL GOING: Good to firm (7.8)
Wind: light across Weather: warm, muggy

5297 DISTANTVISION.CO.UK MEDIAN AUCTION MAIDEN STKS 5f
2:10 (2:10) (Class 6) 2-Y-O **£2,045** (£603; £302) **Stalls** High

Form RPR

5444 1 **Triggerlo**[40] 3955 2-8-10 61 CharlesBishop(7) 1 63
(Mick Channon) *stdd and swtchd lft after s: in tch in last: rdn hands and heels and squeezed through on stands' rail to chal ins fnl f: led and rdr unbalanced fnl 50yds: r.o wl* **7/2**[2]

0623 2 3/4 **Stans Deelyte**[2] 5245 2-8-12 52 AdamKirby 3 55
(Lisa Williamson) *chsd ldng pair: rdn and squeezed between horses to chal wl over 1f out: led over 1f out tl hdd and no ex fnl 50yds* **4/1**[3]

030 3 1/2 **Picura**[25] 4430 2-8-12 54 MartinDwyer 5 54
(William Muir) *taken down early: led: rdn 2f out: hdd over 1f out: stl ev ch tl no ex and one pce fnl 100yds* **14/1**

3066 4 9 **Lord Ali McJones**[54] 3490 2-9-3 65 (p) RichardKingscote 4 26
(Tom Dascombe) *chsd ldrs: rdn and ev ch 2f out: sn struggling: wknd qckly jst over 1f out: tdd fnl f* **4/6**[1]

60.29 secs (0.29) **Going Correction** -0.025s/f (Good) 4 Ran SP% **108.9**
Speed ratings (Par 92): **96,94,94,79**
CSF £16.05 TOTE £5.20; EX 14.10.
Owner Lord Ilsley Racing (Medcroft Syndicate) **Bred** Hesmonds Stud Ltd **Trained** West Ilsley, Berks

FOCUS
Like all races on the card the prize-money was within the tariff set by the Horsemen's Group yet only four lined up here, a quartet already exposed as pretty limited. The pace looked overly strong.

NOTEBOOK
Triggerlo was a beaten favourite in a 7f selling handicap on his previous start, but he had the speed to cope with this sharp 5f and the race set up well for him, helping him gain his first win at the ninth attempt. He was well ridden for the majority of the way, being waited with off the hot pace and then getting a run against the inside rail, although his apprentice became unbalanced near the line. He doesn't appeal as one to follow. (op 11-4)
Stans Deelyte, third in a Polytrack seller two days earlier, had her chance. She would have been 4lb better off with the winner in a handicap. (op 5-1)
Picura did well to last so long considering she was hassled for the lead. (op 9-1 tchd 17-2)
Lord Ali McJones was the pick of the weights, but had cheekpieces and a cross noseband fitted and never travelled. Official explanation: trainer's rep had no explanation for the poor form shown (op 5-6 tchd 10-11, evens in a place)

5298 LAUREN GORDON APPRENTICE H'CAP 7f (S)
2:40 (2:43) (Class 6) (0-60,59) 3-Y-O+ **£2,045** (£603; £302) **Stalls** High

Form RPR

4433 1 **Crown Ridge (IRE)**[6] 5120 3-9-0 59 CharlesBishop(5) 1 66
(Mick Channon) *stdd and swtchd lft after s: hld up in rr: swtchd rt and hdwy wl over 1f out: rdn hands and heels to chal ins fnl f: led fnl 75yds: sn in command: pushed out* **3/1**[2]

3410 2 1 1/4 **Olney Lass**[25] 4444 4-8-10 50 SophieSilvester(5) 4 56
(Lydia Pearce) *chsd ldrs: wnt 2nd 2f out: rdn to chal over 1f out: led ins fnl f: hdd and nt pce of wnr fnl 75yds* **10/3**[3]

2452 3 1 **Jonnie Skull (IRE)**[8] 5037 5-9-8 57 (vt) AdamBeschizza 6 60
(Phil McEntee) *led: pushed along and qcknd 3f out: drvn and hrd pressed over 1f out: hdd ins fnl f: styd on same pce after* **11/4**[1]

6040 4 1 1/2 **Diddums**[8] 5040 5-9-1 57 KatiaScallan(7) 7 56
(Alastair Lidderdale) *in tch: nt clr run and swtchd rt wl over 1f out: hdwy and rdn 1f out: styd on same pce and no imp fnl 100yds* **5/1**

-000 5 1 **Bold Argument (IRE)**[10] 4948 8-8-11 46 SophieDoyle 5 43
(Nerys Dutfield) *awkward leaving stalls: sn rcvrd to chse ldr: rdn and lost 2nd 2f out: unable qck and edgd rt over 1f out: styd on same pce fnl f* **18/1**

0660 6 1 1/2 **Duplicity**[106] 1911 4-9-1 50 MartinHarley 3 43
(Richard Guest) *t.k.h: hld up in last pair: hdwy 3f out: chsd ldng pair and rdn wl over 1f out: drvn and unable qck over 1f out: wknd ins fnl f* **7/1**

1m 26.57s (-0.73) **Going Correction** -0.025s/f (Good)
WFA 3 from 4yo+ 5lb 6 Ran SP% **109.2**
Speed ratings (Par 101): **103,101,100,98,97 95**
toteswingers:1&2:£1.60, 2&3:£2.20, 1&3:£1.90 CSF £12.56 CT £25.97 TOTE £3.60: £1.70, £1.90; EX 12.70 Trifecta £24.80.
Owner M Channon **Bred** Pat Grogan **Trained** West Ilsley, Berks

FOCUS
They all raced stands' side but the rail was not a notable advantage. This was a really moderate race (confined to apprentice riders) and the leader looked to go off too fast.

5299 TOTESWINGER/BRITISH STALLION STUDS EBF MAIDEN FILLIES' STKS 7f (S)
3:10 (3:13) (Class 5) 2-Y-O **£3,557** (£1,058; £529; £264) **Stalls** High

Form RPR

2 1 **Ziefhd**[8] 5048 2-9-0 0 ChrisCatlin 14 78+
(Paul Cole) *mde all: rdn and asserted over 1f out: styd on wl and in command fnl f* **15/8**[1]

06 2 1 3/4 **Viola Da Gamba (IRE)**[24] 4471 2-9-0 0 ShaneKelly 9 74
(William Knight) *chsd wnr thrght: rdn and unable qck wl over 1f out: kpt on same pce u.p fnl f* **8/1**

5 3 1 3/4 **Ashbina**[24] 4474 2-9-0 0 LiamJones 7 69
(William Haggas) *chsd ldrs: rdn and effrt 2f out: drvn to chse ldng pair and sltly hmpd wl over 1f out: no prog ent fnl f: plugged on same pce* **20/1**

4 1 1/2 **Surrey Storm** 2-9-0 0 SebSanders 11 66+
(Roger Teal) *chsd ldrs: rdn ent fnl 2f: drvn and outpcd over 1f out: kpt on same pce fnl f* **66/1**

3 5 1 **Livia's Dream (IRE)**[22] 4525 2-9-0 0 J-PGuillambert 5 63
(Ed Walker) *wnt rt s: in tch: rdn and outpcd over 2f out: rallied ent fnl f: kpt on but no threat to ldrs* **13/2**

6 3/4 **Pretty Pebble (IRE)** 2-9-0 0 MartinDwyer 6 61
(Brian Meehan) *in tch in midfield: pushed along and outpcd 3f out: rallied over 1f out: styd on steadily ins fnl f: no threat to ldrs* **16/1**

0 7 1/2 **Tamima (USA)**[37] 4052 2-9-0 0 TadhgO'Shea 8 60
(Brian Meehan) *chsd ldrs but sn niggled along: rdn over 2f out: wknd over 1f out* **33/1**

00 **8** 1 1/2 **Joyful Spirit (IRE)**[22] 4552 2-9-0 0 IanMongan 1 56
(John Dunlop) *in tch in midfield: rdn and effrt towards centre over 2f out: no prog over 1f out: wknd fnl f: wl hld and eased towards fin* **25/1**

9 1 **Echo Of Thunder (IRE)** 2-9-0 0 LiamKeniry 12 58+
(David Lanigan) *hld up towards rr: switching rt over 2f out: sme hdwy over 1f out: nudged along and kpt on fnl f: nvr trbld ldrs* **80/1**

10 4 **Wild Silk** 2-9-0 0 RichardMullen 4 44
(Sir Michael Stoute) *rn green: in tch in midfield: rdn and outpcd wl over 2f out: wknd and wl btn whn rn green jst over 1f out* **6/1**[3]

11 4 **High Endeavour (IRE)** 2-8-11 0 SeanLevey(3) 13 34
(Robert Mills) *s.i.s: a towards rr: rn green and struggling 3f out: wl btn fnl 2f* **25/1**

00 **12** shd **Better Be Mine (IRE)**[31] 4245 2-9-0 0 AdamKirby 3 33
(John Dunlop) *a bhd: rdn and struggling 4f out: wl bhd over 2f out* **80/1**

13 8 **Dawn Glory** 2-9-0 0 SteveDrowne 2 13
(Roger Charlton) *s.i.s: sn swtchd lft: a in rr: lost tch 3f out:* **11/2**[2]

4 **14** 4 1/2 **Canning Vale**[19] 4646 2-8-11 0 AdamBeschizza(3) 10 —
(Julia Feilden) *racd in midfield: rdn and losing pl 4f out: wl bhd over 2f out: t.o* **150/1**

1m 26.56s (-0.74) **Going Correction** -0.025s/f (Good) **14** Ran SP% **114.8**
Speed ratings (Par 91): **103,101,99,97,96 95,94,93,91,87 82,82,73,68**
toteswingers:1&2:£4.90, 2&3:£18.90, 1&3:£8.80 CSF £14.97 TOTE £2.50: £1.30, £2.80, £4.20; EX 19.00 Trifecta £168.50.
Owner The Fairy Story Partnership **Bred** Deepwood Farm Stud **Trained** Whatcombe, Oxon

FOCUS
Prize-money comfortably over the Horsemen's Group tariff, combined with the yearling bonus being available to most of these, made for an interesting fillies' maiden. However, while there were probably some nice types in the line-up the bare form is not that strong and it paid to be prominent.

NOTEBOOK
Ziefhd showed plenty of ability when runner-up on her debut over 6f at Newbury and confirmed that promise in straightforward fashion. Her dam was a dual Listed winner at 1m for these connections and presumably black type will be the long-term aim with this one. She's considered still a bit weak. (tchd 9-4)
Viola Da Gamba(IRE) had shown ability on her first two starts and did so again. She might find a weaker maiden and nurseries are also now an option. (op 9-1)
Ashbina was never far away and this was a big improvement on the form she showed over 6f on her debut.
Surrey Storm would have been a bit closer had she not been short of room late on, but she wasn't unlucky. She only cost 8,000gns, but is by Montjeu out of a 1m Listed winner and she has ability. (op 50-1)
Livia's Dream(IRE) didn't improve on her debut third at Doncaster, but she was going on at the finish and was best of those from off the pace. There's more to come, although she'll probably want further before long. (op 11-2 tchd 7-1)
Pretty Pebble(IRE) ◆, the first foal of a German 1m2f winner, was running on well in the closing stages without being given a hard ride and is likely to improve a good deal on this next time. (op 25-1)
Echo Of Thunder(IRE) ◆ wasn't subjected to a hard ride and can do better. (tchd 100-1)
Wild Silk, a 165,000gns purchase, carried her head to one side for some of the way and showed little. (op 5-1 tchd 9-2)

5300 TOTEEXACTA (S) STKS — 7f (S)
3:40 (3:41) (Class 6) 3-Y-O+ **£1,908** (£563; £281) **Stalls** High

Form RPR

0412 **1** **Deerslayer (USA)**[9] 4990 5-9-7 72 (p) MartinHarley(3) 6 78
(Richard Guest) *rn wout declared tongue tie: mde all: rdn and asserted over 1f out: clr and pushed out fnl f: easily* **7/4**[1]

0-36 **2** 3 1/2 **Bennelong**[107] 1875 5-9-5 60 PaulDoe 5 64
(Richard Rowe) *chsd wnr: rdn and unable qck wl over 1f out: no ch w wnr but kpt on to hold 2nd fnl f* **12/1**

010 **3** 1 **Lutine Charlie (IRE)**[13] 4865 4-9-5 66 AdamKirby 3 61
(Ronald Harris) *chsd ldrs: rdn and effrt 2f out: outpcd by wnr and btn over 1f out: kpt on same pce fnl f* **13/2**

0046 **4** 1/2 **Paperetto**[8] 5040 3-8-11 58 SeanLevey(3) 4 58
(Robert Mills) *hld up in tch: nt clr run and swtchd rt over 1f out: sme hdwy 1f out: sn no imp and wl hld fnl f* **7/2**[3]

6166 **5** 1 3/4 **Fault**[11] 4897 5-9-10 67 (t) SebSanders 1 60
(Stef Higgins) *stdd and swtchd lft after s: hld up in tch: rdn and effrt over 1f out: fnd virtually nil and sn btn* **5/2**[2]

6 26 **Shannons Brook** 3-8-2 0 AccursioRomeo(7) 7 —
(Brett Johnson) *s.i.s: sn rdn along and a detached in last: lost tch 2f out: t.o* **28/1**

1m 26.44s (-0.86) **Going Correction** -0.025s/f (Good)
WFA 3 from 4yo+ 5lb **6** Ran SP% **111.6**
Speed ratings (Par 101): **103,99,97,97,95 65**
toteswingers:1&2:£2.80, 2&3:£4.10, 1&3:£2.10 CSF £22.68 TOTE £2.30: £1.20, £5.40; EX 19.90.The winner was bought in for 3,600gns
Owner Rakebackmypoker.com **Bred** Bjorn Nielsen **Trained** Stainforth, S Yorks
■ Stewards' Enquiry : Adam Kirby two-day ban: Rule (B)54.2 and improper riding (Sep 6-7)

FOCUS
A weak seller and the runners hardly changed positions, Deerslayer allowed a soft lead and setting a steady pace.

5301 TOTEQUICKPICK H'CAP — 6f
4:10 (4:10) (Class 5) (0-75,75) 3-Y-O+ **£3,067** (£905; £453) **Stalls** High

Form RPR

1611 **1** **Efistorm**[20] 4618 10-9-8 73 HayleyTurner 6 81
(Conor Dore) *led for 1f: outpcd whn gallop qcknd over 4f out: 4th and rdn over 2f out: clsd on ldng pair and rdn hands and heels to chal ins fnl f: kpt on wl to ld last stride* **7/4**[1]

3001 **2** shd **Sermons Mount (USA)**[10] 4960 5-9-5 70 LiamKeniry 2 78
(Peter Hedger) *chsd ldr tl led after 1f: hdd but qcknd clr w rival after 2f: rdn over 1f out: edgd rt u.p but kpt on wl fnl f: hdd last stride* **9/4**[2]

2225 **3** 3 1/2 **Grandmas Dream**[9] 4988 3-9-1 72 (p) RobertLButler(3) 3 69
(Richard Guest) *hld up in rr: outpcd and wl bhd after 2f: rdn and hdwy over 1f out: kpt on to go 3rd nr fin: nvr trbld ldrs* **6/1**

3000 **4** 1/2 **Dream Number (IRE)**[48] 3685 4-8-10 61 MartinDwyer 1 56
(William Muir) *t.k.h: in tch tl jnd ldr over 4f out: led and qcknd clr w rival 4f out: rdn and hdd over 1f out: kpt on and stl ev ch tl wknd qckly fnl 100yds* **17/2**

6020 **5** 3 1/2 **Rum King (USA)**[5] 5155 4-9-7 75 SeanLevey(3) 4 59
(S Donohoe, Ire) *taken down early: s.i.s: sn rcvrd and chsd ldrs: outpcd whn gallop qcknd 4f out: rdn and no prog wl over 1f out: wknd over 1f out* **4/1**[3]

1m 12.08s (-0.62) **Going Correction** -0.025s/f (Good)
WFA 3 from 4yo+ 3lb **5** Ran SP% **111.9**
Speed ratings (Par 103): **103,102,98,97,92**
CSF £6.11 TOTE £2.40: £1.80, £1.30; EX 5.70.
Owner Sean J Murphy **Bred** E Duggan And D Churchman **Trained** Cowbit, Lincs

FOCUS
A modest handicap run at a good gallop.

5302 HP TECHNOLOGY H'CAP — 1m 4f
4:45 (4:46) (Class 6) (0-65,62) 3-Y-O **£2,045** (£603; £302) **Stalls** High

Form RPR

3122 **1** **Come On The Irons (USA)**[4] 5168 3-9-3 61 (t) JamieGoldstein 5 67
(Ralph Smith) *mde all: rdn ent fnl f: kpt on wl and a doing enough fnl f: rdn out* **15/8**[1]

3052 **2** 3/4 **Lady Barastar (IRE)**[18] 4686 3-9-4 62 AdamKirby 4 67
(Walter Swinburn) *chsd ldng pair: effrt whn stmbld and jinked rt jst over 2f out: rdn to press wnr over 1f out: kpt on but a hld fnl f* **4/1**[3]

4403 **3** 3/4 **Hygrove Welshlady (IRE)**[18] 4686 3-9-3 61 MartinDwyer 1 65
(J W Hills) *t.k.h early: hld up in tch in last pair: rdn and hdwy on outer over 1f out: chsd ldng pair ent fnl f: styd on same pce after* **5/1**

1304 **4** 9 **Entrance**[21] 4579 3-8-13 60 AdamBeschizza(3) 2 49
(Julia Feilden) *s.i.s: in tch in last pair: rdn over 2f out: drvn and unable qck over 1f out: wknd 1f out* **5/1**

0330 **5** 6 **Pizzetti (IRE)**[83] 2571 3-9-0 58 SebSanders 3 38
(Sir Mark Prescott Bt) *chsd wnr: rdn over 2f out: drvn and wknd over 1f out: fdd fnl f* **7/2**[2]

2m 42.08s (1.18) **Going Correction** 0.0s/f (Good) **5** Ran SP% **110.3**
Speed ratings (Par 98): **95,94,94,88,84**
CSF £9.60 TOTE £2.00: £1.10, £2.70; EX 5.00.
Owner Mrs H J Fullerton **Bred** Tony Hancock & Rhonda Hancock **Trained** Epsom, Surrey

FOCUS
Another weak race and Come On The Irons benefited from being allowed to dominate. The placed horses are rated close to their recent Yarmouth running.

5303 BRITISH STALLION STUDS SUPPORTING BRITISH RACING EBF FILLIES' H'CAP — 1m 1f 149y
5:15 (5:17) (Class 4) (0-85,85) 3-Y-O+ **£4,851** (£1,443; £721; £360) **Stalls** Centre

Form RPR

-112 **1** **Captivator**[58] 3338 4-10-0 85 HayleyTurner 4 94+
(James Fanshawe) *dwlt: detached in last tl pushed along and clsd over 6f out: rdn and effrt on inner 2f out: drvn to chal ent fnl f: led ins fnl f: kpt on wl* **5/2**[2]

2414 **2** 1/2 **Sacred Shield**[17] 4723 3-9-0 79 IanMongan 3 87
(Sir Henry Cecil) *dwlt: t.k.h: hld up in tch: hdwy to chse ldrs 3f out: rdn to chal on outer over 1f out: led ent fnl f: hdd and kpt on same pce ins fnl f* **7/4**[1]

305 **3** nk **Love Over Gold (FR)**[10] 4962 4-9-9 80 MartinLane 2 87
(Ralph Beckett) *pressed ldr: ev ch and rdn over 2f out: edgd rt u.p 2f out: unable qck u.p ins fnl f: kpt on* **8/1**

1521 **4** 1 1/2 **Medaille D'Or**[31] 4249 3-8-11 76 JackMitchell 6 80
(Roger Varian) *hld up wl in tch: rdn and effrt whn gap clsd and nt clr run 2f out: swtchd lft and drvn over 1f out: edging rt and kpt on same pce ins fnl f: swtchd lft again towards fin* **7/2**[3]

0510 **5** 3 **Goldtrek (USA)**[10] 4971 4-9-7 78 (p) SteveDrowne 1 76
(Roger Charlton) *led: rdn ent fnl 2f: hdd ent fnl f: wknd fnl 150yds* **10/1**

0-60 **6** 21 **Bilidn**[50] 3624 3-9-3 82 PhilipRobinson 5 35
(Clive Brittain) *chsd ldrs on outer: rdn and dropped to last 3f: sn lost tch: t.o and eased ins fnl f* **25/1**

2m 4.38s (-0.52) **Going Correction** 0.0s/f (Good)
WFA 3 from 4yo 8lb **6** Ran SP% **111.2**
Speed ratings (Par 102): **102,101,101,100,97 80**
toteswingers:1&2:£1.40, 2&3:£3.20, 1&3:£4.00; Tote Super 7: Win: £2,028.80. Place: £11.50 CSF £7.15 TOTE £3.40: £1.60, £1.30; EX 8.10.
Owner Lord Vestey **Bred** Stowell Park Stud **Trained** Newmarket, Suffolk

FOCUS
A fair fillies' handicap. The leader seemed to get a breather in at around halfway, but the pace was essentially good. The third is rated to her reappearance form and sets the level.
T/Plt: £65.20 to a £1 stake. Pool:£72,054.36 - 806.64 winning tickets T/Qpdt: £3.80 to a £1 stake. Pool:£5,630.85 - 1,083.76 winning tickets SP

5296 DEAUVILLE (R-H)
Sunday, August 21

OFFICIAL GOING: Turf: good; fibresand: standard

5304a DARLEY PRIX KERGORLAY (GROUP 2) (3YO+) (TURF) — 1m 7f
1:30 (12:00) 3-Y-O+ **£63,879** (£24,655; £11,767; £7,844; £3,922)

RPR

1 **Jukebox Jury (IRE)**[23] 4492 5-9-4 0 NeilCallan 10 117
(Mark Johnston) *broke wl on outside: led: grad moved to inner: mde all: qckrd ins fnl 2 1/2f: c wd to centre of trck st (jst over 2f out): rdn appr fnl f and edgd towards stands' rail: wnt clr fnl f: comfortabl* **5/1**[2]

2 3 **Kasbah Bliss (FR)**[38] 4037 9-9-4 0 MaximeGuyon 5 113
(F Doumen, France) *settled midfield: 5th 1/2-way: 7th and rdn 2f out in centre of trck: styd on between horses (short of room briefly): fnl f: grabbed 2nd cl home* **12/1**

3 1/2 **Brigantin (USA)**[66] 3066 4-9-6 0 Pierre-CharlesBoudot 2 114
(A Fabre, France) *w.w towards rr on ins rail: 11th and pushed along passing 3f marker: hdwy and kpt towards ins fnl bnd: 5th and styng on u.p ins fnl 2f: wnt 3rd appr fnl f: kpt on wl wout qckning* **8/1**[3]

4 nse **Manighar (FR)**[24] 4469 5-9-4 0 KierenFallon 6 112
(Luca Cumani) *chsd ldng gp: 4th and pushed along 2 1/2f out: c drown centre of trck st: 4th and u.p fnl f: no ex* **10/1**

5 snk **Red Cadeaux**[24] 4469 5-9-4 0 TomMcLaughlin 1 112
(Ed Dunlop) *settled in 4th early on rail: relegated to midfield (share of 7th on rail) over 4f out: 6th on ins pushed along and styng on 2 1/2f out: styd on ins rail and chal ldr 2f out: hrd rdn 1 1/2f out: nt qckn ins fnl 150yds* **20/1**

6 shd **Terre Du Vent (FR)**[23] 4524 5-9-1 0 StephanePasquier 7 109
(Y De Nicolay, France) *hld up towards rr: 12th 2 1/2f out: swtchd outside and hdwy u.p down centre of crse fr 2f out: r.o wl appr fnl f: run flattened out last 75yds* **25/1**

7 3/4 **Marinous (FR)**[38] 4037 5-9-6 0 (b) ThierryJarnet 9 113
(F Head, France) *settled in fnl 3rd: 8th and travelling wl 2 1/2f out: rdn 2f out: kpt on wout qckning fnl f* **25/1**

8 3/4 **Tres Rock Danon (FR)**[38] 4037 5-9-4 0 ASuborics 3 110
(W Hickst, Germany) *a.p (2nd for much of the r): cl 4th whn rdn and nt qckn over 1 1/2f out: grad fdd fnl 110yds* **33/1**

9 snk **Dunaden (FR)**[91] 2344 5-9-4 0 JMurtagh 12 110
(M Delzangles, France) *hld up in 6th or 7th towards outside: c wd into st: no imp fnl 2f* **5/1**[2]

10 nse **Americain (USA)**[19] 4653 6-9-8 0 GeraldMosse 4 114
(A De Royer-Dupre, France) *hld up towards rr: 9th and pushed along appr 2 1/2f out: styd towards ins: 6th and styng on 2f out: sltly hmpd 1 1/2f out as gap clsd: no ex fnl f* **10/3**[1]

11 2½ **Ley Hunter (USA)**[19] 4653 4-9-4 0 MickaelBarzalona 11 107
(A Fabre, France) *hld up in last: effrt on wd outside fnl bnd: rdn appr 2f out: no imp* **8/1**[3]

12 5 **Celtic Celeb (IRE)**[77] 2753 4-9-6 0 ChristopheSoumillon 8 103
(F Doumen, France) *a.p: 3rd and pushed along over 2f out: 5th and wkng whn hmpd and snatched up 130yds out: eased* **20/1**

13 4 **Gentoo (FR)**[19] 4653 7-9-8 0 (p) Christophe-PatriceLemaire 13 100
(A Lyon, France) *hld up towards rr on outside: 11th on outside and pushed along 2 1/2f out: no imp in centre of trck fr 2f out: eased fnl f* **16/1**

3m 14.2s (-4.90) **Going Correction** +0.05s/f (Good) **13** Ran SP% **121.5**
Speed ratings: **115,113,113,113,113 112,112,112,112,112 110,108,105**
WIN (incl. 1 euro stake): 10.00. PLACES: 4.00, 7.10, 2.60. DF: 141.20. SF: 440.10.
Owner A D Spence **Bred** Paul Nataf **Trained** Middleham Moor, N Yorks

NOTEBOOK
Jukebox Jury(IRE), narrowly beaten into third at Goodwood last time, made every yard here to return to winning ways. At his best when allowed to dominate, he has the Irish St Leger and the Canadian International on his agenda now.
Manighar(FR) could have done with a stronger pace, but he ran a solid race and will now be prepared for another tilt at the Melbourne Cup.
Americain(USA)wasn't at home on the quick ground and shouldn't be judged too harshly. He'll go into quarantine now before another assault on the Melbourne Cup.

5305a DARLEY PRIX MORNY (GROUP 1) (2YO COLTS & FILLIES) (TURF) 6f
2:40 (12:00) 2-Y-O **£172,405** (£68,974; £34,487; £17,228; £8,629)

RPR

1 **Dabirsim (FR)**[21] 4596 2-9-0 0 FrankieDettori 5 120+
(C Ferland, France) *t.k.h and hld up in 4th: swtchd towards stands' rail and travelling strly appr 2f out: qcknd to ld nring fnl f: pushed clr fnl 120yds: impressive* **5/2**[2]

2 3 **Family One (FR)**[28] 4375 2-9-0 0 IoritzMendizabal 6 111
(Y Barberot, France) *sn led: pressed 2f out: shkn up and hdd appr fnl f: kpt on but no ch w wnr* **3/1**[3]

3 1 **Vladimir (IRE)**[17] 4843 2-9-0 0 MaximeGuyon 1 108
(M Delcher-Sanchez, Spain) *broke wl towards rail: sn settled towards rr but wl in tch: last and pushed along over 2f out: rdn 1 1/2f out: r.o appr fnl f and got up for 3rd cl home* **16/1**

4 shd **Sofast (FR)**[19] 4652 2-9-0 OlivierPeslier 3 108
(F Head, France) *dwlt: last out of stalls and outpcd early: sn in tch: 5th and effrt on outside over 2f out: rdn and r.o 1 1/2f out: no ex fnl f: lost 3rd cl home* **9/1**

5 1½ **Frederick Engels**[14] 4834 2-9-0 0 JMurtagh 4 103
(David Brown) *broke wl and led early: sn settled in 2nd trcking ldr: 3rd and gng wl enough 2 1/2f out: sn pushed along: 3rd and rdn ins fnl 1 1/2f: no ex fnl f* **2/1**[1]

6 3 **Dont Teutch (FR)**[33] 4191 2-8-10 0 Christophe-PatriceLemaire 8 90
(D Smaga, France) *smartly away and t.k.h but sn settled bhd ldng gp: 6th and pushed along appr 2f out: rdn 1 1/2f out: no imp fnl f*

7 1½ **Gatepost (IRE)**[14] 4834 2-9-0 0 JamieSpencer 7 90
(Mick Channon) *a.p: 2nd and pressed ldr 2 1/2f out: shkn up 2f out: wknd fr 1 1/2f out* **14/1**

1m 10.0s (-1.00) **Going Correction** +0.05s/f (Good) **7** Ran SP% **112.4**
Speed ratings: **108,104,102,102,100 96,94**
WIN (incl. 1 euro stake): 2.40. PLACES: 1.10, 1.20, 1.60. DF: 3.00. SF: 5.20.
Owner Simon Springer **Bred** Mme L Monfort **Trained** France

FOCUS
The French had won this race only three times in the previous 17 runnings and Dabirsim was the first French-trained winner since 2004, when Divine Proportions took this as a precursor to four more Group 1s including her domestic Classic wins in the Pouliches and Diane. The likelihood of a home winner was higher this year as there were no Irish-trained contenders (responsible for four overseas winners). The winning time compares favourably with previous runnings, bearing out not only that it was decent ground but also the impression that Family One set an even pace despite both Frederick Engels and Dabirsim taking a strong hold early.

NOTEBOOK
Dabirsim(FR) impressed in stretching his unbeaten record to four, quickening past Family One to win with something in hand and in a style that suggests he will get further, especially if he settles better into his races. He certainly has the physique and pedigree to suggest he will get 1m in time. Connections are targeting the Middle Park and bookmakers gave him a 14-1 quote for the Qipco 2,000 Guineas, which is not the most far-fetched move, especially as Godolphin's jockey Frankie Dettori was highly complimentary.
Family One(FR) was there to be shot at but held the rest comfortably, backing up his Robert Papin win and certainly not failing for stamina over the slightly longer trip.
Vladimir(IRE), dropping back in trip, was on and off the bridle through the race but kept on to snatch third. This Spanish raider looks up to adding a lower Group win to his Listed success in France.
Sofast(FR) was slowly away and always playing catch-up in only his second race. He acquitted himself well and looks a progressive colt to follow this autumn.
Frederick Engels failed to run his race and his trainer reported he gave a cough at the start. He ran around on the ground after taking a keen hold and wilted badly in the final furlong. This was not his running, especially after his Windsor Castle victim Caspar Netscher's Gimcrack success.
Dont Teutch(FR), the only filly in the race, was beaten before the race unfolded.
Gatepost(IRE) ran a second lacklustre race and this leaves him with plenty of questions to answer.

5306a DARLEY PRIX JEAN ROMANET (GROUP 1) (4YO+ FILLIES & MARES) (TURF) 1m 2f
3:10 (12:00) 4-Y-O+ **£123,146** (£49,267; £24,633; £12,306; £6,163)

RPR

1 **Announce**[32] 4223 4-9-0 0 MaximeGuyon 2 115+
(A Fabre, France) *settled in 4th: shkn up 2 1/2f out: jst over 2 l 4th appr 2f out: pushed along appr fnl f: rdn and qcknd ent fnl f to ld 75yds out* **5/2**[2]

2 snk **Timepiece**[21] 4597 4-9-0 0 TomQueally 3 115
(Sir Henry Cecil) *sn settled in share of 2nd on outside: pushed along to chal ldr in centre of trck ent fnl 2f: led appr fnl f: hdd 75yds out: no ex* **1/1**[1]

3 2½ **Lily Of The Valley (FR)**[44] 3822 4-9-0 0 ChristopheSoumillon 4 110
(J-C Rouget, France) *plld hrd and led sn after s: qcknd over 2f out in centre of crse: hdd appr fnl f: kpt on but nt qckn* **10/3**[3]

4 ¾ **Divine Music (IRE)**[24] 4-9-0 0 (b) RonanThomas 5 109
(P Van De Poele, France) *racd in last: scrubbed along over 2f out: abt 4 to 5 l last nring fnl f: kpt on u.p to snatch 4th cl home* **33/1**

5 ¾ **Fleur Enchantee (FR)**[75] 2795 7-9-0 0 (p) GregoryBenoist 1 107
(P Van De Poele, France) *led briefly early: sn hdd and settled in share of 2nd on rail: 3rd and rdn ins fnl 1 1/2f: kpt on at one pce u.p fnl f: lost 4th cl home* **28/1**

2m 10.9s (0.70) **Going Correction** +0.05s/f (Good) **5** Ran SP% **108.0**
Speed ratings: **99,98,96,96,95**
WIN (incl. 1 euro stake): 1.50 (Announce coupled with Timepiece). PLACES: 2.20, 1.30. SF: 6.60.
Owner K Abdulla **Bred** Juddmonte Farms **Trained** Chantilly, France

FOCUS
There are few more ridiculous Group 1 contests in the European Pattern than the Prix Jean Romanet and its third staging as a top-flight event attracted exactly the sort of uninspiring field it deserved. For a Group 1 event so deep in the season to be restricted to 4yos and above is both bizarre and anti-competitive, but for it to come in the same week as the Yorkshire Oaks and just three weeks after the Nassau Stakes is even more ludicrous. The enhancement of the programme for high-class fillies and mares has been welcome and beneficial, but the upgrading of the Jean Romanet is a step too far and of little benefit to the sport save for the small handful of connections that have so shrewdly exploited it. On this occasion only five horses faced the starter, but two of the five were huge outsiders from the same yard, while two members of the trio who could genuinely claim to possess Group 1 talent represented the same owner, Khalid Abdullah.

NOTEBOOK
Announce proved too strong for Timepiece after a typically French home-straight sprint that was the outcome of a race run at a dawdle. The Andre Fabre-trained winner was produced last by Maxime Guyon and ultimately won decisively, adding to a pair of Group 3 victories. Having finished second to Sarafina and Cirrus Des Aigles this season, the daughter of Selkirk had established herself as a high-class individual, but she had not looked like a Group 1 winner waiting to happen. As such, Fabre and Abdullah's racing manager Teddy Grimthorpe should be applauded for making the most of an excellent opportunity. She heads next to the Prix de l'Opera, where a stiffer task will surely await her.
Timepiece has blossomed this season to become the filly Sir Henry Cecil hoped he might have early last season. Her Falmouth Stakes triumph came as a bolt from the blue at the time - not least because she was dropping back to 1m, having previously won the Warwickshire Oaks over 1m3f - but she is plainly versatile. Given her winning form over 1m it was perhaps surprising that she was outpaced by a rival who began her career over 1m4f, and it is debatable whether she was quite at her best. It also seemed that Tom Queally sat quiet for a few strides too long after taking the lead early in the straight, but that was almost certainly because his mount does little once in front. As such, Queally found himself in a difficult situation and he was in no way to blame for the defeat.
Lily Of The Valley(FR), last year's Opera winner, has been a long way below her best this season but this was a step in the right direction, albeit in an unsatisfactory event. She was put under only hands and heels pressure down the straight, which suggests her camp believe improvement is likely in the autumn.
Divine Music(IRE) is a long way below Group 1 material and her proximity to the three principals was due to the steady early gallop. It would be dangerous to assume she has suddenly produced a vastly improved display.

DIELSDORF (R-H)
Sunday, August 21

OFFICIAL GOING: Turf: good

5307a PRIX DE DIANE ELEGANCE (CONDITIONS) (3YO FILLIES) (TURF) 1m 3f 110y
3:00 (12:00) 3-Y-O **£16,275** (£6,344; £4,689; £3,034; £1,655)

RPR

1 **Nayfashion** 3-9-2 0 TonyCastanheira 2 93
(Karin Suter-Weber, Switzerland) **187/10**

2 1 **Pasalsa (FR)**[77] 3-9-2 0 FredericSpanu 4 91
(Carmen Bocskai, Switzerland) **31/5**[2]

3 2 **Madhulika (FR)**[342] 3-9-2 0 NicolasPerret 1 88
(R Mongil, France) **4/5**[1]

4 3 **Zorrita (IRE)** 3-9-2 0 MlleNoemiHerren 10 82
(Carmen Bocskai, Switzerland) **83/10**

5 1½ **Delamour** 3-9-2 0 RobertHavlin 3 80
(M Weiss, Switzerland) **123/10**

6 2½ **Azarra (IRE)**[282] 3-9-2 0 StephaneBreux 5 75
(R Mongil, France) **222/10**

7 1¼ **Pretty Diamond (IRE)**[23] 4515 3-9-2 0 RoystonFfrench 6 73
(Mark Johnston) *w ldrs early: sn settled in 4th on outside: pushed along and lost pl 1/2-way: 10th and scrubbed along 3 1/2f out: styd on u.str.p ins fnl 2f: nt rch ldrs* **13/2**

8 6 **Cresta (SWI)** 3-9-2 0 (b) GeorgBocskai 12 62
(Carmen Bocskai, Switzerland) **218/10**

9 10 **Vuvuzela (SWI)** 3-9-2 0 MKolb 9 44
(H Speck, Switzerland) **141/10**

10 4 **Sabianca (FR)** 3-9-2 0 ChantalZollet 13 37
(Chantal Zollet, Switzerland) **46/1**

11 nk **Aima D'Avril (GER)**[95] 3-9-2 0 (b) MissCBurri 11 36
(P Schaerer, Switzerland) **192/10**

12 1½ **Sunayana (IRE)**[26] 3-9-2 0 Jean-MichelBreux 7 34
(R Mongil, France) **63/10**[3]

13 9 **Prairie Stella (GER)** 3-9-2 0 (b) MathiasSautjeau 8 18
(M Weiss, Switzerland) **30/1**

2m 23.68s (143.68) **13** Ran SP% **145.4**
PARI-MUTUEL (all including 1 swiss franc stake): WIN 19.70; PL 2.80, 2.60, 1.50; DF 35.00.
Owner Maya Suter **Bred** Baroness Bloodstock **Trained** Switzerland

HANOVER (L-H)
Sunday, August 21

OFFICIAL GOING: Turf: good

5308a GROSSER PREIS DES AUDI ZENTRUMS HANNOVER (GROUP 3) (3YO) (TURF) 1m 2f
2:05 (2:10) 3-Y-O
£27,586 (£9,482; £4,741; £2,586; £1,724; £1,293)

RPR

1 **Theo Danon (GER)**[49] 3672 3-9-0 0 FilipMinarik 3 109
(P Schiergen, Germany) *settled 4th on ins rail: travelling wl: r.o wl u.p early in st: tk ld 1 1/2f out: drew clr ins fnl f: easily* **61/10**

2 1 3/4 **Lindenthaler (GER)**[49] 3672 3-9-2 0 .... AStarke 6 107
(P Schiergen, Germany) *broke wl: settled 3rd: flattered briefly early in st: appeared to be wkng but railled to run wl ins fnl f to go 2nd 100yds out* **21/10**[1]
3 hd **Navarra Queen**[14] 4839 3-8-13 0 .... MCadeddu 1 104
(P Schiergen, Germany) *settled as bkmarker: moved forward down bkstretch: r.o u.p in st: chsng ldr: ct for 2nd cl home* **31/5**
4 2 **Gereon (GER)**[28] 4374 3-9-2 0 .... EFrank 5 103
(C Zschache, Germany) *broke fast and led early: then settled bhd ldr: pulling freely: rdn on fnl turn: grabbed ld 2f out: hdd 1 1/2f out: r.o one pce* **31/10**[3]
5 2 1/2 **Aviator (GER)**[42] 3-8-11 0 .... AnthonyCrastus 4 93
(T Mundry, Germany) *settled 6th: r.o in st but nt qckn: no imp* **128/10**
6 3/4 **Sundream (GER)**[69] 3007 3-8-11 0 .... EPedroza 2 91
(A Wohler, Germany) *settled 5th: nvr figured in st* **57/10**
7 1 3/4 **Sinnerman (GER)**[42] 3-9-0 0 .... ADeVries 7 91
(J Hirschberger, Germany) *broke wl and sn led: setting mod pce: began to weaken bef st: sn btn* **13/5**[2]

2m 2.41s (122.41) **7** Ran SP% **134.6**
WIN (incl. 10 euro stake): 71. PLACES: 19, 14, 17. SF: 246.
Owner Guido-Werner Hermann-Schmitt **Bred** Gestut Etzean **Trained** Germany

5202 HAMILTON (R-H)

Monday, August 22

OFFICIAL GOING: Good (good to soft in places on the loop; 7.3)
Wind: Almost nil Weather: Overcast

5309 GLENGOYNE HIGHLAND SINGLE MALT AMATEUR RIDERS' H'CAP 6f 5y

2:30 (2:33) (Class 6) (0-65,63) 4-Y-0+ **£1,646** (£506; £253) **Stalls** High

Form RPR
0046 **1** **Ryedane (IRE)**[9] 5031 9-10-4 **60** ....(b) MrWEasterby(7) 1 72
(Tim Easterby) *hld up: hdwy and edgd lft over 1f out: led wl ins fnl f: r.o* **14/1**
-340 **2** 2 **Ivestar (IRE)**[21] 4600 6-10-4 **58** ....(vt) MissCharlotteHolmes(5) 8 64
(Ben Haslam) *cl up: slt ld over 2f out: hdd wl ins fnl f: r.o* **16/1**
3560 **3** 1/2 **Tournedos (IRE)**[39] 4017 9-10-0 **56** ....(b) MrBHowe(7) 2 60
(Ruth Carr) *prom: effrt and swtchd rt over 1f out: kpt on same pce ins fnl f* **28/1**
3206 **4** 1 1/4 **Two Turtle Doves (IRE)**[21] 4600 5-10-8 **60** .... MissMMullineaux(3) 6 60
(Michael Mullineaux) *cl up: disp ld over 2f out to ins fnl f: hld towards fin* **11/1**
5350 **5** 1 **Hayek**[11] 4945 4-10-9 **63** ....(p) MissRRichardson(5) 5 60
(Tim Easterby) *bhd: hdwy on outside 2f out: sn edgd rt: no imp fnl f* **5/1**[1]
0-45 **6** 1 **Chookie Avon**[10] 4987 4-10-8 **57** ....(p) JackQuinlan 12 51+
(Keith Dalgleish) *bhd: drvn 1/2-way: kpt on fnl f: nvr rchd ldrs* **5/1**[1]
6064 **7** 1/2 **Foreign Rhythm (IRE)**[11] 4942 6-10-8 **62** .... MissVBarr(5) 3 54
(Ron Barr) *prom: pushed along over 2f out: no ex over 1f out* **20/1**
4625 **8** 1 **Burnwynd Boy**[16] 4782 6-10-11 **60** .... MrSWalker 13 49+
(Ian Semple) *hld up: effrt and drvn along over 2f out: no imp over 1f out* **11/2**[2]
6421 **9** 1/2 **Avoncreek**[23] 4563 7-10-0 **49** ....(v) MissSBrotherton 9 37
(Brian Baugh) *early ldr: cl up tl edgd rt and wknd over 1f out* **6/1**[3]
0514 **10** 1 3/4 **Benny The Bear**[13] 4876 4-10-3 **59** .... MrSFeeney(7) 7 41
(Linda Perratt) *fly-jmpd s: sn led: hdd over 2f out: sn wknd* **7/1**
1654 **11** 2 1/4 **Andrasta**[4] 5204 6-10-0 **52** .... MissWGibson(3) 10 27+
(Alan Berry) *bhd: drvn along 1/2-way: sn btn* **50/1**
0-00 **12** shd **Monte Mayor One**[16] 4780 4-10-4 **53** .... MrsCBartley 4 27
(Jim Goldie) *in tch: rdn over 2f out: wknd wl over 1f out* **28/1**

1m 13.08s (0.88) **Going Correction** -0.025s/f (Good) **12** Ran SP% **110.0**
Speed ratings (Par 101): **93,90,89,88,86 85,84,83,82,80 77,77**
toteswingers:1&2:£[illegible], 1&3:£31.60, 2&3:£70.90 CSF £184.14 CT £5261.15 TOTE £15.50: £4.90, £5.50, £12.00; EX 194.30 Trifecta £319.80 Part won. Pool: £432.24 - 0.07 winning units..
Owner Ryedale Partners No 5 **Bred** Tally-Ho Stud **Trained** Great Habton, N Yorks
■ Stewards' Enquiry : Miss W Gibson caution: used whip when out of contention.
Miss Charlotte Holmes three-day ban: used whip with excessive frequency (Sep 20,29,Oct 4)
Jack Quinlan caution: used whip with excessive frequency.

FOCUS
Races on round course were run over 8yds more than advertised. Fresh ground on far side of home straight. The main action unfolded up the middle of the track. This was just a moderate amateur riders' handicap, but the pace was fair. The winner is rated close to his Beverley June form, with the runner-up in line with previous C&D marks.

5310 HAMILTON-PARK.CO.UK TWO YEAR OLD CLAIMING STKS 6f 5y

3:00 (3:04) (Class 6) 2-Y-0 **£1,617** (£481; £240; £120) **Stalls** High

Form RPR
224 **1** **Kimbali (IRE)**[8] 5077 2-9-2 0 .... PaulHanagan 5 75
(Richard Fahey) *chsd ldrs: wnt 2nd over 2f out: effrt and drvn wl over 1f out: led ins fnl f: styd on wl* **8/13**[1]
2161 **2** 2 **Sonko (IRE)**[7] 5105 2-8-7 62 ow1 ....(p) GrahamGibbons 2 60
(Tim Pitt) *led: rdn and edgd rt over 1f out: hdd ins fnl f: kpt on same pce* **13/8**[2]
0 **3** 9 **Reine Du Froid (IRE)**[14] 4853 2-8-7 0 .... PJMcDonald 4 33
(Ben Haslam) *bhd and sn outpcd: plenty to do 1/2-way: sme late hdwy: nvr on terms* **16/1**[3]
3505 **4** 7 **Come To Mind**[16] 4808 2-8-5 47 .... JulieBurke(5) 3 15
(Alan Berry) *chsd ldr to over 2f out: sn rdn and wknd* **100/1**

1m 12.56s (0.36) **Going Correction** -0.025s/f (Good) **4** Ran SP% **106.9**
Speed ratings (Par 92): **96,93,81,72**
CSF £1.81 TOTE £1.50; EX 1.70.
Owner R A Fahey **Bred** P Kelly **Trained** Musley Bank, N Yorks

FOCUS
An uncompetitive claimer with the winner rated to the best view of his earlier form.

NOTEBOOK
Kimbali(IRE), who was down in grade and up in trip, made hard work of gaining his first success at the fourth attempt. He looked held for much of the closing stages, but stayed on stronger than his only serious rival, who had made the running and got noticeably tired. Still, this wasn't a bad effort at the weights considering the runner-up, who was getting 9lb, came into this officially rated 62. (op 4-6 tchd 8-11)
Sonko(IRE), whose two wins to date were gained over 5f, travelled easily in the lead for much of the way and touched 1.01 in-running, but for some reason Graham Gibbons, who put up 1lb overweight, looked around several times in the closing stages and the filly weakened tamely late on, found out by this still 6f. It's likely she would have been beaten regardless of her rider's lack of focus, as she clearly got tired, but it did not make for good viewing. (tchd 6-4)
Reine Du Froid(IRE) was never going on this drop in trip, passing only a beaten rival and appearing to hang right when doing so. (tchd 25-1)

5311 BETFAIR SUPPORTS SCOTTISH RACING H'CAP (BETFAIR BONUS SCOTTISH RACING STAYERS SERIES QUALIFIER) 1m 3f 16y

3:30 (3:32) (Class 5) (0-75,75) 3-Y-0+ **£4,204** (£1,251; £625; £312) **Stalls** High

Form RPR
1531 **1** **Unknown Rebel (IRE)**[22] 4576 3-8-13 **74** ....(p) JulieBurke(5) 1 86
(Kevin Ryan) *mde all: rdn 2f out: kpt on strly fnl f: rdn out* **6/1**
1011 **2** 2 **Carragold**[6] 5150 5-9-3 **64** 6ex .... RobertWinston 4 72
(Mel Brittain) *midfield: rdn and outpcd over 3f out: rallied and chsd (clr) wnr ins fnl f: no imp* **11/2**[3]
564 **3** 1 1/2 **George Adamson (IRE)**[11] 4962 5-10-0 **75** .... PJMcDonald 5 80
(Alan Swinbank) *hld up in tch: hdwy to chse wnr over 2f out to 1f out: kpt on same pce fnl f* **15/2**
0350 **4** 1 1/4 **Royal Straight**[10] 5015 6-8-12 **62** ....(t) DaleSwift(3) 8 65
(Linda Perratt) *hld up: hdwy on ins over 2f out: rdn and kpt on fnl f: nvr able to chal* **25/1**
4602 **5** 1/2 **Jonny Delta**[13] 4879 4-9-3 **67** .... GaryBartley(3) 11 69
(Jim Goldie) *dwlt: hld up: rdn and hdwy over 2f out: kpt on fnl f: nrst fin* **5/1**[2]
0601 **6** 1/2 **Hail Bold Chief (USA)**[9] 5036 4-9-4 **70** .... GarryWhillans(5) 6 71
(Alan Swinbank) *trckd ldrs: effrt over 2f out: sn rdn: outpcd fnl f* **9/1**
5332 **7** 4 **Philharmonic Hall**[12] 4902 3-8-7 **63** ....(p) BarryMcHugh 3 57
(Richard Fahey) *hld up: rdn along 3f out: hdwy over 1f out: nvr rchd ldrs* **8/1**
5003 **8** 3/4 **En Fuego**[36] 4125 4-9-4 **65** .... GrahamGibbons 12 58
(Geoffrey Harker) *towards rr: rdn 4f out: rallied 2f out: sn no imp* **50/1**
0/00 **9** 9 **Lil Ella (IRE)**[9] 5062 4-9-6 **67** .... DuranFentiman 10 44
(Patrick Holmes) *bhd: rdn over 3f out: sn struggling: nvr on terms* **66/1**
0402 **10** nk **Artisan**[19] 4674 3-8-9 **65** .... TomEaves 7 41
(Brian Ellison) *t.k.h: in tch tl rdn and wknd over 2f out* **7/2**[1]
0000 **11** hd **Record Breaker (IRE)**[27] 4407 7-9-9 **70** ....(b) PaulHanagan 13 46
(Mark Johnston) *chsd wnr: rdn over 3f out: wknd over 2f out* **22/1**
300- **12** nk **Northern Acres**[70] 6571 5-9-3 **64** .... DavidAllan 9 39
(Sue Bradburne) *trckd ldrs: drvn over 3f out: sn wknd* **66/1**

2m 24.28s (-1.32) **Going Correction** -0.025s/f (Good)
WFA 3 from 4yo+ 9lb **12** Ran SP% **114.6**
Speed ratings (Par 103): **103,101,100,99,99 98,95,95,88,88 88,88**
toteswingers:1&2:£5.30, 1&3:£9.70, 2&3:£9.40 CSF £35.92 CT £249.01 TOTE £8.20: £2.00, £2.30, £2.90; EX 43.10 Trifecta £450.60 Pool: £805.84 - 1.32 winning units..
Owner D Reilly & Mrs C Reilly **Bred** Kilfrush Stud **Trained** Hambleton, N Yorks

FOCUS
A modest handicap in which the winner made most of the running. The form looks sound enough rated around the placed horses.
Artisan Official explanation: trainer said, regarding running, that the gelding ran too freely early

5312 ST ANDREWS FIRST AID RATING RELATED MAIDEN STKS 1m 3f 16y

4:00 (4:03) (Class 6) 3-Y-0+ **£1,704** (£503; £251) **Stalls** High

Form RPR
-432 **1** **Quails Hollow (IRE)**[34] 4180 3-9-1 70 .... PaulHanagan 3 73+
(William Haggas) *mde all at stdy gallop: qcknd 2f out: easily* **1/9**[1]
0600 **2** 6 **Why So Serious**[14] 4870 5-9-10 47 .... GregFairley 1 51
(Peter Salmon) *t.k.h: prom: hdwy to chse wnr over 2f out: no imp fnl f* **33/1**
436/ **3** nk **Elk Trail (IRE)**[440] 7247 6-9-3 62 .... JosephYoung(7) 2 50
(Michael Mullineaux) *trckd wnr to 2f out: kpt on same pce fnl f* **12/1**[2]
500 **4** 7 **Spread Boy (IRE)**[4] 5208 4-9-5 44 .... JulieBurke(5) 4 38
(Alan Berry) *t.k.h: trckd ldrs: rdn over 2f out: wknd wl over 1f out* **25/1**[3]

2m 28.15s (2.55) **Going Correction** -0.025s/f (Good)
WFA 3 from 4yo+ 9lb **4** Ran SP% **104.5**
Speed ratings (Par 101): **89,84,84,79**
CSF £4.90 TOTE £1.10; EX 3.00.
Owner Liam Sheridan **Bred** Liam Sheridan **Trained** Newmarket, Suffolk

FOCUS
A virtual non-event for first place with the winner value for much more than the official margin.

5313 ISLE OF SKYE 8-Y-O BLENDED SCOTCH WHISKY H'CAP (BETFAIR SCOTTISH RACING SPRINT SERIES QUALIFIER) 5f 4y

4:30 (4:30) (Class 5) (0-70,68) 3-Y-0+ **£4,204** (£1,251; £625; £312) **Stalls** High

Form RPR
/450 **1** **Here Now And Why (IRE)**[6] 5153 4-8-5 **49** oh1 ......(p) DuranFentiman 6 63
(Ian Semple) *trckd ldrs: effrt and rdn over 1f out: led wl ins fnl f: hld on wl* **8/1**[3]
0064 **2** 1/2 **Sharp Shoes**[13] 4881 4-9-2 **63** ....(p) DaleSwift(3) 8 75
(Ann Duffield) *led: rdn over 1f out: hdd wl ins fnl f: kpt on towards fin* **12/1**
3065 **3** 2 3/4 **Ingleby Star (IRE)**[12] 4900 6-9-6 **67** ....(p) PaulPickard(3) 10 69
(Ian McInnes) *cl up: rdn over 1f out: kpt on ins fnl f* **8/1**[3]
1115 **4** hd **Wicked Wilma (IRE)**[6] 5148 7-9-5 **68** .... JulieBurke(5) 2 69
(Alan Berry) *prom: effrt and edgd lft over 1f out: kpt on same pce ins fnl f* **6/1**[2]
2122 **5** 1 **Blown It (USA)**[6] 5148 5-9-7 **65** .... PaulHanagan 4 63
(Keith Dalgleish) *hld up bhd ldng gp: drvn 1/2-way: kpt on fnl f: nvr able to chal* **7/4**[1]
4533 **6** 1 1/4 **Sharp Bullet (IRE)**[10] 4986 5-8-13 **57** ....(p) FrederikTylicki 1 50
(Bruce Hellier) *in tch on outside: rdn 2f out: outpcd fnl f* **10/1**
3201 **7** nk **Sea Salt**[10] 5008 8-9-5 **68** .... GarryWhillans(5) 9 60
(Ron Barr) *cl up: rdn along 1/2-way: no ex over 1f out* **14/1**
0213 **8** nk **Arriva La Diva**[24] 4504 5-9-5 **63** .... DavidAllan 3 54
(Linda Perratt) *fly-jmpd s: hld up: rdn and shortlived effrt over 1f out: btn ins fnl f* **10/1**
2556 **9** 1 1/4 **Saxonette**[13] 4880 3-9-7 **67** .... TomEaves 5 54
(Linda Perratt) *dwlt: hld up: shortlived effrt over 1f out: sn btn* **25/1**
-000 **10** 1/2 **Speedy Senorita (IRE)**[10] 4986 6-8-10 **54** .... PJMcDonald 7 39
(James Moffatt) *dwlt: bhd and outpcd: rdn 1/2-way: nvr on terms* **25/1**

59.53 secs (-0.47) **Going Correction** -0.025s/f (Good)
WFA 3 from 4yo+ 2lb **10** Ran SP% **113.1**
Speed ratings (Par 103): **102,101,96,96,94 92,92,91,89,89**
toteswingers:1&2:£16.90, 1&3:£11.00, 2&3:£11.30 CSF £96.32 CT £786.74 TOTE £11.90: £3.40, £4.60, £3.30; EX 122.20 TRIFECTA Not won..
Owner Kenman Properties **Bred** Mrs Sandra McCarthy **Trained** Carluke, S Lanarks
■ Stewards' Enquiry : Duran Fentiman caution: used whip with excessive frequency.

FOCUS
The pace looked honest, but it can't have been that quick as few got involved. The favourite underperformed and this is ordinary form, although the runner-up has a good record here and is rated back to his best.

5314 LONDON HILL DRY GIN H'CAP (QUALIFIER FOR THE BETFAIR BONUS SCOTTISH RACING MILE FINAL) 1m 65y
5:05 (5:12) (Class 5) (0-75,76) 3-Y-O+ £4,204 (£1,251; £625; £312) Stalls Low

Form RPR

3131 **1** **I'm Super Too (IRE)**[4] 5205 4-9-8 **76** 6ex GarryWhillans(5) 3 89+
(Alan Swinbank) *hld up in midfield: smooth hdwy over 2f out: swtchd lft and led gng wl over 1f out: edgd rt and sn clr: kpt on wl fnl f* **5/2**[1]

00 **2** 3/4 **Master Of Dance (IRE)**[14] 4866 4-8-11 **60** (p) GrahamGibbons 12 69
(Peter Salmon) *prom: drvn and outpcd over 3f out: rallied over 1f out: chsd wnr and edgd rt ins fnl f: kpt on fin* **100/1**

4360 **3** 3 **Botham (USA)**[4] 5205 7-8-10 **62** PaulPickard(3) 6 64
(Jim Goldie) *bhd: hdwy and in tch over 2f out: rdn and kpt on ins fnl f* **20/1**

0524 **4** 1 3/4 **Law To Himself (IRE)**[6] 5150 4-9-3 **66** PJMcDonald 9 64
(Alan Swinbank) *missed break: bhd tl styd on wl fr 2f out: nrst fin* **16/1**

4045 **5** 1 **Fibs And Flannel**[49] 3683 4-9-5 **68** (p) DavidAllan 1 64
(Tim Easterby) *prom: effrt and ev ch 2f out: no ex fnl f* **9/2**[2]

3142 **6** 1 **Seldom (IRE)**[7] 5106 5-8-13 **62** RobertWinston 4 55
(Mel Brittain) *trckd ldrs: effrt and ev ch 2f out: no ex ins fnl f* **7/1**[3]

6126 **7** 1/2 **Solar Spirit (IRE)**[4] 5205 6-9-11 **74** GregFairley 7 66
(Tracy Waggott) *cl up: led over 4f out tl over 1f out: wknd ins fnl f* **16/1**

2503 **8** 1 **Kerrys Requiem (IRE)**[7] 5106 5-9-7 **75** (p) JulieBurke(5) 2 65
(Tim Pitt) *hld up: rdn along over 3f out: outpcd fnl 2f* **7/1**[3]

642 **9** 1 **Andiamo Via**[16] 4813 4-8-11 **60** BarryMcHugh 15 48
(Michael Smith) *s.i.s: hld up: hdwy into midfield 1/2-way: wknd over 2f out* **16/1**

6140 **10** 2 1/2 **Casino Night**[13] 4877 6-9-3 **69** DaleSwift(3) 16 51
(Barry Murtagh) *hld up: rdn and struggling over 2f out: sn btn* **40/1**

6120 **11** 3/4 **Burns Night**[25] 4477 5-9-12 **75** DuranFentiman 5 55
(Geoffrey Harker) *in tch: shuffled bk to rr after 1f: rdn over 3f out: nvr able to chal* **25/1**

2243 **12** 1 **Cono Zur (FR)**[16] 4811 4-9-12 **75** (b) JamesSullivan 10 53
(Ruth Carr) *led to over 4f out: rallied: rdn and wknd over 1f out* **14/1**

5200 **13** 7 **Berbice (IRE)**[9] 5053 6-9-3 **66** FrederikTylicki 13 28
(Linda Perratt) *hld up: effrt on outside over 3f out: rdn and wknd 2f out* **25/1**

61 **14** 1 3/4 **Chookie Royale**[23] 4542 3-9-6 **75** TomEaves 8 33
(Keith Dalgleish) *in tch: effrt on outside over 3f out: wknd wl over 2f out* **16/1**

2662 **15** 23 **Old English (IRE)**[16] 4812 3-8-11 **66** PaulHanagan 11 —
(Linda Perratt) *walked to post: midfield: lost pl qckly 5f out: lost tch fr 3f out* **25/1**

1m 48.17s (-0.23) **Going Correction** -0.025s/f (Good)
WFA 3 from 4yo+ 6lb **15** Ran SP% **121.7**
Speed ratings (Par 103): **100,99,96,94,93 92,92,91,90,87 86,85,78,77,54**
toteswingers:1&2:£45.60, 1&3:£14.80, 2&3:£59.10 CSF £370.92 CT £4299.91 TOTE £3.90: £1.60, £11.80, £3.60; EX 298.40 TRIFECTA Not won..
Owner David C Young **Bred** Norelands Bloodstock, J Hanly & H Lascelles **Trained** Melsonby, N Yorks
■ Stewards' Enquiry : David Allan one-day ban: careless riding (Sep 5)

FOCUS
A modest handicap in which the runner-up sets the standard backed up by the third.

5315 SCOTTISH RACING PUNTERS CLUB H'CAP 1m 1f 36y
5:40 (5:40) (Class 6) (0-60,60) 3-Y-O £1,617 (£481; £240; £120) Stalls Low

Form RPR

102 **1** **Smart Violetta (IRE)**[13] 4878 3-8-9 **51** (t) DaleSwift(3) 5 62
(Ann Duffield) *hld up in tch: checked over 4f out: smooth hdwy to ld over 1f out: sn rdn: edgd rt and kpt on wl fnl f* **11/4**[2]

3643 **2** 3 1/4 **Henrys Gift (IRE)**[13] 4878 3-9-3 **56** TomEaves 6 60
(Michael Dods) *led: rdn over 2f out: hdd over 1f out: kpt on same pce ins fnl f* **11/2**[3]

500- **3** 2 **Way Chief (FR)**[269] 7578 3-9-7 **60** PaulHanagan 1 60
(Richard Fahey) *t.k.h early: trckd ldrs: outpcd over 3f out: kpt on u.p fnl f: no imp* **11/8**[1]

5425 **4** 1/2 **Purkab**[13] 4878 3-8-12 **54** (b[1]) GaryBartley(3) 2 53
(Jim Goldie) *sn cl up: rdn 3f out: outpcd 2f out: no imp after* **7/1**

1060 **5** 3 3/4 **Abernethy (IRE)**[6] 5150 3-8-10 **49** (b[1]) FrederikTylicki 3 39
(Linda Perratt) *hld up in tch: effrt over 2f out: sn no imp: btn fnl f* **11/1**

3053 **U** **Oldmeldrum (IRE)**[26] 4441 3-8-9 **48** GregFairley 4 —
(Peter Salmon) *chsng ldrs whn broke down bdly and uns rdr over 4f out: fatally injured* **10/1**

2m 0.94s (1.24) **Going Correction** -0.025s/f (Good) **6** Ran SP% **114.1**
Speed ratings (Par 98): **93,90,88,87,84** —
toteswingers:1&2:£1.30, 1&3:£2.10, 2&3:£1.90. Totesuper 7: Won: Not won, Place: Not won. CSF £18.33 TOTE £4.30: £4.00, £5.10; EX 10.40.
Owner Six Iron Partnership **Bred** Peter Byrne **Trained** Constable Burton, N Yorks

FOCUS
A weak handicap and muddling form, but rated at face value for now.
T/Plt: £1,815.50 to a £1 stake. Pool:£60,933.92 - 24.50 winning tickets T/Qpdt: £99.00 to a £1 stake. Pool:£5,782.70 - 43.20 winning tickets RY

5140 KEMPTON (A.W) (R-H)
Monday, August 22

OFFICIAL GOING: Standard
Wind: Moderate behind Weather: Sunny

5316 32 ONLINE CASINO NURSERY 5f (P)
2:15 (2:15) (Class 6) (0-65,65) 2-Y-O £1,617 (£481; £240; £120) Stalls Low

Form RPR

6333 **1** **Roy's Legacy**[6] 5147 2-8-9 **53** (t) RobbieFitzpatrick 1 58
(Shaun Harris) *trckd ldrs: wnt 2nd ins fnl 2f: chal fnl f tl led fnl 120yds: drvn out* **7/1**

4356 **2** 1/2 **Balm**[18] 4704 2-9-7 **65** RichardHughes 9 68
(Richard Hannon) *led: rdn and qcknd ins fnl 2f: hdd and outpcd fnl 120yds* **11/2**

5656 **3** 2 **Russian Bullet**[11] 4955 2-8-9 **53** (b) FergusSweeney 4 49
(Jamie Osborne) *broke wl: outpcd: racd on outside and stl last wl over 1f out: str run fnl f and fin wl to take 3rd cl home but nt trble ldng duo* **50/1**

4245 **4** hd **Dressed In Lace**[11] 4955 2-9-5 **63** JimmyFortune 6 58
(Andrew Balding) *chsd ldrs: rdn and one pce 1f out: styd on again fnl f to briefly hold 3rd: kpt on but outpcd into 4th cl home* **4/1**[2]

504 **5** 2 1/4 **Mr Hendrix**[18] 4710 2-8-8 **52** WilliamCarson 10 39
(Brett Johnson) *t.k.h: chsd ldr tl ins fnl 2f: wknd ins fnl f* **10/1**

6601 **6** 3/4 **Selbaar**[12] 4922 2-9-3 **61** (p) AndreaAtzeni 2 45
(Chris Dwyer) *chsd ldrs: rdn over 2f out: wknd wl over 1f out* **3/1**[1]

0006 **7** 1/2 **Compton Bird**[10] 4992 2-8-13 **57** JamesDoyle 8 40
(Hans Adielsson) *broke wl: sn outpcd: rdn and no prog fnl 2f* **20/1**

040 **8** nk **Arabian Flight**[18] 4720 2-8-4 **48** (p) ChrisCatlin 5 30
(Ed Dunlop) *racd on outside: rdn 1/2-way: a in rr* **5/1**[3]

0423 **9** 1 1/2 **Masivo Man (IRE)**[75] 2823 2-8-8 **52** JimmyQuinn 7 28
(Chris Dwyer) *chsd ldrs 3f* **33/1**

006 **10** 4 **Compton Monarch**[11] 4947 2-8-1 **48** SophieDoyle(3) 3 10
(Hans Adielsson) *a outpcd* **16/1**

60.64 secs (0.14) **Going Correction** -0.075s/f (Stan) **10** Ran SP% **114.2**
Speed ratings (Par 92): **95,94,91,90,87 85,85,84,82,75**
toteswingers:1&2:£8.10, 1&3:£20.10, 2&3:£30.10 CSF £43.41 CT £1820.95 TOTE £10.30: £1.80, £2.60, £9.60; EX 43.20.
Owner Karl Blackwell Steve Mohammed S A Harris **Bred** A Christou **Trained** Carburton, Notts

FOCUS
A moderate nursery, mainly dominated by those that raced up with the pace. The form looks sound with the first two clear.

NOTEBOOK
Roy's Legacy has had a few chances and had been running well on a slower surface lately, but he had the plum draw here and that made plenty of difference. He got a nice tow from the two leaders and was able to pounce well inside the last furlong to break his duck at the ninth attempt. The form is modest, but he looks the ideal type to keep on going right through the winter. (op 13-2)
Balm did well to get across from her wide draw in front and made a bold bid to make all, but she was cut down late. She's starting to look exposed. (tchd 5-1)
Russian Bullet bucked the trend as he raced in last early before finishing well after being switched out wide once into the straight, but he had finished unplaced in all six previous starts so it's not worth getting too carried away.
Dressed In Lace merely plugged on having been prominent throughout. (op 9-2)
Mr Hendrix, making his nursery debut after beating a total of two horses in three maidens, was rushed up to press the early leader from the outside stall, but he was keen enough and his earlier exertions eventually told. (op 11-1)
Selbaar, 6lb higher than when success over 6f at Wolverhampton last time in first-time cheekpieces, was another to take a grip in midfield and found little off the bridle. (op 7-2)

5317 32 FOR SLOTS MAIDEN FILLIES' STKS 1m 2f (P)
2:45 (2:45) (Class 5) 3-Y-O+ £2,264 (£673; £336; £168) Stalls Low

Form RPR

2050 **1** **Blaise Chorus (IRE)**[16] 4790 3-8-12 90 MichaelHills 12 87+
(Charles Hills) *mde all: drvn and c clr over 1f out: unchal* **11/4**[1]

2 5 **Sweet Lavender (IRE)** 3-8-12 0 TedDurcan 4 77+
(Saeed Bin Suroor) *chsd ldrs tl rdn and bdly outpcd fr 3f out: styd on again over 1f out: kpt on wl to take 2nd last strides but no ch w wnr* **8/1**

46 **3** nk **Ecossaise**[29] 4370 3-8-12 0 SilvestreDeSousa 13 76+
(Mark Johnston) *chsd ldr: rdn and tried to chal ins fnl 2f: btn and wnt rt over 1f out: lost wl hld 2nd last strides* **18/1**

0 **4** 7 **Perilously (USA)**[98] 2157 3-8-12 0 RichardHughes 2 67+
(Jeremy Noseda) *chsd ldrs: rdn and wkng in 3rd fr 2f out: eased whn btn fnl f* **7/2**[2]

6-25 **5** 4 **Hairstyle**[74] 2840 3-8-12 80 RichardMullen 6 54
(Sir Michael Stoute) *prom tl pushed along and outpcd fr 3f out: mod prog again fnl f* **5/1**[3]

0 **6** 1 **Balandra**[23] 4529 3-8-12 0 AndreaAtzeni 1 52
(Luca Cumani) *ponied to s: chsd ldrs tl wknd fr 2f out* **50/1**

63 **7** 5 **Maz**[12] 4925 3-8-12 0 DavidProbert 3 42
(Alan Bailey) *chsd ldrs: rdn 3f out: sn wknd* **22/1**

8 1 1/4 **Midnight Waltz** 3-8-12 0 SebSanders 7 40+
(Sir Mark Prescott Bt) *slowly away: sn rdn and green: wd into st bnd over 2f out: nvr any ch* **22/1**

0343 **9** 1 1/2 **Dawn Gale (IRE)**[31] 4279 3-8-12 80 SteveDrowne 8 37
(Hughie Morrison) *t.k.h: chsd ldrs: wknd 3f out* **7/2**[2]

10 nk **Cardi Crystal (IRE)** 4-9-6 0 JamesDoyle 9 36
(Ian Wood) *in rr and green: a bhd* **80/1**

00 **11** 10 **Cranworth Quest (IRE)**[23] 4559 3-8-12 0 JimmyQuinn 10 16
(Tim Etherington) *sn in rr* **66/1**

0 **12** 1 1/2 **Lucky Dime**[19] 4663 3-8-12 0 ChrisCatlin 5 13
(Noel Quinlan) *a in rr* **100/1**

06 **13** 1 1/4 **Shikra**[11] 4963 3-8-12 0 (e) WilliamCarson 14 11
(Eugene Stanford) *s.i.s: a in rr* **100/1**

2m 5.50s (-2.50) **Going Correction** -0.075s/f (Stan)
WFA 3 from 4yo 8lb **13** Ran SP% **119.5**
Speed ratings (Par 100): **107,103,102,97,93 93,89,88,86,86 78,77,76**
toteswingers:1&2:£8.20, 1&3:£14.20, 2&3:£17.60 CSF £24.88 TOTE £4.10: £1.60, £3.30, £3.90; EX 31.40.
Owner D J Deer **Bred** D J And Mrs Deer **Trained** Lambourn, Berks
■ A winner with his first runner for Charlie Hils, who has taken over the licence from his father Barry.

FOCUS
Very few ever got into this maiden and they finished well spread out. The winner sets the level rated in line with the balance of her form.
Maz Official explanation: jockey said filly hung left
Dawn Gale(IRE) Official explanation: jockey said filly stopped quickly

5318 32 FOR BLACKJACK H'CAP 1m 2f (P)
3:15 (3:16) (Class 5) (0-70,70) 3-Y-O+ £2,264 (£673; £336; £168) Stalls Low

Form RPR

-004 **1** **Height Of Summer (IRE)**[16] 4800 3-9-4 **69** TedDurcan 6 79+
(Chris Wall) *mid-div: rdn and hdwy on ins fr over 2f out: styd on u.p fnl f to ld fnl 150yds: drvn out* **15/2**

4246 **2** 1 1/4 **Dare To Bare (IRE)**[17] 4755 3-9-2 **67** JimCrowley 7 74
(Amanda Perrett) *sn led: hdd 5f out: styd chsng ldr: rdn to ld again over 1f out: hdd and one pce fnl 150yds* **11/1**

0060 **3** 3 **Tuxedo**[7] 5101 6-9-10 **67** LukeMorris 4 68
(Peter Hiatt) *sn drvn along and in tch: rdn again fr 4f out: styd on to chse ldng trio over 1f out: no ex and btn ins fnl f* **40/1**

0653 **4** 2 3/4 **Jodawes (USA)**[17] 4754 4-9-4 **61** SteveDrowne 1 57
(John Best) *chsd ldrs: rdn 3f out: styd on same pce fr over 1f out* **6/1**[3]

3500 **5** 1/2 **Striding Edge (IRE)**[7] 5101 5-9-8 **65** JamesDoyle 14 60
(Hans Adielsson) *in rr: rdn over 1f out: styd on fnl f but nvr any threat* **20/1**

4/00 **6** 1/2 **Mick's Dancer**[35] 4158 6-9-8 **65** RobertHavlin 12 59
(Richard Phillips) *in rr: drvn and styd on fr over 1f out: nt rch ldrs* **14/1**

-500 **7** 1/2 **Fifty Cents**[74] 2843 7-8-7 **57** BrendanPowell(7) 11 50
(Brendan Powell) *sn chsd ldr: led 5f out: rdn and hdwy over 1f whn n.m.r on ins and wknd qckly* **40/1**

0401 **8** 3/4 **Rio Tinto**[19] 4666 4-9-11 **68** WilliamCarson 5 59
(Giles Bravery) *chsd ldrs: rdn along fr 3f out: styd on over 1f out but no imp: wknd ins fnl f* **9/2**[1]

3056 **9** 3 **Diplomasi**[19] 4664 3-9-2 **67** PhilipRobinson 13 52
(Clive Brittain) *in rr: drvn and sme hdwy 1/2-way: chsd ldrs u.p 2f out: sn btn* **12/1**

3440 **10** shd **Signora Frasi (IRE)**[19] 4656 6-9-3 **60** FergusSweeney 3 45
(Tony Newcombe) *in rr: pushed along and mod prog ins fnl 2f* **14/1**

4650 **11** 3 3/4 **Silverglas (IRE)**[18] 4724 5-9-6 **63** (b[1]) SebSanders 10 40
(William Knight) *chsd ldrs: sn pushed along: rdn to chse ldr 4f out: hung lft and wknd qckly bnd 2f out* **5/1**[2]

2460 **12** 3 1/4 **Lastkingofscotland (IRE)**[10] 4990 5-9-13 **70** (b) HayleyTurner 2 41
(Conor Dore) *chsd ldrs over 6f* **14/1**

-066 **13** 17 **Dalhaan (USA)**[19] 4687 6-9-13 **70** TomMcLaughlin 9 —
(Luke Dace) *a towards rr: eased whn no ch* **20/1**

0030 **14** 2 1/2 **Commerce**[30] 4317 4-9-6 **63** GeorgeBaker 8 —
(Gary Moore) *chsd ldrs: wknd over 3f out: eased* **10/1**

2m 7.42s (-0.58) **Going Correction** -0.075s/f (Stan)
WFA 3 from 4yo+ 8lb **14** Ran SP% **120.4**
Speed ratings (Par 103): **99,98,95,93,93 92,92,91,89,89 86,83,69,67**
toteswingers:1&2:£11.10, 1&3:£47.20, 2&3:£55.60 CSF £83.62 CT £3077.72 TOTE £10.80: £4.30, £3.10, £9.00; EX 43.90.
Owner Hughes, Gibson & Scott **Bred** Sean Murphy **Trained** Newmarket, Suffolk

FOCUS
A modest handicap with a slow-motion finish and the winning time was nearly two seconds slower than the fillies' maiden. The winner is unexposed but the proximity of the placed horses raises doubts about the form.
Lastkingofscotland(IRE) Official explanation: vet said gelding lost a left-fore shoe
Commerce Official explanation: vet said filly lost a left-fore shoe

5319 32 FOR POKER CLAIMING STKS 1m (P)
3:45 (3:45) (Class 6) 3-Y-O+ **£1,617** (£481; £240; £120) **Stalls** Low

Form RPR

400 **1** **Red Somerset (USA)**[10] 5014 8-9-12 77 NeilCallan 8 85
(Mike Murphy) *chsd ldrs: drvn to ld 2f out: drvn out fnl f* **15/2**

042 **2** 1/2 **Pegasus Again (USA)**[35] 4158 6-9-9 78 SeanLevey(3) 1 84
(Robert Mills) *in tch: hdwy 2f out: styd on to chse wnr: fnl f: kpt on clsng stages but a hld* **9/4**[1]

1002 **3** 2 3/4 **Ezdeyaad (USA)**[10] 4997 7-9-5 85 MichaelJMurphy(7) 10 78
(Ed Walker) *chsd ldrs: pushed along and outpcd over 2f out: kpt on again to take 3rd fnl f nt rch ldng duo* **5/2**[2]

-604 **4** 3 **Wisecraic**[10] 4997 4-9-8 70 LiamKeniry 4 67
(J S Moore) *led tl hdd 2f out: wknd over 1f out* **10/1**

100 **5** 3 1/2 **Mcconnell (USA)**[33] 4215 6-9-10 78 (p) GeorgeBaker 6 61
(Gary Moore) *chsd ldr: drvn to chal over 2f out: sn wknd* **14/1**

0000 **6** 3/4 **Herminella**[46] 3782 3-8-13 70 SilvestreDeSousa 3 53
(William Muir) *chsd ldrs: rdn and ev ch 2f out: sn btn* **11/1**

20/6 **7** shd **Dark Islander (IRE)**[23] 4554 8-9-12 92 LukeMorris 5 61
(J S Moore) *t.k.h: rdn fr 3f out: a towards rr* **6/1**[3]

00-6 **8** 12 **Mambo Spirit (IRE)**[32] 4246 7-9-6 69 FergusSweeney 9 27
(Tony Newcombe) *t.k.h: pushed along 3f out: a in rr* **40/1**

0650 **9** 5 **Dichoh**[23] 4544 8-9-6 61 (p) ChrisCatlin 7 16
(Michael Madgwick) *s.i.s: sn rcvrd: rdn and wknd 3f out* **50/1**

10 12 **Davids Dilemma** 3-9-6 0 PatCosgrave 2 —
(Andrew Reid) *s.i.s: rdn 1/2-way: a in rr* **33/1**

1m 38.96s (-0.84) **Going Correction** -0.075s/f (Stan)
WFA 3 from 4yo+ 6lb **10** Ran SP% **116.8**
Speed ratings (Par 101): **101,100,97,94,91 90,90,78,73,61**
toteswingers:1&2:£5.00, 1&3:£4.90, 2&3:£2.50 CSF £24.54 TOTE £6.70: £2.90, £1.50, £1.50; EX 30.80.
Owner M Murphy **Bred** Haras D'Etreham **Trained** Westoning, Beds

FOCUS
Probably not a bad race of its type, featuring as it did a horse rated 92. The pace was ordinary, however, and it paid to be up there. The form looks fair for the grade, rated around the first three.
Mambo Spirit(IRE) Official explanation: trainer said gelding had a breathing problem

5320 32 FOR BINGO EBF MAIDEN FILLIES' STKS 1m (P)
4:15 (4:18) (Class 5) 2-Y-O **£3,234** (£962; £481; £240) **Stalls** Low

Form RPR

1 **Anjaz (USA)** 2-9-0 0 TedDurcan 4 80+
(Saeed Bin Suroor) *trckd ldrs: hdwy whn hmpd over 3f out: drvn and gd hdwy fr 2f out to ld 1f out: r.o strly* **11/4**[1]

2 2 3/4 **Albamara** 2-9-0 0 SebSanders 2 78+
(Sir Mark Prescott Bt) *s.i.s: in rr but clsng whn bdly hmpd on ins after 2f: in rr and stl plenty to do ins fnl 3f: swtchd lft to outside over 2f out: str run fnl f to take 2nd last strides: nt rch wnr: should improve* **3/1**[2]

3 nk **Zenaat** 2-9-0 0 KierenFallon 1 71+
(Sir Michael Stoute) *trckd ldr: rdn and no imp over 2f out: styd on to chse wnr fnl f but a hld: lost 2nd last strides* **11/4**[1]

00 **4** 1/2 **Idols Eye**[19] 4662 2-8-11 0 SeanLevey(3) 7 70
(Richard Hannon) *sn led: rdn and kpt on over 2f out: hdd 1f out: sn one pce* **33/1**

5 **5** 4 **Idyllic Star (IRE)**[45] 3812 2-9-0 0 LiamKeniry 11 61
(J S Moore) *chsd ldrs: rdn 3f out: btn ins fnl 2f* **5/1**[3]

0 **6** 2 1/4 **Tiger Cub**[45] 3812 2-9-0 0 SteveDrowne 3 56
(Roger Charlton) *chsd ldrs: rdn 3f out: wknd 2f out* **12/1**

7 6 **Panettone (IRE)** 2-9-0 0 NeilCallan 9 42+
(Roger Varian) *s.i.s: pushed along and green: a towards rr* **9/1**

8 1/2 **Motheeba (USA)** 2-9-0 0 (v[1]) TadhgO'Shea 8 41+
(Ed Dunlop) *slowly away: in rr: hdwy on outside to get in tch over 3f out: sn wknd* **33/1**

00 **9** 5 **Fox's Ambers (FR)**[19] 4662 2-8-11 0 KieranO'Neill(3) 10 29
(Richard Hannon) *chsd ldrs: riddn 4f out: wknd 3f out* **66/1**

0 **10** 1 3/4 **Mormoran**[65] 3182 2-9-0 0 (p) JimmyQuinn 6 25
(Chris Dwyer) *a towards rr* **100/1**

1m 39.8s **Going Correction** -0.075s/f (Stan) **10** Ran SP% **121.1**
Speed ratings (Par 91): **97,94,93,93,89 87,81,80,75,73**
toteswingers:1&2:£2.80, 1&3:£2.80, 2&3:£3.00 CSF £11.63 TOTE £3.40: £1.10, £1.90, £2.10; EX 12.20.
Owner Godolphin **Bred** Darley **Trained** Newmarket, Suffolk

FOCUS
An interesting maiden and, with the first three places filled by newcomers, form to take a positive view about with the fourth the key to the level.

NOTEBOOK
Anjaz(USA) ◆, a half-sister to a 1m2f Grade 2 winner in the US who was also successful on this surface as a 3-y-o, certainly knew her job as she came home powerfully to nail the leader inside the last furlong. She seems certain to progress and should have little difficulty in getting further. (tchd 9-4)
Albamara ◆ missed the break and then got badly hampered against the inside rail after a couple of furlongs, knocking her back to last. She made up plenty of late ground to take second close to the line and this half-sister to 1m2f winner Albertus Pictor, out of a triple Group 1 winner in Germany, is likely to go one better before too long. (op 13-2)
Zenaat, a 400,000gns half-brother to a winner in Japan, seemed to half-anticipate the start and her rider lost his right iron, but she was still able to take a handy position and had every chance until inside the last furlong. There should be races in her. (op 9-4)
Idols Eye's proximity may be considered to hold the form down as she had been well beaten in her first two starts, but she may have been helped by being left alone in front and she wasn't worn down until a furlong from home. She may be one for nurseries. (op 25-1)
Idyllic Star(IRE), fifth of 13 when 100-1 for a Newbury maiden on her debut that is working out well, made a move 3f from home but could make no further progress. She is another likely to do better in nurseries after one more run. (op 7-1 tchd 9-1)
Panettone(IRE), out of a half-sister to several winners including at Group 3 and Listed level, proved far too green to do herself justice. (op 15-2)

5321 32 FOR BETTING H'CAP 1m 4f (P)
4:45 (4:46) (Class 6) (0-60,60) 3-Y-O **£1,617** (£481; £240; £120) **Stalls** Centre

Form RPR

0211 **1** **Tegan (IRE)**[15] 4827 3-9-2 **58** KieranO'Neill(3) 7 65+
(Richard Hannon) *led tl hdd 7f out: styd trcking ldrs: chal 2f out: sn led: edgd lft u.p over 1f out: in command clsng stages* **5/1**[3]

0350 **2** 1 3/4 **Corvette**[38] 4072 3-9-7 **60** NeilCallan 9 65
(J R Jenkins) *hld up in rr: hdwy 2f out: chsng wnr whn edgd lft over 1f out: kpt on fnl f but a hld* **16/1**

0505 **3** nk **Art Thief**[14] 4847 3-8-11 **50** ChrisCatlin 2 54
(Sylvester Kirk) *in tch: rdn 3f out: styd on fr 2f out and clsng on 2nd nr fin: no imp on wnr* **25/1**

0-00 **4** 3/4 **Cantor**[38] 4065 3-8-13 **52** WilliamCarson 8 55
(Giles Bravery) *pushed along in rr after 2f: in tch: rdn over 4f out and stl towards rr: edgd rt u.p over 2f out: r.o fnl f but nvr gng pce to get to ldng trio* **9/2**[2]

000 **5** 5 **Decana**[35] 4157 3-9-4 **57** SteveDrowne 6 52
(Hughie Morrison) *in rr: rdn and sme hdwy whn nt clr run over 2f out: nvr a danger after* **9/1**

0304 **6** 2 3/4 **Ministry**[6] 5141 3-9-6 **59** (b[1]) LukeMorris 3 50
(John Best) *chsd ldrs: wnt 2nd 5f out: slt ld u.p 2f out: sn hdd: wknd appr fnl f* **5/1**[3]

3632 **7** 1 **Easydoesit (IRE)**[7] 5118 3-8-7 **46** DavidProbert 5 35
(Tony Carroll) *rdn 4f out: a towards rr* **6/1**

5105 **8** 1 3/4 **Rather Cool**[6] 5134 3-9-0 **56** SeanLevey(3) 1 42
(John Bridger) *t.k.h: in tch: rdn to chse ldrs 3f out: wknd ins fnl 2f* **20/1**

5522 **9** 10 **Golestan Palace (IRE)**[32] 4248 3-9-5 **58** NickyMackay 4 35
(Ed Walker) *chsd ldr tl led 7f out: hdd 2f out: wknd qckly* **9/4**[1]

2m 35.23s (0.73) **Going Correction** -0.075s/f (Stan) **9** Ran SP% **121.1**
Speed ratings (Par 98): **94,92,92,92,88 86,86,85,78**
toteswingers:1&2:£10.00, 1&3:£11.50, 2&3:£28.90 CSF £84.11 CT £1844.68 TOTE £5.60: £2.20, £4.70, £4.60; EX 78.50.
Owner Derek And Jean Clee **Bred** D D & Mrs J P Clee **Trained** East Everleigh, Wilts

FOCUS
A moderate handicap with the winner to her recent turf form, backed up by the placed horses.

5322 32 FOR RUMMY H'CAP 7f (P)
5:15 (5:15) (Class 4) (0-85,84) 3-Y-O+ **£4,075** (£1,212; £606; £303) **Stalls** Low

Form RPR

0634 **1** **Golden Tempest (IRE)**[35] 4156 3-9-2 **82** JohnFahy(3) 4 91
(Walter Swinburn) *t.k.h: chsd ldrs: led 2f out: hrd rdn and hld on wl fnl f* **10/1**

3316 **2** 3/4 **Rondeau (GR)**[19] 4656 6-9-8 **80** GeorgeBaker 2 89
(Patrick Chamings) *in rr: hdwy fr over 2f out: styd on u.p over 1f out to chse wnr fnl 120yds but a hld* **11/1**

2143 **3** 1 1/4 **Foxtrot Hotel (IRE)**[29] 4353 3-9-5 **82** LukeMorris 5 86
[illegible] *imp: lost 2nd and one pce fnl 120yds* **7/1**[3]

0604 **4** 1 1/4 **Moretta Blanche**[9] 5043 4-9-5 **77** (t) JimCrowley 8 79
(Ralph Beckett) *in rr: rdn over 2f out: styd on fnl f to take 4th clsng stages but nvr gng pce to rch ldrs* **12/1**

030 **5** nk **Copperwood**[79] 2719 6-9-1 **73** TedDurcan 10 74
(Michael Blanshard) *in rr tl hdwy 4f out: drvn and one pce 2f out: styd on again ins fnl f* **33/1**

2442 **6** 3/4 **Local Singer (IRE)**[30] 4342 3-9-3 **83** LouisBeuzelin(3) 3 80
(Malcolm Saunders) *led 1f: styd chsng ldrs: rdn over 2f out: styd on same pce* **5/1**[2]

0030 **7** 1 3/4 **Douze Points (IRE)**[23] 4566 5-9-2 **77** (b) SeanLevey(3) 14 72
(Ed de Giles) *stdd s: in rr: rdn over 2f out: mod prog fnl f* **14/1**

3506 **8** 1 3/4 **Ocean Legend (IRE)**[14] 4860 6-9-0 **75** MichaelO'Connell(3) 13 65
(Tony Carroll) *in rr: pushed along 3f out: sme prog fnl f* **16/1**

4640 **9** nk **Imprimis Tagula (IRE)**[65] 3162 7-9-4 **83** (v) MissAlexOwen(7) 9 72
(Alan Bailey) *led after 1f: hdd 2f out: sn btn* **40/1**

32-1 **10** 8 **Cape Rambler**[30] 4320 3-9-5 **82** FergusSweeney 11 48+
(Henry Candy) *chsd ldrs: rdn over 2f out and wknd qckly* **16/1**

-050 **11** 2 3/4 **Charles Fosterkane**[5] 5171 3-8-13 **76** SteveDrowne 1 34
(John Best) *plld hrd early: in rr: rdn 4f out: no prog: eased whn no ch fnl f* **16/1**

6004 **12** 3/4 **She Ain't A Saint**[25] 4479 3-9-6 **83** AdamKirby 6 42
(Jane Chapple-Hyam) *rdn 3f out: a towards rr: eased whn no ch fnl f* **12/1**

221 **13** 8 **Kawssaj**[14] 4849 3-9-7 **84** NeilCallan 12 53+
(Roger Varian) *chsd ldrs: rdn 3f out: wknd qckly: eased whn no ch fnl f* **9/4**[1]

1m 25.22s (-0.78) **Going Correction** -0.075s/f (Stan)
WFA 3 from 4yo+ 5lb **13** Ran SP% **122.4**
Speed ratings (Par 105): **101,100,98,97,96 96,94,92,91,82 79,78,69**
toteswingers:1&2:£14.30, 1&3:£12.30, 2&3:£14.60 CSF £118.40 CT £594.08 TOTE £11.70: £3.70, £2.50, £3.00; EX 94.30.
Owner Silver Linings **Bred** Rathasker Stud **Trained** Aldbury, Herts

FOCUS
Quite a decent handicap to end the card, but with a couple of the market leaders flopping the form may not be that strong. However, it looks relatively sound rated around the first four.
She Ain't A Saint Official explanation: jockey said filly never travelled and moved poorly under pressure
Kawssaj Official explanation: jockey said colt lost its action

T/Plt: £304.40 to a £1 stake. Pool:£61,966.18 - 148.60 winning tickets T/Qpdt: £39.30 to a £1 stake. Pool:£4,482.92 - 84.40 winning tickets ST

5110 WINDSOR (R-H)

Monday, August 22

OFFICIAL GOING: Good (7.9)

Wind: Almost nil Weather: Fine, warm

5323 BRITISH STALLION STUDS SUPPORTING BRITISH RACING EBF MAIDEN FILLIES' STKS 6f

5:20 (5:20) (Class 5) 2-Y-O **£3,299** (£981; £490; £245) **Stalls** Low

Form RPR

1 **Cockney Dancer** 2-9-0 0 MichaelHills 3 84+
(Charles Hills) *sn in midfield: pushed along 1/2-way: plld out and prog 2f out: r.o to ld ins fnl f: rdn out* **9/2**[2]

3 2 ¾ **Ladyship**[44] 3865 2-9-0 0 KierenFallon 2 82+
(Sir Michael Stoute) *trckd ldrs against rail: effrt to ld over 1f out: hung lft and hdd ins fnl f: nt qckn* **8/13**[1]

3 5 **Byton** 2-9-0 0 DaneO'Neill 6 64
(Henry Candy) *wl in tch: effrt over 2f out: rdn to chse ldrs over 1f out: sn outpcd* **25/1**

4 1 ½ **Hey Fiddle Fiddle (IRE)** 2-8-9 0 MatthewLawson(5) 4 59+
(Charles Hills) *sn restrained towards rr: shkn up bef 1/2-way and struggling to stay on terms w ldrs: styd on fr over 1f out on outer: n.d* **50/1**

5 nk **Beach Candy (IRE)** 2-9-0 0 RichardHughes 14 58+
(Richard Hannon) *spd fr wd draw to press ldr: upsides and rdn over 1f out: wknd fnl f* **16/1**

3 6 1 ¾ **Esprit Danseur**[18] 4720 2-9-0 0 StephenCraine 12 52
(Jim Boyle) *led to over 1f out: wknd fnl f* **20/1**

4 7 shd **Morning Muse (IRE)**[11] 4954 2-9-0 0 SilvestreDeSousa 15 52
(Peter Winkworth) *wl in tch: shkn up and sing to be outpcd whn short of room over 1f out: fdd* **33/1**

8 ¾ **I See You** 2-9-0 0 AdrianMcCarthy 1 50+
(George Margarson) *s.i.s: t.k.h and sn prom against rail: pushed along over 2f out: wknd over 1f out* **50/1**

3 9 2 ½ **Fairyinthewind (IRE)**[101] 2063 2-9-0 0 JimmyFortune 13 42+
(Paul D'Arcy) *pressed ldrs: shkn up over 2f out: grad wknd over 1f out* **14/1**[3]

10 2 ½ **Bolshoi Melody** 2-9-0 0 RobertHavlin 8 34+
(Jeremy Gask) *sn wl in rr: detached fr ldng gp over 2f out: keeping on at fin* **100/1**

11 ½ **The Games Gone (IRE)** 2-9-0 0 CathyGannon 5 32
(David Evans) *wl in rr: detached fr ldng gp over 2f out: no real prog after* **100/1**

12 shd **Smart Affair** 2-9-0 0 JamesMillman 9 32+
(Rod Millman) *bucking gng to post: rn green in last pair: wl detached over 2f out: keeping on at fin* **100/1**

13 3 ½ **Artful Lady (IRE)** 2-9-0 0 PhilipRobinson 10 20
(George Margarson) *spd to 1/2-way: sn wknd* **50/1**

14 1 ¼ **Perchance** 2-9-0 0 TomQueally 7 16
(Sir Henry Cecil) *a in rr: detached fr ldrs over 2f out and urged along: no prog* **14/1**[3]

15 ½ **Electric Daydream (IRE)** 2-9-0 0 LiamKeniry 16 15
(J S Moore) *t.k.h on outer early: detached in rr gp over 2f out: wknd* **100/1**

16 4 **Sandbanks** 2-9-0 0 JamesDoyle 11 2
(Sylvester Kirk) *a in rr gp: detached fr ldrs over 2f out: wknd* **100/1**

1m 14.26s (1.26) **Going Correction** +0.25s/f (Good) **16** Ran SP% **121.7**

Speed ratings (Par 91): **101,100,93,91,90 88,88,87,84,80 80,80,75,73,73 67**

toteswingers:1&2:£1.60, 2&3:£5.20, 1&3:£21.10 CSF £7.04 TOTE £5.90: £1.80, £1.20, £7.20; EX 11.60 Trifecta £140.00 Pool £1,860.44 - 9.83 winning units..

Owner Phil Cunningham **Bred** P M Cunningham **Trained** Lambourn, Berks

FOCUS

The stands' rail was dolled out three yards at the winning post and eight yards at 6f; the top bend was dolled out three yards from normal configuration, adding 14 yards to race distances at 1m and over. In all probability this was a decent maiden, the front two drawing clear inside the final furlong. The winning time was 3.76secs slower than standard but the first two look decent prospects.

NOTEBOOK

Cockney Dancer ◆, whose trainer had gained his first success since officially taking over the reins at Kempton earlier in the afternoon, had reportedly shaped like a nice filly at home. A half-sister to five winners, most notably the Group 1-placed Gallagher and very useful pair Quick Wit and Roodeye, she is expected to need 7f and it was her extra stamina that saw her home in front, staying on too strongly for the favourite. It will be interesting to see where she goes next, with a race like the Rockfel being a possible long-term target, but first she may take her chance in the big Doncaster sales race early next month. (op 5-1)

Ladyship, third in a good 6f Newmarket maiden last month and strong at the head of the market, had to wait for a run early in the straight, but the gap appeared in plenty of time and the race looked hers when going on over 1f out. She couldn't run straight under pressure, though, and perhaps a seventh furlong will be required for her to get off the mark. (op 4-6 tchd 8-11 in a place)

Byton, half-sister to a 5f 2yo winner, kept on nicely to make a satisfactory debut. Normal progression should see her able to win an ordinary maiden.

Hey Fiddle Fiddle(IRE) ◆, the winner's stablemate and a half-sister to Group 3 winners for the yard Above Average and Sent From Heaven, caught the eye in running on past beaten horses and will be of obvious interest next time upped to 7f. (op 100-1)

Beach Candy(IRE), sister to a 6f 2yo winner, ran better than the bare result, showing pace from a wide draw before fading late on. She should improve enough to win a small maiden.

Esprit Danseur put her experience to use, but was unable to build on a promising first effort. She is probably more of a handicap type.

Morning Muse(IRE) is another who is more of a handicap type. (tchd 40-1)

Smart Affair Official explanation: jockey said filly was hampered leaving stalls

Artful Lady(IRE) Official explanation: jockey said filly ran green and hung left

Perchance, half-sister to a 1m4f winner, out of a 1m2f winner, should leave this form behind in time once granted with a stiffer test. (tchd 16-1)

5324 CITY AIR EXPRESS NURSERY 6f

5:50 (5:51) (Class 5) (0-75,72) 2-Y-O **£2,385** (£704; £352) **Stalls** Low

Form RPR

6024 1 **Karuga**[22] 4581 2-8-13 64 RichardHughes 12 68
(Richard Hannon) *settled in rr: rdn sn after 1/2-way: prog 2f out: drvn and styd on to ld ins fnl f* **15/2**

4546 2 ¾ **Tina's Spirit (IRE)**[23] 4536 2-9-7 72 DaneO'Neill 7 74
(Richard Hannon) *trckd ldrs on outer: led jst over 2f out and sn racd nr far side rail: drvn and hdd ins fnl f: kpt on* **7/1**

0020 3 shd **Middleton Flyer (IRE)**[2] 5270 2-9-7 72 CathyGannon 5 74
(David Evans) *led 1f: w ldrs on outer: chal over 2f out and sn ended towards far rail: upsides 1f out: nt qckn* **25/1**

040 4 2 **Johnson's Cat (IRE)**[46] 3755 2-8-4 55 MartinLane 11 51+
(Richard Guest) *wl in rr towards nr side rail: struggling sn after 1/2-way: drvn and kpt on fr over 1f out in centre: nt pce to chal* **50/1**

0226 5 ½ **Maccabees**[11] 4968 2-9-7 72 JamesMillman 9 66+
(Rod Millman) *hld up in tch: nt clr run over 2f out to over 1f out and styd on centre: rdn and kpt on fnl f: no ch* **9/2**[2]

2100 6 ½ **Royal Blush**[9] 5052 2-9-6 71 SilvestreDeSousa 10 64+
(Paul Cole) *hld up bhd ldrs: nt clr run over 2f out to over 1f out and lost pl: drvn and nt qckn sn after: kpt on fnl f* **13/2**

325 7 ½ **Miss Conduct**[38] 4073 2-9-2 67 JamesDoyle 8 58
(John Spearing) *in tch on outer: rdn to chal 2f out and sn against far rail: wknd jst over 1f out* **25/1**

034 8 nk **Elegant Flight**[14] 4857 2-8-9 63 HarryBentley(3) 2 53
(Alan Jarvis) *rousted along early: sn w ldrs: wknd over 1f out* **4/1**[1]

045 9 1 ¾ **Bewilder**[12] 4912 2-9-2 67 MarcHalford 1 52
(John Gosden) *racd against nr side rail early and in rr: struggling sn after 1/2-way: nvr on terms* **10/1**

0664 10 17 **Lord Ali McJones**[1] 5297 2-8-7 65 (p) CharlesBishop(7) 4 —
(Tom Dascombe) *racd freely: w ldrs to 1/2-way: wknd qckly over 2f out: t.o* **33/1**

3341 11 1 **Red Mischief (IRE)**[39] 4019 2-9-7 72 KierenFallon 3 3
(Harry Dunlop) *led after 1f to jst over 2f out: wknd rapidly and eased: t.o* **6/1**[3]

1m 14.8s (1.80) **Going Correction** +0.25s/f (Good) **11** Ran SP% **111.8**

Speed ratings (Par 94): **98,97,96,94,93 92,92,91,89,66 65**

toteswingers:1&2:£10.30, 2&3:£10.70, 1&3:£14.90 CSF £53.73 CT £1243.26 TOTE £10.70: £2.90, £2.90, £6.90; EX 45.10 Trifecta £716.50 Pool £3,205.32 - 3.31 winning units..

Owner Fairway Racing **Bred** David J Brown, Slatch Farm Stud & J Berry **Trained** East Everleigh, Wilts

FOCUS

A modest nursery that saw Richard Hannon train the first two home. The action unfolded more towards the far side and the winning time was 0.54secs slower than the opening fillies' maiden. The form looks sound rated around the first three.

NOTEBOOK

Karuga had been running well without quite seeing it out over 7f of late and this proved her ideal distance. She readily closed on the leaders having been dropped in from her wide draw and stayed on well. She can continue to pay her way off a slightly higher mark and may win again. (op 7-1)

Tina's Spirit(IRE) ended up against the far rail, running her best race yet, and looks in need of 7f now. (op 8-1)

Middleton Flyer(IRE), well held in a decent conditions race at Chester two days earlier, still has only a selling win to her name in 11 attempts, but her last two efforts in handicaps have been solid. (tchd 20-1)

Johnson's Cat(IRE) ran a much-improved race on this switch to nurseries for the first time and looks capable of winning a small race off his lowly rating.

Maccabees was short of room for the best part of a furlong and was unlucky not to finish closer. (op 5-1 tchd 4-1)

Royal Blush was another who met some trouble and then couldn't pick up. Official explanation: jockey said filly hung left throughout (tchd 6-1 and 15-2)

Elegant Flight was disappointing on this nursery debut, having to be driven to take a forward position and emptying under pressure. She is better than this and probably deserves another chance. Official explanation: trainer said filly finished lame (op 9-2)

Bewilder raced nearest to the stands' rail and was never a threat. (op 9-1 tchd 11-1)

Red Mischief(IRE), raised 7lb for winning a similar race on good to firm ground at Leicester, appeared to exert too much energy through the early stages, but the way she trailed in suggests something may have gone awry. Official explanation: jockey said filly lost its action behind (op 4-1)

5325 TICKETS FOR TROOPS (S) STKS 1m 67y

6:20 (6:20) (Class 6) 2-Y-O **£1,704** (£503; £251) **Stalls** Low

Form RPR

0034 1 **Yammos (IRE)**[17] 4761 2-8-9 65 MatthewDavies(3) 10 62+
(Mick Channon) *hld up in midfield: prog over 3f out: decisive effrt to ld wl over 2f out in centre: in command after: shkn up over 1f out: readily* **9/4**[1]

0006 2 1 ¼ **Make Up**[17] 4761 2-8-8 56 ow1 RichardHughes 1 53
(Richard Hannon) *hld up bhd ldrs: lost pl on inner sn after 1/2-way: prog fr rr over 2f out: rdn to chse wnr fnl f: no imp* **8/1**[3]

3534 3 ¾ **River Nova**[17] 4756 2-8-4 49 HarryBentley(3) 7 50
(Alan Jarvis) *prom: rdn over 2f out: disp 2nd over 1f out: one pce* **11/1**

4 4 ½ **Beacon Lady**[81] 2651 2-8-0 0 JakePayne(7) 12 49
(Bill Turner) *trckd ldrs: rdn to chal wl over 2f out: chsd wnr after: hanging lft and nt qckn: lost 2nd fnl f* **20/1**

043 5 1 ¼ **King Kenobi (IRE)**[17] 4761 2-8-12 61 LiamKeniry 3 52
(J S Moore) *trckd ldrs: pushed along 3f out: sn outpcd: no ch whn shkn up over 1f out: one pce* **5/2**[2]

3350 6 1 **Queen Of The Hop**[12] 4907 2-8-7 55 LukeMorris 13 44
(J S Moore) *towards rr: rdn and sme prog on outer 3f out: no imp on ldrs over 1f out: fdd* **12/1**

000P 7 shd **Bertorella (IRE)**[38] 4069 2-8-7 54 (b[1]) MartinLane 8 44
(Ralph Beckett) *mde most to wl over 2f out: sn outpcd and btn* **20/1**

00 8 shd **Garrarufa (IRE)**[11] 4969 2-8-12 0 JamesMillman 4 49
(Rod Millman) *hld up in midfield: pushed along 3f out: outpcd sn after: hanging lft but kpt on same pce* **33/1**

0 9 7 **Aunty Mavis (IRE)**[33] 4205 2-8-7 0 DavidProbert 14 28
(Ronald Harris) *trckd ldr: chal and upsides fr 1/2-way: sing to lose pl whn squeezed out over 2f out: wknd* **66/1**

0 10 2 ½ **Glitter (IRE)**[11] 4968 2-8-9 0 KieranO'Neill(3) 9 28
(Richard Hannon) *dwlt: t.k.h and hld up in rr: effrt over 3f out: wknd over 2f out* **11/1**

00 11 3 ½ **Cotes Du Rhone (IRE)**[107] 1890 2-8-12 0 CathyGannon 6 20
(David Evans) *dwlt: a wl in rr: struggling fr 1/2-way* **50/1**

12 1 ¾ **Wise Lord** 2-8-12 0 RobertHavlin 5 16
(Andrew Haynes) *a in rr: struggling fr 1/2-way: sn bhd* **25/1**

00 13 1 ¼ **George Tilehurst**[17] 4761 2-8-7 0 RyanPowell(5) 2 14
(J S Moore) *nvr beyond midfield: wknd over 2f out: sn bhd* **100/1**

1m 47.98s (3.28) **Going Correction** -0.10s/f (Good) **13** Ran SP% **115.6**

Speed ratings (Par 92): **79,77,77,76,75 74,74,74,67,64 61,59,58**

toteswingers:1&2:£5.20, 2&3:£7.40, 1&3:£6.30 CSF £18.37 TOTE £4.20: £1.60, £1.70, £2.30; EX 22.20 Trifecta £147.00 Pool £2,224.06 - 11.19 winning units..The winner was bought in for £4,500.

Owner B P York **Bred** The Kathryn Stud **Trained** West Ilsley, Berks

FOCUS

This was a relatively weak seller and the field again came down the centre in the straight. The form is typically weak and best rated around the third and seventh.

NOTEBOOK

Yammos(IRE) got off the mark at the eighth attempt, relishing the step up to the 1m and never looking in any danger once kicked into a clear lead 2f from home. He was bought back in and can prove better than this level. (op 11-4 tchd 3-1)
Make Up was just under 3l behind the winner when they met at Newmarket the time before and she was another to improve for the step up in trip, keeping on again having lost her place. Her rider's overweight made no difference to the result.
River Nova, racing beyond 6f for the first time, put up an improved performance but will remain vulnerable. (op 12-1 tchd 10-1)
Beacon Lady, is probably the one to take from the race, especially as her trainer had warned beforehand she was still quite weak. She showed plenty before getting a little tired late on and should have no trouble winning something similar. (op 18-1)
King Kenobi(IRE) was unable to confirm Newmarket form with the front pair, appearing to have no excuses. (op 9-4 tchd 2-1)
Garrarufa(IRE) was going on late and can do better in time. (op 28-1)
Glitter(IRE) Official explanation: jockey said gelding ran too free

5326 HALLESY H'CAP — 5f 10y

6:50 (6:50) (Class 5) (0-70,70) 3-Y-O+ — **£2,385** (£704; £352) **Stalls** Low

Form				RPR
3323	**1**		**Desert Strike**[13] 4895 5-9-9 **69**....(p) IPoullis 10 (Alan McCabe) *taken down early: slowly away: mostly in last tl taken wdst of all and gd prog over 1f out: led ins fnl f: styd on wl* **8/1**	78
0043	**2**	*1*	**Madam Isshe**[13] 4882 4-8-6 **52**.... CathyGannon 3 (Malcolm Saunders) *w ldr: led 2f out: hdd and outpcd ins fnl f* **5/1**[3]	57+
6121	**3**	*1 1/4*	**Imaginary Diva**[12] 4930 5-8-13 **59**.... TomQueally 6 (George Margarson) *trckd ldrs: looking for room towards nr side rail fr 2f out: effrt to chal 1f out: nt qckn* **4/1**[2]	60+
6626	**4**	*nk*	**Patch Patch**[10] 4988 4-9-2 **62**....(p) RobbieFitzpatrick 9 (Derek Shaw) *taken down early: hld up in rr: taken to outer 2f out: kpt on one pce fnl f: n.d* **33/1**	61
000	**5**	*nse*	**Picansort**[33] 4210 4-9-1 **61**....(p) JimmyQuinn 11 (Brett Johnson) *trckd ldrs: effrt towards outer 2f out: cl enough over 1f out: nt qckn* **8/1**	60
0030	**6**	*nk*	**Whoatealthepius (IRE)**[51] 3635 3-9-3 **65**....(p) ShaneKelly 12 (Dean Ivory) *mde most to 2f out: steadily wknd fnl f* **12/1**	63
0411	**7**	*1 1/2*	**Crimson Queen**[5] 5175 4-9-4 **64** 6ex.... JamesDoyle 2 (Roy Brotherton) *hld up towards rr: looking for room fr wl over 1f out: shkn up ins fnl f: nvr nr ldrs* **10/3**[1]	57+
03	**8**	*shd*	**Leadenhall Lass (IRE)**[25] 4458 5-9-0 **65**.... JemmaMarshall(5) 5 (Pat Phelan) *hld up in last pair: pushed along over 1f out: one pce and no imp* **11/1**	57
0016	**9**	*4 1/2*	**Danzoe (IRE)**[19] 4683 4-9-7 **67**.... SilvestreDeSousa 8 (Christine Dunnett) *pressed ldrs but sn pushed along: no imp over 1f out: wknd sn after* **14/1**	51
0000	**10**	*1/2*	**Cape Royal**[13] 4895 11-9-5 **65**....(bt) KierenFallon 1 (Milton Bradley) *awkward s: sn pressed ldng pair and racd against nr side rail: wknd jst over 1f out: eased* **11/1**	47

61.09 secs (0.79) **Going Correction** +0.25s/f (Good)
WFA 3 from 4yo+ 2lb — **10** Ran SP% **115.9**
Speed ratings (Par 103): **103,101,99,98,98 98,95,95,88,87**
toteswingers:1&2:£9.60, 2&3:£3.90, 1&3:£4.80 CSF £47.48 CT £189.94 TOTE £7.90: £1.90, £3.10, £1.60; EX 60.90 Trifecta £524.20 Pool £2,763.01 - 3.90 winning units..
Owner Mrs M J McCabe **Bred** Mrs Mary Rowlands **Trained** Averham Park, Notts
■ Stewards' Enquiry : I Poullis six-day ban: used whip with excessive frequency without giving gelding time to respond (Sep 5-10)

FOCUS
Back to the stands' rail in the straight for this sprint handicap, but it was perhaps no surprise that the horse who challenged widest of all triumphed. The winner is rted to his turf mark with the placed horses possibly disadvantaged by racing nearer the stands' rail.

5327 SPORTINGBET.COM MAIDEN STKS — 1m 2f 7y

7:20 (7:22) (Class 5) 3-Y-O+ — **£2,385** (£704; £352) **Stalls** Centre

Form				RPR
24	**1**		**Almagest**[81] 2648 3-9-3 0.... RichardHughes 7 (John Gosden) *sweating and coltish bef r: trckd ldr after 2f: led wl over 1f out: rdn and styd on strly* **5/2**[1]	88+
0	**2**	[illegible]	**[illegible] (USA)**[285] [illegible] [illegible].... DaneO'Neill 5 (Saeed Bin Suroor) *prom: shkn up and effrt over 2f out: edgd lft 1f out: kpt on to take 2nd ins fnl f: no ch w wnr* **16/1**	84+
42	**3**	*1 1/4*	**Cairncross (IRE)**[8] 5082 3-8-12 0.... SilvestreDeSousa 3 (Mark Johnston) *restless in stalls: mde most: rdn and hdd wl over 1f out: one pce* **13/2**	76
5	**4**	*1 1/4*	**Rysbrack (USA)**[16] 4805 5-9-11 0.... JimmyFortune 12 (Paul Webber) *hld up towards rr: stdy prog on outer fr 3f out: rdn and kpt on same pce over 1f out* **20/1**	79+
42-	**5**	*3 1/4*	**The Mongoose**[356] 5629 3-9-3 0.... KierenFallon 10 (Sir Michael Stoute) *trckd ldrs: effrt 3f out: shkn up and nt qckn wl over 1f out: pushed along and fdd* **4/1**[2]	72+
	6	*2 1/4*	**Riviera Stars** 3-9-3 0.... HayleyTurner 13 (Michael Bell) *rousted along fr the s: v green and mostly in last: styd on fr over 2f out: nrest at fin* **25/1**	68+
3050	**7**	*1*	**Malanos (IRE)**[45] 3824 3-9-3 70.... NickyMackay 9 (David Elsworth) *trckd ldr 2f: styd prom tl wknd 2f out* **16/1**	66
02-	**8**	*3/4*	**Durante Alighieri**[271] 7559 3-9-3 0.... TomQueally 8 (Sir Henry Cecil) *s.i.s: sn in midfield: outpcd and pushed along over 2f out: fdd* **11/2**	64
	9	*3/4*	**Marshmallow** 3-8-12 0.... CathyGannon 4 (Chris Wall) *difficult to load into stalls: nvr bttr than midfield: outpcd fr 3f out: bttr for r* **50/1**	58+
	10	*3 1/2*	**Ryedale Lass** 3-8-12 0.... EddieCreighton 1 (Joseph Tuite) *dwlt: a in rr: struggling fr 3f out* **125/1**	51
	11	*2 1/2*	**Touching The Stars** 3-9-3 0.... JamesDoyle 11 (Mick Channon) *a in rr: pushed along over 3f out: sn outpcd and btn* **100/1**	51
	12	*2*	**Chapatti (IRE)** 3-8-9 0.... RyanClark(3) 14 (Stuart Williams) *dwlt: a in rr: pushed along in last trio 4f out: no prog* **100/1**	42
	13	*1*	**Race To Dubai (USA)** 3-9-3 0.... TedDurcan 2 (Saeed Bin Suroor) *settled midfield: shkn up over 3f out: sn wknd* **9/2**[3]	45

2m 7.83s (-0.87) **Going Correction** -0.10s/f (Good)
WFA 3 from 5yo 8lb — **13** Ran SP% **120.6**
Speed ratings (Par 103): **99,97,96,95,92 90,90,89,88,86 84,82,81**
toteswingers:1&2:£10.80, 2&3:£11.60, 1&3:£3.60 CSF £45.83 CT £328.20 TOTE £3.70: £1.60, £4.10, £2.50; EX 47.90 Trifecta £328.20 Pool £1,840.59 - 4.15 winning units..
Owner K Abdulla **Bred** Juddmonte Farms Ltd **Trained** Newmarket, Suffolk

FOCUS
The action took place down the centre in what was a fair maiden that should produce winners. The third to his latest form looks the best guide.

5328 SPORTINGBET.COM H'CAP — 1m 2f 7y

7:50 (7:50) (Class 4) (0-85,84) 3-Y-O+ — **£4,075** (£1,212; £606; £303) **Stalls** Centre

Form				RPR
-123	**1**		**Galiando**[19] 4665 3-9-6 **84**.... JimmyFortune 11 (Jeremy Noseda) *taken down early: hld up off the pce in last quartet: prog over 2f out: grabbed far rail and clsd over 1f out: drvn to ld ins fnl f: styd on wl* **15/8**[1]	97+
3010	**2**	*1 3/4*	**On Khee**[11] 4971 4-9-8 **78**....(t) SteveDrowne 2 (Hughie Morrison) *trckd ldrs in 5th: clsd over 2f out: rdn to ld over 1f out: hdd and outpcd ins fnl f* **12/1**	87
664	**3**	*2*	**The Cayterers**[24] 2150 9-9-2 **79**.... RaulDaSilva(7) 6 (Tony Carroll) *dwlt: hld up in last quartet and wl off the pce: effrt 3f out: nt qckn 2f out: kpt on to take 3rd last stride* **8/1**	84
1303	**4**	*shd*	**Miss Bootylishes**[11] 4949 6-8-10 **73**.... DavidKenny(7) 9 (Paul Burgoyne) *hld up off the pce in 8th: prog 3f out: clsd to chal wl over 1f out: one pce fnl f* **33/1**	78
-120	**5**	*6*	**Ken's Girl**[26] 4429 7-9-11 **81**.... FergusSweeney 10 (Stuart Kittow) *taken down early: jockey in stalls bef horse: led at decent pce but pressed: hdd 1/2-way: led again over 3f out: hdd & wknd over 1f out* **17/2**	74
3516	**6**	*2 3/4*	**Abergeldie (USA)**[30] 4313 3-8-8 **72**....(v) DavidProbert 5 (Andrew Balding) *w.w in 6th: rdn 3f out: no prog and struggling 2f out* **6/1**[3]	59
2440	**7**	*hd*	**Moynahan (USA)**[11] 4958 6-10-0 **84**....(p) PaulDoe 3 (Paul Cole) *hld up off the pce in 7th: effrt over 3f out: rdn and no prog 2f out: wknd* **11/1**	71
0060	**8**	*1/2*	**South Cape**[11] 4958 8-9-5 **75**.... GeorgeBaker 4 (Gary Moore) *hld up in last quartet and off the pce: rdn and no real prog wl over 2f out* **20/1**	61
0111	**9**	*5*	**Colinca's Lad (IRE)**[7] 5110 9-8-4 **65** oh3.... RosieJessop(5) 1 (Peter Charalambous) *unable to ld but pressed ldr's str pce: led 1/2-way to over 3f out: wknd* **5/1**[2]	41
0101	**10**	*1 1/2*	**Willow Dancer (IRE)**[19] 4679 7-10-0 **84**....(p) AdamKirby 7 (Walter Swinburn) *chsd ldng pair: rdn and styd along against nr side rail in st: bhd over 2f out* **16/1**	57
0004	**11**	*5*	**Follow The Flag (IRE)**[15] 4818 7-9-1 **71**....(p) IPoullis 12 (Alan McCabe) *hld up in last: sn t.o and styd there* **33/1**	34
2120	**12**	*88*	**Round Won (USA)**[142] 1102 4-10-0 **84**.... ShaneKelly 8 (William Knight) *taken down early: chsd ldrs in 4th: wknd 4f out: t.o whn virtually p.u 2f out* **40/1**	—

2m 6.29s (-2.41) **Going Correction** -0.10s/f (Good)
WFA 3 from 4yo+ 8lb — **12** Ran SP% **122.4**
Speed ratings (Par 105): **105,103,102,101,97 94,94,94,90,89 85,14**
toteswingers:1&2:£9.00, 2&3:£20.80, 1&3:£6.30 CSF £26.85 CT £157.10 TOTE £2.90: £1.40, £4.70, £3.10; EX 33.70 Trifecta £342.70 Pool £745.61 - 1.61 winning units..
Owner Bluehills Racing Limited **Bred** Hesmonds Stud Ltd **Trained** Newmarket, Suffolk

FOCUS
An ordinary handicap, but the pace was strong (time only 0.29secs above standard), and a winner to keep on-side. The winner can do better while the third and fourth set the level.
Round Won(USA) Official explanation: jockey said gelding lost its action
T/Jkpt: £3,550.00 to a £1 stake. Pool £10,000.00 - 2 winning tickets. T/Plt: £52.70 to a £1 stake. Pool £87,751.12 - 1,215.19 winning tickets. T/Qpdt: £10.90 to a £1 stake. Pool £6,946.95 - 469.21 winning tickets. JN

5329 - 5336a (Foreign Racing) - See Raceform Interactive

4815 LEICESTER (R-H)

Tuesday, August 23

OFFICIAL GOING: Good to firm (8.2)
Wind: Light across Weather: Overcast

5337 NEWFOUNDPOOL WMC MAIDEN AUCTION STKS — 7f 9y

2:30 (2:32) (Class 6) 2-Y-O — **£1,617** (£481; £240; £120) **Stalls** High

Form				RPR
0	**1**		**Wyndham Wave**[16] 4815 2-8-10 0.... JamesMillman 12 (Rod Millman) *chsd ldrs: swtchd rt over 2f out: led over 1f out: edgd lft: r.o* **9/2**[1]	74+
0	**2**	*1 1/4*	**Cresta Star**[94] 2309 2-8-9 0.... DaneO'Neill 13 (Richard Hannon) *prom: pushed along 1/2-way: rdn over 1f out: r.o* **9/2**[1]	68+
60	**3**	*2*	**Orwellian**[16] 4815 2-9-0 0.... MartinDwyer 8 (Brian Meehan) *chsd ldrs: rdn and ev ch over 1f out: styd on same pce ins fnl f* **5/1**[2]	68
50	**4**	*1 3/4*	**Loxton Lad (IRE)**[31] 4339 2-9-0 0.... JamesDoyle 11 (Roger Charlton) *hld up: hdwy over 2f out: rdn over 1f out: styd on same pce* **8/1**	63
63	**5**	*hd*	**Baltic Flyer (IRE)**[41] 3981 2-8-7 0.... AndreaAtzeni 2 (Robert Eddery) *chsd ldrs: led over 4f out: rdn and hdd over 1f out: no ex ins fnl f* **13/2**	55
	6	*1 3/4*	**Daghash** 2-8-10 0.... PhilipRobinson 9 (Clive Brittain) *mid-div: sn pushed along: outpcd 1/2-way: n.d after* **12/1**	54
	7	*9*	**Ardmay (IRE)** 2-9-1 0.... PhillipMakin 14 (Kevin Ryan) *sn led: hdd over 4f out: rdn over 2f out: sn wknd* **11/2**[3]	36
	8	*3 3/4*	**One Cool Dancer (IRE)** 2-8-4 0.... SilvestreDeSousa 10 (John Gallagher) *s.i.s: outpcd* **25/1**	15
00	**9**	*1 1/2*	**Remember Rocky**[39] 4068 2-8-11 0.... MartinLane 1 (Steve Gollings) *prom: rdn over 4f out: wknd 1/2-way* **50/1**	18
0	**10**	*1 3/4*	**Recway Striker**[13] 4919 2-8-10 0.... DavidProbert 7 (Des Donovan) *sn pushed along in rr: bhd fr 1/2-way* **100/1**	12
	11	*shd*	**Inch Or Two** 2-8-6 0.... MartinHarley(3) 4 (Des Donovan) *sn outpcd* **66/1**	11
0	**12**	*3/4*	**Princess Tamina (IRE)**[87] 2504 2-8-5 0.... CathyGannon 5 (Patrick Morris) *chsd ldrs tl rdn and wknd 1/2-way* **66/1**	5
	13	*nk*	**Roman Myst (IRE)** 2-8-12 0.... TravisBlock 3 (Sylvester Kirk) *s.i.s: outpcd* **33/1**	11

1m 25.05s (-1.15) **Going Correction** -0.225s/f (Firm) — **13** Ran SP% **113.3**
Speed ratings (Par 92): **97,95,93,91,91 89,78,74,72,70 70,69,69**
toteswingers:1&2:£6.70, 1&3:£6.80, 2&3:£6.50 CSF £22.10 CT £475.90 TOTE £6.10: £2.10, £2.40, £2.40; EX 30.40 Trifecta £475.90 Part won. Pool: £643.23 - 0.90 winning units..
Owner Kentisbeare Racing **Bred** Newsells Park Stud **Trained** Kentisbeare, Devon

FOCUS
Unusually for a maiden like this, the market was wide open though the punters eventually got it right. The draw played its part with the first four drawn eight or higher, and the front six pulled a long way clear of the rest.

NOTEBOOK

Wyndham Wave had finished tenth of 11 on his debut over C&D earlier this month (just behind Orwellian), but he was sent off a much shorter price for this than might have been expected, which suggests he was thought to have come on a lot from that effort. Having travelled to the front smoothly over a furlong from home, he only needed a couple of gentle taps with the whip to make sure of it and he seemed to win with a bit in hand. (op 17-2)

Cresta Star, given a break since finishing tenth of 15 on her Newbury debut back in May, is bred to appreciate this extra furlong and she stayed on well over the last 2f without ever being able to get to the winner. She should be able to win an ordinary maiden over this trip or further. (op 4-1)

Orwellian was well backed to improve on his two previous efforts at this venue and he did so, holding every chance passing the 2f pole but then lacking the pace to take advantage. He now gets a mark. (op 17-2)

Loxton Lad(IRE), well beaten in two 6f Salisbury maidens, made some late progress over this extra furlong and looks another bound for nurseries. (op 17-2 tchd 9-1 and 15-2)

Baltic Flyer(IRE) had shown ability in a couple of 6f maidens on turf and Polytrack and made much of the running, but didn't quite see out the extra furlong. Nurseries now become an option for her too. (op 4-1)

Daghash, retained for 5,000gns as a yearling, was always being niggled along to stay in touch, but he finished well clear of the others and is bred to come into his own over middle-distances next year. (op 8-1 tchd 14-1)

5338 JOHN LIDDINGTON GROUP H'CAP — 5f 218y

3:00 (3:01) (Class 5) (0-70,69) 3-Y-O+ — **£2,264** (£673; £336; £168) **Stalls** High

Form — RPR

6420 **1** **Mount Hollow**[17] 4793 6-8-13 **58**....(p) GrahamGibbons 13 — 69
(Reg Hollinshead) *hood removed late and s.i.s: hld up: nt clr run wl over 1f out: hdwy u.p sn after: r.o to ld wl ins fnl f* — **11/2**[2]

0530 **2** *1 1/4* **Sairaam (IRE)**[10] 5031 5-9-6 **65**.... RobbieFitzpatrick 8 — 72
(Charles Smith) *sn pushed along in rr: hdwy over 1f out: rdn and edgd lft ins fnl f: r.o* — **25/1**

-056 **3** *nse* **Belinsky (IRE)**[17] 4793 4-8-11 **59**.... DaleSwift(3) 2 — 66
(Mark Campion) *chsd ldrs: rdn over 2f out: led over 1f out: hdd wl ins fnl f* — **14/1**

3016 **4** *1/2* **Witchry**[10] 5053 9-9-6 **65**.... DaneO'Neill 4 — 70
(Tony Newcombe) *mid-div: hdwy over 2f out: sn rdn: r.o* — **11/2**[2]

004 **5** *1/2* **Il Battista**[24] 4527 3-8-13 **61**....(p) SebSanders 3 — 66
(Alan McCabe) *a.p: drvn along 1/2-way: styng on same pce whn hmpd towards fin* — **25/1**

0001 **6** *1/2* **Song Of Parkes**[27] 4443 4-9-6 **65**.... DavidAllan 6 — 67
(Eric Alston) *w ldrs: led over 4f out: rdn and hdd over 1f out: edgd rt: styd on same pce ins fnl f* — **8/1**

3426 **7** *nk* **He's A Humbug (IRE)**[14] 4893 7-9-0 **59**....(p) MickyFenton 10 — 60
(Paul Midgley) *hung rt thrght: mid-div: sn pushed along: hdwy whn hmpd 1f out: r.o: nt rch ldrs* — **16/1**

0314 **8** *3/4* **Brave Dream**[20] 4680 3-9-4 **66**.... PhillipMakin 12 — 65
(Kevin Ryan) *led: hdd over 4f out: chsd ldr: rdn and edgd rt over 1f out: no ex ins fnl f* — **15/2**[3]

0214 **9** *3/4* **Mata Hari Blue**[12] 4960 5-9-10 **69**....(t) SilvestreDeSousa 5 — 65
(John Holt) *chsd ldrs: rdn over 2f out: no ex ins fnl f* — **7/2**[1]

3100 **10** *nk* **Gertmegalush (IRE)**[27] 4443 4-9-3 **62**.... BarryMcHugh 9 — 57
(John Harris) *sn outpcd: r.o towards fin: nvr nrr* — **50/1**

5512 **11** *1 1/2* **Delira (IRE)**[25] 4486 3-9-7 **69**.... StephenCraine 7 — 60
(Jonathan Portman) *prom: rdn over 2f out: wknd ins fnl f* — **20/1**

0253 **12** *3* **Watch Chain (IRE)**[10] 5031 4-9-5 **64**....(p) RobertWinston 1 — 45
(Alan McCabe) *hld up: rdn and hung rt over 2f out: wknd fnl f* — **8/1**

1m 11.06s (-1.94) **Going Correction** -0.225s/f (Firm)
WFA 3 from 4yo+ 3lb — **12** Ran SP% **113.9**
Speed ratings (Par 103): **103,101,101,100,99 99,98,97,96,96 94,90**
toteswingers:1&2:£24.50, 1&3:£17.80, 2&3:£53.80 CSF £138.08 CT £1834.84 TOTE £6.10: £2.40, £6.80, £5.30; EX 145.40 TRIFECTA Not won..
Owner Mr and Mrs G Robinson **Bred** G Robinson **Trained** Upper Longdon, Staffs

FOCUS

An ordinary sprint handicap in which the leaders may have gone off too fast and the front pair came from well back.

5339 JOHN SMITH'S EXTRA SMOOTH CLAIMING STKS — 5f 218y

3:30 (3:30) (Class 5) 3-Y-O+ — **£2,264** (£673; £336; £168) **Stalls** High

Form — RPR

1361 **1** **Barons Spy (IRE)**[3] 5262 10-9-4 81.... JamesDoyle 4 — 79
(Richard Price) *hld up in tch: pushed along over 3f out: led 2f out: sn rdn and edgd lft: styd on gamely* — **2/1**[2]

6050 **2** *hd* **Dorback**[15] 4859 4-9-12 83.... DaneO'Neill 6 — 86
(Henry Candy) *chsd ldr to over 4f out: remained handy: hung rt 1/2-way: ev ch fr over 1f out: sn hung rt: nt run on* — **15/8**[1]

6604 **3** *6* **Sophie's Beau (USA)**[16] 4816 4-8-3 50.... ChrisDCogan(5) 3 — 49
(Michael Chapman) *s.i.s: sn prom: rdn over 2f out: sn ev ch: wknd fnl f* — **100/1**

5000 **4** *4 1/2* **Tamagin (USA)**[22] 4609 8-9-12 90....(p) SilvestreDeSousa 5 — 53
(Lydia Pearce) *led: rdn over 2f out: sn hdd & wknd* — **9/1**

-103 **5** *nse* **Spanish Bounty**[77] 2789 6-8-12 85.... StephenCraine 1 — 38
(Jonathan Portman) *s.i.s: hdwy to chse ldr over 4f out: rdn over 2f out: sn wknd* — **5/2**[3]

1m 11.16s (-1.84) **Going Correction** -0.225s/f (Firm)
WFA 3 from 4yo+ 3lb — **5** Ran SP% **107.7**
Speed ratings (Par 103): **103,102,94,88,88**
CSF £5.85 TOTE £3.50: £2.00, £1.10; EX 6.30.Dorback was claimed by Mr N. Wilson for £14,000.
Owner Barry Veasey **Bred** Tally-Ho Stud **Trained** Ullingswick, H'fords

FOCUS

An uncompetitive claimer, but a thrilling finish which purely came down to guts. The race has been rated around the runner-up to this year's handicap form.

Dorback Official explanation: one-day ban: used whip with excessive frequency (Sep 6)

Tamagin(USA) Official explanation: jockey said gelding hung right-handed

5340 REAL BEER AGENCY H'CAP — 1m 3f 183y

4:00 (4:01) (Class 5) (0-75,74) 3-Y-O+ — **£2,264** (£673; £336; £168) **Stalls** Low

Form — RPR

-052 **1** **Flying Power**[18] 4755 3-9-0 **71**....(p) RichardMullen 1 — 80
(David Lanigan) *led after 1f: rdn over 1f out: styd on* — **6/1**[3]

-004 **2** *1/2* **Spensley (IRE)**[46] 3817 5-9-11 **72**.... HayleyTurner 3 — 82+
(James Fanshawe) *hld up: hdwy over 6f out: nt clr run and outpcd over 3f out: rallied over 1f out: r.o: wnt 2nd nr fin: nt rch wnr* — **7/2**[2]

0-64 **3** *1/2* **Sagredo (USA)**[41] 2872 7-9-10 **71**.... GeorgeBaker 2 — 78
(Jonjo O'Neill) *sn pushed along to go prom: chsd wnr over 3f out: rdn over 1f out: styd on* — **14/1**

36 **4** *nse* **Amistress**[12] 4971 3-9-2 **73**.... CathyGannon 6 — 80
(Eve Johnson Houghton) *hld up: pushed along over 4f out: hdwy over 3f out: sn rdn: styd on* — **5/2**[1]

5004 **5** *3 1/4* **Cloudy Start**[14] 4887 5-9-13 **74**....(p) FergusSweeney 7 — 76
(Jamie Osborne) *hld up: hdwy over 3f out: rdn over 2f out: styd on same pce fnl f* — **16/1**

0325 **6** *1 1/2* **Cat O' Nine Tails**[21] 4635 4-9-13 **74**.... SilvestreDeSousa 4 — 73
(Mark Johnston) *chsd ldrs: rdn over 2f out: wknd fnl f* — **13/2**

2120 **7** *1/2* **On The Feather**[12] 4971 5-9-9 **70**.... JamesMillman 8 — 69
(Rod Millman) *hld up: rdn over 2f out: nvr on terms* — **13/2**

-000 **8** *6* **True To Form (IRE)**[48] 3739 4-9-8 **69**....(p) TonyCulhane 5 — 58
(George Baker) *prom: lost pl over 6f out: rdn and wknd over 3f out* — **25/1**

-640 **9** *1 1/2* **Agapanthus (GER)**[22] 4612 6-9-1 **62**.... TomQueally 10 — 49
(Barney Curley) *chsd wnr after 1f tl rdn over 3f out: wknd over 2f out* — **25/1**

2m 32.29s (-1.61) **Going Correction** -0.225s/f (Firm)
WFA 3 from 4yo+ 10lb — **9** Ran SP% **112.0**
Speed ratings (Par 103): **96,95,95,95,93 92,91,87,86**
toteswingers:1&2:£4.60, 1&3:£8.30, 2&3:£8.90 CSF £26.16 CT £277.48 TOTE £6.30: £1.80, £1.70, £3.40; EX 30.00 Trifecta £86.50 Pool: £889.89 - 7.69 winning units..
Owner Saif Ali **Bred** Rabbah Bloodstock Limited **Trained** Newmarket, Suffolk

FOCUS

A modest handicap in which the early pace was steady, which played into the hands of the winner. The race has been rated around the third and fourth.

5341 JOHN SMITH'S H'CAP — 7f 9y

4:30 (4:32) (Class 4) (0-80,78) 3-Y-O+ — **£3,428** (£1,020; £509; £254) **Stalls** High

Form — RPR

1101 **1** **George Baker (IRE)**[39] 4066 4-9-8 **74**.... GeorgeBaker 4 — 86+
(George Baker) *chsd ldrs: led 2f out: rdn ins fnl f: jst hld on* — **5/2**[1]

5402 **2** *shd* **Cornus**[9] 5083 9-9-5 **74**....(be) MartinHarley(3) 2 — 83
(Alan McCabe) *sn prom: rdn to chse wnr over 1f out: r.o* — **7/1**

0230 **3** *2 3/4* **Frognal (IRE)**[25] 4509 5-9-11 **77**....(b) HayleyTurner 8 — 79
(Conor Dore) *hld up and bhd: r.o ins fnl f: wnt 3rd nr fin: nt rch ldrs* — **9/1**

-402 **4** *nk* **Be A Devil**[13] 4910 4-9-6 **72**.... MartinDwyer 5 — 73
(William Muir) *sn pushed along in rr: hdwy u.p 2f out: swtchd rt over 1f out: styd on same pce ins fnl f* — **7/2**[2]

000 **5** *2 1/4* **Not My Choice (IRE)**[37] 4126 6-9-12 **78**.... MichaelStainton 10 — 73
(David C Griffiths) *hood removed sltly late: sn chsng ldrs: rdn over 2f out: no ex fnl f* — **14/1**

4-00 **6** *7* **Gentleman Is Back (USA)**[11] 4994 3-8-13 **73**.... JohnFahy(3) 6 — 47
(Ed de Giles) *dwlt: bhd: hdwy over 2f out: sn rdn: wknd fnl f* — **28/1**

240- **7** *1* **Chris's Ridge**[272] 7554 4-9-3 **72**.... SeanLevey(3) 7 — 45
(Eric Alston) *led 5f: sn rdn: wknd fnl f* — **14/1**

2002 **8** *4* **Roman Dancer (IRE)**[19] 4695 3-8-12 **69**....(v) MartinLane 3 — 29
(John Gallagher) *prom: rdn 1/2-way: wknd over 1f out* — **22/1**

1-25 **9** *15* **Sir Mozart (IRE)**[25] 4509 8-9-6 **72**.... TomQueally 1 — —
(Barney Curley) *chsd ldrs: rdn and wknd over 2f out: eased: t.o* — **4/1**[3]

1m 24.79s (-1.41) **Going Correction** -0.225s/f (Firm)
WFA 3 from 4yo+ 5lb — **9** Ran SP% **114.4**
Speed ratings (Par 105): **99,98,95,95,92 84,83,79,61**
toteswingers:1&2:£4.70, 1&3:£5.60, 2&3:£6.30 CSF £20.41 CT £135.71 TOTE £2.80: £1.20, £2.30, £2.60; EX 23.00 Trifecta £118.20 Pool: £985.69 - 6.17 winning units..
Owner George Baker & Partners **Bred** Mull Enterprises Ltd **Trained** Whitsbury, Hants

FOCUS

A fair handicap run at a solid pace.

Sir Mozart(IRE) Official explanation: trainer's rep had no explanation for the poor form shown

5342 PUB PEOPLE NURSERY (DIV I) — 1m 60y

5:05 (5:07) (Class 6) (0-65,65) 2-Y-O — **£1,617** (£481; £240; £120) **Stalls** Low

Form — RPR

000 **1** **Spirit Of The Law (IRE)**[15] 4864 2-8-7 **51**.... HayleyTurner 3 — 63+
(Ed Dunlop) *a.p: pushed along over 3f out: rdn to ld 1f out: r.o* — **13/2**

334 **2** *1 3/4* **Takeitfromalady (IRE)**[12] 4968 2-9-6 **64**.... GeorgeBaker 11 — 70
(Ralph Beckett) *chsd ldrs: led wl over 1f out: rdn and hdd 1f out: edgd lft: styd on same pce* — **7/2**[2]

0264 **3** *1* **Mcvicar**[7] 5144 2-9-4 **65**.... MartinHarley(3) 8 — 69
(Mick Channon) *hld up: rdn over 3f out: hdwy over 1f out: r.o: nt rch ldrs* — **4/1**[3]

406 **4** *1* **Darling Lexi (IRE)**[18] 4748 2-9-7 **65**.... TonyHamilton 9 — 66
(Richard Fahey) *a.p: rdn over 2f out: hung lft over 1f out: styd on same pce fnl f* — **20/1**

0342 **5** *2* **Mad For Fun (IRE)**[67] 3137 2-8-8 **52**.... MickyFenton 12 — 49
(Paul Midgley) *led: rdn and hdd wl over 1f out: hung lft and wknd ins fnl f* — **50/1**

5500 **6** *1/2* **Enjoying (IRE)**[7] 5144 2-9-2 **63**.... SeanLevey(3) 6 — 59
(Richard Hannon) *hld up: rdn over 2f out: r.o ins fnl f: nvr nrr* — **6/1**

6055 **7** *3/4* **Artistic Thread (IRE)**[13] 4907 2-9-0 **58**.... SebSanders 2 — 52
(Sir Mark Prescott Bt) *chsd ldrs: rdn over 3f out: wknd ins fnl f* — **3/1**[1]

0060 **8** *3 3/4* **Coach Montana (IRE)**[47] 3780 2-8-12 **56**....[1] IvaMilickova 4 — 41
(Jane Chapple-Hyam) *hld up: hdwy over 3f out: rdn and wknd over 1f out* — **28/1**

000 **9** *15* **Festival Spirit**[32] 4292 2-8-1 **45**.... SilvestreDeSousa 10 — —
(Mark Johnston) *chsd ldr tl rdn over 3f out: wknd wl over 1f out* — **12/1**

502 **10** *3 3/4* **Sovereign Waters**[40] 3997 2-8-13 **62**.... AmyScott(5) 7 — —
(Eve Johnson Houghton) *s.i.s: hld up: a in rr: rdn over 3f out: wknd over 2f out* — **25/1**

1m 44.54s (-0.56) **Going Correction** -0.225s/f (Firm) — **10** Ran SP% **116.6**
Speed ratings (Par 92): **93,91,90,89,87 86,86,82,67,63**
toteswingers:1&2:£7.00, 1&3:£4.00, 2&3:£3.30 CSF £28.28 CT £106.18 TOTE £6.30: £1.50, £2.20, £1.30; EX 34.00 Trifecta £130.70 Pool: £646.49 - 3.66 winning units..
Owner R J Arculli **Bred** Georgestown Stud **Trained** Newmarket, Suffolk

FOCUS

A moderate nursery, but a stiff test for these juveniles.

NOTEBOOK

Spirit Of The Law(IRE), one of several making their nursery debuts, had finished well beaten in three maidens over 6f-7f, but his pedigree is all about stamina and he relished this stiffer test, travelling cosily in midfield before being produced to lead a furlong from home. This below-tariff prize was a very small repayment on his 78,000gns purchase price, but he is much better than a 51-rated horse and should be able to win again granted a decent test of stamina. Official explanation: trainer's rep said, regarding apparent improvement in form, that the colt appeared to benefit from racing over 2f further. (op 8-1)

Takeitfromalady(IRE) was another making his nursery debut after showing some ability in three maidens and there is plenty of stamina on the dam' side of his pedigree. He looked to have timed it right when leading over a furlong from home, but the winner saw his race out that much better. He should be up to winning a race like this. (op 3-1 tchd 11-4)

Mcvicar shaped as though this extra furlong would suit when a running-on fourth on his nursery debut at Kempton last time, but as it turned out this wasn't far enough. He took an age to respond to pressure having been held up well off the pace early, but came home strongly and could be of some interest for a 9f or 1m2f nursery before the end of the year. (op 9-2 tchd 11-2 and 7-2)
Darling Lexi(IRE), another making her nursery debut after three starts in maidens, was brought through to hold a chance inside the last 3f, but then proved one-paced. (op 14-1 tchd 12-1)
Mad For Fun(IRE) set the pace until over a furlong from home and ran with credit, but she has already been beaten in selling and claiming company. (op 33-1)
Artistic Thread(IRE)'s prominent position in the market probably owed much to his connections as he had already proved a disappointing favourite on his nursery debut and, after racing prominently here, once again found precious little off the bridle. (op 7-2)

5343 PUB PEOPLE NURSERY (DIV II) — 1m 60y
5:40 (5:41) (Class 6) (0-65,65) 2-Y-O — **£1,617** (£481; £240; £120) **Stalls** Low

Form — RPR

0044 **1** **Moon Trip**[34] 4194 2-9-7 65 .... SilvestreDeSousa 10 80+
(Mark Johnston) *chsd ldr tl led over 6f out: rdn clr over 1f out: easily* **11/4**[1]

043 **2** *7* **Hearts And Minds (IRE)**[14] 4884 2-9-5 63 ....(b[1]) FergusSweeney 12 61
(Jamie Osborne) *a.p: chsd wnr over 3f out: rdn over 2f out: styd on same pce fr over 1f out* **9/1**[3]

030 **3** *1 ¼* **Pond Life (IRE)**[43] 3917 2-9-4 62 .... HayleyTurner 2 56
(Amy Weaver) *chsd ldrs: rdn over 2f out: swtchd lft and styd on same pce fr over 1f out: wnt 3rd nr fin* **11/4**[1]

440 **4** *1* **Daring Damsel (IRE)**[12] 4969 2-8-13 62 ....(p) RyanPowell(5) 3 54
(Paul Cole) *chsd ldrs: rdn over 3f out: styd on same pce fnl 2f* **12/1**

060 **5** *2 ¾* **Milwr**[46] 3816 2-8-1 45 .... AndreaAtzeni 1 31
(Chris Dwyer) *s.i.s: hld up: hdwy and hung lft over 1f out:* **33/1**

060 **6** *1* **Emma Jean Boy**[14] 4884 2-8-9 53 .... TomQueally 6 36
(J S Moore) *sn pushed along in rr: hdwy over 2f out: rdn and wknd over 1f out* **25/1**

000 **7** *5* **Hawkino (IRE)**[15] 4864 2-8-12 56 .... RobbieFitzpatrick 9 28
(Derek Shaw) *hld up: rdn and wknd over 2f out* **18/1**

4500 **8** *1* **Bojangle (IRE)**[13] 4913 2-8-2 49 .... BillyCray(3) 8 18
(Dominic Ffrench Davis) *plld hrd and prom: rdn over 3f out: wknd wl over 1f out* **14/1**

004 **9** *1* **Music Girl**[14] 4884 2-8-7 51 .... FrankieMcDonald 7 18
(Michael Blanshard) *prom over 4f* **50/1**

603 **10** *hd* **Single Girl (IRE)**[19] 4698 2-8-13 57 .... StephenCraine 4 24
(Jonathan Portman) *hld up: a in rr: wknd over 2f out* **22/1**

000 **11** *13* **Astraios (IRE)**[18] 4748 2-9-7 65 .... MartinDwyer 5 2
(Brian Meehan) *a in rr: bhd whn stmbld 5f out: t.o* **5/1**[2]

606 **12** *10* **Revitalise**[61] 3302 2-9-2 60 .... TomEaves 11 —
(Kevin Ryan) *led: hdd over 6f out: chsd wnr tl rdn over 3f out: sn wknd: t.o* **14/1**

1m 44.34s (-0.76) **Going Correction** -0.225s/f (Firm) — **12** Ran SP% **119.4**
Speed ratings (Par 92): **94,87,85,84,82 81,76,75,74,73 60,50**
Totesuper 7 : Win: Not won; Place: £114.30 CSF £28.09 CT £76.54 TOTE £4.30: £1.80, £2.50, £1.10; EX 29.70 Trifecta £89.90 Pool: £612.55 - 5.04 winning units..
Owner Sheikh Hamdan Bin Mohammed Al Maktoum **Bred** Darley **Trained** Middleham Moor, N Yorks

FOCUS
The second leg of this moderate nursery was run 0.2secs faster than the first division. Three-quarters of the field were making their handicap debuts and a number were stepping up in trip, but nothing got into this from off the pace. The runner-up and third help set the level.

NOTEBOOK
Moon Trip failed to handle the soft ground when a beaten favourite on his handicap debut at Catterick last time. However, back on faster ground and given a stiffer test, he galloped his rival into submission, being heavily eased and value for much more than the official margin. Connections will probably have to get him out under a penalty after this, as the handicapper is likely to put him up quite a bit. (op 10-3)
Hearts And Minds(IRE) was fitted with blinkers for this handicap debut and looked a big threat to the winner halfway up the straight. He was well held entering the final furlong, but finished clear of the rest. (tchd 17-2)
Pond Life(IRE), stepping up 2f for this handicap debut, had her chance in the straight but could not sustain the effort. (op 10-3 tchd 7-2)
Daring Damsel(IRE), up in trip and fitted with cheekpieces for this first start in a handicap, was well enough placed early in the straight, but could not pick up. (op 18-1 tchd 20-1)
Bojangle(IRE) Official explanation: jockey said filly did not handle the bend
Astraios(IRE) was backed, but after getting squeezed out early he failed to handle the bend and was always struggling. His rider reported that the colt slipped on the bend. Official explanation: jockey said colt slipped on the bend (op 7-1)
T/Plt: £162.80 to a £1 stake. Pool:£75,091.04 - 336.70 winning tickets T/Qpdt: £7.90 to a £1 stake. Pool:£6,086.83 - 569.00 winning tickets CR

[3779] WARWICK (L-H)
Tuesday, August 23

OFFICIAL GOING: Good to firm (firm in places 1m 2f and further; watered; 8.4)
Wind: Virtually nil Weather: Sunny spells early

5344 ENTERTAIN CLIENTS AT WARWICK APPRENTICE H'CAP — 6f
5:00 (5:00) (Class 6) (0-65,65) 3-Y-O — **£1,772** (£523; £261) **Stalls** Low

Form — RPR

6345 **1** **Blue Deer (IRE)**[38] 4110 3-9-9 64 .... CharlesBishop 1 72
(Mick Channon) *mde all: pushed along over 2f out: drvn and hld on wl fnl f* **5/2**[1]

3361 **2** *2 ¼* **Full Shilling (IRE)**[12] 4950 3-9-2 57 .... MatthewLawson 5 58
(John Spearing) *in rr: drvn along after 2f: hdwy over 1f out: styd on wl fnl f to go 2nd nr fin but no imp on wnr* **11/4**[2]

3526 **3** *¾* **His Grace (IRE)**[10] 5038 3-9-5 60 .... LucyKBarry 8 58
(Andrew Haynes) *sn chsng wnr: rdn and c to r on stands' rail over 2f out: effrt over 1f out and nvr quite on terms: one pce and lost 2nd nr fin* **11/1**

3002 **4** *½* **Atia**[26] 4466 3-9-3 58 ....(p) AntiocoMurgia 9 55
(Jonathan Portman) *chsd ldrs: rdn to dispute 2nd ins fnl f but no rch wnr: wknd clsng stages* **8/1**

3653 **5** *1 ¼* **Lady Excellentia (IRE)**[6] 5176 3-8-2 46 oh1 .... LukeRowe(3) 3 39
(Ronald Harris) *s.i.s: in rr: rdn and sme hdwy whn hmpd appr fnl f: kpt on again cl home* **18/1**

1240 **6** *¾* **Juarla (IRE)**[25] 4486 3-9-10 65 .... RaulDaSilva 7 55
(Ronald Harris) *chsd ldrs: rdn to disute 2nd ins fnl f: sn wknd* **11/2**[3]

0635 **7** *3 ¾* **Vintage Grape (IRE)**[22] 4607 3-8-6 47 .... NathanAlison 6 25
(Eric Alston) *chsd ldrs: rdn over 2f out: wkng whn edgd rt appr fnl f* **12/1**

005 **8** *2 ¾* **Greyemkay**[19] 4706 3-9-0 55 .... DavidKenny 2 25
(Richard Price) *chsd ldrs tl wknd 2f out* **16/1**

3060 **9** *36* **Stravsambition**[21] 4647 3-8-7 53 ....(t) JackDuern(5) 10 —
(Reg Hollinshead) *v. slwly away and rel to r: a t.o* **33/1**

1m 11.75s (-0.05) **Going Correction** -0.25s/f (Firm) course record — **9** Ran SP% **111.8**
Speed ratings (Par 98): **90,87,86,85,83 82,77,74,26**
toteswingers:1&2:£2.10, 1&3:£5.20, 2&3:£7.40 CSF £9.01 CT £59.56 TOTE £2.70: £1.20, £1.80, £2.70; EX 8.60.
Owner M Channon **Bred** Pier House Stud **Trained** West Ilsley, Berks
■ Stewards' Enquiry : Antioco Murgia one-day ban: careless riding (Sep 6)

FOCUS
It was unclear beforehand where the pace would come from in this moderate sprint handicap. The winner has been rated as a length personal best on early maiden promise.

5345 TURFTV (S) STKS — 6f
5:30 (5:30) (Class 5) 3-Y-O+ — **£2,045** (£603; £302) **Stalls** Low

Form — RPR

5000 **1** **Noverre To Go (IRE)**[24] 4531 5-8-13 87 ....(t) NeilCallan 10 72
(Tom Dascombe) *plld hrd: in tch: hdwy 2f out: led jst ins fnl f: drvn and in command whn edgd lft clsng stages* **1/1**[1]

0040 **2** *1 ¼* **Silver Wind**[11] 5012 6-9-5 73 ....(b) RobertWinston 4 74
(Alan McCabe) *in rr: rdn and hdwy fr 2f out: slt ld over 1f out tl hdd jst ins fnl f: styd on but no ch w wnr* **5/1**[3]

3233 **3** *2 ¾* **Could It Be Magic**[57] 3473 4-8-10 72 ....(b) KierenFox(3) 1 59
(Bill Turner) *led tl rdn and hdd over 1f out: sn one pce: rallied u.p to take 3rd clsng stages: no ch w ldng duo* **4/1**[2]

3001 **4** *½* **Dark Lane**[11] 4990 5-9-5 74 .... DavidProbert 7 64
(Tony Carroll) *in rr: rdn over 2f out: styd on u.p fnl f to take one pce 4th clsng stages* **10/1**

3200 **5** *hd* **Our Piccadilly (IRE)**[29] 4387 6-8-5 69 ....(b[1]) LouisBeuzelin(3) 9 52
(Stuart Kittow) *plld hrd in rr: rdn ins fnl 2f: styd on u.p fnl f: nt rch ldrs* **14/1**

0003 **6** *nk* **Memphis Man**[22] 4618 8-9-0 58 .... MatthewCosham(5) 3 62
(David Evans) *in rr: rdn and sme hdwy fr 2f out: styd on same pce ins fnl f* **25/1**

7 *1 ½* **Indian Dumaani**[111] 4-8-8 40 .... DavidAllan 2 46
(David Bridgwater) *chsd ldr: rdn to chal over 2f out tl wknd wl over 1f out* **33/1**

3066 **8** *1 ½* **Eternal Youth (IRE)**[16] 4816 3-9-2 60 ....(b) TomMcLaughlin 8 52
(Ronald Harris) *in rr: styd to r along towards far side and nvr any ch* **66/1**

053 **9** *2 ½* **Little Perisher**[17] 4795 4-8-13 49 ....(b) SteveDrowne 5 38
(Karen George) *chsd ldrs: c to r on stands' side and wknd qckly 2f out* **50/1**

1m 11.05s (-0.75) **Going Correction** -0.25s/f (Firm) course record
WFA 3 from 4yo+ 3lb — **9** Ran SP% **112.7**
Speed ratings (Par 103): **95,93,89,89,88 88,86,84,81**
toteswingers:1&2:£1.90, 1&3:£2.00, 2&3:£3.70 CSF £5.82 TOTE £2.20: £1.60, £1.10, £1.70; EX 8.40.The winner was sold to Ron Harris for 14,000gns.
Owner Duddy Duddy Heeney McBride **Bred** Gestut Gorlsdorf **Trained** Malpas, Cheshire

FOCUS
A decent seller won, as expected, by the 87-rated Noverre To Go.
Could It Be Magic Official explanation: jockey said colt hung right

5346 MERCIA MADE FOR COVENTRY AND WARWICKSHIRE MAIDEN STKS — 5f 110y
6:00 (6:01) (Class 5) 3-Y-O+ — **£2,454** (£724; £362) **Stalls** Low

Form — RPR

5522 **1** **Eshoog (IRE)**[6] 5176 3-8-5 65 ....(bt) LeonnaMayor(7) 1 60
(Phil McEntee) *mde all: shkn up: hung rt and unbalanced jst ins fnl f: sn rcvrd: rdn and edgd lft: hld on wl* **9/2**[2]

0250 **2** *¾* **Adaeze (IRE)**[12] 4950 3-8-12 53 .... JamesDoyle 9 57
(Jonathan Portman) *chsd wnr fr 3f out: rdn over 2f out: kpt on fnl f but no imp* **20/1**

3 *1* **Emkanaat** 3-9-3 0 .... RichardHills 4 59
(Roger Varian) *in tch: rdn and green: outpcd over 2f out: drvn and kpt on fnl f: nt qcknd fnl 120yds* **4/9**[1]

[illegible] **4** [illegible] [illegible] **(IRE)**[15] 4863 3-[illegible] 0 .... KieranFox(3) 3 55
(Karen George) *chsd ldrs: rdn 2f out: wknd fnl 100yds: jst hld on for 4th* **20/1**

-045 **5** *nk* **Amazing Win (IRE)**[12] 4963 3-8-12 66 .... TonyCulhane 8 49
(Mick Channon) *chsd ldrs: rdn and one pce over 1f out: styd on again clsng stages but nvr a threat* **7/1**[3]

5- **6** *1 ¾* **Decimate**[498] 1263 3-9-0 0 .... SophieDoyle(3) 7 48
(Andrew Reid) *sn rdn along in rr and green: nvr in contention but sme prog fnl f* **40/1**

0 **7** *5* **The Flying Cholita (IRE)**[12] 4970 3-8-12 0 .... CathyGannon 5 26
(Eve Johnson Houghton) *early spd: bhd fnl 3f* **33/1**

0 **P** **My Piccadill**[31] 4340 3-8-12 0 .... LiamKeniry 2 —
(Stuart Kittow) *sn drvn: in rr whn p.u 3f out: fatally injured* **20/1**

66.46 secs (0.56) **Going Correction** -0.25s/f (Firm) — **8** Ran SP% **119.6**
Speed ratings (Par 103): **86,85,83,82,81 79,72,—**
toteswingers:1&2:£4.10, 1&3:£1.10, 2&3:£5.30 CSF £81.46 TOTE £3.70: £1.50, £3.90, £1.10; EX 39.50.
Owner S Jakes **Bred** Yeomanstown Stud **Trained** Newmarket, Suffolk
■ Stewards' Enquiry : Leonna Mayor two-day ban: used whip with excessive frequency (Sep 6-7)

FOCUS
A weak sprint maiden.

5347 GEORGE PIG HERE ON 29TH AUGUST MAIDEN STKS — 5f
6:30 (6:34) (Class 5) 2-Y-O — **£2,454** (£724; £362) **Stalls** Low

Form — RPR

3 **1** **Knocker Knowles (IRE)**[21] 4639 2-9-3 0 .... CathyGannon 6 77
(David Evans) *trckd ldr: led ins fnl 2f: pushed clr fnl f: comf* **9/2**[3]

2 *4 ½* **Fantastic Smartie** 2-8-12 0 .... DavidProbert 2 56
(David Evans) *chsd ldrs: pushed along over 2f out: rdn and styd on fr over 1f out: tk 2nd fnl 120yds: no ch w wnr* **20/1**

42 **3** *2* **Samba Night (IRE)**[29] 4377 2-9-3 0 .... RichardMullen 3 54
(Ed McMahon) *led tl hdd ins fnl 2f: no ch w wnr 1f out: wknd and lost 2nd fnl 120yds* **6/4**[1]

00 **4** *2 ¼* **Deduction (IRE)**[10] 5047 2-8-7 0 .... MatthewLawson(5) 5 41
(Charles Hills) *plld hrd: stdd in rr: rn v wd bnd ins fnl 3f and lost any ch but styd on stands' rail and kpt on fnl f: nt rcvr* **3/1**[2]

5 *nk* **Zafonic Star** 2-9-0 0 .... RyanClark(3) 8 44
(Ian Williams) *s.i.s: in rr: pushed along 1/2-way: sme prog fnl f but nvr any ch* **16/1**

6 *nk* **Surrey Spirit** 2-8-9 0 .... JohnFahy(3) 4 38
(Harry Dunlop) *chsd ldrs: rdn over 2f out: sn btn* **13/2**

7 *2* **La Sonadora** 2-8-12 0 .... JamesDoyle 7 31
(John Spearing) *unruly stalls: rdn and green in rr 3f out: a outpcd* **40/1**

60.03 secs (0.43) **Going Correction** -0.25s/f (Firm) **7** Ran SP% **109.6**
Speed ratings (Par 94): **86,78,75,72,71 71,67**
toteswingers:1&2:£8.00, 1&3:£2.40, 2&3:£3.40 CSF £74.30 TOTE £5.20: £1.60, £5.40; EX 47.40.
Owner Shropshire Wolves **Bred** Ballyhane Stud **Trained** Pandy, Monmouths

FOCUS
An ordinary juvenile maiden.

NOTEBOOK
Knocker Knowles(IRE), who was green when a well-beaten third over 6f on debut, had clearly learned plenty from that and stormed home to win the style of a useful type. Things very much went his way and it'll be interesting to see what mark he's given by the handicapper. (op 5-1 tchd 11-2)
Fantastic Smartie, whose dam was a 5f winner, appeared to know her job and she stayed on nicely to finish a clear second. A small maiden should come her way. (op 18-1 tchd 16-1)
Samba Night(IRE) looked likely to prove suited by the drop to 5f, but he got worked up in the preliminaries and emerged from the stalls in something of a lather. Having shown tons of early pace, it was no surprise to see him readily swept aside and, although better than this, he clearly has limitations. (op Evens)
Deduction(IRE) was soon in rear and pulling on this drop to 5f and hung wide into the straight. She did keep on, but is clearly modest. Official explanation: jockey said filly hung badly right (op 5-1)
Zafonic Star, already gelded, is likely to benefit from the experience and an extra furlong. (tchd 20-1)
Surrey Spirit, whose dam is a half-sister to top performers Divine Proportions and Whipper, comes from a yard whose juveniles often benefit greatly from a run and should fare better next time. (op 9-1)

5348 RACING UK NURSERY — 5f
7:00 (7:01) (Class 4) (0-85,88) 2-Y-O — **£3,493** (£1,039; £519; £259) **Stalls** Low

Form — RPR

2013 **1** **Powerful Wind (IRE)**[4] 5237 2-9-7 **82** .... DavidProbert 7 86
(Ronald Harris) *mde all: rdn over 1f out: hrd drvn ins fnl f: hld on wl clsng stages* **9/1**

6034 **2** *¾* **Musical Valley**[17] 4809 2-8-12 **73** ....(t) RichardKingscote 4 74
(Tom Dascombe) *s.i.s: hld up in rr: hdwy over 1f out: rdn and styd on wl to chse wnr ins fnl f: gng on cl home but a hld* **22/1**

02 **3** *2¾* **Lupo D'Oro (IRE)**[38] 4079 2-8-13 **74** .... SteveDrowne 11 65
(John Best) *chsd ldrs: hmpd appr fnl f: styd on again clsng stages to take one pce 3rd* **8/1**

0041 **4** *¾* **Signifer (IRE)**[4] 5237 2-9-13 **88** 6ex .... JamesDoyle 2 77
(Mick Channon) *in tch: hdwy on stands' rails to chse wnr whn veered rt to paddock entrnce over 1f out: kpt on but no imp clsng stages* **7/2**[3]

0422 **5** *¾* **Royal Red**[29] 4386 2-9-0 **75** .... MartinLane 1 61
(Ralph Beckett) *chsd wnr 3f out tl wknd u.p appr fnl f* **10/3**[2]

5103 **6** *2¾* **Courtland King (IRE)**[26] 4460 2-9-3 **78** .... CathyGannon 9 54
(David Evans) *outpcd and rdn in rr 3f out: nt clr run and swtchd lft over 1f out: no prog fnl f* **25/1**

102 **7** *2¾* **Mitie Mouse**[24] 4558 2-9-3 **78** .... NeilCallan 5 44
(Mike Murphy) *chsd ldrs tl rdn hmpd and wknd appr fnl f* **3/1**[1]

10 **8** *2* **Kylesku (IRE)**[11] 4999 2-9-5 **80** .... PhillipMakin 6 39
(Kevin Ryan) *s.i.s: outpcd most of way* **5/1**

58.83 secs (-0.77) **Going Correction** -0.25s/f (Firm) **8** Ran SP% **116.3**
Speed ratings (Par 96): **96,94,90,89,88 83,79,76**
toteswingers:1&2:£7.20, 1&3:£10.00, 2&3:£18.90 CSF £177.72 CT £1662.17 TOTE £13.80: £2.80, £7.20, £3.70; EX 204.20.
Owner Anthony Cooke **Bred** Miss Ciara Doyle **Trained** Earlswood, Monmouths

FOCUS
Not as good a nursery as it promised to be.

NOTEBOOK
Powerful Wind(IRE) is very fast and was always to gain an uncontested lead. He bounced off the fast ground and held on well. He'd finished behind Signifer four days earlier, but put that one in its place on this significantly faster surface, and will remain dangerous when the emphasis is on speed. (tchd 8-1)
Musical Valley stayed on from nearly last to bustle up the winner late on, but he was always booked for second. He's taking his racing well and this looks his trip. (op 28-1)
Lupo D'Oro(IRE)chased the early pace and stayed on again having been impeded over 1f out, taking third. (op 15-2)
Signifer(IRE) had the winner behind when appreciating the soft ground at Sandown the other day, but on 6lb worse terms and faced with a much livelier surface, he was put in his place, costing himself a chance of when hanging sharply right over 1f out. Official explanation: jockey said colt hung right (op 4-1)
Royal Red proved one-paced on this nursery debut and looks worth a try at 6f. Official explanation: jockey said filly hung right (op 7-2 tchd 4-1)
Mitie Mouse's rider was looking down as though something may have gone amiss Official explanation: jockey said colt hung right (op 4-1)
Kylesku(IRE) hasn't gone on at all from her promising debut win. Official explanation: jockey said filly never travelled (op 6-1)

5349 PIMMS AND PUNS ON 16TH SEPTEMBER H'CAP — 1m 2f 188y
7:30 (7:30) (Class 6) (0-60,60) 3-Y-O+ — **£1,772** (£523; £261) **Stalls** Low

Form — RPR

-000 **1** **Fair Breeze**[19] 4705 4-8-12 **46** oh1 .... RobertHavlin 16 53
(Richard Phillips) *chsd ldr off mod pce: drvn to ld wl over 1f out: hrd drvn fnl f: hld on all out* **40/1**

0042 **2** *shd* **Into The Wind**[8] 5112 4-9-5 **53** .... JamesMillman 14 62+
(Rod Millman) *hld up in rr: hdwy on stands' rail over 2f out: str run u.p fnl f: jst failed* **9/2**[1]

6603 **3** *shd* **Kathleen Kennet**[24] 4544 11-8-13 **47** .... LiamKeniry 17 54
(Jonathan Geake) *chsd ldrs off mod pce: rdn and outpcd over 2f out: styd on fnl f: fin strly: nt quite get up* **10/1**

0540 **4** *1¾* **Sir Randolf (IRE)**[25] 4491 3-8-10 **53** ....(t) JamesDoyle 2 56
(Sylvester Kirk) *hld up in mid-div off mod pce: outpcd and dropped towards rr over 3f out: styd on u.p over 1f out: no ex fnl 120yds* **8/1**[3]

00-2 **5** *2½* **Hint Of Honey**[12] 4953 5-8-7 **48** .... DavidKenny(7) 13 47
(Tony Newcombe) *t.k.h: chsd ldrs off mod pce: rdn and hung lft 2f out: outpcd fnl f* **10/1**

0010 **6** *nk* **Reset To Fit**[19] 4716 4-9-9 **57** .... DavidAllan 11 56
(Eric Alston) *t.k.h in rr: hdwy 2f out: styng on whn hmpd 1f out: no ex* **17/2**

-000 **7** *1* **Look For Love**[21] 4647 3-8-3 **46** oh1 .... DavidProbert 15 43
(Reg Hollinshead) *led at mod pce: rdn 3f out: hdd wl over 1f out: sn btn* **50/1**

2443 **8** *½* **Mr Chocolate Drop (IRE)**[14] 4889 7-9-4 **57** ....(t) NathanAlison(5) 12 53
(Mandy Rowland) *in rr: hdwy 1/2-way: styng on whn hmpd 1f out: no prog after* **10/1**

0355 **9** *¾* **Hathaway (IRE)**[8] 5107 4-9-2 **50** .... GrahamGibbons 9 44
(Mark Brisbourne) *plld hrd: chsd ldrs over mod pce: wknd fr 2f out* **9/2**[1]

0050 **10** *1½* **Habsburg**[19] 4705 3-8-11 **53** ow1 ....(b[1]) FergusSweeney 10 46
(Paul Fitzsimons) *chsd ldrs off mod pce: wknd fr 3f out* **20/1**

0103 **11** *1* **Guga (IRE)**[41] 3974 5-9-5 **60** ....(b) RaulDaSilva(7) 7 50
(John Mackie) *in rr: mod prog fnl 2f* **11/2**[2]

-000 **12** *5* **Croeso Mawr**[12] 4948 5-9-1 **49** .... SteveDrowne 6 30
(John Spearing) *a in rr* **16/1**

0-06 **13** *hd* **Applaude**[12] 4946 6-9-6 **54** ....(b) BarryMcHugh 3 35
(Jason Ward) *a in rr* **16/1**

2m 20.96s (-0.14) **Going Correction** -0.25s/f (Firm)
WFA 3 from 4yo+ 9lb **13** Ran SP% **121.6**
Speed ratings (Par 101): **90,89,89,88,86 86,85,85,84,83 83,79,79**
toteswingers:1&2:£20.00, 1&3:£94.60, 2&3:£9.30 CSF £214.34 CT £1999.94 TOTE £61.10: £18.90, £2.00, £4.10; EX 258.20.
Owner Flying Tiger Partnership **Bred** Richard Phillips **Trained** Adlestrop, Gloucs

FOCUS
The pace was a steady one for what looked an open handicap. Perhaps no surprise there was a shock result then. The winner has been rated as running to a small personal best and the level is set around the third.
Fair Breeze Official explanation: trainer said, regarding apparent improvement in form, that the filly appreciated the step up in trip and the better ground
Reset To Fit Official explanation: jockey said gelding was denied a clear run
Mr Chocolate Drop(IRE) Official explanation: jockey said gelding ran too freely
Hathaway(IRE) Official explanation: jockey said filly hung right throughout

5350 1707 H'CAP — 1m 4f 134y
8:00 (8:00) (Class 5) (0-70,70) 3-Y-O — **£2,454** (£724; £362) **Stalls** Low

Form — RPR

0022 **1** **Sugar Hiccup (IRE)**[12] 4971 3-9-1 **67** .... JohnFahy(3) 5 71+
(Clive Cox) *trckd ldr off mod pce: rdn 3f out: styd on u.p fnl f to ld fnl 50yds: drvn out* **8/15**[1]

4040 **2** *nk* **Spanish Plume**[13] 4902 3-9-5 **68** .... GrahamGibbons 2 71
(Reg Hollinshead) *led at mod pce: stl gng wl 3f out: rdn 2f out: kpt on but hdd and no ex fnl 50yds* **7/2**[2]

0053 **3** *2¾* **Imperial Fong**[8] 5118 3-8-2 **51** oh4 .... AndreaAtzeni 6 50
(Chris Dwyer) *racd in 4th off mod pce: rdn fr 4f out: hung rt and styd on fnl f to take 3rd ins fnl f: no ch w ldng duo* **16/1**

0-60 **4** *1½* **Noble Defender**[73] 2930 3-8-13 **62** .... FergusSweeney 3 58
(Stuart Kittow) *t.k.h and chsd ldrs in 3rd of mod pce: rdn and effrt to press for 2nd 3f out: sn wknd* **6/1**[3]

5046 **5** *43* **Sally Anne**[11] 5021 3-8-2 **51** oh6 .... CathyGannon 4 —
(John Harris) *t.k.h in rr off mod pce: rdn and wknd over 4f out: eased fnl 2f: t.o* **33/1**

2m 46.11s (1.51) **Going Correction** -0.25s/f (Firm) **5** Ran SP% **110.6**
Speed ratings (Par 100): **85,84,83,82,55**
CSF £2.73 TOTE £1.60: £1.30, £1.10; EX 2.80.
Owner S R Hope And S W Barrow **Bred** Raysiza Partnership **Trained** Lambourn, Berks

FOCUS
A modest handicap and the pace was steady, resulting in the slowest time of the night compared to standard. The main action unfolded near the stands' rail in the straight. The winner did not need to match her latest Salisbury figure.
Sally Anne Official explanation: jockey said filly hung right
T/Jkpt: Not won. T/Plt: £100.50 to a £1 stake. Pool:£39,586.38 - 287.50 winning tickets T/Qpdt: £48.90 to a £1 stake. Pool:£4,072.60 - 61.60 winning tickets ST

5116 YARMOUTH (L-H)
Tuesday, August 23
OFFICIAL GOING: Good to firm changing to good after race 2 (5:20)
Wind: virtually nil Weather: overcast

5351 ODDSCHECKER.COM MAIDEN AUCTION STKS — 5f 43y
4:45 (4:46) (Class 5) 2-Y-O — **£2,652** (£789; £394; £197) **Stalls** High

Form — RPR

2 **1** **Place In My Heart**[91] 2374 2-8-7 0 .... JamieSpencer 1 84+
(George Baker) *mde all: urged along and readily asserted over 1f out: clr fnl f: easily* **2/1**[2]

0 **2** *4* **Indian Tinker**[8] 5117 2-8-11 0 .... EddieAhern 2 72
(Robert Cowell) *chsd wnr tl over 3f out: styd pressing wnr tl rdn and nt pce of wnr over 1f out: chsd clr wnr and wl hld after* **14/1**[3]

2 **3** *3½* **Gallery**[19] 4720 2-8-10 0 .... KierenFallon 5 58
(William Haggas) *t.k.h: chsd ldrs tl wnt 2nd over3f out: pushed along 2f out: pressed wnr and rdn over 1f out: immediately btn: wknd fnl f* **8/13**[1]

5 **4** *3¾* **Kara's Vision**[12] 4940 2-8-8 0 .... JimmyQuinn 6 43
(Robert Cowell) *dwlt: hld up in last pair: shkn up 1/2-way: rdn over 1f out: sn wknd* **40/1**

063 **5** *3½* **Bookiesindexdotnet**[15] 4848 2-8-8 62 .... ShaneKelly 7 30
(J R Jenkins) *chsd ldrs: rdn over 1f out: sn wknd* **25/1**

0 **6** *9* **Greek Music**[8] 5117 2-8-2 0 .... CagriMetin(3) 3 —
(George Prodromou) *s.i.s: sn bustled along and hung lft: a struggling: hung rt and lost tch ent fnl 2f: t.o* **150/1**

62.19 secs (-0.51) **Going Correction** -0.10s/f (Good) **6** Ran SP% **108.9**
Speed ratings (Par 94): **100,93,88,82,76 62**
toteswingers:1&2:£1.70, 1&3:£1.10, 2&3:£1.70 CSF £23.43 TOTE £2.70: £1.20, £4.50; EX 20.80.
Owner Turf Club 2010 **Bred** Whitsbury Manor Stud **Trained** Whitsbury, Hants
■ Stewards' Enquiry : Jamie Spencer one-day ban: careless riding (Sep 6)

FOCUS
Back straight and bottom bend dolled out 3m up to 4.5f adding 15m to advertised distances. Light rain had fallen overnight, with 3mm more during the morning, but the ground was officially good to firm. Racing began with an interesting juvenile maiden which, though it lacked strength in depth, featured two fillies with sound debut form.

NOTEBOOK
Place In My Heart had been off the course for 91 days since her promising Chepstow debut, but certainly looked sharp here, grabbing the lead from the outset and making all the running. She initially made for the stands' rail, but was eased out towards the centre of the track in the closing stages, by which time she was home and hosed. She should stay further and can win again. (tchd 15-8)
Indian Tinker, seventh of nine over 6f here eight days previously, stepped up on that effort. Fast away and racing a couple of horse widths off the stands rail, he was always chasing the winner and plugged on courageously in the final furlong. A maiden win seems probable. (op 16-1)

Gallery, who stayed on to finish second in a stronger contest at Sandown 19 days earlier, was disappointing. The market indicated she would make a bold bid, as her form suggested she was entitled to do, but she was quite keen early on and found little when put under pressure. She has questions to answer after this run. (op 4-7 tchd 4-6)

Kara's Vision had beaten just one rival at Beverley first time out and was slowly away here. Given those two factors, she did well to finish fourth and this display suggests she might find a little race once handicapped. (op 33-1 tchd 50-1)

Bookiesindexdotnet, thrice-raced and officially rated 62, did not run up to that mark. Second in the early stages, she faded quickly once the winner engaged a higher gear. (op 18-1)

Greek Music was well behind Indian Tinker first time out and again proved no match for that rival. She was never closer than fifth and seems likely to need a drop in grade in order to make any impact.

5352 PROSPECT HANDLING H'CAP — 1m 3y

5:20 (5:22) (Class 6) (0-55,60) 3-Y-O — £1,617 (£481; £240; £120) Stalls High

Form — RPR

40R1 **1** **Arctic Maiden**[6] 5178 3-9-8 **60** 6ex.............................. StevieDonohoe 10 — 69+
(Willie Musson) *towards rr: hdwy 2f out: chsd ldrs and swtchd rt over 1f out: rdn to ld ent fnl f: kpt on u.p: rdn out* **7/4**[1]

00 **2** *1/2* **Gay Gallivanter**[18] 4758 3-8-12 **50**.............................. JamieSpencer 11 — 58+
(Michael Quinn) *stdd s: hld up in rr: hdwy on far side over 2f out: drvn and chsd wnr ent fnl f: pressed wnr fnl 100yds: kpt on* **16/1**

0006 **3** *1 3/4* **Appyjack**[16] 4827 3-8-10 **48**.............................. LukeMorris 6 — 52
(Tony Carroll) *in tch towards rr: lost pl and rdn over 2f out: swtchd rt and hdwy u.p over 1f out: styd on u.p fnl f* **12/1**

0064 **4** *2 3/4* **Ippi N Tombi (IRE)**[19] 4728 3-8-6 **47**.................... AdamBeschizza(3) 14 — 45
(Phil McEntee) *chsd ldrs: rdn over 2f out: drvn and unable qck wl over 1f out: plugged on same pce u.p fnl f* **25/1**

0004 **5** *nk* **Warden Bond**[13] 4927 3-8-3 **46**..............................(p) LauraPike(5) 5 — 43
(William Stone) *t.k.h: hld up in tch in midfield: hdwy 3f out: rdn to chse ldrs 2f out: drvn and unable qck over 1f out: styd on same pce fnl f* **14/1**

5500 **6** *1 1/2* **Talkative Guest (IRE)**[16] 4822 3-9-2 **54**......................(p) KierenFallon 8 — 48
(George Margarson) *led: rdn and hdd wl over 1f out: wknd ins fnl f* **9/1**

0005 **7** *1 1/4* **Indian Wish (USA)**[16] 4827 3-8-8 **46**.............................. SaleemGolam 13 — 37
(Tim McCarthy) *w ldr tl led wl over 1f out: sn rdn and hdd over 1f out: wknd qckly jst ins fnl f* **20/1**

-000 **8** *2 1/2* **Zartina (IRE)**[20] 4657 3-8-7 **48**.............................. KieranO'Neill(3) 9 — 33
(Sylvester Kirk) *t.k.h: hld up in tch: rdn and unable qck over 2f out: kpt on same pce and wl hld fr over 1f out* **40/1**

600 **9** *nk* **Nubian Gem (IRE)**[15] 4849 3-9-0 **52**.............................. LiamJones 3 — 36
(John Best) *in tch in midfield: rdn over 3f out: struggling and btn wl over 1f out: wknd ent fnl f* **33/1**

-300 **10** *2 3/4* **Dililah**[80] 2722 3-8-9 **54**.............................. KristinStubbs(7) 12 — 32
(Linda Stubbs) *taken down early: t.k.h: hld up towards rr: edging lft to far side and effrt over 2f out: no imp and wl hld over 1f out* **66/1**

000 **11** *1 1/2* **Littlepromisedland (IRE)**[8] 5116 3-8-0 **45**............(p) CharlesEddery(7) 1 — 19
(Richard Guest) *chsd ldrs: rdn over 3f out: wknd u.p wl over 1f out: wl btn and eased ins fnl f* **50/1**

506 **12** *hd* **Ability Girl**[98] 2172 3-8-13 **51**.............................. NickyMackay 4 — 25
(Chris Wall) *in tch towards rr: hdwy over 3f out: sn rdn: wknd 2f out: wl btn fnl f* **14/1**

0064 **13** *hd* **Crabbies Gold (IRE)**[14] 4888 3-8-13 **51**.............................. ShaneKelly 2 — 25
(Lisa Williamson) *chsd ldrs: rdn and struggling over 3f out: wknd over 2f out: wl bhd fnl f* **13/2**[3]

3060 **14** *3 1/2* **Crabbies Bay**[25] 4505 3-8-9 **47**.............................. WilliamCarson 7 — 12
(Lisa Williamson) *in tch in midfield: hdwy over 3f out: sn rdn and strugglinng: wknd over 2f out: wl btn ent fnl f* **66/1**

0-06 **15** *14* **Silver Tiger**[91] 2394 3-8-7 **45**.............................. TedDurcan 15 — —
(Chris Wall) *stdd s: a in rr: lost tch over 2f out: eased ins fnl f: t.o* **9/2**[2]

506 **16** *16* **Femme Royale**[13] 4925 3-8-7 **45**.............................. JimmyQuinn 16 — —
(Robert Cowell) *in tch in midfield: lost pl 1/2-way: bhd and lost tch 3f out: t.o and eased ins fnl f* **50/1**

1m 40.18s (-0.42) **Going Correction** -0.10s/f (Good) — **16** Ran SP% **125.7**
Speed ratings (Par 98): **98,97,95,93,92 91,89,87,87,84 82,82,82,79,65 49**
toteswingers:1&2:£7.80, 1&3:£7.40, 2&3:£45.00 CSF £33.03 CT £283.29 TOTE £2.90: £1.10, £4.50, £3.00, £3.90; EX 38.00.
Owner Saville House Thoroughbreds **Bred** Peter Holmes **Trained** Newmarket, Suffolk

FOCUS
A modest handicap, with the top weight rated 60. They initially raced up the centre of the track. The winner did not need to match his Nottingham latest over further.
Littlepromisedland(IRE) Official explanation: jockey said filly lost its action
Femme Royale Official explanation: jockey said filly stopped very quickly

5353 ODDSCHECKER.MOBI (S) STKS — 7f 3y

5:50 (5:54) (Class 6) 2-Y-O — £1,617 (£481; £240; £120) Stalls High

Form — RPR

2450 **1** **Latte**[25] 4512 2-8-12 67..............................(p) KierenFallon 5 — 67+
(Linda Stubbs) *mde all: rdn and reaily asserted over 1f out: r.o strly and drew wl clr fnl f: eased towards fin: easily* **6/4**[1]

4430 **2** *6* **Red Hearts (IRE)**[18] 4756 2-8-10 64.............................. AdamBeschizza(3) 4 — 52
(Julia Feilden) *stdd s: hld up in tch: swtchd lft and hdwy over 2f out: chsd wnr over 1f out: sn outpcd and btn: kpt on to hold 2nd fnl f* **4/1**[2]

356 **3** *1 1/4* **Reina Sofia**[18] 4756 2-8-7 57.............................. LukeMorris 3 — 43
(Tony Carroll) *chsd wnr for 1f: styd prom: rdn over 2f out: wknd u.p over 1f out* **13/2**

5320 **4** *3/4* **Nude (IRE)**[13] 4922 2-8-4 57.............................. KieranO'Neill(3) 7 — 41
(Sylvester Kirk) *t.k.h: hld up in tch: rdn 3f out: drvn and wknd over 1f out* **5/1**[3]

5 *6* **Somemothersdohavem** 2-8-12 0..............................(b[1]) EddieAhern 2 — 31
(John Ryan) *dwlt: sn rcvrd and jnd wnr after 1f tl ent fnl 2f: sn wknd* **12/1**

0020 **6** *9* **Masters Club**[18] 4761 2-8-12 65..............................(b[1]) StevieDonohoe 6 — 7
(John Ryan) *a in rr: rdn 3f out: lost tch 2f out* **7/1**

1m 29.16s (2.56) **Going Correction** -0.05s/f (Good) — **6** Ran SP% **110.2**
Speed ratings (Par 92): **83,76,74,73,67 56**
toteswingers:1&2:£1.60, 1&3:£2.90, 2&3:£4.90 CSF £7.33 TOTE £2.40: £1.60, £1.70; EX 5.50.There was no bid for the winner.
Owner Tyme Partnership **Bred** Edmond And Richard Kent **Trained** Norton, N Yorks

FOCUS
A modest two-year-old event, even by selling standards.

NOTEBOOK
Latte, wearing first-time cheekpieces, bolted up. Fast away, he grabbed the stands' rail soon after the start and was never seriously challenged. He drew away in the closing stages and, while his official rating of 67 is probably slightly flattering, at this level he can find further profitable opportunities. (op 7-4 tchd 11-8)

Red Hearts(IRE), largely disappointing since scoring at Brighton in April, again failed to run close to her official rating of 64. Towards the rear in the early stages, she was asked to quicken at the 2f marker, but, having seemingly travelled sweetly, found little when push came to shove. (tchd 7-2 and 9-2)

Reina Sofia, in selling company for the first time on turf, was second until beyond halfway. She proved one-paced from there on, however, and may not have got home. A drop back in trip and a crack at a selling nursery seems the best course of action now. (op 6-1 tchd 7-1)

Nude(IRE), second of four in a weak Bath maiden two starts back, was never closer than her finishing position. Raced over 5f and 6f previously, she, too, may have found this trip beyond her. (tchd 11-2)

Somemothersdohavem, fitted with blinkers for this first appearance, was boisterous in the paddock beforehand. He was reluctant to enter the stalls too but, after dwelling at the start, showed speed until the 2f marker. He dropped away tamely from there on in, though. (op 10-1 tchd 9-1)

Masters Club, second at this level here two outings ago and fitted with first-time blinkers for this return engagement, ran poorly. Fourth in the very early stages, he soon dropped back to last. (op 13-2 tchd 6-1 and 15-2)

5354 DIGIBET.COM FILLIES' H'CAP — 7f 3y

6:20 (6:22) (Class 4) (0-85,83) 3-Y-O+ — £4,075 (£1,212; £606; £303) Stalls High

Form — RPR

21 **1** **Mundana (IRE)**[62] 3289 3-9-4 **80**.............................. KierenFallon 4 — 93+
(Luca Cumani) *t.k.h: hld up in tch: hdwy to chse ldrs 4f out: rdn and ev ch 2f out: drvn to ld fnl 100yds: kpt on wl* **11/10**[1]

0241 **2** *nk* **Al Mayasah (IRE)**[24] 4559 3-9-2 **78**.............................. JamieSpencer 7 — 90
(David Simcock) *w ldr tl rdn to ld 2f out: drew clr w wnr jst ins fnl f: hdd and styd on same pce fnl 100yds* **2/1**[2]

2525 **3** *4 1/2* **Russian Rave**[11] 5016 5-9-11 **82**.............................. ShaneKelly 5 — 84
(Jonathan Portman) *stdd s: hld up in last pair: rdn and effrt 2f out: 5th and wl hld 1f out: styd on to go 3rd fnl 50yds: no threat to ldng pair* **13/2**[3]

3040 **4** *2* **Strictly Pink (IRE)**[39] 4062 3-8-12 **77**.............................. AmyBaker(3) 2 — 72
(Alan Bailey) *led: rdn and hdd 2f out: styd pressing ldrs tl 1f out: fdd qckly ins fnl f* **33/1**

0616 **5** *3 1/4* **All Honesty**[24] 4544 3-8-1 **66**.............................. HarryBentley(3) 3 — 52
(William Knight) *taken down early: t.k.h: chsd ldrs tl 1/2-way: steadily lost pl: rdn over 2f out: wknd wl over 1f out* **12/1**

01 **6** *1* **Roodle**[75] 2855 4-9-12 **83**..............................(b) EddieAhern 1 — 68
(Eve Johnson Houghton) *stdd s: hld up in last pair: rdn and short-lived effrt ent fnl 2f: wl btn over 1f out* **12/1**

0246 **7** *2* **Noverton**[15] 4849 3-8-10 **72**.............................. LukeMorris 6 — 50
(James Eustace) *in tch in last trio: rdn 1/2-way: wknd wl over 1f out* **25/1**

1m 26.53s (-0.07) **Going Correction** -0.05s/f (Good)
WFA 3 from 4yo+ 5lb — **7** Ran SP% **116.5**
Speed ratings (Par 102): **98,97,92,90,86 85,83**
toteswingers:1&2:£1.30, 1&3:£3.00, 2&3:£2.70 CSF £3.61 TOTE £2.40: £1.80, £1.10; EX 4.10.
Owner Sheikh Mohammed Obaid Al Maktoum **Bred** Scuderia Archi Romani **Trained** Newmarket, Suffolk

FOCUS
A fascinating fillies' handicap featuring three last-time-out scorers. The pace was only modest but the first two came clear and the form has been given a bit of a chance.

5355 JOAN SANDRA OAKLEYS 65TH BIRTHDAY H'CAP — 6f 3y

6:50 (6:51) (Class 6) (0-65,65) 3-Y-O+ — £1,617 (£481; £240; £120) Stalls High

Form — RPR

6313 **1** **Katy's Secret**[13] 4918 4-9-6 **61**.............................. KierenFallon 3 — 71
(William Jarvis) *sn nudged along and struggling to go pce in last trio: hdwy 2f out: chsd clr ldr over 1f out: rdn and kpt on wl ins fnl f: led towards fin* **3/1**[1]

5034 **2** *hd* **Yahafedh Alaih**[13] 4926 3-9-5 **63**..............................(b[1]) ChrisCatlin 4 — 72
(Clive Brittain) *led: rdn and forged clr wl over 1f out: drvn ins fnl f: grad worn down and hdd towards fin* **9/1**

-602 **3** *1/2* **Cool Water Oasis**[6] 5172 3-8-9 **53**.............................. TedDurcan 5 — 60
(Rae Guest) *chsd ldrs: rdn ent fnl 2f: clsd u.p ins fnl f: pressed ldr fnl 75yds: kpt on* **4/1**[3]

-051 **4** *2* **South African Gold (USA)**[20] 4683 4-9-7 **62**.................(p) LukeMorris 7 — 63
(James Eustace) *racd keenly: chsd ldr tl over 1f out: styd on same pce fnl f* **4/1**[3]

-500 **5** *1 1/4* **Clerical (USA)**[20] 4683 5-8-6 **50**..............................(p) KieranO'Neill(3) 1 — 47
(Robert Cowell) *sn pushed along in midfield: rdn and hdwy ent fnl 2f: kpt on same pce and no imp ins fnl f* **25/1**

6325 **6** *hd* **Louphole**[18] 4759 9-9-4 **59**.............................. ShaneKelly 10 — 55
(J R Jenkins) *s.i.s: bhd: hdwy over 1f out: styd on wl and swtchd rt ins fnl f: nvr trbld ldrs* **16/1**

0004 **7** *10* **Angel Of Fashion (IRE)**[20] 4683 4-8-5 **51**.............................. LauraPike(5) 9 — 15
(Peter Charalambous) *chsd ldrs: rdn 1/2-way: wknd qckly wl over 1f out* **16/1**

120- **8** *4 1/2* **Speedyfix**[286] 7390 4-9-7 **65**..............................(v) AdamBeschizza(3) 2 — 15
(Christine Dunnett) *s.i.s: a in rr: lost tch 2f out* **40/1**

0314 **9** *5* **Captainrisk (IRE)**[35] 4187 5-9-6 **61**..............................(v) JamieSpencer 8 — —
(Christine Dunnett) *sn rdn along and nvr gng wl: in tch: steadily lost pl: bhd and eased ent fnl f* **7/2**[2]

1m 13.89s (-0.51) **Going Correction** -0.05s/f (Good)
WFA 3 from 4yo+ 3lb — **9** Ran SP% **115.3**
Speed ratings (Par 101): **101,100,100,97,95 95,82,76,69**
toteswingers:1&2:£8.00, 1&3:£2.80, 2&3:£8.00 CSF £30.84 CT £109.03 TOTE £4.60: £2.10, £2.90, £1.10; EX 23.70.
Owner Miss S E Hall **Bred** Miss S E Hall **Trained** Newmarket, Suffolk

FOCUS
A modest contest, with the top weight rated 65, but competitive on paper and fairly solid form.
Captainrisk(IRE) Official explanation: jockey said gelding never travelled

5356 CHC HELICOPTERS H'CAP — 1m 1f

7:20 (7:20) (Class 5) (0-70,69) 3-Y-O+ — £2,264 (£673; £336; £168) Stalls Low

Form — RPR

3301 **1** **Diverting**[19] 4730 3-9-0 **64**.............................. LeeNewman 4 — 83+
(William Jarvis) *in tch: rdn to chse clr ldr 3f out: led 2f out: sn drvn clr: in n.d fnl f: comf* **7/2**[1]

1110 **2** *7* **Colinca's Lad (IRE)**[1] 5328 9-9-0 **62**.............................. RosieJessop(5) 8 — 64
(Peter Charalambous) *led: clr over 5f out: rdn and c towards centre over 4f out: hdd 2f out: nt pce of wnr and btn over 1f out: no ch w wnr but plugged on to hold 2nd ins fnl f* **7/2**[1]

0-40 **3** *1 1/4* **Encore Un Fois**[20] 4663 3-9-2 **66**.............................. J-PGuillambert 6 — 65
(Luca Cumani) *hld up wl bhd: rdn and effrt 3f out: wnt modest 4th over 1f out: kpt on fnl f to snatch 3rd on post: no ch w wnr* **9/1**

515 **4** *nse* **Cane Cat (IRE)**[4] 5248 4-9-2 **59**..............................(t) LiamJones 5 — 58
(Tony Carroll) *hld up in last pair: rdn and effrt over 2f out: wnt 3rd but no ch w wnr over 1f out: plugged on same pce: lost 3rd on post* **11/2**[3]

523 **5** *11* **Ffajir (IRE)**[15] 4861 3-9-4 **68** ChrisCatlin 3 43
(Clive Brittain) *t.k.h: chsd ldr tl over 6f out: rdn over 3f out: btn 2f out: 5th and wl btn 1f out: wknd* **16/1**

3-62 **6** *2 3/4* **Smirfy's Silver**[19] 4730 7-9-12 **69** StevieDonohoe 7 38
(Deborah Sanderson) *t.k.h: chsd ldrs tl wnt 2nd over 6f out tl 3f out: sn wknd: wl bhd over 1f out* **8/1**

34-0 **7** *3 3/4* **Forks**[19] 4716 4-9-6 **63** LukeMorris 1 23
(Jane Chapple-Hyam) *t.k.h: hld up in last trio: rdn and no prog over 3f out: wl bhd fnl 2f* **11/1**

6364 **R** **Negotiation (IRE)**[15] 4845 5-9-6 **63** JamieSpencer 2 —
(Michael Quinn) *ref to r* **4/1**[2]

1m 55.39s (-0.41) **Going Correction** 0.0s/f (Good)
WFA 3 from 4yo+ 7lb **8** Ran SP% **115.2**
Speed ratings (Par 103): **101,94,93,93,83 81,78,—**
toteswingers:1&2:£3.50, 1&3:£4.40, 2&3:£7.90 CSF £15.97 CT £101.23 TOTE £4.40: £1.10, £2.20, £4.40; EX 19.70.
Owner A Reed **Bred** Anthony Reed **Trained** Newmarket, Suffolk

FOCUS
A trappy-looking handicap featuring a clutch of lightly raced runners, but turned into a procession by the bottom-weight. The form is taken at something like face value.
Forks Official explanation: jockey said gelding hung right-handed throughout

5357 ODDSCHECKER.COM H'CAP 1m 3f 101y
7:50 (7:51) (Class 6) (0-65,65) 4-Y-0+ **£1,617** (£481; £240; £120) **Stalls** Low

Form RPR

5-45 **1** **Iron Condor**[10] 5057 4-9-5 **63** LukeMorris 7 75
(James Eustace) *dwlt: racd in last trio: swtchd rt and hdwy 2f out: rdn to ld jst over 1f out: styd on strly and drew clr fnl 100yds: rdn out* **11/4**[2]

2/24 **2** *3 1/4* **Flame Of Hestia (IRE)**[19] 4730 5-9-7 **65** JamieSpencer 4 71
(James Fanshawe) *hld up in last trio: pushed along and hdwy 3f out: rdn and ev ch ent fnl f: no ex and btn ins fnl f: wknd fnl 100yds* **5/2**[1]

3000 **3** *4* **Yossi (IRE)**[5] 5210 7-8-3 **47** (b) KellyHarrison 8 47
(Richard Guest) *led: rdn over 2f out: hdd jst over 1f out: sn btn: plugged on to hold modest 3rd fnl f* **40/1**

4205 **4** *1 3/4* **Treacle Tart**[20] 4687 6-9-1 **64** (t) LauraPike(5) 10 61
(Peter Charalambous) *stdd s: t.k.h: hld up: hdwy to join ldr 9f out: rdn and unable to quiken over 2f out: lost 2nd over 1f out: sn wknd* **16/1**

-403 **5** *1 3/4* **Toballa**[19] 4730 6-8-2 **46** (t) JimmyQuinn 6 40
(Clifford Lines) *in tch: rdn over 3f out: drvn and no rspnse ent fnl 2f: sn wknd* **13/2**

0004 **6** *hd* **Kames Park (IRE)**[18] 4747 9-8-11 **58** RobertLButler(3) 2 51
(Richard Guest) *s.i.s: hld up in rr: rdn and effrt over 2f out: sltly hmpd 2f out: no prog over 1f out: wknd fnl f* **14/1**

3262 **7** *1/2* **Barbirolli**[20] 4654 9-8-3 **47** WilliamCarson 9 40
(William Stone) *in tch in midfield: rdn over 3f out: drvn and no imp 2f out: sn wknd* **16/1**

0025 **8** *8* **Trecase**[18] 4754 4-8-7 **51** LiamJones 3 30
(Tony Carroll) *t.k.h: led for 1f: chsd ldr tl 9f out: styd chsng ldrs tl wknd qckly wl over 1f out: wl bhd and eased ins fnl f* **14/1**

5030 **9** *14* **Cornish Beau (IRE)**[19] 4697 4-9-5 **63** (b[1]) KierenFallon 11 18
(Mark H Tompkins) *t.k.h: chsd ldrs: rdn and struggling over 3f out: dropped to rr 2f out: eased fnl f: t.o* **11/2**[3]

-554 **10** *nk* **Motarjm (USA)**[44] 3353 7-8-4 **48** (t) ChrisCatlin 12 —
(Lydia Pearce) *hld up in midfield: rdn and dropped to rr 3f out: lost tch 2f out: wl bhd and eased ins fnl f: t.o* **20/1**

2m 28.49s (-0.21) **Going Correction** 0.0s/f (Good) **10** Ran SP% **116.3**
Speed ratings (Par 101): **100,97,94,93,92 92,91,85,75,75**
CSF £10.01 CT £217.51 TOTE £4.80: £1.90, £1.02, £9.60; EX 12.10.
Owner Harold Nass **Bred** Rockville Pike Partnership **Trained** Newmarket, Suffolk

FOCUS
A weak finale, in which the top weight was rated just 65, but they went a decent pace. The form pair finished 1-2.
Cornish Beau(IRE) Official explanation: jockey said gelding stumbled badly
T/Plt: £40.30 to a £1 stake. Pool:£41,555.73 - 751.30 winning tickets T/Qpdt: £4.90 to a £1 stake. Pool:£5,777.51 - 868.40 winning tickets SP

5358 - 5360a (Foreign Racing) - See Raceform Interactive

4026 KILLARNEY (L-H)
Tuesday, August 23
OFFICIAL GOING: Good (good to firm in places; watering)

5361a VINCENT O'BRIEN RUBY STKS (LISTED RACE) 1m 100y
6:40 (6:40) 3-Y-0+ **£22,413** (£6,551; £3,103; £1,034)

RPR

1 **Wild Wind (GER)**[5] 5228 3-8-12 103 CO'Donoghue 7 105+
(A P O'Brien, Ire) *chsd ldrs: mod 5th 1/2-way: drvn along and clsr appr fnl f: edgd lft and led u.p 100yds out: kpt on wl* **5/2**[2]

2 *1 3/4* **Barack (IRE)**[23] 4588 5-9-10 103 (bt) BACurtis 2 107
(Francis Ennis, Ire) *chsd ldrs: mod 3rd 1/2-way: rdn and clsr over 1f out: kpt on wl u.p ins fnl f* **16/1**

3 *shd* **Bay Knight (IRE)**[5] 5226 5-9-7 95 WJLee 8 104
(K J Condon, Ire) *trckd ldr in 2nd: clr of remainder 1/2-way: rdn 2f out: led briefly u.p early fnl f: no ex fnl 100yds* **16/1**

4 *1 3/4* **Marvada (IRE)**[23] 4588 3-8-12 95 JMurtagh 3 97
(K J Condon, Ire) *chsd ldrs on outer: mod 6th 1/2-way: rdn and sme hdwy fr 2f out: kpt on ins fnl f wout troubling ldrs* **8/1**

5 *hd* **Banna Boirche (IRE)**[23] 4588 5-9-7 102 ShaneFoley 5 99
(M Halford, Ire) *hld up: mod 8th 1/2-way: sme hdwy on outer under 2f out: kpt on u.p wout threatening ins fnl f* **16/1**

6 *1/2* **Stunning View (IRE)**[28] 4418 4-9-7 108 PJSmullen 9 98
(D K Weld, Ire) *chsd ldrs: mod 4th 1/2-way: rdn and sme hdwy fr 2f out: no imp u.p fr 1f out* **2/1**[1]

7 *1 3/4* **Gossamer Seed (IRE)**[26] 4481 3-8-12 94 (t) DMGrant 11 92
(John Joseph Murphy, Ire) *towards rr: sme hdwy on outer over 1f out: kpt on one pce* **18/1**

8 *hd* **Lightening Stricks (IRE)**[5] 5226 4-9-7 92 (bt) KLatham 10 94
(Richard Brabazon, Ire) *hld up towards rr: nvr a factor: kpt on one pce in st* **33/1**

9 *shd* **Royal Blue Star (IRE)**[5] 5228 3-8-12 98 FMBerry 6 91
(Mrs John Harrington, Ire) *led: strly pressed fr 2f out: hdd u.p early fnl f: sn wknd and eased* **7/1**[3]

10 *6* **Duchess Of Foxland (IRE)**[113] 1779 4-9-7 101 EJMcNamara 4 81
(Mark L Fagan, Ire) *a towards rr* **33/1**

11 *shd* **Sapphire Pendant (IRE)**[93] 2331 3-8-12 98 (b[1]) WMLordan 1 77
(David Wachman, Ire) *mid-div on inner: mod 7th 1/2-way: nvr a factor: no threat in st* **10/1**

1m 41.81s (-5.29)
WFA 3 from 4yo+ 6lb **11** Ran SP% **123.4**
CSF £45.41 TOTE £3.60: £1.60, £5.20, £4.10; DF 57.60.
Owner Mrs John Magnier **Bred** Ecurie Des Monceaux **Trained** Ballydoyle, Co Tipperary

FOCUS
A competitive Listed race.

NOTEBOOK
Wild Wind(GER) just struggled to go the pace when they turned for home but gradually began to pick up and won quite decisively. She hasn't enjoyed the best of luck, but this was quite impressive and she wouldn't have any difficulty stepping up in trip. (op 10/3)
Barack(IRE) came back to something like his best form. The quick ground was to his benefit and, having been up with the pace the whole way, he sustained his effort inside the final furlong but without the pace to combat the winner. (op 14/1)
Bay Knight(IRE) found plenty for pressure in the straight. He wasn't quite good enough but doesn't look out of place in this grade. (op 11/1)
Marvada(IRE) was held up in mid-division and kept on to pretty decent effect. (op 8/1 tchd 7/1)
Banna Boirche(IRE) kept on fairly strongly from off the pace without threatening. A Listed event on Polytrack will be his principal aim in the coming months. (op 14/1)
Stunning View(IRE) raced close enough to the pace and was well positioned with every chance in the straight. He didn't find a huge amount when for pressure. (op 9/4 tchd 7/4)

5362 - 5364a (Foreign Racing) - See Raceform Interactive

5304 DEAUVILLE (R-H)
Tuesday, August 23
OFFICIAL GOING: Turf: soft; fibresand: standard

5365a CRITERIUM DU FONDS EUROPEEN DE L'ELEVAGE (LISTED RACE) (2YO) (TURF) 1m (R)
1:50 (12:00) 2-Y-0 **£52,586** (£21,034; £15,775; £10,517; £5,258)

RPR

1 **Saint Pellerin (GER)**[18] 2-8-11 0 Christophe-PatriceLemaire 5 99
(J-C Rouget, France) **8/5**[1]

2 *1* **Orcus (FR)** 2-8-11 0 PhilippeSogorb 9 97
(C Ferland, France) **8/1**[3]

3 *3/4* **Humungosaur**[11] 4995 2-8-11 0 ChristopheSoumillon 7 95
(Paul Cole) *settled in 2nd: rdn on turn into st: led 2f out: rdn but nt qckn: hdd 1 1/2f out: rallied and styd on wl* **11/1**

4 *3* **Private Riviera**[8] 5130 2-8-8 0 Pierre-CharlesBoudot 8 86
(C Boutin, France) **25/1**

5 *4* **Rockinante (FR)**[8] 5130 2-9-2 0 RichardHughes 4 85
(Richard Hannon) *settled towards rr: rdn early in st: failed to qckn: no imp fnl 2f* **2/1**[2]

6 *5* **Ruby's Day**[19] 4843 2-8-8 0 IoritzMendizabal 1 66
(E J O'Neill, France) **11/1**

7 *1* **Nadeaud (FR)**[16] 2-8-8 0 ThierryJarnet 6 64
(D Guillemin, France) **83/10**

8 *10* **Silver Northern (FR)**[26] 4484 2-8-11 0 (p) DavyBonilla 3 45
(D Chenu, France) **30/1**

1m 46.0s (5.20) **8** Ran SP% **117.4**
WIN (incl. 1 euro stake): 2.60. PLACES: 1.50, 2.00, 3.00. DF: 9.80. SF: 17.40.
Owner Gerard Augustin-Normand **Bred** Gestut Fahrhof **Trained** Pau, France

5366a PRIX DE LA NONETTE SHADWELL (GROUP 2) (3YO FILLIES) (TURF) 1m 2f
2:55 (12:00) 3-Y-0 **£63,879** (£24,655; £11,767; £7,844; £3,922)

RPR

1 **Dream Peace (IRE)**[24] 4570 3-9-0 0 GeraldMosse 2 114
(Robert Collet, France) *broke wl but settled in midfield early: racd towards rr after 2f: pushed along and hdwy towards ins under 3f out: running on and disputing 4th on heels of ldrs over 2f out: led ins fnl 1 1/2f: r.o wl fnl f* **7/1**

2 *1/2* **Epic Love (IRE)**[72] 2977 3-9-0 0 StephanePasquier 7 113
(P Bary, France) *w.w towards rr: cl 9th over 2 1/2f out: hrd rdn appr 2f out: 8th and styng on u.p whn swtchd outside rival ins fnl 1 1/2f: r.o u.p to go 2nd fnl 100yds: nt quite rch ldr* **7/1**

3 *2* **Haya Landa (FR)**[24] 4570 3-9-0 0 FranckBlondel 4 109
(Mme L Audon, France) *settled on heels of ldrs: in centre of three disputing 3rd 5f out: 5th and scrubbed along ins fnl 2 1/2f: styng on but short of room ins fnl 2f: gap opened 1 1/2f out: r.o to dispute 2nd fnl f: nt qckn last 150yds* **16/1**

4 *1 1/2* **Beatrice Aurore (IRE)**[24] 4570 3-9-0 0 OlivierPeslier 8 106
(John Dunlop) *settled in midfield on outside: t.k.h and moved up to press ldr on outside after 2f: led narrowly on outside 5f out: hdd 3f out: disp ld 2 1/2f out: hdd ins fnl 1 1/2f: no ex* **13/2**[3]

5 *3/4* **Barefoot Lady (IRE)**[24] 4533 3-9-0 0 PaulHanagan 10 105
(Richard Fahey) *broke jst off pce on outside: moved up to ld after 1f: hdd 5f out: 3rd and scrubbed along over 2 1/2f out: one pce fnl f* **9/1**

6 *snk* **Wavering (IRE)**[72] 2977 3-9-0 0 MickaelBarzalona 9 104
(A Fabre, France) *settled in last: hdwy ins fnl 2f: sn rdn: nt pce to chal* **4/1**[1]

7 *1/2* **Joviality**[46] 3822 3-9-0 0 WilliamBuick 3 103
(John Gosden) *trckd ldr early: a.p: led briefly on ins rail passing 3f marker: jnd 2 1/2f out: sn hrd rdn and hdd appr 2f out: grad fdd fr 1 1/2f out* **7/1**

8 *1* **Dalarua (IRE)**[24] 4570 3-9-0 0 ChristopheSoumillon 5 101
(S Wattel, France) *smartly away: chsd ldrs early: sn settled in 7th: outpcd and scrubbed along over 3f out: styd on appr 2f out: rdn and no further imp fnl 1 1/2f* **5/1**[2]

9 *8* **Dorcas Lane**[24] 4570 3-9-0 0 IoritzMendizabal 1 85
(Lucy Wadham) *racd in midfield on rail: ins of three disputing 4th 3f out:: 4th and rdn 2f out: wknd fnl f* **12/1**

10 *snk* **La Pernelle (IRE)**[24] 4570 3-9-0 0 Christophe-PatriceLemaire 11 85
(Y De Nicolay, France) *hld up towards rr: plld wd fnl turn: rdn 2f out: no imp* **20/1**

11 **Cape Dollar (IRE)**[52] 3648 3-9-0 0 MaximeGuyon 6 85
(Sir Michael Stoute) *racd keenly and hmpd after 1 1/2f: sn settled cl up: 4th on outside of three 3f out: rdn and nt qckn 2f out: eased fnl f* **16/1**

2m 9.70s (-0.50) **11** Ran SP% **121.7**
WIN (incl. 1 euro stake): 8.90. PLACES: 2.70, 3.40, 4.40. DF: 30.40. SF: 67.40 CSF: 57.45.
Owner Haras D'Etreham **Bred** Kilfrush Stud Farm **Trained** Chantilly, France

The Form Book, Raceform Ltd, Compton, RG20 6NL

NOTEBOOK
Dream Peace(IRE), narrowly denied here last time, came from off the pace to run down her rivals inside the final 2f. She has the Prix de l'Opera as her next target.
Beatrice Aurore(IRE) beat the winner in the Prix Chloe earlier in the season and finished closer than this to her here last time out, but the ground was softer this time around.
Barefoot Lady(IRE) could do with being dropped back to a mile.

4982 CATTERICK (L-H)
Wednesday, August 24

OFFICIAL GOING: Good (8.3)
Wind: Light behind Weather: Cloudy - sunny periods

5367 YORKSHIRE-OUTDOORS.CO.UK MEDIAN AUCTION MAIDEN STKS 5f
2:20 (2:22) (Class 6) 2-Y-O £1,704 (£503; £251) Stalls Low

Form RPR
0200 1 **Free Zone**[10] 5077 2-9-3 77 TomEaves 10 75
(Bryan Smart) *trckd ldrs: hdwy 1/2-way: rdn over 1f out: drvn ins fnl f: kpt on wl to ld nr fin* **7/1**
000 2 nk **Come On Dave (IRE)**[39] 4105 2-9-3 0 AndrewMullen 11 74
(David Nicholls) *sn led and swtchd lft to inner: clr 1/2-way: rdn over 1f out: drvn ins fnl f: hdd and no ex nr line* **66/1**
03 3 3 **Rusty Rocket (IRE)**[7] 5174 2-9-3 0 SilvestreDeSousa 1 63
(Paul Green) *chsd ldr: pushed along and hung rt 2f out and sn rdn: drvn over 1f out and one pce* **9/2**[3]
32 4 1 3/4 **Towbee**[16] 4851 2-9-3 0 JamesSullivan 5 57
(Michael Easterby) *chsd ldrs: rdn along over 2f out: sn one pce* **7/2**[1]
5 2 1/4 **Gowanharry (IRE)** 2-8-12 0 PhillipMakin 9 44
(Michael Dods) *s.i.s and bhd: hdwy wl over 1f out: kpt on ins fnl f: nrst fin* **4/1**[2]
2253 6 3/4 **Superplex**[26] 4500 2-9-3 72 PaulHanagan 7 46
(John Quinn) *in tch: effrt over 2f out: sn rdn along and no imp* **5/1**
40 7 nk **Indyend**[14] 4899 2-8-12 0 DavidAllan 2 40
(Tim Easterby) *dwlt and towards rr: hdwy on inner over 2f out: sn rdn and no imp fnl f* **22/1**
00 8 1/2 **My New Angel (IRE)**[19] 4748 2-8-9 0 PaulPickard(3) 12 38
(Paul Green) *dwlt and in rr: sme hdwy on outer 1/2-way: sn rdn along and n.d* **66/1**
04 9 1 1/2 **Copp The Lot (USA)**[31] 4365 2-9-3 0 AdrianNicholls 6 38
(David Nicholls) *chsd ldrs: rdn along over 2f out: grad wknd* **13/2**
2 10 1 3/4 **Becksies**[133] 1301 2-8-12 0 MickyFenton 3 26
(Paul Midgley) *a towards rr* **28/1**
6 11 1 3/4 **George Fenton**[8] 5147 2-9-3 0 PaddyAspell 8 25
(Richard Guest) *a towards rr* **66/1**
000 12 1/2 **Mick Slates (IRE)**[53] 3611 2-8-12 0 NeilFarley(5) 4 23
(Declan Carroll) *a towards rr* **125/1**

59.03 secs (-0.77) **Going Correction** -0.225s/f (Firm) 12 Ran SP% **116.0**
Speed ratings (Par 92): **97,96,91,88,85 84,83,82,80,77 74,74**
toteswingers:1&2:£31.00, 2&3:£25.90, 1&3:£8.10 CSF £408.16 TOTE £9.60: £3.60, £9.80, £1.60; EX 144.40 TRIFECTA Not won..
Owner Clipper Logistics **Bred** R G Levin **Trained** Hambleton, N Yorks

FOCUS
The ground had dried out on a bright, breezy day, and was reported to be riding as the official good. The wind was brisk and half behind. An ordinary juvenile maiden and the strong-travelling pacesetter soon had the field spread out.

NOTEBOOK
Free Zone, well beaten on his nursery debut from a mark of 77 when he wore a visor for the first time, was one of just a couple to keep tabs on the leader from his outside draw. He stuck on to show ahead near the line and break his duck at the fifth attempt. (op 6-1)
Come On Dave(IRE), beaten in two sellers and a claimer on his first three starts, had the worst of the draw. He flew out of the traps and set a strong pace against the far side rail. Although starting at 66-1, he actually traded as short as 1.1 in running. Clearly vastly improved, he looks sure to go one better. (op 80-1)
Rusty Rocket(IRE), third in a modest event at Nottingham on his second start, was free to post. He kept tabs on the leader but did not see it out as well as the eventual winner. (tchd 5-1 in a place)
Towbee, placed on his first two starts, struggled to go the pace and a return to 6f in nursery company looks on the cards. (op 9-2)
Gowanharry(IRE) ◆, out of a tough sprinter who did so well for this yard, was on offer at 10-1 in the morning. She completely fluffed her lines at the start and, still last at halfway, made steady late ground under a very considerate ride. She is a lot better than she showed here. (op 9-2 tchd 5-1)
Superplex, on his tenth start, has finished runner-up three times and had been beaten favourite on four of his last five starts. He could never go the pace and is not progressing at all. (op 9-2)
Indyend showed a lot more than on her two previous starts and now qualifies for nurseries. (op 33-1)
My New Angel(IRE) also showed more and now qualifies for nurseries.
Becksies, runner-up in a seller here in April on her only previous start, was sticking on in her own time when running out of racing room inside the final furlong. A claimer or seller looks within her compass. (op 18-1)

5368 ZETLAND MAIDEN STKS 5f 212y
2:50 (2:50) (Class 5) 3-Y-0+ £2,070 (£616; £307; £153) Stalls Low

Form RPR
32 1 **Green Howard**[33] 4282 3-9-3 0 DanielTudhope 3 73
(Robin Bastiman) *in tch on inner: hdwy 1/2-way: swtchd rt over 2f out: chal ent fnl f: sn rdn and led last 50yds* **5/6**[1]
3 2 1/2 **Strong Man**[14] 4923 3-9-3 0 PaddyAspell 4 71
(Michael Easterby) *trckd ldng pair: hdwy over 2f out: sn rdn to chse ldr: drvn to chal ins fnl f and ev ch tl no ex last 50yds* **15/2**[3]
4633 3 3 1/2 **Cheherazad (IRE)**[41] 3998 3-8-12 75 SilvestreDeSousa 5 55
(Paul Cole) *s.i.s: sn rdn along and in tch: hdwy on outer wl over 2f out: sn rdn and edgd lft: kpt on ins fnl f: tk 3rd nr line* **13/8**[2]
4226 4 1 1/4 **Tancred Spirit**[6] 5215 3-8-12 47 (v) TonyHamilton 1 51
(Paul Midgley) *led and sn clr: rdn wl over 1f out: drvn and wknd qckly ins fnl f: hdd fnl 50yds* **10/1**
06 5 5 **Munaa's Dream**[6] 5212 3-8-12 0 AndrewElliott 6 35
(Mrs K Burke) *chsd ldr: rdn along wl over 2f out: sn drvn and wknd* **33/1**
0-00 6 1/2 **Govenor Eliott (IRE)**[29] 4408 6-8-13 34 (v) GeorgeChaloner(7) 9 39
(Alan Lockwood) *chsd ldrs: rdn along 1/2-way: sn wknd* **100/1**
0 7 2 1/4 **Kyllachykov (IRE)**[33] 4286 3-9-3 0 RobertWinston 2 31
(Robin Bastiman) *a towards rr* **33/1**
8 7 **Diumara** 4-8-8 0 TerenceFury(7) 7 —
(Neville Bycroft) *a in rr* **50/1**

5006 9 3 3/4 **Indigo Sands (IRE)**[18] 4813 3-9-3 42 PhillipMakin 10 —
(Alan Berry) *prom: rdn along 1/2-way: sn wknd* **80/1**

1m 13.02s (-0.58) **Going Correction** -0.225s/f (Firm)
WFA 3 from 4yo+ 3lb 9 Ran SP% **123.6**
Speed ratings (Par 103): **94,93,88,87,80 79,76,67,62**
toteswingers:1&2:£3.10, 2&3:£1.30, 1&3:£2.40 CSF £9.15 TOTE £2.70: £1.10, £1.30, £1.30; EX 9.80 Trifecta £20.10 Pool: £612.36 - 22.45 winning units..
Owner Ms M Austerfield **Bred** Miss A J Rawding & P M Crane **Trained** Cowthorpe, N Yorks

FOCUS
Any price bar four in this weak sprint maiden but the first two have the potential to go on to better things.

5369 ABF THE SOLDIERS CHARITY H'CAP 1m 7f 177y
3:20 (3:20) (Class 5) (0-70,68) 3-Y-0+ £2,181 (£644; £322) Stalls Low

Form RPR
-364 1 **Mohawk Ridge**[21] 4671 5-9-10 67 LeeTopliss(3) 3 75
(Michael Dods) *trckd ldr: hdwy over 3f out: rdn to ld 2f out: drvn ent fnl f: kpt on gamely* **5/1**[3]
6402 2 1 1/4 **Danceintothelight**[12] 4982 4-9-8 62 KellyHarrison 8 69
(Micky Hammond) *trckd ldng pair: hdwy wl over 2f out: rdn and edgd lft over 1f out: drvn and kpt on ins fnl f* **4/1**[1]
1443 3 1 **Short Supply (USA)**[16] 4856 5-9-2 56 GrahamGibbons 5 61
(Tim Walford) *led: rdn along 3f out: hdd 2f out and sn drvn: kpt on same pce ins fnl f* **9/2**[2]
2061 4 4 1/2 **Mason Hindmarsh**[21] 4671 4-10-0 68 FrederikTylicki 6 68
(Karen McLintock) *trckd ldrs: hdwy 4f out: rdn along over 2f out: sn drvn and one pce* **5/1**[3]
5-64 5 1 1/2 **Bijou Dan**[16] 4856 10-9-8 62 PJMcDonald 1 60
(George Moore) *hld up towards rr: rdn along over 3f out: styd on u.p fnl 2f: nvr nr ldrs* **7/1**
400 6 3/4 **Miss Ferney**[9] 5107 7-8-10 53 PaulPickard(3) 10 50
(Alan Kirtley) *hld up in rr: hdwy over 4f out: rdn along to chse ldrs 2f out: sn drvn and no imp* **33/1**
2004 7 6 **Dubara Reef (IRE)**[22] 4635 4-9-11 65 SilvestreDeSousa 2 55
(Paul Green) *trckd ldrs: pushed along over 4f out: rdn along 3f out: wknd over 2f out* **11/2**
6015 8 30 **Barnum (USA)**[19] 4751 3-8-2 56 JamesSullivan 4 10
(Michael Easterby) *chsd ldrs: rdn along over 4f out: sn wknd* **14/1**
2240 9 16 **Stadium Of Light (IRE)**[15] 4879 4-9-13 67 PaulHanagan 11 —
(James Given) *hld up in rr: sme hdwy 4f out: rdn along wl over 2f out: sn wknd* **20/1**

3m 29.43s (-2.57) **Going Correction** -0.225s/f (Firm)
WFA 3 from 4yo+ 14lb 9 Ran SP% **113.8**
Speed ratings (Par 103): **97,96,95,93,92 92,89,74,66**
toteswingers:1&2:£5.00, 2&3:£4.30, 1&3:£5.40 CSF £24.91 CT £95.41 TOTE £6.90: £2.60, £2.20, £1.10; EX 33.80 Trifecta £97.40 Pool: £169.83 - 1.29 winning units..
Owner Doug Graham **Bred** Old Mill Stud Ltd And Oomswell Ltd **Trained** Denton, Co Durham

FOCUS
A modest stayers' handicap that proved rather tactical, the first three being in the first three throughout. It's been rated around the front-running third to her turf best.

5370 RACINGUK.COM H'CAP 7f
3:50 (3:50) (Class 4) (0-80,80) 3-Y-0 £4,204 (£1,251; £625; £312) Stalls Low

Form RPR
6141 1 **Roninski (IRE)**[18] 4810 3-9-0 80 JustinNewman(7) 8 91
(Bryan Smart) *stdd s and hld up towards rr: hdwy on outer wl over 2f out: rdn to chal over 1f out: drvn ins fnl f: led nr fin* **5/2**[2]
3112 2 shd **Fast Shot**[17] 4817 3-9-5 78 DavidAllan 4 89
(Tim Easterby) *trckd ldrs: hdwy over 2f out: led 1 1/2f out and sn rdn: drvn ins fnl f: hdd and no ex nr fin* **9/4**[1]
5604 3 3 1/4 **Maverik**[34] 4234 3-9-3 76 TomEaves 5 78
(Michael Dods) *trckd ldrs: hdwy 3f out: cl up over 2f out: sn rdn and ev ch tl drvn and one pce ent fnl f* **12/1**
3636 4 2 3/4 **Breezolini**[7] 5164 3-9-1 74 (p) PaulHanagan 2 69
(Richard Whitaker) *in rr: rdn and hdwy over 2f out: kpt on appr fnl f: nrst fin* **9/1**
2243 5 2 1/2 **Maggie Mey (IRE)**[10] 5081 3-9-2 75 SilvestreDeSousa 3 63
(David O'Meara) *cl up on inner: led 1/2-way: rdn over 2f out: drvn and hdd 1 1/2f out: sn wknd* **4/1**[3]
0000 6 1 3/4 **Iceblast**[12] 5006 3-8-8 74 DavidSimmonson(7) 1 57
(Michael Easterby) *dwlt: a in rr* **16/1**
0301 7 4 1/2 **Auto Mac**[43] 3933 3-9-1 74 (b) AndrewElliott 7 45
(Neville Bycroft) *led to 1/2-way: cl up tl rdn over 2f out and grad wknd* **28/1**
-505 8 9 **Squires Gate (IRE)**[19] 4750 3-8-13 72 RobertWinston 6 19
(Charles Hills) *prom on outer: rdn along 3f out: sn wknd* **12/1**

1m 24.91s (-2.09) **Going Correction** -0.225s/f (Firm) 8 Ran SP% **114.1**
Speed ratings (Par 102): **102,101,98,95,92 90,85,74**
toteswingers:1&2:£2.10, 2&3:£5.60, 1&3:£6.00 CSF £8.51 CT £53.67 TOTE £3.80: £1.10, £1.60, £3.90; EX 10.50 Trifecta £49.50 Pool: £536.74 - 8.02 winning units..
Owner Ron Hull **Bred** Peter Hodgson And Star Pointe Limited **Trained** Hambleton, N Yorks

FOCUS
A competitive 72-80 3yo handicap run at a strong pace and in the end the first two pulled clear.
Squires Gate(IRE) Official explanation: jockey said gelding was unsuited by the track.

5371 BOOK NOW FOR 17TH SEPTEMBER H'CAP 5f 212y
4:20 (4:20) (Class 5) (0-75,80) 3-Y-0+ £2,070 (£616; £307; £153) Stalls Low

Form RPR
0401 1 **Lady Kildare (IRE)**[21] 4669 3-8-6 63 PatrickDonaghy(3) 2 73
(Jedd O'Keeffe) *cl up: led 1 1/2f out: drvn ins fnl f: hld on gamely* **16/1**
2452 2 hd **North Central (USA)**[22] 4634 4-9-2 67 (p) DanielTudhope 3 76
(Jim Goldie) *trckd ldrs on inner: hdwy 2f out: swtchd rt and rdn over 1f out: drvn to chal ins fnl f and ev ch tl no ex nr fin* **7/2**[1]
0636 3 1 1/2 **Black Annis Bower**[47] 3832 3-9-1 69 JamesSullivan 4 73
(Michael Easterby) *chsd ldrs: hdwy 2f out and sn rdn: drvn and kpt on ins fnl f* **16/1**
0401 4 1 3/4 **Last Sovereign**[10] 5083 7-9-12 80 6ex (bt) MichaelO'Connell(3) 9 79+
(Ollie Pears) *s.i.s and bhd: rdn and hdwy over 2f out: swtchd rt over 1f out: kpt on ins fnl f: nrst fin* **5/1**[2]
0626 5 3/4 **Mr Wolf**[21] 4678 10-9-5 70 (p) BarryMcHugh 6 66
(John Quinn) *led: rdn along over 2f out: drvn and hdd 1 1/2f out: grad wknd* **12/1**
2044 6 3/4 **Invincible Force (IRE)**[14] 4921 7-9-10 75 (b) SilvestreDeSousa 7 69+
(Paul Green) *towards rr: hdwy 2f out: sn rdn and no imp* **7/1**
6036 7 1 1/4 **Welcome Approach**[5] 5244 8-8-5 56 oh2 DuranFentiman 5 46
(John Weymes) *midfield: rdn along wl over 2f out: n.d* **33/1**

0-06 **8** *hd* **Spitfire**[40] 4064 6-9-10 **75** TonyCulhane 11 64
(J R Jenkins) *dwlt: a towards rr* **8/1**

2142 **9** *hd* **Royal Blade (IRE)**[15] 4881 4-9-1 **66** PhillipMakin 8 55
(Alan Berry) *chsd ldng pair: rdn along wl over 2f out: sn wknd* **7/1**

01/ **10** *3/4* **Regency Art (IRE)**[688] 6542 4-9-0 **65** AdrianNicholls 10 51
(David Nicholls) *in tch: hdwy to chse ldrs 1/2-way: sn rdn and wknd over 2f out* **16/1**

0410 **11** *4 1/2* **Frequency**[26] 4503 4-9-8 **73** (b) PaulHanagan 1 45
(Keith Dalgleish) *s.i.s: a in rr* **13/2**[3]

1m 12.68s (-0.92) **Going Correction** -0.225s/f (Firm)
WFA 3 from 4yo+ 3lb **11** Ran SP% **116.6**
Speed ratings (Par 103): **97,96,94,92,91 90,88,88,88,87 81**
CSF £70.83 CT £710.22 TOTE £16.60: £3.80, £2.20, £5.90; EX 90.80 Trifecta £222.80 Part won. Pool of £301.19 - 0.20 winnning units..
Owner The Fatalists **Bred** Glending Bloodstock **Trained** Middleham Moor, N Yorks

FOCUS
A competive 6f handicap and again the pace was strong. The winner was in the frist two throughout and has been rated as recording a personal best.
Last Sovereign Official explanation: jockey said gelding missed the break.

5372 GO RACING AT REDCAR ON SATURDAY H'CAP 1m 3f 214y
4:50 (4:51) (Class 6) (0-60,60) 3-Y-O **£1,704** (£503; £251) **Stalls** Low

Form RPR

3015 **1** **Kian's Delight**[14] 4903 3-9-1 **57** MichaelO'Connell(3) 4 65
(Jedd O'Keeffe) *a cl up: chal wl over 2f out and sn rdn: drvn over 1f out: kpt on wl u.p to ld last 50yds* **7/2**[2]

6065 **2** *3/4* **Hernando Torres**[11] 5064 3-9-7 **60** GrahamGibbons 3 67
(Michael Easterby) *led: rdn along over 2f out: drvn over 1f out: hdd and no ex last 50yds* **15/2**

0-02 **3** *1/2* **Al Furat (USA)**[42] 3976 3-8-11 **55** ShaneBKelly(5) 8 61+
(Ron Barr) *hld up towards rr: hdwy over 3f out: rdn 2f out: drvn over 1f out: kpt on u.p ins fnl f: nrst fin* **6/1**[3]

0-06 **4** *3/4* **Lady Intrigue (IRE)**[31] 4363 3-8-7 **46** oh1 PaulHanagan 2 51
(Richard Fahey) *trckd ldrs: hdwy over 3f out: rdn along over 2f out: drvn and kpt on appr fnl f: nrst fin* **16/1**

2321 **5** *hd* **Silver Tigress**[8] 5152 3-9-3 **56** 6ex PJMcDonald 10 60
(George Moore) *hld up in tch: effrt over 3f out: rdn along over 2f out: drvn over 1f out: kpt on ins fnl f* **13/8**[1]

005 **6** *2 1/2* **Shirls Son Sam**[12] 5007 3-8-9 **53** LMcNiff(5) 9 53
(Chris Fairhurst) *dwlt and in rr: hdwy 3f out: rdn over 2f out: kpt on appr fnl f* **33/1**

6043 **7** *1/2* **Black Pond (USA)**[11] 5042 3-9-7 **60** (v) SilvestreDeSousa 5 60
(Mark Johnston) *in tch: hdwy to chse ldrs over 3f out: sn rdn: drvn over 2f out and sn one pce* **13/2**

0040 **8** *2* **Smart Step**[26] 4505 3-8-7 **46** oh1 FrannyNorton 7 42
(Mark Johnston) *chsd ldng pair: rdn along over 3f out: grad wknd* **12/1**

-000 **9** *7* **Srimenanti**[26] 4514 3-8-9 **55** ShirleyTeasdale(7) 6 40
(Brian Rothwell) *a in rr: bhd fr 1/2-way* **66/1**

2m 39.13s (0.23) **Going Correction** 0.0s/f (Good) **9** Ran SP% **117.7**
Speed ratings (Par 98): **99,98,98,97,97 95,95,94,89**
toteswingers:1&2:£5.30, 2&3:£8.80, 1&3:£5.30 CSF £30.63 CT £154.41 TOTE £6.00: £2.10, £2.20, £1.10; EX 37.40 Trifecta £246.60 Part won. Pool of £333.31 - 0.40 winning units..
Owner Jenny & Ray Butler **Bred** Mrs J M Quy **Trained** Middleham Moor, N Yorks

FOCUS
There was a heavy shower ahead of this modest 3yo only 1m4f handicap and significantly the first pair home were one-two throughout. It's been rated around the winner.
Srimenanti Official explanation: jockey said filly stumbled on paddock bend.

5373 CATTERICKBRIDGE.CO.UK H'CAP 5f
5:20 (5:21) (Class 6) (0-65,65) 3-Y-O+ **£1,704** (£503; £251) **Stalls** Low

Form RPR

0550 **1** **Spirit Of Coniston**[12] 5009 8-8-12 **53** MickyFenton 2 63
(Paul Midgley) *qckly away and mde all: sn clr: rdn over 1f out: kpt on wl* **12/1**

3005 **2** *1 1/2* **Silvanus (IRE)**[21] 4678 6-9-8 **63** (p) PaulHanagan 10 68+
(Paul Midgley) *hmpd s and bhd: gd hdwy wl over 1f out: swtchd lft and rdn ent fnl f: kpt on: nt rch wnr* **11/1**

0006 **3** *3/4* **Watts Up Son**[9] 5109 3-8-13 **63** (bt[1]) JasonHart(7) 12 65
(Declan Carroll) *chsd ldrs on outer: pushed along and sltly outpcd 1/2-way: swtchd rt and rdn 2f out: styd on wl ent fnl f: nrst fin* **7/1**

555U **4** *1* **Beautiful Day**[4] 5274 3-9-1 **58** (b) PhillipMakin 5 56
(Kevin Ryan) *chsd ldrs: hdwy 2f out: sn rdn: drvn and kpt on same pce ins fnl f* **8/1**

5300 **5** *nk* **Kalahari Desert (IRE)**[12] 4986 4-8-5 **46** oh1 (v) AndrewMullen 14 43
(Richard Whitaker) *in tch: hdwy 2f out: sn rdn and kpt on same pce ins fnl f* **11/1**

143- **6** *nk* **Mercers Row**[355] 5735 4-9-6 **64** MichaelO'Connell(3) 8 60
(Noel Wilson) *prom: chsd wnr fr 1/2-way: drvn ent fnl f: wknd fnl 100yds* **8/1**

0040 **7** *1 1/4* **Piste**[12] 4986 5-8-2 **46** oh1 BillyCray(3) 15 38
(Tina Jackson) *chsd ldrs on wd outside: rdn along 2f out: sn drvn and grad wknd* **25/1**

0006 **8** *nk* **Rio Sands**[43] 3931 6-8-2 **48** oh1 ow2 ShaneBKelly(5) 13 39
(Richard Whitaker) *dwlt and wnt rt s: towards rr tl sme late hdwy* **18/1**

5535 **9** *hd* **Mr Mo Jo**[38] 4124 3-9-3 **65** (v[1]) LanceBetts(5) 3 55
(Lawrence Mullaney) *in tch on inner: hdwy to chse ldrs over 1f out: sn rdn and wknd ins fnl f* **11/2**[2]

5500 **10** *1* **Red River Boy**[18] 4793 6-8-7 **48** KellyHarrison 4 34
(Chris Fairhurst) *a towards rr* **13/2**[3]

0643 **11** *nk* **Tyrannosaurus Rex (IRE)**[12] 5019 7-8-5 **46** oh1(b[1]) SilvestreDeSousa 11 31
(David O'Meara) *a in rr* **9/2**[1]

000 **12** *2 1/4* **Lovely Lynn (IRE)**[53] 3616 3-7-12 **46** oh1 NeilFarley(5) 9 23
(Declan Carroll) *a towards rr* **50/1**

0-0 **13** *2 1/4* **Windjammer**[54] 3573 7-8-4 **48** (b) DeclanCannon(3) 7 17
(Lawrence Mullaney) *chsd wnr to 1/2-way: rdn along 2f out: wknd over 1f out* **18/1**

59.67 secs (-0.13) **Going Correction** 0.0s/f (Good)
WFA 3 from 4yo+ 2lb **13** Ran SP% **122.3**
Speed ratings (Par 101): **101,98,97,95,95 94,92,92,92,90 89,86,82**
toteswingers:1&2:£25.00, 2&3:£18.70, 1&3:£19.90. Tote Super 7: Win: Not won. Place: Not won. CSF £140.97 CT £1040.92 TOTE £13.40: £3.20, £3.70, £1.70; EX 81.60 TRIFECTA Not won..
Owner P O'Gara & N Kelly **Bred** Green Square Racing **Trained** Westow, N Yorks

FOCUS
They fanned out over two thirds of the track in this wide-open low-grade sprint handicap.

T/Jkpt: Not won. T/Plt: £73.40 to a £1 stake. Pool of £63,680.91- 632.92 winning tickets. T/Qpdt: £17.50 to a £1 stake.Pool of £4,237.65 - 178.20 winning tickets. JR

4947 CHEPSTOW (L-H)
Wednesday, August 24

OFFICIAL GOING: Good to firm (good in places; 8.2) changing to good (good to soft in places) after race 5 (4.00)
Wind: faily light, half against Weather: cloudy, brighter spells

5374 DIGIBET.COM NURSERY 6f 16y
2:00 (2:01) (Class 6) (0-65,65) 2-Y-O **£1,617** (£481; £240; £120) **Stalls** Centre

Form RPR

5644 **1** **Sweet Ovation**[13] 4955 2-8-9 **53** HayleyTurner 12 56
(Mark Usher) *hld up in last trio: rdn and hdwy over 1f out: led fnl 100yds: r.o wl* **6/1**[3]

4055 **2** *1/2* **Night Angel (IRE)**[15] 4892 2-9-6 **64** JamesMillman 10 66
(Rod Millman) *short of room leaving stalls: sn rcvrd and chsd ldr: led jst over 2f out: rdn and hung lft over 1f out: hdd and no ex fnl 100yds* **8/1**

0343 **3** *1/2* **Fast On (IRE)**[25] 4538 2-9-7 **65** (v) RichardMullen 3 65
(Ed McMahon) *hld up in rr: hdwy into midfield 1/2-way: swtchd lft and effrt 2f out: ev ch and drvn jst ins fnl f: styd on same pce fnl 100yds* **4/1**[2]

5235 **4** *2 1/2* **Emma Jean (IRE)**[19] 4756 2-8-10 **54** LukeMorris 9 47
(J S Moore) *in tch: rdn over 2f out: drvn and chsd ldrs over 1f out: outpcd by ldng trio fnl f: kpt on* **8/1**

405 **5** *1/2* **First Rebellion**[9] 5099 2-8-5 **49** LiamJones 11 40
(Tony Carroll) *in tch: rdn jst over 2f out: edgd lft and unable qck over 1f out: styd on same pce fnl f* **14/1**

4550 **6** *1/2* **Gypsy Rider**[14] 4922 2-9-0 **58** DavidProbert 1 48
(Bryn Palling) *chsd ldrs: rdn over 2f out: ev ch 2f out tl jst over 1f out: wknd ins fnl f* **12/1**

1563 **7** *3/4* **Very First Blade**[14] 4922 2-8-10 **57** KieranO'Neill(3) 5 44
(Mark Brisbourne) *in tch towards rr: pushed along after 2f: styd in tch: no imp u.p over 1f out: plugged on same pce fnl f* **6/1**[3]

035 **8** *8* **Two Bridges**[34] 4229 2-8-12 **59** MartinHarley(3) 2 22
(Gary Moore) *racd in midfield: rdn after 2f: struggling 1/2-way: wknd 2f out* **20/1**

230 **9** *3 1/4* **Goal Hanger**[50] 3718 2-9-6 **64** JimCrowley 4 18
(Tom Dascombe) *plld hrd: chsd ldrs tl 2f out: sn wknd* **5/2**[1]

004 **10** *1 3/4* **Joli Colourful (IRE)**[50] 3708 2-8-1 **45** CathyGannon 7 —
(Tony Newcombe) *racd freely: sn led: hdd jst over 2f out: sn lost pl: wl bhd ent fnl f* **20/1**

0000 **11** *3* **Arbeejay**[48] 3779 2-7-8 **45** IanBurns(7) 6 —
(Bill Turner) *a towards rr: rdn and struggling 1/2-way: lost tch 2f out* **66/1**

1m 11.97s (-0.03) **Going Correction** -0.125s/f (Firm) **11** Ran SP% **124.7**
Speed ratings (Par 92): **95,94,93,90,89 89,88,77,73,70 66**
CSF £55.60 CT £224.81 TOTE £6.00: £2.20, £4.40, £1.10; EX 45.10.
Owner The Ridgeway Bloodstock Company Ltd **Bred** Ridgeway Bloodstock **Trained** Upper Lambourn, Berks

FOCUS
A moderate nursery.

NOTEBOOK
Sweet Ovation was held up at the tail of the field on the stands' side and came through to challenge going well before edging ahead inside the last, despite hanging left. The extra furlong helped her and there's room for improvement off her current mark.
Night Angel(IRE), down another 3lb, was never too far off the pace and ran up to her best in defeat. One of the more exposed runners in the line-up, she's a fair guide to the level of the form. (tchd 7-1)
Fast On(IRE) kept on towards the far side but couldn't quite get to the first two. Not for the first time another furlong looks like it will suit him.
Emma Jean(IRE), dropped 4lb since being beaten in a seller last time, is another who has quite an exposed profile now. (op 10-1)
First Rebellion, who was racing from 4lb out of the handicap, didn't help his rider much by continually hanging. (op 16-1)
Goal Hanger ran too freely at Wolverhampton last time and, despite being dropped back a furlong in distance, she again ruined her chance by failing to settle. She also played up before the start and is clearly quite highly strung. (op 7-2)

5375 WEATHERBYS PRIVATE BANKING MAIDEN STKS 1m 14y
2:30 (2:33) (Class 5) 2-Y-O **£2,264** (£673; £336; £168) **Stalls** Centre

Form RPR

332 **1** **Cavaleiro (IRE)**[20] 4722 2-9-3 84 HayleyTurner 5 78+
(Marcus Tregoning) *t.k.h: a travelling wl: chsd ldrs: led on bit 2f out: nudged along and readily qcknd clr 1f out: eased towards fin: easily* **2/7**[1]

00 **2** *3* **Dont Take Me Alive**[14] 4906 2-9-3 0 AdamKirby 9 67
(Clive Cox) *racd in midfield: rdn and hdwy to chse ldng trio 2f out: chsd clr wnr jst ins fnl f: kpt on but no ch w wnr* **9/1**[3]

0 **3** *nk* **Hint Of Mint**[12] 4995 2-9-3 0 LiamKeniry 12 66
(Andrew Balding) *led for over 1f: chsd ldr after tl jst over 2f out: drvn and unable qck over 1f out: battling for 2nd and kpt on ins fnl f: no ch w wnr* **16/1**

0 **4** *3 3/4* **Kings Decree**[12] 4995 2-9-3 0 JamesMillman 1 58
(Rod Millman) *taken down early: racd freely: dashed up to ld over 6f out: hdd and rdn 2f out: styd pressing wnr tl easily brushed aside ent fnl f: wknd* **4/1**[2]

00 **5** *2 3/4* **April Ciel**[12] 4996 2-9-3 0 FergusSweeney 10 51
(Andrew Haynes) *racd in midfield: rdn and effrt to chse ldrs over 2f out: outpcd and struggling ent fnl 2f: 5th and wl btn over 1f out* **16/1**

6 **6** *2 1/4* **Bathwick Street**[69] 3076 2-9-3 0 StevieDonohoe 8 46
(David Evans) *racd in last quartet: rdn 1/2-way: nvr any ch w ldrs but plugged on ins fnl f* **33/1**

0 **7** *1 1/2* **Cash Injection**[39] 4087 2-9-0 0 KierenFox(3) 6 43
(Karen George) *in tch in midfield: rdn and hdwy 1/2-way: struggling and rn green jst over 2f out: wknd wl over 1f out* **50/1**

8 *1/2* **Miss Granger** 2-8-12 0 DavidProbert 11 37
(Ronald Harris) *s.i.s: rn green in last quartet: rdn after 2f: nvr trbld ldrs* **66/1**

9 *5* **Midnight Sequel** 2-8-12 0 MartinLane 4 25
(Andrew Haynes) *rn green and a struggling in rr: wl bhd fnl 2f* **66/1**

50 **10** *33* **Brown Eyed Lass**[13] 4947 2-8-7 0.............................. JamesRogers(5) 2 —
(Laura Young) *a towards rr: lost tch over 2f out: t.o and virtually p.u ins fnl f* **66/1**

1m 37.01s (0.81) **Going Correction** -0.125s/f (Firm) **10** Ran SP% **128.9**
Speed ratings (Par 94): **90,87,86,82,80 77,76,75,70,37**
toteswingers:1&2:£2.40, 2&3:£9.90, 1&3:£3.40 CSF £5.19 TOTE £1.40: £1.02, £2.30, £4.10; EX 7.30.
Owner Guy Brook **Bred** Kildaragh Stud & M Downey **Trained** Lambourn, Berks

FOCUS
The betting suggested this was a straightforward opportunity for Cavaleiro to get off the mark and things couldn't have gone any easier for him, as he only had to be nudged out to win as he pleased.

NOTEBOOK
Cavaleiro(IRE) was entitled to win like this and the handicapper can't raise him beyond his current mark of 84. His trainer mentioned the Haynes, Hanson and Clark as a possible target. (op 1-3 tchd 4-11)
Dont Take Me Alive was under pressure from some way out but did respond and got the mile well. Now eligible for a mark, he should be of more interest in handicaps.
Hint Of Mint, well beaten on his debut at Newbury, showed a lot more here but is another who looks more of a handicap prospect after one more run.
Kings Decree didn't settle that well in front and dropped away tamely once headed.
April Ciel ran his best race so far and nurseries will now be open to him as well.

5376 WEATHERBYS PRIVATE BANKING H'CAP 1m 14y
3:00 (3:03) (Class 5) (0-70,70) 3-Y-O+ **£2,264** (£673; £336; £168) **Stalls** Centre

Form RPR
6501 **1** **Poyle Judy**[13] 4949 3-9-3 **67**.............................. JimCrowley 14 79
(Ralph Beckett) *racd in stands' side trio: chsd ldrs tl overall ldr over 5f out: mde rest: rdn and clr w runner-up wl over 1f out: kpt on wl* **5/1**[1]
3203 **2** *2* **Bold Cross (IRE)**[17] 4821 8-9-4 **65**.............................. KierenFox(3) 13 73
(Edward Bevan) *racd far side gp: hld up in midfield: hdwy 1/2-way: rdn and chsd wnr ent fnl 2f: sn drew clr w wnr: no ex and styd on same pce ins fnl f: 1st of 11 in gp* **12/1**
5035 **3** *3 1/4* **Bidable**[13] 4949 7-9-10 **68**.............................. CathyGannon 10 69
(Bryn Palling) *racd in far side gp: bhd: hdwy u.p past btn horses over 1f out: styd on ins fnl f to go 3rd cl home: no threat to ldrs: 2nd of 11 in gp* **14/1**
1465 **4** *nk* **Sergeant Troy (IRE)**[27] 4479 3-9-6 **70**..............................(t) SteveDrowne 8 69+
(Roger Charlton) *racd in far side gp: stdd s: bhd: stmbld after 1f: hdwy 1/2-way: rdn and no imp and swtchd rt over 1f out: wnt 3rd ins fnl f: lost 3rd cl home: 3rd of 11 in gp* **5/1**[1]
0003 **5** *3/4* **Raghdaan**[12] 5002 4-8-7 **51**.............................. ChrisCatlin 16 49
(Peter Hiatt) *racd in stands' side trio: hld up towards rr overall: rdn and hung lft over 2f out: no ch w ldrs but plugged on ins fnl f: nvr trbld ldrs: 2nd of 3 in gp* **14/1**
4231 **6** *3/4* **Lady Bayside**[20] 4706 3-9-4 **68**.............................. FergusSweeney 11 63
(Malcolm Saunders) *racd in far side gp: hld up tch: rdn and hdwy over 2f out: no imp and no threat to ldrs fr over 1f out: plugged on: 4th of 11 in gp* **5/1**[1]
1106 **7** *1 1/4* **Forward Feline (IRE)**[16] 4865 5-9-1 **59**.............................. DavidProbert 15 53
(Bryn Palling) *racd in stands' side trio: stdd s: hld up towards rr overall: hdwy 1/2-way: chsd ldrs and rdn over 2f out: wknd over 1f out: wl btn fnl f: 3rd of 3 in gp* **14/1**
-000 **8** *3* **Dusty Bluebells (IRE)**[19] 4758 3-8-7 **57**.............................. LukeMorris 4 43
(J S Moore) *racd in far side gp: hld up in midfield: hdwy 1/2-way: rdn and no hdwy jst over 2f out: wknd wl over 1f out: 5th of 11 in gp* **33/1**
0200 **9** *3/4* **Spinning Ridge (IRE)**[11] 5042 6-8-6 **57**..............................(v) RaulDaSilva(7) 3 42
(Ronald Harris) *racd in far side gp: chsd ldrs: led gp and chsd wnr jst over 3f out tl 2f out: wknd and edgd lft over 1f out: fdd ins fnl f: 6th of 11 in gp* **25/1**
5445 **10** *1 1/2* **Mill Mick**[39] 4083 4-9-9 **67**.............................. StephenCraine 7 48
(John Mackie) *racd in far side gp: chsd ldrs tl 3f out: sn struggling: wknd 2f out: 7th of 11 in gp* **10/1**[3]
5244 **11** *1 1/4* **Tap Dance Way (IRE)**[20] 4707 4-9-11 **69**.............................. LiamKeniry 12 48
(Patrick Chamings) *racd in far side gp: prom overall: led gp and chsd wnr over 3f out: sn rdn and losing pl: wknd 2f out: [illegible] of 11 in gp* [illegible]
0600 **12** *7* **Safari Guide**[20] 4701 5-8-4 **51** oh4..............................(p) SophieDoyle(3) 2 13
(Dai Burchell) *racd in far side gp: led gp and prom overall tl over 3f out: sn dropped out u.p: wl bhd over 1f out: 9th of 11 in gp* **66/1**
4500 **13** *hd* **Emerald Girl (IRE)**[168] 802 4-9-5 **66**.............................. RobertLButler(3) 6 28
(Richard Guest) *racd in far side gp: chsd ldrs tl over 3f out: sn lost pl: wl bhd over 1f out: 10th of 11 in gp* **25/1**
0000 **14** *1* **Golden Hinde**[23] 4613 3-9-1 **65**.............................. MartinLane 9 24
(Ronald Harris) *racd in far side gp: prom tl over 3f out: sn struggling: wknd over 2f: wl bhd and eased ins fnl f: 11th of 11 in gp* **14/1**
0-60 **15** *1 3/4* **She's Untouchable**[13] 4953 4-8-3 **52** oh5 ow1..... MatthewLawson(5) 17 —
(Gary Harrison) *racd alone between the gp: racd freely and overall ldr tl over 5f out: rdn and lost pl 1/2-way: wl bhd and eased ins fnl f* **25/1**

1m 34.51s (-1.69) **Going Correction** -0.125s/f (Firm) **15** Ran SP% **120.5**
WFA 3 from 4yo+ 6lb
Speed ratings (Par 103): **103,101,97,97,96 95,94,91,90,89 88,81,81,80,78**
CSF £62.40 CT £801.58 TOTE £6.40: £2.20, £4.20, £3.70; EX 70.50.
Owner Cecil And Miss Alison Wiggins **Bred** Cecil And Miss Alison Wiggins **Trained** Kimpton, Hants

FOCUS
Hard to know if there was an advantage to racing on the stands' side, but Poyle Judy followed up her C&D success from earlier in the month by clinging to the stands' rail in old school fashion and cosily holding off Bold Cross, who was drawn high but raced up the middle.
Sergeant Troy(IRE) Official explanation: jockey said colt stumbled badly after a furlong
Mill Mick Official explanation: trainer said gelding lost a front shoe

5377 FESTIVAL RACING MEDIAN AUCTION MAIDEN STKS 5f 16y
3:30 (3:31) (Class 5) 3-5-Y-O **£2,264** (£673; £336; £168) **Stalls** Centre

Form RPR
2623 **1** **Whitecrest**[9] 5115 3-8-12 67.............................. CathyGannon 4 66
(John Spearing) *mde all: rdn 2f out: kpt on wl and asserted fnl 100yds: rdn out* **6/4**[2]
5000 **2** *1* **Griffin Point (IRE)**[58] 3464 4-8-9 48.............................. JamesRogers(5) 1 62
(William Muir) *pressed wnr tl 2f out: sn rdn and stl ev ch tl no ex fnl 100yds: wnt 2nd again nr fin* **20/1**
4244 **3** *nk* **Ginzan**[14] 4924 3-8-12 57.............................. JimCrowley 5 61
(Malcolm Saunders) *pressed ldrs: wnt 2nd and rdn 2f out: ev ch after tl no ex and btn fnl 100yds: lost 2nd nr fin* **4/1**[3]
22 **4** *6* **Sannibel**[16] 4863 3-8-12 0.............................. ShaneKelly 3 39
(Kevin Morgan) *dwlt: sn rcvrd and jnd ldrs after 2f: wknd jst over 1f out* **5/4**[1]
6 **5** *1 3/4* **Coalburn**[27] 4461 3-9-3 0.............................. MarkLawson 2 38
(Gary Harrison) *awkward leaving stalls and slowly away: rcvrd to press ldrs on outer 1/2-way: rn green: hung lft and wknd over 1f out: eased towards fin* **66/1**

58.75 secs (-0.55) **Going Correction** -0.125s/f (Firm)
WFA 3 from 4yo 2lb **5** Ran SP% **110.7**
Speed ratings (Par 103): **99,97,96,87,84**
CSF £25.12 TOTE £2.00: £1.90, £8.80; EX 31.90.
Owner G M Eales **Bred** J Spearing And Kate Ive **Trained** Kinnersley, Worcs

FOCUS
A moderate maiden and perhaps some more evidence that the stands' rail was an advantage. The winner has been rated well below her best.

5378 RHOMCO H'CAP 5f 16y
4:00 (4:00) (Class 4) (0-80,78) 3-Y-O **£3,234** (£962; £481; £240) **Stalls** Centre

Form RPR
3411 **1** **Swendab (IRE)**[9] 5115 3-9-3 **75** 6ex..............................(v) HayleyTurner 1 84
(John O'Shea) *pressed ldrs tl led 2f out: hrd pressed fr over 1f out: kpt on wl ins fnl f* **7/4**[1]
0604 **2** *shd* **Sugar Beet**[41] 3994 3-9-0 **72**.............................. DavidProbert 2 81
(Ronald Harris) *awkward leaving stalls and slowly away: chsd ldng trio: rdn and hdwy on far side to press ldr over 1f out: kpt on wl u.p but a jst hld ins fnl f* **9/1**
0650 **3** *3 1/4* **Belle Bayardo (IRE)**[17] 4817 3-9-5 **77**.............................. LukeMorris 5 74
(Ronald Harris) *dwlt: sn pushed along and struggling to go pce in rr: drvn 2f out: styd on ins fnl f to go 3rd nr fin: nvr threatened ldrs* **9/1**
125 **4** *nk* **Cruise Tothelimit (IRE)**[15] 4880 3-8-12 **73**.............................. KieranO'Neill(3) 4 69
(Patrick Morris) *pressed ldr tl unable qck and outpcd ent fnl 2f: swtchd lft and rdn wl over 1f out: 3rd and btn ins fnl f: lost 3rd nr fin* **2/1**[2]
0214 **5** *2 3/4* **Bravo King (IRE)**[9] 5119 3-9-3 **78**.............................. RobertLButler(3) 3 64
(Richard Guest) *led: hdd and hung lft 2f out: wknd over 1f out* **4/1**[3]

58.98 secs (-0.32) **Going Correction** -0.125s/f (Firm) **5** Ran SP% **109.7**
Speed ratings (Par 102): **97,96,91,91,86**
CSF £16.54 TOTE £2.60: £1.10, £7.90; EX 7.50.
Owner The Cross Racing Club & Patrick Brady **Bred** P Brady **Trained** Elton, Gloucs
■ Stewards' Enquiry : David Probert caution; excessive use of whip.

FOCUS
A fair sprint and once again the field headed straight for the stands' rail. The winner has been rated as producing a small personal best.

5379 WESTERN DAILY PRESS H'CAP 2m 49y
4:30 (4:31) (Class 6) (0-60,60) 3-Y-O+ **£1,617** (£481; £240; £120) **Stalls** Low

Form RPR
603/ **1** **Whenever**[116] 6400 7-10-0 **60**.............................. FergusSweeney 11 71+
(Richard Phillips) *chsd ldrs: lost pl and pushed along bnd after 2f: hdwy to chse ldrs 7f out: rdn to ld 3f out: forged clr ent fnl f: styd on wl: rdn out* **6/1**[3]
2502 **2** *1 1/2* **Sea The Flames (IRE)**[12] 5022 3-8-9 **55**.............................. HayleyTurner 8 62
(Marcus Tregoning) *hld up in last quartet: hdwy into midfield 6f out: rdn over 3f out: swtchd rt 2f out: racd awkardly but styd on fr over 1f out: wnt 2nd fnl 50yds: nvr gng pce to chal wnr* **9/4**[1]
/530 **3** *1* **Dream Catcher (SWE)**[13] 4974 8-9-12 **58**..............................(p) JimCrowley 10 64
(Jonjo O'Neill) *hld up in midfield: rdn and effrt 4f out: drvn and chsd wnr 2f out: no ex and btn jst ins fnl f: lost 2nd fnl 100yds* **10/1**
000 **4** *2 1/2* **Court Princess**[4] 5267 8-9-1 **47**..............................(p) LukeMorris 1 50
(Richard Price) *chsd ldrs: rdn over 4f out: drvn and plugged on same pce fnl 2f* **18/1**
5-20 **5** *1 3/4* **Picot De Say**[29] 4274 9-9-2 **53**.............................. MatthewLawson(5) 7 54
(Bernard Llewellyn) *s.i.s: hld up in last quartet: hdwy 6f out: chsd ldrs and rdn wl over 2f out: unable qck and no imp fnl 2f* **8/1**
/233 **6** *1/2* **Orbital Orchid**[22] 4630 6-9-9 **55**.............................. ChrisCatlin 9 55
(Nick Williams) *s.i.s: several positions and pushed along thrght: in last quartet: hdwy to [illegible] lost pl over 5f out: drvn and bhd 4f out: hdwy past btn horses over 1f out: styd on ins fnl f* **7/1**
0444 **7** *1 1/2* **Band Of Thunder**[26] 4510 3-8-9 **55**..............................(v) LiamKeniry 5 53
(Andrew Balding) *chsd ldr: rdn 4f out: struggling and lost pl wl over 2f out: plugged on same pce and wl hld over 1f out* **7/2**[2]
0-20 **8** *2 1/2* **Go Amwell**[10] 5079 8-9-3 **49**..............................(v) AdrianMcCarthy 13 44
(J R Jenkins) *s.i.s: bhd: rdn and effrt 4f out: no real hdwy: nvr trbld ldrs* **12/1**
3105 **9** *5* **Annelko**[22] 4630 4-9-13 **59**.............................. MartinLane 6 48
(Andrew Haynes) *led tl 3f out: lost 2nd 2f out: wknd qckly over 1f out* **9/1**
401/ **10** *23* **Acapulco Bay**[123] 2640 7-8-13 **48**.............................. SophieDoyle(3) 3 10
(Dai Burchell) *t.k.h: hld up in midfield: lost pl and bhd over 5f out: rdn and lost tch 4f out: wl bhd and eased ins fnl f: t.o* **50/1**
0060 **11** *1 3/4* **Dubai Miracle (USA)**[29] 3912 4-9-9 **60**.............................. JamesRogers(5) 4 20
(Laura Young) *chsd ldrs: lost pl and dropped in rr 6f out: lost tch 4f out: wl bhd and eased ins fnl f: t.o* **66/1**

3m 41.18s (2.28) **Going Correction** +0.175s/f (Good)
WFA 3 from 4yo+ 14lb **11** Ran SP% **126.4**
Speed ratings (Par 101): **101,100,99,98,97 97,96,95,92,81 80**
toteswingers:1&2:£4.80, 2&3:£8.20, 1&3:£9.80 CSF £21.43 CT £142.76 TOTE £8.80: £2.50, £1.90, £1.90; EX 32.30.
Owner Mr & Mrs W J Williams **Bred** D J And Mrs Deer **Trained** Adlestrop, Gloucs

FOCUS
The rain caused a change in the official going before this race, with the ground being switched to good, good to soft in places. This ordinary staying handicap didn't look like it would take much winning.
Acapulco Bay Official explanation: jockey said gelding lost its action

5380 RHOMCO CONSULTING H'CAP 1m 2f 36y
5:00 (5:00) (Class 6) (0-60,61) 3-Y-O **£1,617** (£481; £240; £120) **Stalls** Low

Form RPR
-600 **1** **Thank You Joy**[28] 4435 3-9-7 **60**.............................. AdrianMcCarthy 8 64
(J R Jenkins) *in tch in midfield: rdn 3f out: rdn hands and heels and hdwy over 1f out: edgd lft and chal ins fnl f: pushed into ld fnl 50yds: eased last strides* **14/1**
2133 **2** *nk* **Ishikawa (IRE)**[19] 4745 3-9-3 **56**.............................. FergusSweeney 4 59
(Alan King) *taken down early: t.k.h: chsd ldrs: trckd ldr 4f out: rdn to ld jst over 1f out: drvn ins fnl f: hdd and no ex fnl 50yds* **3/1**[1]

0051 **3** ½ **Miracle Play (IRE)**[5] 5243 3-9-3 **61** 6ex .... MatthewCosham(5) 6 66+
(David Evans) *hld up off the pce in last pair: clsd and in tch over 4f out: swtchd rt and chsd ldrs 2f out: nt clr run and swtchd rt 1f out: short of room and hmpd ins fnl f: swtchd rt and ralied fnl 75yds: r.o wl* **3/1**[1]

3000 **4** ¾ **Anna Fontenail**[15] 4888 3-9-4 **57** ....(bt[1]) JamesMillman 2 58
(Rod Millman) *taken down early: led: clr 1/2-way: rdn over 2f out: hdd jst over 1f out: kpt on same pce ins fnl f* **14/1**

0402 **5** 2 ¾ **Special Endeavour (IRE)**[16] 4846 3-8-8 **47** ....(p) HayleyTurner 1 42
(William Muir) *chsd ldr tl 4f out: sn rdn: drvn and unable qck over 1f out: wknd ins fnl f* **5/1**[3]

20 **6** 3 **Bella Montagna**[42] 3976 3-9-2 **55** .... ChrisCatlin 11 44
(John Quinn) *hld up off the pce in last pair: rdn: no rspnse and hung lft 4f out: plugged on ins fnl f: nvr trbld ldrs* **9/1**

3051 **7** ½ **Miskin Diamond (IRE)**[13] 4953 3-8-9 **48** .... CathyGannon 9 43+
(Bryn Palling) *chsd ldrs: rdn over 3f out: stl pressing ldrs but plugging on same pce whn squeezed for room and hmpd 1f out: nt rcvr and n.d after* **4/1**[2]

0-00 **8** nse **First Pressing**[17] 4827 3-8-12 **51** .... MartinLane 3 39
(John Berry) *sn pushed along in midfield: rdn over 4f out: struggling u.p 3f out: no threat to ldrs fnl 2f* **20/1**

2m 13.18s (2.58) **Going Correction** +0.175s/f (Good) **8** Ran SP% **114.8**
Speed ratings (Par 98): **96,95,95,94,92 90,89,89**
toteswingers:1&2:£7.60, 2&3:£2.50, 1&3:£10.10 CSF £56.18 CT £163.60 TOTE £22.90: £5.10, £1.70, £1.20; EX 82.20.
Owner Robin Stevens **Bred** D R Tucker **Trained** Royston, Herts
■ Stewards' Enquiry : Adrian McCarthy one-day ban; careless riding (7th Sept)

FOCUS
A fairly open handicap.
Miracle Play(IRE) Official explanation: jockey said filly was denied a clear run
T/Plt: £68.80 to a £1 stake. Pool of £57,567.12 - 610.59 winning tickets. T/Qpdt: £18.40 to a £1 stake. Pool of £3,942.16 - 157.70 winning tickets. SP

5316 KEMPTON (A.W) (R-H)
Wednesday, August 24

OFFICIAL GOING: Standard
Wind: Moderate, behind Weather: Fine

5381 FREE ENTRY FOR BETDAQ MEMBERS H'CAP 1m (P)
6:20 (6:22) (Class 6) (0-65,65) 3-Y-O **£1,617** (£481; £240; £120) **Stalls** Low

Form RPR

4052 **1** **Pearl Opera**[11] 5041 3-8-11 **55** .... KierenFallon 9 62
(Denis Coakley) *trckd ldrs: wnt prom over 2f out: drvn to chse ldr jst over 1f out: clsd to ld last 150yds: styd on* **7/2**[2]

6430 **2** ¾ **Prince Of Passion (CAN)**[12] 4994 3-9-0 **58** .... RobbieFitzpatrick 3 63
(Derek Shaw) *dwlt: hld up in last trio: gd prog on inner fr 2f out: sltly impeded 1f out: styd on to take 2nd nr fin: no ch to chal* **20/1**

-050 **3** ½ **Goodwood Treasure**[34] 4244 3-9-2 **60** .... JimmyFortune 2 64
(John Dunlop) *hld up in midfield: rdn and prog 2f out: hung rt 1f out: styd on: nt pce to chal* **20/1**

1020 **4** hd **Karate (IRE)**[8] 5143 3-9-1 **59** .... JamesDoyle 1 63
(Hans Adielsson) *hld up in last trio: prog towards inner over 2f out: drvn and styd on fnl f: nvr able to chal* **10/1**

6230 **5** nk **Loyal N Trusted**[12] 5014 3-9-5 **63** .... WilliamCarson 11 66
(Michael Wigham) *trblesme to post: led at stdy pce: kicked clr over 2f out: hdd last 150yds: fdd and lost pls nr fin* **14/1**

00-0 **6** 1 **Jibouti (IRE)**[12] 4989 3-9-0 **58** .... KirstyMilczarek 14 59
(Clive Brittain) *chsd ldr to jst over 1f out: fdd fnl f* **25/1**

5002 **7** nse **Rojo Boy**[17] 4829 3-9-6 **64** ....(b) NeilCallan 7 64
(David Elsworth) *hld up in midfield: effrt whn bmpd over 2f out: nt qckn wl over 1f out: styd on: nvr able to chal* **3/1**[1]

0006 **8** 5 **Titan Diamond (IRE)**[8] 5143 3-8-9 **53** .... SteveDrowne 12 42
(Mark Usher) *trckd ldrs: effrt over 2f out: no prog and outpcd over 1f out* **12/1**

0-00 **9** 1 **Sabot D'Or**[9] 5115 3-8-12 **56** .... RobertHavlin 4 43
(Roger Ingram) *prom: rdn wl over 2f out: wkng whn squeezed out 1f out* **20/1**

4565 **10** 2 ¼ **Glass Mountain (IRE)**[14] 4908 3-9-7 **65** ....(v[1]) PatCosgrave 5 46
(James Fanshawe) *dwlt: t.k.h: snatched up after 1f: effrt fr rr whn n.m.r and bmpd over 2f out: no hdwy over 1f out* **4/1**[3]

0000 **11** 2 ½ **A B Celebration**[13] 4970 3-7-13 **46** oh1 .... HarryBentley(3) 6 22
(John Bridger) *dwlt: a in last trio: lft bhd over 2f out* **80/1**

0600 **12** 9 **Fairy Tales**[18] 4796 3-8-13 **60** .... SeanLevey(3) 10 15
(John Bridger) *racd wd: hld up in tch: wknd over 2f out: t.o* **66/1**

0045 **13** 4 ½ **Love For Love**[22] 4638 3-8-2 **46** ....(v[1]) JimmyQuinn 8 —
(David O'Meara) *t.k.h: racd wd: prom tl wknd rapidly wl over 2f out: t.o* **12/1**

1m 40.1s (0.30) **Going Correction** -0.025s/f (Stan) **13** Ran SP% **119.2**
Speed ratings (Par 98): **97,96,95,95,95 94,94,89,88,85 83,74,69**
toteswingers: 1&2 £14.70, 1&3 £16.30, 2&3 £24.40 CSF £79.63 CT £1284.26 TOTE £5.90: £1.10, £4.20, £6.80; EX 57.50.
Owner James Kerr **Bred** Drakenstein Stud **Trained** West Ilsley, Berks

FOCUS
This moderate 3yo handicap was yet another race at this venue run at a muddling pace and there was a blanket finish behind the winner as the hold-up horses closed. The form is rated around the fourth.

5382 BETDAQ.COM EXCHANGE PRICE MULTIPLES MEDIAN AUCTION MAIDEN STKS 1m (P)
6:50 (6:54) (Class 6) 2-Y-O **£1,617** (£481; £240; £120) **Stalls** Low

Form RPR

66 **1** **Gabrial's Gift (IRE)**[17] 4815 2-9-3 0 .... JamesDoyle 1 86
(David Simcock) *pressed ldr: led jst over 2f out gng strly: shkn up and drew clr over 1f out: comf* **4/1**[2]

4 **2** 6 **Amoralist**[20] 4722 2-9-3 0 .... KierenFallon 14 72
(Ed Dunlop) *trckd ldrs: rdn over 2f out disputing 3rd: no imp tl kpt on fnl f to take 2nd last strides* **1/1**[1]

0 **3** nk **Young Prince (IRE)**[31] 4352 2-9-0 0 .... SeanLevey(3) 11 71
(Robert Mills) *led: rdn and hdd jst over 2f out: no ch w wnr after: lost 2nd last strides* **33/1**

4 ¾ **Jack Of Diamonds (IRE)** 2-9-3 0 .... JackMitchell 12 70
(Roger Teal) *wl in tch: outpcd over 2f out: rn green and wandered after: styd on fnl f against nr side rail* **66/1**

00 **5** shd **Shark In The Sea**[13] 4968 2-9-3 0 .... ShaneKelly 13 69
(Brian Meehan) *prom: drvn over 2f out disputing 3rd: kpt on after but lost 4th last strides* **100/1**

06 **6** 2 ¾ **Foster's Road**[11] 5044 2-9-3 0 .... DaneO'Neill 3 63
(Mick Channon) *t.k.h: hld up bhd ldrs: outpcd wl over 2f out: kpt on one pce: n.d* **8/1**[3]

00 **7** 5 **Cato Minor**[18] 4798 2-9-3 0 ....(b[1]) AdamKirby 9 52
(Amanda Perrett) *wl in rr: pushed along sn after 1/2-way: kpt on fnl 2f: nt totally disgracd* **66/1**

00 **8** 5 **Cool Light**[48] 3779 2-8-9 0 .... HarryBentley(3) 2 35
(Alan Jarvis) *prom: rdn over 3f out: steadily wknd fr wl over 2f out* **66/1**

0 **9** 3 **Flight Connection**[32] 4330 2-9-3 0 .... KirstyMilczarek 7 33
(Clive Brittain) *wl in rr: n.d fr over 2f out: modest late prog* **40/1**

00 **10** 2 ½ **The Mighty Lohan (IRE)**[32] 4330 2-9-3 0 .... PatCosgrave 5 27
(Amy Weaver) *wl in rr: outpcd fr 3f out: no ch after* **125/1**

11 2 ½ **Renegotiate** 2-9-3 0 .... JimmyFortune 10 22
(Andrew Balding) *a towards rr: pushed along over 3f out: struggling over 2f out* **9/1**

12 3 ¼ **Beanstalk (IRE)** 2-9-3 0 .... FrankieMcDonald 6 14
(Richard Hannon) *s.i.s: wl in rr: shoved along over 3f out and no real prog: bhd fnl 2f* **25/1**

13 6 **Ali Hope (IRE)** 2-9-3 0 .... SteveDrowne 4 —
(Roger Charlton) *a in last trio: bhd over 2f out* **11/1**

00 **14** 2 ¼ **Fresteem**[83] 2641 2-9-3 0 .... PaulDue 8 —
(Luke Dace) *s.i.s: a wl in rr: bhd over 2f out* **125/1**

1m 39.27s (-0.53) **Going Correction** -0.025s/f (Stan) **14** Ran SP% **115.7**
Speed ratings (Par 92): **101,95,94,93,93 91,86,81,78,75 73,69,63,61**
toteswingers: 1&2 £2.30, 1&3 £19.00, 2&3 £10.00. CSF £7.63 TOTE £4.70: £1.50, £1.50, £3.80; EX 10.40.
Owner Dr Marwan Koukash **Bred** Skymarc Farm **Trained** Newmarket, Suffolk

FOCUS
A modest juvenile maiden in which those held up were at a notable disadvantage as once more the prominent racers dominated.

NOTEBOOK
Gabrial's Gift(IRE) ◆ relished stepping up a furlong on this AW debut and made it third time lucky with a decisive display. He disputed the early lead and once more proved free, but was therefore able to get an ideal sit through the race. He was travelling by far the best 2f out and found plenty when asked to pick up nearing the furling marker. He came right away and is clearly useful. His future probably lies with the handicapper, though, so it will be interesting to see what mark he is now allotted. (tchd 7-2)
Amoralist was a promising fourth on his debut on easy ground over this trip at Sandown and that form got a boost when the third won easily next time out. He was heavily backed, despite being housed on the outside, and lacked the pace to land a telling blow. This test proved too sharp, but he should get off the mark before too long and will be eligible for a mark after his next assignment. (op 11-10 tchd 6-5 in a place)
Young Prince(IRE) cut out the early running with the winner, also proving somewhat keen, and was firmly put in his place by that rival at the furlong marker. This was still a marked improvement on his debut effort and he's clearly going the right way. (op 25-1)
Jack Of Diamonds(IRE) ◆ fared best of the newcomers and would have likely been placed had he kept a straight line inside the final furlong. That was very likely down to inexperience and he travelled like a fair performer prior to being asked for his effort.
Shark In The Sea had finished nearer last than first in two previous outings on turf, so this was obviously a lot more like it from him and nurseries are now an option. Official explanation: stewards held an inquiry into why jockey appeared to drop his hands. jockey said he he was concerned about clipping heels with Young Prince who was drifting left.

5383 LAY BACK AND WIN AT BETDAQ.COM H'CAP (LONDON MILE QUALIFIER) 1m (P)
7:20 (7:22) (Class 4) (0-80,80) 3-Y-O+ **£4,075** (£1,212; £606; £303) **Stalls** Low

Form RPR

041 **1** **Catchanova (IRE)**[9] 5101 4-9-1 **71** 6ex .... NeilCallan 12 83+
(Eve Johnson Houghton) *hld up towards rr: rdn and prog over 2f out: chal over 1f out: led ins fnl f: edgd lft but styd on wl* **8/1**

-214 **2** ½ **Set Me Free (IRE)**[37] 4161 3-9-0 **76** .... KierenFallon 1 85+
(Luca Cumani) *sn wl in tch: rdn and prog over 2f out: led over 1f out: hdd ins fnl f: styd on but jst hld* **6/1**[3]

6630 **3** 1 ½ **Sakhee's Pearl**[55] 3549 5-9-6 **76** ....(b) DaneO'Neill 2 83
(Jo Crowley) *hld up in midfield: prog on inner over 2f out: rdn to chal and upsides over 1f out: edgd lft and one pce fnl f* **16/1**

0-00 **4** 2 **Caldercruix (USA)**[55] 3542 4-9-7 **77** .... SteveDrowne 7 79
(James Evans) *trckd ldrs: effrt over 2f out: rdn to chal wl over 1f out: one pce after: fading at fin* **20/1**

1125 **5** ½ **Powerful Presence (IRE)**[25] 4561 5-9-10 **80** .... JimCrowley 6 81
(David O'Meara) *hld up in midfield: rdn and prog over 2f out: cl enough over 1f out: nt qckn* **5/1**[2]

56/0 **6** nse **Doncosaque (IRE)**[33] 4278 5-9-5 **75** ....(t) ShaneKelly 13 76
(P J O'Gorman) *hld up in rr: rdn over 2f out: hanging but styd on fr jst over 1f out: nrst fin* **100/1**

3545 **7** 2 ½ **Count Bertoni (IRE)**[14] 4901 4-9-0 **70** .... JimmyFortune 8 66
(David O'Meara) *sn trckd ldng pair: chal and upsides wl over 1f out: wknd and eased ins fnl f* **9/2**[1]

0424 **8** 2 **Getcarter**[74] 2910 5-9-3 **73** .... LukeMorris 5 64
(John Best) *hld up in midfield: rdn over 2f out: sn no prog and btn* **20/1**

4056 **9** ½ **The Which Doctor**[14] 4921 6-9-1 **74** ....(e) RobertLButler(3) 14 64
(Richard Guest) *hld up last: rdn and no rspnse wl over 2f out: plugged on fnl f* **25/1**

-100 **10** nse **Tax Break**[14] 4921 4-9-7 **77** .... LeeNewman 10 67
(David Barron) *disp ld at decent pce: led 3f out: hdd wl over 1f out: wknd qckly fnl f* **20/1**

53 **11** nk **Junket**[9] 5100 4-8-13 **72** .... SeanLevey(3) 9 61
(Dr Jon Scargill) *chsd ldrs: rdn over 3f out: wknd jst over 2f out* **5/1**[2]

4042 **12** 2 ¼ **Tewin Wood**[47] 3805 4-9-6 **76** .... LiamJones 3 60
(Alan Bailey) *disp ld at decent pce to 3f out: wknd wl over 1f out* **11/1**

0042 **13** ½ **Satwa Laird**[14] 4926 5-9-6 **76** .... TedDurcan 4 59
(Ed Dunlop) *dwlt: a in rr: rdn and no prog over 2f out* **9/1**

1m 38.48s (-1.32) **Going Correction** -0.025s/f (Stan)
WFA 3 from 4yo+ 6lb **13** Ran SP% **120.2**
Speed ratings (Par 105): **105,104,103,101,100 100,97,95,95,95 95,92,92**
toteswingers: 1&2 £10.40, 1&3 £30.50, 2&3 £29.10. CSF £51.80 CT £790.94 TOTE £8.40: £2.90, £2.90, £6.20; EX 47.10.
Owner Andrew Wyer Darrell Blake Hugh Arthur **Bred** G J King **Trained** Blewbury, Oxon

The Form Book, Raceform Ltd, Compton, RG20 6NL

FOCUS
This was very competitive and sound run and there were any amount of chances in the home straight. Another personal best from the winner.

5384 BRITISH STALLION STUDS SUPPORTING BRITISH RACING E B F MAIDEN STKS 7f (P)
7:50 (7:51) (Class 5) 2-Y-O **£3,169** (£943; £471; £235) **Stalls** Low

Form				RPR
6	1		**Mr Maynard**[35] 4213 2-9-0 0 .... NeilCallan 6 (Sir Michael Stoute) *wnt rt s: trckd ldrs: decisive move to ld wl over 1f out: pushed out and styd on strly* **11/4**[2]	76+
	2	1 ¾	**Sholaan (IRE)** 2-9-0 0 .... LiamJones 2 (William Haggas) *t.k.h: hld up in midfield: outpcd over 2f out: prog wl over 1f out: styd on to take 2nd last strides* **9/1**[3]	71+
0	3	½	**Derfenna Art (IRE)**[16] 4857 2-9-0 0 .... JamesDoyle 9 (Seamus Durack) *chsd ldr 2f: wnt 2nd again over 2f out and sn chalng: wnr swept by wl over 1f out: chsd him after but readily hld: lost 2nd last strides* **25/1**	70
	4	¾	**Muntasir (IRE)** 2-9-0 0 .... TedDurcan 5 (Saeed Bin Suroor) *sn trckd ldrs: outpcd and hanging over 2f out: kpt on fnl f to take 4th nr fin* **5/4**[1]	71+
00	5	¾	**Next Cry (USA)**[16] 4857 2-9-0 0 .... DaneO'Neill 12 (Richard Hannon) *t.k.h: chsd ldr after 2f to over 2f out: cl up whn squeezed out wl over 1f out: fdd* **33/1**	66
	6	2 ¾	**Kiwayu** 2-9-0 0 .... KierenFallon 13 (Luca Cumani) *s.s: rcvrd qckly and prom after 2f: shkn up and outpcd over 2f out: no ch after: fended off clsrs fr rr fnl f* **20/1**	59
0	7	½	**Journalistic (USA)**[51] 3686 2-9-0 0 .... HayleyTurner 11 (Marcus Tregoning) *hld up in last pair: pushed along 3f out: styd on fnl f: no threat* **20/1**	58
0	8	hd	**Men Don't Cry (IRE)**[12] 5013 2-9-0 0 .... (v[1]) AdamKirby 14 (Ed Dunlop) *spd fr wd draw and led: hdd & wknd wl over 1f out* **100/1**	57?
	9	nk	**Rocky Reef** 2-9-0 0 .... JimmyFortune 4 (Andrew Balding) *s.s: t.k.h in last: detached over 2f out: styd on steadily fnl f* **50/1**	57+
0	10	½	**I'm Harry**[12] 4996 2-9-0 0 .... WilliamCarson 1 (Charles Hills) *t.k.h: hld up in rr: outpcd wl over 2f out: pushed along and one pce after* **16/1**	55
00	11	¾	**Songbird Blues**[16] 4864 2-8-9 0 .... RobertHavlin 3 (Mark Usher) *t.k.h: hld up towards rr: outpcd over 2f out but gng wl enough: shuffled along and nvr on terms after* **100/1**	48+
	12	nk	**Seven Veils (IRE)** 2-8-9 0 .... SebSanders 10 (Sir Mark Prescott Bt) *hld up towards rr: outpcd over 2f out: one pce and nvr on terms after* **33/1**	47
5	13	½	**Star Kingdom (IRE)**[9] 5111 2-8-11 0 .... SeanLevey(3) 8 (Robert Mills) *trckd ldrs: outpcd over 2f out: shkn up and steadily fdd* **14/1**	51

1m 27.26s (1.26) **Going Correction** -0.025s/f (Stan) 13 Ran SP% **116.9**
Speed ratings (Par 94): **91,89,88,87,86 83,83,82,82,81 81,80,80**
toteswingers: 1&2 £5.80, 1&3 £23.00, 2&3 £100.40. CSF £24.25 TOTE £4.00: £1.70, £1.60, £8.70; EX 28.50.
Owner Sir Evelyn De Rothschild **Bred** Southcourt Stud **Trained** Newmarket, Suffolk

FOCUS
This looked an above-average juvenile maiden, but it was a messy race and few got seriously involved due to the steady early tempo. Plenty of winners should emerge from this.

NOTEBOOK
Mr Maynard ◆ looked one to follow after finishing sixth on his debut at Sandown last month and he opened his account on this switch to Polytrack with a taking display. He proved somewhat free just off the pace early and got messed about a bit when things became tight nearing the turn. However, he still avoided more trouble than most and found himself ideally placed under his ever-dependable jockey 2f out. He motored once getting himself organised and could have been called the winner some way out. This good-looking colt should only improve as he steps up in trip and could be smart. (op 7-2)
Sholaan(IRE) ◆ was a big eye-catcher. He took time to get the hang of things and stormed home inside the final furlong, but the bird had already flown. This was a promising debut and he should be going one better in the coming weeks. (op 10-1)
Derfenna Art(IRE) was never far away and got the run of the race, but still made a bold bid. This was a big improvement on his debut at Windsor over 6f and, while he is probably more of one for nurseries, will be winning races in due course.
Muntasir(IRE) ◆, a half-brother to a dual 2yo winner for Godolphin, was bidding to extend his trainer's outstanding record with juveniles at this venue. He got a nightmare passage from the start on the inside, however, and that cost him. Looking at the way he responded to pressure off the home turn he would have surely gone close but for that and any losses are merely lent. Indeed he too could be very useful. (tchd 11-8)
Next Cry(USA) well beaten on his two previous outings on turf, was another who proved well suited by racing handy and is a little flattered. He still showed a lot more promise over the extra furlong, though, and looks one to side with when entering nurseries. (op 25-1)
Kiwayu ◆ wasn't done any favours with the draw on his debut and the market strongly suggested the initial experience would be needed. He ran accordingly, but did shape with promise and it wouldn't surprise to see him go very close next time. (op 16-1)

5385 BETDAQ MOBILE APPS H'CAP 6f (P)
8:20 (8:21) (Class 5) (0-75,75) 2-Y-O **£2,264** (£673; £336; £168) **Stalls** Low

Form				RPR
062	1		**Compton Target (IRE)**[13] 4947 2-9-2 **70** .... JamesDoyle 1 (Hans Adielsson) *led 1f: styd prom: led again jst over 2f out: hrd pressed 2f out: drvn out* **16/1**	73
453	2	¾	**Backtrade (IRE)**[16] 4857 2-9-7 **75** .... JimmyFortune 2 (Andrew Balding) *led after 1f to jst over 2f out: drvn to press wnr 1f out: hld last 75yds* **11/8**[1]	76
001	3	1 ¼	**Miserere Mei (IRE)**[19] 4756 2-8-11 **65** .... (p) KierenFallon 3 (Alan McCabe) *trckd ldrs: rdn 2f out: wnt 3rd 1f out: no imp on ldng pair* **7/1**	62
6630	4	¾	**Littlecote Lady**[14] 4922 2-8-3 **57** .... LukeMorris 8 (Mark Usher) *s.i.s: hld up in last pair: shkn up 2f out: styd on fnl f to take 4th nr fin* **40/1**	52
025	5	¾	**Flavius Victor (IRE)**[17] 4815 2-9-7 **75** .... DaneO'Neill 5 (Richard Hannon) *t.k.h: prom: wnt 2nd briefly over 3f out: nt qckn 2f out: fdd fnl f* **3/1**[2]	68
600	6	2 ½	**Chater Garden (IRE)**[17] 4823 2-8-3 **60** .... HarryBentley(3) 7 (Alan Jarvis) *t.k.h: hld up in last pair: no prog over 2f out: nvr on terms* **16/1**	45
543	7	¾	**Invincible Dream (IRE)**[44] 3921 2-9-1 **72** .... SeanLevey(3) 6 (Robert Mills) *t.k.h: hld up in tch: rdn and nt qckn 2f out: wknd fnl f* **13/2**[3]	55
4460	8	12	**Armiger**[20] 4704 2-8-8 **62** .... MartinDwyer 4 (William Muir) *in tch: rdn over 2f out: sn wknd: t.o* **12/1**	9

1m 13.77s (0.67) **Going Correction** -0.025s/f (Stan) 8 Ran SP% **114.8**
Speed ratings (Par 94): **94,93,91,90,89 86,85,69**
toteswingers: 1&2 £8.30, 1&3 £11.90, 2&3 £2.30. CSF £38.84 CT £178.31 TOTE £11.30: £4.60, £1.10, £1.20; EX 40.70.
Owner Erik Penser **Bred** R N Auld **Trained** Kingston Lisle, Oxon

FOCUS
A modest nursery.

NOTEBOOK
Compton Target(IRE), despite proving friendless in the market, shed his maiden tag at the fourth time of asking on this nursery debut under a straightforward ride. He tracked the leader and thus got very much the run of the race, but still saw it out nicely. This looks his ideal trip and he has evidently now found his sort of level.
Backtrade(IRE) proved all the rage ahead of this nursery debut and switch to Polytrack. He took a keen hold to post, though, and then proved far too headstrong once the stalls opened. His rider tried to get a breather into him nearing 2f out, but that enabled the winner to close on him and it was apparent soon after his was in trouble. He bravely rallied under pressure, but really he lost this inside the first furlong. Providing he learns to relax, he is sure to win one of these. (op 2-1)
Miserere Mei(IRE) won a seller in first-time cheekpieces at Lingfield 19 days earlier and, while this rates an improved effort in defeat, she does put the form into some perspective. (op 5-1)
Littlecote Lady would have gone closer had she not made a tardy start from the outside gate.
Flavius Victor(IRE), making his nursery debut, was another who proved too keen for his own good early on and didn't look too straightforward under pressure. (op 7-2 tchd 11-4)

5386 RACING@SKYSPORTS.COM MEDIAN AUCTION MAIDEN STKS 1m 4f (P)
8:50 (8:54) (Class 6) 3-5-Y-O **£1,617** (£481; £240; £120) **Stalls** Centre

Form				RPR
52	1		**My Heart's On Fire (IRE)**[12] 4985 3-8-9 0 .... SebSanders 10 (Tom Dascombe) *hld up in tch: rdn over 2f out: grad clsd u.p over 1f out: styd on to ld last stride* **2/1**[2]	78
4232	2	nse	**Sally Friday (IRE)**[18] 4800 3-8-9 72 .... (p) LukeMorris 6 (Peter Winkworth) *lft in ld over 9f out: hdd 7f out: led again over 2f out gng easily: rdn over 1f out and kpt on same pce: hdd last stride* **6/4**[1]	78
02	3	nk	**Lily In Pink**[17] 4826 3-8-9 0 .... JimCrowley 7 (Jonathan Portman) *t.k.h: hld up in tch: rdn to chse ldr wl over 1f out: clsd fnl f but lost 2nd nr fin* **3/1**[3]	77+
04	4	12	**Colliers Castle (IRE)**[8] 5140 5-9-5 0 .... ShaneKelly 1 (Lisa Williamson) *prom: led 7f out to over 2f out: wknd over 1f out* **25/1**	58
	5	8	**Cardi King** 3-9-0 0 .... NeilCallan 3 (Ian Wood) *awkward s: chsd ldrs: in tch over 2f out: sn wknd* **20/1**	50
00	6	5	**Raynell**[18] 4800 3-9-0 0 .... AdamKirby 9 (Noel Quinlan) *in tch in rr: pushed along 5f out: wknd 3f out* **66/1**	42
65	7	10	**Avon Blaise**[17] 4826 4-9-5 0 .... DaneO'Neill 8 (Peter Hedger) *dwlt: rdn in last at 1/2-way despite modest pce: sn t.o* **33/1**	21
0	U		**Essex Boy**[66] 3206 3-8-11 0 .... (e) RobertLButler(3) 5 (Richard Guest) *led and clr: hanging lft after 1f: veered towards exit to horsewalk and uns rdr over 9f out* **50/1**	—

2m 36.69s (2.19) **Going Correction** -0.025s/f (Stan)
WFA 3 from 4yo+ 10lb 8 Ran SP% **113.3**
Speed ratings (Par 101): **91,90,90,82,77 74,67,—**
toteswingers: 1&2 £1.10, 1&3 £1.40, 2&3 £1.20. CSF £5.04 TOTE £1.90: £1.10, £1.10, £1.10; EX 6.60.
Owner W Chow **Bred** Mount Coote Stud And M Johnston **Trained** Malpas, Cheshire
■ Stewards' Enquiry : Seb Sanders three day ban; excessive use of whip (7th-9th Sept)

FOCUS
There was a blanket finish between the three market leaders in this ordinary fillies' maiden, who finished well clear, and the form is straightforward with the front three close to therir marks.

5387 SKYSPORTS.COM COMPETITION 03.09.11 H'CAP 6f (P)
9:20 (9:22) (Class 5) (0-70,69) 3-Y-O+ **£2,264** (£673; £336; £168) **Stalls** Low

Form				RPR
063	1		**Earlsmedic**[28] 4434 6-9-3 **67** .... (v) WilliamCarson 1 (Stuart Williams) *hld up on inner: prog 2f out: rdn to ld jst over 1f out: styd on wl* **9/4**[1]	78
000	2	1	**Tislaam (IRE)**[11] 5053 4-9-2 **66** .... (p) KierenFallon 5 (Alan McCabe) *t.k.h: hld up bhd ldrs: prog to chal over 1f out: [illegible] fnl f: nt qckn* **9/4**[1]	74
32-4	3	nk	**Daffydowndilly**[28] 4437 3-9-2 **69** .... JimmyFortune 4 (Hughie Morrison) *awkward s: hld up in last: prog on wd outside fr 2f out: styd on to take 3rd fnl f: unable to chal* **7/1**[2]	76
0160	4	½	**Danzoe (IRE)**[2] 5326 4-9-5 **69** .... JamesDoyle 6 (Christine Dunnett) *hld up in rr: prog on outer 2f out: nt qckn over 1f out: kpt on same pce after* **20/1**	74
00	5	2	**Style Margi (IRE)**[13] 4973 3-9-2 **69** .... PatCosgrave 8 (Ed de Giles) *led 1f: styd prom: rdn to ld wl over 1f out to jst over 1f out: wknd fnl f* **33/1**	68
053	6	nk	**Towy Boy (IRE)**[16] 4850 6-9-0 **64** .... (bt) NeilCallan 11 (Ian Wood) *plld hrd: prom: chal gng easily 2f out: nudged along and fdd fnl f* **16/1**	62
0012	7	½	**Valmina**[16] 4850 4-9-0 **64** .... (t) LukeMorris 3 (Tony Carroll) *nvr bttr than midfield: cl enough 2f out: sn nt qckn and outpcd* **8/1**[3]	60
4305	8	1 ¼	**Imjin River (IRE)**[8] 5138 4-9-1 **65** .... (b[1]) SebSanders 9 (Mark H Tompkins) *dwlt: racd wd in midfield: nt qckn and lost pl 2f out: nvr on terms after* **20/1**	57
0300	9	1 ¼	**Dvinsky (USA)**[14] 4910 10-9-2 **66** .... (b) JimmyQuinn 2 (Michael Squance) *hld up in last trio: no prog 2f out: n.d after* **14/1**	54
4006	10	½	**Pippa's Gift**[4] 5279 3-9-1 **68** .... MartinDwyer 7 (William Muir) *sn prom on outer: wknd fr 2f out* **22/1**	55
3366	11	4	**Super Frank (IRE)**[158] 904 8-9-0 **64** .... KirstyMilczarek 12 (Zoe Davison) *led after 1f to wl over 1f out: wknd qckly* **66/1**	38

1m 12.49s (-0.61) **Going Correction** -0.025s/f (Stan)
WFA 3 from 4yo+ 3lb 11 Ran SP% **116.0**
Speed ratings (Par 103): **103,101,101,100,97 97,96,95,93,92 87**
toteswingers: 1&2 £2.60, 1&3 £6.00, 2&3 £4.10. CSF £5.96 CT £29.15 TOTE £4.60: £2.40, £1.02, £3.00; EX 11.00.
Owner Hamill, Ostlere & George **Bred** W N Greig **Trained** Newmarket, Suffolk

FOCUS
Despite this moderate sprint handicap seeing plenty of chances in the home straight, the market principals still fought it out and the form is sound. The winner is back to last autumn's form.
Dvinsky(USA) Official explanation: jopckey said gelding was slowly away.
T/Plt: £45.70 to a £1 stake. Pool of £55,917.79 - 892.48 winning tickets. T/Qpdt: £17.90 to a £1 stake. Pool of £4,170.23 - 171.90 winning tickets. JN

5243 WOLVERHAMPTON (A.W) (L-H)

Wednesday, August 24

OFFICIAL GOING: Standard

Wind: Light to moderate, behind Weather: showers

5388 HOTEL & CONFERENCING AT WOLVERHAMPTON H'CAP 5f 216y(P)

6:10 (6:10) (Class 6) (0-60,60) 3-Y-O **£1,704** (£503; £251) **Stalls** Low

Form RPR

2401 **1** **Dangerous Illusion (IRE)**[21] 4684 3-8-9 **48** AndreaAtzeni 3 57
(Michael Quinn) *led for 1f: chsd ldr after tl regained ld wl over 1f out: wnt clr and in command ins fnl f: r.o wl* **16/1**

-024 **2** 2 ½ **Deslaya (IRE)**[12] 5019 3-9-3 **56** NickyMackay 7 57
(Chris Wall) *towards rr: hdwy on inner 2f out: styd on to take 2nd over 1f out: no imp on wnr fnl f* **10/1**

3243 **3** 1 ¼ **Dictionary**[9] 5121 3-9-7 **60** (bt[1]) JamieSpencer 1 57
(William Haggas) *blindfold removed late and s.s: in rr: rdn and hdwy whn swtchd rt over 1f out: styd on and clsd ins fnl f: nrst fin* **2/1**[1]

6006 **4** nk **Consistant**[14] 4924 3-9-4 **57** J-PGuillambert 4 53
(Brian Baugh) *chsd ldrs: pushed along 3f out: clsd and nt clr run briefly 2f out: rdn and chsd wnr briefly over 1f out: no imp: kpt on same pce ins fnl f* **25/1**

0414 **5** 2 ½ **Silca Conegliano (IRE)**[8] 5138 3-8-10 **52** (v) MartinHarley(3) 5 40
(Mick Channon) *chsd ldrs: rdn over 1f out: one pce and no imp fnl f* **12/1**

0433 **6** ¾ **Valeo Si Vales (IRE)**[8] 5143 3-9-7 **60** (b) EddieAhern 8 46
(Jamie Osborne) *midfield: rdn 2f out: one pce fnl f: nvr able to chal* **9/4**[2]

00-0 **7** 2 ½ **Melody Belle (IRE)**[39] 4112 3-8-10 **49** (t) StevieDonohoe 10 27
(Tobias B P Coles) *midfield: pushed along and outpcd 3f out: bhd fnl 2f* **28/1**

6666 **8** 2 **Running Water**[12] 5009 3-8-0 **46** oh1 VictorSantos(7) 9 17
(Hugh McWilliams) *s.s: a towards rr: outpcd over 2f out* **50/1**

0350 **9** 7 **Too Many Questions (IRE)**[4] 5274 3-9-6 **59** (b[1]) GeorgeBaker 6 —
(David Evans) *gd spd: led after 1f: 5 l clr over 3f out: reduced advantage 2f out: hdd wl over 1f out: sn wknd* **6/1**[3]

365 **U** **Chester Deelyte (IRE)**[4] 5274 3-8-12 **51** (v) SaleemGolam 2 —
(Lisa Williamson) *stmbld and uns rdr leaving stalls* **20/1**

1m 14.78s (-0.22) **Going Correction** -0.075s/f (Stan) **10** Ran SP% **115.1**

Speed ratings (Par 98): **98,94,93,92,89 88,84,82,72,—**

toteswingers: 1&2 £14.50, 1&3 £8.20, 2&3 £5.70. CSF £154.52 CT £472.78 TOTE £22.80: £2.90, £3.60, £1.10; EX 170.90.

Owner M Quinn **Bred** Miss Niamh Hackett **Trained** Newmarket, Suffolk

FOCUS

Mainly exposed performers in a moderate opener. The gallop was a decent one and the third looks better than the bare form. The winner raced centre-to-far side in the straight and the form is not rated too positively.

Dictionary Official explanation: jockey said that the blindfold, although loosened ready for removal, had caught on the geldings blinkers.

Chester Deelyte(IRE) Official explanation: jockey said filly pecked upon jumping out of stalls.

5389 GREAT OFFERS AT WOLVERHAMPTON-RACECOURSE.CO.UK H'CAP 1m 5f 194y(P)

6:40 (6:40) (Class 5) (0-75,75) 3-Y-O+ **£2,264** (£673; £336; £168) **Stalls** Low

Form RPR

5560 **1** **Raktiman (IRE)**[13] 4974 4-9-3 **64** (p) RichardKingscote 6 74
(Tom Dascombe) *midfield: hdwy 2f out: styd on to ld wl ins fnl f: kpt up to work cl home* **28/1**

0-33 **2** ½ **Moment Juste**[65] 3224 3-9-1 **74** WilliamBuick 12 83
(John Gosden) *s.i.s: sn in midfield: hdwy to ld after 6f: hdd over 6f out: remained handy: pushed along 3f out: rdn to ld over 1f out: hdd wl ins fnl f: hld fnl strides* **11/4**[1]

0054 **3** 3 ½ **Sula Two**[11] 5050 4-9-6 **67** DavidProbert 2 71
(Ron Hodges) *hld up: rdn and hdwy on outer 2f out: styd on ins fnl f: nt rch ldrs* **20/1**

0200 **4** nk **Accumulate**[20] 4719 8-9-12 **73** J-PGuillambert 8 77
(Bill Moore) *midfield: hdwy after 6f: chsd ldrs: rdn 3f out: nt qckn over 1f out: kpt on same pce ins fnl f* **16/1**

21-3 **5** ¾ **Mazagee (FR)**[19] 4752 3-9-1 **74** RichardMullen 4 78+
(David Lanigan) *hld up: hdwy whn nt clr run over 1f out: styd on ins fnl f: nt rch ldrs* **7/1**

4112 **6** ¾ **Lemon Drop Red (USA)**[29] 4407 3-9-1 **74** FrederikTylicki 7 76+
(Ed Dunlop) *hld up: hdwy on outer 3f out: rdn and chsd ldrs over 1f out: one pce fnl 100yds* **11/2**[2]

-026 **7** 3 ¾ **Quiz Mistress**[43] 3959 3-9-2 **75** EddieAhern 1 74+
(Gerard Butler) *hld up: hdwy on inner 2f out: nt clr run over 1f out tl eased and swtchd rt ins fnl f: nvr a danger* **14/1**

101 **8** ½ **Sennockian Storm (USA)**[6] 5210 4-8-12 **64** 6ex DarylByrne(5) 10 60
(Mark Johnston) *prom: rdn over 1f out: wknd ins fnl f* **6/1**[3]

0400 **9** 3 **Storm Hawk (IRE)**[9] 5102 4-9-5 **69** (p) JohnFahy(3) 13 61
(Pat Eddery) *s.i.s: bustled along to sn ld: hdd after 6f: remained prom: rdn 2f out: wknd over 1f out* **16/1**

0520 **10** 1 ½ **Cloudy Bay (USA)**[30] 4385 4-8-13 **65** (p) RyanPowell(5) 5 55
(John Flint) *led early: remained handy tl lost pl 6f out: bhd and no imp after* **25/1**

2545 **11** 2 ¼ **See The Smile (USA)**[21] 4664 3-8-10 **69** JamieSpencer 9 55
(Jim Boyle) *hld up: hdwy to go prom after 4f: led over 6f out: rdn 2f out: hdd over 1f out: sn wknd: eased whn btn ins fnl f* **14/1**

-036 **12** 2 ¼ **Dynamic Idol (USA)**[34] 4237 4-10-0 **75** GeorgeBaker 11 58+
(Mikael Magnusson) *chsd ldrs: rdn 2f out: wknd over 1f out: eased whn btn ins fnl f* **8/1**

1045 **13** 2 **Merton Lady**[35] 4209 3-8-4 **63** AndreaAtzeni 3 44
(John Flint) *racd keenly: hld up: struggling over 3f out: nvr on terms* **22/1**

3m 4.03s (-1.97) **Going Correction** -0.075s/f (Stan)

WFA 3 from 4yo+ 12lb **13** Ran SP% **121.5**

Speed ratings (Par 103): **102,101,99,99,99 98,96,96,94,93 92,91,89**

toteswingers: 1&2 £29.80, 1&3 £26.70, 2&3 £21.70. CSF £101.64 CT £1656.74 TOTE £74.70: £17.30, £1.80, £4.30; EX 264.10.

Owner Daniel Perchard **Bred** Kilbride Stud Ltd **Trained** Malpas, Cheshire

■ Stewards' Enquiry : Richard Kingscote one-day ban; careless riding (7th Sept)

FOCUS

A fair handicap for the grade run at just an ordinary gallop. The winner ended up towards the inside rail in the closing stages and the first two pulled clear.

5390 RINGSIDE CONFERENCE SUITE (S) STKS 1m 1f 103y(P)

7:10 (7:10) (Class 6) 3-Y-O+ **£1,636** (£483; £241) **Stalls** Low

Form RPR

5205 **1** **Jordaura**[12] 4990 5-9-11 **72** DavidProbert 3 72
(Tony Carroll) *hld up in rr: hdwy over 1f out: r.o to ld wl ins fnl f: wl on top at fin* **5/2**[1]

004/ **2** 1 ¼ **Agilete**[634] 7583 9-9-5 **77** SaleemGolam 7 63
(Lydia Pearce) *trckd ldrs: rdn to chal over 1f out: led ins fnl f: sn hdd: outpcd by wnr towards fin* **5/1**

4433 **3** 1 **Dream Of Fortune (IRE)**[9] 5112 7-9-5 **56** (bt) StevieDonohoe 6 61
(David Evans) *midfield: hdwy gng wl to chse ldrs over 1f out: rdn ins fnl f: kpt on towards fin: nt gng pce to mount serious chal cl home* **15/2**

4051 **4** ¾ **Empress Leizu (IRE)**[14] 4920 4-9-3 **57** MartinHarley(3) 1 60
(Tony Carroll) *led: rdn over 1f out: hdd ins fnl f: no ex towards fin* **13/2**

000 **5** nk **Smarty Sam (USA)**[13] 4945 4-9-5 **56** (b[1]) RussKennemore 2 59
(Paul Midgley) *midfield: rdn over 2f out: outpcd over 1f out: kpt on ins fnl f: nt gng pce to chal* **22/1**

3515 **6** ¾ **Opus Maximus (IRE)**[14] 4897 6-9-11 **67** (p) StephenCraine 4 63
(Jennie Candlish) *hld up in rr: effrt and hung lft over 1f out: no imp on ldrs ins fnl f* **9/2**[3]

040 **7** 20 **Ahlawy (IRE)**[21] 4679 8-9-11 **81** (bt) AndreaAtzeni 9 21
(Frank Sheridan) *racd keenly: w ldr: rdn and lost 2nd over 2f out: sn wknd* **4/1**[2]

0606 **8** 27 **Henrys Air**[9] 5112 3-9-4 **52** (bt[1]) JamieGoldstein 8 —
(David Bridgwater) *plld hrd: prom tl rdn and wknd over 3f out: wl bhd over 2f out: t.o* **50/1**

2m 1.16s (-0.54) **Going Correction** -0.075s/f (Stan)

WFA 3 from 4yo+ 7lb **8** Ran SP% **114.8**

Speed ratings (Par 101): **99,97,97,96,96 95,77,53**

toteswingers: 1&2 £2.70, 1&3 £3.60, 2&3 £14.50. CSF £15.40 TOTE £3.70: £2.20, £1.10, £3.20; EX 20.30.The winner was sold to Gay Kellaway for 7,000gns.

Owner Carl Hodgson **Bred** Pendley Farm **Trained** Cropthorne, Worcs

FOCUS

A couple of fair sorts and a race run at an ordinary gallop. The winner raced centre-to-far side in the straight and the form is best viewed around the third.

Ahlawy(IRE) Official explanation: jockey said gelding ran too freely.

5391 THE BLACK COUNTRY'S ONLY RACECOURSE FILLIES' H'CAP 1m 1f 103y(P)

7:40 (7:40) (Class 5) (0-75,74) 3-Y-O+ **£2,264** (£673; £336; £168) **Stalls** Low

Form RPR

3264 **1** **Snowy Peak**[19] 4745 3-8-2 **58** (t) JohnFahy(3) 7 69
(Jeremy Noseda) *midfield: u.p fr 3f out: hdwy over 1f out: styd on to ld wl ins fnl f: drvn out* **12/1**

2520 **2** 1 ¼ **Stargazing (IRE)**[99] 2176 5-9-2 **62** AndreaAtzeni 9 70
(Marco Botti) *in tch: effrt 2f out: rdn to ld over 1f out: hdd wl ins fnl f: hld towards fin* **4/1**[2]

064 **3** hd **Convention**[41] 4014 3-9-2 **69** JamieSpencer 5 77
(Ed Dunlop) *hld up in rr: rdn 2f out: hdwy ins fnl f: styd on: nt gng pce to mount serious chal* **7/2**[1]

6364 **4** 1 **Marjury Daw (IRE)**[15] 4877 5-10-0 **74** FrederikTylicki 2 79
(James Given) *led early: trckd ldrs: lost pl over 4f out: in midfield: effrt over 1f out: styd on ins fnl f: nt gng pce to chal ldrs towards fin* **7/1**

3034 **5** 3 ½ **To The Spring**[10] 5082 3-8-12 **68** AdamBeschizza(3) 8 66
(William Haggas) *hld up: rdn and sme hdwy over 1f out: no imp: one pce ins fnl f* **9/2**[3]

1-24 **6** ½ **Midas Moment**[14] 4931 3-9-4 **71** GeorgeBaker 4 68
(William Muir) *prom: led narrowly 2f out: rdn and hdd over 1f out: wknd fnl 100yds* **9/1**

2102 **7** ½ **Full Bloom**[20] 4713 3-9-5 **72** (b) EddieAhern 3 68
(Gerard Butler) *prom: rdn 4f out: wknd over 1f out:* **7/1**

0-65 **8** 4 ½ **Fluvial (IRE)**[16] 4845 3-8-11 **69** DarylByrne(5) 10 56
(Mark Johnston) *wnt sltly rt leaving stalls: sn led: hdd narrowly 2f out: sn rdn: wknd ins fnl f* **20/1**

2503 **9** 10 **Symphonic Dancer (USA)**[16] 4865 4-9-7 **67** J-PGuillambert 1 33+
(Brian Baugh) *hld up: pushed along 3f out: n.m.r over 1f out whn no imp: sn eased* **14/1**

2m 0.28s (-1.42) **Going Correction** -0.075s/f (Stan)

WFA 3 from 4yo+ 7lb **9** Ran SP% **114.5**

Speed ratings (Par 100): **103,101,101,100,97 97,96,92,83**

toteswingers: 1&2 £4.20, 1&3 £8.40, 2&3 £3.60. CSF £59.07 CT £206.74 TOTE £5.50: £1.60, £2.30, £1.60; EX 87.50.

Owner Newsells Park Stud **Bred** Newsells Park Stud Limited **Trained** Newmarket, Suffolk

FOCUS

A fair fillies' handicap but one in which the gallop soon steadied. The winner came down the centre and the first four finished clear. The form is rated slightly positively with the winner and third unexposed.

Symphonic Dancer(USA) Official explanation: jockey said filly hung badly left handed.

5392 WOLVERHAMPTON-RACECOURSE.CO.UK H'CAP 1m 141y(P)

8:10 (8:10) (Class 4) (0-80,79) 3-Y-O **£3,234** (£962; £481; £240) **Stalls** Low

Form RPR

3354 **1** **Climaxfortackle (IRE)**[9] 5121 3-8-5 **63** (v) NickyMackay 4 71
(Derek Shaw) *stdd s: hld up: hdwy wl over 1f out: styd on ins fnl f to get up in fnl stride* **8/1**[3]

2301 **2** hd **Labore**[27] 4479 3-9-7 **79** (b) AndreaAtzeni 8 86
(Marco Botti) *a.p: led over 2f out: kicked over 2 l clr wl over 1f out: u.p whn pressed wl ins fnl f: sn edgd lft: hdd fnl stride* **4/1**[2]

6035 **3** hd **Full Pelt (USA)**[18] 4812 3-8-2 **60** (v) FrannyNorton 3 67
(Tom Dascombe) *dwlt: hld up in rr: hdwy 4f out: rdn to chse ldr 2f out: chalng wl ins fnl f: sn bmpd: hld fnl strides* **20/1**

-003 **4** 3 ¾ **Tedsmore Dame**[14] 4921 3-9-0 **72** (t) RichardKingscote 6 70
(James Unett) *trckd ldrs: rdn over 1f out: no imp on ldrs and one pce ins fnl f* **14/1**

0- **5** 1 ¼ **Newlands Princess (IRE)**[55] 3564 3-9-0 **72** RobertWinston 1 68
(Ollie Pears) *racd keenly: prom: lost pl 4f out: effrt over 1f out: no imp on ldrs* **4/1**[2]

2100 **6** 3 ½ **Hugely Exciting**[47] 3815 3-9-1 **73** (p) LiamKeniry 2 60
(J S Moore) *hld up in tch: rdn wl over 1f out: no imp* **11/1**

4221 **7** 13 **Lucky Legs (IRE)**[16] 4861 3-9-6 **78** MichaelHills 7 36
(Charles Hills) *led: pushed along and hdd over 2f out: wknd over 1f out* **7/2**[1]

021 **8** *16* **Orpen'Arry (IRE)**[13] 4970 3-9-4 **76**.................................. JamieSpencer 5 —
(Andrew Haynes) *racd keenly: prom tl rdn and wknd 2f out: eased whn btn fnl f* **7/2**[1]
1m 49.43s (-1.07) **Going Correction** -0.075s/f (Stan) **8** Ran SP% **115.3**
Speed ratings (Par 102): **101,100,100,97,96 93,81,67**
toteswingers: 1&2 £4.50, 1&3 £32.80, 2&3 £28.00. CSF £40.33 CT £627.11 TOTE £13.40: £2.70, £2.20, £4.60; EX 54.20.
Owner A Flint **Bred** Pat Fullam **Trained** Sproxton, Leics

■ Stewards' Enquiry : Andrea Atzeni four-day ban; two for careless riding, two for using whip with excessive frequency down the shoulder (Sep 7-9, 11)

FOCUS
A fair handicap but one in which a couple of the market leaders disappointed. A reasonable early gallop steadied after around 2f before picking up again turning for home and the first three raced towards the far side in the closing stages. The form is taken at something like face value.

5393 DINE IN HORIZONS MEDIAN AUCTION MAIDEN STKS 7f 32y(P)
8:40 (8:40) (Class 6) 2-Y-O **£1,704** (£503; £251) **Stalls** High

Form RPR
05 **1** **Travelling**[12] 5011 2-8-12 0.. MichaelHills 2 72
(J W Hills) *racd keenly: chsd ldrs: wnt 2nd wl over 1f out: r.o to ld wl ins fnl f: on top cl home* **7/2**[2]
5 **2** *nk* **Chelsea Mick**[20] 4714 2-9-3 0...................................... GrahamGibbons 5 76
(Ed McMahon) *led: rdn over 1f out: hdd wl ins fnl f: jst hld cl home* **8/1**
4 **3** *1 ¼* **Final Delivery**[20] 4708 2-9-3 0.. AndreaAtzeni 3 73
(Marco Botti) *midfield: hdwy on inner over 1f out: chsd ldng 2 jst over 1f out: styd on but unable to chal* **22/1**
4 *1 ½* **Dark Falcon (IRE)** 2-9-3 0.. WilliamBuick 7 70
(Ed Dunlop) *chsd ldrs: rdn over 1f out: styd on same pce ins fnl f: nvr able to land a blow* **11/2**[3]
6 **5** *1* **Ironically (IRE)**[18] 4804 2-8-12 0.................................... RichardMullen 8 62
(David Lanigan) *midfield: hdwy over 3f out: effrt on outer whn chsng ldrs 2f out: wknd 1f out* **5/2**[1]
202 **6** *½* **Rockme Cockney**[16] 4853 2-8-12 75.......................... RoystonFfrench 4 61
(Jeremy Gask) *chsd ldr tl rdn wl over 1f out: wknd fnl 100yds* **5/2**[1]
65 **7** *6* **Astonished Harry (GER)**[14] 4919 2-9-0 0.................. PaulPickard(3) 1 51
(Reg Hollinshead) *hld up: pushed along 2f out: nvr a threat* **40/1**
0 **8** *5* **Three Tenors**[7] 5170 2-9-3 0.. LiamKeniry 9 39
(J S Moore) *hld up: pushed along over 2f out: nvr a threat* **80/1**
0 **9** *4* **Arrow Lake (FR)**[35] 4205 2-8-12 0.................................. JamieSpencer 6 24
(Noel Quinlan) *s.i.s: a bhd: nvr on terms: eased whn wl btn ins fnl f* **12/1**
1m 30.52s (0.92) **Going Correction** -0.075s/f (Stan) **9** Ran SP% **121.6**
Speed ratings (Par 92): **91,90,89,87,86 85,78,73,68**
toteswingers: 1&2 £10.80, 1&3 £12.60, 2&3 £11.70. CSF £32.86 TOTE £4.40: £2.30, £1.10, £3.90; EX 35.90.
Owner Longview Stud & Bloodstock Ltd **Bred** Longview Stud & Bloodstock Ltd **Trained** Upper Lambourn, Berks

FOCUS
Just an ordinary maiden. The gallop was moderate and the winner raced towards the far rail in the straight.

NOTEBOOK
Travelling had shown ability at a modest level on both her turf starts at Newmarket and she bettered those efforts in this less-competitive event on this AW debut. She will be equally effective over 1m and may be able to improve again in ordinary nursery company. (op 4-1 tchd 5-1 and 10-3)

Chelsea Mick had the run of the race and stepped up a fair way on the form shown over 1m on his debut at Haydock. Things were in his favour this time but he should be able to pick up a minor event on this evidence. (op 12-1)

Final Delivery stepped up a fair way on the form shown on his debut at Folkestone. He should have no problems with 1m (dam stayed middle distances) and will be one to take into handicap company in due course. (tchd 25-1)

Dark Falcon(IRE), a 62,000gns half-brother to a dual Wolverhampton (up to 1m1f) winner True Pleasure, showed ability at a modest level on this racecourse debut against more experienced rivals. He'll be suited by 1m and should be able to pick up a small event. (op 7-1)

Ironically(IRE), having her first run on an artificial surface, failed to build on the form shown on her debut but she was by no means disgraced and she looks the type to fare best over further once qualified for a handicap mark. (tchd 11-4)

Rockme Cockney raced with the choke out and was below the form shown on Polytrack on her debut and at Thirsk over this trip on her previous start. She should be able to pick up a small event but is likely to remain vulnerable to the better sorts in this grade. (op 11-4 tchd 7-2 and 9-4)

Arrow Lake(FR) Official explanation: jockey said filly ran too freely.

5394 SPONSOR A RACE BY CALLING 01902 390000 H'CAP 7f 32y(P)
9:10 (9:10) (Class 6) (0-60,60) 3-Y-O+ **£1,704** (£503; £251) **Stalls** High

Form RPR
5000 **1** **Gazboolou**[17] 4822 7-9-1 **53**.. RichardKingscote 1 63
(David Pinder) *chsd ldrs: rdn over 2f out: effrt to chal over 1f out: r.o to ld ins fnl f: gamely* **8/1**
0050 **2** *hd* **Peter Tchaikovsky**[49] 3733 5-8-12 **53**.......................... PaulPickard(3) 8 62
(Ian McInnes) *chsd ldr: rdn to ld over 1f out: hdd ins fnl f: r.o for press but hld cl home* **40/1**
4 **3** *1 ¾* **Tudor Prince (IRE)**[50] 3720 7-9-3 **55**........................ RoystonFfrench 2 59
(Tony Carroll) *racd keenly: in tch: effrt on inner over 1f out: chsd ldrs ins fnl f: no imp fnl 50yds* **7/1**
4523 **4** *1 ¼* **Jonnie Skull (IRE)**[3] 5298 5-9-5 **57**............................(vt) JamieSpencer 3 58+
(Phil McEntee) *s.i.s: hld up in rr: rdn and hdwy over 1f out: styd on ins fnl f: gng on at fin* **3/1**[2]
-000 **5** *½* **July Days (IRE)**[13] 4949 5-9-8 **60**.................................. KellyHarrison 11 60
(Brian Baugh) *hld up: rdn over 1f out: edgd rt ins fnl f: styd on towards fin: nt quite gng pce to rch ldrs* **20/1**
4141 **6** *½* **Sopran Nad (ITY)**[6] 5214 7-9-5 **57** 6ex...................(b) AndreaAtzeni 10 55
(Frank Sheridan) *led: rdn and hdd over 1f out: fdd fnl 75yds* **11/4**[1]
0542 **7** *hd* **Wandering Lad**[28] 4437 3-9-1 **58**.. MickyFenton 7 54
(Paul Midgley) *racd keenly in tch: effrt over 2f out: one pce ins fnl f* **25/1**
00 **8** *½* **Atyaab**[18] 4780 4-9-6 **58**... RobertWinston 4 54
(Alan Swinbank) *hld up: hdwy over 1f out: kpt on tl one pce fnl 100yds* **25/1**
5444 **9** *hd* **West Side (IRE)**[14] 4911 3-9-2 **59**...........................(vt) WilliamBuick 9 53
(Jeremy Noseda) *hld up: rdn 2f out: nvr able to trble ldrs* **4/1**[3]
0663 **10** *3 ½* **Concrete Jungle (IRE)**[7] 5165 3-9-3 **60**........................... MartinLane 6 44
(Andrew Haynes) *sn pushed along towards rr: nvr on terms* **9/1**

2252 **11** *4* **Miss Firefly**[11] 5038 6-9-5 **57**...(p) DavidProbert 5 33
(Ron Hodges) *racd keenly: chsd ldrs: rdn over 1f out: wknd over 1f out* **10/1**
1m 28.93s (-0.67) **Going Correction** -0.075s/f (Stan)
WFA 3 from 4yo+ 5lb **11** Ran SP% **129.3**
Speed ratings (Par 101): **100,99,97,96,95 95,94,94,94,90 85**
toteswingers: 1&2 £38.90, 1&3 £10.90, 2&3 £70.40. CSF £312.72 CT £2415.36 TOTE £8.30: £3.80, £12.10, £3.00; EX 301.60.
Owner Mrs Angela Pinder **Bred** Cheveley Park Stud Ltd **Trained** Kingston Lisle, Oxon

FOCUS
A moderate finale but, although the gallop seemed reasonable, those up with the pace held sway. The winner raced close to the inside rail in the straight. The form is rated around the third's winter form.
Wandering Lad Official explanation: jockey said gelding hung left in the straight.
Miss Firefly Official explanation: jockey said mare hung right handed.
T/Plt: £247.70 to a £1 stake. Pool of £68,591.73 - 202.13 winning tickets. T/Qpdt: £61.00 to a £1 stake. Pool of £5,568.40 - 67.50 winning tickets. DO

5395 - 5397a (Foreign Racing) - See Raceform Interactive

5161 CARLISLE (R-H)
Thursday, August 25

OFFICIAL GOING: Good (good to soft in places; 7.8)
Wind: Almost nil Weather: Cloudy, bright

5398 WATCH RACING UK ON SKY 432 MEDIAN AUCTION MAIDEN STKS 5f 193y
2:10 (2:11) (Class 5) 2-Y-O **£2,385** (£704; £352) **Stalls** Low

Form RPR
1 **Trumpet Voluntary (IRE)** 2-9-3 0................................ TonyHamilton 3 78+
(Richard Fahey) *towards rr and sn pushed along: effrt over 2f out: led ins fnl f: kpt on strly* **33/1**
23 **2** *1* **Star City (IRE)**[31] 4377 2-9-3 0.. TomEaves 6 75
(Michael Dods) *trckd ldrs: rdn and outpcd 2f out: rallied and chsd wnr wl ins fnl f: r.o* **4/1**[1]
3 **3** *nk* **Indego Blues**[36] 4192 2-9-3 0... AdrianNicholls 7 74
(David Nicholls) *towards rr: hdwy on outside 1/2-way: effrt and led over 1f out: edgd rt and hdd ins fnl f: r.o* **4/1**[1]
235 **4** *½* **Pitt Rivers**[48] 3810 2-9-0 75..(v[1]) MartinHarley(3) 5 72
(Mick Channon) *hld up in tch: effrt and drvn 2f out: kpt on ins fnl f: nrst fin* **4/1**[1]
3032 **5** *1* **Just Like Heaven (IRE)**[12] 5058 2-9-3 69......................... DavidAllan 10 69
(Tim Easterby) *led to over 1f out: rdn and kpt on ins fnl f: nt gng pce to chal* **9/2**[2]
05 **6** *4 ½* **Celestial Dawn**[12] 5058 2-8-12 0.................................... PJMcDonald 12 50
(John Weymes) *trckd ldrs tl rdn and wknd over 1f out* **25/1**
7 *½* **Baileys Over Ice** 2-8-12 0... FrederikTylicki 15 48+
(James Given) *bhd: rn green and outpcd 1/2-way: styd on ins fnl f: nvr rchd ldrs* **66/1**
5 **8** *1 ¼* **Alfred George**[24] 4606 2-9-3 0.................................... MichaelStainton 9 49
(Richard Whitaker) *in tch: drvn and outpcd over 3f out: rallied and drifted lft over 2f out: sn no imp* **50/1**
9 *2 ¼* **Colbyor** 2-9-3 0.. PaulHanagan 14 42
(Richard Fahey) *midfield: drvn and outpcd over 3f out: n.d after* **6/1**[3]
10 *5* **Claretintheblood (IRE)** 2-9-0 0.................................... LeeTopliss(3) 4 26
(Richard Fahey) *dwlt: bhd and pushed along: nvr on terms* **12/1**
6 **11** *11* **Madam Bonny (IRE)**[19] 4781 2-8-12 0......................... DanielTudhope 11 —
(Jim Goldie) *cl up tl rdn and wknd fr 2f out* **40/1**
12 *4 ½* **All Good News (IRE)** 2-9-3 0.. BarryMcHugh 8 —
(Lisa Williamson) *bhd and sn outpcd: no ch fr 1/2-way* **100/1**
1m 13.39s (-0.31) **Going Correction** +0.025s/f (Good) **12** Ran SP% **113.8**
Speed ratings (Par 94): **103,101,101,100,99 93,92,90,87,81 66,60**
toteswingers:1&2:£12.70, 2&3:£3.70, 1&3:£25.70 CSF £151.77 TOTE £32.50: £7.30, £2.20, £2.70; EX 177.60.
Owner The RAS Partnership **Bred** Patrick Cassidy **Trained** Musley Bank, N Yorks

FOCUS
The placed horses all had some form to their name so the winner ran to a fair level on his debut.

NOTEBOOK
Trumpet Voluntary(IRE) ◆, for whom there was no market confidence as the betting very much suggested Colbyor was the yard's first string, ran green to past halfway but picked up strongly once he got the hang of things. He can only improve. (tchd 28-1)
Star City(IRE) has now finished placed on all three starts. There's no obvious sign he's getting any better but he looks well worth a try over 7f, doing his best work late on. This also opens up the nursery route for him. (op 7-2)
Indego Blues duly stepped up a little on his debut. There's speed in his pedigree and an easier test than this may suit ideally at this stage. (op 5-1)
Pitt Rivers ran to form but is starting to look exposed, a first-time visor not seeing him pull out any more. (tchd 3-1)
Just Like Heaven(IRE) is proving fairly consistent but is another who's had a few chances now and she'll always be vulnerable to anything with potential in maidens. (tchd 4-1)
Celestial Dawn has hinted at ability on her last two starts and now has nurseries as an option. She's bred to get further.
Colbyor most of the newcomers shaped as if they'll improve for the experience, the Fahey-trained Colbyor one who's clearly thought capable of much better if the betting is any guide. (op 11-2 tchd 13-2)

5399 70'S NIGHT ON 31ST AUGUST NURSERY 5f
2:40 (2:40) (Class 6) (0-65,65) 2-Y-O **£1,704** (£503; £251) **Stalls** Low

Form RPR
0633 **1** **Phoenix Clubs (IRE)**[30] 4406 2-9-1 **59**.......................... BarryMcHugh 2 66+
(Paul Midgley) *hld up: hdwy 2f out: led ins fnl f: edgd rt: kpt on strly* **6/1**[3]
0504 **2** *1 ¾* **Duke Of Aricabeau (IRE)**[10] 5099 2-9-6 **64**............. GrahamGibbons 4 63
(Michael Easterby) *prom: drvn over 2f out: rallied over 1f out: chsd wnr ins fnl f: r.o* **11/4**[1]
5524 **3** *nse* **Yearbook**[80] 2761 2-9-0 **58**.. DavidAllan 5 57
(Tim Easterby) *cl up: led 2f out to ins fnl f: kpt on u.p* **20/1**
030 **4** *1 ¼* **Fifteentwo**[34] 4283 2-9-2 **60**...................................... AdrianNicholls 11 55
(David Nicholls) *hld up: n.m.r over 2f out: hdwy over 1f out: r.o ins fnl f* **20/1**
663 **5** *1* **Jay Kay**[41] 4040 2-9-3 **61**.. JamesSullivan 10 52
(Robert Wylie) *midfield: effrt on outside wl over 1f out: kpt on same pce ins fnl f* **16/1**
5322 **6** *hd* **Justine Time (IRE)**[13] 5005 2-9-1 **59**..............................(b) LeeNewman 3 49
(David Barron) *led to 2f out: rdn and no ex ins fnl f* **5/1**[2]

501 **7** ¾ **True Bond**[14] 4940 2-9-0 **65** .... JustinNewman(7) 1 52
(Geoffrey Oldroyd) *s.i.s: bhd tl hdwy over 1f out: kpt on ins fnl f: nvr able to chal* **9/1**

5601 **8** *hd* **Lord Buffhead**[13] 5005 2-8-10 **57** .... RobertLButler(3) 8 44
(Richard Guest) *in tch: rdn and outpcd over 2f out: n.d after* **15/2**

526 **9** 4 ½ **Oneniteinheaven (IRE)**[103] 2093 2-9-6 **64** .... PaulHanagan 12 34
(Ann Duffield) *hld up: rdn and hung rt over 2f out: sn btn* **16/1**

3604 **10** ¾ **Angel Of Hope (IRE)**[9] 5147 2-9-0 **58** ....(v) TomEaves 9 26
(Bryan Smart) *prom on outside tl rdn and wknd fr 2f out* **10/1**

2506 **11** 1 ½ **Mantuana (IRE)**[14] 4940 2-8-11 **55** .... SilvestreDeSousa 7 17
(David O'Meara) *t.k.h: cl up tl wknd fr 2f out* **12/1**

61.86 secs (1.06) **Going Correction** +0.025s/f (Good) **11** Ran SP% **117.5**
Speed ratings (Par 92): **92,89,89,87,85 85,84,83,76,75 72**
toteswingers:1&2:£4.80, 2&3:£12.90, 1&3:£21.00 CSF £22.75 CT £306.13 TOTE £9.10: £1.60, £1.90, £4.30; EX 28.20.
Owner Williams, Lindley, Turton, Bate **Bred** Mark & Pippa Hackett **Trained** Westow, N Yorks

FOCUS
A modest nursery, though it was at least soundly run and the form should hold up for the level.

NOTEBOOK
Phoenix Clubs(IRE) was returning from a short break and stepped up on her form in maidens to make a winning nursery bow, well suited by the stiff 5f and forging ahead inside the last. She'll be at least as effective at 6f. (op 7-1)
Duke Of Aricabeau(IRE) didn't have things go his way on his nursery bow and this time showed he's on a fair mark, leaving the impression a return to 6f will probably suit him even better. (op 10-3)
Yearbook was back after a mid-season break and arguably ran her best race to date, shaping as if an even sharper test at the trip will suit her better. (op 28-1)
Fifteentwo shaped with more encouragement than previously switched to handicap company for the first time and is one to bear in mind for a similar event, catching the eye with how well he travelled under restraint and keeping on without being unduly knocked about. (op 18-1)
Jay Kay was always caught a bit wider than ideal on his nursery bow and should be up to making more of an impact from this sort of mark another day, travelling comfortably for a long way. (op 18-1 tchd 20-1)
Justine Time(IRE) failed to reproduce the form she showed when runner-up off 1lb lower at Newcastle earlier in the month. (op 6-1)
True Bond won a weak maiden at Beverley and never threatened switched to a nursery, always on the backfoot after a slowish start. (op 8-1)
Lord Buffhead, who'd just edged out Justine Time at Newcastle, was another who did little for the form of that race, never threatening to land a serious blow. (op 6-1)

5400 JOHN SMITH'S NO NONSENSE H'CAP 5f
3:10 (3:11) (Class 5) (0-75,75) 3-Y-0+ **£2,726** (£805; £402) **Stalls** Low

Form RPR

0446 **1** **Invincible Force (IRE)**[1] 5371 7-9-7 **75** ....(b) LeeTopliss(3) 6 85
(Paul Green) *cl up: rdn to ld over 1f out: edgd lft: drvn out fnl f* **18/1**

040 **2** 1 **Sir Nod**[35] 4233 9-9-2 **67** ....(p) PaulHanagan 4 73
(Julie Camacho) *cl up: rdn and ev ch over 1f out: kpt on ins fnl f* **12/1**

6121 **3** 1 **Red Roar (IRE)**[14] 4942 4-8-13 **69** .... JulieBurke(5) 7 72
(Alan Berry) *hld up: hdwy and edgd rt over 1f out: kpt on ins fnl f: nvr able to chal* **11/4**[1]

4036 **4** *nk* **Captain Scooby**[8] 5163 5-9-0 **65** ....(v) SilvestreDeSousa 2 70+
(Richard Whitaker) *bhd: rdn whn n.m.r briefly over 2f out: checked over 1f out: gd hdwy fnl f: nrst fin* **9/2**[2]

0004 **5** *shd* **Commanche Raider (IRE)**[22] 4678 4-9-2 **67** ....(b) TomEaves 10 68
(Michael Dods) *hld up in toucn on outside: effrt over 2f out: edgd lft over 1f out: kpt on ins fnl f* **33/1**

4442 **6** ½ **Bosun Breese**[26] 4539 6-9-3 **73** .... LMcNiff(5) 9 73
(David Barron) *chsd ldrs: rdn and ev ch over 1f out: kpt on same pce fnl f* **11/2**[3]

3540 **7** *shd* **Electioneer (USA)**[29] 4443 4-8-12 **63** ....(b[1]) GrahamGibbons 3 62
(Michael Easterby) *hld up: rdn over 3f out: hdwy over 1f out: nvr able to chal* **8/1**

3020 **8** ¾ **Ballarina**[16] 4881 5-8-11 **62** .... DavidAllan 5 59
(Eric Alston) *prom: rdn over 2f out: swtchd rt over 1f out: sn outpcd* **14/1**

4126 **9** 3 ½ **Carrie's Magic**[47] 3856 4-8-11 **67** .... GarryWhillans(5) 8 51
(Alistair Whillans) *hld up: rdn over 2f out: wknd over 1f out* **6/1**

5020 **10** 6 **Chosen One (IRE)**[15] 4900 6-9-1 **66** ....(b[1]) JamesSullivan 1 28
(Ruth Carr) *led at decent gallop: rdn and hdd over 1f out: sn wknd* **16/1**

60.49 secs (-0.31) **Going Correction** +0.025s/f (Good) **10** Ran SP% **114.1**
Speed ratings (Par 103): **103,101,99,99,99 98,98,97,91,81**
CSF £211.62 CT £780.90 TOTE £21.50: £4.90, £4.60, £1.30; EX 244.00.
Owner Derek A Howard **Bred** Robert Wilson **Trained** Lydiate, Merseyside

FOCUS
Just a run-of-the-mill sprint, though it contained a few potentially well-treated horses. There was no hanging around and the form looks sound with the first four close to recent form.

5401 EXHIBITIONS AT CARLISLE RACECOURSE CLAIMING STKS 7f 200y
3:40 (3:40) (Class 6) 3-Y-0 **£1,704** (£503; £251) **Stalls** Low

Form RPR

2231 **1** **Abidhabidubai**[19] 4812 3-8-11 72 .... PBBeggy 5 73
(John Quinn) *trckd ldrs: rdn to ld over 1f out: kpt on wl ins fnl f* **11/8**[1]

0201 **2** 1 **Sky Diamond (IRE)**[12] 5041 3-8-12 62 ....(b) FrederikTylicki 6 72
(James Given) *led: rdn over 2f out: hdd over 1f out: rallied: kpt on same pce ins fnl f* **8/1**

5535 **3** 3 ½ **Barista (IRE)**[18] 4821 3-8-12 69 .... MartinHarley(3) 7 67
(Mick Channon) *in tch: effrt over 2f out: kpt on same pce appr fnl f* **4/1**[3]

0201 **4** 7 **Deep Applause**[8] 5165 3-9-1 56 ....(p) PJMcDonald 4 51
(Michael Dods) *hld up in tch: rdn and effrt 3f out: wknd over 1f out* **16/1**

1005 **5** 10 **Adlington**[35] 4236 3-9-0 67 .... PaulHanagan 1 27
(Richard Fahey) *chsd ldr tl rdn and wknd fr 2f out* **10/3**[2]

0033 **6** 6 **Fly By White (IRE)**[36] 4200 3-8-2 61 ow1 .... ShaneBKelly(5) 8 —
(Barry Murtagh) *hld up in tch on outside: struggling over 3f out: sn btn* **12/1**

6006 **R** **Ivy And Gold**[7] 5206 3-8-5 40 .... JulieBurke(5) 2 —
(Alan Berry) *s.s: ref to r* **200/1**

1m 39.71s (-0.29) **Going Correction** +0.075s/f (Good) **7** Ran SP% **110.4**
Speed ratings (Par 98): **104,103,99,92,82 76,—**
toteswingers:1&2:£3.10, 2&3:£4.50, 1&3:£2.00 CSF £12.46 TOTE £3.20: £1.40, £5.60; EX 11.60.
Owner Nigel S Cooper **Bred** Brightwalton Stud **Trained** Settrington, N Yorks

FOCUS
A modest claimer and the form is fluid with the first two helping to set the level.

5402 CHRISTMAS PARTY NIGHTS AT CARLISLE RACECOURSE H'CAP (DIV I) 7f 200y
4:10 (4:11) (Class 6) (0-65,63) 3-Y-0+ **£1,617** (£481; £240; £120) **Stalls** Low

Form RPR

6230 **1** **Silly Gilly (IRE)**[14] 4946 7-9-3 **59** .... ShaneBKelly(5) 8 69
(Ron Barr) *hld up in midfield: hdwy on outside to ld wl over 1f out: kpt on wl ins fnl f: r.o* **7/1**[3]

035 **2** *nk* **So Wise (USA)**[12] 5030 3-9-2 **59** .... PaulHanagan 2 68
(Keith Dalgleish) *trckd ldrs: effrt whn n.m.r briefly 2f out: sn rdn: chsd wnr appr fnl f: r.o* **4/1**[1]

5045 **3** 2 **Media Stars**[22] 4673 6-9-7 **58** .... TonyHamilton 6 63
(Robert Johnson) *bhd tl hdwy over 2f out: styd on wl ins fnl f: nrst fin* **14/1**

0660 **4** *shd* **Strong Knight**[10] 5106 4-8-12 **49** ....(p) GrahamGibbons 13 54
(Tim Walford) *cl up: rdn and led briefly 2f out: kpt on same pce ins fnl f* **4/1**[1]

0330 **5** *nk* **Cold Quest (USA)**[19] 4783 7-8-4 **46** .... JulieBurke(5) 12 50
(Linda Perratt) *hld up: rdn over 3f out: hdwy over 1f out: kpt on ins fnl f* **20/1**

6261 **6** 3 **Tanforan**[14] 4948 9-9-7 **58** .... KellyHarrison 10 55
(Brian Baugh) *t.k.h: hld up: rdn and hdwy 2f out: kpt on ins fnl f: nvr able to chal* **10/1**

304- **7** ½ **Ella Woodcock (IRE)**[464] 2204 7-9-12 **63** .... DavidAllan 4 59
(Eric Alston) *hld up: smooth hdwy and in tch over 2f out: rdn and no imp over 1f out* **8/1**

0540 **8** 2 ¼ **Island Chief**[14] 4945 5-9-9 **60** ....(p) JamesSullivan 11 51
(Michael Easterby) *prom on outside: rdn over 2f out: wknd over 1f out* **11/1**

5524 **9** *shd* **Carlitos Spirit (IRE)**[7] 5208 7-9-1 **55** .... LeeTopliss(3) 7 46
(Ian McInnes) *dwlt: bhd: rdn 1/2-way: hdwy over 1f out: nvr able to chal* **13/2**[2]

3050 **10** 4 ½ **Hill Tribe**[7] 5205 4-9-3 **57** .... RobertLButler(3) 3 37
(Richard Guest) *trckd ldrs: effrt over 2f out: wknd over 1f out* **14/1**

0-00 **11** 3 **Hedgerow (IRE)**[113] 229 4-8-8 **45** .... DuranFentiman 5 18
(Dianne Sayer) *led at decent gallop: rdn and hdd 2f out: sn wknd* **50/1**

20-0 **12** ¾ **Funky Munky**[87] 1216 6-8-9 **46** .... PJMcDonald 9 18
(Alistair Whillans) *bhd: struggling over 3f out: sn btn* **20/1**

00-6 **13** 5 **Convitezza**[14] 4945 5-8-8 **45** ....(t) TomEaves 1 5
(Mike Sowersby) *chsd ldr: rdn over 3f out: wknd fr 2f out* **50/1**

1m 40.48s (0.48) **Going Correction** +0.075s/f (Good)
WFA 3 from 4yo+ 6lb **13** Ran SP% **121.1**
Speed ratings (Par 101): **100,99,97,97,97 94,93,91,91,86 83,83,78**
CSF £34.23 CT £402.78 TOTE £10.30: £3.00, £1.60, £5.30; EX 33.00.
Owner D Thomson **Bred** Barronstown Stud **Trained** Seamer, N Yorks
■ Stewards' Enquiry : Lee Topliss caution: failed to take all reasonable and permissable measures to obtain best possible placing.

FOCUS
Modest fare but sound form. The race was run at a strong pace, the field well strung out from an early stage.
Island Chief Official explanation: jockey said cheek pieces were accidentally dislodged before line
Carlitos Spirit(IRE) Official explanation: jockey said gelding missed the berak

5403 CHRISTMAS PARTY NIGHTS AT CARLISLE RACECOURSE H'CAP (DIV II) 7f 200y
4:40 (4:41) (Class 6) (0-65,65) 3-Y-0+ **£1,617** (£481; £240; £120) **Stalls** Low

Form RPR

0031 **1** **Talent Scout (IRE)**[29] 4442 5-9-7 **60** ....(p) GrahamGibbons 11 74
(Tim Walford) *mde all: rdn along 2f out: styd on strly ins fnl f* **6/1**[3]

-364 **2** 5 **Scottish Lake**[17] 4854 3-9-3 **65** .... PatrickDonaghy(3) 3 67
(Jedd O'Keeffe) *midfield: drvn along over 3f out: rallied to chse wnr appr fnl f: kpt on: no imp* **9/2**[1]

656 **3** 1 **Le Chat D'Or**[69] 3138 3-9-1 **60** .... TomEaves 5 59
(Michael Dods) *trckd ldrs: rdn and edgd rt over 2f out: kpt on same pce ins fnl f* **11/1**

5360 **4** *shd* **Sinatramania**[29] 4440 4-9-4 **57** .... FrannyNorton 7 57
(Tracy Waggott) *hld up in midfield: effrt over 2f out: kpt on same pce over 1f out* **13/2**

6042 **5** ¾ **Machir Bay**[7] 5208 4-8-7 **46** oh1 ....(p) PaulHanagan 12 44
(Keith Dalgleish) *chsd wnr: rdn along 3f out: no ex over 1f out* **5/1**[2]

0101 **6** 3 ¼ **Escape Artist**[17] 4852 4-9-5 **58** ....(p) DavidAllan 4 49
(Tim Easterby) *t.k.h: hld up: rdn and effrt over 2f out: no imp over 1f out* **5/1**[2]

6006 **7** 2 ½ **Brisbane (IRE)**[17] 4852 4-8-7 **46** ....(p) DuranFentiman 9 31
(Dianne Sayer) *t.k.h: cl up tl rdn and wknd over 1f out* **16/1**

0012 **8** 2 ¼ **Master Leon**[29] 4441 4-8-13 **59** ....(p) JustinNewman(7) 10 39
(Bryan Smart) *midfield on outside: drvn 3f out: wknd over 1f out* **6/1**[3]

0-00 **9** 2 ¾ **Vittachi**[92] 2400 4-8-11 **50** .... PJMcDonald 1 24
(Alistair Whillans) *bhd: struggling over 3f out: sn btn* **33/1**

-000 **10** 3 **Catawollow**[29] 4441 4-8-7 **46** oh1 ....(e) AndrewMullen 13 13
(Richard Guest) *hld up: rdn over 3f out: btn fnl 2f* **50/1**

00-0 **11** 3 ¼ **French Applause (IRE)**[15] 4904 5-8-7 **46** .... JamesSullivan 6 —
(Mike Sowersby) *bhd: rdn on outside over 3f out: nvr on terms* **66/1**

1m 40.01s (0.01) **Going Correction** +0.075s/f (Good)
WFA 3 from 4yo+ 6lb **11** Ran SP% **114.0**
Speed ratings (Par 101): **102,97,96,95,95 91,89,87,84,81 78**
toteswingers:1&2:£6.10, 2&3:£11.10, 1&3:£12.20 CSF £31.78 CT £293.22 TOTE £7.00: £2.10, £2.00, £4.20; EX 29.90.
Owner John Stacey **Bred** Johnston King **Trained** Sheriff Hutton, N Yorks
■ Stewards' Enquiry : Duran Fentiman caution: used whip without giving gelding time to respond.

FOCUS
The second division of this handicap was much more one-sided than the first. The winner recorded a personal best with the placed horses backing up the form.

5404 CFM RADIO'S CASH FOR KIDS H'CAP 6f 192y
5:10 (5:11) (Class 5) (0-70,70) 3-Y-0+ **£2,264** (£673; £336; £168) **Stalls** Low

Form RPR

2121 **1** **Istiqdaam**[22] 4670 6-9-11 **69** ....(b) PaddyAspell 10 81
(Michael Easterby) *hld up: hdwy on outside and ev ch over 1f out: edgd rt u.p and led wl ins fnl f: kpt on* **7/2**[1]

001 **2** *nk* **Ellies Image**[12] 5034 4-8-13 **57** .... DuranFentiman 2 68
(Brian Baugh) *bhd: rdn over 4f out: gd hdwy on outside 2f out: led to wl ins fnl f: jst hld* **15/2**[3]

532 **3** *3 1/4* **Northern Flyer (GER)**[12] 5031 5-8-11 **60**..................(p) ShaneBKelly(5) 1 62
(John Quinn) *prom: stdy hdwy over 2f out: sn rdn: edgd rt and kpt on same pce ins fnl f* **7/2**[1]

5640 **4** *hd* **Dubai Celebration**[22] 4670 3-9-4 **70**......................(t) PatrickDonaghy(3) 8 70
(Jedd O'Keeffe) *hld up: effrt whn n.m.r appr 2f out and wl over 1f out: sn swtchd rt: kpt on ins fnl f: nrst fin* **10/1**

1500 **5** *2 3/4* **Striker Torres (IRE)**[22] 4670 5-9-12 **70**........................ FrannyNorton 11 67+
(Geoffrey Oldroyd) *hld up: nt clr run and swtchd lft over 1f out: kpt on ins fnl f: nvr able to chal* **12/1**

-456 **6** *shd* **Chookie Avon**[3] 5309 4-8-13 **57**....................................(p) PaulHanagan 3 56+
(Keith Dalgleish) *hld up towards rr: hdwy whn nt clr run wl over 1f out: effrt and styng on but no imp whn hmpd ins fnl f: eased* **9/2**[2]

405 **7** *1/2* **Schoolboy Champ**[9] 5153 4-8-12 **59**............................(v) LeeTopliss(3) 9 52
(Patrick Morris) *cl up: led over 2f out to ent fnl f: sn btn* **11/1**

5005 **8** *2* **Ghost (IRE)**[19] 4810 4-9-9 **67**.. AdrianNicholls 4 66+
(David Nicholls) *trckd ldrs: rdn over 2f out: one pce fr over 1f out: btn whn edgd rt ins fnl f* **14/1**

000 **9** *4* **Born To Be Achamp (BRZ)**[23] 4634 5-9-7 **65**.....(p) SilvestreDeSousa 5 42
(Geoffrey Harker) *w ldr: rdn over 2f out: wknd wl over 1f out* **25/1**

000 **10** *3* **Maharanee (USA)**[22] 4673 3-8-8 **57**...............................(p) TonyHamilton 7 24
(Ann Duffield) *t.k.h: led to over 2f out: sn rdn and wknd* **40/1**

/300 **11** *1 1/2* **Viking Dancer**[115] 1755 4-9-4 **62**.. PJMcDonald 6 26
(Ruth Carr) *in tch: effrt over 2f out: wknd wl over 1f out* **22/1**

1m 26.99s (-0.11) **Going Correction** +0.075s/f (Good)
WFA 3 from 4yo+ 5lb **11** Ran SP% **116.8**
Speed ratings (Par 103): **103,102,98,98,95 95,94,92,88,84 82**
toteswingers:1&2:£5.10, 2&3:£7.00, 1&3:£3.00 CSF £29.21 CT £100.03 TOTE £5.20: £2.50, £3.20, £1.10; EX 31.90.
Owner Two Old Pals **Bred** Cheveley Park Stud Ltd **Trained** Sheriff Hutton, N Yorks
■ Stewards' Enquiry : Shane B Kelly two-day ban: careless riding (Sep 8-9)

FOCUS
Another handicap run at a good pace. The principals all came from off the gallop and a few met trouble as the leaders dropped back through the pack. The principals finished clear and are rated to their best.
Striker Torres(IRE) Official explanation: jockey said gelding was denied a clear run
Ghost(IRE) Official explanation: jockey said gelding suffered interference and lost its action
Born To Be Achamp(BRZ) Official explanation: jockey said gelding hung left

5405 TURFTV.CO.UK H'CAP — 1m 3f 107y
5:40 (5:41) (Class 6) (0-65,61) 3-Y-O+ **£1,704** (£503; £251) **Stalls** High

Form RPR

50-1 **1** **La Bacouetteuse (FR)**[22] 4673 6-9-7 **54**...............(p) SilvestreDeSousa 5 68+
(Iain Jardine) *hld up on ins: rdn over 2f out: gd hdwy to ld wl ins fnl f: comf* **7/2**[1]

0342 **2** *1* **Politbureau**[15] 4904 4-9-4 **51**.. JamesSullivan 3 60
(Michael Easterby) *prom gng wl: smooth hdwy to ld over 1f out: rdn and hdd wl ins fnl f: no ex* **6/1**[2]

663 **3** *1 3/4* **Bavarian Nordic (USA)**[8] 5167 6-9-6 **58**.................. BrianToomey(5) 10 64
(Richard Whitaker) *hld up: rdn and hdwy over 2f out: kpt on same pce ins fnl f* **15/2**

6461 **4** *3/4* **Ferney Boy**[15] 4903 5-9-4 **51**.. KellyHarrison 16 56
(Chris Fairhurst) *hld up: rdn along over 3f out: hdwy on outside 2f out: no imp ins fnl f* **9/1**

3415 **5** *1* **Prince Rhyddarch**[71] 3041 6-9-12 **59**.............................. TomEaves 9 62
(Michael Dods) *cl up: led over 2f to 1f out: no ex ins fnl f* **10/1**

030 **6** *2 1/4* **Dimashq**[13] 4982 9-9-0 **47**.. MickyFenton 4 46
(Paul Midgley) *midfield: effrt and rdn over 2f out: no imp over 1f out* **12/1**

05/0 **7** *2 1/2* **Evelith Regent (IRE)**[29] 4441 8-9-5 **52**.........................(t) PaddyAspell 11 47
(John Davies) *midfield: stdy hdwy over 3f out: rdn and wknd wl over 1f out* **100/1**

/060 **8** *7* **Hada Men (USA)**[39] 4129 6-8-12 **50**...........................(p) JulieBurke(5) 14 33
(Tina Jackson) *midfield on outside: rdn over 4f out: wknd over 2f out* **20/1**

5006 **9** *1* **Birkside**[19] 4785 8-8-13 **46**... BarryMcHugh 8 27
(Linda Perratt) *bhd: sme hdwy 3f out: btn fr 2f out* **28/1**

4345 **10** *1 3/4* **Bright Applause**[15] 4902 3-9-5 **61**................................ FrannyNorton 15 39
(Tracy Waggott) *hld up on outside: struggling over 3f out: btn fnl 2f* **13/2**[3]

00-0 **11** *2 1/4* **Ptolomeos**[40] 4112 8-8-11 **51**.................................... DavidKenny(7) 13 26
(Jean Hogan) *[illegible] towards rr: rdn over 3f out: nvr on terms* **100/1**

0635 **12** *19* **Oddsmaker (IRE)**[8] 5166 10-9-13 **60**............................(t) TonyHamilton [illegible]
(Maurice Barnes) *dwlt: sn pressing ldr: rdn and wknd over 2f out* **14/1**

3240 **13** *14* **Damascus Symphony**[32] 4364 3-9-2 **58**.................. GrahamGibbons 1 —
(James Bethell) *led to over 2f out: sn rdn and wknd* **8/1**

55-4 **14** *6* **Royal Patriot (IRE)**[135] 1297 4-8-9 **45**......................... LeeTopliss(3) 7 —
(Paul Green) *plld hrd early: cl up tl rdn and wknd 3f out* **33/1**

2m 24.74s (1.64) **Going Correction** +0.075s/f (Good)
WFA 3 from 4yo+ 9lb **14** Ran SP% **119.3**
Speed ratings (Par 101): **97,96,95,94,93 92,90,85,84,83 81,67,57,53**
toteswingers:1&2:£5.50, 2&3:£9.90, 1&3:£6.50. Tote Super 7: Win: Not won. Place: 168.40 CSF £22.12 CT £150.27 TOTE £3.80: £1.60, £2.10, £2.60; EX 29.80.
Owner Corsby Racing **Bred** Sarl Classic Breeding & Maria R Mendes **Trained** Hawick, Borders
■ Stewards' Enquiry : Brian Toomey three-day ban: weighed-in 2lb heavy (Sep 8-9)

FOCUS
Form to view quite positively for the grade, a few in-form horses coming to the fore off a sound pace. The fourth and fifth are rated close to their marks and set the level.
Damascus Symphony Official explanation: jockey said filly had no more to give
T/Jkpt: Not won. T/Plt: £35.20 to a £1 stake. Pool £60,517.83 - 1,252.45 winning tickets. T/Qpdt: £11.90 to a £1 stake. Pool of £4,084.89 - 252.76 winning tickets. RY

5037 LINGFIELD (L-H)
Thursday, August 25

OFFICIAL GOING: Turf course - soft; all-weather - standard
Wind: Brisk behind Weather: Sunny spells

5406 OILFIELD INSURANCE AGENCIES H'CAP (TURF) — 1m 2f
2:00 (2:00) (Class 6) (0-65,64) 4-Y-O+ **£1,704** (£503; £251) **Stalls** Low

Form RPR

1336 **1** **Miss Blink**[29] 4440 4-9-7 **64**... KierenFallon 5 76
(Robin Bastiman) *trckd ldrs: pushed along and qcknd to ld appr fnl 2f: pushed out ins fnl f* **11/4**[1]

0042 **2** *3* **Jovial (IRE)**[17] 4847 4-9-5 **62**..(v[1]) EddieAhern 3 68
(Denis Coakley) *in rr: rdn over 3f out: styd on u.p over 2f out to chse wnr ins fnl f but no imp* **10/3**[2]

3000 **3** *1 1/2* **Notabadlad**[18] 4829 4-8-13 **59**.................................. AdamBeschizza(3) 4 62
(Simon Dow) *s.i.s: in rr: stl plenty to do whn rdn over 2f out: str run fr over 1f out to take 3rd fnl 75yds: gng on cl home but nt rch ldng duo* **66/1**

4002 **4** *1 3/4* **Rosy Dawn**[20] 4754 6-8-5 **48**.. WilliamCarson 2 48
(Mark Hoad) *led: rdn 5 l clr over 4f out: hdd appr fnl 2f: no ex fr over 1f out and lost 3rd fnl 75yds* **17/2**

3544 **5** *1/2* **Recalcitrant**[18] 4822 8-9-3 **63**.. KieranO'Neill(3) 9 62
(Simon Dow) *sn chsng ldr: rdn and no imp over 3f out: lost 2nd 2f out: wknd ins fnl f* **6/1**[3]

0000 **6** *1* **Hector The Brave (IRE)**[33] 4322 4-8-6 **49**.................. RichardThomas 8 46
(John E Long) *in tch: drvn along 7f out: sme prog u.p over 2f out: nvr rchd ldrs and sn btn* **25/1**

00-3 **7** *5* **Savaronola (USA)**[233] 40 6-9-1 **58**................................... TomQueally 6 45
(Barney Curley) *a in rr* **12/1**

0242 **8** *1/2* **Vinces**[80] 2759 7-8-12 **55**...(p) J-PGuillambert 10 41
(Tim McCarthy) *chsd ldrs early: sn bhd and n.d* **10/1**

03 **9** *5* **Eastern Gift**[22] 4656 6-9-7 **64**.. NeilCallan 11 40
(Gay Kelleway) *in tch: rdn 5f out: wknd over 3f out* **6/1**[3]

0-60 **10** *7* **Baoli**[13] 5015 4-8-13 **61**... LauraPike(5) 1 23
(Tim McCarthy) *prom early: bhd fr 1/2-way* **33/1**

2m 15.32s (4.82) **Going Correction** +0.425s/f (Yiel) **10** Ran SP% **113.9**
Speed ratings (Par 101): **97,94,93,92,91 90,86,86,82,76**
toteswingers:1&2:£2.50, 2&3:£17.00, 1&3:£18.30 CSF £11.31 CT £469.01 TOTE £3.50: £1.60, £1.30, £10.60; EX 10.90 Trifecta £411.00 Pool: £766.46 - 1.38 winning units..
Owner A Reed **Bred** Anthony Reed **Trained** Cowthorpe, N Yorks

FOCUS
Following 12mm of morning rain, the ground on the turf course had changed significantly from declaration time and was officially soft. A moderate handicap, but the early pace was decent. Another step forward from the winner.

5407 TERSUS LAUNDRY SERVICES H'CAP (TURF) — 1m 2f
2:30 (2:30) (Class 5) (0-75,73) 3-Y-O **£2,385** (£704; £352) **Stalls** Low

Form RPR

4312 **1** **Silken Thoughts**[12] 5049 3-9-0 **69**.................................. CathyGannon 4 82
(John Berry) *broke wl: stdd in rr: stl bhd on outside bnd over 3f out: drvn and hdwy 2f out: qcknd to take slt ld appr fnl f but hanging lft: pushed along and hld on wl clsng stages* **5/2**[1]

3321 **2** *3/4* **Destiny Of Dreams**[21] 4713 3-9-2 **71**................................. DaneO'Neill 7 83
(Jo Crowley) *led: rdn and qcknd 3f out: narrowly hdd appr fnl f: pressed wnr tl no ex fnl 100yds* **8/1**

4343 **3** *2 1/4* **Alshazah**[20] 4751 3-9-1 **70**... JamesMillman 10 77
(Rod Millman) *slowly away: in rr: stl plenty to do whn swtchd rt to outside 2f out: styd on strly ins fnl f to take 3rd nr fin but no imp on ldng duo* **10/1**

5502 **4** *1/2* **Swift Blade (IRE)**[25] 4578 3-9-0 **69**................................ SebSanders 3 75
(Lady Herries) *in tch: drvn and styd on to take 3rd 2f out but nvr gng pce to chal: lost one pce 3rd nr fin* **9/1**

6636 **5** *nk* **Mattoral**[21] 4724 3-9-2 **71**...(b) SteveDrowne 6 76
(Peter Makin) *chsd ldr 6f out: rdn and lost pl over 2f out: styd on again ins fnl f* **4/1**[2]

4644 **6** *1/2* **Kingarrick**[22] 4665 3-9-4 **73**... WilliamBuick 2 77
(Eve Johnson Houghton) *chsd ldr 4f: styd chsng ldrs: rdn over 3f out: sn outpcd: styd on again clsng stages* **13/2**

0011 **7** *10* **Cuckney Bear**[31] 4381 3-9-3 **72**...................................... RichardMullen 8 56
(Ed McMahon) *chsd ldrs: rdn on outer bnd over 3f out: chsd ldrs over 2f out: no imp and sn btn* **5/1**[3]

0256 **8** *1* **Persian Herald**[15] 4905 3-9-4 **73**...................................(b[1]) GeorgeBaker 1 55
(William Muir) *slowly away: in rr tl sme hdwy on ins over 3f out: fnd nil and sn wknd* **25/1**

1006 **9** *14* **Royal Reverie**[38] 4158 3-9-3 **72**.. AdamKirby 5 26
(Walter Swinburn) *chsd ldrs tl wknd and wknd qckly over 3f out* **16/1**

2m 14.57s (4.07) **Going Correction** +0.425s/f (Yiel) **9** Ran SP% **118.5**
Speed ratings (Par 100): **100,99,97,97,96 96,88,87,76**
toteswingers:1&2:£4.70, 2&3:£10.40, 1&3:£5.90 CSF £24.13 CT £174.79 TOTE £3.70: £1.50, £1.90, £3.00; EX 29.10 Trifecta £610.60 Pool: £833.48 - 1.01 winning units..
Owner The Renewal Partnership **Bred** Burton Agnes Stud Co Ltd **Trained** Newmarket, Suffolk

FOCUS
A modest handicap, but the winning time was 0.75 seconds faster than the older horses in the opener. The winner did not need to improve but may do a bit better.
Alshazah Official explanation: jockey said gelding was unsuited by the track
Mattoral Official explanation: jockey said colt hung left
Cuckney Bear Official explanation: jockey said gelding was unsuited by the soft ground
Persian Herald Official explanation: jockey said colt missed the break
Royal Reverie Official explanation: jockey said gelding was unsuited by the soft ground

5408 TERSUS CLAIMING STKS (TURF) — 1m 1f
3:00 (3:00) (Class 6) 3-Y-O+ **£1,533** (£452; £226) **Stalls** Low

Form RPR

2053 **1** **Royal Opera**[15] 4916 3-9-2 67.. JamesMillman 3 72
(Rod Millman) *trckd ldr over 5f out: chal gng wl 2f out: sn slt ld: pushed along fnl f: readily* **6/4**[2]

2230 **2** *1 1/2* **Avon River**[13] 4997 4-9-8 82...(b) KieranO'Neill(3) 2 71
(Richard Hannon) *sn slt ld: jnd 2f out: sn narrowly hdd and hrd drvn: fnd no ex: wknd fnl 120yds* **4/6**[1]

03/0 **3** *13* **Yellow Printer**[6] 5231 5-9-2 63.. EddieAhern 4 33
(Mark Gillard) *w ldr early: dropped to 3rd over 5f out: wknd 3f out* **10/1**[3]

4 *13* **Midnight Tiger** 3-9-3 0... KirstyMilczarek 1 13
(George Prodromou) *slowly away: sme prog to cl over 4f out: sn rdn: wknd qckly 3f out* **40/1**

2m 0.77s (4.17) **Going Correction** +0.425s/f (Yiel)
WFA 3 from 4yo+ 7lb **4** Ran SP% **111.5**
Speed ratings (Par 101): **98,96,85,73**
CSF £2.97 TOTE £2.70; EX 3.30.
Owner The Links Partnership **Bred** Redmyre Bloodstock & Newhall Farm Estate **Trained** Kentisbeare, Devon

FOCUS
Claimers don't get much worse than this. The favourite disappointed and the form is rated around the winner to his recent best.

5409 TERSUS LAUNDRY SERVICES NURSERY — 7f (P)
3:30 (3:31) (Class 5) (0-70,70) 2-Y-O **£2,385** (£704; £352) **Stalls** Low

Form RPR

036 **1** **Vinnie Jones**[13] 5011 2-9-7 **70**.. WilliamBuick 9 73
(John Gosden) *led 2f: styd trcking ldr tl drvn and qcknd on ins to ld bnd 2f out: strly chal thrght fnl f: hld on all out* **3/1**[2]

0005 **2** *nk* **Clone Devil (IRE)**[9] 5144 2-7-12 **47** oh2 JamieMackay 4 49
(Alastair Lidderdale) *led after 2f: hdd 2f out: rallied to chal wnr thrght fnl f: no ex cl home* **33/1**

0024 **3** *1/2* **Dark Ambition (IRE)**[15] 4913 2-9-4 **67** KierenFallon 3 68
(William Haggas) *trckd ldrs on ins: drvn and ev ch 1f out: no ex and one pce ins fnl f* **5/2**[1]

0020 **4** *1/2* **Correct**[26] 4551 2-9-6 **69** TomQueally 7 69
(Michael Bell) *hld up towards rr but in tch: rdn and styd on wl ins fnl f: tk 4th clsng stages: nt rch ldrs* **7/2**[3]

004 **5** *3/4* **Onebytheknows**[15] 4906 2-9-3 **69** SeanLevey(3) 1 67
(Richard Hannon) *in rr: hdwy on ins over 2f out: drvn and styd on fr over 1f out: kpt on clsng stages: nt rch ldrs* **12/1**

4433 **6** *hd* **Kyllasie**[36] 4212 2-9-1 **67** KieranO'Neill(3) 8 64
(Richard Hannon) *t.k.h: chsd ldrs over 2f out: one pce u.p ins fnl f* **8/1**

651 **7** *hd* **Colourful Event (IRE)**[23] 4629 2-8-10 **59** FrankieMcDonald 5 56
(David Arbuthnot) *s.i.s: in rr: hdwy and nt clr run appr fnl f: sn swtchd rt: styd on ins fnl f: gng on cl home* **16/1**

0465 **8** *hd* **Zuzu Angel (IRE)**[18] 4824 2-9-4 **67** ShaneKelly 2 63
(William Knight) *in tch 1/2-way: rdn and outpcd over 2f out: swtchd to outside and hdwy ins fnl f: kpt on cl home* **12/1**

003 **9** *3/4* **Ice Loch**[21] 4708 2-8-8 **57** LukeMorris 6 51
(Michael Blanshard) *chsd ldrs: rdn over 2f out: styd wl there tl outpcd u.p ins fnl f and dropped in rr clsng stages* **25/1**

1m 28.97s (4.17) **Going Correction** +0.225s/f (Slow) **9** Ran SP% **115.0**
Speed ratings (Par 94): **85,84,84,83,82 82,82,81,81**
toteswingers:1&2:£19.50, 2&3:£11.00, 1&3:£2.80 CSF £91.14 CT £282.39 TOTE £3.10: £1.10, £9.50, £1.30; EX 96.30 Trifecta £713.60 Part won. Pool: £964.43 - 0.40 winning units..
Owner C J Murfitt **Bred** C J Murfitt **Trained** Newmarket, Suffolk

FOCUS
A fair little nursery, but dominated by the front pair from the start.

NOTEBOOK
Vinnie Jones was making his nursery debut after showing ability in three maidens and the form of all three has been boosted since. In front early before taking a lead from the runner-up after 2f, he was back in front again on the home turn and proved game in a driving finish. He can't be put up too much for this and there is probably more to come. (tchd 11-4 and 10-3 in a place)
Clone Devil(IRE) improved greatly on his turf efforts when a close fifth of nine in a slowly run nursery over this trip at Kempton last time, but this game effort under a positive ride proved it was no fluke. It could be argued that being 2lb wrong cost him the race, but he can surely still find a small contest on Polytrack. (tchd 40-1)
Dark Ambition(IRE) hasn't looked an easy ride and was again inclined to race with his mouth open in a handy position here. He was also probably not helped by making his effort tight against the usually unfavoured inside rail. (op 11-4)
Correct ran her best previous race when runner-up here two starts back, but she didn't click into gear until it was far too late.
Onebytheknows, another making his nursery debut, improved for the switch to this surface and step up to this trip at Kempton last time, but he could never land a significant blow on this occasion.
Colourful Event(IRE) compromised her chance with a slow start and was never travelling well enough to get close to the leaders. Official explanation: jockey said filly was slowly away (op 20-1 tchd 25-1)
Zuzu Angel(IRE) Official explanation: jockey said filly was denied a clear run

5410 LADBROKES MOBILE MEDIAN AUCTION MAIDEN STKS (DIV I) 6f (P)
4:00 (4:00) (Class 6) 2-Y-O **£1,363** (£402; £201) **Stalls** Low

Form RPR

1 **Integrity (IRE)** 2-9-3 0 WilliamBuick 4 81+
(Jeremy Noseda) *trckd ldrs: travelling wl 2f out: sn trcking ldr: shkn up and qcknd to chal fnl f: led fnl 120yds: comf* **5/6**[1]

5 **2** *1 1/4* **Confucius Elite**[32] 4352 2-9-3 0 PatCosgrave 6 77+
(Jim Boyle) *t.k.h: led: rdn ins fnl 2f: kpt on wl whn chal ins fnl f: hdd and outpcd fnl 120yds but wl clr of 3rd* **5/1**[3]

3 *7* **Persidha** 2-8-12 0 DavidProbert 5 51
(Gay Kelleway) *in tch: rdn and one pce 2f out: styd on again to take wl hld 3rd fnl 120yds* **20/1**

00 **4** *3/4* **True Prince (USA)**[13] 4995 2-9-3 0 TomQueally 10 54
(Amanda Perrett) *chsd ldrs: wnt 2nd briefly over 2f out: styd chsng ldng duo tl lft bhd over 1f out: lost wl hld 3rd fnl 120yds* **20/1**

0 **5** *1/2* **Talya's Storm**[8] 5174 2-8-10 0 RaulDaSilva(7) 3 53
(Jeremy Gask) *s.i.s: in rr: hdwy on ins wl over 1f out: styd on same pce ins fnl f* **50/1**

6 *2* **Twelve Strings (IRE)** 2-9-3 0 KierenFallon 1 48+
(Luca Cumani) *s.i.s: in rr and pushed along 3f out: mod prog fr over 1f out* **7/2**[2]

7 *2 1/4* **Silver Six** 2-9-3 0 SamHitchcott 9 40
(Mick Channon) *s.i.s: in rr: rdn over 3f out: a outpcd* **16/1**

00 **8** *shd* **Compton Shuttle (IRE)**[13] 4992 2-8-12 0 JamesDoyle 7 34
(Hans Adielsson) *chsd ldr tl wknd over 2f out* **50/1**

50 **9** *7* **Dana's Present**[10] 5111 2-9-3 0 TedDurcan 8 18
(George Baker) *chsd ldrs tl wknd qckly over 2f out* **14/1**

0 **10** *16* **Jenndale**[13] 5011 2-9-3 0 NickyMackay 2 —
(Chris Dwyer) *mid-div: rdn over 3f out: wknd qckly ins fnl 2f: eased* **66/1**

1m 12.52s (0.62) **Going Correction** +0.225s/f (Slow) **10** Ran SP% **120.9**
Speed ratings (Par 92): **104,102,93,92,91 88,85,85,76,54**
toteswingers:1&2:£2.10, 2&3:£12.40, 1&3:£5.50 CSF £5.35 TOTE £1.90: £1.10, £1.40, £3.60; EX 5.10 Trifecta £54.10 Pool: £701.83 -9.59 winning units..
Owner Miss Yvonne Jacques **Bred** Mrs Anne Marie Burns **Trained** Newmarket, Suffolk

FOCUS
A modest below-tariff maiden, but featuring a couple of interesting newcomers. The first two pulled well clear.

NOTEBOOK
Integrity(IRE) ◆, a 65,000euros half-brother to four winners (all of them successful over this trip), was clearly expected to make a winning debut and although he had to work a bit in order to get the better of the more experienced runner-up, he picked up stylishly and was well on top at the line. His first-season sire came into this with a record of 5-13 on Polytrack, so the surface was always likely to suit and he should go on to better things. (op 10-11 tchd 4-5 and evens in places)
Confucius Elite ◆, fifth of seven in a valuable Ascot maiden on his debut, tried to make his experience tell and despite racing keenly early, hung in there after being headed and pulled well clear of the rest. A routine Polytrack maiden should be his. (op 9-2)
Persidha ran a pleasing debut. Being by a Derby winner out of a 1m2f winner, she can be expected to improve over further. (op 16-1)
True Prince(USA) had finished well beaten in two maidens at the top tracks. He was bang up there until weakening over a furlong out and now qualifies for nurseries. (op 25-1)
Talya's Storm, who showed nothing on his Nottingham debut the previous week, ran better after missing the break and looks one for the longer term.

Twelve Strings(IRE), a 110,000 yearling but already gelded, proved too green to do himself justice and may be more of a long-term handicap prospect. (op 9-2 tchd 5-1)

5411 LADBROKES MOBILE MEDIAN AUCTION MAIDEN STKS (DIV II) 6f (P)
4:30 (4:30) (Class 6) 2-Y-O **£1,363** (£402; £201) **Stalls** Low

Form RPR

04 **1** **Dishy Guru**[15] 4912 2-9-3 0 LukeMorris 7 74
(Michael Blanshard) *trckd ldrs: led wl over 1f out: rdn fnl f: styd on strly* **6/1**[3]

6 **2** *1* **Princess Of Orange**[24] 4614 2-8-12 0 TedDurcan 3 66
(Rae Guest) *t.k.h: trckd ldrs: chsd led over 3f out tl green and hung bdly rt bnd 2f out and lost many l: styd on again ins fnl f and tk 2nd clsng stages: nt rch wnr and nt rcvr* **11/10**[1]

3 *1/2* **Mister Mackenzie** 2-9-3 0 GeorgeBaker 10 70
(John Best) *led after 1f: hdd wl over 1f out: styd on same pce and lost 2nd clsng stages* **13/2**

02 **4** *2 1/4* **Zain Point (IRE)**[26] 4548 2-9-3 0 (t) NeilCallan 5 65
(Gerard Butler) *t.k.h: trckd ldrs: styng on whn carried bdly rt bnd 2f out and lost many l: nt rcvr but styd on clsng stages* **11/4**[2]

6 **5** *4 1/2* **Trending (IRE)**[27] 4485 2-8-10 0 RaulDaSilva(7) 6 49
(Jeremy Gask) *t.k.h in rr early: pushed along and green 1/2-way: hdwy on ins over 1f out but nvr any ch* **18/1**

00 **6** *4* **Great Mystery (IRE)**[80] 2767 2-9-0 0 PatrickHills(3) 1 37
(J W Hills) *led 1f: styd chaing ldrs: wknd wl over 1f out* **20/1**

00 **7** *1 3/4* **Trisha's Boy (IRE)**[10] 5111 2-9-0 0 AdamBeschizza(3) 8 32
(Simon Dow) *s.i.s: sn rdn and green: a towards rr* **50/1**

8 *3* **Calculated Risk** 2-9-3 0 JamieMackay 2 23
(Willie Musson) *s.i.s: green and a in rr* **25/1**

1m 13.42s (1.52) **Going Correction** +0.225s/f (Slow) **8** Ran SP% **117.7**
Speed ratings (Par 92): **98,96,96,93,87 81,79,75**
toteswingers:1&2:£2.40, 2&3:£3.20, 1&3:£4.30 CSF £13.26 TOTE £3.40: £1.10, £1.10, £2.60; EX 12.10 Trifecta £68.10 Pool: £946.36 - 10.28 winning units..
Owner Clifton Partners **Bred** J W Ford **Trained** Upper Lambourn, Berks

FOCUS
Although there were more horses with solid previous form in this division than the first, it still looked the weaker leg and the winning time was 0.9 seconds slower.

NOTEBOOK
Dishy Guru improved plenty from his first start to his second and progressed again here, quickening up well to lead over a furlong from home, but his cause was greatly aided by the antics of the runner-up. He looks the type for ordinary nurseries. (op 8-1 tchd 11-2)
Princess Of Orange, an eye-catching sixth of 14 on her Windsor debut earlier this month, may well have won had she not hung wide on the home turn as she had travelled beautifully in a prominent position to that point and stayed on well once straightened. She should be able to win a race like this with the extra experience under her belt. Official explanation: jockey said filly hung right (tchd Evens and 6-5)
Mister Mackenzie, a £19,000 colt and one of two newcomers in the field, was soon in front and managed to stay there until over a furlong out. He possesses plenty of stamina on the dam's side of his pedigree, so may appreciate further. (op 15-2 tchd 8-1)
Zain Point(IRE), runner-up to a subsequent winner over 5f here on his second start last month, was already being niggled along when carried very wide by the runner-up turning for home, but he was never going to win. He now gets a mark. (op 5-2 tchd 10-3)
Trending(IRE), last of six on his Bath debut, improved a little on that but looks one for handicaps later on. (op 16-1)

5412 PLAY ROULETTE AT LADBROKES.COM H'CAP 6f (P)
5:00 (5:00) (Class 4) (0-80,80) 3-Y-O+ **£3,238** (£956; £478) **Stalls** Low

Form RPR

-004 **1** **Colorado Gold**[33] 4342 3-9-2 **75** PatCosgrave 7 83
(Ed de Giles) *sn led: rdn and qcknd wl over 1f out: hld on wl u.p ins fnl f* **12/1**

0121 **2** *1/2* **Highland Harvest**[17] 4850 7-9-4 **74** NeilCallan 5 80
(Jamie Poulton) *trckd ldrs: rdn and styd on to press wnr ins fnl f: kpt on but a jst hld* **9/2**[2]

2214 **3** *1 3/4* **Escape To Glory (USA)**[13] 4994 3-9-7 **80** GeorgeBaker 4 80
(Mikael Magnusson) *led briefly: styd trcking ldr on ins: rdn and effrt 1f out: sn struggling and nvr quite on terms: wknd: wl hld 3rd fnl 120yds* **1/1**[1]

024 **4** *1 1/2* **Estonia**[30] 4416 4-9-0 **70** LukeMorris 2 66
(Michael Squance) *t.k.h in rr but in tch: drvn and hdwy appr fnl f: styd on cl home: nvr a threat* **8/1**[3]

4433 **5** *1 1/4* **Chevise (IRE)**[13] 4994 3-9-3 **79** HarryBentley(3) 3 71
(Steve Woodman) *chsd ldrs tl rdn and lost position on ins over 2f out: styd on same pce fr over 1f out and nvr any ch* **9/2**[2]

5602 **6** *1/2* **Saharia (IRE)**[18] 4816 4-9-2 **72** ShaneKelly 8 62
(Michael Attwater) *s.i.s: sn rcvrd towards rr but in tch: chsd ldrs and rdn ins fnl 2f: wknd ins fnl f* **11/1**

1m 13.44s (1.54) **Going Correction** +0.225s/f (Slow)
WFA 3 from 4yo+ 3lb **6** Ran SP% **113.5**
Speed ratings (Par 105): **98,97,95,93,91 90**
toteswingers:1&2:£7.70, 2&3:£1.70, 1&3:£4.80 CSF £64.42 CT £102.90 TOTE £19.00: £2.70, £2.00; EX 82.80 Trifecta £277.90 Pool: £999.20 - 2.66 winning units..
Owner John Manser **Bred** Alan Parker **Trained** Ledbury, Herefordshire

FOCUS
The feature race on the card, albeit still below tariff, but an unsatisfactory contest as the early pace was moderate and the winning time was slower than both divisions of the 2-y-o maiden. Those who raced at the sharp end were hugely favoured and the form is rated around the runner-up.
T/Plt: £40.00 to a £1 stake. Pool of £54,321.12 - 989.79 winning tickets. T/Qpdt: £17.40 to a £1 stake. Pool of £3,322.85 - 141.10 winning tickets. ST

5388 WOLVERHAMPTON (A.W) (L-H)
Thursday, August 25

OFFICIAL GOING: Standard
Wind: Light behind Weather: Cloudy with sunny spells

5413 GREAT OFFERS AT WOLVERHAMPTON-RACECOURSE.CO.UK CLAIMING STKS 1m 141y(P)
6:10 (6:10) (Class 6) 2-Y-O **£1,704** (£503; £251) **Stalls** Low

Form RPR

6040 **1** **Jimmy The Lollipop (IRE)**[14] 4943 2-9-0 68 (b) PhillipMakin 1 67
(Kevin Ryan) *mde all: rdn and edgd rt over 1f out: styd on u.p* **8/1**

2025 **2** *1 1/4* **Sheila's Buddy**[8] 5170 2-9-0 71 LiamKeniry 2 64
(J S Moore) *sn pushed along to chse wnr: rdn over 1f out: styd on* **6/1**[3]

0341 **3** *3/4* **Yammos (IRE)**[3] 5325 2-8-11 65 MatthewDavies(3) 3 63
(Mick Channon) *chsd ldrs: rdn over 3f out: styd on* **85/40**[1]

The Form Book, Raceform Ltd, Compton, RG20 6NL

0503 **4** *hd* **Clean Bowled (IRE)**[15] 4907 2-9-0 58........................(bt) MartinDwyer 9 62
(Brian Meehan) *sn rdn along to chse ldrs: outpcd over 2f out: rallied u.p over 1f out: r.o* **6/1**[3]

00 **5** *2¾* **Alexandra Palace (IRE)**[10] 5097 2-8-4 0........................ JimmyQuinn 10 47
(Mark Johnston) *hld up: hdwy u.p over 1f out: no ex ins fnl f* **20/1**

1122 **6** *5* **Lady Jourdain (IRE)**[6] 5246 2-8-9 66........................ AndrewElliott 11 41
(Mrs K Burke) *prom: rdn over 3f out: wknd over 1f out* **11/4**[2]

0 **7** *14* **Goon Piper**[21] 4714 2-8-7 0........................ RichardKingscote 4 10
(Tom Dascombe) *sn pushed along in rr: rdn 1/2-way: wknd over 3f out* **40/1**

0050 **8** *4* **Sabusa (IRE)**[11] 5077 2-8-6 68........................(p) JohnFahy(3) 8 3
(Alan McCabe) *dwlt: hld up: plld hrd: rdn and wknd over 2f out* **25/1**

1m 50.82s (0.32) **Going Correction** -0.125s/f (Stan) **8** Ran SP% **109.4**
Speed ratings (Par 92): **93,91,91,91,88 84,71,68**
toteswingers:1&2:£7.50, 2&3:£3.00, 1&3:£7.30 CSF £49.45 TOTE £4.70: £2.70, £1.10, £1.30; EX 47.50.
Owner Five Arrows Racing **Bred** Corrin Stud **Trained** Hambleton, N Yorks

FOCUS
This claimer was run at a modest pace.

NOTEBOOK
Jimmy The Lollipop(IRE) had been running over shorter distances in his seven previous starts and his stamina was open to question. This was his first attempt on an artificial surface and, allowed to dictate the pace, he stole a march on his rivals off the final bend. Despite drifting into the middle of the track, he had sufficient reserves of stamina to hold on for his first success. (op 12-1 tchd 15-2)
Sheila's Buddy had only once tried 1m when second at Brighton on his penultimate start. In good form – he'd finished the bridesmaid three times already this year – he was dropping into claiming company for the first time here and ran well, tracking the winner but not finding enough to reel him in. This was only his seventh start and he should not be too long in winning. (op 13-2 tchd 11-2)
Yammos(IRE) broke his duck when stepped up to 1m for the first time in a seller at Windsor three days previously. He didn't find much when asked here, though, and the race may have come a little too quickly. (op 2-1 tchd 9-4)
Clean Bowled(IRE) had improved with every start and upped in distance here, he stayed on late having been one of the first to receive reminders. He's worth another try over the trip. (op 15-2 tchd 11-2)
Alexandra Palace(IRE) hadn't shown much in a couple of maidens, including over 7f on the all-weather at Kempton last time. Stepped up in trip and down in class here, she stayed on at the one pace. The penny dropped a bit too late, however. (op 16-1)
Lady Jourdain(IRE), winner of a Catterick seller over 7f last month and touched off over shorter here last time, blew the start and went wide off the first bend. This didn't help on her first start over this extended trip and she expended too much energy getting into contention. She is consistent in plating company, however. (op 9-4 tchd 2-1)

5414 LADBROKES.COM H'CAP — 1m 141y(P)
6:40 (6:40) (Class 6) (0-65,63) 3-Y-0+ — **£1,704** (£503; £251) **Stalls** Low

Form — RPR

2425 **1** **Kyle Of Bute**[21] 4716 5-9-8 63........................ CathyGannon 13 70
(Brian Baugh) *led 1f: chsd ldr tl led again over 2f out: rdn clr over 1f out: jst hld on* **5/1**[1]

0600 **2** *hd* **Burning Stone (USA)**[13] 5015 4-9-4 62........................ DeclanCannon(3) 4 68
(Gay Kelleway) *chsd ldrs: rdn over 2f out: r.o: jst failed* **6/1**[2]

4430 **3** *nk* **Mr Chocolate Drop (IRE)**[2] 5349 7-9-8 63........................(t) JimmyQuinn 5 68
(Mandy Rowland) *hld up: hdwy over 2f out: rdn over 1f out: r.o* **15/2**

0466 **4** *hd* **Woolston Ferry (IRE)**[22] 4666 5-9-2 62........................ JamesRogers(5) 11 67
(David Pinder) *a.p: chsd wnr 2f out: sn rdn: r.o* **8/1**

4125 **5** *1* **Gemma's Delight (IRE)**[27] 4503 4-9-8 63........................ LiamJones 7 66
(James Unett) *hld up: hdwy over 1f out: r.o* **10/1**

0006 **6** *1¾* **Dazakhee**[44] 3952 4-9-8 63........................ TonyCulhane 8 62+
(Paul Midgley) *hld up: hdwy u.p on outer over 1f out: styd on same pce ins fnl f* **9/1**

20-0 **7** *4* **Monashee Rock (IRE)**[15] 4918 6-9-0 55........................ LiamKeniry 10 44
(Matthew Salaman) *chsd ldrs: rdn over 2f out: wknd ins fnl f* **16/1**

0000 **8** *¾* **Vanilla Rum**[41] 4076 4-9-2 57........................(p) StephenCraine 12 45
(John Mackie) *hld up: hdwy 4f out: rdn over 2f out: wknd over 1f out* **14/1**

0051 **9** *½* **Justcallmehandsome**[59] 3475 9-9-2 62........................(v) LucyKBarry(5) 9 48
(Dominic Ffrench Davis) *dwlt: hld up: hdwy over 3f out: rdn and wknd over 1f out* **13/2**[3]

0660 **10** *5* **Dabbers Ridge (IRE)**[22] 4679 9-9-3 61........................(p) GaryBartley[illegible] 60
(Ian McInnes) *mid-div: rdn over 2f out: sn wknd* **16/1**

3500 **11** *½* **Pie Poudre**[12] 5040 4-9-3 58........................(b) WilliamCarson 6 32
(Roy Brotherton) *s.i.s: hld up: rdn over 1f out: wknd ins fnl f* **7/1**

-000 **12** *7* **Green Agenda**[9] 5143 5-9-0 55........................(v) RobbieFitzpatrick 2 13
(Derek Shaw) *led over 7f out: rdn and hdd over 2f out: wknd over 1f out* **50/1**

1m 49.45s (-1.05) **Going Correction** -0.125s/f (Stan) **12** Ran SP% **119.1**
Speed ratings (Par 101): **99,98,98,98,97 95,92,91,91,86 86,80**
toteswingers:1&2:£7.10, 2&3:£12.40, 1&3:£2.60 CSF £34.27 CT £230.36 TOTE £5.40: £1.80, £2.80, £2.60; EX 39.40.
Owner J H Chrimes And Mr & Mrs G W Hannam **Bred** Chippenham Lodge Stud Ltd **Trained** Audley, Staffs

FOCUS
A modest if competitive handicap for the money, run at a steady clip and it produced an exciting finish. Straightforward form.

5415 ENJOY THE PARTY PACK GROUP OFFER CLAIMING STKS — 1m 4f 50y(P)
7:10 (7:10) (Class 5) 3-Y-0 — **£1,940** (£577; £288; £144) **Stalls** Low

Form — RPR

5060 **1** **Woop Woop (IRE)**[22] 4664 3-7-12 61........................ JimmyQuinn 6 61
(Stef Higgins) *hld up: hdwy over 5f out: led over 1f out: shkn up and r.o wl* **7/2**[3]

1534 **2** *3¾* **Dew Reward (IRE)**[17] 4868 3-8-3 62........................ CathyGannon 2 60
(Bill Turner) *hld up: hdwy over 7f out: chsd ldr over 6f out: rdn and ev ch over 1f out: styd on same pce ins fnl f* **13/2**

0325 **3** *2¾* **Revolutionary**[28] 4476 3-8-0 56........................ SophieDoyle(3) 3 56
(Jamie Osborne) *led: rdn over 2f out: hdd over 1f out: no ex ins fnl f* **11/4**[1]

200 **4** *1* **Elfine (IRE)**[66] 3228 3-8-6 72........................ MartinLane 1 57
(Rae Guest) *plld hrd and prom: losty pl over 5f out: rdn over 2f out: styd on same pce appr fnl f* **3/1**[2]

03 **5** *½* **Fair Dinkum (IRE)**[17] 4868 3-8-3 0........................ ChrisCatlin 4 53
(Jamie Osborne) *hld up: hdwy 2f out: sn rdn: styd on same pce* **7/2**[3]

00- **6** *11* **Safari Sunbeam**[14] 5626 3-8-6 0 ow3........................ RichardKingscote 5 39
(Peter Pritchard) *sn chsng ldr: lost 2nd over 6f out: rdn over 3f out: wknd wl over 1f out* **200/1**

2m 42.46s (1.36) **Going Correction** -0.125s/f (Stan) **6** Ran SP% **109.9**
Speed ratings (Par 100): **90,87,85,85,84 77**
toteswingers:1&2:£2.10, 2&3:£3.20, 1&3:£2.70 CSF £24.37 TOTE £5.90: £1.90, £3.30; EX 18.70.Revolutionary was claimed by Mrs J. B. Pye for £6000.

Owner Lee Westwood & Chubby Chandler **Bred** C Amerian **Trained** Lambourn, Berks

FOCUS
On paper, this was a relatively competitive claimer with the market providing little clue, but it turned into something of a rout. The time was slow and the form is rated around the runner-up.

5416 LADBROKES MOBILE H'CAP — 1m 4f 50y(P)
7:45 (7:45) (Class 5) (0-70,75) 3-Y-0+ — **£1,940** (£577; £288; £144) **Stalls** Low

Form — RPR

-111 **1** **Kepler's Law**[6] 5249 3-9-10 75 6ex........................ SebSanders 3 92+
(Sir Mark Prescott Bt) *mde all: edgd rt and shkn up over 7f out: pushed along over 2f out: sn clr: easily* **1/6**[1]

5540 **2** *4½* **Motarjm (USA)**[2] 5357 7-8-9 50 oh2........................(t) ChrisCatlin 1 55
(Lydia Pearce) *prom: wnt 3rd 3f out: sn rdn: wnt 2nd ins fnl f: no ch w wnr* **14/1**[3]

6020 **3** *2½* **Drawback (IRE)**[68] 3176 8-8-10 51........................(p) FrankieMcDonald 5 52
(Barry Brennan) *hld up: hdwy over 1f out: styd on to go 3rd towards fin: nvr on terms* **40/1**

660 **4** *¾* **Alternative Choice (USA)**[41] 4060 5-9-7 62........................ JimCrowley 2 62
(Nick Littmoden) *prom: chsd wnr over 7f out: rdn over 2f out: sn outpcd: lost 2 pls ins fnl f* **12/1**[2]

055 **5** *30* **Ocean's Dream Day (IRE)**[10] 5118 3-7-10 50 oh2..(p) KieranO'Neill(3) 4 —
(John Ryan) *racd keenly: trckd ldr to over 7f out: sn pushed along: reminders 6f out: rdn and wknd over 2f out: t.o* **16/1**

2m 40.0s (-1.10) **Going Correction** -0.125s/f (Stan)
WFA 3 from 5yo+ 10lb **5** Ran SP% **108.4**
Speed ratings (Par 103): **98,95,93,92,72**
CSF £3.44 TOTE £1.30: £1.02, £4.30; EX 3.30.
Owner Rectory Racing **Bred** Chippenham Lodge Stud Ltd **Trained** Newmarket, Suffolk

FOCUS
A weak handicap run at a sensible pace. The winner's form is still rated more positively than it might have been.

5417 PLAY ROULETTE AT LADBROKES.COM H'CAP — 2m 119y(P)
8:15 (8:15) (Class 4) (0-85,84) 3-Y-0+ — **£3,234** (£962; £481; £240) **Stalls** Low

Form — RPR

511 **1** **Final Liberation (FR)**[22] 4687 3-8-6 76........................ StevieDonohoe 3 90+
(Sir Mark Prescott Bt) *led: rdn and hdd 2f out: rallied to ld 1f out: styd on gamely* **11/8**[2]

6434 **2** *hd* **Rosewood Lad**[10] 5102 4-9-0 70........................ CathyGannon 1 78
(J S Moore) *sn pushed along and prom: rdn over 3f out: styd on gamely* **11/1**[3]

102 **3** *½* **Red Courtier**[10] 5102 4-9-8 78........................(p) JimCrowley 5 91+
(Paul Cole) *chsd wnr: rdn to ld 2f out: hdd 1f out: styd on* **10/11**[1]

200/ **4** *47* **Wine 'n Dine**[612] 2475 6-9-7 84........................ ThomasBrown(7) 4 35
(Bernard Llewellyn) *chsd ldrs: pushed along 1/2-way: wknd over 5f out: t.o* **50/1**

3443 **5** *1* **Gremlin**[17] 4870 7-8-12 68 oh5........................ MartinLane 2 18
(Bernard Llewellyn) *s.i.s: hld up: rdn 7f out: bhd fnl 6f: t.o* **25/1**

3m 36.03s (-5.77) **Going Correction** -0.125s/f (Stan)
WFA 3 from 4yo+ 14lb **5** Ran SP% **108.6**
Speed ratings (Par 105): **108,107,107,85,85**
CSF £14.87 TOTE £3.90: £3.50, £4.80; EX 15.70.
Owner P Bamford **Bred** R & E Bamford Limited **Trained** Newmarket, Suffolk

FOCUS
Poor prize-money and a sub-standard field for the grade, but it produced a thrilling finish. It was run at fair pace. The winner and third were probably a bit better than the bare form compared with the runner-up.
Gremlin Official explanation: jockey said, regarding running and riding, that in view of the fact that he had ridden the gelding hard during the final circuit and being mindful of its welfare, being tired, he rode sympathetically in the home straight.

5418 HORIZONS RESTAURANT MAIDEN AUCTION FILLIES' STKS — 5f 216y(P)
8:45 (8:45) (Class 6) 2-Y-0 — **£1,704** (£503; £251) **Stalls** Low

Form — RPR

4 **1** **Villeneuve**[16] 4883 2-8-9 0........................ MartinDwyer 1 77+
(William Muir) *mde all: clr fr over 1f out: easily* **4/6**[1]

40 **2** *6* **Symphony Time (IRE)**[17] 4853 2-8-9 0........................ ShaneKelly 3 53
(Brian Meehan) *[illegible] thrght: rdn over 2f out: outpcd fr over 1f out* [illegible]

0430 **3** *2* **Spring Daisy (IRE)**[19] 4808 2-8-7 46........................ RichardKingscote 5 45
(Tom Dascombe) *chsd ldrs: rdn over 2f out: styd on same pce* **18/1**

60 **4** *2¼* **Lady Hello (IRE)**[30] 4406 2-8-5 0........................ SamHitchcott 6 36
(Mick Channon) *hld up in tch: wnt 3rd over 2f out: sn rdn: wknd ins fnl f* **14/1**

50 **5** *1* **Vitalicious**[12] 5058 2-8-7 0........................ RoystonFfrench 4 35
(Ed McMahon) *chsd ldrs: rdn 1/2-way: wknd over 1f out* **7/1**[3]

6 *4½* **Geanie Mac (IRE)** 2-8-6 0 ow3........................ SeanLevey(3) 2 24
(Tim Pitt) *dwlt: outpcd* **18/1**

1m 14.31s (-0.69) **Going Correction** -0.125s/f (Stan) **6** Ran SP% **109.7**
Speed ratings (Par 89): **99,91,88,85,84 78**
toteswingers:1&2:£1.70, 2&3:£3.50, 1&3:£1.70 CSF £3.37 TOTE £1.50: £1.10, £3.30; EX 3.80.
Owner Mr & Mrs G Middlebrook **Bred** Mr & Mrs G Middlebrook **Trained** Lambourn, Berks

FOCUS
A reasonable juvenile fillies' sprint for this track.

NOTEBOOK
Villeneuve shaped with plenty of promise on her debut at Ffos Las and put that experience to good use here, bouncing out of the stalls and dictating matters under sensible fractions from her jockey. He took the shortest route and sat quietly on her throughout, without ever having to resort to the whip. She powered clear for an impressive-looking victory although there are obviously question marks over what she actually beat. She will have to show improvement to justify her Fillies' Mile and Cheveley Park entries, but they don't look too fanciful at this stage. (op 4-5)
Symphony Time(IRE) had been beaten a long way over both attempts in 7f maidens, latterly in soft ground, which didn't suit her, at Thirsk. Back a furlong on her AW debut here, she had the winner close up and in her sights throughout, but was made to looked one-paced when Martin Dwyer's mount kicked clear off the final bend. However, she stuck to her task and was dogged in defeat. Connections can now think about nurseries.
Spring Daisy(IRE) clouds the form a little as she's only rated 46. She had six previous races and was barely competitive in a 6f Redcar seller on her previous start. The fact that she stayed on quite well to take third at the death bodes well, but it probably says more about the overall strength of the race. (tchd 20-1)
Lady Hello(IRE), who had shown nothing more than a glimmer of ability in two 5f turf maidens, was slowly away and came wide with her challenge approaching the final 3f. Her run flattened out and a step up in trip might suit. (op 12-1)
Vitalicious had two previous starts and didn't appear to improve for her first when stepped up to 6f at Beverley last time. She showed decent early speed but tired over the last furlong. This was something of an improvement, however. (op 11-2)

Geanie Mac(IRE), a 6,000gns yearling, was very slowly away and outpaced. She made late headway, but she should be swerved until the penny drops. (op 25-1 tchd 16-1)

5419 BET IN-PLAY AT LADBROKES.COM H'CAP 5f 216y(P)
9:15 (9:16) (Class 5) (0-75,75) 3-Y-O **£2,264** (£673; £336; £168) **Stalls** Low

Form RPR
0406 1 **Dasho**[13] 5000 3-9-7 **75** KirstyMilczarek 5 81
(Olivia Maylam) *chsd ldrs: rdn to ld ins fnl f: r.o* 7/2[1]
201 2 *hd* **Showboating (IRE)**[18] 4819 3-9-1 **72** (p) MartinHarley(3) 6 77+
(Alan McCabe) *hld up: hdwy over 1f out: r.o wl: nt rch wnr* 13/2[2]
2000 3 *hd* **Crucis Abbey (IRE)**[36] 4199 3-8-11 **65** LiamJones 9 70
(James Unett) *hld up: hdwy over 2f out: rdn over 1f out: r.o wl* 16/1
2-21 4 *nk* **Supercharged (IRE)**[17] 4863 3-9-4 **72** SebSanders 2 77+
(Chris Wall) *hld up in tch: nt clr run over 1f out: swtchd lft: r.o wl* 7/2[1]
4204 5 *hd* **Dream Catcher (FR)**[28] 4459 3-9-2 **75** JamesRogers(5) 8 78
(David Pinder) *led: hdd over 4f out: chsd ldr tl led again over 2f out: rdn and hdd ins fnl f: styd on* 14/1
0012 6 *1* **Rowan Spirit (IRE)**[10] 5109 3-9-2 **70** (v[1]) ShaneKelly 11 70
(Mark Brisbourne) *prom: rdn over 2f out: styd on* 14/1
2322 7 *3 ½* **Bilko Pak (IRE)**[29] 4431 3-8-13 **67** (p) RobbieFitzpatrick 3 56
(Derek Shaw) *s.i.s: hld up: hdwy over 1f out: nvr trbld ldrs* 8/1
3502 8 *½* **Speightowns Kid (USA)**[13] 4988 3-9-4 **72** LiamKeniry 10 59
(Matthew Salaman) *chsd ldr: led over 4f out to over 2f out: sn rdn: wknd ins fnl f* 7/1[3]
0000 9 *1* **Fettuccine (IRE)**[14] 4973 3-8-8 **62** MartinLane 1 46
(John Gallagher) *s.i.s: sn prom: rdn 1/2-way: wknd ins fnl f* 28/1
0005 10 *nk* **Silly Billy (IRE)**[19] 4799 3-8-7 **66** JemmaMarshall(5) 7 49
(Sylvester Kirk) *hld up: a in rr* 18/1
313 11 *10* **Upper Lambourn (IRE)**[21] 4721 3-9-6 **74** FergusSweeney 4 25
(Jamie Osborne) *hld up: a in rr: rdn over 2f out: sn wknd* 14/1

1m 13.74s (-1.26) **Going Correction** -0.125s/f (Stan) **11** Ran SP% **116.0**
Speed ratings (Par 100): **103,102,102,102,101 100,95,95,93,93 80**
toteswingers:1&2:£5.00, 2&3:£16.70, 1&3:£16.70 CSF £25.43 CT £321.25 TOTE £2.80: £1.10, £2.50, £10.80; EX 49.80.
Owner Mrs P A Clark **Bred** Mrs P A Clark **Trained** Epsom, Surrey

FOCUS
A reasonably competitive sprint handicap and you could throw a blanket over the first six home as they fanned across the track. Ordinary if solid looking form.
T/Plt: £33.00 to a £1 stake. Pool of £53,008.14 - 1,169.74 winning tickets. T/Qpdt: £7.40 to a £1 stake. Pool of £4,768.40 - 472.50 winning tickets. CR

5133 BRIGHTON (L-H)
Friday, August 26

OFFICIAL GOING: Soft (good to soft in places; 6.2)
Wind: Moderate, half behind Weather: Unsettled, rain before racing

5420 TOTEPLACEPOT WIN WITHOUT BACKING A WINNER H'CAP 1m 3f 196y
4:40 (4:41) (Class 5) (0-70,69) 3-Y-O **£2,522** (£750; £375; £187) **Stalls** High

Form RPR
6020 1 **Around The Clock (USA)**[60] 3460 3-9-1 **63** DarrylHolland 7 69
(Amanda Perrett) *mde virtually all: drvn along and hld on wl fnl 2f* 6/1
506 2 *½* **The Calling Curlew**[20] 4800 3-9-7 **69** FergusSweeney 4 74
(Henry Candy) *chsd wnr 5f: lft 2nd again over 3f out: drvn to chal fnl 2f: r.o: jst hld nr fin* 13/2
4203 3 *2 ¼* **Clarion Call**[18] 4845 3-9-7 **69** LiamKeniry 1 73+
(Eve Johnson Houghton) *hld up in 4th: bdly hmpd over 3f out: rallied u.p in centre over 1f out: hung lft: one pce fnl f* 3/1[1]
0-01 4 *1 ½* **Guards Chapel**[85] 2637 3-9-1 **63** GeorgeBaker 3 62+
(Gary Moore) *hld up in 5th: drvn to press ldrs 2f out: no ex 1f out* 4/1[2]
-203 5 *2* **Frederick William**[24] 4627 3-9-5 **67** SebSanders 6 63
(Peter Makin) *hld up in rr: sltly hmpd over 3f out: hrd rdn over 2f out: nvr able to chal* 9/2[3]
0412 U **Peira**[16] 4932 3-9-5 **67** LukeMorris 2 —
(Jane Chapple-Hyam) *chsd ldng pair: wnt 2nd 7f out: hmpd and uns rdr over 3f out* 4/1[2]

2m 38.96s (6.26) **Going Correction** +0.45s/f (Yiel) **6** Ran SP% **110.8**
Speed ratings (Par 100): **97,96,95,94,92** —
toteswingers: 1&2 £6.60, 1&3 £3.10, 2&3 £5.90 CSF £41.41 TOTE £10.80: £4.60, £2.30; EX 32.80.
Owner A D Spence **Bred** Arindel **Trained** Pulborough, W Sussex

FOCUS
Rail dolled out from 6f to 2.5f adding 14yds to distances. As is normally the case when the grounds turns soft they came up the stands' rail in the straight.
Clarion Call Official explanation: jockey said gelding suffered interference in running

5421 TRY TOTEQUICKPICK IF YOU'RE FEELING LUCKY H'CAP 1m 1f 209y
5:10 (5:12) (Class 6) (0-55,56) 3-Y-O+ **£1,811** (£539; £269; £134) **Stalls** High

Form RPR
0303 1 **Abigails Angel**[46] 3916 4-9-6 **54** GeorgeBaker 8 63
(Brett Johnson) *mde virtually all: rdn over 2f out: jnd by runner-up ent fnl f: edgd lft: hld on gamely* 4/1[3]
000 2 *nk* **Reggie Perrin**[34] 4320 3-8-3 **50** JemmaMarshall(5) 3 58
(Pat Phelan) *chsd ldrs: rdn 5f out: drvn level ent fnl f: r.o: jst outpcd nr fin* 9/1
3535 3 *1* **Drumadoon (IRE)**[21] 4745 3-8-12 **54** (p) IanMongan 4 60
(John Dunlop) *hld up in rr: sme hdwy 3f out: hrd rdn and edgd lft fr 2f out: styd on fnl f* 3/1[2]
0000 4 *3 ¼* **Salesiano**[19] 4827 3-8-6 **51** KieranO'Neill(3) 11 51
(Peter Makin) *plld hrd: prom: rdn 4f out: hld whn edgd lft fr 2f out: wknd 1f out* 8/1
2641 5 *1 ½* **Newby Lodge (IRE)**[10] 5134 3-8-9 **56** 6ex LauraPike(5) 2 53
(Alan Bailey) *cl up: jnd ldr 5f out: wknd over 1f out* 9/4[1]
0-00 6 *¾* **Under Fire (IRE)**[15] 4953 8-8-7 **48** GeorgeDowning(7) 7 43
(Tony Carroll) *plld hrd: prom: rdn 5f out: sn lost pl* 14/1
3003 7 *shd* **Corlough Mountain**[22] 4700 7-8-9 **46** oh1 SophieDoyle(3) 14 41
(Paddy Butler) *t.k.h: in tch: rdn 4f out: sn outpcd* 33/1
5000 8 *23* **Ocean Rosie (IRE)**[45] 3942 4-8-12 **46** oh1 LukeMorris 10 —
(Tony Carroll) *in tch: rdn 6f out: drvn along and n.d fnl 4f* 16/1

2m 10.67s (7.07) **Going Correction** +0.45s/f (Yiel)
WFA 3 from 4yo+ 8lb **8** Ran SP% **112.4**
Speed ratings (Par 101): **89,88,87,85,84 83,83,65**
toteswingers: 1&2 £7.60, 1&3 £3.30, 2&3 £6.80 CSF £37.83 CT £120.47 TOTE £4.80: £2.00, £3.00, £1.10; EX 34.10.
Owner B R Johnson **Bred** P Balding **Trained** Ashtead, Surrey

FOCUS
A moderate handicap.

5422 TRY TOTEQUICKPICK ON ALL TOTEPOOL BETS H'CAP 7f 214y
5:40 (5:40) (Class 6) (0-65,65) 3-Y-O+ **£1,811** (£539; £269; £134) **Stalls** Centre

Form RPR
4553 1 **No Larking (IRE)**[10] 5137 3-9-3 **62** FergusSweeney 13 73
(Henry Candy) *mde virtually all: styd alone far side ent st: cut corner while rivals wnt to outside rail: 2 l ahd whn c across to stands' rail over 1f out: drvn out* 7/2[2]
0434 2 *3 ¼* **Inquisitress**[10] 5136 7-8-8 **50** SeanLevey(3) 10 54
(John Bridger) *chsd ldrs: led main gp on stands' rail 3f out: 2 l down whn wnr c across fr far side over 1f out: nt qckn* 11/1
0410 3 *5* **Ocean Countess (IRE)**[15] 4948 5-9-2 **58** (v) MichaelO'Connell(3) 12 50
(Tony Carroll) *s.s: bhd: rdn and hdwy over 2f out: no ex appr fnl f* 4/1[3]
4204 4 *nk* **Salvationist**[21] 4744 3-8-12 **57** IanMongan 14 48
(John Dunlop) *chsd ldrs: briefly led main gp to stands' rail over 3f out: wknd over 1f out* 11/4[1]
056 5 *3 ¾* **Kavachi (IRE)**[22] 4725 8-9-11 **64** GeorgeBaker 8 47
(Gary Moore) *rrd s and missed break: towards rr: rdn 3f out: nvr trbld ldrs* 15/2
0-06 6 *nk* **Ain't Talkin'**[22] 4699 5-8-4 **46** oh1 (p) HarryBentley(3) 4 28
(Michael Attwater) *prom: swtchd rt and rdn over 3f out: wknd over 2f out* 50/1
3042 7 *1* **Khajaaly (IRE)**[18] 4866 4-9-8 **64** AdamBeschizza(3) 2 44
(Julia Feilden) *rrd s and missed break: mid-div: rdn 3f out: sn btn* 5/1
-600 8 *1 ¼* **Private Joke**[45] 3952 4-9-10 **63** AndreaAtzeni 11 40
(Terry Clement) *dwlt: mid-div: rdn and wknd 3f out* 20/1

1m 39.56s (3.56) **Going Correction** +0.45s/f (Yiel)
WFA 3 from 4yo+ 6lb **8** Ran SP% **112.4**
Speed ratings (Par 101): **100,96,91,91,87 87,86,85**
toteswingers: 1&2 £4.90, 1&3 £3.10, 2&3 £7.70 CSF £39.42 CT £157.63 TOTE £5.00: £2.30, £4.00, £1.20; EX 36.90.
Owner Simon Broke And Partners **Bred** Carrigbeg Stud **Trained** Kingston Warren, Oxon

FOCUS
More weak handicap form.
Ocean Countess(IRE) Official explanation: trainer said mare finished distressed

5423 TOTEEXACTA BETTER VALUE FORECAST H'CAP 6f 209y
6:15 (6:16) (Class 5) (0-70,69) 3-Y-O **£2,522** (£750; £375; £187) **Stalls** Centre

Form RPR
5402 1 **High On The Hog (IRE)**[43] 4011 3-9-5 **67** (p) IanMongan 8 76
(John Dunlop) *chsd ldr: led over 2f out: drvn clr 1f out: styd on wl* 9/2[2]
0022 2 *3* **Map Of Heaven**[27] 4559 3-9-4 **69** (b) AdamBeschizza(3) 5 70+
(William Haggas) *hld up in 6th: rdn 3f out: nt clr run and swtchd lft to centre over 2f out: kpt on u.p to take 2nd fnl 75yds* 10/3[1]
0065 3 *¾* **Elegant Muse**[16] 4911 3-8-11 **62** JohnFahy(3) 3 61
(Walter Swinburn) *towards rr: hdwy whn edgd rt and bmpd over 2f out: hrd rdn over 1f out: one pce* 8/1
0500 4 *nk* **Lightning Spirit**[21] 4758 3-8-3 **54** HarryBentley(3) 4 52
(Gary Moore) *in tch: rdn to chse ldrs 2f out: one pce* 5/1[3]
3456 5 *3 ¼* **Prophet In A Dream**[9] 5172 3-8-9 **60** SophieDoyle(3) 2 49
(Paddy Butler) *led tl over 2f out: wknd over 1f out* 33/1
6225 6 *hd* **Arctic Mirage**[16] 4917 3-9-5 **67** LiamKeniry 7 56
(Michael Blanshard) *restless in stalls: s.i.s: hld up in last: shkn up over 2f out: nvr trbld ldrs* 11/2
220 7 *1 ½* **Hawk Moth (IRE)**[20] 4799 3-9-5 **67** ChrisCatlin 10 52
(John Spearing) *chsd ldrs tl wknd 2f out* 5/1[3]
0050 8 *½* **Rafaaf (IRE)**[21] 4765 3-9-5 **67** AndreaAtzeni 1 50
(Robert Eddery) *in tch: rdn 3f out: bmpd over 2f out: sn btn* 8/1

1m 25.92s (2.82) **Going Correction** +0.45s/f (Yiel) **8** Ran SP% **115.1**
Speed ratings (Par 100): **101,97,96,96,92 92,90,90**
toteswingers: 1&2 £2.60, 1&3 £9.30, 2&3 £4.60 CSF £20.07 CT £116.97 TOTE £6.60: £1.90, £1.30, £4.00; EX 19.00.
Owner J L Dunlop **Bred** John Osborne **Trained** Arundel, W Sussex

FOCUS
This looked fairly open on paper.
Arctic Mirage Official explanation: jockey said gelding was upset in stalls and slowly away; vet said gelding had banged its head in stalls

5424 TOTESWINGER MORE WAYS TO WIN MAIDEN AUCTION STKS 5f 213y
6:45 (6:45) (Class 5) 2-Y-O **£2,522** (£750; £375; £187) **Stalls** Centre

Form RPR
56 1 **Red Quartet (IRE)**[18] 4857 2-8-11 0 AndreaAtzeni 5 71
(Robert Eddery) *chsd ldrs: styd far side st: drvn to dispute ld over 1f out: edgd lft: jst ahd of runner-up on stands' side fnl 75yds: rdn out* 6/1
0 2 *¾* **Arctic Stryker**[18] 4848 2-8-11 0 LukeMorris 2 69
(John Best) *disp ld: c stands' side st: jst hld by wnr on far side fnl 75yds: nrly ct for 2nd* 20/1
4 3 *nse* **Theresnoneedfordat (IRE)**[19] 4823 2-8-12 0 SebSanders 7 70
(Lydia Pearce) *in tch: c stands' side st: outpcd 2f out: styd on wl fnl f: nrly snatched 2nd* 15/8[1]
6 4 *1 ½* **Chrissycross (IRE)**[50] 3761 2-8-2 0 KieranO'Neill(3) 8 58
(Roger Teal) *outpcd and bhd: styd far side st: rdn and hdwy 2f out: jst hld whn n.m.r on rail ins fnl f* 11/1
02 5 *1 ¼* **Flamborough Breeze**[25] 4614 2-8-9 0 JackMitchell 1 58
(Edward Vaughan) *disp ld: styd far side st: rdn and hung rt over 2f out: hdd & wknd over 1f out* 9/4[2]
02 6 *¾* **Essexvale (IRE)**[7] 5232 2-8-6 0 SeanLevey(3) 3 56
(Richard Hannon) *in tch: styd far side st: wnt prom 4f out: wknd over 1f out* 9/2[3]
0 7 *hd* **Kaylee**[15] 4954 2-8-5 0 JamieMackay 6 52
(Gary Moore) *prom: c stands' side st: hrd rdn 2f out: wknd 1f out* 33/1

1m 13.9s (3.70) **Going Correction** +0.45s/f (Yiel) **7** Ran SP% **114.1**
Speed ratings (Par 94): **93,92,91,89,88 87,87**
toteswingers: 1&2 £15.60, 1&3 £3.00, 2&3 £4.40 CSF £104.74 TOTE £4.60: £2.00, £10.50; EX 110.90.
Owner Anderson, Donaldson, Keane & Rayment **Bred** Mrs Brid Cosgrove **Trained** Newmarket, Suffolk
■ Stewards' Enquiry : Andrea Atzeni four-day ban: careless riding (Sep 12-15)

FOCUS
A difference of opinion here as only three jockeys decided to come to the stands' side with four sticking to the far rail. As it turned out there was little between all of them at the line. The pace was sound and the form is rated around the winner and third.

The Form Book, Raceform Ltd, Compton, RG20 6NL

NOTEBOOK
Red Quartet(IRE) came home best of the far-side group to score at the third attempt. He wasn't done any favours by Flamborough Breeze at the two pole as that rival veered across him, but he was soon back on an even keel and making headway to lead that group. This looks a slight improvement on what he's shown to date and maybe the easier ground helped. Nurseries are next. (op 8-1)
Arctic Stryker ◆ couldn't get involved over 5f on debut but there was clear evidence that he had come on for that experience and kept on well, shaping like he'll not be long in finding a race.
Theresnoneedfordat(IRE) ◆ came home best of the stands' side trio despite not having the clearest of runs up the rail. He attracted market support beforehand, just as on debut, and is clearly well regarded by connections. Given he is a son of Holy Roman Emperor he'd probably prefer a sounder surface on which to race, but there is obvious ability there and he'll probably soon be winning. (tchd 5-2 in a place)
Flamborough Breeze, who set the standard on her latest Windsor second, was the obvious disappointment, but she looked ill at ease in the conditions (both previous runs on good to firm) and it is probably worth forgiving this. (op 15-8 tchd 5-2)

5425 TOTEPOOL A BETTER WAY TO BET H'CAP — 5f 213y
7:15 (7:15) (Class 5) (0-75,79) 4-Y-O+ — **£2,522** (£750; £375; £187) **Stalls** Centre

Form — RPR
1312 **1** — **Interakt**[15] 4973 4-8-10 **66** .... HarryBentley(3) 7 — 76
(Joseph Tuite) *in tch: c stands' side over 3f out: drvn to ld 2f out: in control fnl 100yds: rdn out* — **7/2**[1]
5023 **2** ½ **Mingun Bell (USA)**[12] 5083 4-9-4 **74** .... JohnFahy(3) 10 — 82
(Ed de Giles) *prom: swtchd towards stands' side pair over 2f out: sn drvn to chal: nt qckn fnl f* — **9/2**[2]
0024 **3** 2¼ **Hand Painted**[13] 5037 5-8-13 **66** .... (p) LiamKeniry 9 — 67
(Anthony Middleton) *dwlt: towards rr: c stands'side over 3f out: rdn over 2f out: styd on u.p fnl f over 1f out* — **9/1**
2023 **4** ¾ **Whiskey Junction**[15] 4967 7-8-13 **69** .... AdamBeschizza(3) 6 — 67
(Michael Quinn) *chsd ldrs: c towards stands' side gp 2f out: hrd rdn over 1f out: one pce* — **7/1**
101 **5** 1 **Italian Tom (IRE)**[7] 5238 4-9-12 **79** 6ex .... LukeMorris 5 — 74
(Ronald Harris) *towards rr: effrt and c towards stands' side gp 2f out: hrd rdn: no ex 1f out* — **5/1**[3]
6400 **6** 1¼ **Imprimis Tagula (IRE)**[4] 5322 7-8-13 **73** .... (v) MissAlexOwen(7) 2 — 64
(Alan Bailey) *in tch: styd alone in centre in st: outpcd fnl 3f* — **5/1**[3]
1420 **7** 2¾ **Bermondsey Bob (IRE)**[15] 4960 5-8-13 **69** .... KierenFox(3) 1 — 51
(John Spearing) *led: c towards stands' side gp and hdd 2f out: drvn along and wknd over 1f out* — **9/2**[2]

1m 12.09s (1.89) **Going Correction** +0.45s/f (Yiel) — **7** Ran SP% **114.4**
Speed ratings (Par 103): **105,104,101,100,99 97,93**
toteswingers: 1&2 £4.10, 1&3 £5.20, 2&3 £11.70 CSF £19.37 CT £128.95 TOTE £3.80: £1.80, £3.40; EX 20.70.
Owner Heart Of The South Racing **Bred** P C Hunt **Trained** Great Shefford, Berkshire
FOCUS
The action unfolded up the stands' side this time.

5426 BET TOTEPOOL ON ALL UK RACING H'CAP — 5f 59y
7:45 (7:45) (Class 6) (0-65,65) 3-Y-O+ — **£1,811** (£539; £269; £134) **Stalls** Low

Form — RPR
5436 **1** — **Stonecrabstomorrow (IRE)**[10] 5138 8-8-9 **56** .... MarkCoumbe(5) 3 — 69+
(Michael Attwater) *hld up off the pce in last: hrd rdn and hdwy over 1f out: drvn to ld fnl 75yds: shade comf* — **7/2**[3]
0265 **2** ½ **Commandingpresence (USA)**[15] 4960 5-9-2 **61** .... SeanLevey(3) 1 — 70
(John Bridger) *led: drvn 2 l ahd 2f out: edgd lft ins fnl f: hdd fnl 75yds: kpt on gamely* — **10/3**[2]
6135 **3** 1¾ **Simple Rhythm**[19] 4828 5-9-1 **57** .... (p) DarryllHolland 7 — 60
(John Ryan) *in tch in 4th: effrt 2f out: one pce fnl f* — **11/4**[1]
3036 **4** 2¼ **Pocket's Pick (IRE)**[10] 5139 5-9-1 **57** .... (bt) PaulDoe 5 — 52
(Jim Best) *t.k.h: cl up: chsd ldr 3f out: drvn along 2f out: wknd fnl f* — **9/1**
5230 **5** ¾ **Kinigi (IRE)**[13] 5053 5-9-2 **65** .... (b) MichaelJMurphy(7) 6 — 57
(Ronald Harris) *chsd ldr 2f: wknd 2f out: 5th and btn whn hung lft ins fnl f* — **11/4**[1]

64.95 secs (2.65) **Going Correction** +0.45s/f (Yiel) — **5** Ran SP% **108.6**
Speed ratings (Par 101): **96,95,92,88,87**
toteswingers: 1&2 £[illegible] CSF £[illegible] TOTE £4.30: £2.80, £1.70; EX 20.00.
Owner Miss Nicola Carroll **Bred** P Dillon **Trained** Epsom, Surrey
FOCUS
A low-grade sprint.
T/Plt: £1,237.70 to a £1 stake. Pool: £48,714.94. 28.73 winning tickets. T/Qpdt: £371.80 to a £1 stake. Pool: £5,226.20. 10.40 winning tickets. LM

4882 FFOS LAS (L-H)
Friday, August 26

OFFICIAL GOING: Flat course - good changing to good to soft after race 3 (3:05); jumps courses - good
Wind: Light, across Weather: showers

5427 TOTEPLACEPOT WIN WITHOUT BACKING A WINNER NURSERY — 6f
2:00 (2:02) (Class 4) (0-85,82) 2-Y-O — **£3,881** (£1,155; £577; £288) **Stalls** High

Form — RPR
3140 **1** — **Imelda Mayhem**[13] 5052 2-9-0 **75** .... ShaneKelly 7 — 81
(J S Moore) *chsd ldrs: pushed along and nt clr run over 2f out: swtchd lft and hdwy 2f out: pushed along and qcknd to ld jst ins fnl f: sn in command: pushed out* — **3/1**[3]
0306 **2** 1¾ **Redair (IRE)**[6] 5270 2-9-1 **76** .... CathyGannon 3 — 76
(David Evans) *led: hdd after 2f: styd upsides ldr and rdn 1/2-way: led again over 1f out: hdd jst ins fnl f: nt pce of wnr and wl hld after: kpt on* — **5/1**
430 **3** 1 **Thirsty Bear**[14] 4995 2-8-12 **73** .... SteveDrowne 4 — 70
(Rebecca Curtis) *sn chsng ldr: led after 2f: rdn and hdd over 1f out: kpt on same pce ins fnl f* — **9/4**[2]
5200 **4** 3¾ **Princess Banu**[27] 4551 2-8-10 **71** .... SamHitchcott 5 — 57
(Mick Channon) *stdd s: sn outpcd in last and pushed along: rdn and clsd 1/2-way: struggling u.p 2f out: wknd ent fnl f* — **14/1**
4312 **5** hd **Molly Jones**[29] 4460 2-8-10 **71** .... MartinLane 1 — 56
(Derek Haydn Jones) *restless in stalls: hld up in tch: hdwy to chal 2f out: sn rdn and unable qck: wknd ent fnl f* — **2/1**[1]

1m 11.4s (1.40) **Going Correction** +0.175s/f (Good) — **5** Ran SP% **112.4**
Speed ratings (Par 96): **96,93,92,87,87**
CSF £17.81 TOTE £4.30: £2.00, £2.10; EX 19.10.
Owner Mrs E O'Leary & J S Moore **Bred** Mrs R Wilson **Trained** Upper Lambourn, Berks
FOCUS
The course had escaped any significant overnight rain though a heavy shower before racing led to there being some cut in the first, an open-looking nursery run at an ordinary pace. Straightforward form, rated around the second and third.
NOTEBOOK
Imelda Mayhem found herself behind a wall of three runners and had to be switched to the centre of the track at the 2f pole, and once clear she was going strongest to pull a little way clear. She never got into it when stepped up to 7f at Newmarket two weeks ago, but that was a better race and set her up for a drop in class and a return to 6f, where she seems more effective at this stage. (op 4-1 tchd 11-4)
Redair(IRE) held a prominent position, but had to be driven from halfway, before staying on a bit. On this evidence she does seem to stay 6f, but it might be that she was more inconvenienced by the ground easing. (op 7-2)
Thirsty Bear held the early lead, but could only find one pace near the finish. After a couple of efforts in tougher assignments this looks more his level, though he has not really progressed from a couple of promising debut runs and this big barrel-looking juvenile might need a bit more time. (op 9-2)
Princess Banu seems to have hit a problem of late, finishing last in her latest two races, and she made it an unfortunate hat-trick with an always-struggling performance. (op 12-1 tchd 16-1)
Molly Jones reared in the stalls but got going readily enough, though she faded after holding a prominent position to question whether she truly saw out this trip in these conditions. Official explanation: trainer said filly was unsuited by the good ground (op 6-4 tchd 9-4)

5428 ACORN CHEMICAL H'CAP — 1m 2f (R)
2:30 (2:30) (Class 5) (0-70,70) 3-Y-O+ — **£2,587** (£770; £384; £192) **Stalls** Low

Form — RPR
5641 **1** — **James Pollard (IRE)**[8] 4674 6-9-9 **65** .... (t) CathyGannon 1 — 71
(Bernard Llewellyn) *t.k.h: hld up in tch: pushed along and hdwy 4f out: rdn to chse ldr over 2f out: drvn and led over 1f out: kpt on and a jst doing enough fnl f* — **4/1**[2]
0563 **2** nk **Chik's Dream**[24] 4645 4-8-10 **52** .... ShaneKelly 8 — 57
(Derek Haydn Jones) *led and set stdy gallop: rdn and qcknd wl over 3f out: hdd over 1f out: kpt battling on but a jst hld fnl f* — **7/1**[3]
-254 **3** 2¾ **Spring Secret**[67] 3215 5-10-0 **70** .... NeilChalmers 3 — 70
(Bryn Palling) *mounted on crse and taken down early: t.k.h: chsd ldr tl 1/2-way: rdn over 3f out: drvn and styd on same pce fnl 2f* — **7/1**[3]
0626 **4** 4½ **Present Story**[16] 4916 4-8-11 **53** .... (v[1]) MarkLawson 9 — 44
(Gary Harrison) *stdd and dropped in bhd after s: hdwy on outer 5f out: rdn over 3f out: drvn and outpcd 2f out: 3rd and wl hld over 1f out: wknd fnl f* — **7/1**[3]
6065 **5** 1½ **Silent Oasis**[22] 4707 5-9-2 **65** .... BrendanPowell(7) 2 — 53
(Brendan Powell) *hld up in tch in rr: hdwy on inner over 3f out: rdn and wknd 2f out* — **9/1**
4020 **6** 4 **Tuscan King**[15] 4948 4-8-10 **52** .... (bt) MartinLane 5 — 32
(Bernard Llewellyn) *dwlt: sn rcvrd and chsd ldng pair: wnt 2nd 1/2-way: drvn over 3f out: lost 2nd over 2f out: wknd 2f out* — **20/1**
3314 **7** 3 **Ice Nelly (IRE)**[26] 4584 3-9-2 **66** .... SteveDrowne 4 — 40
(Hughie Morrison) *hld up in tch: rdn and dropped to last whn pce qcknd over 3f out: wl btn fnl 2f* — **6/4**[1]

2m 17.38s (7.98) **Going Correction** +0.20s/f (Good)
WFA 3 from 4yo+ 8lb — **7** Ran SP% **112.3**
Speed ratings (Par 103): **72,71,69,65,64 61,59**
toteswingers:1&2:£2.10, 1&3:£2.40, 2&3:£8.00 CSF £30.23 CT £186.74 TOTE £4.00: £1.90, £2.70; EX 23.70.
Owner Granville Reynolds **Bred** Gainsborough Stud Management Ltd **Trained** Fochriw, Caerphilly
FOCUS
A steady pace for this ordinary-looking handicap.

5429 TOTEEXACTA YOUR BETTER VALUE FORECAST MAIDEN FILLIES' STKS — 1m (R)
3:05 (3:05) (Class 4) 3-Y-O+ — **£4,528** (£1,347; £673; £336) **Stalls** Low

Form — RPR
3442 **1** — **Swift Bird (IRE)**[22] 4727 3-8-12 72 .... (b) MartinLane 4 — 76
(Noel Quinlan) *chsd ldrs: rdn over 4f out: chsd ldr 3f out: drvn to press wnr and carried rt fr over 1f out: led ins fnl f: kpt on* — **3/1**[2]
02-4 **2** 2 **Vita Lika**[20] 4807 3-8-12 77 .... ShaneKelly 3 — 71
([illegible]) *[illegible] rdn and hung rt fr 2f out: hdd and no ex ins fnl f* — **5/4**[1]
3 7 **Bachelor's Dream** 3-8-12 0 .... CathyGannon 6 — [illegible]
(William Muir) *sn wl bhd in last trio: pushed along over 4f out: styd on fr over 1f out: wnt modest 3rd ins fnl f: nvr trbld ldrs* — **20/1**
4 3½ **Reluctant Heroine (USA)** 3-8-12 0 .... SteveDrowne 7 — 47+
(Mark Johnston) *sn pushed along in midfield: outpcd and dropped to rr over 3f out: plugged on again fr over 1f out to go modest 4th ins fnl f: nvr trbld ldrs* — **4/1**[3]
54 **5** 2¾ **Madam Tessa (IRE)**[24] 4641 3-8-12 0 .... NeilChalmers 8 — 41
(Bryn Palling) *hld up in midfield: rdn and effrt 3f out: struggling and swtchd lft jst over 2f out: sn wknd* — **20/1**
05 **6** 1½ **Main Opinion (IRE)**[7] 5241 3-8-12 0 .... SamHitchcott 1 — 37
(Mick Channon) *chsd ldr tl 3f out: sn struggling u.p: 3rd and wl btn over 1f out: wknd fnl f* — **50/1**
4-2 **7** 1 **Secret Era**[69] 3167 4-8-13 0 .... JamesRogers(5) 5 — 36
(William Muir) *a bhd: rdn and lost tch 4f out* — **6/1**
8 8 **Dreamy Nights** 3-8-12 0 .... MarkLawson 2 — 17
(Gary Harrison) *s.i.s: a wl bhd in last trio: lost tch over 3f out: t.o fnl f* **33/1**

1m 42.97s (1.97) **Going Correction** +0.225s/f (Good)
WFA 3 from 4yo 6lb — **8** Ran SP% **118.2**
Speed ratings (Par 102): **96,94,87,83,80 79,78,70**
toteswingers:1&2:£1.10, 1&3:£13.30, 2&3:£10.90 CSF £7.14 TOTE £3.60: £1.40, £1.10, £4.00; EX 8.50.
Owner Exors Of The Late L Cashman **Bred** Rathbarry Stud **Trained** Newmarket, Suffolk
FOCUS
The two most experienced runners dictated this from the start and had the race between them from some way out, but the result changed in the final furlong as the favourite began to idle and threw away what looked a winning chance. The going continued to ease with ongoing rain.
Vita Lika Official explanation: jockey said filly hung right-handed

5430 TOTESWINGER MORE WAYS TO WIN H'CAP — 6f
3:40 (3:41) (Class 2) (0-100,98) 3-Y-O+ **£11,215** (£3,357; £1,678; £840; £418) **Stalls** High

Form — RPR
0206 **1** — **Colonel Mak**[13] 5060 4-9-6 **94** .... LeeNewman 6 — 106
(David Barron) *chsd ldr tl led 2f out: rdn over 1f out: kpt on wl fnl f: rdn out* — **3/1**[2]
001 **2** 1¼ **Mirza**[20] 4792 4-9-1 **89** .... MartinLane 7 — 97
(Rae Guest) *in tch in rr but sn nudged along: rdn and hdwy 2f out: chsd wnr 1f out: edgd lft ins fnl f: kpt on but no imp on wnr fnl 100yds* — **2/1**[1]

2050 **3** 1 ¼ **Five Star Junior (USA)**[13] 5033 5-9-2 **90**........................... ShaneKelly 3 94
(Linda Stubbs) *hld up in tch in rr: hdwy over 2f out: chsd ldrs and rdn wl over 1f out: drvn and styd on same pce ins fnl f* **16/1**

54-1 **4** nk **Yellow Dandy (IRE)**[17] 4885 3-8-3 **80**........................... JimmyQuinn 11 83
(Liam McAteer, Ire) *chsd ldrs: rdn to chse wnr over 1f out: drvn and unable qck ent fnl f: wknd fnl 100yds* **12/1**

0616 **5** nk **Secret Witness**[6] 5264 5-9-5 **93**...................................(b) MarkLawson 1 95
(Ronald Harris) *chsd ldrs: rdn over 2f out: drvn and pressed ldrs over 1f out: unable qck ent fnl f: wknd fnl 100yds* **13/2**

4044 **6** 2 ¼ **Norville (IRE)**[19] 4836 4-9-10 **98**................................(b) CathyGannon 10 93
(David Evans) *led tl 2f out: sn drvn and unable qck: wknd 1f out* **9/1**

06-4 **7** 4 ½ **Copper Dock (IRE)**[12] 5086 7-8-2 **79** oh4.................. LouisBeuzelin(3) 8 59
(T G McCourt, Ire) *t.k.h early: hld up in tch: rdn and struggling over 2f out: wknd wl over 1f out* **25/1**

0435 **8** nk **Remotelinx (IRE)**[20] 4797 3-8-8 **85**................................. SamHitchcott 9 65
(J W Hills) *in tch in midfield: lost pl and dropped to rr 1/2-way: rdn and wknd 2f out* **16/1**

3143 **9** shd **Star Rover (IRE)**[6] 5264 4-8-11 **90**......................(v) MatthewLawson(5) 4 69
(David Evans) *in tch in midfield: rdn and struggling 1/2-way: dropped to rr ent fnl 2f: n.d after* **6/1**[3]

69.90 secs (-0.10) **Going Correction** +0.25s/f (Good)
WFA 3 from 4yo+ 3lb **9** Ran SP% **119.3**
Speed ratings (Par 109): **109,107,105,105,104 101,95,95,95**
toteswingers: 1&2 £2.20, 1&3 £24.30, 2&3 £10.10 CSF £9.78 CT £82.35 TOTE £2.70: £1.10, £1.80, £4.80; EX 12.00.
Owner Norton Common Farm Racing,O'Kane,Murphy **Bred** Peter Baldwin **Trained** Maunby, N Yorks

■ Stewards' Enquiry : Martin Lane three-day ban: used whip with excessive frequency, down shoulder in the forehand without giving gelding time to respond (Sep 9,11,12)

FOCUS
Three non-runners took some of the edge off this valuable handicap where the field came down the centre of the track and it paid to be up with the early pace.

NOTEBOOK
Colonel Mak ◆ was ridden positively from the outset, sitting half a length behind the leaders before forging on from halfway to hold the others at bay quite comfortably. He had excuses for his last two runs as he had a bad draw at Ripon last time and reportedly hit his head in the stalls and knocked out some teeth at the start of the Stewards' Cup at Goodwood the time before. He had shown signs of coming into form, just as he did at this time of year last season, and with the ground inconveniencing him less than his rivals plus dropping back down to a similar mark to his victory in the Ayr Silver Cup last year, he was able to resume winning ways. Now that he has hit peak form there could well be more to come. (op 5-2)
Mirza landed a gamble when dropped back to 6f to take advantage of some easing of his mark at Haydock three weeks ago. A 7lb rise for that might not have helped, but the rain certainly did, although he was unable to take full advantage. Held up early, he had to be switched towards the stands' side to get a run and was closing all the way to the line. He might not have won, but with a more favourable passage would have finished closer. Official explanation: jockey said gelding hung left (op 5-2)
Five Star Junior(USA) raced prominently and had every chance, but just lacked for pace near the finish. He ran well over 5f at Newmarket last month and though he has otherwise been inconsistent this season, this was another fair effort, especially as the rain would not have helped. (tchd 18-1)
Yellow Dandy(IRE) was a bit fractious beforehand and raced freely. Both her previous wins have come at this track, but she needed to take a massive step forward to have a shout in this and was just found wanting. (op 11-1)
Secret Witness helped set the pace, avoiding the running problems that have plagued him at times in the past, but ultimately he could not keep up the pace on this easier ground. (op 8-1)
Norville(IRE) has been a prolific winner over 6f this year, but the handicapper might have just caught up with him now. (op 10-1 tchd 11-1)

5309 HAMILTON (R-H)
Friday, August 26

OFFICIAL GOING: Good to soft (good in places; 7.6)
Wind: Almost nil Weather: Overcast

5431 EXECUTIVE BENEFIT CONSULTANCY NURSERY 6f 5y
5:30 (5:31) (Class 5) (0-70,69) 2-Y-O **£2,587** (£770; £384; £192) **Stalls** High

Form RPR

01 **1** **Sinai (IRE)**[58] 3505 2-9-5 **67**.. SilvestreDeSousa 3 71+
(Geoffrey Harker) *dwlt: t.k.h: prom: rdn to ld ins fnl f: kpt on wl* **11/10**[1]

1052 **2** ½ **Fayr Fall (IRE)**[20] 4809 2-9-7 **69**.................................... DuranFentiman 4 71+
(Tim Easterby) *t.k.h: led at a modest gallop: rdn: hung rt and hdd over 1f out: kpt on towards fin: bit slipped* **3/1**[3]

6561 **3** 1 ¼ **Dansili Dutch (IRE)**[17] 4892 2-8-13 **61**............................... TomEaves 2 59+
(David Barron) *t.k.h: trckd ldrs: smooth hdwy to ld over 1f out: hdd ins fnl f: no ex towards fin* **5/2**[2]

005 **4** 9 **Burnwynd Spirit (IRE)**[42] 4040 2-8-11 **59** ow1.............. MickyFenton 1 30
(Ian Semple) *dwlt: racd keenly and sn w ldr: rdn over 1f out: wknd ent fnl f: eased whn btn* **14/1**

1m 17.1s (4.90) **Going Correction** +0.425s/f (Yiel) **4** Ran SP% **107.9**
Speed ratings (Par 94): **84,83,81,69**
CSF £4.64 TOTE £2.00; EX 4.60.
Owner Mr & Mrs H Nensey, Saif Nensey **Bred** Con Marnane **Trained** Thirkleby, N Yorks

FOCUS
Rail realignment increased distances by 8yds on round course and there was fresh ground on far side of home straight. A small field and the race became tactical, the pace steady and it effectively developed into a sprint through the final 2f.

NOTEBOOK
Sinai(IRE) was all the rage in the betting and followed up her Catterick win with probably a little more in hand than the margins imply, quickening up nicely once it was opened up for her by the runner-up hanging off the rail. The handicapper can't put her up much and she is one to keep on side. (op 15-8)
Fayr Fall(IRE) has now run well to be runner-up on his last two starts and would have the potential to do a bit better still if he could be kept straight. He had hung left at Redcar and went right this time, letting the winner in up the rail. (op 9-4)
Dansili Dutch(IRE) had gone up 6lb for her Nottingham success and probably ran close to that form, just unable to quicken on this softer ground after being last off the bridle. (op 2-1)
Burnwynd Spirit(IRE) wasn't beaten far on his third start in maidens, but that might flatter him on this evidence as he was soon beaten once the pace increased. (op 10-1 tchd 9-1)

5432 LADBROKES MOBILE OPEN MAIDEN STKS 1m 1f 36y
6:00 (6:00) (Class 5) 3-4-Y-O **£2,587** (£770; £384; £192) **Stalls** Low

Form RPR

532 **1** **Lifetime (IRE)**[14] 5007 3-9-3 79................................. SilvestreDeSousa 5 76+
(Mark Johnston) *prom: hdwy to press ldr after 3f: drvn and slighly outpcd over 3f out: rallied to ld over 2f out: clr whn edgd lft over 1f out: r.o wl* **30/100**[1]

2 5 **Vinniespride (IRE)**[115] 4-9-10 0.................................(t) JamesSullivan 6 60
(Mark Michael McNiff, Ire) *t.k.h: trckd ldrs: chal over 3f out to over 2f out: kpt on same pce appr fnl f* **16/1**

00 **3** 6 **Riczar**[35] 4282 3-8-12 0.. RichardKingscote 1 42
(Tom Dascombe) *led: hung lft over 4f out: rdn and hdd over 2f out: sn outpcd* **12/1**[3]

40 **4** 2 ½ **Takhreej (IRE)**[12] 5082 3-9-3 0... TomEaves 9 41
(Keith Dalgleish) *t.k.h: hld up: pushed along over 2f out: sn outpcd* **7/1**[2]

0-0 **5** 12 **Jack Bell (IRE)**[33] 4363 4-9-10 0...................................... RobertWinston 2 15
(Alan Swinbank) *t.k.h: hld up in tch: rdn over 3f out: sn btn* **16/1**

6 ½ **Carnelian (IRE)** 4-9-10 0... DuranFentiman 3 14
(Ian Semple) *missed break: bhd: drvn 4f out: sn struggling* **25/1**

5 **7** 31 **Miss Pronounce**[8] 5206 3-8-9 0...................................... LeeTopliss(3) 4 —
(Linda Perratt) *trckd ldrs: rdn and ev ch over 3f out: wknd over 2f out* **40/1**

2m 6.30s (6.60) **Going Correction** +0.50s/f (Yiel)
WFA 3 from 4yo 7lb **7** Ran SP% **115.2**
Speed ratings (Par 103): **90,85,80,78,67 66,39**
toteswingers:1&2:£3.90, 1&3:£2.40, 2&3:£7.30 CSF £7.45 TOTE £1.30: £1.10, £6.80; EX 8.80.
Owner Sheikh Hamdan Bin Mohammed Al Maktoum **Bred** Lynn Lodge Stud And Foxtale Farm **Trained** Middleham Moor, N Yorks

FOCUS
A very weak and muddling maiden. Guessy form, with the winner value for further.
Jack Bell(IRE) Official explanation: jockey said gelding ran too free

5433 VARIETY CLUB H'CAP 6f 5y
6:35 (6:35) (Class 6) (0-65,63) 3-Y-O **£1,908** (£563; £281) **Stalls** Centre

Form RPR

0401 **1** **Deliberation (IRE)**[8] 5203 3-9-6 **63** 6ex.......................... JulieBurke(5) 5 76+
(Kevin Ryan) *mde all: rdn along 2f out: kpt on wl fnl f* **5/4**[1]

3564 **2** 1 ½ **Inca Blue**[20] 4812 3-9-0 **52**...(b[1]) RobertWinston 3 58
(Tim Easterby) *hld up: hdwy 1/2-way: effrt and chsd wnr fnl f: kpt on: no imp* **4/1**[2]

1600 **3** 2 **Unwrapit (USA)**[35] 4288 3-9-5 **57**.....................................(p) TomEaves 8 57
(Bryan Smart) *pressed wnr and clr of rest: rdn over 2f out: kpt on same pce fnl f* **7/1**[3]

05-3 **4** 2 ¾ **Cheeky Wee Red**[18] 4863 3-8-12 **53**............................... LeeTopliss(3) 7 44
(Richard Fahey) *chsd clr ldng pair: rdn over 2f out: edgd rt and no ex over 1f out* **8/1**

2061 **5** 4 **Ever Roses**[14] 5010 3-9-7 **59**..(v) MickyFenton 1 37
(Paul Midgley) *sn bhd: drvn along 1/2-way: no imp fnl 2f* **9/1**

6 3 ¼ **Cri Na Mara (IRE)**[26] 4591 3-8-7 **45**..........................(t) JamesSullivan 2 13
(Mark Michael McNiff, Ire) *prom tl rdn and wknd fr 2f out* **20/1**

2433 **7** 3 ½ **Hardrock Diamond**[8] 5206 3-8-11 **49**.......................(p) DuranFentiman 4 —
(Ian Semple) *sn bhd: drvn along 1/2-way: btn fnl 2f* **8/1**

1m 14.88s (2.68) **Going Correction** +0.425s/f (Yiel) **7** Ran SP% **113.9**
Speed ratings (Par 98): **99,97,94,90,85 81,76**
toteswingers:1&2:£1.90, 1&3:£3.00, 2&3:£4.70 CSF £6.33 CT £23.84 TOTE £2.10: £1.20, £1.70; EX 7.70.
Owner Mrs Angie Bailey **Bred** Berkie Brown **Trained** Hambleton, N Yorks

FOCUS
Very much a run-of-the-mill contest and it was easy enough for the favourite who was value for a bit further. The time was relatively good.
Ever Roses Official explanation: jockey said filly never travelled

5434 LADBROKES GAME ON! H'CAP 6f 5y
7:05 (7:06) (Class 4) (0-85,85) 3-Y-O+ **£4,722** (£1,405; £702; £351) **Stalls** Centre

Form RPR

0-33 **1** **Valery Borzov (IRE)**[27] 4531 7-9-7 **85**........................(v) LeeTopliss(3) 12 96
(Richard Fahey) *prom: hdwy over 2f out: ev ch and edgd lft over 1f out: led ins fnl f* **10/3**[1]

0000 **2** ½ **Amenable (IRE)**[33] 4369 4-9-6 **81**................................... AndrewMullen 3 90
(David Nicholls) *led main centre gp: hdd over 2f out: rallied: kpt on to take 2nd nr fin* **20/1**

2000 **3** nk **Klynch**[13] 5032 5-9-10 **85**..(b) JamesSullivan 8 93
(Ruth Carr) *cl up: led main gp over 2f out: hdd ins fnl f: kpt on same pce: lost 2nd nr fin* **10/1**

0-30 **4** 4 **Rasaman (IRE)**[13] 5033 7-9-6 **84**.................................. GaryBartley(3) 13 79
(Jim Goldie) *hld up: hdwy over 2f out: effrt and edgd rt over 1f out: kpt on fnl f: nvr rchd ldrs* **12/1**

0016 **5** 2 **Jobe (USA)**[79] 2806 5-9-5 **80**.......................................(p) PhillipMakin 2 69
(Kevin Ryan) *racd alone far rail: cl up tl rdn and outpcd fr 2f out* **10/1**

1014 **6** shd **Toby Tyler**[12] 5083 5-8-12 **73**...(v) MickyFenton 10 61
(Paul Midgley) *towards rr: drvn along 1/2-way: hdwy over 1f out: nvr able to chal* **7/1**[3]

0-10 **7** 2 **Amazing Amoray (IRE)**[72] 3052 3-9-4 **82**........................ PJMcDonald 7 64
(David Barron) *t.k.h: prom: drvn along over 2f out: sn outpcd: n.d after* **6/1**[2]

-040 **8** nk **Arry's Orse**[118] 1695 4-9-5 **80**......................................(t) TomEaves 4 61
(Bryan Smart) *in tch: drvn along over 2f out: btn over 1f out* **6/1**[2]

0020 **9** 4 **Gap Princess (IRE)**[14] 5012 7-9-6 **81**............................ RobertWinston 5 49
(Geoffrey Harker) *hld up: rdn over 2f out: sn no imp* **14/1**

0000 **10** 1 ½ **Kellys Eye (IRE)**[20] 4802 4-9-2 **84**................................... LeeSwift(7) 9 48
(George Foster) *dwlt: bhd: rdn along 1/2-way: nvr on terms* **10/1**

0000 **11** 2 **Rash Judgement**[9] 5163 6-9-3 **78**..........................(b[1]) SilvestreDeSousa 6 35
(Eric Alston) *t.k.h: prom tl wknd over 2f out* **22/1**

5000 **12** 2 ½ **Befortyfour**[20] 4791 6-9-3 **78**.................................. RobbieFitzpatrick 11 27
(Richard Guest) *dwlt: bhd: drvn towards stands' rail 1/2-way: nvr on terms* **33/1**

1m 13.88s (1.68) **Going Correction** +0.425s/f (Yiel)
WFA 3 from 4yo+ 3lb **12** Ran SP% **117.8**
Speed ratings (Par 105): **105,104,103,98,95 95,93,92,87,85 82,79**
toteswingers:1&2:£14.30, 1&3:£5.10, 2&3:£42.50 CSF £77.82 CT £621.38 TOTE £4.10: £1.80, £7.80, £2.20; EX 82.10.
Owner D R Kilburn/John Nicholls Trading **Bred** Vincent Harrington **Trained** Musley Bank, N Yorks

FOCUS
Quite a few failed to give their running, but it's still form to view fairly positively, at least among the front three who pulled clear off a sound pace. The winner is rated back to last season's form.

5435 LADBROKES LANARK SILVER BELL H'CAP 1m 4f 17y
7:35 (7:41) (Class 3) (0-90,89) 3-Y-0+ **£12,938** (£3,850; £1,924; £962) **Stalls** Low

Form RPR
2161 **1** **Shernando**[26] 4577 4-9-1 **82** .... SilvestreDeSousa 5 96+
(Mark Johnston) *bhd and sn niggled along: hdwy over 3f out: edgd rt over 1f out: led ins fnl f: kpt on strly* **10/1**
4023 **2** *3 ¾* **Hong Kong Island (IRE)**[12] 5078 4-8-11 **83** .... DarylByrne(5) 13 91
(Micky Hammond) *prom: effrt whn hmpd over 3f out: rcvrd and ev ch over 1f out: kpt on same pce ins fnl f* **8/1**
1400 **3** *2 ¼* **Royal Trooper (IRE)**[7] 5250 5-8-10 **82** .... JulieBurke(5) 11 87+
(James Given) *hld up: smooth hdwy to ld 3f out: rdn 2f out: hdd ins fnl f: kpt on same pce* **18/1**
2010 **4** *½* **Lady Chaparral**[7] 5250 4-9-4 **85** .... AndrewMullen 10 89
(George Moore) *hld up midfield: hdwy and cl up over 2f out: sn rdn: kpt on same pce appr fnl f* **15/2**
1044 **5** *¾* **Gogeo (IRE)**[14] 4998 4-9-1 **82** .... RobertWinston 2 85
(Alan Swinbank) *hld up: rdn and outpcd over 4f out: rallied 2f out: kpt on fnl f: nrst fin* **13/2**[3]
060- **6** *8* **Bothy**[141] 7084 5-8-10 **82** .... DanielleMcCreery(5) 7 72
(Brian Ellison) *prom: drvn along fr 1/2-way: rallied and effrt over 2f out: btn fnl f* **6/1**[2]
5002 **7** *2 ¼* **Antigua Sunrise (IRE)**[34] 4344 5-8-11 **81** .... LeeTopliss(3) 8 67
(Richard Fahey) *prom: pushed along 1/2-way: lost pl over 3f out: n.d after* **9/1**
1422 **8** *shd* **Butler (IRE)**[33] 4360 4-9-4 **85** .... TomEaves 1 71
(Luca Cumani) *prom: drvn and outpcd wl over 2f out: sn btn* **7/2**[1]
4421 **9** *1 ¾* **Euston Square**[41] 4109 5-9-1 **82** .... MickyFenton 6 65
(Alistair Whillans) *hld up: struggling over 4f out: nvr on terms* **16/1**
0006 **10** *1 ½* **Becausewecan (USA)**[13] 5057 5-9-3 **84** .... PhillipMakin 12 65
(Mark Johnston) *cl up: led after 3f to over 3f out: sn wknd* **11/1**
020 **11** *7* **Uphold**[34] 4331 4-9-5 **89** .... (b) DeclanCannon(3) 4 59
(Gay Kelleway) *led 3f: cl up: led briefly over 3f out: sn struggling* **28/1**
2m 42.25s (3.65) **Going Correction** +0.50s/f (Yiel) **11** Ran SP% **114.7**
Speed ratings (Par 107): **107,104,103,102,102 96,95,95,94,93 88**
toteswingers:1&2:£15.30, 1&3:£27.50, 2&3:£27.40 CSF £81.50 CT £1232.27 TOTE £7.70: £3.50, £3.50, £6.70; EX 116.00.
Owner The Originals **Bred** Miss K Rausing **Trained** Middleham Moor, N Yorks
■ Stewards' Enquiry : Daryl Byrne one-day ban: careless riding (Sep 9)

FOCUS
A good prize and it attracted a useful and competitive field. The gallop didn't look overly strong but the progressive winner still had them well strung out by the finish. Sound form among the principals.

NOTEBOOK
Shernando had bombed out on soft ground at Sandown a couple of starts back but he showed testing conditions aren't a problem to him as he comfortably made it three wins in his last four starts, looking better the further he went which suggests he is well worth another try at 1m6f before long.
Hong Kong Island(IRE) is proving most consistent and this was another really good effort, sticking on well after getting buffeted about around 3f out. He will continue to give a good account, although there is a danger he will edge up a little further in the weights without winning. (op 17-2)
Royal Trooper(IRE) is well suited by give in the ground and put a couple of poor runs behind him, although arguably not delivering quite the performance that looked likely when he hit the front on the bridle. (op 25-1)
Lady Chaparral wasted no time showing last week's York run to be all wrong, once again a bit keen early on but sticking to her task. Her Carlisle win is solid but an 8lb rise possibly means the handicapper is in control for now. (op 9-1)
Gogeo(IRE) still has time on his side but isn't the easiest to weigh up at present, not looking to be going anywhere for a long way before keeping on late. (op 8-1 tchd 6-1)
Bothy, runner-up in three top handicap hurdles last jumps season, shaped as if he probably needed the run back after a break, fading after working his way into a challenging position 2f out. He is no doubt being prepared for another jumping campaign but he is down to a mark he should be up to making an impact from on the Flat. (op 15-2)
Antigua Sunrise(IRE) had run really well at York last month and clearly didn't get anywhere near that level here, despite having conditions to suit.
Butler(IRE) had a steadily progressive profile this term before this and it is worth forgiving this for now, the softer ground a ready excuse. (op 4-1)

5436 PRESTIGESYNDICATES.CO.UK H'CAP 5f 4y
8:05 (8:06) (Class 6) (0-60,57) 3-Y-0+ **£1,811** (£539; £269; £134) **Stalls** Centre

Form RPR
1300 **1** **Sparking**[43] 4017 4-9-7 **57** .... SilvestreDeSousa 9 69
(David Barron) *prom towards stands' rail: rdn to ld 2f out: kpt on wl fnl f* **7/2**[1]
4550 **2** *2 ¾* **Sandwith**[10] 5148 8-9-3 **56** .... (b[1]) GaryBartley(3) 1 58
(George Foster) *prom towards far side: effrt over 2f out: chsd wnr fnl f: kpt on: no imp* **7/1**
462 **3** *2 ¼* **The Fiery Cross**[48] 3857 4-9-5 **55** .... DuranFentiman 4 49
(Ian Semple) *hld up: rdn and hdwy over 1f out: kpt on fnl f: nrst fin* **5/1**[3]
5005 **4** *½* **El Dececy (USA)**[13] 5031 7-9-5 **55** .... RobbieFitzpatrick 8 47
(Richard Guest) *hld up in tch: rdn over 2f out: sme late hdwy: nvr able to chal* **5/1**[3]
0062 **5** *nse* **Cheyenne Red (IRE)**[14] 5008 5-9-0 **50** .... TomEaves 6 42
(Michael Dods) *cl up: rdn and ev ch 2f out: nt qckn appr fnl f* **4/1**[2]
-600 **6** *1 ¾* **Hitches Dubai (BRZ)**[45] 3937 6-9-5 **55** .... RobertWinston 2 41
(Geoffrey Harker) *prom: drvn and outpcd over 2f out: no imp after* **25/1**
0465 **7** *2 ¼* **Kassaab**[8] 5203 3-9-4 **56** .... (b) PJMcDonald 3 34
(Ian Semple) *led to 2f out: sn rdn and wknd* **20/1**
0000 **8** *14* **Cayman Fox**[17] 4881 6-9-7 **57** .... JamesSullivan 7 —
(Linda Perratt) *rrd and lost best part of 10 l s: nvr on terms* **5/1**[3]
62.52 secs (2.52) **Going Correction** +0.425s/f (Yiel)
WFA 3 from 4yo+ 2lb **8** Ran SP% **113.3**
Speed ratings (Par 101): **96,91,88,87,87 84,80,58**
toteswingers:1&2:£8.80, 1&3:£3.80, 2&3:£8.90 CSF £27.77 CT £121.52 TOTE £4.20: £1.10, £2.20, £2.50; EX 26.80.
Owner P Bamford **Bred** Dandy's Farm **Trained** Maunby, N Yorks

FOCUS
A weak sprint. The winner rates a length personal best.
Cayman Fox Official explanation: jockey said mare reared as stalls opened
T/Plt: £64.90 to a £1 stake. Pool:£41,038.01 - 461.22 winning tickets T/Qpdt: £34.00 to a £1 stake. Pool:£4,539.39 - 98.70 winning tickets RY

5003 NEWCASTLE (L-H)
Friday, August 26

OFFICIAL GOING: Soft (5.5)
Wind: Light, half behind Weather: persistent rain 1st 5

5437 TSG.COM SUPPORTING CHILDREN'S HEART UNIT FUND "HANDS AND HEELS" APPRENTICE SERIES H'CAP 6f
4:45 (4:45) (Class 6) (0-65,58) 3-Y-0+ **£3,234** (£962; £481; £240) **Stalls** Centre

Form RPR
2050 **1** **Brave Battle**[24] 4638 3-9-7 **58** .... JackDuern(3) 7 67
(Ron Barr) *prom: outpcd and lost pl after 2f: hdwy over 2f out: led over 1f out: hld on towards fin* **8/1**
5503 **2** *nk* **Hellbender (IRE)**[14] 5008 5-9-12 **57** .... GeorgeChaloner 8 65
(George Foster) *in rr: hdwy over 2f out: chsd wnr appr fnl f: no ex towards fin* **9/2**[2]
263 **3** *3* **Eeny Mac (IRE)**[41] 4110 4-9-1 **51** .... TerenceFury(5) 1 49
(Neville Bycroft) *sn wl outpcd and bhd: hdwy over 2f out: edgd lft: kpt on to take 3rd last 100yds* **4/1**[1]
0303 **4** *4* **Classlin**[14] 5009 4-9-0 **45** .... NoelGarbutt 4 31
(Jim Goldie) *chsd ldrs: edgd lft 2f out: wknd fnl f* **16/1**
-600 **5** *2 ½* **Angaric (IRE)**[28] 4503 8-9-6 **56** .... EdwardPierce(5) 6 34
(Bryan Smart) *w ldrs: led 2f out: sn hdd: wknd fnl f* **5/1**[3]
500 **6** *1* **Lambrini Lace (IRE)**[35] 4288 6-8-11 **45** .... (b) LauraBarry(3) 9 19
(Lisa Williamson) *w ldrs: led over 3f out: hdd 2f out: sn wknd* **16/1**
6024 **7** *¾* **Just Sam (IRE)**[23] 4672 6-9-9 **57** .... DavidSimmonson(3) 5 29
(Ron Barr) *w ldrs: wknd over 1f out* **9/1**
0100 **8** *8* **Tenancy (IRE)**[24] 4651 7-9-10 **55** .... (e) JakePayne 2 —
(Shaun Harris) *led tl over 3f out: lost pl 2f out: sn bhd* **10/1**
464 **9** *½* **Johannesgray (IRE)**[44] 3972 4-9-10 **58** .... ShirleyTeasdale(3) 3 —
(Noel Wilson) *w ldrs: wknd 2f out: sn bhd* **11/2**
1m 18.56s (3.96) **Going Correction** +0.55s/f (Yiel)
WFA 3 from 4yo+ 3lb **9** Ran SP% **112.2**
Speed ratings (Par 101): **95,94,90,85,81 80,79,68,68**
toteswingers: 1&2 £6.60, 1&3 £9.60, 2&3 £4.00 CSF £42.27 CT £165.59 TOTE £13.40: £3.30, £2.40, £2.00; EX 165.59.
Owner R E Barr **Bred** Lady Whent **Trained** Seamer, N Yorks

FOCUS
A cold, damp evening with further rain changed the going from soft, good to soft in places to soft all round. A modest apprentice sprint with the overall profile of many of the runners an unreliable one. A strong pace in the conditions with the first three all struggling from an early stage and coming from well off the pace with a time nearly 6 seconds outside RPR standard.

5438 PEGASUS SOFTWARE SUPPORTING CHILDREN'S HEART UNIT FUND NURSERY 5f
5:20 (5:20) (Class 5) (0-75,78) 2-Y-O **£3,234** (£962; £481; £240) **Stalls** Centre

Form RPR
0123 **1** **Son Du Silence (IRE)**[13] 5061 2-9-2 **74** .... RyanPowell(5) 5 77
(J S Moore) *trckd ldr: chal over 2f out: led over 1f out: styd on u.p* **7/1**
0221 **2** *¾* **Tip Top Gorgeous (IRE)**[9] 5161 2-9-11 **78** 6ex .... DanielTudhope 4 78
(David O'Meara) *led: hdd over 1f out: kpt on same pce last 50yds* **15/8**[1]
154 **3** *1 ¾* **Dark Ages (IRE)**[41] 4079 2-9-2 **69** .... DavidNolan 6 63
(Noel Quinlan) *chsd ldrs: outpcd after 2f: hdwy over 2f out: kpt on same pce appr fnl f* **12/1**
2233 **4** *nk* **Half A Billion (IRE)**[14] 4984 2-9-6 **73** .... TonyHamilton 2 66
(Michael Dods) *trckd ldrs: kpt on same pce fnl 2f* **7/2**[2]
6540 **5** *1* **Valley Of Hope**[14] 4984 2-8-13 **66** .... PaulHanagan 8 55
(Richard Fahey) *sn trcking ldrs: upsides over 2f out: fdd fnl 150yds* **4/1**[3]
0223 **6** *3 ½* **I'll Be Good**[12] 5077 2-9-7 **74** .... BarryMcHugh 7 51
(Robert Johnson) *chsd ldrs: wknd over 1f out* **13/2**
64.51 secs (3.41) **Going Correction** +0.55s/f (Yiel) **6** Ran SP% **110.5**
Speed ratings (Par 94): **94,92,90,89,87 82**
toteswingers: 1&2 £2.60, 1&3 £4.80, 2&3 £4.70 CSF £19.97 CT £145.79 TOTE £7.30: £4.80, £1.10; EX 14.10.
Owner Ronnie Beggan & Partners **Bred** R J Beggan, S Holt And D Thorpe **Trained** Upper Lambourn, Berks

FOCUS
A good pace for a competitive little nursery with each of the six runners close enough if good enough.

NOTEBOOK
Son Du Silence(IRE) was an easy-ground Windsor winner on his second start but was out of his depth when distant third in a conditions race at Ripon last time. Always up with the pace he kept on well after taking the lead on his first start in a nursery. A starting mark of 74 has proved within his compass and looks a better type when conditions are on the easy side, however, he might just struggle to get his head back in front when reassessed. (tchd 13-2)
Tip Top Gorgeous(IRE)justified strong market support when comfortably getting off the mark in a maiden at Carlise last time. She showed a similar level of form dropped back in trip and, as she was only just held off under her 6lb penalty, she can continue to pay her way. (op 2-1 tchd 7-4, 9-4 in a place)
Dark Ages(IRE) was a 5f quick-ground winner so had something to prove upped in trip in the conditions. He seemed to see out the trip well enough but appears to be on a high enough mark. (op 9-1)
Half A Billion(IRE) has handled similar conditions and has been running consistently in defeat on five occasions but has yet to win and looks vulnerable to a more progressive type. (op 4-1 tchd 9-2, 5-1 in a place)
Valley Of Hope travelled strongly down in trip after being too free over 6f. His effort flattened out at the business end of the race but he certainly looks capable. (op 9-2 tchd 5-1)
I'll Be Good has not run with conditions this soft and appeared not to get home. (op 5-1)

5439 SOPHOS SUPPORTING CHILDREN'S HEART UNIT H'CAP 7f
5:50 (5:50) (Class 5) (0-75,69) 3-Y-O **£3,234** (£962; £481; £240) **Stalls** Centre

Form RPR
121 **1** **Ted's Brother (IRE)**[13] 5031 3-9-7 **69** .... PaulHanagan 5 78+
(Richard Guest) *trckd ldrs: t.k.h: hdwy over 2f out: led wl over 1f out: wandered: wnt rt ins fnl f: drvn out* **4/6**[1]
-360 **2** *1 ¼* **St Oswald**[18] 4854 3-8-13 **61** .... DanielTudhope 4 67
(David O'Meara) *trckd ldr: effrt over 2f out: keeping on same pce whn crooosed and checked ins fnl f* **4/1**[2]
3560 **3** *1 ½* **Lady Gar Gar**[27] 4560 3-9-5 **67** .... (p) TonyHamilton 3 69
(Geoffrey Oldroyd) *drvn to ld: qcknd over 2f out: hdd wl over 1f out: kpt on same pce* **17/2**
1104 **4** *shd* **Monel**[17] 4880 3-8-13 **61** .... BarryMcHugh 6 63
(Jim Goldie) *trckd ldrs: effrt 2f out: 3rd and keeping on same pce whn checked ins fnl f: kpt on towards fin* **11/2**[3]

1000 5 28 **J R Hartley**[28] 4513 3-9-3 **65** ....(p) RoystonFfrench 1 —
(Bryan Smart) *stdd s: t.k.h: sn trcking ldrs: lost pl over 2f out: bhd whn eased: t.o* **28/1**

1m 31.58s (3.78) **Going Correction** +0.55s/f (Yiel) **5** Ran SP% **109.3**
Speed ratings (Par 100): **105,103,101,101,69**
toteswingers: 1&2 £3.10 CSF £3.59 TOTE £1.60: £1.30, £2.10; EX 3.70.
Owner Maze Rattan Limited **Bred** T Counihan **Trained** Stainforth, S Yorks

FOCUS
There was just a reasonable pace, with the ground being reported by the jockeys as soft but hard work and testing.

5440 "HAVE A HEART" TROPHY H'CAP — 1m 4f 93y
6:25 (6:25) (Class 4) (0-80,78) 4-Y-0+ **£6,469** (£1,925; £962; £481) **Stalls** Low

Form RPR

1404 **1** **Red Fama**[31] 4407 7-9-0 **71** .... BarryMcHugh 7 81
(Neville Bycroft) *gave problems gng to s: hld up in rr: hdwy over 2f out: led 1f out: styd on wl towards fin* **8/1**

0100 **2** 1 ½ **Spirit Of A Nation (IRE)**[17] 4879 6-9-2 **73** ....(p) PaddyAspell 9 81
(James Moffatt) *chsd ldrs: upside 1f out: chsd wnr jst ins fnl f: edgd lft and styd on same pce last 75yds* **16/1**

11 **3** 3 ¾ **Hunter Forward (AUS)**[22] 4716 5-9-5 **76** .... KirstyMilczarek 6 78+
(Luca Cumani) *ponied to s: trckd ldrs: quite keen: led on bit over 2f out: hdd 1f out: fdd fnl 100yds* **7/4**[1]

1030 **4** 4 ½ **Amazing Blue Sky**[16] 4901 5-9-4 **75** .... RussKennemore 1 70
(Ruth Carr) *led: hdd over 2f out: wknd appr fnl f* **12/1**

0220 **5** 11 **Rubi Dia**[13] 5035 4-8-5 **65** ow1 ....(tp) PaulPickard(3) 8 42
(Kevin M Prendergast) *hld up in rr: hdwy over 4f out: wknd over 2f out* **20/1**

0-0 **6** 4 **Magic Echo**[34] 4344 7-9-6 **77** .... DanielTudhope 11 48
(Robert Johnson) *hld up in rr: bhd fnl 3f* **33/1**

0051 **7** nk **Lucky Windmill**[27] 4540 4-9-2 **78** .... GarryWhillans(5) 4 48
(Alan Swinbank) *hld up in mid-div: effrt 4f out: wknd 2f out* **13/2**[3]

2056 **8** 6 **Advisor (FR)**[41] 4082 5-9-6 **77** .... PaulHanagan 10 38
(Michael Bell) *trckd ldr: drvn over 4f out: wknd 2f out: eased ins fnl f* **4/1**[2]

1-00 **9** 24 **Best Prospect (IRE)**[62] 3399 9-9-4 **75** ....(vt) TonyHamilton 3 —
(Michael Dods) *hld up in mid-div: hdwy on ins over 2f out: wknd 2f out: bhd whn heavily eased ins fnl f: t.o* **8/1**

2m 54.43s (8.83) **Going Correction** +0.875s/f (Soft) **9** Ran SP% **113.2**
Speed ratings (Par 105): **105,104,101,98,91 88,88,84,68**
toteswingers: 1&2 £25.20, 1&3 £4.30, 2&3 £4.00 CSF £122.62 CT £322.18 TOTE £5.90: £1.30, £6.00, £1.80; EX 199.90.
Owner B F Rayner **Bred** N Bycroft **Trained** Brandsby, N Yorks

FOCUS
A reasonable pace for this ordinary middle-distance handicap with the first four pulling clear.

5441 CLOSE HOUSE SUPPORTING CHILDREN'S HEART UNIT FUND H'CAP — 1m 3y(S)
6:55 (6:56) (Class 5) (0-70,70) 3-Y-0+ **£3,234** (£962; £481; £240) **Stalls** Centre

Form RPR

5102 **1** **Wiseman's Diamond (USA)**[30] 4442 6-9-0 **58** ....(b) RussKennemore 8 68
(Paul Midgley) *trckd one other stands' side rail: drvn over 3f out: led wl over 1f out: edgd lft: drvn rt out* **9/2**[2]

0000 **2** 2 **Christmas Carnival**[13] 5059 4-9-11 **69** .... GrahamGibbons 10 74
(Michael Easterby) *led one other stands' side rail: overall ldr over 3f out: hdd wl over 1f out: edgd lft: kpt on same pce* **4/1**[1]

0062 **3** 2 ¼ **Nolecce**[15] 4946 4-9-3 **64** ....(p) RobertLButler(3) 6 64
(Richard Guest) *chsd ldrs: 3rd over 1f out: kpt on same pce* **9/2**[2]

43-5 **4** 2 ½ **Ad Value (IRE)**[136] 1293 3-8-2 **52** .... FrannyNorton 3 45
(Alan Swinbank) *chsd ldrs: drvn and outpcd over 3f out: kpt on fnl f: tk 4th post* **10/1**

4400 **5** hd **Classic Descent**[15] 4946 6-9-0 **58** ....(bt) FrederikTylicki 1 52
(Ruth Carr) *s.i.s: hld up in rr: effrt over 2f out: chsng ldrs over 1f out: wknd fnl 150yds* **25/1**

4155 **6** 2 **Muwalla**[21] 4747 4-9-7 **65** .... PaulHanagan 2 54
(Chris Grant) *racd wd: chsd ldrs: drvn over 2f out: wknd jst ins fnl f* **4/1**[1]

065- **7** 4 ½ **Makbullet**[224] 5241 4-9-7 **65** .... TonyHamilton 7 44
(Michael Smith) *led centre gp tl over 3f out: wknd over 1f out* **16/1**

4314 **8** 1 ¼ **Thatcherite (IRE)**[20] 4811 3-9-4 **68** ....(t) StephenCraine 5 43
(Tony Coyle) *trckd ldrs: led centre gp over 3f out: wknd over 1f out* **5/1**[3]

40-0 **9** 34 **Penton Hook**[25] 4601 5-8-13 **62** .... GarryWhillans(5) 9 —
(Barry Murtagh) *hld up towards rr: drvn over 4f out: sn lost pl and bhd: eased 2f out: t.o* **25/1**

1m 48.43s (5.03) **Going Correction** +0.55s/f (Yiel)
WFA 3 from 4yo+ 6lb **9** Ran SP% **115.7**
Speed ratings (Par 103): **96,94,91,89,89 87,82,81,47**
toteswingers: 1&2 £4.80, 1&3 £3.00, 2&3 £6.00 CSF £22.92 CT £83.99 TOTE £6.20: £1.70, £1.50, £1.50; EX 32.00.
Owner D I Perry **Bred** Hatta Bloodstock International **Trained** Westow, N Yorks

FOCUS
A competitive handicap with the field splitting into two groups. The majority went towards the centre but it was the pair racing up the stands' side rails who came out on top.

5442 SPEEDFLEX SUPPORTING CHILDREN'S HEART UNIT FUND FILLIES' H'CAP — 6f
7:25 (7:27) (Class 5) (0-75,75) 3-Y-0+ **£3,234** (£962; £481; £240) **Stalls** Centre

Form RPR

1122 **1** **Spinatrix**[17] 4880 3-9-6 **74** .... TonyHamilton 8 82
(Michael Dods) *mde all stands' side rail: kpt on wl fnl f: hld on wl* **7/4**[1]

0244 **2** ¾ **Mango Music**[25] 4609 8-9-10 **75** .... PaulHanagan 6 81
(Richard Fahey) *chsd ldrs: effrt stands' side over 2f out: chsd wnr over 1f out: no ex last 75yds* **9/4**[2]

0640 **3** 2 ½ **Foreign Rhythm (IRE)**[4] 5309 6-8-6 **62** .... ShaneBKelly(5) 7 60
(Ron Barr) *hdwy to chse ldrs over 2f out: one pce fnl f* **13/2**[3]

4003 **4** 2 ½ **Lady Del Sol**[35] 4288 3-8-12 **66** .... BarryMcHugh 1 56
(Marjorie Fife) *wnt lft s: in rr: swtchd stands' side rail after 1f: drvn over 2f out: nvr a threat* **20/1**

6214 **5** ½ **Anjomarba (IRE)**[14] 5018 4-9-5 **70** .... KirstyMilczarek 2 58
(Conor Dore) *w ldr: wknd fnl f* **17/2**

2-35 **6** 38 **Royal Liaison**[65] 3292 3-8-11 **65** .... FrederikTylicki 5 —
(Michael Bell) *chsd ldrs: lost pl over 3f out: bhd whn eased over 1f out: t.o* **7/1**

1m 18.04s (3.44) **Going Correction** +0.55s/f (Yiel)
WFA 3 from 4yo+ 3lb **6** Ran SP% **108.3**
Speed ratings (Par 100): **99,98,94,91,90 40**
toteswingers: 1&2 £1.10, 1&3 £3.40, 2&3 £4.10 CSF £5.42 CT £15.27 TOTE £2.10: £1.10, £2.40; EX 5.30.
Owner Mrs J W Hutchinson & Mrs P A Knox **Bred** T K & Mrs P A Knox **Trained** Denton, Co Durham

FOCUS
Fair fillies' form.

5443 LAIDLER MEMORIAL MAIDEN STKS — 7f
7:55 (7:56) (Class 5) 3-4-Y-0 **£3,234** (£962; £481; £240) **Stalls** Centre

Form RPR

36 **1** **Lady Sledmere (IRE)**[12] 5082 3-8-12 0 .... PaulHanagan 12 68+
(Paul Midgley) *trckd ldrs: led wl over 1f out: drvn out* **13/8**[1]

4 **2** 2 ¼ **Cookieshake**[18] 4849 3-9-3 0 .... KirstyMilczarek 13 67+
(Luca Cumani) *mid-div: drvn 4f out: chsd wnr over 1f out: kpt on same pce* **3/1**[2]

4 **3** 1 **Naafetha (IRE)**[27] 4542 3-8-12 0 .... DanielTudhope 7 59
(George Foster) *mid-div: hdwy on outer over 2f out: wnt 3rd over 1f out: kpt on same pce* **22/1**

00 **4** 2 ½ **Painted Tail (IRE)**[12] 5082 4-8-12 0 .... GarryWhillans(5) 11 62+
(Alan Swinbank) *hld up in rr: hdwy over 2f out: nt clr run 1f out: styd on to take 4th last 75yds* **9/1**

5 2 **Eqtiraab (IRE)** 3-9-3 0 .... BarryMcHugh 2 53
(Tony Coyle) *dwlt: hld up in rr: effrt over 2f out: kpt on: nvr nr ldrs* **16/1**

0 **6** 5 **Bond Blade**[35] 4282 3-9-3 0 .... TonyHamilton 9 40
(Geoffrey Oldroyd) *trckd ldrs: t.k.h: drvn over 2f out: wknd over 1f out* **20/1**

000 **7** 2 ¾ **Stella Marris**[35] 4288 4-9-3 50 .... PaddyAspell 1 30
(Christopher Wilson) *swtchd rt s: led: hdd wl over 1f out: sn wknd* **66/1**

8 7 **Illustration (IRE)** 3-9-3 0 .... FrannyNorton 3 14
(Mark Johnston) *dwlt: in rr and sn drvn along: bhd fnl 3f* **7/2**[3]

0 **9** 6 **Apassionforfashion**[43] 4014 3-8-12 0 .... RoystonFfrench 4 —
(Bryan Smart) *chsd ldrs: wknd over 2f out* **50/1**

1m 33.94s (6.14) **Going Correction** +0.55s/f (Yiel)
WFA 3 from 4yo 5lb **9** Ran SP% **113.8**
Speed ratings (Par 103): **92,89,88,85,83 77,74,66,59**
toteswingers: 1&2 £1.80, 1&3 £5.70, 2&3 £7.40 CSF £6.14 TOTE £2.30: £1.10, £2.30, £5.40; EX 7.40.
Owner John Allan Milburn **Bred** Maddenstown Equine Enterprise Ltd **Trained** Westow, N Yorks

FOCUS
An uncompetitive maiden with the decent pace stringing out the field early on.
T/Plt: £9.50 to a £1 stake. Pool: £39,140.10. 2,989.82 winning tickets. T/Qpdt: £2.70 to a £1 stake. Pool: £4,590.86. 1,248.28 winning tickets. WG

5051 NEWMARKET (R-H)
Friday, August 26

OFFICIAL GOING: Good to soft (good in places) changing to good to soft after race 1 (1:20) changing to soft after race 4 (2:55)
Wind: Light across Weather: Overcast, turning to rain

5444 EBF "RESPLENDENT GLORY" RUSSIAN STANDARD "PLATINUM" MAIDEN FILLIES' STKS (DIV I) — 7f
1:20 (1:22) (Class 4) 2-Y-0 **£4,528** (£1,347; £673; £336) **Stalls** High

Form RPR

0 **1** **Semayyel (IRE)**[39] 4155 2-9-0 0 .... RussellPrice 10 82+
(Clive Brittain) *mde all: rdn over 1f out: edgd lft ins fnl f: styd on* **18/1**

0 **2** ½ **Balady (IRE)**[42] 4061 2-9-0 0 .... RichardHills 8 81
(John Dunlop) *a.p: chsd wnr over 2f out: rdn and ev ch fr over 1f out: hung lft ins fnl f: styd on* **18/1**

3 2 ¼ **Hazel Lavery (IRE)** 2-9-0 0 .... MichaelHills 11 75+
(Charles Hills) *s.i.s: hld up: pushed along over 2f out: hdwy over 1f out: styd on: nt rch ldrs* **7/2**[2]

4 nk **Pearl War (USA)** 2-9-0 0 .... EddieAhern 4 75+
(William Haggas) *hld up in tch: shkn up over 1f out: styd on* **14/1**

4 **5** hd **Candycakes (IRE)**[20] 4804 2-9-0 0 .... JamieSpencer 1 74
(Michael Bell) *chsd ldrs: rdn over 1f out: kpt on* **5/2**[1]

6 3 **Winner's Wish** 2-9-0 0 .... JimmyFortune 13 67+
(Jeremy Noseda) *s.i.s: hld up: hdwy over 2f out: rdn over 1f out: styd on same pce* **11/1**

0 **7** ¾ **Chatterati (USA)**[14] 4992 2-9-0 0 .... MickaelBarzalona 7 65
(Mahmood Al Zarooni) *hld up: swtchd lft over 2f out: hdwy u.p and hung lft sn after: wknd ins fnl f* **22/1**

8 ½ **Seaside Escape (USA)** 2-9-0 0 .... MartinDwyer 9 63+
(Brian Meehan) *hld up: racd keenly: rdn over 2f out: nvr on terms* **25/1**

9 1 ¼ **Amelia May** 2-9-0 0 .... WilliamBuick 2 60
(John Gosden) *hld up: hdwy over 4f out: pushed along 1/2-way: wknd over 2f out* **17/2**

10 1 ¼ **Silver Samba** 2-9-0 0 .... DavidProbert 12 57
(Andrew Balding) *s.i.s: hld up: plld hrd: swtchd rt 5f out: rdn and wknd over 2f out* **33/1**

0 **11** 1 ¾ **Star Of Bombay (FR)**[29] 4471 2-9-0 0 .... RichardHughes 5 53
(Richard Hannon) *s.s: hld up: hdwy over 2f out: rdn and wknd sn after* **14/1**

12 2 ¼ **Al Andaleeb (USA)** 2-9-0 0 .... TedDurcan 6 47
(Saeed Bin Suroor) *chsd wnr 4f: rdn and wknd wl over 1f out* **7/1**[3]

1m 27.53s (1.83) **Going Correction** 0.0s/f (Good) **12** Ran SP% **117.1**
Speed ratings (Par 93): **89,88,85,85,85 81,81,80,79,77 75,73**
toteswingers:1&2:£39.10, 1&3:£22.30, 2&3:£15.80 CSF £295.64 TOTE £22.00: £6.10, £3.90, £1.60; EX 333.90 TRIFECTA Not won..
Owner Saeed Manana **Bred** Rabbah Bloodstock Limited **Trained** Newmarket, Suffolk
■ A first winner as a jockey since 2005 for Russell Price.

FOCUS
Stands' side track used with stalls on far side, except 1m7f centre. Horses were declared on good to firm ground but 7mm of rain fell overnight and that was followed by further rain in the morning, leading to a change in the official going to good to soft, good in places. The winning time of the first race seemed to confirm the change in the going description.

NOTEBOOK
Semayyel(IRE) wouldn't go into the stalls when due to take part in the Sweet Solera here last time, but she was much more amenable down at the start on this occasion, broke well and made the most of her previous experience (promising effort at Windsor first time up) to lead virtually throughout. She was forced to battle by Balady and the form doesn't look anything too special, but she was cosily on top at the finish and her trainer will no doubt now be planning to step her up steeply in grade - she does hold Group 1 entries. (op 20-1 tchd 16-1)
Balady(IRE) showed some ability on her debut despite a slipping saddle and this was a nice step up. She had her chance heading to the final furlong but was outbattled. (op 16-1)

Hazel Lavery(IRE) did best of the newcomers. A Fillies' Mile entry, she showed signs of greenness but kept on well for hands-and-heels riding and should benefit considerably for the experience. (op 5-1)
Pearl War(USA) ◆ travelled best for most of the way and will be of interest in similar company next time with the benefit of this run behind her. (op 16-1)
Candycakes(IRE) was always well placed but couldn't pick up, and perhaps she found the ground softer than ideal. (op 11-4 tchd 3-1 in places)
Winner's Wish, a little awkwardly away, shaped with ability and wasn't knocked about in the closing stages. There should be improvement in her. (op 12-1 tchd 9-1)
Star Of Bombay(FR) didn't settle well enough (later confirmed by rider) and she paid the price. Official explanation: jockey said filly ran keen early (op 16-1)

5445 EBF "RESPLENDENT GLORY" RUSSIAN STANDARD "PLATINUM" MAIDEN FILLIES' STKS (DIV II) 7f
1:50 (1:50) (Class 4) 2-Y-O **£4,528** (£1,347; £673; £336) **Stalls** High

Form RPR
1 **Lyric Of Light** 2-9-0 0 .... MickaelBarzalona 1 79+
(Mahmood Al Zarooni) *hld up in tch: shkn up over 2f out: led wl over 1f out: edgd lft: pushed out* **6/1**
2 *3/4* **Diala (IRE)** 2-9-0 0 .... EddieAhern 4 78+
(William Haggas) *trckd ldrs: nt clr run over 1f out: r.o* **14/1**
3 *2 1/4* **Shada (IRE)** 2-9-0 0 .... KierenFallon 5 71+
(Sir Michael Stoute) *hld up: hdwy 1/2-way: rdn and ev ch over 1f out: styd on same pce ins fnl f* **11/4**[1]
5 **4** *nse* **Fashion's Flight (USA)**[20] 4804 2-9-0 0 .... MartinDwyer 6 71
(Brian Meehan) *chsd ldr: rdn and ev ch over 1f out: edgd rt ins fnl f: styd on same pce* **9/2**[3]
5 *hd* **Toptempo** 2-9-0 0 .... TomQueally 9 71+
(Mark H Tompkins) *pushed along early in rr: reminder over 2f out: r.o wl ins fnl f: nrst fin* **33/1**
6 *hd* **Bana Wu** 2-9-0 0 .... DavidProbert 7 70+
(Andrew Balding) *hld up: hdwy over 2f out: r.o: nt rch ldrs* **33/1**
2632 **7** *1/2* **Show Flower**[17] 4883 2-9-0 77 .... RichardHughes 8 69
(Mick Channon) *a.p: rdn and swtchd lft over 1f out: styd on same pce fnl f* **4/1**[2]
8 *nk* **Quizzed** 2-9-0 0 .... RichardMullen 12 68
(Edward Vaughan) *s.s: swtchd rt sn after s: hdwy over 1f out: r.o* **80/1**
0 **9** *1 1/4* **Marhoona (USA)**[20] 4804 2-9-0 0 .... RichardHills 2 65
(John Dunlop) *chsd ldrs: rdn and ev ch 2f out: styng on same pce whn rdr dropped whip ins fnl f* **8/1**
00 **10** *1 1/4* **Valiant Runner**[25] 4614 2-9-0 0 .... JimmyFortune 3 62
(Jeremy Noseda) *led: rdn and hdd wl over 1f out: no ex fnl f* **100/1**
11 *19* **See Emily Play (IRE)** 2-9-0 0 .... WilliamBuick 10 14
(John Gosden) *sn pushed along in rr: bhd fr 1/2-way* **6/1**

1m 27.48s (1.78) **Going Correction** 0.0s/f (Good) **11 Ran SP% 116.1**
Speed ratings (Par 93): **89,88,85,85,85 85,84,84,82,81 59**
toteswingers:1&2:£15.10, 1&3:£4.60, 2&3:£6.80 CSF £82.82 TOTE £5.90: £2.50, £4.40, £1.50; EX 111.30 Trifecta £382.80 Part won. Pool: £517.41 - 0.44 winning units..
Owner Godolphin **Bred** Darley **Trained** Newmarket, Suffolk

FOCUS
This looked the stronger of the two divisions on paper. The winning time was very marginally the quicker.

NOTEBOOK
Lyric Of Light, a newcomer by Street Cry out of a Cheveley Park runner-up, got first run on the second, who had to wait to be delivered with her challenge, and that may have been the difference in the result, but the winner is from a stable blessed with plenty of talent in this division and she looks another capable of holding her own at a higher level. Perhaps the Rockfel will come under consideration later in the season. (op 9-2)
Diala(IRE) ◆ was travelling strongly in behind horses 2f out, but as the winner went for home down the outside she was stuck waiting for a gap to open up. It finally came inside the last and she quickened up well, but the winner had gone beyond recall and she couldn't make up the lost ground. She shouldn't have any problems going one better. (op 18-1 tchd 20-1)
Shada(IRE) came under pressure some way out but responded quite well. A 290,000gns purchase, she holds a Fillies' Mile entry, is clearly held in some regard and is likely to come on plenty for this debut run. (op 5-2 tchd 9-4)
Fashion's Flight(USA) ran with promise here on her debut and was given every chance to improve on that, being handy throughout. She didn't quite see her race out, though, and perhaps the quicker ground she was declared on would have suited her better. (tchd 5-1)
Toptempo ◆, who is out of a Group 3 winner, looked pretty clueless for much of the race but once she hit the rising ground she began to motor and she'd have been third in a few more yards. This run ought to bring her on plenty, she'll get further as she gets older and she's one to keep an eye on.
Bana Wu, who isn't bred to do much at two, was green but kept on nicely at the finish and will improve with time and distance.
Show Flower, the most exposed runner in the line-up, was up in trip again and too keen to give her a chance of getting home. (op 5-1)

5446 RUSSIAN STANDARD "ORIGINAL" NURSERY 1m
2:20 (2:22) (Class 4) (0-85,83) 2-Y-O **£6,469** (£1,925; £962; £481) **Stalls** High

Form RPR
342 **1** **Devdas (IRE)**[19] 4815 2-8-13 **75** .... AdamKirby 4 81
(Clive Cox) *trckd ldrs: plld hrd: bmpd over 2f out: led over 1f out: drvn out* **11/2**[3]
61 **2** *1 1/4* **Tingo In The Tale (IRE)**[22] 4698 2-8-13 **75** .... JamesDoyle 10 78
(David Arbuthnot) *hld up: hdwy over 2f out: rdn over 1f out: r.o to go 2nd wl ins fnl f: nt rch wnr* **18/1**
6221 **3** *3/4* **Mizbah**[63] 3349 2-8-13 **75** .... TedDurcan 2 77
(Saeed Bin Suroor) *chsd ldrs: rdn over 2f out: edgd lft over 1f out: styd on to go 3rd nr fin* **7/1**
2104 **4** *1/2* **Glee**[13] 5052 2-8-13 **75** .... RichardHughes 11 76
(Richard Hannon) *chsd ldrs: rdn and swtchd rt over 2f out: sn ev ch: no ex and lost 2 pls wl ins fnl f* **16/1**
312 **5** *1 1/4* **Salford Art (IRE)**[13] 5052 2-9-7 **83** .... KierenFallon 8 82
(David Elsworth) *sn pushed along in mid-div: nt clr run and lost pl over 3f out: swtchd rt: r.o ins fnl f: nt rch ldrs* **11/4**[1]
023 **6** *nk* **Benzanno (IRE)**[18] 4853 2-8-13 **75** .... DavidProbert 6 72
(Andrew Balding) *hld up: hdwy over 2f out: rdn and edgd lft over 1f out: styd on* **20/1**
660 **7** *nk* **Manomine**[69] 3152 2-8-3 **65** .... IvaMilickova 5 61
(Clive Brittain) *awkward leaving stalls: sn prom: rdn over 1f out: styd on same pce* **100/1**
633 **8** *1 1/2* **Art Law (IRE)**[20] 4798 2-8-6 **68** .... LiamJones 13 61
(Brian Meehan) *trckd ldrs: plld hrd: rdn over 1f out: no ex fnl f* **25/1**
3050 **9** *1/2* **Come On Blue Chip (IRE)**[18] 4857 2-8-5 **67** .... MartinDwyer 7 59
(Paul D'Arcy) *hld up: rdn over 3f out: hung lft over 1f out: nvr on terms* **9/1**
001 **10** *1 1/4* **Queens Sandridge (IRE)**[18] 4864 2-9-3 **79** .... TomQueally 9 70
(Alan Bailey) *hld up: effrt and nt clr run over 1f out: n.d* **40/1**
0441 **11** *8* **Moon Trip**[3] 5343 2-8-9 **71** 6ex .... MickaelBarzalona 3 43
(Mark Johnston) *led: rdn over 2f out: hdd over 1f out: wknd fnl f* **4/1**[2]
4436 **12** *6* **Tudor Empire (IRE)**[16] 4913 2-8-12 **74** .... WilliamBuick 1 32
(John Gosden) *hld up: rdn 3f out: wknd over 2f out: eased fnl f* **10/1**

1m 40.44s (0.44) **Going Correction** 0.0s/f (Good) **12 Ran SP% 116.8**
Speed ratings (Par 96): **97,95,95,94,93 92,92,91,90,89 81,75**
toteswingers:1&2:£9.80, 1&3:£5.40, 2&3:£10.30 CSF £93.75 CT £714.30 TOTE £6.00: £2.10, £3.30, £2.30; EX 80.60 Trifecta £689.40 Part won. Pool: £931.66 - 0.10 winning units..
Owner H E Sheikh Sultan Bin Khalifa Al Nahyan **Bred** Sheikh Sultan Bin Khalifa Al Nayhan **Trained** Lambourn, Berks

FOCUS
With rain continuing to fall the ground was changed to good to soft before this race. A competitive nursery and the whole field raced up the far-side rail.

NOTEBOOK
Devdas(IRE), pipped at the post at Leicester last time, quickened up well 2f out and stretched clear once he hit the rising ground. The extra furlong really suited this son of Dylan Thomas and the easier ground was clearly no problem for him. (op 13-2)
Tingo In The Tale(IRE), a winner in soft ground at Brighton last time, was at least proven in the conditions and kept on well for second. The least experienced runner in this line-up, he's open to further improvement. (op 16-1)
Mizbah, back from a two-month break, had his chance but this ground might not have been totally ideal (pulled out from intended engagement at Sandown last week when ground was good to soft). (op 9-1)
Glee seemed to handle the ground well enough, but she didn't quite see out the longer trip as well as some. A return to 7f should help. (op 14-1 tchd 12-1)
Salford Art(IRE) ◆ was never travelling. Pushed along from an early stage, she dropped to the tail of the field 3f out and was hampered when still in rear 2f out. She suddenly found her stride once hitting the rising ground, though, and finished with a flourish to take fifth. This was a strange performance, especially considering she won over 6f earlier this month, but she's entitled to be given another chance back on quicker ground. (tchd 5-2)
Benzanno(IRE) ran a solid enough race on his handicap debut and might be the best guide to the level of the form. (op 16-1)
Moon Trip, making a quick reappearance under a penalty, took them along next to the far-side rail, but he was beaten with a furlong and a half to run and he probably needs to get back on fast ground sharpish, as he improved bundles for it at Leicester. (op 3-1)

5447 EBF "DUTCH ART" PIPER-HEIDSIECK CHAMPAGNE MAIDEN STKS 7f
2:55 (2:56) (Class 4) 2-Y-O **£4,528** (£1,347; £673; £336) **Stalls** High

Form RPR
2 **1** **Most Improved (IRE)**[21] 4762 2-9-0 0 .... MartinDwyer 12 93
(Brian Meehan) *w ldr tl led over 2f out: pushed clr fnl f* **4/5**[1]
2 *5* **Welcome Gift** 2-8-9 0 .... AntiocoMurgia(5) 2 81+
(Mahmood Al Zarooni) *s.i.s and wnt rt s: hld up: hdwy over 2f out: rdn over 1f out: hung lft and r.o to go 2nd wl ins fnl f: no ch w wnr* **33/1**
6 **3** *1* **Goldream**[34] 4330 2-9-0 0 .... KierenFallon 4 78
(Luca Cumani) *chsd ldrs: rdn over 1f out: styd on same pce: lost 2nd wl ins fnl f* **5/1**[2]
0 **4** *1 1/2* **Alshmemi (USA)**[21] 4762 2-9-0 0 .... RichardHills 9 74
(John Gosden) *chsd ldrs: rdn over 2f out: no ex fnl f* **33/1**
5 **5** *1 3/4* **Hefner (IRE)**[22] 4722 2-9-0 0 .... RichardHughes 5 70
(Richard Hannon) *led over 4f: sn rdn: wknd fnl f* **7/1**[3]
6 *1/2* **Trois Vallees (USA)** 2-9-0 0 .... MickaelBarzalona 6 69
(Mahmood Al Zarooni) *hld up: rdn and hung lft over 1f out: nvr trbld ldrs* **16/1**
7 *1* **Bank Bonus** 2-9-0 0 .... JimmyFortune 3 66+
(Andrew Balding) *s.s: bhd tl r.o ins fnl f: nvr nrr* **66/1**
8 *3/4* **Mayo Lad (IRE)** 2-9-0 0 .... PatDobbs 14 64+
(Richard Hannon) *hld up: hung lft almost thrght: racd keenly: hdwy over 2f out: wknd over 1f out* **66/1**
9 *nk* **Afaal (USA)** 2-9-0 0 .... LiamJones 13 64+
(William Haggas) *in rr tl styd on ins fnl f: nvr nrr* **100/1**
10 *2* **Colonsay (USA)** 2-9-0 0 .... JamieSpencer 11 59
(Mahmood Al Zarooni) *s.i.s: sn pushed along in rr: n.d* **11/1**
11 *shd* **Alwaaqi** 2-9-0 0 .... TadhgO'Shea 10 58+
(John Dunlop) *dwlt: outpcd: nvr nrr* **80/1**
12 *1 3/4* **Ten On Ten** 2-9-0 0 .... MichaelHills 15 54
(Charles Hills) *mid-div: rdn over 2f out: wknd over 1f out* **40/1**
00 **13** *3/4* **Flugelhorn (IRE)**[14] 5011 2-9-0 0 .... RichardMullen 7 52
(Ed McMahon) *chsd ldrs: rdn over 2f out: sn wknd* **150/1**
14 *nse* **Arte Del Calcio** 2-9-0 0 .... DaneO'Neill 8 52
(David Elsworth) *hld up in tch: plld hrd: rdn over 2f out: sn wknd* **100/1**
15 *7* **Gregorian (IRE)** 2-9-0 0 .... WilliamBuick 1 34
(John Gosden) *prom tl rdn and wknd over 2f out: eased fnl f* **22/1**

1m 25.93s (0.23) **Going Correction** 0.0s/f (Good) **15 Ran SP% 118.5**
Speed ratings (Par 96): **98,92,91,89,87 86,85,84,84,82 82,80,79,79,71**
toteswingers:1&2:£9.20, 1&3:£2.20, 2&3:£25.00 CSF £43.97 TOTE £2.00: £1.10, £7.10, £1.70; EX 32.00 Trifecta £301.00 Pool: £1,310.11 - 3.22 winning units.
Owner Iraj Parvizi **Bred** Skymarc Farm Inc And Ecurie Des Monceaux **Trained** Manton, Wilts

FOCUS
Persistent rain caused the ground to be changed to soft straight after this race. This time the whole field came up the middle-to-stands' side of the track. This had the look of a really interesting maiden on paper, with several well-bred newcomers from top stables taking on a well-regarded favourite with solid form credentials. The winning time compared very favourably with the first two fillies' maidens (over 1.5sec quicker), especially considering the deteriorating ground conditions, and it's a race that's likely to throw up plenty of winners.

NOTEBOOK
Most Improved(IRE) ◆, who routed his rivals, looks a top-notcher in the making. He ran a blinder on his debut when narrowly beaten by the well-bred Godolphin colt Kinglet, and looked sure to take the world of beating here for a yard whose 2-y-os improve plenty for their debut efforts. Despite racing a shade keenly in the front rank, he quickened away heading to the final furlong and drew further clear as the line approached. He coped well with the soft ground, should have no trouble stepping up to a mile and looks well up to winning in Group company. Interestingly, the Racing Post Trophy was mentioned as a possible target for him, a race in which his trainer has a fair recent record - Crowded House won for him in 2008, and Skanky Biscuit (owned at the time by Most Improved's owner Iraj Parvizi) was third the same year, and in 2009 Dancing David finished fourth. (op 8-11 tchd 5-6)
Welcome Gift ◆ looked the stable's third string based on jockey bookings, but he's by Pivotal out of a dual 1m4f Group 1 winner in Germany and these conditions (much softer than had been expected at declaration stage) played to his strengths. He was green but stayed on well up the stands' rail to take the runner-up spot, and there should be plenty more to come from him, especially when stepped up to a mile. (op 25-1)
Goldream, sixth behind subsequent Acomb Stakes winner Entifaadha on his debut here, ran a sound race in contrasting ground conditions and is clearly going the right way. (op 9-1)

Alshmemi(USA) ◆, pulled out from an intended outing at Sandown a week earlier due to unsuitable ground (good to soft) didn't look entirely comfortable on this surface and ran well in the circumstances. It wouldn't be a surprise to see improvement from this $550,000 colt on better ground. (op 22-1)
Hefner(IRE), better away this time, showed up well for a long way but didn't get home. Perhaps the testing ground found him out. (tchd 6-1)
Trois Vallees(USA) was too green to show his true ability, but he was keeping on at the finish and this son of Elusive Quality should know a lot more next time. (op 12-1)
Bank Bonus put in some promising late work and showed more than enough to suggest there'll be races in him, probably over further, in due course. (op 80-1)
Mayo Lad(IRE), a 100,000gns half-brother to Canford Cliffs, was weak in the betting and Richard Hughes was aboard stablemate Hefner. Racing on the outside of the pack, he hung left throughout but showed enough to suggest he has a future.
Colonsay(USA), the shortest priced of the three Godolphin horses, is a half-brother to Vengeance Of Rain, who was a star performer out in Hong Kong, and also won the Dubai Sheema Classic. Another who raced wide of where the main action unfolded, faster ground might well suit him, in line with his sire's statistics (12% Soft, 18% G/F). (op 12-1 tchd 14-1)

5448 PIPER-HEIDSIECK "RARE" H'CAP — 1m 6f 175y
3:30 (3:31) (Class 3) (0-95,92) 3-Y-O+ — **£7,439** (£2,213; £1,106; £553) **Stalls** Centre

Form — RPR
1065 **1** **Cosimo de Medici**[30] 4423 4-9-1 **79** ....(t) RichardHughes 3 — 90
(Hughie Morrison) *hld up: racd centre tunring for home: hdwy over 3f out: led that gp over 2f out: rdn to ld overall over 1f out: hung lft: styd on wl* — **11/1**
0/04 **2** 3 1/4 **Downhiller (IRE)**[20] 4806 6-9-10 **88** .... EddieAhern 14 — 94
(John Dunlop) *mid div: racd centre and hdwy turning for home: rdn and ev ch that gp over 2f out: hung lft over 1f out: styd on same pce: 2nd of 10 in gp* — **13/2**[3]
2533 **3** 1/2 **Regal Park (IRE)**[17] 4890 4-9-8 **86** .... AdamKirby 12 — 91
(Marco Botti) *hld up: racd centre turning for home: hdwy over 2f out: sn rdn: styd on: 3rd of 10 in gp* — **11/2**[2]
0100 **4** *shd* **My Arch**[30] 4423 9-9-10 **88** .... TomQueally 4 — 93
(Ollie Pears) *mid-div: racd centre turning for home: outpcd over 3f out: rallied u.p over 1f out: styd on: 4th of 10 in gp* — **14/1**
1321 **5** 2 3/4 **Danvilla**[20] 4806 4-9-5 **83** .... WilliamCarson 5 — 84
(Paul Webber) *sn led: styd stands' side tuning for home: rdn and hdd over 1f out: styd on same pce: 1st of 2 that side* — **13/2**[3]
5241 **6** 1/2 **Manifestation**[13] 5035 3-8-12 **89** .... WilliamBuick 10 — 90
(John Gosden) *hld up: racd centre turning for home: hdwy over 6f out: rdn over 2f out: styd on same pce: 5th of 10 in gp* — **10/3**[1]
003 **7** 3 **Trovare (USA)**[20] 4806 4-9-4 **82** ....(be[1]) MartinDwyer 1 — 79
(Amanda Perrett) *chsd ldr tl lft in ld of gp in centre turning for home: rdn and hdd over 2f out: hung lft fr over 1f out: wknd fnl f: 6th of 10 in gp* **12/1**
6041 **8** 3/4 **Sherman McCoy**[61] 3428 5-9-6 **84** .... JamesMillman 6 — 80
(Rod Millman) *hld up: racd centre turning for home: rdn over 3f out: nvr on terms: 7th of 10 in gp* — **40/1**
361 **9** 1 3/4 **Pittodrie Star (IRE)**[22] 4719 4-9-1 **79** .... DavidProbert 9 — 73
(Andrew Balding) *chsd ldrs: racd centre turning for home: rdn & hung lft to race alone over 3f out: hung rt well over 1f out, soon hung lft and wknd: 8th of 10 in gp* — **16/1**
5631 **10** 25 **Mister Angry (IRE)**[11] 5102 4-9-4 **82** 6ex.... MickaelBarzalona 13 — 43
(Mark Johnston) *hld up and bhd: racd centre turning for home: rdn over 3f out: wknd over 2f out: t.o: 9th of 10 in gp* — **12/1**
0123 **11** 1 1/2 **Red Kestrel (USA)**[35] 4266 6-9-7 **85** .... PatDobbs 2 — 44
(Kevin Ryan) *chsd ldrs: racd stands' side turning for home and lft 2nd: rdn over 2f out: sn wknd: last of 2 that side: t.o* — **20/1**
1020 **12** 28 **Old Hundred (IRE)**[34] 4348 4-9-10 **88** ....(v) JamieSpencer 7 — 11
(James Fanshawe) *stdd s: hld up: racd centre turning for home rdn over 6f out: no rspnse: t.o fnl 3f: last of 10 in gp* — **12/1**

3m 9.13s (0.73) **Going Correction** +0.20s/f (Good)
WFA 3 from 4yo+ 13lb — **12 Ran SP% 116.3**
Speed ratings (Par 107): **106,104,104,103,102 102,100,100,99,85 85,70**
toteswingers:1&2:£17.50, 1&3:£14.00, 2&3:£9.00 CSF £79.27 CT £441.12 TOTE £13.50: £3.70, £2.50, £2.30; EX 100.00 Trifecta £721.10 Pool: £974.52 - 1.00 winning units.
Owner Bevan, Doyle & Lawrence **Bred** Shortgrove Manor Stud **Trained** East Ilsley, Berks

FOCUS
They seemed to go quite quick early on here considering the ground conditions and the winner came from well off the pace. Straightening for home the majority of the field moved to the centre of the track, while Danvilla and Red Kestrel stayed stands' side. The time suggests that the ground was not that bad, and the third and fourth set the standard.

NOTEBOOK
Cosimo de Medici travelled well into contention, but probably hit the front plenty soon enough as he hung right over to the far side around a furlong out. He's a strong stayer and the quicker they go up front the better it is for him, and the Cesarewitch, for which he's a best price 40-1 with Victor Chandler, should be run to suit him. This success will likely ensure he gets into the race now. (tchd 12-1)
Downhiller(IRE) seems to go on any ground, although he was withdrawn when the ground was soft at Goodwood on his intended reappearance. He's steadily getting back to his best and he reversed course form with Danvilla in this much stronger-run race. (op 12-1)
Regal Park(IRE) doesn't have much margin for error off his current mark but he benefited from being held up in a solidly run contest and posted a solid effort. (op 6-1 tchd 5-1)
My Arch was under pressure some way out, but all he does is stay and he kept on past beaten horses to post a respectable finish. (op 12-1)
Danvilla, running on soft ground for the first time, went too fast in front early on and sticking to the stands' rail in the straight might not have been an advantage either. (tchd 6-1 and 7-1 in places)
Manifestation was the disappointment of the race. The only 3-y-o in the field, he looked one to keep onside when successful at Doncaster last time, but perhaps these conditions were just too testing for him. (tchd 7-2)

5449 PIPER-HEIDSIECK CHAMPAGNE MAIDEN STKS — 1m
4:05 (4:06) (Class 5) 3-Y-O+ — **£3,234** (£962; £481; £240) **Stalls** High

Form — RPR
1 **Tanaami (USA)** 3-8-12 0 .... RichardHills 4 — 80+
(Saeed Bin Suroor) *s.i.s: hld up: hdwy 1/2-way: rdn to ld and hung lft fr over 1f out: r.o* — **10/3**[1]
2 3 1/4 **Upcountry** 3-9-3 0 .... MichaelHills 10 — 78+
(Charles Hills) *a.p: racd keenly: swtchd rt over 2f out: rdn over 1f out: edgd lft and styd on to go 2nd wl ins fnl f* — **12/1**
6-3 **3** *hd* **Looking On**[14] 5021 3-9-3 0 .... DaneO'Neill 11 — 77
(Henry Candy) *led: rdn and hdd over 1f out: styd on same pce ins fnl f* — **10/3**[1]
6 **4** 1/2 **Lieutenant Kojak**[135] 1315 3-8-12 0 .... RosieJessop[(5)] 12 — 76
(Peter Charalambous) *chsd ldrs: rdn and ev ch over 1f out: styd on same pce ins fnl f* — **20/1**
0-4 **5** 2 1/2 **Armoise**[134] 1332 3-8-12 0 ....(t) TomQueally 8 — 65
(Marco Botti) *chsd ldrs: rdn over 1f out: wknd ins fnl f* — **4/1**[2]
6 1 1/4 **Drakes Drum** 3-9-3 0 .... AdamKirby 1 — 67
(Clive Cox) *hld up: hdwy over 2f out: rdn over 1f out: wknd fnl f* — **8/1**
7 2 **Beauchamp Zorro** 3-9-3 0 .... FrankieMcDonald 3 — 63
(Henry Candy) *s.i.s: hld up: hdwy over 2f out: rdn and wknd over 1f out: hung lft fnl f* — **40/1**
4-00 **8** 7 **Fists And Stones**[104] 2103 3-9-3 72 .... RichardHughes 2 — 47
(Mick Channon) *prom tl rdn and wknd over 2f out* — **16/1**
0 **9** *shd* **Monsieur Broughton**[32] 4388 3-9-3 0 .... StevieDonohoe 5 — 46
(Willie Musson) *hld up: a in rr* — **40/1**
10 *hd* **Days In May (IRE)** 3-8-12 0 .... RichardMullen 9 — 41
(Edward Vaughan) *hld up in tch: rdn over 2f out: sn wknd* — **66/1**
00 **11** 13 **Carpentras**[78] 2848 3-8-12 0 .... RobertHavlin 6 — 11
(Dr Jon Scargill) *prom: lost pl over 4f out: wknd over 2f out* — **125/1**
12 3/4 **Sailor's Chant (USA)** 3-9-3 0 .... KierenFallon 7 — 14
(Mark Johnston) *s.i.s: sn prom: rdn and wknd over 2f out* — **6/1**[3]

1m 40.54s (0.54) **Going Correction** +0.20s/f (Good) — **12 Ran SP% 117.1**
Speed ratings (Par 103): **105,101,101,101,98 97,95,88,88,88 75,74**
toteswingers:1&2:£8.30, 1&3:£3.30, 2&3:£8.90 CSF £42.65 TOTE £3.70: £2.10, £4.40, £1.80; EX 43.90 Trifecta £227.50 Pool: £830.16 - 2.70 winning units.
Owner Godolphin **Bred** Shadwell Farm LLC **Trained** Newmarket, Suffolk

FOCUS
Hard to be sure of the value of this form, and the time was slower than the earlier nursery, but there was good support beforehand for the winner. The form is rated around the second and third.

5450 GRANTS WHISKY H'CAP — 7f
4:35 (4:37) (Class 3) (0-90,90) 3-Y-O — **£7,439** (£2,213; £1,106; £553) **Stalls** High

Form — RPR
2-11 **1** **White Frost (IRE)**[15] 4965 3-9-3 **86** .... MichaelHills 5 — 100+
(Charles Hills) *chsd ldrs: led 3f out: rdn and hung lft fr over 1f out: r.o* — **7/2**[1]
-220 **2** 1 3/4 **My Freedom (IRE)**[34] 4313 3-9-7 **90** ....(p) TedDurcan 11 — 96
(Saeed Bin Suroor) *hld up: hdwy 3f out: chsd wnr over 1f out: sn rdn: carried lft ins fnl f: styng on same pce whn nt clr run towards fin* — **5/1**[2]
6312 **3** 3/4 **Saskia's Dream**[14] 4994 3-8-8 **77** ....(p) RichardHughes 1 — 81+
(Jane Chapple-Hyam) *hld up: hdwy over 1f out: edgd lft ins fnl f: r.o: nt rch ldrs* — **16/1**
-051 **4** 1/2 **Capaill Liath (IRE)**[34] 4335 3-9-7 **90** ....(p) JamieSpencer 2 — 93
(Michael Bell) *prom: rdn and hung lft over 2f out: sn outpcd: styd on u.p ins fnl f* — **5/1**[2]
4620 **5** *hd* **Cruiser**[22] 4723 3-9-3 **86** .... MartinDwyer 10 — 88
(William Muir) *prom: rdn over 1f out: styd on same pce fnl f* — **17/2**
-403 **6** 1 1/2 **Tuscania**[14] 5016 3-9-7 **90** .... TomQueally 12 — 88+
(Sir Michael Stoute) *hld up: hdwy over 1f out: sn rdn: no imp ins fnl f* — **11/2**[3]
0130 **7** 2 1/4 **Flynn's Boy**[13] 5054 3-8-10 **79** .... DaneO'Neill 9 — 71
(Rae Guest) *prom: rdn 1/2-way: wknd over 1f out* — **15/2**
1600 **8** 1/2 **Fred Willetts (IRE)**[26] 4574 3-9-2 **90** ....(v) MatthewCosham[(5)] 7 — 81
(David Evans) *led 4f: sn rdn: hung lft and wknd over 1f out* — **50/1**
201 **9** 2 3/4 **Robemaker**[39] 4161 3-9-3 **86** .... WilliamBuick 4 — 69
(John Gosden) *hmpd s: hld up: rdn over 2f out: wknd over 1f out: eased ins fnl f* — **9/1**
1516 **10** 23 **Barkston Ash**[42] 4048 3-8-9 **78** .... PatCosgrave 6 — —
(Eric Alston) *s.i.s: sn prom: rdn: hung lft and wknd over 1f out: eased* — **33/1**

1m 25.97s (0.27) **Going Correction** +0.20s/f (Good) — **10 Ran SP% 114.0**
Speed ratings (Par 104): **106,104,103,102,102 100,98,97,94,68**
toteswingers:1&2:£4.40, 1&3:£4.80, 2&3:£10.70 CSF £20.15 CT £247.47 TOTE £4.10: £1.80, £2.20, £3.50; EX 18.50 Trifecta £114.60 Pool: £884.30 - 5.70 winning units.
Owner Mr And Mrs J D Cotton **Bred** M Henochsberg & Mme D Hazan-Ades **Trained** Lambourn, Berks

FOCUS
A decent handicap and the form makes a fair bit of sense. The winner can better the bare form.

NOTEBOOK
White Frost(IRE) ◆ won impressively in contrasting ground to that he faced here last time. The colt travelled powerfully throughout, clearly relishing the soft ground, and won his race when quickening up approaching the final furlong. Despite edging left all the way over to the far-side rail, he stayed on to record a much easier win than the bare margin might suggest. Firmly on the upgrade, he's likely to stay one step ahead of the handicapper and his trainer suggested he'll be keeping him to 7f for the time being. (tchd 3-1 and 4-1)
My Freedom(IRE) ◆, dropping back to 7f and wearing cheekpieces for the first time, was the only one to make a race of it with the winner. Carried left by him inside the last, he might have finished a little closer had he been allowed to race in a straight line, but he was beaten on merit. It was still a good effort, though, and he won't always bump into one so progressive. (op 11-2)
Saskia's Dream ran right up to her recent best in third, but was never a real threat. (op 14-1)
Capaill Liath(IRE) needed plenty of encouragement to run on but did respond. (op 6-1)
Cruiser ran a better race back on soft ground. (op 8-1 tchd 15-2)
Tuscania seemed to find it hard work in the ground and only made laboured progress from off the pace. (tchd 9-2)

5451 TULLAMORE DEW IRISH WHISKEY H'CAP — 6f
5:05 (5:05) (Class 4) (0-85,85) 3-Y-O+ — **£4,528** (£1,347; £673; £336) **Stalls** High

Form — RPR
2244 **1** **Elusivity (IRE)**[13] 5054 3-9-7 **85** .... JamieSpencer 11 — 96
(Brian Meehan) *racd stands' side: hld up: shkn up and qcknd to ld wl ins fnl f: hung lft towards fin* — **3/1**[1]
0011 **2** 3/4 **Time Medicean**[13] 5053 5-8-9 **77** .... RaulDaSilva[(7)] 3 — 85
(Tony Carroll) *racd stands' side: prom: rdn and edgd lft over 1f out: ev ch ins fnl f: styd on: 2nd of 7 in gp* — **9/2**[2]
-056 **3** *nk* **Requisite**[11] 5100 6-8-13 **74** ....(b) JamesDoyle 4 — 81
(Ian Wood) *racd stands' side: chsd ldr: led overall over 1f out: sn rdn: hdd wl ins fnl f: 3rd of 7 in gp* — **33/1**
1054 **4** 1 **Galatian**[15] 4958 4-9-6 **81** ....(b[1]) JamesMillman 9 — 85
(Rod Millman) *racd far side: chsd ldrs: led that gp over 2f out: sn rdn and hung rt: styd on: 1st of 3 that side* — **8/1**[3]
003 **5** 1/2 **Cardinal**[38] 4188 6-8-13 **74** .... WilliamBuick 2 — 76
(Robert Cowell) *overall ldr stands' side: rdn: edgd lft and hdd over 1f out: styd on same pce ins fnl f: 4th of 7 in gp* — **14/1**
4503 **6** *nk* **Jack My Boy (IRE)**[17] 4886 4-9-2 **77** .... DavidProbert 10 — 78
(David Evans) *racd far side: chsd ldr: rdn and ev ch that gp over 2f out: no ex ins fnl f: 2nd of 3 that side* — **20/1**
-056 **7** 1 1/4 **Loki's Revenge**[14] 5012 3-9-5 **83** .... KierenFallon 6 — 80
(William Jarvis) *racd stands' side: prom: rdn and edgd lft fr over 2f out: no ex fnl f: 5th of 7 in gp* — **9/2**[2]

-006 **8** *3 1/2* **Gaily Noble (IRE)**[107] 2000 5-9-4 **79** RichardHughes 13 65
(Andrew Haynes) *led far side over 3f: wknd fnl f: last of 3 that side* **28/1**
3000 **9** *3* **Bassett Road (IRE)**[14] 5012 3-9-2 **80** StevieDonohoe 1 57
(Willie Musson) *racd stands' side: hld up: plld hrd: wknd 2f out: 6th of 7 in gp* **20/1**
0160 **10** *4* **Divine Call**[34] 4310 4-9-2 **77** JimmyFortune 8 41
(William Haggas) *racd stands' side: s.i.s: hld up: rdn over 2f out: wknd wl over 1f out: last of 7 in gp* **3/1**[1]

1m 12.8s (0.30) **Going Correction** +0.20s/f (Good)
WFA 3 from 4yo+ 3lb **10** Ran SP% **120.1**
Speed ratings (Par 105): **106,105,104,103,102 102,100,95,91,86**
toteswingers:1&2:£3.60, 1&3:£19.50, 2&3:£22.60. Totesuper 7: Win: Not won, Place: Not won. CSF £16.29 CT £389.31 TOTE £4.10: £2.00, £2.00, £6.90; EX 20.70 Trifecta £374.70 Part won. Pool: £506.40 - 0.80 winning units..
Owner Mrs P Good **Bred** J Costello **Trained** Manton, Wilts

FOCUS
The field split for this sprint handicap, with three staying far side and the majority of the field edging over to the stands' side. The first three came from the larger group. A small personal best from the winner.
T/Jkpt: Not won. T/Plt: £329.90 to a £1 stake. Pool:£77,216.62 - 170.86 winning tickets T/Qpdt: £43.40 to a £1 stake. Pool:£6,138.16 - 104.50 winning tickets CR

5104 THIRSK (L-H)
Friday, August 26

OFFICIAL GOING: Good to soft (soft in places) changing to soft after race 2 (2:40) changing to heavy after race 3 (3:15)
Wind: Virtually nil Weather: Overcast and raining

5452 GORMIRE CLASSIFIED (S) STKS 6f
2:10 (2:10) (Class 6) 3-Y-0+ **£2,587** (£770; £384; £192) **Stalls** High

Form RPR
5366 **1** **Go Go Green (IRE)**[11] 5108 5-8-13 74 DanielTudhope 8 76
(Jim Goldie) *hld up in tch: hdwy 2f out and sn pushed along: swtchd lft to outer and rdn over 1f out: drvn and styd on strly ins fnl f: edgd lft and led nr fin* **85/40**[2]
6111 **2** *nk* **Efistorm**[5] 5301 10-9-5 73 KirstyMilczarek 5 81
(Conor Dore) *trckd ldrs: hdwy on outer and cl up 1/2-way: effrt to chal 2f out: rdn to ld jst over 1f out: drvn ins fnl f: edgd lft and hdd nr fin* **15/8**[1]
2253 **3** *2 1/4* **Grandmas Dream**[5] 5301 3-8-13 72 (p) RobertLButler(3) 3 74
(Richard Guest) *cl up: led 2f out: sn rdn and hdd jst over 1f out: sn drvn and one pce* **17/2**
000 **4** *4 1/2* **Tabaret**[42] 4075 8-8-13 75 (v) MichaelStainton 7 53
(Richard Whitaker) *led: hdd and n.m.r on inner over 4f out: effrt to chal over 2f out and ev ch tl rdn and wknd over 1f out* **7/2**[3]
0006 **5** *21* **Olynard (IRE)**[14] 4990 5-8-13 67 (b) PaulHanagan 1 —
(Dr Richard Newland) *prom: led over 4f out: rdn along and hdd 2f out: sn wknd and eased* **15/2**

1m 15.75s (3.05) **Going Correction** +0.60s/f (Yiel)
WFA 3 from 5yo+ 3lb **5** Ran SP% **111.3**
Speed ratings (Par 101): **103,102,99,93,65**
CSF £6.62 TOTE £3.50: £1.10, £1.90; EX 5.70.There was no bid for the winner.
Owner Jim Goldie Racing Club **Bred** Edmond And Richard Kent **Trained** Uplawmoor, E Renfrews
■ Stewards' Enquiry : Kirsty Milczarek caution: used whip with excessive frequency
Daniel Tudhope one-day ban: used whip with excessive frequency (Sep 9)

FOCUS
Not a bad seller, rated around the runner-up. The front pair in the market were a trail-blazer and a hold-up horse, but the tactics of the pair were surprisingly reversed on this occasion, and it was the confirmed front-runner, held up early, who prevailed on a track that generally suits front-runners in sprints.

5453 COXWOLD H'CAP 2m
2:40 (2:40) (Class 4) (0-80,78) 3-Y-O+ **£[illegible]** (£[illegible]; £506; £298) **Stalls** Low

Form RPR
354 **1** **Boss's Destination**[17] 4879 4-9-10 **72** PJMcDonald 5 85
(Alan Swinbank) *trckd ldrs: hdwy over 4f out: led over 3f out: rdn clr over 2f out: drvn ent fnl f and styd on strly* **11/2**[3]
4411 **2** *8* **Beat The Shower**[15] 4941 5-10-0 **76** BarryMcHugh 2 79
(Peter Niven) *hld up in rr: hdwy 4f out: rdn along over 2f out: sn chsng wnr: drvn and no imp fnl f* **11/4**[2]
-211 **3** *6* **Soprano (GER)**[18] 4856 9-9-1 **63** DanielTudhope 4 59
(Jim Goldie) *led 1 1/2f: chsd clr ldr tl led again 7f out: rdn along and hdd over 3f out: drvn over 2f out and grad wknd* **15/8**[1]
5333 **4** *2* **Descaro (USA)**[15] 4941 5-9-10 **72** PhillipMakin 7 66
(David O'Meara) *hld up: hdwy to chse ldrs over 4f out: rdn along 3f out: sn outpcd* **11/1**
/004 **5** *65* **Double Handful (GER)**[22] 4719 5-9-10 **72** PaulHanagan 8 —
(Venetia Williams) *prom: rdn along over 3f out: sn rdn and wknd wl over 2f out: eased* **8/1**
1310 **6** *dist* **Mojolika**[15] 4941 3-8-11 **73** (e) DavidAllan 1 —
(Tim Easterby) *t.k.h: prom: led and hung rt after 1 1/2f: hung bdly rt bnd bef 1/2-way: hdd over 7f out: sn bhd: virtually p.u over 4f out: trotted home* **15/2**

3m 41.68s (13.38) **Going Correction** +0.975s/f (Soft)
WFA 3 from 4yo+ 14lb **6** Ran SP% **108.0**
Speed ratings (Par 105): **105,101,98,97,64** —
toteswingers:1&2:£2.80, 1&3:£2.30, 2&3:£1.10 CSF £19.31 CT £32.95 TOTE £6.80: £3.20, £1.30; EX 21.00.
Owner Ontoawinner 1 **Bred** Overbury Stallions Ltd **Trained** Melsonby, N Yorks

FOCUS
A modest staying handicap run at a steady pace and the time - more than 18 seconds slower than standard - suggested the driving rain, which was into the rider's faces in the straight, had really started to get into the ground. The official going was changed to Soft after this event. The winner rates back to his 3yo best.
Mojolika Official explanation: jockey said gelding was unsteerable

5454 BRITISH STALLION STUDS SUPPORTING BRITISH RACING EBF MAIDEN STKS 1m
3:15 (3:15) (Class 4) 2-Y-0 **£4,398** (£1,309; £654; £327) **Stalls** Low

Form RPR
2342 **1** **Tidal Way (IRE)**[17] 4884 2-9-0 74 MartinHarley(3) 2 79
(Mick Channon) *trckd ldrs: hdwy 1/2-way: cl up 3f out: chal over 2f out and sn rdn: drvn and edgd lft ent fnl f: kpt on to ld last 100yds* **5/1**[3]
52 **2** *1 1/2* **Trail Blaze (IRE)**[20] 4781 2-9-3 0 PhillipMakin 10 76
(Kevin Ryan) *led: jnd 3f out and sn rdn: drvn over 1f out: n.m.r ins fnl f: hdd and no ex last 100yds* **13/2**
0 **3** *2 1/2* **Prepared**[34] 4330 2-9-3 0 RoystonFfrench 8 72+
(Mahmood Al Zarooni) *s.i.s and bhd: hdwy on outer wl over 2f out: rdn wl over 1f out: styd on strly fnl f: nrst fin* **4/1**[2]
4 *1 1/4* **Ahzeemah (IRE)** 2-9-3 0 FrederikTylicki 11 70+
(Saeed Bin Suroor) *s.i.s and bhd: hdwy on outer wl over 2f out: styd on ins fnl f: nrst fin* **10/1**
2 **5** *shd* **Rocktherunway (IRE)**[34] 4323 2-9-3 0 TonyHamilton 1 67
(Michael Dods) *trckd ldrs: effrt 3f out: rdn along over 2f out: sn drvn and no imp* **20/1**
632 **6** *3/4* **Saffa Hill (IRE)**[35] 4292 2-9-3 79 DavidAllan 4 66
(Tim Easterby) *trckd ldr: hdwy to chal 3f out: sn rdn and ev ch tl drvn wl over 1f out and grad wknd* **11/4**[1]
7 *1 3/4* **Princess Caetani (IRE)** 2-8-12 0 FrannyNorton 7 57+
(Mark Johnston) *s.i.s and bhd: hdwy on outer wl over 2f out: sn rdn and kpt on appr fnl f* **16/1**
8 *2 1/4* **Mazeydd** 2-9-3 0 NeilCallan 9 57+
(Roger Varian) *s.i.s and bhd tl styd on fnl 2f: nvr nr ldrs* **8/1**
0 **9** *2* **Istan Star (USA)**[40] 4122 2-9-3 0 BarryMcHugh 14 52
(Julie Camacho) *in rr: sme hdwy over 2f out: n.d* **100/1**
10 *1* **Northern Jewel (IRE)** 2-8-12 0 PaulHanagan 12 45+
(Richard Fahey) *midfield: hdwy on inner 3f out: rdn along over 2f out: sn wknd* **12/1**
63 **11** *4* **Brasingaman Espee**[56] 3570 2-9-3 0 AndrewMullen 13 41
(George Moore) *chsd ldrs: rdn along 1/2-way: sn wknd* **150/1**
00 **12** *4* **Up Ten Down Two (IRE)**[18] 4853 2-9-3 0 PaddyAspell 5 33
(Michael Easterby) *a towards rr* **100/1**
13 *4* **Blue Top** 2-9-3 0 GrahamGibbons 6 24
(Tim Walford) *chsd ldrs: rdn along over 3f out: sn wknd* **66/1**
0 **14** *3 1/4* **Eastern Seel**[16] 4898 2-8-12 0 AdamCarter(5) 3 17
(Tim Easterby) *in tch on inner: rdn along 1/2-way: sn wknd* **150/1**

1m 47.75s (7.65) **Going Correction** +0.975s/f (Soft) **14** Ran SP% **120.0**
Speed ratings (Par 96): **100,98,96,94,94 93,92,89,87,86 82,78,74,71**
toteswingers:1&2:£5.50, 1&3:£7.30, 2&3:£10.20 CSF £36.82 TOTE £8.30: £4.50, £8.30, £6.80; EX 32.10.
Owner Jaber Abdullah **Bred** Tallyho Stud, J Delahooke & P Twoomey **Trained** West Ilsley, Berks
■ Stewards' Enquiry : Martin Harley caution: careless riding.

FOCUS
A weak maiden run at a decent pace in the conditions and two with experience drew clear in the straight.

NOTEBOOK
Tidal Way(IRE) had twice finished runner-up in his five starts, including a narrow second to debutant Montaser at Ffos Las last time. Supervised at the start by his travelling lass Leslie White, he was up with the pace throughout and had enough resolve to get the better of the runner-up in a ding-dong battle. This was the first time he'd encountered ground conditions as easy as this and he was one of the few whose breeding suggested he'd like getting his toe in. So it proved, and he should make his mark in handicaps in future. (op 13-2)
Trail Blaze(IRE) had run well on his second start, just being touched off at Ayr over 7f. Upped in trip here, he made most of the running and battled back when the winner came upside. This was a very creditable effort and he's another who would not have minded the ease underfoot. He won't be long in winning. (op 7-1 tchd 15-2)
Prepared was ninth in what looked a decent 7f Newmarket maiden on his debut, but as he'd done there, he completely missed the break and gave himself plenty to do. He seemed to appreciate the extra distance, as he was eating up the ground late on and time will probably prove he's better than the duo that beat him. Official explanation: jockey said colt reared as stalls opened and missed the break (op 7-2 tchd 9-2)
Ahzeemah(IRE), a 60,000gns yearling, was edgy in the preliminaries for his debut and missed the break. He stayed on nicely, though, in conditions that would be against him. He holds a Derby entry, but while that appears a pipe-dream on this evidence, he should do better with more experience. (tchd 9-1 and 12-1)
Rocktherunway(IRE) produced a decent effort on his debut when second over 7f at Newcastle in a weak, easy-ground affair. Stepped up in trip here, he stayed on quite nicely, and seemed to run to a similar level of form. He has a race or two in him. (op 25-1)
Saffa Hill(IRE) came here on the back of three previous starts, improving on each of them and finishing third in what retrospectively did not look such a strong race as it did at the time. Upped in trip, he was prominent but looked one-paced when the pace was injected. He still shaped as though a stiffer test would suit. (op 7-2)
Princess Caetani(IRE), a 26,000gns yearling making her debut, was slowly away and did very well to get as close as she did. A pleasing first attempt, she is bred to get further and will be better for the experience. (op 18-1)

5455 THIRSK STKS (H'CAP) 7f
3:50 (3:52) (Class 4) (0-80,80) 3-Y-0+ **£4,010** (£1,193; £596; £298) **Stalls** Low

Form RPR
4651 **1** **Glenridding**[18] 4865 7-9-11 **79** FrederikTylicki 10 90
(James Given) *trckd ldrs: hdwy over 3f out: led over 2f out and sn rdn: drvn ent fnl f: kpt on strly* **11/1**
/0-0 **2** *nk* **Silenceofthewind (USA)**[27] 4561 4-9-6 **77** MartinHarley(3) 4 87
(Mrs K Burke) *trckd ldrs: hdwy 3f out: chal 2f out: rdn and ev ch over 1f out: drvn ins fnl f and kpt on* **14/1**
6423 **3** *2 3/4* **Emeralds Spirit (IRE)**[14] 4987 4-8-7 **61** oh1 KellyHarrison 8 64
(John Weymes) *midfield: hdwy 3f out: chsd ldrs 2f out: swtchd lft and rdn over 1f out: styd on wl fnl f: nrst fin* **14/1**
1500 **4** *1/2* **Blue Moon**[27] 4561 4-9-10 **78** NeilCallan 9 80
(Kevin Ryan) *midfield: hdwy and in tch 1/2-way: effrt over 2f out and sn rdn: drvn over 1f out and kpt on same pce fnl f* **7/1**[3]
1100 **5** *nk* **Daring Dream (GER)**[13] 5059 6-9-9 **80** GaryBartley(3) 12 81+
(Jim Goldie) *bhd: hdwy on wd outside over 2f out: sn rdn and kpt on fnl f: nrst fin* **12/1**
2134 **6** *1 3/4* **Tamasou (IRE)**[28] 4503 6-9-6 **74** GrahamGibbons 11 70+
(Ed McMahon) *towards rr and hmpd after 1f: hdwy wl over 2f out: sn rdn and kpt on: nrst fin* **6/1**[2]
0005 **7** *hd* **Besty**[33] 4371 4-8-9 **63** DavidAllan 5 59
(David Nicholls) *trckd ldrs: hdwy 3f out: chal over 2f out and sn rdn: ev ch tl drvn and wknd appr fnl f* **22/1**
2364 **8** *2 3/4* **No Quarter (IRE)**[28] 4517 4-8-8 **62** FrannyNorton 1 51
(Tracy Waggott) *a towards rr* **14/1**
5164 **9** *1 1/2* **Muftarres (IRE)**[13] 5031 6-8-9 **68** (p) LMcNiff(5) 2 53
(Paul Midgley) *a towards rr* **11/2**[1]
2112 **10** *4 1/2* **Dhhamaan (IRE)**[13] 5034 6-8-10 **69** (b) ShaneBKelly(5) 13 42
(Ruth Carr) *prom: hdwy to ld 1/2-way: rdn along and hdd over 2f out: sn wknd* **6/1**[2]
0000 **11** *1* **Without Prejudice (USA)**[23] 4670 6-8-12 **66** PaddyAspell 3 37
(Michael Easterby) *a in rr* **33/1**

4625 **12** *10* **Lindoro**[28] 4517 6-8-7 **64** .... PaulPickard(3) 7 —
(Kevin M Prendergast) *prom: rdn along 3f out: sn wknd* **9/1**

3063 **13** *1 ¼* **Rio Cobolo (IRE)**[20] 4792 5-9-6 **74** .... AdrianNicholls 6 15
(David Nicholls) *led: rdn along and hdd 1/2-way: drvn over 2f out and sn wknd* **9/1**

0000 **14** *4* **Thrust Control (IRE)**[20] 4810 4-9-7 **75** .... PatrickMathers 14 —
(Tracy Waggott) *a in rr* **100/1**

1m 33.02s (5.82) **Going Correction** +0.975s/f (Soft) **14** Ran SP% **120.8**
Speed ratings (Par 105): **105,104,101,100,100 98,98,95,93,88 87,75,74,69**
toteswingers:1&2:£16.30, 1&3:£15.70, 2&3:£36.10 CSF £154.62 CT £2235.13 TOTE £8.30: £4.50, £8.30, £6.80; EX 305.80.
Owner Tremousser Partnership **Bred** Bolton Grange **Trained** Willoughton, Lincs
■ Stewards' Enquiry : Frederik Tylicki caution: used whip with excessive frequency.
Shane B Kelly two-day ban: careless riding (Sep 9,11)

FOCUS
The ground continued to deteriorate and the official description was changed to heavy before this ordinary 7f handicap, which was run at a decent pace. The principals came down the centre of the track, seeking better ground. The winner is rated back to his best.

5456 DON'T MISS LADIES DAY - 3RD SEPTEMBER H'CAP 6f
4:25 (4:26) (Class 4) (0-80,78) 3-Y-O **£4,075** (£1,212; £606; £303) **Stalls** High

Form RPR

2145 **1** **Bravo King (IRE)**[2] 5378 3-9-4 **78** .... RobertLButler(3) 5 86
(Richard Guest) *racd wd: cl up: led 1/2-way: rdn clr 2f out: hung lft ins fnl f: kpt on* **8/1**

0655 **2** *2* **Captain Kolo (IRE)**[14] 5010 3-8-10 **67** .... KellyHarrison 8 69
(Tim Easterby) *led on stands' rail: hdd 1/2-way: rdn along 2f out: drvn over 1f out: kpt on fnl f* **5/1**

3-10 **3** *½* **Lizzie (IRE)**[23] 4680 3-8-13 **70** ....(b) DavidAllan 2 71
(Tim Easterby) *wnt lft s: sn swtchd rt towards stands' rail: trckd ldrs: hdwy 1/2-way: rdn along 2f out: drvn over 1f out: kpt on same pce fnl f* **11/4**[2]

4-36 **4** *shd* **Riverdale (IRE)**[44] 3985 3-9-5 **76** ....(t) GrahamGibbons 3 76
(Nigel Tinkler) *chsd ldrs: pushed along 1/2-way: rdn to chse wnr 2f out: sn drvn and edgd lft ent fnl f: one pce towards fin* **7/2**[3]

0504 **5** *11* **Jack Smudge**[62] 3384 3-9-4 **75** .... FrederikTylicki 6 42
(James Given) *in tch: pushed along 1/2-way: sn rdn and outpcd* **5/2**[1]

-006 **6** *4* **Indian Emperor (IRE)**[38] 4188 3-8-12 **69** .... PBBeggy 4 24
(Peter Niven) *sn outpcd and a in rr* **16/1**

1m 17.14s (4.44) **Going Correction** +0.80s/f (Soft) **6** Ran SP% **111.1**
Speed ratings (Par 102): **102,99,98,98,83 78**
CSF £45.19 CT £133.45 TOTE £8.60: £3.90, £3.00; EX 40.80.
Owner Rakebackmypoker.com **Bred** Celbridge Estates Ltd **Trained** Stainforth, S Yorks

FOCUS
Usually in sprints at Thirsk the stands' side is the place to be, but with the ground easing rapidly, connections of Bravo King elected to correctly plough a lone furrow up the centre of the track in this ordinary 3-y-o handicap for the class. There are questions to answer over the form.
Jack Smudge Official explanation: jockey said gelding never travelled

5457 TURFTV APPRENTICE STKS (H'CAP) 5f
5:00 (5:00) (Class 5) (60-92,75) 3-Y-O+ **£2,911** (£866; £432; £216) **Stalls** High

Form RPR

1154 **1** **Wicked Wilma (IRE)**[4] 5313 7-9-9 **68** .... BrianToomey 9 75
(Alan Berry) *a cl up: led 1/2-way: rdn clr ent fnl f: drvn and hld on wl towards fin* **4/1**[3]

0124 **2** *nk* **Dispol Grand (IRE)**[14] 4986 5-9-0 **59** .... LMcNiff 8 65
(Paul Midgley) *hmpd s: hld up in rr: hdwy wl over 1f out: rdn to chse ldrs ent fnl f: drvn and styd on to chal last 100yds: edgd lft and nt qckn nr fin* **5/2**[1]

4012 **3** *2 ¾* **Grudge**[29] 4475 6-9-6 **68** ....(b) JustinNewman(3) 7 64
(Conor Dore) *hmpd s: sn trcking ldng pair: rdn to chal 2f out: drvn and edgd lft ent fnl f: one pce* **10/1**

6000 **4** *2 ½* **Garstang**[50] 3759 8-8-10 **55** ....(b) AdamCarter 1 42
(Bruce Hellier) *wnt rt s: sn trcking ldng pair: effrt 2f out and sn rdn: drvn over 1f out and kpt on same pce* **20/1**

0462 **5** *1 ¼* **Rio's Girl**[25] 4600 4-8-9 **57** ....(p) LucyKBarry(3) 10 40
(Kevin Ryan) *led: pushed along and hdd 1/2-way: sn rdn and grad wknd* **3/1**[2]

3231 **6** *nk* **Desert Strike**[4] 5326 5-9-11 **75** 6ex ....(p) NoraLooby(5) 6 57
(Alan McCabe) *dwlt and towards rr: hdwy 1/2-way: rdn to chse ldrs wl over 1f out: sn wknd* **5/1**

2501 **7** *4* **Green Warrior**[38] 4172 3-9-2 **66** ....(p) CharlesEddery(3) 4 33
(Richard Guest) *hmpd s: racd wd and cl up tl rdn along 2f out and sn wknd* **9/1**

64.17 secs (4.57) **Going Correction** +0.80s/f (Soft)
WFA 3 from 4yo+ 2lb **7** Ran SP% **114.1**
Speed ratings (Par 103): **95,94,90,86,84 83,77**
toteswingers:1&2:£3.20, 1&3:£6.50, 2&3:£3.70 CSF £14.38 CT £91.15 TOTE £5.60: £3.20, £2.40; EX 20.00.
Owner Mrs Thelma White **Bred** Gerry O'Sullivan **Trained** Cockerham, Lancs

FOCUS
A weak apprentices' sprint handicap restricted to riders who have ridden fewer than 50 winners. The form is rated around the first two.
T/Plt: £582.90 to a £1 stake. Pool:£46,738.25 - 58.53 winning tickets T/Qpdt: £266.20 to a £1 stake. Pool:£3,345.83 - 9.30 winning tickets JR

5458 - 5462a (Foreign Racing) - See Raceform Interactive

5365 DEAUVILLE (R-H)
Friday, August 26

OFFICIAL GOING: Fibresand: standard (turf races were switched to fibresand)

5463a PRIX DE LA HAIE TONDUE (CLAIMER) (3YO) (FIBRESAND) 1m 1f 110y
2:20 (12:00) 3-Y-O **£9,051** (£3,620; £2,715; £1,810; £905)

RPR

1 **Caminar (FR)**[22] 3-8-9 0 ....(p) TheoBachelot(6) 3 86
(S Wattel, France) **31/5**[3]

2 *hd* **Home Run (GER)**[19] 3-9-2 0 .... MaximeGuyon 5 87
(P Schiergen, Germany) **5/2**[1]

3 *3* **Yosha (IRE)**[21] 3-8-11 0 .... ThierryThulliez 7 76
(P Demercastel, France) **23/1**

4 *1 ½* **Black Sheep (USA)**[14] 3-9-1 0 .... IoritzMendizabal 1 77
(G Botti, Italy) **37/1**

5 *½* **Zapatero (GER)**[27] 3-9-4 0 .... Christophe-PatriceLemaire 6 79
(X Nakkachdji, France) **13/1**

6 *shd* **Golden Speed (SPA)**[21] 3-8-11 0 ....(p) JohanVictoire 8 72
(L A Urbano-Grajales, France) **13/2**

7 *½* **Maria Grazie (IRE)**[17] 3-8-10 0 .... MlleLaurieFoulard(6) 13 76
(Mlle C Cardenne, France) **19/1**

8 *½* **Magical Flower**[65] 3267 3-8-11 0 .... FabienLefebvre 17 69
(Mme G Rarick, France) **16/1**

9 *hd* **Fast Draw**[49] 3-8-8 0 .... AnthonyCrastus 4 66
(P Vovcenko, Germany) **84/1**

10 *shd* **Kajsa Kavat (FR)**[19] 3-8-13 0 ....(p) GregoryBenoist 15 71
(Mme Pia Brandt, France) **20/1**

0 **Zack Yield (FR)**[276] 7544 3-9-1 0 ....(p) ThomasMessina 12 —
(A Lamotte D'Argy, France) **28/1**

0 **Iron Green (FR)**[87] 2583 3-8-11 0 .... OlivierPeslier 16 —
(Heather Main) *w.w in midfield: in tch w ldng gp whn rdn and nt qckn over 2f out: wknd fnl 1 1/2f* **45/1**

0 **Giantrio (IRE)**[19] 3-8-10 0 .... AlexisAchard(6) 18 —
(A Althoffer, France) **88/1**

0 **Londinieres**[102] 3-8-11 0 .... TonyPiccone 2 —
(C Lerner, France) **49/1**

0 **Stormbringer (MOR)**[14] 3-9-4 0 .... StephanePasquier 14 —
(P Bary, France) **48/10**[2]

0 **Rova (FR)**[49] 3-8-8 0 ....(p) Pierre-CharlesBoudot 11 —
(P Demercastel, France) **74/1**

0 **Go Jo Go (FR)**[14] 3-8-10 0 .... StevanBourgois(8) 9 —
(Robert Collet, France) **56/1**

0 **Akawy (FR)** 3-8-11 0 .... TristanNormand(4) 10 —
(Mme A Blanchard, France) **111/1**

2m 2.50s (122.50) **18** Ran SP% **116.5**
WIN (incl 1 euro stake): 7.20. PLACES: 2.30, 1.50, 4.60. DF: 12.40. SF:39.50..
Owner Rothschild Family **Bred** Famille Rothschild **Trained** France

4940 BEVERLEY (R-H)
Saturday, August 27

OFFICIAL GOING: Good (good to soft in places) changing to good to soft after race 2 (2:35)
Wind: Light against Weather: Cloudy with showers

5464 MONSIEUR BOND EUROPEAN BREEDERS' FUND MAIDEN FILLIES' STKS 7f 100y
2:00 (2:03) (Class 4) 2-Y-O **£4,463** (£1,328; £663; £331) **Stalls** Low

Form RPR

1 **Witnessed** 2-8-9 0 .... AntiocoMurgia(5) 14 80+
(Mahmood Al Zarooni) *hld up towards rr: smooth hdwy 3f out: swtchd outside and effrt to chse ldrs over 1f out: rdn to chse ldr and edgd rt ins fnl f: styd on wl to ld last 40yds* **17/2**

2423 **2** *1* **Esentepe (IRE)**[51] 3761 2-9-0 **82** .... DaneO'Neill 11 78
(Richard Hannon) *trckd ldrs: hdwy and cl up 1/2-way: led 2f out: rdn clr jst over 1f out: drvn and edgd rt ins fnl f: hdd and no ex last 40yds* **5/2**[1]

0 **3** *2 ½* **Really Lovely (IRE)**[28] 4552 2-8-11 0 .... JohnFahy(3) 1 72+
(Jeremy Noseda) *t.k.h early: trckd ldrs on inner: hdwy 3f out: rdn 2f out: drvn over 1f out and kpt on same pce* **11/4**[2]

45 **4** *1 ¾* **Scarlet Whispers**[14] 5029 2-9-0 0 .... MickyFenton 7 71+
(Pam Sly) *midfield whn n.m.r after 1f: hdwy 3f out: rdn to chse ldrs 2f out: sn drvn and no imp appr fnl f* **5/1**[3]

0 **5** *1 ½* **Spirit Na Heireann (IRE)**[30] 4471 2-9-0 0 .... TonyHamilton 5 64
(Richard Fahey) *midfield: hdwy and n.m.r over 2f out: sn swtchd lft and rdn: kpt on fnl f* **10/1**

6 *nk* **Bond Artist (IRE)** 2-9-0 0 .... TomEaves 2 64
(Geoffrey Oldroyd) *bhd: hdwy on inner wl over 2f out: nt clr run and swtchd lft over 1f out: kpt on ins fnl f: nrst fin* **20/1**

4U34 **7** *hd* **Lady Jameela**[16] 4961 2-9-0 **73** .... SamHitchcott 9 63
(Mick Channon) *sn led: rdn along 3f out: hdd 2f out: sn drvn and wknd* **10/1**

0 **8** *2* **Finity Run (GER)**[14] 5029 2-9-0 0 .... SilvestreDeSousa 6 59
(Mark Johnston) *cl up on inner: rdn along wl over 2f out: grad wknd* **18/1**

44 **9** *¾* **Dorry K (IRE)**[25] 4632 2-9-0 0 .... LeeNewman 3 57
(David Barron) *hld up towards rr: sme hdwy on outer wl over 1f out: nvr a factor* **28/1**

6 **10** *½* **Disco Sensation**[12] 5104 2-9-0 0 .... AdrianNicholls 10 56
(David Nicholls) *a towards rr* **50/1**

06 **11** *½* **Sweet Fairnando**[17] 4898 2-9-0 0 .... DavidAllan 12 54
(Tim Easterby) *dwlt: a in rr* **100/1**

0 **12** *1* **Iberian Rock**[37] 4232 2-9-0 0 .... DavidNolan 13 52
(Ann Duffield) *dwlt: reminders and cl up after 1f: rdn along over 3f out: wknd over 2f out* **100/1**

00 **13** *3 ½* **Bada Bing**[36] 4285 2-8-11 0 .... BillyCray(3) 4 44
(David Nicholls) *towards rr: n.m.r after 1f: bhd after* **100/1**

1m 36.99s (3.19) **Going Correction** +0.475s/f (Yiel) **13** Ran SP% **119.0**
Speed ratings (Par 93): **100,98,96,94,92 91,91,89,88,88 87,86,82**
toteswingers:1&2:£6.20, 1&3:£5.80, 2&3:£1.60 CSF £28.92 TOTE £10.90: £2.90, £1.30, £1.50; EX 44.20.
Owner Godolphin **Bred** Darley **Trained** Newmarket, Suffolk

FOCUS
Rails at innermost configuration. The jockeys after the opener described the ground variously as "dead" and "soft". This was a fair maiden fillies' event, with the runner-up providing the benchmark with an official rating of 82. The winner was quite impressive.

NOTEBOOK
Witnessed had the worst of the draw on the outside and, as a result, was trapped out wide and had to circle the entire field to make her effort, but she powered up the hill to nail the runner-up close to the line. A half-sister to a winning miler out of a US Grade 3 winner, she is from a stable operating at a strike rate of around 33% with its 2-y-o fillies this season and she looks another nice prospect for the yard. (op 11-1 tchd 12-1)
Esentepe(IRE), in the frame in all six previous starts including fourth in the Chesham, looked to have done everything right when stretching clear of her rivals 1f out, but she had the prize snatched from her near the line. She is running out of excuses and has become expensive to follow. (op 2-1 tchd 11-4)
Really Lovely(IRE) showed ability when eighth of 14 on her Newmarket debut last month and that race had already produced two winners from five subsequent runners. She had every chance here, but still showed signs of greenness and may need a bit more time. (op 5-2 tchd 2-1)
Scarlet Whispers, from the stable that won this in 2005 with the subsequent 1,000 Guineas winner Speciosa, had shown ability in a couple of Doncaster maidens and was well backed, but this drop in trip seemed to count against her. She now gets a mark and would be of interest in a nursery back over further. (op 9-1)

Spirit Na Heireann(IRE) showed ability when eighth of 17 on her Goodwood debut last month and would have finished closer here had she not met trouble on a couple of occasions inside the last 2f. (op 11-1 tchd 12-1)
Bond Artist(IRE) ◆, a £55,000 2-y-o and half-brother to four winners at up to 1m, missed the break and raced at the back early, but she showed ability as the contest wore on and should do better with the experience under her belt. (op 16-1)
Lady Jameela, in the frame in all four previous completed outings, set the pace until collared over 1f out and does not seem to be progressing. (tchd 9-1 and 12-1)

5465 TOTEQUICKPICK H'CAP — 7f 100y
2:35 (2:37) (Class 4) (0-85,84) 3-Y-O+ **£5,175** (£1,540; £769; £384) **Stalls** Low

Form — RPR
2310 **1** **Polish World (USA)**[14] 5059 7-9-8 **80** .... MickyFenton 1 — 92
(Paul Midgley) *mde all: rdn wl over 1f out: drvn ent fnl f: kpt on gamely towards fin* **17/2**
5560 **2** *nk* **Mr Rainbow**[21] 4794 5-9-12 **84** .... TomEaves 7 — 95
(Alan Swinbank) *midfield: hdwy and in tch 1/2-way: rdn to chse ldrs 2f out: drvn to chse wnr ins fnl f: edgd rt and kpt on: jst hld* **8/1**[3]
-000 **3** *4* **Oratory (IRE)**[21] 4794 5-9-10 **82** .... RobertWinston 3 — 83
(Geoffrey Harker) *s.i.s and towards rr: stdy hdwy on inner 4f out: nt clr run and swtchd lft over 2f out: rdn to chse ldrs over 1f out: drvn and hung rt ent fnl f: one pce* **12/1**
0000 **4** *6* **Amethyst Dawn (IRE)**[14] 5059 5-9-10 **82** .... DavidAllan 14 — 68
(Tim Easterby) *qckly away and sn cl up: chal over 2f out: sn rdn and ev ch tl drvn and wknd jst over 1f out* **11/1**
0366 **5** *1 ¼* **Diman Waters (IRE)**[36] 4291 4-9-5 **77** .... DaneO'Neill 6 — 60
(Eric Alston) *chsd ldrs: rdn along wl over 2f out: sn one pce* **16/1**
5335 **6** *¾* **Elijah Pepper (USA)**[12] 5106 6-9-2 **74** .... LeeNewman 12 — 55
(David Barron) *towards rr: hdwy wl over 2f out: rdn along wl over 1f out: nvr nr ldrs* **9/1**
0245 **7** *1 ½* **Hacienda (IRE)**[8] 5240 4-9-8 **80** .... SilvestreDeSousa 4 — 57
(Mark Johnston) *in tch on inner: pushed along 3f out: rdn over 2f out: sn drvn and btn* **9/4**[1]
0062 **8** *1* **Robert The Painter (IRE)**[21] 4810 3-9-4 **81** .... TonyHamilton 5 — 56
(Richard Fahey) *chsd ldrs on inner: rdn along 3f out: sn wknd* **7/1**[2]
0041 **9** *1 ¼* **Piceno (IRE)**[9] 5213 3-8-11 **77** ....(p) BillyCray(3) 8 — 49
(David Nicholls) *cl up: rdn along 3f out: drvn over 2f out and grad wknd* **10/1**
1/0- **10** *1 ¾* **Ultimate**[140] 6204 5-9-1 **76** .... PaulPickard(3) 10 — 43
(Brian Ellison) *nvr bttr than midfield* **16/1**
5100 **11** *10* **Powerful Pierre**[13] 5083 4-8-11 **69** ....(v) FrederikTylicki 11 — 11
(Ian McInnes) *dwlt: a in rr: bhd fnl 3f* **40/1**
5514 **12** *¾* **Gala Casino Star (IRE)**[30] 4477 6-8-11 **76** .... LauraBarry(7) 13 — 16
(Richard Fahey) *s.i.s: a bhd* **12/1**
00-0 **13** *23* **Whistledownwind**[26] 4609 6-9-10 **82** .... AdrianNicholls 9 — —
(David Nicholls) *hld up: a in rr: bhd fnl 3f* **40/1**

1m 36.19s (2.39) **Going Correction** +0.475s/f (Yiel)
WFA 3 from 4yo+ 5lb — **13** Ran SP% **124.4**
Speed ratings (Par 105): **105,104,100,93,91 90,89,88,86,84 73,72,46**
toteswingers:1&2:£17.90, 1&3:£31.20, 2&3:£18.50 CSF £78.15 CT £832.09 TOTE £11.40: £2.90, £1.90, £5.70; EX 89.70.
Owner C R Green **Bred** Racehorse Management, Llc **Trained** Westow, N Yorks
■ Stewards' Enquiry : Tom Eaves two-day ban: used whip with excessive frequency (Sep 11-12)

FOCUS
There was a torrential downpour before this race and the going was changed to good to soft after it. They took no prisoners in this fair handicap, with a trio soon scampering clear and very few ever got into it.

5466 TOTESCOOP6 H'CAP — 1m 1f 207y
3:05 (3:07) (Class 2) (0-105,99) 3-Y-O **£12,938** (£3,850; £1,924; £962) **Stalls** Low

Form — RPR
1163 **1** **Sud Pacifique (IRE)**[43] 4058 3-8-10 **91** .... JohnFahy(3) 3 — 106
(Jeremy Noseda) *hld up: smooth hdwy 3f out: chsd ldrs wl over 1f out: effrt and n.m.r ent fnl f: swtchd lft and sn rdn to ld over 100yds out: edgd rt and styd on strly* **9/2**[3]
2134 **2** *3* **Las Verglas Star (IRE)**[30] 4467 3-8-9 **87** .... TonyHamilton 7 — 96
(Richard Fahey) *trckd ldr: effrt and cl up over 2f out: rdn to ld wl over 1f out: drvn ent fnl f: sn hdd and one pce whn sltly hmpd nr fin* **7/2**[2]
2126 **3** *3 ¾* **Arabian Heights**[10] 5177 3-8-7 **85** .... StevieDonohoe 4 — 87
(Sir Mark Prescott Bt) *led: rdn along over 2f out: drvn and hdd wl over 1f out: one pce appr fnl f* **10/1**
0-40 **4** *1 ¼* **Goldenveil (IRE)**[30] 4473 3-8-4 **82** .... PatrickMathers 6 — 81
(Richard Fahey) *trckd ldrs: hdwy wl over 2f out: rdn along over 1f out: sn drvn and one pce* **25/1**
4040 **5** *3 ¼* **Specific Gravity (FR)**[30] 4467 3-9-7 **99** .... IanMongan 9 — 92
(Sir Henry Cecil) *cl up on outer: effrt 3f out: rdn along over 2f out: drvn wl over 1f out: grad wknd* **9/2**[3]
2420 **6** *¾* **Malthouse (GER)**[7] 5275 3-9-6 **98** .... SilvestreDeSousa 1 — 89
(Mark Johnston) *trckd ldrs on inner: pushed along 3f out: rdn over 2f out: sn drvn and wknd* **11/4**[1]
3200 **7** *19* **Tinkertown (IRE)**[30] 4467 3-9-5 **97** .... TomEaves 2 — 50
(Roger Varian) *sn towards rr: rdn along and bhd fnl 3f* **11/2**

2m 11.7s (4.70) **Going Correction** +0.475s/f (Yiel) — **7** Ran SP% **113.6**
Speed ratings (Par 106): **100,97,94,93,91 90,75**
toteswingers:1&2:£3.60, 2&3:£6.00, 1&3:£3.70 CSF £20.28 CT £147.25 TOTE £4.10: £2.00, £2.50; EX 19.80 Trifecta £51.80 Pool: £476.84 - 6.80 winning units..
Owner Sir Robert Ogden **Bred** Eduard Mordukhovitch **Trained** Newmarket, Suffolk

FOCUS
A decent handicap, despite the three non-runners, but this turned into quite a test for these 3-y-os.

NOTEBOOK
Sud Pacifique(IRE) was a disappointing favourite in cheekpieces at Newbury last time and returned to top form here without them. He had to be ridden along for a few strides early, but then settled well at the back of the field before being brought with his effort over 2f out and maintained his relentless progress to lead inside the last furlong. He seemed to relish the ground and could be in for a good autumn. (op 4-1)
Las Verglas Star(IRE) ran well when stepped up to this trip at Goodwood last time and hit the front over 1f out, but didn't last there long and had no answer to the winner. He handles soft ground, but may need a better surface or an easier track over this distance. (tchd 10-3)
Arabian Heights was disappointing stepped up to this trip at Nottingham last time and didn't appear to get home here after making much of the running. (op 17-2 tchd 8-1)
Goldenveil(IRE) met all sorts of trouble at Goodwood last time, but wasn't travelling that well at halfway here and could only plug on. (op 33-1)
Specific Gravity(FR) has faced some stiff tasks this year, but although this ground shouldn't have been a problem he was going nowhere from over 2f out. (tchd 5-1)
Malthouse(GER) has held his form well despite a busy season and the yard has a good recent record in this race, but he found little off the bridle and could have done without the rain. (op 4-1)
Tinkertown(IRE) ran creditably on his debut for the yard at Goodwood last month, but ran poorly here. The trainer's representative reported that the colt was unsuited by the good to soft going. Official explanation: trainer's rep said colt was unsuited by the good to soft ground (op 9-2)

5467 TOTEPOOL BEVERLEY BULLET SPRINT STKS (LISTED RACE) — 5f
3:35 (3:36) (Class 1) 3-Y-O+ **£17,760** (£6,717; £3,357; £1,677) **Stalls** Low

Form — RPR
-100 **1** **Tangerine Trees**[74] 3010 6-9-7 107 ....(v) TomEaves 9 — 116
(Bryan Smart) *mde all on stands' rail: rdn over 1f out: drvn and edgd rt ins fnl f: hld on gamely* **10/1**
1123 **2** *nk* **Duchess Dora (IRE)**[21] 4776 4-8-9 102 .... PBBeggy 4 — 103
(John Quinn) *a cl up: effrt to chal over 1f out: sn rdn: drvn and ev ch ins fnl f: hld whn sltly hmpd nr fin* **7/2**[2]
3321 **3** *nk* **Dinkum Diamond (IRE)**[43] 4063 3-8-12 106 .... DaneO'Neill 12 — 107
(Henry Candy) *trckd ldrs: swtchd rt and rdn to chal over 1f out: drvn and ev ch ins fnl f: nt qckn towards fin* **3/1**[1]
2210 **4** *1* **Captain Dunne (IRE)**[8] 5253 6-9-0 108 ....(p) DavidAllan 14 — 103
(Tim Easterby) *trckd wnr: effrt and n.m.r over 1f out: sn swtchd rt and rdn: drvn and ev ch whn nt clr run ins fnl f: one pce* **4/1**[3]
0060 **5** *2* **Breathless Kiss (USA)**[8] 5253 4-8-9 98 ....(b) SilvestreDeSousa 8 — 91
(Kevin Ryan) *sn outpcd and rdn along in rr: hdwy 1/2-way: drvn wl over 1f out: kpt on ins fnl f: nrst fin* **12/1**
50-0 **6** *5* **Reverence**[21] 4776 10-9-0 98 .... MickyFenton 15 — 78
(Eric Alston) *wnt lft s: chsd ldrs: rdn 2f out: sn one pce* **16/1**
-040 **7** *¾* **Golden Destiny (IRE)**[30] 4468 5-8-9 100 ....(b) RobertWinston 1 — 70
(Peter Makin) *towards rr: hdwy on wd outside to chse ldrs 2f out: sn rdn and wknd appr fnl f* **9/1**
0000 **8** *3 ¼* **Rain Delayed (IRE)**[10] 5180 5-9-0 98 ....(p) TonyHamilton 10 — 64
(Michael Dods) *dwlt: swtchd lft s: a towards rr* **14/1**
1020 **9** *1* **Tax Free (IRE)**[14] 5060 9-9-0 95 .... AdrianNicholls 11 — 60
(David Nicholls) *chsd ldrs: hdwy over 2f out: sn rdn and btn* **9/1**
0642 **10** *10* **Caledonia Princess**[10] 5173 5-8-9 73 .... MarkLawson 5 — 19
(Jo Hughes) *a towards rr: outpcd and bhd fnl 2f* **100/1**

63.14 secs (-0.36) **Going Correction** +0.25s/f (Good)
WFA 3 from 4yo+ 2lb — **10** Ran SP% **117.5**
Speed ratings (Par 111): **112,111,111,109,106 98,97,91,90,74**
toteswingers:1&2:£11.70, 1&3:£3.30, 2&3:£2.60 CSF £45.38 TOTE £11.50: £3.70, £1.80, £1.10; EX 37.10 Trifecta £329.50 Pool: £583.44 - 1.31 winning units..
Owner Tangerine Trees Partnership **Bred** Mrs B A Matthews **Trained** Hambleton, N Yorks

FOCUS
A competitive Listed sprint, despite the five non-runners, in which 3-y-os had been successful in the previous four years, but there was only one representative from the classic generation this year. The runners took the traditional soft-ground route up the stands' rail and the first two home were up with the pace throughout.

NOTEBOOK
Tangerine Trees was found out in both the Group 2 Temple Stakes and Group 1 King's Stand, but he was much more comfortable at this level despite his 7lb penalty for winning the Group 3 Palace House. He was able to get across to the near side from his stall without too much bother and was in front against the stands' rail over 3f from home. He faced several challenges, but despite hanging away to his right late on was always doing just enough. He is now 2-3 over C&D. (op 8-1)
Duchess Dora(IRE) came into this in fine form and had every chance on adjusted official ratings. She was prominent from the start, had every chance, and went down with all guns blazing. She has winning form on soft ground and this was her best effort in Listed company at the fourth attempt. She would be interesting in a race like this confined to her own sex. (op 4-1)
Dinkum Diamond(IRE), the only 3-y-o in the field, was ridden more patiently than the other principals and looked a big danger when switched for his effort over 1f out, but he couldn't quite go through with it. He has run well on soft ground before, but all three of his wins have come on a quicker surface. (op 4-1 tchd 11-4)
Captain Dunne(IRE), best in at the weights and far from disgraced when seventh in the Nunthorpe, didn't have a lot of room to play with when trying to poke his way through inside the last furlong and can be rated a bit better than his finishing position.
Breathless Kiss(USA), unplaced in five previous tries in Pattern company, maintained that record but she still ran with credit as she was completely taken off her feet early and made her finishing effort away from the main action up the centre of the track. (tchd 14-1)
Reverence isn't the horse he was and is only seen rarely these days. The rain would have been welcome, but he never looked like collecting. (tchd 18-1)
Golden Destiny(IRE) raced alone up the centre of the track early before joining the main field, but she never got into it and hasn't managed to win since completing a four-timer two years ago. (op 17-2 tchd 8-1)
Rain Delayed(IRE) was beaten only half a length by Tangerine Trees in the Palace House and was weighted to reverse the form, but he has been disappointing since Newmarket and this was another below-par performance. (op 10-1)

5468 TOTETRIFECTA H'CAP — 5f
4:10 (4:11) (Class 5) (0-75,81) 3-Y-O+ **£2,911** (£866; £432; £216) **Stalls** Low

Form — RPR
0653 **1** **Ingleby Star (IRE)**[5] 5313 6-8-12 **67** ....(p) PaulPickard(3) 11 — 80
(Ian McInnes) *racd on stands' rail: mde all: rdn over 1f out: drvn ins fnl f: styd on wl towards fin* **6/1**[3]
143 **2** *1 ¼* **Sleepy Blue Ocean**[17] 4900 5-9-2 **68** ....(p) GrahamGibbons 15 — 76
(John Balding) *trckd ldrs: swtchd rt and hdwy over 1f out: rdn to chal ent fnl f: sn drvn and ev ch tl one pce towards fin* **10/3**[1]
2126 **3** *hd* **Liberty Ship**[15] 4986 6-9-4 **70** ....(t) RobertWinston 10 — 77
(Mark Buckley) *trckd ldrs: effrt and nt clr run wl over 1f out: swtchd rt and rdn ent fnl f: kpt on wl towards fin* **11/1**
031 **4** *nk* **Northern Bolt**[9] 5204 6-9-4 **70** .... PatrickMathers 6 — 76
(Ian McInnes) *towards rr: rdn along and hdwy 2f out: styd on u.p ins fnl f: nrst fin* **8/1**
2145 **5** *½* **Rylee Mooch**[14] 5053 3-8-12 **73** ....(e) CharlesEddery(7) 4 — 77
(Richard Guest) *chsd ldrs on outer: rdn along 2f out: drvn ent fnl f: kpt on same pce* **8/1**
506 **6** *1 ½* **Select Committee**[17] 4900 6-9-4 **70** ....(v) PBBeggy 7 — 69
(John Quinn) *trckd ldrs: effrt wl over 1f out: sn rdn and one pce* **10/1**
1100 **7** *½* **Choc'A'Moca (IRE)**[49] 3880 4-9-0 **66** ....(v) MickyFenton 9 — 63
(Paul Midgley) *cl up: rdn along wl over 1f out: drvn and wknd ent fnl f* **11/1**
4401 **8** *2* **Green Park (IRE)**[11] 5148 8-9-10 **81** ....(b) NeilFarley(5) 3 — 71
(Declan Carroll) *towards rr: effrt over 2f out: sn rdn and n.d* **13/2**
2253 **9** *15* **Boogie Waltzer**[12] 5108 4-9-4 **73** ....(t) RyanClark(3) 5 — —
(Stuart Williams) *cl up: rdn along 1/2-way: sn drvn and wknd* **9/2**[2]

64.31 secs (0.81) **Going Correction** +0.25s/f (Good)
WFA 3 from 4yo+ 2lb — **9** Ran SP% **116.9**
Speed ratings (Par 103): **103,101,100,100,99 97,96,93,69**
toteswingers:1&2:£6.40, 1&3:£17.80, 2&3:£7.90 CSF £26.67 CT £189.84 TOTE £8.00: £2.20, £1.10, £3.70; EX 33.40 Trifecta £379.30 Part won. Pool: £512.57 - 0.20 winning units..
Owner Stephen Hackney **Bred** Pat Cosgrove **Trained** Catwick, E Yorks
■ Stewards' Enquiry : Graham Gibbons caution: careless riding.

FOCUS
A modest sprint handicap, affected by six non-runners, and again the field came stands' side, but as in the preceding Listed race the horse who bagged the near side rail in front proved successful. The first three were the trio drawn closest to the stands' rail and, as a result, the form is dubious.
Boogie Waltzer Official explanation: trainer's rep had no explanation for the poor form shown

5469 TOTESWINGER MAIDEN STKS — 5f
4:45 (4:48) (Class 5) 3-Y-0+ — **£2,911** (£866; £432; £216) **Stalls** Low

Form — RPR

4022 **1** **Cool In The Shade**[15] 5010 3-8-9 56....(b) JohnFahy(3) 2 — 61
(Paul Midgley) *qckly away: swtchd to stands' rail and mde all: rdn wl over 1f out: drvn ins fnl f: hld on gamely* — **2/1**[1]

000 **2** *nk* **Ingenti**[15] 4986 3-8-7 39.... JulieBurke(5) 3 — 60
(Christopher Wilson) *in tch: hdwy on outer 2f out: sn rdn and styd on to chal ins fnl f: kpt on towards fin* — **33/1**

0502 **3** *hd* **Surely This Time (IRE)**[14] 5063 3-9-3 62....(tp) PhillipMakin 1 — 64
(Kevin Ryan) *chsd wnr: rdn 2f out: drvn to chal over 1f out: kpt on u.p fnl f* — **5/1**[3]

4230 **4** *½* **American Lover (FR)**[46] 3934 4-9-0 58.... PBBeggy 12 — 57
(John Wainwright) *reminders s: in tch: rdn along and outpcd 1/2-way: hdwy on stands' rail over 1f out: fin strly* — **10/1**

4 **5** *1¾* **Libys Dream (IRE)**[14] 5030 3-8-12 0.... DaneO'Neill 8 — 51
(Michael Mullineaux) *chsd ldrs: rdn along over 1f out: drvn and one pce ent fnl f* — **11/2**

-555 **6** *1* **Musnad (USA)**[63] 3377 3-9-0 71.... PaulPickard(3) 5 — 53
(Brian Ellison) *towards rr: hdwy 2f out: sn rdn and kpt on fnl f: nrst fin* **5/2**[2]

45 **7** *2¼* **Boucher Garcon (IRE)**[19] 4863 3-9-3 0.... StevieDonohoe 4 — 44
(Declan Carroll) *a towards rr* — **50/1**

0055 **8** *2¼* **Wing N Prayer (IRE)**[55] 3660 4-8-9 34.... ShaneBKelly(5) 9 — 31
(John Wainwright) *a towards rr* — **40/1**

9 *1½* **Oosisit** 3-8-12 0.... JamesSullivan 6 — 26
(Ruth Carr) *chsd ldrs: rdn along 2f out: sn wknd* — **16/1**

10 *2* **La Danse Champetre** 3-8-12 0.... RobbieFitzpatrick 14 — 19
(Charles Smith) *a bhd* — **33/1**

0 **11** *¾* **Queen's Princess**[14] 5030 3-8-12 0.... PatrickMathers 7 — 16
(John Wainwright) *a bhd* — **100/1**

65.00 secs (1.50) **Going Correction** +0.25s/f (Good)
WFA 3 from 4yo 2lb — **11** Ran SP% **120.2**
Speed ratings (Par 103): **98,97,97,96,93 92,88,84,82,79 78**
toteswingers:1&2:£7.30, 1&3:£2.60, 2&3:£49.50 CSF £81.75 TOTE £2.90: £1.10, £17.30, £2.40; EX 102.90.
Owner The Rumpole Partnership **Bred** R W Gittins **Trained** Westow, N Yorks

FOCUS
A poor sprint maiden, and the nine of these to have raced before had managed to avoid winning a total of 51 times on the Flat between them. It was a familiar story with the winner again being the horse to gain the early advantage against the stands' rail.
Oosisit Official explanation: jockey said filly ran green

5470 STARS OF THE FUTURE APPRENTICE H'CAP — 1m 1f 207y
5:15 (5:18) (Class 6) (0-65,64) 4-Y-0+ — **£2,070** (£616; £307; £153) **Stalls** Low

Form — RPR

0500 **1** **Herrera (IRE)**[24] 4674 6-8-12 **57**.... LauraBarry(3) 4 — 64
(Richard Fahey) *midfield: hdwy 3f out: rdn to chse ldrs 2f out: drvn ent fnl f and styd on wl to ld on line* — **4/1**[1]

0006 **2** *nse* **Petomic (IRE)**[8] 5248 6-9-8 **64**....(p) LukeRowe 10 — 71
(Richard Guest) *chsd ldng pair: smooth hdwy 3f out: led 2f out and sn rdn clr: drvn ins fnl f: wknd towards fin: ct on line* — **7/1**

0000 **3** *7* **Bold Indian (IRE)**[32] 4409 7-8-0 **45**.... ShirleyTeasdale(3) 1 — 38
(Mike Sowersby) *chsd ldrs: rdn along wl over 2f out: styd on u.p appr fnl f* — **25/1**

5-60 **4** *2½* **Penderyn**[34] 4370 4-8-3 **45**.... NoelGarbutt 2 — 33
(Charles Smith) *led 2f: cl up on inner: led 3f out and styd far rail: rdn along and hdd 2f out: drvn and wknd over 1f out* — **28/1**

3346 **5** *5* **Rub Of The Relic (IRE)**[15] 4982 6-8-10 **55**....(v) DavidSimmonson(3) 6 — 33
(Paul Midgley) *hld up: hdwy over 2f out: sn rdn and nvr nr ldrs* — **9/2**[2]

5 **6** *shd* **Desert Nova (IRE)**[35] 4329 9-8-5 **47**.... GeorgeChaloner 13 — 25
(Mark Campion) *in tch: rdn along wl over 2f out: no hdwy* — **8/1**

-000 **7** *2½* **Fama Mac**[72] 3074 4-8-6 **53**.... TerenceFury(5) 8 — 26
(Neville Bycroft) *cl up: led after 2f: hdd 3f out and wd st to stands' rail: sn rdn along and wknd fnl 2f* — **7/1**

/6-1 **8** *1¾* **Freda's Rose (IRE)**[16] 4946 7-8-7 **49**.... NatashaEaton 3 — 18
(Owen Brennan) *unruly in preliminaries: dwlt and in rr: sme hdwy over 2f out: sn rdn and wknd* — **6/1**

0405 **9** *8* **Hits Only Jude (IRE)**[16] 4946 8-8-13 **60**....(v) MichaelKenny(5) 7 — 13
(Declan Carroll) *a in rr* — **5/1**[3]

2m 12.39s (5.39) **Going Correction** +0.475s/f (Yiel) — **9** Ran SP% **112.5**
Speed ratings (Par 101): **97,96,91,89,85 85,83,81,75**
toteswingers:1&2:£4.90, 1&3:£23.20, 2&3:£23.20 CSF £31.12 CT £606.81 TOTE £4.20: £1.20, £2.80, £7.30; EX 27.70.
Owner R A Fahey **Bred** Dr A J F Gillespie **Trained** Musley Bank, N Yorks

FOCUS
A moderate apprentice handicap in which the free-running Fama Mac and Penderyn rather lit each other up and set it up for the closers. The riders made use of the full width of the track on turning in.
Herrera(IRE) Official explanation: trainer's rep said, regarding apparent improvement in form, that the race was run to suit the mare, which possibly saw too much daylight last time.
T/Plt: £93.30 to a £1 stake. Pool:£65,093.29 - 508.98 winning tickets T/Qpdt: £9.40 to a £1 stake. Pool:£3,515.75 - 275.90 winning tickets JR

4954 GOODWOOD (R-H)
Saturday, August 27
OFFICIAL GOING: Good to soft (good in places on round course; 7.4)
Wind: quite strong against at times Weather: cloudy with sunny periods

5471 WINDFLOWER MARCH STKS (LISTED RACE) — 1m 6f
2:15 (2:15) (Class 1) 3-Y-0+ — **£17,013** (£6,450; £3,228; £1,608; £807) **Stalls** High

Form — RPR

2-03 **1** **Motrice**[30] 4470 4-9-2 107.... SebSanders 4 — 108
(Sir Mark Prescott Bt) *sn trcking ldr: rdn to ld jst over 3f out: hung lft briefly over 2f out: styd on strly fnl f: rdn out* — **85/40**[2]

1350 **2** *4½* **Eternal Heart (IRE)**[7] 5271 3-8-7 94.... WilliamBuick 1 — 105
(Mark Johnston) *led briefly early: trckd ldrs: rdn over 4f out: chsd wnr fr over 2f out: nvr quite able to mount chal: leaned rt and no ex fnl f* — **9/2**[3]

6131 **3** *7* **Drunken Sailor (IRE)**[29] 4492 6-9-12 116....(b) KierenFallon 5 — 105
(Luca Cumani) *stdd s: cl up in last pair: rdn over 3f out: wnt 3rd over 2f out: nvr gng pce to get on terms: fdd fnl f* — **10/11**[1]

2305 **4** *12* **Akmal**[56] 3647 5-9-7 103.... TadhgO'Shea 2 — 80
(John Dunlop) *lw: sn led: rdn and hdd jst over 3f out: wknd over 1f out* — **16/1**

2346 **5** *7* **Crocus Rose**[28] 4555 5-9-2 80.... HayleyTurner 3 — 65
(Harry Dunlop) *cl up in last pair: pushed along over 5f out: rdn over 4f out: sn btn* — **66/1**

3m 3.42s (-0.18) **Going Correction** +0.25s/f (Good)
WFA 3 from 4yo+ 12lb — **5** Ran SP% **109.9**
Speed ratings (Par 111): **110,107,103,96,92**
CSF £11.69 TOTE £2.50: £1.60, £2.00; EX 12.10.
Owner Miss K Rausing **Bred** Miss K Rausing **Trained** Newmarket, Suffolk

FOCUS
The ground was on the easy side of good following around 20mm of rain in the week, being officially described as good to soft, with good patches on the round course. The pace was a good one for this Listed contest.

NOTEBOOK
Motrice, who stays much further, was always well positioned to strike under Seb Sanders, who kicked her into a winning lead over 3f out. Despite appearing to idle, she never looked like being passed, and the win confirmed the promise of her last-time-out third in a fillies' Group 3 here. The Long Distance Cup at Ascot in October is presumably the aim. (op 9-4 tchd 2-1)
Eternal Heart(IRE), the sole 3-y-o representative, had been disappointing at Chester a week earlier and had a bit to find at the weights, but he appreciated the good test of stamina and kept on dourly. He has more to offer as a stayer and is entitled to improve from three to four, this being his first season to race. (op 7-1)
Drunken Sailor(IRE), last year's winner, successful in the Group 3 Glorious Stakes over 2f shorter here last month, had to be ridden hard to close and couldn't race on inside the final furlong. The ground was slower than he likes, though, and he was giving plenty of weight under the penalty, so considering his year is being geared towards the Melbourne Cup, this defeat was no great loss. (tchd Evens)
Akmal was driven to take an early lead and ensured it was a proper test. He needs quick ground, but even so it was disappointing to see him fold so tamely. He's been below his best all year. (op 11-1)
Crocus Rose has been held off marks in the low-80s of late, so it was inevitable she was going to struggle. (op 50-1)

5472 WHITELEY CLINIC PRESTIGE STKS (GROUP 3) — 7f
2:50 (2:50) (Class 1) 2-Y-0
£22,684 (£8,600; £4,304; £2,144; £1,076; £540) **Stalls** Low

Form — RPR

12 **1** **Regal Realm**[35] 4312 2-9-0 0.... JimmyFortune 2 — 103+
(Jeremy Noseda) *lw: trckd ldrs: travelling best whn nt clrest of runs over 1f out: swtchd rt: rdn whn swtchd lft ins fnl f: qcknd up wl fnl 100yds: led line* — **2/1**[1]

1 **2** *shd* **Rakasa**[31] 4427 2-9-0 0.... FrankieDettori 3 — 100
(Mahmood Al Zarooni) *lw: trckd ldr: chal jst over 3f out: rdn 2f out: tk v narrow advantage ent fnl f: kpt on wl: hdd line* — **11/2**

1 **3** *hd* **Questing**[67] 3258 2-9-0 0.... WilliamBuick 1 — 99
(John Gosden) *tall: fly-leapt leaving stalls: sn led: rdn whn hrd pressed fr over 2f out: kpt finding: v narrowly hdd ent fnl f: rallied gamely: r.o* — **3/1**[3]

2202 **4** *hd* **Nayarra (IRE)**[13] 5077 2-9-0 78.... KierenFallon 4 — 99?
(Mick Channon) *lw: cl up: rdn over 2f out: disp cl 3rd over 1f out: kpt on wl fnl 100yds: nvr quite getting there* — **33/1**

532 **5** *1¼* **My Queenie (IRE)**[16] 4969 2-9-0 80.... RichardHughes 5 — 96
(Richard Hannon) *hld up 6th but wl in tch: swtchd lft over 2f out: sn rdn: disp cl 3rd over 1f out: no ex fnl f* — **20/1**

5122 **6** *½* **Lily's Angel (IRE)**[21] 4803 2-9-0 100.... PaulHanagan 7 — 94
(Richard Fahey) *cl up: rdn jst over 2f out: disp cl 3rd over 1f out: no ex fnl f* — **5/2**[2]

1m 29.25s (2.35) **Going Correction** +0.25s/f (Good) — **6** Ran SP% **110.0**
Speed ratings (Par 104): **96,95,95,95,94 93**
toteswingers:1&2:£2.80, 1&3:£1.90, 2&3:£3.30 CSF £12.84 TOTE £2.70: £1.70, £2.70; EX 15.20.
Owner Cheveley Park Stud **Bred** Cheveley Park Stud Ltd **Trained** Newmarket, Suffolk
■ Stewards' Enquiry : Jimmy Fortune caution: used whip without giving filly time to respond.

FOCUS
An unsatisfactory race, with the pace being a steady one and the field finishing in a bunch. There are real doubts over the form but the race has been given a chance with the winner value for extra. The fourth's apparent improvement is a big concern.

NOTEBOOK
Regal Realm is much better than the bare result and her performance definitely needs upgrading. Having looked the one to take from the Princess Margaret, when competing for the first time in two months following niggling problems, she was rightly made favourite to see off maiden winners, but Jimmy Fortune started looking anxious when short of room over 2f out, and was denied a way out by Fallon aboard Nayarra approaching the final furlong. She appeared held after this, but having finally seen daylight inside the final 100 yards, she quickened well to get her rider out of trouble. Although this looked far from a Group 1 performance, she's bred to want 1m and it would be no surprise to see her run well in next month's Fillies' Mile. (tchd 15-8 and 9-4)
Rakasa, a 6f maiden winner here on her debut, was handily positioned and stayed on well to just get the better of the front-running third, but Regal Realm's finishing kick was too much. Her yard is strong in the juvenile fillies' department and she may win a Listed race returned to a sounder surface. (tchd 6-1)
Questing, impressive winner of a 7f Newbury maiden in June, set her own tempo and very much had the run of things. It's possible she'd have been better with a lead, in hindsight, this being only her second outing, but she's clearly limited to Listed/Group 3 level. (tchd 11-4 and 7-2)
Nayarra(IRE), 0-5 previously but a four-time runner-up, has been tried in blinkers and a visor, and was beaten five lengths in a 5f Pontefract maiden the time before, so her proximity in the finish is a worry. (op 25-1)
My Queenie(IRE), another without a win, was third to Rakasa in a 6f course maiden last month. She stayed on steadily to be beaten under 2l and ought to win a maiden before long. (op 16-1)
Lily's Angel(IRE), the Sweet Solera runner-up, found little for pressure inside the final 2f and was clearly below form. (op 10-3)

5473 BETFAIR CELEBRATION MILE (GROUP 2) — 1m
3:20 (3:22) (Class 1) 3-Y-0+
£56,710 (£21,500; £10,760; £5,360; £2,690; £1,350) **Stalls** Low

Form — RPR

2264 **1** **Dubawi Gold**[14] 5046 3-8-9 117.... RichardHughes 1 — 119+
(Richard Hannon) *patiently rdn in last: travelling wl but nt clr run fr wl over 1f out tl ent fnl f: qcknd up impressively: led towards fin: readily* — **3/1**[2]

-413 **2** *½* **Set The Trend**[41] 4138 5-9-1 111.... JimmyFortune 2 — 116
(Andrew Balding) *lw: trckd ldrs: rdn 2f out: led ent fnl f: kpt on but nt gng pce of wnr towards fin* — **12/1**

3332 **3** 1/2 **Beacon Lodge (IRE)**[14] 5046 6-9-1 112.............................. AdamKirby 5 115
(Clive Cox) *lw: reluctant gng down: hld up 5th: swtchd lft and rdn 2f out: nipped on hd by Poet's Voice wl over 1f out: kpt on wl fnl f* **5/1**[3]

4210 **4** 1 3/4 **Emerald Commander (IRE)**[16] 4972 4-9-1 113...........(t) WilliamBuick 3 111
(Saeed Bin Suroor) *lw: led: rdn whn hrd pressed fr over 2f out: hdd ent fnl f: no ex* **5/1**[3]

4306 **5** 2 1/4 **Premio Loco (USA)**[16] 4972 7-9-1 115............................ GeorgeBaker 6 106
(Chris Wall) *trckd ldrs: rdn 2f out: kpt on same pce fnl f* **10/1**

0000 **6** 1 1/4 **Riggins (IRE)**[10] 5185 7-9-1 98....................................... HayleyTurner 7 103
(Ed Walker) *trckd ldr: jnd ldr 3f out: rdn over 2f out: fdd ent fnl f* **50/1**

0-20 **7** shd **Poet's Voice**[154] 1002 4-9-1 122....................................(t) FrankieDettori 4 103
(Saeed Bin Suroor) *hld up in last pair: swtchd out for effrt and sme prog over 2f out: rdn and being hassled whn nipped Beacon Lodge wl over 1f out: nt gng pce to chal: fdd fnl f* **15/8**[1]

1m 39.16s (-0.74) **Going Correction** +0.25s/f (Good)
WFA 3 from 4yo+ 6lb **7** Ran SP% **111.9**
Speed ratings (Par 115): **113,112,112,110,108 106,106**
toteswingers:1&2:£4.70, 1&3:£2.40, 2&3:£4.70 CSF £35.40 TOTE £3.70: £1.90, £4.20; EX 37.10.
Owner Andrew Tinkler **Bred** A H Bennett **Trained** East Everleigh, Wilts

FOCUS
The pace appeared solid for this Group 2 contest. The form looks sound but the second did reverse Dusseldorf form with the fourth. Dubawi Gold was value for a bit extra and ran basically to form in what looked a below-par renewal.

NOTEBOOK
Dubawi Gold returned to his best under a Richard Hughes 'special', mowing down his rivals late to win with a bit in hand and further increase the dominance of 3-y-os over their elders in Group races this season. Having run well below par at Royal Ascot, things didn't go right at Newbury last time (behind Beacon Lodge), but he settled nicely out the back and produced a fine burst to come from virtually last to first in just over a furlong. The Prix du Moulin is likely to be next, with the Queen Elizabeth II also an option, but he'll struggle to land his first Group 1 success in either of those. (op 4-1)
Set The Trend, all-the-way winner of a C&D Listed event on fast ground in May, was always well placed and looked to have made a race-winning move when edging ahead inside the final furlong, but despite staying on well, his younger rival's turn of foot was too much. This was still a career-best and he can progress again returned to a genuine sound surface. The Prix Daniel Wildenstein was mentioned as a possible target. (op 11-1)
Beacon Lodge(IRE) has been on his game virtually all season, running well in Group 2s here and at Newbury the last twice. He was unable to repeat last-time-out form with the winner, lacking a change of pace under pressure, but can be rewarded at a slightly lower level. (op 9-2)
Emerald Commander(IRE), a Listed winner at Pontefract in July who was in here to set the pace for his better-fancied stablemate, was run out of the places late on and remains short of this level. (op 17-2)
Premio Loco(USA) was under pressure and beaten inside the final 2f. He needs a sounder surface, so deserves another chance, but his 33-1 Lockinge third has been shown as something of a one-off in subsequent starts. (op 8-1)
Riggins(IRE) was able to hang around until the final furlong and will soon find himself on a very attractive mark with handicaps in mind. (op 28-1)
Poet's Voice, last year's winner, went on to land the Group 1 Queen Elizabeth II at Ascot, hadn't run since finishing last in the Dubai World Cup and he looks one to avoid on the evidence of this. Having travelled kindly enough, he found little for pressure from over 2f out, and even appeared to try and 'nip' at Beacon Lodge before fading. Saeed Bin Suroor had expected him to come on for this, but even so, he's got it all to prove now. (op 13-8 tchd 9-4)

5474 BETFAIR SUMMER DOUBLE SECOND LEG STKS (HERITAGE H'CAP) 7f
3:50 (3:52) (Class 2) 3-Y-O+
£62,250 (£18,640; £9,320; £4,660; £2,330; £1,170) **Stalls** Low

Form RPR
2-54 **1** **Eton Rifles (IRE)**[63] 3394 6-9-4 **97**.................................... KierenFallon 5 109
(David Elsworth) *lw: in tch: waited for clr run tl swtchd lft 2f out: rdn ent fnl f: r.o strly: led fnl 75yds: readily* **5/1**[1]

6221 **2** 1 **Webbow (IRE)**[31] 4428 9-9-2 **95**.. FMBerry 15 104
(Mark Campion) *trckd ldrs: rdn over 2f out: chal wl over 1f out: led ins fnl f: kpt on but no ex whn hdd fnl 75yds* **12/1**

0012 **3** 2 1/4 **Below Zero (IRE)**[7] 5272 4-9-0 **93**.............................. DarrylIHolland 10 96
(Mark Johnston) *led: rdn 2f out: hdd ins fnl f: no ex* **20/1**

0046 **4** 2 **Lowther** [illegible] ....(b) JimCrowley [illegible] [illegible]
(Alan Bailey) *lw: mid-div: pushed along but nt best of runs over 2f out: styd on into 4th ent fnl f* **16/1**

3001 **5** 1 3/4 **Bronze Prince**[35] 4314 4-9-1 **94**.................................... WilliamBuick 19 87
(John Gosden) *mid-div: rdn over 2f out: hdwy over 1f out: styd on same pce fnl f* **11/2**[2]

3056 **6** 1 **Pastoral Player**[28] 4534 4-9-10 **103**.............................. SteveDrowne 13 93
(Hughie Morrison) *stdd s: towards rr: rdn wl over 2f out: no imp tl styd on fnl f: nvr nrr* **10/1**

3014 **7** shd **Chilworth Lad**[30] 4472 3-9-2 **103**.............................. MartinHarley(3) 16 91
(Mick Channon) *hld up towards rr: rdn into midfield wl over 2f out: no further imp tl styd on ins fnl f: nvr a danger* **12/1**

4100 **8** nse **Dunn'o (IRE)**[21] 4774 6-9-3 **96**... AdamKirby 8 86
(Clive Cox) *trckd ldrs: rdn over 2f out: one pce fnl f* **12/1**

5603 **9** 1/2 **Docofthebay (IRE)**[14] 5032 7-8-13 **95**................(p) MichaelO'Connell(3) 4 83
(David Nicholls) *s.i.s: towards rr: rdn 3f out: sme late prog: nvr a threat* **7/1**[3]

6621 **10** 1 3/4 **Casual Glimpse**[30] 4472 3-9-5 **103**.............................. RichardHughes 1 85
(Richard Hannon) *mid-div: nt clrest of runs over 2f out: swtchd lft over 1f out: sn rdn: no imp* **9/1**

0610 **11** 1 1/4 **Brae Hill (IRE)**[35] 4314 5-9-2 **98**................................. LeeTopliss(3) 14 78
(Richard Fahey) *s.i.s: a towards rr* **22/1**

0000 **12** 1 **Brave Prospector**[28] 4534 6-9-4 **97**.................................. JimmyQuinn 3 75
(Richard Fahey) *towards rr: hdwy on ins into midfield over 5f out: rdn wl over 2f out: wknd fnl f* **25/1**

4000 **13** 1 3/4 **Castles In The Air**[35] 4314 6-9-5 **98**............................ PaulHanagan 12 71
(Richard Fahey) *lw: mid-div: rdn over 2f out: nvr any imp: fdd fnl f* **14/1**

0000 **14** 1/2 **Manassas (IRE)**[14] 5032 6-9-5 **98**................................ EddieCreighton 6 70
(Brian Meehan) *a towards rr* **20/1**

-000 **15** 6 **Citrus Star (USA)**[21] 4802 4-9-5 **98**................................ GeorgeBaker 18 53
(Chris Wall) *trckd ldr: rdn wl over 2f out: wknd over 1f out* **25/1**

1m 26.93s (0.03) **Going Correction** +0.25s/f (Good)
WFA 3 from 4yo+ 5lb **15** Ran SP% **120.8**
Speed ratings (Par 109): **109,107,105,103,101 99,99,99,99,97 95,94,92,91,85**
toteswingers:1&2:£15.10, 1&3:£16.80, 2&3:£24.60 CSF £58.46 CT £1128.34 TOTE £6.20: £2.10, £4.20, £5.80; EX 87.40 Trifecta £1649.30 Pool: £36,998.99 - 16.60 winning units..
Owner Transcend Bloodstock LLP **Bred** Grangecon Stud **Trained** Newmarket, Suffolk

FOCUS
Few got into what had looked an open handicap, the first three being in the front five throughout and drawing clear. The pace appeared fair.

NOTEBOOK
Eton Rifles(IRE), lightly raced this season and the subject of good support on this debut for David Elsworth, had been nudged up 3lb for finishing fourth in a 6f Group 3 at Newcastle in June, but he's at least as effective at this longer trip and always looked to have enough forward momentum to get up inside the final furlong. A return to Pattern-level looks likely at some stage and it's probable there's more to come when granted give underfoot. (op 13-2)
Webbow(IRE), a deserved winner over C&D last month, was up just 2lb for this return to handicaps, but no sooner had he got to the front, the winner was bearing down on him. (tchd 11-1)
Below Zero(IRE) is a versatile sort who came into this in good form. Given a fine front-running ride, he briefly looked the winner when skipping a couple of lengths clear inside the final 2f, but was ultimately outstayed.
Lowther was short of room over 2f out and should have been a length or two closer. (op 12-1)
Bronze Prince, chasing a £100,000 Betfair bonus but 5lb higher than when winning a valuable handicap over this trip at Ascot last time, was faced with similar conditions but couldn't pick up in the same manner from an unhelpful draw. (op 8-1)
Pastoral Player, a fast-finisher in the Stewards Cup, isn't straightforward and was asked to make up too much ground on this return to 7f.
Chilworth Lad was unable to get into the race. (op 16-1)
Dunn'o(IRE), often a front-runner, did not lead this time and was again below form.

5475 REVIVAL MAIDEN AUCTION STKS 1m
4:25 (4:28) (Class 5) 2-Y-O **£3,234** (£962; £481; £240) **Stalls** Low

Form RPR
6 **1** **Chil The Kite**[15] 4995 2-8-12 0.. SteveDrowne 7 84+
(Hughie Morrison) *w'like: str: uns rdr gng by flags nr winning post on way to s: mid-div: hdwy 3f out: led over 2f out: sn rdn: edgd sltly rt ins fnl f: kpt on wl: rdn out* **11/4**[1]

03 **2** 1 3/4 **Blue Surf**[16] 4969 2-9-0 0... AdamKirby 3 80
(Amanda Perrett) *in tch: hdwy to hold ev ch 2f out: sn rdn: kpt chsng wnr but a being hld fnl f: no ex fnl 75yds* **4/1**[2]

3 **3** nk **Serene Oasis (IRE)**[14] 5047 2-8-0 0........................ CharlesBishop(7) 8 72+
(Mick Channon) *racd keenly on outside of midfield: rdn over 2f out: hdwy over 1f out: styd on: clsng at fin* **11/2**[3]

0445 **4** 3/4 **Miss Astragal (IRE)**[31] 4427 2-8-10 71...................... RichardHughes 10 74
(Richard Hannon) *hld up bhd: stdy prog whn swtchd rt over 2f out: sn rdn: styd on same pce* **9/1**

0 **5** 2 1/2 **Operation Tracer**[45] 3986 2-8-11 0................................ HayleyTurner 9 69+
(Michael Bell) *w'like: uns rdr gng by flags nr winning post on way to s: prom: led 5f out: rdn and hdd over 2f out: one pce fr over 1f out* **8/1**

65 **6** nk **Viscount Vert (IRE)**[17] 4906 2-8-12 0............................ LiamKeniry 11 70
(Andrew Balding) *sn trcking ldrs: rdn and ch 2f out: sn one pce* **11/1**

7 2 1/2 **Rainbow Gold** 2-8-12 0.. DarrylIHolland 1 64
(Mark Johnston) *lengthy: lw: s.i.s: towards rr of mid-div: rdn over 3f out: nt pce to get on terms* **8/1**

0 **8** 5 **Seemples (IRE)**[15] 4996 2-8-13 0.................................... SebSanders 5 54
(Richard Hannon) *str: lw: prom tl hmpd 5f out: struggling whn short of room 3f out: sn wknd* **20/1**

9 3 **It's A Privilege** 2-8-13 0.. JimCrowley 4 47
(Ralph Beckett) *leggy: s.i.s: a towards rr* **8/1**

65 **10** 20 **Calendar King**[86] 2641 2-8-9 0................................ MartinHarley(3) 2 2
(Mick Channon) *t.k.h: led tl didn't handle bnd and hdd 5f out: rdn over 3f out: wknd 2f out* **50/1**

1m 41.82s (1.92) **Going Correction** +0.25s/f (Good) **10** Ran SP% **120.4**
Speed ratings (Par 94): **100,98,97,97,94 94,91,86,83,63**
toteswingers:1&2:£3.60, 1&3:£4.60, 2&3:£3.20 CSF £14.03 TOTE £3.80: £1.40, £1.60, £1.70; EX 16.60.
Owner Hazel Lawrence & Graham Doyle **Bred** Whitsbury Manor Stud & Pigeon House Stud **Trained** East Ilsley, Berks

FOCUS
Pre-race drama here with several of these juveniles playing up and two, including the winner, unseating in front of the stands on his way down to post. The winner was quite impressive and the runner-up was the best guide to the form.

NOTEBOOK
Chil The Kite ◆, who shaped promisingly following a slow start at Newbury on his debut, was unperturbed by his antics on the way to the start here. He challenged widest of all turning in, but Drowne was full of confidence and, having gone on over 1f out, did only enough in front to score with a bit in hand. He's from a good family, is thought a bit of, and can make his mark in handicaps. (op 9-4 tchd 3-1)
Blue Surf, a bit on edge in the preliminaries, was up to 1m for the first time and saw it out well. He's shown enough to win a minor maiden and now qualifies for a mark also. (op 5-2)
Serene Oasis(IRE) played up badly when mounted, but it didn't affect her performance in the race, staying on having been keen early to confirm the promise of her Newbury debut. (op 7-1)
Miss Astragal(IRE) failed to improve for the step up to 1m, but can be used as a guide to the form. (tchd 8-1)
Operation Tracer, despite pre-race antics, improved on his debut effort under a positive ride. He has scope and is one to watch for in handicaps after another run. (op 11-1)
Viscount Vert(IRE) is now qualified for a mark and should fare better in the handicap arena. (op 16-1)
Rainbow Gold, whose dam is closely related to the yard's German Group 1 winner Lady Jane Digby, wasn't the best away, but is highly likely to improve for the experience, and indeed a longer trip in time. (op 10-1)
It's A Privilege displayed her inexperience in the preliminaries and then in the race itself. (op 9-1 tchd 10-1)

5476 IRISH STALLION FARMS E B F FILLIES' STKS (H'CAP) 6f
5:00 (5:01) (Class 3) (0-95,94) 3-Y-O+ **£9,703** (£2,887; £1,443; £721) **Stalls** High

Form RPR
2510 **1** **Blanche Dubawi (IRE)**[14] 5054 3-9-0 **87**........................ HayleyTurner 9 99+
(Noel Quinlan) *lw: hld up bhd ldrs: str run ent fnl f: led fnl 120yds: comf* **3/1**[1]

4035 **2** 1 1/4 **Hezmah**[15] 5012 3-8-11 **84**.. TadhgO'Shea 4 92
(John Gosden) *lw: cl up: rdn to ld ent fnl f: hdd fnl 120yds: nt pce of wnr* **4/1**[2]

4402 **3** 2 1/2 **Admirable Spirit**[33] 4387 3-8-9 **82**.............................. RichardHughes 6 82
(Richard Hannon) *hld up: nudged along over 2f out: hdwy over 1f out: chsd ldng pair jst ins fnl f: nt pce to get on terms* **11/2**[3]

0640 **4** 3 1/4 **Glas Burn**[21] 4779 3-8-12 **85**.. JimCrowley 1 75
(Jonathan Portman) *prom: led 2f out: sn rdn: hdd ent fnl f: fdd* **20/1**

2145 **5** 1/2 **Millyluvstobouggie**[15] 5000 3-8-3 **76**............................ JimmyQuinn 7 64
(Clive Cox) *trckd ldrs: rdn and edgd rt fr 2f out: fdd ins fnl f* **10/1**

1114 **6** shd **Roodee Queen**[20] 4817 3-8-8 **81**...................................... LiamKeniry 10 69
(Milton Bradley) *led tl rdn 2f out: wknd fnl f* **11/1**

3503 **7** 2 1/4 **Favourite Girl (IRE)**[10] 5180 5-9-10 **94**........................(p) SebSanders 3 74
(Tim Easterby) *little slowly away: sn trcking ldrs: rdn and ev ch 2f out: wknd fnl f* **4/1**[2]

10- **8** *6* **Warm Breeze**[344] 6157 3-9-3 **90**.. SteveDrowne 5 51
(Roger Varian) *hld up in tch: rdn 2f out: wknd ent fnl f* **8/1**

1m 13.04s (0.84) **Going Correction** +0.25s/f (Good)
WFA 3 from 4yo+ 3lb 8 Ran SP% **113.7**
Speed ratings (Par 104): **104,102,99,94,94 93,90,82**
toteswingers:1&2:£3.10, 1&3:£4.10, 2&3:£5.20 CSF £14.84 CT £61.69 TOTE £4.40: £2.00, £1.50, £1.60; EX 17.70.
Owner Burns Farm Racing **Bred** Burns Farm Stud **Trained** Newmarket, Suffolk

FOCUS
A decent fillies' sprint handicap run at just an ordinary pace.

NOTEBOOK
Blanche Dubawi(IRE), although she'd have preferred a stronger gallop to chase, having pulled hard when bombing at Newmarket last time, cruised up over 1f out and stayed on to win with a fair bit in hand. Successful in two of her last three starts, she's got a change of gear, is progressing well, and may be capable of making her mark at Pattern level in time, providing she can settle through the early stages of her race. (op 7-2 tchd 4-1 in places)
Hezmah continues to perform well without suggesting she's thrown in off this sort of mark. She too could have done with a stronger pace at this distance, her maiden win coming over 7f. (op 5-1)
Admirable Spirit hasn't found it easy this year, but her last two efforts have been better and she's capable of winning off this sort of mark when the emphasis is more on stamina. (op 7-1)
Glas Burn was left behind from over 1f out and shows no sign of capitalising on her declining mark. (op 16-1)
Millyluvstobouggie doesn't look up to winning off this mark. (tchd 9-1)
Favourite Girl(IRE), the only older horse, failed to match her last-time-out York third and was disappointing. (op 7-2)
Warm Breeze, returning from 344 days off, has now finished last on both starts since making a successful debut last summer. (op 11-2)

5477 TURFTV IS FOR BETTING SHOPS MAIDEN STKS (H'CAP) 2m

5:35 (5:35) (Class 5) (0-70,70) 3-Y-O £3,234 (£962; £481; £240) Stalls High

Form RPR

0662 **1** **Secret Edge**[11] 5145 3-9-4 **67**.. RichardHughes 5 74
(Alan King) *trckd ldrs: rdn to chal 2f out: tk narrow ld ent fnl f: styd on: drvn out* **3/1**[2]

0600 **2** *nk* **Compassion**[61] 3467 3-9-4 **67**.. HayleyTurner 2 73
(Michael Bell) *led: pushed along whn chal 2f out: rdn and narrowly hdd ent fnl f: styd on* **16/1**

3242 **3** *2* **Veloce (IRE)**[57] 3587 3-9-0 **63**.. JimCrowley 4 67+
(Ralph Beckett) *lw: hld up in last pair: hdwy fr 3f out: sn rdn: styd on but nvr gng pce to chal* **7/4**[1]

0030 **4** *¾* **Strength And Stay (IRE)**[31] 4449 3-8-9 **58**..................(p) LiamKeniry 3 61
(Eve Johnson Houghton) *lw: mid-div: nudged along briefly over 6f out: outpcd 3f out: styd on ent fnl f* **12/1**

4452 **5** *nk* **Handles For Forks (IRE)**[12] 5122 3-8-12 **68**........... CharlesBishop(7) 6 71+
(Mick Channon) *hld up last: swtchd to centre and sme prog over 3f out: rdn over 2f out: styd on ins fnl f: nvr trbld ldrs* **10/1**

0502 **6** *2 ½* **Oculist**[25] 4642 3-9-1 **64**.. FergusSweeney 11 64
(Jamie Osborne) *mid-div: rdn over 3f out: nvr any imp* **14/1**

0-03 **7** *3* **Mancunian (IRE)**[22] 4753 3-8-11 **60**.. SteveDrowne 12 56
(John Best) *prom: rdn 3f out: wknd over 1f out* **8/1**

6634 **8** *1 ¼* **Golden City (IRE)**[45] 3989 3-9-7 **70**.. GeorgeBaker 10 65
(Chris Wall) *mid-div: gd hdwy over 4f out: rdn to chse ldrs over 2f out: wknd jst over 1f out* **6/1**[3]

3m 40.86s (11.86) **Going Correction** +0.25s/f (Good) 8 Ran SP% **116.1**
Speed ratings (Par 100): **80,79,78,78,78 77,75,74**
toteswingers:1&2:£11.10, 1&3:£2.10, 2&3:£8.60 CSF £49.39 CT £107.67 TOTE £4.30: £1.30, £4.40, £1.50; EX 66.20.
Owner Nigel Bunter & David Anderson **Bred** Mrs S M Lee **Trained** Barbury Castle, Wilts

FOCUS
A modest 2m handicap for 3yos in which several of the contenders will no doubt appeal to prospective jumps buyers. They fairly dawdled round and it was nothing like the test of stamina expected beforehand. As a result, the form needs treating with caution.
T/Plt: £153.50 to a £1 stake. Pool:£114,976.52 - 546.66 winning tickets T/Qpdt: £23.90 to a £1 stake. Pool:£6,580.87 - 203.59 winning tickets TM

5444 NEWMARKET (R-H)

Saturday, August 27

OFFICIAL GOING: Good to soft (7.7)
Wind: Light across Weather: Cloudy with sunny spells and showers

5478 NOVAE BLOODSTOCK INSURANCE NURSERY 7f

1:55 (1:55) (Class 3) 2-Y-O £7,762 (£2,310; £1,154; £577) Stalls Low

Form RPR

041 **1** **Amazing Storm (IRE)**[19] 4857 2-9-1 **84**.. PatDobbs 6 87+
(Richard Hannon) *hld up: hdwy over 2f out: chsd ldr over 1f out: rdn to ld ins fnl f: edgd lft: r.o* **9/4**[1]

4232 **2** *nk* **Storming Bernard (USA)**[8] 5254 2-9-4 **87**........................ TomQueally 7 89
(Alan Bailey) *s.i.s: sn chsng ldrs: led over 2f out: rdn over 1f out: edgd lft and hdd ins fnl f: r.o* **9/2**[3]

4220 **3** *nk* **Cravat**[10] 5184 2-9-2 **85**.. NeilCallan 3 87
(Mark Johnston) *led over 2f: chsd ldrs: rdn over 2f out: hung lft ins fnl f: r.o*

21 **4** *½* **Bountiful Girl**[19] 4853 2-8-7 **76**.. BarryMcHugh 2 76+
(Richard Fahey) *prom: lost pl 4f out: sn pushed along: rdn and hung lft over 1f out: r.o wl towards fin* **9/1**

31 **5** *½* **Ruby Night (IRE)**[24] 4668 2-8-10 **79**.. JamieSpencer 1 78
(Michael Bell) *hld up: hdwy over 2f out: sn rdn: styd on same pce wl ins fnl f* **7/2**[2]

6031 **6** *1* **Maroosh**[22] 4760 2-8-8 **77**.. MartinDwyer 5 74
(Brian Meehan) *trckd ldrs: plld hrd: rdn over 1f out: styd on same pce* **13/2**

4201 **7** *½* **Royal Majestic**[17] 4907 2-8-2 **71**.. LukeMorris 4 66
(Mick Channon) *hld up: rdn over 1f out: r.o towards fin: nt trble ldrs* **12/1**

3043 **8** *4* **Hi There (IRE)**[17] 4913 2-7-12 **67** oh1.. CathyGannon 8 52
(J W Hills) *w ldr tl led over 4f out: hdd over 2f out: sn rdn: wknd fnl f* **16/1**

1m 25.84s (0.14) **Going Correction** -0.20s/f (Firm) 8 Ran SP% **114.7**
Speed ratings (Par 98): **91,90,90,89,89 88,87,82**
toteswingers: 1&2:£1.90, 2&3:£14.50, 1&3:£8.20 CSF £12.60 CT £113.12 TOTE £3.20: £1.40, £1.60, £3.70; EX 9.40 Trifecta £150.70 Pool: £625.27 - 3.07 winning units..
Owner W P Drew **Bred** Nore Lee Syndicate **Trained** East Everleigh, Wilts

FOCUS
Stands' side track used with stalls on far side except 1m7f centre. A dry night and the going was given as good to soft, with jockeys returning after the first reporting the ground to be dead and a bit sticky. A competitive little heat featuring five last-time-out winners, but the early pace wasn't hot and they finished in a bit of a bunch. Decent form, limited by the third.

NOTEBOOK
Amazing Storm(IRE) ◆ won nicely at Windsor last time and the step up to 7f promised to suit him. He travelled strongly in behind the leaders and picked up well when they hit the rising ground. Kept up to his work, he won only narrowly, but he was always holding his rivals and the impression left was that he had a bit more in hand than the winning margin suggests. He should be able to deal with a rise in the weights. (op 5-2)
Storming Bernard(USA), runner-up in the Convivial last time out, couldn't quite give 3lb to the winner but he ran another sound race and should be able to pick up a maiden if connections decide to return him to that sort of company. (op 5-1 tchd 4-1)
Cravat, fairly exposed over sprint distances, was trying 7f for the first time and got the trip alright, albeit off a steady enough early pace, but he's likely to remain vulnerable in this sort of company.
Bountiful Girl, one of the first to be niggled along, was putting her best work in at the death and will probably benefit from a step up to a mile in due course - her dam was a three-time winner over 1m4f. (op 15-2)
Ruby Night(IRE), who holds Group race entries, didn't seem to be found out by the trip but he didn't look entirely comfortable on the ground and he can probably be given another chance back on a faster surface. (op 9-2)
Maroosh was keen early and paid the price for that in the closing stages. A stronger gallop would have suited him better and he could well bounce back. (tchd 7-1)

5479 £100,000 TATTERSALLS MILLIONS MEDIAN AUCTION STKS 6f

2:30 (2:34) (Class 2) 2-Y-O

£54,100 (£24,590; £9,840; £4,910; £2,960; £1,970) Stalls Low

Form RPR

2213 **1** **Mehdi (IRE)**[19] 4858 2-8-9 90..(t) ShaneKelly 3 99
(Brian Meehan) *led stands' side: rdn and hung lft fr over 2f out: led ins fnl f: r.o: 1st of 5 in gp* **6/1**[2]

31 **2** *shd* **Samitar**[71] 3104 2-8-10 0.. JamieSpencer 12 100
(Mick Channon) *racd centre: chsd ldrs: led overall and hung rt fr over 1f out: rdn and hdd ins fnl f: r.o: 1st of 10 in gp* **11/10**[1]

010 **3** *3* **Balty Boys (IRE)**[10] 5181 2-8-11 92.. MichaelHills 16 92
(Charles Hills) *overall ldr in centre: rdn: hung rt and hdd over 1f out: stl ev ch whn hmpd ins fnl f: no ex: 2nd of 10 in gp* **6/1**[2]

62 **4** *1* **Chapter Seven**[51] 3761 2-8-7 0.. FrannyNorton 4 85
(Richard Fahey) *racd stands' side: prom: rdn and hung lft over 1f out: r.o: 2nd of 5 in gp* **12/1**

0265 **5** *1* **Orders From Rome (IRE)**[27] 4580 2-8-7 90.................. CathyGannon 5 82
(Eve Johnson Houghton) *racd stands' side: trckd ldrs: hung lft fr over 2f out: rdn over 1f out: styd on same pce: 3rd of 5 in gp* **16/1**

262 **6** *2 ¼* **Lemon Rock**[47] 3915 2-8-4 73.. BACurtis 8 72
(Noel Quinlan) *racd centre: hld up: hdwy over 2f out: sn rdn: wknd ins fnl f: 3rd of 10 in gp* **33/1**

0 **7** *2* **Symphony Star (IRE)**[21] 4804 2-8-2 0.. LukeMorris 15 64
(Paul D'Arcy) *racd centre: prom: rdn over 2f out: wknd fnl f: 4th of 10 in gp* **66/1**

01 **8** *2 ¼* **Jacob Cats**[17] 4912 2-8-7 80.. SeanLevey 7 63
(Richard Hannon) *racd centre: prom: rdn over 2f out: wknd fnl f: 5th of 10 in gp* **17/2**[3]

6 **9** *1 ½* **Soho Rocks**[16] 4961 2-8-2 0.. KirstyMilczarek 9 53
(James Toller) *racd centre: chsd ldrs: rdn over 2f out: wknd over 1f out: 6th of 10 in gp* **66/1**

10 *1 ½* **Sweet Liberta (IRE)** 2-8-4 0.. DavidProbert 17 51
(Andrew Balding) *racd centre: hld up: hdwy over 2f out: rdn and wknd over 1f out: 7th of 10 in gp* **20/1**

021 **11** *1* **Charitable Act (FR)**[17] 4906 2-8-7 82.. MartinDwyer 1 51
(William Muir) *racd stands' side: hld up in tch: racd keenly: rdn over 2f out: hung lft and wknd over 1f out: 4th of 5 in gp* **20/1**

00 **12** *3 ½* **Itsonlymakebelieve (IRE)**[11] 5133 2-8-2 0..............(v[1]) KieranO'Neill 6 35
(Ian Wood) *racd stands' side: prom: rdn 1/2-way: sn hung lft and wknd: last of 5 in gp* **250/1**

4455 **13** *¾* **Busy Bimbo (IRE)**[28] 4557 2-8-0 61.. AdrianMcCarthy 10 31
(Alan Berry) *racd centre: prom tl rdn and wknd over 1f out: 8th of 10 in gp* **150/1**

14 *6* **Popular Choice** 2-8-7 0.. MartinLane 14 20
(Nick Littmoden) *racd centre: s.i.s: outpcd: 9th of 10 in gp* **150/1**

15 *½* **Sir Mike** 2-8-5 0.. RoystonFfrench 11 16
(Amanda Perrett) *racd centre: dwlt: outpcd: last of 10 in gp* **20/1**

1m 11.27s (-1.23) **Going Correction** -0.20s/f (Firm) 15 Ran SP% **119.0**
Speed ratings (Par 100): **100,99,95,94,93 90,87,84,82,80 79,74,73,65,64**
toteswingers:1&2:£3.00, 2&3:£3.30, 1&3:£6.70 CSF £12.00 TOTE £7.50: £2.00, £1.20, £2.00; EX 17.40 Trifecta £39.00 Pool: £1,388.79 - 26.30 winning units..
Owner Iraj Parvizi **Bred** Douglas Taylor **Trained** Manton, Wilts

FOCUS
There was a mix of ability on show for this valuable prize but the market principals came to the fore in the closing stages. They split into two groups initially and, while the winner, along with the fourth and fifth came from the stands' side bunch of five, there at this stage look to be a significant draw bias. Solid, straightforward form, with the sixth the key.

NOTEBOOK
Mehdi(IRE) proved strongest and saw off the filly Samitar, from whom he was getting weight. They split into two groups initially and, while the winner, along with the fourth and fifth came from the stands' side bunch of five, there didn't at this stage look to be a significant draw bias. Mehdi, wearing a tongue-tie for the first time, hadn't been at his best at Windsor last time but his trainer thought that track was a bit sharp for him, and perhaps crucially he was denied the lead that day. He bowled along in front on the stands' side this time before drifting into the middle of the track from 3f out, and battled on strongly to see off the persistent challenge of the favourite. This was a career-best effort from him and, while he'll need to improve further to make his mark in Group company (the Mill Reef was mentioned), it's possible he'll make the leap. (op 13-2 tchd 7-1)
Samitar, the Albany Stakes winner, looked to hold obvious claims in this company and ran well in defeat, but her bigger rival just saw her off close home. She hung right under pressure, doing Balty Boys no favours inside the last, but it made no difference to the result. (tchd Evens, 6-5 and 5-4 in places)
Balty Boys(IRE), who didn't run up to market expectations at York ten days earlier, bounced back with a fine effort in defeat here, and he'd have finished closer, although still in third, had he not been squeezed up between the first two inside the last. (op 7-1)
Chapter Seven is related to plenty of winners and is improving with racing. He shouldn't be long in upholding the family tradition. (op 11-1)
Orders From Rome(IRE), sixth in the Super Sprint earlier in the season, finished third home from the five that raced on the stands' side during the early part of the race and had no problem with the trip. (op 20-1 tchd 25-1)
Lemon Rock probably ran her best race so far, coming out third best from the bigger group that raced towards the far side. Quicker ground ought to suit her better, and she should be up to taking a nursery if her mark doesn't go up too much for this.

Symphony Star(IRE) outran her odds. She's a half-sister to Jersey Stakes runner-up Deposer and should make her mark in handicaps in due course.
Jacob Cats, a winner at Salisbury last time on good to firm ground, may have found conditions here too testing. (op 9-1 tchd 10-1)

5480 RUSSIAN STANDARD VODKA EBF MAIDEN STKS 6f
3:00 (3:02) (Class 4) 2-Y-O **£4,528** (£1,347; £673; £336) **Stalls** Low

Form RPR
020 **1** **Elusive Flame**[19] 4857 2-8-12 72 NickyMackay 15 77
(David Elsworth) *mde all: rdn and edgd lft ins fnl f: r.o* **9/1**
5 **2** *3/4* **Money Never Sleeps**[42] 4098 2-9-3 0 RobertHavlin 11 80
(John Gosden) *trckd ldrs: rdn over 1f out: r.o* **7/2**[2]
04 **3** *1* **Police Force (USA)**[36] 4264 2-9-3 0 RoystonFfrench 16 77
(Mahmood Al Zarooni) *chsd ldrs: rdn and ev ch whn hung lft ins fnl f: no ex towards fin* **7/4**[1]
02 **4** *3/4* **Chapellerie (IRE)**[14] 5047 2-8-12 0 MartinDwyer 14 70
(Brian Meehan) *chsd ldrs: rdn over 1f out: r.o* **8/1**[3]
43 **5** *3 1/4* **Thewinningmachine**[16] 4940 2-8-12 0 BarryMcHugh 10 60
(Richard Fahey) *mid-div: rdn over 2f out: edgd lft and styd on same pce fnl f* **8/1**[3]
6 *3/4* **Berengar (IRE)** 2-9-3 0 ShaneKelly 3 63+
(Brian Meehan) *sn pushed along in rr: pushed along over 2f out: r.o ins fnl f: nvr nrr* **33/1**
04 **7** *shd* **Cheviot Quest (IRE)**[24] 4682 2-9-3 0 TedDurcan 13 62+
(William Jarvis) *chsd ldrs: rdn over 2f out: wknd over 1f out* **100/1**
8 *nk* **Willies Wonder (IRE)** 2-9-3 0 MichaelHills 12 61+
(Charles Hills) *hld up: hdwy over 2f out: rdn and wknd over 1f out* **22/1**
0 **9** *1/2* **Chalk And Cheese (USA)**[22] 4748 2-9-3 0 SaleemGolam 2 60
(John Gosden) *hld up: racd keenly: rdn and hung lft over 1f out: n.d* **40/1**
10 *1 1/4* **Sheikh The Reins (IRE)** 2-9-3 0 LukeMorris 6 56+
(John Best) *s.i.s and hmpd s: sn pushed along in rr: rdn over 1f out: n.d* **14/1**
11 *3/4* **Fareedha (IRE)** 2-8-12 0 RichardHills 7 49
(John Dunlop) *hmpd s: chsd ldrs tl rdn and wknd over 1f out* **20/1**
12 *5* **Sapphire Seeker** 2-9-3 0 CathyGannon 9 39
(Des Donovan) *hld up: rdn over 2f out: sn wknd* **100/1**
13 *nk* **Indiana Guest (IRE)** 2-9-3 0 TomQueally 8 38
(George Margarson) *hmpd s: hld up: wknd over 2f out* **25/1**
0 **14** *1 3/4* **Fallible**[20] 4823 2-9-3 0 NeilCallan 5 33
(Tony Carroll) *wnt lft s: sn prom: rdn over 2f out: wknd over 1f out* **100/1**
15 *5* **Kai** 2-9-3 0 JamieSpencer 1 18
(Michael Bell) *hld up: bhd fr 1/2-way* **14/1**
16 *1 1/4* **Point Made (IRE)** 2-9-3 0 RichardMullen 4 14
(Ed McMahon) *hld up: rdn and wknd over 2f out* **33/1**

1m 12.61s (0.11) **Going Correction** -0.20s/f (Firm) **16** Ran SP% **128.4**
Speed ratings (Par 96): **91,90,88,87,83 82,82,81,81,79 78,71,71,69,62 60**
toteswingers:1&2:£10.60, 2&3:£5.10, 1&3:£6.80 CSF £39.54 TOTE £9.30: £2.70, £2.10, £1.60; EX 78.60 Trifecta £270.50 Pool: £848.32 - 2.32 winning units..
Owner J C Smith **Bred** Littleton Stud **Trained** Newmarket, Suffolk

FOCUS
Run in heavy rain, this was no more than a fair maiden for the track. the pace held up very well. The winner is rated back to form.

NOTEBOOK
Elusive Flame apparently didn't handle the ground when disappointing at Windsor last time, but her second place at the same venue in July gave her every chance in this company and she stayed on strongly once hitting the rising ground. She looks as if she might get a bit further, as her pedigree would suggest, and one would imagine that it'll be nurseries for her next. (op 8-1 tchd 15-2)
Money Never Sleeps, last of five on his debut here last month, knew a lot more this time and finished his race off really well. He might take a maiden but looks more of a handicap prospect. (op 7-1)
Police Force(USA), despite being a half-brother to Dream Ahead, isn't one of his stable's stars, but he ran well enough on this drop back to 6f to suggest he'll have opportunities in nurseries. (op 9-4 tchd 5-2 in places)
Chapellerie(IRE) finished clear of the rest in fourth and will be interesting back on quicker ground in handicap company. (op 7-1)
Thewinningmachine is another who could take advantage of her opening mark back on a quicker surface. (tchd 7-1)
Berengar(IRE), who has already been gelded, showed enough to suggest he'll follow the pattern for his stable's juveniles in improving quite a bit for his debut effort.

5481 CHRIS BLACKWELL MEMORIAL HOPEFUL STKS (LISTED RACE) 6f
3:30 (3:30) (Class 1) 3-Y-O+
£17,013 (£6,450; £3,228; £1,608; £807; £405) **Stalls** Low

Form RPR
4010 **1** **Swiss Dream**[23] 4739 3-8-6 96 NickyMackay 1 104
(David Elsworth) *mde all: rdn and hung lft over 1f out: r.o* **11/2**[3]
0561 **2** *1 1/4* **Son Of The Cat (USA)**[28] 4531 5-9-0 99 (t) FrannyNorton 9 105
(Brian Gubby) *chsd ldrs: pushed along over 2f out: r.o to go 2nd wl ins fnl f: nt trble wnr* **5/1**[2]
6300 **3** *nse* **Royal Rock**[42] 4092 7-9-0 100 TedDurcan 2 105
(Chris Wall) *a.p: rdn to chse wnr over 1f out: hung lft ins fnl f: styd on* **12/1**
2033 **4** *1 3/4* **Mac's Power (IRE)**[28] 4534 5-9-0 100 (t) PatCosgrave 8 99+
(James Fanshawe) *hld up: hdwy over 1f out: sn rdn: no ex wl ins fnl f* **10/3**[1]
4020 **5** *1/2* **Monsieur Chevalier (IRE)**[49] 3863 4-9-0 115 PatDobbs 3 98
(Richard Hannon) *mid-div: rdn over 1f out: nvr trbld ldrs* **10/3**[1]
6500 **6** *1/2* **Cochabamba (IRE)**[7] 5277 3-8-6 96 MartinDwyer 7 91
(Roger Teal) *chsd wnr tl rdn over 1f out: no ex ins fnl f* **20/1**
0-21 **7** *4* **Capone (IRE)**[17] 4909 6-9-0 93 TomQueally 6 83
(David Nicholls) *hld up: swtchd lft over 2f out: rdn over 1f out: edgd rt and wknd ins fnl f* **8/1**
0113 **8** *5* **Cinderkamp**[35] 4333 3-8-11 88 JamieSpencer 5 67
(Edward Vaughan) *hld up: racd keenly: swtchd lft over 2f out: rdn and wknd over 1f out* **9/1**

1m 11.24s (-1.26) **Going Correction** -0.20s/f (Firm)
WFA 3 from 4yo+ 3lb **8** Ran SP% **111.8**
Speed ratings (Par 111): **100,98,98,95,95 94,89,82**
toteswingers:1&2:£4.30, 2&3:£29.80, 1&3:£9.20 CSF £31.46 TOTE £5.20: £1.50, £1.50, £2.80; EX 33.80 Trifecta £419.00 Pool: £1,296.89 - 2.29 winning units..
Owner Lordship Stud **Bred** Lordship Stud **Trained** Newmarket, Suffolk

FOCUS
Not the strongest of Listed races, as apart from Monsieur Chevalier, who disappointed anyway, no horse in the race had an official mark higher than 100.

NOTEBOOK
Swiss Dream was the third winner on the card to make just about all the running. She'd been held up over 5f in France last time but had previously scored twice from the front over this trip earlier this season, and she bounced back to winning ways with a straightforward success. There are no immediate plans for her. (op 7-1)
Son Of The Cat(USA) coped well with the uphill finish and stayed on late to take second. He remains on the upgrade but might prove hard to place off his current mark. (op 13-2 tchd 9-2)
Royal Rock is something of a twilight horse these days and, although he ran a sound enough race with conditions to suit, he's likely to remain so. (op 10-1)
Mac's Power(IRE) didn't run badly in a race not run to suit those held up. He remains on a mark off which he can be competitive in the big handicaps. (op 11-4 tchd 5-2)
Monsieur Chevalier(IRE) held outstanding claims on his Golden Jubilee second, but he was weak in the betting, was niggled along at halfway and made no progress at all. His best form has come in bigger fields, although whether he can be entirely relied on any more is open to question. (op 11-4 tchd 7-2)
Cochabamba(IRE) can't have too many excuses as she was never far off the pace, but she simply gives the impression of not having trained on from two to three. (op 25-1)
Capone(IRE) likes it fast, and perhaps it's worth ignoring this run as his trainer David Nicholls had been worried about the ground for him. (op 9-1)

5482 BURTS CHIPS MADE IN DEVON H'CAP 1m 4f
4:00 (4:03) (Class 3) (0-95,94) 3-Y-O+ **£8,409** (£2,502; £1,250; £625) **Stalls** Centre

Form RPR
-500 **1** **Status Symbol (IRE)**[49] 3867 6-9-2 82 WilliamCarson 7 94
(Giles Bravery) *mde all: rdn over 1f out: styd on wl* **33/1**
3301 **2** *2 3/4* **Qushchi**[28] 4530 3-8-12 88 MartinDwyer 3 95
(William Jarvis) *a.p: rdn to chse wnr over 1f out: styd on same pce ins fnl f* **12/1**
4-31 **3** *shd* **High Jinx (IRE)**[76] 2956 3-9-2 92 PatCosgrave 11 99+
(James Fanshawe) *hld up: hdwy over 3f out: rdn over 1f out: styd on* **5/1**[2]
2000 **4** *1/2* **Nave (USA)**[18] 4890 4-9-6 86 FrannyNorton 14 92
(Mark Johnston) *sn chsng wnr: rdn over 1f out: styd on same pce* **33/1**
3025 **5** *hd* **Trip The Light**[13] 5078 6-9-2 82 (v) BarryMcHugh 17 88
(Richard Fahey) *a.p: rdn over 1f out: styd on* **20/1**
5101 **6** *1/2* **Midnight Oil**[14] 5057 3-9-0 90 KirstyMilczarek 4 96+
(Luca Cumani) *hld up: nt clr run fr over 2f out tl r.o ins fnl f: n.m.r towards fin: nvr trbld ldrs* **8/1**[3]
035 **7** *5* **Chock A Block (IRE)**[21] 4778 5-10-0 94 TedDurcan 10 91
(Saeed Bin Suroor) *hld up: hdwy over 2f out: wknd fnl f* **14/1**
-302 **8** *1 3/4* **Northside Prince (IRE)**[13] 5078 5-9-10 90 PJMcDonald 5 84
(Alan Swinbank) *prom: racd keenly: rdn over 2f out: wknd over 1f out* **12/1**
2412 **9** *3* **Mountain Range (IRE)**[14] 5049 3-8-7 83 JamieSpencer 18 78+
(John Dunlop) *hld up: swtchd lft: hdwy and hmpd rivals over 1f out: eased whn no ch ins fnl f* **9/2**[1]
52-0 **10** *nk* **Mataaleb**[106] 2071 4-9-10 90 LiamJones 13 79
(Lydia Pearce) *hld up: rdn over 2f out: nvr on terms* **50/1**
3520 **11** *1 3/4* **Mcbirney (USA)**[8] 5250 4-9-4 84 ShaneKelly 6 72+
(Paul D'Arcy) *s.i.s: hld up: hdwy whn hmpd over 1f out: sn wknd* **12/1**
-500 **12** *1 1/2* **Chink Of Light**[21] 4775 4-9-5 85 (v) DavidProbert 12 69
(Andrew Balding) *hld up: rdn over 3f out: wknd over 1f out* **25/1**
1203 **13** *nk* **Ittirad (USA)**[42] 4108 3-8-11 87 (b[1]) NeilCallan 19 72+
(Roger Varian) *hld up: plld hrd: hdwy 6f out: rdn and wkng whn hmpd over 1f out* **5/1**[2]
0-35 **14** *hd* **Cobbs Quay**[99] 2258 3-8-0 76 NickyMackay 2 59
(John Gosden) *hld up in tch: racd keenly: pushed along over 3f out: wknd wl over 1f out* **9/1**
0633 **15** *4 1/2* **Chain Of Events**[7] 5281 4-8-9 75 oh1 JackMitchell 15 51
(Neil King) *chsd ldrs tl wknd over 1f out* **25/1**

2m 28.26s (-4.64) **Going Correction** -0.20s/f (Firm)
WFA 3 from 4yo+ 10lb **15** Ran SP% **122.7**
Speed ratings (Par 107): **107,105,105,104,104 104,100,99,97,97 96,95,95,95,92**
toteswingers:1&2:£58.40, 2&3:£17.50, 1&3:£36.70 CSF £372.15 CT £2337.68 TOTE £47.20: £12.10, £3.70, £2.30; EX 1053.40 TRIFECTA Not won..
Owner W H Carson **Bred** Darley **Trained** Cowlinge, Suffolk
■ Stewards' Enquiry : Martin Dwyer one-day ban: careless riding (Sep 11)

FOCUS
Yet another race where it paid to race prominently and another all-the-way winner.

NOTEBOOK
Status Symbol(IRE) had dropped a long way in the weights since the beginning of the season but it was still hard to find much to recommend him beforehand. He was soon in front dictating on the rail though, and as had been the pattern in previous races on the card, it proved very much the place to be. He picked up well inside the final 2f to keep any challengers at bay and came home a comfortable winner in the end. Whether this form will hold up is open to question.
Qushchi made just about all in a five-runner affair last time out but her rider was happy to take a lead this time. She wasn't able to make any inroads into the winner's advantage in the closing stages but held the rest off and probably remains capable of better. (tchd 11-1)
High Jinx(IRE) ◆, back from a break and running in a handicap for the first time, did best of those held up off the pace and as a result he can have his effort upgraded. There is certainly a race to be won with him off his current mark. (op 13-2)
Nave(USA), on the other hand, was never that far away from the leader and had every chance if good enough. This was a big step up on his recent efforts and the pace/draw bias clearly played a part in that.
Trip The Light didn't run badly but he was another to benefit from racing prominently in a race in which it proved hard to make up ground from behind.
Midnight Oil ◆ kept getting blocked in his run as he tried to make up ground from off the pace, so given the bias towards those racing up with the gallop and his troubled passage, he did well in the circumstances. He remains one to be interested in. (op 7-1)
Chock A Block(IRE), another who was held up, didn't make a lot of progress once switched out wide to challenge. He remains opposable off his current mark. (op 12-1)
Mountain Range(IRE), held up out the back, got involved in some bumping and barging when trying to find a way through, but he never got close enough to lay down a meaningful challenge. (op 7-2)
Mcbirney(USA) Official explanation: jockey said gelding lost its action
Ittirad(USA) didn't settle in the first-time blinkers and unsurprisingly failed to get home. (op 13-2)

5483 UNIVERSITY OF CAMBRIDGE VETERINARY SCHOOL TRUST H'CAP 1m 2f
4:35 (4:38) (Class 3) (0-95,94) 3-Y-O+ **£8,409** (£2,502; £1,250; £625) **Stalls** Centre

Form RPR
31 **1** **Dare To Dance (IRE)**[37] 4254 3-8-12 86 JamieSpencer 17 101+
(Jeremy Noseda) *hld up: hdwy over 4f out: rdn over 1f out: led ins fnl f: r.o wl* **3/1**[1]
0125 **2** *2 1/4* **Kirthill (IRE)**[21] 4801 3-9-5 93 KirstyMilczarek 14 102
(Luca Cumani) *a.p: rdn to ld and edgd rt over 1f out: hdd and unable qck ins fnl f* **8/1**[2]

205 **3** *nk* **Viva Vettori**[32] 4415 7-9-4 **84** .... NickyMackay 6 93+
(David Elsworth) *a.p: nt clr run over 1f out: sn rdn: styd on* **10/1**

-010 **4** *½* **Miss Diagnosis (IRE)**[31] 4429 3-9-0 **88** .... JamesDoyle 1 95+
(Ralph Beckett) *hld up: rdn over 1f out: swtchd lft and r.o ins fnl f: nt rch ldrs* **8/1**[2]

21 **5** *1* **Paramour**[13] 5082 4-9-6 **86** .... DanielTudhope 8 91
(David O'Meara) *hld up in tch: rdn over 2f out: styd on same pce ins fnl f* **9/1**[3]

0152 **6** *nk* **Ellemujie**[28] 4553 6-9-6 **86** .... (p) ShaneKelly 10 91
(Dean Ivory) *sn led: rdn and hdd over 1f out: styd on same pce* **25/1**

-134 **7** *nk* **Little Rocky**[35] 4335 3-8-13 **87** .... MartinLane 12 91+
(David Simcock) *hld up: hmpd over 8f out: rdn over 2f out: r.o ins fnl f: nt rch ldrs* **9/1**[3]

5431 **8** *hd* **Sonoran Sands (IRE)**[16] 4962 3-8-13 **87** .... MichaelHills 13 91
(Peter Chapple-Hyam) *chsd ldrs: rdn and ev ch over 1f out: no ex ins fnl f* **22/1**

2602 **9** *nse* **Fadhaa (IRE)**[23] 4723 3-8-10 **84** .... RichardHills 11 88+
(Charles Hills) *hld up: hmpd over 8f out: hdwy over 1f out: rdn and no ex wl ins fnl f* **12/1**

0030 **10** *1 ½* **World Heritage**[10] 5185 5-10-0 **94** .... AndreaAtzeni 9 95
(Robert Eddery) *hld up: hdwy over 2f out: wknd ins fnl f* **16/1**

5100 **11** *½* **Leviathan**[35] 4314 4-9-11 **91** .... BarryMcHugh 3 91
(Tony Newcombe) *hld up in tch: rdn over 2f out: wknd fnl f* **16/1**

051 **12** *5* **Askaud (IRE)**[31] 4429 3-8-13 **87** .... (p) RichardMullen 15 77
(David Nicholls) *hld up: racd keenly: hdwy over 2f out: wknd over 1f out* **25/1**

401 **13** *½* **Tameen**[14] 5062 3-8-3 **77** .... RoystonFfrench 2 66+
(John Dunlop) *prom whn hmpd and lost pl over 8f out: n.d after* **8/1**[2]

0304 **14** *2 ¼* **Suited And Booted (IRE)**[15] 4993 4-9-7 **87** .... TedDurcan 5 71
(Jane Chapple-Hyam) *chsd ldrs: rdn over 2f out: wknd over 1f out* **25/1**

1200 **15** *5* **Oceanway (USA)**[13] 5090 3-9-6 **94** .... FrannyNorton 7 68+
(Mark Johnston) *prom whn hmpd and lost pl over 8f out: n.d after* **16/1**

2m 2.53s (-2.97) **Going Correction** -0.20s/f (Firm)
WFA 3 from 4yo+ 8lb **15** Ran SP% **128.6**
Speed ratings (Par 107): **103,101,100,100,99 99,99,99,99,97 97,93,93,91,87**
toteswingers:1&2:£7.00, 2&3:£19.40, 1&3:£10.70 CSF £26.28 CT £220.18 TOTE £4.00: £1.70, £3.20, £4.30; EX 32.70 Trifecta £289.30 Pool: £1,020.47 - 2.61 winning units..
Owner R A Pegum **Bred** Round Hill Stud **Trained** Newmarket, Suffolk

FOCUS
This looked fairly competitive on paper.

NOTEBOOK
Dare To Dance(IRE) ◆ came in for support for both for this race and for the Cambridgeshire in the morning, and the unexposed son of Danehill Dancer showed himself to be well ahead of the handicapper with a fluent success. To come from midfield and win as he did when previous races had shown that pace was holding up well suggests he's even better than the bare result, and on this evidence 14-1 looks a fair price for the Cambridgeshire. It should be noted that he missed an intended engagement here in July on account of fast ground, so it would appear that he's thought to need cut to show his best. (tchd 11-4 and 7-2)
Kirthill(IRE) was never too far off the pace and so well positioned on a day when the leaders had tended not to come back. He was simply unfortunate to bump into a rival who proved well in on his handicap debut. (op 7-1 tchd 13-2)
Viva Vettori is a consistent sort and he travelled well to 2f out, but he didn't pick up immediately when his rider went for him and the gap that had been there for him closed. He ran on again once in the clear but by that time the race was effectively over and, no doubt frustratingly for connections, he remains a maiden on turf. (op 14-1)
Miss Diagnosis(IRE) ◆ was done no favours at the bend when tightened up badly next to the rail and hampered, and given that she came from the back half of the field to challenge, she did remarkably well to finish where she did. Clearly at home on a softish surface, she's got the ability to win a similar race. (op 9-1 tchd 10-1)
Paramour, stepping up to 1m2f for the first time and tackling easier ground, got the trip well enough and is clearly capable of being competitive off his opening mark. (op 11-1)
Ellemujie enjoyed the benefit of making the running on the stands' rail, which had been such a huge advantage throughout the day. Unfortunately for him, though, he's happier on quicker ground. (op 20-1)
Little Rocky didn't run badly considering he was hampered at the bend and had to make up ground from well off the pace. He got the trip well and he's capable of better than this bare form suggests. Official explanation: vet said colt lost right-fore shoe (op 17-2)
Fadhaa(IRE), done no favours on the bend, didn't run that badly in the circumstances. Official explanation: jockey said colt suffered interference in running (tchd 14-1)
Tameen was hampered on the bend during the general bunching. (op 9-1 tchd 10-1)
Oceanway(USA) was badly hampered on the bend and can be excused this run. Official explanation: jockey said filly suffered interference in running (tchd 14-1)

5484 TURFTV H'CAP 5f
5:10 (5:10) (Class 4) (0-85,84) 3-Y-O+ **£5,175** (£1,540; £769; £384) **Stalls** Low

Form RPR

3405 **1** **Judge 'n Jury**[18] 4886 7-9-8 **82** .... DavidProbert 1 92
(Ronald Harris) *mde all: rdn over 1f out: r.o: edgd lft nr fin* **7/2**[2]

4145 **2** *1 ¾* **Macdillon**[22] 4765 5-9-4 **78** .... ChrisCatlin 3 82
(Stuart Kittow) *chsd ldrs: rdn over 1f out: hung lft ins fnl f: styd on* **4/1**[3]

-146 **3** *hd* **Long Awaited (IRE)**[22] 4765 3-9-6 **82** .... (p) JackMitchell 4 85
(Roger Varian) *a.p: rdn over 1f out: styd on* **5/2**[1]

0500 **4** *1 ½* **Above The Stars**[10] 5163 3-8-13 **75** .... BarryMcHugh 12 73
(Richard Fahey) *hld up: hdwy over 1f out: sn rdn: styd on same pce ins fnl f* **11/1**

2131 **5** *5* **Fair Passion**[15] 4988 4-8-10 **70** .... NickyMackay 8 50
(Derek Shaw) *hld up: rdn and wknd over 1f out* **9/1**

0345 **6** *2 ¾* **Miss Polly Plum**[10] 5173 4-8-8 **68** .... (p) AndreaAtzeni 5 38
(Chris Dwyer) *chsd wnr tl rdn over 1f out: hung lft and wknd ins fnl f* **12/1**

1310 **7** *½* **Bouncy Bouncy (IRE)**[28] 4541 4-7-12 **65** .... (t) IanBurns(7) 2 33
(Michael Bell) *awkward leaving stalls: hld up: swtchd lft 1/2-way: pushed along and wknd over 1f out* **9/2**

58.02 secs (-1.08) **Going Correction** -0.20s/f (Firm)
WFA 3 from 4yo+ 2lb **7** Ran SP% **115.0**
Speed ratings (Par 105): **100,97,96,94,86 82,81**
toteswingers:1&2:£3.10, 2&3:£2.30, 1&3:£2.60 CSF £18.08 CT £40.20 TOTE £5.20: £2.70, £2.40; EX 16.90 Trifecta £55.50 Pool: £525.84 - 7.00 winning units..
Owner Robert & Nina Bailey **Bred** C A Cyzer **Trained** Earlswood, Monmouths

FOCUS
Once again making the running on the stands' rail proved the key.
Fair Passion Official explanation: jockey said filly hung right
T/Jkpt: Not won. T/Plt: £114.60 to a £1 stake. Pool:£109,455.02 - 696.93 winning tickets T/Qpdt: £81.50 to a £1 stake. Pool:£4,210.93 - 38.20 winning tickets CR

4808 REDCAR (L-H)
Saturday, August 27

OFFICIAL GOING: Soft (6.2)
Wind: Virtually nil

5485 KATE FEARNLEY & BAKERS TAILORING FASHION SHOW (LADY AMATEUR RIDERS' H'CAP) 1m 2f
5:20 (5:20) (Class 5) (0-75,74) 3-Y-O+ **£1,871** (£580; £290; £145) **Stalls** Low

Form RPR

0000 **1** **Black Coffee**[14] 5036 6-9-10 **64** .... (b) MissBeckyBrisbourne(5) 5 72
(Mark Brisbourne) *hld up: hdwy over 3f out: swtchd rt over 2f out: sn rdn to chal: kpt on: led post* **16/1**

1002 **2** *shd* **Moody Tunes**[26] 4603 8-10-4 **74** .... MissALMurphy(7) 3 82
(Tom Dascombe) *led: hdd 7f out: prom: rdn over 2f out: led narrowly appr fnl f: kpt on: hdd post* **6/1**[3]

102 **3** *1 ½* **Sartingo (IRE)**[21] 4784 4-10-3 **69** .... LucyAlexander(3) 2 74
(Alan Swinbank) *midfield: pushed along and hdwy over 3f out: led wl over 1f out: hdd appr fnl f: one pce* **4/1**[2]

0051 **4** *2* **Edas**[16] 4945 9-9-10 **62** .... MissHCuthbert(3) 12 63
(Thomas Cuthbert) *hld up in tch: rdn and hdwy over 3f out: ev ch 2f out: no ex fnl f* **9/1**

0030 **5** *2 ¾* **Harare**[8] 5248 10-8-13 **55** oh7 .... (v) MissGTutty(7) 1 51
(Karen Tutty) *midfield: on inner: rdn over 3f out: sn one pce* **33/1**

1-42 **6** *1* **Miereveld**[9] 5210 4-9-9 **58** .... (b) MissSBrotherton 15 52
(Brian Ellison) *wnt rt s: sn prom: led 7f out: rdn whn hdd wl over 2f out: one pce* **13/2**

0005 **7** *2 ¾* **Hurricane Thomas (IRE)**[10] 5178 7-9-1 **55** oh8 .... MissPhillipaTutty(5) 8 43
(Karen Tutty) *prom: rdn to ld wl over 2f out: hdd wl over 1f out: wknd* **20/1**

4314 **8** *6* **Christmas Light**[14] 5062 4-10-2 **72** .... MissRHeptonstall(7) 14 48
(David O'Meara) *hld up towards outer: rdn over 3f out: sn wknd* **15/2**

040 **9** *9* **Tropical Duke (IRE)**[26] 4605 5-9-6 **55** oh8 .... (p) MissLHorner 7 13
(Ron Barr) *midfield: rdn over 3f out: sn wknd* **14/1**

4511 **10** *1 ¼* **Bolodenka (IRE)**[11] 5151 9-10-4 **72** .... MissTSyddall(5) 9 28
(Richard Fahey) *racd keenly: in tch on outer: rdn over 3f out: wknd over 2f out* **7/2**[1]

-060 **11** *10* **Applaude**[4] 5349 6-9-1 **55** oh1 .... (b) MissBAndrews(5) 6 —
(Jason Ward) *trckd ldrs on outer: rdn and hung rt over 3f out: sn wknd* **33/1**

2m 14.06s (6.96) **Going Correction** +0.45s/f (Yiel)
WFA 3 from 4yo+ 8lb **11** Ran SP% **114.8**
Speed ratings (Par 103): **90,89,88,87,84 84,81,77,69,68 60**
toteswingers:1&2:£8.60, 1&3:£17.10, 2&3:£6.20 CSF £104.32 CT £461.47 TOTE £18.90: £5.30, £1.90, £1.80; EX 105.30.
Owner Derek & Mrs Marie Dean **Bred** Mrs M Campbell-Andenaes **Trained** Great Ness, Shropshire

FOCUS
After a wet 24 hours it was a fine and dry evening. The ground was soft. This lady amateur riders' handicap was run at a good pace and the eventual winner was second last turning in.
Black Coffee Official explanation: trainer had no explanation for the apparent improvement in form
Bolodenka(IRE) Official explanation: trainer's rep had no explanation for the poor form shown
Applaude Official explanation: jockey said gelding hung right

5486 MARKET CROSS JEWELLERS MEDIAN AUCTION MAIDEN STKS 6f
5:50 (5:52) (Class 5) 2-Y-O **£1,940** (£577; £288; £144) **Stalls** High

Form RPR

2 **1** **Deepsand (IRE)**[12] 5104 2-9-3 0 .... DavidAllan 5 76+
(Tim Easterby) *w ldr: led 2f out: sn rdn: edgd lft ins fnl f: kpt on* **6/4**[1]

0 **2** *¾* **Master Bond**[117] 1744 2-9-3 0 .... TomEaves 3 72+
(Bryan Smart) *racd keenly: hld up: smooth hdwy over 2f out: rdn to chal over 1f out: kpt on: hld towards fin* **9/2**[2]

3 *2 ¾* **Trioomph** 2-8-12 0 .... FrederikTylicki 12 59
(James Given) *w ldr: rdn over 2f out: stl over ev ch over 1f out: no ex fnl f* **25/1**

0 **4** *1 ¾* **Al Doha**[59] 3504 2-8-12 0 .... StephenCraine 2 53
(Kevin Ryan) *prom: rdn and outpcd over 2f out: kpt on fnl f* **14/1**

0 **5** *1 ¼* **Point At Issue (IRE)**[38] 4192 2-9-3 0 .... AdrianNicholls 9 55
(David Nicholls) *chsd ldrs: rdn over 3f out: one pce* **25/1**

6 *½* **Jay Bee Blue** 2-9-3 0 .... RichardKingscote 10 53+
(Tom Dascombe) *midfield: pushed along over 3f out: kpt on one pce: nvr threatened* **13/2**[3]

7 *1* **Ellastina (IRE)** 2-8-12 0 .... TonyHamilton 11 51+
(Richard Fahey) *hld up: short of room over 2f out: and again 2f out: rdn appr fnl f: kpt on: n.d* **18/1**

8 *¾* **Border Revia (IRE)** 2-9-3 0 .... DavidNolan 1 48
(Richard Fahey) *s.i.s: midfield: pushed along 1/2-way: nvr threatened* **9/1**

9 *shd* **Holy Angel (IRE)** 2-9-3 0 .... DuranFentiman 7 47+
(Tim Easterby) *slowly away: outpcd in rr tl kpt on fr over 1f out: n.d* **20/1**

6406 **10** *1 ¾* **Inya House**[18] 4892 2-9-3 57 .... (v[1]) AndrewMullen 4 42
(Nigel Tinkler) *midfield: pushed along over 2f out: wknd over 1f out* **25/1**

00 **11** *¾* **Time To Excel**[19] 4851 2-9-3 0 .... LeeNewman 13 40
(Michael Dods) *midfield: pushed along over 2f out: wknd over 1f out* **18/1**

0 **12** *1 ¾* **Ferdy (IRE)**[114] 1823 2-8-12 0 .... AntiocoMurgia(5) 6 35
(Paul Green) *led narrowly: rdn whn hdd 2f out: sn wknd* **20/1**

13 *2 ½* **Majestic Bounty** 2-8-12 0 .... KellyHarrison 14 22
(Chris Fairhurst) *midfield: pushed along over 3f out: sn wknd* **66/1**

14 *11* **Brunswick Vale (IRE)** 2-8-9 0 .... DeclanCannon(3) 15 —
(Paul Midgley) *midfield: sn pushed along towards outer: wknd over 3f out* **66/1**

1m 15.49s (3.69) **Going Correction** +0.45s/f (Yiel) **14** Ran SP% **122.8**
Speed ratings (Par 94): **93,92,88,86,84 83,82,81,81,78 77,75,72,57**
toteswingers:1&2:£3.20, 1&3:£14.90, 2&3:£32.60 CSF £6.94 TOTE £2.60: £1.10, £1.60, £14.20; EX 9.70.
Owner Trevor Hemmings **Bred** Gleahill House Stud Ltd **Trained** Great Habton, N Yorks

FOCUS
A run-of-the-mill event but a winner of some potential. The bare form is modest but the winner looks an interesting handicap prospect.

NOTEBOOK
Deepsand(IRE), who has plenty of size and scope, had shaped well when runner-up in a weaker event first time at Thirsk. He took time to gain the upper hand but was firmly in command at the line and will improve again. (op 2-1 tchd 9-4)
Master Bond ◆, who flopped when sent off favourite first time, was back after a three-month break. He travelled strongly before making his way to the outside. He gave the winner a good tussle but was very much second best at the line. He should have little difficulty going one better. (op 5-1 tchd 7-2)

The Form Book, Raceform Ltd, Compton, RG20 6NL

Trioomph, a half-sister to three winners, raced rather isolated from the first two towards the stands' side. She tended to hang left but hopefully this was due to inexperience. Quite stoutly bred on her dams's side, she will be suited by a step up to seven. (op 18-1)

Al Doha, very green first time, knew a lot more this time and is likely to be of more interest once handicapped.

Point At Issue(IRE) was another who showed a lot more than he had done on his debut. He will need another outing before he steps up in trip on his own bow. (op 20-1)

Jay Bee Blue, who changed hands for 52,000gns as a yearling, is a very laid-back individual. He looked fairly clueless but was picking up in his own time at the line. This will have taught him plenty. (op 7-1 tchd 8-1)

Ellastina(IRE) Official explanation: jockey said filly was denied a clear run

Border Revia(IRE) looked in need of this first run and made a satisfactory bow. (op 10-1 tchd 17-2)

Holy Angel(IRE), who lost many lengths at the start, made his way to the far side. Picking up nicely at the death, he looks sure to improve a good deal. (op 22-1 tchd 18-1)

5487 WIN A VIP DAY @ REDCARRACING.CO.UK NOVICE MEDIAN AUCTION STKS 7f

6:25 (6:25) (Class 5) 2-Y-O **£3,881** (£1,155; £577; £288) **Stalls** High

Form RPR

1 **1** **Just Fabulous**[35] [4323] 2-8-13 0 .... AndrewMullen 6 84+
(George Moore) *sn in tch: rdn over 2f out: swtchd lft and hdwy jst ins fnl f: kpt on wl to ld fnl 50yds* **13/2**[3]

312 **2** *1 ¼* **Vital Gold**[14] [5039] 2-9-4 89 .... KellyHarrison 7 86
(William Haggas) *led: pushed along over 2f out: edgd rt appr fnl f: drvn and strly pressed ins fnl f: hdd fnl 50yds* **2/1**[1]

1 **3** *shd* **Counterglow (IRE)**[24] [4655] 2-8-13 0 .... AntiocoMurgia(5) 2 86
(Mahmood Al Zarooni) *trckd ldrs: rdn to chal over 1f out: edgd rt ins fnl f: kpt on one pce* **4/1**[2]

3152 **4** *½* **Elkhart (IRE)**[16] [4964] 2-9-1 92 .... SilvestreDeSousa 4 82
(Mark Johnston) *trckd ldr: rdn and lost pl over 2f out: drvn over 1f out: kpt on one pce: carried lft ins fnl f* **2/1**[1]

5100 **5** *2 ¼* **Barolo Top (IRE)**[49] [3866] 2-9-4 79 .... RichardKingscote 1 79
(Tom Dascombe) *hld up: rdn over 2f out: nvr threatened* **8/1**

0 **6** *11* **Miss Ella Jade**[13] [5077] 2-8-8 0 .... MichaelStainton 5 41
(Richard Whitaker) *trckd ldrs: pushed along and lost pl over 3f out: wknd over 2f out* **100/1**

1m 28.79s (4.29) **Going Correction** +0.45s/f (Yiel) **6** Ran SP% **112.1**
Speed ratings (Par 94): **93,91,91,90,88 75**
CSF £19.91 TOTE £12.00: £6.00, £1.10; EX 26.50.

Owner Sean P Graham **Bred** Palm Tree Thoroughbreds **Trained** Middleham Moor, N Yorks

■ Stewards' Enquiry : Andrew Mullen caution: careless riding.

FOCUS

The two pacesetters seemed to set off to fast in the soft ground. The winner progressed from her debut but a few were below their form on the ground and the fifth limits things.

NOTEBOOK

Just Fabulous ◆, clear-cut winner of a soft ground maiden auction event at Newcastle has plenty of scope. She looked well held soon after halfway but stamina came into play and she showed ahead near the line. She has a most likeable attitude and will be ideally suited by a mile. (op 7-1)

Vital Gold, a late foal, is rated 89 and set the standard here. Quite keen, he ducked right and after getting into a bumping match with the third they were picked off by the winner. He may not want the going as soft as this. (op 9-4)

Counterglow(IRE), who cost just 15,500gns as a foal, had taken an ordinary event on his debut at Brighton. He travelled like the best horse but ducked and dived under pressure and was edged out near the line. A Derby entry, he can do a fair bit better on faster ground. (tchd 9-2)

Elkhart(IRE), rated 92, had the best chance on official figures but looked another at sea on the soft ground. (op 7-4)

Barolo Top(IRE), rated just 79, had plenty on. He gave his rider an anxious moment in the stalls and was never really travelling. (op 11-1 tchd 12-1)

5488 JOHN SMITH'S REDCAR STRAIGHT-MILE CHAMPIONSHIP QUALIFIER STKS (H'CAP) 1m

6:55 (6:56) (Class 4) (0-80,80) 3-Y-O+ **£2,587** (£770; £384; £192) **Stalls** High

Form RPR

1004 **1** **Sweet Child O'Mine**[16] [4959] 4-9-10 78 .... FrederikTylicki 1 89
(Richard Guest) *in tch: hdwy to ld over 2f out: rdn over 1f out: kpt on wl* **8/1**

6004 **2** *2 ¼* **Staff Sergeant**[9] [5205] 4-9-6 77 .... GaryBartley(3) 3 83
(Jim Goldie) *trckd ldr: rdn and ev ch over 2f out: kpt on: a hld by wnr* **7/2**[1]

0140 **3** *1 ¼* **Jonny Lesters Hair (IRE)**[9] [5205] 6-9-11 79 .... DavidAllan 6 82
(Tim Easterby) *led: rdn whn hdd over 2f out: kpt on one pce* **6/1**[3]

5200 **4** *3* **Just The Tonic**[24] [4670] 4-8-10 64 ow2 .... LeeNewman 8 58
(Marjorie Fife) *midfield: rdn and outpcd over 3f out: kpt on fr over 1f out: no threat ldng trio* **25/1**

1003 **5** *2 ½* **Iron Step**[15] [5014] 3-9-1 75 .... (t) GrahamGibbons 4 64
(Nicky Vaughan) *trckd ldrs: rdn over 2f out: wknd ins fnl f* **8/1**

3604 **6** *3 ½* **Sinatramania**[2] [5403] 4-8-8 61 oh4 ow1 .... TomEaves 11 44
(Tracy Waggott) *hld up: rdn over 2f out: no imp* **12/1**

5005 **7** *½* **Striker Torres (IRE)**[2] [5404] 5-9-2 70 .... SilvestreDeSousa 9 51
(Geoffrey Oldroyd) *hld up: rdn over 2f out: no imp* **15/2**

6062 **8** *4 ½* **Sir George (IRE)**[24] [4679] 6-9-10 78 .... PhillipMakin 14 49
(Ollie Pears) *dwlt: hld up: rdn over 2f out: no imp* **11/2**[2]

1-06 **9** *10* **Bond City (IRE)**[35] [4349] 9-9-7 78 .... NataliaGemelova(3) 13 26
(Geoffrey Oldroyd) *trckd ldr: rdn over 2f out: wknd over 1f out* **25/1**

0650 **10** *26* **Jo'Burg (USA)**[9] [5205] 7-9-5 78 .... (b) JulieBurke(5) 2 —
(Ollie Pears) *almost ref to r: t.o thrght* **16/1**

1426 **11** *8* **Seldom (IRE)**[5] [5314] 5-8-10 64 .... RobertWinston 12 —
(Mel Brittain) *midfield: pushed along and lost pl qckly 3f out: eased: t.o* **9/1**

1m 41.74s (3.74) **Going Correction** +0.45s/f (Yiel)
WFA 3 from 4yo+ 6lb **11** Ran SP% **117.1**
Speed ratings (Par 105): **99,96,95,92,90 86,86,81,71,45 37**
toteswingers:1&2:£6.10, 1&3:£13.40, 2&3:£10.20 CSF £35.95 CT £180.36 TOTE £8.30: £3.50, £1.70, £3.30; EX 48.60.

Owner EERC **Bred** A Reid **Trained** Stainforth, S Yorks

■ Stewards' Enquiry : Lee Newman three-day ban: weighed-in 2lb heavy (Sep 11-13)

FOCUS

A competitive mile handicap run at a strong pace in the conditions and a most emphatic winner.

Seldom(IRE) Official explanation: jockey said gelding ran flat and lost its action

5489 HOLD YOUR CHRISTMAS PARTY @ REDCAR RACECOURSE H'CAP 1m 6f 19y

7:25 (7:26) (Class 6) (0-65,62) 3-Y-O **£1,617** (£481; £240; £120) **Stalls** High

Form RPR

2444 **1** **Brook Star (IRE)**[43] [4044] 3-8-11 52 .... TomEaves 8 56
(Michael Dods) *mde all: rdn 3f out: drvn over 1f out: strly pressed fnl f: hld on gamely* **10/1**

-640 **2** *½* **Tigerino (IRE)**[21] [4814] 3-8-4 45 .... DuranFentiman 12 48
(Chris Fairhurst) *trckd wnr: rdn over 2f out: ev ch ins fnl f: kpt on: jst hld* **15/2**[3]

6453 **3** *1 ½* **Cadgers Brig**[11] [5152] 3-9-1 56 .... FrederikTylicki 2 59+
(Keith Dalgleish) *trckd ldr: rdn and outpcd over 3f out: kpt on again over 1f out: disputing 2nd whn short of room on inner fnl 50yds: eased* **7/1**[2]

0454 **4** *1* **Bollin Mandy**[29] [4515] 3-9-6 61 .... DavidAllan 6 61
(Tim Easterby) *v.s.a: sn hld up in tch: swtchd rt over 2f out: sn rdn: kpt on one pce fnl f* **11/4**[1]

2102 **5** *2 ½* **Hal Of A Lover**[11] [5152] 3-9-5 60 .... SilvestreDeSousa 1 56
(David O'Meara) *in tch on inner: rdn and hdwy to chse wnr over 2f out: wknd ins fnl f* **11/4**[1]

-024 **6** *nk* **A Southside Boy (GER)**[11] [5152] 3-8-1 45 .... DeclanCannon(3) 4 41
(Jim Goldie) *hld up in rr: rdn over 3f out: bhd tl kpt on fnl f: nvr trbld ldrs* **25/1**

050 **7** *28* **Indycisive**[84] [2735] 3-8-4 48 ow3 .... PaulPickard(3) 9 —
(Simon West) *midfield: rdn over 4f out: wknd over 2f out: eased: t.o* **9/1**

3m 15.83s (11.13) **Going Correction** +0.45s/f (Yiel) **7** Ran SP% **100.5**
Speed ratings (Par 98): **86,85,84,84,82 82,66**
toteswingers:1&2:£4.70, 1&3:£2.70, 2&3:£6.30 CSF £60.95 CT £378.24 TOTE £16.10: £6.30, £1.20; EX 82.00.

Owner Neale, Wynn-Williams, Woods **Bred** Mrs Eithne Thompson **Trained** Denton, Co Durham

■ Stewards' Enquiry : Tom Eaves three-day ban: careless riding (Sep 13-15)

FOCUS

A low-grade 3-y-o stayers' handicap and a very tactical affair.

A Southside Boy(GER) Official explanation: jockey said gelding hung right-handed throughout

5490 FOLLOW REDCARRACING ON FACEBOOK & TWITTER H'CAP 6f

7:55 (7:57) (Class 6) (0-55,55) 3-Y-O+ **£1,704** (£503; £251) **Stalls** High

Form RPR

0000 **1** **Secret City (IRE)**[18] [4893] 5-9-2 52 .... (b) RobertWinston 4 63
(Robin Bastiman) *prom: drvn to chse ldr over 1f out: kpt on to ld fnl 50yds* **9/1**

0304 **2** *hd* **Winning Draw (IRE)**[10] [5162] 3-8-8 50 .... (b[1]) DeclanCannon(3) 14 60
(Paul Midgley) *prom: led 4f out: rdn over 1f out: hdd fnl 50yds: kpt on: jst hld* **7/1**[3]

0060 **3** *3* **Royal Premium**[26] [4600] 5-8-7 46 oh1 .... (v) BillyCray(3) 10 46
(Bruce Hellier) *racd keenly: hld up: rdn and hdwy over 1f out: wnt 3rd fnl 100yds: kpt on: no threat ldng pair* **33/1**

5030 **4** *½* **Monsieur Pontaven**[18] [4876] 4-9-1 51 .... (b) LeeNewman 11 50
(Robin Bastiman) *chsd ldrs: rdn over 2f out: kpt on* **9/1**

0025 **5** *½* **Isle Of Ellis (IRE)**[21] [4813] 4-8-7 46 oh1 .... (v) PaulPickard(3) 9 43
(Ron Barr) *prom: rdn over 2f out: kpt on one pce* **16/1**

3000 **6** *3* **Bossy Kitty**[37] [4233] 4-8-13 49 .... SilvestreDeSousa 5 37
(Nigel Tinkler) *hld up: pushed along bef 1/2-way: hdwy over 1f out: no ex ins fnl f* **11/2**[2]

1452 **7** *1 ½* **Tahitian Princess (IRE)**[9] [5203] 3-9-2 55 .... (p) DavidNolan 17 38
(Ann Duffield) *chsd ldrs: rdn over 2f out: wknd ins fnl f* **9/2**[1]

1226 **8** *¾* **Hambleton**[38] [4196] 4-9-5 55 .... TomEaves 6 35
(Bryan Smart) *hld up: hdwy to chse ldrs 2f out: wknd ins fnl f* **11/2**[2]

2444 **9** *4* **Majestic Millie (IRE)**[26] [4607] 3-8-2 46 oh1 .... ShaneBKelly(5) 19 14
(David O'Meara) *in tch: rdn over 2f out: wknd over 1f out* **20/1**

0000 **10** *1* **Charles Parnell (IRE)**[18] [4893] 8-9-0 50 .... (b) MichaelStainton 13 14
(Simon Griffiths) *slowly away: hld up: swtchd rt over 2f out: nvr threatened* **20/1**

6000 **11** *¾* **Ellielusive (IRE)**[25] [4640] 4-8-11 47 .... (t) GrahamGibbons 15 9
(Mark Brisbourne) *chsd ldrs: rdn over 2f out: wknd over 1f out* **40/1**

6000 **12** *1 ¼* **Circuitous**[9] [5208] 3-9-0 53 .... DuranFentiman 18 11
(Keith Dalgleish) *chsd ldrs on outer: rdn over 2f out: wknd over 1f out* **10/1**

0406 **13** *1 ¾* **Toffee Nose**[31] [4437] 4-8-10 46 oh1 .... AndrewMullen 8 —
(Ron Barr) *led: hdd 4f out: sn lost pl: wknd over 2f out* **66/1**

5-00 **14** *1 ¼* **Freedom Trail**[14] [5034] 3-9-1 54 .... (v[1]) FrederikTylicki 7 —
(Tim Fitzgerald) *in tch: lost pl over 2f out: wknd over 1f out* **33/1**

-000 **15** *6* **Saxby (IRE)**[46] [3938] 4-8-4 47 .... (v) GeorgeChaloner(7) 20 —
(Alan Lockwood) *a outpcd in rr* **22/1**

1m 14.31s (2.51) **Going Correction** +0.45s/f (Yiel)
WFA 3 from 4yo+ 3lb **15** Ran SP% **120.1**
Speed ratings (Par 101): **101,100,96,96,95 91,89,88,83,81 80,79,76,75,67**
toteswingers:1&2:£14.60, 1&3:£78.60, 2&3:£45.60 CSF £64.38 CT £2047.66 TOTE £6.00: £1.70, £3.10, £23.10; EX 113.70.

Owner Ms M Austerfield **Bred** Miss Karen Theobald **Trained** Cowthorpe, N Yorks

■ Stewards' Enquiry : Lee Newman one-day ban: used whip with excessive frequency (Sep 14)
Declan Cannon one-day ban: used whip in incorrect place (Sep 11)

FOCUS

A low-grade sprint handicap.

Tahitian Princess(IRE) Official explanation: trainer rep had no explanation for the poor form shown

T/Plt: £283.70 to a £1 stake. Pool:£44,858.67 - 115.40 winning tickets T/Qpdt: £213.60 to a £1 stake. Pool:£4,820.98 - 16.70 winning tickets AS

5323 WINDSOR (R-H)

Saturday, August 27

OFFICIAL GOING: Good to soft (7.2)

Wind: medium, behind Weather: bright spells

5491 FEGENTRI WORLD CUP OF NATIONS AN AMATEUR RIDERS' H'CAP (IN MEMORY OF THE LATE JOHN CIECHANOWSKI) 1m 3f 135y

5:05 (5:06) (Class 5) (0-70,78) 3-Y-O+ **£2,963** (£911; £455) **Stalls** Centre

Form RPR

0423 **1** **Waahej**[19] [4862] 5-11-1 61 .... MrSvenSchleppi 4 72
(Peter Hiatt) *hld up in tch in last pair: hdwy on outer over 2f out: rdn to ld over 1f out: kpt on wl fnl f* **11/4**[2]

0206 **2** 3/4 **Ede's Dot Com (IRE)**[15] 5002 7-10-12 **58**........................ JackQuinlan 1 68
(Pat Phelan) *hld up in tch in last pair: swtchd rt and effrt over 2f out: rdn to ld 2f out: hung lft u.p and hdd over 1f out: kpt on but a hld fnl f* **13/2**

0511 **3** 12 **Megalala (IRE)**[9] 5198 10-12-4 **78**.............................. MrMarioBaratti 5 68
(John Bridger) *led: rdn and qcknd over 2f out: hdd 2f out: sn hung lft and struggling: 3rd and wl btn over 1f out* **9/4**[1]

0034 **4** 5 **Maslak (IRE)**[17] 4903 7-11-3 **63**............................ MrDennisSchiergen 2 44
(Peter Hiatt) *chsd ldrs: wnt 2nd over 3f out tl over 2f out: sn rdn and struggling: drvn and wknd qckly ent fnl 2f* **7/2**[3]

0063 **5** 4 **Gower Rules (IRE)**[17] 4905 3-10-6 **62**................. MissGMO'Callaghan 6 36
(John Bridger) *chsd ldr tl over 3f out: rdn and wknd qckly over 2f out: sn bhd* **7/1**

200 **6** shd **Rasam Aldaar**[36] 4280 3-10-9 **65**.........................(p) MlleAlexandraRosa 7 39
(Michael Wigham) *chsd ldrs tl pushed along and struggling 4f out: wknd qckly over 2f out: sn bhd* **20/1**

2m 34.22s (4.72) **Going Correction** +0.20s/f (Good)
WFA 3 from 5yo+ 10lb 6 Ran SP% **110.3**
Speed ratings (Par 103): **92,91,83,80,77 77**
CSF £19.53 TOTE £3.70: £1.70, £2.90; EX 20.00.

Owner Monarch Hose & Hydraulics/ P W Hiatt **Bred** David John Brown **Trained** Hook Norton, Oxon
■ A first British winner for German amateur Sven Schleppi.

FOCUS
Stands' rail dolled out 4yds at 6f and 1yd at the winning post and top bend at normal configuration. A whole raft of non-runners after a prolonged spell of heavy rain turned the ground soft (officially good to soft). The jockeys were pretty unanimous that it was proper soft ground but this opening handicap was run around eight seconds slower than RP standard, suggesting conditions may have been no slower than the official description of good to soft. The front two finished miles clear.

5492 DOREEN RACKHAM, ANGEL OF LAMBOURN, MEMORIAL NOVICE MEDIAN AUCTION STKS 6f
5:40 (5:40) (Class 5) 2-Y-O **£3,067** (£905; £453) **Stalls** Low

Form RPR
13 **1** **Big Note (IRE)**[27] 4575 2-9-5 85...................................... JimmyFortune 1 92
(Andrew Balding) *awkward leaving stalls: sn stdd and t.k.h in 3rd: effrt to press ldr on far side ent fnl 2f: stdd bk and swtchd rt over 1f out: drvn and chal ent fnl f: led fnl 75yds: kpt on* **2/1**[2]

21 **2** 1/2 **Rex Imperator**[15] 5017 2-9-5 0.................................. FrankieDettori 3 90
(Roger Charlton) *racd wd of rivals for over 2f: led: rdn and pressed over 1f out: drvn and flashed tail u.p ins fnl f: hdd and no ex fnl 75yds* **4/7**[1]

146 **3** 14 **Foxtrot India (IRE)**[93] 2437 2-9-5 90.................................. LukeMorris 2 66
(Peter Winkworth) *t.k.h: chsd ldr: rdn over 2f out: dropped to last and drvn 2f out: wknd jst over 1f out: eased ins fnl f* **8/1**[3]

1m 14.49s (1.49) **Going Correction** +0.20s/f (Good) 3 Ran SP% **108.1**
Speed ratings (Par 94): **98,97,78**
CSF £3.66 TOTE £3.30; EX 3.30.

Owner N Botica **Bred** Willow Tree Stud Farm **Trained** Kingsclere, Hants

FOCUS
Only three runners but the outsider of the party had an oficial rating of 90 so it was of good quality. The winner showed improved form but the true merit of this will take time to become clear.

NOTEBOOK
Big Note(IRE) proved too strong despite having raced very free through the early stages. He had been turned over at shortish odds at Chester last time but connections clearly rate him highly given he has Middle Park and Mill Reef entries. However, he needs to learn to settle better if he's to compete at a higher level. (op 9-4 tchd 5-2)

Rex Imperator was sent off a warm order after romping home in a Nottingham maiden but conditions were very different here and he proved vulnerable in the final furlong. It's far too early to be getting negative about him, and he is probably worth forgiving because of the conditions. He doesn't have any Group entries but he's in the Weatherbys sales race at Doncaster and will probably be seen in a much better light back on better ground. (op 8-13 tchd 8-15 tchd 4-6 in places)

Foxtrot India(IRE), tackling 6f for the first time, was too keen early and didn't see his race out. He has now disappointed twice on ground slower than good so is another that needs another chance back on a sound surface. (op 7-1 tchd 13-2)

5493 TOTEEXACTA AUGUST STKS (LISTED RACE) 1m 3f 135y
6:10 (6:10) (Class 1) 3-Y-O+

£17,013 (£6,450; £3,228; £1,608; £807; £405) **Stalls** Centre

Form RPR
3532 **1** **Opera Gal (IRE)**[17] 4915 4-8-11 101.............................. JimmyFortune 4 104
(Andrew Balding) *taken down early: pushed stall open early but c out on terms: mde all: rdn and qcknd clr 3f out: drvn over 1f out: kpt on wl fnl f* **11/4**[2]

1040 **2** 2 3/4 **Sirvino**[7] 5285 6-9-2 96.. TomQueally 2 104
(David Barron) *hld up in midfield: rdn and effrt to chse clr wnr ent fnl 2f: drvn and no imp 1f out: kpt on* **9/2**[3]

3652 **3** 9 **Elusive Pimpernel (USA)**[21] 4789 4-9-2 111.................... EddieAhern 6 89
(John Dunlop) *racd keenly: chsd ldr tl 6f out: wnt 2nd again 4f out: rdn: edgd rt and lost 2nd ent fnl 2f: sn btn: 3rd and no ch over 1f out: tired fnl f* **6/5**[1]

560/ **4** 5 **Enroller (IRE)**[672] 7031 6-9-2 100.................................... FrankieDettori 5 80
(William Muir) *stdd s: hld up in last pair: rdn and no hdwy 3f out: sn wl btn: wnt modest 4th ins fnl f* **9/1**

-005 **5** 4 **Shimmering Surf (IRE)**[27] 4582 4-8-11 94....................(p) LukeMorris 7 68
(Peter Winkworth) *disp 2nd tl chsd wnr 6f out tl 4f out: sn u.p and struggling: 4th and wl btn 2f out: wknd* **12/1**

5140 **6** 19 **Luv U Too**[35] 4335 3-8-1 77.. KieranO'Neill 8 36
(Jo Hughes) *hld up in last: rdn 5f out: lost tch wl over 2f out: t.o and eased ins fnl f* **50/1**

2m 29.63s (0.13) **Going Correction** +0.20s/f (Good)
WFA 3 from 4yo+ 10lb 6 Ran SP% **110.0**
Speed ratings (Par 111): **107,105,99,95,93 80**
toteswingers:1&2:£2.40, 1&3:£1.02, 2&3:£2.30 CSF £14.65 TOTE £3.60: £2.00, £3.50; EX 16.70.

Owner J C Smith **Bred** Littleton Stud **Trained** Kingsclere, Hants

FOCUS
They finished well strung out in this Listed event and conditons proved too testing for most. The winner is rated in line with her Salisbury run, with the favourite disappointing.

NOTEBOOK
Opera Gal(IRE) is a proven performer under these sort of conditions and she poured it on from the front, opening up a useful lead half a mile out before finding plenty to shake off the challenge of Sirvino, who was the only one of her rivals to get anywhere near her in the straight. Given most of her rivals weren't able to run to their best on this ground, this isn't form to be raving about, but she went close in a stronger Listed event at Sandown last time and may still be improving, despite this being her 17th start. She is entered in a Group 3 for fillies at Gowran Park next month. Stewards noted her stall opened early but reported the starter had pressed the start button and that the filly knocked her gate open but then rocked back on her hocks and gained no advantage. (op 3-1 tchd 10-3)

Sirvino is a good-quality handicapper and deserves credit for getting close to the winner despite having to concede the sex allowance to that higher-rated rival. He's a solid handicapper and has a chance of making a breakthrough at this level if pulling out a bit more. (tchd 5-1)

Elusive Pimpernel(USA) had 10lb and upwards in hand of all of his rivals but, having raced keenly early, he was in trouble two furlongs out. Connections later reported he was unsuited by the ground. Official explanation: trainer said colt was unsuited by the good to soft ground (op 5-4 tchd 11-10)

Enroller(IRE) was having his first start since October 2009. He is a proven soft-ground performer and he travelled well through the first mile, but there was little in the locker when push came to shove. He is entitled to come on a bundle for this. (op 15-2 tchd 7-1)

5494 TOTEPOOL WINTER HILL STKS (GROUP 3) 1m 2f 7y
6:40 (6:41) (Class 1) 3-Y-O+

£28,355 (£10,750; £5,380; £2,680; £1,345; £675) **Stalls** Centre

Form RPR
-601 **1** **Prince Siegfried (FR)**[30] 4456 5-9-0 108........................... TedDurcan 4 116
(Saeed Bin Suroor) *hld up wl in tch: hdwy to chse ldrs 4f out: rdn to ld wl over 2f out: drvn and hdd over 1f out: drew clr w runner-up and sustained battle fr over 1f out: led again wl ins fnl f: kpt on wl: gamely* **14/1**

-313 **2** 1/2 **Dux Scholar**[8] 5252 3-8-6 112... WilliamBuick 11 115+
(Sir Michael Stoute) *hld up wl in tch in last trio: hdwy ent fnl 3f: rdn to chse ldr jst over 2f out: drvn to ld and drew clr w wnr over 1f out: kpt on u.p tl hdd and no ex wl ins fnl f* **10/3**[1]

-10U **3** 4 1/2 **Simon De Montfort (IRE)**[21] 4789 4-9-0 113.................. KierenFallon 6 106
(Mahmood Al Zarooni) *stdd s: hld up in last: rdn and hdwy over 2f out: no imp on ldrs over 1f out: plugged on to go 3rd ins fnl f: no threat to ldng pair* **9/2**[3]

6-23 **4** 3 1/4 **Hot Prospect**[21] 4789 4-9-0 110... NeilCallan 9 100
(Roger Varian) *chsd ldrs: carried wd and hmpd bnd 5f out: rdn 3f out: drvn and outpcd by ldng pair over 1f out: wknd and lost 3rd ins fnl f* **6/1**

1233 **5** hd **Mahbooba (AUS)**[14] 5055 4-8-10 103............................... PatCosgrave 5 99
(M F De Kock, South Africa) *t.k.h: chsd ldrs: lost pl and rdn 4f out: no ch w ldrs but plugged on again u.p fr over 1f out* **20/1**

2010 **6** 1 1/4 **Distant Memories (IRE)**[29] 4492 5-9-0 109............... JamieSpencer 12 97
(Tom Tate) *led tl over 7f out: lft in ld 5f out: rdn and hdd wl over 2f out: sn struggling u.p: wknd wl over 1f out* **14/1**

-313 **7** 8 **Principal Role (USA)**[28] 4533 4-8-11 114........................ TomQueally 1 78
(Sir Henry Cecil) *dwlt: sn rcvrd and t.k.h: chsd ldrs: chsd ldr wl over 2f out tl rdn and fnd little over 2f out: wknd wl over 1f out: eased ins fnl f* **7/2**[2]

1-50 **8** 5 **Prince Bishop (IRE)**[154] 1002 4-9-0 117....................... FrankieDettori 8 71
(Saeed Bin Suroor) *hld up in tch: effrt on far side to chse ldrs wl over 2f out: rdn over 2f out: wknd qckly wl over 1f out: wl btn and eased ins fnl f* **5/1**

/0-4 **9** 3/4 **Zafisio (IRE)**[10] 5183 5-9-0 105.. DarryllHolland 7 69
(Jo Hughes) *dwlt: sn rcvrd and chsd ldr: led over 7f out tl hung lft and hdd 5f out: struggling 3f out: sn wknd: wl bhd and eased ins fnl f* **50/1**

3310 **10** 9 **Julienas (IRE)**[16] 4972 4-9-0 100.. AdamKirby 2 51
(Walter Swinburn) *stdd s: hld up in tch: rdn and struggling wl over 2f out: sn wknd: wl bhd and eased ins fnl f: t.o* **14/1**

2m 7.44s (-1.26) **Going Correction** +0.20s/f (Good)
WFA 3 from 4yo+ 8lb 10 Ran SP% **121.2**
Speed ratings (Par 113): **113,112,109,106,106 105,98,94,94,87**
toteswingers:1&2:£16.40, 1&3:£14.00, 2&3:£4.80 CSF £62.83 TOTE £22.40: £5.10, £1.60, £2.90; EX 95.40.

Owner Godolphin **Bred** Haras Saint Pair Du Mont **Trained** Newmarket, Suffolk

FOCUS
Quite a warm Group 3 event with five of the field rated 110+ and a cracking finish. The first pair looked a bit above average to pull clear, with a length personal best from the winner.

NOTEBOOK
Prince Siegfried(FR), despite conceding 8lb to the higher-rated runner-up, saw this out stronger to win in pattern company for the first time. He bounced back to form in a conditions race at Epsom last time but this was a much stronger heat and he ran right up to his best here. His trainer is quoted as saying slow ground is important to him and he deserves a crack at a Group 2 now. (op 16-1)

Dux Scholar caught the eye when finishing strongly in the Strensall Stakes at York last time but, having taken over entering the final furlong he was ultimately seen off by a stronger stayer. That said, he still finshed clear of the rest so this was clearly a cracking effort and he'll not be long in winning at this level. (op 7-2)

Simon De Montfort(IRE) got his career back on track here having clipped heels and unshipped his rider at Haydock last time. He kept on without threatening the front two but he'll need to step up markedly on this if he's to make any kind of impact in the Irish Champion Stakes and Qipco Champion Stakes, both of which he holds entries in. (op 11-2)

Hot Prospect wasn't done any favours on the bend and struggled to land a blow thereafter. He is better than this, as he proved when just over a length behind Dux Scholar at Newbury in July. (op 15-2 tchd 8-1)

Principal Role(USA) was a little too keen for her own good and proved disappointing. (op 10-3 tchd 4-1 in places)

Zafisio(IRE) Official explanation: jockey said horse hung left

Julienas(IRE) Official explanation: trainer said gelding was unsuited by the soft ground

5495 TOTESWINGER H'CAP 1m 67y
7:10 (7:11) (Class 4) (0-85,85) 3-Y-O+ **£5,175** (£1,540; £769; £384) **Stalls** Low

Form RPR
-152 **1** **Pat's Legacy (USA)**[26] 4616 5-9-6 **79**........................... DarryllHolland 14 88+
(Jo Hughes) *led tl hdd 5f out: led again 4f out and sn pushed along: drvn over 1f out: hdd 1f out: kpt on gamely and led again fnl 75yds: styd on wl* **6/1**

500 **2** 1 **Osgood**[14] 5059 4-9-2 **75**.. SamHitchcott 12 82
(Mick Channon) *t.k.h: hld up in tch: hdwy on far side to chse ldrs over 3f out: drvn and ev ch over 1f out: led 1f out: hdd fnl 75yds: no ex* **9/1**

1111 **3** 2 **Starwatch**[9] 5200 4-9-6 **82**.. SeanLevey(3) 8 84
(John Bridger) *in tch: hdwy on inner to chse ldrs 5f out: drvn ent fnl 2f: chsd ldng pair ent fnl f: no ex and plugged on same pce fnl 150yds* **4/1**[2]

/206 **4** *1* **Vimiero (USA)**[16] 4962 4-9-5 **78**.. AdamKirby 13 78
(Walter Swinburn) *urged along leaving stalls: sn chsng ldrs: drvn ent fnl 2f: styd on same pce and hld fnl f* **3/1**[1]

4000 **5** *5* **Prince Of Sorrento**[15] 5002 4-8-3 **67**.......................... NathanAlison(5) 2 55
(John Akehurst) *dwlt: hld up in last: hdwy wl over 3f out: rdn and chsd ldrs 2f out: wknd over 1f out: fdd fnl f* **14/1**

3545 **6** *7* **Huzzah (IRE)**[17] 4921 6-9-3 **76**.. MichaelHills 9 48
(Charles Hills) *taken down early: pushed along early: sn t.k.h and hld up in midfield: rdn and unable qck jst over 2f out: wknd over 1f out: wl btn and eased ins fnl f* **9/2**[3]

0613 **7** *8* **Cultural Desert**[23] 4725 3-8-10 **75**.. MartinLane 1 29
(Ralph Beckett) *t.k.h: chsd ldr tl led on inner bnd 5f out: hdd 4f out and sn struggling u.p: lost tch 2f out: wl bhd and eased ins fnl f* **5/1**

4260 **8** *20* **Hail Promenader (IRE)**[24] 4656 5-9-5 **78**.......................... TomQueally 7 —
(Andrew Haynes) *a in last pair: rdn over 4f out: lost tch 3f out: t.o and eased fnl f* **20/1**

1m 45.12s (0.42) **Going Correction** +0.20s/f (Good)
WFA 3 from 4yo+ 6lb **8** Ran SP% **115.6**
Speed ratings (Par 105): **105,104,102,101,96 89,81,61**
toteswingers:1&2:£8.30, 1&3:£2.70, 2&3:£5.50 CSF £58.50 CT £244.28 TOTE £6.20: £2.40, £2.40, £2.30; EX 61.50.
Owner Mrs Joanna Hughes **Bred** Brereton C Jones **Trained** Lambourn. Berks

FOCUS
This looked a real war of attrition in the closing stages after what looked a reasonable gallop.
Prince Of Sorrento Official explanation: jockey said gelding was slowly away
Cultural Desert Official explanation: jockey said gelding ran too freely

5496 TOTETRIFECTA FILLIES' H'CAP — 1m 67y
7:40 (7:40) (Class 5) (0-75,73) 3-Y-0+ **£3,067** (£905; £453) **Stalls** Low

Form RPR

3034 **1** **Miss Bootylishes**[5] 5328 6-9-5 **73**.. DavidKenny(7) 2 82
(Paul Burgoyne) *hld up in tch in midfield: swtchd lft and effrt wl over 1f out: drvn and ev ch 1f out: led ins fnl f: hld on cl home* **9/2**[2]

6-F1 **2** *hd* **Mrs Dee Bee (IRE)**[30] 4478 3-9-4 **71**.......................... MichaelHills 13 79
(Charles Hills) *stdd s: t.k.h: in tch in midfield: hdwy to press ldrs 3f out: led ent fnl 2f: drvn and hrd pressed over 1f out: hdd ins fnl f: rallied towards fin* **11/4**[1]

5630 **3** *1* **Trend Line (IRE)**[27] 4584 3-9-5 **72**.......................... JimmyFortune 1 77
(Peter Chapple-Hyam) *w ldr: rdn over 2f out: drvn and pressed ldrs ent fnl f: no ex and styd on same pce fnl 100yds* **8/1**

3630 **4** *1 1/4* **Indian Valley (USA)**[16] 4949 4-9-9 **70**.......................(b[1]) NeilCallan 7 73
(Hugo Palmer) *hld up in tch in midfield: hdwy over 2f out: drvn to chse ldrs wl over 1f out: no ex and plugged on same pce ins fnl f* **8/1**

5065 **5** *3/4* **Oh So Saucy**[15] 5014 7-9-12 **73**.......................... GeorgeBaker 10 75
(Chris Wall) *led tl hdd and rdn ent fnl 2f: unable qck u.p and n.m.r ent fnl f: one pce after* **6/1**[3]

423 **6** *3 3/4* **Cahala Dancer (IRE)**[19] 4849 3-9-0 **67**.......................... TomQueally 4 59
(Roger Teal) *hld up in last trio: rdn and effrt ent fnl 2f: no imp: nvr trbld ldrs* **16/1**

-006 **7** *hd* **Ninfea (IRE)**[10] 5179 3-8-12 **65**.......................(p) JamesDoyle 8 57
(Sylvester Kirk) *stdd s: hld up in rr: rdn and effrt ent fnl 2f: no prog: n.d* **20/1**

154 **8** *12* **Treasure Way**[12] 5100 4-9-7 **68**.......................... WilliamBuick 3 33
(Patrick Chamings) *t.k.h: chsd ldrs: rdn and unable qck over 2f out: wknd wl over 1f out: eased ins fnl f* **8/1**

0-05 **9** *4 1/2* **Carcinetto (IRE)**[19] 4865 9-9-4 **65**.......................... KierenFallon 9 20
(David Evans) *t.k.h: hld up in tch in midfield rdn and wknd qckly ent fnl 2f: wl btn and eased ins fnl f* **16/1**

0051 **10** *15* **Adorable Choice (IRE)**[10] 5179 3-9-3 **70**.......................(v) HayleyTurner 5 —
(Tom Dascombe) *bmpd and hmpd s: hld up in rr: rdn and struggling 4f out: lost tch over 2f out: t.o and eased ins fnl f* **17/2**

1m 46.21s (1.51) **Going Correction** +0.20s/f (Good)
WFA 3 from 4yo+ 6lb **10** Ran SP% **119.5**
Speed ratings (Par 100): **100,99,98,97,96 93,92,80,76,61**
toteswingers:1&2:£4.20, 1&3:£6.50, 2&3:£6.80 CSF £17.76 CT £100.36 TOTE £5.30: £1.70, £2.00, £3.30; EX 17.20.
Owner Mrs Helen Adams **Bred** T P Young And D Hanson **Trained** Shepton Montague, Somerset

FOCUS
A modest handicap.
Oh So Saucy Official explanation: vet said mare finished lame
Treasure Way Official explanation: trainer said filly was unsuited by the soft ground
T/Plt: £373.80 to a £1 stake. Pool:£59,620.22 - 116.41 winning tickets T/Qpdt: £23.00 to a £1 stake. Pool:£8,328.01 - 267.70 winning tickets SP

2749 BADEN-BADEN (L-H)
Saturday, August 27

OFFICIAL GOING: Turf: soft

5497a PREIS DER SPARKASSEN FINANZGRUPPE (GROUP 3) (4YO+) (TURF) — 1m 2f
6:15 (12:00) 4-Y-0+
£27,586 (£9,482; £4,741; £2,586; £1,724; £1,293)

RPR

1 **Zazou (GER)**[104] 2134 4-9-0 0.. ASuborics 5 110
(W Hickst, Germany) *dwlt and settled in last: tk clsr order 3f out: wnt 2nd travelling wl on outside appr 2f out (fnl bnd): c wd into st (w whole field): rdn and led 1 1/2f out: rdn out fnl f: eased cl home* **17/5**[2]

2 *1 1/2* **Empire Storm (GER)**[34] 4373 4-9-0 0.......................... EPedroza 2 107
(A Wohler, Germany) *plld in 2nd: led after 4f: stl in front whn tk field towards stands' side fnl bnd: hdd 1 1/2f out: kpt on u.p wout qckning* **6/1**[3]

3 *3/4* **Altair Star (IRE)**[20] 4-9-0 0.. FilipMinarik 4 106
(P Schiergen, Germany) *reluctant early ldr setting v stdy pce: hdd after 4f and trckd new ldr: cl 2nd whn rdn and outpcd over 2 1/2f out: 4th and u.p 1 1/2f out: kpt on again ins fnl f to take 3rd cl home* **147/10**

4 *nk* **Elle Shadow (IRE)**[27] 4599 4-8-13 0.......................... AStarke 3 104
(P Schiergen, Germany) *plld hrd and covered up in 5th towards ins: cl 3rd and stl keen 1/2-way: pushed along 2f out: 3rd and rdn 1f out but nt qckn fnl f: lost 3rd cl home* **3/5**[1]

5 *2* **Abydos (GER)**[20] 6-9-0 0.. ADeVries 7 101
(J Hirschberger, Germany) *racd keenly w ldrs: lost pl over 4f out: last and scrubbed along over 2 1/2f out: styd on at one pce fnl f* **158/10**

6 *2 1/2* **Wheredreamsare**[34] 4373 4-8-11 0.......................... THellier 6 93
(W Figge, Germany) *settled on heels of ldng three: nt qckn whn pce qcknd over 2f out: grad fdd* **172/10**

7 *1* **Val Mondo (GER)**[62] 3446 4-9-2 0.......................... KClijmans 1 96
(Uwe Ostmann, Germany) *settled next to last: rdn over 2f out: no imp* **66/10**

2m 9.19s (4.20) **7** Ran SP% **130.5**
WIN (incl. 10 euro stake): 44. PLACES: 26, 27, 51. SF: 232..
Owner WH Sport Int'l **Bred** Gestut Fahrhof **Trained** Germany

5498 - 5501a - See RI

5464 BEVERLEY (R-H)
Sunday, August 28

OFFICIAL GOING: Good to soft (6.5)
Wind: Fresh, half against Weather: Fine but very breezy

5502 JOHN JENKINS MEMORIAL CLAIMING STKS — 7f 100y
1:50 (1:51) (Class 5) 3-Y-0+ **£2,522** (£750; £375; £187) **Stalls** Low

Form RPR

0424 **1** **Sunnyside Tom (IRE)**[27] 4603 7-9-2 77.......................... LeeTopliss(3) 8 84
(Richard Fahey) *trckd ldr: c stands' side: swtchd rt appr fnl f: styd on to ld nr fin* **9/4**[2]

2534 **2** *1/2* **Academy Blues (USA)**[35] 4361 6-9-5 79.......................... AdrianNicholls 1 82
(David Nicholls) *led: c stands' side: edgd rt and hdd last 50yds* **5/1**[3]

2100 **3** *3 3/4* **Charlie Cool**[22] 4794 8-9-10 83.......................(b) PJMcDonald 6 78+
(Ruth Carr) *wnt rt s: in rr: hdwy and nt clr run over 1f out: swtchd lft to stands' side rail: styd on* **15/8**[1]

0462 **4** *2* **Nicholas Pocock (IRE)**[18] 4920 5-8-9 60.......................... DaleSwift(3) 4 61
(Brian Ellison) *wnt lft s: mid-div: hdwy in centre over 2f out: kpt on same pce over 1f out* **14/1**

00-0 **5** *1 1/2* **Bubber (IRE)**[22] 4783 4-8-4 49.......................... DeclanCannon(3) 10 52
(Ollie Pears) *chsd ldrs: hung rt 2f out: one pce* **66/1**

4434 **6** *2 1/2* **Bonnie Prince Blue**[18] 4897 8-8-10 66.......................(b) PaulPickard(3) 9 52
(Ian McInnes) *hld up in rr: hdwy on outer over 4f out: wknd over 1f out* **33/1**

6332 **7** *5* **Meandmyshadow**[18] 4897 3-8-9 59.......................(p) SilvestreDeSousa 3 39
(Alan Brown) *sn chsng ldrs: wknd 1f out* **9/1**

1006 **8** *1 1/2* **Boga (IRE)**[16] 4987 4-8-7 50.......................... BarryMcHugh 5 30
(Karen Tutty) *hmpd s: sn chsng ldrs: lost pl over 2f out* **66/1**

2303 **9** *1* **Frognal (IRE)**[5] 5341 5-9-4 77.......................(b) J-PGuillambert 2 38
(Conor Dore) *in rr: hdwy in centre 2f out: sn wknd* **8/1**

1m 36.58s (2.78) **Going Correction** +0.525s/f (Yiel)
WFA 3 from 4yo+ 5lb **9** Ran SP% **115.9**
Speed ratings (Par 103): **105,104,100,97,96 93,87,85,84**
toteswingers:1&2:£2.60, 1&3:£1.80, 2&3:£4.00 CSF £14.02 TOTE £2.90: £1.10, £2.20, £1.40; EX 16.30.Nicholas Pocock was claimed by Ian McInnes for £3,000.
Owner The Sunnyside Racing Partnership **Bred** S W D McIlveen **Trained** Musley Bank, N Yorks
■ Stewards' Enquiry : Lee Topliss one-day ban: used whip with excessive frequency (Sep 11)
Adrian Nicholls caution: careless riding.

FOCUS
Rails at innermost configuration.A typical claimer featuring mixed levels of ability. The field came stands' side in the straight and the first two held those positions throughout.

5503 E B F OLD CROSSLEYANS RUGBY UNION FOOTBALL CLUB MEDIAN AUCTION MAIDEN STKS — 1m 100y
2:20 (2:22) (Class 5) 2-Y-0 **£3,169** (£943; £471; £235) **Stalls** Low

Form RPR

4355 **1** **Maastricht (IRE)**[10] 5197 2-9-3 70.......................... SilvestreDeSousa 7 74
(Mark Johnston) *led 2f: chsd ldr: led over 2f out: drvn out* **2/1**[1]

424 **2** *1 1/4* **Naseem Alyasmeen (IRE)**[16] 4992 2-8-12 67.......................... SamHitchcott 1 66
(Mick Channon) *hld up in rr: effrt over 2f out: swtchd rt over 1f out: sn chsng wnr: no imp* **4/1**[3]

32 **3** *2 1/2* **Bapak Pintar**[27] 4606 2-9-3 0.......................... PhillipMakin 8 66
(Kevin Ryan) *wnt lft s: w ldr: t.k.h: led after 2f: hdd over 2f out: kpt on same pce appr fnl f* **9/2**

403 **4** *13* **Curtain Patch (USA)**[18] 4898 2-8-12 58.......................... RoystonFfrench 2 34
(Bryan Smart) *chsd ldrs: drvn over 2f out: wknd over 1f out* **17/2**

030 **5** *4 1/2* **Dr Irv**[20] 4853 2-9-0 70.......................... MichaelO'Connell(3) 5 29
(Kate Walton) *gave problems s: in rr: effrt on outer over 2f out: sn chsng ldrs: wknd over 1f out: eased* **33/1**

4 **6** *3/4* **Double Cee**[43] 4080 2-9-3 0.......................... TonyHamilton 4 28
(Richard Fahey) *chsd ldrs: effrt over 2f out: hung lft and sn outpcd: lost pl over 1f out: eased* **5/2**[2]

1m 53.65s (6.05) **Going Correction** +0.525s/f (Yiel) **6** Ran SP% **113.6**
Speed ratings (Par 94): **90,88,86,73,68 68**
toteswingers:1&2:£1.40, 1&3:£4.50, 2&3:£3.30 CSF £10.63 TOTE £3.30: £2.00, £1.50; EX 10.70.
Owner Sheikh Hamdan Bin Mohammed Al Maktoum **Bred** A G Antoniades **Trained** Middleham Moor, N Yorks
■ Stewards' Enquiry : Michael O'Connell caution: used whip without giving gelding time to respond.

FOCUS
A modest median auction with most having a fair amount of experience and that counted in testing conditions for juveniles. Straightforward form.

NOTEBOOK
Maastricht(IRE), most of whose previous efforts suggested that this stiffer stamina test would be in his favour, proved those assertions correct by galloping on strongly in the straight, having been in the first two throughout. He probably did not have to run much above his official mark here but could well be open to further improvement. (op 5-2)
Naseem Alyasmeen(IRE) up in trip and tackling soft ground for the first time, ran creditably despite the fact she was keen under restraint early. She was the only one to trouble the winner in the closing stages but looked to run close to her mark. (op 7-2 tchd 9-2)
Bapak Pintar, whose Ripon conqueror won the sales race the previous day, was taking a big step up in distance. He showed up throughout but had nothing in reserve in the last 2f. He now qualifies for handicap mark, which is likely to be in the mid-60s.
Curtain Patch(USA) had run well on soft ground on this track previously but could not pick up in the straight. She will be better off in low-grade handicaps. (op 9-1 tchd 8-1)
Dr Irv put up by far his best effort in three starts on this track and did not run badly. He got to the rail in the straight but not in front, and had no more to offer under pressure. He might prefer faster ground. (op 25-1)

Double Cee had run promisingly on his debut six weeks previously but failed to build on it on similar ground here. (tchd 9-4)

5504 BEVERLEY MIDDLE DISTANCE SERIES H'CAP (FINAL ROUND) 1m 4f 16y
2:55 (2:55) (Class 5) (0-75,75) 3-Y-0+ **£5,498** (£1,636; £817; £408) **Stalls** Low

Form / RPR

-042 **1** **Maybeme**[18] 4903 5-8-2 **56** oh2 .... TerenceFury(7) 10 65
(Neville Bycroft) *hood removed v late: dwlt: in rr: hdwy in centre over 2f out: edgd rt and styd on to ld wl ins fnl f* **20/1**

0P13 **2** *1* **Gems**[13] 5107 4-9-0 **66** .... LucyKBarry(5) 2 73
(Peter Hiatt) *led: kpt on fnl 2f: hdd and no ex last 75yds* **4/1**[2]

0046 **3** *2 ½* **Kames Park (IRE)**[5] 5357 9-8-8 **58** .... LeeTopliss(3) 12 61
(Richard Guest) *stdd s: hld up towards rr: stdy hdwy over 2f out: chsng ldrs 1f out: kpt on same pce* **14/1**

3330 **4** *nse* **Golden Future**[14] 5079 8-9-2 **63** .... PhillipMakin 9 66
(Peter Niven) *chsd ldrs: chal over 2f out: hung rt: one pce fnl f* **9/1**

5110 **5** *1* **Bradbury (IRE)**[35] 4366 3-8-11 **68** ....(p) TadhgO'Shea 5 70
(James Bethell) *towards rr: drvn after 4f: hdwy towards centre over 2f out: kpt on one pce* **9/1**

5321 **6** *6* **Jeu De Vivre (IRE)**[10] 5207 3-9-3 **74** .... SilvestreDeSousa 3 66
(Mark Johnston) *mid-div: pushed along over 4f out: chsng ldrs over 1f out: sn wknd* **6/4**[1]

4440 **7** *½* **Saint Thomas (IRE)**[57] 3641 4-9-10 **71** .... GrahamGibbons 1 62
(John Mackie) *chsd ldrs: drvn over 2f out: wknd fnl f* **10/1**

-204 **8** *2 ¼* **Motafarred (IRE)**[25] 4679 9-9-0 **64** .... DaleSwift(3) 4 52
(Micky Hammond) *chsd ldrs: wknd 2f out* **14/1**

0440 **9** *2* **Green Lightning (IRE)**[12] 5149 4-9-2 **63** ....(b) FrannyNorton 8 48
(Mark Johnston) *mid-div: drvn over 5f out: lost pl 2f out* **8/1**[3]

2m 46.19s (6.39) **Going Correction** +0.525s/f (Yiel)
WFA 3 from 4yo+ 10lb **9** Ran SP% **118.3**
Speed ratings (Par 103): **99,98,96,96,95 91,91,90,88**
toteswingers:1&2:£18.90, 1&3:£33.90, 2&3:£16.00 CSF £100.79 CT £1189.02 TOTE £25.30: £3.10, £1.90, £4.80; EX 126.40.
Owner N Bycroft **Bred** Harts Farm And Stud **Trained** Brandsby, N Yorks
■ Terence Fury's first winner.

FOCUS
A competitive-looking handicap that was run at a sound early gallop but it proved a war of attrition and produced a shock result.

5505 JIM AND MARGARET DALY MEMORIAL NURSERY 5f
3:30 (3:30) (Class 4) (0-85,85) 2-Y-0 **£3,881** (£1,155; £577; £288) **Stalls** Low

Form / RPR

0331 **1** **Rent Free**[22] 4787 2-9-0 **78** .... J-PGuillambert 1 83
(Nigel Tinkler) *chsd ldr: outpcd over 3f out: styd on over 1f out: led last 75yds: drvn out* **3/1**[3]

513 **2** *2* **O'Gorman**[22] 4787 2-9-6 **84** .... PhillipMakin 2 82
(Kevin Ryan) *led: clr over 3f out: edgd rt and hdd last 75yds* **11/10**[1]

6450 **3** *5* **Never In (IRE)**[15] 5058 2-7-7 **62** oh11 .... DanielleMcCreery(5) 5 42
(Alan Berry) *chsd ldr: outpcd over 3f out: wknd over 1f out: lft modest 3rd nr line* **33/1**

21 **4** *1* **Key Ambition**[18] 4899 2-9-0 **78** .... RoystonFfrench 4 54
(Bryan Smart) *rrd s: hld up in last: effrt on outer over 2f out: chsng ldr over 1f out: wknd fnl 100yds* **15/8**[2]

66.52 secs (3.02) **Going Correction** +0.525s/f (Yiel) **4** Ran SP% **110.3**
Speed ratings (Par 96): **96,92,84,83**
toteswingers:1&2:£3.10 CSF £6.92 TOTE £4.10; EX 6.30.
Owner Maze Rattan Limited **Bred** L T Roberts **Trained** Langton, N Yorks

FOCUS
An uncompetitive nursery. Straightforward form but the winner is capable of better.

NOTEBOOK
Rent Free, who had handled cut when winning his maiden, confirmed previous form with the runner-up on 2lb worse terms. He struggled to keep up early and was being pushed along 3f out, but he kept finding and proved strongest in the last furlong. He looks tough and genuine and his attitude should enable him to win more races. (op 5-2)
O'Gorman was 2lb better off with the winner for a half-length beating in a nursery at the beginning of the month. He made the running here and got the stands' rail but, after being challenged throughout the last 2f, could not quite hold on. A sounder surface and a flatter track would probably have seen him last home. (op 7-4)
Never In(IRE) ran as well as could have been expected as she was 11lb out of the handicap. (op 16-1)
Key Ambition, who beat a subsequent scorer when winning his maiden over C&D on soft ground, was restless in the stalls, reared as the gates opened and blew the start. He did a lot of running to get into a challenging position inside the last 2f and paid for it late on. He can be given another chance. Official explanation: jockey said colt was restless in stalls and reared as they opened (op 7-4 tchd 2-1)

5506 BEVERLEY LIONS H'CAP 5f
4:05 (4:06) (Class 6) (0-60,61) 3-Y-0 **£1,908** (£563; £281) **Stalls** Low

Form / RPR

6054 **1** **Sleights Boy (IRE)**[10] 5203 3-8-4 **46** oh1 ....(v¹) DeclanCannon(3) 5 55
(Ian McInnes) *chsd ldrs stands' side: led that gp ins fnl f: led overall nr fin* **20/1**

2531 **2** *½* **Rutterkin (USA)**[8] 5274 3-9-3 **61** .... JulieBurke(5) 2 68
(Alan Berry) *dwlt: chsd 1 other far side: drvn over 2f out: led that side 1f out: sn appeared to ld overall: hdd nr fin* **5/2**[2]

0223 **3** *1* **I Got You Babe (IRE)**[9] 5244 3-9-5 **61** .... LeeTopliss(3) 3 64
(Richard Guest) *led one other far side: hdd 1f out: kpt on same pce* **9/4**[1]

5604 **4** *1* **Hootys Agogo**[22] 4786 3-8-3 **49** .... JasonHart(7) 6 49
(Declan Carroll) *trckd ldrs stands' side: overall ldr and edgd lft over 1f out: hdd ins fnl f: wknd* **8/1**

5104 **5** *7* **Dotty Darroch**[26] 4638 3-9-3 **56** .... LeeNewman 1 31
(Robin Bastiman) *chsd ldrs and sn drvn along: c stands' side: outpcd after 2f: wknd 2f out* **10/3**[3]

0423 **6** *4 ½* **Myjestic Melody (IRE)**[16] 5010 3-9-0 **53** .... RobertWinston 8 11
(Noel Wilson) *overall ldr and racd stands' side: hdd over 1f out: sn wknd* **7/1**

67.98 secs (4.48) **Going Correction** +0.525s/f (Yiel) **6** Ran SP% **110.8**
Speed ratings (Par 98): **85,84,82,81,69 62**
toteswingers:1&2:£8.70, 1&3:£6.50, 2&3:£1.10 CSF £67.74 CT £154.65 TOTE £33.30: £8.90, £1.40; EX 71.40.
Owner T Elsey, S A Elsey, R Mustill, J Agar **Bred** Derek Iceton And C F Coxon **Trained** Catwick, E Yorks
■ Stewards' Enquiry : Julie Burke one-day ban: used whip with excessive frequency (Sep 11)

FOCUS
A moderate 3yo sprint run 1.46 secs slower than the preceding nursery. There was a difference of opinion between the jockeys, with two racing far side when the rest came across; they finished second and third.

Sleights Boy(IRE) Official explanation: trainer said, regarding apparent improvement in form, that the gelding seemed to benefit from a change in more forcing tactics.

5507 ANDREW TURNER OH NO FIVE O H'CAP 1m 1f 207y
4:40 (4:41) (Class 6) (0-60,59) 3-Y-0 **£1,811** (£539; £269; £134) **Stalls** Low

Form / RPR

423 **1** **Kodicil (IRE)**[18] 4904 3-9-4 **56** .... GrahamGibbons 2 69
(Tim Walford) *trckd ldrs: led over 1f out: sn jnd: kpt on: all out* **15/8**[1]

021 **2** *shd* **Smart Violetta (IRE)**[6] 5315 3-9-2 **57** 6ex ....(t) DaleSwift(3) 8 70
(Ann Duffield) *in rr: hdwy over 4f out: swtchd rt over 1f out: upsides 1f out: jst failed* **9/2**[3]

5150 **3** *10* **Playful Girl (IRE)**[13] 5107 3-8-10 **48** ....(b) DavidAllan 10 41
(Tim Easterby) *chsd ldrs: one pce appr fnl f* **17/2**

0-63 **4** *5* **Wom**[55] 3676 3-9-7 **59** ....(p) MickyFenton 11 42
(Pam Sly) *racd wd: led hdd over 1f out: sn wknd* **13/2**

0400 **5** *5* **Smart Step**[4] 5372 3-8-7 **45** .... FrannyNorton 7 18
(Mark Johnston) *chsd ldrs: pushed along 6f out: wknd over 1f out* **15/2**

000 **6** *10* **Littlepromisedland (IRE)**[5] 5352 3-8-7 **45** ....(p) KellyHarrison 6 —
(Richard Guest) *in rr-div: rdn and edgd rt 2f out: sn wknd* **33/1**

0304 **7** *10* **Valley Tiger**[11] 5165 3-9-6 **58** .... SilvestreDeSousa 9 —
(William Muir) *s.i.s: in rr: effrt over 3f out: wkng whn sltly hmpd 2f out: eased whn wl bhd* **4/1**[2]

0000 **8** *2 ½* **Go**[33] 4403 3-8-2 **45** ....(p) ShaneBKelly(5) 5 —
(Micky Hammond) *chsd ldrs: drvn 6f out: lost pl 3f out: eased whn wl bhd* **33/1**

2m 11.33s (4.33) **Going Correction** +0.525s/f (Yiel) **8** Ran SP% **114.5**
Speed ratings (Par 98): **103,102,94,90,86 78,70,68**
toteswingers:1&2:£3.10, 1&3:£3.30, 2&3:£4.00 CSF £10.49 CT £54.58 TOTE £2.20: £1.10, £2.20, £2.90; EX 8.90.
Owner D & S Woodall **Bred** Tally-Ho Stud **Trained** Sheriff Hutton, N Yorks
■ Stewards' Enquiry : Graham Gibbons two-day ban: used whip with excessive frequency (Sep 11-12)
Kelly Harrison two-day ban: careless riding (Sep 11-12)

FOCUS
A moderate contest but a good finish between the two market leaders, who came clear on the rest.
Valley Tiger Official explanation: vet said colt bit its tongue
T/Plt: £212.60 to a £1 stake. Pool: £62,710.62. 215.29 winning tickets. T/Qpdt: £91.40 to a £1 stake. Pool: £2,966.48. 24.00 winning tickets. WG

5471 GOODWOOD (R-H)
Sunday, August 28

OFFICIAL GOING: Good (good to soft in places in straight; 7.5)
Wind: Very mild, half across Weather: Sunny with cloudy periods

5508 BANK HOLIDAY STKS (H'CAP) 6f
2:10 (2:10) (Class 3) (0-95,93) 3-Y-0+ **£7,439** (£2,213; £1,106; £553) **Stalls** High

Form / RPR

1451 **1** **Oneladyowner**[16] 5000 3-8-9 **81** .... EddieAhern 8 92
(David Brown) *squeezed up s: towards rr: swtchd rt over 3f out: hdwy in centre over 2f out: rdn to ld jst over 1f out: r.o wl* **9/2**[2]

4100 **2** *1 ¼* **Mac Gille Eoin**[20] 4859 7-9-3 **86** .... IanMongan 2 93
(John Gallagher) *a.p: led 2f out: sn rdn: hdd jst over 1f out: drifted lft: kpt on but nt pce of wnr* **9/1**

0500 **3** *½* **Swilly Ferry (USA)**[20] 4859 4-9-6 **89** ....(b¹) MichaelHills 7 94
(Charles Hills) *in tch: hdwy over 2f out: rdn and ev ch over 1f out: kpt on but nt pce of wnr fnl f* **10/1**

3005 **4** *¾* **Fireback**[29] 4556 4-9-5 **88** .... DavidProbert 3 91
(Andrew Balding) *squeezed out s: sn trcking ldrs: rdn and ev ch over 1f out: kpt on same pce fnl f* **13/2**

0052 **5** *½* **Damika (IRE)**[8] 5278 8-9-7 **90** .... MichaelStainton 1 91
(Richard Whitaker) *chsd ldrs: rdn wl over 3f out: ev ch over 1f out: kpt on same pce* **7/2**[1]

2012 **6** *2 ½* **Quasi Congaree (GER)**[16] 5012 5-9-4 **87** ....(t) RichardHughes 10 80
(Ian Wood) *hld up last: rdn 2f out: passed btn horses ins fnl f but nvr any imp on ldrs* **6/1**[3]

7 *½* **West Coast Dream**[134] 1421 4-9-4 **87** .... WilliamCarson 5 82
(Roy Brotherton) *awkward away: sn led: hdd 2f out: sn rdn: keeping on at sama pce whn carried lft fr jst over 1f out: tight for room ins fnl f: no ch and eased after* **15/2**

1430 **8** *½* **Star Rover (IRE)**[2] 5430 4-9-5 **93** ....(v) MatthewCosham(5) 4 86
(David Evans) *trckd ldrs: rdn over 2f out: keeping on at same pce whn squeezed up on stands' side rails ins fnl f: no ch after: eased* **9/1**

0000 **9** *½* **Tagula Night (IRE)**[20] 4859 5-9-2 **85** ....(vt) AdamKirby 6 74
(Walter Swinburn) *trckd ldrs: rdn over 2f out: wknd ent fnl f* **10/1**

1m 12.49s (0.29) **Going Correction** +0.275s/f (Good)
WFA 3 from 4yo+ 3lb **9** Ran SP% **118.0**
Speed ratings (Par 107): **109,107,106,105,105 101,101,100,99**
toteswingers:1&2:£11.00, 1&3:£10.80, 2&3:£21.80 CSF £45.47 CT £390.62 TOTE £6.30: £2.20, £3.20, £3.80; EX 47.30 Trifecta £336.30 Part won. Pool: £454.41 - 0.10 winning units..
Owner Bolland, Watson, Gregory, Lloyd & Oades **Bred** Barry Minty **Trained** Averham Park, Notts
■ Stewards' Enquiry : Ian Mongan four-day ban: careless riding (Sep 11-14)

FOCUS
Following a dry night the going was given as good, good to soft in places in the straight, and jockeys returning after the first suggested it was sticky, holding and a bit slow. This sprint handicap was made up mostly of horses about which the handicapper knows plenty, but one of the exceptions was the winner.

NOTEBOOK
Oneladyowner was the only 3yo in the field and came here on the back of a win at Newbury on his return from a break. David Brown expected him to have come on for that and predicted the easier ground would suit, and the colt did it well enough in the end, perhaps benefiting from racing more towards the centre of the track than nearer the stands' rail. He's declared to run again at Ripon today, but his trainer nominated the Ayr Silver Cup as his major short-term target. (op 13-2)
Mac Gille Eoin, prominent throughout, did best of those who raced more towards the stands side and kept on well to repeat his result in this race four years ago. He has a good record on downhill tracks. (op 11-1)
Swilly Ferry(USA) hasn't been at his best this season but he has slipped to a fair mark and this was more encouraging in first-time blinkers. He raced more towards the centre, though, which might have been an advantage.
Fireback was another who, along with the first and third, raced towards the outer of the pack, so that may have helped his chance, although the slightly easy ground would not have been in his favour. (op 8-1)
Damika(IRE) held sound claims off a mark 4lb lower than when successful in the Great St Wilfrid last year, but he didn't find a great deal for pressure and carried his head a touch high. It wouldn't be a surprise to see the cheekpieces back on next time. (op 9-2 tchd 5-1)

Quasi Congaree(GER) struggled to make any impression from off the pace and perhaps the ground was against him. (op 5-1)

West Coast Dream, debuting for a new stable, made the running against the stands rail but dropped out in the manner of a horse who needed this first outing since April. (op 13-2)

Star Rover(IRE) Official explanation: jockey said gelding suffered interference at start

5509 FEGENTRI WORLD CHAMPIONSHIP STKS (GENTLEMAN AM RIDERS' H'CAP) (IN MEMORY OF GAY KINDERSLEY) 1m 1f

2:45 (2:45) (Class 5) (0-75,75) 3-Y-O+ **£3,119** (£967; £483; £242) **Stalls** Low

Form RPR

3450 **1** **Loyaliste (FR)**[20] 4862 4-11-5 **68** MrSvenSchleppi 3 73
(Richard Hannon) *hld up bhd ldrs: sltly outpcd over 2f out: r.o strly ent fnl f: led fnl 40yds* **13/2**

6050 **2** ¾ **Byrd In Hand (IRE)**[15] 5040 4-10-7 **56** oh1 MrPMadden 2 59
(John Bridger) *led at crawl: qcknd pce over 2f out whn chal: sn rdn: kpt on gamely: hdd fnl 40yds* **4/1**[3]

5241 **3** 1 ¼ **Shabak Hom (IRE)**[31] 4465 4-11-12 **75** MrNdeBoinville 6 76
(David Simcock) *t.k.h: hld up bhd ldrs: hdwy over 3f out: rdn over 2f out: kpt on same pce fnl f* **11/4**[1]

4024 **4** ¾ **Potentiale (IRE)**[25] 4660 7-11-10 **73** MrMarioBaratti 1 72
(J W Hills) *trckd ldr tl rdn over 2f out: nt pce to chal* **4/1**[3]

4212 **5** nk **Choral Festival**[13] 5110 5-11-8 **71** MrNMKelly 5 69
(John Bridger) *trckd ldrs: chal over 2f out: sn rdn: ev ch tl no ex ins fnl f* **7/2**[2]

0641 **6** 2 ¾ **Gallego**[16] 5002 9-10-13 **62** MrPatrickDeno 4 54
(Richard Price) *slowly away: hld up: hdwy over 3f out: rdn over 2f out: fdd over 1f out* **10/1**

2m 6.99s (10.69) **Going Correction** +0.275s/f (Good) **6** Ran SP% **111.3**
Speed ratings (Par 103): **63,62,61,60,60 57**
toteswingers:1&2:£5.80, 1&3:£4.40, 2&3:£3.10 CSF £31.48 TOTE £8.20: £3.10, £2.60; EX 39.50.
Owner Mrs Sue Brendish **Bred** E A R L Elevage De La Source & F Bozo **Trained** East Everleigh, Wilts

FOCUS
They went a crawl in the early stages of this amateur riders' event and then sprinted up the straight.

5510 SUPREME STKS (GROUP 3) 7f

3:20 (3:21) (Class 1) 3-Y-O+
£28,355 (£10,750; £5,380; £2,012; £2,012; £675) **Stalls** Low

Form RPR

1440 **1** **Libranno**[21] 4838 3-8-13 112 RichardHughes 10 110
(Richard Hannon) *led: rdn and narrowly hdd over 1f out: rallied gamely to regain ld wl ins fnl f: drvn out* **7/2**[2]

-3R4 **2** shd **Jacqueline Quest (IRE)**[22] 4790 4-8-11 99 EddieAhern 5 105
(Ian Williams) *trckd ldrs: travelling best whn swtchd off rails wl over 1f out: sn led and rdn: kpt on but no ex whn hdd wl ins fnl f* **10/1**

2010 **3** 1 **High Standing (USA)**[29] 4534 6-9-0 100 (p) GeorgeBaker 2 105
(William Haggas) *in tch: nt clrest of runs fr 2f out tl swtchd rt ent fnl f: r.o: 3rd and hld whn swtchd lft nring fin* **12/1**

1446 **4** nk **The Cheka (IRE)**[15] 5046 5-9-4 108 (p) TomQueally 7 108
(Eve Johnson Houghton) *trckd ldrs: rdn 2f out: kpt on same pce fnl f* **7/1**[3]

0100 **4** dht **Hooray**[10] 5228 3-8-8 111 ow2 StevieDonohoe 9 101
(Sir Mark Prescott Bt) *trckd ldr tl rdn wl over 1f out: kpt on same pce fnl f: hld in 4th whn sltly hmpd nring fin* **3/1**[1]

4551 **6** ½ **Doncaster Rover (USA)**[8] 5282 5-9-0 108 KierenFallon 8 103
(David Brown) *in tch: pushed along over 3f out but no imp tl rdn and r.o ins fnl f: nvr gng pce to threaten ldrs* **3/1**[1]

-000 **7** ¾ **Balthazaar's Gift (IRE)**[15] 5046 8-9-0 107 AdamKirby 4 101+
(Clive Cox) *hld up: rdn over 2f out: styng on wl ins fnl f whn nt clr run nring fin but nvr gng to threaten* **16/1**

146- **8** ¾ **Karam Albaari (IRE)**[309] 7081 3-8-9 109 MichaelHills 1 97+
(J R Jenkins) *hld up: rdn over 2f out: nvr gng pce to get involved* **20/1**

1m 28.01s (1.11) **Going Correction** +0.275s/f (Good)
WFA 3 from 4yo+ 5lb **8** Ran SP% **112.1**
Speed ratings (Par 113): **104,103,102,102,102 101,100,100**
toteswingers:1&2:£6.00, 1&3:£7.60, 2&3:£11.10 CSF £36.23 TOTE £3.50: £1.10, £2.40, £3.40; EX 45.30 Trifecta £638.70 Part won. Pool: £863.15 - 0.60 winning units..
Owner Mcdowell Racing **Bred** O McDowell **Trained** East Everleigh, Wilts
■ Stewards' Enquiry : Stevie Donohoe three-day ban: weighed-in 2lb heavy (Sep 11-13)

FOCUS
This looked quite a competitive Group 3 on paper.

NOTEBOOK
Libranno gained a huge advantage when granted a free hand soon after the start. Able to dictate his own tempo in front, he was in position A to quicken in the straight and, although briefly headed by Jacqueline Quest inside the last, that filly has promised more than she has delivered in the past and it was the same again as Libranno saw off her challenge to win narrowly but a shade cosily. His record suggests he's a little short of the top level, but he's likely to be given another go at a Group 1 next, with the Prix de la Foret, the only Group 1 in Europe for older horses over this distance, mentioned as a possible target.

Jacqueline Quest(IRE), having her second start for her new stable, got a position tracking the leader on the rail and came there swinging a furlong out. She has done this before and not found a great deal and, while she edged ahead briefly, she doesn't seem to like being in front and soon relinquished the lead back to Libranno. While Ian Williams has done well to get her back to something like her best, she's clearly not an easy ride as her challenge must be delayed until the last possible moment. (op 12-1)

High Standing(USA), three back on the fence entering the straight, was stuck behind a wall of horses when the pace began to pick up and never got a clear run. He would surely have finished closer had he been able to get out and deliver a challenge, but his style of running makes him a hostage to fortune. The Ayr Gold Cup is next up for him and that race should suit his style of running far better. (op 11-1)

Hooray has not reached the levels she showed at two this year and an experiment in holding her up backfired in Ireland last time. She was ridden more prominently here but wasn't able to mount a challenge in the closing stages and carried her head a bit high. She'd probably be better off back racing against her own sex. For some reason her rider weighed in 2lb heavier than he weighed out. (tchd 13-2 and 8-1)

The Cheka(IRE), wearing cheekpieces for the first time this year, had his chance down the outside but tended to edge right under pressure and couldn't make much impression. It was a fair effort under his 4lb penalty. (tchd 13-2 and 8-1)

Doncaster Rover(USA), who got a bit warm beforehand, got outpaced when the sprint for home began before running on late. He could have done with a stronger all-round gallop. (tchd 11-4 and 10-3)

Balthazaar's Gift(IRE) is another who would have benefited from a stronger pace. (op 12-1 tchd 10-1)

Karam Albaari(IRE), making a belated seasonal reappearance, was always at the rear of the field and the race wasn't really run to suit him. He should come on for the outing. (tchd 16-1)

5511 PHILIP OSBORN 60TH BIRTHDAY STKS (H'CAP) 7f

3:55 (3:55) (Class 5) (0-70,70) 3-Y-O+ **£2,587** (£770; £384; £192) **Stalls** Low

Form RPR

2441 **1** **Ellie In The Pink (IRE)**[15] 5040 3-9-3 **66** KierenFallon 2 73+
(Alan Jarvis) *mde all: rdn over 1f out: drifted lft: kpt on wl to assert towards fin: drvn out* **9/4**[1]

0403 **2** ¾ **Billion Dollar Kid**[38] 4255 6-9-12 **70** (bt) RichardKingscote 10 77
(Joanna Davis) *in tch: hdwy whn bmpd over 3f out: rdn over 2f out: ev ch over 1f out: kpt on but no ex ins fnl f* **8/1**

4400 **3** shd **Sunshine Always (IRE)**[10] 5201 5-9-4 **67** MarkCoumbe(5) 9 74
(Michael Attwater) *hld up: in tch whn rdn 2f out: styng on whn sltly hmpd by wnr and swtchd rt wl ins fnl f: wnt 3rd towards fin* **12/1**

-104 **4** ¾ **Saturn Way (GR)**[20] 4866 5-9-8 **66** GeorgeBaker 1 71
(Patrick Chamings) *trckd ldrs: swtchd rt over 1f out: sn rdn: chal ins fnl f: no ex towards fin* **15/2**

0145 **5** ¾ **Push Me (IRE)**[9] 5231 4-9-3 **61** MartinLane 7 64+
(Jamie Poulton) *hld up: hdwy whn nt clr run over 2f out: sn rdn: styd on ent fnl f but nvr gng pce to get on terms* **9/1**

00-0 **6** nk **Xclaim**[134] 1408 3-9-6 **69** AdamKirby 11 69
(Clive Cox) *little slowly away: hld up: rdn 3f out: styd on fnl f: n.d* **13/2**[3]

6013 **7** 8 **Diamond Run**[18] 4911 3-8-10 **59** SebSanders 5 37+
(J W Hills) *w wnr tl rdn over 2f out: hld whn bdly hmpd sn after: wknd fnl f* **7/2**[2]

6560 **8** ¾ **Amber Heights**[38] 4244 3-8-12 **61** EddieAhern 4 37+
(David Pinder) *racd keenly: trckd ldrs: swtchd lft over 3f out: rdn to chal 2f out: stl jst upsides whn lost action ent fnl f* **16/1**

1m 28.5s (1.60) **Going Correction** +0.275s/f (Good)
WFA 3 from 4yo+ 5lb **8** Ran SP% **112.8**
Speed ratings (Par 103): **101,100,100,99,98 97,88,87**
toteswingers:1&2:£4.30, 1&3:£5.80, 2&3:£6.90 CSF £20.33 CT £175.20 TOTE £2.90: £1.30, £2.40, £2.50; EX 20.60 Trifecta £136.50 Part won. Pool: £599.73 - 3.25 winning units..
Owner Jakellie **Bred** J Jamgotchian **Trained** Twyford, Bucks

FOCUS
Just a modest handicap.

Amber Heights Official explanation: jockey said filly lost its action

5512 GOODWOOD (S) STKS 1m 3f

4:30 (4:30) (Class 4) 3-Y-O **£4,528** (£1,347; £673; £336) **Stalls** High

Form RPR

1002 **1** **Zamina (IRE)**[9] 5249 3-8-12 73 JamesDoyle 3 61
(Sylvester Kirk) *trckd ldrs: chal 3f out: rdn to ld jst over 1f out: hld on: all out* **7/4**[1]

3243 **2** shd **Lady Elsie**[9] 5241 3-8-7 70 KierenFallon 7 56
(William Haggas) *led: qcknd pce 3f out: sn rdn and hrd pressed: narrowly hdd jst over 1f out: ev ch thrght fnl f: jst hld* **9/4**[2]

413 **3** 1 ½ **What About Now**[12] 5134 3-8-12 62 (b) MichaelHills 1 58
(J W Hills) *hld up in last pair: hdwy 3f out: sn rdn: styd on same pce fnl f* **13/2**

0043 **4** 1 ¼ **Fastada (IRE)**[17] 4953 3-8-7 48 (v) RichardKingscote 6 51
(Jonathan Portman) *trckd ldr tl 3f out: sn rdn: styd on same pce fnl 2f* **10/1**

4025 **5** 2 ¾ **Special Endeavour (IRE)**[4] 5380 3-8-12 47 (p) SebSanders 5 51
(William Muir) *s.i.s: in last pair: rdn to chse ldrs over 2f out: fdd fnl f* **20/1**

1500 **6** 16 **Loch Fleet (IRE)**[72] 3133 3-9-3 73 GeorgeBaker 2 27
(Gary Moore) *racd keenly: trckd ldrs: rdn over 2f out: sn wknd* **6/1**[3]

2m 32.23s (5.73) **Going Correction** +0.275s/f (Good) **6** Ran SP% **108.6**
Speed ratings (Par 102): **90,89,88,87,85 74**
toteswingers:1&2:£1.60, 1&3:£2.30, 2&3:£2.10 CSF £5.46 TOTE £2.60: £1.50, £1.90; EX 4.30.The winner was bought in for £7,500. Lady Elsie was claimed by Noel Quinlan £7,500.
Owner N Pickett & S Kirk **Bred** Churchtown Bloodstock **Trained** Upper Lambourn, Berks
■ Stewards' Enquiry : James Doyle one-day ban: used whuip with excessive frequency (Sep 11)

FOCUS
There was a tight finish to this seller.

Loch Fleet(IRE) Official explanation: jockey said colt had no more to give

5513 GOODWOOD HOTEL APPRENTICE STKS (H'CAP) 6f

5:05 (5:05) (Class 5) (0-70,70) 3-Y-O+ **£2,587** (£770; £384; £192) **Stalls** High

Form RPR

6060 **1** **Bathwick Xaara**[34] 4387 4-9-0 **60** RossAtkinson 1 68
(Jonathan Portman) *a.p: led 3f out: kpt on wl fnl f: rdn out* **11/1**

0036 **2** ½ **Memphis Man**[5] 5345 8-8-9 **58** MatthewCosham(3) 7 64+
(David Evans) *chsd ldrs: swtchd to centre over 2f out: sn rdn: r.o ent fnl f: nt rch wnr* **12/1**

0452 **3** hd **Seamus Shindig**[17] 4960 9-9-4 **67** AmyScott(3) 5 72
(Henry Candy) *prom: rdn 2f out: ev ch ent fnl f: no ex* **11/4**[1]

0164 **4** hd **Witchry**[5] 5338 9-9-0 **65** DavidKenny(5) 3 70
(Tony Newcombe) *trckd ldrs: rdn over 1f out: ev ch ent fnl f: kpt on but no ex* **3/1**[2]

224 **5** 2 **Even Bolder**[27] 4615 8-9-10 **70** KierenFox 4 68
(Eric Wheeler) *chsd ldrs: rdn over 2f out: nt gng pce to get on terms* **6/1**[3]

004 **6** nk **Gracie's Games**[22] 4793 5-9-0 **60** SophieDoyle 2 57
(Richard Price) *prom: rdn over 2f out: ev ch jst over 1f out: no ex ins fnl f* **13/2**

6105 **7** 6 **Silvee**[15] 5037 4-8-11 **57** SeanLevey 6 35
(John Bridger) *prom: rdn over 2f out: wknd over 1f out* **9/1**

0006 **8** 1 ½ **Rio Royale (IRE)**[20] 4850 5-8-11 **57** (p) KieranO'Neill 9 30
(Amanda Perrett) *led tl rdn 3f out: sn wknd* **9/1**

1m 14.33s (2.13) **Going Correction** +0.275s/f (Good) **8** Ran SP% **115.3**
Speed ratings (Par 103): **96,95,95,94,92 91,83,81**
toteswingers:1&2:£22.10, 1&3:£8.70, 2&3:£6.70 CSF £131.97 CT £471.08 TOTE £12.70: £3.10, £3.50, £1.40; EX 161.40 Trifecta £391.40 Part won. Pool: £529.03 - 0.20 winning units..
Owner Mrs S Clifford **Bred** Charlock Farm Stud **Trained** Compton, Berks

FOCUS
An ordinary sprint handicap.

T/Jkpt: Part won. £44,679.00 to a £1 stake. Pool: £62,928.23. 0.50 winning tickets. T/Plt: £938.20 to a £1 stake. Pool: £86,888.50. 67.60 winning tickets. T/Qpdt: £17.90 to a £1 stake. Pool: £6,760.52. 278.21winning tickets. TM

5351 YARMOUTH (L-H)

Sunday, August 28

OFFICIAL GOING: Soft (6.9)

Wind: Fresh, across Weather: Cloudy with sunny spells

5514 TOTEPLACEPOT WIN WITHOUT BACKING A WINNER E B F MAIDEN FILLIES' STKS 6f 3y

2:00 (2:02) (Class 5) 2-Y-O **£3,557** (£1,058; £529; £264) **Stalls** High

Form RPR

1 **Alsindi (IRE)** 2-9-0 0 .... PhilipRobinson 4 86+
(Clive Brittain) *s.i.s: hld up: hdwy over 2f out: led over 1f out: edgd rt and pushed clr fnl f* **11/2**

04 **2** *3 1/4* **Silke Top**[27] 4614 2-9-0 0 .... SteveDrowne 6 74
(William Jarvis) *chsd ldrs: rdn over 2f out: ev ch over 1f out: styd on same pce* **5/1**[3]

3 *2 1/2* **Darling Grace** 2-9-0 0 .... LiamJones 7 67+
(William Haggas) *s.i.s: sn pushed along in rr: hdwy over 1f out: styd on: nt trble ldrs* **25/1**

4 *2 1/2* **Flaming Ferrari (IRE)** 2-9-0 0 .... PatCosgrave 12 59
(Peter Chapple-Hyam) *chsd ldrs: rdn over 2f out: wknd fnl f* **16/1**

33 **5** *1/2* **Appointee (IRE)**[17] 4961 2-9-0 0 .... WilliamBuick 11 58
(John Gosden) *sn led: rdn and hdd over 1f out: wknd ins fnl f* **5/2**[1]

0 **6** *nk* **I See You**[6] 5323 2-9-0 0 .... AdrianMcCarthy 2 57
(George Margarson) *prom: rdn over 2f out: wknd fnl f* **33/1**

0 **7** *1/2* **Teth**[34] 4386 2-8-9 0 .... AntiocoMurgia(5) 8 55
(Mahmood Al Zarooni) *chsd ldrs: rdn over 2f out: wknd fnl f* **20/1**

0 **8** *nk* **Willow Beauty**[17] 4901 2-9-0 0 .... DarryllHolland 1 54
(J R Jenkins) *prom: rdn over 2f out: wknd over 1f out* **66/1**

9 *1/2* **Mallak (IRE)** 2-8-11 0 .... AdamBeschizza(3) 13 53
(Philip McBride) *s.i.s: sn pushed along: hdwy 1/2-way: rdn and wknd over 1f out* **66/1**

10 *nk* **Adverse (IRE)** 2-9-0 0 .... HayleyTurner 9 52+
(Michael Bell) *prom tl wknd wl over 1f out* **8/1**

11 *18* **Classic Falcon (IRE)** 2-9-0 0 .... RichardHills 10 —
(William Haggas) *s.i.s: sn pushed along and a in rr: bhd fr 1/2-way* **7/2**[2]

12 *1/2* **Fouracres** 2-9-0 0 .... RobbieFitzpatrick 3 —
(Michael Appleby) *sn outpcd* **150/1**

1m 15.48s (1.08) **Going Correction** +0.325s/f (Good) **12** Ran SP% **115.0**
Speed ratings (Par 91): **105,100,97,94,93 92,92,91,91,90 66,66**
toteswingers: 1&2 £5.70, 1&3 £18.20, 2&3 £13.50 CSF £30.29 TOTE £5.60: £1.80, £1.90, £6.10; EX 45.20.

Owner Saeed Manana **Bred** D G Hardisty Bloodstock **Trained** Newmarket, Suffolk

FOCUS
Back straight and bottom bend dolled out 3m up to 4.5f adding 15m to races on round course. The ground was officially soft, with a 6.9 GoingStick reading, after 2mm of overnight rain. Racing began, in bright and breezy weather conditions, with an interesting juvenile fillies' maiden. The winner impressed and the runner-up and time help set the level.

NOTEBOOK
Alsindi(IRE) ◆, bought for 70,000gns as a yearling, won as she liked and looks a bargain on this evidence. Slightly slow to break, she raced in the centre of the track, on the left of the main pack, and made progress at halfway. She quickened nicely to lead approaching the final furlong and drew clear under hands-and- heels riding. She seems set to make a mark in a higher grade. (op 11-1)
Silke Top, fourth at Windsor 27 days earlier, had already established a fair level of form and possibly improved on it here. Always well placed, she stayed on resolutely in the closing stages, even though she was no match for the comfortable winner. (tchd 6-1 in places)
Darling Grace, a newcomer out of a 1m winner, was a market drifter. She ran creditably, however, staying on at the finish after being well back in midfield in the early stages. As her pedigree suggests, she will handle longer trips than this. (op 16-1)
Flaming Ferrari(IRE), a debutante related to sprint winners, also made an encouraging start to her career. Never far away, she plugged on steadily and is likely to improve for the outing.
Appointee(IRE), third in a fair maiden at Newmarket last time out, was rather disappointing. She led soon after the start and took the field along until after halfway. She found little once overtaken, though, and may not have appreciated the easy ground. Official explanation: jockey said, regarding running and riding, that his orders were to try and settle the filly and get it to finish as close as possible, when it came off the bridle it became unbalanced and he had to hold on to it to keep it from rolling on the soft ground. (op 9-4 tchd 11-4)
I See You, eighth of 16 at Windsor on her only previous outing, was always in about the same place. She has ability, although she is no superstar, and may be able to exploit it once handicapped.
Teth, backed before finishing last of eight on her debut a month previously, fared better here. She led briefly early on, stayed prominent until beyond halfway and faded out of contention only in the final furlong. (tchd 22-1)

5515 TOTEEXACTA BETTER VALUE FORECAST H'CAP 1m 3y

2:35 (2:36) (Class 6) (0-60,60) 3-Y-O+ **£1,811** (£539; £269; £134) **Stalls** High

Form RPR

0644 **1** **Ippi N Tombi (IRE)**[5] 5352 3-8-5 **47** .... ChrisCatlin 16 57
(Phil McEntee) *mde all: rdn over 1f out: styd on gamely* **20/1**

40-5 **2** *1/2* **Larkrise Star**[28] 4579 4-9-7 **57** .... ShaneKelly 1 67
(Dean Ivory) *hld up: hdwy over 3f out: rdn and ev ch over 1f out: styd on* **16/1**

321 **3** *hd* **Viking Rose (IRE)**[12] 5137 3-9-4 **60** .... LukeMorris 2 69
(James Eustace) *chsd ldrs: rdn and ev ch over 1f out: styd on* **9/2**[1]

-004 **4** *3 1/2* **Miss Villefranche**[40] 4185 3-9-1 **57** .... (v) HayleyTurner 13 57
(Michael Bell) *hld up in tch: rdn over 1f out: no ex fnl f* **17/2**

4603 **5** *1 1/4* **Strike A Deal (IRE)**[18] 4927 4-9-2 **59** .... DannyBrock(7) 4 58
(Chris Wall) *s.i.s: hdwy over 5f out: rdn and hung rt over 1f out: wknd ins fnl f* **13/2**[3]

4104 **6** *nk* **Princess Gail**[26] 4627 3-8-3 **52** .... RachealKneller(7) 6 49
(Mark Brisbourne) *s.i.s: hld up: styd on fr over 1f out: nvr on terms* **28/1**

2104 **7** *1 1/4* **Border Abby**[12] 5137 3-9-2 **58** .... NeilCallan 7 52
(Rae Guest) *prom: rdn and edgd lft over 2f out: wknd fnl f* **5/1**[2]

0045 **8** *3/4* **Warden Bond**[5] 5352 3-8-1 **48** ow2 .... (p) LauraPike(5) 12 40
(William Stone) *mid-div: sn pushed along: rdn 1/2-way: lost pl 3f out: n.d after* **16/1**

0031 **9** *3 1/4* **Tinkerbell Will**[18] 4928 4-8-13 **49** .... RichardThomas 11 35
(John E Long) *mid-div: rdn 1/2-way: wknd over 1f out* **8/1**

055 **10** *11* **Bell's Ocean (USA)**[20] 4852 4-8-13 **49** .... PhilipRobinson 8 —
(John Ryan) *hld up: rdn 1/2-way: sn bhd* **16/1**

6350 **11** *4* **Exopuntia**[16] 5014 5-9-5 **55** .... DarryllHolland 9 —
(Julia Feilden) *chsd ldrs tl wknd wl over 2f out* **14/1**

0651 **12** *5* **Zaheeb**[18] 4929 3-9-0 **59** .... (p) AdamBeschizza(3) 14 —
(Dave Morris) *prom: rdn over 3f out: wknd over 2f out: eased: t.o* **16/1**

5533 **13** *1 3/4* **Trust Me Boy**[18] 4929 3-8-4 **46** oh1 .... (v) JimmyQuinn 10 —
(John E Long) *hld up: rdn and wknd over 3f out: eased: t.o* **14/1**

6000 **14** *16* **Scruffy Skip (IRE)**[10] 5214 6-8-10 **46** oh1 .... (p) PatCosgrave 15 —
(Christine Dunnett) *chsd ldrs tl rdn and wknd over 3f out: eased fnl 2f: t.o* **40/1**

5000 **15** *1 1/2* **I Hate To Lose (USA)**[18] 4911 3-8-13 **60** .... (t) AntiocoMurgia(5) 5 —
(Philip McBride) *hld up: hdwy 1/2-way: wknd over 2f out: eased: t.o* **28/1**

1m 43.94s (3.34) **Going Correction** +0.325s/f (Good)
WFA 3 from 4yo+ 6lb **15** Ran SP% **120.8**
Speed ratings (Par 101): **96,95,95,91,90 90,89,88,85,74 70,65,63,47,45**
toteswingers: 1&2 £62.20, 1&3 £26.80, 2&3 £14.40 CSF £299.50 CT £1743.83 TOTE £30.10: £9.10, £5.20, £1.10; EX 603.80.

Owner Eventmaker Racehorses **Bred** Olive O'Connor **Trained** Newmarket, Suffolk

FOCUS
A modest contest, with the top weight rated just 59, but few could be confidently discounted. The main action was close to the stands' rail.
Bell's Ocean(USA) Official explanation: trainer said filly was unsuited by the soft ground

5516 TRY TOTEQUICKPICK IF YOU'RE FEELING LUCKY H'CAP 7f 3y

3:10 (3:11) (Class 4) (0-85,85) 3-Y-O+ **£4,528** (£1,347; £673; £336) **Stalls** High

Form RPR

0502 **1** **Cloud Rock**[13] 5119 3-9-5 **83** .... RobertHavlin 11 91+
(Peter Chapple-Hyam) *chsd ldrs: led over 1f out: edgd lft ins fnl f: rdn out* **15/2**

6526 **2** *1* **Fantasy Gladiator**[9] 5240 5-9-7 **80** .... (p) JimmyQuinn 5 87
(Robert Cowell) *s.i.s: hld up: hdwy over 1f out: sn rdn: edgd rt ins fnl f: styd on u.p* **7/1**

1-26 **3** *nk* **Double Dealer**[125] 1571 3-9-0 **83** .... AntiocoMurgia(5) 2 87
(Mahmood Al Zarooni) *chsd ldrs: rdn and ev ch over 1f out: edgd lft ins fnl f: styd on same pce towards fin* **9/2**[2]

1405 **4** *1 1/2* **Rough Rock (IRE)**[13] 5119 6-9-2 **75** .... AndreaAtzeni 4 79+
(Chris Dwyer) *a.p: rdn over 1f out: styng on whn hmpd wl ins fnl f* **16/1**

5032 **5** *1* **Inpursuitoffreedom**[16] 5014 4-8-7 **69** .... AdamBeschizza(3) 1 68
(Philip McBride) *hld up: hdwy over 2f out: sn rdn: no ex ins fnl f* **3/1**[1]

6-53 **6** *1* **Elspeth's Boy (USA)**[13] 5119 4-9-3 **76** .... ShaneKelly 12 73
(William Haggas) *led: rdn and hdd over 1f out: no ex fnl f* **6/1**

0524 **7** *1 1/4* **Cativo Cavallino**[29] 4546 8-8-7 **66** .... RichardThomas 7 59
(John E Long) *sn pushed along in rr: nvr on terms* **25/1**

6000 **8** *8* **Steed**[8] 5272 4-9-4 **80** .... (p) RobertLButler(3) 10 52
(Richard Guest) *hld up: pushed along over 2f out: wknd over 1f out* **16/1**

0303 **9** *15* **Batgirl**[34] 4393 4-9-1 **74** .... WilliamBuick 8 —
(John Berry) *hld up: plld hrd: rdn 1/2-way: wknd 2f out: eased* **11/2**[3]

0-00 **10** *50* **Arteus**[29] 4556 5-9-12 **85** .... PatCosgrave 3 —
(George Margarson) *chsd ldr: rdn over 3f out: wknd over 2f out: eased: t.o* **50/1**

1m 28.75s (2.15) **Going Correction** +0.325s/f (Good)
WFA 3 from 4yo+ 5lb **10** Ran SP% **114.7**
Speed ratings (Par 105): **100,98,98,96,95 94,93,83,66,9**
toteswingers: 1&2 £7.20, 1&3 £7.80, 2&3 £7.10 CSF £58.10 CT £269.87 TOTE £8.80: £2.90, £1.80, £1.90; EX 73.10.

Owner The Coalition **Bred** Lofts Hall Stud **Trained** Newmarket, Suffolk

■ Stewards' Enquiry : Andrea Atzeni three-day ban: used whip down shoulder in the forehand (Sep 16-18)

FOCUS
An open-looking handicap slightly weakened by a couple of withdrawals. Once again, the field congregated close to the stands' rail.
Batgirl Official explanation: jockey said filly never travelled

5517 TRY TOTEQUICKPICK ON ALL TOTEPOOL BETS FILLIES' H'CAP 5f 43y

3:45 (3:45) (Class 5) (0-70,73) 3-Y-O+ **£2,522** (£750; £375; £187) **Stalls** High

Form RPR

1213 **1** **Imaginary Diva**[6] 5326 5-8-8 **59** .... RyanPowell(5) 6 69
(George Margarson) *trckd ldrs: a gng wl: led wl ins fnl f: comf* **7/4**[1]

1353 **2** *1 3/4* **Simple Rhythm**[2] 5426 5-8-11 **57** .... (p) PhilipRobinson 3 61
(John Ryan) *chsd ldrs: led over 1f out: rdn and hdd wl ins fnl f: styd on same pce* **7/4**[1]

1641 **3** *1/2* **Bobby's Doll**[12] 5139 4-9-6 **69** .... AdamBeschizza(3) 7 71+
(Terry Clement) *chsd ldr: n.m.r almost thrght: hmpd 1/2-way: rdn over 1f out: styd on same pce ins fnl f* **11/4**[2]

0505 **4** *9* **Instructress**[25] 4684 3-8-4 **52** .... NickyMackay 1 22
(Robert Cowell) *led: edgd rt 1/2-way: hdd and n.m.r over 1f out: sn wknd* **14/1**[3]

65.15 secs (2.45) **Going Correction** +0.325s/f (Good)
WFA 3 from 4yo+ 2lb **4** Ran SP% **106.1**
Speed ratings (Par 100): **93,90,89,75**
toteswingers: 1&2 £2.20 CSF £4.90 TOTE £2.40; EX 4.10.

Owner Graham Lodge Partnership **Bred** Norcroft Park Stud **Trained** Newmarket, Suffolk

■ Stewards' Enquiry : Nicky Mackay 1st inc three-day ban: careless riding (Sep 11-13); 2nd inc seven-day ban: careless riding (Sep 14-20)

FOCUS
A modest handicap, in which the top weight was rated 73.

5518 TOTESWINGER MORE WAYS TO WIN H'CAP 1m 2f 21y

4:20 (4:20) (Class 5) (0-75,73) 3-Y-O+ **£2,522** (£750; £375; £187) **Stalls** Low

Form RPR

3546 **1** **Minsky Mine (IRE)**[21] 4818 4-9-3 **62** .... RobbieFitzpatrick 5 70
(Michael Appleby) *mde all: rdn over 2f out: styd on u.p: edgd rt nr fin* **28/1**

1064 **2** *1* **Bouggatti**[18] 4902 3-8-13 **66** .... (b1) SteveDrowne 3 72
(William Jarvis) *dwlt: pushed along early: hld up: hdwy u.p 2f out: sn hung rt: styd on* **3/1**[2]

062 **3** *hd* **Spyder**[16] 5004 3-9-6 **73** .... (b) LukeMorris 2 79
(Jane Chapple-Hyam) *chsd wnr 2f: remained handy: rdn over 2f out: styd on* **7/1**

-005 **4** *4 1/2* **Starkat**[8] 5281 5-9-12 **71** .... DarryllHolland 7 68
(George Margarson) *hld up: hdwy over 2f out: rdn over 1f out: styd on same pce* **8/1**

110 **5** *1 3/4* **Mystic Edge**[28] 4584 3-9-6 **73** .... HayleyTurner 8 66
(Michael Bell) *prom: chsd wnr 8f out: rdn over 1f out: wknd ins fnl f* **9/2**[3]

6605 **6** *3 3/4* **Kiss A Prince**[156] 963 5-9-11 **70** .... (p) ShaneKelly 4 56
(Dean Ivory) *hld up: rdn over 2f out: sn wknd* **14/1**

-060 **7** *5* **Myboyalfie (USA)**[16] 5015 4-9-4 **63** .... NeilCallan 6 39
(J R Jenkins) *chsd ldrs tl rdn and wknd over 2f out* **10/1**

2104 **8** *12* **Lady Gabrielle (IRE)**[17] 4971 3-9-5 **72**........................... NickyMackay 1 24
(David Elsworth) *prom: rdn over 2f out: wknd wl over 1f out: eased* **11/4**[1]

2m 12.76s (2.26) **Going Correction** +0.325s/f (Good)
WFA 3 from 4yo+ 8lb **8** Ran SP% **112.7**
Speed ratings (Par 103): **103,102,102,98,97 94,90,80**
toteswingers: 1&2 £14.20, 1&3 £14.00, 2&3 £3.20 CSF £107.64 CT £670.83 TOTE £37.30: £4.80, £1.90, £1.50; EX 164.20.
Owner Terry Pryke **Bred** Moyglare Stud Farm Ltd **Trained** Danethorpe, Notts
■ Stewards' Enquiry : Darryll Holland two-day ban: careless riding (Sep 11-12)

FOCUS
Another modest event, with the top weight rated 71, but it looked competitive.
Lady Gabrielle(IRE) Official explanation: trainer said, regarding running, that the filly was unsuited by the soft ground

5519 TOTEPOOL A BETTER WAY TO BET H'CAP 1m 6f 17y
4:55 (4:55) (Class 6) (0-60,60) 3-Y-0+ **£1,811** (£539; £269; £134) **Stalls** Low

Form RPR
30-6 **1** **Joan D'Arc (IRE)**[26] 4626 4-9-4 **55**........................... AntiocoMurgia(5) 10 69+
(Noel Quinlan) *chsd ldrs: led 3f out: clr over 1f out: comf* **28/1**

0043 **2** *2 ½* **Jinto**[17] 4974 4-9-9 **55**........................... NickyMackay 5 63
(David Elsworth) *a.p: led 4f out: rdn and hdd 3f out: styd on same pce appr fnl f* **7/2**[1]

2633 **3** *3 ¾* **Outland (IRE)**[17] 4952 5-10-0 **60**........................... NeilCallan 7 63
(J R Jenkins) *hld up: hdwy over 3f out: rdn over 2f out: styd on same pce appr fnl f* **4/1**[2]

/0-4 **4** *2* **Astrolibra**[41] 4164 7-9-8 **54**........................... PhilipRobinson 4 54
(Mark H Tompkins) *hld up: hdwy 4f out: rdn over 2f out: styd on same pce* **11/1**

2143 **5** *8* **Nutshell**[34] 4389 3-9-2 **60**........................... JimmyQuinn 9 49
(Harry Dunlop) *prom: rdn over 3f out: wknd over 2f out* **4/1**[2]

5004 **6** *17* **Peaceful Means (IRE)**[11] 5178 8-9-5 **51**...............(t) RobbieFitzpatrick 8 16
(Michael Appleby) *hld up: rdn and wknd over 2f out: t.o* **16/1**

351- **7** *3 ½* **Jennerous Blue**[303] 7213 4-9-5 **51**...........................(p) ShaneKelly 3 11
(Dean Ivory) *prom: rdn over 3f out: sn wknd: t.o* **15/2**

3262 **8** *hd* **Miss Whippy**[24] 4732 4-9-4 **50**...........................(p) HayleyTurner 1 10
(Michael Squance) *chsd ldrs tl wknd over 3f out: t.o* **13/2**[3]

000 **9** *2 ½* **Meshfi**[22] 4805 3-8-8 **52**........................... ChrisCatlin 2 —
(Clive Brittain) *sn led: rdn and hdd 4f out: wknd sn after: t.o* **8/1**

000- **10** *54* **Mater Mater**[162] 7387 4-9-2 **48**...........................(p) PatCosgrave 11 —
(Andrew Reid) *chsd ldr after 2f tl rdn 4f out: sn wknd and eased: t.o* **50/1**

3m 11.92s (4.32) **Going Correction** +0.325s/f (Good)
WFA 3 from 4yo+ 12lb **10** Ran SP% **118.1**
Speed ratings (Par 101): **100,98,96,95,90 81,79,78,77,46**
toteswingers: 1&2 £19.20, 1&3 £20.60, 2&3 £4.40 CSF £125.71 CT £494.82 TOTE £32.50: £4.70, £1.80, £2.00; EX 171.00.
Owner Newtown Anner Stud Farm Ltd **Bred** Lynn Lodge Stud **Trained** Newmarket, Suffolk

FOCUS
A low-grade contest in which the top weight was rated 60. The first three home were the highest trio in the handicap.

5520 BET TOTEPOOL ON ALL UK RACES APPRENTICE H'CAP 1m 2f 21y
5:25 (5:25) (Class 6) (0-60,60) 4-Y-0+ **£1,811** (£539; £269; £134) **Stalls** Low

Form RPR
3622 **1** **Market Puzzle (IRE)**[11] 5178 4-8-5 **47**...........................(p) RachealKneller(3) 4 54
(Mark Brisbourne) *chsd ldrs: led on bit wl ins fnl f: rdn out* **3/1**[2]

2563 **2** *¾* **Locum**[47] 3960 6-9-3 **56**........................... CharlesEddery 6 62
(Mark H Tompkins) *dwlt: hld up: hdwy over 3f out: rdn to ld over 1f out: hdd and unable qck wl ins fnl f* **5/1**

4662 **3** *hd* **Derby Desire (IRE)**[13] 5116 7-8-0 **46**........................... RichardOld(7) 7 51
(Des Donovan) *chsd ldrs: led 3f out: rdn and hdd over 1f out: styd on* **9/2**[3]

5635 **4** *2 ½* **Olimamu (IRE)**[20] 4869 4-8-11 **50**...........................(t) AntiocoMurgia 5 50
(Lydia Pearce) *sn chsng ldr: ev ch over 2f out: sn rdn: no ex ins fnl f* **11/4**[1]

000 **5** *1 ½* **Visions Of Johanna (USA)**[33] 4408 6-9-4 **60**...............(p) LukeRowe(3) 3 57
(Richard Guest) *hld up: hdwy 2f out: rdn over 1f out: no ex fnl f* **9/1**

550- **6** *17* **Storming Redd**[263] 7760 4-8-11 **50**........................... CharlesBishop 1 13
([illegible]) *led at stdy pce: pckd over 3f out: sn hdd: wknd 2f out* **11/2**

2m 18.75s (8.25) **Going Correction** +0.325s/f (Good) **6** Ran SP% **111.9**
Speed ratings (Par 101): **80,79,79,77,76 62**
toteswingers: 1&2 £2.30, 1&3 £3.30, 2&3 £2.30. Totesuper7: Win: Not won; Place: £370.30 CSF £17.90 TOTE £3.30: £1.40, £2.40; EX 11.60.
Owner Mark Brisbourne **Bred** Yeomanstown Stud **Trained** Great Ness, Shropshire

FOCUS
A poor finale, weakened by the withdrawal of the likely favourite.
T/Plt: £690.00 to a £1 stake. Pool: £67,912.35. 71.84 winning tickets. T/Qpdt: £32.10 to a £1 stake. Pool: £5,789.07. 133.45 winning tickets. CR

5521 - (Foreign Racing) - See Raceform Interactive

[5289]CURRAGH (R-H)
Sunday, August 28

OFFICIAL GOING: Good (good to firm in places on round course)

5522a GO AND GO ROUND TOWER STKS (GROUP 3) 6f
2:45 (2:45) 2-Y-0 **£29,418** (£8,599; £4,073; £1,357)

RPR
1 **Lightening Pearl (IRE)**[21] 4833 2-8-12 107........................... JMurtagh 7 111+
(G M Lyons, Ire) *a.p: led over 2f out: asserted over 1f out: styd on strly to draw clr fnl f: easily* **6/4**[1]

2 *5* **Experience (IRE)**[8] 5290 2-9-1 99........................... WJLee 6 99
(David Wachman, Ire) *hld up in rr: wnt 4th 2f out: no imp on wnr fr over 1f out: kpt on one pce to go 2nd ins fnl f* **9/2**[3]

3 *¾* **An Ghalanta (IRE)**[8] 5290 2-8-12 97...........................(t) KJManning 3 94
(J S Bolger, Ire) *trckd ldrs in 3rd: 2nd and no imp on wnr fr wl over 1f out: kpt on one pce* **4/1**[2]

4 *3* **Boris Grigoriev (IRE)**[8] 5290 2-9-1 99...............(b) SeamieHeffernan 2 88
(A P O'Brien, Ire) *chsd ldrs on stands' side rail: 4th 1/2-way: sn drvn along: no imp and kpt on one pce fr wl over 1f out* **9/2**[3]

5 *2 ½* **Captain Obvious (IRE)**[53] 3748 2-9-1........................... WMLordan 1 80
(David Wachman, Ire) *chsd ldrs on outer: 5th 1/2-way: no threat fr 1 1/2f out* **15/2**

6 *½* **Lady Pastrana (IRE)**[23] 4770 2-8-12 84........................... NGMcCullagh 5 76
(B P Galvin, Ire) *led: strly pressed and hdd over 2f out: sn no ex: wknd* **33/1**

1m 11.17s (-3.83) **Going Correction** -0.50s/f (Hard) **6** Ran SP% **111.1**
Speed ratings: **105,98,97,93,90 89**
CSF £8.39 TOTE £2.30: £1.50, £2.30; DF 10.60.
Owner Pearl Bloodstock Ltd **Bred** Castlemartin Stud And Skymarc Farm **Trained** Dunsany, Co. Meath

FOCUS
The winner was entitled to prevail given that she was rated well above her rivals but she produced an impressive display. The level of the form is solid.

NOTEBOOK
Lightening Pearl(IRE) ◆ was entitled to win this race well and was deeply impressive. Content to take a lead, she went to the front inside the 2f pole and when asked to quicken nothing could live with her. Her trainer was of the opinion she needs at least 7f. Whether what he saw here will lead to a change of opinion remains to be seen, but if she produced this sort of toe over the extra furlong she would be close to the highest class. She's probably a bit unlucky to be around in a particularly strong year for juvenile fillies. Winning trainer Ger Lyons: "She was unlucky not to be second in the Debutante Stakes when she was beaten by a very good filly [Maybe]. I think the fillies are better than the colts this year. She's now Group 2-placed and a Group 3 winner, she's done all we've asked of her. She's in the Cheveley Park and the Redcar 2-y-o Trophy, we'll sit down and have a think about it." (op 6/4 tchd 11/8)
Experience(IRE) went some way towards putting a couple of sub-standard displays behind her. Held up, she started to make up her ground inside the final 2f, and while the winner got first run, she couldn't lay a glove on her and was well beaten. She did keep on to pretty decent effect, though. (op 6/1)
An Ghalanta(IRE) was also well beaten but there wouldn't be much to suggest she ran below her mark. Tracking the pace, she couldn't quicken with the winner over 1f out and kept on at the same pace inside the last. (op 7/2)
Boris Grigoriev(IRE) was in a reasonable position from which to challenge at halfway but was left behind when they quickened. (op 7/2)
Captain Obvious(IRE) may want a bit further. He was struggling a bit to go the pace at halfway and looked one-paced in this company over this trip. (op 13/2 tchd 8/1)
Lady Pastrana(IRE) faded badly once headed inside the last 2f as she ran about as well as she was entitled to. (op 33/1 tchd 50/1)

5523a DANCE DESIGN STKS (GROUP 3) (F&M) 1m 1f
3:15 (3:16) 3-Y-0+ **£37,823** (£11,056; £5,237; £1,745)

RPR
1 **Bible Belt (IRE)**[18] 4936 3-8-12 111........................... FMBerry 2 111+
(Mrs John Harrington, Ire) *settled in mid-div: 8th 1/2-way: nt clr run and swtchd lft 2f out: gd hdwy to ld 1f out: kpt on wl ins fnl f* **15/8**[1]

2 *1 ¼* **Wild Wind (GER)**[5] 5361 3-8-12 103........................... CO'Donoghue 10 108
(A P O'Brien, Ire) *settled in rr of mid-div: gd hdwy on outer to go 2nd 1f out: no imp on wnr ins fnl f: kpt on same pce* **5/1**[2]

3 *¾* **Look At Me (IRE)**[10] 5228 3-8-12 101........................... WJSupple 11 106
(A P O'Brien, Ire) *hld up in rr: gd hdwy between horses fr early st: chal 1f out: sn no imp and kpt on one pce* **20/1**

4 *2* **Obama Rule (IRE)**[29] 4566 4-9-5 98........................... JPO'Brien 3 102
(Ms Joanna Morgan, Ire) *hld up towards rr: hdwy into 6th 1f out: kpt on same pce ins fnl f* **20/1**

5 *shd* **Blaze Brightly (IRE)**[28] 4588 4-9-5 100........................... KLatham 13 102
(Mrs John Harrington, Ire) *hld up towards rr: hdwy on outer early st: 7th 1f out: kpt on one pce* **33/1**

6 *1 ½* **Marvada (IRE)**[5] 5361 3-8-12 95........................... ShaneFoley 15 99
(K J Condon, Ire) *mid-div: 9th ent st: drvn along in 5th over 1f out: no imp ins fnl f* **16/1**

7 *nk* **Duchess Of Foxland (IRE)**[5] 5361 4-9-5 98................. EJMcNamara 1 98
(Mark L Fagan, Ire) *trckd ldrs on inner: 6th appr st: short of room and swtchd lft under 2f out: 9th over 1f out: kpt on one pce* **50/1**

8 *shd* **One Spirit (IRE)**[18] 4936 3-8-12 98........................... NGMcCullagh 7 98
(F Dunne, Ire) *trckd ldrs: 5th 1/2-way: hdwy to chal ent st: led 2f out: strly pressed and hdd 1f out: no ex ins fnl f* **20/1**

9 *8* **Primevere (IRE)**[18] 4915 3-8-12........................... KJManning 4 81
(Roger Charlton) *trckd ldrs: 3rd 1/2-way: no imp fr wl over 1f out: wknd fnl f* **11/2**[3]

10 *2* **Contredanse (IRE)**[37] 4293 4-9-5........................... KirstyMilczarek 9 77
(Luca Cumani) *in rr of mid-div: reminders on outer 1/2-way: no threat fr under 2f out* **10/1**

11 *shd* **Gemstone (IRE)**[21] 4831 3-8-12 106........................... WJLee 16 77
(A P O'Brien, Ire) *chsd ldrs on outer: 6th 1/2-way: no ex fr wl over 1f out* **28/1**

12 *1 ¾* **Field Day (IRE)**[29] 4533 4-9-5...........................(t) PJSmullen 5 73
(Brian Meehan) *prom: 2nd 1/2-way: led briefly early st: hdd 2f out: sn no ex and wknd* **12/1**

13 *2* **Aoife Alainn (IRE)**[21] 4831 4-9-5 108..................... SeamieHeffernan 12 69
(Tracey Collins, Ire) *trckd ldrs: 4th 1/2-way: drvn along ent st: no ex fr 2f out* **20/1**

14 *2 ½* **Good Time Sue (IRE)**[10] 5226 7-9-5 86...........................(t) GFCarroll 14 64
(Ms M Dowdall Blake, Ire) *chsd ldrs: 9th appr st: no ex fr 2f out* **66/1**

15 *9* **Haziyna (IRE)**[28] 4589 3-8-12 102...........................(p) JMurtagh 8 45
(John M Oxx, Ire) *led: strly pressed and hdd early st: no ex fr 1 1/2f out: wknd* **8/1**

1m 55.48s (0.58) **Going Correction** +0.25s/f (Good)
WFA 3 from 4yo+ 7lb **15** Ran SP% **129.5**
Speed ratings: **107,105,105,103,103 102,101,101,94,92 92,91,89,87,79**
CSF £10.03 TOTE £2.50: £1.50, £2.00, £8.60; DF 13.90.
Owner Anamoine Limited **Bred** Anamoine Ltd **Trained** Moone, Co Kildare

FOCUS
The form generally looks sound but the third is a bit dubious.

NOTEBOOK
Bible Belt(IRE) apparently wasn't travelling that well early on but when asked for her effort in the straight quickened up smartly. With her ears pricked inside the last, it was obvious she had plenty left should it have been required. It wasn't. She's better than a Group 3 performer on this evidence and it wouldn't be a surprise should she be a Group 1 filly later in the autumn, maybe in time for a Sun Chariot or a Prix de l'Opera bid. At her rate of progress anything is possible. (op 9/4)
Wild Wind(GER) had come back to form at Killarney during the week and ran at least equally as well here. Held up, she followed the winner through with her run and that sort of momentum would have been more than good enough on another day. She was beaten by a better filly and there was no disgrace. (op 6/1)
Look At Me(IRE) made good ground to get into contention 1f from the finish but her effort flattened out late as the first two went past. It is a run that will provide encouragement.
Obama Rule(IRE) faced a stiffer task this time but probably ran a better race. She was never a factor but stayed on to be nearest at the death.
Blaze Brightly(IRE) kept going well from mid-division. (op 25/1)
Marvada(IRE) challenged briefly in the straight until her effort ran out of steam.
Duchess Of Foxland(IRE) ran a reasonably encouraging race.

Contredanse(IRE) Official explanation: jockey said filly never travelled
Haziyna(IRE) Official explanation: jockey said filly ran keenly throughout

5524a MARKET SLIDE FLYING FIVE STKS (GROUP 3) 5f
3:50 (3:50) 3-Y-O+ **£32,219** (£9,418; £4,461; £1,487)

RPR

1 **Amour Propre**[31] 4468 5-9-3 .... DaneO'Neill 4 114
(Henry Candy) *a.p: disp ld 1/2-way: led 1f out: drvn out and kpt on wl ins fnl f* **15/8**[1]

2 *1 3/4* **Sole Power**[23] 4768 4-9-8 117 .... KLatham 9 113
(Edward Lynam, Ire) *prom on stands' side rail: disp ld 1/2-way: hdd wl over 1f out: no imp on wnr ins fnl f: kpt on same pce* **5/1**[3]

3 *nk* **Roicead (USA)**[6] 5331 4-9-3 108 ....(t) WJSupple 5 107
(Brendan W Duke, Ire) *led early and a.p: jnd 1/2-way: hdd u.p 1f out: no imp on wnr ins fnl f* **7/2**[2]

4 *1* **Move In Time**[23] 4768 3-9-1 .... TomEaves 1 103
(Bryan Smart) *chsd ldrs: 4th 2f out: no imp u.p over 1f out: kpt on one pce* **8/1**

5 *1 1/4* **Invincible Ash (IRE)**[23] 4768 6-9-3 107 ....(p) GFCarroll 8 99
(M Halford, Ire) *chsd ldrs: 6th 1/2-way: no imp u.p over 1f out: kpt on one pce* **8/1**

6 *nk* **Celerina (IRE)**[23] 4768 4-9-0 100 .... WMLordan 6 94
(T Stack, Ire) *chsd ldrs: 5th 2f out: rdn and sn no imp: kpt on one pce* **14/1**

7 *1 1/4* **Empowering (IRE)**[21] 4836 3-9-1 103 .... JPO'Brien 3 93
(A P O'Brien, Ire) *chsd ldrs on outer: 7th 1/2-way: no threat fr under 2f out* **7/1**

8 *2* **Anadolu (IRE)**[6] 5331 3-9-12 90 ....(b) MCHussey 7 83
(Tracey Collins, Ire) *a bhd: nvr a factor* **33/1**

58.34 secs (-4.16) **Going Correction** -0.50s/f (Hard)
WFA 3 from 4yo+ 2lb **8** Ran SP% **118.0**
Speed ratings: **113,110,109,108,106 105,103,100**
CSF £12.08 TOTE £2.60: £1.02, £1.90, £1.60; DF 10.70.
Owner Simon Broke And Partners **Bred** Mrs Sheila Oakes **Trained** Kingston Warren, Oxon

FOCUS
British stables continued their dominance of this particular race. Amour Propre got closer to his 2009 form and Sole Power produced his best run outside his two British wins.

NOTEBOOK
Amour Propre, always in the first three, he sustained his effort from over 1f out and kept on strongly all the way to the line. He's been a good and honest performer this season and this was a deserved success and a good opportunity. (op 2/1 tchd 7/4)
Sole Power has been an enigma this season and possibly saves his best for the best company. He showed great speed towards the stands' rail and, while he couldn't really pick up when the winner went on, he stuck at it well enough to suggest his season might not be over yet. (op 4/1)
Roicead(USA) performed with great credit. He was up there the whole way and did sustain his effort inside the last furlong, but in this company that wasn't quite enough. Perhaps an extra furlong might suit him better in stakes company. (op 5/1)
Move In Time ran on reasonably well but could never get on terms, having been waited with in mid-division. (op 8/1 tchd 9/1)
Invincible Ash(IRE) managed to get herself back into contention after a slightly tardy start but in the end wasn't able to sustain her effort inside the last furlong. Official explanation: trainer said mare showed signs of being in season post-race (op 7/1)

5525a MOYGLARE STUD STKS (GROUP 1) (FILLIES) 7f
4:25 (4:25) 2-Y-O **£112,500** (£36,853; £17,456; £5,818; £3,879; £1,939)

RPR

1 **Maybe (IRE)**[21] 4833 2-9-1 113 ow1 .... JPO'Brien 8 114+
(A P O'Brien, Ire) *trckd ldr in 2nd: travelling best to ld 2f out: sn rdn to assert: drvn out and kpt on wl fnl f* **8/13**[1]

2 *1 3/4* **Fire Lily (IRE)**[10] 5217 2-9-0 105 .... WMLordan 9 109+
(David Wachman, Ire) *trckd ldrs: 6th 1/2-way: 4th 2f out: rdn to go 2nd over 1f out: kpt on u.p but no imp on wnr fnl f* **8/1**[3]

3 *3* **La Collina (IRE)**[21] 4834 2-9-0 114 .... DPMcDonogh 4 102
(Kevin Prendergast, Ire) *broke wl and settled to trck ldrs: 4th 1/2-way: rdn over 2f out: no imp in 4th over 1f out: kpt on one pce fnl f* **3/1**[2]

4 *shd* **Rubina (IRE)**[21] 4833 2-9-0 .... JMurtagh 5 101
(John M Oxx, Ire) *chsd ldrs: 5th 1/2-way: no imp u.p 1 1/2f out: kpt on one pce fnl f* **16/1**

5 *shd* **Princess Sinead (IRE)**[64] 3415 2-9-0 99 .... FMBerry 10 101
(Mrs John Harrington, Ire) *trckd ldrs: 3rd 1/2-way: 2nd and rdn 2f out: sn no imp on wnr: no ex ins fnl f* **12/1**

6 *3/4* **Teolane (IRE)**[21] 4833 2-9-0 104 .... KJManning 11 99
(J S Bolger, Ire) *towards rr: drvn along 3f out: kpt on one pce u.p fr over 1f out* **25/1**

7 *nk* **Criostal (IRE)**[9] 5256 2-9-0 ....(t) RPCleary 2 98
(J S Bolger, Ire) *a bhd: no threat fr over 2f out: kpt on one pce* **100/1**

8 *8* **Soon (IRE)**[8] 5292 2-9-0 99 .... SeamieHeffernan 1 93+
(A P O'Brien, Ire) *led: hdd 2f out: sn no ex: eased whn btn fnl f* **33/1**

1m 24.26s (-6.54) **Going Correction** -0.80s/f (Hard) **8** Ran SP% **119.4**
Speed ratings: **105,103,99,99,99 98,98,89**
CSF £7.13 TOTE £1.50: £1.02, £2.30, £2.40; DF 7.90.
Owner Michael Tabor **Bred** Epona Bloodstock Ltd **Trained** Ballydoyle, Co Tipperary

FOCUS
A contest worthy of its Group 1 billing witnessed another smart performance by Maybe. She is holding her form really well and did not need to improve much. La Collina was below her Phoenix Stakes form.

NOTEBOOK
Maybe(IRE) ◆ is now unbeaten in five starts and will finish the season as a leading 1,000 Guineas candidate providing she negotiates a final juvenile engagement. That is likely to be in either the Prix Marcel Boussac, won last year by the stable's Misty For Me after landing this prize, or the Fillies' Mile at Ascot. The pacemaker fulfilled her role, and the Galileo filly, who has now won successively at each level of the Pattern since triumphing in the Chesham Stakes, took control of the race through the final quarter-mile. She takes her racing well and should continue to thrive. Aidan O'Brien, winning trainer: "She is very uncomplicated. She goes her own pace and picks up when she wants. She has gears and everything went smoothly". (op 8/11)
Fire Lily(IRE) finished a bit closer than when she was second to the unbeaten Queen Mary winner Best Terms in the Lowther, but it would be unwise to base any firm conclusions on a differential that is marginal. One thing is fairly sure, Fire Lily has now run up against both of the best two juvenile fillies in Britain and Ireland.
La Collina(IRE) was beaten quite comprehensively in third this time against Maybe, who had beaten her a neck last time. It certainly looked as if she ran below the level of her last run.
Rubina(IRE)'s running was broadly in line with her fourth place behind Maybe in the Debutante Stakes at the venue three weeks ago.
Princess Sinead(IRE) weakened after failing to get to grips when the winner began to raise the tempo.
Teolane(IRE) has been worryingly regressive since beating Princess Sinead at Naas in early June and this was a further disappointment.
Criostal(IRE) was out of her depth in this company.

5526 - 5527a (Foreign Racing) - See Raceform Interactive

5497 BADEN-BADEN (L-H)
Sunday, August 28

OFFICIAL GOING: Turf: soft

5528a BESTWETTEN.DE GOLDENE PEITSCHE (GROUP 2) (3YO+) (TURF) 6f
3:50 (12:00) 3-Y-O+

£34,482 (£13,362; £5,603; £3,448; £2,155; £1,293)

RPR

1 **Silverside (USA)**[31] 4483 5-9-4 0 .... JulienGrosjean 6 111
(F Sanchez, France) *broke fast: a.p: chal and tk ld 2f out: r.o wl: drew clr ins fnl f* **173/10**

2 *2 1/2* **Smooth Operator (GER)**[21] 4838 5-9-4 0 ....(b) THellier 10 103
(Mario Hofer, Germany) *broke fast: racd promly: r.o wl in st: led briefly 2 1/2f out: kpt on wl fnl f but no ch w wnr* **3/1**[3]

3 *hd* **Clairvoyance (IRE)**[60] 3531 4-9-1 0 .... FilipMinarik 5 99
(H-A Pantall, France) *hld up bhd: produced to chal in st: shkn up: qcknd wl 1 1/2f out: fin wl* **66/10**

4 *1* **Rose Blossom**[14] 5080 4-9-1 0 .... PaulHanagan 9 96
(Richard Fahey) *broke slowly: flattered briefly in st but r.o one pce fnl 1 1/2f* **13/5**[2]

5 *nse* **Aslana (IRE)**[7] 4-9-1 0 .... AStarke 2 96
(P Schiergen, Germany) *bkmarker fr s: swung wd into st: qcknd wl ent fnl f: nrest at fin* **94/10**

6 *nk* **Amico Fritz (GER)**[50] 3863 5-9-4 0 .... FabriceVeron 7 98
(H-A Pantall, France) *broke wl to ld: rdn ent st: hdd 2 1/2f out: sn wknd* **9/5**[1]

7 *hd* **Golden Eagle**[43] 4121 5-9-4 0 .... EPedroza 8 97
(A Savujev, Czech Republic) *broke slowly: hld up in midfield: nvr threatened* **116/10**

8 *1 1/4* **Mood Music**[35] 7-9-4 0 ....(b) AHelfenbein 4 93
(Mario Hofer, Germany) *hld up bhd: r.o wl ent st but sn wknd* **14/1**

69.61 secs (-0.68) **8** Ran SP% **131.3**
WIN (incl. 10 euro stake): 183. PLACES: 43, 19, 23. SF: 863.
Owner Safsaf Canarias Srl **Bred** Edward P Evans **Trained** France

NOTEBOOK
Silverside(USA), who stays further than this, drew clear in the closing stages for a cosy success. He could well come over to Ascot on Champions Day next.
Rose Blossom didn't have ground conditions to suit and wasn't best away following problems removing her blindfold at the start.

5463 DEAUVILLE (R-H)
Sunday, August 28

OFFICIAL GOING: Turf: very soft; fibresand: standard

5529a PRIX HOTEL NORMANDY BARRIERE DE DEAUVILLE (CLAIMER) (3YO COLTS & GELDINGS) (FIBRESAND) 7f 110y
12:30 (12:00) 3-Y-O **£9,051** (£3,620; £2,715; £1,810; £905)

RPR

1 **Jag War (FR)**[24] 3-8-9 0 .... MaximeGuyon 13 60
(H-A Pantall, France) **10/1**

2 *hd* **Rovos (FR)**[23] 3-8-8 0 .... TheoBachelot[(6)] 6 64
(S Wattel, France) **63/10**[3]

3 *nk* **Beautiful Lando (FR)**[18] 4908 3-9-0 0 ....(b) OlivierPeslier 1 63
(Heather Main) *sn led: hld clr ld 1 1/2f out: hdd wl ins fnl f: r.o* **11/1**

4 *1/2* **Moncofar (IRE)**[28] 3-8-2 0 .... ThomasHenderson[(7)] 7 57
(J-C Rouget, France) **2/1**[1]

5 *1/2* **Nova Valorem (IRE)**[11] 3-8-13 0 ....(p) Francois-XavierBertras 11 60
(F Rohaut, France) **5/1**[2]

6 *nse* **Mister Segway (IRE)**[24] 3-8-4 0 ....(b) EddyHardouin[(5)] 5 56
(Robert Collet, France) **42/1**

7 *3* **Domino Rock (FR)**[35] 3-9-2 0 ....(p) Christophe-PatriceLemaire 8 55
(C Boutin, France) **14/1**

8 *snk* **Mister Par Coeur (FR)**[110] 3-9-3 0 .... MatthieuAutier[(3)] 12 59
(D Allard, France) **49/1**

9 *1 1/2* **Andreino (IRE)**[28] 3-8-9 0 .... IoritzMendizabal 4 44
(G Botti, Italy) **9/1**

10 *1/2* **Valerius Maximus**[14] 3-8-7 0 .... MathieuTavaresDaSilva[(6)] 2 47
(F Doumen, France) **45/1**

0 **Prime Preacher (USA)**[170] 3-8-9 0 .... Roberto-CarlosMontenegro 14 —
(X Thomas-Demeaulte, France) **34/1**

0 **Bread Loft (FR)**[24] 3-8-9 0 .... AlexisBadel 3 —
(Mme M Bollack-Badel, France) **26/1**

0 **Flying Tomato (FR)**[35] 3-8-13 0 ....(p) SylvainRuis 10 —
(T Lemer, France) **33/1**

0 **Undeux Croixnoire (FR)** 3-9-2 0 .... JohanVictoire 9 —
(C Baillet, France) **25/1**

1m 31.3s (91.30) **14** Ran SP% **117.6**
WIN (incl. 1 euro stake): 11.00. PLACES: 3.50, 2.50, 4.60. DF: 27.30. SF: 73.80.
Owner Erich Schmid **Bred** E Schmid **Trained** France

5530a PRIX QUINCEY LUCIEN BARRIERE (GROUP 3) (3YO+) (TURF) 1m (R)
1:30 (12:00) 3-Y-O+ **£34,482** (£13,793; £10,344; £6,896; £3,448)

RPR

1 **Zinabaa (FR)**[39] 4223 6-9-0 0 .... YannickLetondeur 4 111
(M Mace, France) *a.p: effrt and chsd ldr over 1f out: kpt on wl u.p fnl f: led towards fin* **14/1**

2 *snk* **Sandy's Charm (FR)**[16] 5028 3-8-11 0 .... Francois-XavierBertras 5 113
(F Rohaut, France) *led at ordinary gallop: pushed along and qcknd over 1f out: rdn and edgd rt ins fnl f: kpt on: hdd towards fin* **15/8**[1]

3 *1 1/2* **African Story**[57] 3654 4-9-2 0 .... MaximeGuyon 1 109
(A Fabre, France) *hld up in tch: niggled along over 3f out: effrt and drvn over 2f out: kpt on fnl f: nt rch first two* **5/2**[2]

4 *nk* **Salto (IRE)**[21] 3-8-10 0.. OlivierPeslier 2 108
(F Head, France) *hld up off ordinary gallop: rdn and hdwy over 1f out: kpt on fnl f: nvr able to chal* **4/1**[3]

5 *hd* **Big Hunter (FR)**[21] 4-9-0 0....................................(p) MickaelBarzalona 6 106
(E Kurdu, Germany) *t.k.h: hld up towards rr in r run at ordinary gallop: rdn and hdwy over 1f out: kpt on fnl f* **25/1**

6 *2 ½* **Unnefer (FR)**[77] 2980 6-9-0 0.................................... StephanePasquier 9 100
(P Bary, France) *stdd s: hld up last off ordinary gallop: rdn along 2f out: kpt on fnl f: nvr able to chal* **8/1**

7 *1 ½* **Handsome Maestro (IRE)**[11] 5195 5-9-0 0............. SebastienMaillot 7 97
(Robert Collet, France) *t.k.h: trckd ldr tl rdn: edgd rt and wknd over 1f out* **22/1**

8 *1 ½* **Garde Slickly (FR)**[35] 3-8-8 0.. ThierryJarnet 8 92
(Mlle Valerie Boussin, France) *hld up off ordinary gallop: rdn and edgd rt wl over 1f out: sn wknd* **20/1**

9 *20* **Usbeke (GER)**[21] 5-9-0 0..(b[1]) ThierryThulliez 3 47
(J-P Carvalho, Germany) *trckd ldrs: drvn along over 2f out: sn wknd* **16/1**

1m 39.5s (-1.30) **Going Correction** +0.175s/f (Good)
WFA 3 from 4yo+ 6lb **9** Ran SP% **120.0**
Speed ratings: **113,112,111,111,110 108,106,105,85**
WIN (incl. 1 euro stake): 15.10. PLACES: 2.00, 1.20, 1.30. DF: 14.50. SF: 51.40.
Owner Ecurie Victoria Dreams **Bred** Mlle V Dubois, J Dubois & E Dubois **Trained** France

5531a LUCIEN BARRIERE GRAND PRIX DE DEAUVILLE (GROUP 2) (3YO+) (TURF) 1m 4f 110y

2:40 (12:00) 3-Y-0+ **£98,275** (£37,931; £18,103; £12,068; £6,034)

RPR

1 **Cirrus Des Aigles (FR)**[14] 5094 5-9-6 0........................ FranckBlondel 4 125+
(Mme C Barande-Barbe, France) *racd wd: pressed ldr: taken to outside rail in bk st: overall ldr 1/2-way: shkn up and qcknd clr fr 2f out: readily* **1/2**[1]

2 *10* **Silver Pond (FR)**[63] 3448 4-9-6 0.................................... OlivierPeslier 2 111
(C Laffon-Parias, France) *trckd ldrs: styd cl to ins rail thrght: effrt and chsd (clr) wnr over 1f out: kpt on ins fnl f: no imp* **9/2**[2]

3 *shd* **Marinous (FR)**[7] 5304 5-9-3 0.......................................(b) ThierryJarnet 6 108
(F Head, France) *t.k.h: hld up in tch: taken to outside rail in bk st: effrt and disp 2nd pl whn carried hd high and hung rt over 1f out: kpt on same pce fnl f* **12/1**

4 *5* **Ted Spread**[8] 5285 4-9-3 0.......................... Christophe-PatriceLemaire 1 100
(Mark H Tompkins) *led at ordinary gallop: styd cl to ins rail thrght: hdd 1/2-way: chsd wnr tl rdn and wknd over 1f out* **20/1**

5 *½* **Agent Secret (IRE)**[39] 4223 5-9-3 0................. Francois-XavierBertras 5 99
(F Rohaut, France) *t.k.h: cl up on outside: taken to outside rail in bk st: effrt and chsd (clr) wnr briefly over 1f out: wknd fnl f* **14/1**

6 *dist* **Ivory Land (FR)**[84] 2753 4-9-3 0.......................... ChristopheSoumillon 3 —
(A De Royer-Dupre, France) *in tch: taken to outside rail in bk st: rdn over 3f out: wknd 2f out: sn lost tch and eased* **8/1**[3]

2m 45.0s (-1.40) **Going Correction** +0.175s/f (Good) **6** Ran SP% **115.1**
Speed ratings: **111,104,104,101,101** —
WIN (incl. 1 euro stake): 1.40. PLACES: 1.10, 1.50. SF: 2.80.
Owner Jean-Claude-Alain Dupouy **Bred** Y Lelimouzin And B Deschamps **Trained** France

NOTEBOOK
Cirrus Des Aigles(FR) would have won his last five starts had he not bumped into Sarafina in the Grand Prix de Saint-Cloud back in June, and he showed here that he gets 1m4f well, even in testing ground. The Prix Dollar at Longchamp on October 1 could be next up for him, with the Champion Stakes at Ascot two weeks later also a possibility.

5532a PRIX DE MEAUTRY LUCIEN BARRIERE (GROUP 3) (3YO+) (TURF) 6f

3:10 (12:00) 3-Y-0+ **£34,482** (£13,793; £10,344; £6,896; £3,448)

RPR

1 **Marchand D'Or (FR)**[21] 4838 8-9-1 0................................ DavyBonilla 4 107
(M Delzangles, France) *s.i.s: hld up: gd hdwy over 1f out: rdn to ld ins fnl f: kpt on wl* **11/4**[1]

2 *½* **Definightly**[71] 3154 5-9-1 0..(b) ThierryThulliez 10 [illegible]
(Roger Charlton) *t.k.h: led: rdn 2f out: hdd ins fnl f: kpt on u.p towards fin* **17/2**

3 *nk* **Le Valentin (FR)**[24] 4739 5-9-1 0................................ AnthonyCrastus 6 104
(Y De Nicolay, France) *hld up towards rr nr side: effrt and edgd rt over 1f out: kpt on strly fnl f: nrst fin* **20/1**

4 *1 ½* **Fred Lalloupet**[43] 4121 4-9-1 0...................................... OlivierPeslier 2 99
(D Smaga, France) *hld up towards nr side: rdn and gd hdwy fnl f: kpt on: nrst fin* **12/1**

5 *shd* **Morache Music**[22] 4779 3-8-11 0.......................... ChristopheSoumillon 7 98
(Peter Makin) *midfield: drvn and outpcd over 2f out: rallied u.p fnl f: kpt on: nt pce to chal* **7/1**[3]

6 *shd* **Stark Danon (FR)**[28] 3-8-11 0.. RonanThomas 13 98
(W Hickst, Germany) *trckd ldrs: drvn along over 2f out: kpt on same pce ins fnl f* **14/1**

7 *shd* **Nuit De Glace (FR)**[8] 7-8-11 0.................................... SebastienMaillot 9 94?
(Mlle Valerie Boussin, France) *hld up: effrt and rdn over 1f out: kpt on ins fnl f: nvr able to chal* **33/1**

8 *nk* **Time Prisoner (USA)**[43] 4121 4-9-5 0........................ MaximeGuyon 14 101
(A Fabre, France) *prom: effrt and drvn over 2f out: edgd rt over 1f out: kpt on same pce fnl f* **13/2**[2]

9 *½* **Split Trois (FR)**[21] 4838 3-8-8 0........................... Pierre-CharlesBoudot 5 92
(Y De Nicolay, France) *hld up and bhd: pushed along whn n.m.r briefly appr fnl f: kpt on fnl f: no imp* **12/1**

10 *nk* **Rock Jock (IRE)**[28] 4573 4-9-1 0.. PShanahan 11 95
(Tracey Collins, Ire) *in tch: rdn over 2f out: edgd rt over 1f out: sn btn* **14/1**

0 **Mariol (FR)**[8] 8-9-1 0.. IoritzMendizabal 3 —
(Robert Collet, France) *hld up and bhd: pushed along over 1f out: kpt on fnl f: nvr on terms* **22/1**

0 **Bluster (FR)**[7] 5-9-1 0................................ Christophe-PatriceLemaire 15 —
(Robert Collet, France) *in tch: drvn over 2f out: wknd over 1f out: eased whn btn ins fnl f* **20/1**

0 **Chopouest (FR)**[110] 4-9-1 0.......................................(b[1]) FredericSpanu 1 —
(A Spanu, France) *dwlt: sn prom on outside of gp: rdn 2f out: sn wknd: eased whn no ch fnl f* **40/1**

0 **Poppet's Treasure**[35] 4-8-11 0.. GeraldMosse 16 —
(R Pritchard-Gordon, France) *plld hrd: hld up on outside of gp: rdn and wknd wl over 1f out: eased whn no ch ins fnl f* **25/1**

0 **Izalia (FR)**[49] 3898 3-8-8 0.. FranckBlondel 8 —
(F Rossi, France) *trckd ldrs: rdn over 2f out: wkng whn checked over 1f out: eased and lost tch fnl f* **7/1**[3]

1m 12.1s (1.10) **Going Correction** +0.525s/f (Yiel)
WFA 3 from 4yo+ 3lb **15** Ran SP% **127.3**
Speed ratings: **113,112,111,109,109 109,109,109,108,108** —,—,—,—,—
WIN (incl. 1 euro stake): 3.70. PLACES: 1.70, 3.10, 4.50. DF: 17.20. SF: 27.50.
Owner Mme Jean-Louis Giral **Bred** Mme C Giral **Trained** France

FOCUS
A blanket finish.

NOTEBOOK
Marchand D'Or(FR), third in the Maurice de Gheest last time out, found this easier and came with a late rattle to win his first race since May 2010. The Prix de l'Abbaye and the Prix de la Foret will now come under consideration.
Definightly, down the field in the Golden Jubilee last time out, bounced back to form with a solid effort in defeat.

5533 - (Foreign Racing) - See Raceform Interactive

[5374] CHEPSTOW (L-H)

Monday, August 29

OFFICIAL GOING: Good to soft (soft in places; 6.4)
Wind: Moderate across Weather: Overcast

5534 GRAND PIER WESTON-SUPER-MARE APPRENTICE H'CAP 5f 16y

2:05 (2:05) (Class 6) (0-60,60) 3-Y-0+ **£1,617** (£481; £240; £120) **Stalls** Centre

Form RPR

2064 1 **Two Turtle Doves (IRE)**[7] 5309 5-9-4 **60**.................. JosephYoung[(3)] 6 67
(Michael Mullineaux) *trckd ldrs: drvn and qcknd between horses ins fnl f: kpt on u.p to ld cl home* **7/1**

6231 2 *½* **Colourbearer (IRE)**[10] 5244 4-9-5 **58**................................(t) LukeRowe 3 63+
(Milton Bradley) *rrd stalls: sltly hmpd and sn bhd: swtchd lft on outside 2f out and stdy run fr over 1f out: slt ld fnl 120yds: hdd and outpcd cl home* **3/1**[1]

0354 3 *nse* **Festival Dance**[27] 4628 3-9-2 **60**.. IanBurns[(3)] 8 65
(Ron Hodges) *chsd ldrs: chal fr 1/2-way tl slt ld wl over 1f out: jnd ins fnl f and hdd 120yds out: styd on same pce clsng stages* **25/1**

0432 4 *nse* **Madam Isshe**[7] 5326 4-8-13 **52**.. JakePayne 9 57
(Malcolm Saunders) *led: jnd fr 1/2-way: narrowly hdd wl over 1f out: rallied and kpt on fnl 120yds but nt quite pce to chal* **13/2**

6000 5 *2* **Riflessione**[10] 5244 5-9-4 **57**....................................(b) MichaelJMurphy 1 55
(Ronald Harris) *chsd ldrs: rdn over 2f out: wknd ins fnl f* **9/2**[3]

004 6 *½* **Lithaam (IRE)**[19] 4930 7-8-2 **46** oh1......................(tp) BrendanPowell[(5)] 7 42
(Milton Bradley) *outpcd and sn pushed along: sme prog fnl f* **14/1**

7 *1* **Wheatfield (IRE)**[71] 5482 7-8-5 **47** oh1 ow1............(t) ThomasBrown[(3)] 5 39
(Thomas McGivern, Ire) *rdn and outpcd 3f out: nvr in contention after* **16/1**

4503 8 *2 ½* **The Jailer**[11] 5204 8-9-7 **60**..(p) NoelGarbutt 4 43
(John O'Shea) *chsd ldrs: rdn 1/2-way: wknd appr fnl f* **14/1**

0-42 9 *1* **Beachwood Bay**[11] 5206 3-8-7 **55**.............................. JoshBaudains[(7)] 2 35
(Jo Hughes) *chsd ldrs 3f* **4/1**[2]

59.98 secs (0.68) **Going Correction** +0.05s/f (Good)
WFA 3 from 4yo+ 2lb **9** Ran SP% **112.1**
Speed ratings (Par 101): **96,95,95,95,91 91,89,85,83**
toteswingers:1&2:£6.70, 1&3:£29.10, 2&3:£19.90 CSF £27.19 CT £493.42 TOTE £10.20: £4.60, £1.80, £7.20; EX 40.40.
Owner George Cornes **Bred** M Sharkey **Trained** Alpraham, Cheshire

FOCUS
They came stands' side despite the stalls being in the centre. Modewst form, the winner rated back to her best, but the second looked unlucky.

5535 ACTIONGROUP.CO.UK NURSERY 5f 16y

2:40 (2:40) (Class 6) (0-60,64) 2-Y-0 **£1,704** (£503; £251) **Stalls** Centre

Form RPR

4055 1 **First Rebellion**[5] 5374 2-8-8 **45**.. DavidProbert 5 50
(Tony Carroll) *chsesd ldrs: rdn to chal ins fnl f: styd on wl u.p to ld clsng stages: all out* **9/2**[2]

0464 2 *shd* **Thorpe Bay**[19] 4922 2-9-7 **58**.. [illegible] 1 [illegible]
(Mark Rimmer) *chsd ldsers: rdn to chal 1f out: sn led but qckly jnd: kpt slt advantage tl hdd and no ex clsng stages* **7/2**[1]

000 3 *2 ½* **Jawim**[54] 3722 2-8-9 **46** ow1.. SamHitchcott 6 41
(Malcolm Saunders) *chsd ldrs: rdn to take slt ld over 1f out: hdd jst ins fnl f: outpcd by ldng duo fnl 120yds* **16/1**

2354 4 *1 ½* **Emma Jean (IRE)**[5] 5374 2-9-3 **54**.. AdamKirby 9 44
(J S Moore) *s.i.s and n.m.r s: in rr: rdn and hdwy over 1f out: styd on fnl f: nt rch ldrs* **7/2**[1]

5436 5 *¾* **Lady Caprice**[10] 5245 2-9-6 **57**..................................(b) DarryllHolland 11 44
(Ann Duffield) *led after 1f: rdn 2f out: hdd appr fnl f: sn btn* **13/2**[3]

0040 6 *1* **Joli Colourful (IRE)**[5] 5374 2-8-8 **45**.............................. RobertHavlin 3 29
(Tony Newcombe) *disp ld early: styd chsng ldrs: rdn 1/2-way: wknd fnl f* **22/1**

6563 7 *1 ¾* **Russian Bullet**[7] 5316 2-9-2 **53**..................................(b) FergusSweeney 2 30
(Jamie Osborne) *in rr: sn pushed along: sme prog clsng stages* **9/1**

056 8 *2 ¾* **Kathryn Perry (IRE)**[65] 3408 2-9-4 **55**...................... RobbieFitzpatrick 8 23
(Andrew Haynes) *in tch: rdn and btn 1/2-way* **8/1**

6020 9 *4 ½* **Concordia Notte (IRE)**[19] 4922 2-9-3 **54**.......................... JimCrowley 4 —
(Richard Guest) *sn outpcd* **20/1**

660 10 *7* **Professor Tim (IRE)**[35] 4377 2-8-3 **45**.......................... RyanPowell[(5)] 10 —
(Patrick Morris) *s.i.s: a outpcd* **66/1**

60.59 secs (1.29) **Going Correction** +0.05s/f (Good) **10** Ran SP% **113.6**
Speed ratings (Par 92): **91,90,86,84,83 81,78,74,67,56**
toteswingers:1&2:£3.20, 1&3:£12.50, 2&3:£8.60 CSF £19.56 CT £232.88 TOTE £5.80: £2.40, £1.10, £7.50; EX 26.50.
Owner J Dewhurst **Bred** Mayden Stud, J A And D S Dewhurst **Trained** Cropthorne, Worcs

FOCUS
A weak nursery but the time was reasonable and the first three all improved.

NOTEBOOK
First Rebellion had done all of his racing on a sound surface up to now but he has improved for tackling this softer surface and he showed a good attitude under pressure, something he hasn't always done in the past. This isn't strong form though. (op 11-2 tchd 4-1)
Thorpe Bay has also shown improved form and the drop back to this trip worked well. The removal of the headgear he has been wearing recently proved no issue and he looks capable of winning one of these under similar conditions. (op 9-2)
Jawim hadn't showed much on three maiden starts on quick ground, but she fared better here and only gave way in the final furlong. She looks quite speedy so could be interesting over a sharper 5f off a light weight. (op 12-1)

Emma Jean(IRE) is more exposed having had nine previous starts and she didn't really show enough speed to cope with the drop back to the minimum trip. She made good late headway to suggest she'll be seen to better effect back up in trip. (tchd 4-1)

5536 BRITISH STALLION STUDS SUPPORTING BRITISH RACING E B F MAIDEN STKS 1m 14y

3:15 (3:17) (Class 5) 2-Y-O **£3,169** (£943; £471; £235) **Stalls** Centre

Form				RPR
2	**1**		**Kid Suitor (IRE)**[10] [5239] 2-9-0 .... RichardHughes 8 (Richard Hannon) *hld up in tch: shkn up and qckd appr fnl f: led fnl 150yds: edgd lft: readily* **4/7**[1]	80+
00	**2**	*1*	**Hyperlink (IRE)**[30] [4535] 2-9-0 .... DarryllHolland 2 (Mark Johnston) *led: drvn and qcknd 2f out: hdd 150yds out: edgd lft: one pce* **13/2**[3]	78+
0	**3**	*8*	**Wayne Manor (IRE)**[24] [4762] 2-9-0 .... JimCrowley 9 (Ralph Beckett) *chsd ldrs and racd wd 1st 2f: jnd main gp and chsd ldr 3f out: sn rdn: wknd into wl hld 3rd over 1f out* **7/2**[2]	60+
66	**4**	*1 1/2*	**Bathwick Street**[5] [5375] 2-9-0 .... EddieCreighton 7 (David Evans) *chsd ldrs: rdn 1/2-way: no ch w ldrs fnl 2f* **50/1**	57
	5	*2*	**Tushuk Tash (USA)** 2-9-0 .... SamHitchcott 1 (Mick Channon) *s.i.s: green and sn t.o: drvn and hdwy fr 2f out: styng on in clsng stages: nvr a threat* **16/1**	53
0	**6**	*1/2*	**Kingscombe (USA)**[47] [3986] 2-9-0 .... AdamKirby 10 (Pat Eddery) *chsd ldrs: rdn 3f out: wknd 2f out* **25/1**	51
	7	*3/4*	**Khan Of Khans (IRE)** 2-9-0 .... FergusSweeney 5 (Rebecca Curtis) *s.i.s: rdn and in tch 3f out: wknd 2f out* **20/1**	50
00	**8**	*4 1/2*	**Recway Striker**[6] [5337] 2-9-0 .... DavidProbert 4 (Des Donovan) *in rr: rdn 1/2-way: nvr in contention* **100/1**	40
6	**9**	*26*	**Dubai Rythm**[11] [5202] 2-9-0 .... RobbieFitzpatrick 3 (Michael Appleby) *chsd ldr 4f: wknd qckly 3f out* **25/1**	—

1m 36.59s (0.39) **Going Correction** +0.05s/f (Good) **9** Ran SP% **120.5**
Speed ratings (Par 94): **100,99,91,89,87 87,86,81,55**
toteswingers:1&2:£1.90, 1&3:£1.50, 2&3:£2.00 CSF £5.00 TOTE £1.60: £1.02, £1.90, £1.70; EX 5.10.
Owner Byerley Thoroughbred Racing **Bred** Brian Dolan **Trained** East Everleigh, Wilts

FOCUS
No depth to this maiden and the first two pulled a mile clear. The winner built on his good debut.

NOTEBOOK
Kid Suitor(IRE), who shaped with so much promise at Sandown on debut, went one better and although he took a while to master Hyperlink, he was well on top at the finish. He still looks quite green and raw, a point emphasised by Richard Hughes after the race, so having to work for his victory will have done him good and he's a horse for the future. (op 8-15 tchd 4-9, tchd 8-13 in a place)
Hyperlink(IRE) made a bold bid from the front and left his previous two runs a long way behind in keeping on so well. He was different class to everything bar the winner and shouldn't be long in getting off the mark. (op 6-1 tchd 7-1)
Wayne Manor(IRE) was best of the rest, but he was left trailing in the wake of the front two and has only marginally improved on his Newmarket debut. There was plenty of money for him beforehand, suggesting better was expected. (op 13-2)
Tushuk Tash(USA) shaped with some promise in making headway from well off the pace having looked very green early. He is from a decent family and should derive plenty from this initial experience.

5537 BRITISH STALLION STUDS SUPPORTING BRITISH RACING E B F MEDIAN AUCTION MAIDEN FILLIES' STKS 1m 14y

3:50 (3:51) (Class 5) 2-Y-O **£3,169** (£943; £471; £235) **Stalls** Centre

Form				RPR
	1		**Little Dutch Girl** 2-9-0 .... (b[1]) AdamKirby 10 (Clive Cox) *slowly away: green: sn rdn and detached: hdwy u.p 3f out: styd on to chal fnl 75yds: led last strides* **7/2**[2]	73
	2	*hd*	**Good Morning Star (IRE)** 2-9-0 .... DarryllHolland 5 (Mark Johnston) *sn led: rdn and kpt on wl fnl 2f: jnd on either side fnl 75yds: hdd last strides* **13/2**	72
4332	**3**	*nse*	**Roedean (IRE)**[24] [4760] 2-9-0 79 .... RichardHughes 1 (Richard Hannon) *pushed along 3f out: styd on wl fr over 1f out to chal fnl 75yds: styd upsides tl no ex last strides* **6/4**[1]	72
	4	*4 1/2*	**Fleur De La Vie (IRE)** 2-9-0 .... JimCrowley 4 (Ralph Beckett) *t.k.h early: trckd ldrs: pushed along and kpt on fr over 1f out: nt clr run ins fnl f: sn one pce* **4/1**[3]	62+
	5	*2*	**Johanna Fosie (IRE)** 2-9-0 .... SamHitchcott 3 (Mick Channon) *in tch: rdn 3f out: wknd over 1f out* **25/1**	58
	6	*3/4*	**Abundantly** 2-9-0 .... RobertHavlin 8 (Hughie Morrison) *s.i.s: in rr: green and outpcd: hdwy fr 2f out: no imp on ldrs and styd on same pce fnl f* **18/1**	56+
	7	*1 3/4*	**Annaluna (IRE)** 2-9-0 .... EddieCreighton 7 (David Evans) *in rr: rdn and sme prog 3f out: wknd fr 2f out* **40/1**	52
	8	*2 1/4*	**Brundon** 2-9-0 .... FergusSweeney 6 (Henry Candy) *in tch: pushed along and green 3f out: wknd ins fnl 2f* **10/1**	47
0	**9**	*8*	**Kozmina Bay**[47] [3986] 2-8-11 .... MatthewDavies(3) 9 (Jonathan Portman) *in tch: rdn 1/2-way: wknd fr 3f out* **100/1**	30
0	**10**	*36*	**Sammie Fallon (IRE)**[17] [4995] 2-9-0 .... RobbieFitzpatrick 2 (Andrew Haynes) *pressed ldr 4f out: wknd qckly over 3f out: t.o* **100/1**	—

1m 37.35s (1.15) **Going Correction** +0.05s/f (Good) **10** Ran SP% **118.2**
Speed ratings (Par 91): **96,95,95,91,89 88,86,84,76,40**
toteswingers:1&2:£5.10, 1&3:£2.40, 2&3:£3.00 CSF £26.44 TOTE £5.50: £1.50, £2.50, £1.20; EX 44.70.
Owner Mrs Hugh Maitland-Jones **Bred** Mrs Hugh Maitland-Jones **Trained** Lambourn, Berks
■ Stewards' Enquiry : Darryll Holland two-day ban: used whip down shoulder in the forehand (Sep 13-14)

FOCUS
A much more interesting maiden than the previous contest. The third, time and averages set the level.

NOTEBOOK
Little Dutch Girl broke slowly and found herself at the back of the field in the early stages, but she made relentless progress towards the stands' side of the field, responding to all of her rider's urgings to get on top close home. The fact that she was wearing blinkers on debut sounded something of a warning note, but she hails from a family laden with stamina and the further she went the better she looked. She already looks like she'll be even better over further and has a bright future. (op 8-1)
Good Morning Star(IRE) ran a blinder on debut, battling on really bravely with the more experienced Roedean before being collared by the late thrust of Little Dutch Girl. She should have little trouble finding a maiden before going on to better things. (op 9-2)
Roedean(IRE) set quite a useful the standard with an official rating of 77 and it's impossible to knock this effort. She is vulnerable to anything above average in maiden company but is clearly capable of winning races. (op 5-4 tchd 6-5)
Fleur De La Vie(IRE) travelled strongly for a long way and wasn't knocked about in the closing stages. (op 9-2)
Johanna Fosie(IRE) is another who showed ability and looks one for the future. (op 33-1)
Brundon is from a good middle-distance family, but she raced too freely in the early stages. (op 12-1 tchd 14-1)

5538 WYVERN ICES H'CAP 1m 14y

4:25 (4:26) (Class 5) (0-70,69) 3-Y-O+ **£2,264** (£673; £336; £168) **Stalls** Centre

Form				RPR
6002	**1**		**Ashkalara**[18] [4949] 4-9-0 57 .... JimCrowley 9 (Stuart Howe) *in tch: hdwy 3f out: rdn to ld over 1f out: hrd drvn fnl f: in command and pushed out fnl 120yds* **5/2**[1]	69
0245	**2**	*2 1/2*	**Lockantanks**[14] [5101] 4-9-10 67 .... JamesDoyle 2 (Michael Appleby) *in tch: hdwy 3f out: n.m.r ins fnl 2f: styd on u.p fnl f to chse wnr fnl 120yds: no imp* **7/2**[2]	73
-345	**3**	*1*	**Final Verse**[194] [562] 8-9-12 69 .... AdamKirby 5 (Matthew Salaman) *sn ldng main gp in centre and overall ldr ins fnl 3f: rdn 2f out: hdd over 1f out: kpt on same pce* **10/1**	73
3040	**4**	*3*	**My Sister**[18] [4949] 4-8-7 50 .... EddieCreighton 1 (Mark Usher) *chsd ldrs: rdn over 2f out: wknd ins fnl f* **10/1**	47
1010	**5**	*3/4*	**Fleetwoodsands (IRE)**[21] [4866] 4-9-10 67 .... (t) FergusSweeney 12 (Milton Bradley) *t.k.h in rr: hdwy fr 3f out: chsd ldrs fr 2f out: wknd ins fnl f* **18/1**	62
60-4	**6**	*5*	**Omnipotent (IRE)**[37] [4320] 3-9-3 66 .... RichardHughes 8 (Richard Hannon) *chsd ldrs: rdn 3f out: wknd 2f out* **9/2**[3]	50
0065	**7**	*4*	**Luv U Noo**[48] [3944] 4-8-8 51 oh1 ow1 .... RobbieFitzpatrick 4 (Brian Baugh) *s.i.s: in rr: sme prog 2f out: nvr in contention* **9/1**	25
6000	**8**	*hd*	**Safari Guide**[5] [5376] 5-8-9 52 oh3 ow2 .... SamHitchcott 10 (Dai Burchell) *t.k.h: chsd ldrs: rdn and btn 3f out* **40/1**	26
0000	**9**	*12*	**Unbreak My Heart (IRE)**[13] [5149] 6-8-8 58 .... (tp) JakePayne(7) 6 (Richard Guest) *racd alone far side and led overall tl hdd & wknd ins fnl 3f* **20/1**	—
10-0	**10**	*8*	**Callie's Angel**[91] [2550] 3-8-9 58 .... DavidProbert 11 (Bryn Palling) *chsd ldrs 5f* **14/1**	—

1m 36.42s (0.22) **Going Correction** +0.05s/f (Good)
WFA 3 from 4yo+ 6lb **10** Ran SP% **116.3**
Speed ratings (Par 103): **100,97,96,93,92 87,83,83,71,63**
toteswingers:1&2:£4.00, 1&3:£6.70, 2&3:£5.80 CSF £10.98 CT £75.24 TOTE £4.70: £2.30, £2.40, £1.40; EX 14.30.
Owner C R Hollands Industrial Supplies **Bred** R G Levin **Trained** Oakford, Devon

FOCUS
A modest handicap but a decent enough gallop and the form is fairly sound.
Omnipotent(IRE) Official explanation: jockey said colt lost its action

5539 ROBERT MOTTRAM MEMORIAL H'CAP 7f 16y

5:00 (5:00) (Class 6) (0-65,65) 3-Y-O+ **£1,617** (£481; £240; £120) **Stalls** Centre

Form				RPR
3005	**1**		**Cape Kimberley**[13] [5143] 4-9-6 59 .... RobertHavlin 10 (Tony Newcombe) *chsd ldrs: rdn over 2f out: led jst ins fnl f: drvn out* **16/1**	71
131	**2**	*1 1/2*	**Royal Box**[19] [4918] 4-9-5 58 .... (p) KellyHarrison 8 (Dai Burchell) *led: rdn over 2f out: hdd jst ins fnl f: sn one pce but hld on wl for 2nd* **13/2**[2]	66
-604	**3**	*shd*	**Farmers Dream (IRE)**[13] [5143] 4-8-2 46 .... RyanPowell(5) 7 (Richard Price) *in tch: rdn and styd on fr 2f out: kpt on fnl f to cl on 2nd last strides: no imp on wnr* **12/1**	54
0351	**4**	*4*	**Katmai River (IRE)**[11] [5201] 4-9-10 63 .... (v) DavidProbert 3 (Mark Usher) *chsd ldrs towards far side: rdn over 2f out: wknd fnl f* **10/1**	60
2212	**5**	*hd*	**George Thisby**[10] [5231] 5-9-5 65 .... LukeRowe(7) 2 (Rod Millman) *chsd ldrs towards far side: ev ch over 2f out: wknd fnl f* **6/1**[1]	61
0000	**6**	*1*	**Golden Hinde**[5] [5376] 3-9-0 65 .... (p) MichaelJMurphy(7) 13 (Ronald Harris) *in rr: rdn over 3f out: styd on fnl f: nt rch ldrs* **25/1**	57
4046	**7**	*hd*	**Kyllachy Storm**[10] [5231] 7-9-6 62 .... MatthewDavies(3) 6 (Ron Hodges) *in tch: rdn to chse ldrs 3f out: no prog fnl 2f* **33/1**	55
0543	**8**	*1/2*	**Babich Bay (IRE)**[11] [5203] 3-8-13 57 .... (p) RobbieFitzpatrick 11 (Jo Hughes) *towards rr: rdn over 3f out: mod prog fr over 1f out* **20/1**	47
0-50	**9**	*1 1/2*	**Grandad Mac**[21] [4861] 3-9-0 58 .... RichardHughes 1 (Jane Chapple-Hyam) *racd towards far side: rdn fr 3f out and in tch: no prog u.p over 1f out: sn btn* **14/1**	44
0042	**10**	*1 3/4*	**Obiter Dicta**[18] [4970] 3-9-2 65 .... AmyScott(5) 17 (Henry Candy) *in rr: pushed along over 3f out: mod prog fnl f* **10/1**	46
301	**11**	*nk*	**Abacist (IRE)**[38] [4271] 3-9-4 62 .... JimCrowley 5 (Ralph Beckett) *racd towards far aside: w ldr 1/2-way: wknd fr 2f out* **15/2**[3]	42
3433	**12**	*3/4*	**Justbookie Dot Com (IRE)**[9] [5274] 3-9-1 59 .... (v) JamesDoyle 9 (David Evans) *chsd ldrs: rdn 3f out: wknd over 2f out* **14/1**	37
0405	**13**	*1 1/4*	**Valentino Swing (IRE)**[11] [5208] 8-8-0 46 .... (p) IanBurns(7) 16 (Michael Appleby) *hrd rdn in mid-div 1/2-way: nvr in contention* **25/1**	23
0000	**14**	*4*	**Realt Na Mara (IRE)**[41] [4183] 8-9-0 53 .... DarryllHolland 4 (Hughie Morrison) *racd towards far side and pressed ldrs to 1/2-way: wknd 2f out: eased fnl f* **40/1**	19
0402	**15**	*1 1/2*	**Kenswick**[25] [4705] 4-9-3 56 .... (v) AdamKirby 14 (Pat Eddery) *rdn over 3f out: a towards rr* **11/1**	18
0540	**16**	*1 1/4*	**Lennoxwood (IRE)**[112] [1952] 3-7-13 50 .... RachealKneller(7) 12 (Mark Usher) *s.i.s: a in rr* **25/1**	—
0156	**17**	*6*	**Euroquip Boy (IRE)**[21] [4866] 4-9-7 60 .... EddieCreighton 15 (Michael Scudamore) *in tch early: bhd fr 1/2-way* **9/1**	—

1m 23.55s (0.35) **Going Correction** +0.05s/f (Good)
WFA 3 from 4yo+ 5lb **17** Ran SP% **124.5**
Speed ratings (Par 101): **100,98,98,93,93 92,92,91,89,87 87,86,85,80,78 77,70**
toteswingers:1&2:£36.30, 1&3:£61.00, 2&3:£9.50 CSF £108.53 CT £1326.77 TOTE £21.20: £4.30, £2.70, £3.80, £3.20; EX 235.40.
Owner J R Salter **Bred** Heather Raw **Trained** Yarnscombe, Devon

FOCUS
Competitive for the grade. The middle of the track was the place to be and the winner showed his best form since he was a 2yo.

5540 GRANDPIER.CO.UK H'CAP 6f 16y

5:35 (5:36) (Class 6) (0-55,55) 3-Y-O+ **£1,617** (£481; £240; £120) **Stalls** Centre

Form				RPR
5000	**1**		**Mary's Pet**[39] [4255] 4-9-2 55 .... (p) AdamKirby 16 (John Akehurst) *led: sn clr: stl 3 l in front whn rdn appr fnl f: hld on to diminishing ld cl home* **8/1**	65
023	**2**	*nk*	**Mucky Molly**[23] [4796] 3-8-10 52 .... SamHitchcott 12 (Olivia Maylam) *chsd ldrs: rdn and kpt on to go 2nd ins fnl f: clsng on wnr nr fin but a hld* **12/1**	61

3563 **3** 1/2 **Doctor Hilary**[16] 5038 9-9-0 **53**......(v) RobertHavlin 10 60
(Mark Hoad) *in tch: drvn and hdwy over 1f out: styd on ins fnl f and clsng nr fin but a hld* **20/1**

5134 **4** 1 **Flaxen Lake**[20] 4893 4-8-11 **50**...... RichardHughes 5 54
(Milton Bradley) *broke wl and c towards stands' side: chsd clr ldr 2f out: sn rdn and no imp: styd on same pce fnl f* **11/2**[2]

4136 **5** 1/2 **Dancing Welcome**[18] 4948 5-8-9 **53**......(b) LucyKBarry(5) 6 55
(Milton Bradley) *racd towards centre of crse: in tch: rdn over 2f out: kpt on fnl f but nvr gng pce to rch ldrs* **3/1**[1]

0305 **6** 2 **Charlie Delta**[11] 5204 8-8-8 **54**......(b) BrendanPowell(7) 13 50
(John O'Shea) *towards rr and rdn 3f out: kpt on insuide fnl f: nt rch ldrs* **40/1**

6066 **7** 1 1/2 **Lethal**[137] 1336 8-8-13 **52**...... JamesDoyle 7 43
(Richard Price) *sn chsng clr ldr: rdn and no imp over 2f out: wknd over 1f out* **20/1**

0050 **8** 1/2 **Cwmni**[19] 4918 5-9-0 **53**...... DavidProbert 14 42
(Bryn Palling) *in rr: rdn 1/2-way: kpt on fnl f but nvr a threat* **9/1**

0003 **9** 1 **Avon Light**[18] 4950 3-7-12 **47**......(p) RachealKneller(7) 15 33
(Milton Bradley) *chsd ldrs: rdn over 2f out: styd on same pce tl wknd fnl f* **16/1**

065- **10** nk **Northern Genes (AUS)**[397] 4488 5-8-8 **47** ow1..(p) RobbieFitzpatrick 11 32
(Michael Appleby) *s.i.s: bhd: sn drvn alomg: sme prog fnl f* **16/1**

006 **11** 3/4 **Poyle Todream**[25] 4706 3-8-12 **54**...... JimCrowley 17 37
(Ralph Beckett) *drvn along towards rr 1/2-way: a outpcd* **13/2**[3]

0-04 **12** 3/4 **Disco Doll**[26] 4657 3-8-13 **55**...... FergusSweeney 1 35
(Patrick Chamings) *racd towards centre of crse: sme prog 3f out: sn wknd* **16/1**

215/ **13** 1 **Perfect Honour (IRE)**[856] 1529 5-8-13 **52**...... KellyHarrison 4 29
(Des Donovan) *racd towards centre of crse: outpcd fr 1/2-way* **28/1**

0000 **14** 1 1/2 **Three Scoops**[19] 4917 3-7-13 **46** oh1...... RyanPowell(5) 9 18
(Dominic Ffrench Davis) *chsd ldrs over 3f* **40/1**

0055 **15** 1 1/2 **Danzig Fox**[20] 4893 6-8-7 **46** oh1......(be) EddieCreighton 2 14
(Michael Mullineaux) *racd towards centre of crse: outpcd fr 1/2-way* **66/1**

6406 **16** 1 **Slatey Hen (IRE)**[14] 5120 3-8-6 **55**...... JakePayne(7) 8 19
(Richard Guest) *chsd ldrs over 3f* **33/1**

0-00 **17** 7 **Transeggselence**[54] 3726 4-8-11 **50**...... MarcHalford 3 —
(Gary Harrison) *racd towards centre of crse: sn outpcd* **50/1**

1m 12.03s (0.03) **Going Correction** +0.05s/f (Good)
WFA 3 from 4yo+ 3lb **17** Ran SP% **124.4**
Speed ratings (Par 101): **101,100,99,98,97 95,93,92,91,90 89,88,87,85,83 82,72**
toteswingers:1&2:£22.20, 1&3:£42.40, 2&3:£49.80 CSF £93.22 CT £1881.37 TOTE £12.20: £3.00, £2.90, £4.30, £1.50; EX 82.90.
Owner Mrs I Marshall **Bred** Green Pastures Farm **Trained** Epsom, Surrey

FOCUS
Modest fare and a high draw proved important. The winner's first turf form, a length off her AW best.
Danzig Fox Official explanation: jockey said gelding hung right
T/Plt: £24.20 to a £1 stake. Pool of £50,242.27 - 1,514.73 winning tickets. T/Qpdt: £5.30 to a £1 stake. Pool of £3,335.25 - 461.58 winning tickets. ST

5196 EPSOM (L-H)
Monday, August 29

OFFICIAL GOING: Round course - good to soft (good in places; 7.2); 5f course - good (good to soft in places; 7.6; home straight: stands' side 7.6; far side 7.7)
Wind: Light, against Weather: Fine

5541 JRA/BRITISH STALLION STUDS E B F MEDIAN AUCTION MAIDEN STKS 7f
2:00 (2:00) (Class 5) 2-Y-O **£3,881** (£1,155; £577; £288) **Stalls** Low

Form RPR

645 **1** **Stateos (IRE)**[13] 5142 2-9-3 70...... TomQueally 9 78
(Sir Henry Cecil) *led: rdn over 1f out: narrowly hdd 50yds out: rallied to ld last strides* **15/2**

063 **2** shd **Blank Czech (IRE)**[17] 4996 2-9-3 78...... StevieDonohoe 7 78
(Amanda Perrett) *prom [illegible] to chse wnr over 1f out: clsd to ld narrowly 50yds out: hdd last strides* **10/3**

53 **3** 2 **Ashbina**[8] 5299 2-8-12 0...... EddieAhern 4 68
(William Haggas) *chsd wnr to 4f out: disp 2nd again jst over 3f out to over 1f out: one pce* **7/1**

24 **4** 1 1/2 **Gunner Will (IRE)**[45] 4053 2-9-3 0...... HayleyTurner 8 69
(George Baker) *hld up in midfield: cl enough in 6th st: rdn 2f out: one pce and nvr able to chal* **9/4**[1]

0 **5** 2 1/4 **Swift Cat**[19] 4906 2-9-3 0...... ChrisCatlin 3 63
(John Best) *t.k.h: hld up in 5th: jst pushed along fr 2f out: no imp* **33/1**

05 **6** 2 1/4 **Northern Territory (IRE)**[23] 4798 2-9-3 0...... PatCosgrave 5 57
(Jim Boyle) *dwlt: t.k.h: prom: chsd wnr 4f out to jst over 3f out: sn lost pl and hanging* **100/1**

05 **7** 3/4 **Mount St Mistress**[25] 4698 2-8-7 0...... AntiocoMurgia(5) 10 50
(George Baker) *t.k.h: hld up in last pair: struggling over 2f out: no prog after* **80/1**

0 **8** 2 3/4 **Regal Gold**[24] 4762 2-9-3 0...... PatDobbs 1 48
(Richard Hannon) *hld up in last: pushed along over 2f out: no prog* **14/1**

3 **9** 1/2 **Gulf Of Alaska**[38] 4292 2-9-3 0...... WilliamBuick 2 47
(Mahmood Al Zarooni) *a in rr: 7th and pushed along st: no prog and wl btn 2f out* **7/2**[3]

1m 27.38s (4.08) **Going Correction** +0.30s/f (Good) **9** Ran SP% **112.2**
Speed ratings (Par 94): **88,87,85,83,81 78,77,74,74**
toteswingers:1&2:£5.70, 2&3:£5.00, 1&3:£4.40 CSF £31.45 TOTE £8.50: £2.40, £1.30, £2.30; EX 43.20 Trifecta £432.30 Part won. Pool of £584.20 - 0.81 winning units..
Owner Niarchos Family **Bred** Islanmore Stud & A Cooper **Trained** Newmarket, Suffolk

FOCUS
Rail dolled out 3yds from 1m to 6f and 4yds from 6f to winning post which added about 10yds to Round course distances. All of these 2-y-os had run before so not many would have been unexposed, but although the ground was on the easy side the winning time was still slow. Sound form, with improvement from the winner.

NOTEBOOK
Stateos(IRE) had shown ability in his first three starts but didn't seem to be progressing. However, he got the run of the race out in front here and proved very game when looking sure to be caught well inside the last furlong. He was 8lb badly in with the runner-up, so may well be put up for this. (op 7-1 tchd 8-1)
Blank Czech(IRE) appeared to have delivered his challenge at just the right time 50yds from the line and was matched at 1.02 in running, but the winner pulled out a little more. This was a chance missed as he would have been giving the winner 8lb in a handicap, but any horse can be given the benefit of the doubt on this track.
Ashbina had every chance when getting short of room between the front pair over a furlong from home, was she wasn't unlucky. Nurseries look the way forward with her. (op 11-2)
Gunner Will(IRE) had already shown ability in his first two starts and the form of both races has worked out extremely well, but he didn't pick up this time. He is worth another chance back on a more conventional track with nurseries now an option.
Swift Cat showed some ability when seventh of 11 on his Kempton debut and did so again here, despite racing keenly early. He may come into his own once handicapped.
Mount St Mistress Official explanation: jockey said filly hung left
Gulf Of Alaska was a beaten favourite on his York debut, but that was mainly due to greenness and he still showed plenty of ability. However, despite being well backed, he never looked happy at the back of the field on this occasion and held his head high. He is given the benefit of the doubt on this demanding track. (op 11-2)

5542 DOWNLOAD THE EPSOM IPHONE APP H'CAP 6f
2:30 (2:32) (Class 5) (0-75,73) 3-Y-O **£3,234** (£962; £481; £240) **Stalls** High

Form RPR

02 **1** **Celtic Sixpence (IRE)**[25] 4715 3-9-7 **73**...... TomQueally 2 83
(Noel Quinlan) *led 2f: pressed ldr: led again over 2f out: shkn up to assert over 1f out: styd on wl* **9/2**[3]

3451 **2** 1 1/2 **Blue Deer (IRE)**[6] 5344 3-8-5 **64**...... CharlesBishop(7) 6 69
(Mick Channon) *trckd ldrs: cl 4th st: rdn 2f out: styd on to take 2nd last 100yds: no imp on wnr* **11/4**[1]

1-53 **3** 3/4 **Mon Visage**[23] 4799 3-9-7 **73**...... WilliamBuick 4 76+
(Chris Wall) *wl off the pce in last trio and nt handling the trck: 8th st: sn rdn: prog u.p 2f out: styd on to take 3rd nr fin* **7/2**[2]

1330 **4** 1 **Welsh Inlet (IRE)**[14] 5115 3-9-3 **69**...... NeilChalmers 5 69
(John Bridger) *pressed ldng pair and racd on outer: nt qckn over 2f out: disp 2nd over 1f out: one pce after* **8/1**

6042 **5** shd **Sugar Beet**[5] 5378 3-9-6 **72**...... KirstyMilczarek 1 71
(Ronald Harris) *pressed ldr: led after 2f to over 2f out: nt qckn and hld over 1f out: fdd and lost several pls last 100yds* **12/1**

00 **6** nse **Mixed Emotions (IRE)**[37] 4321 3-8-13 **65**...... PatDobbs 3 64
(Richard Hannon) *s.i.s: wl off the pce in last trio: 7th st: sn rdn: no prog tl styd on fnl f: nrst fin* **12/1**

0522 **7** nse **Diamond Vine (IRE)**[20] 4885 3-9-4 **70**......(p) PatCosgrave 9 69
(Ronald Harris) *chsd ldrs: cl 5th st: rdn and nt qckn 2f out: fdd over 1f out* **12/1**

4003 **8** 1 **One Cool Chick**[24] 4759 3-7-13 **54** oh5...... KieranO'Neill(3) 7 50+
(John Bridger) *s.s: wl off the pce in last and nt handling trck that wl: no prog tl styd on fnl f: n.m.r nr fin* **20/1**

5221 **9** 10 **Eshoog (IRE)**[6] 5346 3-9-3 **69** 6ex......(bt) JackMitchell 8 33
(Phil McEntee) *chsd ldrs: 6th st: wknd 3f out: t.o* **12/1**

1m 11.37s (1.97) **Going Correction** +0.30s/f (Good) **9** Ran SP% **113.7**
Speed ratings (Par 100): **98,96,95,93,93 93,93,92,78**
toteswingers:1&2:£3.20, 1&3:£4.30, 2&3:£3.60 CSF £16.98 CT £47.64 TOTE £4.90: £1.90, £1.20, £1.90; EX 18.40 Trifecta £45.10 Pool: £595.28 - 9.76 winning units..
Owner Burns Farm Racing **Bred** Burns Farm Stud **Trained** Newmarket, Suffolk

FOCUS
A modest sprint handicap and not many got into it. Fair form for the grade, the winner posting a small personal best.

5543 TRY TOTEQUICKPICK IF YOU'RE FEELING LUCKY H'CAP 5f
3:05 (3:05) (Class 2) (0-100,99) 3-Y-O+
£9,960 (£2,982; £1,491; £559; £559; £187) **Stalls** High

Form RPR

435 **1** **Your Gifted (IRE)**[16] 5033 4-8-3 **85**...... DavidKenny(7) 6 94
(Patrick Morris) *dwlt: prog fr rr after 2f and wdst of all: sustained effrt over 1f out to ld ins fnl f: hld on wl* **12/1**

0-00 **2** hd **Moorhouse Lad**[117] 1809 8-8-11 **93**...... JustinNewman(7) 14 101
(Bryan Smart) *w ldr and racd one off rail: led 1/2-way: hanging lft fr over 1f out: hdd ins fnl f: r.o* **8/1**[3]

0206 **3** 1/2 **Sohraab**[23] 4776 7-8-12 **90**...... KieranO'Neill(3) 10 96
(Hughie Morrison) *rdn and struggling to go the pce after 2f: no prog fr rr tl styd on wl fnl f nr rail: tk 3rd last strides* **4/1**[1]

0430 **4** 1/2 **Fathom Five (IRE)**[16] 5033 7-8-12 **87**...... NeilChalmers 5 91
(David Nicholls) *towards outer and in rr: effrt 2f out: styd on fr over 1f out: nvr able to chal* **8/1**[3]

3526 **4** dht **La Fortunata**[9] 5278 4-8-6 **84** 6w1...... [illegible] 9 [illegible]
(Mike Murphy) *spd fr wdst draw and pressed ldrs: nt qckn over 1f out: cl up bhd ldng trio whn nt clr run ins fnl f: kpt on* **9/1**

35-4 **6** hd **Crimea (IRE)**[16] 5033 5-8-11 **86**...... AdrianNicholls 9 90
(David Nicholls) *pressed ldng pair and racd three off rail: rdn to chal over 1f out: upsides ent fnl f: fdd* **11/2**[2]

0210 **7** 1/2 **Strike Up The Band**[12] 5180 8-8-5 **87**...... ShirleyTeasdale(7) 15 89
(David Nicholls) *racd against rail: led to 1/2-way: steadily lost pl over 1f out* **16/1**

0060 **8** 1 **Indian Trail**[76] 3028 11-8-9 **84** ow2......(v) WilliamBuick 12 85+
(David Nicholls) *hld up in last trio: bustled along 2f out: no prog whn hmpd jst over 1f out: no ch after* **11/1**

0000 **9** nk **Stone Of Folca**[25] 4739 3-9-8 **99**...... TomQueally 4 96
(John Best) *chsd ldrs: rdn 2f out: no prog over 1f out: one pce after* **16/1**

0021 **10** 2 **Diamond Charlie (IRE)**[39] 4238 3-8-7 **84**...... HayleyTurner 13 74
(Simon Dow) *spd and cl up bhd ldrs tl wknd over 1f out* **11/2**[2]

-050 **11** 3 1/2 **Rowe Park**[100] 2288 8-9-6 **95**......(v[1]) StevieDonohoe 11 72
(Linda Jewell) *outpcd in last after 2f: bhd rest of way* **28/1**

56.02 secs (0.32) **Going Correction** +0.30s/f (Good)
WFA 3 from 4yo+ 2lb **11** Ran SP% **114.2**
Speed ratings (Par 109): **109,108,107,107,107 106,105,104,103,100 95**
toteswingers:1&2:£22.70, 1&3:£9.90, 2&3:£10.30 CSF £101.62 CT £463.94 TOTE £13.20: £3.70, £3.50, £2.00; EX 166.60 Trifecta £996.40 Part won. Pool of £1346.61 - 0.71 winning units..
Owner Mrs S Morris **Bred** Rathasker Stud **Trained** Tarporley, Cheshire

FOCUS
A decent sprint handicap, even with the four non-runners, but the usual bias towards high-drawn horses didn't really materialise. The winner continued her remarkable progress.

NOTEBOOK
Your Gifted(IRE), closely matched with Crimea on recent Doncaster running and with winning form on soft ground, wasn't best away but she travelled very nicely and made smooth progress to reach a challenging position on the wide outside at halfway. She maintained her effort to lead well inside the last furlong and the fact that she was 6lb above her last winning mark suggests she is still improving. (tchd 14-1)
Moorhouse Lad hasn't been in much form recently, but he was down to the same mark as for his last handicap success. In front over 2f from home, he had every chance but was inclined to hang away down the camber and couldn't quite hold off the filly's finishing burst. (op 9-1)

Sohraab is still 6lb higher than when scoring at Salisbury in June, though he has twice scored off a higher mark than this in the past. Not much went right for him here, though, as he was having to be ridden along from an early stage and didn't find his stride until switched to the stands' rail over a furlong from home. He prefers tracks with a stiffer finish. (op 9-2)
Fathom Five(IRE) hasn't scored since winning off 4lb higher on his reappearance here last year, but came into this 2-6 over C&D and this was another creditable effort as he didn't enjoy the clearest of runs and had to be switched very wide for his final effort. (op 15-2)
La Fortunata, 1lb higher than when runner-up in this last year, had been placed in all three previous tries over C&D and she ran well again as she was always seeing plenty of daylight on the outside of the leaders. She had already run her race when getting short of room inside the last furlong and may have preferred quicker ground. (op 15-2)
Crimea(IRE) ran a cracker on his return from over a year off at Doncaster earlier this month and was brought through to hold every chance over a furlong from home before his effort flattened out. This may have come soon enough and he is another who could probably have done with quicker ground.
Strike Up The Band, off the same mark as when third in this last year, appeared to have the plum draw and led early, but he was struggling once headed by the runner-up just after halfway and started to hang. He is a hard horse to win with these days. (op 14-1)
Indian Trail didn't get the gaps when he needed them, but has only managed to win one of his last 46 starts. Official explanation: jockey said gelding suffered interference in running (tchd 10-1)

5544 TRY TOTEQUICKPICK ON ALL TOTEPOOL BETS CONDITIONS STKS — 1m 2f 18y

3:40 (3:41) (Class 3) 3-Y-O+

£6,411 (£1,919; £959; £479; £239; £120) **Stalls** Low

Form — RPR

5-00 **1** **Vesuve (IRE)**[59] [3591] 5-9-2 104........ WilliamBuick 8 — 105
(Saeed Bin Suroor) *racd wd: pressed ldng pair: pushed along 3f out: sustained chal fr 2f out: drvn ahd ins fnl f* **9/1**

2300 **2** ¾ **Measuring Time**[34] [4411] 3-8-5 100........ KieranO'Neill(3) 4 — 103
(Richard Hannon) *hld up bhd ldrs: prog to chal 3f out: narrow ld 2f out but hrd pressed: hdd and one pce ins fnl f* **13/2**

00 **3** *nk* **Forte Dei Marmi**[34] [4410] 5-9-2 106........ J-PGuillambert 7 — 106+
(Luca Cumani) *hld up in last pair: pushed along 3f out: prog 2f out: jnd ldng trio 1f out: wandered u.p: nt qckn last 100yds* **4/1**[2]

-530 **4** *nse* **Picture Editor**[74] [3069] 3-8-8 99........ TomQueally 6 — 102
(Sir Henry Cecil) *pressed ldr: led narrowly 3f out: hdd 2f out: styd upsides tl no ex ins fnl f* **7/2**[1]

1006 **5** 1¼ **Resurge (IRE)**[23] [4788] 6-9-2 100........ PatCosgrave 3 — 100
(Stuart Kittow) *taken down early: hld up in tch: effrt on inner 3f out and cl up: nt qckn 2f out: styd on ins fnl f* **5/1**[3]

1000 **6** *nse* **Spanish Duke (IRE)**[34] [4410] 4-9-2 101........ EddieAhern 2 — 100
(John Dunlop) *trckd ldrs: cl enough and pushed along over 2f out: light reminders arnd 1f: styd on same pce* **5/1**[3]

6060 **7** 1½ **Al Shemali**[156] [1001] 7-9-9 112........ HayleyTurner 5 — 104
(Mahmood Al Zarooni) *hld up in last: pushed along over 2f out: kpt on one pce after: nvr nr ldrs* **14/1**

1230 **8** *13* **Spring Of Fame (USA)**[44] [4095] 5-9-2 112........ ChrisCatlin 1 — 71
(Saeed Bin Suroor) *led to 3f out: sn wknd: t.o* **10/1**

2m 10.75s (1.05) **Going Correction** +0.30s/f (Good)
WFA 3 from 4yo+ 8lb — **8** Ran SP% **114.6**
Speed ratings (Par 107): **107,106,106,106,105 105,103,93**
toteswingers:1&2:£8.20, 1&3:£9.50, 2&3:£8.00 CSF £65.83 TOTE £10.40: £2.90, £2.60, £2.00; EX 79.20 Trifecta £691.50 Pool: £1037.25 - 1.11 winning units..
Owner Godolphin **Bred** Dayton Investments Ltd **Trained** Newmarket, Suffolk

FOCUS
A few had questions marks against them in this conditions event and the early pace wasn't strong, resulting in a dash down the home straight. They finished in a bit of a heap, suggesting the form isn't that strong, albeit the race was more competitive than most for the grade. Godolphin had taken six of the last eight runnings of this race and launched a three-pronged attack this time, albeit split between their two trainers, and extended their domination of the event.

NOTEBOOK
Vesuve(IRE) hadn't beaten a rival in two previous starts this year, but this was a marked drop in class. Always handy before being brought to challenge over 2f from home, it looked a case of him wanting it more than some of his nearest rivals, but he will need to progress again to be competitive back in Pattern company. (op 8-1)
Measuring Time, still without a win since landing his first two starts at two, started the season off promisingly enough but seemed to have gone the wrong way. However, he was well backed here and despite not coming down the hill too well, had every chance and was just run out of it. (op 10-1)
Forte Dei Marmi hasn't hit the heights that seemed possible at the start of the year and probably needs quicker ground, but he still looked to have been produced with a race-winning challenge on the outside over a furlong from home (hit 1.07 in-running). However, he then hung in towards his rivals and failed to go through with it. He probably prefers bigger fields and he may not have handled the track, but this still didn't look good. (op 9-2 after 6-1 in a place)
Picture Editor could be excused his performance at Royal Ascot and the form of his previous third at Goodwood has worked out very well. Always handy, he went to the front over 2f from home, but didn't last there long though he did battle back gamely once headed. The drop back in trip may not have been ideal. (op 9-2)
Resurge(IRE) had a bit to find with a few of these on official ratings, but he has a wonderful record here (3-5 over C&D and runner-up on the other two occasions). He had every chance when sneaking between the inside rail and the weakening Spring Of Fame over 2f from home, but lacked the speed to take full advantage. (tchd 11-2)
Spanish Duke(IRE) came into this 1-1 here having beaten Resurge in the City And Suburban over C&D back in April, but although he met trouble rounding Tattenham Corner, it was lack of a turn of foot in this better company that did for him. (op 6-1)
Al Shemali, returning from 156 days off and having his first start in this country in three years, was never competitive but neither was he given a hard race. (op 9-1)
Spring Of Fame(USA) Official explanation: trainer's rep said horse was unsuited by track

5545 MAY FAMILY AMATEUR DERBY (H'CAP) (FOR GENTLEMAN AMATEUR RIDERS) — 1m 4f 10y

4:15 (4:16) (Class 4) (0-85,85) 4-Y-O+ — **£4,991** (£1,548; £773; £387) **Stalls** Centre

Form — RPR

-350 **1** **Bramalea**[32] [4470] 6-11-2 85........ MrRPooles(5) 4 — 96
(Hughie Morrison) *trckd ldng pair: wnt 2nd st: led 3f out and sn kicked clr: styd on wl: unchal* **9/2**[2]

02 **2** *3* **Epsom Salts**[31] [4488] 6-9-12 67........ MrFMitchell(5) 5 — 73
(Pat Phelan) *hld up in last pair: prog on outer 3f out: chsd wnr jst over 2f out: styd on but no imp* **11/2**[3]

5113 **3** *8* **Megalala (IRE)**[2] [5491] 10-10-9 78........ ThomasGarner(5) 3 — 71
(John Bridger) *led at decent pce: hdd 3f out: lost 2nd jst over 2f out: hld on for modest 3rd* **9/1**

6401 **4** *1* **Resplendent Light**[14] [5112] 6-9-11 66........(t) MrJWilliams(5) 6 — 58
(Bernard Llewellyn) *hld up in 5th: effrt to go 3rd briefly over 2f out: sn rdn and no hdwy* **12/1**

200 **5** ½ **Rowan Tiger**[25] [4724] 5-10-12 76........ MrSWalker 1 — 67
(Jim Boyle) *chsd ldng trio: rdn over 2f out: hanging and wl btn fnl 2f* **8/1**

3344 **6** *7* **Sancho Panza**[11] [5198] 4-10-3 67........ MrRBirkett 2 — 47
(Julia Feilden) *nvr gng wl: dropped to last 1/2-way: wl bhd over 2f out* **4/1**[1]

0501 **7** *8* **Maybe I Wont**[20] [4889] 6-10-2 66........ MrPCollington 8 — 33
(Lucinda Featherstone) *hld up in last pair: no prog 3f out: wl bhd fnl 2f* **4/1**[1]

6442 **8** *19* **If I Were A Boy (IRE)**[46] [4008] 4-10-4 71........ MrCMartin(3) 7 — —
(Dominic Ffrench Davis) *chsd ldr: lost 2nd ent st and wknd rapidly: t.o* **8/1**

2m 42.51s (3.61) **Going Correction** +0.30s/f (Good) — **8** Ran SP% **113.5**
Speed ratings (Par 105): **99,97,91,91,90 86,80,68**
toteswingers:1&2:£5.90, 1&3:£8.30, 2&3:£7.80 CSF £28.86 CT £211.26 TOTE £6.40: £2.00, £2.20, £2.20; EX 45.20 Trifecta £467.00 Pool: £791.96 - 1.25 winning units..
Owner P J Cave **Bred** P J Cave **Trained** East Ilsley, Berks

FOCUS
The early pace was solid enough for this famous old contest, but few ever got into it and there were a couple of major disappointments. Bramalea showed last year's Ascot win didn't flatter her.

5546 BET TOTEPOOL ON ALL UK RACES H'CAP — 1m 2f 18y

4:50 (4:52) (Class 3) (0-90,90) 3-Y-O+ — **£6,663** (£1,982; £990; £495) **Stalls** Low

Form — RPR

2041 **1** **Celestial Girl**[13] [5135] 4-8-9 71........ ChrisCatlin 3 — 80
(Hughie Morrison) *hld up in last pair: prog on outer over 2f out: clsd to ld 1f out: edgd lft but rdn clr* **16/1**

-520 **2** 2¼ **Fanny May**[33] [4429] 3-9-1 85........ EddieAhern 5 — 90+
(Denis Coakley) *trckd ldng trio: prog to chal 2f out: led briefly jst over 1f out: edgd lft fnl f: hld whn sltly tightened up last 100yds* **8/1**

2424 **3** ½ **Ramona Chase**[9] [5275] 6-8-13 80........(t) MarkCoumbe(5) 9 — 85+
(Michael Attwater) *s.i.s: trckd ldrs in 5th: rdn wl over 2f out: tried to cl wl over 1f out: nt clr run jst ins fnl f: swtchd and styd on to take 3rd nr fin* **6/1**[2]

-416 **4** ½ **Tiger Webb**[80] [2877] 3-8-7 84........ CharlesEddery(7) 4 — 86
(Sir Henry Cecil) *hld up in last quartet: 7th st: prog u.p on wd outside jst over 2f out: nt qckn over 1f out: kpt on* **12/1**

0111 **5** *1* **Tenby Lady (USA)**[25] [4723] 3-9-6 90........ StevieDonohoe 1 — 92+
(Sir Mark Prescott Bt) *pressed ldr: rdn to ld over 2f out: hdd jst over 1f out: hld in 3rd whn hmpd last 100yds and lost 2 pls* **11/4**[1]

2054 **6** 2¼ **Wiggy Smith**[33] [4432] 12-8-13 75........ FrankieMcDonald 6 — 71
(Henry Candy) *hld up in last pair: rdn wl over 2f out: plugged on one pce: n.d* **25/1**

1510 **7** *7* **You've Been Mowed**[14] [5101] 5-8-13 82........ CharlesBishop(7) 7 — 64
(Richard Price) *t.k.h: led to over 2f out: wknd qckly over 1f out* **25/1**

3223 **8** *8* **Licence To Till (USA)**[9] [5275] 4-9-5 81........ WilliamBuick 8 — 47
(Mark Johnston) *pressed ldng pair on outer: rdn and lost pl over 3f out: sn btn* **11/4**[1]

3433 **9** *10* **Don't Call Me (IRE)**[16] [5059] 4-10-0 90........ AdrianNicholls 2 — 36
(David Nicholls) *hld up in last quartet: 6th st: rdn and wknd over 2f out: t.o* **7/1**[3]

2m 10.55s (0.85) **Going Correction** +0.30s/f (Good)
WFA 3 from 4yo+ 8lb — **9** Ran SP% **112.5**
Speed ratings (Par 107): **108,106,105,105,104 102,97,90,82**
toteswingers:1&2:£11.50, 1&3:£10.90, 2&3:£9.10 CSF £133.03 CT £857.80 TOTE £13.90: £3.60, £3.00, £1.30; EX 86.10 Trifecta £633.30 Part won. Pool of £855.90 - 0.84 winning units..
Owner Helena Springfield Ltd **Bred** Meon Valley Stud **Trained** East Ilsley, Berks

FOCUS
A decent handicap. The early pace was modest but the time was reasonable. The winner recorded a 4lb personal best.

NOTEBOOK
Celestial Girl was put up 2lb for her recent Brighton success (her third win there) which gave encouragement that she would handle this roller coaster of a track. Patiently ridden, she was brought through to lead a furlong out and, although hanging over to the inside rail and causing problems for three of her rivals in behind, she was the best horse on merit. (op 14-1)
Fanny May didn't find the cards falling right for her on her handicap debut at Goodwood last time, but had every chance here. Brought to challenge for the lead 2f out, no sooner had she poked her head in front than the winner was delivered with her effort and, although she was intimidated by her rival inside the last furlong, it made no difference to the result. (op 9-1 tchd 10-1 and 11-1 in places)
Ramona Chase had a strike-rate of 2-54 on the Flat coming into this, though he often runs well here including a success over C&D just under a year ago. He can be rated a bit closer as he ran out of room completely when trying for a passage up the inside rail a furlong out and he needs a stronger gallop in any case, but his overall record doesn't make him an attractive proposition. Official explanation: jockey said gelding was denied a clear run (op 7-1)
Tiger Webb was brought very wide starting up the home straight and, although he made up plenty of late ground, he also tended to hang down the camber. He still looks on a stiff mark. (tchd 11-1)
Tenby Lady(USA) was bidding for a four-timer off a 6lb higher mark and had her chance when leading over 2f out, but only lasted in front for a furlong and was already beaten when badly hampered.
You've Been Mowed, successful in her last two starts on turf and 5lb higher (1-1 at the track), didn't seem to stay in her only previous try at this trip and having raced keenly in front under restraint early, gave herself little chance of seeing it out. (op 22-1)
Licence To Till(USA) found little off the bridle over 3f from home and is now 0-13 for the year. (tchd 5-2 and 100-30 in a place and 3-1 in places)

5547 CHANTILLY H'CAP — 1m 114y

5:25 (5:25) (Class 4) (0-80,78) 3-Y-O+ — **£4,528** (£1,347; £673; £336) **Stalls** Low

Form — RPR

4055 **1** **Orientalist**[21] [4860] 3-9-1 72........ TomQueally 10 — 83
(Eve Johnson Houghton) *hld up in midfield: lost pl sltly and 8th st: prog on outer 2f out: drvn to ld last 150yds: drvn out* **5/1**[3]

3210 **2** ½ **Whitby Jet (IRE)**[17] [5014] 3-8-10 72........ AntiocoMurgia(5) 4 — 82+
(Edward Vaughan) *hld up in midfield: 6th st: prog and n.m.r 2f out: drvn to chal and upsides 1f out: jst hld last 100yds* **9/2**[2]

0220 **3** *3* **Danehill Dante (IRE)**[37] [4335] 3-9-1 75........ KieranO'Neill(3) 7 — 78
(Richard Hannon) *chsd ldrs: 5th and rdn st: prog u.p over 2f out: led briefly 1f out: wknd last 100yds* **7/2**[1]

2326 **4** *1* **Cat Hunter**[18] [4949] 4-9-2 66........ KirstyMilczarek 5 — 69+
(Ronald Harris) *slowly away: hld up in last pair: 9th st: prog on inner after to ld jst over 2f out: hdd 1f out: wkng whn hmpd ins fnl f* **9/1**

0-00 **5** 2½ **Botanist**[59] [3592] 4-9-9 73........(t) StevieDonohoe 6 — 68
(Tobias B P Coles) *dwlt: hld up in last pair: stl there 3f out: hanging bdly lft 2f out: late prog fnl f: no ch* **14/1**

152 **6** *hd* **Green Earth (IRE)**[26] [4656] 4-9-2 66........ EddieAhern 8 — 61+
(Pat Phelan) *hld up: 7th st: nt clr run 3f out and dropped to last pair: bmpd wl over 1f out: kpt on after: no ch* **6/1**

0-04 **7** 4½ **My Name Is Bert**[17] 4987 5-8-2 **59** oh5 NoelGarbutt(7) 11 43
(Lucinda Featherstone) *trckd ldng pair: lost pl sn after: n.d fnl 2f* **18/1**
1350 **8** 3 **Salient**[18] 4958 7-9-9 **73** J-PGuillambert 2 51
(Michael Attwater) *led 1f: chsd ldr to jst over 2f out: short of room briefly sn after and wknd* **10/1**
0530 **9** 1 **Buxfizz (USA)**[70] 3231 3-9-4 **78** SeanLevey(3) 3 53
(Robert Mills) *trckd ldrs: 4th st: lost pl over 2f out and sn wknd* **12/1**
3-00 **10** 2¾ **King's Colour**[10] 5240 6-10-0 **78** PatCosgrave 1 47
(Brett Johnson) *t.k.h: led after 1f: hdd & wknd qckly jst over 2f out* **16/1**

1m 48.12s (2.02) **Going Correction** +0.30s/f (Good)
WFA 3 from 4yo+ 7lb **10** Ran SP% **116.0**
Speed ratings (Par 105): **103,102,99,99,96 96,92,89,89,86**
toteswingers:1&2:£4.90, 1&3:£4.50, 2&3:£4.40. Tote Super 7: Win: Not won. Place: £462.00 CSF £27.63 CT £90.74 TOTE £6.30: £2.30, £2.00, £1.80; EX 26.50 Trifecta £132.90 Pool: £618.17 - 3.44 winning units..
Owner Eden Racing IV **Bred** Whitsbury Manor Stud **Trained** Blewbury, Oxon

FOCUS
An ordinary handicap and the pace looked modest despite a contested lead. A typical Epsom finish, with plenty meeting trouble and horses hanging all over the place. The winner is rated to this year's form.
T/Plt: £388.90 to a £1 stake. Pool:£66,012.39 - 123.90 winning tickets T/Qpdt: £78.30 to a £1 stake. Pool:£3,612.28 - 34.10 winning tickets JN

5437 NEWCASTLE (L-H)
Monday, August 29

OFFICIAL GOING: Soft (5.4)
Wind: Fresh, against Weather: Overcast

5548 BRITISH STALLION STUDS SUPPORTING BRITISH RACING E B F MAIDEN STKS 7f
2:15 (2:17) (Class 4) 2-Y-O **£4,528** (£1,347; £673; £336) **Stalls** High

Form RPR
36 **1** **Zakreet**[16] 5058 2-9-3 0 StephenCraine 4 83
(Kevin Ryan) *mde all: rdn over 2f out: edgd lft ins fnl f: drvn out* **20/1**
4230 **2** 1 **Choisan (IRE)**[37] 4347 2-9-3 81 DuranFentiman 5 80
(Tim Easterby) *chsd wnr to over 1f out: sn drvn: rallied and regained 2nd last 100yds: kpt on* **10/1**[3]
3 1¼ **Talk Of The North** 2-8-12 0 LukeMorris 8 72
(Hugo Palmer) *dwlt: sn hld up in tch: effrt and hung lft fr over 2f out: ev ch over 1f out: lost 2nd and no ex last 100yds* **14/1**
4 2½ **Never Perfect (IRE)** 2-9-3 0 JamieSpencer 3 71+
(Tom Tate) *missed break: hld up: shkn up and hdwy over 2f out: kpt on ins fnl f: bttr for r* **9/2**[2]
0 **5** ½ **Party Line**[46] 4002 2-8-12 0 FrannyNorton 7 64
(Mark Johnston) *trckd ldrs: drvn and outpcd over 2f out: n.d after* **25/1**
0 **6** ¾ **Warcrown (IRE)**[34] 4414 2-9-3 0 PaulHanagan 10 68
(Richard Fahey) *in tch: rdn and hdwy over 2f out: wknd appr fnl f* **4/6**[1]
7 2½ **Silver Blaze** 2-8-12 0 GarryWhillans(5) 6 61
(Alan Swinbank) *dwlt: hld up: rdn over 2f out: edgd lft and wknd wl over 1f out* **12/1**
6 **8** 4 **Fine Altomis**[44] 4080 2-9-3 0 TomEaves 1 51
(Michael Dods) *plld hrd: hld up: struggling 1/2-way: sn btn* **33/1**
9 3 **Lady Romanza (IRE)** 2-8-12 0 BarryMcHugh 2 39
(Tim Easterby) *dwlt: bhd: drvn along 1/2-way: sn wknd* **50/1**
10 nk **Firefly** 2-9-3 0 JamesSullivan 9 43
(John Weymes) *hld up: struggling 1/2-way: sn wknd* **100/1**

1m 31.7s (3.90) **Going Correction** +0.50s/f (Yiel) **10** Ran SP% **116.1**
Speed ratings (Par 96): **97,95,94,91,91 90,87,82,79,78**
toteswingers:1&2:£8.30, 1&3:£54.40, 2&3:£17.00 CSF £194.07 TOTE £20.80: £4.10, £2.20, £3.00; EX 59.90.
Owner Mubarak Al Naimi **Bred** M R M Bloodstock 3 **Trained** Hambleton, N Yorks

FOCUS
An ordinary juvenile maiden rated tentatively around the runner-up and the race averages. The winner was a significant improver.

NOTEBOOK
Zakreet, comfortably held on both previous attempts over 6f, is bred to cope with some give underfoot and he relished the extra yardage, dictating under a positive ride and staying on well. Nurseries will presumably be next, although in beating an 81-rated rival it remains to be seen how generous a mark he receives from the handicapper. (op 16-1 tchd 14-1)
Choisan(IRE), the most experienced of these, was up to 7f for the first time and saw it out well, but won't find handicap life easy off his current mark. (op 7-1 tchd 13-2)
Talk Of The North, a half-sister to a 1m4f winner, is very much bred to be a middle-distance filly, so it was obviously encouraging she could overcome a sluggish start to finish where she did. (op 18-1 tchd 20-1)
Never Perfect(IRE), a Racing Post Trophy entrant who blew the start and looked as though the experience would do him the world of good. He'll be well suited by 1m and can win a standard maiden. (op 4-1)
Party Line improved considerably on her debut effort and will be one for nurseries over 1m following another start. (op 33-1)
Warcrown(IRE), well backed prior to flopping on his debut at Goodwood (had excuses), had been given a short break and the money again came, but soft ground presented a possible problem, and he never looked like justifying short odds. Clearly held in some regard, hence Derby, Champagne and Royal Lodge entries, he can show this running to be wrong in time, but for now at least has a sizeable amount to prove. Official explanation: jockey said colt never travelled (op 4-5 tchd 5-6)

5549 CHILD TRUST FUND CLAIMING STKS 1m 3y(S)
2:50 (2:50) (Class 6) 3-Y-O+ **£1,617** (£481; £240; £120) **Stalls** High

Form RPR
002 **1** **Master Of Dance (IRE)**[7] 5314 4-9-5 60 (p) GregFairley 9 71
(Peter Salmon) *trckd ldrs: led over 2f out: drvn clr ins fnl f: eased nr fin* **3/1**[3]
3260 **2** 9 **The Osteopath (IRE)**[23] 4811 8-9-11 76 TomEaves 6 56
(Michael Dods) *t.k.h early: trckd ldrs: rdn over 2f out: rallied to chse (clr) wnr ins fnl f: r.o* **15/8**[1]
1005 **3** nk **Dechiper (IRE)**[26] 4671 9-9-9 49 TonyHamilton 5 54
(Robert Johnson) *hld up in tch: drvn and outpcd over 2f out: rallied ins fnl f: kpt on: nrst fin* **25/1**
20/0 **4** 3½ **Monthly Medal**[19] 4897 8-8-13 72 (t) JamesSullivan 8 36
(Wilf Storey) *hld up: hdwy and ev ch over 2f out: sn rdn: wknd and lost two pls ins fnl f* **14/1**
560 **5** 7 **Isheforreal (IRE)**[22] 4816 4-9-0 57 PaulPickard(3) 2 23
(Brian Ellison) *trckd ldr: effrt and ev ch over 2f out: sn rdn: wknd wl over 1f out* **20/1**
4100 **6** 15 **Bold Marc (IRE)**[26] 4656 9-9-13 77 AndrewElliott 3 —
(Mrs K Burke) *led to over 2f out: sn drvn: wknd over 1f out: eased whn btn ins fnl f* **2/1**[2]
0050 **7** 9 **Charity Fair**[28] 4601 4-8-3 36 (v) ShaneBKelly(5) 1 —
(Ron Barr) *dwlt: bhd: drvn 1/2-way: sn struggling: t.o* **100/1**

1m 46.8s (3.40) **Going Correction** +0.50s/f (Yiel) **7** Ran SP% **109.4**
Speed ratings (Par 101): **103,94,93,90,83 68,59**
.Master of Dance was claimed by K. W. Dalgleish for £6000.\n\x\x
Owner Leods Contracts Limited **Bred** Mick McGinn **Trained** Kirk Deighton, West Yorks
■ Stewards' Enquiry : Greg Fairley caution: used whip when clearly winning

FOCUS
A surprisingly easy victory in this claimer for the 60-rated Master Of Dance, who handled conditions best. The third and the time limit the form.
Bold Marc(IRE) Official explanation: jockey said gelding ran flat

5550 SANTANDER FOUNDATION BLAYDON RACE (NURSERY) 1m 3y(S)
3:25 (3:25) (Class 2) 2-Y-O **£8,086** (£2,406; £1,202; £601) **Stalls** High

Form RPR
4221 **1** **Quick Bite (IRE)**[17] 5003 2-8-11 **75** LukeMorris 6 79
(Hugo Palmer) *prom: smooth hdwy to ld over 2f out: rdn and hung rt ent fnl f: edgd lft and kpt on wl* **6/1**[3]
2643 **2** 1 **Mcvicar**[6] 5342 2-8-2 **66** DuranFentiman 7 69
(Mick Channon) *hld up: smooth hdwy over 2f out: rdn and chse wnr over 1f out: styng on whn nt clr run ins fnl f: kpt on towards fin* **6/1**[3]
1301 **3** 2 **Loyal Master (IRE)**[18] 4943 2-8-13 **77** JamieSpencer 3 75
(George Foster) *hld up: drvn and hdwy over 2f out: kpt on same pce ins fnl f* **5/1**[2]
502 **4** 1½ **Alborz (IRE)**[27] 4646 2-8-4 **68** PaulHanagan 4 62
(Mark Johnston) *cl up: rdn and ev ch over 2f out: kpt on same pce ent fnl f* **14/1**
031 **5** 8 **New Decade**[48] 3947 2-8-9 **73** FrannyNorton 1 50
(Mark Johnston) *cl up: drvn along over 2f out: wknd over 1f out* **9/1**
01 **6** 11 **Position**[27] 4646 2-9-7 **85** SebSanders 8 38
(Sir Mark Prescott Bt) *racd alone stands' side: sn cl up: drvn over 3f out: wknd over 2f out* **6/5**[1]
251 **7** 1¾ **Flurry Of Hands (IRE)**[26] 4667 2-7-12 **62** oh1 (p) JamesSullivan 5 11
(Ann Duffield) *led tl rdn and hdd over 2f out: sn wknd* **16/1**

1m 47.17s (3.77) **Going Correction** +0.50s/f (Yiel) **7** Ran SP% **113.2**
Speed ratings (Par 100): **101,100,98,96,88 77,75**
toteswingers:1&2:£4.50, 2&3:£6.10, 1&3:£3.20 CSF £40.20 CT £191.97 TOTE £8.90: £2.70, £3.20; EX 42.50.
Owner Chisholm, Vestey, Warrender, Kerr-Dineen **Bred** Lodge Park Stud **Trained** Newmarket, Suffolk
■ Stewards' Enquiry : Luke Morris three-day ban: careless riding (Sep 12-14)

FOCUS
A modest nursery and several of these looked to struggle in the ground. Sound form around the front trio.

NOTEBOOK
Quick Bite(IRE) had no worries with the going, having shed her maiden tag at the fourth attempt in heavy ground over 7f here last time (also first run on turf), and she just found enough to hold on, although it would have been very close had she not drifted right and squeezed the runner-up against the rail. This is as far as she wants to go distance-wise. (op 11-2 tchd 5-1)
Mcvicar had run well on both previous handicap ventures off 1lb lower, and he was staying on well, certainly looking set to run the winner close, when denied a run against the rail. He looked unlucky but may gain compensation, with 1m2f likely to suit. (op 15-2)
Loyal Master(IRE) has already won twice this season, including in soft ground, but he found the 5lb rise for his latest success enough to stop a follow up. (op 7-1)
Alborz(IRE), beaten 10l by Position at Southwell last time, again looked one paced under pressure and is clearly in need of 1m2f. He can win a small race over that trip. (op 12-1 tchd 16-1)
New Decade found little for pressure, but should have been fine in the ground, being a son of Pivotal who'd run well on a similar surface on his second start. Official explanation: jockey said colt had no more to give (tchd 11-1)
Position elected to race alone stands' side after a slow start and was beaten and eased with over 2f to run. He'd looked good at Southwell previously and deserves another chance returned to a sounder surface. Official explanation: trainer's rep had no explanation for the poor form shown (op 5-4 tchd 11-10)

5551 FLEXIBLE ISA FILLIES' H'CAP 7f
4:00 (4:00) (Class 5) (0-75,75) 3-Y-O+ **£2,264** (£673; £336; £168) **Stalls** High

Form RPR
0355 **1** **Layla Jamil (IRE)**[9] 5268 3-9-7 **75** JamieSpencer 2 75
(Mick Channon) *in tch centre: smooth hdwy to trck ldr over 2f out: rdn to ld appr fnl f: hld on wl u.p* **3/1**[2]
254 **2** ¾ **Eilean Eeve**[13] 5153 5-8-7 **56** oh6 (p) PaulHanagan 1 55
(George Foster) *cl up centre: outpcd and hung to stands' side over 2f out: rallied to chse wnr ins fnl f: kpt on: hld nr fin* **12/1**
6414 **3** 1 **Fenella Fudge**[14] 5109 3-8-12 **69** (b) DaleSwift(3) 3 63
(James Given) *led centre: rdn over 2f out: hdd appr fnl f: kpt on same pce last 100yds* **4/1**
0003 **4** 1 **Ishiadancer**[12] 5164 6-9-4 **72** LMcNiff(5) 5 66
(Eric Alston) *cl up stands' side: rdn along over 2f out: kpt on same pce ins fnl f* **7/2**[3]
2420 **5** 24 **Clumber Place**[10] 5255 5-9-7 **73** RobertLButler(3) 4 —
(Richard Guest) *cl up stands' side: drvn along wl over 2f out: sn lost tch* **7/4**[1]

1m 34.35s (6.55) **Going Correction** +0.50s/f (Yiel)
WFA 3 from 5yo+ 5lb **5** Ran SP% **111.3**
Speed ratings (Par 100): **82,81,80,78,51**
CSF £32.36 TOTE £3.60: £2.60, £2.90; EX 35.40.
Owner Dr Marwan Koukash **Bred** Patrick Gleeson **Trained** West Ilsley, Berks

FOCUS
A weak fillies' handicap with the runner-up a dubious improver. The main action unfolded centre-field.
Clumber Place Official explanation: jockey said mare never travelled

5552 DAISY CHAIN H'CAP 5f
4:35 (4:35) (Class 6) (0-65,65) 3-Y-O+ **£1,617** (£481; £240; £120) **Stalls** High

Form RPR
3305 **1** **Mission Impossible**[37] 4328 6-8-5 **46** PatrickMathers 4 59
(Tracy Waggott) *in tch: rdn to ld over 1f out: kpt on wl ins fnl f* **13/2**
0063 **2** 1½ **Watts Up Son**[5] 5373 3-8-13 **63** (bt) JasonHart(7) 2 71
(Declan Carroll) *taken early to post: led to over 1f out: edgd rt and kpt on ins fnl f* **10/3**[2]
6411 **3** 5 **Cross Of Lorraine (IRE)**[17] 5009 8-9-10 **65** (b) TonyHamilton 3 55
(Chris Grant) *cl up: rdn and ev ch over 2f out: no ex fr over 1f out* **9/2**[3]

025- **4** *2* **Danum Dancer**[316] 6965 7-9-1 **56** .... BarryMcHugh 7 38
(Neville Bycroft) *prom: drvn and outpcd over 2f out: n.d after* **5/1**

0642 **5** *15* **Sharp Shoes**[7] 5313 4-9-8 **63** ....(p) PaulHanagan 5 —
(Ann Duffield) *chsd ldrs tl rdn and wknd over 2f out* **5/2**[1]

5560 **6** *10* **Ignatieff (IRE)**[17] 4988 4-9-10 **65** .... DuranFentiman 9 —
(Linda Stubbs) *cl up tl hung lft and wknd over 2f out* **17/2**

63.59 secs (2.49) **Going Correction** +0.50s/f (Yiel)
WFA 3 from 4yo+ 2lb 6 Ran SP% **110.4**
Speed ratings (Par 101): **100,97,89,86,62 46**
toteswingers:1&2:£3.40, 2&3:£2.20, 1&3:£4.20 CSF £27.15 CT £100.71 TOTE £8.60: £2.80, £2.30; EX 40.70.
Owner H Conlon **Bred** Rodney Meredith **Trained** Spennymoor, Co Durham

FOCUS
The soft-ground performers came to the fore in this moderate handicap. The winner's best form since November 2009.

5553 ASSET FINANCE H'CAP — 1m 4f 93y
5:10 (5:10) (Class 5) (0-70,69) 3-Y-O **£2,264** (£673; £336; £168) **Stalls** Low

Form RPR

0-31 **1** **Lordofthehouse (IRE)**[24] 4752 3-9-2 **64** .... PaulHanagan 1 84+
(William Haggas) *dwlt: sn led: mde rest: pushed clr over 3f out: unchal* **1/2**[1]

2400 **2** *6* **Damascus Symphony**[4] 5405 3-8-10 **58** .... AndrewElliott 2 66
(James Bethell) *hld up in last but in tch: hdwy against ins rail to chse (clr) wnr over 2f out: kpt on: no imp* **12/1**

3044 **3** *17* **Madrasa (IRE)**[40] 4209 3-9-4 **66** .... TomEaves 3 47
(Keith Reveley) *trckd ldng pair: rdn over 3f out: wknd over 2f out: t.o* **9/1**[3]

663 **4** *35* **Tourtiere**[28] 4611 3-9-7 **69** .... JamieSpencer 4 —
(George Moore) *early ldr: chsd ldr: pushed along after 4f: drvn and outpcd over 4f out: wknd over 2f out: eased whn no ch* **7/2**[2]

2m 49.5s (3.90) **Going Correction** +0.325s/f (Good) 4 Ran SP% **106.6**
Speed ratings (Par 100): **100,96,84,61**
CSF £6.73 TOTE £1.10; EX 5.80.
Owner Lael Stable **Bred** Lael Stables **Trained** Newmarket, Suffolk

FOCUS
An uncompetitive handicap. The winner had little to beat but the time was fair considering the early dawdle. He probably has more to offer.
Tourtiere Official explanation: jockey said gelding never travelled

5554 SUPER BOND H'CAP — 6f
5:45 (5:45) (Class 4) (0-80,80) 3-Y-O+ **£3,234** (£962; £481; £240) **Stalls** High

Form RPR

443 **1** **Layla's Hero (IRE)**[23] 4810 4-9-10 **80** .... JamieSpencer 6 93+
(John Quinn) *hld up and bhd: smooth hdwy and swtchd rt over 1f out: rdn to ld ins fnl f: kpt on wl* **11/4**[1]

113 **2** *1 1/4* **Little Jimmy Odsox (IRE)**[26] 4669 3-8-13 **72** .... DuranFentiman 1 81+
(Tim Easterby) *prom: drvn and outpcd over 2f out: rallied on outside over 1f out: chsd wnr last 75yds: kpt on fin* **10/1**

1221 **3** *1* **Spinatrix**[3] 5442 3-9-4 **80** 6ex........ DaleSwift(3) 4 86
(Michael Dods) *sn cl up: led 1/2-way: rdn 2f out: hdd ins fnl f: kpt on same pce towards fin* **4/1**[2]

0314 **4** *5* **Northern Bolt**[2] 5468 6-9-0 **70** .... PatrickMathers 8 60
(Ian McInnes) *prom: drvn and outpcd 1/2-way: rallied over 1f out: kpt on fnl f: nt pce of first three* **16/1**

0002 **5** *1 1/4* **Tadalavil**[16] 5053 6-8-10 **66** .... BarryMcHugh 2 52
(Linda Perratt) *cl up tl rdn: edgd lft and wknd appr fnl f* **8/1**

3503 **6** *1/2* **Ingleby Arch (USA)**[42] 4145 8-8-10 **66** .... SebSanders 5 50
(David Barron) *in tch: drvn along 1/2-way: no imp fr 2f out* **11/1**

0004 **7** *1 1/2* **Nadeen (IRE)**[14] 5108 4-9-4 **74** .... PaulHanagan 9 53
(Michael Smith) *hld up: drvn over 2f out: nvr able to chal* **14/1**

625 **8** *nk* **Ursula (IRE)**[23] 4791 5-9-10 **80** .... AndrewElliott 7 58
(Mrs K Burke) *prom: effrt over 2f out: edgd lft and wknd over 1f out* **8/1**

0000 **9** *shd* **Durham Express (IRE)**[36] 4362 4-8-6 **62** oh1 ow1........(p) TomEaves 3 40
(Michael Dods) *led to 1/2-way: rdn and wknd over 1f out* **20/1**

551 **10** *4 1/2* **Mawjoodah**[19] 4923 3-8-6 **68** .... PaulPickard(3) 10 32
(Brian Ellison) *hld up: struggling over 2f out: sn btn* **15/2**[3]

1m 16.79s (2.19) **Going Correction** +0.50s/f (Yiel)
WFA 3 from 4yo+ 3lb 10 Ran SP% **115.4**
Speed ratings (Par 105): **105,103,102,95,93 93,91,90,90,84**
toteswingers:1&2:£4.70, 2&3:£6.40, 1&3:£3.30 CSF £30.90 CT £112.35 TOTE £3.70: £1.40, £3.30, £1.70; EX 36.10.
Owner Dr Marwan Koukash **Bred** Epona Bloodstock Ltd **Trained** Settrington, N Yorks

FOCUS
The right horses came clear in this sprint handicap, with two in-form 3yos chasing home the well handicapped winner. The third helps set the standard.
T/Plt: £984.20 to £1 stake. Pool of £43,618.61 - 32.35 winning tickets. T/Qpdt: £139.60 to a £1 stake. Pool of £2,924.89 - 15.50 winning tickets. RY

5058 RIPON (R-H)
Monday, August 29

OFFICIAL GOING: Good to soft (7.4)
Wind: Light across Weather: Overcast

5555 RACING AGAIN TOMORROW (S) STKS — 6f
2:25 (2:26) (Class 6) 2-Y-O **£2,045** (£603; £302) **Stalls** High

Form RPR

000 **1** **Lady Advocate (IRE)**[31] 4512 2-8-11 **40** ....(b) RobertWinston 12 57
(Tim Easterby) *overall ldrs stands' side: pushed along and jnd over 2f out: sn rdn and hdd wl over 1f out: sn n.m.r: drvn and hmpd ent fnl f: rallied and edgd rt: kpt on to ld again last 50yds* **40/1**

550 **2** *1* **Look Here's Lady**[53] 3755 2-8-11 **51** .... GrahamGibbons 11 54
(Ed McMahon) *prom stands' side: hdwy to chal over 2f out: led wl over 1f out: sn rdn and edgd lft: drvn and hung lft ent fnl f: hdd and no ex last 50yds 2nd of 9 in gp* **5/1**[2]

0050 **3** *2* **Dylan's Dream (IRE)**[18] 4943 2-8-11 **47** .... DavidAllan 10 48
(Tim Easterby) *prom stands' side: effrt over 2f out: rdn to chse ldng pair over 1f out: drvn and kpt on fnl f: 3rd of 9 in gp* **16/1**

60 **4** *3/4* **Crimson Sea (IRE)**[19] 4899 2-8-11 **0** .... PJMcDonald 7 46
(Ben Haslam) *in rr stands' side: hdwy over 2f out and sn rdn along: swtchd rt over 1f out: kpt on fnl f: nrst fin: 4th of 9 in gp* **25/1**

666 **5** *1/2* **Uncle Timmy**[21] 4851 2-9-2 **56** .... PBBeggy 9 49
(John Quinn) *chsd ldrs stands' side: rdn along 2f out: sn drvn and kpt on same pce appr fnl f: 5th of 9 in gp* **16/1**

20 **6** *4 1/2* **Becksies**[5] 5367 2-8-8 **0** .... JohnFahy(3) 6 31
(Paul Midgley) *midfield stands' side: rdn along 1/2-way: n.d: 6th of 8 in gp* **9/1**

564 **7** *nk* **Bellechance**[10] 5246 2-9-2 **60** .... PhillipMakin 2 35+
(Nigel Tinkler) *racd far side: chsd ldr: led that gp 2f out: n.d: 1st of 3 in gp* **9/1**

5060 **8** *3* **In A Jiffy (IRE)**[18] 4943 2-8-11 **45** .... LeeNewman 1 21+
(David Barron) *led far side gp: rdn along 1/2-way: sn hdd & wknd: 2nd of 3 in gp* **16/1**

2145 **9** *3/4* **Arcticality (IRE)**[62] 3491 2-8-13 **58** .... LeeTopliss(3) 13 24
(Richard Fahey) *a in rr stands' side: 7th of 9 in gp* **7/1**[3]

6252 **10** *nse* **Koalition (IRE)**[17] 4983 2-9-2 **64** .... SilvestreDeSousa 8 23
(Deborah Sanderson) *trckd ldrs stands' side: pushed along after 2f: rdn along 1/2-way: sn lost pl and bhd: 8th of 9 in gp* **13/8**[1]

0066 **11** *1 1/2* **Nadia's Place**[14] 5105 2-8-8 **37** .... DeclanCannon(3) 3 14+
(Nigel Tinkler) *in rr far side: rdn along and sme hdwy 2f out: nvr a factor: 3rd of 3 in gp* **66/1**

0304 **12** *7* **Angel Kiss (IRE)**[17] 4983 2-8-11 **51** ....(b[1]) DanielTudhope 4 —
(David O'Meara) *s.i.s and reminders s: a bhd stands' side: last of 9 in gp* **12/1**

1m 16.32s (3.32) **Going Correction** +0.15s/f (Good) 12 Ran SP% **120.4**
Speed ratings (Par 92): **83,81,79,78,77 71,70,66,65,65 63,54**
toteswingers:1&2:£9.70, 1&3:£5.10, 2&3:£7.40 CSF £232.65 TOTE £49.60: £14.60, £2.20, £5.10; EX 130.30.There was no bid for the winner.
Owner S A Heley **Bred** Michael O'Dwyer & Knockainey Stud **Trained** Great Habton, N Yorks

FOCUS
Rail at innermost position and distances as advertised. A few failed to run anywhere near their form in a seller which not many ever threatened to get into, the first two home sharing those positions throughout. Those in the three lowest stalls went over to the far side, but it was clear from halfway that they were well behind those on the stands' side. The jockeys reported the ground was 'holding'. Surprise improvement from the winner with the ground and draw likely factors.

NOTEBOOK
Lady Advocate(IRE) had shown little previously, including in a claimer with this headgear on last time, so the softer ground is a possible explanation for the improvement, as she finally got the better of the runner-up inside the last. She only had an official rating of 40 prior to this, so will look well treated if connections can get her in a low-grade nursery under a penalty before she's reassessed. Official explanation: trainer had no explanation for the apparent improvement in form
Look Here's Lady has progressed with each start and won't have to wait much longer for her first success if kept to this level, travelling best for a long way but still hinting at inexperience off the bridle (wandered about a bit). (op 6-1 tchd 13-2)
Dylan's Dream(IRE) is a stable-companion of the winner and, like that one, comfortably bettered her previous efforts here, always to the fore. She's another who also has a very low handicap mark to work with. (op 18-1)
Crimson Sea(IRE) offered a bit more than previously dropped to a seller, though it's hardly anything to write home about. (op 20-1)
Uncle Timmy has a bit of ability but there's no indication at this stage that he's going to prove any better than modest.
Bellechance fared best of the trio that raced far side and almost certainly remains in form. (op 6-1)
Arcticality(IRE), who was returning from a couple of months off, was well below the form she'd shown on a sounder surface earlier in the summer, never going with any fluency. (tchd 13-2)
Koalition(IRE) wasn't quite the good thing the betting suggested but might still have been expected to do a lot better, beaten by halfway back in trip. Perhaps the soft ground didn't suit. Official explanation: jockey said gelding hung left (op 5-2)
Angel Kiss(IRE) seems to be going backwards, not facing the first-time blinkers at all. (op 16-1)

5556 PAUL LAURA AND OLIVIA CELEBRATION MAIDEN STKS — 1m
3:00 (3:03) (Class 5) 3-4-Y-O **£2,264** (£673; £336; £168) **Stalls** Low

Form RPR

5 **1** **Neutrafa (IRE)**[15] 5082 3-8-9 **0** .... MichaelO'Connell(3) 9 77+
(John Mackie) *in tch: hdwy to trck ldrs 4f out: cl up and swtchd lft 3f out: rdn to ld 2f out: edgd rt ent fnl f: sn clr* **16/1**

410 **2** *6* **Quadrant (IRE)**[93] 2506 3-9-3 **82** .... MartinDwyer 5 67
(Brian Meehan) *trckd ldr: cl up 1/2-way: chal over 3f out and sn rdn: ev ch 2f out: sn drvn: n.m.r ent fnl f: kpt on one pce* **6/4**[1]

4035 **3** *3* **Chadford**[43] 4128 3-9-3 **48** ....(p) DanielTudhope 7 60
(Tim Walford) *led: pushed along 4f out: rdn 2f out: hdd 2f out and sn drvn: one pce* **50/1**

03- **4** *2 3/4* **Albert Bridge**[306] 7178 3-9-3 **0** .... MartinLane 4 53
(Ralph Beckett) *reminders s and sn rdn along in midfield: lost pl and bhd 1/2-way: rdn and kpt on fnl 2f: nrst fin* **4/1**[3]

2 **5** *1/2* **Landaman (IRE)**[12] 5169 3-9-3 **0** .... SilvestreDeSousa 6 52
(Mark Johnston) *trckd ldrs on inner: swtchd lft and hdwy over 3f out: rdn along over 2f out: sn drvn and wknd* **7/4**[2]

6 *1 1/2* **Maven** 3-8-12 **0** .... RobertWinston 3 44
(Tim Easterby) *unruly in stalls: green and sn detached in last: pushed along 1/2-way: hdwy over 2f out: kpt on appr fnl f: nrst fin* **20/1**

36 **7** *3 3/4* **Lord Emerson**[38] 4282 3-9-0 **0** .... LeeTopliss(3) 10 40
(Richard Fahey) *chsd ldrs: rdn along over 3f out: drvn over 2f out and sn wknd* **25/1**

0 **8** *4* **Sendarose (IRE)**[23] 4813 3-9-3 **0** .... DavidAllan 8 30
(Tim Easterby) *a in rr* **33/1**

1m 41.64s (0.24) **Going Correction** +0.10s/f (Good) 8 Ran SP% **115.8**
Speed ratings (Par 103): **102,96,93,90,89 88,84,80**
toteswingers:1&2:£8.90, 1&3:£27.60, 2&3:£17.80 CSF £40.12 TOTE £22.20: £3.90, £1.10, £8.90; EX 54.70.
Owner Tony Ashley **Bred** Twelve Oaks Stud & Deerpark Stud **Trained** Church Broughton , Derbys

FOCUS
The presence of a 48-rated horse in third holds the level of this form down a bit but it's still hard not to be taken with the performance of the winner. She could be rated higher at face value.

5557 RIPON ROWELS H'CAP — 1m
3:35 (3:35) (Class 2) (0-100,97) 3-Y-O+ **£10,081** (£3,017; £1,508; £755; £376) **Stalls** Low

Form RPR

0-01 **1** **Stevie Thunder**[31] 4506 6-9-0 **88** .... RyanClark(3) 2 97
(Ian Williams) *hld up towards rr: stdy hdwy on inner over 3f out: trckd ldrs 2f out: swtchd lft and rdn over 1f out: styd on to chal jst ins fnl f: led last 100yds* **14/1**

2434 **2** *3/4* **Dolphin Rock**[23] 4794 4-8-13 **84** .... LeeNewman 6 91
(David Barron) *a.p: cl up 3f out: led over 2f out: rdn over 1f out: drvn ent fnl f: hdd and one pce last 100yds* **7/1**[1]

0316 **3** *nk* **Shavansky**[33] 4428 7-9-9 **94** .... JamesMillman 8 101
(Rod Millman) *hld up in rr: hdwy on inner over 3f out: chsd ldrs whn nt clr run wl over 1f out: swtchd lft and rdn ent fnl f: swtchd rt and styd on wl last 100yds* **9/1**

0001 **4** 2½ **Osteopathic Remedy (IRE)**^{30} 4561 7-9-9 **94**........... RobertWinston 5 95
(Michael Dods) *in tch: hdwy to chse ldrs over 2f out: rdn over 1f out: ev ch ent fnl f: sn drvn and one pce* **12/1**

2050 **5** *nse* **Lord Aeryn (IRE)**^{34} 4415 4-8-13 **87**.............................(p) LeeTopliss(3) 1 88
(Richard Fahey) *trckd ldrs on inner: hdwy over 2f out: rdn and nt clr run over 1f out: drvn and kpt on same pce fnl f* **$8/1^{3}$**

0004 **6** 1¼ **Wannabe King**^{23} 4774 5-9-12 **97**...................................(b) TedDurcan 17 95
(David Lanigan) *swtchd rt and hld up: hdwy over 3f out: trckd ldrs over 2f out: swtchd lft and effrt over 1f out: rdn to chal ent fnl f and ev ch: sn drvn and wknd* **16/1**

3004 **7** 5 **Desert Romance (IRE)**^{16} 5059 5-9-4 **89**.................. DanielTudhope 11 75
(David O'Meara) *dwlt and bhd: hdwy 3f out: rdn over 2f out: kpt on: nt rch ldrs* **16/1**

-501 **8** 1½ **Silvery Moon (IRE)**^{23} 4811 4-8-8 **79**................................ DavidAllan 10 62
(Tim Easterby) *midfield: hdwy to trck ldrs 1/2-way: effrt on outer 3f out: rdn wl over 1f out and grad wknd* **$15/2^{2}$**

3250 **9** *shd* **Snow Bay**^{23} 4774 5-9-6 **94**............................ MichaelO'Connell(3) 15 77+
(David Nicholls) *led: pushed along and hdd over 4f out: cl up and rdn over 2f out: drvn and wknd over 1f out* **16/1**

-610 **10** 2 **Xilerator (IRE)**^{65} 3397 4-9-6 **91**..................................... AndrewMullen 9 69
(David Nicholls) *prom: led over 4f out: rdn along 3f out: drvn and hdd over 2f out: sn wknd* **25/1**

0300 **11** 1½ **Dubai Dynamo**^{9} 5272 6-9-9 **94**.. PJMcDonald 16 69
(Ruth Carr) *s.i.s: a in rr* **16/1**

312 **12** 1¾ **Shalloon (IRE)**^{11} 5199 3-8-4 **81**................................. MartinLane 7 52
(Mark Johnston) *chsd ldrs: rdn along 1/2-way: sn wknd* **10/1**

-031 **13** ¾ **City Of The Kings (IRE)**^{75} 3051 6-9-3 **88**............(p) GrahamGibbons 3 57
(Geoffrey Harker) *hld up: hdwy over 3f out: rdn to chse ldrs over 2f out: sn drvn and wknd* **14/1**

0100 **14** 1¼ **Masked Dance (IRE)**^{11} 5218 4-9-6 **91**........................(p) PhillipMakin 13 57
(Kevin Ryan) *midfield: hdwy on outer over 3f out: rdn along over 2f out: sn wknd* **33/1**

-645 **15** ¾ **Desert Kiss**^{33} 4429 6-9-4 **92**... JohnFahy(3) 14 56
(Walter Swinburn) *nvr bttr than midfield* **16/1**

0003 **16** ½ **Dream Lodge (IRE)**^{60} 3537 7-8-10 **84**.............................. BillyCray(3) 4 47
(David Nicholls) *a in rr* **28/1**

0-60 **17** 8 **Master Of Arts (USA)**^{12} 5185 6-9-5 **90**................ SilvestreDeSousa 12 35
(Mark Johnston) *prom: rdn along 3f out: drvn over 2f out: sn wknd* **$8/1^{3}$**

1m 40.3s (-1.10) **Going Correction** +0.10s/f (Good)
WFA 3 from 4yo+ 6lb **17** Ran SP% **126.3**
Speed ratings (Par 109): **109,108,107,105,105 104,99,97,97,95 94,92,91,90,89 89,81**
toteswingers:1&2:£25.40, 1&3:£17.80, 2&3:£9.30 CSF £109.63 CT £959.59 TOTE £15.40: £4.60, £2.00, £2.60, £2.70; EX 137.60.
Owner Steve Gray **Bred** Sir Eric Parker **Trained** Portway, Worcs

FOCUS
A useful and competitive affair and no reason why the form won't hold up, the pace a sound one to boot. Low draws were best.

NOTEBOOK
Stevie Thunder is clearly back as good as he's ever been, up 10lb and in a much stronger race than last time yet still able to follow up. He's got a potentially very lenient hurdling mark to expolit once the handicapper gets the better of him in this sphere.
Dolphin Rock is as tough and consistent as they come and gave it his all yet again. He deserves to get his head in front but is going to edge up a bit more in the weights without winning. (op 17-2)
Shavansky is in just about the form of his life right now and will remain one to bear in mind, briefly messed about a bit approaching the final furlong and finishing well. (op 10-1)
Osteopathic Remedy(IRE) won this last year but was 7lb higher this time round and ran just as well in defeat without having any excuses. He goes well in the mud and there's no reason why he won't have another profitable autumn. (op 9-1)
Lord Aeryn(IRE) had cheekpieces on instead of blinkers this time and showed he's still in good heart without suggesting he's a winner in waiting, soon well positioned from his good draw. (op 17-2 tchd 9-1)
Wannabe King is back in form but doesn't have much room for manoeuvre off this mark and was one paced after being produced with every chance. (tchd 18-1)
Desert Romance(IRE) was caught quite a long way back and probably remains in a bit better heart than the bare result might suggest. Official explanation: jockey said gelding missed the break
Silvery Moon(IRE) had gone up 10lb for winning a lesser race at Redcar and came up quite a long way short in the end, though being caught wide didn't help and he's lightly enough raced to get back on the up at some stage. (op 8-1)
Xilerator(IRE) didn't get home upped in trip so shouldn't be judged too harshly.
Shalloon(IRE) was much more lightly raced than the rest of these but this was a totally different test to anything he'd faced previously and he was beaten at halfway. It's still early days, though.
City Of The Kings(IRE) Official explanation: jockey said gelding never travelled
Master Of Arts(USA) hasn't stood much racing in recent years and hasn't gone on from his comeback effort so far, dropping out pretty tamely. (op 9-1)

5558 RIPON CHAMPION TWO YRS OLD TROPHY, 2011 (LISTED RACE) 6f
4:10 (4:11) (Class 1) 2-Y-O
£15,311 (£5,805; £2,905; £1,447; £726; £364) **Stalls** High

Form RPR

213 **1** **Gerfalcon**^{11} 5216 2-9-2 95.. MartinDwyer 2 98+
(Brian Meehan) *hld up towards rr: hdwy over 2f out: sn swtchd rt and rdn over 1f out: styd on to chal ins fnl f: led last 50yds* **$4/1^{1}$**

11 **2** ½ **Gold City (IRE)**^{20} 4891 2-9-2 0.. TedDurcan 5 97+
(Saeed Bin Suroor) *trckd ldrs: hdwy and cl up 2f out: rdn to ld over 1f out: drvn and edgd lft ins fnl f: hdd and no ex last 50yds* **$11/2^{3}$**

12 **3** 2 **Compton**^{21} 4858 2-9-2 0..(p) MartinLane 8 91
(Ralph Beckett) *cl up: led after 2f: rdn along 2f out: drvn and hdd over 1f out: n.m.r ins fnl f: kpt on* **7/1**

1110 **4** ½ **Roger Sez (IRE)**^{11} 5216 2-8-11 84.............................. DanielTudhope 9 84
(Tim Easterby) *hld up: hdwy over 2f out: sn swtchd rt and rdn over 1f out: styd on to chse ldrs ent fnl f: sn drvn and one pce* **20/1**

1162 **5** 2 **Last Bid**^{9} 5286 2-8-11 98.. DavidAllan 6 78
(Tim Easterby) *prom: cl up 1/2-way: rdn and ev ch 2f out tl drvn and wknd appr fnl f* **8/1**

314 **6** 1¾ **Gusto**^{9} 5286 2-9-2 97.. SilvestreDeSousa 7 78
(Richard Hannon) *trckd ldng pair: effrt over 2f out and sn rdn: drvn and wknd over 1f out* **$4/1^{1}$**

0056 **7** 1 **On The Dark Side (IRE)**^{17} 4999 2-8-11 98...................... PhillipMakin 11 70
(Kevin Ryan) *led 2f: prom tl rdn along over 2f out and sn wknd* **12/1**

114 **8** *hd* **Redact (IRE)**^{44} 4094 2-9-2 97.. RobertWinston 1 74
(Richard Hannon) *s.i.s and swtchd lft s: a in rr* **$9/2^{2}$**

4113 **9** ¾ **Mister Musicmaster**^{12} 5184 2-9-2 87........................... JamesMillman 3 72
(Rod Millman) *chsd ldrs on outer: cl up 1/2-way: rdn along over 2f out: sn wknd* **11/1**

1m 13.89s (0.89) **Going Correction** +0.15s/f (Good) **9** Ran SP% **118.0**
Speed ratings (Par 102): **100,99,96,96,93 91,89,89,88**
toteswingers:1&2:£4.10, 1&3:£7.20, 2&3:£11.00 CSF £26.76 TOTE £5.10: £1.50, £1.90, £2.90; EX 32.50.
Owner Michael Buckley **Bred** Enterprise B'Stock & Newsells Park Stud **Trained** Manton, Wilts

FOCUS
Always a useful affair and this looks an up-to-scratch renewal. The pace was sound enough and the fourth helps with the form.

NOTEBOOK
Gerfalcon has got better by the race, stepping up a little on the form he showed when placed in a valuable event at York earlier this month, not ideally drawn and keen enough early on but still coming with a sustained run on the outer to get on top late on. He holds an entry in the Mill Reef and will be well worth his place, though that will demand a fair bit more again. (op 9-2 tchd 7-2)
Gold City(IRE) couldn't maintain his unbeaten record but lost little in defeat, showing himself versatile regards ground into the bargain. He's got an entry in the Two-Year-Old Trophy at Redcar and appeals as the type to go well in that. (op 5-1 tchd 9-2)
Compton ran well in the first-time cheekpieces, up there throughout and sticking to his task despite hanging right. He'll be winning again dropped back to a conditions event, and this pays a compliment to his Windsor conqueror Rebellious Guest. Official explanation: jockey said colt hung right (op 9-1)
Roger Sez(IRE) has proved progressive bar her York run (well behind Gerfalcon that day) and there'll be weaker Listed races for her to contest among her own sex. (tchd 18-1)
Last Bid was just about the form pick on her recent second in the Roses at York but couldn't reproduce that effort, beaten a bit too far out to suggest lack of stamina was the sole reason (raced only at 5f previously). (op 7-1)
Gusto was another who didn't do much for the form of the Roses, fading after being produced with every chance approaching the final furlong. (op 6-1)
On The Dark Side(IRE)'s close fifth in the Molecomb is starting to look a bit of a stand-out, certainly nowhere near reproducing it in two starts since. (op 10-1)
Redact(IRE) was disappointing on the day but probably deserves another chance, dropping in after missing the break from the widest stall and never looking entirely at ease on this undulating track. Official explanation: jockey said colt missed the break (op 4-1 tchd 5-1)

5559 BILLY NEVETT MEMORIAL H'CAP 6f
4:45 (4:45) (Class 4) (0-85,87) 3-Y-O **£4,204** (£1,251; £625; £312) **Stalls** High

Form RPR

0062 **1** **Elusive Prince**^{16} 5054 3-9-7 **85**......................................(v) LeeNewman 6 97
(David Barron) *trckd ldrs: pushed along 1/2-way: hdwy and cl up 2f out: sn led and rdn clr: styd on strly* **$7/4^{1}$**

0060 **2** 3¼ **Boundaries**^{21} 4855 3-9-0 **78**.. TedDurcan 4 80
(Tim Easterby) *in rr and pushed along after 2f: hdwy 1/2-way: swtchd rt to outer 2f out: sn rdn and kpt on ins fnl f: no ch w wnr* **22/1**

0236 **3** 3¼ **Indian Ballad (IRE)**^{22} 4817 3-9-7 **85**........................ GrahamGibbons 8 76
(Ed McMahon) *hld up: pushed along and outpcd in rr bef 1/2-way: hdwy 2f out: sn rdn and styd on ins fnl f: nrst fin* **$9/2^{3}$**

5021 **4** ¾ **Another Citizen (IRE)**^{20} 4880 3-9-2 **80**..........................(p) DavidAllan 3 69
(Tim Easterby) *trckd ldrs: effrt over 2f out: rdn wl over 1f out: drvn and wknd ent fnl f* **$9/4^{2}$**

-505 **5** *nk* **Nasharra (IRE)**^{36} 4353 3-9-0 **78**..................................(b1) PhillipMakin 1 66
(Kevin Ryan) *in tch: effrt 1/2-way: sn rdn along and wknd over 2f out* **12/1**

504 **6** 6 **On The High Tops (IRE)**^{9} 5268 3-9-2 **80**........................ PJMcDonald 2 49
(Ruth Carr) *cl up: rdn along 2f out: sn wknd* **16/1**

2030 **7** 5 **Bay Of Fires (IRE)**^{14} 5109 3-8-7 **71**........................ SilvestreDeSousa 7 24
(David O'Meara) *led: rdn along 1/2-way: drvn over 2f out: sn hdd & wknd* **10/1**

1m 13.47s (0.47) **Going Correction** +0.15s/f (Good) **7** Ran SP% **112.3**
Speed ratings (Par 102): **102,97,93,92,91 83,77**
toteswingers:1&2:£12.30, 1&3:£2.00, 2&3:£16.30 CSF £38.57 CT £149.93 TOTE £2.60: £2.10, £5.00; EX 55.50.
Owner Bridge Extraction Systems Ltd **Bred** Usk Valley Stud **Trained** Maunby, N Yorks

FOCUS
They went hard in front in this sprint, the field well strung out at halfway, setting it up for those coming from a little further back. Improved form again from the winner.

5560 TOTEPOOL A BETTER WAY TO BET H'CAP 1m 1f 170y
5:20 (5:21) (Class 5) (0-75,73) 3-Y-O [illegible] **Stalls** Low

Form RPR

3313 **1** **Sangar**^{31} 4515 3-8-9 **61**.. GrahamGibbons 8 76
(Ollie Pears) *trckd ldng pair on inner: hdwy over 3f out: swtchd lft and chal over 2f out: rdn to ld wl over 1f out: drvn ins fnl f and kpt on gamely* **$6/1^{2}$**

2163 **2** ½ **Icebuster**^{19} 4914 3-9-6 **72**.. JamesMillman 2 86+
(Rod Millman) *hld up in rr: hdwy on inner 3f out: nt clr run 2f out and sn swtchd lft: rdn and hdwy to chse wnr appr fnl f: drvn and edgd rt last 100yds: no imp towards fin* **$5/2^{1}$**

6503 **3** 10 **Free Art**^{42} 4142 3-9-4 **70**.. SilvestreDeSousa 3 64
(Geoffrey Harker) *trckd ldrs: effrt 3f out: rdn along over 2f out: drvn wl over 1f out and one pce* **$8/1^{3}$**

6410 **4** 2 **Ventura Sands (IRE)**^{30} 4560 3-9-0 **69**............................ LeeTopliss(3) 7 58
(Richard Fahey) *t.k.h: early hld up towards rr: hdwy 3f out: rdn along over 2f out: sn drvn and one pce* **10/1**

2000 **5** ¾ **Baby Driver**^{21} 4866 3-8-8 **63**...................................... RossAtkinson(3) 1 51
(Tom Dascombe) *t.k.h: led: rdn along 3f out: jnd and drvn over 2f out: hdd wl over 1f out and sn wknd* **25/1**

1365 **6** 7 **Honest Deal**^{49} 3904 3-9-7 **73**.. PJMcDonald 4 47
(Alan Swinbank) *trckd ldrs: effrt over 3f out: sn rdn and wknd 2f out* **$6/1^{2}$**

0564 **7** 3 **Kalahaag (IRE)**^{11} 5213 3-9-1 **70**... BillyCray(3) 5 37
(David Nicholls) *s.i.s: a in rr* **16/1**

332 **8** 18 **Pivot Bridge**^{25} 4716 3-9-1 **67**... RobertWinston 9 —
(Charles Hills) *trckd ldr: effrt and cl up 4f out: rdn along over 3f out and sn wknd* **$5/2^{1}$**

2m 5.22s (-0.18) **Going Correction** +0.10s/f (Good) **8** Ran SP% **115.6**
Speed ratings (Par 100): **104,103,95,94,93 87,85,71**
toteswingers:1&2:£4.30, 1&3:£5.90, 2&3:£3.40 CSF £21.69 CT £121.59 TOTE £6.50: £1.80, £1.60, £2.10; EX 25.50.
Owner Timothy O'Gram **Bred** L C And Mrs A E Sigsworth **Trained** Norton, N Yorks

FOCUS
A few underperformed in this but the leading pair still deserve credit for pulling a long way clear. They have been given credit but it's hard to know how literally to take the form.
Pivot Bridge Official explanation: jockey said colt had no more to give
T/Jkpt: Not won. T/Plt: £277.90 to a £1 stake. Pool:£72,936.59 - 191.58 winning tickets T/Qpdt: £14.20 to £1 stake. Pool:£5,534.38 - 286.55 winning tickets JR

5344 WARWICK (L-H)

Monday, August 29

OFFICIAL GOING: Good (good to soft in places; 6.8)

Wind: Fresh half-behind Weather: Overcast

5561 TURFTV H'CAP 6f

2:10 (2:10) (Class 5) (0-70,69) 3-Y-0+ **£2,264** (£673; £336; £168) **Stalls** Low

Form RPR

5031 **1** **Paradise Spectre**[14] 5121 4-9-0 **62**.............................. HarryBentley(3) 2 75
(Mrs K Burke) *trckd ldrs: rdn to ld over 1f out: r.o* **5/1**[1]

2501 **2** *1 ½* **Oh So Spicy**[25] 4729 4-9-6 **65**.............................. GeorgeBaker 10 73
(Chris Wall) *chsd ldrs: rdn over 2f out: hung lft ins fnl f: r.o: nt trble wnr* **13/2**[2]

0225 **3** *1 ½* **Steel City Boy (IRE)**[39] 4233 8-8-13 **58**.............................. JimmyQuinn 1 61
(Garry Woodward) *led: rdn and hdd over 1f out: styd on same pce ins fnl f* **8/1**

4200 **4** *1 ¼* **Bermondsey Bob (IRE)**[3] 5425 5-9-10 **69**.............................. CathyGannon 9 68
(John Spearing) *sn drvn along to chse ldr tl over 2f out: no exTra fnl f* **7/1**[3]

3405 **5** *¾* **Make My Dream**[23] 4795 8-9-6 **65**.............................. TadhgO'Shea 5 62+
(John Gallagher) *prom: lost pl over 3f out: rdn over 2f out: r.o ins fnl f* **25/1**

0136 **6** *hd* **Downhill Skier (IRE)**[11] 5201 7-9-7 **66**.............................. ShaneKelly 8 62
(Mark Brisbourne) *hld up: rdn over 2f out: styd on ins fnl f: nvr nrr* **7/1**[3]

1106 **7** *nse* **Dead Cool**[18] 4973 3-9-7 **69**.............................. SteveDrowne 11 65
(Hughie Morrison) *s.i.s: sn pushed along in rr: hdwy u.p and hung lft fr over 1f out: nt trble ldrs* **8/1**

0155 **8** *nk* **Shostakovich (IRE)**[39] 4238 3-9-6 **68**..............................(tp) JamesDoyle 12 63
(Sylvester Kirk) *chsd ldrs: rdn over 2f out: styd on same pce fr over 1f out* **14/1**

0065 **9** *1 ½* **Penny's Pearl (IRE)**[9] 5265 3-9-2 **69**.............................. MatthewCosham(5) 3 59
(David Evans) *mid-div: rdn 1/2-way: wknd fnl f* **18/1**

5535 **10** *½* **Dualagi**[18] 4973 7-9-2 **61**.............................. DaneO'Neill 6 50
(Martin Bosley) *hld up: rdn over 2f out: nvr on terms* **25/1**

5012 **11** *nk* **Rainy Night**[10] 5244 5-9-1 **67**..............................(v) JackDuern(7) 7 55
(Reg Hollinshead) *sn pushed along in rr: rdn over 2f out: nvr on terms* **15/2**

0-06 **12** *20* **Jibouti (IRE)**[5] 5381 3-8-10 **58**.............................. NeilCallan 4 —
(Clive Brittain) *sn rdn along to chse ldrs: wknd over 2f out: eased over 1f out* **10/1**

1m 11.41s (-0.39) **Going Correction** -0.175s/f (Firm) course record

WFA 3 from 4yo+ 3lb **12** Ran SP% **117.7**

Speed ratings (Par 103): **95,93,91,89,88 88,88,87,85,84 84,57**

toteswingers:1&2:£8.60, 1&3:£14.30, 2&3:£11.10 CSF £36.10 CT £257.55 TOTE £6.40: £2.20, £1.50, £3.20; EX 31.30.

Owner The Paradise Partnership **Bred** Bearstone Stud **Trained** Middleham Moor, North Yorks

FOCUS

It was dry overnight and the going was good, good to soft in places. An ordinary sprint handicap. Three of the first four raced prominently and the field came centre to stands' side in the straight. The winner was close to his 2yo best.

Dualagi Official explanation: trainer said mare was struck into

5562 AVON TOYS LEAMINGTON NURSERY 5f 110y

2:45 (2:48) (Class 5) (0-75,74) 2-Y-0 **£2,264** (£673; £336; £168) **Stalls** Low

Form RPR

2551 **1** **Stepper Point**[18] 4955 2-9-6 **73**.............................. GeorgeBaker 16 95+
(William Muir) *trckd ldrs: a gng wl: led over 2f out: clr fnl f: easily* **14/1**

21 **2** *5* **Baltic Fizz (IRE)**[37] 4319 2-8-13 **69**.............................. MartinHarley(3) 6 72
(Mrs K Burke) *s.i.s: hdwy 1/2-way: rdn and swtchd rt over 1f out: styd on to go 2nd wl ins fnl f: no ch w wnr* **13/2**[2]

332 **3** *1 ½* **School Fees**[25] 4710 2-9-7 **74**.............................. DaneO'Neill 8 72
(Henry Candy) *led: rdn and hdd over 2f out: no ex fnl f* **7/1**[3]

5462 **4** *¾* **Tina's Spirit (IRE)**[7] 5324 2-9-5 **72**.............................. JimmyFortune 3 68
(Richard Hannon) *chsd ldrs: rdn over 2f out: styd on same pce fr over 1f out* **6/1**[1]

445 **5** *½* **Ashpan Sam**[22] 4823 2-8-11 **64**.............................. NeilCallan 4 58
(John Spearing) *s.i.s: hdwy over 3f out: rdn over 1f out: wknd ins fnl f* **7/1**[3]

1510 **6** *1 ½* **Silvas Romana (IRE)**[11] 5197 2-9-2 **72**.............................. HarryBentley(3) 10 61
(Mark Brisbourne) *prom: outpcd over 3f out: styd on u.p ins fnl f* **12/1**

3534 **7** *½* **The Rising (IRE)**[12] 5174 2-9-3 **70**..............................(v) RichardMullen 5 57
(Ed McMahon) *prom: rdn over 2f out: wknd fnl f* **12/1**

0421 **8** *1* **Worth**[14] 5099 2-9-4 **71**..............................(b) ShaneKelly 7 55
(Brian Meehan) *chsd ldrs: rdn over 2f out: wknd fnl f* **11/1**

0342 **9** *½* **Musical Valley**[6] 5348 2-9-6 **73**..............................(t) RichardKingscote 15 55
(Tom Dascombe) *dwlt: sn pushed along in rr: sme hdwy over 1f out: nvr on terms* **14/1**

1442 **10** *½* **Ocean Myth**[18] 4955 2-9-3 **70**.............................. LiamJones 11 51
(William Haggas) *chsd ldrs tl rdn and wknd over 1f out* **9/1**

1044 **11** *shd* **I'm Still The Man (IRE)**[54] 3745 2-9-2 **72**..............................(t) KierenFox(3) 9 52
(Bill Turner) *hld up: rdn over 1f out: a in rr* **33/1**

3521 **12** *1 ¾* **Aquasulis (IRE)**[10] 5245 2-9-1 **68**.............................. CathyGannon 2 43
(David Evans) *prom: rdn 1/2-way: wknd over 1f out* **16/1**

4502 **13** *1 ¾* **Cataract**[45] 4069 2-7-13 **52**..............................(b) JimmyQuinn 1 21
(John Weymes) *s.i.s: sn pushed along in rr: n.d* **25/1**

222 **14** *2 ½* **Excavator**[60] 3539 2-9-6 **73**..............................(b[1]) SteveDrowne 12 34
(Roger Charlton) *prom: lost pl over 3f out: sn bhd* **14/1**

65.69 secs (-0.21) **Going Correction** -0.175s/f (Firm) **14** Ran SP% **119.0**

Speed ratings (Par 94): **94,87,85,84,83 81,81,79,79,78 78,75,73,70**

toteswingers:1&2:£5.80, 1&3:£13.40, 2&3:£10.90 CSF £101.13 CT £723.18 TOTE £14.20: £4.40, £3.80, £1.80; EX 156.10.

Owner C L A Edginton **Bred** Whitsbury Manor Stud **Trained** Lambourn, Berks

FOCUS

This looked a very competitive nursery but the winner absolutely blitzed his rivals before cruising to victory in a race where the four market leaders chased him home. He might be up to making his mark in a Listed race. The next two help with the level.

NOTEBOOK

Stepper Point was looking fairly exposed after a Sandown disappointment but he reportedly scoped dirty after that run and found a big surge of improvement to win six-runner Goodwood nursery with something in hand last time. Racing off 5lb higher, he travelled powerfully out wide before seizing the initiative and coasting clear against the stands' rail. He will face a sharp race after this demolition job but something has really clicked recently and could continue to improve. (op 12-1)

Baltic Fizz(IRE) stayed on in determined style to win the race for second on her nursery debut back from five weeks off. The form of her odds-on win in a 5f good-ground maiden auction at Lingfield has taken some knocks, but this very lightly raced filly has potential for further progress and could appreciate a stiffer test. (op 7-1 tchd 15-2)

School Fees, placed in three sprint maidens, ran a solid race under a prominent ride on nursery debut. Out of a 1m1f winning half-sister to decent multiple 6f-7f winners, she looks a willing type who should have more to offer. (op 13-2 tchd 11-2)

Tina's Spirit(IRE) hit personal best when a close second in a Windsor nursery last week and ran respectably off the same mark here, particularly as she may have been at a disadvantage racing on the far side in the straight. (op 13-2 tchd 11-2)

Ashpan Sam showed ability in maidens and gave a decent account of himself dropped slightly in trip on nursery debut. (op 12-1 tchd 13-2)

Musical Valley Official explanation: jockey said gelding was slowly away

5563 LEAMINGTON FOOD AND DRINK FESTIVAL CONDITIONS STKS 7f 26y

3:20 (3:20) (Class 3) 3-Y-0+ **£6,663** (£1,982; £990; £495) **Stalls** Low

Form RPR

0534 **1** **Colonial (IRE)**[16] 5032 4-9-0 105.............................. FrankieDettori 5 112
(Saeed Bin Suroor) *mde all: rdn over 1f out: r.o wl: eased nr fin* **9/4**[1]

4002 **2** *2* **Forjatt (IRE)**[18] 4965 3-8-7 102 ow1.............................. NeilCallan 8 103
(Roger Varian) *a.p: chsd winned wnr 1/2-way: rdn over 1f out: styd on* **7/2**[2]

00-2 **3** *4* **Al Aasifh (IRE)**[30] 4526 3-8-6 104.............................. RichardMullen 9 91
(Saeed Bin Suroor) *chsd ldrs: rdn over 2f out: styd on same pce fr over 1f out:* **10/1**

-000 **4** *½* **Rodrigo De Torres**[9] 5282 4-8-8 95.............................. MartinHarley(3) 3 91
(Mrs K Burke) *chsd wnr to 1/2-way: sn rdn: wknd ins fnl f* **20/1**

5040 **5** *¾* **Inler (IRE)**[65] 3404 4-9-0 104.............................. ShaneKelly 6 92
(Brian Meehan) *hld up: hdwy over 2f out: shkn up over 1f out: no imp* **7/1**

6-20 **6** *¾* **Mia's Boy**[16] 5032 7-8-11 100.............................. AndreaAtzeni 1 87
(Chris Dwyer) *hld up: rdn over 2f out: nvr on terms* **8/1**

F205 **7** *½* **Mon Cadeaux**[9] 5272 4-8-11 98.............................. LiamKeniry 7 86
(Andrew Balding) *hld up: plld hrd: rdn over 1f out: n.d* **11/2**[3]

0300 **8** *2 ¾* **Invincible Soul (IRE)**[68] 3290 4-8-11 97.............................. JimmyFortune 2 79
(Richard Hannon) *chsd ldrs: rdn 1/2-way: wknd over 1f out* **20/1**

1m 21.71s (-2.89) **Going Correction** -0.175s/f (Firm)

WFA 3 from 4yo+ 5lb **8** Ran SP% **110.6**

Speed ratings (Par 107): **109,106,102,101,100 99,99,96**

toteswingers:1&2:£2.10, 1&3:£1.90, 2&3:£1.70 CSF £9.32 TOTE £2.40: £1.30, £2.20, £3.60; EX 6.10.

Owner Godolphin **Bred** Darley **Trained** Newmarket, Suffolk

FOCUS

A useful conditions event. The 105-rated favourite scored with something in hand over his main market rival who pulled clear of the rest. It was the best of the C&D times but the form has not been rated too positively.

NOTEBOOK

Colonial(IRE) was a triple Listed winner over 7f/1m for Andre Fabre, and ran a huge race when fourth off 105 in a Doncaster handicap last time. He had decent claims reunited with Frankie Dettori and put in a power-packed front-running display to justify strong support and improve his strike-rate to 5-16. He looks well worth his current mark and could make a big impact back in Group 3 company. (opened 9-4 after early 5-2 in places and 11-4 in a place, tchd 7-4)

Forjatt(IRE) recorded two sprint wins in maiden/novice company as a juvenile. He had come up a bit short in handicaps this time around but his latest second off 98 at Newmarket was a personal best and the form was boosted by the progressive winner going in again off 6lb higher next time. He had a fair chance at the weights and kept fighting to finish clear of the third. A gelded son of Iffraaj, he is unexposed at this trip and could find some more improvement. (op 4-1 tchd 9-2)

Al Aasifh(IRE), forced wide for most of the way, ran respectably behind his stablemate on just his second run this season. A maiden/Listed winner on good or slower ground last summer, this 3yo son of Invincible Spirit is still very lightly raced. (op 8-1)

Rodrigo De Torres won a 7f Doncaster conditions event for Sir Henry Cecil last May but he has struggled since for a couple of different yards. This run represents an upturn in form but he was well held and remains some way below his best. (op 25-1 tchd 28-1)

Inler(IRE) ended 2010 with a decisive win in hot conditions race at Doncaster. He had shown mixed form in Group/Listed company this season but had claims on his fourth in a Group 3 at Haydock two runs back. Things looked promising when he travelled well just off the pace early in the straight but this market drifter didn't pick up and may have needed the run back from a short break and gelding operation. He should improve next time and it is interesting that both of his wins have been in the autumn. (op 13-2 tchd 8-1)

Mia's Boy confirmed that he retains all of ability when dividing 110 and 104-rated rivals in conditions event at Newbury on comeback but he has not fired in two runs since. (op 15-2)

Mon Cadeaux hit a form high when runner-up in 7f Chester Listed race before a creditable fifth off 98 last time, but he was keen and never competitive with a bit to find in this company. (tchd 6-1)

5564 BRITISH STALLION STUDS SUPPORTING BRITISH RACING E B F MAIDEN STKS (DIV I) 7f 26y

3:55 (3:59) (Class 5) 2-Y-0 **£2,975** (£885; £442; £221) **Stalls** Low

Form RPR

2 **1** **Farraaj (IRE)**[33] 4446 2-9-3 0.............................. NeilCallan 5 88+
(Roger Varian) *a.p: chsd ldr over 2f out: rdn to ld ins fnl f: edgd rt: r.o* **13/8**[1]

3 **2** *1 ½* **She Spirit Di Su (IRE)**[16] 5048 2-8-12 0.............................. JimmyFortune 14 77
(Peter Chapple-Hyam) *chsd ldr tl led over 4f out: shkn up over 1f out: hdd and unable qck ins fnl f* **7/1**

23 **3** *3* **Surfer (USA)**[33] 4446 2-9-3 0.............................. FrankieDettori 4 75
(Mahmood Al Zarooni) *hld up in tch: rdn over 1f out: no ex ins fnl f* **5/2**[2]

02 **4** *1* **Endowing (IRE)**[17] 5013 2-9-3 0.............................. DaneO'Neill 11 72+
(Richard Hannon) *s.i.s: hld up: rdn and r.o ins fnl f: nvr nrr* **7/2**[3]

0 **5** *1 ½* **Romantic (IRE)**[23] 4798 2-9-3 0.............................. IanMongan 9 69+
(Sir Henry Cecil) *prom: rdn over 2f out: wknd fnl f* **28/1**

00 **6** *¾* **Darrow (IRE)**[17] 4996 2-9-3 0.............................. ShaneKelly 12 67
(William Knight) *hld up in tch: rdn over 2f out: wknd fnl f* **66/1**

0 **7** *2* **Never Satisfied**[17] 4995 2-9-3 0.............................. MichaelHills 1 62
(Charles Hills) *hld up: shkn up over 1f out: nvr nr to chal* **12/1**

00 **8** *¾* **Romany Spirit (IRE)**[14] 5111 2-8-12 0.............................. SteveDrowne 8 55
(Jim Boyle) *led: hdd over 4f out: chsd ldr tl rdn over 2f out: wknd over 1f out* **100/1**

00 **9** *½* **Methaen (USA)**[23] 4798 2-9-3 0.............................. TadhgO'Shea 3 59
(Ed Dunlop) *hld up: rdn over 1f out: nvr on terms* **80/1**

10 *2* **Emman Bee (IRE)** 2-8-12 0.............................. CathyGannon 2 49
(John Gallagher) *s.s: a in rr* **66/1**

11 *2* **Shot In The Dark (IRE)** 2-9-3 0.............................. LiamKeniry 10 49
(Andrew Balding) *s.i.s: hdwy into mid-div over 4f out: wknd over 2f out* **33/1**

0 **12** *2 ¾* **Norfolk Sky**[18] 4961 2-8-12 0.............................. NickyMackay 13 37
(Chris Wall) *hld up: a in rr* **100/1**

0 **13** *6* **Ashes Star**[35] 4384 2-9-3 0.............................. RichardKingscote 7 27
(Jonathan Portman) *chsd ldrs tl rdn over 2f out: sn wknd* **100/1**

1m 24.73s (0.13) **Going Correction** -0.175s/f (Firm) **13** Ran SP% **122.7**

Speed ratings (Par 94): **92,90,86,85,84 83,80,80,79,77 74,71,64**

toteswingers:1&2:£4.30, 1&3:£1.30, 2&3:£5.90 CSF £14.45 TOTE £2.70: £1.50, £2.80, £1.10; EX 14.60.

Owner Sheikh Ahmed Al Maktoum **Bred** Darley **Trained** Newmarket, Suffolk

FOCUS

A useful maiden. It was run at a strong pace and the four market leaders filled the first four positions. The winner can go on and rate higher, with those down the field anchoring the level.

NOTEBOOK

Farraaj(IRE) ran green but was just held by a rival who raced closer to the steady pace when a solid 3-1 chance in a 7f Sandown maiden on debut. A weak favourite, he kept the leaders in his sights and showed a good attitude to deliver on his second start. A brother to useful 7f winner Taqdeyr and half-brother to top-class 6f/7f performer Iffraaj, he looks a decent prospect and is clearly well regarded as he holds an entry in the Group 1 Racing Post Trophy. (op 11-10 tchd 7-4)

She Spirit Di Su(IRE) showed good early pace and rallied well under pressure when a promising third in a 6f Newbury maiden on debut and she ran a similar race to chase home the market leader here. A late foal who was retained for 80,000gns as a yearling, she is from successful Italian family and should be able to win races. (op 8-1)

Surfer(USA) was well backed but he finished 3l further behind Farraaj than he did last time. However, that rival looks useful and progressive, and this $350,000 brother to 6f 2yo winner Baffled has achieved decent form in three maidens and should find a good opening. (op 4-1)

Endowing(IRE) took a huge step forward on his debut form when 50-1 second behind useful Jeremy Noseda-trained odds-on favourite in 1m Newmarket maiden. He couldn't pose a threat back in trip but did catch the eye staying on strongly and should appreciate a return to 1m. (tchd 3-1)

Romantic(IRE) was always behind after losing plenty of ground in flip start of 1m AW maiden on debut but he showed some promise this time. Related to stacks of winners, notably Grand Criterium winner Second Empire, he is quite a late foal and should go forward from this. (tchd 33-1)

Never Satisfied was a market springer but couldn't get into the main action on his second start. (op 20-1)

5565 BRITISH STALLION STUDS SUPPORTING BRITISH RACING E B F MAIDEN STKS (DIV II) 7f 26y

4:30 (4:33) (Class 5) 2-Y-O £2,975 (£885; £442; £221) Stalls Low

Form RPR

243 **1** **Pickled Pelican (IRE)**[21] 4864 2-9-3 75 ..... LiamJones 8 82
(William Haggas) *mde all: rdn clr over 2f out: styd on* **17/2**

0 **2** *2 ¼* **Strictly Silver (IRE)**[10] 5254 2-9-3 0 ..... CathyGannon 5 76
(Alan Bailey) *trckd ldrs: rdn over 2f out: edgd lft and wnt 2nd wl ins fnl f: nt rch wnr* **11/2[3]**

3 **3** *shd* **Spoke To Carlo**[13] 5133 2-9-3 0 ..... NeilCallan 12 76
(Eve Johnson Houghton) *a.p: chsd wnr over 4f out: rdn over 2f out: styd on: lost 2nd wl ins fnl f* **4/1[2]**

2 **4** *½* **Everlong**[23] 4804 2-8-12 0 ..... JimmyFortune 1 72+
(Peter Chapple-Hyam) *hld up in tch: hmpd after 1f: rdn and swtchd lft over 1f out: kpt on* **85/40[1]**

34 **5** *2 ¼* **Always Et Toujours**[89] 2617 2-9-3 0 ..... FrederikTylicki 2 69
(Mark Johnston) *chsd ldrs: rdn over 2f out: wknd ins fnl f* **28/1**

6 *3 ¾* **Asifa (IRE)** 2-9-3 0 ..... FrankieDettori 7 60+
(Saeed Bin Suroor) *dwlt: outpcd: nvr nrr* **6/1**

364 **7** *½* **Represent (IRE)**[89] 2606 2-8-12 72 ..... SteveDrowne 11 54
(Mick Channon) *sn outpcd: hdwy over 2f out: wknd over 1f out* **25/1**

0 **8** *1 ¾* **Saratoga Slew (IRE)**[23] 4804 2-8-12 0 ..... MichaelHills 10 49
(Charles Hills) *outpcd* **16/1**

52 **9** *2 ¼* **Cool Hand Luke (IRE)**[19] 4919 2-9-3 0 ..... RichardKingscote 3 49
(Tom Dascombe) *chsd wnr over 2f: sn rdn: wknd over 2f out* **16/1**

0 **10** *1 ¼* **Bountiful Catch**[48] 3954 2-9-3 0 ..... MickyFenton 6 46+
(Pam Sly) *hld up: wknd over 2f out* **100/1**

0 **11** *10* **Quixote**[24] 4762 2-9-3 0 ..... RoystonFfrench 13 21
(Clive Brittain) *s.s: outpcd* **40/1**

1m 24.02s (-0.58) **Going Correction** -0.175s/f (Firm) 11 Ran SP% **114.7**

Speed ratings (Par 94): **96,93,93,92,90 85,85,83,80,79 67**

toteswingers:1&2:£34.40, 1&3:£4.00, 2&3:£7.80 CSF £51.81 TOTE £10.60: £3.40, £2.20, £1.20; EX 64.70.

Owner D I Scott & L K Piggott **Bred** T Hirschfeld **Trained** Newmarket, Suffolk

■ Stewards' Enquiry : Liam Jones two-day ban: careless riding (Sep 12-13)

FOCUS

This didn't look quite as strong as the first division. The pace was fairly solid but a runner who raced prominently made a race winning move when kicking clear off the final turn. He has been accorded a personal best.

NOTEBOOK

Pickled Pelican(IRE) was a promising 7-2 second behind a potentially useful/well backed newcomer in a 6f Yarmouth maiden on debut, but he pulled hard when held at odds-on at Brighton next time and could only plug on for third when a strong form contender on AW last time on return from a break and gelding operation. He had a bit to prove but attracted support and scored with something in hand under an attacking ride. This continued a trend of front-running winners against the stands' rail on this card but there was still a lot to like about the performance from this half-brother to smart/highly progressive Alexander Pope. (op 11-1)

Strictly Silver(IRE) holds entries in Champagne Stakes/Racing Post Trophy but this 40,000gns half-brother to fair 6f winner Chaussini made no impact at a biggish price on his debut at York. However, he was big market mover throughout the day and showed plenty of improvement on this second run. There were still signs of inexperience as he went a bit in snatches, and he should progress again next time. (op 5-1)

Spoke To Carlo, a promising 12-1 third behind two useful market leaders in 7f Brighton maiden on debut, was never far away and ran a decent run on his second outing. (op 11-2 tchd 7-2)

Everlong was sent off at 11-2 when promising 4l second behind an impressive newcomer in 7f Newmarket fillies' maiden on debut. She had decent claims but this Fillies' Mile entry got caught out when the winner kicked on before staying on in a race that didn't set up for the hold-up runners. She could be worth another chance next time. (op 7-4 tchd 13-8)

Always Et Toujours was unsold at 9,500gns as a yearling but he is out of a 7f 2yo winning half-sister to a 7f Listed placed 2yo winner Celestial Lagoon and has shown some pace and promise and three maidens. (op 25-1)

Asifa(IRE), a 110,000euros Green Desert colt, looked inexperienced before doing some late work on debut. (op 13-2 tchd 7-1)

5566 TIM STACEY 40TH BIRTHDAY H'CAP 1m 6f 213y

5:05 (5:07) (Class 6) (0-60,60) 3-Y-O+ £2,385 (£704; £352) Stalls Low

Form RPR

511 **1** **Mina's Boy**[25] 4732 3-9-1 60 ..... RoystonFfrench 1 68+
(Ed Dunlop) *chsd ldrs: pushed along over 3f out: hrd rdn fr over 1f out: jnd ldr 110yds out where rdr mistk the winning line and eased for a few strides: rallied to ld post* **3/1[1]**

0650 **2** *nse* **Drawn Gold**[37] 4341 7-10-0 60 ..... GeorgeBaker 8 66
(Reg Hollinshead) *trckd ldrs: led 2f out: sn rdn: styd on: hdd post* **8/1**

0005 **3** *2 ¼* **Dhampas**[17] 5022 3-8-1 46 oh1 ..... (b) NickyMackay 4 49
(Jim Boyle) *s.i.s: hld up: hdwy over 2f out: rdn and edgd rt over 1f out: styd on same pce ins fnl f* **18/1**

0645 **4** *1 ¾* **Green Future (USA)**[18] 4974 3-8-13 58 ..... NeilCallan 12 59
(Amanda Perrett) *hld up: hdwy over 4f out: rdn over 1f out: styd on same pce* **6/1[3]**

0031 **5** *½* **Blazing Buck**[38] 4274 5-9-8 54 ..... LiamJones 6 54
(Tony Carroll) *led: rdn over 3f out: hdd 2f out: no ex fnl f* **17/2**

4323 **6** *½* **Arctic Reach**[20] 4491 3-8-2 47 ..... (p) CathyGannon 10 47
(Brendan Powell) *hld up: hdwy over 6f out: rdn over 3f out: nt clr run and swtchd lft over 1f out: styd on same pce* **11/2[2]**

0045 **7** *nk* **Neighbourhood (USA)**[49] 3922 3-7-12 50 ..... RaulDaSilva(7) 7 49
(James Evans) *chsd ldrs: lost pl 9f out: last 6f out: rallied and swtchd lft over 1f out: nt rch ldrs* **28/1**

6504 **8** *6* **Astromoon**[14] 5122 4-9-1 47 ..... JimmyQuinn 3 38
(Mark H Tompkins) *mid-div: rdn over 3f out: wknd over 2f out* **16/1**

0043 **9** *1* **Mountain Myst**[17] 5022 3-8-4 49 ..... WilliamCarson 9 39
(William Muir) *chsd ldr: rdn over 4f out: wknd over 1f out* **12/1**

0530 **10** *2* **Can Can Dancer**[11] 5209 6-9-0 46 ..... AndreaAtzeni 5 33
(Charles Smith) *hld up: rdn over 2f out: a in rr* **20/1**

0006 **11** *¾* **Dixie Land Band**[9] 5267 3-8-3 48 oh1 ow2 ..... RichardThomas 2 34
(Bill Turner) *hld up in tch: rdn over 3f out: wknd over 2f out* **40/1**

3m 20.65s (1.65) **Going Correction** -0.175s/f (Firm)

WFA 3 from 4yo+ 13lb 11 Ran SP% **105.8**

Speed ratings (Par 101): **88,87,86,85,85 85,85,81,81,80 79**

toteswingers:1&2:£3.60, 1&3:£19.50, 2&3:£16.70 CSF £21.19 CT £264.27 TOTE £3.60: £1.60, £2.40, £6.90; EX 27.50.

Owner P A Deal, G Lowe & M J Silver **Bred** Hermes Services Ltd **Trained** Newmarket, Suffolk

FOCUS

The first two had a good battle and finished clear in this minor staying handicap. The form is best viewed around the runner-up but the third holds it down. Tiger Tess got very worked up at the start and refused to enter the stalls.

Mountain Myst Official explanation: vet said gelding lost a hind shoe

5567 WARWICKSHIRE COLLEGE'S CAREERS OUTSIDE CLASSROOM MAIDEN STKS 7f 26y

5:40 (5:42) (Class 5) 3-Y-O+ £4,204 (£1,251; £625; £312) Stalls Low

Form RPR

-04 **1** **Backstreet Fighter (IRE)**[18] 4970 3-8-12 0 ..... MatthewLawson(5) 4 78+
(Gary Harrison) *hld up: hdwy u.p over 2f out: styd on to ld nr fin* **66/1**

2 *nk* **Wadha (IRE)** 3-8-12 0 ..... FrankieDettori 2 72
(Saeed Bin Suroor) *chsd ldrs: rdn to ld wl ins fnl f: hdd nr fin* **11/4[2]**

4 **3** *½* **Ziraun**[146] 1155 3-8-12 0 ..... RoystonFfrench 10 71
(Clive Brittain) *led: rdn over 1f out: hdd and unable qck wl ins fnl f* **10/1**

0-2 **4** *1 ½* **Russian Affair**[14] 5114 3-9-3 0 ..... NeilCallan 7 72
(Roger Varian) *chsd ldr: rdn over 2f out: no ex towards fin* **9/4[1]**

5 *1 ¼* **Triple Charm** 3-8-12 0 ..... JimmyFortune 12 64+
(Jeremy Noseda) *hld up in tch: nt clr run over 1f out: no ex ins fnl f* **7/2[3]**

5 **6** *2* **En Hiver**[17] 4991 3-8-12 0 ..... RichardKingscote 11 58
(Ralph Beckett) *mid-div: hdwy over press over 1f out: no imp fnl f* **14/1**

2 **7** *2* **Tenavon**[10] 5241 3-8-12 0 ..... ShaneKelly 13 53
(William Knight) *chsd ldrs: rdn over 2f out: wknd ins fnl f* **8/1**

000 **8** *2* **Lechlade Lass**[14] 5114 3-8-7 0 ..... JamesRogers(5) 8 47
(Adrian Chamberlain) *s.i.s: sn rcvrd into mid-div: rdn 1/2-way: sn wknd* **150/1**

60 **9** *2* **Gennie**[102] 2223 3-8-12 0 ..... DaneO'Neill 9 42
(Richard Hannon) *chsd ldrs: rdn over 2f out: wknd over 1f out* **25/1**

0 **10** *½* **Peace Seeker**[17] 5021 3-9-3 0 ..... WilliamCarson 3 46
(Giles Bravery) *s.i.s: hld up: swtchd rt and hdwy 1/2-way: rdn and wknd over 1f out* **66/1**

11 *2* **Moonlark** 3-8-12 0 ..... AndreaAtzeni 5 35
(John Holt) *hld up: plld hrd: wknd over 2f out* **100/1**

12 *nk* **Glastonberry** 3-8-9 0 ..... SophieDoyle(3) 6 34
(Geoffrey Deacon) *s.s: outpcd* **50/1**

04 **13** *¾* **The Right Time**[21] 4861 3-8-12 0 ..... LiamJones 1 32
(Tony Carroll) *sn pushed along and a in rr* **66/1**

1m 25.27s (0.67) **Going Correction** -0.175s/f (Firm) 13 Ran SP% **118.5**

Speed ratings (Par 103): **89,88,88,86,84 82,80,78,75,75 72,72,71**

toteswingers:1&2:£28.70, 1&3:Not won, 2&3:£6.80 CSF £240.86 TOTE £71.20: £16.90, £1.10, £3.30; EX 330.70.

Owner Gary Harrison **Bred** Mr & Mrs David Wilson **Trained** Llandeilo, Carmarthens

FOCUS

There was a big-priced winner in this fair maiden but it was no fluke even though the pace was slow. There is a bit of doubt over what the form is worth.

5568 STRATFORD H'CAP 1m 2f 188y

6:10 (6:12) (Class 4) (0-80,80) 3-Y-O+ £4,075 (£1,212; £606; £303) Stalls Low

Form RPR

0463 **1** **Significant Move**[64] 3434 4-9-11 77 ..... IanMongan 10 87+
(Stuart Kittow) *s.i.s: hld up: hdwy 1/2-way: rdn to chse ldr over 1f out: edgd rt and styd on to ld nr fin* **9/2[1]**

0414 **2** *¾* **Battle Of Britain**[32] 4457 3-9-1 76 ..... (t) WilliamCarson 15 84
(Giles Bravery) *led: rdn over 1f out: edgd lft and hdd nr fin* **12/1**

0114 **3** *¾* **Broughtons Swinger**[17] 5015 4-8-12 67 ..... AdamBeschizza(3) 13 74
(Willie Musson) *hld up: hdwy over 4f out: rdn over 1f out: styd on* **15/2**

5226 **4** *2* **Standpoint**[32] 4477 5-9-12 78 ..... GeorgeBaker 6 82
(Reg Hollinshead) *chsd ldrs: rdn over 2f out: styd on same pce fnl f* **14/1**

2212 **5** *1 ¾* **Number Theory**[16] 5064 3-9-2 77 ..... AndreaAtzeni 2 78+
(John Holt) *hld up: rdn over 2f out: styd on fnl f: nvr nrr* **13/2[3]**

531- **6** *nk* **Corsican Boy**[250] 7962 3-9-2 77 ..... SteveDrowne 1 77+
(Roger Charlton) *s.i.s: hld up: hdwy over 2f out: nt trble ldrs* **9/2[1]**

0612 **7** *hd* **Mariners Lodge (USA)**[27] 4625 3-9-5 80 ..... NeilCallan 5 80
(Mark Johnston) *plld hrd and prom: trckd ldr over 8f out: rdn over 2f out: wknd ins fnl f* **5/1[2]**

0433 **8** *½* **Scamperdale**[22] 4818 9-9-9 80 ..... JamesRogers(5) 3 79
(Brian Baugh) *hld up: hdwy over 5f out: rdn over 2f out: styd on same pce* **16/1**

260- **9** *1 ½* **Gross Prophet**[9] 6832 6-9-2 71 ..... SophieDoyle(3) 9 67
(Alastair Lidderdale) *chsd ldrs: rdn over 3f out: styd far side fnl 3f: styd on same pce* **33/1**

4113 **10** *nk* **One Hit Wonder**[22] 4825 4-9-3 69 ..... LiamKeniry 8 65
(Jonathan Portman) *trckd ldrs: rdn over 2f out: sn wknd* **12/1**

0300 **11** *½* **King Zeal (IRE)**[58] 3641 7-9-9 75 ..... (t) CathyGannon 7 70
(Barry Leavy) *hld up: rdn over 2f out: n.d* **22/1**

15 **12** *6* **Archie Rice (USA)**[32] 3244 5-9-0 66 ..... JimmyQuinn 12 50
(Tom Keddy) *mid-div: lost pl over 3f out: sn bhd* **50/1**

1656 **13** *29* **Oriental Cavalier**[29] 4577 5-9-10 **76**.......................(v) RoystonFfrench 14 10
(Mark Buckley) *chsd ldrs tl rdn and wknd over 3f out* **25/1**

2m 19.35s (-1.75) **Going Correction** -0.175s/f (Firm)
WFA 3 from 4yo+ 9lb **13** Ran SP% **119.2**
Speed ratings (Par 105): **99,98,97,96,95 94,94,94,93,93 92,88,67**
toteswingers:1&2:£11.30, 1&3:£4.50, 2&3:£24.60 CSF £56.50 CT £402.52 TOTE £4.60: £1.70, £3.20, £2.20; EX 79.30.
Owner Midd Shire Racing **Bred** Juddmonte Farms Ltd **Trained** Blackborough, Devon

FOCUS
A fair middle-distance handicap run at a reasonable pace. The winner was not as exposed as most and the form is the best guide.
Corsican Boy Official explanation: jockey said gelding hung left
Oriental Cavalier Official explanation: jockey said gelding stopped very quickly
T/Plt: £67.50 to a £1 stake. Pool of £44,430.55 - 480.32 winning tickets. T/Qpdt: £13.30 to a £1 stake Pool of £2,084.60 - 115.92 w. tckts CR

5569 - 5576 (Foreign Racing) - See RI

5541 EPSOM (L-H)

Tuesday, August 30

OFFICIAL GOING: Good (good to soft in back straight; overall & home straight 7.5, far side 7.8, stands' side 8.0)
Wind: light, half against Weather: overcast

5577 TOTEPLACEPOT WIN WITHOUT BACKING A WINNER NURSERY 7f
2:10 (2:10) (Class 5) (0-75,75) 2-Y-O **£3,234** (£962; £481; £240) **Stalls** Low

Form RPR

61 **1** **Producer**[33] 4455 2-9-4 **72**....................................... PatDobbs 1 83+
(Richard Hannon) *lw: chsd ldng pair: pushed along and hdwy to ld wl over 1f out: clr ent fnl f: r.o strly: comf* **4/5**[1]

3065 **2** *2 3/4* **Always Ends Well (IRE)**[31] 4538 2-8-5 **59**.................... FrannyNorton 6 61
(Mark Johnston) *chsd ldng trio: edgd lft over 5f out: rdn and unable qck over 2f out: hdwy u.p over 1f out: chsd clr wnr ins fnl f: kpt on but no ch w wnr* **16/1**

5052 **3** *3 3/4* **Ermyn Flyer**[12] 5197 2-7-13 **58**.............................. JemmaMarshall(5) 8 50
(Pat Phelan) *racd in midfield: edgd lft over 5f out: rdn and unable qck 2f out: no prog tl kpt on ins fnl f to go 3rd towards fin: no ch w wnr* **10/1**

2516 **4** *3/4* **Rooknrasbryripple**[60] 3584 2-8-9 **66**........................... MartinHarley(3) 4 56
(Mick Channon) *led: rdn ent fnl 2f: hdd wl over 1f out: sn outpcd by wnr and btn ent fnl f: wknd and lost 2 pls ins fnl f* **33/1**

2360 **5** *1 1/4* **Ivor's Princess**[20] 4913 2-9-4 **72**................................. JamesMillman 7 59
(Rod Millman) *sn outpcd in last: sme hdwy over 1f out: kpt on fnl f but n.d* **14/1**

453 **6** *3* **Choisirez (IRE)**[109] 2053 2-8-11 **65**............................... CathyGannon 5 44
(David Evans) *racd in last trio: hmpd over 5f out: a outpcd and struggling after* **25/1**

0323 **7** *3/4* **Lady Gibraltar**[23] 4824 2-9-4 **75**.............................. MatthewDavies(3) 2 52
(Alan Jarvis) *sn chsng ldr: lost 2nd 2f out and hanging bdly lft: wknd wl over 1f out: eased ins fnl f* **7/1**[3]

005 **8** *2 3/4* **Laurel Lad (IRE)**[22] 4857 2-8-11 **65**............................ DarryllHolland 3 35
(Charles Hills) *lw: racd in last trio: hmpd over 5f out: outpcd and n.d after* **5/1**[2]

1m 24.02s (0.72) **Going Correction** +0.225s/f (Good) **8** Ran SP% **113.1**
Speed ratings (Par 94): **104,100,96,95,94 90,90,86**
Tote Swingers: 1&2 £4.70, 1&3 £3.20, 2&3 £15.20 CSF £15.84 CT £78.93 TOTE £1.60: £1.10, £3.10, £2.70; EX 17.20.
Owner J Palmer-Brown **Bred** Cheveley Park Stud Ltd **Trained** East Everleigh, Wilts
■ Stewards' Enquiry : Jemma Marshall four-day ban: careless riding (Sep 13-16)

FOCUS
Course at innermost configuration and distances as advertised. After a dry night and morning the ground had dried out a little compared with the previous day. The consensus amongst the jockeys was that the ground was just on the easy side of good. A fair nursery run at a decent gallop.

NOTEBOOK
Producer ◆ had built on his promising debut when taking a C&D maiden in easy fashion and was backed in to odds-on to repeat that. He picked up really well when asked and swept past the leaders to put the race to bed with over a furlong still to run. He will go up a fair amount for this but looks sure to make his mark in a higher grade. (op Evens tchd 11-10 in places)
Always Ends Well(IRE) was stepping up in trip and was close enough early in the straight, but she could not go with the winner when that one committed and merely followed him though. It was better than recent efforts, however. (op 20-1)
Ermyn Flyer ran well when a close second over C&D earlier in the month, but could never pick up sufficiently to deliver a challenge this time, despite staying on. (op 8-1)
Rooknrasbryripple ran well from the front on this step up in trip, without convincing that the extra distance suited. (op 40-1)
Ivor's Princess was held up at the back early before staying on without ever getting involved. (op 16-1)
Choisirez(IRE)'s trainer reported that the filly suffered interference in running. Official explanation: trainer said filly suffered interference in running (op 16-1)
Lady Gibraltar's rider reported that the filly hung badly left. Official explanation: jockey said filly hung badly left (tchd 13-2 and 15-2)
Laurel Lad(IRE) is from a decent family and was expected to improve for the step up in trip on this handicap debut. However, he was always out the back and failed to figure. (op 9-2 tchd 4-1)

5578 TOTESWINGER MORE WAYS TO WIN H'CAP 6f
2:40 (2:40) (Class 4) (0-85,84) 3-Y-O+ **£5,822** (£1,732; £865; £432) **Stalls** High

Form RPR

0100 **1** **Baldemar**[29] 4609 6-9-5 **82**... LeeTopliss(3) 8 89
(Richard Fahey) *chsd ldrs: rdn and effrt 2f out: drvn to chal jst ins fnl f: r.o wl u.p to ld fnl 50yds* **4/1**[3]

1104 **2** *hd* **Clear Ice (IRE)**[13] 5173 4-8-13 **73**.............................(b) DavidProbert 5 79
(Gay Kelleway) *w ldr: ev ch and rdn 2f out: drvn over 1f out: kpt on u.p: no ex cl home* **12/1**

1-53 **3** *nk* **Gentle Lord**[18] 5012 3-9-7 **84**..................................(t) RichardKingscote 3 89
(Tom Dascombe) *lw: sn pushed along to ld: rdn jst over 1f out: kpt on wl tl hdd and lost 2 pls fnl 50yds* **11/4**[1]

1202 **4** *1 1/4* **Another Try (IRE)**[20] 4909 6-9-5 **82**............................ HarryBentley(3) 6 83+
(Alan Jarvis) *hld up in tch: n.m.r ent fnl 2f: hdwy to chse ldrs and pushed along over 1f out: kpt on same pce ins fnl f: swtchd rt wl ins fnl f* **7/2**[2]

5020 **5** *1* **Stevie Gee (IRE)**[37] 4369 7-8-9 **74**.............................. RyanPowell(5) 1 72
(Ian Williams) *dwlt: sn bustled along: in tch towards rr: rdn and hdwy on inner over 2f out: styd on same pce and no imp fnl f* **17/2**

0-50 **6** *1 1/4* **Baby Dottie**[83] 2822 4-8-3 **68**................................... JemmaMarshall(5) 9 62+
(Pat Phelan) *in tch in midfield on outer: effrt but hanging lft ent fnl 2f: no imp and stl hanging over 1f out* **11/1**

4546 **7** *nse* **Scarlet Rocks (IRE)**[10] 5268 3-8-8 **71**............................ CathyGannon 7 68+
(David Evans) *stdd s: hld up in rr: rdn and clsd over 2f out: nt clr run over 1f out: hmpd and snatched up jst ins fnl f: swtchd rt and r.o fnl 50yds* **16/1**

0450 **8** *3/4* **Clear Praise (USA)**[25] 4765 4-9-1 **75**.............................. HayleyTurner 4 66
(Simon Dow) *chsd ldng pair: rdn and struggling ent fnl 2f: wknd over 1f out* **15/2**

1m 10.34s (0.94) **Going Correction** +0.225s/f (Good)
WFA 3 from 4yo+ 3lb **8** Ran SP% **113.1**
Speed ratings (Par 105): **102,101,101,99,98 96,96,95**
Tote Swingers: 1&2 £6.90, 1&3 £3.30, 2&3 £4.70 CSF £48.77 CT £152.64 TOTE £5.70: £1.70, £3.50, £1.10; EX 40.40.
Owner A Rhodes Haulage And P Timmins **Bred** Hellwood Stud Farm **Trained** Musley Bank, N Yorks

FOCUS
A decent sprint handicap in which Richard Fahey followed up last year's success.
Baby Dottie Official explanation: jockey said filly hyung left
Scarlet Rocks(IRE) Official explanation: trainer said filly did not handle the track

5579 EBF "SAKHEE'S SECRET" MAIDEN STKS 1m 114y
3:15 (3:16) (Class 5) 2-Y-O **£3,881** (£1,155; £577; £288) **Stalls** Low

Form RPR

2 **1** **Albamara**[8] 5320 2-8-12 0.. SebSanders 2 79+
(Sir Mark Prescott Bt) *mde all: rdn and readily drew clr 2f out: r.o wl: easily* **4/7**[1]

6 **2** *4* **Dynamic Duo (IRE)**[18] 5013 2-9-3 0.................................... PatDobbs 6 73+
(Richard Hannon) *lw: chsd wnr: rdn and outpcd 2f out: no ch w wnr but kpt on to hold 2nd fnl f* **11/4**[2]

0 **3** *hd* **Paloma's Prince (IRE)**[26] 4722 2-9-3 0.......................... JackMitchell 1 71
(Jim Boyle) *chsd ldng pair: rdn and outpcd by wnr ent fnl 2f: no ch w wnr but ev ch of 2nd fr over 1f out: kpt on* **50/1**

0 **4** *1 1/4* **Tallevu (IRE)**[18] 5011 2-9-3 0..................................... RichardKingscote 3 68
(Tom Dascombe) *w'like: leggy: in tch in last trio: rdn and outpcd over 2f out: wnt modest 4th jst over 1f out: kpt on ins fnl f but no ch w wnr* **10/1**[3]

0 **5** *1 1/4* **Shivsingh**[17] 5044 2-9-3 0... ChrisCatlin 8 65
(Mick Channon) *dwlt: in rr: rdn and struggling ent fnl 3f: plugged on same pce and wl hld fnl 2f* **25/1**

0 **6** *shd* **Le Cagnard**[31] 4535 2-9-3 0.. HayleyTurner 7 65
(Michael Bell) *lw: chsd ldrs: rdn and unable qck 3f out: outpcd and no ch w wnr 2f out: wknd over 1f out* **20/1**

0 **7** *11* **Edensor (IRE)**[88] 2687 2-9-3 0... EddieAhern 5 42
(John Dunlop) *str: in tch in last trio: rdn and struggling 3f out: wknd jst over 2f out: wl bhd and eased ins fnl f* **50/1**

1m 48.47s (2.37) **Going Correction** +0.225s/f (Good) **7** Ran SP% **111.9**
Speed ratings (Par 94): **98,94,94,93,92 91,82**
Tote Swingers: 1&2 £1.50, 1&3 £9.80, 2&3 £12.60 CSF £2.13 TOTE £1.60: £1.10, £1.40; EX 2.70.
Owner Miss K Rausing **Bred** Miss K Rausing **Trained** Newmarket, Suffolk

FOCUS
No more than a reasonable maiden.

NOTEBOOK
Albamara ◆, a beautifully bred filly who had shown plenty of promise when running on late on her debut at Kempton, was much sharper here, despite still showing signs of greenness. She was ridden to get the early lead, but her rider did not go that fast and then got a breather into her around halfway. When asked she picked up well and ran on strongly all the way to the line. She has a Fillies' Mile entry and on breeding could make up into an Oaks filly for next year, when the course experience could prove invaluable. (op 1-2)
Dynamic Duo(IRE), a half-brother to the smart Cai Shen who had shown promise in a good Newmarket maiden on his debut, kept the winner company early but could not go with her once she quickened and only just hung on for second. (op 3-1 tchd 10-3 in places)
Paloma's Prince(IRE) tracked the first two from the start and stuck to his task under pressure. This was a decent step up on his debut effort.
Tallevu(IRE) had been keen on his debut in a Newmarket maiden that has already produced two subsequent winners. He was backed here but, despite settling better this time, never got into contention. He can be given a bit more time to prove himself. (op 16-1 tchd 20-1 in places)
Le Cagnard had shown nothing on his debut, but this Derby entry showed a little more here, giving the impression better will be seen of him next season. (op 25-1)

5580 TOTEEXACTA THE BETTER VALUE FORECAST H'CAP 1m 4f 10y
3:50 (3:53) (Class 5) (0-75,75) 3-Y-O+ **£3,881** (£1,155; £577; £288) **Stalls** Centre

Form RPR

6001 **1** **Shesha Bear**[40] 4242 6-8-13 **60**....................................(p) HayleyTurner 2 73+
(Jonathan Portman) *hld up in tch in last trio: rdn and hdwy ent fnl 2f: led jst over 1f out: r.o wl u.p fnl f* **4/1**[2]

0034 **2** *1/2* **Brouhaha**[10] 5266 7-9-10 **71**...................................... RichardKingscote 9 83
(Tom Dascombe) *hld up in tch in midfield: effrt on outer and edging lft 2f out: ev ch jst over 1f out: r.o wl u.p but a hld ins fnl f* **6/1**[3]

0000 **3** *3* **The Bells O Peover**[10] 5283 3-9-4 **75**............................ DarryllHolland 5 82
(Mark Johnston) *t.k.h: chsd ldng pair tl led over 8f out: hrd pressed and rdn over 2f out: hdd jst over 1f out: outpcd by ldng pair and btn fnl 150yds* **3/1**[1]

2240 **4** *1* **Wily Fox**[18] 5015 4-9-6 **67**.. JackMitchell 3 73
(James Eustace) *led for 1f: chsd ldrs after: rdn and effrt to press ldr on inner over 2f out: no ex 1f out: wknd ins fnl f* **8/1**

235 **5** *1 3/4* **Penang Cinta**[33] 4465 8-8-13 **60**..................................... CathyGannon 1 63
(David Evans) *sn pushed up to chse ldr: led after 1f tl over 8f out: drvn 3f out: unable qck and outpcd 2f out: styd on same pce u.p fr over 1f out* **16/1**

0230 **6** *1/2* **Bubbly Braveheart (IRE)**[54] 3760 4-9-4 **65**...................... IanMongan 8 67
(Pat Phelan) *t.k.h: hld up in midfield: rdn and effrt over 2f out: chsng ldrs but unable qck u.p over 1f out: outpcd and btn 1f out* **16/1**

5431 **7** *nk* **Dancing Storm**[54] 3762 8-9-4 **65**...................................... ChrisCatlin 4 67
(Stuart Kittow) *swtg: t.k.h: hld up in last pair: swtchd rt and effrt u.p 2f out: kpt on ins fnl f but never gng pce to trble ldrs* **7/1**

4652 **8** *2* **Beat Route**[15] 5103 4-9-1 **67**.................................. JemmaMarshall(5) 7 65
(Michael Attwater) *in tch: rdn and unable qck 3f out: wknd over 1f out* **14/1**

1132 **9** *18* **Filun**[61] 3533 6-9-7 **73**.. RyanPowell(5) 6 43
(Anthony Middleton) *t.k.h: hld up in rr: rdn over 2f out: wknd qckly 2f out: wl bhd and eased ins fnl f* **7/1**

2m 40.6s (1.70) **Going Correction** +0.225s/f (Good)
WFA 3 from 4yo+ 10lb **9** Ran SP% **113.8**
Speed ratings (Par 103): **103,102,100,100,98 98,98,96,84**
Tote Swingers: 1&2 £5.90, 1&3 £3.20, 2&3 £5.10 CSF £27.79 CT £80.62 TOTE £4.30: £1.70, £2.00, £1.10; EX 33.20.
Owner RWH Partnership **Bred** Beechgrove Stud Farm Ltd & Catridge Farm Stud **Trained** Compton, Berks

FOCUS
A competitive handicap run at a fair gallop.
Filun Official explanation: jockey said gelding never travelled

5581 DOWNLOAD THE EPSOM IPHONE APP H'CAP 7f
4:20 (4:21) (Class 4) (0-80,80) 3-Y-O **£5,822** (£1,732; £865; £432) **Stalls** Low

Form RPR
3321 **1** **Konstantin (IRE)**[14] 5136 3-9-0 **73**.................................. HayleyTurner 2 84+
(Marcus Tregoning) *lw: chsd ldr: jnd ldr and travelling strly 3f out: led 2f out: rdn and readily asserted ent fnl f: r.o wl: eased cl home* **2/1**[1]
0600 **2** *3/4* **Sonning Rose (IRE)**[19] 4965 3-9-5 **78**............................. ChrisCatlin 10 84
(Mick Channon) *hld up in last trio: gd hdwy to press ldrs 3f out: rdn and sltly outpcd 2f out: chsd wnr and drvn 1f out: kpt on but no threat to wnr* **7/1**
6106 **3** *1* **Loving Thought**[24] 4807 3-8-8 **67**....................................... EddieAhern 3 70
(Sir Henry Cecil) *in tch: rdn and effrt over 1f out: kpt on to go 3rd fnl 75yds: nvr gng pce to trble wnr* **14/1**
1351 **4** *3/4* **Silverware (USA)**[13] 5171 3-9-5 **78**....................................... PatDobbs 4 79
(Richard Hannon) *led: drvn and hdd 2f out: outpcd u.p ent fnl f: styd on same pce after* **6/1**
1305 **5** *nse* **Chosen Character (IRE)**[16] 5081 3-9-7 **80**.........(vt) RichardKingscote 5 81
(Tom Dascombe) *hld up in last trio: hdwy on outer over 4f out: drvn to chse ldrs and edgd lft over 1f out: styd on same pce fnl f* **11/2**[3]
0613 **6** *1 1/4* **Songsmith**[17] 5040 3-8-4 **66**.. LouisBeuzelin(3) 8 64
(Lucy Wadham) *in tch in midfield: shuffled bk towards rr over 3f out: drvn 2f out: kpt on ins fnl f: no threat to wnr* **9/2**[2]
2101 **7** *shd* **Cootehill Lass (IRE)**[34] 4431 3-8-11 **70**........................... CathyGannon 11 67
(David Evans) *stdd s: hld up in last: rdn and swtchd rt 2f out: kpt on ins fnl f: nvr trbld ldrs* **16/1**
004 **8** *9* **Rafella (IRE)**[24] 4799 3-8-4 **68** ow1........................ MatthewCosham(5) 9 41
(Simon Dow) *chsd ldrs: rdn and struggling over 2f out: wknd qckly over 1f out* **33/1**
30 **9** *3 1/2* **Primo Lady**[18] 5016 3-9-4 **80**..(b) LeeTopliss(3) 7 44
(Gay Kelleway) *in tch: rdn and no imp over 2f out: wknd wl over 1f out* **20/1**

1m 24.41s (1.11) **Going Correction** +0.225s/f (Good) **9** Ran SP% **113.9**
Speed ratings (Par 102): **102,101,100,99,99 97,97,87,83**
Tote Swingers: 1&2 £4.10, 1&3 £6.50, 2&3 £8.50 CSF £16.26 CT £153.07 TOTE £3.00: £1.20, £2.50, £2.00; EX 17.20.
Owner Lady Tennant **Bred** Miss Annmarie Burke **Trained** Lambourn, Berks

FOCUS
Another competitive event but run 0.39secs slower than the opening juvenile contest.
Chosen Character(IRE) Official explanation: jockey said gelding had no more to give

5582 TOTEPOOL AUTUMN MEETING 25TH SEPTEMBER APPRENTICE H'CAP 1m 2f 18y
4:55 (4:55) (Class 5) (0-75,75) 3-Y-0+ **£3,234** (£962; £481; £240) **Stalls** Low

Form RPR
1213 **1** **Highlife Dancer**[14] 5135 3-9-4 **73**.................................. CharlesBishop 5 80
(Mick Channon) *in tch: pushed along and hdwy to chse ldr ent fnl 2f: rdn hands and heels to ld ins fnl f: sn in command: pushed out* **5/1**[2]
25-0 **2** *1 3/4* **Ullswater (IRE)**[12] 5205 3-9-6 **75**.. DarylByrne 4 79
(Mark Johnston) *led: rdn and fnd ex over 2f out: clr w wnr over 1f out: hdd ins fnl f: sn btn but kpt on* **11/2**[3]
0352 **3** *1 3/4* **Ermyntrude**[33] 4454 4-8-11 **58**.. LucyKBarry 7 58
(Pat Phelan) *dwlt: rcvrd to chse ldr after 2f tl ent fnl 2f: sn drvn and outpcd by ldng pair: kpt on again ins fnl f but no threat to wnr* **8/1**
0513 **4** *2* **Miracle Play (IRE)**[6] 5380 3-8-4 **59**........................... MatthewCosham 1 55
(David Evans) *b: chsd ldr for 2f: styd chsng ldrs: rdn and outpcd jst over 2f out: edgd rt and styd on same pce u.p fr over 1f out* **2/1**[1]
0440 **5** *1/2* **Effigy**[26] 4724 7-9-12 **73**.. AmyScott 6 68
(Henry Candy) *t.k.h: stdd after s: hld up wl in tch in last trio: rdn and effrt 3f out: edgd lft and outpcd ent fnl 2f: no threat to ldrs after: kpt on ins fnl f* **8/1**
0-53 **6** *5* **Penchesco (IRE)**[41] 4211 6-9-5 **66**............................... JustinNewman 3 51
(Amanda Perrett) *lw: sn niggled along in last trio: rdn and edgd rt 3f out: sn struggling: wknd 2f out* **6/1**
0244 **7** *5* **Potentiale (IRE)**[2] 5509 7-9-9 **73**............................ BrendanPowell(3) 2 48
(J W Hills) *in tch: dropped to last trio but stl wl in tch 3f out: rdn and [illegible] 3f out: sn struggling: wknd 2f out* **11/2**[3]

2m 11.33s (1.63) **Going Correction** +0.225s/f (Good)
WFA 3 from 4yo+ 8lb **7** Ran SP% **117.3**
Speed ratings (Par 103): **102,100,99,97,97 93,89**
CSF £33.46 TOTE £3.80: £1.40, £3.80; EX 43.50.
Owner The Highlife Racing Club **Bred** Imperial & Mike Channon Bloodstock Ltd **Trained** West Ilsley, Berks

FOCUS
An ordinary apprentice handicap
T/Jkpt: £832.40 to a £1 stake. Pool:£115,724.47 - 98.70 winning tickets T/Plt: £28.20 to a £1 stake. Pool:£65,284.43 - 1,688.06 winning tickets T/Qpdt: £12.40 to a £1 stake. Pool:£3,487.65 - 207.30 winning tickets SP

[5508] GOODWOOD (R-H)
Tuesday, August 30

OFFICIAL GOING: Good (7.8)
Wind: Light, across Weather: Cloudy

5583 EBF RACING UK MAIDEN FILLIES' STKS 1m
2:20 (2:20) (Class 5) 2-Y-0 **£3,234** (£962; £481; £240) **Stalls** Low

Form RPR
4 **1** **Swingland**[33] 4471 2-9-0 0.. JimmyFortune 4 78+
(Paul Cole) *mde all: kicked on over 2f out: rdn over 1f out: styd on wl: readily* **3/1**[1]
64 **2** *2 1/2* **Savanna Days (IRE)**[53] 3812 2-9-0 0............................... TedDurcan 11 72
(Mick Channon) *hld up in last trio: prog on outer to chse wnr over 1f out: edgd rt and no imp fnl f* **10/1**
6 **3** *3/4* **Defy The Odds**[31] 4552 2-9-0 0.. TomQueally 3 70
(Sir Henry Cecil) *hld up in midfield: sltly impeded over 2f out: shkn up and nt qckn sn after: styd on to take 3rd jst ins fnl f* **7/2**[2]
5 **4** *2* **Specific (IRE)**[31] 4552 2-9-0 0.................................... FrankieDettori 7 65
(Mahmood Al Zarooni) *mostly chsd wnr to over 1f out: fdd fnl f* **7/2**[2]
2 **5** *1/2* **Amber Silk (IRE)**[33] 4471 2-9-0 0.................................. MichaelHills 9 64
(Charles Hills) *racd wd: trckd ldrs: effrt over 2f out: disp 2nd briefly over 1f out: wknd sn after* **6/1**[3]
60 **6** *1 1/2* **Perfect Paradise**[18] 4992 2-9-0 0................................. WilliamBuick 10 61
(John Gosden) *hld up in last pair: shkn up 2f out: no prog tl kpt on fnl f: nrst fin* **20/1**
7 *1/2* **Fearless Dream** 2-9-0 0... NickyMackay 6 60
(John Gosden) *s.s: hld up in last pair: pushed along and rn green 3f out: nvr on terms but kpt on* **25/1**
0 **8** *nk* **Estedaama (IRE)**[33] 4471 2-9-0 0................................. RichardHills 2 59
(Marcus Tregoning) *hld up in midfield: pushed along whn sltly impeded over 2f out: steadily outpcd* **14/1**
9 *1 1/2* **Napoleon's Muse (IRE)** 2-9-0 0....................................... JimCrowley 1 56
(Ralph Beckett) *prom: disp 2nd and reminder 3f out: wknd wl over 1f out* **33/1**
0 **10** *1* **Dalacara**[19] 4968 2-9-0 0.. AdamKirby 5 54
(Clive Cox) *in tch: pushed along 1/2-way: lost pl and dropped to rr 3f out: sn struggling* **33/1**

1m 40.37s (0.47) **Going Correction** 0.0s/f (Good) **10** Ran SP% **114.0**
Speed ratings (Par 91): **97,94,93,91,91 89,89,88,87,86**
Tote Swingers: 1&2 £4.20, 1&3 £4.30, 2&3 £7.10 CSF £31.15 TOTE £4.10: £1.80, £2.90, £1.50; EX 31.90 Trifecta £201.90 Pool: £474.90 - 1.74 winning units..
Owner Ben & Sir Martyn Arbib **Bred** Arbib Bloodstock Partnership **Trained** Whatcombe, Oxon

FOCUS
Lower bend dolled out 5yds increasing distances by 8yds. This looked a fair fillies' maiden, though the winner was allowed to set a steady pace.

NOTEBOOK
Swingland was behind Amber Silk when fourth over 7f here on her debut, but this time enjoyed a much better trip than her old rival. She might be a touch flattered by the manner of her win, but it was no surprise the step up in trip suited - there's loads of stamina on the dam's side of her pedigree - and she should continue to progress. A Fillies' Mile entry shows how highly she's regarded. (op 10-3)
Savanna Days(IRE), returning from 53 days off and stepped up in trip, raced off the speed following a sluggish start, but she ran on quite well, deserving extra credit considering the lack of pace. Handicaps are now an option. (op 9-1)
Defy The Odds ◆ reversed debut form with the slightly disappointing Specific on this step up from 7f, but she still looked green from an early stage. She would have been slightly closer had she not been short of room in the straight and there's a lot more to come. Like the winner, she's well enough regarded to be in the Fillies' Mile. (tchd 4-1)
Specific(IRE) was well placed throughout but failed to build on her debut. (op 4-1)
Amber Silk(IRE) didn't build on her debut (ahead of Swingland), but shouldn't be harshly judged. She was stuck wide without cover for much of the way and was a bit keen. (op 5-1)
Perfect Paradise was going on at the finish and can now go handicapping. (op 25-1)
Fearless Dream made some late progress after a slow start, looking as though she'll be better for this first experience. (tchd 28-1)
Dalacara Official explanation: jockey said filly ran too free

5584 PARMNICK SMYTHBURY NURSERY STKS (H'CAP) 6f
2:50 (2:51) (Class 4) (0-85,84) 2-Y-O **£3,428** (£1,020; £509; £254) **Stalls** High

Form RPR
016 **1** **Gung Ho Jack**[22] 4858 2-9-2 **79**... AdamKirby 1 82
(John Best) *mde all and led field down centre: rdn 2f out: wandered over 1f out: hrd pressed fnl f: edgd rt but styd on wl* **3/1**[2]
014 **2** *1* **Mahkama (USA)**[27] 4661 2-9-6 **83**............................. FrankieDettori 6 83
(Saeed Bin Suroor) *dwlt: hld up in last pair: prog over 2f out: chsd wnr over 1f out: drvn and str chal jst ins fnl f: edgd rt and nt qckn 100yds out: fading at fin* **3/1**[2]
10 **3** *1/2* **Free Verse**[18] 4999 2-9-7 **84**.. RichardHughes 3 83
(Richard Hannon) *chsd ldng pair: pushed along sn after 1/2-way: nt qckn wl over 1f out: one pce after* **5/2**[1]
51 **4** *nse* **The Noble Ord**[11] 5232 2-8-8 **74**................................. SophieDoyle(3) 4 72
(Sylvester Kirk) *n.m.r s: hld up in last pair: pushed along over 2f out: no prog tl styd on wl last 150yds* **17/2**
003 **5** *2 1/4* **Majestic Rose**[40] 4228 2-8-9 **72**.. TedDurcan 2 64
(Mick Channon) *chsd ldng trio: rdn jst over 2f out: no imp over 1f out: fdd fnl f* **25/1**
4134 **6** *3 1/4* **Safari Storm (USA)**[11] 5237 2-9-0 **77**...............................(t) ShaneKelly 5 59
(Brian Meehan) *chsd wnr: stl 2nd and gng wl enough over 1f out: sn wknd qckly* **7/2**[3]

1m 12.71s (0.31) **Going Correction** 0.03s/f (Good) **6** Ran SP% **115.0**
Speed ratings (Par 96): **96,94,94,93,90 86**
Tote Swingers: 1&2 £2.40, 1&3 £2.40, 2&3 £1.40 CSF £12.87 TOTE £3.10: £1.30, £2.60; EX 13.50.
Owner John Fletcher **Bred** D R Tucker **Trained** Hucking, Kent

FOCUS
A fair nursery run at an even pace, and the time was good, being 0.07 seconds quicker than the later older-horse Class 4 handicap. The action unfolded centre-field.

NOTEBOOK
Gung Ho Jack showed good speed throughout and found extra under a strong ride when looking sure to be passed by the Godolphin runner late on. Having won his maiden on his second start, he failed to beat a rival at Windsor next time, but that was a strong race. The third placed finisher was Mehdi, who picked up a sales race next time, and the winner, Rebellious Guest, looks Group class and is one to keep in mind. It wouldn't surprise if Gung Ho Jack defied a rise. (op 5-1)
Mahkama(USA) has shown a tendency to move quite freely through her races, including when winning her maiden from the front and then when a beaten favourite under a waiting ride last time. As such, exaggerated hold-up tactics were no surprise on this occasion and she came through in good time to have every chance, but once more her finishing effort was weak. Despite her pedigree perhaps a drop to 5f will help. (op 5-2 tchd 10-3)
Free Verse was beaten over 2f out when coming off the bridle, but she kept on surprisingly well, leaving the impression she needs further. (op 11-4 tchd 3-1 in places)
The Noble Ord stayed on late to win a maiden over this trip on his previous start, but he took too long to get going this time. He's still learning and there should be better to come. (op 11-1 tchd 8-1)
Safari Storm(USA), who was a bit free, again disappointed. (tchd 4-1)

5585 BUY A £10,000 RACING POST BONUS YEARLING MAIDEN STKS 1m 1f 192y
3:25 (3:25) (Class 5) 3-Y-O **£2,587** (£770; £384; £192) **Stalls** Low

Form RPR
1 **Late Telegraph (IRE)** 3-9-3 0...[1] TomQueally 6 91+
(Sir Henry Cecil) *dwlt: hld up in tch: prog 3f out: shkn up to chal jst over 1f out: green but r.o fnl f: bmpd 50yds out: led last stride* **6/1**[3]
3 **2** *hd* **Dick Doughtywylie**[53] 3824 3-9-3 0............................... WilliamBuick 8 90+
(John Gosden) *sn led: pushed along and pressed fr over 2f out: drvn over 1f out: edgd lft 75yds out: hdd last stride* **8/11**[1]
2-46 **3** *nk* **Always The Lady**[115] 1894 3-8-12 82.................................. AdamKirby 4 84
(Clive Cox) *mostly pressed ldr: shkn up to chal over 2f out: stl pressing hrd ins fnl f: bmpd and lost 2nd last 50yds* **3/1**[2]

5-0 **4** *8* **Mafeteng**[102] 2258 3-8-12 0........ RichardHughes 3 68+
(John Dunlop) *prom: rdn and nt qckn jst over 2f out: hanging and wknd qckly jst over 1f out* **14/1**
00 **5** *3¾* **Red Lago (IRE)**[136] 1408 3-9-3 0........ MichaelHills 5 66
(Charles Hills) *dwlt: hld up in tch: shkn up 3f out: sn lft bhd* **14/1**
-606 **6** *2* **Royal Reason**[71] 3220 3-8-12 55........ EddieCreighton 7 57
(Joseph Tuite) *sn heavily restrained into last: shkn up 3f out: no prog and btn after* **100/1**
0 **7** *1½* **Touching The Stars**[8] 5327 3-9-3 0........ TedDurcan 1 59
(Mick Channon) *dwlt: chsd ldrs: rdn 3f out: wknd qckly 2f out* **66/1**

2m 9.42s (1.42) **Going Correction** 0.0s/f (Good) 7 Ran SP% **113.0**
Speed ratings (Par 100): **94,93,93,87,84 82,81**
Tote Swingers: 1&2 £1.70, 1&3 £2.40, 2&3 £1.10 CSF £10.54 TOTE £6.80: £2.50, £1.40; EX 11.20 Trifecta £23.00 Pool: £593.65 - 19.02 winning units..
Owner Thomas Barr **Bred** Storm Bloodstock **Trained** Newmarket, Suffolk
FOCUS
Only three of these seriously counted, but the trio all look at least useful.

5586 BETTING SHOPS BACK TURFTV STKS (H'CAP) 1m
4:00 (4:00) (Class 4) (0-80,85) 3-Y-0+ **£4,075** (£1,212; £606; £303) **Stalls** Low

Form RPR
1521 **1** **Pat's Legacy (USA)**[3] 5495 5-9-12 **85** 6ex........ JamesRogers(5) 7 95
(Jo Hughes) *mde all: dictated stdy pce to 1/2-way: rdn 2f out: styd on wl fnl f* **2/1**[1]
2334 **2** *½* **Uppercut**[20] 4914 3-9-4 **78**........ DaneO'Neill 5 86+
(Stuart Kittow) *hld up in 4th: prog 2f out: rdn to chse wnr 1f out: no imp 100yds out: kpt on nr fin* **3/1**[2]
142 **3** *2½* **Jewelled**[20] 4931 5-9-5 **76**........ AdamBeschizza(3) 2 79
(Lady Herries) *chsd wnr: rdn 2f out: nt qckn and lost 2nd 1f out: fdd* **7/2**[3]
0061 **4** *¾* **Uncle Fred**[29] 4616 6-9-12 **80**........ JimCrowley 4 81
(Patrick Chamings) *stdd s: t.k.h and hld up last: effrt on inner over 2f out: nt qckn over 1f out: fdd fnl f* **15/2**
3605 **5** *2¾* **Compton Blue**[12] 5200 5-9-7 **75**........(b) RichardHughes 1 70
(Richard Hannon) *trckd ldng pair: looking for room over 2f out: sn dropped to last: no prog fnl f* **9/2**

1m 41.83s (1.93) **Going Correction** 0.0s/f (Good)
WFA 3 from 4yo+ 6lb 5 Ran SP% **110.5**
Speed ratings (Par 105): **90,89,87,86,83**
CSF £8.27 TOTE £3.20: £1.80, £1.90; EX 9.70.
Owner Mrs Joanna Hughes **Bred** Brereton C Jones **Trained** Lambourn, Berks
FOCUS
An ordinary handicap in which Pat's Legacy took advantage of being allowed an uncontested lead, setting a steady pace that resulted in a time much slower than the earlier 2yo maiden.

5587 AMP STKS (H'CAP) 6f
4:30 (4:30) (Class 4) (0-80,80) 3-Y-0+ **£4,075** (£1,212; £606; £303) **Stalls** High

Form RPR
5244 **1** **Sluggsy Morant**[13] 5171 3-9-5 **78**........ DaneO'Neill 2 86+
(Henry Candy) *dwlt: hld up in 6th: plenty to do whn shkn up and effrt 2f out: prog over 1f out: wl-timed run to ld last 75yds* **3/1**[2]
5226 **2** *½* **Perfect Pastime**[18] 4994 3-9-6 **79**........ AdamKirby 5 85
(Walter Swinburn) *mostly chsd ldr: clsd over 1f out: led briefly ins fnl f: outpcd nr fin* **5/1**[3]
0011 **3** *nk* **Night Trade (IRE)**[23] 4816 4-9-1 **78**........ RaulDaSilva(7) 3 83
(Ronald Harris) *led: tk fierce hold downhill after 1f: edgd lft over 2f out and urged along: hdd and nt qckn ins fnl f* **7/1**
0132 **4** *1* **Aye Aye Digby (IRE)**[25] 4742 6-9-10 **80**........ GeorgeBaker 1 82
(Patrick Chamings) *t.k.h: hld up bhd ldrs: rdn and nt qckn wl over 1f out: kpt on: nvr able to chal* **11/4**[1]
2106 **5** *1¼* **Volito**[34] 4434 5-8-11 **67**........ RichardHughes 7 65
(Anabel K Murphy) *s.s: hld up in last: cajoled along wl over 1f out: hd high and limited rspnse: kpt on fnl f: eased nr fin* **15/2**
-341 **6** *¾* **Minety Lass**[23] 4828 3-8-6 **70**........ JamesRogers(5) 4 65
(Adrian Chamberlain) *prom: carried lft over 2f out whn cl enough: wknd jst over 1f out* **14/1**
0011 **7** *1¾* **Kings 'n Dreams**[24] 4793 4-9-3 **73**........(b) ShaneKelly 8 63
(Dean Ivory) *hld up in 5th: rdn over 1f out: fnd nil and sn btn* **15/2**

1m 12.78s (0.58) **Going Correction** 0.0s/f (Good)
WFA 3 from 4yo+ 3lb 7 Ran SP% **111.0**
Speed ratings (Par 105): **96,95,94,93,91 90,88**
Tote Swingers: 1&2 £3.80, 1&3 £4.70, 2&3 £5.10 CSF £17.17 CT £90.52 TOTE £4.10: £2.40, £1.80; EX 21.80 Trifecta £217.20 Pool: £631.17 - 2.15 winning units..
Owner Henry Candy & Partners II **Bred** A B Barraclough **Trained** Kingston Warren, Oxon
FOCUS
This looked an ordinary handicap for the class. The main action unfolded towards the middle of the track.

5588 HALNAKER GENTLEMAN AMATEUR RIDERS' H'CAP 1m 3f
5:05 (5:06) (Class 5) (0-70,69) 4-Y-0+ **£2,495** (£774; £386; £193) **Stalls** High

Form RPR
5000 **1** **Boston Blue**[31] 4562 4-11-0 **69**........ MrCCarroll(7) 4 81+
(Tony Carroll) *hld up in last trio: prog on outer over 2f out: led over 1f out: r.o wl and sn clr* **9/4**[1]
1203 **2** *2¾* **Mustajed**[30] 4579 10-10-6 **59**........(b) MrPMillman(5) 5 66
(Rod Millman) *racd wd: led: rdn 3f out: hdd and outpcd over 1f out: kpt on* **6/1**[3]
5300 **3** *3* **Belle Boleyn**[12] 5210 4-10-2 **55** oh1........ MrFrazerWilliams(5) 3 57
(Chris Wall) *dwlt: hld up in last trio: effrt on inner 3f out: nt qckn wl over 1f out: plugged on to take 3rd nr fin* **12/1**
2113 **4** *½* **Transfer**[61] 3546 6-11-0 **65**........ MrMPrice(3) 8 66
(Richard Price) *hld up in last trio: effrt on outer over 2f out: hanging and nt qckn over 1f out: one pce after* **9/4**[1]
0600 **5** *hd* **Sail Home**[28] 4649 4-10-12 **60**........ MrRBirkett 7 60
(Julia Feilden) *trckd ldrs: prog to chal 2f out: nrly upsides over 1f out: wknd qckly fnl f* **10/1**
1050 **6** *6* **Mr Plod**[36] 4389 6-10-0 **55** oh3........(p) MrAJones(7) 6 45
(Andrew Reid) *t.k.h: hld up in midfield: urged along 3f out: wknd u.p 2f out* **12/1**
0-60 **7** *3* **Sweet Seville (FR)**[135] 118 7-10-0 **55** oh7........ MrGrahamCarson(7) 2 39
(Terry Clement) *mostly chsd ldr: chal over 4f out: wknd over 2f out* **80/1**
5003 **8** *7* **Taste The Wine (IRE)**[13] 5168 5-10-5 **58**........ MrRJWilliams(5) 1 30
(Bernard Llewellyn) *s.s: sn prom: chal and upsides 4f out: wknd 3f out* **9/2**[2]

2m 31.74s (5.24) **Going Correction** 0.0s/f (Good) 8 Ran SP% **119.7**
Speed ratings (Par 103): **80,78,75,75,75 70,68,63**
CSF £17.65 CT £136.98 TOTE £3.10: £1.40, £1.30, £5.20; EX 24.70 Trifecta £391.30 Pool: £872.57 - 1.65 winning units..
Owner B J Millen **Bred** Ballykilbride Stud **Trained** Cropthorne, Worcs
■ The first winner for Charlie Carroll, son of trainer Tony Carroll.
■ Stewards' Enquiry : Mr A Jones one-day ban: used whip when out of contention (Sep 13)
FOCUS
A modest amateur riders' handicap run at a steady pace.
T/Plt: £57.60 to a £1 stake. Pool:£52,422.44 - 663.41 winning tickets T/Qpdt: £20.00 to a £1 stake. Pool:£3,756.97 - 138.80 winning tickets JN

5555 RIPON (R-H)
Tuesday, August 30

OFFICIAL GOING: Good to soft (good in places) changing to soft after race 5 (4.10)
Wind: light 1/2 behind Weather: raining

5589 RIPON-RACES.CO.UK (S) STKS 1m 1f 170y
2:00 (2:06) (Class 6) 3-4-Y-0 **£2,045** (£603; £302) **Stalls** Low

Form RPR
3142 **1** **Janet's Pearl (IRE)**[26] 4728 3-8-7 69........ PaulHanagan 2 53
(Paul Midgley) *led 1f: chsd ldr: effrt over 3f out: kpt on to ld 1f out: drvn out* **1/3**[1]
0165 **2** *3¼* **Yorksters Prince (IRE)**[19] 4944 4-9-7 51........(b) BrianToomey(5) 5 57
(Tony Coyle) *led after 1f: clr over 5f out: rdn over 2f out: hdd 1f out: no ex* **12/1**[3]
0030 **3** *11* **En Fuego**[8] 5311 4-9-12 65........ RobertWinston 9 45
(Geoffrey Harker) *trckd ldng pair: t.k.h: drvn over 3f out: hung rt and no imp: eased last 100yds* **4/1**[2]
004 **4** *7* **Spread Boy (IRE)**[8] 5312 4-9-1 44........(p) JulieBurke(5) 7 14
(Alan Berry) *t.k.h in rr: effrt over 4f out: wnt modest 4th over 2f out* **33/1**
0465 **5** *17* **Sally Anne**[7] 5350 3-8-7 32........ AndrewElliott 8 —
(John Harris) *s.i.s: bhd and drvn over 6f out* **80/1**
6066 **6** *¾* **May Burnett (IRE)**[32] 4515 3-8-7 37........(bt[1]) BarryMcHugh 1 —
(Brian Rothwell) *chsd ldrs: rdn over 4f out: sn lost pl* **50/1**
7 *3¼* **Umbonga** 3-8-7 0........ TomEaves 4 —
(Neville Bycroft) *in rr: drvn along and lost tch over 3f out* **25/1**

2m 6.04s (0.64) **Going Correction** +0.025s/f (Good)
WFA 3 from 4yo 8lb 7 Ran SP% **112.7**
Speed ratings (Par 101): **98,95,86,81,67 66,64**
Tote Swingers: 1&2 £1.50, 1&3 £1.02, 2&3 £2.50 CSF £5.28 TOTE £1.40: £1.10, £4.60; EX 5.40.The winner was bought by Mrs Wright for £6,000.
Owner Sandfield Racing **Bred** Roundhill Stud & Gleadhill House Stud Ltd **Trained** Westow, N Yorks
FOCUS
Rail at innermost position and distances as advertised. No strength-in-depth to this seller, run at a good clip.

5590 TOTESWINGER FILLIES' MAIDEN AUCTION STKS 5f
2:30 (2:31) (Class 5) 2-Y-0 **£2,264** (£673; £336; £168) **Stalls** High

Form RPR
0004 **1** **Elusive Bonus (IRE)**[20] 4899 2-8-1 55........ DeclanCannon(3) 10 58
(David O'Meara) *mde virtually all: jst hld on* **11/2**
2003 **2** *nse* **Red Shadow**[20] 4899 2-8-4 57........ AndrewMullen 6 58
(Alan Brown) *chsd ldrs: upsides 1f out: jst failed* **5/1**[3]
6005 **3** *½* **Economic Crisis (IRE)**[14] 5147 2-8-4 53........(p) PatrickMathers 3 56
(Alan Berry) *chsd ldrs: effrt over 2f out: kpt on wl fnl f* **28/1**
630 **4** *¾* **Trust Fund Babe (IRE)**[13] 5161 2-8-4 62........ DuranFentiman 9 54
(Tim Easterby) *hld up: hdwy over 2f out: nt clr run 1f out: keeping on same pce when n.m.r nr fin.* **7/2**[2]
0 **5** *1¾* **Bitter Lemon**[113] 1957 2-8-0 0 ow1........ JulieBurke(5) 7 48
(Kevin Ryan) *sn outpcd and in rr: gd hdwy on outer over 2f out: sn chsng ldrs: wknd fnl f* **10/1**
54 **6** *1¼* **Kara's Vision**[7] 5351 2-8-7 0........ GrahamGibbons 11 46
(Robert Cowell) *w ldr: wknd fnl f* **16/1**
7 *2¾* **Dream Lioness** 2-8-4 0........ JamesSullivan 4 33
(Ben Haslam) *mid-div: effrt over 2f out: wknd over 1f out* **33/1**
5 **8** *¾* **Majestic Breeze (IRE)**[22] 4851 2-8-7 0........ PaulHanagan 1 33
(Brian Ellison) *chsd ldrs on outer: wknd over 1f out* **11/4**[1]
0 **9** *1¼* **Show Of Faith (IRE)**[45] 4106 2-8-11 0........ RichardMullen 5 33
(Ed McMahon) *in rr: sn drvn along: nvr on terms* **20/1**
10 *1¾* **Takealookatmenow (IRE)** 2-8-4 0........ AdrianNicholls 8 19
(David Nicholls) *s.v.s: a last* **8/1**

61.84 secs (1.14) **Going Correction** +0.075s/f (Good) 10 Ran SP% **118.2**
Speed ratings (Par 91): **93,92,92,90,88 86,81,80,78,75**
Tote Swingers: 1&2 £3.20, 1&3 £51.60, 2&3 £29.40 CSF £32.86 TOTE £4.50: £1.80, £1.70, £9.40; EX 31.00.
Owner The Three County Partnership **Bred** T Jones **Trained** Nawton, N Yorks
■ Stewards' Enquiry : Andrew Mullen two-day ban: used whip with excessive frequency (Sep 13-14)
FOCUS
A weak juvenile maiden that was fought out by the three most exposed runners.
NOTEBOOK
Elusive Bonus(IRE) improved enough on her previous efforts to narrowly prevail, helped no doubt by having the stands' rail to race against throughout. She'll need to better this form to win a nursery. (op 15-2 tchd 5-1)
Red Shadow has now run better the last twice, seemingly helped by easy ground, but she'll remain vulnerable to something less exposed, whether it be a maiden or nursery. (tchd 9-2 and 11-2)
Economic Crisis(IRE), rated 53, bounced back to the sort of form shown earlier in the season, but like the runner-up, she will remain vulnerable wherever she runs. (op 33-1)
Trust Fund Babe(IRE) bounced back from a poor effort at Carlisle and should have gone close to winning the race, being short of room inside the final furlong and then squeezed out again near the line having run into the back of horses. (op 4-1 tchd 9-2)
Bitter Lemon will be of interest for low-grade nurseries following another run. (op 17-2 tchd 8-1)
Majestic Breeze(IRE) took a backward step having made a promising debut at Thirsk, but it's quite possible the easy ground was no use to her, so another chance has to be given. Official explanation: jockey said filly was unsuited by the track (tchd 10-3)

5591 SIS LIVE NURSERY 6f
3:00 (3:00) (Class 4) (0-85,83) 2-Y-0 **£3,557** (£1,058; £529; £264) **Stalls** High

Form RPR
2305 **1** **Tell Dad**[31] 4536 2-9-4 **83**........ KieranO'Neill(3) 5 94+
(Richard Hannon) *trckd ldrs: swtchd outside over 2f out: led 1f out: drvn clr* **15/8**[1]
5201 **2** *5* **Blue Shoes (IRE)**[17] 5058 2-8-4 **66**........ PaulHanagan 4 62
(Tim Easterby) *led: hdd 1f out: edgd rt: no ch w wnr* **5/2**[2]

The Form Book, Raceform Ltd, Compton, RG20 6NL

15 **3** 2¾ **Class Monitor**[32] 4502 2-8-8 **70**.......... AndrewElliott 3 58
(Mrs K Burke) *dwlt: sn chsng ldrs: drvn over 2f out: wandered: one pce* **9/2**

6010 **4** 20 **Lord Buffhead**[5] 5399 2-7-12 **60** oh3.......... JamesSullivan 2 —
(Richard Guest) *sn pushed along and wl outpcd: bhd fnl 2f: lft poor 4th 1f out* **20/1**

4105 **P** **Almond Branches**[31] 4558 2-8-12 **74**.......... PJMcDonald 6 —
(George Moore) *trckd ldrs: swtchd outside after 1f: wknd and heavily eased over 1f out: p.u and dismntd ins fnl f* **7/2**[3]

1m 14.48s (1.48) **Going Correction** +0.075s/f (Good) **5** Ran SP% **108.5**
Speed ratings (Par 96): **93,86,82,56,—**
CSF £6.62 TOTE £2.40: £1.10, £1.40; EX 5.20.

Owner Andrew Tinkler **Bred** Wallace Holmes & Partners **Trained** East Everleigh, Wilts

FOCUS
An ordinary nursery won in authoritative fashion by the top weight.

NOTEBOOK
Tell Dad seemed well at home with some cut in the ground and proved much too good. He ought to stay 7f, but seems perfectly at home over this trip for the time being and earned himself a rise in grade with this display, but along with it will come a hike in the ratings. (op 5-2)
Blue Shoes(IRE), an all-the-way winner of a C&D maiden last time, attempted to repeat those tactics, but was blown away by a far classier rival. A similar performance ought to see him win a slightly lesser race. (op 3-1)
Class Monitor doesn't look up to winning off this mark. (op 7-2)
Almond Branches, encountering a slow surface for the first time, came to a standstill and was dismounted, her rider reporting she was never happy and had lost her action. Official explanation: jockey said filly lost its action (op 3-1)

5592 SAPPER CONDITIONS STKS 5f
3:35 (3:35) (Class 3) 2-Y-O **£5,670** (£1,697; £848; £424; £211) **Stalls** High

Form RPR

4106 **1** **Ponty Acclaim (IRE)**[12] 5216 2-9-1 85.......... DavidAllan 2 95
(Tim Easterby) *chsd ldrs: effrt over 2f out: edgd rt and led 1f out: edgd lft and drvn clr: readily* **2/1**[1]

1223 **2** 3¾ **Kool Henry (IRE)**[31] 4558 2-9-4 85.......... DanielTudhope 1 85
(David O'Meara) *led: edgd rt and hdd 1f out: kpt on same pce* **3/1**[2]

0414 **3** 2½ **Signifer (IRE)**[7] 5348 2-9-2 87.......... AdrianNicholls 4 74
(Mick Channon) *trckd ldr: effrt and hung rt 2f out: one pce fnl f* **4/1**[3]

213 **4** ½ **Quite A Thing**[10] 5263 2-8-13 89.......... StevieDonohoe 6 69
(Sir Mark Prescott Bt) *chsd ldrs: sn drvn along: outpcd appr fnl f* **4/1**[3]

4132 **5** 3 **Mr Majeika (IRE)**[25] 4757 2-9-4 90.......... PaulHanagan 5 63
(Richard Hannon) *t.k.h early: trckd ldrs: drvn over 2f out: lost pl over 1f out* **8/1**

6 **6** ½ **Endless Applause**[39] 4283 2-8-9 0.......... MichaelStainton 3 52
(Richard Whitaker) *dwlt: outpcd and in rr: nvr on terms* **66/1**

61.23 secs (0.53) **Going Correction** +0.075s/f (Good) **6** Ran SP% **110.9**
Speed ratings (Par 98): **98,92,88,87,82 81**
Tote Swingers: 1&2 £2.00, 1&3 £2.10, 2&3 £1.50 CSF £8.04 TOTE £3.50: £2.00, £1.10; EX 8.00.

Owner Rapcalone **Bred** T Darcy & Vincent McCarthy **Trained** Great Habton, N Yorks

FOCUS
What had looked quite a tight conditions race was won with ease by Ponty Acclaim.

NOTEBOOK
Ponty Acclaim(IRE) had performed well in highly valuable sales races the last twice and found this easier, going on over 1f out and drawing clear. She's in the Two-Year-Old Trophy at Redcar in early October and could easily play a prominent role in that contest. All ground conditions seem to come alike. (op 5-2 tchd 11-4 in a place)
Kool Henry(IRE) was soon in front and looked to run his race, giving the form a solid look. He deserves to win another race, but often leaves himself vulnerable late on. (op 10-3 tchd 11-4)
Signifer(IRE), a handicap winner off 82 two starts back, had finished behind the winner in the Super Sprint and wasn't good enough. (op 9-2 tchd 7-2)
Quite A Thing isn't progressing and was ineffective faced with this ground for the first time. (op 7-2)
Mr Majeika(IRE) had finished behind Quite A Thing at Lingfield last time and didn't look worth his official rating of 90 coming into this. (tchd 9-1)
Endless Applause, having only her second start, had been withdrawn due to soft ground in the past and ran about as well as could have been expected. She'll find easier opportunities. (op 50-1)

5593 CITY OF RIPON STKS (H'CAP) 1m 1f 170y
4:10 (4:10) (Class 3) (0-90,89) 3-Y-0+ **£6,616** (£1,980; £990; £495; £246) **Stalls** Low

Form RPR

0-54 **1** **Scrapper Smith (IRE)**[45] 4107 5-8-10 **76**.......... GarryWhillans(5) 8 92
(Alistair Whillans) *hld up in rr: hdwy and nt clr run over 2f out: swtchd lft: led over 1f out: drew clr* **20/1**

0650 **2** 4½ **Mirrored**[11] 5250 5-9-10 **85**.......... DuranFentiman 10 91
(Tim Easterby) *stdd s: hld up in rr: hdwy and nt clr run over 2f out: styd on wl to take 2nd last 50yds* **16/1**

-664 **3** 1¾ **Classic Colori (IRE)**[61] 3542 4-9-11 **86**.......... DanielTudhope 7 89
(David O'Meara) *mid-div: effrt on outside over 2f out: sn chsng ldrs and pushed lft: styd on same pce fnl f* **14/1**

1000 **4** nk **Pleasant Day (IRE)**[24] 4788 4-10-0 **89**..........(b) PaulHanagan 3 91+
(Richard Fahey) *chsd ldrs: wnt 2nd 1f out: kpt on one pce* **8/1**[3]

6201 **5** 1¼ **Ailsa Craig (IRE)**[20] 4901 5-9-2 **77**.......... JamesSullivan 13 77
(Edwin Tuer) *hld up in rr: effrt on outer whn pushed wd 3f out: slty hmpd over 2f out: kpt on same pce* **13/2**[2]

4312 **6** 2¼ **King Of The Celts (IRE)**[45] 4108 3-8-9 **78**.......... DavidAllan 2 73+
(Tim Easterby) *w ldr: led over 5f out: hdd over 1f out: wknd fnl 150yds* **7/2**[1]

0620 **7** 4½ **Fastnet Storm (IRE)**[31] 4537 5-9-11 **86**.......... LeeNewman 11 72
(David Barron) *led: hdd over 5f out: lost pl over 1f out* **12/1**

0225 **8** ½ **Destiny Blue (IRE)**[26] 4724 4-9-8 **83**.......... PJMcDonald 1 68
(Jamie Osborne) *chsd ldrs: wknd over 1f out* **9/1**

0245 **9** ½ **Hidden Glory**[34] 4440 4-8-12 **73**.......... FrederikTylicki 9 57
(James Given) *in rr: swtchd lft 3f out: nvr a factor* **25/1**

0003 **10** 2 **Ginger Jack**[35] 4404 4-9-9 **84**.......... RobertWinston 6 64
(Geoffrey Harker) *in rr: sme hdwy on ins over 3f out: nvr a factor: wknd over 1f out* **14/1**

430- **11** 10 **Rumble Of Thunder (IRE)**[109] 6428 5-8-13 **77**.......... MichaelO'Connell(3) 4 36
(Kate Walton) *chsd ldrs: rdn over 4f: wknd over 2f out: bhd whn eased* **25/1**

1062 **12** 13 **Kensei (IRE)**[29] 4608 4-9-3 **78**.......... DavidNolan 5 —
(David O'Meara) *chsd ldrs: wknd over 2f out: sn bhd and eased* **12/1**

2122 **13** 10 **Epernay**[39] 4275 4-8-10 **71**..........(t) TomEaves 12 —
(Ian Williams) *chsd ldrs: wkng whn hmpd 3f out: sn bhd: eased* **13/2**[2]

2m 6.00s (0.60) **Going Correction** +0.25s/f (Good)
WFA 3 from 4yo+ 8lb **13** Ran SP% **117.1**
Speed ratings (Par 107): **107,103,102,101,100 98,95,94,94,92 84,74,66**
Tote Swingers: 1&2 £50.00, 1&3 £54.60, 2&3 £56.50 CSF £296.83 CT £4546.13 TOTE £22.90: £7.30, £6.80, £5.80; EX 138.70.

Owner A C Whillans **Bred** John Costello **Trained** Newmill-On-Slitrig, Borders
■ Stewards' Enquiry : Garry Whillans one-day ban: careless riding (Sep 13)

FOCUS
A race in which it seemed an advantage to come from the rear, the early pace being a good one.

NOTEBOOK
Scrapper Smith(IRE) recovered having been denied a clear run to power away on this first try at 1m2f. He'd been expected to improve for it and the soft ground was certainly in his favour. He'll be forced up in grade now, but is unexposed over this trip and could have more to offer. (op 16-1)
Mirrored, back on the same mark as when winning at Doncaster on his reappearance in April, stayed on from off the pace and will be of obvious interest next time. (op 12-1)
Classic Colori(IRE) continues to ease down the weights and his last two efforts have been better, suggesting his new yard can get a win out of him.
Pleasant Day(IRE), 1lb higher than when winning at the course in June, left several dismal efforts behind in finishing fourth.
Ailsa Craig(IRE), up 2lb for winning at Beverley, was forced a bit wide and didn't get the best of runs, so probably should have finished closer. (op 8-1)
King Of The Celts(IRE) stays further than this, but in wanting to ensure it was proper test at the distance got involved in going too fast early. (op 4-1)
Fastnet Storm(IRE) got involved in going too fast early.
Epernay has been running well all year, but he was under pressure and looked awkward rounding the final bend, eventually dropping right out. This wasn't her true form. (op 7-1 tchd 6-1)

5594 ATTHERACES.COM IS FREE H'CAP 1m
4:45 (4:45) (Class 5) (0-75,75) 3-Y-0+ **£2,264** (£673; £336; £168) **Stalls** Low

Form RPR

0111 **1** **Hot Rod Mamma (IRE)**[29] 4603 4-9-6 **74**.......... ShaneBKelly(5) 12 90+
(Dianne Sayer) *hld up in rr-div: hdwy 3f out: wnt 2nd over 1f out: r.o wl to ld last 75yds* **3/1**[1]

6640 **2** 1¼ **Come Here Yew (IRE)**[17] 5056 3-9-5 **74**.......... DanielTudhope 8 83
(Declan Carroll) *in rr: gd hdwy over 1f out: edgd rt and styd on wl to take 2nd last 50yds* **14/1**

3032 **3** 3 **Jupiter Fidius**[14] 5150 4-8-10 **62**..........(p) MichaelO'Connell(3) 9 65
(Kate Walton) *trckd ldrs: brought wd over 3f out: led over 2f out: edgd rt: hdd ins fnl f: wknd* **6/1**[2]

1455 **4** 1¼ **Spavento (IRE)**[21] 4877 5-9-0 **63**..........(p) DavidAllan 1 63
(Eric Alston) *dwlt: sn mid-div: effrt and n.m.r over 2f out: one pced* **11/1**

3160 **5** 2½ **Shadowtime**[38] 4349 6-9-12 **75**.......... AndrewMullen 2 69
(Tracy Waggott) *led: hdd over 2f out: wknd over 1f out* **12/1**

0000 **6** shd **Call Of Duty (IRE)**[15] 5106 6-8-11 **60**.......... DuranFentiman 7 54
(Dianne Sayer) *mid-div: hdwy over 3f out: one pce fnl 2f* **16/1**

0420 **7** 1½ **Ours (IRE)**[35] 4404 8-9-11 **74**..........(p) BarryMcHugh 5 65
(John Harris) *s.i.s: hdwy on outer over 2f out: nvr nr ldrs* **10/1**

6600 **8** 1¼ **Rosbay (IRE)**[15] 5106 7-9-1 **64**..........(p) RobertWinston 4 52
(Tim Easterby) *w ldrs: brought wd over 3f out: wknd 2f out: eased towards fin* **6/1**[2]

0040 **9** 1¼ **Keys Of Cyprus**[15] 5106 9-9-1 **71**.......... ShirleyTeasdale(7) 3 56
(David Nicholls) *chsd ldrs: lost pl wl over 1f out* **12/1**

1000 **10** 1¾ **Global**[66] 3386 5-9-2 **65**.......... PaulHanagan 6 46
(Brian Ellison) *trckd ldrs: lost pl over 1f out* **8/1**[3]

040- **11** 4½ **Snoqualmie Boy**[416] 3889 8-9-10 **73**.......... AdrianNicholls 11 44
(David Nicholls) *a towards rr: bhd fnl 2f* **16/1**

000- **12** 3½ **Shotley Mac**[301] 7283 7-9-3 **73**.......... TerenceFury(7) 10 36
(Neville Bycroft) *hld up in rr: bhd fnl 2f* **16/1**

1m 42.94s (1.54) **Going Correction** +0.25s/f (Good)
WFA 3 from 4yo+ 6lb **12** Ran SP% **121.8**
Speed ratings (Par 103): **102,100,97,96,94 93,92,91,89,88 83,80**
Tote Swingers: 1&2 £15.40, 1&3 £3.60, 2&3 £21.30 CSF £49.84 CT £246.79 TOTE £3.30: £1.50, £5.70, £2.60; EX 63.70.

Owner A Slack **Bred** Philip Hore Jnr **Trained** Hackthorpe, Cumbria

FOCUS
They appeared to go a reasonable gallop and the first two came from the second half of the field.

5595 WAKEMAN STAYERS H'CAP 2m
5:15 (5:15) (Class 6) (0-65,65) 3-Y-0+ **£2,264** (£673; £336; £168) **Stalls** Low

Form RPR

/4-2 **1** **Spice Bar**[26] 4703 7-8-5 **49** oh1.......... JasonHart(7) 8 56+
(Declan Carroll) *trckd ldrs: t.k.h: led over 2f out: edgd rt: forged clr fnl f* **7/2**[2]

4530 **2** 2¾ **Spruzzo**[16] 5079 5-9-5 **56**.......... TomEaves 1 60
(Chris Fairhurst) *led tl 10f out: chal over 3f out: kpt on same pce fnl f* **11/2**[3]

3456 **3** 1¼ **Strikemaster (IRE)**[24] 4814 5-8-12 **49**..........(t) DuranFentiman 2 52
(Lee James) *dwlt: in rr: swtchd outside and hdwy over 1f out: styd on to take 3rd nr fin* **20/1**

460 **4** ¾ **River Dragon (IRE)**[18] 4985 6-9-5 **61**.......... BrianToomey(5) 6 63
(Tony Coyle) *w ldr: led 10f out: hdd over 2f out: one pce* **20/1**

3422 **5** shd **Simple Jim (FR)**[16] 5079 7-9-6 **57**.......... DanielTudhope 9 58
(David O'Meara) *hld up in rr: hdwy 4f out: sn drvn: kpt on ins fnl f: nvr nr ldrs* **2/1**[1]

0122 **6** 2 **White Deer (USA)**[34] 4438 7-10-0 **65**..........(p) RobertWinston 3 64
(Geoffrey Harker) *hld up in rr: drvn 4f out: nvr a factor* **14/1**

400U **7** ¾ **Valdan (IRE)**[29] 4602 7-9-7 **58**..........(p) JamesSullivan 10 56
(Ruth Carr) *hld up in mid-div: hdwy 7f out: wknd fnl 150yds* **20/1**

1252 **8** 4½ **Terenzium (IRE)**[13] 5167 9-9-4 **55**..........(p) FrederikTylicki 4 48
(Micky Hammond) *t.k.h: trckd ldrs: outpcd over 5f out: lost pl over 3f out* **14/1**

3101 **9** 4 **Brasingaman Eric**[13] 5167 4-9-10 **61**.......... PJMcDonald 7 49
(George Moore) *chsd ldrs: wknd 2f out* **7/2**[2]

3m 43.79s (11.99) **Going Correction** +0.25s/f (Good) **9** Ran SP% **120.8**
Speed ratings (Par 101): **80,78,78,77,77 76,76,73,71**
Tote Swingers: 1&2 £7.90, 1&3 £17.60, 2&3 £11.10. Tote Super 7: Win: Not won. Place: Not won. CSF £23.50 CT £326.68 TOTE £6.90: £1.90, £2.00, £3.80; EX 44.10.

Owner K McConnell **Bred** Littleton Stud **Trained** Sledmere, E Yorks
■ Stewards' Enquiry : Jason Hart one-day ban: used whip in incorrect place (Sep 13)

FOCUS
This 2m handicap was by no means the test of stamina it promised to be, with the pace being steady.
T/Plt: £138.90 to a £1 stake. Pool:£61,068.25 - 320.93 winning tickets T/Qpdt: £20.00 to a £1 stake. Pool:£3,756.97 - 138.80 winning tickets WG

5209 SOUTHWELL (L-H)

Tuesday, August 30

OFFICIAL GOING: Standard

Wind: moderate half behind Weather: Overcast

5596 TOTEPLACEPOT WIN WITHOUT BACKING A WINNER MAIDEN STKS 6f (F)

4:40 (4:41) (Class 5) 2-Y-O £2,385 (£704; £352) **Stalls** Low

Form RPR

1 **Three Sugars (AUS)** 2-8-12 0 NeilCallan 4 68+
(Jeremy Noseda) *chsd ldng pair: green and rdn along 1/2-way: drvn and hdwy over 1f out: styd on wl ent fnl f: led last 100yds* **5/6**[1]

05 **2** ¾ **Bengaline**[15] 5104 2-9-3 0 RichardMullen 8 71
(David Nicholls) *cl up: rdn to ld over 2f out: drvn over 1f out: hdd and no ex last 100yds* **20/1**

2302 **3** 2¼ **Scrooby Doo**[12] 5211 2-8-9 63 BillyCray(3) 3 59
(David Nicholls) *led: rdn along and hdd over 2f out: drvn over 1f out and kpt on same pce* **3/1**[2]

65 **4** 10 **New Romantic**[21] 4875 2-8-12 0 TonyHamilton 5 29
(Julie Camacho) *in tch: hdwy to chse ldrs 1/2-way: rdn over 2f out: sn one pce* **33/1**

5 **5** 2 **Ghost Train (IRE)**[34] 4433 2-9-3 0 SilvestreDeSousa 7 28
(Mark Johnston) *s.i.s and sn rdn along: hdwy and in tch over 3f out: rdn along wl over 2f out: sn drvn and edgd lft over 1f out: wknd* **4/1**[3]

4 **6** nk **Bogey Hole (IRE)**[28] 4648 2-8-12 0 RussKennemore 2 22
(Tom Dascombe) *in rr: rdn along 1/2-way: nvr a factor* **25/1**

0 **7** 10 **Echo Of Dubai (IRE)**[87] 2718 2-8-12 0 RoystonFfrench 6 —
(Clive Brittain) *a in rr: outpcd and bhd fr 1/2-way* **12/1**

8 20 **Gilly's Giant (IRE)** 2-9-3 0 StephenCraine 1 —
(Patrick Morris) *in tch: rdn along bef 1/2-way: sn outpcd and bhd* **100/1**

1m 18.21s (1.71) **Going Correction** +0.125s/f (Slow) **8** Ran SP% **119.8**

Speed ratings (Par 94): **93,92,89,75,73 72,59,32**

Tote Swingers: 1&2 £4.00, 1&3 £1.80, 2&3 £4.90 CSF £25.32 TOTE £2.20: £1.60, £4.30, £1.10; EX 22.40.

Owner P Makin **Bred** Paulyn Investments Pty Ltd, Qld **Trained** Newmarket, Suffolk

FOCUS

A modest juvenile maiden.

NOTEBOOK

Three Sugars(AUS), a choicely-bred debutante from a powerful stable, stayed on well to score. Only third in the early stages and still well adrift of the front two turning into the straight, she took time to engage top gear, but hit the front approaching the final furlong and came home strongly. The bare form of this victory is nothing special, but she should improve and make an impact in nurseries later on. (op Evens tchd 6-5 in places)

Bengaline had shown only modest form in two previous starts, but seemed to step up on those efforts on his first Fibresand run. He was fast out of the stalls and disputed the lead from outset, but could not match the winner's finishing thrust. (op 14-1 tchd 12-1)

Scrooby Doo, four-times raced previously and rated 63, appeared to run her race. She vied with Bengaline for the lead until the final furlong, but failed to quicken in the closing stages. (op 7-2 tchd 11-4)

New Romantic, dropped in trip after weakening over 7f three weeks earlier, was never in a better position than at the finish. She finished well beaten, but this is probably her ideal distance at this stage. (op 18-1)

Ghost Train(IRE), fifth of six on his only previous run, was not helped by a slow start. He was soon rushed up to take a prominent position, but began to tread water shortly after the field turned into the straight. (op 11-2)

Bogey Hole(IRE), fourth of six here first time out, never threatened the principals. She will be better off once receiving a mark for handicaps. Official explanation: jockey said filly was slowly into stride (op 20-1 tchd 28-1)

5597 TOTEEXACTA THE BETTER VALUE FORECAST NURSERY 7f (F)

5:10 (5:12) (Class 6) (0-65,65) 2-Y-O £1,704 (£503; £251) **Stalls** Low

Form RPR

655 **1** **Bitaphon (IRE)**[35] 4402 2-9-3 **61** SteveDrowne 2 69
(Deborah Sanderson) *trckd ldrs on inner: hdwy to chse ldr over 2f out: rdn wl over 1f out: drvn ent fnl f: styd on to take ld last 30yds* **22/1**

2124 **2** ½ **Flying Pickets (IRE)**[48] 3973 2-9-0 **58** NeilCallan 5 65
(Alan McCabe) *led: rdn clr over 2f out: drvn over 1f out: hdd and no ex last 30yds* **11/1**

034 **3** 12 **Rano Pano (USA)**[12] 5211 2-8-12 **59** PaulPickard(3) 11 35
(Brian Ellison) *prom: rdn along over 2f out: sn drvn: edgd lft and one pce fr wl over 1f out* **13/8**[1]

0003 **4** 1 **Emley Moor**[24] 4808 2-9-1 **59** RoystonFfrench 1 32
(Chris Fairhurst) *midfield: hdwy wl over 2f out: sn rdn and kpt on ins fnl f: nrst fin* **25/1**

0004 **5** shd **Peters Pursuit (IRE)**[19] 4943 2-9-2 **60** TonyHamilton 10 33
(Richard Fahey) *in rr: rdn along 1/2-way: hdwy over 2f out: kpt on appr fnl f: nrst fin* **14/1**

0004 **6** 1½ **Man Of My Word**[15] 5104 2-9-4 **65** BillyCray(3) 6 34
(David Nicholls) *dwlt and in rr: wd st: gd hdwy on outer 2f out: rdn and edgd lft over 1f out: sn no imp* **16/1**

0404 **7** 1¾ **Johnson's Cat (IRE)**[8] 5324 2-8-8 **55** RobertLButler(3) 12 19
(Richard Guest) *prom: rdn along to chse ldng pair 3f out: drvn over 2f out and grad wknd* **20/1**

050 **8** 7 **Grippa**[79] 2953 2-9-5 **63** (b[1]) RichardMullen 7 —
(David Brown) *dwlt and rdn along in rr: nvr a factor* **22/1**

000 **9** 1¾ **Bea Persuasive**[18] 4983 2-7-10 **45** (e[1]) DanielleMcCreery(5) 9 —
(Shaun Harris) *a towards rr* **100/1**

0052 **10** 1 **Clone Devil (IRE)**[5] 5409 2-7-11 **46** RosieJessop(5) 13 —
(Alastair Lidderdale) *in tch: rdn along to chse ldrs over 2f out: wknd wl over 1f out* **12/1**

5030 **11** 4 **Electrickery**[20] 4907 2-9-3 **61** SilvestreDeSousa 3 —
(Mark Johnston) *midfield on inner: rdn along 1/2-way: n.m.r 3f out: sn drvn and wknd* **6/1**[3]

0432 **12** 3 **Hearts And Minds (IRE)**[7] 5343 2-9-5 **63** (b) FergusSweeney 4 —
(Jamie Osborne) *midfield: sme hdwy 1/2-way: rdn along wl over 2f out and sn wknd* **7/2**[2]

040 **13** 15 **After Timer (IRE)**[17] 5058 2-8-2 **46** PatrickMathers 14 —
(Julie Camacho) *dwlt: sn chsng ldrs on outer: rdn along wl over 2f out: wknd wl over 1f out* **33/1**

205 **14** 23 **Lady Tycoon**[21] 4884 2-8-11 **55** RobbieFitzpatrick 8 —
(Mark Brisbourne) *reminders s and sn rdn along into midfield: drvn 3f out and sn wknd* **40/1**

1m 30.71s (0.41) **Going Correction** +0.125s/f (Slow) **14** Ran SP% **126.9**

Speed ratings (Par 92): **102,101,87,86,86 84,82,74,72,71 67,63,46,20**

Tote Swingers: 1&2 £46.50, 1&3 £20.00, 2&3 £5.80 CSF £243.57 CT £640.36 TOTE £54.00: £12.80, £4.20, £1.10; EX 247.60.

Owner Mrs Caren Walsh **Bred** Pitrizzia Partnership **Trained** Sturton le Steeple, Notts

FOCUS

A moderate nusery where the first pair came well clear.

NOTEBOOK

Bitaphon(IRE), making his handicap debut after three runs in maidens, battled on bravely to grab the prize in the dying strides. Always in the leading trio, he made his challenge up the middle of the track and led well inside the final furlong. On this evidence, he will stay further Official explanation: trainer said, regarding apparent improvement in form, that the gelding appeared to benefit from racing on Fibresand for the first time. (tchd 20-1 and 25-1)

Flying Pickets(IRE), runner-up in a claimer over 6f here in June, again showed his liking for this surface. In front after a furlong, he led into the home straight and stuck steadfastly to the inside rail. Hard ridden in the closing stages, he was overhauled only very late on. This was a game effort (op 9-1 tchd 12-1)

Rano Pano(USA), making her handicap debut after three runs in 5/6f maidens, was heavily backed beforehand. She was always in the leading quartet and seemingly had no excuses, but was left well behind in the home straight once the principals locked horns. (op 5-2)

Emley Moor, third in a Redcar seller on her previous outing, was another towards the front in the first half of the race. She looked one-paced, though, when the pace quickened in the home straight. (op 22-1)

Peters Pursuit(IRE), 2lb higher than when fourth at Beverley 19 days earlier, was never in serious contention. A longer distance may help him. (tchd 16-1)

Man Of My Word, a half-brother to a Fibresand sprint winner, was making his handicap debut. Judged on this, he does not look particularly well-treated. (op 10-1)

After Timer(IRE) Official explanation: trainer's rep said filly was unsuited by the Fibresand

Lady Tycoon

5598 TRY TOTEQUICKPICK IF YOU'RE FEELING LUCKY MAIDEN STKS 1m (F)

5:40 (5:44) (Class 5) 3-Y-O £2,385 (£704; £352) **Stalls** Low

Form RPR

065 **1** **Outpost (IRE)**[12] 5212 3-9-3 0 TonyHamilton 2 78
(Alan Bailey) *led: pushed along and jnd over 2f out: hdd wl over 1f out: cl up: rallied ins fnl f to ld nr fin* **66/1**

2323 **2** ½ **Burj Hatta (USA)**[32] 4514 3-9-3 77 (p) RoystonFfrench 12 77
(Saeed Bin Suroor) *trckd ldrs: smooth hdwy over 3f out: chal over 2f out: rdn to take slt ld wl over 1f out and sn edgd lft: drvn ins fnl f: sn edgd lft: hdd and no ex nr fin* **9/4**[1]

3 **3** 4½ **Ampleforth**[12] 5212 3-9-3 0 SilvestreDeSousa 3 67+
(Mark Johnston) *in tch: hdwy 1/2-way: rdn along 3f out: drvn 2f out and kpt on same pce* **11/4**[2]

-355 **4** 1 **Crystal Etoile**[41] 4215 3-8-12 73 RichardMullen 10 59
(Sir Michael Stoute) *midfield: hdwy on outer to chse ldrs 3f out: rdn along over 2f out: sn drvn and plugged on same pce* **13/2**

0 **5** 6 **Dffra (IRE)**[138] 1338 3-8-12 0 SaleemGolam 5 46
(Clive Brittain) *dwlt: hdwy and in tch after 3f: rdn along wl over 2f out and n.d* **14/1**

4 **6** 9 **Mazij**[23] 4826 3-8-12 0 WilliamCarson 6 25
(Peter Hiatt) *a towards rr* **33/1**

0 **7** hd **Pronounce**[37] 4370 3-9-3 0 RobbieFitzpatrick 4 29
(Michael Appleby) *dwlt: nvr bttr than midfield* **200/1**

503 **8** ½ **Indian Mist (IRE)**[23] 4826 3-8-12 71 (p) NeilCallan 8 23
(Roger Varian) *chsd ldng pair: rdn along and edgd lft over 2f out: drvn wl over 1f out and sn wknd* **17/2**

2605 **9** ¾ **Discovery Bay**[20] 4914 3-9-3 75 (b[1]) SteveDrowne 7 27
(Roger Charlton) *sn rdn along and a in rr* **9/2**[3]

53 **10** 3 **Munaawib**[63] 3478 3-9-3 0 FergusSweeney 13 20
(David C Griffiths) *dwlt: hdwy on outer into midfield 1/2-way: sn rdn along and wknd 3f out* **40/1**

6 **11** 2½ **Classical Chloe**[73] 3191 3-8-9 0 RobertLButler(3) 9 —
(Richard Guest) *dwlt: a in rr* **150/1**

0030 **12** 11 **Totally Trusted**[22] 4854 3-8-9 58 (p) BillyCray(3) 1 —
(David Nicholls) *cl up: rdn along over 3f out and sn wknd* **80/1**

1m 44.66s (0.96) **Going Correction** +0.125s/f (Slow) **12** Ran SP% **115.4**

Speed ratings (Par 100): **100,99,95,94,88 79,78,78,77,74 72,61**

Tote Swingers: 1&2 £18.20, 1&3 £18.60, 2&3 £2.40 CSF £208.06 TOTE £80.70: £13.00, £1.10, £2.00; EX 166.50.

Owner Rathordan Partnership **Bred** Martin Dunne **Trained** Newmarket, Suffolk

FOCUS

A modest maiden, rated around the placed horses.

5599 TOTESWINGER MORE WAYS TO WIN H'CAP 1m 6f (F)

6:10 (6:10) (Class 5) (0-75,71) 3-Y-O+ £2,385 (£704; £352) **Stalls** Low

Form RPR

0603 **1** **All My Heart**[40] 4251 3-8-13 **68** StevieDonohoe 1 91+
(Sir Mark Prescott Bt) *mde all: pushed clr over 3f out: styd on strly: unchal* **2/1**[1]

0000 **2** 20 **Record Breaker (IRE)**[8] 5311 7-9-13 **70** (b) SilvestreDeSousa 6 65
(Mark Johnston) *chsd ldrs: rdn along after 5f: hdwy and cl up 6f out: rdn along to chse wnr over 3f out: drvn wl over 2f out: plugged on but no ch w wnr* **12/1**

6002 **3** 6 **Why So Serious**[8] 5312 5-8-10 **53** oh6 GregFairley 4 40
(Peter Salmon) *towards rr: hdwy to chse ldrs 4f out: rdn along over 3f out: sn drvn and plugged on to take remote 3rd ins fnl f* **50/1**

-426 **4** 7 **Miereveld**[3] 5485 4-8-12 **58** (be) PaulPickard(3) 3 35
(Brian Ellison) *reminders s and pushed along to chse ldrs after 2f: rdn along 1/2-way: drvn along 4f out: outpcd fnl 3f: lost remote 3rd ins fnl f* **6/1**

0100 **5** 23 **Trojan Gift (USA)**[22] 4856 4-9-6 **63** (v[1]) TonyHamilton 5 —
(Julie Camacho) *trckd ldrs: rdn along over 5f out: drvn 4f out: sn outpcd and eased over 2f out* **15/2**

0021 **6** 19 **Native Colony**[15] 5122 3-9-2 **71** NeilCallan 2 —
(Roger Varian) *chsd ldrs 4f: lost pl and rr after 6f: sn rdn along: outpcd and bhd fr 5f out: t.o fnl 3f* **7/2**[3]

2221 **7** 34 **May Contain Nuts**[19] 4974 3-9-2 **71** FergusSweeney 7 —
(Brendan Powell) *prom: rdn along 6f out: drvn and wknd over 4f out: sn bhd: eased and t.o fnl 3f* **3/1**[2]

3m 10.65s (2.35) **Going Correction** +0.125s/f (Slow)

WFA 3 from 4yo+ 12lb **7** Ran SP% **116.3**

Speed ratings (Par 103): **98,86,83,79,66 55,35**

Tote Swingers: 1&2 £4.80, 1&3 £14.20, 2&3 £12.60 CSF £28.19 TOTE £2.80: £1.10, £5.90; EX 22.90.

The Form Book, Raceform Ltd, Compton, RG20 6NL

Owner Miss K Rausing **Bred** Miss K Rausing And Shellin Blk **Trained** Newmarket, Suffolk
FOCUS
A moderate staying handicap dominated by the winner.
Native Colony Official explanation: trainer's rep said colt was unsuited by the Fibresand
May Contain Nuts Official explanation: trainer said gelding was unsuited by the Fibresand

5600 FOLLOW AT THE RACES ON TWITTER H'CAP — 5f (F)
6:40 (6:41) (Class 6) (0-65,64) 3-Y-0+ — **£1,617** (£481; £240; £120) **Stalls** High

Form — RPR
2312 **1** — **Colourbearer (IRE)**[1] 5534 4-9-2 **58**..........(t) SilvestreDeSousa 3 — 75
(Milton Bradley) *dwlt: reminders and swtchd lft to outer after 1f: hdwy 1/2-way: rdn over 1f out: led jst ins fnl f: r.o strly* **7/4**[1]
5501 **2** 2¾ **Spirit Of Coniston**[6] 5373 8-9-3 **59** 6ex.......... RussKennemore 7 — 66
(Paul Midgley) *led 2f: cl up: rdn along wl over 1f out: sn hung bdly lft: to far rail: kpt on* **7/1**
5222 **3** 1 **Elusive Warrior (USA)**[28] 4651 8-8-9 **58**..........(p) NoraLooby(7) 2 — 63+
(Alan McCabe) *prom: rdn along 2f out: nt clr run on far rail ins fnl f: swtchd rt and one pce* **6/1**[3]
1003 **4** ½ **Premier League**[42] 4182 4-9-2 **58**..........(p) RoystonFfrench 8 — 60
(Julia Feilden) *racd alone on stands' rail: prom: rdn 2f out and ev ch tl one pce fnl f* **9/2**[2]
2153 **5** ¾ **Spic 'n Span**[13] 5175 6-9-1 **64**..........(b) MichaelJMurphy(7) 1 — 63
(Ronald Harris) *prom: led after 2f: rdn over 1f out: hdd jst ins fnl f: sn wknd* **6/1**[3]
6264 **6** shd **Patch Patch**[8] 5326 4-9-6 **62**..........(v[1]) RobbieFitzpatrick 5 — 61
(Derek Shaw) *cl up: rdn along over 2f out: drvn and wknd over 1f out* **8/1**
5160 **7** 2½ **Princess Dayna**[12] 5215 3-8-11 **58**.......... RossAtkinson(3) 6 — 48
(Tom Dascombe) *a in rr* **33/1**
0500 **8** 7 **Je Suis Unrockstar**[38] 4328 3-9-0 **61**..........(b[1]) BillyCray(3) 4 — 25
(David Nicholls) *dwlt: sn chsng ldrs: rdn along 1/2-way: sn wknd* **14/1**

59.70 secs **Going Correction** +0.025s/f (Slow)
WFA 3 from 4yo+ 2lb — **8** Ran SP% **116.3**
Speed ratings (Par 101): **101,96,95,94,93 92,88,77**
Tote Swingers: 1&2 £4.30, 1&3 £2.50, 2&3 £6.80 CSF £15.08 CT £61.74 TOTE £2.70: £1.10, £4.60, £1.60; EX 17.60.
Owner E A Hayward **Bred** Corduff Stud & J Corcorcan **Trained** Sedbury, Gloucs
■ Stewards' Enquiry : Russ Kennemore three-day ban: careless riding (Sep 13-15)
FOCUS
A very weak handicap.

5601 BRAND NEW ATR PREDICTOR H'CAP — 7f (F)
7:10 (7:10) (Class 6) (0-55,55) 3-Y-0+ — **£1,704** (£503; £251) **Stalls** Low

Form — RPR
3422 **1** — **Scarborough Lily**[20] 4927 3-9-0 **55**..........(b) NeilCallan 7 — 64
(Edward Vaughan) *in tch: smooth hdwy to trck ldrs 1/2-way: chal on bit over 2f out: led wl over 1f out and sn rdn: drvn and hung bdly rt ins fnl f: jst hld on* **5/1**[2]
2040 **2** shd **Lujano**[22] 4852 6-9-2 **52**.......... BarryMcHugh 3 — 62
(Ollie Pears) *prom on inner: rdn along and sltly outpcd 3f out: swtchd rt and hdwy wl over 1f out: drvn ent fnl f and styd on to chal: ev ch whn hmpd nr line* **5/1**[2]
0052 **3** 2¼ **Spacecraft (IRE)**[12] 5214 4-8-7 **46** oh1.......... PaulPickard(3) 11 — 50
(Christopher Kellett) *dwlt and in rr: hdwy wl over 2f out: sn rdn and styd on wl appr fnl f: nrst fin* **13/2**[3]
0164 **4** nk **Norcroft**[15] 5116 9-8-6 **49**..........(p) DanielHarris(7) 13 — 52
(Christine Dunnett) *chsd ldrs: hdwy 2f out: sn rdn and kpt on u.p fnl f: nrst fin* **20/1**
0130 **5** 1¼ **Twennyshortkid**[28] 4638 3-8-10 **51**..........(v) RoystonFfrench 12 — 49
(Paul Midgley) *cl up: rdn along 2f out: drvn over 1f out: one pce ent fnl f* **11/1**
652 **6** 4½ **Anrheg**[12] 5212 3-8-13 **54**.......... SilvestreDeSousa 14 — 40
(David Brown) *chsd ldrs on outer: effrt over 2f out: rdn and hung lft over 1f out: sn drvn and wknd* **9/4**[1]
5560 **7** 3½ **Vogarth**[28] 4651 7-8-5 **46**..........(b) ChrisDCogan(5) 1 — 24
(Michael Chapman) *midfield: rdn along on inner 3f out: drvn over 2f out: n.d* **66/1**
0000 **8** 4½ **Scruffy Skip (IRE)**[0] [illegible]..........(p) WilliamCarson 6 — 16
(Christine Dunnett) *dwlt: a towards rr* **20/1**
0004 **9** ½ **Fathey (IRE)**[12] 5214 5-8-10 **46**.......... RobbieFitzpatrick 9 — 11
(Charles Smith) *prom: rdn along 1/2-way: sn wknd* **25/1**
6606 **10** ½ **Duplicity**[9] 5298 4-8-11 **50**..........(tp) RobertLButler(3) 5 — 13
(Richard Guest) *led: rdn along over 2f out: drvn and hdd over 1f out: wknd* **28/1**
3500 **11** ¾ **Crocodile Bay (IRE)**[12] 5214 8-8-10 **46** oh1..........(be) AndrewMullen 2 — —
(Richard Guest) *a towards rr* **25/1**
6000 **12** 3¼ **Gracie's Gift (IRE)**[17] 5034 9-9-2 **55**..........(e) RossAtkinson(3) 8 — —
(Richard Guest) *towards rr fr 1/2-way* **25/1**
-060 **13** 4½ **High Class Lady**[113] 1953 3-8-9 **50**.......... FergusSweeney 4 — —
(Walter Swinburn) *dwlt: a in rr* **25/1**
000- **14** 6 **Stay On Track (IRE)**[469] 2200 4-8-9 **48**.......... BillyCray(3) 10 — —
(Garry Woodward) *a in rr* **33/1**

1m 31.46s (1.16) **Going Correction** +0.125s/f (Slow)
WFA 3 from 4yo+ 5lb — **14** Ran SP% **118.6**
Speed ratings (Par 101): **98,97,95,94,93 88,84,79,78,78 77,73,68,61**
Tote Swingers: 1&2 £5.20, 1&3 £4.80, 2&3 £8.90 CSF £25.20 CT £170.81 TOTE £5.20: £1.10, £1.40, £2.70; EX 35.50.
Owner A M Pickering **Bred** Stowell Park Stud **Trained** Newmarket, Suffolk
■ Stewards' Enquiry : Neil Callan two-day ban: careless riding (Sep 13-14)
FOCUS
A weak handicap.

5602 GOLF AND RACING AT SOUTHWELL APPRENTICE H'CAP — 1m (F)
7:40 (7:41) (Class 5) (0-75,71) 3-Y-0 — **£2,385** (£704; £352) **Stalls** Low

Form — RPR
050 **1** — **Caledonia Prince**[57] 3690 3-7-12 **52** oh7..........(p) JoshBaudains(7) 6 — 57
(Jo Hughes) *cl up: led after 2f: pushed along and hdd briefly 3f out: led again wl over 2f out: hdd wl over 1f out: styd cl up and rallied to ld again wl ins fnl f: kpt on gamely* **20/1**
-102 **2** hd **Golden Creek (USA)**[12] 5213 3-9-7 **71**.......... MatthewLawson(3) 1 — 76
(Mrs K Burke) *in rr and rdn along over 3f out: gd hdwy to chal over 2f out: led wl over 1f out and sn drvn: hdd wl ins fnl f: no ex towards fin* **15/8**[1]
106 **3** 1½ **William Haigh (IRE)**[18] 5004 3-9-6 **70**.......... GarryWhillans(3) 3 — 74+
(Alan Swinbank) *trckd ldrs: rdn along 3f out: styd on u.p fr over 1f out: clsd up to chal whn edgd lft and sltly hmpd ins fnl f: one pce after* **11/2**[3]
-320 **4** 3¼ **Lion Court (IRE)**[15] 5103 3-9-7 **68**.......... RosieJessop 4 — 62
(Sir Mark Prescott Bt) *dwlt: hdwy on outer and cl up after 2f: rdn and led briefly 3f out: sn hdd and drvn: wknd fnl 2f* **2/1**[2]
413 **5** 9 **Cheylesmore (IRE)**[14] 5136 3-9-7 **68**..........(v) TobyAtkinson 2 — 41
(Stuart Williams) *led 2f: prom tl rdn along wl over 2f out and grad wknd* **11/2**[3]
4400 **6** 8 **Ad Vitam (IRE)**[57] 3683 3-8-2 **56**.......... ClaireMurray(7) 5 — 11
(David C Griffiths) *in tch on outer: rdn along over 3f out and sn wknd* **16/1**

1m 44.32s (0.62) **Going Correction** +0.125s/f (Slow) — **6** Ran SP% **109.5**
Speed ratings (Par 100): **101,100,99,96,87 79**
Tote Swingers: 1&2 £10.40, 1&3 £8.80, 2&3 £2.50 CSF £55.23 TOTE £35.20: £17.00, £3.30; EX 86.30.
Owner Isla & Colin Cage **Bred** Mrs I M Cage And C J Cage **Trained** Lambourn, Berks
FOCUS
A competitive finale, albeit it at a modest form level.
Caledonia Prince Official explanation: trainer said, regarding apparent improvement in form, that the gelding appeared to be suited by racing on Fibresand for the first time.
T/Plt: £42.70 to a £1 stake. Pool:£44,047.23 - 751.84 winning tickets T/Qpdt: £11.90 to a £1 stake. Pool:£4,279.29 - 265.55 winning tickets JR

5413 WOLVERHAMPTON (A.W) (L-H)
Tuesday, August 30

OFFICIAL GOING: Standard
Wind: Light across Weather: Overcast

5603 ATTHERACES.COM EXCLUSIVE HUGH TAYLOR TIPPING H'CAP — 5f 216y(P)
5:55 (5:56) (Class 6) (0-60,59) 3-Y-0+ — **£1,704** (£503; £251) **Stalls** Low

Form — RPR
1500 **1** — **Almaty Express**[11] 5244 9-9-5 **57**.......... JamieSpencer 3 — 67
(John Weymes) *mde all: rdn over 1f out: styd on u.p* **17/2**
0644 **2** 1½ **Cadmium Loch**[10] 5274 3-8-11 **59**..........(p) JackDuern(7) 2 — 64
(Reg Hollinshead) *a.p: chsd wnr 1/2-way: rdn over 1f out: styd on* **11/2**[1]
5514 **3** nse **Francis Albert**[13] 5175 5-8-10 **55**.......... JosephYoung(7) 7 — 60
(Michael Mullineaux) *sn prom: rdn over 1f out: r.o* **12/1**
5350 **4** 1 **Itsthursdayalready**[11] 5244 4-9-5 **57**.......... TomMcLaughlin 1 — 59
(Mark Brisbourne) *hld up: hdwy over 1f out: r.o: nt rch ldrs* **15/2**[3]
0004 **5** ½ **Dingaan (IRE)**[11] 5244 8-9-2 **54**.......... AndreaAtzeni 4 — 54
(Peter Grayson) *mid-div: hdwy over 2f out: rdn over 1f out: styd on* **15/2**[3]
4035 **6** 1 **Ghost Dancer**[71] 3234 7-8-8 **49**..........(p) RyanClark(3) 11 — 46
(Milton Bradley) *s.s: hld up: nt clr run wl over 1f out: edgd lft and r.o ins fnl f: nt rch ldrs* **16/1**
6303 **7** 2 **Boldinor**[14] 5138 8-9-6 **58**.......... RobertHavlin 5 — 49
(Martin Bosley) *chsd ldrs: n.m.r over 3f out: rdn over 1f out: styd on same pce* **12/1**
0360 **8** ½ **Welcome Approach**[6] 5371 8-9-7 **59**.......... JimmyQuinn 6 — 48
(John Weymes) *hood removed late: s.i.s: hld up: r.o ins fnl f: nvr nrr* **6/1**[2]
0-24 **9** 2¼ **Kristollini**[222] 233 3-9-0 **55**.......... JamesDoyle 12 — 37
(William Muir) *prom: rdn over 2f out: wknd over 1f out* **16/1**
000 **10** 2 **Replicator**[66] 3412 6-8-9 **52**..........(e) AntiocoMurgia(5) 8 — 27
(Patrick Gilligan) *chsd ldrs: rdn over 1f out: wknd fnl f* **25/1**
0040 **11** 2 **Lily Wood**[56] 3720 5-8-11 **49**..........(p) LiamJones 10 — 18
(James Unett) *hld up: rdn 1/2-way: wknd over 2f out* **17/2**
5006 **12** ¾ **Mark Anthony (IRE)**[17] 5034 4-9-6 **58**.......... FrannyNorton 9 — 25
(Shaun Harris) *chsd ldrs: rdn over 2f out: wknd over 1f out* **17/2**

1m 13.39s (-1.61) **Going Correction** -0.25s/f (Stan)
WFA 3 from 4yo+ 3lb — **12** Ran SP% **115.8**
Speed ratings (Par 101): **100,98,97,96,95 94,91,91,88,85 82,81**
Tote Swingers: 1&2 £13.00, 1&3 £12.50, 2&3 £9.20 CSF £53.39 CT £572.50 TOTE £10.30: £5.00, £1.10, £6.00; EX 59.70.
Owner Highmoor Racing 4 & Tag Racing **Bred** P G Airey **Trained** Middleham Moor, N Yorks
FOCUS
Mainly exposed performers in a moderate opener. Although the gallop seemed reasonable, those held up were at a disadvantage and the winner raced just off the inside rail in the straight.
Welcome Approach Official explanation: jockey said blindfold had been tightly fitted and had not loosened prior to start resulting in gelding being slowly away
Replicator Official explanation: vet said gelding was struck into on its left-hind leg

5604 WOLVERHAMPTON-RACECOURSE.CO.UK (S) STKS — 5f 20y(P)
6:25 (6:25) (Class 6) 3-5-Y-O — **£1,567** (£462; £231) **Stalls** Low

Form — RPR
4121 **1** — **Deerslayer (USA)**[9] 5300 5-9-3 72..........(p) MartinHarley(3) 5 — 87+
(Richard Guest) *mde all: pushed clr fnl f: comf* **13/8**[1]
0203 **2** 4½ **Brynfa Boy**[18] 4990 5-8-11 73.......... MatthewDavies(3) 4 — 65
(Paul D'Arcy) *hld up: hdwy to chse wnr over 1f out: sn rdn and edgd lft: no imp* **15/8**[2]
2502 **3** 3½ **Polemica (IRE)**[22] 4865 5-9-1 64..........(bt) JamesDoyle 3 — 53
(Frank Sheridan) *chsd wnr tl over 3f out: rdn 1/2-way: wknd fnl f* **8/1**
0014 **4** ¾ **Dark Lane**[7] 5345 5-9-6 74.......... JamieSpencer 6 — 56
(Tony Carroll) *prom: pushed along 3f out: sn outpcd: n.d after* **4/1**[3]
0065 **5** 1 **Olynard (IRE)**[4] 5452 5-9-0 67..........(vt) AndreaAtzeni 7 — 46
(Dr Richard Newland) *s.i.s: hdwy to chse wnr over 3f out tl rdn over 1f out: sn wknd* **14/1**

60.22 secs (-2.08) **Going Correction** -0.25s/f (Stan) course record
WFA 3 from 5yo 2lb — **5** Ran SP% **110.7**
Speed ratings (Par 101): **106,98,93,92,90**
CSF £5.02 TOTE £1.80: £1.40, £1.70; EX 5.20.The winner was bought in for 6,400gns.
Owner Rakebackmypoker.com **Bred** Bjorn Nielsen **Trained** Stainforth, S Yorks
FOCUS
A couple of fair sorts but not a competitive event. An ordinary gallop lifted turning for home and the winner came down the centre in the straight.

5605 ENJOY THE PARTY PACK GROUP OFFER MAIDEN AUCTION STKS — 7f 32y(P)
6:55 (6:57) (Class 5) 2-Y-0 — **£2,385** (£704; £352) **Stalls** High

Form — RPR
0220 **1** — **Red Aggressor (IRE)**[77] 3012 2-9-1 90.......... PhilipRobinson 3 — 74+
(Clive Brittain) *chsd ldr: shkn up over 1f out: led ins fnl f: edgd rt: rdn out* **1/2**[1]
2 1¼ **Let Your Love Flow (IRE)** 2-8-9 0.......... JamesDoyle 2 — 59+
(Sylvester Kirk) *led: rdn over 1f out: hdd and unable qck ins fnl f* **8/1**[3]
466 **3** 1¼ **Moment In The Sun**[19] 4954 2-8-5 49.......... FrannyNorton 1 — 52
(William Muir) *trckd ldrs: plld hrd: rdn over 1f out: styd on same pce ins fnl f* **25/1**
4 **4** hd **Enery (IRE)**[13] 5170 2-8-7 0.......... AntiocoMurgia(5) 4 — 59
(Mahmood Al Zarooni) *prom: rdn over 1f out: r.o: nt rch ldrs* **11/4**[2]

5300 **5** *18* **Bit A Craic**[15] 5099 2-8-4 46.. JamieMackay 5 6
(John Ryan) *s.i.s: hld up: wknd 1/2-way* **50/1**
1m 30.64s (1.04) **Going Correction** -0.25s/f (Stan) 5 Ran SP% **110.3**
Speed ratings (Par 94): **84,82,81,80,60**
CSF £5.44 TOTE £1.30: £1.02, £5.80; EX 5.90.
Owner C E Brittain **Bred** John Foley & Miss A Foley **Trained** Newmarket, Suffolk

FOCUS
An uncompetitive maiden won in workmanlike fashion by the short-priced favourite. The steady gallop and the proximity of the 49-rated third confirms this bare form is shaky and the winner came down the centre in the straight.

NOTEBOOK
Red Aggressor(IRE), far from disgraced when ninth in the Coventry, didn't have to run to that level to get off the mark in workmanlike fashion in this uncompetitive event on this all-weather debut. He's almost certainly better than he was able to show in this muddling event on this first run over 7f and has physical scope, but he will have to raise his game by some way to follow up in a nursery or if returned to Pattern company. (op 4-7 tchd 4-9 tchd 8-13 in places)
Let Your Love Flow(IRE), a 19,000gns half-sister to modest triple Polytrack winner Suhayl Star and to 7f juvenile turf winner Annamay, was allowed an easy lead but showed ability to chase home a useful sort on this racecourse debut. She's entitled to improve for this experience and should be able to pick up a small race at some point. (op 12-1 tchd 20-1)
Moment In The Sun, who faced a very stiff task at the weights, turned in easily her best effort in terms of form on this all-weather debut. However her proximity to the useful winner owes plenty to the steady gallop and it will be interesting to see how the handicapper reacts. (op 14-1)
Enery(IRE), who showed ability at a moderate level on his debut, failed to build on that form but left the impression that a stronger gallop over 7f or the step up to 1m would see him in a more favourable light. He should be able to step up on these bare facts in ordinary handicaps in due course. (op 5-2 tchd 3-1)

5606 READ PAUL HANAGAN'S BLOG ON ATR H'CAP 1m 141y(P)
7:25 (7:26) (Class 6) (0-60,60) 3-Y-O+ **£1,704** (£503; £251) **Stalls** Low

Form RPR
6604 **1** **Excellent Vision**[9] 5248 4-8-11 **48**..(t) RyanClark(3) 8 56
(Milton Bradley) *s.s: hld up: hdwy over 1f out: rdn to ld and edgd lft wl ins fnl f: r.o* **10/1**
2000 **2** *hd* **Spinning Ridge (IRE)**[6] 5376 6-9-9 **57**....................(v) TomMcLaughlin 3 65
(Ronald Harris) *s.i.s: hld up: hdwy over 1f out: hung lft and led ins fnl f: sn hdd: r.o* **14/1**
0600 **3** *3/4* **Queenie's Star (IRE)**[31] 4549 4-8-8 **47**........................ MarkCoumbe(5) 4 53
(Michael Attwater) *chsd ldrs: rdn to ld 1f out: edgd lft and sn hdd: styd on* **20/1**
4606 **4** *shd* **Beach Babe**[21] 4888 3-9-4 **59**.. NickyMackay 7 65
(Jonathan Portman) *hld up in tch: rdn over 1f out: styd on* **10/1**
6650 **5** *1/2* **Twisted**[35] 4408 5-9-11 **59**..(b) PaddyAspell 11 64
(Michael Easterby) *chsd ldrs: rdn over 3f out: outpcd over 1f out: r.o towards fin* **20/1**
54 **6** *1 3/4* **Supa Seeker (USA)**[25] 4755 5-9-12 **60**........................ JamieSpencer 6 63+
(Tony Carroll) *trckd ldr: led on bit 2 out: rdn and hdd 1f out: btn whn hmpd towards fin* **5/2**[1]
520 **7** *1/2* **Lilli Palmer (IRE)**[17] 5040 4-9-8 **56**........................ MartinLane 2 58+
(Mike Murphy) *chsd ldrs: nt clr run wl over 1f out: sn rdn: styd on same pce ins fnl f* **9/1**
4340 **8** *1 1/2* **So Is She (IRE)**[11] 5248 3-9-1 **59**..............................(b) AmyBaker(3) 5 62+
(Alan Bailey) *hld up: nt clr run fr over 1f out: nvr able to chal* **14/1**
4521 **9** *nk* **Putin (IRE)**[14] 5143 3-8-13 **54**.. AndreaAtzeni 1 52+
(Derek Haydn Jones) *led: rdn and hdd 2f out: btn whn hmpd ins fnl f* **5/1**[2]
2430 **10** *4 1/2* **Scoglio**[13] 5179 3-9-5 **60**..(bt) JamesDoyle 10 45
(Frank Sheridan) *s.s: hld up: hdwy over 2f out: wknd over 1f out* **8/1**[3]
045 **11** *7* **Saktoon (USA)**[24] 4796 3-9-2 **57**.................................... PhilipRobinson 9 26
(Clive Brittain) *prom: rdn over 3f out: wknd over 2f out* **14/1**
0-60 **12** *41* **Ime Not Bitter**[11] 5248 3-8-7 **48**..............................(t) JamieMackay 13 —
(Bill Moore) *hld up: lost tch fnl 3f: t.o* **100/1**
1m 49.37s (-1.13) **Going Correction** -0.25s/f (Stan)
WFA 3 from 4yo+ 7lb 12 Ran SP% **115.0**
Speed ratings (Par 101): **95,94,94,94,93 92,91,90,90,86 79,43**
Tote Swingers: 1&2 £18.20, 1&3 £43.30, 2&3 £18.70 CSF £134.46 CT £2763.61 TOTE £16.70: £5.70, £6.10, £13.60; EX 123.80.
Owner E A Hayward **Bred** Manor Farm Stud (rutland) **Trained** Sedbury, Gloucs

FOCUS
A moderate handicap but, although the gallop was no more than fair, the first two placings were filled by those that came from off the pace. The winner raced centre to far side in the straight.

5607 SPONSOR RACE BY CALLING 01902 390000 MAIDEN STKS 1m 1f 103y(P)
7:55 (7:56) (Class 5) 3-Y-O+ **£2,045** (£603; £302) **Stalls** Low

Form RPR
4-30 **1** **Kyllachy Spirit**[74] 3118 3-9-3 70.. JamieSpencer 11 89+
(William Knight) *mde all: clr fr over 5f out: rdn over 1f out: styd on wl* **6/1**[2]
0 **2** *8* **Midnight Waltz**[8] 5317 3-8-12 0.. SebSanders 10 67
(Sir Mark Prescott Bt) *a.p: chsd wnr 4f out: rdn over 2f out: styd on same pce* **9/1**
0304 **3** *1 3/4* **Change The Subject (USA)**[17] 5056 3-9-3 74.............(b) IanMongan 2 69
(Sir Henry Cecil) *a.p: wnt 3rd over 2f out: sn rdn: no imp whn rdr dropped whip over 1f out* **4/7**[1]
0 **4** *3 1/4* **Fairest Isle (IRE)**[112] 1991 3-8-12 0..............................(t) MartinLane 12 57
(James Fanshawe) *s.i.s: hld up: styd on fr over 1f out: nvr nr ldrs* **33/1**
5 *5* **Mahfal (FR)**[106] 3-9-0 0.. DaleSwift(3) 7 51
(Brian Ellison) *hld up: rdn over 1f out: nvr on terms* **15/2**[3]
6 *1/2* **Swooping Hawk (IRE)**[96] 2443 4-9-10 0........................ StephenCraine 3 50
(Sylvester Kirk) *hld up in tch: rdn and wknd wl over 1f out* **25/1**
0 **7** *1 1/4* **Novirak (IRE)**[14] 5140 3-9-3 0.. PatCosgrave 8 48
(James Fanshawe) *chsd wnr over 5f: rdn and wknd over 2f out* **33/1**
00 **8** *3* **Akarana (IRE)**[12] 5212 4-9-10 0.. JamieMackay 4 41
(Willie Musson) *hld up: nvr nr to chal* **50/1**
9 *12* **Our Freedom** 3-8-12 0.. ChrisCatlin 5 —
(David Lanigan) *s.i.s: sn pushed along in rr: bhd fnl 5f: t.o* **22/1**
0 **10** *1 1/4* **Millers Dhustone**[26] 4706 5-8-12 0.............................. RachealKneller(7) 13 —
(Pam Ford) *chsd ldrs tl rdn and wknd over 3f out: t.o* **125/1**
11 *2 1/2* **My Cherie Amour** 3-8-9 0.. MartinHarley(3) 9 —
(Richard Guest) *s.i.s: hld up: plld hrd early: bhd fnl 5f: t.o* **100/1**
12 *1 3/4* **Noneedtofret** 3-8-5 0.. MatthewMcGhee(7) 6 —
(Bill Moore) *s.i.s: a in rr: bhd fnl 5f: t.o* **100/1**
1m 58.29s (-3.41) **Going Correction** -0.25s/f (Stan)
WFA 3 from 4yo+ 7lb 12 Ran SP% **118.5**
Speed ratings (Par 103): **105,97,96,93,89 88,87,84,74,73 70,69**
Tote Swingers: 1&2 £3.20, 1&3 £1.90, 2&3 £2.50 CSF £53.99 TOTE £6.00: £1.40, £3.90, £1.02; EX 43.80.
Owner Mrs J R Jenrick & R D Jenrick **Bred** Mrs H I S Calzini **Trained** Patching, W Sussex

FOCUS
Several unexposed sorts but no more than a fair maiden. The gallop was soon reasonable and the 70-rated winner came centre to far side in the straight.

5608 BETTER WIN PRICES EVERY RACE AT CORAL.CO.UK H'CAP 1m 1f 103y(P)
8:25 (8:25) (Class 4) (0-80,79) 3-Y-O+ **£3,557** (£1,058; £529; £264) **Stalls** Low

Form RPR
3000 **1** **Totally Ours**[15] 5113 4-10-0 **79**.. FrannyNorton 7 89
(William Muir) *chsd ldrs: rdn to ld over 1f out: r.o* **7/1**[3]
12 **2** *1 1/2* **Satwa Pearl**[112] 1992 5-10-0 **79**.. HayleyTurner 6 86
(Ed Dunlop) *hld up: hdwy over 2f out: rdn to chse wnr ins fnl f: r.o* **11/4**[1]
-100 **3** *1/2* **African Cheetah**[101] 2301 5-9-12 **77**..............................(p) IanMongan 1 83
(Reg Hollinshead) *hld up: hdwy over 2f out: swtchd rt over 1f out: sn rdn: r.o* **16/1**
0630 **4** *2 1/4* **Mazamorra (USA)**[46] 4066 4-9-9 **79**........................ AntiocoMurgia(5) 10 80
(Marco Botti) *a.p: chsd ldr over 6f out: led over 2f out: rdn ant: hdd over 1f out: no ex ins fnl f* **12/1**
3-31 **5** *1* **Tarooq (USA)**[105] 2178 5-9-9 **74**.. TonyHamilton 3 73
(Richard Fahey) *chsd ldrs: rdn over 1f out: no ex ins fnl f* **3/1**[2]
5005 **6** *2* **Striding Edge (IRE)**[8] 5318 5-8-11 **62**.. JamesDoyle 2 57
(Hans Adielsson) *hld up: hdwy 2f out: sn rdn: nt trble ldrs* **20/1**
4600 **7** *6* **Champagne Style (USA)**[19] 4958 4-8-11 **65**........(tp) MartinHarley(3) 11 47
(Richard Guest) *hld up: rdn over 2f out: nvr on terms* **25/1**
1566 **8** *1/2* **El Djebena (IRE)**[12] 5213 3-8-12 **70**.. SebSanders 9 51
(Sir Mark Prescott Bt) *sn led: rdn 4f out: hdd over 2f out: wknd over 1f out* **8/1**
0036 **9** *10* **Kidlat**[27] 4660 6-10-0 **79**.. PatCosgrave 5 39
(Alan Bailey) *pushed along early to go prom: rdn over 3f out: wknd over 2f out* **12/1**
0430 **10** *5* **Sirgarfieldsobers (IRE)**[17] 5036 5-9-6 **76**........................ NeilFarley(5) 8 26
(Declan Carroll) *trckd ldrs: plld hrd: rdn and wknd over 2f out* **16/1**
1100 **11** *15* **Strong Vigilance (IRE)**[59] 3641 4-9-10 **75**........................ JamieSpencer 12 —
(Michael Bell) *hld up: rdn 3f out: no rspnse and sn wknd: t.o* **12/1**
1m 57.82s (-3.88) **Going Correction** -0.25s/f (Stan)
WFA 3 from 4yo+ 7lb 11 Ran SP% **118.7**
Speed ratings (Par 105): **107,105,105,103,102 100,95,94,85,81 68**
Tote Swingers: 1&2 £7.80, 1&3 £39.10, 2&3 £12.70 CSF £26.77 CT £305.43 TOTE £4.50: £1.10, £2.30, £7.40; EX 23.00.
Owner Foursome Thoroughbreds **Bred** W Muir And Foursome Thoroughbreds **Trained** Lambourn, Berks

FOCUS
A fair handicap in which the gallop was just an ordinary one. The first six finished clear and the winner raced towards the centre in the straight.
Strong Vigilance(IRE) Official explanation: jockey said gelding never travelled

5609 ENHANCED WIN ODDS FROM NOON AT CORAL.CO.UK H'CAP 1m 4f 50y(P)
8:55 (8:56) (Class 6) (0-65,65) 3-Y-O+ **£1,704** (£503; £251) **Stalls** Low

Form RPR
0000 **1** **Epic (IRE)**[16] 5078 4-9-11 **65**.. FrannyNorton 1 77
(Mark Johnston) *chsd ldrs: pushed along over 5f out: rdn to chse wnr over 1f out: led ins fnl f: r.o wl* **9/1**
4333 **2** *2* **Boa**[11] 4626 6-9-11 **65**.. JamieSpencer 8 74
(Reg Hollinshead) *chsd ldrs: led over 8f out: rdn over 1f out: hdd and unable qck ins fnl f* **9/2**[3]
2350 **3** *2 3/4* **Wrecking Crew (IRE)**[12] 5198 7-9-4 **58**........................ JamesMillman 2 63+
(Rod Millman) *hld up: nt clr run over 2f out: hdwy over 1f out: edgd rt and styd on ins fnl f: nt trble ldrs* **4/1**[2]
5000 **4** *3* **Beauchamp Xiara**[11] 5248 5-9-3 **57**.. JamesDoyle 6 57
(Hans Adielsson) *prom: chsd ldr over 2f out tl rdn over 1f out: wknd ins fnl f* **12/1**
4100 **5** *1/2* **Turjuman (USA)**[15] 5103 6-9-0 **61**........................ ShannonEdmondson(7) 3 60
(Willie Musson) *hld up: r.o ins fnl f: nvr nrr* **14/1**
1264 **6** *3/4* **Dane Cottage**[17] 5036 4-8-11 **54**.. DaleSwift(3) 7 52
(Brian Ellison) *s.i.s: hld up: hdwy over 3f out: rdn and wknd over 1f out* **7/2**[1]
3634 **7** *7* **Maoi Chinn Tire (IRE)**[11] 5249 4-9-11 **65**................(p) StephenCraine 4 52
(Jennie Candlish) *led 1f: chsd ldr to over 8f out: wnt 2nd again over 6f out to over 2f out: sn rdn: wknd over 1f out:* **7/2**[1]
6-00 **8** *19* **Into The Light**[11] 4562 6-9-1 **55**..............................(b) RussKennemore 5 —
(Philip Kirby) *pushed along to ld after 1f: hdd over 8f out: chsd ldr to over 6f out: rdn and wknd over 3f out: t.o* **16/1**
2m 37.16s (-3.94) **Going Correction** -0.25s/f (Stan) 8 Ran SP% **112.9**
Speed ratings (Par 101): **103,101,99,97,97 97,92,79**
Tote Swingers: 1&2 £5.70, 1&3 £6.90, 2&3 £4.60 CSF £47.79 CT £187.94 TOTE £16.50: £3.90, £1.10, £2.30; EX 49.20.
Owner Racegoers Club Owners Group **Bred** P D Savill **Trained** Middleham Moor, N Yorks

FOCUS
A modest handicap in which the two market leaders underperformed. The gallop was an ordinary one and the winner came down the centre in the straight.
T/Plt: £56.30 to a £1 stake. Pool:£59,885.01 - 776.12 winning tickets T/Qpdt: £24.40 to a £1 stake. Pool:£5,353.49 - 162.30 winning tickets CR

5528 BADEN-BADEN (L-H)
Tuesday, August 30

OFFICIAL GOING: Turf: good

5610a AMERICAN EXPRESS ZUKUNFTS-RENNEN (GROUP 3) (2YO) (TURF) 7f
5:15 (12:00) 2-Y-O
£27,586 (£9,482; £4,741; £2,586; £1,724; £1,293)

RPR
1 **Amaron**[37] 4372 2-9-2 0.. AHelfenbein 2 104
(Andreas Lowe, Germany) *broke fast: sn led: set gd pce: r.o wl in st: chal and hdd by Pakal 2f out: rallied: rdn to chal ldr 1f out: regained ld 100yds out: edgd clr* **9/10**[1]
2 *1* **Pakal (GER)**[16] 2-9-0 0.. THellier 8 99
(Mario Hofer, Germany) *racd bhd ldr: chal early in st: tk ld 2f out: rdn 1 1/2f out: ct and hdd 100yds out: r.o* **68/10**
3 *1* **Sun Of Jamaica**[37] 4372 2-8-10 0.. StefanieHofer 4 92
(Mario Hofer, Germany) *settled in 5th: rdn to chal on home turn: r.o wl fnl 2f* **184/10**

 The Form Book, Raceform Ltd, Compton, RG20 6NL

4 ½ **Caitania (IRE)** 2-8-10 0 ADeVries 7 91
(H-W Hiller, Germany) *bkmarker fr s: proged early in st: shkn up 2f out: r.o wl past tiring horses* **194/10**

5 ½ **Spirit Danon (IRE)** 2-9-0 0 ASuborics 1 94
(P Schiergen, Germany) *racd in 3rd: r.o wl on ins rail in st: briefly threatened ldrs: rdn but wknd fnl f* **162/10**

6 hd **Amarillo (IRE)**[37] 4372 2-9-0 0 AStarke 3 93
(P Schiergen, Germany) *racd in 4th: rdn to chal early in st: no ex: no imp on ldrs* **10/1**

7 nse **Percy Jackson**[37] 4372 2-9-0 0 JohnFahy 5 93
(Denis Coakley) *a towards rr: rdn but no ex in st: no imp on ldrs* **48/10**[3]

8 4 **Fashion (GER)** 2-8-10 0 EPedroza 6 78
(A Wohler, Germany) *broke wl then settled un 6th: gd prog ent st: rdn but sn wknd: dropped away* **3/1**[2]

1m 25.97s (2.07) **8** Ran SP% **132.7**
WIN (incl. 10 euro stake): 19. PLACES: 14, 19, 23. SF: 135.
Owner Gestut Winterhauch **Bred** Genesis Green Stud Ltd **Trained** Germany

5262 BATH (L-H)

Wednesday, August 31

OFFICIAL GOING: Good (8.1)
Wind: Virtually nil Weather: Overcast

5611 PERTEMPS PEOPLE DEVELOPMENT GROUP H'CAP — 1m 2f 46y
2:30 (2:31) (Class 6) (0-65,65) 4-Y-0+ **£1,617** (£481; £240; £120) **Stalls** Low

Form RPR

6033 **1** **Kathleen Kennet**[8] 5349 11-7-10 **47** KatiaScallan(7) 10 62
(Jonathan Geake) *in tch: hdwy on outside fr 4f out: trckd ldr over 3f out: led over 2f out: sn pushed clr: easily* **16/1**

2032 **2** 4 ½ **Bold Cross (IRE)**[7] 5376 8-9-4 **65** KierenFox(3) 13 70
(Edward Bevan) *in rr: hdwy on outside fr 4f out: styd on to chse wnr appr fnl f: nvr any ch but clr of 3rd* **11/2**[2]

1460 **3** 3 **Corrib (IRE)**[14] 5178 8-8-10 **54** (p) CathyGannon 5 53
(Bryn Palling) *in rr: hdwy towards outside over 3f out: styd on to take 3rd appr fnl f but nvr any ch w ldng duo* **8/1**

6-25 **4** ¾ **Cuckoo Rock (IRE)**[40] 4273 4-9-4 **62** StephenCraine 11 60
(Jonathan Portman) *chsd ldrs: rdn and one pce fnl 2f* **7/1**[3]

-565 **5** hd **Mister Fantastic**[13] 2872 5-8-3 **47** KellyHarrison 3 44
(Dai Burchell) *led after 2f: hdd over 2f out: wknd over 1f out* **9/1**

4333 **6** 1 ¼ **Dream Of Fortune (IRE)**[7] 5390 7-8-12 **56** (bt) GrahamGibbons 2 51
(David Evans) *in rr: rdn and hdwy over 2f out: nvr rchd ldrs and styd on same pce* **16/1**

6600 **7** ¾ **El Libertador (USA)**[15] 5143 5-8-5 **52** (b) KieranO'Neill(3) 6 45
(Eric Wheeler) *mid-div tl rdn and dropped to rr over 3f out: sme prog u.p fnl 2f but nvr any ch* **25/1**

3452 **8** 2 **Beneath**[18] 4605 4-9-4 **62** AdamKirby 14 51
(Neil Mulholland) *in rr: mod prog u.p fnl 2f* **7/1**[3]

5355 **9** 6 **Regal Rave (USA)**[24] 4829 4-8-12 **56** ow1 DaneO'Neill 8 33
(Peter Hedger) *chsd ldrs tl wknd fr 3f out* **20/1**

0330 **10** ¾ **Aflaam (IRE)**[14] 5178 6-9-3 **61** (p) DavidProbert 7 37
(Ronald Harris) *chsd ldrs tl wknd over 2f out* **16/1**

000 **11** 11 **Lord Theo**[13] 5198 7-9-5 **63** TomMcLaughlin 1 17
(Nick Littmoden) *chsd ldrs to 3f out: sn wknd* **28/1**

-235 **12** 51 **Pennfield Pirate**[15] 5141 4-9-3 **61** NickyMackay 4 —
(Hughie Morrison) *led 2f: styd chsng ldr tl over 3f out: sn wknd: virtually p.u fnl f* **3/1**[1]

2m 9.98s (-1.02) **Going Correction** -0.175s/f (Firm) **12** Ran SP% **116.2**
Speed ratings (Par 101): **97,93,91,90,90 89,88,87,82,81 72,32**
toteswingers:1&2:£9.60, 1&3:£13.70, 2&3:£8.20 CSF £97.28 CT £768.87 TOTE £19.20: £4.90, £2.30, £2.90; EX 78.20.
Owner R W Floyd **Bred** Richard William Floyd **Trained** Marlborough, Wilts
■ Stewards' Enquiry : Kieran O'Neill four-day ban: improper riding (Sep 14-17)

FOCUS
All races that included the bottom bend turning into straight were increased by 12.5yds due to bend realignment. A weak handicap. The early pace was sound, but the leader slowed things right up nearing the turn for home and most took a keen hold at that stage.
Pennfield Pirate Official explanation: jockey said gelding would not let itself down on the good ground

5612 GRANGE 3YR FREE SERVICING SEPTEMBER GRANGE.CO.UK H'CAP — 1m 5f 22y
3:00 (3:06) (Class 6) (0-60,60) 4-Y-0+ **£1,704** (£503; £251) **Stalls** High

Form RPR

3154 **1** **Maydream**[63] 3516 4-8-6 **48** KieranO'Neill(3) 6 57
(Jimmy Fox) *in rr tl hdwy 5f out to chse clr ldr 4f out: styd on u.p fr 2f out: gaining on fading ldr fnl 120yds: hung lft under hand driving: led clsng stages* **10/3**[1]

3306 **2** ¾ **Dove Cottage (IRE)**[49] 3978 9-9-1 **54** (b) FergusSweeney 10 62
(Stuart Kittow) *sn led: 10 l clr after 5f: 20 l clr 6f out: pushed along: stl clr but beginning to fade fr 2f out: wknd fnl 120yds: hdd clsng stages* **13/2**

0203 **3** 3 ¾ **Drawback (IRE)**[6] 5416 8-8-12 **51** (p) StephenCraine 2 53
(Barry Brennan) *in tch w main gp bhd clr ldr: hdwy 4f out: styd on u.p to take 3rd over 1f out: one pce ins fnl f* **16/1**

5640 **4** hd **Squad**[13] 5198 5-9-7 **60** (v) EddieAhern 11 62
(Simon Dow) *s.i.s: in rr: hdwy 4f out: rdn and lost pl 3f out: styd on again fnl f: kpt on cl home* **5/1**[3]

5042 **5** 6 **Bahkov (IRE)**[11] 5267 5-9-0 **53** (b) DavidProbert 7 46
(Eric Wheeler) *chsd ldrs in main gp bhd clr ldr: rdn over 3f out: no imp and no ch fnl 2f* **4/1**[2]

2400 **6** 1 ¼ **Oak Leaves**[20] 4952 4-8-10 **49** AndreaAtzeni 12 40
(Nikki Evans) *sn chsng ldr: rdn and dropped to cl 3rd 4f out: sn rdn: wknd wl over 1f out* **13/2**

004 **7** 4 **Court Princess**[7] 5379 8-8-7 **46** oh1 (p) MartinLane 9 31
(Richard Price) *prom early: bhd fnl 4f* **12/1**

6033 **8** 2 **Holden Eagle**[15] 5141 6-9-5 **58** SteveDrowne 1 40
(Tony Newcombe) *a towards rr* **7/1**

4000 **9** 2 ¼ **Bussell Along (IRE)**[20] 4952 5-8-0 **46** oh1 RachealKneller(7) 5 25
(Pam Ford) *a in rr* **33/1**

2m 51.53s (-0.47) **Going Correction** -0.175s/f (Firm) **9** Ran SP% **115.4**
Speed ratings (Par 101): **94,93,91,91,87 86,84,82,81**
toteswingers:1&2:£5.40, 1&3:£8.80, 2&3:£12.20 CSF £25.31 CT £302.27 TOTE £3.00: £1.30, £2.50, £4.10; EX 30.10.
Owner The Dancing Partners **Bred** The Dancing Partners **Trained** Collingbourne Ducis, Wilts

FOCUS
A staying handicap run at a strong pace thanks to a tearaway leader and the majority were given too much to do.

5613 DIGIBET.COM MAIDEN AUCTION STKS — 5f 161y
3:30 (3:35) (Class 5) 2-Y-O **£2,385** (£704; £352) **Stalls** Centre

Form RPR

3 **1** **Royal Reyah**[85] 2788 2-8-9 0 FergusSweeney 5 68+
(Stuart Kittow) *s.i.s: hdwy 3f out: nt clr run and swtchd rt 2f out: styng on to press ldrs whn bmpd jst ins fnl f: sn rcvrd and kpt on wl to ld fnl 75yds: readily* **7/2**[2]

0552 **2** ¾ **Night Angel (IRE)**[7] 5374 2-8-10 64 JamesMillman 7 67
(Rod Millman) *chsd ldrs: rdn and outpcd 3f out: rallied and styd on to chal whn bmpd jst ins fnl f: slt ld u.p fnl 120yds: hdd and nt qckn fnl 75yds* **8/1**

6 **3** ½ **Royal Trix**[56] 3722 2-8-10 0 EddieAhern 11 65
(Marcus Tregoning) *led after 1f: jnd but kpt slt advantage fr over 1f out: narrowly hdd fnl 120yds: one pce* **22/1**

523 **4** ¾ **Shout For Joy (IRE)**[20] 4954 2-8-5 65 KieranO'Neill(3) 2 61
(Richard Hannon) *pressed ldrs: chal fr over 1f out: edgd rt whn upsides jst ins fnl f: stl upsides fnl 120yds: wknd fnl 50yds* **9/1**

20 **5** 1 ¾ **Dutch Rose (IRE)**[39] 4339 2-8-4 0 MartinLane 6 51
(Ralph Beckett) *sn drvn along to chse ldrs: kpt on fnl f but nvr gng pce to chal* **3/1**[1]

6 **6** 2 **Blackburn**[21] 4912 2-8-13 0 AdamKirby 3 54
(Clive Cox) *led 1f: styd pressing ldrs to 2f out: wknd u.p ins fnl f* **9/2**[3]

7 nse **Dangerous To Know** 2-8-4 0 NickyMackay 9 44
(Hughie Morrison) *sn pushed along towards rr: styd on fr over 1f out: nt rch ldrs* **20/1**

0 **8** 1 ½ **Roman Senate (IRE)**[40] 4269 2-9-1 0 SteveDrowne 12 50
(Martin Bosley) *in rr: drvn along over 2f out: styd on fnl f but nvr a threat* **40/1**

9 ¾ **Chicarito** 2-8-6 0 SophieDoyle(3) 8 42
(John Gallagher) *s.i.s: in rr: n.m.r on ins 2f out: kpt on ins fnl f* **66/1**

5 **10** 8 **Tenbridge**[29] 4639 2-8-4 0 (p) AndreaAtzeni 13 11
(Derek Haydn Jones) *s.i.s: outpcd* **100/1**

11 ¾ **My Name Is Sam** 2-9-1 0 DavidProbert 1 19
(Ronald Harris) *pressed ldrs 3f* **50/1**

46 **12** 1 ½ **Perfecto Tiempo (IRE)**[107] 2160 2-8-11 0 CathyGannon 10 10
(Ronald Harris) *s.i.s: a outpcd* **66/1**

252 **13** nk **Key Addition (IRE)**[14] 5161 2-9-1 71 MartinDwyer 4 13
(William Muir) *chsd ldrs tl rdn and wknd over 2f out* **7/1**

1m 11.31s (0.11) **Going Correction** -0.175s/f (Firm) **13** Ran SP% **116.5**
Speed ratings (Par 94): **92,91,90,89,87 84,84,82,81,70 69,67,67**
toteswingers:1&2:£6.40, 1&3:£8.50, 2&3:£26.50 CSF £28.97 TOTE £2.90: £1.10, £2.70, £6.90; EX 41.30.
Owner S Kittow, R Perry, B Hopkins **Bred** Hopkins, Kittow & Mrs Perry **Trained** Blackborough, Devon

FOCUS
This juvenile maiden was run at a frantic early pace and there was a bunched finish.

NOTEBOOK
Royal Reyah got on top near the finish and, building on his debut third when last seen in June, opened his account at the second attempt. He was rather taken off his feet early, but hit top gear at the furlong pole and did well to get on top after being hampered around 200yards out. Reverting to another half furlong should prove ideal and this lightly raced son of Royal Applause should make his mark in nurseries as he is entitled to improve again for the outing. (op 4-1 tchd 9-2 and 10-3)
Night Angel(IRE), another that got outpaced a fair way out, finished second off 64 in a nursery a week earlier so rates a decent guide for this form. She wasn't done any favours by the fourth late on and proved game, but it didn't change the overall result. (op 7-1)
Royal Trix ◆ was soon at the head of affairs and was still travelling sweetly nearing the final furlong. She felt the pinch shortly afterwards, though, and ultimately paid for her early exertions. She's bred to get further, but is clearly speedy and should be winning before long. (op 20-1 tchd 25-1)
Shout For Joy(IRE), placed on her two previous outings, held every chance back down half a furlong in trip and was responsible for hampering the first two home when jinking to her right. She'll probably be better off back over the bare 5f. (op 17-2 tchd 8-1 and 10-1)
Dutch Rose(IRE) was outpaced before turning into the home straight, but posted a better effort in defeat and will be suited by a return to 6f. Nurseries are now an option. (op 11-4 tchd 9-4)
Blackburn was supported to improve on his debut sixth at Salisbury and showed decent early dash, but paid for those exertions from the furlong marker. (op 8-1)
Dangerous To Know, bred to enjoy longer trips, was noted doing some fair late work and ought to show the benefit of this debut experience next time out. (op 28-1)

5614 CRABBIES ALCOHOLIC GINGER BEER FILLIES' H'CAP — 1m 2f 46y
4:00 (4:02) (Class 5) (0-75,75) 3-Y-0+ **£2,264** (£673; £336; £168) **Stalls** Low

Form RPR

05-5 **1** **History Repeating**[35] 4448 3-8-1 **56** oh3 DavidProbert 5 63
(Mark Usher) *in rr but in tch: hdwy 4f out: rdn 3f out: chsd ldr over 1f out: styd on to ld fnl 150yds: rdn out* **18/1**

111 **2** ½ **Dubawi Dancer**[26] 4751 3-9-3 **75** AdamBeschizza(3) 1 81+
(William Haggas) *t.k.h: hld up towards rr: rdn along towards outside 3f out: styd on fr over 1f out to chse wnr fnl 120yds: kpt on but a jst hld* **4/6**[1]

4065 **3** 2 ¼ **Levantera (IRE)**[18] 5049 3-8-9 **64** EddieAhern 3 66
(Clive Cox) *led: rdn 2f out: styd on tl hdd & wknd fnl 150yds* **5/1**[2]

6240 **4** ½ **Oriental Girl**[21] 4916 6-9-7 **68** (p) SteveDrowne 4 69
(Jonathan Geake) *chsd ldrs tl rdn and outpcd ins fnl 3f: styd on again fnl f but nvr a danger* **9/1**

0000 **5** 1 ¼ **Miss Chicane**[35] 4448 3-9-1 **70** [1] AdamKirby 7 68
(Walter Swinburn) *chsd ldrs: wnt 2nd 6f out: rdn over 2f out: wknd 1f out* **20/1**

5122 **6** hd **Only You Maggie (IRE)**[19] 5002 4-9-7 **68** (v) MarkLawson 2 66
(Gary Harrison) *t.k.h: rdn 3f out: mod prog clsng stages* **8/1**[3]

0406 **7** 3 ½ **Galloping Queen (IRE)**[12] 5243 3-8-6 **61** FrannyNorton 8 52
(Mick Channon) *chsd ldr to 6f out: wknd 2f out* **20/1**

2m 14.36s (3.36) **Going Correction** -0.175s/f (Firm)
WFA 3 from 4yo+ 8lb **7** Ran SP% **112.6**
Speed ratings (Par 100): **79,78,76,76,75 75,72**
toteswingers:1&2:£4.30, 1&3:£9.80, 2&3:£1.80 CSF £29.95 CT £75.55 TOTE £26.60: £7.30, £1.10; EX 51.50.
Owner M D I Usher **Bred** Usk Valley Stud **Trained** Upper Lambourn, Berks

FOCUS
Not a bad handicap for the class. It was run at an uneven pace, though, which resulted in something of a dash for home from 3f out and the overall form is worth treating with a degree of caution.

5615 SIS LIVE H'CAP — 5f 11y
4:30 (4:33) (Class 5) (0-70,70) 3-Y-O — £2,264 (£673; £336; £168) Stalls Centre

Form — RPR

3323 **1** **Best Be Careful (IRE)**[11] 5265 3-8-12 **61** ... DaneO'Neill 3 — 72
(Mark Usher) *t.k.h and trckd ldrs: qcknd to chal between horses ins fnl 2f: drvn to ld appr fnl f: rdn clr fnl 120yds* **8/1**

2443 **2** 2 **Ginzan**[7] 5377 3-8-8 **57** ... CathyGannon 4 — 61
(Malcolm Saunders) *pressed ldrs: chal 2f out and sn led u.p: hdd appr fnl f: kpt on but no ch w wnr fnl 120yds* **16/1**

23 **3** hd **Till Dawn (IRE)**[21] 4924 3-8-8 **57** ... DavidProbert 9 — 60
(Tony Carroll) *pressed ldrs 3f out: stl ev ch fr 2f out tl 1f out: styd on same pce ins fnl f* **11/1**

6465 **4** nk **Catalinas Diamond (IRE)**[16] 5115 3-8-11 **60** ... SteveDrowne 2 — 62
(Pat Murphy) *in rr: rdn and hdwy towards outside over 2f out: kpt on ins fnl f and gng on cl home but no ch w wnr* **11/1**

1112 **5** 2 1/4 **Dreams Of Glory**[11] 5279 3-8-8 **64** ... CharlesBishop(7) 1 — 58
(Ron Hodges) *slt ld tl hdd over 3f out: ev ch fr 2f out: wknd fnl f* **9/2**[2]

5135 **6** 1 **Madame Kintyre**[60] 3635 3-9-1 **64** ... JamesMillman 6 — 54
(Rod Millman) *in rr: drvn and styd on fnl 2f: nvr gng pce to rch ldrs* **7/1**[3]

0055 **7** nk **Look Who's Kool**[22] 4895 3-9-2 **65** ... (b) GrahamGibbons 7 — 54
(Ed McMahon) *led over 3f out: jnd 2f out: sn hdd: wknd fnl f* **16/1**

4512 **8** 1 1/4 **Blue Deer (IRE)**[2] 5542 3-9-1 **64** ... FrannyNorton 5 — 49+
(Mick Channon) *outpcd and sn pushed along: styd on fnl f but nvr any ch* **2/1**[1]

61.76 secs (-0.74) **Going Correction** -0.175s/f (Firm) — **8** Ran SP% **103.6**
Speed ratings (Par 100): **98,94,94,94,90 88,88,86**
toteswingers:1&2:£10.20, 1&3:£4.60, 2&3:£10.50 CSF £98.53 CT £1030.50 TOTE £7.70: £2.40, £4.40, £3.00; EX 89.40.
Owner Mrs Jill Pellett **Bred** M Phelan **Trained** Upper Lambourn, Berks

FOCUS
This was weakened by the late withdrawal, but it was still competitive enough for the class and there was no hanging about from the gates.
Madame Kintyre Official explanation: jockey said filly never travelled
Blue Deer(IRE) Official explanation: jockey said gelding suffered interference at start

5616 BATH CHRONICLE H'CAP — 5f 161y
5:00 (5:00) (Class 5) (0-75,75) 4-Y-O+ — £2,264 (£673; £336; £168) Stalls Centre

Form — RPR

0240 **1** **The Name Is Frank**[24] 4828 6-8-7 **61** ow1 ... (t) FergusSweeney 12 — 72
(Mark Gillard) *in tch: hdwy on outside fr 2f out: rdn and styd on strly fnl f to ld last strides* **11/1**

0012 **2** hd **Sermons Mount (USA)**[10] 5301 5-9-2 **70** ... DaneO'Neill 10 — 80
(Peter Hedger) *sn chsng ldrs: styd on u.p to take slt ld fnl 100yds: ct last strides* **5/1**[2]

3344 **3** 1 **Wooden King (IRE)**[11] 5262 6-9-6 **74** ... TomMcLaughlin 7 — 81
(Malcolm Saunders) *pressed ldrs tl tk slt ld appr 2f out: kpt narrow ld u.p tl hdd and nt qckn fnl 100yds* **6/1**[3]

5623 **4** 3/4 **Piddie's Power**[20] 4973 4-9-5 **73** ... GrahamGibbons 4 — 78
(Ed McMahon) *chsd ldrs: rdn over 2f out: kpt on fnl f: no imp and one pce clsng stages* **9/2**[1]

4215 **5** 1/2 **Emiratesdotcom**[11] 5262 5-9-0 **68** ... StephenCraine 13 — 71+
(Milton Bradley) *in rr: rdn and hdwy fr 2f out: kpt on fnl f: nt gng pce to rch ldrs* **5/1**[2]

1455 **6** 4 **Interchoice Star**[23] 4850 6-8-0 **57** oh1 ow1 ... (p) BillyCray(3) 6 — 47
(Ray Peacock) *sn led: hdd appr fnl 2f but styd pressing ldrs tl wknd ins fnl f* **20/1**

2155 **7** nk **Equuleus Pictor**[27] 4731 7-9-7 **75** ... (p) SteveDrowne 9 — 64
(John Spearing) *chsd ldrs: rdn and one pce 2f out: n.d after* **16/1**

4055 **8** 1/2 **Make My Dream**[2] 5561 8-8-11 **65** ... MartinLane 2 — 52
(John Gallagher) *in rr: rdn along fr 3f out: styng on one pce on ins whn rdr dropped whip over 1f out* **16/1**

0500 **9** 2 3/4 **Brandywell Boy (IRE)**[22] 4895 8-8-6 **65** ow1 ... (b) MatthewLawson(5) 5 — 43
(Dominic Ffrench Davis) *in rr: nt clr run and swtchd rt to outside over 1f out: nvr in contention* **25/1**

00-0 **10** 1 **Johnstown Lad (IRE)**[53] 3886 7-9-2 **70** ... (t) AndreaAtzeni 8 — 45
(Daniel Mark Loughnane, Ire) *outpcd most of way* **14/1**

0342 **11** 1 **Bateleur**[15] 5139 7-8-3 **57** ... FrannyNorton 11 — 28
(Mick Channon) *s.i.s: outpcd most of way* **12/1**

2466 **12** 2 1/4 **Steelcut**[29] 4644 7-9-5 **73** ... (p) CathyGannon 3 — 37
(David Evans) *outpcd* **16/1**

3-00 **13** 2 3/4 **Superior Edge**[27] 4707 4-9-5 **73** ... DavidProbert 1 — 28
(Christopher Mason) *chsd ldrs to 1/2-way* **28/1**

1m 10.45s (-0.75) **Going Correction** -0.175s/f (Firm) — **13** Ran SP% **118.2**
Speed ratings (Par 103): **98,97,96,95,94 89,89,88,84,83 82,79,75**
toteswingers:1&2:£10.90, 1&3:£13.70, 2&3:£7.90 CSF £62.85 CT £368.84 TOTE £17.40: £5.30, £2.50, £2.70; EX 87.30.
Owner Don Hazzard **Bred** Fifehead Farms M C Denning **Trained** Holwell, Dorset

FOCUS
An ordinary sprint handicap that was wide open. It paid to race handily.

5617 BETFAIR RACING EXCELLENCE APPRENTICE TRAINING SERIES H'CAP — 5f 161y
5:30 (5:30) (Class 6) (0-55,58) 4-Y-O+ — £1,617 (£481; £240; £120) Stalls Centre

Form — RPR

3600 **1** **Welcome Approach**[1] 5603 8-9-2 **53** ... JustinNewman 9 — 62
(John Weymes) *in rr but in tch: hdwy on outside to ld ins fnl 2f: drvn and styd on wl fnl f* **6/1**[2]

6040 **2** nk **Trade Centre**[27] 4705 6-8-11 **48** ... MatthewLawson 11 — 56
(Milton Bradley) *chsd ldrs: rdn and styd on to go 2nd ins fnl f: kpt on clsng stages but a jst hld* **6/1**[2]

0 **3** 1 1/2 **Wheatfield (IRE)**[2] 5534 7-8-5 **47** ow2 ... (t) ThomasBrown(5) 8 — 50
(Thomas McGivern, Ire) *chsd ldr tl led briefly 2f out: sn hdd: styd chsng wnr tl ins fnl f: wknd nr fin* **11/1**[3]

0066 **4** 3/4 **Best One**[22] 4882 7-8-8 **45** ... (v) RaulDaSilva 3 — 46+
(Ronald Harris) *bmpd s: sn towards rr: hdwy over 1f out: kpt on fnl f: nt rch ldrs* **16/1**

0401 **5** nk **Ridgeway Sapphire**[15] 5138 4-8-11 **51** ... (v) RachealKneller(3) 10 — 51
(Mark Usher) *s.i.s: in rr: pushed along and styd on fnl f but nvr gng pce to rch ldrs* **6/1**[2]

6- **6** 1 1/2 **Lovestoned (IRE)**[14] 5191 5-8-6 **48** ... SAGray(5) 4 — 43
(G A Kingston, Ire) *chsd ldrs: rdn over 2f out: wknd ins fnl f* **6/1**[2]

1344 **7** 1/2 **Flaxen Lake**[2] 5540 4-8-13 **50** ... LucyKBarry 1 — 43
(Milton Bradley) *chsd ldrs: rdn over 2f out: wknd fnl f* **9/4**[1]

3400 **8** 1 **What Katie Did (IRE)**[33] 4487 6-8-8 **45** ... (p) MatthewCosham 7 — 35
(Milton Bradley) *led tl hdd 2f out: wknd appr fnl f* **20/1**

540- **9** 4 1/2 **Like For Like (IRE)**[366] 5579 5-8-5 **45** ... JakePayne(3) 2 — 20
(Ron Hodges) *outpcd most of way* **22/1**

5006 **10** 1 1/4 **Ishipink**[10] 3939 4-8-8 **45** ... CharlesBishop 5 — 16
(Ron Hodges) *chsd ldrs 3f* **25/1**

69.90 secs (-1.30) **Going Correction** -0.175s/f (Firm) — **10** Ran SP% **115.1**
Speed ratings (Par 101): **101,100,98,97,97 95,94,93,87,85**
toteswingers:1&2:£6.50, 1&3:£12.20, 2&3:£14.50. Totesuper 7: Win: Not won, Place: Not won. CSF £39.99 CT £306.21 TOTE £8.60: £2.70, £1.30, £3.40; EX 42.60.
Owner T A Scothern & Tag Racing **Bred** P Wyatt And Ranby Hall **Trained** Middleham Moor, N Yorks

FOCUS
A typically weak sprint handicap for apprentice riders. It was run in a quicker time than the preceding Class 5 handicap over the same C&D.
T/Jkpt: Not won. T/Plt: £240.60 to a £1 stake. Pool:£74,353.46 - 225.53 winning tickets T/Qpdt: £58.80 to a £1 stake. Pool:£5,363.94 - 67.50 winning tickets ST

5398 CARLISLE (R-H)
Wednesday, August 31

OFFICIAL GOING: Good (good to soft in places; 7.5)
Wind: Almost nil Weather: Overcast

5618 WATCH RACING UK ON SKY432 MAIDEN STKS — 5f 193y
5:05 (5:05) (Class 5) 2-Y-O — £2,264 (£673; £336; £168) Stalls Low

Form — RPR

3 **1** **Duke Of Firenze**[37] 4384 2-9-3 0 ... PaulHanagan 3 — 82+
(Sir Michael Stoute) *hld up in midfield: n.m.r briefly over 2f out: shkn up and hdwy wl over 1f out: led ins fnl f: comf* **4/6**[1]

4 **2** 2 **Glamorous Angel (IRE)**[13] 5202 2-9-3 0 ... AndrewElliott 14 — 74
(Alan Swinbank) *prom: effrt and ev ch appr fnl f: edgd rt: chsd wnr ins fnl f: r.o* **7/1**[2]

0 **3** 1 1/4 **Findhornbay**[35] 4436 2-8-12 0 ... SilvestreDeSousa 12 — 65
(Mark Johnston) *unruly in paddock: led: rdn 2f out: hdd ins fnl f: kpt on same pce* **40/1**

4 **4** 3 **Dubious Escapade (IRE)**[77] 3035 2-8-12 0 ... FrederikTylicki 7 — 56
(Ann Duffield) *midfield: drvn and outpcd over 2f out: styd on wl fnl f: nrst fin* **16/1**

5 1 1/4 **Stepharlie** 2-8-12 0 ... TomEaves 6 — 52
(Bryan Smart) *bhd: struggling 1/2-way: styd on wl fnl f: nvr able to chal* **12/1**[3]

0 **6** 1/2 **Roll Of Thunder**[69] 3314 2-9-3 0 ... PBBeggy 11 — 55
(John Quinn) *sn pushed along towards rr: outpcd 1/2-way: styd on fnl f: nrst fin* **100/1**

05 **7** 3/4 **Giorgio's Dragon (IRE)**[91] 2617 2-9-3 0 ... TonyHamilton 9 — 53
(Richard Fahey) *trckd ldrs: effrt over 2f out: edgd rt and wknd appr fnl f* **14/1**

020 **8** 1/2 **Premier Choice**[12] 5254 2-9-3 73 ... DavidAllan 5 — 51
(Tim Easterby) *hld up: drvn over 2f out: sn edgd rt: no imp over 1f out* **7/1**[2]

9 4 1/2 **Emily Hall** 2-8-12 0 ... RoystonFfrench 1 — 32
(Bryan Smart) *chsd ldrs: drvn over 2f out: wknd over 1f out* **40/1**

0 **10** 5 **Cherchedi (IRE)**[14] 5161 2-8-7 0 ... JulieBurke(5) 4 — 17
(Alan Berry) *s.i.s: bhd: struggling 1/2-way: nvr on terms* **150/1**

0 **11** 6 **Bu Samra (IRE)**[13] 5202 2-9-3 0 ... PhillipMakin 10 — 3
(Kevin Ryan) *cl up: rdn over 2f out: sn wknd* **33/1**

12 nk **Gran Canaria Queen** 2-8-12 0 ... BarryMcHugh 13 — —
(Ian Semple) *towards rr: struggling after 2f: nvr on terms* **100/1**

1m 14.4s (0.70) **Going Correction** +0.025s/f (Good) — **12** Ran SP% **115.7**
Speed ratings (Par 94): **96,93,91,87,86 85,84,83,77,71 63,62**
toteswingers:1&2:£2.00, 1&3:£6.60, 2&3:£30.90 CSF £5.23 TOTE £1.60: £1.20, £1.80, £5.20; EX 6.20.
Owner Cheveley Park Stud **Bred** Cheveley Park Stud Ltd **Trained** Newmarket, Suffolk

FOCUS
Old Stable bend moved out 4yds from inside adding 8yds to race of 1m and over. After 6mm of rain over the previous two days, a dry day enabled the ground to dry out and ride just on the easy side of good. An interesting juvenile maiden and they raced in one group towards the far side.

NOTEBOOK
Duke Of Firenze, first foal of a Coronation Stakes winner, had finished a promising third in a weak Windsor maiden first time. After a troubled passage early on he had to bide his time racing hard against the far side rail. He quickened up well and was firmly in command at the line. A step up to 7f will suit him and there will be plenty of tempting targets this backend. (tchd 8-11)
Glamorous Angel(IRE), a 105,000gns yearling, had shaped well before tiring when fourth first time at Hamilton. He travelled strongly and was by no means knocked about when it was clear he had met one better. He looks sure to improve again and looks a fair long-term prospect. (op 15-2 tchd 8-1)
Findhornbay, who blew her chance at the start first time, took them along but edged off the rail and left the door open for the winner. She will improve again and should be able to find a race.
Dubious Escapade(IRE), fourth at Hamilton on her bow, stayed on nicely on his first start for ten weeks. She should make her mark in handicap company at three. (op 14-1)
Stepharlie, a newcomer from the family of the 1,000 Guineas winner On The House, is not that big. After a slow start and still last but one 1f out, she came home to some effect.
Roll Of Thunder, gelded since his debut two months ago, was another to make significant late ground. He will improve again over a bit further.
Giorgio's Dragon(IRE), rejected by Paul Hanagan, cost 130,000gns. He shaped nicely on his first start for three months and is now qualified for a nursery mark. (op 12-1)
Premier Choice, back over 6f, seemed quite keen racing towards the rear. He carried his head high and has something to prove now. (tchd 6-1)

5619 CHRISTMAS PARTIES AT CARLISLE H'CAP — 5f 193y
5:35 (5:35) (Class 6) (0-60,60) 3-Y-O — £1,704 (£503; £251) Stalls Low

Form — RPR

0000 **1** **Circuitous**[4] 5490 3-9-0 **53** ... (b[1]) TomEaves 8 — 62
(Keith Dalgleish) *mde all: rdn 2f out: hrd pressed ins fnl f: hld on gamely towards fin* **28/1**

033 **2** nk **Salik Tag (USA)**[18] 5063 3-9-7 **60** ... (t) AdrianNicholls 11 — 68
(David Nicholls) *in tch: hdwy to chse wnr 2f out: sn rdn and edgd rt: disp ld ins fnl f: hld cl home* **14/1**

3320 **3** 2 1/4 **Meandmyshadow**[3] 5502 3-9-6 **59** ... SilvestreDeSousa 4 — 60
(Alan Brown) *chsd wnr to 2f out: sn drvn: kpt on same pce fnl f* **8/1**

5642 **4** *1 3/4* **Inca Blue**[5] 5433 3-8-13 **52**...........................(b) DavidAllan 7 47+
(Tim Easterby) *hld up: rdn and hdwy over 2f out: kpt on fnl f: nvr able to chal* **3/1**[2]

2434 **5** *nk* **Cathcart Castle**[27] 4729 3-8-12 **54**.............. MatthewDavies(3) 6 48
(Mick Channon) *taken early to post: prom: effrt and rdn over 2f out: nt qckn over 1f out* **14/1**

0-00 **6** *3* **Uncle Bryn**[90] 2650 3-9-4 **57**.............................. PBBeggy 9 42+
(John Quinn) *sn pushed along towards rr: effrt u.p 1/2-way: no imp fr 2f out* **2/1**[1]

0656 **7** *nk* **Valentine's Gift**[14] 5165 3-9-2 **55**..................... AndrewElliott 1 39
(Neville Bycroft) *taken early to post: hld up: hdwy on outside 2f out: no imp fnl f* **12/1**

4520 **8** *3 1/2* **Tahitian Princess (IRE)**[4] 5490 3-9-2 **55**..........(b[1]) PaulHanagan 10 27
(Ann Duffield) *s.i.s: hld up: rdn and edgd rt over 2f out: nvr on terms* **11/2**[3]

004 **9** *11* **Tootie Flutie**[32] 4559 3-8-10 **49**.................... MichaelStainton 12 —
(Richard Whitaker) *chsd ldrs tl rdn and wknd fr 2f out* **40/1**

563 **10** *1 3/4* **Needwood Park**[25] 4813 3-9-6 **59**.................. RoystonFfrench 2 —
(Ray Craggs) *t.k.h: hld up on ins: struggling over 2f out: sn btn* **66/1**

4004 **11** *3/4* **Guinea Seeker**[18] 5063 3-9-2 **55**.................... DuranFentiman 3 —
(Tim Easterby) *hld up: drvn 1/2-way: btn fnl 2f* **28/1**

0306 **R** **Tinzo (IRE)**[13] 5203 3-8-2 **46** oh1......................... JulieBurke(5) 5 —
(Alan Berry) *ref to r* **150/1**

1m 14.07s (0.37) **Going Correction** +0.025s/f (Good) **12** Ran SP% **117.3**
Speed ratings (Par 98): **98,97,94,92,91 87,87,82,68,65 64,—**
toteswingers:1&2:£51.70, 1&3:£36.10, 2&3:£7.00 CSF £362.00 CT £3460.37 TOTE £37.20: £12.90, £3.00, £2.80; EX 630.10.
Owner A R M Galbraith **Bred** Deepwood Farm Stud **Trained** Carluke, South Lanarkshire

FOCUS
A low-grade 3yo sprint handicap and very few got into it.
Circuitous Official explanation: trainer said, regarding apparent improvement in form, that the gelding benefited from the first-time blinkers.

5620 70'S NIGHT TONIGHT H'CAP 5f
6:05 (6:06) (Class 6) (0-60,58) 3-Y-O+ £1,704 (£503; £251) Stalls Low

Form RPR

002 **1** **Ingenti**[4] 5469 3-8-6 **46** oh1................................ TomEaves 9 56
(Christopher Wilson) *t.k.h: cl up: rdn to ld over 1f out: kpt on wl fnl f* **4/1**[1]

0030 **2** *1 1/2* **Fair Bunny**[19] 4987 4-8-8 **45**..................(b) SilvestreDeSousa 3 51
(Alan Brown) *bhd: pushed along 1/2-way: hdwy and hung rt 2f out: chsd wnr ins fnl f: r.o* **8/1**

6540 **3** *3/4* **Andrasta**[9] 5309 6-8-9 **51**.............................. JulieBurke(5) 5 54
(Alan Berry) *bhd and pushed along after 2f: hdwy over 1f out: styd on fnl f: nrst fin* **25/1**

3005 **4** *1 1/2* **Kalahari Desert (IRE)**[7] 5373 4-8-8 **45**..............(b[1]) AndrewMullen 4 43
(Richard Whitaker) *trckd ldrs: effrt and rdn 2f out: kpt on same pce fnl f* **9/1**

4066 **5** *1 1/2* **King Of Swords (IRE)**[24] 4820 7-8-5 **45**..........(v[1]) DeclanCannon(3) 2 38
(Nigel Tinkler) *trckd ldrs tl rdn and nt qckn over 1f out* **12/1**

0403 **5** *dht* **See Vermont**[28] 4684 3-9-0 **53**.......................... LeeNewman 12 46
(Robin Bastiman) *midfield: drvn and outpcd over 2f out: styd on fnl f: nvr able to chal* **6/1**[2]

5502 **7** *1 1/4* **Sandwith**[5] 5436 8-9-1 **55**......................(b) GaryBartley(3) 7 43
(George Foster) *led: edgd lft and hdd over 1f out: continued to drift to stands' rail and sn outpcd* **7/1**[3]

0645 **8** *3 1/4* **Triskaidekaphobia**[58] 3678 8-8-8 **45**..............(t) JamesSullivan 10 21
(Wilf Storey) *bhd: effrt and drvn towards far side over 2f out: btn over 1f out* **25/1**

1400 **9** *hd* **Media Jury**[21] 4900 4-9-6 **57**.............................(v) DavidNolan 14 33
(John Wainwright) *midfield on outside: struggling 1/2-way: nvr on terms* **12/1**

6000 **10** *6* **Sensational Love (IRE)**[15] 5153 3-9-5 **58**............. PaulHanagan 1 12
(Keith Dalgleish) *trckd ldrs tl rdn and wknd 2f out* **8/1**

62.16 secs (1.36) **Going Correction** +0.025s/f (Good)
WFA 3 from 4yo+ 2lb **10** Ran SP% **102.1**
Speed ratings (Par 101): [illegible]
toteswingers:1&2:£51.70, 1&3:£36.10, 2&3:£7.00 CSF £28.05 CT £495.41 TOTE £5.00: £1.40, £2.20, £4.80; EX 33.50.
Owner David Bartlett **Bred** Mrs Andrea Bartlett **Trained** Manfield, N Yorks

FOCUS
Another low-grade sprint handicap and they ended up racing across the entire width of the track.
Sandwith Official explanation: jockey said gelding hung left throughout

5621 CARLISLE FOR CONFERENCES H'CAP 6f 192y
6:35 (6:36) (Class 4) (0-85,82) 3-Y-O £4,204 (£1,251; £625; £312) Stalls Low

Form RPR

-500 **1** **Try The Chance**[21] 4914 3-9-4 **82**.................. MatthewDavies(3) 4 91
(Mick Channon) *hld up: hdwy to ld over 1f out: rdn and edgd rt: kpt on wl fnl f* **7/1**[3]

4663 **2** *1/2* **My Single Malt (IRE)**[23] 4854 3-9-0 **75**..........(b[1]) SilvestreDeSousa 2 83
(Tom Tate) *dwlt: t.k.h and sn cl up: effrt and ev ch over 1f out: edgd rt and kpt on ins fnl f* **7/2**[2]

5024 **3** *2 1/2* **Youhavecontrol (IRE)**[28] 4676 3-9-0 **75**..................... TomEaves 1 76
(Michael Dods) *led at ordinary gallop: rdn and hdd over 1f out: kpt on same pce ins fnl f* **20/1**

1122 **4** *1 1/4* **Fast Shot**[7] 5370 3-9-3 **78**................................ DavidAllan 5 76+
(Tim Easterby) *hld up: effrt and swtchd rt over 1f out: kpt on fnl f: nvr able to chal* **11/8**[1]

0100 **5** *1/2* **Spes Nostra**[32] 4550 3-8-12 **73**.............................. LeeNewman 7 70
(David Barron) *cl up: hung rt and outpcd over 2f out: kpt on fnl f: no imp* **14/1**

2211 **6** *3 1/4* **Icy Blue**[16] 5109 3-8-10 **71**............................ RobertWinston 3 59
(Richard Whitaker) *stdd in tch: effrt and rdn over 2f out: no imp whn blkd over 1f out* **7/1**[3]

5002 **7** *4* **Tamareen (IRE)**[11] 5274 3-8-13 **74**..................... PaulHanagan 6 51
(Richard Fahey) *t.k.h: trckd ldrs: rdn over 2f out: wknd wl over 1f out* **11/1**

1m 27.67s (0.57) **Going Correction** +0.175s/f (Good) **7** Ran SP% **109.1**
Speed ratings (Par 102): **103,102,99,98,97 93,89**
toteswingers:1&2:£33.90, 1&3:£4.00, 2&3:£8.80 CSF £28.66 TOTE £12.00: £4.10, £2.80; EX 32.30.
Owner Jaber Abdullah **Bred** Ms Jon Horley & C A Vanner **Trained** West Ilsley, Berks

FOCUS
A decent handicap. The pace was steady until past the halfway mark.
Try The Chance Official explanation: trainer's rep said, regarding apparent improvement in form, that the colt was better suited by being ridden from of the pace and given a chance early.

5622 EDWARDS AND PRINGLE INVESTMENT CONSULTANTS H'CAP 1m 1f 61y
7:05 (7:05) (Class 5) (0-70,69) 3-Y-O+ £2,264 (£673; £336; £168) Stalls Low

Form RPR

0003 **1** **Desert Vision**[35] 4442 7-9-8 **63**.....................(v) JamesSullivan 9 74
(Michael Easterby) *mde all: rdn 2f out: hld on wl fnl f* **9/1**

234 **2** *1/2* **Petsas Pleasure**[37] 4380 5-9-4 **59**.............................. TomEaves 2 68
(Ollie Pears) *hld up and bhd: gd hdwy on outside wl over 2f out: chsd wnr and edgd rt appr fnl f: kpt on fin* **8/1**[2]

5105 **3** *1 1/4* **Key Breeze**[13] 5205 4-9-4 **64**............................(t) PhillipMakin 13 71
(Kevin Ryan) *missed break: hld up and bhd: weaved through and in tch over 1f out: rdn and kpt on fnl f* **10/1**

3603 **4** *1 1/2* **Botham (USA)**[9] 5314 7-9-3 **61**.................... PaulPickard(3) 15 65
(Jim Goldie) *hld up on outside: effrt over 2f out: kpt on ins fnl f: no imp* **12/1**

3223 **5** *1 3/4* **Amtired**[29] 4651 5-8-12 **56**................................ DaleSwift(3) 8 56
(Brian Ellison) *midfield: drvn and outpcd wl over 2f out: rallied over 1f out: kpt on ins fnl f* **8/1**[2]

2660 **6** *1/2* **Zaplamation (IRE)**[48] 3456 6-9-4 **64**.................. ShaneBKelly(5) 10 63
(John Quinn) *midfield: rdn along over 2f out: no imp over 1f out* **17/2**[3]

5244 **7** *3/4* **Law To Himself (IRE)**[9] 5314 4-9-5 **65**.............. GarryWhillans(5) 6 62
(Alan Swinbank) *hld up on ins: rdn along over 2f out: hdwy over 1f out: kpt on: nrst fin* **5/1**[1]

4425 **8** *1/2* **Lady Excel (IRE)**[35] 4441 5-8-9 **50**........................ BarryMcHugh 11 46
(Brian Rothwell) *pressed wnr: rdn over 2f out: wknd appr fnl f* **20/1**

1400 **9** *1/2* **Casino Night**[9] 5314 6-9-9 **69**............................ NeilFarley(5) 1 64
(Barry Murtagh) *prom: drvn along 3f out: wknd over 1f out* **33/1**

3305 **10** *1 3/4* **Ollon (USA)**[19] 5004 3-9-0 **62**.......................... PaulHanagan 12 54
(Richard Fahey) *hld up: rdn whn n.m.r wl over 2f out: sn n.d* **14/1**

5020 **11** *hd* **Dean Iarracht (IRE)**[45] 4123 5-9-1 **56**...............(p) PatrickMathers 4 47
(Tracy Waggott) *t.k.h: trckd ldrs tl rdn and wknd wl over 1f out* **18/1**

1016 **12** *3/4* **Escape Artist**[6] 5403 4-9-3 **58**..........................(p) DavidAllan 7 48
(Tim Easterby) *plld hrd: in tch tl rdn and wknd over 1f out* **10/1**

-000 **13** *1 3/4* **Blue Spinnaker (IRE)**[65] 3456 12-9-0 **55**.................. PaddyAspell 5 41
(Michael Easterby) *hld up in midfield: lost pl over 2f out: n.d after* **25/1**

2446 **14** *2 3/4* **Desert Hunter (IRE)**[28] 4674 8-9-0 **55**...............(p) FrederikTylicki 3 35
(Micky Hammond) *t.k.h: trckd ldrs tl rdn and wknd over 2f out* **16/1**

-004 **15** *3/4* **Captain Peachey**[28] 4673 5-8-9 **50** oh5............. SilvestreDeSousa 14 29
(Alistair Whillans) *midfield on outside: struggling over 2f out: sn btn* **20/1**

1m 58.5s (0.90) **Going Correction** +0.175s/f (Good)
WFA 3 from 4yo+ 7lb **15** Ran SP% **119.4**
Speed ratings (Par 103): **103,102,101,100,98 98,97,97,96,95 94,94,92,90,89**
toteswingers:1&2:£15.00, 1&3:£25.70, 2&3:£6.70 CSF £73.87 CT £744.25 TOTE £13.90: £4.10, £3.30, £3.20; EX 107.80.
Owner A Black,R Edmonds,J Holdroyd,J Quickfall **Bred** Gainsborough Stud Management Ltd **Trained** Sheriff Hutton, N Yorks

FOCUS
A modest handicap run at a sound pace. The winner made all yet the placed horses were the last two turning for home.

5623 TURFTV.CO.UK H'CAP 1m 3f 107y
7:35 (7:37) (Class 6) (0-65,64) 3-Y-O £1,704 (£503; £251) Stalls High

Form RPR

0001 **1** **Sharp Relief (IRE)**[19] 5022 3-9-7 **64**..................... PaulHanagan 3 79+
(Hughie Morrison) *dwlt: t.k.h and sn trcking ldrs: led gng wl 3f out: pushed clr fr 2f out: eased towards fin* **11/10**[1]

5400 **2** *3 3/4* **Rapturous Applause**[23] 4852 3-8-9 **52**............... FrederikTylicki 4 56
(Micky Hammond) *prom: rdn over 3f out: effrt and hung rt over 1f out: chsd (clr) wnr last 100yds: kpt on: no imp* **12/1**

0000 **3** *1 3/4* **Srimenanti**[7] 5372 3-8-12 **55**........................(p) BarryMcHugh 7 56
(Brian Rothwell) *plld hrd: cl up: disp ld after 3f to 3f out: sn rdn and chsd wnr to last 100yds: kpt on same pce* **50/1**

6623 **4** *1 1/2* **Royal Bonsai**[11] 4612 3-9-1 **58**................................ PBBeggy 6 56
(John Quinn) *slt ld to 3f out: sn rdn: outpcd fnl f* **2/1**[2]

005 **5** *6* **Joe Rocco (IRE)**[108] 2125 3-8-7 **50**.................... AndrewElliott 5 37
(Alan Swinbank) *plld hrd early: trckd ldrs tl rdn and outpcd over 3f out: [illegible]*

-060 **6** *9* **Red Lite (IRE)**[79] 3002 3-9-2 **59**....................... JamesSullivan 1 30
(Wilf Storey) *hld up in tch: rdn over 3f out: sn wknd* **20/1**

0066 **7** *12* **Langtoon Lass**[33] 4505 3-8-6 **49** ow1......................... TomEaves 2 —
(Brian Storey) *t.k.h: stdd in tch: struggling over 3f out: sn btn* **50/1**

2m 30.34s (7.24) **Going Correction** +0.175s/f (Good) **7** Ran SP% **108.4**
Speed ratings (Par 98): **80,77,76,74,70 64,55**
toteswingers:1&2:£2.00, 1&3:£10.00, 2&3:£9.30 CSF £13.62 CT £346.93 TOTE £2.10: £1.30, £2.10; EX 11.90.
Owner The Hon W H Smith & Partners **Bred** Declan Gardiner **Trained** East Ilsley, Berks

FOCUS
A weak 3yo stayers' handicap but a most decisive winner of some potential.
T/Plt: £440.10 to a £1 stake. Pool:£39,642.72 - 65.75 winning tickets T/Qpdt: £63.90 to a £1 stake. Pool:£5,207.54 - 60.30 winning tickets RY

5297 FOLKESTONE (R-H)
Wednesday, August 31

OFFICIAL GOING: Good to firm (8.7)
Wind: virtually nil Weather: overcast

5624 BEST OFFERS AT JUSTBOOKIES.COM H'CAP 7f (S)
2:20 (2:20) (Class 6) (0-65,65) 3-Y-O £2,045 (£603; £302) Stalls High

Form RPR

4056 **1** **National Hope (IRE)**[27] 4707 3-9-5 **63**...............(t) KierenFallon 9 71
(George Baker) *stdd s: racd in last trio: rdn and hdwy 3f out: drvn and swtchd rt over 1f out: chsd ldr ent fnl f: r.o wl u.p to ld cl home* **4/1**[2]

0255 **2** *nk* **Links Drive Lady**[18] 5040 3-9-3 **64**...........(b) LouisBeuzelin(3) 10 71
(Mark Rimmer) *w ldr tl led travelling strly wl over 1f out: rdn over 1f out: drvn and kpt on wl ins fnl f tl hdd and no ex cl home* **8/1**

4356 **3** *3 3/4* **Thunda**[15] 5136 3-9-7 **65**................................ TomQueally 4 62
(Eve Johnson Houghton) *stdd s: racd in last trio: effrt and rdn 2f out: modest 6th and nt clr run over 1f out: swtchd lft ent fnl f: squeezed through on rail and styd on to go 3rd wl ins fnl f: no ch w ldrs* **9/1**

5001 **4** *1/2* **Spirit Of Oakdale (IRE)**[16] 5120 3-9-3 **61**...........(v) JamieSpencer 5 57
(Walter Swinburn) *chsd ldrs: drvn and effrt to press ldrs wl over 1f out: btn jst ins fnl f: fdd fnl 100yds* **9/2**[3]

00-2 **5** 5 **Poppy**[19] 4991 3-8-13 **60** .... SeanLevey(3) 7 42
(Richard Hannon) *led: rdn 2f out: sn hdd: wknd qckly ent fnl f* **11/1**

01 **6** 1 ¾ **Edgware Road**[13] 5206 3-9-7 **65** .... NeilCallan 1 42+
(Keith Dalgleish) *broke wl and crossed towards stands' side: chsd ldrs: rdn and unable qck ent fnl f: btn over 1f out: wknd and edgd lft fnl f* **7/4**[1]

7 ¾ **Money Note**[67] 3-9-5 **63** .... StevieDonohoe 8 38
(Tobias B P Coles) *s.i.s: a struggling to go pce and rdn thrght: wknd and lost tch 2f out* **28/1**

4021 **8** 11 **Piccoluck**[24] 4840 3-9-7 **65** ....(b) PatCosgrave 2 11
(Amy Weaver) *in tch: effrt and drvn wl over 1f out: sn btn and wknd: wl bhd and eased ins fnl f* **20/1**

0-40 **9** 20 **Manasha**[50] 3943 3-8-4 **51** oh6........ JohnFahy(3) 3 —
(John Dunlop) *dwlt: sn rcvrd and pressed ldrs on outer: rdn and struggling 1/2-way: wknd and lost tch over 2f out: t.o* **66/1**

1m 27.95s (0.65) **Going Correction** +0.025s/f (Good) 9 Ran SP% **113.7**
Speed ratings (Par 98): **97,96,92,91,86 84,83,70,47**
toteswingers:1&2:£8.60, 1&3:£8.80, 2&3:£19.80 CSF £34.30 CT £270.66 TOTE £4.30: £1.50, £2.60, £2.70; EX 44.00 Trifecta £418.90 Part won. Pool: £566.10 - 0.10 winning units..
Owner The No Hope Partnership **Bred** Oghill House Stud & Jimmy Hyland **Trained** Whitsbury, Hants

FOCUS
A modest handicap run at a fair pace.

5625 JUSTBOOKIES.COM (S) STKS — 6f
2:50 (2:50) (Class 6) 2-Y-O £1,704 (£503; £251) **Stalls** High

Form RPR

4302 **1** **Rod Hearts (IRE)**[8] 5353 2-8-13 **64** .... JimmyQuinn 8 62
(Julia Feilden) *t.k.h: hld up in tch: travelling but nt clr run on stands' rail over 1f out: swtchd rt arnd 4 horses ent fnl f: r.o wl u.p to ld wl ins fnl f* **8/1**

1036 **2** ¾ **Courtland King (IRE)**[8] 5348 2-9-4 **78** .... KierenFallon 4 65
(David Evans) *in tch: pushed along and effrt to chse ldrs 3f out: rdn to ld over 1f out: drvn ins fnl f: hdd and no ex wl ins fnl f* **6/4**[1]

0640 **3** ½ **The Name Is Don (IRE)**[24] 4823 2-8-11 **64** .... TomQueally 7 56
(Mark Gillard) *taken down early: s.i.s: bdly hmpd sn after s and wl bhd: hdwy and in tch 1/2-way: rdn and effrt to chse ldrs over 1f out: drvn and pressing ldrs ent fnl f: styd on same pce fnl 100yds* **8/1**

00 **4** hd **Anginola (IRE)**[44] 4155 2-8-6 0........ EddieCreighton 1 51
(Joseph Tuite) *s.i.s: immediately swtchd sharply lft and rdn along: clsd and in tch 1/2-way: sltly hmpd and swtchd lft over 1f out: swtchd rt ins fnl f: r.o strly fnl 100yds: nt rch ldrs* **4/1**[2]

1450 **5** ¾ **Faraway**[34] 4460 2-8-13 **64** ....(v[1]) RyanPowell(5) 9 60
(David Evans) *led: rdn 2f out: hdd over 1f out: no ex and styd on same pce ins fnl f* **14/1**

5445 **6** hd **Guava**[12] 5245 2-8-6 **60** .... FrankieMcDonald 3 48
(Richard Hannon) *chsd ldrs: rdn and unable qck over 1f out: nt clr run and swtchd rt jst ins fnl f: keeping on same pce whn nt clr run and eased towards fin* **6/1**[3]

0056 **7** 4 **High Five Prince (IRE)**[16] 5099 2-8-11 **45** ....(p) RobertHavlin 2 41
(Mark Usher) *taken down early: chsd ldr tl 2f out: stl chsng ldrs but wkng whn hmpd jst over 1f out: fdd ins fnl f* **40/1**

6 **8** 10 **Captain Baldwin**[118] 1827 2-8-11 0........ WilliamBuick 6 11
(David Evans) *sn outpcd in rr: lost tch over 2f out* **14/1**

0000 **9** hd **Arbeejay**[7] 5374 2-8-3 **31** ....(b[1]) JohnFahy(3) 5 5
(Bill Turner) *a towards rr: drvn and struggling 1/2-way: lost tch over 2f out* **150/1**

1m 14.57s (1.87) **Going Correction** +0.025s/f (Good) 9 Ran SP% **112.9**
Speed ratings (Par 92): **88,87,86,86,85 84,79,66,65**
toteswingers:1&2:£1.70, 1&3:£7.00, 2&3:£2.50 CSF £19.90 TOTE £6.70: £1.80, £1.10, £1.70; EX 21.80 Trifecta £66.70 Pool: £571.04 - 6.33 winning units..There was no bid for the winner. Anginola was subject to a friendly claim of £6,000.
Owner R J Creese **Bred** Tally-Ho Stud **Trained** Exning, Suffolk
■ Stewards' Enquiry : Jimmy Quinn one-day ban: careless riding (Sep 14)
Eddie Creighton five-day ban: careless riding (Sep 14-18)

FOCUS
A messy race, with a few of these finding trouble, and the form is moderate.

NOTEBOOK
Red Hearts(IRE) had to be switched wide around a furlong out, well away from the stands' rail, but she had raced against the often-favoured fence for most of the way and that may have been a help. This isn't form to get carried away with, but the drop from 7f helped and she travelled through the race like a filly in really good order. (op 13-2)
Courtland King(IRE), who was stepping up in trip, had upwards of 7lb in hand over those with official figures, but despite being produced with every chance, he was below his best. He raced off the near rail. (op 13-8 tchd 7-4 and 11-8)
The Name Is Don(IRE) did well to finish so close as he was hampered soon after the start, then raced keenly and made headway out wide without much cover. He's only had five starts and has the ability to win, though he could do with settling better in future. (op 7-1)
Anginola(IRE) was switched to race close to the stands' rail soon after the start, so she may have been on the best ground. She had to wait for a run and then took a while to pick up when in the clear, but she was really going on at the finish. (op 11-2)
Guava, up in trip, was continually denied a clear run in the closing stages and otherwise would have gone close to winning. (op 13-2 tchd 7-1)
Captain Baldwin Official explanation: jockey said gelding was hampered at start.

5626 JUSTBOOKIES.COM MAIDEN STKS — 6f
3:20 (3:20) (Class 5) 3-Y-O £2,590 (£764; £382) **Stalls** High

Form RPR

2 **1** **Passing Stranger (IRE)**[65] 3465 3-8-12 0........ WilliamBuick 3 72+
(Jeremy Noseda) *hld up in tch: hdwy to join ldrs on bit over 1f out: pushed into narrow ld ins fnl f: rdn and a jst holding rival fnl 100yds* **1/5**[1]

0- **2** nse **Shadow Of The Sun**[337] 6441 3-8-12 0........ EddieCreighton 6 68+
(Joseph Tuite) *t.k.h: chsd ldrs: rdn and ev ch over 1f out: whip knocked out of rdrs hand 1f out: edgd rt ins fnl f: kpt on wl but a jst hld* **33/1**

0360 **3** 2 ¾ **Choose The Moment**[54] 3818 3-8-12 **56** ....(p) NeilCallan 7 59
(Eve Johnson Houghton) *pushed along early: led after 1f: rdn and hrd pressed wl over 1f out: drvn and hdd ins fnl f: outpcd and btn fnl 150yds* **10/1**[2]

4 2 ¼ **Enchanted Dream** 3-8-12 0........ TomQueally 1 52
(George Margarson) *hld up in tch: pushed along and outpcd wl over 1f out: rdn and styd on ins fnl f* **20/1**

-045 **5** 1 **Dualite (IRE)**[26] 4743 3-8-12 **62** .... TedDurcan 2 49
(John Dunlop) *hld up in tch in rr: rdn and effrt over 1f out: no hdwy ent fnl f: wknd ins fnl f* **10/1**[2]

4 **6** 5 **Dolly Bay**[21] 4925 3-8-12 0........ JimmyQuinn 4 33
(Julia Feilden) *restless in stalls: led for 1f: pressed ldr after: rdn and ev ch over 1f out: struggling whn n.m.r ent fnl f: wknd rapidly fnl f* **16/1**[3]

7 1 ¾ **Suffolini** 3-8-7 0........ LauraPike(5) 5 27
(William Stone) *s.i.s: pushed along early: clsd and in tch whn hit rail and lost pl over 3f out: n.d after* **66/1**

1m 14.05s (1.35) **Going Correction** +0.025s/f (Good) 7 Ran SP% **116.6**
Speed ratings (Par 100): **92,91,88,85,83 77,74**
toteswingers:1&2:£6.30, 1&3:£1.70, 2&3:£10.60 CSF £15.41 TOTE £1.10: £1.02, £11.30; EX 11.80.
Owner Mrs Susan Roy **Bred** Atha Bloodstock **Trained** Newmarket, Suffolk

FOCUS
This isn't strong form, but the front two can probably rate higher.

5627 JUSTBOOKIES.COM H'CAP — 5f
3:50 (3:50) (Class 4) (0-80,80) 3-Y-O+ £4,771 (£1,409; £704) **Stalls** High

Form RPR

340 **1** **Fair Value (IRE)**[16] 5115 3-9-0 **72** .... NeilCallan 7 90
(Simon Dow) *mde all: clr 2f out: rdn and drew wl clr over 1f out: hung rt but r.o strly fnl f: easily* **4/1**[3]

0213 **2** 4 ½ **Go Nani Go**[12] 5238 5-9-5 **75** .... PatCosgrave 2 77
(Ed de Giles) *wnt rt s and slowly away: sn swtchd rt: bhd: hdwy 1/2-way: drvn and chsd clr wnr jst ins fnl f: kpt on but no imp* **4/1**[3]

55/0 **3** 1 ¾ **Miss Chamanda (IRE)**[30] 4618 5-9-2 **72** .... KierenFallon 6 68
(David Evans) *chsd ldrs: pushed along 1/2-way: drvn and unable qck over 1f out: no ch w wnr and plugged on same pce fnl f* **11/4**[1]

0453 **4** nk **Magical Speedfit (IRE)**[14] 5173 6-8-13 **74** .... RyanPowell(5) 8 69
(George Margarson) *sn outpcd in last pair: rdn and struggling 3f out: edgd rt fr 2f out: kpt on u.p ins fnl f: no ch w wnr* **8/1**

0006 **5** ¾ **Style And Panache (IRE)**[10] 5115 3-9-1 **73** .... WilliamBuick 3 65
(David Evans) *chsd ldng trio: pushed along and struggling 1/2-way: no ch w wnr but kpt on u.p ins fnl f* **6/1**

3465 **6** ¾ **Osiris Way**[31] 4583 9-9-7 **80** .... JohnFahy(3) 4 69
(Patrick Chamings) *chsd wnr: rdn and outpcd over 1f out: wl btn 1f out: wknd ins fnl f* **7/2**[2]

59.42 secs (-0.58) **Going Correction** +0.025s/f (Good)
WFA 3 from 4yo+ 2lb 6 Ran SP% **114.3**
Speed ratings (Par 105): **105,97,95,94,93 92**
toteswingers:1&2:£4.70, 1&3:£1.60, 2&3:£3.50 CSF £20.61 CT £50.27 TOTE £5.80: £3.30, £1.70; EX 26.60 Trifecta £124.00 Pool: £360.41 - 2.15 winning units..
Owner Edward Hyde **Bred** Edward Hyde **Trained** Epsom, Surrey

FOCUS
Few of these ran to their best and this was an uncompetitive sprint handicap.

5628 BEST OFFERS AT JUSTBOOKIES.COM H'CAP — 2m 93y
4:20 (4:20) (Class 6) (0-65,69) 3-Y-O+ £2,045 (£603; £302) **Stalls** High

Form RPR

3-31 **1** **Red Current**[11] 5267 7-8-12 **54** .... DavidKenny(5) 2 60
(Michael Scudamore) *hld up in last pair: gd hdwy on outer over 2f out: rdn and ev ch over 1f out: led 1f out: kpt on wl ins fnl f* **6/1**[3]

2341 **2** hd **Dr Finley (IRE)**[37] 4396 4-10-0 **65** .... KierenFallon 4 70
(Lydia Pearce) *chsd ldr tl 12f out: wnt 2nd again 4f out: rdn and ev ch over 1f out: drvn and kpt on wl ins fnl f* **15/8**[1]

2054 **3** 3 ¼ **Treacle Tart**[8] 5357 6-9-8 **64** ....(t) RosieJessop(5) 5 65
(Peter Charalambous) *t.k.h: hld up in tch towards rr: plld out and hdwy to ld 12f out: sn clr: rdn and hrd pressed wl over 1f out: hdd 1f out: no ex and btn fnl 100yds* **8/1**

-045 **4** 2 ¾ **Winning Show**[14] 5168 7-8-12 **49** oh3........(vt) LiamJones 7 47
(Chris Gordon) *in tch: chsd ldng pair wl over 3f out: rdn and unable qck over 2f out: kpt on same pce u.p fr over 1f out* **14/1**

-526 **5** ½ **Astrovenus**[27] 4732 4-8-13 **50** .... TomQueally 3 47
(Mark H Tompkins) *in tch: lost pl and dropped to last pair over 3f out: hdwy over 2f out: unable qck and outpcd 2f out: one pce after* **13/2**

1221 **6** 2 ¼ **Come On The Irons (USA)**[10] 5302 3-8-13 **69** 6ex.(t) MarkCoumbe(5) 1 64
(Ralph Smith) *led tl 12f out: chsd ldr after tl 4f out: lost pl and dropped to last 3f out: rdn and btn 2f out* **3/1**[2]

3305 **7** 2 **Pizzetti (IRE)**[10] 5302 3-8-7 **58** .... StevieDonohoe 6 50
(Sir Mark Prescott Bt) *hld up in tch in rr: hdwy to chse ldng trio 3f out: rdn and lost pl over 2f out: wknd 2f out* **10/1**

3m 49.99s (12.79) **Going Correction** +0.025s/f (Good)
WFA 3 from 4yo+ 14lb 7 Ran SP% **114.3**
Speed ratings (Par 101): **69,68,67,65,65 64,63**
toteswingers:1&2:£2.20, 1&3:£10.70, 2&3:£3.00 CSF £17.70 TOTE £2.90: £1.20, £1.20; EX 13.40.
Owner M Scudamore **Bred** Wretham Stud **Trained** Bromsash, Herefordshire
■ Stewards' Enquiry : Kieren Fallon one-day ban: used whip with excessive frequency (Sep 14)

FOCUS
A moderate staying handicap and they didn't seem to go that quick, resulting in a time almost 13secs above standard.

5629 CLAIM YOUR BONUSES AT JUSTBOOKIES.COM MAIDEN STKS — 1m 4f
4:50 (4:50) (Class 5) 3-Y-O+ £2,590 (£764; £382) **Stalls** High

Form RPR

62-3 **1** **Protaras (USA)**[18] 5057 4-9-13 **78** .... TomQueally 1 80
(Sir Henry Cecil) *hld up in midfield: rdn to chse ldrs over 2f out: drvn and edgd rt over 1f out: chal ins fnl f: kpt on u.p to ld cl home* **11/4**[1]

-222 **2** nk **Whispered**[19] 5001 3-8-12 **79** ....(v[1]) KierenFallon 8 75
(Sir Michael Stoute) *t.k.h: led: rdn 2f out: drvn and kpt on u.p tl hdd cl home* **10/3**[3]

4 **3** hd **Yasir (USA)**[14] 5169 3-9-3 0........ TadhgO'Shea 2 80+
(Saeed Bin Suroor) *hld up bhd: outpcd but nt pushed 3f out: hdwy in 7th and swtchd rt over 1f out: rdn and running on strly jst over 1f out: clsng but bhd wall of horses and swtchd lft fnl 100yds: r.o wl:nt quite get up: too much to do* **12/1**

0-00 **4** shd **Kid Charlemagne (IRE)**[81] 2931 8-9-13 **79** ....(vt[1]) WilliamBuick 3 80
(Warren Greatrex) *t.k.h: hld up in midfield: hdwy to chse ldrs 3f out: rdn over 2f out: drvn and kpt on over 1f out: ev ch ins fnl f: unable qck towards fin* **16/1**

52 **5** 1 ¼ **Shaqira**[29] 4641 3-8-12 0........ RichardHills 10 73
(Marcus Tregoning) *pressed ldr: rdn and ev ch wl over 1f out: no ex and btn fnl 100yds* **18/1**

42 **6** 2 **Figaro**[26] 4763 3-9-3 **78** .... LiamJones 5 74
(William Haggas) *chsd ldrs: rdn and struggling over 2f out: plugging on u.p but btn whn hmpd ins fnl f* **3/1**[2]

7 2 ¾ **Mahayogin (USA)** 3-9-3 0........ JimmyQuinn 4 70
(Sir Henry Cecil) *dwlt and bustled along leaving stalls: hld up in tch towards rr: outpcd wl over 2f out: kpt on same pce fnl 2f* **33/1**

62 **8** *1 ¾* **Viva Diva**[30] 4611 3-8-12 0........................ TedDurcan 7 62
(David Lanigan) *hld up in midfield: rdn and struggling over 2f out: wknd 2f out* **20/1**

9 *42* **Royal Alcor (IRE)**[56] 4-9-13 0........................(t) RobertHavlin 6 —
(Alastair Lidderdale) *v.s.a: sn rcvrd and in tch in rr: shkn up over 4f out: wknd qckly ent fnl 3f: t.o and eased fnl f* **100/1**

5-26 **10** *32* **Jamr**[26] 4753 3-9-3 79........................(v) FrankieDettori 9 —
(Saeed Bin Suroor) *chsd ldng trio tl lost pl rapidly over 3f out: virtually p.u fr over 2f out: wl t.o* **6/1**

2m 40.37s (-0.53) **Going Correction** +0.025s/f (Good)
WFA 3 from 4yo+ 10lb **10** Ran SP% **116.6**
Speed ratings (Par 103): **102,101,101,101,100 99,97,96,68,47**
toteswingers:1&2:£3.70, 1&3:£6.50, 2&3:£9.20 CSF £11.91 TOTE £4.30: £1.70, £1.10, £4.10; EX 15.30 Trifecta £140.40 Pool: £622.37 - 3.28 winning units..
Owner Niarchos Family **Bred** Flaxman Holdings Ltd **Trained** Newmarket, Suffolk
■ Stewards' Enquiry : Tadhg O'Shea two-day ban: careless riding (Sep 14-15)

FOCUS
Plenty of powerful connections were represented and this was a fair maiden, although some of these had already had a few chances.
Jamr Official explanation: jockey said gelding lost its action
T/Plt: £64.50 to a £1 stake. Pool:£53,317.70 - 603.10 winning tickets T/Qpdt: £6.40 to a £1 stake. Pool:£3,921.25 - 449.02 winning tickets SP

5381 KEMPTON (A.W) (R-H)

Wednesday, August 31

OFFICIAL GOING: Standard
Wind: Almost nil Weather: Fine

5630 FREE ENTRY FOR BETDAQ MEMBERS H'CAP — 1m 2f (P)

5:50 (5:51) (Class 5) (0-70,70) 3-Y-O **£2,264** (£673; £336; £168) **Stalls** Low

Form RPR

0054 **1** **Sit Tight**[12] 5247 3-9-4 **67**........................ GeorgeBaker 3 81
(Chris Wall) *trckd ldr 3f: styd prom: wnt 2nd again 2f out gng wl: chal over 1f out: rdn to ld last 75yds* **14/1**

2462 **2** *½* **Dare To Bare (IRE)**[9] 5318 3-9-4 **67**........................ JimCrowley 13 80
(Amanda Perrett) *led: rdn 2f out: kpt on wl but hdd and jst hld last 75yds* **6/1**[2]

364- **3** *4* **Waltzing Cat (USA)**[300] 7312 3-9-0 **63**........................ SebSanders 1 68
(Sir Mark Prescott Bt) *s.i.s: sn t.k.h chsng ldrs: rdn over 2f out: wnt 3rd jst over 1f out but wl outpcd* **7/2**[1]

-055 **4** *hd* **For What (USA)**[16] 5103 3-9-7 **70**........................ ChrisCatlin 8 75
(David Lanigan) *prom: rdn over 2f out: disp 3rd over 1f out: outpcd after* **15/2**[3]

3623 **5** *2* **Mrs Neat (IRE)**[18] 5050 3-9-4 **67**........................(p) JamesDoyle 9 68
(Sylvester Kirk) *hld up in midfield: rdn over 2f out: kpt on fr over 1f out to take 5th last strides: n.d* **10/1**

-305 **6** *nk* **Mia Madonna**[51] 3907 3-9-3 **66**........................ ShaneKelly 7 66
(Brian Meehan) *prog on outer to chse ldr after 3f: lost 2nd 2f out: wknd fnl f* **14/1**

0400 **7** *hd* **My Vindication (USA)**[24] 4825 3-9-3 **69**........................ SeanLevey(3) 2 69
(Richard Hannon) *awkward s: towards rr on inner: rdn and tried to make prog over 2f out: one pce after* **16/1**

5650 **8** *1* **Wordiness**[24] 4825 3-8-12 **68**........................ BrendanPowell(7) 11 66
(Barry Brennan) *towards rr and racd wd: effrt on bnd 3f out: plugged on: nvr a real factor* **8/1**

2033 **9** *nse* **Clarion Call**[5] 5420 3-9-6 **69**........................(p) DarryllHolland 5 67
(Eve Johnson Houghton) *a in midfield: rdn over 2f out: no prog over 1f out* **8/1**

364 **10** *¾* **Carinya (IRE)**[19] 5007 3-9-5 **68**........................ RichardMullen 14 64
(Amy Weaver) *dwlt: hld up in last pair: rdn over 2f out and stl there: modest late prog* **50/1**

645 **11** *2* **Tamara Bay**[28] 4663 3-8-8 **60**........................ GilmarPereira(3) 6 52
(William Haggas) *hld up: a abt same pl: pushed along 3f out and no prog* **8/1**

6124 **12** *½* **Double Duchess**[101] 750 3-9-4 **67**........................ WilliamCarson 4 58
(Paul D'Arcy) *taken down early: chsd ldrs: rdn 3f out: steadily wknd wl over 1f out* **33/1**

1050 **13** *4* **Rather Cool**[9] 5321 3-8-2 **54**........................(t) HarryBentley(3) 10 37
(John Bridger) *a wl in rr: struggling fnl 3f* **50/1**

0360 **14** *1 ½* **Roman Flame**[56] 3742 3-8-11 **60**........................(b) JamieSpencer 12 40
(Michael Quinn) *stdd s: hld up in last: briefest of effrts 3f out: sn btn* **33/1**

2m 6.68s (-1.32) **Going Correction** -0.10s/f (Stan) **14** Ran SP% **119.7**
Speed ratings (Par 100): **101,100,97,97,95 95,95,94,94,93 92,91,88,87**
toteswingers:1&2:£9.00, 1&3:£13.30, 2&3:£3.80 CSF £93.31 CT £365.94 TOTE £22.20: £6.70, £1.60, £1.80; EX 132.30 TRIFECTA Not won..
Owner Des Thurlby **Bred** Mrs D O Joly **Trained** Newmarket, Suffolk

FOCUS
A modest but very competitive-looking handicap with plenty supported in the pre-race market. However, one of the less fancied runners prevailed.

5631 LAY BACK AND WIN AT BETDAQ.COM (S) STKS — 1m (P)

6:20 (6:23) (Class 6) 3-Y-O **£1,617** (£481; £240; £120) **Stalls** Low

Form RPR

2012 **1** **Sky Diamond (IRE)**[6] 5401 3-9-8 62........................(b) JimCrowley 5 69
(James Given) *mde all: hrd rdn fnl 2f: hld on wl* **6/1**[3]

2421 **2** *½* **Chilledtothebone**[27] 4728 3-9-8 63........................(tp) KierenFallon 4 68
(Linda Stubbs) *pushed along in midfield 1/2-way: nt qckn over 2f out: hrd rdn and styd on wl fr over 1f out: tk 2nd nr fin and clsd on wnr* **4/1**[2]

0006 **3** *½* **Herminella**[9] 5319 3-8-12 70........................ MartinDwyer 8 57
(William Muir) *chsd wnr after 2f: rdn 2f out: kpt on but hld fnl f: lost 2nd nr fin* **10/1**

0052 **4** *nk* **Conducting**[28] 4685 3-9-3 70........................(b) JamieSpencer 6 61
(Brian Meehan) *trckd ldrs: wnt 3rd over 2f out: sn rdn: tried to chal jst over 1f out: nt qckn* **5/4**[1]

0303 **5** *3* **Granny Anne (IRE)**[13] 5213 3-9-3 60........................(p) JamesDoyle 7 54
(Alan Bailey) *towards rr: rdn over 2f out: plugged on one pce fr over 1f out* **20/1**

3400 **6** *1* **So Is She (IRE)**[1] 5606 3-9-0 59........................(b) AmyBaker(3) 1 52
(Alan Bailey) *reluctant to enter stalls: mostly in last pair and nt gng that wl: plugged on fr over 1f out* **16/1**

345 **7** *4 ½* **Flying Phoenix**[27] 4713 3-9-3 65........................(b) DarryllHolland 2 42
(Gay Kelleway) *chsd wnr 2f: racd in 3rd after tl wknd over 2f out* **8/1**

4005 **8** *3 ¼* **Endaxi Mana Mou**[57] 3710 3-8-12 62........................ KellyHarrison 3 29
(Noel Quinlan) *mostly in last pair: pushed along and no prog over 2f out* **33/1**

1m 39.4s (-0.40) **Going Correction** -0.10s/f (Stan) **8** Ran SP% **112.5**
Speed ratings (Par 98): **98,97,97,96,93 92,88,84**
toteswingers:1&2:£3.70, 1&3:£5.20, 2&3:£4.00 CSF £29.18 TOTE £7.20: £2.00, £1.10, £2.40; EX 21.30 Trifecta £134.00 Pool: £5350.19 - 29.53 winning units..There was no bid for the winner.
Owner Danethorpe Racing Partnership **Bred** David Bourke **Trained** Willoughton, Lincs

FOCUS
Not a bad seller and quite competitive on paper, with the runners officially rated 59-70, but one at the lower end of the ratings scored.

5632 BRITISH STALLION STUDS SUPPORTING BRITISH RACING E B F MEDIAN AUCTION MAIDEN STKS — 6f (P)

6:50 (6:51) (Class 5) 2-Y-O **£3,169** (£943; £471; £235) **Stalls** Low

Form RPR

65 **1** **Roman Seal (IRE)**[18] 5047 2-8-12 0........................ RichardKingscote 2 75
(Tom Dascombe) *trckd ldng pair: rdn to ld wl over 1f out: styd on fnl f* **16/1**

2 *½* **Poseidon Grey (IRE)** 2-9-3 0........................ AdamKirby 9 79
(Walter Swinburn) *chsd ldrs in 5th: pushed along to cl 2f out: chsd wnr jst over 1f out: hung bdly lft after or might wl have won* **25/1**

3 **3** *1 ¼* **Performing Pocket (USA)**[21] 4912 2-9-3 0........................ FrankieDettori 5 75
(George Baker) *hld up in 7th: prog on inner 2f out: wnt 3rd 1f out: kpt on one pce after* **4/7**[1]

4 *2* **Feelthedifference** 2-8-12 0........................ IanMongan 1 64
(Sir Henry Cecil) *dwlt: wl in rr and rn green: pushed along on inner over 2f out: styd on steadily after to take 4th last strides* **14/1**

0232 **5** *nk* **King Of Wing (IRE)**[20] 4954 2-9-0 74........................ SeanLevey(3) 11 68
(Richard Hannon) *prom: shkn up over 2f out: outpcd fr over 1f out: lost 4th last strides* **7/1**[3]

6 *½* **Fine Painting (IRE)** 2-8-12 0........................ RichardMullen 7 61
(Gary Moore) *wl in tch in 6th: shkn up jst over 2f out: outpcd after but pushed along and kpt on* **50/1**

4 **7** *2* **La Bocca (USA)**[16] 5111 2-8-12 0........................ JamesDoyle 3 55
(Roger Charlton) *led: edgd lft jst over 2f out: hdd & wknd wl over 1f out* **4/1**[2]

04 **8** *½* **Welsh Royale**[29] 4639 2-9-3 0........................ MartinDwyer 6 59
(William Muir) *chsd ldr: rdn whn squeezed out 2f out: sn wknd* **66/1**

9 *2* **Picalily** 2-8-9 0........................ LouisBeuzelin(3) 8 48
(Sylvester Kirk) *rn v green and shoved along thrght: a in rr* **100/1**

4 **10** *¾* **Purley Queen (IRE)**[48] 3997 2-8-12 0........................ JamieSpencer 4 46
(Sylvester Kirk) *sn hld up in last: nudged along over 2f out: nvr a factor* **50/1**

11 *12* **Dingle Two (IRE)** 2-8-12 0........................ ShaneKelly 10 10
(David Evans) *s.i.s: a in rr: v wd bnd 3f out: t.o* **40/1**

1m 13.23s (0.13) **Going Correction** -0.10s/f (Stan) **11** Ran SP% **121.4**
Speed ratings (Par 94): **95,94,92,90,89 88,86,85,82,81 65**
toteswingers:1&2:£33.90, 1&3:£4.00, 2&3:£8.80 CSF £342.91 TOTE £22.50: £3.80, £7.10, £1.60; EX 519.50 Trifecta £2495.00 Part won. Pool: £3,371.66 - 0.50 winning units..
Owner Bellman Black Owen **Bred** Lynchbages Edgeridge Ltd & Glenvale Stud **Trained** Malpas, Cheshire

FOCUS
Some newcomers of interest in this juvenile maiden but they went 14/1 bar three, suggesting few were fancied, although there was a surprise result.

NOTEBOOK
Roman Seal(IRE) had improved on her debut second time and this switch to Polytrack seemed to suit, as she stepped up again to get off the mark. She has yet to race on soft ground on turf, which suited her relatives, so could be of interest in a nursery given those conditions.
Poseidon Grey(IRE) ◆, a half-brother to a 5f juvenile winner who cost 42,000euros at the breeze-ups, is possibly the horse to take out of this. He tracked the pace but when he came through to challenge hung all over the place, and his rider had to more or less just keep hold of his head near the finish. As it was he was beaten only narrowly and would have won had he kept straight. This can be put down to greenness but the fact that he was already gelded before this debut suggests he could be quirky. He can be given a chance as he clearly has a fair amount of ability. Official explanation: jockey said gelding hung left and ran green (tchd 33-1)
Performing Pocket(USA) was sent off at odds-on here, having made a promising debut at Salisbury, and the runner-up and fourth from that contest had won since. He had to come from quite a way back but got a good split at the junction of the courses, only to be unable to find more when in the clear. George Baker reported that the colt was unsuited by the all-weather surface. Official explanation: trainer said colt was unsuited by the all-weather surface (op 4-6 tchd 8-11 in places)
Feelthedifference, the daughter of a 1m winner, missed the break from her inside stall and was at the rear before staying on in the straight. She should be better for the experience. (op 12-1)
King Of Wing(IRE) set the standard and had run well on Polytrack before. However, he raced wide from his draw and faded in the closing stages. (op 13-2)
Fine Painting(IRE), a £45,000 half-sister to a 6f-1m2f winner, showed a bit of promise on this debut and can be expected to do better in due course.
La Bocca(USA) had run promisingly on her debut on fast turf and made the running this time. However, she could not pick up under pressure and faded quite badly in the last furlong.

5633 BETDAQ.COM EXCHANGE PRICE MULTIPLES MAIDEN STKS — 7f (P)

7:20 (7:21) (Class 5) 3-Y-O+ **£2,264** (£673; £336; £168) **Stalls** Low

Form RPR

542 **1** **Eclipseoftheheart**[19] 5021 3-8-12 72........................ KierenFallon 11 76+
(James Fanshawe) *prom fr wd draw: chsd ldr after 2f: led jst over 2f out: edgd rt over 1f out: drew clr fnl f* **1/1**[1]

2- **2** *2 ¼* **Always Like This (IRE)**[271] 7682 3-8-12 0........................ JamieSpencer 8 72+
(Marco Botti) *led: shkn up and hdd jst over 2f out: edgd rt over 1f out: hld whn swtchd lft ins fnl f* **3/1**[2]

3 *1 ½* **Darsan (IRE)** 3-8-12 0........................ SebSanders 12 66+
(Chris Wall) *dwlt: wl in rr: prog on outer over 2f out but rn green: wnt modest 3rd over 1f out: styd on: nrst fin* **16/1**

6 **4** *½* **George Guru**[19] 4991 4-9-3 0........................ MarkCoumbe(5) 6 72+
(Michael Attwater) *dwlt: settled in last pair: prog on inner 2f out: wl outpcd by front pair but styd on steadily* **40/1**

5 *7* **Fastnette (IRE)** 4-9-3 0........................ JamesDoyle 1 48
(Ian Wood) *mostly in midfield: rdn and outpcd fr over 2f out: n.d after* **66/1**

3/0 **6** *¾* **Spring Buck (IRE)**[13] 5212 6-9-8 0........................ ChrisCatlin 5 51
(Paul Cole) *trckd ldrs: wl outpcd fnl 2f: fdd* **25/1**

052 **7** *hd* **Jumeira Field (USA)**[23] 4849 3-9-3 74........................ JimCrowley 9 48
(Robert Cowell) *chsd ldrs: rdn over 2f out: sn outpcd: fdd* **5/1**[3]

8 *2 ½* **Kampai** 3-8-12 0........................ IanMongan 3 36
(John Akehurst) *slowest away: mostly in last pair: rdn 3f out: modest late prog on inner* **16/1**

9 hd **Heavenly Games** 4-9-3 0 .... RobertHavlin 4 38
(Jeremy Gask) *dwlt: a in rr: lft wl bhd fnl 2f* **50/1**

000 10 1 **Pastoral Jet**[23] 4849 3-8-10 52 .... LukeRowe(7) 10 38
(Richard Rowe) *prog fr rr on outer to go prom over 4f out: wknd wl over 2f out* **100/1**

00 11 1 **Prana (USA)**[20] 4970 3-8-9 0 .... KieranO'Neill(3) 7 30
(Jeremy Gask) *plld hrd bhd ldrs: wknd wl over 2f out* **66/1**

12 2 ¼ **Nially Noo** 3-9-3 0 .... NickyMackay 2 29
(Derek Shaw) *chsd ldr 2f: styd prom to over 2f out: wknd rapidly over 1f out* **33/1**

1m 26.13s (0.13) **Going Correction** -0.10s/f (Stan)
WFA 3 from 4yo+ 5lb 12 Ran SP% **118.6**
Speed ratings (Par 103): **95,92,90,90,82 81,81,78,77,76 75,73**
toteswingers:1&2:£1.40, 1&3:£5.50, 2&3:£5.60 CSF £3.70 TOTE £2.80: £1.10, £1.40, £5.80; EX 5.20 Trifecta £45.10 Pool: £3,835.68 - 62.84 winning units..
Owner Landseer Racing **Bred** B Smith & Miss I Williams **Trained** Newmarket, Suffolk

FOCUS
A modest-looking older horse maiden and fairly uncompetitive, as they went 16/1 bar three.

5634 BETDAQ MOBILE APPS NURSERY 1m (P)
7:50 (7:52) (Class 6) (0-65,65) 2-Y-O £1,617 (£481; £240; £120) **Stalls** Low

Form RPR

0004 1 **Shannon Spree**[12] 5233 2-9-4 65 .... KieranO'Neill(3) 3 70
(Richard Hannon) *prom but pushed along aty several stages: rdn and effrt to ld wl over 1f out: styd on wl* **5/1**[2]

605 2 1 ¼ **Spunky**[27] 4710 2-9-2 60 .... KierenFallon 4 62
(Luca Cumani) *sweating: lost midfield pl after 2f and sn in last trio: prog on inner jst over 2f out: drvn and styd on wl to tako 2nd nr fin* **6/2**[1]

0000 3 shd **Doctor Banner**[13] 5197 2-9-1 59 .... SamHitchcott 5 61
(Mick Channon) *settled in midfield: effrt over 2f out: styd on fr over 1f out: tk 3rd wl ins fnl f* **40/1**

6600 4 nk **Manomine**[5] 5446 2-9-7 65 .... PhilipRobinson 11 66
(Clive Brittain) *racd wd thrght including on bnds: in tch: prog over 2f out: rdn to chse wnr briefly ins fnl f: one pce after* **8/1**

600 5 2 **Finley Connolly (IRE)**[23] 4857 2-9-2 60 .... MartinDwyer 12 56
(Brian Meehan) *wl in rr: effrt on outer over 3f out: stl in rr and rdn over 2f out: styd on wl fnl f: nrst fin* **10/1**

6006 6 nk **Tigers Tale (IRE)**[12] 5233 2-9-5 63 .... JamesDoyle 6 59
(Roger Teal) *pressed ldr: led briefly 2f out: btn over 1f out: wknd fnl f* **8/1**

004 7 1 ¾ **Rocco Breeze (IRE)**[35] 4433 2-8-3 50 .... AdamBeschizza(3) 8 42
(Philip McBride) *mostly in midfield: nt qckn over 2f out: one pce after and n.d* **12/1**

605 8 hd **Milwr**[8] 5343 2-8-1 45 ....(p) AndreaAtzeni 7 36
(Chris Dwyer) *led to 2f out: steadily wknd over 1f out* **40/1**

006 9 ½ **Always A Sinner (USA)**[21] 4906 2-9-7 65 .... ShaneKelly 1 55
(William Knight) *mostly in last trio: shkn up on inner over 2f out: kpt on but nvr a threat* **6/1**[3]

0640 10 1 ¼ **Raspberry Fizz**[15] 5144 2-8-7 51 ....(b[1]) CathyGannon 2 38
(Eve Johnson Houghton) *mostly in last trio: no prog over 2f out: no ch after* **20/1**

0000 11 nk **Astraios (IRE)**[8] 5343 2-9-7 65 ....(b[1]) JamieSpencer 13 52
(Brian Meehan) *racd wd: prog to chse ldng pair over 5f out: hrd rdn and hanging over 2f out: wkng whn wobbled over 1f out* **20/1**

0463 12 5 **Flying Kitty**[39] 4319 2-8-6 53 .... SeanLevey(3) 9 28
(John Bridger) *prom tl wknd qckly over 2f out* **40/1**

5343 13 nk **River Nova**[9] 5325 2-8-2 49 .... HarryBentley(3) 14 23
(Alan Jarvis) *chsd ldng pair to over 5f out: wknd qckly over 2f out* **20/1**

1m 39.83s (0.03) **Going Correction** -0.10s/f (Stan) 13 Ran SP% **120.1**
Speed ratings (Par 92): **95,93,93,93,91 91,89,89,88,87 87,82,81**
toteswingers:1&2:£3.40, 1&3:£44.30, 2&3:£23.50 CSF £16.30 CT £393.89 TOTE £5.40: £2.00, £1.50, £12.30; EX 22.90 Trifecta £214.70 Pool: £1,939.44 - 2.01 winning units..
Owner Denis J Barry **Bred** Peter W Harris **Trained** East Everleigh, Wilts

FOCUS
A low-grade but quite competitive nursery run 0.43secs slower than the earlier 3yo seller.

NOTEBOOK
Shannon Spree had improved for longer trips on her two previous starts and she handled the switch to Polytrack well, tracking the pace before striking for home halfway up the straight and running on strongly. This surface or easy turf seems to suit her best. (op 11-2)
Spunky was sent off favourite on this handicap debut over a longer trip but sweated up and was coltish beforehand then missed the break and got rather carried back on the rail. He got a gap at the intersection of the courses but, despite staying on, could not produce sufficient pace to trouble the winner. (op 9-4)
Doctor Banner had not troubled the judge in four starts on varying turf but ran much better on this surface over a longer trip, following the winner through and staying on under pressure. (op 66-1)
Manomine had run his best race on his handicap debut on his previous start but had to race wide from his outside stall here. He did well to get into contention over 1f out before his effort flattened out and can be given another chance from a better draw. (op 10-1)
Finley Connolly(IRE), another stepping up in trip on his handicap debut, ran his best race yet. He was drawn wide and had to come from a fair way back, but finished to good effect. (op 12-1)
Tigers Tale(IRE) had shown minor promise in a nursery over this trip last time and adopted different tactics here, going on early in the straight having been up there throughout, but fading late.
Always A Sinner(USA) had the inside draw, was backed but never got involved on this handicap debut. (op 15-2)

5635 OFF LIMITS TEAM BUILDING THROUGH EVENTS H'CAP (LONDON MILE QUALIFIER) 1m (P)
8:20 (8:21) (Class 4) (0-85,85) 3-Y-O £4,075 (£1,212; £606; £303) **Stalls** Low

Form RPR

3106 1 **Trumpington Street (IRE)**[26] 4763 3-8-13 77 .... WilliamBuick 2 93
(John Gosden) *trckd ldng pair: swtchd lft over 2f out: rdn to ld over 1f out: drvn clr and r.o wl* **8/1**

220 2 3 ½ **Little Black Book (IRE)**[18] 5056 3-8-12 79 ....(t) SeanLevey(3) 13 87
(Gerard Butler) *pressed ldr: led wl over 2f out: hdd over 1f out: clr of rest fnl f but no match for wnr* **7/1**[3]

051 3 2 ¼ **Point Du Jour (FR)**[21] 4908 3-8-8 72 oh1 ow1 .... JamesDoyle 1 75
(Ian Wood) *settled in midfield: erffort whn outpcd over 2f out: styd on to take 3rd jst ins fnl f* **14/1**

0262 4 ¾ **Switchback**[28] 4665 3-8-7 71 .... RichardMullen 7 72+
(Sir Michael Stoute) *racd wd: hld up towards rr: rdn over 2f out: styd on fr over 1f out to take 4th wl ins fnl f* **5/1**[2]

63-1 5 shd **Shooting Line (IRE)**[72] 3232 3-9-7 85 .... KierenFallon 5 86+
(Walter Swinburn) *t.k.h: hld up in rr: effrt over 2f out but sn outpcd: drvn and kpt on: n.d* **3/1**[1]

1523 6 1 ¾ **Wiqaaya (IRE)**[44] 4161 3-9-6 84 .... RichardHills 3 81
(Ed Dunlop) *s.i.s: hld up in last pair: outpcd whn effrt over 2f out: sme prog on inner over 1f out: no threat* **14/1**

31 7 1 ¼ **Social Forum (IRE)**[130] 1532 3-9-1 79 .... DaneO'Neill 10 73
(David Elsworth) *chsd ldng trio: outpcd over 2f out: steadily wknd over 1f out* **10/1**

1-04 8 nk **Orange Ace**[117] 1862 3-9-0 78 .... ShaneKelly 9 71
(Paul Cole) *sn pushed along in last pair: outpcd wl over 2f out: v modest late prog* **20/1**

0-60 9 shd **Secret Love (IRE)**[77] 3034 3-9-7 85 .... GeorgeBaker 11 78
(Mikael Magnusson) *led at gd pce to wl over 2f out: wknd qckly wl over 1f out* **15/2**

-206 10 ½ **General Synod**[30] 4617 3-9-3 81 .... JimCrowley 6 73
(Richard Hannon) *mostly in midfield: outpcd over 2f out: wl btn whn nt clrest of runs wl over 1f out: wknd* **12/1**

21-2 11 7 **If You Whisper (IRE)**[235] 101 3-9-1 79 .... TonyCulhane 8 55
(Mike Murphy) *racd wd: chsd ldrs: rowed along over 2f out: sn wknd* **28/1**

1m 37.21s (-2.59) **Going Correction** -0.10s/f (Stan) 11 Ran SP% **115.4**
Speed ratings (Par 102): **108,104,102,101,101 99,98,98,98,97 90**
toteswingers:1&2:£9.50, 1&3:£18.50, 2&3:£15.10 CSF £61.79 CT £786.69 TOTE £11.80: £3.60, £2.00, £6.40; EX 63.10 Trifecta £519.10 Part won. Pool: £701.53 - 0.70 winning units..
Owner Bailey, Hall & Hood **Bred** Eimear Mulhern J Flynn & Abbeville Stud **Trained** Newmarket, Suffolk

FOCUS
A decent handicap run 2.19secs faster than the quicker of the two earlier races over the trip, and an impressive winner.

5636 LADIES DAY AT KEMPTON ON SATURDAY APPRENTICE H'CAP 1m 3f (P)
8:50 (8:50) (Class 6) (0-60,56) 3-Y-O £1,617 (£481; £240; £120) **Stalls** Low

Form RPR

6415 1 **Newby Lodge (IRE)**[5] 5421 3-9-1 55 .... ThomasBrown(5) 5 66
(Alan Bailey) *disp ld to 5f out: rdn over 2f out: kpt on to ld jst over 1f out: sn clr* **7/2**[1]

3602 2 2 ¾ **If What And Maybe**[18] 5042 3-9-7 56 ....(v[1]) RyanPowell 7 62
(John Ryan) *disp ld tl definitie advantage 5f out: hrd rdn over 2f out: sltly impeded by loose horse over 1f out: sn wknd and hdd* **4/1**[2]

5160 3 ½ **Hi Note**[20] 3958 3-8-11 53 .... MartinLeonard(7) 3 58
(Sheena West) *hld up off the pce: prog to go 3rd 4f out: looked dangerous 3f out: nt qckn over 2f out: plugged on over 1f out* **15/2**

5404 4 8 **Sir Randolf (IRE)**[8] 5349 3-9-1 53 ....(t) MatthewLawson(3) 4 44
(Sylvester Kirk) *s.s: detached in last and nt gng wl: wnt 4th u.p over 3f out: no hdwy after* **11/2**[3]

0300 5 19 **Tommy Tiger**[19] 5022 3-9-0 49 ....(b[1]) TobyAtkinson 6 —
(Stuart Williams) *chsd ldrs: u.p and lost pls 4f out: wl btn after: t.o* **6/1**

555 6 7 **Ocean's Dream Day (IRE)**[6] 5416 3-8-6 48 ....(b[1]) BradleyBosley(7) 2 —
(John Ryan) *plld hrd early: stmbld after 150yds: hld up in tch: wknd over 3f out: t.o* **25/1**

0-06 7 53 **Pani Ash**[20] 4956 3-8-7 45 .... NathanAlison(3) 8 —
(Pat Phelan) *rdn to stay in tch 1/2-way: sn wknd: wl t.o* **20/1**

0001 U **Librettela**[18] 5042 3-8-12 54 .... JordanUys(7) 1 —
(Alan Jarvis) *trckd ldrs: hit rail and uns rdr after 2f* **4/1**[2]

2m 22.95s (1.05) **Going Correction** -0.10s/f (Stan) 8 Ran SP% **112.3**
Speed ratings (Par 98): **92,90,89,83,70 64,26,—**
toteswingers:1&2:£3.30, 1&3:£10.00, 2&3:£6.10 CSF £16.93 CT £95.68 TOTE £4.10: £1.20, £1.80, £1.80; EX 26.70 Trifecta £201.80 Pool: £703.71 - 2.58 winning units..
Owner A J H **Bred** S McCann **Trained** Newmarket, Suffolk

FOCUS
A moderate apprentice handicap in which three of the jockeys were having their first ride in public. Unfortunately two of them rather bumped each other on the turn away from the stands and Librettela lost her rider. Fortunately Jordan Uys appeared none the worse. They did not appear to go that quick and the time was on the slow side, but they finished well strung out.
Sir Randolf(IRE) Official explanation: jockey said gelding suffered interference from a loose horse
T/Plt: £207.30 to a £1 stake. Pool:£57,262.95 - 201.59 winning tickets T/Qpdt: £31.70 to a £1 stake. Pool:£6,011.49 - 140.00 winning tickets JN

5630 KEMPTON (A.W) (R-H)
Thursday, September 1

OFFICIAL GOING: Standard
Wind: Fresh, half behind Weather: Fine, warm

5637 32 ONLINE CASINO CLAIMING STKS 7f (P)
5:40 (5:41) (Class 6) 2-Y-O £1,617 (£481; £240; £120) **Stalls** Low

Form RPR

3000 1 **Mr Knightley (IRE)**[13] 5233 2-9-1 68 ....(b[1]) KieranO'Neill(3) 9 81+
(Richard Hannon) *pressed ldr: led 3f out: sn kicked wl clr: kpt up to work tl eased last 100yds* **7/2**[2]

00 2 10 **Mormoran**[10] 5320 2-8-3 0 ....(p) AndreaAtzeni 8 40
(Chris Dwyer) *plld hrd early in midfield but rdn in 5th 4f out: prog and hung rt over 2f out: chsd clr wnr over 1f out: no imp* **40/1**

0540 3 1 ¾ **Emerald Smile (IRE)**[13] 5245 2-7-11 59 .... RyanPowell(5) 1 34
(J S Moore) *chsd ldng trio: rdn to chse clr wnr over 2f out and carried hd high: lost 2nd over 1f out: one pce* **7/1**[3]

3204 4 3 ½ **Nude (IRE)**[9] 5353 2-8-2 55 ....(b[1]) NickyMackay 3 25
(Sylvester Kirk) *rdn in 6th 4f out and off the pce: nvr on terms: passed wkng rivals fnl f* **12/1**

0 5 ¾ **Notnowstanley**[17] 5111 2-8-1 0 .... RachealKneller(7) 2 29
(J S Moore) *s.i.s: wl off the pce in last pair: nvr a factor: plugged past wkng rivals fnl f* **11/1**

6100 6 2 ¼ **Greatest Dancer (IRE)**[14] 5197 2-9-3 77 ....(b[1]) KierenFallon 4 33
(Jamie Osborne) *wnt lft s: sn chsd ldng pair: rdn 3f out: lost pl and wl btn over 2f out* **11/10**[1]

0 7 ¾ **King Fong**[152] 1095 2-8-7 0 .... JackMitchell 7 21
(John Ryan) *a in rr: rdn and struggling in 7th 4f out: nvr a factor* **16/1**

00P0 8 1 ¾ **Bertorella (IRE)**[10] 5325 2-8-2 54 ....(b) MartinLane 6 11
(Ralph Beckett) *led to 3f out: wknd qckly* **11/1**

50 9 1 ½ **Bridgets Call**[21] 4961 2-8-2 0 .... KellyHarrison 5 7
(Des Donovan) *bmpd s: a in last pair: wl bhd fnl 3f* **25/1**

1m 25.66s (-0.34) **Going Correction** -0.125s/f (Stan) 9 Ran SP% **118.9**
Speed ratings (Par 93): **96,84,82,78,77 75,74,72,70**
toteswingers: 1&2 £26.70, 1&3 £4.70, 2&3 £36.60 CSF £126.41 TOTE £2.50: £1.02, £13.90, £3.70; EX 155.60.
Owner P A Deal **Bred** Miss Deirdre Cogan **Trained** East Everleigh, Wilts

FOCUS
An uncompetitive claimer that took less winning than seemed likely with the market leader disappointing. The runner-up will help put this form in perspective in time. The gallop was an ordinary one and the winner raced close to the inside rail in the straight. The winner was a big improver on this Polytrack debut.

NOTEBOOK
Mr Knightley(IRE), dropped in grade and fitted with blinkers for this all-weather debut, raced with the choke out but took advantage of a couple of below-par performances from his main rivals to win with plenty in hand. He should be able to win again in this company. (op 4-1)
Mormoran, who had shown precious little in two maiden starts, doesn't look entirely straightforward (fitted with stalls blanket and failed to settle) but turned in her best effort in this uncompetitive event. She has a bit of size about her and may do better in low-grade handicaps. (op 33-1)
Emerald Smile(IRE), who had shown a modicum of ability over sprint distances on turf, seemed beaten through lack of ability rather than lack of stamina on her first run over this trip. Her best chance of success is likely to be in modest handicaps. (op 8-1 tchd 9-1)
Nude(IRE) has had plenty of chances and again had her limitations exposed returned to Polytrack in first-time blinkers. She reportedly lost a left-hind shoe. Official explanation: vet said filly lost left-hind shoe
Greatest Dancer(IRE), who had a good chance at the weights, was well backed but was again below the form of her Fibresand win returned to Polytrack with the blinkers on for the first time. She has plenty to prove at present. (tchd 6-5 and 5-4 in places)

5638 32 FOR SLOTS NOVICE AUCTION STKS 7f (P)
6:10 (6:11) (Class 5) 2-Y-O £2,264 (£673; £336; £168) Stalls Low

Form RPR
012 **1** **Jubilance (IRE)**[34] 4508 2-9-0 84 .... WilliamBuick 1 87+
(Jeremy Noseda) *trckd ldr: chal 2f out: disp ld over 1f out: drvn to ld narrowly last 50yds* **1/1**[1]
3341 **2** *hd* **Shere Khan**[29] 4661 2-8-11 82 .... KieranO'Neill(3) 2 85
(Richard Hannon) *trckd ldng pair: shkn up over 2f out: clsd to dispute ld over 1f out: kpt on wl: narrowly hdd last 50yds* **4/1**[3]
012 **3** *5* **Hamble**[12] 5280 2-8-11 85 .... KierenFallon 3 69
(William Haggas) *led at gd pce: drvn and hdd over 1f out: fdd* **13/8**[2]
50 **4** *29* **Fen Flyer**[76] 3132 2-8-9 0 ....(p) AndreaAtzeni 4 —
(Chris Dwyer) *awkward s: in tch: rdn and wknd 3f out: t.o* **100/1**
1m 25.44s (-0.56) **Going Correction** -0.125s/f (Stan) 4 Ran SP% **109.1**
Speed ratings (Par 95): **98,97,92,58**
CSF £5.39 TOTE £2.30; EX 5.30.
Owner Miss Yvonne Jacques **Bred** Old Carhue & Graeng Bloodstock **Trained** Newmarket, Suffolk

FOCUS
Only four runners but a useful novice event, despite the below-par showing of the second favourite. The gallop was an ordinary one and the winner raced centre-to-far-side in the straight.

NOTEBOOK
Jubilance(IRE) ◆ is a useful and steadily progressive sort who had the run of the race and showed a good attitude on this all-weather debut to confirm himself fully effective on Polytrack. He again showed his effectiveness in a tactical event and remains the type to win more races. (op 11-10 tchd 11-8 in places)
Shere Khan's record is one of improvement and this recent course winner posted his best effort on this first run over 7f to make the useful market leader fight all the way to the line. It'll be a surprise if he isn't able to win again. (op 7-2 tchd 9-2)
Hamble proved disappointing, especially as he was allowed to do his own thing in front. However he's a scopey sort who, with hindsight, may not really have been best suited by a tactical race over this trip and he'll be well worth another try on this surface granted a more suitable stamina test. (tchd 6-4 and 7-4)
Fen Flyer had a very stiff task on these terms and was predictably outclassed.

5639 32 FOR BLACKJACK MEDIAN AUCTION MAIDEN STKS 1m (P)
6:40 (6:43) (Class 6) 3-5-Y-O £1,617 (£481; £240; £120) Stalls Low

Form RPR
0 **1** **Princess Icicle**[29] 4663 3-8-10 0 .... JohnFahy(3) 4 75
(Jo Crowley) *sn pressed ldr: rdn to ld narrowly wl over 1f out: hld on wl fnl f* **50/1**
6433 **2** *hd* **Tanmawy (IRE)**[13] 5247 3-9-4 70 .... RichardHills 7 80
(Ed Dunlop) *led: hrd pressed over 2f out: narrowly hdd wl over 1f out and clr of rest: upsides after but leaning lft into wnr: nt qckn nr fin* **11/8**[1]
4 **3** *12* **Love Your Looks**[13] 5241 3-8-13 0 .... TonyCulhane 5 47+
(Mike Murphy) *s.i.s: t.k.h: hld up in 11th: stl there over 2f out: pushed along and gd prog to take remote 3rd over 1f out: encouraging effrt* **25/1**
0 **4** *5* **Conesuala**[104] 2258 4-9-1 0 .... MatthewDavies(3) 6 36
(Alan Jarvis) *wl in rr: outpcd fr 3f out: pushed along and kpt on to take remote 4th last stride* **40/1**
40 **5** *nse* **Long Live Love (USA)**[64] 3513 3-9-4 0 .... NeilCallan 3 41
(Mark Johnston) *chsd ldng pair: hrd rdn and lft bhd over 2f out: lost remote 3rd over 1f out* **10/1**
5-0 **6** *¾* **Cyber Star**[115] 1950 3-8-13 0 .... PatCosgrave 13 34
(James Fanshawe) *chsd ldrs: wl outpcd and hanging wl over 2f out: no ch after* **7/1**[2]
25-4 **7** *3 ¾* **Sinchiroka (FR)**[20] 4991 5-9-9 65 .... JamieGoldstein 11 30
(Ralph Smith) *racd wd in midfield: dropped to rr bnd 3f out: sn no ch* **16/1**
6-0 **8** *¾* **Queen's Silk**[31] 4617 3-8-13 0 .... WilliamCarson 8 24
(Brett Johnson) *t.k.h: trckd ldrs: outpcd wl over 2f out: shuffled along and steadily fdd* **14/1**
5205 **9** *9* **Brinmore**[24] 4849 3-8-13 72 .... ShaneKelly 9 —
(William Knight) *cl up: wl outpcd fr 3f out: wknd: t.o* **15/2**[3]
U6 **10** *2 ¾* **Kantata**[44] 4186 3-8-8 0 ....(t) MatthewCosham(5) 2 —
(James Toller) *unruly in stalls: in tch: rdn towards rr fr 1/2-way: wknd over 2f out: t.o* **100/1**
/ **11** *4 ½* **Balesteem** 4-9-9 0 .... JamesDoyle 1 —
(Clifford Lines) *in tch in midfield: wknd 3f out: eased 2f out: t.o* **20/1**
12 *3 ¾* **Young Dr Jekyll** 3-9-4 0 .... DaneO'Neill 10 —
(Henry Candy) *v s.i.s: rn green in last: t.o* **17/2**
3440 **13** *6* **Major Domo (FR)**[40] 4337 3-9-4 66 .... KierenFallon 12 —
(Harry Dunlop) *racd wd in last pair and a detached: pushed along and no prog over 2f out: t.o* **12/1**
1m 38.8s (-1.00) **Going Correction** -0.125s/f (Stan)
WFA 3 from 4yo+ 5lb 13 Ran SP% **120.2**
Speed ratings (Par 101): **100,99,87,82,82 82,78,77,68,65 61,57,51**
toteswingers: 1&2 £38.40, 1&3 £107.20, 2&3 £9.00 CSF £117.10 TOTE £51.20: £14.40, £1.20, £5.10; EX 280.60.
Owner Kilstone Limited **Bred** Hedsor Stud **Trained** Whitcombe, Dorset

FOCUS
No strength at all to this ordinary maiden in which the first two, who came down the centre, pulled a long way clear. The gallop was no more than fair and the runner-up looks the best guide to the form, rated around his Wolverhampton run.
Brinmore Official explanation: trainer said filly finished distressed
Major Domo(FR) Official explanation: jockey said gelding did not feel right

5640 32 FOR POKER H'CAP 6f (P)
7:10 (7:10) (Class 5) (0-70,70) 3-Y-O+ £2,264 (£673; £336; £168) Stalls Low

Form RPR
0-00 **1** **Aldermoor (USA)**[99] 2398 5-9-3 66 .... WilliamCarson 9 76+
(Stuart Williams) *towards rr on outer: prog over 2f out: rdn to chse ldr over 1f out: clsd to ld jst ins fnl f: edgd lft: hld on* **5/2**[1]
6302 **2** *nk* **Tislaam (IRE)**[8] 5387 4-9-3 66 ....(p) RobertWinston 6 75
(Alan McCabe) *hld up in 10th: prog on outer 2f out: chsd wnr ins fnl f: carried sltly lft as tried to chal: a jst hld* **7/2**[2]
3000 **3** *1 ¾* **Dvinsky (USA)**[8] 5387 10-9-3 66 ....(b) ShaneKelly 1 69
(Michael Squance) *drvn to ld: clr after 2f: hdd and one pce jst ins fnl f* **28/1**
2-43 **4** *1 ¼* **Daffydowndilly**[8] 5387 3-9-4 69 .... JimmyFortune 10 68
(Hughie Morrison) *chsd ldr to over 2f out: kpt on same pce fr over 1f out* **6/1**[3]
2464 **5** *½* **Nezami (IRE)**[14] 5201 6-9-7 70 .... NeilCallan 2 68
(John Akehurst) *chsd ldrs: rdn and nt qckn over 2f out: kpt on same pce fnl f* **13/2**
2100 **6** *½* **My Own Way Home**[17] 5119 3-9-2 67 .... CathyGannon 7 63
(Des Donovan) *chsd ldrs: nt qckn over 2f out and lost pl: kpt on again fnl f* **20/1**
1- **7** *hd* **Torres Del Paine**[274] 7655 4-8-12 64 .... SeanLevey(3) 4 60
(Jimmy Fox) *s.s: hld up in last: shkn up over 2f out: stl last over 1f out: styd on fnl f* **15/2**
0400 **8** *nk* **Perlachy**[57] 3721 7-9-0 63 ....(v) LukeMorris 5 58
(Ronald Harris) *wl in rr: prog on inner 2f out: effrt petered out fnl f* **40/1**
3524 **9** *¾* **Sherjawy (IRE)**[98] 2422 7-9-5 68 .... SamHitchcott 8 60
(Zoe Davison) *t.k.h: hld up towards rr: rdn and nt qckn over 2f out: sn btn* **28/1**
1604 **10** *1 ¼* **Danzoe (IRE)**[8] 5387 4-9-6 69 .... JamesDoyle 12 57
(Christine Dunnett) *chsd ldrs: rdn 1/2-way: wknd 2f out* **16/1**
3050 **11** *8* **Imjin River (IRE)**[8] 5387 4-9-1 64 ....(b) KierenFallon 3 27
(Mark H Tompkins) *prom: chsd ldr wl over 2f out to over 1f out: wknd rapidly and eased* **14/1**
1m 12.21s (-0.89) **Going Correction** -0.125s/f (Stan)
WFA 3 from 4yo+ 2lb 11 Ran SP% **116.8**
Speed ratings (Par 103): **100,99,97,95,94 94,94,93,92,90 80**
toteswingers: 1&2 £3.40, 1&3 £29.00, 2&3 £13.60 CSF £10.33 CT £198.19 TOTE £2.10: £1.10, £2.10, £6.50; EX 19.00.
Owner Phil & Frances Kendall **Bred** Gulf Coast Farms LLC **Trained** Newmarket, Suffolk
■ Stewards' Enquiry : William Carson two-day ban: careless riding (Sep 15-16)

FOCUS
Exposed performers in a modest handicap. The gallop was sound and the winner came down the centre in the straight. The winner returned to form after plummeting in the weights.
Imjin River(IRE) Official explanation: jockey said gelding stopped quickly

5641 32 FOR BINGO H'CAP 1m 4f (P)
7:40 (7:40) (Class 4) (0-85,85) 3-Y-O £4,075 (£1,212; £606; £303) Stalls Centre

Form RPR
-212 **1** **A Boy Named Suzi**[21] 4966 3-8-12 76 .... LukeMorris 5 87
(James Eustace) *hld up disputing 6th: pushed along over 3f out: rdn and effrt over 2f out: c wd up st and styd on wl to ld last 75yds* **7/1**[3]
531 **2** *1* **Qahriman**[30] 4641 3-9-7 85 .... KierenFallon 2 94
(Luca Cumani) *trckd ldng pair: wnt 2nd 5f out: clsd to ld wl over 1f out: styd on but hdd and outpcd last 75yds* **5/2**[1]
0-50 **3** *¾* **Ryton Runner (IRE)**[27] 4763 3-8-9 73 .... WilliamBuick 3 81
(John Gosden) *hld up disputing 4th: rdn 4f out: cl up but flat out over 2f out: styd on after: nvr quite able to chal* **7/1**[3]
11 **4** *hd* **Planetoid (IRE)**[21] 4966 3-9-6 84 .... TedDurcan 7 92
(David Lanigan) *hld up disputing 6th: prog 4f out: clsd on ldrs over 2f out: rdn to chal over 1f out: nt qckn and readily hld fnl f* **5/2**[1]
0441 **5** *¾* **Twice Bitten**[22] 4905 3-8-12 81 .... MatthewCosham(5) 6 88
(James Toller) *t.k.h: pressed ldr: led over 5f out and upped the pce: shkn up and hdd wl over 1f out and rdr in a tangle: one pce fnl f* **9/2**[2]
3106 **6** *13* **Aldedash (USA)**[19] 5049 3-8-1 72 .... CharlesEddery(7) 8 58
(Sir Henry Cecil) *stdd s: hld up in last: shkn up 3f out: no prog and sn bhd* **14/1**
16 **7** *6* **Val O'Hara (IRE)**[39] 4355 3-9-3 81 .... JimCrowley 4 57
(Peter Winkworth) *hld up disputing 4th: rdn wl over 4f out: wknd over 2f out* **16/1**
400 **8** *3 ½* **Suzi's A Class Act**[13] 5242 3-8-7 71 .... JackMitchell 1 42
(James Eustace) *led to over 5f out: sn lost pl: wknd over 2f out: eased* **25/1**
2m 31.69s (-2.81) **Going Correction** -0.125s/f (Stan) 8 Ran SP% **116.7**
Speed ratings (Par 103): **104,103,102,102,102 93,89,87**
toteswingers: 1&2 £2.60, 1&3 £8.50, 2&3 £7.10 CSF £25.46 CT £129.58 TOTE £8.00: £2.30, £1.50, £1.80; EX 27.10.
Owner Greenstead Hall Racing Ltd **Bred** Greenstead Hall Racing **Trained** Newmarket, Suffolk

FOCUS
Several recent winners in a useful handicap. The gallop to the home straight was no more than fair and the winner edged from the centre towards the stands rail late on.
Planetoid(IRE) Official explanation: jockey said colt hung right

5642 32 FOR BETTING H'CAP (DIV I) 1m 3f (P)
8:10 (8:10) (Class 6) (0-55,55) 3-Y-O+ £1,293 (£385; £192; £96) Stalls Low

Form RPR
032 **1** **Professor John (IRE)**[16] 5135 4-9-7 55 ....(v) JamesDoyle 6 67+
(Ian Wood) *hld up in midfield: smooth prog 3f out: cruised through to ld jst over 1f out: shkn up and fnd enough to assert fnl f* **7/2**[1]
6645 **2** *1* **The Absent Mare**[14] 2379 3-8-4 46 .... MartinLane 1 56
(Robin Dickin) *hld up towards rr: smooth prog on inner 3f out: led 2f out: rdn and hdd jst over 1f out: styd on wl but readily hld* **20/1**
3601 **3** *4 ½* **Prince Blue**[24] 4847 4-9-5 53 .... SamHitchcott 7 55
(John E Long) *trckd ldr 2f: styd prom: rdn to chal 2f out: outpcd sn after: one pce* **7/1**
0063 **4** *hd* **Appyjack**[9] 5352 3-8-6 48 .... LukeMorris 2 50
(Tony Carroll) *sn settled to trck ldrs: rdn and lost pl on outer 3f out: outpcd sn after: kpt on fnl f to press for 3rd nr fin* **6/1**
4151 **5** *4 ½* **Newby Lodge (IRE)**[1] 5636 3-8-6 55 .... ThomasBrown(7) 11 48
(Alan Bailey) *trckd ldr after 2f: rdn to ld over 3f out: hdd 2f out: wknd* **11/2**[3]
333/ **6** *hd* **Salybia Bay**[147] 7392 5-9-7 55 .... DaneO'Neill 4 48
(Andy Turnell) *hld up in rr: rdn and nt qckn wl over 2f out and sn wl outpcd: plugged on fr over 1f out* **14/1**

604/ **7** 4 ½ **Ray Diamond**[290] 120 6-8-12 **46** oh1........................ FrankieMcDonald 9 31
(Michael Madgwick) *hld up in last trio: shkn up 1/2-way: struggling 4f out: nvr on terms* **25/1**

005 **8** 1 **Price Of Retrieval**[49] 4023 4-9-2 **50**............................ JimmyFortune 10 33
(Peter Chapple-Hyam) *hld up in last pair: gng bttr than sme 4f out: outpcd 3f out: drvn and no hdwy 2f out* **5/1**[2]

0003 **9** 1 ¾ **Yossi (IRE)**[9] 5357 7-9-0 **48**..(b) KellyHarrison 3 28
(Richard Guest) *led at decent pce: hdd and rdn over 3f out: wknd 2f out* **8/1**

0510 **10** 29 **Miskin Diamond (IRE)**[8] 5380 3-8-6 **48**......................... CathyGannon 8 —
(Bryn Palling) *prom: pushed along 5f out: wknd qckly over 3f out: t.o* **16/1**

0-00 **11** *dist* **Bonamassa**[71] 3281 4-8-12 **46** oh1.....................................(p) TomQueally 5 —
(Michael Attwater) *in tch on outer: rdn and wknd over 4f out: wl t.o fnl 2f and virtually p.u* **66/1**

2m 20.55s (-1.35) **Going Correction** -0.125s/f (Stan)
WFA 3 from 4yo+ 8lb **11** Ran SP% **114.8**
Speed ratings (Par 101): **99,98,95,94,91 91,88,87,86,65** —
toteswingers: 1&2 £36.90, 1&3 £3.20, 2&3 £35.60 CSF £77.37 CT £465.58 TOTE £4.10: £1.60, £7.20, £3.70; EX 55.30.
Owner Paddy Barrett **Bred** Manfred Wurtenberger **Trained** Upper Lambourn, Berks

FOCUS
Division one of a moderate handicap. A reasonable pace saw those held up come to the fore late on and the winner and second, who pulled clear, raced in the centre. It was faster than division II and the winner is rated close to his winter Polytrack form.
Prince Blue Official explanation: jockey said gelding hung left
Miskin Diamond(IRE) Official explanation: jockey said filly had no more to give

5643 32 FOR RUMMY H'CAP (DIV II) 1m 3f (P)
8:40 (8:41) (Class 6) (0-55,55) 3-Y-0+ **£1,293** (£385; £192; £96) **Stalls** Low

Form RPR

006- **1** **Single Lady**[286] 7516 4-8-13 **47**.................................... JamieSpencer 11 55+
(Emmet Michael Butterly, Ire) *hld up in midfield: shkn up and prog to chse ldng pair 2f: hrd rdn and r.o to ld last 150yds: sn clr* **7/4**[1]

3-36 **2** 1 ½ **Zelos Diktator**[24] 4847 5-9-5 **53**.....................................(p) GeorgeBaker 2 58
(Gary Moore) *trckd ldng pair: wnt 2nd over 3f out: rdn to ld narrowly over 2f out: hdd and outpcd last 150yds* **11/2**[3]

4035 **3** 1 ¼ **Toballa**[9] 5357 6-8-9 **46**..(t) AdamBeschizza(3) 4 49
(Clifford Lines) *dwlt: sn prom: effrt over 3f out: hrd rdn to chal and upsides over 2f out: stl there 1f out: one pce* **10/1**

5064 **4** 3 ¾ **Prince Of Thebes (IRE)**[19] 5042 10-9-7 **55**................... TomQueally 10 51
(Michael Attwater) *dwlt: hld up in last pair: pushed along over 3f out: prog to chse ldrs over 1f out: nt qckn and outpcd after* **15/2**

0000 **5** 3 **Laffraaj (IRE)**[14] 5210 3-8-2 **47**.......................................(v) JohnFahy(3) 9 38
(Pat Eddery) *led 1f: chsd ldr: led again over 3f out: hdd over 2f out: hanging and carried hd high: immediately btn* **12/1**

4000 **6** 1 **Burnbrake**[62] 3599 6-9-4 **52**...(b) JamesMillman 1 41
(Les Hall) *hld up in last pair: nvr on terms: shkn up and no prog over 2f out: kpt on after* **12/1**

06 **7** ½ **Wodian (IRE)**[22] 4927 3-8-8 **50**..(t) TedDurcan 3 38
(David Lanigan) *trckd ldrs: rdn and sing to lose pl whn squeezed out over 2f out: wknd* **9/2**[2]

4463 **8** 3 ¼ **Rigid**[25] 4829 4-8-12 **46** oh1.. DavidProbert 6 28
(Tony Carroll) *trckd ldrs: cl enough 3f out: rdn and nt qckn over 2f out: wknd* **10/1**

5006 **9** 11 **Dunaskin (IRE)**[14] 5209 11-8-12 **49**..........................(b) RobertLButler(3) 8 11
(Richard Guest) *led after 1f: hdd & wknd over 3f out* **25/1**

000 **10** 10 **Lady Valtas**[24] 4861 3-8-4 **46** oh1.................................... AndreaAtzeni 5 —
(Robert Eddery) *reminders after 2f and at several stages: a in rr: wknd 3f out: t.o* **66/1**

2m 21.44s (-0.46) **Going Correction** -0.125s/f (Stan)
WFA 3 from 4yo+ 8lb **10** Ran SP% **120.6**
Speed ratings (Par 101): **96,94,94,91,89 88,88,85,77,70**
toteswingers: 1&2 £2.40, 1&3 £10.60, 2&3 £14.60 CSF £11.90 CT £78.39 TOTE £2.70: £1.20, £2.50, £3.90; EX 16.30.
Owner Peader Browne **Bred** Miss Alison Jones **Trained** Letterkenny, Co Donegal
■ Stewards' Enquiry : Jamie Spencer two-day ban: careless riding (Sep 15-16)

FOCUS
Another moderate handicap in which the gallop was soon reasonable. The time was 0.89sec slower than division I. The winner came down the centre in the straight and the first three pulled clear. The form is rated around the second and third.
Lady Valtas Official explanation: jockey said filly never travelled

5644 KEMPTON FOR OUTDOOR EVENTS H'CAP 6f (P)
9:10 (9:12) (Class 6) (0-65,65) 3-Y-O **£1,617** (£481; £240; £120) **Stalls** Low

Form RPR

2132 **1** **Golden Compass**[17] 5120 3-8-12 **56**............................ WilliamCarson 5 62+
(Giles Bravery) *trckd ldr: led 2f out: rdn and styd on fr over 1f out: in command fnl f* **9/4**[1]

-130 **2** 1 ¼ **Magic Cross**[76] 3136 3-9-4 **65**.................................. AdamBeschizza(3) 9 67
(Philip McBride) *hld up in last trio: prog on inner over 2f out: drvn to chse wnr over 1f out: kpt on but no imp* **15/2**

3065 **3** *nse* **Saucy Buck (IRE)**[50] 3983 3-9-5 **63**.............................. JamieGoldstein 4 65
(Ralph Smith) *chsd ldrs: pushed along 1/2-way: prog u.p 2f out: tk 3rd 1f out: kpt on but no imp* **8/1**

0660 **4** 1 **Eternal Youth (IRE)**[9] 5345 3-9-2 **60**................................(v) LukeMorris 7 59
(Ronald Harris) *s.s and rousted along early in last: rdn and prog on inner over 2f out: kpt on same pce to take 4th nr fin* **20/1**

0000 **5** *nk* **Avalon Bay**[22] 4911 3-8-11 **58**.......................................(p) SeanLevey(3) 6 56
(Pat Eddery) *wnt lft s: mostly in last trio: rdn and struggling over 2f out: prog over 1f out and threatened briefly: one pce ins fnl f* **14/1**

0306 **6** ¾ **Whoateallthepius (IRE)**[10] 5326 3-9-7 **65**......................(p) ShaneKelly 3 60
(Dean Ivory) *led to 2f out: steadily fdd over 1f out* **7/1**[3]

60 **7** 2 ¾ **Osgoodisgood**[166] 909 3-8-7 **51** oh4.............................(t) SaleemGolam 2 37
(Stuart Williams) *trckd ldrs: disp cl 3rd 1/2-way: rdn over 2f out: wknd over 1f out* **8/1**

022 **8** 5 **Comrade Bond**[17] 5121 3-9-2 **60**.. KierenFallon 10 30
(Mark H Tompkins) *prom: drvn over 2f out: wknd qckly over 1f out* **3/1**[2]

0400 **9** 5 **Dark Pegasus**[21] 4950 3-8-5 **52** oh4 ow1.......................... KierenFox(3) 8 —
(Karen George) *racd wd: rdn in rr after 2f: bhd fnl 2f* **50/1**

1m 12.35s (-0.75) **Going Correction** -0.125s/f (Stan) **9** Ran SP% **115.6**
Speed ratings (Par 99): **100,98,98,96,96 95,91,85,78**
toteswingers: 1&2 £4.30, 1&3 £7.20, 2&3 £12.70 CSF £19.94 CT £116.05 TOTE £4.40: £1.50, £2.40, £2.60; EX 20.70.
Owner J P Carrington **Bred** Mrs F Bravery **Trained** Cowlinge, Suffolk

FOCUS
Not too many in-form sorts in this modest handicap and one that took less winning than seemed likely with the second favourite disappointing. It's doubtful the winner had to improve on his recent turf form. The gallop was sound and the winner was another to race in the centre in the straight.
T/Plt: £71.60 to a £1 stake. Pool: £54,175.17. 552.34 winning tickets. T/Qpdt: £6.40 to a £1 stake. Pool: £8,694.26. 996.61 winning tickets. JN

5485 REDCAR (L-H)
Thursday, September 1

OFFICIAL GOING: Good (good to soft in places; 8.0)
Wind: Light, across Weather: Overcast

5645 WIN A VIP DAY @ REDCARRACING.CO.UK NURSERY 7f
2:00 (2:01) (Class 5) (0-75,75) 2-Y-O **£2,102** (£625; £312; £156) **Stalls** High

Form RPR

1 **1** **Nemushka**[60] 3656 2-9-3 **71**... PaulHanagan 7 77+
(Richard Fahey) *s.i.s towards rr: hdwy 1/2-way: chal over 2f out: sn edgd lft and led wl over 1f out: rdn and hung bdly lft to far rail over 1f out: kpt on* **2/1**[1]

1200 **2** 1 **Indepub**[15] 5184 2-9-2 **75**...(p) JulieBurke(5) 4 76
(Kevin Ryan) *trckd ldrs: hdwy and n.m.r wl over 1f out: sn rdn: styd on ins fnl f: nt rch wnr* **13/2**[3]

640 **3** *nk* **Karma Chameleon**[38] 4390 2-8-2 **56**............................ AndrewMullen 8 57
(Richard Guest) *trckd ldrs: hdwy 1/2 way: rdn along 2f out: n.m.r and swtchd lft over 1f out: kpt on ins fnl f* **16/1**

2204 **4** *nse* **Joshua The First**[15] 5161 2-9-2 **70**................................ PJMcDonald 6 70
(Keith Dalgleish) *prom: effrt over 2f out: rdn and edgd rt over 1f out: drvn and hung lft ins fnl f: kpt on towards fin* **8/1**

5410 **5** 1 **Lolita Lebron (IRE)**[12] 5287 2-8-10 **67**.................. DeclanCannon(3) 11 67
(Lawrence Mullaney) *led: rdn along over 2f out: hdd and drvn wl over 1f out: sn edgd lft: carried lft and hmpd appr fnl f: one pce after* **14/1**

004 **6** 5 **Chevanah (IRE)**[33] 4538 2-8-12 **66**..................................... TomEaves 5 51
(Ann Duffield) *in rr: effrt and sme hdwy 2f out: nvr a factor* **20/1**

6004 **7** 2 ¾ **Arrowroot**[23] 4892 2-7-7 **52** oh2.................................... NeilFarley(5) 10 30
(Tim Easterby) *chsd ldrs: rdn along over 3f out: sn wknd* **12/1**

3026 **8** 2 ¾ **Al Jemailiya (IRE)**[43] 4194 2-8-13 **67**............................ TonyHamilton 1 38
(Kevin Ryan) *wnt rt s: prom: cl up after 2f: rdn along over 3f out and grad wknd* **17/2**

500 **9** ¾ **Gabrial's Princess (IRE)**[12] 5269 2-8-2 **56**............. SilvestreDeSousa 2 25
(Bryan Smart) *bmpd s and in rr: rdn along 1/2-way: sn bhd* **9/2**[2]

4460 **10** *nk* **Pearl Catcher (IRE)**[21] 4943 2-8-0 **54**......................... DuranFentiman 3 22
(Tim Easterby) *in tch on outer: rdn along over 3f out: sn wknd* **33/1**

1m 25.74s (1.24) **Going Correction** -0.075s/f (Good) **10** Ran SP% **114.4**
Speed ratings (Par 95): **89,87,87,87,86 80,77,74,73,73**
toteswingers: 1&2 £3.40, 1&3 £9.70, 2&3 £11.20 CSF £14.67 CT £160.45 TOTE £2.50: £1.40, £2.10, £4.40; EX 12.20.
Owner The G-Guck Group **Bred** Avenue Farm Stud **Trained** Musley Bank, N Yorks

FOCUS
The ground had dried out and was riding just on the dead side.

NOTEBOOK
Nemushka, who defeated Joshua The First a length and a half when making a winning debut at Ayr two months earlier, met that rival on 6lb worse terms. After moving on to the heels of the leader she hung left then went badly left carrying the pacesetter to the far rail. Hopefully it was just inexperience as she looks to have a fair bit more ability than her mark of just 71 here. (op 6-4)
Indepub, 1lb higher than when runner-up over 6f at Pontefract two outings ago, wore first-time cheekpieces. She stayed on to close the errant winner down at the line and clearly appreciated the step up to seven. (op 7-1 tchd 6-1)
Karma Chameleon, who showed little in three qualifying starts, finished best of all and will be suited by a step up to a mile. (op 14-1 tchd 12-1)
Joshua The First, runner-up five times including when chasing home the winner at Ayr, again ran without the visor. He basically does little wrong but that first win is proving highly elusive.
Lolita Lebron(IRE), with her 3rd trainer already, took them along but was carried badly left by the winner and then hampered by her. She still finished clear of the remainder. (op 16-1)
Gabrial's Princess(IRE) was well supported to make a winning nursery debut, but after a slow start she never went a yard. Official explanation: jockey said filly never travelled (op 7-1)

5646 RACING UK ON CHANNEL 432 MAIDEN AUCTION STKS 5f
2:30 (2:33) (Class 6) 2-Y-O **£1,704** (£503; £251) **Stalls** High

Form RPR

3202 **1** **Rougini (IRE)**[17] 5105 2-8-6 66......................................(v) AndrewElliott 3 64
(Mrs K Burke) *cl up: led 1/2-way: rdn wl over 1f out: drvn and edgd lft ins fnl f: kpt on* **7/2**[3]

4230 **2** ¾ **One Kool Dude**[40] 4343 2-8-13 71...................................... PaulHanagan 8 68
(Richard Fahey) *sn chsng ldng pair: rdn along 1/2-way: edgd lft and drvn wl over 1f out: drvn to chal ins fnl f: hld whn n.m.r nr fin* **9/4**[1]

0 **3** *nk* **Sir Windsorlot (IRE)**[22] 4899 2-8-11 0............................. PBBeggy 7 65
(John Quinn) *dwlt: sn in tch: hdwy to chse ldrs 1/2-way: rdn wl over 1f out: kpt on ins fnl f* **10/1**

4 1 **Annie Beach (IRE)** 2-8-4 0... LeeNewman 6 55
(David Barron) *led: hdd 1/2-way and sn pushed along: rdn over 1f out: green and edgd lft ent fnl f: one pce* **5/2**[2]

5 2 ½ **Wood Nymph (IRE)** 2-8-8 0.. DavidAllan 4 50
(Tim Easterby) *towards rr: hdwy on wd outside 1/2-way: rdn to chse ldrs wl over 1f out: sn one pce* **8/1**

6 ½ **Taffe** 2-9-1 0.. FrederikTylicki 1 55
(James Given) *a towards rr* **20/1**

400 **7** 3 **Indyend**[8] 5367 2-8-4 0.. DuranFentiman 5 33
(Tim Easterby) *in tch: rdn along 1/2-way: sn outpcd* **33/1**

0430 **8** *nk* **Koolgreycat (IRE)**[16] 5147 2-8-6 62.......................... SilvestreDeSousa 2 34
(Noel Wilson) *broke wl: sn lost pl and rdn along: bhd fnl 2f* **14/1**

59.18 secs (0.58) **Going Correction** -0.075s/f (Good) **8** Ran SP% **116.1**
Speed ratings (Par 93): **92,90,90,88,84 83,79,78**
toteswingers: 1&2 £2.20, 1&3 £5.80, 2&3 £5.90 CSF £12.04 TOTE £4.70: £1.20, £1.10, £3.20; EX 12.30.
Owner McKeown & Wotherspoon **Bred** John Graham **Trained** Middleham Moor, North Yorks

FOCUS
A weak maiden auction race and the first two home had already run 14 times between them.

NOTEBOOK
Rougini(IRE), visored for the first time when runner-up in a claiming race at Thirsk, had 3lb in hand of the runner-up on official figures. She is all speed and in the end did just enough despite a tendency to edge left. A return to claiming company is on the cards. (op 11-4)
One Kool Dude, in the frame on his first seven starts, could not make any impression from a mark of 71 on his nursery debut. He did nothing wrong but was held when slightly hampered near the line and that initial success is proving highly elusive. (tchd 2-1)

Sir Windsorlot(IRE), a half-brother to three winners, gave plenty of problems at the stalls. After missing a beat he stuck on strongly. It is to be hoped his temperament does not get the better of him. (op 9-1 tchd 8-1)
Annie Beach(IRE), a neat, well made newcomer, was a cheap buy. A half-sister to three winners, she matched strides with the winner until tiring late on. She had clearly been showing something at home and should improve and find a similar event. (op 7-2)
Wood Nymph(IRE), a 10,000gns purchase, is a half-sister to three winners. After a tardy start all she wanted to do was hang left. She has plenty to learn. (op 12-1 tchd 16-1)
Taffe, a 12,000gns purchase, was hopelessly outpaced. She appeared very late on the scene and can do better given a much stiffer test. (op 16-1)
Koolgreycat(IRE) Official explanation: jockey said filly had no more to give

5647 ROY WELSH BIRTHDAY H'CAP 6f
3:05 (3:05) (Class 5) (0-75,75) 3-Y-0+ **£2,102** (£625; £312; £156) **Stalls** High

Form RPR
0146 **1** **Toby Tyler**[6] 5434 5-9-5 **73**.....(v) PJMcDonald 7 80
(Paul Midgley) *towards rr: hdwy 1/2-way: chsd ldrs over 1f out: sn rdn and styd on to ld nr fin* **9/2**[2]
5036 **2** *nk* **Ingleby Arch (USA)**[3] 5554 8-8-7 **66**..... LMcNiff(5) 3 72
(David Barron) *towards rr: hdwy 1/2-way: rdn over 1f out: styd on ins fnl f: ev ch tl drvn and nt qckn nr fin* **4/1**[1]
2010 **3** *hd* **Sea Salt**[10] 5313 8-8-9 **68**..... ShaneBKelly(5) 6 73
(Ron Barr) *chsd ldng pair: edgd lft to far rail 1/2-way: rdn and hdwy to ld ent fnl f: drvn: nt qckn and hdd nr fin* **10/1**
6403 **4** *nk* **Foreign Rhythm (IRE)**[6] 5442 6-8-6 **63** ow1..... DaleSwift(3) 9 67
(Ron Barr) *towards rr: rdn along 1/2-way: hdwy wl over 1f out: styd on ins fnl f: nrst fin* **12/1**
4210 **5** *1 1/2* **Nine Before Ten (IRE)**[12] 5268 3-9-5 **75**.....(t) RobbieFitzpatrick 2 75+
(Richard Guest) *chsd clr ldr: cl up 2f out: sn rdn and ev ch tl drvn and one pce ins fnl f* **8/1**
0364 **6** *3/4* **Captain Scooby**[7] 5400 5-8-11 **65**.....(v) SilvestreDeSousa 4 62
(Richard Whitaker) *dwlt and in rr: hdwy 2f out: sn rdn and kpt on ins fnl f: nt rch ldrs* **4/1**[1]
0030 **7** *1 1/4* **Haadeeth**[18] 5083 4-8-11 **65**.....(b) PaulHanagan 1 58
(Richard Fahey) *led and sn clr: jnd 2f out: sn rdn: hdd & wknd ent fnl f* **13/2**[3]
0461 **8** *1 1/4* **Ryedane (IRE)**[10] 5309 9-8-7 **66** 6ex.....(b) AdamCarter(5) 10 55
(Tim Easterby) *dwlt: a in rr* **15/2**
0000 **9** *1* **Thrust Control (IRE)**[6] 5455 4-9-7 **75**..... PatrickMathers 5 61
(Tracy Waggott) *a in rr* **40/1**

1m 11.35s (-0.45) **Going Correction** -0.075s/f (Good)
WFA 3 from 4yo+ 2lb **9** Ran SP% **113.6**
Speed ratings (Par 103): **100,99,99,98,96 95,94,92,91**
toteswingers: 1&2 £5.30, 1&3 £8.40, 2&3 £10.70 CSF £22.45 CT £169.47 TOTE £5.50: £1.60, £1.10, £4.20; EX 32.30.
Owner Anthony D Copley **Bred** Whitsbury Manor Stud **Trained** Westow, N Yorks

FOCUS
The two leaders went off too fast for their own good in this 63-75 sprint handicap. A small personal best from the winner.

5648 JOHN SMITH'S REDCAR STRAIGHT-MILE CHAMPIONSHIP (QUALIFIER) (H'CAP) 1m
3:40 (3:40) (Class 4) (0-85,85) 3-Y-0+ **£2,587** (£770; £384; £192) **Stalls** High

Form RPR
1003 **1** **Charlie Cool**[4] 5502 8-9-8 **83**.....(b) PJMcDonald 4 94
(Ruth Carr) *hld up in tch: hdwy 1/2-way: led wl over 1f out: rdn clr ent fnl f: styd on strly* **7/2**[1]
5060 **2** *4* **Kiwi Bay**[26] 4794 6-9-10 **85**..... TomEaves 8 87
(Michael Dods) *stdd s: hld up in rr: hdwy wl over 2f out: rdn wl over 1f out: styd on to chse wnr ins fnl f: no imp* **5/1**[3]
10-2 **3** *2* **Soccerjackpot (USA)**[87] 2768 7-9-0 **75**..... RussKennemore 9 72
(Paul Midgley) *prom: hdwy over 3f out: led wl over 2f out: rdn and hdd wl over 1f out: kpt on same pce appr fnl f* **16/1**
2135 **4** *1* **Koo And The Gang (IRE)**[19] 5059 4-8-13 **77**..... PaulPickard(3) 3 72
(Brian Ellison) *led: rdn along 3f out: sn hdd and grad wknd* **9/2**[2]
1010 **5** *3/4* **Munsarim (IRE)**[37] 4415 4-9-6 **81**..... DavidAllan 6 74
(Keith Dalgleish) *in tch: hdwy to chse ldrs 3f out: rdn over 2f out: sn one* **11/1**
1110 **6** *1* **Regimental (IRE)**[40] 4325 3-8-11 **80**..... DaleSwift(3) 2 71
(Ann Duffield) *chsd ldrs: rdn along 3f out: sn drvn and wknd* **9/1**
000- **7** *1 1/4* **Huntingfortreasure**[318] 6984 4-8-10 **71** oh4..... PaulHanagan 1 59
(Philip Kirby) *wnt lft s: sn prom on outer: rdn along 3f out: grad wknd* **16/1**
1016 **8** *5* **Toto Skyllachy**[37] 4404 6-9-7 **82**..... SilvestreDeSousa 7 59
(Ollie Pears) *dwlt: towards rr and reminders after 1f: sn in tch: niggled along 1/2-way: rdn on outer to chse ldrs wl over 2f out: sn wknd* **5/1**[3]
400 **9** *11* **Majuro (IRE)**[26] 4794 7-9-6 **81**.....(t) RobbieFitzpatrick 5 32
(Richard Guest) *chsd ldrs: rdn along 1/2-way: sn wknd* **25/1**

1m 36.37s (-1.63) **Going Correction** -0.075s/f (Good)
WFA 3 from 4yo+ 5lb **9** Ran SP% **114.7**
Speed ratings (Par 105): **105,101,99,98,97 96,95,90,79**
toteswingers: 1&2 £5.20, 1&3 £12.90, 2&3 £11.60 CSF £20.85 CT £245.99 TOTE £4.40: £2.00, £1.20, £4.90; EX 16.10.
Owner Middleham Park Racing Xxiv **Bred** Middle Park Stud Ltd **Trained** Huby, N Yorks

FOCUS
Quite a competitive 71-85 handicap but £2,300 below tariff and the form isn't the strongest for the grade. The winner is rated back to this year's best.
Koo And The Gang(IRE) Official explanation: jockey said gelding hung left

5649 FOLLOW REDCARRACING ON FACEBOOK & TWITTER MAIDEN STKS 6f
4:15 (4:20) (Class 5) 3-Y-0+ **£1,940** (£577; £288; £144) **Stalls** High

Form RPR
6640 **1** **Stilettoesinthemud (IRE)**[30] 4638 3-8-12 56..... FrederikTylicki 10 63
(James Given) *trckd ldr: led 1/2-way: rdn 2f out and sn edgd lft: drvn ins fnl f: jst hld on* **6/1**[3]
0030 **2** *nse* **Llewellyn**[22] 4910 3-9-3 70..... StevieDonohoe 5 68
(James Fanshawe) *chsd ldrs: hdwy over 2f out: swtchd rt and rdn wl over 1f out: styd on to chse wnr ins fnl f: kpt on wl towards fin: jst failed* **3/1**[1]
0 **3** *3* **Violet's Gift (IRE)**[29] 4663 3-8-12 0..... SilvestreDeSousa 7 53
(James Fanshawe) *chsd ldng pair: rdn along and sltly outpcd over 2f out: styd on ins fnl f* **3/1**[1]
005 **4** *1/2* **Merito**[50] 3977 3-9-3 60..... PaulHanagan 6 57
(Kevin Ryan) *led to 1/2-way: rdn along and cl up whn carried lft wl over 1f out: drvn and wknd appr fnl f* **3/1**[1]
2304 **5** *1 3/4* **American Lover (FR)**[5] 5469 4-9-0 58..... DavidNolan 8 46
(John Wainwright) *dwlt: sn chsng ldrs: rdn along wl over 2f out and sn one pce* **5/1**[2]
5300 **6** *9* **Chardonnay Star (IRE)**[20] 4987 4-8-9 46.....(v) LanceBetts(5) 9 17
(Colin Teague) *a towards rr* **50/1**
0 **7** *1 3/4* **Peteron**[41] 4282 3-9-0 0..... DaleSwift(3) 3 17
(Colin Teague) *s.i.s: a in rr* **100/1**
0-0P **8** *1 1/4* **Musical Leap**[20] 5021 3-8-12 0..... DanielleMcCreery(5) 2 13
(Shaun Harris) *chsd ldrs: rdn along bef 1/2-way: sn wknd* **150/1**
00 **9** *3 1/2* **Queen's Princess**[5] 5469 3-8-9 0..... DeclanCannon(3) 1 —
(John Wainwright) *s.i.s: a bhd* **100/1**

1m 11.51s (-0.29) **Going Correction** -0.075s/f (Good)
WFA 3 from 4yo 2lb **9** Ran SP% **110.6**
Speed ratings (Par 103): **98,97,93,93,90 78,76,74,70**
toteswingers: 1&2 £3.90, 1&3 £3.40, 2&3 £2.40 CSF £22.68 TOTE £4.30: £1.50, £1.70, £1.20; EX 24.80.
Owner Andrew Gray **Bred** Blackdown Stud **Trained** Willoughton, Lincs
■ Stewards' Enquiry : Robbie Fitzpatrick two-day ban: struck horse at start (tbn)

FOCUS
A very weak 3-y-o sprint maiden. The eexposed winner rates a small personal best.

5650 HOLD YOUR CHRISTMAS PARTY @ REDCAR RACECOURSE H'CAP (DIV I) 1m 6f 19y
4:50 (4:51) (Class 6) (0-65,64) 3-Y-0+ **£1,363** (£402; £201) **Stalls** Low

Form RPR
023 **1** **Al Furat (USA)**[8] 5372 3-8-3 **55**..... ShaneBKelly(5) 7 69+
(Ron Barr) *hld up towards rr: stdy hdwy over 4f out: chsd ldrs 3f out: chal on outer and hung lft 2f out: sn led and hung bdly lft: clr ent fnl f: styd on strly* **3/1**[1]
5420 **2** *4 1/2* **Body Language (IRE)**[29] 4671 3-9-3 **64**..... DavidNolan 8 69
(Ann Duffield) *led: pushed along 4f out: rdn 3f out: drvn and hdd wl over 1f out: kpt on: no ch w wnr* **11/2**[2]
0003 **3** *1 3/4* **They All Laughed**[21] 4944 8-8-12 **48**..... BarryMcHugh 6 51
(Marjorie Fife) *hld up in rr: hdwy 4f out: rdn along over 2f out: styd on appr fnl f: nrst fin* **12/1**
4-00 **4** *2 1/4* **Master Nimbus**[22] 4903 11-9-5 **55**..... PBBeggy 4 54
(John Quinn) *in tch: hdwy 5f out: chsd ldrs over 3f out: rdn along over 2f out: sn drvn and one pce* **12/1**
2152 **5** *1/2* **Amir Pasha (UAE)**[27] 4747 6-10-0 **64**.....(p) TomEaves 11 63
(Micky Hammond) *in tch: hdwy 4f out: rdn to chse ldrs wl over 2f out: drvn and one pce fr wl over 1f out* **11/2**[2]
-000 **6** *2 1/2* **Tayacoba (CAN)**[79] 3023 4-9-8 **58**.....(p) PJMcDonald 10 53
(Martin Todhunter) *hld up: hdwy over 3f out: rdn along over 2f out: kpt on: nvr nr ldrs* **14/1**
0600 **7** *2* **Hada Men (USA)**[7] 5405 6-8-9 **50**.....(p) JulieBurke(5) 1 42
(Tina Jackson) *midfield: effrt and sme hdwy over 4f out: sn rdn along and n.d* **14/1**
-600 **8** *9* **Fantino**[42] 4237 5-9-11 **61**..... PaulHanagan 12 41
(John Mackie) *trckd ldrs: smooth hdwy 5f out: cl up 4f out: rdn to chal 3f out: drvn over 2f out and sn btn* **7/1**[3]
0450 **9** *1* **Geminus (IRE)**[35] 4476 3-8-3 **50**.....(b) SilvestreDeSousa 5 28
(Jedd O'Keeffe) *cl up: rdn along over 4f out: sn wknd* **8/1**
500 **10** *2* **Revolving World (IRE)**[14] 5209 8-8-9 **45**..... DuranFentiman 9 21
(Lee James) *dwlt: a in rr* **66/1**
0044 **11** *6* **Ballade De La Mer**[26] 4785 5-8-9 **45**.....(v) LeeNewman 3 12
(George Foster) *chsd ldng pair: rdn along over 4f out: sn wknd* **20/1**
1600 **12** *28* **Without Equal**[17] 5107 5-8-11 **52**.....(p) NeilFarley(5) 2 —
(David Thompson) *dwlt: a in rr: bhd fnl 4f* **33/1**

3m 4.53s (-0.17) **Going Correction** -0.075s/f (Good)
WFA 3 from 4yo+ 11lb **12** Ran SP% **117.3**
Speed ratings (Par 101): **97,94,93,92,91 90,89,84,83,82 79,63**
toteswingers: 1&2 £5.10, 1&3 £8.50, 2&3 £7.10 CSF £18.04 CT £174.28 TOTE £5.20: £1.90, £1.70, £4.10; EX 21.30.
Owner P Cartmell **Bred** Philip Brown **Trained** Seamer, N Yorks

FOCUS
Part one of a low-grade stayers' handicap run at just a steady pace until the final 5f. The winner improved, woth the runner-up to form.

5651 HOLD YOUR CHRISTMAS PARTY @ REDCAR RACECOURSE H'CAP (DIV II) 1m 6f 19y
5:20 (5:21) (Class 6) (0-65,64) 3-Y-0+ **£1,363** (£402; £201) **Stalls** Low

Form RPR
4006 **1** **Miss Ferney**[8] 5369 7-8-11 **50**..... PaulPickard(3) 6 61+
(Alan Kirtley) *hld up in rr: stdy hdwy on outer 4f out: led over 2f out: rdn clr over 1f out: styd on* **8/1**
5223 **2** *3* **Falcun**[29] 4671 4-9-8 **58**.....(v[1]) PaulHanagan 4 63
(Micky Hammond) *bmpd s and in rr: pushed along 4f out: rdn over 3f out: swtchd rt and drvn 2f out: styd on appr fnl f: nt rch wnr* **7/2**[1]
0056 **3** *nk* **Shirls Son Sam**[8] 5372 3-8-6 **53**..... DuranFentiman 9 58
(Chris Fairhurst) *dwlt and hld up in rr: pushed along and hdwy over 3f out: rdn 2f out: styd on to chse wnr appr fnl f: one pce* **20/1**
6033 **4** *1 3/4* **Light The City (IRE)**[14] 5210 4-9-5 **55**..... JamesSullivan 7 58
(Ruth Carr) *hld up: stdy hdwy over 4f out: effrt to chse wnr over 2f out and sn rdn: drvn appr fnl f: kpt on same pce* **10/1**
5123 **5** *3 3/4* **Colonel Sherman (USA)**[13] 5249 6-9-2 **52**.....(t) SilvestreDeSousa 11 49
(Philip Kirby) *chsd ldrs: effrt 4f out: rdn along over 3f out: sn drvn and grad wknd* **4/1**[2]
6035 **6** *1* **Denison Flyer**[22] 4904 4-8-8 **49**..... LanceBetts(5) 8 45
(Lawrence Mullaney) *trckd ldrs on inner: hdwy over 3f out: rdn to chse wnr 2f out: sn drvn and grad wknd* **16/1**
1501 **7** *9* **Zefooha (FR)**[26] 4814 7-10-0 **64**.....(b) GrahamGibbons 5 47
(Tim Walford) *trckd ldrs: hdwy 4f out: nt clr run over 2f out: sn rdn and btn* **9/2**[3]
5220 **8** *12* **Golestan Palace (IRE)**[10] 5321 3-8-11 **58**..... J-PGuillambert 1 25
(Ed Walker) *trckd ldng pair: hdwy to ld over 3f out: rdn along and hdd over 2f out: sn wknd* **5/1**
-026 **9** *16* **Clueless**[15] 5167 9-9-4 **54**..... DavidAllan 10 —
(Keith Dalgleish) *cl up: rdn along over 3f out: sn wknd* **16/1**
0600 **10** *30* **Bunacurry**[29] 4673 6-8-9 **45**..... BarryMcHugh 2 —
(Barry Murtagh) *wnt rt s: led: rdn along over 4f out: hdd over 3f out and sn wknd* **50/1**

3m 4.92s (0.22) **Going Correction** -0.075s/f (Good)
WFA 3 from 4yo+ 11lb **10** Ran SP% **115.8**
Speed ratings (Par 101): **96,94,94,93,90 90,85,78,69,52**
toteswingers: 1&2 £7.40, 1&3 £23.30, 2&3 £11.10 CSF £35.87 CT £546.31 TOTE £10.70: £4.00, £1.80, £8.50; EX 49.00.
Owner Mrs P J Taylor-Garthwaite **Bred** K And P J Garthwaite **Trained** West Auckland, Co Durham

FOCUS
Part two and more of the same, but with the two pacesetters taking each other on the gallop was much more generous, though in the end the overall time was fractionally slower than division one. The first four came from the rear and it was the winner's best effort this season.

5652 GO RACING IN YORKSHIRE APPRENTICE H'CAP 7f
5:50 (5:50) (Class 5) (0-70,70) 3-Y-0+ **£1,940** (£577; £288; £144) **Stalls** Low

Form RPR

0151 **1** **Broctune Papa Gio**[36] 4441 4-9-0 **60**........................ DeclanCannon 9 65+
(Keith Reveley) *cl up: chal 3f out: sn led: rdn wl over 1f out: drvn ins fnl f and kpt on wl towards fin* **5/2**[1]

5-36 **2** ½ **Glenmuir (IRE)**[17] 5106 8-9-0 **65**........................(p) ShaneBKelly(5) 4 68
(John Quinn) *trckd ldrs: pushed along and sltly outpcd over 2f out: rdn and n.m.r over 1f out: drvn and kpt on ins fnl f* **7/2**[2]

0464 **3** ¾ **Red Scintilla**[20] 5008 4-8-10 **56** oh1........................ MartinHarley 8 57
(Nigel Tinkler) *hld up in tch: hdwy wl over 2f out: rdn over 1f out: kpt on fnl f* **4/1**[3]

003 **4** *shd* **Uddy Mac**[34] 4518 4-8-3 **56** oh7........................(b) TerenceFury(7) 2 57
(Neville Bycroft) *hld up in rr: gd hdwy on outer 3f out: rdn to chal wl over 1f out and ev ch tl drvn and one pce ins fnl f* **16/1**

5 1½ **Thoroughly Red (IRE)**[292] 5706 6-9-10 **70**........................ JamesSullivan 1 67
(Linda Stubbs) *trckd ldrs: hdwy 3f out: rdn to chse ldrs 2f out: sn rdn and edgd rt wl over 1f out: drvn and one pce fnl f* **50/1**

3305 **6** *nse* **Izzet**[15] 5165 3-8-7 **57**........................ PaulPickard 6 52
(Ron Barr) *hld up towards rr: hdwy over 2f out: chsd ldrs whn hmpd wl over 1f out: swtchd lft and rdn fnl f: no imp* **11/2**

0056 **7** ½ **Indieslad**[18] 5083 3-9-6 **70**........................ LeeTopliss 7 63
(Ann Duffield) *chsd ldrs: rdn along over 2f out: drvn and one pce fr over 1f out* **6/1**

-050 **8** 3¾ **Peppercorn Rent (IRE)**[57] 3732 3-8-3 **56** oh11........(be[1]) JulieBurke(3) 5 39
(John Davies) *t.k.h: sn led: rdn along over 3f out: hdd wl over 2f out and sn wknd* **33/1**

040- **9** 9 **Ten To The Dozen**[346] 6261 8-8-7 **56** oh11........................ NeilFarley(3) 3 17
(David Thompson) *chsd ldr: rdn along over 2f out: wkng whn hmpd wl over 1f out* **66/1**

1m 24.98s (0.48) **Going Correction** -0.075s/f (Good)
WFA 3 from 4yo+ 4lb **9** Ran SP% **112.7**
Speed ratings (Par 103): **94,93,92,92,90 90,90,85,75**
toteswingers: 1&2 £2.70, 1&3 £3.60, 2&3 £4.10; Totesuper7: Win: Not Won; Place: £1,402.80 CSF £10.88 CT £32.52 TOTE £3.90: £1.80, £1.60, £2.70; EX 10.40.
Owner Broctune Partners I **Bred** Lesley Winn And Reveley Farms **Trained** Lingdale, Redcar & Cleveland

FOCUS
A modest apprentice handicap and an unexposed winner of some potential. The form is a bit muddling with the fourth 7lb out of the handicap.
T/Jkpt: Part won. £7,100.00 to a £1 stake. Pool: £8,866.70. 0.50 winning tickets. T/Plt: £26.00 to a £1 stake. Pool: £62,735.41. 1,758.41 winning tickets. T/Qpdt: £11.50 to a £1 stake. Pool: £3,610.34. 230.80 winning tickets. JR

5231 SALISBURY (R-H)
Thursday, September 1

OFFICIAL GOING: Good (good to firm in places; 8.2)
Wind: Virtually nil Weather: Sunny

5653 AXMINSTER CARPETS RACING EXCELLENCE APPRENTICE H'CAP (WHIPS SHALL BE CARRIED BUT NOT USED) 1m
2:10 (2:10) (Class 5) (0-70,69) 3-Y-0+ **£2,425** (£721; £360; £180) **Stalls** Low

Form RPR

6416 **1** **Gallego**[4] 5509 9-9-3 **62**........................ RachealKneller 11 70
(Richard Price) *hld up in rr: stdy hdwy on outside over 2f out: led jst ins fnl f: comf* **13/2**[3]

0-00 **2** 2¼ **Whitechapel**[19] 5053 4-9-3 **67**........................ ThomasBrown(5) 7 70
(Andrew Balding) *towards rr but in tch: hdwy fr 3f out: drvn to take slt ld 1f out: sn hdd: styd on but nt pce of wnr* **8/1**

-050 **3** 2¼ **Carcinetto (IRE)**[5] 5496 9-9-1 **65**........................ KevinLundie(5) 1 63
(David Evans) *led 1f: styd chsng ldr: rdn over 2f out: styd on to ld again over 1f out: sn hdd: one pce fnl f* **16/1**

0535 **4** 1½ **Batchworth Blaise**[33] 4544 8-8-10 **55** oh8........................(b) RaulDaSilva 4 50+
(Eric Wheeler) *s.i.s: sn chsng ldrs: rdn over 2f out: nt clr run and hung rt over 1f out: sn no ex* **20/1**

0502 **5** *nk* **Byrd In Hand (IRE)**[4] 5509 4-8-10 **55**........................ CharlesBishop 6 49
(John Bridger) *led after 1f: rdn along 3f out: hdd over 1f out and sn btn* **11/4**[1]

-406 **6** 1 **My Jeanie (IRE)**[22] 4928 7-8-10 **55** oh10........................ JustinNewman 8 46
(Jimmy Fox) *s.i.s towards rr: drvn and hdwy fr 3f out: nvr rchd ldrs and one pce fnl 2f* **50/1**

2455 **7** *hd* **Edgeworth (IRE)**[17] 5110 5-9-5 **69**........................ JoshBaudains(5) 2 60
(David Bridgwater) *chsd ldrs: pushed along over 2f out and styd on same pce* **8/1**

3000 **8** 1½ **Qeethaara (USA)**[14] 5200 7-9-3 **67**........................ JackDuern(5) 10 54
(Mark Brisbourne) *towards rr: pushed along and sme prog 3f out: nvr rchd ldrs and sn one pce* **14/1**

-600 **9** *nk* **Cotswold Village (AUS)**[21] 4949 5-8-12 **62**........... BrendanPowell(5) 3 49
(Adrian Chamberlain) *chsd ldrs: rdn 3f out: wknd fr 2f out* **16/1**

1011 **10** 12 **Dannios**[17] 5116 5-9-7 **69**........................(t) MichaelJMurphy(3) 9 28
(Ed Walker) *pushed along over 3f out: nvr travelling and a bhd* **7/2**[2]

6-13 **11** 21 **Futurism**[147] 1194 3-9-5 **69**........................ CharlesEddery 5 —
(Richard Hannon) *chsd ldrs tl wknd 3f out: eased whn no ch fnl 2f* **17/2**

1m 43.28s (-0.22) **Going Correction** -0.125s/f (Firm)
WFA 3 from 4yo+ 5lb **11** Ran SP% **120.1**
Speed ratings (Par 103): **96,93,91,90,89 88,88,87,86,74 53**
toteswingers: 1&2 £9.30, 1&3 £26.10, 2&3 £31.50 CSF £59.05 CT £826.15 TOTE £9.70: £2.40, £3.50, £4.80; EX 68.20 TRIFECTA Not won..
Owner My Left Foot Racing Syndicate **Bred** Mrs C Regalado-Gonzalez **Trained** Ullingswick, H'fords

FOCUS
There was a rail up 8ft off the permanent far-side rail between 6f and 4f. The pace was too strong in this modest handicap, a race in which these apprentices were not allowed to use their whips. The pace collapsed and the form is a bit shaky.

5654 E B F WHITSBURY MANOR STUD NOVICE STKS 1m
2:40 (2:41) (Class 4) 2-Y-0 **£4,528** (£1,347; £673; £336) **Stalls** Low

Form RPR

21 **1** **Farhaan (USA)**[20] 5011 2-9-0 0........................ RichardHills 5 91+
(John Dunlop) *trckd ldr: drvn to chal fr 3f out: slt ld fr 2f out but strly chal thrght fnl f: kpt on wl u.p: asserted last strides* **9/4**[2]

0134 **2** *nk* **Mister Music**[19] 5044 2-9-0 84........................ DaneO'Neill 1 90+
(Richard Hannon) *led: rdn and qcknd pce over 3f out: sn jnd and narrowly hdd 2f out: styd pressing wnr and remained upsides u.p thrght fnl f tl no ex last strides* **16/1**

1 **3** 2 **Kinglet (USA)**[27] 4762 2-9-3 0........................ FrankieDettori 2 88
(Mahmood Al Zarooni) *chsd ldrs: rdn and swtchd rt ins fnl 3f: swtchd lft and drvn 2f out: no imp on ldng duo and one pce fnl f* **6/5**[1]

1232 **4** 3¼ **Lord Ofthe Shadows (IRE)**[13] 5234 2-9-3 97........... RichardHughes 3 81
(Richard Hannon) *hld up towards rr but in tch: hdwy to disp 3rd over 2f out: no imp on ldng duo and wknd fnl f* **7/2**[3]

5 2 **Stature (IRE)** 2-8-12 0........................ DavidProbert 6 71+
(Andrew Balding) *t.k.h and stdd in rr: rdn along 3f out: kpt on fnl 2f but nvr gng pce to get into contention* **22/1**

6 **6** 3 **Daghash**[9] 5337 2-8-12 0........................ PhilipRobinson 7 64
(Clive Brittain) *trckd ldrs: rdn 3f out: wknd fr 2f out* **80/1**

1m 43.25s (-0.25) **Going Correction** -0.125s/f (Firm) **6** Ran SP% **109.9**
Speed ratings (Par 97): **96,95,93,90,88 85**
toteswingers: 1&2 £3.50, 1&3 £1.40, 2&3 £2.60 CSF £32.39 TOTE £4.00: £1.20, £2.40; EX 31.40.
Owner Hamdan Al Maktoum **Bred** Shadwell Farm LLC **Trained** Arundel, W Sussex
■ Stewards' Enquiry : Dane O'Neill one-day ban: used whip down shoulder in the forehand (Sep 15)

FOCUS
Often a good race, the most notable winners in the last decade being Punctilious (later won Yorkshire Oaks) and the Group-class miler Cityscape. The bare form of this year's running can't be considered particularly strong considering the runner-up, who came into this officially rated just 84, was allowed to set what looked a pretty modest pace. The time, though, was 0.03 seconds quicker than the earlier Class 5 handicap for older-horses, a race in which the pace was overly quick.

NOTEBOOK
Farhaan(USA) had improved a good deal on his debut when a clear-cut winner over 7f at the July course, and the fifth and sixth-placed finishers both won next time. A number of Group-race entries showed the regard in which he's held and he was good enough to gradually wear down a runner who had the run of the race. It remains to be seen exactly what he achieved, especially as he was better placed than most, and it's doubtful he's up to winning a Group race this term, but he's a nice long-term prospect. He's very much still learning and has the size and scope to improve, while he's likely to appreciate further in time, the colt appearing to have inherited plenty of stamina from his first-season sire Jazil, who won the 2006 Belmont Stakes. (tchd 11-4 in a place)
Mister Music was outclassed behind Fencing in a 7f Listed race on his previous start (reported to have hung left), but he stepped up on that form, helped by the extra furlong and an uncontested lead. Surely he's flattered. (tchd 18-1)
Kinglet(USA) created a good impression when a winner on his debut over 7f at the July course, narrowly defeating Most Improved, who won well next time, and he is his trainer's only entry in the Beresford Stakes (only big-race entry in Britain or Ireland). It's therefore hard not to be disappointed with this. Admittedly he was conceding 3lb to the first two and didn't enjoy quite as smooth a trip as that pair, but he was essentially one-paced. Maybe this ground was slower than ideal. (op 5-4)
Lord Ofthe Shadows(IRE), second in an ordinary C&D Listed race last time, struggled on this drop in class. (op 10-3)
Stature(IRE) ◆, a 28,000gns purchase, has a nice middle-distance pedigree, being by Montjeu out of Darshaan mare, a highly successful nick that notably produced this year's Derby hero Pour Moi. He was green for much of the way and lacked the required speed to get competitive from off this steady gallop, but it was taking how well he galloped out after the line - he was soon well clear. There's a lot better to come when the emphasis is on stamina. (op 25-1)

5655 E B F "NORSE DANCER" QUIDHAMPTON MAIDEN FILLIES' STKS 6f 212y
3:15 (3:17) (Class 3) 2-Y-0 **£6,469** (£1,925; £962; £481) **Stalls** Centre

Form RPR

2 **1** **Firdaws (USA)**[20] 4995 2-9-0 0........................ RichardHills 18 86+
(Roger Varian) *trckd ldrs: rdn fr 2f out: pressed ldr fnl f tl led fnl 120yds: styd on strly clsng stages* **2/5**[1]

6 **2** 2 **Whimsical (IRE)**[19] 5047 2-9-0 0........................ RichardHughes 12 81
(Richard Hannon) *pressed ldrs: chal fr 3f out tl slt ld 2f out: sn rdn: jnd 1f out: kpt slt ld tl hdd and outpcd fnl 120yds* **14/1**

3 3¾ **Rhagori** 2-9-0 0........................ JimCrowley 5 71
(Ralph Beckett) *sn led: rdn 3f out: hdd 2f out: outpcd fnl f but kpt on wl for 3rd* **33/1**

4 *shd* **Dulkashe (IRE)** 2-9-0 0........................ KierenFallon 1 71+
(Luca Cumani) *prom: chsd ldrs: 3f out: rdn and one pce 2f out: kpt on fnl f to cl on 3rd nr fin: nt trble ldng duo* **11/1**[2]

5 *hd* **Miss Cap Estel** 2-9-0 0........................ JimmyFortune 7 70+
(Andrew Balding) *in tch whn hmpd ins fnl 4f and sn pushed along: swtchd lft to outside over 2f out: kpt on wl fnl f but nt rch ldrs* **28/1**

6 1½ **Safarjal (IRE)** 2-9-0 0........................ TadhgO'Shea 6 66+
(Charles Hills) *s.i.s: in rr: pushed along and hdwy fr 2f out: styd on ins fnl f: nt rch ldrs* **33/1**

7 *hd* **Baheeja** 2-9-0 0........................ NeilCallan 15 66
(Roger Varian) *chsd ldrs: edgd rt ins fnl 4f: chsd ldrs fr 3f out: one pce fnl 2f* **33/1**

8 1¼ **Biba Diva (IRE)** 2-9-0 0........................ FrankieDettori 11 63
(Jeremy Noseda) *chsd ldrs: rdn 3f out: wknd fnl f* **12/1**[3]

9 *nk* **Forgive** 2-9-0 0........................ DaneO'Neill 8 62+
(Richard Hannon) *towards rr and rdn 3f out: styd on fnl f: nt rch ldrs* **22/1**

10 2¼ **Kaylena** 2-9-0 0........................ JamieSpencer 3 56+
(Jeremy Noseda) *bmpd s and bhd: swtchd lft to outside 3f out: kpt on fnl 2f but nvr gng pce to rch ldrs* **20/1**

11 ¾ **Monopoli** 2-9-0 0........................ RichardThomas 14 59+
(Ralph Beckett) *t.k.h: chsd ldrs: hmpd ins fnl 4f: sn drvn and green but sme hdwy over 2f out: no imp and no ch after* **100/1**

12 4 **Watanee** 2-9-0 0........................ PhilipRobinson 13 44
(Clive Brittain) *nvr bttr than mid-div* **50/1**

13 4 **Moody Dancer** 2-9-0 0........................ MartinDwyer 2 33
(William Muir) *chsd ldrs: rdn over 3f out: sn btn* **80/1**

14 1½ **La Passionata** 2-9-0 0........................ TomQueally 4 29
(Robert Mills) *wnt rt s and s.i.s: a outpcd* **100/1**

The Form Book, Raceform Ltd, Compton, RG20 6NL

15 ½ **Pearls From Sydney** 2-9-0 0 .... PhillipMakin 17 28
(Paul Cole) *s.i.s: sn in tch: rdn and effrt 3f out: sn wknd* **50/1**

16 4 ½ **Afnoon (USA)** 2-9-0 0 .... IanMongan 16 16
(John Dunlop) *a in rr* **66/1**

17 13 **Arkadia** 2-9-0 0 .... JamesMillman 10 —
(Rod Millman) *a in rr* **100/1**

1m 28.56s (-0.04) **Going Correction** -0.125s/f (Firm) **17** Ran SP% **125.1**
Speed ratings (Par 96): **95,92,88,88,88 86,86,84,84,81 80,76,71,70,69 64,49**
toteswingers: 1&2 £4.50, 1&3 £7.60, 2&3 £16.00 CSF £5.99 TOTE £1.50: £1.10, £3.00, £6.00; EX 10.90 Trifecta £232.30 Pool: £1,076.87 - 3.43 winning units..

Owner Hamdan Al Maktoum **Bred** Shadwell Farm LLC **Trained** Newmarket, Suffolk

FOCUS

A maiden of above-average class. The 2011 UAE Oaks and UAE Derby winner Khawlah was runner-up in a division of this last year, and in 2008 subsequent US Grade 1-winner Ave was only fourth. This time for a change the race wasn't divided, meaning it was packed full of interesting types, and surely plenty of nice winners will emerge. The first two finishers were the only runners with previous experience.

NOTEBOOK

Firdaws(USA) is out of 2005 Oaks winner Eswarah and had only just failed to make a winning debut when runner-up over this trip at Newbury (form already been boosted). She made hard enough work of going one place better, but in fairness the widest draw was no help and the further she went the better she looked, her dam clearly a key influence. There should be a lot more to come when she goes up in trip, and she's in the Fillies' Mile. (tchd 8-15 in a place)

Whimsical(IRE) improved a good deal on the form she showed behind stable companion Dreamwriter (not get run of race in following Listed contest) on her debut over 6f at Newbury. She had the edge on experience over those behind her, but still looks quite useful.

Rhagori ◆ had been due to make her debut at the July course (non-runner owing to unsuitable ground) and instead came here for another decent maiden, indicating she's well regarded. She's the first foal of a useful winner at around 1m4f, but is by a speedy sire and showed plenty of pace before getting tired. There should be more to come. (op 25-1)

Dulkashe(IRE), a 120,000euros purchase, is a half-sister to a few winners of quite varying ability. She ran well for a long way on this debut and is from a stable whose newcomers often improve plenty. (op 12-1)

Miss Cap Estel ◆ is bred to stay well and this was a taking debut. Having met some trouble at around halfway, she was going on well at the finish and galloped out strongly after the line. (op 25-1)

Safarjal(IRE) ◆ is from a decent family, notably being a sister to Oriental Fashion, a 1m Group 2 winner in Italy, and she kept on nicely from well off the place to make a pleasing start. A May foal, there should be a lot better to come in time.

Baheeja, a 50,000gns half-sister to a couple of winners, out of a 5f juvenile winner who later won a Listed race at 1m, showed ability and is likely to be better for the run. (op 25-1)

Biba Diva(IRE), an 80,000euros half-sister to winners at 6f-1m, out of a 1m Listed scorer, showed up to a point but faded to be well held. (op 11-1 tchd 10-1)

Kaylena ◆, who is out of Kootenay (triple Listed winner at around 1m), raced well off the pace for much of the way, but despite not being given a hard time late on she galloped out much stronger than most. Significant improvement is expected next time. (op 18-1)

Monopoli, the Ralph Beckett second string, met some trouble and should be capable of better.

Arkadia Official explanation: jockey said filly hung left

5656 IRISH STALLION FARMS E B F DICK POOLE FILLIES' STKS (LISTED RACE) 6f

3:50 (3:52) (Class 1) 2-Y-O

£14,177 (£5,375; £2,690; £1,340; £672; £337) **Stalls** Low

Form RPR

105 **1** **Sajwah (IRE)**[55] 3821 2-8-12 101 .... RichardHills 2 100
(Charles Hills) *dispute ld tl led over 2f out: drvn over 1f out: styd on strly fnl f* **8/1**

1135 **2** 1 ½ **Misty Conquest (IRE)**[49] 4036 2-8-12 92 .... RichardKingscote 9 96
(Tom Dascombe) *disp ld tl drvn over 2f out: nt pce of wnr fnl f but kpt on wl for 2nd* **28/1**

121 **3** nk **Pimpernel (IRE)**[19] 5052 2-8-12 95 .... FrankieDettori 1 95
(Mahmood Al Zarooni) *chsd ldrs: drvn to dispute 2nd fr over 1f out: nvr gng pce to rch wnr and one pce ins fnl f* **4/1**[2]

1246 **4** 1 ¼ **Inetrobil (IRE)**[14] 5217 2-8-12 102 .... PhillipMakin 8 91
(Kevin Ryan) *chsd ldrs: rdn over 2f out: kpt on ins fnl f to take 4th last strides but nt rch ldng trio* **5/1**[3]

612 **5** shd **Responsive**[54] 3842 2-8-12 84 .... JimmyFortune 3 91
(Hughie Morrison) *in tch: drvn to chse ldrs fr 2f out: no imp and styd on same pce fnl f* **22/1**

13 **6** ½ **Mary Fildes (IRE)**[20] 4999 2-8-12 0 .... LukeMorris 5 89
(J S Moore) *in rr: rdn and hung bdly rt over 3f out: stl hanging and hd high fr 2f out: r.o u.p clsng stages but nvr a threat* **11/1**

1 **7** 1 ¾ **Miss Azeza**[23] 4883 2-8-12 0 .... JamieSpencer 4 84
(David Simcock) *n.m.r s and s.i.s: in rr: swtchd lft to outside then veered lft wl over 1f out: styd on clsng stages* **10/1**

0133 **8** nk **Hidden Passion (USA)**[12] 5270 2-8-12 80 .... (t) ShaneKelly 11 83
(Brian Meehan) *chsd ldrs: rdn 2f out: wknd fnl f* **50/1**

615 **9** ½ **Elbe**[9] 5039 2-8-12 79 .... [1] TomQueally 10 82
(Sir Henry Cecil) *s.i.s: t.k.h: hdwy to chse ldrs over 2f out: sn hung rt: wknd fnl f* **16/1**

110 **10** ¾ **Cockney Fire**[20] 4999 2-8-12 86 .... CathyGannon 7 80
(David Evans) *t.k.h: rdn 3f out: nvr gng pce to get into contention* **40/1**

1 **11** nk **Dreamwriter (USA)**[19] 5047 2-8-12 0 .... RichardHughes 6 79
(Richard Hannon) *s.i.s: t.k.h and hld up in rr: shkn up and pushed along 2f out: wnt rt over 1f out: eased whn nt clr run ins fnl f* **7/4**[1]

1m 14.54s (-0.26) **Going Correction** -0.125s/f (Firm) **11** Ran SP% **119.6**
Speed ratings (Par 100): **96,94,93,91,91 91,88,88,87,86 86**
toteswingers: 1&2 £31.80, 1&3 £5.30, 2&3 £19.80 CSF £216.34 TOTE £10.30: £2.60, £6.10, £2.20; EX 261.10 TRIFECTA Not won..

Owner Hamdan Al Maktoum **Bred** Shadwell Estate Company Limited **Trained** Lambourn, Berks

FOCUS

A race that's worked out really well in recent seasons. Last year the runner-up was Rimth (later won Fred Darling) and the third was Margot Did (Nunthorpe), while the winner Brevity could yet prove to be pretty smart. In 2008 it was won by Serious Attitude, who followed up in the Cheveley Park, as well as later adding the Nearctic Stakes, a Canadian Grade 1. This time around the pace, or seemingly a lack of it, dictates that the bare form cannot be considered anything out of the ordinary. The first two filled the front two positions pretty much throughout, while the third and fourth-placed finishers tracked the leaders. The runner-up came here officially rated only 92.

NOTEBOOK

Sajwah(IRE) hadn't gone on as expected from a taking debut win at Warwick, finishing behind Inetrobil in both the Albany and the Cherry Hinton, though she had the odd excuse, finding the ground easier than ideal at Ascot and also racing keenly on both occasions. She had been given 55 days off and proved a different proposition on her return. Having gone early to post, she was allowed to stride on this time, and although a touch keen early and having Misty Conquest for company, she was conducive enough to the new tactics to have plenty left for the closing stages. All things considered, her connections deserve plenty of credit for getting this filly back on track, and while she had the run of the race, she's clearly going the right way again now and is worthy of her Cheveley Park entry. (op 15-2)

Misty Conquest(IRE), dropped in trip, returned to something like her best form, helped by the run of the race. She's apparently being aimed at the Firth of Clyde at Ayr. (tchd 33-1)

Pimpernel(IRE), dropped in trip after winning over a stiff 7f off a mark of 90 last time, was never far away and kept on. She probably would have preferred more of a test. (op 9-2 tchd 5-1)

Inetrobil(IRE) hasn't progressed since finishing runner-up in a weak running of the Albany Stakes, subsequently managing only fourth in the Cherry Hinton and sixth in the Lowther. (op 6-1)

Responsive fared best of those from off the pace. She's probably up to gaining black type at some stage.

Mary Fildes(IRE), third in a 5f Listed race on her second start, looked a hard ride. She needed strong whip pressure from an early stage, seemingly to stop her hanging right, and it was a surprise she finished so close. Official explanation: jockey said filly hung right (op 12-1 tchd 14-1)

Miss Azeza ◆'s debut win over this trip at Ffos Las was hard to weigh up, but it indicated she was pretty useful. She lost her chance when squeezed out at the start, but kept on gradually out wide and can do a fair bit better. (op 14-1)

Elbe, who has been keen over 7f, had a hood on for the first time on this drop in trip, but she was inclined to run around and looked awkward. (op 12-1)

Dreamwriter(USA), who had Whimsical (runner-up in maiden earlier on this card) well behind when bolting up in a 6f maiden at Newbury on her debut, had nothing go right for her and is probably best excused. The way the race unfolded meant she had little chance of getting involved under a hold-up ride, and having initially struggled when first asked for her challenge, she found trouble when not being switched wide late on, leaving her to coast home with something left. Official explanation: jockey said filly was denied a clear run (op 15-8 tchd 2-1)

5657 E B F "COMPTON PLACE" LOCHSONG FILLIES' STKS (H'CAP) 6f 212y

4:25 (4:25) (Class 2) (0-100,95) 3-Y-0+

£12,450 (£3,728; £1,864; £932; £466; £234) **Stalls** Centre

Form RPR

0126 **1** **Golden Delicious**[26] 4790 3-8-8 83 .... RichardHughes 6 92
(Hughie Morrison) *towards rr: hdwy fr 3f out: rdn 2f out: chalng whn edgd rt sn after: led appr fnl f: sn drvn: hld on wl clsng stages* **13/2**

1224 **2** ¾ **Dubai Queen (USA)**[61] 3648 3-9-6 95 .... KierenFallon 9 102
(Luca Cumani) *in tch: pushed along and hdwy fr 2f out: drvn to chal fr 1f out: stl ev ch fnl 120yds: no ex clsng stages but hld on wl for 2nd* **3/1**[1]

1124 **3** hd **Chokurei (IRE)**[20] 5016 3-8-4 82 .... JohnFahy[(3)] 12 88
(Clive Cox) *chsd ldrs: rdn 3f out: hung rt u.p and str chal 1f out: stl ev ch ins fnl f: no ex clsng stages and lost struggle for 2nd last strides* **12/1**

3122 **4** 1 ¼ **Romantic Wish**[21] 4958 3-8-8 86 .... SeanLevey[(3)] 11 89
(Robert Mills) *s.i.s and swtchd rt s: in rr: rdn and hdwy over 2f out: edgd rt over 1f out: r.o to take 4th clsng stages: no imp on ldrs* **9/1**

5253 **5** ½ **Russian Rave**[9] 5354 5-8-11 82 .... StephenCraine 4 86
(Jonathan Portman) *chsd ldrs: rdn over 2f out: styng on whn bmpd wl over 1f out: styd on same pce ins fnl f* **28/1**

4336 **6** ½ **Perfect Silence**[13] 5255 6-8-13 89 .... LucyKBarry[(5)] 7 91
(Clive Cox) *in rr: hrd rdn fr over 2f out: hdwy but hanging rt over 1f out: styd on clsng stages: nt rch ldrs* **10/1**

2412 **7** shd **Al Mayasah (IRE)**[9] 5354 3-8-6 81 oh3 .... JamieSpencer 1 81
(David Simcock) *led: rdn over 2f out: hdd appr fnl f: wknd fnl 150yds* **7/2**[2]

3165 **8** 2 ½ **Gobama**[58] 3703 4-9-8 93 .... SebSanders 3 88
(J W Hills) *in rr: pushed along 3f out: sme hdwy whn bmpd over 1f out: no ch after* **25/1**

0000 **9** ½ **Yer Woman (IRE)**[24] 4859 4-8-12 83 .... (b[1]) DaneO'Neill 10 77
(Richard Hannon) *rdn 3f out: outpcd* **25/1**

-345 **10** 12 **Ishbelle**[18] 5080 3-9-4 93 .... (p) JimCrowley 2 53
(Ralph Beckett) *chsd ldrs: rdn 3f out: wkng whn bmpd over 1f out: eased whn no ch* **14/1**

10/1 **11** 2 ½ **Theladyinquestion**[20] 5016 4-8-10 81 oh2 .... DavidProbert 8 36
(Andrew Balding) *pressed ldrs to 2f out: sn wknd: eased whn no ch fnl f* **6/1**[3]

1m 26.51s (-2.09) **Going Correction** -0.125s/f (Firm)
WFA 3 from 4yo+ 4lb **11** Ran SP% **119.4**
Speed ratings (Par 96): **106,105,104,103,102 102,102,99,98,85 82**
toteswingers: 1&2 £7.40, 1&3 £15.00, 2&3 £12.10 CSF £26.13 CT £239.27 TOTE £8.00: £3.30, £1.10, £5.80; EX 33.40 Trifecta £216.10 Pool: £812.20 - 2.78 winning units..

Owner Nicholas Jones **Bred** Coln Valley Stud **Trained** East Ilsley, Berks

FOCUS

A race won two years ago by Tropical Paradise, a subsequent Group 3 winner, and this looked another classy running of this fillies' handicap. Sound form. The pace was strong and the time was much quicker than the earlier juvenile maiden. They raced towards the stands' side in the closing stages.

NOTEBOOK

Golden Delicious might have found 1m too far and Listed company a bit hot last time, and she was helped by this drop in grade as well as a strongly run 7f on a stiff track. She did, however, shape as though she may yet get a bit further in time and this was only her eighth start, so there should be more to come. (tchd 6-1)

Dubai Queen(USA) is in danger of becoming something of a nearly horse, but to be fair this represents something like her best form, and she had been off for two months, so there could yet be better to come. A half-sister to Dubawi, this was only her seventh start. (tchd 9-2 in places)

Chokurei(IRE) was never far away from the hot pace and deserves credit. (tchd 14-1)

Romantic Wish missed the break, but then stayed on strongly, helped by the leaders coming back.

Russian Rave, due to be eased 1lb, was going on strongly at the line, helped by the quick pace and the stiff finish.

Perfect Silence stayed on from a long way back, but she never looked like winning and was probably passing mainly beaten horses. Easier ground might have helped.

Al Mayasah(IRE) was 3lb out of the handicap yet still well in, but she couldn't confirm recent Yarmouth form with Russian Rave and looked to pay for going off too fast. (op 9-2)

Gobama ◆ had apparently injured herself in a swimming pool recently and was expected by John Hills to need the run, her first for two months. She looked a bit fresh early and found trouble late on, so can do better. Official explanation: vet said filly lost its left-hind shoe (op 20-1)

Theladyinquestion had a couple of these behind when winning on her belated reappearance at the July course earlier in month, but she ran no sort of race this time and seemingly bounced. (tchd 13-2 in a place)

5658 SYDENHAMS H'CAP 5f

5:00 (5:00) (Class 5) (0-70,70) 3-Y-0+ **£2,425** (£721; £360; £180) **Stalls** Low

Form RPR

2652 **1** **Commandingpresence (USA)**[6] 5426 5-8-9 **61**........... SeanLevey(3) 7 70
(John Bridger) *trckd ldrs in 3rd tl wnt 2nd ins fnl 2f: styd on u.p fnl f to ld cl home* **15/2**

3411 **2** *nk* **Rebecca Romero**[31] 4615 4-9-2 **65**........................... RichardHughes 4 73+
(Denis Coakley) *hld up towards rr but in tch: rdn and hdwy over 1f out: str run ins fnl f to take 2nd clsng stages and gaining in wnr but nt quite get up* **5/2**[1]

336 **3** *hd* **Athwaab**[23] 4895 4-8-10 **64**.. LauraPike(5) 8 71
(Tim McCarthy) *sn led: drvn 3 l clr 2f out: kpt on fnl f tl wknd and hdd cl home: lost 2nd last strides* **14/1**

2245 **4** 2 ¾ **Even Bolder**[4] 5513 8-9-4 **70**................................ KierenFox(3) 5 67
(Eric Wheeler) *in rr: rdn over 2f out: hung rt u.p over 1f out but kpt on fnl f: nt rch ldrs* **8/1**

4004 **5** 1 **Bilash**[23] 4895 4-9-2 **65**.. JamieSpencer 2 59
(Reg Hollinshead) *n.m.r s and s.i.s: in rr: rdn over 2f out: sme prog fnl f* **4/1**[2]

6301 **6** 7 **Straboe (USA)**[15] 5173 5-8-6 **58**..........................(v) RyanClark(3) 6 27
(Stuart Williams) *chsd ldrs: rdn and hung rt 2f out: wknd over 1f out* **17/2**

0624 **7** ½ **Atlantic Beach**[58] 3713 6-9-5 **68**.................... RichardKingscote 3 35
(Milton Bradley) *chsd ldrs to 1/2-way: sn wknd* **11/2**[3]

-606 **8** 3 **Avrilo**[12] 5265 5-9-0 **63**.. TomMcLaughlin 1 19
(Malcolm Saunders) *pressed ldr early and styd in 2nd to 1/2-way: wknd ins fnl 2f* **11/1**

60.83 secs (-0.17) **Going Correction** -0.125s/f (Firm) **8** Ran SP% **112.4**
Speed ratings (Par 103): **96,95,95,90,89 78,77,72**
toteswingers: 1&2 £3.30, 1&3 £19.90, 2&3 £7.30 CSF £25.68 CT £258.49 TOTE £9.30: £2.40, £1.30, £4.30; EX 18.70 Trifecta £573.30 Part won. Pool: £774.76 - 0.62 winning units..
Owner Mrs Liz Gardner **Bred** Lazy Lane Farms Inc **Trained** Liphook, Hants

FOCUS
A modest sprint handicap and they were soon strung out owing to a strong pace set by Athwaab. Small personal bests from the first two.

5659 CGA "PERSIAN PUNCH" CONDITIONS STKS 1m 6f 21y

5:30 (5:31) (Class 2) 3-Y-0+

£9,960 (£2,982; £1,491; £745; £372; £187)

Form RPR

1150 **1** **Highland Castle**[12] 5284 3-8-7 100.......................... JamieSpencer 10 113+
(David Elsworth) *stdd s and wl bhd early: hdwy 3f out: swtchd lft over 2f out and trckd ldr sn after: drvn to ld appr fnl f: sn clr: eased clsng stages* **3/1**[1]

4460 **2** 2 ½ **Roxy Flyer (IRE)**[12] 5271 4-8-11 97.......................... JimmyQuinn 4 98
(Amanda Perrett) *in tch: rdn and kpt on fr 3f out: styng on whn crossed appr fnl 2f: styd on u.p fnl f to take 2nd fnl 120yds but no ch w eased down wnr* **10/1**

-002 **3** 1 ½ **Woolfall Treasure**[26] 4775 6-9-2 96..........................(v) RichardHughes 9 101
(Gary Moore) *trckd ldr tl led over 7f out: rdn 3f out: kpt on fr 2f out tl hdd appr fnl f and sn outpcd: lost 2nd fnl 120yds* **14/1**

5005 **4** 2 ½ **Sabotage (UAE)**[12] 5271 5-9-2 103................................ FrankieDettori 2 98
(Saeed Bin Suroor) *chsd ldrs: drvn to chse ldr 4f out: no imp: wknd fnl f* **3/1**[1]

0324 **5** ¾ **Mountain Hiker (IRE)**[41] 4266 4-9-2 95........................(v) GeorgeBaker 6 96
(Jeremy Noseda) *rel to r and sn wl bhd: hdwy to cl on main gp fr 7f out: pushed along over 3f out: styd on fnl 2f but nvr gng pce to get into contention* **6/1**[3]

50 **6** 13 **Kidnapped (AUS)**[61] 3625 5-9-8 106..............................(v) TedDurcan 1 84
(Saeed Bin Suroor) *in rr but in tch: hdwy 6f out: rdn 3f out: sn btn* **12/1**

305 **7** ¾ **Mystery Star (IRE)**[33] 4532 6-9-2 96........................ PhilipRobinson 7 77
(Mark H Tompkins) *chsd ldrs: rdn 4f out: wknd fr 3f out* **16/1**

1124 **8** 15 **Colour Vision (FR)**[17] 5131 3-8-5 101.......................... FrannyNorton 3 56
(Mark Johnston) *chsd ldrs: rdn 6f out: sn btn* **7/2**[2]

9 15 **Radetsky March (IRE)**[167] 8-9-2 0.......................... FergusSweeney 8 35
(Mark Bradstock) *led tl hdd over 7f out: wknd 3f out* **100/1**

3m 5.09s (-2.31) **Going Correction** -0.125s/f (Firm)
WFA 3 from 4yo+ 11lb **9** Ran SP% **116.8**
Speed ratings (Par 109): **101,99,98,97,96 89,89,80,71**
toteswingers: 1&2 £9.00, 1&3 £7.10, 2&3 £11.70 CSF £34.54 TOTE £3.80: £1.40, £1.50, £2.60; EX 37.90 Trifecta £499.90 Part won. Pool: £675.55 - 0.90 winning units..
Owner J Wotherspoon & W Harrison-Allan **Bred** John Wotherspoon **Trained** Newmarket, Suffolk

FOCUS
A race that has almost always gone to a classy type in recent years, most notably in 2002 when it was won by old favourite Persian Punch, who has the race named in his honour these days. It's a surprise the race doesn't have a higher grade. As usual for this distance at Salisbury, a flip-start was used, and the pace was good. The fiorm may not be the most reliable but the winner impressed and is value for extra.

NOTEBOOK
Highland Castle ◆ lost several lengths when briefly getting stuck behind the reluctant Mountain Hiker. As it turned out, that was no bad thing considering the gallop was sound, and he gradually eased his way into the race. He was still on the bridle when going to the front in the straight and found more than enough when asked, despite wandering a bit and basically still looking raw. This fine, scopey individual has faced some tough tasks recently, including finishing down the field in the Lonsdale Cup just 12 days earlier, but he showed he's still going forward and really should make a terrific older stayer as he matures both mentally and physically. Representing the trainer of Persian Punch, he'll surely win Cup races. Incidentally, he's now 2-2 for Jamie Spencer, whose ability to help him settle is a big positive. (op 5-1)
Roxy Flyer(IRE) travelled well for a fair way, and then having found a bit of trouble when first asked to make her bid she kept on. She wasn't unlucky, but this was a good effort behind an improving type. (op 8-1)
Woolfall Treasure ran a solid race under a positive ride. (op 12-1)
Sabotage(UAE) was disappointing, not really picking up after being produced with every chance. (op 5-2 tchd 9-4)
Mountain Hiker(IRE), who had to be withdrawn at York in August having been unruly at the start, didn't want to know at all this time. He was flashing his tail even before the tape went up and took an age to jump off with the others, so it was a surprise he finished so close. Official explanation: jockey said gelding was reluctant to race (op 7-1 tchd 15-2)
Colour Vision(FR) was beaten a long way out and did not give his true running. (tchd 9-2 in a place)
T/Plt: £350.60 to a £1 stake. Pool: £55,518.51. 115.57 winning tickets. T/Qpdt: £19.40 to a £1 stake. Pool: £4,945.83. 188.60 winning tickets. ST

5660 - 5663a (Foreign Racing) - See Raceform Interactive

5610 BADEN-BADEN (L-H)

Thursday, September 1

OFFICIAL GOING: Turf: good

5664a DARLEY OETTINGEN-RENNEN (GROUP 2) (3YO+) (TURF) 1m

6:00 (6:03) 3-Y-0+

£34,482 (£13,362; £5,603; £3,448; £2,155; £1,293)

RPR

1 **Shamalgan (FR)**[47] 4120 4-9-1 0.......................... FilipMinarik 1 112
(A Savujev, Czech Republic) *broke slowly: settled in midfield on ins rail: a travelling smoothly: shkn up ent st: nt qckn immediately but once fnd stride r.o strly to catch and hd ldr under 1f out: wnt clr: easily* **76/10**

2 1 ¾ **Alianthus (GER)**[46] 4138 6-9-4 0.......................... ADeVries 6 111
(J Hirschberger, Germany) *sn led: set gd pce: led into st: r.o wl but ct and hdd under 1f out: styd on* **3/5**[1]

3 1 **Blue Panis (FR)**[41] 4-9-1 0.......................... Christophe-PatriceLemaire 8 106
(F Chappet, France) *broke wl to r bhd ldr: r.o wl in st wout threatening ldrs* **49/10**[2]

4 ½ **Sir Oscar (GER)**[25] 4-9-1 0.......................... ASuborics 7 105
(T Potters, Germany) *hld up in midfield: full of running ent st but nt qckn to chal ldrs: styd on wl fnl f* **19/2**

5 *nk* **Le Big (GER)**[32] 7-9-1 0.......................... AHelfenbein 4 104
(U Stoltefuss, Germany) *bkmarker fr s: swung wd into st: rdn and styd on fnl f* **181/10**

6 5 **Point Blank (GER)**[39] 4373 3-8-10 0.......................... StefanieHofer 91
(Mario Hofer, Germany) *broke fast and settled on ins rail bhd ldr: flattered briefly ent st but nt qckn and sn wknd* **99/10**

7 2 ½ **Neatico (GER)**[25] 4-9-1 0.......................... AStarke 9 87
(P Schiergen, Germany) *broke fast then settled 4th: rdn but no ex in st: wknd* **66/10**[3]

8 3 ½ **Walero (GER)**[25] 5-9-1 0.......................... KClijmans 2 79
(Uwe Ostmann, Germany) *settled in 3rd: rdn bef st: no ex: wknd* **178/10**

1m 37.48s (-1.63)
WFA 3 from 4yo+ 5lb **8** Ran SP% **133.5**
WIN (incl. 10 euro stake): 86. PLACES: 18, 11, 17. SF: 170.
Owner Ardak Amirkulov **Bred** M Daguzan-Garros & Rolling Hills Farm **Trained** Czech Republic

5420 BRIGHTON (L-H)

Friday, September 2

OFFICIAL GOING: Good (good to firm in places; watered; 7.2) (visibility reduced for last four races due to sea fret)
Sea mist reduced visability for Race 4 (3:50) to final 5f out, for race 5 (4:20) 1f out, for race 6 (4:50) just over 1f, for race 7 (5:20) just over 2f
Wind: Light against Weather: bright and sunny

5665 DEREK HUNNISETT MEMORIAL DAY H'CAP 1m 3f 196y

2:20 (2:20) (Class 6) (0-60,64) 3-Y-0 **£1,811** (£539; £269; £134) **Stalls** High

Form RPR

400 **1** **Fairling**[32] 4617 3-9-7 **59**.......................... SteveDrowne 6 69+
(Hughie Morrison) *mde all: hrd pressed and rdn jst over 2f out: kpt on v gamely and forged clr 1f out: in command and styd on wl fnl f* **9/2**[3]

2111 **2** 1 ¾ **Tegan (IRE)**[11] 5321 3-9-9 **64** 6ex.......................... KieranO'Neill(3) 7 71+
(Richard Hannon) *hld up wl in tch: plld out in to centre and effrt 2f out: hdwy u.p over 1f out: chsd wnr fnl 150yds: kpt on but no imp* **85/40**[1]

3562 **3** 2 ½ **Dolly Colman (IRE)**[17] 5134 3-8-9 **47**.......................... LukeMorris 1 50
(Andrew Haynes) *stdd s: hld up in tch: hdwy to chse press ldr over 5f out: ev ch and rdn over 2f out: no ex and btn ent fnl f: lost 2nd ins fnl f and wknd fnl 100yds* **3/1**[2]

0535 **4** *shd* **Heart Of Dixie (IRE)**[14] 5243 3-8-9 **52**.......................... RyanPowell(5) 5 55
(Paul Cole) *chsd wnr tl over 5f out: styd handy: rdn and pressing ldrs 2f out: unable qck u.p over 1f out: wknd fnl 100yds* **5/1**

0553 **5** 3 ½ **Disturbia (IRE)**[25] 4847 3-8-9 **47**.......................... KierenFallon 2 44
(J W Hills) *hld up in tch: hdwy over 4f out: chsd ldrs and rdn ent 2f out: edgd lft u.p and btn over 1f out: wknd fnl f: sddle slipped* **5/1**

-000 **6** 17 **Sabot D'Or**[9] 5381 3-9-1 **53**.......................... JackMitchell 4 23
(Roger Ingram) *in tch: dropped to last over 4f out: rdn and effrt on inner 2f out: wknd over 1f out: wl btn and eased ins fnl f* **25/1**

2m 39.82s (7.12) **Going Correction** +0.075s/f (Good) **6** Ran SP% **112.4**
Speed ratings (Par 99): **79,77,76,76,73 62**
toteswingers:1&2:£2.40, 1&3:£4.10, 2&3:£1.20 CSF £14.54 CT £31.89 TOTE £5.10: £1.70, £1.30; EX 27.00.
Owner The Fairy Story Partnership **Bred** Deepwood Farm Stud **Trained** East Ilsley, Berks
■ Stewards' Enquiry : Ryan Powell ten-day ban: failed to ride out for 3rd (Sep 16-25)

FOCUS
After a dry night the going was good, good to firm in places. The rail was dolled out from 6f to 2.5f, adding 16 yards to race distances. There was a lively market for this low-grade handicap which was run at a steady pace. Reasonable form for the grade, rated around the fourth.
Disturbia(IRE) Official explanation: jockey said saddle slipped

5666 SUPPORT THE MARTLETS HOSPICE FILLIES' H'CAP 1m 1f 209y

2:50 (2:51) (Class 5) (0-70,69) 3-Y-0+ **£2,522** (£750; £375; £187) **Stalls** High

Form RPR

1520 **1** **Golden Waters**[17] 5135 4-9-12 **69**.......................... SebSanders 6 78
(Eve Johnson Houghton) *hld up in tch in last trio: hdwy to chse ldr over 4f out: led wl over 2f out: drvn and flashed tail u.p fr over 1f out: forged clr fnl 100yds: styd on wl* **11/4**[2]

2251 **2** 2 ½ **Empress Charlotte**[29] 4727 3-9-4 **68**.......................... LukeMorris 1 72
(Michael Bell) *hld up in tch: nt clr run and hmpd on bnd over 4f out: hdwy to chse ldrs and rdn ent 3f out: chsd ldng pair 2f out: styd on u.p ins fnl f to snatch 2nd on post: no threat to wnr* **2/1**[1]

515 **3** *shd* **Out Of The Storm**[17] 5135 3-8-11 **61**.......................... KierenFallon 4 65
(Simon Dow) *led: hdd and rdn wl over 2f out: stl pressing wnr and drvn over 1f out: btn fnl 150yds: wknd fnl 100yds and lost 2nd on post* **7/2**[3]

6300 **4** *hd* **Very Well Red**[21] 5002 8-9-11 **68**.......................... ChrisCatlin 3 71
(Peter Hiatt) *chsd ldr tl over 4f out: rdn and unable qck wl over 2f out: 4th and btn over 1f out: no threat to wnr but kpt on u.p ins fnl f* **14/1**

The Form Book, Raceform Ltd, Compton, RG20 6NL

3044 **5** *5* **Entrance**[12] 5302 3-8-10 **60**........ JimmyQuinn 2 53
(Julia Feilden) *stdd s and awkward leaving stalls: hld up in tch in rr: rdn and effrt 4f out: wknd wl over 2f out* **14/1**

-555 **6** *18* **Always De One**[115] 1233 4-8-12 **55** oh10........(p) JamieMackay 7 12
(K F Clutterbuck) *chsd ldrs: rdn and lost pl 4f out: lost tch 2f out: wl btn and eased ins fnl f* **50/1**

304 **7** *12* **Flaming Nora**[18] 5098 3-9-0 **64**........(v[1]) JackMitchell 5 —
(James Fanshawe) *chsd ldrs tl lost pl and dropped to last 4f out: rdn and lost tch 3f out: t.o and eased 1f out* **7/1**

2m 5.65s (2.05) **Going Correction** +0.075s/f (Good)
WFA 3 from 4yo+ 7lb **7** Ran SP% **110.0**
Speed ratings (Par 100): **94,92,91,91,87 73,63**
toteswingers:1&2:£1.10, 1&3:£2.40, 2&3:£1.10 CSF £7.96 TOTE £4.30: £2.20, £1.40; EX 10.10.
Owner R Crutchley **Bred** R E Crutchley **Trained** Blewbury, Oxon

FOCUS
A minor fillies' handicap run at a sedate pace. Modest form, with a length personal best from the winner.

5667 DONATELLO RISTORANTE SUPPORTS THE MARTLETS HOSPICE APPRENTICE H'CAP 7f 214y
3:20 (3:20) (Class 6) (0-60,60) 4-Y-0+ **£1,811** (£539; £269; £134) **Stalls** Centre

Form RPR

4102 **1** **Olney Lass**[12] 5298 4-8-8 **50**........ SophieSilvester(3) 7 61
(Lydia Pearce) *hld up off the pce towards rr: hdwy on outer over 1f out: rdn to chal and wnt clr w rival 1f out: led ins fnl f: pushed along and r.o wl* **6/1**[3]

0234 **2** *1 1/4* **Indian Violet (IRE)**[29] 4699 5-9-3 **59**........ LukeRowe(3) 8 67
(Ralph Smith) *t.k.h: chsd ldrs tl stdd into midfield after 2f: rdn and gd hdwy to ld over 1f out: drew clr w wnr 1f out: hdd and stdy on same pce ins fnl f* **8/1**

004 **3** *4 1/2* **Hierarch (IRE)**[23] 4928 4-9-1 **57**........ MichaelJMurphy(3) 2 55
(David Simcock) *hld up off the pce towards rr: rdn and effrt over 1f out: outpcd by ldng pair 1f out: wnt 3rd wl ins fnl f: no threat to ldrs* **10/3**[1]

6634 **4** *1 1/4* **King Columbo (IRE)**[14] 5231 6-8-10 **49**........(p) CharlesBishop 5 44
(Julia Feilden) *t.k.h: hld up off the pce in rr: clsd over 3f out: effrt on inner and swtchd rt wl over 1f out: chsd ldng and outpcd 1f out: wknd ins fnl f* **12/1**

3522 **5** *5* **Annes Rocket (IRE)**[17] 5143 6-9-2 **60**........(p) ThomasBrown(5) 9 43
(Jimmy Fox) *v.s.a: wl detached in last tl clsd and tagged on to bk of field 3f out: rdn and effrt wl over 1f out: sn wknd* **9/2**[2]

4456 **6** *hd* **Musashi (IRE)**[22] 4445 6-8-11 **57**........(b) CharlotteJenner(7) 4 40
(Laura Mongan) *chsd ldrs tl dashed up to ld after 1f: sn clr: hdd 2f out: wknd over 1f out: fdd ins fnl f* **40/1**

6623 **7** *nk* **Derby Desire (IRE)**[5] 5520 7-8-7 **46**........ RaulDaSilva 6 28
(Des Donovan) *led for 1f: chsd ldr tl 4f out: rdn and struggling jst over 2f out: wkng whn n.m.r wl over 1f out* **6/1**[3]

4342 **8** *3/4* **Inquisitress**[7] 5422 7-8-10 **49**........ RachealKneller 1 29
(John Bridger) *hld up off the pce in midfield: pushed along and effrt over 2f out: wknd over 1f out: fdd fnl f* **9/2**[2]

0060 **9** *6* **Carlcol Girl**[23] 4927 4-8-2 **46** oh1........ DanielHarris(5) 3 13
(Christine Dunnett) *dwlt: sn rdn along and hdwy to chse ldrs after 1f: wnt 2nd 4f out: rdn to ld 2f out: hdd over 1f out: sn wknd: fdd fnl f* **100/1**

1m 36.27s (0.27) **Going Correction** +0.075s/f (Good) **9** Ran SP% **110.2**
Speed ratings (Par 101): **101,99,95,94,89 88,88,87,81**
toteswingers:1&2:£7.70, 1&3:£8.20, 2&3:£3.80 CSF £49.22 CT £175.13 TOTE £7.50: £2.20, £2.10, £1.70; EX 58.60.
Owner T H Rossiter **Bred** T H Rossiter **Trained** Newmarket, Suffolk

FOCUS
Mist was rolling in before this ordinary apprentice handicap. It was run at a strong pace and the first two pulled clear. The runner-up sets the standard.

5668 BRITISH STALLION STUDS E.B.F./DEREK HUNNISETT MEMORIAL MAIDEN STKS 6f 209y
3:50 (3:50) (Class 5) 2-Y-0 **£3,234** (£962; £481; £240) **Stalls** Centre

Form RPR

2322 **1** **Storming Bernard (USA)**[6] 5478 2-9-3 87........ IanMongan 3 81+
(Alan Bailey) *mde all: rdn and readily asserted 1f out: in command after: eased cl home: comf* **5/4**[1]

5 **2** *1 1/4* **Strident Force**[42] 4264 2-9-3 0........ KierenFallon 5 78+
(Sir Michael Stoute) *t.k.h: hld up in tch: chsd wnr wl over 2f out: rdn and unable qck over 1f out: outpcd and btn jst ins fnl f: kpt on same pce* **11/8**[2]

3 *1 3/4* **Representation (USA)** 2-8-12 0........ AntiocoMurgia(5) 4 73+
(Mahmood Al Zarooni) *dwlt and sltly hmpd s: rn green and hld up in tch in rr: hdwy to chse ldrs wl over 2f out: unable qck and btn over 1f out: hung lft ins fnl f* **15/2**[3]

005 **4** *3* **Next Cry (USA)**[9] 5384 2-9-0 0........ KieranO'Neill(3) 2 66
(Richard Hannon) *awkward leaving stalls: t.k.h early: hld up in tch: hdwy over 2f out: outpcd wl over 1f out: wknd jst over 1f out* **22/1**

354 **5** *hd* **Pitt Rivers**[8] 5398 2-9-3 75........(v) SamHitchcott 1 65
(Mick Channon) *in tch: rdn and effrt on inner over 2f out: no imp and btn jst over 1f out* **16/1**

0 **6** *45* **Flatford Mill**[115] 1988 2-9-3 0........ ChrisCatlin 7 —
(K F Clutterbuck) *racd freely: styd wd: chsd ldr tl wl over 2f out: sn dropped out and t.o fr wl over 1f out* **150/1**

1m 24.56s (1.46) **Going Correction** +0.075s/f (Good) **6** Ran SP% **109.2**
Speed ratings (Par 95): **94,92,90,87,86 35**
toteswingers:1&2:£1.10, 1&3:£3.00, 2&3:£2.80 CSF £3.02 TOTE £1.60: £1.10, £1.70; EX 3.20.
Owner John Stocker **Bred** Hill 'N' Dale Equine Holdings Inc & Netp **Trained** Newmarket, Suffolk

FOCUS
A useful maiden run at a slow tempo. It was won with authority by the 87-rated favourite but he probably didn't need to match his previous best. There was plenty of promise from the placed horses.

NOTEBOOK
Storming Bernard(USA) set a useful/clear standard on his peak form which included a front-running second to subsequent Group 3 winner at Newmarket and a close call off a mark of 87 on nursery debut last time. Ridden positively, he gradually wound things up and powered to a decisive success on his sixth attempt. He is proving generally progressive and seems equally effective on fast and slow ground, and on stiff and sharp tracks. (tchd 6-4)
Strident Force is bred to make a 2yo at about this trip and showed plenty of promise when staying on to hunt up those in the frame in decent 7f Ascot maiden on debut in July. He had something to find but attracted a landslide of support and gave it a decent try without ever looking a big threat to main form contender. However, this form looks decent and this scopey Refuse To Bend colt should have no trouble striking in maiden company before possibly going on to better things. (op 11-10 tchd Evens)
Representation(USA), a Derby entered Street Cry colt who is out of a 6f 2yo/1m2f (Listed) winner, looked inexperienced but ran a big race with a decent target to aim at on debut. He should have learned a lot and should improve next time. (op 12-1 tchd 13-2)
Next Cry(USA) ran respectably with quite a bit to find. Related to some useful US winners, he has found some improvement in four runs and a switch to nurseries should broaden his horizons. (op 33-1 tchd 20-1)
Pitt Rivers finished close up in his four previous maiden runs and ran a fair race stepped up in trip in a second-time visor. He is not really progressing, but is a consistent 75-rated gelding who looks a fairly solid marker for the form. (op 20-1)

5669 INSURANCE AND MORTGAGES ON TAP 08002 983 666 H'CAP 6f 209y
4:20 (4:20) (Class 5) (0-75,75) 3-Y-0+ **£2,522** (£750; £375; £187) **Stalls** Centre

Form RPR

2235 **1** **Mandhooma**[17] 5136 5-9-0 **65**........ ChrisCatlin 4 74
(Peter Hiatt) *hmpd sn after s: hld up in last trio: chalng on stands' rail and u.p 1f out: r.o wl to ld wl ins fnl f* **9/2**[3]

5120 **2** *nk* **Blue Deer (IRE)**[2] 5615 3-8-2 **64**........ CharlesBishop(7) 8 70
(Mick Channon) *led: racing nr stands' rail and hrd pressed u.p 1f out: hdd and no ex wl ins fnl f* **4/1**[2]

-313 **3** *2* **Patavium Prince (IRE)**[60] 3674 8-9-8 **73**........ DaneO'Neill 2 76
(Jo Crowley) *chsd ldrs: 3rd and pressing ldrs but hrd drvn 1f out: no ex ins fnl f* **15/2**

00 **4** *3/4* **Miss Dutee**[22] 4973 3-8-3 **61** oh2........ KieranO'Neill(3) 9 60
(Richard Hannon) *in tch: 4th and racing towards centre u.p 1f out: styd on same pce after* **22/1**

6000 **5** *1 1/2* **Buxton**[25] 4865 7-9-6 **71**........(t) MartinLane 6 68
(Roger Ingram) *hld up in last trio: 8th and u.p towards stands' rail 1f out: styd on ins fnl f: nt rch ldrs* **25/1**

4021 **6** *1/2* **High On The Hog (IRE)**[7] 5423 3-9-4 **73** 6ex........(p) IanMongan 3 66
(John Dunlop) *chsd ldrs: 5th and struggling u.p 1f out: wknd fnl 150yds* **7/2**[1]

51 **7** *1* **Main Beach**[111] 2094 4-9-10 **75**........(t) StevieDonohoe 7 68
(Tobias B P Coles) *taken down early: awkward leaving stalls and s.i.s: in tch towards rr: hdwy and in tch whn hung lft over 1f out: 6th 1f out: wknd ins fnl f: fin lame* **11/2**

1212 **8** *3/4* **Highland Harvest**[8] 5412 7-9-2 **67**........ SteveDrowne 1 58
(Jamie Poulton) *chsd ldr tl 4f out: 7th and btn 1f out: wknd ins fnl f: eased towards fin* **9/1**

303 **9** *hd* **Aspectus (IRE)**[15] 5200 8-9-6 **74**........(b) SophieDoyle(3) 5 64
(Jamie Osborne) *in tch in midfield: styd far side st: last and btn 1f out* **10/1**

1m 24.66s (1.56) **Going Correction** +0.075s/f (Good)
WFA 3 from 4yo+ 4lb **9** Ran SP% **114.8**
Speed ratings (Par 103): **94,93,91,90,88 88,87,86,86**
toteswingers:1&2:£5.00, 1&3:£6.10, 2&3:£6.70 CSF £22.73 CT £131.92 TOTE £4.00: £2.70, £1.30, £2.90; EX 27.30.
Owner P W Hiatt **Bred** Shadwell Estate Company Limited **Trained** Hook Norton, Oxon

FOCUS
It was very misty during this competitive handicap. The field were spread across the track in the straight and there was a tight finish. It's doubtful the winner had to improve much
Main Beach Official explanation: trainer said gelding returned lame
Aspectus(IRE) Official explanation: jockey said horse ran too free early stages

5670 HUNNISETT HIGHLAND CHIEFTAIN H'CAP 5f 213y
4:50 (4:50) (Class 6) (0-55,55) 3-Y-0 **£1,811** (£539; £269; £134) **Stalls** Centre

Form RPR

0050 **1** **Microlight**[23] 4930 3-8-7 **46** oh1........(b) RichardThomas 4 50
(John E Long) *chsd ldr: in ld racing towards stands' rail over 1f out: hld on wl u.p fnl f* **13/2**[3]

5450 **2** *nk* **Bambika**[58] 3724 3-9-0 **53**........ DaneO'Neill 7 56
(Jo Crowley) *in tch in midfield: racing towards stands' rail and chsng wnr u.p over 1f out: ev ch thrght fnl f: kpt on wl* **7/2**[2]

055 **3** *2 1/2* **Acclamatory**[43] 4247 3-8-4 **50**........ CharlesBishop(7) 11 45
(Stuart Williams) *chsd ldng trio: chsng ldng pair and racing against stands' rail over 1f out: wknd ins fnl f* **13/2**[3]

5006 **4** *1/2* **Talkative Guest (IRE)**[10] 5352 3-9-1 **54**........(tp) KierenFallon 9 47
(George Margarson) [illegible] *racing in centre jst over 1f out: hung lft and kpt on same pce ins fnl f* **5/2**[1]

000 **5** *1 3/4* **Elite Syncopations**[17] 5137 3-8-7 **46** oh1........ MartinLane 10 34
(Andrew Haynes) *awkward leaving stalls and slowly away: sn detached in last and rdn along: stl wl bhd in last over 1f out: styd on wl ins fnl f: nvr trbld ldrs* **14/1**

4060 **6** *3/4* **Slatey Hen (IRE)**[4] 5540 3-8-13 **55**........ RobertLButler(3) 3 40
(Richard Guest) *chsd ldrs: styd far side st: 4th and u.p over 1f out: wknd ins fnl f* **7/1**

-005 **7** *3 1/2* **Bella Nemica**[22] 4950 3-8-7 **46** oh1........ EddieCreighton 2 20
(Edward Creighton) *led: styd towards far side st: 6th and btn over 1f out: wknd fnl f* **22/1**

5060 **8** *2 1/2* **Femme Royale**[10] 5352 3-8-7 **46** oh1........(t) ChrisCatlin 5 12
(Robert Cowell) *dwlt: sn rdn along in last quartet: styd far side st: 7th and wl btn over 1f out* **40/1**

0400 **9** *3/4* **Blazing Apostle (IRE)**[23] 4929 3-8-0 **46** oh1........(p) DanielHarris(7) 6 10
(Christine Dunnett) *s.i.s: a struggling in rr: styd far side st: 8th and wl btn over 1f out* **8/1**

1m 11.97s (1.77) **Going Correction** +0.075s/f (Good) **9** Ran SP% **114.5**
Speed ratings (Par 99): **91,90,87,86,84 83,78,75,74**
toteswingers:1&2:£4.10, 1&3:£5.60, 2&3:£2.70 CSF £29.25 CT £155.00 TOTE £6.00: £1.50, £1.50, £1.80; EX 32.80.
Owner R D John **Bred** Newsells Park Stud **Trained** Caterham, Surrey

FOCUS
A very modest handicap, and poor visibility. Most of the runners were still maidens and they had all been beaten 6l+ on their latest run. They split into two groups in the straight and the first three raced near the stands' side.
Blazing Apostle(IRE) Official explanation: jockey said filly hung left

5671 DEREK HUNNISETT MEMORIAL FILLIES' H'CAP 5f 213y
5:20 (5:20) (Class 5) (0-75,75) 3-Y-0+ **£2,522** (£750; £375; £187) **Stalls** Centre

Form RPR

363 **1** **Yurituni**[21] 5018 4-9-4 **75**........(v) LouisBeuzelin(3) 4 83
(Eve Johnson Houghton) *chsd ldrs: ev ch and hrd drvn wl over 1f out: led ins fnl f: styd on strly and drew clr fnl 75yds* **7/2**[2]

3121 **2** *2 1/2* **Interakt**[7] 5425 4-8-11 **72** 6ex........ CharlesBishop(7) 2 72
(Joseph Tuite) *dwlt: in rr: hdwy to chal 2f out: led narrowly wl over 1f out: sn rdn: hdd ins fnl f: wknd fnl 75yds: eased cl home* **11/10**[1]

5120 **3** *2* **Delira (IRE)**[10] 5338 3-8-10 **69**.................................... RossAtkinson(3) 1 63
(Jonathan Portman) *in tch in last pair: effrt to chal 2f out: pressing ldrs and hung rt ent fnl f: wknd ins fnl f* **10/1**

-001 **4** *1 1/2* **Jahanara (IRE)**[16] 5172 3-8-8 **67**.................................... KieranO'Neill(3) 3 56
(Richard Hannon) *led: hdd wl over 1f out: wknd 1f out* **11/2**[3]

160 **5** *3/4* **Chaussini**[23] 4909 4-9-6 **74**.................................... StevieDonohoe 5 60
(James Toller) *w ldr tl 2f out: struggling over 1f out: wknd fnl f* **6/1**

1m 10.95s (0.75) **Going Correction** +0.075s/f (Good)
WFA 3 from 4yo 2lb **5** Ran SP% **108.6**
Speed ratings (Par 100): **98,94,92,90,89**
CSF £7.61 TOTE £3.40: £1.40, £1.10; EX 9.30.
Owner Mrs R F Johnson Houghton **Bred** Jeremy Green And Sons **Trained** Blewbury, Oxon

FOCUS
The runners stayed centre to far side in this sprint handicap and the well handicapped winner scored with quite a bit in hand. Modest form, rated around her.
T/Plt: £60.10 to a £1 stake. Pool:£64,582.70 - 784.25 winning tickets T/Qpdt: £18.90 to a £1 stake. Pool:£5,399.33 - 210.40 winning tickets SP

5534 CHEPSTOW (L-H)
Friday, September 2

OFFICIAL GOING: Good (7.5)
Wind: Moderate across Weather: Sunny periods

5672 LIFE MUSIC FOUNDATION MAIDEN AUCTION STKS 1m 14y
2:30 (2:30) (Class 6) 2-Y-O **£1,811** (£539; £269; £134) **Stalls** Centre

Form RPR

36 **1** **Titus Star (IRE)**[22] 4969 2-8-9 0.................................... JamesDoyle 6 77+
(J S Moore) *trckd ldr: drvn to chal over 1f out: styd on wl fnl f to ld fnl 75yds: readily* **5/1**[3]

05 **2** *1* **Beau Duke (IRE)**[22] 4968 2-8-11 0.................................... JimmyFortune 3 77
(Andrew Balding) *led: drvn ins fnl 2f: jnd over 1f out: hdd and no ex fnl 75yds* **15/8**[1]

00 **3** *6* **Strictly Mine**[73] 3258 2-8-5 0 ow1.................................... TadhgO'Shea 5 57
(Jonathan Portman) *chsd ldrs: rdn along fr 3f out: styd on to chse ldng duo appr fnl f but no imp* **33/1**

0 **4** *1 3/4* **Lone Foot Laddie (IRE)**[22] 4968 2-8-13 0.................... StephenCraine 4 61
(Sylvester Kirk) *chsd ldrs: rdn: hung lft and v green fr over 2f out: sn no ex: lost 3rd appr fnl f* **7/2**[2]

5 *6* **Stickleback** 2-8-1 0.................................... JohnFahy(3) 12 38
(Harry Dunlop) *s.i.s: in rr and wl bhd 1/2-way: hdwy fr 3f out: styd on wl fnl f and gng on cl home but nvr any ch* **16/1**

6 *3/4* **Elavssom (IRE)** 2-8-11 0.................................... MarkLawson 10 44+
(Jo Hughes) *hdwy 4f out: rdn to chse ldrs 3f out: no imp and wknd ins fnl 2f* **25/1**

0 **7** *3* **Singmeasong**[27] 4804 2-8-6 0.................................... WilliamCarson 11 32
(J W Hills) *in tch: rdn and dropped to rr 4f out: mod prog again fnl f* **20/1**

0 **8** *3 1/4* **Silver Six**[8] 5410 2-8-10 0.................................... MartinHarley(3) 9 31
(Mick Channon) *chsd ldrs over 4f* **22/1**

9 *2 1/4* **Isola Bella** 2-8-7 0 ow1.................................... NeilChalmers 1 20
(Jonathan Portman) *s.i.s: in rr: sme hdwy 4f out: wknd fr 3f out* **28/1**

10 *1* **Rowan Sun** 2-8-9 0.................................... CathyGannon 7 20
(Eve Johnson Houghton) *a outpcd in rr* **12/1**

11 *hd* **Grande Illusion** 2-9-2 0.................................... EddieAhern 8 26
(J W Hills) *broke wl: sn stdd in rr: pushed along: green and hung lft 3f out: no ch after* **7/1**

1m 37.08s (0.88) **Going Correction** -0.05s/f (Good) **11** Ran SP% **119.1**
Speed ratings (Par 93): **93,92,86,84,78 77,74,71,69,68 67**
toteswingers:1&2:£2.30, 1&3:£26.20, 2&3:£13.00 CSF £13.87 TOTE £7.30: £2.10, £1.10, £10.50; EX 18.30.
Owner Ray Styles & J S Moore **Bred** A M F Persse **Trained** Upper Lambourn, Berks

FOCUS
All the races were on the straight track, in ascending order of trip. The traces of good to firm had been removed from the official going description, and riders in the first reported that the ground was "a bit loose on top" and "on the slow side of good". This was a very modest maiden in which all the male runners had already been gelded. The time was around four seconds outside the standard. The stalls were in the centre but the first pair, who came clear, ended up on the stands' side. Improvement from the first two.

NOTEBOOK
Titus Star(IRE) produced a sustained challenge to the favourite and, after grabbing the rail, got on top late on. Beaten in a seller first time out, he has his limitations, but his attitude is good and he should continue to pay his way at the right level. He may go to Fairyhouse later this month for a valuable sales race. (op 7-1 tchd 8-1 in a place)
Beau Duke(IRE), the form pick on his Salisbury fifth, became a little keyed up in the preliminaries. After making the running, he edged to his right when let down and could not fend off a persistent rival. He's now qualified for handicaps. (op 2-1 tchd 9-4 in places)
Strictly Mine was returning from a break. She was under pressure a good way out and was readily left behind by the first two. (op 25-1)
Lone Foot Laddie(IRE), who looked green and carried his head a little high when the pressure was on, was beaten further by Beau Duke than he had been at Salisbury. (tchd 4-1)
Stickleback was well beaten in the end, but did make a little late progress. A half-sister to the durable handicapper Marjury Daw, she should improve with time and a longer trip. (op 14-1)
Elavssom(IRE) is by a sprinter and is a half-brother to the smart 5f performer Dragon Flyer, and he weakened out of things over a trip that probably stretched him. (tchd 28-1)
Grande Illusion Official explanation: jockey said, regarding running and riding, that his orders were to give the gelding a chance, get it organised into a rhythm and finish as best he could, adding that the gelding was very green and threw its head in the air each time it hit a ridge.

5673 EURO COMMERCIALS MERCEDES-BENZ COMMERCIAL VEHICLES H'CAP 1m 14y
3:00 (3:02) (Class 6) (0-65,64) 3-Y-O+ **£1,811** (£539; £269; £134) **Stalls** Centre

Form RPR

-351 **1** **Quite A Catch (IRE)**[44] 4200 3-9-4 **63**.................(v) StephenCraine 12 73
(Jonathan Portman) *mde virtually all: drvn along fr 2f out: strly chal fr over 1f out: kpt finding u.p thrght fnl f: hld on gamely* **20/1**

0-05 **2** *hd* **Makyaal (IRE)**[23] 4916 3-8-5 **50** oh1.................................... TadhgO'Shea 8 60
(John Dunlop) *trckd ldrs: wnt 2nd over 2f out: drvn to chal wnr fr over 1f out and stl upsides ins fnl f but hanging rt and fnd no ex clsng stages* **10/1**

4250 **3** *2* **Duquesa (IRE)**[60] 3688 3-9-5 **64**.................................(v) CathyGannon 7 71+
(David Evans) *hld up in rr: shkn up over 3f out: nt clr run fr 2f out tl 1f out whn drvn and rapid hdwy fnl 150yds to take 3rd cl home but nt rch ldng duo* **10/1**

3212 **4** *1/2* **Daneside (IRE)**[22] 4948 4-9-4 **63**.................................... MatthewLawson(5) 2 68
(Gary Harrison) *chsd ldrs: tk cl 3rd u.p 2f out but nvr gong pce to chal: one pce fnl f and lost 3rd cl home* **15/8**[1]

-206 **5** *1 1/2* **Genes Of A Dancer (AUS)**[41] 4337 5-9-0 **54**.................... NeilChalmers 1 56
(Adrian Chamberlain) *chsd wnr tl over 2f out: sn rdn: wknd over 1f out* **20/1**

6622 **6** *2 1/4* **Adelina Patti**[17] 5137 3-9-3 **62**.................................... EddieAhern 4 58
(Walter Swinburn) *t.k.h: chsd ldrs: rdn over 2f out: styd on same pce fnl f* **9/2**[2]

3430 **7** *2* **Wishformore (IRE)**[21] 5002 4-9-8 **62**.................................(p) JamesDoyle 9 54
(J S Moore) *in tch: rdn and no imp fr 3f out: styd on same pce fnl 2f* **13/2**[3]

2616 **8** *2 1/4* **Tanforan**[8] 5402 9-9-4 **58**.................................... KellyHarrison 11 45
(Brian Baugh) *in rr tl drvn and sme hdwy 3f out: wknd fr 2f out* **9/1**

-400 **9** *3 3/4* **Slumbering Sioux**[41] 4317 3-8-12 **60**.................................... JohnFahy(3) 6 37
(Harry Dunlop) *chsd ldrs: rdn over 2f out: wknd rapidly wl over 1f out* **25/1**

6264 **10** *8* **Present Story**[7] 5428 4-8-13 **53**.................................(v) MarkLawson 5 13
(Gary Harrison) *t.k.h in rr: rdn and bhd fr 1/2-way* **20/1**

1m 35.51s (-0.69) **Going Correction** -0.05s/f (Good)
WFA 3 from 4yo+ 5lb **10** Ran SP% **112.6**
Speed ratings (Par 101): **101,100,98,98,96 94,92,90,86,78**
toteswingers:1&2:£19.60, 1&3:£19.20, 2&3:£19.20 CSF £188.50 CT £2113.96 TOTE £14.60: £5.00, £2.80, £2.30; EX 250.10.
Owner J G B Portman **Bred** Yeomanstown Stud **Trained** Compton, Berks

FOCUS
A very modest event, one of four Class 6 handicaps on the card. Again the runners gravitated towards the stands' side late on. The fourth sets the level rated just shy of previous C&D form.
Present Story Official explanation: jockey said filly never travelled

5674 NEWPORT COUNTY LOTTERY H'CAP 7f 16y
3:30 (3:30) (Class 6) (0-60,60) 3-Y-O+ **£1,811** (£539; £269; £134) **Stalls** Centre

Form RPR

012 **1** **Ellies Image**[8] 5404 4-9-7 **57**.................................... JimmyFortune 13 67+
(Brian Baugh) *s.i.s: in rr tl drvn: swtchd lft to far side of gp and gd hdwy fr 2f out: styd on to chse ldr 1f out: led fnl 120yds: styd on wl* **7/2**[1]

1365 **2** *1 1/4* **Dancing Welcome**[4] 5540 5-9-3 **53**.................(b) RoystonFfrench 17 60
(Milton Bradley) *chsd ldrs: rdn over 2f out: styd on u.p fnl f to take 2nd fnl 50yds but no ch w wnr* **6/1**[3]

1033 **3** *2 3/4* **Sienna Blue**[56] 3803 3-9-6 **60**.................................... CathyGannon 12 58
(Malcolm Saunders) *w ldr tl led over 3f out: rdn 2 l clr appr fnl f: hdd and no ex fnl 120yds: lost 2nd fnl 50yds* **16/1**

0345 **4** *nse* **Tourist**[22] 4948 6-9-1 **51**.................................... LiamJones 10 50
(Ian Williams) *t.k.h: hld up in rr: hdwy 2f out: sn nt clr run: styd on u.p fnl f to chal for 3rd last strides but no imp on ldng duo* **15/2**

0030 **5** *1 3/4* **Avon Light**[4] 5540 3-8-2 **47**.................................(p) JamesRogers(5) 2 40
(Milton Bradley) *led tl narrowly hdd and rdn over 3f out: kpt on same pce u.p fnl 2f* **33/1**

6043 **6** *1 1/4* **Farmers Dream (IRE)**[4] 5539 4-8-5 **46**...............(p) MatthewLawson(5) 5 37
(Richard Price) *in rr: rdn along fr 3f out: chsd ldrs fr 2f out but nvr on terms: styd on same pce* **4/1**[2]

0402 **7** *1* **Trade Centre**[2] 5617 6-8-12 **48**.................................... KellyHarrison 8 37
(Milton Bradley) *chsd ldrs: drvn along fr 4f out: outpcd fnl 2f* **7/1**

0043 **8** *3/4* **Timpanist (USA)**[15] 5201 4-9-7 **57**.................................... GeorgeBaker 16 44
(Simon Dow) *in tch: rdn over 2f out: no ch after* **16/1**

-062 **9** *nk* **All In A Paddy**[23] 4929 3-8-9 **52**.................................(b) MartinHarley(3) 11 36
(Ed McMahon) *broke wl: stdd in rr: drvn fr 3f out: styd on same pce fnl f* **16/1**

0-60 **10** *1/2* **Piccolete**[87] 2792 3-8-8 **51**.................................... SeanLevey(3) 15 36
(Richard Hannon) *chsd ldrs: rdn 2f out: eased whn hld ins fnl f* **28/1**

0000 **11** *1/2* **Dusty Bluebells (IRE)**[9] 5376 3-9-3 **57**.................(b[1]) JamesDoyle 1 38
(J S Moore) *chsd ldrs: rdn over 2f out: wknd over 1f out* **25/1**

65-0 **12** *2 1/2* **Northern Genes (AUS)**[4] 5540 5-8-10 **46**.................(p) RobbieFitzpatrick 4 22
(Michael Appleby) *chsd ldrs tl wknd over 2f out* **20/1**

3000 **13** *2* **Frosty Reception**[22] 4950 3-8-10 **50**.................................... NeilChalmers 7 19
(Michael Appleby) *s.i.s: a outpcd* **100/1**

5430 **14** *3* **Babich Bay (IRE)**[4] 5539 3-9-3 **57**.................................(b) TadhgO'Shea 9 18
(Jo Hughes) *chsd ldrs over 3f* **14/1**

-000 **15** *hd* **Transeggselence**[4] 5540 4-9-0 **50**.................................... MarkLawson 14 12
(Gary Harrison) *chsd ldrs to 1/2-way* **66/1**

5000 **16** *3/4* **Talamahana**[14] 5244 6-9-0 **50**.................................(v) EddieAhern 3 10
(Andrew Haynes) *s.i.s: outpcd most of way* **40/1**

1m 23.44s (0.24) **Going Correction** -0.05s/f (Good)
WFA 3 from 4yo+ 4lb **16** Ran SP% **125.0**
Speed ratings (Par 101): **96,94,91,91,89 87,86,85,85,85 84,81,79,75,75 74**
toteswingers:1&2:£7.50, 1&3:£25.80, 2&3:£17.20 CSF £23.28 CT £255.39 TOTE £4.90: £1.90, £1.80, £3.60, £2.80; EX 27.50.
Owner F Gillespie **Bred** Miss S M Potts **Trained** Audley, Staffs

FOCUS
An open handicap but the form looks sound enough rated around the reliable runner-up.
Tourist Official explanation: jockey said gelding reared and injured itself leaving stalls
Babich Bay(IRE) Official explanation: jockey said gelding stumbled and lost its action
Talamahana Official explanation: jockey said mare reared leaving stalls

5675 ACORN GROUP APPRENTICE (S) STKS 7f 16y
4:00 (4:00) (Class 6) 3-4-Y-O **£1,811** (£539; £269; £134) **Stalls** Centre

Form RPR

5353 **1** **Barista (IRE)**[8] 5401 3-8-13 69.................................... MartinHarley 6 72
(Mick Channon) *hld up in rr but wl in tch: drvn and qcknd to chal ins fnl 2f tl def ld wl over 1f out: rdn clr fnl f* **11/8**[1]

2333 **2** *2 1/2* **Could It Be Magic**[10] 5345 4-8-12 72.................................(b) JakePayne(5) 7 67
(Bill Turner) *t.k.h trckd ldr 4f out: qckned travelling wl to chal ins fnl 2f: stl upsides tl outpcd over 1f out: no ch w wnr fnl f but styd on for clr 2nd* **5/2**[2]

020 **3** *4* **Mister Ben Vereen**[23] 4911 3-8-10 63.................................... AmyScott(3) 4 54
(Eve Johnson Houghton) *trckd ldrs: drvn and qcknd to chal 2f out: wknd into wl hld 3rd fnl f* **5/1**[3]

0524 **4** *8* **Control Chief**[16] 5176 3-8-13 57.................................... SeanLevey 2 33
(Ralph Beckett) *plunged leaving stalls: sn rcvrd and led over 5f out: jnd u.p 2f out: wknd over 1f out* **13/2**

3463 **5** *11* **Novabridge**[16] 5172 3-9-4 60.................................... PatrickHills 1 —
(Andrew Haynes) *led tl over 5f out: styd chsng ldrs tl wknd over 2f out* **12/1**

00 **6** 2 3/4 **Adaero Star**[25] 4861 3-8-3 0....................................(v[1]) NathanAlison(5) 5 —
(Karen George) *a outpcd and wl bhd* **66/1**
1m 23.96s (0.76) **Going Correction** -0.05s/f (Good)
WFA 3 from 4yo 4lb **6** Ran SP% **109.9**
Speed ratings (Par 101): **93,90,85,76,63 60**
toteswingers:1&2:£1.02, 1&3:£1.90, 2&3:£3.40 CSF £4.75 TOTE £2.50: £1.50, £1.90; EX 5.60.There was no bid for the winner.
Owner Mrs T Burns **Bred** Rathasker Stud **Trained** West Ilsley, Berks
FOCUS
A modest seller, and not form to treat too seriously with nothing solid. The pace was ordinary.

5676 NEWPORT COUNTY AMBER ADVANCE SCHEME FILLIES' H'CAP 7f 16y
4:30 (4:30) (Class 5) (0-75,75) 3-Y-0+ **£2,522** (£750; £375; £187) **Stalls** Centre

Form RPR
2021 **1** **Mrs Greeley**[23] 4925 3-9-1 **70**.. WilliamCarson 5 82
(Eve Johnson Houghton) *in tch: hdwy 2f out: led over 1f out: drvn clr ins fnl f* **3/1[2]**
200 **2** 3 1/4 **Song Of The Siren**[21] 4994 3-9-6 **75**........................(v[1]) JimmyFortune 3 78
(Andrew Balding) *racd alone far side and hrd drvn fnl 2f: kpt on wl for 2nd fnl f but no ch w wnr* **6/1**
1-5 **3** 1 1/2 **Swift Breeze**[18] 5100 3-9-2 **71**... LiamJones 1 70
(William Haggas) *crossed sn after s: t.k.h and in tch: drvn and hdwy to chse ldrs over 2f out: styd on u.p fnl f to take one pce 3rd last strides* **15/8[1]**
3600 **4** shd **Cape Melody**[18] 5100 5-9-5 **70**... GeorgeBaker 2 71
(George Baker) *s.i.s: in rr: rdn and kpt on fr 2f out to press for one pce 3rd clsng stages* **15/2**
3-31 **5** 1/2 **Lucky Meadows (IRE)**[161] 959 3-9-0 **72**...................... SeanLevey(3) 4 69
(Richard Hannon) *led over 5f out tl hdd over 1f out: sn btn* **5/1[3]**
0205 **6** 1 3/4 **Tinaheely (IRE)**[56] 3803 3-8-12 **67**................................ StephenCraine 7 60
(Jonathan Portman) *led untol over 5f out: wknd fr 2f out* **16/1**
1m 23.47s (0.27) **Going Correction** -0.05s/f (Good)
WFA 3 from 5yo 4lb **6** Ran SP% **108.4**
Speed ratings (Par 100): **96,92,90,90,89 87**
toteswingers:1&2:£2.00, 1&3:£1.80, 2&3:£3.80 CSF £19.20 TOTE £5.40: £3.10, £2.20; EX 17.30.
Owner Mrs Romilla Arber **Bred** Minster Stud **Trained** Blewbury, Oxon
FOCUS
Just a modest fillies' handicap. The runner-up raced alone on the fair rail, with the remainder down the centre. She is rated close to her best and sets the level.
Swift Breeze Official explanation: jockey said filly clipped heels shortly after start
Cape Melody Official explanation: jockey said mare was slow into stride

5677 EASYODDS.COM H'CAP 6f 16y
5:00 (5:00) (Class 6) (0-60,64) 3-Y-0+ **£1,811** (£539; £269; £134) **Stalls** Centre

Form RPR
0004 **1** **Darcey**[39] 4394 5-9-7 **60**.. GeorgeBaker 12 70
(Amy Weaver) *towards rr but in tch on stands' rail: drvn and hdwy over 2f out: styd on u.p to take slt ld fnl 100yds: hld on all out* **5/1[3]**
3440 **2** shd **Flaxen Lake**[2] 5617 4-8-8 **50**... SeanLevey(3) 7 60
(Milton Bradley) *chsd ldrs towards middle of crse: styd on u.p fnl f to chal fnl 150yds: stl upsides clsng stages: no ex last strides* **5/1[3]**
0330 **3** 1 1/2 **Athaakeel (IRE)**[22] 4973 5-9-5 **58**................................(b) CathyGannon 6 63
(Ronald Harris) *racd towards far side and sn slt ld: rdn over 2f out to maintan slt advantage tl hdd and no ex fnl 100yds* **25/1**
4210 **4** 1 **Avoncreek**[11] 5309 7-8-10 **49**......................................(v) KellyHarrison 10 51
(Brian Baugh) *racd towards stands' side and pressed ldr tl rdn and hung lft 2f out: stl ev ch ins fnl f: no ex fnl 100yds* **20/1**
0362 **5** 1/2 **Memphis Man**[5] 5513 8-9-0 **58**.............................. MatthewCosham(5) 9 58
(David Evans) *chsd ldrs towards stands' side: rdn and outpcd over 2f out: kpt on again fnl 120yds: nvr a threat* **10/1**
3121 **6** 1/2 **Colourbearer (IRE)**[3] 5600 4-9-11 **64** 6ex................(t) RoystonFfrench 1 68+
(Milton Bradley) *racd towards far side: in tch: hdwy 2f out but sn hmpd and outpcd: mod prog again ins fnl f* **5/2[1]**
0356 **7** 3/4 **Ghost Dancer**[3] 5603 7-8-10 **49**....................................(p) EddieAhern 3 45
(Milton Bradley) *chsd ldrs towards far side: ev ch fr 2f out tl wknd jst ins fnl f* **16/1**
[illegible] **8** nk **Full Chilling (IRE)**[10] [illegible] .... [illegible]
(John Spearing) *s.i.s: in rr: rdn and hdwy towards centre crse to chse ldrs and ev ch 2f out: wknd ins fnl f* **9/2[2]**
4015 **9** 2 3/4 **Ridgeway Sapphire**[2] 5617 4-8-12 **51**......................(v) JimmyFortune 11 38
(Mark Usher) *chsd ldrs on stands' side: rdn 2f out: wknd fnl f* **9/1**
0005 **10** 2 **Bold Argument (IRE)**[12] 5298 8-8-7 **46**................. FrankieMcDonald 13 26
(Nerys Dutfield) *slowly away: a outpcd towards stands' side* **33/1**
1m 11.69s (-0.31) **Going Correction** -0.05s/f (Good)
WFA 3 from 4yo+ 2lb **10** Ran SP% **116.6**
Speed ratings (Par 101): **100,99,97,96,95 95,94,93,90,87**
toteswingers:1&2:£3.90, 1&3:£21.70, 2&3:£17.50 CSF £29.46 CT £584.94 TOTE £8.90: £4.00, £1.20, £8.60; EX 37.60.
Owner Bringloe, Spain, Parkin & Lennox **Bred** Raymond Cowie **Trained** Newmarket, Suffolk
■ Stewards' Enquiry : Sean Levey one-day ban: used whip with excessive freqauency (Sep 16)
FOCUS
Another very modest event. A group of four raced separately from the others, towards the far rail, before the groups merged. The placed horses set the level and the form looks straightforward for the grade.
Bold Argument(IRE) Official explanation: jockey said gelding was slowly away

5678 FESTIVAL RACING H'CAP 5f 16y
5:30 (5:30) (Class 6) (0-55,54) 3-Y-0+ **£1,811** (£539; £269; £134) **Stalls** Centre

Form RPR
0002 **1** **Griffin Point (IRE)**[9] 5377 4-8-8 **48**............................ JamesRogers(5) 3 58
(William Muir) *bmpd after s: in tch: hdwy towards centre of crse over 2f out to ld over 1f out: sn rdn: hld on all out* **4/1[2]**
0664 **2** 1/2 **Best One**[2] 5617 7-8-10 **45**..(v) JamesDoyle 6 53
(Ronald Harris) *in rr but in tch on stands' side: rdn and hdwy over 1f out: styd on unde press fnl f: chsd wnr fnl 100yds: a jst hld* **7/1**
-000 **3** 2 **Rich Harvest (USA)**[29] 4705 6-8-10 **45**............................... KellyHarrison 9 46
(Ray Peacock) *chsd ldrs towards stands' side: rdn 2f out: styd on fnl f to take 3rd last strides* **50/1**
530 **4** nse **Little Perisher**[10] 5345 4-9-0 **49**....................................(b) TadhgO'Shea 1 50
(Karen George) *racd alone far side: rdn along half way and in tch: styd on fnl f but nvr quite on terms w main gp: one pce and lost 3rd last strides* **20/1**
1535 **5** nk **Spic 'n Span**[3] 5600 6-9-5 **54**....................................(v) GeorgeBaker 10 54
(Ronald Harris) *racd on stands' rail and led 3f out: rdn 2f out: hdd over 1f out: wknd ins fnl f* **11/2[3]**

4324 **6** 1 3/4 **Madam Isshe**[4] 5534 4-9-3 **52**... CathyGannon 4 45
(Malcolm Saunders) *towards rr and racd towards centre of crse: rdn 2f out: styd on fnl f: nt trble ldrs* **2/1[1]**
0046 **7** 3/4 **Lithaam (IRE)**[4] 5534 7-8-10 **45**..............................(tp) RoystonFfrench 11 36
(Milton Bradley) *chsd ldrs: wkng whn hmpd 1f out* **10/1**
006 **8** 2 **Lambrini Lace (IRE)**[7] 5437 6-8-10 **45**........................(b) NeilChalmers 7 29
(Lisa Williamson) *outpcd fr 1/2-way* **28/1**
4000 **9** 1 1/4 **What Katie Did (IRE)**[2] 5617 6-8-10 **45**..........................(p) EddieAhern 8 24
(Milton Bradley) *led 2f: wknd ins fnl 2f* **12/1**
4242 **10** 3 1/2 **Ladydolly**[15] 5215 3-9-3 **53**......................................(b) WilliamCarson 5 19
(Roy Brotherton) *broke fast and wnt lft to press for ld in centre crse: wknd qckly over 1f out: eased whn no ch ins fnl f* **8/1**
59.52 secs (0.22) **Going Correction** -0.05s/f (Good)
WFA 3 from 4yo+ 1lb **10** Ran SP% **119.3**
Speed ratings (Par 101): **96,95,92,91,91 88,87,84,82,76**
toteswingers:1&2:£6.40, 1&3:£57.10, 2&3:£37.50. Totesuper 7: Win: Not won, Place: Not won. CSF £32.30 CT £1253.01 TOTE £3.80: £1.30, £2.70, £22.30; EX 39.40.
Owner F Hope **Bred** Vincent Dunne **Trained** Lambourn, Berks
FOCUS
A weak sprint handicap rated around the first two.
T/Plt: £403.70 to a £1 stake. Pool:£57,189.43 103.40 winning tickets T/Qpdt: £52.10 to a £1 stake. Pool:£5,014.60 71.10 winning tickets ST

4787 HAYDOCK (L-H)
Friday, September 2

OFFICIAL GOING: Good (good to firm in places over 1m 2f & 1m 6f; 7.5)
Wind: Light to moderate half against Weather: Fine

5679 BETFRED BIG SOCIETY H'CAP (DIV I) 5f
1:40 (1:43) (Class 4) (0-85,85) 3-Y-0+ **£4,528** (£1,347; £673; £336) **Stalls** Centre

Form RPR
4355 **1** **Mayoman (IRE)**[18] 5108 6-8-4 **73**.................................... NeilFarley(5) 6 81
(Declan Carroll) *in tch: sn niggled along: rdn over 1f out: r.o ins fnl f: led fnl 110yds: wl on top cl home* **6/1[3]**
6000 **2** 1/2 **Invincible Lad (IRE)**[18] 5108 7-8-12 **76**........................ AdrianNicholls 3 82
(David Nicholls) *dwlt: hld up: hdwy whn swtchd lft ins fnl f: r.o: hld cl home* **20/1**
21 **3** nse **Beauty Pageant (IRE)**[31] 4628 4-9-1 **79**..................... RichardMullen 1 85
(Ed McMahon) *chsd ldrs: rdn to chal over 1f out: nt qckn cl home* **4/1[1]**
1562 **4** 1/2 **Bronze Beau**[24] 4886 4-9-7 **85**......................................(t) JamesSullivan 5 89
(Linda Stubbs) *led: rdn ins fnl f: hdd fnl 110yds: kpt on same pce towards fin* **11/1**
0002 **5** 1/2 **Oldjoesaid**[18] 5108 7-9-4 **82**...(b) PhillipMakin 4 85+
(Kevin Ryan) *in rr: rdn whn nt clr run and snatched up jst over 1f out: sn swtchd lft: carried lft ins fnl f: kpt on: nt get to ldrs and eased towards fin* **6/1[3]**
050 **6** 1/2 **Walvis Bay (IRE)**[18] 5108 4-8-12 **76**................................ TomQueally 10 76
(Tom Tate) *prom: rdn to chal over 1f out: no ex fnl 75yds* **11/2[2]**
0164 **7** nk **Gottcher**[25] 4855 3-8-12 **77**... LeeNewman 9 76
(David Barron) *dwlt: towards rr: rdn over 1f out: one pce ins fnl f* **11/2[2]**
1052 **8** 2 3/4 **Lucky Art (USA)**[44] 4195 5-9-2 **80**.................................. PJMcDonald 2 69
(Ruth Carr) *w ldr: rdn over 1f out: wknd ins fnl f* **12/1**
5123 **9** 1 3/4 **Nomoreblondes**[42] 4291 7-8-11 **75**........................(v) RussKennemore 8 58
(Paul Midgley) *stmbld s: chsd ldrs: pushed along 1/2-way: rdn 2f out: wknd over 1f out* **7/1**
61.34 secs (0.54) **Going Correction** +0.025s/f (Good)
WFA 3 from 4yo+ 1lb **9** Ran SP% **112.6**
Speed ratings (Par 105): **96,95,95,94,93 92,92,87,85**
toteswingers:1&2:£26.50, 1&3:£4.50, 2&3:£16.60 CSF £111.58 CT £535.38 TOTE £7.80: £2.40, £4.70, £1.10; EX 113.50 Trifecta £401.10 Part won. Pool: £542.11 - 0.44 winning units..
Owner Tom Tuohy **Bred** James Cosgrove **Trained** Sledmere, E Yorks
FOCUS
All races were run over the stands'-side home straight. Actual races distances were: 5f, 6f, 7f 50yds, 1m2f 45yds, 1m6f 50yds. After the first race Adrian Nicholls said it was "beautiful ground". The pace was strong yet they still finished in a bunch and this was evidently a competitive sprint handicap. The time was 0.57 seconds slower than the second division and the action unfolded towards the far-side rail. The fourth is taken at face value.
Gottcher Official explanation: vet said gelding lost a hind shoe

5680 BETFRED SHARPLES GROUP H'CAP (DIV II OF 1.40) 5f
2:10 (2:12) (Class 4) (0-85,85) 3-Y-0+ **£4,528** (£1,347; £673; £336) **Stalls** Centre

Form RPR
1242 **1** **Pelmanism**[27] 4792 4-8-9 **76**... DaleSwift(3) 4 86
(Brian Ellison) *hld up: niggled along 3f out: hdwy over 1f out: r.o to ld and edgd lft wl ins fnl f: won gng away* **2/1[1]**
6006 **2** 1 1/4 **Even Stevens**[25] 4855 3-8-9 **77**.. BillyCray(3) 5 83+
(David Nicholls) *led: rdn and hung lft fr over 1f out: hdd wl ins fnl f: nt pce of wnr cl home* **33/1**
4600 **3** 1 1/4 **Beat The Bell**[20] 5033 6-9-7 **85**................................ GrahamGibbons 2 86
(David Barron) *trckd ldrs: rdn over 1f out: tried to chal ins fnl f: styd on same pce fnl 75yds* **5/1[2]**
1263 **4** shd **Liberty Ship**[6] 5468 6-8-7 **71** oh1..........................(t) SilvestreDeSousa 9 72
(Mark Buckley) *pushed along towards rr: hdwy over 2f out: rdn to chal over 1f out: no ex fnl 50yds* **7/1**
0653 **5** 2 1/2 **The Nifty Fox**[16] 5163 7-9-2 **80**.......................................(v) DavidAllan 6 72
(Tim Easterby) *in tch: rdn over 1f out: one pce fnl 75yds* **6/1[3]**
2050 **6** 1 **Legal Eagle (IRE)**[27] 4792 6-8-12 **76**........................(p) PaulHanagan 3 64
(Paul Green) *w ldr tl rdn over 1f out: wknd ins fnl f* **12/1**
54U2 **7** 1/2 **Restless Bay (IRE)**[13] 5262 3-8-9 **77**......................(p) PaulPickard(3) 8 63
(Reg Hollinshead) *strumbled s and slowly away: a rdn along and bhd: nvr able to get to ldrs* **8/1**
0220 **8** 2 3/4 **Pavershooz**[27] 4792 6-9-5 **83**.. DuranFentiman 1 59
(Noel Wilson) *racd alone on far-side: prom: rdn 2f out: wknd fnl 120yds: b.b.v* **10/1**
3300 **9** 10 **Sir Geoffrey (IRE)**[119] 1878 5-9-1 **79**..............................(b) NeilCallan 10 19
(David Nicholls) *chsd ldrs: rdn 2f out: wknd over 1f out* **12/1**
60.77 secs (-0.03) **Going Correction** +0.025s/f (Good)
WFA 3 from 4yo+ 1lb **9** Ran SP% **115.3**
Speed ratings (Par 105): **101,99,97,96,92 91,90,86,70**
totewingers:1&2:£15.20, 1&3:£3.30, 2&3:£25.90 CSF £78.78 CT £297.95 TOTE £3.40: £1.50, £6.20, £2.20; EX 58.70 Trifecta £430.00 Part won. Pool: £581.12 - 0.10 winning units..
Owner Koo's Racing Club **Bred** Guy Reed **Trained** Norton, N Yorks
FOCUS
The pace was fair and the time was 0.57 seconds quicker than the first division. They raced middle to far side. The winner is improving and it was the runner-up's best turf run.

Liberty Ship Official explanation: jockey said gelding hung left
Restless Bay(IRE) Official explanation: jockey said gelding slipped on leaving stalls
Pavershooz Official explanation: vet said gelding bled from the nose

5681 BETFRED E B F "BEAT ALL" PRECISION LEGAL SERVICES GROUP MAIDEN STKS 6f

2:40 (2:42) (Class 5) 2-Y-O £3,234 (£962; £481; £240) **Stalls** Centre

Form RPR

1 **Radio Gaga** 2-8-12 0 GrahamGibbons 9 81+
(Ed McMahon) *midfield: shkn up over 2f out: nt clr run and hdwy wl over 1f out: r.o ins fnl f: green and swtchd rt to go arnd ldrs wl ins fnl f: sn qcknd to ld and edgd lft: wl on top at fin* **14/1**

2 1 ¼ **Accession (IRE)** 2-9-3 0 AdamKirby 11 82+
(Clive Cox) *midfield: rdn and hdwy over 2f out: edgd lft u.p over 1f out: edgd rt and r.o to ld briefly wl ins fnl f: hld cl home* **3/1²**

322 3 shd **Van Der Art**[18] 5117 2-8-12 0 PaulHanagan 8 77
(Alan Jarvis) *in tch: effrt over 2f out: rdn over 1f out: chalng wl ins fnl f: styd on but hld cl home* **4/1³**

330 4 2 ¼ **Ballesteros**[80] 3014 2-9-3 82 ShaneKelly 10 75
(Brian Meehan) *displayed plenty of pce to ld: rdn over 1f out: hdd wl ins fnl f: no ex towards fin* **11/4¹**

5 4 ½ **Lawn Jamil (USA)** 2-9-3 0 DarryllHolland 15 62+
(Charles Hills) *missed break: in rr: rn green: hdwy over 1f out: kpt on ins fnl f: no imp on ldrs: should improve* **9/1**

40 6 2 ¼ **My Pearl (IRE)**[16] 5161 2-9-3 0 PhillipMakin 5 55
(Kevin Ryan) *trckd ldrs: rdn 2f out: outpcd by ldrs ins fnl f* **25/1**

05 7 1 **Siberian Belle (IRE)**[44] 4192 2-8-12 0 TonyHamilton 12 50+
(Richard Fahey) *bhd: outpcd 4f out: kpt on ins fnl f: nt pce to trble ldrs* **50/1**

40 8 1 ¼ **Rapid Heat Lad (IRE)**[13] 5269 2-9-0 0 PaulPickard(3) 17 48
(Reg Hollinshead) *hld up: outpcd 1/2-way: kpt on modly ins fnl f: nvr on terms w ldrs* **25/1**

40 9 1 ¼ **Elusive Island (USA)**[37] 4436 2-9-3 0 (p) DavidNolan 4 44
(Ann Duffield) *chsd ldrs: pushed along 2f out: fdd ins fnl f* **33/1**

00 10 nk **Small Steps (IRE)**[25] 4864 2-8-12 0 RichardMullen 6 38
(Ed McMahon) *in tch: pushed along and outpcd by ldrs 2f out: no imp after* **16/1**

11 1 ¾ **Generalyse** 2-9-3 0 RobertHavlin 14 38
(Ben De Haan) *missed break: hld up: sme hdwy u.p over 1f out: nvr able to chal* **100/1**

12 1 ¼ **Miriam's Song** 2-8-12 0 DavidAllan 3 29
(Stuart Kittow) *bmpd s: in tch: pushed along 4f out: rdn and wknd over 1f out* **25/1**

13 1 ¾ **Twenty One Choice (IRE)** 2-9-3 0 PatCosgrave 2 29
(Ed de Giles) *missed break: sn in midfield: outpcd fnl 2f* **28/1**

14 nk **Pelican Rock (IRE)** 2-9-3 0 RussKennemore 7 28
(Tom Dascombe) *missed break: midfield: sn niggled along: outpcd fnl 2f* **16/1**

15 2 ¼ **Love Island** 2-8-12 0 MichaelStainton 13 16
(Richard Whitaker) *prom: rdn over 2f out: wknd over 1f out* **20/1**

00 16 1 ¼ **Ferdy (IRE)**[6] 5486 2-9-3 0 SilvestreDeSousa 16 18
(Paul Green) *midfield: pushed along 4f out: rdn 2f out: wknd over 1f out* **40/1**

0 17 8 **Oakbrook**[16] 5174 2-9-0 0 DaleSwift(3) 1 —
(Ann Duffield) *midfield: rdn and wknd wl over 1f out* **100/1**

1m 14.01s (0.21) **Going Correction** +0.025s/f (Good) **17** Ran SP% **129.2**
Speed ratings (Par 95): **99,97,97,94,88 85,83,82,80,80 77,76,73,73,70 68,58**
toteswingers:1&2:£16.50, 1&3:£9.10, 2&3:£5.30 CSF £53.85 TOTE £21.70: £4.60, £1.90, £2.00; EX 97.30 Trifecta £384.20 Pool: £685.33 - 1.32 winning units.
Owner Multiplex Racing **Bred** Mickley Stud **Trained** Lichfield, Staffs

FOCUS
They raced up the middle in what looked a decent maiden. A couple of promising newcomers finished one-two, and there were a few in behind who help give the form a solid look. The pace was good.

NOTEBOOK
Radio Gaga is a half-sister to a number of winners, and her dam won regularly over 5f as a juvenile. She was relatively unfancied in the market, but moved nicely off the hot pace and quickened impressively without having to be subjected to a hard ride. It would not surprise if she were up to gaining black type at some stage. (op 20-1)
Accession(IRE), a 68,000euros first foal of a multiple 5f scorer, is in the Mill Reef. He travelled quite well in a similar position to the winner and looked likely to take this when picking up nicely in the latter stages, but Radio Gaga soon pounced. Still, he kept on to hold second from some more experienced rivals and should soon be winning. (op 7-2)
Van Der Art made it four straight top-three finishes. She did nothing wrong and this might represent improved form. A lesser race should come her way. (op 7-2 tchd 3-1)
Ballesteros was having his first start since finishing well beaten in the Windsor Castle, having earlier shown promise. His finishing bid was slightly disappointing considering he had an uncontested lead, but he was entitled to need the run and probably went off fast enough on a day when front runners struggled on the straight track. A drop back to 5f might help. (op 7-2)
Lawn Jamil(USA) ◆ shaped really well. He's by first-season sire Jazil, who won the 2006 Belmont Stakes, out of a sister to Sakhee, and it's a pedigree that indicates he'll stay well (holds Derby entry). Clearly this trip was likely to be on the short side and he was green throughout, looking likely to finish up well beaten, but it was quite taking how well he stayed on under a tender ride. There should be significant improvement to come. (op 8-1 tchd 10-1)
My Pearl(IRE) showed a bit of promise on what was his third start and can be expected to progress in nurseries. (op 33-1)

5682 BETFRED BOLTON LADS & GIRLS CLUB H'CAP (DIV I) 6f

3:10 (3:11) (Class 4) (0-85,85) 3-Y-O+ £4,528 (£1,347; £673; £336) **Stalls** Centre

Form RPR

104 1 **Marvellous Value (IRE)**[40] 4369 6-9-6 84 TomEaves 11 97
(Michael Dods) *hld up: sn trcking ldrs: gng wl whn nt clr run and swtchd lft 2f out: led jst ins fnl f: pushed out* **8/1**

0630 2 2 ¼ **Rio Cobolo (IRE)**[7] 5455 5-8-10 74 AdrianNicholls 9 80
(David Nicholls) *mid-div: hdwy over 2f out: sn chsng ldrs: kpt on same pce ins fnl f* **20/1**

034 3 nk **Ryan Style (IRE)**[27] 4792 5-9-2 80 SilvestreDeSousa 8 85
(Lisa Williamson) *hld up towards rr: swtchd rt and hdwy over 2f out: kpt on same pce ins fnl f* **15/2³**

423 4 1 ¼ **River Falcon**[55] 3880 11-9-1 79 DanielTudhope 10 80
(Jim Goldie) *in rr: hdwy over 2f out: styd on same pce fnl f* **17/2**

4461 5 nk **Invincible Force (IRE)**[8] 5400 7-9-0 81 6ex (b) LeeTopliss(3) 13 81+
(Paul Green) *chsd ldrs: led over 1f out: edgd lft and hdd ins fnl f: fdd* **14/1**

0165 6 2 **Jobe (USA)**[7] 5434 5-9-2 80 (p) PhillipMakin 5 74
(Kevin Ryan) *led: hdd over 1f out: sn wknd* **8/1**

060 7 ½ **Flowing Cape (IRE)**[13] 5264 6-9-3 84 PaulPickard(3) 12 76
(Reg Hollinshead) *chsd ldrs: wknd fnl f* **8/1**

2344 8 ½ **Tro Nesa (IRE)**[50] 4016 3-8-7 73 PaulHanagan 7 63
(Ann Duffield) *in rr: effrt over 2f out: edgd lft fnl f: nvr nr ldrs* **25/1**

4022 9 1 ½ **Cornus**[10] 5341 9-8-11 75 (be) ShaneKelly 3 61
(Alan McCabe) *s.i.s: a in rr* **8/1**

0003 10 1 ¼ **Klynch**[7] 5434 5-9-7 85 (b) JamesSullivan 4 67
(Ruth Carr) *mid-div: effrt over 2f out: wkng whn hmpd and swtchd rt ins fnl f* **5/1¹**

-040 11 ¾ **La Zamora**[14] 5255 5-9-4 82 GrahamGibbons 1 61
(David Barron) *sn trcking ldr: wknd over 1f out* **6/1²**

1m 13.2s (-0.60) **Going Correction** +0.025s/f (Good)
WFA 3 from 4yo+ 2lb **11** Ran SP% **113.0**
Speed ratings (Par 105): **105,103,103,101,101 98,97,97,95,93 92**
toteswingers:1&2:£22.80, 1&3:£11.50, 2&3:£22.90 CSF £149.32 CT £1238.37 TOTE £10.70: £3.10, £5.20, £2.80; EX 175.50 Trifecta £402.30 Part won. Pool: £543.78 - 0.10 winning units..
Owner A J Henderson **Bred** John Cullinan **Trained** Denton, Co Durham

FOCUS
A fair sprint handicap run at a good gallop, and again those who were waited with came to the fore. The time was just 0.03 seconds slower than the second leg. The winner rates back to his early best.
La Zamora Official explanation: trainer's rep said mare was unsuited by the good ground

5683 BETFRED SPRINT FESTIVAL H'CAP (DIV II OF 3.10) 6f

3:40 (3:40) (Class 4) (0-85,85) 3-Y-O+ £4,528 (£1,347; £673; £336) **Stalls** Centre

Form RPR

0/03 1 **Fabreze**[28] 4765 6-9-2 80 TomQueally 8 90
(Peter Makin) *hld up: pushed along 4f out: rdn and hdwy over 1f out: r.o ins fnl f to ld towards fin* **7/1³**

2260 2 ½ **Ballinargh Girl (IRE)**[19] 5083 3-8-6 72 SilvestreDeSousa 12 80
(Robert Wylie) *in tch: rdn wl over 1f out: r.o to ld wl ins fnl f: sn hdd: hld cl home* **12/1**

61 3 1 ¼ **Ganas (IRE)**[20] 5030 3-9-5 85 AdamKirby 4 89+
(Clive Cox) *led: rdn and edgd rt over 1f out: hdd wl ins fnl f: kpt on same pce towards fin* **6/1²**

-400 4 ½ **Misplaced Fortune**[14] 5255 6-9-1 82 (v) DaleSwift(3) 7 84
(Nigel Tinkler) *midfield: rdn and hdwy over 1f out: chalng ins fnl f: no ex cl home* **3/1¹**

2621 5 1 ¼ **Hotham**[35] 4516 8-9-3 81 PaulHanagan 11 79
(Noel Wilson) *prom: rdn and nt qckn over 1f out: kpt on same pce fnl 100yds* **10/1**

0052 6 1 **Lucky Numbers (IRE)**[16] 5163 5-9-6 84 JamesSullivan 9 79
(Paul Green) *hld up: rdn over 1f out: kpt on ins fnl f: nt pce to chal* **12/1**

2015 7 1 ½ **Victorian Bounty**[25] 4859 6-9-6 84 NeilCallan 2 74
(Stef Higgins) *prom: rdn 2f out: wknd fnl 120yds* **10/1**

0005 8 hd **Who's Shirl**[47] 4126 5-8-12 76 TedDurcan 3 66
(Chris Fairhurst) *bhd: outpcd 1/2-way: nvr on terms* **10/1**

0613 9 ¾ **Jarrow (IRE)**[35] 4516 4-9-3 81 AdrianNicholls 1 68
(David Nicholls) *trckd ldrs: rdn 2f out: wknd 1f out* **7/1³**

2316 10 nk **Desert Strike**[7] 5457 5-8-11 75 6ex (p) ShaneKelly 10 61
(Alan McCabe) *missed break: bhd: hdwy into midfield over 2f out: wknd fnl f* **25/1**

004 11 4 ½ **Tabaret**[7] 5452 8-8-11 75 (v) MichaelStainton 6 47
(Richard Whitaker) *trckd ldrs: pushed along over 2f out: wknd over 1f out* **40/1**

4100 12 1 ¼ **Red Cape (FR)**[18] 5108 8-9-0 78 PJMcDonald 5 46
(Ruth Carr) *hld up: pushed along 2f out: nvr on terms* **22/1**

1m 13.17s (-0.63) **Going Correction** +0.025s/f (Good)
WFA 3 from 4yo+ 2lb **12** Ran SP% **117.6**
Speed ratings (Par 105): **105,104,102,102,100 99,97,96,95,95 89,87**
toteswingers:1&2:£19.40, 1&3:£7.50, 2&3:£12.80 CSF £85.31 CT £545.49 TOTE £8.50: £3.00, £2.40, £2.20; EX 114.30 Trifecta £605.60 Part won. Pool: £818.37 - 0.40 winning units..
Owner Weldspec Glasgow Limited **Bred** D Brocklehurst **Trained** Ogbourne Maisey, Wilts

FOCUS
The time was almost identical to the first division, and again the front-runners struggled. They raced middle-to-stands' side. The winner got a bit closer to his 3yo form.
Ganas(IRE) Official explanation: jockey said colt hung right-handed

5684 BETFRED EVENTURA H'CAP 7f

4:10 (4:10) (Class 3) (0-90,90) 3-Y-O+ £7,439 (£2,213; £1,106; £553) **Stalls** Low

Form RPR

4202 1 **One Scoop Or Two**[33] 4574 5-8-12 78 (p) GrahamGibbons 14 88
(Reg Hollinshead) *swtchd lft s: mde all: rdn ins fnl f: r.o and a in control ins fnl f* **7/2¹**

3004 2 1 ¼ **Prime Exhibit**[15] 5218 6-9-7 90 LeeTopliss(3) 7 96+
(Richard Fahey) *hld up: pushed along over 2f out: hdwy on outer over 1f out: styd on to take 2nd wl ins fnl f: unable to rch wnr* **5/1²**

0000 3 ¾ **Bawaardi (IRE)**[20] 5032 5-9-7 87 PaulHanagan 8 91
(Richard Fahey) *a.p: rdn over 1f out: styd on same pce ins fnl f* **10/1**

2316 4 nk **Karaka Jack**[27] 4794 4-9-5 85 AdrianNicholls 13 88+
(David Nicholls) *hld up: swtchd rt and hdwy over 1f out: styd on ins fnl f: nt quite get to ldrs* **6/1³**

3-00 5 1 **Amitola (IRE)**[67] 3459 4-9-7 87 LeeNewman 1 87
(David Barron) *prom: rdn over 1f out: one pce fnl 100yds* **20/1**

335 6 1 ¼ **Imaginary World (IRE)**[14] 5255 3-8-8 78 ow2 (be) ShaneKelly 12 71+
(Alan McCabe) *hld up: nt clr run over 1f out: nt clr run ins fnl f: kpt on wout threatening* **9/1**

0020 7 ¾ **Mujaadel (USA)**[20] 5059 6-8-11 77 (p) JamieGoldstein 10 72
(David Nicholls) *midfield: rdn over 1f out: one pce and no imp ins fnl f* **25/1**

2000 8 nk **Everymanforhimself (IRE)**[32] 4609 7-9-6 86 (b) PhillipMakin 11 80
(Kevin Ryan) *midfield: pushed along over 2f out: rdn over 1f out: no imp* **12/1**

9 2 ¾ **Naabegha**[95] 4-9-10 90 PatCosgrave 5 76
(Ed de Giles) *plld hrd: hld up in midfield: dropped away over 1f out* **33/1**

0044 10 ½ **Silver Rime (FR)**[20] 5053 6-9-2 85 DaleSwift(3) 2 70
(Linda Perratt) *prom: rdn over 1f out: wknd ent fnl f* **15/2**

5030 11 2 ¾ **King Of Eden (IRE)**[32] 4609 5-9-6 86 TomQueally 6 64
(Eric Alston) *rrd s: bhd: pushed along over 3f out: nvr on terms* **9/1**

1m 32.23s (1.33) **Going Correction** +0.375s/f (Good)
WFA 3 from 4yo+ 4lb **11** Ran SP% **113.3**
Speed ratings (Par 107): **107,105,104,104,103 101,100,100,97,96 93**
toteswingers:1&2:£3.90, 1&3:£6.90, 2&3:£8.60 CSF £18.88 CT £159.46 TOTE £4.60: £1.80, £1.70, £4.20; EX 20.00 Trifecta £78.70 Pool: £764.12 - 7.18 winning units.
Owner Showtime Ice Cream Concessionaire **Bred** S And R Ewart **Trained** Upper Longdon, Staffs

FOCUS
A handicap that should produce some winners in the coming weeks. Front-runners struggled on the straight course on this card, but it was a different story in this first race run on the round track. The winner posted a length personal best.

NOTEBOOK
One Scoop Or Two made most of an uncontested lead. He was drawn widest, but got to the front without taking too much out of himself and, although a bit free early, was able to save plenty. He won't always get the run of the race like this and will be higher in the weights next time. (op 5-1 tchd 10-3)
Prime Exhibit ◆ was ridden much more patiently than is usually the case these days. The tactics were perhaps understandable considering the earlier results on the straight course, but it meant the winner got his own way, and as well as this one stayed on out wide after travelling well, he was always held. This confirmed the good impression he made at York last time and he's ready to win again. (tchd 11-2)
Bawaardi(IRE) ◆ travelled really well and kept on at the one pace after having to wait for a run. He's back on a good mark and is another who looks ready to win again. (op 8-1)
Karaka Jack ◆ didn't have the race run to suit but stayed on from a long way back. This mark is not beyond him. (op 13-2 tchd 11-2)
Amitola(IRE) faded after racing handily, but this was an encouraging performance after 67 days off, certainly a big improvement on her two previous efforts this term. (op 14-1)
Imaginary World(IRE) would have finished slightly closer with a better trip. (op 8-1 tchd 10-1)
King Of Eden(IRE) Official explanation: jockey said gelding reared up leaving stalls

5685 BETFRED DIGICOMM 10 YEAR CELEBRATION H'CAP 1m 6f
4:40 (4:41) (Class 4) (0-85,85) 3-Y-O+ **£4,528** (£1,347; £673; £336) **Stalls** Low

Form RPR
044 **1** **Palazzo Bianco**[21] 4989 3-8-8 **76** ... RobertHavlin 5 88+
(John Gosden) *trckd ldrs: drvn over 4f out: rdn and outpcd over 3f out: swtchd rt over 1f out: styd on to ld ins fnl f: kpt on wl* **7/2**[1]
1403 **2** *1 1/2* **Huff And Puff**[13] 5266 4-9-7 **78** ...(p) NeilCallan 7 84
(Amanda Perrett) *sn led: hdd 10f out: led 3f out: hdd ins fnl f: no ex* **9/1**
3055 **3** *nk* **Gordonsville**[38] 4043 8-9-8 **79** ... DanielTudhope 3 85
(Jim Goldie) *sn chsng ldrs: led 1f out tl 3f out: styd on same pce fnl f* **22/1**
4415 **4** *1 1/2* **Baltimore Clipper (USA)**[27] 4806 4-9-9 **80** ... TomEaves 1 83+
(Paul Cole) *hld up in rr: effrt on outside over 3f out: edgd lft and one pce fnl f* **25/1**
2213 **5** *hd* **Harvey's Hope**[43] 4237 5-9-4 **75** ... PaulHanagan 11 78+
(Keith Reveley) *hld up: hdwy over 3f out: nt clr run 1f out: kpt on wl towards fin* **7/1**[3]
/465 **6** *1/2* **Spiekeroog**[20] 5035 5-8-13 **70** ... SilvestreDeSousa 9 73+
(David O'Meara) *hld up in rr: hdwy on inner whn nt clr run over 2f out: kpt on fnl f* **7/1**[3]
2-40 **7** *nk* **Abergavenny**[100] 2107 4-9-9 **83** ... DaleSwift(3) 13 85
(Brian Ellison) *hld up in rr: hdwy on inner over 3f out: nt clr run and swtchd rt over 1f out: styng on at fin* **6/1**[2]
5-01 **8** *nk* **Dr Livingstone (IRE)**[24] 4887 6-10-0 **85** ... PatCosgrave 4 87
(Charles Egerton) *led early: trckd ldrs: drvn on inner 4f out: one pce over 1f out* **25/1**
610 **9** *1* **Pittodrie Star (IRE)**[7] 5448 4-9-8 **79** ... DavidProbert 14 79
(Andrew Balding) *chsd ldrs: drvn over 3f out: one pce whn nt clr run ins fnl f* **10/1**
2030 **10** *7* **Rare Ruby (IRE)**[29] 4719 7-9-5 **76** ... TomQueally 2 66
(Jennie Candlish) *hld up in rr: effrt over 3f out: sn chsng ldrs: wknd 2f out* **33/1**
3265 **11** *1/2* **Hallstatt (IRE)**[13] 5273 5-8-12 **69** ...(tp) PhillipMakin 10 59
(John Mackie) *sn chsng ldrs: nt clr run 3f out: wknd 2f out* **25/1**
1210 **12** *nse* **Carter**[47] 1855 5-9-8 **79** ... GrahamGibbons 8 69
(Ian Williams) *s.i.s: hdwy on outer 9f out: nt clr run over 2f out: sn wknd* **16/1**
2004 **13** *1 3/4* **Kitty Wells**[20] 5035 4-9-11 **82** ... KirstyMilczarek 15 69
(Luca Cumani) *s.s: hdwy on outer 8f out: drvn over 4f out: edgd lft and lost pl 2f out* **8/1**

3m 2.05s (0.85) **Going Correction** +0.20s/f (Good)
WFA 3 from 4yo+ 11lb **13** Ran SP% **116.4**
Speed ratings (Par 105): **105,104,103,103,103 102,102,102,101,97 97,97,96**
toteswingers:1&2:£9.90, 1&3:£16.40, 2&3:£25.70 CSF £31.35 CT £604.19 TOTE £5.50: £2.40, £4.00, £2.80; EX 46.00 Trifecta £78.40 Pool: £903.20 - 8.51 winning units..
Owner H R H Princess Haya Of Jordan **Bred** Cheveley Park Stud Ltd **Trained** Newmarket, Suffolk

FOCUS
A fair handicap, but those ridden prominently dominated, and it went to the only 3-y-o in the line-up. The unexposed winner is better than the bare form.
Kitty Wells Official explanation: jockey said filly was slowly away

5686 BETFRED DR BECKMANN GLOWHITE H'CAP 1m 2f 95y
5:10 (5:13) (Class 3) (0-90,89) 3-Y-O+ **£7,439** (£2,213; £1,106; £553) **Stalls** Centre

Form RPR
0050 **1** **Taqleed (IRE)**[27] 4801 4-9-9 **87** ... RobertHavlin 8 98
(John Gosden) *mde all: rdn over 1f out: r.o and a in control ins fnl f* **17/2**
31-2 **2** *2* **On Her Way**[63] 3585 4-9-4 **82** ... J-PGuillambert 6 91+
(Luca Cumani) *hld up: rdn and swtchd rt over 1f out: hdwy ins fnl f: r.o to take 2nd towards fin: nt rch wnr* **8/1**[3]
1314 **3** *1/2* **Barren Brook**[16] 5185 4-9-11 **89** ... JamesSullivan 17 95
(Michael Easterby) *missed break: hld up: rdn and hdwy over 1f out: styd on ins fnl f: unable to threaten wnr* **13/2**[2]
1231 **4** *nk* **Take It To The Max**[22] 4958 4-9-4 **82** ... PaulHanagan 4 88
(Richard Fahey) *trckd ldrs: n.m.r and plld out to take 2nd over 1f out: styd on same pce and lost 2nd fnl 75yds* **7/2**[1]
2541 **5** *shd* **Tres Coronas (IRE)**[69] 3399 4-9-7 **85** ... LeeNewman 5 90+
(David Barron) *rrd jst bef s: hld up: rdn and hdwy over 1f out: kpt on ins fnl f: nt quite pce to chal* **12/1**
5-00 **6** *3/4* **Colour Scheme (IRE)**[106] 2217 4-9-5 **83** ...(t) ShaneKelly 16 87
(Brian Meehan) *prom: rdn and carried rt over 1f out: one pce ins fnl f* **20/1**
0000 **7** *1 1/4* **Snow Dancer (IRE)**[19] 5078 7-9-3 **81** ... PhillipMakin 2 84+
(Hugh McWilliams) *hld up: nt clr run over 1f out: kpt on: nvr able to chal* **50/1**
0000 **8** *hd* **Breakheart (IRE)**[38] 4415 4-9-5 **83** ... TomEaves 12 84
(Michael Dods) *midfield: rdn 2f out: no imp fnl f* **16/1**
614- **9** *2* **Tamanaco (IRE)**[151] 6677 4-9-0 **78** ... GrahamGibbons 14 75
(Tim Walford) *prom: rdn whn sltly hmpd over 1f out: wknd ins fnl f* **16/1**
4020 **10** *hd* **Dhaular Dhar (IRE)**[27] 4788 9-9-6 **84** ... DanielTudhope 10 81
(Jim Goldie) *hld up: pushed along over 2f out: nvr a threat* **20/1**
4104 **11** *2 1/4* **Eltheeb**[34] 4528 4-9-2 **80** ... PJMcDonald 15 72
(George Moore) *midfield: plld along over 2f out: wknd entreting fnl f* **20/1**
0034 **12** *nse* **Baptist (USA)**[19] 5081 3-9-2 **87** ... DavidProbert 11 79
(Andrew Balding) *plld hrd: trckd ldrs: rdn 2f out: wknd ent fnl f* **9/1**
2151 **13** *27* **First Post (IRE)**[14] 5240 4-9-9 **87** ... TomQueally 9 27
(Derek Haydn Jones) *midfield: rdn and no imp whn hit rail and stmbld bdly over 1f out: sn eased and bhd* **14/1**

2m 13.39s (-2.61) **Going Correction** -0.075s/f (Good)
WFA 3 from 4yo+ 7lb **13** Ran SP% **109.6**
Speed ratings (Par 107): **107,105,105,104,104 104,103,102,101,101 99,99,77**
toteswingers:1&2:£11.50, 1&3:£11.20, 2&3:£7.00 CSF £55.56 CT £303.16 TOTE £8.30: £3.90, £2.50, £1.50; EX 71.70 Trifecta £420.10 Part won. Pool: £567.70 - 0.71 winning units..
Owner Hamdan Al Maktoum **Bred** Shadwell Estate Co Ltd **Trained** Newmarket, Suffolk

FOCUS
A good handicap run in a fair time. The winner bounced back and the form makes sense overall.

NOTEBOOK
Taqleed(IRE) was soon able to establish a relatively easy lead, setting what looked no more than a modest gallop. He hasn't had the season many expected, coming into this 0-4 for 2011, but he found plenty for pressure to take full advantage of having the run of the race. The handicapper had given him a chance - he was 8lb lower than at the start of the campaign - and maybe he's well and truly back on track now, but he'll still have it to prove when he doesn't get the ideal run of a race. (op 10-1 tchd 8-1)
On Her Way was far from straightforward and she didn't give herself much of a chance by racing in snatches, but she again advertised she's a pretty talented filly by running on strongly from off the modest pace to take second. She had also looked awkward when runner-up over C&D on her reappearance two months earlier.
Barren Brook did well to get so close as he lost several lengths with a slow start and was then a bit keen off the modest gallop. He has more to offer. (op 7-1 tchd 8-1)
Take It To The Max was well placed, but proved held off 3lb higher than when successful over 1m at Goodwood last time. (op 5-1)
Tres Coronas(IRE) had been off for over two months since winning at Newcastle off 4lb lower, and he might be better for the run. (op 14-1 tchd 16-1)
Snow Dancer(IRE) travelled powerfully, as is often the case, but the lack of pace gave her little hope and she also found trouble.
Tamanaco(IRE) Official explanation: trainer said gelding was unsuited by the good ground
T/Jkpt: Not won. T/Plt: £548.90 to a £1 stake. Pool:£79,019.57 - 105.09 winning tickets T/Qpdt: £107.80 to a £1 stake. Pool:£5,013.09 - 34.40 winning tickets DO

5637 KEMPTON (A.W) (R-H)
Friday, September 2

OFFICIAL GOING: Standard
Wind: Light, behind Weather: Sunny, warm

5687 MIDLAND FACILITIES APPRENTICE H'CAP 1m (P)
6:20 (6:20) (Class 4) (0-85,84) 3-Y-O+ **£4,528** (£1,347; £673; £336) **Stalls** Low

Form RPR
0600 **1** **Emerald Wilderness (IRE)**[13] 5275 7-9-4 **78** ...(p) JohnFahy 8 89
(Robert Cowell) *in tch disputing 5th: rdn over 2f out: prog over 1f out: styd on between rivals to ld last 100yds* **15/2**
6040 **2** *1* **Den's Gift (IRE)**[20] 5053 7-8-13 **78** ...(b) LucyKBarry(5) 6 87
(Clive Cox) *pressed ldr: led wl over 2f out: hrd pressed fnl 2f: hdd and one pce last 100yds* **7/1**[3]
0-02 **3** *1/2* **Silenceofthewind (USA)**[7] 5455 4-9-0 **77** ... JulieBurke(3) 7 85
(Mrs K Burke) *hld up disputing 5th: prog wl over 2f out: rdn to chal and w ldr over 1f out: nt qckn ins fnl f* **4/1**[1]
3000 **4** *3 1/2* **Marajaa (IRE)**[20] 5043 9-9-6 **80** ... AdamBeschizza 2 80
(Willie Musson) *s.s: towards rr: rdn and struggling 3f out: plugged on fr over 1f out: snatched 4th post* **9/2**[2]
6520 **5** *hd* **Nahab**[43] 4253 4-9-5 **84** ... AntiocoMurgia(5) 5 83
(David Lanigan) *awkward s: sn chsd ldng pair: rdn and nt qckn 2f out: fdd jst over 1f out* **4/1**[1]
0420 **6** *1/2* **Tewin Wood**[9] 5383 4-9-2 **76** ... AmyBaker 4 74
(Alan Bailey) *led to wl over 2f out: wknd over 1f out* **9/1**
6254 **7** *1 1/2* **Brick Dust (IRE)**[36] 4478 3-8-2 **74** ... SAJackson(7) 3 68
(Luca Cumani) *chsd ldng pair: steadily wknd fnl 2f* **14/1**
313 **8** *16* **Scary Movie (IRE)**[33] 4593 6-9-2 **76** ... AlanCreighton 9 34
(Emmet Michael Butterly, Ire) *sn last of main gp: rdn and wknd 3f out: t.o* **12/1**
4001 **9** *8* **Red Somerset (USA)**[11] 5319 8-9-6 **83** 6ex ... RyanPowell(3) 1 23
(Mike Murphy) *rel to r and lost all ch: nvr wl in tch of main gp: t.o* **11/1**

1m 38.43s (-1.37) **Going Correction** 0.0s/f (Stan)
WFA 3 from 4yo+ 5lb **9** Ran SP% **115.1**
Speed ratings (Par 105): **106,105,104,101,100 100,98,82,74**
toteswingers:1&2:£9.70, 1&3:£4.60, 2&3:£6.00 CSF £58.68 CT £240.72 TOTE £11.80: £1.50, £4.30, £2.90; EX 71.50.
Owner Mrs J Morley & Khalifa Dasmal **Bred** Mrs Joan Murphy **Trained** Six Mile Bottom, Cambs

FOCUS
Not too many in-form or progressive sorts in a useful handicap. The gallop was sound and the winner raced just off the inside rail in the straight.
Red Somerset(USA) Official explanation: jockey said gelding was slowly away

5688 LETCHWORTH COURIERS E B F MAIDEN STKS 1m (P)
6:50 (6:51) (Class 5) 2-Y-O **£3,299** (£981; £490; £245) **Stalls** Low

Form RPR
3 **1** **Validus**[21] 5011 2-9-3 0 ... KierenFallon 8 94+
(Luca Cumani) *prom: trckd ldr 1/2-way: led and edgd rt jst over 2f out: sn clr: readily* **7/2**[2]
2 **2** *6* **Pulverize (USA)**[21] 4996 2-9-3 0 ... RichardHills 5 80
(Sir Michael Stoute) *trckd ldrs: shkn up in 3rd over 2f out and sn wl outpcd: kpt on to chse wnr ins fnl f: no ch* **10/11**[1]
3 *shd* **Almaas (USA)** 2-9-3 0 ... FrankieDettori 7 81+
(Saeed Bin Suroor) *trckd ldrs: bmpd 5f out: shkn up and outpcd in 5th over 2f out: styd on wl over 1f out: nrly snatched 2nd* **9/2**[3]
02 **4** *2 1/2* **Strictly Silver (IRE)**[4] 5565 2-9-3 0 ... IanMongan 1 74
(Alan Bailey) *led: bmpd and hdd jst over 2f out: steadily fdd and lost 2nd ins fnl f* **8/1**
50 **5** *4 1/2* **Paladin (IRE)**[41] 4330 2-8-12 0 ... AntiocoMurgia(5) 4 64
(Mahmood Al Zarooni) *sweating: chsd ldrs: hung lft 5f out: rdn over 2f out: sn lft bhd: wknd fnl f* **16/1**
565 **6** *10* **Perfect Gratitude (USA)**[14] 5239 2-9-3 0 ... TomMcLaughlin 12 41
(Ed Dunlop) *chsd ldr to 1/2-way: wknd rapidly fnl 2f* **50/1**
00 **7** *1/2* **Flight Connection**[9] 5382 2-9-3 0 ... PhilipRobinson 9 40
(Clive Brittain) *nvr on terms w ldrs: struggling over 3f out: wl bhd fnl 2f* **100/1**
0 **8** *2 1/2* **Shek O Lad**[21] 5011 2-9-0 0 ... HarryBentley(3) 6 34
(Alan Jarvis) *a towards rr: struggling sn after 1/2-way: wl bhd fnl 2f* **100/1**
9 *1* **Art Of Gold** 2-8-12 0 ... FergusSweeney 2 27
(Amy Weaver) *dwlt: a wl in rr: wl bhd fnl 2f* **66/1**

0 **10** *5* **Pack Of Cards (IRE)**[64] 3553 2-9-3 0 MarcHalford 10 20
(Terry Clement) *sn struggling in last pair: t.o fnl 2f* **80/1**

11 *4* **Bevis Marks (USA)** 2-9-3 0 FrannyNorton 3 11
(Mark Johnston) *rn v green and sn dropped to rr: struggling fr 1/2-way: t.o* **40/1**

1m 38.88s (-0.92) **Going Correction** 0.0s/f (Stan) **11** Ran SP% **118.9**
Speed ratings (Par 95): **104,98,97,95,90 80,80,77,76,71 67**
CSF £7.09 TOTE £3.40: £1.10, £1.10, £1.40; EX 7.70.

Owner S Stuckey **Bred** Stuart Stuckey **Trained** Newmarket, Suffolk

FOCUS
A maiden that has thrown up smart sorts in Monzante (2006), Crowded House (2008) and Mendip (2009) and this year's ready winner, who already looks very useful, appeals as the sort to hold his own in stronger company. Quite a positive view has been taken of the form. The gallop was no more than fair in the first half of the race but the field finished well strung out and the winner edged to the far rail late on. The form is treated positively, although the runner-up is rated a slightly below his debut form, with the fourth helping to set the level.

NOTEBOOK
Validus ◆, a good-looker who holds an entry in the Derby, had shaped with plenty of promise in a race that is working out really well at Newmarket on his debut and he duly stepped up a fair bit on that effort to win a useful-looking maiden over this longer trip with plenty in hand. There was plenty to like about the manner of this victory, he should have no problems with 1m2f and he appeals strongly as the sort to hold his own in a higher grade. (tchd 3-1 and 4-1)

Pulverize(USA), the well-backed market leader, had also shaped with plenty of promise on turf and whose pedigree suggested he would be at least as effective on this synthetic surface. Despite getting warm between his hind legs beforehand, he probably wasn't far off that debut form and looks sure to pick up a run-of-the-mill maiden at the very least. (op 6-5)

Almaas(USA) ◆, a $160,000 yearling out of an unraced half-sister to July Cup/Abbaye winner Agnes World and to a leading Japanese sprinter/miler, was relatively easy to back on this debut but showed a useful level of form, despite his apparent greenness. He'll come on a good deal for this and is sure to pick up a maiden before stepping up in grade. (op 4-1)

Strictly Silver(IRE) who was well supported when showing improved form at Warwick, had the run of the race and probably ran to a similar (fair) level on this all-weather debut. There will be easier opportunities in this grade and he now also has the option of stepping into nurseries. (op 7-1)

Paladin(IRE) had failed to build on his debut promise (in a race that worked out well) at Newbury in July but fared better in this above-average maiden on this all-weather debut. He has a bit of size and scope about him and he too will be of interest in nursery company. (op 20-1)

Perfect Gratitude(USA) again had his limitations exposed in maiden company. He should be able to step up on what he has achieved to date once he goes into ordinary nursery company.

Flight Connection Official explanation: jockey said colt suffered interference on bend

Bevis Marks(USA), a half-brother to useful 1m2f winner Blue Leader (also won over hurdles) and to modest 1m2f winner Blue Symphony, ran noticeably green on this debut and should improve a fair bit for the experience.

5689 EVENTMASTERS.CO.UK E B F MAIDEN FILLIES' STKS 6f (P)
7:20 (7:20) (Class 5) 2-Y-O **£3,299** (£981; £490; £245) **Stalls** Low

Form RPR
422 **1** **Al Mahmeyah**[36] 4474 2-9-0 76 PatDobbs 8 76
(Richard Hannon) *mde all: pushed along and in command over 1f out: hld on to dwindling ld nr fin* **9/4**[1]

2 *3/4* **Riot Of Colour** 2-9-0 0 JimCrowley 9 76+
(Ralph Beckett) *s.v.s: rcvrd and chsd ldrs on outer after 2f: shkn up 2f out: r.o to take 2nd last 150yds: clsd on wnr fin* **11/2**

6320 **3** *1 1/4* **Show Flower**[7] 5445 2-9-0 77 FrannyNorton 6 70
(Mick Channon) *t.k.h: trckd ldrs: rdn and nt qckn 2f out: styd on fnl f: nt pce to chal* **5/2**[2]

604 **4** *nk* **Iced Opal**[30] 4662 2-9-0 70 DaneO'Neill 3 69
(Michael Blanshard) *in tch: rdn and outpcd over 2f out: styd on again over 1f out: nrly tk 3rd* **16/1**

5 **5** *1 3/4* **Art Show**[18] 5117 2-9-0 0 KierenFallon 1 64
(Ed Dunlop) *dwlt: t.k.h and sn chsd wnr: shkn up and no imp 2f out: wknd ins fnl f* **11/4**[3]

6 *nk* **Words Come Easy** 2-8-11 0 AdamBeschizza[(3)] 4 63
(Philip McBride) *dwlt: wl in rr and pushed along bef 1/2-way: prog on inner 2f out: no hdwy 1f out: fdd* **66/1**

40 **7** *4 1/2* **Morning Muse (IRE)**[11] 5323 2-9-0 0 LukeMorris 5 49
(Peter Winkworth) *a in rr: lost tch 2f out* **40/1**

8 *1/2* **Atmanna** 2-9-0 0 RussellPrice 7 48
(Clive Brittain) *s.s: rn green and a in rr: lost tch 2f out* **40/1**

0 **9** *3 1/2* **Corn Rigs**[18] 5111 2-9-0 0 TomMcLaughlin 2 37
(Ed Dunlop) *chsd ldrs: rdn over 2f out: wknd rapidly over 1f out* **66/1**

1m 14.08s (0.98) **Going Correction** 0.0s/f (Stan) **9** Ran SP% **115.1**
Speed ratings (Par 92): **93,92,90,89,87 87,81,80,75**
toteswingers:1&2:£3.80, 1&3:£2.60, 2&3:£3.70 CSF £14.96 TOTE £2.80: £1.10, £2.50, £1.50; EX 12.60.

Owner Hamed Rashed Bin Ghadayer **Bred** Windymains Farm Ltd **Trained** East Everleigh, Wilts

FOCUS
A race that has thrown up three very useful sorts since the first running in 2006 but this looks no more than a fair renewal. The gallop was an ordinary one and the winner raced towards the centre in the straight. Straightforward form, the winner to her mark. The form looks straightforward rated through the winner.

NOTEBOOK
Al Mahmeyah, uneasy in the market, was allowed an easy lead and probably didn't have to improve to get off the mark. She'd be no good thing to confirm placings with the runner-up should the pair meet again but she's a consistent sort who should continue to go well. (op 7-4)

Riot Of Colour ◆, the first foal of a winning sprinter, who shaped well after missing the break from the widest draw and after running green on this debut and is the one to take from the race. She shapes as though she'll stay 7f and looks sure to pick up a similar event before going into handicaps. (op 15-2)

Show Flower, who still holds a highly optimistic entry in the Fillies' Mile, wasn't far off her best and is another fair yardstick but, while she should be suited by the return to 7f, she's likely to remain vulnerable against the better types in this grade and she'll have to improve to win a competitive nursery from her current mark of 77. (op 11-4 tchd 3-1)

Iced Opal's form is one of steady improvement and she was far from disgraced over this shorter trip. The return to 7f and the step into ordinary nursery company should provide her with her best chance of success. (tchd 20-1)

Art Show attracted support and bettered her debut form on this first run on an artificial surface, despite racing with the choke out for much of the way. She should be able to step up on this level as she learns to settle. Official explanation: jockey said filly ran too freely (op 3-1)

Words Come Easy, a half-sister to the yard's smart 7f-1m performer Audacity Of Hope, was far from disgraced after running green on this debut. She should be able to step up in due course.

5690 EVENTMASTERS.CO.UK NURSERY 6f (P)
7:50 (7:51) (Class 5) (0-70,70) 2-Y-O **£2,522** (£750; £375; £187) **Stalls** Low

Form RPR
6353 **1** **Darnathean**[17] 5144 2-9-4 67 (b) LukeMorris 5 75
(Paul D'Arcy) *mde all at str pce: clr 2f out: hrd rdn over 1f out: styd on: unchal* **12/1**

5343 **2** *2 1/2* **Khazium (IRE)**[18] 5099 2-9-7 70 DaneO'Neill 2 71
(Pat Eddery) *dwlt: hld up in last: prog on inner fr 2f out: hanging lft but styd on to take 2nd last 100yds* **7/2**[2]

305 **3** *1/2* **Sunley Valentine**[16] 5174 2-9-1 64 SamHitchcott 1 63
(Mick Channon) *towards rr: rdn and prog over 2f out: disp 2nd ins fnl f: one pce* **25/1**

363 **4** *1* **Eightfold**[18] 5111 2-9-7 70 PatDobbs 3 66
(Richard Hannon) *chsd ldrs: effrt over 2f out: disp 2nd briefly ins fnl f: fdd nr fin* **5/2**[1]

0013 **5** *2* **Miserere Mei (IRE)**[9] 5385 2-8-13 65 MartinHarley[(3)] 12 55
(Alan McCabe) *slowly ino stride: rapid prog on outer to chse wnr over 4f out: rdn and no imp over 2f out: wknd last 100yds* **14/1**

060 **6** *3/4* **Camrock Star (IRE)**[20] 5047 2-8-10 62 [1] HarryBentley[(3)] 7 50
(William Knight) *dwlt: towards rr: rdn fr 1/2-way: plugged on u.p fnl 2f: n.d* **20/1**

603 **7** *3/4* **Rock Of Monet**[22] 4947 2-9-1 64 (b) WilliamBuick 11 50
(David Simcock) *chsd ldrs: rdn to dispute 3rd over 2f out: no hdwy after: wknd over 1f out* **10/1**

0340 **8** *4 1/2* **Elegant Flight**[11] 5324 2-8-13 62 KierenFallon 8 34
(Alan Jarvis) *awkward s: a in rr: wd bnd 3f out: no ch after* **15/2**

230 **9** *21* **Wolf Spirit (IRE)**[38] 4414 2-9-2 70 JulieBurke[(5)] 4 —
(Kevin Ryan) *sn pushed along in midfield: lost pl over 3f out: wl in rr and btn 2f out: eased and t.o* **9/2**[3]

001 **10** *11* **Laura's Bairn**[31] 4648 2-9-3 66 (v) FrannyNorton 6 —
(J R Jenkins) *chsd wnr to over 4f out: wknd v rapidly over 2f out: t.o* **25/1**

1m 12.92s (-0.18) **Going Correction** 0.0s/f (Stan) **10** Ran SP% **116.6**
Speed ratings (Par 95): **101,97,97,95,93 92,91,85,57,42**
toteswingers:1&2:£8.60, 1&3:£20.90, 2&3:£12.60 CSF £52.54 CT £1037.14 TOTE £15.50: £5.70, £1.10, £11.60; EX 70.70.

Owner K Snell **Bred** K Snell **Trained** Newmarket, Suffolk

■ Stewards' Enquiry : Dane O'Neill one-day ban: used whip down shoulder in the forehand (Sep 16)

FOCUS
Several unexposed sorts in a modest nursery. The gallop was sound throughout and the winner came down the centre in the straight. Straightforward nursery form rated around the placed horses.

NOTEBOOK
Darnathean settled better under a more forceful ride than he had been under restraint over 7f on his two previous turf runs and he turned in his best effort back on Polytrack. He has bags of foot and it wouldn't be a surprise if he was just as effective over 5f. (tchd 14-1)

Khazium(IRE) had shown improved form over course and distance on his previous start and he ran to a similar level back at this track, despite edging left late on. He is well worth another try over 7f and should be able to pick up a small event. (op 5-2 tchd 9-4)

Sunley Valentine, having her first run over this trip, ran as well as she has done on this all-weather debut. There is a small race to be won with her at some point. (op 28-1 tchd 33-1)

Eightfold attracted support but failed to build on his previous turf form on this nursery and all-weather debut. However, he is in good hands, should be better suited by 7f and may do better. (op 3-1)

Miserere Mei(IRE) had shown improved form in cheekpieces on her two previous all-weather starts but failed to build on that with the equipment left off from the widest draw. She will be worth another chance in similar company with the cheekpieces refitted.

Elegant Flight Official explanation: jockey said filly had no more to give

Wolf Spirit(IRE) attracted support but was below debut form for the third time in succession on this all-weather and nursery debut. He looks one to tread very carefully with at present. (op 15-2)

Laura's Bairn Official explanation: jockey said colt ran too freely

5691 FIRST CALL CONTRACT SERVICES E B F "KYLLACHY" FILLIES' CONDITIONS STKS 7f (P)
8:20 (8:20) (Class 3) 2-Y-O
£5,602 (£1,677; £838; £419; £209; £105) **Stalls** Low

Form RPR
2 **1** **Island Paradise (IRE)**[18] 5097 2-8-12 0 LukeMorris 5 84
(Peter Winkworth) *t.k.h early: trckd ldr: pushed up to chal 2f out and continually edgd lft after: hrd rdn fnl f: eventually r.o to ld last 50yds* **9/2**[3]

21 **2** *1/2* **Ziefhd**[12] 5299 2-9-2 0 ChrisCatlin 4 87
(Paul Cole) *led at mod pce: continually edgd lft fr over 2f out: rdn and pressed wl over 1f out: worn down last 50yds* **5/2**[1]

33 **3** *4 1/2* **Serene Oasis (IRE)**[6] 5475 2-8-12 0 WilliamBuick 3 71
(Mick Channon) *t.k.h: trckd ldng pair: rdn over 2f out: no imp u.p over 1f out* **7/1**

2 **4** *1 1/2* **Alhira**[22] 4961 2-8-12 0 DaneO'Neill 6 67
(David Simcock) *t.k.h: hld up bhd ldng pair: rdn and nt qckn over 2f out: fdd* **5/2**[1]

5 *4* **Porcini** 2-8-9 0 AdamBeschizza[(3)] 2 57
(Philip McBride) *dwlt and awkward s: a in last pair: rdn 3f out: sn lft bhd* **40/1**

6 *9* **Dalkova** 2-8-12 0 KierenFallon 1 33
(Sir Michael Stoute) *hld up in last pair: shkn up over 2f out: no prog and sn eased* **7/2**[2]

1m 27.33s (1.33) **Going Correction** 0.0s/f (Stan) **6** Ran SP% **112.5**
Speed ratings (Par 96): **92,91,86,84,80 69**
toteswingers:1&2:£2.60, 1&3:£3.60, 2&3:£2.90 CSF £16.21 TOTE £2.30: £1.70, £1.10; EX 15.50.

Owner P Winkworth & Rupert Williams **Bred** Larry And Billy Moran **Trained** Chiddingfold, Surrey

FOCUS
A useful conditions event that has thrown up a smart winner on three of the last four runnings but a race in which a couple of the market leaders proved disappointing. A moderate gallop only picked up passing the intersection and the first two, who drifted towards the stands rail late on, did well to pull clear. They both produced improved, solid efforts.

NOTEBOOK
Island Paradise(IRE), who showed promise at a fair level over course and distance last month, duly stepped up on that level and showed a pleasing attitude - despite still showing signs of greenness - to overhaul one that got an uncontested lead. She'll be equally effective over 1m and appeals as the sort to win more races. (op 5-1 tchd 6-1)

Ziefhd, who had shown fair form on both turf starts, had the run of the race and turned in her best effort conceding 4lb to one who had shown promise on her debut. This was a useful effort from a filly who should have no problems staying a bit further and she should be able to pick up another race either on turf or on Polytrack. (tchd 2-1)

Serene Oasis(IRE) had shown a similar level of fair form on her two previous efforts on grass and who left the impression that a stiffer overall test of stamina at this trip would have suited. She may be seen to best effect in ordinary handicaps. (op 8-1 tchd 13-2)
Alhira caught the eye in no uncertain terms at Newmarket on her debut but that race has taken several knocks and, although she attracted plenty of support, she proved disappointing. However it's worth noting she failed to settle in this muddling event and she's probably worth another chance when a better gallop looks likely. (op 2-1 tchd 11-4 and 15-8 in a place)
Porcini, who cost 9,500gns and is the first foal of a smart dam (from 7f-1m4f), herself a half-sister to winners, was easy to back and had her limitations exposed in this useful event on her debut. There will be easier opportunities than this. (op 66-1)
Dalkova, a 150,000gns first foal of a half-sister to Derby/Irish Derby runner-up Daliapour (who later won Group 1 Coronation Cup and Hong Kong Vase) and to Queen's Vase scorer Dalampour, took the eye in the paddock and attracted support but offered little immediate promise and was allowed to coast home when clearly held. However, she is in good hands and should leave this bare form well behind in due course. (op 9-2)

5692 LADIES DAY TOMORROW H'CAP — 2m (P)
8:50 (8:50) (Class 5) (0-75,75) 4-Y-0+ — **£2,522** (£750; £375; £187) **Stalls** Low

Form — RPR

0503 **1** **Where's Susie**[18] 5102 6-9-2 **70** ... DaneO'Neill 4 — 79
(Michael Madgwick) *hld up in last trio: nt clr run wl over 2f out and swtchd lft: gd prog to chse ldr 1f out: r.o wl to ld last 75yds: rdn out* **9/1**

1505 **2** *1* **Addwaitya**[15] 5198 6-9-7 **75** ... IanMongan 3 — 83
(Laura Mongan) *hld up in last trio: gd prog on outer to ld 2f out: r.o but hdd and outpcd last 75yds* **13/2**[3]

4610 **3** *3 1/4* **Soundbyte**[14] 5236 6-8-10 **67** ... JohnFahy(3) 7 — 71
(John Gallagher) *early reminders to get gng: racd wd in midfield: prog to try to chal jst over 2f out but sn outpcd: kpt on* **8/1**

-300 **4** *1/2* **Andorn (GER)**[10] 4562 7-8-11 **65** ... SebSanders 5 — 70+
(Philip Kirby) *trckd ldrs: nt clr run over 2f out jst as r was unfolding: rdn and styd on fr over 1f out: nt rcvr* **10/1**

4420 **5** *1 1/4* **Penangdouble O One**[20] 5035 4-9-5 **73** ...(tp) JimCrowley 2 — 75
(Ralph Beckett) *trckd ldng pair: rdn to chal jst over 2f out: sn outpcd: fdd fnl f* **5/2**[1]

21-0 **6** *1/2* **Perception (IRE)**[18] 5102 5-9-2 **70** ... FergusSweeney 1 — 71
(Alan King) *hld up in midfield: effrt on inner over 2f out: outpcd wl over 1f out: fdd fnl f* **13/2**[3]

0111 **7** *1 1/2* **Brabazon (IRE)**[14] 4568 8-8-13 **70** ...(bt) MartinHarley(3) 10 — 69
(Emmet Michael Butterly, Ire) *s.v.s: ct up at bk of field after 3f: rdn wl over 2f out: kpt on one pce over 1f out* **6/1**[2]

-320 **8** *1 3/4* **Motirani**[97] 2496 4-8-12 **66** ... ChrisCatlin 6 — 63
(Lydia Pearce) *hld up in midfield: first to be rdn over 3f out: wknd over 2f out* **16/1**

40-2 **9** *7* **Croix Rouge (USA)**[44] 4211 9-8-3 **57** ... NickyMackay 9 — 46
(Ralph Smith) *led at seemingly mod pce to 2f out: wknd qckly* **14/1**

0200 **10** *20* **Coda Agency**[58] 3738 8-9-0 **68** ... KierenFallon 11 — 33
(Brendan Powell) *pressed ldr to wl over 2f out: dropped out qckly and eased: t.o* **16/1**

0-00 **11** *1 1/2* **Balletlou (IRE)**[48] 4083 4-8-13 **67** ... LukeMorris 8 — 30
(John Best) *trckd ldrs: wknd rapidly over 2f out: t.o* **33/1**

3m 30.98s (0.88) **Going Correction** 0.0s/f (Stan) — **11** Ran SP% **121.1**
Speed ratings (Par 103): **97,96,94,94,94 93,93,92,88,78 77**
toteswingers:1&2:£10.30, 1&3:£16.60, 2&3:£13.70 CSF £68.51 CT £498.86 TOTE £8.60: £2.80, £3.30, £4.80; EX 68.10.
Owner Recycled Products Limited **Bred** Mrs L R Burrage **Trained** Denmead, Hants

FOCUS
A fair handicap featuring mainly exposed sorts. Although the gallop was only modest until the turn for home the first two, who pulled clear in the centre late on, both came from off the pace.
Croix Rouge(USA) Official explanation: jockey said gelding hung left

5693 BUNGE H'CAP — 1m 3f (P)
9:20 (9:22) (Class 3) (0-95,94) 3-Y-0+
£7,158 (£2,143; £1,071; £535; £267; £134) **Stalls** Low

Form — RPR

0042 **1** **Spensley (IRE)**[10] 5340 5-9-4 **86** ... KierenFallon 12 — 98+
(James Fanshawe) *restless in stalls: slwd s: hld up in last: eff t 3f out: hanging over 2f out: prog on outer wl over 1f out: drvn to ld last 100yds: cajoled along to hold on* **11/4**[2]

0505 **2** *nk* **Art History (IRE)**[16] 5177 3-8-8 **84** ... FrannyNorton 7 — 93
(Mark Johnston) *prom: chsd ldr over 3f out: rdn to ld wl over 1f out: hdd last 100yds: styd on* **8/1**

056 **3** *1 1/4* **Greylami (IRE)**[84] 2884 6-9-12 **94** ... JimCrowley 2 — 101
(Robert Mills) *hld up in rr: prog but nt clr run over 2f out: clsd on ldrs over 1f out: styd on to take 3rd last 50yds but nvr gng pce to chal* **11/1**

1-0 **4** *1/2* **Kristalette (IRE)**[91] 2676 4-9-6 **88** ... IanMongan 3 — 94
(Walter Swinburn) *led: kicked on over 3f out: hdd wl over 1f out: styd on same pce* **20/1**

4330 **5** *nk* **Scamperdale**[4] 5568 9-9-8 **90** ... JackMitchell 10 — 95
(Brian Baugh) *stdd s: hld up in last pair: rdn over 2f out: prog on outer over 1f out and looked dangerous ent fnl f: effrt petered out* **25/1**

42-1 **6** *hd* **Direct Answer (USA)**[16] 5169 4-8-12 **80** ... PatDobbs 1 — 85+
(Sir Michael Stoute) *trckd ldr to over 3f out: styd cl up: rdn wen nt clr run briefly jst over 1f out: one pce after* **5/2**[1]

2201 **7** *1 3/4* **Haylaman (IRE)**[34] 4553 3-8-13 **89** ... WilliamBuick 9 — 91
(Ed Dunlop) *trckd ldrs: rdn over 3f out: styd chsng but nt qckn 2f out: fdd fnl f* **5/1**[3]

4140 **8** *3 1/4* **Star In Flight**[20] 5057 4-9-0 **82** ... SebSanders 11 — 78
(Brian Meehan) *t.k.h: hld up in last trio: prog on outer to go prom 4f out: wknd 2f out* **16/1**

0006 **9** *nk* **Beaubrav**[17] 5135 5-9-12 **94** ...(t) ChrisCatlin 6 — 89
(Michael Madgwick) *hld up in rr: rdn over 3f out: no prog over 2f out: wl btn after* **40/1**

561 **10** *6* **Saint Helena (IRE)**[36] 4464 3-8-3 **82** ... JohnFahy(3) 5 — 67
(Harry Dunlop) *prom: lost pl on inner over 3f out u.p: sn btn* **20/1**

2m 19.67s (-2.23) **Going Correction** 0.0s/f (Stan)
WFA 3 from 4yo+ 8lb — **10** Ran SP% **113.0**
Speed ratings (Par 107): **108,107,106,106,106 106,104,102,102,97**
toteswingers:1&2:£5.40, 1&3:£6.80, 2&3:£9.00 CSF £22.57 CT £205.90 TOTE £3.40: £1.70, £1.80, £2.40; EX 26.80.
Owner Axom (XV) **Bred** Mount Coote Stud And M H Dixon **Trained** Newmarket, Suffolk

FOCUS
A useful-looking handicap in which an ordinary gallop picked up turning for home. The winner came down the centre in the straight.

NOTEBOOK
Spensley(IRE) had run well in a tactical turf race on his previous start and, although he'd have preferred a stronger overall gallop, he showed a good attitude to win his fourth consecutive victory over middle distances at this course. He may be a bit better than the bare form and, as he shouldn't be going up too much for this, can add to his tally on this surface. (op 15-8 tchd 7-4)
Art History(IRE) had been disappointing on his last four starts on turf but he had the run of the race and fared much better back on Polytrack for only the third time. He's still not fully exposed and should be able to pick up another race on this surface. (op 14-1)
Greylami(IRE) ran another solid race in defeat returned to Polytrack and is a good marker for the worth of the form but he has only won once since early 2009 and his consistency means he is unlikely to get any short-term respite from the handicapper, leaving him vulnerable to the more progressive or better handicapped sorts in this grade. (op 9-1 tchd 8-1)
Kristalette(IRE) ◆, a maiden winner over 1m4f at this course nearly a year ago, had the run of the race and stepped up a fair way on her reappearance (turf) and handicap debut form in early June. She shapes as though the return to further will suit and this lightly raced sort is capable of winning again. (tchd 25-1)
Scamperdale is another exposed but consistent sort who ran right up to his best returned to his favoured Polytrack surface. However he is another who has very little margin for error from this mark and he'll have to raise his game to win a competitive handicap.
Direct Answer(USA), who showed he retains all his ability when winning a Folkestone maiden on his reappearance, was understandably popular and was far from disgraced after racing with the choke out on this handicap and all-weather debut. He's the type to step up on this bare form in due course. (op 3-1)
Haylaman(IRE), raised 4lb for winning at Newmarket on his previous start, wasn't disgraced in a race run at just an ordinary gallop returned to Polytrack. He'll be better suited by a more truly run race over this trip and he's lightly raced enough to be worth another chance. (op 11-2 tchd 6-1)
T/Plt: £81.40 to a £1 stake. Pool:£69,067.94 - 619.08 winning tickets T/Qpdt: £26.70 to a £1 stake. Pool:£6,316.39 - 174.60 winning tickets JN

5694a & 5696a - (Foreign Racing) - See Raceform Interactive

4036 LONGCHAMP (R-H)
Friday, September 2

OFFICIAL GOING: Turf: good

5695a PRIX DE LA COCHERE (LISTED RACE) (3YO FILLIES) (TURF) — 1m
1:50 (12:00) 3-Y-0 — **£23,706** (£9,482; £7,112; £4,741; £2,370)

RPR

1 **Mixed Intention (IRE)**[21] 5028 3-9-2 0 ...... Christophe-PatriceLemaire 1 — 106
(F Vermeulen, France) **6/5**[1]

2 *1/2* **Rosa Bonheur (USA)**[38] 4422 3-8-11 0 ... ChristopheSoumillon 6 — 100
(E Lellouche, France) **10/1**

3 *1* **Solar Midnight (USA)**[26] 3-8-11 0 ... StephanePasquier 4 — 98
(P Bary, France) **15/2**

4 *shd* **Splendido (FR)**[47] 4139 3-9-2 0 ... FranckBlondel 3 — 102
(F Rossi, France) **14/1**

5 *1 1/2* **Blue Blue Sea**[51] 3-8-11 0 ... GregoryBenoist 8 — 94
(Y De Nicolay, France) **63/10**[3]

6 *nse* **Stella Point (IRE)**[50] 4015 3-8-11 0 ... GeraldMosse 2 — 94
(Mick Channon) *racd in midfield on ins rail: dropped bk ent st: rallied and styd on wl u.p fnl 1 1/2f* **19/1**

7 *hd* **Cerveza**[38] 4422 3-9-2 0 ... MaximeGuyon 7 — 98
(Mme Pia Brandt, France) **13/1**

8 *1 1/2* **Brevity (USA)**[13] 5277 3-8-11 0 ... MartinDwyer 9 — 90
(Brian Meehan) *racd towards rr on outside: rdn early in st: nt qckn: no imp fnl 1 1/2f: fdd* **43/10**[2]

1m 41.16s (2.76) — **8** Ran SP% **117.7**
WIN (incl. 1 euro stake): 2.20. PLACES: 1.20, 2.20, 2.00. DF: 9.00. SF: 11.70.
Owner Gerard Augustin-Normand **Bred** Oghill House Stud **Trained** France

NOTEBOOK
Mixed Intention(IRE), who had been running consistently without reward this season, got on top in the last half-furlong after a good tussle.
Stella Point(IRE), down in trip, was tapped for speed a little when the front two pulled clear off the slow early pace.

4774 ASCOT (R-H)
Saturday, September 3

OFFICIAL GOING: Good (good to firm in places on straight course; straight 8.8; round 8.0)
Wind: Light, across Weather: Fine, warm

5697 ARK BUILD MAIDEN STKS — 7f
2:05 (2:07) (Class 4) 2-Y-0 — **£5,175** (£1,540; £769; £384) **Stalls** High

Form — RPR

1 **Ortac Rock (IRE)** 2-9-3 0 ... AdamKirby 10 — 85+
(Richard Hannon) *hld up in tch: prog over 2f out: rdn and swtchd lft jst over 1f out: sltly impeded jst ins fnl f: r.o to ld last 120yds: sn clr* **66/1**

2 *1 1/4* **Electrician** 2-9-3 0 ... MarcHalford 6 — 82
(John Gosden) *slowest away: hld up in rr: prog 3f out: led briefly wl over 1f out: stl upsides whn bmpd jst ins fnl f: styd on same pce* **66/1**

4230 **3** *hd* **Firestarter**[15] 5254 2-9-3 75 ... MickaelBarzalona 3 — 81
(David Elsworth) *trckd ldrs: rdn and prog to ld over 1f out: hung bdly lft jst ins fnl f: hdd and nt qckn last 100yds* **10/1**

0 **4** *3 1/4* **Eurystheus (IRE)**[35] 4535 2-9-3 0 ... PatDobbs 9 — 73+
(Richard Hannon) *hld up in rr: prog over 2f out: chsd ldrs jst over 1f out: pushed along and one pce after* **28/1**

4 **5** *1* **Cryptic Choice (IRE)**[29] 4762 2-9-3 0 ... MichaelHills 4 — 70
(Charles Hills) *sweating: hld up in rr: prog over 2f out: shkn up and one pce over 1f out* **9/1**

6 *3/4* **Starboard** 2-9-3 0 ... NickyMackay 11 — 68+
(John Gosden) *s.i.s: hld up in last: smooth prog 3f out: shkn up and nt qckn 2f out: outpcd after* **2/1**[1]

003 **7** *2* **Il Pazzo**[27] 4815 2-9-3 69 ... FergusSweeney 7 — 63
(Mike Murphy) *trckd ldrs: effrt to dispute ld over 2f out to wl over 1f out: sn wknd* **40/1**

3 **8** *1/2* **Big Johnny D (IRE)**[29] 4762 2-9-3 0 ... TedDurcan 12 — 62
(John Dunlop) *dwlt: hld up in rr: prog over 2f out: shkn up and no hdwy over 1f out: fdd* **9/4**[2]

03 **9** *3 3/4* **Derfenna Art (IRE)**[10] 5384 2-9-3 0 ... MarkLawson 8 — 52
(Seamus Durack) *w ldrs but sn pushed along: disp ld over 2f out to wl over 1f out: wknd qckly* **28/1**

10 3 3/4 **Emperor Vespasian** 2-9-3 0 .... JimmyFortune 2 42
(Andrew Balding) *dwlt: hld up in rr: prog on outer 3f out: no hdwy 2f out: sn wknd* **33/1**

65 **11** 6 **Always Eager**[14] 5269 2-9-3 0 .... FrannyNorton 1 26
(Mark Johnston) *stl green in preliminaries: led or disp to over 2f out: wknd qckly* **50/1**

12 17 **His Royal Highness (CAN)** 2-9-3 0 .... JamesDoyle 13 —
(Mikael Magnusson) *green in preliminaries: racd alone towards nr side: pushed along and hanging 1/2-way: sn wknd: t.o* **20/1**

13 2 3/4 **Scrupul (IRE)** 2-9-3 0 .... KierenFallon 5 —
(Luca Cumani) *disp ld to 3f out: wknd qckly and eased: t.o* **6/1**[3]

1m 29.31s (2.11) **Going Correction** +0.05s/f (Good) **13** Ran SP% **119.5**
Speed ratings (Par 97): **89,87,87,83,82 81,79,78,74,70 63,43,40**
toteswingers:1&2:£129.40, 1&3:£75.50, 2&3:£25.50 CSF £2164.05 TOTE £64.60: £9.30, £6.90, £2.90; EX 1237.10 TRIFECTA Not won..
Owner Coriolan Links Partnership Iii **Bred** Liam Queally **Trained** East Everleigh, Wilts

FOCUS
Rail movement increased Old (round) Mile by 6yds and 12f races by 16yds. This looked no more than a fair maiden for the course, despite representatives from some big yards who hold some fancy entries. Run at a fair pace, it produced a shock winner with the third the best guide to the level.

NOTEBOOK
Ortac Rock(IRE), a son of Aussie Rules, has no fancy engagements but had been working well according to his trainer and on jockey bookings he looked the stable's second-string. He travelled kindly, getting plenty of cover, and once he saw daylight after being switched inside the leading pair, he showed a neat turn of foot to win comfortably. He may get a bit further in time. (tchd 50-1)
Electrician ◆ did not appear to be his stable's leading light but the Echo Of Light newcomer produced a very pleasing debut. He received a bump as the third lugged into him inside the final furlong and ran on again to take second. There looked to be plenty left to work on, so he could be interesting next time.
Firestarter hung violently left in a 7f Kempton maiden last month and as he came through with his challenge, he did so again, clouting the runner-up. He holds Racing Post Trophy and Derby entries and, while they look optimistic, he clearly has the talent to win a decent race. (op 9-1)
Eurystheus(IRE) had learned plenty from a nondescript effort on his Goodwood debut in July. He came home well up the middle of the track, suggesting he will be happier when stepped up in trip. (op 25-1 tchd 33-1)
Cryptic Choice(IRE) was a little warm in the paddock beforehand, although his trainer said that was usually the case with him. He'd made a promising debut when fourth in a Newmarket maiden and probably built on that here, finishing nicely. He will get further. (op 7-1)
Starboard, a Zamindar colt who looked very strong through the neck and shoulder, was the subject of good support. He travelled very well and seemed to be cruising approaching the 3f marker, but didn't find much. There was plenty left to work on - he'll be much fitter for this - and he is clearly one for the future. (tchd 7-4 and 9-4 in places)
Big Johnny D(IRE), who had Cryptic Choice narrowly behind him at Newmarket on his debut, travelled well early on but didn't pick up. He needs further on this evidence. (op 7-2)

5698 CARRAIG INSURANCE HYPERION FILLIES' CONDITIONS STKS 1m (R)
2:40 (2:41) (Class 2) 2-Y-O **£9,703** (£2,887; £1,443; £721) **Stalls** Low

Form RPR
2104 **1** **Falls Of Lora (IRE)**[56] 3866 2-8-12 90 .... KierenFallon 4 94+
(Mahmood Al Zarooni) *hld up last: rapid prog on outer to ld 2f out and sn clr: pushed out: v decisive* **5/2**[1]

1 **2** 3 1/2 **Kunooz (IRE)**[50] 4061 2-8-12 0 .... MickaelBarzalona 7 86+
(Mahmood Al Zarooni) *sltly awkward s: trckd ldr after 2f: coming to chal as wnr swept by 2f out: unavailing pursuit after* **3/1**[2]

1 **3** 3 3/4 **Ittasal**[22] 4992 2-8-12 80 .... TedDurcan 1 77+
(Saeed Bin Suroor) *hld up in 5th: effrt whn n.m.r and bmpd 2f out jst as wnr swept into the ld: disp 3rd and wl outpcd after* **9/2**[3]

51 **4** 3/4 **Sugarformyhoney (IRE)**[19] 5097 2-8-12 85 .... PatDobbs 5 76
(Richard Hannon) *led 1f: settled in 3rd: nt clr run then bmpd 2f out as wnr swept into the ld: disp 3rd and wl outpcd after* **5/2**[1]

62 **5** 9 **Lady Bellatrix**[18] 5142 2-8-12 0 .... MichaelHills 6 55
(Mark H Tompkins) *hld up in 4th: cl up jst over 2f out: wknd over 1f out* **33/1**

1 **6** 13 **Daraa (IRE)**[30] 4726 2-8-12 0 .... PhilipRobinson 3 25+
(Clive Brittain) *plld way into ld over 6f out: hdd 2f out: wkng qucikly whn n.m.r sn after* **12/1**

1m 43.41s (2.71) **Going Correction** +0.225s/f (Good) **6** Ran SP% **111.0**
Speed ratings (Par 98): **95,91,87,87,78 65**
toteswingers:1&2:£1.90, 1&3:£3.00, 2&3:£2.50 CSF £10.05 TOTE £3.10: £1.90, £2.20; EX 9.70 Trifecta £19.50 Pool: £909.25 - 34.38 winning units..
Owner Godolphin **Bred** Darley **Trained** Newmarket, Suffolk

FOCUS
An unsatisfactory early pace for a decent fillies' conditions event and it was a muddling, tactical affair which means the race has been rated cautiously. They'd crawled along until turning into the home straight where the complexion of the race quickly changed.

NOTEBOOK
Falls Of Lora(IRE) ◆ was delivered with a sweeping move up the outside which caught her rivals napping. She put the race quickly to bed and ran out a very comfortable winner. Having disappointed in a Listed race here, she'd upped her game with a decent fourth in Newmarket nursery last time. Clearly benefiting from that, she showed she is a filly to follow with this latest effort and can handle a step up in class. (op 3-1 tchd 9-4)
Kunooz(IRE), narrow winner of a 7f fillies' maiden in July, was stepping up in trip here and, while the race wasn't run to suit, she looks worth another try over it. She ran on well, despite having no chance with the winner. (op 10-3 tchd 7-2)
Ittasal looked a useful prospect when justifying favouritism in a 7f Kempton fillies' maiden on her debut, was taking a jump in trip and class, but the result told us very little because she was caught flat-footed. Another try at this trip beckons. (tchd 5-1)
Sugarformyhoney(IRE) had won well a 7f Kempton fillies' maiden in style. Speedily bred, but stepped up in trip here, she battled well, although one could not conclusively say she got the trip, such was the muddling nature of the race. (op 3-1)
Lady Bellatrix was beaten a long way and didn't really improve from her improved second in a 1m Kempton event against a decent colt. (op 20-1)
Daraa(IRE) had won a steadily run four-runner maiden at Yarmouth and was keen in front but her rider appeared to have steering problems round the bend and she eventually finished tailed off. Official explanation: jockey said filly hung badly left (op 9-1 tchd 8-1)

5699 FLY LONDON SOUTHEND AIRPORT H'CAP 7f
3:15 (3:16) (Class 2) 3-Y-O+ **£51,752** (£15,400; £7,696; £3,848) **Stalls** High

Form RPR
0032 **1** **Smarty Socks (IRE)**[16] 5218 7-9-0 95 .... DanielTudhope 12 107
(David O'Meara) *dwlt: hld up wl in rr: stdy prog gng wl fr over 2f out: led 1f out gng strly: rdn and styd on wl* **11/2**[2]

P0-5 **2** 1 **Gramercy (IRE)**[77] 3155 4-9-2 97 .... TomQueally 3 106
(Michael Bell) *hld up towards rr: stdy prog over 2f out gng easily: rdn to chse wnr ins fnl f: styd on but a hld* **9/1**

-541 **3** 2 **Eton Rifles (IRE)**[7] 5474 6-9-7 102 .... KierenFallon 6 106
(David Elsworth) *pressed ldng pair: led over 2f out: drvn and hdd 1f out: one pce* **7/2**[1]

0566 **4** 1 1/4 **Pastoral Player**[7] 5474 4-9-7 102 .... DarrylHolland 16 102+
(Hughie Morrison) *trckd ldrs: hrd rdn and nt qckn wl over 1f out: styd on fnl f: unable to chal* **7/1**[3]

6500 **5** 3/4 **Atlantic Sport (USA)**[21] 5060 6-9-3 98 .... TedDurcan 2 96
(Mick Channon) *hld up in last pair: rdn over 2f out: styd on fnl 2f: gng on at fin but nvr gng pce to be involved* **14/1**

4030 **6** nk **Mr David (USA)**[14] 5272 4-9-0 95 .... FergusSweeney 1 92
(Jamie Osborne) *settled in rr: rdn on outer over 2f out: styd on fr over 1f out: nt pce to threaten* **25/1**

5016 **7** 3 1/4 **Bridgefield (USA)**[37] 4472 3-9-3 102 .... MickaelBarzalona 7 89
(Mahmood Al Zarooni) *dwlt: hld up in rr: effrt over 2f out: rdn and kpt on one pce fr over 1f out: n.d* **17/2**

0200 **8** hd **King Of Jazz (IRE)**[21] 5054 3-9-0 99 .... PatDobbs 14 85
(Richard Hannon) *prom: rdn over 2f out: steadily wknd over 1f out* **28/1**

25-5 **9** 2 1/4 **Swift Gift**[28] 4774 6-9-3 98 .... JimmyFortune 15 80
(Ed Dunlop) *dwlt: hld up in rr: rdn over 2f out: no real prog after* **10/1**

4-50 **10** 1 **Bohemian Melody**[14] 5272 4-9-0 95 .... FrannyNorton 11 74
(Marco Botti) *disp ld: led 1/2-way tl over 2f out: sn wknd* **16/1**

0100 **11** 1/2 **Reignier**[21] 5032 4-9-0 98 .... MartinHarley(3) 4 76
(Mrs K Burke) *wl in tch: pushed along 3f out: cl enough 2f out: sn wknd u.p* **33/1**

4045 **12** 1 **King Of Dixie (USA)**[21] 5032 7-9-2 97 .... TadhgO'Shea 9 75
(William Knight) *chsd ldrs: rdn over 2f out: sn wknd* **25/1**

4 **13** 3 1/4 **Palace Moon**[35] 4526 6-9-5 100 .... (t) AdamKirby 8 66
(William Knight) *trckd ldrs: rdn over 2f out: sn lost pl and btn* **28/1**

6100 **14** 3 1/4 **Brae Hill (IRE)**[7] 5474 5-9-1 96 .... BarryMcHugh 13 54
(Richard Fahey) *racd against nr side rail: disp ld to 1/2-way: sn wknd* **20/1**

0464 **15** 14 **Lowther**[7] 5474 6-9-3 98 .... (be) JamesDoyle 10 18
(Alan Bailey) *blindfold stl on as stalls opened and completely missed break: in tch in last pair after 2f: wknd over 2f out: t.o* **14/1**

1m 27.06s (-0.14) **Going Correction** +0.05s/f (Good)
WFA 3 from 4yo+ 4lb **15** Ran SP% **121.2**
Speed ratings (Par 109): **102,100,98,97,96 95,92,92,89,88 87,86,82,79,63**
toteswingers:1&2:£4.90, 1&3:£3.50, 2&3:£4.70 CSF £49.03 CT £205.59 TOTE £5.60: £2.10, £2.60, £1.80; EX 37.80 Trifecta £51.50 Pool: £2,538.84 - 34.48 winning units..
Owner R Fell & K Everitt **Bred** Mick McGinn **Trained** Nawton, N Yorks

FOCUS
A competitive handicap and the pace was true. The form looks solid.

NOTEBOOK
Smarty Socks(IRE) had been in the form of his life this summer, winning a 7f race at Doncaster, and excellent placed efforts at Goodwood and York on his last two outings. He has a tendency to start slowly and he can mess about in the stalls, but was away well here. Drawn near the rail, he was waited with as his rider wanted him to get a clear run, so he eased him towards the centre of the track. Thereafter, he travelled supremely well and came through with a powerful late run to win off a career-high mark of 95. Things will get tougher from here on, but he is still improving. (op 13-2 tchd 5-1)
Gramercy(IRE) ◆ opened his campaign with a good fifth in the Wokingham Handicap in ground that was easy enough for him. Like the winner, he was travelling very sweetly throughout but took a while to respond when his rider asked the question. He should improve for the run and will be interesting if he goes for the Ayr Gold Cup. (op 15-2)
Eton Rifles(IRE) had produced a very taking performance when winning a 15-runner 7f event at Goodwood last weekend and consequently gone up 5lb. That didn't seem too harsh considering the manner of his victory, but the ground was a bit faster here and he is a horse whose best form is with cut. It was still a very solid run and there were no excuses. (op 9-2 tchd 5-1 in places)
Pastoral Player was beaten eight lengths by Eton Rifles at Goodwood last week. All grounds seem to come alike to him and he ran another fine race, despite looking as though a slightly longer trip might suit him. He has not won off a mark this high, but still appears to have a decent handicap in him. (op 17-2)
Atlantic Sport(USA) didn't show in a 6f handicap at Ripon last time and has not scored since taking a conditions event at Newbury over three years ago. Upped in trip here, he ran his best race for a long while and perhaps a revival in form is on the cards. (op 18-1)
Mr David(USA) has not tried this trip often but when he has he's run well (fourth in the Bunbury Cup at Newmarket and when running there again in a handicap on his penultimate start). Dropping back from a mile after a disappointing effort at Chester, he stayed on resolutely. He has yet to win off a mark this high, but probably has the ability to do so.
King Of Dixie(USA) Official explanation: jockey said gelding lost its action
Lowther Official explanation: jockey said he was slow to remove blindfold as it had become stuck on the eye-shield/blinkers.

5700 LADBROKES MOBILE H'CAP (HERITAGE HANDICAP) 1m 4f
3:45 (3:48) (Class 2) 3-Y-O **£97,035** (£28,875; £14,430; £7,215) **Stalls** Low

Form RPR
4251 **1** **Barbican**[29] 4764 3-9-7 100 .... DarrylHolland 15 110
(Alan Bailey) *mostly trckd ldng trio: effrt 2f out: hrd rdn to chal 1f out: led last 150yds: hld on* **16/1**

-122 **2** shd **Spifer (IRE)**[56] 3867 3-8-9 88 .... J-PGuillambert 10 98+
(Luca Cumani) *dwlt: hld up in last trio: taken wd and gd prog jst over 2f out: drvn to chal fnl f: hanging lft and threw it away* **6/1**[2]

2033 **3** 1/2 **Swift Alhaarth (IRE)**[28] 4777 3-8-7 86 .... FrannyNorton 8 95
(Mark Johnston) *trckd ldr: led wl over 2f out and kicked on: hdd last 150yds: styd on* **12/1**

1305 **4** 3/4 **Seelo (USA)**[28] 4777 3-8-12 91 .... NickyMackay 3 99
(John Gosden) *mostly trckd ldng pair: wnt 2nd jst over 2f out and sn chalng: one pce fnl f* **9/1**

1320 **5** 1/2 **Arch Fire (USA)**[14] 5275 3-8-13 92 .... (v) JimmyFortune 7 99
(Sir Michael Stoute) *hld up towards rr: prog over 2f out: rdn to chse ldrs over 1f out: styd on same pce* **14/1**

3016 **6** shd **Bridle Belle**[38] 4426 3-8-10 89 .... BarryMcHugh 5 96
(Richard Fahey) *wl plcd bhd ldrs: effrt over 2f out: drvn to disp 3rd over 1f out: one pce after* **33/1**

4411 **7** 1 1/4 **Parlour Games**[14] 5283 3-9-3 96 .... MickaelBarzalona 16 101+
(Mahmood Al Zarooni) *hld up in rr and racd wd: prog 4f out: chsd ldrs 2f out and cl enough: nt qckn and btn jst over 1f out* **13/2**[3]

1350 **8** nse **Well Sharp**[39] 4411 3-8-12 91 .... JimmyQuinn 11 96+
(Michael Dods) *s.i.s: hld up last: stl there over 2f out: prog on inner over 1f out: styd on: hopeless task* **22/1**

3515 **9** 3/4 **Fulgur**[37] 4467 3-9-5 98 .... KierenFallon 14 102+
(Luca Cumani) *hld up in last trio: shkn up over 2f out and plenty to do: styd on fr over 1f out: nvr rchd ldrs* **5/1**[1]

-301 **10** *shd* **Rain Mac**[20] [5078] 3-9-0 **93**.. PatDobbs 9 96
(John Gosden) *settled towards rr: rdn over 3f out: kpt on one pce fnl 2f: no threat* **6/1**[2]

112 **11** *2* **Halfsin (IRE)**[29] [4764] 3-9-5 **98**.. AdamKirby 12 98
(Marco Botti) *racd quite wd: wl in tch: rdn and no imp 2f out: wknd fnl f* **14/1**

1120 **12** *5* **Ithoughtitwasover (IRE)**[17] [5185] 3-8-10 **89**.................. MichaelHills 13 81+
(Mark Johnston) *forced to r wd in midfield: prog and jnd ldrs 4f out: wknd 2f out* **14/1**

3210 **13** *hd* **Thimaar (USA)**[17] [5182] 3-8-13 **92**.. TedDurcan 2 84
(John Gosden) *led: rdn and hdd wl over 2f out: wknd qckly jst over 1f out* **16/1**

1415 **14** *nse* **Tanfeeth**[38] [4426] 3-9-2 **95**.. TadhgO'Shea 4 87
(Ed Dunlop) *dwlt: hld up towards rr: effrt on inner over 2f out: sn no prog and wknd* **16/1**

2140 **15** *2 1/4* **Communicator**[14] [5283] 3-8-8 **87**.. MartinLane 6 75
(Michael Bell) *trckd ldrs on inner: wknd 2f out* **20/1**

2m 32.5s **Going Correction** +0.225s/f (Good) **15** Ran SP% **126.0**
Speed ratings (Par 107): **109,108,108,108,107 107,106,106,106,106 104,101,101,101,99**
Tote Swingers: 1&2 £15.20, 1&3 £31.80, 2&3 £11.20 CSF £110.79 CT £1231.15 TOTE £20.40: £5.00, £2.40, £3.90; EX 207.30 TRIFECTA Not won..
Owner John Stocker **Bred** Hascombe And Valiant Studs **Trained** Newmarket, Suffolk
■ Stewards' Enquiry : J-P Guillambert two-day ban: used whip in incorrect place (Sep 17-18)

FOCUS
An ultra-competitive handicap for good prize-money, but run at only a modest early pace. It produced a blanket finish but the form makes sense, with the third to sixth placed horses pretty much to their marks.

NOTEBOOK
Barbican had looked very useful over 1m2f last season and took a step forward when beating Halfsin at level weights at Newmarket last month, previously having lost a shoe when disappointing there on his penultimate run in May. Carrying top weight and having his first crack at 1m4f, he didn't have the best draw, but the steady early pace helped him and he was soon in among the main group. Settled in fifth off the bend, he found daylight approaching 2f out, and once he hit the front he stuck doggedly to his task. His rider intimated that he could be a Melbourne Cup horse next year. With expected progression - this was only his seventh career start - that assessment looks possible. (op 18-1 tchd 20-1 in a place)
Spifer(IRE) threw away a 1m4f handicap at Newmarket by swerving left last time and he did a similar thing here, coming very wide to throw down a challenge. Although he stuck doggedly to the task, he could not reel in the winner. Connections were rightly frustrated but he is definitely on an upward curve. (op 15-2 tchd 8-1)
Swift Alhaarth(IRE) has been very competitive in good handicaps this summer, including when third to Parlour Games here over C&D on his latest start. He got first run on his rivals and perhaps idled in front but stayed on in gritty fashion, just being worn down late on. He has not won off a mark this high but is likely to be punished for his consistency.
Seelo(USA) was a good staying-on fifth to Parlour Games here a month ago when stepped up to this trip. He ran to a similar level of form, tracing the leading pair but being found wanting at the business end. He has a progressive profile, however. (op 10-1)
Arch Fire(USA) got going too late over 1m3f here in July but improved last time at Goodwood on this first try at this 1m4f trip. Held up, he made good progress from halfway to get into contention, but his run petered out. This was a solid display and he may need a little further. (op 16-1)
Bridle Belle had won a decent Ripon 1m4f handicap before a creditable defeat at Goodwood last time. This was a tougher assignment, but she handled it well and was bang in contention with 3f to run, before fading. (tchd 28-1)
Parlour Games was looking for a hat-trick after his C&D and York victories, but having been held up and having to race wide, it only compounded a stiff task under this 7lb rise in the weights. (op 7-1)

5701 DJP INTERNATIONAL NURSERY 5f
4:20 (4:20) (Class 2) 2-Y-O **£9,703** (£2,887; £1,443; £721) **Stalls** High

Form RPR

5510 **1** **Chunky Diamond (IRE)**[39] [4413] 2-9-3 **79**.................... JimmyFortune 9 86
(Peter Chapple-Hyam) *dwlt: t.k.h and sn trckd ldrs: smooth prog to ld 1f out: rdn out and a holding on* **6/1**

1211 **2** *nk* **Fanrouge (IRE)**[44] [4226] 2-9-5 **81**.................................. TomMcLaughlin 8 87
(Malcolm Saunders) *in tch in rr: rdn and prog fr 2f out: r.o to go 2nd last 100yds: clsd on wnr fin* **16/1**

6311 **3** *2 1/4* **Sea Odyssey (IRE)**[31] [4658] 2-9-5 **81**.............................. MichaelHills 2 79
(Charles Hills) *[illegible] upsides ent fnl f: one pce* **11/2**[3]

4225 **4** *hd* **Royal Red**[11] [5348] 2-8-13 **75**... NickyMackay 3 72
(Ralph Beckett) *prom: led 2f out: sn drvn: hdd 1f out: outpcd after* **12/1**

0156 **5** *1 1/4* **Springinmystep (IRE)**[14] [5286] 2-9-7 **83**........................(t) TomQueally 4 76+
(Michael Dods) *dwlt: outpcd in last: rdn 1/2-way: styd on fnl f: nrst fin* **8/1**

4441 **6** *1 1/2* **Triggerlo**[13] [5297] 2-8-2 **64**.. FrannyNorton 1 51
(Mick Channon) *in tch on outer: rdn 2f out: cl enough over 1f out: wknd qckly sn after* **25/1**

6412 **7** *3/4* **Guru Girl**[28] [4787] 2-8-12 **77**... MartinHarley(3) 6 62
(Mrs K Burke) *led to 2f out: wknd over 1f out* **7/2**[2]

2410 **8** *9* **Moustache (IRE)**[16] [5216] 2-9-7 **83**.................................. KierenFallon 5 35
(Richard Hannon) *chsd ldrs: rdn bef 1/2-way: sn dropped to rr and hanging rt: t.o* **5/2**[1]

020 **9** *1/2* **Mitie Mouse**[11] [5348] 2-9-2 **78**.. TonyCulhane 7 28
(Mike Murphy) *chsd ldr to 1/2-way: sn wknd: t.o* **16/1**

61.61 secs (0.41) **Going Correction** +0.05s/f (Good) **9** Ran SP% **114.9**
Speed ratings (Par 101): **98,97,93,93,91 89,88,73,72**
toteswingers:1&2:£15.50, 1&3:£4.90, 2&3:£5.20 CSF £94.67 CT £562.22 TOTE £7.00: £2.50, £3.60, £2.20; EX 85.60 Trifecta £414.80 Pool: £1,339.96 - 2.39 winning units..
Owner Rebel Racing **Bred** Mrs E Comer **Trained** Newmarket, Suffolk

FOCUS
A reasonable nursery run at a decent pace. The form looks reliable.

NOTEBOOK
Chunky Diamond(IRE) hung right on his last run in the Group 3 Molecomb at Goodwood, but his previous Windsor maiden form had been well advertised. He travelled very strongly, if a little keen in the early stages here, and put the race to bed in great style. This track suited him much better and it would be no surprise to see him drop back to 5f since he shows plenty of natural speed. He's progressive, no question. (op 8-1 tchd 9-1 in a place)
Fanrouge(IRE) came here on the back of three wins in four starts, after victory in a 5.7f Bath nursery. This was a much hotter race and on a 3lb higher mark, she acquitted herself really well, powering home up the stands' side late on. She is still on the upgrade. (op 11-1)
Sea Odyssey(IRE) won a small-field AW maiden and followed up in a Brighton nursery and was also bidding for a three-timer. Up 4lb, he travelled well on the outside and stuck to the task when the principals quickened. He wasn't beaten far and this was another sprightly effort. (op 4-1)
Royal Red had questions to answer after a poor fifth at Warwick off this mark last time, but appeared to answer them, for this was a pleasing effort. This straighter track helped and she appears to have a race or two in her. (op 11-1)

Springinmystep(IRE) had run fairly well in Listed company after being fitted with a tongue-tie last time. Back down in class, he found himself outpaced early, but made significant late headway, really catching the eye. (tchd 9-1 in a place)

5702 WEAR IT PINK FILLIES' H'CAP 1m (S)
4:50 (4:52) (Class 3) (0-90,90) 3-Y-O+ **£8,409** (£2,502; £1,250; £625) **Stalls** High

Form RPR

112 **1** **Electra Star**[24] [4914] 3-8-12 **86**.................................. AdamBeschizza(3) 2 98+
(William Haggas) *dwlt: hld up at bk of main gp: looking for room 2f out: weaved through fr over 1f out: ean on strly to ld last 75yds: won gng away* **7/2**[1]

2124 **2** *1 3/4* **Valencha**[38] [4429] 4-9-1 **81**.. TomQueally 9 88
(Hughie Morrison) *hld up in midfield: prog over 2f out: led over 1f out: hdd and outpcd last 75yds: jst hld on for 2nd* **6/1**[3]

2010 **3** *shd* **Our Gal**[22] [5016] 3-8-5 **76** oh1.. MartinLane 6 82
(Noel Quinlan) *hld up in rr: swtchd rt and prog wl over 1f out: hrd rdn and styd on fnl f: nrly snatched 2nd* **33/1**

-011 **4** *3/4* **Azameera (IRE)**[56] [3873] 3-9-4 **89**.................................... AdamKirby 13 93
(Clive Cox) *dwlt: sn chsd ldng pair: clsd to ld 2f out: hdd over 1f out: kpt on same pce* **9/2**[2]

-026 **5** *1/2* **Avon Lady**[22] [5016] 4-8-13 **79**...................................... MickaelBarzalona 3 83
(James Fanshawe) *hld up in rr: shkn up and prog over 2f out: chsd ldrs over 1f out: fdd last 100yds* **9/1**

4110 **6** *3 1/2* **Submission**[28] [4790] 3-9-5 **90**.. KierenFallon 8 85
(Luca Cumani) *trckd ldng pair: rdn over 2f out: cl enough over 1f out: wl hld whn sltly hmpd ins fnl f* **9/2**[2]

0050 **7** *1 1/4* **Gouray Girl (IRE)**[22] [4993] 4-9-7 **90**...........................(t) JohnFahy(3) 5 83
(Walter Swinburn) *hld up in last pair of main gp: rdn and effrt 2f out: limited prog over 1f out: no hdwy fnl f* **18/1**

434 **8** *3* **Bella Noir**[17] [5164] 4-8-7 **76**..(v) MartinHarley(3) 10 62
(Mrs K Burke) *chsd ldr: upsides jst over 2f out: sn wknd qckly* **12/1**

1430 **9** *3* **Certral**[16] [5220] 3-8-7 **78**... JimmyQuinn 7 56
(Brian Ellison) *hld up in midfield: effrt over 2f out: wknd qckly wl over 1f out* **10/1**

06-0 **10** *3/4* **Madam Macie (IRE)**[15] [5255] 4-9-5 **85**........................ DanielTudhope 11 63
(David O'Meara) *led to 2f out: wknd qckly* **14/1**

4330 **11** *13* **Byrony (IRE)**[49] [4093] 3-9-2 **87**.. PatDobbs 1 34
(Richard Hannon) *chsd ldrs: wknd qckly over 2f out: sn bhd* **33/1**

16 **12** *43* **Roodle**[11] [5354] 4-9-1 **81**...(b) JimmyFortune 4 —
(Eve Johnson Houghton) *rel to r and a wl bhd: allowed to amble home: t.o* **33/1**

1m 40.28s (-0.32) **Going Correction** +0.05s/f (Good)
WFA 3 from 4yo 5lb **12** Ran SP% **120.4**
Speed ratings (Par 104): **103,101,101,100,99 96,95,92,89,88 75,32**
toteswingers:1&2:£5.90, 1&3:£38.40, 2&3:£45.80 CSF £24.37 CT £594.12 TOTE £4.20: £1.70, £2.10, £9.00; EX 32.20 Trifecta £271.90 Pool: £1,495.78 - 4.07 winning units..
Owner Mohamed Obaida **Bred** Rabbah Bloodstock Limited **Trained** Newmarket, Suffolk
■ Stewards' Enquiry : Adam Beschizza two-day ban: careless riding (Sep 17-18)

FOCUS
A decent and competitive fillies' handicap, run at a satisfactory pace. A slight personal best from the runner-up and the third to the best view of her previous form set the level.

NOTEBOOK
Electra Star ◆ had shown plenty of ability when winning a 1m Windsor maiden and a 1m Sandown handicap before being touched off by Godolphin's unexposed Terdaad at Salisbury last month. That form had been upheld by the third home, and she naturally had plenty of support here. However, those supporters had their hearts in their mouths for a while as she found gaps closing several times. Once she was eventually switched inside to find daylight, she ate up the ground impressively and won a shade cosily. There's much more to come on this evidence. (op 5-1)
Valencha is a consistent filly who found a little trouble in running at Goodwood last time. Up 3lb here, she did not have the same excuses. She got first run on her rivals and looked to have poached a winning lead, but was scythed down near the line. She remains progressive.
Our Gal had proved she stays a mile and had disappointed over 7f at Newmarket last time. Back up in trip, she was staying on quite well at the finish and this was much more like her true form. (tchd 40-1 in a place)
Azameera(IRE) had won three times from five starts and was one of the first to kick on. Her run petered out late on, possibly the 3lb rise finding her out. She had had a bit of a break since her last run and perhaps needed this. (op 5-1)
Avon Lady had a progressive profile until disappointing off a career-high mark at Yarmouth last time. She ran much better here, but was a little one paced in the closing stages. (tchd 10-1)
Submission had found easy ground and a step into Listed company too much at Haydock last time. Dropped in class and on ground that would have suited, she appeared to have no obvious excuses for another relatively lacklustre display. (tchd 5-1 in a place)
Roodle Official explanation: jockey said filly was reluctant to race

5703 GOODING GROUP H'CAP 5f
5:20 (5:22) (Class 3) (0-90,90) 3-Y-O+ **£8,409** (£2,502; £1,250; £625) **Stalls** High

Form RPR

030 **1** **Elna Bright**[21] [5043] 6-8-12 **81**.. JimmyQuinn 4 92
(Brett Johnson) *hld up towards rr in centre: prog 2f out: rdn to chal ins fnl f: styd on wl to ld post* **20/1**

3360 **2** *nse* **Sutton Veny (IRE)**[21] [5053] 5-8-7 **83**........................ RaulDaSilva(7) 10 94
(Jeremy Gask) *trckd ldng pair nr side: effrt over 1f out: shkn up to ld ins fnl f: pushed along and hdd post* **6/1**[1]

4051 **3** *1 3/4* **Judge 'n Jury**[7] [5484] 7-9-4 **87**.. LukeMorris 13 92
(Ronald Harris) *overall ldr nr side: edgd rt fr 2f out: hdd u.p ins fnl f: one pce* **13/2**[2]

343 **4** *hd* **Ryan Style (IRE)**[1] [5682] 5-8-11 **80**................................ DanielTudhope 5 84
(Lisa Williamson) *dwlt: hld up in last pair in centre: effrt 2f out: weaved through over 1f out: styd on same pce last 150yds* **11/1**

1200 **5** *2 1/2* **Solemn**[56] [3846] 6-9-5 **88**...(b) KierenFallon 12 83
(Milton Bradley) *pressed overall ldr nr side: rdn whn carried rt 2f out: fdd jst over 1f out* **12/1**

4-00 **6** *1 1/2* **Lenny Bee**[21] [5033] 5-9-3 **86**..(t) JimmyFortune 11 75
(George Foster) *last of nr side gp and early reminders: struggling to stay in tch: kpt on fr over 1f out: n.d* **14/1**

6004 **7** *2 1/4* **Button Moon (IRE)**[14] [5264] 3-8-12 **85**......................(p) MartinHarley(3) 1 66
(Ian Wood) *racd centre: chsd ldrs: rdn 2f out: nt qckn over 1f out: nvr on terms after* **12/1**

114 **8** *1/2* **Living It Large (FR)**[14] [5278] 4-9-1 **87**............................ JohnFahy(3) 7 67
(Ed de Giles) *pressed ldr in centre: rdn and wknd fr over 1f out* **9/1**

4112 **9** *nk* **Tyfos**[23] [4967] 6-9-5 **88**.. TomMcLaughlin 9 66
(Brian Baugh) *chsd ldrs in centre: lost pl u.p wl over 1f out: wl btn after* **8/1**

0-00 **10** *nk* **Gallagher**[21] [5060] 5-9-5 **88**.. FrannyNorton 6 65
(David Nicholls) *awkward s: mostly in last pair and nvr gng the pce: nvr a factor* **7/1**[3]

1503 **11** *nk* **Poppy Seed**[25] 4894 4-9-7 **90**........ PatDobbs 8 66
(Richard Hannon) *led gp in centre to wl over 1f out: steadily wknd* **9/1**

2061 **12** *1 ½* **Magical Macey (USA)**[19] 5108 4-9-2 **85**........(b) TomQueally 2 56
(David Barron) *dwlt: racd centre: sn chsd ldrs: wkng whn squeezed out over 1f out* **10/1**

0342 **13** *½* **Yahafedh Alaih**[11] 5355 3-8-6 **76** oh9........(b) NickyMackay 3 45
(Clive Brittain) *hld up in centre: effrt to cl on ldrs 1/2-way: wknd over 1f out* **25/1**

60.49 secs (-0.71) **Going Correction** +0.05s/f (Good)
WFA 3 from 4yo+ 1lb **13** Ran SP% **119.3**
Speed ratings (Par 107): **107,106,104,103,99 97,93,93,92,92 91,89,88**
toteswingers:1&2:£23.50, 1&3:£23.20, 2&3:£6.90 CSF £135.68 CT £915.56 TOTE £25.50: £7.40, £2.60, £2.20; EX 187.10 TRIFECTA Not won..
Owner Peter Crate **Bred** D R Tucker **Trained** Ashtead, Surrey

FOCUS
A tight sprint handicap and they initially split into two groups, with a quartet near the stands' rail and the remainder going up the centre of the track. They merged towards the centre towards the finish, where there was a head-bobbing finish. The form looks sound with the third the best guide.

NOTEBOOK
Elna Bright is better known as an AW performer these days but he has turf ability and plenty of speed, as shown when a front-running third over 1m at Windsor on his penultimate start. He had not run over the minimum trip since his 2-y-o campaign but was on his lowest turf mark in two years. The drop back in trip now looks an inspired move, as he stayed on towards the centre of the track to get the verdict on the nod. He may have been a little fortunate, but this really gives connections a few more options.
Sutton Veny(IRE), who had been a close-up sixth of 17 over 5f on her penultimate start at Goodwood, can rightly be considered unlucky. One of the four who elected to stay stands' side, the grey came there to win the race and was in front a stride from the line, but was done on the bob of heads. The fact that she edged right in the dying strides, plus her rider did not appear to be as aggressive as he perhaps could have been, undoubtedly cost her the race. She is a consistent sort and should pay to follow. (op 11-2 tchd 5-1)
Judge 'n Jury had earned his first in for over two years at Newmarket last Saturday and showed he remains in great heart. The ground came up too fast for him here. (op 6-1 tchd 11-2)
Ryan Style(IRE) was having his second run in 24 hours, having finished a good third at Haydock on Friday. He stayed on well until the final half a furlong, where he was found wanting for finishing speed. This was another decent effort (op 16-1)
Solemn was taking a drop in class, having twice disappointed, including over C&D last time. This was a much better effort on ground he would have probably preferred. He wasn't hard ridden once his chance had gone and remains interesting. (op 14-1)
Lenny Bee had plenty of decent form last year but had shown precious little in two starts this season. Equipped again with tongue-tie that was first fitted on his last run, he was outpaced on the stands' side early but made good late headway. He is only 1lb higher than his last winning mark. (op 16-1 tchd 18-1)
T/Plt: £452.60 to a £1 stake. Pool:£113,767.19 - 183.46 winning tickets T/Qpdt: £24.60 to a £1 stake. Pool:£9,807.07 - 294.03 winning tickets JN

5679 HAYDOCK (L-H)
Saturday, September 3

OFFICIAL GOING: Good to firm (good in places; sprint: 8.8; round 8.0)
Wind: light across Weather: overcast, light rain, shower race 6

5704 BETFRED "GOALS GALORE" SUPERIOR MILE (LISTED RACE) 1m
2:00 (2:01) (Class 1) 3-Y-O+
£17,013 (£6,450; £3,228; £1,608; £807; £405) **Stalls** Low

Form RPR

10-4 **1** **King Torus (IRE)**[14] 5282 3-8-11 110........ RichardHughes 1 113+
(Richard Hannon) *trckd ldr: drvn to chse ldr over 3f out: led appr fnl f: hld on nr fin* **3/1**[1]

3530 **2** *nk* **Questioning (IRE)**[36] 4493 3-8-11 99........(p) WilliamBuick 9 112
(John Gosden) *hld up towards rr: drvn over 3f out: hdwy over 1f out: carried hd high: styd on to take 2nd nr fin* **9/1**

1-14 **3** *1* **Dark Promise**[60] 3703 4-8-11 99........ NeilCallan 3 106
(Roger Varian) *led: hdd appr fnl f: kpt on same pce fnl 150yds* **11/2**

13-6 **4** *3* **Rainfall (IRE)**[96] 2558 4-8-11 112........(t) FrankieDettori 6 99
(Saeed Bin Suroor) *hld up in mid-div: hdwy over 2f out: chsng ldrs over 1f out: wknd last 150yds* **5/1**[3]

2334 **5** *3 ¼* **First City**[34] 4597 5-8-11 110........ JamieSpencer 8 92
(David Simcock) *swtchd rt s: hld up in rr: effrt over 2f out: wknd fnl f* **7/2**[2]

0200 **6** *1* **Fontley**[34] 4582 4-8-11 99........ PhillipMakin 7 89
(Eve Johnson Houghton) *trckd ldrs: drvn over 3f out: wknd fnl f* **25/1**

-662 **7** *6* **Sahara Kingdom (IRE)**[191] 679 4-9-2 103........ EddieAhern 4 81
(Saeed Bin Suroor) *hld up in mid-div: drvn over 3f out: wknd over 2f out* **20/1**

-000 **8** *¾* **Atlantis Star**[177] 827 4-9-2 100........ SilvestreDeSousa 2 79
(Mahmood Al Zarooni) *hld up in mid-div: drvn over 3f out: wknd over 2f out* **40/1**

5161 **9** *7* **Navajo Chief**[16] 5218 4-9-2 107........ HarryBentley 5 63
(Alan Jarvis) *chsd ldr: drvn 3f out: lost pl over 2f out: sn bhd* **6/1**

1m 43.11s (0.21) **Going Correction** +0.125s/f (Good)
WFA 3 from 4yo+ 5lb **9** Ran SP% **114.6**
Speed ratings (Par 111): **103,102,101,98,95 94,88,87,80**
toteswingers:1&2:£4.20, 1&3:£2.40, 2&3:£11.90 CSF £29.55 TOTE £3.80: £1.10, £3.20, £2.00; EX 30.10 Trifecta £308.50 Pool: £750.43 - 1.80 winning units..
Owner Sir Robert Ogden **Bred** Whisperview Trading Ltd **Trained** East Everleigh, Wilts

FOCUS
Sprints run on inner home straight and races on Round course finished on outer (stands' side) home straight and distances on Round course increased by 57yds. The ground after a dry night was good to firm, good in places. This decent Listed race contained the usual mixture of exposed and improving types. The field came up the centre of the track in the straight and the two 3-y-os filled the first two placings. The form is decent for the grade, and sound enough.

NOTEBOOK
King Torus(IRE), a dual Group winner as a juvenile, had run well on his belated return to action at York. He tracked the leader from the start but came under pressure around 2f from home before staying on to lead in the closing stages. He won with a little more in hand than the official margin suggests and should be able to hold his own in Group races for the remainder of the season. (op 7-2 tchd 4-1 in places)
Questioning(IRE) ◆, whose only success came on Polytrack, had been held in Group and Listed company. Wearing first-time cheekpieces, he came from well back to deliver the last challenge and should not be long in winning at this level, judged on this performance. (tchd 15-2)
Dark Promise had progressed on the AW over the winter and built on that over 1m back on turf this summer. Up in grade, she made the running and only gave best inside the final furlong. This was a sound effort and the black type will be valuable from a breeding point of view. (op 13-2)
Rainfall(IRE), who has gained all her wins at 7f, had been well beaten on her only previous start this year, in May, and had been absent since. Wearing a first-time tongue tie, she moved up from the back to challenge around 2f out but her effort petered out. A drop back to 7f looks likely after this. (op 4-1 tchd 11-2)
First City doesn't win very often but had finished in the frame in Group races against fillies this summer and had the joint-highest official rating. Held up at the back, this was probably not the place to be as she never got close enough to deliver a challenge. (op 9-2)
Fontley, one of the three lowest rated in the line-up, dropped away when the race began in earnest.
Sahara Kingdom(IRE) one of two Godolphin runners having their first outings since running in Dubai over the winter, never figured having been held up. (op 16-1)
Navajo Chief, who had won well in a handicap at the Ebor meeting on his return from a trip to Meydan, dropped away quickly over 2f out and may have 'bounced'. The trainer subsequently reported that the gelding was unsuited by the good/firm, good places going. Official explanation: trainer said gelding was unsuited by the good to firm (good in places) ground (op 7-1)

5705 BETFRED BUNDLES OLD BOROUGH CUP (H'CAP) 1m 6f
2:30 (2:30) (Class 2) (0-105,103) 3-Y-O+**£32,345** (£9,625; £4,810; £2,405) **Stalls** Low

Form RPR

54-0 **1** **Bauer (IRE)**[28] 4788 8-9-7 **100**........ NeilCallan 12 110
(Luca Cumani) *mid-div: hdwy over 3f out: styd on to ld last 100yds* **16/1**

/010 **2** *1 ¼* **Nehaam**[14] 5285 5-9-10 **103**........ RichardHills 7 111
(John Gosden) *hld up in rr: t.k.h: hdwy over 3f out: led and edgd rt over 1f out: hdd and no ex ins fnl f* **14/1**

4342 **3** *nk* **Zuider Zee (GER)**[28] 4778 4-8-13 **92**........ WilliamBuick 6 100
(John Gosden) *trckd ldrs: chal 3f out: styd on same pce last 150yds* **13/2**[1]

0-30 **4** *3 ¾* **Ajaan**[56] 3875 7-9-5 **98**........(b) IanMongan 13 100
(Sir Henry Cecil) *hld up towards rr: hdwy on outside 7f: effrt over 3f out: led over 2f out: hdd over 1f out: kpt on same pce* **33/1**

3102 **5** *½* **Tominator**[14] 5271 4-9-4 **100**........ PaulPickard(3) 3 102
(Reg Hollinshead) *hld up in rr hdwy over 3f out: upsides over 1f out: kpt on same pce* **8/1**[3]

1-50 **6** *2 ¾* **Ashbrittle**[81] 3013 4-8-11 **90**........ StevieDonohoe 17 88
(Ralph Beckett) *hld up in rr: hdwy on outside 7f out: drvn 4f out: hung bdly lft and hmpd 1f out: one pce* **16/1**

4343 **7** *¾* **Deauville Flyer**[16] 5221 5-9-2 **95**........(b[1]) GrahamGibbons 5 92
(Tim Easterby) *mid-div: hdwy over 3f out: one pce whn hmpd 1f out* **11/1**

500 **8** *2* **Merchant Of Dubai**[56] 3876 6-9-4 **97**........ FrankieDettori 2 93+
(Jim Goldie) *trckd ldr: chal over 3f out: edgd lft and wknd appr fnl f* **8/1**[3]

1001 **9** *½* **Crackentorp**[15] 5250 6-8-13 **92**........ DavidAllan 9 85
(Tim Easterby) *hld up in rr: kpt on fnl 2f: nvr a factor* **25/1**

-220 **10** *3 ¾* **Blissful Moment (USA)**[14] 5285 4-9-5 **98**........ RichardHughes 15 88+
(Sir Michael Stoute) *trckd ldrs: lost pl over 6f out: sme hdwy over 2f out: eased last 100yds* **7/1**[2]

-10B **11** *½* **Activate**[35] 4532 4-9-3 **96**........ JamieSpencer 10 87+
(Michael Bell) *hld up in rr: drvn 4f out: hdwy on ins over 2f out: no imp whn hmpd 1f out: eased* **10/1**

/614 **12** *1 ¼* **Ile De Re (FR)**[14] 5271 5-9-1 **94**........ PaulHanagan 8 80
(Ian Williams) *prom: t.k.h: effrt 4f out: wknd 2f out* **7/1**[2]

0004 **13** *nk* **Nave (USA)**[7] 5482 4-8-7 **86**........ RoystonFfrench 16 71
(Mark Johnston) *chsd ldrs: lost pl over 3f out* **33/1**

0300 **14** *½* **Exemplary**[16] 5221 4-8-6 **85**........ DavidProbert 1 69
(Mark Johnston) *led: hdd over 2f out: lost pl over 1f out* **33/1**

1611 **15** *1* **Shernando**[6] 5435 4-8-12 **91**........ SilvestreDeSousa 4 86+
(Mark Johnston) *mid-div: drvn 4f out: hung lft, wknd and hmpd 1f out* **10/1**

213 **16** *14* **Line Of Duty (IRE)**[77] 3163 4-8-10 **89**........ AndrewElliott 14 52
(Alan Swinbank) *mid-div: effrt 4f out: wknd over 2f out: heavily eased last 150yds* **22/1**

2m 59.51s (-1.69) **Going Correction** +0.125s/f (Good) course record**16** Ran SP% **122.5**
Speed ratings (Par 109): **109,108,108,105,105 104,103,102,102,100 99,99,98,98,98 90**
toteswingers:1&2:£44.60, 1&3:£13.00, 2&3:£14.00 CSF £212.13 CT £1608.83 TOTE £22.40: £4.40, £3.70, £1.60, £8.00; EX 362.10 Trifecta £1028.70 Part won. Pool: £1,390.24 - 0.40 winning units..
Owner Aston House Stud & O T I Racing **Bred** Aston House Stud **Trained** Newmarket, Suffolk
■ Stewards' Enquiry : Frankie Dettori one-day ban: careless riding (Sep 17)

FOCUS
A high-class, competitive handicap that usually features horses who took part in one of the big middle-distance or staying handicaps at York. The pace looked sound and three drew clear in the last furlong. Bauer is rated to last year's form.

NOTEBOOK
Bauer(IRE), touched off in the Melbourne Cup in 2008 but rarely seen since, was back to a more suitable trip here having been racing over shorter. Racing off his lowest mark since 2007, he gradually got into the action and proved the strongest in the last furlong. This was a terrific piece of training and it will be interesting to see where the gelding goes next.
Nehaam, placed in Listed and Group company in 2009, came back from a long absence to win a handicap off 99 on his second appearance. He finished 12th in the Ebor off 4lb higher but, at this slightly lower level, ran well off the same mark, making headway from the rear to deliver his challenge and only being run out of it late on. (op 16-1)
Zuider Zee(GER) had gained his wins at around 1m4f but appeared to stay this trip in three previous attempts. Never far away, he came to have every chance but was just outstayed. He has been held off this sort of mark for the past year but the handicapper is unlikely to relent if he continues to run this well. (op 7-1 tchd 6-1)
Ajaan seems best at extreme distances these days, having been a winner at 2m2f and third in the Queen Alexandra in the past year. He proved he still has the pace for this trip, aided by the good gallop, and he only faded late on.
Tominator, the Northumberland Plate winner off 90, had run well at Chester last time, handles fast and easy ground but is 10lb higher now and, although running well, that seemed to find him out. (op 7-1)
Ashbrittle, a winner at this trip in a first-time visor last autumn off 2lb lower, has not worn the headgear since. He ran a decent race, although he did several rivals no favours when ducking left under pressure inside the last 2f. (op 20-1 tchd 22-1)
Deauville Flyer is well suited by a flat track and has been running well but is 11lb above his last winning mark. He travelled better than usual in the first-time blinkers but was beginning to struggle when broadsided by Ashbrittle. (op 10-1)
Merchant Of Dubai, a capable sort in handicaps at up to this trip, made much of the running but could not sustain the effort. (op 9-1)
Blissful Moment(USA), a dual winner in 2010 who had run well this year, finishing second in the Duke of Edinburgh at Royal Ascot, lost a prominent pitch at around halfway and his chance had gone turning for home. (op 9-1)
Activate scored twice at this trip last autumn, including the 3-y-o handicap on this card, but had been well beaten in Northumberland Plate and brought down next time. Held up in the rear, he never got competitive. (op 9-1)

Ile De Re(FR) improved for a step up in trip to score over 2m at Ascot last month but had finished behind Tominator last time. He was a little keen early and paid for it in the straight. (op 9-1)

5706 BETFRED "THE BONUS KING" BE FRIENDLY H'CAP 5f

3:00 (3:00) (Class 2) (0-100,94) 3-Y-0+ **£12,938** (£3,850; £1,924; £962) **Stalls** Centre

Form RPR

21 **1** **Zero Money (IRE)**[35] 4556 5-9-7 **94**..........(b) SteveDrowne 1 108+
(Roger Charlton) *mde all: edgd lft 100yds out: hld on wl: eased cl home* **9/4**[1]

0103 **2** ¾ **Master Rooney (IRE)**[21] 5033 5-8-12 **85**.......... RoystonFfrench 8 94
(Bryan Smart) *tubed: led to s: chsd ldrs: wnt 2nd over 2f out: kpt on wl last 75yds* **14/1**

6006 **3** 2 **Courageous (IRE)**[21] 5033 5-8-13 **86**.......... PhillipMakin 12 88+
(Kevin Ryan) *in rr: hdwy over 2f out: kpt on same pce fnl f* **12/1**

0000 **4** hd **Cheveton**[56] 3846 7-9-0 **87**.......... SilvestreDeSousa 9 88
(Richard Price) *rrd s: sn chsng ldrs: kpt on same pce fnl f* **15/2**[3]

2000 **5** ½ **Ballista (IRE)**[36] 4498 3-9-0 **88**.......... RussKennemore 3 87
(Tom Dascombe) *chsd ldrs: hung rt and kpt on same pce fnl f* **33/1**

034 **6** 1¼ **Secret Millionaire (IRE)**[29] 4767 4-8-11 **84**.......... RichardHughes 7 79
(Patrick Morris) *trckd ldrs: t.k.h: effrt 2f out: kpt on same pce: fdd nr fin* **8/1**

0622 **7** ½ **Hazelrigg (IRE)**[21] 5033 6-9-1 **88**..........(be) DavidAllan 5 81
(Tim Easterby) *in rr: hdwy 2f out: kpt on fnl f* **7/1**[2]

4351 **8** shd **Your Gifted (IRE)**[5] 5543 4-8-11 **91** 6ex.......... CharlesBishop(7) 6 84
(Patrick Morris) *trckd ldrs: chal 2f out: wknd fnl f* **8/1**

140 **9** nk **Medici Time**[42] 4346 6-9-2 **89**..........(v) GrahamGibbons 2 81
(Tim Easterby) *sn outpcd and in rr: sme hdwy over 2f out: nvr a factor* **12/1**

-425 **10** 2 **Piscean (USA)**[175] 848 6-9-4 **91**.......... GeorgeBaker 11 75
(Tom Keddy) *dwlt: a towards rr* **22/1**

0020 **11** ½ **Julius Geezer (IRE)**[28] 4779 3-8-12 **86**.......... NeilCallan 4 69
(Tom Dascombe) *chsd ldrs: wknd over 1f out* **33/1**

2030 **12** 2½ **The Thrill Is Gone**[14] 5288 3-9-4 **92**.......... EddieAhern 10 66
(Mick Channon) *racd virtually alone stands' side: chsd ldrs: hung lft and lost pl 2f out* **25/1**

6200 **13** 3¼ **Falasteen (IRE)**[17] 5180 4-9-7 **94**.......... JamieSpencer 13 56
(Kevin Ryan) *a in rr: bhd whn eased last 150yds* **16/1**

58.56 secs (-2.24) **Going Correction** -0.175s/f (Firm) course record
WFA 3 from 4yo+ 1lb **13** Ran SP% **119.3**
Speed ratings (Par 109): **110,108,105,105,104 102,101,101,101,97 97,93,87**
toteswingers:1&2:£9.50, 1&3:£8.90, 2&3:£43.50 CSF £34.89 CT £325.93 TOTE £3.30: £1.40, £4.10, £5.00; EX 41.90 Trifecta £192.80 Pool: £1,467.36 - 5.63 winning units..
Owner Ms Gillian Khosla **Bred** Carrigbeg Stud **Trained** Beckhampton, Wilts

FOCUS

A good, tight-looking sprint handicap in which the field raced up the centre. The first two were 1-2 almost throughout, byut the form is taken at face value, with the winner posting another personal best.

NOTEBOOK

Zero Money(IRE) ◆ had improved recently for the addition of blinkers but was dropping in trip and had been raised 6lb for his last-time-out success. He was soon in front and, finding extra when asked, was in control entering the final furlong. He looks more than capable of going in again, despite a rise in the handicap. (op 11-4 tchd 3-1 in places)

Master Rooney(IRE) beat Hazelrigg at Beverley in June and the pair were closely matched on that form. He kept the winner company from the start but that rival had his measure in the later stages. He beat the others well enough.

Courageous(IRE) ◆ has not won since his debut back in July 2008 but was third in this race last season and weighted to get the better of Cheveton on their running in last year's Ayr Bronze Cup. He finished well to uphold that form and looks one to keep in mind if returning to Ayr later in the month. (tchd 14-1)

Cheveton ◆, whose last two wins were in September last year, was 5lb below that last winning mark and came here with a record of 3-3 over C&D (including this race in 2009). He ran a race full of promise, considering he reared as the gates opened and all his wins have been on softer ground, so is one to keep on side for the rest of the autumn. (op 10-1)

Ballista(IRE) scored over C&D on his racecourse debut and this was his first visit since. Back on a competitive mark, he ran well in the slipstream of the winner, especially as he was quite keen early on. The rider later reported that the gelding hung right-handed. Official explanation: jockey said gelding hung right-handed (op 40-1)

Secret Millionaire(IRE) ◆ whose last win was gained a year ago, had put up some decent efforts since. Racing off 3lb below his last winning mark, he showed enough to suggest his turn is not far away. (tchd 7-1)

Hazelrigg(IRE), whose last two wins were gained in September last year, tracked the pace but looked held when short of room entering the last furlong. He is currently 9lb above his last winning mark but is finishing too close for the handicapper to give him much leeway. (tchd 15-2 and 8-1 in places)

Your Gifted(IRE), a progressive in-foal filly who scored at Epsom on Bank Holiday Monday, had a 6lb penalty here but was 2-2 over C&D. She tried to stay close to the principals but paid for her efforts in the closing stages. (op 7-1)

5707 BETFRED SPRINT CUP (GROUP 1) 6f

3:35 (3:36) (Class 1) 3-Y-0+

£133,722 (£50,697; £25,372; £12,638; £6,343; £3,183) **Stalls** Centre

Form RPR

-510 **1** **Dream Ahead (USA)**[27] 4838 3-9-1 124.......... WilliamBuick 9 122+
(David Simcock) *w ldrs: led over 2f out: rdn and wandered: edgd rt wl ins fnl f: bmpd: all out* **4/1**[1]

1520 **2** nse **Bated Breath**[15] 5253 4-9-3 118.......... SteveDrowne 15 122
(Roger Charlton) *w ldr: chal over 1f out: edgd lft ins fnl f: bmpd: jst denied* **5/1**[2]

0116 **3** hd **Hoof It**[15] 5253 4-9-3 119.......... GrahamGibbons 13 121+
(Michael Easterby) *hld up in mid-div: travelled strly: effrt over 1f out: chsng ldng pair whn forced lft ins fnl f: kpt on wl: jst hld* **5/1**[2]

0164 **4** 1¼ **Genki (IRE)**[27] 4838 7-9-3 111..........(v) GeorgeBaker 14 117
(Roger Charlton) *stdd s: hld up in rr: effrt stands' side over 2f out: edgd lft 1f out: kpt on wl* **20/1**

5140 **5** 2 **Elzaam (AUS)**[56] 3863 3-9-1 112.......... RichardHills 12 111
(Roger Varian) *s.i.s: towards rr: hdwy and swtchd lft over 1f out: hung lft and kpt on wl* **16/1**

0212 **6** 1¼ **Society Rock (IRE)**[27] 4838 4-9-3 117.......... PatCosgrave 1 107
(James Fanshawe) *dwlt: racd far side: hdwy over 2f out: kpt on same pce fnl f* **9/1**[3]

6006 **7** ¾ **Dalghar (FR)**[39] 4412 5-9-3 107..........[1] DavidProbert 16 105
(Andrew Balding) *chsd ldrs: fdd appr fnl f* **25/1**

1-10 **8** shd **Bewitched (IRE)**[77] 3154 4-9-0 111..........(t) RichardHughes 6 101+
(Charles O'Brien, Ire) *s.i.s: hld up in rr: hdwy and n.m.r over 2f out: nt clr run 1f out: kpt on wl clsng stages* **14/1**

4103 **9** 1 **Hitchens (IRE)**[56] 3863 6-9-3 114.......... FMBerry 2 101
(David Barron) *racd towards far side: chsd ldrs: effrt over 2f out: wknd fnl f* **25/1**

0604 **10** 1½ **Kingsgate Native (IRE)**[15] 5253 6-9-3 113.......... NeilCallan 8 96
(Sir Michael Stoute) *chsd ldrs: drvn over 2f out: wknd over 1f out* **20/1**

5516 **11** hd **Doncaster Rover (USA)**[6] 5510 5-9-3 108.......... SilvestreDeSousa 11 96+
(David Brown) *in rr and sn drvn along: nvr a factor* **33/1**

1052 **12** 2¾ **Sole Power**[6] 5524 4-9-3 117.......... KLatham 4 87
(Edward Lynam, Ire) *racd far side: w ldr: wknd appr fnl f* **20/1**

-505 **13** ¾ **Wootton Bassett**[27] 4838 3-9-1 113.......... PaulHanagan 10 84
(Richard Fahey) *w ldrs: led over 4f out: hdd over 2f out: wknd over 1f out* **16/1**

150 **14** 1½ **Delegator**[39] 4412 5-9-3 112.......... FrankieDettori 5 80
(Saeed Bin Suroor) *in rr: drvn over 2f out: no imp whn n.m.r 1f out: wknd* **9/1**[3]

0110 **15** 6 **Masamah (IRE)**[15] 5253 5-9-3 112.......... JamieSpencer 7 60
(Kevin Ryan) *racd towards far side: led over 1f: hung lft and wknd wl over 1f out: eased* **25/1**

0010 **16** 9 **Tiddliwinks**[15] 5253 5-9-3 104.......... PhillipMakin 3 32
(Kevin Ryan) *racd far side: chsd ldrs: lost pl 2f out: bhd whn heavily eased* **66/1**

1m 10.36s (-3.44) **Going Correction** -0.175s/f (Firm)
WFA 3 from 4yo+ 2lb **16** Ran SP% **122.0**
Speed ratings (Par 117): **115,114,114,113,110 108,107,107,106,104 103,100,99,97,89 77**
toteswingers:1&2:£7.20, 1&3:£9.00, 2&3:£9.40 CSF £19.88 CT £105.24 TOTE £4.80: £1.80, £2.10, £2.60; EX 26.70 Trifecta £162.50 Pool: £39,290.89 - 178.92 winning units..
Owner Khalifa Dasmal **Bred** Darley **Trained** Newmarket, Suffolk

FOCUS

A big field for one of the major 6f sprints of the season and it produced a dramatic and close finish, with the July Cup proving the key. Sound if not outstanding form amongst the principals, Dream Ahead a length off his July Cup figure. Bated Breath ran to form and Hoof It was possibly unlucky. A personal best from Genki.

NOTEBOOK

Dream Ahead(USA) dropped back in trip to win the July Cup on fast ground from Bated Breath but had since been well held in the Maurice de Gheest on soft ground that should have suited. He bounced back here, being never far away and then just doing enough to hang on despite again showing a tendency to wander around under pressure, with the fast ground probably a factor. He hampered the third more than the runner-up in the closing stages but the result was allowed to stand. (op 5-1)

Bated Breath, a progressive sprinter who is best on fast, had finished runner-up to Dream Ahead in the July Cup and the weight for age was less here. He came through to challenge the winner and kept straighter than his rival, only to lose out by the width of a cigarette paper. He deserves to win a Group 1 sprint but his options this season are few, although he might be kept in training. (op 6-1 tchd 13-2 in places)

Hoof It ◆, an extremely progressive sort who had proved suited by this track in the past, had won the Stewards' Cup under a record burden before finding things not going right for him in the Nunthorpe. He tracked the pace before being produced late, only to be carried left by the winner inside the last furlong. He was in front soon after the line and can be considered an unlucky loser. He has proved himself up to this level now and he will no doubt be back contesting all the big sprints again next year. (op 9-2 tchd 4-1)

Genki(IRE) is a reliable sort who came here with a course record of one win and two places, including third in this race last season. With the visor back on instead of the blinkers he wore last time, he missed the break and was last until around halfway, but then stayed on well in the closing stages to finish on the heels of the principals. He looks sure to find another opportunity before the season is out.

Elzaam(AUS) found the drop back to 6f helping him win a Listed race in May and had posted decent efforts in the Golden Jubilee and July Cup since. He had a bit to find on that form but ran another sound race, if no threat to those in the frame. He can make his mark at a slightly lower level.

Society Rock(IRE) has made up into a top-class sprinter this season, winning the Golden Jubilee and finishing second in the Maurice de Gheest. He had a bit to find with Bated Breath on previous C&D form, and did not help his chance with a tardy start. (tchd 10-1)

Dalghar(FR) ◆ had put up a decent effort over 7f last time but had previously been well held in the Golden Jubilee and the July Cup and had a bit to find. Wearing a hood for the first time, he ran well for a long way and is the sort who could make his mark in something like the Prix de la Foret, where softer ground will be in his favour.

Bewitched(IRE), a multiple winner at up to Group 3 level who handles any ground, had reportedly pulled a muscle when a well-beaten favourite in the Golden Jubilee. Having her first run since, she was held up out the back before doing her best work in the closing stages. She can win again at Group level, if not in the top grade. (op 12-1)

Hitchens(IRE), in the form of his life this season, beating Tiddliwinks at the Curragh and finishing third in the July Cup, was having his first run since the July Cup and performed creditably. He normally benefits from a recent outing and is one to bear in mind when he next appears.

Kingsgate Native(IRE), who finished ahead of Hoof It when fourth in the Nunthorpe, had been first and second in the Temple Stakes on two previous visits here. He had his chance but faded late on. (op 22-1 tchd 16-1)

Sole Power won last season's Nunthorpe and beat Kingsgate Native in the Temple Stakes over 5f here in May, but was beaten in a Group 3 the previous weekend. Having his first try over 6f since 2009, he showed up well before appearing not to last home.

Wootton Bassett, an unbeaten juvenile who finished fifth in the Poulains on his return, had been held in both the St James's Palace and Maurice de Gheest since and was dropping back further in trip. He showed up early before fading and, although not up to winning at the top level on this evidence, owes nobody anything.

5708 BETFRED 1350 SHOPS NATIONWIDE NURSERY 6f

4:05 (4:07) (Class 2) 2-Y-0 **£9,703** (£2,887; £1,443; £721) **Stalls** Centre

Form RPR

0162 **1** **Democretes**[31] 4661 2-8-9 **78**.......... RichardHughes 1 87
(Richard Hannon) *mde all racing towards far side: edgd rt over 1f out: kpt rt up to work to forge clr* **13/2**[2]

1401 **2** 2¼ **Imelda Mayhem**[8] 5427 2-8-12 **81**.......... NeilCallan 2 83
(J S Moore) *chsd wnr on far side: drvn over 2f out: kpt on same pce fnl f* **16/1**

513 **3** hd **Nimiety**[21] 5052 2-8-4 **73**.......... SilvestreDeSousa 6 74
(Mark Johnston) *chsd ldrs: drvn over 2f out: kpt on same pce fnl f* **5/2**[1]

13 **4** hd **Chooseday (IRE)**[25] 4891 2-8-10 **79**.......... PhillipMakin 10 80
(Kevin Ryan) *hld up towards stands' side: hdwy over 2f out: chsd wnr over 1f out: edgd lft and kpt on same pce* **10/1**[3]

1160 **5** 3 **Piranha (IRE)**[22] 4999 2-8-13 **82**.......... JamieSpencer 7 76+
(Ed Dunlop) *1/2 rrd s: hld up in last: effrt 2f out: sn drvn: kpt on: nvr rchd ldrs* **14/1**

1410 **6** 4 **Mabroor (USA)**[36] 4496 2-9-7 **90**.......... RichardHills 9 70
(Mark Johnston) *chsd ldrs towards stands' side: lost pl 2f out: kpt on again last 100yds* **12/1**

1 **7** *1* **Brickfielder (IRE)**[30] 4708 2-8-2 **74**.............................. HarryBentley(3) 3 51
(Roger Charlton) *hld up: effrt over 2f out: edgd lft and lost pl over 1f out* **5/2**[1]

6120 **8** *½* **Nearly A Gift (IRE)**[17] 5184 2-9-0 **83**..............................(p) DavidAllan 8 58
(Tim Easterby) *chsd ldrs: rdn over 2f out: wknd over 1f out* **12/1**

010 **9** *3* **Sanad (IRE)**[17] 5184 2-8-6 **75**.. PaulHanagan 5 47
(Brian Meehan) *chsd ldrs: hung lft and wknd over 1f out: eased* **14/1**

1m 12.78s (-1.02) **Going Correction** -0.175s/f (Firm) **9** Ran SP% **114.2**
Speed ratings (Par 101): **99,96,95,95,91 86,84,84,80**
toteswingers:1&2:£9.80, 1&3:£3.40, 2&3:£6.80 CSF £101.50 CT £329.56 TOTE £7.50: £1.90, £4.10, £1.30; EX 75.40.
Owner The High Flyers **Bred** R J Cornelius **Trained** East Everleigh, Wilts

FOCUS
A decent nursery that is usually won by an improving sort and that was the case again. The first two raced more towards the far side and the winner built on his good maiden win with the placed horses helping to st the level.

NOTEBOOK
Democretes, a 6f maiden winner in the spring, this colt had only fair nursery form since but had made the running last time and was suited by doing so again, this time not finding himself vulnerable to a late challenge. He could progress again from here. (op 6-1 tchd 7-1)
Imelda Mayhem, a dual winner over a sharp 6f on good ground, had been raised 6lb for her win last time but chased the winner throughout and stuck to her task under pressure. (op 14-1)
Nimiety, a 6f winner on fast ground in May, had made a good return over 7f last time and was dropping back in trip. Racing off 2lb higher, she raced up with the pace and came again after looking held. A return to 7f will be in her favour. (op 11-4 tchd 9-4)
Chooseday(IRE), the winner of a C&D maiden on debut in July, finished last of three in a novice stakes next time, although the winner of that race finished runner-up in a Listed race on his next start. He looked reasonably treated now handicapping and ran his race, just losing out in a three-way battle for second. (op 8-1)
Piranha(IRE), a dual Polytrack winner, was out the back early after dwelling in the stalls and, although she ran on late, never got close enough to land a blow. (op 10-1)
Brickfielder(IRE) had won an ordinary Folkestone maiden over 7f on easy ground early last month and did not appear to appreciate the drop in trip and faster ground on this handicap debut. (op 3-1 tchd 10-3)

5709 BETFRED TREBLE ODDS ON ALL LUCKY'S STKS (REGISTERED AS THE ASCENDANT STAKES) (LISTED RACE) 1m
4:40 (4:41) (Class 1) 2-Y-O

£12,192 (£4,622; £2,313; £1,152; £578; £290) **Stalls** Low

Form RPR

3014 **1** **Caledonian Spring (IRE)**[17] 5181 2-9-0 97....................... EddieAhern 5 106+
(Paul D'Arcy) *trckd ldrs: led over 2f out: kpt on wl to forge clr fnl f* **10/3**[2]

112 **2** *3* **Crius (IRE)**[14] 5287 2-9-0 91.. RichardHughes 1 98
(Richard Hannon) *led hdd over 2f out: kpt on same pce appr fnl f* **3/1**[1]

123 **3** *¾* **Leqqaa (USA)**[21] 5044 2-9-0 91... RichardHills 2 96
(Mark Johnston) *s.i.s: hdwy on ins over 3f out: sn chsng ldrs: kpt on same pce appr fnl f* **8/1**

1 **4** *1* **Stipulate**[27] 4815 2-9-0 79.. IanMongan 4 94
(Sir Henry Cecil) *trckd ldrs: t.k.h: chal over 2f out: one pce over 1f out* **5/1**[3]

51 **5** *½* **Martin Chuzzlewit (IRE)**[30] 4722 2-9-0 90..................... WilliamBuick 7 93
(Sir Michael Stoute) *chsd ldrs: drvn 4f out: sn outpcd: lost pl over 2f out: crowded over 1f out: kpt on ins fnl f* **3/1**[1]

31 **6** *2 ¼* **Noor Zabeel (USA)**[114] 2033 2-9-0 91.......................... JamieSpencer 8 88
(Mick Channon) *hld up in rr: hdwy over 3f out: wknd over 1f out* **16/1**

0214 **7** *1 ½* **Goldoni (IRE)**[15] 5234 2-9-0 87.. DavidProbert 6 84
(Andrew Balding) *chsd ldrs: drvn 4f out: edgd lft and lost pl over 2f out* **16/1**

1m 43.68s (0.78) **Going Correction** +0.125s/f (Good) **7** Ran SP% **112.6**
Speed ratings (Par 103): **101,98,97,96,95 93,92**
toteswingers:1&2:£2.40, 1&3:£4.90, 2&3:£3.30 CSF £13.33 TOTE £4.10: £2.40, £1.80; EX 11.30.
Owner Dr J S Kinnear **Bred** Patrick Cosgrove **Trained** Newmarket, Suffolk

FOCUS
Not the strongest Listed race for juveniles on the calendar but a decisive winner. Straightforward form.

NOTEBOOK
Caledonian Spring(IRE) had the highest official rating, having beaten a subsequent sales-race winner at Ascot before finishing fourth in the Group 3 Acomb at York. Always travelling well, he was kicked for home around the 2f pole and soon had the race in safe keeping. He could be competitive back in Group races. (op 7-2)
Crius(IRE) had won his first two starts before finishing second in a nursery at the Ebor meeting. Under a change of tactics, he made the running but was easily seen off by the winner before keeping on well to retain second place. The 1m nursery at Doncaster might be a suitable target for him. (op 7-2 tchd 11-4)
Leqqaa(USA) had some decent form at up to Listed level but took time to find his stride here. He ran on from around 2f out but could not get past the runner-up, let alone trouble the winner. (op 10-1)
Stipulate narrowly beat a subsequent winner on his debut at Leicester but was easy in the market on this step up in grade. He tracked the pace early but failed to pick up under pressure. (op 4-1 tchd 11-2)
Martin Chuzzlewit(IRE) was prominent early but came under pressure early in the straight before keeping on again. His win was gained on an easy surface and he might have not been entirely happy on this fast ground. (op 7-2)
Noor Zabeel(USA), returning from four months off, was always at the rear and never figured. (op 11-1)
Goldoni(IRE) was being ridden along over 2f out and failed to respond. This was disappointing. (op 14-1)

5710 BETFRED MACHINE FREEPLAY H'CAP 1m 6f
5:10 (5:11) (Class 3) (0-90,88) 3-Y-O **£8,409** (£2,502; £1,250; £625) **Stalls** Centre

Form RPR

1250 **1** **Motivado**[14] 5283 3-9-6 **87**.. StevieDonohoe 10 105+
(Sir Mark Prescott Bt) *hld up in rr: effrt 4f out: drivcen to ld 2f out: drew clr fnl f: eased towards fin* **9/1**

2542 **2** *7* **Four Nations (USA)**[21] 5035 3-8-13 **80**.......................... EddieAhern 2 88
(Amanda Perrett) *trckd ldrs: chal over 2f out: kpt on same pce over 1f out* **5/1**[3]

0410 **3** *2* **Elrasheed**[21] 5035 3-8-8 **75**... RichardHills 8 80
(John Dunlop) *trckd ldr: led over 10f out tl 2f out: kpt on same pce* **10/1**

3141 **4** *¾* **Getabuzz**[21] 5064 3-8-11 **78**... DavidAllan 4 82
(Tim Easterby) *hld up in rr: effrt 4f out: kpt on one pce fnl 2f* **14/1**

0314 **5** *½* **Lexington Bay (IRE)**[79] 3084 3-8-12 **79**....................... PaulHanagan 3 82
(Richard Fahey) *chsd ldrs: drvn over 5f out: one pce whn sltly hmpd over 2f out* **18/1**

21 **6** *nk* **Cops And Robbers**[28] 4805 3-9-7 **88**........................... RichardHughes 7 91
(Sir Michael Stoute) *sn trcking ldrs: drvn over 3f out: one pce fnl 2f* **5/2**[1]

01 **7** *3 ¾* **Gulf Of Naples (IRE)**[22] 4985 3-9-1 **82**.................... SilvestreDeSousa 5 84
(Mark Johnston) *in rr: drvn after 3f: sme hdwy on ins over 2f out: wknd and eased 1f out* **16/1**

2311 **8** *22* **Watered Silk**[24] 4932 3-9-1 **82**...(b) NeilCallan 11 —
(Marcus Tregoning) *led over 3f: w ldrs: drvn over 3f out: edgd rt and lost pl 2f out: sn bhd: heavily eased last 100yds* **11/1**

3-01 **9** *24* **Suhaili**[99] 2458 3-9-2 **83**... WilliamBuick 6 —
(Roger Varian) *hld up in mid-div: drvn 5f out: lost pl over 2f out: bhd and eased 1f out: virtually p.u* **11/4**[2]

3m 0.12s (-1.08) **Going Correction** +0.125s/f (Good) **9** Ran SP% **117.1**
Speed ratings (Par 105): **108,104,102,102,102 101,99,87,73**
toteswingers:1&2:£11.10, 1&3:£25.50, 2&3:£14.90 CSF £54.30 CT £465.35 TOTE £10.20: £3.20, £1.80, £3.80; EX 59.60.
Owner Syndicate 2009 **Bred** Newsells Park Stud **Trained** Newmarket, Suffolk

FOCUS
A decent staying handicap for 3yos, run 0.61sec slower than the earlier Class 2 older-horse handicap over the trip. The winner produced a clear personal best and the form looks sound.

NOTEBOOK
Motivado, who had not really gone on from winning on his seasonal reappearance, was held up at the rear but made good headway through the field to lead over 2f out and soon came clear. This was much more like the horse we saw early in the season and hopefully he can go on again from this, with the Mallard Handicap at Doncaster later in the month a possible target. (op 11-1)
Four Nations(USA) goes well on fast ground and appreciated the step up to this sort of trip when runner-up on his previous outing. He travelled well throughout and delivered his challenge at the same time as the winner, only to be unable to go with that rival. He should be able to win again off this sort of mark. (op 9-2 tchd 11-2)
Elrasheed took over in front entering the back straight and maintained the gallop until the principals went by. He looks a solid stayer given a sound surface. (op 16-1)
Getabuzz has gained his wins on easier ground than this and, after being held up at the rear, could only run on at one pace in the straight. (tchd 11-1)
Lexington Bay(IRE), stepping up in trip, had beaten today's winner at Musselburgh in May and was weighted to finish upsides. He was, however, 6lb above his last winning mark and, although he ran reasonably, may have needed the outing after 11 weeks off. (op 16-1)
Cops And Robbers progressed from his debut to take a 1m4f Newmarket maiden last month but, after getting into contention leaving the back straight, could only muster one pace when the race began in earnest. He is bred to stay but gave the impression he found the trip too far at this stage of his development. (op 11-4)
Gulf Of Naples(IRE), an easy-ground maiden winner, lost his place and was being ridden before halfway, so probably did not handle the surface, being eased late on. (op 12-1)
Watered Silk, who had gone up a stone for his two wins in a lower grade last month, led early but then chased the leader before challenging 2f out. However, he was soon in trouble and dropped right away. (op 15-2)
Suhaili, returning after a three-month absence since his maiden success, was backed and was close enough turning in, but soon came under pressure and could not respond, eventually finishing tailed off. (op 7-2)
T/Jkpt: Not won. T/Plt: £77.00 to a £1 stake. Pool:£146,255.73 - 1,386.06 winning tickets T/Qpdt: £11.10 to a £1 stake. Pool:£7,313.66 - 483.32 winning tickets WG

5687 KEMPTON (A.W) (R-H)
Saturday, September 3

OFFICIAL GOING: Standard (watered)
Wind: light, across Weather: bright and sunny

5711 BETFRED SEPTEMBER STKS (GROUP 3) 1m 4f (P)
2:15 (2:15) (Class 1) 3-Y-O+

£28,355 (£10,750; £5,380; £2,680; £1,345; £675) **Stalls** Centre

Form RPR

0224 **1** **Modun (IRE)**[14] 5285 4-9-4 105... ShaneKelly 8 113+
(Sir Michael Stoute) *hld up in tch: hdwy to chse ldng trio over 6f out: edgd rt and effrt ent fnl 2f: led over 1f out: rdn clr 1f out: styd on wl: rdn out* **2/1**[2]

0100 **2** *1 ½* **Bronze Cannon (USA)**[177] 824 6-9-4 105....................... TomQueally 5 109
(Gary Moore) *hld up wl in tch in last trio: n.m.r over 2f out: rdn and hdwy over 1f out: chsd wnr ins fnl f: kpt on wl but nt pce to threaten wnr* **16/1**

3224 **3** *1 ¾* **Harris Tweed**[14] 5284 4-9-4 115.. LiamJones 2 106
(William Haggas) *led: rdn and qcknd over 2f out: drvn and hdd over 1f out: styd on same pce after: lost 2nd ins fnl f* **15/8**[1]

0260 **4** *½* **Myplacelater**[20] 5093 4-9-1 107.. LukeMorris 4 102
(David Elsworth) *stdd s: hld up wl in tch in last pair: rdn and outpcd whn pce qcknd over 2f out: rallied u.p 1f out: styd on wl ins fnl f* **17/2**

41 **5** *1 ¼* **Classic Punch (IRE)**[28] 4801 8-9-4 104........................... DaneO'Neill 6 103
(David Elsworth) *chsd ldr: rdn over 2f out: drvn and stl pressing ldrs 2f out: unable qck over 1f out and btn ent fnl f: styd on same pce fnl f* **10/1**

0-56 **6** *1 ¾* **Brushing**[16] 5219 5-9-1 102... SebSanders 1 97
(Mark H Tompkins) *chsd ldrs: rdn whn pce qcknd over 2f out: unbale to qckn u.p 2f out: styd on same pce and no threat to ldrs fr over 1f out* **25/1**

10U3 **7** *2 ¼* **Simon De Montfort (IRE)**[7] 5494 4-9-4 113..................... ChrisCatlin 7 97
(Mahmood Al Zarooni) *stdd s: hld up in tch in last trio: rdn over 3f out: drvn and struggling over 2f out: wknd 2f out* **13/2**[3]

2m 31.1s (-3.40) **Going Correction** +0.025s/f (Slow) **7** Ran SP% **110.8**
Speed ratings (Par 113): **112,111,109,109,108 107,106**
Tote Swingers: 1&2 £14.60, 1&3 £1.10, 2&3 £8.10 CSF £30.23 TOTE £2.90: £1.50, £5.00; EX 43.40 Trifecta £195.60 Pool: £496.94 - 1.88 winning units..
Owner Ballymacoll Stud **Bred** Ballymacoll Stud Farm Ltd **Trained** Newmarket, Suffolk

FOCUS
The sixth running of the September Stakes on Polytrack. The early pace wasn't by any means strong and it developed into something of a 3f sprint. The form looks s bit muddling and could prove shaky.

NOTEBOOK
Modun(IRE), back in trip after not quite seeing out the extra 2f in the Ebor, handled this surface well enough when beaten a short head by Spensley (a winner back here the previous evening) on his only previous try over C&D 11 months ago. Wide early on, he was taken inside to make his effort between horses after turning for home and quickened up well once leading over a furlong out. Whether he can prove effective at this level back on turf remains to be seen, but if not he could benefit by continuing his career on sand overseas. (op 9-4 tchd 15-8)
Bronze Cannon(USA), a dual Group 2 winner for John Gosden and twice successful here earlier in his career, was making his debut for Gary Moore on this first run since enjoying mixed fortunes in Dubai at the start of the year. He has won after a similar absence in the past, but it was still pleasing to see him run on so strongly after getting outpaced starting up the home straight and this gives his new connections something to build on. (tchd 20-1)

Harris Tweed has improved plenty on turf since finishing unplaced on Polytrack in his first two racecourse appearances, but he stays further than this so may have been better off setting a stronger pace out in front. As it was, he tried to wind things up off the home bend yet still proved a sitting duck. (op 2-1 tchd 7-4)
Myplacelater, a prolific winner at three including on Polytrack, has found things harder this time around and she didn't find her stride until it was far too late. (op 10-1 tchd 11-1)
Classic Punch(IRE), placed a couple of times here last year including in this race, usually likes to go from the front but he wasn't asked to lead this time and was never going to find the required turn of foot once off the bridle. (op 11-1 tchd 12-1)
Brushing, making her all-weather debut, was dropping in class compared with her two previous outings this season, but was still firmly put in her place from over a furlong out. (op 16-1)
Simon De Montfort(IRE) was in trouble over 3f from home and then showed an awkward head-carriage before hanging to the far rail after the intersection. He seems to have lost his way. (op 5-1)

5712 BETFRED LONDON MILE H'CAP (SERIES FINAL) 1m (P)
2:45 (2:45) (Class 2) 3-Y-0+

£27,265 (£8,164; £4,082; £2,041; £1,020; £512) **Stalls** Low

Form RPR
2012 **1** **Red Gulch**[22] 4993 4-9-8 **96** J-PGuillambert 12 108+
(Ed Walker) *broke wl: sn stdd and t.k.h: hld up in tch: rdn and qcknd to ld over 1f out: r.o wl fnl f: rdn out* **8/1**[2]
3003 **2** *1 ½* **Kajima**[22] 4993 4-9-5 **93** DaneO'Neill 9 102
(Richard Hannon) *in tch in midfield: rdn and effrt ent fnl 2f: hdwy over 1f out: r.o wl u.p fnl f: wnt 2nd fnl 50yds: nt pce to threaten wnr* **16/1**
5262 **3** *¾* **Fantasy Gladiator**[6] 5516 5-8-12 **86** (p) JimmyQuinn 6 93
(Robert Cowell) *t.k.h: hld up in midfield: swtchd ins and effrt 2f out: drvn and kpt on fnl f: wnt 3rd cl home: nt pce to threaten wnr* **12/1**
0401 **4** *hd* **Primaeval**[22] 4993 5-9-10 **98** (v) JimCrowley 7 105
(James Fanshawe) *in tch: swtchd ins and effrt ent fnl 2f: drvn to chse wnr jst over 1f out: no ex and btn ins fnl f: lost 2 pls fnl 50yds* **4/1**[1]
6000 **5** *1 ¼* **Chapter And Verse (IRE)**[22] 4993 5-9-5 **93** TonyCulhane 8 97+
(Mike Murphy) *towards rr: rdn and effrt 2f out: hdd over 1f out: styd on u.p fnl f: nvr able to chal* **8/1**[2]
1100 **6** *nk* **Indian Jack (IRE)**[105] 2296 3-8-9 **88** LukeMorris 16 91
(Alan Bailey) *racd in midfield: rdn and effrt on outer ent fnl 2f: styd on u.p fnl f: unable to chal* **12/1**
1250 **7** *¾* **Night Lily (IRE)**[22] 4993 5-9-5 **93** LiamJones 13 95
(Paul D'Arcy) *chsd ldrs: rdn to ld over 2f out: drvn and hdd over 1f out: wknd ins fnl f* **20/1**
0320 **8** *1 ½* **Loyalty**[56] 3848 4-8-8 **82** (v) RobbieFitzpatrick 2 80
(Derek Shaw) *chsd ldrs: rdn and lost pl 1/2-way: rallied u.p on inner 2f out: wknd jst ins fnl f* **20/1**
0025 **9** *½* **Benandonner (USA)**[22] 4993 8-9-4 **92** AndreaAtzeni 4 89
(Mike Murphy) *led tl rdn and hdd over 2f out: wknd ent fnl f* **20/1**
1210 **10** *1 ¾* **Sinfonico (IRE)**[37] 4472 3-8-8 **90** SeanLevey(3) 14 83
(Richard Hannon) *hld up towards rr: rdn ent fnl f: kpt on ins fnl f: nvr trbld ldrs* **20/1**
6106 **11** *shd* **Shamir**[23] 4958 4-9-0 **88** ShaneKelly 3 81
(Jo Crowley) *in tch in midfield: hmpd and lost pl over 6f out: drvn over 1f out: no imp and styd on same pce after* **17/2**[3]
00 **12** *shd* **Nelson's Bounty**[49] 4100 4-8-11 **85** SebSanders 15 77
(Paul D'Arcy) *chsd ldrs on outer: rdn over 2f out: wknd u.p jst over 1f out* **16/1**
1010 **13** *¾* **Willow Dancer (IRE)**[12] 5328 7-8-7 **84** (p) JohnFahy(3) 10 75
(Walter Swinburn) *in tch in midfield: rdn over 3f out: no prog and no threat to ldrs fnl 2f* **25/1**
3040 **14** *1 ½* **Merchant Of Medici**[22] 5012 4-8-8 **82** MartinDwyer 5 69+
(William Muir) *taken down early: dwlt: towards rr: hmpd over 6f out: n.d* **8/1**[2]
1203 **15** *½* **Crown Counsel (IRE)**[14] 5272 3-9-1 **94** WJSupple 11 80
(Mark Johnston) *chsd ldrs: effrt u.p and ev ch over 2f out: wknd over 1f out* **16/1**
0516 **16** *6* **Layline (IRE)**[22] 4993 4-9-1 **92** KieranO'Neill(3) 1 64
(Gay Kelleway) *dwlt: towards rr: hmpd and dropped to last over 6f out: n.d after* **16/1**

1m 37.77s (-2.03) **Going Correction** +0.025s/f (Slow)
WFA 3 from 4yo+ 5lb **16** Ran SP% **125.7**
Speed ratings (Par 109): **111,109,108,108,107 107,106,104,104,102 102,102,101,100,99 93**
Tote Swingers: 1&2 £11.10, 1&3 £13.90, 2&3 £63.60 CSF £121.70 CT £1555.64 TOTE £9.60: £3.30, £3.90, £3.20, £1.40; EX 120.40 Trifecta £382.10 Part won. Pool: £516.44 - 0.50 winning units..
Owner S Al Ansari **Bred** Cheveley Park Stud Ltd **Trained** Newmarket, Suffolk

FOCUS
Seven of these ran in the same qualifier just over three weeks earlier and that race provided the winner, second, fourth and fifth here. The early pace was solid enough, but this was a rough race with some serious crowding after a furlong which badly affected the chances of at least four horses. The main sufferers were Shamir, Chapter and Verse, Merchant Of Medici and Layline, with the last pair very fortunate to stay on their feet. Nevertheless the form looks sound rated around the principals.

NOTEBOOK
Red Gulch was beaten just over 2l by Primaeval in the qualifier over C&D three weeks ago and was 6lb better off. Although he broke well from his high draw, he was steadied to track the pace but was travelling much the best coming to the last 2f and when switched out for his effort over a furlong out, there was only going to be one winner. He may not be the easiest to place now having won this off 96, but he is a half-brother to a 1m2f winner so may be worth a go in the Cambridgeshire. (tchd 15-2)
Kajima, third behind Primaeval and Red Gulch in that qualifier last month and closely matched with the pair on these revised terms, sat in midfield before running on strongly inside the last furlong, but the winner had already gone beyond recall.
Fantasy Gladiator was 6lb higher than for the second of two victories here towards the end of last year, but he ran a blinder this time, making progress before the intersection and finishing strongly against the inside rail. (op 14-1)
Primaeval came into this 3-5 here and was put up 7lb for winning the qualifier last month. He was always in a good position behind the leaders and had every chance after the intersection, but couldn't produce the same turn of foot this time. (op 9-2)
Chapter And Verse(IRE) was 6lb higher than when winning this race last year and fared worst of the seven that ran in the qualifier here 22 days earlier, but in view of the trouble he suffered early on here, which cost him valuable ground, he did very well to finish where he did. With more luck he would have gone closer to winning. (op 10-1)
Indian Jack(IRE) had run poorly in his last two starts on turf and was returning from an absence of 105 days, but he came into this 3-3 here and he was finishing as well as anything having been given plenty to do. (op 16-1)
Night Lily(IRE) had to be ridden to take a prominent position early and was in front over 2f out, but she didn't get home. She still looks on a stiff mark. (tchd 18-1)
Shamir Official explanation: jockey said gelding suffered interference in running
Merchant Of Medici Official explanation: jockey said gelding was hampered at start

5713 BETFRED BONUS COUPON CONDITIONS STKS 7f (P)
3:20 (3:20) (Class 4) 2-Y-0 **£4,398** (£1,309; £654) **Stalls** Low

Form RPR
1 **1** **Tidentime (USA)**[21] 5051 2-9-2 0 ChrisCatlin 4 80+
(Mick Channon) *wnt lft s: w ldr: rdn wl over 2f out: led jst over 1f out: r.o wl under hands and heels riding ins fnl f* **11/8**[1]
6 **2** *¾* **Samuel Pickwick (IRE)**[15] 5239 2-8-12 0 ShaneKelly 1 74+
(Sir Michael Stoute) *stdd s: trckd rivals: effrt and nt clr run over 1f out: swtchd lft and sltly outpcd jst over 1f out: rdn and hdwy ins fnl f: wnt 2nd fnl 100yds: r.o* **7/4**[2]
63 **3** *½* **Juvenal (IRE)**[15] 5239 2-8-12 0 DaneO'Neill 3 73
(Richard Hannon) *led and set stdy gallop: rdn and qcknd over 2f out: hdd jst over 1f out: kpt on same pce and lost 2nd fnl 100yds* **5/2**[3]

1m 29.61s (3.61) **Going Correction** +0.025s/f (Slow) **3** Ran SP% **107.0**
Speed ratings (Par 97): **80,79,78**
CSF £3.95 TOTE £1.70; EX 2.80.
Owner Jon and Julia Aisbitt **Bred** Big C Farms **Trained** West Ilsley, Berks

FOCUS
For the second year running just three went to post for this conditions event. The form is difficult to pin down but the first two look as if they can do better.

NOTEBOOK
Tidentime(USA)'s chances didn't look great at halfway as he was the first of the trio to be niggled along at halfway whilst in second place, but there is stamina on the dam's side of his pedigree and he ground his way to the front over a furlong from home. A strongly run race over this trip may see him in an even better light. (op 10-11)
Samuel Pickwick(IRE) finished behind Juvenal on his Sandown debut last month and turned that form around, but having been settled in last he took time in finding top gear and could never get to the winner. (op 5-2)
Juvenal(IRE) had the run of the race out in front until collared over a furlong from home and perhaps lacks the scope of the other pair. (op 3-1)

5714 BETFRED TEXT "FRED" TO 89660 H'CAP 2m (P)
3:50 (3:50) (Class 4) (0-80,78) 3-Y-0 **£5,175** (£1,540; £769; £384) **Stalls** Low

Form RPR
6031 **1** **All My Heart**[4] 5599 3-9-3 **74** 6ex SebSanders 4 82
(Sir Mark Prescott Bt) *led: jnd and rdn 6f out: hdd 5f out: switching lft over 1f out: rallied gamely u.p to chal ins fnl f: led fnl 50yds: styd on* **4/5**[1]
0260 **2** *1* **Quiz Mistress**[10] 5389 3-9-4 **75** DaneO'Neill 7 82
(Gerard Butler) *hld up in last pair: hdwy and stl travelling wl 4f out: chsd ldr over 2f out: rdn to ld over 1f out: forged ahd u.p and edgd lft ins fnl f: hdd and no ex fnl 50yds* **10/1**
3160 **3** *2 ¼* **Mungo Park**[23] 4941 3-9-7 **78** WJSupple 8 82
(Mark Johnston) *chsd ldr tl wnt upsides wnr travelling wl 6f out: led 5f out: rdn 3f out: drvn and hdd over 1f out: wknd ins fnl f* **14/1**
1-0 **4** *3 ¾* **Mahab El Shamaal**[73] 3291 3-8-11 **71** KieranO'Neill(3) 1 71
(David Simcock) *chsd ldrs: rdn 6f out: struggling u.p 3f out: 4th and btn whn veered rt u.p over 1f out* **4/1**[2]
006 **5** *12* **Rasam Aldaar**[7] 5491 3-8-7 **64** (v[1]) LukeMorris 6 49
(Michael Wigham) *chsd ldrs: rdn 6f out: struggling u.p 4f out: 5th and wl btn over 2f out* **33/1**
0131 **6** *4* **Susan Stroman**[18] 5145 3-9-6 **77** ChrisCatlin 5 58
(Ed Dunlop) *hld up in last pair: rdn 6f out: wknd and wl bhd fnl 3f* **9/2**[3]

3m 30.26s (0.16) **Going Correction** +0.025s/f (Slow) **6** Ran SP% **112.4**
Speed ratings (Par 103): **100,99,98,96,90 88**
Tote Swingers: 1&2 £2.40, 1&3 £1.20, 2&3 £53.00 CSF £10.13 CT £63.85 TOTE £1.70: £1.10, £3.00; EX 9.70.
Owner Miss K Rausing **Bred** Miss K Rausing And Shellin Blk **Trained** Newmarket, Suffolk
■ Stewards' Enquiry : Seb Sanders two-day ban: used whip with excessive frequency (Sep 17-18)

FOCUS
Not the strongest of handicaps, but staying was very much the name of the game. The winner battled well but the form looks shaky.
Susan Stroman Official explanation: trainer said filly was in season

5715 BETFRED BONUS KING SIRENIA STKS (GROUP 3) 6f (P)
4:25 (4:25) (Class 1) 2-Y-0

£19,281 (£7,310; £3,658; £1,822; £914; £459) **Stalls** Low

Form RPR
1230 **1** **Shumoos (USA)**[16] 5217 2-8-11 103 MartinDwyer 4 103
(Brian Meehan) *stdd s: hld up in tch: rdn and effrt 2f out: chsd wnr jst over 1f out: r.o wl to ld towards fin* **9/4**[1]
0165 **2** *hd* **Vocational (USA)**[14] 5286 2-8-11 98 WJSupple 9 102
(Mark Johnston) *wnt lft s: sn led: stdd gallop 1/2-way: rdn and qcknd over 2f out: drvn 1f out: kpt on wl u.p tl hdd and no ex towards fin* **16/1**
115 **3** *½* **Saigon**[36] 4495 2-9-0 103 KirstyMilczarek 2 104
(James Toller) *hld up in last pair: rdn and outpcd over 2f out: drvn 2f out: 6th and looked wl hld over 1f out: hdwy jst ins fnl f: r.o strly fnl 100yds: nt quite rch ldrs* **3/1**[2]
3011 **4** *1 ¾* **Bayleyf (IRE)**[35] 4536 2-9-0 94 LukeMorris 3 99
(John Best) *chsd ldrs tl chsd wnr over 2f out: rdn ent fnl 2f: drvn and unable qck over 1f out: wknd ins fnl f* **13/2**
1340 **5** *1* **Crown Dependency (IRE)**[16] 5216 2-9-0 102 DaneO'Neill 1 96
(Richard Hannon) *stdd s: hld up in tch: rdn and effrt on inner over 2f out: no imp over 1f out: kpt on same pce u.p fnl f* **7/2**[3]
31 **6** *4* **Heeraat (IRE)**[31] 4675 2-9-0 0 ShaneKelly 6 84
(William Haggas) *chsd ldr tl over 2f out: sn drvn and struggling to qckn: wknd over 1f out* **7/1**
15 **7** *6* **Pearl Charm (USA)**[42] 4311 2-9-0 86 JimCrowley 7 66
(Richard Hannon) *dwlt: rdn along thrght and a struggling: lost tch jst over 2f out* **20/1**

1m 12.04s (-1.06) **Going Correction** +0.025s/f (Slow) **7** Ran SP% **114.5**
Speed ratings (Par 105): **108,107,107,104,103 98,90**
Tote Swingers: 1&2 £42.30, 2&3 £1.40 CSF £38.54 TOTE £3.50: £2.50, £11.50; EX 47.50.
Owner Fawzi Abdulla Nass **Bred** Brushwood Stable **Trained** Manton, Wilts

FOCUS
None of the seven runners had raced on sand before and this year's renewal of the Sirenia was dominated by the only two fillies in the field. The form looks straightforward withn the winner roughly to her mark backed up by the third.

NOTEBOOK
Shumoos(USA) failed to fire in the Lowther last time out, but her previous placed efforts in the Queen Mary and Cherry Hinton were still the best form on offer here. Switched inside after the intersection, she had to fight hard to get on terms with the pace-setter, but she has already proved that she gets this trip and managed to poke her head in front close to the line. The Cheveley Park looks the obvious target next, in which she will try to match the exploits of last year's winner Hooray. (op 7-2)

Vocational(USA) finished well behind Shumoos in the Queen Mary and was racing beyond the minimum trip for the first time in her eighth outing. Add to that the outside stall, and she did incredibly well to make all the running until the last few strides. She doesn't possess much in the way of scope, but she is well worth another try at the trip and the Firth Of Clyde may be the race for her.

Saigon ◆ looked as though he needed further than this when fifth in the Richmond last time and this performance rather backed that up. Given plenty to do, he became outpaced at the back of the field over 2f from home, but then found his feet and was flying home down the outside at the line. He will be very interesting over 7f. (op 10-3 tchd 7-2)

Bayleyf(IRE) was bidding for a hat-trick, but had plenty on at this level and, although he had every chance, probably just ran close to his official mark. (op 6-1 tchd 5-1 and 7-1 in a place)

Crown Dependency(IRE) was a bitterly disappointing favourite for the big sales race at York last month, but his previous good runs in the Norfolk and Molecomb gave him a big chance here, so this was disappointing. He isn't progressing.

Heeraat(IRE) barely had to break sweat in order to land the odds in a five-runner Pontefract maiden last month, but this level proved well beyond him. (op 6-1 tchd 11-2)

Pearl Charm(USA) had raced over 7f in his two previous starts and was never travelling at any stage. (op 16-1)

5716 BETFRED "10 BEST ODDS RACES DAILY" H'CAP — 1m 3f (P)

4:55 (4:55) (Class 4) (0-85,82) 3-Y-O+ — **£5,175** (£1,540; £769; £384) **Stalls** Low

Form			Horse	Jockey	RPR
1043	1		**Yes Chef**[25] 4887 4-9-7 **77**	JamesMillman 5	86
			(Rod Millman) *taken down early: hld up in tch: hdwy to chse ldrs and carried bdly lft over 2f out: racd against stands' rail after: kpt on wl fnl f to ld last strides* **8/1**		
33-0	2	hd	**Estourah (IRE)**[126] 1692 3-9-4 **82**	(t) DaneO'Neill 7	91
			(Saeed Bin Suroor) *dwlt: t.k.h early: hld up in tch: swtchd rt and effrt over 2f out: rdn to ld over 1f out: kpt on wl fnl f tl hdd last strides* **11/2**[3]		
0326	3	3 ¾	**Elmfield Giant (USA)**[19] 5103 4-8-12 **68**	ShaneKelly 8	70
			(Richard Fahey) *hld up in tch in last trio: rdn and hdwy towards inner over 2f out: pressed ldr and drvn over 1f out: wknd ins fnl f* **11/1**		
3-00	4	1 ¼	**Tenessee**[49] 4097 4-9-6 **76**	JimCrowley 4	76
			(Peter Makin) *chsd ldr: ev ch whn carried lft and hmpd over 2f out: rdn to ld 2f out: hdd over 1f out: wknd ins fnl f* **11/2**[3]		
0112	5	2 ½	**Street Secret (USA)**[22] 5020 3-9-4 **82**	JackMitchell 9	77
			(Roger Varian) *dwlt: rcvrd to ld after 2f: rdn and hung bdly lft over 2f out: hdd 2f out: wknd jst over 1f out* **4/1**[1]		
5-02	6	14	**Ullswater (IRE)**[4] 5582 3-8-11 **75**	WJSupple 1	45
			(Mark Johnston) *led for 2f: chsd ldr after tl over 2f out: wknd wl over 1f out: wl btn and eased ins fnl f* **9/2**[2]		
3241	7	3	**Star Commander**[18] 5140 3-9-4 **82**	MartinDwyer 3	47
			(Mark H Tompkins) *in tch: pushed along 1/2-way: drvn and no imp over 2f out: wknd 2f out: wl btn and eased ins fnl f* **12/1**		
0135	8	13	**Granny McPhee**[34] 4577 5-9-3 **73**	JamesDoyle 2	14
			(Alan Bailey) *dwlt: hld up in tch in last trio: rdn and no hdwy over 2f out: wl bhd and eased ins fnl f: t.o* **11/1**		
-200	P		**Isolate**[37] 4473 3-9-2 **80**	DarryllHolland 6	—
			(Hughie Morrison) *taken down early: chsd ldrs tl lost action over 4f out: eased and p.u 4f out: dismntd* **9/1**		

2m 19.34s (-2.56) **Going Correction** +0.025s/f (Slow)
WFA 3 from 4yo+ 8lb — **9** Ran SP% **114.4**
Speed ratings (Par 105): **110,109,107,106,104 94,92,82,—**
Tote Swingers: 1&2 £10.50, 1&3 £8.00, 2&3 £13.30 CSF £50.98 CT £486.12 TOTE £10.70: £2.90, £1.60, £4.50; EX 42.20.
Owner Coombeshead Racing **Bred** Percys (north Harrow) Ltd **Trained** Kentisbeare, Devon

FOCUS
A fair handicap, but something of a messy race. The third sets the level rated close to his non-claiming race best.

5717 BETFRED.COM H'CAP (DIV I) — 7f (P)

5:25 (5:26) (Class 4) (0-85,85) 3-Y-O+ — **£4,851** (£1,443; £721; £360) **Stalls** Low

Form			Horse	Jockey	RPR
4-00	1		**Greensward**[99] 2470 5-9-3 **85**	JadeMuggeridge(7) 4	99
			(Brian Meehan) *hld up towards rr: pushed along and hdwy ent fnl 2f: str run fr over 1f out to ld fnl 100yds: sn in command: comf* **12/1**		
0356	2	1 ¾	**Regal Approval**[37] 4459 3-8-10 **75**	DarryllHolland 5	82
			(Hughie Morrison) *chsd ldrs: rdn to chal 2f out: drvn ent fnl f: hdd and nt pce of wnr fnl 100yds* **12/1**		
60	3	2 ¼	**Summer Dancer (IRE)**[42] 4310 7-8-12 **73**	TedDurcan 3	76
			(Paul Midgley) *in tch in midfield: effrt u.p ent fnl 2f: drvn and kpt on same pce fnl f* **11/1**		
1000	4	½	**Tax Break**[10] 5383 4-8-13 **74**	JackMitchell 2	76
			(David Barron) *broke fast and led: drvn and hrd pressed 2f out: hdd over 1f out: wknd ins fnl f* **13/2**[3]		
3155	5	hd	**Tiradito (USA)**[80] 3045 4-9-7 **82**	(v[1]) ShaneKelly 12	83+
			(Michael Attwater) *wnt rt s: stdd and hld up in rr: nt clr run ent fnl 2f: hdwy and rdn over 1f out: kpt on fnl f: nvr able to chal* **20/1**		
2012	6	nk	**Showboating (IRE)**[9] 5419 3-8-8 **73**	(p) JamesDoyle 6	71+
			(Alan McCabe) *in tch in midfield on outer: rdn and hdwy over 2f out: drvn and styd on same pce fr over 1f out* **8/1**		
2001	7	1 ¾	**Reposer (IRE)**[22] 4994 3-9-1 **83**	KierenFox(3) 7	77
			(John Best) *chsd ldr tl 2f out: hrd drvn and btn over 1f out: wknd fnl f* **8/1**		
4024	8	hd	**Be A Devil**[11] 5341 4-8-11 **72**	MartinDwyer 10	67+
			(William Muir) *in tch in midfield on outer: lost pl and rdn over 3f out: rallied u.p wl over 1f out: no imp fnl f* **9/2**[1]		
3105	9	2 ¼	**My Son Max**[21] 5056 3-8-11 **79**	SeanLevey(3) 11	66
			(Richard Hannon) *hmpd and swtchd rt s: hld up in tch in rr: effrt u.p on inner ent fnl 2f: no prog over 1f out: wknd 1f out* **11/2**[2]		
0045	10	3 ½	**Diriculous**[24] 4909 7-9-5 **80**	JimCrowley 9	59
			(Robert Mills) *stdd s: t.k.h: hld up in rr: rdn and no prog wl over 1f out: n.d* **20/1**		
0202	11	20	**All Right Now**[24] 4921 4-9-2 **77**	FergusSweeney 1	—
			(Derek Haydn Jones) *chsd ldrs tl wknd over 2f out: wl bhd and virtually p.u ins fnl f* **13/2**[3]		

1m 25.26s (-0.74) **Going Correction** +0.025s/f (Slow)
WFA 3 from 4yo+ 4lb — **11** Ran SP% **115.7**
Speed ratings (Par 105): **105,103,100,99,99 99,97,97,94,90 67**
Tote Swingers: 1&2 £43.60, 1&3 £25.00, 2&3 £11.40 CSF £145.21 CT £1617.64 TOTE £14.60: £3.60, £4.30, £4.20; EX 291.80.
Owner Smoke & Mirrors **Bred** Kincorth Investments Inc **Trained** Manton, Wilts
■ Stewards' Enquiry : Darryll Holland caution: used whip down shoulder in the forehand.

FOCUS
Another fair handicap in which the fourth set a good pace and is rated to his handicap best.

5718 BETFRED.COM H'CAP (DIV II) — 7f (P)

5:55 (5:55) (Class 4) (0-85,84) 3-Y-O+ — **£4,851** (£1,443; £721; £360) **Stalls** Low

Form			Horse	Jockey	RPR
0563	1		**Requisite**[8] 5451 6-9-0 **74**	(b) JamesDoyle 10	83
			(Ian Wood) *wnt rt s: swtchd rt and dropped in bhd after s: hld up in last trio: rdn and hdwy wl over 1f out: led 1f out: r.o wl u.p fnl f* **12/1**		
0014	2	½	**Great Acclaim**[24] 4909 3-9-2 **80**	JackMitchell 2	86
			(James Fanshawe) *hld up in tch towards rr: rdn and gd hdwy on inner wl over 1f out: ev ch 1f out: r.o but a hld ins fnl f* **5/1**[3]		
1430	3	1	**Choral**[35] 4550 3-8-6 **73**	KieranO'Neill(3) 5	77+
			(Richard Hannon) *in tch: pushed along 4f out: rdn and lost pl over 2f out: rallied and styd on wl ins fnl f: wnt 3rd last strides* **13/2**		
0230	4	hd	**Dukes Art**[21] 5043 5-9-7 **81**	KirstyMilczarek 3	85
			(James Toller) *chsd ldrs: rdn and pressing ldrs over 1f out: styd on same pce ins fnl f* **5/1**[3]		
6131	5	1	**The Guru Of Gloom (IRE)**[28] 4799 3-8-13 **77**	MartinDwyer 4	77
			(William Muir) *t.k.h: chsd ldr: rdn to ld wl over 1f out: hdd 1f out: no ex and btn fnl 100yds* **4/1**[1]		
1534	6	1	**Arctic Lynx (IRE)**[22] 5012 4-9-4 **78**	TedDurcan 1	77
			(John Best) *led: rdn and hrd pressed over 2f out: hdd wl over 1f out: wknd jst ins fnl f* **9/2**[2]		
000	7	hd	**Vitznau (IRE)**[42] 4310 7-9-5 **79**	JamesMillman 11	77
			(Robert Cowell) *stdd s: hld up in tch in rr: effrt on inner over 1f out: kpt on but no imp fnl f* **20/1**		
0311	8	nk	**Master Mylo (IRE)**[57] 3815 4-9-10 **84**	ShaneKelly 7	82
			(Dean Ivory) *t.k.h: in tch on outer: hdwy to chal and rdn over 2f out: drvn and unable qck over 1f out: wknd 1f out* **7/1**		
045	9	5	**Il Battista**[11] 5338 3-8-13 **77**	(p) DarryllHolland 9	59
			(Alan McCabe) *chsd ldrs: rdn and unable qck over 2f out: wknd 2f out:* **25/1**		
1-00	10	8	**Premium Coffee**[47] 4156 3-8-11 **75**	DaneO'Neill 6	36
			(Joseph Tuite) *t.k.h: hld up in tch: rdn and struggling over 2f out: sn wknd* **33/1**		

1m 26.34s (0.34) **Going Correction** +0.025s/f (Slow)
WFA 3 from 4yo+ 4lb — **10** Ran SP% **116.6**
Speed ratings (Par 105): **99,98,97,97,95 94,94,94,88,79**
Tote Swingers: 1&2 £31.20, 1&3 £11.70, 2&3 £50.80 CSF £69.34 CT £440.20 TOTE £11.10: £3.60, £2.20, £2.20; EX 73.00.
Owner Paddy Barrett **Bred** Darley **Trained** Upper Lambourn, Berks

FOCUS
The winning time was 1.08 seconds slower than the first division. The winner put up just about her best effort since her 3-y-o days and the third is rated pretty much to form.
T/Plt: £261.10 to a £1 stake. Pool: £55,423.00. 154.95 winning tickets. T/Qpdt: £28.30 to a £1 stake. Pool: £2,397.00. 62.60 winning tickets. SP

5147 MUSSELBURGH (R-H)

Saturday, September 3

OFFICIAL GOING: Good (good to soft in places on straight course; 6.3)
Wind: Light, half against Weather: Overcast

5719 BETFAIR BONUS SCOTTISH RACING SPRINT SERIES CONSOLATION H'CAP — 5f

2:35 (2:36) (Class 4) 3-Y-O+ — **£4,918** (£1,475; £984; £492) **Stalls** High

Form			Horse	Jockey	RPR
-000	1		**Monte Mayor One**[12] 5309 4-8-9 **50**	LeeNewman 12	64
			(Jim Goldie) *in tch: rdn 1/2-way: hdwy to ld ins fnl f: r.o strly* **14/1**		
0060	2	1 ½	**Distant Sun (USA)**[28] 4780 7-8-4 **50**	(p) ShaneBKelly(5) 8	59
			(Linda Perratt) *bhd: drvn and hdwy over 1f out: styd on to take 2nd nr fin: nt rch wnr* **22/1**		
0200	3	¾	**Ballarina**[9] 5400 5-8-12 **60**	JustinNewman(7) 14	66
			(Eric Alston) *taken early to post: chsd ldrs: led and edgd rt over 1f out: hdd ins fnl f: kpt on same pce* **9/2**[1]		
5560	4	1 ¾	**Saxonette**[12] 5313 3-9-9 **65**	FrederikTylicki 11	65
			(Linda Perratt) *in tch: drvn over 2f out: styd on fnl f: nvr able to chal* **16/1**		
5336	5	nk	**Sharp Bullet (IRE)**[12] 5313 5-8-9 **55**	(p) GarryWhillans(5) 5	54+
			(Bruce Hellier) *prom: drvn 1/2-way: effrt over 1f out: kpt on same pce ins fnl f* **11/2**[2]		
0125	6	¾	**Irish Boy (IRE)**[43] 4295 3-9-10 **66**	DuranFentiman 7	62
			(Noel Wilson) *slt ld tl drvn and hdd over 1f out: outpcd fnl f* **9/2**[1]		
1045	7	nk	**Dotty Darroch**[6] 5506 3-8-9 **56**	JulieBurke(5) 10	51+
			(Robin Bastiman) *dwlt: bhd and outpcd: hdwy and edgd rt over 1f out: no imp fnl f* **12/1**		
0000	8	nse	**Cayman Fox**[8] 5436 6-8-12 **56**	RobertLButler(3) 6	51
			(Linda Perratt) *taken early to post: cl up tl rdn and outpcd appr fnl f* **25/1**		
3000	9	2 ¾	**Eternal Instinct**[18] 5148 4-9-6 **64**	GaryBartley(3) 3	49+
			(Jim Goldie) *dwlt: bhd and pushed along: hdwy over 1f out: kpt on fin* **12/1**		
03	10	hd	**Brian Sprout**[33] 4607 3-8-4 **51**	NeilFarley(5) 9	35
			(John Weymes) *sn drvn along towards rr: effrt 1/2-way: sn no imp* **20/1**		
2130	11	1	**Arriva La Diva**[12] 5313 5-9-4 **62**	DaleSwift(3) 4	43
			(Linda Perratt) *w ldrs: rdn 1/2-way: wknd appr fnl f* **8/1**[3]		
0200	12	shd	**Chosen One (IRE)**[9] 5400 6-9-10 **65**	(p) JamesSullivan 1	45
			(Ruth Carr) *prom on outside: drifted to far side to r alone after 2f: rdn and wknd fr 2f out* **16/1**		
5350	13	7	**Mr Mo Jo**[10] 5373 3-9-7 **63**	(p) DavidNolan 2	18
			(Lawrence Mullaney) *prom: rdn after 2f: wknd fr 2f out* **14/1**		

60.11 secs (-0.29) **Going Correction** +0.075s/f (Good)
WFA 3 from 4yo+ 1lb — **13** Ran SP% **116.3**
Speed ratings (Par 105): **105,102,101,98,98 96,96,96,91,91 90,89,78**
Tote Swingers: 1&2 £32.80, 1&3 £20.40, 2&3 £24.50 CSF £288.57 CT £1607.98 TOTE £19.10: £4.80, £10.00, £2.20; EX 403.20.
Owner The Dregs Of Humanity **Bred** Mrs D J Hughes **Trained** Uplawmoor, E Renfrews

FOCUS
Rail in same position as at last meeting on August 16th. This moderate opening sprint handicap was run at a decent pace and the main action was towards the stands' rail.

Arriva La Diva Official explanation: jockey said mare hung right

5720 BETFAIR BONUS SCOTTISH RACING SPRINT SERIES FINAL H'CAP 5f

3:05 (3:06) (Class 4) 3-Y-O+

£14,755 (£4,427; £2,460; £1,475; £982; £492) **Stalls** High

Form RPR

6531 **1** **Ingleby Star (IRE)**[7] 5468 6-8-8 **73** ow2................(p) JustinNewman(7) 10 82
(Ian McInnes) *trckd ldrs: rdn to ld over 1f out: styd on strly fnl f* **9/2**[2]

1541 **2** *2 1/2* **Wicked Wilma (IRE)**[8] 5457 7-8-8 **73**................ DavidSimmonson(7) 11 73
(Alan Berry) *prom: rdn and hdwy to chse wnr over 1f out: kpt on fnl f: no imp* **10/1**

1620 **3** *1* **Rothesay Chancer**[21] 5054 3-9-1 **77**................ GaryBartley(3) 14 73+
(Jim Goldie) *bhd: swtchd rt and hdwy over 1f out: kpt on fnl f: nrst fin* **4/1**[1]

0-00 **4** *hd* **Igoyougo**[18] 5148 5-8-10 **68**................ PaulQuinn 12 64
(Noel Wilson) *prom: hung rt thrght: rdn and kpt on same pce fnl f* **25/1**

0025 **5** *1/2* **Tadalavil**[5] 5554 6-8-1 **66**................ GeorgeChaloner(7) 4 60+
(Linda Perratt) *in tch: drvn 1/2-way: kpt on same pce fnl f* **16/1**

3100 **6** *1 3/4* **Senate Majority**[25] 4895 4-8-11 **69**................(b) DuranFentiman 7 57
(Tim Easterby) *sn led: rdn and hdd over 1f out: sn no ex* **25/1**

0160 **7** *1/2* **Midnight Dynamo**[18] 5148 4-8-12 **70**................ JamesSullivan 2 56+
(Jim Goldie) *bhd and sn pushed along: hdwy over 1f out: kpt on: nvr able to chal* **20/1**

1225 **8** *2* **Blown It (USA)**[12] 5313 5-8-11 **69**................ FrederikTylicki 3 48+
(Keith Dalgleish) *towards rr: sn drvn along: no imp wl over 1f out* **12/1**

510 **9** *shd* **Hypnosis**[36] 4504 8-8-6 **69**................ NeilFarley(5) 13 47+
(Noel Wilson) *dwlt: bhd and pushed along: hdwy on outside 2f out: sn no imp* **20/1**

3060 **10** *nk* **Doc Hay (USA)**[17] 5163 4-9-7 **82**................ DaleSwift(3) 1 59+
(Keith Dalgleish) *dwlt: bhd on outside: rdn 1/2-way: nvr on terms* **9/1**[3]

1420 **11** *3/4* **Royal Blade (IRE)**[10] 5371 4-8-3 **66**................ JulieBurke(5) 6 40
(Alan Berry) *cl up tl rdn and wknd appr fnl f* **9/1**[3]

4426 **12** *1 1/4* **Bosun Breese**[9] 5400 6-9-0 **72**................ LeeNewman 5 42
(David Barron) *early ldr: cl up tl rdn and wknd over 1f out* **9/1**[3]

3103 **13** *nse* **Dancing Freddy (IRE)**[18] 5148 4-8-11 **72**................(tp) RobertLButler(3) 8 42
(Richard Guest) *cl up: rdn over 1f out: sn wknd* **16/1**

4522 **14** *4* **North Central (USA)**[10] 5371 4-8-8 **71**................(p) ShaneBKelly(5) 9 26
(Jim Goldie) *bhd and sn drvn along: nvr on terms* **10/1**

60.34 secs (-0.06) **Going Correction** +0.075s/f (Good)
WFA 3 from 4yo+ 1lb **14 Ran SP% 123.0**
Speed ratings (Par 105): **103,99,97,97,96 93,92,89,89,88 87,85,85,79**
Tote Swingers: 1&2 £9.30, 1&3 £2.40, 2&3 £4.20 CSF £47.45 CT £172.92 TOTE £7.30: £2.60, £3.10, £1.10; EX 43.50.
Owner Stephen Hackney **Bred** Pat Cosgrove **Trained** Catwick, E Yorks

FOCUS
Once again a high draw proved an advantage in this modest handicap and it was run to suit the closers. The winning time was marginally slower than the preceding C&D handicap. Tthe runner-up and fourth help set the level.

5721 BETFAIR BONUS SCOTTISH RACING MILE SERIES CONSOLATION H'CAP 1m

3:40 (3:41) (Class 4) 3-Y-O+ **£4,918** (£1,475; £984; £492) **Stalls** Low

Form RPR

2004 **1** **Just The Tonic**[7] 5488 4-8-13 **61**................ JulieBurke(5) 5 70
(Marjorie Fife) *hld up towards rr: rdn and hdwy 2f out: led ins fnl f: r.o wl* **8/1**[3]

15 **2** *3/4* **Military Call**[28] 4783 4-8-9 **59**................(p) JustinNewman(7) 3 66
(Alistair Whillans) *midfield: hdwy to ld over 2f out: hdd ins fnl f: r.o same pce towards fin* **8/1**[3]

0000 **3** *1 1/4* **Social Rhythm**[17] 5164 7-8-11 **59**................ GarryWhillans(5) 14 63
(Alistair Whillans) *bhd tl rdn and hdwy wl over 1f out: kpt on fnl f: nrst fin* **14/1**

4233 **4** *3/4* **Emeralds Spirit (IRE)**[8] 5455 4-8-12 **60**................ ShaneBKelly(5) 8 62+
(John Weymes) *in tch: effrt whn nt clr run over 2f out: rallied over 1f out: kpt on same pce ins fnl f* **6/1**[1]

1010 **5** *hd* **Drive Home (USA)**[40] 4379 4-9-2 **59**................(p) DuranFentiman 1 61
(Noel Wilson) *in tch: smooth hdwy and ev ch over 2f out: edgd rt: one pce fnl f* **12/1**

5605 **6** *nk* **Isheforreal (IRE)**[5] 5549 4-8-11 **57**................ DaleSwift(3) 10 58
(Brian Ellison) *bhd: rdn over 2f out: styd on wl fnl f: nrst fin* **25/1**

323 **7** *2 1/2* **Glenluji**[47] 4143 6-9-0 **60**................ GaryBartley(3) 4 56
(Jim Goldie) *dwlt: hld up: effrt whn nt clr run briefly over 2f out: no imp over 1f out* **7/1**[2]

4050 **8** *1 1/4* **Monkton Vale (IRE)**[21] 3905 4-8-8 **58**................ GeorgeChaloner(7) 2 51
(Noel Wilson) *towards rr: drvn 3f out: sme late hdwy: nvr able to chal* **12/1**

4554 **9** *nse* **Spavento (IRE)**[4] 5594 5-9-1 **63**................ NeilFarley(5) 13 56
(Eric Alston) *hld up in midfield on outside: hdwy and ev ch over 2f out: sn rdn: wknd over 1f out* **17/2**

4005 **10** *4 1/2* **Classic Descent**[8] 5441 6-9-0 **57**................(bt) JamesSullivan 6 39+
(Ruth Carr) *bhd: hdwy against ins rail whn no room wl over 1f out: nt rcvr and sn eased* **20/1**

5140 **11** *2* **Benny The Bear**[12] 5309 4-9-2 **59**................ FrederikTylicki 11 37
(Linda Perratt) *disp ld and clr of rest: rdn and led briefly over 2f out: sn wknd* **14/1**

105 **12** *5* **On The Cusp (IRE)**[18] 5150 4-9-4 **64**................(p) RobertLButler(3) 7 30
(Richard Guest) *led at str gallop to over 2f out: wknd wl over 1f out* **16/1**

1626 **P** **Mangham (IRE)**[18] 5150 6-9-7 **64**................(p) LeeNewman 9 —
(George Foster) *prom tl broke down and p.u ent st* **8/1**[3]

6620 **P** **Old English (IRE)**[12] 5314 3-9-1 **63**................ DavidNolan 12 —
(Linda Perratt) *rdr lost irons sn after s: sn wl bhd: t.o whn p.u 1/2-way* **20/1**

1m 42.16s (0.96) **Going Correction** +0.075s/f (Good)
WFA 3 from 4yo+ 5lb **14 Ran SP% 118.6**
Speed ratings (Par 105): **98,97,96,95,95 94,92,91,90,86 84,79,—,—**
Tote Swingers: 1&2 £29.60, 1&3 £29.60, 2&3 £20.40 CSF £67.49 CT £914.62 TOTE £10.10: £4.10, £6.50, £9.00; EX 68.40.
Owner R W Fife **Bred** West Dereham Abbey Stud **Trained** Stillington, N Yorks

FOCUS
A moderate and wide-open handicap. It was run at a strong pace and the form looks sound enough.
Mangham(IRE) Official explanation: jockey said gelding finished distressed

Old English(IRE) Official explanation: jockey said buckle on stirrup leather broke on leaving stalls

5722 BETFAIR BONUS SCOTTISH RACING MILE SERIES FINAL H'CAP 1m

4:15 (4:16) (Class 4) 3-Y-O+

£14,755 (£4,427; £2,460; £1,475; £982; £492) **Stalls** Low

Form RPR

120 **1** **Focail Eile**[43] 4278 6-8-7 **67**................ FrederikTylicki 10 84
(John Ryan) *midfield on outside: hdwy to ld 1f out: kpt on strly fnl f* **18/1**

6041 **2** *3 1/4* **Imperator Augustus (IRE)**[63] 3621 3-8-1 **73**................ NoelGarbutt(7) 3 82
(Patrick Holmes) *trckd ldrs: chal after 3f: led over 3f out to 1f out: kpt on same pce fnl f* **20/1**

0011 **3** *3/4* **Swiftly Done (IRE)**[25] 4877 4-9-1 **80**................(b) NeilFarley(5) 7 90+
(Declan Carroll) *hld up: rdn over 2f out: hdwy over 1f out: kpt on fnl f: nvr able to chal* **15/2**[3]

1260 **4** *1* **Solar Spirit (IRE)**[12] 5314 6-8-8 **73**................ ShaneBKelly(5) 1 79
(Tracy Waggott) *hld up: hdwy against ins rail over 2f out: kpt on same pce ins fnl f* **12/1**

6522 **5** *1* **Music Festival (USA)**[25] 4877 4-8-7 **67**................ LeeNewman 12 70
(Jim Goldie) *chsd ldrs: drvn 3f out: kpt on same pce over 1f out* **10/1**

0455 **6** *3/4* **Fibs And Flannel**[12] 5314 4-8-3 **66**................(p) RossAtkinson(3) 4 67
(Tim Easterby) *in tch: rdn 3f out: kpt on same pce over 1f out* **11/1**

2000 **7** *1* **Berbice (IRE)**[12] 5314 6-8-5 **65**................ PaulQuinn 14 64
(Linda Perratt) *s.i.s: hld up: stdy hdwy over 2f out: effrt over 1f out: no imp* **33/1**

2430 **8** *1 1/4* **Cono Zur (FR)**[12] 5314 4-9-0 **74**................(b) JamesSullivan 5 70
(Ruth Carr) *towards rr: drvn over 2f out: no imp over 1f out* **20/1**

311 **9** *2 1/2* **I'm Super Too (IRE)**[12] 5314 4-9-5 **84**................ GarryWhillans(5) 9 75
(Alan Swinbank) *t.k.h: midfield on outside: drvn over 2f out: wknd over 1f out* **4/1**[1]

4130 **10** *1 1/2* **Ravi River (IRE)**[15] 3828 7-9-3 **80**................ DaleSwift(3) 6 67
(Brian Ellison) *prom: rdn along over 3f out: wknd wl over 1f out* **11/1**

6511 **11** *1 1/4* **Sabratha (IRE)**[46] 4176 3-8-0 **70**................ JulieBurke(5) 2 53
(Linda Perratt) *towards rr: drvn along 1/2-way: nvr able to chal* **14/1**

2121 **12** *1 3/4* **Thinking**[19] 5106 4-8-11 **71**................ DuranFentiman 8 51
(Tim Easterby) *prom tl rdn and wknd fr 2f out* **9/2**[2]

5260 **13** *1* **High Resolution**[16] 5205 4-8-11 **74**................ GaryBartley(3) 13 52
(Linda Perratt) *s.i.s: bhd: effrt on outside over 2f out: sn btn* **20/1**

0000 **14** *3* **Global**[4] 5594 5-8-0 **65**................ DanielleMcCreery(5) 11 36
(Brian Ellison) *led to over 3f out: rdn and wknd fr 2f out* **14/1**

1m 40.61s (-0.59) **Going Correction** +0.075s/f (Good)
WFA 3 from 4yo+ 5lb **14 Ran SP% 119.2**
Speed ratings (Par 105): **105,101,101,100,99 98,97,96,93,92 90,89,88,85**
Tote Swingers: 1&2 £40.00, 2&3 £29.40 CSF £342.04 CT £3017.50 TOTE £23.40: £10.50, £13.40, £4.30; EX 340.50.
Owner Cathal Fegan **Bred** D Robb **Trained** Newmarket, Suffolk

FOCUS
A competitive affair. There was a sound pace on and it was a creditable winning time for the class, so the form looks decent and sound for the grade, rated around the placed horses.
Imperator Augustus(IRE) ◆ Official explanation: jockey said gelding hung left
Thinking Official explanation: jockey said gelding ran flat

5723 BETFAIR BONUS SCOTTISH RACING STAYERS' SERIES CONSOLATION H'CAP 1m 5f

4:45 (4:45) (Class 4) 3-Y-O+ **£4,918** (£1,475; £984; £492) **Stalls** Low

Form RPR

6123 **1** **Think Its All Over (USA)**[18] 5149 4-9-6 **63**................ FrederikTylicki 3 73
(Julie Camacho) *mde all at ordinary gallop: rdn over 2f out: hld on wl fnl f* **9/2**[1]

1525 **2** *1 3/4* **Amir Pasha (UAE)**[2] 5650 6-9-2 **64**................(p) ShaneBKelly(5) 4 71
(Micky Hammond) *prom: effrt and chsd wnr over 2f out: rdn wl over 1f out: kpt on same pce ins fnl f* **10/1**

1320 **3** *1 3/4* **Pokfulham (IRE)**[46] 4173 5-9-8 **65**................(v) LeeNewman 12 69
(Jim Goldie) *t.k.h: prom: effrt and rdn over 2f out: kpt on ins fnl f* **6/1**[2]

2646 **4** *hd* **Dane Cottage**[4] 5609 4-8-4 **54**................ JacobButterfield 9 60+
(Brian Ellison) *hld up: rdn 3f out: gd hdwy on outside over 1f out: kpt on wl fnl f* **12/1**

0340 **5** *1 1/2* **Hawdyerwheesht**[25] 4879 3-9-1 **68**................(p) DuranFentiman 13 70
(Mark Johnston) *hld up: rdn and hdwy on outside over 2f out: edgd rt and no imp over 1f out* **12/1**

4-61 **6** *1* **Grandad Bill (IRE)**[14] 4879 8-8-11 **61**................ JustinNewman(7) 6 61
(Jim Goldie) *midfield: lost pl 1/2-way: sn rdn: rallied over 1f out: nvr able to chal* **7/1**[3]

0052 **7** *1/2* **Stags Leap (IRE)**[16] 5207 4-9-2 **64**................(v) GarryWhillans(5) 14 64
(Alistair Whillans) *hld up: hdwy and in tch 1/2-way: rdn over 2f out: no ex over 1f out* **7/1**[3]

3504 **8** *4* **Royal Straight**[12] 5311 6-9-0 **62**................(t) JulieBurke(5) 2 56
(Linda Perratt) *hld up: rdn over 2f out: sn no imp* **16/1**

60-5 **9** *1/2* **Ananda Kanda (USA)**[18] 5149 4-9-7 **67**................ DaleSwift(3) 10 60
(Brian Ellison) *midfield: rdn over 3f out: wknd wl over 1f out* **20/1**

1400 **10** *hd* **Maid Of Meft**[42] 4326 4-9-2 **62**................ RobertLButler(3) 5 55
(Linda Perratt) *hld up: hdwy on outside wl over 2f out: wknd over 1f out* **14/1**

3066 **11** *1* **Grand Diamond (IRE)**[18] 5149 7-9-3 **63**................ GaryBartley(3) 1 54
(Jim Goldie) *in tch: rdn over 3f out: wknd fr 2f out* **20/1**

00U0 **12** *nk* **Valdan (IRE)**[4] 5595 7-9-1 **58**................(p) JamesSullivan 8 49
(Ruth Carr) *hld up: stdy hdwy whn n.m.r over 2f out: sn rdn: btn over 1f out* **22/1**

6504 **13** *1* **Kingsdale Orion (IRE)**[17] 5167 7-9-2 **59**................ DavidNolan 11 48
(Brian Ellison) *hld up in midfield: drvn over 4f out: rallied wl over 2f out: sn btn* **11/1**

0-00 **14** *5* **Red Skipper (IRE)**[71] 3129 6-8-8 **51**................ PaulQuinn 7 33
(Noel Wilson) *chsd wnr tl rdn and wknd over 2f out* **40/1**

2m 51.72s (-0.28) **Going Correction** +0.075s/f (Good)
WFA 3 from 4yo+ 10lb **14 Ran SP% 119.1**
Speed ratings (Par 105): **103,101,100,100,99 99,98,96,96,95 95,95,94,91**
Tote Swingers: 1&2 £5.70, 1&3 £11.70, 2&3 £9.60 CSF £45.90 CT £276.42 TOTE £5.40: £2.00, £4.30, £1.90; EX 51.90.
Owner Terry Warner **Bred** B Wayne Hughes **Trained** Norton, N Yorks

FOCUS
This staying handicap was yet another wide-open event. It was run at an uneven pace, however, and it paid to race handily. The placed horses set the standard.

5724 BETFAIR BONUS SCOTTISH RACING STAYERS' SERIES FINAL H'CAP — 1m 5f
5:15 (5:16) (Class 4) 3-Y-0+

£14,755 (£4,427; £2,460; £1,475; £982; £492) **Stalls** Low

Form				RPR
6025	**1**		**Jonny Delta**[12] 5311 4-8-10 **67** GaryBartley(3) 7 (Jim Goldie) *hld up: faltered after 2f: hdwy on outside to ld 2f out: sn rdn and edgd both ways: kpt on wl fnl f* **2/1**[1]	77+
3042	**2**	1 ¼	**Meetings Man (IRE)**[18] 5149 4-9-5 **78** GarryWhillans(5) 6 (Micky Hammond) *t.k.h: effrt and hdwy to chse wnr over 1f out: edgd rt ins fnl f: kpt on* **8/1**	86
5120	**3**	½	**Los Nadis (GER)**[14] 4562 7-8-13 **72** ShaneBKelly(5) 3 (Jim Goldie) *hld up in midfield: effrt and rdn over 2f out: kpt on ins fnl f* **16/1**	79
1202	**4**	4	**Zennor**[16] 5198 4-9-6 **77** RossAtkinson(3) 9 (Tom Dascombe) *hld up: rdn 3f out: kpt on fr 2f out: nvr able to chal* **7/1**[3]	78
0601	**5**	½	**Chookie Hamilton**[18] 5149 7-9-8 **76** FrederikTylicki 11 (Keith Dalgleish) *hld up: pushed along and effrt over 2f out: nvr able to chal* **9/1**	77
0614	**6**	1 ¼	**Mason Hindmarsh**[10] 5369 4-9-0 **68** JamesSullivan 10 (Karen McLintock) *hld up on outside: hdwy and prom after 3f: rdn 3f out: nt qckn fnl 2f* **16/1**	67
5311	**7**	¾	**Unknown Rebel (IRE)**[12] 5311 3-8-12 **81** (p) JulieBurke(5) 2 (Kevin Ryan) *led: rdn and hdd over 2f out: wknd wl over 1f out* **5/1**[2]	79
0005	**8**	2 ¼	**The Galloping Shoe**[35] 4540 6-8-11 **72** JustinNewman(7) 5 (Ian Semple) *missed break: hld up: hmpd after 2f: rdn and effrt over 2f out: n.d* **20/1**	66
-414	**9**	2 ½	**Forrest Flyer (IRE)**[40] 4382 7-8-13 **70** (p) RobertLButler(3) 8 (Jim Goldie) *trckd ldrs: drvn along 3f out: wknd wl over 1f out* **16/1**	60
1546	**9**	dht	**Simonside**[25] 4879 8-9-4 **75** DaleSwift(3) 1 (Brian Ellison) *trckd ldrs tl rdn and wknd fr 2f out* **12/1**	65
6223	**11**	¾	**Sharp Sovereign (USA)**[16] 5207 5-8-13 **67** LeeNewman 12 (David Barron) *sn chsng ldr: ev ch and rdn over 3f out: wknd fnl 2f* **18/1**	56
4110	**12**	3	**Jewelled Dagger (IRE)**[21] 5035 7-9-0 **75** EdmondLinehan(7) 4 (Keith Dalgleish) *in tch: rdn and outpcd over 4f out: shortlived effrt wl over 2f out: sn btn* **16/1**	60

2m 51.5s (-0.50) **Going Correction** +0.075s/f (Good)
WFA 3 from 4yo+ 10lb — 12 Ran SP% **124.9**
Speed ratings (Par 105): **104,103,102,100,100 99,98,97,96,96 95,93**
Tote Swingers: 1&2 £6.80, 1&3 £4.30, 2&3 £4.50 CSF £19.41 CT £216.52 TOTE £3.50: £1.90, £2.30, £4.70; EX 27.90.

Owner Johnnie Delta Racing **Bred** Miss Gill Quincey **Trained** Uplawmoor, E Renfrews

FOCUS
A fair handicap for the class and there was a sound pace on. Solid form with the third rated to his former best.

Jewelled Dagger(IRE) Official explanation: trainer said gelding had been struck into

5725 BETFAIR BONUS SCOTTISH RACING APPRENTICE H'CAP — 7f 30y
5:50 (5:50) (Class 5) (0-70,68) 3-Y-0+ **£2,587** (£770; £384; £192) **Stalls** Low

Form				RPR
6422	**1**		**Catallout (IRE)**[22] 4987 3-8-13 **62** JasonHart(3) 4 (Declan Carroll) *in tch: effrt and cl up whn n.m.r and swtchd rt over 1f out: edgd rt and led ins fnl f: r.o wl* **11/4**[1]	73
0523	**2**	½	**Goninodaethat**[25] 4876 3-8-6 **52** GeorgeDowning 9 (Jim Goldie) *chsd ldng pair: hdwy to ld whn edgd lft over 1f out: edgd rt and hdd ins fnl f: kpt on fin* **6/1**[3]	62
4566	**3**	1 ½	**Chookie Avon**[9] 5404 4-8-10 **55** (p) LauraBarry(3) 2 (Keith Dalgleish) *hld up in tch: wd bnd over 3f out: effrt and ev ch over 1f out: kpt on same pce ins fnl f* **7/2**[2]	63
6250	**4**	4	**Burnwynd Boy**[12] 5309 6-9-0 **59** DavidSimmonson(3) 5 (Ian Semple) *s.s: bhd: hdwy over 2f out: no imp over 1f out* **16/1**	56
3000	**5**	¾	**Shunkawakhan (IRE)**[18] 5153 8-8-2 **49** oh1...(tp) CherylArmstrong(5) 11 (Linda Perratt) *towards rr: hdwy over 1f out: nvr able to chal* **33/1**	44
0400	**6**	2 ¼	**Ya Boy Sir (IRE)**[18] 5153 4-8-4 **49** oh4 (b) JacobButterfield(3) 1 (Ian Semple) *t.k.h: w ldr: led over 2f tl over 1f out: sn btn* **33/1**	38
2026	**7**	2 ½	**Cannon Bolt (IRE)**[24] 4929 3-8-3 **52** ShirleyTeasdale(3) 10 (Robin Bastiman) *led at decent gallop: hdd over 2f out: wknd over 1f out* **8/1**	32
0605	**8**	3 ¼	**Abernethy (IRE)**[12] 5315 3-8-0 **49** oh3 (b) HannahNunn(3) 7 (Linda Perratt) *missed break: bhd: shkn up over 2f out: n.d* **40/1**	21
5032	**9**	2	**Hellbender (IRE)**[8] 5437 5-9-5 **61** (p) GeorgeChaloner 12 (George Foster) *sn drvn along in rr: nvr on terms* **8/1**	29
4250	**10**	shd	**Coax**[66] 3508 3-9-8 **68** NoelGarbutt 6 (Patrick Holmes) *hld up: drvn along 1/2-way: btn fnl 2f* **12/1**	34
1260	**11**	3 ½	**Carrie's Magic**[9] 5400 4-9-7 **66** (b) DannyBrock(3) 8 (Alistair Whillans) *t.k.h: prom tl rdn and wknd fr 2f out* **12/1**	24
3305	**12**	1	**Cold Quest (USA)**[9] 5402 7-8-7 **49** oh4 JakePayne 3 (Linda Perratt) *bhd: pushed along 1/2-way: nvr on terms* **25/1**	—

1m 30.82s (1.82) **Going Correction** +0.075s/f (Good)
WFA 3 from 4yo+ 4lb — 12 Ran SP% **118.8**
Speed ratings (Par 103): **92,91,89,85,84 81,78,75,72,72 68,67**
Tote Swingers: 1&2 £6.80, 1&3 £4.30, 2&3 £4.50 CSF £18.67 CT £60.69 TOTE £2.80: £1.10, £4.30, £2.80; EX 20.20.

Owner Ferrari Racing **Bred** K McConnell **Trained** Sledmere, E Yorks

FOCUS
A weak handicap, confined to apprentice riders. It was run at a strong pace and the principals came clear. The winner did not need to improve much on her Catterick form to score.

Cold Quest(USA) Official explanation: jockey said, regarding slowness to remove blindfold, that it had become stuck in the bridle and the gelding reared.

T/Plt: £1,912.80 to a £1 stake. Pool: £44,180.00. 16.86 winning tickets. T/Qpdt: £87.20 to a £1 stake. Pool: £2,993.00. 25.40 winning tickets. RY

5452 THIRSK (L-H)
Saturday, September 3

OFFICIAL GOING: Good (8.3)
Wind: Light half behind Weather: Cloudy

5726 HAPPY BIRTHDAY MARC FINDLAY AND TOM SLOANS MAIDEN AUCTION STKS — 6f
2:25 (2:26) (Class 5) 2-Y-0 **£4,204** (£1,251; £625; £312) **Stalls** High

Form				RPR
6	**1**		**Taro Tywod (IRE)**[43] 4285 2-8-4 0 WilliamCarson 2 (Ann Duffield) *sn prom: effrt on outer 2f out: rdn over 1f out: led jst ins fnl f and kpt on wl* **22/1**	73
0	**2**	1 ¼	**Diamond Belle**[47] 4155 2-8-8 0 PJMcDonald 1 (Noel Quinlan) *prom: cl up 1/2-way: rdn to ld over 1f out: drvn and hdd jst ins fnl f: kpt on same pce* **8/1**	73
2334	**3**	2 ¼	**Half A Billion (IRE)**[8] 5438 2-8-10 73 LeeTopliss(3) 3 (Michael Dods) *trckd ldrs: swtchd lft and hdwy to chal over 1f out: sn rdn and one pce ent fnl f* **9/2**[2]	72
0	**4**	3	**Holy Angel (IRE)**[7] 5486 2-8-8 0 LanceBetts(5) 9 (Tim Easterby) *in tch: hdwy 2f out: sn rdn and kpt on same pce appr fnl f* **12/1**	63
0325	**5**	4 ½	**Just Like Heaven (IRE)**[9] 5398 2-8-9 69 RobertWinston 5 (Tim Easterby) *led: rdn along over 2f out: hdd over 1f out and sn wknd* **7/2**[1]	45
	6	¾	**Gibraltar Road** 2-8-9 0 PBBeggy 12 (John Quinn) *towards rr: sme hdwy fnl 2f: n.d* **7/1**	43
	7	½	**Gulf Storm (IRE)** 2-8-13 0 TomEaves 6 (Bryan Smart) *wnt rt s: midfield: rdn along wl over 2f out: sn wknd* **6/1**[3]	45
	8	7	**Pacific Trader** 2-8-9 0 CathyGannon 7 (William Haggas) *sltly hmpd s: a towards rr* **6/1**[3]	20
03	**9**	4	**Reine Du Froid (IRE)**[12] 5310 2-8-4 0 PatrickMathers 4 (Ben Haslam) *dwlt and towards rr: hdwy on wd outside 1/2-way: sn rdn and wknd* **66/1**	3
	10	1 ¾	**Ottavino (IRE)** 2-8-10 0 DeclanCannon(3) 10 (Nigel Tinkler) *chsd ldrs: rdn along 1/2-way: sn wknd* **28/1**	7
05	**11**	6	**Point At Issue (IRE)**[7] 5486 2-8-13 0 AdrianNicholls 11 (David Nicholls) *a in rr: bhd fr 1/2-way* **16/1**	—

1m 12.73s (0.03) **Going Correction** +0.10s/f (Good) — 11 Ran SP% **115.4**
Speed ratings (Par 95): **103,101,98,94,88 87,86,77,72,69 61**
Tote Swingers: 1&2 £9.60, 1&3 £16.60, 2&3 £7.30 CSF £182.71 TOTE £19.80: £4.70, £2.80, £1.20; EX 204.30.

Owner Rasio Cymru Racing 1 **Bred** Pat Fullam **Trained** Constable Burton, N Yorks

FOCUS
Following a dry night the ground was given as good (GoingStick 8.3). After riding in the first race Adrian Nicholls agreed with the official description and Cathy Gannon said it was "good, though a little dead in places". A modest maiden and it paid to race prominently. The first three came out of the three lowest stalls and the third and time limit the level.

NOTEBOOK
Taro Tywod(IRE) didn't quite see her race out when sixth over 7f here on her debut, but the second and third from that race won next time out so the form hadn't worked out badly. She showed enough speed to bag a position tracking the front two and, while she got a little outpaced heading to the 2f marker, she stayed on strongly at the finish and was well on top at the line. She's bred to appreciate further and should be okay over 7f as she matures. (op 18-1)
Diamond Belle, twice a non-runner due to softish ground since debuting at Windsor, travelled strongly to the leader's outer and had her chance, but the winner just saw her race out better. There could be a similar race in her, but she'll also have the nursery option after one more outing. (tchd 7-1)
Half A Billion(IRE) has an official mark of 73 and although he was a bit keen early there seems no reason to suppose he hasn't run fairly close to that mark in defeat. (op 10-3)
Holy Angel(IRE) showed some ability on his debut and this was a big step up. He'll be of more interest once eligible for a mark. (op 14-1)
Just Like Heaven(IRE) showed his usual early speed to cross over and make the running on the stands' rail but he dropped out tamely approaching the last. (tchd 4-1)
Gibraltar Road had a good draw and was well backed, but he got outpaced before halfway and struggled to land a blow. He's out of a 2-y-o 5f winner and should do better with this experience behind him. (op 25-1)

5727 E B F "IKTIBAS" MAIDEN STKS — 7f
2:55 (2:56) (Class 5) 2-Y-0 **£4,528** (£1,347; £673; £336) **Stalls** Low

Form				RPR
4	**1**		**Unex Michelangelo (IRE)**[22] 4996 2-9-3 0 RobertHavlin 3 (John Gosden) *trckd ldr: cl up 3f out: led wl over 1f out: rdn clr fnl f* **11/8**[1]	82+
	2	3 ¾	**Blades Lad** 2-9-0 0 LeeTopliss(3) 12 (Richard Fahey) *in tch: hdwy on outer 1/2-way: chsd ldrs and swtchd lft to inner over 2f out: rdn over 1f out: kpt on wl fnl f to take 2nd last 100yds* **22/1**	70+
0	**3**	nk	**Byron Blue (IRE)**[22] 4995 2-9-3 0 SaleemGolam 14 (Jamie Osborne) *stdd and swtchd lft s: hld up in rr: hdwy wl over 2f out: rdn wl over 1f out: styd on wl fnl f* **14/1**	69
460	**4**	½	**Sygnature**[21] 5058 2-9-3 62 PJMcDonald 10 (Alan Swinbank) *chsd ldrs: hdwy 3f out: rdn wl over 1f out: styd on u.p fnl f* **25/1**	68
344	**5**	¾	**Marching On (IRE)**[42] 4323 2-9-3 78 StephenCraine 5 (Kevin Ryan) *led: rdn along 3f out: drvn and hdd wl over 1f out: wknd ins fnl f* **6/1**[3]	66
0	**6**	½	**Absolute Fun (IRE)**[21] 5029 2-8-7 0 AdamCarter(5) 7 (Tim Easterby) *towards rr: hdwy on wd outside over 2f out: sn rdn and styd on appr fnl f: nrst fin* **66/1**	60
	7	3	**Confirmed** 2-9-3 0 (t) CathyGannon 11 (Marco Botti) *s.i.s and bhd: hdwy wl over 2f out: kpt on appr fnl f: nrst fin* **15/2**	67+
	8	4	**Last Zak** 2-9-3 0 PaddyAspell 6 (Michael Easterby) *in tch: rdn along wl over 2f out: grad wknd* **66/1**	47
00	**9**	1 ¼	**Pontius Pilate (IRE)**[94] 2617 2-9-3 0 (p) TomEaves 1 (Bryan Smart) *a midfield* **50/1**	43
02	**10**	3 ¾	**Bollin Tommy**[22] 5003 2-9-3 0 RobertWinston 13 (Tim Easterby) *a in rr* **14/1**	34+
04	**11**	6	**Abhaath (USA)**[27] 4815 2-8-12 0 AntiocoMurgia(5) 4 (Saeed Bin Suroor) *chsd ldrs: rdn along and edgd rt over 2f out: sn wknd* **7/2**[2]	18
	12	3 ¼	**Demolition Blue (IRE)** 2-8-9 0 PatrickDonaghy(3) 8 (Ben Haslam) *sltly hmpd s: a in rr* **100/1**	—

13 ½ **Artlana** 2-8-12 0 PBBeggy 9 —
(Julie Camacho) *awkward and hmpd s: a bhd* **100/1**

0335 14 9 **Ave Sofia**[24] 4922 2-8-7 56 JamesRogers(5) 2 —
(John Holt) *prom: rdn along 1/2-way: sn wknd* **100/1**

1m 28.46s (1.26) **Going Correction** +0.10s/f (Good) 14 Ran SP% **119.8**
Speed ratings (Par 95): **96,91,91,90,89 89,85,81,79,75 68,65,64,54**
Tote Swingers: 1&2 £8.70, 1&3 £7.90, 2&3 £45.20 CSF £41.65 TOTE £2.00: £1.30, £6.80, £5.80; EX 41.60.
Owner W J Gredley **Bred** Chenchikova Syndicate **Trained** Newmarket, Suffolk

FOCUS
Questionable whether there was much strength in depth to this maiden, but there's more to come from the winner who can rate a good bit higher.

NOTEBOOK
Unex Michelangelo(IRE) had finished fourth in a decent Newbury race on his debut and looks a useful type on this evidence. Never too far off the pace, he stretched clear inside the last, won eased down and this well-bred colt looks to have a future. (op 6-4, tchd 7-4 in a place)
Blades Lad ◆, who is already gelded, was keen and caught wide on the bend. In the circumstances he kept on well to take second, and he looks sure to learn plenty from this. (op 16-1)
Byron Blue(IRE), who hinted at ability on his debut, finished with some purpose. He's closely related to high-class sprinter Society Rock but seems to have inherited more stamina from his sire Dylan Thomas. (op 20-1 tchd 22-1)
Sygnature, who had promised to be suited by the return to 7f, probably paid for taking on the leader and the winner from some way out as he faltered inside the last. (op 20-1)
Marching On(IRE) had to do a lot of early running to get to the front and he paid for that effort in the latter stages. (tchd 11-2)
Absolute Fun(IRE) showed more than on her debut. (op 50-1)
Confirmed ◆, a son of Authorized, lost several lengths at the start and then raced keenly in rear. He stayed on nicely in the straight while running green and there's plenty more to come from him. Official explanation: jockey said colt missed the break (op 9-1 tchd 10-1)
Bollin Tommy needed this for a mark and he should do better in handicaps. (op 10-1)
Abhaath(USA) didn't settle early on and weakened in the straight. Official explanation: trainer's rep had no explanation for the poor form shown (op 4-1)

5728 ADORN HATS H'CAP (DIV I) 1m
3:30 (3:30) (Class 5) (0-75,80) 4-Y-0+ **£2,587** (£770; £384; £192) **Stalls** Low

Form RPR

1111 1 **Hot Rod Mamma (IRE)**[4] 5594 4-9-10 **80** 6ex LeeTopliss(3) 10 96+
(Dianne Sayer) *hld up: gd hdwy over 2f out: led on bit over 1f out: pushed clr: eased towards fin: comf* **11/4**[1]

0340 2 4½ **Violent Velocity (IRE)**[31] 4679 8-9-2 **69** PBBeggy 3 72
(John Quinn) *hld up in tch: rdn over 2f out: hdwy over 1f out: kpt on to go 2nd fnl 100yds: no ch w wnr* **12/1**

3644 3 2 **Marjury Daw (IRE)**[10] 5391 5-9-6 **73** CathyGannon 8 71
(James Given) *trckd ldr: rdn to ld over 2f out: hdd over 1f out: sn no ch w wnr: one pce and lost 2nd fnl 100yds* **4/1**[2]

0100 4 3¼ **Legal Legacy**[19] 5106 5-9-5 **72** TomEaves 2 63
(Michael Dods) *in tch: rdn 2f out: sn one pce* **13/2**[3]

1200 5 hd **Burns Night**[12] 5314 5-9-7 **74** PJMcDonald 6 64
(Geoffrey Harker) *dwlt: hld up: rdn and hdwy 2f out: one pce fnl f* **18/1**

4051 6 3¾ **West End Lad**[27] 4821 8-9-6 **73** (b) RobertWinston 4 55
(Roy Bowring) *led: rdn whn hdd over 2f out: wknd fnl f* **14/1**

0062 7 ¾ **Petomic (IRE)**[7] 5470 6-9-0 **67** (p) AndrewMullen 7 47
(Richard Guest) *midfield: rdn over 2f out: wknd over 1f out* **14/1**

5052 8 hd **Marvo**[46] 4170 7-9-1 **68** SaleemGolam 5 48
(Mark H Tompkins) *hld up: rdn over 3f out: sn no imp* **10/1**

003- 9 4 **Steel Stockholder**[347] 6267 5-8-12 **65** AdrianNicholls 9 35
(Mel Brittain) *midfield on outer: hdwy to chse ldr 4f out: rdn over 2f out: wknd over 1f out* **14/1**

0002 10 3½ **Christmas Carnival**[8] 5441 4-9-4 **71** (b) PaddyAspell 1 33
(Michael Easterby) *trckd ldr: rdn 3f out: sn wknd* **13/2**[3]

1m 40.8s (0.70) **Going Correction** +0.10s/f (Good) 10 Ran SP% **115.4**
Speed ratings (Par 103): **100,95,93,90,90 86,85,85,81,77**
Tote Swingers: 1&2 £3.20, 1&3 £3.70, 2&3 £10.70 CSF £36.94 CT £134.17 TOTE £3.10: £1.50, £3.50, £1.60; EX 31.20.
Owner A Slack **Bred** Philip Hore Jnr **Trained** Hackthorpe, Cumbria

FOCUS
Just a modest handicap but a decisive winner who was value for at least 6l. The time was good.

5729 TOTEPOOL HAMBLETON CUP H'CAP 1m 4f
4:00 (4:00) (Class 4) (0-85,84) 3-Y-0+ **£3,881** (£1,155; £577; £288) **Stalls** Low

Form RPR

1200 1 **War Poet**[20] 5078 4-9-10 **82** RobertWinston 12 93+
(David O'Meara) *hld up in rr: smooth hdwy on wd outside 3f out: led 1 1/2f out: sn rdn and edgd lft fnl f: kpt on wl* **3/1**[1]

1133 2 nk **Persian Peril**[16] 5205 7-9-8 **80** PJMcDonald 10 90
(Alan Swinbank) *t.k.h: in tch: hdwy 3f out: chal 2f out: rdn and ev ch over 1f out: drvn and n.m.r ins fnl f: no ex towards fin* **7/1**

0400 3 3 **Ethics Girl (IRE)**[21] 5057 5-9-7 **79** (t) RobertHavlin 8 84
(John Berry) *hld up: hdwy and nt clr run over 2f out: sn swtchd lft and rdn to chse ldng pair appr fnl f: kpt on same pce* **14/1**

4041 4 nk **Red Fama**[8] 5440 7-9-6 **78** AndrewMullen 6 83
(Neville Bycroft) *hld up towards rr: hdwy 3f out: rdn to chse ldrs wl over 1f out: edgd lft ins fnl f: kpt on* **10/1**

4003 5 3¼ **Royal Trooper (IRE)**[8] 5435 5-9-7 **82** LeeTopliss(3) 1 81
(James Given) *hld up in rr: hdwy wl over 2f out: rdn wl over 1f out: kpt on ins fnl f: nrst fin* **13/2**[3]

1103 6 2½ **Cotton King**[16] 5198 4-9-5 **77** (vt) CathyGannon 7 72
(Tobias B P Coles) *trckd ldrs tl led 1/2-way: rdn over 2f out: drvn and hdd wl over 1f out: grad wknd* **8/1**

0304 7 1¼ **Amazing Blue Sky**[8] 5440 5-9-2 **74** PaddyAspell 4 67
(Ruth Carr) *chsd ldrs on inner: rdn along over 3f out: grad wknd* **20/1**

4250 8 hd **Kathleen Frances**[35] 4537 4-9-9 **81** SaleemGolam 5 74
(Mark H Tompkins) *trckd ldrs: hdwy to chse ldr 3f out: rdn 2f out: sn drvn and grad wknd* **6/1**[2]

-300 9 11 **Beat The Rush**[65] 3544 4-9-7 **79** TomEaves 11 54
(Julie Camacho) *trckd ldrs: cl up 1/2-way: rdn along over 3f out and sn wknd* **14/1**

1 10 7 **Jawaab (IRE)**[176] 835 7-9-12 **84** (e) StephenCraine 9 48
(Richard Guest) *sn led: hdd 1/2-way: cl up tl rdn along over 3f out and sn wknd* **9/1**

0604 11 ¾ **Raleigh Quay (IRE)**[28] 4784 4-8-9 **70** oh9 (p) MichaelO'Connell(3) 2 33
(Micky Hammond) *a in rr* **40/1**

550- 12 3 **Lochiel**[414] 4086 7-9-6 **78** PBBeggy 3 36
(Ian Semple) *prom: rdn along over 3f out and sn wknd* **28/1**

2m 38.14s (1.94) **Going Correction** +0.10s/f (Good)
WFA 3 from 4yo+ 9lb 12 Ran SP% **119.3**
Speed ratings (Par 105): **97,96,94,94,92 90,89,89,82,77 77,75**
Tote Swingers: 1&2 £2.80, 1&3 £11.80, 2&3 £3.10 CSF £23.14 CT £259.90 TOTE £3.40: £1.50, £2.50, £4.00; EX 29.90.
Owner Mike Kirby & Andrew Crowther **Bred** Darley **Trained** Nawton, N Yorks

FOCUS
They didn't seem to go that quick here but the winner came from last to first.
War Poet Official explanation: trainer's rep said, regarding apparent improvement in form, that the gelding was better suited by the slower ground and a return to the track as a previous winner.

5730 "DRESSED OF HARROGATE" H'CAP 1m
4:35 (4:37) (Class 3) (0-95,95) 3-Y-0 **£12,938** (£3,850; £1,924; £962) **Stalls** Low

Form RPR

2501 1 **Belle Royale (IRE)**[14] 5272 3-9-4 **95** RyanClark(3) 4 109
(Mark Brisbourne) *midfield: gd hdwy over 2f out: rdn to ld wl over 1f out and rdr dropped whip: edgd rt ins fnl f: kpt on* **18/1**

3-1 2 1¾ **Skilful**[105] 2306 3-9-2 **90** RobertHavlin 12 100+
(John Gosden) *towards rr: gd hdwy on outer over 3f out: rdn to chal and edgd rt 2f out: drvn and ev ch ent fnl f: one pce* **9/2**[1]

1100 3 ½ **Good Boy Jackson**[37] 4473 3-8-6 **80** CathyGannon 9 89
(Kevin Ryan) *hld up in rr: gd hdwy on outer over 2f out: rdn to chse ldng pair whn swtchd lft over 1f out: drvn and one pce ins fnl f* **22/1**

-120 4 5 **Anoint**[42] 4335 3-8-12 **86** (t) PJMcDonald 11 84
(William Haggas) *hld up in rr: gd hdwy over 3f out: rdn over 2f out: drvn and no imp appr fnl f* **12/1**

1312 5 5 **Ingleby Exceed (IRE)**[30] 4718 3-8-0 **77** DeclanCannon(3) 14 63
(David O'Meara) *in tch: pushed along and sltly outpcd 3f out: rdn to chse ldrs 2f out: sn drvn and no imp* **16/1**

0410 6 2 **Piceno (IRE)**[7] 5465 3-7-13 **76** oh1 (b[1]) BillyCray(3) 3 57
(David Nicholls) *led and sn clr: rdn over 2f out: drvn and hdd wl over 1f out: grad wknd* **33/1**

0321 7 2 **Federation**[36] 4514 3-8-11 **85** TomEaves 16 62
(Roger Charlton) *chsd clr ldr: effrt 3f out: rdn along 2f out: sn drvn: edgd lft and wknd* **11/2**[3]

0100 8 3 **Kingscroft (IRE)**[14] 5272 3-8-13 **92** DarylByrne(5) 8 62
(Mark Johnston) *nvr bttr than midfield* **14/1**

1230 9 7 **Metropolitain Miss (IRE)**[108] 2189 3-8-13 **87** SamHitchcott 6 41
(Mick Channon) *midfield: effrt and sme hdwy 3f out: sn rdn and wknd* **33/1**

1202 10 7 **Tullius (IRE)**[20] 5081 3-9-2 **90** RobertWinston 5 28
(Peter Winkworth) *chsd ldrs: rdn along 3f out: sn wknd* **5/1**[2]

-264 11 3¼ **Fieldgunner Kirkup (GER)**[57] 3830 3-8-6 **80** AndrewMullen 10 —
(David Barron) *a in rr* **16/1**

510 12 4 **Askaud (IRE)**[7] 5483 3-8-10 **87** (p) MichaelO'Connell(3) 7 —
(David Nicholls) *prom: hdwy to chse clr ldr over 3f out: sn rdn and wknd over 2f out* **16/1**

1046 13 15 **Midsummer Fair (USA)**[30] 4718 3-8-12 **91** AntiocoMurgia(5) 2 —
(Mahmood Al Zarooni) *midfield: rdn along 1/2-way: sn wknd* **16/1**

1601 14 4 **Polar Kite (IRE)**[20] 5081 3-8-13 **90** LeeTopliss(3) 1 —
(Richard Fahey) *dwlt: a in rr* **11/2**[3]

5123 15 ½ **Izzy The Ozzy (IRE)**[21] 5062 3-8-5 **79** WilliamCarson 13 —
(David Barron) *chsd ldrs to 1/2-way: sn wknd* **10/1**

1m 39.44s (-0.66) **Going Correction** +0.10s/f (Good) 15 Ran SP% **124.9**
Speed ratings (Par 105): **107,105,104,99,94 92,90,87,80,73 70,66,51,47,47**
Tote Swingers: 1&2 £19.30, 1&3 £96.20, 2&3 £38.10 CSF £96.57 CT £1872.72 TOTE £24.00: £5.60, £2.40, £6.10; EX 143.80.
Owner Peter Mort **Bred** Dxb Bloodstock Ltd **Trained** Great Ness, Shropshire

FOCUS
A strong handicap on paper but, with the future in mind, it's worth noting that there was a mad dash up front early, they went off miles too fast and three of the first four home were held up in the last four places early on. The winner proved herself a smart filly.

NOTEBOOK
Belle Royale(IRE) found her rivals stopping in front and threaded her way through the pack to follow up her recent Chester win, defying a 5lb higher mark in the process. Another rise for this will take some defying unless she comes across a similar pace scenario. Chasing some black type will apparently be the priority now. (op 16-1)
Skilful was probably the best horse in the race. Not seen since taking an AW maiden back in May, he was drawn out in stall 12 and was trapped wide in midfield going round the bend. He moved up to fourth place, travelling well, on straightening up, but the winner, who had been ridden far more patiently, went by him approaching the final furlong. To his credit he kept on well, but the race had been lost in the first half of the race. He undoubtedly has the ability to win a similar race. (op 5-1)
Good Boy Jackson won twice from the front earlier in the season but he benefited from being dropped right out the back this time as the leaders went off too fast and he was able to sweep past the majority of the field in the straight.
Anoint, who lost his action at Newmarket last time, wore a tongue-tie for the first time. Held up in last, he was another who kept on to take a place thanks mainly to the overly strong pace up front. (op 14-1)
Ingleby Exceed(IRE) has been running well lately and did so again despite racing a little too close to the fast pace.
Piceno(IRE), blinkered for the first time, was responsible for setting the scorching gallop. That he didn't drop out much further than he did was creditable in the circumstances. (op 25-1)
Federation led the chasing pack and paid the price for going too quick early. It would be wrong to judge her too harshly on this effort and she remains open to improvement. (op 5-1)
Tullius(IRE) was another who raced too close to the pace. (op 17-2)
Fieldgunner Kirkup(GER)'s rider reported that the gelding was never travelling. Official explanation: jockey said gelding never travelled
Askaud(IRE) was reported as having hung right throughout. Official explanation: jockey said filly hung right-handed throughout (op 18-1 tchd 14-1)
Polar Kite(IRE) seems more comfortable in smaller fields. (op 6-1 tchd 13-2)

5731 HUMPHREY AND TILLY H'CAP 1m
5:05 (5:06) (Class 5) (0-70,70) 3-Y-0 **£2,911** (£866; £432; £216) **Stalls** Low

Form RPR

3140 1 **Thatcherite (IRE)**[8] 5441 3-9-4 **67** (t) StephenCraine 12 74
(Tony Coyle) *dwlt: hld up: gd hdwy 3f out: trckd ldr whn short of room 2f out: sn swtchd lft: rdn to ld appr fnl f: drvn and hld on wl* **14/1**

2205 2 hd **Save The Bees**[35] 4560 3-9-6 **69** TomEaves 14 76
(Declan Carroll) *midfield on outer: rdn and hdwy over 2f out: led wl over 1f out: sn edgd lft: hdd appr fnl f: kpt on: jst hld* **7/1**[3]

0633 3 nse **Ibiza Sunset (IRE)**[24] 4908 3-9-6 **69** CathyGannon 13 76
(Peter Winkworth) *hld up in rr: rdn and hdwy over 2f out: chsd ldng pair over 1f out: kpt on wl fnl f* **12/1**

3602 **4** *4 1/2* **St Oswald**[8] 5439 3-8-9 **61** DeclanCannon(3) 11 58
(David O'Meara) *midfield: hdwy to chse ldrs over 2f out: drvn over 1f out: kpt on one pce* **9/2**[1]

-666 **5** *3/4* **Sam Nombulist**[25] 4877 3-9-6 **69** RobertHavlin 4 64
(Richard Whitaker) *hld up in tch: hdwy and n.m.r 3f out: rdn over 1f out: kpt on one pce* **25/1**

4213 **6** *3/4* **Starbound (IRE)**[30] 4727 3-9-5 **68** PJMcDonald 6 61
(William Haggas) *trckd ldr: hdwy to ld over 3f out: sn rdn: hdd wl over 1f out: no ex* **7/1**[3]

6404 **7** *7* **Dubai Celebration**[9] 5404 3-9-4 **70** (t) PatrickDonaghy(3) 8 47
(Jedd O'Keeffe) *in tch: rdn over 2f out: wknd appr fnl f* **12/1**

0022 **8** *3* **The Buska (IRE)**[17] 5179 3-9-3 **69** MichaelO'Connell(3) 7 39
(Declan Carroll) *chsd ldrs: rdn over 3f out: wknd over 1f out* **8/1**

1143 **9** *1 1/2* **Ryedale Dancer (IRE)**[19] 5109 3-9-3 **66** (t) RobertWinston 10 33
(Tim Easterby) *chsd ldrs on outer: rdn and ev ch over 2f out: wknd over 1f out* **5/1**[2]

010- **10** *2 3/4* **Newport Arch**[320] 6979 3-9-4 **67** PBBeggy 9 27
(John Quinn) *hld up: pushed along 4f out: n.d* **40/1**

3503 **11** *10* **Magic Rhythm**[25] 4880 3-8-11 **60** (p) AndrewElliott 2 —
(Mrs K Burke) *trckd ldrs: rdn over 3f out: wknd over 2f out* **12/1**

0105 **12** *4* **Alluring Star**[17] 5164 3-9-7 **70** PaddyAspell 3 —
(Michael Easterby) *hld up: rdn over 3f out: a towards rr* **22/1**

001 **13** *37* **Roman Ruler (IRE)**[15] 5248 3-8-7 **56** GregFairley 5 —
(Chris Fairhurst) *prom: rdn and lost pl over 3f out: wknd over 2f out: eased* **22/1**

5030 **14** *5* **Greenhead High**[151] 1149 3-9-0 **63** AdrianNicholls 1 —
(David Nicholls) *led: hanging whn hdd over 3f out: sn wknd and eased* **25/1**

1m 41.71s (1.61) **Going Correction** +0.10s/f (Good) **14** Ran SP% **119.5**
Speed ratings (Par 101): **95,94,94,90,89 88,81,78,77,74 64,60,23,18**
Tote Swingers: 1&2 £17.40, 1&3 £29.70, 2&3 £10.60 CSF £100.82 CT £830.35 TOTE £21.90: £5.70, £2.80, £3.90; EX 142.30.
Owner Brian Kerr & Tony Coyle **Bred** Taroka Equine Investments **Trained** Norton, N Yorks

FOCUS
Just a modest handicap, but sound form with a 4lb personal best from the winner.
Thatcherite(IRE) Official explanation: trainer's rep said, regarding apparent improvement in form, that the gelding appreciated the better ground.
Roman Ruler(IRE) Official explanation: jockey said gelding bled from the nose
Greenhead High Official explanation: jockey said gelding hung right-handed throughout

5732 "GOOD LUCK KATIE!" H'CAP 6f
5:35 (5:37) (Class 5) (0-70,70) 4-Y-0+ **£2,911** (£866; £432; £216) **Stalls** High

Form RPR

1366 **1** **Downhill Skier (IRE)**[5] 5561 7-8-10 **66** JackDuern(3) 3 74
(Mark Brisbourne) *hld up towards rr: gd hdwy 2f out: rdn to chse ldrs over 1f out: rdn to chse ldrs over 1f out: kpt on ins fnl f to ld nr fin* **5/1**[2]

0045 **2** *nk* **Commanche Raider (IRE)**[9] 5400 4-9-0 **66** (p) LeeTopliss(3) 11 73
(Michael Dods) *cl up: led over 2f out: rdn over 1f out: drvn ins fnl f: hdd and no ex nr fin* **9/1**

5400 **3** *2* **Electioneer (USA)**[9] 5400 4-8-13 **62** (b) PaddyAspell 5 63
(Michael Easterby) *midfield: hdwy to chse ldrs over 1f out: swtchd rt and rdn ins fnl f: kpt on towards fin* **10/1**

0563 **4** *nk* **Belinsky (IRE)**[11] 5338 4-8-11 **60** RobertWinston 2 60
(Mark Campion) *trckd ldrs: hdwy on outer 2f out: rdn and ch over 1f out: drvn and one pce ins fnl f* **3/1**[1]

/000 **5** *nk* **Half A Crown (IRE)**[26] 4869 6-8-7 **56** oh7 AndrewElliott 12 55
(Peter Salmon) *in tch: hdwy nr stands over 1f out: swtchd lft and rdn ent fnl f: kpt on: nrst fin* **18/1**

0020 **6** *1/2* **Elhamri**[22] 4988 7-8-10 **59** PJMcDonald 9 56
(Conor Dore) *in rr: hdwy wl over 1f out: rdn and kpt on ins fnl f: nrst fin* **18/1**

0240 **7** *nk* **Just Sam (IRE)**[8] 5437 6-8-7 **56** AndrewMullen 1 52
(Ron Barr) *prom: hdwy and cl up 1/2-way: rdn to chal over 1f out: ev ch tl drvn: edgd rt and wknd ins fnl f* **16/1**

405 **8** *3 1/2* **Alis Aquilae (IRE)**[39] 4405 5-9-5 **68** GregFairley 7 53
(Tim Etherington) *sltly hmpd s: a in rr* **10/1**

0650 **9** *nk* **Avertuoso**[35] 4539 7-9-0 **63** (v) TomEaves 10 47
(Bryan Smart) *trckd ldrs on inner: effrt over 2f out: sn rdn and wknd* **25/1**

0200 **10** *1 1/4* **Sonny Red (IRE)**[20] 5083 7-9-4 **70** (v[1]) MichaelO'Connell(3) 4 50
(David Nicholls) *towards rr: hdwy on wd outside to chse ldrs 1/2-way: sn rdn and wknd* **10/1**

3000 **11** *1/2* **Incomparable**[119] 1907 6-9-5 **68** (tp) CathyGannon 8 46
(David Nicholls) *cl up: rdn 2f out: sn drvn and wknd* **20/1**

0050 **12** *3/4* **Besty**[8] 5455 4-8-12 **61** (v) AdrianNicholls 13 37
(David Nicholls) *led: rdn along 1/2-way: sn hdd: drvn wl over 1f out and sn wknd* **6/1**[3]

2000 **13** *9* **Punching**[22] 4988 7-8-8 **60** DeclanCannon(3) 6 7
(Conor Dore) *cl up: rdn along over 2f out: sn wknd* **20/1**

1m 12.8s (0.10) **Going Correction** +0.10s/f (Good) **13** Ran SP% **123.0**
Speed ratings (Par 103): **103,102,99,99,99 98,98,93,93,91 90,89,77**
Tote Swingers: 1&2 £4.90, 1&3 £8.60, 2&3 £16.30 CSF £49.75 CT £458.54 TOTE £5.80: £2.30, £2.80, £3.70; EX 32.10.
Owner Miss P D Insull **Bred** Swettenham Stud **Trained** Great Ness, Shropshire
■ Stewards' Enquiry : Michael O'Connell caution: used whip without giving gelding time to respond.

FOCUS
Another standard handicap, which was well run. The winner enhanced his good record here.
Sonny Red(IRE) Official explanation: jockey said gelding hung left throughout
Besty Official explanation: jockey said gelding hung left throughout

5733 ADORN HATS H'CAP (DIV II OF 3.30) 1m
6:05 (6:05) (Class 5) (0-75,77) 4-Y-0+ **£2,587** (£770; £384; £192) **Stalls** Low

Form RPR

0600 **1** **Horatio Carter**[47] 4141 6-8-13 **67** RobertWinston 9 75
(David O'Meara) *prom: led over 2f out: sn rdn: drvn ent fnl f: hld on gamely* **8/1**

1040 **2** *hd* **Fazza**[21] 5059 4-9-6 **74** PBBeggy 6 82
(Edwin Tuer) *trckd ldrs on inner: effrt over 2f out: rdn to chal over 1f out: drvn and ev ch ins fnl f: jst hld* **9/4**[1]

3356 **3** *nse* **Elijah Pepper (USA)**[7] 5465 6-9-0 **73** LMcNiff(5) 2 81
(David Barron) *towards rr: pushed along and hdwy 2f out: rdn to chse ldrs over 1f out: swtchd rt and drvn ins fnl f: styd on strly: jst failed* **5/1**[2]

2300 **4** *3 1/2* **Lord Of The Dance (IRE)**[27] 4821 5-9-2 **70** WilliamCarson 8 70
(Mark Brisbourne) *in tch: hdwy on outer over 2f out: chal wl over 1f out: sn rdn and ev ch tl drvn and wknd ent fnl f* **22/1**

2301 **5** *5* **Silly Gilly (IRE)**[9] 5402 7-8-2 **63** JackDuern(7) 4 51
(Ron Barr) *towards rr: effrt and sme hdwy on inner 2f out: sn rdn and n.d* **10/1**

0000 **6** *1* **Thrust Control (IRE)**[2] 5647 4-9-4 **72** PatrickMathers 10 58
(Tracy Waggott) *led: rdn along 3f out: hdd over 2f out and grad wknd* **33/1**

0004 **7** *4* **Tukitinyasok (IRE)**[36] 4501 4-8-12 **66** (p) PaddyAspell 5 43
(Clive Mulhall) *dwlt: sn chsng ldrs on inner: rdn along over 3f out and sn wknd* **11/2**[3]

002 **8** *8* **Osgood**[7] 5495 4-9-9 **77** SamHitchcott 1 35
(Mick Channon) *chsd ldrs: rdn along wl over 2f out: sn wknd* **13/2**

0110 **9** *3 1/2* **High Five Society**[50] 4070 7-9-1 **72** (b) RyanClark(3) 3 22
(Roy Bowring) *a in rr* **14/1**

1610 **10** *2 1/2* **Postman**[19] 5106 5-9-0 **68** (p) TomEaves 7 13
(Bryan Smart) *a in rr* **12/1**

1m 41.76s (1.66) **Going Correction** +0.10s/f (Good) **10** Ran SP% **118.0**
Speed ratings (Par 103): **95,94,94,91,86 85,81,73,69,67**
Tote Swingers: 1&2 £9.20, 1&3 £9.80, 2&3 £4.10 CSF £26.65 CT £105.57 TOTE £7.30: £2.30, £1.10, £2.00; EX 43.80.
Owner R G Fell **Bred** Mrs T Brudenell **Trained** Nawton, N Yorks
■ Stewards' Enquiry : Robert Winston two-day ban: used whip with excessive frequency (Sep 17-18)
P B Beggy caution: used whip with excessive frequency.

FOCUS
The slower of the two divisions by almost a second. The second and third set the standard and the winner will still be on a good mark after this.
High Five Society Official explanation: jockey said gelding never travelled
T/Plt: £308.60 to a £1 stake. Pool: £43,718.00. 103.40 winning tickets. T/Qpdt: £137.70 to a £1 stake. Pool: £2,140.00. 11.50 winning tickets. JR

5603 WOLVERHAMPTON (A.W) (L-H)
Saturday, September 3

OFFICIAL GOING: Standard
Wind: Fresh behind Weather: Overcast

5734 CLEANEVENT CLAIMING STKS 7f 32y(P)
6:00 (6:00) (Class 5) 3-Y-0+ **£1,704** (£503; £251) **Stalls** High

Form RPR

1022 **1** **Cavitie**[45] 4206 5-8-6 67 (p) LouisBeuzelin(3) 2 75
(Andrew Reid) *trckd ldrs: racd keenly: nt clr run over 2f out: swtchd rt over 1f out: led ins fnl f: rdn out* **4/1**[2]

3421 **2** *1 3/4* **Unlimited**[24] 4921 9-9-1 80 LiamJones 6 76
(Tony Carroll) *s.i.s: hld up: rdn over 2f out: hdwy over 1f out: edgd lft and r.o ins fnl f: nt rch wnr* **6/5**[1]

1010 **3** *2 1/2* **Orpenindeed (IRE)**[24] 4921 8-9-4 80 (t) RobbieFitzpatrick 1 72
(Frank Sheridan) *led: rdn over 2f out: hdd and no ex ins fnl f* **8/1**[3]

0023 **4** *1 1/2* **Ezdeyaad (USA)**[12] 5319 7-9-6 80 MichaelJMurphy(7) 8 77
(Ed Walker) *sn prom: pushed along to chse ldr over 2f out: sn rdn and ev ch: no ex fnl f* **4/1**[2]

4260 **5** *3/4* **He's A Humbug (IRE)**[11] 5338 7-9-1 58 (p) RussKennemore 5 63
(Paul Midgley) *hld up in tch: rdn 1/2-way: styd on same pce fnl 2f* **25/1**

0205 **6** *4* **Rum King (USA)**[13] 5301 4-8-9 72 SteveDrowne 7 46
(S Donohoe, Ire) *sn outpcd: nvr on terms* **20/1**

520 **7** *5* **Brio**[16] 5215 3-8-5 58 (p) AndreaAtzeni 3 31
(Alan McCabe) *chsd ldr tl rdn over 2f out: wknd over 1f out* **16/1**

1m 27.64s (-1.96) **Going Correction** -0.25s/f (Stan)
WFA 3 from 4yo+ 4lb **7** Ran SP% **111.1**
Speed ratings (Par 103): **101,99,96,94,93 89,83**
Tote Swingers: 1&2 £1.60, 1&3 £3.90, 2&3 £3.40 CSF £8.65 TOTE £6.30: £3.40, £2.10; EX 11.90.The winner was claimed by Diamond Racing for £5,000.
Owner A S Reid **Bred** A S Reid **Trained** Mill Hill, London NW7
■ Stewards' Enquiry : Louis Beuzelin one-day ban: careless riding (Sep 17)

FOCUS
Fair form in a claimer in which a few Polytrack specialists came to the fore. The pace was sound but those in the frame behind the winner were below their best and the fifth limits the form.

5735 RENAULT WOLVERHAMPTON MEGANE COUPE CABRIOLET H'CAP 7f 32y(P)
6:30 (6:32) (Class 5) (0-75,77) 3-Y-O **£2,385** (£704; £352) **Stalls** High

Form RPR

1103 **1** **Sound Amigo (IRE)**[31] 4680 3-9-6 **74** BarryMcHugh 8 83
(Ollie Pears) *trckd ldr: racd keenly: rdn over 1f out: led and edgd lft ins fnl f: r.o* **3/1**[1]

4061 **2** *1/2* **Dasho**[9] 5419 3-9-4 **77** LucyKBarry(5) 10 85
(Olivia Maylam) *led: rdn and hdd ins fnl f: styd on* **9/2**[3]

050 **3** *1 1/4* **Ducal**[84] 2924 3-8-8 **67** RosieJessop(5) 12 72+
(Sir Mark Prescott Bt) *s.i.s: hld up: rdn over 2f out: hdwy over 1f out: edgd lft and r.o ins fnl f: wnt 3rd post: nt rch ldrs* **13/2**

510 **4** *shd* **Mawjoodah**[5] 5554 3-9-1 **72** PaulPickard(3) 2 76
(Brian Ellison) *chsd ldrs: rdn over 1f out: styd on same pce ins fnl f: lost 3rd post* **8/1**

1006 **5** *1 1/4* **Hugely Exciting**[10] 5392 3-9-2 **70** (b[1]) PatCosgrave 4 71
(J S Moore) *mid-div: hdwy over 2f out: rdn over 1f out: styd on same pce* **20/1**

2530 **6** *1/2* **Dark Isle**[28] 4799 3-9-1 **72** PatrickHills(3) 11 72
(J W Hills) *s.i.s: hld up: hdwy u.p over 1f out: styd on same pce ins fnl f* **14/1**

200 **7** *1 1/4* **Hawk Moth (IRE)**[8] 5423 3-8-12 **66** LiamJones 3 62
(John Spearing) *hld up: rdn over 1f out: nvr trbld ldrs* **20/1**

2165 **8** *hd* **Jibaal (IRE)**[71] 3358 3-9-7 **75** AndreaAtzeni 6 71
(Marco Botti) *trckd ldrs: racd keenly: rdn over 1f out: hung lft and no ex fnl f* **7/2**[2]

0000 **9** *4 1/2* **Adaria**[21] 5056 3-9-4 **72** SteveDrowne 7 56
(David C Griffiths) *sn pushed along in rr: nvr on terms* **28/1**

0066 **10** *nk* **Indian Emperor (IRE)**[8] 5456 3-9-1 **69** RoystonFfrench 5 52
(Peter Niven) *hld up: rdn 1/2-way: n.d* **80/1**

0126 **11** *3/4* **Rowan Spirit (IRE)**[9] 5419 3-9-2 **70** RobbieFitzpatrick 9 51
(Mark Brisbourne) *prom: rdn over 2f out: wknd wl over 1f out* **22/1**

1m 28.01s (-1.59) **Going Correction** -0.25s/f (Stan) **11** Ran SP% **115.1**
Speed ratings (Par 101): **99,98,97,96,95 94,93,93,88,87 86**
Tote Swingers: 1&2 £2.30, 1&3 £5.00, 2&3 £8.40 CSF £14.83 CT £80.67 TOTE £2.90: £1.10, £1.10, £4.50; EX 14.90.
Owner Tom McManus **Bred** Sherbourne Lodge **Trained** Norton, N Yorks

FOCUS
The pace steadied early in this handicap and it paid to race handily, the first two sharing those positions throughout. The performance of the third, who came from well off the pace, is definitely worth marking up. the second and fourth set the level with slight improvements on recent form.

5736 CLEANDOMAIN H'CAP 5f 216y(P)
7:00 (7:02) (Class 6) (0-65,66) 3-Y-O+ **£1,704** (£503; £251) **Stalls** Low

Form RPR
0120 **1** **Valmina**[10] 5387 4-9-5 **63**..............................(t) SteveDrowne 8 73
(Tony Carroll) *hld up: hdwy over 1f out: led ins fnl f: pushed out* **15/2**[3]
2210 **2** *1 ½* **Eshoog (IRE)**[5] 5542 3-8-10 **63**..............................(bt) LeonnaMayor(7) 11 68
(Phil McEntee) *led: rdn clr over 1f out: hdd and unable qck ins fnl f* **16/1**
0653 **3** *hd* **Elegant Muse**[8] 5423 3-9-0 **60**.............................. IanMongan 1 65
(Walter Swinburn) *s.i.s: hld up: hdwy u.p over 1f out: r.o* **8/1**
0045 **4** *½* **Bond Fastrac**[28] 4793 4-9-7 **65**..............................(v) SilvestreDeSousa 4 68
(Geoffrey Oldroyd) *trckd ldrs: racd keenly: rdn to chse wnr 1f out: styd on same pce ins fnl f* **5/2**[1]
01 **5** *1 ¾* **Kipchak (IRE)**[30] 4709 6-9-2 **65**..............................(b) LucyKBarry(5) 9 62
(Conor Dore) *chsd ldr: rdn over 1f out: no ex ins fnl f* **20/1**
23-0 **6** *½* **First In Command (IRE)**[92] 2703 6-9-6 **64**..............................(t) AndreaAtzeni 13 60
(Daniel Mark Loughnane, Ire) *hld up: rdn and r.o ins fnl f: nrst fin* **9/1**
0260 **7** *½* **Wolf Slayer**[14] 5274 3-9-5 **65**.............................. RussKennemore 3 59
(Tom Dascombe) *chsd ldrs: rdn over 2f out: no ex fnl f* **25/1**
6001 **8** *1 ¼* **Welcome Approach**[3] 5617 8-9-1 **59**.............................. ChrisCatlin 5 49
(John Weymes) *mid-div: pushed along over 2f out: no imp fnl f* **6/1**[2]
0003 **9** *1* **Crucis Abbey (IRE)**[9] 5419 3-9-6 **66**.............................. LiamJones 7 53
(James Unett) *sn pushed along in rr: hdwy over 2f out: sn rdn: styd on same pce appr fnl f* **8/1**
40 **10** *1* **Fantasy Fighter (IRE)**[45] 4206 6-9-5 **63**..............................(v) PatCosgrave 12 47
(John E Long) *hld up: nvr on terms* **16/1**
2530 **11** *1 ¼* **Watch Chain (IRE)**[11] 5338 4-9-5 **63**..............................(p) SebSanders 10 43
(Alan McCabe) *prom: rdn over 2f out: wknd fnl f* **14/1**
0000 **12** *10* **Takajan (IRE)**[25] 4893 4-9-2 **65**.............................. JamesRogers(5) 6 13
(Mark Brisbourne) *chsd ldrs tl rdn and wknd over 2f out* **50/1**

1m 13.74s (-1.26) **Going Correction** -0.25s/f (Stan)
WFA 3 from 4yo+ 2lb **12** Ran SP% **115.8**
Speed ratings (Par 101): **98,96,95,95,92 92,91,89,88,87 85,72**
Tote Swingers: 1&2 £12.00, 1&3 £31.50, 2&3 £19.10 CSF £115.30 CT £998.39 TOTE £6.60: £2.30, £8.70, £5.10; EX 158.40.
Owner Mayden Stud **Bred** Mayden Stud, J A And D S Dewhurst **Trained** Cropthorne, Worcs

FOCUS
Just modest fare, though it was at least soundly run. The third set the level rated to her best C&D mark.

5737 E B F WHITTINGHAM MAIDEN STKS 5f 20y(P)
7:30 (7:30) (Class 5) 2-Y-O **£3,234** (£962; £481; £240) **Stalls** Low

Form RPR
1 **Relentless Harry (IRE)** 2-9-3 0..............................(t) TonyCulhane 4 76+
(George Baker) *s.i.s: sn hld up in tch: shkn up to ld 1f out: rdn and hung lft ins fnl f: r.o wl* **9/2**
2 *2 ½* **Regal Lady** 2-8-12 0.............................. EddieAhern 3 60
(David Brown) *led: rdn and hdd 1f out: styd on same pce* **5/2**[2]
044 **3** *hd* **White Spirit (IRE)**[52] 3981 2-8-12 67.............................. SilvestreDeSousa 1 59
(Marco Botti) *chsd ldrs: rdn over 1f out: styd on same pce ins fnl f* **6/4**[1]
0400 **4** *½* **Arabian Flight**[12] 5316 2-8-12 45.............................. RoystonFfrench 2 57
(Ed Dunlop) *hld up: r.o ins fnl f: nt rch ldrs* **25/1**
2243 **5** *nse* **Gin Twist**[35] 4548 2-8-12 66.............................. RussKennemore 7 57
(Tom Dascombe) *chsd ldrs: pushed along 1/2-way: rdn and hung lft over 1f out: styd on same pce* **7/2**[3]
0003 **6** *1 ¼* **Wake Up Sioux (IRE)**[16] 5211 2-8-12 55.............................. SteveDrowne 6 52
(David C Griffiths) *w ldr tl rdn over 1f out: no ex fnl f* **20/1**

61.35 secs (-0.95) **Going Correction** -0.25s/f (Stan) **6** Ran SP% **117.6**
Speed ratings (Par 95): **97,93,92,91,91 89**
Tote Swingers: 1&2 £1.90, 1&3 £1.60, 2&3 £2.10 CSF £17.11 TOTE £5.10: £2.70, £1.10; EX 12.30.
Owner PJL Racing **Bred** Corduff Stud Ltd & J Corcoran **Trained** Whitsbury, Hants

FOCUS
Those to have run hardly set an exacting standard so it was no big surprise a couple of newcomers came to the fore. The winner has more to offer but the form is limited by the proximity of the fourth and sixth.

NOTEBOOK
Relentless Harry(IRE), who was fitted with a tongue strap, cost a few quid at the breeze-ups and made an encouraging start, nicely on top by the finish. The handicapper can't go crazy on him and he appeals as the type to do better, particularly up at 6f+.
Regal Lady, a daughter of Captain Rio, was no match for the winner in the end, but made a promising enough start and is entitled to improve, for all she seemed to know her job fairly well. (op 9-4 tchd 2-1)
White Spirit(IRE) has now run to a similar level to fill the frame on her last three starts, not obviously shaping as if she'll have much more to come, though it's clearly still early days. (op 9-4 tchd 5-2 in a place)
Arabian Flight put a slightly disappointing effort on her nursery bow behind her, but connections would surely have been better off sticking with that route as a mark of 45 is sure to take a hit (third rated 67).
Gin Twist already looks pretty exposed and it will be a really weak maiden she wins. (op 9-2 tchd 6-1)

5738 RENAULT WOLVERHAMPTON WIND ROADSTER (S) STKS 1m 4f 50y(P)
8:00 (8:00) (Class 6) 3-5-Y-O **£1,533** (£452; £226) **Stalls** Low

Form RPR
243- **1** **Reality Show (IRE)**[52] 5922 4-9-1 79.............................. MatthewDavies(3) 4 56
(Brian Ellison) *hld up: pushed along over 3f out: hdwy over 2f out: rdn to ld over 1f out: edgd lft ins fnl f: styd on* **5/6**[1]
2 *1 ½* **Kingston Tiger**[121] 3-9-0 73..............................(p) GrahamGibbons 3 58
(Peter Niven) *hld up: hdwy over 3f out: chsd ldr over 2f out: sn rdn: styd on same pce ins fnl f* **2/1**[2]
66 **3** *shd* **Mayan Flight (IRE)**[21] 5064 3-8-9 48..............................(b) MichaelStainton 6 53
(Richard Whitaker) *chsd ldr tl led 4f out: rdn over 2f out: hdd over 1f out: styd on same pce* **33/1**
005 **4** *3 ¾* **Smarty Sam (USA)**[10] 5390 4-9-4 55..............................(b) RussKennemore 2 47
(Paul Midgley) *chsd ldrs: rdn over 2f out: styd on same pce fr over 1f out* **16/1**
2400 **5** *9* **Stadium Of Light (IRE)**[10] 5369 4-9-4 63.............................. SilvestreDeSousa 1 33
(James Given) *led 8f: sn rdn: wknd over 1f out* **7/1**[3]

2m 38.28s (-2.82) **Going Correction** -0.25s/f (Stan)
WFA 3 from 4yo 9lb **5** Ran SP% **109.2**
Speed ratings (Par 101): **99,98,97,95,89**
CSF £2.65 TOTE £1.80: £1.70, £1.10; EX 3.20.The winner was bought by Mr Joe Singh for 6,200gns. Kingston Tiger was claimed by Mr Michael Wigham £6,000.
Owner M Khan X2 **Bred** Highfort Stud **Trained** Norton, N Yorks

FOCUS
This seller was always going to revolve around the winner but the third probably improved for teh switch to Polytrack but anchoring the form at the same time.

5739 SPOTLESS FACILITY SERVICES H'CAP 1m 4f 50y(P)
8:30 (8:30) (Class 6) (0-60,62) 3-Y-O+ **£2,181** (£644; £322) **Stalls** Low

Form RPR
5053 **1** **Art Thief**[12] 5321 3-8-8 **51**.............................. SilvestreDeSousa 3 59
(Sylvester Kirk) *hld up: hdwy over 2f out: rdn to ld ins fnl f: styd on u.p* **9/2**[3]
204 **2** *¾* **Saloon (USA)**[19] 5112 7-9-5 **53**..............................(p) IvaMilickova 8 59
(Jane Chapple-Hyam) *hld up: hdwy and nt clr run over 1f out: rdn and r.o ins fnl f: wnt 2nd post: nt rch wnr* **18/1**
023 **3** *hd* **Laconicos (IRE)**[22] 5015 9-9-3 **56**..............................(t) LauraPike(5) 9 62
(William Stone) *trckd ldrs: led 2f out: rdn and hdd ins fnl f: styd on* **9/1**
06-1 **4** *¾* **Single Lady**[2] 5643 4-9-2 **53** 6ex.............................. MartinHarley(3) 4 58
(Emmet Michael Butterly, Ire) *hld up in tch: rdn over 1f out: edgd lft and styd on same pce ins fnl f* **5/2**[2]
0046 **5** *1 ½* **Peaceful Means (IRE)**[6] 5519 8-9-3 **51**..............................(t) RobbieFitzpatrick 6 53
(Michael Appleby) *s.i.s: hld up: hdwy u.p over 1f out: styd on same pce ins fnl f* **33/1**
3422 **6** *¾* **Politbureau**[9] 5405 4-9-6 **54**.............................. GrahamGibbons 1 55
(Michael Easterby) *chsd ldrs: rdn over 1f out: no ex fnl f* **15/8**[1]
5402 **7** *nk* **Motarjm (USA)**[9] 5416 7-9-2 **50**..............................(t) ChrisCatlin 7 51
(Lydia Pearce) *hld up: hdwy over 1f out: no ex fnl f* **16/1**
0353 **8** *4 ½* **Full Pelt (USA)**[10] 5392 3-9-5 **62**..............................(v) FrannyNorton 5 56
(Tom Dascombe) *hld up in tch: shkn up 7f out: rdn over 2f out: wknd over 1f out* **13/2**
6000 **9** *1 ½* **Swords**[14] 5267 9-8-12 **46** oh1.............................. AndreaAtzeni 2 37
(Ray Peacock) *led: rdn and hdd 2f out: wknd fnl f* **50/1**
6/ **10** *11* **Le Reveur**[47] 4319 9-8-12 **46** oh1.............................. KellyHarrison 10 20
(Richard Guest) *chsd ldr tl rdn over 2f out: wknd over 1f out* **66/1**

2m 38.35s (-2.75) **Going Correction** -0.25s/f (Stan)
WFA 3 from 4yo+ 9lb **10** Ran SP% **122.4**
Speed ratings (Par 101): **99,98,98,97,96 96,96,93,92,84**
Tote Swingers: 1&2 £19.50, 1&3 £8.90, 2&3 £7.90 CSF £83.79 CT £717.07 TOTE £4.10: £1.10, £8.00, £4.90; EX 123.30.
Owner Antoniades Family **Bred** A G Antoniades **Trained** Upper Lambourn, Berks
■ Stewards' Enquiry : Iva Milickova caution: used whip without giving gelding time to respond.

FOCUS
Run-of-the-mill fare, though one of the less-exposed sorts did at least come out on top. Moderate form and the placed horses set the level.
Swords Official explanation: jockey said gelding hung right

5740 EVENT MANAGEMENT CATERING H'CAP 1m 141y(P)
9:00 (9:00) (Class 6) (0-65,64) 3-Y-O+ **£1,704** (£503; £251) **Stalls** Low

Form RPR
0352 **1** **So Wise (USA)**[9] 5402 3-9-2 **62**.............................. PatCosgrave 1 71+
(Keith Dalgleish) *chsd ldrs: rdn to ld 1f out: r.o u.p* **9/4**[1]
0302 **2** *½* **Aussie Blue (IRE)**[15] 5248 7-9-4 **58**..............................(v) TonyCulhane 2 66
(Richard Whitaker) *chsd ldrs: rdn over 1f out: r.o* **8/1**[3]
3336 **3** *nk* **Dream Of Fortune (IRE)**[3] 5611 7-9-3 **57**.........(bt) SilvestreDeSousa 10 64
(David Evans) *s.i.s: hld up: hdwy over 2f out: rdn and edgd rt over 1f out: r.o* **5/1**[2]
4060 **4** *¾* **Knowe Head (NZ)**[21] 5040 4-9-3 **57**.............................. LiamJones 9 63+
(James Unett) *hld up: hdwy and hung lft fr over 1f out: r.o* **16/1**
4624 **5** *½* **Nicholas Pocock (IRE)**[6] 5502 5-9-3 **60**.............................. PaulPickard(3) 5 64
(Ian McInnes) *hld up: hdwy over 1f out: r.o: nt rch ldrs* **16/1**
0 **6** *¾* **Eastern Gift**[9] 5406 6-9-7 **64**.............................. DeclanCannon(3) 6 67
(Gay Kelleway) *hld up: hdwy over 1f out: sn rdn: styd on* **9/1**
0514 **7** *2 ½* **Empress Leizu (IRE)**[10] 5390 4-9-3 **57**.............................. AndreaAtzeni 7 54
(Tony Carroll) *led: rdn and hdd 1f out: no ex ins fnl f* **11/1**
0500 **8** *½* **Hill Tribe**[9] 5402 4-9-8 **62**.............................. RoystonFfrench 13 58
(Richard Guest) *chsd ldr tl rdn over 1f out: no ex fnl f* **40/1**
0510 **9** *2* **Justcallmehandsome**[9] 5414 9-9-3 **62**..............................(v) LucyKBarry(5) 4 53
(Dominic Ffrench Davis) *hld up: rdn over 1f out: nvr trbld ldrs* **12/1**
362 **10** *3 ¾* **Bennelong**[13] 5300 5-9-6 **60**.............................. PaulDoe 12 43
(Richard Rowe) *chsd ldrs: rdn over 2f out: wknd over 1f out* **14/1**
0005 **11** *2 ¾* **July Days (IRE)**[10] 5394 5-9-4 **58**.............................. KellyHarrison 8 34
(Brian Baugh) *mid-div: pushed along 1/2-way: rdn over 2f out: sn wknd* **12/1**
4424 **12** *1* **McCool Bannanas**[116] 1974 3-9-1 **64**.............................. MatthewDavies(3) 11 38
(James Unett) *s.i.s: plld hrd and sn prom: rdn over 2f out: wknd wl over 1f out* **20/1**

1m 47.95s (-2.55) **Going Correction** -0.25s/f (Stan)
WFA 3 from 4yo+ 6lb **12** Ran SP% **117.9**
Speed ratings (Par 101): **101,100,100,99,99 98,96,95,94,90 88,87**
Tote Swingers: 1&2 £4.20, 1&3 £2.00, 2&3 £4.40 CSF £19.96 CT £84.64 TOTE £3.30: £1.60, £1.30, £1.50; EX 14.90.
Owner S Laffan **Bred** Juddmonte Farms Inc **Trained** Carluke, South Lanarkshire
■ Stewards' Enquiry : Matthew Davies two-day ban: careless riding (Sep 17-18)

FOCUS
An ordinary handicap, and again one of the unexposed sorts came to the fore. The runner-up looks the best guide to the level, backed up by the fourth.
T/Plt: £324.20 to a £1 stake. Pool: £67,727.00. 152.49 winning tickets. T/Qpdt: £75.00 to a £1 stake. Pool: £7,193.00. 70.90 winning tickets. CR

5741 - 5743a (Foreign Racing) - See Raceform Interactive

^{4975}LEOPARDSTOWN (L-H)

Saturday, September 3

OFFICIAL GOING: Good

5744a KILTERNAN STKS (GROUP 3) 1m 2f

5:10 (5:10) 3-Y-O+ **£32,219** (£9,418; £4,461; £1,487)

			RPR
1		**Galileo's Choice (IRE)**^{8} 5461 5-9-8 102 .... PJSmullen 7 (D K Weld, Ire) *prom: led 3f out: rdn clr ent st: kpt on wl fnl f* **13/2**	111
2	1 1/4	**Look At Me (IRE)**^{6} 5523 3-8-12 105 .... SeamieHeffernan 5 (A P O'Brien, Ire) *hld up in last: 6th 3f out: rdn in 4th 2f out: wnt 2nd 1f out: kpt on wl fnl f wout troubling wnr* **9/2**^{3}	106+
3	2 1/2	**Freedom (IRE)**^{55} 3894 3-9-1 95 .... DavidMcCabe 2 (A P O'Brien, Ire) *led: rdn and hdd 3f out: dropped to 5th ent st: rallied to regain 3rd fnl f* **20/1**	103
4	1/2	**Mutahadee (IRE)**^{27} 4831 3-9-1 107 .... WMLordan 3 (T Stack, Ire) *hld up in tch: prog into 2nd and rdn ent st: no imp fr 1 1/2f out* **11/4**^{2}	102
5	2	**Kissable (IRE)**^{24} 4936 3-8-12 110 .... DPMcDonogh 6 (Kevin Prendergast, Ire) *chsd ldrs on outer: rdn 3f out: no imp st* **8/1**	95
6	nk	**Northgate (IRE)**^{6} 5526 6-9-8 93 .... CDHayes 4 (Joseph G Murphy, Ire) *chsd ldrs: rdn and no imp fr 3f out* **16/1**	97
7	2	**Viscount Nelson (USA)**^{84} 2949 4-9-8 114 ....(b) CO'Donoghue 1 (A P O'Brien, Ire) *chsd ldrs: rdn in 3rd ent st: wknd fr 2f out* **13/8**^{1}	96

2m 5.68s (-2.52) **Going Correction** +0.025s/f (Good)
WFA 3 from 4yo+ 7lb 7 Ran SP% **118.0**
Speed ratings: **111,110,108,107,106 105,104**
CSF £37.14 TOTE £6.20: £2.10, £3.00; DF 39.30.
Owner Dr Michael Smurfit **Bred** Patrick F Kelly **Trained** The Curragh, Co Kildare

FOCUS

The quality of this Group 3 may well be somewhat questionable and it has been rated to the low end of the averages.

NOTEBOOK

Galileo's Choice(IRE) had his stamina used to good effect, was sent to the front 3f out and stretched the opposition from there. They couldn't live with him and any inroads the opposition made into his lead was of the slow variety. His versatility and his ability to run at a high level over various trips is now proven and it could be an exciting couple of months ahead. Winning trainer Dermot Weld: "Hopefully he could go to the top over hurdles and we'll also see what weight he gets in the Melbourne Cup. I thought he'd take a lot of beating today and I wouldn't totally rule him out of running in the Irish St Leger next week." (op 6/1)

Look At Me(IRE) came back to some sort of form at the Curragh the previous week and continued that here. It would be somewhat disappointing if she couldn't win a stakes race in the remaining couple of months of the season. Held up in last place, she picked up in the straight and ran on well inside the last furlong or so without reaching the winner. She probably wants 1m2f or more, has an engine although she does possess a somewhat ungainly style of running, and one would imagine a race like the Blandford Stakes would suit her well. (op 5/1 tchd 4/1)

Freedom(IRE) battled back having lost his place, which probably showed how much racing a couple of others did both to get to him in the first place and then when pursuing the winner. It was certainly a fair step up on a disappointing effort in a Fairyhouse winners' event two months previously.

Mutahadee(IRE) had to race wide enough to get towards the front but didn't appear to find a huge amount off the bridle once getting there and got tired inside the last. (op 7/2)

Kissable(IRE) ran a more straightforward race here than at Gowran the previous month. She just wasn't good enough. (op 15/2 tchd 10/1)

Viscount Nelson(USA) isn't the most trustworthy but he ran no race whatsoever, coming off the bridle when the winner went on and finding nothing. Official explanation: vet said colt was found to be blowing hard post-race (op 6/4 tchd 7/4)

5745a COOLMORE FUSAICHI PEGASUS MATRON STKS (GROUP 1) (F&M) 1m

5:40 (5:40) 3-Y-O+ **£106,465** (£31,120; £14,741; £4,913)

			RPR
1		**Emulous**^{66} 3527 4-9-5 112 .... PJSmullen 8 (D K Weld, Ire) *in tch in rr: gd prog on outer ent st: rdn to ld 1f out: qckly clr and styd on wl: comf* **9/2**^{3}	120+
2	3	**Together (IRE)**^{78} 3106 3-9-0 112 .... CO'Donoghue 7 (A P O'Brien, Ire) *chsd ldrs: rdn in 5th 2f out: wnt 2nd ins fnl f: kpt on wout threatening wnr* **3/1**^{2}	112
3	1	**Misty For Me (IRE)**^{70} 3417 3-9-0 120 .... SeamieHeffernan 2 (A P O'Brien, Ire) *prom: disp ld fr 4f out: rdn ent st: led briefly over 1f out: sn hdd and kpt on one pce in 3rd fnl f* **6/4**^{1}	110
4	hd	**Barefoot Lady (IRE)**^{11} 5366 3-9-0 .... TonyHamilton 6 (Richard Fahey) *chsd ldrs: rdn ent st: kpt on same pce fr 2f out* **12/1**	109
5	nk	**Wild Wind (GER)**^{6} 5523 3-9-0 106 .... JPO'Brien 5 (A P O'Brien, Ire) *hld up in rr: rdn ent st: kpt on same pce fr 1 1/2f out* **16/1**	109
6	2	**Ballybacka Lady (IRE)**^{24} 4936 3-9-0 100 .... FMBerry 1 (P A Fahy, Ire) *led: jnd 4f out: rdn to ld again ent st: hdd over 1f out and sn wknd* **50/1**	104
7	1 3/4	**Lolly For Dolly (IRE)**^{16} 5228 4-9-5 112 ....(b) WMLordan 3 (T Stack, Ire) *bmpd leaving stalls: chsd ldrs: rdn and no imp fr 3f out* **10/1**	101
8	3	**Emiyna (USA)**^{23} 4978 3-9-0 109 ....(b^{1}) JMurtagh 4 (John M Oxx, Ire) *chsd ldrs: 4th 3f out: sn rdn and no imp* **10/1**	93

1m 38.47s (-2.73) **Going Correction** +0.025s/f (Good)
WFA 3 from 4yo 5lb 8 Ran SP% **116.9**
Speed ratings: **115,112,111,110,110 108,106,103**
CSF £18.90 TOTE £6.10: £2.30, £2.00, £1.02; DF 30.40.
Owner K Abdulla **Bred** Juddmonte Farms Ltd **Trained** The Curragh, Co Kildare

FOCUS

With an illustrious list of previous winners that includes household names like Soviet Song, Attraction, Lush Lashes and Rainbow View in the last decade, this year's renewal looked slightly substandard beforehand. However, the winner looks like a new star in the making. It has been rated around the fourth, fifth and sixth.

NOTEBOOK

Emulous ◆ could hardly have been more impressive in winning on her first try at Group 1 level. Given her style of running, the wide draw didn't prove too much of an inconvenience as her rider was content to settle her at the rear of the field. She remained there until switched to the outside in the home straight and unleashing a devastating turn of foot to leave some proven Group 1 performers trailing in her wake. To come from last to first in a race where the pacesetters didn't cut each others' throats was a fine performance and she looks a filly with an extremely bright future. The Sun Chariot at Newmarket could be next. (op 5/1)

Together(IRE) finished runner-up in the Irish and English 1,000 Guineas and gives the form a solid look. She ran another good race here and looked primed to mount a serious challenge when coming with her challenge on the inside 2f out. But she was unable to match the acceleration of the winner and was firmly put in her place. She deserves to pick up a Group 1 but could struggle to find a suitable opportunity before the season draws to a close. (op 10/3 tchd 11/4)

Misty For Me(IRE) was sent off favourite on the back of her 6l thumping of Midday in the Pretty Polly Stakes but there was always a suspicion that she was flattered by that performance and the drop down to 1m proved her undoing here. She was never travelling with the same fluency as she did at the Curragh and looked in trouble turning into the home straight. She just plugged on at the one pace to hold onto third and evidently needs a longer trip to be seen at her best. (op 5/4)

Barefoot Lady(IRE) raced prominently but got outpaced on the home turn before plugging on in the final furlong. She had been outclassed on her previous tries at the top table so it was no surprise to see her do so again here. She is another who looks ideally suited by 1m2f. (op 14/1)

Wild Wind(GER), the least well-fancied of the Ballydoyle trio, was held up towards the rear but did stay on well enough in the home straight without ever troubling the principals. (op 20/1)

Ballybacka Lady(IRE) ran a brave race from the front and remained at the head of affairs until swallowed up passing the 1f pole.

Lolly For Dolly(IRE) disappointed last time at Tipperary and did so again here. She was bumped shortly after leaving the stalls but that was no excuse for her tame effort and she may be feeling the effects of a long hard season. (op 8/1)

Emiyna(USA) seemed to travel well into the home straight but found nothing when pressure was applied and question marks hang over her now. (op 10/1 tchd 11/1)

5746a THETOTE.COM SEPTEMBER H'CAP (PREMIER HANDICAP) 7f

6:10 (6:14) 3-Y-O+ **£41,379** (£13,103; £6,206; £2,068; £1,379; £689)

			RPR
1		**Below Zero (IRE)**^{7} 5474 4-9-2 95 .... FMBerry 2 (Mark Johnston) *mde all: rdn clr ent st: styd on wl fnl f: reduced advantage fnl f but a in command* **4/1**^{1}	103+
2	1 1/4	**Hujaylea (IRE)**^{6} 5526 8-9-12 105 ....(p) ShaneFoley 6 (M Halford, Ire) *in rr of mid-div: rdn in mod 13th on inner 2f out: styd on strly to go 2nd ins fnl f: nt trble wnr: nvr nrr* **12/1**	110
3	1 1/2	**Northern Rocked (IRE)**^{16} 5226 5-9-1 99 ....(b) LFRoche$^{(5)}$ 7 (D K Weld, Ire) *chsd ldrs: 5th 3f out: sn rdn: mod 3rd 1f out: kpt on same pce* **10/1**^{3}	100
4	2	**Peahen**^{55} 3892 3-9-4 101 .... KLatham 4 (G M Lyons, Ire) *mid-div on inner: rdn in 6th ent st: kpt on same pce fr 2f out* **14/1**	94
5	shd	**Luisant**^{20} 5086 8-9-7 103 .... JPO'Brien$^{(3)}$ 3 (J A Nash, Ire) *mid-div: rdn ent st: 10th 1f out: kpt on wout threatening* **10/1**^{3}	98
6	nk	**Jamesie (IRE)**^{35} 4566 3-8-13 96 .... CO'Donoghue 12 (David Marnane, Ire) *mid-div: rdn in 7th 3f out: kpt on same pce st* **9/2**^{2}	88
7	1/2	**Barack (IRE)**^{11} 5361 5-9-12 105 ....(bt) BACurtis 1 (Francis Ennis, Ire) *chsd ldrs: rdn ent st: sn no imp* **14/1**	98
8	1 1/2	**Iron Major (IRE)**^{19} 5124 4-8-8 87 ....(p) PJSmullen 9 (Edward Lynam, Ire) *in rr of mid-div: rdn and kpt on same pce fr 3f out* **14/1**	76
9	nk	**Star Links (USA)**^{23} 4976 5-7-9 84 ....(b) GJPhillips$^{(10)}$ 14 (S Donohoe, Ire) *mid-div on outer: rdn and kpt on same pce st* **25/1**	72
10	1/2	**Collingwood (IRE)**^{23} 4976 9-8-11 90 ....(t) WMLordan 17 (T M Walsh, Ire) *towards rr: rdn ent st: 12th 1f out: no ex* **16/1**	77
11	2	**Six Of Hearts**^{27} 4836 7-9-9 107 ....(p) SHJames$^{(5)}$ 11 (Cecil Ross, Ire) *mid-div: no imp fr 3f out* **22/1**	88
12	1	**Duff (IRE)**^{23} 4978 8-9-9 102 .... DPMcDonogh 8 (Edward Lynam, Ire) *prom: 3rd 3f out: sn rdn and no imp* **14/1**	80
13	shd	**Spirit Of Xaar (IRE)**^{6} 5526 5-7-9 84 .... DHBergin$^{(10)}$ 13 (David Marnane, Ire) *s.i.s and in rr: rdn and no imp fr 3f out* **14/1**	62
14	shd	**Jembatt (IRE)**^{12} 5331 4-8-5 84 ....(tp) CDHayes 10 (Michael Mulvany, Ire) *prom: 2nd 1/2-way: rdn and wknd ent st* **25/1**	62
15	2 1/2	**Sharisse (IRE)**^{27} 4835 5-9-1 94 .... JMurtagh 5 (W T Farrell, Ire) *in rr of mid-div on inner: rdn ent st: bhd ldrs u.p on rail whn checked 1f out: eased* **10/1**^{3}	65
16	4 1/2	**Music In The Rain (IRE)**^{342} 6403 3-8-4 87 ....(t) RPCleary 18 (J S Bolger, Ire) *sn pushed along into prom position on outer: rdn and wknd ent st* **12/1**	44
17	3/4	**Simla Sunset (IRE)**^{6} 5526 5-8-11 95 ....(p) RPWhelan$^{(5)}$ 15 (P J Prendergast, Ire) *chsd ldrs: rdn and wknd fr 3f out* **16/1**	52
18	13	**The Tooth Fairy (IRE)**^{19} 5124 5-7-13 85 .... SAGray$^{(7)}$ 16 (Michael Mulvany, Ire) *uns rdr and rn loose bef s: slowly away and a bhd* **25/1**	7

1m 27.27s (-1.43) **Going Correction** +0.025s/f (Good)
WFA 3 from 4yo+ 4lb 18 Ran SP% **141.8**
Speed ratings: **109,107,105,103,103 103,102,100,100,99 97,96,96,96,93 88,87,72**
CSF £58.04 CT £481.65 TOTE £4.10: £1.60, £2.80, £3.60, £3.70; DF 89.50.
Owner Sheikh Hamdan Bin Mohammed Al Maktoum **Bred** Darley **Trained** Middleham Moor, N Yorks

FOCUS

What looked a wide-open handicap on paper was turned into something of a procession by the sole British representative, who looks destined for Listed or Group level. It has been rated around the third and fourth as just off their best.

NOTEBOOK

Below Zero(IRE) ◆ was again allowed to dictate the fractions and could be called the winner a long way from home. In hindsight, he probably should have got more than 10lb for that Dundalk triumph given the ease with which he won and this was a similarly impressive display of front running. His rider made full use of the good draw and was soon at the head of affairs. He was kicked clear turning into the home straight and that proved the decisive move. He never looked in danger of being reeled in and was value for more than the winning margin. He looks well up to contesting Listed races. (op 5/1)

Hujaylea(IRE) looked to have gone off the boil a little on his last two starts but this was a much-improved showing and he stayed on stoutly in the home straight to grab second. He never looked like catching the winner, though. (op 12/1 tchd 11/1)

Northern Rocked(IRE) racked up a string of victories at the end of last season and has struggled a little with his higher rating this term. But this was a fine display and he stayed on well to suggest a victory off this mark is possible.

Peahen was one of many to be left sitting when the winner kicked for home rounding the final bend but he did stick on well enough. He may need to come back down the weights a little to register a second career success. (op 16/1)

Luisant looked to be going nowhere turning into the home straight but kept galloping and passed several beaten horses in the final furlong. (op 12/1)

Jamesie(IRE) has been a model of consistency all season and while his string of placed efforts ended here, it was another solid display. (op 9/2 tchd 5/1)

The Tooth Fairy(IRE) ran loose before the start and started slowly which ended any hopes of landing a blow.

5747a RED MILLS IRISH CHAMPION STKS (GROUP 1) 1m 2f

6:45 (6:45) 3-Y-O+

£374,568 (£122,413; £57,758; £18,965; £12,500; £6,034)

RPR

1 **So You Think (NZ)**[63] 3646 5-9-7 127 SeamieHeffernan 3 128+
(A P O'Brien, Ire) *chsd ldr in mod 2nd: impr to ld 2f out: sn rdn and strly pressed: maintained ld and kpt on wl fr 1 1/2f out* **1/4**[1]

2 ½ **Snow Fairy (IRE)**[35] 4533 4-9-4 FrankieDettori 1 124
(Ed Dunlop) *chsd ldrs in 3rd: wnt 2nd and rdn 2f out: sn strly pressed wnr: kpt on wl fr 1 1/2f out wout rching wnr* **6/1**[2]

3 6 **Famous Name**[34] 4599 6-9-7 117 PJSmullen 4 115
(D K Weld, Ire) *chsd ldrs in 4th: rdn ent st: wnt mod 3rd 1 1/2f out: kpt on same pce fnl f* **14/1**[3]

4 4 **Dunboyne Express (IRE)**[19] 5128 3-9-0 110 (t) DPMcDonogh 2 107
(Kevin Prendergast, Ire) *hld up in 5th: rdn and no imp fr 3f out* **50/1**

5 2 ½ **Roderic O'Connor (IRE)**[69] 3442 3-9-0 117 JPO'Brien 5 102
(A P O'Brien, Ire) *led at fast pce and sn clr: reduced advantage ent st: rdn and hdd 2f out: sn wknd* **20/1**

6 17 **Recital (FR)**[91] 2715 3-9-0 115 CO'Donoghue 6 68
(A P O'Brien, Ire) *hld up in last and plld hrd: rdn and no imp fr 3f out: eased fnl f* **14/1**[3]

2m 4.20s (-4.00) **Going Correction** +0.025s/f (Good)
WFA 3 from 4yo+ 7lb **6** Ran SP% **114.3**
Speed ratings: **117,116,111,108,106 93**
CSF £2.49 TOTE £1.10: £1.02, £2.00; DF 2.60.
Owner D Smith, Mrs J Magnier, M Tabor **Bred** M J Moran & Piper Farm Ltd **Trained** Ballydoyle, Co Tipperary

FOCUS
What we learned was questionable, but the expected stroll for So You Think didn't materialise and the filly Snow Fairy made a real race of it. The form looks solid rated around the third.

NOTEBOOK
So You Think(NZ) knuckled down pretty well under pressure and come what may Snow Fairy wasn't going to get past, indeed it looked a case of him doing enough and something to himself should a more potent challenge arise. It wasn't the performance of a superstar, it's hard to be even too definitive about whether it was the performance of a truly top-class horse, and the question once again is what did we learn? The answer is little enough. The horse had the luxury of running a few pounds below his official best and still won. His defeat of Workforce at Sandown is still the only evidence this season of his supposed star quality - one imagines the true extent of it will be revealed later in the autumn. His trainer didn't rule out a tilt at the Arc, especially now the same owners have lost Pour Moi. (op 1/4 tchd 2/9)
Snow Fairy(IRE) ◆ proved herself a filly of the highest calibre with what on paper was her best run of the season. She consigned to the dustbin her disappointing effort in the Eclipse and managed to step up on her second to Midday in the Nassau Stakes with this performance. She took a little bit of stoking up before they turned in but she built up quite a head of steam with which to lay down her challenge. She just wasn't good enough to get past the winner and was always being held, but connections can surely look forward to taking on the colts in Group 1 company with a bit more confidence after this.
Famous Name ran up to his best. He travelled well for most of the journey but once the gauntlet was thrown down he couldn't make an impression. The servant he has been to his connections makes one almost root for them to find that elusive winnable Group 1.
Dunboyne Express(IRE) ran just about up to his best and earned some decent prize-money to boot. It certainly wasn't a waste of time but he belongs in a grade below this one.
Roderic O'Connor(IRE) was used as a pacemaker but he didn't go off at such an insane pace that the others could ignore him. Unfortunately though he could only tow his stable companion to the turn into the straight, which left that horse with a huge task.
Recital(FR) hadn't run since failing to handle the undulations at Epsom in June. He was entitled to need it coming back from a break and raced a bit keenly in last place but he barely raised a gallop inside the final half-mile. Official explanation: jockey said colt ran free throughout (op 16/1)

5748a IRISH STALLION FARMS EUROPEAN BREEDERS FUND AUTUMN FILLIES H'CAP (PREMIER HANDICAP) 1m 4f

7:20 (7:23) 3-Y-O+

£38,793 (£12,284; £5,818; £1,939; £1,293; £646)

RPR

1 **Goldplated (IRE)**[5] 5574 3-7-8 82 5ex oh3 MMMonaghan(10) 18 [illegible]
(John Joseph Murphy, Ire) *mid-div on outer: rdn in 13th and outpcd 3f out: 9th 1f out: rapid hdwy to ld ins fnl f: edgd rt and styd on wl cl home* **20/1**

2 1 ¼ **Asiya (IRE)**[31] 4691 5-8-5 81 RDawson(7) 19 85
(Norman Cassidy, Ire) *mid-div on outer: prog into 3rd and rdn 2f out: disp ld over 1f out: hdd and no ex ins fnl f* **16/1**

3 ¾ **Fleur De Nuit (IRE)**[10] 5397 6-8-11 87 DJBenson(7) 8 90
(J Bleahen, Ire) *chsd ldrs: clsr in 2nd and rdn 2f out: disp ld over 1f out: sn hdd: no ex cl home* **11/2**[2]

4 ¾ **Plum Sugar (IRE)**[20] 5090 4-9-3 86 FMBerry 13 88
(P J Prendergast, Ire) *chsd ldrs: rdn in 3rd 3f out: led briefly under 2f out: sn hdd: no ex fnl f* **20/1**

5 ¾ **Benefit Of Porter (IRE)**[15] 5260 7-8-2 78 RADoyle(7) 20 78
(Patrick Sinnott, Ire) *in rr: hdwy bef st: rdn in 5th under 2f out: kpt on same pce* **20/1**

6 ½ **Mohedian Lady (IRE)**[17] 5177 3-9-4 96 PJSmullen 12 96
(Luca Cumani) *in rr of mid-div: prog fr 3f out: rdn and kpt on wout threatening st* **3/1**[1]

7 1 ¾ **Elyaadi**[14] 5284 7-9-7 95 RPWhelan(5) 6 92
(John Queally, Ire) *mid-div: rdn ent st: kpt on same pce fr 2f out* **12/1**

8 hd **Mojita (IRE)**[11] 5364 3-7-11 82 oh6 RossCoakley(7) 2 78
(K J Condon, Ire) *chsd ldrs: rdn and kpt on same pce fr 3f out* **16/1**

9 nk **Sceal Nua (IRE)**[31] 4691 3-8-10 88 (p) NGMcCullagh 15 84
(John M Oxx, Ire) *chsd ldrs: 5th 3f out: sn rdn and no imp* **8/1**[3]

10 2 ½ **Ideal**[52] 3991 3-8-5 83 (p) CDHayes 17 75
(David Wachman, Ire) *chsd ldrs: rdn to ld briefly over 2f out: sn hdd & wknd* **20/1**

11 1 ¾ **Syann (IRE)**[31] 4691 4-9-4 92 SHJames(5) 14 81
(David Marnane, Ire) *mid-div: rdn and no imp fr 3f out* **20/1**

12 ½ **Quaintly (USA)**[17] 5192 3-8-7 85 (p) ShaneFoley 5 73
(David Wachman, Ire) *led: rdn and hdd over 2f out: sn wknd* **12/1**

13 nk **Strandfield Lady (IRE)**[19] 5125 6-9-5 88 (b) SeamieHeffernan 3 76
(H Rogers, Ire) *in rr: no imp fr 4f out* **16/1**

14 ¾ **Lovers Peace (IRE)**[11] 5363 3-8-4 82 oh3 DMGrant 11 69
(Edmond Kent, Ire) *chsd ldrs: 6th 3f out: sn wknd* **25/1**

15 2 **Rising Wind (IRE)**[14] 5291 3-9-2 94 DPMcDonogh 1 78
(Kevin Prendergast, Ire) *chsd ldrs on inner: rdn and wknd fr 4f out* **16/1**

16 1 ¼ **Make My Heart Sing (IRE)**[34] 4589 3-8-10 88 CO'Donoghue 4 70
(A P O'Brien, Ire) *in rr of mid-div: no imp fr 4f out* **25/1**

17 1 ¼ **Gypsie Queen (IRE)**[16] 5229 4-8-5 74 (b) BACurtis 10 54
(Ms Joanna Morgan, Ire) *s.i.s and pushed along in last early: sme hdwy into 11th and rdn ent st: wknd* **20/1**

18 8 **Cnocandancer (IRE)**[113] 2082 4-9-3 86 WMLordan 16 53
(T Stack, Ire) *a towards rr* **10/1**

19 7 **Hurricane Havoc (IRE)**[24] 4936 3-9-8 100 (bt) KJManning 9 56
(J S Bolger, Ire) *prom: rdn in 4th 3f out: sn wknd* **20/1**

20 1 ¼ **Reach The Stars (IRE)**[35] 4568 4-7-13 73 oh4 (b) LFRoche(5) 7 27
(D K Weld, Ire) *mid-div: 10th 3f out: sn wknd* **11/1**

2m 31.97s (-3.33) **Going Correction** +0.025s/f (Good)
WFA 3 from 4yo+ 9lb **20** Ran SP% **148.9**
Speed ratings: **112,111,110,110,109 109,108,108,107,106 105,104,104,103,102 101,100,95,90,90**
Daily Double: 118.50 to a 5 euro stake. CSF £321.00 CT £2054.15 TOTE £18.30: £3.80, £5.60, £1.90, £5.30; DF 893.80.
Owner Mrs M B O'Sullivan **Bred** Corrin Stud **Trained** Upton, Co. Cork

FOCUS
The race is rated around the third and fourth although the winner won with plenty in hand.

NOTEBOOK
Goldplated(IRE) confirmed her improvement here by posting her fourth win of the season. Her 5lb mandatory penalty for her win over the trip at Galway five days previously still left her 3lb out of the handicap, but under her 10lb claiming rider she made rapid headway from over 1f out to get on top inside the final furlong and was well on top towards the finish despite drifting right.
Asiya(IRE) acquitted herself well, making headway from mid division before the straight and challenging to dispute the lead over 1f out. She stayed on but could not match the winner's finishing surge. (op 14/1)
Fleur De Nuit(IRE), back in trip having finished sixth on her handicap debut over 1m6f at Killarney last month, attracted market support in the morning and on track. Fifth into the straight, she arrived with every chance 1f out where she was vying for the lead until finding no extra late on. (op 8/1)
Plum Sugar(IRE) had lost her form following a couple of placed efforts this season and this was more encouraging on her part. Third and ridden before the straight, she hit the front under 2f out but her lead proved short-lived and she could raise no extra inside the final furlong.
Benefit Of Porter(IRE) was making her handicap debut. She made headway from behind to stay on steadily in the straight and will improve on this effort when going back up in distance.
Mohedian Lady(IRE) was tackling this trip for the first time. Held up, she made headway in mid-division into the straight and kept on steadily without ever travelling well enough to mount a serious challenge. (op 10/3 tchd 3/1)
T/Jkpt: @11,250.00. Pool of @15,000.00 - 1 winning ticket. T/Plt: @134.00. Pool of @18,985.70 - 106 winning tickets. II

5664 BADEN-BADEN (L-H)

Saturday, September 3

OFFICIAL GOING: Turf: good

5749a MERCEDES-BENZ STUTEN-PREIS VON BADEN (GROUP 3) (3YO+ FILLIES & MARES) (TURF) 1m 3f

5:30 (5:36) 3-Y-O+

£27,586 (£9,482; £4,741; £2,586; £1,724; £1,293)

RPR

1 **February Sun**[71] 3-8-11 0 IoritzMendizabal 6 111
(J-C Rouget, France) *settled in midfield: clsd on ldrs travelling smoothly down bk st: r.o wl u.p as field crossed to stands' rail: tk ld 1 1/2f out: sn chal hrd by Djumama: hld on wl fnl f* **42/10**[2]

2 nk **Djumama (IRE)**[27] 4839 3-8-11 0 AHelfenbein 10 110
(Andreas Lowe, Germany) *settled 6th: shkn up turning into st: jnd ldr 1 1/2f out: chal hrd thrght fnl f: a hld* **9/10**[1]

3 2 ½ **Nicea (GER)**[19] 4-9-5 0 FilipMinarik 5 106
(P Schiergen, Germany) *settled in midfield: r.o wl to go 3rd 2f out: styd on wl wout threatening ldrs* **216/10**

4 ¾ **Indian Breeze (GER)**[63] 4-9-5 0 ADeVries 7 105
(J Hirschberger, Germany) *a.p bhd ldr: rdn early in st: r.o wl wout threatening ldrs* **96/10**

5 [illegible] **[illegible] (GER)**[11] [illegible] [illegible] 2 103
(A Wohler, Germany) *broke fast: sn led: set mod pce: led into st: hdd over 1 1/2f out: rdn but no ex: styd on* **218/10**

6 shd **Vertana (IRE)**[31] 4-9-5 0 FabriceVeron 3 103
(H-A Pantall, France) *settled towards rr: rdn and r.o in st but only passed btn horses* **131/10**

7 nk **Lagalp (GER)**[20] 5093 4-9-5 0 MircoDemuro 4 103
(P Schiergen, Germany) *settled 4th: rdn and effrt early in st: no imp* **29/1**

8 3 **Not For Sale (GER)**[91] 4-9-5 0 EFrank 9 97
(T Mundry, Germany) *a towards rr: nvr figured* **11/2**

9 9 **Aigrette Garzette (IRE)**[27] 4839 3-8-11 0 AStarke 1 81
(P Schiergen, Germany) *prom in 3rd on ins rail bhd ldrs: threatened briefly turning into st: rdn but no ex: wknd qckly* **53/10**[3]

2m 21.27s (2.00)
WFA 3 from 4yo 8lb **9** Ran SP% **131.8**
WIN (incl. 10 euro stake): 52. PLACES: 16, 11, 26. SF: 106.
Owner Rashit Shaykhutdinov **Bred** Newsells Park Stud **Trained** Pau, France

5750 - 5752a (Foreign Racing) - See Raceform Interactive

VELIEFENDI

Saturday, September 3

OFFICIAL GOING: Turf: good; polytrack: standard

5753a INTERNATIONAL ISTANBUL EUROPEAN CAPITAL OF CULTURE TROPHY (LOCAL GROUP 2) (F&M) (TURF) 1m

5:00 (12:00) 3-Y-O+ **£99,137** (£39,655; £19,827; £9,913)

RPR

1 **Vanjura (GER)**[34] 4597 4-9-6 0 APietsch 4 113
(R Dzubasz, Germany) *chsd clr ldr: abt 15 l 2nd 4f out: grad reeled in clr ldr: 4 l down and rdn 2f out: led appr fnl f: r.o wl* **7/10**[1]

2 2 **Rhythm Of Light**[22] 5028 3-8-13 0 RichardKingscote 7 105
(Tom Dascombe) *w.w towards rr: tk clsr order and 6th 4f out: 5th: pushed along and running on 2f out: swtchd outside wkng pcesetter to take 2nd ins fnl f: nt pce to chal ldr: run flattened out cl home* **7/1**

3 hd **Antara (GER)**[57] 3822 5-9-6 0 (p) RichardMullen 5 108
(Saeed Bin Suroor) *midfield early: 4th 4f out: effrt and wnt 3rd appr 2f out: sn rdn and nt qckn 1 1/2f out: styd on again ins fnl 100yds: jst failed to snatch 2nd* **11/5**[3]
4 2 **Music Show (IRE)**[80] 3030 4-9-6 0 AlanMunro 2 103
(Mick Channon) *a.p in gp chsng clr ldr: 3rd and rdn 2f out: kpt on wout qckning fnl f* **7/4**[2]
5 2 1/2 **Actionmax (TUR)**[364] 5782 6-9-6 0 HalisKaratas 8 98
(B Dag, Turkey) *racd towards rr: 9th and effrt on outside over 2f out: styd on u.p fnl f: nvr rchd ldrs* **68/10**
6 hd **Mystical Storm (TUR)** 4-9-6 0 SelimKaya 9 97
(H Caliskan, Turkey) *w.w in midfield on outside: 7th and pushed along ins fnl 3f: hrd rdn appr 2f out: kpt on fnl f: nvr able to chal* **101/20**
7 1 **The Rising (TUR)**[364] 5782 7-9-6 0 AkinSozen 10 95
(S Aydogdi, Turkey) *a bhd: last and hrd rdn 2f out: sme late hdwy: nvr in contention* **7/1**
8 hd **Princess Zahra (IRE)** 4-9-6 0 MehmetKaya 1 94
(S Demiral, Turkey) *broke wl and led: 15 l clr 4f out: rdn and coming bk to field over 2f out: tiring and hdd over 1f out: wknd fnl f* **41/5**
9 5 1/2 **Rudolph Schmidt (IRE)**[701] 6442 5-9-6 0 (bt) MarioChristofis 3 82
(A Mykoniatis, Greece) *nvr in contention: bhd whn hrd rdn 2f out: no imp* **222/10**
10 1/2 **Rockatella (IRE)**[36] 4497 4-9-6 0 ASuborics 6 81
(W Hefter, Germany) *racd in 5th much of r: pushed along to keep pl 3 1/2f out: hrd rdn and no imp ins fnl 2f: wl btn whn eased fnl f* **185/10**

1m 34.22s (-1.11)
WFA 3 from 4yo+ 5lb **10** Ran SP% **201.1**
PARI-MUTUEL (including 1Turkish lira stakes): WIN: 1.70; remaining totes N/A.
Owner M Barth **Bred** J-C Haimet & J-P Liberge **Trained** Germany

NOTEBOOK
Vanjura(GER) landed this for the second year running.
Rhythm Of Light kept on well to secure second, but never looked like troubling the winner.
Antara(GER), who had been handy in the main pack, stayed on and nearly claimed second.
Music Show(IRE) could not quicken up and had to settle for fourth.

5754a INTERNATIONAL FRANCE GALOP FRBC ANATOLIA TROPHY (LOCAL GROUP 2) (3YO+) (POLYTRACK) 1m 2f (P)
7:00 (12:00) 3-Y-O+ **£99,137** (£39,655; £19,827; £9,913)

RPR
1 **Dordogne (IRE)**[58] 3775 3-8-11 0 AlanMunro 5 109
(Mark Johnston) *dwlt and short of room first f: once in clr trckd ldr on outside: shkn up to ld over 2f out: rdn appr fnl f and styd on strly* **13/2**
2 1 1/2 **Belgian Bill**[16] 5230 3-8-11 0 (t) ASuborics 4 106
(George Baker) *a.p: 3 l 3rd 4f out: pushed along 3f out and prog on outside: rdn and wnt 2nd 2f out: effrt and rchd wnr's quarters 1f out: r.o gamely* **96/10**
3 5 **Emirates Champion**[64] 3591 5-9-6 0 (t) RichardMullen 6 98
(Saeed Bin Suroor) *dwlt and pushed along to get position: settled 6th: 5th and pushed along to hold pl 4f out: styd on 2 1/2f out: hrd rdn appr 2f marker: tk 3rd ins foinal f but no imp on first two* **3/5**[2]
4 4 **Buenos Aires (TUR)** 4-9-6 0 (bt) AhmetCelik 8 90
(S Karagoz, Turkey) *led tl hdd appr 2f out: rdn and wknd over 1f out* **68/10**
5 2 1/2 **Amfitryon**[841] 6-9-6 0 (b) MarioChristofis 7 85
(A Mykoniatis, Greece) *towards rr: 6th 2f out: plugged on u.p fnl f: nvr threatened but tk 5th cl home* **6/1**[3]
6 1/2 **Dervis Aga (TUR)**[364] 5781 6-9-6 0 (b) YalcinAkagac 3 84
(S Mutlu, Turkey) *w.w towards rr: 7th and rdn 3f out: no imp on ldrs fnl 2f: lost 5th cl home* **9/20**[1]
7 16 **Mavi Kumsal (TUR)** 4-9-6 0 FuatCakar 2 52
(A Isgoren, Turkey) *bhd: detached last over 3f out: modest late hdwy: nvr a factor* **8/1**
8 1 **Babayigit (TUR)**[364] 5781 7-9-6 0 GokhanKocakaya 1 50
(A Gokce, Turkey) *prom: 4th and rdn 2 1/2f out: wknd u.p fnl 2f* **104/10**

2m 2.62s (-2.38)
WFA 3 from 4yo+ 7lb **8** Ran SP% **201.2**
PARI-MUTUEL (including 1Turkish lira stakes): WIN: 7.50; PL: N/A; DF 24.75; SF 44.25.
Owner Sheikh Hamdan Bin Mohammed Al Maktoum **Bred** Mr & Mrs G Middlebrook **Trained** Middleham Moor, N Yorks
■ A 1-2-3 for British-based trainers.

NOTEBOOK
Dordogne(IRE), who gets further, found more for Alan Munro, who has a fine record at this big meeting.
Belgian Bill was always handy and kept on well for second.
Emirates Champion was well held in third on this rise in grade.

5282 YORK (L-H)
Sunday, September 4

OFFICIAL GOING: Good (6.7)
Wind: almost nil Weather: dull and overcast, light drizzle 1st 4

5755 JUDITH MARSHALL MEMORIAL STKS (NURSERY) 7f
1:50 (1:51) (Class 4) (0-85,80) 2-Y-O **£5,239** (£1,559; £779; £389) **Stalls** Low

Form RPR
31 1 **Lady Layla**[26] 4875 2-9-0 **73** TomEaves 3 79+
(Bryan Smart) *mde all: hld on wl* **9/2**[2]
0522 2 1 1/4 **Fayr Fall (IRE)**[9] 5431 2-8-11 **70** DavidAllan 1 73
(Tim Easterby) *trckd ldrs: chal over 1f out: styd on same pce last 100yds* **14/1**
315 3 1 1/2 **Satanic Beat (IRE)**[18] 5184 2-9-7 **80** PJMcDonald 4 79
(Jedd O'Keeffe) *dwlt: hld up: hdwy over 2f out: hung lft: kpt on same pce last 150yds* **5/2**[1]
0534 4 6 **On The Hoof**[18] 5184 2-9-2 **75** (b[1]) GrahamGibbons 2 59
(Michael Easterby) *chsd ldrs: sltly hmpd 2f out: one pce* **5/1**[3]
5133 5 2 **Ladykin (IRE)**[27] 4867 2-9-5 **78** PaulHanagan 9 57
(Richard Fahey) *mid-div: drvn and outpcd over 3f out: kpt on fnl f* **11/2**
6300 6 3 1/2 **Dicky Mint**[18] 5184 2-8-5 **64** JamesSullivan 8 35
(Michael Easterby) *trckd ldrs: t.k.h: drvn and outpcd over 3f out: lost pl over 2f out* **16/1**
143 7 3 1/2 **Citizen's Charter (USA)**[30] 4760 2-9-5 **78** PhillipMakin 7 40
(Mahmood Al Zarooni) *gave problems in stalls: dwlt: hld up in rr: rdn 3f out: nvr a factor* **13/2**
4054 8 2 3/4 **Drummoyne (USA)**[15] 5280 2-8-8 **67** SilvestreDeSousa 5 22
(Mark Johnston) *w wnr: lost pl over 1f out* **11/1**
060 9 3/4 **Farzan (IRE)**[18] 5161 2-8-6 **65** KellyHarrison 6 18
(Tim Easterby) *in rr: drvn and outpcd over 3f out: sn bhd* **50/1**

1m 27.27s (1.97) **Going Correction** +0.375s/f (Good) **9** Ran SP% **115.0**
Speed ratings (Par 97): **103,101,99,93,90 86,82,79,78**
Tote Swingers: 1&2 £9.00, 1&3 £2.80, 2&3 £6.90 CSF £64.41 CT £190.44 TOTE £4.70: £1.90, £3.30, £1.10; EX 38.70 Trifecta £89.60 Pool: £569.50 - 4.70 winning units..
Owner Dr Marwan Koukash **Bred** H Q Spooner **Trained** Hambleton, N Yorks

FOCUS
Rail moved in from 9f to entrance to home straight reducing distances of 10f and over by 27yds. The official going was described as Good (Goingstick 6.7). The GoingStick readings in the straight were 6.6 in the centre and 6.5 on both flanks, but the 2-y-os in this opening nursery seemed to find it tough going and one rider described the ground as a little on the soft side of good. They raced up the centre of the track starting up the home straight, but edged back towards the inside rail as they got tired. The form looks straightforward, rated around the placed horses.

NOTEBOOK
Lady Layla ◆, making her nursery debut off a mark of 73, was the least exposed in the field and was proven at the trip having made just about all to win an Ayr maiden on her second start last month. She faced competition for the early lead from Drummoyne here, but it made no difference and, having edged her way to the front at halfway, saw her race out gamely. She is entitled to improve again from this. (op 4-1)
Fayr Fall(IRE), the most experienced in the field, was trying this trip for the first time. Always up there, he tried very hard to get to the winner but was always being held and had to settle for his third consecutive runner's-up spot.
Satanic Beat(IRE) was up to 7f for the first time having met trouble when fifth of 16 (just behind On The Hoof and 3lb better off) in a much stronger nursery over 6f here last month. All the rage in the market, he looked dangerous when brought to challenge over 2f out, but then repeatedly hung in behind the winner and was never doing enough. He did become restless in the stalls beforehand, so may be worth another chance. (op 3-1)
On The Hoof, like his old rival up in trip, had blinkers on for the first time but he raced keenly in the early stages and when an effort was asked for the response was limited. (op 9-2 tchd 11-2)
Ladykin(IRE) had run well in a couple of nurseries over this trip in her last two starts, but she never got involved this time and was disappointing. (op 6-1)
Citizen's Charter(USA) got himself into a state in the stalls and never figured in the race itself. (op 7-1 tchd 15-2)

5756 MINSTER ALARMS 30TH ANNIVERSARY E B F MAIDEN STKS 5f 89y
2:25 (2:26) (Class 3) 2-Y-O **£6,469** (£1,925; £962; £481) **Stalls** Centre

Form RPR
235 1 **Pea Shooter**[30] 4748 2-9-3 0 PhillipMakin 2 98+
(Kevin Ryan) *mde all: edgd rt and drew clr fnl f* **6/1**
2 6 **Lisiere (IRE)** 2-8-12 0 PaulHanagan 7 72+
(Richard Fahey) *in rr: n.m.r and dropped detached last after 1f: hdwy over 2f out: styd on to take 2nd last 100yds: edgd lft: no ch w wnr* **7/2**[2]
06 3 3 **Rio Grande**[99] 2510 2-9-0 0 JohnFahy[(3)] 1 67
(Jeremy Noseda) *hood removed v late: dwlt: sn trcking ldrs: upsides over 2f out: rdn over 1f out: wknd fnl 75yds* **11/10**[1]
2 4 nk **Personal Touch**[17] 5202 2-9-0 0 LeeTopliss[(3)] 3 65
(Richard Fahey) *trckd ldrs: upsides over 2f out: wknd jst ins fnl f* **9/2**[3]
2236 5 2 1/4 **I'll Be Good**[9] 5438 2-9-0 72 GaryBartley[(3)] 6 58
(Robert Johnson) *chsd ldrs: upsides over 2f out: wknd jst ins fnl f* **20/1**
2 6 1 3/4 **First Phase**[24] 4940 2-8-12 0 DavidAllan 5 46
(Mel Brittain) *chsd ldrs: lost pl 2f out* **25/1**

65.72 secs (1.62) **Going Correction** +0.375s/f (Good) **6** Ran SP% **110.9**
Speed ratings (Par 99): **102,92,87,87,83 80**
Tote Swingers: 1&2 £2.80, 1&3 £2.40, 2&3 £1.80 CSF £26.27 TOTE £5.60: £2.40, £1.90; EX 22.80.
Owner Mrs Margaret Forsyth **Bred** R F And S D Knipe **Trained** Hambleton, N Yorks

FOCUS
Not the strongest of York maidens, but an impressive winner and the form behind looks reasonable.

NOTEBOOK
Pea Shooter ◆ was disappointing on his return from a three-month absence at Haydock last month, but was placed in his first two starts in April and the form of both races has worked out, especially his second to subsequent Group 2-winner Lilbourne Lad on his Doncaster debut. Soon in front, he stretched clear in impressive fashion when asked and looks capable of winning something rather better than this. (tchd 11-2)
Lisiere(IRE), a 65,000gns filly related to some smart sprinters on the dam's side of her pedigree, including Owington, represented the yard responsible for the last two winners of this race. Green and clueless early, she eventually got the message and kept on to finish a clear second, albeit at a respectful distance behind the winner. An ordinary maiden should be hers for the taking. (op 4-1 tchd 9-2 and 5-1 in a place)
Rio Grande, not seen since finishing unplaced in two starts back in May, didn't break too well but made up the ground smoothly mid-race and looked sure to cause the winner problems, but he showed an awkward head-carriage under pressure and folded tamely. He looks one to treat with caution. (op 5-4 tchd Evens and 11-8 in places)
Personal Touch, a stablemate of the runner-up, ran well to finish second under today's rider on his Hamilton debut last month, but this slightly shorter trip on a flatter track seemed to count against him. He should do better when again faced with a stiffer test. (op 4-1)
I'll Be Good was firmly put in his place by his less-exposed rivals, though his mark of 72 provides the benchmark. (op 14-1)
First Phase was just beaten in a six-runner Beverley maiden on her debut last month, but she became upset in the stalls and appeared to run her race before she had even started. (op 20-1)

5757 FUTURE SELECT RECRUITMENT CLAIMING STKS 1m 2f 88y
3:00 (3:00) (Class 4) 3-Y-O+ **£5,239** (£1,559; £779; £389) **Stalls** Low

Form RPR
0340 1 **Demolition**[18] 5185 7-9-4 90 PaulHanagan 9 90
(Richard Fahey) *trckd ldr: chal over 3f out: led over 1f out: drvn rt out* **5/4**[1]
6000 2 1/2 **Space War**[18] 5185 4-9-5 85 JamesSullivan 8 90
(Michael Easterby) *hld up in mid-div: effrt 3f out: styd on to chse wnr ins fnl f: no ex* **16/1**
0411 3 2 1/4 **Malice Or Mischief (IRE)**[20] 5118 3-8-7 78 LukeMorris 6 81
(J S Moore) *s.s: hld up: hdwy over 3f out: sn rdn: styd on fnl f: tk 3rd nr fin* **20/1**
0350 4 1/2 **Porgy**[16] 5250 6-9-0 86 ShaneKelly 3 80
(David Simcock) *t.k.h in rr: hdwy on ins 4f out: upsides over 1f out: sn rdn and fnd little* **9/2**[2]
6005 5 2 3/4 **Changing The Guard**[24] 4959 5-8-13 78 FrederikTylicki 10 74
(Richard Fahey) *mid-div: effrt on outside over 3f out: one pce fnl 2f* **9/1**
0526 6 nk **Overrule (USA)**[22] 5050 7-8-8 76 SeanLevey[(3)] 1 71
(Brian Ellison) *mid-div: effrt over 3f out: one pce fnl 2f* **14/1**
5111 7 1/2 **Stand Guard**[27] 4868 7-8-11 73 StevieDonohoe 5 70
(Noel Quinlan) *chsd ldrs: drvn over 3f out: hung rt over 1f out: one pce* **16/1**

2010 **8** *5* **Doctor Zhivago**[16] 5250 4-8-11 80 .... DeclanCannon(3) 12 64
(Ian McInnes) *led: edgd lft and hdd over 1f out: sn wknd* **18/1**

4100 **9** *2* **Quite Sparky**[43] 4325 4-8-11 83 .... (p) SilvestreDeSousa 13 57
(David O'Meara) *chsd ldrs: drvn over 3f out: lost pl over 1f out* **6/1**[3]

-000 **10** *15* **Best Prospect (IRE)**[9] 5440 9-8-11 71 .... (vt) PhillipMakin 7 28
(Michael Dods) *hood removed v late: s.s: hld up in last: drvn 3f out: no rspnse: bhd whn eased ins fnl f* **33/1**

2m 11.42s (-1.08) **Going Correction** +0.025s/f (Good)
WFA 3 from 4yo+ 7lb **10** Ran SP% **118.3**
Speed ratings (Par 105): **105,104,102,102,100 99,99,95,93,81**
Tote Swingers: 1&2 £7.30, 1&3 £5.30, 2&3 £33.60 CSF £25.58 TOTE £2.10: £1.20, £4.80, £2.20; EX 26.30 Trifecta £556.60 Pool: £932.70 - 1.24 winning units..Quite Sparky claimed by Mr M. E. Sowersby for £10,000.
Owner M Wormald **Bred** P D And Mrs Player **Trained** Musley Bank, N Yorks

FOCUS
This was quite a decent claimer featuring horses rated 71-91. The early pace was modest and it developed into a bit of a sprint. They raced centre-to-stands' side in the straight.
Stand Guard Official explanation: jockey said gelding hung right final 1 1/2f
Best Prospect(IRE) Official explanation: jockey said gelding was fractious in stalls, blindfold was caught on bridle and he failed to remove it first time.

5758 BETFAIR SUPPORTS GO RACING IN YORKSHIRE STKS (H'CAP) 6f
3:30 (3:31) (Class 2) (0-100,95) 3-Y-O+ **£11,644** (£3,465; £1,731; £865) **Stalls** Centre

Form RPR

6360 **1** **Internationaldebut (IRE)**[22] 5032 6-8-13 87 .... FrederikTylicki 13 98
(Paul Midgley) *mid-div: hdwy and nt clr run 2f out: styd on wl fnl f: led nr fin* **12/1**

0034 **2** *½* **Parisian Pyramid (IRE)**[22] 5060 5-9-5 93 .... PhillipMakin 2 102+
(Kevin Ryan) *mid-div: towards far side: gd hdwy and n.m.r over 1f out: sn chsng ldrs: tk 3rd nr line* **9/2**[1]

3301 **3** *¾* **Verinco**[18] 5163 5-8-12 93 .... (v) JustinNewman(7) 8 100
(Bryan Smart) *led: wnt clr over 2f out: wknd and hdd fnl 50yds* **18/1**

3000 **4** *1 ½* **Johannes (IRE)**[18] 5180 8-9-1 89 .... TonyHamilton 11 91
(Richard Fahey) *mid-div: hdwy over 1f out: styd on same pce last 100yds* **25/1**

3400 **5** *nse* **Fathsta (IRE)**[22] 5060 6-9-3 91 .... SilvestreDeSousa 12 93
(David Simcock) *mid-div: stands' side: hdwy 2f out: styd on wl last 150yds* **13/2**[2]

0000 **6** *¾* **Mass Rally (IRE)**[22] 5032 4-9-0 88 .... (v) TomEaves 15 88
(Michael Dods) *s.i.s: in rr stands' side: hdwy 2f out: kpt on ins fnl f* **50/1**

2503 **7** *nk* **Baby Strange**[15] 5278 7-9-0 88 .... RobbieFitzpatrick 7 87
(Derek Shaw) *mid-div: swtchd lft and hdwy on outer over 1f out: kpt on: nvr nr to chal* **18/1**

1100 **8** *1* **Orpsie Boy (IRE)**[22] 5032 8-8-13 87 .... JamesSullivan 17 82
(Ruth Carr) *in rr: hdwy over 1f out: kpt on last 100yds* **50/1**

210 **9** *hd* **Capone (IRE)**[8] 5481 6-9-5 93 .... ShaneKelly 16 88
(David Nicholls) *dwlt: mid-div: kpt on fnl 2f: nvr a threat* **25/1**

6030 **10** *nk* **Midnight Martini**[18] 5180 4-9-0 88 .... GrahamGibbons 1 82
(Tim Easterby) *chsd ldr: fdd appr fnl f* **12/1**

2320 **11** *1 ½* **Whozthecat (IRE)**[22] 5033 4-8-13 87 .... (v) SebSanders 6 76
(Declan Carroll) *chsd ldrs: wknd jst ins fnl f* **14/1**

0300 **12** *1* **King Of Eden (IRE)**[2] 5684 5-8-12 86 .... AndrewMullen 19 72
(Eric Alston) *s.i.s: in rr: hdwy stands' side 2f out: nvr nr ldrs* **40/1**

2500 **13** *½* **Singeur (IRE)**[43] 4346 4-9-6 94 .... LeeNewman 3 78
(Robin Bastiman) *mid-div: towards far side: effrt over 2f out: wknd over 1f out* **16/1**

3000 **14** *shd* **Striking Spirit**[22] 5060 6-9-0 91 .... JohnFahy(3) 14 75
(Tim Easterby) *chsd ldrs stands' side: lost pl over 1f out* **16/1**

2260 **15** *2 ½* **Cocktail Charlie**[15] 5288 3-9-4 94 .... (p) DavidAllan 10 70
(Tim Easterby) *prom: drvn over 2f out: wknd 2f out* **12/1**

331 **16** *2 ¼* **Valery Borzov (IRE)**[9] 5434 7-9-2 90 .... (v) PaulHanagan 18 59
(Richard Fahey) *chsd ldr: wknd fnl f* **8/1**[3]

000- **17** *6* **Ingleby Lady**[400] 4576 5-9-7 95 .... DanielTudhope 9 45
(David O'Meara) *chsd ldrs: wknd over 1f out* **16/1**

4105 **18** *nk* **Piazza San Pietro**[52] 3996 5-9-5 93 .... MartinLane 20 42
(Andrew Haynes) *s.i.s: a bhd* **33/1**

0504 **19** *8* **Joseph Henry**[36] 4531 9-9-2 90 .... AdrianNicholls 5 13
(David Nicholls) *[illegible] hung lft and wknd over 1f out: eased towards fin* **20/1**

5003 **20** *10* **Swilly Ferry (USA)**[7] 5508 4-9-1 89 .... (b) WilliamCarson 4 —
(Charles Hills) *chsd ldrs towards far side: lost pl over 2f out: bhd whn eased ins fnl f* **14/1**

1m 12.99s (1.09) **Going Correction** +0.375s/f (Good)
WFA 3 from 4yo+ 2lb **20** Ran SP% **129.0**
Speed ratings (Par 109): **107,106,105,103,103 102,101,100,100,99 97,96,95,95,92 89,81,81,70,57**
Tote Swingers: 1&2 £15.10, 1&3 £52.10, 2&3 £13.70 CSF £62.51 CT £1030.84 TOTE £15.70: £3.80, £1.70, £3.90, £6.80; EX 94.30 Trifecta £1755.30 Part won. Pool: £932.70 - 0.60 winning units..
Owner A Taylor Jnr **Bred** Ennistown Stud **Trained** Westow, N Yorks

FOCUS
A red-hot sprint handicap in which the main action unfolded down the centre of the track. There was no hanging about.

NOTEBOOK
Internationaldebut(IRE) came into this on a losing run of 31 and appeared to need a stiffer test than this, but the strong pace gave him something to run at. He did have to rather thread his way through to make his effort, but was out in the clear in plenty of time and came home strongly. His overall profile doesn't make him an ideal candidate for a follow up, however. (op 14-1)
Parisian Pyramid(IRE) was off the same mark as when 'winning' the race on his side in the Great St Wilfrid and he did well to finish so close here as he still had plenty to do 1f out, but finished in great style. He isn't enjoying much luck at present, but could be just the type to pop up in one of the big sprint handicaps at Ayr. (op 5-1)
Verinco ◆ set a scorching pace and, having established a clear advantage at halfway, it seemed as though he might not be caught, but he became legless well inside the last furlong and was swamped by the front pair inside the last 50 yards. This was still a smart effort considering he was put up 10lb for last month's easy Carlisle success and, as he has gained all five career victories over the minimum trip, he could take some catching back at 5f even off this sort of mark. (tchd 16-1)
Johannes(IRE) is now on a losing run of 17, but this was an improvement on recent efforts as he was still there with every chance 1f out. He still looks to have a decent prize in him.
Fathsta(IRE) ◆, in the same ownership as the runner-up, hasn't enjoyed much luck recently and seemed to struggle to go the pace here, but finished well towards the near side. He could be another interesting one for Ayr, especially as he seems to go on any ground. (op 7-1)
Mass Rally(IRE) ◆ hadn't shown much for his new yard this year and had never raced over a trip this short before, so he did well as he missed the break before running on late. He is one to keep an eye on.
Baby Strange, back over probably his best trip, can be given credit as he was forced to switch towards the far side of the field to make his final effort, away from the main action. (op 16-1)
Orpsie Boy(IRE) still looks on a stiff mark, but he was noted doing some good late work and as he has won over 7f may be worth returning to that trip.
Capone(IRE) ◆, 8lb higher than when winning on Polytrack two starts back, travelled strongly into the race and looked a danger 1f out before his effort flattened out. This was only his fourth start for the Nicholls yard and he could be another one to keep in mind for something at Ayr.
Joseph Henry Official explanation: jockey said gelding hung left-handed

5759 CASTLES UK EDUCATIONAL AND RESIDENTIAL FURNITURE STKS (H'CAP) 2m 88y
4:00 (4:00) (Class 4) (0-85,83) 3-Y-O+ **£5,239** (£1,559; £779; £389) **Stalls** Low

Form RPR

0246 **1** **Bow To No One (IRE)**[17] 5221 5-9-10 79 .... MartinLane 13 87
(Alan Jarvis) *hld up in rr: hdwy stands' side over 2f out: chsng ldrs appr fnl f: styd on to ld last 50yds* **8/1**[3]

3333 **2** *½* **Bollin Greta**[22] 5035 6-9-13 82 .... (t) DavidAllan 11 89
(Tim Easterby) *s.i.s: sn mid-div: hdwy over 3f out: edgd lft and led over 1f out: hdd and no ex clsng stages* **6/1**[2]

4112 **3** *½* **Beat The Shower**[9] 5453 5-9-7 76 .... PaulHanagan 8 82
(Peter Niven) *hld up in rr: drvn over 4f out: gd hdwy over 1f out: styd on wl towards fin* **8/1**[3]

1525 **4** *hd* **Riptide**[21] 5079 5-9-1 70 .... (v) JamieGoldstein 3 76
(Michael Scudamore) *trckd ldr: led after 3f: hdd over 1f out: kpt on same pce ins fnl f* **12/1**

2060 **5** *nk* **Magicalmysterytour (IRE)**[17] 5221 8-9-8 77 .... StevieDonohoe 5 83
(Willie Musson) *hld up in mid-div: effrt over 3f out: styd on fnl f: nt rch ldrs* **12/1**

541 **6** *3 ¼* **Boss's Destination**[9] 5453 4-9-10 79 .... PJMcDonald 2 81
(Alan Swinbank) *t.k.h: led 3f: chal over 3f out: wknd appr fnl f* **2/1**[1]

5000 **7** *1 ¾* **L Frank Baum (IRE)**[20] 5102 4-9-11 80 .... DavidProbert 12 80
(Gay Kelleway) *sn chsng ldrs: wknd over 1f out* **20/1**

043/ **8** *½* **Mr Crystal (FR)**[574] 6676 7-9-7 76 .... FrederikTylicki 9 75
(Micky Hammond) *mid-div: hdwy 7f out: sn chsng ldrs: wknd over 1f out* **33/1**

3334 **9** *hd* **Descaro (USA)**[9] 5453 5-9-1 70 .... DanielTudhope 6 69
(David O'Meara) *hld up in rr: effrt 3f out: nvr nr ldrs* **12/1**

0050 **10** *2 ¼* **Ejteyaaz**[26] 4879 4-8-11 69 .... LeeTopliss(3) 4 65
(Richard Fahey) *hld up in tch: hdwy 6f out: chsng ldrs over 3f out: wknd wl over 1f out* **16/1**

6310 **11** *20* **Mister Angry (IRE)**[9] 5448 4-10-0 83 .... SilvestreDeSousa 1 55
(Mark Johnston) *chsd ldrs: drvn over 4f out: lost pl over 3f out: eased whn bhd ins fnl f: t.o* **9/1**

023- **12** *16* **Sphinx (FR)**[193] 7226 13-9-1 70 .... (b) TonyHamilton 10 23
(Edwin Tuer) *trckd ldrs: drvn 4f out: lost pl over 2f out: bhd whn eased ins fnl f: t.o* **33/1**

3m 41.88s (7.38) **Going Correction** +0.025s/f (Good) **12** Ran SP% **119.4**
Speed ratings (Par 105): **82,81,81,81,81 79,78,78,78,77 67,59**
Tote Swingers: 1&2 £10.00, 1&3 £8.00, 2&3 £4.40 CSF £54.71 CT £400.47 TOTE £9.80: £2.10, £2.60, £2.40; EX 63.20 Trifecta £253.30 Pool: £958.70 - 2.80 winning units..
Owner A L R Morton **Bred** Albert Conneally **Trained** Twyford, Bucks

FOCUS
This staying event was run at a dawdle and the first five finished in a heap, so not form to rely on. Despite that, the first three home came from well off the pace.

5760 WATT FENCES STKS (H'CAP) 7f
4:30 (4:32) (Class 4) (0-80,84) 3-Y-O+ **£5,239** (£1,559; £779; £389) **Stalls** Low

Form RPR

1111 **1** **Blues Jazz**[26] 4876 5-8-12 71 .... GarryWhillans(5) 18 87+
(Ian Semple) *in rr: gd hdwy on outer 2f out: styd on strly to ld and forged clr fnl 75yds* **8/1**[3]

3565 **2** *2 ¼* **Illustrious Prince (IRE)**[21] 5083 4-8-13 72 .... NeilFarley(5) 9 82
(Declan Carroll) *chsd ldrs: drvn over 3f out: kpt on to ld last 100yds: sn hdd and no ex* **11/1**

2265 **3** *1 ¼* **Sunrise Safari (IRE)**[18] 5162 8-9-7 78 .... (v) LeeTopliss(3) 13 85
(Richard Fahey) *chsd ldrs on outer: styd on same pce ins fnl f* **16/1**

2101 **4** *½* **Caranbola**[25] 4900 5-9-10 78 .... TomEaves 5 83
(Mel Brittain) *chsd ldr: led over 1f out: led: hdd and no ex last 100yds* **14/1**

4054 **5** *½* **Rough Rock (IRE)**[7] 5516 6-9-4 75 .... KieranO'Neill(3) 12 79
(Chris Dwyer) *in rr: hdwy over 2f out: styd on ins fnl f* **12/1**

6005 **6** *2* **Fishforcompliments**[43] 4310 7-9-3 71 .... PaulHanagan 2 69
(Richard Fahey) *drvn to chse ldrs: dropped bk over 4f out: hdwy over 2f out: chal over 1f out: fdd last 75yds* **9/2**[1]

03-0 **7** *1 ½* **Steel Stockholder**[1] 5728 5-8-11 65 .... PhillipMakin 1 59
(Mel Brittain) *trckd ldrs on inner: keen and stdd towards rr after 1f: hdwy 2f out: kpt on ins fnl f* **20/1**

0021 **8** *½* **Diablo Dancer**[18] 5164 3-8-13 71 .... DanielTudhope 17 62
(Tim Walford) *mid-div: on outer: drvn over 2f out: nvr a factor* **5/1**[2]

-364 **9** *½* **Riverdale (IRE)**[9] 5456 3-9-3 75 .... (v[1]) SilvestreDeSousa 3 65
(Nigel Tinkler) *chsd ldrs: rdn and hung lft over 2f out: fdd appr fnl f* **10/1**

0110 **10** *2 ¾* **Mandalay King (IRE)**[52] 4013 6-9-2 77 .... (p) JustinNewman(7) 4 61
(Marjorie Fife) *in rr: gd hdwy over 2f out: chsng ldrs over 1f out: wknd jst ins fnl f* **20/1**

3665 **11** *2 ¼* **Diman Waters (IRE)**[8] 5465 4-9-7 75 .... ShaneKelly 14 53
(Eric Alston) *chsd ldrs on outer: wknd wl over 1f out* **18/1**

1000 **12** *1 ¾* **Powerful Pierre**[8] 5465 4-8-11 68 .... (v) DeclanCannon(3) 20 41
(Ian McInnes) *in rr on outer: sn drvn along: nvr on terms* **50/1**

1120 **13** *¾* **Dhhamaan (IRE)**[9] 5455 6-9-1 69 .... (b) PJMcDonald 10 40
(Ruth Carr) *led: hdd over 1f out: 8th and wkng whn heavily eased last 75yds* **16/1**

0006 **14** *nk* **Iceblast**[11] 5370 3-8-7 72 .... DavidSimmonson(7) 7 41
(Michael Easterby) *in rr: sme hdwy over 2f out: nvr on terms* **16/1**

110- **15** *2* **Signore Momento (IRE)**[373] 5495 5-9-9 77 .... (tp) AndrewElliott 6 42
(Amy Weaver) *a towards rr* **33/1**

2410 **16** *2* **Moral Issue**[20] 5109 3-8-10 71 .... PatrickDonaghy(3) 8 29
(Jedd O'Keeffe) *chsd ldrs: lost pl over 1f out* **28/1**

005 **17** *½* **Not My Choice (IRE)**[12] 5341 6-9-9 77 .... MichaelStainton 11 35
(David C Griffiths) *prom: effrt over 2f out: sn wknd* **33/1**

0630 **18** *2 ¼* **My Gacho (IRE)**[36] 4537 9-9-9 77 .... (b) AdrianNicholls 15 29
(David Nicholls) *rrd s: in rr on outer* **20/1**

1m 27.0s (1.70) **Going Correction** +0.375s/f (Good)
WFA 3 from 4yo+ 4lb **18** Ran SP% **126.2**
Speed ratings (Par 105): **105,102,101,100,99 97,95,95,94,91 89,87,86,85,83 81,80,78**
Tote Swingers: 1&2 £19.70, 1&3 £16.70, 2&3 £32.80 CSF £86.83 CT £1442.22 TOTE £9.60: £2.90, £2.90, £4.70, £4.80; EX 122.60 Trifecta £586.90 Part won. Pool: £793.22 - 0.10 winning units..

Owner Robert Reid **Bred** David Sugars And Bob Parker **Trained** Carluke, S Lanarks
■ Stewards' Enquiry : Neil Farley caution: used whip with excessive frequency.
FOCUS
A fair handicap run at a decent pace and fiercely competitive.
Riverdale(IRE) Official explanation: jockey said gelding hung left-handed
Dhhamaan(IRE) Official explanation: trainer said gelding finished distressed

5761 FUTURE CLEANING SERVICES APPRENTICE STKS (H'CAP) 1m 4f
5:00 (5:04) (Class 4) (0-80,80) 4-Y-0+ £5,239 (£1,559; £779; £389) Stalls Low

Form RPR
160- **1** **Alsahil (USA)**[296] 7061 5-8-7 **69**........ JamesRogers(3) 3 80
(Micky Hammond) *mde all: rdn over 2f out: hld on gamely* **25/1**
606- **2** ½ **Red Jade**[274] 7698 6-9-7 **80**........ LeeTopliss 10 90
(Richard Fahey) *chsd ldrs: chal over 1f out: no ex towards fin* **5/1**[2]
2400 **3** 11 **Comedy Act**[17] 5221 4-9-2 **80**........ DarylByrne(5) 9 72
(Mark Johnston) *chsd ldrs: drvn over 3f out: one pce over 1f out* **9/1**
514 **4** ¾ **Fossgate**[25] 4901 10-8-13 **75**........ ShaneBKelly(3) 11 66
(James Bethell) *hld up in rr: hdwy over 5f out: brought stands' side to r alone 3f out: sn chsng ldrs: one pce over 1f out* **11/1**
0112 **5** ½ **Carragold**[13] 5311 5-8-7 **66**........ JamesSullivan 12 56
(Mel Brittain) *chsd ldrs: outpcd and lost pl over 2f out: kpt on fnl f* **6/1**[3]
3312 **6** ½ **Broughtons Paradis (IRE)**[24] 4962 5-8-13 **72**........ AdamBeschizza 2 62
(Willie Musson) *hld up in rr: hdwy whn hmpd and swtchd rt over 2f out: one pce over 1f out* **5/1**[2]
-225 **7** 4 ½ **Royal Swain (IRE)**[114] 2071 5-9-0 **78**........ GarryWhillans(5) 5 60
(Alan Swinbank) *trckd ldrs: edgd lft over 2f out: wknd over 1f out* **3/1**[1]
1036 **8** nk **Cotton King**[1] 5729 4-9-4 **77**........(vt) SophieDoyle 7 59
(Tobias B P Coles) *rrd s: chsd ldrs: checked over 6f out: outpcd over 3f out: wknd over 1f out* **10/1**
055 **9** 1 ¼ **Jacob McCandles**[23] 4985 4-8-7 **66**........ JohnFahy 4 46
(David Barron) *t.k.h in rr: hdwy on inner over 3f out: wknd over 1f out* **11/1**
0016 **10** 4 ½ **Urban Space**[20] 5110 5-8-9 **71**........ RyanPowell(3) 1 44
(John Flint) *chsd ldrs: drvn over 3f out: hmpd over 2f out: sn wknd* **16/1**
2m 31.9s (-1.30) **Going Correction** +0.025s/f (Good) 10 Ran SP% **118.1**
Speed ratings (Par 105): **105,104,97,96,96 96,93,92,92,89**
Tote Swingers: 1&2 £19.30, 1&3 £28.60, 2&3 £10.20 CSF £147.63 CT £1240.30 TOTE £35.70: £7.40, £2.20, £3.20; EX 229.80 Trifecta £725.70 Part won. Pool: £980.75 - 0.54 winning units..
Owner R D Bickenson **Bred** Shadwell Farm LLC **Trained** Middleham Moor, N Yorks
■ Stewards' Enquiry : Garry Whillans two-day ban: careless riding (Sep 18-19)
FOCUS
An ordinary apprentice handicap in which the riders made use of the full width of the track in the home straight and the first two, who were both reappearing from long absences, pulled miles clear.
T/Jkpt: Not won. T/Plt: £119.30 to a £1 stake. Pool:£130,519.00 - 798.47 winning tickets T/Qpdt: £30.80 to a £1 stake. Pool:£11,153.00 - 267.72 winning tickets WG

5762 - 5769a (Foreign Racing) - See Raceform Interactive

5694 LONGCHAMP (R-H)
Sunday, September 4

OFFICIAL GOING: Turf: very soft

5770a PRIX LA ROCHETTE (GROUP 3) (2YO) (TURF) 7f
1:00 (12:00) 2-Y-0 £39,310 (£15,172; £7,241; £4,827; £2,413)

RPR
1 **Sofast (FR)**[14] 5305 2-8-11 0........ OlivierPeslier 6 112+
(F Head, France) *settled 6th: shkn up over 1 1/2f out: str run on outside fnl f to ld cl home under hands and heels* **3/1**[2]
2 ½ **Mac Row (IRE)**[18] 5194 2-8-11 0........ IoritzMendizabal 1 111
(J-C Rouget, France) *racd freely in 2nd: moved out to chal ldr 1f out: led fnl 110yds: r.o but hdd cl home* **8/1**
3 ¾ **American Devil (FR)**[52] 4036 2-8-11 0........ RonanThomas 3 109
(J Van Handenhove, France) *led: qcknd ins fnl 1 1/2f: sn rdn: hdd fnl 110yds: no ex* **6/4**[1]
4 2 ½ **Regina Ejina (FR)**[26] 2-8-8 0........ GregoryBenoist 4 100
(M Delzangles, France) *broke wl and t.k.h: sn restrained on outside in 4th: in tch and niggled ins fnl 2f: rdn and nt quickien fnl f* **14/1**
5 ½ **Lidari (FR)**[20] 5130 2-8-11 0........ GeraldMosse 7 101
(J-C Rouget, France) *slowly away: settled in last: swtchd outside and rdn 2f out: kpt on fnl f but nt pce to rch ldrs* **6/1**[3]
6 shd **Vaniloquio (IRE)**[20] 5130 2-8-11 0........ ThierryThulliez 5 101
(N Clement, France) *settled in 3rd: effrt on outside of two ldrs ins fnl 2f: rdn and outpcd appr fnl f* **13/2**
7 2 **Private Riviera**[12] 5365 2-8-8 0........ Pierre-CharlesBoudot 2 93
(C Boutin, France) *w.w in tch (4th or 5th much of the way): pushed along 1 1/2f out: nt qckn fnl f* **25/1**
1m 25.24s (4.54) **Going Correction** +0.80s/f (Soft) 7 Ran SP% **114.2**
Speed ratings: **106,105,104,101,101 101,98**
WIN (incl. 1 euro stake): 3.20. PLACES: 2.30, 5.80. SF: 31.90.
Owner Wertheimer & Frere **Bred** Wertheimer Et Frere **Trained** France
FOCUS
This race has posted strong averages for the grade over the last five years and this form is rated positively with that in mind.
NOTEBOOK
Sofast(FR) paid a quick tribute to his Prix Morny conqueror Dabirsim. The winner did it in good style and may gor for the Prix Jean-Luc Lagardere.

5771a PRIX DE LUTECE (GROUP 3) (3YO) (TURF) 1m 7f
1:30 (12:00) 3-Y-0 £34,482 (£13,793; £10,344; £6,896; £3,448)

RPR
1 **Pacifique (IRE)**[23] 5027 3-8-8 0........ GeraldMosse 4 104
(A De Royer-Dupre, France) *broke wl and racd keenly: racd w bk trio: last and pushed along ins fnl 3f: styng on whn sltly impeded and swtchd outside rival over 1 1/2f out: rdn and wnt 2nd ins fnl f: led 110yds out: a holding runner-up* **6/4**[1]
2 nk **Miss Lago (IRE)**[20] 5131 3-8-6 0........ AnthonyCrastus 1 102
(E Lellouche, France) *w.w in last but in tch: effrt on outside ins fnl 3f: hdwy u.p fr 2f out: wnt 4th appr fnl f: styd on u.p but a hld by wnr* **10/1**
3 ½ **Ibicenco (GER)**[63] 3672 3-8-11 0........ ADeVries 6 106
(J Hirschberger, Germany) *trckd ldr on outside: wnt upside ldr 4f out: led 3f out: pushed along and hdd 2 1/2f out: rallied u.p to ld again 1 1/2f out: hdd fnl 110yds: no ex* **6/1**[3]
4 4 **Miss Crissy (IRE)**[21] 5093 3-8-8 0........ GregoryBenoist 5 99
(M Delzangles, France) *slowly away but sn rcvrd grnd and settled 3rd: rdn and responded to ld 2 1/2f out: hdd 1 1/2f out: wknd u.p fnl f* **11/4**[2]
5 2 ½ **Manjakani**[20] 5131 3-8-9 0........ MickaelBarzalona 2 97
(A Fabre, France) *settled midfield (disp 3rd at times early on): pushed along and nt qckn over 1 1/2f out: fdd ins fnl f* **10/1**
6 3 **Landscape (FR)**[31] 3-8-10 0 ow1........(p) OlivierPeslier 7 95
(J E Pease, France) *in bk three in tch: hrd rdn over 1 1/2f out: no imp* **12/1**
7 dist **Girevole**[27] 3-8-9 0........ MaximeGuyon 3 —
(A Fabre, France) *led: jnd 4f out: hdd 3f out: pushed along and nt qckn 2 1/2f out: wknd fnl 1 1/2f* **10/1**
3m 22.06s (6.06) **Going Correction** +0.80s/f (Soft) 7 Ran SP% **115.9**
Speed ratings: **115,114,114,112,111 109,—**
WIN (incl. 1 euro stake): 2.50. PLACES: 1.60, 3.00. SF: 12.20.
Owner Skymarc Farm & Ecurie des Monceaux **Bred** Skymarc Farm, Ecurie Des Monceaux **Trained** Chantilly, France

NOTEBOOK
Pacifique(IRE), upped in distance, ran out a cosy winner. A progressive filly, she may drop back in trip for the Prix de Royallieu.

5772a PRIX DU PIN (GROUP 3) (3YO+) (TURF) 7f
2:40 (12:00) 3-Y-0+ £34,482 (£13,793; £10,344; £6,896; £3,448)

RPR
1 **Best Dating (IRE)**[20] 5127 4-9-1 0........ GregoryBenoist 7 114
(S Wattel, France) *niggled early to go pce: racd towards rr: last and pushed along ins fnl 2f: r.o wl on outside fnl f: led cl home* **9/2**[3]
2 ¾ **Evaporation (FR)**[28] 4838 4-8-11 0........ OlivierPeslier 5 108
(C Laffon-Parias, France) *racd keenly in midfield: settled 5th at 1/2-way: cl 4th gng wl ent fnl f: sn rdn: qcknd to ld 110yds out: hdd cl home* **9/4**[1]
3 ¾ **Sommerabend**[62] 3699 4-9-1 0........ GeraldMosse 3 110
(U Stoltefuss, Germany) *w ldrs early: settled midfield 1/2-way: 5th and in tch 2f out: pushed along and styng on fr 1 1/2f out: 3rd and hrd rdn ins fnl f: no ex fnl 50yds* **6/1**
4 nk **Blue Soave (FR)**[35] 4595 3-8-11 0........ ThierryThulliez 6 107
(F Chappet, France) *w ldrs: trcking ldr 3f out: gng wl and led ins fnl 2f: 2 l ld appr fnl f: hdd 110yds out: no ex* **9/1**
5 nk **Venomous**[35] 4595 3-8-11 0........ ThierryJarnet 9 106
(T Clout, France) *settled towards rr on outside: hdwy 2f out: sn hrd rdn: nt pce to chal ldrs* **3/1**[2]
6 1 ½ **Konig Concorde (GER)**[35] 6-9-1 0........ DPorcu 4 104
(C Sprengel, Germany) *wl away and racd w ldrs: 3rd and gng wl enough over 2f out: 2nd and rdn appr fnl f: nt qckn* **20/1**
7 nse **Nova Step**[23] 5028 3-8-8 0........ StephanePasquier 8 99
(F Rohaut, France) *settled towards rr: 6th and gng smoothly 2 1/2f out: pushed along and effrt ent fnl f: wknd last 100yds* **12/1**
8 10 **Espirita (FR)**[23] 5028 3-8-8 0........ AnthonyCrastus 2 72
(E Lellouche, France) *racd towards rr: rdn 2f out: no imp: wl btn ent fnl f: heavily eased* **12/1**
9 8 **Invincible Viking (IRE)**[24] 3-8-11 0........(b) DominiqueBoeuf 1 54
(Y Barberot, France) *led: hrd rdn over 2f out: sn hdd: wknd qckly: eased* **33/1**
1m 24.02s (3.32) **Going Correction** +0.80s/f (Soft)
WFA 3 from 4yo+ 4lb 9 Ran SP% **121.3**
Speed ratings: **113,112,111,110,110 108,108,97,88**
WIN (incl. 1 euro stake): 5.80. PLACES: 1.60, 1.30, 1.70. DF: 7.20. SF: 19.10.
Owner Jean-Jacques Rabineau **Bred** Gerrardstown Stud **Trained** France

NOTEBOOK
Best Dating(IRE) stormed down the outside to score, and may return for the Prix Daniel Wildenstein on Arc weekend.

5749 BADEN-BADEN (L-H)
Sunday, September 4

OFFICIAL GOING: Turf: very soft

5773a LONGINES GROSSER PREIS VON BADEN (GROUP 1) (3YO+) (TURF) 1m 4f
3:50 (3:56) 3-Y-0+ £129,310 (£51,724; £21,551; £12,931)

RPR
1 **Danedream (GER)**[42] 4374 3-8-8 0........ AStarke 2 124
(P Schiergen, Germany) *settled 2nd: 3 l bhd ldr: travelled smoothly through fnl turn: cruised into ld 2f out: sn wnt clr: extended advantage all the way to fin: easily* **19/10**[2]
2 6 **Night Magic (GER)**[42] 4374 5-9-3 0........ KKerekes 1 114
(W Figge, Germany) *broke fast: sn led: set str pce: sn clr: led into st: hdd 2f out: r.o but no answer to wnr: easily 2nd best* **22/5**[3]
3 7 **Joshua Tree (IRE)**[22] 5055 4-9-6 0........ WilliamBuick 5 106
(Marco Botti) *settled 4th: rdn and r.o wl in st to go 3rd but no match for first two: jst hld on for 3rd on line* **23/5**
4 hd **Maria Royal (IRE)**[33] 4653 4-9-3 0........ THellier 6 103
(A De Royer-Dupre, France) *bkmarker fr s: rdn and r.o in st: jst missed 3rd on line* **71/10**
5 4 ½ **Silvaner (GER)**[21] 5092 3-8-11 0........ FilipMinarik 1 99
(P Schiergen, Germany) *settled 3rd: rdn and sn btn in st* **10/1**
6 hd **Waldpark (GER)**[20] 5128 3-8-11 0........ EPedroza 3 98
(A Wohler, Germany) *unsettled during preliminaries: settled towards rr: rdn but no ex in st: sn btn* **8/5**[1]
2m 37.52s (4.06)
WFA 3 from 4yo+ 9lb 6 Ran SP% **130.8**
WIN (incl. 10 euro stake): 29. PLACES: 17, 20. SF: 123.
Owner Gestut Burg Eberstein **Bred** Gestut Brummerhof **Trained** Germany

NOTEBOOK
Danedream(GER) has really hit form with a vengeance and is a filly well worth following wherever she runs next. One option would be to supplement her for the Arc or the Breeders Cup Filly & Mare Turf, but she is also entered in two very valuable races in Japan.
Night Magic(GER) hasn't quite looked as good as she has done in the past, but she ensured the race was run at a good gallop and did more than enough to suggest she was second best on the day.
Joshua Tree(IRE) wouldn't have liked this going and was one-paced when the tempo increased.
Waldpark(GER), said to be upset during the preliminaries, ran terribly and is starting to look over the top.

5774 - 5775a & 5778a - (Foreign Racing) - See Raceform Interactive

5753 VELIEFENDI

Sunday, September 4

OFFICIAL GOING: Turf: good

5776a INTERNATIONAL BOSPHORUS CUP (GROUP 2) (3YO+) (TURF) 1m 4f
2:00 (12:00) 3-Y-0+ £155,172 (£62,068; £31,034; £15,517)

RPR

1 **Indian Days**[37] 4492 6-9-6 0 AlanMunro 4 114
(James Given) *settled towards rr: 6th and rail 3f out: shkn up and swtchd outside over 2f out: styng on u.p whn gap clsd and forced to switch ins: blocked again and swtchd outside appr last f: r.o wl fnl 150yds to ld* **4/1**

2 nk **Campanologist (USA)**[37] 4492 6-9-6 0 FrankieDettori 8 114
(Saeed Bin Suroor) *w.w in 7th: 5th and styng on ent fnl 3f: pushed along and swtchd outside over 2f out: styd on to ld appr fnl f: r.o but hdd fnl strides* **31/20**[2]

3 1 1/2 **Superstition (FR)**[42] 4374 5-9-3 0 ASuborics 5 108
(Markus Klug, Germany) *led after 1 1/2f: hdd sn after and trckd ldr on rail: stl 2nd ent fnl 3f: led appr 2f out: sn rdn: hdd 1 1/2f out: 4th ent fnl f: kpt on again to claim 3rd cl home* **27/10**[3]

4 nk **Afsare**[59] 3775 4-9-6 0 (b) KierenFallon 2 111
(Luca Cumani) *t.k.h early: settled in 6th: 4th and travelling wl on rail 3f out: smooth prog to be cl 3rd 2f out: led briefly 1 1/2f out: hdd appr fnl f: nt qckn and lost 3rd cl home* **7/5**[1]

5 1 1/2 **Halicarnassus (IRE)**[15] 5285 7-9-6 0 HalisKaratas 1 108
(Mick Channon) *led early: hdd after 1 1/2f: settled in 4th: 3rd and pushed along 3f out: hrd rdn appr 2f out: nt qckn and one pce fnl f* **22/5**

6 1/2 **Hakkar (TUR)** 4-9-6 0 (b) YalcinAkagac 6 107
(B Dag, Turkey) *hld up in rr: 8th and hdwy u.p over 2 1/2f out: sn hrd rdn: kpt on wout qckning fnl 1 1/2f* **15/4**

7 11 **Smerc (TUR)** 4-9-6 0 AhmetCelik 7 90
(S Coskun, Turkey) *bhd: short-lived effrt on outside 3f out: wl btn fnl 2f* **18/1**

8 4 **Inspector (TUR)**[364] 5804 7-9-6 0 (b) SelimKaya 10 83
(K Saglam, Turkey) *led after 2f: hrd rdn 2 1/2f out: hdd appr 2f out: wknd and heavily eased fnl f* **18/5**

9 8 1/2 **Aydemirhan (TUR)** 4-9-6 0 (b) ErhanYavuz 3 70
(G Subasi, Turkey) *a bhd: eased fnl f* **138/10**

10 21 1/2 **Bambino (TUR)** 4-9-3 0 GokhanYildiz 9 32
(B Dag, Turkey) *w ldrs: rdn and wknd qckly over 4f out: t.o* **15/4**

2m 26.44s (-2.36) **10** Ran SP% **222.3**
PARI-MUTUEL (including 1Turkish lira stakes): WIN: 5.00; PLACE (first two): 1.10, 1.35; DF 10.45; SF 18.30.

Owner D J Fish **Bred** Mrs C Regalado-Gonzalez **Trained** Willoughton, Lincs

NOTEBOOK
Indian Days came from well off the pace to repeat last year's victory in this richly endowed event, sweeping down the outside when a gap came to nail Campanologist close home.
Campanologist(USA) forged ahead at the furlong marker and looked sure win, only to be denied on the line.
Afsare, tried in blinkers, travelled well before taking it up but could not hold off the challengers.
Halicarnassus(IRE), the 2009 winner and fourth last year, was having his final start before taking up stallion duties in Turkey.

5777a INTERNATIONAL TOPKAPI TROPHY (GROUP 2) (3YO+) (TURF) 1m
3:30 (12:00) 3-Y-0+ £232,758 (£93,103; £46,551; £23,275)

RPR

1 **Musir (AUS)**[22] 5046 5-9-6 0 ChristopheSoumillon 6 114+
(M F De Kock, South Africa) *hld up towards rr: smooth hdwy on outside 2 1/2f out: pushed along and qcknd to ld ins fnl 2f: wnt clr fnl f: eased cl home* **30/100**[1]

2 3 1/2 **Invisible Man**[17] 5218 5-9-6 0 (b) FrankieDettori 3 106
(Saeed Bin Suroor) *settled towards rr: 7th abt 10 l off ldr 3f out: tk clsr order: abt 4 l 5th and rdn 1 1/2f out: styd on u.p fnl f to take 2nd cl home: nt pce to trble wnr* **67/10**

3 nk **Indomito (GER)**[42] 4373 5-9-6 0 ASuborics 5 105
(A Wohler, Germany) *a in first four: 2nd and styng on appr 2f out: kpt on u.p but nt pce to chal wnr: lost 2nd cl home* **596/100**

4 3 1/2 **Dream Eater (IRE)**[15] 5282 6-9-6 0 (t) JimmyFortune 4 97
(Andrew Balding) *hld up in midfield: 6th on rail 3f out: rdn and nt qckn 2f out: kpt on fnl f but nt pce to rch ldrs* **63/20**[3]

5 2 **Midas Touch (TUR)** 4-9-6 0 (b) GokhanKocakaya 8 93
(S Tasbek, Turkey) *slowly away: last and hrd rdn over 3f out: kpt on fr 2f: nvr able to chal* **152/10**

6 1 1/2 **Kurtiniadis (IRE)**[71] 8-9-6 0 YalcinAkagac 1 89
(S Kulak, Turkey) *chsd ldrs: 3rd and rdn 3f out: nt qckn w ldrs over 1 1/2f out: wknd ins fnl f* **111/10**

7 1/2 **Astrakhan (TUR)**[71] 4-9-6 0 (b) HalisKaratas 2 88
(Z Temucin, Turkey) *led: shkn up and hdd ins fnl 2f: wknd last f and eased last 100yds* **31/20**[2]

8 4 **Vagabond Shoes (IRE)**[50] 4120 4-9-6 0 KierenFallon 7 79
(Y Durepaire, Spain) *rushed up to trck ldr: racd keenly: 2nd and bustled up 3f out: rdn and nt qckn 2f out: sn btn: last and eased fnl f* **77/20**

1m 33.58s (-1.75) **8** Ran SP% **202.6**
PARI-MUTUEL (including 1Turkish lira stakes): WIN: 1.30; DF 6.50; SF 6.65.

Owner Sheikh Mohammed Bin Khalifa Al Maktoum **Bred** Sheikh Mohammad Bin Khalifa Al Maktoum **Trained** South Africa

NOTEBOOK
Musir(AUS), who spent the summer in Newmarket and shaped with promise after a layoff in the Hungerford Stakes, slammed his rivals for an easy win in this valuable event.
Invisible Man bounced back from a disappointing run at York, just getting up for second.
Dream Eater(IRE), runner-up to Pressing in the last two runnings, was never able to mount a serious challenge but stayed on and only just missed the places.

5611 BATH (L-H)

Monday, September 5

OFFICIAL GOING: Good (8.3)
Wind: Strong half ahead Weather: Overcast, sunny periods

5779 LINDLEY GROUP MAIDEN AUCTION STKS 5f 11y
2:10 (2:15) (Class 6) 2-Y-0 £1,617 (£481; £240; £120) Stalls Centre

Form RPR

545 1 **Courtland Avenue (IRE)**[25] 4947 2-8-8 63 RichardKingscote 8 72+
(Jonathan Portman) *trckd ldr: drvn and styd on to ld fnl 120yds: readily* **4/1**

U340 2 1 1/2 **Lady Jameela**[9] 5464 2-8-9 73 EddieAhern 5 68
(Mick Channon) *sn slt ld: rdn over 1f out: hdd and outpcd fnl 120yds* **5/2**[2]

3 3/4 **Rode Two Destiny (IRE)** 2-8-9 0 FergusSweeney 6 65
(Peter Makin) *in tch: pushed along over 2f out: styd on towards outside over 1f out: kpt on ins fnl f nvr gng pce to chal* **9/4**[1]

0 4 shd **Trusting (IRE)**[17] 5232 2-8-3 0 CathyGannon 4 59
(Eve Johnson Houghton) *chsd ldrs: rdn and ev ch over 1f out: one pce ins fnl f* **12/1**

2 5 6 **Verus Delicia (IRE)**[20] 5147 2-8-2 0 KieranO'Neill(3) 1 39
(Patrick Morris) *pressed ldet: and stl ev ch over 1f out: wknd ins fnl f* **7/2**[3]

6 nk **Allegra Byron** 2-8-3 0 ow1 RossAtkinson(3) 9 39
(Jonathan Portman) *s.i.s: a outpcd* **16/1**

00 7 2 **Four Poorer (IRE)**[25] 4954 2-8-6 0 SophieDoyle(3) 7 35
(Jamie Osborne) *outpcd fr 1/2-way* **66/1**

8 14 **Cool Ice** 2-7-10 0 IanBurns(7) 2 —
(Ron Hodges) *led to s: green and wnt lft s: a wl bhd* **50/1**

64.69 secs (2.19) **Going Correction** +0.15s/f (Good) **8** Ran SP% **118.6**
Speed ratings (Par 93): **88,85,84,84,74 74,70,48**
toteswingers:1&2:£2.50, 2&3:£2.20, 1&3:£3.40 CSF £15.07 TOTE £5.00: £1.30, £1.20, £1.30; EX 17.40.

Owner Prof C D Green **Bred** Mrs Caroline Green **Trained** Compton, Berks

FOCUS
Rail realignment increased distances by about 12.5yds. After 3mm of rain overnight and 3mm more before racing the official going description was changed to Good. There was a fresh crosswind, half against the runners in the straight. A fair maiden auction and a fairly lively betting market.

NOTEBOOK
Courtland Avenue(IRE), the only non-female and rated 63 after three reasonable efforts, tracked the pace before coming through to get the better of his rivals fairly emphatically. He should be competitive in handicaps off a mark in the high-60s. (op 9-2)
Lady Jameela, who unseated her rider leaving the stalls when 1-5 on her only previous visit, set the standard after some fair efforts and ran her race but is not progressing. (op 9-4 tchd 3-1)
Rode Two Destiny(IRE), related to several good sprinters, including Golden Destiny, was heavily backed shortly before the off but missed the break slightly and was always struggling to catch up after that. She finished quite well though and can be expected to be sharper next time. (op 6-1)
Trusting(IRE) improved on her debut, keeping the winner company for much of the way, but was not able to stay with him in the closing stages. (op 10-1 tchd 9-1)
Verus Delicia(IRE), runner-up on her debut behind a very experienced rival, drifted out from favouritism but jumped well and helped make the running with the second before fading quite quickly late on. (op 11-4 tchd 5-2)

5780 AJK PREMIER FOOD COURTS MAIDEN STKS 5f 161y
2:40 (2:46) (Class 5) 3-Y-0+ £2,264 (£673; £336; £168) Stalls Centre

Form RPR

2242 1 **Suzy Alexander**[32] 4711 4-9-0 58 ChrisCatlin 2 69
(David Simcock) *mde all: pushed clr over 1f out: eased cl home: unchal* **11/8**[1]

0024 2 5 **Atia**[13] 5344 3-8-12 58 (p) RichardKingscote 8 52
(Jonathan Portman) *chsd wnr thrght: no ch fnl f and jst hld on for 2nd clsng stages* **5/2**[2]

3 shd **Sleep Dance** 3-8-12 0 CathyGannon 3 52+
(Eve Johnson Houghton) *s.i.s: towards rr: pushed along and hdwy fr 2f out: styd on wl ins fnl f to press for 2nd in the clsng stages: nvr any ch w wnr* **6/1**[3]

545 4 3 1/4 **Miakora**[19] 5176 3-8-12 52 ShaneKelly 4 41
(Michael Quinn) *t.k.h: chsd ldrs: rdn over 1f out: wknd ins fnl f* **14/1**

6535 5 shd **Lady Excellentia (IRE)**[13] 5344 3-8-12 43 LukeMorris 6 41
(Ronald Harris) *s.i.s: in rr: rdn and sme hdwy 2f out: nvr rchd ldrs: wknd ins fnl f* **20/1**

0525 6 3 **Lough Corrib (USA)**[125] 1801 3-9-3 53 (p) FrankieMcDonald 5 36
(Alastair Lidderdale) *in rr: rdn and swtchd to outside over 2f out: nvr gng pce to rch ldrs* **20/1**

65 7 2 **Coalburn**[12] 5377 3-9-3 0 MarkLawson 7 29
(Gary Harrison) *in rr: hdwy on outside over 2f out: sn in tch w ldrs: rdn and wknd over 1f out* **40/1**

0 8 6 **Two Bucks More**[55] 3950 3-8-10 0 JakePayne(7) 9 10
(Bill Turner) *chsd ldrs: rdn 3f out: wknd qckly 2f out* **80/1**

-000 9 3 **Ivory Trilogy (IRE)**[28] 4863 3-9-3 47 (b) JamesMillman 1 —
(Tim Etherington) *sn pushed along: wknd 3f out* **50/1**

1m 12.12s (0.92) **Going Correction** +0.15s/f (Good)
WFA 3 from 4yo 2lb **9** Ran SP% **110.7**
Speed ratings (Par 103): **99,92,92,87,87 83,81,73,69**
toteswingers:1&2:£1.90, 2&3:£2.50, 1&3:£2.20 CSF £4.27 TOTE £2.10: £1.10, £1.30, £1.80; EX 4.90.

Owner Mrs T A Foreman **Bred** Mrs T A Foreman **Trained** Newmarket, Suffolk

FOCUS
A very moderate maiden, with all bar one 3yos. That one was favourite, while they bet 16-1 bar three. The race went exactly as the market expected with the five fillies beating the four geldings. The time was reasonable and the winner rates back to his best.

5781 WEATHERBYS BLOODSTOCK INSURANCE H'CAP 5f 161y
3:10 (3:11) (Class 5) (0-75,75) 3-Y-0+ £2,264 (£673; £336; £168) Stalls Centre

Form RPR

4523 1 **Seamus Shindig**[8] 5513 9-8-8 67 AmyScott(5) 8 78
(Henry Candy) *in rr: hdwy over 1f out: qcknd to chse ldr ins fnl f: styd on wl to ld last stride* **7/1**[3]

-333 2 shd **Seeking Magic**[16] 5279 3-9-0 73 JohnFahy(3) 11 84
(Clive Cox) *in tch: hdwy 2f out: led appr fnl f: styd on u.p: ct last stride* **5/2**[1]

5666 3 1 3/4 **Shifting Star (IRE)**[25] 4967 6-9-7 75 (p) ChrisCatlin 3 80
(Walter Swinburn) *chsd ldrs rdn 2f out: one pce appr fnl f: styd on clsng stages to take one pce 3rd* **16/1**

6044 **4** 1 ¾ **Diapason (IRE)**[16] 5265 5-8-13 **67**..........................(t) RichardKingscote 6 66
(Tom Dascombe) *in rr: hdwy towards outside over 1f out: styd to take one pce 4th clsng stages* **14/1**

5000 **5** ¾ **Brandywell Boy (IRE)**[5] 5616 8-8-7 **64**..........................(p) BillyCray(3) 9 61
(Dominic Ffrench Davis) *sn in tch: drvn to chal 2f out: wknd jst ins fnl f* **40/1**

2103 **6** *shd* **Titus Gent**[31] 4742 6-8-11 **72**.......................... RaulDaSilva(7) 2 68
(Jeremy Gask) *restless stalls: broke wl: sn led: hdd appr fnl f: sn btn* **9/1**

0234 **7** ½ **Whiskey Junction**[10] 5425 7-9-0 **68**.......................... SebSanders 12 63
(Michael Quinn) *chsd ldrs on outside: rdn over 2f out: wknd ins fnl f* **11/1**

6503 **8** 1 **Belle Bayardo (IRE)**[12] 5378 3-9-5 **75**.......................... CathyGannon 4 66
(Ronald Harris) *in rr: hdwy on inner whn hmpd appr fnl f: no ch after* **28/1**

0122 **9** 3 ¼ **Sermons Mount (USA)**[5] 5616 5-9-5 **73**.......................... DaneO'Neill 5 54
(Peter Hedger) *w ldr: rdn 2f out: wknd over 1f out* **4/1**[2]

1640 **10** 2 ½ **Indian Shuffle (IRE)**[24] 5000 3-9-1 **71**.......................... EddieAhern 10 43
(Jonathan Portman) *chsd ldrs: rdn over 2f out: sn wknd* **22/1**

4522 **11** ½ **Triple Dream**[17] 5238 6-9-4 **72**..........................(tp) LiamKeniry 7 43
(Milton Bradley) *pressed ldrs tl upsides over 2f out: wknd rapidly wl over 1f out* **15/2**

1m 11.6s (0.40) **Going Correction** +0.15s/f (Good)
WFA 3 from 4yo+ 2lb 11 Ran SP% **114.0**
Speed ratings (Par 103): **103,102,100,98,97 97,96,95,90,87 86**
toteswingers:1&2:£3.90, 2&3:£9.40, 1&3:£13.10 CSF £23.46 CT £275.63 TOTE £8.90: £3.10, £1.20, £3.40; EX 27.80.
Owner Henry Candy **Bred** R S A Urquhart **Trained** Kingston Warren, Oxon

FOCUS
A fair handicap run 0.52secs faster than the preceding maiden and a close finish. Pretty straightforward form.
Triple Dream Official explanation: jockey said gelding moved poorly throughout

5782 WEATHERBYS BLOODSTOCK INSURANCE FILLIES' H'CAP 1m 3f 144y
3:40 (3:40) (Class 5) (0-75,75) 3-Y-O+ **£2,264** (£673; £336; £168) **Stalls** Low

Form RPR

023 **1** **Lily In Pink**[12] 5386 3-9-3 **75**.......................... EddieAhern 3 82
(Jonathan Portman) *hld up in rr: pushed along 3f out: hrd drvn fr 2f out: styd on towards outside over 1f out: r.o u.p: edgd lft clsng stages and bmpd: led last strides* **13/2**

-440 **2** *hd* **Shades Of Grey**[98] 2552 4-8-11 **63**.......................... JohnFahy(3) 7 70
(Clive Cox) *chsd ldrs: chal fr 2f out tl slt advantage 1f out: stl hrd pressed: jnd: edgd rt and bmpd clsng stages: hdd last strides* **9/1**

1220 **3** ½ **Undulant Way**[25] 4971 3-9-3 **75**.......................... PatDobbs 4 81
(Amanda Perrett) *in rr but in tch: rdn and hdwy fr 2f out: styd on wl clsng stages to take clsng 3rd last strides* **11/4**[1]

0641 **4** ½ **One Lucky Lady**[16] 5266 3-8-10 **73**.......................... MatthewLawson(5) 5 78
(Charles Hills) *chsd ldr to 5f out: pushed along 3f out: sn one pce: rallied and styd on again clsng stages whn n.m.r: nt rch ldrs* **11/4**[1]

412U **5** *shd* **Peira**[10] 5420 3-8-9 **67**.......................... LukeMorris 6 72
(Jane Chapple-Hyam) *chsd ldrs: wnt 2nd over 5f out: slt ld over 2f out: sn rdn and jnd: narrowly hdd 1f out: styd chalng tl fnl 120yds: no ex* **4/1**[3]

0165 **6** 5 **Sasheen**[24] 5002 4-9-4 **67**..........................(p) KierenFallon 8 63
(Jeremy Gask) *led tl hdd over 2f out: sn btn* **5/1**[2]

2m 32.05s (1.45) **Going Correction** +0.15s/f (Good)
WFA 3 from 4yo 9lb 6 Ran SP% **107.6**
Speed ratings (Par 100): **101,100,100,100,100 96**
toteswingers:1&2:£6.30, 2&3:£4.30, 1&3:£2.70 CSF £53.96 CT £171.12 TOTE £7.00: £2.30, £4.10; EX 40.40.
Owner Miss Sarah Lloyd **Bred** J Ford & Peter J Skinner **Trained** Compton, Berks

FOCUS
An ordinary but quite competitive fillies' handicap and the first five finished in a bunch. Improvement from the winner.

5783 DIGIBET.COM NURSERY 1m 2f 46y
4:10 (4:10) (Class 5) (0-75,76) 2-Y-O **£2,264** (£673; £336; £168) **Stalls** Low

Form RPR

5006 **1** **Enjoying (IRE)**[13] 5342 2-8-4 **61**..........................(b[1]) KieranO'Neill(3) 2 64
(Richard Hannon) *in rr: drvn along fr 3f out: styd on towards outside fnl f and str run fnl 100yds: pushed rt clsng stages: led last strides* **10/1**

3551 **2** *shd* **Maastricht (IRE)**[8] 5503 2-9-8 **76** 6ex.......................... RoystonFfrench 8 79
(Mark Johnston) *pressed ldr and str chal fr 3f out tl slt ld fnl 100yds: edgd rt u.p clsng stages: hdd last strides* **9/2**[3]

066 **3** ½ **Foster's Road**[12] 5382 2-8-13 **70**.......................... MartinHarley(3) 6 72+
(Mick Channon) *chsd ldrs: rdn 3f out: one pce appr fnl f: styd on wl u.p to take 3rd clsng stages* **10/1**

060 **4** ¾ **Welsh Nayber**[25] 4968 2-8-8 **62**.......................... EddieAhern 7 63
(Amanda Perrett) *chsd ldrs: rdn 2f out: sn one pce: kpt on again fnl f: nt clr run clsng stages* **7/2**[2]

3201 **5** *shd* **Snowed In (IRE)**[17] 5246 2-9-4 **72**.......................... LukeMorris 4 72
(J S Moore) *in rr but in tch: rdn over 3f out: chsd ldrs over 1f out: nvr quite gng pce to chal and styd on same pce clsng stages* **16/1**

1044 **6** *nk* **Glee**[10] 5446 2-9-7 **75**.......................... PatDobbs 3 75
(Richard Hannon) *slt ld but jnd fr 4f out: strly chal fr 3f out tl narrowly hdd fnl 100yds: wknd fnl 50yds* **3/1**[1]

5034 **7** 3 ½ **Clean Bowled (IRE)**[11] 5413 2-8-10 **64**..........................(bt) EddieCreighton 5 58
(Brian Meehan) *in rr: rdn 4f out: nvr gng pce to rch ldrs* **20/1**

5020 **8** *shd* **Accustomed**[20] 5144 2-8-13 **67**.......................... LiamKeniry 9 60
(Sylvester Kirk) *in rr but in tch: rdn and effrt on outside over 2f out: nvr gng pce to chal: sn wknd* **8/1**

005 **9** 14 **Shark In The Sea**[12] 5382 2-9-2 **70**..........................(b[1]) ShaneKelly 1 38
(Brian Meehan) *chsd ldrs: rdn and wknd over 2f out: eased whn no ch fnl f* **10/1**

2m 13.85s (2.85) **Going Correction** +0.15s/f (Good) 9 Ran SP% **114.4**
Speed ratings (Par 95): **94,93,93,92,92 92,89,89,78**
toteswingers:1&2:£8.80, 2&3:£8.90, 1&3:£20.50 CSF £54.06 CT £465.77 TOTE £21.30: £4.40, £1.10, £4.00; EX 71.90.
Owner Ben CM Wong **Bred** Gerry Smith **Trained** East Everleigh, Wilts

FOCUS
A stiff test for juveniles in this 1m2f nursery and the winner came from last to get up near the line.

NOTEBOOK
Enjoying(IRE), whose best previous effort came on Polytrack, was wearing blinkers for the first time but was soon being pushed along and was given a reminder after only 2f. Despite still being last 3f out, his rider persisted with his urgings and his mount eventually consented to run on, and swept down the outside to lead almost on the line. Official explanation: trainer's rep said, regarding apparent improvement in form, that the colt had benefited from the step up in trip and first-time blinkers. (op 12-1)

Maastricht(IRE) ran a terrific race from up front and did not deserve to be beaten. He fought off the challenge of the winner's stable companion after a protracted duel, but then drifted right in the closing stages and was just run down. He had a hard race here, but a return to slightly easier ground might enable him to gain compensation. (op 7-2 tchd 5-1)

Foster's Road, making his handicap debut off 70, ran pretty well and stayed the extra trip without ever looking like getting to the front. (op 12-1)

Welsh Nayber, stepping up from 7f on this handicap debut, tracked the pace throughout but could not find a change of gear. (op 9-2)

Snowed In(IRE), another stepping up from 7f, did not get the clearest of runs but was staying on all the way to the line. Both his wins came on Polytrack and he might be more potent back on that surface. (op 18-1)

Glee disputed the lead with the runner-up for much of the way, but was eventually worn down by that rival and did not appear to get home. (op 4-1)

Accustomed's rider reported that the filly hung right. Official explanation: jockey said filly hung right (op 11-2)

5784 EVENTS BAR MANAGEMENT MAIDEN H'CAP 1m 5f 22y
4:40 (4:40) (Class 5) (0-70,70) 3-Y-O+ **£2,264** (£673; £336; £168) **Stalls** High

Form RPR

-650 **1** **Dark And Dangerous (IRE)**[72] 3393 3-8-4 **56** oh2.......... CathyGannon 4 63
(Peter Winkworth) *in tch tl lost position and in rr 3f out: hdwy on ins fr 2f out: str run fr over 1f out to ld ins fnl f: drvn out* **18/1**

4525 **2** ½ **Handles For Forks (IRE)**[9] 5477 3-8-13 **68**.......................... MartinHarley(3) 9 76+
(Mick Channon) *in rr: hdwy 3f out: styng on whn nt clr run fr 2f out tl impr over 1f out: sn n.m.r again: fnlly got clr ins fnl f and r.o u.p to take 2nd last strides but nt rch wnr* **13/2**[3]

0536 **3** *nk* **Evergreen Forest (IRE)**[20] 5141 3-9-1 **67**.......................... FergusSweeney 3 73
(Alastair Lidderdale) *towards rr tl hdwy fr 4f out: pressed ldrs 3f out: slt ld fr 2f out: edgd lft 1f out and sn hdd: styd on but nt gng pce of wnr: lost 2nd last strides* **15/2**

0522 **4** 1 ½ **Lady Barastar (IRE)**[15] 5302 3-8-11 **63**.......................... ChrisCatlin 8 66
(Walter Swinburn) *chsd ldrs: rdn over 3f out: drvn and ev ch ins fnl 2f: no ex fnl 120yds* **12/1**

50-6 **5** ¾ **Sansili**[11] 3911 4-9-4 **60**..........................(p) WilliamCarson 11 62
(Peter Bowen) *pushed along to chse ldr after 2f: drvn to chal 2f out: wknd ins fnl f* **9/4**[1]

5440 **6** 2 **High Samana**[31] 4753 3-9-4 **70**..........................(b[1]) JimCrowley 7 69
(Ralph Beckett) *in rr: hdwy on outside fr 3f out to chal 2f out: wknd appr fnl f* **13/2**[3]

0533 **7** ½ **Imperial Fong**[13] 5350 3-8-1 **56** oh6.......................... KieranO'Neill(3) 1 54
(Chris Dwyer) *in rr: t.k.h: hdwy to chse ldrs fr 3f out: wknd ins fnl f* **40/1**

0033 **8** 1 ½ **Reillys Daughter**[20] 5145 3-8-13 **65**.......................... LukeMorris 14 61
(J S Moore) *in rr: rdn and sme hdwy on outside over 2f out: wknd over 1f out* **16/1**

0033 **9** 1 **Indochina**[21] 5122 4-9-10 **66**..........................(v[1]) KierenFallon 5 61
(Ian Williams) *sn led: rdn 2f out: sn hdd: btn whn hmpd 1f out* **7/2**[2]

0430 **10** 1 ¾ **Black Pond (USA)**[12] 5372 3-8-5 **57**.......................... RoystonFfrench 13 49
(Mark Johnston) *chsd ldrs to 3f out: wknd qckly wl over 2f out* **20/1**

2m 56.21s (4.21) **Going Correction** +0.15s/f (Good)
WFA 3 from 4yo 10lb 10 Ran SP% **117.5**
Speed ratings (Par 103): **93,92,92,91,91 89,89,88,88,86**
toteswingers:1&2:£20.30, 2&3:£10.10, 1&3:£26.00 CSF £131.37 CT £969.69 TOTE £33.40: £6.70, £1.80, £3.70; EX 173.10.
Owner North South Alliance **Bred** Roundhill Stud And A Stroud **Trained** Chiddingfold, Surrey

FOCUS
A modest but quite competitive staying handicap, although made less so by four non-runners. They appeared to go a sound gallop and the early leaders weakened in the straight. The unlucky second has been rated a narrow winner.

Dark And Dangerous(IRE) Official explanation: trainer's rep said, regarding apparent improvement in form, that the gelding did not face the headgear on its previous run and benefited from a rest and change of routine.

Handles For Forks(IRE) Official explanation: jockey said filly was denied a clear run

5785 UNIVERSITY & LITERARY CLUB BRISTOL H'CAP 1m 3f 144y
5:10 (5:10) (Class 6) (0-60,57) 4-Y-O+ **£1,617** (£481; £240; £120) **Stalls** Low

Form RPR

0331 **1** **Kathleen Kennet**[5] 5611 11-8-13 **56** 6ex.......................... KatiaScallan(7) 4 69+
(Jonathan Geake) *hld up in rr but in tch: hdwy 6f out to ld over 4f out: drvn clr over 2f out: styd on strly* **11/4**[2]

54-6 **2** 4 **Rose Aurora**[154] 1135 4-8-9 **45**..........................(vt) RichardMullen 3 49
(Marcus Tregoning) *s.i.s: sn chsng ldrs: rdn to go 2nd 3f out: no imp on wnr fr over 2f out whn edgd rt: styd on u.p to hold 2nd clsng stages* **11/2**

6-56 **3** ½ **Cruise Control**[25] 4953 5-8-2 **45**.......................... RachealKneller(7) 1 48
(Richard Price) *chsd ldrs: rdn and kpt on to press for 2nd ins fnl f but nvr any ch w wnr: one pce into 3rd cl home* **15/2**

0035 **4** 1 ¼ **Raghdaan**[12] 5376 4-8-13 **49**.......................... ChrisCatlin 2 50
(Peter Hiatt) *t.k.h in rr: rdn and styd on fr 2f out to take n.d 4th ins fnl f* **9/2**[3]

0422 **5** ¾ **Into The Wind**[13] 5349 4-9-7 **57**.......................... JamesMillman 7 57
(Rod Millman) *in rr but in tch: rdn and hdwy to cl on ldrs over 2f out: nvr nr wnr and wknd ins fnl f* **2/1**[1]

-006 **6** 8 **Under Fire (IRE)**[10] 5421 8-8-10 **46**.......................... LukeMorris 8 32
(Tony Carroll) *chsd ldr tl slt ld 6f out: hdd over 4f out: wknd over 2f out* **20/1**

3005 **7** 32 **Warrior Nation (FR)**[39] 3094 5-8-9 **45**.......................... NeilChalmers 6 —
(Adrian Chamberlain) *led tl hdd 6f out: wknd ins fnl 4f* **66/1**

2m 32.45s (1.85) **Going Correction** +0.15s/f (Good) 7 Ran SP% **111.6**
Speed ratings (Par 101): **99,96,96,95,94 89,68**
toteswingers:1&2:£2.80, 2&3:£5.30, 1&3:£3.50 CSF £17.23 CT £97.14 TOTE £3.20: £1.10, £4.10; EX 18.30.
Owner R W Floyd **Bred** Richard William Floyd **Trained** Marlborough, Wilts

FOCUS
A very moderate handicap but another success for the veteran mare, who was bettering even her early form.

T/Plt: £304.10 to a £1 stake. Pool of £62,354.32 - 149.66 winning tickets. T/Qpdt: £529.20 to a £1 stake. Pool of £3,647.73 - 5.10 winning tickets ST

The Form Book, Raceform Ltd, Compton, RG20 6NL

[5548]NEWCASTLE (L-H)

Monday, September 5

OFFICIAL GOING: Soft (5.7)

Wind: Breezy, half against Weather: Cloudy and showers

5786 BET365 E B F MAIDEN STKS 6f

2:20 (2:22) (Class 5) 2-Y-O **£3,234** (£962; £481; £240) **Stalls** Low

Form				RPR
4	**1**		**Mr Spiggott (IRE)**[21] 5117 2-9-3 0 TonyCulhane 6 (Mick Channon) *towards rr: hdwy over 2f out: rdn over 1f out: str run ins fnl f to ld nr line* **9/1**[3]	77
22	**2**	*hd*	**Signor Sassi**[21] 5111 2-9-3 0 NeilCallan 7 (Roger Varian) *led: rdn clr wl over 1f out: drvn ins fnl f: hdd and no ex nr line* **11/8**[1]	76
24	**3**	*nk*	**Grizzle**[38] 4507 2-8-12 0 AntiocoMurgia(5) 10 (Mahmood Al Zarooni) *in tch: hdwy wl over 2f out: rdn to chse ldrs wl over 1f out: drvn and ch wl ins fnl f: no ex towards fin* **5/2**[2]	75
2365	**4**	*1*	**I'll Be Good**[1] 5756 2-9-0 72 GaryBartley(3) 3 (Robert Johnson) *midfield: gd hdwy on outer 2f out: rdn over 1f out: styd on to chal ins fnl f: sn drvn and one pce* **33/1**	72
0	**5**	*5*	**Ardmay (IRE)**[13] 5337 2-9-3 0 PhillipMakin 15 (Kevin Ryan) *prom: rdn along over 2f out: grad wknd* **25/1**	57
	6	*hd*	**Untold Melody** 2-8-12 0 StephenCraine 2 (Kevin Ryan) *hld up towards rr: hdwy on outer 2f out: styd on appr fnl f: nrst fin* **50/1**	52
4	**7**	*½*	**Be Calm**[75] 3274 2-8-12 0 JamesSullivan 9 (Michael Easterby) *midfield: pushed along wl over 2f out: rdn over 1f out: one pce* **16/1**	50
0	**8**	*1 ½*	**Border Revia (IRE)**[9] 5486 2-9-3 0 PaulHanagan 8 (Richard Fahey) *in tch: effrt wl over 2f out: sn rdn along and n.d* **25/1**	51
	9	*shd*	**Kieron's Rock (IRE)** 2-9-0 0 PatrickDonaghy(3) 14 (Jedd O'Keeffe) *dwlt and towards rr: pushed along 1/2-way and sme hdwy: sn rdn and n.d* **100/1**	50
0035	**10**	*nk*	**Dazzlin Bluebell (IRE)**[19] 5161 2-8-12 57 RobertWinston 13 (Tim Easterby) *chsd ldr: rdn along over 2f out: drvn wl over 1f out: sn wknd* **33/1**	44
	11	*½*	**Feeling Good** 2-9-0 0 DaleSwift(3) 11 (Brian Ellison) *dwlt: a in rr* **33/1**	48
6	**12**	*4 ½*	**Sabhan (IRE)**[40] 4436 2-9-3 0 SilvestreDeSousa 5 (Geoffrey Harker) *chsd ldrs: rdn along 1/2-way: sn wknd* **12/1**	34
4503	**13**	*½*	**Never In (IRE)**[8] 5505 2-8-7 51 DanielleMcCreery(5) 12 (Alan Berry) *chsd ldrs: rdn along wl over 2f out: sn wknd* **100/1**	28
	14	*7*	**Serendipity Blue** 2-8-12 0 DuranFentiman 4 (John Weymes) *dwlt: a in rr* **100/1**	7
3	**15**	*11*	**Medam**[95] 2651 2-8-12 0 RobbieFitzpatrick 1 (Shaun Harris) *a in rr: bhd fr 1/2-way* **100/1**	—

1m 18.19s (3.59) **Going Correction** +0.475s/f (Yiel) **15** Ran **SP% 116.7**

Speed ratings (Par 95): **95,94,94,93,86 86,85,83,83,82 82,76,75,66,51**

toteswingers:1&2:£4.30, 2&3:£2.20, 1&3:£5.70 CSF £19.62 TOTE £12.60: £2.20, £1.10, £1.40; EX 32.40 Trifecta £84.30 Pool: £526.56 - 4.62 winning units..

Owner M Channon **Bred** Martin Francis Ltd **Trained** West Ilsley, Berks

■ Stewards' Enquiry : Neil Callan two-day ban: careless riding (Sep 19-20); one-day ban: failed to ride to draw (Sep 21)

FOCUS

Rail moved to provide fresh ground and 1m4f race increased by 5yds and 2m by 7yds. They raced centre-field for this ordinary juvenile maiden. Straightforward form rated around the second and fourth.

NOTEBOOK

Mr Spiggott(IRE) came between runners to win. Slowly away and in need of the experience when fourth of six at Yarmouth on debut, he was faced with a slower surface this time and the greater emphasis on stamina suited. He'll stay 7f and can make his mark in nurseries. (op 8-1 tchd 15-2)

Signor Sassi travelled much the best, but it's three seconds in a row now. His rider will no doubt wish he'd have held on to him for longer, but the horse can surely pick up a small race, with a return to quicker ground likely to be of benefit. (op 6-4)

Grizzle kept on dourly to challenge inside the final furlong and he'll be helped by a step up to 7f in nurseries. (op 11-4)

I'll Be Good, rated 72 and reappearing just one day after finishing a well-beaten fifth at York, ran better, but isn't going to be easy to win with. (op 50-1)

Ardmay(IRE) improved on his initial effort and will be qualified for a mark following one more run. (op 28-1 tchd 33-1)

Untold Melody, a half-sister to the useful Mappin Time, made some late headway without being given a hard time and should improve.

5787 BET365.COM H'CAP 6f

2:50 (2:53) (Class 6) (0-55,55) 3-Y-O+ **£1,617** (£481; £240; £120) **Stalls** Low

Form				RPR
3051	**1**		**Mission Impossible**[7] 5552 6-8-13 52 6ex PatrickMathers 8 (Tracy Waggott) *in tch: effrt 2f out: rdn to ld ins fnl f: kpt on strly* **11/2**[3]	64
0232	**2**	*¾*	**Mucky Molly**[7] 5540 3-8-11 52 NeilCallan 4 (Olivia Maylam) *trckd ldrs: rdn to ld wl over 1f out: hdd ins fnl f: kpt on wl* **5/1**[2]	62+
0000	**3**	*2 ¼*	**Charles Parnell (IRE)**[9] 5490 8-8-9 48 MichaelStainton 9 (Simon Griffiths) *missed break: bhd: hdwy over 2f out: kpt on wl ins fnl f: nt rch first two* **40/1**	51
625	**4**	*2 ¼*	**Cheyenne Red (IRE)**[10] 5436 5-8-9 48 TomEaves 5 (Michael Dods) *led 2f: cl up: rdn and ev ch over 2f out: kpt on same pce ins fnl f* **16/1**	44
0434	**5**	*2 ¼*	**Jackie Love (IRE)**[23] 5041 3-8-4 50 (b) JulieBurke(5) 10 (Olivia Maylam) *towards rr: shkn up and hdwy over 1f out: kpt on ins fnl f: nrst fin* **25/1**	39
6424	**6**	*shd*	**Inca Blue**[5] 5619 3-8-11 52 (b) RobertWinston 6 (Tim Easterby) *dwlt: bhd: hdwy over 2f out: no imp over 1f out* **9/2**[1]	41
4501	**7**	*1 ¾*	**Here Now And Why (IRE)**[14] 5313 4-9-2 55 (p) DuranFentiman 1 (Ian Semple) *cl up: led after 2f: rdn and hdd wl over 1f out: sn btn* **17/2**	39
0606	**8**	*hd*	**Slatey Hen (IRE)**[3] 5670 3-8-11 55 RobertLButler(3) 11 (Richard Guest) *trckd ldrs tl rdn and wknd over 1f out* **40/1**	38
3042	**9**	*5*	**Winning Draw (IRE)**[9] 5490 3-8-11 55 (b) DeclanCannon(3) 13 (Paul Midgley) *racd towards stands' side: in tch: drvn and outpcd 1/2-way: n.d after* **5/1**[2]	23
-000	**10**	*1 ¼*	**Freedom Trail**[9] 5490 3-8-10 51 FrederikTylicki 16 (Tim Fitzgerald) *bhd and sn struggling stands' side: nvr on terms* **50/1**	15
060	**11**	*4 ½*	**Bahamian Kid**[35] 4600 6-8-9 48 (v) LeeNewman 2 (George Foster) *in tch: drvn over 2f out: wknd wl over 1f out* **20/1**	—
0206	**12**	*1 ½*	**Bahamian Jazz (IRE)**[21] 5121 4-9-1 54 DanielTudhope 15 (Robin Bastiman) *racd stands' side: rdn and struggling fr over 3f out* **12/1**	—
6006	**13**	*12*	**Hitches Dubai (BRZ)**[10] 5436 6-8-13 52 SilvestreDeSousa 12 (Geoffrey Harker) *in tch towards stands' side: drvn and outpcd 1/2-way: sn btn: t.o* **50/1**	—
5/5-	**14**	*22*	**Manana Manana**[605] 86 5-8-13 52 TonyCulhane 7 (Richard Guest) *bhd: struggling 1/2-way: sn btn: t.o* **33/1**	—
006	**15**	*8*	**Yungaburra (IRE)**[139] 1471 7-9-2 55 (t) PaulHanagan 14 (David C Griffiths) *walked to s: racd towards stands' side: midfield: struggling 1/2-way: sn btn: t.o* **33/1**	—

1m 18.03s (3.43) **Going Correction** +0.475s/f (Yiel)

WFA 3 from 4yo+ 2lb **15** Ran **SP% 114.3**

Speed ratings (Par 101): **96,95,92,89,86 85,83,83,76,74 68,66,50,21,10**

toteswingers:1&2:£4.60, 2&3:£37.80, 1&3:£39.70 CSF £28.14 CT £982.47 TOTE £5.40: £2.10, £1.70, £9.20; EX 17.90 TRIFECTA Not won..

Owner H Conlon **Bred** Rodney Meredith **Trained** Spennymoor, Co Durham

FOCUS

The main action unfolded centre-field once more, the few who raced stands' side finishing well held. Just a low-grade sprint handicap and few showed their form on the bad ground. The winner's best form since he was a 3yo.

Bahamian Kid Official explanation: jockey said gelding hung left-handed

5788 BET365 H'CAP (DIV I) 7f

3:20 (3:21) (Class 6) (0-60,60) 3-Y-O+ **£1,617** (£481; £240; £120) **Stalls** Low

Form				RPR
634	**1**		**Reason To Believe (IRE)**[24] 5004 3-9-4 58 (b[1]) PaulHanagan 7 (Ben Haslam) *mde all: rdn along wl over 1f out: drvn ins fnl f: edgd rt and kpt on wl towards fin* **7/1**[3]	68
0-60	**2**	*hd*	**Moonlight Mystery**[89] 2821 3-9-6 60 GrahamGibbons 8 (Chris Wall) *prom: trckd wnr fr 1/2-way: rdn to chal over 1f out: drvn and ev ch ins fnl f: no ex towards fin* **14/1**	69
633	**3**	*1 ¾*	**Eeny Mac (IRE)**[10] 5437 4-9-0 50 SilvestreDeSousa 15 (Neville Bycroft) *hld up towards rr: hdwy 1/2-way: chsd ldrs over 2f out: rdn wl over 1f out: drvn to chse ldng pair and edgd lft ins fnl f: no imp* **7/1**[3]	57
/402	**4**	*3*	**Billy Cadiz**[56] 3903 6-8-10 46 oh1 RobertWinston 14 (Mark Campion) *hld up towards rr: hdwy 3f out: rdn along to chse ldrs 2f out: drvn and no imp ins fnl f* **16/1**	45
0060	**5**	*1 ½*	**Brisbane (IRE)**[11] 5403 4-8-5 46 oh1 ShaneBKelly(5) 13 (Dianne Sayer) *s.i.s and in rr: hdwy over 3f out: rdn to chse ldrs and n.m.r wl over 1f out: kpt on u.p ins fnl f: nrst fin* **22/1**	41
2504	**6**	*5*	**Burnwynd Boy**[2] 5725 6-9-4 59 GarryWhillans(5) 1 (Ian Semple) *dwlt and in rr: hdwy over 2f out: kpt on appr fnl f: nvr nr ldrs* **16/1**	41
4005	**7**	*nk*	**Spahi (FR)**[19] 5167 5-9-0 50 DanielTudhope 3 (David O'Meara) *hld up in rr: hdwy 1/2-way: chsd ldrs wl over 2f out: sn rdn and wknd* **6/1**[2]	31
0353	**8**	*nk*	**Chadford**[7] 5556 3-8-8 48 (p) DuranFentiman 11 (Tim Walford) *chsd ldrs: rdn along wl over 2f out: sn wknd* **7/1**[3]	27
1511	**9**	*1*	**Broctune Papa Gio**[4] 5652 4-9-7 60 DeclanCannon(3) 2 (Keith Reveley) *trckd ldrs: effrt wl over 2f out and sn rdn along: wknd wl over 1f out and eased* **3/1**[1]	38
3260	**10**	*3*	**Jamarjo (IRE)**[62] 3709 4-8-12 51 LeeTopliss(3) 10 (Steve Gollings) *chsd ldrs: rdn along 1/2-way: sn wknd* **40/1**	21
00-0	**11**	*¾*	**Cut The Cackle (IRE)**[26] 4918 5-9-5 58 (t[1]) RobertLButler(3) 9 (Richard Guest) *dwlt: sn in tch: effrt and sme hdwy 3f out: sn rdn and wknd* **50/1**	26
604	**12**	*9*	**Blue Noodles**[28] 4852 5-9-2 52 (p) PaddyAspell 6 (John Wainwright) *chsd ldrs: rdn along 1/2-way: sn wknd* **20/1**	—
6033	**13**	*4 ½*	**Broughtons Silk**[18] 5208 6-8-10 46 oh1 PJMcDonald 5 (Alistair Whillans) *chsd ldrs: rdn along 3f out: sn wknd* **20/1**	—

1m 31.74s (3.94) **Going Correction** +0.475s/f (Yiel)

WFA 3 from 4yo+ 4lb **13** Ran **SP% 113.5**

Speed ratings (Par 101): **96,95,93,90,88 82,82,82,81,77 76,66,61**

toteswingers:1&2:£16.40, 2&3:£13.80, 1&3:£4.70 CSF £87.87 CT £730.33 TOTE £7.40: £2.50, £4.90, £1.50; EX 107.20 TRIFECTA Not won..

Owner Mrs Carol Aldridge **Bred** Yeomanstown Stud **Trained** Middleham Moor, N Yorks

FOCUS

Few got into the first division of this low-grade handicap. The entire field raced down the middle of the track. The time compared well with that for division II, and the winner rates back to his 2yo best.

Chadford Official explanation: jockey said gelding hung left-handed from halfway.

Broctune Papa Gio Official explanation: jockey said gelding was unsuited by the soft ground

5789 BET365 H'CAP (DIV II) 7f

3:50 (3:51) (Class 6) (0-60,60) 3-Y-O+ **£1,617** (£481; £240; £120) **Stalls** Low

Form				RPR
5663	**1**		**Chookie Avon**[2] 5725 4-9-5 55 (p) TomEaves 13 (Keith Dalgleish) *in tch: effrt over 2f out: led ins fnl f: kpt on strly* **7/2**[2]	66
0415	**2**	*1 ¾*	**Whispering Spirit (IRE)**[26] 4920 5-9-10 60 (p) SilvestreDeSousa 2 (Ann Duffield) *hld up: hdwy over 2f out: rdn and ev ch ins fnl f: kpt on* **14/1**	66
0304	**3**	*½*	**Monsieur Pontaven**[9] 5490 4-9-0 50 (b) LeeNewman 9 (Robin Bastiman) *prom: hdwy to ld over 2f out: hdd ins fnl f: kpt on same pce* **12/1**	55
-600	**4**	*1 ¼*	**Fulford**[24] 5009 6-8-10 46 oh1 RobertWinston 5 (Mel Brittain) *prom: effrt and drvn over 2f out: one pce over 1f out* **40/1**	48
5600	**5**	*nk*	**Phair Winter**[19] 5165 3-8-4 47 PaulPickard(3) 14 (Alan Brown) *dwlt: bhd: hdwy over 2f out: kpt on ins fnl f: nrst fin* **20/1**	46
0603	**6**	*2*	**Royal Premium**[9] 5490 5-8-5 46 oh1 (v) AdamCarter(5) 7 (Bruce Hellier) *dwlt: bhd: rdn and kpt on fr 2f out: nvr able to chal* **20/1**	42
6311	**7**	*2 ½*	**Whats For Pudding (IRE)**[20] 5153 3-8-10 55 NeilFarley(5) 16 (Declan Carroll) *sn drvn along towards rr: sme late hdwy: nvr on terms* **10/3**[1]	42
1000	**8**	*3 ¼*	**Tenancy (IRE)**[10] 5437 7-9-3 53 RobbieFitzpatrick 6 (Shaun Harris) *led to over 2f out: rdn and wknd over 1f out* **50/1**	34
5000	**9**	*¾*	**Crocodile Bay (IRE)**[6] 5601 8-8-10 46 oh1 (bt) AndrewMullen 10 (Richard Guest) *in tch: rdn whn hmpd over 2f out: sn btn* **50/1**	25
3000	**10**	*3*	**Viking Dancer**[11] 5404 4-9-8 58 PJMcDonald 15 (Ruth Carr) *hld up: rdn over 2f out: sn btn* **25/1**	29
4600	**11**	*2 ¼*	**Honest Buck**[18] 5214 4-8-11 50 (p) MichaelO'Connell(3) 8 (Kate Walton) *prom: drvn along whn hmpd over 2f out: sn btn* **20/1**	15
506	**12**	*13*	**King Bertolini (IRE)**[20] 5153 4-8-10 46 oh1 (p) TonyHamilton 3 (Alan Berry) *sn drvn along towards rr: struggling fr over 2f out: t.o* **50/1**	—
0304	**13**	*½*	**Caldermud (IRE)**[23] 5040 4-9-2 59 (t) HarryPoulton(7) 4 (Olivia Maylam) *hld up in midfield: struggling 3f out: sn btn: t.o* **15/2**	—

542 **14** *3 ¼* **Eilean Eeve**[7] 5551 5-9-0 **50**..............................(p) PaulHanagan 12 —
(George Foster) *prom tl rdn and wknd fr 3f out: t.o* **5/1**[3]

000 **15** *22* **Alpha Tauri (USA)**[23] 5034 5-9-7 **57**....................(t[1]) TonyCulhane 11 —
(Richard Guest) *pressed ldr tl rdn and wknd wl over 2f out: sn btn* **50/1**

1m 33.73s (5.93) **Going Correction** +0.475s/f (Yiel)
WFA 3 from 4yo+ 4lb **15** Ran SP% **116.5**
Speed ratings (Par 101): **85,83,82,81,80 78,75,71,70,67 64,50,49,45,20**
toteswingers:1&2:£7.80, 2&3:£9.20, 1&3:£10.10 CSF £42.41 CT £530.45 TOTE £4.10: £1.10, £3.60, £4.10; EX 60.20 Trifecta £377.40 Pool: £530.42 - 1.04 winning units..
Owner Carleton Boys Of Carlisle **Bred** D And J Raeburn **Trained** Carluke, South Lanarkshire
■ Stewards' Enquiry : Lee Newman two-day ban: careless riding (Sep 19-20)

FOCUS
The winning time was considerably slower than the first division, but the form looks more straightforward with the winner back to his best.
Whats For Pudding(IRE) Official explanation: jockey said filly never travelled
Tenancy(IRE) Official explanation: trainer said gelding lost both front shoes
Eilean Eeve Official explanation: jockey said mare hung right-handed

5790 POKER AT BET365 H'CAP — 2m 19y
4:20 (4:20) (Class 6) (0-65,64) 3-Y-O+ **£2,264** (£673; £336; £168) **Stalls** Low

Form RPR

4365 **1** **Puy D'Arnac (FR)**[9] 4562 8-9-9 **64**.............................. JulieBurke[(5)] 1 74
(George Moore) *hld up: hdwy over 2f out: led over 1f out: rdn and r.o wl ins fnl f* **12/1**

4-21 **2** *¾* **Spice Bar**[6] 5595 7-8-11 **54** 6ex.............................. JasonHart[(7)] 8 63
(Declan Carroll) *hld up: hdwy over 2f out: chsd wnr ins fnl f: r.o* **9/2**[2]

6/12 **3** *3 ¾* **Circus Clown (IRE)**[19] 5166 6-9-9 **59**.................... DanielTudhope 15 64
(Jim Goldie) *hld up in midfield on outside: niggled along 1/2-way: no imp tl hdwy appr 2f out: kpt on wl ins fnl f: nt rch first two* **4/1**[1]

4225 **4** *½* **Simple Jim (FR)**[6] 5595 7-9-7 **57**.......................... SilvestreDeSousa 12 61
(David O'Meara) *hld up: hdwy on ins over 2f out: n.m.r briefly over 1f out: rdn and kpt on ins fnl f* **6/1**[3]

1301 **5** *nk* **Ivanov (IRE)**[18] 5209 3-8-10 **59**..................................(p) TomEaves 6 63
(K F Clutterbuck) *in tch: effrt over 2f out: rdn and kpt on same pce ins fnl f* **12/1**

4604 **6** *3 ¼* **River Dragon (IRE)**[6] 5595 6-9-6 **61**.................... BrianToomey[(5)] 11 61
(Tony Coyle) *sn trcking ldrs: led 1/2-way and sn clr: rdn over 2f out: hdd over 1f out: wknd ins fnl f* **20/1**

6000 **7** *½* **Hada Men (USA)**[4] 5650 6-8-6 **47** oh1....................(p) DaleSwift[(3)] 10 46
(Tina Jackson) *midfield: rdn and outpcd over 4f out: plugged on fnl 2f: nvr able to chal* **40/1**

6402 **8** *3 ½* **Tigerino (IRE)**[9] 5489 3-7-12 **47** oh1.......................... DuranFentiman 2 42
(Chris Fairhurst) *hld up: rdn over 4f out: hdwy over 2f out: no imp over 1f out* **33/1**

0053 **9** *4* **Dechiper (IRE)**[7] 5549 9-8-13 **49**................................ TonyHamilton 3 39
(Robert Johnson) *hld up in midfield: rdn and outpcd over 2f out: n.d after* **33/1**

0-61 **10** *2 ½* **Joan D'Arc (IRE)**[8] 5519 4-9-6 **61** 6ex.................... AntiocoMurgia[(5)] 7 48
(Noel Quinlan) *chsd ldrs: smooth hdwy to chse wnr over 2f out: wknd over 1f out* **10/1**

0030 **11** *¾* **Silent Lucidity (IRE)**[28] 4856 7-8-10 **49**..............(p) DeclanCannon[(3)] 13 35
(Peter Niven) *hld up: rdn over 4f out: hdwy on outside wl over 2f out: sn no imp* **16/1**

4433 **12** *¾* **Short Supply (USA)**[12] 5369 5-9-6 **56**........................ GrahamGibbons 4 41
(Tim Walford) *led 4f: cl up tl rdn and wknd over 2f out* **12/1**

-643 **13** *29* **Rosie Raymond**[42] 4396 6-8-12 **48**........................ RobbieFitzpatrick 14 —
(Charles Smith) *hld up: struggling over 4f out: lost tch fnl 2f: eased* **66/1**

4533 **14** *9* **Cadgers Brig**[9] 5489 3-8-8 **57**.................................... PaulHanagan 5 —
(Keith Dalgleish) *t.k.h: cl up: led after 4f to 1/2-way: rdn and wknd wl over 1f out: t.o* **10/1**

4544 **15** *17* **Bollin Mandy**[9] 5489 3-8-12 **61**................................ RobertWinston 9 —
(Tim Easterby) *t.k.h: in tch tl rdn and wknd over 3f out: t.o* **14/1**

/0-0 **16** *98* **Strobe**[13] 4382 7-9-4 **54**..(p) PaddyAspell 16 —
(Lucy Normile) *prom tl wknd qckly over 4f out: virtually p.u fnl 3f* **100/1**

3m 46.47s (7.07) **Going Correction** +0.475s/f (Yiel)
WFA 3 from 4yo+ 13lb **16** Ran SP% **121.8**
Speed ratings (Par 101): **101,100,98,98,98 96,96,94,92,91 91,90,76,71,63 14**
toteswingers:1&2:£10.90, 2&3:£5.00, 1&3:£12.30 CSF £61.93 CT £263.54 TOTE £16.00: £2.80, £1.80, £1.50, £1.90; EX 75.70 Trifecta £167.60 Pool: £693.38 - 3.06 winning units..
Owner Barrow Brook Racing **Bred** Mrs Axelle Du Verdier **Trained** Middleham Moor, N Yorks

FOCUS
The pace increased a fair way out in this staying handicap and those held up early seemed at an advantage. The winner is rated back to something like last year's form.

5791 CASINO AT BET365.COM H'CAP — 1m 4f 93y
4:50 (4:50) (Class 6) (0-65,62) 3-Y-O+ **£1,617** (£481; £240; £120) **Stalls** Low

Form RPR

0520 **1** **Aegean Destiny**[21] 5107 4-9-1 **54**.............................. DeclanCannon[(3)] 5 65
(John Mackie) *in tch: hdwy to ld over 2f out: sn rdn: styd on wl ins fnl f* **11/1**

0-00 **2** *2 ¼* **Dzesmin (POL)**[87] 2892 9-9-9 **62**..........................(p) RobertLButler[(3)] 10 69
(Richard Guest) *in tch: smooth hdwy and ev ch over 2f out: sn chsd wnr and rdn: kpt on same pce ins fnl f* **40/1**

4614 **3** *½* **Ferney Boy**[11] 5405 5-9-1 **51**.................................... RobertWinston 16 57
(Chris Fairhurst) *hld up in midfield on outside: hdwy over 2f out: kpt on u.p ins fnl f* **11/2**[2]

0334 **4** *3 ½* **Light The City (IRE)**[4] 5651 4-9-5 **55**........................ JamesSullivan 9 56
(Ruth Carr) *t.k.h: trckd ldrs: effrt and rdn over 2f out: kpt on same pce ins fnl f* **14/1**

4600 **5** *nk* **Child Of Our Time (IRE)**[44] 4329 4-8-12 **48** oh2........ PatrickMathers 14 48
(Tracy Waggott) *hld up: hdwy over 2f out: rdn and kpt on same pce ins fnl f* **25/1**

0061 **6** *hd* **Miss Ferney**[4] 5651 7-9-3 **56** 6ex.............................. PaulPickard[(3)] 7 56
(Alan Kirtley) *hld up: hdwy over 2f out: rdn and no imp fr over 1f out* **6/1**[3]

3241 **7** *2 ¼* **Lady Norlela**[21] 5107 5-9-5 **60**................................ ShaneBKelly[(5)] 13 56
(Brian Rothwell) *hld up in midfield: rdn and outpcd 3f out: plugged on ins fnl f: n.d* **9/2**[1]

0240 **8** *2* **Rockweiller**[19] 5178 4-9-7 **60**..(v) LeeTopliss[(3)] 2 53
(Steve Gollings) *cl up: rdn along over 3f out: wknd over 1f out* **9/1**

3640 **9** *1 ¾* **Donna Elvira**[66] 3574 4-9-6 **56**...................................... PaulHanagan 6 46
(Edwin Tuer) *led to over 2f out: wknd over 1f out* **8/1**

-000 **10** *1 ¾* **Vittachi**[11] 5403 4-8-12 **48** oh2.. TomEaves 1 35
(Alistair Whillans) *hld up: drvn along fr 3f out: nvr on terms* **66/1**

500 **11** *¾* **Gilt (USA)**[68] 3519 3-8-4 **49**...................................... AndreaAtzeni 8 35
(Ed Dunlop) *prom: rdn along over 4f out: wknd fr 3f out* **16/1**

6633 **12** *nk* **Bavarian Nordic (USA)**[11] 5405 6-9-6 **61**................ BrianToomey[(5)] 15 47
(Richard Whitaker) *hld up: rdn and effrt 3f out: btn over 1f out* **6/1**[3]

535/ **13** *69* **Molesden Glen (IRE)**[437] 7660 5-9-10 **60**.................... AndrewElliott 4 —
(Simon Waugh) *bhd: lost tch 1/2-way: t.o* **100/1**

0150 **14** *28* **Barnum (USA)**[12] 5369 3-8-9 **54**................................ GrahamGibbons 12 —
(Michael Easterby) *t.k.h: trckd ldrs tl wknd over 3f out: sn lost tch: t.o* **33/1**

2m 51.7s (6.10) **Going Correction** +0.475s/f (Yiel)
WFA 3 from 4yo+ 9lb **14** Ran SP% **115.8**
Speed ratings (Par 101): **98,96,96,93,93 93,92,90,89,88 87,87,41,22**
toteswingers:1&2:£41.60, 2&3:£36.70, 1&3:£17.60 CSF £400.57 CT £2659.84 TOTE £13.10: £4.90, £9.80, £1.60; EX 566.90 TRIFECTA Not won..
Owner Derbyshire Racing III **Bred** Theobalds Stud **Trained** Church Broughton , Derbys

FOCUS
A moderate handicap but a proper test on the ground. Sound form, the winner only needing to match this year's efforts.
Bavarian Nordic(USA) Official explanation: jockey said gelding stopped quickly
Barnum(USA) Official explanation: jockey gelding lost its action

5792 BET365.COM MAIDEN STKS — 1m (R)
5:20 (5:22) (Class 5) 3-Y-O+ **£2,264** (£673; £336; £168) **Stalls** Low

Form RPR

0- **1** **Jawhar (IRE)**[311] 7201 3-9-3 0.................................... TonyCulhane 4 81+
(William Haggas) *trckd ldrs: smooth hdwy to ld over 2f out: rdn clr over 1f out: drvn out* **9/4**[1]

4 **2** *1 ¼* **Tadabeer**[79] 3183 3-9-3 0.. PaulHanagan 13 75
(Ian Williams) *in tch: hdwy over 3f out: chsd ldrs 2f out: rdn over 1f out: drvn ins fnl f: kpt on:* **5/2**[2]

3 **3** *nk* **Alfred Hutchinson**[22] 5082 3-9-0 0............................ DaleSwift[(3)] 14 74
(Geoffrey Oldroyd) *hld up: hdwy on wd outside over 2f out: rdn wl over 1f out: chsd wnr ent fnl f: kpt on same pce towards fin* **9/2**[3]

0 **4** *10* **Illustration (IRE)**[10] 5443 3-9-3 0.......................... SilvestreDeSousa 9 51
(Mark Johnston) *towards rr: pushed along 1/2-way: rdn over 2f out: styd on u.p appr fnl f: nrst fin* **10/1**

4 **5** *nk* **Think**[30] 4813 4-9-8 0.. PaddyAspell 1 51
(Clive Mulhall) *cl up: led after 1 1/2f: rdn 3f out: drvn over 2f out and sn hdd: grad wknd* **40/1**

6 *hd* **Stillington** 5-9-8 0.. RobbieFitzpatrick 6 50
(Mel Brittain) *trckd ldrs on inner: pushed along 3f out: rdn over 2f out and grad wknd* **50/1**

30- **7** *2 ½* **Pursuing**[310] 7235 3-8-12 0.. PhillipMakin 5 39
(Nigel Tinkler) *chsd ldrs: effrt to chse wnr 2f out: sn rdn and wknd over 1f out* **16/1**

00 **8** *6* **Sendarose (IRE)**[7] 5556 3-9-3 0................................ DuranFentiman 8 31
(Tim Easterby) *trckd ldrs: rdn along 3f out: wknd fnl 2f* **66/1**

9 *2* **Jordans Chrissy (IRE)** 3-8-12 0.......................... GrahamGibbons 10 21
(Tim Pitt) *a towards rr* **25/1**

43 **10** *4 ½* **Naafetha (IRE)**[10] 5443 3-8-12 0.............................. DanielTudhope 16 —
(George Foster) *a towards rr* **8/1**

11 *½* **Camina** 3-8-12 0.. TomEaves 15 —
(Michael Smith) *s.i.s: a in rr* **66/1**

12 *5* **Eila Wheeler**[73] 4-9-0 0...................................... GaryBartley[(3)] 3 —
(Robert Johnson) *s.i.s: a in rr* **100/1**

60 **13** *½* **Classical Chloe**[6] 5598 3-8-9 0.............................. RobertLButler[(3)] 7 —
(Richard Guest) *midfield: rdn along 1/2-way: sn wknd* **100/1**

0 **14** *4 ½* **Titch The Witch**[66] 3577 3-8-12 0.............................. AndrewElliott 2 —
(David C Griffiths) *led 1 1/2f: cl up: rdn along and hung bdly lft wl over 2f out: sn wknd* **150/1**

1m 48.43s (3.13) **Going Correction** +0.475s/f (Yiel)
WFA 3 from 4yo+ 5lb **14** Ran SP% **117.5**
Speed ratings (Par 103): **103,101,101,91,91 90,88,82,80,75 75,70,69,65**
toteswingers:1&2:£2.90, 2&3:£4.40, 1&3:£6.50 CSF £7.42 TOTE £4.10: £1.90, £2.00, £1.10; EX 11.50 Trifecta £29.20 Pool: £345.29 - 8.75 winning units..
Owner Hamdan Al Maktoum **Bred** Shadwell Estate Company Limited **Trained** Newmarket, Suffolk

FOCUS
A modest maiden lacking strength-in-depth, though the front three, who pulled 10l clear of the remainder, ought to win races in future. It's hard to know exactly what they achieved.
Naafetha(IRE) Official explanation: jockey said filly never travelled

5793 MOBILE AT BET365 MAIDEN STKS — 5f
5:50 (5:51) (Class 5) 3-Y-O+ **£2,264** (£673; £336; £168) **Stalls** Low

Form RPR

5023 **1** **Surely This Time (IRE)**[9] 5469 3-9-3 62....................(tp) PhillipMakin 7 67
(Kevin Ryan) *prom: led 1/2-way: rdn wl over 1f out: drvn ins fnl f: hld on wl* **11/4**[1]

2 *hd* **Cool Rhythm** 3-9-3 0.. SilvestreDeSousa 10 66
(David O'Meara) *dwlt: sn in tch: hdwy 2f out: sn chsng wnr and rdn: drvn to chal ins fnl f kpt on* **11/4**[1]

0- **3** *2 ¼* **Avoncharm**[405] 4451 3-8-12 0.................................... GrahamGibbons 12 53
(Mel Brittain) *chsd ldrs: hdwy 1/2-way: rdn wl over 1f out: drvn ent fnl f: kpt on same pce* **8/1**[3]

500- **4** *2 ¾* **Monte Cassino (IRE)**[497] 1569 6-9-4 50............................ TomEaves 2 48
(Bryan Smart) *towards rr: hdwy on wd outside 2f out: sn rdn and kpt on ins fnl f: nrst fin* **8/1**[3]

50 **5** *1* **Miss Pronounce**[10] 5432 3-8-7 0................................ ShaneBKelly[(5)] 14 39
(Linda Perratt) *dwlt and in rr: hdwy 2f out: sn rdn and kpt on ins fnl f: nt rch ldrs* **66/1**

00 **6** *1* **Kyllachykov (IRE)**[12] 5368 3-9-3 0..............................(b[1]) LeeNewman 13 41
(Robin Bastiman) *chsd ldrs: rdn along over 2f out: sn wknd* **40/1**

00 **7** *nse* **Our Princess Ellie (USA)**[17] 5247 3-8-12 0.................. RobbieFitzpatrick 15 36
(Derek Shaw) *towards rr: sme hdwy 2f out: sn rdn and n.d* **66/1**

0455 **8** *nk* **Amazing Win (IRE)**[13] 5346 3-8-12 63............................ TonyCulhane 1 35
(Mick Channon) *chsd ldrs: rdn along over 2f out: sn drvn and wknd* **4/1**[2]

0 **9** *1 ¼* **Oosisit**[9] 5469 3-8-12 0.. JamesSullivan 8 30
(Ruth Carr) *chsd ldrs to 1/2-way: sn wknd* **16/1**

000- **10** *½* **Clanachy**[403] 4516 5-8-13 38.. DanielTudhope 9 28
(George Foster) *led: rdn along and hdd 1/2-way: sn wknd* **100/1**

0645 **11** *½* **Bygones For Coins (IRE)**[23] 5063 3-8-7 42.................... JulieBurke[(5)] 6 26
(Alan Berry) *a towards rr* **28/1**

12 *21* **Exceeded** 3-8-9 0.. DeclanCannon[(3)] 4 —
(Robert Johnson) *s.i.s: sn outpcd in rr and wl bhd fr 1/2-way* **20/1**

64.34 secs (3.24) **Going Correction** +0.475s/f (Yiel)
WFA 3 from 4yo+ 1lb **12** Ran SP% **116.1**
Speed ratings (Par 103): **93,92,89,84,83 81,81,80,78,78 77,43**
Totesuper 7: Win: Not won. Place: £1332.80 CSF £9.22 TOTE £5.30: £2.30, £1.10, £4.50; EX 12.10 Trifecta £110.00 Pool: £364.26 - 2.45 winning units..
Owner F Gillespie **Bred** S J Macdonald **Trained** Hambleton, N Yorks
■ Stewards' Enquiry : Silvestre De Sousa one-day ban: used whip in incorrect place (Sep 19)

FOCUS
A typically weak 3yo-plus sprint maiden in the north. The winner is the best guide.
T/Jkpt: Not won. T/Plt: £272.30 to a £1 stake. Pool of £82,277.90 - 220.50 winning tickets.
T/Qpdt: £77.40 to a £1 stake. Pool of £4,916.81 - 47.00 winning tickets. RY

5794a, 5797 - 5800a (Foreign Racing) - See Raceform Interactive

5337 LEICESTER (R-H)
Tuesday, September 6

OFFICIAL GOING: Good to firm (good in places; 7.6)
Wind: Strong behind Weather: Overcast

5801 BRITISH STALLION STUDS E B F APOLLO MAIDEN STKS 7f 9y
2:00 (2:00) (Class 4) 2-Y-O **£4,334** (£1,289; £644; £322) **Stalls** High

Form RPR
1 **Oscan (USA)** 2-9-3 0 .... AhmedAjtebi 16 77+
(Mahmood Al Zarooni) *s.i.s: hld up: hdwy over 2f out: rdn to ld wl ins fnl f: hung rt nr fin* **5/1**[2]
3500 **2** 1 1/4 **Verse Of Love**[27] 4913 2-9-3 68 .... GrahamGibbons 7 74
(David Evans) *mid-div: hdwy 1/2-way: rdn to ld over 1f out: hdd wl ins fnl f* **25/1**
0 **3** 1 1/2 **Uprise**[45] 4330 2-9-0 0 .... LouisBeuzelin(3) 8 70+
(Sir Michael Stoute) *chsd ldrs: rdn over 1f out: styd on same pce ins fnl f* **11/2**[3]
0 **4** 1 1/2 **Dark Don (IRE)**[18] 5254 2-9-3 0 .... MichaelHills 13 66
(Charles Hills) *sn led: rdn and hdd over 1f out: no ex ins fnl f* **9/1**
0 **5** 1/2 **Andalieb**[25] 5011 2-9-3 0 .... NeilCallan 4 65
(David Simcock) *plld hrd and prom: rdn over 2f out: styd on same pce fr over 1f out* **9/2**[1]
6 3/4 **Counsel (IRE)** 2-9-3 0 .... RichardMullen 9 63+
(Sir Michael Stoute) *s.i.s: hdwy 1/2-way: styd on same pce appr fnl f* **15/2**
04 **7** 1 **Love Tale**[40] 4474 2-8-12 0 .... PJMcDonald 3 55
(Mark Rimell) *chsd ldrs: rdn over 1f out: wknd ins fnl f* **125/1**
8 1 1/4 **Mr Churchill (IRE)** 2-9-3 0 .... SilvestreDeSousa 10 57
(Mahmood Al Zarooni) *dwlt: sn pushed along in rr: styd on fnl f: nvr nrr* **15/2**
9 3 1/4 **Multilateral (USA)** 2-9-3 0 .... IanMongan 15 49+
(Amanda Perrett) *hld up: pushed along 1/2-way: wknd wl over 1f out* **28/1**
10 1 1/2 **Fisher** 2-9-3 0 .... PatDobbs 6 45
(Richard Hannon) *chsd ldrs tl rdn and wknd over 1f out* **12/1**
11 2 **Tigertoo (IRE)** 2-9-0 0 .... RyanClark(3) 12 40
(Stuart Williams) *sn pushed along and a in rr* **80/1**
12 3 3/4 **Aleksandar** 2-9-3 0 .... KierenFallon 2 41+
(Luca Cumani) *prom: pushed along over 2f out: sn wknd* **8/1**
00 **13** 1/2 **Men Don't Cry (IRE)**[13] 5384 2-9-3 0 .... ChrisCatlin 11 29
(Ed Dunlop) *sn pushed along in rr: bhd fr 1/2-way* **25/1**

1m 24.0s (-2.20) **Going Correction** -0.30s/f (Firm) **13** Ran SP% **115.7**
Speed ratings (Par 97): **100,98,96,95,94 93,92,91,87,85 83,79,78**
toteswingers:1&2:£32.10, 1&3:£8.30, 2&3:£33.70 CSF £130.36 TOTE £7.10: £2.40, £8.20, £3.50; EX 204.50.
Owner Godolphin **Bred** Darley **Trained** Newmarket, Suffolk

FOCUS
The driest summer in the midlands since 1976 and after just over 4mm rain during the night and in the morning, it was a bright, blustery day. There was a strong tail wind and the going was described as 'good' by the winning rider after the opener. Plenty of well-bred newcomers from powerful stables and a winner of real potential, but the exposed 68-rated runner-up puts a big question mark over the exact value of the form.

NOTEBOOK
Oscan(USA), a big, well made half-brother to Godolphin's St Leger winner Mastery, took time to pick up racing towards the stands' side. In the end, he won with some authority and looks sure to develop into a good 1m2f performer at three. (op 11-2)
Verse Of Love, having her fifth start and already well beaten in nursery company from a mark of 72, seemed to run out of her skin. On face value a quick return to nursery company from a mark of just 68 would make her very hard to beat. (op 33-1)
Uprise, well beaten first time, was backed at 16/1 in the morning. He gave a good account of himself and normal improvement will see him get off the mark. (op [illegible] tchd [illegible])
Dark Don(IRE) again travelled strongly but did not get home. A drop back to 6f might suit him better at this early stage of his career. (tchd 8-1 and 10-1)
Andalieb, who shaped nicely on his debut, again showed ability racing towards the far side. The best of him has yet to be seen. (op 6-1)
Counsel(IRE), a Derby entry and related to St Leger candidate Sea Moon, cost 200,000gns. After a slow start he picked up in encouraging fashion late on and looks capable of a lot better. (op 5-1)
Love Tale stepped up markedly on his first two efforts, showing good speed down the outside. This may have blown a possible lenient nursery mark out of the water. (op 150-1)
Mr Churchill(IRE) made significant late ground after a very slow start and looks sure to fare much better next time. (op 10-1 tchd 7-1)
Multilateral(USA), a rangy, backward-looking newcomer, looks as though he needs another year over his head. (op 25-1)

5802 ILLSTON-ON-THE-HILL (S) STKS 7f 9y
2:30 (2:30) (Class 6) 2-Y-O **£1,617** (£481; £240; £120) **Stalls** High

Form RPR
0435 **1** **King Kenobi (IRE)**[15] 5325 2-8-12 61 .... LiamKeniry 5 61
(J S Moore) *chsd ldrs: rdn over 2f out: led ins fnl f: styd on u.p* **13/2**
0062 **2** nk **Make Up**[15] 5325 2-8-4 56 .... KieranO'Neill(3) 8 56
(Richard Hannon) *a.p: nt clr run over 2f out: rdn and swtchd lft over 1f out: r.o* **6/1**[3]
000 **3** hd **Garrarufa (IRE)**[15] 5325 2-8-12 53 .... JamesMillman 7 60
(Rod Millman) *sn pushed along in rr: hdwy over 2f out: rdn and ev ch 1f out: styd on* **11/1**
4501 **4** 2 1/2 **Latte**[14] 5353 2-9-3 70 ....(p) KierenFallon 9 58
(Linda Stubbs) *chsd ldr: rdn over 2f out: ev ch 1f out: no ex ins fnl f* **13/8**[1]
0500 **5** 3/4 **Sabusa (IRE)**[12] 5413 2-8-12 58 ....(p) RobertWinston 10 51
(Alan McCabe) *led: rdn and hung rt over 1f out: hdd and no ex ins fnl f* **28/1**
00 **6** 6 **Three Tenors**[13] 5393 2-8-12 0 ....(p) CathyGannon 4 36
(J S Moore) *s.i.s: sn pushed along in rr: hdwy over 2f out: wknd over 1f out* **66/1**
0426 **7** 6 **Bajan Hero**[40] 4462 2-8-12 68 ....(v[1]) SilvestreDeSousa 3 20
(David Evans) *prom: rdn 1/2-way: wknd 2f out* **11/4**[2]
00 **8** 23 **Aunty Mavis (IRE)**[15] 5325 2-8-7 0 .... DavidProbert 2 —
(Ronald Harris) *prom: rdn 1/2-way: wknd over 2f out: t.o* **100/1**
00 **9** 2 1/4 **Loving Emma**[31] 4808 2-8-7 0 .... DuranFentiman 6 —
(John Weymes) *sn pushed along in rr: rdn and wknd 1/2-way: t.o* **100/1**
00 **10** 65 **Edensor (IRE)**[7] 5579 2-8-12 0 .... IanMongan 1 —
(John Dunlop) *dwlt: sn outpcd: t.o fnl 5f* **16/1**

1m 24.33s (-1.87) **Going Correction** -0.30s/f (Firm) **10** Ran SP% **113.5**
Speed ratings (Par 93): **98,97,97,94,93 86,80,53,51,—**
toteswingers:1&2:£3.50, 1&3:£6.20, 2&3:£6.20 CSF £43.31 TOTE £6.80: £1.90, £1.60, £3.20; EX 33.30.There was no bid for the winner. Make Up was claimed by Mr N Wilson for £6,000.
Owner G V March & J S Moore **Bred** John Burke **Trained** Upper Lambourn, Berks
■ Stewards' Enquiry : Liam Keniry two-day ban: used whip with excessive frequency (Sep 20-21)

FOCUS
A standard backend juvenile seller with little to choose between the first three at the line, and the first five finished clear of the remainder.

NOTEBOOK
King Kenobi(IRE), whose five runs now have been in selling company, had finished fifth when Make Up was second at Windsor two weeks earlier. He has the right attitude, but may have had luck on his side here. (tchd 11-2)
Make Up, over 3l ahead of the winner at Windsor, missed a beat at the start. Short of room and forced to switch to the stands' rail, she would have prevailed in a few more strides. She was claimed by Noel Wilson. (op 5-1)
Garrarufa(IRE), only eighth behind today's first two at Windsor, seemed to turn in a much improved effort on his fourth start. (tchd 9-1 and 12-1)
Latte, who sported cheekpieces for the first time when making all for a wide-margin success at Yarmouth, didn't get his own way this time and found the penalty too much in the end. (op 11-8 tchd 5-4 and 7-4)
Sabusa(IRE), last of eight in first-time cheekpieces over an extended 1m in claiming company at Wolverhampton on his previous start, towed them along and may be able to pick up a seller over 6f. (op 40-1)
Bajan Hero, visored on his first try in selling company, had the best chance on official ratings but he looks to be going the wrong way. (op 4-1 tchd 9-2)

5803 SIS LIVE H'CAP 7f 9y
3:00 (3:01) (Class 5) (0-70,70) 3-Y-0+ **£2,264** (£673; £336; £168) **Stalls** High

Form RPR
0000 **1** **Without Prejudice (USA)**[11] 5455 6-9-5 63 .... JamesSullivan 1 74
(Michael Easterby) *hld up: hdwy over 2f out: sn rdn: styd on to ld nr fin* **33/1**
1010 **2** nk **Cootehill Lass (IRE)**[7] 5581 3-9-8 70 ....(p) SilvestreDeSousa 11 78
(David Evans) *chsd ldrs: rdn over 2f out: led over 1f out: hdd nr fin* **9/2**[3]
3531 **3** 4 1/2 **Barista (IRE)**[4] 5675 3-9-2 67 .... MartinHarley(3) 4 63
(Mick Channon) *hld up: rdn over 2f out: hdwy and swtchd rt over 1f out: styd on to go 3rd post: nvr nrr* **3/1**[1]
5302 **4** hd **Sairaam (IRE)**[14] 5338 5-9-8 66 .... RobbieFitzpatrick 5 63
(Charles Smith) *hld up: hdwy over 2f out: edgd lft and no ex ins fnl f: lost 3rd post* **10/1**
5000 **5** 2 1/4 **Micky P**[48] 4206 4-9-4 62 ....(vt) SaleemGolam 12 53
(Stuart Williams) *chsd ldrs: rdn over 2f out: wknd ins fnl f* **12/1**
5040 **6** 3 1/2 **Faith And Hope (IRE)**[66] 3633 3-9-5 67 ....(t) KierenFallon 2 47
(James Fanshawe) *prom: led wl over 2f out: rdn and hdd over 1f out: wknd ins fnl f* **12/1**
6024 **7** 3/4 **Fluctuation (IRE)**[32] 4743 3-8-6 57 ....(v[1]) RyanClark(3) 15 35
(Ian Williams) *trckd ldrs: racd keenly: rdn over 2f out: wknd over 1f out* **16/1**
1300 **8** 2 1/2 **Bertie Blu Boy**[100] 2527 3-8-12 60 .... CathyGannon 10 31
(Paul Green) *led: rdn and hdd wl over 2f out: wknd over 1f out* **25/1**
6136 **9** 4 **Songsmith**[7] 5581 3-9-4 66 ....(p) IanMongan 7 26
(Lucy Wadham) *prom: rdn over 2f out: wknd over 1f out* **7/2**[2]
-006 **10** 3 1/4 **Elegant Dancer (IRE)**[25] 5008 4-8-2 51 oh6 ....(v[1]) ShaneBKelly(5) 6 —
(Paul Green) *mid-div: rdn 1/2-way: wknd over 2f out* **100/1**
6520 **11** 1 1/4 **Cuthbert (IRE)**[50] 4160 4-9-7 70 ....(v) MarkCoumbe(5) 3 —
(William Jarvis) *mid-div on outer: rdn over 2f out: wknd over 1f out* **12/1**
1405 **12** 3 3/4 **Here To Eternity (USA)**[27] 4926 3-9-6 68 .... WilliamBuick 8 —
(Peter Chapple-Hyam) *hld up in tch: wknd over 1f out* **14/1**
-035 **13** 1/2 **Queen's Choice (IRE)**[50] 4149 3-8-3 54 .... KieranO'Neill(3) 9 —
(Anabel K Murphy) *s.i.s: sn pushed along and a in rr: wknd over 2f out* **20/1**

1m 23.41s (-2.79) **Going Correction** -0.30s/f (Firm)
WFA 3 from 4yo+ 4lb **13** Ran SP% **122.7**
Speed ratings (Par 103): **103,102,97,97,94 90,89,87,83,78 77,73,72**
toteswingers:1&2:£25.40, 1&3:£26.70, 2&3:£4.40 CSF £176.68 CT £621.95 TOTE £30.20: £7.40, £1.50, £1.70; EX 233.40.
Owner Tri Nations Racing Syndicate **Bred** Castlemartin Stud And Skymarc Farm **Trained** Sheriff Hutton, N Yorks

FOCUS
A modest 7f handicap and the winner was hard to predict.
Without Prejudice(USA) Official explanation: trainer's rep said, regarding apparent improvement in form, that the gelding was better suited by the quicker ground.
Faith And Hope(IRE) Official explanation: jockey said filly was unsuited by the good to firm (good in places) ground
Songsmith Official explanation: jockey said gelding never travelled
Here To Eternity(USA) Official explanation: jockey said filly was unsuited by the good to firm (good in places) ground

5804 KIEREN FALLON WRITES FOR THE WEEKENDER H'CAP 1m 3f 183y
3:30 (3:30) (Class 5) (0-70,70) 3-Y-0+ **£2,264** (£673; £336; £168) **Stalls** Low

Form RPR
6105 **1** **Hot Spice**[25] 5015 3-9-0 67 .... PhillipMakin 15 83+
(John Dunlop) *hld up: hdwy 3f out: rdn to ld and hung rt ins fnl f: r.o: comf* **11/2**[1]
1 **2** 2 **O Ma Lad (IRE)**[31] 4800 3-9-3 70 .... NeilCallan 2 83
(Sylvester Kirk) *hld up: hdwy 1/2-way: led over 1f out: rdn and hdd ins fnl f: styd on same pce* **13/2**[2]
0133 **3** 1 **Chatterer (IRE)**[37] 4584 3-9-1 68 ....(t) RichardMullen 14 79
(Marcus Tregoning) *s.i.s: hld up: hdwy and hung rt fr over 2f out: styd on: nt rch ldrs* **11/2**[1]
2604 **4** 7 **Eastern Magic**[48] 4204 4-9-4 62 ....(p) GrahamGibbons 11 62
(Reg Hollinshead) *prom: led 10f out: hung lft 8f out: rdn and hdd over 1f out: wknd fnl f* **15/2**[3]
0040 **5** 1 1/4 **Dubara Reef (IRE)**[13] 5369 4-9-4 62 ....(p) SilvestreDeSousa 10 60
(Paul Green) *mid-div: lost pl 1/2-way: rdn over 4f out: sn hung rt: bhd whn nt clr run over 2f out: styd on u.p ins fnl f* **16/1**
1200 **6** nse **On The Feather**[14] 5340 5-9-11 69 .... JamesMillman 7 67
(Rod Millman) *hld up: hdwy over 2f out: nvr trbld ldrs* **14/1**
2543 **7** 1 **Spring Secret**[11] 5428 5-9-12 70 .... DavidProbert 12 66
(Bryn Palling) *prom: chsd ldr 8f out tl rdn over 2f out: wknd over 1f out* **25/1**

1/4 **8** ½ **King's Road**[20] 5168 6-9-2 **60**....(t) JimCrowley 1 55
(Anabel K Murphy) *hld up: hdwy over 3f out: rdn and wknd over 1f out* **12/1**
0463 **9** 1 **Kames Park (IRE)**[9] 5504 9-8-9 **56**....RobertLButler(3) 6 50
(Richard Guest) *s.i.s: hld up: nt clr run over 2f out: nvr trbld ldrs* **25/1**
6201 **10** 1 **Lauberhorn**[32] 4746 4-9-4 **62**....(b) CathyGannon 5 54
(Eve Johnson Houghton) *hld up: hdwy over 5f out: rdn and wknd over 1f out* **14/1**
003 **11** 7 **Sister Andrea**[20] 5169 3-9-0 **67**.... ShaneKelly 4 48
(James Fanshawe) *led 1f: chsd ldrs tl rdn and wknd over 2f out* **12/1**
263 **12** 4½ **Tiny Temper (IRE)**[25] 4985 3-9-0 **70**.... LeeTopliss(3) 8 44
(Richard Fahey) *s.i.s: sn rcvrd into mid-div: rdn and wknd over 2f out* **10/1**
0344 **13** ¾ **Maslak (IRE)**[10] 5491 7-9-4 **62**....(p) ChrisCatlin 13 35
(Peter Hiatt) *chsd ldrs: rdn over 3f out: wknd over 2f out* **33/1**
00-2 **14** 9 **Bolanderi (USA)**[27] 4916 6-9-8 **66**.... WilliamBuick 3 24
(Andy Turnell) *led 11f out to 10f out: chsd ldrs: rdn over 2f out: wknd and eased over 1f out* **14/1**

2m 32.7s (-1.20) **Going Correction** -0.125s/f (Firm)
WFA 3 from 4yo+ 9lb **14** Ran SP% **116.9**
Speed ratings (Par 103): **99,97,97,92,91 91,90,90,89,89 84,81,80,74**
toteswingers:1&2:£6.20, 1&3:£6.70, 2&3:£7.70 CSF £37.47 CT £207.38 TOTE £6.40: £2.00, £2.80, £2.70; EX 42.80.
Owner David & Jennifer Sieff & Partner **Bred** J L Dunlop **Trained** Arundel, W Sussex

FOCUS
Another modest handicap and the first three finished clear.
O Ma Lad(IRE) Official explanation: vet said gelding finished lame near-fore
Eastern Magic Official explanation: jockey said gelding hung left
Dubara Reef(IRE) Official explanation: jockey said gelding hung right
Spring Secret Official explanation: jockey said gelding slipped on bend

5805 PRESTWOLD CONDITIONS STKS 5f 2y
4:00 (4:00) (Class 4) 3-Y-O+ **£5,355** (£1,603; £801; £401; £199) **Stalls** High

Form RPR
0500 **1** **Mister Manannan (IRE)**[31] 4776 4-8-9 92.... AdrianNicholls 8 101
(David Nicholls) *awkward leaving stalls: rcvrd to ld 4f out: rdn over 1f out: r.o wl* **15/2**[3]
0450 **2** 1¼ **Bathwick Bear (IRE)**[17] 5264 3-8-8 93.... GrahamGibbons 1 96
(David Evans) *led 1f: chsd ldr: rdn 1/2-way: ev ch over 1f out: styd on same pce ins fnl f* **18/1**
6020 **3** ½ **Pabusar**[24] 5054 3-8-8 104.... JimCrowley 7 94
(Ralph Beckett) *s.i.s: hdwy over 3f out: rdn over 1f out: styd on same pce ins fnl f* **7/4**[2]
2030 **4** shd **Monsieur Joe (IRE)**[106] 2370 4-8-9 105.... SilvestreDeSousa 3 94
(Walter Swinburn) *prom: pushed along 3f out: swtchd rt 1/2-way: sn rdn: styd on same pce ins fnl f* **5/4**[1]
0000 **5** 6 **Stone Of Folca**[8] 5543 3-8-11 99.... FrederikTylicki 5 75
(John Best) *chsd ldrs: rdn 1/2-way: wknd over 1f out* **8/1**

58.15 secs (-1.85) **Going Correction** -0.30s/f (Firm)
WFA 3 from 4yo+ 1lb **5** Ran SP% **108.9**
Speed ratings (Par 105): **102,100,99,99,89**
CSF £92.53 TOTE £8.00: £2.90, £5.60; EX 72.60.
Owner Mrs M Schofield **Bred** Mull Enterprises Ltd **Trained** Sessay, N Yorks

FOCUS
A depleted field for this Class 4 sprint.

5806 BRITISH STALLION STUDS SUPPORTING BRITISH RACING E B F MAIDEN FILLIES' STKS (DIV I) 1m 60y
4:30 (4:31) (Class 4) 2-Y-O **£4,010** (£1,193; £596; £298) **Stalls** Low

Form RPR
5325 **1** **My Queenie (IRE)**[10] 5472 2-9-0 93.... PatDobbs 11 80+
(Richard Hannon) *chsd ldr tl led over 1f out: pushed clr fnl f* **5/2**[2]
56 **2** 1¾ **Protect**[53] 4061 2-8-11 0.... LouisBeuzelin(3) 1 76
(Sir Michael Stoute) *set stdy pce tl qcknd over 2f out: rdn and hdd over 1f out: styd on same pce* **10/1**[3]
00 **3** 1½ **Aliante**[25] 4992 2-9-0 0.... SilvestreDeSousa 2 72+
(Mark Johnston) *sn prom: rdn over 2f out: styd on* **66/1**
4 nk **Saytara (IRE)** 2-9-0 0.... RichardMullen 4 71+
(Saeed Bin Suroor) *s.i.s: hld up: swtchd lft over 1f out: r.o ins fnl f: nrst fin* **11/1**
3 **5** hd **Buzkashi (IRE)**[38] 4552 2-9-0 0.... NeilCallan 6 73+
(Roger Varian) *chsd ldrs: nt clr run and stmbld bdly 2f out: nt rcvr* **11/10**[1]
6 1½ **Egretta (IRE)** 2-9-0 0.... JimCrowley 7 68+
(Hughie Morrison) *hld up: racd keenly: hdwy and hung rt over 1f out: styd on* **33/1**
06 **7** 3¼ **Tiger Cub**[15] 5320 2-9-0 0.... RichardKingscote 8 60
(Roger Charlton) *hld up in tch: rdn over 2f out: wknd fnl f* **66/1**
8 4½ **Khione** 2-9-0 0.... KierenFallon 12 50
(Luca Cumani) *chsd ldrs: pushed along over 2f out: wknd over 1f out* **18/1**
04 **9** 3¼ **Maliha (IRE)**[24] 5029 2-9-0 0.... PhillipMakin 10 42
(Kevin Ryan) *hld up in tch: plld hrd: rdn over 3f out: wknd over 1f out* **28/1**
0 **10** 17 **Amelia May**[11] 5444 2-9-0 0.... WilliamBuick 5 —
(John Gosden) *hld up: nvr on terms: lost tch fnl 2f: t.o* **16/1**
0 **11** ½ **Tresabella**[53] 4061 2-9-0 0.... RobbieFitzpatrick 9 —
(Michael Appleby) *sn pushed along and a in rr: bhd fr 1/2-way: t.o* **200/1**

1m 46.1s (1.00) **Going Correction** -0.125s/f (Firm) **11** Ran SP% **114.6**
Speed ratings (Par 94): **90,88,86,86,86 84,81,77,73,56 56**
CSF £26.02 TOTE £2.00: £1.10, £2.20, £11.10; EX 24.00.
Owner N A Woodcock **Bred** Rathbarry Stud **Trained** East Everleigh, Wilts

FOCUS
No strength in depth in part one of this maiden juvenile fillies' event and the pace was very steady to past halfway.

NOTEBOOK
My Queenie(IRE), rated 93 after her fifth in the Group 3 Prestige Stakes at Goodwood, had the leader covered and in the end opened her account at the fifth attempt with the minimum of fuss. (op 9-4)
Protect, the reluctant leader, had finished a neck behind My Queenie at Newmarket in July. She quickened up the pace soon after the half way mark but in the end proved no match. (op 9-1 tchd 11-1)
Aliante, a daughter of Sir Percy, is bred to come good over middle-distances. On her third start, she picked up in good style late on and can certainly take a nursery if that is the chosen option.
Saytara(IRE), a well-related newcomer, missed the break but put in some highly pleasing late work. This will have taught her plenty. (op 9-1 tchd 12-1)
Buzkashi(IRE), a well-related newcomer, missed the break but put in some highly pleasing late work. This will have taught her plenty. (op 11-8 tchd 6-4 in places)
Egretta(IRE) got the hang of things very late on and is the type to do much better at three. (op 50-1)
Tiger Cub went well until tiring and this opens up the nursery route for her.

5807 BRITISH STALLION STUDS SUPPORTING BRITISH RACING E B F MAIDEN FILLIES' STKS (DIV II) 1m 60y
5:00 (5:01) (Class 4) 2-Y-O **£4,010** (£1,193; £596; £298) **Stalls** Low

Form RPR
4232 **1** **Esentepe (IRE)**[10] 5464 2-9-0 80.... PatDobbs 1 79
(Richard Hannon) *trckd ldrs: racd keenly: shkn up to ld ins fnl f: r.o wl* **2/1**[1]
632 **2** 1¾ **Perfect Delight**[24] 5029 2-8-11 74.... JohnFahy(3) 12 75
(Clive Cox) *led: rdn and hdd ins fnl f: unable qck* **4/1**[2]
3 3 **Corsetry (USA)** 2-9-0 0.... IanMongan 11 68
(Sir Henry Cecil) *chsd ldrs: rdn over 3f out: styd on same pce fnl f* **5/1**[3]
4 nk **Dinvar Diva** 2-9-0 0.... WilliamBuick 3 67+
(John Gosden) *hld up: hdwy over 3f out: rdn and edgd rt over 1f out: styd on same pce* **7/1**
0 **5** 1¾ **The Giving Tree (IRE)**[60] 3813 2-9-0 0.... LiamKeniry 10 63
(Sylvester Kirk) *chsd ldr tl rdn over 1f out: no ex fnl f* **50/1**
0 **6** nse **Princess Caetani (IRE)**[11] 5454 2-9-0 0.... SilvestreDeSousa 2 63+
(Mark Johnston) *prom: rdn over 2f out: edgd rt and no ex fnl f* **11/1**
7 1 **Estimate (IRE)** 2-9-0 0.... RichardMullen 4 61+
(Sir Michael Stoute) *s.i.s: sn pushed along in rr: nvr nrr* **12/1**
8 2¼ **Moment In Time (IRE)** 2-9-0 0.... MartinLane 5 56
(David Simcock) *dwlt: rdn over 2f out: n.d* **17/2**
0 **9** 6 **Smart Affair**[15] 5323 2-9-0 0.... JamesMillman 8 42
(Rod Millman) *hld up: hdwy over 4f out: wknd over 1f out* **125/1**
10 2¼ **Velvet Star (IRE)** 2-9-0 0.... ChrisCatlin 6 37
(Paul Cole) *hld up: plld hrd: hdwy over 2f out: sn wknd* **20/1**
0 **11** 5 **Motheeba (USA)**[15] 5320 2-9-0 0.... TadhgO'Shea 7 25
(Ed Dunlop) *s.i.s: hld up: pushed along over 3f out: wknd over 2f out* **66/1**

1m 45.07s (-0.03) **Going Correction** -0.125s/f (Firm) **11** Ran SP% **118.1**
Speed ratings (Par 94): **95,93,90,89,88 88,87,84,78,76 71**
toteswingers:1&2:£2.10, 1&3:£4.00, 2&3:£7.90 CSF £9.57 TOTE £2.90: £1.20, £1.10, £3.50; EX 8.70.
Owner Middleham Park Racing XXXVIII **Bred** Peter Kelly And Ms Wendy Daly **Trained** East Everleigh, Wilts

FOCUS
Division two and again the gallop was steady until the final 3f.

NOTEBOOK
Esentepe(IRE), rated 80, made it eighth time lucky. Tucked in on the rail on the heels of the leader, she had to bide her time but when the gap came she grasped it with both hands. No-one could say she did not deserve this first success. (op 15-8)
Perfect Delight, rated 74, had the run of the race from the front but could not match the winner's finishing burst. Though limited, she does absolutely nothing wrong. (tchd 7-2)
Corsetry(USA), a half-sister to connections' Oaks winner Light Shift, made a pleasing bow and normal improvement should see her make her mark. (op 10-1)
Dinvar Diva, who cost 105,000gns, is likewise from the family of Light Shift. Pushed along before there was any injection of pace, she stuck on strongly and will do better over further next year. (op 15-2 tchd 8-1)
The Giving Tree(IRE) stepped up on her debut effort at Newbury but she is another backward type who will not reveal her full potential until next season. (op 66-1 tchd 80-1)
Princess Caetani(IRE) was being driven along turning in and looks more of a middle-distance type at three. (op 12-1 tchd 10-1)
Estimate(IRE), a half-sister to three smart performers including the Ascot Gold Cup winner Enzei, was slow to break. She picked up in her own time late on and will do better over further next year. (op 10-1 tchd 9-1)

5808 STAG APPRENTICE H'CAP 1m 1f 218y
5:30 (5:31) (Class 5) (0-70,68) 4-Y-O+ **£1,940** (£577; £288; £144) **Stalls** Low

Form RPR
0-03 **1** **Bowsers Brave (USA)**[83] 3042 5-9-1 **64**....(t) KatiaScallan(3) 5 75
(Marcus Tregoning) *hld up: hdwy over 2f out: led over 1f out: r.o wl* **7/2**[2]
5461 **2** 6 **Minsky Mine (IRE)**[9] 5518 4-9-8 **68** 6ex.... JustinNewman 3 67
(Michael Appleby) *led: pushed along over 3f out: rdn and hdd over 1f out: styd on same pce* **9/4**[1]
0655 **3** shd **Silent Oasis**[11] 5428 5-9-2 **62**....(tp) EdmondLinehan 8 61
(Brendan Powell) *dwlt and reluctant early: clsd on to the rr of the gp 7f out: hdwy over 3f out: rdn over 1f out: styd on same pce* **10/1**
0266 **4** 1½ **Sweet Secret**[30] 4825 4-9-6 **66**.... RaulDaSilva 4 62
(Jeremy Gask) *chsd ldr: chal 3f out: rdn over 1f out: no ex ins fnl f* **6/1**
5010 **5** 14 **Maybe I Wont**[8] 5545 6-9-3 **66**.... NoelGarbutt(3) 6 34
(Lucinda Featherstone) *prom: pushed along over 4f out: wknd over 2f out* **15/2**
0353 **6** 1½ **Bidable**[13] 5376 7-9-4 **67**.... ThomasBrown(3) 1 32
(Bryn Palling) *hld up: racd keenly: rdn and wknd over 2f out* **12/1**
6221 **7** 3 **Market Puzzle (IRE)**[9] 5520 4-8-7 **53** 6ex....(p) RachealKneller 2 12
(Mark Brisbourne) *chsd ldrs tl rdn and wknd over 2f out* **11/2**[3]

2m 5.87s (-2.03) **Going Correction** -0.125s/f (Firm) **7** Ran SP% **111.2**
Speed ratings (Par 103): **103,98,98,96,85 84,82**
toteswingers:1&2:£1.90, 1&3:£7.10, 2&3:£4.50 CSF £11.13 CT £65.96 TOTE £4.60: £1.70, £1.10; EX 11.50.
Owner Mrs Simon Aldridge **Bred** Shadwell Farm LLC **Trained** Lambourn, Berks

FOCUS
A very modest apprentice handicap and the two leaders took each other on some way from home leaving them vulnerable to a strong finisher.
T/Jkpt: Not won. T/Plt: £2,361.70 to a £1 stake. Pool:£74,574.11 - 23.05 winning tickets T/Qpdt: £216.60 to a £1 stake. Pool:£6,254.82 - 21.36 winning tickets CR

5406 LINGFIELD (L-H)
Tuesday, September 6

OFFICIAL GOING: Turf course - good to soft changing to soft after race 2 (2:40); all-weather - standard
Wind: very strong, half behind Weather: windy and wet

5809 FREE REPLAYS AT ATTHERACES.COM NURSERY (TURF) 7f
2:10 (2:12) (Class 5) (0-75,75) 2-Y-O **£2,385** (£704; £352) **Stalls** High

Form RPR
630 **1** **Poetic Lord**[33] 4722 2-9-4 **72**.... DaneO'Neill 11 80
(Richard Hannon) *chsd ldr: rdn to chal over 1f out: kpt on wl fnl f to ld towards fin: edgd rt cl home* **7/2**[1]

The Form Book, Raceform Ltd, Compton, RG20 6NL

310 **2** ¾ **Long Lost Love**[28] 4892 2-9-0 **68** J-PGuillambert 3 74
(Mark Johnston) *broke wl and crossed to r against stands' rail: led: rdn and drew clr w wnr over 1f out: hdd towards fin: hld whn n.m.r nr fin* **12/1**
0243 **3** 4 **Dark Ambition (IRE)**[12] 5409 2-8-10 **67** AdamBeschizza(3) 1 63
(William Haggas) *racd in midfield: swtchd lft and effrt over 2f out: kpt on u.p to chse ldng pair ins fnl f: no threat to ldrs* **7/1**
1460 **4** 7 **Lady Victory (IRE)**[24] 5052 2-9-0 **68** (v[1]) SamHitchcott 13 47
(Mick Channon) *chsd ldrs: rdn over 2f out: wknd over 1f out: 3rd and wl btn 1f out: fdd and lost 3rd ins fnl f* **20/1**
000 **5** ¾ **Joyful Spirit (IRE)**[16] 5299 2-8-8 **62** EddieAhern 4 39
(John Dunlop) *chsd ldrs: rdn and struggling over 2f out: 4th and wl btn over 1f out: wknd fnl f* **5/1**[2]
0010 **6** 2 ¼ **Queens Sandridge (IRE)**[11] 5446 2-9-7 **75** DarryllHolland 9 46
(Alan Bailey) *chsd ldrs: rdn and struggling jst over 2f out: wknd wl over 1f out* **8/1**
2346 **7** 1 ¼ **Siouxperhero (IRE)**[21] 5133 2-9-2 **70** MartinDwyer 8 38
(William Muir) *towards rr: rdn along and barging match w rival 4f out: struggling 3f out: sn btn* **14/1**
1330 **8** shd **Xinbama (IRE)**[19] 5197 2-9-1 **69** SebSanders 7 37
(J W Hills) *towards rr: barging match w rival 4f out: pushed along and struggling 1/2-way: no threat to ldrs fnl 2f* **11/1**
3456 **9** ½ **Rock Canyon (IRE)**[19] 5197 2-9-0 **71** SeanLevey(3) 12 37
(Robert Mills) *chsd ldrs: rdn and struggling over 2f out: wknd 2f out* **11/2**[3]
0003 **10** 12 **Angel Cake (IRE)**[30] 4841 2-8-8 **62** FergusSweeney 10 —
(Amy Weaver) *racd in midfield: rdn and lost pl 3f out: sn bhd: t.o fnl f* **12/1**
000 **11** 18 **Fresteem**[13] 5382 2-7-11 **54** oh4 ow2 (b[1]) HarryBentley(3) 5 —
(Luke Dace) *bhd: lost tch 1/2-way: t.o fnl 2f* **66/1**

1m 24.14s (0.84) **Going Correction** 0.0s/f (Good) 11 Ran SP% **114.5**
Speed ratings (Par 95): **95,94,89,81,80 78,76,76,76,62 41**
toteswingers:1&2:£5.80, 1&3:£5.30, 2&3:£7.40 CSF £45.72 CT £283.01 TOTE £4.80: £1.40, £3.00, £2.10; EX 31.20 Trifecta £96.20 Pool: £312.31 - 2.40 winning units..
Owner Mrs John Lee **Bred** Howard Barton Stud **Trained** East Everleigh, Wilts

FOCUS
The stands' running rail was as per August 13, in two meters from the traditional line. There was a lot of rain around and following the opener Dane O'Neill and Fergus Sweeney respectively described the ground as "more soft than good to soft" and "soft". There was a fierce wind behind the runners. This race was run in gloomy conditions and visibility was poor for much of the way. The stands' rail was a help, as is usually the case here, and plenty of these won't have handled the ground, so not obviously strong form.

NOTEBOOK
Poetic Lord stepped up a good deal on his maiden form, justifying market support in the process. He may be worthy of extra credit considering he didn't have the rail and gradually wore down a rival who was racing against the fence. (tchd 3-1)
Long Lost Love flopped when dropped back to 6f at Nottingham last time, having previously won a 1m maiden, and the return to more of a stamina test evidently suited. She was quite possibly helped by having the stands' rail to race against, and also a tailwind, although she did have to use up energy to get across from a low draw. (op 17-2)
Dark Ambition(IRE) has shown a tendency to race with his mouth open, but the gloomy conditions made it difficult to tell if that was the case this time. The lowest draw was no help, but he kept on from well back and has the ability to win a race when things go his way. (op 13-2 tchd 15-2)
Lady Victory(IRE) didn't improve for a first-time visor, but she might want better ground. (op 22-1 tchd 25-1)
Joyful Spirit(IRE) ◆ was stuck out wide and could make no real impression. She'll probably do better over further (half-sister to two 1m4f winners, out of a 1m4f winner) and it's unlikely we'll see the best of her this season. (op 7-1 tchd 9-2)
Queens Sandridge(IRE), who won an alright 6f maiden before being denied a clear run (off 4lb higher) over 1m, attracted early market support, but presumably didn't really like the ground. (op 11-2)

5810 BRAND NEW ATR PREDICTOR MAIDEN STKS (TURF) 7f
2:40 (2:41) (Class 5) 3-Y-0+ **£2,385** (£704; £352) **Stalls** High

Form RPR
3 **1** **Emkanaat**[14] 5346 3-9-3 0 RichardHills 6 79+
(Roger Varian) *mde all: readily c clr 2f out: eased ins fnl f: v easily* **7/4**[2]
03 **2** 5 **Princess Willow**[25] 4991 3-8-12 0 RichardThomas 7 60
(John E Long) *in tch: chsd wnr 2f out: sn rdn and edgd lft: no prog and wl btn over 1f out: eased ins fnl f* **20/1**
42 **3** 6 **Cookieshake**[11] 5443 3-9-3 0 KirstyMilczarek 3 50
(Luca Cumani) *pushed along early: chsd ldrs: wnt 2nd 3f out tl rdn and edgd lft ent fnl 2f: 3rd and wl btn over 1f out* **5/4**[1]
5 **4** nk **Harvest Mist (IRE)**[45] 4320 3-8-12 0 NeilChalmers 2 44
(Michael Blanshard) *t.k.h: chsd wnr tl 3f out: sn rdn and edgd lft: wknd ent fnl 2f* **9/2**[3]
0 **5** 6 **Bunkered Again**[26] 4970 4-9-2 0 SteveDrowne 4 28
(Jeremy Gask) *in tch in rr: rdn and struggling 3f out: lost tch 2f out* **33/1**

1m 24.94s (1.64) **Going Correction** 0.0s/f (Good)
WFA 3 from 4yo 4lb 5 Ran SP% **106.7**
Speed ratings (Par 103): **90,84,77,77,70**
CSF £26.54 TOTE £2.70: £1.40, £4.30; EX 18.00.
Owner Hamdan Al Maktoum **Bred** C J Mills **Trained** Newmarket, Suffolk

FOCUS
A seriously uncompetitive maiden with a couple of these disappointing. They raced towards the stands' side. It's hard to know what the winner achieved but he's potentially better than this.

5811 CARAVAN CLUB H'CAP (TURF) 7f
3:10 (3:10) (Class 4) (0-85,85) 3-Y-0+ **£3,234** (£962; £481; £240) **Stalls** High

Form RPR
5653 **1** **Yair Hill (IRE)**[20] 5171 3-8-12 **77** TedDurcan 11 89+
(John Dunlop) *hld up in tch and hugged stands' rail: hdwy to trck ldng pair but nt clr run over 1f out: gap opened and rdn to ld ins fnl f: r.o wl and sn in command* **11/4**[1]
4405 **2** 1 ¼ **Oil Strike**[17] 5278 4-9-9 **84** WilliamCarson 8 90
(Peter Winkworth) *led and crossed to r against stands' rail: rdn over 1f out: hanging lft ent fnl f: continued to hang and hdd ins fnl f: no ex* **11/2**[3]
3036 **3** ½ **Camache Queen (IRE)**[61] 3782 3-8-10 **75** EddieAhern 10 78
(Denis Coakley) *t.k.h: hld up in tch: nt clr run over 2f out: effrt to chse ldr 2f out: pressing ldr and rdn jst over 1f out: carried lft and kpt on same pce fnl f* **7/2**[2]
0016 **4** 4 ½ **Watch Amigo (IRE)**[60] 3797 5-9-10 **85** JimmyFortune 4 78
(Walter Swinburn) *in tch on outer: rdn and effrt over 2f out: struggling u.p wl over 1f out: 4th and wl btn fnl f* **11/2**[3]
0005 **5** 3 ½ **Alhaban (IRE)**[153] 1183 5-9-1 **76** LukeMorris 9 60
(Ronald Harris) *dwlt: in tch in rr: u.p and no prog over 2f out: plugged on but wl btn over 1f out* **20/1**
0600 **6** ½ **Amwell Pinot**[25] 4993 3-9-2 **81** (b) DarryllHolland 2 62
(Alan Bailey) *chsd ldr: drvn 3f out: lost 2nd 2f out: sn wknd u.p* **9/1**
-616 **7** 3 ¾ **Dominium (USA)**[24] 5043 4-9-2 **77** SteveDrowne 6 50
(Jeremy Gask) *t.k.h: hld up in tch: rdn over 2f out: sn struggling: wknd 2f out* **8/1**
-000 **8** 3 **King's Colour**[8] 5547 6-9-3 **78** FergusSweeney 5 43
(Brett Johnson) *hld up in tch: rdn and struggling over 2f out: sn wknd* **28/1**
1100 **9** 13 **Bajan Bear**[38] 4550 3-8-10 **75** ow1 DaneO'Neill 1 —
(Michael Blanshard) *v.s.a: a bhd* **16/1**

1m 23.84s (0.54) **Going Correction** +0.225s/f (Good)
WFA 3 from 4yo+ 4lb 9 Ran SP% **114.9**
Speed ratings (Par 105): **105,103,103,97,93 93,89,85,70**
toteswingers:1&2:£4.30, 1&3:£3.20, 2&3:£7.00 CSF £18.03 CT £53.38 TOTE £3.20: £1.50, £2.10, £1.70; EX 14.00 Trifecta £33.70 Pool: £385.99 - 8.40 winning units..
Owner The Earl Cadogan **Bred** The Earl Cadogan **Trained** Arundel, W Sussex
■ Stewards' Enquiry : William Carson three-day ban: careless riding (Sep 20-22)

FOCUS
The going was changed to soft all over ahead of this race. The stands' rail yet again provided an advantage and this is form to treat with caution, although the winner is value for extra. The form is rated around the second and third.
Bajan Bear Official explanation: jockey said gelding was slowly away

5812 ASPEN MEDIAN AUCTION MAIDEN STKS (TURF) 6f
3:40 (3:41) (Class 5) 2-Y-0 **£2,385** (£704; £352) **Stalls** High

Form RPR
62 **1** **Princess Of Orange**[12] 5411 2-8-12 0 TedDurcan 14 82+
(Rae Guest) *mde all and racd against stands' rail: pushed clr wl over 1f out: eased ins fnl f: easily* **15/8**[2]
2 3 **Gabriel's Lad (IRE)** 2-9-3 0 EddieAhern 12 72
(Denis Coakley) *chsd ldrs: rdn and effrt to chse clr wnr over 1f out: no imp: kpt on* **4/1**[3]
42 **3** 2 **Sir Fredlot (IRE)**[29] 4857 2-9-3 0 LukeMorris 2 66+
(Peter Winkworth) *broke wl and crossed to chse ldrs towards stands' rail: chsd wnr and rdn over 2f out: outpcd and btn whn lost 2nd over 1f out* **7/4**[1]
50 **4** 1 ¼ **Al's Memory (IRE)**[29] 4864 2-9-3 0 StevieDonohoe 7 62
(David Evans) *chsd ldr tl over 3f out: rdn and struggling over 2f out: wl btn and swtchd lft over 1f out: no ch but plugged on fnl f* **40/1**
5 1 ¼ **Jane Lachatte (IRE)** 2-8-12 0 WilliamCarson 5 53+
(Stuart Williams) *s.i.s: rn green in rr: pushed along and hdwy 2f out: kpt on ins fnl f: n.d* **80/1**
0 **6** shd **Justbookies Dotnet**[64] 3686 2-9-3 0 FrankieMcDonald 3 58
(Louise Best) *chsd ldrs: wnt 2nd over 3f out tl over 2f out: sn wandering u.p: wknd wl over 1f out* **100/1**
0 **7** nk **Bolshoi Melody**[15] 5323 2-8-12 0 FergusSweeney 11 52+
(Jeremy Gask) *in tch: outpcd and pushed along over 2f out: swtchd lft 2f out: one pce and no imp after* **50/1**
40 **8** 4 **Denton Dancer**[78] 3229 2-9-3 0 JackMitchell 9 45
(James Eustace) *racd off the pce in midfield: rdn and struggling 1/2-way: no ch fnl 2f* **33/1**
9 ½ **Ailanthus** 2-8-12 0 DaneO'Neill 10 39
(Henry Candy) *in tch: rn green and hung lft over 2f out: wknd 2f out* **11/1**
10 ½ **Silent Mistress** 2-8-12 0 AdrianMcCarthy 1 37
(J R Jenkins) *stdd s: hld up in rr: rn green and struggling 3f out: n.d* **100/1**
55 **11** hd **Atlantis Crossing (IRE)**[40] 4455 2-9-3 0 StephenCraine 6 41
(Jim Boyle) *sn outpcd towards rr: n.d* **50/1**
12 2 ¼ **Lady Arabella (IRE)** 2-8-12 0 SteveDrowne 4 30
(Alastair Lidderdale) *sn outpcd in last quartet: n.d* **25/1**
13 3 **Hesperides** 2-8-9 0 HarryBentley(3) 13 21
(Harry Dunlop) *s.i.s: a struggling in rr: rn green and hung lft 1/2-way* **50/1**

1m 12.8s (1.60) **Going Correction** +0.225s/f (Good) 13 Ran SP% **117.8**
Speed ratings (Par 95): **98,94,91,89,88 87,87,82,81,80 80,77,73**
toteswingers:1&2:£3.30, 1&3:£1.70, 2&3:£2.80 CSF £9.09 TOTE £2.20: £1.02, £3.00, £1.50; EX 9.30 Trifecta £43.50 Pool: £569.31 - 9.67 winning units..
Owner Colin Joseph **Bred** Cheveley Park Stud Ltd **Trained** Newmarket, Suffolk

FOCUS
The stands' rail again provided a major advantage and this form needs treating with caution.

NOTEBOOK
Princess Of Orange showed ability at Windsor on her debut and again when runner-up here on the Polytrack (both over 6f), and she made full use of being drawn against the favoured rail this time, winning with a lot in hand on ground that evidently suited. It's hard to overstate how much of an advantage the rail provided and consequently she'll be difficult to support next time, but she is well regarded. (op 2-1)
Gabriel's Lad(IRE), a 17,000gns half-brother to a 6f winner, out of a multiple sprint scorer, has already been gelded. There was plenty of money around for him, although presumably much of it was owing to his draw. He lacked the knowhow of the winner but kept on gradually, all the while racing against the rail, and galloped out well after the line. Clearly he has ability, but he was helped by where he raced. (op 10-3 tchd 3-1)
Sir Fredlot(IRE), poorly drawn, raced off the rail and couldn't repeat the form he showed when runner-up to Amazing Storm (followed up off 84, albeit over an extra furlong) last time. He can be given another chance and is now eligible for a handicap mark. (op 15-8 tchd 9-4)
Al's Memory(IRE) ran creditably and now has the option of nurseries. (op 66-1)
Jane Lachatte(IRE) ◆ is very much one to take from the race. The first foal of a middle-distance winner, she needed the experience and raced furthest away from the favoured rail, but was going on nicely at the finish. We might not see the best of her until she's handicapping over further, but it would be dangerous to underestimate her in maiden company. (op 100-1 tchd 66-1)

5813 BRITISH STALLION STUDS SUPPORTING BRITISH RACING E B F MAIDEN FILLIES' STKS (DIV I) 7f (P)
4:10 (4:11) (Class 5) 2-Y-0 **£2,911** (£866; £432; £216) **Stalls** Low

Form RPR
1 **Ihsas (USA)** 2-9-0 0 FrankieDettori 5 84+
(Saeed Bin Suroor) *dwlt: sn swtchd rt and hdwy into midfield: clsd to trck ldr over 2f out: led over 1f out: sn pushed clr: comf* **10/11**[1]
2 3 ¼ **Medea (IRE)** 2-9-0 0 JimmyFortune 6 75+
(Sir Michael Stoute) *hld up in last trio: hdwy over 2f out: rdn to chse clr ldng pair jst over 1f out: kpt on to go 2nd wl ins fnl f: no ch w wnr* **9/4**[2]
3 hd **Berwin (IRE)** 2-9-0 0 DaneO'Neill 3 74+
(Sylvester Kirk) *hld up in tch: rdn and effrt wl over 1f out: rn green over 1f out: r.o wl ins fnl f to go 3rd last strides: no ch w wnr* **20/1**
4 nk **Silver Marizah (IRE)** 2-9-0 0 TomQueally 9 73
(Gary Moore) *chsd ldr tl led over 2f out: rdn and clr w wnr wl over 1f out: sn hdd and outpcd by wnr: wl hld but kpt on: lost 2 pls nr fin* **25/1**

5 1 1/4 **Wye Valley** 2-9-0 0 EddieAhern 2 70+
(Amanda Perrett) *in tch: rdn and outpcd ent fnl 2f: swtchd lft over 1f out: no ch w wnr but kpt on again ins fnl f* **16/1**

6 3 1/2 **Lazeez (USA)** 2-9-0 0 PhilipRobinson 10 61
(Clive Brittain) *dwlt: sn rcvrd to chse ldrs: rdn and unable qck ent fnl 2f: wknd over 1f out* **20/1**

0 7 7 **Echo Of Thunder (IRE)**[16] 5299 2-9-0 0 TedDurcan 1 43
(David Lanigan) *led tl over 2f out: sn wknd: wl btn and eased ins fnl f* **14/1**[3]

00 8 2 1/4 **Waspy**[27] 4906 2-9-0 0 JamieSpencer 7 37
(Ed Dunlop) *stdd s: a bhd: pushed and sme hdwy on outer jst over 2f out: wd bnd 2f out and sn bhd* **20/1**

00 9 3 **La Confession**[38] 4525 2-8-11 0 PatrickHills(3) 8 29
(J W Hills) *in tch: lost pl and rdn 3f out: wl bhd over 1f out* **25/1**

10 2 **My Liberty** 2-9-0 0 AndreaAtzeni 4 24
(Chris Dwyer) *in tch towards rr: rdn over 3f out: wknd wl over 2f out* **100/1**

1m 25.57s (0.77) **Going Correction** +0.10s/f (Slow) **10 Ran SP% 118.7**
Speed ratings (Par 92): **99,95,95,94,93 89,81,78,75,73**
toteswingers:1&2:£1.80, 1&3:£6.10, 2&3:£8.90 CSF £2.62 TOTE £2.00: £1.10, £1.50, £5.00; EX 3.30 Trifecta £32.90 Pool: £739.41 - 16.59 winning units..
Owner Godolphin **Bred** Darley **Trained** Newmarket, Suffolk

FOCUS
The market only wanted to know two of these fillies, both of whom were newcomers representing powerful connections, and one of them created a fine first impression. It's hard to know the exact worth of the form, but the winner looks smart and there were a few in behind who should do alright. The time was 1.51 seconds quicker than the slowly run second division.

NOTEBOOK
Ihsas(USA) ◆ was ridden with confidence. The filly was slowest away, but her rider was content to take her wide, covering more ground than most but ensuring a smooth trip, and she travelled well before finding plenty without being given a hard time. The winner, a sister to the stable's Group 1 performer Rio De La Plata, is not that big and still has some filling out to do, so the suggestion is she might not have many more runs this year, but she looks up to pattern company. (op 11-8)
Medea(IRE) took the eye on breeding and was popular in the market, but she was no match at all for the winner and only just hung on for second from some seemingly unfancied rivals. Maybe she needed the run. (op 2-1 tchd 5-2)
Berwin(IRE), a 34,000euros half-sister to very useful 6f winner Gramercy, out of a French 1m1f scorer, showed a deal of ability. She should come on for this and looks a useful prospect. (tchd 25-1)
Silver Marizah(IRE), a 20,000gns half-sister to a few winners, including the smart Joe Bear (1m and 1m2f, Grade 1 placed in US), seemed reasonably well educated, showing up well for a long way and only losing second late on. (op 20-1)
Wye Valley ◆, a half-sister to among others smart 1m1f winner Rainwashed Gold, out of a smart performer at around 1m, needed the experience but was going on at the finish. She has plenty of size and should progress in time. (op 11-1)
La Confession Official explanation: jockey said filly hung left

5814 BRITISH STALLION STUDS SUPPORTING BRITISH RACING E B F MAIDEN FILLIES' STKS (DIV II) 7f (P)
4:40 (4:40) (Class 5) 2-Y-O **£2,911** (£866; £432; £216) **Stalls** Low

Form RPR

1 **Punita (USA)** 2-9-0 0 FrankieDettori 1 79+
(Mahmood Al Zarooni) *hld up in tch in midfield: stl plenty to do 2f out: pushed along and effrt on inner over 1f out: qcknd and str run to ld fnl 100yds: sn in command: easily* **13/8**[1]

2 1 1/4 **Invasor Girl (USA)** 2-9-0 0[1] RichardHills 3 73
(William Haggas) *chsd ldr: rdn 2f out: drvn and unable qck over 1f out: chsd wnr wl ins fnl f: no imp* **22/1**

004 3 1 1/4 **Idols Eye**[15] 5320 2-9-0 70 DaneO'Neill 9 70
(Richard Hannon) *led at stdy gallop: rdn ent fnl 2f: drvn and hdd fnl 100yds: sn btn: wknd fnl 75yds* **6/1**[3]

4 3/4 **King's Guest (IRE)** 2-9-0 0 JimmyFortune 7 68
(Sir Michael Stoute) *dwlt: sn rcvrd and in tch on outer: rdn and unable qck over 1f out: kpt on same pce ins fnl f* **6/1**[3]

36 5 1/2 **Esprit Danseur**[15] 5323 2-9-0 0 StephenCraine 4 67
(Jim Boyle) *t.k.h: hld up in tch: chsd ldrs and rdn wl over 1f out: styd on same pce ins fnl f* **14/1**

6 nk **Mixora (USA)** 2-9-0 0 TomQueally 8 66+
(Sir Henry Cecil) *s.i.s: hmpd sn after s: sn pushed along in rr: rdn and outpcd 2f out: rallied 1f out: no ch w wnr but kpt on fnl f* **6/1**[3]

0 7 2 1/4 **Navajo Charm**[25] 4996 2-8-11 0 HarryBentley(3) 2 60
(Alan Jarvis) *chsd ldrs: rdn and unable qck 2f out: wknd 1f out* **33/1**

8 6 **Herbaceous** 2-9-0 0 (t) JamieSpencer 6 45
(Jeremy Noseda) *s.i.s: swtchd rt sn after s: hld up in tch towards rr: rdn and rn green bnd jst over 2f out: sn wknd* **5/1**[2]

9 11 **Oratrix (IRE)** 2-9-0 0 EddieAhern 10 16
(Denis Coakley) *s.i.s: sn detached in last: lost tch 3f out: t.o* **25/1**

1m 27.08s (2.28) **Going Correction** +0.10s/f (Slow) **9 Ran SP% 115.4**
Speed ratings (Par 92): **90,88,87,86,85 85,82,75,63**
toteswingers:1&2:£6.00, 1&3:£3.90, 2&3:£13.20 CSF £45.51 TOTE £3.30: £1.60, £4.90, £1.10; EX 39.40 Trifecta £354.80 Pool: £642.50 - 1.34 winning units..
Owner Godolphin **Bred** Darley **Trained** Newmarket, Suffolk

FOCUS
A few newcomers representing top stables lined up and this should produce a few winners. The time was 1.51 seconds slower than the previous race, confirming the visual impression that they didn't go quick. A Saeed Bin Suroor newcomer landed the first division in impressive fashion, and Godolphin's other trainer, Mahmood Al Zarooni, sent out a winning debutante in this leg.

NOTEBOOK
Punita(USA) ◆, who is out of a 1m1f Grade 1 winner on turf in US, won in contrasting style to Ihsas, but was just as taking. The winner wasn't quite as short a price as the winner of the previous race, but was still solid considering plenty of others seemed fancied. She was kept to the inside throughout and lost ground when having to wait for a run on the final bend, but she had travelled well throughout and her rider always looked confident. Once in line for the finish, she stuck to the fence, which may or may not have been a disadvantage, and had plenty of ground to make up from off the slow pace, yet she quickened nicely. All things considered, she did well to win so tidily and, like Ihsas, looks pattern-class material. (op 7-4 tchd 2-1)
Invasor Girl(USA) had the increasingly popular hood fitted for her debut. A daughter of the brilliant dirt performer Invasor (first-season sire), she was always well placed considering how the race unfolded and kept on admirably. (op 33-1)
Idols Eye came into this with an official rating of just 70, but she was allowed to set a modest pace and it would probably be wrong to use her to hold the form down. (op 9-2)
King's Guest(IRE), a half-sister to Queen Mary winner Langs Lash, was well enough placed but found only the one pace. (op 5-1 tchd 9-2)
Esprit Danseur again showed ability and should find her level in nurseries. (op 12-1 tchd 16-1)
Mixora(USA), a daughter of Mizzen Mast, missed the break and made only limited progress in the straight, but she should be a lot better for this. (op 8-1)
Herbaceous, the first foal of a 1m1f winner, had a tongue-tie fitted for this debut. She missed the break and came wide in the straight, but made no real progress. (op 7-1)

5815 LADBROKES MOBILE (S) STKS 1m 2f (P)
5:10 (5:10) (Class 6) 3-Y-0+ **£1,533** (£452; £226) **Stalls** Low

Form RPR

-400 1 **Safari Team (IRE)**[33] 4724 3-8-11 78 (p) LukeMorris 7 71
(Peter Winkworth) *in tch: rdn and effrt to press ldrs 2f out: led jst ins fnl f: sn in command: r.o wl* **5/2**[1]

3363 2 2 3/4 **Dream Of Fortune (IRE)**[3] 5740 7-9-4 57 (bt) StevieDonohoe 8 65
(David Evans) *stdd after s: hld up in rr: c wd and effrt over 1f out: r.o strly to go 2nd wl ins fnl f: no threat to wnr* **4/1**[3]

04/2 3 1 **Agilete**[13] 5390 9-9-4 75 JackMitchell 4 63
(Lydia Pearce) *chsd ldng pair: rdn and effrt on inner wl over 1f out: ev ch tl nt pce of wnr jst ins fnl f: kpt on same pce after* **7/2**[2]

1336 4 3/4 **Carlton Scroop (FR)**[20] 5168 8-9-9 65 AndreaAtzeni 1 67
(Paddy Butler) *led: rdn ent fnl 2f: edgd rt wl over 1f out: hdd jst ins fnl f: sn outpcd* **8/1**

4060 5 nk **Galloping Queen (IRE)**[6] 5614 3-8-6 61 (v) SamHitchcott 6 56
(Mick Channon) *t.k.h: hld up in tch: effrt and rdn ent fnl 2f: drvn and nt qckn ent fnl f: one pce after* **10/1**

6600 6 1/2 **Mujood**[25] 4997 8-9-4 62 TomQueally 2 60
(Eve Johnson Houghton) *chsd ldr: rdn to press ldr over 2f out: unable qck over 1f out: one pce and btn whn n.m.r ins fnl f* **8/1**

5006 7 6 **Loch Fleet (IRE)**[9] 5512 3-9-2 73 JimmyFortune 3 53
(Gary Moore) *stdd s: t.k.h: hld up in tch in midfield: rdn and effrt 2f out: btn jst over 1f out: wknd fnl f* **7/1**

1065 8 6 **Sunset Boulevard (IRE)**[24] 5042 8-9-4 58 (b) DavidKenny(5) 5 41
(Paddy Butler) *hld up in last pair: rdn and struggling over 2f out: wknd wl over 1f out* **25/1**

2m 7.85s (1.25) **Going Correction** +0.10s/f (Slow)
WFA 3 from 7yo+ 7lb **8 Ran SP% 118.5**
Speed ratings (Par 101): **99,96,96,95,95 94,89,85**
toteswingers:1&2:£3.30, 1&3:£4.00, 2&3:£3.00 CSF £13.23 TOTE £3.40: £1.10, £1.90, £2.60; EX 13.90 Trifecta £31.20 Pool: £732.93 - 17.34 winning units..The winner was bought by P Wheatly for 8,800gns. Galloping Queen was claimed by Miss Sheena West for £6,000.
Owner The Ascot Colts & Fillies Club **Bred** Fortbarrington Stud **Trained** Chiddingfold, Surrey

FOCUS
Not a bad seller on paper, but there were doubts over most. The form's rated around the second and third.

5816 PLAY ROULETTE AT LADBROKES.COM MEDIAN AUCTION MAIDEN STKS 1m 2f (P)
5:40 (5:42) (Class 6) 3-4-Y-O **£1,704** (£503; £251) **Stalls** Low

Form RPR

0230 1 **Satwa Dream (IRE)**[25] 5014 4-9-10 74 JamieSpencer 3 83
(Ed Dunlop) *hld up in midfield: hdwy to chse ldr over 2f out: clsd over 1f out: rdn to ld ins fnl f: sn in command* **3/1**[1]

5 2 4 **Grand Theft Equine**[31] 4800 3-9-0 0 MatthewDavies(3) 8 75+
(Jim Boyle) *hld up in tch towards rr: hdwy on outer over 2f out: led 3f out and sn rdn clr: hdd ins fnl f: sn btn* **4/1**[3]

4-03 3 2 1/2 **Rocky Rebel**[21] 5140 3-9-3 72 (p) StevieDonohoe 9 70
(Ralph Beckett) *in tch: outpcd and drvn over 2f out: chsd ldng pair 2f out: no imp* **13/2**

6 4 5 **Millennium Star (IRE)**[36] 4611 3-8-12 0 TomQueally 7 55+
(Sir Henry Cecil) *t.k.h: hld up in tch: shuffled bk and dropped to rr over 4f out: nt clr run over 3f out: swtchd rt and rallied 2f out: hung lft and styd on same pce fr over 1f out* **7/2**[2]

05 5 3 1/4 **Dollar Deal**[80] 3167 3-9-3 0 J-PGuillambert 6 54
(Luca Cumani) *chsd ldrs: stdd bk but stl wl in tch 8f out: rdn and struggling over 2f out: sn wknd* **14/1**

0-35 6 nk **Knightly Escapade**[26] 4956 3-9-3 75 DaneO'Neill 2 53
(John Dunlop) *s.i.s: sn in tch in midfield: rdn and outpcd over 2f out: wknd 2f out* **13/2**

05 7 nk **Full Stretch (USA)**[21] 5140 3-9-3 0 SteveDrowne 10 52
(Pat Eddery) *sn rdn along to ld: hdd over 3f out: drvn and struggling over 2f out: wknd u.p wl over 1f out* **33/1**

8 6 **Tunduce (IRE)** 3-8-12 0 JackMitchell 5 35
(Noel Quinlan) *stdd s: t.k.h: hld up in tch in rr: outpcd over 2f out: pushed along and no imp fr over 1f out* **50/1**

05 9 1 1/4 **In The Long Grass (IRE)**[25] 4989 3-9-3 0 StephenCraine 12 38
(Jim Boyle) *hld up in tch in rr: rdn and outpcd 3f out: wl btn fnl 2f* **100/1**

00 10 13 **Polly Adler**[41] 4445 4-9-5 0 FergusSweeney 11 —
(Alastair Lidderdale) *dwlt: sn dashed up on outer to chse ldrs: led over 3f out: rdn and hdd over 2f out: sn wknd: wl bhd and eased ins fnl f: t.o* **100/1**

-03F 11 16 **Steely**[21] 5140 3-9-3 0 PaulDoe 13 —
(Jim Best) *chsd ldr tl rn wd bnd 9f out: chsd ldrs after: lost pl over 4f out: bhd and lost tch 3f out: wl t.o fnl 2f* **20/1**

0 12 37 **Broken Eagle (USA)**[36] 4617 3-9-3 0 (b) GeorgeBaker 14 —
(Mikael Magnusson) *chsd ldrs: carried wd bnd 9f out: sn chsng ldr tl over 3f out: immediately dropped out: t.o and virtually p.u fr over 2f out* **14/1**

2m 7.06s (0.46) **Going Correction** +0.10s/f (Slow)
WFA 3 from 4yo 7lb **12 Ran SP% 118.9**
Speed ratings (Par 101): **102,98,96,92,90 89,89,84,83,73 60,31**
Totesuper 7: Win: Not won. Place: £462.00. toteswingers:1&2:£4.90, 1&3:£4.50, 2&3:£6.70 CSF £14.57 TOTE £3.80: £1.50, £1.50, £1.10; EX 20.10 Trifecta £77.90 Pool: £514.24 - 5.83 winning units..
Owner The Lamprell Partnership **Bred** Mayfair Stud Sa **Trained** Newmarket, Suffolk

FOCUS
An ordinary maiden but the form seems sound. The winner is rated back to his French form.
Steely Official explanation: jockey said gelding hung right
Broken Eagle(USA) Official explanation: jockey said colt stopped quickly

T/Plt: £12.30 to a £1 stake. Pool:£56,865.13 - 3,363.87 winning tickets T/Qpdt: £2.40 to a £1 stake. Pool:£4,362.14 - 1,300.17 winning tickets SP

^{5618}CARLISLE (R-H)

Wednesday, September 7

OFFICIAL GOING: Soft (good to soft in places) changing to heavy after race 6 (5:00)

Wind: Strong, half against Weather: Cloudy, heavy rain between races 5 and 6

5817 CARLISLE-RACES.CO.UK NURSERY — 5f 193y

2:10 (2:11) (Class 6) (0-65,65) 2-Y-O **£1,617** (£481; £240; £120) **Stalls** Low

Form RPR

060 **1** **Regal Acclaim (IRE)**^{60} 3878 2-8-1 **45** DuranFentiman 7 52+
(Tim Easterby) *cl up: rdn and ev ch over 2f out: led wl ins fnl f: kpt on wl* **14/1**

056 **2** *½* **Celestial Dawn**^{13} 5398 2-8-9 **53** PJMcDonald 1 59+
(John Weymes) *led: pushed along 2f out: hdd wl ins fnl f: hld cl home* **10/1**

3053 **3** *3 ½* **Sunley Valentine**^{5} 5690 2-9-3 **64** MatthewDavies$^{(3)}$ 9 59
(Mick Channon) *bhd: gd hdwy on outside to chse clr ldng pair appr fnl f: kpt on: no imp* **5/1**^{1}

324 **4** *1 ½* **Towbee**^{14} 5367 2-9-7 **65** JamesSullivan 4 55
(Michael Easterby) *t.k.h: trckd ldrs: effrt over 2f out: kpt on same pce over 1f out* **7/1**^{2}

446 **5** *nk* **Summer Lane (IRE)**^{30} 4864 2-8-13 **57** PaulHanagan 14 46
(Richard Fahey) *in tch: effrt and rdn over 2f out: no imp over 1f out* **5/1**^{1}

334 **6** *1 ½* **Oddysey (IRE)**^{25} 5058 2-9-7 **65** TonyHamilton 2 50
(Michael Dods) *cl up tl rdn and wknd over 1f out* **5/1**^{1}

2666 **7** *4 ½* **Ingleby Angel (IRE)**^{32} 4809 2-8-7 **54** DeclanCannon$^{(3)}$ 3 25
(David O'Meara) *dwlt: sn drvn along in midfield: rdn and wknd wl over 1f out* **12/1**

0455 **8** *1 ¼* **Spoken Words**^{32} 4809 2-8-12 **56** FrederikTylicki 6 23
(Hugh McWilliams) *towards rr: rdn over 2f out: hdwy over 1f out: n.d* **25/1**

000 **9** *1* **Sir Elmo (IRE)**^{67} 3618 2-8-8 **57** NeilFarley$^{(5)}$ 13 21
(Declan Carroll) *midfield: pushed along over 2f out: sn outpcd* **8/1**^{3}

0053 **10** *1 ½* **Economic Crisis (IRE)**^{8} 5590 2-8-9 **53** PatrickMathers 12 12
(Alan Berry) *towards rr on outside: struggling 1/2-way: sn btn* **16/1**

505 **11** *4 ½* **No More Games**^{23} 5105 2-8-7 **56** (b^{1}) JulieBurke$^{(5)}$ 10 1
(Kevin Ryan) *bhd on outside: struggling 1/2-way: sn btn* **16/1**

000 **12** *3* **My New Angel (IRE)**^{14} 5367 2-8-8 **52** BarryMcHugh 5 —
(Paul Green) *s.i.s: sn drvn along in rr: nvr on terms* **100/1**

5243 **13** *15* **Yearbook**^{13} 5399 2-8-12 **59** LeeTopliss$^{(3)}$ 15 —
(Tim Easterby) *trckd ldrs tl rdn and wknd 2f out: t.o* **16/1**

1m 17.09s (3.39) **Going Correction** +0.40s/f (Good) **13** Ran SP% **119.5**

Speed ratings (Par 93): **93,92,87,85,85 83,77,75,74,72 66,62,42**

toteswingers:1&2:£42.30, 1&3:£27.30, 2&3:£13.80 CSF £147.35 CT £834.29 TOTE £20.70: £5.20, £3.50, £2.40; EX 153.10.

Owner Mr And Mrs J D Cotton **Bred** Mrs H A Jellett **Trained** Great Habton, N Yorks

■ Stewards' Enquiry : Duran Fentiman caution: used whip with excessive frequency.

FOCUS

Course at normal configuration and distances as advertised. Testing ground and hard work for the horses, with a headwind not helping. The opening time, 4.59 sec outside the standard, confirmed that conditions were riding soft. There were no previous winners in this weak nursery. The runners remained on the far side once into the straight and it proved difficult to make up ground from off the pace, with the first pair always prominent. There is probably better to come from the winner.

NOTEBOOK

Regal Acclaim(IRE) ◆ delivered a sustained challenge to the leader and got on top late on, winning a shade more easily than the narrow margin would imply. Gelded since his last run, he was making his nursery debut off a plater's mark - he was 2lb out of the weights - and has further improvement to come. Official explanation: trainer's rep said, regarding apparent improvement in form, that it had benefited from being gelded. (op 16-1)

Celestial Dawn, drawn in the inside stall, was quickly away and attempted to make all, only giving best after trying hard to fend off the winner. This was a creditable effort on her nursery bow. (op 12-1)

Sunley Valentine performed best of those who came from the rear, staying on down the outside for a well-held third. Third on Polytrack on her nursery debut, she was encountering easy ground for the first time here. (op 9-2 tchd 11-2)

Towbee, back up in trip for his nursery debut, plugged on after coming under pressure before halfway. (op 15-2 tchd 8-1)

Summer Lane(IRE), another nursery debutante, has improvement in her when tackling further. (op 13-2)

Oddysey(IRE) faded after chasing the pace and her best trip is still open to debate. (tchd 9-2 and 11-2)

Ingleby Angel(IRE) could not cash in on a 5lb drop since her recent nursery debut.

Sir Elmo(IRE), given a break since three quick runs in maidens, came in for support, but he was never seen with a chance. (op 17-2 tchd 9-1)

5818 BRITISH STALLION STUDS SUPPORTING BRITISH RACING E B F MAIDEN STKS — 7f 200y

2:45 (2:46) (Class 5) 2-Y-O **£3,408** (£1,006; £503) **Stalls** Low

Form RPR

4625 **1** **Ventura Spirit**^{18} 5287 2-9-3 71 PaulHanagan 8 71
(Richard Fahey) *cl up: led over 2f out: sn hrd pressed: hld on gamely u.p fnl f* **1/1**^{1}

4242 **2** *nk* **Naseem Alyasmeen (IRE)**^{10} 5503 2-8-9 67 MatthewDavies$^{(3)}$ 5 65
(Mick Channon) *hld up: hdwy to chal over 2f out: sn rdn: kpt on fnl f: jst hld* **2/1**^{2}

23 **3** *4* **Behlul (IRE)**^{36} 4646 2-9-3 0 TonyHamilton 3 61
(Gerard Butler) *led to over 2f out: sn rdn along: kpt on same pce over 1f out* **9/1**^{3}

0 **4** *3* **Catramis**^{52} 4122 2-9-0 0 DaleSwift$^{(3)}$ 9 54
(Geoffrey Oldroyd) *bhd: detached after 3f: styd on wl fnl 2f: nvr able to chal* **50/1**

6 **5** *1 ½* **More Bottle (IRE)**^{80} 3200 2-8-12 0 FrederikTylicki 6 46
(Tom Tate) *prom: drvn over 3f out: edgd rt and wknd over 1f out* **12/1**

00 **6** *5* **Eastern Seel**^{12} 5454 2-9-3 0 DuranFentiman 7 39
(Tim Easterby) *hld up on outside: struggling over 3f out: n.d after* **100/1**

0500 **7** *1 ¼* **Grippa**^{8} 5597 2-9-0 63 DeclanCannon$^{(3)}$ 1 36
(David Brown) *sn trcking ldrs: drvn over 3f out: sn wknd* **33/1**

00 **8** *hd* **Istan Star (USA)**^{12} 5454 2-9-3 0 BarryMcHugh 4 36
(Julie Camacho) *in tch: rdn along over 3f out: wknd over 2f out* **20/1**

1m 45.34s (5.34) **Going Correction** +0.55s/f (Yiel) **8** Ran SP% **111.7**

Speed ratings (Par 95): **95,94,90,87,86 81,79,79**

toteswingers:1&2:£1.20, 1&3:£2.30, 2&3:£2.10 CSF £2.88 TOTE £2.00: £1.10, £1.10, £1.50; EX 3.40.

Owner Keith Denham **Bred** The National Stud Never Say Die Club Ltd **Trained** Musley Bank, N Yorks

FOCUS

No depth to this maiden, which always had the look of a two-horse race. Straightforward form, the winner close to his mark.

NOTEBOOK

Ventura Spirit, back in this grade after contesting a warm nursery at York, reverted to prominent tactics. This time he saw out the mile dourly, fighting off a persistent challenge from his market rival. He handles soft ground well and may get a bit further next year. (op 11-8 tchd 6-4 in a place)

Naseem Alyasmeen(IRE) made swift improvement turning in to serve it up to the winner, but could not get by her much bigger rival. A consistent filly, she has finished runner-up three times now and should find a race before the end of the season. (op 6-4)

Behlul(IRE) was suited by the soft conditions on this turf debut and probably stepped up on the very modest placed form he posted at Southwell on his first two starts. (op 10-1 tchd 11-1)

Catramis was virtually tailed off at halfway and still last a furlong and a half out, but he stayed on past beaten rivals from there. The bare form is very modest and it would not do to get carried away, but there were positives to be taken from this. (op 40-1)

More Bottle(IRE) showed more than she had on her debut over 6f in June but her stamina was waning late on. (tchd 14-1)

5819 TOM SEGAL WRITES FOR THE WEEKENDER MAIDEN FILLIES' STKS — 6f 192y

3:20 (3:22) (Class 5) 2-Y-O **£2,264** (£673; £336; £168) **Stalls** Low

Form RPR

1 **Albaspina (IRE)** 2-9-0 0 PaulHanagan 2 81+
(Sir Mark Prescott Bt) *s.i.s: rn green in midfield: hdwy on outside to ld 2f out: sn drifted rt: kpt on strly fnl f: improve* **5/4**^{1}

3 **2** *2 ¾* **Aleut**^{21} 5161 2-9-0 0 JamesSullivan 7 70
(James Given) *cl up: effrt and ev ch 2f out: kpt on fnl f: nt gng pce of wnr* **11/2**^{3}

U3 **3** *3 ¼* **Mistress Of Rome**^{29} 4875 2-9-0 0 PJMcDonald 13 61
(Michael Dods) *sn cl up: rdn and ev ch over 2f out: kpt on same pce appr fnl f* **15/2**

0 **4** *2 ½* **Sugarpine (IRE)**^{18} 5269 2-9-0 0 TonyHamilton 8 54
(Richard Fahey) *prom: effrt over 2f out: nt qckn over 1f out* **7/2**^{2}

02 **5** *4 ½* **Champagne Valley**^{35} 4675 2-8-11 0 MichaelO'Connell$^{(3)}$ 6 42
(Sharon Watt) *led to 2f out: sn rdn: wknd appr fnl f* **25/1**

0 **6** *7* **Lady Romanza (IRE)**^{9} 5548 2-9-0 0 DuranFentiman 4 23
(Tim Easterby) *s.i.s: bhd and sn pushed along: drvn 1/2-way: nvr on terms* **40/1**

7 *2 ½* **Lizzie Drippin** 2-9-0 0 PaddyAspell 11 16
(Michael Easterby) *bhd: outpcd after 2f: sme late hdwy: nvr on terms* **50/1**

003 **8** *1 ¾* **Landaho**^{26} 5003 2-8-7 51 VictorSantos$^{(7)}$ 5 12
(Hugh McWilliams) *in tch: rdn over 3f out: wknd over 2f out* **100/1**

6 **9** *¾* **Cloud Cuckooland (IRE)**^{21} 5161 2-9-0 0 FrederikTylicki 3 10
(James Given) *s.i.s: bhd and sn outpcd: no ch fr 1/2-way* **9/1**

00 **10** *4 ½* **Cherchedi (IRE)**^{7} 5618 2-9-0 0 PatrickMathers 9 —
(Alan Berry) *towards rr: drvn along 1/2-way: wknd wl over 2f out* **200/1**

1m 31.23s (4.13) **Going Correction** +0.55s/f (Yiel) **10** Ran SP% **113.5**

Speed ratings (Par 92): **98,94,91,88,83 75,72,70,69,64**

toteswingers:1&2:£3.20, 1&3:£3.00, 2&3:£4.70 CSF £8.03 TOTE £2.10: £1.10, £2.20, £2.10; EX 8.50.

Owner Miss K Rausing **Bred** Miss K Rausing And Mrs S M Rogers **Trained** Newmarket, Suffolk

FOCUS

Just a modest fillies' maiden overall, but the winner looks useful and was value for extra. The third helps with the form.

NOTEBOOK

Albaspina(IRE) made a pleasing start to her career. A little slow to break, she was soon being niggled along in midfield, looking decidedly green, but she made good progress to challenge and won going away in the end, seeing out the trip strongly. From a superb family long associated with Sir Mark Prescott and Kirsten Rausing, she holds an entry in the Fillies' Mile at Newmarket and is sure to improve considerably on this bare form with the experience to draw upon. (op Evens)

Aleut, third over a furlong shorter on her debut here three weeks ago, ran another sound race and got the extra yardage well, but was no match for the winner. (op 5-1 tchd 7-2)

Mistress Of Rome, having her third run, broke well this time from the widest stall and was always up with the pace. She stuck on well enough and it will be interesting to see how she fares on a sounder surface. (op 9-1)

Sugarpine(IRE), rejected by Paul Hanagan in favour of the winner, improved for her debut experience at Chester but lacked a change of pace in the holding ground. (op 6-1 tchd 11-2)

Champagne Valley was beaten 11l when runner-up at Pontefract on her second start. She made the running but didn't see out the trip in the testing conditions. (op 20-1)

Cloud Cuckooland(IRE) was slowly away and could never get into it. She finished much further behind Aleut than she had on her debut over shorter here, with the ground a likely factor. (op 10-1)

5820 COMLONGON CASTLE H'CAP — 6f 192y

3:55 (3:55) (Class 4) (0-85,88) 3-Y-O **£5,822** (£1,732; £865; £432) **Stalls** Low

Form RPR

5001 **1** **Try The Chance**^{7} 5621 3-9-9 **88** 6ex MatthewDavies$^{(3)}$ 2 97
(Mick Channon) *hld up: hdwy over 2f out: chsd ldr over 1f out: led ins fnl f: kpt on wl* **5/1**^{2}

5-30 **2** *nk* **Honeymead (IRE)**^{81} 3159 3-9-7 **83** PaulHanagan 3 91+
(Richard Fahey) *early ldr: trckd ldrs: hdwy to ld 2f out: sn rdn: hdd ins fnl f: r.o* **10/3**^{1}

3125 **3** *4 ½* **Ingleby Exceed (IRE)**^{4} 5730 3-9-1 **77** DanielTudhope 5 73
(David O'Meara) *hld up in tch: hdwy on outside and cl up over 2f out: no ex ent fnl f* **10/3**^{1}

2250 **4** *¾* **No Poppy (IRE)**^{19} 5255 3-9-5 **81** DuranFentiman 1 75
(Tim Easterby) *prom: drvn along and outpcd over 2f out: n.d after* **14/1**

6632 **5** *3 ¼* **My Single Malt (IRE)**^{7} 5621 3-8-13 **75** (b) FrederikTylicki 6 61
(Tom Tate) *cl up: rdn over 2f out: wknd over 1f out* **10/3**^{1}

5055 **6** *4* **Nasharra (IRE)**^{9} 5559 3-9-2 **78** (b) StephenCraine 7 54
(Kevin Ryan) *t.k.h: sn led: hung lft over 4f out: hdd 2f out: edgd rt and sn wknd* **28/1**

-210 **7** *8* **Easy Over (IRE)**^{39} 4550 3-9-1 **77** RoystonFfrench 4 32
(Ed McMahon) *hld up: struggling over 3f out: sn btn* **6/1**^{3}

1m 30.41s (3.31) **Going Correction** +0.55s/f (Yiel) **7** Ran SP% **110.3**

Speed ratings (Par 103): **103,102,97,96,92 88,79**

toteswingers:1&2:£3.90, 1&3:£5.20, 2&3:£3.00 CSF £20.36 TOTE £6.40: £4.10, £1.30; EX 27.90.

Owner Jaber Abdullah **Bred** Ms Jon Horley & C A Vanner **Trained** West Ilsley, Berks

FOCUS

A fair handicap run at a brisk pace. The first two came clear and showed decent form for the grade.

My Single Malt(IRE) Official explanation: trainer's rep said, regarding running, that the race may have come too soon for the gelding

Easy Over(IRE) Official explanation: jockey said gelding never travelled

5821 HAPPY BIRTHDAY SUE ELLIS H'CAP 6f 192y
4:30 (4:31) (Class 5) (0-75,73) 3-Y-O £2,385 (£704; £352) Stalls Low

Form RPR

0632 **1** **Watts Up Son**[9] 5552 3-8-4 **63**....(bt) JasonHart(7) 6 72
(Declan Carroll) *t.k.h: pressed ldr: led over 2f out: drvn and drifted rt fr over 1f out: hld on wl fnl f* **7/2**[2]

5313 **2** *nk* **Barista (IRE)**[1] 5803 3-8-12 **67**.... MatthewDavies(3) 2 75
(Mick Channon) *bhd: hdwy over 2f out: checked over 1f out: chsd wnr ins fnl f: r.o: jst hld* **85/40**[1]

30P2 **3** *2 1/4* **Chokidar (IRE)**[25] 5030 3-9-4 **73**....(b[1]) MichaelO'Connell(3) 4 75
(David Nicholls) *prom: stdy hdwy 3f out: rdn and chsd wnr over 1f out: hung rt and lost 2nd ins fnl f* **14/1**

016 **4** *3* **Edgware Road**[7] 5624 3-8-13 **65**.... RoystonFfrench 5 60
(Keith Dalgleish) *in tch: outpcd over 3f out: kpt on fnl 2f: nvr able to chal* **13/2**

6552 **5** *1 3/4* **Captain Kolo (IRE)**[12] 5456 3-9-1 **67**.... KellyHarrison 3 57
(Tim Easterby) *t.k.h: led to over 2f out: wknd over 1f out* **12/1**

5603 **6** *3/4* **Lady Gar Gar**[12] 5439 3-8-11 **66**....(p) DaleSwift(3) 1 54
(Geoffrey Oldroyd) *chsd ldrs: rdn over 2f out: wknd wl over 1f out* **11/2**[3]

3-30 **7** *25* **Indian Giver**[21] 5164 3-8-12 **64**.... PaulHanagan 8 —
(Hugh McWilliams) *hld up: rdn over 3f out: wknd fr over 2f out* **12/1**

620P **8** *28* **Old English (IRE)**[4] 5721 3-8-11 **63**.... PJMcDonald 7 —
(Linda Perratt) *ponied to s: in tch: struggling over 3f out: lost tch fnl 2f* **20/1**

1m 31.08s (3.98) **Going Correction** +0.55s/f (Yiel) **8** Ran SP% **112.1**
Speed ratings (Par 101): **99,98,96,92,90 89,61,29**
toteswingers:1&2:£2.20, 1&3:£8.70, 2&3:£4.90 CSF £10.87 CT £87.79 TOTE £3.50: £1.20, £1.20, £4.50; EX 10.60.
Owner L Ibbotson, D Watts & J Syme **Bred** West Dereham Abbey Stud **Trained** Sledmere, E Yorks

FOCUS
A modest handicap, run at a sound pace and in a time 0.67 sec slower than the preceding 71-85 handicap, also for 3yos.
Indian Giver Official explanation: jockey said filly never travelled

5822 WATCH RACING UK ON SKY432 H'CAP (DIV I) 1m 1f 61y
5:00 (5:00) (Class 6) (0-60,60) 3-Y-O+ £1,704 (£503; £251) Stalls Low

Form RPR

0212 **1** **Smart Violetta (IRE)**[10] 5507 3-9-2 **58**....(t) PaulHanagan 12 67+
(Ann Duffield) *hld up in midfield: rdn along over 4f out: hdwy over 2f out: led over 1f out: kpt on wl* **7/4**[1]

3450 **2** *1 1/4* **Bright Applause**[13] 5405 3-9-4 **60**.... PatrickMathers 15 65
(Tracy Waggott) *stdd in rr: effrt and hdwy 3f out: chsd wnr ins fnl f: r.o* **13/2**[3]

5400 **3** *1* **Island Chief**[13] 5402 5-9-1 **58**.... DavidSimmonson(7) 6 61
(Michael Easterby) *trckd ldrs: effrt and led briefly over 1f out: kpt on same pce ins fnl f* **20/1**

6-00 **4** *2* **Sister Sioux (IRE)**[20] 5214 3-7-13 **46** oh1.... ChrisDCogan(5) 4 45
(Robin Bastiman) *midfield: rdn and effrt 3f out: kpt on same pce over 1f out* **80/1**

4600 **5** *nk* **Fairy Mist (IRE)**[21] 5178 4-9-0 **50**.... FrederikTylicki 13 48
(Brian Rothwell) *trckd ldrs: rdn and effrt 3f out: one pce over 1f out* **14/1**

0425 **6** *4 1/2* **Machir Bay**[13] 5403 4-8-7 **46**....(p) MichaelO'Connell(3) 11 35
(Keith Dalgleish) *led to over 1f out: sn btn* **9/1**

5240 **7** *3* **Carlitos Spirit (IRE)**[13] 5402 7-9-1 **54**.... DaleSwift(3) 2 36
(Ian McInnes) *in tch: styd far side ent st: outpcd fr 2f out* **10/1**

0305 **8** *nse* **Harare**[11] 5485 10-8-12 **48**....(v) StephenCraine 1 30
(Karen Tutty) *hld up: rdn over 3f out: nvr able to chal* **28/1**

0332 **9** *2 1/2* **Syncopated Lady (IRE)**[21] 5165 3-8-12 **54** ow1....(e) DanielTudhope 7 31
(David O'Meara) *t.k.h: hld up: rdn and effrt far side over 2f out: nvr on terms: eased whn btn fnl f* **11/2**[2]

03-0 **10** *1 1/4* **Renege The Joker**[108] 1993 8-8-10 **46** oh1.... RussKennemore 10 20
(Sean Regan) *hld up: rdn over 3f out: nvr on terms* **100/1**

0-00 **11** *2 1/4* **Funky Munky**[13] 5402 6-8-8 **47** oh1 ow1.... LeeTopliss(3) 3 17
(Alistair Whillans) *trckd ldrs tl edgd rt and wknd fnl 2f* **20/1**

1050 **12** *1 1/4* **Poppy Golightly**[175] 862 4-8-11 **52**.... NeilFarley(5) 9 19
(Declan Carroll) *midfield: struggling over 3f out: sn btn* **9/1**

0453 **13** *10* **Media Stars**[13] 5402 6-9-7 **57**.... TonyHamilton 16 —
(Robert Johnson) *hld up: struggling over 4f out: sn lost tch* **20/1**

2m 7.34s (9.74) **Going Correction** +1.125s/f (Soft)
WFA 3 from 4yo+ 6lb **13** Ran SP% **120.8**
Speed ratings (Par 101): **101,99,99,97,96 92,90,90,88,86 84,83,74**
toteswingers:1&2:£7.60, 1&3:£9.50, 2&3:£30.10 CSF £11.83 CT £178.09 TOTE £1.90: £1.20, £3.00, £4.00; EX 18.60.
Owner Six Iron Partnership **Bred** Peter Byrne **Trained** Constable Burton, N Yorks

FOCUS
It started to rain very heavily prior to this event, and the official going description was changed to heavy after the race. Visibility was poor for this low-grade handicap. The principals raced down the centre of the track in the home straight, with those staying on the inside rail well beaten.
Carlitos Spirit(IRE) Official explanation: jockey said gelding was unsuited by the heavy ground

5823 WATCH RACING UK ON SKY432 H'CAP (DIV II) 1m 1f 61y
5:30 (5:30) (Class 6) (0-60,59) 3-Y-O+ £1,704 (£503; £251) Stalls Low

Form RPR

4005 **1** **Smart Step**[10] 5507 3-8-4 **45**.... PaulHanagan 7 59
(Mark Johnston) *trckd ldr: led over 4f out: rdn and styd on gamely fnl 2f* **12/1**

2014 **2** *1 3/4* **Deep Applause**[13] 5401 3-9-3 **58**....(p) PJMcDonald 8 68
(Michael Dods) *hld up: hdwy to chse wnr and rdn 2f out: kpt on fnl f: hld nr fin* **12/1**

-400 **3** *6* **Phoenix Flame**[21] 5179 3-9-0 **55**.... DanielTudhope 9 52
(Alan McCabe) *in tch: outpcd over 3f out: styd on fnl 2f: nt pce of first two* **16/1**

0106 **4** *2 1/2* **Reset To Fit**[15] 5349 4-9-1 **57**.... JustinNewman(7) 15 49
(Eric Alston) *dwlt: sn midfield on outside: outpcd over 3f out: plugged on fnl 2f: no imp* **9/1**

6604 **5** *nk* **Strong Knight**[13] 5402 4-8-13 **48**....(p) DuranFentiman 2 40
(Tim Walford) *midfield: effrt and rdn towards far side over 3f out: styd on fnl 2f: nrst fin* **6/1**[2]

044 **6** *5* **Spread Boy (IRE)**[8] 5589 4-8-10 **45**....(p) RoystonFfrench 16 26
(Alan Berry) *trckd ldrs: ev ch over 3f out: wknd over 1f out* **25/1**

020 **7** *shd* **Celtic Step**[28] 4902 7-8-13 **51**.... LeeTopliss(3) 3 32
(Peter Niven) *trckd ldrs tl rdn and wknd over 2f out* **12/1**

6046 **8** *4 1/2* **Sinatramania**[11] 5488 4-9-7 **56**.... PatrickMathers 12 27
(Tracy Waggott) *dwlt: hld up: rdn over 3f out: hdwy 2f out: nvr able to chal* **4/1**[1]

0000 **9** *1 1/2* **Blue Spinnaker (IRE)**[7] 5622 12-9-6 **55**.... PaddyAspell 10 23
(Michael Easterby) *midfield: drvn and outpcd over 3f out: sn btn* **7/1**[3]

0650 **10** *9* **Luv U Noo**[9] 5538 4-8-11 **49**.... DaleSwift(3) 1 —
(Brian Baugh) *dwlt: bhd: rdn and wd over 3f out: nvr able to chal* **8/1**

1503 **11** *1 1/2* **Playful Girl (IRE)**[10] 5507 3-8-7 **48**....(b) KellyHarrison 6 —
(Tim Easterby) *led to over 4f out: rdn and wknd over 2f out* **9/1**

0-00 **12** *1/2* **Ptolomeos**[13] 5405 8-8-11 **46**.... RussKennemore 4 —
(Sean Regan) *hld up: struggling over 3f out: sn btn* **25/1**

0606 **13** *26* **Red Lite (IRE)**[7] 5623 3-9-4 **59**.... JamesSullivan 5 —
(Wilf Storey) *midfield: rdn along over 4f out: wknd over 3f out* **40/1**

0603 **14** *24* **Second Reef**[27] 4946 9-8-10 **45**....(p) LeeNewman 14 —
(Thomas Cuthbert) *trckd ldrs tl rdn and wknd 3f out* **33/1**

2m 7.61s (10.01) **Going Correction** +1.125s/f (Soft)
WFA 3 from 4yo+ 6lb **14** Ran SP% **119.9**
Speed ratings (Par 101): **100,98,93,90,90 86,86,82,80,72 71,70,47,26**
toteswingers:1&2:£12.50, 1&3:£7.90, 2&3:£14.40 CSF £142.47 CT £2317.02 TOTE £18.00: £3.30, £3.00, £7.30; EX 82.80.
Owner S R Counsell **Bred** Hascombe And Valiant Studs **Trained** Middleham Moor, N Yorks

FOCUS
The rain had eased prior to this event, which was run in a marginally slower time than the first division. This is not form to take too seriously. Again the leading players came up the centre of the track in the home straight, and the first pair came clear.
Smart Step Official explanation: trainer's rep had no explanation for the apparent improvement in form
Playful Girl(IRE) Official explanation: jockey said filly was unsuited by the heavy ground
Ptolomeos Official explanation: jockey said gelding hung right-handed throughout

5824 LLOYD BMW H'CAP 5f
6:00 (6:01) (Class 6) (0-65,65) 3-Y-O+ £1,617 (£481; £240; £120) Stalls Low

Form RPR

0454 **1** **Bond Fastrac**[4] 5736 4-9-4 **65**.... DaleSwift(3) 5 77
(Geoffrey Oldroyd) *hld up in midfield: hdwy to ld over 1f out: rdn and r.o wl fnl f* **11/4**[2]

0511 **2** *1 3/4* **Mission Impossible**[2] 5787 6-9-0 **58** 12ex.... PatrickMathers 3 64
(Tracy Waggott) *hld up: hdwy on outside of gp over 1f out: rdn and pressed wnr ins fnl f: kpt on: hld nr fin* **2/1**[1]

1321 **3** *4 1/2* **Novalist**[20] 5215 3-8-11 **56**....(b) LeeNewman 4 46
(Robin Bastiman) *in tch: effrt over 2f out: kpt on same pce fnl f* **8/1**[3]

5403 **4** *3/4* **Andrasta**[7] 5620 6-8-7 **51** oh1.... RoystonFfrench 7 38
(Alan Berry) *prom: effrt over 2f out: kpt on same pce fnl f* **25/1**

0034 **5** *nse* **Lady Del Sol**[12] 5442 3-9-5 **64**.... DanielTudhope 9 51
(Marjorie Fife) *hld up in midfield: hdwy and ev ch over 1f out: wknd ins fnl f* **12/1**

0541 **6** *3/4* **Sleights Boy (IRE)**[10] 5506 3-8-3 **51** 6ex....(v) DeclanCannon(3) 2 35
(Ian McInnes) *midfield: drvn over 2f out: no imp tl kpt on fnl f: n.d* **25/1**

0000 **7** *nk* **Tenancy (IRE)**[2] 5789 7-8-9 **53**.... KellyHarrison 10 36
(Shaun Harris) *led tl over 1f out: sn rdn and no ex* **16/1**

300- **8** *3 1/4* **Drumpellier (IRE)**[315] 7170 4-8-6 **53**.... PaulPickard(3) 8 24
(Simon West) *w ldr tl rdn and wknd over 1f out* **33/1**

4113 **9** *4 1/2* **Cross Of Lorraine (IRE)**[9] 5552 8-9-7 **65**....(b) TonyHamilton 11 20
(Chris Grant) *chsd ldrs: effrt over 2f out: wknd over 1f out* **9/1**

0065 **10** *3/4* **Kinlochrannoch**[27] 4942 3-9-1 **65**....(p) ShaneBKelly(5) 6 18
(Ben Haslam) *hld up: effrt and c nr side over 2f out: btn fnl f* **16/1**

0015 **11** *5* **Suddenly Susan (IRE)**[20] 5215 3-8-9 **57**....(b) MichaelO'Connell(3) 1 —
(David Nicholls) *sn chsng ldrs: rdn and wknd wl over 1f out* **8/1**[3]

65.23 secs (4.43) **Going Correction** +0.925s/f (Soft)
WFA 3 from 4yo+ 1lb **11** Ran SP% **122.3**
Speed ratings (Par 101): **101,98,91,89,89 88,88,82,75,74 66**
toteswingers:1&2:£2.10, 1&3:£4.70, 2&3:£1.70 CSF £8.85 CT £40.33 TOTE £4.20: £1.70, £1.50, £2.00; EX 12.40.
Owner R C Bond **Bred** Bond Thoroughbred Corporation **Trained** Brawby, N Yorks

FOCUS
An ordinary sprint handicap. The runners came centre to stands' side on turning in and were fanned across the course at the two pole, with the first two home, who came clear, ending up down the centre.
Suddenly Susan(IRE) Official explanation: jockey said filly never travelled
T/Plt: £42.20 to a £1 stake. Pool:£45,089.15 - 779.78 winning tickets T/Qpdt: £7.90 to a £1 stake. Pool:£3,869.62 - 361.12 winning tickets RY

5029 DONCASTER (L-H)
Wednesday, September 7

OFFICIAL GOING: Good (good to firm in places) changing to good after race 1 (2:00)
Wind: fresh 1/2 against Weather: overcast, breezy

5825 ARENA STRUCTURES NURSERY 7f
2:00 (2:02) (Class 2) 2-Y-O £9,703 (£2,887; £1,443; £721) Stalls High

Form RPR

10 **1** **Ghostwriting (USA)**[60] 3861 2-9-4 **85**.... WilliamBuick 9 92
(John Gosden) *wnt rt s: in rr-div: drvn over 3f out: gd hdwy to chse ldr 1f out: styd on to ld last 50yds* **9/2**[1]

2125 **2** *1 1/4* **The Blue Banana (IRE)**[18] 5280 2-8-10 **77**....(b[1]) ShaneKelly 3 81
(Brian Meehan) *s.i.s: hdwy on outside over 2f out: led over 1f out: hung bdly lft and ended up far side rail: hdd clsng stages* **10/1**

3020 **3** *1 3/4* **Magic City (IRE)**[20] 5216 2-9-7 **88**.... RichardHughes 10 92
(Richard Hannon) *dwlt: hld up in last: hdwy over 2f out: nt clr run and hmpd over 1f out: styd on wl fnl f: fin strly* **11/2**[2]

2120 **4** *shd* **West Leake Hare (IRE)**[21] 5184 2-8-11 **78**.... MichaelHills 6 77
(Charles Hills) *chsd ldrs: kpt on same pce appr fnl f* **6/1**[3]

2002 **5** *1 3/4* **Indepub**[6] 5645 2-8-8 **75**....(p) PhillipMakin 8 70
(Kevin Ryan) *chsd ldrs: hung lft and one pce appr fnl f* **20/1**

11 **6** *4 1/2* **Jessie's Spirit (IRE)**[25] 5061 2-9-4 **85**.... DavidNolan 12 69
(Ann Duffield) *hld up in rr stands' side: nt clr run over 3f out tl over 1f out: kpt on ins fnl f: nvr nr ldrs* **6/1**[3]

1224 **7** *nse* **Wolfgang (IRE)**[18] 5287 2-9-4 **88**.... KieranO'Neill(3) 7 72
(Richard Hannon) *chsd ldrs: drvn 3f out: outpcd and lost pl 2f out: kpt on ins fnl f* **7/1**

0520 **8** *2* **Es Que Love (IRE)**[21] 5184 2-9-5 **86**.... SilvestreDeSousa 4 65
(Mark Johnston) *led after 2f: hdd over 1f out: sn wknd* **9/1**

3102 **9** *1 1/2* **Nameitwhatyoulike**[27] 4943 2-8-7 **74**....(b) GrahamGibbons 2 49
(Michael Easterby) *chsd ldrs: lost pl over 1f out* **33/1**

2140 **10** *½* **Travis County (IRE)**^{39} 4536 2-8-5 **75**........................... PaulPickard$^{(3)}$ 1 49
(Brian Ellison) *racd wd: led 2f: edgd lft and lost pl over 1f out* **12/1**

0046 **11** *hd* **Man Of My Word**^{8} 5597 2-7-11 **67** ow2............................ BillyCray$^{(3)}$ 5 40
(David Nicholls) *dwlt: sn chsng ldrs: sn drvn along: wknd wl over 1f out* **66/1**

6161 **12** *2¾* **See Clearly**^{26} 4984 2-8-9 **76**.. RobertWinston 11 42
(Tim Easterby) *mid-div: drvn over 2f out: lost pl over 1f out* **16/1**

1m 27.73s (1.43) **Going Correction** +0.025s/f (Good) **12** Ran SP% **116.5**
Speed ratings (Par 101): **92,90,88,88,86 81,81,78,77,76 76,73**
toteswingers:1&2:£8.60, 1&3:£7.60, 2&3:£13.80 CSF £48.06 CT £257.21 TOTE £5.00: £1.80, £3.20, £2.60; EX 59.20 Trifecta £271.50 Pool: £932.23 - 2.54 winning units..

Owner H R H Princess Haya Of Jordan **Bred** Darley **Trained** Newmarket, Suffolk

FOCUS
Following morning rain, the ground had eased slightly and was officially described as good, good to firm in places (GoingStick 6.7). The horses were running into a strong headwind. A decent nursery, run at a fair pace, and the first three came from the back. The form is best rated around the third.

NOTEBOOK
Ghostwriting(USA) was thrown in at the deep end in the Group 2 Superlative Stakes at the July Meeting following his Wolverhampton debut win, but found that too much of an ask. However, given a 60-day break since then and back in more suitable company, he returned to winning ways but it didn't seem likely when he was being niggled along to stay in touch before halfway. It was a similar story when he won at Wolverhampton, though, and the further they went the stronger he became. He was undoubtedly helped by the antics of the runner-up, but this was still a nice performance and 1m should be no problem at all. (op 5-1)

The Blue Banana(IRE) lost a shoe when disappointing on his first try at the trip at Sandown last time and was tried in first-time blinkers here, but despite the headgear he looked a hard ride. Following a tardy start, his rider was having to give him little taps with the whip in order to keep him honest at various stages of the contest, but he still made smooth progress on the outside of the field to take over in front over a furlong from home. However, once there he started to hang violently away to his left under pressure, ending up against the far rail, and basically threw it away. He has questions to answer. (tchd 9-1)

Magic City(IRE) looked a potential star when winning on his debut at Newbury back in April, but hasn't reached the heights that seemed possible then. Making his nursery debut on this first try at 7f, the ride he was given was puzzling to say the least. Slow to break and then heavily restrained, he seemed to travel very well at the back of the field, but being ridden with such confidence was always going to rely on him getting the gaps when he needed them, and his luck ran out when he got squeezed out when trying for a run between Travis Bounty and Man Of My Word over a furlong from home. He already had plenty to do at that stage, and the interference made a difficult task impossible. He finished strongly to just snatch third, but he must have gone close to winning had things worked out more in his favour. Official explanation: jockey said colt was denied a clear run (tchd 5-1)

West Leake Hare(IRE) didn't seem to handle York's easy ground last time and ran better here, holding every chance over a furlong out before finding just the one pace. He may prefer genuinely quick ground. (op 11-2)

Indepub ran better in first-time cheekpieces on his first try at the trip at Redcar last time, but he had previously been twice well beaten in this class. He plugged on up the stands rail under pressure and can win nurseries at a more suitable level, though he is already due to go up another 1lb.

Jessie's Spirit(IRE), previously unbeaten after two wins over 6f in a Leicester maiden and a Ripon conditions event, had a wall of horses in front of her when trying for a run passing the 2f pole, but she didn't exactly take off when eventually in the clear. (op 11-2 tchd 7-1)

Es Que Love(IRE) didn't get home in his only previous try at the trip and it was a similar story here after making the early running. (op 12-1)

5826 NAPOLEONS SHEFFIELD CONDITIONS STKS 6f
2:35 (2:35) (Class 2) 2-Y-O **£9,337** (£2,796; £1,398; £699; £349) **Stalls** High

Form RPR

1156 **1** **Eureka (IRE)**^{40} 4495 2-9-3 102.................................. RichardHughes 3 101
(Richard Hannon) *led: shkn up 2f out: edgd lft ins fnl f: hld on gamely* **7/2**^{3}

112 **2** *½* **Gold City (IRE)**^{9} 5558 2-9-1 94.............................. FrankieDettori 1 98
(Saeed Bin Suroor) *trckd wnr: drvn and upsides wl over 1f out: no ex nr fin* **2/1**^{1}

15 **3** *shd* **Artistic Jewel (IRE)**^{26} 4999 2-8-8 90........................ GrahamGibbons 2 90
(Ed McMahon) *hld up: hdwy over 2f out: chsng ldrs 1f out: n.m.r: hld whn hmpd nr fin* **11/2**

1 **4** *1* **Foxtrot Romeo (IRE)**^{20} 5202 2-8-13 0.............................. TomEaves 5 92
(Bryan Smart) *trckd ldrs: drvn 2f out: kpt on same pce fnl f* **12/1**

1 **5** *2¾* **Alaskan Bullet (IRE)**^{23} 5117 2-8-11 0......................... JamieSpencer 4 82
(Michael Bell) *s.s: hld up in last: hdwy over 2f out: drvn over 1f out: no rspnse* **5/2**^{2}

1m 14.14s (0.54) **Going Correction** +0.025s/f (Good) **5** Ran SP% **107.2**
Speed ratings (Par 101): **97,96,96,94,91**
CSF £10.30 TOTE £4.30: £2.00, £1.30; EX 6.80.

Owner Noodles Racing **Bred** Jerry Murphy **Trained** East Everleigh, Wilts

FOCUS
The going was changed to Good before this race. A decent juvenile conditions race in which six of the last seven winners have gone on to be competitive at Listed and Group level. They went steadily into the headwind before it became a 2f sprint. Straightforward form.

NOTEBOOK
Eureka(IRE) won his first two starts over this trip and ran well in the Super Sprint back at 5f but was then outclassed in the Richmond. He had the highest official rating here and, even though he had to give weight away, appreciated the drop in grade and made all the running. Richard Hughes dictated the pace but went steadily and was able to pick up from the front. He kept on gamely to the line to score narrowly. He is entered in the Mill Reef later in the month but a Listed race might be a more feasible option. (op 3-1)

Gold City(IRE) won his first two over 6f on fast ground but was narrowly beaten in Listed race at Ripon over 6f on easy going. He got shelter in behind the winner for most of the way but could not pick up well enough to get past. He might need fast ground to give of his best. (op 9-4)

Artistic Jewel(IRE) won an ordinary 5f maiden on her debut at Windsor in July but ran well in a Listed race after being bumped at the start next time. She tried to come between the first two in the latter stages, but there was not much room and couple of slight bumps prevented her from doing so.

Foxtrot Romeo(IRE), a 90,000euros brother to the high-class Air Chief Marshall and Misu Bond, won a 6f Hamilton maiden from modest sorts on his debut. Stepping up in grade, he was close enough throughout but could not produce and extra gear in the last furlong. He would have preferred a stiffer test at the trip and another furlong might be in his favour.

Alaskan Bullet(IRE) had made all to win a maiden over 6f on fast ground and was another up in grade. He briefly got upset in the saddling boxes beforehand and then went right and rather blew the start. He was then keen at the back of the field and, although still close enough over a furlong out, appeared to want to edge right when ridden and was eventually eased down. He clearly has a good deal of ability and it is hoped he can put this behind him. (op 11-4)

5827 SCARBROUGH STKS (LISTED RACE) 5f
3:10 (3:10) (Class 1) 2-Y-O+ **£23,680** (£8,956; £4,476; £2,236) **Stalls** High

Form RPR

535 **1** **Humidor (IRE)**^{41} 4468 4-9-9 102..................................(t) FrankieDettori 6 113
(George Baker) *s.i.s: hld up in rr: hdwy and swtchd outside over 1f out: r.o wl to ld last 100yds: hld on wl* **14/1**

3213 **2** *½* **Dinkum Diamond (IRE)**^{11} 5467 3-9-8 106........................ DaneO'Neill 7 111
(Henry Candy) *trckd ldrs: led 1f out: hdd ins fnl f: no ex* **5/1**^{2}

2112 **3** *1* **Medicean Man**^{32} 4776 5-9-9 109..............................(p) RichardHughes 3 107
(Jeremy Gask) *dwlt: stmbld sn after s: in rr: hdwy over 1f out: swtchd lft ins fnl f: kpt on* **11/4**^{1}

0534 **4** *hd* **Group Therapy**^{33} 4768 6-9-9 105................................ JamieSpencer 11 107
(David Barron) *dwlt: hld up in rr: effrt 2f out: styd on fnl f* **7/1**^{3}

2104 **5** *2¼* **Captain Dunne (IRE)**^{11} 5467 6-9-9 108..........................(p) DavidAllan 2 99
(Tim Easterby) *sn trcking ldr: led 2f out: hdd 1f out: wknd last 100yds* **7/1**^{3}

3402 **6** *¾* **Bear Behind (IRE)**^{21} 5194 2-8-3 99......................... RichardKingscote 1 91
(Tom Dascombe) *led: hdd 2f out: fdd appr fnl f* **16/1**

0202 **7** *nk* **Aneedah (IRE)**^{75} 3365 3-9-3 97.................................. WilliamBuick 10 90
(John Gosden) *hld up in rr: effrt 2f out: kpt on last 150yds* **14/1**

1465 **8** *shd* **Anne Of Kiev (IRE)**^{38} 4573 6-9-7 100............................(t) LukeMorris 4 92
(Jeremy Gask) *s.i.s: sme hdwy 2f out: sn wknd* **20/1**

0605 **9** *½* **Breathless Kiss (USA)**^{11} 5467 4-9-4 95........................ PhillipMakin 5 88
(Kevin Ryan) *chsd ldrs: wknd over 1f out* **33/1**

1232 **10** *3* **Duchess Dora (IRE)**^{11} 5467 4-9-4 102............................... PBBeggy 9 77
(John Quinn) *chsd ldrs: lost pl over 1f out* **7/1**^{3}

5014 **11** *1* **Shoshoni Wind**^{32} 4776 3-9-3 96..................................... KierenFallon 12 73
(Kevin Ryan) *trckd ldrs: lost pl over 1f out* **14/1**

59.48 secs (-1.02) **Going Correction** +0.025s/f (Good) **11** Ran SP% **114.4**
Speed ratings: **109,108,106,106,102 101,101,100,100,95 93**
toteswingers:1&2:£10.50, 1&3:£6.60, 2&3:£5.10 CSF £80.39 TOTE £14.50: £4.00, £1.60, £1.80; EX 98.60 Trifecta £1122.40 Pool: £2,325.87 - 1.53 winning units..

Owner M Khan X2 **Bred** Yeomanstown Stud **Trained** Whitsbury, Hants

FOCUS
A good Listed sprint that fell to the subsequent Group 1 winner Prohibit in 2010. As in the previous race they came up the centre. Ordinary form for the grade, with the winner continuing his progress.

NOTEBOOK
Humidor(IRE), who missed a race at Leicester the day before because the ground was considered too fast, had been upped from handicaps into Group races the last twice and run well. Dropping slightly in grade, he came with a good run to lead well inside the last furlong and improved his record to 2-2 here. He entered in a Listed race at Goodwood at the weekend and connections might be tempted to go there, as the gelding has a good record at that track as well.

Dinkum Diamond(IRE) is well suited by 5f on fast ground but also handles cut and put up another decent effort. He looks more than capable of winning a similar contest this autumn. (op 11-2)

Medicean Man, a progressive handicapper who has risen a stone in the ratings since returning to turf in the spring, was up in grade. He missed the break and then stumbled after less than half a furlong, so was left with a lot to do. He made good late headway without ever looking likely to reach the principals and this effort can be ignored. Richard Hughes reported that the gelding stumbled leaving the stalls and the trainer reported that the gelding scoped dirty post-race. Official explanation: jockey said gelding stumbled leaving stalls; trainer said gelding scoped dirty (op 3-1 tchd 7-2 in a place)

Group Therapy had not won since June 2010 when returning from a long absence but did finish third in this last year. Bought for 85,000gns last October and running well in Group and Listed races since, he was not helped by missing the break but came with a run, only for it to peter out late. (op 6-1)

Captain Dunne(IRE), fourth in this last year; had been in good form this season and had stepped up from handicaps into Group and Listed company. However, he was easy in the market and, although he came through to show in front 2f out, he could not sustain the effort. (op 6-1 tchd 15-2)

Bear Behind(IRE), the only juvenile runner, had been placed in Listed company and run well in Group races. He made the running but was headed 2f out and gradually faded. (op 20-1)

Duchess Dora(IRE), a consistent performer in handicaps who went down narrowly in a Beverley Listed race with today's second, fifth and Breathless Kiss behind, had a good chance with Medicean Man on previous handicap form but, after showing up until beyond halfway, she dropped away tamely. (op 8-1)

Shoshoni Wind raced nearest the stands' side and was in contention 2f out before fading. (op 16-1)

5828 CLIPPER LOGISTICS LEGER LEGENDS CLASSIFIED STKS 1m (S)
3:45 (3:49) (Class 5) 3-Y-O+ **£6,469** (£1,925; £962; £481) **Stalls** High

Form RPR

0141 **1** **Invincible Hero (IRE)**^{32} 4783 4-11-5 70...........................(t) JulieKrone 1 83+
(Declan Carroll) *trckd ldrs: c stands' side over 4f out: edgd lft to centre and led over 2f out: styd on strly to forge clr fnl f* **4/1**^{1}

0046 **2** *3½* **Skyfire**^{26} 5014 4-11-5 70.. CharlieSwan 13 75
(Ed de Giles) *mid-div: hdwy over 2f out: chsng wnr 1f out: kpt on same pce* **9/1**^{3}

-452 **3** *nk* **Dialogue**^{40} 4513 5-11-5 69.. GeorgeDuffield 6 74
(Ollie Pears) *t.k.h in rr: hdwy over 2f out: chsng ldrs 1f out: styd on same pce* **6/1**^{2}

0325 **4** *2* **Inpursuitoffreedom**^{10} 5516 4-11-5 69.......................... RayCochrane 10 70
(Philip McBride) *in rr: hdwy over 2f out: kpt on same pce appr fnl f* **9/1**^{3}

2452 **5** *3* **Lockantanks**^{9} 5538 4-11-5 67... ThierryGillet 19 63
(Michael Appleby) *hld up in rr: hdwy to chse ldrs over 2f out: fdd last 100yds* **12/1**

0524 **6** *4* **Conducting**^{7} 5631 3-11-0 70.. GayKelleway 15 54
(Gay Kelleway) *racd stands' side: lft alone 3f out: towards rr tl kpt on fnl 2f: nvr a factor* **20/1**

4203 **7** *¾* **Dr Red Eye**^{22} 5151 3-11-0 68.. JohnReid 18 52
(David Nicholls) *chsd ldrs: wknd over 1f out* **12/1**

-002 **8** *nse* **Whitechapel**^{6} 5653 4-11-5 67.. ErnieJohnson 7 52
(Andrew Balding) *towards rr: hdwy over 2f out: wknd over 1f out* **14/1**

6044 **9** *5* **Wisecraic**^{16} 5319 4-11-5 68..................................(p) SteveSmith-Eccles 12 40
(J S Moore) *mid-division: effrt over 2f out: sn wknd* **33/1**

2603 **10** *nk* **Ginger Grey (IRE)**^{28} 4897 4-11-5 70................................ DaleGibson 8 40
(David O'Meara) *trckd ldrs: t.k.h: wknd over 1f out* **14/1**

5640 **11** *3* **Kalahaag (IRE)**^{9} 5560 3-11-0 70..................................(b) LukeHarvey 14 33
(David Nicholls) *chsd ldrs: wknd 2f out* **33/1**

0154 **12** *8* **Tribal Myth (IRE)**^{78} 3244 4-11-5 70.............................. KevinDarley 11 14
(Kevin Ryan) *chsd ldrs: drvn over 2f out: sn wknd* **11/1**

006 **13** *1 ½* **Aquilifer (IRE)**[32] 4812 3-11-0 70 NormanWilliamson 4 11
(Mrs K Burke) *mid-div: rdn and hung rt over 2f out: sn lost pl* **40/1**
5060 **14** *6* **Ocean Legend (IRE)**[16] 5322 6-11-5 70 GrahamBradley 2 —
(Tony Carroll) *chsd ldrs far side: wknd over 1f out* **25/1**
400 **15** *3* **Ahlawy (IRE)**[14] 5390 8-11-5 70 (bt) JamieOsborne 17 —
(Frank Sheridan) *s.i.s: a in rr* **50/1**
0311 **16** *2 ¼* **Talent Scout (IRE)**[13] 5403 5-11-5 69 (b) TomO'Ryan 5 —
(Tim Walford) *led: wnt clr after 2f: hdd over 2f out: sn lost pl and bhd* **9/1**[3]

1m 42.23s (2.93) **Going Correction** +0.025s/f (Good)
WFA 3 from 4yo+ 5lb **16** Ran SP% **120.2**
Speed ratings (Par 103): **86,82,82,80,77 73,72,72,67,67 64,56,54,48,45 43**
toteswingers:1&2:£10.20, 1&3:£8.30, 2&3:£19.50 CSF £35.37 TOTE £4.70: £1.80, £3.80, £2.80; EX 50.20 Trifecta £319.60 Pool: £1,114.34 - 2.58 winning units..
Owner Mrs Sarah Bryan **Bred** Fortbarrington Stud **Trained** Sledmere, E Yorks
■ Winner 3,708 for Julie Krone, who rode a treble on her one previous trip to Britain, at Redcar in 1992.

FOCUS
The second running of this legends contest and few of these horses had ever been asked to carry anything like these sorts of weights in a race before, even in amateur riders' events. In most races where the field split into two, they do so from the start and then sometimes merge, but this was different. The field started off as one bunch, then split over 5f out, only to merge again over 2f from home. The form is sound, with further improvement from the winner.

5829 COOPERS MARQUEES CONDITIONS STKS 1m 2f 60y
4:20 (4:20) (Class 2) 3-5-Y-0
£12,450 (£3,728; £1,864; £932; £466; £234) **Stalls** Low

Form RPR
2300 **1** **Cai Shen (IRE)**[18] 5275 3-8-11 103 RichardHughes 1 109
(Richard Hannon) *led: jnd 3f out: shkn up 1f out: a doing jst enough* **7/1**
11/3 **2** *½* **Zeitoper**[230] 242 4-9-2 100 FrankieDettori 3 106
(Mahmood Al Zarooni) *trckd ldrs: t.k.h: effrt over 2f out: styd on to chse wnr last 75yds: kpt on towards fin* **6/1**[3]
2036 **3** *1* **Black Spirit (USA)**[53] 4095 4-9-2 108 (t) LukeMorris 8 104
(Clive Cox) *mid-div: drvn over 3f out: styd on wl fnl f: tk 3rd nr line* **11/1**
-551 **4** *hd* **Fallen Idol**[18] 5275 4-9-2 108 WilliamBuick 7 104+
(John Gosden) *in rr: drvn over 3f out: hdwy over 1f out: kpt on wl* **15/8**[1]
6523 **5** *nk* **Elusive Pimpernel (USA)**[11] 5493 4-9-2 108 EddieAhern 4 103
(John Dunlop) *trckd wnr: chal 3f out: rdn 2f out: wknd fnl 100yds* **7/2**[2]
6 *shd* **Sahara Sun (CHI)**[213] 4-9-8 107 (t) KierenFallon 2 109
(Luca Cumani) *t.k.h towards rr: effrt 3f out: hdwy over 2f out: kpt on wl ins fnl f* **14/1**
-000 **7** *8* **Wealthy (IRE)**[53] 4095 4-9-2 105 (t) TedDurcan 5 88
(Saeed Bin Suroor) *dwlt: hld up in rr: effrt over 3f out: wknd 2f out* **33/1**
3-06 **8** *3* **Rasmy**[40] 4492 4-9-2 107 RichardHills 9 82
(Marcus Tregoning) *trckd ldrs: t.k.h: rdn and wknd 2f out* **8/1**

2m 8.68s (-0.72) **Going Correction** +0.175s/f (Good)
WFA 3 from 4yo 7lb **8** Ran SP% **112.8**
Speed ratings (Par 109): **109,108,107,107,107 107,100,98**
toteswingers:1&2:£7.90, 1&3:£10.80, 2&3:£9.50 CSF £46.93 TOTE £9.40: £2.50, £2.10, £2.60; EX 55.60 Trifecta £880.60 Pool: £1,261.49 - 1.06 winning units..
Owner Mrs J Wood **Bred** Wardstown Stud Ltd **Trained** East Everleigh, Wilts
■ Stewards' Enquiry : Luke Morris caution: used whip down shoulder in the forehand.

FOCUS
A competitive conditions race whose best recent winner was the subsequent multiple Group 1 winner Twice Over and a good standard for the grade, with every runner rated 100 or more. It fell to the only 3yo in the race who is rated back to his Britannia form. The form may not prove the most reliable though.

NOTEBOOK
Cai Shen(IRE) was progressive last autumn and in the spring and was placed in Listed company at this trip, although his best previous effort was when narrowly beaten in the Britannia at Royal Ascot. He made the running and, although being taken on by Elusive Pimpernel early and then again 3f out, his rider sat still and did not ask him to win his race until entering the last furlong. He found enough to hold his rivals, most of whom finished in a bunch.
Zeitoper, an unbeaten Group 3 winning juvenile in 2009 but not seen last season, had put up a fair effort on his return to action at Meydan in January but had been absent again since. He ran well and finished clear second-best, so can be expected to build on this if remaining fit and healthy. (op 5-1)
Black Spirit(USA) finished fourth in this last year and just managed to go one better. He had been touched off in a 1m2f Group 3 in the spring but had not confirmed that effort since, so this was at least a step in the right direction. (op 14-1)
Fallen Idol, a Listed winner but held by a couple of these in Group races before returning to form when dropped back into a handicap, was patiently ridden but was being pushed along more than 3f from home before staying on well late. He seems best suited by Sandown, where he is 3-4. (op 5-2)
Elusive Pimpernel(USA), a dual Group 3 winner who had not won since taking the Craven Stakes in spring 2010, kept the winner company and might have briefly headed him around 3f out. However, he could not get past and faded in the last furlong. He ideally needs a sounder surface.
Sahara Sun(CHI), a high-class Chilean import who had proved effective between 1m and 1m4f, was giving weight all round on this first outing since February and did not fare badly. He has apparently been bought with the Melbourne Cup in mind and this should help bring him on. (op 11-1)
Wealthy(IRE), runner-up in Group races on soft ground in France, had shown little for his current trainer in Dubai and back here since and it was the same story here. (op 28-1)
Rasmy, whose only win was at 1m, was dropping back from 1m4f but was too keen under restraint and paid for it late on.

5830 QUATTROVALLI LUXURY WINE CHAMPIONS H'CAP 7f
4:50 (4:51) (Class 2) (0-100,99) 3-Y-O
£12,450 (£3,728; £1,864; £932; £466; £234) **Stalls** High

Form RPR
4112 **1** **Lightning Cloud (IRE)**[46] 4310 3-8-11 89 PhillipMakin 9 103+
(Kevin Ryan) *hld up in mid-div: smooth hdwy over 2f out: squeezed through to ld and qckn over 1f out: sn hung lft and ended up far side rail: jst hld on* **8/1**
1113 **2** *hd* **Louis The Pious**[25] 5054 3-8-11 89 FrankieDettori 10 100+
(Kevin Ryan) *hld up in rr: hdwy stands' side over 2f out: styd on fnl f: jst hld* **9/2**[2]
2110 **3** *½* **Johnny Castle**[67] 3649 3-9-0 92 WilliamBuick 1 103+
(John Gosden) *hld up in rr: hdwy over 2f out: chsng wnr whn sltly hmpd jst ins fnl f: hung bdly rt: kpt on towards fin* **7/1**[3]
5P66 **4** *2* **Trade Storm**[27] 4965 3-9-6 98 SilvestreDeSousa 12 102
(John Gallagher) *hld up in mid-div: effrt over 2f out: kpt on same pce appr fnl f* **25/1**
20 **5** *1 ¼* **Rigolleto (IRE)**[25] 5043 3-8-10 88 RichardHughes 11 89
(Mick Channon) *hld up in rr: effrt over 2f out: one pce appr fnl f* **33/1**
-111 **6** *2 ¾* **White Frost (IRE)**[12] 5450 3-9-0 92 MichaelHills 5 85
(Charles Hills) *trckd ldrs: t.k.h: effrt 2f out: sn wknd* **4/1**[1]
4131 **7** *½* **Shesastar**[19] 5255 3-8-8 86 JamieSpencer 7 78
(David Barron) *in rr: dropped bk in detached last after 1f: hdwy 2f out: nvr nr ldrs* **4/1**[1]
213 **8** *1 ¾* **Sea Soldier (IRE)**[27] 4965 3-8-7 85 oh1 DavidProbert 13 72
(Andrew Balding) *trckd ldrs: effrt 2f out: sn wknd* **12/1**
6151 **9** *1* **Sacrosanctus**[26] 5012 3-8-9 87 TomQueally 4 72
(David Nicholls) *led: narrowly hdd over 2f out: wknd over 1f out* **25/1**
1411 **10** *nk* **Roninski (IRE)**[14] 5370 3-8-8 86 TomEaves 14 70
(Bryan Smart) *hld up in mid-div: hdwy over 2f out: wknd over 1f out* **20/1**
3310 **11** *1 ¾* **Levitate**[25] 5054 3-8-4 85 oh2 (p) MartinHarley(3) 3 64
(Alan McCabe) *w ldr: led narrowly over 2f out: hdd & wknd over 1f out* **16/1**
42-0 **12** *8* **Mawaakef (IRE)**[57] 3969 3-8-12 90 KierenFallon 6 48
(J R Jenkins) *trckd ldrs: drvn over 2f out: sn lost pl: eased whn bhd ins fnl f* **20/1**

1m 26.67s (0.37) **Going Correction** +0.025s/f (Good) **12** Ran SP% **115.5**
Speed ratings (Par 107): **98,97,97,94,93 90,89,87,86,86 84,75**
toteswingers:1&2:£8.40, 1&3:£10.70, 2&3:£6.90 CSF £39.26 CT £271.31 TOTE £10.40: £3.60, £1.70, £2.80; EX 37.10 Trifecta £327.30 Pool: £1,601.29 - 3.62 winning units..
Owner Hambleton Racing Ltd XVIII **Bred** John Cullinan **Trained** Hambleton, N Yorks

FOCUS
A strong 3yo handicap in which the four previous winners have been rated between 88 and 98, and the sequence was maintained here. The time was 1.06secs faster than the opening race and the principals all came from off the pace. The first three were on the up and the winner rates slightly better than the bare form.

NOTEBOOK
Lightning Cloud(IRE) had gained four wins from six previous starts this season, all at this trip, and had risen 20lb in the weights. Freshened up by a short break, he moved up going well and got a nice split through the centre of the pack to take the lead. However, he hung sharply left once in front, crossing the third and ending up on the rail, but just managing to hold off his stablemate on the stands' side. He looks capable of further success.
Louis The Pious, a stable companion of the winner, had also won four of his six previous starts this season but all those had been at 6f and he had been beaten on his only try at this trip. Racing off 6lb above his last winning mark, he came with a strong run in the last furlong and was only just denied. (op 5-1 tchd 4-1)
Johnny Castle broke his maiden over C&D after finishing runner-up on his first four starts, but built on that by beating two subsequent winners at Newmarket next time. He had been given a break since finishing well beaten off this 8lb higher mark last time at the beginning of July and ran well, not being helped by the winner cutting across him inside the last furlong, although he himself went right late on. (op 8-1)
Trade Storm, who had finished fifth in the Britannia and had run well in Listed company a couple of times, had gained his last win over C&D and was only 1lb higher here. He ran creditably without being able to peg back the principals in the last furlong. (op 22-1)
Rigolleto(IRE) had not won since taking his maiden over this trip on easy ground 13 months ago but had run well off similar marks this season and did so again, if unable to land a serious blow.
White Frost(IRE) had won all three of his previous outings this season, all at this trip; and, although he had gone up 6lb for his last success, looked set to make it four when coming through to join the leaders going well. However, no sooner than he arrived on the scene than so did the winner, going even better, and he could not respond. (tchd 9-2)
Shesastar, a progressive filly who had won two of three starts here, both over 6f; had won on her first try at 7f last time and Jamie Spencer was 2-2 on her. She was held up out the back but never appeared to be going that well and was unable to get involved, although those that raced immediately in front of her early filled the first three placings. This was not her true running. (op 7-2)

5831 GOFFS/DBS ST LEGER CARNIVAL SALES H'CAP 5f
5:20 (5:24) (Class 4) (0-85,85) 3-Y-O+ **£6,469** (£1,925; £962; £481) **Stalls** High

Form RPR
042 **1** **Haajes**[28] 4900 7-9-0 78 TomQueally 19 88
(Paul Midgley) *trckd ldrs stands' side: effrt over 1f out: r.o to ld last 100yds: hld on towards fin* **9/1**[2]
1226 **2** *¾* **Eland Ally**[37] 4610 3-9-2 81 RichardHughes 22 88
(Tom Tate) *trckd ldrs stands' side: swtchd lft over 1f out: styd on strly last 150yds: jst hld* **14/1**
0236 **3** *shd* **Lujeanie**[39] 4556 5-9-4 82 (p) FrankieDettori 13 89
(Dean Ivory) *hld up in rr: hdwy 2f out: chsng ldrs 1f out: styd on same pce last 50yds* **9/1**[2]
0600 **4** *hd* **Indian Trail**[9] 5543 11-9-4 82 (b) PaulQuinn 15 88
(David Nicholls) *hld up: hdwy 2f out: w ldrs 1f out: edgd rt and no ex clsng stages* **14/1**
3000 **5** *½* **Rocket Rob (IRE)**[25] 5033 5-9-3 81 StevieDonohoe 7 85
(Willie Musson) *s.i.s: in rr: hdwy over 1f out: styd on last 100yds: hmpd nr fin* **9/2**[1]
012 **6** *½* **Picabo (IRE)**[18] 5265 3-8-11 76 DaneO'Neill 17 78
(Lucy Wadham) *s.i.s: last stands' side gp: hdwy over 1f out: kpt on ins fnl f* **10/1**[3]
14-0 **7** *1 ¾* **Drift And Dream**[18] 5278 4-9-2 80 TedDurcan 14 76
(Chris Wall) *mid-div: hdwy 2f out: wnt rt over 1f out: kpt on same pce* **11/1**
0062 **8** *½* **Even Stevens**[5] 5680 3-8-9 77 (p) BillyCray(3) 9 71+
(David Nicholls) *w ldrs: led over 1f out: hdd 100yds out: fdd* **20/1**
1300 **9** *¾* **Lost In Paris (IRE)**[25] 5033 5-9-7 85 (p) DavidAllan 20 77+
(Tim Easterby) *chsd ldr stands' side: kpt on same pce appr fnl f* **16/1**
3160 **10** *1 ½* **Desert Strike**[5] 5683 5-8-3 74 (p) RyanTate(7) 18 60
(Alan McCabe) *s.s: sn swtchd lft to centre: kpt on fnl 2f: nvr a factor* **33/1**
0130 **11** *½* **Berberana (IRE)**[18] 5288 3-9-1 80 RobertWinston 12 64
(Tim Easterby) *led tl over 1f out: wknd fnl 150yds* **33/1**
0025 **12** *shd* **Oldjoesaid**[5] 5679 7-9-4 82 (b) PhillipMakin 2 66
(Kevin Ryan) *mid-div: drvn over 2f out: nvr a factor* **9/1**[2]
4-30 **13** *2* **Major Muscari (IRE)**[102] 2505 3-9-0 79 SilvestreDeSousa 10 56
(Geoffrey Oldroyd) *mid-div: effrt over 2f out: nvr nr ldrs* **25/1**
0065 **14** *1 ½* **Style And Panache (IRE)**[7] 5627 3-8-8 73 DavidProbert 6 44
(David Evans) *chsd ldrs: wknd over 1f out* **50/1**
6003 **15** *hd* **Beat The Bell**[5] 5680 6-9-7 85 (b[1]) GrahamGibbons 3 56
(David Barron) *mid-div: effrt over 2f out: nvr a factor* **14/1**
3000 **16** *hd* **Sir Geoffrey (IRE)**[5] 5680 5-9-1 79 (b) ShaneKelly 11 49
(David Nicholls) *chsd ldrs: wknd over 1f out* **66/1**
1211 **17** *nk* **Deerslayer (USA)**[8] 5604 5-8-11 78 6ex (p) MartinHarley(3) 5 47
(Richard Guest) *w ldrs: wknd over 1f out* **10/1**[3]
020 **18** *1 ½* **Best Trip (IRE)**[28] 4909 4-8-10 74 AndrewMullen 21 37
(Richard Guest) *led stands' side gp: hdd over 1f out: sn lost pl* **33/1**
2140 **19** *¾* **Jack Rackham**[26] 5012 7-8-11 75 (v) TomEaves 16 36
(Bryan Smart) *towards rr: wnt rt 2f out: nvr on terms* **28/1**

5612 **20** *2 1/4* **Fol Hollow (IRE)**[20] 5204 6-9-2 **80**................................ AdrianNicholls 1 33
(David Nicholls) *mid-div: effrt far side 2f out: sn wknd* **20/1**
2550 **21** *8* **Taurus Twins**[60] 3847 5-9-4 **82**.....................................(b) WilliamBuick 8 6
(Richard Price) *w ldrs: rdr lost irons 3f out: sn eased and bhd* **25/1**
60.82 secs (0.32) **Going Correction** +0.025s/f (Good)
WFA 3 from 4yo+ 1lb **21** Ran SP% **133.5**
Speed ratings (Par 105): **98,96,96,96,95 94,91,91,89,87 86,86,83,80,80 80,79,77,76,72 59**
toteswingers:1&2:£26.30, 1&3:£22.00, 2&3:£22.50. Totesuper 7: Win:Not won, Place: Not won. CSF £122.62 CT £1224.51 TOTE £8.90: £2.30, £4.10, £2.50, £3.80; EX 142.80 Trifecta £1376.10 Part won. Pool: £1,859.60 - 0.64 winning units..
Owner N Lomas, A Taylor Snr, A Taylor Jnr **Bred** Irish National Stud **Trained** Westow, N Yorks
■ Stewards' Enquiry : Paul Quinn one-day ban: careless riding (Sep 21)

FOCUS
A wide-open sprint handicap, won by Reverence in 2005 before he went on to much better things. The field soon split into two with the larger group of 16 racing centre-to-far side, whilst five raced up the stands' rail but that quintet provided the winner, second and sixth. The form has a pretty straightforward look to it.
T/Jkpt: Not won. T/Plt: £134.30 to a £1 stake. Pool:£139,688.77 - 758.97 winning tickets T/Qpdt: £52.70 to a £1 stake. Pool:£7,931.38 - 111.34 winning tickets WG

5711 KEMPTON (A.W) (R-H)

Wednesday, September 7

OFFICIAL GOING: Standard
Wind: Fresh, across (away from stands) Weather: Cloudy

5832 FREE ENTRY FOR BETDAQ MEMBERS CLASSIFIED STKS — 1m 2f (P)
5:50 (5:51) (Class 6) 3-Y-O+ **£1,617** (£481; £240; £120) **Stalls** Low

Form RPR
0634 **1** **Appyjack**[6] 5642 3-8-11 48... NeilCallan 4 62
(Tony Carroll) *led 1f: settled in 5th: prog on inner to chse ldr 2f out: rdn to ld over 1f out: didn't find much but asserted v grad* **6/1**[3]
-001 **2** *3/4* **Distant Waters**[33] 4755 4-9-4 51.. JimCrowley 5 60
(Alan Jarvis) *t.k.h: hld up in rr: gng bttr than most over 2f out: prog wl over 1f out: styd on wl to take 2nd nr fin: unable to chal* **9/1**
5000 **3** *1/2* **Fifty Cents**[16] 5318 7-9-4 52.. DarryllHolland 11 59
(Brendan Powell) *led after 1f: kicked on 3f out: hdd over 1f out: kpt on same pce: lost 2nd nr fin* **16/1**
0040 **4** *2 1/2* **Minortransgression (USA)**[19] 5248 4-9-1 54...... AdamBeschizza(3) 13 54
(Paul Rich) *hld up in midfield: lost pl on inner 3f out: prog again 2f out: chsd ldrs and ch jst over 1f out: one pce* **20/1**
-004 **5** *1 3/4* **Cantor**[16] 5321 3-8-11 52.. WilliamCarson 8 51
(Giles Bravery) *wl in rr: pushed along after 2f: nvr gng wl after: no prog whn wdst of all bnd 2f out: styd on over 1f out: nrst fin* **3/1**[1]
3-54 **6** *1 1/2* **Ad Value (IRE)**[12] 5441 3-8-11 51.................................... CathyGannon 2 48
(Alan Swinbank) *wl in rr: shoved along fr 1/2-way: struggling after: plugged on fnl 2f: nrst fin* **8/1**
200/ **7** *1 3/4* **Den Maschine**[451] 5679 6-9-4 49.. MartinLane 1 44
(John Flint) *sn trckd ldng pair: rdn 3f out: fdd fnl 2f* **4/1**[2]
4044 **8** *3/4* **Sir Randolf (IRE)**[7] 5636 3-8-11 54.............................(t) JamesDoyle 14 43
(Sylvester Kirk) *chsd ldr after 1f to after 3f: wnt 2nd again briefly over 2f out and rdr dropped whip: grad wknd* **25/1**
0000 **9** *1 1/4* **Iztaccihuatl**[34] 4705 3-8-11 44.................................... JamieGoldstein 6 40
(Michael Scudamore) *racd wd in midfield: prog arnd field on bnd 3f out: wknd wl over 2f out* **40/1**
0-40 **10** *14* **My Mate Les (IRE)**[31] 4827 3-8-8 50.................................. KierenFox(3) 3 12
(John Best) *in tch tl wknd qckly wl over 2f out: t.o* **40/1**
035 **11** *1/2* **Fair Dinkum (IRE)**[13] 5415 3-8-11 54.......................... FergusSweeney 7 11
(Jamie Osborne) *hld up in midfield: cl enough disputing 5th 3f out: wknd rapidly: t.o* **16/1**
5354 **12** *1 1/2* **Heart Of Dixie (IRE)**[5] 5665 3-8-6 52.......................... RyanPowell(5) 10 8
(Paul Cole) *s.i.s and rousted along: prog to join ldr after 4f: wknd rapidly over 2f out: t.o* **11/1**
0006 **13** *1 3/4* **Hector The Brave (IRE)**[13] 5406 4-9-4 47................. RichardThomas 9 —
(John E Long) *a in rr: detached in last 4f out: t.o* **40/1**
2m 6.25s (-1.75) **Going Correction** -0.125s/f (Stan)
WFA 3 from 4yo+ 7lb **13** Ran SP% **116.4**
Speed ratings (Par 101): **102,101,101,99,97 96,95,94,93,82 81,80,79**
toteswingers: 1&2 £8.80, 1&3 £19.40, 2&3 £24.70. CSF £53.95 TOTE £9.70: £2.10, £2.80, £6.40; EX 40.80.
Owner Mayden Stud **Bred** Mayden Stud, J A And D S Dewhurst **Trained** Cropthorne, Worcs

FOCUS
Conditions were dry but there was a brisk wind blowing across the track into the stands. There was a fair gallop in this classified stakes. The winner rates back to his best.

5833 BETDAQ.COM EXCHANGE PRICE MULTIPLES NURSERY — 5f (P)
6:20 (6:20) (Class 5) (0-70,70) 2-Y-O **£2,264** (£673; £336; £168) **Stalls** Low

Form RPR
3331 **1** **Roy's Legacy**[16] 5316 2-8-9 **58**...............................(t) RobbieFitzpatrick 8 70
(Shaun Harris) *dwlt: gd spd to ld after 150yds: mde rest: rdn clr over 1f out: styd on wl* **13/2**
0642 **2** *3 1/2* **Meloneras**[34] 4702 2-9-7 **70**... JamesMillman 4 69
(Rod Millman) *chsd ldrs: rdn to chse wnr 2f out: no imp at all* **5/1**
0551 **3** *1/2* **First Rebellion**[9] 5535 2-7-9 **51** 6ex............................. RaulDaSilva(7) 1 48
(Tony Carroll) *in tch: effrt on inner 2f out: chsd ldng pair over 1f out: kpt on same pce* **4/1**[2]
4642 **4** *1* **Thorpe Bay**[9] 5535 2-8-6 **58**... LouisBeuzelin(3) 9 52
(Mark Rimmer) *hld up at rr of gp: gng bttr than most 2f out: wnt 4th and asked for effrt 1f out: no rspnse* **9/2**[3]
0443 **5** *1 1/2* **White Spirit (IRE)**[4] 5737 2-9-4 **67**.................................. JimmyQuinn 6 55
(Marco Botti) *racd wd: chsd ldrs: pushed along and nt qckn in 5th 1f out: reminders and fdd* **6/1**
543 **6** *2 1/2* **Dark Ages (IRE)**[12] 5438 2-9-4 **67**.. NeilCallan 2 46
(Noel Quinlan) *in tch in rr: rdn 1/2-way: no prog* **7/2**[1]
2004 **7** *1 1/2* **Princess Banu**[12] 5427 2-9-5 **68**.. ChrisCatlin 7 42
(Mick Channon) *led 150yds: lost pl rapidly and dropping to last whn squeezed out after 2f: bhd after* **16/1**
6460 **8** *1* **Imperial Weapon (IRE)**[23] 5099 2-7-12 **47** oh2..........(p) CathyGannon 5 17
(John Spearing) *racd freely: chsd wnr after 1f to 2f out: wknd rapidly* **50/1**
60.61 secs (0.11) **Going Correction** -0.125s/f (Stan) **8** Ran SP% **112.5**
Speed ratings (Par 95): **94,88,87,86,83 79,77,75**
toteswingers: 1&2 £8.50, 1&3 £6.10, 2&3 £5.00. CSF £37.54 CT £146.14 TOTE £4.20: £1.10, £2.60, £1.80; EX 37.00.
Owner Karl Blackwell Steve Mohammed S A Harris **Bred** A Christou **Trained** Carburton, Notts

FOCUS
A modest nursery that was won at the start. The winner will face a fair rise for this and the form is straightforward in behind.

NOTEBOOK
Roy's Legacy won from the best draw over C&D last time and looked to face a stiffer task here off 5lb higher and from a wide draw. However, he broke best of all, crossed over to the rail and made just about all to win far easier than last time. This track clearly suits him and, while he's sure to go up a few pounds now, there could yet be more improvement to come from him on this surface. (op 9-2)
Meloneras has led in the past but wasn't quick enough to do so here and, while she kept on for second, the winner comfortably maintained his advantage over her in the closing stages. (op 13-2 tchd 7-1)
First Rebellion, 2lb wrong under his penalty, had the best draw but jinked slightly leaving the stalls and had to settle for a midfield position on the rail. He got a nice run through turning in but could make no significant inroads. Perhaps he needs a stiffer 5f to be seen at his best. (op 5-1)
Thorpe Bay, narrowly beaten by First Rebellion at Chepstow last time, was drawn worst of all, got trapped a shade wide on the bend and had to wait for a gap to open up in the straight. He kept on once in the clear but looked to find this trip on this track a bit sharp. (tchd 4-1)
White Spirit(IRE) got caught widest rounding the bend into the straight, which was no help. (op 11-2)
Dark Ages(IRE), who was not that well away, was disappointing considering this quick 5f should have suited her better than the soft ground she faced at Newcastle last time. (op 4-1, tchd 9-2 in a place)
Princess Banu Official explanation: jockey said filly failed to handle the bend

5834 LAY BACK AND WIN AT BETDAQ.COM MAIDEN AUCTION STKS — 6f (P)
6:50 (6:51) (Class 5) 2-Y-O **£2,264** (£673; £336; £168) **Stalls** Low

Form RPR
2 **1** **Heyward Girl (IRE)**[142] 1441 2-8-2 0..................... AdamBeschizza(3) 12 71+
(Robert Eddery) *gd spd fr wdst draw: mde all: clr 2f out: shkn up and edgd lft but in n.d after* **4/5**[1]
5 **2** *3* **Planet I T (IRE)**[20] 5211 2-8-10 0....................................... LiamKeniry 11 67
(Mark Usher) *rcvrd fr wd draw to chse wnr after 1f: hung lft towards nr side and outpcd 2f out: no imp after: kpt on* **40/1**
3 *3/4* **Navaho Spirit** 2-8-11 0.. MarcHalford 4 66
(Terry Clement) *chsd wnr 1f: styd prom: outpcd over 2f out: kpt on same pce after* **50/1**
64 **4** *hd* **Chrissycross (IRE)**[12] 5424 2-8-1 0............................ HarryBentley(3) 5 58
(Roger Teal) *prom: drvn and outpcd in 4th over 2f out: styd on fnl f* **15/2**[3]
6 **5** *2 1/2* **Haafhd Handsome**[31] 4823 2-8-8 0................................ SeanLevey(3) 8 58
(Richard Hannon) *settled in midfield: effrt to chse ldng quartet over 2f out: one pce and no real imp* **8/1**
6 *1 1/4* **Future Wonder (IRE)** 2-8-5 0...................................... MartinLane 10 48+
(Rae Guest) *s.s: hld up in last: pushed along over 2f out: styd on steadily fnl 2f: nrst fin* **66/1**
0 **7** *1* **Emirates Jack (IRE)**[46] 4339 2-8-12 0............................ TonyCulhane 3 52
(George Baker) *mostly in midfield and off the pce: rdn to dispute 5th over 2f out to over 1f out: wknd* **16/1**
2 **8** *hd* **Molamento (IRE)**[19] 5245 2-8-5 0.................................. CathyGannon 7 44
(Gary Moore) *hld up off the pce in midfield: sltly awkward over 3f out: no prog 2f out: fdd* **7/1**[2]
9 *2 3/4* **Cincinnati Kit** 2-8-7 0... WilliamCarson 1 38
(Stuart Williams) *mounted on crse: wl in rr: rdn and effrt on outer over 2f out: sn no prog* **20/1**
10 *2* **Wordismybond** 2-8-13 0... FergusSweeney 2 38+
(Peter Makin) *wl in rr: brief effrt on inner over 2f out: wknd over 1f out* **14/1**
11 *hd* **Awesome Rock (IRE)** 2-8-13 0.. IanMongan 9 37
(Louise Best) *nvr beyond midfield: rdn and wknd on outer over 2f out* **50/1**
00 **12** *6* **Peering**[100] 2556 2-8-3 0... RichardOld(7) 6 16
(Nick Littmoden) *chsd ldng quartet to over 2f out: hanging bdly and wknd rapidly* **100/1**
1m 13.15s (0.05) **Going Correction** -0.125s/f (Stan) **12** Ran SP% **117.1**
Speed ratings (Par 95): **94,90,89,88,85 83,82,82,78,75 75,67**
toteswingers: 1&2 £12.90, 1&3 £29.90, 2&3 £153.90. CSF £57.60 TOTE £2.00: £1.10, £8.50, £11.30; EX 38.70.
Owner Phillips,Donaldson,Matthews,Smith & Kerve **Bred** Ballykilbride Stud **Trained** Newmarket, Suffolk

FOCUS
Not much strength in depth to this maiden and the first four filled those positions throughout. The winner didn't need to match her debut effort.

NOTEBOOK
Heyward Girl(IRE), despite the wide draw, looked to have been found a straightforward opportunity to get off the mark, as on her debut back in April, in a race that has worked out very well, she'd finished second to Queen Mary and Lowther winner Best Terms. Fairly quick away from the stalls, she had little difficulty getting to the front and crossing over to the rail before the first bend and she proceeded to make every yard for an easy success. She didn't cost much but she's by Bertolini out of a mare who was a prolific winning sprinter, and she looks to have inherited plenty of her parents' speed. There should be more races to be won with her, and her trainer earmarked a novice race here early next month as her short-term target. (op 10-11, tchd Evens in places)
Planet I T(IRE) showed some ability on his debut at Southwell and this was another step in the right direction. Drawn next door to the winner, he was able to take up a position racing in second to her outer and, while unable to live with her in the straight, kept on well enough to suggest he'll be paying his way once eligible for handicaps. (op 50-1)
Navaho Spirit did best of the newcomers, showing good early speed to bag a position tracking the winner on the rail. He also kept on well to hold off the more experienced Chrissycross for third, hinting at improvement for a longer trip (half-brother to 1m2f winner). (op 66-1)
Chrissycross(IRE) ran a sound enough race and can now have his attentions turned to modest nursery company. (op 7-1 tchd 8-1)
Haafhd Handsome is a half-brother to Linas Selection, who won at up to 1m6f, so one should expect him to improve once stepped up in distance. (op 12-1)
Future Wonder(IRE) ◆, a half-sister to six winners including Group 3-winning juvenile Soul City, was worst away from the stalls and trailed the field for much of the race, but she was keeping on quite nicely at the finish and is likely to come on quite a bit for this.

5835 BETDAQ MOBILE APPS H'CAP — 1m (P)
7:20 (7:20) (Class 5) (0-75,75) 3-Y-O+ **£2,264** (£673; £336; £168) **Stalls** Low

Form RPR
0035 **1** **Iron Step**[11] 5488 3-9-4 **74**..(t) DarryllHolland 1 83
(Nicky Vaughan) *mde most: set mod pce tl kicked on over 2f out: hrd rdn over 1f out: styd on* **8/1**
2022 **2** *1 1/4* **Ferruccio (IRE)**[23] 5101 3-9-5 **75**.. KierenFallon 9 81
(James Fanshawe) *trckd ldrs: rdn over 2f out: drvn to dispute 2nd fr over 1f out: kpt on: nvr able to chal* **3/1**[1]

0513 **3** *hd* **Point Du Jour (FR)**[7] 5635 3-9-0 **70** JamesDoyle 6 76
(Ian Wood) *mostly chsd wnr: rdn and nt qckn over 2f out: kpt on but nvr able to chal after: lost 2nd nr fin* **5/1**[3]

2510 **4** *3* **Dazeen**[35] 4656 4-9-8 **73** (b[1]) TonyCulhane 8 73
(David Flood) *t.k.h: hld up in last trio: prog over 2f out: chsd ldng trio over 1f out: no imp after* **16/1**

3514 **5** *1* **Oetzi**[42] 4447 3-8-8 **67** HarryBentley(3) 10 63
(Alan Jarvis) *hld up towards rr: nt qckn over 2f out and dropped to last trio: kpt on again fr over 1f out* **14/1**

0103 **6** *2* **Exchange**[25] 5041 3-9-3 **73** GeorgeBaker 5 65
(Andrew Haynes) *hld up in last trio: taken wd of rest in home st: rdn and sme late prog: n.d* **33/1**

0411 **7** *nk* **Catchanova (IRE)**[14] 5383 4-9-10 **75** NeilCallan 2 67
(Eve Johnson Houghton) *hld up in midfield: outpcd over 2f out: drvn and no imp on ldrs over 1f out* **4/1**[2]

1-50 **8** *hd* **The Holyman (IRE)**[44] 4385 3-9-5 **75** IanMongan 11 66
(Jo Crowley) *chsd ldrs: rdn 3f out: sn lost pl: no ch over 1f out* **14/1**

5403 **9** *½* **Cool Hand Jake**[23] 5101 5-9-5 **70** FergusSweeney 7 60
(Peter Makin) *hld up early: prog on outer to dispute 2nd 5f out to 3f out: sn wknd* **15/2**

0305 **10** *1 ¾* **Copperwood**[16] 5322 6-9-7 **72** LiamKeniry 4 58
(Michael Blanshard) *chsd ldrs: rdn and outpcd over 2f out: wknd qckly over 1f out on inner* **50/1**

5534 **11** *1 ½* **Hereford Boy**[28] 4910 7-9-4 **69** (b) RobertHavlin 3 52
(Dean Ivory) *hld up in last trio: outpcd over 2f out: effrt but no ch whn hmpd over 1f out* **12/1**

1m 38.55s (-1.25) **Going Correction** -0.125s/f (Stan)
WFA 3 from 4yo+ 5lb 11 Ran SP% **116.4**
Speed ratings (Par 103): **101,99,99,96,95 93,93,93,92,90 89**
toteswingers: 1&2 £11.00, 1&3 £12.10, 2&3 £5.80. CSF £31.80 CT £137.02 TOTE £14.60: £3.20, £1.40, £2.30; EX 61.60.
Owner Andrew Tinkler **Bred** Brook Stud Bloodstock Ltd **Trained** Helshaw Grange, Shropshire

FOCUS
Most of these wanted to be held up so there was always a chance that there'd be a false pace. That's how it turned out, with very few getting into it and Darryll Holland doing what he does best, setting a pace to suit himself out in front. Sound enough form amongst the front three, even though the winner was another to make all.
Cool Hand Jake Official explanation: jockey said gelding was slowly away
Hereford Boy Official explanation: jockey said gelding was denied a clear run

5836 ALLAN PULLEN MEMORIAL CLASSIFIED CLAIMING STKS 1m (P)
7:50 (7:52) (Class 6) 3-Y-O+ **£1,617** (£481; £240; £120) **Stalls** Low

Form RPR

0066 **1** **Dazakhee**[13] 5414 4-9-2 61 TonyCulhane 5 71
(David Flood) *hld up in last quartet: prog on outer over 2f out: urged along and clsd over 1f out: led last 150yds: styd on* **20/1**

0121 **2** *1* **Sky Diamond (IRE)**[7] 5631 3-9-1 65 (b) JimCrowley 11 72
(James Given) *trckd ldrs in 5th: gng strly over 2f out: sn clsd: drvn to ld jst over 1f out: hdd and one pce last 150yds* **9/2**[1]

6500 **3** *1 ¾* **Dichoh**[16] 5319 8-8-10 59 (p) KirstyMilczarek 8 58
(Michael Madgwick) *trckd ldng pair: wnt 2nd wl over 2f out: led wl over 1f out to jst over 1f out: one pce* **50/1**

4300 **4** *1 ¾* **Wishformore (IRE)**[5] 5673 4-8-7 62 (p) RyanPowell(5) 6 56
(J S Moore) *settled midfield: rdn in 8th 1/2-way: struggling over 2f out: styd on fr over 1f out: tk 4th post* **12/1**

0001 **5** *hd* **Gazboolou**[14] 5394 7-8-11 57 JamesRogers(5) 14 60
(David Pinder) *racd wd in midfield to 1/2-way: 7th over 3f out: swtchd to inner and effrt over 2f out: one pce over 1f out* **25/1**

103 **6** *nk* **Lutine Charlie (IRE)**[17] 5300 4-8-6 65 CathyGannon 2 49+
(Ronald Harris) *hld up in last quartet: nt clr run 3f out to 2f out: gd prog over 1f out: styd on same pce fnl f* **10/1**

334 **7** *3 ½* **Dr Wintringham (IRE)**[42] 4445 5-8-12 66 DarryllHolland 13 47
(Karen George) *hld up in last and sn detached: rdn over 2f out: prog u.p over 1f out: no ch w ldrs* **15/2**

6000 **8** *½* **Fivefold (USA)**[28] 4910 4-8-6 65 (p) ChrisCatlin 7 40
(John Akehurst) *led at gd pce: hdd wl over 1f out: wknd qckly fnl f* **20/1**

6400 **9** *2 ¼* **Querido (GER)**[23] 5103 7-8-13 60 RobertLButler(3) 12 45
(Paddy Butler) *hld up and sn wl adrift in last pair: shkn up and hanging over 2f out: kpt on fr over 1f out: no ch* **66/1**

3563 **10** *5* **Thunda**[7] 5624 3-8-11 65 NeilCallan 9 32
(Eve Johnson Houghton) *chsd ldng trio: wknd wl over 1f out: eased whn no ch fnl f* **7/1**[3]

6103 **11** *1 ¾* **Grand Piano (IRE)**[26] 4997 4-8-7 68 ow1 (v) LiamKeniry 3 20
(Andrew Balding) *hld up in rr: rdn and no prog over 2f out: wknd: t.o* **11/2**[2]

0-46 **12** *1* **Alqaahir (USA)**[53] 4088 9-8-6 62 (p) LiamJones 10 17
(Paddy Butler) *a towards rr: no prog over 2f out: wl bhd after* **50/1**

0632 **13** *nk* **Enriching (USA)**[18] 3916 3-8-7 68 (t) KierenFallon 1 21
(Noel Quinlan) *pressed ldr to wl over 2f out: sn wknd: eased whn no ch over 1f out* **8/1**

2-50 **14** *½* **Suzhou**[89] 2869 4-8-3 60 JohnFahy(3) 4 15
(Denis Coakley) *chsd ldrs in 6th: lost pl over 2f out: wknd qckly over 1f out: sn bhd* **11/2**[2]

1m 38.44s (-1.36) **Going Correction** -0.125s/f (Stan)
WFA 3 from 4yo+ 5lb 14 Ran SP% **119.9**
Speed ratings (Par 101): **101,100,98,96,96 96,92,92,89,84 83,82,81,81**
toteswingers: 1&2 £19.40, 1&3 £64.20, 2&3 £33.00. CSF £102.28 TOTE £43.80: £9.20, £1.30, £8.00; EX 199.90.
Owner Darren & Annaley Yates **Bred** M Kerr-Dineen **Trained** Exning, Suffolk

FOCUS
There was a fair gallop and the winner came from well off the pace. The winning time was marginally quicker than the previous Class 5 handicap and Dazakhee could have improvement in her.

5837 SIMON HOLT WRITES FOR THE WEEKENDER H'CAP 1m 4f (P)
8:20 (8:22) (Class 4) (0-85,84) 3-Y-O+ **£4,075** (£1,212; £606; £303) **Stalls** Centre

Form RPR

0060 **1** **Becausewecan (USA)**[12] 5435 5-9-10 **82** NeilCallan 5 91
(Mark Johnston) *racd keenly: led at modest pce: kicked on over 2f out: drvn wl over 1f out: styd on wl whn pressed fnl f* **7/1**

2525 **2** *1 ¼* **Incendo**[39] 4555 5-9-12 **84** (t) KierenFallon 2 91
(James Fanshawe) *t.k.h: hld up in midfield: prog over 2f out to chse wnr over 1f out: sn chalng: nt qckn ins fnl f* **4/1**[2]

3602 **3** *3* **Viking Storm**[49] 4209 3-8-12 **79** ChrisCatlin 1 81
(Harry Dunlop) *trckd ldng pair: chsd wnr wl over 2f out to over 1f out: outpcd after* **10/1**

-203 **4** *1 ¼* **Ajeeb (USA)**[49] 4208 3-8-12 **79** JamieSpencer 3 79
(David Simcock) *trckd ldng trio: hanging and nt qckn over 2f out: stl cl enough on inner over 1f out: fdd tamely* **7/2**[1]

-305 **5** *1* **Warneford**[19] 5242 3-8-4 **71** (b[1]) LiamJones 7 70
(Brian Meehan) *t.k.h: trckd wnr: racd awkwardly and pushed along over 4f out: hung bdly lft and lost pl wl over 2f out: no ch after* **13/2**[3]

451 **6** *¾* **Iron Condor**[15] 5357 4-9-6 **78** LukeMorris 9 75
(James Eustace) *hld up in last pair: rdn whn pce lifted over 2f out: one pce and nvr on terms* **4/1**[2]

2656 **7** *2* **Nibani (IRE)**[68] 3593 4-9-2 **79** AmyScott(5) 6 73
(Alastair Lidderdale) *hld up in midfield: prog to chse ldrs 5f out: pushed along over 3f out: fdd fnl 2f* **25/1**

0305 **8** *1* **Dynamic Drive (IRE)**[27] 4957 4-9-0 **75** SeanLevey(3) 4 68
(Walter Swinburn) *stmbld s: t.k.h: hld up towards rr: rdn and no prog whn pce lifted over 2f out: fdd* **13/2**[3]

6056 **9** *shd* **Kiss A Prince**[10] 5518 5-9-6 **78** (p) JimCrowley 8 70
(Dean Ivory) *s.i.s: hld up in last pair: shkn up and no prog over 2f out* **33/1**

2m 33.95s (-0.55) **Going Correction** -0.125s/f (Stan)
WFA 3 from 4yo+ 9lb 9 Ran SP% **117.3**
Speed ratings (Par 105): **96,95,93,92,91 91,89,89,89**
toteswingers: 1&2 £4.10, 1&3 £14.40, 2&3 £7.60. CSF £35.72 CT £283.85 TOTE £3.30: £1.10, £1.90, £3.90; EX 38.90.
Owner Douglas Livingston **Bred** Tony Holmes & Walter Zent **Trained** Middleham Moor, N Yorks

FOCUS
Another race in which the leader was not taken on in front and was able to dictate throughout. The form is a bit shaky.
Warneford Official explanation: jockey said colt hung left
Dynamic Drive(IRE) Official explanation: jockey said gelding stumbled at start

5838 RACING@SKYSPORTS.COM H'CAP 1m 3f (P)
8:50 (8:55) (Class 6) (0-65,65) 3-Y-O **£1,617** (£481; £240; £120) **Stalls** Low

Form RPR

005 **1** **Ambala**[103] 2457 3-9-2 **60** GeorgeBaker 4 73+
(Chris Wall) *trckd ldrs: smooth prog to go 2nd over 2f out: led over 1f out: in command after and jst nudged along fnl f* **7/1**

64-3 **2** *1 ¼* **Waltzing Cat (USA)**[7] 5630 3-9-5 **63** StevieDonohoe 9 69+
(Sir Mark Prescott Bt) *settled in rr: pushed along over 3f out: prog u.p over 2f out: r.o to take 2nd ins fnl f: clsd on wnr fin but no ch* **9/4**[1]

0635 **3** *3 ½* **Gower Rules (IRE)**[11] 5491 3-9-0 **61** SeanLevey(3) 6 61
(John Bridger) *pressed ldr despite decent pce: led over 3f out: tried to kick clr over 2f out: hdd over 1f out: fdd and lost 2nd ins fnl f* **20/1**

001U **4** *¾* **Librettela**[7] 5636 3-8-7 **54** HarryBentley(3) 10 52
(Alan Jarvis) *racd on outer: trckd ldrs: effrt over 2f out: nt qckn wl over 1f out: one pce after* **16/1**

0005 **5** *6* **Decana**[16] 5321 3-8-12 **56** DarryllHolland 2 44
(Hughie Morrison) *trckd ldrs: effrt 3f out: nt qckn over 2f out: fdd over 1f out* **14/1**

5450 **6** *20* **See The Smile (USA)**[14] 5389 3-9-7 **65** (v[1]) JamieSpencer 3 17
(Jim Boyle) *hld up in last: rdn and no prog 3f out: t.o* **17/2**

030 **7** *10* **Lupa Montana (USA)**[21] 5169 3-9-5 **63** JimCrowley 1 —
(Ralph Beckett) *led at gd pce but pressed: hdd & wknd over 3f out: t.o* **12/1**

5354 **8** *8* **Crystal Sky (IRE)**[19] 5243 3-9-4 **62** NeilCallan 7 —
(Andrew Haynes) *trckd ldrs: wknd rapidly 3f out: t.o* **20/1**

0000 **9** *6* **Hard Bargain (IRE)**[19] 5243 3-9-2 **60** TadhgO'Shea 8 —
(Denis Coakley) *a in rr: wknd 4f out: sn t.o* **50/1**

4363 **R** **Kalendar Girl (IRE)**[21] 5179 3-9-5 **63** KierenFallon 5 —
(Willie Musson) *led to post and mounted at s: ref to r: tk no part* **11/4**[2]

2m 19.27s (-2.63) **Going Correction** -0.125s/f (Stan) 10 Ran SP% **117.0**
Speed ratings (Par 99): **104,103,100,100,95 81,73,68,63,—**
toteswingers: 1&2 £6.10, 1&3 £19.50, 2&3 £10.40. CSF £22.68 CT £307.08 TOTE £13.50: £3.00, £1.10, £3.40; EX 31.90.
Owner Mrs Claude Lilley **Bred** Mrs David Low **Trained** Newmarket, Suffolk

FOCUS
Just a modest handicap but they finished well strung out behind the first four and this looks solid form for the grade. The winner rates value for extra.
Ambala ◆ Official explanation: trainer's rep said, regarding apparent improvement in form, that the filly had strengthened up, improved since having a virus and was having its first run on the all-weather.
T/Plt: £197.00 to a £1 stake. Pool:£64,020.94 - 237.23 winning tickets. T/Qpdt: £26.50 to a £1 stake. Pool:£9,204.24 - 256.14 winning tickets. JN

3447 SAINT-CLOUD (L-H)
Wednesday, September 7

OFFICIAL GOING: Turf: soft

5839a PRIX DES TOURELLES (LISTED RACE) (3YO+ FILLIES & MARES) (TURF) 1m 4f 110y
5:15 (12:00) 3-Y-O+ **£22,413** (£8,965; £6,724; £4,482; £2,241)

RPR

1 **Bernieres (IRE)**[55] 4036 3-8-7 0 Christophe-PatriceLemaire 6 104
(Mme Pia Brandt, France) **213/10**

2 *¾* **Solemia (IRE)**[91] 3-8-7 0 MickaelBarzalona 7 103
(C Laffon-Parias, France) **16/1**

3 *nk* **Cill Rialaig**[18] 5285 6-9-3 0 SteveDrowne 1 103
(Hughie Morrison) *settled in midfield on rail: a travelling easily: gd prog early in st: briefly short of room over 1 1/2f out whn swtchd away fr rail to chse eventual wnr: fnd daylight under 1f out: fin wl: nrest at fin* **17/2**

4 *1 ½* **Toi Et Moi (IRE)**[24] 5093 4-9-3 0 ThierryThulliez 2 100
(P Bary, France) **33/10**[2]

5 *1* **Terre Du Vent (FR)**[17] 5304 5-9-3 0 StephanePasquier 5 99
(Y De Nicolay, France) **6/1**[3]

6 *1 ½* **Oekaki (FR)**[24] 5093 4-9-3 0 IoritzMendizabal 3 97
(Y Barberot, France) **10/1**

7 *2* **Gradara**[36] 4-9-3 0 ChristopheSoumillon 11 94
(S Wattel, France) **68/10**

8 *3* **Sandslide**[67] 6-9-3 0 MaximeGuyon 10 89
(M Trybuhl, Germany) **28/1**

9 *hd* **Sinndarina (FR)**[10] 4-9-3 0 OlivierPeslier 8 89
(P Demercastel, France) **45/1**

10 1 1/2 **Polygon (USA)**[26] 5027 3-8-7 0.. ThierryJarnet 9 87
(John Gosden) *settled in 3rd: dropped back to 4th bef st: sn rdn: no ex u.p: eased ent fnl f* **5/2**[1]

11 **Venise Jelois (FR)**[11] 5498 3-8-7 0............................ SebastienMaillot 4 87
(Robert Collet, France) **36/1**

2m 37.9s (157.90)
WFA 3 from 4yo+ 9lb **11** Ran SP% **117.2**
WIN (incl. 1 euro stake): 22.30. PLACES: 6.70, 5.60, 3.70. DF: 104.40. SF: 301.20.
Owner Gerard Augustin-Normand **Bred** Grangemore Stud **Trained** France

NOTEBOOK
Cill Rialaig finished with some gusto for third. Connections will try to win a Listed race with her.
Polygon(USA) was up with the pace for much of the way before fading.

5672 CHEPSTOW (L-H)

Thursday, September 8

OFFICIAL GOING: Soft (6.4)
Wind: Moderate across Weather: Overcast

5840 DIGIBET.COM NURSERY 6f 16y
2:05 (2:06) (Class 5) (0-75,75) 2-Y-O **£2,264** (£673; £336; £168) **Stalls** Centre

Form RPR

2454 **1** **Dressed In Lace**[17] 5316 2-8-8 **62**.. LiamKeniry 2 66
(Andrew Balding) *pressed ldrs: upsides fr over 2f out tl drvn to take slt ld over 1f out: kpt on whn chal ins fnl f: asserted clsng stages* **9/1**

0203 **2** *1* **Middleton Flyer (IRE)**[17] 5324 2-9-5 **73**.............................. JamesDoyle 7 74
(David Evans) *w ldr tl led after 2f: rdn and jnd over 2f out: narrowly hdd over 1f out: styd chalng ins fnl f: no ex cl home* **14/1**

4632 **3** *3/4* **Daunt (IRE)**[20] 5237 2-9-4 **75**.. SeanLevey(3) 3 74
(Richard Hannon) *trckd ldrs: rdn to take 3rd appr fnl 2f: styd on u.p fnl f: no imp whn edgd rt clsng stages* **5/1**[1]

4303 **4** *3 1/4* **Thirsty Bear**[13] 5427 2-9-2 **70**..................................(p) J-PGuillambert 4 59
(Rebecca Curtis) *chsd ldrs: rdn over 2f out: outpcd fnl f* **6/1**[2]

5106 **5** *hd* **Silvas Romana (IRE)**[10] 5562 2-9-4 **72**...................... TomMcLaughlin 9 60
(Mark Brisbourne) *chsd ldrs: rdn over 2f out: styd on same pce fnl f* **10/1**

6441 **6** *3 1/2* **Sweet Ovation**[15] 5374 2-8-2 **56**.................................... MartinLane 13 34
(Mark Usher) *s.i.s: in rr: hdwy 3f out: nvr gng pce to rch ldrs and no ch fnl 2f* **9/1**

5522 **7** *6* **Night Angel (IRE)**[8] 5613 2-8-11 **65**.............................. JamesMillman 8 25
(Rod Millman) *chsd ldrs: rdn over 2f out: sn btn* **6/1**[2]

5164 **8** *1 1/2* **Rooknrasbryripple**[9] 5577 2-8-12 **66**........................... SamHitchcott 5 21
(Mick Channon) *in rr and sn rdn along: mod prog u.p fnl 2f* **16/1**

0U20 **9** *1/2* **Berlusca (IRE)**[31] 4857 2-9-0 **68**.................................. LiamJones 10 22
(William Jarvis) *outpcd most of way* **13/2**[3]

041 **10** *13* **Subtle Embrace (IRE)**[28] 4947 2-8-12 **66**........................ LukeMorris 1 —
(Harry Dunlop) *chsd ldrs over 3f* **12/1**

005 **11** *2 1/4* **Ionwy**[30] 4883 2-8-1 **58**... HarryBentley(3) 6 —
(Derek Haydn Jones) *pressed ldrs: rdn 1/2-way and wknd qckly* **20/1**

2520 **12** *1* **Key Addition (IRE)**[8] 5613 2-8-12 **71**..................(b[1]) JamesRogers(5) 11 —
(William Muir) *led 2f: sn rdn: wknd 1/2-way* **25/1**

1m 15.11s (3.11) **Going Correction** +0.50s/f (Yiel) **12** Ran SP% **116.5**
Speed ratings (Par 95): **99,97,96,92,92 87,79,77,76,59 56,55**
toteswingers:1&2:£43.60, 1&3:£7.00, 2&3:£17.20 CSF £126.22 CT £711.86 TOTE £9.40: £2.90, £6.20, £1.70; EX 105.30.
Owner J K Gale & D F Powell **Bred** R F And S D Knipe **Trained** Kingsclere, Hants

FOCUS
After some light rain overnight the ground remained soft. An ordinary nursery with a strong pace considering the conditions. The first four home were always at the head of affairs, racing predominantly in the centre of the track.

NOTEBOOK
Dressed In Lace had been looking a bit one-paced in nurseries over 5f so this step up in trip proved to be to her liking having previously run well with plenty of give in the ground. Always up with the pace, she stuck to her task well to fend off the runner up, going on at the finish. With similar conditions underfoot she can remain competitive if realistically reassessed. (op 15-2 tchd 10-1)
Middleton Flyer(IRE) has been performing creditably since winning a seller back in May. Again this was a solid effort from the front as she only gave best in the closing stages, but she looks fairly exposed now.
Daunt(IRE) ran respectably but looks to be on a stiff enough mark at present. However, he appeared to handled the conditions and appreciated the return to 6f. (op 11-2 tchd 6-1)
Thirsty Bear looks to be on a stiff enough mark as he has failed to build on initial promise and was now being tried in cheekpieces. He pressed the leaders for much of the way before fading entering the final furlong. (op 9-1)
Silvas Romana(IRE) did best of those racing nearer to the stands' side and. She could never get competitive but was staying on nicely in the final furlong. (op 8-1)
Sweet Ovation missed the break and could never recover but confirmed placings with Night Angel. (tchd 8-1)
Night Angel(IRE), after chasing the pace, failed to get home. (op 13-2 tchd 11-2)

5841 BRITISH STALLION STUDS SUPPORTING BRITISH RACING E B F MAIDEN STKS 7f 16y
2:35 (2:35) (Class 5) 2-Y-O **£3,169** (£943; £471; £235) **Stalls** Centre

Form RPR

56 **1** **Amadeus Wolfe Tone (IRE)**[19] 5269 2-9-3 0............ FergusSweeney 3 74+
(Jamie Osborne) *sn racing alone towards far side and led 4f out: drvn clr fnl f: readily* **2/1**[1]

0 **2** *2 3/4* **Shot In The Dark (IRE)**[10] 5564 2-9-3 0............................ LiamKeniry 6 67
(Andrew Balding) *s.i.s: in rr: hdwy fr 3f out: styd on to chse wnr over 1f out: edgd lft u.p ins fnl f: no imp* **3/1**[2]

4 **3** *2 1/4* **Lady Percy (IRE)**[20] 5232 2-8-9 0.................................. SeanLevey(3) 7 57
(Mark Usher) *led towards centre of crse tl hdd by wnr 4f out: rdn and no imp fr 2f out: lost 2nd over 1f out and sn one pce* **13/2**

00 **4** *1 1/2* **Special Boy (IRE)**[90] 2882 2-9-3 0...........................(p) RoystonFfrench 4 58+
(Saeed Bin Suroor) *t.k.h: in rr but in tch: hdwy: carried hd awkwardly and sn rdn 2f out: faltered and plld off heels over 1f out: styd on clsng stages* **11/2**[3]

0 **5** *1* **Our Phylli Vera (IRE)**[24] 5097 2-8-9 0............................ HarryBentley(3) 9 50
(Harry Dunlop) *chsd ldrs: rdn fr 3f out: wknd wl over 1f out* **25/1**

0 **6** *2 3/4* **Annaluna (IRE)**[10] 5537 2-8-12 0...................................... JamesDoyle 2 43
(David Evans) *in rr: detached at 1/2-way: pushed along 2f out: styd on wl clsng stages and gng on cl home* **8/1**

0 **7** *nk* **My Boy Ginger**[63] 3779 2-9-3 0.................................... JamesMillman 8 48
(Rod Millman) *chsd ldrs: rdn over 2f out: wknd ins fnl 2f* **16/1**

8 *1 1/4* **Poetry Writer** 2-9-3 0... NeilChalmers 5 45
(Michael Blanshard) *sn chsng ldr: rdn over 2f out and sn wknd* **40/1**

0 **9** *1/2* **Miss Granger**[15] 5375 2-8-12 0.. LukeMorris 1 38
(Ronald Harris) *in rr early: hdwy 4f out: drvn to chse ldrs 3f out: wknd qckly wl over 1f out* **33/1**

1m 27.35s (4.15) **Going Correction** +0.50s/f (Yiel) **9** Ran SP% **113.3**
Speed ratings (Par 95): **96,92,90,88,87 84,83,82,81**
toteswingers:1&2:£2.00, 1&3:£1.30, 2&3:£4.90 CSF £7.61 TOTE £2.70: £1.40, £1.20, £1.30; EX 12.20.
Owner John Duddy **Bred** Brian Williamson **Trained** Upper Lambourn, Berks

FOCUS
A weak maiden with the majority of the runners grouping to the centre of the track except for the comfortable winner.

NOTEBOOK
Amadeus Wolfe Tone(IRE) cut a lone furrow closer to the far side, eventually finishing right up on the rails. He had shaped with promise when upped to this trip last time and on paper looked the one to beat here, as it proved. He travelled well on the ground and could be called the winner from a fair way out. He has plenty of scope for further improvement as he beat a modest looking bunch here and should not be too harshly treated for this. (op 9-4 tchd 15-8)
Shot In The Dark(IRE) never figured on her debut but that had been won by a potentially useful sort and with any improvement she was entitled to fare better here. She came in for some considerable support during the morning and, after being held up just off the pace, stayed on to chase the winner entering the final furlong but never held a chance. She should find an opening when handicapped. (tchd 7-2)
Lady Percy(IRE) ran with promise when staying on at Salisbury and shaped with encouragement again here. She should continue to improve with experience. (op 6-1)
Special Boy(IRE), a 2012 Derby entrant, was being tried in first-time cheekpieces after two disappointing efforts so far. He was staying on after feeling the pinch halfway but the headgear did not appear to have the desired effect and he is looking modest. (op 5-1 tchd 6-1)
Our Phylli Vera(IRE) had little more to offer entering the final furlong but showed a degree of promise. (op 33-1)

5842 BRITISH HEART FOUNDATION MENDING BROKEN HEARTS MAIDEN FILLIES' STKS 7f 16y
3:10 (3:10) (Class 5) 3-Y-O **£2,264** (£673; £336; £168) **Stalls** Centre

Form RPR

0222 **1** **Map Of Heaven**[13] 5423 3-9-0 69.......................................(b) LiamJones 5 73
(William Haggas) *broke fast and wnt sharply rt to grab stands' rail: mde rest and drvn rt out to go clr fnl f whn in n.d: eased clsng stages: unchal* **2/5**[1]

6333 **2** *16* **Cheherazad (IRE)**[15] 5368 3-9-0 72............................... FergusSweeney 4 31
(Paul Cole) *sn trcking wnr on stands' rail: rdn and edgd lft ins fnl 3f and nvr any ch after but kpt on for modest 2nd* **5/2**[2]

056 **3** *1 3/4* **Main Opinion (IRE)**[13] 5429 3-9-0 46.............................. SamHitchcott 3 27
(Mick Channon) *rced promly and rdn 4f out: nvr nr unchal w and styd on for modest 3rd clsng stages* **20/1**[3]

0 **4** *nk* **Dreamy Nights**[13] 5429 3-9-0 0...................................... MarkLawson 2 26
(Gary Harrison) *chsd wnr: rdn over 3f out and nvr any ch wknd over 2f out and lost mod 3rd clsng stages* **66/1**

0 **5** *10* **Ellephil (IRE)**[29] 4920 3-9-0 0... LukeMorris 1 —
(Bryn Palling) *chsd ldrs towards centre crse early: rdden 4f out: sn btn: no ch fnl 3f* **33/1**

1m 26.47s (3.27) **Going Correction** +0.50s/f (Yiel) **5** Ran SP% **109.2**
Speed ratings (Par 98): **101,82,80,80,68**
CSF £1.57 TOTE £1.50: £1.02, £1.40; EX 1.40.
Owner Lael Stable **Bred** Lael Stables **Trained** Newmarket, Suffolk
■ Stewards' Enquiry : Liam Jones caution: used whip when clearly winning

FOCUS
A weak maiden fillies' race with the winner again disappointing. The winner probably didn't need to improve too much.
Dreamy Nights Official explanation: jockey said filly hung right

5843 KILSBY AND WILLIAMS CHARTERED ACCOUNTANTS H'CAP 7f 16y
3:45 (3:45) (Class 6) (0-60,60) 3-Y-O+ **£1,617** (£481; £240; £120) **Stalls** Centre

Form RPR

0002 **1** **Spinning Ridge (IRE)**[9] 5606 6-9-6 **56**.....................(v) TomMcLaughlin 6 67
(Ronald Harris) *racd far side and towards rr tl hdwy over 2f out: led wl over 1f out: drvn out fnl f* **16/1**

5633 **2** *2* **Doctor Hilary**[10] 5540 9-9-0 **53**...(v) KierenFox(3) 1 59
(Mark Hoad) *racd far side and chsd ldrs: rdn over 2f out: styd on fnl f to take 2nd fnl 120yds but nvr any ch w wnr* **8/1**[3]

0 **3** *2 1/4* **Indian Dumaani**[16] 5345 4-8-9 **50**................................ RyanPowell(5) 7 50
(David Bridgwater) *racd far side and chsd ldrs: rdn over 2f out and sn one pce: kpt on again clsng stages to take wl hld 3rd clsng stages* **16/1**

4020 **4** *nk* **Kenswick**[10] 5539 4-9-3 **56**..(v) SeanLevey(3) 8 55
(Pat Eddery) *racd far side and trckd ldr tl led over 5f out: rdn over 3f out: styd on tl hdd wl over 1f out: wknd fnl f and dropped two pls fnl 120yds* **9/1**

3652 **5** *1 3/4* **Dancing Welcome**[6] 5674 5-9-3 **53**...........................(b) RoystonFfrench 5 48
(Milton Bradley) *racd far side and in tch tl rdn and lost position over 3f out: styd on again u.p fr over 1f out: nvr gng pce to trble ldrs* **11/4**[2]

1416 **6** *7* **Sopran Nad (ITY)**[15] 5394 7-9-7 **57**...................................(b) JamesDoyle 2 34
(Frank Sheridan) *racd far side and led tl hdd over 5f out: rdn over 3f out and no imp on ldr: wknd fr 2f out* **9/4**[1]

6350 **7** *3/4* **Flying Cherry (IRE)**[89] 2921 4-8-10 **46**....................(t) FergusSweeney 12 21
(Jo Crowley) *racd stands' side and outpcd: styd on to ld that gp 1f out but nvr any ch w main gp far side* **25/1**

3620 **8** *1/2* **Beating Harmony**[160] 1082 3-8-9 **56**........................ GeorgeDowning(7) 11 27
(Tony Carroll) *racd stands' side and wl bhd tl styd on fr over 1f out to take 2nd in gp ins fnl f but nvr any ch w main gp far side* **22/1**

0500 **9** *2 3/4* **Cwmni**[10] 5540 5-9-3 **53**... MartinLane 10 19
(Bryn Palling) *racd far side: rdn and sme prog over 3f out: nvr rchd ldrs and wknd over 2f out: fin seventh in gp* **16/1**

0-00 **10** *nk* **Justice Walk (IRE)**[117] 2103 3-9-3 **57**........................ FrankieMcDonald 15 20
(Paul Fitzsimons) *racd stands' side and disp ld of that gp tl 2f out but nvr on terms w main gp far side: wknd over 1f out: fin 3rd in gp* **40/1**

5400 **11** *3/4* **Lennoxwood (IRE)**[10] 5539 3-8-10 **50**...............................(p) LiamKeniry 9 11
(Mark Usher) *racd far side: chsd ldrs 3f out: sn rdn: wknd over 2f out: fin 8th in gp* **28/1**

00- **12** *2* **Gibraltar Lass (USA)**[310] 7288 4-8-10 **46** oh1......... RussKennemore 13 —
(Mike Murphy) *racd stands' side and led that gp most of way tl over 1f out but nvr on terms w main bunch far side: wknd rapidly: fin 4th and last in gp* **33/1**

5354 **13** *21* **Zalano**[30] 4885 3-9-3 **60**......................................(b[1]) HarryBentley(3) 3 —
(Derek Haydn Jones) *racd far side: rdn and wknd 3f out: eased whn no ch fnl f: t.o: fin 9th and last in gp* **16/1**

1m 27.47s (4.27) **Going Correction** +0.50s/f (Yiel)
WFA 3 from 4yo+ 4lb **13** Ran SP% **119.1**
Speed ratings (Par 101): **95,92,90,89,87 79,78,78,75,74 74,71,47**
toteswingers:1&2:£12.30, 1&3:£21.70, 2&3:£41.10 CSF £130.05 CT £2098.35 TOTE £16.10: £3.90, £2.60, £4.80; EX 67.80.
Owner Robert & Nina Bailey **Bred** Eddie O'Leary **Trained** Earlswood, Monmouths

FOCUS
An open low-grade handicap and the field split into two groups. Those racing up the stands' side were never on terms with the more favoured far side, ultimately, all finishing soundly beaten. The winner is up a length on his recent AW form.
Lennoxwood(IRE) Official explanation: jockey said gelding had no more to give

5844 BLOOR HOMES NURSERY 1m 14y
4:20 (4:20) (Class 6) (0-65,71) 2-Y-O **£1,617** (£481; £240; £120) **Stalls** Centre

Form RPR
000 **1** **Remember Rocky**[16] 5337 2-8-5 **49**.................................... LiamJones 1 58+
(Steve Gollings) *trckd ldr: hrd drvn and one pce 3f out: styd disputing 2nd: edgd rt over 1f out: led ins fnl f: styng on strly whn edgd rt clsng stages* **16/1**
0652 **2** *3 ¼* **Always Ends Well (IRE)**[9] 5577 2-9-1 **59**.................. RoystonFfrench 3 61
(Mark Johnston) *led: rdn appr fnl 2f: hdd ins fnl f: nt pce of wnr but hld on wl for 2nd* **3/1**[1]
6400 **3** *1* **Raspberry Fizz**[8] 5634 2-8-4 **51**..............................(b) LouisBeuzelin(3) 12 51
(Eve Johnson Houghton) *towards rr: drvn and hdwy over 2f out and sn disputing 2nd: kpt on same pce u.p fnl f* **12/1**
0003 **4** *2 ¼* **Doctor Banner**[8] 5634 2-9-1 **59**.................................... SamHitchcott 11 54
(Mick Channon) *sn in tch: hdwy 3f out: styng on to chse ldrs whn edgd lft and hmpd over 1f out: hung bdly lft u.p ins fnl f: styd on same pce* **11/2**[3]
0041 **5** *1* **Shannon Spree**[8] 5634 2-9-10 **71** 6ex............................. SeanLevey(3) 7 64
(Richard Hannon) *in rr but in tch: pushed along 3f out and one pce: styd on ins fnl f: nt trble ldrs* **4/1**[2]
600 **6** *1 ½* **Rainbow Chorus**[23] 5133 2-8-5 **54**................................. RyanPowell(5) 4 43
(Paul Cole) *s.i.s: in rr tl drvn and hdwy 3f out: disp 2nd over 2f out: wknd fnl f* **9/1**
4536 **7** *shd* **Choisirez (IRE)**[9] 5577 2-9-7 **65**.................................. FergusSweeney 9 54
(David Evans) *in rr: sme hdwy over 3f out: nvr rchd ldrs: hung lft over 1f out* **20/1**
4663 **8** *4 ½* **Moment In The Sun**[9] 5605 2-8-5 **49**.................................. MartinLane 5 28
(William Muir) *chsd ldrs: disp 2nd over 2f out: wknd qckly appr fnl f* **13/2**
3506 **9** *8* **Queen Of The Hop**[17] 5325 2-8-9 **53**.............................(p) LukeMorris 8 15
(J S Moore) *chsd ldrs 5f: wknd qckly* **22/1**
000 **10** *4* **Fox's Ambers (FR)**[17] 5320 2-7-12 **45**......................... HarryBentley(3) 10 —
(Richard Hannon) *a in rr* **7/1**

1m 40.35s (4.15) **Going Correction** +0.50s/f (Yiel) **10** Ran SP% **118.9**
Speed ratings (Par 93): **99,95,94,92,91 90,89,85,77,73**
toteswingers:1&2:£17.00, 1&3:Not won, 2&3:£11.80 CSF £65.09 CT £634.18 TOTE £27.70: £5.10, £2.60, £6.00; EX 77.80.
Owner Richard Swift **Bred** Cherry Park Stud **Trained** Scamblesby, Lincs

FOCUS
An ordinary mile nursery run at a fair pace.

NOTEBOOK
Remember Rocky was not disgraced in a fair maiden on debut but had been slightly disappointing in two runs since. He chased the long-time leader throughout until, eventually, wearing him down inside the final furlong to win going away. Starting life off a lowly mark of 46, he is at the right end of the handicap and, being open to further improvement, he should handle a rise. He's one to keep on side at this level in similar conditions. Official explanation: trainer's rep said, regarding the apparent improvement in form shown, colt was suited by the soft ground and step up in trip (op 25-1)
Always Ends Well(IRE) dictated a reasonable pace and had the rest of the field under pressure from a fair way out before being collared in the final furlong. He acquitted himself well on this step up in trip and is becoming of more interest now, stringing together some consistency. (op 10-3 tchd 7-2)
Raspberry Fizz looks fairly exposed and showed little when tried in blinkers last time, but this was the first time she has encountered soft ground and it appears to have brought about some improvement.
Doctor Banner had not shown a great deal in four runs on turf but shaped with more promise stepped up to a mile last time on the AW. This was an encouraging enough effort, but he did hang, although, to be fair, he did get hampered when coming with his run so it would be rather harsh to fault his attitude. He looks capable of finding a little handicap. (op 7-1)
Shannon Spree had come good since switching to nurseries and got off the mark (Doctor Banner behind) on the AW last time. Conditions should have been suitable, so it was a little disappointing she could never get competitive under her penalty. (op 7-2)

5845 BRITISH HEART FOUNDATION H'CAP 1m 14y
4:50 (4:50) (Class 6) (0-65,64) 3-Y-0+ **£1,617** (£481; £240; £120) **Stalls** Centre

Form RPR
0501 **1** **Mr Udagawa**[35] 4701 5-9-10 **64**.......................................(p) MartinLane 10 72
(Bernard Llewellyn) *chsd ldrs and racd towards centre of crse: drvn to chal 2f out: led sn after: styd on u.p fnl f: jst hld on* **15/2**
3640 **2** *hd* **Advertise**[20] 5231 5-9-2 **56**.. LiamKeniry 11 63
(Joseph Tuite) *s.i.s: in rr: racd towards centre of crse and hdwy fr 3f out: styd on u.p to take 2nd fnl 30yds: clsng on wnr: nt quite get up* **6/1**[3]
0006 **3** *1 ½* **Golden Hinde**[10] 5539 3-8-13 **58**..........................(p) TomMcLaughlin 4 60
(Ronald Harris) *towards rr: racd towards centre of crse: hdwy 4f out: drvn to chal 2f out: no ex ins fnl f and lost 2nd fnl 30yds* **10/1**
600 **4** *1* **Myboyalfie (USA)**[11] 5518 4-9-9 **63**........................(v[1]) FergusSweeney 9 64
(J R Jenkins) *disp ld tl led towards far side 4f out: jnd 2f out: hdd sn after: styd wl there tl wknd fnl 50yds* **12/1**
-040 **5** *nk* **Another Whisper (IRE)**[74] 3430 3-9-0 **62**...................... SeanLevey(3) 2 61
(Richard Hannon) *racd towards far side and wl in tch: rdn and one pce 1/2-way: styd on fr over 1f out: kpt on: nt rch ldrs* **4/1**[1]
1060 **6** *1 ½* **Forward Feline (IRE)**[15] 5376 5-9-3 **57**........................... LukeMorris 7 54
(Bryn Palling) *chsd ldrs towards centre crse: rdn 2f out: hanging lft and btn sn after* **8/1**
0206 **7** *1 ¼* **Tuscan King**[13] 5428 4-8-6 **51**..............................(bt) JamesRogers(5) 6 45
(Bernard Llewellyn) *bhd: drvn and plenty to do over 2f out: drvn and styd on fr over 1f out: keeping on clsng stages but nvr a threat* **14/1**
1305 **8** *7* **Phluke**[21] 5201 10-9-7 **64**...................................... LouisBeuzelin(3) 12 42
(Eve Johnson Houghton) *rdn 1/2-way: bhd most of way* **11/1**
0000 **9** *4* **Hertford Street**[34] 4758 3-8-5 **50** oh3................................ LiamJones 8 18
(Peter Makin) *rdn and bhd fnl 3f* **40/1**
0060 **10** *shd* **Ninfea (IRE)**[12] 5496 3-9-4 **63**......................................(p) JamesDoyle 3 30
(Sylvester Kirk) *rdn 5f out: nvr gng w any fluency: a wl bhd* **11/2**[2]
0004 **11** *36* **Anna Fontenail**[15] 5380 3-8-11 **56**..............................(bt) JamesMillman 1 —
(Rod Millman) *disp ld 4f: wknd qckly over 3f out: eased whn no ch: t.o* **11/1**

1m 39.99s (3.79) **Going Correction** +0.50s/f (Yiel)
WFA 3 from 4yo+ 5lb **11** Ran SP% **115.1**
Speed ratings (Par 101): **101,100,99,98,98 96,95,88,84,84 48**
toteswingers:1&2:£7.30, 1&3:£12.50, 2&3:£12.60 CSF £50.89 CT £460.64 TOTE £6.30: £2.60, £1.80, £4.70; EX 33.90.
Owner B J Llewellyn **Bred** Richard C J Manning **Trained** Fochriw, Caerphilly

FOCUS
An ordinary handicap. The winner's best form since he was a 3yo with the second to this year's form.
Phluke Official explanation: jockey said gelding was never travelling

5846 BLUE CHIP FEED H'CAP 5f 16y
5:25 (5:25) (Class 6) (0-65,65) 3-Y-0+ **£1,617** (£481; £240; £120) **Stalls** Centre

Form RPR
0641 **1** **Two Turtle Doves (IRE)**[10] 5534 5-8-11 **58**................ HarryBentley(3) 1 68
(Michael Mullineaux) *trckd ldrs: wnt 2nd 2f out: drvn and qcknd to ld ins fnl f: pushed along and styd on strly clsng stages* **9/4**[2]
0000 **2** *nk* **Cape Royal**[17] 5326 11-9-1 **62**....................................(tp) SeanLevey(3) 4 71
(Milton Bradley) *led: rdn wl over 1f out: hdd ins fnl f: kpt on but nt pce of wnr clsng stages* **16/1**
1216 **3** *3 ¼* **Colourbearer (IRE)**[6] 5677 4-9-6 **64** 6ex..................(t) RoystonFfrench 3 61
(Milton Bradley) *slowly into strde: in rr but in tch: hdwy over 1f out: swtchd rt sn after and kpt on same pce ins fnl f* **2/1**[1]
4654 **4** *1 ½* **Catalinas Diamond (IRE)**[8] 5615 3-8-12 **60**............... SophieDoyle(3) 5 52
(Pat Murphy) *chsd ldrs: rdn one pce whn n.m.r 1f out: kpt on again clsng stages to take 4th last strides* **17/2**
0422 **5** *shd* **Adventure Story**[37] 4628 4-9-7 **65**................................. FergusSweeney 8 56
(Peter Makin) *t.k.h: chsd ldr to 1/2-way: rdn 2f out: wknd ins fnl f: lost 4th last strides* **11/2**[3]
0005 **6** *2 ¼* **Riflessione**[10] 5534 5-8-13 **57**..(v) TomMcLaughlin 2 40
(Ronald Harris) *chsd ldrs: rdn 1/2-way: wknd over 1f out* **12/1**
1624 **7** *½* **The Tatling (IRE)**[32] 4820 14-9-6 **64**.................................. LukeMorris 7 46
(Milton Bradley) *in tch tl rdn: hung lft and btn over 2f out* **20/1**
3456 **8** *3 ¾* **Bookiesindex Boy**[29] 4930 7-8-7 **51** oh3................. FrankieMcDonald 6 19
(J R Jenkins) *t.k.h: hld up in rr: rdn and swtchd lft to far rail over 1f out: a outpcd* **28/1**

61.71 secs (2.41) **Going Correction** +0.50s/f (Yiel)
WFA 3 from 4yo+ 1lb **8** Ran SP% **111.8**
Speed ratings (Par 101): **100,99,94,91,91 88,87,81**
toteswingers:1&2:£10.50, 1&3:£1.90, 2&3:£7.80 CSF £35.43 CT £80.30 TOTE £4.60: £2.10, £7.30, £1.02; EX 43.10.
Owner George Cornes **Bred** M Sharkey **Trained** Alpraham, Cheshire

FOCUS
A low-grade sprint handicap.
T/Plt: £50.10 to a £1 stake. Pool:£53,497.93 - 778.30 winning tickets T/Qpdt: £12.10 to a £1 stake. Pool:£3,731.54 - 228.00 winning tickets ST

5825 DONCASTER (L-H)
Thursday, September 8

OFFICIAL GOING: Good (8.2; far side 8.6; stands' side 8.5)
Wind: fresh 1/2 against Weather: fine

5847 IRISH STALLION FARMS E B F CARRIE RED FILLIES' NURSERY 6f 110y
1:25 (1:26) (Class 2) 2-Y-O **£19,407** (£5,775; £2,886; £1,443) **Stalls** High

Form RPR
0201 **1** **Elusive Flame**[12] 5480 2-8-13 **79**.................................... JamieSpencer 1 87
(David Elsworth) *trckd ldrs: hdwy over 2f out: chal 1f out: sn rdn and edgd lft: drvn to ld wl ins fnl f: kpt on wl* **13/2**[3]
3136 **2** *hd* **Poetic Dancer**[41] 4496 2-8-10 **79**.................................. JohnFahy(3) 4 86
(Clive Cox) *trckd ldrs: hdwy 3f out: effrt to ld wl over 1f out and sn rdn: jnd and drvn 1f out: edgd lft and hdd wl ins fnl f: no ex towards fin* **13/2**[3]
6125 **3** *2 ½* **Responsive**[7] 5656 2-9-4 **84**.. JimmyFortune 5 85
(Hughie Morrison) *trckd ldrs: n.m.r and swtchd lft after 1 1/2f: hdwy wl over 2f out: rdn to chse ldng pair over 1f out: sn drvn and no imp fnl f* **9/2**[1]
1104 **4** *½* **Roger Sez (IRE)**[10] 5558 2-9-4 **84**................................... DavidAllan 8 83
(Tim Easterby) *towards rr: rdn along 1/2-way: hdwy on outer 2f out and sn rdn: drvn and kpt on fnl f: nrst fin* **15/2**
2415 **5** *2 ¼* **Alabanda (IRE)**[31] 4867 2-8-11 **77**............................. DuranFentiman 9 70+
(Tim Easterby) *in rr: hdwy over 2f out: rdn wl over 1f out: styd on wl fnl f: nrst fin* **40/1**
3023 **6** *1 ¾* **Scrooby Doo**[9] 5596 2-7-13 **68**....................................... BillyCray(3) 2 56
(David Nicholls) *sn led: rdn along over 2f out: hdd wl over 1f out and grad wknd* **33/1**
521 **7** *½* **Besito (IRE)**[28] 4961 2-9-7 **87**....................................... KierenFallon 7 76
(William Jarvis) *t.k.h: trckd ldrs whn n.m.r after 1 1/2f: swtchd rt and effrt to chse ldrs over 2f out: sn rdn and wknd over 1f out* **9/2**[1]
2114 **8** *nk* **Amis Reunis**[40] 4536 2-8-11 **77**.............................. RichardHughes 12 63
(Richard Hannon) *t.k.h early: hld up towards rr: swtchd rt to stands' rails and hdwy over 2f out: sn rdn and nvr rchd ldrs* **6/1**[2]
2001 **9** *4* **Toffee Tart**[32] 4824 2-8-8 **74**.. EddieAhern 10 49
(J W Hills) *hld up in midfield: rdn along wl over 2f out: sn btn* **18/1**
2012 **10** *3 ¼* **Blue Shoes (IRE)**[9] 5591 2-8-0 **66**.......................(p) SilvestreDeSousa 11 32
(Tim Easterby) *disp ld early: cl up: rdn along 3f out: sn wknd* **20/1**
100 **11** *¾* **Ebony Clarets**[54] 4094 2-8-6 **72**.................................. PaulHanagan 14 36
(Richard Fahey) *chsd ldrs on outer: rdn along over 3f out: sn wknd* **20/1**
1006 **12** *2* **Royal Blush**[17] 5324 2-8-4 **70**.. ChrisCatlin 6 28
(Paul Cole) *t.k.h: trckd ldrs: hung rt after 1 1/2f: pushed along 1/2-way: rdn and wknd wl over 2f out* **28/1**
3315 **13** *½* **Vassaria (IRE)**[49] 4252 2-9-2 **82**.................................... TomEaves 3 39
(Michael Dods) *dwlt and towards rr: sme hdwy on wd outside bef 1/2-way: sn rdn: hung rt and nvr a factor* **25/1**

1m 20.0s (0.10) **Going Correction** +0.025s/f (Good) **13** Ran SP% **116.5**
Speed ratings (Par 98): **100,99,96,96,93 91,91,90,86,82 81,79,78**
toteswingers:1&2:£8.00, 1&3:£6.80, 2&3:£8.00 CSF £42.38 CT £180.42 TOTE £7.10: £2.50, £2.50, £2.10; EX 59.30 Trifecta £236.50 Pool: £894.88 - 2.80 winning units..
Owner J C Smith **Bred** Littleton Stud **Trained** Newmarket, Suffolk

FOCUS
The opening contest looked quite competitive but it would be surprising if it was really strong form. A few recent winners have tried their luck in Group company subsequently without any success.

NOTEBOOK

Elusive Flame, who has always been highly regarded, could have been given a chance on the best of her form and, under a waiting ride, stayed on really well to collect a second career victory. Her maiden success came when she made all the running, so it appears that she is quite tactically versatile. (op 15-2)

Poetic Dancer didn't run too badly on her previous outing (first try in a handicap) from a modest draw and proved she is heading in the right direction with a solid performance. She only went down narrowly and looks a tough sort. (op 7-1 tchd 6-1)

Responsive, officially 9lb well in, had every chance here once in the clear before being caught one-paced. (op 5-1)

Roger Sez(IRE), 2lb well in, was under strong pressure early before coming home strongly. It was noticeable that she flashed her tail a couple of times in the final stages. (op 6-1)

Alabanda(IRE), who'd been running over 7f recently, ran disappointingly when tried on Polytrack for her handicap debut, but did better here, although looking in need of further. (tchd 50-1)

Scrooby Doo, who has done most of her racing on the Fibresand, showed lots of pace again but didn't get home.

Besito(IRE), who has a Cheveley Park entry, didn't look to have too many excuses under top weight. She has quite a bit of size about her so can be given another chance as she develops.

Amis Reunis was beaten on her first try at 6f, which was also her nursery debut, when last seen at Goodwood in July, so it still remains to seen whether this trip suits. (op 7-1 tchd 15-2)

5848 JAPAN RACING ASSOCIATION SCEPTRE STKS (GROUP 3) (F&M) 7f

1:55 (1:56) (Class 1) 3-Y-0+ £29,600 (£11,195; £5,595; £2,795) Stalls High

Form RPR

1 **1** **Alanza (IRE)**[21] 5228 3-8-10 109 JMurtagh 7 112+
(John M Oxx, Ire) *trckd ldrs: effrt 2f out: edgd rt 1f out: r.o to ld nr fin* **11/4**[2]

224 **2** *nk* **Dever Dream**[25] 5080 4-9-0 105 EddieAhern 6 111
(William Haggas) *sn trcking ldrs: effrt over 2f out: edgd lft 1f out: styd on to chal wl ins fnl f: no ex* **13/2**

3121 **3** *hd* **Chachamaidee (IRE)**[41] 4497 4-9-3 113 TomQueally 1 113
(Sir Henry Cecil) *racd wd: trckd ldrs: smooth hdwy to ld over 1f out: hdd and no ex nr fin* **5/2**[1]

0-46 **4** *2 1/4* **Marvada (IRE)**[11] 5523 3-8-10 98 ShaneFoley 8 102
(K J Condon, Ire) *hld up in rr: hdwy over 1f out: styng on at fin* **50/1**

-103 **5** *2* **Seta**[29] 4915 4-9-0 109 KierenFallon 2 99
(Luca Cumani) *dwlt: racd wd: sn trcking ldr: led after 2f: qcknd over 3f out: hdd over 1f out: fdd* **6/1**[3]

-120 **6** *nk* **Flambeau**[75] 3404 4-9-0 107 DaneO'Neill 5 98
(Henry Candy) *hld up in mid-div: drvn and outpcd over 2f out: kpt on fnl f* **7/1**

0010 **7** *2* **Crying Lightening (IRE)**[148] 1319 3-8-10 102 JamieSpencer 9 93
(Peter Chapple-Hyam) *led 2f: chsd ldrs: wkng whn n.m.r 1f out* **66/1**

1040 **8** *3/4* **Rimth**[25] 5080 3-8-13 107 (p) FrankieDettori 3 92
(Paul Cole) *slowly away and swvd bdly lft: bhd: effrt over 2f out: kpt on fnl f: nvr a factor* **16/1**

6360 **9** *7* **Magic Eye (IRE)**[19] 5277 6-9-0 101 WilliamBuick 10 72
(Marco Botti) *trckd ldrs: drvn over 3f out: lost pl 2f out* **40/1**

3325 **10** *4 1/2* **Off Chance**[19] 5277 5-9-0 99 DuranFentiman 4 60
(Tim Easterby) *ponied to s: racd wd: chsd ldr: drvn over 3f out: wknd 2f out* **33/1**

3R42 **11** *3 1/4* **Jacqueline Quest (IRE)**[11] 5510 4-9-0 99 RichardHughes 11 51
(Ian Williams) *swtchd lft after s: hld up in rr: swtchd wd over 4f out: effrt over 2f out: sn wknd* **16/1**

1m 25.53s (-0.77) **Going Correction** +0.025s/f (Good)
WFA 3 from 4yo+ 4lb 11 Ran SP% **116.0**
Speed ratings (Par 113): **105,104,104,101,99 99,96,96,88,82 79**
toteswingers:1&2:£5.30, 1&3:£2.20, 2&3:£4.50 CSF £20.31 TOTE £3.70: £1.60, £2.40, £1.40; EX 24.20 Trifecta £41.50 Pool: £2,106.10 - 37.52 winning units..

Owner H H Aga Khan **Bred** His Highness The Aga Khan's Studs S C **Trained** Currabeg, Co Kildare

FOCUS

The first running of the Sceptre Stakes as a Group 3 and the pace seemed solid enough. The field split into two early with seven racing centre-to-stands' side, whilst four came up the centre. The two groups had merged just after halfway. Sound enough form amongst the principals.

NOTEBOOK

Alanza(IRE) ◆ was the least exposed in the field, having had just five previous outings, and was her trainer's first runner in Britain this year. Settled in the nearside group, she settled particularly well and, as she has won over 1m, the solid pace was in her favour. She picked up well when asked to move closer over a furlong from home and maintained her effort to hit the front around 50 yards from the line, meaning that 3yos have now won nine of the last ten runnings of this and making it 24-30 in the contest overall. She has done nothing but improve and there is surely even better to come from her, possibly next year. (tchd 5-2)

Dever Dream, winner of this race last year, was beaten nearly 3l by Chachamaidee at Glorious Goodwood and had a 3lb pull. Prominent in the nearside group, she was off the bridle over 2f from home and responded to the pressure to just get up and pip her old rival, but the winner proved just too good for the pair of them. (op 7-1 tchd 15-2)

Chachamaidee(IRE) had three of today's rivals behind her when winning the Goodwood contest and looked likely to follow up when hitting the front over a furlong from home, but she may have got there just too soon and was mugged inside the last 50 yards. (op 3-1)

Marvada(IRE) had fallen short since moving up into Pattern company and had work to do in order to reverse Cork July running with Alanza, but she still ran well as she was off the bridle at the back of the field a fair way out before finishing well. (op 66-1)

Seta, back over a more suitable trip, is a triple Listed winner who hasn't reached the heights that once seemed possible when pitched into higher Group company, though this was her first try in a Group 3. Not only did she lead the centre group early, she held the overall advantage but was in trouble as soon as Chachamaidee ranged alongside over a furlong out and was run right out of it. (op 11-2)

Flambeau was reported to have never been travelling when disappointing at Newmarket in June and could only plug on under pressure here, but she probably needs faster ground. (op 8-1)

Crying Lightening(IRE) led the nearside group for a long way and was entitled to need it as she hadn't been seen since running moderately in the Nell Gwyn. Official explanation: jockey said filly had no more to give

Rimth, in first-time cheekpieces, lost all chance at the start. Official explanation: jockey said filly missed the break

Jacqueline Quest(IRE) will always be remembered as the filly that lost the 1000 Guineas in the stewards' room and not for the first time since she proved very disappointing. (op 14-1 tchd 12-1)

5849 WEATHERBYS INSURANCE £300,000 2-Y-O STKS 6f 110y

2:25 (2:29) (Class 2) 2-Y-0

£207,293 (£82,951; £41,475; £20,695; £10,368; £10,368) Stalls High

Form RPR

156 **1** **Reply (IRE)**[20] 5251 2-9-2 0 JPO'Brien 13 107
(A P O'Brien, Ire) *trckd ldrs: effrt wl over 1f out: rdn to chal over 1f out: led jst ins fnl f: drvn out* **20/1**

1300 **2** *1/2* **Factory Time (IRE)**[19] 5286 2-8-3 96 ChrisCatlin 4 93
(Mick Channon) *t.k.h: hld up in rr: gd hdwy on wd outside 3f out: rdn over 1f out: chsd wnr ins fnl f: sn drvn and kpt on* **33/1**

2240 **3** *hd* **Letsgoroundagain (IRE)**[21] 5216 2-8-3 85 JimmyQuinn 19 92
(Charles Hills) *wnt rt s: towards rr: pushed along 1/2-way: rdn 2f out: styd on strly u.p appr fnl f: nrst fin* **66/1**

10 **4** *1/2* **Moon Pearl (USA)**[22] 5181 2-8-9 0 JimCrowley 20 98
(Ralph Beckett) *hmpd s and towards rr: pushed along 1/2-way: rdn over 2f out: styd on wl appr fnl f: nrst fin* **16/1**

12 **5** *3/4* **Ladys First**[19] 5270 2-8-1 84 PaulHanagan 2 87
(Richard Fahey) *midfield: effrt whn n.m.r and sltly outpcd 2f out: sn swtchd lft and rdn: styd on ins fnl f: nrst fin* **10/1**

101 **6** *shd* **Bogart**[21] 5216 2-8-6 103 PhillipMakin 15 92
(Kevin Ryan) *led: rdn along wl over 1f out: sn edgd lft: drvn and hdd jst ins fnl f: sn edgd rt and wknd* **9/4**[1]

0136 **7** *hd* **Campanology**[22] 5184 2-8-9 85 (v[1]) RichardHughes 6 95
(Richard Hannon) *hld up: hdwy and n.m.r over 2f out: sn swtchd rt and rdn: drvn and kpt on ins fnl f: nrst fin* **22/1**

21 **8** *3/4* **Top Cop**[19] 5263 2-8-12 87 JimmyFortune 9 95
(Andrew Balding) *prom: hdwy to chal over 2f out: sn rdn and ev ch tl drvn and wknd over 1f out* **14/1**

0444 **9** *hd* **North Star Boy (IRE)**[31] 4858 2-8-12 97 (b[1]) KierenFallon 16 95
(Richard Hannon) *midfield: hdwy over 2f out: sn rdn and kpt on ins fnl f: nrst fin* **25/1**

2131 **10** *1/2* **Mehdi (IRE)**[12] 5479 2-8-12 96 (t) ShaneKelly 11 93
(Brian Meehan) *hld up towards rr: hdwy over 2f out: rdn over 1f out: kpt on ins fnl f: nrst fin* **9/1**[3]

3101 **11** *1* **Alejandro (IRE)**[39] 4575 2-8-6 94 LeeTopliss 10 84
(Richard Fahey) *midfield: rdn along 3f out: no hdwy* **25/1**

110 **12** *1/2* **West Leake Diman (IRE)**[21] 5216 2-8-3 90 WilliamCarson 7 84+
(Charles Hills) *t.k.h: hld up in rr: hdwy 1/2-way: n.m.r and swtchd rt 2f out: sn rdn and no imp* **25/1**

212 **13** *nk* **Rex Imperator**[12] 5492 2-8-9 93 SteveDrowne 5 85
(Roger Charlton) *t.k.h: hld up: hdwy whn n.m.r and hmpd 2f out: swtchd lft and rdn: kpt on same pce* **16/1**

304 **14** *1/2* **Boris Grigoriev (IRE)**[11] 5522 2-8-12 0 (v) CO'Donoghue 21 87
(A P O'Brien, Ire) *hld up: gd hdwy on outer to chse ldrs over 2f out: sn rdn and hung lft: wknd over 1f out* **28/1**

1 **15** *1 3/4* **Cockney Dancer**[17] 5323 2-8-1 0 SilvestreDeSousa 12 71
(Charles Hills) *towards rr: hdwy over 2f out: sn swtchd rt and rdn: n.d* **6/1**[2]

62 **16** *shd* **Whimsical (IRE)**[7] 5655 2-8-1 0 KieranO'Neill 17 71
(Richard Hannon) *prom: rdn along 1/2-way: drvn and wknd wl over 2f out* **33/1**

3113 **17** *shd* **Sea Odyssey (IRE)**[5] 5701 2-8-7 81 ow1 RobertWinston 1 77
(Charles Hills) *cl up on wd outside: pushed along 1/2-way: sn rdn and wknd over 2f out* **66/1**

2 **18** *nk* **Shevington**[153] 1209 2-8-6 0 BarryMcHugh 8 75
(Richard Fahey) *dwlt: a in rr* **100/1**

1040 **19** *8* **Betty Fontaine (IRE)**[27] 4999 2-7-12 93 CathyGannon 22 45
(Mick Channon) *chsd ldrs on outer to 1/2-way: sn wknd* **25/1**

45 **20** *1 1/2* **Cryptic Choice (IRE)**[5] 5697 2-8-9 0 MichaelHills 18 52
(Charles Hills) *a in rr* **100/1**

131 **21** *1* **Big Note (IRE)**[12] 5492 2-8-9 94 DavidProbert 3 49
(Andrew Balding) *t.k.h: in tch on wd outside: rdn along 1/2-way: sn lost pl and bhd* **14/1**

1m 19.85s (-0.05) **Going Correction** +0.025s/f (Good) **21** Ran SP% **128.0**
Speed ratings (Par 101): **101,100,100,99,98 98,98,97,97,96 95,95,94,94,92 92,91,91,82,80 79**
toteswingers:1&2:£29.10, 1&3:£106.10, 2&3: Not won CSF £552.40 TOTE £17.60: £6.20, £11.50, £17.80; EX 1005.80 TRIFECTA Not won..

Owner Mrs John Magnier **Bred** Mrs C Regalado-Gonzalez **Trained** Ballydoyle, Co Tipperary

FOCUS

A hugely competitive event for the money on offer, and the form should turn out to be strong considering the level of ability and potential on show.

NOTEBOOK

Reply(IRE) is a classy individual who looked sure to be suited by this step up in distance and, after always being prominent, kept on really well to win at surprisingly long odds. He should get a bit further and a return to Group company looks assured. (op 14-1)

Factory Time(IRE) didn't have much to find with the favourite on their Richmond Stakes running and comfortably reversed that form with a staying-on effort, as the weights suggested he would. The horse seems to go well for Chris Catlin.

Letsgoroundagain(IRE), who'd twice finished behind the market leader in the past, finished well off his low weight from a midfield position and did the best of the Charlie Hills-trained quintet.

Moon Pearl(USA) ran much the same sort of race as the third and can hopefully continue his upward course again after a modest effort in the Group 3 Acomb Stakes. (op 25-1)

Ladys First, representing last year's winning trainer/jockey, suggested that she has more to come with a staying-on performance from midfield. (tchd 9-1)

Bogart was following the same route Wootton Bassett took last year in sales races after landing the DBS Premier Yearling Stakes at York on his previous outing. However, this looked a stronger contest on paper than his Knavesmire success and he wasn't able to see it out after leading early. He was wandering in the final stages, so presumably got tired. (op 5-2)

Campanology had a visor tried in an attempt to boost his credentials and he travelled really well for much of the race until finding a bit of trouble in running. On a line through the third, whom he beat before being disqualified earlier in the year, he can be rated better than his final position suggests. (op 28-1)

Top Cop probably ran pretty well on only his third start under a fairly big weight. (op 12-1)

North Star Boy(IRE), blinkered for the first time, was a place behind Mehdi at Windsor on his last outing but reversed that form after holding every chance. (op 33-1)

Mehdi(IRE), who won a valuable prize on his previous outing when a tongue-tie was added for the first time, lost his place a little when the tempo increased before staying on powerfully towards the middle of the track. (op 10-1 tchd 8-1)

Cockney Dancer is from a successful family so it wasn't a huge surprise to see that she had inherited a winning mentality on her debut when getting the better of an odds-on favourite. However, she found this an altogether different task and looked too inexperienced under pressure to play a part. (op 15-2 tchd 8-1)

Shevington ◆ hadn't been out since making his debut in April, where he finished runner-up. Soon ridden along in behind, the penny dropped over 2f out and, although in no position to make any impression on the main body of the field, he made up plenty of ground to run a lot better than his rear-division finish implies.

Big Note(IRE) Official explanation: jockey said colt became upset in the stalls

5850 DFS PARK HILL STKS (GROUP 2) (F&M) 1m 6f 132y
3:00 (3:00) (Class 1) 3-Y-O+
£45,368 (£17,200; £8,608; £4,288; £2,152; £1,080) **Stalls** Low

Form				RPR
3210	1		**Meeznah (USA)**[26] 5045 4-9-4 113 ... FrankieDettori 1 (David Lanigan) *trckd ldrs: smooth hdwy to ld appr fnl 2f: rdn over 1f out: styd on strly: v readily* **5/2**[2]	115
1111	2	3 ½	**Set To Music (IRE)**[21] 5220 3-8-6 110 ... JamieSpencer 5 (Michael Bell) *trckd ldrs: chsd wnr 2f out: styd on: no imp* **9/4**[1]	110
4543	3	5	**Polly's Mark (IRE)**[21] 5220 5-9-4 105 ... RichardHughes 3 (Clive Cox) *trckd ldrs: hdwy over 3f out: wnt 3rd 1f out: kpt on one pce* **8/1**	104
6002	4	2 ¼	**Cracking Lass (IRE)**[21] 5220 4-9-4 107 ...(b) PaulHanagan 4 (Richard Fahey) *dwlt: racd in last: drvn 7f out: reminders over 4f out: stl last 1f out: kpt on to snatch 4th nr fin* **16/1**	101
1	5	½	**Goldplated (IRE)**[5] 5748 3-8-6 74 ... DMGrant 6 (John Joseph Murphy, Ire) *t.k.h in rr: hdwy 3f out: 4th over 1f out: wknd last 100yds* **25/1**	100
-204	6	2 ¼	**Spin (IRE)**[10] 5573 3-8-6 101 ... CO'Donoghue 2 (A P O'Brien, Ire) *trckd ldr: led over 2f out: sn hdd: wknd appr fnl f* **8/1**	97
5211	7	13	**Sense Of Purpose (IRE)**[35] 4737 4-9-4 105 ... PJSmullen 7 (D K Weld, Ire) *led: drvn 3f out: sn hdd: wknd over 1f out: heavily eased last 100yds* **7/2**[3]	88

3m 5.53s (-1.87) **Going Correction** +0.15s/f (Good)
WFA 3 from 4yo+ 12lb **7 Ran SP% 113.5**
Speed ratings (Par 115): **110,108,105,104,104 102,95**
toteswingers:1&2:£1.70, 1&3:£4.50, 2&3:£3.60 CSF £8.44 TOTE £3.40: £1.70, £1.90; EX 8.90.
Owner Saif Ali & Saeed H Altayer **Bred** Swettenham Stud **Trained** Newmarket, Suffolk

FOCUS
A decent renewal of the Park Hill, with three coming into this on a winning streak and a strong challenge from across the Irish Sea. Recent winners of the race were a fairly even split between the 3yos and the older horses. The pace was strong from the off, so this was a proper test at the trip and they finished well spread out. Sound form, Meeznah rated to her best.

NOTEBOOK
Meeznah(USA) finished third in this race last year and was a winner over this trip at Goodwood in July, but ran too badly to be true when favourite for the Geoffrey Freer last time. She bounced back to her very best here, though, racing comfortably in mid-division before being sent for home over 2f out. She lengthened very nicely when asked to go and win her race and took this with real authority. She is now beginning to confirm the form she showed when beaten a neck by Snow Fairy in last year's Oaks and it will be interesting to see where she goes next. (op 11-4 tchd 3-1)
Set To Music(IRE) was bidding for a five-timer and had three of these behind her when successfully stepping up to 1m4f in the Galtres Stakes at York last month. She looked to be travelling better than the winner when slipstreaming her passing the 2f pole, but she was moving into unknown territory distance-wise at that stage and she could make no further impression on her rival.
Polly's Mark(IRE) had a bit to find with a few of today's rivals on her last two efforts and finished behind Meeznah in this last year. Off the bridle over 2f out, she shied away to her right and may have been caught by a rival's whip, but then bumped into another rival and hung back the other way. She was third-best on merit, however, and probably ran her race. (op 11-1)
Cracking Lass(IRE) ran poorly in both previous tries over this trip, but seemed to respond well to blinkers when chasing home Set To Music at York last month. However, she didn't repeat the performance in the headgear, dropping herself out and hanging before the home straight before running on past beaten rivals. (tchd 18-1)
Goldplated(IRE) has been in cracking form in handicaps over shorter in Ireland lately, but she never made much impression here and held her head high when off the bridle over 2f from home. She had upwards of 10lb to find with her rivals, so faced a stiff task in any case. (op 20-1)
Spin(IRE), who finished behind three of these when fourth in the Galtres, probably paid for chasing the strong pace. (op 12-1)
Sense Of Purpose(IRE) was already proven at the trip and likes to dominate, so it was understandable that she was ridden positively, but she may have gone off too quickly as she was running on empty when headed over 2f from home. Official explanation: jockey said filly ran flat (op 3-1 tchd 11-4 and 4-1)

5851 CROWNHOTEL-BAWTRY.COM EBF "GREEN DESERT" MAIDEN STKS 1m (S)
3:35 (3:36) (Class 3) 2-Y-O
£7,439 (£2,213; £1,106; £553) **Stalls** High

Form				RPR
	1		**Perennial** 2-9-3 0 ... MichaelHills 5 (Charles Hills) *trckd ldrs: effrt on inner over 1f out: r.o to ld nr fin* **12/1**	88+
	2	½	**Encke (USA)** 2-9-3 0 ... FrankieDettori 16 (Mahmood Al Zarooni) *hld up towards rr: smooth hdwy on ins over 2f out: led last 150yds: hdd nr fin* **7/2**[2]	87+
4	3	hd	**Rawaafed (IRE)**[26] 5051 2-9-3 0 ... RichardHills 8 (Brian Meehan) *trckd ldrs: effrt over 2f out: upsides ins fnl f: no ex nr fin* **11/4**[1]	86+
	4	4	**Curzon Line** 2-9-3 0 ... AhmedAjtebi 14 (Mahmood Al Zarooni) *trckd ldrs: hung bdly lft over 1f out: wknd towards fin* **20/1**	77+
	5	nk	**Brailsford (IRE)** 2-9-3 0 ... KierenFallon 10 (Mahmood Al Zarooni) *hld up in mid-div: outpcd over 2f out: kpt on fnl f* **14/1**	77+
	6	¾	**Deia Sunrise (IRE)** 2-9-3 0 ... WilliamBuick 1 (John Gosden) *s.i.s: sn mid-div: hdwy on outer to chse ldrs over 1f out: one pce whn crowded last 100yds: hmpd nr fin* **20/1**	76+
62	7	hd	**Dynamic Duo (IRE)**[9] 5579 2-9-3 0 ... DaneO'Neill 3 (Richard Hannon) *w ldr: led 2f out: sn hdd and hmpd: one pce* **10/1**	75
0	8	¾	**Imperial Order (IRE)**[20] 5254 2-9-3 0 ... RichardHughes 11 (Richard Hannon) *trckd ldrs: keeping on same pce whn hmpd over 1f out: fdd* **4/1**[3]	75+
	9	1	**Venegazzu (IRE)** 2-9-3 0 ... JackMitchell 13 (Peter Chapple-Hyam) *in rr: kpt on fnl 2f: nvr nr to chal* **25/1**	70
	10	1 ½	**Kung Hei Fat Choy (USA)** 2-9-3 0 ... FrederikTylicki 2 (James Given) *led: hdd 2f out: sn wknd* **66/1**	67
	11	¾	**Kaiser Wilhelm (IRE)** 2-9-3 0 ... ChrisCatlin 4 (Paul Cole) *chsd ldrs: wknd over 1f out* **40/1**	65
	12	7	**Bridgehampton** 2-9-3 0 ... JamieSpencer 7 (Michael Bell) *s.s: reminder after 2f: sme hdwy over 3f out: sn lost pl* **33/1**	49
04	13	1 ½	**Dutchman's Field**[58] 3941 2-9-0 0 ... BillyCray(3) 9 (David Nicholls) *mid-div: drvn over 3f out: lost pl 2f out* **100/1**	46
	14	12	**Tantalized** 2-8-12 0 ... DavidProbert 15 (Andrew Balding) *in rr: bhd fnl 2f* **33/1**	13
	15	7	**Bells Of Berlin** 2-9-3 0 ... RobertWinston 6 (Alan McCabe) *s.i.s: sn rdn along: sme hdwy over 3f out: sn lost pl and bhd* **14/1**	2

1m 40.88s (1.58) **Going Correction** +0.025s/f (Good) **15 Ran SP% 123.2**
Speed ratings (Par 99): **93,92,92,88,88 87,87,86,85,83 83,76,74,62,55**
toteswingers:1&2:£9.40, 1&3:£8.90, 2&3:£4.00 CSF £50.43 TOTE £13.60: £3.20, £2.10, £1.60; EX 51.60 Trifecta £245.50 Pool: £1,284.23 - 3.87 winning units..
Owner K Abdulla **Bred** Juddmonte Farms Ltd **Trained** Lambourn, Berks

FOCUS
This has proved to be a really decent maiden down the years, and last season's renewal illustrated that perfectly. Winner Picture Editor may not have hit the heights since, but just behind him was both King George winner Nathaniel and Sandown Classic Trial winner Genuis Beast, among seven subsequent winners. One would imagine that this is strong maiden form.

NOTEBOOK
Perennial made plenty of appeal on breeding, being a Motivator half-brother to the stable's high-class middle-distance performer Redwood, who won his only 2yo start. Settled in midfield, he took time to hit top gear but kept on well and got up in good style to win in pleasing fashion. He doesn't hold any fancy entries at this stage, so it remains to be seen in what direction he's aimed.
Encke(USA) ◆, a brother to stablemate Genius Beast, who finished third in this very race last year, looked to be ridden in the manner of a good horse and gave the firm impression that he was as he moved up stylishly to pass horses in order to get involved. He didn't go on as it looked, but that shouldn't detract from a highly promising debut, and it would be a surprise if he didn't turn out to be at least smart. (tchd 3-1)
Rawaafed(IRE) made a promising debut in a Newmarket maiden in the middle of last month over 6f (winner has won again since) and helps to make the form look sound. He should easily land any ordinary contest. (op 10-3 tchd 7-2 in places)
Curzon Line, a half-brother to eight winners, notably useful dual 2-y-o 7f winner Queen Of Poland, who was also with the Godolphin, ran extremely green in the final stages and hung violently left across some of his rivals. He then got hampered himself inside the last half a furlong, so is better than his final position suggests, although one will have to wait and see if he's quirky or not. Official explanation: jockey said colt hung left
Brailsford(IRE) ◆, who cost 48,000gns, looks a nice long-term middle-distance prospect with this staying-on effort. He took a while to find his stride as the race developed but stayed on pleasingly to catch the eye. Official explanation: jockey said colt ran green (op 12-1 tchd 16-1)
Deia Sunrise(IRE), an already gelded half-brother to several winners, notably useful French 1m1f-11.5f winner Ivy League, came through to have a chance but didn't get home. He was eased in the closing stages. (op 16-1)
Dynamic Duo(IRE), who already had some fair form behind him, was in the process of losing a bit of ground when badly hampered by Curzon Line. He kept on again when in the clear but probably didn't lose too many positions as a result of the trouble he encountered. (op 8-1)
Imperial Order(IRE) ran respectably in the Convivial Maiden on his debut and was running well again until being badly baulked by Curzon Line. (op 9-2)
Venegazzu(IRE), out of Irish Oaks winner Vintage Tipple, has a lot of size about him and will no doubt improve for this initial experience. (op 20-1)

5852 ELEMENTS MEDISPA H'CAP 6f
4:10 (4:12) (Class 3) (0-90,93) 3-Y-O+ **£8,409** (£2,502; £1,250; £625) **Stalls** High

Form				RPR
3601	1		**Internationaldebut (IRE)**[4] 5758 6-9-9 93 6ex ... FrederikTylicki 16 (Paul Midgley) *midfield: smooth hdwy 2f out: rdn to ld jst ins fnl f: sn edgd lft and clr* **7/1**[2]	108
0036	2	2 ¾	**Marine Commando**[19] 5288 3-9-1 87 ... PaulHanagan 20 (Richard Fahey) *chsd ldrs: hdwy to ld wl over 1f out and sn rdn: drvn and hdd jst ins fnl f: kpt on same pce* **16/1**	93
0503	3	nk	**Five Star Junior (USA)**[13] 5430 5-9-5 89 ... ShaneKelly 18 (Linda Stubbs) *stdd and swtchd lft s: hld up towards rr: gd hdwy 2f out: rdn to chse ldrs over 1f out: kpt on ins fnl f* **28/1**	94
3600	4	1 ¼	**Shropshire (IRE)**[22] 5180 3-9-1 87 ... MichaelHills 13 (Charles Hills) *hld up towards rr: stdy hdwy 2f out: rdn to chse ldrs over 1f out: drvn and kpt on fnl f:* **33/1**	88
0454	5	½	**Barnet Fair**[19] 5288 3-9-4 90 ... RichardHughes 15 (Richard Guest) *hld up and bhd: swtchd lft to wd outside bef 1/2-way: hdwy 2f out: rdn over 1f out: kpt on ins fnl f: nrst fin* **15/2**[3]	90+
622	6	½	**Dimension**[42] 4472 3-9-4 90 ... KierenFallon 6 (James Fanshawe) *in tch: effrt and hdwy 2f out: sn rdn and one pce appr fnl f* **3/1**[1]	88
3100	7	½	**Ivory Silk**[54] 4101 6-8-7 84 ...(b) RaulDaSilva(7) 4 (Jeremy Gask) *in tch: hdwy on wd outside to chse ldrs 1/2-way: rdn along wl over 1f out: grad wknd* **50/1**	80
0004	8	nk	**Advanced**[19] 5272 8-9-6 90 ... JamieSpencer 12 (Kevin Ryan) *chsd ldrs: rdn along 2f out: drvn over 1f out: sn one pce* **11/1**	85
1412	9	hd	**Farlow (IRE)**[27] 5000 3-9-1 87 ... JimCrowley 1 (Ralph Beckett) *towards rr: hdwy 2f out: rdn over 1f out: kpt on: nt rch ldrs* **10/1**	82
2000	10	hd	**Mon Brav**[22] 5180 4-9-2 86 ... SilvestreDeSousa 19 (Brian Ellison) *midfield: hdwy on wd outside 2f out: rdn to chse ldrs over 1f out and sn ev ch: wknd ins fnl f* **16/1**	80
-605	11	1 ½	**Waking Warrior**[75] 3378 3-9-0 86 ... PhillipMakin 14 (Kevin Ryan) *bhd: hdwy 2f out: sn rdn and kpt on fnl f: nvr nr ldrs* **40/1**	75
14	12	¾	**Azzurra Du Caprio (IRE)**[33] 4779 3-9-1 87 ... PJMcDonald 2 (Ben Haslam) *chsd ldrs: rdn along wl over 2f out: sn wknd* **20/1**	74
1104	13	1	**Pravda Street**[47] 4314 6-9-0 87 ... DaleSwift(3) 10 (Brian Ellison) *towards rr: effrt and sme hdwy over 2f out: sn rdn and wknd* **16/1**	71
0-00	14	hd	**Able Master (IRE)**[57] 3982 5-9-1 85 ...(p) SteveDrowne 11 (Jeremy Gask) *a towards rr* **33/1**	68
00-0	15	¾	**Summerinthecity (IRE)**[117] 2099 4-9-6 90 ... PatCosgrave 3 (Ed de Giles) *s.i.s and bhd: hdwy whn nt clr run 2f out: nvr a factor* **50/1**	71
5602	16	shd	**We Have A Dream**[31] 4859 6-9-4 88 ... GeorgeBaker 5 (William Muir) *chsd ldrs: rdn along 1/2-way: sn wknd* **25/1**	68
0525	17	1 ½	**Damika (IRE)**[11] 5508 8-9-6 90 ...(p) MichaelStainton 8 (Richard Whitaker) *towards rr: rdn along 1/2-way: nvr a factor* **14/1**	66
0000	18	1	**Discanti (IRE)**[26] 5033 6-9-1 85 ...(t) DavidAllan 17 (Tim Easterby) *chsd ldrs: rdn along over 2f out: sn wknd* **66/1**	57
0030	19	½	**Novellen Lad (IRE)**[19] 5278 6-9-5 89 ... TomQueally 7 (Willie Musson) *midfield: rdn along 1/2-way: sn wknd* **33/1**	60
0100	20	10	**Cadeaux Pearl**[26] 5033 3-8-12 87 ...(b) BillyCray(3) 21 (David Nicholls) *led and sn clr: rdn along over 2f out: drvn and hdd wl over 1f out: sn wknd* **50/1**	26

0000 **21** *2¼* **Barney McGrew (IRE)**[46] 4369 8-9-3 **87**......................(b[1]) TomEaves 22 19
(Michael Dods) *chsd clr ldr: rdn along wl over 2f out: sn wknd* **14/1**

1m 12.69s (-0.91) **Going Correction** +0.025s/f (Good)
WFA 3 from 4yo+ 2lb **21** Ran SP% **128.4**
Speed ratings (Par 107): **107,103,102,101,100 99,99,98,98,98 96,95,94,93,92 92,90,89,88,75 72**
toteswingers:1&2:£24.00, 1&3:£30.60, 2&3:£85.50 CSF £104.44 CT £3001.37 TOTE £8.10: £2.10, £2.30, £8.40, £9.80; EX 254.40 Trifecta £1739.30 Part won. Pool: £2,350.53 - 0.10 winning units..
Owner A Taylor Jnr **Bred** Ennistown Stud **Trained** Westow, N Yorks

FOCUS
A hot sprint handicap in which the main bulk of the field raced up the centre, but in the end the winner took this in some style. The early pace was frenetic with Cadeaux Pearl and Barney McGrew tearing off in front, but they did far too much and eventually dropped right out to finish a well-beaten last and last but one. The winner is impressed and the form is rated around the third.

NOTEBOOK
Internationaldebut(IRE), from a stable that can do little wrong at present, was carrying a 6lb penalty after ending a 31-race losing run at York four days earlier, but he could have carried two penalties and still won this. He travelled like a Group horse amongst a bunch of handicappers and found plenty for pressure to win going away. He will take another hike in the ratings after this, but in his current mood he looks capable of winning something much better, though it does appear that he needs them to go hard up front. (op 17-2 tchd 9-1)
Marine Commando ◆ hasn't scored since taking last year's Windsor Castle, though he didn't run badly in his last two starts over 5f and was down another 2lb. He travelled every bit as well as the winner, if ridden closer to the pace, and hit the front briefly over a furlong out before the winner was unleashed. He looks poised to return to winning form. (op 14-1)
Five Star Junior(USA), 2-30 on turf coming into this, may be best over the minimum trip on grass and was held up for a late run. He did finish his race off well, but the front pair were already home and hosed. (op 25-1)
Shropshire(IRE) ◆ had done nothing since finishing a distant third behind Frankel and Excelebration in the Greenham on his reappearance, but this was much more promising. He didn't enjoy the smoothest of passages in the early stages and found himself at the back of the field, but he travelled strongly into contention as the race progressed and was one of those fighting for the lead over a furlong from home before his effort flattened out. Still relatively unexposed, he can win a race like this.
Barnet Fair was another to run into a bit of trouble in the early stages and had to be switched left to the far side of the field in order to see daylight, but he ran on well in the closing stages. He has been in good form all year and still looks capable off this sort of mark. (tchd 7-1 and 8-1)
Dimension, racing over a shorter trip than he had attempted before, was bang there over a furlong from home but was then completely done for foot. (op 7-2)
Ivory Silk made an effort towards the far side coming to the last furlong, but then emptied. She is still 5lb higher than when winning at Newmarket in June, her only turf win in 21 attempts. (tchd 40-1)
Advanced was never too far off the pace and still has the ability to run well in big-field handicaps like this, but is now on a losing run of 28. (op 12-1 tchd 14-1)
Farlow(IRE) was up another 4lb having been unlucky not to make it four wins from five starts this season at Newbury last time (winner and sixth have scored since), but he didn't find a great deal once coming off the bridle over 2f from home. (op 11-1)
Mon Brav had been below par in his previous three starts, but the form of his second to Dungannon over C&D in June has worked out very well since. Racing closest to the stands' rail, this was a bit more like it despite finishing only tenth.
Able Master(IRE) Official explanation: jockey said gelding hung left

5853 DFS H'CAP — 1m 2f 60y
4:40 (4:40) (Class 2) (0-110,99) 3-Y-O+ **£16,172** (£4,812; £2,405; £1,202) **Stalls** Low

Form RPR
1013 **1** **Club Oceanic**[22] 5185 3-9-1 **97**.....................................(p) JamieSpencer 7 107+
(Jeremy Noseda) *dwlt: hld up: hdwy 9f out: drvn on outer over 3f out: hung lft and styd on to ld last 50yds* **10/3[2]**
0225 **2** *nk* **Chain Lightning**[19] 5275 3-9-0 **96**.................................. RichardHughes 5 106
(Richard Hannon) *trckd ldr: drvn over 2f out: led narrowly last 75yds: hdd and no ex nr fin* **9/4[1]**
0005 **3** *nk* **Sharaayeen**[20] 5250 4-9-4 **93**... RichardHills 4 102
(Charles Hills) *led: drvn over 3f out: narrowly hdd last 75yds: no ex clsng stages* **9/2[3]**
125 **4** *2* **Prince Of Johanne (IRE)**[44] 4410 5-9-2 **91**.............(p) RobertWinston 8 96
(Tom Tate) [illegible] *drvn 3f out: n.m.r over 1f out: keeping on same pce whn hmpd last 50yds* **12/1**
0044 **5** *½* **Jutland**[33] 4788 4-9-9 **98**... SilvestreDeSousa 1 102
(Mark Johnston) *trckd ldrs: drvn on ins 3f out: n.m.r over 1f out: kpt on same pce fnl f* **15/2**
-450 **6** *11* **Janood (IRE)**[147] 1339 3-9-1 **97**....................................... WilliamBuick 3 88
(Saeed Bin Suroor) *sn trcking ldrs: one pce whn bdly hmpd 100yds out: eased* **28/1**
0-50 **7** *nse* **Total Command**[61] 3875 4-9-6 **95**..................................... TomQueally 6 78
(Sir Michael Stoute) *t.k.h in rr: drvn over 2f out: hung lft and lost pl over 1f out* **25/1**
/100 **8** *1¼* **Burj Nahar**[33] 4788 4-9-10 **99**..............................(t) FrankieDettori 2 80
(Saeed Bin Suroor) *hld up in rr: effrt over 3f out: nvr a factor: wknd over 1f out* **7/1**

2m 8.48s (-0.92) **Going Correction** +0.025s/f (Good)
WFA 3 from 4yo+ 7lb **8** Ran SP% **111.3**
Speed ratings (Par 109): **109,108,108,106,106 97,97,96**
toteswingers:1&2:£2.20, 1&3:£4.50, 2&3:£3.00 CSF £10.60 CT £31.08 TOTE £4.10: £1.70, £1.60, £1.60; EX 9.90 Trifecta £42.40 Pool: £1,843.65 - 32.16 winning units..
Owner Sir Robert Ogden **Bred** Card Bloodstock **Trained** Newmarket, Suffolk
■ Stewards' Enquiry : Jamie Spencer one-day ban: careless riding (Sep 22); caution: used whip without giving colt time to respond

FOCUS
A few of these had question marks hanging over them, so the form may not be the strongest for a class 2 event. It wasn't strong run. The winner continues to progress.

NOTEBOOK
Club Oceanic hasn't done a lot wrong throughout his career, and collected another success to add to his previous four victories. He doesn't give the impression he's the easiest of rides but he cannot be faulted for his attitude at the business end of a race. Considering his winning profile, one would imagine that connections will carefully consider a try at the Cambridgeshire if the going is to his advantage, although afterwards they did suggest that a Listed contest might be next on the agenda if one can be found. They also believe he'll stay further, and his pedigree supports that view. (op 3-1 tchd 7-2)
Chain Lightning was mugged close to the line after being given a prominent ride. He has been in mainly good heart this season and may have a decent handicap in him. (op 3-1 tchd 2-1)
Sharaayeen, taking another ease in trip, is capable of running well off this mark, although it is 15lb above his only success in handicaps. Looking a bit warm, his jockey set fractions in front to suit himself and, as a result, he wasn't beaten far. (op 11-2 tchd 6-1 in places)
Prince Of Johanne(IRE) has enjoyed a good season at this sort of trip, but had risen through the weights accordingly. He kept on but wasn't quite good enough. (op 9-1 tchd 8-1)
Jutland stayed on up the inside rail and had every chance. This was a fair effort but he hasn't always been the most predictable of performers. (op 6-1 tchd 8-1)
Janood(IRE), absent since mid-April, and without the headgear he'd worn on his previous two starts, wasn't beaten when badly hampered inside the final furlong. There was no way back from that point and his jockey eased him. (op 25-1)
Total Command was taking a sharp drop in distance after a string of moderate performances, but did not run any better. One would imagine that he may go through the sales ring later in the year. (op 18-1)
Burj Nahar continues to disappoint and wearing a tongue-tie for the first time didn't improve him. Official explanation: jockey said colt lost its action (op 6-1)
T/Jkpt: Not won. T/Plt: £911.40 to a £1 stake. Pool:£169,486.38 - 135.75 winning tickets T/Qpdt: £290.10 to a £1 stake. Pool:£10,823.51 - 27.60 winning tickets JR

5577 EPSOM (L-H)
Thursday, September 8

OFFICIAL GOING: Good to soft (good in places; 7.1; home straight: stands' side 7.6; far side 7.1)
Wind: fresh, half against Weather: overcast

5854 CHROMAAGENCY.COM WEBSITE EXPERTS MEDIAN AUCTION MAIDEN FILLIES' STKS — 6f
2:15 (2:15) (Class 5) 2-Y-O **£3,234** (£962; £481; £240) **Stalls** High

Form RPR
335 **1** **Appointee (IRE)**[11] 5514 2-9-0 0...................................... RobertHavlin 9 74+
(John Gosden) *racd wd: chsd ldr: c to r in centre st: rdn to chal ent fnl f: led fnl 150yds: r.o wl* **10/3[2]**
3640 **2** *1* **Represent (IRE)**[10] 5565 2-8-11 72.............................. MartinHarley(3) 1 71
(Mick Channon) *led early: chsd ldrs: styd far side st: led wl over 1f out: drvn and edgd rt ent fnl f: hdd fnl 150yds: kpt on same pce* **11/2**
00 **3** *1¼* **Tamima (USA)**[18] 5299 2-9-0 0.. TadhgO'Shea 5 67+
(Brian Meehan) *stdd s: racd wl off the pce in last trio: c centre st: hdwy 2f out: rdn and chsd ldng pair over 1f out: kpt on wl ins fnl f: nt rch ldrs* **14/1**
04 **4** *1* **Lovage**[52] 4155 2-9-0 0... RichardMullen 3 65
(Roger Charlton) *sn bhd in last trio: styd far side st: rdn and hdwy 2f out: chsd ldng trio 1f out: kpt on ins fnl f: nvr able to chal* **3/1[1]**
5 **5** *5* **Princess Palmer**[112] 2227 2-9-0 0................................. DarryllHolland 6 49
(Hugo Palmer) *t.k.h: chsd ldrs: c to r against stands' rail and outpcd 3f out: no prog and btn whn hung lft over 1f out* **25/1**
6 *1¼* **Pawprints (IRE)** 2-8-11 0.. AdamBeschizza(3) 2 46+
(William Haggas) *s.i.s: sn outpcd in rr: styd far side st: sme hdwy but unbalanced over 1f out: swtchd rt 1f out: kpt on ins fnl f: nvr trbld ldrs* **15/2**
60 **7** *1¾* **More Is To Come (USA)**[70] 3547 2-9-0 0..................... StevieDonohoe 8 40
(Ralph Beckett) *led: styd far side st: rdn and hdd wl over 1f out: wknd qckly over 1f out* **20/1**
00 **8** *1¼* **First Of February (IRE)**[115] 2153 2-8-9 0.................. NathanAlison(5) 4 37
(Jim Boyle) *racd off the pce in midfield: styd far side st: rdn and no prog over 2f out: wknd wl over 1f out* **66/1**
9 *14* **Murmur (IRE)** 2-9-0 0... IanMongan 7 —
(Sir Henry Cecil) *racd in midfield: styd far side st: wknd 2f out: wl btn and eased fnl f* **4/1[3]**

1m 12.42s (3.02) **Going Correction** +0.275s/f (Good) **9** Ran SP% **112.0**
Speed ratings (Par 92): **90,88,87,85,79 77,75,73,54**
toteswingers:1&2:£8.90, 1&3:£9.60, 2&3:£16.70 CSF £20.74 TOTE £3.50: £2.00, £1.60, £3.20; EX 22.30.
Owner H R H Princess Haya Of Jordan **Bred** Darley **Trained** Newmarket, Suffolk

FOCUS
Rail dolled out 2yds from 6f to Winning Post adding circa 4yds to distances. After a dry morning, the ground was officially good to soft, good in places, with a GoingStick reading of 7.1. This was a run-of-the-mill juvenile maiden.

NOTEBOOK
Appointee(IRE), officially rated 77, was well below that level on softer ground last time out. Here, however, she returned to something like her earlier form to notch a snug success. Fast away, she [illegible] wide early on and was brought towards the stands' side in the straight. She was only second with 1f left, where the runner-up had the lead, but stayed on well and was nicely on top at the finish. (op 3-1 tchd 7-2)
Represent(IRE), rather disappointing in three starts since her encouraging debut, was quick to break and set out to make all the running. She was still in front at the 1f pole, by then gradually working her way out into the centre of the track, but could not match the winner's finishing kick. (op 9-2)
Tamima(USA), dropped in trip after fading over 7f last time, found this distance more to her liking. Never far away, she followed Appointee down the stands' side and plugged on gamely in the closing stages. She seems to be improving and qualifies for a mark now. (op 16-1 tchd 12-1)
Lovage, off for 52 days since finishing fourth at Windsor on her second run, did not seem to handle Epsom's cambers as well as the first three. She was well adrift of the principals with 2f left, racing close to the far rail, but was making ground on them at the finish. She now qualifies for nurseries and may have something to offer punters in those. (op 4-1)
Princess Palmer, fifth of seven on her only previous run, was another to follow the winner over towards the stands' side. She had proved keen in the early stages, though, and got tired in the final furlong. Official explanation: jockey said filly ran too free (op 33-1)
Pawprints(IRE), a newcomer whose dam was placed over 7f, was never really in contention. She will probably do better when trying a longer trip. (op 9-1)

5855 CHROMAAGENCY.COM APP EXPERTS/BRITISH STALLION STUDS E B F MEDIAN AUCTION MAIDEN STKS — 7f
2:45 (2:45) (Class 5) 2-Y-O **£3,881** (£1,155; £577; £288) **Stalls** Low

Form RPR
4330 **1** **Tidy Affair (IRE)**[27] 4996 2-9-3 77.. NeilCallan 9 79
(Richard Hannon) *sn chsng ldr: rdn to chal over 2f out: led over 1f out: edgd lft ins fnl f: styd on wl and forged ahd fnl 100yds* **13/2[3]**
2 **2** *1¼* **Presburg (IRE)**[28] 4968 2-9-3 0..................................... EddieCreighton 1 76
(Joseph Tuite) *dwlt: pushed along and sn rcvrd to chse ldrs: rdn jst over 2f out: drvn and ev ch 1f out: no ex and styd on same pce fnl 100yds* **11/1**
3 *hd* **Zaeem** 2-8-12 0.. AnticoMurgia(5) 3 75+
(Mahmood Al Zarooni) *chsd ldrs: effrt 2f out: rdn and ev ch 1f out: unable qck ins fnl f: styd on same pce and btn fnl 100yds* **14/1**
52 **4** *2¼* **Money Never Sleeps**[12] 5480 2-9-3 0.............................. RobertHavlin 6 70
(John Gosden) *led: jnd over 2f out: rdn and hdd over 1f out: stl ev ch jst ins fnl f: wknd fnl 100yds* **11/8[1]**
5 *1½* **Famous Poet (IRE)** 2-9-3 0.. TadhgO'Shea 2 66+
(Saeed Bin Suroor) *hld up in tch: outpcd: rn green and pushed along 2f out: kpt on steadily ins fnl f: nvr trbld ldrs* **16/1**

20 **6** *1 ½* **Roman Province (IRE)**[36] 4662 2-8-9 0.................. AdamBeschizza(3) 8 57
(Roger Teal) *in tch in last trio: pushed along 4f out: rdn and no prog over 3f out: styd on same pce and no threat to ldrs fnl 2f* **33/1**

0 **7** *1* **Mayo Lad (IRE)**[13] 5447 2-9-3 0.................. PatDobbs 5 60
(Richard Hannon) *s.i.s: t.k.h: hld up in last pair: rdn and no hdwy 2f out: one pce and no imp after* **20/1**

34 **8** *2 ¼* **Right Regal (IRE)**[62] 3823 2-9-3 0.................. AdamKirby 7 54
(Marco Botti) *chsd ldrs: rdn and unable qck over 2f out: wknd wl over 1f out* **5/2**[2]

9 *6* **Good Luck Charm** 2-9-3 0.................. DarryllHolland 4 39
(Gary Moore) *s.i.s: t.k.h: hld up in rr: struggling over 3f out: lost tch 2f out* **50/1**

1m 26.45s (3.15) **Going Correction** +0.275s/f (Good) **9** Ran SP% **114.6**
Speed ratings (Par 95): **93,91,91,88,87 85,84,81,74**
toteswingers:1&2:£7.00, 1&3:£11.30, 2&3:£7.90 CSF £71.89 TOTE £5.00: £1.30, £2.80, £3.80; EX 80.10.
Owner Gallagher Equine & Des O'Rourke **Bred** Jim McCormack **Trained** East Everleigh, Wilts

FOCUS
An interesting 2yo maiden, featuring a clutch of runners with fair form and some choicely-bred newcomers. The whole field raced up the middle of the course in the straight.

NOTEBOOK
Tidy Affair(IRE), twice third before a below-par effort last time out, was entitled to win this with his official mark of 75. Backed at each-way prices beforehand, he was always in the leading group and second at halfway. He stayed on strongest from that point on and should now be competitive in nurseries at this trip or slightly longer. Official explanation: trainer said, regarding the apparent improvement in form shown, colt was better suited by the softer ground (op 9-1 tchd 5-1)
Presburg(IRE), a 100-1 runner-up at Salisbury on his only previous start, proved that effort was no fluke. Always in the leading trio, he battled on gamely in the closing stages and snatched second in the dying strides. (op 10-1 tchd 12-1)
Zaeem, a first-time-out half-brother to a 1m winner, posted an encouraging performance. Another in the vanguard virtually throughout, he led briefly before the final furlong, but was just run out of it close home. (op 9-1)
Money Never Sleeps, second in a 6f Newmarket maiden 12 days earlier, appeared to find this trip beyond him. Fastest away, he led 3f out, but dropped away as the principals fought out first prize in the closing stages. (op 13-8, tchd 7-4 in places)
Famous Poet(IRE), a newcomer related to several winners at 1m-plus, plugged on dourly and made ground in the final furlong. He will surely benefit from a longer distance. (op 10-1)
Roman Province(IRE), disappointing on Polytrack after finishing second on her only previous turf outing, again showed this surface suits her better than the all-weather. She is no superstar, but qualifies for nurseries now and can probably be placed to advantage at some stage. (op 25-1)

5856 WEATHERBYS BANK H'CAP — 1m 114y
3:20 (3:20) (Class 5) (0-75,75) 3-Y-O **£3,234** (£962; £481; £240) **Stalls** Low

Form RPR

3050 **1** **Yojimbo (IRE)**[26] 5056 3-9-0 **71**.................. MatthewDavies(3) 4 79
(Mick Channon) *chsd ldr: rdn to chal over 2f out: drvn ahd over 1f out: kpt on wl ins fnl f* **8/1**

3541 **2** *1 ½* **Climaxfortackle (IRE)**[15] 5392 3-8-12 **66**..................(v) NickyMackay 2 71
(Derek Shaw) *hld up in tch in midfield: rdn and switching rt 2f out: drvn to chse ldng pair 1f out: chsd wnr wl ins fnl f: no imp* **20/1**

1020 **3** *¾* **Full Bloom**[15] 5391 3-9-0 **71**..................(tp) MartinHarley(3) 3 74
(Gerard Butler) *chsd ldng pair: effrt and waiting for gap between ldrs over 2f out: drvn and hdwy to chse wnr jst over 1f out: styd on same pce u.p ins fnl f* **16/1**

2102 **4** *hd* **Whitby Jet (IRE)**[10] 5547 3-8-13 **72**.................. AntiocoMurgia(5) 8 72+
(Edward Vaughan) *s.i.s: in tch towards rr: rdn and effrt whn n.m.r wl over 2f out: hdwy u.p over 1f out: kpt on ins fnl f: unable to chal: fin 5th: plcd 4th* **11/4**[1]

5024 **5** *¾* **Swift Blade (IRE)**[14] 5407 3-8-11 **68**.................. AdamBeschizza(3) 7 66
(Lady Herries) *hld up in last pair: rdn 4f out: hdwy and edging lft over 1f out: kpt on ins fnl f: nvr trbld ldrs: fin 6th: plcd 5th* **8/1**

423 **6** *5* **Cairncross (IRE)**[17] 5327 3-9-5 **73**.................. NeilCallan 1 60
(Mark Johnston) *led: flashed tail leaving stalls: rdn over 2f out: hdd over 1f out: wknd ent fnl f: fin 7th: plcd 6th* **9/2**[2]

6035 **7** *2 ¼* **Tagansky**[23] 5137 3-8-7 **61** oh2.................. EddieCreighton 10 43
(Simon Dow) *stdd and dropped in bhd after s: rdn 4f out: drvn and no prog over 2f out: sn wknd fin 8th: plcd 7th* **50/1**

U413 **8** *5* **Numeral (IRE)**[33] 4797 3-9-4 **72**.................. PatDobbs 5 42
(Richard Hannon) *in tch: shkn up and unable qck 3f out: rdn and struggling over 2f out: sn wknd: fin 9th: plcd 8th* **15/2**

1255 **9** *20* **Baqaat (USA)**[27] 5020 3-9-7 **75**.................. TadhgO'Shea 9 —
(Ed Dunlop) *in tch tl lost pl and dropped to last over 2f out: sn lost tch: eased ins fnl f: t.o: fin 10th: plcd 9th* **10/1**

5011 **D** *1* **Poyle Judy**[15] 5376 3-9-5 **73**.................. StevieDonohoe 6 74
(Ralph Beckett) *t.k.h: chsd ldrs: rdn and unable qck over 2f out: kpt on same pce ins fnl f: disqualified: jockey failed to weigh in* **13/2**[3]

1m 48.32s (2.22) **Going Correction** +0.275s/f (Good) **10** Ran SP% **113.9**
Speed ratings (Par 101): **101,99,99,97,97 92,90,86,68,98**
CSF £149.94 CT £1617.81 TOTE £8.50: £2.30, £4.30, £7.40; EX 146.40.
Owner Jon and Julia Aisbitt **Bred** Peter Kelly And Ms Wendy Daly **Trained** West Ilsley, Berks
■ Matthew Davies rode out his claim with this victory.
■ Stewards' Enquiry : Stevie Donohoe three-day ban: jockey failed to weigh in (Sep 22, 25-26)

FOCUS
Just a middling 3yo handicap, with the top weight rated 75, but it looked competitive on paper. the winner rates back to his best.
Baqaat(USA) Official explanation: jockey said filly lost its action

5857 MAY FAMILY JUMP JOCKEYS DERBY H'CAP (TO BE RIDDEN BY NATIONAL HUNT JOCKEYS) — 1m 4f 10y
3:55 (3:58) (Class 4) (0-80,80) 4-Y-O+ **£6,469** (£1,925; £962; £481) **Stalls** Centre

Form RPR

0011 **1** **Shesha Bear**[9] 5580 6-10-10 **66** 6ex..................(p) HaddenFrost 10 77
(Jonathan Portman) *hld up in last trio: gd hdwy on outer over 2f out: rdn to ld over 1f out: r.o wl and in command ins fnl f* **5/1**[2]

2312 **2** *2 ½* **Mohanad (IRE)**[19] 4844 5-11-7 **77**.................. LeightonAspell 3 84
(Sheena West) *chsd ldrs: rdn and effrt on inner 3f out: pressed ldrs and drvn 2f out: nt pce of wnr and kpt on same pce fnl f* **14/1**

0-00 **3** *¾* **Kings Troop**[120] 2006 5-11-10 **80**.................. JimmyMcCarthy 4 86
(Alan King) *hld up in midfield: swtchd rt and rdn 4f out: hdwy over 2f out: kpt on u.p ins fnl f: snatched 3rd last strides: no threat to wnr* **14/1**

022 **4** *hd* **Epsom Salts**[10] 5545 6-10-11 **67**.................. DenisO'Regan 6 73
(Pat Phelan) *in tch in midfield: hdwy over 3f out: led 2f out: drvn and hdd over 1f out: pushed along and styd on same pce fnl f: lost 3rd last strides* **11/2**[3]

0001 **5** *1 ¾* **Boston Blue**[9] 5588 4-11-5 **75** 6ex.................. WayneHutchinson 1 78
(Tony Carroll) *hld up in last quartet: hdwy towards inner over 2f out: kpt on same pce and no imp ins fnl f* **4/1**[1]

32-2 **6** *7* **Palawi (IRE)**[154] 11 4-11-5 **75**.................. DougieCostello 7 67
(John Quinn) *chsd ldrs: rdn and unable qck 3f out: wknd over 1f out* **4/1**[1]

6-06 **7** *¾* **Herschel (IRE)**[26] 3479 5-10-10 **66** oh2.................. JamieMoore 11 56
(Gary Moore) *hld up in last quartet: rdn and no hdwy over 2f out: kpt on past btn horses fnl f: nvr trbld ldrs* **66/1**

3624 **8** *1 ¼* **Nobunaga**[26] 5057 6-11-5 **75**.................. AidanColeman 5 63
(Venetia Williams) *chsd ldr tl led ent fnl 3f: drvn and hdd 2f out: wknd over 1f out: fdd fnl f* **7/1**

0153 **9** *hd* **Kings Bayonet**[28] 4957 4-11-6 **76**.................. RobertThornton 8 64
(Alan King) *stdd s: hld up in rr: rdn and effrt towards inner over 2f out: no prog over 1f out: wknd fnl f* **12/1**

3540 **10** *7* **Lang Shining (IRE)**[24] 5110 7-10-13 **69**..................(b) AndrewTinkler 12 46
(Jamie Osborne) *in tch in midfield: rdn 4f out: wknd over 2f out: wl bhd and hung lft ins fnl f* **33/1**

3060 **11** *2* **Solicitor**[21] 5198 4-11-6 **76**..................(b[1]) TomScudamore 2 50
(Mark Johnston) *led tl hdd and drvn 3f out: wknd qckly over 1f out* **16/1**

2m 45.09s (6.19) **Going Correction** +0.275s/f (Good) **11** Ran SP% **115.9**
Speed ratings (Par 105): **90,88,87,87,86 81,81,80,80,75 74**
toteswingers:1&2:£8.90, 1&3:£9.60, 2&3:£16.70 CSF £71.78 CT £919.50 TOTE £8.50: £2.90, £3.90, £4.30; EX 80.60.
Owner RWH Partnership **Bred** Beechgrove Stud Farm Ltd & Catridge Farm Stud **Trained** Compton, Berks

FOCUS
A novelty event, for jump jockeys only, but it featured several decent performers and looked wide open. The pace was decent and the form looks sound enough.

5858 PONY CLUB H'CAP — 7f
4:30 (4:31) (Class 5) (0-75,75) 3-Y-O+ **£3,234** (£962; £481; £240) **Stalls** Low

Form RPR

4361 **1** **Stonecrabstomorrow (IRE)**[13] 5426 8-8-5 **61**.......... MarkCoumbe(5) 4 69
(Michael Attwater) *sn detached in last: rdn and clsng 2f out: hdwy u.p over 1f out: nt clr run and swtchd lft ins fnl f: r.o wl to ld cl home* **9/1**

0430 **2** *hd* **Timpanist (USA)**[6] 5674 4-8-7 **61** oh4..................(b[1]) AdamBeschizza(3) 2 68
(Simon Dow) *chsd ldrs: rdn to chal 2f out: drvn to ld 1f out: kpt on wl u.p tl hdd cl home* **10/1**

1640 **3** *2 ¼* **Speak The Truth (IRE)**[31] 4850 5-8-8 **62**.................. MatthewDavies(3) 3 63
(Jim Boyle) *hld up in tch: rdn and effrt jst over 2f out: edging lft and unable qck over 1f out: kpt on same pce ins fnl f* **14/1**

526 **4** *½* **Green Earth (IRE)**[10] 5547 4-9-1 **66**.................. IanMongan 1 66
(Pat Phelan) *chsd ldr tl rdn to ld over 2f out: drvn and hdd 1f out: edgd lft and wknd fnl 100yds* **15/8**[1]

4003 **5** *1 ¾* **Sunshine Always (IRE)**[11] 5511 5-9-2 **67**.................. NeilCallan 6 62
(Michael Attwater) *chsd ldrs: rdn and effrt 2f out: unable qck u.p over 1f out: wknd ins fnl f* **2/1**[2]

1000 **6** *1 ¾* **Guilded Warrior**[21] 5198 8-9-7 **75**.................. RobertLButler(3) 7 66
(Paddy Butler) *led: hdd and rdn over 1f out: drvn and wknd over 1f out* **10/1**

0606 **7** *11* **Golden Taurus (IRE)**[22] 5171 3-9-0 **69**.................. AdamKirby 5 28
(J W Hills) *s.i.s: a towards rr: rdn and no prog over 3f out: wknd over 1f out* **8/1**[3]

1m 26.81s (3.51) **Going Correction** +0.275s/f (Good)
WFA 3 from 4yo+ 4lb **7** Ran SP% **114.1**
Speed ratings (Par 103): **90,89,87,86,84 82,70**
toteswingers:1&2:£7.90, 1&3:£9.40, 2&3:£9.30 CSF £90.14 TOTE £7.60: £3.00, £5.70; EX 45.60.
Owner Miss Nicola Carroll **Bred** P Dillon **Trained** Epsom, Surrey

FOCUS
No better than an ordinary handicap, with the top weight rated 75, but few could be confidently discounted. Modest form, with plenty of doubts over the field.

5859 EPSOM SEASON FINALE 25.9.11 H'CAP — 6f
5:00 (5:00) (Class 5) (0-75,75) 3-Y-O **£3,234** (£962; £481; £240) **Stalls** High

Form RPR

4011 **1** **Deliberation (IRE)**[13] 5433 3-8-9 **68**.................. JulieBurke(5) 6 77+
(Kevin Ryan) *mde all: rdn and fnd ex over 1f out: in command and pushed out ins fnl f: eased cl home* **15/8**[1]

1202 **2** *1* **Blue Deer (IRE)**[6] 5669 3-8-9 **70**.................. CharlesBishop(7) 7 72
(Mick Channon) *chsd ldrs: drvn over 1f out: chsd wnr ins fnl f: kpt on but no real threat to wnr* **4/1**[2]

2233 **3** *hd* **I Got You Babe (IRE)**[11] 5506 3-8-7 **61**.................. RichardMullen 1 62+
(Richard Guest) *hld up off the pce in last trio: rdn over 3f out: hdwy u.p over 1f out: running on whn nt clr run and swtchd rt ins fnl f: fin wl but no threat to wnr* **9/1**

0653 **4** *hd* **Saucy Buck (IRE)**[7] 5644 3-8-10 **64** ow1.................. JamieGoldstein 8 65
(Ralph Smith) *chsd wnr: rdn and pressing wnr 2f out: unable qck over 1f out: kpt on same pce ins fnl f* **12/1**

5030 **5** *1 ¼* **Belle Bayardo (IRE)**[3] 5781 3-9-7 **75**.................. RobertHavlin 4 72
(Ronald Harris) *chsd ldrs: lost pl and rdn 3f out: kpt on same pce u.p fr over 1f out* **14/1**

5312 **6** *1 ½* **Rutterkin (USA)**[11] 5506 3-8-4 **61**.................. PaulPickard(3) 5 53
(Alan Berry) *in tch: rdn and effrt over 2f out: unable qck over 1f out: styng on same pce and btn whn pushed rt jst ins fnl f: wknd fnl 100yds* **7/1**

040- **7** *18* **Mirabile Visu**[329] 6875 3-8-5 **62**.................. AdamBeschizza(3) 2 —
(Heather Main) *s.i.s: a in rr: rdn and struggling over 3f out: lost tch over 1f out: eased ins fnl f* **25/1**

2220 **8** *33* **Ceffyl Gwell**[27] 5000 3-9-7 **75**.................. PatDobbs 3 —
(Richard Hannon) *stdd s: hld up in rr: struggling 1/2-way: btn and eased 2f out: t.o over 1f out* **9/2**[3]

1m 12.23s (2.83) **Going Correction** +0.275s/f (Good) **8** Ran SP% **113.7**
Speed ratings (Par 101): **92,90,90,90,88 86,62,18**
toteswingers:1&2:£2.40, 1&3:£3.70, 2&3:£4.80. Totesuper 7: Win: Not won, Place: £203.00 CSF £9.20 CT £51.99 TOTE £2.70: £2.20, £1.20, £3.20; EX 9.00.
Owner Mrs Angie Bailey **Bred** Berkie Brown **Trained** Hambleton, N Yorks
■ Stewards' Enquiry : Richard Mullen one-day ban: careless riding (Sep 22)

FOCUS
A seemingly competitive finale in which, once again, the main action took place in the centre of the track. Straightforward form. The winner had something to spare.
I Got You Babe(IRE) Official explanation: jockey saif filly hung right on the bend
Ceffyl Gwell Official explanation: jockey said colt lost its action
T/Plt: £2,639.30 to a £1 stake. Pool:£50,617.62 - 14.00 winning tickets T/Qpdt: £123.40 to a £1 stake. Pool:£5,270.32 - 31.60 winning tickets SP

5734 WOLVERHAMPTON (A.W) (L-H)

Thursday, September 8

OFFICIAL GOING: Standard

Wind: Fresh behind Weather: Cloudy with sunny spells

5860 WILLIAM HILL - THE HOME OF BETTING APPRENTICE H'CAP 1m 1f 103y(P)

5:40 (5:40) (Class 6) (0-60,64) 3-Y-O+ **£1,533** (£452; £226) **Stalls Low**

Form | | | | RPR

000 **1** **Ulla**[33] 4805 3-8-12 **58**........ DannyBrock(5) 11 68
(Chris Wall) *chsd ldrs: rdn to ld ins fnl f: styd on* **10/1**

6064 **2** *hd* **Beach Babe**[9] 5606 3-9-4 **59**........ MatthewLawson 2 68
(Jonathan Portman) *hld up: pushed along over 3f out: hdwy over 1f out: rdn and ev ch ins fnl f: styd on* **9/2**[2]

6505 **3** *shd* **Twisted**[9] 5606 5-9-5 **59**........(b) DavidSimmonson(5) 10 68
(Michael Easterby) *a.p: rdn to ld over 1f out: hdd ins fnl f: styd on* **11/2**[3]

3550 **4** *2 1/4* **Hathaway (IRE)**[16] 5349 4-9-0 **49**........ RachealKneller 5 53
(Mark Brisbourne) *s.i.s: hld up: hdwy over 2f out: rdn and ev ch over 1f out: styd on same pce ins fnl f* **9/2**[2]

5630 **5** *1/2* **Star Addition**[29] 4902 5-9-4 **53**........ DarylByrne 3 56
(Eric Alston) *chsd ldrs: rdn over 3f out: styd on same pce fnl f* **8/1**

000 **6** *7* **Honest And True (IRE)**[40] 4543 4-9-1 **50**........(b[1]) JustinNewman 9 39+
(Ian Semple) *chsd ldr tl led 4f out: rdn and hdd over 1f out: wknd ins fnl f* **4/1**[1]

0004 **7** *2 1/2* **Beauchamp Xiara**[9] 5609 5-9-8 **57**........ LucyKBarry 7 40
(Hans Adielsson) *s.i.s: hld up: rdn over 2f out: nvr on terms* **15/2**

0000 **8** *2 1/4* **Flyjack (USA)**[33] 4783 4-8-7 **45**........ NatashaEaton(3) 12 24
(Lisa Williamson) *prom: rdn over 2f out: hung lft and wknd over 1f out* **100/1**

060- **9** *1 3/4* **Hits Only Cash**[254] 7996 9-9-4 **53**........(p) DavidKenny 4 28
(Lydia Pearce) *hld up: a in rr* **25/1**

3606 **10** *5* **Danceyourselfdizzy (IRE)**[26] 5041 3-9-4 **59**........ LeonnaMayor 1 23
(Phil McEntee) *hld up: a in rr: bhd fnl 4f* **40/1**

6050 **11** *8* **Gessabelle**[20] 5231 4-8-5 **45**........(tp) HayleyBurton(5) 6 —
(Phil McEntee) *led: pushed along over 5f out: hdd 4f out: wknd over 2f out* **80/1**

2m 0.40s (-1.30) **Going Correction** -0.15s/f (Stan)
WFA 3 from 4yo+ 6lb **11** Ran SP% **112.2**
Speed ratings (Par 101): **99,98,98,96,96 90,87,85,84,79 72**
toteswingers:1&2:£11.10, 2&3:£2.80, 1&3:£10.30 CSF £51.18 CT £273.31 TOTE £16.00: £6.60, £1.20, £1.70; EX 66.80.

Owner J Targett **Bred** J Targett **Trained** Newmarket, Suffolk

FOCUS
Not too many in-form horses in a moderate handicap. The gallop was reasonable, the first five finished clear and the winner came down the centre in the straight. The winner was unexposed and the next two set a modest standard.

Ulla Official explanation: trainer said, regarding the apparent improvement in form shown, filly appeared to benefit from a drop in class

5861 VISIT ATTHERACES.COM/STLEGER MAIDEN STKS 7f 32y(P)

6:10 (6:13) (Class 5) 2-Y-O **£2,264** (£673; £336; £168) **Stalls High**

Form | | | | RPR

1 **Three Am Tour (IRE)** 2-8-9 0........ KieranO'Neill(3) 4 73+
(Richard Hannon) *a.p: n.m.r wl over 3f out: rdn to ld wl ins fnl f: r.o* **9/2**[2]

42 **2** *1/2* **Fa'Iz (IRE)**[19] 5269 2-9-3 0........ TedDurcan 10 77
(Saeed Bin Suroor) *chsd ldr tl led over 5f out: rdn and edgd lft fr over 1f out: hdd wl ins fnl f* **8/13**[1]

6 **3** *1 1/4* **Berengar (IRE)**[12] 5480 2-9-3 0........ MartinDwyer 7 74
(Brian Meehan) *led: hdd over 5f out: chsd ldr: rdn over 1f out: hung lft and styd on same pce ins fnl f* **9/2**[2]

6 **4** *3 1/4* **Kiwayu** [illegible]........ KirstyMilczarek 3 66
(Luca Cumani) *trckd ldrs: racd keenly: pushed along over 2f out: edgd lft and styd on same pce fr over 1f out* **15/2**[3]

5 *4* **Yes It's The Boy (USA)** 2-9-3 0........ J-PGuillambert 5 56
(Ed Walker) *s.i.s: hld up: plld hrd: hdwy 3f out: rdn over 1f out: wknd ins fnl f* **40/1**

00 **6** *2 1/2* **Big Time Charlie (IRE)**[32] 4815 2-9-3 0........ CathyGannon 1 50
(Richard Hannon) *chsd ldrs tl rdn and wknd over 2f out* **66/1**

7 *hd* **Hector's Chance** 2-9-3 0........ RichardKingscote 11 50
(Heather Main) *hld up in tch: wknd over 2f out* **80/1**

8 *4* **Tokyo Brown (USA)** 2-9-3 0........ EddieAhern 6 40
(Heather Main) *s.i.s: outpcd* **33/1**

60 **9** *3 3/4* **Captain Baldwin**[8] 5625 2-8-12 0........(v[1]) MatthewCosham(5) 9 31
(David Evans) *chsd ldrs: pushed along over 5f out: wknd 3f out* **100/1**

00 **10** *9* **Mexican Wave**[40] 4525 2-8-10 0........ IanBurns(7) 2 9
(Michael Bell) *sn outpcd* **80/1**

1m 28.54s (-1.06) **Going Correction** -0.15s/f (Stan) **10** Ran SP% **120.4**
Speed ratings (Par 95): **100,99,98,94,89 86,86,82,77,67**
toteswingers:1&2:£1.80, 2&3:£1.40, 1&3:£3.10 CSF £7.92 TOTE £4.80: £1.30, £1.02, £1.60; EX 17.10.

Owner Adam Victor **Bred** Mrs T Stack **Trained** East Everleigh, Wilts

FOCUS
Not the most competitive of maidens but fair form from the first three. The gallop was an ordinary one and the winner raced against the inside rail in the straight.

NOTEBOOK

Three Am Tour(IRE) ◆, a 32,000euro second foal of a half-sister to smart 7f-1m4f winner Falak and to useful 1m winner Eshaarat and the only filly in the race, attracted support in the day but turned in a fair performance to beat a couple of more experienced rivals on this racecourse debut. He should have no problems with 1m and should be able to build on this. (op 7-2)

Fa'Iz(IRE) had to race wide early on but he was soon enjoying the rub of things on this all-weather debut and he probably ran to a similar mark as at Chester on his previous start. This looks as good as he is but he's capable of picking up a small event. (tchd 4-6)

Berengar(IRE) had shown ability at a modest level on his debut and duly stepped up on that level over this longer trip on this all-weather debut. He too should be able to pick up a minor event at some point. (op 5-1)

Kiwayu ◆ stepped up on his initial effort over this trip at Kempton. His pedigree suggests he'll be suited by a much stiffer stamina test and he's capable of winning races. (op 7-1)

Yes It's The Boy(USA), a $50,000 yearling and first foal of an unraced half-sister to numerous winners, including three US Grade 1 winners up to 1m2f and to the dam of triple Group 1 winner David Junior, showed ability at an ordinary level after a slow start on this racecourse debut. He should improve for the experience. (op 33-1)

5862 WILLIAMHILL.COM FILLIES' H'CAP 7f 32y(P)

6:40 (6:41) (Class 4) (0-80,80) 3-Y-O+ **£3,234** (£962; £481; £240) **Stalls High**

Form | | | | RPR

1303 **1** **Close To The Edge (IRE)**[32] 4817 3-8-13 **76**........ MartinHarley(3) 7 87
(Alan McCabe) *hld up: hdwy over 2f out: swtchd rt over 1f out: rdn and r.o to ld post* **12/1**

3131 **2** *hd* **Katy's Secret**[16] 5355 4-8-10 **66**........ KierenFallon 3 78
(William Jarvis) *hld up in tch: swtchd rt over 2f out: rdn to ld 1f out: hdd post* **5/1**[3]

1214 **3** *2 3/4* **Caelis**[20] 5255 3-9-3 **77**........(v) JimCrowley 1 80
(Ralph Beckett) *chsd ldrs: rdn and ev ch over 1f out: styd on same pce ins fnl f* **7/4**[1]

0050 **4** *nse* **Who's Shirl**[6] 5683 5-9-6 **76**........ TedDurcan 10 80
(Chris Fairhurst) *hld up: rdn over 1f out: r.o wl ins fnl f: nrst fin* **16/1**

0503 **5** *1/2* **Carcinetto (IRE)**[7] 5653 9-8-10 **66** oh3........ CathyGannon 11 69
(David Evans) *hld up: rdn over 1f out: r.o ins fnl f: nvr nrr* **25/1**

0200 **6** *3/4* **Gap Princess (IRE)**[13] 5434 7-9-10 **80**........(p) GrahamGibbons 5 81
(Geoffrey Harker) *hld up in tch: rdn over 1f out: styd on same pce* **14/1**

0404 **7** *shd* **Strictly Pink (IRE)**[16] 5354 3-9-1 **75**........ PaulHanagan 4 74
(Alan Bailey) *chsd ldrs: rdn to ld over 1f out: sn hung lft and hdd: no ex ins fnl f* **4/1**[2]

0034 **8** *3/4* **Ishiadancer**[10] 5551 6-8-11 **72**........ LMcNiff(5) 12 71
(Eric Alston) *chsd ldr tl led over 2f out: rdn and hdd over 1f out: no ex ins fnl f* **14/1**

1146 **9** *1 1/2* **Roodee Queen**[12] 5476 3-9-6 **80**........ RichardKingscote 6 73
(Milton Bradley) *hld up: rdn over 1f out: nvr on terms* **12/1**

1406 **10** *1/2* **Blaraafa (IRE)**[50] 4202 3-9-1 **75**........ EddieAhern 8 66
(Michael Bell) *hld up: rdn over 1f out: n.d* **10/1**

4260 **11** *5* **First Class Favour (IRE)**[22] 5164 3-8-9 **74**........ LanceBetts(5) 2 52
(Tim Easterby) *led over 4f: wknd over 1f out* **14/1**

1m 27.44s (-2.16) **Going Correction** -0.15s/f (Stan)
WFA 3 from 4yo+ 4lb **11** Ran SP% **127.2**
Speed ratings (Par 102): **106,105,102,102,102 101,101,100,98,97 92**
toteswingers:1&2:£11.90, 2&3:£3.30, 1&3:£5.50 CSF £76.96 CT £165.13 TOTE £18.30: £4.70, £2.80, £1.10; EX 64.20.

Owner Charles Wentworth **Bred** Martin Francis **Trained** Averham Park, Notts

FOCUS
A fair fillies' handicap in which the gallop was reasonable. The first two, who pulled clear late on, edged towards the stands side in the straight. The winner produced a 5lb personal best.

5863 THE BLACK COUNTRY'S ONLY RACECOURSE MAIDEN STKS 5f 216y(P)

7:10 (7:11) (Class 5) 2-Y-O **£2,264** (£673; £336; £168) **Stalls Low**

Form | | | | RPR

4420 **1** **Lucky Money**[20] 5233 2-9-3 75........(b[1]) StevieDonohoe 11 74
(Sir Mark Prescott Bt) *a.p: chsd ldr 3f out: r.o u.p to ld nr fin* **6/4**[1]

6620 **2** *3/4* **Chillie Billie**[61] 3879 2-9-3 74........ KirstyMilczarek 7 72
(Phil McEntee) *led: rdn over 1f out: hdd nr fin* **11/1**

40 **3** *1* **Purley Queen (IRE)**[8] 5632 2-8-12 0........ JamesDoyle 5 64+
(Sylvester Kirk) *mid-div: hdwy over 2f out: rdn and r.o ins fnl f: wnt 3rd post: nt rch ldrs* **66/1**

2 **4** *nse* **Fantastic Smartie**[16] 5347 2-8-12 0........ DavidProbert 4 64
(David Evans) *chsd ldr to 1/2-way: rdn over 2f out: styd on: lost 3rd post* **4/1**[3]

6 **5** *2* **Twelve Strings (IRE)**[14] 5410 2-9-3 0........ KierenFallon 1 63+
(Luca Cumani) *sn pushed along and prom: outpcd over 2f out: rdn and hung lft over 1f out: styd on ins fnl f* **5/2**[2]

5 **6** *nk* **Zafonic Star**[16] 5347 2-9-0 0........ RyanClark(3) 10 62+
(Ian Williams) *s.s: bhd: racd wd turning for home: r.o ins fnl f: nrst fin* **33/1**

0 **7** *1 1/4* **Refreshestheparts (USA)**[illegible] [illegible] 2-8-12 0........ [illegible] 10 [illegible]
(George Baker) *mid-div: rdn over 2f out: styd on ins fnl f: nt trble ldrs* **25/1**

8 *4 1/2* **Black Douglas** 2-9-3 0........ SteveDrowne 12 44
(William Jarvis) *dwlt: sn pushed along in rr: rdn over 1f out: nvr nrr* **6/1**

5 **9** *8* **Hatha Zain (IRE)**[19] 5263 2-9-3 0........ RichardKingscote 9 19
(Milton Bradley) *chsd ldrs tl wknd 2f out* **66/1**

10 *1* **South Kenter (USA)** 2-9-3 0........ EddieAhern 6 16
(Heather Main) *s.s: a in rr* **16/1**

11 *1 1/2* **Gone To Ground** 2-8-10 0........ RaulDaSilva(7) 8 11
(Jeremy Gask) *s.s: a in rr* **50/1**

12 *3/4* **Stoneacre Wigan** 2-8-12 0........ SladeO'Hara(5) 3 9
(Peter Grayson) *s.s: a in rr* **66/1**

1m 14.9s (-0.10) **Going Correction** -0.15s/f (Stan) **12** Ran SP% **130.3**
Speed ratings (Par 95): **94,93,91,91,88 88,86,80,70,68 66,65**
toteswingers:1&2:£3.80, 2&3:£76.00, 1&3:£15.90 CSF £22.51 TOTE £3.80: £1.50, £2.60, £9.70; EX 14.30.

Owner J M Brown **Bred** Whitley Stud **Trained** Newmarket, Suffolk

■ Stewards' Enquiry : Pat Cosgrave one-day ban: careless riding (Sep 22)

FOCUS
No more than a fair maiden. The gallop was again reasonable and the winner came down the centre in the straight.

NOTEBOOK

Lucky Money, fitted with blinkers for this drop in trip, didn't have to better his previous course form to get off the mark in a fairly uncompetitive maiden. He'll be suited by the return to 7f and has the scope to improve a little. (op 13-8 tchd 15-8)

Chillie Billie, 1lb behind the winner on official ratings, ran up to his best after a two-month break on this all-weather debut back over this longer trip. He's had a few chances but this showed he should be able to win an ordinary event. (op 10-1 tchd 12-1)

Purley Queen(IRE) hadn't shown much in two previous starts but fared considerably better under considerate handling against two rivals rated in the 70's. This won't have done her mark any good but she'll be of interest upped to 7f in nurseries. (op 50-1)

Fantastic Smartie, upped in trip for this all-weather debut, had the run of the race and turned in an improved effort. She is likely to remain vulnerable against the better types in this grade but will be worth a second look in nurseries. (op 9-2)

Twelve Strings(IRE) was never really travelling but tuned in an improved effort in terms of form and is another that will make more appeal over further in nurseries. (op 9-4 tchd 11-4 in places)

Zafonic Star caught the eye after a tardy start. He wasn't knocked about, is open to improvement and should be able to pick up a race in due course. Official explanation: jockey said gelding jumped awkwardly from the stalls

5864 ATR ST LEGER MICROSITE NOW LIVE H'CAP 5f 216y(P)
7:40 (7:41) (Class 6) (0-60,62) 3-Y-O £1,704 (£503; £251) Stalls Low

Form RPR

4330 **1** **Justbookie Dot Com (IRE)**[10] 5539 3-9-6 **59**..............(v) KierenFallon 5 71
(David Evans) *hld up in tch: rdn over 1f out: r.o to ld wl ins fnl f* **3/1**[1]

6442 **2** ½ **Cadmium Loch**[9] 5603 3-8-13 **59**..............(p) JackDuern(7) 12 69
(Reg Hollinshead) *led: rdn over 1f out: hdd wl ins fnl f* **5/1**[2]

2550 **3** 2¾ **Trojan Rocket (IRE)**[34] 4758 3-9-2 **55**.............. AdrianMcCarthy 3 56+
(George Prodromou) *prom: nt clr run and lost pl 4f out: hmpd 1/2-way: nt clr run wl over 1f out: hung lft and r.o ins fnl f: nt rch ldrs* **22/1**

0001 **4** 2¾ **Circuitous**[8] 5619 3-9-3 **56** 6ex..............(b) TomEaves 1 48
(Keith Dalgleish) *chsd ldrs: rdn and nt clr run over 2f out: styd on same pce fr over 1f out* **6/1**[3]

0064 **5** nk **Consistant**[15] 5388 3-9-2 **55**.............. J-PGuillambert 2 46
(Brian Baugh) *chsd ldr to 1/2-way: sn rdn: no ex ins fnl f* **20/1**

0000 **6** nk **Maharanee (USA)**[14] 5404 3-8-11 **53**..............(p) DaleSwift(3) 6 43
(Ann Duffield) *hld up in tch: rdn over 1f out: no imp* **20/1**

0305 **7** ¾ **Avon Light**[6] 5674 3-8-8 **47**..............(p) RichardKingscote 4 35
(Milton Bradley) *s.i.s: in rr tl styd on fr over 1f out: nvr on terms* **10/1**

6401 **8** 1¾ **Stilettoesinthemud (IRE)**[7] 5649 3-9-9 **62** 6ex.......... FrederikTylicki 13 44
(James Given) *prom: lost pl 4f out: n.d after* **9/1**

6044 **9** ½ **Hootys Agogo**[11] 5506 3-8-5 **49**.............. NeilFarley(5) 10 30
(Declan Carroll) *s.i.s: hld up: rdn over 1f out: n.d* **20/1**

3600 **10** ½ **Ballinargh Boy**[55] 4041 3-8-10 **49**.............. StevieDonohoe 9 28
(Robert Wylie) *prom: rdn over 2f out: wknd over 1f out* **16/1**

2433 **11** ½ **Dictionary**[15] 5388 3-9-7 **60**..............(bt) PaulHanagan 7 38
(William Haggas) *prom: chsd ldr 1/2-way: rdn and wknd over 1f out* **3/1**[1]

1m 13.84s (-1.16) **Going Correction** -0.15s/f (Stan) 11 Ran SP% **124.6**
Speed ratings (Par 99): **101,100,96,93,92 92,91,88,88,87 86**
toteswingers:1&2:£6.70, 2&3:£31.60, 1&3:£15.40 CSF £17.95 CT £299.42 TOTE £2.50: £1.10, £3.40, £12.00; EX 21.50.
Owner J A Wilcox **Bred** Haydock Park Stud **Trained** Pandy, Monmouths
■ Stewards' Enquiry : Jack Duern three-day ban: careless riding (Sep 22, 25-26)

FOCUS
A moderate handicap in which the gallop was soon sound. The winner edged towards the far side late on. He rates back to his early best.
Avon Light Official explanation: jockey said gelding missed the break
Dictionary Official explanation: jockey said gelding hung left throughout

5865 DINE IN HORIZONS H'CAP 5f 20y(P)
8:10 (8:10) (Class 6) (0-55,55) 3-Y-O+ £1,533 (£452; £226) Stalls Low

Form RPR

5504 **1** **Rightcar**[50] 4207 4-8-7 **46** oh1.............. RobbieFitzpatrick 6 53
(Peter Grayson) *dwlt: hld up: hdwy 1/2-way: led over 1f out: drvn out* **12/1**

0 **2** 1 **Lake Wanaka (IRE)**[17] 5336 3-8-6 **46** oh1..............(t) CathyGannon 3 49
(Ms Joanna Morgan, Ire) *hld up: plld hrd: hdwy over 1f out: rdn to chse wnr ins fnl f: r.o* **12/1**

5143 **3** 1½ **Francis Albert**[9] 5603 5-9-2 **55**.............. KierenFallon 1 53
(Michael Mullineaux) *a.p: rdn and ev ch over 1f out: styd on same pce ins fnl f* **15/8**[1]

6560 **4** 1¾ **Mi Sun Donk**[36] 4657 3-8-8 **48**.............. WilliamCarson 2 40
(Brett Johnson) *led: reminder 2f out: hdd over 1f out: edgd rt and styd on same pce* **25/1**

0460 **5** ¾ **Lithaam (IRE)**[6] 5678 7-8-7 **46** oh1..............(tp) RichardKingscote 4 35
(Milton Bradley) *prom: rdn over 1f out: styd on same pce* **16/1**

5-34 **6** nk **Cheeky Wee Red**[13] 5433 3-8-11 **51**.............. PaulHanagan 7 39
(Richard Fahey) *sn outpcd: hdwy u.p over 1f out: nt rch ldrs* **11/2**

23 **7** 1¼ **The Fiery Cross**[13] 5436 4-9-0 **53**..............(v[1]) TomEaves 9 36
(Ian Semple) *chsd ldrs: hung lft fr 1/2-way: wknd over 1f out* **5/1**[3]

450 **8** ½ **Boucher Garcon (IRE)**[12] 5469 3-8-7 **47**.............. StevieDonohoe 8 29
(Declan Carroll) *prom: hmpd and lost pl over 3f out: n.d after* **4/1**[2]

5405 **9** shd **Cloth Ears**[51] 4189 5-8-13 **52**..............(be) KirstyMilczarek 5 33
(Phil McEntee) *trckd ldrs: racd keenly: wknd over 1f out* **16/1**

0000 **10** 1¾ **Ellielusive (IRE)**[12] 5490 4-8-8 **47** oh1 ow1..........(t) GrahamGibbons 10 22
(Mark Brisbourne) *chsd ldrs: rdn 1/2-way: wknd over 1f out* **33/1**

61.45 secs (-0.85) **Going Correction** -0.15s/f (Stan)
WFA 3 from 4yo+ 1lb 10 Ran SP% **120.8**
Speed ratings (Par 101): **100,98,96,93,92 91,89,88,88,85**
toteswingers:1&2:£9.00, 2&3:£6.40, 1&3:£7.70 CSF £151.65 CT £403.49 TOTE £13.50: £4.20, £3.70, £1.60; EX 155.00.
Owner Richard Teatum **Bred** J M Beever **Trained** Formby, Lancs

FOCUS
A very weak handicap in which the three unexposed sorts proved disappointing. The gallop was a reasonable one and the winner raced centre-to-far side in the straight.
The Fiery Cross Official explanation: jockey said gelding hung left from 2f out

5866 MOBET.WILLIAMHILL.COM H'CAP 1m 4f 50y(P)
8:40 (8:40) (Class 5) (0-75,75) 4-Y-O+ £2,264 (£673; £336; £168) Stalls Low

Form RPR

6112 **1** **Eagle Nebula**[27] 5015 7-9-1 **69**.............. GeorgeBaker 3 78+
(Brett Johnson) *hld up: hdwy over 1f out: styd on to ld wl ins fnl f: comf* **4/1**[2]

3162 **2** 1¼ **Ghufa (IRE)**[36] 4687 7-9-2 **70**.............. KierenFallon 1 76
(Lydia Pearce) *a.p: pushed along over 3f out: rdn to ld ins fnl f: sn hdd and unable qck* **4/1**[2]

0360 **3** 1¼ **Dynamic Idol (USA)**[15] 5389 4-9-5 **73**..............(b) PaulHanagan 4 77
(Mikael Magnusson) *led: rdn over 1f out: hdd ins fnl f: styd on same pce* **13/2**

4000 **4** ½ **Langley**[24] 5102 4-9-2 **70**.............. SteveDrowne 2 73
(Pat Murphy) *chsd ldr 4f: remained handy: wnt 2nd again 2f out: rdn and ev ch ins fnl f: styd on same pce* **33/1**

5601 **5** 1 **Raktiman (IRE)**[15] 5389 4-9-1 **69**..............(p) RichardKingscote 5 71
(Tom Dascombe) *hld up in tch: rdn over 2f out: styd on same pce ins fnl f* **11/2**[3]

13-2 **6** 1¼ **Albertus Pictor**[245] 67 4-9-7 **75**.............. StevieDonohoe 8 75
(Sir Mark Prescott Bt) *prom: chsd ldr 8f out tl rdn 2f out: no ex ins fnl f* **7/4**[1]

6140 **7** 1¾ **Irish Jugger (USA)**[110] 2312 4-9-0 **68**.............. JamesMillman 7 65
(Rod Millman) *hld up: rdn over 1f out: n.d* **14/1**

1061 **8** 2 **Bavarica**[22] 5168 9-9-2 **73**.............. AdamBeschizza(3) 6 67
(Julia Feilden) *hld up: rdn over 2f out: nvr on terms* **14/1**

2m 39.97s (-1.13) **Going Correction** -0.15s/f (Stan) 8 Ran SP% **121.4**
Speed ratings (Par 103): **97,96,95,95,94 93,92,91**
toteswingers:1&2:£3.30, 2&3:£4.80, 1&3:£7.10 CSF £21.84 CT £104.95 TOTE £4.10: £1.10, £1.30, £2.70; EX 22.80.
Owner Tann Racing **Bred** Juddmonte Farms Ltd **Trained** Ashtead, Surrey

FOCUS
A fair handicap but, although the gallop to the home turn was on the steady side, the first two came from just off the pace. The winner raced towards the inside rail in the straight. The level is set around the second and third.
T/Plt: £51.40 to a £1 stake. Pool of £82,323.90 - 1,167.43 winning tickets. T/Qpdt: £22.80 to a £1 stake. Pool of £8,994.11 - 291.00 winning tickets. CR

5867 - 5872a & 5874a (Foreign Racing) - See Raceform Interactive

5770 LONGCHAMP (R-H)
Thursday, September 8

OFFICIAL GOING: Turf: good to soft

5873a PRIX D'AUMALE (GROUP 3) (2YO FILLIES) (TURF) 1m
1:50 (12:00) 2-Y-O £34,482 (£13,793; £10,344; £6,896; £3,448)

RPR

1 **Zantenda**[16] 2-8-9 0.............. OlivierPeslier 2 104+
(F Head, France) *settled at rr and wl off ld ent st: rdn 1 1/2f out: qcknd wl on wd outside fnl f: ct ldrs ins fnl 100yds: sltly impeded 50yds out but qcknd again to get up cl home: comf* **7/5**[1]

2 nk **Rajastani (IRE)**[40] 2-8-9 0.............. StephanePasquier 4 103
(S Wattel, France) *settled 6th: rdn 2f out: fnd split 1 1/2f out: chsd ldr and hrd rdn ent fnl f: ct ldr 100yds out: sltly impeded eventual wnr 50yds out: hdd cl home* **43/10**[3]

3 2 **Kinetica**[33] 4803 2-8-9 0.............. Jean-BernardEyquem 5 98
(Sir Mark Prescott Bt) *sn led and wnt clr: hld clr ld ent fnl f: r.o u.p: ct under 100yds out: r.o wl* **9/2**

4 2½ **Iceni Girl**[49] 4245 2-8-9 0.............. GeraldMosse 1 92
(John Gosden) *settled in 2nd: hrd rdn 1 1/2f out: nt qckn: styd on fnl f* **21/1**

5 3 **Absolutely True**[30] 2-8-9 0.............. ChristopheSoumillon 3 85
(E Lellouche, France) *settled towards rr: r.o u.p 1 1/2f out: nt qckn fnl f* **33/10**[2]

6 6 **Nimohe (FR)**[19] 5296 2-8-9 0.............. SylvainRuis 7 72
(J Heloury, France) *settled 3rd: hrd rdn 1 1/2f out: nt qckn: eased ins fnl f* **20/1**

7 nk **Enjoy The Life**[25] 2-8-9 0.............. FilipMinarik 6 71
(Mario Hofer, Germany) *settled 4th and moved into 3rd ent st: hrd rdn but nt qckn: eased ins fnl f* **17/1**

1m 40.7s (2.30) 7 Ran SP% **116.8**
WIN (incl. 1 euro stake): 2.40. PLACES: 1.70, 2.50. SF: 9.80.
Owner Wertheimer & Frere **Bred** Wertheimer & Frere **Trained** France

FOCUS
The third and fourth's British form dictate the level.

NOTEBOOK
Zantenda's rider was in no hurry, and having pulled Zantenda to the outside, the response wasn't instant, but the daughter of Zamindar always looked to have the measure of the runner-up. Still green here, she could go for the Prix Marcel Boussac on Arc day.
Rajastani(IRE), unbeaten in two previous starts, was collared close home.
Kinetica, upped in trip, may have gone a shade quickly up front. She was adding a second placed effort at this level, having finished third to the impressive Discourse in the Sweet Solera Stakes at Newmarket.
Iceni Girl stayed on well for fourth after following the early pace. Connections will chase black type with her.

5268 CHESTER (L-H)
Friday, September 9

OFFICIAL GOING: Good (7.4)
Wind: Light to moderate, half-behind Weather: Cloudy

5875 EUROPEAN BREEDERS FUND MAIDEN STKS (C&G) 7f 122y
2:00 (2:00) (Class 4) 2-Y-O £4,851 (£1,443; £721; £360) Stalls High

Form RPR

6432 **1** **Mcvicar**[11] 5550 2-8-11 **66**.............. MartinHarley(3) 1 77
(Mick Channon) *trckd ldrs: rdn and swtchd rt over 1f out: r.o ins fnl f: led towards fin* **7/1**

002 **2** nk **Hyperlink (IRE)**[11] 5536 2-9-0 0.............. SilvestreDeSousa 6 76
(Mark Johnston) *led: rdn whn pressed over 1f out: hdd towards fin* **2/1**[2]

4 **3** 1 **Sir Trevor (IRE)**[20] 5269 2-9-0 0.............. RussKennemore 4 74
(Tom Dascombe) *racd keenly: a.p: rdn whn chalng over 1f out: ev ch tl no ex towards fin* **5/1**[3]

2 **4** 2 **Sholaan (IRE)**[16] 5384 2-9-0 0.............. LiamJones 3 69
(William Haggas) *s.i.s: hld up: effrt 2f out: unable to mount serious chal: one pce ins fnl f* **13/8**[1]

0 **5** 17 **Tectonic (IRE)**[21] 5239 2-9-0 0..............(v[1]) RichardMullen 2 28
(Sir Michael Stoute) *racd keenly: hld up: u.p and outpcd over 2f out: sn lft bhd* **14/1**

060 **P** **Eagle Of Rome (IRE)**[71] 3553 2-9-0 **67**..............(v[1]) TomMcLaughlin 5 —
(Nick Littmoden) *prom tl wnt wrong after 1f and p.u* **40/1**

1m 34.98s (1.18) **Going Correction** 0.0s/f (Good) 6 Ran SP% **109.7**
Speed ratings (Par 97): **94,93,92,90,73** —
CSF £20.47 TOTE £4.70: £2.30, £1.60; EX 14.70.
Owner M Channon **Bred** J Breslin **Trained** West Ilsley, Berks

FOCUS
Rail out 3yds from 6f to top of home straight with drop in at that point. Races up to 10.5f increased by 13yds and 2m race by 26yds. No more than a fair maiden and that it should be won by a horse with an official rating of 66 who has had six runs already suggests it's not form to be rating highly, although it reads straightforward enough. The gallop was steady.

NOTEBOOK
Mcvicar almost certainly improved on his previous form in making amends for a slightly unlucky run at Newcastle last time, while leaving the impression a return to further will suit, gradually getting on top close home. Even so, he'll probably be vulnerable back in nurseries if the handicapper hikes up his mark on a line through the runner-up. (op 11-2)
Hyperlink(IRE) set the standard on form and was soon best placed in front, but he looks a galloper above all else and in hindsight connections may regret not making much more use of his proven stamina. (tchd 15-8)

Sir Trevor(IRE) had shown promise on his debut and probably improved on that level a bit without impressing as anything out of the ordinary or up to winning a maiden race next time out. He won't have any trouble with a step up to 1m. (op 9-2, tchd 4-1 in a place)

Sholaan(IRE) attracted plenty of support after his promising debut, but the early signs are that the Kempton maiden he contested then may not have been much of a race, for all he may not have been helped here by a bump at the start or the very tight track. He's got an extravagant round action and for all he might do better back on a more galloping track, he's no superstar clearly. (op 2-1 tchd 9-4)

Tectonic(IRE) is plainly one of the stable lesser-lights, showing little more here in a first-time visor on just his second start than he did at Sandown on his debut.

5876 MS SUPPORT & POLYMORPH IT SERVICES NURSERY — 7f 2y

2:35 (2:35) (Class 3) (0-95,94) 2-Y-O — **£7,115** (£2,117; £1,058; £529) **Stalls High**

Form			Horse	Jockey	RPR
2203	**1**		**Cravat**[13] 5478 2-8-12 **85** (Mark Johnston) *trckd ldrs: rdn to ld on inner over 1f out: qcknd clr ins fnl 100yds: comf* **2/1**[1]	SilvestreDeSousa 1	92
2241	**2**	*3 ¼*	**Kimbali (IRE)**[18] 5310 2-8-6 **79** (Richard Fahey) *a.p: rdn to chal over 1f out: outpcd by wnr fnl 100yds* **13/2**[3]	BarryMcHugh 6	78
0015	**3**	*1 ¾*	**Bling King**[32] 4858 2-9-7 **94** (Eve Johnson Houghton) *hld up: hdwy to chse ldrs 2f out: nt gng pce to chal over 1f out: edgd rt ins fnl f: styd on towards fin* **7/1**	TomQueally 4	89
3531	**4**	*shd*	**Darnathean**[7] 5690 2-8-0 **73** 6ex (Paul D'Arcy) *led: rdn and hdd over 1f out: stl ch ent fnl f: no ex fnl 100yds* **4/1**[2]	(b) LukeMorris 2	67
5034	**5**	*2 ½*	**Jack Who's He (IRE)**[40] 4575 2-9-0 **87** (David Evans) *racd keenly: hld up: n.m.r briefly over 5f out: sn hung rt and looked totally ill at ease on trck: effrt and in tch 4f out: wl outpcd over 2f out: v wd ent st wl over 1f out: no imp after* **10/1**	PatCosgrave 7	75+
2240	**6**	*1 ¼*	**Tight Lipped (IRE)**[20] 5287 2-8-5 **78** (David Brown) *cl up: lost pl over 4f out: outpcd over 2f out: n.d after* **7/1**	RichardMullen 3	63
3214	**7**	*2 ¼*	**Stellar Express (IRE)**[32] 4867 2-8-0 **73** (Michael Appleby) *prom: u.p over 2f out: sn wknd* **11/1**	JimmyQuinn 5	52

1m 26.52s (0.02) **Going Correction** 0.0s/f (Good) — **7** Ran SP% **109.1**
Speed ratings (Par 99): **99,95,93,93,90 88,86**
toteswingers:1&2:£4.10, 2&3:£4.90, 1&3:£2.60 CSF £13.84 TOTE £2.90: £1.90, £1.80; EX 10.00.

Owner Sheikh Hamdan Bin Mohammed Al Maktoum **Bred** Darley **Trained** Middleham Moor, N Yorks

FOCUS

A tight-looking nursery beforehand, but a wide-margin winner as things turned out at the conclusion of a well-run race. Three of the next four home all ran better than the result suggests and the bare form looks slightly misleading. The runner-up helps with the level.

NOTEBOOK

Cravat, who's out of a mare by Sadler's Wells, looks all about stamina and was never stronger than at the finish after getting a good tow round on the rail in the slipstream of the strong pace. He'll almost certainly fare even better over 1m before the season is out, though whether he'll have things drop as perfectly again as they did here has to be open to doubt. The handicapper is sure to go to town with his rating too, so it might be that he'll be seen out again very quickly. (op 5-2 tchd 11-4)

Kimbali(IRE) ran very well considering he had very little cover, made his effort from too wide on the track, and probably too early too. Given a level playing field he'd have run the winner close and he's sure to win a nursery off his current mark. (op 5-1 tchd 9-2)

Bling King seemed to be ridden with suspect stamina in mind and for all he snatched third late on, was never a threat. The trip didn't look an issue and he can be ridden more positively at it next time. (op 6-1)

Darnathean was ridden in similar fashion to his recent win at Kempton. There's little reason to doubt that form, but the combination of the extra furlong and being harried in front took its toll and he just lost third. Probably 6f is his best trip for now. (op 7-2)

Jack Who's He(IRE) was another whose position didn't do him justice. Too wide throughout and seemingly ill at ease on the track, hanging right out on one occasion, he still put in some good late work and probably figures on a decent mark. He could go well at a big price back on a more conventional track next time. Official explanation: jockey said gelding hung right throughout (tchd 8-1)

Tight Lipped(IRE) now has two disappointing runs to his name. (op 9-1 tchd 10-1)

Stellar Express(IRE) is looking increasingly flattered by her win here in July when presented with a soft lead. (op 9-1)

5877 AXON RESOURCING MAIDEN FILLIES' STKS — 1m 2f 75y

3:10 (3:12) (Class 5) 3-Y-O+ — **£4,043** (£1,203; £601; £300) **Stalls Low**

Form			Horse	Jockey	RPR
324	**1**		**Floral Beauty**[28] 4985 3-8-12 81 (Sir Michael Stoute) *racd keenly: hld up: hdwy 4f out: chsd ldrs 2f out: r.o to ld wl ins fnl f: on top cl home* **7/1**[3]	RichardMullen 7	82+
3	**2**	*½*	**Kahraba (USA)**[28] 5001 3-8-12 0 (Saeed Bin Suroor) *trckd ldrs: chalng 3f out: upsides 2f out: led over 1f out: sn edgd rt: hdd wl ins fnl f: kpt on cl home* **6/4**[2]	PatCosgrave 2	81+
335	**3**	*4 ½*	**Shuhra (IRE)**[25] 5098 3-8-12 75 (William Haggas) *led: rdn and hdd over 1f out: no ch w front 2 fnl 100yds* **11/1**	LiamJones 3	72
205-	**4**	*1*	**Spey Song (IRE)**[322] 7057 3-8-12 73 (James Bethell) *dwlt: bhd: niggled along 4f out: styd on ins fnl f: tk 4th cl home: nvr gng pce to threaten* **25/1**	TomEaves 4	70
06	**5**	*½*	**Balandra**[18] 5317 3-8-12 0 (Luca Cumani) *hld up: tk cl order to chse ldrs 3f out: outpcd 2f out: one pce and n.d ins fnl f*	KirstyMilczarek 6	69+
3	**6**	*9*	**Night And Dance (IRE)**[119] 2068 3-8-12 0 (Sir Henry Cecil) *trckd ldrs: effrt on outer over 3f out: wknd 2f out* **11/8**[1]	TomQueally 5	51
	7	*23*	**Gorau Glas** 3-8-12 0 (Mark Brisbourne) *s.i.s: a bhd: struggling to keep up over 4f out: nvr on terms* **50/1**	RobbieFitzpatrick 1	—
4	**8**	*1*	**Reluctant Heroine (USA)**[14] 5429 3-8-12 0 (Mark Johnston) *prom: rdn over 4f out: wknd over 2f out* **20/1**	SilvestreDeSousa 8	—

2m 11.82s (0.62) **Going Correction** 0.0s/f (Good) — **8** Ran SP% **115.5**
Speed ratings (Par 100): **97,96,93,92,91 84,66,65**
toteswingers:1&2:£4.50, 2&3:£5.60, 1&3:£12.80 CSF £17.74 TOTE £6.90: £1.60, £1.30, £2.30; EX 21.60.

Owner Saeed Suhail **Bred** Rabbah Bloodstock Limited **Trained** Newmarket, Suffolk

■ Stewards' Enquiry : Silvestre De Sousa caution; used whip without giving mount time to respond

FOCUS

Just a fair maiden run at something of an uneven gallop.

5878 DEEPBRIDGE CAPITAL LLP H'CAP — 1m 7f 195y

3:45 (3:46) (Class 3) (0-95,93) 3-Y-O+ — **£7,762** (£2,310; £1,154; £577) **Stalls High**

Form			Horse	Jockey	RPR
212	**1**		**Never Can Tell (IRE)**[62] 3851 4-9-7 **85** (Jamie Osborne) *mde all: rdn over 1f out: pressed fnl f: kpt finding more cl home: hld on wl* **11/1**	TonyHamilton 9	92
0012	**2**	*nk*	**Kazbow (IRE)**[31] 4890 5-10-0 **92** (Luca Cumani) *chsd ldrs: pushed along over 3f out: wnt 2nd over 1f out: str chal ins fnl f: hld fnl strides* **7/1**[2]	J-PGuillambert 8	98
3650	**3**	*hd*	**Bowdler's Magic**[21] 5250 4-9-6 **84** (Mark Johnston) *hld up: hdwy over 1f out: styd on to chal between horses fnl 75yds: jst hld* **7/1**[2]	FrederikTylicki 1	90+
3421	**4**	*1 ¾*	**Slight Advantage (IRE)**[21] 5236 3-8-3 **83** (Clive Cox) *midfield: clsd to chse ldrs over 2f out: nt clr run over 1f out: styd on ins fnl f: unable to chal front trio* **3/1**[1]	JohnFahy(3) 6	87+
0060	**5**	*¾*	**English Summer**[34] 4778 4-9-12 **90** (Mark Johnston) *hld up in rr: nt clr run over 1f out: sn rdn: styd on to chse ldrs ins fnl f: no imp fnl 75yds* **12/1**	SilvestreDeSousa 5	93+
2350	**6**	*1*	**Plato (JPN)**[22] 5221 4-9-9 **87** (Sir Henry Cecil) *chsd ldr: pushed along 3f out: rdn 2f out: lost 2nd over 1f out: fdd fnl 100yds* **7/1**[2]	(b) TomQueally 2	89
0032	**7**	*1 ¼*	**Chilly Filly (IRE)**[22] 5221 5-9-4 **82** (Brian Ellison) *hld up: effrt over 1f out: one pce fnl f: nvr able to chal* **3/1**[1]	TomEaves 4	82
3215	**8**	*2 ½*	**Danvilla**[14] 5448 4-9-5 **83** (Paul Webber) *in tch: pushed along over 3f out: rdn 2f out: wknd 1f out: eased whn wl btn fnl 75yds* **17/2**[3]	RichardMullen 7	80

3m 29.41s (1.41) **Going Correction** 0.0s/f (Good)
WFA 3 from 4yo+ 13lb — **8** Ran SP% **114.1**
Speed ratings (Par 107): **96,95,95,94,94 94,93,92**
toteswingers:1&2:£11.20, 2&3:£12.80, 1&3:£18.90 CSF £84.21 CT £580.49 TOTE £9.30: £2.60, £2.30, £2.40; EX 24.40.

Owner Dr Marwan Koukash **Bred** Shaanara Syndicate **Trained** Upper Lambourn, Berks

■ Stewards' Enquiry : Frederik Tylicki caution; used whip without giving mount sufficient time to respond

FOCUS

A useful handicap, but one run at a steady pace for the most part despite several front-runners in opposition. There looked a couple of hard-luck stories and the form might not be reliable.

NOTEBOOK

Never Can Tell(IRE) has a good record here and extended that under what was a smart ride given she'd the pace to win at 1m4f here earlier in the summer, steadying the gallop once she got to the front and saving enough to just hold on in a tight finish. Things are unlikely to drop as kindly next time elsewhere off what will be a career-high mark. (op 8-1)

Kazbow(IRE) usually makes the running, but was dropped in behind the winner saving ground on the rail. He lost nothing in defeat, proving he stays 2m in the process, and continues to make gradual progress. (tchd 6-1)

Bowdler's Magic looked a shade unlucky not to land his first win of the season. He was poorly placed albeit still going well turning for home, but had his path blocked more than once including well inside the last when running into a blind alley behind the winner. That said, the emphasis on speed would have suited him given his form at shorter trips, and his overall record isn't one to back on reproducing it next time. (op 8-1)

Slight Advantage(IRE) ◆ looked to be travelling strongly turning for home, but was another whose path was blocked just at the point she needed a clear run. She took some time to pick up and left the impression she would have been suited by a much stronger gallop. (op 7-2 tchd 4-1)

English Summer was another whose effort can be marked up. He was well back turning for home, but like his stable-mate never had much room or time to hit top stride and ended up being given a very considerate ride. (op 11-1)

Plato(JPN) was again below his best in blinkers, albeit not by much, and it wouldn't be a surprise to see them discarded next time. (op 13-2 tchd 6-1)

Chilly Filly(IRE) is potentially well handicapped, but she's going to need her stamina tested more than it was here. (op 7-2)

5879 HAWKER BEECHCRAFT H'CAP — 7f 2y

4:20 (4:22) (Class 3) (0-95,94) 3-Y-O+ — **£7,762** (£2,310; £1,154; £577) **Stalls High**

Form			Horse	Jockey	RPR
5-	**1**		**Alakhan (IRE)**[522] 1117 5-8-10 **80** (Ian Williams) *racd keenly: hld up in midfield: hdwy over 1f out: r.o to ld wl ins fnl f: wl in command towards fin* **14/1**	LiamJones 6	91+
5030	**2**	*1 ¾*	**Baby Strange**[5] 5758 7-9-4 **88** (Derek Shaw) *towards rr: hdwy over 1f out: styd on towards fin: nt rch wnr* **12/1**	RobbieFitzpatrick 7	94
2021	**3**	*hd*	**One Scoop Or Two**[7] 5684 5-9-0 **84** 6ex (Reg Hollinshead) *racd keenly: a.p: led over 1f out: hdd wl ins fnl f: hld cl home* **5/1**[1]	(p) J-PGuillambert 12	89+
5530	**4**	*1*	**Capercaillie (USA)**[26] 5080 4-9-4 **91** (Clive Cox) *midfield: hdwy over 1f out: ch ins fnl f: nt qckn* **9/1**	JohnFahy(3) 10	94
6511	**5**	*nk*	**Glenridding**[14] 5455 7-8-13 **83** (James Given) *led: hdd over 5f out: chsd ldr tl regained ld briefly over 1f out: one pce fnl 75yds* **7/1**[3]	FrederikTylicki 1	85
0000	**6**	*nk*	**Rulesn'regulations**[20] 5264 5-9-2 **86** (Matthew Salaman) *trckd ldrs: rdn over 1f out: styd on same pce ins fnl f* **16/1**	(b) LukeMorris 8	87
3000	**7**	*shd*	**Corporal Maddox**[28] 4997 4-9-1 **85** (Jamie Osborne) *swtchd lft sn after s: hld up: hdwy ins fnl f: sn swtchd lft: styd on wl towards fin* **28/1**	TonyHamilton 14	86+
0000	**8**	*2 ¼*	**Kyllachy Star**[20] 5272 5-9-7 **94** (Richard Fahey) *midfield: rdn and hdwy over 1f out: styng on for press whn swtchd lft and bdly hmpd wl ins fnl f: no ch after* **7/1**[3]	LeeTopliss(3) 5	94+
1000	**9**	*hd*	**Orpsie Boy (IRE)**[5] 5758 8-9-3 **87** (Ruth Carr) *midfield: wknd over 2f out* **20/1**	JamesSullivan 9	81
000	**10**	*1 ¼*	**Global City (IRE)**[41] 4534 5-9-8 **92** (Saeed Bin Suroor) *dwlt: towards rr: hdwy whn nt clr run over 1f out: one pce ins fnl f* **10/1**	(t) RichardMullen 4	83+
-230	**11**	*1 ¾*	**No Hubris (USA)**[70] 3578 4-9-8 **92** (Roger Varian) *prom: pushed along 3f out: rdn over 1f out: styng on same pce whn hmpd wl ins fnl f* **13/2**[2]	TomEaves 2	93+
4014	**12**	*¾*	**Last Sovereign**[16] 5371 7-8-11 **81** (Ollie Pears) *missed break: swtchd lft sn after s: nvr gng wl: a bhd* **16/1**	(bt) TomQueally 11	65
0000	**13**	*4 ½*	**Celtic Sultan (IRE)**[20] 5272 7-8-12 **82** (Tom Tate) *prom: led over 5f out: rdn and hdd over 1f out: wknd ins fnl f* **20/1**	(b) SilvestreDeSousa 13	54

0300 **14** *6* **Douze Points (IRE)**[18] 5322 5-9-0 **84**............................(p) PatCosgrave 3 40
(Ed de Giles) *s.i.s: midfield: outpcd over 1f out* **16/1**

1m 26.68s (0.18) **Going Correction** 0.0s/f (Good) **14** Ran SP% **119.1**
Speed ratings (Par 107): **98,96,95,94,94 93,93,91,91,89 87,86,81,74**
toteswingers:1&2:£49.80, 2&3:£10.40, 1&3:£15.80 CSF £165.90 CT £989.98 TOTE £18.10: £5.10, £4.30, £2.20; EX 281.00.
Owner Patrick Kelly **Bred** Juergen Imm **Trained** Portway, Worcs
■ Stewards' Enquiry : Lee Topliss three-day ban; careless riding (25th-27th Sep)

FOCUS
A useful handicap run at a strong pace, but one in which luck in running played its part with one or two ill-fated in behind.

NOTEBOOK
Alakhan(IRE) ◆ hadn't been seen since April 2010 and clearly hasn't been easy to train, but he's clearly well ahead of his current mark and settled this with a bit to spare after showing a good turn of foot having been waited with. He might not be one to tread warily with if turned out again quickly, but is still lightly raced and looks the sort that might start making up for lost time in decent handicaps next year at this trip or 1m. (op 10-1)
Baby Strange has always looked best at up to 6f, but the strong pace more than anything else played to his strengths and he saw the trip out well with a strong finish. He's in good form right now (won this same week last year) and is worth looking out for next time. (op 11-1)
One Scoop Or Two continues in excellent form and confirmed much of his season has been wasted trying 1m2f, faring best here of those that were up there all the way. (op 8-1)
Capercaillie(USA) ran a fine race considering he raced wider than pretty much anything else for most of the trip. (op 12-1)
Glenridding also shaped as if he's still in form despite being not dominating as he's best doing. (op 5-1)
Rulesn'regulations had every chance back at a more suitable trip and doesn't need any excuses.
Corporal Maddox can have his effort upgraded a little as he didn't have an entirely clear run in the straight having been switched sharply to the rail on leaving the stalls. (tchd 25-1)
Kyllachy Star had little luck in running in the straight, twice denied a run. He would probably have finished fourth or fifth had he not been snatched up inside the last. (op 9-1)
Global City(IRE) had little luck in running. Official explanation: jockey said horse was denied a clear run (op 17-2 tchd 8-1)
Last Sovereign blew his chance with a very slow start.
Celtic Sultan(IRE) had no chance of lasting home given the suicidal gallop he set. (op 22-1)

5880 EQUESTRIAN ART H'CAP — 1m 2f 75y
4:50 (4:50) (Class 3) (0-90,90) 3-Y-O **£7,762** (£2,310; £1,154; £577) **Stalls** Low

Form — RPR

10 **1** **Midsummer Sun**[85] 3068 3-9-5 **88**.................................. TomQueally 1 100+
(Sir Henry Cecil) *racd keenly: hld up: hdwy to go prom 6f out: led over 1f out: r.o wl: in full control towards fin* **7/4**[1]

2210 **2** *1 ½* **Calaf**[43] 4467 3-8-9 **78**.. TonyHamilton 4 87
(Richard Fahey) *hld up: rdn and hdwy over 1f out: styd on to take 2nd towards fin: nt trble wnr* **4/1**[2]

-546 **3** *nk* **Poplin**[92] 2839 3-9-7 **90**.. KirstyMilczarek 7 98
(Luca Cumani) *racd keenly: prom: stdd 7f out: hdwy over 2f out: tried to chal ins fnl f: styd on same pce fnl 75yds* **16/1**

5321 **4** *4 ½* **Lifetime (IRE)**[14] 5432 3-8-10 **79**............................... SilvestreDeSousa 3 79
(Mark Johnston) *hld up: hdwy after 2f: handy: rdn over 1f out: one pce ins fnl f* **17/2**

0105 **5** *¾* **Abdicate (IRE)**[27] 5062 3-8-7 **76**.................................... BarryMcHugh 6 74
(Richard Fahey) *led: rdn and hdd over 1f out: wknd fnl 100yds* **20/1**

31 **6** *3 ¾* **Gobooll**[28] 4989 3-9-1 **84**.. LiamJones 8 75
(William Haggas) *prom: rdn over 2f out: wknd over 1f out* **6/1**[3]

2131 **7** *1 ½* **Highlife Dancer**[10] 5582 3-8-0 **76** oh3........................ CharlesBishop(7) 5 64
(Mick Channon) *hld up in rr: rdn 2f out: nvr able to get on terms* **8/1**

0034 **8** *2* **Sergeant Ablett (IRE)**[23] 5177 3-9-6 **89**...................... FrederikTylicki 2 74
(James Given) *prom tl wknd 3f out* **8/1**

2m 11.9s (0.70) **Going Correction** 0.0s/f (Good) **8** Ran SP% **114.0**
Speed ratings (Par 105): **97,95,95,91,91 88,87,85**
toteswingers:1&2:£2.80, 2&3:£13.70, 1&3:£4.80 CSF £8.61 CT £80.51 TOTE £2.90: £1.10, £1.80, £4.60; EX 10.00.
Owner K Abdulla **Bred** Juddmonte Farms Ltd **Trained** Newmarket, Suffolk

FOCUS
A fairly useful handicap run at a stop-start gallop, but won in impressive fashion by a late-developing half-brother to Midday.

NOTEBOOK
Midsummer Sun looks the sort that will live up to his tall home reputation with another winter behind him. Thought good enough to run in the Tercentenary Stakes at Royal Ascot when last seen, he made light work of his handicap mark of 88 with an authoritative performance, travelling smoothly then always doing enough after sweeping to the front. He'll be even more effective back at 1m4f in time and might have a good handicap in him before making the step up in grade. (op 2-1, tchd 9-4 in places)
Calaf ran well considering he had to make his effort from further back than the winner. He might have more to offer not having been with his current handler long and will no doubt be laid out for a handicap here early next year. (op 5-1 tchd 7-2)
Poplin also let the winner get first run to some extent, but time will show she was facing a stiff task conceding him weight. She looks more of a stayer than she did earlier in the year and looks worth stepping up to 1m4f now. (op 12-1)
Lifetime(IRE) might need his mark coming down a little, but he still looked inexperienced so might still do better in the lower grade for which he's eligible back on a more conventional track. (op 9-1 tchd 8-1)
Abdicate(IRE) looks to have gone off the boil for now and ought to have been favoured given that she was able to dictate taking the shortest route round. (op 18-1)
Gobooll looked open to progress going handicapping after his Kempton win, but perhaps found this too tough a race too quickly on this tricky track. He created a good impression when winning and shouldn't be written off yet. (tchd 13-2)
Highlife Dancer found this company far tougher than the ordinary handicaps he's been contesting. (op 13-2)
Sergeant Ablett(IRE) looks to be finishing his season tamely. (op 9-1)

5881 STELLAR GROUP H'CAP (FOR GENTLEMAN AMATEUR RIDERS) — 6f 18y
5:25 (5:28) (Class 5) (0-70,72) 3-Y-O+ **£3,899** (£1,209; £604; £302) **Stalls** High

Form — RPR

1312 **1** **Royal Box**[11] 5539 4-10-5 **58**..................................(p) MrRJWilliams(5) 11 67+
(Dai Burchell) *in tch: effrt whn n.m.r and hmpd 1f out: r.o ins fnl f to ld towards fin* **4/1**[1]

3625 **2** *½* **Memphis Man**[7] 5677 8-10-5 **58**..................................... MrFMitchell(5) 5 63
(David Evans) *hld up in midfield: rdn and hdwy 1f out: r.o to take 2nd towards fin* **10/1**

4556 **3** *½* **Interchoice Star**[9] 5616 6-10-2 **55**.........................(p) MrJohnWilley(5) 12 58
(Ray Peacock) *in tch: rdn over 2f out: effrt whn edgd lft over 1f out: sn led: hdd towards fin and sn lost 2nd* **14/1**

0003 **4** *1 ¼* **Bahamian Lad**[32] 4866 6-11-0 **65**....................(p) MrStephenHarrison(3) 4 64
(Reg Hollinshead) *led: rdn and hdd 1f out: one pce fnl 50yds* **6/1**[3]

0060 **5** *hd* **Mark Anthony (IRE)**[10] 5603 4-10-12 **65**.....................(p) MrOGarner(5) 7 64
(Shaun Harris) *trckd ldrs: rdn over 1f out: kpt on same pce fnl 100yds* **33/1**

3661 **6** *1 ¼* **Downhill Skier (IRE)**[6] 5732 7-11-5 **72** 6ex.............. MrNdeBoinville(5) 1 67
(Mark Brisbourne) *midfield: rdn over 1f out: kpt on same pce ins fnl f* **11/2**[2]

050 **7** *nk* **Schoolboy Champ**[15] 5404 4-10-5 **58**....................(v) ThomasGarner(5) 2 52
(Patrick Morris) *chsd ldrs: rdn 3f out: one pce ins fnl f* **7/1**

2104 **8** *½* **Avoncreek**[7] 5677 7-10-0 **55** oh6..................................(v) RyanWhile(7) 10 47
(Brian Baugh) *dwlt: hld up: kpt on ins fnl f: nt gng pce to chal* **25/1**

402 **9** *1 ¼* **Sir Nod**[15] 5400 9-11-7 **69**..(p) MrSWalker 13 57
(Julie Camacho) *midfield: effrt over 1f out: no ex fnl 75yds* **10/1**

4200 **10** *nk* **Royal Blade (IRE)**[6] 5720 4-10-11 **66**........................... MrMGrossett(7) 8 53
(Alan Berry) *displayed gd spd: prom: chalng 2f out: wknd ins fnl f* **16/1**

4610 **11** *¾* **Ryedane (IRE)**[8] 5647 9-10-13 **66**..............................(b) MrWEasterby(5) 6 51
(Tim Easterby) *missed break: a bhd: nvr on terms* **9/1**

640 **12** *¾* **Johannesgray (IRE)**[14] 5437 4-10-4 **55**.......................(p) MrJHamer(3) 9 37
(Noel Wilson) *hld up: rdn over 1f out: nvr able to get on terms* **25/1**

3504 **13** *1 ¾* **Itsthursdayalready**[10] 5603 4-10-7 **55** oh2.................. MrPCollington 14 32
(Mark Brisbourne) *midfield on outer: wknd over 2f out* **14/1**

1m 16.82s (3.02) **Going Correction** 0.0s/f (Good) **13** Ran SP% **120.2**
Speed ratings (Par 103): **79,78,77,76,75 74,73,73,71,70 69,68,66**
toteswingers:1&2:£8.50, 2&3:£39.50, 1&3:£17.70 CSF £43.69 CT £534.28 TOTE £5.30: £1.70, £3.20, £5.80; EX 52.00.
Owner T R Pearson **Bred** The Queen **Trained** Briery Hill, Blaenau Gwent

FOCUS
A modest finale, but one run at a strong gallop.
Interchoice Star Official explanation: jockey said regarding why he apparently stopped riding close to line, his horse had lost momentum and had already been passed by a fast finisher for second.
T/Plt: £164.90 to a £1 stake. Pool of £57,164.34 - 253.06 winning tickets. T/Qpdt: £38.50 to a £1 stake. Pool of £4,169.56 - 80.00 winning tickets. DO

5847 DONCASTER (L-H)
Friday, September 9

OFFICIAL GOING: Good (good to firm in places; overall 8.6; far side 8.5; stands' side 8.7)
Wind: Breezy against Weather: Sunny

5882 POLYPIPE FLYING CHILDERS STKS (GROUP 2) — 5f
1:25 (1:26) (Class 1) 2-Y-O
£39,697 (£15,050; £7,532; £3,752; £1,883; £945) **Stalls** High

Form — RPR

5110 **1** **Requinto (IRE)**[21] 5253 2-9-0 110.. WMLordan 2 110
(David Wachman, Ire) *trckd ldr: cl up 2f out: rdn to ld over 1f out: drvn ins fnl f: hld on wl* **10/3**[1]

4223 **2** *shd* **Burwaaz**[21] 5251 2-9-0 109... RichardHills 4 110
(Ed Dunlop) *trckd ldng pair: effrt 2f out: rdn to chal jst over 1f out: carried sltly lft ent fnl f: sn drvn and styd on: jst failed* **6/1**

3034 **3** *½* **Caledonia Lady**[22] 5217 2-8-11 96................................. PaulHanagan 1 105
(Jo Hughes) *hld up in rr: hdwy 2f out: swtchd rt and rdn whn n.m.r ent fnl f: sn drvn and kpt on* **20/1**

1142 **4** *nk* **Lilbourne Lad (IRE)**[21] 5251 2-9-3 111...................... RichardHughes 10 110
(Richard Hannon) *hld up in rr: gd hdwy on wd outside 2f out: rdn to chse ldrs over 1f out: drvn and ch ins fnl f: nt qckn towards fin* **5/1**[2]

1521 **5** *2* **Kohala (IRE)**[28] 4999 2-8-11 99....................................... JimmyFortune 5 97
(David Barron) *hld up in rr: swtchd lft and hdwy 2f out: rdn over 1f out: kpt on same pce u.p ins fnl f* **10/1**

1652 **6** *nk* **Vocational (USA)**[6] 5715 2-8-11 98................................. WilliamBuick 7 95
(Mark Johnston) *led: rdn along 2f out: hdd over 1f out: sn drvn and edgd rt ent fnl f: wknd* **14/1**

110 **7** *1 ½* **Angels Will Fall (IRE)**[22] 5217 2-8-11 104.................. RobertWinston 6 90
(Charles Hills) *dwlt: t.k.h and in tch: rdn along 2f out: sn wknd* **5/1**[2]

101 **8** *2 ½* **My Propeller (IRE)**[20] 5286 2-8-11 101.......................... JamieSpencer 3 83
(Peter Chapple-Hyam) *stmbld bdly s: sn in tch: hdwy to chse ldrs 2f out: sn rdn and wknd over 1f out* **11/2**[3]

5314 **9** *6* **Miss Lahar**[28] 4999 2-8-11 96.. KierenFallon 9 59
(Mick Channon) *in tch: hdwy to chse ldrs over 2f out: sn rdn and wknd wl over 1f out* **20/1**

0560 **10** *1 ¼* **On The Dark Side (IRE)**[11] 5558 2-8-11 98.................... PhillipMakin 8 55
(Kevin Ryan) *chsd ldrs: rdn along 2f out: sn wknd* **66/1**

59.23 secs (-1.27) **Going Correction** 0.0s/f (Good) **10** Ran SP% **112.9**
Speed ratings (Par 107): **110,109,109,108,105 104,102,98,88,86**
toteswingers:1&2:£4.50, 2&3:£21.00, 1&3:£11.50 CSF £21.88 TOTE £3.00: £1.10, £2.10, £5.90; EX 16.00 Trifecta £95.70 Pool: £5452.83 - 42.14 winning units..
Owner M Tabor, D Smith & Mrs John Magnier **Bred** Liberty Bloodstock **Trained** Goolds Cross, Co Tipperary
■ Stewards' Enquiry : William Buick two-day ban; careless riding (25th-26th Sep)

FOCUS
Drying ground led to a going change before racing, and riders in the first agreed that the ground was on the fast side of good. There was a headwind up the straight. The time was a respectable 0.73sec outside the standard. This looked a decent renewal of this Group 2 prize. Fleeting Spirit, successful in 2007, has been the only recent winner to go on to top-level victory, and neither of the last two winners has run at three. The runners raced down the centre of the track and the first four finished in a heap. Straightforward, solid form.

NOTEBOOK
Requinto(IRE) emulated Fleeting Spirit and last year's scorer Zebedee as Molecomb Stakes winners to add this race. He was found wanting against the top older sprinters in the Nunthorpe Stakes on his latest start, but the easy ground was against him at York. Always in the first pair here, he moved ahead a furlong out and held on well, although it was pretty tight in the end. A tough colt and a real sprinting type, he is in the Middle Park but could remain at 5f and tackle his elders in the Prix de l'Abbaye. The ground will determine where he runs. (op 7-2 tchd 3-1)
Burwaaz ran another solid race and was gaining close home on Requinto, who beat him more easily in the Molecomb. He reversed Gimcrack form with Lilbourne Lad over this shorter trip and deserves to pick up a Group race, having made the frame in four of them now. The Mill Reef Stakes and the Middle Park are options open to him, but it may be that he is best over 5f. (op 13-2)
Caledonia Lady did best of the fillies, who have a good record in this race with nine victories in the last two decades, and outnumbered the males this year by seven to three. She ran on well from the rear to be beaten narrowly, despite needing to switch. Twice third at this level, she is clearly a very useful filly, but she remains a maiden and threw away a good opportunity at Ffos Las last month. This looks her best trip. (op 22-1)

Lilbourne Lad(IRE)'s Railway Stakes victory in the summer meant he carried a 3lb penalty here. A head in front of Burwaaz when they were second and third to Caspar Netscher in the Gimcrack, he was down at 5f for the first time since winning over this C&D on his debut in April. Held up this time, he came with a sustained run down the near side of the bunch and was gaining steadily at the finish.
Kohala(IRE) landed Newbury's St Hugh's Stakes last month, and two recent winners of that fillies' race have gone on to land this event. Switched to the outer and finishing well, if too late, she did confirm Newbury form with Miss Lahar and On The Dark Side, both of whom were well held here.
Vocational(USA) ran a cracker from the front in the Sirenia Stakes at Kempton on Saturday, and showed her usual fine pace back down at 5f. She was still holding second at the furlong pole before running out of steam. (op 16-1)
Angels Will Fall(IRE) pulled too hard when a beaten favourite in the Lowther Stakes and it was a similar story back down at 5f as she failed to quicken once let down. She needs to settle better. (op 9-2 tchd 11-2 in a place)
My Propeller(IRE), successful in York's Roses Stakes last time, stumbled badly leaving the stalls which cannot have helped her chances, although she quickly raced in touch. She did not pick up for pressure and Jamie Spencer eased her in the last half-furlong. Official explanation: jockey said filly stumbled at the start

5883 LADBROKES MALLARD STKS (H'CAP) 1m 6f 132y
1:55 (1:55) (Class 2) 3-Y-0+ **£25,876** (£7,700; £3,848; £1,924) **Stalls** Low

Form RPR
0200 **1** **Old Hundred (IRE)**[14] 5448 4-8-10 **86**.........................(v) EddieAhern 10 92+
(James Fanshawe) *trckd ldrs: hdwy 2f out: effrt and nt clr run over 1f out: rdn to ld last 100yds: jst hld on* **16/1**
0100 **2** *hd* **Nanton (USA)**[20] 5285 9-9-12 **102**................................ DanielTudhope 1 108
(Jim Goldie) *hld up in rr: hdwy on outer 2f out: rdn and str run ent fnl f: jst failed* **25/1**
1020 **3** *½* **Bourne**[41] 4528 5-8-13 **89**.. KierenFallon 6 94
(Luca Cumani) *in tch: hdwy to trck ldrs over 4f out: cl up 2f out: rdn to ld 1 1/2f out: drvn ins fnl f: hdd and no ex last 100yds* **6/1**[2]
1025 **4** *hd* **Tominator**[6] 5705 4-9-7 **100**.. PaulPickard(3) 4 105
(Reg Hollinshead) *hld up in rr: stdy hdwy on outer over 3f out: chsd ldrs over 1f out and sn rdn: drvn and ev ch ins fnl f tl no ex towards fin* **8/1**
1060 **5** *1 ½* **Harlestone Times (IRE)**[20] 5285 4-9-10 **100**...................... TedDurcan 9 103
(John Dunlop) *hld up: hdwy to trck ldrs over 3f out: rdn along 2f out: drvn and kpt on same pce ins fnl f* **10/1**
6110 **6** *nse* **Shernando**[6] 5705 4-9-1 **91**.. PaulHanagan 11 95+
(Mark Johnston) *hld up towards rr: hdwy on outer 3f out: rdn to chal wl over 1f out and ev ch tl drvn and wknd ins fnl f* **16/1**
00-0 **7** *nk* **Precision Break (USA)**[20] 5271 6-9-5 **95**...................... JamieSpencer 5 98
(David Simcock) *trckd ldr: effrt over 2f out: sn pushed along: rdn and n.m.r wl over 1f out: grad wknd appr fnl f* **13/2**[3]
6203 **8** *hd* **Theology**[20] 5271 4-10-0 **104**.. RichardHughes 3 108+
(Jeremy Noseda) *trckd ldrs on inner: pushed along over 2f out: rdn and n.m.r over 1f out: one pce* **13/2**[3]
2304 **9** *3 ¼* **Hawk Mountain (UAE)**[22] 5221 6-9-0 **90**...................... JimmyFortune 8 88
(John Quinn) *prom: trckd ldr fr 1/2-way: rdn to ld briefly 2f out: sn hdd: drvn and wknd over 1f out* **9/1**
0315 **10** *1 ¼* **Itlaaq**[22] 5221 5-9-4 **94**..(t) GrahamGibbons 7 90
(Michael Easterby) *hld up: hdwy on inner over 2f out and sn chsng ldrs: rdn and n.m.r wl over 1f out: wknd appr fnl f* **10/1**
3502 **11** *¾* **Eternal Heart (IRE)**[13] 5471 3-8-12 **100**........................ WilliamBuick 2 95
(Mark Johnston) *led: rdn along over 3f out: hdd 2f out and sn wknd* **9/2**[1]

3m 12.28s (4.88) **Going Correction** +0.05s/f (Good)
WFA 3 from 4yo+ 12lb **11** Ran SP% **114.0**
Speed ratings (Par 109): **88,87,87,87,86 86,86,86,84,84 83**
toteswingers:1&2:£57.70, 2&3:£29.70, 1&3:£18.50 CSF £347.52 CT £2652.03 TOTE £22.70: £5.80, £6.00, £2.10; EX 315.90 Trifecta £905.10 Pool: £1712.44 - 1.40 winning units..
Owner Lael Stable **Bred** Lael Stables **Trained** Newmarket, Suffolk

FOCUS
This looked a tight handicap on paper, they went no gallop early on and it turned into a sprint. With something of a bunch finish the form needs treating with caution.

NOTEBOOK
Old Hundred(IRE) has been in and out since winning over this C&D on his reappearance, but he was on a going day this time, got plenty of cover, travelled strongly to a furlong out and quickened up well when asked. He might not be one to entirely trust, but he's a capable performer at his best, and his record suggests this is one of the tracks for which he reserves his best (form figures now read 32121).
Nanton(USA) has 1m2f speed so, while in theory a stronger pace should have suited this hold-up performer, the way the race was run actually played into his hands and he showcased his finishing kick by coming from last place 2f out to take second on the line.
Bourne had never previously run beyond 1m4f but he's always looked to want a trip and this race wasn't run to suit him, as he's essentially a one-paced galloper. He can do better off a stronger pace. (op 5-1 tchd 9-2)
Tominator, winner of the Northumberland Plate, wouldn't have been ideally suited by the way the race was run over this shorter trip, but he had an uninterrupted passage down the outside and posted another sound effort in defeat. (op 15-2)
Harlestone Times(IRE) doesn't look to have much margin for error off his current mark, but he shouldn't be too harshly judged on this effort as he was stuck behind horses and didn't have much room for manoeuvre from 2f out. (op 12-1)
Shernando had every chance a furlong out, but didn't seem to quite see out the trip. (tchd 18-1, 20-1 in a place)
Precision Break(USA), three from three in his previous starts here, was travelling just about as well as the winner 2f out but he was beaten to the gap by Old Hundred, and then got slightly outpaced before running on again late. A stronger all-round gallop would have suited him and he's on a mark he should be able to win off. (op 6-1 tchd 11-2)
Theology didn't get much of a clear run and his jockey was never able to quite go for everything. It's not worth dwelling too much on this performance. (op 7-1 tchd 15-2)
Eternal Heart(IRE) was the only 3yo in the field, a generation successful in twelve of the last 20 renewals. Despite enjoying the run of things out in front, though, he was unable to take advantage. His form appears to have hit a plateau. Official explanation: trainer's rep had no explanation for the poor form shown (op 11-2)

5884 STOBART DONCASTER CUP (GROUP 2) 2m 2f
2:25 (2:25) (Class 1) 3-Y-0+ **£56,710** (£21,500; £10,760; £5,360; £2,690; £1,350) **Stalls** Low

Form RPR
3 **1** **Saddler's Rock (IRE)**[20] 5291 3-8-1 101......................(t) NGMcCullagh 2 122
(John M Oxx, Ire) *towards rr: pushed along after 4f: niggled along 1/2-way: rdn and sltly outpcd over 5f out: hdwy to chse ldrs 3f out: swtchd rt and rdn over 1f out: styd on to ld ins fnl f: r.o strly and sn clr* **11/2**[3]
4211 **2** *4* **Opinion Poll (IRE)**[20] 5284 5-9-4 116............................ FrankieDettori 4 119
(Mahmood Al Zarooni) *hld up in rr: stdy hdwy 4f out: chal over 2f out: rdn to ld over 1f out: drvn and hdd ins fnl f: sn edgd lft and one pce* **11/8**[1]
-031 **3** *1 ¼* **Motrice**[13] 5471 4-8-12 107.. PaulHanagan 5 112
(Sir Mark Prescott Bt) *trckd ldrs: hdwy 6f out: cl up 4f out: rdn to ld wl over 2f out: drvn and hdd over 1f out: one pce fnl f* **9/2**[2]
0253 **4** *8* **Bergo (GER)**[20] 5284 8-9-1 108.. GeorgeBaker 1 106
(Gary Moore) *trckd ldng pair: pushed along 4f out: rdn and outpcd 3f out: plugged on u.p fnl 2f* **12/1**
-2P0 **5** *1* **Tastahil (IRE)**[43] 4469 7-9-1 113...................................... RichardHills 6 105
(Charles Hills) *trckd ldr: cl up 1/2-way: disp ld 6f out tl rdn along and outpcd 3f out: plugged on one pce u.p fnl 2f* **12/1**
1030 **6** *10* **Blue Bajan (IRE)**[20] 5284 9-9-4 113.............................. DanielTudhope 7 97
(David O'Meara) *hld up in rr: hdwy on outer 4f out: rdn along wl over 2f out: sn wknd* **14/1**
-212 **7** *½* **Tactician**[20] 5285 4-9-1 108.. EddieAhern 8 93
(Michael Bell) *mde most tl rdn along and hdd wl over 2f out: sn drvn and wknd* **13/2**

3m 49.83s (-5.17) **Going Correction** +0.05s/f (Good) course record
WFA 3 from 4yo+ 14lb **7** Ran SP% **111.1**
Speed ratings (Par 115): **113,111,110,107,106 102,102**
toteswingers:1&2:£3.10, 2&3:£1.60, 1&3:£3.80 CSF £12.72 TOTE £8.70: £3.20, £1.20; EX 17.70 Trifecta £62.80 Pool: £4328.17 - 50.95 winning units..
Owner Michael O'Flynn **Bred** Rockfield Farm **Trained** Currabeg, Co Kildare

FOCUS
A reasonable edition of this long-established event, which has held Group 2 status since 2003. The pace was solid and the form should hold up.

NOTEBOOK
Saddler's Rock(IRE) ◆ was being niggled along on the approach to the home turn, but he came back on the bridle halfway up the home straight. Switched out with two to run and wound up for a strong run, he cut down the favourite to win going away, although the official margin of four lengths looked on the long side. Having just the sixth race of his life, he had been third to Irish St Leger candidates Fictional Account and Fame And Glory at the Curragh last time and was tackling an extra half-mile here. Only the second 3yo successful in the last 22 runnings, following Alleluia in 2001, his trainer John Oxx won this race with the previous year's Gold Cup winner Enzeli in 2000 and had not had a runner in it since. The colt may not appear again this year, as he well at home on decent ground, but looks sure to prove a real contender for the Cup races next year. There is definitely further improvement in him and on this evidence the 2m4f of the Gold Cup would pose him few problems. (tchd 13-2 after early 15-2 in places)
Opinion Poll(IRE) has now twice failed to enhance the fine record of Lonsdale Cup winners in this (five others have followed up since 2002), having finished fourth, to Lonsdale second Samuel, here last year for Michael Jarvis. He carried a 3lb penalty for the York success, which followed a second to Fame And Glory at Ascot and victory in the Goodwood Cup. Contesting fifth place with Saddler's Rock before cruising up in the slipstream of Motrice in the straight, he was shaken up to lead but quickly mastered by the winner, to whom he was conceding 17lb. He did little wrong and his target remains the very valuable Long Distance Cup on British Champions Day at Ascot, where he is sure to give another good account of himself. (op 6-4 tchd 5-4)
Motrice, also third in this last year, represented the connections of Alleluia. Going on with just under three to run, she could not repel the runner-up before the winner went past the pair of them, but finished clear of the remainder. She came here on the back of a Listed victory over 1m6f at Goodwood, but has been placed without winning on each of her five tries at Group 2 or 3 level.
Bergo(GER) was behind Opinion Poll at both Goodwood and York, and ran creditably again without showing that he is quite good enough to win a race at this level. The longer trip was no problem to this thorough stayer and he kept on again having dropped to last place at the two pole, where he was rether hemmed in on the rail.
Tastahil(IRE) was runner-up in this 12 months ago before taking the final running of the Jockey Club Cup at Newmarket. Seeking to put poor runs at Ascot and Goodwood behind him but joint top on official ratings with Opinion Poll, he raced close up but proved unable to raise his game when the race took shape in the straight.
Blue Bajan(IRE), still penalised for May's Henry II Stakes win, was held up at the back and, although he was close enough with half a mile to run, never landed a blow at the leaders. He has been rather hit and miss this year. (tchd 16-1)
Tactician, the Ebor runner-up, was taking a rise in grade, and a step up in trip too for a horse who had never tacked further than an extended 1m6f (when fifth in the Mallard Handicap on this card a year ago). After setting a sound pace, he gradually faded once tackled in the straight. He is in the Long Distance Cup and the Cesarewitch, but may prove tricky to place from now on. Official explanation: jockey said gelding had no more to give (tchd 6-1)

5885 BARRETT STEEL MAY HILL STKS (GROUP 2) (FILLIES) 1m (S)
3:00 (3:01) (Class 1) 2-Y-0 **£39,697** (£15,050; £7,532; £3,752; £1,883; £945) **Stalls** High

Form RPR
1 **1** **Lyric Of Light**[14] 5445 2-8-12 0.. FrankieDettori 2 111+
(Mahmood Al Zarooni) *hld up towards rr: stdy hdwy over 3f out: trckd ldrs 2f out: led over 1f out: sn rdn: rn green and hung rt appr fnl f: kpt on wl* **9/1**
1 **2** *nk* **Fallen For You**[41] 4552 2-8-12 85.................................... WilliamBuick 8 110
(John Gosden) *hld up in rr: hdwy over 3f out: rdn to chse ldrs over 1f out: chal whn carried rt ent fnl f: sn drvn and one pce towards fin* **2/1**[1]
312 **3** *3 ¼* **Samitar**[13] 5479 2-8-12 105.. JamieSpencer 5 103
(Mick Channon) *hld up towards rr: hdwy wl over 2f out: rdn over 1f out: edgd rt and kpt on ins fnl f: nrst fin* **9/2**[3]
121 **4** *2* **Regal Realm**[13] 5472 2-8-12 102.................................... JimmyFortune 4 98
(Jeremy Noseda) *trckd ldrs: hdwy 1/2-way: rdn and cl up whn n.m.r appr fnl f: sn wknd* **9/4**[2]
01 **5** *4* **Semayyel (IRE)**[14] 5444 2-8-12 0...................................... KierenFallon 3 89
(Clive Brittain) *led and sn clr: rdn along wl over 2f out: drvn and hdd wl over 1f out: wknd* **33/1**
24 **6** *½* **Everlong**[11] 5565 2-8-12 0.. RichardHughes 6 88
(Peter Chapple-Hyam) *racd wd early: trckd ldrs 1/2-way: rdn along 3f out and sn wknd* **25/1**
221 **7** *1 ¾* **Na Zdorovie**[20] 5269 2-8-12 83.. MichaelHills 1 84
(Charles Hills) *chsd ldng pair: rdn along over 2f out: grad wknd* **20/1**
143 **8** *1 ½* **Switcher (IRE)**[20] 5296 2-8-12 99................................ RichardKingscote 7 80
(Tom Dascombe) *chsd ldr: rdn along 3f out: sn wknd* **10/1**

1m 38.39s (-0.91) **Going Correction** 0.0s/f (Good) **8** Ran SP% **112.9**
Speed ratings (Par 104): **104,103,100,98,94 93,92,90**
toteswingers:1&2:£4.90, 2&3:£2.80, 1&3:£3.90 CSF £26.55 TOTE £4.40: £1.30, £1.20, £1.80; EX 15.00 Trifecta £58.00 Pool: £9366.19 - 119.34 winning units..
Owner Godolphin **Bred** Darley **Trained** Newmarket, Suffolk
■ Stewards' Enquiry : Frankie Dettori two-day ban; careless riding (25th-26th Sep)

FOCUS
This looked an informative race, and it was run at a strong gallop, which no doubt helped the first three, who raced in the last three places early on. At least the joint second-best renewal in the last decade with the winner another smart filly for Godolphin.

NOTEBOOK

Lyric Of Light, despite having a bit to prove up in grade, highlighted once again the strength in depth her stable can boast in this division (Dettori commented how they are bringing each other on at home). Travelling best into contention, she hit the front approaching the furlong marker and soon ran green, edging right under pressure and carrying the runner-up over to the stands' side in the process. She won on merit, though, and it will now be a case of finding the right Group 1 for her. Four of the last seven winners of this race have followed up in the Fillies' Mile, but Discourse has already been earmarked for that race, so perhaps Lyric Of Light will go for the Marcel Boussac instead. She's a general 16-1 shot for the Guineas. (op 8-1)

Fallen For You, despite looking green, still picked up well to give the winner plenty to think about from a furlong out. She was carried right and slightly intimidated by the Godolphin filly, which won't have helped her cause, but she looked second-best on the day anyway. With plenty of scope to improve for a winter on her back, it wouldn't be a surprise to see her make the leap to the top level next year, but several bookmakers eased her slightly for the Guineas after this defeat, with Paddy Power going biggest at 20-1. (op 15-8)

Samitar, narrowly beaten in a sales race last time out, had previously taken the Albany Stakes over 6f. This was a big step up in distance for her and, while not quite able to challenge the first two, she ran well enough to suggest she'll be a player in the Rockfel over 7f if given her chance. (op 11-2)

Regal Realm, who took the Prestige Stakes in a bunch finish last time out, was up a furlong in distance in a much stronger-run race, and it found her out. She came to challenge 1 1/2f out but was soon put in her place by the first two (squeezed up slightly in between the pair as well) and was outpaced. The Rockfel might also be an option for her as on this evidence there wouldn't be much point running in the Fillies' Mile. (op 85-40 tchd 2-1)

Semayyel(IRE) set a strong gallop and simply couldn't sustain it. She has ability but needs her energy conserving better. (tchd 40-1 in a place)

Everlong faced a stiff task anyway but her job was made harder by going round the houses. She was brought to the stands' rail soon after the start but the rest of the field stayed up the centre of the track, and her rider then elected to slowly edge over to rejoin them, so ground was given up for no good reason. (op 40-1)

Na Zdorovie, who got off the mark at the third attempt last time, raced closer to the pace than ideal and found this steep rise in class all too much. (tchd 18-1)

Switcher(IRE) raced closest to the leader in what was a strongly-run affair, before stopping quickly 2f out. She's probably had enough for the year. (op 14-1)

5886 FRANK WHITTLE PARTNERSHIP CONDITIONS STKS 7f

3:35 (3:36) (Class 2) 2-Y-O £10,893 (£3,262; £1,631; £815; £407) Stalls Low

Form			Horse	RPR
1	1		**Ektihaam (IRE)**[56] 4053 2-9-2 89 RichardHills 3 (Roger Varian) *trckd ldng pair: hdwy on outer over 2f out: rdn to chal over 1f out: led appr fnl f: sn drvn and edgd rt: kpt on* **8/15**[1]	98+
6	2	4	**Mizwaaj (IRE)**[21] 5254 2-8-12 0 FrankieDettori 1 (Saeed Bin Suroor) *hld up towards rr: hdwy 3f out: swtchd rt to stands' rail and smooth hdwy to ld wl over 1f out: sn jnd and rdn: hdd appr fnl f: hld whn n.m.r ins fnl f* **11/4**[2]	82+
14	3	3/4	**Waseem Faris (IRE)**[35] 4757 2-9-2 82 JamieSpencer 2 (Mick Channon) *hld up in rr: hdwy over 2f out: rdn to chse ldng pair over 1f out: sn drvn and no imp* **20/1**	83
12	4	3 3/4	**Hot Sugar (USA)**[27] 5061 2-9-2 88 PhillipMakin 5 (Kevin Ryan) *led: rdn along 3f out: drvn over 2f out: sn hdd & wknd* **8/1**[3]	73
04	5	10	**Abshir Zain (IRE)**[63] 3795 2-8-12 0 PhilipRobinson 6 (Clive Brittain) *chsd ldr: rdn along wl over 2f out: sn wknd* **50/1**	43

1m 26.66s (0.36) **Going Correction** 0.0s/f (Good) **5 Ran SP% 109.7**

Speed ratings (Par 101): **97,92,91,87,75**

CSF £2.23 TOTE £1.70: £1.10, £1.40; EX 2.20.

Owner Hamdan Al Maktoum **Bred** Bernard Cooke **Trained** Newmarket, Suffolk

FOCUS

Frankel announced himself a Classic contender when bolting up in this race last year. It was unrealistic to expect a similar performance this time around but Ektihaam impressed and could be smart, up to winning Listed races at least. The third helps with the level.

NOTEBOOK

Ektihaam(IRE) won with authority, giving 4lb to the runner-up, and showed enough to suggest he's a smart colt in the making. The bookmakers certainly think so, as he was promptly cut to a best price of 20-1 for the 2000 Guineas, although that might have more to do with the lack of realistic contenders on the scene at the moment. He was briefly challenged by the runner-up approaching the last, but he soon found more to draw clear, while still showing signs of greenness. A long-striding sort with plenty of size who still has some developing to do, despite being by Invincible Spirit he promises to stay a mile (dam won over as far as 1m4f), and the quicker they go the better he'll be as he's a strong traveller. He holds Group-race entries and could run again before the season's out, but his trainer said he'd be equally happy to rough him off for the year. (op 4-6b tchd 8-11 in places)

Mizwaaj(IRE), sixth in the Convivial maiden on his debut, looked to be slightly intimidated when the winner drew up alongside, but it was still a good effort in defeat (albeit in receipt of 4lb) and he should be well up to finding a maiden. (op 10-3 tchd 7-2)

Waseem Faris(IRE) kept on reasonably well considering the concerns about his stamina, and remains open to further improvement having had just the three starts. (op 14-1)

Hot Sugar(USA), stepping up another furlong in distance, took them along to 2f out but then dropped away tamely. (op 6-1 tchd 11-2)

Abshir Zain(IRE), returning from a two-month break, was outclassed and would be better employed from now on in handicaps. (op 33-1)

5887 UNIVERSAL RECYCLING H'CAP 6f 110y

4:10 (4:11) (Class 2) (0-105,99) 3-Y-O+ £12,938 (£3,850; £1,924; £962) Stalls High

Form			Horse	RPR
0210	1		**Sirius Prospect (USA)**[48] 4333 3-8-10 88 JimCrowley 3 (Dean Ivory) *s.i.s and in rr: gd hdwy over 2f out: swtchd rt and rdn to ld over 1f out: kpt on wl* **12/1**	98
6220	2	1 3/4	**Lutine Bell**[44] 4428 4-9-6 94 RichardHughes 2 (Mike Murphy) *s.i.s and in rr: gd hdwy 2f out: chsd ldrs whn rdn and hung bdly rt over 1f out: sn ev ch tl one pce wl ins fnl f* **11/1**	100
4005	3	nk	**Fathsta (IRE)**[5] 5758 6-9-3 91 JamieSpencer 10 (David Simcock) *towards rr: pushed along and hdwy over 2f out: n.m.r and swtchd rt wl over 1f out: sn rdn: styd on ins fnl f: tk 3rd nr line* **6/1**[2]	96
0000	4	hd	**Castles In The Air**[13] 5474 6-9-7 95 DavidNolan 15 (Richard Fahey) *midfield: hdwy wl over 2f out: rdn to chal over 1f out and ev ch tl drvn and one pce ins fnl f* **33/1**	100
0000	5	1 1/4	**Citrus Star (USA)**[13] 5474 4-9-6 94 GeorgeBaker 8 (Chris Wall) *hld up towards rr: swtchd lft ahd hdwy 2f out: rdn to chse ldrs whn carried lft over 1f out: kpt on ins fnl f* **16/1**	95
2155	6	nk	**Kanaf (IRE)**[23] 5180 4-9-10 98 RichardHills 1 (Ed Dunlop) *trckd ldrs: hdwy over 2f out: rdn and ev ch over 1f out: sn drvn and one pce ins fnl f* **4/1**[1]	98+
2511	7	3/4	**Grissom (IRE)**[27] 5032 5-9-4 92 DavidAllan 9 (Tim Easterby) *hld up towards rr: hdwy and nt clr run wl over 1f out: sn swtchd lft and rdn: kpt on ins fnl f: nrst fin* **15/2**	92+
1231	8	1 1/4	**Below Zero (IRE)**[6] 5746 4-9-11 99 6ex KierenFallon 12 (Mark Johnston) *chsd ldrs: rdn along 2f out: drvn wl over 1f out and grad wknd* **8/1**	93
6030	9	hd	**Docofthebay (IRE)**[13] 5474 7-9-7 95 (p) GrahamGibbons 5 (David Nicholls) *midfield: effrt over 2f out: sn rdn and n.d* **10/1**	88
005	10	2	**Kuanyao (IRE)**[27] 5043 5-9-3 91 JimmyFortune 13 (Peter Makin) *nvr bttr than midfield* **20/1**	79
0054	11	3/4	**Fireback**[12] 5508 4-9-0 88 (v[1]) DavidProbert 11 (Andrew Balding) *prom: rdn along over 2f out: grad wknd* **16/1**	73+
1100	12	nse	**Thunderball**[27] 5032 5-8-11 92 (b) LeonnaMayor[(7)] 6 (David Nicholls) *cl up: led 1/2-way: rdn over 2f out: hung bdly lft and hdd over 1f out: wknd* **28/1**	77+
0013	13	1/2	**Noble Citizen (USA)**[48] 4314 6-9-5 93 (b) PhillipMakin 4 (David Simcock) *chsd ldrs: rdn along over 2f out: sn wknd* **7/1**[3]	77+
1300	14	8	**Swiss Franc**[23] 5180 6-9-7 95 WilliamBuick 14 (David Elsworth) *led to 1/2-way: prom tl rdn along and wkng whn hmpd wl over 1f out* **16/1**	55+
0000	15	7	**Prince Shaun (IRE)**[44] 4428 6-9-2 90 EddieAhern 7 (Richard Guest) *s.i.s: a in rr* **100/1**	29

1m 18.23s (-1.67) **Going Correction** 0.0s/f (Good)

WFA 3 from 4yo+ 2lb **15 Ran SP% 124.6**

Speed ratings (Par 109): **109,107,106,106,105 104,103,102,102,99 99,98,98,89,81**

toteswingers:1&2:£24.90, 2&3:£10.50, 1&3:£19.00 CSF £137.29 CT £906.30 TOTE £14.70: £4.50, £3.60, £2.60; EX 192.20 Trifecta £1729.10 Part won. Pool of £2336.71 - 0.20 winning units..

Owner Miss N Yarrow **Bred** Brookdale And Dr Ted Folkerth **Trained** Radlett, Herts

■ Stewards' Enquiry : Leonna Mayor three day ban; careless riding (25th-27th Sep)

FOCUS

The third running of this good handicap, run over an intermediate trip. The gallop was a strong one and the first three home all came from the rear.

NOTEBOOK

Sirius Prospect(USA) was the only 3yo in the line-up. Racing off the pace down the centre following a slow start, he picked up to lead a furlong out and was well in command from there. He had looked a nice prospect when winning at Windsor in July and his subsequent defeat at Newmarket can be attributed to the race coming too soon. Although not straightforward, he is getting it together now and rates a useful sprint handicap prospect for next season. (op 16-1)

Lutine Bell raced without the regular headgear for the first time in over a year. Dropped in at the back and travelling strongly, he cut through the field late on but the winner was in the clear. This was a fine run off a career-high mark, but despite numerous good efforts he is without a win on turf since scoring off 70 in July last year. (op 14-1)

Fathsta(IRE) is effective at both 6f and 7f, so this trip was fine. Making a quick return to the track after his fifth at York on Saturday, he had a lot of ground to make up at the two pole but finished well. This was a good effort with Ayr in mind. (op 15-2)

Castles In The Air was runner-up in this race in 2009, when running off 5lb lower, and his stable also won the race last year. Things have not been going his way this season but he ran a solid race at Ascot two runs back. Chasing the pace, he came under pressure at halfway but stuck on and was momentarily in second before the closers went by. (op 28-1)

Citrus Star(USA), beaten favourite in this last year, was another who had not been at his best this season. He was starting his run when he was carried badly across the track by the hanging Thunderball, and did well to finish fifth in the circumstances. (op 14-1)

Kanaf(IRE) had come in for plenty of support for Saturday's Portland Handicap, following a pair of eye-catching runs where he failed to get the breaks, but his connections opted to run him here over a furlong or so more. Drawn widest, he raced in the centre prior to edging over and had his chance, before fading late on. He gets 6f, but this trip looked to stretch him. (op 9-2 tchd 5-1 in a place)

Grissom(IRE) came here on a hat-trick, but was up another 4lb. He found himself trapped in on the approach to the furlong pole, but ran on well and would have finished closer to the placed horses with a trouble-free passage. Official explanation: jockey said gelding was denied a clear run (op 7-1 tchd 13-2)

Below Zero(IRE) has developed into a smart performer, but his good recent efforts had been from the front and he could not get to the lead here. He is due for a 6lb hike to a mark of 105 now, which won't make him easy to place. (op 6-1)

Kuanyao(IRE) hinted at a return to form at Newbury, but was unable to step up on that. (op 16-1)

Thunderball was clear in the centre with two furlongs to run, but then began to hang badly to his left, his rider not helping by persisting to use the stick in her incorrect hand. Someting may have been amiss with the gelding. (op 25-1)

Noble Citizen(USA)'s best efforts tend to come at Ascot. His highest winning rating is 87 and he has been beaten more than 20 times from marks in the 90s. (op 11-1)

Swiss Franc Official explanation: jockey said gelding hung right

5888 MOLLART COX CLASSIFIED STKS 1m 2f 60y

4:40 (4:42) (Class 3) 3-Y-O+

£8,092 (£2,423; £1,211; £605; £302; £152) Stalls Low

Form			Horse	RPR
1	1		**Beaten Up**[146] 1415 3-8-11 85 RichardHughes 7 (William Haggas) *trckd ldr: smooth hdwy 3f out: led wl over 1f out: pushed clr fnl f: comf* **9/4**[1]	106+
6142	2	4	**Mashaaref**[62] 3844 3-8-11 85 RichardHills 12 (Roger Varian) *trckd ldrs: hdwy 3f out: rdn to chse wnr over 1f out: drvn ent fnl f and kpt on same pce* **4/1**[2]	93
516-	3	3 1/2	**Valid Reason**[177] 7876 4-9-4 80 JimCrowley 9 (Dean Ivory) *led: rdn along 3f out: drvn over 2f out: hdd wl over 1f out and sn one pce* **66/1**	86
2112	4	3/4	**Kenyan Cat**[27] 5062 4-8-10 80 NeilFarley[(5)] 15 (Ed McMahon) *in tch: hdwy to chse ldrs over 2f out and sn rdn: drvn over 1f out: no imp* **16/1**	82
30	5	nk	**Audemar (IRE)**[41] 4537 5-9-4 85 TedDurcan 3 (Edward Vaughan) *chsd ldrs: rdn along over 3f out: drvn 2f out and grad wknd* **20/1**	84
5052	6	hd	**Art History (IRE)**[7] 5693 3-8-11 84 WilliamBuick 11 (Mark Johnston) *towards rr: hdwy on wd outside 3f out: rdn along over 2f out: kpt on appr fnl f: nrst fin* **12/1**	84+
2310	7	2	**King Kurt (IRE)**[41] 4553 3-8-11 83 PhillipMakin 13 (Kevin Ryan) *nvr bttr than midfield* **25/1**	80
0000	8	nse	**Snow Dancer (IRE)**[7] 5686 7-9-1 81 DavidAllan 4 (Hugh McWilliams) *hld up in rr: sme hdwy 3f out: rdn along and n.m.r over 2f out: n.d* **33/1**	77
1004	9	3/4	**Pass Muster**[26] 5078 4-9-1 85 MichaelO'Connell[(3)] 14 (Ollie Pears) *hld up towards rr: sme hdwy 3f out: rdn along over 2f out: n.d* **14/1**	79
0200	10	2 1/2	**Dhaular Dhar (IRE)**[7] 5686 9-9-4 84 DanielTudhope 5 (Jim Goldie) *hld up in rr: sme hdwy over 2f out: sn rdn and n.d* **20/1**	74
6502	11	1/2	**Mirrored**[10] 5593 5-9-4 85 DuranFentiman 10 (Tim Easterby) *dwlt: a towards rr* **10/1**	73
	12	1 3/4	**Red Anthem**[57] 4-9-4 84 JimmyFortune 17 (Gerard Butler) *awkward s: a in rr* **50/1**	70

0 **13** *1* **Jawaab (IRE)**[6] 5729 7-8-11 84......................................(e) JasonHart(7) 1 68
(Richard Guest) *in tch: rdn along over 3f out: drvn over 2f out and sn wknd* **40/1**

053 **14** *1 ½* **Viva Vettori**[13] 5483 7-9-4 85... JamieSpencer 2 65
(David Elsworth) *a towards rr* **6/1**[3]

0002 **15** *1* **Camerooney**[39] 4601 8-9-1 84... DaleSwift(3) 8 63
(Brian Ellison) *a bhd* **40/1**

6-10 **16** *1* **Dumbarton (IRE)**[27] 5049 3-8-11 82................................ KierenFallon 16 61
(Sir Michael Stoute) *s.i.s and in rr: effrt and sme hdwy over 4f out: sn rdn and wknd* **9/1**

2m 8.13s (-1.27) **Going Correction** +0.05s/f (Good)
WFA 3 from 4yo+ 7lb **16** Ran SP% **129.0**
Speed ratings (Par 107): **107,103,101,100,100 100,98,98,97,95 95,93,93,91,91 90**
toteswingers:1&2:£3.20, 2&3:£60.60, 1&3:£35.00 CSF £10.09 TOTE £3.40: £1.70, £2.20, £16.00; EX 15.00 Trifecta £1391.00 Part won. Pool of £1879.85 - 0.94 winning units..
Owner B Haggas **Bred** J B Haggas **Trained** Newmarket, Suffolk

FOCUS

In theory this should have been a very competitive race on paper, as just 6lb separated the entire field based on adjusted official ratings, but the market suggested otherwise and the finish was dominated by the first two in the betting - a couple of lightly raced 3yos who showed themselves to be nicely handicapped. They went a dawdle early on and the pace held up.

NOTEBOOK

Beaten Up, the least exposed runner in the line-up having only had the one previous start, when successful at Ripon back in April, travelled up going supremely well 2f out and his rider only had to nudge him out to win by a clear margin. In hindsight this half-brother to Harris Tweed was thrown in and, while the bare form might be a little unreliable, he can still expect a significant rise in the weights now. However, he's unexposed and should be able to deal with it. It's likely he'll get further in time. (op 11-4 tchd 10-3 in places)

Mashaaref, returning from a two-month break, was well placed tracking the winner but had no chance with him in the closing stages. He beat the rest well enough, though, and should be able to go close in a handicap off around his current mark. (op 11-2 tchd 6-1)

Valid Reason, last seen running over hurdles in March, was worst in at the weights, albeit not by a great deal, but he enjoyed the run of things out in front and perhaps his finishing position flatters him a touch. (op 100-1)

Kenyan Cat got a bit warm beforehand and was a keen in the race, but he was closer to the pace than some and put up a fair effort.

Audemar(IRE) is arguably better over shorter so the steady early pace probably helped him preserve his stamina. (tchd 22-1)

Art History(IRE) deserves some credit for doing best of those trying to close from well off the pace. (op 11-1)

King Kurt(IRE), who has won over 1m4f, no doubt found this steadily run affair all against him.

Viva Vettori raced far too keenly off the steady early gallop, and that ruined any chance he had. (tchd 13-2)

Dumbarton(IRE) ran way below form and this couldn't have been his true running. (op 11-1)

T/Jkpt: £195,451.41 to a £1 stake. Pool of £275,283.72 - 1.00 winning tickets. T/Plt: £193.40 to a £1 stake. Pool of £165,302.64 - 623.74 winning tickets T/Qpdt: £15.30 to a £1 stake. Pool of £10,883.00 - 523.00 winning tickets. JR

5275 SANDOWN (R-H)

Friday, September 9

OFFICIAL GOING: Good (good to soft in places on sprint course)

Wind: Light, half against Weather: Cloudy, quite humid

5889 TRANSLLOYD DEVELOPMENTS SUPPORTING THE RACEHORSE SANCTUARY E B F MAIDEN STKS 5f 6y

2:15 (2:16) (Class 5) 2-Y-O **£3,881** (£1,155; £577; £288) **Stalls** Low

Form RPR

02 **1** **Indian Tinker**[17] 5351 2-9-3 0.. ShaneKelly 12 81
(Robert Cowell) *hld up bhd ldrs: prog to chse ldng pair 2f out: rdn and [illegible]* **12/1**

3304 **2** *½* **Ballesteros**[7] 5681 2-9-3 82.. MartinDwyer 11 79
(Brian Meehan) *taken down early and ponied to s: spd fr wd draw to press ldr: led 2f out: drvn fnl f: hdd and no ex last 75yds* **5/2**[1]

04 **3** *2* **Venetian View (IRE)**[24] 5133 2-9-3 0............................ FergusSweeney 7 72+
(Gary Moore) *hld up wl in rr: stdy prog gng wl fr 2f out: nudged along and styd on to take 3rd nr fin* **66/1**

0 **4** *¾* **Elite**[84] 3132 2-8-12 0... NeilCallan 10 64
(Sir Michael Stoute) *s.i.s: sn chsd ldrs: outpcd fr 2f out: kpt on ins fnl f: nt gng pce to chal* **8/1**

06 **5** *nk* **Larwood (IRE)**[26] 5077 2-9-3 0... DaneO'Neill 8 68+
(Henry Candy) *stdd s: hld up wl in rr: pushed along 2f out: styd on steadily fr over 1f out: nrst fin* **12/1**

0 **6** *½* **Sandfrankskipsgo**[40] 4580 2-9-3 0.................................... IanMongan 1 66
(Brett Johnson) *led against rail: rdn and hdd 2f out: lost 2nd and wknd ins fnl f* **25/1**

5 **7** *½* **Beach Candy (IRE)**[18] 5323 2-8-12 0...................................... PatDobbs 3 62+
(Richard Hannon) *chsd ldrs against rail: pushed along after 2f: nt clr run and swtchd lft 2f out: drvn and kpt on one pce* **4/1**[2]

8 *hd* **Million Faces** 2-8-12 0... SteveDrowne 5 64+
(Rae Guest) *stdd s: hld up wl in rr: nt clr run and swtchd lft wl over 1f out: prog into midfield after but hanging: kpt on steadily: do bttr* **11/1**

9 *nk* **Shamakat** 2-8-12 0.. WilliamCarson 6 58+
(Rae Guest) *stdd s: hld up in last: taken to outer and pushed along 2f out: styd on: nt disgracd* **40/1**

66 **10** *¾* **Blackburn**[9] 5613 2-9-3 0.. AdamKirby 2 60
(Clive Cox) *pressed ldr to 1/2-way: rdn and steadily wknd fnl 2f* **12/1**

06 **11** *1 ¼* **Look At Me Now**[23] 5174 2-9-0 0................................ MatthewDavies(3) 14 55
(Jim Boyle) *hld up wl in rr on outer: pushed along and sme prog over 1f out: no hdwy and fdd ins fnl f* **100/1**

6 **12** *8* **Surrey Spirit**[17] 5347 2-8-12 0.. ChrisCatlin 4 22
(Harry Dunlop) *a in rr: struggling 2f out: t.o* **80/1**

00 **13** *nse* **Fallible**[13] 5480 2-9-3 0.. JamesDoyle 13 26
(Tony Carroll) *racd wd: pushed up to chse ldrs: wknd 2f out: t.o* **150/1**

2 **14** *2 ¾* **Poseidon Grey (IRE)**[9] 5632 2-9-3 0.................................. JackMitchell 9 17
(Walter Swinburn) *pressed ldrs: wknd rapidly over 2f out: t.o* **6/1**[3]

63.34 secs (1.74) **Going Correction** +0.175s/f (Good) **14** Ran SP% **116.0**
Speed ratings (Par 95): **93,92,89,87,87 86,85,85,84,83 81,68,68,64**
toteswingers:1&2:£9.00, 2&3:£40.20, 1&3:£90.50 CSF £39.79 TOTE £13.50: £3.90, £1.10, £10.70; EX 59.00.
Owner J Sargeant **Bred** R S Cockerill (farms) Ltd **Trained** Six Mile Bottom, Cambs

FOCUS

Rail dolled out from 7f to 2.5f and drop in at that point adding 5yds to distances on Round course. A decent juvenile maiden in which the pacesetters appeared to go too fast. There were eyecatchers aplenty and the race should produce its share of winners. The runner-up helps with the opening level of the form. The time was 1.25 seconds slower than the following sprint handicap for older horses.

NOTEBOOK

Indian Tinker, brushed aside by a potentially decent sort at Yarmouth last time, may have been helped by the easier ground and certainly relished the stiff finish. He'll be suited by 6f and ought to get competitive in nurseries, with his trainer expecting further improvement. (op 11-1 tchd 10-1)

Ballesteros is flattered by his official rating, but still seems capable of fair form, looking the winner for much of the final 2f here only to be reeled in late on. (tchd 3-1 in places)

Venetian View(IRE) ◆showed much-improved form on this third run and gave the impression he'd have gone close with more vigorous riding. He was strong at the finish, taking third, and looks almost certain to win races at the right level, although a potentially reasonable handicap mark has probably been blown.

Elite, keen when disappointing over 6f on debut, was going on well following a sluggish start and may be best kept to this distance for the time being. She can win a small maiden.

Larwood(IRE) ◆ looks a nice type and, having had only one behind with 2f to run, he really started to motor home once switched. He has a long, raking stride and will benefit from a stiffer test in future. One to keep on side. (op 10-1)

Sandfrankskipsgo had learned plenty from his first start and showed plenty of pace before fading. Faster ground ought to help in future.

Beach Candy(IRE) didn't get the clearest of runs and can be rated better than the bare form. (op 5-1 tchd 11-2)

Million Faces ◆, from a sprinting family her yard knows well, was another to give a noteworthy performance. Allowed to find her stride early, she found herself quite a way back and was then stopped in her tracks when making headway 2f out. Her chance had gone, but she stayed on nicely without being given a hard time and should learn plenty from the experience. Her rider reported she suffered interference at the start. Official explanation: jockey said filly suffered interference at the start (op 14-1)

Shamakat, bred to need further and slowest into stride, shaped with some promise also and should improve. (tchd 50-1)

Blackburn slowly dropped away, but is now qualified for a mark.

Poseidon Grey(IRE), another up there early, was too keen and failed to build on his debut effort. (op 5-1)

5890 CAPITAL STOCK SUPPORTING THE RACEHORSE SANCTUARY H'CAP 5f 6y

2:45 (2:54) (Class 5) (0-75,75) 3-Y-O+ **£2,587** (£770; £384; £192) **Stalls** Low

Form RPR

0500 **1** **Rafaaf (IRE)**[14] 5423 3-8-10 65.. NickyMackay 8 78
(Robert Eddery) *hld up in midfield: prog on outer 2f out: rdn to ld last 150yds: styd on strly* **20/1**

4-51 **2** *1 ¾* **Gooseberry Bush**[31] 4882 4-8-11 65................................ SteveDrowne 11 72
(Peter Makin) *trckd ldrs: stdy prog 2f out: rdn to ld 1f out: sn hdd: styd on but outpcd* **15/2**

2140 **3** *2 ¼* **Mata Hari Blue**[17] 5338 5-9-0 68....................................(t) MartinDwyer 2 67
(John Holt) *pressed ldrs: rdn to chal jst over 1f out: wl outpcd fnl f* **11/2**[1]

6040 **4** *½* **Danzoe (IRE)**[8] 5640 4-8-12 66.. IanMongan 15 63
(Christine Dunnett) *stdd s: dropped in fr wd draw and hld up last: effrt 1/2-way: plld out wd and rdn wl over 1f out: styd on fnl f: nrst fin* **25/1**

030 **5** *shd* **Leadenhall Lass (IRE)**[18] 5326 5-8-4 63............. JemmaMarshall(5) 13 60
(Pat Phelan) *hld up wl in rr: pushed along 2f out: styd on wl ins fnl f: nrst fin* **20/1**

1550 **6** *shd* **Equuleus Pictor**[9] 5616 7-9-7 75..................................(b1) CathyGannon 4 71
(John Spearing) *w ldr: led over 3f out: hrd rdn and hdd 1f out: wknd* **9/1**

0035 **7** *2 ¾* **Cardinal**[14] 5451 6-9-5 73.. ShaneKelly 12 59
(Robert Cowell) *wl in rr: rdn and dropped to last pair 1/2-way: n.d after: styd on ins fnl f* **6/1**[2]

1550 **8** *1 ½* **Shostakovich (IRE)**[11] 5561 3-8-13 68......................(tp) JamesDoyle 1 49
(Sylvester Kirk) *rdn to stay in tch bhd ldrs over 3f out: nvr gng wl after: fdd over 1f out* **10/1**

2530 **9** *nk* **Boogie Waltzer**[13] 5468 4-9-1 72.............................(t) RyanClark(3) 3 52
(Stuart Williams) *racd against rail: led to over 3f out: styd w ldrs tl wknd 1f out* **15/2**

[illegible] **10** *shd* **Triple Dream**[4] 5781 6-9-1 72...........................(tp) SeanLevey(3) 10 52
(Milton Bradley) *trckd ldrs: rdn 2f out: sn wknd* **[illegible]**

0000 **11** *2 ¼* **Plume**[25] 5100 4-9-4 72..(b1) JackMitchell 7 44
(Roger Teal) *checked by vet bef s: awkward leaving stalls and slowly away: wl in rr: effrt and sme prog 1/2-way: wknd and eased over 1f out* **25/1**

-016 **12** *¾* **Sulis Minerva (IRE)**[31] 4886 4-8-11 72...............(t) RaulDaSilva(7) 14 41
(Jeremy Gask) *stdd s: hld up in last pair and racd wd: nudged along 2f out: no prog* **16/1**

62.09 secs (0.49) **Going Correction** +0.175s/f (Good)
WFA 3 from 4yo+ 1lb **12** Ran SP% **107.9**
Speed ratings (Par 103): **103,100,96,95,95 95,91,88,88,88 84,83**
toteswingers:1&2:£14.20, 2&3:£7.10, 1&3:£30.20 CSF £135.24 CT £825.59 TOTE £27.70: £6.30, £2.00, £2.30; EX 171.20.
Owner Aitken & Phillips **Bred** Oscar Stud **Trained** Newmarket, Suffolk
■ Stratton Banker was withdrawn (12/1, unruly in stalls). R4 applies.

FOCUS

An ordinary sprint handicap that was delayed after Stratton Banker ducked down under the stalls and got lodged for a brief time. The winning time was 1.25 seconds quicker than the opening juvenile maiden.

Cardinal Official explanation: trainer said horse lost a front shoe

Sulis Minerva(IRE) Official explanation: trainer said filly had a breathing problem

5891 PKF BRITISH STALLION STUDS E B F MAIDEN STKS 1m 14y

3:20 (3:24) (Class 5) 2-Y-O **£3,881** (£1,155; £577; £288) **Stalls** Low

Form RPR

02 **1** **Emmuska**[28] 4992 2-8-12 0... PatDobbs 15 76
(Richard Hannon) *trckd ldr: rdn to ld over 1f out: drvn ins fnl f: jst hld on* **9/1**[3]

2 *nse* **Shantaram** 2-9-3 0... RobertHavlin 10 81+
(John Gosden) *hld up in last trio: stdy prog on outer over 2f out: pushed along over 1f out: r.o to take 2nd ins fnl f: clsd on wnr: jst failed* **11/2**[2]

3 *2* **Cape Rainbow** 2-9-3 0.. DaneO'Neill 11 76
(Mark Usher) *hld up towards rr: pushed along and prog on outer 2f out: styd on ins fnl f: tk 3rd last stride* **66/1**

2 **4** *hd* **El Greco (IRE)**[51] 4213 2-9-3 0.. NeilCallan 9 76
(Sir Michael Stoute) *trckd ldrs in 6th: prog to chse ldng pair over 1f out: sn rdn and nt qckn: wl hld ins fnl f* **4/7**[1]

50 **5** *1 ¼* **Drummond**[56] 4053 2-9-3 0... AdamKirby 3 73
(Clive Cox) *led: rdn and hdd over 1f out: fdd ins fnl f* **16/1**

00 **6** ½ **Cades Reef (IRE)**[20] 5269 2-9-3 0 .... LiamKeniry 14 72
(Andrew Balding) *trckd ldng pair: rdn 2f out: lost 3rd and grad fdd over 1f out* **25/1**

7 ½ **Eshaab (USA)** 2-9-3 0 .... ShaneKelly 4 71+
(Ed Dunlop) *dwlt: hld up in rr: pushed along on inner and kpt on fnl 2f: nrst fin* **40/1**

5 **8** 1 ½ **Tushuk Tash (USA)**[11] 5536 2-9-3 0 .... SamHitchcott 8 67
(Mick Channon) *in tch in midfield: shkn up over 2f out: kpt on same pce after: n.d* **40/1**

0 **9** 9 **Season Spirit**[28] 4996 2-9-3 0 .... SteveDrowne 13 47+
(James Given) *s.s: pushed up to go prom after 2f: rdn wl over 2f out: wknd rapidly over 1f out* **100/1**

60 **10** ½ **Mitch Rapp (USA)**[21] 5254 2-9-3 0 .... ChrisCatlin 6 46
(Harry Dunlop) *sn detached in last pair: shkn up and no prog over 2f out: bhd after* **50/1**

00 **11** hd **King Fong**[8] 5637 2-9-0 0 .... KieranO'Neill(3) 16 45
(John Ryan) *towards rr and rn in snatches: effrt over 2f out: wknd over 1f out* **150/1**

12 3 ¾ **Mawaqeet (USA)** 2-9-3 0 .... TadhgO'Shea 12 36+
(Sir Michael Stoute) *s.v.s: rn green and detached in last: nvr a factor* **14/1**

13 hd **Autarch (USA)** 2-9-3 0 .... MartinDwyer 1 36
(Amanda Perrett) *dwlt: sn prom on inner: rdn and wknd rapidly 2f out* **20/1**

1m 46.07s (2.77) **Going Correction** +0.075s/f (Good) **13** Ran SP% **120.2**
Speed ratings (Par 95): **89,88,86,86,85 85,84,83,74,73 73,69,69**
toteswingers:1&2:£5.40, 2&3:£26.20, 1&3:£56.40 CSF £55.15 TOTE £11.90: £2.30, £2.10, £5.90; EX 53.30.
Owner Martin A Collins **Bred** Martin A Collins **Trained** East Everleigh, Wilts

FOCUS
A fair juvenile maiden.

NOTEBOOK
Emmuska has improved with each run and was well suited by the step up to 1m. She wouldn't want to go any further for the time being and can make an impact in nurseries. (op 8-1 tchd 10-1)
Shantaram ◆, a brother to 2,000 Guineas third Gan Amhras, is in the Racing Post Trophy and Derby. A touch keen early, he was settled towards the back and the winner ended up with quite a head start, but began to run on nicely down the outside from over 2f out and, whilst understandable connections would want him looked after on debut, it likely would have taken no more than one light tap for him to make a winning debut. A fine-looking son of Galileo, he's going to relish 1m2f in time, but can win a maiden over this trip first. (op 15-2)
Cape Rainbow, half-brother to a 6f Listed winner, is from a yard whose juvenile often improve plenty for a run, so this had to go down as a hugely encouraging effort. Although bred to be no more than a miler on pedigree, he was strong at the finish of his race and a minor maiden can surely come his way.
El Greco(IRE), who found only one too good in a 7f course maiden on debut (form mixed), should have relished the extra yardage, but having travelled well he couldn't pick up. This was most disappointing. (op 8-13)
Drummond is now qualified for a mark. (op 18-1)
Cades Reef(IRE) ◆ is now qualified for a mark, a sphere he should do much better in.
Eshaab(USA), entered in the Derby, kept on under an educational ride.
Mawaqeet(USA), a stablemate of the disappointing favourite, was weak in the market, soon trailed following a slow start whilst also running green, and made no headway. Evidently badly in need of the experience, this expensive purchase should improve markedly, but obviously needs to.

5892 SUNGARD SECURITIES FINANCE H'CAP 1m 14y
3:55 (3:55) (Class 4) (0-85,85) 3-Y-O **£4,528** (£1,347; £673; £336) **Stalls** Low

Form RPR

2402 **1** **Sure Route**[25] 5113 3-9-4 **82** .... PatDobbs 10 97
(Richard Hannon) *t.k.h: hld up bhd ldrs: prog over 2f out: rdn to ld over 1f out: hrd pressed last 100yds: hld on wl* **6/1**[2]

-263 **2** nk **Double Dealer**[12] 5516 3-9-0 **83** .... AntiocoMurgia(5) 9 97+
(Mahmood Al Zarooni) *stdd s: hld up in last trio: prog on outer over 2f out: rdn over 1f out: wnt 2nd ins fnl f and clsd on wnr: nrly upsides last 75yds: n.g.t* **6/1**[2]

5613 **3** 4 **Arabian Star (IRE)**[29] 4959 3-9-2 **80** .... LiamKeniry 4 85
(Andrew Balding) *trckd ldr 2f: styd prom: rdn to chal over 1f out: fdd ins fnl f but hld on for 3rd* **10/1**

6630 **4** hd **Muntasib (USA)**[27] 5049 3-9-4 **82** .... MartinDwyer 5 87
(Marcus Tregoning) *hld up in rr: prog towards inner over 2f out: clsd on ldrs to chal over 1f out: fdd ins fnl f* **14/1**

0602 **5** 3 ¼ **Mutajare (IRE)**[27] 5056 3-9-2 **80** .... TadhgO'Shea 8 77
(Mark Johnston) *trckd ldr after 2f: led 3f out but pressed after: hdd over 1f out: wknd qckly ins fnl f* **16/1**

6205 **6** ½ **Cruiser**[14] 5450 3-9-7 **85** .... NeilCallan 11 84+
(William Muir) *t.k.h: trckd ldrs: cl up whn rdn and nt qckn over 2f out: renewed effrt and pressing ldrs whn squeezed out over 1f out: nt rcvr and wknd* **9/2**[1]

2253 **7** ½ **Focail Maith**[28] 5004 3-8-4 **71** oh1 ....(b) KieranO'Neill(3) 1 66
(John Ryan) *settled midfield: 8th whn hmpd on inner 1/2-way: nvr really rcvrd: struggling 2f out: kpt on* **14/1**

0551 **8** ¾ **Orientalist**[11] 5547 3-9-0 **78** 6ex .... CathyGannon 6 71
(Eve Johnson Houghton) *mostly in last trio and nt gng wl: no prog over 2f out: kpt on ins fnl f: no ch* **8/1**

2100 **9** hd **Whistle On By**[37] 4665 3-9-2 **80** .... WilliamCarson 3 73
(Charles Hills) *led: narrowly hdd 3f out but kpt pressing ldr: stl upsides over 1f out: sn wknd rapidly* **20/1**

6-33 **10** ½ **Looking On**[14] 5449 3-8-11 **75** .... DaneO'Neill 12 66
(Henry Candy) *trckd ldrs on outer: cl enough 3f out: wknd 2f out* **8/1**

1122 **11** 12 **Hurricane Lady (IRE)**[34] 4807 3-8-13 **80** .... SeanLevey(3) 2 44
(Walter Swinburn) *prom: rdn 3f out: wknd rapidly 2f out* **7/1**[3]

3525 **12** 15 **Cocohatchee**[43] 4459 3-8-11 **75** ....(p) IanMongan 7 —
(Pat Phelan) *hld up in last: scrubbed along over 3f out: no prog: eased over 1f out: t.o* **40/1**

1m 42.62s (-0.68) **Going Correction** +0.075s/f (Good) **12** Ran SP% **117.0**
Speed ratings (Par 103): **106,105,101,101,98 97,97,96,96,95 83,68**
toteswingers:1&2:£10.90, 2&3:£17.70, 1&3:£17.30 CSF £41.30 CT £361.25 TOTE £8.50: £2.30, £2.60, £3.80; EX 51.00.
Owner Malih Lahej Al Basti **Bred** Malih L Al Basti **Trained** East Everleigh, Wilts

FOCUS
The front pair drew 4l clear in what looked a fairly ordinary handicap.
Orientalist Official explanation: jockey said gelding was never travelling
Cocohatchee Official explanation: jockey said colt was never travelling

5893 WILDWOOD GOLF & COUNTRY CLUB H'CAP (SUPPORTING THE RACEHORSE SANCTUARY) 1m 2f 7y
4:30 (4:30) (Class 4) (0-80,80) 3-Y-O+ **£5,175** (£1,540; £769; £384) **Stalls** Low

Form RPR

1632 **1** **Icebuster**[11] 5560 3-8-11 **72** .... JamesMillman 3 89
(Rod Millman) *dwlt: hld up: last 1/2-way: stl there 3f out: swtchd out wd jst over 2f out: rapid prog to ld over 1f out: sn rdn wl clr* **7/4**[1]

2-41 **2** 6 **Dean Swift**[29] 4956 3-9-5 **80** .... MartinDwyer 12 85
(Brian Meehan) *hld up in midfield: prog fr 3f out: rdn to chal over 1f out: unavailing chse of wnr after* **8/1**[3]

0546 **3** 2 **Wiggy Smith**[11] 5546 12-9-7 **75** .... DaneO'Neill 10 76
(Henry Candy) *stdd s: hld up in last trio: prog on outer over 2f out: styd on to take 3rd ins fnl f but no ch* **12/1**

1143 **4** 1 **Broughtons Swinger**[11] 5568 4-8-10 **67** .... AdamBeschizza(3) 5 66
(Willie Musson) *hld up towards rr: prog over 2f out: drvn to chse ldrs over 1f out: kpt on: wl outpcd* **9/1**

6446 **5** 1 **Kingarrick**[15] 5407 3-8-11 **72** .... FergusSweeney 8 73+
(Eve Johnson Houghton) *trckd ldrs: lost pl 3f out then repeatedly hmpd: rdn and plugged on whn fnlly in the clr ins fnl f* **16/1**

-536 **6** 5 **Penchesco (IRE)**[10] 5582 6-8-12 **66** ....(b[1]) PatDobbs 1 53
(Amanda Perrett) *dwlt: hld up in last trio: effrt gng strly jst over 2f out: cajoled along over 1f out and fnd nthing: n.d* **33/1**

5003 **7** 2 **Stentorian (IRE)**[42] 4489 3-9-2 **77** .... NeilCallan 7 60
(Mark Johnston) *nvr really gng sweetly but chsd ldrs: drvn to chal over 2f out: wknd over 1f out* **20/1**

55-6 **8** 2 ¼ **Spirit Of Gondree (IRE)**[21] 5242 3-8-6 **67** .... ChrisCatlin 2 46
(John Dunlop) *nvr bttr than midfield: u.p wl over 2f out: no imp over 1f out: wknd* **7/1**[2]

0023 **9** ½ **Blue Spartan (IRE)**[25] 5110 6-8-13 **70** .... LouisBeuzelin(3) 6 48
(Brian Meehan) *led 1f: chsd ldr: drvn 3f out: stl chalng 2f out: sn wknd rapidly* **12/1**

5002 **10** ¾ **Understory (USA)**[33] 4825 4-9-7 **78** .... KieranO'Neill(3) 4 54
(Tim McCarthy) *trckd ldrs in abt 4th: gng strly over 3f out: prog to ld over 2f out: hdd over 1f out: wknd rapidly* **25/1**

-006 **11** 2 ¼ **Sohcahtoa (IRE)**[77] 3354 5-9-1 **72** .... SeanLevey(3) 11 44
(Robert Mills) *prom: chsd ldng pair 1/2-way: rdn and cl enough jst over 2f out: sn wknd rapidly* **16/1**

2064 **12** 3 ¼ **Vimiero (USA)**[13] 5495 4-9-9 **77** ....(p) AdamKirby 9 42
(Walter Swinburn) *led after 1f at str pce: hdd & wknd rapidly over 2f out* **9/1**

2m 9.86s (-0.64) **Going Correction** +0.075s/f (Good)
WFA 3 from 4yo+ 7lb **12** Ran SP% **118.7**
Speed ratings (Par 105): **105,100,98,97,97 93,91,89,89,88 86,84**
toteswingers:1&2:£3.60, 2&3:£18.40, 1&3:£7.00 CSF £15.21 CT £133.83 TOTE £2.30: £1.40, £2.90, £3.90; EX 15.30.
Owner The Links Partnership **Bred** Cheveley Park Stud Ltd **Trained** Kentisbeare, Devon
■ Stewards' Enquiry : Dane O'Neill two-day ban; careless riding (25th-26th Sep)

FOCUS
The gallop was a good one in this 1m2f handicap.
Kingarrick Official explanation: jockey said gelding was denied a clear run

5894 LONDON BUSINESS CENTRES SUPPORTING THE RACEHORSE SANCTUARY H'CAP 1m 14y
5:00 (5:01) (Class 4) (0-80,80) 3-Y-O+ **£4,528** (£1,347; £673; £336) **Stalls** Low

Form RPR

2124 **1** **Daneside (IRE)**[7] 5673 4-8-5 **66** oh3 .... MatthewLawson(5) 6 77+
(Gary Harrison) *trckd ldrs: wnt prom over 3f out: led over 2f out and kicked on: in command over 1f out: rdn out* **9/1**

201 **2** 2 ¼ **Focail Eile**[6] 5722 6-9-0 **73** 6ex .... KieranO'Neill(3) 3 79
(John Ryan) *hld up in midfield: prog on inner jst over 2f out: drvn and styd on to take 2nd ins fnl f: no ch w wnr* **5/1**[3]

3500 **3** ½ **Salient**[11] 5547 7-9-3 **73** .... PaulDoe 12 78
(Michael Attwater) *trckd ldr: led 3f out to over 2f out: no ch w wnr over 1f out: lost 2nd ins fnl f* **33/1**

230- **4** nk **Peponi**[405] 4579 5-9-6 **76** .... SteveDrowne 16 80+
(Peter Makin) *hld up in rr: effrt over 2f out: prog over 1f out: styd on: nrly snatched a pl: rn wl* **16/1**

0625 **5** 1 **Muqtarrib (IRE)**[23] 5169 3-9-0 **75** ....(b) TadhgO'Shea 5 76
(Brian Meehan) *hld up in midfield: prog over 2f out: sn rdn: no imp on ldrs over 1f out: kpt on* **12/1**

4645 **6** 2 ¾ **First Cat**[29] 4958 4-9-9 **79** .... PatDobbs 4 75
(Richard Hannon) *hld up in last trio: prog over 2f out: rdn over 1f out: nt qckn and no imp after* **9/2**[2]

0421 **7** 1 **Eastern Breeze (IRE)**[25] 5114 3-8-13 **79** .... AntiocoMurgia(5) 10 71
(Saeed Bin Suroor) *trckd ldrs: rdn and nt qckn over 2f out: no imp over 1f out: fdd* **4/1**[1]

6001 **8** 1 ¼ **Emerald Wilderness (IRE)**[7] 5687 7-9-5 **78**.....(p) AdamBeschizza(3) 11 68
(Robert Cowell) *s.s: t.k.h in last trio: rdn and no prog over 2f out: kpt on fr over 1f out* **9/2**[2]

1040 **9** 2 **Hip Hip Hooray**[20] 5281 5-8-10 **66** oh3 .... WilliamCarson 14 58
(Luke Dace) *hld up in midfield: effrt on outer over 2f out: sn no prog: wknd and eased ins fnl f* **25/1**

0005 **10** 3 ¼ **Prince Of Sorrento**[13] 5495 4-8-5 **66** oh1 .... NathanAlison(5) 15 44
(John Akehurst) *hld up in midfield on outer: rdn and no prog over 2f out: n.d after: wknd over 1f out* **25/1**

4-00 **11** nse **Forks**[17] 5356 4-8-10 **66** oh6 .... ChrisCatlin 7 44
(Jane Chapple-Hyam) *racd keenly: led to 3f out: wknd 2f out* **33/1**

4236 **12** 1 ¼ **Cahala Dancer (IRE)**[13] 5496 3-8-5 **66** oh1 .... CathyGannon 2 40
(Roger Teal) *prom: u.p 3f out: wknd fr 2f out* **16/1**

0504 **13** 1 ¾ **Hurricane Spirit (IRE)**[32] 4860 7-9-10 **80** .... RobertHavlin 8 51
(Terry Clement) *s.s: a in last trio: no prog over 2f out: eased over 1f out* **25/1**

1m 44.06s (0.76) **Going Correction** +0.075s/f (Good)
WFA 3 from 4yo+ 5lb **13** Ran SP% **119.9**
Speed ratings (Par 105): **99,96,96,95,94 92,91,89,87,84 84,83,81**
toteswingers:1&2:£7.80, 2&3:£25.20, 1&3:£42.90. Tote Super 7: Win: Not won. Place: Not won. CSF £50.49 CT £1476.22 TOTE £11.20: £2.40, £2.40, £3.80; EX 66.10.
Owner Gary Harrison **Bred** Iona Equine **Trained** Llandeilo, Carmarthens

FOCUS
A competitive handicap, or at least it was on paper.
T/Plt: £476.60 to a £1 stake. Pool of £65,555.84 - 100.41 winning tickets. T/Qpdt: £73.00 to a £1 stake. Pool of £4,449.36 - 45.10 winning tickets. JN

[5860] WOLVERHAMPTON (A.W) (L-H)

Friday, September 9

OFFICIAL GOING: Standard changing to standard to fast after race 1 (5.10)

Wind: Fresh behind Weather: Showers

5895 WILLIAM HILL - THE HOME OF BETTING H'CAP — 5f 216y(P)

5:10 (5:11) (Class 5) (0-70,68) 3-Y-O+ **£2,522** (£750; £375; £187) **Stalls** Low

Form RPR

2155 **1** **Emiratesdotcom**[9] [5616] 5-9-5 **68** .... RoystonFfrench 2 80
(Milton Bradley) *s.i.s and hmpd sn after s: pushed along into mid-div 5f out: hdwy over 2f out: swtchd rt over 1f out: led 1f out: drvn out* **9/2**[2]

4360 **2** *hd* **Ishetoo**[27] [5031] 7-9-3 **66** .... PJMcDonald 5 77
(Ollie Pears) *prom: outpcd 1/2-way: hdwy over 1f out: rdn and r.o wl ins fnl f: nt quite get up* **4/1**[1]

0536 **3** *2 1/4* **Towy Boy (IRE)**[16] [5387] 6-9-0 **63** .... (bt) RobertWinston 1 67
(Ian Wood) *chsd ldrs: pushed along over 2f out: rdn and ev ch over 1f out: no ex ins fnl f* **6/1**[3]

00 **4** *1* **Fantasy Fighter (IRE)**[6] [5736] 6-9-0 **63** .... (p) JimmyQuinn 9 64
(John E Long) *hld up: hdwy over 2f out: rdn and edgd lft ins fnl f: styd on* **11/1**

4040 **5** *1* **Bertie Southstreet**[31] [4895] 8-9-3 **66** .... (v) RussKennemore 12 63
(Paul Midgley) *prom: rdn over 1f out: styd on same pce fnl f* **20/1**

0000 **6** *nk* **Takajan (IRE)**[6] [5736] 4-8-11 **65** .... JamesRogers(5) 4 61
(Mark Brisbourne) *dwlt: hld up: r.o ins fnl f: nrst fin* **50/1**

0120 **7** *1/2* **Rainy Night**[11] [5561] 5-8-11 **67** .... (v) JackDuern(7) 3 62
(Reg Hollinshead) *led: rdn and hdd 1f out: no ex* **6/1**[3]

55U4 **8** *nk* **Beautiful Day**[16] [5373] 3-9-1 **66** .... (p) PaulHanagan 6 60
(Kevin Ryan) *w ldr: rdn and ev ch over 1f out: no ex fnl f* **9/1**

6625 **9** *nse* **Ace Of Spies (IRE)**[24] [5139] 6-9-2 **68** .... (b) MartinHarley(3) 11 62
(Conor Dore) *s.i.s: styd on ins fnl f: nvr nrr* **33/1**

0020 **10** *1 1/2* **Roman Dancer (IRE)**[17] [5341] 3-9-2 **67** .... AndrewElliott 7 56
(John Gallagher) *prom: nt clr run and lost pl over 2f out: n.d after* **14/1**

5001 **11** *nk* **Almaty Express**[10] [5603] 9-9-0 **63** 6ex .... (b) DarryllHolland 8 51
(John Weymes) *chsd ldrs tl wknd over 1f out* **9/1**

4000 **12** *3/4* **Perlachy**[8] [5640] 7-9-0 **63** .... (v) KellyHarrison 13 49
(Ronald Harris) *sn outpcd* **20/1**

0206 **13** *nk* **Elhamri**[6] [5732] 7-8-13 **67** .... LucyKBarry(5) 10 52
(Conor Dore) *sn outpcd: no ch whn nt clr run ins fnl f* **12/1**

1m 13.96s (-1.04) **Going Correction** -0.10s/f (Stan)
WFA 3 from 4yo+ 2lb **13 Ran SP% 123.9**
Speed ratings (Par 103): **102,101,98,97,96 95,95,94,94,92 92,91,90**
Tote Swingers:1&2:£4.10, 2&3:£4.70, 1&3:£5.20 CSF £22.73 CT £105.36 TOTE £3.90: £1.10, £2.80, £2.50; EX 24.60.
Owner Ms S Howell **Bred** Newsells Park Stud **Trained** Sedbury, Gloucs

FOCUS
It was fast and furious in this sprint handicap in which the leaders went off too hard.
Roman Dancer(IRE) Official explanation: jockey said gelding hung badly right

5896 JOHN ROBERTS CO-OPERATIVE GOODBYE CLASSIC CLAIMING STKS — 5f 216y(P)

5:40 (5:41) (Class 6) 2-Y-O **£2,045** (£603; £302) **Stalls** Low

Form RPR

5210 **1** **Aquasulis (IRE)**[11] [5562] 2-8-3 68 .... PaulHanagan 8 70
(David Evans) *chsd ldr: shkn up to ld 1f out: rdn out* **10/3**[2]

1213 **2** *1 1/4* **Pint Size**[37] [4661] 2-8-12 84 .... RobertWinston 5 75
(Gay Kelleway) *led: rdn and hdd 1f out: styd on same pce* **4/6**[1]

00 **3** *6* **Wrapped Up**[65] [3736] 2-8-7 0 .... FrankieMcDonald 4 52
(Heather Main) *hld up: hdwy over 1f out: r.o to go 3rd nr fin: nt trble ldrs* **20/1**

4000 **4** *1/2* **Liebesziel**[91] [2889] 2-8-6 66 ow1 .... (p) MartinHarley(3) 1 53
(Alan McCabe) *s.i.s: sn chsng ldrs: rdn over 1f out: wknd ins fnl f: lost 3rd nr fin* **14/1**

60 **5** *1 1/2* **Aglaia**[21] [5246] 2-8-5 0 .... SophieDoyle(3) 6 47
(Frank Sheridan) *chsd ldrs: pushed along 1/2-way: wknd over 1f out* **33/1**

6400 **6** *hd* **J Cunningham**[25] [5099] 2-7-11 42 .... RyanPowell(5) 7 41
(Mark Usher) *hld up: nvr on terms* **50/1**

153 **7** *3 1/4* **Class Monitor**[10] [5591] 2-8-5 70 .... AndrewElliott 3 34
(Mrs K Burke) *prom whn hmpd and lost pl over 5f out: sn pushed along towards rr: nt clr run over 2f out: n.d* **9/2**[3]

60 **8** *2 1/4* **Dubai Rythm**[11] [5536] 2-8-10 0 .... NeilChalmers 2 32
(Michael Appleby) *chsd ldrs tl wknd over 2f out* **40/1**

1m 15.08s (0.08) **Going Correction** -0.10s/f (Stan) **8 Ran SP% 120.0**
Speed ratings (Par 93): **95,93,85,84,82 82,78,75**
Tote Swingers:1&2:£1.70, 2&3:£4.30, 1&3:£9.10 CSF £6.11 TOTE £5.90: £1.70, £1.10, £5.70; EX 10.20.The winner was the subject of a friendly claim.
Owner Bathwick Gold Partnership **Bred** Rathasker Stud **Trained** Pandy, Monmouths

FOCUS
The going was changed to standard to fast. A fair claimer for 2-y-os. The first two pulled clear and the odds-on favourite was turned over. Straightforward form.

NOTEBOOK
Aquasulis(IRE) kept close tabs on the front-running favourite and responded well to pressure to score with something in hand. She is an exposed 68-rated filly but is a genuine type who has a record of 221211 in sellers/claimers and should have some more good opportunities for her shrewd trainer. (op 3-1 tchd 7-2)
Pint Size was a runaway winner in claimers on three of his last five starts and was third off 84 in a Kempton nursery last time. He set a decent standard but was a bit lacklustre and wayward in this bid to make it four wins from nine starts. His peak efforts have been at Southwell and he may be most potent on Fibresand. (tchd 8-11)
Wrapped Up, well beaten in two 6f maidens, made some encouarging late headway and shaped like a step up in trip should suit. (tchd 25-1)
Liebesziel had failed to progress after showing ability in decent 5f maidens in the spring, and this 66-rated performer was a bit keen and faded on return from a break and gelding operation.
Class Monitor pulled hard under a hold-up ride and couldn't find a finishing effort. She won a Beverley claimer on debut in July, but has looked a bit of a tricky ride since then and current mark of 70 for nurseries looks prohibitive.

5897 MOBET.WILLIAMHILL.COM H'CAP — 1m 5f 194y(P)

6:10 (6:10) (Class 5) (0-70,80) 3-Y-O **£2,522** (£750; £375; £187) **Stalls** Low

Form RPR

0311 **1** **All My Heart**[6] [5714] 3-10-2 **80** 12ex .... StevieDonohoe 3 91+
(Sir Mark Prescott Bt) *chsd ldr: pushed along over 7f out: rdn to ld over 1f out: styd on* **4/6**[1]

0230 **2** *1 3/4* **Maher (USA)**[20] [5266] 3-9-1 **70** .... LucyKBarry(5) 2 76
(David Simcock) *hld up: hdwy over 2f out: rdn to chse wnr fnl f: styd on same pce* **5/1**[3]

0201 **3** *2 1/4* **Around The Clock (USA)**[14] [5420] 3-9-1 **65** .... DarryllHolland 1 68
(Amanda Perrett) *led: rdn over 2f out: hdd over 1f out: no ex* **10/3**[2]

0601 **4** *44* **Woop Woop (IRE)**[15] [5415] 3-9-0 **64** .... JimmyQuinn 5 —
(Stef Higgins) *chsd ldrs tl wknd over 2f out: t.o* **11/1**

3m 3.40s (-2.60) **Going Correction** -0.10s/f (Stan) **4 Ran SP% 108.1**
Speed ratings (Par 101): **103,102,100,75**
CSF £4.34 TOTE £1.20; EX 3.40.
Owner Miss K Rausing **Bred** Miss K Rausing And Shellin Blk **Trained** Newmarket, Suffolk

FOCUS
Three last-time-out winners lined-up in this small field handicap. The pace was fair and the hot favourite did the job in professional style.

5898 VISIT ATTHERACES.COM/STLEGER H'CAP — 1m 4f 50y(P)

6:40 (6:42) (Class 6) (0-55,55) 3-Y-O **£1,567** (£462; £231) **Stalls** Low

Form RPR

0-50 **1** **Castlemorris King**[97] [2715] 3-8-8 **52** .... MarkCoumbe(5) 10 69
(Michael Attwater) *a.p: chsd ldr over 6f out: led over 2f out: rdn clr over 1f out: styd on* **4/1**[2]

6452 **2** *2* **The Absent Mare**[8] [5642] 3-8-7 **46** .... RoystonFfrench 12 60
(Robin Dickin) *a.p: rdn to chse wnr over 1f out: styd on* **4/1**[2]

-005 **3** *5* **Black Iceman**[37] [4686] 3-8-11 **50** .... SaleemGolam 2 56
(Lydia Pearce) *chsd ldrs: rdn over 2f out: styd on same pce* **33/1**

63 **4** *1 3/4* **Mayan Flight (IRE)**[6] [5738] 3-8-9 **48** .... (b) MichaelStainton 7 51
(Richard Whitaker) *led: hdd over 10f out: led again over 8f out: rdn and hdd over 2f out: wknd fnl f* **6/1**[3]

000 **5** *2 1/4* **Azurinta (IRE)**[126] [1873] 3-9-2 **55** .... GeorgeBaker 5 54
(Michael Bell) *hld up: rdn over 2f out: nvr trbld ldrs* **9/4**[1]

1046 **6** *2 1/4* **Princess Gail**[12] [5515] 3-8-13 **52** .... GrahamGibbons 9 48
(Mark Brisbourne) *hld up: hdwy over 2f out: wknd over 1f out* **7/1**

300 **7** *14* **Chillianwallah**[42] [4505] 3-8-7 **46** oh1 .... PatrickMathers 6 19
(James Unett) *mid-div: pushed along over 6f out: rdn and wknd over 4f out* **50/1**

0005 **8** *3/4* **Laffraaj (IRE)**[8] [5643] 3-8-5 **47** .... (v) JohnFahy(3) 1 19
(Pat Eddery) *sn drvn along to chse ldr: led over 10f out to over 8f out: chsd ldr then tl over 6f out: remained handy tl rdn and wknd over 2f out* **9/1**

06 **9** *3/4* **Bella Montagna**[16] [5380] 3-8-12 **51** .... (v1) PBBeggy 8 22
(John Quinn) *s.i.s: sn drvn along and a in rr* **16/1**

006 **10** *1 1/4* **Raynell**[16] [5386] 3-8-9 **48** .... PJMcDonald 11 17
(Noel Quinlan) *hld up: hdwy 5f out: rdn and wknd over 2f out* **20/1**

00-6 **11** *14* **Safari Sunbeam**[15] [5415] 3-8-7 **46** oh1 .... (p) FrankieMcDonald 4 —
(Peter Pritchard) *sn pushed along in rr: rdn over 6f out: bhd fnl 5f: t.o* **50/1**

0650 **12** *25* **Unbeatable**[20] [5267] 3-8-7 **46** oh1 .... PaulHanagan 3 —
(William Knight) *hld up in tch: rdn and wknd over 3f out: t.o* **14/1**

2m 38.58s (-2.52) **Going Correction** -0.10s/f (Stan) **12 Ran SP% 131.7**
Speed ratings (Par 99): **104,102,99,98,96 95,85,85,84,84 74,58**
Tote Swingers:1&2:£7.90, 2&3:£42.70, 1&3:£25.90 CSF £22.41 CT £496.30 TOTE £5.60: £1.50, £1.60, £13.30; EX 34.00.
Owner C O'Connell **Bred** Peter Storey **Trained** Epsom, Surrey

FOCUS
They finished well strung out in this low-grade middle-distance handicap.
Castlemorris King Official explanation: trainer said regarding apparent improvement in form, colt had benefited from a drop in class.
Azurinta(IRE) Official explanation: jockey said filly hung left-handed

5899 ST LEGER LIVE ON ATR MEDIAN AUCTION MAIDEN STKS — 1m 141y(P)

7:10 (7:12) (Class 6) 2-Y-O **£1,908** (£563; £140; £140) **Stalls** Low

Form RPR

533 **1** **Swing Alone (IRE)**[36] [4722] 2-9-3 82 .... RobertWinston 2 72
(Gay Kelleway) *chsd ldrs: led over 6f out: rdn over 1f out: styd on* **5/2**[1]

0 **2** *1 3/4* **Ballyheigue (IRE)**[75] [3424] 2-9-3 0 .... ShaneKelly 1 68
(Brian Meehan) *a.p: chsd wnr over 2f out: rdn over 1f out: styd on* **20/1**

426 **3** *1/2* **Juno The Muffinman (IRE)**[56] [4068] 2-9-3 0 .... PaulHanagan 5 68+
(Tom Dascombe) *hld up: hdwy over 1f out: r.o* **11/4**

43 **3** *dht* **Final Delivery**[16] [5393] 2-9-3 0 .... JimmyQuinn 10 70+
(Marco Botti) *s.i.s and hmpd s: hld up: hdwy over 1f out: swtchd lft ins fnl f: r.o* **9/1**

005 **5** *1/2* **Voodoo Rhythm (USA)**[42] [4507] 2-9-3 72 .... KierenFallon 13 66
(Brian Meehan) *led 1f: chsd ldrs: rdn over 1f out: styd on: n.m.r nr fin* **8/1**

6 *1/2* **Inqadh (USA)** 2-9-3 0 .... RoystonFfrench 11 65
(Saeed Bin Suroor) *chsd ldr: led over 7f out: stmbld and hdd sn after: rn green and pushed along at various stages: rdn over 2f out: styd on same pce fr over 1f out* **13/2**

6500 **7** *2 1/4* **Adranian (IRE)**[30] [4922] 2-9-3 55 .... (v) StevieDonohoe 3 60
(David Evans) *chsd ldrs: rdn over 2f out: no ex fnl f* **80/1**

65 **8** *3/4* **Ironically (IRE)**[16] [5393] 2-8-12 0 .... RichardMullen 8 54+
(David Lanigan) *hld up: rdn over 3f out: n.d* **20/1**

0 **9** *1 1/2* **No Plan B (IRE)**[20] [5269] 2-8-9 0 .... MartinHarley(3) 4 50+
(Noel Quinlan) *s.i.s: hld up: n.d* **100/1**

6 **10** *1* **Compton Bell**[24] [5142] 2-9-0 0 .... SophieDoyle(3) 6 53+
(Hans Adielsson) *s.i.s: hld up: racd keenly: a in rr* **50/1**

11 *1/2* **Echo Of Dream** 2-9-3 0 .... AhmedAjtebi 9 52+
(Mahmood Al Zarooni) *hld up: plld hrd: a in rr* **9/2**[3]

00 **12** *1 3/4* **Echo Of Dubai (IRE)**[10] [5596] 2-8-12 0 .... JamesSullivan 7 44
(Clive Brittain) *mid-div: rdn over 3f out: wknd over 2f out* **50/1**

1m 51.74s (1.24) **Going Correction** -0.10s/f (Stan) **12 Ran SP% 123.5**
Speed ratings (Par 93): **90,88,88,88,87 87,85,84,83,82 81,80**
Place: JTM £0.50, FD £2.20. Tote Swingers:1&2:£13.60, 2&3:£13.00, 1&3:£3.90, 2&3:£3.40, 1&3:£1.10 CSF £61.13 TOTE £3.00: £1.10, £8.40; EX 62.70.
Owner Whatley,Stanbrook,Bowles & Krolikowski **Bred** M Sinanan **Trained** Exning, Suffolk
■ Stewards' Enquiry : Jimmy Quinn jockey said gelding was slowly away.

FOCUS
A decent maiden on paper but the early pace was very steady. A few are likely flattered and this is form to rate negatively.

NOTEBOOK
Swing Alone(IRE) was a highly promising fifth in the Chesham at Royal Ascot on debut and showed a fair level of ability without confirming that form in a couple of maidens since. Officially rated 82, he had leading form claims and delivered in decent style under an attacking ride. It is a slight concern that he has not really progressed and his current mark looks on the high side, but he is very well regarded and looks a willing and uncomplicated type. (op 3-1)
Ballyheigue(IRE), a 42,000gns High Chaparral half-brother to useful 6f 2yo winner Abraxas Antelope, stayed on steadily in a much improved second effort. (op 25-1)

Juno The Muffinman(IRE) entered the reckoning on his close call over 7f here in June and was prominent in the betting, but he got caught out when the pace increased and got going too late. However, this was an encouraging return from a break and gelding operation and he shaped like a stiffer test and stronger pace would suit. (op 3-1)
Final Delivery left his debut form well behind when a 22-1 third over 7f here last time and confirmed that promise with creditable staying-on effort over this longer distance. Out of 1m-1m3f winner, he is open to further progress. Official explanation: jockey said gelding was slowly away (op 3-1)
Voodoo Rhythm(USA) finished a creditable 66-1 fifth dropped to 6f at Newmarket last time. His US pedigree suggests he will stay at least 1m and he looked suited by this stiffer test, staying on nicely to finish in the chasing pack. (tchd 15-2)
Inqadh(USA), a Derby entered half-brother to promising 3-y-o Deraasa, looked very inexperienced near the pace but did really well to hang in there on debut and should have learned a lot. (op 5-1)
Compton Bell Official explanation: jockey said gelding was slowly away
Echo Of Dream ran green and was always in rear on debut. (tchd 11-2)

5900 ENJOY THE PARTY PACK GROUP OFFER MAIDEN STKS 1m 141y(P)
7:40 (7:40) (Class 5) 3-Y-O+ **£1,908** (£563; £281) **Stalls** Low

Form RPR
4-20 **1** **Secret Era**[14] 5429 4-8-11 64 JamesRogers(5) 4 64
(William Muir) *a.p: rdn and swtchd rt ins fnl f: r.o to ld nr fin* **10/1**
2500 **2** ½ **Iron Green (FR)**[14] 5463 3-9-1 61 KierenFallon 8 68
(Heather Main) *chsd ldr tl led over 2f out: rdn ins fnl f: hdd nr fin* **5/1[2]**
004 **3** ½ **Painted Tail (IRE)**[14] 5443 4-9-2 0 PJMcDonald 3 62
(Alan Swinbank) *hld up: hdwy over 1f out: r.o* **11/1**
5030 **4** ½ **Symphonic Dancer (USA)**[16] 5391 4-9-2 65 J-PGuillambert 11 61
(Brian Baugh) *a.p: rdn over 2f out: styd on* **7/1[3]**
5 **5** *shd* **Triple Charm**[11] 5567 3-8-7 0 JohnFahy(3) 6 60
(Jeremy Noseda) *trckd ldrs: racd keenly: rdn over 1f out: styd on same pce ins fnl f* **8/11[1]**
5 **6** 1½ **Mahfal (FR)**[10] 5607 3-8-12 0 PaulPickard(3) 5 62
(Brian Ellison) *hld up: hdwy over 1f out: r.o* **14/1**
0605 **7** 1 **Tigerbill**[22] 5214 3-9-1 46 JamesDoyle 7 60
(Nicky Vaughan) *led: rdn and hdd over 2f out: no ex ins fnl f* **33/1**
00 **8** 11 **Monsieur Broughton**[14] 5449 3-9-1 0 StevieDonohoe 1 34
(Willie Musson) *s.i.s: a in rr: wknd over 3f out* **50/1**
00 **9** 13 **Pronounce**[10] 5598 3-9-1 0 RobbieFitzpatrick 2 —
(Michael Appleby) *s.s: hld up: hung rt 4f out: effrt over 2f out: sn wknd* **100/1**
00 **10** 2¼ **Millers Dhustone**[10] 5607 5-8-9 0 RachealKneller(7) 13 —
(Pam Ford) *sn outpcd* **100/1**
0 **11** 15 **Femme D'Espere**[32] 4861 5-9-2 0 NeilChalmers 9 —
(Christopher Kellett) *mid-div: rdn and wknd over 3f out: t.o* **100/1**

1m 49.89s (-0.61) **Going Correction** -0.10s/f (Stan)
WFA 3 from 4yo+ 6lb **11** Ran SP% **119.0**
Speed ratings (Par 103): **98,97,97,96,96 95,94,84,73,71 57**
Tote Swingers:1&2:£8.20, 2&3:£7.30, 1&3:£13.40 CSF £59.53 TOTE £21.80: £4.70, £2.30, £5.30; EX 89.00.
Owner Carmel Stud **Bred** Carmel Stud **Trained** Lambourn, Berks
FOCUS
An ordinary maiden. The odds-on favourite was held and they finished in a bunch.

5901 WILLIAMHILL.COM H'CAP (DIV I) 7f 32y(P)
8:10 (8:14) (Class 6) (0-65,65) 3-Y-O+ **£1,567** (£462; £231) **Stalls** High

Form RPR
5023 **1** **Polemica (IRE)**[10] 5604 5-9-9 64 (bt) JamesDoyle 8 74
(Frank Sheridan) *hld up: hdwy over 1f out: rdn to ld and edgd rt ins fnl f: r.o* **15/2**
-450 **2** 1¼ **Holiday Snap**[72] 3512 5-9-6 61 (t) GeorgeBaker 7 68
(Mary Hambro) *led: rdn over 1f out: hdd and unable qck ins fnl f* **5/2[1]**
4636 **3** *nk* **Piccolo Express**[30] 4918 5-9-1 56 J-PGuillambert 1 62
(Brian Baugh) *chsd ldrs: rdn over 1f out: styd on* **6/1[3]**
0524 **4** 1 **Army Of Stars (IRE)**[32] 4865 5-9-4 62 (b) RyanClark(3) 2 65
(Michael Blake) *chsd ldrs: rdn over 2f out: styd on same pce ins fnl f* **11/2[2]**
0050 **5** *nk* **Silly Billy (IRE)**[15] 5419 3-9-0 64 JemmaMarshall(5) 10 64
(Sylvester Kirk) *hld up: hdwy over 2f out: nt clr run over 1f out: r.o* **18/1**
0005 **6** ½ **Avalon Bay**[8] 5644 3-8-10 58 (p) JohnFahy(3) 6 57
(Pat Eddery) *hld up: bhd and rdn 1/2-way: r.o fnl f: nvr trbld ldrs* **9/1**
15 **7** 1¼ **Kipchak (IRE)**[6] 5736 6-9-5 65 (b) LucyKBarry(5) 3 63
(Conor Dore) *chsd ldr: rdn over 2f out: no ex fnl f* **7/1**
5256 **8** ¾ **Lough Corrib (USA)**[4] 5780 3-8-13 58 (p) FrankieMcDonald 9 52
(Alastair Lidderdale) *s.i.s: outpcd: r.o ins fnl f: nvr nrr* **33/1**
0100 **9** 4½ **Meydan Style (USA)**[39] 4604 5-8-10 51 StevieDonohoe 5 34
(Bruce Hellier) *chsd ldrs: rdn over 1f out: wknd fnl f* **14/1**
2605 **10** 1¾ **He's A Humbug (IRE)**[6] 5734 7-9-3 58 (p) RussKennemore 11 37
(Paul Midgley) *hld up: hdwy over 2f out: sn rdn: wknd fnl f* **8/1**

1m 28.69s (-0.91) **Going Correction** -0.10s/f (Stan)
WFA 3 from 5yo+ 4lb **10** Ran SP% **118.5**
Speed ratings (Par 101): **101,99,99,98,97 97,95,94,89,87**
Tote Swingers:1&2:£5.00, 2&3:£4.90, 1&3:£8.30 TOTE £8.10: £2.30, £1.10, £2.90; EX 28.10.
Owner Diamond Racing Ltd **Bred** Mervyn Stewkesbury **Trained** Wolverhampton, W Midlands
FOCUS
A modest handicap run at a good pace. Kiss N Kick refused to enter the stalls and was withdrawn.

5902 WILLIAMHILL.COM H'CAP (DIV II) 7f 32y(P)
8:40 (8:41) (Class 6) (0-65,65) 3-Y-O+ **£1,567** (£462; £231) **Stalls** High

Form RPR
5043 **1** **Beautiful Lando (FR)**[12] 5529 3-9-1 60 (b) KierenFallon 9 70
(Heather Main) *sn led: clr 3f out: rdn over 1f out: styd on* **10/3[1]**
0204 **2** 2¼ **Karate (IRE)**[16] 5381 3-9-0 59 JamesDoyle 7 63
(Hans Adielsson) *hld up: hdwy over 2f out: rdn over 1f out: edgd lft and r.o ins fnl f: nt rch wnr* **8/1**
6165 **3** ¾ **All Honesty**[17] 5354 3-9-6 65 GeorgeBaker 1 67
(William Knight) *hld up: hdwy and n.m.r over 1f out: r.o: nt rch ldrs* **11/1**
0060 **4** *shd* **Titan Diamond (IRE)**[16] 5381 3-7-13 51 oh2 RachealKneller(7) 4 53
(Mark Usher) *prom: chsd wnr over 5f out: rdn over 1f out: styd on same pce ins fnl f* **10/1**
5210 **5** *nk* **Putin (IRE)**[10] 5606 3-8-9 54 ShaneKelly 3 55
(Derek Haydn Jones) *chsd ldrs: rdn over 2f out: styd on same pce fnl f* **5/1[3]**
1220 **6** ½ **Fortunate Bid (IRE)**[24] 5143 5-9-5 60 (p) JamesSullivan 8 61
(Linda Stubbs) *hld up: rdn over 1f out: r.o ins fnl f: nt clr run and swtchd rt towards fin: nt rch ldrs* **13/2**
4303 **7** 1¼ **Mr Chocolate Drop (IRE)**[15] 5414 7-9-9 64 (t) JimmyQuinn 10 62
(Mandy Rowland) *hld up: rdn over 2f out: styd on ins fnl f: nvr nrr* **12/1**
-040 **8** ½ **My Name Is Bert**[11] 5547 5-8-8 54 ChrisDCogan(5) 2 51
(Lucinda Featherstone) *chsd ldrs: rdn over 2f out: wknd ins fnl f* **20/1**
3151 **9** 2¼ **This Ones For Eddy**[59] 3953 6-9-7 62 GrahamGibbons 5 53
(John Balding) *hld up: rdn over 2f out: nt trble ldrs* **4/1[2]**
2000 **10** 10 **Hab Reeh**[74] 3462 3-9-6 65 (bt) RoystonFfrench 6 27
(Clive Brittain) *hld up: a in rr: wknd over 2f out* **33/1**

1m 28.67s (-0.93) **Going Correction** -0.10s/f (Stan)
WFA 3 from 5yo+ 4lb **10** Ran SP% **117.0**
Speed ratings (Par 101): **101,98,97,97,97 96,95,94,91,80**
Tote Swingers:1&2:£7.10, 2&3:£11.00, 1&3:£6.40 CSF £30.64 CT £271.57 TOTE £2.70: £1.10, £3.00, £4.00; EX 47.00.
Owner Les Chevaliers **Bred** Jean-Pierre Deroubaix **Trained** Kingston Lisle, Oxon
FOCUS
There was a dominant trailblazing winner in the second division of this minor handicap.
Fortunate Bid(IRE) Official explanation: jockey said gelding was denied a clear run
T/Plt: £69.70 to a £1 stake. Pool £66,913.10. 700.02 winning units. T/Qpdt: £22.50 to a £1 stake. Pool £8,312.14. 272.90 winning units. CR

5903 - 5910a (Foreign Racing) - See Raceform Interactive

5779 BATH (L-H)
Saturday, September 10

OFFICIAL GOING: Good to soft (7.4)
Wind: strong half across Weather: overcast

5911 CASINO AT BET365.COM MAIDEN STKS 1m 3f 144y
2:15 (2:17) (Class 5) 3-Y-O+ **£2,911** (£866; £432; £216) **Stalls** Low

Form RPR
-23 **1** **Tmaam (USA)**[91] 2930 3-9-4 0 LukeMorris 13 94+
(Mark Johnston) *trckd ldrs: rdn to chse ldr over 3f out: chal over 2f out: led over 1f out: styd on strly to assert fnl f* **10/1**
4320 **2** 3¾ **Lidar (FR)**[71] 3593 6-9-10 82 MartinHarley(3) 8 86
(Alan King) *led: rdn whn chal over 2f out: hdd over 1f out: kpt on tl no ex ins fnl f* **22/1**
2 **3** 3¾ **Asaid**[35] 4805 3-8-13 0 AntiocoMurgia(5) 4 79
(Saeed Bin Suroor) *s.i.s: sn mid-div: pushed along to chse ldng trio 3f out: sn rdn: edgd lft: wnt 3rd over 1f out: styd on same pce* **4/1[2]**
4 6 **Enthusiastic** 3-9-4 0 J-PGuillambert 10 69
(Luca Cumani) *mid-div: sme hdwy over 3f out: sn rdn: styd on same pce fnl 2f: nvr trbld ldrs* **40/1**
3- **5** ½ **Tonnerre (IRE)**[322] 7094 3-9-4 0 ShaneKelly 3 68
(Sir Michael Stoute) *s.i.s: sn mid-div: rdn 3f out: styd on same pce: nvr threatened ldrs* **15/2**
523 **6** 1¼ **Moment Of Time**[93] 2839 3-8-13 90 LiamKeniry 7 61
(Andrew Balding) *trckd ldrs: rdn over 4f out: one pce fnl 2f* **9/4[1]**
3443 **7** ½ **Monopolize**[35] 4805 3-9-4 78 IanMongan 6 65
(Sir Henry Cecil) *trckd ldr tl rdn over 3f out: styd 3rd tl wknd over 1f out* **6/1**
6 **8** 5 **Riviera Stars**[19] 5327 3-9-4 0 PatCosgrave 1 57
(Michael Bell) *s.i.s: towards rr: hdwy 3f out: sn rdn: wknd over 1f out* **25/1**
9 14 **Vasily** 3-9-4 0 AndreaAtzeni 9 33
(Robert Eddery) *mid-div: rdn over 2f out: wknd over 1f out* **9/2[3]**
10 2 **Lily Le Braz**[19] 6-9-8 0 MarkLawson 11 25
(Gary Harrison) *s.i.s: rdn over 4f out: a towards rr* **100/1**
11 ¾ **High Carol (IRE)**[639] 9-9-13 0 CathyGannon 12 28
(Andy Turnell) *a towards rr* **150/1**
12 17 **On Alert** 3-9-4 0 TravisBlock 2 —
(Seamus Durack) *a towards rr: t.o 3f out* **150/1**
5 **13** 38 **Pacific Reach**[22] 5247 3-9-4 0 ChrisCatlin 5 —
(Andrew Balding) *t.k.h: trckd ldrs tl over 5f out: sn bhd: t.o* **100/1**

2m 32.97s (2.37) **Going Correction** +0.35s/f (Good)
WFA 3 from 6yo+ 9lb **13** Ran SP% **118.0**
Speed ratings (Par 103): **106,103,101,97,96 95,95,92,82,81 81,69,44**
toteswingers:1&2:£22.80, 2&3:£59.90, 1&3:£16.00 CSF £207.16 TOTE £11.00: £3.80, £5.40, £1.80; EX 172.00.
Owner Jaber Abdullah **Bred** Claiborne Farm **Trained** Middleham Moor, N Yorks
FOCUS
Rail movement increased distances by about 12.5yds. Quite a deep maiden for the track. The field was quite well strung out from an early stage but the gallop didn't appear to be that strong.
Monopolize Official explanation: jockey said colt hung left

5912 BET365.COM H'CAP 1m 2f 46y
2:45 (2:49) (Class 6) (0-60,62) 3-Y-O+ **£2,070** (£616; £307; £153) **Stalls** Low

Form RPR
3311 **1** **Kathleen Kennet**[5] 5785 11-9-7 62 6ex KatiaScallan(7) 5 82+
(Jonathan Geake) *hld up in rr: gd prog on outer on bnd fr over 5f out: led over 3f out: wl in command sn after: readily* **9/4[1]**
2 10 **Homebrew (IRE)**[18] 5362 6-9-3 54 MartinHarley(3) 13 54
(M A Molloy, Ire) *trckd ldrs: rdn to chse wnr fr over 3f out: styd on but no ch w wnr fnl 2f* **8/1[2]**
4400 **3** ¾ **Signora Frasi (IRE)**[19] 5318 6-9-4 57 DavidKenny(5) 2 56
(Tony Newcombe) *hld up in last pair w wnr: pushed along and stdy prog fr over 3f out: styd on to go 3rd ins fnl f* **25/1**
04/0 **4** 1¼ **Nina Rose**[64] 3814 4-9-12 60 LukeMorris 7 56
(Clive Cox) *trckd ldrs: rdn 3f out: styd on same pce fnl 2f* **10/1**
0-00 **5** 1½ **Jody Bear**[82] 3226 3-8-8 52 HarryBentley(3) 8 45
(Jonathan Portman) *mid-div: rdn 3f out: nvr threatened ldrs: styd on same pce* **25/1**
0404 **6** ¾ **My Sister**[12] 5538 4-9-0 48 LiamKeniry 4 40
(Mark Usher) *mid-div: short of room on bnd and lost pl over 4f out: rdn whn swtchd rt over 2f out: styd on but nvr bk on terms* **12/1**
6000 **7** *hd* **El Libertador (USA)**[10] 5611 5-8-13 50 (b) KierenFox(3) 6 41
(Eric Wheeler) *hld up towards rr: pushed along over 4f out: sme prog whn nt clr run briefly over 2f out: sn rdn: no further imp* **28/1**
605 **8** *nk* **Indefinite Hope (ITY)**[30] 4953 4-8-11 48 (t) LouisBeuzelin(3) 1 39
(Frank Sheridan) *nvr bttr than mid-div* **14/1**
3600 **9** 1¼ **Madame Boot (FR)**[33] 4869 4-9-5 53 (b[1]) IanMongan 12 41
(Peter Makin) *pushed along in midfield early: rdn over 4f out: wknd over 1f out* **16/1**
2640 **10** ¾ **Present Story**[8] 5673 4-9-2 50 (b[1]) MarkLawson 14 37
(Gary Harrison) *mid-div: rdn 3f out: wknd ins fnl f* **33/1**
4603 **11** 9 **Corrib (IRE)**[10] 5611 8-9-5 53 (p) CathyGannon 9 22
(Bryn Palling) *trckd ldr: rdn wl over 3f out: nt gng pce to chal: wknd ins fnl f* **17/2[3]**
0-60 **12** 1¼ **Illustrious Forest**[99] 2677 3-9-0 55 PatCosgrave 3 21
(John Mackie) *trckd ldrs tl rdn 3f out: grad fdd* **10/1**

 The Form Book, Raceform Ltd, Compton, RG20 6NL

0354 13 1 1/4 **Raghdaan**[5] [5785] 4-9-1 **49** ChrisCatlin 11 13
(Peter Hiatt) *a towards rr* **9/1**

0001 14 29 **Fair Breeze**[18] [5349] 4-9-2 **50** WilliamCarson 10 —
(Richard Phillips) *led tl rdn over 3f out: wknd over 2f out* **14/1**

2m 14.03s (3.03) **Going Correction** +0.35s/f (Good)
WFA 3 from 4yo+ 7lb **14** Ran SP% **121.6**
Speed ratings (Par 101): **101,93,92,91,90 89,89,89,88,87 80,79,78,55**
toteswingers:1&2:£11.80, 2&3:£84.30, 1&3:£110.50 CSF £18.72 CT £371.84 TOTE £3.00: £1.20, £2.50, £7.40; EX 20.70.
Owner R W Floyd **Bred** Richard William Floyd **Trained** Marlborough, Wilts

FOCUS
A weak handicap.
Indefinite Hope(ITY) Official explanation: jockey said filly was never travelling

5913 GET MOBILE AT BET365.COM NURSERY 5f 161y

3:20 (3:22) (Class 4) (0-85,78) 2-Y-O **£3,881** (£1,155; £577; £288) **Stalls** Centre

Form RPR

1623 1 **Marygold**[23] [5197] 2-9-3 **77** HarryBentley(3) 4 80
(John Akehurst) *mde all: kpt on wl: rdn out* **9/4[1]**

5401 2 1 3/4 **Whisky Bravo**[23] [5211] 2-8-11 **68** ChrisCatlin 6 65
(David Brown) *chsd ldrs: rdn over 2f out: chsd wnr jst ins fnl f: kpt on: a being hld* **8/1**

0621 3 1 1/4 **Compton Target (IRE)**[17] [5385] 2-8-13 **75** JamesRogers(5) 2 68
(Hans Adielsson) *trckd ldrs: pushed along over 2f out: swtchd rt ent fnl f: kpt on but nt gng pce to chal* **11/2[3]**

0040 4 1 1/2 **Princess Banu**[3] [5833] 2-8-4 **68** CharlesBishop(7) 5 56
(Mick Channon) *trckd wnr: rdn over 2f out: edgd lft over 1f out: one pce ins fnl f* **14/1**

2U1 5 1 **Uncle Roger (IRE)**[43] [4485] 2-9-6 **77** CathyGannon 3 62
(Eve Johnson Houghton) *slowly away and bmpd s: chsd ldrs: rdn 3f out: wknd ins fnl f* **7/2[2]**

041 6 3/4 **Dishy Guru**[16] [5411] 2-9-4 **75** LukeMorris 7 57
(Michael Blanshard) *outpcd in last: hdwy to chse ldrs 2f out: wknd ins fnl f* **7/2[2]**

1m 13.46s (2.26) **Going Correction** +0.175s/f (Good) **6** Ran SP% **108.4**
Speed ratings (Par 97): **91,88,87,85,83 82**
toteswingers:1&2:£11.80, 2&3:£84.30, 1&3:£110.50 CSF £18.94 TOTE £3.00: £1.10, £3.60; EX 24.50.
Owner The No Water Partnership **Bred** Green Pastures Farm **Trained** Epsom, Surrey

FOCUS
A weakish race and not form to take too literally. The winner got a good ride from the front.

NOTEBOOK
Marygold blitzed them from the front, setting a strong pace and keeping on relentlessly in the straight to prove way too good. The drop back from 7f proved ideal for this speedball of a filly and she had proved at Brighton earlier in the season that slow ground was no problem for her, so everything came together. She is better than a 77-rated horse under these conditions and could be a real force on speed-favouring tracks. (op 3-1 tchd 2-1)
Whisky Bravo shed his maiden tag in a weak race on the Fibresand at Southwell and was hard to evaluate under these very different conditions, but he acquitted himself with a deal of credit and this late foal looks capable of winning off this sort of mark, especially as he appears to be progressing. (op 6-1)
Compton Target(IRE) lacked the gears to challenge in the straight but he ran on well in the closing stages and looks like he'll be a force back up in trip (several of his relatives won over 1m+, while his dam stayed 1m4f). (op 4-1 tchd 6-1)
Princess Banu dropped away and just isn't the same filly as earlier in the season. (op 12-1 tchd 10-1)
Uncle Roger(IRE) struggled to get into it and his opening mark looks high enough. (op 9-2)
Dishy Guru, who had only raced over 6f previously, was taken off his feet early and looks the type to fare better over slightly further, but he doesn't appear particularly well treated off 75. (op 10-3, tchd 4-1 in places)

5914 POKER AT BET365.COM H'CAP 5f 11y

3:55 (3:56) (Class 4) (0-80,79) 3-Y-O+ **£3,881** (£1,155; £577; £288) **Stalls** Centre

Form RPR

5106 1 **Maze (IRE)**[21] [5262] 6-9-3 **78** HarryBentley(3) 8 88
(Tony Carroll) *hld up: rdn and hdwy over 1f out: led jst ins fnl f: r.o wl* **6/1[2]**

5501 2 1 3/4 **Crew Cut (IRE)**[24] [5176] 3-8-4 **70** RaulDaSilva(7) 9 74+
(Jeremy Gask) *trckd ldrs: rdn 2f out: nt clr run whn abt to mount chal 1f out: r.o whn clr sn after: snatched 2nd fnl stride* **17/2**

1452 3 nse **Macdillon**[14] [5484] 5-9-6 **78** IanMongan 4 82
(Stuart Kittow) *trckd ldr: rdn for str chal fr over 2f out: led briefly ent fnl f: nt gng pce of wnr: lost 2nd fnl stride* **7/4[1]**

3443 4 1 1/2 **Wooden King (IRE)**[10] [5616] 6-8-9 **74** JakePayne(7) 1 72
(Malcolm Saunders) *led: rdn whn chal over 2f out: hdd ent fnl f: no ex* **8/1**

3231 5 nse **Best Be Careful (IRE)**[10] [5615] 3-8-8 **67** LiamKeniry 11 65
(Mark Usher) *in tch: hdwy over 2f out: sn rdn: ev ch ent fnl f: kpt on same pce* **13/2[3]**

0045 6 shd **Bilash**[9] [5658] 4-8-8 **66** oh2 ow1 ShaneKelly 10 64
(Reg Hollinshead) *hld up: rdn over 2f out: sme late prog: n.d* **14/1**

2401 7 1 **The Name Is Frank**[10] [5616] 6-8-4 **65** (t) AmyBaker(3) 5 59
(Mark Gillard) *chsd ldrs: rdn over 2f out: nvr gng pce to chal* **11/1**

2311 8 2 **Comptonspirit**[21] [5265] 7-9-1 **78** JamesRogers(5) 3 65
(Brian Baugh) *in tch: rdn over 2f out: wknd ins fnl f* **8/1**

44 9 5 **Estonia**[16] [5412] 4-8-11 **69** CathyGannon 2 38
(Michael Squance) *hld up: rdn over 2f out: wknd over 1f out* **20/1**

62.69 secs (0.19) **Going Correction** +0.175s/f (Good)
WFA 3 from 4yo+ 1lb **9** Ran SP% **116.5**
Speed ratings (Par 105): **105,102,102,99,99 99,97,94,86**
toteswingers:1&2:£14.80, 2&3:£11.20, 1&3:£5.30 CSF £56.29 CT £126.23 TOTE £10.00: £3.50, £5.00, £1.20; EX 100.50.
Owner Centaur Global Partnership I **Bred** Millsec Limited **Trained** Cropthorne, Worcs

FOCUS
A competitive sprint handicap featuring a host of in-form runners.
Crew Cut(IRE) Official explanation: vet said gelding lost it's left-fore shoe
The Name Is Frank Official explanation: vet said gelding lost it's right-hind shoe

5915 BET365.COM FILLIES' H'CAP 1m 2f 46y

4:30 (4:30) (Class 5) (0-75,75) 3-Y-O+ **£2,911** (£866; £432; £216) **Stalls** Low

Form RPR

3212 1 **Destiny Of Dreams**[16] [5407] 3-9-5 **75** IanMongan 7 87
(Jo Crowley) *prom for 1f: trckd ldrs: wnt 2nd over 6f out: rdn to ld over 2f out: styd on wl: rdn out* **5/2[1]**

463 2 3 1/2 **Ecossaise**[19] [5317] 3-9-4 **74** J-PGuillambert 5 79
(Mark Johnston) *led for 1f: trckd ldr tl 6f out: pushed along to chse ldrs over 4f out: rdn 3f out: chsd wnr over 1f out: a being hld* **5/1[2]**

5350 3 3/4 **Countess Comet (IRE)**[76] [3434] 4-9-9 **72** (p) StevieDonohoe 2 76
(Ralph Beckett) *trckd ldrs: rdn wl over 2f out: styd on ins fnl f* **6/1[3]**

2404 4 1 3/4 **Oriental Girl**[10] [5614] 6-9-4 **67** (p) LiamKeniry 4 67
(Jonathan Geake) *trckd ldrs tl dropped to rr: pushed along 6f out: rdn and hdwy over 3f out: styd on same pce fnl 2f* **6/1[3]**

1226 5 1/2 **Only You Maggie (IRE)**[10] [5614] 4-8-13 **67** (v) MatthewLawson(5) 1 66
(Gary Harrison) *slowly away: hdwy to ld after 1f: rdn and hdd over 2f out: no ex ins fnl f* **8/1**

3056 6 hd **Mia Madonna**[10] [5630] 3-8-8 **64** ow1 (b1) ShaneKelly 6 63
(Brian Meehan) *hld up: rdn 3f out: styd on but nvr gng pce to get involved* **6/1[3]**

0504 7 3 **Rose Of Sarratt (IRE)**[25] [5134] 3-8-2 **61** HarryBentley(3) 3 54
(Rae Guest) *s.i.s: a towards rr* **12/1**

0350 8 1 **Little Cottonsocks**[28] [5049] 3-9-1 **71** (t) LukeMorris 10 62
(Clive Cox) *in tch: rdn 3f out: wknd ins fnl f* **12/1**

2m 13.52s (2.52) **Going Correction** +0.35s/f (Good)
WFA 3 from 4yo+ 7lb **8** Ran SP% **114.6**
Speed ratings (Par 100): **103,100,99,98,97 97,95,94**
toteswingers:1&2:£1.10, 2&3:£6.10, 1&3:£3.70 CSF £15.01 CT £66.77 TOTE £2.70: £1.30, £1.50, £2.10; EX 10.00.
Owner Kilstone Limited **Bred** Black Horse Farm **Trained** Whitcombe, Dorset

FOCUS
An ordinary fillies' handicap.

5916 BET365 H'CAP 1m 5f 22y

5:00 (5:00) (Class 6) (0-60,59) 3-Y-O+ **£2,181** (£644; £322) **Stalls** High

Form RPR

1541 1 **Maydream**[10] [5612] 4-9-0 **52** JustinNewman(7) 13 64+
(Jimmy Fox) *mid-div: rdn and hdwy to chse ldr 3f out: led over 2f out: styd on wl* **9/4[1]**

3062 2 3 **Dove Cottage (IRE)**[10] [5612] 9-9-11 **56** (v1) ShaneKelly 6 63
(Stuart Kittow) *led: clr after 2f: rdn over 2f out: hdd over 1f out: hld whn hmpd sn after* **3/1[2]**

3050 3 1 3/4 **Stormy Morning**[47] [4396] 5-9-9 **59** (p) JamesRogers(5) 3 63
(Pat Eddery) *trckd ldrs: rdn to chse ldr briefly over 3f out: styd on same pce fnl 2f* **14/1**

1514 4 nk **Lucky Diva**[21] [5267] 4-9-1 **53** (p) JakePayne(7) 14 57
(Bill Turner) *mid-div: rdn and hdwy over 3f out: styd on same pce fnl 2f* **11/1**

2565 5 8 **Dot's Delight**[21] [5267] 7-9-2 **47** LukeMorris 8 39
(Mark Rimell) *mid-div: hdwy 6f out: rdn 4f out: nvr threatened ldrs: fdd fnl f* **14/1**

2435 6 13 **Minder**[135] [1631] 5-9-3 **51** (p) HarryBentley(3) 9 23
(Jonathan Portman) *mid-div: rdn over 3f out: wknd over 1f out* **10/1[3]**

05-6 7 1 1/2 **Drivemode**[32] [4889] 4-8-11 **45** KierenFox(3) 2 15
(Dr Jon Scargill) *hld up towards rr: rdn 3f out: sme late prog: nvr a factor* **40/1**

-604 8 1 1/2 **Noble Defender**[18] [5350] 3-9-4 **59** (b1) IanMongan 1 27
(Stuart Kittow) *mid-div: rdn over 4f out: nvr threatened ldrs: wknd over 1f out* **14/1**

006 9 5 **Farmers Hill**[29] [4989] 3-8-4 **45** WilliamCarson 4 —
(Mark Hoad) *chsd ldrs: rdn over 3f out: wknd over 2f out* **14/1**

00-0 10 6 **Aureate**[191] [596] 7-9-6 **54** SophieDoyle(3) 12 —
(Brian Forsey) *chsd clr ldr in clr 2nd tl rdn over 3f out: wknd over 2f out* **33/1**

00-2 11 1 1/2 **Waldsee (GER)**[59] [2905] 6-9-9 **54** J-PGuillambert 10 —
(Joanna Davis) *in tch tl wknd over 2f out* **12/1**

33/6 12 24 **Salybia Bay**[9] [5642] 5-9-10 **55** RichardThomas 11 —
(Andy Turnell) *pushed along fr 1/2-way: a towards rr: t.o* **28/1**

0-56 13 1/2 **Romantic Girl (IRE)**[29] [5022] 3-8-4 **45** KellyHarrison 7 —
(Alan Juckes) *a towards rr* **40/1**

650 14 10 **Avon Blaise**[17] [5386] 4-9-3 **53** DavidKenny(5) 5 —
(Peter Hedger) *a struggling in rr: t.o* **50/1**

2m 57.83s (5.83) **Going Correction** +0.35s/f (Good)
WFA 3 from 4yo+ 10lb **14** Ran SP% **120.8**
Speed ratings (Par 101): **96,94,93,92,87 79,79,78,75,71 70,55,55,49**
toteswingers:1&2:£6.50, 2&3:£1.10, 1&3:£26.90 CSF £8.12 CT £78.20 TOTE £3.10: £1.10, £1.80, £3.30; EX 11.90.
Owner The Dancing Partners **Bred** The Dancing Partners **Trained** Collingbourne Ducis, Wilts

FOCUS
Almost identical circumstances to a C&D handicap ten days ago.
Salybia Bay Official explanation: jockey said mare was never travelling

5917 BET365.COM APPRENTICE H'CAP 5f 161y

5:35 (5:36) (Class 6) (0-60,64) 3-Y-O+ **£2,070** (£616; £307; £153) **Stalls** Centre

Form RPR

4432 1 **Ginzan**[10] [5615] 3-9-2 **57** LouisBeuzelin 14 67
(Malcolm Saunders) *sn prom: c in centre 3f out: sn led: rdn 2f out: hld on wl thrght fnl f: on top nring fin* **3/1[1]**

2161 2 1 **My Meteor**[43] [4487] 4-9-0 **58** DavidKenny(5) 11 64
(Tony Newcombe) *mid-div: hdwy over 3f out: sn swtchd to r in centre: chal jst over 1f out: ev ch ins fnl f: no ex fnl 75yds* **6/1[3]**

304 3 1 1/4 **Little Perisher**[8] [5678] 4-8-1 **47** (b) JulieCumine(7) 5 49
(Karen George) *s.i.s: bhd: swtchd to centre 3f out: hdwy over 2f out: hung lft over 1f out: kpt on but nt gng pce of ldrs* **16/1**

1201 4 1 1/2 **Valmina**[7] [5736] 4-9-2 **60** (t) GeorgeDowning(5) 10 57
(Tony Carroll) *hld up towards rr: hdwy 3f out: sn swtchd rt and rdn: drifted lft over 1f out: kpt on same pce ins fnl f* **13/2**

3543 5 shd **Festival Dance**[12] [5534] 3-9-0 **62** IanBurns(7) 12 58
(Ron Hodges) *awkward leaving stalls: towards rr: c centre 3f out: rdn and hdwy sn after: kpt on same pce fnl f* **14/1**

0001 6 6 **Mary's Pet**[12] [5540] 4-9-5 **58** (p) HarryBentley 7 34
(John Akehurst) *s.i.s: towards rr: nt clrest of runs over 2f out: hmpd over 1f out: styd on ins fnl f: nvr trbld ldrs* **7/2[2]**

050 7 2 1/4 **Anathena**[99] [2673] 3-8-7 **55** JackDuern(7) 13 24
(Reg Hollinshead) *chsd ldrs: rdn over 2f out: wknd jst over 1f out* **16/1**

0003 8 3/4 **Rich Harvest (USA)**[8] [5678] 6-8-4 **46** oh1 MatthewCosham(3) 9 13
(Ray Peacock) *chsd ldrs: rdn over 2f out: keeping on at same pce whn hmpd over 1f out* **25/1**

0/2- 9 1 1/4 **Nordic Light (USA)**[12] 7-8-0 **46** oh1 TimClark(7) 1 8
(Mrs A Malzard, Jersey) *led tl wl over 2f out: wknd ent fnl f* **33/1**

444 10 1 3/4 **Howyadoingnotsobad (IRE)**[18] [5346] 3-8-13 **54** BillyCray 8 11
(Karen George) *prom: rdn over 2f out: wkng whn hmpd over 1f out* **16/1**

-634 11 3 1/2 **Whitstable Native**[24] [5172] 3-9-3 **58** KierenFox 3 —
(John Best) *mid-div tl 3f out: wknd over 1f out* **16/1**

046 **12** *1 ¼* **Gracie's Games**[13] 5513 5-9-6 **59**....................(v) SophieDoyle 2 —
(Richard Price) *mid-div: rdn over 2f out: hld whn hmpd over 1f out* **10/1**

1m 12.37s (1.17) **Going Correction** +0.175s/f (Good)
WFA 3 from 4yo+ 2lb **12 Ran SP% 120.9**
Speed ratings (Par 101): **99,97,96,94,93 85,82,81,80,77 73,71**
toteswingers:1&2:£4.10, 2&3:£20.00, 1&3:£12.50 CSF £21.55 CT £258.27 TOTE £3.40: £1.10, £2.10, £5.30; EX 21.00.
Owner Paul Nicholas **Bred** Hedsor Stud **Trained** Green Ore, Somerset
■ Stewards' Enquiry : Julie Cumine three-day ban: careless riding (Sep 25-27)

FOCUS
A modest sprint handicap in which the well-backed winner came down the middle of the track and the first five came home clear.
T/Plt: £53.20 to a £1 stake. Pool of £51,600.25 - 707.35 winning tickets. T/Qpdt: £9.60 to a £1 stake. Pool of £3,697.23 - 284.60 winning tickets. TM

5875 CHESTER (L-H)
Saturday, September 10

OFFICIAL GOING: Good (7.4)
Wind: Fairly strong, across Weather: Fine.

5918 POMMERY CHAMPAGNE H'CAP (DIV 1) 5f 16y
2:00 (2:01) (Class 4) (0-85,84) 3-Y-0+ **£4,851** (£1,443; £721; £360) **Stalls** High

Form RPR

0250 **1** **Foxy Music**[28] 5033 7-9-7 **84**.................... GrahamGibbons 10 92
(Eric Alston) *gd spd fr the gate and sn swtchd across to rail: mde all: hung rt and drifted off fence fr over 3f out: rdn over 1f out: all out cl home* **14/1**

0506 **2** *hd* **Legal Eagle (IRE)**[8] 5680 6-8-12 **75**....................(p) FrannyNorton 3 82
(Paul Green) *in tch: effrt over 1f out: wnt 2nd ins fnl f: pressed wnr: r.o towards fin* **14/1**

432 **3** *¾* **Sleepy Blue Ocean**[14] 5468 5-8-7 **70** oh2....................(p) RobertWinston 4 75+
(John Balding) *in rr: hdwy whn nt clr run 2f out: prog over 1f out: r.o ins fnl f: nvr gng to get there: hld cl home* **9/2**[3]

0020 **4** *½* **Tamareen (IRE)**[10] 5621 3-8-10 **74**.................... PaulHanagan 7 77
(Richard Fahey) *midfield: rdn and hdwy over 1f out: chsd ldrs ins fnl f: styd on wl towards fin: nt quite pce of ldrs* **12/1**

3006 **5** *1 ½* **Tillys Tale**[74] 3493 4-8-7 **73**.................... MichaelO'Connell(3) 2 70
(Paul Midgley) *chsd wnr: rdn and ch over 1f out: lost 2nd ins fnl f: no ex fnl 75yds* **10/1**

3551 **6** *½* **Mayoman (IRE)**[8] 5679 6-8-8 **76**.................... NeilFarley(5) 5 72
(Declan Carroll) *pushed along in rr: hdwy and swtchd lft ins fnl f: kpt on but unable to trble ldrs* **4/1**[2]

254 **7** *1* **Cruise Tothelimit (IRE)**[17] 5378 3-8-8 **72**.................... JamesSullivan 8 64
(Patrick Morris) *chsd ldrs: rdn and hung rt over 2f out: wknd over 1f out* **28/1**

3-24 **8** *¾* **Flash City (ITY)**[147] 1391 3-9-6 **84**....................(p) TomEaves 6 73
(Bryan Smart) *racd on outer: chsd ldrs: u.p 2f out: sn outpcd: dropped away fnl 100yds* **7/1**

6215 **9** *¾* **Hotham**[8] 5683 8-9-3 **80**.................... BarryMcHugh 11 67
(Noel Wilson) *stdd s: hld up: u.p over 2f out: nvr on terms* **16/1**

1451 **10** *hd* **Bravo King (IRE)**[15] 5456 3-9-3 **84**.................... RobertLButler(3) 9 70
(Richard Guest) *s.i.s: pushed along briefly in rr: hdwy to go in tch over 3f out: rdn and wknd over 1f out* **33/1**

1213 **11** *5* **Red Roar (IRE)**[16] 5400 4-8-2 **70** oh1.................... JulieBurke(5) 1 38
(Alan Berry) *midfield: lost pl over 3f out and sn hmpd whn n.m.r: bhd after* **7/2**[1]

61.41 secs (0.41) **Going Correction** +0.225s/f (Good)
WFA 3 from 4yo+ 1lb **11 Ran SP% 115.3**
Speed ratings (Par 105): **105,104,103,102,100 99,97,96,95,95 87**
Tote Swingers:1&2:£8.20, 2&3:£12.00, 1&3:£23.80 CSF £191.24 CT £1046.89 TOTE £15.90: £3.40, £3.50, £1.70; EX 137.60.
Owner G M & Mrs C Baillie **Bred** G M & C Baillie & Springs Equestrian **Trained** Longton, Lancs
■ Stewards' Enquiry : Graham Gibbons three-day ban: careless riding (Sep 25-27)

FOCUS
Rail out 6yds from 6f to top of home straight with drop in at that point. 5f race increased by 20yds, 5.5f by 22yds, 7.5f by 24yds, 1m 2f by 25yds and 1m 4f by 38yds. A fair handicap run at a strong pace as expected, but few got into contention.
Cruise Tothelimit(IRE) Official explanation: jockey said gelding hung right throughout
Red Roar(IRE) Official explanation: trainer said filly was unsuited by the goood ground

5919 YORK BREWERY MAIDEN STKS 7f 2y
2:30 (2:31) (Class 4) 2-Y-0 **£4,851** (£1,443; £721; £360) **Stalls** High

Form RPR

3 **1** **Mabaany**[48] 4352 2-9-3 0.................... TadhgO'Shea 5 88+
(William Haggas) *racd in 2nd pl: led over 2f out: qcknd clr fr over 1f out: r.o strly: eased towards fin* **4/5**[1]

52 **2** *10* **Chelsea Mick**[17] 5393 2-9-3 0.................... GrahamGibbons 4 72
(Ed McMahon) *led: hdd over 2f out: rdn and outpcd by wnr over 1f out: eased whn no ch fnl 110yds* **5/2**[2]

06 **3** *9* **Zammy**[103] 2559 2-9-3 0.................... RobertWinston 2 49
(Charles Hills) *racd keenly: hld up: chsd front 2 jst over 3f out but no imp: wl outpcd over 1f out* **5/1**[3]

4 *10* **Latenfast** 2-9-3 0.................... JamesSullivan 1 20
(Michael Easterby) *chsd ldrs: rdn and rn green over 3f out: wknd over 2f out: lost tch over 1f out* **25/1**

5 *8* **Beckfield Point** 2-9-0 0.................... RyanClark(3) 3 —
(Stuart Williams) *slowly away: a bhd: lost tch over 1f out* **22/1**

1m 28.1s (1.60) **Going Correction** +0.225s/f (Good) **5 Ran SP% 109.0**
Speed ratings (Par 97): **99,87,77,65,56**
CSF £2.94 TOTE £1.90: £1.10, £1.60; EX 2.40.
Owner Hamdan Al Maktoum **Bred** Shadwell Estate Company Limited **Trained** Newmarket, Suffolk
■ Stewards' Enquiry : Tadhg O'Shea two-day ban: careless riding (Sep 25-26)

FOCUS
An uncompetitive maiden in which the runners finished well strung out despite the pace being on the steady side. The winner might be a good bit better than this but a conservative vire has been taken of the form.

NOTEBOOK
Mabaany looked much more worth his lofty entries here than he did at Ascot on his debut, for all that form has been franked since by Zumbi's third in the Acomb, and he did it while still looking green and not totally at ease on the track, really getting into his stride only in the short straight and being never stronger than at the finish. On this evidence, though, he looks as if he might need a bit more experience before being thrown in at the deep end. (tchd Evens)
Chelsea Mick ran as well as could have been expected, never being a match for the winner but beating the rest as easily as he was entitled to, and that while being eased. He's probably not quite up to winning a maiden so it's likely to be nurseries now. (op 3-1)
Zammy was in trouble a long way out and did not achieve much in a remote third, but this first run since May will have tuned him up nicely for modest nurseries and he may yet do better. Official explanation: jockey said colt was hampered at the start (op 6-1 tchd 9-2)
Latenfast didn't show much on his debut. Official explanation: jockey said gelding hung right-handed throughout (op 14-1)
Beckfield Point also didn't show much on this debut after being particularly slowly away. (op 12-1 tchd 25-1)

5920 TETLEY'S BITTER H'CAP 7f 122y
3:00 (3:01) (Class 3) (0-90,90) 3-Y-0+ **£8,409** (£2,502; £1,250; £625) **Stalls** High

Form RPR

2450 **1** **Hacienda (IRE)**[14] 5465 4-8-13 **79**.................... FrannyNorton 14 88
(Mark Johnston) *mde all: rdn over 1f out: styd on gamely: in control towards fin* **14/1**

6300 **2** *1 ¼* **My Gacho (IRE)**[6] 5760 9-8-8 **77**....................(b) MichaelO'Connell(3) 6 83
(David Nicholls) *in tch: effrt over 1f out: styd on ins fnl f: nvr quite gng pce of wnr* **40/1**

3101 **3** *shd* **Weapon Of Choice (IRE)**[23] 5199 3-8-11 **87**.................... JulieBurke(5) 4 92+
(David Simcock) *hld up: hdwy over 3f out: rdn and r.o ins fnl f: gng on at fin* **11/2**[3]

4110 **4** *nk* **Queen Of Cash (IRE)**[22] 5255 3-8-13 **84**.................... RobertWinston 12 88
(Hughie Morrison) *racd keenly: prom: rdn to chal over 1f out: styd on same pce towards fin* **14/1**

0302 **5** *3 ½* **Venutius**[35] 4794 4-9-7 **87**.................... GrahamGibbons 7 83
(Ed McMahon) *prom: rdn over 1f out: nt qckn whn intimidated and drifted rt wl ins fnl f: one pce fnl 75yds* **5/1**[2]

0022 **6** *1 ¼* **Moody Tunes**[14] 5485 8-8-7 **76**.................... RossAtkinson(3) 3 69
(Tom Dascombe) *midfield: pushed along most of way: nvr able to chal* **16/1**

0213 **7** *nk* **One Scoop Or Two**[1] 5879 5-9-2 **82**....................(p) TonyCulhane 8 74
(Reg Hollinshead) *chsd ldrs: rdn over 1f out: carried hd to one side: one pce fnl 100yds* **9/2**[1]

0000 **8** *2* **Everymanforhimself (IRE)**[8] 5684 7-9-3 **83**....................(p) TomEaves 1 70
(Kevin Ryan) *chsd ldrs: rdn and outpcd over 2f out: no imp after* **16/1**

0650 **9** *1* **Kay Gee Be (IRE)**[24] 5185 7-9-10 **90**.................... TonyHamilton 11 75
(Richard Fahey) *s.i.s: hld up: pushed along over 2f out: nvr on terms* **10/1**

1030 **9** *dht* **Viva Ronaldo (IRE)**[21] 5272 5-9-7 **87**.................... PaulHanagan 13 72
(Richard Fahey) *in tch: lost pl 6f out: sn in rr div: n.d after* **8/1**

6002 **11** *2 ¼* **Sonning Rose (IRE)**[11] 5581 3-8-9 **80**.................... DuranFentiman 9 58
(Mick Channon) *s.i.s: hld up: u.p 2f out: nvr on terms* **17/2**

0000 **12** *½* **Steed**[13] 5516 4-8-8 **77**....................(p) RobertLButler(3) 2 55
(Richard Guest) *racd keenly in midfield: rdn and wknd over 1f out* **20/1**

3055 **13** *2* **Chosen Character (IRE)**[11] 5581 3-8-8 **79**....................(vt) TadhgO'Shea 5 51
(Tom Dascombe) *swtchd lft s: hld up: nvr able to get on terms* **14/1**

1m 34.01s (0.21) **Going Correction** +0.225s/f (Good)
WFA 3 from 4yo+ 5lb **13 Ran SP% 119.9**
Speed ratings (Par 107): **107,105,105,105,101 100,100,98,97,97 95,94,92**
Tote Swingers:1&2:£83.30, 2&3:£72.80, 1&3:£19.50 CSF £474.04 CT £3549.86 TOTE £16.30: £4.30, £12.30, £2.40; EX 231.40.
Owner Sheikh Hamdan Bin Mohammed Al Maktoum **Bred** Yeomanstown Stud **Trained** Middleham Moor, N Yorks
■ Stewards' Enquiry : Michael O'Connell caution: used whip without giving gelding sufficient time to respond

FOCUS
What looked an open handicap beforehand ended up concerning only a handful of runners, with those held up never able to land a blow. The gallop wasn't strong.

NOTEBOOK
Hacienda(IRE) came here on a long losing run in handicaps and looked to be poorly drawn but, as with the winner of the opener, the decision to break quickly and get across to the rail paid dividends as he ended up being left alone in front. Things are not going to fall as ideally next time and his overall record suggests he will struggle to follow up. (op 12-1)
My Gacho(IRE) did not get to the front as he often does but that did not seem to affect him and he ran as well as he has for a while, albeit being well placed throughout. His record this year has been patchy, though, so he is no sure thing to repeat this next time. (op 33-1)
Weapon Of Choice(IRE) ◆ continues in fine form and was arguably unlucky not to have followed up his recent Epsom win as he fared best of those just off the pace and probably gave the winner too much rope. The ground might not have been soft enough for him either, so he has good prospects of winning again this autumn. (op 6-1)
Queen Of Cash(IRE) was another soon well placed close to the rail despite a wide draw and she does not need any excuses. (op 12-1)
Venutius is another who does not need an excuse, for all he might have finished a tad closer had he not been bumped in the straight. (op 11-2 tchd 6-1)
Moody Tunes almost certainly remains in form as he found the drop in trip and rise in grade very much against him. (op 12-1)
One Scoop Or Two has run well turned out very quickly before, so the fact he ran well the day before should not have been an issue in respect of his effort here. Probably more importantly, he was forced to race wide and that seemed to tell on him as he faded. (op 13-2)
Everymanforhimself(IRE) could not take advantage of his inside draw and faded late on. (tchd 18-1)

5921 STAR SPORTS STAND CUP (LISTED RACE) 1m 4f 66y
3:30 (3:33) (Class 1) 3-Y-0+ **£17,760** (£6,717; £3,357; £1,677) **Stalls** High

Form RPR

0004 **1** **Debussy (IRE)**[49] 4315 5-9-1 110.................... PaulHanagan 2 104+
(Mahmood Al Zarooni) *racd keenly: a.p: led over 1f out: drew clr ins fnl f: r.o wl: eased cl home* **15/8**[1]

1122 **2** *2 ½* **Kiama Bay (IRE)**[22] 5250 5-9-1 99.................... TomEaves 5 97
(John Quinn) *hld up: hdwy 2f out: chsd ldng pair and edgd lft over 1f out: styd on to take 2nd post: no ch w wnr* **4/1**[3]

2024 **3** *hd* **Zennor**[7] 5724 4-8-10 77.................... GrahamGibbons 1 92
(Tom Dascombe) *led: rdn and hdd over 1f out: no ch w wnr ins fnl f: no ex: lost 2nd post* **25/1**

2411 **4** *3 ½* **Berling (IRE)**[21] 5271 4-9-6 99.................... RichardMullen 4 96
(John Dunlop) *hld up: pushed along over 3f out: chsd ldrs over 1f out: no imp* **10/3**[2]

1240 **5** *8* **Colour Vision (FR)**[9] 5659 3-8-6 100.................... FrannyNorton 3 79
(Mark Johnston) *prom tl rdn and wknd over 2f out* **7/1**

-500 **6** *13* **Prince Bishop (IRE)**[14] 5494 4-9-1 114....................(v[1]) RobertWinston 6 58
(Saeed Bin Suroor) *hld up in tch: tk clsr order over 4f out: rdn over 2f out: wknd over 1f out* **11/2**

2m 37.39s (-1.11) **Going Correction** +0.225s/f (Good)
WFA 3 from 4yo+ 9lb **6 Ran SP% 109.6**
Speed ratings (Par 111): **112,110,110,107,102 93**
Tote Swingers:1&2:£2.40, 2&3:£2.70, 1&3:£6.50 CSF £9.13 TOTE £2.80: £1.80, £2.00; EX 8.70.
Owner Godolphin **Bred** Darley **Trained** Newmarket, Suffolk

FOCUS
A variety of abilities on show in an uncompetitive Listed race. The pace was only steady and the form has a very muddling look, with the third a doubt. The winner did not need to be anywhere near his best.

NOTEBOOK
Debussy(IRE) had stamina doubts to answer at the trip and questions about his current wellbeing too after being employed as a pacemaker in recent starts, but the 2010 Arlington Million winner was far too good for these, as his best form suggested he would be, in a race where the steady pace played right into his hands. This form does not confirm he is back to his best, but he clearly retains more than enough ability for a fruitful autumn. (op 5-2)
Kiama Bay(IRE) had been running well in good handicaps lately but had 11lb to find with Debussy on official ratings and the steady gallop only made his task even harder. In the circumstances, it was a respectable effort and he will probably end up taking his chance in the November Handicap. (op 7-2)
Zennor seems to have run very well on the face of it but with the three behind her all well below form for one reason or another quite what she achieved having had the run of race out in front is not easy to know. Her handicap mark is sure to suffer as a consequence, but that might not worry her connections now she has some black type. (op 16-1)
Berling(IRE) came here on a roll but ran a flat race for all he faced a stiff task giving weight all round. He would have been better suited by a strong gallop with his rivals coming back to him, and should not be judged on this. (op 3-1 tchd 11-4)
Colour Vision(FR) has plenty of questions to answer now after this second poor run in a row, for all the steady gallop at a trip shorter than ideal would not have tested his stamina enough. (op 13-2)
Prince Bishop(IRE) dropped out very tamely in first-time headgear and would appear to be a pale shadow of the horse he was last season. (tchd 13-2)

5922 CHESHIRE LIFE NURSERY — 5f 110y
4:10 (4:10) (Class 3) (0-95,87) 2-Y-O **£7,561** (£2,263; £1,131; £566; £282) **Stalls** High

Form	Pos	Dist	Horse	RPR
1045	**1**		**Bubbly Ballerina**[21] 5270 2-9-0 **80** .... RichardMullen 4 (Alan Bailey) *racd keenly: chsd ldrs: rdn to chal over 1f out: led wl ins fnl f: r.o* **7/1**	83
2001	**2**	*nk*	**Free Zone**[17] 5367 2-8-10 **76** .... TomEaves 7 (Bryan Smart) *chsd ldr: rdn to chal strly fr over 1f out: r.o: jst hld* **7/1**	78
4143	**3**	*1 ¼*	**Signifer (IRE)**[11] 5592 2-9-7 **87** .... TonyCulhane 10 (Mick Channon) *hld up in rr: rdn and hdwy over 1f out: r.o ins fnl f: gng on at fin* **15/2**	87
1612	**4**	*½*	**Sonko (IRE)**[19] 5310 2-8-4 **70** ....(p) FrannyNorton 3 (Tim Pitt) *led: rdn whn pressed over 1f out: hdd wl ins fnl f: no ex towards fin* **7/1**	66
0142	**5**	*3*	**Mahkama (USA)**[11] 5584 2-9-5 **85** .... RobertWinston 6 (Saeed Bin Suroor) *s.i.s: hld up: pushed along over 2f out: effrt to chse ldrs over 1f out: one pce ins fnl f* **3/1**[1]	71
3451	**6**	*1 ¾*	**Beau Mistral (IRE)**[24] 5174 2-8-7 **73** .... JamesSullivan 8 (Paul Green) *racd on outer: chsd ldrs: rdn 2f out: wknd over 1f out* **14/1**	54
1351	**7**	*1 ½*	**Amadeus Denton (IRE)**[43] 4500 2-9-0 **85** .... JulieBurke(5) 9 (Michael Dods) *towards rr: rdn 2f out: nvr on terms* **13/2**[3]	64
023	**8**	*4 ½*	**Forest Edge (IRE)**[21] 5269 2-9-2 **82** .... GrahamGibbons 2 (David Evans) *s.i.s: midfield: pushed along over 3f out: wknd over 2f out* **4/1**[2]	43

67.48 secs (1.28) **Going Correction** +0.225s/f (Good) **8** Ran SP% **114.3**
Speed ratings (Par 99): **100,99,97,97,93 90,88,82**
Tote Swingers: 1&2 £11.10, 1&3 £10.80, 2&3 £11.00 CSF £54.53 CT £381.45 TOTE £6.00: £1.80, £2.30, £2.80; EX 51.70.
Owner The Champagne Club **Bred** Whitsbury Manor Stud **Trained** Newmarket, Suffolk

FOCUS
No more than a fair nursery, despite it being a 0-95, and once again it was difficult to get involved from off the pace. The winner was very well treated on her best efforts. Limited but straightforward form.

NOTEBOOK
Bubbly Ballerina ran in the Queen Mary earlier in the season but still looked to have a bit to find off an official rating of 80 on her nursery debut. She only just scrambled home, having taken the shortest route throughout, and is unlikely to find another opening as weak as this. (op 11-2)
Free Zone was never far away and continued his good recent form without suggesting he is suddenly going to find the improvement he will need to get his head in front. (op 11-2)
Signifer(IRE) bounced back from a couple of lesser efforts and was a bit unfortunate. It was not the fact that he was drawn widest that seemed to hold him back, but that he lost his position at halfway and found the post coming too soon. (op 10-1)
Sonko(IRE)'s last win had come in a claimer and she probably ran right up to her best. (op 8-1)
Mahkama(USA) once again did not see her race out as seemed likely, having moved smoothly into contention after a slowish start, and has a bit to prove now. (op 4-1)
Beau Mistral(IRE) found this tougher than when landing a weak maiden at Nottingham last time but, that said, was not helped by racing wide throughout. (op 11-1)

5923 POMMERY CHAMPAGNE H'CAP (DIV II) — 5f 16y
4:45 (4:45) (Class 4) (0-85,85) 3-Y-0+ **£4,851** (£1,443; £721; £360) **Stalls** Low

Form	Pos	Dist	Horse	RPR
4060	**1**		**Bertoliver**[65] 3778 7-8-10 **77** .... RyanClark(3) 3 (Stuart Williams) *mde all: rdn ins fnl f: r.o: in control towards fin* **11/2**[3]	85
0526	**2**	*½*	**Lucky Numbers (IRE)**[8] 5683 5-9-5 **83** .... JamesSullivan 4 (Paul Green) *slowly away: hld up: plld to wd outside and hdwy over 1f out: r.o ins fnl f: gng on at fin but nt quite get to wnr* **6/1**	89+
1455	**3**	*nk*	**Rylee Mooch**[14] 5468 3-8-7 **72** ....(e) GrahamGibbons 5 (Richard Guest) *chsd ldrs: effrt on inner to take 2nd pl over 1f out: nvr quite got to wnr: lost 2nd fnl stride* **8/1**	77
4010	**4**	*½*	**Green Park (IRE)**[14] 5468 8-8-11 **80** ....(b) NeilFarley(5) 7 (Declan Carroll) *hld up: rdn and hdwy over 1f out: styd on ins fnl f: nt rch ldrs* **11/1**	83
5412	**5**	*1*	**Wicked Wilma (IRE)**[7] 5720 7-8-4 **73** .... JulieBurke(5) 8 (Alan Berry) *chsd ldr tl rdn over 1f out: no ex fnl 75yds* **5/1**[2]	73
-156	**6**	*hd*	**Lucky Dan (IRE)**[35] 4791 5-8-10 **74** .... PaulHanagan 2 (Paul Green) *hld up in rr: rdn and hdwy ins fnl f: kpt on: unable to get to ldrs* **9/4**[1]	73+
2650	**7**	*4 ½*	**Bold Bidder**[43] 4498 3-9-6 **85** .... FrannyNorton 6 (Kevin Ryan) *chsd ldrs: rdn 2f out: wknd ins fnl f* **17/2**	68
046	**8**	*1*	**On The High Tops (IRE)**[12] 5559 3-8-13 **78** .... PJMcDonald 9 (Ruth Carr) *prom on outer tl wknd over 1f out* **20/1**	57

61.50 secs (0.50) **Going Correction** +0.225s/f (Good)
WFA 3 from 5yo+ 1lb **8** Ran SP% **111.8**
Speed ratings (Par 105): **105,104,103,102,101 101,93,92**
Tote Swingers: 1&2 £4.10, 1&3 £7.80, 2&3 £6.90 CSF £36.45 CT £258.12 TOTE £7.20: £1.70, £2.30, £2.50; EX 45.40.
Owner Mrs A Shone **Bred** Pillar To Post Racing **Trained** Newmarket, Suffolk

FOCUS
The second division of the sprint handicap was not as fiercely run as the opener and the winner was able to dictate fairly comfortably.

5924 BARTON ROUGE H'CAP — 7f 122y
5:15 (5:16) (Class 5) (0-75,75) 3-Y-0+ **£4,043** (£1,203; £601; £300) **Stalls** High

Form	Pos	Dist	Horse	RPR
5652	**1**		**Illustrious Prince (IRE)**[6] 5760 4-9-2 **72** .... NeilFarley(5) 6 (Declan Carroll) *chsd ldrs: kicked into ld 2f out: r.o wl to draw clr ins fnl f: eased towards fin* **4/1**[2]	85+
3300	**2**	*4 ½*	**Hoppy's Flyer (FR)**[50] 4290 3-8-7 **66** ow1 .... MichaelO'Connell(3) 8 (Paul Midgley) *bmpd s: in midfield: nt clr run 2f out: hdwy over 1f out: styd on ins fnl f: tk 2nd fnl stride: no ch w wnr* **10/1**	65+
0126	**3**	*hd*	**Jungle Bay**[24] 5195 4-9-9 **74** ....(p) FrannyNorton 1 (Jane Chapple-Hyam) *led: rdn and hdd 2f out: outpcd by wnr ins fnl f: lost 2nd fnl stride* **11/4**[1]	73
1255	**4**	*¾*	**Gemma's Delight (IRE)**[16] 5414 4-8-12 **63** ....(p) LiamJones 16 (James Unett) *towards rr: hdwy over 1f out: styd on for press ins fnl f: nt quite get to ldrs* **8/1**	60
0-5R	**5**	*nk*	**Timeteam (IRE)**[224] 351 5-9-6 **71** .... RichardMullen 2 (Alan Bailey) *missed break: in rr: hdwy 2f out: styd on ins fnl f: nt quite pce to get to ldrs* **25/1**	68
5035	**6**	*nk*	**Carcinetto (IRE)**[2] 5862 9-8-9 **63** .... RossAtkinson(3) 4 (David Evans) *hmpd 6f out: in rr and rdn along after: hdwy ins fnl f: styd on: nvr nrr* **12/1**	59
3004	**7**	*5*	**Lord Of The Dance (IRE)**[7] 5733 5-9-0 **68** .... RyanClark(3) 15 (Mark Brisbourne) *in tch: effrt over 2f out: chsd ldrs over 1f out: no imp: wknd ins fnl f* **16/1**	51
0-5	**8**	*1 ¼*	**Newlands Princess (IRE)**[17] 5392 3-9-1 **71** .... RobertWinston 5 (Ollie Pears) *chsd ldrs: rdn over 2f out: outpcd over 1f out: wl btn fnl f* **6/1**[3]	50
3000	**9**	*1*	**Bertie Blu Boy**[4] 5803 3-8-5 **61** oh1 .... JamesSullivan 13 (Paul Green) *midfield: rdn over 4f out: wknd fnl f* **25/1**	38
2062	**10**	*1*	**Georgebernardshaw (IRE)**[43] 4501 6-9-8 **73** .... PBBeggy 14 (John Quinn) *chsd ldrs: rdn 2f out: wknd over 1f out* **14/1**	48
0105	**11**	*14*	**Drive Home (USA)**[7] 5721 4-8-10 **61** oh2 ....(p) DuranFentiman 3 (Noel Wilson) *w ldr to 3f out: rdn and wknd over 2f out* **12/1**	—
0000	**12**	*14*	**Insolenceofoffice (IRE)**[113] 2250 3-9-0 **70** .... FrederikTylicki 11 (Bruce Hellier) *hmpd s: a bhd: nvr on terms* **40/1**	—
40-0	**13**	*5*	**Chris's Ridge**[18] 5341 4-9-5 **70** .... GrahamGibbons 7 (Eric Alston) *racd keenly in midfield: rdn and wknd wl over 2f out: eased whn wl btn over 1f out* **25/1**	—

1m 35.53s (1.73) **Going Correction** +0.225s/f (Good)
WFA 3 from 4yo+ 5lb **13** Ran SP% **123.1**
Speed ratings (Par 103): **100,95,95,94,94 93,88,87,86,85 71,57,52**
Tote Swingers:1&2:£10.50, 2&3:£10.80, 1&3:£2.70 CSF £43.41 CT £136.10 TOTE £5.00: £2.10, £3.80, £1.70; EX 73.20.
Owner P J Dolan **Bred** Rathbarry Stud **Trained** Sledmere, E Yorks

FOCUS
A run-of-the-mill handicap that was turned into a procession by the well-handicapped winner. There was a bit of early trouble in running and the runners were soon well strung out.

5925 CRUISE NIGHTSPOT H'CAP — 1m 2f 75y
5:50 (5:50) (Class 5) (0-75,78) 3-Y-O **£4,043** (£1,203; £601; £300) **Stalls** Low

Form	Pos	Dist	Horse	RPR
0402	**1**		**Spanish Plume**[18] 5350 3-9-2 **70** .... RobertWinston 1 (Reg Hollinshead) *hld up: swtchd rt and hdwy on outer over 1f out: r.o ins fnl f: got up to ld fnl strides* **9/1**	77
5363	**2**	*hd*	**Glyn Ceiriog**[41] 4576 3-8-12 **66** ....(p) TonyCulhane 4 (George Baker) *hld up in midfield: hdwy 2f out: nt clr run over 1f out: sn swtchd lft: r.o to chal wl ins fnl f: jst denied in driving fin* **8/1**	72+
0540	**3**	*hd*	**Tapis Libre**[28] 5064 3-8-11 **65** .... JamesSullivan 11 (Michael Easterby) *led after 1 1/2f: rdn over 1f out: hrd pressed ins fnl f: hdd fnl strides* **25/1**	71
3131	**4**	*shd*	**Sangar**[12] 5560 3-8-13 **67** .... GrahamGibbons 12 (Ollie Pears) *a.p: rdn over 1f out: str chal ins fnl f: r.o in driving fin* **11/4**[1]	73
3351	**5**	*1 ½*	**She's Got The Luck (IRE)**[32] 4878 3-9-1 **69** .... PaulHanagan 3 (Richard Fahey) *in tch: lost pl over 2f out: rallied ins fnl f: styd on but unable to chal front quartet* **13/2**	72+
0041	**6**	*1 ¼*	**Red Inca**[21] 5281 3-9-5 **73** .... TadhgO'Shea 9 (Brian Meehan) *s.i.s: in rr: pushed along 3f out: effrt on outer over 1f out: styd on but no real imp on ldrs ins fnl f* **4/1**[2]	74
4542	**7**	*nk*	**Cadore (IRE)**[41] 4576 3-9-6 **74** .... JackMitchell 7 (Peter Chapple-Hyam) *trckd ldrs: tried to chal 2f out: nt qckn over 1f out: one pce fnl 75yds* **6/1**[3]	74
50	**8**	*1 ¼*	**Regal Kiss**[29] 5020 3-9-3 **71** .... FrannyNorton 6 (Mark Johnston) *led for 1 1/2f: continued to trck ldrs: rdn over 1f out: kpt on tl eased and no ex fnl 75yds* **12/1**	69
4040	**9**	*2 ½*	**Dubai Celebration**[7] 5731 3-8-11 **68** .... PatrickDonaghy(3) 5 (Jedd O'Keeffe) *hld up: u.p over 2f out: nvr on terms* **22/1**	61
0110	**10**	*16*	**Cuckney Bear**[16] 5407 3-9-4 **72** .... RichardMullen 10 (Ed McMahon) *racd keenly: sn in tch on outer: clsd 3f out: wknd u.p 2f out* **14/1**	34

2m 13.65s (2.45) **Going Correction** +0.225s/f (Good) **10** Ran SP% **117.9**
Speed ratings (Par 101): **99,98,98,98,97 96,96,95,93,80**
Tote Swingers:1&2:£10.30, 2&3:£29.00, 1&3:£57.80 CSF £79.84 CT £1744.04 TOTE £12.30: £2.70, £2.90, £8.10; EX 90.10.
Owner The Three R'S **Bred** Mrs J A Prescott **Trained** Upper Longdon, Staffs

■ Stewards' Enquiry : Tony Culhane two-day ban: used whip without giving filly sufficient time to respond (Sep 25-26)

FOCUS
An ordinary handicap to end proceedings. It was run at no more than a fair gallop and there was never much between the runners throughout.

Cuckney Bear Official explanation: trainer said gelding was unsuited by the track

T/Plt: £321.80 to a £1 stake. Pool £59,321.47. 134.54 winning tickets. T/Qpdt: £86.90 to a £1 stake. Pool £3,736.18. 31.80 winning tickets. DO

5882 DONCASTER (L-H)

Saturday, September 10

OFFICIAL GOING: Good to firm (8.8)

Wind: Strong against Weather: Cloudy - sunny periods

5926 ONE CALL INSURANCE CHAMPAGNE STKS (GROUP 2) (C&G) 7f

2:05 (2:05) (Class 1) 2-Y-O **£42,532** (£16,125; £8,070; £4,020; £2,017) **Stalls** High

Form				RPR
0214	**1**		**Trumpet Major (IRE)**[21] 5276 2-8-12 104 RichardHughes 4 *(Richard Hannon) trckd ldng pair: hdwy and cl up 2f out: rdn to ld 1 1/2f out: kpt on wl ins fnl f* **7/1**	111+
3113	**2**	*1 1/4*	**Red Duke (USA)**[45] 4424 2-9-1 107 KierenFallon 3 *(John Quinn) hld up in rr: hdwy over 2f out: rdn over 1f out: chsd wnr ins fnl f: kpt on* **11/4**[2]	111
11	**3**	*1*	**Entifaadha**[24] 5181 2-8-12 105 RichardHills 5 *(William Haggas) led: pushed along over 2f out: rdn and hdd 1 1/2f out: sn edgd lft and one pce* **11/10**[1]	105
	4	*1/2*	**Daddy Long Legs (USA)**[31] 4933 2-8-12 0 JPO'Brien 2 *(A P O'Brien, Ire) trckd ldr: cl up 1/2-way: rdn along 2f out: sn drvn and kpt on same pce* **5/1**[3]	104
15	**5**	*6*	**Al Khan (IRE)**[24] 5181 2-8-12 91 FrankieDettori 1 *(Peter Chapple-Hyam) hld up: swtchd lft and gd hdwy 2f out: chal and ev ch 1 1/2f out: sn rdn and btn* **10/1**	89

1m 25.86s (-0.44) **Going Correction** -0.075s/f (Good) **5** Ran SP% **112.5**

Speed ratings (Par 107): **99,97,96,95,89**

toteswingers:1&2:£1.90, 2&3:£1.10, 1&3:£2.70 CSF £26.62 TOTE £8.40: £3.80, £2.10; EX 26.70.

Owner John Manley **Bred** John Cullinan **Trained** East Everleigh, Wilts

FOCUS

There was quite a strong headwind in the straight, and they didn't go overly fast in this opening contest. Historically a good race, but it's had little impact on the following season's Classics for a while now and this looked an ordinary renewal, rated slightly below the race average. Trumpet Major posted an effort in keeping with his Newmarket win.

NOTEBOOK

Trumpet Major(IRE), unable to act in soft ground when favourite for a Group 3 at Sandown the time before, had earlier been a particularly impressive winner at Newmarket, and the return to a faster surface enabled him to record a career-best, tracking the early speed centre-field and showing a decent change of pace to get first run on the runner-up. This looks his best trip for the time being, although he is bred to stay further on the dam's side of his pedigree and he's entitled to take his chance in next month's Dewhurst, for all that he'd be an unlikely winner. (op 17-2)

Red Duke(USA), saddled with a 3lb penalty for having previously won at this level, marginally prevails as the best horse at the weights on strict interpretations. As had been the case at Goodwood the time before, the race didn't pan out for him, briefly being caught flat-footed when the pace lifted before staying on well. A stiffer test will suit and he'll now be trained for the Breeders' Cup, where the longer trip and more frenetic pace is expected to suit. (tchd 3-1 in places)

Entifaadha had created a fine impression in going unbeaten in two previous starts, and the form of his last-time-out Group 3 success at York had worked out well. He seemed something of a reluctant leader, though, and considering there was a headwind, it was no surprise to see him brushed aside. This wasn't him at his best and his trainer expects him to prove suited by 1m. (tchd 6-5, 5-4 in places)

Daddy Long Legs(USA), whose yard don't tend to aim their better ones at this, is unlikely to be a star, but there's a fair bit of scope to him and he can leave this form behind in time, with a more truly run race likely to suit. (tchd 11-2)

Al Khan(IRE), as had been the case at York last time, travelled strongly into contention before fading. He's by a sprinter, out of a sprinter, and his maiden win came over 6f, so it's probable this trip is too far. It's likely we've still to see the best of him. (op 12-1 tchd 14-1)

5927 LADBROKES PORTLAND (H'CAP) 5f 140y

2:35 (2:38) (Class 2) 3-Y-O+

£37,350 (£11,184; £5,592; £2,796; £1,398; £702) **Stalls** High

Form				RPR
00	**1**		**Nocturnal Affair (SAF)**[19] 5331 5-9-5 **101** NeilCallan 15 *(David Marnane, Ire) dwlt: sn in midfield: hdwy over 2f out: rdn to ld jst ins fnl f: drvn out* **14/1**	111+
3020	**2**	*1/2*	**Confessional**[28] 5060 4-8-13 **95** (e) SilvestreDeSousa 7 *(Tim Easterby) in tch: rdn along 2f out: drvn and styd on to chal ins fnl f: ev ch whn hung lft and no ex towards fin* **14/1**	103
4550	**3**	*nse*	**Addictive Dream (IRE)**[28] 5060 4-9-1 **97** FrankieDettori 16 *(Walter Swinburn) trckd ldrs: hdwy 2f out: rdn to chal over 1f out and ev ch: drvn ins fnl f: kpt on same pce towards fin* **14/1**	105
3106	**4**	*nk*	**Ancient Cross**[24] 5180 7-9-4 **100** (t) PaddyAspell 19 *(Michael Easterby) midfield: hdwy over 2f out: swtchd rt and rdn over 1f out: styd on ins fnl f* **20/1**	107
2211	**5**	*hd*	**York Glory (USA)**[21] 5288 3-8-11 **95** (b) PhillipMakin 21 *(Kevin Ryan) dwlt and towards rr: hdwy 1/2-way: rdn and styng on whn nt clr run ent fnl f: kpt on wl: nrst fin* **11/2**[1]	101+
0030	**6**	*1/2*	**Jimmy Styles**[42] 4534 7-9-10 **106** (p) AdamKirby 18 *(Clive Cox) midfield: hdwy 2f out: nt clr run and swtchd lft ent fnl f: sn rdn and fin wl* **16/1**	110
3013	**7**	*3/4*	**Verinco**[6] 5758 5-8-11 **93** (v) RoystonFfrench 11 *(Bryan Smart) led: rdn wl over 1f out: drvn and hdd jst ins fnl f: grad wknd* **16/1**	95
0200	**8**	*1/2*	**Tax Free (IRE)**[14] 5467 9-8-13 **95** AdrianNicholls 17 *(David Nicholls) towards rr: hdwy wl over 1f out: sn rdn and n.m.r appr fnl f: styd on: nrst fin* **25/1**	95
6101	**9**	*1/2*	**Dungannon**[35] 4776 4-9-3 **99** WilliamBuick 6 *(Andrew Balding) midfield: effrt and hdwy wl over 1f out: sn rdn and no imp ins fnl f* **11/1**	97
6165	**10**	*3/4*	**Secret Witness**[15] 5430 5-8-10 **92** (b) RichardHills 20 *(Ronald Harris) chsd ldrs: prom 1/2-way: rdn along 2f out and grad wknd* **20/1**	88
1246	**11**	*1/2*	**Lexi's Hero (IRE)**[28] 5054 3-9-5 **103** (b) StephenCraine 12 *(Kevin Ryan) chsd ldrs: rdn 2f out: drvn and wkng whn n.m.r and hmpd ent fnl f* **25/1**	97
4250	**12**	*1 3/4*	**Waffle (IRE)**[28] 5060 5-9-9 **105** (v[1]) RichardHughes 4 *(David Barron) a towards rr* **8/1**[3]	93
2400	**13**	*1 1/4*	**Doctor Parkes**[35] 4776 5-9-0 **96** SebSanders 13 *(Eric Alston) chsd ldrs: rdn along over 2f out: grad wknd* **33/1**	80
0012	**14**	*1*	**Joe Packet**[21] 5264 4-9-0 **96** RichardKingscote 14 *(Jonathan Portman) s.i.s: a in rr* **12/1**	77
11	**15**	*nk*	**Zero Money (IRE)**[7] 5706 5-9-6 **102** (b) GeorgeBaker 2 *(Roger Charlton) racd wd: prom: rdn along over 2f out: sn wknd* **7/1**[2]	82
5030	**16**	*1/2*	**Favourite Girl (IRE)**[14] 5476 5-8-12 **94** (v) DavidAllan 10 *(Tim Easterby) prom: rdn along over 2f out: sn drvn and wknd wl over 1f out* **33/1**	72
0500	**17**	*5*	**Lui Rei (ITY)**[42] 4534 5-8-10 **95** LeeTopliss(3) 22 *(Robert Cowell) dwlt: a in rr* **25/1**	56
0101	**18**	*3 1/2*	**Swiss Dream**[14] 5481 3-9-0 **98** OlivierPeslier 8 *(David Elsworth) prom: rdn along over 2f out: sn drvn and wknd wl over 1f out* **8/1**[3]	47
0000	**19**	*1/2*	**Burning Thread (IRE)**[35] 4776 4-8-12 **94** JackMitchell 9 *(Tim Etherington) chsd ldrs: rdn along over 2f out: sn wknd* **66/1**	41
5-03	**20**	*4 1/2*	**Bajan Tryst (USA)**[27] 5086 5-9-3 **99** KierenFallon 3 *(Kevin Ryan) in rr fr 1/2-way* **16/1**	31
0000	**21**	*14*	**Rain Delayed (IRE)**[14] 5467 5-9-0 **96** TomQueally 1 *(Michael Dods) racd wd: in tch: rdn along 1/2-way: sn wknd and bhd* **33/1**	—

66.69 secs (-2.11) **Going Correction** -0.075s/f (Good)

WFA 3 from 4yo+ 2lb **21** Ran SP% **135.2**

Speed ratings (Par 109): **111,110,110,109,109 108,107,107,106,105 104,102,100,99,99 98,91,87,86,80 61**

toteswingers:1&2:£43.70, 2&3:£94.80, 1&3:£63.50 CSF £188.76 CT £2887.46 TOTE £19.20: £4.10, £4.10, £3.90, £4.50; EX 412.80 Trifecta £8736.10 Pool: £51944.80 - 4.40 winning units..

Owner Mrs Emma Bifova **Bred** T D Andrews **Trained** Bansha, Co Tipperary

FOCUS

A typically open running of this historic sprint handicap. There was plenty of pace in the race and the time was just under a second inside the standard. The main bulk of the field raced towards the stands' side, with a pair in isolation near to the far rail. There was a bunch finish and those drawn high emerged on top, with five of the first six home coming from stalls 15 or higher. The winner looks up to Listed races at least.

NOTEBOOK

Nocturnal Affair(SAF), a Group 3 winner for Greg Ennion in his native South Africa, had run well on his debut for the Marnane yard at Cork and was relatively unexposed at sprint distances. He broke awkwardly from the stalls, but soon raced strongly tracking the pace and found sufficient after easing to the front entering the last furlong. The winner should prove competitive in Listed and Group 3 races and his South African record suggests he will not mind some ease in the ground.

Confessional came through to challenge but then hung left in the dying stages, throwing away his chance. Also runner-up in the Stewards' Cup consolation race at Goodwood, he is capable of winning a big pot when things go his way. He did best of those racing from a single-figure draw. (op 16-1)

Addictive Dream(IRE) came close to giving Walter Swinburn a big-race success in the last few weeks before he relinquishes his training licence. Without the cheekpieces he's worn on his previous two starts, the chestnut travelled well before delivering his challenge nearest to the stands' rail, but was just held. (op 16-1)

Ancient Cross had run well despite finishing unplaced at Goodwood and York and he again finished strongly, if just too late. He remains 5lb above his latest winning mark. (op 16-1)

York Glory(USA) did best of the three from that age group, tracking the winner through and running on for pressure without quickening sufficiently. He has had a fine season and this is the first time he's been unplaced in his career. There should be more to come from him next year. (op 6-1 tchd 5-1)

Jimmy Styles threaded his way through and ran on late. He's a smart sprinter, but from a mark of 106 he's not easy to place and he has been beaten in all nine handicaps he's contested since taking the Ayr Gold Cup two years ago. (op 22-1)

Verinco, only caught late on at York on Saturday, once again showed fine pace. He could not hold off the pursuers and needs the bare 5f.

Tax Free(IRE) retains some of his dash, and after encountering a bit of trouble he came home well, without ever threatening the leaders. (op 28-1)

Dungannon, after coming with his run on the outside of the bunch, was held when he was eased in the last few strides. He had gone up 4lb for his Shergar Cup Dash win at Ascot. (tchd 12-1)

Waffle(IRE), in a first-time visor, raced on the far side of the group and was never a factor. He remains without a win since his 2yo debut. Richard Hughes later reported he was unsuited by the good to firm ground. Official explanation: jockey said gelding was unsuited by the good to firm ground

Joe Packet dented his chance with a tardy start. Official explanation: jockey said gelding reared at the start (tchd 14-1, tchd 16-1 in places)

Zero Money(IRE) had the ground in his favour for this hat-trick bid. From stall 2, he led the pair who raced apart from the remainder and had no chance the way the race panned out. He can be forgiven this. (op 15-2)

Swiss Dream was unable to dominate. (op 12-1)

Bajan Tryst(USA), last year's runner-up, never figured from what turned out to be a bad draw.

5928 LADBROKES ST LEGER STKS (GROUP 1) (ENTIRE COLTS & FILLIES) 1m 6f 132y

3:10 (3:13) (Class 1) 3-Y-O

£306,262 (£116,110; £58,109; £28,946; £14,527; £7,290) **Stalls** Low

Form				RPR
5101	**1**		**Masked Marvel**[65] 3772 3-9-0 109 WilliamBuick 3 *(John Gosden) hld up in tch: smooth hdwy over 4f out: cl up 3f out: rdn to ld 1 1/2f out: clr ins fnl f: styd on strly* **15/2**	124+
1152	**2**	*3*	**Brown Panther**[28] 5045 3-9-0 115 KierenFallon 2 *(Tom Dascombe) towards rr and niggled along 10f out: pushed along over 5f out: rdn and hdwy 3f out: drvn 2f out: kpt on to chse wnr ins fnl f: no imp* **15/2**	119
1-11	**3**	*1/2*	**Sea Moon**[24] 5182 3-9-0 121 OlivierPeslier 1 *(Sir Michael Stoute) hld up in rr: hdwy over 3f out: effrt on inner to chse ldrs 2f out and sn n.m.r: nt clr run and hmpd over 1f out: swtchd rt and rdn ent fnl f: kpt on* **2/1**[1]	121+
0223	**4**	*1 1/2*	**Seville (GER)**[24] 5182 3-9-0 120 JPO'Brien 5 *(A P O'Brien, Ire) trckd ldng pair: hdwy over 4f out: sn cl up: led wl over 2f out: sn rdn: hdd and drvn 1 1/2f out: sn one pce* **17/2**	116
1221	**5**	*2 1/2*	**Census (IRE)**[28] 5045 3-9-0 117 RichardHughes 9 *(Richard Hannon) hld up in rr: niggled along over 6f out: hdwy on outer over 3f out: rdn over 2f out: drvn wl over 1f out and one pce* **11/2**[3]	113
1411	**6**	*6*	**Blue Bunting (USA)**[23] 5219 3-8-11 118 FrankieDettori 7 *(Mahmood Al Zarooni) hld up and bhd: sme hdwy over 3f out: sn rdn along and nvr a factor* **7/2**[2]	102
2334	**7**	*8*	**Buthelezi (USA)**[28] 5045 3-9-0 105 [1] RobertHavlin 6 *(John Gosden) sn led and set str pce: rdn along 4f out: drvn over 3f out: sn hdd & wknd* **40/1**	94
1364	**8**	*12*	**Genius Beast (USA)**[24] 5182 3-9-0 110 SilvestreDeSousa 4 *(Mahmood Al Zarooni) chsd ldrs on inner: rdn along over 4f out and sn wknd* **25/1**	78
1600	**9**	*15*	**Rumh (GER)**[23] 5219 3-8-11 103 RichardHills 8 *(Saeed Bin Suroor) chsd ldr: cl up over 5f out: drvn along 4f out: sn wknd* **100/1**	55

3m 0.44s (-6.96) **Going Correction** -0.375s/f (Firm) course record **9** Ran SP% **112.3**

Speed ratings (Par 115): **103,101,101,100,99 95,91,85,77**

toteswingers:1&2:£6.50, 2&3:£3.90, 1&3:£3.60 CSF £59.42 CT £153.31 TOTE £8.80: £2.40, £2.80, £1.10; EX 60.00 Trifecta £288.80 Pool: £7427.27 - 19.03 winning units..

The Form Book, Raceform Ltd, Compton, RG20 6NL

Owner B E Nielsen **Bred** Newsells Park Stud **Trained** Newmarket, Suffolk

FOCUS

A good edition of the year's final Classic, judged on recent runnings anyway. It's hard to remember a St Leger run at such a strong gallop, leading to a track record despite there being a headwind in the straight, and the market principals were wisely ridden under restraint. Masked Marvel rates John Gosden's best Leger winner at this stage of his career. The form is rated around the runner-up and the fifth, and Sea Moon would have been second with a clear run.

NOTEBOOK

Masked Marvel, whose trainer was bidding for a fourth win in the race, and third in five years following last season's triumph with Arctic Cosmos, was put aside specifically for this race and the son of Montjeu ran out an impressive winner in the circumstances. William Buick rode a fine race, and whilst others were under pressure trying to make their move rounding the final bend, he was sitting relatively motionless. Considering the headwind, it was a good decision not to commit too soon, but once he did, the response was impressive and the pair were never in any danger from over 1f out, the colt galloping on strongly to the point where his rider struggled pulling him up. He'd been a bit hit and miss up until this point, albeit his Derby eighth at a relatively early stage was a fair effort, and Gosden deserves all the credit for given him the time he so clearly needed to reach a peak. Although a grandson of a German St Leger winner, by a sire who's an influence for stamina, there's little doubt he's got the pace, and certainly the ability, to prove as effective back at 1m4f, and it'll be fascinating to see which route he takes, for the remainder of this season and next, with the stable also housing King George winner Nathaniel. (op 7-1)

Brown Panther has progressed from a mark of just 73 this season, and bounced back from a below-par run on heavy ground in the German Derby when chasing home Census at Newbury. He'd earlier beaten that rival at Royal Ascot, though, and did so again here, responding to pressure (niggled at quite an early stage), despite the ground possibly being too quick, and keeping on dourly without ever looking like reeling in the winner. The fact he was second can be owed to his rider, who kept the favourite in against the rail at a critical stage, and he deserves a rest now following a long season that began in early April. The Ormonde Stakes at Chester will presumably be the aim for next year's comeback. (op 10-1)

Sea Moon was considered a Derby contender at two, but didn't get back to the track until winning off a mark of 92 in a 1m2f handicap at York in June. He leapt to favouritism for this following his rampant Voltigeur victory last month and was bidding to help banish memories of what has so far been a desperate year by his legendary trainer's standards. He only added to Stoute's woes, however, his rider beginning to look for room from over 3f out and then being squeezed out against the rail approaching the distance. He wouldn't have won, not racing with the same exuberance as he had done on the Knavesmire, but almost certainly would have claimed second, and along with the winner, is the one to take from the race with next year in mind. (op 15-8)

Seville(GER), barring a below-par run behind the favourite last time, would have entered this as a strong fancy for many, judged on his placed efforts in the Irish Derby and Grand Prix de Paris. It's not hard to forgive a horse a poor run at York these days, his effort deserves to be upgraded significantly, for not only did he sit too close to the fast early pace, ending up in front little under 3f out, but he also lost a shoe. Ridden with a touch more restraint, it's hard not to think he'd have placed, and he gives the form a solid look, this effort being back to something like his best. (op 8-1 tchd 10-1)

Census(IRE) had beaten Brown Panther over 1f shorter in the Geofrey Freer at Newbury last month, but couldn't confirm the form faced with this stiffer test, picking up well to challenge before fading from 1f out. Connections felt the he wouldn't let himself down on the ground, which is feasible, but it's probable 1m4f will prove his best trip. (op 5-1)

Blue Bunting(USA), who had events not worked against her at Epsom, may have come into this unbeaten at three, having notched a notable hat-trick of the 1,000 Guineas, Irish and Yorkshire Oaks aside from that reverse, was a major disappointment. With plenty of stamina in her pedigree, and possessing a die hard attitude, she seemed certain to run well, but was last and being ridden before they straightened for home, and could never pick up, being eased from over 1f out. She had a hard race at York previously, and Frankie Dettori felt it had left it's mark. The Stewards ordered the filly to be routine tested. It emerged that she might have been in season. Official explanation: trainer said filly was suffering from a long season and in need of a break (op 10-3 tchd 3-1)

Buthelezi(USA), a well held fourth behind Census and Brown Panther in the Geoffrey Freer, is in different ownership to the winner and appeared to be making the running in his own right. He went far too quick in the first-time hood, even leading the pacemaker, and predictably stopped to nothing. (op 50-1)

Genius Beast(USA) had the winner behind when landing the Sandown Classic Trial earlier in the season, but hasn't really gone on and, having finished a well-held fourth in the Voltigeur, was beaten out of sight here having chased the early pace. (op 33-1)

Rumh(GER), supplemented for £45,000 to make the pace for Blue Bunting, was unable to lead.

5929 AGRIARGO UK TRACTOR CHALLENGE H'CAP — 1m (S)

3:45 (3:46) (Class 2) (0-110,103) 3-Y-0+ **£12,938** (£3,850; £1,924; £962) **Stalls** High

Form				RPR
-066	**1**		**Man Of Action (USA)**[43] 4494 4-9-2 **95**......(v) FrankieDettori 11 (Saeed Bin Suroor) *hld up in rr: swtchd rt and gd hdwy 2f out: chal ent fnl f: rdn and qcknd to ld last 100yds: sn clr* **13/2**	107+
-145	**2**	*1 1/2*	**Eton Forever (IRE)**[87] 3032 4-9-10 **103**...... NeilCallan 7 (Roger Varian) *trckd ldrs: hdwy 2f out: rdn to ld ent fnl f: sn drvn: hdd and one pce last 100yds* **9/4**[1]	109
6210	**3**	*hd*	**Casual Glimpse**[14] 5474 3-9-5 **103**...... RichardHughes 12 (Richard Hannon) *trckd ldrs: hdwy 2f out: rdn over 1f out: kpt on u.p ins fnl f* **12/1**	108
0314	**4**	*nk*	**Sooraah**[43] 4494 4-9-5 **98**...... KierenFallon 3 (William Haggas) *hld up in tch: hdwy over 2f out: rdn to chal over 1f out and ev ch tl drvn and one pce ins fnl f* **9/2**[3]	103
2030	**5**	*hd*	**Crown Counsel (IRE)**[7] 5712 3-8-10 **94**...... SilvestreDeSousa 10 (Mark Johnston) *led 3f: cl up tl led again wl over 2f out and sn rdn: hdd and drvn ent fnl f: kpt on same pce* **16/1**	97
2006	**6**	*shd*	**Vainglory (USA)**[23] 5218 7-8-10 **89**...... FergusSweeney 9 (David Simcock) *hld up in tch: hdwy over 2f out: rdn over 1f out: kpt on same pce* **10/1**	93
-206	**7**	*nk*	**Mia's Boy**[12] 5563 7-9-5 **98**...... GeorgeBaker 5 (Chris Dwyer) *hld up in rr: hdwy on outer over 2f out: rdn and ch over 1f out: drvn and one pce fnl f* **18/1**	101
-151	**8**	*3/4*	**Cry Fury**[30] 4959 3-8-13 **97**...... WilliamBuick 4 (Roger Charlton) *in tch: pushed along 3f out: rdn 2f out: drvn appr fnl f and one pce* **7/2**[2]	98
1200	**9**	*6*	**Just Bond (IRE)**[35] 4794 9-8-10 **89** oh4...... AndrewElliott 2 (Geoffrey Oldroyd) *cl up: led after 3f: rdn along and hdd wl over 2f out: sn wknd* **28/1**	76
000	**10**	*15*	**Majuro (IRE)**[9] 5648 7-8-3 **89** oh11......(t) JasonHart(7) 1 (Richard Guest) *chsd ldrs: rdn along 3f out: sn wknd* **66/1**	40

1m 39.62s (0.32) **Going Correction** -0.075s/f (Good)
WFA 3 from 4yo+ 5lb — **10** Ran SP% **117.4**
Speed ratings (Par 109): **95,93,93,93,92 92,92,91,85,70**
toteswingers:1&2:£4.30, 2&3:£6.80, 1&3:£10.70 CSF £21.62 CT £175.24 TOTE £6.70: £2.00, £1.20, £3.60; EX 24.10 Trifecta £178.10 Pool: £1908.61 - 7.93 winning units..

Owner Godolphin **Bred** Gainesway Thoroughbreds Ltd **Trained** Newmarket, Suffolk

FOCUS

A decent handicap, if not the strongest for the grade. They raced in the centre of the track and the pace was only modest, resulting in a bit of a sprint finish. They finished in a heap behind the winner and the form is a little suspect, although it has been taken at face value. The winner is perhaps worth a bit extra.

NOTEBOOK

Man Of Action(USA) was partnered by Frankie Dettori, who replaced Robert Havlin when Godolphin's other runner Sarrsar was taken out because of the fast ground. Covered up at the rear of the field, the gelding was switched to the stands' rail before producing a fine turn of foot to burst to the front and win easily. He'd had run well in the face of a bad draw in the totesport Mile at Goodwood and there is more to come from him at this sort of trip. He could go for the Cambridgeshire provided the ground has not gone against him. (op 6-1 tchd 11-2)

Eton Forever(IRE), off since finishing fifth in the Royal Hunt Cup at Royal Ascot, was back at the scene of his impressive Spring Mile win at the start of the season. He was well placed when the pace quickened approaching the two pole and got the verdict in a bunch finish for second. He holds an entry in a valuable 7f handicap at Ascot at the beginning of October, and that trip may suit him there. (op 11-4 tchd 3-1)

Casual Glimpse, held up on the near side of the group, had his chance without quickening up. Suited by this ground, he is equally effective at this trip and 7f. (op 10-1)

Sooraah, two places ahead of Man Of Action at Goodwood, raced a little keenly off the steady gallop and stuck on at the same pace in the final sprint. Her reported aim is a Listed fillies' race at Ascot next month.

Crown Counsel(IRE), representing last year's winning connections, was up there from the off and still battling away inside the last. He is very useful on his day but not especially consistent. (op 18-1 tchd 20-1)

Vainglory(USA), after being held up towards the back, was running on when it was too late. He is consistent and is still in decent heart, but remains without a win since May last year and is still 2lb above that mark. (op 9-1)

Mia's Boy, back up in trip, delivered his run on the far side of the bunch, which was perhaps disadvantageous. He hasn't won a handicap since May 2008. (op 16-1)

Cry Fury, raised 9lb for his win at Goodwood, was down two furlongs in trip. The steadily run race was against him and he failed to pick up when the pace lifted. This didn't enhance his Cambridgeshire credentials, but that race, should he be allowed to take his chance, would play more to his strengths than this one. (op 4-1 tchd 10-3, tchd 9-2 in places)

5930 APC INDUSTRIAL SERVICES PARK STKS (GROUP 2) — 7f

4:15 (4:16) (Class 1) 3-Y-O+ **£56,710** (£21,500; £10,760; £5,360; £2,690) **Stalls** High

Form				RPR
3065	**1**		**Premio Loco (USA)**[14] 5473 7-9-4 114...... GeorgeBaker 4 (Chris Wall) *trckd ldrs: hdwy wl over 1f out: chal ent fnl f: rdn and qcknd to ld last 100yds* **15/8**[1]	113
32-5	**2**	*1/2*	**Dafeef**[21] 5282 4-9-4 105...... RichardHills 5 (William Haggas) *s.i.s and bhd: tk cl order after 2f: hdwy to chse ldng pair 3f out: rdn to chal over 1f out: drvn ins fnl f and ev ch tl nt qckn towards fin* **7/2**[3]	112
4464	**3**	*1/2*	**The Cheka (IRE)**[13] 5510 5-9-4 108......(p) TomQueally 3 (Eve Johnson Houghton) *trckd ldr: hdwy to ld over 2f out: rdn wl over 1f out: drvn ent fnl f: hdd and one pce last 100yds* **11/4**[2]	111
0000	**4**	*3 1/4*	**Balthazaar's Gift (IRE)**[13] 5510 8-9-4 103...... AdamKirby 2 (Clive Cox) *hld up in rr: hdwy on outer over 2f out: rdn along wl over 1f out: sn drvn and btn appr fnl f* **8/1**	102
6650	**5**	*6*	**Duff (IRE)**[7] 5746 8-9-4 99......(v) RichardHughes 1 (Edward Lynam, Ire) *sn led: rdn along and hdd over 2f out: drvn and wknd over 1f out* **13/2**	86

1m 25.93s (-0.37) **Going Correction** -0.075s/f (Good) — **5** Ran SP% **108.1**
Speed ratings (Par 115): **99,98,97,94,87**
CSF £8.32 TOTE £2.90: £1.80, £1.40; EX 9.30.

Owner Bernard Westley **Bred** Kidder, Cole & Griggs **Trained** Newmarket, Suffolk

FOCUS

This was quite a weak race for the grade. In contrast to the opening small-field event over the same trip, the runners raced against the stands' rail with the pace set by Duff being relatively steady. As a result, the winning time was 0.07 seconds slower than the Champagne. There was near enough four in a line approaching the final furlong. There are doubts over the form, which could rate higher at face value.

NOTEBOOK

Premio Loco(USA), the highest-rated runner in the field, got up late on. Placed in the Lockinge earlier in the season, he'd been below that level since, but this was a weak race for the grade and he stayed on strongest inside the final 100 yards, appreciating the quick ground. The Joel Stakes at Newmarket was mentioned as his next possible target, and his trainer wasn't ruling out a trip to Dubai next year either, assuming he retains his form. (op 9-4)

Dafeef ran a promising race on his recent reappearance at York and built on that to go close here, indeed he may well have won had he not bungled the start. He effortlessly recovered the ground, though, with the pace being steady, and held every chance. For a horse who prefers some dig underfoot, this was a fine effort, and he can win at Pattern-level before long. (op 4-1)

The Cheka(IRE) raced enthusiastically in tracking the early leader and was allowed to stride into the lead over 2f out, but he always looked vulnerable and could only keep on at the one pace, possibly not helped by the headwind. He's a Group 3 horse.

Balthazaar's Gift(IRE) should have found this easier and came to challenge widest of all, but he had nothing left from soon inside the final furlong. (op 11-2)

Duff(IRE) isn't the horse he was when winning this in 2009 and, despite a brief rally having been headed, was ultimately eased late on once beaten. He was reported to have lost his action. Official explanation: jockey said gelding lost it's action (op 6-1, thcd 13-2 in a place)

5931 STRATSTONE ENDURANCE NURSERY — 1m (S)

4:50 (4:50) (Class 2) 2-Y-O **£9,703** (£2,887; £1,443; £721) **Stalls** High

Form				RPR
1	**1**		**Anjaz (USA)**[19] 5320 2-9-2 **82**...... FrankieDettori 5 (Saeed Bin Suroor) *hld up in rr: smooth hdwy on outer wl over 2f out: chal over 1f out: rdn to ld ins fnl f: edgd rt and kpt on* **7/2**[1]	88+
245	**2**	*1/2*	**Burano (IRE)**[22] 5254 2-9-4 **84**...... NeilCallan 4 (Brian Meehan) *trckd ldr: cl up 1/2-way: led 2f out: rdn and edgd rt over 1f out: drvn and hdd ins fnl f: kpt on* **7/2**[1]	89
4120	**3**	*3/4*	**That's Dangerous**[31] 4913 2-8-9 **75**...... RichardKingscote 10 (Roger Charlton) *hld up: hdwy on inner over 2f out: swtchd lft over 1f out and sn rdn to chse ldrs: n.m.r ent fnl f: sn drvn and kpt on* **25/1**	78+
0411	**4**	*1/2*	**Amazing Storm (IRE)**[14] 5478 2-9-6 **86**...... RichardHughes 8 (Richard Hannon) *t.k.h: hld up in rr: hdwy on outer over 2f out: rdn over 1f out: kpt on ins fnl f: nrst fin* **4/1**[2]	89
13	**5**	*shd*	**Dance The Rain**[30] 4964 2-8-10 **76**...... RoystonFfrench 6 (Bryan Smart) *prom: rdn along 2f out: edgd lft over 1f out: drvn and edgd rt ent fnl f: one pce* **25/1**	78
1511	**6**	*2 3/4*	**Pride And Joy (IRE)**[21] 5280 2-9-6 **86**...... FergusSweeney 9 (Jamie Osborne) *dwlt and in rr: hdwy over 3f out: rdn to chse ldrs 2f out: drvn and wknd appr fnl f* **15/2**[3]	82

331 **7** *1¾* **Repeater**[58] 4007 2-8-12 **78**........ SebSanders 2 69
(Sir Mark Prescott Bt) *plld hrd: chsd ldrs: rdn along 2f out: wkng whn n.m.r over 1f out* **4/1**[2]

150 **8** *nk* **Pearl Charm (USA)**[7] 5715 2-9-3 **83**........ TomQueally 1 74
(Richard Hannon) *in tch: effrt over 3f out: sn rdn along and wknd wl over 1f out* **20/1**

4410 **9** *2¾* **Moon Trip**[15] 5446 2-8-11 **77**........ SilvestreDeSousa 3 61+
(Mark Johnston) *led: rdn along 3f out: hdd 2f out and sn wknd* **17/2**

0100 **10** *½* **Captain Cardington (IRE)**[22] 5233 2-8-6 **72**........ SamHitchcott 11 55
(Mick Channon) *a in rr* **40/1**

1m 40.22s (0.92) **Going Correction** -0.075s/f (Good) **10** Ran SP% **121.6**
Speed ratings (Par 101): **92,91,90,90,90 87,85,85,82,82**
toteswingers:1&2:£4.00, 2&3:£19.90, 1&3:£18.50 CSF £15.87 CT £278.73 TOTE £3.50: £1.90, £1.40, £5.60; EX 20.90 Trifecta £999.10 Part won. Pool: £1350.27 - 0.40 winning units..
Owner Godolphin **Bred** Darley **Trained** Newmarket, Suffolk

FOCUS
A good nursery won last year by St Leger also-ran Buthelezi. Leger hero Bollin Eric himself won this in in 2001, and the race was also taken by that good filly Anna Pavlova three years later. The form is rated positively and the winner can do better.

NOTEBOOK
Anjaz(USA) was switched to the outside before unleashing a smooth run. She edged to her right when in front and won a shade more easily than the margin would imply. A daughter of Playful Act, who won the May Hill Stakes and Fillies' Mile in 2004, she was retaining her unbeaten record following a winning debut on Polytrack and showed she handles quick turf well. She could well be worth a step up in class. (op 11-4)

Burano(IRE) had run three solid races in maidens and this was another commendable effort on his nursery debut. Well at home over the extra furlong, he was up with the pace throughout and briefly nosed ahead before the filly claimed him. (op 6-1)

That's Dangerous was running on determinedly against the rail in the latter stages after not enjoying an entirely clear passage. He saw out the mile well.

Amazing Storm(IRE) was a bit free, something he had been in his early races. Bidding for a hat-trick off a mark just 2lb higher than when winning at Newmarket, he was held up at the back and was slightly short of room when beginning to run on. It did not cost him victory, but he would have finished a little closer. The extra furlong was fine for him. (op 5-1)

Dance The Rain was third of four to Champagne Stakes winner Trumpet Major at Newmarket on her previous start. She ran respectably on this nursery debut without seeing out the longer trip as well as some of the others. (op 18-1)

Pride And Joy(IRE), the most experienced in the line-up, was aiming for a hat-trick off 9lb higher than for his first nursery win. He was slightly hampered in the final furlong, but for which he would have finished closer to the placed horses. (op 8-1 tchd 7-1)

Repeater threw his head about in the early stages and his rider did well to settle him by halfway. The colt was chasing the pace but already being pushed along when he was hampered at the furlong pole. The longer trip had promised to suit him and this was disappointing. (op 9-2)

Pearl Charm(USA) has now disappointed on each of his three starts since his taking debut win. (op 16-1)

Moon Trip's Leicester win now stands out amongst several lesser efforts. He had his ground here but was leading into a headwind. (tchd 8-1)

5932 POWELL ENGINEERING H'CAP 1m 4f
5:25 (5:25) (Class 2) (0-105,100) 3-Y-O+ **£12,938** (£3,850; £1,924; £962) **Stalls** Low

Form RPR

0333 **1** **Swift Alhaarth (IRE)**[7] 5700 3-8-4 **87**........ SilvestreDeSousa 2 100
(Mark Johnston) *mde all: rdn along wl over 2f out: drvn over 1f out: styd on gamely u.p ins fnl f* **9/4**[1]

1016 **2** *1¾* **Midnight Oil**[14] 5482 3-8-7 **90**........ KierenFallon 3 101
(Luca Cumani) *trckd ldrs: hdwy over 3f out: rdn to chal wl over 1f out and sn ev ch tl drvn and one pce ins fnl f* **9/4**[1]

0016 **3** *2¼* **Agent Archie (USA)**[22] 5250 4-9-0 **88**........[1] RichardHughes 4 95
(William Haggas) *trckd wnr: effrt over 3f out: rdn along over 2f out: drvn and one pce fr over 1f out* **6/1**[3]

5304 **4** *2½* **Picture Editor**[12] 5544 3-9-2 **99**........ TomQueally 10 102
(Sir Henry Cecil) *hld up in rr: hdwy 4f out: rdn to chse ldrs 2f out: sn one pce* **11/2**[2]

-240 **5** *1¾* **Waldvogel (IRE)**[22] 5250 7-9-4 **92**........ WilliamBuick 6 92
(Nicky Richards) *dwlt and hld up in rr: hdwy 4f out: rdn along wl over 2f out: kpt on u.p appr fnl f: nrst fin* **12/1**

0-10 **6** *1½* **Tepmokea (IRE)**[63] 3876 5-9-6 **97**........ LeeTopliss(3) 9 95
(Richard Fahey) *in tch: rdn along wl over 3f out: hdwy over 2f out: sn drvn and btn* **12/1**

2060 **7** *10* **Dansili Dancer**[70] 3625 9-8-13 **87**........ AdamKirby 5 69
(Clive Cox) *hld up in tch: sme hdwy over 3f out: rdn along over 2f out and sn wknd* **10/1**

/0-0 **8** *51* **Almail (USA)**[21] 5271 5-9-12 **100**........(b[1]) GeorgeBaker 1 —
(Jamie Osborne) *chsd ldng pair: rdn along over 3f out: sn wknd* **33/1**

2m 27.48s (-7.42) **Going Correction** -0.375s/f (Firm) course record
WFA 3 from 4yo+ 9lb **8** Ran SP% **118.6**
Speed ratings (Par 109): **109,107,106,104,103 102,95,61**
toteswingers:1&2:£2.20, 2&3:£4.40, 1&3:£2.80 CSF £7.28 CT £26.35 TOTE £3.70: £1.40, £1.30, £2.00; EX 6.80 Trifecta £33.60 Pool: £1413.64 - 31.11 winning units..
Owner Dr Marwan Koukash **Bred** Mrs Joan Murphy **Trained** Middleham Moor, N Yorks

FOCUS
The 3yos were always likely to dominate this handicap.

NOTEBOOK
Swift Alhaarth(IRE), granted an easy lead, has been running well in defeat of late and he galloped on relentlessly for a thoroughly deserved victory, wanting it more than the runner-up when things got tough. There wasn't much strength in depth to the race so the winner may struggle to defy much of a rise, but there's little doubt this tough sort will continue to give a good account. (op 7-2)

Midnight Oil, who received little luck at Newmarket last time, having won there previously, appeared the likely winner when challenging inside the final 2f, but he has rather a high head carriage, and having got to within half a length of the winner, either couldn't or wouldn't go past. He's a fine horse physically and it's hoped he goes the right way. (op 2-1 tchd 15-8 and 5-2 and 9-4 in a place)

Agent Archie(USA) bounced back from his York disappointment with a hood applied for the first time, simply being unable to match two progressive 3yos. (op 8-1)

Picture Editor hasn't met with expectations this year, possibly suffering as a result of being used as a pacemaker for Frankel on his return. His stamina for this trip remains in question. (op 5-1 tchd 6-1)

Waldvogel(IRE) never got into it from the rear and would have preferred a stronger pace to run at.

Tepmokea(IRE) Official explanation: jockey said gelding hung right

Almail(USA) Official explanation: jockey said horse had no more to give

T/Jkpt: Not won. T/Plt: £209.80 to a £1 stake. Pool of £190,359.06 - 662.11 winning tickets
T/Qpdt: £10.20 to a £1 stake. Pool of £11,142.90 - 803.31 winning tickets. JR

5583 GOODWOOD (R-H)
Saturday, September 10

OFFICIAL GOING: Good to soft (7.3)
Wind: Brisk, across (away from stands) Weather: Cloudy, drizzly

5933 PETER WILLETT STKS (REGISTERED AS THE STARDOM STAKES) (LISTED RACE) 7f
1:45 (1:45) (Class 1) 2-Y-O
£12,192 (£4,622; £2,313; £1,152; £578; £290) **Stalls** Low

Form RPR

1 **1** **Bronterre**[63] 3870 2-9-0 0........ PatDobbs 1 111+
(Richard Hannon) *dwlt: hld up in last pair: smooth prog over 2f out: led over 1f out: shkn up and drew rt away ins fnl f* **11/4**[2]

3214 **2** *5* **Justineo**[22] 5251 2-9-0 106........ MichaelHills 2 97
(William Haggas) *trckd ldng pair: clsd to chal 2f out: upsides over 1f out: sn lft bhd by wnr: fdd and jst hld on for 2nd* **6/5**[1]

2024 **3** *nse* **Nayarra (IRE)**[14] 5472 2-8-9 95........ TedDurcan 3 92
(Mick Channon) *hld up in 4th: rdn over 2f out: nt qckn and outpcd wl over 1f out: styd on ins fnl f: nrly snatched 2nd* **5/1**[3]

2201 **4** *2¼* **Red Aggressor (IRE)**[11] 5605 2-9-0 90........ PhilipRobinson 5 91
(Clive Brittain) *trckd ldr: clsd to chal jst over 2f out: rdn wl over 1f out: sn easily outpcd* **11/1**

1462 **5** *¾* **Sixx**[64] 3795 2-9-0 89........ DaneO'Neill 4 89
(Richard Hannon) *led: rdn over 2f out: hdd & wknd over 1f out* **20/1**

3331 **6** *4½* **My Lucky Liz (IRE)**[21] 5270 2-8-9 85........ MartinLane 6 73
(David Simcock) *t.k.h: hld up in last pair: rdn and wknd over 2f out* **9/1**

1m 28.94s (2.04) **Going Correction** +0.30s/f (Good) **6** Ran SP% **111.9**
Speed ratings (Par 103): **100,94,94,91,90 85**
toteswingers:1&2:£1.90, 2&3:£1.10, 1&3:£2.70 CSF £6.40 TOTE £4.10: £2.10, £1.10; EX 6.40.
Owner Michael Pescod **Bred** Swettenham Stud & Lofts Hall Stud **Trained** East Everleigh, Wilts

FOCUS
An interesting race, which produced a horse that seems likely to hold his own against classier types. The promising Titus Mills won this last year before a down-the-field run in the Racing Post Trophy (absent since), while 2009 winner Vale Of York held his own in Group company before taking the Breeders' Cup Juvenile at Santa Anita. Bronterre impressed but there may not have been much depth in behind.

NOTEBOOK
Bronterre ◆, who has a Dewhurst entry, made a winning debut back in early July over roughly the same trip at Salisbury, but hadn't been seen since. Held up early here, he produced a telling turn-of-foot when put into an attacking position and won in the manner of a horse destined for better things. He doesn't lack size, so should continue to progress until his level is found. (op 5-2 tchd 3-1)

Justineo, entered in the Middle Park and Dewhurst, was the clear pick on his Gimcrack effort, form boosted during the previous week by Burwaaz and Reply, but this was a step up in distance and it didn't appear to suit in this ground, as he only just held on for second. (op 5-4 tchd 11-8 in a place)

Nayarra(IRE) took a while to hit full speed here, and was staying on well inside the final furlong. One would imagine connections will be desperate to get a win of any sort into this daughter of Cape Cross now she has placed third in Listed company. (op 7-1)

Red Aggressor(IRE) chased the leader early but had little to offer in the final stages. (op 12-1 tchd 10-1)

Sixx, trying the trip for the first time, made the running but was one-paced at the end. (op 25-1)

My Lucky Liz(IRE) was the most experienced of these and had a good level of form, but she raced too freely early in the easy ground to have much left at the end. (op 8-1)

5934 BETFRED BONUS KING SELECT STKS (GROUP 3) 1m 1f 192y
2:20 (2:20) (Class 1) 3-Y-O+
£28,355 (£10,750; £5,380; £2,680; £1,345; £675) **Stalls** Low

Form RPR

15-1 **1** **French Navy**[28] 5055 3-8-7 110........ AhmedAjtebi 8 113+
(Mahmood Al Zarooni) *hld up in last: quick move against nr side rail to ld over 2f out: rdn and in command over 1f out: styd on wl* **2/1**[1]

1330 **2** *2½* **Slumber**[46] 4411 3-8-7 101........ MichaelHills 4 106
(Charles Hills) *trckd ldr 1f: styd handy: tried to chal over 2f out: chsd wnr wl over 1f out: readily hld* **9/2**[3]

3002 **3** *nk* **Measuring Time**[12] 5544 3-8-7 100........ PatDobbs 7 105
(Richard Hannon) *trckd ldr after 1f to over 4f out: lost pl and outpcd 3f out: styd on again over 1f out: pressed for 2nd nr fin* **20/1**

5321 **4** *1¼* **Opera Gal (IRE)**[14] 5493 4-8-11 101........ DavidProbert 3 100
(Andrew Balding) *taken down early: led: brought field to nr side in st: rdn and hdd over 2f out: fdd over 1f out* **4/1**[2]

-416 **5** *1¾* **Nationalism**[22] 5252 4-9-0 107........ NickyMackay 1 99
(John Gosden) *cl up: chsd ldr over 4f out to 3f out: sn rdn: fdd over 1f out* **9/2**[3]

1-3 **6** *15* **Ceilidh House**[89] 2994 4-8-11 102........(t) JimCrowley 5 66
(Ralph Beckett) *hld up in 5th: moved clsr to ldrs 3f out: wknd qckly 2f out: t.o* **13/2**

46-0 **7** *1¼* **Karam Albaari (IRE)**[13] 5510 3-8-7 104........ MartinDwyer 6 67
(J R Jenkins) *hld up in last pair: shkn up over 3f out: sn btn: t.o* **22/1**

2m 8.15s (0.15) **Going Correction** +0.30s/f (Good)
WFA 3 from 4yo+ 7lb **7** Ran SP% **112.1**
Speed ratings (Par 113): **111,109,108,107,106 94,93**
toteswingers:1&2:£1.60, 2&3:£9.70, 1&3:£6.20 CSF £10.79 TOTE £2.40: £1.70, £2.10; EX 7.50 Trifecta £339.60 Pool: £762.00 - 1.66 winning units..
Owner Godolphin **Bred** Darley **Trained** Newmarket, Suffolk

FOCUS
After the first race, Roger Charlton withdrew Mac Love due the ground, but that still left a strong contest for the grade, one that the 3-y-os dominated. The early leader set what looked ordinary fractions and brought the field towards the stands' side down the home straight.

NOTEBOOK
French Navy ◆ was potentially the classiest of these on his best efforts, he'd also held a Prix Niel entry for this weekend, but the concern was whether he'd bounce after a winning comeback at Newmarket after injury. Held up, he was able to make his effort closest to the rail and won comfortably once getting to the front. He is in the Champion Stakes but has plenty to find yet to have a chance at that level, and Longchamp's Prix Dollar is a possible option. (tchd 9-4)

Slumber, unsurprisingly dropped in trip after appearing not to get home in the Gordon Stakes, moved up stylishly again over 2f out but, although keeping on, didn't really quicken. That said, he kept on well to post a respectable effort.

Measuring Time finished behind Slumber when they met in the Gordon Stakes but got closer here, confirming he is back to his best. (op 16-1)

Opera Gal(IRE), down in trip after a brave success in a Windsor Listed event, had it her own way out in front and rallied for pressure to collect an honest fourth. (op 11-2)

Nationalism, a previous course winner, didn't get home as well as some here after coming with a promising effort early in the home straight. (tchd 4-1 and 5-1)
Ceilidh House, off since mid-June, ran a similar race to Nationalism but was eased in the final stages. She is quite capable of much better form, but isn't always the most consistent. (op 7-1 tchd 15-2)

5935 BETFRED STARLIT STKS (LISTED RACE) 6f
2:50 (2:51) (Class 1) 3-Y-O+

£17,013 (£6,450; £3,228; £1,608; £807; £405) **Stalls** High

Form RPR

0205 **1** **Monsieur Chevalier (IRE)**^{14} 5481 4-9-0 115 SteveDrowne 3 110
(Richard Hannon) *hld up at rr of main gp: effrt on outer 2f out: drvn and r.o fnl f: led post* **6/1**

2213 **2** *nse* **Desert Poppy (IRE)**^{27} 5080 4-8-9 99 JimCrowley 4 105
(Walter Swinburn) *trckd ldrs in centre: rdn 2f out: prog to ld ent fnl f: r.o: hdd post* **12/1**

5101 **3** *¾* **Blanche Dubawi (IRE)**^{14} 5476 3-8-7 94 MartinLane 8 103+
(Noel Quinlan) *dwlt: hld up last of main gp in centre: hrd rdn and prog over 1f out: styd on to take 3rd wl ins fnl f: unable to chal* **6/1**

0020 **4** *½* **Markab**^{34} 4838 8-9-0 114 DaneO'Neill 6 106
(Henry Candy) *led main gp in centre of crse: rdn 2f out: hdd and one pce ent fnl f* **11/4**^{1}

5612 **5** *1 ½* **Son Of The Cat (USA)**^{14} 5481 5-9-0 100 (t) DarryllHolland 7 101
(Brian Gubby) *trckd ldrs in main gp: effrt over 1f out and rn into trble: nt clr run again jst ins fnl f: nt rcvr* **9/2**^{3}

0421 **6** *½* **Desert Law (IRE)**^{21} 5264 3-8-12 100 DavidProbert 2 100
(Andrew Balding) *t.k.h: hld up bhd ldrs in centre: gng strly and cl up 2f out: fdd fnl f* **4/1**^{2}

0040 **7** *1 ½* **Elshabakiya (IRE)**^{85} 3106 3-8-7 94 PhilipRobinson 5 93+
(Clive Brittain) *pressed ldr in centre: rdn 2f out: sing to lose pl whn hmpd over 1f out: no ch after* **16/1**

-150 **8** *3* **Retainer (IRE)**^{56} 4092 3-8-12 100 PatDobbs 10 85
(Richard Hannon) *racd alone towards nr side rail: on terms w overall ldr to over 2f out: wknd* **25/1**

1130 **9** *2 ¼* **Cinderkamp**^{14} 5481 3-8-12 88 TedDurcan 9 78
(Edward Vaughan) *hld up at rr of main gp: effrt towards nr side over 2f out: sn wknd* **33/1**

1002 **10** *7* **Mac Gille Eoin**^{13} 5508 7-9-0 87 JohnFahy 1 56
(John Gallagher) *dropped in fr wd draw to r against rails: immediately wl bhd and styd there* **40/1**

1m 11.62s (-0.58) **Going Correction** +0.175s/f (Good)
WFA 3 from 4yo+ 2lb **10** Ran SP% **116.2**
Speed ratings (Par 111): **110,109,108,108,106 105,103,99,96,87**
toteswingers:1&2:£16.20, 2&3:£10.50, 1&3:£8.40 CSF £73.20 TOTE £5.80: £2.10, £2.30, £2.30; EX 69.20 Trifecta £620.80 Part won. Pool of £838.97 - 0.40 winning units..
Owner Mrs Valerie Hubbard & Ian Higginson **Bred** Tally-Ho Stud **Trained** East Everleigh, Wilts
■ Stewards' Enquiry : David Probert caution: careless riding

FOCUS
Not a race for 3-y-os in the past (only one winner in last ten) and so it proved again. The pace looked decent.

NOTEBOOK
Monsieur Chevalier(IRE), who won the Molecomb here, had a couple of decent efforts behind him this season after he'd been off the course for 596 days. However, he was not going the best here at around halfway, but does stay well and motored home to win in a driving finish. He reportedly needs soft ground and may head to Longchamp next, especially if the ground comes up heavy. (tchd 5-1)
Desert Poppy(IRE) has been running well during the summer but this was a step up in form again. She looked certain to collect as she got to the front late on but was mugged in the final strides. (op 8-1 tchd 15-2)
Blanche Dubawi(IRE), a C&D winner last time, brought useful handicap form into this and came home well after sitting towards the rear. She is clearly in great heart and could win at this level if a suitable opportunity can be found soon. (op 8-1)
Markab looked to have a big chance after some reasonable efforts this year, and had no penalty to carry from his Group 1 Haydock success, but he failed to hold a couple of rivals that operate at a much lower level in the final stages. (op 4-1)
Son Of The Cat(USA) finished in front of a couple of these in the Hopeful Stakes last time at Newmarket, including the winner, and had a good record at this course, but he met trouble in running at a crucial time and couldn't recover. (tchd 5-1)
Desert Law(IRE) gained a well-deserved first victory of the season at Bath on his previous start in a conditions event, but was comfortably held in this. (op 7-2)

5936 SHELL HOUSE STKS (H'CAP) 7f
3:25 (3:29) (Class 2) (0-100,99) 3-Y-O+

£12,450 (£3,728; £1,864; £932; £466; £234) **Stalls** Low

Form RPR

4405 **1** **Decent Fella (IRE)**^{45} 4428 5-9-4 **93** (vt) DavidProbert 10 102
(Andrew Balding) *trckd ldng pair: c towards nr side in st: rdn 2f out: styd on to ld ins fnl f: drvn out* **9/1**

-302 **2** *hd* **Wake Up Call**^{29} 5016 5-9-3 **92** TedDurcan 12 100
(Chris Wall) *trckd ldrs in 6th: rdn 2f out: c towards nr side rail and r.o 1f out: clsd on wnr fin: jst hld* **12/1**

-302 **3** *¾* **The Confessor**^{49} 4314 4-9-1 **90** DaneO'Neill 7 96
(Henry Candy) *trckd ldr: rdn to ld in centre over 1f out: hdd ins fnl f: kpt on* **11/4**^{1}

-421 **4** *nk* **Woodcote Place**^{29} 4997 8-8-13 **88** NickyMackay 8 93
(Patrick Chamings) *hld up in last quartet: effrt 2f out: prog and wdst of all over 1f out: styd on ins fnl f: nvr quite on terms w nr side pair* **20/1**

2300 **5** *nk* **Captain Bertie (IRE)**^{63} 3877 3-8-9 **88** MichaelHills 9 90
(Charles Hills) *hld up in midfield on outer in 8th: effrt towards nr side 2f out: chsng ldrs and cl enough 1f out: styd on but nt gng pce to chal* **5/1**^{2}

0020 **6** *½* **Axiom**^{23} 5218 7-9-3 **99** MichaelJMurphy$^{(7)}$ 5 102
(Ed Walker) *dwlt and stdd s: hld up in last pair: prog on outer over 2f out: drvn to chal fnl f: no ex last 100yds* **11/1**

-005 **7** *hd* **Al Khaleej (IRE)**^{42} 4554 7-9-7 **96** MartinLane 4 98
(David Simcock) *dwlt: hld up in 10th: prog on outer over 2f out: drvn to chal fnl f: no ex last 150yds* **12/1**

0400 **8** *nk* **Golden Desert (IRE)**^{28} 5043 7-9-3 **92** MartinDwyer 2 94
(Robert Mills) *trckd ldng quartet: cl enough 2f out: rdn and nt qckn over 1f out: one pce* **20/1**

1-00 **9** *1 ½* **Kalk Bay (IRE)**^{85} 3109 4-8-12 **90** (t) AdamBeschizza$^{(3)}$ 13 88
(William Haggas) *stdd after s: hld up in last quartet: rdn 3f out: no prog tl styd on towards nr side fnl f* **8/1**^{3}

0133 **10** *hd* **Truism**^{42} 4537 5-9-2 **91** JimCrowley 6 88
(Amanda Perrett) *hld up in midfield in 9th: rdn and nt qckn 2f out: sn lost pl and btn* **12/1**

0103 **11** *½* **Space Station**^{28} 5043 5-8-13 **88** (b) PatDobbs 1 84
(Simon Dow) *trckd ldrs in 7th: effrt over 2f out: rdn and cl enough over 1f out: wknd ins fnl f* **14/1**

0100 **12** *2* **Norse Blues**^{44} 4472 3-8-9 **88** JamesDoyle 11 76
(Sylvester Kirk) *led: c centre in st: hung bdly lft 2f out: hung rt and hdd over 1f out: wknd* **28/1**

1000 **13** *1 ½* **Kingscroft (IRE)**^{7} 5730 3-8-11 **90** DarryllHolland 3 74
(Mark Johnston) *trckd ldng trio: cl up whn hmpd over 1f out: losing pl whn squeezed out sn after* **25/1**

000 **14** *2* **Freeforaday (USA)**^{29} 4993 4-9-1 **90** SteveDrowne 14 71
(John Best) *t.k.h: hld up in last quartet: rdn and no prog over 2f out: wknd* **40/1**

1m 28.55s (1.65) **Going Correction** +0.375s/f (Good)
WFA 3 from 4yo+ 4lb **14** Ran SP% **121.8**
Speed ratings (Par 109): **105,104,103,103,103 102,102,102,100,100 99,97,95,93**
toteswingers:1&2:£20.80, 2&3:£9.10, 1&3:£7.40 CSF £105.46 CT £381.89 TOTE £9.60: £2.90, £3.50, £1.30; EX 114.90.
Owner One Carat Partnership **Bred** Michael Dalton **Trained** Kingsclere, Hants

FOCUS
A strong handicap run at a good pace, which saw plenty of horses have a chance approaching the final furlong.

NOTEBOOK
Decent Fella(IRE), with a tongue-tie on for the first time since May 2010, was always close up and kept on well after coming towards the stands' side, after seeing plenty of daylight in the latter stages. He is being aimed towards the totescoop6 Challenge Cup at Ascot on the 1st October.
Wake Up Call, who had been carrying big weights in handicaps on her previous two outings, came home really well for a stable in form and only narrowly failed to get up. (op 14-1 tchd 16-1)
The Confessor, 3lb higher after finishing a fine second in an Ascot heritage handicap, put up another sterling performance after always being prominent.He has plenty of options left this season. (op 10-3 tchd 5-2)
Woodcote Place, who has been running in claimers recently, including a success in one, goes well here and kept on nicely towards the centre of the track.
Captain Bertie(IRE) ◆ had plenty of scope for improvement being a lightly raced 3-y-o, and didn't run too badly on his return from a 63-day break. He will be interesting in a quality handicap before the end of the season, and is in the totescoop6 Challenge Cup at Ascot. (op 9-2 tchd 13-2)
Axiom has a good record at this course and came into the picture going well but didn't find as much as looked likely. (op 12-1 tchd 9-1)
Al Khaleej(IRE), who has gone well here in the past, gave the impression here he needs to come down the weights a bit to have a chance of being involved in the finish. (op 11-1)
Kalk Bay(IRE) had been well beaten in two previous starts this season, but had been given plenty of time to recover from a moderate effort at Royal Ascot. A tongue-tied was added in an attempt to improve his chances, but it appeared to have little effect and he has a lot to prove now. (op 12-1 tchd 15-2)

5937 SEB MERCHANT BANK E B F MAIDEN STKS 1m 1f 192y
4:00 (4:03) (Class 4) 2-Y-O **£4,528** (£1,347; £673; £336) **Stalls** Low

Form RPR

0 **1** **Daneking**^{29} 5013 2-9-3 0 NickyMackay 5 80+
(John Gosden) *mde all: set stdy pce tl kicked on over 2f out: styd on wl whn pressed fnl 2f: rdn out* **5/4**^{1}

3 **2** *1 ½* **Cherry Street**^{25} 5142 2-9-3 0 DavidProbert 8 75+
(Andrew Balding) *chsd wnr: rdn to chal against nr side rail 2f out: hld whn swtchd rt ins fnl f: styd on* **9/2**^{3}

05 **3** *4 ½* **Shivsingh**^{11} 5579 2-9-3 0 TedDurcan 4 67
(Mick Channon) *hld up in tch: rdn and effrt over 2f out: outpcd over 1f out* **17/2**

435 **4** *1* **Nant Saeson (IRE)**^{29} 4995 2-9-3 76 PatDobbs 6 65
(Richard Hannon) *hld up in tch: cl up over 2f out: wknd over 1f out* **3/1**^{2}

5 *1 ½* **News Show** 2-8-12 0 MartinLane 1 57+
(David Simcock) *hld up in last pair: pushed along over 3f out: outpcd 2f out: no ch after: kpt on towards fin* **16/1**

6 *4 ½* **Ctappers** 2-9-3 0 SteveDrowne 3 54
(Mick Channon) *dwlt: hld up in last pair: rdn and wknd over 2f out* **16/1**

0 **7** *27* **Beanstalk (IRE)**^{17} 5382 2-9-3 0 DaneO'Neill 2 6
(Richard Hannon) *chsd wnr: rdn and wknd rapidly wl over 2f out: t.o and eased over 1f out* **25/1**

2m 13.78s (5.78) **Going Correction** +0.375s/f (Good) **7** Ran SP% **113.8**
Speed ratings (Par 97): **91,89,86,85,84 80,59**
toteswingers:1&2:£2.80, 2&3:£17.30, 1&3:£2.10 CSF £7.19 TOTE £2.20: £1.20, £3.40; EX 7.40.
Owner Sir Eric Parker & Rachel Hood **Bred** Sir Eric Parker **Trained** Newmarket, Suffolk

FOCUS
Probably nothing more than a fair maiden, and a stamina test. The early pace didn't look strong, and the pair that sat prominent may well have had an advantage. They came clear. It's hard to rate the bare form any higher but the winner can do better.

NOTEBOOK
Daneking, who is in the Derby, displayed a good attitude under pressure, after leading for much of the contest, to hold off the runner-up. A promising seventh on his debut in the 'Frankel maiden' at Newmarket (started 20/1), this is a step in the right direction and he'll undoubtedly stay middle-distances next season. (op 15-8)
Cherry Street, a Derby entrant, showed a good attitude on his debut (1m at Kempton) and fought on well again here despite being a bit short of room in the final stages. He's another who looks certain to stay well. (op 4-1 tchd 5-1)
Shivsingh, who is in the Racing Post Trophy and Derby, came to hold every chance here before weakening. He'll find his level in handicaps. (op 8-1 tchd 15-2)
Nant Saeson(IRE) had the most experience but didn't appear to set a high level to beat on his 7f efforts. Officially rated 76, he gives the race a marker. (op 7-2)
News Show is stoutly bred and only really got going in the final stages. If she comes on for this experience, she can be given a chance in a race over a similar trip as a juvenile. (op 11-1)

5938 BETFRED GOALS GALORE STKS (H'CAP) 1m 4f
4:35 (4:37) (Class 4) (0-80,80) 3-Y-O **£5,175** (£1,540; £769; £384) **Stalls** High

Form RPR

1431 **1** **Covert Decree**^{28} 5050 3-9-2 **78** JohnFahy$^{(3)}$ 11 90+
(Clive Cox) *trckd ldr 1f: settled in 5th: rdn and clsd over 2f out: led over 1f out: idled in front and looking arnd: hrd rdn and styd on* **13/2**^{3}

4113 **2** *nk* **Franciscan**^{30} 4966 3-9-4 **77** KirstyMilczarek 6 89
(Luca Cumani) *hld up in 8th: rdn and prog over 2f out: styd on u.p to chse wnr fnl f: clsd at fin: jst hld* **10/1**

321 **3** *1 ¼* **Quails Hollow (IRE)**^{19} 5312 3-8-11 **70** MichaelHills 12 80
(William Haggas) *led 4f: trckd ldr: led again 4f out: drvn and hdd over 1f out: one pce* **6/1**^{2}

0021 **4** *¾* **Zamina (IRE)**^{13} 5512 3-9-0 **73** JamesDoyle 8 81
(Sylvester Kirk) *trckd ldrs in 6th: rdn wl over 2f out: tried to cl over 1f out: kpt on one pce* **25/1**

2204 **5** 4 1/2 **Hidden Valley**[26] 5103 3-8-11 **70**...(v1) DavidProbert 2 71
(Andrew Balding) *trckd ldrs in 4th: rdn and effrt over 2f out whn cl enough: wknd over 1f out* **22/1**

313 **6** 3/4 **Korngold**[28] 5064 3-8-12 **71**... DaneO'Neill 3 71
(John Dunlop) *settled in 7th: prog on outer 3f out: sn rdn: no hdwy and btn 2f out: wknd* **2/1**[1]

-350 **7** 3 1/4 **Cobbs Quay**[14] 5482 3-9-0 **73**... PhilipRobinson 10 68
(John Gosden) *trckd ldng pair: wnt 2nd and cl enough 3f out: wknd wl over 1f out* **7/1**

2203 **8** 12 **Danehill Dante (IRE)**[12] 5547 3-9-2 **75**... PatDobbs 5 51
(Richard Hannon) *hld up in last pair: rdn and no prog 3f out: sn wknd and bhd* **12/1**

3343 **9** nk **Orthodox Lad**[22] 5242 3-8-12 **71**... MartinDwyer 1 46
(John Best) *dwlt: rousted along to chse ldr after 1f: led after 4f: hdd 4f out: wknd 3f out: sn bhd* **12/1**

301 **10** 3 **Deck Walk (USA)**[29] 5001 3-9-7 **80**... SteveDrowne 9 50
(Roger Charlton) *hld up in last pair: rdn and no prog 3f out: sn wknd and bhd* **12/1**

0041 **11** 68 **Height Of Summer (IRE)**[19] 5318 3-9-3 **76**... TedDurcan 4 —
(Chris Wall) *hld up in 9th: wknd rapidly wl over 2f out: t.o* **16/1**

2m 40.99s (2.59) **Going Correction** +0.375s/f (Good) **11** Ran SP% **119.7**
Speed ratings (Par 103): **106,105,104,104,101 100,98,90,90,88 43**
toteswingers:1&2:£8.40, 2&3:£8.00, 1&3:£7.00 CSF £71.24 CT £416.31 TOTE £6.60: £1.60, £3.20, £2.40; EX 46.70.

Owner Lakes Bathrooms Ltd **Bred** A M Tombs **Trained** Lambourn, Berks

■ Stewards' Enquiry : Kirsty Milczarek four-day ban: used whip with excessive frequency without giving gelding time to respond (Sep 25-28)

FOCUS
A few of these looked like they had a bit more improvement to come, but four came nicely clear in the end and the favourite disappointed, so this is probably modest form for the class.
Deck Walk(USA) Official explanation: trainer said filly was unsuited by the track

5939 COUNTRYSIDE ALLIANCE STKS (H'CAP) 5f
5:05 (5:08) (Class 5) (0-75,79) 3-Y-O **£3,234** (£962; £481; £240) **Stalls** High

Form RPR

0425 **1** **Sugar Beet**[12] 5542 3-9-7 **75**... DavidProbert 6 87
(Ronald Harris) *stdd s: hld up last as ldrs blasted off: gd prog wl over 1f out: led jst ins fnl f: drvn clr* **12/1**

5010 **2** 2 3/4 **Green Warrior**[15] 5457 3-8-12 **66**...(p) PatDobbs 8 68
(Richard Guest) *w.w bhd str pce: prog 2f out: chal 1f out: sn outpcd by wnr* **16/1**

021 **3** 1 **Celtic Sixpence (IRE)**[12] 5542 3-9-11 **79**... MartinLane 2 77+
(Noel Quinlan) *w ldrs at str pce: led 1/2-way: hdd and fdd jst ins fnl f* **5/2**[1]

6231 **4** 2 1/2 **Whitecrest**[17] 5377 3-8-13 **67**... NickyMackay 7 56
(John Spearing) *w ldr to 1/2-way: lost pl wl over 1f out: n.d after* **6/1**[3]

3304 **5** nk **Welsh Inlet (IRE)**[12] 5542 3-9-0 **68**... NeilChalmers 1 56
(John Bridger) *racd in centre: on terms w ldrs: nrly upsides over 1f out: wknd* **8/1**

3066 **6** 2 1/2 **Whoateallthepius (IRE)**[9] 5644 3-8-9 **63**...(b1) MartinDwyer 4 42
(Dean Ivory) *mde most at str pce to 1/2-way: wknd over 1f out* **11/1**

3403 **7** 1 **Royal Bajan (USA)**[33] 4855 3-9-2 **70**... JimCrowley 3 46
(James Given) *trckd ldrs: cl enough 2f out: wknd over 1f out* **3/1**[2]

5045 **8** 6 **Jack Smudge**[15] 5456 3-9-4 **72**...(p) SteveDrowne 5 26
(James Given) *a in last trio: rdn and struggling over 2f out: sn bhd* **8/1**

59.45 secs (1.05) **Going Correction** +0.25s/f (Good) **8** Ran SP% **112.0**
Speed ratings (Par 101): **101,96,95,91,90 86,84,75**
toteswingers:1&2:£14.30, 2&3:£8.10, 1&3:£6.50 CSF £172.04 CT £635.80 TOTE £15.70: £3.50, £5.00, £1.10; EX 137.80.

Owner Ridge House Stables Ltd **Bred** Coln Valley Stud **Trained** Earlswood, Monmouths

FOCUS
A good gallop was set by the leading bunch, so the form should be sound for this level. The first two home came from off the pace.

5940 GOLF AT GOODWOOD STKS (H'CAP) 1m 1f
5:40 (5:42) (Class 2) (0-100,96) 3-Y-O+
£12,450 (£3,728; £1,864; £932; £466; £234) **Stalls** Low

Form RPR

6026 **1** **Circumvent**[21] 5275 4-9-9 **95**...(p) PatDobbs 10 105
(Paul Cole) *trckd ldng pair: rdn towards nr side over 2f out: led over 1f out: drvn out* **14/1**

010 **2** 1 **Robemaker**[15] 5450 3-8-7 **85**... NickyMackay 6 93
(John Gosden) *hld up in rr: effrt over 2f out: prog and swtchd rt over 1f out: styd on wl ins fnl f to take 2nd last 100yds* **20/1**

4141 **3** nk **Thistle Bird**[26] 5113 3-9-1 **93**... SteveDrowne 11 100+
(Roger Charlton) *reluctant to enter stalls: hld up in midfield: lost pl and dropped in rr 3f out: rdn and prog 2f out: styd on to take 3rd nr fin* **6/1**

2000 **4** 3/4 **Oceanway (USA)**[14] 5483 3-9-2 **94**... DarryllHolland 8 99
(Mark Johnston) *trckd ldrs on inner: rdn and effrt over 2f out: cl enough wl over 1f out: styd on same pce* **16/1**

6-11 **5** shd **Making Eyes (IRE)**[66] 3739 3-8-8 **86**... MichaelHills 5 91
(Hugo Palmer) *hld up in last trio: stdy prog on outer fr 3f out: rdn 2f out and cl enough: nt qckn over 1f out: one pce* **7/2**[1]

0040 **6** 1/2 **Brick Red**[87] 3032 4-9-4 **90**... DavidProbert 13 94
(Andrew Balding) *hld up in rr: rdn and struggling towards nr side 3f out: styd on u.p over 1f out: nrst fin* **15/2**

6450 **7** 2 1/4 **Desert Kiss**[12] 5557 6-9-1 **90**... SeanLevey(3) 4 89
(Walter Swinburn) *led: stretched on 1/2-way: hdd & wknd over 1f out* **25/1**

3163 **8** 1 **Shavansky**[12] 5557 7-9-8 **94**... JamesMillman 2 91
(Rod Millman) *dwlt: hld up in last pair: effrt on outer over 2f out: no prog over 1f out: fdd* **9/2**[2]

341- **9** 1/2 **Credit Swap**[212] 6562 6-9-8 **94**... JimCrowley 14 90
(Venetia Williams) *stdd fr wd draw and dropped in: hld up in last: pushed along and no great prog over 2f out: plugged on* **20/1**

0250 **10** 1 1/4 **Benandonner (USA)**[7] 5712 8-9-4 **90**... MartinLane 7 83
(Mike Murphy) *chsd ldr tl wknd u.p over 2f out* **33/1**

1060 **11** 3 1/2 **Sam Sharp (USA)**[35] 4788 5-9-0 **86**... MartinDwyer 9 71
(Ian Williams) *trckd ldrs: rdn wl over 2f out: wknd wl over 1f out* **14/1**

1525 **12** 3/4 **Duster**[46] 4415 4-9-3 **89**... DaneO'Neill 3 73
(Hughie Morrison) *t.k.h: trckd ldng pair: wnt 2nd briefly over 2f out: wknd rapidly wl over 1f out* **11/2**[3]

3000 **13** 7 **Invincible Soul (IRE)**[12] 5563 4-9-5 **94**... KieranO'Neill(3) 12 62
(Richard Hannon) *racd wd bhd ldrs: rdn 3f out: sn wknd* **40/1**

1m 58.2s (1.90) **Going Correction** +0.45s/f (Yiel)
WFA 3 from 4yo+ 6lb **13** Ran SP% **119.8**
Speed ratings (Par 109): **109,108,107,107,107 106,104,103,103,102 99,98,92**
toteswingers:1&2:£38.80, 2&3:£27.50, 1&3:£8.70 CSF £272.47 CT £1867.12 TOTE £16.50: £4.40, £5.50, £2.40; EX 316.70.

Owner The Fairy Story Partnership **Bred** Deepwood Farm Stud **Trained** Whatcombe, Oxon

FOCUS
A useful contest in which plenty of these had a chance. It's best to rate the race positively until proven otherwise.

NOTEBOOK
Circumvent had gone a long time without winning and had come down the weights as a result. Cheekpieces were back on after an experiment with blinkers, and possibly that made the difference as he won with a bit in hand. He is in the Cambridgeshire and one would imagine he'll go there for another try (he was a far from disgraced 16th last season off a mark of 107) all being well. (op 16-1)
Robemaker, up 2f in distance after an ordinary effort over 7f at Newmarket, represented a trainer who'd won two of the last four renewals of this, and he ran well, albeit without ever looking likely to win after meeting a little bit of trouble when the tempo lifted. He is in the Cambridgeshire.
Thistle Bird ran well for a fairly inexperienced filly. She is still one to remain interested in if connections keep her on the go. (op 5-1)
Oceanway(USA) came from a stable with a good record in this contest and had excuses for a couple of recent modest performances. This was obviously better but he doesn't appear to have anything in hand over the handicapper.
Making Eyes(IRE), off since winning at Kempton in early July, and 6lb higher, appeared to have been given the perfect ride considering the way the race had been run, so the fact she couldn't go on when looking a big danger suggests she either just needed it or is on her correct mark. It might be wise to allow her the chance to prove it was the former reason next time. (tchd 4-1)
Brick Red ◆, absent since a modest effort in the Royal Hunt Cup, needed strong driving once in the home straight towards the stands' rail and kept on. Entered in the Cambridgeshire, he would be of interest in that race if building on this, as he won a 1m handicap at Newmarket in October last season, and ran well during late autumn. (op 9-1)
Shavansky hadn't run over this sort of trip for a while and never really got into this after getting away slowly. (op 11-2)
Credit Swap ◆ caught the eye on his first start since February and will be interesting for the rest of the season in similar races.
Duster raced keenly while close up and then dropped away quickly when most were keeping on. (op 7-1)
T/Plt: £38.70 to a £1 stake. Pool of £74,829.64 - 1,410.40 winning tickets. T/Qpdt: £18.60 to a £1 stake. Pool of £3,648.03 - 144.65 winning tickets. JN

5832 KEMPTON (A.W) (R-H)
Saturday, September 10

OFFICIAL GOING: Standard
Wind: Light, half-against. Weather: cloudy

5941 BETFRED H'CAP 5f (P)
5:20 (5:20) (Class 6) (0-60,60) 3-Y-O **£1,617** (£481; £240; £120) **Stalls** Low

Form RPR

6003 **1** **Porthgwidden Beach (USA)**[23] 5215 3-8-12 **51**...(t) LeeNewman 5 58+
(Anthony Middleton) *in tch in midfield: swtchd lft and effrt over 1f out: drvn and r.o wl fnl f to ld fnl 50yds* **7/1**

4011 **2** 1/2 **Dangerous Illusion (IRE)**[17] 5388 3-9-1 **54**... AndreaAtzeni 8 57
(Michael Quinn) *chsd ldrs: swtchd lft and effrt over 1f out: rdn to ld ent fnl f: drvn and hrd pressed ins fnl f: hdd and no ex fnl 50yds* **11/4**[1]

5054 **3** hd **Instructress**[13] 5517 3-8-7 **49**... AdamBeschizza(3) 9 51
(Robert Cowell) *stdd s: t.k.h: hld up in last trio: hdwy over 1f out: rdn and gd hdwy ent fnl f: chal fnl 100yds: unable qck fnl 50yds* **25/1**

6060 **4** 2 3/4 **Slatey Hen (IRE)**[5] 5787 3-8-10 **52**...(p) MartinHarley(3) 2 45
(Richard Guest) *led for 1f: w ldr tl led again 1/2-way: rdn wl over 1f out: hdd ent fnl f: wknd ins fnl f* **5/1**[3]

4310 **5** nk **Nafa (IRE)**[21] 5274 3-9-3 **56**... JimmyQuinn 1 48+
(Michael Mullineaux) *chsd ldrs: travelling wl but nt clr run fr wl over 1f out tl swtchd lft jst ins fnl f: kpt on but nvr able to chal* **11/2**

6-00 **6** hd **Future Impact (IRE)**[30] 4950 3-9-5 **58**... PatCosgrave 7 49
(Ed de Giles) *in tch in midfield: rdn and unable qck over 1f out: kpt on same pce fnl f* **7/2**[2]

0150 **7** 1 1/2 **My Love Fajer (IRE)**[22] 5244 3-9-2 **60**... TobyAtkinson(5) 6 45
(Alan McCabe) *taken down early: stdd s: hld up in rr: rdn and effrt over 1f out: kpt on same pce* **8/1**

6065 **8** 3 **Aurivorous**[24] 5172 3-9-2 **55**...(p) RussKennemore 4 30
(Anabel K Murphy) *w ldr tl led after 1f: hdd 1/2-way: stl pressing ldr and drvn over 1f out: wknd ent fnl f* **40/1**

6006 **9** 7 **Stoneacre Joe Joe**[176] 892 3-8-8 **47** oh1 ow1... RobbieFitzpatrick 3 —
(Peter Grayson) *s.i.s: a in rr: rdn and struggling 1/2-way: wknd 2f out* **50/1**

60.93 secs (0.43) **Going Correction** +0.075s/f (Slow) **9** Ran SP% **112.8**
Speed ratings (Par 99): **99,98,97,93,93 92,90,85,74**
Tote Swingers: 1&2 £3.30, 1&3 £40.10, 2&3 £11.90 CSF £25.60 CT £454.06 TOTE £8.20: £3.20, £1.10, £3.30; EX 25.60.

Owner Macable Partnership **Bred** John Kerber & Jeff Kerber **Trained** Granborough, Bucks

FOCUS
A moderate handicap run at a decent gallop. The winner raced centre-to-far-side in the straight.
Nafa(IRE) Official explanation: jockey said filly was denied a clear run

5942 BETFRED "THE BONUS KING" H'CAP 1m 2f (P)
5:55 (5:56) (Class 5) (0-70,78) 3-Y-O+ **£2,264** (£673; £336; £168) **Stalls** Low

Form RPR

-301 **1** **Kyllachy Spirit**[11] 5607 3-9-6 **78**... MichaelJMurphy(7) 4 89
(William Knight) *mde all: drew clr w runner-up over 3f out: rdn over 1f out: battled on gamely fnl f* **4/1**[2]

4622 **2** hd **Dare To Bare (IRE)**[10] 5630 3-9-6 **71**...(v1) PatCosgrave 8 81
(Amanda Perrett) *chsd wnr thrght: drew clr w wnr over 3f out: ev ch after and drvn wl over 1f out: a jst hld fnl f* **5/2**[1]

0642 **3** 3 3/4 **Bouggatti**[13] 5518 3-9-3 **68**... LeeNewman 5 71
(William Jarvis) *bustled along thrght: in tch: rdn and outpcd by ldng pair over 3f out: wnt modest 3rd over 1f out: styd on but no threat to ldrs* **9/2**[3]

4664 **4** 1 3/4 **Woolston Ferry (IRE)**[16] 5414 5-9-2 **63**... AdamBeschizza(3) 9 62
(David Pinder) *hld up towards rr: rdn: swtchd lft and hdwy over 2f out: wnt modest 4th 1f out: no imp fnl f: nvr trbld ldrs* **16/1**

6406 **5** 3 3/4 **Rosco Flyer (IRE)**[26] 5102 5-9-2 **65**...(b1) TobyAtkinson(5) 7 57
(Roger Teal) *in tch in midfield: rdn and outpcd over 3f out: plugged on fnl f: nvr trbld ldrs* **14/1**

0300 **6** *hd* **Commerce**[19] 5318 4-9-2 **63** MartinHarley(3) 6 54
(Gary Moore) *chsd ldrs: rdn and outpcd over 3f out: 3rd and no imp 2f out: wknd ent fnl f* **25/1**

5042 **7** *½* **Lakota Ghost (USA)**[176] 898 3-8-11 **62** MarkLawson 10 52
(Seamus Durack) *hld up in rr: rdn over 2f out: swtchd lft and styd on ins fnl f: n.d* **16/1**

0200 **8** *½* **Lisahane Bog**[38] 4660 4-9-12 **70** (p) RobbieFitzpatrick 1 59
(Peter Hedger) *v.s.a and drvn along early: bhd: rdn and struggling 4f out: no ch fnl 2f* **33/1**

0-46 **9** *4* **Omnipotent (IRE)**[12] 5538 3-9-0 **65** JimmyQuinn 11 46
(Richard Hannon) *s.i.s: rdn along early: towards rr and stuck wd: rdn and toiling 4f out: wl btn fnl 2f* **11/1**

1000 **10** *2¾* **May Be Some Time**[22] 5242 3-9-1 **66** ChrisCatlin 12 42
(Stuart Kittow) *chsd ldrs: rdn and struggling over 4f out: wknd 3f out* **20/1**

0322 **11** *2½* **Bold Cross (IRE)**[10] 5611 8-9-2 **67** RaulDaSilva(7) 2 38
(Edward Bevan) *t.k.h early: in midfield early: dropped bk to rr 7f out: lost tch over 2f out* **9/1**

2m 6.54s (-1.46) **Going Correction** +0.075s/f (Slow)
WFA 3 from 4yo+ 7lb **11** Ran SP% **115.1**
Speed ratings (Par 103): **108,107,104,103,100 100,99,99,96,94 92**
Tote Swingers:1&2:£1.20, 2&3:£2.70, 1&3:£4.90 CSF £13.63 CT £45.95 TOTE £4.40: £2.90, £2.00, £1.10; EX 12.50.
Owner Mrs J R Jenrick & R D Jenrick **Bred** Mrs H I S Calzini **Trained** Patching, W Sussex

FOCUS
An ordinary handicap run at just an ordinary gallop and one in which the two market leaders pulled clear in the last two and a half furlongs. The winner raced against the inside rail in the straight.
Commerce Official explanation: vet said filly lost a near hind shoe

5943 BETFRED BINGO H'CAP (DIV I) 1m (P)
6:25 (6:25) (Class 6) (0-55,55) 3-Y-O+ **£1,293** (£385; £192; £96) **Stalls** Low

Form RPR

2065 **1** **Genes Of A Dancer (AUS)**[8] 5673 5-8-10 **51** LucyKBarry(5) 11 62
(Adrian Chamberlain) *dropped to rr after 1f: swtchd to outer and hdwy into midfield after 2f: rdn and effrt over 2f out: led and edgd rt over 1f out: clr ins fnl f: r.o wl* **5/1**[1]

6003 **2** *2¼* **Queenie's Star (IRE)**[11] 5606 4-8-6 **47** MarkCoumbe(5) 10 53
(Michael Attwater) *s.i.s: rdn and effrt jst over 2f out: edging rt and hdwy over 1f out: r.o to chse wnr fnl 75yds: no imp and nvr a threat to wnr* **6/1**[2]

6441 **3** *1½* **Ippi N Tombi (IRE)**[13] 5515 3-8-9 **50** ChrisCatlin 2 53
(Phil McEntee) *w ldr tl led over 3f out: rdn over 2f out: hdd over 1f out and sn outpcd by wnr: wknd ins fnl f* **8/1**

000 **4** *hd* **Gala Spirit (IRE)**[48] 4371 4-9-2 **52** AndreaAtzeni 12 54
(Peter Niven) *t.k.h: pressed ldrs: ev ch over 2f out: rdn and nt qckn 2f out: wknd jst ins fnl f* **20/1**

0250 **5** *2¼* **Trecase**[18] 5357 4-9-0 **50** (t) JimmyQuinn 7 47
(Tony Carroll) *in tch towards rr: drvn and effrt on outer over 2f out: styd on same pce and no real imp fnl f* **8/1**

0045 **6** *¾* **Dingaan (IRE)**[11] 5603 8-8-13 **54** SladeO'Hara(5) 1 49
(Peter Grayson) *hld up in tch towards rr: swtchd ins and effrt ent fnl 2f: no prog over 1f out and wl hld fnl f* **11/1**

0054 **7** *1* **Smarty Sam (USA)**[7] 5738 4-9-5 **55** (b) RussKennemore 4 48+
(Paul Midgley) *in tch in midfield: lost pl and dropped to rr wl over 2f out: nt clr run and hmpd ent fnl 2f: swtchd lft over 1f out: kpt on fnl f: no threat to ldrs* **8/1**

6041 **8** *1* **Excellent Vision**[11] 5606 4-9-1 **51** (t) CathyGannon 5 42
(Milton Bradley) *stdd s: hld up in rr: nt clr run over 2f out: swtchd ins and effrt ent fnl 2f: drvn and no hdwy over 1f out: wknd fnl f* **6/1**[2]

3/5 **9** *10* **Surwaki (USA)**[91] 2922 9-9-4 **54** PatCosgrave 3 22
(Robert Cowell) *in tch: rdn and nt qckn 2f out: btn over 1f out: eased fnl f* **13/2**[3]

00-0 **10** *3½* **Floating Angel (USA)**[30] 4948 4-8-10 **46** oh1 KirstyMilczarek 8 —
(John Best) *chsd ldrs: struggling u.p over 3f out: wknd over 2f out: wl bhd and eased ins fnl f* **33/1**

003 **11** *2* **Riczar**[15] 5432 3-8-9 **50** JamesDoyle 9 —
(Tom Dascombe) *led tl over 3f out: drvn and struggling over 2f out: wknd qckly wl over 1f out: wl btn and eased ins fnl f* **14/1**

1m 39.89s (0.09) **Going Correction** +0.075s/f (Slow)
WFA 3 from 4yo+ 5lb **11** Ran SP% **114.6**
Speed ratings (Par 101): **102,99,98,98,95 95,94,93,83,79 77**
Tote Swingers:1&2:£8.00, 2&3:£5.30, 1&3:£14.80 CSF £33.31 CT £239.62 TOTE £8.00: £2.40, £2.20, £2.50; EX 39.20.
Owner Colin Rogers **Bred** C Rogers **Trained** Ashton Keynes, Wilts

FOCUS
A moderate handicap run at a reasonable gallop. The winner came down the centre in the straight.
Queenie's Star(IRE) Official explanation: jockey said filly suffered interference shortly after the start
Smarty Sam(USA) Official explanation: jockey said gelding was denied a clear run
Riczar Official explanation: jockey said filly lost it's action

5944 BETFRED BINGO H'CAP (DIV II) 1m (P)
6:55 (6:55) (Class 6) (0-55,55) 3-Y-O+ **£1,293** (£385; £192; £96) **Stalls** Low

Form RPR

3226 **1** **Love Nest**[36] 4758 3-8-12 **53** LiamKeniry 1 61+
(John Dunlop) *chsd ldrs: rdn and ev ch fnl 2f: led ins fnl f: hdd towards fin: led again last stride* **9/4**[1]

6040 **2** *shd* **Shaunas Spirit (IRE)**[82] 3223 3-8-5 **46** WilliamCarson 7 53
(Dean Ivory) *dwlt: sn in tch in midfield: swtchd lft and effrt over 1f out: ev ch 1f out: drvn ins fnl f: led towards fin: hdd last stride* **25/1**

03-0 **3** *nse* **Qaraqum (USA)**[42] 4549 4-9-4 **54** CathyGannon 9 61+
(Denis Coakley) *in tch on outer: rdn 1/2-way: hdwy u.p and ev ch 2f out: led 1f out: hdd ins fnl f: no ex cl home* **8/1**[3]

4630 **4** *nk* **Rigid**[9] 5643 4-8-10 **46** oh1 JamesDoyle 3 52
(Tony Carroll) *hld up in midfield: clsd to trck ldrs and gng wl 2f out: swtchd rt and effrt jst over 1f out: rdn and ev ch ins fnl f: unable qck fnl 75yds* **11/1**

504 **5** *2½* **My Flame**[60] 3942 6-9-1 **51** StephenCraine 5 52
(J R Jenkins) *t.k.h: chsd ldrs: jnd ldrs and travelling wl over 2f out: rdn and fnd little wl over 1f out: wknd ins fnl f* **15/2**[2]

0-00 **6** *nse* **Monashee Rock (IRE)**[16] 5414 6-8-11 **52** LeeNewnes(5) 11 52+
(Matthew Salaman) *stdd s: hld up in rr: rdn and effrt but stl plenty to do 2f out: pushed along and styd on wl ins fnl f: nvr trbld ldrs* **10/1**

0606 **7** *nk* **Prime Circle**[23] 5214 5-9-0 **50** PatCosgrave 2 50
(Alan Brown) *in tch in midfield: drvn and effrt on inner to chse ldrs over 1f out: wknd ins fnl f* **12/1**

0000 **8** *nk* **Diplomatic (IRE)**[33] 4865 6-9-5 **55** (b[1]) KirstyMilczarek 8 54
(Michael Squance) *w ldr: rdn and ev ch over 2f out: wknd jst ins fnl f* **20/1**

550 **9** *1¼* **Bell's Ocean (USA)**[13] 5515 4-9-1 **51** JimmyQuinn 12 47
(John Ryan) *in tch towards rr: rdn and effrt 2f out: kpt on same pce and no real imp fr over 1f out* **14/1**

6000 **10** *nk* **Nubian Gem (IRE)**[18] 5352 3-8-9 **50** LukeMorris 4 46
(John Best) *in tch in midfield: rdn 1/2-way: outpcd and drvn over 2f out: plugged on same pce fnl 2f* **25/1**

0100 **11** *2¾* **Litotes**[31] 4908 3-8-7 **53** [1] MarkCoumbe(5) 6 42
(Michael Attwater) *led: rdn ent fnl 2f: wknd ent fnl f: fdd ins fnl f* **12/1**

0000 **12** *1¾* **Richo**[14] 4654 5-8-10 **46** oh1 (p) RobbieFitzpatrick 13 31
(Shaun Harris) *stdd s: t.k.h: hld up in rr: rdn and no prog over 2f out* **22/1**

5000 **13** *4½* **Emerald Girl (IRE)**[17] 5376 4-9-2 **55** MartinHarley(3) 10 30
(Richard Guest) *stdd s: hld up in rr: rdn and no prog over 2f out: wknd wl over 1f out* **12/1**

1m 40.02s (0.22) **Going Correction** +0.075s/f (Slow)
WFA 3 from 4yo+ 5lb **13** Ran SP% **117.6**
Speed ratings (Par 101): **101,100,100,100,98 98,97,97,96,95 93,91,86**
Tote Swingers:1&2:£8.30, 2&3:£75.40, 1&3:£2.00 CSF £72.96 CT £396.68 TOTE £3.40: £1.20, £11.90, £2.60; EX 86.30.
Owner Mrs Mark Burrell **Bred** Dragon's Stud **Trained** Arundel, W Sussex

FOCUS
Division two of a moderate handicap. The gallop was just fair and the winner raced towards the centre in the straight.

5945 TOTEPOOL FILLIES' NURSERY 1m (P)
7:25 (7:25) (Class 5) (0-75,71) 2-Y-O **£2,264** (£673; £336; £168) **Stalls** Low

Form RPR

5621 **1** **Tweet Lady**[25] 5144 2-9-3 **67** JamesMillman 3 69
(Rod Millman) *t.k.h: mde all and set stdy gallop: rdn and qcknd over 2f out: battled on wl fnl f: gamely* **7/2**[3]

5213 **2** *½* **My Sharona**[22] 5233 2-9-7 **71** LiamKeniry 4 72
(Sylvester Kirk) *w wnr thrght: rdn and ev ch over 2f out: drvn fnl f: kpt on but no ex fnl 50yds* **15/8**[1]

000 **3** *shd* **Better Be Mine (IRE)**[20] 5299 2-7-12 **48** oh3 CathyGannon 5 49+
(John Dunlop) *dwlt: bustled along early: in tch: rdn over 2f out: hdwy to chse ldng pair and edging rt jst over 1f out: kpt on wl ins fnl f: nt quite pce to rch wnr* **10/1**

026 **4** *5* **Essexvale (IRE)**[15] 5424 2-9-0 **67** SeanLevey(3) 2 56
(Richard Hannon) *in tch: rdn over 2f out: unable qck and outpcd over 1f out: wknd 1f out* **15/2**

0204 **5** *1* **Correct**[16] 5409 2-9-1 **68** JohnFahy(3) 6 55
(Michael Bell) *t.k.h: chsd ldrs: rdn and unable qck jst over 2f out: hung rt and wknd over 1f out* **9/4**[2]

1m 41.46s (1.66) **Going Correction** +0.075s/f (Slow) **5** Ran SP% **108.6**
Speed ratings (Par 92): **94,93,93,88,87**
CSF £10.20 TOTE £2.70: £2.20, £1.10; EX 9.70.
Owner The People's Horse **Bred** D J And Mrs Deer **Trained** Kentisbeare, Devon

FOCUS
A weakish nursery and a steady pace means the bare form isn't entirely reliable. The winner raced close to the inside rail throughout.

NOTEBOOK
Tweet Lady was again allowed a very easy lead but she showed a good attitude over this longer trip to extend her unbeaten record in nurseries at this course. She won't be going up much for this and, although things were in her favour, she will remain of interest when it looks as though she will be allowed to dominate in a similar manner. (op 3-1)
My Sharona was also well placed given the way things unfolded and she ran up to her best on this all-weather debut. A stronger gallop would have suited better but this consistent sort should continue to give a good account. (op 9-4 tchd 7-4)
Better Be Mine(IRE) ◆ showed her first worthwhile form from out of the handicap on this nursery and all-weather debut and is the one to take from the race. She'll be much better suited by the step up to 1m2f in a more truly run race and it'll be a surprise if she can't take advantage of her current mark at some point. (op 9-1 tchd 11-1)
Essexvale(IRE) didn't improve for the step up to this trip in this muddling event on this all-weather debut after taking a good hold. She may be best in a more strongly run race over shorter. (op 6-1 tchd 8-1)
Correct had shaped as though worth a try at this trip but she pulled too hard in this falsely run race and was a long way below her best. This wasn't her true form and she'll be worth another chance when a better gallop looks likely. (op 5-2 tchd 11-4)

5946 BETFRED "TEXT FRED TO 89660" MAIDEN FILLIES' STKS 6f (P)
7:55 (7:55) (Class 5) 3-Y-O+ **£2,264** (£673; £336; £168) **Stalls** Low

Form RPR

45 **1** **Libys Dream (IRE)**[14] 5469 3-8-12 0 JimmyQuinn 7 70
(Michael Mullineaux) *t.k.h: hld up in tch: rdn and effrt over 1f out: drvn to chal ins fnl f: r.o wl to ld cl home* **12/1**

6023 **2** *hd* **Cool Water Oasis**[18] 5355 3-8-12 58 DavidProbert 1 69
(Rae Guest) *t.k.h: chsd ldrs: rdn and effrt ent fnl 2f: led 1f out: r.o u.p tl hdd and no ex cl home* **8/1**[3]

0-2 **3** *1¾* **Shadow Of The Sun**[10] 5626 3-8-12 0 SteveDrowne 2 63
(Joseph Tuite) *sn led: rdn ent fnl 2f: hdd 1f out: no ex and one pce fnl 150yds* **7/2**[2]

2-2 **4** *2* **Always Like This (IRE)**[10] 5633 3-8-12 0 AndreaAtzeni 8 57
(Marco Botti) *chsd ldrs: rdn and effrt wl over 1f out: fnd little u.p and styd on same pce fr over 1f out* **8/13**[1]

66 **5** *nse* **Hollie**[58] 3998 3-8-12 0 TravisBlock 9 57
(Peter Makin) *taken down early: rn green: t.k.h: hld up in tch on outer: rdn and effrt ent fnl 2f: kpt on same pce fr over 1f out*

0 **6** *½* **Glastonberry**[12] 5567 3-8-9 0 SophieDoyle(3) 6 55
(Geoffrey Deacon) *hld up in tch in rr: pushed along and unable qck 2f out: kpt on same pce fr over 1f out* **66/1**

4040 **7** *4* **Lady Ellice**[169] 967 3-8-12 48 (p) ChrisCatlin 5 42
(Phil McEntee) *chsd ldr tl jst over 2f out: wknd u.p over 1f out: fdd ins fnl f* **50/1**

5 **8** *10* **Goldstorm**[31] 4923 3-8-12 0 WilliamCarson 3 —
(Brian Baugh) *fly leapt after leaving stalls and immediately detached in last: reminder and sn swtchd to outer: v wd but clsd bnd over 3f out: no hdwy and btn 2f out: eased fnl f* **33/1**

1m 13.36s (0.26) **Going Correction** +0.075s/f (Slow) **8** Ran SP% **117.0**
Speed ratings (Par 100): **101,100,98,95,95 95,89,76**
Tote Swingers:1&2:£6.20, 2&3:£3.20, 1&3:£6.20 CSF £102.34 TOTE £20.10: £6.00, £3.70, £2.90; EX 100.30.
Owner Michael Mullineaux **Bred** Irish National Stud **Trained** Alpraham, Cheshire

FOCUS
A moderate and uncompetitive fillies' maiden that didn't take as much winning as seemed likely with the short-priced favourite disappointing. The gallop was only fair and the winner raced centre-to-far-side in the straight.

Goldstorm Official explanation: jockey said filly hung left throughout

5947 TOTESCOOP6 H'CAP 2m (P)
8:25 (8:26) (Class 6) (0-65,65) 3-Y-O+ £1,617 (£481; £240; £120) Stalls Low

Form RPR

/005 **1** **Katies Tuitor**[33] 4870 8-9-6 **57**.......................................(p) LiamKeniry 5 68+
(J S Moore) *led tl 10f out: styd chsng ldr tl led again over 2f out: sn rdn clr: in command fnl f: pushed out fnl 100yds* **16/1**

0432 **2** *2* **Jinto**[13] 5519 4-9-6 **57**....................................... NickyMackay 6 63
(David Elsworth) *hld up towards rr: hdwy 4f out: hanging rt and swtchd lft 2f out: battling for 2nd and edgd rt 1f out: chsd wnr fnl 50yds: kpt on but nvr looked like getting to wnr* **3/1**[1]

03/1 **3** *½* **Whenever**[17] 5379 7-10-0 **65**....................................... SteveDrowne 10 70
(Richard Phillips) *s.i.s: rdn along and sn swtchd to outer: hdwy into midfield after 3f: chsd ldrs 10f out: rdn and outpcd over 3f out: rallied to chse clr wnr 1f out: kpt on but nvr able to chal: lost 2nd fnl 50yds* **11/2**[3]

6454 **4** *3 ¼* **Green Future (USA)**[12] 5566 3-8-9 **59** ow1..................(b[1]) PatCosgrave 8 61
(Amanda Perrett) *t.k.h: hld up in tch: rdn and effrt over 2f out: chsd clr wnr 2f out: no imp: lost 2 pls 1f out: plugged on* **7/1**

4000 **5** *1* **Storm Hawk (IRE)**[17] 5389 4-9-11 **65**..........................(p) JohnFahy(3) 4 65
(Pat Eddery) *dwlt: hld up in last piar: hdwy on outer over 3f out: no prog u.p over 2f out: kpt on ins fnl f: nvr trbld ldrs* **8/1**

3004 **6** *2* **Andorn (GER)**[8] 5692 7-10-0 **65**....................................... IanMongan 12 63
(Philip Kirby) *chsd ldr tl led 10f out: hdd and rdn over 2f out: sn outpcd by wnr: wknd over 1f out* **5/1**[2]

500- **7** *4 ½* **Tallulah Mai**[17] 7475 4-9-2 **53**....................................... LukeMorris 9 46
(Matthew Salaman) *chsd ldrs: rdn over 4f out: wknd u.p 2f out* **16/1**

5442 **8** *10* **Mediterranean Sea (IRE)**[25] 5141 5-9-13 **64**.............. StephenCraine 3 45
(J R Jenkins) *in tch in midfield: rdn and struggling 3f out: wknd over 2f out* **12/1**

3400 **9** *1 ½* **William's Way**[26] 5102 9-9-9 **63**..................................(t) MartinHarley(3) 2 42
(Ian Wood) *stdd s: hld up in rr: rdn and toiling over 3f out: wl bhd over 2f out* **25/1**

5026 **10** *10* **Oculist**[14] 5477 3-8-13 **63**....................................... FergusSweeney 7 30
(Jamie Osborne) *chsd ldrs tl lost pl rapidly u.p over 3f out: wl bhd fnl 2f: t.o* **11/1**

0040 **11** *21* **Himalayan Moon**[23] 5209 4-9-0 **51**.................................. JamesDoyle 1 —
(Ian Wood) *hld up in last trio: rdn 6f out: lost tch 4f out: t.o* **16/1**

/0-0 **12** *nk* **Nesnaas (USA)**[46] 3311 10-8-6 **48** oh3.........................(t) AmyScott(5) 11 —
(Mark Rimell) *in tch in midfield tl lost pl and rdn 8f out: in rr and lost tch 4f out: t.o* **50/1**

3m 30.23s (0.13) **Going Correction** +0.075s/f (Slow)
WFA 3 from 4yo+ 13lb 12 Ran SP% **120.1**
Speed ratings (Par 101): **102,101,100,99,98 97,95,90,89,84 74,73**
Tote Swingers:1&2:£7.20, 2&3:£4.10, 1&3:£12.20 CSF £64.49 CT £311.95 TOTE £28.30: £8.50, £1.60, £2.80; EX 126.90.
Owner Bill Adams **Bred** Brendan W Duke **Trained** Upper Lambourn, Berks

FOCUS
A modest handicap in which an ordinary gallop to the home straight meant very few figured. The winner raced towards the inside rail in the straight.
Whenever Official explanation: jockey said gelding hung left
Himalayan Moon Official explanation: vet said filly lost a right fore shoe

5948 BETFRED 1350 SHOPS NATIONWIDE H'CAP 7f (P)
8:55 (8:56) (Class 4) (0-80,80) 3-Y-O+ £4,075 (£1,212; £606; £303) Stalls Low

Form RPR

140 **1** **Kakapuka**[70] 3634 4-9-5 **76**....................................... IanMongan 1 86
(Anabel K Murphy) *t.k.h: chsd ldrs: rdn and swtchd lft 2f out: led jst over 1f out: clr ins fnl f: r.o wl: eased cl home* **25/1**

2031 **2** *1 ½* **Ongoodform (IRE)**[26] 5119 4-9-6 **77**..............................(v) LukeMorris 7 83
(Paul D'Arcy) *hld up in last trio: swtchd ins and effrt ent fnl 2f: hdwy over 1f out: swtchd lft 1f out: chsd clr wnr ins fnl f: kpt on but nvr able to chal* **11/2**[2]

0520 **3** *½* **Gallant Eagle (IRE)**[26] 5106 4-9-9 **80**.............................. PatCosgrave 9 85
(Ed de Giles) *hld up in last quartet: pushed along along wl over 2f out: hdwy u.p over 1f out: swtchd lft jst ins fnl f: r.o: nt rch wnr* **7/1**[3]

1341 **4** *shd* **Dashwood**[31] 4926 4-9-5 **76**.......................................(t) WilliamCarson 2 80+
(Giles Bravery) *in tch: rdn and unable qck ent fnl 2f: hdwy u.p 1f out: kpt on u.p but nvr gng pce to chal wnr* **11/4**[1]

5631 **5** *½* **Requisite**[7] 5718 6-9-5 **76**.......................................(b) JamesDoyle 10 79+
(Ian Wood) *hld up in last trio: effrt and swtchd ins ent fnl 2f: nt clr run over 1f out: r.o wl ins fnl f: unable to chal* **15/2**

03 **6** *nse* **Summer Dancer (IRE)**[7] 5717 7-9-1 **72**.................. RussKennemore 4 75
(Paul Midgley) *taken down early: t.k.h: hld up in tch: swtchd to outer and effrt 2f out: kpt on u.p fnl f: nt pce to threaten wnr* **8/1**

0300 **7** *¾* **Zip Lock (IRE)**[31] 4909 5-9-1 **77**.................................(t) LucyKBarry(5) 3 78
(Olivia Maylam) *chsd ldr: ev ch and rdn over 2f out: nt pce of wnr jst over 1f out: chsd wnr 1f out tl ins fnl f: no ex* **25/1**

0040 **8** *nse* **She Ain't A Saint**[19] 5322 3-9-5 **80**.............................. RobertHavlin 5 79
(Jane Chapple-Hyam) *hld up in tch in midfield: rdn and effrt jst over 2f out: kpt on same pce fnl f* **16/1**

0110 **9** *1 ¼* **Kings 'n Dreams**[11] 5587 4-9-2 **73**..............................(b) ShaneKelly 8 70
(Dean Ivory) *t.k.h: chsd ldrs: rdn and unable qck ent fnl 2f: wknd 1f out* **16/1**

2045 **10** *3* **Dream Catcher (FR)**[16] 5419 3-8-9 **75**.................... JamesRogers(5) 11 62
(David Pinder) *led: rdn over 2f out: hdd and nt pce of wnr jst over 1f out: wknd fnl f* **16/1**

0560 **11** *shd* **The Which Doctor**[17] 5383 6-8-12 **72**........................(e) MartinHarley(3) 12 61
(Richard Guest) *stdd s: hld up in rr: rdn and no imp over 2f out: kpt on but n.d* **20/1**

1130 **12** *1* **Rezwaan**[136] 1603 4-9-6 **77**....................................... FergusSweeney 6 63
(Gary Moore) *in tch in midfield: rdn and lost pl over 2f out: bhd and no hdwy over 1f out* **10/1**

1m 25.66s (-0.34) **Going Correction** +0.075s/f (Slow)
WFA 3 from 4yo+ 4lb 12 Ran SP% **116.6**
Speed ratings (Par 105): **104,102,101,101,101 100,100,100,98,95 95,93**
Tote Swingers:1&2:£25.70, 2&3:£7.00, 1&3:£40.10 CSF £151.81 CT £1092.88 TOTE £38.30: £7.60, £1.20, £2.90; EX 354.80.
Owner Mrs E Mills & A Murphy **Bred** Paradime Ltd **Trained** Wilmcote, Warwicks

FOCUS
Mainly exposed performers in a fair handicap but a moderate gallop meant very few figured. The winner raced just off the inside rail in the straight.
T/Plt: £57.30 to a £1 stake. Pool £56,561.60. 719.78 winning tickets. T/Qpdt: £16.70 to a £1 stake. Pool £7,576.49. 334.60 winning tickets. SP

5949 - (Foreign Racing) - See Raceform Interactive

5521 CURRAGH (R-H)
Saturday, September 10

OFFICIAL GOING: Yielding to soft

5950a THE IRISH FIELD BLENHEIM STKS (LISTED RACE) 6f
2:40 (2:40) 2-Y-O £22,413 (£6,551; £3,103; £1,034)

RPR

1 **Born To Sea (IRE)** 2-9-1 .... JMurtagh 6 104+
(John M Oxx, Ire) *sn in tch towards rr: clsd fr 1 1/2f out: got in the clr 1f out: rdn and qcknd wl fnl f to ld fr over 50yds out* **5/2**[1]

2 *1 ½* **Pearl In The Sand (IRE)**[13] 5521 2-8-12 .... NGMcCullagh 7 94
(G M Lyons, Ire) *s.i.s: clsd on rail 1f out: kpt on u.p wout matching wnr ins fnl f* **10/1**

3 *¾* **An Ghalanta (IRE)**[13] 5522 2-9-1 97..............................(t) KJManning 3 95
(J S Bolger, Ire) *sn led: pressed fr 2f out: hdd and kpt on same pce fr over 50yds out* **5/1**[3]

4 *2 ½* **Experience (IRE)**[13] 5522 2-9-3 99.............................. WMLordan 1 90
(David Wachman, Ire) *w.w: clsd travelling wl fr over 2f out: sn 2nd: no imp and kpt on same pce fnl f* **3/1**[2]

5 *½* **Lanett Lady (IRE)**[41] 4585 2-8-12 .... ShaneFoley 5 83
(M Halford, Ire) *sn in tch towards rr: swtchd and kpt on same pce u.p fr over 1f out* **14/1**

6 *2* **Bible Black (IRE)**[21] 5290 2-9-1 95.............................. KLatham 9 80
(G M Lyons, Ire) *prom: struggling fr over 2f out: no imp and kpt on same pce fr over 1f out* **11/2**

7 *8* **Pierre D'Or (IRE)**[21] 5289 2-9-1 .... CDHayes 4 56
(J T Gorman, Ire) *trckd ldrs: struggling fr over 2f out: sn no imp: no ex fr 1f out* **14/1**

8 *9* **Gush (USA)**[13] 5521 2-8-12 .... FMBerry 2 26
(Mrs John Harrington, Ire) *trckd ldrs: rdn over 2f out: sn no imp: no ex 1f out* **10/1**

1m 16.01s (1.01) **Going Correction** +0.15s/f (Good) 8 Ran SP% **117.1**
Speed ratings: **99,97,96,92,92 89,78,66**
CSF £29.17 TOTE £2.70: £1.10, £3.40, £1.20; DF 46.60.
Owner Christopher Tsui **Bred** Sunderland Holdings Ltd **Trained** Currabeg, Co Kildare

FOCUS
The winner made an impressive debut, while the runner-up has improved. The third is the best guide, along with the fifth.

NOTEBOOK
Born To Sea(IRE) ◆ got plenty of cover and, despite running green and tending to drift a little bit to his right inside the final furlong, displayed a turn of foot that was far too much for some decent juveniles to handle. Comparisons to his half-brother Sea The Stars are unavoidable, and the tentative evidence of this race would suggest Born To Sea possesses a more potent turn of foot than his sibling did at this very early stage of his career. That makes him potentially very exciting. The Group 3 Killavullan Stakes at Leopardstown in October will probably be his only other run this season. (op 7/2 tchd 9/4)
Pearl In The Sand(IRE) shouldn't be forgotten as she ran probably her best race to date. Missing the break a fraction, possibly on purpose, she got plenty of cover against the strong headwind and picked up well to chase the winner inside the final furlong. She didn't possess the same level of speed but it was a big run and she'll win a good race. (op 9/1)
An Ghalanta(IRE) seemed to run up to her mark. She saw plenty of early daylight as she raced prominently but was quite comfortably outpaced inside the last furlong. (op 9/2)
Experience(IRE) improved to challenge over a furlong out but faded inside the last. She does seem to be more effective at 5f. (op 10/3 tchd 7/2)
Lanett Lady(IRE) coped reasonably with her step up to this level as she kept on from the rear of the small field.

5951a GOFFS NATIONAL STKS (GROUP 1) (C&F) 7f
3:15 (3:15) 2-Y-O
£100,000 (£32,758; £15,517; £5,172; £3,448; £1,724)

RPR

1 **Power**[34] 4834 2-9-1 116.. SeamieHeffernan 7 118
(A P O'Brien, Ire) *sn trckd ldrs in 4th: rdn fr 2f out: mod 2nd over 1f out: clsd and led fr over 50yds out: styd on wl* **11/4**[2]

2 *½* **Dragon Pulse (IRE)**[21] 5293 2-9-1 110.............................. FMBerry 5 117
(Mrs John Harrington, Ire) *w.w: 6th 1/2-way: rdn fr 2f out: mod 4th over 1f out: clsd and styd on wl ins fnl f: 2nd fnl 50yds: nt quite get to wnr* **5/2**[1]

3 *1 ¼* **David Livingston (IRE)**[21] 5293 2-9-1 104.............................. PJSmullen 4 114
(A P O'Brien, Ire) *sn led: attempted to assert and wnt on fr 2f out: reduced ld and hdd fr over 50yds out: sn dropped to 3rd* **8/1**[3]

4 *nk* **Furner's Green (IRE)**[24] 5181 2-9-1 .... CO'Donoghue 6 113
(A P O'Brien, Ire) *towards rr: rdn to go mod 5th over 1f out: styd on wl wout threatening fnl f* **9/1**

5 *6* **Tough As Nails (IRE)**[34] 4834 2-9-1 112.............................. GFCarroll 2 98
(Michael Mulvany, Ire) *towards rr: rdn to go mod 6th over 1f out: kpt on same pce* **14/1**

6 *¾* **Strait Of Zanzibar (USA)**[21] 5293 2-9-1 101................(b[1]) ShaneFoley 9 96
(K J Condon, Ire) *prom: dropped to mod 3rd over 1f out: no ex* **50/1**

7 *4 ½* **Whip Rule (IRE)**[6] 5763 2-9-1 96..............................(p) KJManning 1 85
(J S Bolger, Ire) *sn trckd ldrs in 5th: pushed along fr 1/2-way: sn no imp* **33/1**

8 *3* **Vault (IRE)**[21] 5293 2-9-1 101.............................. JamieSpencer 8 77
(A P O'Brien, Ire) *prom: 3rd 1/2-way: no ex fr under 2f out* **25/1**

9 *3* **Talwar (IRE)**[21] 5276 2-9-1 .... JimmyFortune 3 70
(Jeremy Noseda) *sn chsd ldrs in 6th: struggling fr after 1/2-way: no ex fr under 2f out* **11/4**[2]

1m 27.74s (-3.06) **Going Correction** -0.20s/f (Firm) 9 Ran SP% **118.4**
Speed ratings: **109,108,107,106,99 98,93,90,86**
CSF £10.23 TOTE £2.90: £1.02, £1.10, £3.00; DF 9.60.
Owner Michael Tabor **Bred** Norelands & Hugo Lascelles **Trained** Ballydoyle, Co Tipperary

FOCUS
Far from a vintage renewal, but there was a decent pace on and the form should be reliable enough.

NOTEBOOK
Power was tackling this trip for the first time having lost his unbeaten record when collared late on in the Group 1 Phoenix Stakes over 6f here last month. This event has been won by many horses who went to achieve major success at three and while this might not have been a vintage renewal, the winner did the job well on ground slower than he had experienced previously. He had been ridden prominently on his previous start and different tactics were used here. He tracked the leaders and began his effort under 2f out before responding well when asked to step up a gear and lead well inside the final furlong. It will be interesting to see whether he sticks to 7f next time but he should have reasonable prospects of getting 1m on quicker ground.

Dragon Pulse(IRE), winner of the Group 2 Futurity Stakes over the course and trip last month, was attempting to complete the same double achieved by his stablemate Pathfork a year ago when he landed this Group 1 event. Well suited by ease and supplemented here, he produced a good effort, making steady progress from 2f out and finishing well without quite getting to the winner who got first run on him. (op 3/1)
David Livingston(IRE), a stablemate of the winner and one of four Ballydoyle colts in the line-up, had won his maiden over the course and trip before finishing fourth in the Futurity Stakes, This time he had plenty of use made of him and was soon in front before being ridden clear 2f out. However, he was reeled in inside the final furlong and could raise no extra in the closing stages. (op 7/1)
Furner's Green(IRE), another of the Aidan O'Brien team, had won his maiden over a slightly longer trip on debut at Tipperary before making little impact on his second start at York. He showed more here and, after being held up out the back, he began to close over 1f out and finished out the race well. (op 8/1)
Tough As Nails(IRE), a consistent performer who had been touched off by Power in a 5f Listed race here in May before being placed in both the Group 2 Railway Stakes and the Group 1 Phoenix Stakes, was tackling the trip for the first time and was never able to mount a serious challenge. He should benefit from dropping back in trip. (op 12/1)
Talwar(IRE), the winner of three of his four previous starts, had easily landed the Solario Stakes on his previous start and had had the form of a previous Ascot win boosted earlier in the day when the runner-up Trumpet Major won the Champagne Stakes at Doncaster. Supplemented to this race and with the ground to suit, he ran well below expectations and was struggling by halfway before trailing in last. It will be a surprise if something does not come to light to explain his performance. Official explanation: jockey said he was unhappy with the colt's action during the race

5952a THE IRISH FIELD ST. LEGER (GROUP 1) 1m 6f
3:50 (3:50) 3-Y-O+
£73,017 (£73,017; £17,068; £5,689; £3,793; £1,896)

RPR

1 **Duncan**[21] 5284 6-9-11 .... EddieAhern 3 119
(John Gosden) *trckd ldr in 2nd: chal and on terms fr 2f out: styd on wl u.p: dead-heated* **5/1**[3]

1 *dht* **Jukebox Jury (IRE)**[20] 5304 5-9-11 .... JMurtagh 1 119
(Mark Johnston) *attempted to make all: jnd fr 2f out: styd on wl u.p: dead-heated* **4/1**[2]

3 *1* **Red Cadeaux**[20] 5304 5-9-11 .... TomMcLaughlin 5 118
(Ed Dunlop) *chsd ldrs: mainly in 4th: u.p fr 5f out: mod 3rd under 3f out: styd on wl fnl f wout getting to dead-heaters* **12/1**

4 *22* **Fame And Glory**[21] 5291 5-9-11 120........ JamieSpencer 2 91
(A P O'Brien, Ire) *trckd ldrs in 3rd: struggling fr bef st: dropped to mod 4th under 3f out: no ex* **8/13**[1]

5 *9* **Waydownsouth (IRE)**[21] 5291 4-9-11 101........ DMGrant 6 74
(Patrick J Flynn, Ire) *racd last of the 6: struggling fr over 5f out: sn no imp* **100/1**

6 *3 ¾* **Fictional Account (IRE)**[21] 5291 6-9-8 103........ FMBerry 4 66
(V C Ward, Ire) *racd 5th of the 6 for much: no ex fr bef st* **14/1**

3m 8.01s (-1.39) **Going Correction** +0.25s/f (Good) **6** Ran SP% **113.9**
Speed ratings: **113,113,112,99,94 92**
WIN: JJ 1.50, D 2.00; PLACE: JJ 1.70, D 2.20; EXACTA: D & JJ 8.00, JJ & D 6.60; CSF D & JJ 12.71, JJ & D 12.11.
Owner A D Spence **Bred** Paul Nataf **Trained** Middleham Moor, N Yorks
■ The first ever dead-heat in this event, and the first in an Irish Classic since the 1988 Irish Oaks. Eddie Ahern's first Classic win.
Owner Normandie Stud Ltd **Bred** Normandie Stud Ltd **Trained** Newmarket, Suffolk
■ The first ever dead-heat in this event, and the first in an Irish Classic since the 1988 Irish Oaks. Eddie Ahern's first Classic win.

FOCUS
It wasn't a race that promised to be a classic Classic beforehand but how wrong that was proved to be as two dour stayers battled it out from the top of the straight to finish in a dead heat. The race is rated around the third, with a cautious view taken over the form.

NOTEBOOK
Duncan has been a standing dish in Cup races this season, winning the Yorkshire Cup and running a big race in the Ascot Gold Cup. He took a lead from Jukebox Jury and sustained his challenge from the top of the straight. It was a tremendously game effort from him as well. While his main protagonist maybe deserved it a shade more, the result couldn't really be complained about. Connections retired him after the race. (op 9/2)
Jukebox Jury(IRE) was the one that least deserved to lose. He did all of the donkey work in front, albeit under a terrific tactical front-running ride from Johnny Murtagh, who managed to bag the inside rail from an early stage. When he upped the tempo before the turn into the straight he looked for a while to have stolen it, and while he didn't quite do that he continued to find a bit more. It was a tremendous effort to try to make all and he deserved at least a share of the spoils. It's the culmination of an excellent season for this tough individual following his victory at Deauville in August. (op 9/2)
Red Cadeaux came back to the level of form he showed when running away with the Curragh Cup on similar ground over C&D back in June. Held up early on, he made ground to be on the heels of the leaders before the straight. He was then caught a bit flat-footed before they turned in, but kept staying on in the straight. He didn't help his rider by drifting towards the centre of the track. (op 12/1 tchd 11/1)
Fame And Glory capitulated completely once the pace quickened before the turn into the straight. It's a performance that can be completely forgotten. Official explanation: jockey said gelding never travelled theroughout (op 8/11)

5953 - 5957a (Foreign Racing) - See Raceform Interactive

BORDEAUX LE BOUSCAT (R-H)
Saturday, September 10
OFFICIAL GOING: Turf: soft

5958a PRIX OCCITANIE (LISTED RACE) (3YO FILLIES) (TURF) 1m 1f 110y
3:55 (12:00) 3-Y-O **£23,706** (£9,482; £7,112; £4,741; £2,370)

RPR

1 **Skallet (FR)**[37] 3-9-0 0........(b) StephanePasquier 1 103
(S Wattel, France) **81/10**[2]

2 *hd* **Brasileira**[94] 3-9-0 0........ MaximeGuyon 2 103
(J-M Beguigne, France) **15/1**

3 *¾* **Futurista (USA)**[29] 5028 3-9-0 0........ MickaelBarzalona 5 101
(F Head, France) **14/1**

4 *snk* **Humdrum**[21] 5277 3-9-0 0........ ThierryThulliez 9 101
(Richard Hannon) *broke wl: settled 4th on outside: gng wl: rdn early in st: chsd ldrs: nt qckn fnl f: styd on* **17/1**

5 *1* **Private Eye (FR)**[23] 5230 3-9-0 0........ GregoryBenoist 4 99
(E Libaud, France) **12/1**

6 *nk* **Angalia (IRE)**[42] 4570 3-9-0 0........ AnthonyCrastus 11 98
(E Lellouche, France) **29/1**

7 *½* **Lyrique (IRE)**[46] 4422 3-9-0 0........ ChristianHanotel 8 97
(A Fabre, France) **15/1**

8 *1* **Dinner's Out**[21] 3-9-0 0........(b) Jean-BernardEyquem 7 95
(J-C Rouget, France) **9/1**[3]

9 *¾* **Cesseras (IRE)**[82] 3-9-0 0........ PhilippeSogorb 13 94
(M Delzangles, France) **20/1**

10 *nk* **Galaxie Sud (USA)**[43] 3-9-0 0........ Francois-XavierBertras 3 93
(J-C Rouget, France) **15/1**

0 **Peinture Abstraite**[69] 3671 3-9-0 0........ ChristopheSoumillon 10 —
(A De Royer-Dupre, France) **1/1**[1]

0 **Satcat (FR)** 3-9-0 0........ CharlesNora 6 —
(R Martin Sanchez, Spain) **100/1**

2m 7.07s (127.07) **12** Ran SP% **118.7**
WIN (incl. 1 euro stake): 9.10. PLACES: 2.90, 4.40, 4.40. DF: 48.00. SF: 160.80.
Owner Guy Pariente **Bred** Ecurie Jarlan **Trained** France

NOTEBOOK
Skallet(FR), bought out of a claimer two starts back, got the better of a duel with the runner-up.
Humdrum was soon tracking the pace. Turning for home she was pulled wide to mount her challenge, and in doing so virtually stopped the even money favourite Peinture Abstraite in her tracks. The Queen's runner could never get on terms with the front two.

5427 FFOS LAS (L-H)
Sunday, September 11
OFFICIAL GOING: Good to soft (7.6)
Wind: Fresh, against Weather: Sunny spells

5959 BRITISH STALLION STUDS SUPPORTING BRITISH RACING E B F MAIDEN STKS 1m (R)
2:20 (2:20) (Class 4) 2-Y-O **£4,528** (£1,347; £673; £336) **Stalls** Low

Form RPR

5 **1** **Silver Lime (USA)**[46] 4446 2-9-3 0........ MartinDwyer 6 81
(Roger Charlton) *racd in 4th: rdn and hdwy over 2f out: styd on to ld nr fin* **5/6**[1]

00 **2** *hd* **Journalistic (USA)**[18] 5384 2-8-10 0........ KatiaScallan(7) 8 80
(Marcus Tregoning) *in tch: rdn over 2f out: r.o to ld ent fnl f: pushed along: hdd nr fin* **16/1**

03 **3** *7* **City Dazzler (IRE)**[43] 4545 2-8-12 0........ DaneO'Neill 2 60
(Richard Hannon) *cl up: tk narrow ld over 3f out: rdn over 1f out: sn hdd and one pce* **11/2**[3]

4 *4 ½* **Gucci D'Oro (USA)** 2-9-3 0........ FrankieMcDonald 5 55
(David Simcock) *s.i.s: in rr: rdn 3f out: styd on fnl 2f: nvr nr ldrs* **16/1**

024 **5** *5* **Macdonald Mor (IRE)**[78] 3408 2-9-3 83........ PaulHanagan 1 44
(David Simcock) *led: hdd over 3f out but remained cl up: rdn over 2f out: wknd over 1f out* **11/4**[2]

0 **6** *20* **Ali Hope (IRE)**[18] 5382 2-9-3 0........ RichardKingscote 4 —
(Roger Charlton) *in rr: niggled along over 4f out: grad lost tch: t.o* **28/1**

0 **7** *¾* **Khan Of Khans (IRE)**[13] 5536 2-8-12 0........ RyanPowell(5) 7 —
(Rebecca Curtis) *trckd ldrs: rdn over 3f out: sn edgd rt and wknd: t.o* **50/1**

1m 46.09s (5.09) **Going Correction** +0.575s/f (Yiel) **7** Ran SP% **113.8**
Speed ratings (Par 97): **97,96,89,85,80 60,59**
toteswingers: 1&2 £15.00, 1&3 £6.10, 2&3 £46.40 CSF £17.14 TOTE £1.80: £1.10, £5.90; EX 12.50.
Owner K Abdulla **Bred** Millsec Ltd **Trained** Beckhampton, Wilts

FOCUS
Fair form from the principals in a maiden where the field ended up quite well stretched out on the rain-softened ground. The winner built on his debut effort and the first pair came clear.

NOTEBOOK
Silver Lime(USA) had shaped nicely on his Sandown debut and duly improved, though he had to work hard to land the odds, needing virtually all of this longer trip to prevail. He's bred to stay further and there should be more to come. (op 10-11 tchd 6-5)
Journalistic(USA) has improved a chunk with each outing, so there's a good chance he'll do better still, worn down at the finish but pulling a long way clear of the rest. He'll be winning before long. (op 18-1)
City Dazzler(IRE) probably ran to a similar level as at Lingfield, fading as though her stamina may have just been stretched in the end. She'll need to step up a little on what she's achieved so far to win a maiden but this does at least open up the handicap route for her. (tchd 5-1 and 6-1)
Gucci D'Oro(USA), a Medaglia d'Oro colt, needed the experience but he did show ability by the finish, and should be all the better with this behind him. (op 14-1)
Macdonald Mor(IRE) had chased home Trumpet Major when second at Goodwood back in May but hasn't come close to repeating that in two starts since, this his first in nearly three months/since leaving Paul Cole, though stamina seemed an issue up 2f in trip and he is probably worth another chance to show what he can do for his new yard back over shorter. (op 3-1 tchd 2-1)

5960 FELINFOEL DRAGON STOUT MAIDEN STKS 1m (R)
2:50 (2:51) (Class 4) 3-Y-O+ **£4,528** (£1,347; £673; £336) **Stalls** Low

Form RPR

4102 **1** **Quadrant (IRE)**[13] 5556 3-9-3 78........(b[1]) MartinDwyer 6 83
(Brian Meehan) *trckd ldr: led over 1f out: drvn clr fnl f* **9/4**[1]

3043 **2** *4* **Change The Subject (USA)**[12] 5607 3-9-3 73........(b) PaulHanagan 1 74
(Sir Henry Cecil) *led: set str pce: rdn over 2f out: hdd and hung rt over 1f out: sn one pce* **5/2**[2]

6 **3** *¾* **Drakes Drum**[16] 5449 3-9-0 0........ JohnFahy(3) 7 72+
(Clive Cox) *chsd ldng pair: clsd over 1f out: rdn and one pce fnl f* **7/2**[3]

0 **4** *6* **Beauchamp Zorro**[16] 5449 3-9-3 0........ DaneO'Neill 8 58
(Henry Candy) *hld up in 4th: clsd over 2f out: nvr trbld ldrs: wknd ins fnl f* **17/2**

5 *4* **Nakhutha (FR)** 3-9-3 0........ RichardKingscote 3 49
(Mahmood Al Zarooni) *racd in mod 6th: rdn over 3f out: nvr rchd ldrs: wknd over 1f out* **11/2**

0 **6** *5* **Young Dr Jekyll**[10] 5639 3-9-3 0........ FrankieMcDonald 2 38
(Henry Candy) *midfield: rdn over 4f out: wknd over 2f out* **66/1**

7 *19* **Daisy Crazy** 4-8-12 0........ RyanPowell(5) 4 —
(Gary Harrison) *s.s: a in rr: t.o fnl 3f* **40/1**

00/ **8** *73* **Indared**[26] 6070 7-9-1 0........(v) DannyBrock(7) 5 —
(Tracey Barfoot-Saunt) *a in rr: struggling over 4f out: sn wl t.o* **150/1**

1m 45.88s (4.88) **Going Correction** +0.70s/f (Yiel)
WFA 3 from 4yo+ 5lb **8** Ran SP% **112.1**
Speed ratings (Par 105): **103,99,98,92,88 83,64,—**
toteswingers: 1&2 £3.00, 1&3 £5.10, 2&3 £4.80 CSF £7.78 TOTE £3.60: £1.70, £1.10, £1.20; EX 8.20.
Owner Highclere Thoroughbred Racing-Masquerade **Bred** Trebles Holford Farm Thoroughbreds **Trained** Manton, Wilts

FOCUS
A fairly useful effort from the winner.

5961 CELTIC GOLD NURSERY 5f
3:25 (3:26) (Class 4) (0-85,82) 2-Y-O £3,881 (£1,155; £577; £288) Stalls High

Form RPR
641 1 **Royal Award**[34] 4848 2-9-1 78 MartinDwyer 2 82
(Ian Wood) *cl up: led over 3f out: shkn up 2f out: drvn out ins fnl f* 4/1[3]
1231 2 1 **Son Du Silence (IRE)**[16] 5438 2-8-9 77 RyanPowell(5) 4 77
(J S Moore) *trckd ldng pair: n.m.r on rail over 2f out but sn in 2nd: chal wnr over 1f out: unable qck ins fnl f* 2/1[1]
1605 3 1 1/4 **Piranha (IRE)**[8] 5708 2-9-2 79 PaulHanagan 1 75
(Ed Dunlop) *racd in last: swtchd lft over 2f out and sn chsd ldng pair: styd on same pce ins fnl f* 10/3[2]
610 4 16 **Huma Bird**[89] 3014 2-9-5 82 DaneO'Neill 3 50
(Mahmood Al Zarooni) *led over 1f: remained cl up tl hung rt and wknd qckly 2f out: eased ent fnl f: t.o* 2/1[1]

62.60 secs (4.30) **Going Correction** +0.70s/f (Yiel) 4 Ran SP% 109.7
Speed ratings (Par 97): **93,91,89,63**
CSF £12.25 TOTE £2.90; EX 9.20.
Owner Miss Jacqueline Goodearl **Bred** Miss Jacqueline Goodearl **Trained** Upper Lambourn, Berks

FOCUS
Hardly the most competitive of nurseries, and not really form to trust.

NOTEBOOK
Royal Award hails from a yard which has refound some form of late and improved again to follow up her Lingfield maiden success. She's speedy and potentially useful the way she's going. (op 11-4)
Son Du Silence(IRE) ran well from a 3lb higher mark than Newcastle, just running into a progressive one in the winner. He hasn't finished out of the first three since his debut and there's no reason why he won't continue to give a good account. (op 5-2)
Piranha(IRE) wasn't discredited, but hasn't progressed since her pair of Polytrack wins in mid-summer, unable to pick up from off the pace. (op 7-2 tchd 3-1)
Huma Bird, who had been off the track since finishing well beaten in the Windsor Castle, backed out of things pretty tamely, the softish ground a possible excuse, but she will still have a bit to prove next time, her Lingfield success (raced against favoured rail) a standout at present. (op 5-2)

5962 DOUBLE DRAGON - NATIONAL ALE OF WALES FILLIES' H'CAP 1m 2f (R)
4:00 (4:01) (Class 4) (0-80,80) 3-Y-O+ £4,528 (£1,347; £673; £336) Stalls Low

Form RPR
122 1 **Satwa Pearl**[12] 5608 5-9-12 80 PaulHanagan 8 87
(Ed Dunlop) *trckd ldng pair: rdn 2f out: sn chal ldr: led 1f out: drvn out* 5/2[1]
3103 2 3/4 **Miss Aix**[30] 5020 3-9-5 80 FrankieMcDonald 9 85
(Michael Bell) *led after 1f: set mod pce: rdn along and qcknd over 2f out: hdd 1f out: jockey momentarily stopped riding sn after as rgoer rn across crse: kpt on same pce* 5/1[2]
-414 3 3/4 **Baisse**[113] 2287 3-9-3 78 MartinDwyer 3 82
(Sir Henry Cecil) *racd in 4th: rdn over 2f out: styd on fnl f* 6/1[3]
3160 4 3/4 **Misty Isles**[45] 4473 3-8-10 74 JohnFahy(3) 1 76
(Heather Main) *towards rr: clsd 3f out: styd on fnl 2f: unable to chal ldrs* 12/1
234 5 3/4 **Hayaku (USA)**[31] 4956 3-8-12 73 (t) RichardKingscote 5 74
(Ralph Beckett) *led 1f: trckd ldr: pushed along 4f out: rdn over 2f out: kpt on one pce* 7/1
1540 6 1 **Countermarch**[27] 5113 3-9-1 76 DaneO'Neill 6 75
(Richard Hannon) *wnt rt s: midfield: hdwy 3f out: no imp on ldrs fr over 1f out* 17/2
3016 7 3 1/2 **Lady of Burgundy**[33] 4887 5-9-2 75 LeeNewnes(5) 7 67
(Mark Usher) *s.i.s: in rr: clsd over 2f out: sn rdn and outpcd by ldrs* 25/1
0021 8 1/2 **Ashkalara**[13] 5538 4-8-7 66 oh4 RyanPowell(5) 4 57
(Stuart Howe) *hld up in rr: niggled along over 2f out: unable qck and sn wknd* 8/1
0341 9 6 **Miss Bootylishes**[15] 5496 6-9-4 77 DavidKenny(5) 2 56
(Paul Burgoyne) *towards rr: rdn and hung lft over 2f out: wknd over 1f out* 9/1

2m 19.11s (9.71) **Going Correction** +0.70s/f (Yiel)
WFA 3 from 4yo+ 7lb 9 Ran SP% 115.2
Speed ratings (Par 102): **89,88,87,87,86 85,83,82,77**
toteswingers: 1&2 £2.30, 1&3 £2.20, 2&3 £7.80 CSF £14.69 CT £67.12 TOTE £2.80: £1.20, £2.10, £1.80; EX 18.00.
Owner The Lamprell Partnership **Bred** E Puerari And Dominique Ades-Hazan **Trained** Newmarket, Suffolk

FOCUS
A fillies' event which wasn't run at a strong gallop and it paid to race handily, very few ever threatening to get into it.

5963 CELTIC PRIDE H'CAP 1m 4f (R)
4:30 (4:30) (Class 3) (0-95,94) 3-Y-O+ £7,439 (£2,213; £1,106; £553) Stalls Low

Form RPR
0060 1 **Classic Vintage (USA)**[23] 5250 5-9-9 91 (b1) FrankieMcDonald 5 98
(Amanda Perrett) *sn led: dictated pce: qckng over 3f out: sn rdn along: drvn out fnl f and styd on wl* 11/2[3]
2-31 2 1 1/2 **Protaras (USA)**[11] 5629 4-8-10 81 JohnFahy(3) 1 86
(Sir Henry Cecil) *midfield: hdwy into 2nd over 4f out: drvn 2f out: styd on but hld by wnr ins fnl f* 3/1[2]
60/4 3 11 **Enroller (IRE)**[15] 5493 6-9-12 94 MartinDwyer 7 81
(William Muir) *hld up in last: hdwy over 3f out: wnt mod 3rd over 2f out: sn rdn and no imp on first two* 9/1
6-26 4 10 **Jivry**[33] 4890 4-9-1 83 DaneO'Neill 8 54
(Henry Candy) *chsd ldrs: rdn and outpcd 3f out: wknd over 1f out* 15/8[1]
2-00 5 5 **Mataaleb**[15] 5482 4-9-5 87 RichardKingscote 2 50
(Lydia Pearce) *towards rr: hdwy to dispute modest 3rd over 3f out: sn rdn along: grad wknd fnl 2f* 14/1
6431 6 17 **Zafarana**[27] 5098 3-8-8 85 PaulHanagan 3 21
(Ed Dunlop) *towards rr: pushed along 4f out: wknd over 2f out: t.o* 11/2[3]
7 8 **Platinum (IRE)**[390] 4-9-5 92 RyanPowell(5) 6 15
(Rebecca Curtis) *led early: trckd wnr tl rdn and lost pl over 4f out: wknd qckly: t.o* 16/1

2m 44.44s (7.04) **Going Correction** +0.70s/f (Yiel)
WFA 3 from 4yo+ 9lb 7 Ran SP% 113.1
Speed ratings (Par 107): **104,103,95,89,85 74,69**
toteswingers: 1&2 £3.90, 1&3 £6.20, 2&3 £3.40 CSF £21.83 CT £144.36 TOTE £8.60: £3.00, £1.80; EX 35.70.
Owner R & P Scott A & J Powell Gallagher Stud **Bred** Gallagher's Stud **Trained** Pulborough, W Sussex

FOCUS
Few got into this handicap and they finished strung out behind the first two.

NOTEBOOK
Classic Vintage(USA) quickened the pace at the top of the straight, and responded really well to the first-time blinkers, this probably a career-best for all he's performed well in some competitive handicaps in the past. His immediate prospects will depend to some degree on how the handicapper reacts to the leading pair pulling so far clear. (op 13-2 tchd 7-1)
Protaras(USA) has almost certainly shown improved form, never quite able to get on terms with the winner but staying on strongly to pull well clear of the remainder. He'll look well treated if turned out before being reassessed (has until a week on Friday). (op 11-4)
Enroller(IRE) has been given a chance by the handicapper and there were signs here he still retains plenty of ability. He'll come down a bit more for this and there's a chance he'll strip fitter again next time, this just his second outing in two years. (op 10-1)
Jivry was well backed, her Nottingham win last year having come on an easy surface, but she was disappointing, beaten early in the straight. She's still very lightly raced but will have a bit to prove next time after this. (op 5-2)
Mataaleb has yet to show much for his new yard this term. (op 16-1 tchd 18-1)
Zafarana got a mark in the mid-80s after her wide-margin Polytrack maiden success but has yet to get near that level on turf and was soon beaten under pressure in the straight. (op 4-1)
Platinum(IRE) had some fairly useful form to his name for Andre Fabre in France last year but offered nothing starting out for his new yard. (op 14-1)

5964 CAMBRIAN BEST BITTER H'CAP 1m 4f (R)
5:05 (5:05) (Class 5) (0-70,70) 3-Y-O+ £2,587 (£770; £384; £192) Stalls Low

Form RPR
02-0 1 **Durante Alighieri**[20] 5327 3-9-2 69 MartinDwyer 2 79+
(Sir Henry Cecil) *s.i.s: sn trcking ldrs: racd alone on ins fr over 4f out: drvn and ev ch fr over 2f out: led 1f out: styd on wl to pull clr fnl 50yds* 5/4[1]
0643 2 2 3/4 **Convention**[18] 5391 3-9-3 70 PaulHanagan 5 76
(Ed Dunlop) *trckd ldrs: nudged along over 4f out: styd on u.p fnl 2f: wnt 2nd nr fin* 11/4[2]
62 3 1/2 **Yourinthewill (USA)**[33] 4888 3-8-6 62 JohnFahy(3) 4 67
(Daniel Mark Loughnane, Ire) *hld up in last: hdwy 3f out: led 2f out and edgd lft u.p: hdd 1f out: no ex towards fin* 13/2
5632 4 7 **Chik's Dream**[16] 5428 4-8-8 57 RyanPowell(5) 1 51
(Derek Haydn Jones) *led: drvn and edgd lft over 2f out: sn hdd: wknd appr fnl f* 8/1
5-55 5 12 **Rosairlie (IRE)**[62] 3912 3-9-1 68 DaneO'Neill 3 43
(Harry Dunlop) *bustled along fr stalls to trck ldr: rdn and lost pl over 3f out: wknd over 1f out* 11/2[3]

2m 48.06s (10.66) **Going Correction** +0.70s/f (Yiel)
WFA 3 from 4yo 9lb 5 Ran SP% 110.9
Speed ratings (Par 103): **92,90,89,85,77**
CSF £4.96 TOTE £1.90: £1.30, £1.60; EX 5.20.
Owner H E Sheikh Sultan Bin Khalifa Al Nahyan **Bred** Newsells Park Stud **Trained** Newmarket, Suffolk

FOCUS
A maiden handicap in all but name.

5965 HOLSTEN VIER H'CAP 5f
5:40 (5:41) (Class 6) (0-60,60) 3-Y-O+ £1,908 (£563; £281) Stalls High

Form RPR
-561 1 **Steel Rain**[104] 2549 3-9-1 55 PaulHanagan 5 63
(Nikki Evans) *trckd ldrs: swtchd lft over 1f out: rdr dropped whip ins fnl f: r.o to ld cl home* 7/2[2]
02 2 shd **Lake Wanaka (IRE)**[3] 5865 3-8-6 46 oh1 (t) MartinDwyer 4 54
(Ms Joanna Morgan, Ire) *led: drvn 1f out: hdd cl home* 5/1
3 3 nk **Queen Grace (IRE)**[25] 5191 4-9-4 60 JohnFahy(3) 1 67
(Michael J Browne, Ire) *chsd ldrs: hdwy over 1f out: sn drvn and ev ch: unable qck nr fin* 5/2[1]
0021 4 1 3/4 **Griffin Point (IRE)**[9] 5678 4-8-11 55 JamesRogers(5) 7 56+
(William Muir) *chsd ldrs: pushed along and lost pl over 2f out: r.o u.p ins fnl f: nt rch ldrs* 4/1[3]
6-6 5 1/2 **Lovestoned (IRE)**[3] 5869 5-8-8 47 RichardKingscote 3 46
(G A Kingston, Ire) *in rr: outpcd after 1f: hdwy on outer over 1f out: drvn and r.o ins fnl f* 5/1
0050 6 3/4 **Greyemkay**[19] 5344 3-8-7 52 DavidKenny(5) 6 48
(Richard Price) *sed awkwardly: in rr: swtchd lft and rdn 1/2-way: one pce u.p ins fnl f* 28/1
5030 7 1 1/2 **The Jailer**[13] 5534 8-9-0 58 RyanPowell(5) 2 49
(John O'Shea) *w ldr: drvn 2f out: wknd ins fnl f* 14/1

61.57 secs (3.27) **Going Correction** +0.70s/f (Yiel)
WFA 3 from 4yo+ 1lb 7 Ran SP% 114.2
Speed ratings (Par 101): **101,100,100,97,96 95,93**
toteswingers: 1&2 £2.90, 1&3 £2.20, 2&3 £2.30; totesuper7: Win: Not won, Place: Not won CSF £21.16 TOTE £4.40: £3.20, £2.50; EX 15.50.
Owner John Berry (Gwent) **Bred** L T Roberts **Trained** Pandy, Monmouths

FOCUS
Modest fare, but in-form horses came to the fore and it represents solid form for the level.
T/Plt: £23.20 to a £1 stake. Pool: £70,815.26. 2,221.61winning tickets. T/Qpdt: £11.30 to a £1 stake. Pool: £5,203.68. 340.60 winning tickets. RL

5933 GOODWOOD (R-H)
Sunday, September 11

OFFICIAL GOING: Soft (7.0)
Wind: Strong, half against Weather: Fine

5966 RACING UK ON SKY 432 BONUS STKS (H'CAP) 2m
1:55 (1:55) (Class 4) (0-85,86) 3-Y-O+ £4,528 (£1,347; £673; £336) Stalls High

Form RPR
1310 1 **Cunning Act**[22] 5283 3-8-13 83 StephenCraine 10 97+
(Jonathan Portman) *hld up in midfield: smooth prog towards nr side to trck ldr 3f out: led 2f out: shkn up and sn clr: eased last 75yds* 5/1[2]
2100 2 4 **Galivant (IRE)**[30] 4998 3-8-5 75 ChrisCatlin 4 82
(J W Hills) *settled in rr: rdn and prog fr over 3f out: styd on to take 2nd jst over 1f out: no ch w wnr* 10/1
21-U 3 3 1/2 **Tuscan Gold**[24] 5221 4-10-1 86 SebSanders 8 89+
(Sir Mark Prescott Bt) *lw: prom: led 4f out and c towards nr side: rdn 3f out: hdd 2f out and no ch w wnr after: lost 2nd jst over 1f out: fdd* 13/2[3]
5422 4 1 **Four Nations (USA)**[8] 5710 3-8-11 81 NeilCallan 9 83
(Amanda Perrett) *trckd ldrs: c towards nr side st: rdn 3f out: outpcd fnl 2f* 11/4[1]
1042 5 2 3/4 **Schism**[23] 5236 3-8-4 74 CathyGannon 1 72
(Henry Candy) *hld up towards rr: rdn over 3f out: modest prog over 2f out: nvr on terms* 7/1

315/ **6** *hd* **Mobaasher (USA)**[156] 5758 8-9-11 **82**.......................... JamesMillman 3 80
(Rod Millman) *hld up in last: struggling 5f out: lost tch 4f out and in danger of tailing off: pushed along and styd on fnl 2f: nrst fin* **25/1**

3653 **7** *1¾* **Time To Work (IRE)**[30] 4998 3-9-1 **85**........................(v) JimmyFortune 6 81
(Andrew Balding) *swtg: in tch: trckd ldrs 4f out: prog in centre and wl on terms 3f out: wknd 2f out* **7/1**

5364 **8** *¾* **Hawridge King**[23] 5236 9-8-12 **69**..................................(b[1]) LukeMorris 2 64
(Stuart Kittow) *hld up in last pair: rdn and struggling 4f out: modest prog over 2f out: nvr on terms* **20/1**

6315 **9** *9* **Cluain Dara (IRE)**[39] 4677 3-8-6 **76**........................ SilvestreDeSousa 12 60
(Mark Johnston) *pressed ldrs: upsides 5f out to over 3f out: wknd rapidly wl over 2f out* **18/1**

3 **10** *5* **Kahsabelle (FR)**[23] 5236 6-8-9 **66**.................................. DavidProbert 5 44
(Venetia Williams) *pressed ldr: led 5f out to 4f out: wknd rapidly 3f out* **14/1**

1220 **11** *19* **Jacobs Son**[50] 4336 3-8-6 **79**.......................... SeanLevey(3) 11 34
(Robert Mills) *mde most to 5f out: wknd rapidly over 3f out: t.o* **20/1**

3m 35.85s (6.85) **Going Correction** +0.575s/f (Yiel)
WFA 3 from 4yo+ 13lb 11 Ran SP% **116.1**
Speed ratings (Par 105): **105,103,101,100,99 99,98,98,93,91 81**
toteswingers: 1&2 £13.80, 1&3 £6.60, 2&3 £10.50 CSF £51.66 CT £329.41 TOTE £7.10: £2.00, £3.10, £2.00; EX 55.10 Trifecta £360.50 Part won. Pool: £487.19 - 0.63 winning units..
Owner M J Vandenberghe **Bred** The Hon Mrs R Pease **Trained** Compton, Berks

FOCUS
The ground conditions certainly played a part in the opening staying contest, especially as the pace looked fair.

5967 NICK BROOKS STKS (NURSERY) 7f
2:30 (2:30) (Class 4) (0-85,79) 2-Y-O **£4,528** (£1,347; £673; £336) **Stalls** Low

Form RPR

0242 **1** **Freddy Q (IRE)**[24] 5196 2-9-3 **78**..................................... SeanLevey(3) 2 83
(Richard Hannon) *trckd ldng pair: rdn to ld over 1f out: hrd pressed ins fnl f: hld on wl* **14/1**

0632 **2** *nk* **Blank Czech (IRE)**[13] 5541 2-9-4 **76**.................................... NeilCallan 7 80
(Amanda Perrett) *swtg: trckd ldr: tried to grab initiative against nr side rail 3f out but ldr got there first: swtchd rt 2f out: drvn to press wnr ins fnl f: nt qckn nr fin* **10/3**[2]

0066 **3** *1½* **Tigers Tale (IRE)**[11] 5634 2-7-13 **60**.........................(v[1]) KieranO'Neill(3) 5 60
(Roger Teal) *t.k.h: hld up in last trio and racd wd: struggling over 2f out: styd on over 1f out: tk 3rd last stride* **7/1**

3026 **4** *nse* **Vociferous (USA)**[26] 5144 2-8-3 **61**.......................... SilvestreDeSousa 1 61
(Mark Johnston) *led: grabbed nr side rail 3f out: hdd over 1f out: fdd ins fnl f* **12/1**

2212 **5** *1* **Tip Top Gorgeous (IRE)**[16] 5438 2-9-7 **79**................. DanielTudhope 6 78
(David O'Meara) *hld up in last pair: effrt 3f out: swtchd rt 2f out: sme prog over 1f out: one pce fnl f* **13/2**

034 **6** *1¼* **Gold Sceptre (FR)**[42] 4580 2-9-1 **73**.................................... PatDobbs 8 68
(Richard Hannon) *trckd ldng trio: cl enough 2f out: nt qckn over 1f out: wknd* **3/1**[1]

2265 **7** *5* **Maccabees**[20] 5324 2-8-12 **70**.. JamesMillman 4 52
(Rod Millman) *hld up in last pair: prog on outer 3f out: chsd ldrs 2f out: sn wknd* **9/2**[3]

003 **8** *1¼* **Dollar Bill**[24] 5196 2-9-3 **75**.. JimmyFortune 3 54
(Andrew Balding) *trckd ldrs in 5th: rdn and lost pl over 2f out: wknd over 1f out* **20/1**

1m 31.73s (4.83) **Going Correction** +0.575s/f (Yiel) 8 Ran SP% **111.2**
Speed ratings (Par 97): **95,94,92,92,91 90,84,83**
toteswingers: 1&2 £5.50, 1&3 £15.10, 2&3 £5.70 CSF £57.10 CT £353.25 TOTE £12.90: £3.20, £1.90, £2.30; EX 58.50 Trifecta £347.00 Part won. Pool: £468.96 - 0.30 winning units..
Owner H R Hunt **Bred** John Martin McLoughney **Trained** East Everleigh, Wilts

FOCUS
A fair-looking contest. A personal best from the winner to beat the frustrating runner-up.

NOTEBOOK
Freddy Q(IRE) had some fair form at this distance and went off at surprisingly long odds considering his connections. Never far away, he found plenty when Sean Levey went for him, and did enough to claim a first success. One mile should be within his range. (op 12-1 tchd 16-1)
Blank Czech(IRE), whose first two runs, both [illegible], came at this course, was having his first try in handicaps and ran a funny race. In prime position turning in, he headed towards the stands' rail but didn't utilise that position and was forced to come round a couple of horses to make a final, but ultimately unsuccessful, challenge. (op 7-2 tchd 3-1)
Tigers Tale(IRE), back down in distance, and with a visor tried for the first time, was keen early but stayed on well to take third right on the line. (op 13-2)
Vociferous(USA) has to be considered disappointing given her really nice pedigree (dam was a Group 2 winner as a juvenile), but she should have been third here with a little more effort in the final strides.
Tip Top Gorgeous(IRE), up 2f in trip, was far from disgraced on her first venture into handicaps last time (1lb higher here despite finishing second) but couldn't get on terms in this after making her challenge wide. (op 5-1)
Gold Sceptre(FR), off since late July, was back up in trip for his handicap debut but ran as though this was needed. (op 10-3 tchd 7-2)

5968 TURFTV BONUS STKS (H'CAP) 1m 1f 192y
3:05 (3:06) (Class 4) (0-85,84) 3-Y-O+ **£4,528** (£1,347; £673; £336) **Stalls** Low

Form RPR

4243 **1** **Ramona Chase**[13] 5546 6-9-5 **80**...............................(t) MarkCoumbe(5) 5 91
(Michael Attwater) *trckd ldrs: rdn over 2f out: wnt 2nd over 1f out: upsides ent fnl f: looked hld last 100yds: rallied to ld last strides* **5/1**[2]

6120 **2** *hd* **Mariners Lodge (USA)**[13] 5568 3-9-3 **80**.............. SilvestreDeSousa 11 91
(Mark Johnston) *trckd ldr: grabbed nr side rail in st: led jst over 2f out: drvn and jnd 1f out: narrow ld last 100yds: hdd fnl strides* **6/1**

1132 **3** *4* **Grumeti**[49] 4355 3-9-7 **84**.. JimmyFortune 4 87
(Michael Bell) *lw: trckd ldrs: effrt over 2f out: hrd rdn and cl enough wl over 1f out: chsd ldng pair fnl f but readily outpcd* **2/1**[1]

4405 **4** *1¾* **Effigy**[12] 5582 7-8-10 **71**.. AmyScott(5) 1 71
(Henry Candy) *dwlt: hld up in last and sn detached: urged along 1/2-way: prog over 2f out: styd on to take 4th ins fnl f* **14/1**

2125 **5** *1* **Choral Festival**[14] 5509 5-9-1 **71**...................................... NeilChalmers 7 69
(John Bridger) *hld up disputing 6th: gng wl enough over 2f out and in tch: sn shkn up and nt qckn: wl hld after* **25/1**

1205 **6** *shd* **Ken's Girl**[20] 5328 7-9-10 **80**.. FergusSweeney 9 77
(Stuart Kittow) *lw: led at gd pce: c to nr side in st but nt against rail: hdd jst over 2f out: wknd over 1f out* **11/2**[3]

2560 **7** *7* **Persian Herald**[17] 5407 3-8-6 **69**.................................. WilliamCarson 8 52
(William Muir) *s.s: hld up in 8th: drvn and tried to make prog against nr side rail 3f out: no hdwy 2f out: wknd* **20/1**

4501 **8** *½* **Loyaliste (FR)**[14] 5509 4-9-1 **71**.. PatDobbs 10 53
(Richard Hannon) *dwlt: hld up disputing 6th: dropped to last and struggling 2f out: sn btn* **9/1**

1003 **9** *20* **African Cheetah**[12] 5608 5-9-7 **77**.......................................(p) NeilCallan 6 19
(Reg Hollinshead) *chsd ldng pair: rdn 3f out: wknd over 2f out: t.o* **11/1**

2m 11.96s (3.96) **Going Correction** +0.575s/f (Yiel)
WFA 3 from 4yo+ 7lb 9 Ran SP% **113.3**
Speed ratings (Par 105): **107,106,103,102,101 101,95,95,79**
toteswingers: 1&2 £5.30, 1&3 £3.20, 2&3 £2.40 CSF £34.28 CT £78.08 TOTE £5.60: £2.00, £2.10, £1.60; EX 41.70 Trifecta £90.50 Pool: £643.68 - 5.26 winning units..
Owner Bagden Wood Building Services Limited **Bred** Ridgecourt Stud **Trained** Epsom, Surrey

FOCUS
Quite a few of the older runners were disappointing or hard to win with, so it looked at the mercy of a 3-y-o.

5969 GOODWOOD.COM BONUS STKS (H'CAP) 1m
3:35 (3:35) (Class 4) (0-85,85) 3-Y-O+ **£4,528** (£1,347; £673; £336) **Stalls** Low

Form RPR

1113 **1** **Starwatch**[15] 5495 4-9-8 **82**... SeanLevey(3) 11 90
(John Bridger) *t.k.h: sn trckd ldr: rdn over 2f out: led over 1f out: drvn and kpt on wl fnl f* **9/1**

520 **2** *½* **Tilsworth Glenboy**[27] 5101 4-8-11 **68**...................... SilvestreDeSousa 5 75
(J R Jenkins) *hld up in last pair: stdy prog on outer 2f out: drvn over 1f out: styd on to take 2nd ins fnl f: a hld* **10/1**

0050 **3** *¾* **Mahadee (IRE)**[34] 4860 6-9-9 **83**...............................(p) HarryBentley(3) 8 88
(Ed de Giles) *trckd ldng pair: rdn 2f out: nt qckn over 1f out: kpt on again last 100yds* **33/1**

0420 **4** *nk* **Satwa Laird**[18] 5383 5-9-4 **75**... GeorgeBaker 3 80
(Ed Dunlop) *trckd ldng trio: effrt towards outer 2f out: drvn and tried to chal jst over 1f out: one pce fnl f* **8/1**[3]

215 **5** *nk* **Paramour**[15] 5483 4-10-0 **85**.. DanielTudhope 7 89
(David O'Meara) *led: c to nr side rail in st: rdn and hdd over 1f out: one pce and lost pls fnl f* **11/8**[1]

0041 **6** *2* **Sweet Child O'Mine**[15] 5488 4-9-8 **82**.................. MartinHarley(3) 4 81
(Richard Guest) *trckd ldrs in 5th: cl up against nr side rail over 2f out: nt qckn nr fin: no prog after* **3/1**[2]

0600 **7** *1½* **South Cape**[20] 5328 8-9-0 **71**... TadhgO'Shea 2 67
(Gary Moore) *t.k.h: hld up in last pair: rdn and no prog jst over 2f out: wl btn after* **11/1**

000 **8** *¾* **Vitznau (IRE)**[8] 5718 7-9-5 **76**.. JamesMillman 6 70
(Robert Cowell) *lw: hld up in 6th and racd wd: c to nr side rail 3f out but sn no prog: n.d after* **25/1**

1m 44.77s (4.87) **Going Correction** +0.575s/f (Yiel) 8 Ran SP% **112.4**
Speed ratings (Par 105): **98,97,96,96,96 94,92,91**
toteswingers: 1&2 £5.80, 1&3 £19.30, 2&3 £18.40 CSF £90.06 CT £2805.36 TOTE £7.00: £2.20, £2.40, £6.80; EX 55.30 Trifecta £212.70 Pool: £629.64 - 2.19 winning units..
Owner J J Bridger **Bred** Mrs J A Chapman **Trained** Liphook, Hants

FOCUS
Plenty of these looked easy to oppose, so this is probably only modest form, especially as the fancied horses disappointed.

5970 TURFTV FOR BETTING SHOPS BONUS STKS (H'CAP) 7f
4:10 (4:10) (Class 4) (0-85,82) 3-Y-O+ **£4,528** (£1,347; £673; £336) **Stalls** Low

Form RPR

2100 **1** **Tariq Too**[44] 4509 4-9-8 **79**... AdamBeschizza(3) 5 92+
(David Simcock) *s.s: hld up in last: gd prog over 2f out gng strly: led over 1f out: shkn up and sn in command* **13/2**

1242 **2** *2¼* **Valencha**[8] 5702 4-10-0 **82**... JimmyFortune 9 89+
(Hughie Morrison) *lw: trckd ldrs: prog to go 2nd over 2f out: effrt to chal over 1f out: chsd wnr after but no imp* **15/8**[1]

0035 **3** *1* **Sunshine Always (IRE)**[3] 5858 5-8-8 **67**.................. MarkCoumbe(5) 2 71
(Michael Attwater) *hld up in last trio: rdn over 2f out: prog and swtchd sharply rt over 1f out: kpt on to take 3rd fnl f* **12/1**

2006 **4** *shd* **Mubtadi**[43] 4550 3-9-7 **82**...............................(t) KieranO'Neill(3) 6 84
(David Simcock) *hld up in last pair: effrt over 2f out: hanging rt over 1f out: kpt on to press for 3rd nr fin* **7/2**[2]

0100 **5** [illegible] **April Fool**[32] 4010 7-10-0 **82**...............................(b) DavidProbert 4 82
(Ronald Harris) *lw: led at gd pce: c towards nr side in st: hdd over 1f out: fdd fnl f* **16/1**

0055 **6** *2½* **Alhaban (IRE)**[5] 5811 5-9-8 **76**..(p) LukeMorris 3 69
(Ronald Harris) *in tch: hrd rdn and nt qckn 2f out: wl hld whn carried rt over 1f out* **25/1**

0544 **7** *½* **Galatian**[16] 5451 4-9-12 **80**...(b) JamesMillman 1 72+
(Rod Millman) *chsd ldrs: racd awkwardly fr 1/2-way: struggling down centre of crse over 2f out: sn btn: sddle slipped* **5/1**[3]

4205 **8** *6* **Clumber Place**[13] 5551 5-9-0 **71**............................ RobertLButler(3) 8 47
(Richard Guest) *chsd ldr: hanging rt and wknd over 2f out* **20/1**

2256 **9** *1¾* **Arctic Mirage**[16] 5423 3-8-9 **67**.. LiamKeniry 7 37
(Michael Blanshard) *chsd ldng pair tl wknd qckly over 2f out* **22/1**

1m 31.14s (4.24) **Going Correction** +0.575s/f (Yiel)
WFA 3 from 4yo+ 4lb 9 Ran SP% **113.5**
Speed ratings (Par 105): **98,95,94,94,92 89,88,81,79**
toteswingers: 1&2 £3.30, 1&3 £10.70, 2&3 £2.70 CSF £18.23 CT £143.41 TOTE £9.10: £2.20, £1.40, £2.90; EX 23.00 Trifecta £336.50 Part won. Pool: £454.85 - 0.73 winning units..
Owner Saleh Al Homaizi & Imad Al Sagar **Bred** D R Botterill **Trained** Newmarket, Suffolk

FOCUS
The runners stayed towards the centre of the course in the home straight, having headed straight to the stands' rail earlier in the day.

5971 GOODWOOD RACEHORSE OWNERS' GROUP STKS (H'CAP) 1m 4f
4:40 (4:40) (Class 4) (0-85,85) 3-Y-O+ **£4,528** (£1,347; £673; £336) **Stalls** High

Form RPR

010 **1** **Tameen**[15] 5483 3-8-11 **77**.. TadhgO'Shea 1 93
(John Dunlop) *lw: hld up in 4th: clsd over 3f out: led wl over 2f out: sn rdn clr: in n.d over 1f out* **7/2**[1]

120 **2** *8* **Achalas (IRE)**[26] 5149 3-8-8 **74**.. CathyGannon 6 77
(Heather Main) *hld up in 5th: rdn over 3f out: outpcd over 2f out: styd on fr over 1f out to take 2nd last strides* **14/1**

6210 **3** *nk* **Romeo Montague**[22] 5283 3-9-0 **80**...............................(v) ChrisCatlin 7 83
(Ed Dunlop) *t.k.h: hld up in last trio: pushed along and prog 3f out: chsd clr wnr over 1f out: no imp: fdd and lost 2nd last strides* **6/1**

0012 **4** *1* **Spice Fair**[30] 4998 4-9-8 **79**... GeorgeBaker 4 80
(Mark Usher) *lw: t.k.h: hld up in last trio: shkn up 3f out: outpcd over 2f out: styd on fnl f* **5/1**[3]

4631 **5** *1 ½* **Significant Move**[13] 5568 4-9-11 **82**............................ FergusSweeney 8 81
(Stuart Kittow) *taken down early: trckd clr ldng trio: cl up over 3f out: sn outpcd: fdd* **7/2**[1]

0300 **6** *¾* **Pivotman**[22] 5283 3-9-5 **85**............................ NeilCallan 10 82
(Amanda Perrett) *trckd ldr and clr of rest: styd alone far side over 3f out: on terms to over 2f out: wknd qckly over 1f out: fin tired* **9/2**[2]

1133 **7** *5* **Megalala (IRE)**[13] 5545 10-9-5 **76**............................ NeilChalmers 9 65
(John Bridger) *led and sn spreadeagled field: tk main body towards nr side in st: hdd & wknd wl over 2f out* **16/1**

606- **8** *2 ¾* **Numide (FR)**[183] 7252 8-9-4 **75**............................ JamesMillman 11 60
(Rod Millman) *s.s: a last: rdn and no prog 3f out* **12/1**

2m 44.68s (6.28) **Going Correction** +0.575s/f (Yiel)
WFA 3 from 4yo+ 9lb **8** Ran SP% **113.8**
Speed ratings (Par 105): **102,96,96,95,94 94,90,89**
toteswingers: 1&2 £9.80, 1&3 £5.50, 2&3 £6.20 CSF £52.48 CT £283.45 TOTE £5.80: £2.30, £3.20, £1.50; EX 52.10 Trifecta £133.60 Pool: £646.36 - 3.58 winning units..
Owner Hamdan Al Maktoum **Bred** Shadwell Estate Company Limited **Trained** Arundel, W Sussex

FOCUS
There was a difference of opinion as the field swept round the bend.

5972 GOODWOOD REVIVAL 16-18TH SEPTEMBER BONUS STKS (H'CAP) 6f

5:15 (5:15) (Class 4) (0-85,85) 3-Y-0+
£4,357 (£1,304; £652; £326; £163; £81) **Stalls** High

Form RPR

0000 **1** **Tagula Night (IRE)**[14] 5508 5-9-4 **82**............................[1] SeanLevey(3) 5 91
(Walter Swinburn) *lw: pressed ldr: led 1/2-way: rdn 2f out: edgd lft over 1f out: styd on wl* **11/1**

0113 **2** *¾* **Night Trade (IRE)**[12] 5587 4-9-4 **79**............................ DavidProbert 7 86
(Ronald Harris) *trckd ldrs: rdn to chal 2f out: sn nt qckn: styd on again to take 2nd fnl f: a hld* **14/1**

4511 **3** *hd* **Oneladyowner**[14] 5508 3-9-8 **85**............................ SebSanders 8 91+
(David Brown) *lw: s.i.s: hld up towards rr: nt clr run briefly over 2f out: prog over 1f out: styd on to take 3rd nr fin* **7/2**[1]

3611 **4** *nk* **Barons Spy (IRE)**[19] 5339 10-9-8 **83**............................ SilvestreDeSousa 11 88
(Richard Price) *in tch in midfield: rdn over 2f out: prog u.p over 1f out: wnt 3rd ins fnl f: hld whn n.m.r nr fin* **12/1**

0112 **5** *¾* **Time Medicean**[16] 5451 5-8-10 **78**............................ RaulDaSilva(7) 2 81+
(Tony Carroll) *t.k.h: hld up last and sn detached: shuffled along 2f out: gd prog fnl f: nvr nrr* **9/2**[2]

0140 **6** *1* **Alfresco**[37] 4742 7-8-13 **74**............................(b) JimmyFortune 3 73
(John Best) *dwlt: t.k.h: hld up in last pair: shkn up 2f out: styd on fnl f: nrst fin* **16/1**

0560 **7** *hd* **Loki's Revenge**[16] 5451 3-9-1 **81**............................ HarryBentley(3) 15 80
(William Jarvis) *lw: s.i.s: hld up towards rr: prog nr side over 2f out: drvn to chal over 1f out: wknd ins fnl f* **15/2**

0606 **8** *¾* **Avonmore Star**[36] 4779 3-9-8 **85**............................ PatDobbs 9 81
(Richard Hannon) *hld up in midfield: effrt 2f out: chsd ldrs on outer over 1f out: fdd ins fnl f* **16/1**

4023 **9** *½* **Admirable Spirit**[15] 5476 3-9-1 **81**............................ KieranO'Neill(3) 6 76
(Richard Hannon) *lw: hld up in rr: prog on outer 2f out: tried to cl on ldrs 1f out: sn fdd* **6/1**[3]

0220 **10** *hd* **Cornus**[9] 5682 9-9-0 **78**............................(be) MartinHarley(3) 14 72
(Alan McCabe) *taken down early and free to post: prom: losing pl whn hmpd over 1f out: no ch after* **25/1**

015 **11** *1 ¾* **Italian Tom (IRE)**[16] 5425 4-9-4 **79**............................ LukeMorris 1 68
(Ronald Harris) *pressed ldrs: rdn to chal 2f out: wknd over 1f out* **12/1**

40-0 **12** *nse* **Mirabile Visu**[3] 5859 3-8-3 **66** oh4............................(b[1]) CathyGannon 12 54
(Heather Main) *chsd ldrs to 2f out: sn lost pl and btn* **66/1**

116 **13** *1* **Redvers (IRE)**[44] 4498 3-9-8 **85**............................ GeorgeBaker 10 70
(Ralph Beckett) *n.m.r after 1f: towards rr after: n.m.r again over 1f out: sn btn* **16/1**

1060 **14** *10* **Dolly Parton (IRE)**[88] 3049 3-8-4 **67** oh1 ow1............................ ChrisCatlin 13 20
(John Bridger) *led to 1/2-way: wkng rapidly whn short of room over 2f out: t.o* **50/1**

1m 15.03s (2.83) **Going Correction** +0.575s/f (Yiel)
WFA 3 from 4yo+ 2lb **14** Ran SP% **121.8**
Speed ratings (Par 105): **104,103,102,102,101 100,99,98,98,97 95,95,94,80**
toteswingers: 1&2 £27.60, 1&3 £11.20, 2&3 £11.80 CSF £156.38 CT £659.79 TOTE £14.50: £4.50, £3.90, £1.50; EX 163.40 TRIFECTA Not won..
Owner Hufford, Moss & Papworth **Bred** Carpet Lady Partnership **Trained** Aldbury, Herts
■ Stewards' Enquiry : Sean Levey three-day ban: careless riding (Sep 27-29)

FOCUS
A really competitive handicap to conclude the two-day meeting with.
T/Jkpt: Not won. T/Plt: £235.40 to a £1 stake. Pool: £89,831.39. 278.54 winning tickets. T/Qpdt: £37.20 to a £1 stake. Pool: £7,645.63. 151.85 winning tickets. JN

5973a & 5975a - (Foreign Racing) - See Raceform Interactive

[5949] CURRAGH (R-H)

Sunday, September 11

OFFICIAL GOING: Straight course - soft; round course - yielding

5974a FLAME OF TARA EUROPEAN BREEDERS FUND STKS (LISTED RACE) (FILLIES) 1m

2:40 (2:42) 2-Y-0
£33,620 (£9,827; £4,655; £1,551)

RPR

1 **Coral Wave (IRE)**[22] 5292 2-8-12............................ DPMcDonogh 5 104+
(P J Prendergast, Ire) *sn led: rdn and kpt on strly fr over 1f out: comf* **9/2**[2]

2 *3 ½* **Lady Wingshot (IRE)**[31] 4975 2-8-12............................ KJManning 6 97
(J S Bolger, Ire) *chsd ldrs in 4th: rdn in 3rd 2f out: styd on into 2nd 1f out: no imp on wnr fnl f: kpt on same pce* **5/1**[3]

3 *2* **Rubina (IRE)**[14] 5525 2-8-12 105............................(t) JMurtagh 2 92
(John M Oxx, Ire) *sn chsd ldr in 2nd: rdn 2f out: no imp on ldr over 1f out: 3rd 1f out: kpt on same pce fnl f* **6/5**[1]

4 *½* **Devotion (IRE)**[73] 3561 2-8-12 86............................ SeamieHeffernan 7 91
(A P O'Brien, Ire) *settled 5th: rdn 2f out: 4th over 1f out: no imp: kpt on same pce* **11/2**

5 *2 ½* **Soon (IRE)**[14] 5525 2-8-12 96............................ CO'Donoghue 1 86
(A P O'Brien, Ire) *chsd ldrs in 3rd: rdn in 4th 2f out: sn no ex and kpt on one pce* **8/1**

6 *3 ¼* **Lady Rochford (IRE)**[22] 5290 2-8-12 86............................ KLatham 3 78
(G M Lyons, Ire) *a towards rr: rdn and no imp 2f out* **14/1**

1m 43.3s (-2.70) **Going Correction** -0.175s/f (Firm) **6** Ran SP% **113.5**
Speed ratings: **106,102,100,100,97 94**
CSF £26.98 TOTE £5.60: £2.10, £1.90; DF 29.10.
Owner Richard Barnes **Bred** Grangecon Stud **Trained** Melitta Lodge, Co Kildare

FOCUS
The winner dictated and pulled away to win well in a race in which the order changed little.

NOTEBOOK
Coral Wave(IRE), ruled out of the Moyglare due to unsuitable ground, appreciated the ease in the going here, making all the running and stretching clear from over a furlong down. (op 4/1 tchd 7/2)
Lady Wingshot(IRE) coped well enough with the step up in class despite proving no match for the winner. She was a clear second-best. (op 5/1 tchd 11/2)
Rubina(IRE) was sent off a warm favourite on the strength of two fourth placings in Pattern company, both behind Maybe, in the Debutante Stakes and in the Moyglare. She did not run up to her best on the ground. (op 11/10 tchd 5/4)
Devotion(IRE) won a maiden at Leopardstown in June but was unable to raise her effort on soft here. (op 6/1 tchd 7/1)
Soon(IRE) is now the more exposed, this being her fourth run since she won a maiden at Galway towards the end of July. (op 9/1)

5976a WWW.THETOTE.COM BLANDFORD STKS (GROUP 2) (F&M) 1m 2f

3:45 (3:46) 3-Y-0+
£53,232 (£15,560; £7,370; £2,456)

RPR

1 **Manieree (IRE)**[56] 4132 3-8-12 105............................(b) NGMcCullagh 4 112
(John M Oxx, Ire) *mde all: kicked clr 3f out: rdn under 2f out: kpt on strly fr over 1f out* **9/1**

2 *3 ¼* **Sapphire (IRE)**[32] 4936 3-8-12 103............................(b) PJSmullen 3 105+
(D K Weld, Ire) *chsd ldrs: 5th 1/2-way: hdwy into 3rd 3f out: rdn in 2nd 2f out: no imp on wnr: kpt on same pce fr over 1f out* **12/1**

3 *4* **Look At Me (IRE)**[8] 5744 3-8-12 105............................ SeamieHeffernan 6 97+
(A P O'Brien, Ire) *mid-div: hdwy into 5th 3f out: rdn into 3rd 2f out: no imp and kpt on same pce fr over 1f out* **11/2**[2]

4 *4 ½* **Flowers Of Spring (IRE)**[44] 4520 4-9-5 97............................(p) CDHayes 7 88+
(Andrew Oliver, Ire) *mid-div: rdn into 5th 2f out: no imp in 4th 1f out: kpt on same pce* **14/1**

5 *2 ¾* **Eleanora Duse (IRE)**[50] 4345 4-9-5............................ DPMcDonogh 11 83+
(Sir Michael Stoute) *chsd ldrs: 3rd 1/2-way: rdn in 4th 3f out: no ex in 6th 2f out: kpt on one pce* **7/1**

6 *1 ¼* **Chrysanthemum (IRE)**[78] 3417 3-8-12 104............................ WMLordan 12 80+
(David Wachman, Ire) *chsd ldrs: 4th 1/2-way: rdn in 6th 3f out: u.p in 8th 2f out: kpt on one pce fr over 1f out* **13/2**[3]

7 *1* **Bible Belt (IRE)**[14] 5523 3-8-12 111............................ FMBerry 9 78+
(Mrs John Harrington, Ire) *chsd ldrs: 6th 1/2-way: rdn 3f out: no ex in 7th 2f out: kpt on one pce* **11/8**[1]

8 *3 ¼* **Kirinda (IRE)**[32] 4936 3-8-12 102............................ JMurtagh 8 72
(John M Oxx, Ire) *chsd ldr in 2nd: rdn 3f out: no ex in 4th 2f out: wknd over 1f out* **10/1**

9 *2 ¼* **Obama Rule (IRE)**[14] 5523 4-9-5 101............................ JPO'Brien 5 67
(Ms Joanna Morgan, Ire) *mid-div: rdn in 9th 3f out: no ex and kpt on one pce* **33/1**

10 *4 ¾* **Siren's Song (IRE)**[42] 4589 3-8-12 99............................(b[1]) ShaneFoley 2 58
(Mrs John Harrington, Ire) *a towards rr* **25/1**

11 *17* **Mid Mon Lady (IRE)**[47] 4418 6-9-5 100............................(b) CO'Donoghue 10 24
(H Rogers, Ire) *a towards rr: wknd over 2f out* **40/1**

2m 12.0s (-2.30) **Going Correction** +0.075s/f (Good)
WFA 3 from 4yo+ 7lb **11** Ran SP% **126.0**
Speed ratings: **112,109,106,102,100 99,98,96,94,90 76**
CSF £117.50 TOTE £12.50: £3.20, £3.00, £2.60; DF 140.40.
Owner Maxwell Morris **Bred** Max Morris **Trained** Currabeg, Co Kildare

FOCUS
The winner was 3l clear from the outset and had stretched her lead to 5l turning in. Few got involved and the runner-up is the best guide to the level.

NOTEBOOK
Manieree(IRE) put up a smart performance to continue a tremendous run of form for John Oxx, who had two Pattern winners at Doncaster and a double at his home track on Saturday. Ridden in the same way when winning a Group 3 event over a furlong shorter at this venue in July, the winner won with considerable authority. (op 10/1 tchd 8/1)
Sapphire(IRE) maintained the progression that she had shown when third in a Listed event at Gowran last month.
Look At Me(IRE) finished in isolation in third, well adrift of the first two and with a slightly longer gap to the fourth. She is being kept busy (this was her fifth run in just over a month) and seems to take her racing well. (op 6/1 tchd 5/1)
Flowers Of Spring(IRE), who has been a progressive handicapper since the end of last season, justified the decision to let her take her chance at this level by making the frame. (op 16/1)
Eleanora Duse(IRE), the winner of this last year, has not managed to reach the same heights this season and could make no impression here. (op 6/1 tchd 15/2)
Chrysanthemum(IRE) was well beaten on her first run since finishing third in the Pretty Polly in June. A promising juvenile last season, she has been lightly campaigned this year, though at a high level. (op 8/1)
Bible Belt(IRE) was unable to sustain the progression that had yielded successive wins in a handicap, a Listed race and a Group 3 event. Though last season's Roscommon maiden win had suggested that the conditions would not be a problem, it seems fair to assume that the going proved her undoing. Official explanation: jockey said filly never travelled on today's ground (op 6/4)

5977a WOODIES DIY SUPPORTING IRISH AUTISM SOLONAWAY STKS (GROUP 3) 1m

4:15 (4:15) 3-Y-0+
£32,219 (£9,418; £4,461; £1,487)

RPR

1 **Cityscape**[27] 5129 5-9-6............................ SteveDrowne 8 121+
(Roger Charlton) *trckd ldr in 2nd: rdn to chal 1 1/2f out: sn led: kpt on strly fnl f: eased cl home* **2/5**[1]

2 *2 ½* **Wild Wind (GER)**[8] 5745 3-8-12 108............................ CO'Donoghue 3 110+
(A P O'Brien, Ire) *chsd ldrs in 3rd: rdn 1 1/2f out: styd on into 2nd fnl f: no imp on wnr* **5/1**[2]

3 *2 ½* **Across The Rhine (USA)**[22] 5282 5-9-9 109............................ PShanahan 4 111
(Tracey Collins, Ire) *led: rdn and chal 1 1/2f out: sn hdd: no ex and kpt on same pce* **16/1**

4 *2 ¾* **One Spirit (IRE)**[14] 5523 3-8-12 98............................ NGMcCullagh 7 98
(F Dunne, Ire) *chsd ldrs in 4th: rdn over 2f out: no ex 1 1/2f out: kpt on same pce* **33/1**

5 *3 ½* **Emiyna (USA)**[8] 5745 3-9-1 109............................ JMurtagh 6 93
(John M Oxx, Ire) *hld up in last: 5th 3f out: rdn and no imp over 2f out: kpt on one pce* **7/1**[3]

6 *1 1/2* **Taameer**^{22} [5291] 5-9-6 102 .... PJSmullen 5 90
(D K Weld, Ire) *hld up in 5th: last 3f out: rdn and no imp under 2f out* **16/1**

1m 43.7s (-2.30) **Going Correction** -0.175s/f (Firm)
WFA 3 from 5yo+ 5lb **6** Ran SP% **115.3**
Speed ratings: **104,101,99,96,92 91**
CSF £3.09 TOTE £1.30: £1.02, £2.90; DF 3.40.
Owner K Abdulla **Bred** Juddmonte Farms Ltd **Trained** Beckhampton, Wilts

FOCUS
The winner did not need to be at his best to score, and the second and third help set the level.

NOTEBOOK
Cityscape, whose form this season has featured a fine third behind Canford Cliffs and Goldikova in the Queen Anne Stakes, duly won with plenty to spare, his first success since landing a Group 3 at Newmarket last October. He has several options in the future that include the Daniel Wildenstein Group 2 at Arc weekend at Longschamp or the Premio Vittorio Capua, a Group 1 at Milan on September 24. (op 4/9)
Wild Wind(GER) was having her 12th outing of the season and fifth inside a month. Though she won a Listed race at Kilarney last month, and has run some good races in defeat, she looks a fully exposed type at this stage. (op 8/1)
Across The Rhine(USA) was a front-running Group 3 winner over 7f at the venue last month and similar tactics were tried here. He could not raise his effort in the last furlong after being headed. (op 14/1)
One Spirit(IRE) looked up against it at this level, but below-par displays by the higher-rated pair Emiyna and Tameer enabled her to complete the frame. (op 25/1)
Emiyna(USA) wants quicker ground. (op 6/1)

5979a WWW.THETOTE.COM RENAISSANCE STKS (GROUP 3) 6f
5:20 (5:22) 3-Y-O+ **£32,219** (£9,418; £4,461; £1,487)

RPR

1 **Bewitched (IRE)**^{8} [5707] 4-9-3 111 ....(t) JMurtagh 10 112+
(Charles O'Brien, Ire) *hld up in last: hdwy in 6th and swtchd over 1f out: rdn to ld last 150yds: kpt on wl* **13/8**^{1}

2 *3/4* **Definightly**^{14} [5532] 5-9-3 ....(b) SteveDrowne 2 108
(Roger Charlton) *led: chal 2f out: rdn over 1f out: hdd last 150yds: no ex and kpt on same pce* **5/2**^{2}

3 *1/2* **Croisultan (IRE)**^{31} [4978] 5-9-3 100 .... NGMcCullagh 6 106
(Liam McAteer, Ire) *chsd ldrs: 4th 1/2-way: rdn 2f out: u.p in 5th 1f out: kpt on same pce fnl f* **16/1**

4 *1/2* **Empowering (IRE)**^{14} [5524] 3-9-1 103 .... JPO'Brien 1 104
(A P O'Brien, Ire) *chsd ldrs: 3rd 1/2-way: impr to chal 2f out: rdn over 1f out: no ex ins fnl f: kpt on same pce* **12/1**

5 *hd* **Dawn Eclipse (IRE)**^{24} [5228] 6-9-0 102 .... CO'Donoghue 9 101
(T G McCourt, Ire) *mid-div: 7th 1/2-way: rdn into 4th 1f out: no ex ins fnl f: kpt on same pce* **33/1**

6 *1 3/4* **Arctic (IRE)**^{35} [4836] 4-9-3 105 .... PJSmullen 3 98
(Tracey Collins, Ire) *chsd ldr in 2nd: rdn in 3rd 2f out: no ex ins fnl f* **8/1**

7 *3 1/4* **Rock Jock (IRE)**^{14} [5532] 4-9-3 104 .... PShanahan 7 88
(Tracey Collins, Ire) *hld up towards rr early: 5th 1/2-way: rdn in 7th 2f out: no ex over 1f out* **16/1**

8 *1 1/4* **Knock Stars (IRE)**^{28} [5086] 3-8-12 94 .... CDHayes 4 81
(Patrick Martin, Ire) *hld up towards rr: rdn into 6th 2f out: no ex over 1f out* **33/1**

9 *1 1/2* **Rose Bonheur**^{24} [5228] 3-8-12 107 .... DPMcDonogh 5 76
(Kevin Prendergast, Ire) *chsd ldrs: pushed along in 6th 1/2-way: rdn in 5th 2f out: wknd over 1f out* **5/1**^{3}

1m 13.7s (-1.30) **Going Correction** +0.075s/f (Good)
WFA 3 from 4yo+ 2lb **9** Ran SP% **119.8**
Speed ratings: **111,110,109,108,108 106,101,100,98**
Daily Double: Not won. CSF £6.00 TOTE £2.30: £1.10, £1.10, £4.20; DF 7.00.
Owner Mrs John Magnier **Bred** Monsieur J C Coude **Trained** Straffan, Co Kildare

FOCUS
The winner quickened up well to score cosily, and the race has been rated around the third, fourth and fifth.

NOTEBOOK
Bewitched(IRE) won the same event a year ago. She got no sort of run in a Group 1 at Haydock eight days previously on her first start back following the Golden Jubillee at Royal Ascot from which she returned lame, but she was well up to the task here. Held up in rear as she has often been in the past, the winner began to make headway when switched right over 1f out and she picked up well to get on top well inside the final furlong. She has won on most types of ground and, while connections are keen to give her another shot at a Group 1, they are running very short of options. (op 7/4)
Definightly, a winner at this level in France last year and runner-up to Marchand D'Or in another Group 3 at Deauville last month, is suited by plenty of cut and he made the running here, shaking off his rivals until the winner took his measure well inside the final furlong. (op 5/2 tchd 9/4)
Croisultan(IRE), another with a preference for this sort of ground, ran his best race for some time. He tracked the leaders and, after looking well held in fifth entering the final furlong, kept on quite well in the closing stages.
Empowering(IRE), a winner over 7f at this level early in the season, was going back up in trip following a run over 5f here last month. She raced close up and had every chance from 2f out before failing to raise any extra for pressure over the final furlong. (op 10/1)
Dawn Eclipse(IRE), dropping down in trip having run fourth behind Alanza over an extended 7f at Tipperary last month, made headway on the outside well over 1f out and kept on without finding enough to pose a serious threat.
Arctic(IRE) had conditions to his liking but, after racing prominently, he had no more to offer from 1f out. (op 8/1 tchd 7/1)
Rose Bonheur has shown her best form on quicker ground and, having raced close up for much of the journey, her effort petered out inside the last 2f. (op 6/1)
T/Jkpt: @3,750.00. Pool of @5,000.00 - 1 winning unit. T/Plt: @4,508.70. Pool of @28,466.90 - 5 winning units. II

5978a (Foreign Racing) - See Raceform Interactive

5308 HANOVER (L-H)
Sunday, September 11
OFFICIAL GOING: Turf: good

5980a GROSSER PREIS DER METALLBAU BURCKHARDT GMBH (LISTED RACE) (3YO+ FILLIES & MARES) (TURF) 1m
4:05 (12:00) 3-Y-O+ **£10,344** (£3,793; £2,068; £1,034)

RPR

1 **Glady Romana (GER)**^{7} 4-9-0 0 .... GaetanMasure 5 103+
(W Baltromei, Germany) **73/10**

2 *1* **Mosqueras Romance**^{162} [1104] 5-9-0 0 .... AndreBest 4 101
(Marco Botti) *broke fast: racd keenly bhd ldr then settled in 4th: proged to 3rd in bk st: qcknd wl early in st: grabbed ld under 2f out: sn chal by wnr: battled hrd tl wl ins fnl f: hdd 50yds out* **33/10**^{2}

3 *5* **Wolkenburg (GER)**^{21} 3-8-13 0 .... FilipMinarik 3 92
(P Schiergen, Germany) **13/10**^{1}

4 *hd* **Shining Glory (GER)**^{21} 4-9-3 0 .... EFrank 7 92
(W Hickst, Germany) **17/2**

5 *2 1/2* **Julie's Love**^{71} [3651] 3-8-13 0 .... KClijmans 11 86
(Manfred Hofer, Germany) **5/1**^{3}

6 *1 1/2* **C'Est L'Amour (GER)**^{42} 4-9-0 0 ....(b) VSchulepov 6 80
(Frau E Mader, Germany) **209/10**

7 *3* **Waldjagd**^{21} 4-9-0 0 .... JBojko 1 73
(A Wohler, Germany) **126/10**

8 *4* **Adorna (GER)**^{21} 4-9-3 0 .... WPanov 9 67
(C Sprengel, Germany) **147/10**

9 *4 1/2* **Kaya Belle (GER)**^{21} 4-9-0 0 .... PJWerning 2 53
(Stanislav Otruba, Germany) **166/10**

10 *27* **Seduisant (GER)**^{37} 3-8-9 0 .... MrDennisSchiergen 8 —
(Frau M Weber, Germany) **217/10**

1m 40.24s (100.24)
WFA 3 from 4yo+ 5lb **10** Ran SP% **134.4**
WIN (incl. 10 euro stake): 83. PLACES: 22, 15, 15. SF: 578.
Owner Stall Oberlausitz **Bred** Gestut Auenquelle **Trained** Germany

NOTEBOOK
Mosqueras Romance had been off since April. Always well placed, she looked the likely winner when taking the lead one and a half furlongs out but was run out of it in the final stages. She has now been runner-up five times in Listed races without winning one.

2601 TABY (R-H)
Sunday, September 11
OFFICIAL GOING: Dirt: sloppy; turf: good

5981a TATTERSALLS NICKES MINNESLOPNING (LISTED RACE) (3YO+) (DIRT) 1m (D)
2:00 (12:00) 3-Y-O+ **£28,735** (£14,367; £6,896; £4,597; £2,873)

RPR

1 **Energia Colonial (BRZ)**^{199} [680] 4-9-4 0 .... RomarMeloDeBarros 11 104
(Fabricio Borges, Sweden) **178/10**

2 *2 1/2* **Oroveso (BRZ)**^{182} 5-9-4 0 .... ValmirDeAzeredo 3 99
(Fabricio Borges, Sweden) **241/10**

3 *1/2* **Peas And Carrots (DEN)**^{35} [4842] 8-9-4 0 .... FJohansson 1 98
(Lennart Reuterskiold Jr, Sweden) **39/10**^{3}

4 *1* **La Zona (IRE)**^{14} 5-9-1 0 .... Jan-ErikNeuroth 5 93
(Wido Neuroth, Norway) **16/5**^{2}

5 *1 1/2* **Luca Brasi (FR)**^{121} 7-9-4 0 .... ElioneChaves 7 93
(Francisco Castro, Sweden) **6/5**^{1}

6 *4* **Maybach**^{336} [6792] 10-9-4 0 .... YvonneDurant 4 85
(Lars Bexell, Sweden) **153/10**

7 *1/2* **Amazing Tiger (GER)**^{62} 5-9-4 0 .... ShaneKarlsson 9 84
(Peter Jardby, Sweden) **35/1**

8 *1 1/2* **Frontier Star (USA)**^{315} 4-9-4 0 ....(b) NikolajStott 6 81
(Fredrik Reuterskiold, Sweden) **69/1**

9 *nk* **Buen Rumbero (USA)**^{488} [2019] 5-9-4 0 .... Per-AndersGraberg 2 80
(Niels Petersen, Norway) **105/10**

10 *5* **Layline (IRE)**^{8} [5712] 4-9-4 0 .... RobertWinston 8 70
[illegible] *out: nt qckn: sltly hmpd whn struggling to hold pl 1 1/2f out: eased ins fnl f* **39/1**

11 *2* **Perks (IRE)**^{66} 6-9-4 0 .... EspenSki 10 66
(Jessica Long, Sweden) **175/10**

1m 37.7s (97.70) **11** Ran SP% **125.9**
PARI-MUTUEL (all including 1sek stake): WIN 18.76; PLACE 3.22, 5.58, 1.95; DF 484.62.
Owner Energi Dupla Racing AB **Bred** Haras Estrela Energia **Trained** Sweden

NOTEBOOK
Layline(IRE) could never get into the action.

5982a COOLMORE MATCHMAKER STKS (LISTED RACE) (3YO+ FILLIES & MARES) (TURF) 1m 1f 165y
2:25 (12:00) 3-Y-O+ **£19,157** (£9,578; £4,597; £3,065; £1,915)

RPR

1 **Grafitti**^{14} 6-9-6 0 .... Per-AndersGraberg 4 96
(Niels Petersen, Norway) **89/20**^{2}

2 *nk* **Entangle**^{14} 5-9-6 0 .... JacobJohansen 2 96
(Arnfinn Lund, Norway) **30/100**^{1}

3 *7* **Bea Remembered**^{32} [4915] 4-9-6 0 .... RobertWinston 3 81
(Brian Meehan) *racd freely in 2nd off stdy gallop: pushed along as ldr qcknd clr 3 1/2f out: chal ldr and led over 2f out: sn hdd: no ex as first two wnt clr fnl f* **101/10**^{3}

4 *4* **Mariyca (IRE)**^{14} 5-9-6 0 .... DinaDanekilde 1 73
(Ole Larsen, Sweden) **161/10**

5 *3* **Madam Markievicz (IRE)**^{38} 3-9-0 0 ....(b) YvonneDurant 7 68
(Yvonne Durant, Sweden) **237/10**

6 *2 1/2* **Geordie Iris (IRE)**^{14} 3-9-0 0 .... Jan-ErikNeuroth 8 63
(Wido Neuroth, Norway) **136/10**

7 *1 1/2* **Balsha (USA)**^{28} [5096] 4-9-6 0 .... RafaelSchistl 6 59
(Roy Arne Kvisla, Sweden) **51/1**

8 *3* **Catch Me A Dream (IRE)**^{38} 3-9-0 0 .... ElioneChaves 5 54
(Barry McGann, Sweden) **179/10**

2m 0.50s (1.20)
WFA 3 from 4yo+ 7lb **8** Ran SP% **128.2**
PARI-MUTUEL (all including 1sek stake): WIN 5.44; PLACE 1.02, 1.00, 1.07; DF 16.53.
Owner E Nagell-Erichsen Family **Bred** Newsells Park Stud Limited **Trained** Norway

NOTEBOOK
Bea Remembered was unable to go with the first two once push came to shove in the final 300 yards.

5983a BRITTFURN AMACITALPNING (CONDITIONS RACE) (2YO FILLIES) (TURF) 5f 165y
2:51 (12:00) 2-Y-0 **£19,157** (£9,578; £4,597; £3,065; £1,915)

RPR

1 **Judas Jo (FR)**[43] 4551 2-9-4 0 RobertWinston 8 —
(Gay Kelleway) *midfield early: smooth prog 1/2-way into 5th: rdn whn short of room and hmpd ins fnl 2f: swtiched outside appr fnl f: r.o to ld last half-f: won gng away* **81/10**

2 1 ½ **Musical Contest (SWE)** 2-9-4 0 GustavoSolis 9 —
(Kerstin Helander, Sweden) **144/10**

3 ½ **Ko Zin (IRE)** 2-9-4 0 YvonneDurant 2 —
(Yvonne Durant, Sweden) **13/10**[1]

4 ½ **Hope On Earth (FR)**[109] 2-9-4 0 FernandoDiaz 10 —
(Jens Erik Lindstol, Norway) **16/1**

5 shd **Goldinova (USA)** 2-9-4 0 JacobJohansen 3 —
(Lennart Reuterskiold Jr, Sweden) **32/5**

6 1 ½ **Domo Arigato (SWE)** 2-9-4 0 ValmirDeAzeredo 6 —
(Caroline Malmborg, Sweden) **63/10**[3]

7 1 ½ **Oaksana (SWE)** 2-9-4 0 DannyPatil 5 —
(Bo Neuman, Sweden) **75/1**

8 nk **Royal Purse**[119] 2121 2-9-4 0 (b) RebeccaColldin 1 —
(Claes Bjorling, Sweden) **30/1**

9 shd **Kanzee Gold (SWE)** 2-9-4 0 ManuelSantos 4 —
(Henrik Engblom, Sweden) **48/1**

10 1 ½ **Fool Too Cool (IRE)** 2-9-4 0 (b) Per-AndersGraberg 11 —
(Niels Petersen, Norway) **39/10**[2]

11 1 **Mountain Onyx (SWE)** 2-9-4 0 TinaLangstrom 7 —
(Tina Langstrom, Sweden) **80/1**

12 7 **Celine (SWE)** 2-9-4 0 RafaelSchistl 12 —
(Roy Arne Kvisla, Sweden) **30/1**

13 nk **Merlot (SWE)** 2-9-4 0 NathalieMortensen 13 —
(Henrik Engblom, Sweden) **78/1**

69.50 secs (2.80) **13** Ran SP% **126.8**
PARI-MUTUEL (all including 1sek stake): WIN 9.07; PLACE 3.95, 2.73, 1.38; DF 156.49.
Owner Mrs G Lamprell **Bred** Ashbrittle Stud **Trained** Exning, Suffolk

NOTEBOOK
Judas Jo(FR) easily landed this decent prize. She will be a much better filly next year, according to her trainer.

5984a JR FORVALTNING STOCKHOLM CUP INTERNATIONAL (GROUP 3) (3YO+) (TURF) 1m 4f
3:43 (12:00) 3-Y-0+ **£95,785** (£33,524; £11,494; £7,662; £4,789)

RPR

1 **Bank Of Burden (USA)**[14] 4-9-4 0 (b) Per-AndersGraberg 1 100
(Niels Petersen, Norway) *broke wl but settled in midfield on rail: pushed along and tk clsr order over 2 1/2f out: hdwy on outside to ld appr fnl f: r.o wl: eased cl home* **77/20**[2]

2 ½ **Mores Wells**[29] 5045 7-9-4 0 (b) SebastienMaillot 5 99
(M Delzangles, France) *chsd ldng gp: effrt u.p 2f out: wnt 2nd appr fnl f: nt pce to go w wnr but styd on* **39/10**[3]

3 2 **Hot Six (BRZ)**[192] 758 6-9-4 0 ValmirDeAzeredo 7 96
(Fabricio Borges, Sweden) *hld up: hdwy 2f out: styd on wl fnl f: nrest at fin* **23/5**

4 ½ **Sir Lando**[14] 4-9-4 0 (b) FJohansson 4 95
(Wido Neuroth, Norway) *dwlt: settled towards rr: hdwy on outside over 3 1/2f out: 6th and pushed along over 2 1/2f out: short of room and sltly hmpd 2f out: sn swtchd outside: styd on fnl f: nt able to chal ldrs* **17/10**[1]

5 1 ½ **Palermo (GER)**[14] 5-9-4 0 EspenSki 3 93
(Cathrine Erichsen, Norway) *pressed ldr: led 2f out: sn rdn and hdd appr fnl f: no ex* **31/1**

6 shd **Mulan (GER)**[14] 4-9-4 0 ManuelSantos 6 93
(Elisabeth Gautier, Sweden) *chsd ldng pair: rdn to hold pl over 2 1/2f out: one pce fnl 1 1/2f* **32/1**

7 1 ½ **Boxing Day**[14] 4-9-4 0 JacobJohansen 2 90
(Bent Olsen, Denmark) *racd in midfield towards outside: kpt on ins fnl 1 1/2f but nvr plcd to chal* **25/1**

8 hd **Aces Star (USA)**[66] 4-9-4 0 (b) NikolajStott 9 90
(Fredrik Reuterskiold, Sweden) *racd in midfield: 8th 4f out: rdn and no imp fnl 2f* **40/1**

9 3 **Handsome Hawk (IRE)**[14] 5-9-4 0 (b) Jan-ErikNeuroth 11 85
(Wido Neuroth, Norway) *led: rdn and hdd 2f out: sn wknd* **28/1**

10 2 ½ **Theocritus (USA)**[103] 2601 6-9-4 0 (b) ElioneChaves 8 81
(Claes Bjorling, Sweden) *racd in fnl 3rd of field: rdn and nt qckn appr fnl 2f: eased fnl f* **71/1**

11 5 **Theatrical Award (NOR)**[14] 6-9-1 0 CarlosLopez 12 70
(Michael Taylor, Norway) *settled towards rr: effrt and c wd fnl bnd: sn btn and eased* **9/1**

12 7 **Woy Woy (IRE)**[666] 7406 7-9-4 0 ManuelMartinez 10 62
(Johan Reuterskiold, Sweden) *a bhd: n.d* **32/1**

2m 31.5s (2.30) **12** Ran SP% **126.2**
PARI-MUTUEL (all including 1sek stake): WIN 4.87; PLACE 1.77, 2.01, 2.46; DF 26.68.
Owner Oslo Racing Stables & IORR Stables **Bred** Bjarne Minde **Trained** Norway

5873 LONGCHAMP (R-H)
Sunday, September 11
OFFICIAL GOING: Turf: good to soft changing to very soft after race 4 (2.08)

5985a QATAR PRIX DU PETIT COUVERT (GROUP 3) (3YO+) (TURF) 5f (S)
12:30 (12:00) 3-Y-0+ **£34,482** (£13,793; £10,344; £6,896; £3,448)

RPR

1 **Prohibit**[23] 5253 6-9-6 0 (p) JimCrowley 9 121
(Robert Cowell) *broke wl and chsd ldrs towards outside: 2nd and rdn over 2f out: r.o u.p fnl f: bmpd w runner-up: led cl home* **9/2**[3]

2 hd **Mar Adentro (FR)**[38] 4739 5-8-13 0 (p) ChristopheSoumillon 3 113
(R Chotard, France) *wl away and pressed ldr: led 1/2-way: pushed along over 1 1/2f out: r.o fnl f: bmpd w wnr: hdd cl home* **8/1**

3 1 ½ **Hamish McGonagall**[23] 5253 6-8-13 0 DavidAllan 5 108
(Tim Easterby) *led: scrubbed along and hdd 1/2-way: remained 3rd and kpt on wout qckning fnl 1 1/2f* **7/2**[1]

4 1 ½ **So Long Malpic (FR)**[22] 4-8-9 0 OlivierPeslier 3 98
(T Lemer, France) *settled in midfield in tch: 5th and pushed along ins fnl 2f: r.o over 1f out: nt pce to chal fnl 150yds* **16/1**

5 nk **Dam D'Augy (FR)**[21] 6-8-9 0 (b) FranckBlondel 4 97
(Mlle S-V Tarrou, France) *dwlt: racd towards rr: pushed along and hdwy on rail 2f out: swtchd off rail and r.o wl fnl f: nvr nrr* **28/1**

6 snk **Bluster (FR)**[14] 5532 5-8-13 0 Christophe-PatriceLemaire 2 101
(Robert Collet, France) *racd in midfield in tch: effrt over 1 1/2f out: sn rdn and one pce fnl f* **20/1**

7 1 ½ **Chinese Wall (IRE)**[38] 4739 3-8-8 0 ThierryJarnet 1 91
(D Guillemin, France) *broke wl and racd keenly on rail on heels of ldrs: pushed along to hold pl 1/2-way: fdd fnl 1 1/2f* **18/1**

8 nk **Exciting Life (IRE)**[28] 3-8-11 0 GeraldMosse 6 93
(Adam Wyrzyk, Poland) *scrubbed along to go pce: racd in rr: last and pushed along 1/2-way: styd on past btn horses ins fnl f* **25/1**

9 snk **Spectacle Du Mars (FR)**[21] 4-8-13 0 GregoryBenoist 7 94
(X Nakkachdji, France) *midfield: hmpd and squeezed out after 2f: towards rr: pushed along and styd on past btn horses ins fnl 150yds* **4/1**[2]

10 1 **Le Valentin (FR)**[14] 5532 5-8-13 0 AnthonyCrastus 11 90
(Y De Nicolay, France) *towards rr on outside: rdn and no imp fnl 1 1/2f* **11/1**

11 shd **War Artist (AUS)**[64] 3863 8-8-13 0 ASuborics 12 90
(Markus Klug, Germany) *chsd ldng gp on outside: pushed along 1/2-way: rdn and nt qckn fnl f: wknd and eased fnl 110yds* **7/1**

12 1 **Lisselan Diva (IRE)**[38] 4739 5-8-9 0 WilliamsSaraiva 10 86
(Mme J Bidgood, France) *chsd ldrs early: midfield and rdn 1/2-way: nt qckn: wknd ins fnl f* **16/1**

55.35 secs (-0.95) **Going Correction** +0.15s/f (Good)
WFA 3 from 4yo+ 1lb **12** Ran SP% **121.4**
Speed ratings: **113,112,110,107,107 107,104,104,104,102 102,100**
WIN (incl. 1 euro stake): 6.00. PLACES: 1.90, 2.10, 1.70. DF: 21.10. SF: 43.90.
Owner Dasmal, Rix, Barr, Morley, Mrs Penney **Bred** Juddmonte Farms Ltd **Trained** Six Mile Bottom, Cambs

FOCUS
A recognised trial for the Prix de L'Abbaye on Arc day that has been dominated by British runners over the years. Nothing got into the race from off the pace, possibly aided by a tailwind in the straight (time was good), and it was no surprise then that one of the two English-based runners triumphed.

NOTEBOOK
Prohibit put up a heck of a performance under his Group 1 penalty. Wisely ridden more positively than usual, it was clear from inside the final 2f that it was between the front two, and he always just looked to be coming out on top. Sixth beaten over 4l in last season's Abbaye, he's a better horse now, and the fact he doesn't have to be held up these days will only help when he returns here at the one to beat next month.

Mar Adentro(FR), a 66-1 third in last season's Abbaye, has been in good form at a lower level and he showed this C&D suits him well with a bold run in second. He'll again have place claims next month.

Hamish McGonagall, the Nunthorpe runner-up, was always have to be kept up to his work having got to the front and couldn't match the front pair for pace. Perhaps a pair of blinkers would sharpen him up.

Spectacle Du Mars(FR) soon found himself behind having been interfered with and was unable to make up any significant ground afterwards. He's well worth giving another chance to.

War Artist(AUS) found little for pressure and was disappointing.

5986a QATAR PRIX FOY (GROUP 2) (4YO+) (TURF) 1m 4f
1:00 (12:00) 4-Y-0+ **£63,879** (£24,655; £11,767; £7,844)

RPR

1 **Sarafina (FR)**[77] 3448 4-8-13 0 Christophe-PatriceLemaire 2 122+
(A De Royer-Dupre, France) *hld up last as field racd in single file: pushed along and hdwy over 1 1/2f out: chal under hands and heels ride between horses ins fnl f: led fnl 50yds* **4/6**[1]

2 snk **Hiruno D'Amour (JPN)**[133] 4-9-2 0 ShinjiFujita 1 125
(Mitsugu Kon, Japan) *trckd clr ldr early: relegated to 3rd after 2f: effrt but briefly outpcd over 2f out: r.o u.p fnl 1 1/2f and led 165yds out: hdd last 50yds* **9/1**

3 2 ½ **St Nicholas Abbey (IRE)**[50] 4315 4-9-2 0 ChristopheSoumillon 4 121
(A P O'Brien, Ire) *racd in 3rd early: rushed up to trck ldr after 2f: remained 2nd and pressed ldr over 2f out: led narrowly appr fnl 1 1/2f: hdd 165yds out: no ex* **10/3**[2]

4 ½ **Nakayama Festa (JPN)**[287] 7615 5-9-2 0 MasayoshiEbina 3 120
(Yoshitaka Ninomiya, Japan) *led and sn clr: others tk clsr order after 2f but continued to make running: pressed appr 2f out: hdd narrowly over 1 1/2f out: rallied but nt qckn fnl f* **6/1**[3]

2m 32.28s (1.88) **Going Correction** +0.50s/f (Yiel) **4** Ran SP% **107.4**
Speed ratings: **113,112,111,110**
WIN (incl. 1 euro stake): 1.70. PLACES: 1.10, 1.50. SF: 5.10.
Owner H H Aga Khan **Bred** H H Aga Khan **Trained** Chantilly, France

FOCUS
A race that's produced five Arc winners, and it's worth noting only two of those, Allez France in 1974 and Sagace in 1984, were actually victorious in this. Just the four runners and a surprisingly decent early gallop set, last year's Arc runner-up Nakayama Festa soon making his way to the front and ensuring there was no hanging around. The winning time was 0.15 seconds quicker than the Niel.

NOTEBOOK
Sarafina(FR)was an unlucky third in last year's Arc, having almost been knocked over, and her entire season has been geared towards gaining compensation in the autumn showpiece. Despite her trainer emphasising this was no more than a prep, her sheer class led her to victory. Christophe Lemaire took a gamble in going for an incredibly narrow gap between the second and third, but the daughter of Refuse To Bend willingly went through, despite having a whip flailing in her face, and won with much more in hand than the official margin suggests. She's done nothing but impress this season and it was no surprise to see her Arc odds shorten to a general 7-2. She'll head there as the one to beat, but is sure to be given a race by the pick of the 3yos.

Hiruno D'Amour(JPN), off since winning the big 2m Grade 1 race at Kyoto in May, picked up well to challenge and got his head in front inside the final furlong, but was unable to keep Sarafina in, and was predictably done for toe by the filly close home. This was a highly encouraging European debut, and one that suggests he's capable of hitting the frame in the big one next month.

St Nicholas Abbey(IRE), who got warm beforehand, wouldn't have been suited by the way things panned out in the 'shambles' that was the King George last time, and he appeared perfectly positioned in tracking the early leader. However, having taken a narrow lead inside the final 2f, he couldn't get away and was ultimately left trailing by the front pair. With the recent failings of Fame And Glory, he should be trained with next year's Ascot Gold Cup in mind.

Nakayama Festa(JPN), runner-up in both this and the Arc last year, hadn't run since getting injured in last November's Japan Cup and was expected to need the run by connections. All things considering, he ran really well after setting a decent early gallop, but it's hard to see him repeating last season's prominent placing in the big one.

5987a QATAR PRIX NIEL (GROUP 2) (3YO COLTS & FILLIES) (TURF) 1m 4f

1:30 (12:00) 3-Y-O **£63,879** (£24,655; £11,767; £7,844; £3,922)

RPR

1 **Reliable Man**[59] [4038] 3-9-2 0 GeraldMosse 3 123+
(A De Royer-Dupre, France) *settled in 3rd: effrt on outside of two ldrs ins fnl 2f: led 1 1/2f out: shkn up and r.o wl ent fnl f: eased cl home* **5/2**[2]

2 *2* **Meandre (FR)**[59] [4038] 3-9-2 0 MaximeGuyon 5 120
(A Fabre, France) *in rr on outside racing keenly: settled towards rr 1/2-way: 4th and effrt on outside 2f out: wnt 2nd appr fnl 110yds: nt pce to trble wnr* **1/1**[1]

3 *snk* **Vadamar (FR)**[99] [2715] 3-9-2 0 Christophe-PatriceLemaire 2 119
(A De Royer-Dupre, France) *settled in 4th: 5th towards rail 2f out: styd on fnl f: nvr able to chal ldrs* **13/2**[3]

4 *1* **Colombian (IRE)**[27] [5128] 3-9-2 0 WilliamBuick 6 117
(John Gosden) *trckd ldr: pressed ldr on outside 2 1/2f out: led narrowly over 2f out: hdd fnl 1 1/2f: nt qckn fnl f* **18/1**

5 *3* **King Of Arnor**[50] [4351] 3-9-2 0 Pierre-CharlesBoudot 1 112
(A Fabre, France) *led: hdd narrowly over 2f out: 3rd ent fnl f: fdd fnl 150yds* **14/1**

6 *4* **Nakayama Knight (JPN)**[105] 3-9-2 0 YoshitomiShibata 4 106
(Yoshitaka Ninomiya, Japan) *in rr on ins: last and pushed along 2f out: no imp: bhd fnl 1 1/2f* **16/1**

2m 32.43s (2.03) **Going Correction** +0.50s/f (Yiel) **6** Ran SP% **109.7**
Speed ratings: **113,111,111,110,108 106**
WIN (incl. 1 euro stake): 3.40. PLACES: 1.20, 1.10. SF: 7.00.
Owner Pride Racing Club **Bred** N P Bloodstock Ltd **Trained** Chantilly, France

FOCUS
Undoubtedly the best Arc trial, with no less than 12 winners going on to land the big one the following month, the pick of them in recent years being Montjeu, Sinndar, Dalakhani and Rail Link, who was the most recent in 2006. It's also worth noting that Bago, only third in this in 2004, also went on to land the Arc. The pace was no more than an even one, which may explain why the time was 0.15 seconds slower than the earlier Foy won by Sarafina.

NOTEBOOK
Reliable Mana touch disappointing when given plenty of ground to make up by Gerald Mosse in the Grand Prix de Paris, only finishing third to Meandre, was nicely positioned in third this time, ahead of his old rival, and picked up takingly to lead before staying on strongly for an impressive success, without his rider having to so much as tap him with the whip. Alain De Royer-Dupre, also responsible for Sarafina, had predictably said beforehand he wouldn't be at a peak, so it's reasonable to expect further improvement, and the trainer is shaping up to have a very strong hand in the Arc. The son of Dalakhani was having only his fifth race and still makes plenty of appeal at a general 8-1, compared to the likes of Workforce and So You Think, who are ahead of him in the market.\n
Meandre(FR) had been forced to miss some work after running a temperature a couple of weeks earlier and confidence in him had waned in recent days, largely due to rumours that Andre Fabre's stable, or at least part of it, had been hit with a virus. A horse who took seven starts to get off the mark, his sudden improvement has been remarkable, but whereas the race panned out perfectly for him when beating Reliable Man last time, he was a touch keen on this occasion and couldn't match his old rival from 1f out. He appeared to get a little tired, but was wisely looked after by Maxime Guyon and, if supplemented for the Arc, it would be no surprise to see him make the frame, though whether he can reverse form with the winner is doubtful. His odds were pushed out to 14-1.
Vadamar(FR), the winner's stablemate, hadn't run since finishing midfield in the Epsom Derby. He'd reportedly been working well, but as had been the case earlier in the season, his lack of tactical speed found him out. He stayed on nicely for third and we've still to see the best of him, with a more truly-run race almost certain to bring improvement. The Prix de Conseil de Paris, two weeks after the Arc, is the aim.
Colombian(IRE) has been running well all season in France since winning his Chester maiden. He provides a line of form comparison between Reliable Man and Galikova and can also give his trainer a guide as to what Nathaniel will have to beat next month. He can be rewarded dropped to Group 3/Listed level.
King Of Arnor has been progressing well at a lower level and is considered more of a horse for next year by Andre Fabre.
Nakayama Knight(JPN), a Japanese runner, just wasn't up to it.

5988a QATAR PRIX DU MOULIN DE LONGCHAMP (GROUP 1) (3YO+ COLTS, FILLIES & MARES) (TURF) 1m

2:40 (12:00) 3-Y-O+ **£221,663** (£88,681; £44,340; £22,150; £11,094)

RPR

1 **Excelebration (IRE)**[29] [5046] 3-8-11 0 JamieSpencer 1 121+
(Marco Botti) *settled in 3rd abt 4 l off 2nd: tk clsr order over 2 1/2f out: hdwy on outside ins fnl 2f: disputing 2nd and pushed along 1 1/2f out: led appr fnl f: r.o wl fnl f: edgd rt to ins rail fnl 110yds* **11/8**[1]

2 *1 1/2* **Rio De La Plata (USA)**[46] [4425] 6-9-2 0 FrankieDettori 8 119
(Saeed Bin Suroor) *broke wl enough on outside: sn settled in 2nd bhd clr ldr: tk clsr order over 2 1/2f out: chal ldr and led under 1 1/2f out: hdd appr fnl f: kpt on u.p wout qckning* **14/1**

3 *1/2* **Rajsaman (FR)**[46] [4425] 4-9-2 0 (b) ThierryJarnet 3 118+
(F Head, France) *racd in 4th: 5th on outside of two rivals 2 1/2f out: pushed along and r.o over 1 1/2f out: wnt 3rd ins fnl f: run flattened out and kpt on wout qckning* **11/1**

4 *1* **Dubawi Gold**[15] [5473] 3-8-11 0 RichardHughes 2 115+
(Richard Hannon) *hld up in last: scrubbed along and hdwy towards rail over 2f out: forced to switch outside ins fnl 2f and again over 1 1/2f out: styd on ins fnl f but no imp fnl 100yds* **11/2**[2]

5 *3* **Royal Bench (IRE)**[27] [5129] 4-9-2 0 OlivierPeslier 5 109
(Robert Collet, France) *hld up towards rr: 6th towards ins over 2f out: swtchd outside 2f out: sn rdn and no imp over 1 1/2f out* **7/1**[3]

6 *1 1/2* **Handsome Maestro (IRE)**[14] [5530] 5-9-2 0 FranckBlondel 4 105
(Robert Collet, France) *led: sn clr: hdd under 1 1/2f out: rdn and wknd fnl f: eased fnl 100yds* **150/1**

7 *2* **Tin Horse (IRE)**[27] [5129] 3-8-11 0 Christophe-PatriceLemaire 7 100
(D Guillemin, France) *w.w towards rr: 7th and pushed along 2 1/2f out: sn rdn and no imp: nvr trbld ldrs* **7/1**[3]

8 *8* **Planteur (IRE)**[27] [5129] 4-9-2 0 ChristopheSoumillon 6 82
(E Lellouche, France) *settled in 5th: 4th and rdn ins fnl 2 1/2f: nt qckn u.p: btn ins fnl 1 1/2f: eased fnl f* **11/2**[2]

1m 37.74s (-0.66) **Going Correction** +0.25s/f (Good)
WFA 3 from 4yo+ 5lb **8** Ran SP% **113.5**
Speed ratings: **113,111,111,110,107 105,103,95**
WIN (incl. 1 euro stake): 3.20. PLACES: 1.60, 1.90, 2.50. DF: 6.30. SF: 22.10.
Owner Manfredini, Tabor, Smith & Magnier **Bred** Owenstown Stud **Trained** Newmarket, Suffolk

FOCUS
There was a heavy and continual downpour following the Prix Niel, which led to the ground cutting up, and conditions became quite tough for this Group 1 contest. This didn't look as strong as last month's Jacques Le Marois, with no Immortal Verse, Goldikova or Sahpresa, and Andre Fabre's Golden Lilac was missing also. Despite this, the form still looks solid enough, with rank outsider Handsome Maestro tearing off and making it a well-run race. It actually proved hard to make ground from the rear. The pacemaker limits the form.

NOTEBOOK
Excelebration(IRE) had twice bustled up Frankel this season, and ran out a deeply impressive winner on his two other starts, scoring by 7l and 6l respectively in Group 2s at Cologne and Newbury, on the latter occasion finishing ahead of Dubawi Gold for the second time this season. This was a major test for him, but he passed in emphatic fashion, having no problems with the ground and picking up smartly to lead inside the final furlong. In a year when Goldikova has shown signs of weakness, he, along with Immortal Verse if that's the route she takes, will make it awfully hard for the great mare to win a fourth straight Breeders' Cup Mile.
Rio De La Plata(USA), runner-up last year, again filled that position. He found this easier than when blown away by Frankel in the Sussex Stakes, running to form with Rajsaman, and the rain was certainly in his favour. It was no disgrace being beaten by a younger, classier rival.
Rajsaman(FR) has improved for the fitting of blinkers this season and he ran better than when last of four in the Sussex.
Dubawi Gold, winner of an ordinary Group 2 at Goodwood last time, got closer to the winner than he had done previously, despite having to come from last, but still gives the impression he'll struggle to win a good Group 1.
Royal Bench(IRE) was not at his best, struggling to get into it having been held up.
Tin Horse(IRE) was not at his best, struggling to get into it having been held up.
Planteur(IRE) had the ground come right for him and was returning to his favourite track, but he found little for pressure and was right off late on. He's now left with a lot to prove.

5989a QATAR PRIX VERMEILLE (GROUP 1) (3YO+ FILLIES & MARES) (TURF) 1m 4f

3:15 (12:00) 3-Y-O+ **£172,405** (£68,974; £34,487; £17,228; £8,629)

RPR

1 **Galikova (FR)**[27] [5128] 3-8-8 0 OlivierPeslier 2 121+
(F Head, France) *broke wl and prom early racing keenly: sn hld up in 4th in tch: 3rd and shkn up over 1 1/2f out: rdn 1f out: r.o fnl f to ld fnl 110yds: sn clr: comf* **5/6**[1]

2 *2 1/2* **Testosterone (IRE)**[77] [3447] 3-8-8 0 StephanePasquier 1 116
(P Bary, France) *racd in 3rd on rail ins Wonder Of Wonders: pushed along 2 1/2f out: n.m.r between horses 2f out: rdn and styng on fr 1 1/2f out: grabbed 2nd cl home: no ch w wnr* **9/1**[3]

3 *nk* **Shareta (IRE)**[30] [5027] 3-8-8 0 Christophe-PatriceLemaire 3 116
(A De Royer-Dupre, France) *led: rdn and 2 l clr over 1 1/2f out: kpt on wout qckning: hdd fnl 110yds: lost 2nd cl home* **9/2**[2]

4 *2* **Sarah Lynx (IRE)**[28] [5093] 4-9-3 0 (b) FrankieDettori 5 112
(J E Hammond, France) *hld up in rr: effrt 2f out but no gap: swtchd outside and sltly impeded 1 1/2f out: nt qckn fnl f* **20/1**

5 *5* **Wonder Of Wonders (USA)**[24] [5219] 3-8-8 0.... ChristopheSoumillon 6 104
(A P O'Brien, Ire) *trckd ldr on outside of Testosterone: shkn up 2 1/2f out but nt qckn: wknd fnl f* **9/2**[2]

6 *3* **Wavering (IRE)**[19] [5366] 3-8-8 0 MickaelBarzalona 4 100
(A Fabre, France) *hld up in rr: tk clsr order 2 1/2f out: rdn and no imp over 1 1/2f out: eased fnl 110yds* **20/1**

2m 34.38s (3.98) **Going Correction** +0.60s/f (Yiel)
WFA 3 from 4yo 9lb **6** Ran SP% **110.4**
Speed ratings: **110,108,108,106,103 101**
WIN (incl. 1 euro stake): 1.80. PLACES: 1.30, 1.60. SF: 7.50.
Owner Wertheimer & Frere **Bred** Wertheimer & Frere **Trained** France

FOCUS
The rain had stopped by this point, but the ground was still softer than for the earlier trials, which explains why the time was around 2 seconds slower. Although a top race in its own right, carrying Group 1 status, this is very much considered an Arc trial for fillies and mares. The great Zarkava, in 2008, became the fifth horse to win this and the big one in the same season. The pace seemed a fair one. Personal bests from the first three.

NOTEBOOK
Galikova(FR) stated her Arc claims with a likeable display, getting well on top inside the final furlong and appearing to please her rider. As a half-sister to the brilliant Goldikova, expectations are always going to be high, but apart from her Diane second to top-notcher Golden Lilac, when subsequently found to be in season, she's been pretty flawless this season. Finally given a chance to strut her stuff over 1m4f, the daughter of Galileo didn't pick up immediately, but really found her stride from over 1f out, and the further they went the better she looked. A tough filly with a likeable attitude, she's should be well suited to the demands of an Arc, and still makes plenty of appeal at a top-priced 8-1 for next month's showpiece.
Testosterone(IRE) surprisingly didn't lead, but this progressive filly showed she doesn't need to by staying on take second. She was no match for the classy winner, but remains capable of better.
Shareta(IRE) had already finished behind the winner twice this season and, having taken them along for much of the way, she was found wanting for pace/class by her old rival. She's bred to stay well and should probably go up in trip now.
Sarah Lynx(IRE), beaten just over 1l in the race last year, ran well considering she lost many lengths at the start.
Wonder Of Wonders(USA), placed in each of the Epsom, Irish and Yorkshire Oaks, couldn't respond when asked to quicken and dropped right away. This clearly wasn't her form.
Wavering(IRE) hasn't built on May's Group 1 Saint-Alary win, the step up to 1m4f failing to improve for the daughter of Refuse To Bend.

5990a QATAR PRIX GLADIATEUR (GROUP 3) (4YO+) (TURF) 1m 7f 110y

4:20 (12:00) 4-Y-O+ **£34,482** (£13,793; £10,344; £6,896; £3,448)

RPR

1 **Ley Hunter (USA)**[21] [5304] 4-9-0 0 MickaelBarzalona 6 112
(A Fabre, France) *t.k.h towards rr first 4f: 8th towards rail 2 1/2f out: hdwy on to heels of ldrs 2f out: sn rdn: 4th and u.p ent fnl f: styd on to ld on line* **7/1**[3]

2 *shd* **Tac De Boistron (FR)**[39] 4-8-11 0 FranckBlondel 2 109
(A Lyon, France) *in first four thrght: effrt between horses under 2f out: led 1 1/2f out: r.o u.p fnl f: ct on line* **28/1**

3 *nk* **Shamanova (IRE)**[28] [5093] 4-8-10 0 Christophe-PatriceLemaire 9 108
(A De Royer-Dupre, France) *w.w towards rr: moved clsr 2 1/2f out: 5th and styd on appr fnl f: no ex cl home* **7/4**[1]

4 *2* **Silver Valny (FR)**[19] 5-8-11 0 ThomasMessina 7 107
(Mlle M-L Mortier, France) *midfield: effrt to go 4th appr 2f out: sn rdn: one pce fnl f* **14/1**

5 *1/2* **Celtic Celeb (IRE)**[21] [5304] 4-9-4 0 ChristopheSoumillon 3 113
(F Doumen, France) *led at stdy gallop: rdn and qcknd 2 1/2f out: hdd 1 1/2f out: no ex appr fnl f: wknd fnl 110yds* **10/1**

6 *3* **Flamingo Fantasy (GER)**[14] 6-9-0 0 DominiqueBoeuf 5 106
(S Smrczek, Germany) *midfield: 7th and rdn 1 1/2f out: no imp* **14/1**

7 snk **Brigantin (USA)**[21] 5304 4-9-4 0 .... Pierre-CharlesBoudot 10 110
(A Fabre, France) *a.p: pressed ldr on outside over 2f out: rdn and nt qckn 1 1/2f out: wknd fnl 150yds* **11/4**[2]
8 2 ½ **Allied Powers (IRE)**[22] 5284 6-9-0 0 .... JamieSpencer 1 103
(Michael Bell) *settled in rr: rdn and no imp ins fnl 2f* **9/1**
9 15 **Talgado**[59] 4037 4-8-11 0 .... MariaMagdalenaRossak 4 84
(F Neuberg, Czech Republic) *racd in first four: c wd fnl bnd: rdn and wknd fr 2f out* **33/1**

3m 33.99s (12.49) **Going Correction** +0.60s/f (Yiel) 9 Ran SP% **114.3**
Speed ratings: **92,91,91,90,90 89,88,87,80**
WIN (incl. 1 euro stake): 14.60. PLACES: 2.80, 2.50, 1.30. DF: 67.30. SF: 217.40.
Owner Godolphin SNC **Bred** Gainsborough Farm Inc **Trained** Chantilly, France

FOCUS
A race often used as a stepping stone to the Prix du Cadran on Arc day. It was predictably run at a steady pace and there was something of a dash to the line. The form is worth little.

NOTEBOOK
Ley Hunter(USA)'s trainer hasn't been enjoying the best of runs, but the colt lunged late to record his first win of the year, and first victory over this sort of trip. Whether he's got the stamina for the 2m4f of the Cadran remains to be seen, however.
Tac De Boistron(FR), a progressive handicapper, looked the winner when striking on, only to be cruelly denied in the final strides. This was a big step up on his previous efforts.
Shamanova(IRE) looked at first glance to have been given too much to do, but she was actually ahead of the winner turning in, and just lacked the same acceleration. She stayed on well, albeit without ever looking likely to get there.
Celtic Celeb(IRE) has a turn of foot so doesn't seem particularly well suited to making the running. He had the run of the race, but is better having something to aim at. He could bounce back in the Cadran if ridden with restraint.
Brigantin(USA) was always prominent, but couldn't pick up for pressure and ultimately dropped away.
Allied Powers(IRE) failed to pick up and has now been below par on each of his last two starts.

5665 BRIGHTON (L-H)
Monday, September 12

OFFICIAL GOING: Soft (good to soft in places; 6.0)
Wind: Strong, half against Weather: Sunny

5991 BRITISH STALLION STUDS SUPPORTING BRITISH RACING EBF MEDIAN AUCTION MAIDEN STKS 6f 209y
2:00 (2:00) (Class 6) 2-Y-O **£2,458** (£731; £365; £182) **Stalls** Centre

Form RPR
23 1 **Go Dutch (IRE)**[30] 5051 2-9-3 0 .... NeilCallan 4 82+
(Roger Varian) *hld up in 3rd: wnt 2nd 3f out: led wl over 1f out: rdn clr: readily* **2/5**[1]
4322 2 4 ½ **Tidal's Baby**[26] 5170 2-9-3 75 ....(p) DaneO'Neill 1 70
(Noel Quinlan) *hld up in rr: rdn and hdwy 2f out: chsd wnr over 1f out: nt qckn* **3/1**[2]
0252 3 3 ½ **Sheila's Buddy**[18] 5413 2-9-3 68 .... LiamKeniry 3 60
(J S Moore) *led tl wl over 1f out: sn outpcd* **10/1**[3]
0 4 9 **Hollywood All Star (IRE)**[117] 2194 2-8-12 0 .... JamesRogers(5) 6 36
(William Muir) *chsd ldr tl 3f out: rdn and wknd 2f out* **100/1**

1m 27.61s (4.51) **Going Correction** +0.55s/f (Yiel) 4 Ran SP% **106.5**
Speed ratings (Par 93): **96,90,86,76**
CSF £1.79 TOTE £1.50; EX 1.80.
Owner K Allen, R Marchant, G Moss & M Jarvis **Bred** Wiji Bloodstock & Gerry Mullins **Trained** Newmarket, Suffolk

FOCUS
After 4mm of rain overnight, the going was changed to soft, good to soft in places. There was a very strong headwind which was gusting to around 30 m.p.h., but racing was allowed to go ahead after an inspection of the track. The unexposed hot favourite delivered in decent style in this small-field maiden auction, recording a persoanl best in the process. The runners shifted to the stands' rail in the straight.

NOTEBOOK
Go Dutch(IRE) set the standard on his second behind subsequent Gimcrack fourth Justineo on 6f debut at Newmarket and a third behind a next-time-out conditions winner over the same C&D last time. The step up in trip looked likely to suit and he travelled well just off the pace before kicking clear to comfortably justify odds-on favouritism. A Dutch Art half-brother to French 6.5f Listed winner Peach Pearl, out of 2-y-o 1m winner, he is scopey type who seems versatile regarding ground and should be open to further progress. (op 4-9)
Tidal's Baby has had quite a few chances but he showed fair form when collared late on after looking the likely winner in a fast-ground 7f maiden at Folkestone last time and ran a fair race in second-time cheekpieces on the switch to slower ground. His current mark of 75 looks on the high side on the balance of his form, but he is consistent and should find a small opening. (tchd 16-5 tchd 100-30 in places)
Sheila's Buddy is an exposed 68-rated performer but he ran respectably under prominent ride with something to find back at 7f on turf. (op 9-1)
Hollywood All Star(IRE) is a gelded half-brother to three 2-y-o winners, but he has been a well beaten last in both of his runs. (tchd 80-1)

5992 FROSTS FUN AT THE FIREWORKS 4TH NOVEMBER H'CAP 7f 214y
2:30 (2:30) (Class 5) (0-70,70) 3-Y-O+ **£2,264** (£673; £336; £168) **Stalls** Centre

Form RPR
560 1 **Ancient Greece**[47] 4444 4-9-6 66 ....(t) TonyCulhane 6 80
(George Baker) *mid-div: hdwy over 2f out: led over 1f out: hld on wl whn strly chal fnl f* **33/1**
-403 2 shd **Encore Un Fois**[20] 5356 3-9-0 65 .... J-PGuillambert 8 78
(Luca Cumani) *towards rr: hdwy 2f out: str chal fnl f: kpt on wl* **8/1**
0055 3 5 **Silver Alliance**[26] 5179 3-8-13 67 .... SeanLevey(3) 1 68
(Walter Swinburn) *hld up in rr: hdwy 2f out: chsd ldrs over 1f out: one pce* **16/1**
5504 4 1 ¼ **Rosedale**[28] 5113 4-9-8 68 .... TedDurcan 4 67
(James Toller) *hld up in rr: hdwy 2f out: no imp fnl f* **9/2**[2]
3264 5 shd **Cat Hunter**[14] 5547 4-9-5 65 .... KirstyMilczarek 13 64
(Ronald Harris) *sn chsng ldrs: led over 3f out tl over 1f out: sn wknd* **9/1**
5531 6 1 ¾ **No Larking (IRE)**[17] 5422 3-9-2 67 .... DaneO'Neill 3 61
(Henry Candy) *led 2f: prom tl wknd over 1f out* **7/2**[1]
6214 7 2 ½ **Blue Maisey**[26] 5179 3-9-3 68 .... CathyGannon 7 56
(Peter Makin) *pushed along towards rr: rdn and no hdwy fnl 3f* **10/1**
0500 8 16 **Malanos (IRE)**[21] 5327 3-8-12 70 .... CharlesBishop(7) 9 22
(David Elsworth) *chsd ldrs tl wknd over 3f out* **5/1**[3]
135 9 1 ¼ **Cheylesmore (IRE)**[13] 5602 3-9-3 68 ....(v) WilliamCarson 2 17
(Stuart Williams) *in tch tl wknd 2f out* **14/1**
3453 10 13 **Final Verse**[14] 5538 8-9-8 68 .... PatCosgrave 10 —
(Matthew Salaman) *prom: led after 2f tl over 3f out: sn wknd: bhd and eased over 1f out* **14/1**
0/6- 11 11 **Biancarosa (IRE)**[341] 4-9-4 64 .... NeilCallan 11 —
(Simon Dow) *mid-div: wknd 3f out: wl bhd whn virtually p.u fnl f* **20/1**

1m 39.78s (3.78) **Going Correction** +0.55s/f (Yiel)
WFA 3 from 4yo+ 5lb 11 Ran SP% **114.2**
Speed ratings (Par 103): **103,102,97,96,96 94,92,76,75,62 51**
toteswingers:1&2:£64.00, 2&3:£32.30, 1&3:£63.90 CSF £270.76 CT £4422.79 TOTE £29.40: £8.90, £2.90, £5.20; EX 587.80 TRIFECTA Not won..
Owner Inkin, Inkin, Byng, Baker & Partners **Bred** Darley **Trained** Whitsbury, Hants

FOCUS
The went a decent pace in this 1m handicap, which played into the hands of the hold-up performers and the first two pulled clear. A shock winner but the time was decent.
Ancient Greece Official explanation: trainer said, regarding the apparent improvement of form, that the gelding was better suited by the easier ground

5993 PERCY CUNLIFFE H'CAP 1m 3f 196y
3:00 (3:01) (Class 6) (0-60,57) 3-Y-O+ **£1,617** (£481; £240; £120) **Stalls** High

Form RPR
1354 1 **Royal Defence (IRE)**[35] 4847 5-9-8 56 .... SeanLevey(3) 1 62
(Michael Quinn) *chsd ldr: led 3f out: disp ld fnl 2f: hung lft over 1f out: hung rt ins fnl f: all out* **10/3**[2]
0530 2 ½ **Rowan Ridge**[40] 4686 3-9-3 57 ....(v[1]) PatCosgrave 6 62
(Jim Boyle) *prom: jnd wnr and wandered fnl 2f: kpt on u.p: jst hld nr fin* **8/1**
5353 3 2 ½ **Drumadoon (IRE)**[17] 5421 3-9-1 55 ....(p) TedDurcan 7 61+
(John Dunlop) *mid-div: drvn and hdwy 2f out: styng on into cl 3rd whn nt clr run on stands' rail ins fnl f: nt rcvr* **5/2**[1]
0-10 4 ¾ **Steady Gaze**[73] 3600 6-9-4 49 .... PaulDoe 4 49
(Richard Rowe) *in tch: drvn to chse ldrs over 2f out: nt qckn fnl f* **10/1**
2420 5 2 ½ **Vinces**[18] 5406 7-9-4 54 .... TobyAtkinson(5) 10 50
(Tim McCarthy) *bhd: rdn over 3f out: sme late hdwy* **14/1**
0024 6 5 **Rosy Dawn**[18] 5406 6-9-2 47 .... WilliamCarson 5 35
(Mark Hoad) *led tl 3f out: wknd 2f out* **5/1**[3]
50-6 7 5 **Storming Redd**[15] 5520 4-9-1 46 .... JackMitchell 8 26
(James Eustace) *chsd ldrs: rdn 4f out: wknd over 2f out* **14/1**
0004 8 8 **Salesiano**[17] 5421 3-8-10 50 .... TravisBlock 2 17
(Peter Makin) *towards rr: pushed along 5f out: n.d fnl 3f* **8/1**

2m 43.33s (10.63) **Going Correction** +0.725s/f (Yiel)
WFA 3 from 4yo+ 9lb 8 Ran SP% **113.0**
Speed ratings (Par 101): **93,92,91,90,88 85,82,76**
toteswingers:1&2:£4.00, 2&3:£4.20, 1&3:£2.30 CSF £29.15 CT £75.73 TOTE £5.70: £2.20, £3.20, £1.10; EX 33.30 Trifecta £57.10 Pool £685.33 - 8.87 winning units..
Owner M Quinn **Bred** Joseph Rogers **Trained** Newmarket, Suffolk
■ Stewards' Enquiry : Pat Cosgrave two-day ban: careless riding (26-27 Sep)

FOCUS
The favourite looked unlucky in this steadily run middle-distance handicap. The form is muddling and looks weak, with the placed horses th best guides to the level.
Vinces Official explanation: jockey said the gelding was upset in the stalls and never travelling in the race

5994 IAN CARNABY APPRENTICE (S) H'CAP 1m 1f 209y
3:30 (3:32) (Class 6) (0-65,62) 3-Y-O+ **£1,617** (£481; £240; £120) **Stalls** High

Form RPR
3620 1 **Bennelong**[9] 5740 5-9-7 60 .... LukeRowe(3) 8 66
(Richard Rowe) *t.k.h: prom: led after 2f: hdd 2f out: rallied gamely: drvn to regain ld fnl 50yds* **8/1**
6344 2 nk **King Columbo (IRE)**[10] 5667 6-8-12 48 oh1 ....(p) LucyKBarry 5 53
(Julia Feilden) *prom: drvn to ld 1f out: kpt on u.p: hdd fnl 50yds* **9/2**[2]
565 3 1 ¾ **Kavachi (IRE)**[17] 5422 8-9-9 62 .... MichaelJMurphy(3) 6 64
(Gary Moore) *hld up in 6th: hdwy 3f out: led 2f out tl 1f out: one pce* **15/2**
6354 4 7 **Olimamu (IRE)**[15] 5520 4-8-13 49 ....(t) DavidKenny 7 37
(Lydia Pearce) *s.i.s: towards rr: rdn 5f out: hrd rdn and sme hdwy 2f out: wknd 1f out* **4/1**[1]
6230 5 2 ½ **Derby Desire (IRE)**[10] 5667 7-8-7 48 oh2 .... IanBurns(5) 4 31
(Des Donovan) *in tch: rdn over 3f out: wknd over 1f out* **13/2**
-065 6 nk **Prince Golan (IRE)**[196] 711 7-9-4 54 .... RachealKneller 9 36
(Richard Price) *trckd ldrs and gng wl: rdn over 2f out: wknd wl over 1f out* **16/1**
4-00 7 ½ **Munich (IRE)**[22] 317 7-9-3 53 ....(p) MatthewLawson 1 34
(Barry Brennan) *led 2f: prom: rdn 4f out: wknd over 2f out* **11/1**
2060 8 nk **Tuscan King**[4] 5845 4-8-12 51 ....(tp) ThomasBrown(3) 3 31
(Bernard Llewellyn) *bhd: rdn 4f out: hdwy and in tch in centre 2f out: wknd 1f out* **13/2**
1044 R **Command Marshal (FR)**[34] 4889 8-9-8 61 .... SophieSilvester(3) 2 —
(Ed de Giles) *ref to r shortly after s: uns rdr* **6/1**[3]

2m 13.44s (9.84) **Going Correction** +0.725s/f (Yiel) 9 Ran SP% **116.2**
Speed ratings (Par 101): **89,88,87,81,79 79,79,78,—**
toteswingers:1&2:£10.60, 2&3:£5.20, 1&3:£10.00 CSF £44.17 CT £284.32 TOTE £8.40: £2.00, £2.00, £2.10; EX 58.80 Trifecta £364.00 Part won. Pool £491.40 - 0.40 winning units..There was no bid for the winner.
Owner Miss Victoria Baalham **Bred** The National Stud **Trained** Sullington, W Sussex

FOCUS
A selling handicap run at a fair pace. It looked hard work in the closing stages and there was a tight finish. The form is weak and best rated around the first two to this year's form.

5995 SELECT SURVEYS LTD H'CAP 6f 209y
4:00 (4:00) (Class 6) (0-65,65) 3-Y-O+ **£1,617** (£481; £240; £120) **Stalls** Centre

Form RPR
1021 1 **Olney Lass**[10] 5667 4-9-0 55 .... SaleemGolam 10 67+
(Lydia Pearce) *towards rr: hdwy over 2f out: led ins fnl f: pushed out* **11/8**[1]
4302 2 ½ **Timpanist (USA)**[4] 5858 4-8-13 57 ....(b) AdamBeschizza(3) 3 68+
(Simon Dow) *bhd: hdwy and n.m.r 2f out: swtchd lft: swtchd rt and r.o nr fin: a hld* **10/3**[2]
3420 3 2 ¼ **Inquisitress**[10] 5667 7-8-3 51 oh2 .... CharlesBishop(7) 6 56
(John Bridger) *chsd ldrs: led 3f out tl ins fnl f: no ex* **7/1**
0024 4 ¾ **Comadoir (IRE)**[36] 4828 5-9-5 63 ....(p) JohnFahy(3) 9 66
(Jo Crowley) *prom: led over 5f out tl 3f out: wknd 1f out* **4/1**[3]
556 5 14 **Demoiselle Bond**[167] 1020 3-8-6 51 oh3 .... RichardThomas 5 16
(Lydia Richards) *prom tl wknd over 2f out* **50/1**
0600 6 4 **High Class Lady**[13] 5601 3-8-12 60 ....[1] SeanLevey(3) 4 14
(Walter Swinburn) *hld up in 5th: rdn and wknd over 2f out* **22/1**

005 **7** *27* **Style Margi (IRE)**^{19} [5387] 3-9-2 **61**.................................. PatCosgrave 7 —
(Ed de Giles) *led over 1f: prom tl wknd over 2f out* **16/1**
1m 27.86s (4.76) **Going Correction** +0.725s/f (Yiel)
WFA 3 from 4yo+ 4lb **7** Ran SP% **109.9**
Speed ratings (Par 101): **101,100,97,97,81 76,45**
toteswingers:1&2:£2.10, 2&3:£3.60, 1&3:£2.50 CSF £5.53 CT £19.50 TOTE £3.50: £1.70, £2.30; EX 6.30 Trifecta £25.20 Pool £567.09 - 16.60 winning units..
Owner T H Rossiter **Bred** T H Rossiter **Trained** Newmarket, Suffolk
FOCUS
There were plenty of withdrawals in this ordinary handicap but the two in-form market leaders pulled clear from off the decent pace and the form looks solid with the third setting the standard.

5996 BEER AND BALTI RACEDAY HERE 13TH OCTOBER H'CAP 5f 213y
4:30 (4:30) (Class 6) (0-55,55) 3-Y-0+ **£1,617** (£481; £240; £120) **Stalls** Centre

Form RPR
3050 **1** **Avon Light**^{4} [5864] 3-8-5 **46** oh1................................(p) RichardKingscote 8 55
(Milton Bradley) *w ldr: led over 1f out: hung lft: drvn out* **11/1**
2322 **2** *3/4* **Mucky Molly**^{7} [5787] 3-8-13 **54**.. SamHitchcott 1 61+
(Olivia Maylam) *towards rr: rdn 3f out: hdwy in centre 2f out: drvn to chal fnl f: kpt on* **13/8^{1}**
4402 **3** *nk* **Flaxen Lake**^{10} [5677] 4-8-11 **53**.. SeanLevey$^{(3)}$ 2 59
(Milton Bradley) *towards rr: hrd rdn and hdwy fr over 1f out: nrst fin* **3/1^{2}**
15/0 **4** *1* **Perfect Honour (IRE)**^{14} [5540] 5-8-10 **52**............. AdamBeschizza$^{(3)}$ 11 55
(Des Donovan) *stdd s: plld hrd in rr: rdn and hdwy over 1f out: styd on fnl f* **22/1**
0660 **5** *hd* **Lethal**^{14} [5540] 8-8-7 **51**... JamesRogers$^{(5)}$ 12 53
(Richard Price) *led 3f: w ldrs tl no ex ins fnl f* **11/1**
6642 **6** *1* **Best One**^{10} [5678] 7-8-10 **49**..(v) CathyGannon 10 48
(Ronald Harris) *prom: led 3f out tl over 1f out: no ex* **10/1**
4502 **7** *1 1/4* **Bambika**^{10} [5670] 3-9-0 **55**.. DaneO'Neill 3 53+
(Jo Crowley) *chsd ldrs: outpcd and squeezed for room over 2f out: tried to rally over 1f out: sn btn* **7/1^{3}**
0304 **8** *1/2* **Jemimaville (IRE)**^{55} [4189] 4-8-7 **46** oh1....................(v) WilliamCarson 4 39
(Giles Bravery) *towards rr: hdwy over 3f out: wknd over 1f out* **16/1**
400 **9** *nk* **Heavenly Pursuit**^{38} [4759] 3-8-3 **51**........................... DanielCremin$^{(7)}$ 9 43
(Jim Boyle) *in tch: rdn over 2f out: wknd over 1f out* **33/1**
-0P0 **10** *26* **Musical Leap**^{11} [5649] 3-8-5 **46** oh1..............................(b^{1}) ChrisCatlin 13 —
(Shaun Harris) *chsd ldrs: lost pl over 3f out: sn bhd* **66/1**
1m 15.04s (4.84) **Going Correction** +0.725s/f (Yiel)
WFA 3 from 4yo+ 2lb **10** Ran SP% **116.0**
Speed ratings (Par 101): **96,95,94,93,93 91,90,89,88,54**
toteswingers:1&2:£4.60, 2&3:£3.20, 1&3:£10.30 CSF £28.73 CT £70.14 TOTE £13.90: £3.90, £1.10, £1.40; EX 50.70 Trifecta £449.50 Pool £813.99 - 1.34 winning units..
Owner Ms S Howell **Bred** D J And Mrs Deer **Trained** Sedbury, Gloucs
FOCUS
An ordinary handicap. It was fast and furious and the heavily backed favourite came up a bit short. The third is the best guide to the level.
Best One Official explanation: jockey said that the gelding hung left

5997 BRASSERIE ITALIAN MARINA SQUARE H'CAP 5f 59y
5:00 (5:00) (Class 6) (0-65,65) 3-Y-0+ **£1,617** (£481; £240; £120) **Stalls** Low

Form RPR
6521 **1** **Commandingpresence (USA)**^{11} [5658] 5-9-4 **65**.......... SeanLevey$^{(3)}$ 7 75
(John Bridger) *chsd ldng pair: led over 1f out: drvn out* **9/4^{1}**
100 **2** *1 1/4* **Bouncy Bouncy (IRE)**^{16} [5484] 4-9-6 **64**...........................(t) ChrisCatlin 2 70
(Michael Bell) *off the pce in 5th: hdwy over 1f out: r.o to take 2nd ins fnl f* **7/2^{2}**
4050 **3** *shd* **Cloth Ears**^{4} [5865] 5-8-5 **52**......................................(be) AdamBeschizza$^{(3)}$ 8 58
(Phil McEntee) *led tl over 1f out: kpt on u.p* **25/1**
2120 **4** *1 1/2* **Highland Harvest**^{10} [5669] 7-9-7 **65**................................. RobertHavlin 3 65
(Jamie Poulton) *modest 4th tl effrt over 1f out: hung lft: one pce fnl f* **5/1^{3}**
6240 **5** *2 1/2* **The Tatling (IRE)**^{4} [5846] 14-9-6 **64**.................................. CathyGannon 4 56
(Milton Bradley) *s.i.s: sn wl bhd: nvr rchd ldrs* **9/1**
0002 **6** *1* **Cape Royal**^{4} [5846] 11-9-4 **62**...................................(tp) RichardKingscote 1 50
(Milton Bradley) *chsd ldr tl wknd over 1f out* **7/2^{2}**
0364 **7** *4 1/2* **Pocket's Pick (IRE)**^{17} [5426] 5-8-8 **55** ow1.............(bt) RobertLButler$^{(3)}$ 5 27
(Jim Best) *awkward s: outpcd* **20/1**
66.21 secs (3.91) **Going Correction** +0.725s/f (Yiel) **7** Ran SP% **110.5**
Speed ratings (Par 101): **97,95,94,92,88 86,79**
toteswingers:1&2:£2.20, 2&3:£11.30, 1&3:£8.20; totesuper7: Win: Not won; Place: £18.70 CSF £9.52 CT £137.02 TOTE £2.10: £1.10, £1.90; EX 9.00 Trifecta £137.80 Pool £620.53 - 3.33 winning units..
Owner Mrs Liz Gardner **Bred** Lazy Lane Farms Inc **Trained** Liphook, Hants
FOCUS
A sprint handicap. It was run at a fast pace and they were well strung out in the early stages. The winner recorded a personal best and the runner-up sets the standard.
The Tatling(IRE) Official explanation: jockey said that the gelding jumped awkwardly
T/Jkpt: Not won. T/Plt: £134.50 to a £1 stake. Pool:£69,099.92 - 374.90 winning tickets T/Qpdt: £5.80 to a £1 stake. Pool:£7,008.08 - 879.10 winning tickets LM

5941 KEMPTON (A.W) (R-H)
Monday, September 12

OFFICIAL GOING: Standard
Wind: Strong half across Weather: Sunny spells

5998 32 ONLINE CASINO NURSERY 6f (P)
2:10 (2:11) (Class 6) (0-60,60) 2-Y-0 **£1,617** (£481; £240; £120) **Stalls** Low

Form RPR
6304 **1** **Littlecote Lady**^{19} [5385] 2-9-1 **55**....................................... DavidProbert 3 57
(Mark Usher) *trckd ldrs: chal ins fnl 2f tl slt ld appr fnl f: jst hld on* **11/2^{1}**
4060 **2** *nk* **Inya House**^{16} [5486] 2-9-0 **54**... SebSanders 1 55
(Nigel Tinkler) *in tch tl rdn and lost position 4f out: swtchd lft to outside bnd 3f out: styd on u.p fr over 1f out: fin wl fnl f: nt quite get up* **8/1**
000 **3** *nse* **Romany Spirit (IRE)**^{14} [5564] 2-9-5 **59**............................. GeorgeBaker 11 60+
(Jim Boyle) *in tch: pushed along and gd hdwy fr 2f out: drvn and str chal fnl f: no ex last strides* **15/2**
066 **4** *shd* **The Wicked Lord**^{24} [5232] 2-9-6 **60**...................................... FergusSweeney 7 61
(Stuart Kittow) *in tch tl drvn and outpcd 3f out: styd on fr 2f out and str chal fnl f: no ex last strides* **11/2^{1}**
4130 **5** *2 3/4* **Lady Nickandy (IRE)**^{34} [4892] 2-8-12 **59**............................... NoraLooby$^{(7)}$ 4 51
(Alan McCabe) *t.k.h: trckd ldrs: styd on fnl f: nt pce to trble ldng quartet* **25/1**
000 **6** *nk* **Cat Queen**^{32} [4961] 2-9-6 **60**.. AdamKirby 5 52
(Gay Kelleway) *in rr: hrd drvn over 3f out: styd on fnl f: nt rch ldrs* **7/1^{3}**
006 **7** *1* **Mount McLeod (IRE)**^{101} [2661] 2-8-12 **55**.................. SophieDoyle$^{(3)}$ 12 45
(Jamie Osborne) *slowly away and swtchd rt to rails s: hmpd after 1f: rapid hdwy on ins over 2f out to take slt ld over 1f out: sn hdd: wknd fnl 120yds* **22/1**
5445 **8** *1/2* **Flosse**^{60} [4019] 2-9-2 **56**... JimCrowley 2 43
(Ed Walker) *chsd ldrs: slt ld fr 3f out tl hdd over 1f out: wknd ins fnl f* **13/2^{2}**
6236 **9** *3/4* **Sea Poet**^{91} [2998] 2-9-4 **58**.. NeilChalmers 6 43
(John Bridger) *in rr: rdn over 2f out: styd on fnl f: nvr a threat* **33/1**
4600 **10** *15* **Armiger**^{19} [5385] 2-9-5 **59**..(p) MartinDwyer 10 —
(William Muir) *sn led: hdd 3f out: wknd qckly ins fnl 2f* **16/1**
6016 **11** *1/2* **Selbaar**^{21} [5316] 2-9-2 **59**...(p) MartinHarley$^{(3)}$ 9 —
(Chris Dwyer) *chsd ldrs: wkng whn sltly hmpd 2f out: t.o* **11/2^{1}**
0206 **12** *16* **Masters Club**^{20} [5353] 2-9-6 **60**.. KierenFallon 8 —
(John Ryan) *sn bhd: t.o* **11/1**
1m 14.58s (1.48) **Going Correction** +0.05s/f (Slow) **12** Ran SP% **120.2**
Speed ratings (Par 93): **92,91,91,91,87 87,86,85,84,64 63,42**
toteswingers:1&2:£9.80, 2&3:£18.30, 1&3:£9.80 CSF £48.76 CT £342.05 TOTE £6.80: £2.10, £3.80, £3.70; EX 67.00.
Owner Littlecote House Racing **Bred** Ridgeway Bloodstock **Trained** Upper Lambourn, Berks
FOCUS
A very weak nursery with only two of these having tasted success before and, with the first four horses finishing in a line across the track, the form looks modest with the winner the best guide.
NOTEBOOK
Littlecote Lady had plenty to find with Selbaar on last month's Wolverhampton running, but she ran much better over this C&D last time, so obviously likes it here and her sire has a decent record at this venue. She proved very game after leading over a furlong out, coming out best in a four-way photo, but any significant rise in her mark will leave her in trouble. (op 9-2)
Inya House, making his AW debut, struggled to go the early pace but finished with quite a flourish down the wide outside and it looked at one stage as though he might get there. On this evidence he may prefer another furlong. (op 10-1 tchd 11-1)
Romany Spirit(IRE), making her AW/nursery debut after finishing well beaten in three turf maidens, had every chance and deserves credit as she was always trapped out wide from her high draw. She can win a similar nursery on Polytrack. (op 8-1)
The Wicked Lord, another making his AW/nursery debut, having shown some ability in three turf maidens, kept staying on to go down only narrowly and may find an opportunity in a similarly weak affair. (op 6-1 tchd 13-2)
Lady Nickandy(IRE), making her AW debut, had twice run poorly since justifying long odds-on in a four-runner Yarmouth maiden and was another who seemed to struggle to go the early pace. She may need dropping into a seller. (op 20-1)
Sea Poet was making his AW/nursery debut on this first start for the yard following a three-month absence, but never got much of a chance after receiving a broadside from both sides exiting the stalls. Official explanation: jockey said that the gelding suffered interference shortly after the start (op 25-1)
Selbaar was up there early, but dropped away very tamely before the furlong pole.

5999 32 FOR SLOTS MAIDEN FILLIES' STKS 1m (P)
2:40 (2:41) (Class 5) 3-4-Y-0 **£2,264** (£673; £336; £168) **Stalls** Low

Form RPR
33 **1** **Fabulouslyspirited**^{30} [5030] 3-9-0 0.................................. JimCrowley 5 84+
(Ralph Beckett) *w ldr 2f: styd prom: pushed along to chse ldrs over 2f out: led over 1f out: pushed clr fnl f* **11/2^{3}**
2025 **2** *4 1/2* **Barathea Dancer (IRE)**^{60} [4009] 3-9-0 76....................(t) JamesDoyle 12 73
(Roger Teal) *w ldr 6f out: slt ld 3f out: rdn 2f out: hdd over 1f out: nt pce of wnr but hld on wl for 2nd* **9/2^{2}**
0- **3** *1/2* **Huwayit (IRE)**^{439} [3562] 3-9-0 0....................................... PhilipRobinson 2 72+
(Clive Brittain) *chsd ldrs: rdn and nt qckn 2f out: styd on again fnl f: gng on clsng stages* **16/1**
2 **4** *1 1/4* **Wadha (IRE)**^{14} [5567] 3-9-0 0... FrankieDettori 9 69
(Saeed Bin Suroor) *sn slt ld: narrowly hdd 3f out: rallied and ev ch over 1f out: wknd ins fnl f* **11/10^{1}**
5 *3 3/4* **Appeal (IRE)** 3-9-0 0.. SebSanders 10 60+
(Sir Mark Prescott Bt) *slowly away: in rr: pushed along and green pushed along 4f out: stl plenty to do over 2f out: styd on wl clsng stages: should improve* **12/1**
6 *1 1/2* **Hairpin (USA)** 3-9-0 0.. AhmedAjtebi 6 56+
(Mahmood Al Zarooni) *in rr: sn green: stl green and wd bnd 3f out: styd on fr over 1f out: nt rch ldrs* **11/2^{3}**
0- **7** *1 1/2* **Callisto Light**^{459} [2890] 4-9-5 0...................................... AdrianMcCarthy 7 53
(George Prodromou) *mid-div: drvn along over 2f out: styd on same pce fr over 1f out* **100/1**
0 **8** *4 1/2* **Moonlark**^{14} [5567] 3-9-0 0.. RussKennemore 3 42
(John Holt) *in rr: sme prog fnl 2f* **100/1**
3 **9** *nse* **Tetbury Lass**^{28} [5114] 3-9-0 0.. NeilChalmers 8 42
(Adrian Chamberlain) *chsd ldrs 5f* **50/1**
04 **10** *13* **Conesuala**^{11} [5639] 4-9-5 0... MatthewDavies 1 10
(Alan Jarvis) *rdn and bhd fr 1/2-way* **33/1**
00 **11** *2 1/4* **The Flying Cholita (IRE)**^{20} [5346] 3-8-9 0........................ AmyScott$^{(5)}$ 11 —
(Eve Johnson Houghton) *chsd ldrs 4f* **100/1**
1m 39.27s (-0.53) **Going Correction** +0.05s/f (Slow)
WFA 3 from 4yo 5lb **11** Ran SP% **118.0**
Speed ratings (Par 100): **104,99,99,97,94 92,91,86,86,73 71**
toteswingers:1&2:£9.90, 2&3:£23.00, 1&3:£10.10 CSF £30.29 TOTE £5.10: £1.60, £1.30, £4.20; EX 33.60.
Owner Newsells Park Stud **Bred** Newsells Park Stud **Trained** Kimpton, Hants
FOCUS
Older-horse maidens at this time of year can be moderate affairs, but this was made a bit more interesting by the presence of three very expensive yearlings. The form looks a buit shaky with the runner-up rated to her AW best.
Barathea Dancer(IRE) Official explanation: jockey said that the filly hung right

6000 32 FOR BLACKJACK/E B F MAIDEN FILLIES' STKS 1m (P)
3:10 (3:11) (Class 5) 2-Y-0 **£3,299** (£981; £490; £245) **Stalls** Low

Form RPR
1 **Misdemeanour (IRE)** 2-9-0 0.. PatDobbs 7 81+
(Richard Hannon) *hld up in tch: stdy hdwy fr 2f out: rdn 1f out: qcknd to ld fnl 120yds: comf* **15/2**
43 **2** *2* **Parisian Princess (IRE)**^{40} [4662] 2-9-0 0.............................. KierenFallon 5 74
(George Baker) *chsd ldr 4f out: drvn to chal 2f out: led sn after: rdn over 1f out: hdd and nt qckn fnl 120yds* **15/8^{1}**
6 **3** *3/4* **Winner's Wish**^{17} [5444] 2-9-0 0.. FrankieDettori 3 73
(Jeremy Noseda) *chsd ldr 4f: styd chsng ldrs: drvn and flashed tail fr over 2f out: sn str chal: one pce fnl 120yds* **11/4^{2}**
4 *1/2* **Coquet** 2-9-0 0... JimCrowley 9 72
(Hughie Morrison) *s.i.s: in rr: drvn and hdwy over 2f out: styd on appr fnl f: one pce fnl 120yds* **14/1**

0 **5** 2 ¾ **Winter Dress**^{28} 5097 2-8-11 0 .... KieranO'Neill(3) 8 65
(Roger Teal) *chsd ldrs: rdn on outside bnd 3f out: styd on same pce fnl 2f* **25/1**

65 **6** 4 ½ **Zamarelle**^{32} 4969 2-9-0 0 .... JamesDoyle 2 55
(Roger Charlton) *in rr: drvn along ins fnl 3f: no prog tl mod hdwy fnl f* **6/1**^{3}

0 **7** 1 **Emman Bee (IRE)**^{14} 5564 2-9-0 0 .... FrankieMcDonald 6 53
(John Gallagher) *sn led: continually flashed tail: hdd ins fnl 2f: wknd qckly over 1f out* **66/1**

6 **8** 14 **Abundantly**^{14} 5537 2-9-0 0 .... SteveDrowne 1 20
(Hughie Morrison) *in rr: rdn along in mid-div 1/2-way: wknd fr 3f out* **8/1**

00 **9** hd **She's Flawless (USA)**^{100} 2709 2-9-0 0 .... MartinDwyer 4 20
(Brian Meehan) *in tch: rdn 4f out: sn wknd* **33/1**

1m 40.26s (0.46) **Going Correction** +0.05s/f (Slow) **9** Ran SP% **113.6**
Speed ratings (Par 92): **99,97,96,95,93 88,87,73,73**
toteswingers:1&2:£2.00, 2&3:£1.20, 1&3:£7.00 CSF £21.33 TOTE £13.10: £3.30, £1.10, £1.70; EX 14.80.
Owner Thurloe Thoroughbreds XXIX **Bred** Ceka Ireland Limited **Trained** East Everleigh, Wilts

FOCUS
Nothing more than an ordinary fillies' maiden although the winner was quite impressive.

NOTEBOOK
Misdemeanour(IRE), a daughter of Azamour whose half-sister won over 7f at three, wasn't particularly strong in the market, but travelled up smoothly under Pat Dobbs and readily asserted. This was a very promising start and she'll presumably take the nursery route. (op 10-1)
Parisian Princess(IRE) improved for the step up to 1m without proving a match for the classier winner late on. She now has the option of nurseries. (op 13-8)
Winner's Wish looked in need of this longer trip when sixth over 7f at Newmarket on debut, and she duly improved. She can win a small race. (op 5-2 tchd 9-4 and 3-1 in places)
Coquet, a half-sister to the useful Midnight Oil, is from a good family and she stayed on late to register an encouraging first effort. Natural progress should see her winning a minor maiden, with 1m2f and more likely to suit. (op 10-1)
Abundantly was under pressure rounding the final bend and dropped out as though something was amiss, failing to build on her debut effort. (op 12-1)
She's Flawless(USA) Official explanation: jockey said that the filly hung badly right

6001 32 FOR POKER NURSERY (DIV I) 7f (P)
3:40 (3:43) (Class 6) (0-65,65) 2-Y-O £1,293 (£385; £192; £96) Stalls Low

Form RPR

000 **1** **Inniscastle Boy**^{47} 4446 2-9-2 **60** .... MartinDwyer 7 61
(William Muir) *towards rr: hdwy 3f out: drvn and str chal u.p thrght fnl f: led last strides* **14/1**

004 **2** nse **Anginola (IRE)**^{12} 5625 2-9-1 **59** .... KierenFallon 3 60
(Joseph Tuite) *slt ld tl narrowly hdd after 2f: styd pressing ldr tl led again over 2f out: rdn and jnd fnl f: hdd and no ex last strides* **7/2**^{1}

004 **3** ½ **True Prince (USA)**^{18} 5410 2-8-10 **54** .... EddieAhern 11 54
(Amanda Perrett) *trckd ldrs: drvn to chal appr fnl f and stl ev ch tl no ex clsng stages* **4/1**^{2}

05 **4** 1 ¼ **Samasana (IRE)**^{27} 5133 2-8-10 **54** ow2 ....(v) JamesDoyle 8 53
(Ian Wood) *towards rr: hdwy fr 2f out: styng on whn nt clr run and swtchd lft fnl 100yds: kpt on: nt rcvr* **25/1**

1226 **5** hd **Lady Jourdain (IRE)**^{18} 5413 2-9-6 **64** .... RoystonFfrench 9 61
(Mrs K Burke) *in rr: rdn over 2f out: styd on over 1f out: kpt on clsng stages: nt rch ldrs* **8/1**

6050 **6** hd **Milwr**^{12} 5634 2-8-1 **45** .... JimmyQuinn 1 41
(Chris Dwyer) *chsd ldrs: drvn to chal over 2f out: wkng whn bmpd fnl 120yds* **14/1**

3544 **7** 1 ½ **Emma Jean (IRE)**^{14} 5535 2-8-3 **50** ....(p) HarryBentley(3) 4 42
(J S Moore) *in tch: rdn and one pce over 2f out: kpt on again clsng stages* **11/2**

506 **8** 2 **Tangtastic (IRE)**^{84} 3237 2-8-12 **56** .... EddieCreighton 10 43
(Edward Creighton) *s.i.s: in rr: sme hdwy on ouside fr 3f out: nvr rchd ldrs and wknd fnl f* **66/1**

0135 **9** 1 ¼ **Miserere Mei (IRE)**^{10} 5690 2-9-4 **65** ....(p) MartinHarley(3) 2 48
(Alan McCabe) *t.k.h: chsd ldrs 5f* **8/1**

500 **10** 2 **Rain Dance**^{24} 5232 2-9-3 **64** .... KieranO'Neill(3) 5 42
(Richard Hannon) *w ldr: led after 2f: rdn 3f out: hdd over 2f out: sn btn* **5/1**^{3}

0520 **11** 1 ¾ **Clone Devil (IRE)**^{13} 5597 2-8-4 **48** .... FrankieMcDonald 6 22
(Alastair Lidderdale) *s.i.s: in rr: sme hdwy 3f out: wknd 2f out* **16/1**

1m 28.25s (2.25) **Going Correction** +0.05s/f (Slow) **11** Ran SP% **121.1**
Speed ratings (Par 93): **89,88,88,86,86 86,84,82,81,78 76**
toteswingers:1&2:£19.50, 2&3:£3.60, 1&3:£12.70 CSF £64.48 CT £246.43 TOTE £28.50: £7.80, £1.40, £2.50; EX 71.30.
Owner The Lavelle Family **Bred** Carmel Stud **Trained** Lambourn, Berks

FOCUS
Just two previous winners amongst the 11 runners for this moderate nursery and the form looks weak.

NOTEBOOK
Inniscastle Boy, making his AW/nursery debut after beating a total of three horses in three turf maidens, left his previous form well behind and just managed to prevail by the skin of his teeth following a protracted duel with the runner-up. He can't be put up much for this and may have more to offer on Polytrack, possibly over a bit further. Official explanation: trainer said, regarding the apparent improvement in form, that the colt, who is a lazy individual, may have benefitted from racing for the first time on the all weather surface
Anginola(IRE), also making her AW/nursery debut after showing improved form to finish fourth in a Folkestone seller, was trying this trip for the first time. She battled back gamely after being headed, but her proximity doesn't do a great deal for the form. (op 9-2)
True Prince(USA) ran his best race so far when switched to Polytrack at Lingfield last time. He was off the bridle over 2f from home, but kept battling on and this was a fair effort from the outside stall. He may be capable of better. (op 5-1 tchd 11-2)
Samasana(IRE), unplaced in six turf maidens, stayed on to record her best effort yet and the surface may have helped her, but she is unlikely to have much in the way of further improvement.
Lady Jourdain(IRE), winner of two sellers, came off the bridle at the back of the field a fair way out but didn't find her stride until it was too late. (op 13-2)
Milwr Official explanation: jockey said that the gelding hung left

6002 32 FOR POKER NURSERY (DIV II) 7f (P)
4:10 (4:10) (Class 6) (0-65,65) 2-Y-O £1,293 (£385; £192; £96) Stalls Low

Form RPR

000 **1** **Outlaw Torn (IRE)**^{35} 4864 2-8-8 **52** .... KierenFallon 10 60+
(Alan McCabe) *stdd s: t.k.h off mod pce: dropped to rr and pushed along towards outside fr over 2f out: str run fr over 1f out: led fnl 120yds: won gng away* **4/1**^{3}

000 **2** 1 ½ **Doc Hill**^{32} 4969 2-8-1 **45** .... JimmyQuinn 6 49+
(Michael Blanshard) *in rr: hdwy on ins to take slt ld ins fnl 2f: drvn over 1f out: hdd and outpcd fnl 120yds* **20/1**

006 **3** 1 ¼ **Great Mystery (IRE)**^{18} 5411 2-8-11 **55** .... SebSanders 7 56
(J W Hills) *t.k.h off mod pce: in tch: pushed along: edgd rt and nt clr run over 2f out: styd on fnl f: nt rch ldrs* **11/1**

0533 **4** 2 ¾ **Sunley Valentine**^{5} 5817 2-9-6 **64** .... MatthewDavies 3 58
(Mick Channon) *t.k.h off mod pce: hdwy and nt clr run over 2f out: styd on again fnl f but no ch w ldrs* **13/8**^{1}

3430 **5** ¾ **River Nova**^{12} 5634 2-8-4 **51** .... HarryBentley(3) 1 43
(Alan Jarvis) *chsd ldrs: slt ld u.p 2f out: sn hdd: wknd fnl f* **14/1**

400 **6** 1 **Morning Muse (IRE)**^{10} 5689 2-9-1 **59** .... JimCrowley 8 48
(Peter Winkworth) *w ldr: chal fr over 3f out tl 2f out: wknd over 1f out* **3/1**^{2}

002 **7** 2 ¾ **Mormoran**^{11} 5637 2-8-3 **50** ....(p) KieranO'Neill(3) 5 32
(Chris Dwyer) *sn led: jnd over 3f out: hdd 2f out: wknd sn after* **9/1**

1m 28.79s (2.79) **Going Correction** +0.05s/f (Slow) **7** Ran SP% **112.9**
Speed ratings (Par 93): **86,84,82,79,78 77,74**
toteswingers:1&2:£12.20, 2&3:£13.10, 1&3:£7.50 CSF £70.56 CT £806.64 TOTE £5.10: £3.20, £13.30; EX 81.50.
Owner Charles Wentworth **Bred** Derek Veitch & Rory O'Brien **Trained** Averham Park, Notts

FOCUS
This division was contested by seven maidens. They didn't go much of a pace early and a few took a pull. The winning time was 0.54 seconds slower than the first leg and the form looks far from solid, with the third the best guide.

NOTEBOOK
Outlaw Torn(IRE) was making his nursery debut after finishing well beaten in three maidens over shorter, though he met trouble in running at Wolverhampton last time. Despite the extra furlong here, he was being ridden along a fair way out here but eventually found his stride down the centre of the track and maintained his effort to hit the front half a furlong from home. This was a very weak race, but he can probably do better. Official explanation: trainer said, regarding the apparent improvment of form, that gelding was hampered last time, and that he was dropped in class (op 5-1 tchd 11-2)
Doc Hill, beaten a long way in three turf maidens, was off the bridle at the back of the field before halfway but responded to pressure and found himself in front after diving for the far rail after the cutaway. He couldn't cope with the winner, but although finishing a clear second best, he was effectively 9lb wrong here, which doesn't say much for those behind him. (op 25-1)
Great Mystery(IRE), well beaten in three 6f maidens, was one of those to take a hold early. He had every chance over a furlong from home, but then proved one-paced and will do well to find a weaker nursery. (op 14-1)
Sunley Valentine's third in a 6f nursery here two starts back was the best form coming into this and, though she pulled hard early, she was travelling best of all behind the leaders 2f home. It just looked a question of her finding a gap, but when she did her response off the bridle was very disappointing. (op 7-4 tchd 2-1)
River Nova, the most experienced in the field, has shown her best form so far in sellers and looks to need a return to that level. (op 12-1)

6003 32 FOR BINGO H'CAP 7f (P)
4:40 (4:40) (Class 4) (0-85,84) 3-Y-O £4,075 (£1,212; £606; £303) Stalls Low

Form RPR

1315 **1** **The Guru Of Gloom (IRE)**^{9} 5718 3-9-0 **77** .... MartinDwyer 6 87
(William Muir) *hld up in rr: stl plenty to do whn rdn ins fnl 2f: str run fnl f: sn swtchd rt: kpt on u.p to ld fnl 75yds* **8/1**

-543 **2** 1 **Birdolini**^{28} 5113 3-8-9 **72** .... FergusSweeney 8 79
(Alan King) *chsd ldrs: rdn and one pce 2f out: styd on wl u.p clsng stages to take 2nd but no imp on wnr* **5/1**^{2}

2143 **3** ½ **Escape To Glory (USA)**^{18} 5412 3-9-2 **79** ....(b^{1}) GeorgeBaker 1 85
(Mikael Magnusson) *led: rdn 2f out: kpt on fnl f tl hdd and no ex fnl 75yds: lost 2nd cl home* **11/2**^{3}

4335 **4** hd **Chevise (IRE)**^{18} 5412 3-9-1 **78** .... MatthewDavies 9 83
(Steve Woodman) *chsd ldrs: rdn and outpcd over 2f out: styd on again fnl f* **25/1**

2202 **5** 1 ½ **Little Black Book (IRE)**^{12} 5635 3-9-2 **79** ....(t) NeilCallan 2 80
(Gerard Butler) *chsd ldr: rdn and lost 2nd over 1f out: sn outpcd* **13/8**^{1}

4200 **6** shd **Majestic Dream (IRE)**^{24} 5240 3-9-7 **84** ....(v) AdamKirby 7 85
(Walter Swinburn) *in rr but in tch: rdn and hdwy 2f out: nvr quite on terms and one pce fnl f* **11/1**

-156 **7** 1 **Munaaseb**^{33} 4909 3-9-4 **81** .... RichardHills 10 79+
(Ed Dunlop) *in rr: hdwy on outside fr 3f out: drvn to chse ldr over 1f out: no imp and wknd fnl f* **13/2**

4350 **8** 8 **Remotelinx (IRE)**^{17} 5430 3-9-7 **84** .... SebSanders 4 61
(J W Hills) *bhd most of way* **25/1**

1000 **9** nse **May's Boy**^{25} 5201 3-9-1 **81** ....(p) HarryBentley(3) 5 58
(Mark Usher) *chsd ldrs 4f* **33/1**

1m 26.21s (0.21) **Going Correction** +0.05s/f (Slow) **9** Ran SP% **113.6**
Speed ratings (Par 103): **100,98,98,98,96 96,95,85,85**
toteswingers:1&2:£4.90, 2&3:£4.70, 1&3:£4.10 CSF £45.74 CT £239.93 TOTE £7.40: £1.90, £2.10, £1.60; EX 59.20.
Owner R Haim **Bred** Oak Lodge Bloodstock **Trained** Lambourn, Berks
■ Stewards' Enquiry : Matthew Davies one-day ban: careless riding (26 Sep)

FOCUS
A decent handicap run at a scorching early pace, which played into the hands of the hold-up horses. The solid runner-up is rated to her latest turf mark and sets the level.

6004 32 FOR BETTING (S) STKS 1m 3f (P)
5:10 (5:12) (Class 6) 3-Y-O £1,617 (£481; £240; £120) Stalls Low

Form RPR

0063 **1** **Herminella**^{12} 5631 3-8-12 56 .... MartinDwyer 7 60
(William Muir) *trckd ldr: led over 3f out: hrd drvn over 1f out: jnd ins fnl f: styd on dourly u.p and on top cl home* **11/4**^{3}

133 **2** ½ **What About Now**^{15} 5512 3-9-4 62 ....(b) SebSanders 8 65
(J W Hills) *hld up in tch: stdy hdwy to trck wnr 2f out: stl travelling wl appr fnl f: rdn to chal ins fnl f but fnd no ex and hld fnl 50yds* **9/4**^{2}

004 **3** 14 **Elfine (IRE)**^{18} 5415 3-8-12 67 .... NeilCallan 1 34
(Rae Guest) *led tl hdd over 3f out: wknd qckly wl over 1f out* **7/4**^{1}

5342 **4** 4 **Dew Reward (IRE)**^{18} 5415 3-9-9 62 .... AdamKirby 6 38
(Bill Turner) *chsd ldrs: rdn 4f out: wknd fr 3f out* **5/1**

5600 **5** 4 **Chillie Peppar**^{28} 5120 3-8-12 47 .... MarinosKyriakides(5) 4 24
(George Prodromou) *in rr: rdn and sme prog 4f out: nvr anywhere nr ldrs and sn wknd* **33/1**

0050 **6** 23 **Bella Nemica**^{10} 5670 3-8-12 40 .... EddieCreighton 3 —
(Edward Creighton) *in rr: rdn and lost tch over 3f out* **66/1**

2m 22.21s (0.31) **Going Correction** +0.05s/f (Slow) **6** Ran SP% **114.9**
Speed ratings (Par 99): **100,99,89,86,83 66**
toteswingers:1&2:£1.90, 2&3:£1.60, 1&3:£1.90 CSF £9.72 TOTE £4.10: £3.70, £3.10; EX 11.50.There was no bid for the winner.
Owner Dulverton Equine **Bred** Herminoe Partnership **Trained** Lambourn, Berks

The Form Book, Raceform Ltd, Compton, RG20 6NL

FOCUS
A weak seller, but it was run at a solid gallop. The winner built on her latest form ahead of the runner-up, who is rated to her mark.

6005 32 FOR RUMMY H'CAP 1m 3f (P)
5:40 (5:42) (Class 5) (0-75,74) 3-Y-0+ £2,264 (£673; £336; £168) Stalls Low

Form RPR
3433 1 **Alshazah**[18] 5407 3-9-0 70 .... JamesMillman 11 82
(Rod Millman) *hld up in rr: hdwy on outside 3f out: styng on whn hmpd appr fnl 2f: qckng appr fnl f: led fnl 120yds: readily* **3/1**[1]
4420 2 1 **If I Were A Boy (IRE)**[14] 5545 4-9-8 70 .... (p) SebSanders 7 80
(Dominic Ffrench Davis) *chsd ldrs: rdn and slt ld ins fnl f: hdd fnl 120yds: one pce* **20/1**
1405 3 1 1/4 **Two Certainties**[45] 4506 4-9-0 62 .... JimCrowley 10 70
(Stuart Williams) *towards rr: hdwy over 3f out: rdn and styd on fnl 2f: tk 3rd fnl 120yds but no imp on ldng duo* **14/1**
0540 4 2 3/4 **Classically (IRE)**[26] 5178 5-9-10 72 .... (e[1]) SteveDrowne 3 74
(Peter Hedger) *sn trcking ldr: rdn to ld over 2f out: hdd ins fnl f: sn btn fnl 120yds* **20/1**
4230 5 4 **Alfouzy**[30] 5064 3-9-4 74 .... (p) NeilCallan 5 68
(Roger Varian) *chsd ldrs: rdn over 2f out: wknd fnl f* **6/1**[3]
0-55 6 3 **Eastern Paramour (IRE)**[30] 5050 6-9-12 74 .... KierenFallon 12 62
(Rod Millman) *in rr: racd on outside: rdn and sme hdwy 2f out: nvr quite gng pce to rch ldrs and wknd over 1f out* **12/1**
0422 7 1 1/4 **Jovial (IRE)**[18] 5406 4-9-1 63 .... EddieAhern 6 49
(Denis Coakley) *in rr: pushed along 3f out: styd on same pce fnl 2f* **5/1**[2]
/006 8 1/2 **Mick's Dancer**[21] 5318 6-9-2 64 .... MartinDwyer 8 49
(Richard Phillips) *racd towards outside: rdn and styd on to chse ldrs fr 3f out: no imp and wknd 2f out* **12/1**
1120 9 3 1/2 **Addikt (IRE)**[95] 2843 6-9-9 71 .... EddieCreighton 1 49
(Michael Scudamore) *s.i.s: in rr: rdn over 3f out: nvr in contention* **20/1**
50 10 1 **Archie Rice (USA)**[14] 5568 5-9-5 67 .... GeorgeBaker 2 43
(Tom Keddy) *sn slt ld: hdd & wknd over 2f out* **20/1**
0321 11 1 1/2 **Professor John (IRE)**[11] 5642 4-8-13 61 .... (v) JamesDoyle 9 34
(Ian Wood) *in tch on ins: rdn and wknd over 1f out* **5/1**[2]
24-4 12 nk **Nothing To Hide (IRE)**[247] 95 3-8-13 69 .... MarkLawson 4 41
(Dominic Ffrench Davis) *nvr bttr than mid-div* **50/1**
-100 13 3/4 **Halyard (IRE)**[28] 5110 4-9-10 72 ....[1] AdamKirby 13 42
(Walter Swinburn) *chsd ldrs: rdn over 4f out: wknd qckly fr 2f out* **16/1**

2m 19.85s (-2.05) **Going Correction** +0.05s/f (Slow)
WFA 3 from 4yo+ 8lb **13** Ran SP% **121.6**
Speed ratings (Par 103): **109,108,107,105,102 100,99,99,96,95 94,94,93**
toteswingers:1&2:£20.40, 2&3:£27.00, 1&3:£11.50 CSF £73.96 CT £753.40 TOTE £4.10: £1.70, £9.00, £6.40; EX 109.00.
Owner The Links Partnership **Bred** Brookside Breeders Club **Trained** Kentisbeare, Devon

FOCUS
An ordinary handicap, but the pace was good and the winning time was 2.36 seconds quicker than the seller. The form looks solid and should work out.
Jovial(IRE) Official explanation: jockey said the gelding was unsuited by the kickback
T/Plt: £595.80 to a £1 stake. Pool:£49,828.10 - 61.05 winning tickets T/Qpdt: £79.30 to a £1 stake. Pool:£5,049.86 - 47.10 winning tickets ST

5719 MUSSELBURGH (R-H)
Monday, September 12

OFFICIAL GOING: Good to soft (6.8) (meeting abandoned after race 1 (2.20) due to high winds)
Wind: Very strong across Weather: Rain and gales

6006 SUBSCRIBE ONLINE AT RACINGUK.COM CLAIMING STKS 1m 1f
2:20 (2:20) (Class 6) 3-Y-0+ £1,617 (£481; £240; £120) Stalls Low

Form RPR
30-1 1 **Just Lille (IRE)**[114] 2314 8-9-9 89 .... (p) SilvestreDeSousa 7 93
(Ann Duffield) *cl up: rdn to ld 2f out: drvn and edgd rt ent fnl f: styd on strly* **10/3**[3]
4241 2 3 3/4 **Sunnyside Tom (IRE)**[15] 5502 7-9-5 80 .... PaulHanagan 8 81
(Richard Fahey) *trckd ldrs on outer: hdwy wl over 2f out: effrt to chal wl over 1f out and sn rdn: drvn and edgd rt ent fnl f: kpt on same pce* **2/1**[2]
1355 3 2 3/4 **Fremen (USA)**[45] 4501 11-9-0 73 .... AdrianNicholls 1 70
(David Nicholls) *led: rdn along over 3f out: drvn and hdd 2f out: grad wknd* **14/1**
0031 4 4 **Charlie Cool**[11] 5648 8-9-11 91 .... (b) PJMcDonald 4 72
(Ruth Carr) *trckd ldrs: effrt wl over 2f out and sn rdn: drvn wl over 1f out and sn btn* **13/8**[1]
0/04 5 1 **Monthly Medal**[14] 5549 8-8-6 66 .... (t) JulieBurke[(5)] 3 56
(Wilf Storey) *hld up in rr: hdwy 3f out: sn rdn and n.d* **20/1**
400- 6 20 **Nesno (USA)**[58] 2902 8-8-13 51 .... (p) PhillipMakin 5 14
(Chris Grant) *chsd ldrs: rdn along 3f out: sn wknd* **80/1**

1m 54.64s (0.74) **Going Correction** +0.275s/f (Good) **6** Ran SP% **107.2**
Speed ratings (Par 101): **107,103,101,97,96 79**
toteswingers:1&2:£1.60, 2&3:£2.60, 1&3:£3.00 CSF £9.43 TOTE £3.80: £1.50, £1.20; EX 11.80.
Owner Middleham Park Racing XLVI **Bred** Sweetmans Bloodstock **Trained** Constable Burton, N Yorks

FOCUS
After 2mm rain overnight and a further 2mm in the lead up to racing the ground was described as 'just on the easy side'. The tailend of Hurricane Katia resulted in a 32mph crosswind with gusts of around 40mph making conditions even more difficult. Paul Hanagan said conditions were 'horrendous', Adrian Nicholls said 'it was not good at all in the home straight'. A claimer run at a sound pace in the conditions, the runners being buffeted by the crosswind in the home straight.

6007 TURFTV (S) STKS 7f 30y
() (Class 6) 2-Y-0 £

6008 CMYK DIGITAL SOLUTIONS H'CAP 1m 6f
() (Class 5) (0-75,) 3-Y-0+ £

6009 TOTEPLACEPOT H'CAP (DIV I) 7f 30y
() (Class 6) (0-65,) 3-Y-0+ £

6010 TOTEPLACEPOT H'CAP (DIV II) 7f 30y
() (Class 6) (0-65,) 3-Y-0+ £

6011 TURFTV NURSERY 5f
() (Class 4) (0-85,) 2-Y-0 £

6012 WATCH RACING UK ONLINE AT RACINGUK.COM H'CAP 5f
() (Class 5) (0-70,) 3-Y-0+ £

6013 SCOTTISH RACING YOUR BETTER BET H'CAP 1m 4f 100y
() (Class 6) (0-65,) 3-Y-0+ £

T/Plt: £1.30 to £1 Pool:£52,991.33 - 29,430.67 w. tckts JR 6014 - 6016a - See RI

5624 FOLKESTONE (R-H)
Tuesday, September 13

OFFICIAL GOING: Good to soft (6.4)
Wind: Very strong, 3/4 behind, races 1-5; easing remainder. Weather: Fine early, changeable after with heavy showers races 4 & 5

6017 EASTWELL MANOR CLAIMING STKS 1m 1f 149y
2:20 (2:20) (Class 6) 3-Y-0+ £1,704 (£503; £251) Stalls Centre

Form RPR
2302 1 **Avon River**[19] 5408 4-9-6 80 .... RichardHughes 2 78+
(Richard Hannon) *led: stdd pce 3f out: drvn and narrowly hdd 2f out: sn led again and asserted: 2 l up ins fnl f: eased nr fin* **11/4**[2]
0531 2 1/2 **Royal Opera**[19] 5408 3-8-11 70 .... JamesMillman 5 72
(Rod Millman) *pressed wnr: chal over 2f out: sn nt qckn and dropped to 3rd: styd on again to take 2nd nr fin: safely hld* **5/2**[1]
1006 3 3/4 **Bold Marc (IRE)**[15] 5549 9-9-0 75 .... SeanLevey[(3)] 1 69
(Mrs K Burke) *trckd ldng pair: nt qckn whn sprint sed over 2f out: shkn up and styd on wl fnl f to take 3rd last strides* **7/1**
4 nk **Ashammar (FR)**[10] 6-9-3 0 .... (t) DaneO'Neill 7 69
(Paul Webber) *hld up in last pair: quick move arnd outer to ld narrowly 2f out: sn hdd: wl hld fnl f: fdd and lost 2 pls nr fin* **25/1**
5643 5 2 1/2 **Ajdaad (USA)**[24] 5036 4-9-1 65 .... MartinHarley[(3)] 6 65
(Alan McCabe) *s.s: hld up in last pair: nt qckn whn sprint sed over 2f out: one pce after* **12/1**
1130 6 3/4 **One Hit Wonder**[15] 5568 4-9-6 68 .... LiamKeniry 8 65
(Jonathan Portman) *hld up in 4th: nt qckn whn sprint sed over 2f out: one pce and no imp after* **3/1**[3]
005 7 9 **Mcconnell (USA)**[22] 5319 6-9-2 73 .... (b) GeorgeBaker 4 42
(Gary Moore) *hld up in 5th: snatched up 3f out: outpcd over 2f out: wknd* **14/1**

2m 9.38s (4.48) **Going Correction** +0.375s/f (Good)
WFA 3 from 4yo+ 7lb **7** Ran SP% **110.9**
Speed ratings (Par 101): **97,96,96,95,93 93,85**
Tote Swingers: 1&2 £1.40, 1&3 £5.20, 2&3 £9.10 CSF £9.42 TOTE £3.00: £1.40, £2.00; EX 7.10.
Owner Jim Horgan **Bred** Poulton Stud **Trained** East Everleigh, Wilts

FOCUS
A total of 6mm of rain fell overnight and there was a further 4mm on the day, but the going remained good to soft. There was a tailwind helping the runners up the straight. A decent little claimer, albeit the gallop was a slow one and the form looks muddling, with the runner-up to this year's form.
Royal Opera Official explanation: trainer said the gelding had cut his near fore leg

6018 LADBROKES.COM MAIDEN STKS (DIV I) 7f (S)
2:50 (2:52) (Class 5) 2-Y-0 £2,385 (£704; £352) Stalls High

Form RPR
00 1 **Holiday Reading (USA)**[32] 5013 2-9-3 0 .... MartinDwyer 6 77
(Brian Meehan) *ponied to post: pressed ldr and one off the rail: rdn over 2f out: narrow ld over 1f out: grad asserted ins fnl f* **11/4**[2]
2203 2 1 1/4 **Marcus Augustus (IRE)**[41] 4655 2-9-3 72 .... RichardHughes 10 74
(Richard Hannon) *led against nr side rail: rdn over 2f out: narrowly hdd over 1f out: pressed wnr tl no ex last 100yds* **5/2**[1]
6 3 1/2 **Asifa (IRE)**[15] 5565 2-9-3 0 .... PatCosgrave 11 73
(Saeed Bin Suroor) *s.s: sn chsd ldng trio: wnt 3rd 1/2-way: rdn and nt qckn over 2f out: styd on fnl f: clsng at fin* **11/4**[2]
6 4 2 3/4 **Jasie Jac (IRE)**[79] 3424 2-9-0 0 .... SeanLevey[(3)] 9 66+
(Robert Mills) *chsd ldrs: wnt 4th 1/2-way: outpcd by ldng trio over 2f out: shkn up and styd on* **7/1**[3]
00 5 6 **Roman Senate (IRE)**[13] 5613 2-9-3 0 .... GeorgeBaker 1 51
(Martin Bosley) *pressed ldng pair: lost pl and dropped to midfield by 1/2-way: n.d after: plugged on fnl f* **40/1**
6 hd **Emperors Waltz (IRE)** 2-8-12 0 .... LiamKeniry 5 45+
(Rae Guest) *wl in rr: outpcd fr 1/2-way: sme prog over 2f out: nvr on terms* **50/1**
00 7 1/2 **Silver Six**[11] 5672 2-9-0 0 .... MartinHarley[(3)] 12 49
(Mick Channon) *chsd ldrs: outpcd and rdn 3f out: nvr on terms after* **66/1**
06 8 5 **Le Cagnard**[14] 5579 2-9-3 0 .... DaneO'Neill 7 37
(Michael Bell) *chsd ldrs: outpcd and dropped to rr by 1/2-way: no ch after* **10/1**
9 1/2 **Astroscarlet** 2-8-12 0 .... JimmyQuinn 2 30
(Mark H Tompkins) *a in rr: outpcd fr 1/2-way* **100/1**

00 **10** *33* **Auntie Kathryn (IRE)**[57] 4155 2-8-12 0........................(t) WilliamCarson 4 —
(Stuart Williams) *dwlt: racd wd: a in last trio: bhd 3f out: t.o* **66/1**

1m 28.0s (0.70) **Going Correction** +0.125s/f (Good) **10** Ran SP% **111.9**
Speed ratings (Par 95): **101,99,99,95,89 88,88,82,81,44**
Tote Swingers: 1&2 £1.50, 1&3 £2.20, 2&3 £2.60 CSF £9.43 TOTE £2.50: £1.10, £1.80, £1.20; EX 10.70.
Owner Timeform Betfair Racing Club & Sangster Family **Bred** Shell Bloodstock **Trained** Manton, Wilts

FOCUS
Few got into the first division of what was an ordinary maiden. The time was 0.99 seconds quicker than division two and the runner-up sets a reasonable standard.

NOTEBOOK
Holiday Reading(USA), ponied to post having boiled over on the way to start previously, had run creditably in a considerably stronger maiden than this over 1m at Newmarket last time and, despite conceding the favoured rail to the runner-up, he still proved too strong. He's in the Group 1 Racing Post Trophy, but nurseries will presumably be the route he takes, and there should be more to come. (op 3-1 tchd 5-2)
Marcus Augustus(IRE) was given every possible chance to win by Hughes, grabbing the favoured rail, but he couldn't stay on as strongly and is now 0-5. (op 11-4 tchd 3-1)
Asifa(IRE) improved on last month's debut effort at Warwick, going on best at the finish, and can win a minor maiden upped to 1m on faster ground. (tchd 5-2 and 3-1)
Jasie Jac(IRE), a mildly promising sixth at Salisbury in June, will be of interest over 1m, especially once handicapping. (op 17-2)
Roman Senate(IRE) ought to do better now qualified for a mark. (op 28-1)
Le Cagnard is another who ought to do better now qualified for a mark. (op 9-1 tchd 8-1)

6019 LADBROKES.COM MAIDEN STKS (DIV II) 7f (S)
3:20 (3:22) (Class 5) 2-Y-O **£2,385** (£704; £352) **Stalls** High

Form RPR
2325 **1** **King Of Wing (IRE)**[13] 5632 2-9-3 73.......................... RichardHughes 4 73
(Richard Hannon) *pressed ldr: led over 2f out and grabbed rail: sn hrd pressed and rdn: gained upper hand fnl f* **3/1**[2]
0 **2** *1* **Alwaaqi**[18] 5447 2-9-3 0.. TadhgO'Shea 5 71
(John Dunlop) *prom towards outer: wnt 2nd over 2f out and sn chalng: upsides over 1f out: nt qckn fnl f* **20/1**
54 **3** *2 ¾* **Piers Gaveston (IRE)**[40] 4698 2-9-3 0.............................. DaneO'Neill 9 64
(George Baker) *prom: rdn sn after 1/2-way: kpt on to take 3rd over 1f out: nvr able to chal* **8/1**
4 **4** *nk* **Hey Fiddle Fiddle (IRE)**[22] 5323 2-8-12 0...................... MichaelHills 8 58+
(Charles Hills) *t.k.h: hld up in midfield against rail: outpcd and shkn up over 2f out: styd on over 1f out: no imp fnl f* **5/2**[1]
0 **5** *6* **Rogue Reporter (IRE)**[32] 5011 2-9-3 0......................... KierenFallon 1 50+
(Luca Cumani) *racd wd: chsd ldrs: rdn over 2f out: no imp over 1f out: wknd fnl f* **5/1**[3]
0 **6** *2 ¼* **Colonsay (USA)**[18] 5447 2-9-3 0.................................... AhmedAjtebi 6 42+
(Mahmood Al Zarooni) *racd wd: hld up towards rr: effrt 3f out: no prog and wl btn 2f out* **5/1**[3]
00 **7** *2 ¾* **Smart Affair**[7] 5807 2-8-12 0.. JamesMillman 2 30
(Rod Millman) *hld up in rr on outer: wl outpcd fr 1/2-way: kpt on fnl f* **100/1**
8 *1* **Titus Bolt (IRE)** 2-9-3 0.. PatCosgrave 3 33
(Jim Boyle) *dwlt: hld up in last: nvr on terms: no ch fnl 2f* **150/1**
00 **9** *½* **Doctor Dalek (IRE)**[26] 5211 2-9-3 0............................ EddieCreighton 11 32
(Edward Creighton) *racd against rail: led to over 2f out: wknd rapidly* **200/1**
10 *1 ¾* **Statementofintent (IRE)** 2-9-3 0.................................. MartinDwyer 12 27
(Brian Meehan) *rn green in rr: no prog 1/2-way: wl btn after* **14/1**
11 *6* **Knoydart (USA)** 2-9-3 0.. JimCrowley 10 12
(Amanda Perrett) *chsd ldng pair to 1/2-way: wknd rapidly* **16/1**
00 **12** *16* **Welease Bwian (IRE)**[62] 3984 2-9-3 0............................(t) SaleemGolam 7 —
(Stuart Williams) *stdd s: hld up towards rr: wknd over 2f out: t.o* **125/1**

1m 28.99s (1.69) **Going Correction** +0.125s/f (Good) **12** Ran SP% **118.3**
Speed ratings (Par 95): **95,93,90,90,83 80,77,76,76,74 67,48**
Tote Swingers: 1&2 £4.10, 1&3 £34.10, 2&3 £28.90 CSF £66.30 TOTE £4.80: £1.70, £7.40, £2.80; EX 53.80.
Owner Andrew Russell **Bred** Anthony Hanahoe **Trained** East Everleigh, Wilts

FOCUS
The front two had this between them from 2f out. The time was 0.99 seconds slower than division one and the winner is rated just above his pre-race mark.

NOTEBOOK
King Of Wing(IRE) stayed on too strongly for the less experienced runner-up. Up to 7f for the first time, it's taken him six attempts to get off the mark, but he seems genuine despite many by his sire not being that way, and should pay his way in nurseries. (op 5-2 tchd 9-4)
Alwaaqi, very inexperienced when beaten 14l on debut at Newmarket, had clearly learned a good deal and looked the likely winner when drawing alongside over 1f out, but was ultimately found wanting. He'll benefit from 1m and can win something similar. (op 16-1 tchd 22-1)
Piers Gaveston(IRE) wasn't necessarily helped by the drop to 7f, despite his pedigree, but still fared better than last time and is now qualified for a mark. (op 7-1 tchd 6-1)
Hey Fiddle Fiddle(IRE) proved one-paced under pressure, having appeared to have an ideal early sit. (op 11-4 tchd 3-1)
Rogue Reporter(IRE) wasn't best positioned and could never make a challenge. He'll be of more interest in handicaps next season. (op 8-1)
Colonsay(USA), just ahead of the runner-up on debut, was never involved and ought to do better next season over middle distances on faster ground. (op 8-1)
Titus Bolt(IRE) Official explanation: jockey said that the gelding ran green

6020 LADBROKES.COM ON YOUR MOBILE MAIDEN STKS 7f (S)
3:50 (3:52) (Class 5) 3-Y-O+ **£2,726** (£805; £402) **Stalls** High

Form RPR
0023 **1** **Semmsu (IRE)**[33] 4970 3-9-1 75.. KierenFallon 3 83
(Luca Cumani) *chsd ldng trio: pushed along 1/2-way: effrt to go 2nd 2f out: drvn to ld jst over 1f out: styd on wl to draw clr* **9/2**[3]
2 **2** *4 ½* **Upcountry**[18] 5449 3-9-1 0.. MichaelHills 2 70+
(Charles Hills) *pressed ldr at str pce: led after 2f: drvn and hdd jst over 1f out: sn btn* **10/11**[1]
2060 **3** *2 ¾* **General Synod**[13] 5635 3-9-1 78.......................................(b[1]) RichardHughes 6 63
(Richard Hannon) *rousted along and str reminder to ld against rail: hdd after 2f: chsd ldr to 2f out: sn btn* **9/4**[2]
4 *5* **Master Jack** 3-9-1 0.. MartinDwyer 7 50
(Bill Turner) *hld up and sn wl off the pce: nudged along 1/2-way: kpt on steadily to take 4th fnl f: nrst fin* **66/1**
3 **5** *1 ½* **Sleep Dance**[8] 5780 3-8-10 0.. WilliamCarson 8 40
(Eve Johnson Houghton) *chsd ldng pair in strly run r: wknd over 2f out* **12/1**
05 **6** *6* **Fleetwoodmaxi (USA)**[33] 4970 4-9-5 0.............................. FergusSweeney 4 29
(Peter Makin) *hld up: sn wl off the pce: nudged along 1/2-way: nvr a factor* **25/1**
7 *4 ½* **Mufasa Rules (USA)** 3-9-1 0...(t) LiamKeniry 5 17
(Sylvester Kirk) *hld up and sn wl off the pce: pushed along and no prog 3f out* **50/1**
0 **8** *9* **Kampai**[13] 5633 3-8-12 0 ow2.. DaneO'Neill 1 —
(John Akehurst) *a last: pushed along and struggling bef 1/2-way* **50/1**

1m 28.52s (1.22) **Going Correction** +0.125s/f (Good)
WFA 3 from 4yo 4lb **8** Ran SP% **118.3**
Speed ratings (Par 103): **98,92,89,84,82 75,70,60**
Tote Swingers: 1&2 £1.70, 1&3 £1.90, 2&3 £1.02 CSF £9.29 TOTE £8.20: £2.10, £1.02, £1.10; EX 8.80.
Owner Scuderia Rencati Srl **Bred** Hardys Of Kilkeel Ltd **Trained** Newmarket, Suffolk

FOCUS
A fair maiden run at a strong enough gallop, and that played into the hands of the winner. The form shouldn't be taken at face value as it is not easy to pin down.

6021 LADBROKESGAMES.COM NURSERY 6f
4:20 (4:21) (Class 5) (0-70,70) 2-Y-O **£2,726** (£805; £402) **Stalls** High

Form RPR
5104 **1** **Chandigarh (IRE)**[24] 5263 2-9-6 69.............................. FrankieMcDonald 4 76
(Paul Fitzsimons) *qckly away and grabbed nr side rail: disp ld: rdn to take def advantage over 1f out: styd on wl* **33/1**
0241 **2** *2 ½* **Karuga**[22] 5324 2-9-5 68.. RichardHughes 2 68
(Richard Hannon) *chsd ldng pair and racd away fr rail: rdn over 2f out: kpt on to take 2nd jst over 1f out: no imp on wnr* **3/1**[1]
565 **3** *1 ¾* **Galilee Chapel (IRE)**[83] 3273 2-9-0 63............................ DaneO'Neill 8 57
(David Elsworth) *chsd ldrs: shkn up and nt qckn 2f out: pushed along and styd on to take 3rd wl ins fnl f* **3/1**[1]
4416 **4** *¾* **Triggerlo**[10] 5701 2-8-6 62.. CharlesBishop[(7)] 1 54
(Mick Channon) *t.k.h: racd one off the rail: disp ld tl wknd over 1f out* **13/2**
0560 **5** *2 ½* **High Five Prince (IRE)**[13] 5625 2-7-12 47..................... JamieMackay 5 31
(Mark Usher) *racd wd: in tch: shkn up and outpcd 2f out: reminder and flashed tail over 1f out: no imp* **20/1**
0300 **6** *½* **Storm Fairy**[39] 4749 2-8-2 51..(p) WilliamCarson 7 34
(Mrs K Burke) *in tch: rdn and nt qckn over 2f out: nvr on terms after* **33/1**
000 **7** *4 ½* **Our Boy Billy**[62] 3984 2-8-2 51......................................(p) JimmyQuinn 10 20
(Robert Cowell) *a in rr: outpcd over 2f out: no ch after* **28/1**
043 **8** *½* **Gold Coin**[29] 5097 2-9-7 70.. MichaelHills 6 38
(J W Hills) *racd wd: a in last pair: wl off the pce 1/2-way: no prog after* **9/2**[2]
002 **9** *5* **Dine Out**[68] 3767 2-9-4 67.. KierenFallon 9 20
(Mark H Tompkins) *a towards rr: rdn and struggling bef 1/2-way: nvr a factor* **5/1**[3]
0406 **U** **Joli Colourful (IRE)**[15] 5535 2-7-9 49 oh2 ow2............ RyanPowell[(5)] 3 —
(Tony Newcombe) *stmbld: swvd and uns rdr sn after s* **66/1**

1m 15.1s (2.40) **Going Correction** +0.125s/f (Good) **10** Ran SP% **113.8**
Speed ratings (Par 95): **89,85,83,82,79 78,72,71,65,—**
Tote Swingers: 1&2 £9.90, 1&3 £5.70, 2&3 £2.90 CSF £123.03 CT £408.62 TOTE £59.20: £14.80, £1.20, £1.10; EX 153.00.
Owner Bal Sohal **Bred** Secret Justice Syndicate **Trained** Upper Lambourn, Berks

FOCUS
The stands' rail again played a huge part in the outcome of this nursery. The winner weas quite impressive and the runner-up sets the standard.

NOTEBOOK
Chandigarh(IRE) soon led against the rail and surged on close home for a first handicap win. The slower ground was clearly in her favour, but with the future in mind it's worth noting she was favoured by a bias here.
Karuga, up 4lb for winning at Windsor, ran well considering she couldn't get to the rail from stall two. There are still races to be won with her off this mark. (op 11-4 tchd 5-2)
Galilee Chapel(IRE), unplaced in three maidens for Howard Johnson, showed improved form on his debut for David Elsworth, going on best at the finish and shaping as though he'll be winning something minor once upped to 7f. (op 4-1)
Triggerlo, a 5f fast-ground maiden winner here last month, was soon disputing it one off the rail, but the combination of slower ground over this longer trip proved too much late on. (op 7-1 tchd 6-1)
High Five Prince(IRE) stood little chance racing wide. (tchd 22-1)
Gold Coin, who was dropping in trip and was entitled to run well, had little chance in racing out wide. He can be given another chance. (op 11-2)
Dine Out can be given another chance on faster ground, which is the preferred going of his sire's progeny. (op 9-2 tchd 11-2)

6022 BOURNE AMENITY H'CAP 6f
4:50 (4:50) (Class 5) (0-75,74) 3-Y-O+ **£2,726** (£805; £402) **Stalls** High

Form RPR
6626 **1** **Silenzio**[43] 4618 3-8-13 68.. RichardHughes 8 78+
(Richard Hannon) *dwlt: sn chsd ldrs against rail: gap appeared and rdn to ld jst over 1f out: drvn out* **10/11**[1]
0042 **2** *1 ¼* **Flameoftheforest (IRE)**[26] 5201 4-9-7 74....................(p) PatCosgrave 5 80
(Ed de Giles) *s.i.s: mostly last: pushed along 1/2-way: prog wl over 1f out: styd on u.p to take 2nd last strides* **9/2**[3]
-060 **3** *nk* **Spitfire**[20] 5371 6-9-5 72.. TonyCulhane 6 77
(J R Jenkins) *chsd ldr tl edgd rt wl over 1f out: chsd wnr fnl f: no imp: lost 2nd last strides* **18/1**
2552 **4** *2* **Links Drive Lady**[13] 5624 3-8-9 67...........................(b) LouisBeuzelin[(3)] 7 66
(Mark Rimmer) *led against rail to over 1f out: wknd fnl f* **12/1**
0402 **5** *¾* **Silver Wind**[21] 5345 6-9-3 73......................................(b) MartinHarley[(3)] 4 69
(Alan McCabe) *racd away fr rail: pressed ldrs: rdn sn after 1/2-way: lost pl and btn 2f out* **10/1**
4032 **6** *5* **Billion Dollar Kid**[16] 5511 6-9-3 70..............................(bt) KierenFallon 1 50
(Joanna Davis) *taken to r alone in centre: on terms whn jnd main gp after 2f: rdn and wknd over 2f out* **3/1**[2]
0243 **7** *½* **Hand Painted**[18] 5425 5-8-12 65....................................(p) LiamKeniry 2 44
(Anthony Middleton) *a in last pair: rdn and struggling over 2f out: wknd* **20/1**

1m 14.39s (1.69) **Going Correction** +0.125s/f (Good)
WFA 3 from 4yo+ 2lb **7** Ran SP% **122.4**
Speed ratings (Par 103): **93,91,90,88,87 80,79**
Tote Swingers: 1&2 £2.50, 1&3 £6.90, 2&3 £5.90 CSF £6.23 CT £48.30 TOTE £1.80: £1.10, £3.60; EX 8.30.
Owner White Beech Farm **Bred** Lady Whent **Trained** East Everleigh, Wilts

FOCUS
A modest and uncompetitive sprint handicap that went the way the market suggested it would. The runner-up sets the standard rated close to recent marks.

Billion Dollar Kid Official explanation: jockey said that the gelding hung left

6023 GARDENSCAPEDIRECT.CO.UK H'CAP — 1m 4f
5:20 (5:20) (Class 5) (0-75,74) 3-Y-O+ — **£2,726** (£805; £402) **Stalls** High

Form — RPR

11-1 **1** **Rhythm Stick**[239] 190 4-9-9 **71** .... JimCrowley 1 — 87+
(John Berry) *trckd ldng trio: lost pl over 3f out: gd prog on inner fr 2f out to ld over 1f out: drvn clr* — **11/1**

2404 **2** *3* **Wily Fox**[14] 5580 4-9-4 **66** .... MickyFenton 9 — 73
(James Eustace) *pushed up to ld: 3 l clr 1/2-way: drvn and jnd 2f out: hdd over 1f out: kpt on* — **10/1**

2005 **3** *nk* **Rowan Tiger**[15] 5545 5-9-12 **74** .... PatCosgrave 2 — 81
(Jim Boyle) *trckd ldrs in 5th: prog 3f out: drvn to chal 2f out: upsides over 1f out: nt qckn* — **18/1**

5062 **4** *1 1/2* **The Calling Curlew**[18] 5420 3-8-13 **70** .... DaneO'Neill 7 — 74
(Henry Candy) *prom: trckd ldr 5f out: rdn to chal over 2f out: upsides over 1f out: fdd* — **11/2**[3]

254/ **5** *3/4* **Gilded Age**[123] 6203 5-9-1 **70** ....(p) BrendanPowell(7) 5 — 73
(Chris Gordon) *chsd ldr to 5f out: lost pl and rdn 4f out: kpt on same pce after: unable to chal* — **33/1**

0521 **6** *3/4* **Flying Power**[21] 5340 3-9-2 **73** ....(p) RichardHughes 11 — 75
(David Lanigan) *hld up in last trio: looking for room 3f out: rdn and prog over 1f out: kpt on but nvr any ch* — **9/4**[1]

0266 **7** *2 1/2* **Hurakan (IRE)**[50] 4385 5-9-9 **71** ....(t) KierenFallon 8 — 69
(George Baker) *hld up in midfield: rdn to chse ldrs in 5th over 2f out: no imp over 1f out: fdd* — **11/1**

0015 **8** *4* **Shy**[25] 5236 6-9-3 **65** ....(b) JamesMillman 10 — 56
(Rod Millman) *hld up towards rr: reminder 1/2-way: effrt u.p on outer 3f out: wknd over 1f out* — **17/2**

P132 **9** *3 1/4* **Gems**[16] 5504 4-9-1 **68** .... LucyKBarry(5) 3 — 54
(Peter Hiatt) *hld up in midfield: nt clr run and lost pl on inner over 3f out: struggling after: wl btn fnl 2f* — **9/2**[2]

0045 **10** *8* **Cloudy Start**[21] 5340 5-9-11 **73** ....(p) FergusSweeney 4 — 46
(Jamie Osborne) *hld up last: shkn up and no prog 3f out* — **18/1**

0000 **11** *8* **Admirable Duque (IRE)**[67] 3817 5-9-5 **70** ....(p) BillyCray(3) 12 — 31
(Dominic Ffrench Davis) *settled in last trio: rdn on outer 4f out: sn btn and bhd* — **66/1**

2m 44.26s (3.36) **Going Correction** +0.375s/f (Good)
WFA 3 from 4yo+ 9lb — **11** Ran SP% **115.6**
Speed ratings (Par 103): **103,101,100,99,99 98,97,94,92,86 81**
Tote Swingers: 1&2 £9.10, 1&3 £20.20, 2&3 £17.10. Totesuper7: Win: Not won; Place: £118.40 CSF £114.17 CT £1958.36 TOTE £10.00: £3.50, £3.60, £6.40; EX 117.80.
Owner Red Furlongs Partnership **Bred** Mrs M L Parry & P M Steele-Mortimer **Trained** Newmarket, Suffolk

FOCUS
A fairly moderate middle-distance handicap with the placed horses setting the standard backed up by the fourth.
T/Plt: £5.60 to a £1 stake. Pool:£60,813.57 - 7,883.41 winning tickets T/Qpdt: £4.70 to a £1 stake. Pool:£4,163.07 - 652.65 winning tickets JN

5704 HAYDOCK (L-H)
Tuesday, September 13

OFFICIAL GOING: Good to soft (good in places; 7.0)
Wind: fresh 1/2 against Weather: fine but very breezy, shower after race 2

6024 KING'S REGIMENT CUP H'CAP — 1m 3f 200y
2:30 (2:30) (Class 4) (0-85,82) 3-Y-O+ — **£5,822** (£1,732; £865; £432) **Stalls** Centre

Form — RPR

6012 **1** **Snow Hill**[36] 4862 3-8-10 **75** .... JackMitchell 5 — 86+
(Chris Wall) *hld up in rr: hdwy on outer over 3f out: led and hung bdly lft 1f out: drvn out* — **3/1**[1]

1332 **2** *1/2* **Persian Peril**[10] 5729 7-9-12 **82** .... PJMcDonald 3 — 90
(Alan Swinbank) *hld up in mid [illegible] ldrs 2f out: chsd wnr 1f out: hmpd and swtchd rt 100yds out: r.o* — **9/2**[3]

1311 **3** *1* **Judicious**[48] 4432 4-9-9 **79** .... RobertWinston 6 — 85
(Geoffrey Harker) *hld up in rr: hdwy 3f out: swtchd rt 1f out: r.o to take 3rd last 100yds* — **10/1**

0255 **4** *1 1/4* **Trip The Light**[17] 5482 6-9-9 **82** ....(v) LeeTopliss(3) 1 — 86
(Richard Fahey) *led early: trckd ldrs: drvn on ins over 2f out: led briefly over 1f out: one pce* — **6/1**

6635 **5** *1/2* **Lunar Phase (IRE)**[25] 5235 3-8-5 **73** .... JohnFahy(3) 10 — 77
(Clive Cox) *trcked ldrs: t.k.h: chal over 2f out: one pce fnl f* — **8/1**

0414 **6** *1 1/2* **Red Fama**[10] 5729 7-9-8 **78** .... BarryMcHugh 4 — 79
(Neville Bycroft) *dwlt: hld up in rr: effrt over 2f out: one pce* — **8/1**

4F60 **7** *1* **Embsay Crag**[44] 4577 5-9-1 **76** .... ShaneBKelly(5) 8 — 76
(Kate Walton) *sn trcking ldrs: t.k.h: hdwy over 3f out: drvn 2f out: fdd appr fnl f* — **28/1**

60-1 **8** *10* **Alsahil (USA)**[9] 5761 5-8-8 **69** .... JamesRogers(5) 9 — 53
(Micky Hammond) *hdwy to ld after 100yds: t.k.h: hdd over 1f out: sn wknd: eased towards fin* — **4/1**[2]

2m 32.98s (-1.02) **Going Correction** -0.10s/f (Good)
WFA 3 from 4yo+ 9lb — **8** Ran SP% **112.2**
Speed ratings (Par 105): **99,98,98,97,96 95,95,88**
Tote Swingers: 1&2 £3.20, 1&3 £5.10, 2&3 £4.40 CSF £15.91 CT £115.68 TOTE £3.60: £1.80, £1.80, £2.80; EX 13.40.
Owner Mollers Racing **Bred** Old Mill Stud **Trained** Newmarket, Suffolk
■ Stewards' Enquiry : Jack Mitchell two-day ban: careless riding (27-28 Sep)

FOCUS
A fair handicap run at a reasonable gallop, although the time was nearly 4secs outside the standard. The form looks sound enough rated around the second and fourth.
Alsahil(USA) Official explanation: jockey said that the gelding ran too free

6025 IRISH STALLION FARMS E B F SMOOTH RADIO MAIDEN STKS — 6f
3:00 (3:00) (Class 5) 2-Y-O — **£3,234** (£962; £481; £240) **Stalls** Centre

Form — RPR

0 **1** **Point Made (IRE)**[17] 5480 2-9-3 0 .... RichardMullen 6 — 75
(Ed McMahon) *chsd ldrs: wnt 2nd over 1f out: kpt on to ld nr fin* — **16/1**

6 **2** *1/2* **Jay Bee Blue**[17] 5486 2-9-3 0 .... RichardKingscote 1 — 74
(Tom Dascombe) *dwlt: hdwy to chse ldrs on outer 2f out: kpt on fnl f: no ex nr fin* — **11/4**[2]

3 *hd* **Anton Chigurh** 2-9-3 0 .... StephenCraine 7 — 73+
(Tom Dascombe) *dwlt: hdwy on ins over 2f out: led wl over 1f out: hdd and no ex towards fin* — **9/1**[3]

65 **4** *8* **Trending (IRE)**[19] 5411 2-9-3 0 .... EddieAhern 10 — 49
(Jeremy Gask) *mid-div: swtchd rt over 1f out: nvr nr ldrs* — **20/1**

0 **5** *3* **Lord Franklin**[24] 5269 2-9-3 0 .... DavidAllan 2 — 40
(Eric Alston) *chsd ldrs: wknd fnl 2f* — **33/1**

05 **6** *3/4* **Talya's Storm**[19] 5410 2-8-10 0 .... RaulDaSilva(7) 8 — 38
(Jeremy Gask) *dwlt: in rr: sme hdwy whn hmpd and swtchd rt over 1f out: nvr nr ldrs* — **14/1**

7 *15* **Confused Sphere (IRE)** 2-9-3 0 .... BarryMcHugh 5 — —
(Noel Wilson) *sn outpcd and in rr: bhd fnl 2f* — **50/1**

8 *6* **Valiant Blue (IRE)** 2-9-3 0 .... JamesDoyle 4 — —
(Nicky Vaughan) *chsd ldrs: lost pl over 1f out* — **20/1**

6U **9** *nk* **Blue Tiger**[29] 5104 2-9-3 0 ....(v[1]) RoystonFfrench 11 — —
(Saeed Bin Suroor) *led: t.k.h and sn clr: wknd rapidly and hdd wl over 1f out: sn bhd* — **1/1**[1]

10 *18* **Red All Over (IRE)** 2-8-7 0 .... JulieBurke(5) 9 — —
(Alan Berry) *dwlt: sn wl outpcd and bhd: t.o after 2f* — **50/1**

1m 17.69s (3.89) **Going Correction** +0.50s/f (Yiel) — **10** Ran SP% **115.6**
Speed ratings (Par 95): **94,93,93,82,78 77,57,49,49,25**
Tote Swingers: 1&2 £7.40, 1&3 £7.30, 2&3 £3.30 CSF £56.57 TOTE £20.80: £3.30, £1.30, £2.30; EX 88.20.
Owner J C Fretwell **Bred** J Costello **Trained** Lichfield, Staffs

FOCUS
Not much previous form to go on in this maiden and they went 14-1 bar three. It was hard work for these juveniles into the headwind, experience told in the end, and the time was 6.69secs slower than standard. The form is difficult to rate with the first two both stepping up on moderate debut promise.

NOTEBOOK
Point Made(IRE), who was easy in the market, had finished last on his debut but that experience stood him on good stead, as he was able to rally well under pressure to run down the debutant near the line. This form is difficult to assess but there was nothing wrong with his attitude. (op 12-1)
Jay Bee Blue built on the promise of his debut, having raced on the outside of his field before staying on well near the finish. He can step up on this next time. (op 3-1 tchd 5-2)
Anton Chigurh ◆, a 38,000gns yearling who is related to several winners at 6f-7f, is probably the one to take out of the race. He was held up early, but cruised up to take the lead only to lose out due to inexperience racing into the headwind well inside the last furlong. He was well clear of the remainder and should be more street-wise next time. (op 10-1)
Trending(IRE) had shown only moderate ability in two previous starts but did better here, although beaten some way by the leading trio. He now qualifies for handicaps and can find a race at a low level.
Blue Tiger had shown signs of temperament on his previous start and the first-time visor lit him up so much that he bolted off in front. However, he was racing into a headwind and stopped to nothing around 2f from home, so much so that horses nearly ran into the back of him. He looks one to avoid after this and seems unlikely to remain in his current yard for long. Royston Ffrench reported that the colt was unsuited by the first-time visor. Official explanation: jockey said that the colt was unsuited by the first-time visors (op 11-10, tchd 6-5 in places)

6026 E B F "MIND GAMES" REAL RADIO MAIDEN STKS — 5f
3:30 (3:31) (Class 5) 2-Y-O — **£3,234** (£962; £481; £240) **Stalls** Centre

Form — RPR

0043 **1** **Idols Eye**[7] 5814 2-8-12 70 .... PatDobbs 5 — 65+
(Richard Hannon) *trckd ldrs: effrt over 1f out: styd on to ld fnl strides: all out* — **15/8**[1]

2 *shd* **Sheer Vanity (USA)** 2-8-12 0 ....(t) RichardMullen 6 — 65+
(Ed McMahon) *s.i.s: sn trcking ldrs: t.k.h: swtchd lft ins fnl f: kpt on: jst failed* — **3/1**[2]

4 **3** *nk* **Annie Beach (IRE)**[12] 5646 2-8-12 0 .... GrahamGibbons 3 — 64+
(David Barron) *led: shkn up over 1f out: hdd and no ex nr fin* — **3/1**[2]

0 **4** *1/2* **Love Island**[11] 5681 2-8-12 0 .... MichaelStainton 4 — 62
(Richard Whitaker) *w ldr: rdn over 1f out: kpt on same pce last 100yds* — **5/1**[3]

5030 **5** *6* **Never In (IRE)**[8] 5786 2-8-7 51 .... DanielleMcCreery(5) 2 — 40
(Alan Berry) *hld up: effrt 2f out: wknd over 1f out* — **66/1**

6 *20* **Pavers Star** 2-9-3 0 .... PaulQuinn 1 — —
(Noel Wilson) *dwlt and wnt lft s: sn chsng ldrs: lost pl over 2f out: sn bhd* — **16/1**

63.04 secs (3.04) **Going Correction** +0.50s/f (Yiel) — **6** Ran SP% **108.8**
Speed ratings (Par 95): **95,94,94,93,83 51**
Tote Swingers: 1&2 £8.00, 1&3 £3.40, 2&3 £8.80 CSF £7.23 TOTE £2.30: £1.30, £1.20; EX 7.40.
Owner D Farrington, D Cox, R St J Brophy **Bred** Mrs Maria Ferguson **Trained** East Everleigh, Wilts

FOCUS
A fair maiden but hard to be positive with the first four finishing in a heap.

NOTEBOOK
Idols Eye set a modest standard in this maiden, having been running reasonably in similar races at 7f and a mile on Polytrack, and this was therefore a big drop in trip. She tracked the pace but struggled to go with the two leaders when they quickened over 2f out, then her stamina came into play as that pair faltered racing into the headwind and she got up virtually on the post. A return to further should be in her favour. (op 9-4 tchd 7-4 and 5-2 in a place)
Sheer Vanity(USA) ◆, who was backed just before the off, made a very encouraging debut, being slowly away and then racing keenly under restraint. She was left with a fair bit to do when the leaders quickened, but ran on really well under pressure and just lost out. Her turn should not be long delayed. (op 7-2 tchd 11-4)
Annie Beach(IRE) made a bold bid from the front, and was unlucky to be collared virtually on the line, having raced into the teeth of the gale for most of the way. This is her trip and compensation surely awaits. (op 9-4 tchd 10-3)
Love Island improved considerably on her debut, having raced with the leader virtually throughout and was not beaten far. (op 6-1)

6027 E B F "MULTIPLEX" GEORGE FORMBY SOCIETY GOLDEN JUBILEE CONDITIONS STKS — 7f
4:00 (4:00) (Class 3) 3-Y-O+ — **£6,663** (£1,982; £990; £495) **Stalls** Low

Form — RPR

3113 **1** **Firebeam**[38] 4779 3-8-11 **99** .... EddieAhern 3 — 109+
(William Haggas) *led: shkn up and qcknd over 1f out: drvn out: unchal* — **11/10**[1]

0-23 **2** *2* **Al Aasifh (IRE)**[15] 5563 3-8-8 **101** ....(p) RichardMullen 1 — 101
(Saeed Bin Suroor) *trckd ldrs: wnt 2nd over 1f out: kpt on same pce: no imp* — **6/1**

2400 **3** *hd* **Field Of Dream**[33] 4972 4-8-12 **103** .... J-PGuillambert 4 — 102+
(Luca Cumani) *sn drvn along in rr: hdwy over 2f out: styd on to take 3rd 100yds out: kpt on towards fin* — **4/1**[2]

2000 **4** *1* **Cape To Rio (IRE)**[45] 4534 3-8-8 **97** .... PatDobbs 2 — 98
(Richard Hannon) *hld up in rr: hdwy on ins over 2f out: kpt on same pce over 1f out* — **11/1**

5350 **5** *1* **Toolain (IRE)**[73] 3645 3-8-8 103..........................(p) JackMitchell 7 95
(Roger Varian) *drvn along early to chse ldrs: wnt 2nd 3f out: rdn and hubng lft 2f out: one pce* **5/1**[3]

0004 **6** *4* **Rodrigo De Torres**[15] 5563 4-8-12 92.................. RobertWinston 6 86
(Mrs K Burke) *sn trcking ldrs: effrt over 2f out: wknd fnl f* **20/1**

7 *2* **Fugnina**[79] 3-8-6 94 ow2.......................... AntiocoMurgia(5) 8 82
(Marco Botti) *sn trcking ldrs: effrt over 3f out: wknd 2f out* **40/1**

0 **8** *17* **Nially Noo**[13] 5633 3-8-8 0.......................... BarryMcHugh 5 33
(Derek Shaw) *hld up in rr: lost pl 2f out: sn bhd: t.o* **200/1**

1m 28.51s (-2.39) **Going Correction** -0.10s/f (Good)
WFA 3 from 4yo 4lb **8** Ran SP% **114.6**
Speed ratings (Par 107): **109,106,106,105,104 99,97,77**
Tote Swingers: 1&2 £2.20, 1&3 £2.40, 2&3 £3.30 CSF £8.25 TOTE £2.20: £1.10, £1.60, £2.20; EX 7.90.
Owner Highclere Thoroughbred Racing-Blue Peter **Bred** Dukes Stud & Overbury Stallions Ltd **Trained** Newmarket, Suffolk
■ Stewards' Enquiry : Antioco Murgia two-day ban: weighed in 2lb more than when he weighed out (27-28 Sep)

FOCUS
A good standard in this competitive conditions stakes with three of the field rated in the 100s, although several had something to prove. The form is rated around the runner-up and fourth to this year's form.

NOTEBOOK
Firebeam has been progressive in a relatively short career. The step back up to 7f here suited him and he made all the running. He kicked for home at the quarter-mile pole and, despite swishing his tail under pressure, held on well. He looks ready for the step up into Listed company now. (op 6-5 tchd 5-4)
Al Aasifh(IRE), with the cheekpieces back on, was keen early but tracked the winner throughout and went in pursuit of that rival 2f out. He could make no impression, but ran up to his form. (op 13-2 tchd 7-1)
Field Of Dream was held up at the back but was being ridden soon after turning for home. He responded though and stayed on well, despite not getting the clearest of runs, and would have been second in another few strides. The drop in class from Group level probably helped him rediscover his form. (op 11-2 tchd 6-1)
Cape To Rio(IRE), another who had been below his best this summer, put up a better effort on this step up in trip without totally proving he stays. (op 10-1)
Toolain(IRE) had been gelded since his previous appearance, but had to be ridden to race prominently. He had every chance in the straight, but faded and now has something to prove, although easy ground might not suit him as well as fast does. (op 4-1)

6028 BETDAQ THE BETTING EXCHANGE HAYDOCK PARK APPRENTICE TRAINING SERIES H'CAP 1m 2f 95y
4:30 (4:30) (Class 5) (0-75,75) 4-Y-0+ **£2,587** (£770; £384; £192) **Stalls** Centre

Form RPR

0342 **1** **Brouhaha**[14] 5580 7-9-7 75.......................... HarryBentley 3 87
(Tom Dascombe) *hld up in mid-div: smooth hdwy 4f out: led on bit appr fnl 2f: r.o wl: comf: eased towards fin* **5/1**[2]

4450 **2** *3 ¾* **Mill Mick**[20] 5376 4-8-12 66.......................... ShaneBKelly 8 70
(John Mackie) *hld up in rr: hdwy over 3f out: chsd wnr appr fnl f: no imp* **7/1**

0323 **3** *1 ¾* **Jupiter Fidius**[14] 5594 4-8-8 62..........................(p) JulieBurke 5 63
(Kate Walton) *trckd ldrs: drvn and lost pl over 6f out: rallied over 2f out: wnt 3rd appr fnl f: kpt on same pce* **7/1**

3000 **4** *1 ½* **King Zeal (IRE)**[15] 5568 7-9-4 72..........................(t) JamesRogers 9 70
(Barry Leavy) *chsd ldr: led wl over 2f out: sn hdd: one pce appr fnl f* **7/2**[1]

1630 **5** *nse* **Mighty Clarets (IRE)**[29] 5106 4-9-4 72.......................... LeeTopliss 2 69
(Richard Fahey) *trckd ldrs: effrt on inner 3f out: one pce* **7/1**

0001 **6** *hd* **Black Coffee**[17] 5485 6-8-13 67..........................(b) RyanClark 7 64
(Mark Brisbourne) *s.i.s: hdwy over 3f out: one pce fnl 2f* **10/1**

-006 **7** *1 ¾* **Gritstone**[34] 4901 4-9-0 73.......................... GeorgeChaloner(5) 6 67
(Richard Fahey) *chsd ldrs: wknd fnl f* **11/2**[3]

4300 **8** *4 ½* **Sirgarfieldsobers (IRE)**[14] 5608 5-9-6 74.......................... NeilFarley 4 59
(Declan Carroll) *s.i.s: effrt over 3f out: lost pl 2f out* **9/1**

0060 **9** *16* **Idealism**[60] 4077 4-8-7 61 oh11.......................... LMcNiff 1 14
(Micky Hammond) *led: hdd wl over 2f out: wknd 2f out* **66/1**

2m 13.96s (-2.04) **Going Correction** -0.10s/f (Good) **9** Ran SP% **112.4**
Speed ratings (Par 103): **104,101,99,98,98 96,96,93,80**
Tote Swingers: 1&2 £8.00, 1&3 £3.40, 2&3 £8.80 CSF £38.38 CT £241.94 TOTE £5.30: £1.90, £4.00, £3.10; EX 30.00.
Owner Grant Thornton Racing Club **Bred** Mrs Rosamund Furlong **Trained** Malpas, Cheshire

FOCUS
A tightly knit apprentice handicap but the time was respectable in the conditions. The placed horses set the level.

6029 HAPPYFEETUK.COM H'CAP (FOR GENTLEMAN AMATEUR RIDERS) 1m 3f 200y
5:00 (5:00) (Class 5) (0-70,66) 4-Y-0+ **£2,183** (£677; £338; £169) **Stalls** Centre

Form RPR

2210 **1** **Dancing Primo**[35] 4887 5-11-7 66.......................... MrPCollington 6 77
(Mark Brisbourne) *mid-div: hdwy to chse ldrs over 3f out: wnt 2nd last 100yds: hrd rdn to ld nr fin* **7/1**[3]

5201 **2** *½* **Aegean Destiny**[8] 5791 4-11-1 60 6ex.......................... MrSWalker 13 70
(John Mackie) *trckd ldrs: led over 1f out: hung lft ins fnl f: hdd towards fin* **5/1**[1]

1134 **3** *1 ¼* **Transfer**[14] 5588 6-11-2 64.......................... MrMPrice(3) 4 72
(Richard Price) *hld up towards rr: hdwy over 3f out: wnt 3rd last 75yds: kpt on same pce* **15/2**

4231 **4** *1 ¾* **Waahej**[17] 5491 5-11-2 66.......................... MrFMitchell(5) 3 71
(Peter Hiatt) *chsd ldrs: upsides over 6f out: one pcer appr fnl f* **13/2**[2]

36/3 **5** *½* **Elk Trail (IRE)**[22] 5312 6-10-5 57.......................... MrMAllan(7) 7 61
(Michael Mullineaux) *led: qcknd over 3f out: hdd over 1f out: one pce* **25/1**

5252 **6** *1* **Amir Pasha (UAE)**[10] 5723 6-11-3 65..........................(p) MrJHamer(3) 8 68
(Micky Hammond) *chsd ldrs: wnt 2nd over 3f out: chal over 2f out: one pce appr fnl f* **7/1**[3]

0421 **7** *3 ¼* **Maybeme**[16] 5504 5-10-10 60.......................... MrSebSpencer(5) 5 58
(Neville Bycroft) *s.i.s: hld up: hdwy over 2f out: kpt on: nvr rchd ldrs* **10/1**

3003 **8** *1 ¾* **Belle Boleyn**[14] 5588 4-10-4 54.......................... MrFrazerWilliams(5) 11 49
(Chris Wall) *s.i.s: sme hdwy over 3f out: one pce fnl 2f* **10/1**

2032 **9** *6* **Mustajed**[14] 5588 10-10-11 61..........................(b) MrPMillman(5) 2 46
(Rod Millman) *mid-div: drvn 3f out: hung lft and sn lost pl* **14/1**

6502 **10** *hd* **Drawn Gold**[15] 5566 7-11-1 63.......................... MrStephenHarrison(3) 1 48
(Reg Hollinshead) *trckd ldrs: drvn 4f out: lost pl over 2f out* **8/1**

0000 **11** *11* **Swords**[10] 5739 9-10-2 52 oh7.......................... MrJohnWilley(5) 10 19
(Ray Peacock) *hld up in rr: hdwy to chse ldrs after 2f: edgd rt and wknd over 2f out: sn bhd* **100/1**

0-25 **12** *3 ½* **Prickles**[235] 252 6-10-4 52 oh3.......................... JamesBest(3) 9 14
(Derek Shaw) *hld up in rr: bhd whn hmpd over 2f out* **20/1**

3554 **13** *2* **Grethel (IRE)**[15] 4605 7-10-0 52 oh4.......................... MrMGrossett(7) 12 10
(Alan Berry) *in rr: effrt over 3f out: hung lft and sn lost pl: bhd fnl 2f* **28/1**

2m 34.6s (0.60) **Going Correction** -0.10s/f (Good) **13** Ran SP% **115.8**
Speed ratings (Par 103): **94,93,92,91,91 90,88,87,83,83 75,73,72**
Tote Swingers: 1&2 £4.60, 1&3 £7.80, 2&3 £8.20 CSF £38.88 CT £271.98 TOTE £9.10: £2.70, £2.20, £2.20; EX 19.90.
Owner L R Owen **Bred** L R Owen **Trained** Great Ness, Shropshire
■ Stewards' Enquiry : Mr John Willey two-day ban: careless riding (28-29 Sep)

FOCUS
Plenty of runners in this modest amateurs' handicap and a good finish between two near the head of the market. The time was 1.62secs slower than the opening race but the form looks reasonably sound with the third and fourth to recent marks.
T/Plt: £25.70 to a £1 stake. Pool:£58,207.14 - 1,647.72 winning tickets T/Qpdt: £7.50 to a £1 stake. Pool:£3,864.24 - 378.80 winning tickets WG

5514 YARMOUTH (L-H)
Tuesday, September 13

OFFICIAL GOING: Good to firm changing to good (good to soft in places) after race 2 (2.40)
Wind: strong, half against Weather: showers

6030 BRITISH STALLION STUDS SUPPORTING BRITISH RACING EBF MAIDEN FILLIES' STKS 6f 3y
2:10 (2:12) (Class 5) 2-Y-O **£3,687** (£1,097; £548; £274) **Stalls** Centre

Form RPR

1 **Ultrasonic (USA)** 2-9-0 0.......................... TomQueally 9 80+
(Sir Michael Stoute) *hld up in tch and travelled wl: hdwy to trck ldrs over 2f out: chal over 1f out: shkn up and qcknd to ld ins fnl f: rdn wl ins fnl f: pressed and kpt on towards fin* **7/2**[1]

2 *hd* **Shaleek** 2-9-0 0.......................... TedDurcan 3 79+
(Roger Varian) *s.i.s: bhd: hdwy over 2f out: chsd ldng trio ent fnl f: r.o wl under hands and heels riding to chse wnr fnl 75yds: pressing wnr cl home but a jst hld* **15/2**

3 **3** *2 ½* **Persidha**[19] 5410 2-9-0 0.......................... DavidProbert 5 69
(Gay Kelleway) *led for 1f: chsd ldr after: ev ch and rdn over 1f out: styd on same pce and btn fnl 100yds* **25/1**

0 **4** *½* **Fareedha (IRE)**[17] 5480 2-9-0 0.......................... RichardHills 14 67
(John Dunlop) *w ldr tl led after 1f: rdn over 1f out: hdd ins fnl f: nt pce of wnr and styd on same pce after* **6/1**[3]

5 *½* **Jellicle (IRE)** 2-9-0 0.......................... WilliamBuick 7 68+
(John Gosden) *s.i.s: bhd: pushed along 1/2-way: hdwy over 1f out: styng on and swtchd lft ins fnl f: gng on fin but nvr trbld ldrs* **6/1**[3]

6 **6** *1 ½* **Pretty Pebble (IRE)**[23] 5299 2-9-0 0.......................... ShaneKelly 11 61
(Brian Meehan) *in tch in midfield: rdn and outpcd wl over 1f out: no threat to ldrs but kpt on ins fnl f* **8/1**

7 *½* **Graser (IRE)** 2-9-0 0.......................... AdamKirby 2 60+
(Marco Botti) *s.i.s: bhd and rn green in rr: pushed along and hdwy over 1f out: styd on ins fnl f: nvr trbld ldrs* **40/1**

24 **8** *¾* **Alhira**[11] 5691 2-9-0 0.......................... MartinLane 6 58
(David Simcock) *in tch: drvn and unable qck over 1f out: sn outpcd and btn: wl hld and plugged on same pce fnl f* **9/2**[2]

9 *nk* **Jamhara** 2-9-0 0.......................... RussellPrice 4 57
(Clive Brittain) *rn green: hld up in tch: rdn and unable qck wl over 1f out: sn outpcd and btn ent fnl f: wl hld and styd on same pce after* **20/1**

10 *3* **Crazy Too (IRE)** 2-9-0 0.......................... JamieSpencer 8 48
(David Simcock) *s.i.s: bhd: pushed along and sme hdwy over 1f out: nvr trbld ldrs* **9/1**

0 **11** *4* **Artful Lady (IRE)**[22] 5323 2-9-0 0.......................... PhilipRobinson 10 36
(George Margarson) *in tch towards rr: pushed along and struggling whn unbalanced over 2f out: wknd 2f out* **100/1**

00 **12** *1 ¼* **Willow Beauty**[16] 5514 2-9-0 0.......................... AdrianMcCarthy 12 32
(J R Jenkins) *chsd ldrs tl rdn and wknd qckly wl over 1f out: fdd fnl f* **100/1**

13 *13* **Peters Pleasure** 2-9-0 0.......................... SteveDrowne 16 —
(Robert Cowell) *chsd ldrs: reminders 1/2-way: sn lost pl: wl bhd and eased ins fnl f* **125/1**

14 *7* **Skyblue** 2-9-0 0.......................... RobertHavlin 1 —
(Tobias B P Coles) *dwlt and reminders early: sn rcvrd and chsd ldrs: rdn and wknd qckly ent fnl 2f: wl bhd and eased ins fnl f: t.o* **125/1**

1m 14.43s (0.03) **Going Correction** -0.25s/f (Firm) **14** Ran SP% **116.5**
Speed ratings (Par 92): **89,88,85,84,84 82,81,80,80,76 70,69,51,42**
Tote Swingers: 1&2 £6.80, 1&3 £12.00, 2&3 £18.20 CSF £27.84 TOTE £4.80: £1.70, £3.20, £3.80; EX 36.60 Trifecta £302.40 Part won. Pool: £408.74 - 0.53 winning units..
Owner K Abdulla **Bred** Juddmonte Farms Inc **Trained** Newmarket, Suffolk

FOCUS
There was a strong westerly cross-wind that was half against slightly hindering runners, rather than assisting. The track was watered in the morning with 3mm being applied to the straight. This was followed by a short, sharp shower that fell just before and during the first. The jockeys reported that the ground was riding on the slow side of good. Given the conditions, the time, which was just over three seconds slower than standard, was respectable for the two-year-olds in the opener, several of whom were unraced and the first two should go on to better things.

NOTEBOOK
Ultrasonic(USA) ◆, a half-sister to a 1m2f winner, won in taking style. She was given a clever ride away from the worst of the slanting rain and travelled smoothly under hands and heals. Just shaken up by Tom Queally, she breezed to the front and left the impression that she had plenty left in the tank, despite only winning by a head. The Oh So Sharp Stakes, a race Sir Michael Stoute has won in each of the past two years, may well come too soon for her, but she left the impression that she is a filly destined for bigger things and 7f will be well within her compass. (op 3-1)
Shaleek ◆, a half-sister to a 6f winner from a family that produced some smart types, put up a very promising debut display. There were signs of inexperience early in the race as she broke slowly, but at the business end she quickened up without being knocked about, passing rivals with ease. A maiden looks hers for the taking next time, given the improvement one would expect from a first outing. (op 17-2)
Persidha, in the frame on her debut but well beaten, ran a very creditable race here given that she was on the front end for much of this, giving way only when challenged by two exciting prospects. She should win a maiden and progress further.
Fareedha(IRE), who probably ran a little better than the bare form of her debut at Newmarket where she was hampered at the start, was well supported. She led after a furlong and didn't wilt after being headed late on. This was a step in the right direction and she is another who is likely to take the beating next time. (op 8-1 tchd 17-2)

Jellicle(IRE) ◆ is a half-sister to a Grade 1 winner at 9f. The dam also scored in Grade company at the trip. This filly ran as if she will appreciate going further in time. Not given an unduly hard time, she showed a lovely flowing stride in the closing stages and it would be no surprise if she made rapid improvement from this run. She was green in the paddock beforehand and will know much more next time. (op 11-2 tchd 5-1)
Pretty Pebble(IRE) wasn't able to quicken up with the leading duo, but stayed on nicely enough late on. She will probably appreciate going back up to 7f. (op 12-1)
Graser(IRE), the first foal of an unraced mare, was slowly into stride but shaped well enough once the penny dropped. (op 50-1)
Alhira has not progressed since her encouraging second on debut at Newmarket. She was a well beaten favourite over 7f in a novices' race and was dropped back in trip here, but was one of the first off the bridle. She also unshipped jockey Martin Lane behind the stalls and there are one or two questions to answer after this. (op 7-2 tchd 3-1)
Peters Pleasure Official explanation: jockey said that the filly hung left

6031 MOULTON NURSERIES NURSERY (FOR THE JACK LEADER CHALLENGE TROPHY) 1m 3y

2:40 (2:42) (Class 4) (0-85,85) 2-Y-O **£3,428** (£1,020; £509; £254) **Stalls** Centre

Form RPR
2431 **1** **Pickled Pelican (IRE)**[15] 5565 2-9-2 **83**............... AdamBeschizza(3) 10 94+
(William Haggas) *mde all and racd alone against stands' rail: clr and rdn 2f out: wl clr over 1f out: pushed out* **4/1**[2]
012 **2** *7* **Clare Island Boy (IRE)**[40] 4717 2-9-3 **84**.................... KieranO'Neill(3) 7 79+
(Richard Hannon) *racd in centre: hld up in tch in rr: rdn over 3f out: hdwy u.p but no ch w wnr over 1f out: edgd lft 1f out: wnt modest 2nd ins fnl f* **12/1**
2213 **3** *3/4* **Mizbah**[18] 5446 2-8-12 **76**.. JamieSpencer 4 69
(Saeed Bin Suroor) *stdd s: racd in centre: hld up in tch in rr: hdwy to chse ldrs over 3f out: rdn to chse clr wnr over 1f out: plugged on same pce u.p and wl hld fnl f* **11/4**[1]
416 **4** *nk* **Shamaal Nibras (USA)**[39] 4760 2-9-7 **85**........................ TomQueally 2 78
(Ed Dunlop) *racd in centre: hld up in tch in last trio: hdwy 3f out: rdn and pressing for placings but no ch w wnr over 1f out: kpt on same pce ins fnl f* **16/1**
6004 **5** *1* **Manomine**[13] 5634 2-8-3 **67** ow2.. ChrisCatlin 1 57
(Clive Brittain) *racd in centre: chsd ldrs: rdn over 3f out: pressing for placings but no ch w wnr over 1f out: plugged on same pce fnl f* **11/1**
4360 **6** *1/2* **Tudor Empire (IRE)**[18] 5446 2-8-7 **71**............................ RobertHavlin 5 60
(John Gosden) *racd in centre: in tch: rdn and over 2f out: no ch w wnr and plugged on same pce u.p fr over 1f out* **16/1**
213 **7** *1 1/4* **Croquembouche (IRE)**[24] 5280 2-8-13 **77**.................. JimmyFortune 8 63
(Sir Michael Stoute) *racd in centre: chsd wnr: drvn and no imp ent fnl 2f: wl btn over 1f out: wknd ins fnl f* **4/1**[2]
3160 **8** *17* **Comical**[24] 5287 2-9-1 **79**.. AdamKirby 9 26
(Mark Johnston) *racd in centre: chsd ldrs tl rdn 3f out: sn struggling: wknd 2f: wl bhd and eased ins fnl f: t.o* **12/1**
054 **9** *1 1/4* **Ex Oriente (IRE)**[34] 4919 2-8-10 **74**...........................(b[1]) WilliamBuick 3 18
(John Gosden) *racd in centre: rdn 1/2-way: drvn and dropped out over 3f out: lost tch 2f out: t.o ins fnl f* **10/1**[3]

1m 39.15s (-1.45) **Going Correction** -0.25s/f (Firm) **9** Ran SP% **111.2**
Speed ratings (Par 97): **97,90,89,88,87 87,86,69,67**
Tote Swingers: 1&2 £6.10, 1&3 £3.50, 2&3 £3.00 CSF £47.90 CT £148.03 TOTE £5.60: £2.00, £2.80, £1.70; EX 35.40 Trifecta £222.00 Pool: £348.11 - 1.16 winning units..
Owner D I Scott & L K Piggott **Bred** T Hirschfeld **Trained** Newmarket, Suffolk

FOCUS
The time was slower than standard by only 1.95seconds. The winner probably enjoyed a track advantage and is rated 3l lower than a strict reading of the result.

NOTEBOOK
Pickled Pelican(IRE) benefited from a shrewd decision by rider Adam Beschizza to race alone on the stands' rail. This had looked a tight nursery on paper, but the William Haggas-trained improver turned it into a procession, leading every step of the way. The victory margin suggests that Beschizza had identified the best strip of ground and, indeed, the going was changed to good, good to soft in places, after this race. Given that the ground probably played a key part in the winning distance, the form needs careful assessment. Even so, there was plenty to like about the willing way the gelding went about his job as he built on a 7f success in what appears to be a strong-looking Warwick maiden. He gets 1m well and as long as the handicapper doesn't take the victory margin literally, should have further good days ahead of him. (tchd 7-2)
Clare Island Boy(IRE) fared beat of the rest. He stayed on well after travelling towards the rear, appreciating the give in the ground more than several of the others did. (tchd 10-1)
Mizbah was third in a 1m nursery at Newmarket last time and again ran another satisfactory race, but was never in a position to deliver a meaningful blow. (op 10-3 tchd 4-1)
Shamaal Nibras(USA) was disappointing on his previous start when beaten favourite at Newmarket just over a month ago. This was more encouraging, although he may need some respite from the handicapper. (op 12-1)
Manomine ran his best race to date when fourth in a Kempton nursery at this trip 13 days earlier and once again ran respectably enough. (op 17-2 tchd 13-2)
Croquembouche(IRE) had form with cut in the ground, but didn't pick up here. This was the first time he'd finished outside the first three and he should be given another chance. (tchd 7-2)
Comical has not progressed since making a winning start to his career over 7f at Yarmouth. (op 14-1)
Ex Oriente(IRE) Official explanation: jockey said that the colt hung right

6032 NICHOLSONS OF STALHAM JCB DEALERS H'CAP (DIV I) 1m 3y

3:10 (3:11) (Class 6) (0-60,60) 3-Y-O+ **£1,704** (£503; £251) **Stalls** Centre

Form RPR
0-52 **1** **Larkrise Star**[16] 5515 4-9-9 **59**... ShaneKelly 10 69+
(Dean Ivory) *hld up in tch: hdwy 2f out: pushed along to ld ins fnl f: edgd rt but sn in command: pushed out: comf* **4/1**[2]
6534 **2** *2* **Jodawes (USA)**[22] 5318 4-9-10 **60**.................................. SteveDrowne 9 65
(John Best) *w ldr tl led after 2f: rdn 2f out: edgd lft u.p over 1f out: hdd ins fnl f: nt pce of wnr and sn btn* **7/1**
0450 **3** *1/2* **Warden Bond**[16] 5515 3-8-5 **46** oh1.............................(p) CathyGannon 8 50
(William Stone) *in tch: effrt u.p over 1f out: kpt on u.p ins fnl f: nt pce to threaten wnr* **16/1**
-052 **4** *2 1/4* **Makyaal (IRE)**[11] 5673 3-8-12 **53**................................... RichardHills 1 52+
(John Dunlop) *chsd ldrs: effrt 2f out: pressing ldr and drvn over 1f out: unable qck ent fnl f: wknd fnl 100yds* **2/1**[1]
6604 **5** *1/2* **Yakama (IRE)**[41] 4681 6-8-11 **47**..............................(p) SebSanders 12 45
(Christine Dunnett) *stdd s: hld up in tch in rr: effrt and nt clr run over 1f out: rdn and no real imp fnl f* **20/1**
060 **6** *1 1/2* **Arkaim**[96] 2848 3-9-0 **55**.. JimmyFortune 6 49
(Ed Walker) *led for 2f: styd upsides ldr: rdn and fnd little 2f out: wknd u.p over 1f out* **9/2**[3]
6510 **7** *1 1/2* **Zaheeb**[16] 5515 3-9-1 **59**..(p) AdamBeschizza(3) 3 50
(Dave Morris) *w ldrs: rdn and lost pl jst over 2f out: plugged on same pce and wl hld over 1f out* **14/1**

55 **8** *1* **Nuba (IRE)**[36] 4861 3-9-2 **57**.. AdamKirby 4 46
(Luke Dace) *dwlt: sn pushed along and in tch in midfield: rdn and struggling over 2f out: wknd over 1f out* **9/1**
-005 **9** *3 1/2* **Hilltop Artistry**[34] 4928 5-8-10 **46** oh1..........................(v[1]) ChrisCatlin 11 27
(J R Jenkins) *in tch: rdn and struggling over 2f out: drvn and wknd wl over 1f out* **33/1**
0000 **10** *22* **Lady Valtas**[12] 5643 3-8-5 **46** oh1.. MartinLane 13 —
(Robert Eddery) *rrd as stalls opened and v.s.a: rdn thrght and a last: lost tch 3f out: t.o* **80/1**

1m 41.45s (0.85) **Going Correction** -0.10s/f (Good)
WFA 3 from 4yo+ 5lb **10** Ran SP% **115.5**
Speed ratings (Par 101): **91,89,88,86,85 84,82,81,78,56**
Tote Swingers: 1&2 £4.30, 1&3 £11.90, 2&3 £18.50 CSF £31.22 CT £403.42 TOTE £4.70: £1.20, £2.50, £4.10; EX 25.00 TRIFECTA Not won..
Owner Radlett Racing **Bred** D K Ivory **Trained** Radlett, Herts

FOCUS
This was more than two seconds slower than the preceding nursery and, while the overall form rates as modest. The placed horses set the level.

6033 NICHOLSONS OF STALHAM JCB DEALERS H'CAP (DIV II) 1m 3y

3:40 (3:42) (Class 6) (0-60,60) 3-Y-O+ **£1,704** (£503; £251) **Stalls** Centre

Form RPR
0036 **1** **Desert Chieftain**[27] 5178 3-8-12 **53**.............................(b) KirstyMilczarek 6 66+
(Luca Cumani) *chsd ldng trio: effrt to ld over 2f out: rdn and drew wl clr over 1f out: pushed out ins fnl f* **9/2**[2]
0000 **2** *1 3/4* **Croeso Mawr**[21] 5349 5-8-10 **46**.................................... SteveDrowne 11 55
(John Spearing) *taken down early: in tch towards rr: swtchd lft and hdwy ent fnl f: chsd clr wnr over 1f out: kpt on ins fnl f but nvr able to chal* **16/1**
3605 **3** *10* **Makheelah**[40] 4696 3-9-5 **60**...................................(p) PhilipRobinson 10 46
(Clive Brittain) *in tch in midfield: pushed along 1/2-way: rdn and outpcd over 2f out: wl btn over 1f out: plugged on ins fnl f to go modest 3rd towards fin* **17/2**
4302 **4** *1/2* **Prince Of Passion (CAN)**[20] 5381 3-9-4 **59**............ RobbieFitzpatrick 3 44
(Derek Shaw) *hld up in tch in last trio: hdwy whn edgd rt and barging match w rival over 2f out: sn outpcd: 4th and wl btn over 1f out* **8/1**
4413 **4** *dht* **Ippi N Tombi (IRE)**[3] 5943 3-8-9 **50**................................... ChrisCatlin 7 35
(Phil McEntee) *led for 2f: chsd ldr tl led again over 3f out: hdd over 2f out: sn rdn and outpcd by wnr: wl btn and lost 2nd over 1f out* **3/1**[1]
300 **6** *3 1/4* **Come And Go (UAE)**[27] 5178 5-9-3 **53**..................... PatrickMathers 12 30
(Ian McInnes) *hld up in tch in last trio: rdn and effrt over 2f out: no prog and btn 2f out: sn wknd* **8/1**
000 **7** *1 1/4* **Carpentras**[18] 5449 3-9-0 **55**.. RobertHavlin 4 30
(Dr Jon Scargill) *hld up in tch: nt clr run and hmpd over 2f out: rdn and wknd 2f out: sn wl btn* **40/1**
S340 **8** *10* **Aviso (GER)**[32] 5002 7-9-7 **60**..................................... RichardEvans(3) 2 12
(David Evans) *taken down early: grad crossed towards stands' rail: chsd ldrs tl led after 2f: hdd over 3f out: wkng u.p whn hmpd over 2f out: wl bhd fnl 2f* **5/1**[3]
060 **9** *4* **Ability Girl**[21] 5352 3-8-7 **48**... TedDurcan 5 —
(Chris Wall) *s.i.s: in tch in rr: rdn and struggling 3f out: wknd over 2f out: t.o* **16/1**
5-00 **10** *5* **Alioonagh (USA)**[40] 4730 4-9-8 **58**............................... JimmyFortune 8 —
(Peter Chapple-Hyam) *w ldrs tl wl over 2f out: sn struggling and dropped out: wl bhd and eased ins fnl f: t.o* **12/1**

1m 40.78s (0.18) **Going Correction** -0.10s/f (Good)
WFA 3 from 4yo+ 5lb **10** Ran SP% **114.5**
Speed ratings (Par 101): **95,93,83,82,82 79,78,68,64,59**
Tote Swingers: 1&2 £18.60, 1&3 £7.50, 2&3 £43.60 CSF £72.13 CT £588.76 TOTE £5.00: £1.60, £7.30, £3.70; EX 120.80 Trifecta £282.20 Part won. Pool: £381.42 - 0.20 winning units..
Owner Lady Juliet Tadgell **Bred** Lady Juliet Tadgell **Trained** Newmarket, Suffolk

FOCUS
The time was 0.67 seconds quicker than the first division, but was still more than a second-and-a-half slower than the nursery. The form is tricky to pin down but the time compared with the nursery helps set the level.
Aviso(GER) Official explanation: jockey said that the gelding was unsuited by the good, good to soft in places, ground

6034 THOMAS PRIOR MEMORIAL MAIDEN STKS 6f 3y

4:10 (4:13) (Class 5) 3-Y-O+ **£2,264** (£673; £336; £168) **Stalls** Centre

Form RPR
43 **1** **Ziraun**[15] 5567 3-8-12 0.. PhilipRobinson 4 64
(Clive Brittain) *t.k.h: chsd ldrs: hdwy to join ldrs gng wl 2f out: led over 1f out: r.o wl u.p ins fnl f: edgd rt fnl 75yds* **2/1**[2]
42-4 **2** *1/2* **Question Times**[115] 2281 3-8-12 96.............................. JimmyFortune 3 62
(Peter Chapple-Hyam) *taken down early: hld up in midfield: hdwy 2f out: chsd ldrs and rdn 1f out: nt clr run: swtchd lft and forced way out ins fnl f: rdn and pressed wnr fnl 50yds: no imp towards fin* **5/6**[1]
5-6 **3** *1* **Decimate**[21] 5346 3-9-0 0.. KieranO'Neill(3) 6 64
(Andrew Reid) *w ldrs: rdn to ld 2f out: hdd over 1f out: styd on same pce ins fnl f* **25/1**
4434 **4** *nk* **Tiberius Claudius (IRE)**[40] 4695 3-9-3 73....................... TomQueally 1 63
(George Margarson) *s.i.s: hld up in last pair: hdwy over 2f out: rdn to chse ldrs over 1f out: pressing ldrs but unable qck whn pushed lft fnl 100yds: one pce after* **11/2**[3]
0- **5** *12* **Itum**[364] 6060 4-9-5 0.. SebSanders 5 25
(Christine Dunnett) *led tl 2f out: sn rdn: wknd jst over 1f out: fdd fnl f* **66/1**
0066 **6** *11* **Mrs Medley**[42] 4650 5-9-0 30... ShaneKelly 2 —
(Garry Woodward) *t.k.h: chsd ldr tl jst over 2f out: sn wknd: wl btn and eased wl ins fnl f* **250/1**
0 **7** *18* **Suffolini**[13] 5626 3-8-9 0... AdamBeschizza(3) 7 —
(William Stone) *s.i.s: a in rr: rdn and lost tch 1/2-way: t.o fnl 2f* **100/1**

1m 14.56s (0.16) **Going Correction** -0.10s/f (Good)
WFA 3 from 4yo+ 2lb **7** Ran SP% **110.0**
Speed ratings (Par 103): **94,93,92,91,75 60,36**
Tote Swingers: 1&2 £1.10, 1&3 £4.00, 2&3 £2.90 CSF £3.68 TOTE £2.90: £1.60, £1.10; EX 4.50.
Owner Saeed Manana **Bred** Miss A Shaykhutdinova **Trained** Newmarket, Suffolk

FOCUS
The race lacked depth and the finish was fought out by the two market leaders with the time 3.26 seconds slower than standard. the form is rated negatively with the proximity of the third raising doubts.

6035 AT THE RACES CONDITIONS STKS 6f 3y
4:40 (4:40) (Class 3) 3-Y-O+ **£6,490** (£1,942; £971; £486; £242) **Stalls** Centre

Form RPR
3003 **1** **Royal Rock**[17] 5481 7-8-9 100 TedDurcan 2 96+
(Chris Wall) *chsd ldng trio: clsd to chse ldrs 2f out: rdn to ld jst over 1f out: r.o wl and in command fnl 100yds: pushed out* **9/4**[2]
4502 **2** 1 ½ **Bathwick Bear (IRE)**[7] 5805 3-8-7 93 CathyGannon 7 91+
(David Evans) *chsd ldrs: rdn ent fnl 2f: chsd wnr ins fnl f: kpt on but no imp fnl 100yds* **25/1**
0505 **3** ½ **Imperial Guest**[38] 4802 5-8-9 97 PhilipRobinson 4 89+
(George Margarson) *hld up in last pair: hdwy and chsd ldrs over 1f out: swtchd lft 1f out: drvn and styd on same pce fnl 100yds* **9/2**[3]
0-52 **4** 1 **Gramercy (IRE)**[10] 5699 4-8-9 101 JamieSpencer 3 86+
(Michael Bell) *stdd s: hld up in last: clsd and swtchd lft jst over 2f out: rdn to chse ldrs over 1f out: drvn and no ex ins fnl f: wknd fnl 100yds* **5/4**[1]
6330 **5** 6 **Masaya**[67] 3822 3-8-3 96 ow1 ChrisCatlin 1 63
(Clive Brittain) *chsd ldr tl led over 2f out: drvn and hdd jst over 1f out: wknd qckly fnl 150yds* **7/1**
2253 **6** 1 ¼ **Steel City Boy (IRE)**[15] 5561 8-8-6 57 KieranO'Neill(3) 5 63
(Garry Woodward) *led and sn clr: hdd and rdn over 2f out: wknd over 1f out* **200/1**

1m 12.45s (-1.95) **Going Correction** -0.10s/f (Good)
WFA 3 from 4yo+ 2lb **6 Ran SP% 110.2**
Speed ratings (Par 107): **109,107,106,105,97 95**
Tote Swingers: 1&2 £4.90, 1&3 £2.10, 2&3 £4.50 CSF £45.09 TOTE £3.90: £2.10, £7.10; EX 35.30.
Owner Ms Aida Fustoq **Bred** Deerfield Farm **Trained** Newmarket, Suffolk

FOCUS
A decent but muddlin conditions race with the sixth limiting the form.

NOTEBOOK
Royal Rock won this a shade comfortably in a time that was almost two seconds quicker than the opening juvenile fillies' maiden. The time was 1.15 seconds slower than standard, reflecting the underfoot ease triggered by the early-afternoon shower. It was a first victory in almost two years for the 7-y-o gelding, but prior to this he showed he was back on song when third in Listed company at Newmarket 17 days ago. He stalked Masaya and then took over at the front, grabbing the favoured stands' rail. Once there, he never looked like giving up pole position and triumphed with some authority. He is now likely to head back into Group company with the Bengough Stakes at Ascot his possible target. (tchd 15-8)
Bathwick Bear(IRE) had showed his wellbeing when second at Leicester over 5f a week earlier and underlined it with another fine effort over a furlong further. (tchd 28-1)
Imperial Guest has been running respectably in good handicaps without winning over the summer. He again ran to his form, but is probably a difficult horse to place now, rated 97 as he is. (tchd 7-2)
Gramercy(IRE)'s run was something of a disappointment. After two really good displays during a light campaign, he didn't find sufficient to ever suggest that he'd threaten Royal Rock. The pair ran off level weights here, with only 1lb splitting them on official figures, but Gramercy was soundly beaten and probably didn't run to his best. (op 6-4 tchd 7-4, 15-8 in places)
Masaya, back in class and trip after finding the Group 1 Falmouth Stakes beyond her, is best treated with caution for the time being. (op 6-1 tchd 8-1 in places)
Steel City Boy(IRE) ensured this was a proper test by jumping swiftly and leading them along early on. (op 150-1)

6036 IDEAL FLOORING AND LA CONTINENTAL CAFE H'CAP 5f 43y
5:10 (5:10) (Class 4) (0-85,85) 3-Y-O+ **£4,075** (£1,212; £606; £303) **Stalls** Centre

Form RPR
346 **1** **Secret Millionaire (IRE)**[10] 5706 4-9-1 82 KieranO'Neill(3) 7 93
(Patrick Morris) *sn pressing ldr: led over 3f out: edgd lft but rdn clr wl over 1f out: in command and pushed out ins fnl f* **11/2**
4003 **2** 1 ¾ **Soap Wars**[24] 5262 6-9-7 85 SebSanders 6 90
(Hugo Palmer) *hld up off the pce in last trio: rdn and effrt ent fnl 2f: chsd clr wnr 1f out: r.o wl but nvr able to chal wnr* **5/1**
5624 **3** 5 **Bronze Beau**[11] 5679 4-9-7 85 (t) JamesSullivan 3 72
(Linda Stubbs) *led tl over 3f out: rdn and outpcd by wnr wl over 1f out: lost 2nd jst and wknd jst ins fnl f* **9/1**
2431 **4** ½ **Midnight Rider (IRE)**[40] 4731 3-8-11 76 (p) TedDurcan 2 61+
(Chris Wall) *racd off the pce in last pair: clsd over 2f out: swtchd rt and rdn over 1f out: kpt on same pce and no ch w wnr ins fnl f* **9/2**[3]
2363 **5** nk **Lujeanie**[6] 5831 5-9-4 82 (p) PhilipRobinson 4 66
(Dean Ivory) *s.i.s: sn rdn along and outpcd in rr: sme hdwy and swtchd lft jst ins fnl f: styd on fnl 100yds: nvr trbld ldrs* **7/2**[1]
434 **6** 2 **Ryan Style (IRE)**[10] 5703 5-9-2 80 AdamKirby 1 57
(Lisa Williamson) *dwlt: sn chsng ldrs: rdn and outpcd jst over 2f out: wknd over 1f out* **4/1**[2]
1042 **7** ½ **Clear Ice (IRE)**[14] 5578 4-8-12 76 (b) DavidProbert 8 51
(Gay Kelleway) *chsd ldng pair: rdn 1/2-way: unable qckn and struggling 2f out: wknd over 1f out* **8/1**

62.49 secs (-0.21) **Going Correction** +0.10s/f (Good)
WFA 3 from 4yo+ 1lb **7 Ran SP% 113.6**
Speed ratings (Par 105): **105,102,94,93,92 89,88**
Tote Swingers: 1&2 £5.80, 1&3 £10.10, 2&3 £7.90 CSF £32.25 CT £241.80 TOTE £5.70: £2.70, £3.50; EX 43.40 TRIFECTA Not won..
Owner Secret Millionaire Syndicate **Bred** James Delaney **Trained** Tarporley, Cheshire

FOCUS
A decent handicap that was run at a true pace and the time was slow by 1.79 seconds in comparison with the standard. The runner-up is rated to her latest mark and the form is taken at face value.
Lujeanie Official explanation: jockey saidn the gelding was unsuited by the good, good to soft in places, ground
Ryan Style(IRE) Official explanation: jockey said that the gelding stopped quickly

6037 AVENUE PUB BEATTY ROAD H'CAP 1m 3f 101y
5:40 (5:41) (Class 5) (0-70,69) 3-Y-O+ **£2,264** (£673; £336; £168) **Stalls** Low

Form RPR
0-45 **1** **Armoise**[18] 5449 3-9-1 66 (t) AdamKirby 2 81+
(Marco Botti) *chsd ldr tl 6f out: cl up whn short of room and bdly hmpd 3f out: rallied to chse ldrs 2f out: rdn and qcknd to ld over 1f out: clr and r.o strly fnl f: eased towards fin* **9/4**[1]
/242 **2** 3 ¼ **Flame Of Hestia (IRE)**[21] 5357 5-9-12 69 JamieSpencer 1 76
(James Fanshawe) *in tch in midfield: hdwy to chse ldrs 3f out: rdn and pressed ldrs over 2f out: chsd wnr over 1f out: sn outpcd and styd on same pce fnl f* **9/4**[1]
4033 **3** 3 ¼ **Hygrove Welshlady (IRE)**[23] 5302 3-8-10 61 SebSanders 9 62
(J W Hills) *t.k.h: hld up in tch in last quartet: hdwy on outer to join ldrs and lft in ld 3f out: rdn and edgd lft over 2f out: hdd over 1f out: wknd fnl f* **12/1**
6400 **4** 1 ½ **Agapanthus (GER)**[21] 5340 6-9-1 58 (p) TomQueally 6 57
(Barney Curley) *hld up in last trio: swtchd rt 3f out: rdn and no prigress 2f out: wnt modest 4th 1f out: nvr trbld ldrs* **22/1**
-440 **5** 3 ¼ **Divinite Green (IRE)**[102] 2677 3-9-4 69 JimmyFortune 11 62
(Peter Chapple-Hyam) *chsd ldrs tl wnt 2nd 6f out: lft w ev ch and sltly hmpd 3f out: wknd over 1f out: fdd fnl f* **16/1**
000 **6** 2 **Suzi's A Class Act**[12] 5641 3-9-2 67 ChrisCatlin 10 57
(James Eustace) *stdd s: t.k.h: hld up in last trio: rdn and short-lived effrt over 2f out: wknd 2f out* **8/1**[3]
00-0 **7** 5 **Mater Mater**[16] 5519 4-8-9 55 oh10 (p) KieranO'Neill(3) 3 37
(Andrew Reid) *in tch in midfield: hdwy to chse ldrs 4f out: sn rdn and struggling: wknd over 2f out* **100/1**
0001 **P** **Epic (IRE)**[14] 5609 4-9-12 69 WilliamBuick 8 —
(Mark Johnston) *led tl rdn: lost action and eased 3f out: p.u and dismntd* **7/1**[2]
5614 **P** **Little Jazz**[33] 4966 3-9-4 69 CathyGannon 5 —
(Paul D'Arcy) *hld up in tch in last quartet: hdwy on far rail whn bdly hmpd and lost any ch 3f out: p.u over 2f out* **10/1**

2m 30.9s (2.20) **Going Correction** +0.10s/f (Good)
WFA 3 from 4yo+ 8lb **9 Ran SP% 113.2**
Speed ratings (Par 103): **96,93,91,90,87 86,82,—,—**
Tote Swingers: 1&2 £2.10, 1&3 £6.90, 2&3 £3.30 CSF £6.56 CT £45.60 TOTE £3.10: £1.10, £1.40, £3.70; EX 8.80 Trifecta £79.20 Pool: £923.95 - 8.63 winning units..
Owner Scuderia Vittadini Srl **Bred** Grundy Bloodstock Srl **Trained** Newmarket, Suffolk

FOCUS
This was only run at a steady gallop and the time was almost six seconds slower than standard. The form is a bit muddling with the third close to previous C&D form.
Little Jazz Official explanation: jockey said that the filly suffered interference in running
T/Jkpt: £12,172.90 to a £1 stake. Pool:£60,007.38 - 3.50 winning tickets T/Plt: £357.70 to a £1 stake. Pool:£72,661.36 - 148.25 winning tickets T/Qpdt: £66.30 to a £1 stake. Pool:£4,617.72 - 51.50 winning tickets SP

6038 - 6041a (Foreign Racing) - See Raceform Interactive

4422 MAISONS-LAFFITTE (R-H)
Tuesday, September 13

OFFICIAL GOING: Turf: soft

6042a PRIX D'ARENBERG (GROUP 3) (2YO) (TURF) 5f 110y
1:50 (12:00) 2-Y-O **£34,482** (£13,793; £10,344; £6,896; £3,448)

RPR
1 **Restiadargent (FR)**[45] 4569 2-8-8 0 MaximeGuyon 5 101+
(H-A Pantall, France) *racd in 4th on outside: rdn and chal 1 1/2f out: qcknd wl to assert 100yds out: r.o wl: comf* **9/1**
2 ¾ **Kendam (FR)**[11] 2-8-8 0 FabriceVeron 8 98
(H-A Pantall, France) *followed eventual wnr fr s: outpcd 1 1/2f out: rallied u.p to fin wl fnl 100yds* **23/1**
3 snk **Calahorra (FR)**[27] 5194 2-8-8 0 GeraldMosse 9 98
(C Baillet, France) *in rr fr s: suddenly swtchd to wd outside over 2f out: qcknd wl 1 1/2f out: ev ch and r.o wl fnl f: nrest at fin* **15/2**[3]
4 1 ½ **Luv U Forever**[24] 5270 2-8-8 0 DominiqueBoeuf 7 93
(Jo Hughes) *racd in 2nd on outside of ldr: shkn up 2 1/2f out: chal for ld 1 1/2f out: hdd and nt qckn fnl 110yds* **15/1**
5 ¾ **Dont Teutch (FR)**[23] 5305 2-8-8 0 Christophe-PatriceLemaire 2 91
(D Smaga, France) *racd in 3rd on rail bhd ldr: rdn 2f out: nt qckn tl swtchd away fr rail: r.o fnl f but no threat to ldrs* **19/5**[2]
6 nk **Hi Molly (FR)**[44] 4596 2-8-11 0 ThierryJarnet 4 93
(D Guillemin, France) *racd towards rr: rdn over 2f out: nt qckn: no imp fnl f* **13/1**
7 ½ **Eden's Drift**[46] 2-8-11 0 ChristopheSoumillon 1 93
(M Delzangles, France) *sn led: set ordinary pce: rdn 2f out: hdd and nt qckn 1 1/2f out: sn fdd: eased clsng stages* **6/4**[1]
8 ½ **Louve Rouge (FR)**[37] 2-8-8 0 JohanVictoire 6 86
(C Boutin, France) *a towards rr: rdn but no rspnse 2f out: no imp* **17/2**
9 ¾ **Pyman's Theory (IRE)**[49] 4413 2-8-8 0 StephanePasquier 3 84
(Tom Dascombe) *settled in midfield: rdn over 2f out: no rspnse: fdd to rr of field fnl f* **19/1**

66.20 secs (-1.10) **9 Ran SP% 115.7**
WIN (incl. 1 euro stake): 7.30 (Restiadargent coupled with Kendam). PLACES: 3.30, 6.70, 3.00. DF: 39.20. SF: 82.20.
Owner Guy Pariente **Bred** G Pariente **Trained** France

5502 BEVERLEY (R-H)
Wednesday, September 14

OFFICIAL GOING: Good to firm (7.9)
Wind: Strong, against Weather: Overcast, sunny periods

6043 BEVERLEY ANNUAL BADGEHOLDERS (S) NURSERY 5f
2:00 (2:01) (Class 6) (0-65,63) 2-Y-O **£1,704** (£503; £251) **Stalls** Low

Form RPR
5502 **1** **Look Here's Lady**[16] 5555 2-8-11 53 GrahamGibbons 3 57
(Ed McMahon) *trckd ldr on inner: swtchd lft 2f out and sn cl up: rdn to ld appr fnl f: kpt on wl* **3/1**[1]
5050 **2** ¾ **No More Games**[7] 5817 2-9-0 56 (p) PhillipMakin 13 57
(Kevin Ryan) *in rr and rdn along after 1f: swtchd lft 1/2-way: hdwy on wd outside wl over 1f out: sn rdn and styd on wl fnl f: nrst fin* **20/1**
604 **3** 1 **Lady Hello (IRE)**[20] 5418 2-8-8 50 TonyCulhane 7 47
(Mick Channon) *t.k.h: hld up towards rr: hdwy and n.m.r over 2f out: effrt and nt clr run wl over 1f out: sn swtchd lft and rdn: styd on ins fnl f: nrst fin* **16/1**
006 **4** ¾ **Headstight (IRE)**[117] 2248 2-8-10 52 BarryMcHugh 12 47
(Paul Midgley) *in tch: hdwy on inner whn nt clr run over 1f out: sn swtchd lft and rdn: kpt on ins fnl f: nrst fin* **12/1**
5405 **5** shd **Valley Of Hope**[19] 5438 2-9-7 63 PaulHanagan 9 57
(Richard Fahey) *towards rr: swtchd lft and hdwy on outer 2f out: rdn to chse ldrs and hung rt ent fnl f: sn drvn and one pce* **9/2**[2]

The Form Book, Raceform Ltd, Compton, RG20 6NL

6665 **6** *1 1/4* **Uncle Timmy**[16] 5555 2-8-7 **54**..................(p) ShaneBKelly(5) 17 48
(John Quinn) *towards rr: hdwy whn hmpd and stmbld bdly 2f out: sn swtchd lft and rdn: styd on wl fnl f: nrst fin* **22/1**

3226 **7** *1 1/4* **Justine Time (IRE)**[20] 5399 2-9-3 **59**..................(b) LeeNewman 2 44
(David Barron) *chsd ldrs: rdn and edgd rt wl over 1f out: sn drvn and wknd fnl f* **7/1**[3]

4000 **8** *2* **Indyend**[13] 5646 2-8-10 **52**..................(b[1]) DuranFentiman 1 30
(Tim Easterby) *in rr and rdn along 1/2-way: swtchd rt to inner wl over 1f out: kpt on u.p: nrst fin* **25/1**

6640 **9** *1 1/2* **Lord Ali McJones**[23] 5324 2-9-4 **60**..................(p) RichardKingscote 4 33
(Tom Dascombe) *led: rdn along 2f out: drvn and hdd appr fnl f: wknd* **16/1**

0064 **10** *6* **Maria Medecis (IRE)**[26] 5245 2-8-9 **51**..................(v) RoystonFfrench 8 —
(Ann Duffield) *chsd ldrs: rdn along bef 1/2-way: sn wknd* **10/1**

0041 **11** *1 3/4* **Elusive Bonus (IRE)**[15] 5590 2-9-1 **57**.................. DanielTudhope 15 —
(David O'Meara) *towards rr: hdwy on wd outside 1/2-way: in tch and rdn wl over 1f out: sn wknd* **8/1**

5005 **12** *1/2* **Sabusa (IRE)**[8] 5802 2-9-2 **58**..................(p) RobertWinston 10 —
(Alan McCabe) *chsd ldrs: prom 1/2-way: sn rdn and wknd wl over 1f out* **16/1**

540 **13** *3 3/4* **Just Dixie**[26] 5245 2-8-2 **49** ow2..................(p) JulieBurke(5) 11 —
(John Weymes) *a in rr* **50/1**

4230 **14** *2 3/4* **Masivo Man (IRE)**[23] 5316 2-8-8 **50**.................. AndrewElliott 5 —
(Chris Dwyer) *chsd ldrs: rdn along 1/2-way: sn wknd* **25/1**

5260 **15** *nk* **Oneniteinheaven (IRE)**[20] 5399 2-9-4 **60**..................(tp) DavidNolan 6 —
(Ann Duffield) *chsd ldrs: rdn along 1/2-way: sn wknd* **16/1**

65.87 secs (2.37) **Going Correction** +0.20s/f (Good) **15** Ran SP% **125.9**
Speed ratings (Par 93): **89,87,86,85,84 82,80,77,75,65 62,62,56,51,51**
toteswingers: 1&2 £24.50, 1&3 £10.30, 2&3 £60.90 CSF £74.21 CT £888.37 TOTE £4.00: £1.80, £10.30, £5.60; EX 118.40.The winner was bought in for £7,000.
Owner S L Edwards **Bred** S L Edwards **Trained** Lichfield, Staffs
■ Stewards' Enquiry : Tony Culhane one-day ban: careless riding (Sep 28)

FOCUS
A modest race.

NOTEBOOK
Look Here's Lady won a shade cosily and looks capable of defying a higher mark. She was always travelling well towards the far side and, while she was being closed down at the line, she was never going to be caught. An easier 5f will probably suit her even better. She was bought in for £7,000.
No More Games, who ran no sort of race in soft ground at Carlisle last time when wearing blinkers for the first time, had cheekpieces on here. Slowly away and not travelling early, he really got going once switched to the outer inside the last furlong. He has ability, but doesn't look the most straightforward.
Lady Hello(IRE), running in a handicap for the first time, didn't settle through the early stages so it's to her credit that she was able to finish where she did. There's room for some improvement.
Headstight(IRE), another making her handicap debut having been off the track since May, was drawn in stall 12 but ended up on the far rail heading into the last 1 1/2f. She couldn't get the clearest of runs and didn't run badly. (op 16-1)
Valley Of Hope, held in handicaps the last twice, was 3lb lower but still found a few too good. (op 11-2)
Uncle Timmy, who was drawn widest of all and was hampered, causing him to stumble 2f out, shaped better than his finishing position suggests. (tchd 25-1)

6044 PONY RACING HERE ON 2 OCTOBER H'CAP 5f
2:35 (2:36) (Class 5) (0-75,75) 3-Y-O+ **£2,264** (£673; £336; £168) **Stalls** Low

Form RPR

066 **1** **Select Committee**[18] 5468 6-8-13 **67**..................(v) PBBeggy 9 79
(John Quinn) *chsd ldrs: led jst ins fnl f: all out* **8/1**[3]

400- **2** *nk* **Trade Secret**[418] 4349 4-9-2 **70**.................. RobertWinston 10 81
(Mel Brittain) *in rr: nt clr run over 1f out: styd on strly fnl f: jst hld* **10/1**

134 **3** *2 1/4* **Diamond Blue**[41] 4715 3-8-13 **68**.................. MichaelStainton 13 71+
(Richard Whitaker) *towards rr on outer: hdwy 2f out: w ldrs 1f out: styd on same pce* **16/1**

3646 **4** *hd* **Captain Scooby**[13] 5647 5-8-7 **64**.................. AmyRyan(3) 2 66
(Richard Whitaker) *chsd ldrs: outpcd over 2f out: hdwy and n.m.r over 1f out: kpt on same pce* **5/1**[1]

2610 **5** *1/2* **Forever's Girl**[illegible] 4200 [illegible].................. [illegible] 68
(Geoffrey Oldroyd) *sn last and drvn along: swtchd outside over 1f out: kpt on wl* **6/1**[2]

1131 **6** *hd* **Boy The Bell**[44] 4604 4-9-0 **71**.................. DaleSwift(3) 6 71
(Brian Ellison) *in rr-div: hdwy over 1f out: edgd rt: styd on same pce last 100yds* **5/1**[1]

1030 **7** *3 1/2* **Dancing Freddy (IRE)**[11] 5720 4-9-0 **71**..................(tp) RobertLButler(3) 12 58
(Richard Guest) *t.k.h: sn w ldrs: led over 1f out: hdd and rdr dropped whip 150yds out: sn wknd* **25/1**

2145 **8** *1/2* **Anjomarba (IRE)**[19] 5442 4-9-1 **69**.................. JoeFanning 3 54
(Conor Dore) *chsd ldrs: one pce whn nt clr run over 1f out* **12/1**

2546 **9** *1* **Argentine (IRE)**[36] 4881 7-8-2 **61** oh7..................(b) JulieBurke(5) 7 43
(Ian Semple) *hld up in rr on inner: nt clr run over 1f out: kpt on ins fnl f* **14/1**

040 **10** *6* **Tabaret**[12] 5683 8-9-2 **70**..................(v) TonyCulhane 14 30
(Richard Whitaker) *sn chsng ldrs on outer: wknd appr fnl f* **40/1**

1230 **11** *1 1/2* **Nomoreblondes**[12] 5679 7-9-1 **74**..................(v) LMcNiff(5) 5 29
(Paul Midgley) *led tl over 2f out: wknd over 1f out* **8/1**[3]

6420 **12** *1 1/2* **Ice Trooper**[30] 5115 3-9-6 **75**.................. DuranFentiman 1 24
(Linda Stubbs) *taken quitely to post: chsd ldrs: wkng whn n.m.r over 1f out* **14/1**

4011 **13** *4* **Lady Kildare (IRE)**[21] 5371 3-8-10 **68**.................. PatrickDonaghy(3) 11 —
(Jedd O'Keeffe) *towards rr: eased over 1f out: sn bhd* **9/1**

64.11 secs (0.61) **Going Correction** +0.20s/f (Good)
WFA 3 from 4yo+ 1lb **13** Ran SP% **123.5**
Speed ratings (Par 103): **103,102,98,98,97 97,91,91,89,79 77,75,68**
toteswingers: 1&2 £24.70, 1&3 £34.90, 2&3 £39.60 CSF £88.73 CT £1273.17 TOTE £9.60: £3.00, £3.60, £4.80; EX 138.90.
Owner Which Bits Mine Syndicate **Bred** Llety Stud **Trained** Settrington, N Yorks
■ Stewards' Enquiry : Julie Burke two-day ban: careless riding (Sep 28-29)
Robert Winston two-day ban: careless riding (Sep 28-29)

FOCUS
This looked a competitive heat and it was run in a relatively good time. Pretty solid form.
Lady Kildare(IRE) Official explanation: jockey said filly suffered interference in running

6045 WATCH RACING UK ON SKY CHANNEL 432 MAIDEN STKS 5f
3:10 (3:12) (Class 5) 2-Y-O **£2,264** (£673; £336; £168) **Stalls** Low

Form RPR

5340 **1** **The Rising (IRE)**[16] 5562 2-9-3 67..................(v) GrahamGibbons 3 74
(Ed McMahon) *cl up: led after 2f: rdn clr ent fnl f: kpt on strly* **3/1**[1]

2 *4 1/2* **Dreaming Of Rubies** 2-8-12 0.................. PaulHanagan 7 53+
(Ben Haslam) *trckd ldrs: hdwy to chse wnr 2f out: rdn over 1f out: kpt on same pce fnl f* **4/1**[2]

6 **3** *nk* **Untold Melody**[9] 5786 2-8-12 0.................. StephenCraine 2 52
(Kevin Ryan) *hld up towards rr: swtchd lft and hdwy 2f out: rdn over 1f out: kpt on ins fnl f: nrst fin* **4/1**[2]

50 **4** *nk* **I'm A Doughnut**[28] 5161 2-9-3 0.................. RichardKingscote 4 56
(Tom Dascombe) *hld up towards rr: swtchd lft and hdwy 2f out: sn rdn and styd on wl fnl f* **20/1**

052 **5** *1 3/4* **Bengaline**[15] 5596 2-9-0 70.................. BillyCray(3) 8 49
(David Nicholls) *led: pushed along and hdd after 2f: rdn 2f out: sn drvn: hung lft and wknd over 1f out* **6/1**[3]

6 *nk* **Code Six (IRE)** 2-8-12 0.................. RoystonFfrench 6 43
(Bryan Smart) *dwlt: t.k.h and sn trcking ldrs: effrt 2f out: sn rdn and edgd rt over 1f out: one pce* **14/1**

5445 **7** *3/4* **Baltic Bomber (IRE)**[35] 4899 2-9-3 67.................. PBBeggy 9 46
(John Quinn) *chsd ldrs: rdn along wl over 1f out: grad wknd* **10/1**

8 *1* **Indivisible** 2-8-12 0.................. DavidAllan 13 37
(Tim Easterby) *dwlt and swtchd rt s: bhd tl sme late hdwy* **25/1**

0 **9** *2* **Brunswick Vale (IRE)**[18] 5486 2-8-12 0.................. FrederikTylicki 1 30
(Paul Midgley) *in tch on inner: rdn along over 2f out and grad wknd* **50/1**

0 **10** *1 1/2* **Emily Hall**[14] 5618 2-8-8 0 ow3.................. JustinNewman(7) 12 27
(Bryan Smart) *racd wd: a in rr* **33/1**

26 **11** *8* **First Phase**[10] 5756 2-8-12 0.................. RobertWinston 11 —
(Mel Brittain) *racd wd: a towards rr* **9/1**

00 **12** *1 1/2* **Bu Samra (IRE)**[14] 5618 2-9-3 0..................(b[1]) PhillipMakin 5 —
(Kevin Ryan) *midfield: whn n.m.r and lost pl after 1f: towards rr: rdn along over 2f out and sn outpcd* **50/1**

65.66 secs (2.16) **Going Correction** +0.20s/f (Good) **12** Ran SP% **120.5**
Speed ratings (Par 95): **90,82,82,81,79 78,77,75,72,70 57,54**
toteswingers: 1&2 £4.00, 1&3 £4.00, 2&3 £5.30 CSF £14.19 TOTE £4.00: £1.60, £1.60, £2.00; EX 17.60.
Owner C Cheng & J Coleman **Bred** Denis Brosnan **Trained** Lichfield, Staffs
■ Stewards' Enquiry : Phillip Makin caution: used whip when out of contention.

FOCUS
A modest maiden.

NOTEBOOK
The Rising(IRE), who came into the race officially rated 67 following five previous starts, make all from his low draw. If he hasn't improved out of nowhere then it doesn't say a lot for those he beat. (old market op 4-1 new market)
Dreaming Of Rubies, who cost 130,000gns at the breeze-ups, was never too far off the leader but couldn't stay with him in the closing stages. He's entitled to come on for the experience, but will need to. (old market op 4-1 new market)
Untold Melody finished all too late after the winner had kicked off the front. She looks one for nurseries over further after one more run. (old market op 6-1 tchd 13-2 new market)
I'm A Doughnut appreciated being back on quick ground and was another keeping on late. This was his best effort to date and handicaps should now be open to him. (new market)
Bengaline disappointed on his return to turf and should get back on the Fibresand sharpish. (old market op 9-2 new market)
Code Six(IRE) didn't set the world alight on her debut. (old market tchd 16-1 new market)
First Phase Official explanation: jockey said filly hung left

6046 COMEDY CURRY NIGHT ON 24TH SEPTEMBER H'CAP 1m 4f 16y
3:45 (3:45) (Class 4) (0-85,84) 3-Y-O **£4,528** (£1,347; £673; £336) **Stalls** Low

Form RPR

0003 **1** **The Bells O Peover**[15] 5580 3-8-12 **75**..................(b[1]) FrederikTylicki 7 88
(Mark Johnston) *a.p: effrt 3f out: rdn to ld 2f out: drvn and hung bdly lft over 1f out: styd on* **5/1**[3]

112 **2** *3 1/2* **Dubawi Dancer**[14] 5614 3-9-0 **77**.................. PaulHanagan 2 84+
(William Haggas) *hld up towards rr: hdwy over 2f out: rdn over 1f out: drvn and kpt on ins fnl f* **9/4**[1]

3126 **3** *2* **King Of The Celts (IRE)**[15] 5593 3-9-0 **77**.................. PJMcDonald 4 81
(Tim Easterby) *trckd ldrs: hdwy on inner over 2f out: rdn and ev ch wl over 1f out: sn drvn and kpt on same pce* **4/1**[2]

3030 **4** *1* **Waltz Darling (IRE)**[25] 5283 3-9-3 **80**.................. TonyHamilton 1 83
(Richard Fahey) *in tch: hdwy on inner wl over 1f out: sn rdn and kpt on ins fnl f: nrst fin* **12/1**

0151 **5** *hd* **Gottany O'S**[20] 5235 3-9-7 **84**.................. [illegible] [illegible]
(Mick Channon) *hld up in rr: hdwy 2f out: rdn over 1f out: kpt on ins fnl f: n.d* **6/1**

254 **6** *1 1/4* **Light Blow (USA)**[39] 4805 3-8-10 **73**.................. EddieAhern 5 73
(Sir Henry Cecil) *led: rdn along over 3f out: drvn and hdd 2f out: grad wknd* **7/1**

0040 **7** *1 1/2* **Greyfriars Drummer**[49] 4426 3-9-4 **81**.................. JoeFanning 6 79
(Mark Johnston) *cl up: effrt 3f out: rdn along 2f out: drvn: edgd lft and wknd wl over 1f out* **7/1**

2m 38.94s (-0.86) **Going Correction** +0.025s/f (Good) **7** Ran SP% **114.4**
Speed ratings (Par 103): **103,100,99,98,98 97,96**
toteswingers: 1&2 £3.10, 1&3 £4.30, 2&3 £2.60 CSF £16.72 TOTE £8.00: £3.20, £1.70; EX 22.90.
Owner D & G Mercer **Bred** Belgrave Bloodstock Ltd **Trained** Middleham Moor, N Yorks
■ Stewards' Enquiry : Paul Hanagan one-day ban: careless riding (Sep 28)

FOCUS
A decent race for the grade. The winner rates back to his earlier maiden best.

6047 EUROPEAN BREEDERS' FUND MAIDEN FILLIES' STKS 7f 100y
4:20 (4:21) (Class 5) 2-Y-O **£3,169** (£943; £471; £235) **Stalls** Low

Form RPR

4 **1** **Feelthedifference**[14] 5632 2-9-0 0.................. EddieAhern 3 72+
(Sir Henry Cecil) *trckd ldrs: effrt over 2f out: hung rt and led appr fnl f: drvn clr* **3/1**[2]

25 **2** *3 1/4* **Ghalaa (IRE)**[35] 4898 2-9-0 0.................. JoeFanning 7 64
(Mark Johnston) *mde most: hdd appr fnl f: kpt on same pce* **7/2**[3]

0 **3** *nk* **Baileys Over Ice**[20] 5398 2-9-0 0.................. FrederikTylicki 11 63
(James Given) *in tch: effrt on outside over 2f out: styd on fnl f* **22/1**

0 **4** *1 1/4* **Northern Jewel (IRE)**[19] 5454 2-9-0 0.................. PaulHanagan 10 60
(Richard Fahey) *chsd ldrs: kpt on one pce fnl 2f* **11/1**

4034 **5** *nk* **Curtain Patch (USA)**[17] 5503 2-9-0 58..................(p) RoystonFfrench 5 59
(Bryan Smart) *in tch: effrt over 2f out: kpt on: nvr a threat* **25/1**

06 **6** *1 1/2* **Absolute Fun (IRE)**[11] 5727 2-9-0 0.................. DavidAllan 2 55
(Tim Easterby) *dwlt: in rr: drvn over 2f out: kpt on: nvr nr ldrs* **8/1**

00 **7** *3/4* **Iberian Rock**[18] 5464 2-9-0 0..................(p) DavidNolan 4 53
(Ann Duffield) *in rr: hung rt at bnd 6f out: hdwy on ins over 2f out: nvr nr ldrs* **66/1**

8 *5* **Naturalmente (IRE)** 2-9-0 0.................. PhillipMakin 1 41
(Kevin Ryan) *w ldr: drvn over 2f out: wknd over 1f out* **11/1**

0 **9** *15* **Demolition Blue (IRE)**[11] 5727 2-9-0 0 PJMcDonald 6 —
(Ben Haslam) *s.i.s: sn bhd: t.o* **100/1**

6 **U** **Bond Artist (IRE)**[18] 5464 2-8-11 0 DaleSwift(3) 9 —
(Geoffrey Oldroyd) *dropped to rr and pushed along whn clipped heels and uns rdr 6f out* **15/8**[1]

1m 34.28s (0.48) **Going Correction** +0.025s/f (Good) 10 Ran SP% **120.5**
Speed ratings (Par 92): **98,94,93,92,92 90,89,83,66,—**
toteswingers: 1&2 £3.70, 1&3 £16.00, 2&3 £19.30 CSF £14.15 TOTE £4.60: £1.90, £1.10, £7.20; EX 10.40.
Owner Friends Of The Pink Rose **Bred** Mill Farm Stud **Trained** Newmarket, Suffolk

FOCUS
A modest maiden.

NOTEBOOK
Feelthedifference finished fourth over 6f on her debut (fifth won next time out), shaping very much like a filly who would appreciate a step up in distance. In the box seat behind the two leaders, she picked up well when asked and saw the trip out in good style. The handicapper can't be too harsh on her for this and she'll be of interest in handicap company. (op 7-4)
Ghalaa(IRE), runner-up here on her debut but a disappointing favourite on soft ground when returning to the track a fortnight later, bounced back to form returned to what appears to be her favoured surface, and as a sister to a 1m3f winner, she can be expected to improve as she steps up in distance, especially next year. (op 4-1 tchd 9-2)
Baileys Over Ice, too green to do herself justice on her debut, ran a lot better this time and is heading in the right direction. (op 25-1)
Northern Jewel(IRE) showed a lot more than on her first outing, perhaps benefiting from getting to race on quicker ground this time. (op 14-1)
Curtain Patch(USA), who was wearing cheekpieces for the first time, has a pedigree that will make her very interesting if she turns up on the Fibresand at Southwell, where her trainer as a good record. (op 22-1)
Absolute Fun(IRE) kept on without perhaps getting the clearest of runs, but she's now eligible for a mark and figures to do better in handicap company. (tchd 9-1)
Bond Artist(IRE) clipped heels early on and her rider had no chance of staying on board. (op 7-2 after early 9-2)

6048 BEVERLEY ANNUAL BADGEHOLDERS MAIDEN AUCTION STKS 7f 100y
4:50 (4:53) (Class 5) 2-Y-O £2,264 (£673; £336; £168) Stalls Low

Form RPR

66 **1** **Daghash**[13] 5654 2-8-9 0 RoystonFfrench 7 79+
(Clive Brittain) *in tch: hdwy over 2f out: swtchd lft and rdn over 1f out: styd on wl to ld ins fnl f* **16/1**

2 **2** *2 ¼* **Blades Lad**[11] 5727 2-8-9 0 PaulHanagan 5 73
(Richard Fahey) *t.k.h: trckd ldr: effrt to chal wl over 1f out: rdn to ld ent fnl f: sn drvn and hdd: one pce towards fin* **11/10**[1]

44 **3** *4 ½* **Landown Littlerock**[37] 4853 2-8-6 0 PaulPickard(3) 1 62
(Reg Hollinshead) *led: rdn along 2f out: drvn over 1f out: hdd & wknd ent fnl f* **12/1**

0 **4** *hd* **Hareby (IRE)**[61] 4073 2-8-11 0 DavidAllan 4 64
(Tim Easterby) *in tch: effrt over 2f out and sn rdn along: kpt on fnl f: nrst fin* **25/1**

05 **5** *½* **Operation Tracer**[18] 5475 2-8-11 0 PhillipMakin 12 62
(Michael Bell) *trckd ldrs: hdwy over 2f out: rdn wl over 1f out: drvn and no imp appr fnl f* **9/2**[3]

0 **6** *1 ½* **Kieron's Rock (IRE)**[9] 5786 2-8-10 0 PatrickDonaghy(3) 2 61
(Jedd O'Keeffe) *t.k.h: chsd ldng pair: cl up over 2f out: rdn along wl over 1f out: wknd appr fnl f* **33/1**

05 **7** *nse* **Allegri (IRE)**[53] 4323 2-8-11 0 TonyHamilton 3 59
(Ann Duffield) *t.k.h: chsd ldrs: rdn along over 2f out: grad wknd* **100/1**

8 *2 ¼* **Hunting Gonk** 2-8-11 0 FrederikTylicki 13 53
(James Given) *a towards rr* **50/1**

9 *3* **Running Deer (IRE)** 2-8-7 0 ow1 EddieAhern 10 41
(Sir Henry Cecil) *s.i.s: a in rr* **4/1**[2]

60 **10** *2 ¾* **Disco Sensation**[18] 5464 2-8-5 0 BillyCray(3) 6 36
(David Nicholls) *a towards rr* **33/1**

50 **11** *nk* **Rock On Candy**[48] 4471 2-8-10 0 TravisBlock 8 37
(Sylvester Kirk) *a in rr* **11/1**

12 *¾* **Duchesse Satin (IRE)** 2-8-4 0 DuranFentiman 11 29
(Tim Easterby) *s.i.s: a in rr* **66/1**

60 **13** *31* **Dubai Destiny**[59] 4122 2-9-1 0 RobertWinston 14 —
(Tim Easterby) *s.i.s: a bhd: t.o and eased fnl 2f* **66/1**

1m 33.93s (0.13) **Going Correction** +0.025s/f (Good) 13 Ran SP% **123.4**
Speed ratings (Par 95): **100,97,92,92,91 89,89,87,83,80 80,79,43**
toteswingers: 1&2 £10.30, 1&3 £11.20, 2&3 £3.60 CSF £34.25 TOTE £28.10: £4.90, £1.20, £2.40; EX 54.60.
Owner Mohammed Al Nabouda **Bred** Rabbah Bloodstock Limited **Trained** Newmarket, Suffolk

FOCUS
Another modest contest.

NOTEBOOK
Daghash was taking a drop in class having competed against some useful rivals in a novice race at Salisbury last time. She got the job done well enough, although the bare form is nothing special. (op 12-1)
Blades Lad, just like on his debut, was a bit keen early and that may have been his undoing in the end, especially as this race was over an extra 100yds on a stiffer track. (op 11-8 tchd 6-4)
Landown Littlerock was also a little keen in front and that prevented him from seeing out his race. He's now eligible for a mark. (op 11-1 tchd 10-1)
Hareby(IRE) still looked in need of the experience but he was staying on nicely at the finish and took a step in the right direction.
Operation Tracer didn't improve on his previous efforts but is another for whom handicaps are now an option. (op 6-1)
Running Deer(IRE) struggled to get involved on her debut and must be one of her yard's lesser lights. Official explanation: jockey said filly ran green (op 7-2 tchd 9-2)
Dubai Destiny Official explanation: jockey said gelding moved poorly

6049 BETFAIR RACING EXCELLENCE APPRENTICE TRAINING SERIES CLASSIFIED STKS (DIV I) 1m 100y
5:20 (5:23) (Class 6) 3-Y-O+ £1,363 (£402; £201) Stalls Low

Form RPR

04 **1** **Diamond Sunrise (IRE)**[47] 4505 3-8-4 49 ShirleyTeasdale(5) 9 54
(Noel Wilson) *mde all: edgd lft to stands' side rail 1f out: styd on wl towards fin* **20/1**

0000 **2** *2* **Look For Love**[22] 5349 3-8-4 45 JackDuern(5) 3 49
(Reg Hollinshead) *chsd ldrs: kpt on same pce last 150yds* **14/1**

0550 **3** *nk* **Wing N Prayer (IRE)**[18] 5469 4-9-0 36 JustinNewman 5 48
(John Wainwright) *in rr: hdwy over 2f out: edgd lft and styd on fnl f* **66/1**

0006 **4** *shd* **Honest And True (IRE)**[6] 5860 4-9-0 50 (b) DarylByrne 8 48
(Ian Semple) *chsd ldrs: kpt on one pce fnl f* **9/1**

360 **5** *½* **Lord Emerson**[16] 5556 3-8-4 55 LauraBarry(5) 7 47
(Richard Fahey) *unruly and uns rdr bhd stalls: trckd ldrs: edgd rt towards far rail over 1f out: kpt on one pce* **11/2**[3]

143 **6** *hd* **Byron Bear (IRE)**[42] 4676 3-8-4 55 DavidSimmonson(5) 10 46
(Paul Midgley) *hld up in tch: effrt over 2f out: edgd rt and kpt on one pce fnl f* **3/1**[2]

0600 **7** *1* **Cabal**[44] 4612 4-9-0 55 (p) ShaneBKelly 2 44
(Andrew Crook) *mid-div: hdwy over 2f out: kpt on one pce fnl f* **9/1**

0-06 **8** *hd* **Chicamia**[41] 4701 7-8-11 48 SophieSilvester(3) 11 44
(Michael Mullineaux) *s.i.s: hdwy far side 2f out: kpt on fnl f: nvr trbld ldrs* **25/1**

3223 **9** *nk* **Master Of Song**[27] 5214 4-9-0 52 (bt) DavidKenny 6 43
(Roy Bowring) *chsd ldrs: hung bdly lft 2f out: wknd appr fnl f* **5/2**[1]

6-10 **10** *1 ¾* **Freda's Rose (IRE)**[18] 5470 7-8-11 49 KatiaScallan(3) 12 39
(Owen Brennan) *s.i.s: kpt on clsng stages: nvr a factor* **17/2**

0-60 **11** *4* **Convitezza**[20] 5402 5-8-9 33 JasonHart(5) 1 30
(Mike Sowersby) *mid-div: hdwy far side over 2f out: wknd over 1f out* **66/1**

0000 **12** *1 ¾* **Catawollow**[20] 5403 4-8-9 42 (e) TerenceFury(5) 13 26
(Richard Guest) *s.i.s: swtchd rt s: a in rr* **40/1**

5/6- **13** *12* **Fairys In A Storm (IRE)**[302] 7472 4-8-11 42 GeorgeChaloner(3) 4 —
(Alan Lockwood) *in rr: drvn over 4f out: sn bhd* **33/1**

1m 47.85s (0.25) **Going Correction** +0.025s/f (Good)
WFA 3 from 4yo+ 5lb 13 Ran SP% **123.1**
Speed ratings (Par 101): **99,97,96,96,96 95,94,94,94,92 88,86,74**
toteswingers: 1&2 £20.50, 1&3 £30.80, 2&3 £52.10 CSF £268.03 TOTE £18.20: £3.90, £6.80, £6.80, EX 254.30.
Owner Noel Wilson & Lauren Stapley **Bred** Denis And Mrs Teresa Bergin **Trained** Sandhutton, N Yorks
■ Stewards' Enquiry : Justin Newman two-day ban: careless riding (Sep 28-29)

FOCUS
The early pace wasn't great and it paid to race handily. It was half a second quicker than the second division. Weak form with nothing solid.

6050 BETFAIR RACING EXCELLENCE APPRENTICE TRAINING SERIES CLASSIFIED STKS (DIV II) 1m 100y
5:50 (5:53) (Class 6) 3-Y-O+ £1,363 (£402; £201) Stalls Low

Form RPR

6005 **1** **Fairy Mist (IRE)**[7] 5822 4-8-9 50 (p) JasonHart(5) 9 54
(Brian Rothwell) *mde all: rdn and clr whn hung bdly lft over 1f out: drvn ins fnl f: jst hld on* **7/1**

4030 **2** *nk* **Kheskianto (IRE)**[34] 4945 5-8-11 44 (b) NoelGarbutt(3) 3 53
(Michael Chapman) *dwlt and towards rr: gd hdwy 1/2-way: chsd ldrs over 2f out: rdn to chse wnr ins fnl f: sn drvn and ev ch tl no ex nr fin* **20/1**

333 **3** *2* **Eeny Mac (IRE)**[9] 5788 4-8-9 50 TerenceFury(5) 8 49
(Neville Bycroft) *hld up: hdwy wl over 2f out: rdn wl over 1f out: styd on ins fnl f: nrst fin* **7/2**[2]

3056 **4** *1 ¼* **Izzet**[13] 5652 3-8-9 55 JustinNewman 1 46
(Ron Barr) *hld up: hdwy over 2f out: swtchd lft and rdn over 1f out: drvn and kpt on ins fnl f* **11/4**[1]

000- **5** *½* **Northgate Lodge (USA)**[498] 1812 6-8-11 42 GeorgeChaloner(3) 10 45
(Mel Brittain) *plld hrd: cl up: rdn along 2f out: drvn and edgd rt appr fnl f: grad wknd* **5/1**[3]

500 **6** *1 ¼* **Luv U Noo**[7] 5823 4-9-0 48 DavidKenny 4 42
(Brian Baugh) *in rr: hdwy on wd outside wl over 2f out: rdn to chse ldrs over 1f out: drvn and no imp ins fnl f* **11/1**

0345 **7** *1 ½* **Northumberland**[59] 398 5-8-9 42 LauraBarry(5) 2 38
(Owen Brennan) *chsd ldrs on inner: rdn along wl over 2f out: grad wknd* **40/1**

240 **8** *3 ¼* **See The Storm**[35] 4929 3-8-9 51 DarylByrne 6 31
(Patrick Morris) *chsd ldng pair: rdn along over 2f out: drvn and wkng whn n.m.r over 1f out* **7/1**

0446 **9** *nk* **Spread Boy (IRE)**[7] 5823 4-8-9 40 (p) DavidSimmonson(5) 12 30
(Alan Berry) *in tch: rdn along wl over 2f out: sn wknd* **33/1**

0000 **10** *¾* **Fitzwarren**[50] 4408 10-8-11 36 (tp) SophieSilvester(3) 7 28
(Alan Brown) *v.s.a and bhd: rdn along 3f out: sme late hdwy* **50/1**

0400 **11** *¾* **Morning Air (IRE)**[42] 4673 3-8-9 52 ShaneBKelly 5 27
(Ann Duffield) *a towards rr* **12/1**

006 **12** *13* **Littlepromisedland (IRE)**[17] 5507 3-8-9 33 (v1) CharlesEddery 11 —
(Richard Guest) *a in rr: bhd fnl 2f* **66/1**

1m 48.35s (0.75) **Going Correction** +0.025s/f (Good)
WFA 3 from 4yo+ 5lb 12 Ran SP% **120.2**
Speed ratings (Par 101): **97,96,94,93,92 91,90,86,86,85 85,72**
toteswingers: 1&2 £23.10, 1&3 £5.60, 2&3 £15.70 CSF £143.59 TOTE £8.30: £2.70, £6.40, £1.70; EX 68.00.
Owner Brian Rothwell **Bred** Sandro Garavelli **Trained** Norton, N Yorks

FOCUS
The slower of the two divisions by 0.5sec, and just like in the previous race the winner made all. Limited form.
T/Jkpt: Not won. T/Plt: £85.10 to a £1 stake. Pool: £50,765.37. 435.15 winning tickets. T/Qpdt: £5.80 to a £1 stake. Pool: £4,126.07. 520.50 winning tickets. JR

5998 KEMPTON (A.W) (R-H)
Wednesday, September 14

OFFICIAL GOING: Standard
Wind: Moderate, across Weather: Sunny early

6051 FREE ENTRY FOR BETDAQ MEMBERS H'CAP 7f (P)
5:40 (5:40) (Class 5) (0-75,75) 3-Y-O+ £2,264 (£673; £336; £168) Stalls Low

Form RPR

0603 **1** **Mishrif (USA)**[35] 4910 5-9-5 70 (b) RichardHughes 5 80
(J R Jenkins) *trckd ldrs: drvn to ld over 1f out: edgd rt ins fnl f: pushed out* **8/1**

0102 **2** *1* **Cootehill Lass (IRE)**[8] 5803 3-8-10 65 (p) JamesDoyle 8 71
(David Evans) *in tch: rdn and one 3f out: styd on again fr 2f out: r.o u.p to chse wnr ins fnl f: no imp* **6/1**[2]

5240 **3** *1 ¾* **Cativo Cavallino**[17] 5516 8-9-0 65 RichardThomas 9 68
(John E Long) *towards rr: hdwy 3f out: sn rdn: styd on fnl 2f to take 3rd jst ins fnl f: one pce* **16/1**

5225 **4** *¾* **Annes Rocket (IRE)**[12] 5667 6-8-7 61 oh1 (p) SeanLevey(3) 7 62
(Jimmy Fox) *s.i.s towards rr: nt clr run 2f out: hdwy over 1f out: styd on fnl f to take 4th fnl 50yds* **11/1**

540 **5** *½* **Treasure Way**[18] 5496 4-9-2 67 LiamKeniry 4 67
(Patrick Chamings) *in tch: chsd ldrs and rdn 2f out: wknd ins fnl f* **16/1**

The Form Book, Raceform Ltd, Compton, RG20 6NL

4416 **6** *4 ½* **Aleqa**[30] 5119 4-9-9 **74**.. GeorgeBaker 1 61
(Chris Wall) *trckd ldrs: pushed along and n.m.r towards ins fr 2f out: wknd fnl f* **15/2**[3]
6026 **7** *½* **Saharia (IRE)**[20] 5412 4-9-5 **70**.............................(v[1]) RobbieFitzpatrick 12 56
(Michael Attwater) *s.i.s towards rr: rdn over 2f out: mod prog fnl f* **20/1**
0004 **8** *½* **Tax Break**[11] 5717 4-9-7 **72**.. JackMitchell 3 57
(David Barron) *sn led: goined fr 3f out: hdd ins fnl 2f: wknd sn after* **8/1**
001 **9** *shd* **Aldermoor (USA)**[13] 5640 5-9-6 **71**.......................... WilliamCarson 2 56+
(Stuart Williams) *slowly away: nt rcvr and a bhd* **13/8**[1]
-000 **10** *nk* **Seneschal**[33] 4997 10-8-6 **64**.................................... RachealKneller(7) 13 48
(Adrian Chamberlain) *sn pressing ldr: ev ch fr 3f out tl led ins fnl 2f: hdd sn after and wknd qckly* **66/1**
-006 **11** *12* **Gentleman Is Back (USA)**[22] 5341 3-8-11 **69**................. JohnFahy(3) 6 18
(Ed de Giles) *s.i.s: a in rr* **33/1**

1m 24.79s (-1.21) **Going Correction** -0.15s/f (Stan)
WFA 3 from 4yo+ 4lb **11** Ran SP% **115.7**
Speed ratings (Par 103): **100,98,96,96,95 90,89,89,89,88 74**
toteswingers: 1&2 £8.00, 1&3 £20.00, 2&3 £17.40 CSF £53.52 CT £753.14 TOTE £6.00: £1.70, £1.60, £4.60; EX 32.60 Trifecta £5132.40 Part won. Pool: £6,935.68 - 0.63 winning units..
Owner Mrs Wendy Jenkins **Bred** Mr & Mrs Theodore Kuster Et Al **Trained** Royston, Herts
■ Stewards' Enquiry : James Doyle one-day ban: used whip with excessive frequency (Sep 28)

FOCUS
A fair and quite competitive handicap, although the favourite blew the start. The form looks sound enough.
Treasure Way Official explanation: jockey said filly hung left
Aldermoor(USA) Official explanation: jockey said gelding missed the break

6052 BETDAQ MULTIPLES H'CAP 1m 4f (P)
6:10 (6:14) (Class 6) (0-65,65) 3-Y-O **£1,617** (£481; £240; £120) **Stalls** Centre

Form RPR
0003 **1** **Bright Abbey**[47] 4510 3-9-1 **62**...(v[1]) JohnFahy(3) 5 73
(Walter Swinburn) *rdn fr stalls: sn in tch: pushed along and lost position ins fnl 3f: styd on u.p fr 2f out: chsd ldr 1f out: kpt on to ld fnl 100yds: won gng away* **12/1**
5302 **2** *1 ¾* **Rowan Ridge**[2] 5993 3-8-13 **57**..(v) PatCosgrave 9 65
(Jim Boyle) *chsd ldrs: led over 2f out: drvn 3f clr over 1f out: hdd u.p fnl 100yds but hld on for 2nd* **13/2**[2]
3502 **3** *1 ½* **Corvette**[23] 5321 3-9-4 **62**.......................................(v[1]) SilvestreDeSousa 12 68
(J R Jenkins) *in rr tl drvn and hdwy fr 3f out: chsd wnr ins fnl 2f: no imp and outpcd into 3rd fnl f* **8/1**[3]
3343 **4** *3* **Joe Strummer (IRE)**[28] 5178 3-9-4 **62**......................... JamieSpencer 11 65
(Michael Bell) *towards rr but in tch: hdwy fr 3f out: rdn: hung rt and styd on fnl f: sn no imp: eased whn no ch w first three clsng stages* **4/1**[1]
6353 **5** *2 ¾* **Gower Rules (IRE)**[7] 5838 3-9-0 **61**................................ SeanLevey(3) 7 57
(John Bridger) *sn led: hdd 1m out: styd chsng ldrs and disp ld over 2f out: wknd fnl f* **8/1**[3]
-014 **6** *nk* **Guards Chapel**[10] 5420 3-9-4 **62**...................................... GeorgeBaker 4 58
(Gary Moore) *in rr: pushed along 3f out: hdwy over 1f out: kpt on: nt rch ldrs* **12/1**
6235 **7** *1 ½* **Mrs Neat (IRE)**[14] 5630 3-9-7 **65**.....................................(p) JamesDoyle 2 59
(Sylvester Kirk) *chsd ldrs: rdn over 2f out: wknd over 1f out* **8/1**[3]
-460 **8** *2* **Omnipotent (IRE)**[4] 5942 3-9-7 **65**................................... RichardHughes 3 55
(Richard Hannon) *chsd ldrs to 3f out: wknd 2f out* **8/1**[3]
2216 **9** *5* **Come On The Irons (USA)**[14] 5628 3-9-6 **64**..........(t) JamieGoldstein 6 46
(Ralph Smith) *in rr: rdn and hdwy on outside3f out: wknd 2f out* **9/1**
-634 **10** *2 ¾* **Wom**[17] 5507 3-9-0 **58**...(p) MickyFenton 8 36
(Pam Sly) *led after 4f: rdn 3f out: hdd & wknd over 2f out* **20/1**
0006 **11** *7* **Blue Cossack (IRE)**[26] 5249 3-8-13 **57**............................ LiamKeniry 10 33
(Mark Usher) *nvr bttr than mid-div* **25/1**
065 **12** *8* **Rasam Aldaar**[11] 5714 3-8-13 **60**............................(v) AdamBeschizza(3) 1 24
(Michael Wigham) *rdn along fr 1/2-way: sn bhd* **33/1**

2m 32.6s (-1.90) **Going Correction** -0.15s/f (Stan) **12** Ran SP% **114.7**
Speed ratings (Par 99): **100,98,97,95,94 93,92,91,88,86 85,80**
toteswingers: 1&2 £8.30, 1&3 £13.40, 2&3 £6.10 CSF £83.07 CT £666.76 TOTE £13.80: £5.20, £3.70, £3.00; EX 157.50 Trifecta £635.20 Pool: £7,297.19 - 8.50 winning units..
Owner P W Harris **Bred** Pendley Farm **Trained** Aldbury, Herts

FOCUS
A modest 3-y-o handicap but with only 8lb covering the whole field on official ratings it looked quite competitive, and it was sound run. Big improvement from the winner.
Corvette Official explanation: jockey said filly hung right from 3f out

6053 BACK OR LAY AT BETDAQ.COM NURSERY 1m (P)
6:40 (6:41) (Class 6) (0-65,65) 2-Y-O **£1,617** (£481; £240; £120) **Stalls** Low

Form RPR
0001 **1** **Spirit Of The Law (IRE)**[22] 5342 2-8-13 **57**.................. JamieSpencer 8 70+
(Ed Dunlop) *hld up in tch: shkn up and qcknd to ld on bit over 1f out: shkn up fnl 120yds: easily* **7/2**[1]
0450 **2** *2 ¼* **Bewilder**[23] 5324 2-9-6 **64**.. RobertHavlin 12 70+
(John Gosden) *hld up in rr: hdwy over 2f qcknd to chse wnr fnl f: no impresison but wl clr of 3rd* **11/1**
3413 **3** *5* **Yammos (IRE)**[20] 5413 2-9-7 **65**.................................. MatthewDavies 7 59
(Mick Channon) *chsd ldrs: rdn to dispute 2nd 2f out: sn no imp on ldng duo: wl btn 3rd fnl f* **9/1**
000 **4** *1* **Valiant Runner**[19] 5445 2-9-3 **64**...................................... JohnFahy(3) 2 56
(Jeremy Noseda) *in rr: hdwy over 2f out: styd on fnl f to cl on 3rd nr fin but nvr any ch w ldng duo* **8/1**
504 **5** *hd* **Loxton Lad (IRE)**[22] 5337 2-9-6 **64**.............................. SteveDrowne 10 55
(Roger Charlton) *in tch: pushed along and hdwy towards outer fr 2f out: styd on clsng stages* **11/2**[3]
6510 **6** *2 ¼* **Colourful Event (IRE)**[20] 5409 2-9-1 **59**................. FrankieMcDonald 5 45
(David Arbuthnot) *in rr: pushed along and sltly hmpd 4f out: styd on fnl f* **33/1**
000 **7** *nk* **Cato Minor**[21] 5382 2-8-12 **56**...(b) JimCrowley 14 41
(Amanda Perrett) *in tch: rdn and one pce 3f out: sme prog fnl f* **33/1**
5060 **8** *¾* **Tangtastic (IRE)**[2] 6001 2-8-12 **56**.................................. MarcHalford 4 40
(Edward Creighton) *led tl hdd over 1f out: sn btn* **50/1**
6006 **9** *1* **Rainbow Chorus**[6] 5844 2-8-10 **54**.........................(p) SilvestreDeSousa 3 35
(Paul Cole) *in rr: rdn and sme hdwy fr 3f out: wknd u.p ins fnl 2f* **16/1**
1242 **10** *3* **Flying Pickets (IRE)**[15] 5597 2-9-5 **63**.......................... KierenFallon 1 37
(Alan McCabe) *chsd ldrs: rdn over 2f out: wknd qckly over 1f out* **5/1**[2]
000 **11** *7* **Highly Likely (IRE)**[33] 5011 2-9-0 **58**........................ RichardHughes 13 16
(John Dunlop) *chsd ldr tl wknd 2f out* **7/1**
060 **12** *14* **Superinjunction**[58] 4155 2-9-4 **62**................................ MartinDwyer 6 —
(Brian Meehan) *slowly away: a in rr* **16/1**
326 **13** *nse* **Monessa (IRE)**[28] 5170 2-9-4 **65**.................................. AlanCreighton(3) 9 —
(Edward Creighton) *in rr: sme hdwy into mid-div over 3f out: sn bhd* **50/1**

1m 39.78s (-0.02) **Going Correction** -0.15s/f (Stan) **13** Ran SP% **117.8**
Speed ratings (Par 93): **94,91,86,85,85 83,83,82,81,78 71,57,57**
toteswingers: 1&2 £16.90, 1&3 £7.10, 2&3 £27.10 CSF £41.61 CT £320.88 TOTE £5.00: £2.00, £4.60, £2.70; EX 43.20 Trifecta £326.80 Pool: £2,893.23 - 6.55 winning units..
Owner R J Arculli **Bred** Georgestown Stud **Trained** Newmarket, Suffolk

FOCUS
A modest nursery but it threw up a couple of colts who might be able to go on to better things.

NOTEBOOK
Spirit Of The Law(IRE), a winner on turf who had been well beaten in both previous tries on Polytrack, tracked the pace before cruising up to join the leaders inside the last 2f, and was then ridden out to make sure of success. He is clearly progressing, having started life in handicaps at a low level, and the hat-trick is by no means out of the question. (op 10-3 tchd 3-1)
Bewilder was held up near the back going well but, despite making good headway in the straight, was unable to close the gap on the winner who got first run. He was well clear of the rest, though, and a similar race should be his before long on this evidence. (op 12-1)
Yammos(IRE) stays this trip and handles the surface, so probably sets the standard. He was never far away but was unable to match the pace of the first two in the straight. (op 14-1)
Valiant Runner ◆ caught the eye on this nursery debut, having been held up out the back before making good late progress through his field, despite still showing signs of inexperience. He can do better at this level.
Loxton Lad(IRE), making his handicap debut, did not get the clearest of runs on the home turn but was being ridden along soon after straightening for home and just stayed on past beaten rivals. (tchd 6-1)
Flying Pickets(IRE)'s rider reported that the gelding hung left. Official explanation: jockey said gelding hung left (op 7-2)
Highly Likely(IRE)'s rider reported that the colt hung left. Official explanation: jockey said colt hung left (op 8-1)
Superinjunction was reported by the Veterinary Officer as being stiff behind. Official explanation: vet said filly was stiff behind (op 20-1)

6054 BETDAQ MOBILE APPS MAIDEN FILLIES' STKS 1m 4f (P)
7:10 (7:10) (Class 4) 3-4-Y-O **£4,075** (£1,212; £606; £303) **Stalls** Centre

Form RPR
05 **1** **Asterism**[77] 3519 3-8-12 0... RichardHughes 9 82+
(Sir Henry Cecil) *hld up towards rr: rdn and hdwy towards outside over 2f out: styd on wl to ld appr fnl f: won gng away: easily* **14/1**
2 **2** *1 ½* **Sweet Lavender (IRE)**[23] 5317 3-8-12 0......................... FrankieDettori 7 77
(Saeed Bin Suroor) *sn trcking ldr: drvn to chal wl over 1f out: sn narrowly hdd: nt pce of wnr ins fnl f: hld on wl for 2nd cl home* **11/10**[1]
3 *shd* **Chabada (JPN)** 3-8-12 0... PatCosgrave 4 77+
(Sir Henry Cecil) *in tch: rdn and outpcd 3f out: styd on u.p fr over 1f out: kpt on to cl for 2nd last strides but no ch w wnr* **33/1**
022 **4** *hd* **Deraasa (USA)**[33] 4989 3-8-12 **77**................................... MartinDwyer 8 77
(Saeed Bin Suroor) *sn led: drvn and jnd wl over 1f out: styd on same pce fnl f* **9/1**
-332 **5** *1 ½* **Moment Juste**[21] 5389 3-8-12 **78**...................................... RobertHavlin 3 75+
(John Gosden) *in tch: n.m.r on ins fr 3f out: edgd rt wl over 2f out: drvn and styd on fr over 1f out: nvr gng pce to rch ldrs* **4/1**[2]
55 **6** *½* **Cape Princess**[137] 1692 3-8-12 0.. JamieSpencer 5 74+
(Michael Bell) *hld up in rr: nt clr run 2f out: styd on ins fnl f: nt rch ldrs* **33/1**
2222 **7** *1 ½* **Whispered**[14] 5629 3-8-12 **78**..(e[1]) KierenFallon 1 71
(Sir Michael Stoute) *chsd ldrs: rdn over 2f out: wknd over 1f out* **9/2**[3]
0-5 **8** *nse* **Tafaneen (USA)**[118] 2218 3-8-12 0.................................... JackMitchell 2 71?
(Roger Varian) *chsd ldrs: rdn over 2f out: sn one pce: wknd fnl f* **33/1**
65 **9** *5* **Silent Ninja**[33] 5001 3-8-12 0... SteveDrowne 10 63
(Hughie Morrison) *towards rr most of way* **66/1**

2m 35.71s (1.21) **Going Correction** -0.15s/f (Stan) **9** Ran SP% **112.8**
Speed ratings (Par 102): **89,88,87,87,86 86,85,85,82**
toteswingers: 1&2 £4.70, 1&3 £23.20, 2&3 £11.40 CSF £28.86 TOTE £13.50: £2.60, £1.10, £7.10; EX 34.00 Trifecta £566.80 Pool: £7,069.63 - 9.22 winning units..
Owner K Abdulla **Bred** Juddmonte Farms Ltd **Trained** Newmarket, Suffolk

FOCUS
Those who had official marks were all rated in the high 70s, so this looked a reasonable contest for a 3-4yo maiden at this time of year, although only 3-y-os took part. The pace slowed to a crawl in the back straight and then became something of a 3f sprint, as confirmed by the time, which was 3.11sec slower than the earlier handicap. The form is taken at something like face value.
Cape Princess Official explanation: jockey said filly hung left

6055 TFM NETWORKS CONDITIONS STKS 7f (P)
7:40 (7:41) (Class 4) 2-Y-O **£3,428** (£1,020; £509; £254) **Stalls** Low

Form RPR
614 **1** **Graphic (IRE)**[32] 5039 2-9-0 **86**...................................... RichardHughes 3 98+
(Richard Hannon) *hld up towards rr but in tch: stdy hdwy to chal 2f out: slt ld sn after: pushed clr fnl f: comf* **9/1**
316 **2** *3* **Noor Zabeel (USA)**[11] 5709 2-9-0 **91**............................ MatthewDavies 5 88
(Mick Channon) *chsd ldr: rdn to chal 2f out: led briefly sn after: styd chsng wnr but no ch fnl f: jst hld on for 2nd clsng stages* **5/1**[3]
13 **3** *hd* **Counterglow (IRE)**[18] 5487 2-9-0 **89**............................ FrankieDettori 6 87
(Mahmood Al Zarooni) *hld up towards rr: hdwy 3f out: drvn and hung rt fr 2f out: styd on to press for 2nd cl home but no ch w wnr* **5/1**[3]
1200 **4** *1 ½* **Sir Glanton (IRE)**[47] 4496 2-9-0 **86**................................. LiamKeniry 2 83
(Amanda Perrett) *towards rr: rdn along 3f out: styd on to take 4th fnl f* **14/1**
123 **5** *8* **Compton**[16] 5558 2-9-0 **92**...(p) JimCrowley 1 61
(Ralph Beckett) *chsd ldrs: rdn and ev ch 2f out: wknd over 1f out* **5/2**[2]
31 **6** *2 ¼* **Gabrial The King (USA)**[43] 4639 2-9-0 0........................ JamieSpencer 4 63
(Michael Bell) *sn led: rdn and hdd ins fnl 2f: sn btn: eased whn no ch fnl f* **9/4**[1]

1m 24.82s (-1.18) **Going Correction** -0.15s/f (Stan) **6** Ran SP% **109.3**
Speed ratings (Par 97): **100,96,96,94,85 82**
toteswingers: 1&2 £12.50, 1&3 £1.10, 2&3 £3.60 CSF £49.08 TOTE £7.70: £3.50, £3.40; EX 47.10.
Owner The Royal Ascot Racing Club **Bred** Kevin & Meta Cullen **Trained** East Everleigh, Wilts

FOCUS
A decent juvenile conditions stakes with those with ratings having marks between 86 and 92 and the time was just 0.03sec slower than the opening older-horse handicap.

NOTEBOOK
Graphic(IRE) had disappointed on his previous start when reportedly failing to handle the track after winning his maiden, but bounced back in emphatic style. Always travelling smoothly on this AW debut, he hit the front inside the last quarter-mile and stretched away to score nicely. He looks capable of further improvement. (op 8-1)
Noor Zabeel(USA) had been well held in a Listed race on his return from a break since May but ran better at this lower level, if no match for the winner. (op 9-2 tchd 11-2)

Counterglow(IRE) was held up early but moved up to have his chance in the straight before being unable to find an extra gear. His best effort was on fast turf and he is worth returning to that sort of surface. He could be the sort to do well at Meydan in the new year. (op 6-1 tchd 9-2)
Sir Glanton(IRE) has not really gone on after a good start to his career and only ran on past beaten rivals here. (op 16-1 tchd 12-1)
Compton had looked progressive on turf but was never travelling that well, although close enough early, before dropping away. The surface might not have suited him. (tchd 9-4)
Gabrial The King(USA), making his AW debut, made the running but probably did too much early and faded when challenged on all sides in the straight. Jamie Spencer reported that the colt ran too free and the Stewards ordered the colt to be routine tested. Official explanation: jockey said colt ran too free (tchd 5-2)

6056 KIEREN FALLON WRITES FOR THE WEEKENDER CLASSIFIED CLAIMING STKS 6f (P)

8:10 (8:11) (Class 5) 3-Y-0+ **£2,264** (£673; £336; £168) **Stalls** Low

Form | RPR
2533 **1** **Grandmas Dream**[19] [5452] 3-8-6 72..........................(p) MartinHarley(3) 7 74
(Richard Guest) *led 1f: styd trcking ldrs: led appr fnl 2f: rdn fnl f: jst hld on* **11/1**
3004 **2** *shd* **Co Dependent (USA)**[33] [4990] 5-8-2 67...................... SophieDoyle(3) 9 68+
(Jamie Osborne) *s.i.s: hld up in rr: rapid hdwy appr fnl f: str run clsng stages and edgd rt: nt quite get up* **12/1**
2351 **3** *nk* **Desert Icon (IRE)**[32] [5037] 5-8-5 68.................................... MartinLane 6 67
(David Simcock) *s.i.s: in rr: hdwy fr over 1f ou: drvn and styd on wl clsng stages: carried rt whn gng on last strides* **5/1**[3]
0005 **4** *1 1/4* **Brandywell Boy (IRE)**[9] [5781] 8-8-7 62.................. SilvestreDeSousa 5 65
(Dominic Ffrench Davis) *chsd ldrs: rdn fr 2f out: nvr gng pce to chal and styd on same pce fnl f* **12/1**
4660 **5** *hd* **Steelcut**[14] [5616] 7-8-9 71....................................(p) KierenFallon 8 66
(David Evans) *t.k.h: trckd ldrs: rdn to press wnr appr fnl f: no imp: wknd and lost 3 pls clsng stages* **4/1**[1]
4645 **6** *1/2* **Nezami (IRE)**[13] [5640] 6-8-2 70..................................... JohnFahy(3) 2 60
(John Akehurst) *in rr: rdn and hdwy towards outside over 1f out: kpt on cl home: nvr a threat* **9/2**[2]
0600 **7** *3/4* **Lucky Mellor**[163] [1140] 4-8-4 74.. PaulBooth(7) 4 64
(Dean Ivory) *t.k.h led after 1f tl hdd appr fnl 2f: wknd ins fnl f* **8/1**
3030 **8** *5* **Frognal (IRE)**[17] [5502] 5-8-13 71...............................(b) RichardHughes 3 50
(Conor Dore) *s.i.s: sn chsng ldrs: wknd appr fnl 2f* **4/1**[1]
-000 **9** *4 1/2* **Premium Coffee**[11] [5718] 3-8-0 70...........................(b[1]) RyanPowell(5) 1 30
(Joseph Tuite) *in tch: rdn 3f out: wknd over 2f out* **25/1**

1m 12.18s (-0.92) **Going Correction** -0.15s/f (Stan)
WFA 3 from 4yo+ 2lb **9** Ran SP% **113.5**
Speed ratings (Par 103): **100,99,99,97,97 96,95,89,83**
toteswingers: 1&2 £11.20, 1&3 £4.80, 2&3 £8.60 CSF £131.17 TOTE £12.00: £3.70, £3.60, £1.50; EX 69.20 Trifecta £188.30 Pool: £745.87 - 2.93 winning units..
Owner Rakebackmypoker.com **Bred** Mrs Mary Taylor **Trained** Stainforth, S Yorks
■ Stewards' Enquiry : Sophie Doyle caution: careless riding

FOCUS
A tight classified claimer with all but one having marks in a 6lb range. It was steadily run and the form is rated cautiously.

6057 RACING@SKYSPORTS.COM H'CAP 2m (P)

8:40 (8:40) (Class 5) (0-75,75) 3-Y-0 **£2,264** (£673; £336; £168) **Stalls** Low

Form | RPR
2110 **1** **Fire Fighter (IRE)**[31] [5079] 3-9-7 **75**.................................. SebSanders 3 89+
(Sir Mark Prescott Bt) *hld up in rr: hdwy and nt clr run 2f out: swtchd rt and qcknd to ld 1f out: sn clr: easily* **11/10**[1]
6-02 **2** *3 3/4* **Rien Ne Vas Plus (IRE)**[40] [4753] 3-9-3 **71**...................... KierenFallon 5 76
(Sir Michael Stoute) *disp 3rd tl trckd ldr 3f out: led over 2f out: sn drvn: hdd 1f out: sn no ch w wnr but styd on for clr 2nd* **7/2**[3]
6621 **3** *7* **Secret Edge**[18] [5477] 3-9-3 **71**...................................... RichardHughes 1 68
(Alan King) *sn led: hdd after 4f: chsd ldrs: rdn and n.m.r on ins over 2f out: effrt over 1f out: nvr on terms: sn wknd* **3/1**[2]
0430 **4** *2* **Mountain Myst**[16] [5566] 3-8-2 **56** oh7.............................. WilliamCarson 2 51?
(William Muir) *disp 3rd: rdn over 5f out: styd in tch tl wknd u.p appr fnl 2f* **20/1**
6002 **5** *14* **Compassion**[18] [5477] 3-9-2 **70**...................................... JamieSpencer 4 48
(Michael Bell) *led after 4th: rdn 3f out: hdd over 2f out: sn wknd* **8/1**

3m 27.08s (-3.02) **Going Correction** -0.15s/f (Stan) **5** Ran SP% **110.7**
Speed ratings (Par 101): **101,99,95,94,87**
CSF £5.32 TOTE £1.90: £1.10, £2.40; EX 5.30.
Owner J Fishpool - Osborne House **Bred** Airlie Stud And Sir Thomas Pilkington **Trained** Newmarket, Suffolk

FOCUS
A fairly tight 3yo stayers' event on paper despite the small field, but it was won in emphatic style with the winner back on track. The form is a little muddling.
T/Plt: £595.60 to a £1 stake. Pool: £53,867.30. 66.02 winning tickets. T/Qpdt: £60.40 to a £1 stake. Pool: £7,221.61. 88.40 winning tickets. ST

5889 SANDOWN (R-H)

Wednesday, September 14

OFFICIAL GOING: Good (good to firm in places on round course; sprint 7.7, round 8.1)
Wind: Moderate, against Weather: Fine

6058 SEPTEMBER NURSERY 5f 6y

2:20 (2:21) (Class 5) (0-75,75) 2-Y-0 **£2,264** (£673; £336; £168) **Stalls** Low

Form | RPR
364 **1** **Billyrayvalentine (CAN)**[37] [4864] 2-9-0 **68**.................(t) FrankieDettori 9 82+
(George Baker) *dropped in fr wd draw: w.w in rr: stylish prog fr 1/2-way: chsd ldr over 1f out: jst pushed along to cl and ld last 150yds: v comf* **7/4**[1]
23 **2** *2 1/4* **Lupo D'Oro (IRE)**[22] [5348] 2-9-6 **74**................................. SteveDrowne 8 77
(John Best) *lw: w ldr: led over 3f out: kicked on 1/2-way: styd7 on wl fnl f but hdd and readily outpcd last 150yds* **7/1**[3]
503 **3** *4* **Our Cool Cat (IRE)**[47] [4485] 2-8-9 **63**..........................(b) JamesDoyle 11 52
(Gary Moore) *racd wd in rr: rdn and prog over 1f out: styd on to take 3rd last 100yds* **40/1**
436 **4** *3/4* **Dark Ages (IRE)**[7] [5833] 2-9-0 **68** ow1...........................(b[1]) AdamKirby 2 54
(Noel Quinlan) *trckd ldng trio: prog to chse ldr 2f out to over 1f out: fdd ins fnl f* **14/1**
5430 **5** *2 3/4* **Invincible Dream (IRE)**[21] [5385] 2-9-2 **70**......................... KierenFallon 1 46+
(Robert Mills) *dwlt: no room and snatched up sn after s: mostly last tl sme prog over 1f out: one pce and no hdwy ins fnl f* **7/1**[3]
004 **6** *1* **Deduction (IRE)**[22] [5347] 2-8-3 **62** ow1................ MatthewLawson(5) 10 35
(Charles Hills) *taken down early: racd wd towards rr: outpcd fr 2f out: nvr on terms after* **20/1**
4210 **7** *3/4* **Worth**[16] [5562] 2-9-3 **71**...(b) MartinDwyer 3 41+
(Brian Meehan) *no room and snatched up sn after s: mostly in last pair: no ch whn nowhere to go 1f out: nvr in it* **8/1**
0404 **8** *1 1/2* **Princess Banu**[4] [5913] 2-8-11 **68**.................................. MartinHarley(3) 7 33
(Mick Channon) *led to over 3f out: wknd wl over 1f out* **33/1**
3130 **9** *1 1/4* **Ballyea (IRE)**[46] [4551] 2-9-7 **75**...................................... RichardHughes 6 35
(Richard Hannon) *w ldr to 1/2-way: shkn up 2f out: sn wknd qckly* **15/2**
3311 **10** *14* **Roy's Legacy**[7] [5833] 2-8-10 **64** 6ex.......................(t) RobbieFitzpatrick 4 —
(Shaun Harris) *chsd ldrs but nvr gng wl: rdn and wknd sn after 1/2-way: no ch whn hmpd jst over 1f out: t.o* **11/2**[2]

62.56 secs (0.96) **Going Correction** +0.075s/f (Good) **10** Ran SP% **116.4**
Speed ratings (Par 95): **95,91,85,83,79 77,76,74,72,49**
toteswingers: 1&2 £3.10, 1&3 £14.70, 2&3 £62.40 CSF £13.97 CT £331.41 TOTE £2.70: £1.20, £1.80, £6.80; EX 13.70.
Owner Russell, Wheeler, Vail Partnership **Bred** Windfields Farm **Trained** Whitsbury, Hants
■ Stewards' Enquiry : Martin Harley two-day ban: careless riding (Sep 28-29)

FOCUS
The ground was described as good, with some good to firm places on the round course. The usual bias towards low-drawn horses was turned on its head in this nursery with the first three coming from stalls 9, 8 and 11.

NOTEBOOK
Billyrayvalentine(CAN) was back to the minimum trip for this nursery debut and was sent off a very well-backed favourite. He always looked the likely winner too, racing kindly off the pace and quickening up nicely to collar the leader well inside the last furlong. This shows that his opening mark of 68 was lenient and he should be able to win something a bit better. (op 9-4 tchd 13-8)
Lupo D'Oro(IRE) had run well in nurseries on his previous two starts and, although beaten again, this was his best effort to date. One of three to share the early pace, he held the advantage on his own at halfway and went clear, but was cut down by the progressive winner up the final climb. He still finished clear of the others, though, and can find a race like this. (op 13-2 tchd 6-1)
Our Cool Cat(IRE), making his nursery debut after finishing third of six in a Bath claimer, was dropped in from the outside stall but ran on to finish a never-dangerous third. He looks capable of finding a small race. (op 25-1)
Dark Ages(IRE) hadn't sparkled in nurseries since winning a Nottingham maiden and was tried in blinkers, but she raced keenly enough in them and although holding every chance over a furlong out, she didn't get up the hill. (op 10-1)
Invincible Dream(IRE) was seriously hampered after exiting the stalls and his effort can be upgraded. (op 10-1)
Worth was another to get badly hampered after leaving the stalls. Official explanation: jockey said filly suffered interference shortly after start and was denied a clear run (op 9-1)
Roy's Legacy was bidding for a hat-trick under a 6lb penalty following two recent successes on the Kempton Polytrack, but ran appallingly and was almost pulled up. It would be easy to label him as just an all-weather horse, but this was too bad to be true even based on the pick of his turf efforts. Official explanation: trainer's rep said colt was struck into left-fore (op 9-2 tchd 6-1)

6059 BAM/BRITISH STALLION STUDS E B F MAIDEN STKS 1m 14y

2:55 (2:55) (Class 5) 2-Y-0 **£3,881** (£1,155; £577; £288) **Stalls** Low

Form | RPR
1 **Open Water (FR)** 2-9-3 0... JimmyFortune 4 80+
(Andrew Balding) *unf: scope: settled in midfield: shkn up over 2f out: prog over 1f out: rdn to ld last 100yds: edgd rt but styd on wl* **20/1**
54 **2** *1/2* **Greek War (IRE)**[33] [5013] 2-9-3 0................................... FrankieDettori 10 79
(Mahmood Al Zarooni) *lw: trckd ldng trio: chsd ldr wl over 2f out and sn shkn up: nt qckn over 1f out: kpt on ins fnl f as wnr wnt by* **11/4**[1]
04 **3** *nk* **Alshmemi (USA)**[19] [5447] 2-9-3 0.. RichardHills 3 78
(John Gosden) *lengthy: led: gng bttr than rest 2f out: shkn up jst over 1f out and edgd lft: hdd and nt qckn last 100yds* **7/1**[3]
4 *1* **Rosslyn Castle** 2-9-3 0.. SteveDrowne 9 76+
(Roger Charlton) *leggy: on toes: mostly in last pair and rn green: reminder over 2f out: no prog tl r.o fnl f: fin best of all* **40/1**
0 **5** *1/2* **Free House**[33] [5011] 2-9-3 0... MartinDwyer 1 75
(Brian Meehan) *leggy: athletic: trckd ldng pair on inner: rdn over 2f out: kpt on same pce and nvr able to chal* **3/1**[2]
6 *1/2* **Dynastic** 2-9-3 0.. KierenFallon 6 74+
(Sir Michael Stoute) *str: settled in midfield: brought wd and shkn up over 2f out: kpt on fr over 1f out: nt pce to threaten* **3/1**[2]
7 *shd* **Pilgrims Rest (IRE)** 2-9-3 0.. RichardHughes 11 73
(Richard Hannon) *w'like: attr: sn trckd ldrs on outer: shkn up over 2f out: no imp jst over 1f out: one pce and lost pls fnl f* **9/1**
8 *shd* **Galleon** 2-9-3 0.. DavidProbert 5 73
(Sir Michael Stoute) *leggy: attr: settled towards rr: shkn up and no prog over 2f out: kpt on fnl f* **14/1**
9 *5* **Man Of Plenty** 2-9-3 0.. AdamKirby 8 62
(John Dunlop) *tall: attr: on toes: sn in last: reminder over 3f out: nvr on terms* **100/1**
0 **10** *6* **Bevis Marks (USA)**[12] [5688] 2-9-3 0.......................... SilvestreDeSousa 7 48
(Mark Johnston) *w'like: str: chsd ldr to wl over 2f out: sn wknd* **50/1**
P **High Miswaki (FR)** 2-9-3 0.. JamieSpencer 2 —
(Jeremy Noseda) *w'like: lengthy: p.u after 2f: lame* **20/1**

1m 43.98s (0.68) **Going Correction** -0.225s/f (Firm) **11** Ran SP% **120.7**
Speed ratings (Par 95): **87,86,86,85,84 84,84,84,79,73** —
toteswingers: 1&2 £6.50, 1&3 £17.90, 2&3 £4.20 CSF £74.24 TOTE £22.40: £3.80, £1.60, £2.70; EX 75.30.
Owner Thurloe Thoroughbreds XXVI **Bred** Edy S R L & Azienda Agr La Cucchetta **Trained** Kingsclere, Hants

FOCUS
This maiden was won by the St Leger winner Masked Marvel on his debut last year and some fascinating types lined up for the race this time.

NOTEBOOK
Open Water(FR) ◆ wasn't strong in the market, but he still proved too good for these rivals on his racecourse debut and quickened up nicely after not having much room to play with entering the last 2f. A 47,000gns colt out of a dual winner in Italy, who is a half-sister to the Prix Vermeille/Park Hill winner Sweet Stream, he should improve and looks a nice prospect. (op 16-1)
Greek War(IRE) had already shown ability in maidens here and at Newmarket, finishing ahead of subsequent winners on both occasions. Never far away, he kept on all the way to the line, but he did have the advantage of race fitness and he isn't progressing as quickly as might have been expected. (op 9-4 tchd 2-1)
Alshmemi(USA) had also run twice before, improving plenty from his first start to his second, and tried to make all here. He managed to stay there until collared around 50 yards from the line and can certainly win a maiden, but he doesn't look anything special. (op 13-2 tchd 6-1)

The Form Book, Raceform Ltd, Compton, RG20 6NL

Rosslyn Castle ◆ was the main eye-catcher as he raced green at the back of the field early and didn't look like figuring at all when first put under pressure, but he really found his stride inside the final furlong and finished with a flourish. A brother to a 1m3f winner and a half-brother to a winner over 1m4f, we should be hearing plenty of him over middle distances next season. (op 50-1)
Free House finished seventh of 17 on his Newmarket debut last month and the four of those that finished ahead of him to have run since all won, so better might have been expected, but despite holding a decent position just behind the leaders he didn't produce as much off the bridle as had looked likely. (op 4-1 tchd 9-2)
Dynastic, a 150,000euros half-brother to four winners including the smart pair Il Waard and Coy, was rather on and off the bridle but he did make up some ground when switched out wide. Connections had warned that he might need it, so better can be expected. (op 9-2 tchd 11-2)
Pilgrims Rest(IRE), a 95,000euros brother to a Group 2 winner in South Africa and a half-brother to winners in Greece and Denmark, showed enough on this debut to suggest that he has a future. (op 11-1)
Galleon hinted at ability on this debut and this half-brother to four winners, including the useful pair Promotion and Tactician, is bred to appreciate middle distances next season. (op 10-1)
High Miswaki(FR) Official explanation: vet said colt pulled up lame left-hind

6060 VVB ENGINEERING NOVICE STKS — 7f 16y
3:30 (3:30) (Class 4) 2-Y-O — **£3,557** (£1,058; £529; £264) **Stalls** Low

Form — RPR
21 **1** — **Farraaj (IRE)**[16] 5564 2-9-3 88 .... RichardHills 2 — 105+
(Roger Varian) *lw: mde all: pushed along whn pressed over 2f out: in command over 1f out: r.o wl fnl f* **5/4**[1]
3051 **2** *5* **Tell Dad**[15] 5591 2-9-3 91 .... RichardHughes 5 — 93
(Richard Hannon) *hld up last: prog wl over 2f out: rdn to chse wnr over 1f out: no imp and jst pushed along fnl f* **10/3**[3]
13 **3** *1* **Kinglet (USA)**[13] 5654 2-9-3 92 .... FrankieDettori 3 — 88
(Mahmood Al Zarooni) *chsd wnr: tried to chal over 2f out: sn nt qckn and hld: lost 2nd over 1f out: one pce* **7/4**[2]
1005 **4** *7* **Barolo Top (IRE)**[18] 5487 2-9-3 79 .... SebSanders 1 — 69
(Tom Dascombe) *chsd ldng pair: rdn 3f out: sn dropped to last and wknd* **33/1**

1m 28.84s (-0.66) **Going Correction** -0.225s/f (Firm) — **4** Ran SP% **106.8**
Speed ratings (Par 97): **94,88,87,79**
CSF £5.55 TOTE £2.10; EX 4.60.
Owner Sheikh Ahmed Al Maktoum **Bred** Darley **Trained** Newmarket, Suffolk

FOCUS
Just the four runners, but an interesting contest nonetheless. Seven of the nine previous winners of this race were sent off favourite and the same number had won their previous start. That statistic was extended.

NOTEBOOK
Farraaj(IRE) ◆ had been narrowly beaten in a C&D maiden on his debut in July, which has worked out very well since, and made no mistake when justifying favouritism at Warwick next time. Soon in front under Richard Hills, he dictated throughout and once shaken up entering the last 2f, was never in any danger of defeat. He still showed some signs of greenness inside the last furlong, which strongly suggests there is still plenty of improvement in him, and this Racing Post Trophy entry looks destined for better things. (op 6-5 tchd 11-10 and 11-8 in places)
Tell Dad was back in hotter company after bolting up in a five-runner Ripon nursery and was held up on this first attempt at the trip. He stayed on under pressure from over a furlong out, but was never a threat to the winner and may not be easy to place now that he is officially rated 91. (op 3-1)
Kinglet(USA) was a disappointing favourite in a similar event at Salisbury last time, having narrowly beaten an impressive subsequent winner on his Newmarket debut, and was again below-par here. He was keen enough early and when he was asked to take on the winner over 2f from home, the response was limited. He has an awful lot to prove now. (op 2-1 tchd 9-4 in places)
Barolo Top(IRE), disappointing since winning a Haydock maiden in June, was beaten just after halfway. (op 28-1 tchd 25-1)

6061 FORTUNE STKS (LISTED RACE) — 1m 14y
4:05 (4:05) (Class 1) 3-Y-O+
£17,013 (£6,450; £3,228; £1,608; £807; £405) **Stalls** Low

Form — RPR
-124 **1** — **Lay Time**[25] 5277 3-8-8 103 .... DavidProbert 4 — 111+
(Andrew Balding) *lw: trckd ldng quartet: stdy prog wl over 2f out: led over [illegible]* **4/1**[3]
2006 **2** *3 ½* **Fontley**[11] 5704 4-8-13 99 .... SilvestreDeSousa 7 — 103
(Eve Johnson Houghton) *swtg: pushed along in last trio after 3f: prog u.p fr 3f out: chal wl over 1f out: sn nt qckn: kpt on* **33/1**
2104 **3** *¾* **Emerald Commander (IRE)**[18] 5473 4-9-7 113 .... (t) FrankieDettori 5 — 109
(Saeed Bin Suroor) *warm: pressed ldr: chal over 2f out: upsides wl over 1f out: nt qckn and wl hld after* **10/3**[2]
5524 **4** *nk* **Mikhail Glinka (IRE)**[188] 826 4-9-4 110 .... (t) GeorgeBaker 2 — 106+
(Gary Moore) *settled in last trio: rdn and no prog over 2f out: styd on fr over 1f out: nrst fin* **40/1**
3440 **5** *9* **Critical Moment (USA)**[26] 5252 4-9-4 104 .... (b[1]) MichaelHills 10 — 85
(Charles Hills) *swtg: t.k.h: trckd ldng trio: lost pl wl over 2f out: sn btn* **12/1**
64 **6** *3 ½* **Lieutenant Kojak**[19] 5449 3-8-13 0 .... MartinDwyer 6 — 77?
(Peter Charalambous) *s.i.s: mostly in last: struggling 3f out: passed two toiling rivals fnl f* **100/1**
0-41 **7** *22* **King Torus (IRE)**[11] 5704 3-9-2 110 .... RichardHughes 1 — 29+
(Richard Hannon) *trckd ldng pair: cl up 2f out: sn wknd rapidly: virtually p.u fnl f* **7/4**[1]
4223 **8** *2 ¾* **The Rectifier (USA)**[34] 4972 4-9-4 106 .... MickyFenton 8 — 20+
(Jim Boyle) *lw: led at gd pce: rdn and pressed over 2f out: hdd & wknd qckly over 1f out: virtually p.u* **4/1**[3]

1m 39.69s (-3.61) **Going Correction** -0.225s/f (Firm)
WFA 3 from 4yo+ 5lb — **8** Ran SP% **113.5**
Speed ratings (Par 111): **109,105,104,104,95 91,69,67**
toteswingers: 1&2 £13.60, 1&3 £2.70, 2&3 £8.80 CSF £109.71 TOTE £5.00: £1.70, £4.00, £1.50; EX 119.00.
Owner R Barnett **Bred** W And R Barnett Ltd **Trained** Kingsclere, Hants

FOCUS
The third running of this race since the distance was increased to 1m. The previous two runnings were won by older horses, but this was one for the Classic generation. Ordinary form for the grade, but the winner continues to improve.

NOTEBOOK
Lay Time had run well in a similar event confined to fillies over C&D last month and this performance suggests she is still progressing. In front over a furlong from home, she powered right away in the closing stages and her best days may well still be ahead of her. (op 5-1)
Fontley, safely held by King Torus on recent Haydock running, was 3-6 at the track coming into this and that was probably the reason for this huge effort. Although off the bridle over 3f out, she responded to the pressure and it looked a furlong out as though she might cause a major upset, but the winner proved different class. Official explanation: jockey said filly hung right (op 28-1)
Emerald Commander(IRE) came into this 2-2 in Listed company and had every chance when leading 2f out, but he wasn't in front for long and was done for finishing pace. He needs softer ground. (op 4-1)
Mikhail Glinka(IRE), returning from 188 days off and back with Gary Moore for whom he made just one appearance a year ago, was always going to find this trip too short having won last season's Queen's Vase. Not surprisingly he was doing all his best work late, but he did well to finish so close and this was encouraging. (op 33-1)
Critical Moment(USA) had found Group company too much since needing the race in Listed company on his reappearance. Blinkered for the first time, he pulled far too hard in the early stages and gave himself little chance.
King Torus(IRE), a dual Group 2 winner as a juvenile, came into this fresher than most having only made his reappearance last month. He was close enough if good enough but saw little daylight over 2f out before getting caught behind the eased-off The Rectifier, but he was already under strong pressure by then. His rider reported that the colt stopped quickly. Official explanation: jockey said colt stopped quickly (op 6-4 tchd 15-8 in places and 11-8 in places)
The Rectifier(USA) Official explanation: jockey said colt lost its action halfway up straight

6062 ERITH GROUP FILLIES' H'CAP — 1m 14y
4:40 (4:40) (Class 4) (0-85,85) 3-Y-O — **£4,075** (£1,212; £606; £303) **Stalls** Low

Form — RPR
3011 **1** — **Diverting**[22] 5356 3-8-8 75 .... HarryBentley(3) 13 — 87+
(William Jarvis) *hld up in last trio: gd prog on outer over 2f out: led over 1f out: drvn and styd on wl* **9/1**
6341 **2** *1 ½* **Golden Tempest (IRE)**[23] 5322 3-9-7 85 ....[1] KierenFallon 5 — 93
(Walter Swinburn) *on toes: restrained into last after 1f: rdn 3f out: gd prog wl over 1f out: drvn to chse wnr ins fnl f: styd on but no imp* **14/1**
2300 **3** *hd* **Metropolitain Miss (IRE)**[11] 5730 3-9-1 82 .... MartinHarley(3) 11 — 91+
(Mick Channon) *trckd ldng pair: short of room and hemmed in 2f out: rdn and styd on fr over 1f out: tk 3rd last 100yds* **40/1**
011 **4** *1 ¾* **Jiwen (CAN)**[35] 4931 3-9-5 83 .... RichardHills 12 — 86
(Roger Varian) *str: trckd ldr's str pce: led over 2f out: rdn and hdd over 1f out: fdd last 100yds* **13/2**[3]
1500 **5** *½* **Doricemay (IRE)**[60] 4093 3-8-7 74 .... JohnFahy(3) 9 — 76
(Clive Cox) *settled towards rr: rdn over 2f out: kpt on u.p fnl 2f: nvr able to chal* **40/1**
4125 **6** *1 ½* **Bakoura**[39] 4807 3-8-12 76 .... LiamKeniry 7 — 74+
(John Dunlop) *n.m.r s: hld up in last pair: stl there and looking for room 2f out: shkn up over 1f out: styd on: nvr nr ldrs* **20/1**
5166 **7** *¾* **Abergeldie (USA)**[23] 5328 3-8-7 71 .... (v) DavidProbert 3 — 68
(Andrew Balding) *trckd ldrs in 6th: gng strly and cl up 3f out: swtchd lft wl over 1f out: sn rdn and no rspnse* **10/1**
1-22 **8** *2 ¼* **Present Danger**[28] 5164 3-8-13 77 .... (v[1]) SebSanders 6 — 69
(Tom Dascombe) *settled towards rr: rdn 3f out: no prog and struggling 2f out* **6/1**[2]
1 **9** *4 ½* **Tanaami (USA)**[19] 5449 3-9-0 78 .... FrankieDettori 4 — 59
(Saeed Bin Suroor) *lengthy: hld up towards rr: effrt over 2f out: limited prog over 1f out: sn btn: wknd qckly last 100yds* **9/4**[1]
51 **10** *½* **Neutrafa (IRE)**[16] 5556 3-8-6 77 .... CharlesBishop(7) 10 — 57
(John Mackie) *racd wd: sn pressed ldrs: tried to chal over 2f out: wknd rapidly wl over 1f out* **12/1**
2311 **11** *8* **Moone's My Name**[56] 4202 3-9-1 79 .... JimCrowley 8 — 41
(Ralph Beckett) *t.k.h: trckd ldrs: wl there over 2f out: sn wknd rapidly* **6/1**[2]
3300 **12** *7* **Byrony (IRE)**[11] 5702 3-9-6 84 .... RichardHughes 2 — 30
(Richard Hannon) *lw: led at str pce: hdd over 2f out: wknd rapidly wl over 1f out: eased* **33/1**

1m 41.16s (-2.14) **Going Correction** -0.225s/f (Firm) — **12** Ran SP% **118.7**
Speed ratings (Par 100): **101,99,99,97,97 95,94,92,88,87 79,72**
toteswingers: 1&2 £13.00, 1&3 £37.20, 2&3 £96.40 CSF £122.87 CT £4766.07 TOTE £9.30: £2.80, £4.70, £10.90; EX 114.50.
Owner A Reed **Bred** Anthony Reed **Trained** Newmarket, Suffolk

FOCUS
A competitive handicap run at a decent gallop, and good fillies' form for the grade. The first two came from well off the strong pace.
Golden Tempest(IRE) Official explanation: jockey said filly hung right

6063 HWFA WILLIAMS H'CAP — 1m 2f 7y
5:10 (5:11) (Class 4) (0-85,84) 3-Y-O — [illegible] **Stalls** [illegible]

Form — RPR
3120 **1** — **Shalloon (IRE)**[16] 5557 3-9-3 80 .... SilvestreDeSousa 8 — 89
(Mark Johnston) *led to over 6f out: rdn to ld narrowly over 2f out and clr of remainder: drvn and hld on wl fr over 1f out* **6/1**
6020 **2** *¾* **Fadhaa (IRE)**[18] 5483 3-9-6 83 .... RichardHills 6 — 90
(Charles Hills) *prog to ld over 6f out: hdd over 2f out and clr of rest: gd battle w wnr after tl no ex last 100yds* **7/2**[2]
0026 **3** *½* **Heatherbird**[28] 5169 3-8-7 73 .... HarryBentley(3) 1 — 79
(William Jarvis) *awkward and stdd s: hld up in last pair: smooth prog to chse clr ldng pair jst over 2f out: sn rdn: clsd grad fnl f but nvr rchd them* **12/1**
-101 **4** *1 ¼* **Groomed (IRE)**[26] 5242 3-9-3 83 .... AdamBeschizza(3) 3 — 87
(William Haggas) *hld up disputing 5th: rdn 3f out: styd on fr over 1f out: nrst fin but unable to chal* **6/1**
3322 **5** *2 ¼* **Aerial Acclaim (IRE)**[25] 5281 3-9-5 82 .... AdamKirby 7 — 81
(Clive Cox) *s.i.s: hld up in last pair: rdn 3f out: no prog 2f out: plugged on over 1f out* **10/3**[1]
10 **6** *8* **Look Left**[26] 5235 3-9-4 81 .... RobertHavlin 2 — 64
(John Gosden) *dwlt: hld up disputing 5th: slt stumble over 4f out: rdn 3f out: wknd over 2f out* **8/1**
-040 **7** *¾* **Orange Ace**[14] 5635 3-8-7 70 oh1 .... (p) MartinDwyer 9 — 52
(Paul Cole) *prom: rdn 3f out: sn struggling and btn* **25/1**
3-15 **8** *1 ½* **Shooting Line (IRE)**[14] 5635 3-9-7 84 .... KierenFallon 4 — 63
(Walter Swinburn) *lw: prom: rdn 3f out: sn wknd and btn* **9/2**[3]

2m 9.21s (-1.29) **Going Correction** -0.225s/f (Firm) — **8** Ran SP% **114.7**
Speed ratings (Par 103): **96,95,95,94,92 85,85,84**
toteswingers: 1&2 £4.80, 1&3 £11.40, 2&3 £6.60 CSF £27.39 CT £244.18 TOTE £9.20: £2.20, £1.10, £3.80; EX 29.70.
Owner Sheikh Hamdan Bin Mohammed Al Maktoum **Bred** Gigginstown House Stud & Lynn Lodge Stud **Trained** Middleham Moor, N Yorks

FOCUS
The early pace was modest in this 3yo handicap and the place to be in such an event is at the front, which is exactly where the first two were. The form makes plenty of sense.
Look Left Official explanation: jockey said colt lost its action
Shooting Line(IRE) Official explanation: jockey said colt never travelled
T/Plt: £1,657.60 to a £1 stake. Pool: £56,541.84. 24.90 winning tickets. T/Qpdt: £369.10 to a £1 stake. Pool: £4,340.18. 8.70 winning tickets. JN

[6030]YARMOUTH (L-H)

Wednesday, September 14

OFFICIAL GOING: Good (7.6)

Wind: Medium, half against Weather: Light cloud, brighter spells

6064 BRITISH STALLION STUDS SUPPORTING BRITISH RACING E B F MAIDEN STKS 7f 3y

2:10 (2:12) (Class 5) 2-Y-O **£3,234** (£962; £481; £240) **Stalls** Centre

Form RPR

2 **1** **Electrician**[11] 5697 2-9-3 0 ..... WilliamBuick 10 86+
(John Gosden) *chsd ldr tl led 4f out: pushed clr and edgd lft wl over 1f out: in command fnl f: eased towards fin: easily* **8/11**[1]

4 **2** 3 ¾ **Debating Society (IRE)**[26] 5239 2-9-3 0 ..... RichardMullen 1 76
(Sir Michael Stoute) *chsd ldrs: rdn and nt pce of wnr wl over 1f out: chsd clr wnr over 1f out: kpt on but no imp* **11/2**[3]

3 1 ½ **Excellent Jem** 2-9-3 0 ..... TomQueally 3 72
(George Margarson) *sn led: hdd 4f out: chsd wnr after: rdn and outpcd wl over 1f out: 3rd and kpt on same pce fr over 1f out* **25/1**

0 **4** 2 ½ **Protanto (IRE)**[53] 4330 2-9-3 0 ..... TedDurcan 5 65+
(David Lanigan) *s.i.s: in tch: rdn: rn green and outpcd ent fnl 2f: edgd lft and sme hdwy over 1f out: n.d but kpt on ins fnl f* **9/2**[2]

303 **5** 1 ½ **Cockney Rocker**[82] 3349 2-9-3 69 ..... FrannyNorton 7 61
(Jane Chapple-Hyam) *plld hrd: hld up wl in tch: rdn and outpcd ent fnl 2f: 4th and wl btn over 1f out* **14/1**

6 nk **Arabic** 2-9-3 0 ..... ShaneKelly 6 60
(James Fanshawe) *dwlt: rn green and pushed along leaving stalls: hld up in tch towards rr: sme hdwy 1/2-way: rdn and outpcd over 2f out: no ch w wnr but rallied 1f out: swtchd lft and kpt on ins fnl f* **40/1**

7 ½ **Opinion (IRE)** 2-9-3 0 ..... StevieDonohoe 9 61+
(Sir Michael Stoute) *s.i.s: rn v green early: in tch towards rr: hdwy into midfield after 2f out: lost pl and bhd whn rn green u.p over 2f out: no ch w wnr but rallied 1f out: kpt on ins fnl f* **16/1**

8 ¾ **Plastiki** 2-9-0 0 ..... LouisBeuzelin(3) 4 57
(Sir Michael Stoute) *t.k.h: hld up wl in tch: rdn and struggling over 2f out: sn outpcd and wl btn fnl 2f* **22/1**

9 10 **Thecornishcowboy** 2-9-0 0 ..... MichaelO'Connell(3) 11 30
(John Ryan) *t.k.h: hld up wl in tch: rdn: rn green and struggling over 2f out: sn wknd: wl bhd fnl f* **150/1**

1m 26.69s (0.09) **Going Correction** -0.30s/f (Firm) **9** Ran SP% **115.3**

Speed ratings (Par 95): **87,82,81,78,76 76,75,74,63**

toteswingers: 1&2 £1.30, 1&3 £9.20, 2&3 £10.50 CSF £4.87 TOTE £1.70: £1.10, £1.40, £3.70; EX 5.60 Trifecta £45.90 Pool: £546.58 - 8.81 winning units..

Owner H R H Princess Haya Of Jordan **Bred** Darley **Trained** Newmarket, Suffolk

FOCUS

There were several good Newmarket stables involved in this, with some interesting and unexposed runners on display, but the winner trounced the rest of them. It remains to be seen just how good this race turns out to be, but he looks a fair sort in the making.

NOTEBOOK

Electrician learnt plenty on his debut and had this in the bag more than 2f from home, though Buick had to keep him up to his work all the way home. Rated something of a baby, he should continue to progress. (op 5-6 after early 10-11 and evens in places)

Debating Society(IRE) has now twice run respectably at 7f, but he is a half-brother to four winners around 1m2f and 1m-plus will suit him. He should come into his own next season. (op 4-1)

Excellent Jem showed plenty of speed and should put that to good use. His dam won eight times from 1m1f-1m4f, but this son of the sprinter Exceed and Excel ought to be capable of winning at shorter distances. (op 16-1)

Protanto(IRE) did not step up significantly from his debut, and needs to do better to win a maiden. (op 6-1)

Cockney Rocker has some ability but maidens have proved beyond him. A switch to nurseries would be a good move. (tchd 12-1)

Arabic, whose dam won over 6f, is a half-brother to two winners from 7f-1m2f. He began to pick up too late, but there was some encouragement in the way he finished. (op 33-1)

Opinion(IRE), a 210,000gns Oasis Dream half-brother to the useful middle-distance handicapper Fox Hunt, ought to have benefited from the outing. However, improvement is needed to feature more prominently, so he needs to be monitored next time

6065 AVENUE PUB FILLIES' H'CAP 6f 3y

2:45 (2:47) (Class 5) (0-75,75) 3-Y-O+ **£2,264** (£673; £336; £168) **Stalls** Centre

Form RPR

0041 **1** **Darcey**[12] 5677 5-8-10 **64** ..... CathyGannon 7 77
(Amy Weaver) *sn pushed along in midfield: rdn and effrt to chse ldrs ent fnl 2f: led over 1f out: clr and kpt on wl fnl f* **10/1**

1312 **2** 2 **Katy's Secret**[6] 5862 4-8-9 **66** ..... RyanClark(3) 4 73
(William Jarvis) *hld up in midfield: pushed along and hdwy to chse ldrs over 1f out: drvn and kpt on to chse wnr ins fnl f: kpt on* **7/2**[2]

5012 **3** 1 **Oh So Spicy**[16] 5561 4-8-13 **67** ..... TedDurcan 12 70
(Chris Wall) *racd on stands' rail hld up in rr: hdwy and swtchd lft 2f out: drvn and chsd ldng pair over 1f out: kpt on same pce ins fnl f* **10/3**[1]

2421 **4** 2 ¾ **Suzy Alexander**[9] 5780 4-8-10 **64** 6ex ..... ChrisCatlin 2 59
(David Simcock) *chsd ldrs: rdn and effrt to press ldrs 2f out: chsd wnr and nt qckn u.p over 1f out: wknd ins fnl f* **15/2**[3]

4651 **5** 2 **Bianca De Medici**[51] 4387 4-9-7 **75** ..... TomQueally 11 63
(Hughie Morrison) *sn pushed along and outpcd in last trio: hdwy over 1f out: kpt on past btn horses ins fnl f: nvr trbld ldrs* **10/3**[1]

0006 **6** 2 **Breedj (IRE)**[33] 5018 3-9-5 **75** ..... PhilipRobinson 8 57
(Clive Brittain) *awkward leaving stalls and dropped to last sn after s: bhd and detached: rdn over 1f out: styd on past btn horses fnl f: nvr trbld ldrs* **40/1**

-030 **7** 1 **Supreme Spirit (IRE)**[104] 2633 4-9-4 **72** ..... FrannyNorton 10 51
(George Margarson) *racd in midfield: pushed along and unable qck 2f out: sn outpcd and no threat to ldrs fr over 1f out* **25/1**

2102 **8** ½ **Eshoog (IRE)**[11] 5736 3-8-1 **64** ow1 ..... (bt) LeonnaMayor(7) 13 41
(Phil McEntee) *racd against stands' rail chsd overall ldr tl led 2f out: rdn and hdd over 1f out: wknd fnl f* **14/1**

3456 **9** 6 **Miss Polly Plum**[18] 5484 4-8-11 **65** ..... (p) MartinLane 3 23
(Chris Dwyer) *taken down early: led tl 2f: sn rdn and wknd over 1f out: fdd fnl f* **22/1**

5426 **10** 2 ¾ **Black Baccara**[119] 2193 4-8-3 **64** ow1 ..... DannyBrock(7) 6 13
(Phil McEntee) *swtchd to r towards stands' rail after 1f: chsd ldrs: rdn and struggling over 2f out: wknd wl over 1f out* **40/1**

5/03 **11** 14 **Miss Chamanda (IRE)**[14] 5627 5-9-2 **70** ..... StevieDonohoe 5 —
(David Evans) *chsd ldrs: rdn and struggling wl over 2f out: sn wknd: wl bhd and virtually p.u ins fnl f: t.o* **20/1**

1m 12.5s (-1.90) **Going Correction** -0.30s/f (Firm)

WFA 3 from 4yo+ 2lb **11** Ran SP% **113.7**

Speed ratings (Par 100): **100,97,96,92,89 87,85,85,77,73 54**

toteswingers: 1&2 £5.80, 1&3 £4.40, 2&3 £1.40 CSF £40.65 CT £143.91 TOTE £9.30: £2.70, £1.60, £1.40; EX 47.00 Trifecta £128.00 Pool: £576.34 - 3.33 winning units..

Owner Bringloe, Spain, Parkin & Lennox **Bred** Raymond Cowie **Trained** Newmarket, Suffolk

FOCUS

They raced wide apart, from the middle to the stands' rail, with the winner forming part of the main group in the centre.

Breedj(IRE) Official explanation: jockey said filly suffered interference at start

Miss Chamanda(IRE) Official explanation: jockey said mare lost its action

6066 IRISH E B F AT RACES JOHN MUSKER FILLIES' STKS (FOR THE JOHN MUSKER TROPHY) (LISTED RACE) 1m 2f 21y

3:20 (3:21) (Class 1) 3-Y-O+

£16,866 (£6,420; £3,213; £1,602; £804; £405) **Stalls** Low

Form RPR

3130 **1** **Principal Role (USA)**[18] 5494 4-9-6 114 ..... TomQueally 4 109+
(Sir Henry Cecil) *hld up in midfield: swtchd rt and hdwy 4f out: pushed along and effrt to press ldr 2f out: rdn to ld over 1f out: readily asserted 1f out: in command and pushed out fnl 100yds: comf* **4/1**[2]

10-2 **2** 2 **Modeyra**[25] 5277 4-9-2 108 ..... TedDurcan 5 101
(Saeed Bin Suroor) *chsd ldr for 1f: chsd ldng pair after tl hdwy to ld over 2f out: rdn and hdd over 1f out: nt pce of wnr 1f out and btn jst ins fnl f: kpt on same pce after* **6/4**[1]

1121 **3** 1 ¾ **Captivator**[24] 5303 4-9-2 87 ..... CathyGannon 6 97
(James Fanshawe) *stdd s: t.k.h: hld up in last trio: gd hdwy on inner 4f out: chsd ldng pair and rdn wl over 1f out: unable qck and swtchd rt jst ins fnl f: kpt on same pce after* **16/1**

-035 **4** 2 ¼ **Date With Destiny (IRE)**[119] 2189 3-8-9 90 ..... PatDobbs 7 94+
(Richard Hannon) *chsd ldng trio: clsd on ldr 4f out: rdn and effrt whn stmbld 2f out: sn outpcd by ldng trio and kpt on same pce after* **33/1**

1534 **5** 1 ¾ **Piano**[35] 4915 4-9-2 99 ..... WilliamBuick 11 89
(John Gosden) *hld up in last quartet: clsd on ldrs 4f out: rdn and effrt jst over 2f out: sn drvn and unable qck: kpt on same pce and wl hld after* **5/1**[3]

-460 **6** ¾ **Nouriya**[47] 4492 4-9-2 99 ..... RichardMullen 12 88
(Sir Michael Stoute) *hld up in midfield: clsd on ldrs 4f out: in tch and rdn jst over 2f out: unable qck 2f out: one pce and no threat to ldrs fr over 1f out* **10/1**

1115 **7** 1 ½ **Tenby Lady (USA)**[16] 5546 3-8-9 88 ..... StevieDonohoe 10 85
(Sir Mark Prescott Bt) *stdd s: t.k.h: hld up in last trio: hdwy on outer 4f out: rdn and unable qck over 2f out: sn outpcd and wl hld over 1f out* **17/2**

0411 **8** ½ **Celestial Girl**[16] 5546 4-9-2 77 ..... ChrisCatlin 2 84
(Hughie Morrison) *stdd s: t.k.h: hld up in rr: clsd and nt clr run 3f out: rdn and no prog over jst over 2f out: sn outpcd and wl btn over 1f out* **33/1**

5 **9** 4 ½ **Skyway (IRE)**[27] 5226 4-9-2 88 ..... KLatham 1 75
(Takashi Kodama, Ire) *led and sn clr: c bk to field 4f out: rdn and hdd over 2f out: wknd u.p 2f out: eased wl ins fnl f* **33/1**

05 **10** 7 **Dffra (IRE)**[15] 5598 3-8-9 0 ..... PhilipRobinson 9 61
(Clive Brittain) *s.i.s: gd hdwy to chse ldr after 1f tl 3f out: wknd over 2f out: wl bhd fnl f* **250/1**

2m 4.65s (-5.85) **Going Correction** -0.375s/f (Firm)

WFA 3 from 4yo 7lb **10** Ran SP% **111.4**

Speed ratings (Par 108): **108,106,105,103,101 101,100,99,96,90**

toteswingers: 1&2 £1.50, 1&3 £13.40, 2&3 £7.20 CSF £9.62 TOTE £4.90: £1.60, £1.10, £3.00; EX 10.60 Trifecta £69.10 Pool: £1,063.77 - 11.39 winning units..

Owner K Abdulla **Bred** Juddmonte Farms Inc **Trained** Newmarket, Suffolk

FOCUS

A fine turnout for Yarmouth's top race of the year. They went a decent gallop, which played into the hands of the classier performers, and were stretched out by a good 15l by halfway. The first two are rated a few pounds off their best.

NOTEBOOK

Principal Role(USA) bounced back after a disappointing run last time, when the ground was probably too soft. The drop to Listed grade proved the ideal opportunity to get her back on track, with her class shining through in the last 2f, and she looks capable of winning a Group 3 at least. (tchd 7-2)

Modeyra, who has already won at this level, showed again that she has trained on well despite being lightly raced. Finishing second to the classy winner was a good effort. (op 11-8 tchd 5-4)

Captivator, who has done well since being fitted with a hood, was a bit short of room on the rail but that did not seriously affect her final placing. This big step up in class was just beyond her, but she performed with credit. (tchd 18-1)

Date With Destiny(IRE), unraced since May, has had a largely disappointing season, running here as if she needs at least 1m4f. However, one attempt around that trip earlier in the season was unproductive and it looks as if she is just finding things a bit tough at this level. However, the black type gained here will further increase this uniquely bred filly's value. (op 28-1)

Piano runs well in Listed company, but she keeps finding a few too good for her. Rated 99, she has few attractive options in handicaps but needs to find a little more to win in this grade. (op 13-2)

Nouriya, the winner of this race last year, has not recaptured that form this season. (op 9-1)

Tenby Lady(USA), yet to win outside maiden and handicap company, found this too tough. (op 10-1)

Celestial Girl, winner of two recent handicaps, found this too hard off a mark of 77. (op 28-1)

Skyway(IRE)'s stamina ran out after setting a good gallop. Official explanation: jockey said filly hung right

6067 DANNY WRIGHT MEMORIAL (S) STKS 1m 2f 21y

3:55 (3:56) (Class 6) 3-4-Y-O **£1,704** (£503; £251) **Stalls** Low

Form RPR

440 **1** **Harry Lime**[58] 4164 3-8-12 53 ..... CathyGannon 8 62
(William Jarvis) *in tch: rdn 4f out: hdwy u.p 3f out: chsd clr ldr wl over 1f out: kpt on dourly to ld ins fnl f: styd on wl* **4/1**[2]

0030 **2** 2 **Sister Andrea**[8] 5804 3-8-7 67 ..... ShaneKelly 9 53
(James Fanshawe) *taken down early: stdd s: rn in snatches in rr: rdn 4f out: sme hdwy into modest 5th 2f out: swtchd rt and chsd ldng pair jst over 1f out: styd on to chse wnr fnl 50yds: nvr looked like chalng* **5/4**[1]

0-64 **3** 1 ¼ **Lord Of The Storm**[34] 4576 3-8-9 62 ..... (t) KierenFox(3) 6 56
(Bill Turner) *chsd ldr tl rdn to ld 4f out: clr 3f out: drvn over 1f out: hdd ins fnl f: wknd fnl 75yds* **14/1**

6060 **4** 7 **Danceyourselfdizzy (IRE)**[6] 5860 3-8-12 59 ..... ChrisCatlin 3 42
(Phil McEntee) *led tl 4f out: sn drvn and outpcd: wknd u.p over 1f out: fdd fnl f* **25/1**

450 **5** *2 ¾* **Flying Phoenix**^{14} 5631 3-8-5 61 .... NatashaEaton(7) 7 36
(Gay Kelleway) *taken down early: t.k.h: chsd ldrs: wnt 2nd 4f out: rdn and no imp over 2f out: lost 2nd wl over 1f out: sn wknd: fdd ins fnl f* **8/1^{3}**

0 **6** *7* **Cardi Crystal (IRE)**^{23} 5317 4-8-9 0 .... AntiocoMurgia(5) 1 17
(Ian Wood) *t.k.h: chsd ldrs: struggling and drvn wl over 2f out: sn wknd and wl btn fnl 2f* **12/1**

3540 **7** *3 ¾* **Crystal Sky (IRE)**^{7} 5838 3-8-12 62 .... (p) MartinLane 2 15
(Andrew Haynes) *in tch in midfield: rdn and effrt 4f out: drvn and struggling 3f out: edgd lft and wknd over 2f out: sn wl btn* **8/1^{3}**

4 **8** *3 ¾* **Midnight Tiger**^{20} 5408 3-8-12 0 .... AdrianMcCarthy 5 —
(George Prodromou) *dwlt: hld up in tch towards rr: rdn and struggling over 3f out: wknd over 2f out: sn bhd* **100/1**

9 *39* **Loganberry** 3-8-7 0 .... RichardMullen 4 —
(Robert Cowell) *in tch in midfield: pushed along and lost pl after 3f: last and lost tch 5f out: t.o and eased fnl 2f* **12/1**

2m 8.57s (-1.93) **Going Correction** -0.375s/f (Firm)
WFA 3 from 4yo 7lb **9** Ran SP% **113.6**
Speed ratings (Par 101): **92,90,89,83,81 76,73,70,38**
toteswingers: 1&2 £2.30, 1&3 £4.80, 2&3 £4.40 CSF £9.15 TOTE £4.20: £1.40, £1.30, £2.40; EX 9.10 Trifecta £101.40 Pool: £853.08 - 6.22 winning units..The winner was sold to Michael Foulger for 6,000gns.
Owner Michael Payton,A Briam & I Robertson **Bred** Car Colston Hall Stud **Trained** Newmarket, Suffolk

FOCUS
A weak seller in which the third tried to slip the field 3f from home, but in doing so he only set the finish up for two stronger finishers. The time was not bad and the for is rated around that, with the second a stone+ off.

6068 VAUXHALL HOLIDAY PARK H'CAP (FOR THE GOLDEN JUBILEE TROPHY) 1m 2f 21y
4:30 (4:30) (Class 3) (0-90,89) 3-Y-O+ **£6,490** (£1,942; £971; £486; £242) **Stalls** Low

Form RPR

-006 **1** **Colour Scheme (IRE)**^{12} 5686 4-9-5 **82** .... (t) ShaneKelly 1 93
(Brian Meehan) *chsd ldr: rdn and qcknd to ld ent fnl f: in command and r.o wl ins fnl f* **11/2^{3}**

2-16 **2** *1 ½* **Direct Answer (USA)**^{12} 5693 4-9-2 **79** .... RichardMullen 8 87
(Sir Michael Stoute) *led: rdn over 2f out: drvn and hdd ent fnl f: kpt on but a hld fnl f* **11/2^{3}**

051 **3** *2 ½* **Junoob**^{100} 2760 3-9-3 **87** .... TomQueally 7 90
(John Dunlop) *chsd ldng pair: effrt and rdn 2f out: unable qck w ldrs ent fnl f: styd on same pce after* **9/2^{2}**

1526 **4** *hd* **Ellemujie**^{18} 5483 6-9-9 **86** .... (p) PhilipRobinson 3 89
(Dean Ivory) *chsd ldng trio: clsde to chse ldrs and rdn over 1f out: unable qck w ldrs ent fnl f: styd on same pce after* **8/1**

1155 **5** *hd* **Art Scholar (IRE)**^{38} 4818 4-9-0 **77** .... NeilChalmers 4 79
(Michael Appleby) *hld up in tch in last pair: swtchd rt and effrt over 1f out: unable qck and no imp on ldrs ent fnl f: one pce after* **16/1**

241 **6** *29* **Almagest**^{23} 5327 3-9-3 **87** .... WilliamBuick 2 31+
(John Gosden) *dwlt and pushed along leaving stalls: nvr looked to be travelling: in tch in last pair: pushed along over 4f out: rdn 3f out: sn hung lft and btn: eased wl over 1f out: virtually p.u ins fnl f* **11/10^{1}**

2m 6.82s (-3.68) **Going Correction** -0.375s/f (Firm)
WFA 3 from 4yo+ 7lb **6** Ran SP% **113.6**
Speed ratings (Par 107): **99,97,95,95,95 72**
toteswingers: 1&2 £3.20, 1&3 £4.40, 2&3 £2.80 CSF £35.14 CT £146.39 TOTE £6.40: £2.90, £3.20; EX 30.20 Trifecta £119.20 Pool: £755.73 - 4.69 winning units..
Owner Paul & Jenny Green **Bred** Paul And Mrs Jenny Green **Trained** Manton, Wilts

FOCUS
Despite the smallish field, this was run at a solid, medium gallop which gave everyone a chance. Decent form, with personal bests from the first two.

NOTEBOOK
Colour Scheme(IRE) has had a quiet season, but he picked up willingly when asked and should go on from here. This was his first win on turf, but with only eight races behind him he is fresher than most. (op 6-1 tchd 5-1)
Direct Answer(USA) ran a sound race in defeat, being beaten only by a relatively unknown [illegible] He, too, is lightly [illegible], and should find more opportunities at this sort of level. (op 6-1 tchd 13-2)
Junoob, off since June, had a testing mark for this first handicap run. Though well held in the last 2f, he does have ability and can improve on this a bit. (op 5-1 tchd 11-2)
Ellemujie ran respectably as usual, but he was not at his most effective against some relatively unexposed rivals. (tchd 9-1)
Art Scholar(IRE) has been heading up the handicap during the course of a fine season, so things are tougher for him now. (op 12-1)
Almagest was never comfortable and, after racing awkwardly in the straight in a manner which suggested some sort of problem, he was eased down. He showed at Windsor that he is capable of much better. Official explanation: jockey said colt moved poorly (op 6-5 tchd 5-4 in a place and 11-8 in places)

6069 SEA-DEER H'CAP 1m 3y
5:00 (5:00) (Class 4) (0-85,85) 3-Y-O+ **£4,075** (£1,212; £606; £303) **Stalls** Centre

Form RPR

2-14 **1** **Mujrayaat (IRE)**^{50} 4404 3-9-2 **82** .... ^{1} J-PGuillambert 1 94
(Roger Varian) *chsd ldrs: rdn over 2f out: ev ch over 1f out: led 1f out: edgd rt but r.o strly ins fnl f* **7/2^{1}**

00 **2** *2* **Nelson's Bounty**^{11} 5712 4-9-8 **83** .... WilliamBuick 9 91
(Paul D'Arcy) *hld up in tch in midfield: rdn and effrt 2f out: ev ch ent fnl f: nt pce of wnr and btn whn sltly hmpd ins fnl f* **7/2^{1}**

0012 **3** *¾* **Top Diktat**^{26} 5240 3-8-9 **75** .... RichardMullen 12 80
(Sir Michael Stoute) *hld up in tch in last trio: edging lft and effrt u.p over 1f out: kpt on but nvr gng pce to chal wnr* **9/2^{2}**

1334 **4** *hd* **Hawaana (IRE)**^{25} 5281 6-9-1 **79** .... DeclanCannon(3) 7 84
(Gay Kelleway) *hld up in tch: rdn 2f out: unable qck and n.m.r over 1f out: kpt on ins fnl f: nt pce to threaten wnr* **14/1**

0545 **5** *hd* **Rough Rock (IRE)**^{10} 5760 6-8-10 **74** .... RyanClark(3) 6 78
(Chris Dwyer) *chsd ldng trio: rdn whn gallop qcknd 2f out: kpt on same pce ins fnl f* **12/1**

2623 **6** *¾* **Fantasy Gladiator**^{11} 5712 5-9-6 **81** .... (p) ShaneKelly 10 84
(Robert Cowell) *hld up in tch in last trio: effrt and rdn over 1f out: styd on same pce under ins fnl f* **13/2**

2-22 **7** *½* **Afkar (IRE)**^{140} 1606 3-9-5 **85** .... PhilipRobinson 3 85
(Clive Brittain) *led at stdy gallop: rdn and qcknd 2f out: hdd 1f out: no ex and wknd fnl 100yds* **11/2^{3}**

6510 **8** *¾* **Amoya (GER)**^{39} 4807 4-8-13 **74** .... PatDobbs 11 74
(Philip McBride) *t.k.h: chsd ldr tl wl over 1f out: sn rdn and unable qck: wknd ins fnl f* **20/1**

-250 **9** *6* **Sir Mozart (IRE)**^{22} 5341 8-8-11 **72** .... TomQueally 4 58
(Barney Curley) *awkward leaving stalls and slowly away: hld up in tch in rr: pushed along and brief effrt jst over 2f out: rdn and wknd over 1f out* **33/1**

1m 39.35s (-1.25) **Going Correction** -0.30s/f (Firm)
WFA 3 from 4yo+ 5lb **9** Ran SP% **113.4**
Speed ratings (Par 105): **94,92,91,91,90 90,89,88,82**
toteswingers: 1&2 £3.60, 1&3 £5.20, 2&3 £5.40 CSF £15.21 CT £54.77 TOTE £5.00: £1.70, £2.00, £1.20; EX 19.90 Trifecta £111.50 Pool: £693.69 - 4.60 winning units..
Owner Hamdan Al Maktoum **Bred** Lady Richard Wellesley **Trained** Newmarket, Suffolk

FOCUS
The field raced in one bunch in the middle of the track, and the pace was ordinary. Decent form, with a clear personal best from the winner.

6070 REEVE PROPERTY RESTORATION H'CAP (DIV I) 7f 3y
5:30 (5:31) (Class 6) (0-60,60) 3-Y-O+ **£1,704** (£503; £251) **Stalls** Centre

Form RPR

500 **1** **Swansea Jack**^{95} 2920 4-9-2 **55** .... (vt^{1}) RyanClark(3) 7 70
(Stuart Williams) *hld up in tch: edgd lft and effrt over 1f out: drvn and chal ins fnl f: led fnl 75yds: r.o wl* **8/1**

2230 **2** *½* **Zafeen's Pearl**^{33} 5014 4-9-10 **60** .... ShaneKelly 5 74
(Dean Ivory) *hld up in tch: hdwy and rdn to ld wl over 1f out: drvn fnl f: hdd and no ex fnl 75yds* **3/1^{1}**

0204 **3** *4 ½* **Fedora (IRE)**^{64} 3943 5-9-3 **53** .... (t) CathyGannon 11 55
(Olivia Maylam) *hld up in tch: rdn and effrt to chse ldrs over 1f out: hld hd high and hung lft u.p over 1f out: wknd ins fnl f* **7/2^{2}**

0343 **4** *3* **Avec Moi**^{41} 4729 4-8-3 **46** oh1 .... DanielHarris(7) 10 40
(Christine Dunnett) *w ldrs tl led 4f out: rdn 1/2-way: hdd wl over 1f out: no ex u.p and btn jst over 1f out: wknd fnl f* **16/1**

0040 **5** *shd* **Fathey (IRE)**^{15} 5601 5-8-7 **46** oh1 .... (t) MichaelO'Connell(3) 4 39
(Charles Smith) *w ldrs: ev ch and rdn 3f out: no ex and btn jst over 1f out: wknd fnl f* **28/1**

-600 **6** *5* **Piccolete**^{12} 5674 3-8-9 **49** ow1 .... PatDobbs 3 27
(Richard Hannon) *in tch in midfield: rdn and effrt on far side ent fnl 2f: wknd over 1f out: fdd ins fnl f* **10/1**

5234 **7** *¾* **Jonnie Skull (IRE)**^{21} 5394 5-9-6 **56** .... (vt) ChrisCatlin 9 34
(Phil McEntee) *led tl 4f out: rdn and struggling 3f out: wknd 2f out: wl bhd fnl f* **7/1^{3}**

3603 **8** *1 ¼* **Choose The Moment**^{14} 5626 3-9-2 **56** .... (p) TomQueally 13 29
(Eve Johnson Houghton) *hld up in rr: rdn and no hdwy over 2f out: wl btn and hung lft over 1f out* **8/1**

4000 **9** *1* **Blazing Apostle (IRE)**^{12} 5670 3-8-6 **46** oh1 .... (p) AdrianMcCarthy 8 16
(Christine Dunnett) *t.k.h: hld up wl in tch: rdn wl over 2f out: wknd u.p wl over 1f out* **50/1**

2005 **10** *7* **Hackett (IRE)**^{98} 2825 3-9-1 **55** .... (v) FrannyNorton 12 —
(Michael Quinn) *reminders sn after s: in tch towards rr: rdn and little rspnse over 2f out: wknd wl over 1f out* **25/1**

006 **11** *2* **Come And Go (UAE)**^{1} 6033 5-9-3 **53** .... PatrickMathers 1 —
(Ian McInnes) *chsd ldrs: rdn 4f out: wknd u.p 2f out: wl bhd over 1f out* **11/1**

1m 25.59s (-1.01) **Going Correction** -0.30s/f (Firm)
WFA 3 from 4yo+ 4lb **11** Ran SP% **114.5**
Speed ratings (Par 101): **93,92,87,83,83 78,77,75,74,66 64**
toteswingers: 1&2 £7.10, 1&3 £12.90, 2&3 £4.10 CSF £30.77 CT £101.77 TOTE £11.10: £3.40, £1.50, £1.60; EX 42.30 Trifecta £120.50 Pool: £545.51 - 3.35 winning units..
Owner K J Mercer **Bred** Usk Valley Stud **Trained** Newmarket, Suffolk

FOCUS
A modest event, but one with many still in contention on the run to the last furlong. The first pair were clear.

6071 REEVE PROPERTY RESTORATION H'CAP (DIV II) 7f 3y
6:00 (6:00) (Class 6) (0-60,60) 3-Y-O+ **£1,704** (£503; £251) **Stalls** Centre

Form RPR

0130 **1** **Diamond Run**^{17} 5511 3-9-3 **57** .... PatDobbs 10 68+
(J W Hills) *mde all: rdn and hrd pressed over 1f out: edgd rt but kpt on wl ins fnl f* **7/2^{1}**

3040 **2** *1* **Caldermud (IRE)**^{9} 5789 4-9-9 **59** .... (t) CathyGannon 11 69
(Olivia Maylam) *taken down early: [illegible] 1f out: no ex and btn fnl 100yds* **13/2^{3}**

1644 **3** *2 ¾* **Norcroft**^{15} 5601 9-8-3 **46** oh1 .... (p) DanielHarris(7) 4 49
(Christine Dunnett) *dwlt: hld up in tch: hdwy 2f out: chsd ldng pair and rdn 1f out: no imp ins fnl f* **14/1**

3400 **4** *¾* **Pearly Wey**^{26} 5244 8-9-2 **52** .... PatrickMathers 2 53
(Ian McInnes) *taken down early: stdd and dropped in bhd after s: hld up in rr: hdwy 2f out: drvn and kpt on ins fnl f: nvr able able to chal* **16/1**

3340 **5** *2 ¼* **Pytheas (USA)**^{64} 3944 4-9-1 **56** .... MarkCoumbe(5) 5 50
(Michael Attwater) *hld up in tch: effrt 2f out: drvn and chsd ldrs over 1f out: nt qckn ent fnl f: wknd fnl 150yds* **4/1^{2}**

0064 **6** *3 ½* **Talkative Guest (IRE)**^{12} 5670 3-8-11 **51** .... AdrianMcCarthy 6 34
(George Margarson) *chsd ldrs: rdn and nt qckn over 1f out: wknd fnl f* **10/1**

0 **7** *2 ¼* **Money Note**^{14} 5624 3-9-6 **60** .... StevieDonohoe 8 37
(Tobias B P Coles) *dwlt and short of room s: in rr: rdn and effrt 2f out: sn outpcd and wl btn over 1f out: no ch but styd on past btn horses ins fnl f* **22/1**

0010 **8** *1 ¼* **Rileys Crane**^{64} 3956 4-9-3 **53** .... (v) SaleemGolam 7 29
(Christine Dunnett) *wnt rt s: chsd ldrs tl rdn 2f out: wknd qckly over 1f out* **16/1**

43 **9** *1 ½* **Tudor Prince (IRE)**^{21} 5394 7-9-5 **55** .... TomQueally 9 27
(Tony Carroll) *t.k.h: hld up wl in tch: rdn and unable qck wl over 1f out: sn wknd: fdd fnl f* **7/2^{1}**

-060 **10** *1 ½* **Jibouti (IRE)**^{16} 5561 3-9-1 **55** .... PhilipRobinson 1 20
(Clive Brittain) *chsd ldrs: rdn and struggling over 2f out: wknd wl over 1f out* **14/1**

0500 **11** *¾* **Gessabelle**^{6} 5860 4-8-10 **46** oh1 .... (tp) ChrisCatlin 3 —
(Phil McEntee) *taken down early: chsd ldrs: wkng u.p whn short of room over 1f out: fdd fnl f* **66/1**

0600 **12** *14* **Femme Royale**^{12} 5670 3-8-6 **46** oh1 .... (tp) LiamJones 12 —
(Robert Cowell) *in tch in midfield: rdn and struggling 1/2-way: bhd and lost tch 2f out: t.o* **66/1**

1m 25.64s (-0.96) **Going Correction** -0.30s/f (Firm)
WFA 3 from 4yo+ 4lb **12** Ran SP% **119.3**
Speed ratings (Par 101): **93,91,88,87,85 81,78,77,75,73 73,57**
toteswingers: 1&2 £3.90, 1&3 £8.40, 2&3 £10.70. ToteSuper7 Win: Not won; Place: Not won CSF £26.35 CT £290.32 TOTE £4.90: £2.20, £2.00, £3.70; EX 18.80 Trifecta £269.90 Part won. Pool: £364.74 - 0.63 winning units..
Owner Hills' Angels **Bred** T W Bloodstock Ltd **Trained** Upper Lambourn, Berks

FOCUS
The time was similar to division I. It was won by one of the less-exposed runners in the field, and the only horse on the card to make all. She was back to her best here.
Jibouti(IRE) Official explanation: jockey said gelding hung right
T/Plt: £21.00 to a £1 stake. Pool: £64,571.67. 2,243.41 winning tickets. T/Qpdt: £18.20 to a £1 stake. Pool: £4,116.89. 166.95 winning tickets. SP

6072 - 6074a (Foreign Racing) - See Raceform Interactive

4875 **AYR** (L-H)
Thursday, September 15

OFFICIAL GOING: Good to soft (soft in places; 8.4; sprint course: far side 8.4; centre 8.4; stands' side 8.2)
Wind: Light, half against Weather: Sunny, hot

6075 FLY RYANAIR MAIDEN AUCTION STKS 6f
1:50 (1:50) (Class 5) 2-Y-O **£2,328** (£693; £346; £173) **Stalls** Centre

Form RPR
63 **1** **Farang Kondiew**[110] 2504 2-8-11 0 DanielTudhope 6 80+
(Declan Carroll) *prom: pushed along over 2f out: hdwy to ld appr fnl f: r.o wl: comf* **1/1**[1]
U33 **2** 2 1/4 **Mistress Of Rome**[8] 5819 2-8-7 0 ow1 PJMcDonald 5 66+
(Michael Dods) *cl up: rdn and outpcd 2f out: rallied to chse wnr ins fnl f: edgd lft: kpt on* **7/1**
0 **3** 1 1/2 **Takealookatmenow (IRE)**[16] 5590 2-8-4 0 AdrianNicholls 9 59
(David Nicholls) *trckd ldrs: led and edgd lft 2f out: hdd appr fnl f: kpt on same pce* **50/1**
3230 **4** 2 **Lady Gibraltar**[15] 5577 2-8-3 73 (v[1]) HarryBentley(3) 3 55
(Alan Jarvis) *t.k.h: cl up: ev ch 2f out: sn one pce* **4/1**[2]
2302 **5** 1/2 **One Kool Dude**[14] 5646 2-8-11 70 (p) PaulHanagan 2 58
(Richard Fahey) *led to 2f out: sn drvn and nt qckn* **9/2**[3]
5 **6** 4 1/2 **Stepharlie**[15] 5618 2-8-8 0 RoystonFfrench 1 42
(Bryan Smart) *prom tl rdn and wknd over 1f out* **12/1**
7 1 **Red Shimmer (IRE)** 2-8-9 0 DarryllHolland 4 40
(Jo Hughes) *towards rr: drvn and outpcd over 2f out: sn btn* **33/1**
60 **8** 19 **Madam Bonny (IRE)**[21] 5398 2-8-4 0 JamesSullivan 7 —
(Jim Goldie) *bhd: struggling over 2f out: lost tch over 1f out: t.o* **100/1**

1m 14.15s (1.75) **Going Correction** +0.25s/f (Good) **8 Ran SP% 114.3**
Speed ratings (Par 95): **98,95,93,90,89 83,82,57**
toteswingers:1&2:£3.40, 1&3:£11.40, 2&3:£13.00 CSF £8.84 TOTE £2.20: £1.10, £2.20, £4.30; EX 7.00.
Owner Kenny Mackay & Lee Ibbotson **Bred** The Lavington Stud **Trained** Sledmere, E Yorks

FOCUS
After 55mm of rain over the last two weeks, and 22 of those over the previous six days, the three-day Western meeting started on easy ground described as 'very dead'. This was a weak maiden auction maiden and they raced in one group towards the centre of the track.

NOTEBOOK
Farang Kondiew, a tall, leggy individual, had been absent since finishing third on quick ground behind two subsequent Group winners at Haydock in May. He took time to get his act together, but after making his way towards the far side he ran out a most decisive winner. He stands over 17hh and still needs to strengthen and will not be see at his best until next year. (op 11-8 tchd 13-8 in a place)
Mistress Of Rome, placed in maidens here and at Carlisle over 7f, stayed on strongly after getting outpaced and will need a return to the extra furlong in nursery company. (op 13-2 tchd 6-1)
Takealookatmenow(IRE), a bargain basement yearling, showed a lot more than on her debut. She is only small and connections may be tempted to drop her into claiming company. (op 66-1)
Lady Gibraltar, in a first-time visor, has proved a tricky customer but at least the addition of the headgear persuaded her to run in a straight line.
One Kool Dude, fully exposed and fitted with cheekpieces, he took them along but came up well short. (op 4-1 tchd 5-1)
Stepharlie lacks size and scope and did not improve on her promising first run. (op 11-1)

6076 BREWIN DOLPHIN INVESTMENT MANAGEMENT H'CAP 5f
2:20 (2:21) (Class 5) (0-70,69) 3-Y-O+ **£2,328** (£693; £346; £173) **Stalls** Centre

Form RPR
3666 **1** **Hinton Admiral**[30] 5151 7-9-7 69 JoeFanning 4 82
(Keith Dalgleish) *cl up: swtchd to r alone towards far rail after 1f: overall ldr 2f out: styd on strly* **28/1**
4314 **2** nk **Tongalooma**[30] 5148 5-8-12 60 PJMcDonald 1 72
(James Moffatt) *cl up centre: effrt and ev ch over 1f out: kpt on towards fin* **10/1**[3]
0221 **3** 2 1/4 **Cool In The Shade**[19] 5469 3-8-9 58 (b) TonyHamilton 8 62
(Paul Midgley) *cl up centre: effrt and chal 2f out: kpt on same pce ins fnl f* **8/1**[2]
1006 **4** nk **Senate Majority**[12] 5720 4-9-5 67 (b) DavidAllan 14 70
(Tim Easterby) *pressed stands' side ldr: led that quintet 2f out: kpt on fnl f: nt rch far and centre ldrs* **14/1**
2000 **5** 1 **Sonny Red (IRE)**[12] 5732 7-8-12 67 ShirleyTeasdale(7) 2 66
(David Nicholls) *towards rr on outside of centre gp: rdn over 2f out: kpt on fnl f: nrst fin* **14/1**
0255 **6** nk **Tadalavil**[12] 5720 6-9-3 65 PhillipMakin 16 63
(Linda Perratt) *trckd stands' side ldrs: drvn over 2f out: kpt on u.p fnl f* **12/1**
1600 **7** 1/2 **Midnight Dynamo**[12] 5720 4-9-6 68 DanielTudhope 18 64
(Jim Goldie) *in tch stands' side: rdn over 2f out: kpt on fnl f: no imp* **12/1**
2250 **8** shd **Blown It (USA)**[12] 5720 5-9-1 68 ShaneBKelly(5) 12 64
(Keith Dalgleish) *hld up in tch centre: effrt over 2f out: edgd lft fnl f: one pce* **10/1**[3]
2000 **9** nk **Chosen One (IRE)**[12] 5719 6-8-11 64 (p) JulieBurke(5) 6 59
(Ruth Carr) *led and overall ldr centre to 2f out: sn one pce* **25/1**
6363 **10** 1 **Black Annis Bower**[22] 5371 3-9-6 69 JamesSullivan 10 60
(Michael Easterby) *hld up centre: rdn over 2f out: kpt on fnl f: nvr able to chal* **9/2**[1]
0000 **11** 1/2 **Eternal Instinct**[12] 5719 4-8-11 62 GaryBartley(3) 3 52
(Jim Goldie) *hld up on outside of centre gp: rdn and hdwy over 1f out: edgd lft: no imp fnl f* **20/1**
0300 **12** nk **Haadeeth**[14] 5647 4-9-2 64 (v[1]) PaulHanagan 9 52
(Richard Fahey) *prom centre: drvn over 2f out: no ex over 1f out* **8/1**[2]
0001 **13** 1 **Monte Mayor One**[12] 5719 4-8-9 57 LeeNewman 11 42
(Jim Goldie) *midfield centre: rdn 1/2-way: no imp wl over 1f out* **8/1**[2]
0602 **14** 1/2 **Distant Sun (USA)**[12] 5719 7-8-7 55 oh3 (p) RoystonFfrench 5 38
(Linda Perratt) *bhd centre: rdn over 2f out: nvr able to chal* **40/1**
5604 **15** 2 **Saxonette**[12] 5719 3-8-12 64 LeeTopliss(3) 7 40
(Linda Perratt) *midfield centre: outpcd over 2f out: sn btn* **18/1**
0154 **16** 5 **Ridley Didley (IRE)**[55] 4289 6-9-2 69 NeilFarley(5) 15 27
(Noel Wilson) *led stands' side quintet to 2f out: sn wknd* **22/1**
3034 **17** nk **Classlin**[20] 5437 4-8-7 55 oh10 AndrewElliott 17 12
(Jim Goldie) *hld up stands' side: rdn over 2f out: nvr on terms* **100/1**

60.27 secs (0.87) **Going Correction** +0.25s/f (Good)
WFA 3 from 4yo+ 1lb **17 Ran SP% 123.5**
Speed ratings (Par 103): **103,102,98,98,96 96,95,95,94,93 92,92,90,89,86 78,77**
toteswingers:1&2:£32.20, 1&3:£27.80, 2&3:£10.30 CSF £274.13 CT £2566.66 TOTE £40.20: £6.40, £2.40, £1.90, £3.70; EX 374.60.
Owner William Brand & Gordon McDowall **Bred** Gainsborough Stud Management Ltd **Trained** Carluke, South Lanarkshire

FOCUS
A low-grade sprint handicap. Five came to race stands' side but the winner went to race virtually alone against the far rail. Not many got involved. The winner showed his best form so far for this yard.
Black Annis Bower Official explanation: jockey said filly never travelled

6077 BRITISH STALLION STUDS SUPPORTING BRITISH RACING E B F NOVICE STKS 1m
2:50 (2:51) (Class 4) 2-Y-O **£4,463** (£1,328; £663; £331) **Stalls** High

Form RPR
3221 **1** **Storming Bernard (USA)**[13] 5668 2-9-5 88 DarryllHolland 5 92
(Alan Bailey) *mde all: rdn and qcknd clr over 2f out: kpt on wl: unchal* **7/4**[1]
214 **2** 2 1/4 **Bountiful Girl**[19] 5478 2-8-11 76 PaulHanagan 7 78
(Richard Fahey) *chsd wnr: rdn along 3f out: kpt on fnl f: no imp* **6/1**
1043 **3** 3/4 **Sound Advice**[27] 5234 2-9-5 88 DavidAllan 1 84
(Keith Dalgleish) *hld up in tch: rdn and edgd lft over 1f out: kpt on fnl f: no imp* **6/1**
13 **4** 10 **Shamrocked (IRE)**[61] 4091 2-9-5 86 MatthewDavies 6 61
(Mick Channon) *prom on outside: effrt and rdn over 2f out: wknd over 1f out* **7/2**[2]
10 **5** hd **John Lightbody**[68] 3861 2-9-5 81 JoeFanning 4 61
(Mark Johnston) *cl up: checked after 1f: drvn and lost pl wl over 2f out: n.d after* **4/1**[3]

1m 44.37s (0.57) **Going Correction** -0.05s/f (Good) **5 Ran SP% 107.2**
Speed ratings (Par 97): **95,92,92,82,81**
CSF £11.61 TOTE £2.00: £1.80, £2.30; EX 8.20.
Owner John Stocker **Bred** Hill 'N' Dale Equine Holdings Inc & Netp **Trained** Newmarket, Suffolk
■ Stewards' Enquiry : Darryll Holland caution: careless riding.

FOCUS
The overall time suggested the ground on the round course may have been slightly easier, although the winner was allowed an uncontested lead.

NOTEBOOK
Storming Bernard(USA), a tough type, was having his seventh start having won a maiden at Brighton on his previous outing. A resolute galloper, his action suggests he needs easy ground and, winding up the pace once in line for home, he had this won some way from home, in the end being able to ease up. He is just the hard-working type his trainer has excelled with over the years. (op 2-1 tchd 13-8)
Bountiful Girl, who had something to find with the winner on Newmarket 7f nursery running, never gave up trying but was never going to come off anything but second best. (op 5-1 tchd 13-2, 7-1 in a place)
Sound Advice was on and off the bridle but in the end finished well clear of the remainder. (op 9-2 tchd 4-1)
Shamrocked(IRE), encountering easy ground for the first time, made a brief effort once in line for home but in the end the extra furlong proved way beyond him at this stage. (tchd 4-1)
John Lightbody, a big type, had disappointed behind Sound Advice in a Group 2 at Newmarket after his first-time out Sandown maiden win. He has a long, fluent action and the ground was probably against him here. Even so he has something to prove now. (op 5-1 tchd 11-2)

6078 ISLE OF SKYE 8-Y-O BLENDED SCOTCH WHISKY H'CAP (DIV I) 1m
3:20 (3:20) (Class 4) (0-85,85) 3-Y-O+ **£4,204** (£1,251; £625; £312) **Stalls** High

Form RPR
5010 **1** **Silvery Moon (IRE)**[17] 5557 4-9-2 77 DavidAllan 8 90+
(Tim Easterby) *hld up in tch: hdwy over 2f out: led and edgd lft over 1f out: clr ins fnl f: hld on towards fin* **11/2**[2]
0113 **2** nk **Swiftly Done (IRE)**[12] 5722 4-9-5 80 (b) DanielTudhope 13 92+
(Declan Carroll) *hld up on ins: nt clr run over 2f out: gd hdwy over 1f out: kpt on wl fnl f: jst hld* **5/1**[1]
0440 **3** 3 1/2 **Silver Rime (FR)**[13] 5684 6-9-9 84 PhillipMakin 12 88
(Linda Perratt) *hld up: hdwy on outside 2f out: kpt on fnl f: no imp* **20/1**
6016 **4** nk **Hail Bold Chief (USA)**[24] 5311 4-8-10 71 oh1 PJMcDonald 10 74
(Alan Swinbank) *hld up in midfield: rdn over 2f out: hdwy over 1f out: kpt on ins fnl f* **16/1**
0042 **5** shd **Staff Sergeant**[19] 5488 4-9-2 77 LeeNewman 11 80
(Jim Goldie) *prom: led fr over 3f tl over 1f out: kpt on same pce fnl f* **5/1**[1]
0422 **6** 3/4 **Veiled Applause**[28] 5200 8-8-9 75 ShaneBKelly(5) 7 76
(John Quinn) *hld up in midfield: rdn and effrt on outside over 2f out: no imp fnl f* **8/1**[3]
2250 **7** 1 **She's A Character**[40] 4794 4-9-5 80 PaulHanagan 2 79
(Richard Fahey) *towards rr: drvn 3f out: hdwy over 1f out: nvr able to chal* **14/1**
3160 **8** 2 1/4 **Magic Cat**[54] 4325 5-9-10 85 AndrewElliott 1 79
(Mrs K Burke) *s.i.s: bhd tl sme late hdwy: nvr on terms* **17/2**
1406 **9** 4 1/2 **Luv U Too**[19] 5493 3-8-8 77 HarryBentley(3) 5 61
(Jo Hughes) *led 2f: cl up tl rdn and wknd wl over 1f out* **20/1**
623- **10** hd **Battle Honour**[145] 5150 4-8-11 72 PaddyAspell 9 55
(Sue Bradburne) *towards rr: drvn along over 3f out: nvr on terms* **100/1**
0006 **11** 2 1/4 **Desert Creek (IRE)**[34] 5006 5-9-7 82 AdrianNicholls 4 60
(David Nicholls) *cl up: chal over 3f out: wknd over 1f out* **22/1**
0000 **12** 13 **Breakheart (IRE)**[13] 5686 4-9-6 81 TonyHamilton 6 29
(Michael Dods) *midfield: rdn and edgd lft over 2f out: sn struggling: t.o* **8/1**[3]
0651 **13** 17 **Outpost (IRE)**[16] 5598 3-8-12 78 (v[1]) DarryllHolland 3 —
(Alan Bailey) *t.k.h: led after 2f to over 3f out: lost tch fnl 2f: t.o* **8/1**[3]

1m 42.21s (-1.59) **Going Correction** -0.05s/f (Good)
WFA 3 from 4yo+ 5lb **13 Ran SP% 120.0**
Speed ratings (Par 105): **105,104,101,100,100 100,99,96,92,92 89,76,59**
toteswingers:1&2:£5.20, 1&3:£21.70, 2&3:£21.10 CSF £31.71 CT £522.13 TOTE £6.60: £2.00, £2.00, £7.60; EX 36.40.
Owner R J Swinbourne **Bred** Colin Kennedy **Trained** Great Habton, N Yorks
■ Stewards' Enquiry : Daniel Tudhope two-day ban: careless riding (Sep 29-30)

FOCUS
A strong gallop with four horses keen to make the pace. A similar time to division II. There are grounds for thinking the first two can do better, with the form rated around the third.

Outpost(IRE) Official explanation: jockey said colt failed to stride out when it came off the bridle

6079 ISLE OF SKYE 8-Y-O BLENDED SCOTCH WHISKY H'CAP (DIV II) — 1m
3:50 (3:51) (Class 4) (0-85,85) 3-Y-0+ **£4,204** (£1,251; £625; £312) **Stalls** High

Form | RPR

2314 **1** **Take It To The Max**[13] [5686] 4-9-7 **82**..........(p) PaulHanagan 8 — 93
(Richard Fahey) *trckd ldrs: smooth hdwy to ld 2f out: rdn and edgd lft: kpt on wl fnl f* **11/4**[1]

6402 **2** *1 ½* **Come Here Yew (IRE)**[16] [5594] 3-8-11 **77**.......... DanielTudhope 4 — 84+
(Declan Carroll) *midfield: drvn and sltly outpcd over 2f out: styd on wl fnl f: tk 2nd cl home: nt rch wnr* **7/1**[3]

1003 **3** *hd* **Good Boy Jackson**[12] [5730] 3-9-2 **82**.......... PhillipMakin 2 — 89
(Kevin Ryan) *in tch: rdn and hdwy to chse wnr over 1f out: kpt on fnl f: lost 2nd cl home* **4/1**[2]

211 **4** *2* **Ted's Brother (IRE)**[20] [5439] 3-8-7 **73**.......... RoystonFfrench 3 — 75
(Richard Guest) *hld up: rdn and hdwy 2f out: kpt on fnl f: nrst fin* **8/1**

4206 **5** *3 ¼* **Tewin Wood**[13] [5687] 4-9-0 **75**.......... DarryllHolland 5 — 70
(Alan Bailey) *led to over 3f out: sn drvn: rallied: no ex over 1f out* **20/1**

0004 **6** *¾* **Amethyst Dawn (IRE)**[19] [5465] 5-9-5 **80**.......... DavidAllan 11 — 74
(Tim Easterby) *midfield: effrt and drvn on outside over 2f out: no imp over 1f out* **16/1**

0602 **7** *1* **Kiwi Bay**[14] [5648] 6-9-10 **85**.......... TonyHamilton 10 — 76
(Michael Dods) *hld up: rdn over 2f out: kpt on fnl f: nvr able to chal* **12/1**

2600 **8** *nk* **High Resolution**[12] [5722] 4-8-11 **72**.......... JamesSullivan 7 — 63
(Linda Perratt) *t.k.h: hld up: rdn over 2f out: sme late hdwy: nvr on terms* **33/1**

4210 **9** *nk* **Euston Square**[20] [5435] 5-8-13 **81**.......... JustinNewman(7) 12 — 71
(Alistair Whillans) *hld up on outside: struggling over 2f out: n.d after* **12/1**

1005 **10** *nk* **Daring Dream (GER)**[20] [5455] 6-9-1 **79**.......... GaryBartley(3) 9 — 68
(Jim Goldie) *hld up: rdn over 2f out: no imp over 1f out* **16/1**

0020 **11** *2 ½* **Osgood**[12] [5733] 4-9-2 **77**.......... MatthewDavies 13 — 61
(Mick Channon) *cl up: led fr over 3f tl over 1f out: sn wknd* **20/1**

002- **12** *9* **Full Toss**[524] [1208] 5-9-7 **82**.......... LeeNewman 6 — 45
(Jim Goldie) *trckd ldrs tl wknd over 2f out* **16/1**

6060 **13** *¾* **Rasselas (IRE)**[54] [4349] 4-8-10 **71**.......... AdrianNicholls 1 — 32
(David Nicholls) *midfield: drvn 1/2-way: wknd fnl 2f* **20/1**

1m 42.27s (-1.53) **Going Correction** -0.05s/f (Good)
WFA 3 from 4yo+ 5lb **13** Ran SP% **120.5**
Speed ratings (Par 105): **105,103,103,101,98 97,96,96,95,95 92,83,83**
toteswingers:1&2:£5.50, 1&3:£4.10, 2&3:£5.30 CSF £20.63 CT £81.50 TOTE £2.50: £1.10, £2.10, £2.20; EX 18.60.
Owner Mrs Phillipa Davies **Bred** Whatton Manor Stud **Trained** Musley Bank, N Yorks

FOCUS
Part two and more of the same. The time was only fractionally slower than division one. The form is sound with the winner back to his old best.

6080 WILLIAMHILL.COM H'CAP (FOR THE KILKERRAN CUP) — 1m 2f
4:20 (4:20) (Class 2) (0-100,97) 3-Y-0+
£9,835 (£2,945; £1,472; £736; £368; £184) **Stalls** High

Form | RPR

-541 **1** **Scrapper Smith (IRE)**[16] [5593] 5-8-9 **85**.......... JulieBurke(5) 1 — 93+
(Alistair Whillans) *s.i.s: hld up: weaved through over 1f out: styd on wl fnl f: led cl home* **7/1**[3]

1542 **2** *shd* **Las Verglas Star (IRE)**[19] [5466] 3-8-9 **87**.......... PaulHanagan 10 — 95
(Richard Fahey) *t.k.h: cl up: led over 2f out: sn rdn: kpt on wl fnl f: hdd cl home* **11/4**[1]

5020 **3** *hd* **Mirrored**[6] [5888] 5-9-1 **86**.......... DuranFentiman 11 — 93
(Tim Easterby) *hld up in midfield on outside: hdwy over 2f out: kpt on fnl f: jst hld* **16/1**

5043 **4** *nk* **Seattle Drive (IRE)**[42] [4718] 3-8-11 **89**.......... DavidAllan 9 — 95
(David Elsworth) *t.k.h: hld up: hdwy and ev ch over 1f out: edgd rt ins fnl f: hld cl home* **9/2**[2]

3020 **5** *nk* **Northside Prince (IRE)**[19] [5482] 5-9-5 **90**.......... PJMcDonald 6 — 96
(Alan Swinbank) *in tch: effrt and rdn over 2f out: kpt on u.p ins fnl f* **9/1**

[illegible] **6** [illegible] [illegible] **(IRE)**[16] [illegible] [illegible]..........(b) TonyHamilton [illegible] — [illegible]
(Richard Fahey) *trckd ldrs: rdn 3f out: wknd over 1f out* **16/1**

0002 **7** *½* **Space War**[11] [5757] 4-9-0 **85**.......... JamesSullivan 8 — 78
(Michael Easterby) *hld up: rdn over 2f out: nvr able to chal* **14/1**

06-0 **8** *1 ½* **Emirates Dream (USA)**[28] [5218] 4-9-12 **97**..........(p) DarryllHolland 7 — 87
(Saeed Bin Suroor) *in tch: drvn over 2f out: wknd over 1f out* **9/1**

01-0 **9** *10* **Medicinal Compound**[166] [1092] 4-9-5 **90**.......... PhillipMakin 2 — 60
(Kevin Ryan) *trckd ldrs: rdn 4f out: wknd over 2f out* **25/1**

600 **10** *2 ¾* **Zenella**[27] [5255] 3-8-9 **87**..........(p) RoystonFfrench 3 — 52
(Ann Duffield) *led to over 2f out: sn rdn and btn* **20/1**

1111 **11** *17* **Hot Rod Mamma (IRE)**[12] [5728] 4-9-4 **92**.......... LeeTopliss(3) 4 — 23
(Dianne Sayer) *hld up: stmbld home bnd over 3f out: sn rdn: wknd fnl 2f* **8/1**

2m 11.2s (-0.80) **Going Correction** -0.05s/f (Good)
WFA 3 from 4yo+ 7lb **11** Ran SP% **115.5**
Speed ratings (Par 109): **101,100,100,100,100 95,95,93,85,83 70**
toteswingers:1&2:£3.70, 1&3:£20.70, 2&3:£11.80 CSF £25.98 CT £300.26 TOTE £9.10: £2.60, £1.50, £4.90; EX 30.80.
Owner A C Whillans **Bred** John Costello **Trained** Newmill-On-Slitrig, Borders

FOCUS
Quite a valuable handicap run at a sound pace and there wasn't much separating the first five at the line. Sound but ordinary form for the grade.

NOTEBOOK
Scrapper Smith(IRE), last away, had work to do and was in need of luck in running. He had to search for an opening and was only fifth 100yds out, but he put his head in front on the line. He needs easy ground and is a credit to connections. (op 13-2)
Las Verglas Star(IRE), a winner first time out this year from a mark of 70, raced from 87 here. He struck for home coming to the final quarter mile only to be nailed right on the line. He is a dependable tough-type. (op 7-2)
Mirrored, who chased home Scrapper Smith at Ripon, enjoyed a 13lb pull. He needs a strongly run race and has just the one short, sharp burst. Things very nearly worked out for him here.
Seattle Drive(IRE), stepping up in trip, made ground down the outer travelling well. After looking a real threat he had to settle for fourth. He has a good engine but needs everything to fall just right. (op 4-1)
Northside Prince(IRE), runner-up a year ago from a 7lb lower mark, had flopped over 1m2f last time. He has a good record here and this plucky effort was right up to his very best. (op 8-1)
Hot Rod Mamma(IRE), who had run up a five-timer in Class 5 and 6 handicaps, was 12lb higher than for her latest victory and an incredible 44lb higher than for her initial success this year. She was just starting her effort when she stumbled once in line for home. After making her way to the outside in the end she was eased right up. It remains to be seen if she can be effective from an inflated mark of 92. Official explanation: jockey said filly clipped heels on bend turning into home straight and never travelled thereafter (op 15-2)

6081 TOM ALLAN MEMORIAL H'CAP — 7f 50y
4:50 (4:51) (Class 5) (0-75,78) 3-Y-0+ **£2,716** (£808; £404; £202) **Stalls** High

Form | RPR

0400 **1** **Keys Of Cyprus**[16] [5594] 9-8-11 **69**.......... ShirleyTeasdale(7) 3 — 81
(David Nicholls) *in tch: hdwy over 2f out: edgd lft and led over 1f out: kpt on wl fnl f* **14/1**

0056 **2** *½* **Fishforcompliments**[11] [5760] 7-9-6 **71**..........(v) PaulHanagan 10 — 81
(Richard Fahey) *awkward s: hld up towards rr: effrt and hdwy over 1f out: chsd wnr wl ins fnl f: kpt on* **15/2**[3]

6302 **3** *1 ¼* **Rio Cobolo (IRE)**[13] [5682] 5-9-9 **74**.......... AdrianNicholls 7 — 81
(David Nicholls) *cl up: led over 2f tl over 1f out: kpt on same pce ins fnl f* **14/1**

6665 **4** *shd* **Sam Nombulist**[12] [5731] 3-8-12 **67**..........(v[1]) TonyHamilton 5 — 73
(Richard Whitaker) *led to over 2f out: rallied: kpt on same pce fnl f* **12/1**

310 **5** *2* **Social Forum (IRE)**[15] [5635] 3-9-5 **74**.......... DavidAllan 8 — 75
(David Elsworth) *towards rr: pushed along 1/2-way: hdwy over 1f out: kpt on fnl f* **14/1**

3505 **6** *hd* **Hayek**[24] [5309] 4-8-6 **62**..........(b) JulieBurke(5) 2 — 63
(Tim Easterby) *midfield on ins: rdn over 2f out: kpt on same pce fnl f* **12/1**

6521 **7** *¾* **Illustrious Prince (IRE)**[5] [5924] 4-9-8 **78** 6ex.......... NeilFarley(5) 12 — 77
(Declan Carroll) *in tch: effrt over 2f out: edgd lft and kpt on same pce over 1f out* **11/4**[1]

0000 **8** *1* **Berbice (IRE)**[12] [5722] 6-8-12 **63**.......... PhillipMakin 11 — 59+
(Linda Perratt) *hld up: no room on ins fr over 2f out to ent fnl f: nt rcvr* **20/1**

3222 **9** *shd* **Beckermet (IRE)**[34] [5006] 9-9-3 **68**.......... PJMcDonald 1 — 64
(Ruth Carr) *trckd ldrs: drvn over 2f out: nt qckn over 1f out* **5/1**[2]

5 **10** *¾* **Thoroughly Red (IRE)**[14] [5652] 6-9-3 **68**.......... JamesSullivan 6 — 62
(Linda Stubbs) *midfield: drvn and outpcd over 3f out: rallied over 1f out: no imp* **25/1**

5220 **11** *5* **North Central (USA)**[12] [5720] 4-9-6 **71**.......... DanielTudhope 9 — 52
(Jim Goldie) *towards rr: rdn whn n.m.r briefly over 2f out: sn btn* **25/1**

1350 **12** *¾* **Frontline Girl (IRE)**[53] [4361] 5-9-9 **74**.......... AndrewElliott 13 — 53
(Mrs K Burke) *bhd: drvn along over 3f out: nvr on terms* **8/1**

4100 **13** *2 ¾* **Frequency**[22] [5371] 4-9-7 **72**.......... JoeFanning 14 — 44
(Keith Dalgleish) *hld up on outside: rdn over 2f out: sn btn* **20/1**

4040 **14** *6* **Strictly Pink (IRE)**[7] [5862] 3-9-6 **75**..........(v[1]) DarryllHolland 4 — 31
(Alan Bailey) *trckd ldr: rdn and wandered over 2f out: sn wknd* **16/1**

1m 33.41s (0.01) **Going Correction** -0.05s/f (Good)
WFA 3 from 4yo+ 4lb **14** Ran SP% **124.7**
Speed ratings (Par 103): **97,96,95,94,92 92,91,90,90,89 83,82,79,72**
toteswingers:1&2:£23.90, 1&3:£31.90, 2&3:£15.10 CSF £113.40 CT £1552.87 TOTE £13.10: £4.20, £2.40, £4.80; EX 160.10.
Owner The Beasley Gees **Bred** Juddmonte Farms **Trained** Sessay, N Yorks

■ Stewards' Enquiry : Shirley Teasdale three-day ban: used whip with excessive frequency (Sep 29-30, Oct 1)

FOCUS
A wide-open handicap with many of the runners coming into this in indifferent form. The winner's best effort of the year with the third helping set the standard.
Keys Of Cyprus Official explanation: trainer had no explanation for the apparent improvement in form
Berbice(IRE) Official explanation: jockey said gelding was denied a clear run
Frontline Girl(IRE) Official explanation: jockey said mare never travelled
Strictly Pink(IRE) Official explanation: jockey said filly hung left in straight

6082 JOHN SMITH'S H'CAP — 1m 5f 13y
5:20 (5:20) (Class 5) (0-70,69) 3-Y-0+ **£2,587** (£770; £384; £192) **Stalls** Low

Form | RPR

4500 **1** **The Oil Magnate**[33] [5036] 6-9-13 **68**.......... TonyHamilton 10 — 78
(Michael Dods) *hld up: smooth hdwy over 2f out: effrt and drvn fnl f: styd on to ld cl home* **12/1**

5001 **2** *nk* **Herrera (IRE)**[19] [5470] 6-9-4 **59**.......... PaulHanagan 8 — 68
(Richard Fahey) *cl up: rdn 3f out: led ins fnl f: edgd lft: hdd cl home* **10/3**[1]

0012 **3** *1 ¾* **Distant Waters**[8] [5832] 4-8-11 **55**.......... HarryBentley(3) 3 — 62
(Alan Jarvis) *in tch: smooth hdwy to ld over 1f out: sn rdn: hdd ins fnl f: one pce* **4/1**[3]

4140 **4** *½* **Forrest Flyer (IRE)**[12] [5724] 7-10-0 **69**.......... PhillipMakin 6 — 75
(Jim Goldie) *chsd ldrs: rdn over 3f out: rallied 2f out: kpt on same pce fnl f* **13/2**

3215 **5** *13* **Silver Tigress**[22] [5372] 3-8-9 **60**.......... PJMcDonald 7 — 47
(George Moore) *cl up: led over 3f tl over 1f out: sn wknd* **7/2**[2]

0000 **6** *½* **Vittachi**[10] [5791] 4-9-0 **55** oh9.......... PaddyAspell 2 — 41
(Alistair Whillans) *in tch: drvn and outpcd over 2f out: btn over 1f out* **50/1**

5040 **7** *2* **Royal Straight**[17] [5723] 6-9-0 **60**..........(t) JulieBurke(5) 9 — 43
(Linda Perratt) *hld up: shortlived effrt over 2f out: btn over 1f out* **12/1**

-616 **8** *½* **Grandad Bill (IRE)**[12] [5723] 8-9-6 **61**.......... DanielTudhope 1 — 43
(Jim Goldie) *led to over 3f out: wknd fr 2f out* **9/2**

2m 59.51s (5.51) **Going Correction** -0.05s/f (Good)
WFA 3 from 4yo+ 10lb **8** Ran SP% **114.2**
Speed ratings (Par 103): **81,80,79,79,71 71,69,69**
toteswingers:1&2:£7.30, 1&3:£7.10, 2&3:£3.10. Totesuper 7: Win: Not won, Place: Not won CSF £51.71 CT £191.77 TOTE £17.20: £3.60, £1.60, £1.10; EX 71.30.
Owner Smith & Allan Racing **Bred** Wheelersland Stud **Trained** Denton, Co Durham

FOCUS
A modest stayers' handicap run at just a steady pace. The winner is basically rated to his best form since he was a 3yo.
The Oil Magnate Official explanation: trainer had no explanation for the apparent improvement in form
Silver Tigress Official explanation: jockey said filly ran too free

T/Jkpt: Not won. T/Plt: £71.80 to a £1 stake. Pool:£66,025.04 - 671.25 winning tickets T/Qpdt: £8.40 to a £1 stake. Pool:£4,305.25 - 378.55 winning tickets RY

6051 KEMPTON (A.W) (R-H)

Thursday, September 15

OFFICIAL GOING: Standard

Wind: Moderate across Weather: Early sun

6083 BOOK NOW FOR JUMP SUNDAY 16.10.11 H'CAP (DIV I) 1m (P)

5:40 (5:42) (Class 6) (0-55,55) 3-Y-0+ £1,293 (£385; £192; £96) Stalls Low

Form RPR

0000 **1** **Gee Major**[35] 4948 4-8-13 **49** LukeMorris 12 58
(Nicky Vaughan) *chsd ldrs: led over 2f out: drvn and styd on strly thrght fnl f* **14/1**

0402 **2** 1 ¼ **Shaunas Spirit (IRE)**[5] 5944 3-8-5 **46** JimmyQuinn 4 51
(Dean Ivory) *chsd ldrs: rdn and one pce appr fnl 2f: rallied and styd on u.p to chse wnr ins fnl f: no mprssion but hld on all out for 2nd* **11/2**[1]

3/03 **3** nse **Yellow Printer**[21] 5408 5-9-5 **55** (b[1]) AdamKirby 10 61
(Mark Gillard) *towards rr on outside and rdn over 2f out: styd on u.p thrght fnl f to press for 2nd last strides but no imp on wnr* **11/1**

4000 **4** hd **Lennoxwood (IRE)**[7] 5843 3-8-7 **48** (be[1]) RichardKingscote 13 52
(Mark Usher) *in rr: pushed along and hdwy between horses ins fnl 2f: edgd rt and styd on ins fnl f: kpt on cl home but no imp on wnr* **20/1**

0000 **5** hd **Warbond**[11] 4827 3-8-13 **54** (v[1]) FrankieMcDonald 6 58
(Michael Madgwick) *prom: rdn 2f out: hung rt and one pce sn after: rallied and kpt on again ins fnl f: nt rch ldrs* **66/1**

0032 **6** ½ **Queenie's Star (IRE)**[5] 5943 4-8-6 **47** MarkCoumbe[(5)] 9 51
(Michael Attwater) *chsd ldrs towards outside: drvn to dispute 2nd fnl 120yds: wknd sn after* **11/2**[1]

4203 **7** hd **Inquisitress**[3] 5995 7-8-7 **46** oh1 SeanLevey[(3)] 14 49
(John Bridger) *hld up in rr: hdwy and qcknd fr 2f out to dispute 2nd fnl 120yds: wknd sn after* **13/2**[3]

0353 **8** 2 ¼ **Toballa**[14] 5643 6-8-7 **46** (t) AdamBeschizza[(3)] 5 44
(Clifford Lines) *mid-div: rdn: edgd rt and hdwy towards far rail over 2f out: nvr quite gng pce to rch ldrs and wknd ins fnl f* **10/1**

045 **9** ½ **My Flame**[5] 5944 6-9-1 **51** PatDobbs 7 48
(J R Jenkins) *led tl hdd over 2f out: wknd ins fnl f* **6/1**[2]

0410 **10** hd **Excellent Vision**[5] 5943 4-8-12 **51** (t) RyanClark[(3)] 1 48
(Milton Bradley) *slowly away and bhd: hdwy to cl on main gp 2f out: n.m.r over 1f out: sn fdd* **10/1**

5200 **11** hd **Lilli Palmer (IRE)**[16] 5606 4-9-4 **54** TonyCulhane 2 50
(Mike Murphy) *chsd ldrs: rdn 2f out: wkng whn n.m.r ins fnl f* **15/2**

3550 **12** 1 ¾ **Regal Rave (USA)**[15] 5611 4-9-2 **52** (e[1]) LiamKeniry 11 44
(Peter Hedger) *chsd ldrs: wknd ins fnl 2f: eased clsng stages* **14/1**

1m 39.71s (-0.09) **Going Correction** -0.025s/f (Stan)
WFA 3 from 4yo+ 5lb 12 Ran SP% **116.3**
Speed ratings (Par 101): **99,97,97,97,97 96,96,94,93,93 93,91**
toteswingers:1&2:£20.80, 2&3:£7.50, 1&3:£32.70 CSF £87.48 CT £902.73 TOTE £31.00 : £7.10, £3.40, £2.90; EX 149.90.
Owner David Sykes **Bred** D Sykes **Trained** Helshaw Grange, Shropshire

FOCUS
A very modest event. The pace was fairly steady and the first seven finished in a heap, but the form reads sound enough. The time was just under two seconds outside the standard, and slightly slower than division two. Half a dozen of these had been in action in two divisions of a very similar event over C&D five days earlier.

6084 BOOK NOW FOR JUMP SUNDAY 16.10.11 H'CAP (DIV II) 1m (P)

6:10 (6:10) (Class 6) (0-55,55) 3-Y-0+ £1,293 (£385; £192; £96) Stalls Low

Form RPR

5655 **1** **Mister Fantastic**[15] 5611 5-8-5 **46** oh1 RyanPowell[(5)] 7 56
(Dai Burchell) *sn chsng ldr: led 2f out: drvn and styd on strly ins fnl f* **6/1**[2]

040 **2** 1 ½ **Blue Noodles**[10] 5788 5-9-2 **52** (p) LukeMorris 3 59
(John Wainwright) *chsd ldrs: rdn to go 2nd wl over 1f out: kpt on but no imp on wnr* **8/1**

0000 **3** 2 ¾ **Lechlade Lass**[17] 5567 3-8-6 **54** RachealKneller[(7)] 10 53
(Adrian Chamberlain) *in tch early: sn lost pl and in rr: swtchd lft to outside over 1f out: styd on wl ins fnl f to take 3rd fnl 120yds: nt rch ldng duo* **66/1**

3500 **4** nk **Flying Cherry (IRE)**[7] 5843 4-8-7 **46** (t) JohnFahy[(3)] 9 46
(Jo Crowley) *in rr: rdn and hdwy on outside fr 2f out: styd on ins fnl f to press for 3rd cl home but no ch w ldng duo* **10/1**

0000 **5** ¾ **Hertford Street**[7] 5845 3-8-6 **47** MartinDwyer 14 44
(Peter Makin) *chsd ldrs: rdn 3f out: hung rt fr 2f out and again ins fnl f: nt look resolute* **14/1**

6 **6** 4 ½ **Swooping Hawk (IRE)**[16] 5607 4-9-4 **54** JamesDoyle 12 41
(Sylvester Kirk) *in tch: rdn over 2f out: no imp: wknd over 1f out* **11/4**[1]

600 **7** 2 ½ **Gennie**[17] 5567 3-8-10 **54** SeanLevey[(3)] 2 35
(Richard Hannon) *chsd ldrs: rdn over 2f out: wknd over 1f out* **9/1**

500 **8** nk **Bell's Ocean (USA)**[5] 5944 4-9-1 **51** StevieDonohoe 4 32
(John Ryan) *in tch whn hmpd and dropped in rr after 1f: rdn and effrt on ins wl over 2f out but no imp: wknd ins fnl f* **10/1**

-066 **9** 2 ½ **Ain't Talkin'**[20] 5422 5-8-5 **46** oh1 (p) MarkCoumbe[(5)] 1 21
(Michael Attwater) *rdn along fr 3f out: a bhd* **16/1**

0060 **10** 1 ¾ **Poyle Todream**[17] 5540 3-8-11 **52** JimCrowley 6 22
(Ralph Beckett) *sn led: rdn and hdd 2f out: wknd qckly* **13/2**[3]

0000 **11** 2 ¼ **A B Celebration**[22] 5381 3-8-5 **46** oh1 NeilChalmers 5 11
(John Bridger) *a towards rr* **66/1**

000 **12** 15 **Atyaab**[22] 5394 4-9-5 **55** RichardKingscote 13 —
(Alan Swinbank) *chsd ldrs tl over 2f out: wknd and eased appr fnl f* **8/1**

1m 39.35s (-0.45) **Going Correction** -0.025s/f (Stan)
WFA 3 from 4yo+ 5lb 12 Ran SP% **120.2**
Speed ratings (Par 101): **101,99,96,96,95 91,88,88,85,84 81,66**
toteswingers:1&2:£5.20, 2&3:£30.70, 1&3:£36.00 CSF £54.30 CT £2917.98 TOTE £3.60 : £1.20, £3.40, £20.70; EX 29.40.
Owner C Friel **Bred** Mascalls Stud **Trained** Briery Hill, Blaenau Gwent

FOCUS
Division two of this weak handicap was also steadily run, but they finished more strung out and the time was 0.36sec quicker than the first. The principals all raced down the centre of the track, some way from the inside rail. The winner's best Flat form since his 3yo reappearance.

Atyaab Official explanation: jockey said filly had a breathing problem

6085 TURFTV MAIDEN STKS 1m (P)

6:40 (6:44) (Class 5) 3-Y-0+ £2,264 (£673; £336; £168) Stalls Low

Form RPR

6 **1** **Songburst**[222] 437 3-9-3 0 PatDobbs 14 82+
(Richard Hannon) *racd in 2nd over 4f out: rdn and one pce whn ldr qcknd fr 2f out: rallied and r.o strly ins fnl f to ld fnl 30yds: in command clsng strides* **16/1**

6 **2** ¾ **Press Office (USA)**[111] 2469 3-9-3 0 FrankieDettori 11 81+
(Mahmood Al Zarooni) *led: rdn and qcknd 3 l clr 2f out: stl looked ok whn rdn ins fnl f: wknd fnl 120yds: hdd fnl 30yds and narrowly hld on for 2nd* **6/4**[1]

2- **3** ½ **Moonscape**[338] 6828 3-9-3 0 ShaneKelly 5 79+
(Sir Michael Stoute) *in tch: rdn 2f out: styd on appr fnl f: qckmd fnl 120yds gng on cl home* **15/8**[2]

4 shd **Moannaa** 3-9-3 0 JackMitchell 2 79+
(Roger Varian) *chsd ldr tl over 4f out: styd disputing 2nd tl one pce whn ldr qcknd fr 2f out: rallied and styd on ins fnl f: kpt on in the clsng stages* **15/2**[3]

64 **5** ½ **George Guru**[15] 5633 4-9-3 0 MarkCoumbe[(5)] 3 78
(Michael Attwater) *in tch tl pushed along and outpcd ins fnl 3f: styd on again ins fnl f: gng on cl home* **11/1**

0 **6** 5 **Treasure Act**[40] 4800 3-8-12 0 LiamKeniry 9 61
(Patrick Chamings) *chsd ldrs: rdn over 2f out: wknd appr fnl f* **100/1**

7 ½ **Sadeek's Song (USA)** 3-9-3 0 AhmedAjtebi 10 65+
(Mahmood Al Zarooni) *slowly away: in rr: drvn along fr 3f out: wnt rt to far rail: rdn and green fr 2f out but styd on wl ins fnl f: kpt on cl home but nvr a threat* **11/1**

8 6 **Russian Storm** 3-8-12 0 FrankieMcDonald 13 45
(Pat Phelan) *green and plld hrd towards rr: sme prog fr 3f out and in tch whn v green and veered lft 2f out: no ch after* **40/1**

9 ½ **Glens Wobbly** 3-9-3 0 RobertHavlin 4 49
(Jonathan Geake) *slowly away: in rr early: rcvrd and in tch 1/2-way: wknd fr 3f out* **80/1**

10 6 **Red Marksman** 3-9-0 0 JohnFahy[(3)] 8 35
(James Evans) *sn towards rr* **50/1**

11 7 **Grand Sort** 3-9-3 0 IanMongan 12 18
(Tony Newcombe) *s.i.s: in rr: mod prog 3f out: sn wknd* **80/1**

12 1 ¾ **Turbulent Priest** 3-9-3 0 KirstyMilczarek 6 14
(Zoe Davison) *slowly away: a in rr* **100/1**

1m 40.29s (0.49) **Going Correction** -0.025s/f (Stan)
WFA 3 from 4yo 5lb 12 Ran SP% **117.9**
Speed ratings (Par 103): **96,95,94,94,94 89,88,82,82,76 69,67**
toteswingers:1&2:£7.20, 2&3:£1.10, 1&3:£7.50 CSF £40.34 TOTE £14.10 : £3.30, £1.40, £1.10; EX 63.50.
Owner Axom (XXIV) **Bred** Paulyn Limited **Trained** East Everleigh, Wilts
■ Stewards' Enquiry : Frankie McDonald one-day ban: used whip down shoulder in the forehand (Sep 29)

FOCUS
Quite an interesting maiden, but slowly run in a time around a second slower than the second division of the 0-55 handicap. The principals were always to the fore and the picture changed rapidly in the last half-furlong. The form can probably be taken at face value.

Russian Storm Official explanation: jockey said filly hung badly left
Turbulent Priest Official explanation: jockey said colt was slowly away

6086 BOOK YOUR CHRISTMAS PARTY AT KEMPTON MEDIAN AUCTION MAIDEN STKS 1m 4f (P)

7:10 (7:15) (Class 6) 3-4-Y-0 £1,617 (£481; £240; £120) Stalls Centre

Form RPR

0-3 **1** **Passion Play**[31] 5098 3-8-12 0 JimCrowley 7 57
(William Knight) *trckd ldrs: drvn to ld 2f out: hrd drvn and jnd fnl 120yds: kpt finding and asserted again in clsng stages* **15/2**[2]

0 **2** nk **Magic Minstrel**[66] 3925 3-9-3 0 LiamKeniry 11 62
(Andrew Balding) *in rr: rdn on outside over 2f out: hdwy appr fnl f: styd on to chal fnl 120yds: outpcd by wnr cl to home* **14/1**

04 **3** 1 **Fairest Isle (IRE)**[16] 5607 3-8-12 0 (t) StevieDonohoe 9 55
(James Fanshawe) *in rr: rdn and hdwy 3f out: styd on u.p ins fnl f to chal fnl 120yds: no ex and one pce into 3rd in clsng stages* **10/1**[3]

0-6 **4** 1 ½ **Samanda (IRE)**[70] 3766 3-9-3 0 (v[1]) KirstyMilczarek 2 58
(Luca Cumani) *in tch: hdwy and rdn fr 2f out: nt clr run and swtchd sharply rt jst ins fnl f: kpt on but nt gng pce to rch ldrs* **20/1**

5 ½ **Ultimate Best** 3-8-12 0 JimmyQuinn 10 52
(Michael Mullineaux) *s.i.s: in rr: drvn and sme prog on inner over 2f out: nvr gng pce to rch ldrs* **25/1**

60 **6** hd **Ballina Blue**[63] 4023 3-8-10 0 MartinLeonard[(7)] 5 56
(Sheena West) *sn led: rdn 3f out: hdd 2f out: wknd ins fnl f* **66/1**

5 **7** 2 **Cardi King**[22] 5386 3-9-3 0 JamesDoyle 8 53
(Ian Wood) *mid-div: rdn and in tch 2f out: green and edgd rt over 1f out: sn wknd* **33/1**

06 **8** nk **Graceful Act**[81] 3437 3-8-12 0 RobertHavlin 1 48
(James Toller) *chsd ldrs: rdn to chal 2f out: wknd ins fnl f* **12/1**

2322 **9** nk **Sally Friday (IRE)**[22] 5386 3-8-12 75 (p) LukeMorris 6 47
(Peter Winkworth) *in tch: rdn: n.m.r and one pce appr fnl 2f: rallied and styng on whn bdly hmpd jst ins fnl f: nt rcvr* **8/13**[1]

10 11 **Lady Sefton** 3-8-12 0 SteveDrowne 3 30
(James Given) *w ldr to 1/2-way: rdn 4f out: wknd fr 3f out* **16/1**

0 **11** 18 **Royal Alcor (IRE)**[15] 5629 4-9-12 0 (t) FrankieMcDonald 4 —
(Alastair Lidderdale) *a in rr: eased whn t.o ins fnl f* **66/1**

2m 36.27s (1.77) **Going Correction** -0.025s/f (Stan)
WFA 3 from 4yo 9lb 11 Ran SP% **117.6**
Speed ratings (Par 101): **93,92,92,91,90 90,89,89,88,81 69**
toteswingers:1&2:£11.80, 2&3:£16.10, 1&3:£3.60 CSF £98.75 TOTE £8.30 : £2.90, £5.80, £5.20; EX 100.00.
Owner Mascalls Stud **Bred** Mascalls Stud **Trained** Patching, W Sussex
■ Stewards' Enquiry : Kirsty Milczarek two-day ban: careless riding (Sep 29-30)

FOCUS
They went no pace in this weak maiden event, and the form is dubious and unlikely to prove too solid.

Royal Alcor(IRE) Official explanation: jockey said gelding hung left from home turn

6087 WATCH RACING UK ON SKY 432 H'CAP 2m (P)
7:40 (7:44) (Class 6) (0-60,63) 3-Y-0+ £1,617 (£481; £240; £120) Stalls Low

Form RPR
3046 **1** **Ministry**[24] [5321] 3-8-13 **56**........ LukeMorris 8 71+
(John Best) *trckd ldrs: drvn to go 2nd over 2f out: led over 1f out: sn clr: eased fnl 120yds* **6/1**[3]
5544 **2** *4* **Delorain (IRE)**[28] [5209] 8-9-1 **50**........(v) LauraPike(5) 10 55
(William Stone) *chsd ldrs: rdn to go 2nd over 4f out: no imp and dropped to 3rd over 2f out: kpt on again to chse eased down wnr last strides* **14/1**
0051 **3** *½* **Katies Tuitor**[5] [5947] 8-10-5 **63** 6ex........(p) LiamKeniry 7 67
(J S Moore) *led after 1f: rdn and qckd fr 3f out: hdd over 1f out: sn no ch w wnr: wknd in clsng stages and lost 2nd last strides* **6/4**[1]
4544 **4** *1* **Green Future (USA)**[5] [5947] 3-9-1 **58**........(b) PatCosgrave 2 61
(Amanda Perrett) *chsd ldrs: rdn and outpcd fr over 2f out: styd on again clsng stages: nvr nr eased down wnr* **9/2**[2]
5022 **5** *¾* **Sea The Flames (IRE)**[22] [5379] 3-9-0 **57**........(b) MartinDwyer 12 59
(Marcus Tregoning) *impr to chse ldrs after 4f: rdn towards outside and lost position 3f out: styd on again ins fnl f but nvr nr eased down wnr* **6/1**[3]
51-0 **6** *¾* **Jennerous Blue**[18] [5519] 4-9-6 **50**........(p) PaulQuinn 5 51
(Dean Ivory) *in rr: rdn and hdwy fr 3f out: styd on ins fnl f* **11/1**
5660 **7** *¾* **Prince Charlemagne (IRE)**[35] [4974] 8-9-3 **52**...(p) MatthewCosham(5) 4 52
(Dr Jeremy Naylor) *mid-div: rdn and outpcd 4f out: styd on again fr over 1f out* **25/1**
/-33 **8** *5* **Henry Holmes**[223] [419] 8-9-2 **46**........ RichardThomas 13 40
(Lydia Richards) *in rr: sme hdwy over 4f out: no ch over 2f out* **33/1**
0450 **9** *½* **Neighbourhood (USA)**[17] [5566] 3-8-6 **49**........ ChrisCatlin 3 43
(James Evans) *led 1f: chsd ldrs: rdn 5f out: sn wknd* **20/1**
0-05 **10** *20* **Happy Fleet**[11] [2659] 8-9-7 **51**........ JimCrowley 11 21
(Natalie Lloyd-Beavis) *rdn over 3f out: a in rr* **25/1**
0600 **11** *25* **Dubai Miracle (USA)**[22] [5379] 4-9-9 **58**........(b) DavidKenny(5) 6 —
(Laura Young) *rdn and wl bhd over 4f out* **50/1**

3m 29.32s (-0.78) **Going Correction** -0.025s/f (Stan)
WFA 3 from 4yo+ 13lb **11** Ran SP% **119.1**
Speed ratings (Par 101): **100,98,97,97,96 96,96,93,93,83 70**
toteswingers:1&2:£20.00, 2&3:£9.30, 1&3:£3.40 CSF £79.60 CT £190.27 TOTE £5.70: £1.50, £4.20, £1.40; EX 118.80.
Owner Malt, Adams & Gurney **Bred** Cheveley Park Stud Ltd **Trained** Hucking, Kent

FOCUS
A very ordinary staying handicap, but probably decent form for the grade with the winner value for at least twice as far. They went a reasonable pace.

6088 KEMPTON.CO.UK CONDITIONS STKS 1m (P)
8:10 (8:13) (Class 4) 3-Y-0+ £4,075 (£1,212; £606; £303) Stalls Low

Form RPR
1330 **1** **Western Aristocrat (USA)**[27] [5252] 3-8-9 107........ ShaneKelly 2 109+
(Jeremy Noseda) *trckd ldrs: wnt 2nd over 3f out: drvn and qcknd to chal 1f out: sn led and clr: easily* **6/4**[1]
0450 **2** *1 ¾* **King Of Dixie (USA)**[12] [5699] 7-9-0 96........ JimCrowley 4 106
(William Knight) *trckd ldr: led 4f out: drvn and jnd 1f out: sn hdd and no ch w wnr: styd on same pce for 2nd* **5/1**[3]
2203 **3** *3 ½* **Enak (ARG)**[49] [4456] 5-9-0 107........(t) RobertHavlin 10 98
(Saeed Bin Suroor) *in rr but in tch: drvn and styd on fr over 1f out: tk one pce 3rd ins fnl f* **12/1**
6620 **4** *hd* **Sahara Kingdom (IRE)**[12] [5704] 4-9-0 103........(v[1]) IanMongan 8 97
(Saeed Bin Suroor) *in rr but in tch: drvn and styd on fr over 1f out: nvr any ch* **10/1**
2300 **5** *7* **Spring Of Fame (USA)**[17] [5544] 5-9-0 112........ FrankieDettori 5 81
(Saeed Bin Suroor) *chsd ldrs: rdn over 2f out: wknd qckly 2f out* **5/2**[2]
103/ **6** *nk* **Sos Brillante (CHI)**[545] 6-8-9 84........ LukeMorris 1 76
(Terry Clement) *in rr: sme prog over 2f out: nvr any ch and sn wknd* **50/1**
1205 **7** *8* **Sylvestris (IRE)**[40] [4790] 3-8-4 93........[1] RichardKingscote 3 56
(Ralph Beckett) *led tl hdd 4f out: wknd quicky over 2f out* **12/1**

1m 35.73s (-4.07) **Going Correction** -0.025s/f (Stan) course record
WFA 3 from 4yo+ 5lb **7** Ran SP% **111.7**
Speed ratings (Par 105): **119,117,113,113,106 106,98**
toteswingers:1&2:£2.10, 2&3:£3.70, 1&3:£4.10 CSF £8.01 TOTE [illegible]: £1.10, £2.40; EX 10.40.
Owner Tom Ludt **Bred** Grapestock Llc **Trained** Newmarket, Suffolk

FOCUS
A fair conditions event but there were question marks over the majority of the field. In the event we saw a smart performance from the winner, who broke the course record with a time around two seconds inside the standard. Those behind the second were 10lb+ off.

6089 BOOK KEMPTON TICKETS ON 0844 579 3008 H'CAP 1m (P)
8:40 (8:40) (Class 5) (0-75,74) 3-Y-0 £2,264 (£673; £336; £168) Stalls Low

Form RPR
6222 **1** **Dare To Bare (IRE)**[5] [5942] 3-9-4 **71**........(v) PatCosgrave 10 82
(Amanda Perrett) *mde all: rdn over 1f out: styd on wl ins fnl f: unchal* **5/2**[2]
0503 **2** *1 ¼* **Ducal**[12] [5735] 3-9-1 **68**........ SebSanders 3 76
(Sir Mark Prescott Bt) *s.i.s: in rr: drvn and hdwy on outside fr 2f out: chsd wnr over 1f out: kpt on but no imp fnl 120yds* **9/4**[1]
4303 **3** *1 ½* **Choral**[12] [5718] 3-9-6 **73**........ PatDobbs 4 78
(Richard Hannon) *in tch: drvn to chse ldrs fr 2f out: sn one pce: styd on to take one 3rd ins fnl f* **9/1**
4143 **4** *1* **Fenella Fudge**[17] [5551] 3-9-0 **67**........(b) JimCrowley 11 69
(James Given) *sn chsng wnr: rdn over 2f out: lost 2nd over 2f out and sn wknd* **20/1**
0560 **5** *2 ½* **Diplomasi**[24] [5318] 3-8-11 **64**........(p) PhilipRobinson 7 61
(Clive Brittain) *t.k.h: stdd in rr: rdn over 1f out: styd on ins fnl f: nvr any ch w ldrs* **20/1**
45-2 **6** *shd* **Ebony Song (USA)**[50] [4435] 3-9-3 **70**........ LiamKeniry 5 66
(Jo Crowley) *chsd ldrs: rdn to chse wnr over 2f out: no imp: wknd ins fnl f* **10/1**
3045 **7** *1* **Dunseverick (IRE)**[28] [5213] 3-9-4 **71**........ ChrisCatlin 8 65
(David Lanigan) *s.i.s: in rr: hdwy and drvn along 3f out: wknd fr 2f out* **10/1**
6141 **8** *1* **Russian Ice**[36] [4911] 3-8-13 **66**........(b) ShaneKelly 2 58
(Dean Ivory) *in rr: rdn 3f out: sn wknd* **11/1**
6333 **9** *5* **Ibiza Sunset (IRE)**[12] [5731] 3-9-5 **72**........ IanMongan 13 52
(Peter Winkworth) *chsd ldrs: rdn 3f out: wknd qckly over 1f out* **6/1**[3]

1m 38.67s (-1.13) **Going Correction** -0.025s/f (Stan) **9** Ran SP% **119.7**
Speed ratings (Par 101): **104,102,101,100,97 97,96,95,90**
toteswingers:1&2:£2.30, 2&3:£4.20, 1&3:£3.90 CSF £8.95 CT £41.45 TOTE £4.10: £1.80, £1.10, £2.50; EX 10.20.
Owner Mr & Mrs F Cotton Mrs S Conway **Bred** Mrs E Thompson **Trained** Pulborough, W Sussex

FOCUS
A fair handicap for the grade. The winner is rated in line with his recent 1m2f efforts.
Russian Ice Official explanation: jockey said filly never travelled

6090 KEMPTON FOR OUTDOOR EVENTS H'CAP 6f (P)
9:10 (9:11) (Class 6) (0-65,65) 3-Y-0+ £1,617 (£481; £240; £120) Stalls Low

Form RPR
1302 **1** **Magic Cross**[14] [5644] 3-9-2 **65**........ AdamBeschizza(3) 9 74
(Philip McBride) *in rr: rdn and hdwy over 1f out: str run to ld ins fnl f: drvn out* **6/1**[3]
1-0 **2** *1 ¼* **Torres Del Paine**[14] [5640] 4-9-3 **64**........ SeanLevey(3) 4 69
(Jimmy Fox) *bmpd s: sn rcvrd to chse ldrs: drvn to ld appr over 2f out: hdd ins fnl f: nt qckn: jst hld on for 2nd last strides* **5/1**[2]
4336 **3** *shd* **Valeo Si Vales (IRE)**[22] [5388] 3-9-0 **60**........(b) JamesDoyle 12 65
(Jamie Osborne) *stdd s: hld up in rr: rdn and hdwy over 1f out: styd on to take 3rd ins fnl f: clsd on 2nd in last strides: could nt rch wnr* **7/1**
1005 **4** *¾* **Paphos**[36] [4910] 4-9-4 **65**........(v) RyanClark(3) 3 67
(Stuart Williams) *bmpd s: sn chsng ldrs: rdn over 2f out: styd on same pce ins fnl f* **7/2**[1]
0060 **5** *1* **Rio Royale (IRE)**[18] [5513] 5-9-2 **60**........(v[1]) JimCrowley 11 59
(Amanda Perrett) *chsd ldrs: rdn over 2f out: wknd ins fnl f* **14/1**
6534 **6** *1* **Saucy Buck (IRE)**[7] [5859] 3-9-3 **63**........ JamieGoldstein 8 59
(Ralph Smith) *chsd ldrs: rdn along 3f out: wknd ins fnl f* **6/1**[3]
0-60 **7** *½* **Mambo Spirit (IRE)**[24] [5319] 7-9-7 **65**........(t) SteveDrowne 2 59
(Tony Newcombe) *bmpd s: in rr: pushed along and n.m.r over 1f out: drvn and sme prog ins fnl f* **8/1**
3/06 **8** *2 ¼* **Spring Buck (IRE)**[15] [5633] 6-9-1 **59**........ PatDobbs 6 46
(Paul Cole) *rdn over 2f out: a outpcd* **15/2**
3230 **9** *4 ½* **Abadejo**[81] [3433] 3-9-3 **63**........ AdamKirby 7 36
(J R Jenkins) *t.k.h: sn led: hdd appr over 2f out: sn btn* **14/1**
3660 **10** *3 ¾* **Super Frank (IRE)**[22] [5387] 8-9-4 **62**........ IanMongan 1 23
(Zoe Davison) *chsd ldrs over 3f out* **20/1**

1m 12.15s (-0.95) **Going Correction** -0.025s/f (Stan)
WFA 3 from 4yo+ 2lb **10** Ran SP% **120.9**
Speed ratings (Par 101): **105,103,103,102,100 99,98,95,89,84**
toteswingers:1&2:£5.40, 2&3:£6.90, 1&3:£7.20 CSF £37.56 CT £224.55 TOTE £6.20: £2.00, £1.60, £1.50; EX 34.80.
Owner P J McBride **Bred** J W P Clark **Trained** Newmarket, Suffolk

FOCUS
Modest but sound sprint handicap form. They went a strong pace.
Abadejo Official explanation: jockey said bit slipped through gelding's mouth
T/Plt: £427.70 to a £1 stake. Pool of £56,334.00 - 96.15 winning tickets. T/Qpdt: £26.90 to a £1 stake. Pool of £8,004.17 - 219.60 winning tickets. ST

5077 PONTEFRACT (L-H)
Thursday, September 15
OFFICIAL GOING: Good to firm (watered; 8.3)
Wind: light across Weather: Fine and dry

6091 PONTEFRACT APPRENTICE H'CAP 6f
2:30 (2:30) (Class 5) (0-70,70) 3-Y-0+ £2,264 (£673; £336; £168) Stalls Low

Form RPR
4201 **1** **Mount Hollow**[23] [5338] 6-8-12 **64**........(p) JackDuern(3) 7 71
(Reg Hollinshead) *stdd s and hld up in rr: stdy hdwy over 2f out: swtchd rt and effrt appr fnl f: sn rdn and styd on wl to ld nr fin* **4/1**[3]
0005 **2** *nk* **Half A Crown (IRE)**[12] [5732] 6-8-2 **56** oh2........ HannahNunn(5) 2 62
(Peter Salmon) *trckd ldr: cl up 2f out: rdn to ld 1f out: sn drvn: hdd and no ex nr fin* **14/1**
3022 **3** *hd* **Tislaam (IRE)**[14] [5640] 4-8-12 **66**........(p) RyanTate(5) 6 71
(Alan McCabe) *trckd ldrs: smooth hdwy 2f out: chal ent fnl f: sn rdn and ev ch tl nt qckn nr fin* **7/2**[2]
0311 **4** *¾* **Paradise Spectre**[17] [5561] 4-9-0 **68**........ JasonHart(5) 5 71
(Mrs K Burke) *trckd ldrs: hdwy on outer 2f out: rdn and ev ch whn edgd lft 1f out: kpt on* **3/1**
6265 **5** *3 ¾* **Mr Wolf**[22] [5371] 10-9-1 **69**........(p) DavidSimmonson(5) 3 60
(John Quinn) *led: rdn along 2f out: hdd 1f out: grad wknd* **7/1**
1000 **6** *1 ¼* **Gertmegalush (IRE)**[23] [5338] 4-8-11 **60**........ GeorgeChaloner 1 47
(John Harris) *dwlt: sn chsng ldng pair on inner: rdn along wl over 2f out and sn wknd* **14/1**
351 **7** *¾* **Mandhooma**[13] [5669] 5-9-4 **70**........ IanBurns(3) 4 54
(Peter Hiatt) *hld up: a towards rr* **8/1**
034 **8** *3 ¼* **Uddy Mac**[14] [5652] 4-8-2 **56**........(b) TerenceFury(5) 8 30
(Neville Bycroft) *hld up in rr: hdwy and rn wd bnd 2f out: sn rdn and n.d* **12/1**

1m 16.42s (-0.48) **Going Correction** -0.125s/f (Firm) **8** Ran SP% **111.9**
Speed ratings (Par 103): **98,97,97,96,91 89,88,84**
toteswingers:1&2:£13.80, 1&3:£4.20, 2&3:£16.50 CSF £54.23 CT £212.15 TOTE £4.10: £1.30, £3.90, £1.80; EX 47.50.
Owner R Hollinshead **Bred** G Robinson **Trained** Upper Longdon, Staffs
■ Stewards' Enquiry : Jason Hart one-day ban: used whip in incorrect place (Sep 29)

FOCUS
The ground was officially described as good to firm. An ordinary apprentice handicap and the pace was by no means breakneck. The form is rated around the winner and third.

6092 TOTEQUICKPICK MEDIAN AUCTION MAIDEN STKS 5f
3:00 (3:01) (Class 5) 2-Y-0 £2,264 (£673; £336; £168) Stalls Low

Form RPR
2 **1** **Passionada**[43] [4668] 2-8-12 0........ BarryMcHugh 4 71
(Ollie Pears) *mde all: qcknd wl over 1f out: rdn: rn green and edgd rt fnl f: kpt on* **2/1**[1]
63 **2** *hd* **Royal Trix**[15] [5613] 2-8-12 0........ CathyGannon 10 71
(Marcus Tregoning) *trckd ldrs: hdwy over 2f out: rdn to chse wnr over 1f out: drvn and ev ch ins fnl f: kpt on* **7/1**
5 **3** *2 ¾* **Archers Prize (IRE)**[62] [4068] 2-9-3 0........ RichardMullen 5 66
(Ed McMahon) *in tch: pushed along 1/2-way: sn rdn: hdwy over 1f out: kpt on u.p fnl f* **11/4**[2]
0600 **4** *1* **Farzan (IRE)**[11] [5755] 2-9-3 65........(b[1]) DavidNolan 2 62
(Tim Easterby) *trckd ldrs on inner: effrt over 2f out and sn rdn along: drvn over 1f out and one pce* **66/1**
545 **5** *nse* **Pitt Rivers**[13] [5668] 2-9-0 71........ MartinHarley(3) 3 62
(Mick Channon) *chsd ldrs: rdn along 2f out: drvn over 1f out and kpt on same pce* **10/3**[3]

3 **6** *hd* **Trioomph**[19] 5486 2-8-12 0 ...... FrederikTylicki 7 56
(James Given) *cl up: rdn along over 2f out: drvn over 1f out and grad wknd* **10/1**

6304 **7** *½* **Trust Fund Babe (IRE)**[16] 5590 2-8-12 59 ...... RobertWinston 11 54
(Tim Easterby) *dwlt: a in rr* **20/1**

05 **8** *3* **Bitter Lemon**[16] 5590 2-8-12 0 ...... FrannyNorton 6 47
(Kevin Ryan) *a towards rr* **25/1**

63.27 secs (-0.03) **Going Correction** -0.125s/f (Firm) **8** Ran SP% **114.8**
Speed ratings (Par 95): **95,94,90,88,88 88,87,82**
toteswingers:1&2:£8.30, 1&3:£1.10, 2&3:£2.60 CSF £16.51 TOTE £3.40: £1.20, £1.50, £1.30; EX 12.80.
Owner Mia Racing **Bred** Mia Racing **Trained** Norton, N Yorks

FOCUS
An ordinary maiden.

NOTEBOOK
Passionada finished clear of the rest when narrowly beaten by a 1-4 shot on her debut last month and only needed to run close to that form to go one better. Soon in front, she railed like a greyhound but had to dig deep to withstand the persistent challenge of the runner-up. She wasn't impressive, but at least she showed she can battle and will now head for the Redcar Two-Year-Old Trophy. (tchd 9-4, 15-8 in places)
Royal Trix improved plenty from her first start to her second and probably stepped up again here. Trapped out wide from the outside stall, she kept snapping away at the favourite like a terrier all the way up the home straight and should be able to find an ordinary race, with nurseries now a possibility.
Archers Prize(IRE), a half-brother to Masta Plasta, showed speed for a long way on his debut over 6f at Nottingham in July, but he was always being taken off his feet over this trip and didn't get into stride until it was too late. (op 3-1)
Farzan(IRE) improved a bit for the first-time blinkers, but doesn't look a winner waiting to happen.
Pitt Rivers, placed twice over this trip in the spring, attracted market support but he became restless in the stalls and never threatened to make an impact. He is looking totally exposed now. (op 5-1)
Trioomph, an encouraging third over 6f on her Redcar debut, isn't bred to have appreciated this drop in trip. She raced up with the pace for a long way, but carried her head to one side as she faded from over a furlong out. (op 17-2)

6093 RACING UK ON SKY CHANNEL 432 H'CAP — 1m 4y
3:30 (3:31) (Class 4) (0-80,80) 3-Y-O+ **£4,075** (£1,212; £606; £303) **Stalls** Low

Form RPR

3356 **1** **Imaginary World (IRE)**[13] 5684 3-9-1 76 ......(be) RobertWinston 13 84
(Alan McCabe) *dwlt: hld up on inner: gd hdwy over 1f out: kpt on ins fnl f to ld nr fin* **9/1**[3]

2604 **2** *nk* **Solar Spirit (IRE)**[12] 5722 6-9-3 73 ...... PatrickMathers 3 81
(Tracy Waggott) *trckd ldrs and t.k.h: hdwy to chal over 1f out: ev ch ins fnl f: kpt on: jst hld* **10/1**

264 **3** *½* **Standpoint**[17] 5568 5-9-7 77 ......(p) GrahamGibbons 5 84
(Reg Hollinshead) *trckd ldr: led wl over 1f out: kpt on: hdd nr fin* **6/1**[1]

0620 **4** *1½* **Robert The Painter (IRE)**[19] 5465 3-9-5 80 ...... FrederikTylicki 17 82+
(Richard Fahey) *hld up in midfield: rdn over 2f out: hdwy on outer over 1f out: kpt on: wnt 4th nr fin* **11/1**

1403 **5** *shd* **Jonny Lesters Hair (IRE)**[19] 5488 6-9-8 78 ...... DavidNolan 15 81
(Tim Easterby) *midfield: rdn over 2f out: chsd ldrs over 1f out: kpt on one pce* **10/1**

0620 **6** *1* **Sir George (IRE)**[19] 5488 6-9-7 77 ......(p) BarryMcHugh 7 78
(Ollie Pears) *hld up in midfield on inner: hdwy over 2f out: sn rdn: briefly short of room ent fnl f: kpt on one pce* **12/1**

1605 **7** *2* **Shadowtime**[16] 5594 6-9-4 74 ...... AndrewMullen 4 70
(Tracy Waggott) *in tch: pushed along whn short of room and lost pl over 2f out: kpt on fnl f* **11/1**

0-53 **8** *¾* **Duke Of Burgundy (FR)**[15] 3170 8-8-12 68 ...... StephenCraine 9 63
(Jennie Candlish) *hld up: rdn over 2f out: one pce* **25/1**

5412 **9** *1¾* **Climaxfortackle (IRE)**[7] 5856 3-8-5 66 ......(v) RichardMullen 16 56
(Derek Shaw) *slowly away: hld up: pushed along over 2f out: n.d* **9/1**[3]

-606 **10** *nk* **Bilidn**[25] 5303 3-9-1 76 ...... FrannyNorton 10 65
(Clive Brittain) *midfield: rdn over 2f out: no imp* **25/1**

1540 **11** *½* **Tribal Myth (IRE)**[8] 5828 4-8-11 70 ......(p) AmyRyan(3) 11 59
(Kevin Ryan) *trckd ldrs on outer: rdn over 2f out: wknd over 1f out* **20/1**

4300 **12** *2¾* **Cono Zur (FR)**[12] 5722 4-8-13 72 ......(b) DaleSwift(3) 8 54
(Ruth Carr) *led: rdn whn hdd wl over 1f out: sn wknd* **14/1**

0030 **13** *¾* **Dream Lodge (IRE)**[17] 5557 7-9-9 79 ...... TomQueally 1 60
(David Nicholls) *midfield: rdn over 2f out: wknd over 1f out* **8/1**[2]

0050 **14** *3* **Not My Choice (IRE)**[11] 5760 6-9-7 77 ...... MichaelStainton 2 51
(David C Griffiths) *trckd ldr: short of room on inner 2f out: sn lost pl and wknd* **33/1**

2435 **15** *3¾* **Maggie Mey (IRE)**[22] 5370 3-8-10 74 ...... DeclanCannon(3) 14 38
(David O'Meara) *prom: rdn over 2f out: wknd over 1f out* **12/1**

0-00 **16** *3½* **Whistledownwind**[19] 5465 6-9-4 77 ...... MichaelO'Connell(3) 12 34
(David Nicholls) *hld up: nvr threatened* **50/1**

5600 **17** *6* **The Which Doctor**[5] 5948 6-8-13 72 ......(e) RobertLButler(3) 6 15
(Richard Guest) *s.i.s: in midfield on outer: rdn over 2f out: sn wknd* **22/1**

1m 43.33s (-2.57) **Going Correction** -0.125s/f (Firm)
WFA 3 from 4yo+ 5lb **17** Ran SP% **124.0**
Speed ratings (Par 105): **107,106,106,104,104 103,101,100,99,98 98,95,94,91,88 84,78**
toteswingers:1&2:£27.80, 1&3:£11.10, 2&3:£16.50 CSF £88.54 CT £615.22 TOTE £7.90: £1.80, £2.30, £2.10, £2.50; EX 90.20.
Owner Hairy Gorrilaz **Bred** Denis McDonnell **Trained** Averham Park, Notts
■ Stewards' Enquiry : Patrick Mathers caution: used whip with excessive frequency.

FOCUS
A competitive handicap run at a strong pace thanks to the freely sweating Cono Zur tearing off in front, but he had run himself into the ground before the furlong pole. The winner always looked like having an effort like this in her.

6094 PONTEFRACT PARK FILLIES' H'CAP — 6f
4:00 (4:01) (Class 3) (0-90,82) 3-Y-O+
£6,411 (£1,919; £959; £479; £239; £120) **Stalls** Low

Form RPR

4004 **1** **Misplaced Fortune**[13] 5683 6-9-6 81 ......(v) DaleSwift(3) 6 93
(Nigel Tinkler) *hld up towards rr: gd hdwy wl over 1f out: rdn and styd on strly ent fnl f to ld last 100yds* **7/2**[1]

5520 **2** *½* **Jade**[32] 5081 3-9-1 75 ...... GrahamGibbons 4 85
(Ollie Pears) *dwlt and in rr: hmpd over 2f out: gd hdwy on inner over 1f out: rdn to ld jst ins fnl f: hdd and no ex last 100yds* **6/1**[2]

1014 **3** *1¼* **Caranbola**[11] 5760 5-9-6 78 ...... RobertWinston 1 84
(Mel Brittain) *a.p: rdn 2f out: drvn and ev ch ent fnl f: kpt on same pce* **7/1**

3031 **4** *hd* **Close To The Edge (IRE)**[7] 5862 3-9-8 82 6ex ...... FrederikTylicki 8 87+
(Alan McCabe) *chsd ldrs on outer: cl up 2f out: sn rdn: led briefly ent fnl f: sn drvn and hdd: kpt on same pce* **15/2**

6364 **5** *3¼* **Breezolini**[22] 5370 3-8-9 72 ......(v[1]) AmyRyan(3) 12 67
(Richard Whitaker) *swtchd lft s and sn pushed along in rr: sltly hmpd over 2f out: swtchd wd and hdwy wl over 1f out: sn rdn and edgd lft ent fnl f: kpt on: nrst fin* **16/1**

3551 **6** *nse* **Layla Jamil (IRE)**[17] 5551 3-9-0 77 ...... MartinHarley(3) 2 72
(Mick Channon) *chsd ldrs: rdn along 2f out: sn drvn and no imp* **9/1**

030 **7** *1½* **Cloud's End**[47] 4556 4-9-5 77 ...... TomQueally 10 67
(Robert Cowell) *led: rdn along over 2f out: drvn over 1f out: hdd & wknd ent fnl f* **14/1**

6-00 **8** *nk* **Madam Macie (IRE)**[12] 5702 4-9-8 80 ...... CathyGannon 9 69
(David O'Meara) *chsd ldrs: effrt 2f out: sn rdn and wknd over 1f out* **13/2**[3]

6000 **9** *2½* **Mey Blossom**[31] 5108 6-8-13 71 ......(b[1]) MichaelStainton 3 52
(Richard Whitaker) *towards rr: rdn along whn hmpd wl over 1f out: nvr a factor* **33/1**

6404 **10** *11* **Glas Burn**[19] 5476 3-9-8 82 ...... StephenCraine 7 28
(Jonathan Portman) *a towards rr* **20/1**

631 **11** *nk* **Yurituni**[13] 5671 4-9-6 81 ......(v) LouisBeuzelin(3) 5 26
(Eve Johnson Houghton) *dwlt and towards rr: hdwy on inner and in tch 1/2-way: sn rdn and wknd over 2f out* **12/1**

5104 **12** *½* **Mawjoodah**[12] 5735 3-8-3 66 ...... DeclanCannon(3) 11 —
(Brian Ellison) *cl up: rdn along over 2f out: sn wknd* **14/1**

1m 15.23s (-1.67) **Going Correction** -0.125s/f (Firm)
WFA 3 from 4yo+ 2lb **12** Ran SP% **118.7**
Speed ratings (Par 104): **106,105,103,103,99 99,97,96,93,78 78,77**
toteswingers:1&2:£5.10, 1&3:£7.70, 2&3:£7.40 CSF £23.43 CT £143.86 TOTE £5.40: £1.10, £2.00, £3.20; EX 28.20.
Owner W F Burton **Bred** Adrian Smith **Trained** Langton, N Yorks

FOCUS
A useful fillies' handicap for the grade and though the early pace didn't look overly strong, the principals came from the back of the field. The winner rates back to something like her best.

NOTEBOOK
Misplaced Fortune hadn't won since May of last year, but she is much better handicapped now. She had a lot to do at halfway, but was nonetheless travelling well and produced a telling finish in the straight to lead well inside the last furlong. She is worth keeping in mind now that she has regained winning form and may head to Hamilton at the weekend, but she will need the ground to remain on the fast side. (op 9-2 tchd 5-1)
Jade's two previous tries over this C&D resulted in a win and a narrow defeat and this was another decent effort. Held up well off the pace alongside the winner, she finished strongly against the inside rail, but her rival's finishing effort was just too strong. She deserves to get her head back in front. (op 7-1)
Caranbola was always up there and had every chance, but the last half-furlong seemed to find her out. She needs an easier 6f than this or a return to the minimum trip. (tchd 13-2 and 15-2)
Close To The Edge(IRE), a dual C&D winner this year and carrying a 6lb penalty for her recent Polytrack success, got herself into a state in the stalls. She was in front out in the centre of the track over a furlong out, but the nervous energy she had expended earlier may have made the difference. (op 6-1)
Breezolini, tried in a visor, was being ridden along in last place early, but she was running on well at the end.
Layla Jamil(IRE), 2lb higher than for last month's Newcastle success, lacked the pace to worry the principals and probably needs further than this now. (op 8-1)

6095 PONTEFRACT STAYERS CHAMPIONSHIP H'CAP (ROUND 6) — 2m 1f 22y
4:30 (4:31) (Class 6) (0-75,74) 3-Y-O+ **£4,204** (£1,251; £625; £312) **Stalls** Low

Form RPR

2210 **1** **May Contain Nuts**[16] 5599 3-8-12 71 ...... FergusSweeney 6 80
(Brendan Powell) *chsd clr ldr: tk clsr order over 5f out: led 2f out: rdn clr over 1f out: drvn out* **11/1**

3412 **2** *1½* **Dr Finley (IRE)**[15] 5628 4-9-7 67 ...... CathyGannon 3 74+
(Lydia Pearce) *hld up towards rr: tk clsr order 1/2-way: hdwy on inner 2f out: sn rdn: styd on wl fnl f: nt rch wnr* **11/1**

-000 **3** *1¾* **Dan Buoy (FR)**[101] 2762 8-8-13 62 ......(b) BillyCray(3) 9 67
(Richard Guest) *led and sn wl clr: pushed along over 4f out: rdn and hdd 2f out: drvn and rallied ent fnl f: sn edgd rt and kpt on* **25/1**

5252 **4** *hd* **Handles For Forks (IRE)**[10] 5784 3-8-6 68 ...... MartinHarley(3) 4 73
(Mick Channon) *hld up and bhd: stdy hdwy 5f out: rdn to chse ldrs 2f out: drvn over 1f out and kpt on same pce* **5/1**[2]

1460 **5** *2½* **Tillietudlem (FR)**[32] 5079 5-9-1 61 ...... GrahamGibbons 1 63
(Jim Goldie) *hld up in midfield: hdwy over 4f out: rdn along 3f out: kpt on same pce u.p fnl 2f* **11/2**[3]

5460 **6** *1¼* **Simonside**[12] 5724 8-9-11 74 ...... DaleSwift(3) 10 75
(Brian Ellison) *trckd ldrs: effrt 4f out: rdn along 3f out: drvn and one pce fnl 2f* **16/1**

1534 **7** *shd* **Spiders Star**[65] 3935 8-9-1 64 ......(p) PaulPickard(3) 13 65
(Simon West) *hld up and bhd: effrt 3f out and sn rdn along: styd on appr fnl f: nrst fin* **16/1**

2241 **8** *1½* **Petella**[32] 5079 5-9-8 68 ...... TomQueally 5 67
(George Moore) *hld up: hdwy and in tch 1/2-way: effrt on wd outside 4f out: rdn along 3f out: wknd wl over 1f out* **3/1**[1]

256 **9** *nk* **Cat O' Nine Tails**[23] 5340 4-9-13 73 ...... FrannyNorton 7 72
(Mark Johnston) *chsd ldrs: hdwy over 4f out: rdn along 3f out: sn drvn and weak ened wl over 1f out* **14/1**

5302 **10** *4½* **Spruzzo**[16] 5595 5-8-12 58 ...... FrederikTylicki 11 52
(Chris Fairhurst) *prom: rdn along over 3f out: drvn over 2f out and sn wknd* **12/1**

3340 **11** *3½* **Descaro (USA)**[11] 5759 5-9-10 70 ...... RobertWinston 2 60
(David O'Meara) *hld up: a in rr* **13/2**

3244 **12** *2¼* **Heart Of Dubai (USA)**[9] 5166 6-8-9 55 ......(p) KellyHarrison 8 42
(Micky Hammond) *hld up towards rr: sme hdwy 5f out: rdn along over 3f out and nvr a factor* **20/1**

3m 46.57s (1.97) **Going Correction** -0.125s/f (Firm)
WFA 3 from 4yo+ 13lb **12** Ran SP% **121.8**
Speed ratings (Par 101): **90,89,88,88,87 86,86,85,85,83 81,80**
toteswingers:1&2:£11.90, 1&3:£38.30, 2&3:£32.60 CSF £129.84 CT £2965.28 TOTE £14.70: £3.40, £3.30, £7.50; EX 131.30.
Owner I S Smith **Bred** S A Douch **Trained** Upper Lambourn, Berks
■ Stewards' Enquiry : Fergus Sweeney two-day ban: used whip in incorrect place (Sep 29-30)

FOCUS
Round six of this stayers' series and, with Dan Buoy in the field, this race was only going to be run one way. Sound enough form, with a 6lb personal best from the winner.

6096 BOOK YOUR 17TH OCTOBER TOTESPORT PACKAGE MAIDEN STKS (DIV I) 1m 2f 6y
5:00 (5:03) (Class 5) 3-Y-O+ **£2,264** (£673; £336; £168) **Stalls** Low

Form RPR
3-2 **1** **Jameel (USA)**[24] 5327 3-9-0 0 .... LouisBeuzelin(3) 3 92+
(Saeed Bin Suroor) *trckd ldr: rdn to ld over 1f out: drvn 2 l clr bef rdr tk things easy fnl 75yds: jst hld on* **11/4**[2]
426 **2** *hd* **Figaro**[15] 5629 3-9-3 78 .... LiamJones 2 87
(William Haggas) *led: rdn whn hdd over 1f out: kpt on: clsd on eased wnr towards fin* **9/4**[1]
25- **3** *6* **Academy (IRE)**[323] 7179 3-9-3 0 .... RichardMullen 11 73
(Sir Michael Stoute) *in tch: wnt 3rd 3f out: sn rdn: kpt on one pce: no threat ldng pair* **5/1**
0 **4** *3* **Korithi**[141] 1605 3-8-12 0 .... GrahamGibbons 6 61+
(Roger Charlton) *hld up in midfield: pushed along and hdwy over 2f out: kpt on fnl f* **25/1**
525 **5** *shd* **Shaqira**[15] 5629 3-8-12 74 .... CathyGannon 12 61
(Marcus Tregoning) *in tch: rdn wl over 2f out: sn one pce: no ex fnl f* **13/2**
0 **6** *8* **Mahayogin (USA)**[15] 5629 3-9-3 0 .... TomQueally 10 48
(Sir Henry Cecil) *midfield: pushed along over 3f out: sn no imp* **7/2**[3]
6 **7** *21* **Stillington**[10] 5792 5-9-10 0 .... RobertWinston 9 —
(Mel Brittain) *dwlt: hld up: bhd fr 1/2-way* **100/1**
6660 **8** *4 1/2* **Carrside Lady**[143] 1567 5-9-5 35 .... (b) FergusSweeney 8 —
(Garry Woodward) *midfield: pushed along over 3f out: wknd over 2f out* **100/1**
9 *2 1/4* **Ohwhatalady (IRE)**[300] 7509 3-8-9 0 .... MartinHarley(3) 7 —
(Noel Quinlan) *trckd ldrs tl wknd qckly over 3f out* **100/1**
0 **10** *10* **Ferroviere**[32] 5082 3-9-3 0 .... BarryMcHugh 4 —
(Ollie Pears) *hld up in rr: t.o 1/2 way* **100/1**
0 **11** *50* **My Cherie Amour**[16] 5607 3-8-12 0 .... FrederikTylicki 1 —
(Richard Guest) *plld hrd in midfield early: lost pl after 2f: hung rt over 6f out: sn bhd: t.o* **100/1**
0 **12** *hd* **Camina**[10] 5792 3-8-12 0 .... StephenCraine 5 —
(Michael Smith) *s.i.s: sn reminders in rr: t.o 1/2-way* **100/1**

2m 10.37s (-3.33) **Going Correction** -0.125s/f (Firm)
WFA 3 from 5yo 7lb **12** Ran SP% **119.4**
Speed ratings (Par 103): **108,107,103,100,100 94,77,73,71,63 23,23**
toteswingers:1&2:£2.40, 1&3:£3.60, 2&3:£3.80 CSF £9.40 TOTE £4.40: £1.90, £1.30, £2.00; EX 10.20.
Owner Godolphin **Bred** Darley **Trained** Newmarket, Suffolk

FOCUS
Less than half the field could be given any sort of chance in this maiden and only the front pair were ever in it. It turned out to be a rather controversial race. Decent maiden form from the front pair.
My Cherie Amour Official explanation: jockey said filly hung badly right-handed

6097 BOOK YOUR 17TH OCTOBER TOTESPORT PACKAGE MAIDEN STKS (DIV II) 1m 2f 6y
5:30 (5:31) (Class 5) 3-Y-O+ **£2,264** (£673; £252; £252) **Stalls** Low

Form RPR
25 **1** **Landaman (IRE)**[17] 5556 3-9-3 0 .... FrannyNorton 8 91+
(Mark Johnston) *trckd ldr: hdwy to ld 3f out: clr wl over 1f out: easily* **7/4**[1]
005 **2** *8* **Red Lago (IRE)**[16] 5585 3-9-3 68 .... RobertWinston 6 68
(Charles Hills) *a.p: hdwy to chse wnr 2f out and sn rdn: drvn appr fnl f: kpt on: no ch w wnr* **11/2**[3]
3 *1 1/2* **Montefeltro** 3-9-3 0 .... RichardMullen 10 65+
(Mahmood Al Zarooni) *towards rr: hdwy on inner over 3f out: swtchd rt and rdn to chse ldrs wl over 1f out: sn hung lft: drvn and kpt on same pce* **6/1**
000- **3** *dht* **Cottam Donny**[328] 7058 3-9-3 40 .... (t) GrahamGibbons 4 65
(Mel Brittain) *trckd ldrs: hdwy 3f out: rdn wl over 1f out: sn drvn and one pce* **9/1**
5 *5* **Avison (IRE)** 3-9-3 0 .... DavidNolan 3 [illegible]
(Richard Fahey) *towards rr: hdwy 1/2-way: rdn along and in tch 3f out: sn drvn and no imp* **16/1**
0- **6** *9* **Fantastic Times**[528] 1119 5-9-3 0 .... JohnCavanagh(7) 1 32
(Mel Brittain) *led: and sn clr: rdn along 4f out: hdd 3f out: grad wknd* **100/1**
7 *5* **Thackeray**[46] 4-9-10 0 .... KellyHarrison 2 21
(Chris Fairhurst) *a bhd* **33/1**
8 *1 1/2* **Sky High Diver (IRE)** 3-8-7 0 .... GarryWhillans(5) 7 12
(Alan Swinbank) *a in rr* **10/1**
00- **9** *1 1/2* **Nella Sofia**[336] 6873 3-8-12 0 .... FrederikTylicki 9 9
(James Given) *chsd ldrs: rdn along 4f out: sn wknd* **100/1**
0 **10** *7* **Secret Lodge**[40] 4813 3-8-12 0 .... FergusSweeney 11 —
(Garry Woodward) *a in rr* **150/1**
0 **11** *11* **Labroc (IRE)**[143] 1568 3-9-3 0 .... LiamJones 3 —
(William Haggas) *in tch: rdn along over 4f out: sn wknd* **9/2**[2]

2m 10.73s (-2.97) **Going Correction** -0.125s/f (Firm)
WFA 3 from 4yo+ 7lb **11** Ran SP% **114.8**
Speed ratings (Par 103): **106,99,98,98,94 87,83,82,80,75 66**
toteswingers:1&2:£3.60, 2&CD:£4.00, 1&CD:£2.20, 2&MF:£2.20, 1&MF:£1.90 CSF £11.06 TOTE £2.60: £1.40, £1.20; EX 12.90 TRIFECTA PL: Montefeltro £1.20, Cottam Donny £1.50.
Owner Sheikh Hamdan Bin Mohammed Al Maktoum **Bred** Darley **Trained** Middleham Moor, N Yorks

FOCUS
This was even less competitive than the first division and the winning time was 0.36 seconds slower. The winner impressed and the form is taken at face value.
Labroc(IRE) Official explanation: trainer's rep had no explanation for the poor form shown other than the gelding never travelled

6098 BOOK YOUR CHRISTMAS PARTY HERE ON 0113 2876387 H'CAP 1m 4y
6:00 (6:01) (Class 5) (0-70,69) 3-Y-O+ **£2,264** (£673; £336; £168) **Stalls** Low

Form RPR
0510 **1** **Adorable Choice (IRE)**[19] 5496 3-9-5 69 .... (v) StephenCraine 2 76
(Tom Dascombe) *trckd ldrs: hdwy wl over 1f out: swtchd lft and rdn to ld ins fnl f: sn drvn and jst hld on* **25/1**
5156 **2** *hd* **Opus Maximus (IRE)**[22] 5390 6-9-3 65 .... (p) SophieDoyle(3) 9 73+
(Jennie Candlish) *dwlt: t.k.h in rr: hdwy wl over 1f out: swtchd rt and rdn ent fnl f: styd on strly: jst failed* **14/1**
213 **3** *3/4* **Viking Rose (IRE)**[18] 5515 3-8-11 61 .... CathyGannon 17 66
(James Eustace) *prom: chal 3f out: rdn to ld 2f out: drvn and hdd ins fnl f: no ex last 75yds* **12/1**
0050 **4** *1/2* **Classic Descent**[12] 5721 6-8-12 57 .... (bt) FrederikTylicki 10 62
(Ruth Carr) *towards rr: hdwy 2f out: rdn over 1f out: styd on strly fnl f: nrst fin* **33/1**
342 **5** *1* **Petsas Pleasure**[15] 5622 5-9-2 61 .... GrahamGibbons 14 64+
(Ollie Pears) *hld up in rr: hdwy on wd outside over 2f out: rdn to chse ldrs over 1f out: drvn and one pce fnl f* **7/1**[2]
4050 **6** *1 1/2* **Hits Only Jude (IRE)**[19] 5470 8-8-6 58 .... (v) MichaelKenny(7) 7 57
(Declan Carroll) *midfield: hdwy over 2f out: chsd ldrs wl over 1f out: swtchd lft and drvn ent fnl f: kpt on same pce* **25/1**
5556 **7** *1 3/4* **Musnad (USA)**[19] 5469 3-9-1 68 .... DaleSwift(3) 3 62
(Brian Ellison) *in rr: hdwy wl over 1f out: sn rdn and styd on ins fnl f: nrst fin* **7/1**[2]
3022 **8** *nk* **Aussie Blue (IRE)**[12] 5740 7-9-0 59 .... (v) MichaelStainton 4 54
(Richard Whitaker) *a.p: effrt over 2f out: rdn to chal over 1f out and ev ch tl drvn and wknd ins fnl f* **8/1**
5225 **9** *5* **Music Festival (USA)**[12] 5722 4-9-8 67 .... TomQueally 12 50
(Jim Goldie) *nvr bttr than midfield* **15/2**[3]
56-1 **10** *nk* **Shayla**[66] 3902 4-9-3 67 .... GarryWhillans(5) 1 49+
(Alan Swinbank) *in tch: rdn along over 3f out: sn wknd* **5/1**[1]
4260 **11** *shd* **Seldom (IRE)**[19] 5488 5-9-4 63 .... RobertWinston 16 45
(Mel Brittain) *chsd ldrs: rdn along wl over 2f out: grad wknd* **22/1**
0402 **12** *3 1/2* **Lujano**[16] 5601 6-8-10 55 .... BarryMcHugh 6 29
(Ollie Pears) *sn led: rdn along and jnd 3f out: hdd 2f out: sn drvn and wknd* **11/1**
0006 **13** *1 1/4* **Thrust Control (IRE)**[12] 5733 4-9-8 67 .... PatrickMathers 13 38
(Tracy Waggott) *in tch on wd outside: rdn along 1/2-way: sn wknd* **40/1**
3004 **14** *shd* **Very Well Red**[13] 5666 8-9-3 67 .... LucyKBarry(5) 11 38
(Peter Hiatt) *chsd ldrs: rdn along 3f out: sn wknd* **14/1**
2040 **15** *1 1/4* **Motafarred (IRE)**[18] 5504 9-8-12 62 .... JamesRogers(5) 15 30
(Micky Hammond) *a in rr* **14/1**
00-0 **16** *17* **Bavarian Princess (USA)**[53] 4370 3-9-1 65 .... FrannyNorton 5 —
(Mrs K Burke) *prom: rdn along 1/2-way: sn wknd* **40/1**

1m 44.35s (-1.55) **Going Correction** -0.125s/f (Firm)
WFA 3 from 4yo+ 5lb **16** Ran SP% **120.4**
Speed ratings (Par 103): **102,101,101,100,99 98,96,96,91,90 90,87,85,85,84 67**
toteswingers:1&2:£49.50, 1&3:£41.10, 2&3:£34.40 CSF £319.65 CT £4529.97 TOTE £30.30: £6.80, £3.50, £2.50, £7.40; EX 735.90.
Owner John Brown **Bred** John O'Connor **Trained** Malpas, Cheshire
■ Stewards' Enquiry : Stephen Craine three-day ban: used whip with excessive frequency in incorrect place without giving filly time to respond (Sep 29-30,Oct 1)

FOCUS
A competitive if ordinary handicap and the pace was solid with four horses disputing the advantage for a long way. A 3lb personal best from the winner.
Adorable Choice(IRE) Official explanation: trainer's rep said, regarding apparent improvement in form, that the filly was better suited by the faster ground and in its previous race, suffered interference leaving stalls.
Bavarian Princess(USA) Official explanation: jockey said filly ran too free
T/Plt: £55.90 to a £1 stake. Pool:£46,482.68 - 606.80 winning tickets T/Qpdt: £21.90 to a £1 stake. Pool:£4,008.76 - 135.25 winning tickets JR

6064 YARMOUTH (L-H)
Thursday, September 15

OFFICIAL GOING: Good (good to firm in places; 7.8)
Wind: light, across Weather: light cloud

6099 BRITISH STALLION STUDS E B F BARTHOLOMEWS JEWELLERS SPRINT MAIDEN STKS 6f 3y
2:10 (2:14) (Class 5) 2-Y-O **£3,654** (£1,093; £546; £273; £136) **Stalls** Centre

Form RPR
0 **1** **Biba Diva (IRE)**[14] 5655 2-8-12 0 .... TedDurcan 8 74+
(Jeremy Noseda) *unf: hld up in tch: bmpd over 4f out: nt clr run and swtchd rt ent fnl 2f: rdn and chsd ldng pair over 1f out: led wl ins fnl f: r.o wl* [illegible]
4 **2** *1* **Idler (IRE)**[167] 1071 2-9-3 0 .... SilvestreDeSousa 9 76
(Mark Johnston) *str: gd bodied: s.i.s: t.k.h: hld up in tch: hdwy to ld ent fnl 2f: rdn over 1f out: hdd and no ex wl ins fnl f* **4/1**[3]
043 **3** *1* **Poker Hospital**[39] 4823 2-8-12 74 .... KierenFallon 1 68
(George Baker) *on toes: t.k.h: chsd ldrs: rdn and effrt jst over 2f out: ev ch over 1f out: unable qck ins fnl f: one pce fnl 100yds* **9/4**[1]
00 **4** *2 1/4* **Chalk And Cheese (USA)**[19] 5480 2-9-3 0 .... WilliamBuick 3 65
(John Gosden) *w'like: on toes: s.i.s: bhd: hdwy ent fnl 2f: chsd ldng trio and rdn over 1f out: racd awkwardly and no imp ins fnl f* **5/1**
0 **5** *5* **Indiana Guest (IRE)**[19] 5480 2-9-3 0 .... NeilCallan 2 49
(George Margarson) *unf: scope: in tch in midfield: rdn 4f out: struggling and lost pl over 2f out: plugged on but no treat to ldrs fnl 2f* **20/1**
0 **6** *nk* **Conowen**[39] 4823 2-9-3 0 .... MartinLane 6 48
(William Jarvis) *unf: racd freely: w ldrs tl over 2f out: sn rdn and unable qck: wknd over 1f out* **100/1**
04 **7** *hd* **Kings Decree**[22] 5375 2-9-3 0 .... JamesMillman 5 48
(Rod Millman) *taken down early: t.k.h: hdwy to ld over 4f out: hdd and rdn jst over 2f out: wknd and bhd whn wandered wl over 1f out* **9/1**
8 *2 3/4* **Brother Tiger** 2-9-3 0 .... AdrianMcCarthy 4 39
(George Margarson) *str: bit bkwd: m green: in tch tl lost pl and dropped to rr after 2f out: rdn and btn over 2f out* **100/1**
000 **9** *2 1/2* **Ooi Long**[65] 3954 2-9-3 46 .... TomMcLaughlin 10 31
(Mark Rimmer) *racd against stands' rail: led tl over 4f out: lost pl and in rr whn hmpd 2f out: sn bhd* **200/1**

1m 13.02s (-1.38) **Going Correction** -0.25s/f (Firm) **9** Ran SP% **113.2**
Speed ratings (Par 95): **99,97,96,93,86 86,86,82,79**
toteswingers:1&2:£2.40, 1&3:£2.20, 2&3:£2.70 CSF £12.51 TOTE £3.40: £1.10, £1.60, £1.30; EX 13.20 Trifecta £33.90 Pool: £858.46 - 18.73 winning units..
Owner Mrs Susan Roy **Bred** Barronstown Stud **Trained** Newmarket, Suffolk

FOCUS
An ordinary maiden. Somemothersdohavem, who was ponied early to the start, really misbehaved at the stalls and was withdrawn after getting plenty of assistance.

NOTEBOOK
Biba Diva(IRE), down about a furlong in trip, travelled strongly for much of the race before showing a good attitude in the final stages, down the stands' rail, to win by a comfortable margin. It remains to be seen quite how good she is. (op 7-2)
Idler(IRE) made a promising debut in a race that has worked out well back in April, and put up another pleasing performance after a lengthy break. He gave the impression he should get further.

Poker Hospital, who has an official rating of 74, was readily outpaced once getting into at least a share of the lead over 1f out, so is seemingly going to find it difficult to win a maiden at this trip unless it's really weak. (op 2-1 tchd 15-8)
Chalk And Cheese(USA) started slowly and wasn't able to put in a big challenge. One got the suspicion that he wasn't an easy ride considering his head carriage inside the final furlong. (op 9-2)

6100 BRITISH STALLION STUDS SUPPORTING BRITISH RACING E B F MAIDEN STKS 1m 3y

2:40 (2:46) (Class 5) 2-Y-O **£3,465** (£1,037; £518; £259; £129) **Stalls** Centre

Form RPR

1 **Main Sequence (USA)** 2-9-3 0 .... GeorgeBaker 2 80+
(David Lanigan) *w'like: s.i.s: bhd: hdwy but stl plenty to do over 1f out: rn green and hung lft jst over 1f out: str run ins fnl f to ld fnl 50yds: sn in command* **50/1**

6 2 1 1/4 **Almuftarris (USA)**[69] 3823 2-9-3 0 .... RichardHills 9 75
(Ed Dunlop) *edgy: chsd ldrs: rdn to ld over 1f out: hdd and nt pce of wnr fnl 50yds* **9/4**[1]

3 *hd* **Yaa Salam** 2-9-3 0 .... SilvestreDeSousa 12 75
(Mahmood Al Zarooni) *w'like: lengthy: scope: in tch: rdn over 2f out: chsd ldrs u.p over 1f out: kpt on ins fnl f* **11/1**

4 4 1 1/2 **Muntasir (IRE)**[22] 5384 2-9-3 0 .... TedDurcan 6 71
(Saeed Bin Suroor) *str: lw: led tl over 6f out: styd chsng ldrs: rdn wl over 1f out: styd on same pce u.p fnl f* **11/4**[2]

5 *1* **Handsome Ransom** 2-9-3 0 .... WilliamBuick 5 69+
(John Gosden) *w'like: scope: towards rr: pushed along and hdwy over 2f out: rdn over 1f out: kpt on same pce ins fnl f* **5/1**[3]

6 3 1/4 **Tafawuk (USA)** 2-9-3 0 .... NeilCallan 13 61+
(Roger Varian) *w'like: scope: lw: awkward leaving stalls: sn rcvrd and in tch: led jst over 2f out tl rdn and hdd over 1f out: wknd fnl f* **18/1**

05L5 7 2 1/4 **Thecornishcockney**[27] 5234 2-9-3 79 .... EddieAhern 1 56
(John Ryan) *taken down early and ponied to s: t.k.h: chsd ldrs tl led over 6f out: hdd jst over 2f out: wknd u.p ent fnl f* **11/1**

0 8 *1* **Bank On Me**[34] 5013 2-9-3 0 .... MartinLane 3 54
(Philip McBride) *s.i.s: bhd: struggling whn hmpd jst over 2f out: nvr trbld ldrs* **100/1**

0 9 2 1/4 **Hartside (GER)**[27] 5239 2-9-3 0 .... KierenFallon 10 49
(Sir Michael Stoute) *w'like: attr: in tch: rdn 1/2-way: wknd over 2f out: wl bhd fnl 2f* **8/1**

0 10 *7* **Inch Or Two**[23] 5337 2-9-3 0 .... DavidProbert 7 33
(Des Donovan) *neat: towards rr: pushed along after 2f: wknd and rn green over 2f out* **250/1**

00 11 *1/2* **Singspiel Spirit**[42] 4698 2-9-3 0 .... (p) ChrisCatlin 4 32
(Clive Brittain) *chsd ldrs: rdn 1/2-way: wknd over 2f out: wl bhd over 1f out* **100/1**

00 12 *12* **Pack Of Cards (IRE)**[13] 5688 2-9-3 0 .... MarcHalford 11 —
(Terry Clement) *lt-f: in tch in midfield: lost pl and rdn 3f out: lost tch 2f out* **250/1**

1m 39.67s (-0.93) **Going Correction** -0.25s/f (Firm) 12 Ran SP% **111.9**
Speed ratings (Par 95): **94,92,92,91,90 86,84,83,81,74 73,61**
toteswingers:1&2:£25.20, 1&3:£33.10, 2&3:£6.20 CSF £155.47 TOTE £61.50: £9.90, £1.60, £3.40; EX 286.50 Trifecta £665.90 Part won. Pool: £899.97 - 0.20 winning units..
Owner Niarchos Family **Bred** Flaxman Holdings Ltd **Trained** Newmarket, Suffolk

FOCUS
The odd nice type has taken this maiden in the past, so there will be no surprise if the winner develops into a useful handicapper at least with time.

NOTEBOOK
Main Sequence(USA) ◆, the first foal of Group-placed 2-y-o who was a 7f winner, took a little while to get loaded and settle into the race but he really got to grips with things inside the final furlong and won really nicely. It looked the performance of an above-average type. (op 33-1)
Almuftarris(USA) ◆ made a promising start to his career in July at Newmarket over 7f (not seen since) and looked certain to win deep inside the final furlong, but he was reeled in by the strong-finishing challenger. A similar contest would appear to be a formality on decent ground. (op 3-1)
Yaa Salam, whose dam was a Group 2 winner in Australia, looked incredibly green and got behind, but the further he went the more he learnt and this was a solid effort, although he will need to be wiser in the early stages next time to have a chance of winning. (op 16-1)
Muntasir(IRE), who made an unsuccessful debut on the Polytrack when a well backed 5-4 shot, was never far away and had every chance. However, this was a decent event and he isn't one to give up on yet. (tchd 5-2 and 3-1)
Handsome Ransom ◆, who is related to plenty of winners, made a pleasing debut and should come on for the experience. (op 4-1 tchd 11-2)
Tafawuk(USA) ◆ loomed up travelling well things looked good. However, he found little for pressure and, after looking assured of a place at least, managed to be outside the first five. Possibly a drop in trip might help but one will want to see him finish better next time. (op 16-1)
Thecornishcockney, without blinkers this time and ponied to the start, wasn't beaten that far in a Listed event last time, and although that effort and his official rating may flatter him, he does give the race a marker to rate it through. (op 7-1 tchd 12-1)

6101 SEAJACKS (S) NURSERY 1m 3y

3:10 (3:13) (Class 6) (0-65,60) 2-Y-O **£1,617** (£481; £240; £120) **Stalls** Centre

Form RPR

0600 1 **Coach Montana (IRE)**[23] 5342 2-8-12 **51** .... IvaMilickova 6 56
(Jane Chapple-Hyam) *lw: chsd ldr tl led ent fnl 2f: rdn over 1f out: styd on wl and clr ins fnl f* **20/1**

005 2 *3* **Alexandra Palace (IRE)**[21] 5413 2-8-10 **54** .... DarylByrne(5) 2 52
(Mark Johnston) *chsd ldrs: effrt u.p ent fnl 2f: drvn and chsd wnr ent fnl f: no imp* **12/1**

3544 3 *1/2* **Manderston**[77] 3554 2-9-1 **54** .... SilvestreDeSousa 8 51
(Mark Johnston) *chsd ldrs: rdn over 2f out: styd on same pce u.p fnl f* **11/1**

0034 4 *1* **Doctor Banner**[7] 5844 2-9-7 **60** .... SamHitchcott 1 55
(Mick Channon) *hld up in last trio: hdwy over 2f out: hld hd high u.p over 1f out: kpt on ins fnl f: nvr able to chal* **9/2**[2]

6265 5 *3/4* **Jaci Uzzi (IRE)**[27] 5246 2-8-12 **51** .... KierenFallon 7 44
(David Evans) *in tch towards rr: rdn and effrt over 2f out: no imp tl styd on ins fnl f: nvr trbld ldrs* **8/1**

504 6 1 1/2 **Fen Flyer**[14] 5638 2-8-6 **45** .... (b[1]) MartinLane 9 35
(Chris Dwyer) *led and racd against stands' rail thrght: hdd ent fnl 2f: drvn over 1f out: wknd fnl f* **25/1**

0003 7 *nk* **Garrarufa (IRE)**[9] 5802 2-9-0 **53** .... JamesMillman 11 42
(Rod Millman) *hld up in last trio: pushed along and edging lft fr over 2f out: no pogress and n.d* **2/1**[1]

2044 8 1 1/4 **Nude (IRE)**[14] 5637 2-9-0 **53** .... (b) ChrisCatlin 10 39
(Sylvester Kirk) *in tch in midfield: rdn and no rspnse over 2f out: wknd u.p over 1f out* **20/1**

050 9 3 1/4 **Mount St Mistress**[17] 5541 2-9-1 **54** .... TedDurcan 4 32
(George Baker) *a in rr: rdn and btn ent fnl 2f: wl btn over 1f out* **7/1**[3]

000 10 *1* **The Mighty Lohan (IRE)**[22] 5382 2-8-6 **45** .... JamieMackay 5 21
(Amy Weaver) *t.k.h: rdn and struggling over 2f out: wkng whn n.m.r wl over 1f out: no ch after* **9/1**

000 11 *20* **Recway Striker**[17] 5536 2-8-12 **51** .... DavidProbert 3 —
(Des Donovan) *lw: in tch in midfield: rdn 1/2-way: wknd and lost tch 2f out: t.o* **33/1**

1m 41.52s (0.92) **Going Correction** -0.25s/f (Firm) 11 Ran SP% **117.5**
Speed ratings (Par 93): **85,82,81,80,79 78,77,76,73,72 52**
toteswingers:1&2:£38.30, 1&3:£32.40, 2&3:£14.60 CSF £229.50 CT £2816.26 TOTE £40.10: £7.50, £4.20, £2.50; EX 443.10 TRIFECTA Not won..The winner was bought by Karl Moore for 4,000gns.
Owner Mrs Jane Chapple-Hyam **Bred** Summerhill & J Osborne **Trained** Dalham, Suffolk

FOCUS
The whole field came across to the stands' side quite early, and a couple of these met a bit of trouble.

NOTEBOOK
Coach Montana(IRE), who was backed to win a Polytrack maiden in June, had been well beaten on virtually every previous outing so, as his starting price suggests, this was a fairly big shock. The drop in grade must have made all the difference as he appeared to take this comfortably. Official explanation: trainer said, regharding apparent improvement in form, that the gelding benefited from running in lower class. (op 18-1)
Alexandra Palace(IRE), a half-sister to Manyriverstwocross, was always thereabouts and stayed on. (op 11-1)
Manderston, beaten in a 6f seller at this track last time, was returning from a break and ran a similar race to the runner-up. (op 8-1 tchd 15-2)
Doctor Banner hadn't been running too badly in handicaps so was obviously interesting here, but he got short of room on occasions when the race took shape, and he seemed to hang a bit as well. (op 13-2)
Jaci Uzzi(IRE), back down in grade, had the visor she was tried in last time removed, but it didn't improve her chances. Official explanation: jockey said filly lost its action (tchd 17-2)
Garrarufa(IRE), 7lb well in, was having his third successive start at this level but got behind and never featured. Official explanation: jockey said colt never travelled (op 9-4)
Nude(IRE) looked to be going okay when finding little room. That was enough to end any chance she had. (tchd 22-1)

6102 AT THE RACES NURSERY 7f 3y

3:40 (3:40) (Class 4) (0-80,79) 2-Y-O **£3,428** (£1,020; £509; £254) **Stalls** Centre

Form RPR

345 1 **Always Et Toujours**[17] 5565 2-8-13 **71** .... SilvestreDeSousa 1 77
(Mark Johnston) *lw: led tl hdd and wnt lft wl over 1f out: stl ev ch and drvn over 1f out: led again wl ins fnl f: kpt on wl* **4/1**[2]

5002 2 *shd* **Verse Of Love**[9] 5801 2-8-10 **68** .... KierenFallon 6 74
(David Evans) *wnt lft s: w wnr tl led wl over 1f out: sn rdn: drvn fnl f: hdd and no ex wl ins fnl f* **4/1**[2]

0361 3 *1* **Vinnie Jones**[21] 5409 2-9-0 **72** .... WilliamBuick 8 75
(John Gosden) *in tch: hdwy to chse ldrs 2f out: rdn and effrt wl over 1f out: styd on same pce ins fnl f* **11/2**[3]

011 4 2 1/4 **Bu Naaji (IRE)**[36] 4913 2-9-4 **76** .... NeilCallan 5 73
(Roger Varian) *in tch: rdn and unable qck 2f out: drvn and styd on same pce fr over 1f out* **11/4**[1]

0340 5 *3/4* **Flying Trader (USA)**[34] 5013 2-9-0 **72** .... TedDurcan 7 67
(Jane Chapple-Hyam) *hld up in last pair: rdn and outpcd 2f out: rallied ins fnl f: kpt on* **8/1**

040 6 1 1/2 **Cheviot Quest (IRE)**[19] 5480 2-8-7 **65** .... MartinLane 2 56
(William Jarvis) *in tch: rdn and unable qck wl over 1f out: wknd 1f out* **16/1**

3013 7 *41* **Singalat**[33] 5039 2-9-7 **79** .... GeorgeBaker 4 —
(James Given) *hmpd s: hld up in rr: lost tch 2f out: virtually p.u ins fnl f: t.o* **7/1**

1m 25.72s (-0.88) **Going Correction** -0.25s/f (Firm) 7 Ran SP% **111.5**
Speed ratings (Par 97): **95,94,93,91,90 88,41**
toteswingers:1&2:£3.80, 1&3:£2.60, 2&3:£4.10 CSF £19.24 CT £84.48 TOTE £5.40: £2.40, £2.70; EX 17.60 Trifecta £136.70 Pool: £548.81 - 2.97 winning units..
Owner Always Trying Partnership VIII (E) **Bred** Southcourt Stud **Trained** Middleham Moor, N Yorks

FOCUS
With so many of these trying handicaps for the first time it's difficult to know how to evaluate the form accurately. The early pace looked far from strong.

NOTEBOOK
Always Et Toujours, making his handicap debut, was ideally placed considering how the race was run and showed a fine attitude under pressure to collect. One would imagine that 1m will be no problem in due course. (op 9-2 tchd 7-2)
Verse Of Love, held by Bu Naaji on form earlier in the season, and due to go up 4lb from the weekend, ran all the way to the line but couldn't keep his head in front once there. He seems gutsy enough so deserves a victory soon. (op 9-2)
Vinnie Jones won on his nursery debut (7f) at Lingfield's AW surface and had been raised 2lb. He was always in the first three, as had been the two who finished in front of him, but he didn't have the same acceleration. (op 5-1 tchd 6-1)
Bu Naaji(IRE) was chasing a hat-trick after wins at Lingfield (AW) and Salisbury, but looked the one most inconvenienced by the slow early tempo and burnt himself out. He should be allowed another chance. (op 9-4)
Flying Trader(USA), making his handicap debut down in trip, kept on well from the rear but never looked like getting to the leaders. (op 10-1)
Singalat Official explanation: jockey said gelding lost its action

6103 BOODLES DIAMOND H'CAP 1m 6f 17y

4:10 (4:10) (Class 2) (0-100,96) 3-Y-O+ **£9,955** (£2,979; £1,489; £745; £371) **Stalls** Low

Form RPR

6503 1 **Bowdler's Magic**[6] 5878 4-9-2 **84** .... SilvestreDeSousa 4 93
(Mark Johnston) *in tch: hdwy on inner over 3f out: chsd ldrs and swtchd rt over 1f out: drvn to ld fnl 100yds: r.o wl* **6/1**[3]

2121 2 *3/4* **A Boy Named Suzi**[14] 5641 3-8-1 **80** .... MartinLane 8 88
(James Eustace) *hld up in tch: hdwy on outer 3f out: chsng ldrs and edgd lft over 1f out: pressed ldrs ins fnl f: kpt on* **8/1**

0023 3 *1/2* **Woolfall Treasure**[14] 5659 6-10-0 **96** .... (v) GeorgeBaker 5 103
(Gary Moore) *led: rdn over 1f out: drvn ent fnl f: hdd and styd on same pce fnl 100yds* **20/1**

2140 4 1 3/4 **Thubiaan (USA)**[26] 5283 3-8-6 **85** .... RichardHills 3 90
(William Haggas) *t.k.h: hld up in last trio: hdwy and chsd ldrs 9f out: chsd ldr over 2f out: rdn wl over 1f out: unable qck 1f out: wknd fnl 100yds* **2/1**[1]

4-46 5 *2* **Hayzoom**[110] 2512 4-8-10 **78** .... DavidProbert 1 80
(Peter Chapple-Hyam) *hld up in tch in rr: rdn and effrt on outer over 2f out: no imp over 1f out: kpt on but nvr gng pce to rch ldrs* **14/1**

3423 **6** ½ **Zuider Zee (GER)**[12] 5705 4-9-11 **93**.............................. WilliamBuick 7 94
(John Gosden) *lw: in tch in midfield: rdn and unable qck 3f out: styd on same pce and no imp fr over 1f out* **7/2**[2]

4032 **7** ¾ **Huff And Puff**[13] 5685 4-8-12 **80**.............................(v[1]) KierenFallon 9 80
(Amanda Perrett) *lw: chsd ldr tl 11f out: lost pl and pushed along 5f out: dropped to last and swtchd rt 2f out: kpt on but no threat to ldrs fnl f* **8/1**

3000 **8** 2½ **Bay Willow (IRE)**[27] 5250 4-9-10 **92**.............................. TedDurcan 6 89
(Saeed Bin Suroor) *in tch in midfield: rdn and effrt 3f out: unable qck and struggling 2f out: no imp fr over 1f out: wl hld and eased towards fin* **22/1**

1631 **9** 2 **Rockfella**[34] 4998 5-8-11 **79**.............................. EddieAhern 2 73
(Denis Coakley) *lw: chsd ldrs tl wnt 2nd 11f out: lost 2nd over 2f out: sn lost pl and bhd over 1f out* **12/1**

3m 1.19s (-6.41) **Going Correction** -0.20s/f (Firm)
WFA 3 from 4yo+ 11lb **9** Ran SP% **115.5**
Speed ratings (Par 109): **110,109,109,108,107 106,106,105,103**
toteswingers:1&2:£2.10, 1&3:£3.10, 2&3:£2.60 CSF £53.03 CT £901.06 TOTE £6.60: £1.90, £3.00, £4.60; EX 66.90 TRIFECTA Not won..
Owner Paul Dean **Bred** Miss K Rausing **Trained** Middleham Moor, N Yorks

FOCUS
On official ratings this was the best race on the card and it was competitive with plenty of these holding a chance at one stage. It was sound run and the winner is rated basically to this year's form.

NOTEBOOK
Bowdler's Magic ran really well at Chester recently but needed plenty of pushing here and only got on top in the final stages. This victory came off his last winning handicap mark (also his highest one) which was back in July 2010, so a follow up doesn't look obvious, although one should never discount a Johnston-trained horse to find a bit more. He is in the Cesarewitch. (tchd 11-2)
A Boy Named Suzi, up 4lb for winning on the Polytrack last time, has been in good heart this year and continued his upward profile with a solid performance. (op 10-1 tchd 12-1)
Woolfall Treasure had been running well this season after an inauspicious start at York in July, and did well again after dominating. (op 16-1)
Thubiaan(USA) was a little disappointing when tried over this trip for the first time at York in the Melrose, and didn't seem to get home again after arriving on the scene going well. He may be worth another try at 1m4f. (op 7-2)
Hayzoom, off since the end of May, stayed on nicely from the back of the field and will surely improve for the outing. (op 25-1 tchd 28-1)
Zuider Zee(GER) came into this race off the back of a solid effort in the Old Borough Cup, so better could have been expected. Official explanation: trainer's rep said gelding was unsuited by the good (good to firm places) ground (op 9-4)
Rockfella Official explanation: jockey said gelding ran too free

6104 YOUR MORTGAGE SOLUTIONS GORLESTON H'CAP 2m
4:40 (4:41) (Class 5) (0-70,70) 3-Y-0+ **£2,264** (£673; £336; £168) **Stalls** Low

Form RPR

522 **1** **Astromagick**[58] 4190 3-8-11 **66**.............................. WilliamBuick 6 77+
(Mark H Tompkins) *lw: hld up in rr: hdwy and swtchd ins 3f out: upsides ldrs on bit 2f out: rdn and qcknd to ld over 1f out: in comnand fnl f: comf* **2/1**[2]

0045 **2** 2½ **Double Handful (GER)**[20] 5453 5-10-0 **70**.............. SilvestreDeSousa 5 74
(Venetia Williams) *stdd s: in tch: chsd ldr over 7f out: ev ch and rdn 4f out: led over 3f out: hdd over 1f out and immediately outpcd by wnr: plugged on same pce after* **9/1**

6535 **3** 1½ **Ugalla**[31] 5102 4-9-13 **69**.............................. EddieAhern 3 71
(Jane Chapple-Hyam) *hld up in tch: hdwy to chse ldrs 3f out: ev ch and rdn jst over 2f out: outpcd by wnr and one pce fr over 1f out* **8/1**[3]

4415 **4** 2¾ **Twice Bitten**[14] 5641 3-9-1 **70**.............................. KierenFallon 2 71
(James Toller) *lw: t.k.h: chsd ldr tl led 1/2-way: hdd and hanging rt 3f out: wknd over 1f out: wl hld and eased fnl 50yds* **5/4**[1]

0010 **5** 12 **Torran Sound**[17] 2526 4-9-1 **57**..............................(b) MartinLane 1 42
(James Eustace) *chsd ldrs: rdn 5f out: lost tch 3f out* **16/1**

3200 **6** 30 **Motirani**[13] 5692 4-9-9 **65**.............................. MickyFenton 7 14
(Lydia Pearce) *sn led: hdd 1/2-way: rdn and lost pl 6f out: lost tch 4f out: t.o* **12/1**

3m 29.79s (-2.61) **Going Correction** -0.20s/f (Firm)
WFA 3 from 4yo+ 13lb **6** Ran SP% **112.5**
Speed ratings (Par 103): **98,96,96,94,88 73**
toteswingers:1&2:£2.10, 1&3:£3.10, 2&3:£2.60 CSF £19.61 TOTE £2.80: £1.50, £2.30; EX 19.10 TRIFECTA Not won.
Owner Mystic Meg Limited **Bred** Mystic Meg Limited **Trained** Newmarket, Suffolk

FOCUS
The early gallop looked modest at best. The winner came from the rear and there looks more to come, but this form is shaky.
Twice Bitten Official explanation: jockey said gelding ran too free and hung very badly right

6105 PLAY MECCA BINGO ON YOUR IPHONE H'CAP 6f 3y
5:10 (5:11) (Class 6) (0-60,57) 3-Y-0+ **£1,617** (£481; £240; £120) **Stalls** Centre

Form RPR

3500 **1** **Too Many Questions (IRE)**[22] 5388 3-9-5 **57**............(p) KierenFallon 10 68
(David Evans) *mde all: sn clr and grad crossed over to r against stands' rail: pressed and drvn over 1f out: fnd ex and forged clr ins fnl f: r.o wl* **18/1**

0232 **2** 2 **Cool Water Oasis**[5] 5946 3-9-4 **56**.............................. MartinLane 6 61
(Rae Guest) *racd in midfield: rdn and no imp 1/2-way: swtchd lft over 1f out: kpt on wl u.p to chse wnr fnl 50yds: unable to chal* **11/2**[2]

6-45 **3** 1¾ **Mr Skipiton (IRE)**[27] 5244 6-9-6 **56**.............................. TomMcLaughlin 7 55
(Brian McMath) *prom in main gp: clsd on wnr over 2f out: rdn pressed wnr over 1f out: no ex and btn ins fnl f: wknd fnl 75yds* **7/1**

233 **4** nk **Till Dawn (IRE)**[15] 5615 3-9-5 **57**.............................. DavidProbert 13 55
(Tony Carroll) *chsd ldrs: wnt 2nd 1/2-way and clsd on wnr: pressed wnr and drvn over 1f out: no ex and btn jst ins fnl f: one pce after* **13/2**

0242 **5** nse **Deslaya (IRE)**[22] 5388 3-9-4 **56**.............................. TedDurcan 3 54
(Chris Wall) *in tch in midfield: rdn 1/2-way: no imp tl styd on u.p ins fnl f: nvr trbld wnr* **11/2**[2]

4004 **6** shd **Pearly Wey**[1] 6071 8-8-11 **52**.............................. DarylByrne(5) 8 50
(Ian McInnes) *v slow away: bhd: rdn 2f out: styd on wl ins fnl f: nvr trbld ldrs* **10/1**

2043 **7** nk **Fedora (IRE)**[1] 6070 5-9-3 **53**..............................(t) SilvestreDeSousa 1 50
(Olivia Maylam) *dwlt: hld up in last trio: hdwy on far side over 1f out: drvn and kpt on ins fnl f: nvr trbld ldrs* **5/1**[1]

3532 **8** hd **Simple Rhythm**[18] 5517 5-9-6 **56**.............................. GeorgeBaker 2 52
(John Ryan) *racd in midfield: rdn and effrt 2f out: hdwy 1f out: kpt on ins fnl f: nvr able to chal* **6/1**[3]

5005 **9** ¾ **Clerical (USA)**[23] 5355 5-8-13 **49**..............................(p) J-PGuillambert 4 43
(Robert Cowell) *prom in main gp: rdn and no imp 1/2-way: outpcd and btn wl over 1f out: plugged on same pce after* **14/1**

600 **10** 1¾ **Osgoodisgood**[14] 5644 3-8-9 **47**..............................(t) SaleemGolam 11 35
(Stuart Williams) *chsd ldr tl 1/2-way: sn rdn and no imp: styd on same pce and wl hld fr over 1f out* **16/1**

0240 **11** 12 **Look Twice**[57] 4199 3-9-4 **56**.............................. EddieAhern 12 —
(Alex Hales) *in tch tl lost pl qckly 1/2-way: lost tch wl over 1f out* **25/1**

1m 12.83s (-1.57) **Going Correction** -0.25s/f (Firm)
WFA 3 from 4yo+ 2lb **11** Ran SP% **118.3**
Speed ratings (Par 101): **100,97,95,94,94 94,94,93,92,90 74**
toteswingers:1&2:£22.40, 1&3:£32.90, 2&3:£7.60 CSF £114.82 CT £776.70 TOTE £17.10: £5.30, £2.20, £2.50; EX 130.70.
Owner Nick Shutts **Bred** R N Auld **Trained** Pandy, Monmouths

FOCUS
A modest affair. The winner got across and made all on the rail, rating back to his early AW maiden form.
Look Twice Official explanation: jockey said filly hung badly left
T/Plt: £327.60 to a £1 stake. Pool:£63,657.11 - 141.83 winning tickets T/Qpdt: £111.00 to a £1 stake. Pool:£4,304.18 - 28.68 winning tickets SP

6106 - 6109a (Foreign Racing) - See Raceform Interactive

6075 AYR (L-H)
Friday, September 16

OFFICIAL GOING: Good to soft changing to good to soft (soft in places) after race 3 (3:55) changing to soft (good to soft in places) after race 5 (4:30)
Wind: Fresh, half behind Weather: Overcast, dull

6110 WEST SOUND AND WEST FM/IRISH E B F MAIDEN STKS 7f 50y
2:10 (2:10) (Class 4) 2-Y-O **£4,463** (£1,328; £663; £331) **Stalls** High

Form RPR

024 **1** **Strictly Silver (IRE)**[14] 5688 2-9-0 78.............................. DominicFox(3) 8 82
(Alan Bailey) *hld up on ins: hdwy 2f out: rdn to ld wl ins fnl f: kpt on* **5/2**[1]

522 **2** 1 **Trail Blaze (IRE)**[21] 5454 2-9-3 75.............................. PhillipMakin 14 80
(Kevin Ryan) *led: rdn 2f out: hdd wl ins fnl f: kpt on same pce* **7/2**[2]

333 **3** 1¾ **Serene Oasis (IRE)**[14] 5691 2-8-12 72.............................. TonyCulhane 1 70
(Mick Channon) *t.k.h in midfield: effrt and swtchd rt over 2f out: effrt and cl up appr fnl f: edgd lft: one pce last 100yds* **13/2**

23 **4** ½ **Magic Destiny**[42] 4748 2-8-12 0.............................. AndrewElliott 3 69
(Mrs K Burke) *trckd ldrs: effrt and rdn over 2f out: kpt on same pce ins fnl f* **9/1**

46 **5** 7 **Double Cee**[19] 5503 2-9-3 0.............................. PaulHanagan 2 57
(Richard Fahey) *s.i.s: bhd tl kpt on fnl 2f: nvr able to chal* **16/1**

232 **6** 2 **Star City (IRE)**[22] 5398 2-9-3 72.............................. TomEaves 5 52
(Michael Dods) *in tch: rdn over 2f out: wknd wl over 1f out* **5/1**[3]

7 ½ **Happy Sun Percy** 2-9-3 0.............................. DarryllHolland 13 51
(Jo Hughes) *s.i.s: bhd: rdn over 3f out: sme late hdwy: nvr on terms* **50/1**

020 **8** ¾ **Daddy Warbucks (IRE)**[48] 4535 2-9-3 67.............................. AdrianNicholls 12 49
(David Nicholls) *chsd ldr: rdn over 2f out: wknd over 1f out* **14/1**

0 **9** ½ **Son Of May**[54] 4365 2-9-3 0..............................(b[1]) DanielTudhope 10 48+
(Jo Hughes) *s.i.s: bhd: pushed along over 2f out: nvr on terms* **25/1**

04 **10** ¾ **Sugarpine (IRE)**[9] 5819 2-8-12 0.............................. TonyHamilton 11 41
(Richard Fahey) *chsd ldrs: drvn over 2f out: wknd over 1f out* **33/1**

00 **11** 24 **Shek O Lad**[14] 5688 2-9-3 0.............................. MartinLane 9 —
(Alan Jarvis) *towards rr: struggling over 2f out: sn btn: t.o* **100/1**

40 **U** **Be Calm**[11] 5786 2-8-12 0.............................. JamesSullivan 6 —
(Michael Easterby) *midfield whn stmbld and uns rdr after 1f* **16/1**

1m 33.81s (0.41) **Going Correction** +0.10s/f (Good) **12** Ran SP% **119.0**
Speed ratings (Par 97): **101,99,97,97,89 87,86,85,85,84 56,—**
toteswingers:1&2:£3.80, 1&3:£4.00, 2&3:£6.10 CSF £10.67 TOTE £3.10: £1.50, £1.60, £2.10; EX 11.10.
Owner A J H **Bred** Langton Stud **Trained** Newmarket, Suffolk
■ A winner for Dominic Fox on his return from two years out of the saddle.

FOCUS
After a dry night the going was amended to Good to soft. Both bends had been moved out, adding six yards to race distances on the round course. The best winner of this event in the past decade or so was Franklins Gardens, who went on to take the Yorkshire Cup. This looked fair maiden form, and it appears straightforward. They went a reasonable pace and the time was 4.31sec outside the standard, confirming that the ground was slow.

NOTEBOOK
Strictly Silver(IRE) had just about the best previous form on offer with a BHA rating of 78. Picking up ground a quarter-mile out, he took time to master the leader but was nicely on top close home, giving his rider a comeback winner after two years out of the saddle. The grey has been declared for a nursery here on Saturday and the return to a mile should be fine for him. (op 3-1 tchd 7-2 in places)
Trail Blaze(IRE), rated 75, found one too good for the third successive start. He tried to make all from the outside stall and fought on well, but had to succumb to the winner close home. There didn't appear to be anything wrong with his attitude. (op 4-1)
Serene Oasis(IRE) has finished third on all four of her starts and is a consistent filly whose turn will come. She has already proved that she stays a mile. (op 7-1 tchd 15-2)
Magic Destiny is a half-sister to Magic Cat, who won the Harry Rosebery Trophy on this card for the same connections in 2008. The filly switched back to the rail and battled on well, but her stamina was just waning late on. (op 7-1)
Double Cee, who was one of the first off the bridle but stayed on late for pressure. He had run no sort of race at Beverley following an encouraging debut, and this was more like it.
Star City(IRE) represented a stable with a good recent record in this event and had shown fair placed form on his first three starts, but he weakened after racing a shade keenly.
Son Of May was last on his debut at Pontefract after a slow start, and had blinkers fitted now for this rise in trip. He again forfeited ground leaving the stalls and was never able to get to the leaders, but was keeping on in his own time in the latter stages and gave the distinct impression that he is capable of bettering this.

6111 S.T. ANDREW PLANT HIRE NURSERY 6f
2:45 (2:46) (Class 3) (0-95,84) 2-Y-O **£5,498** (£1,636; £817; £408) **Stalls** Centre

Form RPR

21 **1** **Deepsand (IRE)**[20] 5486 2-8-12 **75**.............................. DavidAllan 1 81+
(Tim Easterby) *prom far side: pushed along over 2f out: hdwy to ld ins fnl f: kpt on strly* **5/2**[1]

1020 **2** hd **Nameitwhatyoulike**[9] 5825 2-8-10 **73**.............................. JamesSullivan 3 78
(Michael Easterby) *disp ld far side: rdn and led over 2f out: hdd ins fnl f: kpt on towards fin* **28/1**

134 **3** ½ **Chooseday (IRE)**[13] 5708 2-9-2 **79**.............................. PhillipMakin 8 83+
(Kevin Ryan) *trckd centre ldrs: edgd lft and smooth hdwy over 2f out: chal over 1f out to ins fnl f: sn rdn: nt qckn last 75yds* **9/2**[3]

4126 **4** 3¼ **Act Your Shoe Size**[27] 5287 2-9-0 **77**.............................. JoeFanning 4 71
(Keith Dalgleish) *slt ld far side to over 2f out: sn rdn: kpt on same pce appr fnl f* **9/1**

150 **5** *1* **Mitchum**[94] 3012 2-9-7 **84** .... LeeNewman 6 75
(David Barron) *t.k.h: cl up far side: ev ch 2f out: sn rdn: outpcd appr fnl f* **6/1**

1 **6** *1* **Trumpet Voluntary (IRE)**[22] 5398 2-8-13 **76** .... PaulHanagan 2 64
(Richard Fahey) *s.i.s: chsd ldng gp far side: drvn 1/2-way: outpcd fnl 2f* **11/4**[2]

3106 **7** *4 1/2* **Pen Bal Crag (IRE)**[48] 4538 2-8-9 **72** .... TonyHamilton 7 47
(Richard Fahey) *disp ld centre tl edgd lft and wknd fr 2f out* **14/1**

144 **8** *hd* **Al Shaqab (IRE)**[35] 4984 2-9-5 **82** .... StephenCraine 9 56
(Kevin Ryan) *disp ld centre to 2f out: edgd lft and sn wknd* **20/1**

0106 **9** *9* **Queens Sandridge (IRE)**[10] 5809 2-8-12 **75** .... DarryllHolland 5 22
(Alan Bailey) *bhd and sn drvn along: lost tch fr 2f out* **16/1**

1m 13.5s (1.10) **Going Correction** +0.175s/f (Good) **9** Ran SP% **118.5**
Speed ratings (Par 99): **99,98,98,93,92 91,85,84,72**
toteswingers:1&2:£9.10, 1&3:£3.20, 2&3:£16.40 CSF £74.07 CT £310.11 TOTE £3.60: £1.30, £6.30, £1.80; EX 86.30.
Owner Trevor Hemmings **Bred** Gleahill House Stud Ltd **Trained** Great Habton, N Yorks
■ Stewards' Enquiry : James Sullivan one-day ban: used whip with erxcessive frequency (Sep 30)
David Allan caution: used whip with excessive frequency.

FOCUS
A reasonable nursery. The field split into two from the stalls, with three runners racing down the centre and the other half dozen going up the far rail. The pace was strong and the two groups merged at around the two marker. The winner continues to progress and the second is the key to the form.

NOTEBOOK
Deepsand(IRE) was off the bridle by halfway, but stuck on well for pressure against the rail and forged to the front late on. He is tough and progressive, and will get further. (op 11-4 tchd 9-4 and 3-1 in a place)
Nameitwhatyoulike was up with the pace all the way and battled on well. Without the blinkers he has been wearing, he was down in trip here and was due to be dropped a pound by the handicapper before this. Easy ground suits him well. (op 33-1)
Chooseday(IRE) tracked the other pair to race down the centre, still travelling when all his opponents were hard at work. It appeared a matter of how far, but although he may have taken a narrow lead, once let down he did not find as much as he'd promised and was run out of it. He could have done with getting a tow into the race for longer. (tchd 5-1)
Act Your Shoe Size ran a reasonable race back over 6f and on an easier surface again, but after showing pace she could not sustain it. (op 8-1)
Mitchum, running for the first time since finishing down the field in the Coventry Stakes at Royal Ascot, may have found the ground a bit dead on this nursery debut. (op 10-1)
Trumpet Voluntary(IRE)'s debut win at Carlisle was not boosted when runner-up Star City was well held in the opening maiden. The Fahey yard had won this with the smart Utmost Respect back in 2006, but this colt found things happening too quickly for him here. (op 3-1)

6112 M & CO H'CAP — 5f

3:20 (3:22) (Class 4) (0-85,85) 3-Y-0+ **£4,851** (£1,443; £721; £360) **Stalls** Centre

Form RPR

0610 **1** **Magical Macey (USA)**[13] 5703 4-9-7 **85** ....(b) GrahamGibbons 3 96
(David Barron) *w ldrs far side: styd on to ld last 100yds: 1st of 12 that gp* **18/1**

6120 **2** *1 1/2* **Fol Hollow (IRE)**[9] 5831 6-8-13 **80** .... MichaelO'Connell(3) 4 86
(David Nicholls) *racd far side: chsd ldrs: overall ldr over 1f out: hdd and no ex last 100yds: 2nd of 12 that gp* **28/1**

4553 **3** *3/4* **Rylee Mooch**[6] 5923 3-8-0 **72** ....(e) CharlesEddery(7) 19 75
(Richard Guest) *led stands' side gp: edgd lft and styd on same pce last 150yds: 1st of 10 that gp* **25/1**

5516 **4** *nk* **Mayoman (IRE)**[6] 5918 6-8-7 **76** .... NeilFarley(5) 22 78
(Declan Carroll) *racd stands' side: w ldr: styd on ins fnl f: 2nd of 10 that gp* **14/1**

421 **5** *nk* **Haajes**[9] 5831 7-9-6 **84** 6ex........ PJMcDonald 6 85
(Paul Midgley) *racd far side in mid-div: hdwy to chse ldrs over 2f out: kpt on same pce fnl f: 3rd of 12 in gp* **7/1**[2]

6203 **6** *1/2* **Rothesay Chancer**[13] 5720 3-8-8 **76** .... GaryBartley(3) 14 75
(Jim Goldie) *racd stands' side: in rr: hdwy 2f out: styd on wl fnl 100yds: 3rd of 10 that gp* **14/1**

6535 **7** *hd* **The Nifty Fox**[14] 5680 7-9-1 **79** .... DavidAllan 20 78
(Tim Easterby) *racd stands' side: trckd ldrs: kpt on wl fnl f: 4th of 10 that gp* **18/1**

4323 **8** *1/2* **Sleepy Blue Ocean**[6] 5918 5-8-7 **71** oh3........(p) MartinLane 9 68
(John Balding) *racd far side: hld up towards rr: effrt over 1f out: styd on wl clsng stages: 4th of 12 that gp* **16/1**

3025 **9** *hd* **Arganil (USA)**[30] 5163 6-9-3 **84** ....(p) AmyRyan(3) 12 80
(Kevin Ryan) *racd far side: in rr: hdwy 2f out: swtchd wd: styd on fnl f: 5th of 12 that gp* **22/1**

3320 **10** *nk* **Crimson Knot (IRE)**[27] 5268 3-8-5 **75** .... JulieBurke(5) 11 70
(Alan Berry) *racd far side: in rr: kpt on fnl 2f: nvr a factor: 6th of 12 that gp* **33/1**

0030 **11** *1* **Beat The Bell**[9] 5831 6-9-6 **84** .... LeeNewman 10 75
(David Barron) *racd far side: mid-div: one pce fnl 2f: 7th of 12 that gp* **25/1**

5004 **12** *nk* **Above The Stars**[20] 5484 3-8-8 **73** .... PaulHanagan 23 63
(Richard Fahey) *racd stands' side rail: chsd ldrs: one pce fnl 2f: 5th of 10 that gp* **12/1**[3]

-0U1 **13** *1/2* **Thats A Fret (IRE)**[6] 5955 5-8-13 **77** ....(b) JoeFanning 2 66
(Liam McAteer, Ire) *led far side gp tl over 1f out: fdd: 8th of 12 that gp* **20/1**

1000 **14** *3/4* **Mr Optimistic**[34] 5054 3-9-1 **83** .... LeeTopliss(3) 5 69
(Richard Fahey) *racd far side: chsd ldrs: one pce fnl 2f: 9th of 12 that gp* **5/1**[1]

2150 **15** *1/2* **Hotham**[6] 5918 8-9-2 **80** .... BarryMcHugh 21 64
(Noel Wilson) *racd stands' side: in tch: one pce fnl 2f: 6th of 10 that gp* **25/1**

3661 **16** *1/2* **Go Go Green (IRE)**[21] 5452 5-8-10 **74** ow2........(t) DanielTudhope 7 56
(Jim Goldie) *racd far side: in rr: kpt on fnl 2f: nvr a factor: 10th of 12 that gp* **16/1**

0063 **17** *1/2* **Courageous (IRE)**[13] 5706 5-9-7 **85** .... PhillipMakin 15 65
(Kevin Ryan) *swtchd rt after s to r stands' side: chsd ldrs: wknd appr fnl f: 7th of 10 that gp* **7/1**[2]

0250 **18** *nk* **Oldjoesaid**[9] 5831 7-9-4 **82** ....(b) StephenCraine 13 61
(Kevin Ryan) *swtchd lft after s to r far side: a towards rr: 11th of 12 that gp* **20/1**

0002 **18** *dht* **Invincible Lad (IRE)**[14] 5679 7-8-13 **77** .... AdrianNicholls 16 56
(David Nicholls) *s.i.s: racd stands' side: hld up towarda rr: effrt 2f out: sn wknd: 8th of 10 that gp* **20/1**

0620 **20** *2 1/4* **Even Stevens**[9] 5831 3-8-11 **79** .... BillyCray(3) 18 50
(David Nicholls) *racd stands' side: chsd ldrs: lost pl over 1f out: 9th of 10 that gp* **16/1**

6004 **21** *1 1/2* **Indian Trail**[9] 5831 11-9-2 **80** ....(b) PaulQuinn 17 46
(David Nicholls) *racd stands' side: in rr: bhd fnl 2f: last of 10 that gp* **16/1**

1640 **22** *1* **Gottcher**[14] 5679 3-8-11 **76** .... TomEaves 8 38
(David Barron) *racd far side: chsd ldrs: wknd 2f out: last of 12 that gp* **33/1**

60.01 secs (0.61) **Going Correction** +0.25s/f (Good)
WFA 3 from 4yo+ 1lb **22** Ran SP% **136.3**
Speed ratings (Par 105): **105,102,101,100,100 99,99,98,98,97 96,95,94,93,92 92,91,90,90,87 84,83**
toteswingers:1&2:£52.40, 1&3: Not won, 2&3:£104.90 CSF £472.86 CT £12090.90 TOTE £25.30: £6.20, £10.40, £7.20, £4.00; EX 344.10.
Owner K J Alderson **Bred** Silver Springs Stud Farm Inc & Mrs J Costelloe **Trained** Maunby, N Yorks

FOCUS
A competitive handicap for the grade. The field split into two groups and although the first two home raced on the far side, there did not appear to be too much in it, with the first eight equally split between the two flanks. Not many became involved. The winner posted a length personal best.

6113 WILLIAM HILL AYR BRONZE CUP (H'CAP) — 6f

3:55 (3:57) (Class 2) 3-Y-0+

£12,450 (£3,728; £1,864; £932; £466; £234) **Stalls** Centre

Form RPR

3010 **1** **Coolminx (IRE)**[28] 5255 4-9-6 **83** .... BarryMcHugh 3 95
(Richard Fahey) *mde all far side: rdn 2f out: hrd pressed fnl f: hld on gamely: 1st of 11 in gp* **12/1**

4463 **2** *shd* **Jeannie Galloway (IRE)**[28] 5255 4-9-5 **82** .... PaulHanagan 15 94+
(Richard Fahey) *trckd stands' side ldrs: led that gp over 1f out: styd on strly to pull clr of remainder of gp ins fnl f: jst hld by far side wnr: 1st of 14 in gp* **13/2**[1]

5201 **3** *1/2* **Esprit De Midas**[30] 5162 5-9-8 **85** .... AdrianNicholls 9 95
(David Nicholls) *in tch far side gp: hdwy to press wnr over 1f out: kpt on fnl f: hld nr fin: 2nd of 11 in gp* **16/1**

1100 **4** *2 1/2* **Mandalay King (IRE)**[12] 5760 6-8-9 **77** ....(p) JulieBurke(5) 19 79
(Marjorie Fife) *dwlt: hld up on outside of stands' side gp: hdwy over 1f out: kpt on fnl f: no imp: 2nd of 14 in gp* **66/1**

0000 **5** *2* **Mon Brav**[8] 5852 4-9-9 **86** .... PhillipMakin 27 82+
(Brian Ellison) *hld up stands' side: nt clr run over 2f and over 1f out: kpt on fnl f: nrst fin: 3rd of 14 in gp* **18/1**

431 **6** *1/2* **Layla's Hero (IRE)**[18] 5554 4-9-8 **85** 5ex........ PBBeggy 25 79
(John Quinn) *towards rr stands' side: rdn over 2f out: hdwy over 1f out: kpt on: 4th of 14 in gp* **17/2**[3]

3100 **7** *hd* **Levitate**[9] 5830 3-9-4 **83** ....(p) PaddyAspell 11 76
(Alan McCabe) *bhd and sn pushed along far side: hdwy over 1f out: kpt on: nvr able to chal: 3rd of 11 in gp* **25/1**

3164 **8** *1/2* **Karaka Jack**[14] 5684 4-9-5 **85** .... MichaelO'Connell(3) 14 77
(David Nicholls) *prom stands' side gp: rdn over 2f out: kpt on same pce over 1f out: 5th of 14 in gp* **12/1**

1440 **9** *nk* **Namwahjobo (IRE)**[34] 5054 3-9-3 **82** .... DanielTudhope 26 73
(Jim Goldie) *bhd stands' side gp: rdn over 2f out: kpt on fnl f: no imp: 6th of 14 in gp* **20/1**

5600 **10** *shd* **Loki's Revenge**[5] 5972 3-9-4 **81** .... DarryllHolland 2 74
(William Jarvis) *towards rr far side: rdn and hdwy wl over 1f out: no imp fnl f: 4th of 11 in gp* **20/1**

250 **11** *2 1/4* **Ursula (IRE)**[18] 5554 5-9-3 **80** ....(p) AndrewElliott 7 63
(Mrs K Burke) *bhd and rdn along far side: hdwy appr fnl f: nvr able to chal: 5th of 11 in gp* **25/1**

-100 **12** *1/2* **Amazing Amoray (IRE)**[21] 5434 3-9-3 **82** .... LeeNewman 17 64
(David Barron) *towards rr stands' side: rdn over 2f out: nvr able to chal: 7th of 14 in gp* **28/1**

0115 **13** *nse* **Zomerlust**[35] 4997 9-9-8 **85** ....(v) TomEaves 18 67
(John Quinn) *midfield stands' side: drvn along 1/2-way: outpcd fnl 2f: 8th of 14 in gp* **33/1**

0400 **14** *nse* **La Zamora**[14] 5682 5-9-5 **82** .... GrahamGibbons 16 63
(David Barron) *led stands' side to over 1f out: sn btn: 9th of 14 in gp* **28/1**

346 **15** *nse* **Ryan Style (IRE)**[3] 6036 5-9-0 **80** .... LeeTopliss(3) 13 61
(Lisa Williamson) *sn prom far side gp: drvn over 2f out: wknd over 1f out: 6th of 11 in gp* **33/1**

0214 **16** *nse* **Another Citizen (IRE)**[18] 5559 3-9-1 **80** ....(p) DavidAllan 24 61
(Tim Easterby) *chsd stands' side ldr: drvn over 2f out: wknd over 1f out: 10th of 14 in gp* **10/1**

0030 **17** *nk* **Klynch**[14] 5682 5-9-8 **85** ....(b) JamesSullivan 23 65
(Ruth Carr) *prom stands' side: drvn over 2f out: wknd over 1f out: 11th of 14 in gp* **25/1**

2653 **18** *3/4* **Sunrise Safari (IRE)**[12] 5760 8-9-1 **78** ....(v) TonyHamilton 8 56
(Richard Fahey) *prom far side: drvn over 2f out: wknd over 1f out: 7th of 11 in gp* **20/1**

3002 **19** *1/2* **My Gacho (IRE)**[6] 5920 9-9-0 **77** ....(b) PaulQuinn 12 53
(David Nicholls) *s.i.s: bhd and rdn along far side: nvr on terms: 8th of 11 in gp* **25/1**

-304 **20** *nk* **Rasaman (IRE)**[21] 5434 7-9-4 **84** .... GaryBartley(3) 21 59+
(Jim Goldie) *hld up stands' side gp: no room fr over 2f out: nt rcvr: 12th of 14 in gp* **33/1**

0060 **20** *dht* **Desert Creek (IRE)**[1] 6078 5-8-12 **82** .... ShirleyTeasdale(7) 1 57
(David Nicholls) *cl up far side tl rdn and wknd over 1f out: 9th of 11 in gp* **25/1**

4234 **22** *1 1/4* **River Falcon**[14] 5682 11-8-9 **79** .... JustinNewman(7) 22 50
(Jim Goldie) *bhd and sn drvn along stands' side: no ch fr 1/2-way: 13th of 14 in gp* **25/1**

0002 **23** *1 1/2* **Amenable (IRE)**[21] 5434 4-9-4 **81** .... AndrewMullen 10 47
(David Nicholls) *midfield far side gp: drvn over 2f out: wknd over 1f out: 10th of 11 in gp* **14/1**

0060 **24** *2 1/4* **Cara's Request (AUS)**[34] 5059 6-9-1 **78** .... JoeFanning 6 37
(David Nicholls) *cl up far side tl rdn and wknd fr 2f out: last of 11 in gp* **8/1**[2]

5631 **25** *6* **Mappin Time (IRE)**[27] 5268 3-9-3 **82** ....(p) DuranFentiman 20 22
(Tim Easterby) *dwlt: bhd and rdn along: struggling 1/2-way: nvr on terms: last of 14 in gp* **33/1**

1m 13.76s (1.36) **Going Correction** +0.325s/f (Good)
WFA 3 from 4yo+ 2lb **25** Ran SP% **134.8**
Speed ratings (Par 109): **103,102,102,98,96 95,95,94,94,94 91,90,90,90,90 90,89,88,88,87 87,86,84,81,73**
toteswingers:1&2:£20.20, 1&3:£15.00, 2&3:£19.60 CSF £72.77 CT £1321.36 TOTE £14.00: £3.60, £2.00, £4.40, £15.90; EX 137.20.
Owner Mrs H Steel **Bred** D Couper Snr **Trained** Musley Bank, N Yorks
■ Stewards' Enquiry : Barry McHugh one-day ban: used whip with excessive frequency (Sep 30)

FOCUS
Rain began to fall prior to this race. This consolation event for the Gold and Silver Cups was inaugurated in 2009, since when the winner's prize has fallen by around a third. The topweight's mark of 86 equated to 8st 1lb in the long handicap, and there was a spread of only 9lb between the 25 runners, meaning that a rating of 77 was required to get a run even in this third tier. Predictably, they split into two groups. As in the previous sprint handicap the far side just about came out on top, but there was hardly anything in it. Richard Fahey won the first running with Baldemar and was responsible for the first two here, both fillies who had been well beaten in this event 12 months ago. Not many showed their form in the worsening ground, but the winner is rated back to her old best.

NOTEBOOK
Coolminx(IRE), the beaten favourite last year, made just about all up the far side, gamely holding off the third after edging away from the rail and just getting the verdict from her stablemate on the opposite flank. She did not look badly treated off 6lb higher than when winning at Newcastle last month and was proven in soft conditions. (op 14-1)

Jeannie Galloway(IRE) ◆, only 25th a year ago, was down at 6f for only the second time since. Leading her group with over a furlong to run and claiming the fence, she was just pipped by the filly on the other side of the track. She finished clear on her side and can be counted a little unlucky, as she had nothing to race against in the final furlong. She may run again at Hamilton on Sunday. (op 17-2)

Esprit De Midas, successful in a claimer last time and racing from his last winning mark, had every chance on the far side but could not claw back a tough winner. It is surely just a matter of time before his trainer David Nicholls wins his first Bronze Cup. (op 14-1)

Mandalay King(IRE) raced on the outside of the larger stands'-side group and stuck on for fourth, albeit comfortably held by the principals. He has had a good season.

Mon Brav travelled well on the stands' side and ran on for a creditable fifth. He remains in good heart and is due to be dropped a pound now. (op 20-1)

Layla's Hero(IRE), carrying a penalty, kept on from the back of the field for a never-nearer sixth. (op 9-1)

Levitate bounced back from a disappointing effort over 7f.

Karaka Jack, another of the David Nicholls six, ran creditably over a trip on the short side for him. (tchd 14-1)

Namwahjobo(IRE) ◆ caught the eye finishing well once switched away from the rail. (op 22-1)

Ryan Style(IRE) Official explanation: jockey said gelding hung right final furlong

Another Citizen(IRE) could not get to the front and dropped out after chasing the pace. (op 12-1)

Klynch Official explanation: jockey said gelding was denied a clear run

Rasaman(IRE) Official explanation: jockey said gelding was denied a clear run

Cara's Request(AUS), who usually runs over further, was another to fade out of things. (op 17-2 tchd 9-1)

6114 BAM PROPERTIES HARRY ROSEBERY STKS (FOR THE SOUTH AYRSHIRE CUP) (LISTED RACE) 5f
4:30 (4:31) (Class 1) 2-Y-O

£13,043 (£4,945; £2,474; £1,232; £618; £310) **Stalls** Centre

Form RPR

0343 **1** **Caledonia Lady**[7] 5882 2-8-12 96 .... PaulHanagan 1 101+
(Jo Hughes) *s.i.s: hdwy over 2f out: squeezed through to ld over 1f out: r.o strly: readily* **5/4**[1]

40 **2** *1 3/4* **Hexagonal (IRE)**[7] 5903 2-9-3 0 .... PhillipMakin 6 96
(Lee Smyth, Ire) *chsd ldrs: wnt 2nd 1f out: no imp* **25/1**

2312 **3** *1 3/4* **Son Du Silence (IRE)**[5] 5961 2-9-3 77 ....(b[1]) GrahamGibbons 4 89
(J S Moore) *led early: chsd ldr: kpt on same pce fnl f* **33/1**

2232 **4** *3/4* **Kool Henry (IRE)**[17] 5592 2-9-3 87 .... DanielTudhope 2 87
(David O'Meara) *hld up towards rr: effrt 2f out: swtchd rt 1f out: kpt on* **11/1**[3]

1010 **5** *1/2* **Alejandro (IRE)**[8] 5849 2-9-3 94 .... TonyHamilton 3 85
(Richard Fahey) *chsd ldrs: drvn over 2f out: one pce and edgd rt fnl f* **11/1**[3]

1061 **6** *2 1/2* **Ponty Acclaim (IRE)**[17] 5592 2-8-12 94 .... DavidAllan 7 71
(Tim Easterby) *t.k.h in rr: effrt 2f out: sn wknd* **9/4**[2]

1100 **7** [illegible] **Sig[illegible] (IRE)**[6] [illegible] [illegible] 87 .... TonyCulhane 8 75
(Mick Channon) *in rr: effrt 2f out: nvr a factor* **16/1**

0131 **8** *3* **Powerful Wind (IRE)**[24] 5348 2-9-3 87 .... JoeFanning 5 64
(Ronald Harris) *sn led: hdd over 1f out: sn wknd* **16/1**

60.98 secs (1.58) **Going Correction** +0.40s/f (Good) **8** Ran SP% **110.4**
Speed ratings (Par 103): **103,100,97,96,95 91,90,86**
toteswingers:1&2:£5.90, 1&3:£7.80, 2&3:£12.90 CSF £33.82 TOTE £2.10: £1.10, £5.10, £4.70; EX 34.90.

Owner Isla & Colin Cage **Bred** Mrs I M Cage And C J Cage **Trained** Lambourn, Berks

FOCUS
No more than average form for the grade, a race contested by some exposed juveniles. The first two home were the only maidens in the line-up. They all headed over to the fair rail and the pace was strong. A deserved victory from the winner.

NOTEBOOK
Caledonia Lady was a healthy 11lb clear on adjusted official figures and she belatedly got off the mark. After starting slowly she then had to show courage to go through a fairly small gap, but quickened to the front and won pretty comfortably. She handled the ground well and deserved this after making the frame in a higher grade three times. The Cornwallis Stakes at Newmarket is her target. (op 6-4 tchd 13-8 in a place)

Hexagonal(IRE) ran a solid race but the filly proved too strong. He was a beaten favourite in a Down Royal maiden a week earlier but showed that running to be all wrong and bagged himself some black type. (op 20-1)

Son Du Silence(IRE) chased the strong pace, himself showing bags of speed, and stuck on surprisingly well for third. He can be lazy according to his trainer, hence why blinkers were applied, and outran his rating as he was worst in by 10lb on official figures.

Kool Henry(IRE) is a pacey colt but was held up on this rise in grade. He was running on at the end but missed a place for the first time in eight starts. (op 9-1 tchd 8-1)

Alejandro(IRE), whose trainer won this prize 12 months ago with Arctic Feeling, is usually partnered by Paul Hanagan who opted for Caledonia Lady here. The colt chased the tearaway leading pair and plugged on at the business end. This was his first run on easy ground. (op 10-1)

Ponty Acclaim(IRE), second top rated on official figures but with a fair bit to find with the favourite, was always at the back of the field. She had Kool Henry behind when winning at Ripon last time but could not confirm that form despite being 2lb better off. David Allan reported that the filly ran too free. Official explanation: jockey said filly ran too free

Signifer(IRE) had been third in that Ripon race and he was well held here after racing on the outside from the highest stall.

Powerful Wind(IRE) showed his customary blinding pace but dropped away once headed to finish last.

6115 RICHARD MCLEAN RETIREMENT CELEBRATION H'CAP (FOR THE EGLINTON & WINTON CHALLENGE CUP) 2m 1f 105y
5:05 (5:06) (Class 4) (0-85,85) 4-Y-O+ **£5,175** (£1,540; £769; £384) **Stalls** Low

Form RPR

51 **1** **Taikoo**[157] 1291 6-9-0 78 .... DarryllHolland 4 87
(Hughie Morrison) *racd wd first 5f: mde all: brought centre in st: rdn and styd on strly fnl 2f* **9/2**[1]

23-0 **2** *2* **Sphinx (FR)**[12] 5759 13-8-6 70 ....(b) JamesSullivan 9 77
(Edwin Tuer) *hld up: hdwy in centre 3f out: rdn and chsd wnr ins fnl f: kpt on: no imp towards fin* **16/1**

3641 **3** *4 1/2* **Mohawk Ridge**[23] 5369 5-8-7 71 .... TomEaves 1 73
(Michael Dods) *t.k.h: chsd wnr: effrt and styd cl to far rail in st: no ex and lost 2nd ins fnl f* **12/1**

2113 **4** *3* **Soprano (GER)**[21] 5453 9-7-11 66 oh4 .... NeilFarley(5) 6 65
(Jim Goldie) *prom: drvn and outpcd 4f out: plugged on fnl 2f: no imp* **11/1**

1304 **5** *1 1/4* **John Forbes**[31] 5149 9-8-7 71 .... PBBeggy 8 68
(Brian Ellison) *t.k.h: in tch tl edgd lft and outpcd fnl 2f* **10/1**

3651 **6** *1 1/4* **Puy D'Arnac (FR)**[11] 5790 8-8-1 70 6ex .... JulieBurke(5) 2 66
(George Moore) *hld up: effrt over 2f out: sn outpcd: n.d after* **9/2**[1]

3203 **7** *12* **Pokfulham (IRE)**[13] 5723 5-8-2 66 oh1 ....(v) PaulHanagan 5 49
(Jim Goldie) *midfield: dropped to rr over 5f out: n.d after* **13/2**[3]

1501 **8** *4* **Bollin Judith**[38] 4890 5-9-7 85 ....(t) DavidAllan 7 63
(Tim Easterby) *hld up: effrt and in tch over 3f out: styd far rail in st: wknd over 2f out* **6/1**[2]

5416 **9** *3* **Boss's Destination**[12] 5759 4-9-1 79 .... PJMcDonald 3 54
(Alan Swinbank) *trckd ldrs tl rdn and wknd over 2f out* **9/2**[1]

4m 3.70s (3.20) **Going Correction** +0.325s/f (Good) **9** Ran SP% **113.2**
Speed ratings (Par 105): **105,104,101,100,99 99,93,91,90**
toteswingers:1&2:£14.70, 1&3:£6.20, 2&3:£14.30 CSF £75.96 CT £800.64 TOTE £6.10: £2.20, £4.00, £3.80; EX 86.50.

Owner Mrs M D W Morrison **Bred** Miss B Swire **Trained** East Ilsley, Berks

FOCUS
This staying event was run at a fairly steady pace, but still proved a test of stamina in rain-affected ground which was by now officially described as Soft, good to soft in places. The winner was allowed to make his own running and is rated back to his old turf best.

Bollin Judith Official explanation: jockey said mare was unsuited by the soft (good to soft in places) ground

6116 DUNNE GROUP H'CAP 1m
5:40 (5:41) (Class 5) (0-70,70) 3-Y-O **£2,587** (£770; £384; £192) **Stalls** High

Form RPR

4104 **1** **Ventura Sands (IRE)**[18] 5560 3-9-5 68 .... PaulHanagan 9 77
(Richard Fahey) *midfield: hdwy to chal over 1f out: edgd lft u.p: led ins fnl f: drvn out* **11/2**[2]

2030 **2** *1* **Dr Red Eye**[9] 5828 3-9-2 68 .... BillyCray(3) 8 75
(David Nicholls) *cl up: rdn 3f out: led over 1f out to ins fnl f: kpt on same pce towards fin* **9/1**

3642 **3** *3 1/2* **Scottish Lake**[22] 5403 3-8-13 65 .... PatrickDonaghy(3) 2 64
(Jedd O'Keeffe) *prom: effrt and drvn over 2f out: kpt on same pce appr fnl f* **6/1**[3]

630 **4** *hd* **Maz**[25] 5317 3-8-10 62 .... DominicFox(3) 13 60
(Alan Bailey) *s.i.s: bhd and sn pushed along: hdwy u.p over 2f out: styd on fnl f: nrst fin* **20/1**

5232 **5** *2 1/4* **Goninodaethat**[13] 5725 3-8-7 56 oh1 .... LeeNewman 3 49
(Jim Goldie) *t.k.h: led after 2f to over 1f out: kpt on same pce* **4/1**[1]

6432 **6** *2 1/2* **Henrys Gift (IRE)**[25] 5315 3-8-7 56 .... TomEaves 5 43
(Michael Dods) *trckd ldr: drvn over 2f out: wknd over 1f out* **10/1**

1063 **7** *4 1/2* **William Haigh (IRE)**[17] 5602 3-9-0 68 .... GarryWhillans(5) 7 45
(Alan Swinbank) *sn pushed along in rr: struggling over 3f out: sme late hdwy: nvr on terms* **10/1**

1044 **8** *1 3/4* **Monel**[21] 5439 3-8-11 60 .... DanielTudhope 14 33
(Jim Goldie) *hld up in tch on outside: effrt over 2f out: wknd over 1f out* **8/1**

9 *1/2* **Qubuh (IRE)**[141] 1644 3-9-7 70 .... DarryllHolland 12 42
(Linda Stubbs) *in tch: rdn and wknd wl over 1f out* **33/1**

6506 **10** *11* **Cosmic Moon**[41] 4784 3-8-13 65 .... LeeTopliss(3) 1 11
(Richard Fahey) *prom: drvn over 2f out: sn wknd* **8/1**

5-00 **11** *3 3/4* **Golden Blaze**[56] 4290 3-8-13 62 .... PhillipMakin 4 —
(James Moffatt) *midfield: struggling 1/2-way: sn btn: eased whn no ch fnl f* **14/1**

110 **12** *1/2* **Last Destination (IRE)**[37] 4908 3-9-0 68 .... ShaneBKelly(5) 11 —
(Nigel Tinkler) *bhd: drvn along 1/2-way: btn fnl 2f* **16/1**

1m 47.32s (3.52) **Going Correction** +0.40s/f (Good) **12** Ran SP% **120.3**
Speed ratings (Par 101): **98,97,93,93,91 88,84,82,81,70 67,66**
toteswingers:1&2:£10.30, 1&3:£6.40, 2&3:£11.50 CSF £55.33 CT £317.08 TOTE £6.30: £2.10, £3.10, £2.30; EX 65.10.

Owner Keith Denham **Bred** J Jamgotchian **Trained** Musley Bank, N Yorks

FOCUS
An ordinary handicap run at a sound early tempo and in testing ground. The runners came up the centre of the course off the home turn. The first two were closely matched on Haydock July form.

Qubuh(IRE) Official explanation: jockey said gelding hung left

T/Jkpt: Not won. T/Plt: £844.80 to a £1 stake. Pool:£92,108.90 - 79.59 winning tickets T/Qpdt: £258.80 to a £1 stake. Pool:£6,996.54 - 20.00 winning tickets RY

5809 LINGFIELD (L-H)
Friday, September 16

OFFICIAL GOING: Turf course - good to firm (good in places; 8.0); all-weather - standard
Wind: virtually nil Weather: fine

6117 CABLESHEER MAIDEN AUCTION FILLIES' STKS 7f 140y
2:25 (2:27) (Class 6) 2-Y-O **£1,908** (£563; £281) **Stalls** Centre

Form RPR

1 **Four Better** 2-8-10 0 .... FergusSweeney 3 74
(Jamie Osborne) *in tch: swtchd lft and effrt 2f out: rdn to ld 1f out: keeping on and looked to be holding runner-up whn edgd lft u.p wl ins fnl f: rdn out* **28/1**

3 **2** *1 ¼* **Talk Of The North**[18] 5548 2-8-4 0.................................. LukeMorris 12 67+
(Hugo Palmer) *chsd ldng pair: trying to chal between horses whn nt clr run and swtchd lft over 1f out: nt clr run and swtchd lft again ins fnl f: r.o wl fnl 100yds: unable to chal* **5/4**[1]

4 **3** *¾* **Surrey Storm**[26] 5299 2-8-8 0.. SebSanders 1 69
(Roger Teal) *in tch: and grad crossed over to r against stands' rail: pushed along after 2f: rdn over 1f out: styng on wl and clsng whn nt clr run and swtchd lft fnl 100yds: r.o wl to snatch 3rd cl home* **9/2**[2]

06 **4** *nk* **Elbow Beach**[32] 5097 2-8-10 0.. LiamKeniry 2 68
(Dr Jon Scargill) *chsd ldng pair: chal 2f out: rdn over 1f out: chsd wnr fnl 100yds: pressing wnr but looked hld whn squeezed out and snatched up wl ins fnl f: nt rcvr and lost 2 pls towards fin* **25/1**

00 **5** *2 ¼* **Arrow Lake (FR)**[23] 5393 2-8-9 0 ow1.......................... PatCosgrave 14 62
(Noel Quinlan) *led: rdn over 1f out: hdd 1f out: no ex and btn ins fnl f: wknd fnl 100yds* **66/1**

6 *1 ¼* **Sweetscot (IRE)** 2-8-6 0.. KirstyMilczarek 9 56
(Amy Weaver) *dwlt: hld up in midfield: hdwy on outer to chse ldrs and rdn wl over 1f out: wknd jst ins fnl f* **33/1**

7 *½* **La Romantique (IRE)** 2-8-6 0.. JimmyQuinn 4 55+
(Marco Botti) *dwlt: bhd and rn green early: pushed along and sme hdwy 1/2-way: kpt on steadily fnl f: nvr trbld ldrs* **10/1**

8 *3 ½* **Tinzapeas** 2-8-4 0.. FrannyNorton 15 44+
(Mick Channon) *s.i.s: in rr and rn green: pushed along and sme hdwy 2f out: swtchd lft and styd on steadily ins fnl f: nvr trbld ldrs* **14/1**

0 **9** *2 ¼* **Isola Bella**[14] 5672 2-8-8 0.. JamesDoyle 8 45
(Jonathan Portman) *chsd ldr tl over 2f out: wkng whn bdly hmpd over 1f out: sn fdd* **66/1**

10 *2* **Synfonica** 2-8-4 0.. FrankieMcDonald 7 34
(Richard Hannon) *v.s.a: a bhd: nvr on terms* **14/1**

5 **11** *1 ½* **Stickleback**[14] 5672 2-8-7 0 ow1.............................. MatthewDavies 11 34
(Harry Dunlop) *dwlt: a in rr: rn green and edgd rt jst over 5f out: wl bhd fnl 3f* **20/1**

12 *1 ½* **Enthrall (IRE)** 2-8-8 0.. TedDurcan 10 31
(Denis Coakley) *racd in midfield: lost pl and rdn 4f out: wl bhd fnl 3f* **7/1**[3]

13 *17* **Delishuss** 2-8-1 0.. SophieDoyle(3) 13 —
(Dominic Ffrench Davis) *dwlt: towards rr: hmpd and dropped to last jst over 5f out: lost tch 1/2-way: t.o* **66/1**

1m 29.7s (-2.60) **Going Correction** -0.65s/f (Hard) 2y crse rec **13** Ran SP% **117.0**
Speed ratings (Par 90): **87,85,85,84,82 81,80,77,74,72 71,69,52**
toteswingers:1&2:£24.20, 1&3:£89.40, 2&3:£2.30 CSF £60.00 TOTE £48.50: £7.60, £1.10, £1.70; EX 132.90.

Owner C Woollett P Hearn & Mr & Mrs J Wilson **Bred** Lordship Stud **Trained** Upper Lambourn, Berks

■ Stewards' Enquiry : Luke Morris one-day ban: careless riding (Oct 1)

FOCUS
Times were quick on the turf course, which suggests the ground may have been riding faster than advertised. An ordinary fillies' maiden. Connections of both the second and third will feel unlucky, with neither horse getting much of a run inside the final 2f. The form could rate higher in time.

NOTEBOOK
Four Better, whose dam is a sister to Oaks winner Love Divine, has clearly inherited some of her sire's speed and she picked up well to make a surprise winning debut, her trainer having not had a 2yo go in on debut all season. With the placed horses looking unlucky, it would be unwise to get carried away, but this was still a positive start. (op 25-1)
Talk Of The North, well backed, was soon tracking the leading pair on the rail, appearing to hold the ideal sit, but Luke Morris found he had little room to manoeuvre from over 2f out, being blocked off by Elbow Beach when trying to squeeze through a gap, and despite picking up well once switched wide, the winner had got away. She ought to win a maiden, but may be over-bet next time as a result of this unfortunate defeat. (op 11-10 tchd 11-8)
Surrey Storm did well to get across from stall one to race three back on the rail, but she too had nowhere to go for much of the final 2f, and was another staying on well at the finish. Seb Sanders wasn't at all hard on her, realising her winning chance had gone, and she can gain compensation in something similar, with a slightly stiffer test likely to help. (tchd 7-2)
Elbow Beach was soon prominent and stuck on better than expected, hampering the runner-up's chance in the process. She's now qualified for a mark and may pick up a small nursery. (op 20-1)
Arrow Lake(FR), who made a lot of the running against the rail, is another now qualified for a mark. She may be the type to do better next year.
La Romantique(IRE) wasn't given a hard time on debut and should improve. (op 8-1)
Tinzapeas is related to numerous winners. (op 12-1 tchd 16-1)
Isola Bella was impeded when the runner-up switched sharply left and can do better in time. (op 50-1)
Synfonica didn't offer much encouragement, but she's entitled to do better with the experience behind her. Official explanation: jockey said filly was slowly away

6118 KEVIN GOLSON MEMORIAL BRITISH STALLION STUDS E B F MEDIAN AUCTION MAIDEN STKS — 5f

3:00 (3:05) (Class 6) 2-Y-O **£3,340** (£986; £493) **Stalls** High

Form RPR

20 **1** **Molamento (IRE)**[9] 5834 2-8-12 0.................................. FergusSweeney 10 69
(Gary Moore) *pressed ldr thrght: rdn over 1f out: led ins fnl f: kpt on wl* **16/1**

40 **2** *½* **La Bocca (USA)**[16] 5632 2-8-12 0.................................... JamesDoyle 12 67
(Roger Charlton) *led and clr w wnr thrght: rdn over 1f out: hdd ins fnl f: kpt on but a jst hld after* **11/4**[2]

3 **3** *2 ½* **Mister Mackenzie**[22] 5411 2-9-3 0................................ LukeMorris 11 63
(John Best) *chsd clr ldng pair: rdn 1/2-way: drvn and styd on same pce fr over 1f out* **5/2**[1]

34 **4** *1 ¾* **Lana (IRE)**[65] 3984 2-8-5 0.. IanBurns(7) 8 52
(Michael Bell) *chsd ldrs: rdn over 1f out: no imp: wl hld whn hung rt wl ins fnl f* **6/1**

5 *1 ¼* **Purple 'n Gold (IRE)** 2-9-3 0.. PatCosgrave 9 53+
(George Baker) *dwlt: pushed along early: hdwy into midfield and rdn 2f out: 5th and no imp fnl f: hmpd and snatched up towards fin* **11/2**[3]

60 **6** *¾* **Ishiamiracle**[51] 4427 2-8-12 0... LiamKeniry 5 45
(Andrew Balding) *s.i.s: sn rdn and nvr gng wl in rr: sme hdwy into modest 6th and hung lft ent fnl f: n.d* **12/1**

50 **7** *3 ½* **Hatha Zain (IRE)**[8] 5863 2-9-3 0.............................. RichardKingscote 4 37
(Milton Bradley) *stdd s: hld up in rr: rdn and strugglong over 2f out: wknd 2f out* **100/1**

00 **8** *6* **King's Future**[71] 3761 2-9-3 0....................................... IanMongan 3 15
(John Akehurst) *a towards rr: struggling 1/2-way: sn wknd* **25/1**

9 *3* **Johnny Splash (IRE)** 2-9-3 0.. SebSanders 7 5
(Roger Teal) *sn pushed along in midfield: wknd over 2f out: wl bhd over 1f out* **13/2**

10 *49* **Here Comes Jeanie** 2-8-12 0..................................... KirstyMilczarek 2 —
(Michael Madgwick) *v.s.a: immediately t.o* **100/1**

57.42 secs (-0.78) **Going Correction** -0.65s/f (Hard) **10** Ran SP% **117.6**
Speed ratings (Par 93): **80,79,75,72,70 69,63,54,49,—**
toteswingers:1&2:£7.90, 1&3:£8.00, 2&3:£1.90 CSF £60.31 TOTE £15.20: £3.30, £1.30, £1.10; EX 71.70.

Owner R A Green **Bred** Michael Wiley **Trained** Lower Beeding, W Sussex

FOCUS
A modest maiden, with the winner having been beaten in a seller on her debut, and few managed to get involved, the front pair soon being a couple of lengths clear and staying there. Fairly solid form as rated.

NOTEBOOK
Molamento(IRE), weak in the market, was disappointing over 6f on her debut for this yard, but a proper test of speed suited her much better and, despite conceding the rail to the runner-up, was still good enough. She looks a likely type for nurseries and may have more to offer. (op 9-1)
La Bocca(USA), another down in trip having disappointed over 6f the time before, was quickly away and bagged the rail, but despite keeping on well, the winner proved too strong. She's limited, but seems capable of winning a minor race. (tchd 3-1)
Mister Mackenzie showed speed when third over 6f on Polytrack here on debut, but following an awkward start, he was quickly outpaced and never looked like winning. He's clearly in need of a stiffer test. (tchd 11-4)
Lana(IRE) should do better now qualified to run in handicaps, with a longer trip likely to be of assistance. (op 11-2)
Purple 'n Gold(IRE) is the one to take from the race. A 46,000gns purchase whose dam is a half-sister to Breeders' Cup Juvenile Turf winner Pounced, he has a bit of size about him and, having been unable to go the early pace, stayed on nicely inside the final furlong without being given anything like a hard time. A maiden should come his way, with a step up to 6f, or maybe even 7f, in order. (op 5-1 tchd 7-1)
Ishiamiracle was another going on nicely at the finish and is one to watch for in a low-grade nursery. (op 14-1 tchd 8-1)
Johnny Splash(IRE), for whom there was plenty of money, is from a yard that remains without a winner since May. (op 16-1)
Here Comes Jeanie Official explanation: jockey said filly was slowly away

6119 ANGLIA FORWARDING RUBY H'CAP — 5f

3:35 (3:36) (Class 5) (0-70,71) 3-Y-O+ **£2,658** (£785; £392) **Stalls** High

Form RPR

2314 **1** **Whitecrest**[6] 5939 3-9-4 **67**... PatCosgrave 14 76
(John Spearing) *in tch: rdn and effrt to chse ldng pair wl over 1f out: drvn and chal between horses 1f out: edgd lft u.p fnl f: led fnl 50yds: stl edging lft but r.o wl* **5/1**[2]

2354 **2** *nk* **Billy Red**[80] 3482 7-9-4 **66**.............................(b) FergusSweeney 6 74
(J R Jenkins) *broke fast: led and grad crossed over to r against stands' rail: rdn jst over 1f out: hdd and no ex fnl 50yds* **14/1**

0164 **3** *2 ½* **Atlantic Cycle (IRE)**[28] 5238 4-9-6 **68**..................(t) RichardKingscote 5 67
(Milton Bradley) *dwlt and short of room sn after s: sn rcvrd and chsd ldr: rdn and pressing ldr over 1f out: wknd ins fnl f* **25/1**

131 **4** *½* **Imaginary Diva**[19] 5517 5-9-3 **65**................................. FrannyNorton 13 62
(George Margarson) *in tch: effrt wl over 1f out: no imp and rdn 1f out: kpt on ins fnl f: nt pce to chal ldrs* **9/2**[1]

0404 **5** *¾* **Danzoe (IRE)**[7] 5890 4-9-3 **65**... IanMongan 2 59+
(Christine Dunnett) *bhd: rdn and hdwy in centre over 1f out: styd on wl ins fnl f: nt rch ldrs* **16/1**

2454 **6** *nk* **Even Bolder**[15] 5658 8-9-4 **69**.. KierenFox(3) 9 62+
(Eric Wheeler) *wl bhd: swtchd lft and effrt in centre 2f out: hdwy over 1f out: kpt on wl ins fnl f: nt rch ldrs* **16/1**

3335 **7** *½* **Star Twilight**[36] 4967 4-9-0 **62**.......................................(p) LiamKeniry 4 54
(Derek Shaw) *chsd ldrs: rdn and chsd ldng pair 2f out: unable qck over 1f out: wknd ins fnl f* **20/1**

250- **8** *¾* **Amosite**[472] 2635 5-9-1 **63**.. AdrianMcCarthy 15 52
(J R Jenkins) *towards rr: hdwy u.p jst over 1f out: kpt on ins fnl f: nvr able to chal* **14/1**

2340 **9** *1 ¾* **Whiskey Junction**[11] 5781 7-9-6 **68**.............................(v) SebSanders 8 51
(Michael Quinn) *in tch in midfield: rdn and no imp 2f out: wknd 1f out* **14/1**

1356 **10** *½* **Madame Kintyre**[16] 5615 3-9-0 **63**................................ JamesMillman 12 44
(Rod Millman) *in tch in midfield: rdn and no rspnse ent fnl 2f: styd on same pce and n.d after* **9/1**

5211 **11** *nk* **Commandingpresence (USA)**[4] 5997 5-9-2 **71** 6ex CharlesBishop(7) 3 51
(John Bridger) *racd off the pce towards rr: effrt in centre and rdn 2f out: no imp and btn ent fnl f: wknd* **6/1**[3]

6060 **12** *3 ½* **Avrilo**[15] 5658 5-8-12 **60**... TomMcLaughlin 7 27
(Malcolm Saunders) *a towards rr: rdn and no prog ent fnl 2f: wknd over 1f out* **33/1**

0514 **13** *¾* **South African Gold (USA)**[24] 5355 4-9-0 **62**..............(p) LukeMorris 10 26
(James Eustace) *sn outpcd and rdn in rr: n.d* **8/1**

0123 **14** *3 ¾* **Grudge**[21] 5457 6-9-6 **68**..(b) JamesDoyle 11 19
(Conor Dore) *taken down early: chsd ldrs: rdn and struggling 1/2-way: wknd 2f out: wl bhd fnl f* **12/1**

56.09 secs (-2.11) **Going Correction** -0.65s/f (Hard) course record
WFA 3 from 4yo+ 1lb **14** Ran SP% **121.3**
Speed ratings (Par 103): **90,89,85,84,83 83,82,81,78,77 76,71,70,64**
toteswingers:1&2:£16.30, 1&3:£29.90, 2&3:£60.00 CSF £72.18 CT £1655.50 TOTE £6.80: £2.50, £3.20, £9.00; EX 108.60.

Owner G M Eales **Bred** J Spearing And Kate Ive **Trained** Kinnersley, Worcs

FOCUS
Few got into what had initially looked quite a competitive handicap, with the pace being strong and leading to a course record.
Grudge Official explanation: jockey said gelding was unsettled in stalls and raced for first 3f with lead rein attached

6120 DECUS INSURANCE BROKERS CLAIMING STKS — 1m (P)

4:10 (4:10) (Class 6) 3-Y-O **£1,533** (£452; £226) **Stalls** High

Form RPR

0065 **1** **Hugely Exciting**[13] 5735 3-8-13 68.................................(b) LiamKeniry 4 70
(J S Moore) *chsd ldr fr 2f out: in tch after: rdn and effrt over 1f out: pressed ldr 1f out: led ins fnl f: kpt on wl* **5/1**

1212 **2** *½* **Sky Diamond (IRE)**[9] 5836 3-8-13 66.....................(b) RichardKingscote 2 69
(James Given) *dwlt: sn rcvrd and pressed ldr after 2f out: rdn to ld 2f out: drvn over 1f out: hdd and no ex ins fnl f* **2/1**[1]

5306 **3** *¾* **Dark Isle**[13] 5735 3-8-13 70.. SebSanders 3 67
(J W Hills) *in tch: rdn and effrt 2f out: drvn to press ldrs ent fnl f: styd on same pce ins fnl f* **9/2**[3]

3132 **4** 3/4 **Barista (IRE)**[9] 5821 3-8-11 73 MatthewDavies 1 63
(Mick Channon) *in tch: rdn over 2f out: no imp tl styd on ins fnl f: nt pce to rch ldrs* **5/2**[2]

4345 **5** 1/2 **Jackie Love (IRE)**[11] 5787 3-7-7 50 (v[1]) HeidiHolder(7) 6 51?
(Olivia Maylam) *stdd s: hld up in tch in last: rdn and effrt over 1f out: edgd lft u.p jst ins fnl f: kpt on but nt pce to rch ldrs* **50/1**

0500 **6** hd **Charles Fosterkane**[25] 5322 3-8-8 73 LukeMorris 5 59
(John Best) *t.k.h: led tl hdd and rdn 2f out: wknd ins fnl f* **7/1**

1m 39.46s (1.26) **Going Correction** +0.025s/f (Slow) **6** Ran SP% **111.2**
Speed ratings (Par 99): **94,93,92,92,91 91**
toteswingers:1&2:£2.90, 1&3:£7.40, 2&3:£1.70 CSF £15.16 TOTE £7.50: £2.40, £2.10; EX 17.40.
Owner The Insurance Boys **Bred** Snowdrop Stud Co Limited **Trained** Upper Lambourn, Berks

FOCUS
A steadily-run claimer and the field finished in a bunch.

6121 DECOR SOLUTIONS H'CAP 1m 5f (P)
4:45 (4:45) (Class 5) (0-75,75) 3-Y-0+ **£2,658** (£785; £392) **Stalls** Low

Form RPR

1-35 **1** **Mazagee (FR)**[23] 5389 3-9-2 **74** TedDurcan 10 88+
(David Lanigan) *in tch in midfield: hdwy to press ldr and drew clr 2f out: rdn to ld over 1f out: drvn and wnt clr 1f out: styd on strly: eased towards fin* **7/2**[2]

0002 **2** 3 3/4 **Record Breaker (IRE)**[17] 5599 7-9-4 **67** (b) FrannyNorton 4 71
(Mark Johnston) *rn in snatches: sn pushed along: in tch: reminders 10f out: hdwy u.p 3f out: wnt modest 4th wl over 1f out: kpt on to go 2nd wl ins fnl f: no ch w wnr* **14/1**

1126 **3** 1 **Lemon Drop Red (USA)**[23] 5389 3-9-1 **73** TomMcLaughlin 2 76
(Ed Dunlop) *in tch: rdn to chse ldrs 4f out: drvn and outpcd by ldng pair 2f out: no threat to wnr but plugged on u.p fnl f* **6/1**

2203 **4** 1 **Undulant Way**[11] 5782 3-8-10 **75** (p) LukeRowe(7) 6 76
(Amanda Perrett) *chsd ldrs: wnt 2nd 4f out: led ent fnl 3f: rdn and drew clr w wnr 2f out: hdd over 1f out: btn 1f out: wknd and lost 2 pls wl ins fnl f* **9/2**[3]

044 **5** 16 **Colliers Castle (IRE)**[23] 5386 5-8-12 **61** oh1 ShaneKelly 11 38
(Lisa Williamson) *racd wd: hld up in last pair: rdn and sme hdwy wl over 3f out: wknd and wl btn over 2f out* **33/1**

3-26 **6** 4 1/2 **Albertus Pictor**[8] 5866 4-9-12 **75** SebSanders 8 46
(Sir Mark Prescott Bt) *s.i.s: sn swtchd lft and rdn along early: in tch in midfield: swtchd rt 6f out: rdn and effrt to chse ldrs 4f out: 5th and wknd 2f out: fdd over 1f out* **10/3**[1]

4/2- **7** 5 **Sumani (FR)**[539] 989 5-9-4 **67** LukeMorris 3 30
(Simon Dow) *led tl rdn and hdd ent fnl 3f: wknd qckly 2f out: 6th and wl btn over 1f out* **8/1**

3603 **8** 9 **Dynamic Idol (USA)**[8] 5866 4-9-10 **73** IanMongan 7 23
(Mikael Magnusson) *chsd ldr tl rdn and lost pl 4f out: lost tch 3f out: t.o and virtually p.u fnl f* **8/1**

-0 **9** 12 **Promised Wings (GER)**[174] 271 4-9-0 **70** BrendanPowell(7) 1 —
(Chris Gordon) *chsd ldrs tl lost pl qckly u.p and dropped to last 5f out: sn lost tch and wl t.o fnl 3f* **66/1**

2000 **10** 7 **Coda Agency**[14] 5692 8-9-3 **66** FergusSweeney 9 —
(Brendan Powell) *chsd ldrs: rdn and struggling over 4f out: dropped out qckly over 3f out: t.o and virtually p.u fr wl over 1f out* **25/1**

2m 45.09s (-0.91) **Going Correction** +0.025s/f (Slow)
WFA 3 from 4yo+ 9lb **10** Ran SP% **114.9**
Speed ratings (Par 103): **103,100,100,99,89 86,83,78,70,66**
toteswingers:1&2:£9.10, 1&3:£4.60, 2&3:£10.90 CSF £49.49 CT £285.05 TOTE £5.40: £2.00, £3.70, £1.50; EX 39.40.
Owner Saif Ali & Saeed H Altayer **Bred** Jean-Philippe Dubois **Trained** Newmarket, Suffolk

FOCUS
A modest handicap run at a sound pace. The first four were well clear and the winner was value for around 6l.

6122 JUSTBOOKIES.COM H'CAP 1m 2f (P)
5:20 (5:20) (Class 6) (0-60,60) 3-Y-0 **£1,908** (£563; £281) **Stalls** Low

Form RPR

0503 **1** **Goodwood Treasure**[23] 5381 3-9-7 **60** TedDurcan 3 68
(John Dunlop) *hld up in midfield: hdwy to chse ldrs over 2f out: rdn to chal ent fnl f: led ins fnl f: idled and edgd rt wl ins fnl f: rdn out* **8/1**

3600 **2** 1 **Roman Flame**[16] 5630 3-9-4 **57** SebSanders 4 63
(Michael Quinn) *in tch: hdwy to chse ldr 3f out: drvn over 1f out: ev ch ins fnl f: kpt on same pce fnl 100yds: wnt 2nd last strides* **25/1**

6022 **3** nk **If What And Maybe**[16] 5636 3-9-4 **57** (b) PatCosgrave 6 62
(John Ryan) *sn rdn along to ld: drvn 2f out: hrd pressed but kpt on u.p tl hdd ins fnl f: no ex and kpt on same pce: lost 2nd last strides* **5/1**[2]

0002 **4** shd **Reggie Perrin**[21] 5421 3-9-0 **53** IanMongan 11 58
(Pat Phelan) *in tch in midfield: rdn over 4f out: drvn to chse ldng trio 2f out: kpt on u.p ins fnl f* **6/1**[3]

2042 **5** 8 **Karate (IRE)**[7] 5902 3-9-6 **59** JamesDoyle 9 48
(Hans Adielsson) *hld up towards rr: hdwy jst over 2f out: 6th and drvn wl over 1f out: no imp and no ch w ldrs fr over 1f out* **6/1**[3]

1435 **6** 1 1/4 **Nutshell**[19] 5519 3-9-6 **59** JimmyQuinn 1 46
(Harry Dunlop) *in tch: rdn and fnd little ent fnl 2f: wknd wl over 1f out* **4/1**[1]

0523 **7** 2 **Take A Spin**[63] 4071 3-9-7 **60** LiamKeniry 13 43
(Paul Cole) *s.i.s: hld up in tch in rr: hdwy over 2f out: sltly hmpd bnd jst over 2f out: sn rdn and wknd: wl btn over 1f out* **9/1**

000 **8** 1 **Beggers Belief**[39] 4861 3-8-0 **46** oh1 RaulDaSilva(7) 8 27
(Eric Wheeler) *s.i.s: bustled along early: in tch in rr: rdn and struggling over 2f out: wknd ent fnl 2f and wl btn after* **50/1**

0000 **9** 8 **Three Scoops**[18] 5540 3-8-4 **46** oh1 (t) SophieDoyle(3) 12 11
(Dominic Ffrench Davis) *in tch: rdn and effrt to chse ldrs on outer 3f out: sn struggling: wknd qckly jst over 2f out: wl bhd fnl f* **33/1**

46 **10** 3 1/4 **Mazij**[17] 5598 3-9-7 **60** LukeMorris 14 18
(Peter Hiatt) *s.i.s: in tch in rr: rdn and struggling over 4f out: lost tch over 3f out: no ch whn hmpd and swtchd rt bnd jst over 2f out* **25/1**

0051 **11** 5 **Smart Step**[9] 5823 3-8-12 **51** 6ex FrannyNorton 7 —
(Mark Johnston) *chsd ldrs tl lost pl qckly u.p over 3f out: wl bhd fnl 2f: t.o* **9/1**

5330 **12** 14 **Imperial Fong**[11] 5784 3-8-11 **50** KellyHarrison 2 —
(Chris Dwyer) *nvr gng wl: sn dropped to last: swtchd rt and rdn w no rspnse 6f out: lost tch and t.o fr over 3f out* **16/1**

0000 **13** 11 **Diamond Bob**[28] 5243 3-9-7 **60** TomMcLaughlin 10 —
(Ed Dunlop) *chsd ldr tl over 3f out: sn struggling u.p: dropped out rapidly bnd jst over 2f out: sn eased and virtually p.u fr over 1f out: t.o* **20/1**

2m 6.17s (-0.43) **Going Correction** +0.025s/f (Slow) **13** Ran SP% **119.6**
Speed ratings (Par 99): **102,101,100,100,94 93,91,91,84,82 78,66,58**
toteswingers:1&2:£29.20, 1&3:£5.40, 2&3:£25.40 CSF £200.96 CT £1108.83 TOTE £11.30: £2.50, £4.60, £1.70; EX 224.80.
Owner Goodwood Racehorse Owners Group (17)Ltd **Bred** Jeremy Green And Sons **Trained** Arundel, W Sussex

FOCUS
A moderate 3yo handicap in which the first four pulled 8l clear. Sound if limited form.
T/Plt: £128.10 to a £1 stake. Pool:£57,731.01 - 328.93 winning tickets T/Qpdt: £87.00 to a £1 stake. Pool:£3,671.26 - 31.20 winning tickets SP

5043 NEWBURY (L-H)
Friday, September 16

OFFICIAL GOING: Good to soft (good in places; 6.3)
Wind: virtually nil Weather: Sunny spells

6123 DOWNLOAD THE BLUE SQUARE BET IPHONE APP E B F MAIDEN STKS (DIV I) 6f 8y
2:00 (2:00) (Class 4) 2-Y-0 **£4,398** (£1,309; £654; £327) **Stalls** Centre

Form RPR

0 **1** **Mince**[47] 4580 2-8-12 0 SteveDrowne 6 78+
(Roger Charlton) *str: gd bodied: rrd s and slowly away: sn rcvrd and in tch w main gp 1/2-way: hdwy over 2f out: swtchd rt over 1f out: str run ins fnl f to ld cl home* **10/1**

0 **2** 1/2 **Swing It**[56] 4276 2-9-3 0 RichardHughes 7 80
(Richard Hannon) *lengthy: chsd ldrs: rdn over 2f out: chal ins fnl 2f tl slt ld ins fnl f: hdd cl home* **5/2**[1]

3 1 **Lucky Henry** 2-9-3 0 AdamKirby 10 77+
(Clive Cox) *unf: in tch: drvn along over 2f out: str run ins fnl f: tk 3rd last strides: nt rch ldng duo* **9/1**

06 **4** nse **Amphora**[32] 5111 2-8-12 0 JimmyFortune 8 71
(Andrew Balding) *pressed ldr: drvn and ev ch fr 2f out and stl upsides u.p ins fnl f: no ex clsng stages and lost 3rd on line* **5/1**[3]

0 **5** 1 **Generalyse**[14] 5681 2-9-0 0 JohnFahy(3) 4 73
(Ben De Haan) *str: sn slt ld: rdn and maintained narrow advantage tl hdd ins fnl f: wknd fnl 120yds* **100/1**

6 2 1/4 **Fourth Of June (IRE)** 2-9-3 0 FrankieDettori 12 67+
(Ed Dunlop) *w'like: scope: warm: towards rr and pushed along over 2f out: styd on ins fnl f: gng on clsng stages but nt a threat* **4/1**[2]

4 **7** 1/2 **Marah Music**[53] 4384 2-9-3 0 TomQueally 3 65
(Peter Makin) *w'like: pressed ldrs: ev ch fr over 2f out tl wknd jst ins fnl f* **5/1**[3]

8 3 1/2 **Barn Dance (FR)** 2-9-0 0 RossAtkinson(3) 5 55
(Jonathan Portman) *w'like: bit bkwd: s.i.s: in rr: rdn and sme prog over 2f out: kpt on same pce fnl f* **33/1**

9 2 1/4 **Keepax** 2-9-3 0 GeorgeBaker 9 48
(Chris Wall) *w'like: towards rr: rdn along and outpcd fnl 3f* **16/1**

00 **10** 4 **Aussie Guest (IRE)**[56] 4264 2-9-3 0 SamHitchcott 11 36
(Mick Channon) *rdn over 2f out: outpcd most of way* **25/1**

11 1 **Seraphiel** 2-9-3 0 DaneO'Neill 2 33
(Chris Down) *w'like: bit bkwd: swtg: rdn and outpcd fr 1/2-way* **80/1**

1m 14.4s (1.40) **Going Correction** +0.125s/f (Good) **11** Ran SP% **115.9**
Speed ratings (Par 97): **95,94,93,92,91 88,87,83,80,74 73**
toteswingers:1&2:£6.50, 1&3:£17.10, 2&3:£6.00 CSF £34.16 TOTE £12.10: £3.10, £1.20, £2.40; EX 52.80 Trifecta £193.50 Part won. Pool: £261.59 - 0.10 winning units..
Owner Lady Rothschild **Bred** The Rt Hon Lord Rothschild **Trained** Beckhampton, Wilts
■ Valley Of Destiny (10/1) was withdrawn on vet's advice. Deduct 5p in the £ under R4.

FOCUS
The rail had not been moved since the last meeting, so all round course races were six metres longer than normal. Notable recent winners of this maiden include the likes of Stimulation and Paco Boy, who were in separate divisions in 2007. There was no real buzz about this year's bunch and the form doesn't look anything special by Newbury's standards, but the winner, who went 0.33 seconds quicker than the later division, is a nice prospect. They raced middle to near side and they finished somewhat compressed.

NOTEBOOK
Mince ◆ was far too green on her debut over C&D 47 days earlier, but despite again still looking in need of the experience, she was good enough to win. She was slowest away from the stalls, and although recovering well enough, took a while to pick up when first asked. In the last furlong, however, she really got going and had her ears pricked on crossing the line. While the form is nothing out of the ordinary, she has a lot of growing up to do and is a potentially smart long-term prospect. (new market op 14-1)
Swing It hinted at ability when green on his debut over this trip at Newmarket in July. Racing in the Paco Boy colours, he took a while to pick up but kept on at the one pace. He might be sharper for the run. (new market op 3-1 tchd 10-3)
Lucky Henry, a half-brother to a 7f scorer, out of a winner at around 1m, was under pressure a fair way out but gradually got the idea and was going on at the finish. (new market op 8-1)
Amphora seems to be learning with each start and now has the option of handicaps. (new market op 11-2)
Generalyse is well regarded and stepped up a good deal on his debut performance. There should be more to come. (new market)
Fourth Of June(IRE), a 50,000gns half-sister to a 5f winner in Italy, took too long to pick up but was running on well at the line and should do a lot better next time. (new market op 7-2)
Marah Music, a well-beaten fourth on his debut over this trip at Windsor in July, showed pace until getting tired and seemed to need the run. (new market op 4-1)
Barn Dance(FR) ran green but hinted at ability. (new market tchd 40-1)

6124 DUBAI DUTY FREE FINEST SURPRISE STKS (H'CAP) 1m 2f 6y
2:35 (2:35) (Class 4) (0-85,85) 3-Y-0+ **£4,528** (£1,347; £673; £336) **Stalls** Low

Form RPR

0-50 **1** **Sour Mash (IRE)**[41] 4801 4-9-7 **82** FrankieDettori 6 93
(Ed Dunlop) *t.k.h: hld up in rr: drvn and hdwy over 2f out: str run appr fnl f to ld u.p fnl 120yds: styd on wl* **20/1**

1-13 **2** 1/2 **Fine Threads**[87] 3260 3-8-13 **80** MichaelHills 5 90
(Charles Hills) *swtg: t.k.h towards rr: hdwy on outside fr 2f out: styd on wl fnl f: chsd wnr fnl 50yds but no imp* **4/1**[1]

2230 **3** 1 3/4 **Licence To Till (USA)**[18] 5546 4-9-6 **81** NeilCallan 9 88
(Mark Johnston) *swtg: trckd ldr: led appr fnl 3f: rdn over 2f out: hdd fnl 120yds: lost 2nd fnl 50yds* **7/1**

0143 **4** 1 1/2 **The Only Key**[41] 4788 5-9-10 **85** AdamKirby 10 89
(Jane Chapple-Hyam) *chsd ldrs: drvn to go 2nd over 1f out: no imp and one pce fnl 150yds* **5/1**[2]

541 **5** *5* **Elraabeya (CAN)**28 5241 3-8-10 **77** ...... RichardHills 8 71
(Sir Michael Stoute) *swtg: t.k.h: in tch: chsd ldrs 4f out: rdn over 2f out: wknd over 1f out* **14/1**

1344 **6** *nse* **Great Shot**28 5242 3-8-9 **76** ...... DaneO'Neill 2 69
(Sylvester Kirk) *in tch: swtchd towards outside over 2f out: sn drvn: no imp* **16/1**

0564 **7** *2 ½* **Spectait**28 5240 9-9-6 **81** ...... GeorgeBaker 4 69
(Jonjo O'Neill) *pushed along fr 3f out: nvr beyond mid-div* **20/1**

2300 **8** *3 ¼* **Shallow Bay**89 3203 4-9-8 **83** ...... KierenFallon 7 65
(David Pipe) *led tl hdd appr fnl 3f: wknd 2f out* **11/2**3

0540 **9** *¾* **Nazreef**69 3840 4-9-8 **83** ......(t) SteveDrowne 3 63
(Hughie Morrison) *chsd ldrs: wknd qckly 2f out* **9/1**

31-6 **10** *¾* **Corsican Boy**18 5568 3-8-10 **77** ......(b1) EddieAhern 1 56
(Roger Charlton) *in rr: sme hdwy on ins 3f out: wknd sn after* **10/1**

-150 **11** *27* **Laughing Jack**88 3231 3-9-1 **82** ...... RichardHughes 11 —
(Ed Dunlop) *stdd s: t.k.h: pushed along and sme prog 4f out: wknd 3f out: eased fnl 2f* **12/1**

2m 8.72s (-0.08) **Going Correction** +0.125s/f (Good)
WFA 3 from 4yo+ 6lb **11** Ran SP% **113.4**
Speed ratings (Par 105): **105,104,103,102,98 97,95,93,92,92 70**
toteswingers:1&2:£14.40, 1&3:£24.60, 2&3:£5.40 CSF £95.07 CT £625.00 TOTE £22.40: £5.70, £1.70, £2.80; EX 146.70 Trifecta £504.50 Part won. Pool: £681.79 - 0.10 winning units..
Owner The Honorable Earle I Mack **Bred** Epona Bloodstock Ltd **Trained** Newmarket, Suffolk
■ Stewards' Enquiry : Adam Kirby caution: careless riding.

FOCUS
Visually the pace set by Shallow Bay looked only modest, but the winner came from well back and the first four finished clear. This is probably quite solid handicap form, with the winner back towards his best.

Sour Mash(IRE) Official explanation: trainer said, regarding apparent improvement in form, that the gelding had pulled too hard previously but had settled better under a more patient ride.
Shallow Bay Official explanation: jockey said gelding had no more to give
Nazreef Official explanation: jockey said saddle slipped

6125 DUBAI DUTY FREE CONDITIONS STKS 1m 1f
3:10 (3:10) (Class 3) 3-Y-0+ **£7,158** (£2,143; £1,071; £535; £267) **Stalls** Low

Form RPR

1- **1** **Dubai Prince (IRE)**326 7135 3-8-6 0 ...... KierenFallon 1 114+
(Mahmood Al Zarooni) *trckd ldr to 4f out: styd cl up tl led 2f out: pushed clr fnl f: comf* **4/6**1

-120 **2** *2 ½* **Jet Away**77 3591 4-9-4 108 ...... TomQueally 2 112
(Sir Henry Cecil) *swtg: s.i.s: in tch tl t.k.h 5f out and hdwy to chse ldr 4f out: rdn and styd on to chse wnr over 1f out: no ch fnl f whn followed ldr rt: kpt on for 2nd* **8/1**3

4355 **3** *2 ¼* **Penitent**28 5252 5-8-11 108 ......(p) RichardHughes 4 100
(William Haggas) *lw: led tl hdd 2f out: styd disputing 2nd fnl f but no ch w wnr and kpt on same pce clsng stages* **2/1**2

002- **4** *2* **Togiak (IRE)**94 6552 4-8-11 90 ...... NeilCallan 5 96?
(David Pipe) *towards rr but a wl in tch tl rdn and outpcd fnl 2f but kpt on for 4th cl home* **66/1**

200/ **5** *½* **Bolivia (GER)**684 5-8-6 98 ......1 RichardMullen 6 90
(Lucy Wadham) *t.k.h: chsd ldrs: rdn over 2f out: hung lft and bhd sn after: lost 4th cl home* **25/1**

1m 54.87s (-0.63) **Going Correction** +0.125s/f (Good)
WFA 3 from 4yo+ 5lb **5** Ran SP% **109.8**
Speed ratings (Par 107): **107,104,102,101,100**
CSF £6.92 TOTE £2.10: £1.20, £2.40; EX 4.10.
Owner Godolphin **Bred** Mrs Eithne Hamilton **Trained** Newmarket, Suffolk

FOCUS
This is typically muddling conditions race form and the winner was getting weight from his four rivals, but he confirmed he retains plenty of ability and Kieren Fallon sounded seriously impressed. He can only be rated to his 2yo form but could be a lot better.

NOTEBOOK
Dubai Prince(IRE), who won both his starts for Dermot Weld last year, including the 7f Group 3 Killavullan Stakes, missed the Classics owing to a hairline fracture of his pelvic region. The first-time fitting of a sizeable sheepskin noseband for his return was a touch disconcerting, but he's done well physically for his time off and in the race itself he did everything that was asked of him in a professional manner. The pace, set by Penitent, seemed a bit stop-start, but Dubai Prince travelled on the bridle until asked for his challenge and only had to be shown the whip to draw away and comfortably take his record to 3-3. This looked the sort of performance he should go forward from and his next start should tell us more. (op 8-11)
Jet Away didn't go on as expected after winning a decent conditions race on his return, but he'd been given 77 days off and returned to form. Time may show this was a really smart performance considering he was conceding 12lb to the winner. (op 7-1)
Penitent, with cheekpieces replacing a visor, didn't see his race out despite being allowed to dominate. He's better at 1m, but looks best watched for now regardless of the trip. (op 5-2)
Togiak(IRE) had plenty to find on his return to the Flat. He ran pretty well but may be flattered. (op 50-1)
Bolivia(GER), Group 2-placed over 1m2f in Germany, had a hood fitted on her debut for a new stable. She wasn't beaten all that far, despite hanging, and might come on for this, but the form may not be trustworthy. (op 20-1)

6126 HAYNES, HANSON & CLARK CONDITIONS STKS (C&G) 1m (S)
3:45 (3:45) (Class 2) 2-Y-0
£9,337 (£2,796; £1,398; £699; £349; £175) **Stalls** Centre

Form RPR

3321 **1** **Cavaleiro (IRE)**23 5375 2-9-2 84 ...... RichardMullen 3 93+
(Marcus Tregoning) *swtg: trckd ldrs: drvn to challange ins fnl 2f: slt ld 1f out: hld on to narrow ld ins fnl f: all out* **11/1**3

21 **2** *nk* **Harvard N Yale (USA)**35 5013 2-9-2 86 ...... GeorgeBaker 4 92+
(Jeremy Noseda) *lw: led main gp towards centre of crse and upsides w sole ldr on stands' rail tl gp merged 2f out and sn led: narrowly hdd 1f out: styd chalng thrght fnl f tl no ex last strides* **4/7**1

33 **3** *3 ½* **Spoke To Carlo**18 5565 2-8-12 0 ...... NeilCallan 6 80
(Eve Johnson Houghton) *unf: scope: sn wl in tch: drvn and hdwy over 2f out: tk 3rd u.p fnl f: kpt on but no ch w ldng duo* **12/1**

4 *½* **Mysterious Man (IRE)** 2-8-12 0 ...... DavidProbert 7 79+
(Andrew Balding) *angular: s.i.s: towards rr: rdn and green over 2f out: kpt on over 1f out: styd on for 4th ins fnl f* **33/1**

5 *2 ¼* **Linkable** 2-8-12 0 ...... MichaelHills 2 74+
(Charles Hills) *unf: scope: lengthy: towards rr but in tch: hdwy 3f out: qcknd to trck ldrs 2f out: shkn up over 1f out: fdd fnl f* **11/1**3

33 **6** *15* **Performing Pocket (USA)**16 5632 2-8-12 0 ...... KierenFallon 1 41
(George Baker) *w'like: t.k.h: trckd ldrs: wknd qckly 2f out: eased whn no ch fnl f* **16/1**

1 **7** *6* **Oscan (USA)**10 5801 2-9-2 0 ...... FrankieDettori 8 32
(Mahmood Al Zarooni) *str: sn racd alone stands' side and overall ldr tl jnd by main gp over 2f out: hdd sn after: wknd qckly over 1f out: eased whn btn* **6/1**2

1m 41.85s (2.15) **Going Correction** +0.125s/f (Good) **7** Ran SP% **111.1**
Speed ratings (Par 101): **94,93,90,89,87 72,66**
toteswingers:1&2:£2.50, 1&3:£4.90, 2&3:£2.60 CSF £16.87 TOTE £9.20: £2.80, £1.20; EX 18.80 Trifecta £66.00 Pool: £1,012.22 - 11.34 winning units..
Owner Guy Brook **Bred** Kildaragh Stud & M Downey **Trained** Lambourn, Berks
■ Stewards' Enquiry : Frankie Dettori one-day ban: failed to ride out for 6th (Sep 30)

FOCUS
A race with a famous history of producing top-class horses, although not so much lately, with Authorized (third in 2006) the only star to emerge in recent times, and it's doubtful we saw a top notcher on this occasion. The form is good all the same, with improvement from the winner. The main bunch raced towards the middle early, but the action ultimately unfolded towards the near side.

NOTEBOOK
Cavaleiro(IRE) took four goes to get off the mark, winning easily at Chepstow last time, and this represents a significant step forward. A lack of juvenile Group-race entries suggests his progress has taken connections by surprise, although Marcus Tregoning said afterwards he's been patient with the colt, and consequently he may yet go on improving. A pedigree that suggests middle-distances could be within reach next year offers further hope of more to come and this son of the stable's 2006 Epsom hero Sir Percy might be worth a shot in a Derby trial. (op 9-1)
Harvard N Yale(USA) came here with a tall reputation, but his form (runner-up to the smart Ektihaam before winning a traditionally red-hot maiden) was decent rather than spectacular. This has to go down as a disappointing performance, even if he was forced to race handier than ideal, as he simply lacked the winner's finishing speed. A big horse, it's doubtful we've seen the best of him, but so far he's been just the type who is over bet.
Spoke To Carlo had run to just a fair level at minor tracks on his first two starts. This was probably an improved performance on this step up from 7f, and he looks a useful type, but his proximity adds weight to the theory that this form is nothing special compared with some of the previous runnings. Handicaps are now an option. (op 16-1)
Mysterious Man(IRE) ◆'s dam won the 7f Group 1 Moyglare Stud Stakes at two, but otherwise this is a colt with a stout pedigree. Considering he can be expected to relish middle-distances next year, and was one of only two newcomers, this was a promising start. (tchd 28-1)
Linkable, who is out of a 1m2f Listed winner, showed ability and should do better in the long term. (op 20-1 tchd 25-1)
Oscan(USA), a half-brother to St Leger winner Mastery, won an ordinary 7f maiden at Leicester on his debut, but he ran poorly on this step up in class. Possible excuses include him being at a disadvantage in racing alone against the stands' rail until the others edged over, and also that this may have come too soon, but he'll still have plenty to prove next time. (op 5-1)

6127 DOWNLOAD THE BLUE SQUARE BET IPHONE APP E B F MAIDEN STKS (DIV II) 6f 8y
4:20 (4:20) (Class 4) 2-Y-0 **£4,398** (£1,309; £654; £327) **Stalls** Centre

Form RPR

2 **1** **Accession (IRE)**14 5681 2-9-3 0 ...... AdamKirby 7 85+
(Clive Cox) *w'like: scope: lw: pressed ldrs: chal over 2f out tl drvn to ld wl over 1f out: styd on strly ins fnl f* **5/4**1

22 **2** *2 ¼* **Glen Moss (IRE)**42 4748 2-9-3 0 ...... MichaelHills 11 75
(Charles Hills) *sn led: pushed along and jnd over 2f out: hdd wl over 1f out: kpt on fnl f but nt pce of wnr* **15/8**2

3 *1 ½* **Our Merv (IRE)** 2-9-3 0 ...... DaneO'Neill 6 71+
(Terry Clement) *leggy: slowly away: bhd and hdwy over 2f out: drvn whn green and hung lft over 1f out: styd on wl fnl f to take 3rd fnl 120yds: nt rch ldng duo* **33/1**

0 **4** *¾* **Authora (IRE)**46 4614 2-8-12 0 ...... PatDobbs 1 63
(Richard Hannon) *unf: sn pressing ldrs: stl ev ch fr 2f out tl outpcd ins fnl f* **40/1**

50 **5** *shd* **Star Kingdom (IRE)**23 5384 2-9-3 0 ...... StevieDonohoe 3 68
(Robert Mills) *chsd ldrs: rdn ins fnl 2f: styd on same pce appr fnl f* **40/1**

0 **6** *½* **Wordismybond**9 5834 2-9-3 0 ...... TomQueally 2 66
(Peter Makin) *str: towards rr: rdn and outpcd over 2f out: styd on ins fnl f: kpt on cl home* **80/1**

0 **7** *½* **Rocky Reef**23 5384 2-9-3 0 ...... JimmyFortune 9 65
(Andrew Balding) *in rr: rdn and hdwy over 2f out: nvr rchd ldrs and styd on same pce fnl f* **16/1**

8 *4* **Coup De Grace (IRE)** 2-9-3 0 ...... EddieAhern 4 53
(Amanda Perrett) *w'like: in tch: rdn 2f out: wknd appr fnl f* **33/1**

9 *1 ½* **Smacker (IRE)** 2-9-3 0 ...... JimCrowley 5 48
(Hughie Morrison) *athletic: chsd ldrs 4f* **16/1**

10 *6* **Royal Prospector** 2-9-3 0 ...... RichardHughes 8 30
(Richard Hannon) *w'like: chsd ldrs: rdn and wknd 2f out: eased whn btn fnl f* **8/1**3

11 *4 ½* **Foot Tapper** 2-9-3 0 ...... GeorgeBaker 10 17
(Chris Wall) *unf: bit bkwd: s.i.s: a outpcd* **33/1**

1m 14.73s (1.73) **Going Correction** +0.125s/f (Good) **11** Ran SP% **117.0**
Speed ratings (Par 97): **93,90,88,87,86 86,85,80,78,70 64**
toteswingers:1&2:£1.70, 1&3:£12.20, 2&3:£15.90 CSF £3.38 TOTE £1.70: £1.10, £1.40, £7.10; EX 3.80 Trifecta £78.70 Pool: £1,105.25 - 10.38 winning units..
Owner Brighthelm Racing **Bred** Corduff Stud Ltd **Trained** Lambourn, Berks

FOCUS
The time was 0.33 seconds slower than Mince recorded in the first division and the form doesn't look that strong, but the winenr impressed and has more to offer. They raced middle to near side.

NOTEBOOK
Accession(IRE), a promising second in a fair 6f Haydock maiden on his recent debut, improved on that form with a straightforward, clear-cut success. He's bred to be a sprinter, but was really strong at the line and, while he'll doubtless face tougher tasks, he looks decent. (tchd 11-8)
Glen Moss(IRE) didn't progress from his debut second when runner-up over 6f at Haydock last time (got warm, overraced on the lead), and he again found one too good. Like last time he was a bit warm and did a bit too much early. He's not really progressing but time is on his side and at the moment he looks a 5f horse. Also, judging by his fluent action, a quicker surface might help. (op 9-4)
Our Merv(IRE) was slowest away but recovered to travel quite well and had he not run green under pressure (went left), he would have finished a deal closer. He cost only 1,800euros, but is a half-brother to a 6f juvenile winner in Italy and looks at least a fair type in the making. Quick going would be a concern, though, as he displayed a knee action and really grabbed the ground.
Authora(IRE) improved on her debut form after a 46-day break. (op 50-1)
Star Kingdom(IRE) again showed ability. He can now switch to handicaps.

Wordismybond stayed on from some way back and can do better.

6128 DUBAI DUTY FREE FULL OF SURPRISES E B F "PIVOTAL' FILLIES" CONDITIONS STKS 7f (S)

4:55 (4:58) (Class 2) 2-Y-O

£9,337 (£2,796; £1,398; £699; £349; £175) **Stalls** Centre

Form RPR

3 **1** **Hazel Lavery (IRE)**[21] 5444 2-8-12 0 MichaelHills 3 90+
(Charles Hills) *lw: trckd ldrs: wnt 2nd 2f out: drvn to ld wl over 1f out: qckndd ins fnl f: comf* **5/2**[1]

2 *2* **Dank** 2-8-12 0 KierenFallon 1 85+
(Sir Michael Stoute) *athletic: attr: hld up in rr but in tch: qcknd to chse ldrs 2f out: wnt 2nd ins fnl f and kpt on wl clsng stages but nt pce of wnr* **9/2**

3 *2* **Coplow** 2-8-12 0 PatDobbs 5 80+
(Richard Hannon) *leggy: scope: s.i.s: sn rcvrd to trck ldrs: outpcd by ldng duo fnl f but kpt on wl for 3rd* **16/1**

3251 **4** *1 3/4* **My Queenie (IRE)**[10] 5806 2-9-2 93 RichardHughes 4 81
(Richard Hannon) *lw: trckd ldrs: rdn and one pce 2f out: no imp fnl f* **11/4**[2]

5 *1 1/4* **Westwiththenight (IRE)** 2-8-12 0 EddieAhern 6 73+
(William Haggas) *w'like: str: s.i.s: in rr and t.k.h: effrt and sme prog 2f out: wknd sn after* **4/1**[3]

01 **6** *2 1/4* **What's Up (IRE)**[30] 5170 2-8-12 75 TomQueally 7 67
(Jim Boyle) *lw: led: rdn over 2f out: hdd wl over 1f out: sn btn* **16/1**

7 *11* **Intense Pink** 2-8-12 0 WilliamBuick 2 42
(Chris Wall) *unf: in tch: drvn along 3f out: wknd fr 2f out: eased whn no ch ins fnl f* **11/1**

1m 26.39s (0.69) **Going Correction** +0.125s/f (Good) 7 Ran SP% **113.5**
Speed ratings (Par 101): **101,98,96,94,93 90,77**
toteswingers:1&2:£2.70, 1&3:£10.60, 2&3:£14.60 CSF £13.93 TOTE £3.50: £2.10, £3.30; EX 17.70.
Owner R Morecombe, E O'Leary, R Scarborough **Bred** Longueville Bloodstock **Trained** Lambourn, Berks

FOCUS
A decent fillies' conditions event. They raced up the middle of the track. The winner impressed and this form is likely to work out well.

NOTEBOOK
Hazel Lavery(IRE) ◆, third in a 7f maiden on her debut at the Newmarket July course, improved to justify strong market support in tidy fashion. She looks pattern class and that's the direction her trainer is looking, suggesting the Rockfel could be the target. (op 3-1)
Dank is a half-sister to some smart types, notably Hong Kong Cup winner Eagle Mountain, out of a triple 1m2f winner. She raced freely under restraint, but picked up for pressure to briefly threaten and should come on plenty for this. (op 7-2)
Coplow ◆, a 78,000gns half-sister to some smart types, including 7f-1m2f winner (including Group 3) Middle Club, out of a 1m2f scorer, was apparently passed over by Richard Hughes, but she looks a lovely filly in the making. She seemed to float over the ground, displaying a really light action, but was green under pressure and that cost her a winning chance. There ought to be a deal more to come. (op 22-1 tchd 25-1)
My Queenie(IRE), fifth in an ordinary running of the Prestige Stakes before winning a 1m maiden at Leicester, struggled under her penalty against less-exposed types. She didn't get a clear run, but was not unlucky. (op 9-4 tchd 2-1)
Westwiththenight(IRE), a half-sister to a 1m3f winner, out of a Cheshire Oaks winner, was the only one of these with an entry in the Irish 1,000 Guineas. She never seriously threatened but will be worth another chance. (op 11-2 tchd 6-1)
What's Up(IRE) escaped a penalty for her win in a weak 7f maiden at Folkestone on her second start, but she was outclassed. (op 12-1 tchd 11-1)

6129 DUBAI DUTY FREE CUP (LISTED RACE) 7f (S)

5:30 (5:30) (Class 1) 3-Y-O+

£17,013 (£6,450; £3,228; £1,608; £807; £405) **Stalls** Centre

Form RPR

0140 **1** **Chilworth Lad**[20] 5474 3-8-13 102 RichardHughes 4 110
(Mick Channon) *hld up in rr: drvn and rapid hdwy over 2f out to take narrow ld ins fnl f: styd on strly to assert fnl 75yds* **8/1**[3]

5341 **2** *3/4* **Colonial (IRE)**[18] 5563 4-9-2 108 FrankieDettori 1 109
(Saeed Bin Suroor) *led: pushed along 2f out: hdd ins fnl f: styd chalng tl outpcd fnl 75yds* **9/4**[2]

0120 **3** *3/4* **Joe Packet**[6] 5927 4-9-2 96 JimCrowley 3 107
(Jonathan Portman) *lw: hld up in rr: drvn and hdwy over 1f out: tk 3rd fnl f and kpt on but no imp on ldng duo* **20/1**

0010 **4** *3/4* **Yaa Wayl (IRE)**[27] 5282 4-9-2 108 (v) WilliamBuick 6 105
(Saeed Bin Suroor) *trckd ldrs: rdn and one pce 2f out: rdn and hd sltly high fr over 1f out: kpt on u.p to take wl hld 4th clsng stages* **16/1**

3323 **5** *1* **Beacon Lodge (IRE)**[20] 5473 6-9-2 112 AdamKirby 5 102
(Clive Cox) *lw: chsd ldrs: rdn over 2f out: wknd ins fnl f* **11/8**[1]

1610 **6** *3/4* **Navajo Chief**[13] 5704 4-9-2 107 HarryBentley 2 100
(Alan Jarvis) *chsd ldr tl rdn over 2f out: wknd over 1f out* **8/1**[3]

0000 **7** *27* **Himalya (IRE)**[27] 5282 5-9-2 100[1] GeorgeBaker 7 27
(Roger Charlton) *racd alone stands' side: no ch fnl 3f: t.o* **33/1**

1m 25.06s (-0.64) **Going Correction** +0.125s/f (Good)
WFA 3 from 4yo+ 3lb 7 Ran SP% **108.7**
Speed ratings (Par 111): **108,107,106,105,104 103,72**
toteswingers:1&2:£2.40, 1&3:£4.50, 2&3:£3.50 CSF £23.79 TOTE £10.00: £2.60, £1.60; EX 33.50.
Owner 7Rus **Bred** Phil Jen Racing **Trained** West Ilsley, Berks

FOCUS
More like a conditions race than a Listed contest, plenty of these not giving their true running and the form seems very ordinary for the grade. A fair winning time suggests they went an even enough pace, and the majority of these raced up the middle of the track. Chilworth Lad posted a small personal best.

NOTEBOOK
Chilworth Lad, the only 3yo in the race, was keen early but still stayed on best. In a handicap he would have been 6lb better off with the runner-up, but 6lb worse off with the third. This tough sort seems to have run to something like his official mark of 102 and was improving his C&D record to 2-2. (op 10-1)
Colonial(IRE) won a conditions race at Warwick on his previous start, but he was sweating this time and didn't run up to his official mark of 108. (tchd 2-1)
Joe Packet usually races over sprint trips but he got this distance well enough to apparently run right up to his best, albeit he didn't find quite as much as expected after moving strongly. (op 14-1)
Yaa Wayl(IRE) raced with his tongue out under pressure and again looked awkward. He was below his official rating of 108. (op 12-1)

Beacon Lodge(IRE) had been contesting Group races (without success) since taking a Listed race last May and had upwards of 4lb in hand on this drop in class, but he found disappointingly little after travelling okay. He seemed a bit moody on the way to post and will be best watched next time. (tchd 11-10)

6130 BET AT BLUESQ.COM ON YOUR MOBILE H'CAP 1m 4f 5y

6:00 (6:01) (Class 4) (0-85,85) 3-Y-O+ **£4,528** (£1,347; £673; £336) **Stalls** Low

Form RPR

03-4 **1** **Albert Bridge**[18] 5556 3-8-8 75 JimCrowley 7 83
(Ralph Beckett) *trckd ldrs: drvn to chal fr 3f out tl led appr fnl 2f: styd on gamely ins fnl f and kpt on fnl clsng stages* **15/2**

0221 **2** *3/4* **Sugar Hiccup (IRE)**[24] 5350 3-8-1 71 JohnFahy(3) 5 78
(Clive Cox) *chsd ldrs: drvn to chal fr 2f out and kpt on u.p to take 2nd fnl 100yds but a hld by wnr* **9/1**

133- **3** *nk* **Shubaat**[389] 5371 4-9-9 82 NeilCallan 4 88
(Roger Varian) *chsd ldrs: rdn and one pce 2f out: rallied u.p fnl f to take 3rd last strides* **6/1**[3]

6334 **4** *shd* **Unex Renoir**[58] 4208 3-9-1 82 WilliamBuick 3 88
(John Gosden) *lw: chsd ldr: slt ld and rdn fr 3f out: narrowly hdd appr fnl 2f: kpt on to dispute cl 2nd u.p fnl f tl wknd and dropped to 4th clsng stages* **6/1**[3]

-454 **5** *1* **Foxhaven**[36] 4957 9-9-5 78 (v) GeorgeBaker 14 83
(Patrick Chamings) *in rr: hdwy towards outside over 2f out but sn hanging bdly lft u.p: one pce ins fnl f* **14/1**

4120 **6** *2 1/2* **Mountain Range (IRE)**[20] 5482 3-9-2 83 EddieAhern 10 84
(John Dunlop) *in rr tl hdwy on ins over 2f out: nvr gng pce to chal and styd on same pce fnl f* **7/2**[1]

6100 **7** *3 3/4* **Pittodrie Star (IRE)**[14] 5685 4-9-5 78 DavidProbert 2 73
(Andrew Balding) *led tl hdd 3f out: wknd u.p wl over 1f out* **9/1**

6023 **8** *1/2* **Viking Storm**[9] 5837 3-8-12 79 ChrisCatlin 9 73
(Harry Dunlop) *chsd ldrs: rdn over 2f out: sn wknd* **33/1**

-010 **9** *1/2* **Dr Livingstone (IRE)**[14] 5685 6-9-9 85 HarryBentley(3) 13 78
(Charles Egerton) *in rr: rdn and sme prog towards outside over 2f out: nvr rchd ldrs and sn wknd* **12/1**

3426 **10** *1/2* **Aldwick Bay (IRE)**[36] 4957 3-9-0 81 RichardHughes 12 73
(Richard Hannon) *hld up in rr: rdn and no imp wl over 2f out* **11/2**[2]

5202 **11** *39* **Time Square (FR)**[160] 1243 4-9-2 75 (t) TomQueally 6 —
(Tony Carroll) *t.k.h: chsd ldrs tl wknd qckly fr 3f out: virtually p.u fnl f* **25/1**

2m 37.63s (2.13) **Going Correction** +0.125s/f (Good)
WFA 3 from 4yo+ 8lb 11 Ran SP% **119.1**
Speed ratings (Par 105): **97,96,96,96,95 93,91,91,90,90 64**
toteswingers:1&2:£14.00, 1&3:£10.30, 2&3:£8.30. totesuper7: WIN: Not won. PLACE: Not won. CSF £74.28 CT £437.43 TOTE £8.90: £3.20, £3.10, £2.40; EX 42.90 Trifecta £489.30 Part won. Pool: £661.25 - 0.20 winning units..
Owner The Cheyne Walkers **Bred** Miss K Rausing **Trained** Kimpton, Hants
■ Stewards' Enquiry : John Fahy three-day ban: used whip with excessive frequency (Sep 30, Oct 1,3)

FOCUS
A fair handicap, although they didn't go that quick and those held up were at a disadvantage. The form still seems well enough.
Mountain Range(IRE) Official explanation: jockey said gelding never travelled
Dr Livingstone(IRE) Official explanation: jockey said saddle slipped
Aldwick Bay(IRE) Official explanation: jockey said colt ran flat
Time Square(FR) Official explanation: jockey said gelding ran too freely
T/Plt: £12.70 to a £1 stake. Pool:£54,540.67 - 3,111.98 winning tickets T/Qpdt: £2.70 to a £1 stake. Pool:£4,310.93 - 1,149.37 winning tickets ST

5895 WOLVERHAMPTON (A.W) (L-H)

Friday, September 16

OFFICIAL GOING: Standard
Wind: Fresh, behind Weather: shower

6131 THE BLACK COUNTRY'S ONLY RACECOURSE MEDIAN AUCTION MAIDEN FILLIES' STKS 5f 216y(P)

5:15 (5:16) (Class 5) 2-Y-O **£1,908** (£563; £281) **Stalls** Low

Form RPR

2553 **1** **Blodwen Abbey**[69] 3849 2-9-0 63 LiamJones 6 69
(James Unett) *racd keenly: chsd ldrs: effrt to take 2nd over 1f out: led ins fnl f: r.o and drvn out* **6/1**[2]

042 **2** *1* **Silke Top**[19] 5514 2-9-0 74 SteveDrowne 10 66
(William Jarvis) *chsd ldr: rdn to ld over 1f out: hdd ins fnl f: kpt on but hld towards fin* **1/1**[1]

50 **3** *1 1/2* **Tenbridge**[16] 5613 2-9-0 0 (p) RobertWinston 5 62
(Derek Haydn Jones) *in tch: pushed along over 3f out: outpcd over 2f out: rallied u.p over 1f out: styd on: no imp on front 2* **100/1**

0 **4** *nse* **Remix (IRE)**[60] 4155 2-9-0 0 SilvestreDeSousa 7 61
(J W Hills) *midfield: rdn 1/2-way: prog to chse ldrs over 1f out: styd on: nt quite get to ldrs* **11/1**

054 **5** *4 1/2* **Get The Trip**[39] 4848 2-9-0 53 RoystonFfrench 9 48
(James Toller) *led: rdn and hdd over 1f out: wknd ins fnl f* **33/1**

30 **6** *1 1/2* **Fairyinthewind (IRE)**[25] 5323 2-9-0 0 CathyGannon 4 43
(Paul D'Arcy) *bhd: styd on u.p fr over 1f out: no imp on ldrs* **7/1**[3]

7 *1 1/2* **Sangrail** 2-9-0 0 MartinDwyer 11 39
(William Muir) *hld up: u.p over 3f ou: kpt on fr over 1f out: no imp on ldrs* **14/1**

8 *1/2* **Bellinda** 2-8-9 0 AntiocoMurgia(5) 1 37
(Ian Wood) *midfield: outpcd 1/2-way: nvr a threat* **40/1**

0 **9** *hd* **Dora's Sister (IRE)**[153] 1414 2-8-11 0 DeclanCannon(3) 12 37
(John Quinn) *racd on outer: chsd ldrs: rdn 2f out: wknd over 1f out* **6/1**[2]

10 *1 1/4* **Dare I Ask** 2-8-7 0 JakePayne(7) 2 33
(Bill Turner) *sn wl outpcd and bhd: nvr on terms* **14/1**

11 *17* **Nani Jani** 2-9-0 0 FrederikTylicki 8 —
(Bruce Hellier) *hld up: struggling over 2f out: wl bhd fnl f* **66/1**

1m 14.95s (-0.05) **Going Correction** -0.10s/f (Stan) 11 Ran SP% **120.6**
Speed ratings (Par 92): **96,94,92,92,86 84,82,81,81,80 57**
toteswingers:1&2:£2.40, 1&3:£42.40, 2&3:£17.20 CSF £12.54 TOTE £5.40: £1.30, £1.30, £15.10; EX 19.00.
Owner J M Davies **Bred** Bearstone Stud **Trained** Tedsmore Hall, Shropshire

FOCUS
The 63-rated second favourite overhauled the market leader in this fillies' auction maiden.

NOTEBOOK

Blodwen Abbey has had a few chances and was returning from a break, but she travelled enthusiastically just behind the leaders and found a change of gear back at 6f to get off the mark on the fifth attempt. She didn't progress in her four previous runs, but this looks a step forward and she is related to 7f-1m2f winners, so could find some further improvement as she continues to go up in trip. (tchd 11-2)

Silke Top was quietly progressive in three 6f maidens on fast and soft turf, the latest when just over 3l second behind impressive newcomer at Yarmouth. She had strong form claims and was always well positioned near the steady pace, but it was a bit disappointing that she couldn't repel a rival with an 11lb lower official mark. (op 10-11)

Tenbridge virtually refused to race on debut and was always outpaced with cheekpieces tried last time, but she showed promise staying-on well against the far rail on this third run.

Remix(IRE) finished well out wide in an improved second run. She is out of a 6f Fibresand winner who is a half-sister to useful 1m/1m1f handicapper Champion Lodge, and should continue to go the right way.

Get The Trip has been beaten 7l+ in four sprint maidens and has a BHA rating of just 53, but she showed up well for a long way and her trainer should have something to work with in minor handicaps.

Fairyinthewind(IRE) was never involved in a second heavy defeat since a close third of four at Newmarket on debut. (op 8-1)

6132 WILLIAMHILL.COM NURSERY 7f 32y(P)
5:50 (5:52) (Class 5) (0-70,70) 2-Y-O £2,522 (£750; £375; £187) Stalls High

Form RPR

5645 **1** **Fiction Or Fact (IRE)**[92] 3070 2-9-2 **65**.....................(p) FrederikTylicki 11 68
(Kevin Ryan) *chsd ldrs on outer: rdn over 1f out: r.o to ld fnl 75yds: a doing enough cl home* **25/1**

040 **2** ½ **Abhaath (USA)**[13] 5727 2-9-5 **68**....................................... TadhgO'Shea 1 70
(Saeed Bin Suroor) *midfield: rdn and hdwy over 1f out: r.o ins fnl f: gng on at fin* **13/2**[3]

4105 **3** *nk* **Lolita Lebron (IRE)**[15] 5645 2-9-4 **67**.......................... RobertWinston 9 68
(Lawrence Mullaney) *led: rdn and edgd rt over 1f out: hdd fnl 75yds: one pce fnl strides* **18/1**

000 **4** ½ **Saint Irene**[32] 5097 2-9-0 **63**... JackMitchell 8 63
(Michael Blanshard) *s.i.s: in rr: reminder 4f out: hld up: rdn and hung bdly rt ent st wl over 1f out: racd on stands' side hdwy 1f out: r.o ins fnl f: nt quite get to ldrs* **40/1**

0500 **5** *hd* **Come On Blue Chip (IRE)**[21] 5446 2-9-1 **64**...........(b[1]) CathyGannon 5 64
(Paul D'Arcy) *s.i.s: in rr: nt clr run over 1f out: hdwy ins fnl f: fin strly* **3/1**[2]

3300 **6** *hd* **Xinbama (IRE)**[10] 5809 2-9-6 **69**.. LiamJones 2 68
(J W Hills) *midfield: rdn and hdwy over 1f out: styd on ins fnl f: nt quite pce to shake-up ldrs: no further prog cl home* **33/1**

3102 **7** 2¾ **Long Lost Love**[10] 5809 2-9-5 **68**............................. SilvestreDeSousa 4 60
(Mark Johnston) *trckd ldrs: rdn over 2f out: kpt on same pce fr over 1f out: nt pce to threaten* **15/8**[1]

0320 **8** ¾ **Dickens Rules (IRE)**[47] 4581 2-9-5 **68**............................ SteveDrowne 6 58
(Sylvester Kirk) *midfield: rdn over 2f out: one pce fr over 1f out: no imp* **10/1**

245 **9** ½ **Slenningford**[85] 3314 2-9-0 **66**.................................... MartinHarley[(3)] 10 55
(Ollie Pears) *chsd ldr tl rdn over 1f out: sn wknd* **13/2**[3]

3460 **10** *nk* **Siouxperhero (IRE)**[10] 5809 2-9-7 **70**...........................(b) MartinDwyer 7 58
(William Muir) *midfield: rdn over 1f out: kpt on fnl f: nvr able to chal* **28/1**

025 **11** 6 **Monty Fay (IRE)**[50] 4462 2-9-3 **66**................................ J-PGuillambert 3 40
(Derek Haydn Jones) *racd keenly: chsd ldrs: rdn over 1f out: sn wknd* **20/1**

5656 **12** 2½ **Perfect Gratitude (USA)**[14] 5688 2-9-3 **66**................. RoystonFfrench 12 33
(Ed Dunlop) *a bhd: struggling over 2f out: nvr on terms* **20/1**

1m 29.66s (0.06) **Going Correction** -0.10s/f (Stan) 12 Ran SP% **123.0**

Speed ratings (Par 95): **95,94,94,93,93 93,89,89,88,88 81,78**

toteswingers:1&2:£32.70, 1&3:£21.50, 2&3:£24.00 CSF £173.61 CT £3079.94 TOTE £26.70: £5.30, £2.20, £2.80; EX 122.40.

Owner Mrs Margaret Forsyth **Bred** Michael O'Mahony **Trained** Hambleton, N Yorks

FOCUS

The went a fair pace in this nursery.

NOTEBOOK

Fiction Or Fact(IRE) was disappointing as favourite in a Beverley maiden when last seen in June, but he burst back to form to strike with cheekpieces applied on nursery debut back from a break and gelding operation. He has looked unruly and bit difficult at times, but he showed a good attitude here and there should be more to come from a horse who is related to a useful 1m1f US winner.

Abhaath(USA) flopped on two of his three maiden runs, but this $400,000 half-brother to US 7f Grade 1 2yo winner Hot Dixie, ran a big race to go close on nursery/AW debut. The blots in his profile are not easy to ignore but he has potential now he has got his act together and could have quite a bit of leeway to successfully operate off this mark. (op 6-1 tchd 11-2)

Lolita Lebron(IRE) set a fair pace and kept fighting on AW debut. She won a Thirsk claimer for Tim Pitt in July and has been close up in her last two nursery runs. (op 16-1)

Saint Irene was a well held eighth at big prices in three maidens, and looked difficult and wayward on nursery debut, but she eventually stayed on strongly after racing solo against the near rail in the closing stages. Official explanation: jockey said filly hung right (op 50-1)

Come On Blue Chip(IRE), a big market springer, ran into some trouble before finishing fast from a long way back with blinkers tried on AW debut. (op 11-2)

Long Lost Love hit a personal best when a clear second in a 7f nursery on good to soft at Lingfield last time. She looked well treated off the same mark and was a strong favourite but she couldn't adopt a prominent position like she did last time and was lacklustre in a bid to improve her strike-rate to 2-5. (op 6-4)

Dickens Rules(IRE) Official explanation: jockey said colt suffered interference at start

Slenningford raced near the pace but faded, stepped up in trip and switched to AW on nursery debut. (op 11-2 tchd 7-1)

Perfect Gratitude(USA) Official explanation: jockey said colt hung right

6133 RINGSIDE CONFERENCE SUITE - 700 THEATRE STYLE CLASSIFIED CLAIMING STKS 7f 32y(P)
6:20 (6:20) (Class 5) 3-Y-O+ £1,908 (£563; £281) Stalls High

Form RPR

0205 **1** **Stevie Gee (IRE)**[17] 5578 7-8-5 68.................................... RyanClark[(3)] 6 74
(Ian Williams) *midfield: hdwy 2f out: led ent fnl f: hrd pressed clsng stages: hld on wl* **10/1**

2032 **2** *shd* **Brynfa Boy**[17] 5604 5-8-3 70....................................... SilvestreDeSousa 5 69
(Paul D'Arcy) *racd keenly: hld up: hdwy 2f out: r.o ins fnl f: pressed wnr fnl 100yds: jst hld* **9/2**[3]

6002 **3** 1¾ **Burning Stone (USA)**[22] 5414 4-8-9 63............................ RobertWinston 2 70
(Gay Kelleway) *midfield: hdwy whn nt clr run over 1f out: sn swtchd lft: chsd ldrs ins fnl f: nt quite pce of front 2* **12/1**

5035 **4** 1 **Mottley Crewe**[53] 4393 4-8-4 70....................................... CathyGannon 1 63
(Richard Guest) *a.p: rdn to ld briefly over 1f out: styd on same pce fnl 100yds* **10/1**

560 **5** 1½ **Indieslad**[15] 5652 3-8-10 68....................................... RussKennemore 3 67
(Ann Duffield) *hld up: hdwy 2f out: chsd ldrs ins fnl f: kpt on same pce fnl 100yds* **22/1**

4152 **6** ¾ **Whispering Spirit (IRE)**[11] 5789 5-8-7 70...............(v) RoystonFfrench 9 60
(Ann Duffield) *bustled along in rr: kpt on u.p fnl f: nt pce to chal* **14/1**

323 **7** *hd* **Northern Flyer (GER)**[22] 5404 5-8-0 63.................(p) DeclanCannon[(3)] 8 55
(John Quinn) *midfield: clsd 4f out: effrt 2f out: chalng over 1f out: no ex fnl 100yds* **9/1**

0540 **8** 2¾ **Defector (IRE)**[32] 5101 5-8-9 69.............................. FrankieMcDonald 12 54
(Seamus Durack) *prom: led over 2f out: rdn and hdd over 1f out: wknd ins fnl f* **25/1**

0240 **9** 1¾ **Be A Devil**[13] 5717 4-8-9 70.. MartinDwyer 11 49
(William Muir) *hld up: hdwy 5f out: effrt 4 wd 3f out: wknd over 1f out* **4/1**[2]

10- **10** 1½ **Striking Priorite**[336] 6901 3-8-8 70.............................. FrederikTylicki 4 46
(Tim Fitzgerald) *a bhd* **40/1**

0221 **11** *hd* **Cavitie**[13] 5734 5-8-2 69..(p) LouisBeuzelin[(3)] 7 40
(Frank Sheridan) *racd keenly: trckd ldrs: rdn over 1f out: sn wknd* **11/4**[1]

50 **12** ½ **Il Battista**[13] 5718 3-8-11 70...................................(p) MartinHarley[(3)] 10 50
(Alan McCabe) *led: pushed along and hdd over 2f out: wknd over 1f out* **22/1**

1m 28.33s (-1.27) **Going Correction** -0.10s/f (Stan)

WFA 3 from 4yo+ 3lb 12 Ran SP% **122.4**

Speed ratings (Par 103): **103,102,100,99,98 97,96,93,91,90 89,89**

toteswingers:1&2:£12.40, 1&3:£28.80, 2&3:£10.10 CSF £54.04 TOTE £16.50: £3.90, £2.00, £4.90; EX 96.30.Brynfa Boy was claimed by Patrick Morris for £6,000.

Owner Steve Gray **Bred** Irish National Stud **Trained** Portway, Worcs

FOCUS

Ten of the runners had BHA ratings between 68 and 70 in this fair claimer. The pace was decent and the first two came from some way back. The winner is rated close to his reappearance effort.

Indieslad Official explanation: jockey said gelding was denied a clear run

Cavitie Official explanation: jockey said gelding stopped quickly

6134 WILLIAM HILL - THE HOME OF BETTING H'CAP (DIV I) 1m 1f 103y(P)
6:50 (6:50) (Class 6) (0-65,65) 3-Y-O+ £1,908 (£563; £281) Stalls Low

Form RPR

0604 **1** **Knowe Head (NZ)**[13] 5740 4-9-1 **56**.................................. LiamJones 10 66+
(James Unett) *hld up: sltly hmpd under 4f out: rdn and hdwy over 1f out: led ins fnl f: r.o: in command towards fin* **10/3**[2]

2503 **2** 1½ **Duquesa (IRE)**[14] 5673 3-9-4 **64**....................................(v) KierenFallon 3 71
(David Evans) *trckd ldrs: effrt 2f out: chalng ins fnl f: nt qckn fnl 100yds* **4/1**[3]

0460 **3** ½ **Dandarrell**[85] 3317 4-8-10 **51** oh1.................................(p) FrederikTylicki 7 57
(Julie Camacho) *in tch: effrt over 1f out: ev ch ent fnl f: styd on same pce fnl 75yds* **16/1**

4251 **4** 1½ **Kyle Of Bute**[22] 5414 5-9-10 **65**....................................... CathyGannon 9 68
(Brian Baugh) *racd keenly: chsd ldr: led 2f out: rdn over 1f out: hdd ins fnl f: no ex fnl 75yds* **9/2**

6245 **5** 1½ **Nicholas Pocock (IRE)**[13] 5740 5-9-1 **59**................ DeclanCannon[(3)] 8 59
(Ian McInnes) *hld up: forced sltly wd under 4f out: effrt 2f out: chsd ldrs and edgd lft ins fnl f: one pce* **9/1**

0000 **6** 1 **Vanilla Rum**[22] 5414 4-9-0 **55**.....................................(p) RoystonFfrench 6 53
(John Mackie) *midfield: u.p 3f out: effrt to chse ldrs over 1f out: no imp fnl f* **14/1**

2400 **7** 4½ **Carnival Dream**[54] 4361 6-8-10 **51** oh6..................(p) SilvestreDeSousa 2 39
(Hugh McWilliams) *led: rdn 3f out: hdd 2f out: wknd 1f out: eased whn wl btn ins fnl f* **25/1**

2642 **8** ¾ **Ride The Wind**[28] 5243 3-9-3 **63**...................................... MartinDwyer 11 50
(Chris Wall) *racd keenly on outer: prom tl rdn and wknd over 2f out* **3/1**[1]

P066 **9** 3¼ **Moonlight Fantasy (IRE)**[48] 4549 8-8-5 **51** oh6......... ChrisDCogan[(5)] 1 31
(Lucinda Featherstone) *a bhd: u.p over 2f out: nvr a threat* **33/1**

2m 1.14s (-0.56) **Going Correction** -0.10s/f (Stan)

WFA 3 from 4yo+ 5lb 9 Ran SP% **115.6**

Speed ratings (Par 101): **98,96,96,94,93 92,88,88,85**

CSF £17.16 CT £184.83 TOTE £4.00: £1.80, £2.00, £4.00; EX 14.10.

Owner Stuart J Stone **Bred** Glazeley Farms Trust **Trained** Tedsmore Hall, Shropshire

FOCUS

An ordinary handicap and the slower of the two divisions. It was run at just a fair pace and was a race of changing fortunes in the closing stages.

6135 WILLIAM HILL - THE HOME OF BETTING H'CAP (DIV II) 1m 1f 103y(P)
7:20 (7:20) (Class 6) (0-65,65) 3-Y-O+ £1,908 (£563; £281) Stalls Low

Form RPR

3136 **1** **Monster Munchie (JPN)**[27] 5266 3-9-4 **64**...................... KierenFallon 7 74+
(William Knight) *hld up: hdwy over 3f out: led over 1f out: r.o ins fnl f: a in full control* **5/2**[1]

-650 **2** 1 **Fluvial (IRE)**[23] 5391 3-9-5 **65**.................................. SilvestreDeSousa 1 73
(Mark Johnston) *chsd ldrs: wnt 2nd 3f out: rdn to chal fr 2f out: nt qckn 1f out: kpt on ins fnl f but a hld* **15/2**[3]

3250 **3** 1¾ **Aldo**[35] 5002 4-9-8 **63**..(t) FrankieMcDonald 6 67
(Alastair Lidderdale) *in tch: dropped to midfield 6f out: pushed along and outpcd over 3f out: rdn and hdwy over 1f out: styd on ins fnl f: nt pce to threaten front 2* **4/1**[2]

0540 **4** *shd* **Smarty Sam (USA)**[6] 5943 4-9-0 **55**.....................(b) RussKennemore 3 59
(Paul Midgley) *led: rdn 2f out: hdd over 1f out: kpt on same pce fnl 75yds* **11/1**

060 **5** 2 **Lunar River (FR)**[36] 4953 8-8-7 **53**...........................(t) JamesRogers[(5)] 9 53
(David Pinder) *hld up: effrt over 1f out: kpt on ins fnl f: nvr able to chal* **14/1**

46 **6** 1½ **Supa Seeker (USA)**[17] 5606 5-9-4 **59**...........................(t) SteveDrowne 5 55
(Tony Carroll) *prom: rdn 3f out: wknd fnl f: eased whn wl btn towards fin* **5/2**[1]

4520 **7** 1 **Beneath**[16] 5611 4-9-6 **61**.. CathyGannon 2 55
(Neil Mulholland) *bhd: u.p over 3f out: effrt over 2f out: nvr able to trble ldrs* **9/1**

506/ **8** 17 **Circus Polka (USA)**[1267] 1064 7-8-7 **51** oh5.......... DeclanCannon[(3)] 10 10
(Owen Brennan) *in tch: rdn and wknd over 3f out: eased whn wl btn over 1f out* **25/1**

000 **9** 9 **Charmouth Girl**[29] 5212 5-8-10 **51** oh6........................ RoystonFfrench 8 —
(John Mackie) *racd keenly: prom tl rdn and wknd wl over 2f out: eased whn wl btn over 1f out* **40/1**

2m 0.65s (-1.05) **Going Correction** -0.10s/f (Stan)

WFA 3 from 4yo+ 5lb 9 Ran SP% **120.2**

Speed ratings (Par 101): **100,99,97,97,95 94,93,78,70**

toteswingers:1&2:£4.40, 1&3:£5.00, 2&3:£8.00 CSF £23.56 CT £75.32 TOTE £3.30: £2.00, £2.70, £1.70; EX 16.00.

Owner A Black **Bred** Shadai Farm **Trained** Patching, W Sussex

FOCUS
The winner defied a huge market drift to win the second division of a modest handicap. The time was 0.49sec quicker than the first and the winner recorded a 6lb personal best.
Supa Seeker(USA) Official explanation: jockey said gelding hung left
Charmouth Girl Official explanation: jockey said mare ran too freely

6136 BOOK NOW FOR CHRISTMAS H'CAP 1m 4f 50y(P)
7:50 (7:50) (Class 5) (0-75,75) 3-Y-O £2,522 (£750; £375; £187) Stalls Low

Form RPR
4114 **1** **Caravan Rolls On**[114] 2407 3-9-6 **74** .... JackMitchell 1 84
(Peter Chapple-Hyam) *in tch: effrt over 2f out: sn wnt lft and led: over 2 l clr over 1f out: r.o wl: in command fnl f* **11/2**[3]

2023 **2** *2 ½* **Sunday Bess (JPN)**[36] 4971 3-9-7 **75** .... (v) KierenFallon 6 81
(Tom Dascombe) *trckd ldrs: n.m.r and hmpd jst over 2f out: wnt 2nd u.p wl over 1f out: no imp on wnr after* **3/1**[1]

614P **3** *4 ½* **Little Jazz**[3] 6037 3-9-1 **69** .... CathyGannon 2 68
(Paul D'Arcy) *in rr: pushed along over 3f out: effrt over 2f out: chsd ldrs over 1f out: one pce ins fnl f* **7/1**

5134 **4** *nk* **Miracle Play (IRE)**[17] 5582 3-8-3 **62** .... MatthewCosham(5) 7 60
(David Evans) *hld up in rr: rdn whn hmpd jst over 2f out: kpt on fnl f: nvr able to chal* **17/2**

6340 **5** *1 ¼* **Golden City (IRE)**[20] 5477 3-8-7 **68** .... DannyBrock(7) 3 64
(Chris Wall) *in tch: rdn 3f out: effrt to chal on outer over 2f out: outpcd wl over 1f out: btn after* **8/1**

4001 **6** *22* **Fairling**[14] 5665 3-8-12 **66** .... SteveDrowne 8 27
(Hughie Morrison) *led: rdn and hdd jst over 2f out: wknd qckly wl over 1f out: sn eased* **6/1**

-11P **7** *32* **Birdwatcher (IRE)**[133] 1872 3-9-0 **68** .... SilvestreDeSousa 5 —
(Mark Johnston) *hld up: niggled along 7f out: rdn over 5f out: sn wl outpcd: wl bhd fnl 3f: t.o* **7/2**[2]

034 **U** **Daruband**[89] 3206 3-9-0 **73** .... ChrisDCogan(5) 4 —
(Michael Chapman) *chsd ldr: w ldr over 6f out: rdn whn n.m.r: bdly hmpd and uns rdr jst over 2f out* **20/1**

2m 38.32s (-2.78) **Going Correction** -0.10s/f (Stan) 8 Ran SP% **115.8**
Speed ratings (Par 101): **105,103,100,100,99 84,63,—**
toteswingers:1&2:£3.80, 1&3:£4.70, 2&3:£6.00 CSF £22.71 CT £117.42 TOTE £8.20: £2.70, £1.10, £2.60; EX 22.90.
Owner Paul Hancock **Bred** Miss K Rausing **Trained** Newmarket, Suffolk
■ Stewards' Enquiry : Jack Mitchell five-day ban: careless riding (Sep 30, Oct 1, 3-5)

FOCUS
A middle-distance handicap. The pace was decent and they finished fairly strung out. The winner resumed his progress.

6137 MOBET.WILLIAMHILL.COM MAIDEN FILLIES' STKS 1m 141y(P)
8:20 (8:21) (Class 5) 3-Y-O+ £2,522 (£750; £375; £187) Stalls Low

Form RPR
1 **Dubai Bay (FR)**[124] 2133 3-8-12 73 .... RussKennemore 6 75
(Paul Midgley) *mde all: qcknd up 2f out: clr over 1f out: r.o wl: in command fnl f* **7/1**

3 **2** *3 ¼* **Double Trouble**[50] 4478 3-8-12 0 .... SilvestreDeSousa 8 68
(Marco Botti) *chsd wnr: pushed along over 3f out: rdn over 2f out: outpcd by wnr wl over 1f out: no imp* **11/4**[2]

0- **3** *1 ¾* **Moon Over Water (IRE)**[321] 7231 3-8-12 0 .... JackMitchell 5 64+
(Roger Varian) *midfield: pushed along 3f out: hdwy over 2f out: styd on ins fnl f: no imp on front 2* **6/1**

0433 **4** *2 ¾* **Golden Slipper**[37] 4931 3-8-12 75 .... KierenFallon 4 57
(Ed Dunlop) *chsd ldrs: pushed along over 2f out: outpcd by ldrs and no imp wl over 1f out: no ex fnl f* **15/8**[1]

0 **5** *nse* **Days In May (IRE)**[21] 5449 3-8-7 0 .... AntiocoMurgia(5) 7 57+
(Edward Vaughan) *hld up: pushed along over 2f out: styd on fr over 1f out: nvr trbld ldrs* **33/1**

6 *½* **Belenkaya (USA)** 3-8-12 0 .... AhmedAjtebi 2 56+
(Mahmood Al Zarooni) *hld up: outpcd 3f out: styd on fnl f: nvr able to go pce to trble ldrs* **5/1**[3]

005- **7** *2 ¼* **Arisea (IRE)**[107] 3669 8-9-3 44 .... FrederikTylicki 9 51
(James Moffatt) *midfield: u.p and outpcd 3f out: nvr a danger* **28/1**

8 *hd* **Soho Star** 3-8-12 0 .... MartinDwyer 11 50
(Gerard Butler) [illegible] *struggling 3f out: nvr on terms* **16/1**

-00 **9** *2 ¼* **Polly McGinty**[129] 1985 3-8-12 0 .... (t) RoystonFfrench 3 45
(Nicky Vaughan) *chsd ldrs tl rdn and wknd wl over 1f out:* **50/1**

000- **10** *9* **Georgina Bailey (IRE)**[323] 7197 3-8-9 49 .... MartinHarley(3) 1 24
(Alan McCabe) *hld up: toiling 3f out: nvr on terms* **66/1**

1m 50.29s (-0.21) **Going Correction** -0.10s/f (Stan)
WFA 3 from 4yo+ 5lb 10 Ran SP% **120.6**
Speed ratings (Par 100): **96,93,91,89,89 88,86,86,84,76**
toteswingers:1&2:£4.00, 1&3:£6.60, 2&3:£3.10 CSF £27.08 TOTE £9.10: £2.50, £1.10, £1.40; EX 32.10.
Owner D I Perry **Bred** Rabbah Bloodstock Ltd **Trained** Westow, N Yorks

FOCUS
A 73-rated runner hammered her rivals under a front-running ride in this fillies' maiden. It was steadily run and the form is only modest.

6138 HAPPY BIRTHDAY DIANE HENNESSEY H'CAP 7f 32y(P)
8:50 (8:50) (Class 6) (0-65,64) 3-Y-O+ £1,567 (£462; £231) Stalls High

Form RPR
2340 **1** **Jonnie Skull (IRE)**[2] 6070 5-8-13 **56** .... (vt) KierenFallon 6 65
(Phil McEntee) *mde all: rdn over 1f out: edgd lft ins fnl f: a doing enough cl home* **8/1**

0356 **2** *½* **Carcinetto (IRE)**[6] 5924 9-9-6 **63** .... SilvestreDeSousa 11 71
(David Evans) *a.p: rdn over 2f out: r.o towards fin but nvr gng to get there* **13/2**

06 **3** *1* **Eastern Gift**[13] 5740 6-9-5 **62** .... RobertWinston 1 67
(Gay Kelleway) *hld up: rdn and hdwy over 1f out: styd on towards fin* **8/1**

0121 **4** *nk* **Ellies Image**[14] 5674 4-9-6 **63** .... CathyGannon 10 67
(Brian Baugh) *dwlt: bhd: hdwy on outer over 1f out: styd on and edgd lft whn chsng ldrs ins fnl f: one pce fnl strides* **4/1**[2]

0600 **5** *shd* **Global Village (IRE)**[162] 1198 6-9-4 **64** .... RyanClark(3) 5 68
(Michael Blake) *midfield: rdn and hdwy on inner 2f out: effrt over 1f out: styd on same pce fnl 75yds* **3/1**[1]

5040 **6** *1 ½* **Itsthursdayalready**[7] 5881 4-8-11 **57** .... MartinHarley(3) 8 57
(Mark Brisbourne) *hld up in midfield: rdn over 2f out: hdwy over 1f out: nt clr run briefly ins fnl f: kpt on but unable to get to ldrs* **16/1**

1000 **7** *2* **Meydan Style (USA)**[7] 5901 5-8-8 **51** .... FrederikTylicki 2 46
(Bruce Hellier) *a.p: rdn over 1f out: wknd ins fnl f* **25/1**

060 **8** *3 ¼* **Yungaburra (IRE)**[11] 5787 7-9-3 **60** .... (p) SteveDrowne 9 46
(David C Griffiths) *midfield: rdn 2f out: wknd over 1f out* **66/1**

0015 **9** *1* **Gazboolou**[9] 5836 7-8-9 **57** .... JamesRogers(5) 12 40
(David Pinder) *in tch: rdn 3f out: wknd over 2f out* **9/1**

6363 **10** *1* **Piccolo Express**[7] 5901 5-8-13 **56** .... J-PGuillambert 7 37
(Brian Baugh) *chsd ldrs: rdn 2f out: wknd wl over 1f out* **6/1**[3]

2050 **11** *29* **Royal Acclamation (IRE)**[155] 1336 6-8-6 **54** .... DavidKenny(5) 3 —
(Michael Scudamore) *hld up: u.p over 3f out: wl bhd fnl 2f: t.o* **25/1**

1m 28.58s (-1.02) **Going Correction** -0.10s/f (Stan) 11 Ran SP% **119.9**
Speed ratings (Par 101): **101,100,99,98,98 97,94,91,89,88 55**
toteswingers:1&2:£9.20, 1&3:£3.30, 2&3:£3.60 CSF £59.44 CT £445.28 TOTE £10.60: £2.60, £2.90, £2.20; EX 44.10.
Owner Eventmaker Racehorses **Bred** Canice Farrell Jnr **Trained** Newmarket, Suffolk

FOCUS
A minor handicap and there was another all-the-way winner, showing his best Polytrack form since early last year. The time was good compared with the earlier 7f races.
Jonnie Skull(IRE) Official explanation: trainer said, regarding apparent improvement in form, that the gelding may have been inconvenienced by the loose ground on its previous run.
T/Plt: £177.70 to a £1 stake. Pool:£67,571.73 - 277.56 winning tickets T/Qpdt: £21.30 to a £1 stake. Pool:£9,954.90 - 344.60 winning tickets DO

6106 LISTOWEL (L-H)
Friday, September 16

OFFICIAL GOING: Flat course - heavy (soft to heavy in places) changing to heavy after race 2 (2:45); jumps courses - heavy

6139a JOHN & TERRY MORIARTY MEMORIAL H'CAP 6f 60y
2:15 (2:15) (47-65,69) 3-Y-O+ £5,056 (£1,172; £512; £293)

RPR
1 **Bonnie Acclamation (IRE)**[4] 6015 3-10-3 69 5ex .... DMGrant 12 79
(Patrick J Flynn, Ire) *sn disp ld: in front into st: forged on u.p fnl f: styd on* **5/6**[1]

2 *2* **Mountain Mama (IRE)**[25] 5335 4-9-3 53 .... (t) RPCleary 4 56
(C W J Farrell, Ire) *trckd ldrs: mod 3rd into st: chsd wnr fnl f: nt getting there and kpt on same pce clsng stages* **7/1**[2]

3 *1 ¾* **Style Majic (USA)**[66] 3965 3-8-2 47 .... SAGray(7) 5 45
(Michael F Brassil, Ire) *sn mid-div: 8th early: kpt on same pce u.p wout threatening st* **50/1**

4 *½* **If Paradise**[7] 5906 10-8-10 53 .... (p) MAEnright(7) 14 49
(Charles Coakley, Ire) *sn disp ld: 2nd into st: no ex and kpt on same pce fnl f* **16/1**

5 *¾* **Sable (IRE)**[7] 5906 5-9-2 52 .... (tp) CDHayes 13 46
(Adrian McGuinness, Ire) *trckd ldrs: mod 5th into st: sn no imp u.p: kpt on same pce* **16/1**

6 *1 ¾* **Pagan Steps (IRE)**[42] 4771 4-8-7 50 .... (p) CTKeane(7) 7 38
(Stephen Michael Cox, Ire) *chsd ldrs: 7th early: kpt on same pce u.p st* **14/1**

7 *½* **Florry Knox (IRE)**[33] 5089 3-9-10 62 .... WMLordan 9 48
(Patrick J Flynn, Ire) *towards rr: no imp and kpt on wout threatening u.p st* **9/1**

8 *1 ½* **Miss Fantastick (IRE)**[31] 5157 4-8-11 47 .... (t) BACurtis 8 29
(M McDonagh, Ire) *towards rr: no imp and kpt on wout threatening u.p st* **50/1**

9 *nk* **Polar Explorer (IRE)**[69] 3882 5-9-5 55 .... (b) FMBerry 3 36
(Niall Madden, Ire) *towards rr: no imp and kpt on wout threatening u.p st* **14/1**

10 *¾* **Tara Tartan (IRE)**[66] 3899 5-8-11 47 .... GFCarroll 2 25
(Michael Mulvany, Ire) *chsd ldrs: 6th early: no imp u.p into st* **20/1**

11 *4 ¾* **Captain James (IRE)**[126] 2080 4-8-11 47 .... MCHussey 6 10
(Emmanuel Hughes, Ire) *prom: mod 4th into st: sn no ex* **16/1**

12 *2 ¼* **Hello Man (IRE)**[46] 4621 8-9-12 62 .... (t) WJSupple 11 18
(S M Duffy, Ire) *in rr of mid-div: no ex u.p appr st* **8/1**[3]

13 *6 ½* **Under Review (IRE)**[46] 4621 5-9-10 60 .... (t) SeamieHeffernan 1 —
(Michael J Browne, Ire) *s.i.s: nvr bttr than mid-div* **14/1**

1m 29.8s (89.80)
WFA 3 from 4yo+ 2lb 13 Ran SP% **134.5**
CSF £8.31 CT £223.13 TOTE £1.80: £1.10, £2.30, £19.80; DF 9.70.
Owner Alan Macalister **Bred** J Donnelly **Trained** Carrick-On-Suir, Co Waterford
■ Stewards' Enquiry : M A Enright two-day ban: used whip with excessive frequency (Sep 30, Oct 2)

FOCUS
The winner was chucked in under a small penalty and plenty of his rivals looked exposed.

NOTEBOOK
Bonnie Acclamation(IRE), raised 16lb for his seven-and-a-half length win over the course and distance four days previously, was a warm order here with only a mandatory 5lb penalty to contend with and with the form of Monday's win having been boosted by the third winning since. The tactics used were similar to those employed on Monday and although his high draw appeared a possible negative, he was soon disputing the lead before forging ahead on the final bend. Kept up to his work, he was never in any real danger. Expect to see him bid for a hat-trick before long.\ (op 9/10 tchd 1/1)
Mountain Mama(IRE), winner of a maiden over the same trip on easy ground at Leopardstown two seasons back, had failed to trouble the judge since and, while her run at Cork last month was mildly encouraging, she was down 2lb here. Soon close up, she threw down a sustained challenge in the straight and kept on for second well inside the final furlong without ever threatening the winner. (op 10/1)
Style Majic(USA), tailed off over 1m at Dundalk on her handicap debut in July, fared better for this drop down in trip. She made headway in the straight and kept on for pressure to take third place close home. (op 33/1)
If Paradise, a six-time winner but without a victory for over two years, has been dropping gradually down the ratings. This ground was more testing than anything he had won on and after racing prominently and vying for the lead for much of the journey, he came under pressure in second turning for home and could raise no extra from over 1f out.
Sable(IRE), whose only first-three placing was achieved in the same race a year ago, had cheekpieces on here. She chased the leading group and kept plugging away without ever posing a threat. (op 16/1 tchd 14/1)

6140 - 6143a (Foreign Racing) - See Raceform Interactive

[6110]AYR (L-H)

Saturday, September 17

OFFICIAL GOING: Soft (heavy in places in back straight; overall 8.0; sprint course: far side 7.7, centre 7.7, stands' side 7.6)
Wind: Fresh, half-against. Weather: Cloudy

6144 JACKY MCKINNON 50TH BIRTHDAY NURSERY 1m

1:40 (1:40) (Class 2) 2-Y-O

£6,847 (£2,050; £1,025; £512; £256; £128) **Stalls** Low

Form RPR

361 **1** **Zakreet**[19] 5548 2-9-5 **79**.................... PhillipMakin 2 86
(Kevin Ryan) *mde virtually all: rdn 2f out: kpt on strly fnl f* **5/1**

1 **2** 2 ¾ **Montaser (IRE)**[39] 4884 2-9-5 **79**.................... SilvestreDeSousa 10 80
(David Simcock) *hld up: effrt and edgd lft fr 2f out: kpt on to chse wnr wl ins fnl f: kpt on* **11/4**[1]

2044 **3** *nk* **Joshua The First**[16] 5645 2-8-10 **70**.................... DavidAllan 1 70
(Keith Dalgleish) *trckd ldrs: effrt over 2f out: chsd wnr over 1f out to wl ins fnl f: one pce* **12/1**

1541 **4** 3 ½ **Risky Art**[28] 5287 2-9-4 **81**.................... JPO'Brien(3) 3 74
(Michael Easterby) *in tch: effrt and drifted rt 2f out: kpt on same pce fnl f* **10/3**[2]

3013 **5** 1 ¼ **Loyal Master (IRE)**[19] 5550 2-9-2 **76**.................... LeeNewman 9 66
(George Foster) *cl up tl rdn and no ex over 1f out* **17/2**

2410 **6** 3 **Holy Roman Warrior (IRE)**[28] 5287 2-9-3 **77**.................... PaulHanagan 5 60
(Richard Fahey) *t.k.h: hld up in tch: rdn over 2f out: edgd lft: wknd over 1f out* **9/2**[3]

0343 **7** 7 **Rano Pano (USA)**[18] 5597 2-7-13 **62** ow3.................... BillyCray(3) 6 30
(Brian Ellison) *bhd and sn pushed along: rdn 3f out: btn over 1f out* **16/1**

0622 **8** 1 ¾ **Make Up**[11] 5802 2-7-10 **59** oh2 ow1.................... NataliaGemelova(3) 11 23
(Noel Wilson) *cl up on outside: rdn over 2f out: wknd over 1f out* **25/1**

1m 48.84s (5.04) **Going Correction** +0.475s/f (Yiel) **8** Ran SP% **112.5**
Speed ratings (Par 101): **93,90,89,86,85 82,75,73**
Tote Swingers:1&2:£4.00, 2&3:£6.40, 1&3:£7.40 CSF £18.52 CT £154.20 TOTE £5.40: £1.70, £1.80, £2.70; EX 20.50.
Owner Mubarak Al Naimi **Bred** M R M Bloodstock 3 **Trained** Hambleton, N Yorks

FOCUS

The bends were 4m out adding approximately 12 yards to race distances on the round course. The ground had eased further overnight and was officially changed to soft, heavy in places in the back straight, but the juveniles in the first seemed to go through it reasonably well even if the time was over 10secs outside standard. This race has thrown up several decent performers amongst its winners. The 2004 winner Comic Strip found fame as Viva Pataca when exported to Hong Kong, while Smokey Oakey went on to win the Lincoln. This looked just a fair renewal and the field raced centre to far side in the straight. Straightforward form.

NOTEBOOK

Zakreet ◆, a 7f soft-ground maiden winner on his third start, was making his handicap debut off 79. He made the running and, although challenged by several in the last 2f, found plenty for pressure to draw away in the final furlong. He clearly relishes soft conditions and might be able to complete the hat-trick on similar going. (op 9-2)

Montaser(IRE), a half-brother to four winners from the family of Zilzal, beat a more experienced subsequent winner on his debut over 1m on fast ground last month. He was short of room 3f out but got in the clear and appeared to have his chance inside the last quarter-mile before his effort flattened out. (op 3-1, tchd 10-3 in a place)

Joshua The First came into this having had ten starts without winning, but had posted a good effort off this mark last time. Stepping up in trip, he ran pretty well but was unable to hold the less-exposed pair. (tchd 14-1)

Risky Art, the winner of 1m nursery last time on good, was 6lb higher and came nearest the stands' side in the straight, but did not pick up in the ground. (op 11-4)

Loyal Master(IRE) had gained both his wins over an extended 7f at Beverley, one on fast, one on soft. He was ridden to race prominently from the start, but weakened entering the closing stages. (op 10-1 tchd 8-1)

Holy Roman Warrior(IRE), runner-up here on his debut to subsequent sales-race winner Bogart, had since won a 7f maiden on easy ground. He had a lot to find with Risky Art on York nursery form although 9lb better off, and never really got involved having been held up. (op 6-1)

6145 WILLIAM HILL AYR SILVER CUP (H'CAP) 6f

2:15 (2:15) (Class 2) 3-Y-O+

£21,787 (£6,524; £3,262; £1,631; £815; £409) **Stalls** Centre

Form RPR

0004 **1** **Cheveton**[14] 5706 7-8-11 **87**.................... DaleSwift(3) 21 100
(Richard Price) *mde all stands' side: rdn over 1f out: edgd lft: kpt on wl fnl f: 1st of 13 in gp* **12/1**[3]

1041 **2** ½ **Marvellous Value (IRE)**[15] 5682 6-9-2 **89** 5ex.................... LiamKeniry 24 100
(Michael Dods) *hld up in tch stands' side: effrt over 1f out: kpt on wl fnl f: 2nd of 13 in gp* **20/1**

0040 **3** 1 ¼ **Advanced**[9] 5852 8-9-0 **90**.................... AmyRyan(3) 14 97
(Kevin Ryan) *racd alone in centre: rdn and hung lft 2f out: kpt on same pce wl ins fnl f* **25/1**

650 **4** *shd* **Maarek**[34] 5086 4-9-2 **89**.................... AndrewElliott 15 96
(David Peter Nagle, Ire) *prom on outside of stands' side gp: effrt and drifted lft fr over 1f out: kpt on fnl f: 3rd of 13 in gp* **25/1**

0006 **5** *hd* **Mass Rally (IRE)**[13] 5758 4-9-1 **88**....................(v) DanielTudhope 17 94
(Michael Dods) *bhd stands' side: effrt on outside of gp 2f out: kpt on fnl f: nrst fin: 4th of 13 in gp* **28/1**

012 **6** ½ **Mirza**[22] 5430 4-9-2 **89**.................... AdamKirby 22 93
(Rae Guest) *in tch stands' side: effrt 2f out: hung lft fnl f: kpt on same pce: 5th of 13 in gp* **12/1**[3]

3151 **7** ¾ **Bertiewhittle**[35] 5054 3-9-1 **90**.................... FMBerry 4 92+
(David Barron) *hld up bhd ldng gp far side: effrt over 2f out: led that gp ins fnl f: nt rch stands' side ldrs: 1st of 10 in gp* **13/2**[1]

0042 **8** ½ **Prime Exhibit**[15] 5684 6-9-0 **90**.................... LeeTopliss(3) 12 90
(Richard Fahey) *racd on outside of far side gp: hld up in tch: effrt and cl up over 1f out: kpt on same pce fnl f: 2nd of 10 in gp* **16/1**

0053 **9** 1 **Fathsta (IRE)**[8] 5887 6-9-4 **91**.................... SilvestreDeSousa 18 88
(David Simcock) *cl up stands' side gp: rdn over 2f out: one pce over 1f out: 6th of 13 in gp* **8/1**[2]

5110 **10** *shd* **Grissom (IRE)**[8] 5887 5-9-5 **92**.................... DavidAllan 11 89
(Tim Easterby) *prom on outside of far side gp: rdn and ev ch over 1f out: kpt on same pce ins fnl f: 3rd of 10 in gp* **12/1**[3]

5040 **11** *nk* **Joseph Henry**[13] 5758 9-9-0 **90**.................... MichaelO'Connell(3) 10 86
(David Nicholls) *cl up far side: led that gp 1/2-way to ins fnl f: one pce: 4th of 10 in gp* **40/1**

0005 **12** *hd* **Arctic Feeling (IRE)**[28] 5288 3-8-8 **90**.................... LauraBarry(7) 2 85
(Richard Fahey) *prom far side gp: rdn over 2f out: no ex over 1f out: 5th of 10 in gp* **50/1**

2000 **13** *shd* **Tax Free (IRE)**[7] 5927 9-9-8 **95**.................... AdrianNicholls 19 90
(David Nicholls) *hld up stands' side: effrt and drvn over 2f out: no imp over 1f out: 7th of 13 in gp* **20/1**

-000 **14** *nk* **Gallagher**[14] 5703 5-9-1 **88**.................... TedDurcan 26 82
(Ruth Carr) *dwlt: bhd stands' side: rdn over 2f out: kpt on fnl f: no imp: 8th of 13 in gp* **50/1**

2100 **15** 1 ¾ **Capone (IRE)**[13] 5758 6-9-1 **93**.................... LMcNiff(5) 27 81
(David Nicholls) *hld up in midfield stands' side: rdn over 2f out: btn over 1f out: 9th of 13 in gp* **40/1**

0100 **16** ¾ **Edinburgh Knight (IRE)**[35] 5060 4-9-7 **94**.................... EddieAhern 1 80
(Paul D'Arcy) *hld up in tch far side: rdn over 2f out: btn fnl f: 6th of 10 in gp* **12/1**[3]

310 **17** ½ **Valery Borzov (IRE)**[13] 5758 7-9-3 **90** 5ex....................(v) PaulHanagan 9 74
(Richard Fahey) *w far side ldrs tl rdn and no ex over 1f out: 7th of 10 in gp* **16/1**

1001 **18** 5 **Baldemar**[18] 5578 6-8-7 **87** 5ex.................... GeorgeChaloner(7) 16 55
(Richard Fahey) *cl up stands' side tl rdn and wknd wl over 1f out: 10th of 13 in gp* **33/1**

0662 **19** *nk* **Sioux Rising (IRE)**[29] 5255 5-9-6 **96**.................... JPO'Brien(3) 7 63
(Richard Fahey) *in tch far side tl rdn and wknd wl over 1f out: 11th of 13 in gp* **20/1**

0342 **20** 1 ¾ **Parisian Pyramid (IRE)**[13] 5758 5-9-6 **93**.................... PhillipMakin 3 55
(Kevin Ryan) *led far side to 1/2-way: struggling fnl 2f: 12th of 13 in gp* **8/1**[2]

4135 **21** 4 ½ **El Viento (FR)**[37] 4965 3-9-4 **93**....................(b) TonyHamilton 25 40
(Richard Fahey) *chsd stands' side ldrs: rdn 1/2-way: wknd fnl 2f: 11th of 13 in gp* **40/1**

0621 **22** *nk* **Elusive Prince**[19] 5559 3-9-1 **90** 5ex....................(v) LeeNewman 23 37
(David Barron) *towards rr stands' side: drvn along 1/2-way: nvr on terms: 12th of 13 in gp* **14/1**

0046 **23** 1 ¼ **Rodrigo De Torres**[4] 6027 4-9-5 **95**....................(p) MartinHarley(3) 20 38
(Mrs K Burke) *chsd stands' side ldrs tl rdn and wknd over 2f out: last of 13 in gp* **50/1**

0300 **24** 2 **Ginger Ted (IRE)**[31] 5180 4-9-1 **88**....................(b) DarryllHolland 13 24
(Richard Guest) *t.k.h: hld up in tch far side: rdn and wknd over 2f out: eased whn btn fnl f: last of 10 in gp* **18/1**

1m 16.17s (3.77) **Going Correction** +0.775s/f (Yiel)
WFA 3 from 4yo+ 2lb **24** Ran SP% **131.6**
Speed ratings (Par 109): **105,104,102,102,102 101,100,99,98,98 98,97,97,97,94 93,93,86,86,83 77,77,75,73**
Tote Swingers:1&2:£72.90, 2&3:£70.20, 1&3:£47.70 CSF £240.63 CT £5884.65 TOTE £13.50: £3.30, £7.80, £5.90, £6.80; EX 563.50 Trifecta £1890.00 Part won. Pool £2,554.17 - 0.10 winning units..
Owner Mrs K Oseman **Bred** Miss K Rausing **Trained** Ullingswick, H'fords
■ Stewards' Enquiry : Adam Kirby four-day ban: used whip with excessive frequency without giving gelding time to respond (Oct 1,3-5)

FOCUS

They split into two main groups, while Advanced, the eventual third, came up the middle of the course alone. Those racing stands' side had the edge over the far-side group at the finish. Cheveton showed similar form to last year's Bronze Cup. The form is sound among the principals, but not many gave their running in the ground and those on the far side could rate 10lb+ higher at face value.

NOTEBOOK

Cheveton won the Bronze Cup last year and got to race off just a 2lb higher mark this time around. He'd hinted at a return to form at Haydock last time and, with the ground more in his favour here, returned to his best, holding a position in the front rank all along and staying on strongly. He followed up in the 5f Lester Piggott 'Start To Finish' Handicap at Haydock last year, beating Hoof It into second, and it wouldn't be a surprise to see him try and repeat the feat.

Marvellous Value(IRE), penalised for his win at Haydock last time, was fifth in this race in 2008 prior to almost two years on the sidelines. He travelled strongly in behind the winner and kept on well, but just couldn't get past him. Although he doesn't want the ground fast, in an ideal world he might not want it this testing either. (op 18-1)

Advanced, a previous Ayr Gold Cup winner and fourth in this race last year, got to race off 5lb lower this time around. Making his own way up the centre of the track proved far from a disadvantage and he ran another fine race in defeat. (op 28-1)

Maarek, who raced on the outer of the stands' side group, drifted left under pressure but kept on well to record a career-best effort. The ground really suited him.

Mass Rally(IRE), who has not always looked the most straightforward, has done most of his racing over further and, predictably, he was putting in his best work at the finish.

Mirza was given the full treatment - his rider got four days for excessive frequency - but he couldn't quite take advantage of being 2lb well in following his second at Ffos Las last time out.

Bertiewhittle, a well-supported favourite, won his race on his side and was just unlucky to be in the wrong group. He remains firmly on the upgrade and quite capable of winning off his new mark. (op 7-1, tchd 15-2 in a place)

Prime Exhibit, who raced towards the outer of the far-side group, had ground conditions to suit and came out second best on his side. His best trip is 7f, though. (tchd 18-1)

Fathsta(IRE) looked to be on a competitive mark and had every chance 2f out before weakening. (op 9-1)

Grissom(IRE) was another who didn't quite get home in the testing ground. (op 16-1)

Joseph Henry's style of running means he's there to be shot at in these big handicaps.

Arctic Feeling(IRE) didn't run badly given that this trip on this ground would have been testing his stamina to the limit.

Edinburgh Knight(IRE), who raced on the 'wrong' side, shouldn't be judged too harshly as he probably found conditions too soft. (tchd 11-1 and 14-1 in a place)

Parisian Pyramid(IRE) Official explanation: jockey said gelding never travelled

6146 LAUNDRY COTTAGE STUD FIRTH OF CLYDE STKS (GROUP 3) (FILLIES) 6f

2:45 (2:48) (Class 1) 2-Y-O

£31,190 (£11,825; £5,918; £2,948; £1,479; £742) **Stalls** Centre

Form RPR

1044 **1** **Roger Sez (IRE)**[9] 5847 2-8-12 86....................(b[1]) DavidAllan 11 106
(Tim Easterby) *mid-div: effrt and swtchd outside 2f out: styd on wl to ld jst ins fnl f: drvn clr: eased towards fin* **14/1**

1002 **2** 4 **Miss Work Of Art**[30] 5216 2-8-12 98.................... PaulHanagan 6 95
(Richard Fahey) *w ldrs: drvn over 2f out: led over 1f out: hdd jst ins fnl f: no ex* **9/4**[1]

136 **3** 3 ¼ **Mary Fildes (IRE)**[16] 5656 2-8-12 94.................... LiamKeniry 9 86
(J S Moore) *in rr: hdwy on outer over 2f out: kpt on fnl f: tk 3rd nr line* **6/1**[2]

1352 **4** *nk* **Misty Conquest (IRE)**[16] 5656 2-8-12 97.................... RichardKingscote 4 85
(Tom Dascombe) *chsd ldrs: upsides over 2f out: kpt on ins fnl f to snatch 4th nr line* **6/1**[2]

3140 **5** *hd* **Miss Lahar**[8] 5882 2-8-12 95.. MartinHarley 2 85
(Mick Channon) *w ldrs: chal over 1f out: wknd and lost 2 pls nr line* **16/1**

4031 **6** *2¾* **Kune Kune**[34] 5077 2-8-12 85.............................. SilvestreDeSousa 8 77
(Marco Botti) *dwlt: sn trcking ldrs: hung lft and wknd over 1f out: fin 7th: plcd 6th* **13/2**[3]

4244 **7** *2* **Luv U Forever**[4] 6042 2-8-12 95.............................. DarryllHolland 10 72
(Jo Hughes) *chsd ldrs: drvn and lost pl over 3f out: fin 8th: plcd 7th* **10/1**

1 **8** *1* **Cafe Express (IRE)**[54] 4377 2-8-12 74.............................. FMBerry 5 69
(Linda Perratt) *dwlt: in rr whn hmpd over 3f out: nvr on terms: fin 9th: plcd 8th* **33/1**

621 **9** *1¼* **Princess Of Orange**[11] 5812 2-8-12 86.............................. TedDurcan 3 65
(Rae Guest) *dwlt: in rr: hdwy over 2f out: lost pl and heavily eased appr fnl f: fin 10th: plcd 9th* **15/2**

5210 **D** *4½* **Besito (IRE)**[9] 5847 2-8-12 83.............................. EddieAhern 7 71
(William Jarvis) *led tl hdd & wknd over 1f out: fin 6th: disqualified: jockey failed to weigh in* **14/1**

1m 17.71s (5.31) **Going Correction** +0.775s/f (Yiel) **10** Ran SP% **115.7**
Speed ratings (Par 102): **95,89,85,84,84 75,72,71,69,78**
Tote Swingers:1&2:£13.90, 2&3:£4.30, 1&3:£13.30 CSF £45.34 TOTE £17.70: £3.50, £1.40, £2.30; EX 45.50 Trifecta £610.50 Part won. Pool £825.04 - 0.20 winning units..
Owner R Sidebottom **Bred** B Kennedy **Trained** Great Habton, N Yorks
■ Stewards' Enquiry : Eddie Ahern three-day ban: failed to weigh-in (Oct 1,3-4)

FOCUS
This Group 3 has proved a career highlight for the majority of its recent winners, but it did throw up the Nell Gwyn winner Misterah and Temple Stakes heroine Airwave early in the century. This year's contest may not have been the strongest although it looked a pretty competitive affair on paper. However it was turned into a procession by the winner. Few showed their form in the ground, but Roger Sez is amongst the better winners of this race as rated.

NOTEBOOK
Roger Sez(IRE), a three-time previous winner - once at 5f on easy ground, twice at 6f on fast - had since posted a fair effort in Listed company on easy ground, but was up in grade here. However, blinkered for the first time, she picked up really well from the back when asked and once in front drew right away. She had a fair amount to do on the ratings beforehand and it remains to be seen if the headgear works as well next time, but that said it is job done as far as her breeding prospects are concerned. (op 16-1)
Miss Work Of Art had won her first three over 5f, including in Listed company, and posted a good effort behind Bogart in a sales race last time over 6f on easy ground. That made her the pick on ratings and she had every chance, but could not go with the winner. (op 5-2 tchd 11-4)
Mary Fildes(IRE), a winner on her debut over an extended 5f on fast ground, had finished third in a Listed race at Newbury next time but was a little disappointing in similar event over 6f on her latest start. Untried on soft, she ran on late to snatch the minor placing but never threatened to win. (op 9-1)
Misty Conquest(IRE), a dual 6f winner on fast ground and placed twice in Listed company since (once on easy ground) made the early running but looked set to drop away when headed only to rally in the last furlong. On this evidence she might be worth another go at 7f. (op 5-1)
Miss Lahar, whose only win came on easy ground over 5f following a third in a Group 3 at Ascot, showed up for a good way but was just run out of the placings near the finish. A return to 5f looks likely if she runs again this season.
Kune Kune got off the mark at fourth attempt over 5f on fast ground, but she was up in trip and grade and untried on softer than good, and never figured. Silvestre De Sousa reported that the filly hung left in the final 2f. Official explanation: jockey said filly hung left final 2f (tchd 7-1)
Luv U Forever Official explanation: jockey said filly lost its action
Princess Of Orange Official explanation: jockey said filly had no more to give
Besito(IRE)'s rider failed to weigh in after the race and picked up a three-day ban.

6147 WILLIAM HILL AYR GOLD CUP (HERITAGE H'CAP) 6f
3:20 (3:22) (Class 2) 3-Y-O+

£74,700 (£22,368; £11,184; £5,592; £2,796; £1,404) **Stalls** Centre

Form RPR

0562 **1** **Our Jonathan**[35] 5060 4-9-6 105.............................. FrannyNorton 12 117
(Kevin Ryan) *hld up on outside of far side gp: gd hdwy to ld over 1f out: kpt on strly fnl f: 1st of 11 in gp* **11/1**[3]

5413 **2** *2* **Eton Rifles (IRE)**[14] 5699 6-9-3 102 5ex.............................. TedDurcan 16 108
(David Elsworth) *in tch stands' side: effrt 2f out: led that gp ins fnl f: kpt on wl: nt pce of wnr: 1st of 15 in gp* **6/1**[1]

[illegible] **3** *1½* **Son Of The Cat (USA)**[7] [illegible] 5-9-0 99 (t) SilvestreDeSousa 9 101
(Brian Gubby) *hld up on outside of far side gp: effrt and hdwy 2f out: kpt on fnl f: 2nd of 11 in gp* **18/1**

2061 **4** *nk* **Colonel Mak**[22] 5430 4-9-0 99 5ex.............................. LeeNewman 15 100
(David Barron) *led stands' side tl hung lft and hdd ins fnl f: kpt on: 2nd of 15 in gp* **16/1**

5664 **5** *nse* **Pastoral Player**[14] 5699 4-9-4 103.............................. DarryllHolland 22 103+
(Hughie Morrison) *hld up stands' side: n.m.r briefly over 1f out: gd hdwy fnl f: nrst fin: 3rd of 15 in gp* **18/1**

0000 **6** *½* **Evens And Odds (IRE)**[35] 5060 7-8-8 98..................(t) JulieBurke[(5)] 19 97
(Kevin Ryan) *cl up stands' side: rdn over 2f out: kpt on same pce over 1f out: 4th of 15 in gp* **33/1**

0063 **7** *½* **Croisultan (IRE)**[6] 5979 5-9-1 100.............................. NGMcCullagh 7 97
(Liam McAteer, Ire) *led far side gp to over 1f out: outpcd ins fnl f: 3rd of 11 in gp* **10/1**[2]

2500 **8** *2¼* **Waffle (IRE)**[7] 5927 5-9-6 105..............................(v) PhillipMakin 17 96
(David Barron) *hld up stands' side: rdn and hdwy over 1f out: kpt on fnl f: 5th of 15 in gp* **20/1**

5200 **9** *½* **Tajneed (IRE)**[35] 5060 8-9-1 103.............................. MichaelO'Connell[(3)] 21 92
(David Nicholls) *prom stands' side: rdn over 2f out: kpt on same pce fr over 1f out: 6th of 15 in gp* **25/1**

-410 **10** *½* **Hawkeyethenoo (IRE)**[56] 4314 5-9-2 104.............................. GaryBartley[(3)] 20 92+
(Jim Goldie) *hld up in midfield stands' side: rdn over 2f out: nvr able to chal: 7th of 15 in gp* **12/1**

3040 **11** *nk* **Regal Parade**[28] 5282 7-9-9 108.............................. AdrianNicholls 27 95
(David Nicholls) *bhd stands' side: drvn along 1/2-way: sme late hdwy: nvr able to chal: 8th of 15 in gp* **12/1**

0103 **12** *nk* **High Standing (USA)**[20] 5510 6-9-1 100.....................(p) TonyCulhane 6 86
(William Haggas) *hld up far side: effrt and hdwy over 1f out: kpt on same pce fnl f: 4th of 11 in gp* **20/1**

0102 **13** *½* **Majestic Myles (IRE)**[28] 5282 3-9-7 111.............................. JPO'Brien[(3)] 10 95
(Richard Fahey) *prom far side: drvn over 2f out: no ex over 1f out: 5th of 11 in gp* **25/1**

1064 **14** *½* **Ancient Cross**[7] 5927 7-9-1 100..............................(t) PaddyAspell 13 83
(Michael Easterby) *upset in stalls: dwlt: bhd stands' side: rdn and hdwy over 1f out: n.d: 9th of 15 in gp* **28/1**

6050 **15** *½* **Breathless Kiss (USA)**[10] 5827 4-8-10 98.................... AmyRyan[(3)] 26 79
(Kevin Ryan) *bhd stands' side: drvn 1/2-way: nvr able to chal: 10th of 15 in gp* **66/1**

1010 **16** *2¼* **Dungannon**[7] 5927 4-9-0 99.............................. LiamKeniry 18 74
(Andrew Balding) *hld up stands' side: rdn wl over 1f out: sn wknd: 11th of 15 in gp* **20/1**

1000 **17** *1½* **Light From Mars**[77] 3645 6-8-11 99.............................. DaleSwift[(3)] 2 69
(John Quinn) *cl up far side: rdn over 2f out: wknd over 1f out: 6th of 11 in gp* **50/1**

-003 **18** *½* **Kaldoun Kingdom (IRE)**[105] 2727 6-8-10 98................ LeeTopliss[(3)] 4 67
(Richard Fahey) *prom far side tl rdn and wknd over 1f out: 7th of 11 in gp* **16/1**

4650 **19** *1¼* **Anne Of Kiev (IRE)**[10] 5827 6-9-1 100..............................(t) AdamKirby 25 65
(Jeremy Gask) *bhd stands' side: rdn over 2f out: sn btn: 12th of 15 in gp* **28/1**

0004 **20** *¾* **Castles In The Air**[8] 5887 6-8-6 98.............................. GeorgeChaloner[(7)] 1 61
(Richard Fahey) *cl up far side: drvn along over 2f out: wknd over 1f out: 8th of 11 in gp* **40/1**

26-3 **21** *1¾* **Mayson**[35] 5060 3-8-13 100.............................. PaulHanagan 5 57
(Richard Fahey) *hld up far side: hdwy over 2f out: rdn and wknd over 1f out: 9th of 11 in gp* **14/1**

0111 **22** *1* **Pepper Lane**[35] 5060 4-9-4 103.............................. DanielTudhope 11 57
(David O'Meara) *cl up far side tl rdn and wknd 2f out: 10th of 11 in gp* **14/1**

0000 **23** *¾* **Brave Prospector**[21] 5474 6-8-12 97.............................. TonyHamilton 3 49
(Richard Fahey) *hld up far side: rdn over 2f out: sn btn: last of 11 in gp* **40/1**

0542 **24** *½* **Darajaat (USA)**[34] 5080 3-8-13 100.............................. RoystonFfrench 14 51
(Marcus Tregoning) *cl up stands' side tl rdn and wknd over 1f out: 13th of 15 in gp* **40/1**

0334 **25** *10* **Mac's Power (IRE)**[21] 5481 5-9-1 100..............................(t) EddieAhern 8 21
(James Fanshawe) *sn swtchd to r on outside of stands' side gp: hld up: rdn over 2f out: sn btn: 14th of 15 in gp* **12/1**

2310 **26** *6* **Below Zero (IRE)**[8] 5887 4-8-13 98 5ex.............................. FMBerry 23 1
(Mark Johnston) *cl up stands' side tl wknd over 2f out: eased whn no ch fnl f: last of 15 in gp* **28/1**

1m 15.35s (2.95) **Going Correction** +0.775s/f (Yiel)
WFA 3 from 4yo+ 2lb **26** Ran SP% **136.4**
Speed ratings (Par 109): **111,108,106,105,105 105,104,101,100,100 99,99,98,98,97 94,92,91,90,89 86,85,84,83,70 62**
Tote Swingers:1&2:£30.20, 2&3:£73.00, 1&3:£30.60 CSF £66.47 CT £1252.69 TOTE £14.40: £3.30, £2.00, £5.00, £5.80; EX 75.10 Trifecta £4074.60 Pool £37,883.34 - 6.88 winning units..
Owner Dr Marwan Koukash **Bred** W G M Turner **Trained** Hambleton, N Yorks

FOCUS
One of the top sprint handicaps of the season with nearly two thirds of the field rated 100 or more and highly competitive, with two consolation races for those not making the cut also run at the meeting. The field split into two almost even groups but the winner, third and sixth raced far side, while the second, fourth and fifth raced in the bunch towards the stands' rail. The time was 0.82secs faster than the earlier Silver Cup. A smart effort from the winner, but the ground was bad and there may be a doubt about him repeating this.

NOTEBOOK
Our Jonathan, winner of a 7f Chester handicap in May but 10lb higher here, had put up a good effort when second to Pepper Lane in the Great St Wilfrid and was 5lb better off with that filly here. Held up on the far side early, he got a good lead into the race and once he struck the front the result was never in doubt. He is clearly in good form at present and will go to Ascot for a valuable 7f handicap following this emphatic success. (op 14-1)
Eton Rifles(IRE), a four-time winner at 6-7f who has won on heavy, has been running well for his new yard and travelled strongly into the race, but he could make no impression on the winner racing on the other side of the track in the latter stages. He has risen 8lb in the handicap as a result of those recent efforts, but it probably did not make the difference between winning and finishing runner-up this time. (op 8-1, tchd 10-1 in a place)
Son Of The Cat(USA) had been in decent form in Listed company on easy ground of late and the flat track suited. He handled the heavy ground, coming out of the pack in the wake of the winner, and this was a decent effort. (op 22-1)
Colonel Mak is suited by some ease and won the Silver Cup here last year when he had scored on his previous start. Following a similar pattern again, he was up with the pace all the way in the stands' side group, and only gave best inside the last furlong.
Pastoral Player ◆ had gained all his wins at 6f on a sound surface but finished third in the Wokingham on soft (his only previous try on it). Held up out the back, he was noted running on really well in the latter stages, just missing out on a place in the frame. There is a race to be won with him on this surface and he may take on Our Jonathan at Ascot. (tchd 10-1)
Evens And Odds(IRE) won the Stewards' Cup in 2010 (still 2lb higher here) and was fourth in this race in 2009, his best run in three attempts. He put up another sound effort under a positive ride.
Croisultan(IRE) has not won for well over a year but is well suited by soft ground and this trip, and finished a good third in a 6f Group 3 on soft last time. He went for home on the far side around 2f from home, but only succeeded in providing the winner with a tow into the race and had nothing in reserve when challenged. This was still a creditable run. (op 14-1)
Waffle(IRE) has not won since his debut back in 2008 but has run lots of decent races since, including finishing a neck second to Deacon Blues in the Wokingham. Racing off 5lb higher and wearing a visor for the second time, he raced more towards the centre than most and could never get close enough to land a blow. (tchd 25-1 in a place)
Tajneed(IRE), runner-up to Regal Parade in this on heavy ground in 2008 and 2lb better off here, had gained all four wins in this country over 6f at Ripon but had not scored for over a year and was still 6lb above that last winning mark. He ran his race, but could not find any extra in the last couple of furlongs.
Hawkeyethenoo(IRE) won the Victoria Cup over 7f in May, but he was 8lb higher here and had been beaten off this mark since. He might need that extra furlong judging by the way he finished. (op 14-1)
Regal Parade, the 2008 winner, was taking his chance again, having gone on to win at Group 1 level twice in the meantime. He was having his first run in a handicap since, but was still rated 9lb higher and struggled to go the pace early before staying on late. (op 14-1)
High Standing(USA) is best at 6f and won a Group 3 on soft in the past, but he had a bit to find with a couple of these on Wokingham form and ran reasonably without offering a major threat.
Majestic Myles(IRE) has a good strike-rate (5-12 coming into this) and has continued his progression this season, winning twice, including in Listed company. However, all that form was on good and fast ground, so in the circumstances he performed reasonably under top weight.
Ancient Cross Official explanation: jockey said gelding hit its head on the gates causing it to be slowly away
Anne Of Kiev(IRE) Official explanation: trainer's rep said mare was unsuited by the soft ground
Mayson, a lightly raced 3yo but Listed placed and third in the Great St Wilfrid on his belated reappearance, was better off with Pepper Lane and Our Jonathan here, but failed to get involved, having been held up in the same group as that pair.
Pepper Lane has been a highly progressive filly this season, having won four times and gone up 29lb since scoring on her reappearance. She had beaten several of these in the Great St Wilfrid, but was 8lb higher here and, not helped by anticipating the start and rearing slightly as the gates opened, might have found conditions softer than ideal. The stewards noted the trainer could offer no explanation for the filly's performance and they ordered her to be routine tested. Official explanation: trainer had no explanation for the poor form shown (tchd 16-1)

Mac's Power(IRE) finished third in Stewards' Cup, but he had a bit to find with a couple of these on Wokingham form. He was drawn low in stall 8, but his rider took the decision to come stands' side, which he may have subsequently regretted as the winner and third were drawn higher than he was and raced far side. Official explanation: jockey said gelding was unsuited by the soft ground

6148 ERIC GUNN, THURSO - 50TH BIRTHDAY CELEBRATION H'CAP 7f 50y

3:55 (3:56) (Class 3) (0-95,92) 3-Y-O+

£6,225 (£1,864; £932; £466; £233; £117) **Stalls** High

Form RPR

6100 **1** **Xilerator (IRE)**[19] 5557 4-9-4 **89** AdrianNicholls 6 105
(David Nicholls) *mde all: styd on strly to forge clr fnl f* **12/1**

0425 **2** *5* **Staff Sergeant**[2] 6078 4-8-7 **78** oh1 LeeNewman 11 81
(Jim Goldie) *trckd wnr: chal over 2f out: kpt on same pce appr fnl f* **13/2**[3]

5602 **3** *nk* **Mr Rainbow**[21] 5465 5-9-4 **89** SilvestreDeSousa 10 91
(Alan Swinbank) *mid-div: effrt over 2f out: styd on wl fnl f: tk 3rd towards fin* **6/1**[2]

-302 **4** *¾* **Honeymead (IRE)**[10] 5820 3-8-13 **87** PaulHanagan 4 87
(Richard Fahey) *trckd ldrs: effrt 3f out: kpt on one pce over 1f out* **9/4**[1]

1000 **5** *½* **Masked Dance (IRE)**[19] 5557 4-9-5 **90** (p) PhillipMakin 12 89
(Kevin Ryan) *trckd ldrs: edgd rt over 1f out: one pce* **16/1**

-023 **6** *3* **Silenceofthewind (USA)**[15] 5687 4-8-7 **81** ow1 MartinHarley(3) 5 72
(Mrs K Burke) *hld up in rr: keeping on whn n.m.r over 1f out: nt rch ldrs* **12/1**

4403 **7** *shd* **Silver Rime (FR)**[2] 6078 6-8-8 **84** JulieBurke(5) 9 76
(Linda Perratt) *s.i.s: effrt on outside 3f out: nvr a factor: eased and lost 6th line* **12/1**

0050 **8** *5* **Daring Dream (GER)**[2] 6079 6-8-10 **81** ow2 DanielTudhope 2 59
(Jim Goldie) *s.i.s: sn trcking ldrs: wknd over 1f out* **11/1**

5000 **9** *2½* **Lovelace**[30] 5218 7-9-4 **92** LeeTopliss(3) 8 63
(Richard Fahey) *hood removed v late: s.i.s: a in rr* **20/1**

02-1 **10** *1¾* **Mullins Way (USA)**[52] 4439 3-8-13 **87** DarryllHolland 14 54
(Jo Hughes) *mid-div: drvn over 3f out: sn lost pl* **10/1**

0500 **11** *1¼* **Imperial Djay (IRE)**[42] 4802 6-9-3 **91** DaleSwift(3) 7 55
(Ruth Carr) *s.s: a in rr* **25/1**

3220 **12** *2¼* **Thirteen Shivers**[28] 5288 3-8-13 **87** PaddyAspell 3 45
(Michael Easterby) *trckd ldrs: wknd 2f out* **16/1**

1m 35.49s (2.09) **Going Correction** +0.475s/f (Yiel)
WFA 3 from 4yo+ 3lb **12** Ran SP% **119.3**
Speed ratings (Par 107): **107,101,100,100,99 96,95,90,87,85 83,81**
Tote Swingers:1&2:£42.60, 2&3:£6.70, 1&3:£19.60 CSF £88.56 CT £530.46 TOTE £13.70: £3.70, £2.40, £1.90; EX 113.40.
Owner J Law **Bred** Denis And Mrs Teresa Bergin **Trained** Sessay, N Yorks
■ Stewards' Enquiry : Julie Burke two-day ban: failed to ride out for 6th (Oct 1,3)

FOCUS
Not a bad handicap and it was won in impressive fashion, but not many got involved and there is a doubt over how literally to take this form in the ground.

NOTEBOOK
Xilerator(IRE) hadn't been able to dominate in his last two starts since bolting up at Newcastle in May, but was allowed to do his own thing in front again this time and quickened off the front heading to the final furlong to win as he pleased. Lightly raced for a 4yo, the winner's from a family that improves with age (half-brother to Tax Free and Inxile) and it'll be a surprise if he doesn't win a big race down the line. He's clearly very dangerous when left alone in front and is something to look forward to next year.
Staff Sergeant, making a quick reappearance after running fifth here on Thursday, tracked the leader throughout but couldn't live with him when he quickened. He hadn't run over a trip this short since his racecourse debut, but he coped with it well. (op 8-1)
Mr Rainbow, 5lb higher for his latest second, posted a solid effort, keeping on from midfield to take third in a race dominated by those that raced up front. (op 11-2 tchd 5-1)
Honeymead(IRE), having only her fourth outing of the campaign, had conditions to suit and was a shade disappointing. She ran poorly here in June and perhaps the track isn't really to her liking. (op 11-4)
Masked Dance(IRE) bounced back to form at a track where he has run well in the past, although his current mark doesn't make things easy for him. (tchd 20-1)
Silenceofthewind(USA), another who is fresher than most at this time of year, having had only three previous outings this term, looked to be travelling well heading to the 2f marker, but the gap he went for was soon closed off and his response afterwards was limited. He acts on Polytrack so that's always an option for connections this backend. (tchd 14-1)
Silver Rime(FR), who was narrowly in front of Staff Sergeant over 1m here on Thursday, could have done with a disputed lead up front to set things up for his closing style. (op 9-1)
Daring Dream(GER), whose rider put up 2lb overweight, was another who could have done with a stronger pace. (op 12-1)
Lovelace Official explanation: jockey said, regarding running, that the horse became restless and he missed the handle of blindfold at first attempt.
Mullins Way(USA) Official explanation: jockey said gelding was unsuited by the soft ground

6149 WILLIAMHILL.COM DOONSIDE CUP STKS (LISTED RACE) 1m 2f

4:30 (4:30) (Class 1) 3-Y-O+ **£22,684** (£8,600; £4,304; £2,144; £1,076) **Stalls** Low

Form RPR

2604 **1** **Poet**[34] 5094 6-9-0 114 AdamKirby 2 117
(Clive Cox) *mde all: rdn clr 2f out: kpt on strly fnl f: unchal* **5/4**[1]

-001 **2** *4* **Vesuve (IRE)**[19] 5544 5-9-0 104 SilvestreDeSousa 5 109
(Saeed Bin Suroor) *trckd ldrs: rdn and outpcd over 2f out: rallied to chse clr wnr ins fnl f: no imp* **9/2**[3]

-234 **3** *1¼* **Hot Prospect**[21] 5494 4-9-0 110 EddieAhern 4 107
(Roger Varian) *in tch: hdwy to chse wnr over 2f out: sn rdn and edgd lft: one pce fr over 1f out: lost 2nd ins fnl f* **9/4**[2]

0024 **4** *2* **Cracking Lass (IRE)**[9] 5850 4-8-9 107 (b) PaulHanagan 3 98
(Richard Fahey) *s.i.s: bhd and sn drvn along: lost tch after 3f: rallied whn hung bdly lft over 1f out: kpt on fnl f* **7/1**

0-40 **5** *13* **Zafisio (IRE)**[21] 5494 5-9-0 99 (p) DarryllHolland 1 77
(Jo Hughes) *chsd wnr to over 2f out: rdn and wknd wl over 1f out* **16/1**

2m 15.63s (3.63) **Going Correction** +0.475s/f (Yiel) **5** Ran SP% **111.8**
Speed ratings (Par 111): **104,100,99,98,87**
CSF £7.45 TOTE £2.20: £1.30, £1.90; EX 6.20.
Owner H E Sheikh Sultan Bin Khalifa Al Nahyan **Bred** Meon Valley Stud **Trained** Lambourn, Berks

FOCUS
A decent Listed race judged on the ratings. The mudlark winner has been rated back to his best.

NOTEBOOK
Poet is well suited by soft ground but had been held on it in better company of late, so the drop to Listed class was clearly of benefit. He made the running as usual and, when he kicked for home, soon had his rivals in trouble and scored at his leisure. This should give him a nice confidence-boost before another crack at either the Prix Dollar or the St Simon Stakes, both of which he contested last season. (tchd 11-10 and 11-8 and 6-4 in a place)
Vesuve(IRE) was trying to follow up last year's success. However, this was arguably a stronger renewal and the ground was softer than ideal for him, so he was unable to offer a meaningful challenge to the winner, having been close enough turning for home. (op 4-1)
Hot Prospect has been Group 3 placed and goes well on soft, but has not won for over a year and found disappointingly little after appearing to have every chance here. (op 11-4 tchd 3-1)
Cracking Lass(IRE) has won on soft and heavy ground but stays 1m4f well and the drop in trip raised questions. However, it was more her attitude that was the problem here, as her rider was soon bustling her along after a tardy start and she took very little interest, hanging left under pressure in the straight and looking unco-operative. Connections might decide to retire her to stud following this. (op 13-2 tchd 15-2)
Zafisio(IRE), a former Group 1 juvenile winner who is well suited by testing ground but had not had much racing in recent seasons, had a chance on his 2009 form wearing cheekpieces for the first time, but he faded tamely in the straight and looks a shadow of his former self. (op 20-1 tchd 14-1)

6150 WILLIAMHILL.COM AYRSHIRE H'CAP 1m

5:00 (5:00) (Class 2) (0-105,103) 3-Y-O+

£12,450 (£3,728; £1,864; £932; £466; £234) **Stalls** Low

Form RPR

4330 **1** **Don't Call Me (IRE)**[19] 5546 4-8-10 **89** oh1 (t) AdrianNicholls 13 101
(David Nicholls) *hld up: gd hdwy to ld 2f out: sn rdn and edgd lft: kpt on wl fnl f* **12/1**

4236 **2** *3* **Extraterrestrial**[35] 5059 7-8-10 **89** oh1 PaulHanagan 6 94
(Richard Fahey) *hld up in tch: hdwy to chse wnr over 1f out: kpt on ins fnl f* **8/1**[3]

0505 **3** *hd* **Lord Aeryn (IRE)**[19] 5557 4-8-10 **89** oh3 TonyHamilton 11 94
(Richard Fahey) *hld up: rdn and hdwy over 1f out: kpt on same pce wl ins fnl f* **11/1**

0000 **4** *1¼* **Harrison George (IRE)**[30] 5218 6-9-1 **97** JPO'Brien(3) 3 99+
(Richard Fahey) *towards rr: rdn and hdwy over 3f out: n.m.r and lost pl over 2f out: kpt on fnl f* **5/1**[2]

5200 **5** *hd* **Tiger Reigns**[31] 5185 5-9-0 **93** PhillipMakin 4 95
(Michael Dods) *in tch: effrt and rdn over 2f out: outpcd ins fnl f* **5/1**[2]

1600 **6** *2* **Magic Cat**[2] 6078 5-8-10 **89** oh4 DavidAllan 5 86
(Mrs K Burke) *in tch: effrt over 2f out: wknd ins fnl f* **11/1**

0014 **7** *2¼* **Osteopathic Remedy (IRE)**[19] 5557 7-9-0 **93** DanielTudhope 2 85
(Michael Dods) *hld up: hdwy and prom over 2f out: wknd fnl f* **8/1**[3]

5211 **8** *6* **Pat's Legacy (USA)**[18] 5586 5-8-10 **89** oh1 DarryllHolland 9 67+
(Jo Hughes) *led to 2f out: sn rdn and wknd* **14/1**

6- **9** *1¼* **Memory Cloth**[495] 1985 4-8-13 **95** DaleSwift(3) 1 70
(Brian Ellison) *bhd: drvn along 1/2-way: nvr on terms* **25/1**

2500 **10** *3¼* **Snow Bay**[19] 5557 5-8-13 **92** FrannyNorton 10 60
(David Nicholls) *rrd s: bhd: rdn over 2f out: sn btn* **14/1**

4101 **11** *9* **Miami Gator (IRE)**[52] 4445 4-8-10 **89** oh2 (v) AndrewElliott 8 36
(Mrs K Burke) *cl up: rdn and outpcd whn hmpd over 2f out: sn btn* **25/1**

0201 **12** *3¼* **Sarrsar**[42] 4774 4-9-10 **103** (v) SilvestreDeSousa 7 43
(Saeed Bin Suroor) *trckd ldrs: rdn and effrt over 2f out: wknd wl over 1f out* **7/2**[1]

1m 46.36s (2.56) **Going Correction** +0.475s/f (Yiel) **12** Ran SP% **123.2**
Speed ratings (Par 109): **106,103,102,101,101 99,97,91,89,86 77,74**
Tote Swingers:1&2:£23.50, 2&3:£20.50, 1&3:£22.60 CSF £108.86 CT £1116.09 TOTE £15.90: £3.20, £2.80, £4.10; EX 107.40.
Owner Matt Morgan & Lauren Stapley **Bred** Darley **Trained** Sessay, N Yorks

FOCUS
The leaders went off too fast this time and that set the race up for a closer. A 4lb personal best from the winner with the next two close to their marks.

NOTEBOOK
Don't Call Me(IRE) ran poorly at Epsom last time, but he'd been very consistent throughout the season prior to that and the big change this time was that the tongue-tie, which he wore to success four times when with Bryan Smart last year, was back on for the first time since joining his current yard. He came with a sweeping run from off the pace to run out a clear winner, and there might yet be more to come from him with the headgear in place. Official explanation: trainer said, regarding apparent improvement in form, that the gelding had benefited from the reapplication of a tongue strap.
Extraterrestrial, who took this race in 2009 but was only ninth last year, had the race run to suit, but the winner got first run on him and he was always playing catch-up thereafter.
Lord Aeryn(IRE), racing from 3lb out of the handicap, ran well considering the ground was probably on the soft side for him. (op 12-1)
Harrison George(IRE), who has had a disappointing season, might have threatened for one of the minor placings with a clearer run. (op 13-2 tchd 7-1)
Tiger Reigns, another who hasn't enjoyed much luck this season, never really threatened to repeat despite being 4lb lower this time around. (op 6-1)
Magic Cat had conditions were in his favour, but he was 4lb out of the handicap and this was a tougher race than the one he was eighth in here on Thursday. (op 14-1)
Osteopathic Remedy(IRE) had every chance 2f out, but he proved one-paced in the finish.
Pat's Legacy(USA) Official explanation: jockey said gelding hung left-handed final 2f
Snow Bay Official explanation: jockey said gelding reared as stalls opened
Sarrsar sat in third early and dropped right out inside the final 2f. This was disappointing as he looked to have conditions to suit, but he probably raced too close to the pace. Official explanation: trainer had no explanation for the poor form shown (tchd 10-3)

6151 WILSONS AUCTIONS H'CAP 1m 5f 13y

5:35 (5:35) (Class 3) (0-90,89) 3-Y-O+

£6,225 (£1,864; £932; £466; £233; £117) **Stalls** Low

Form RPR

3145 **1** **Lexington Bay (IRE)**[14] 5710 3-8-8 **78** PaulHanagan 4 87
(Richard Fahey) *hld up: hdwy over 2f out: drvn to ld ins fnl f: r.o* **5/1**[2]

3332 **2** *1½* **Bollin Greta**[13] 5759 6-9-8 **83** (t) DavidAllan 6 90
(Tim Easterby) *hld up: hdwy over 2f out: kpt on fnl f: tk 2nd cl home* **7/1**

3100 **3** *nk* **King Kurt (IRE)**[8] 5888 3-8-11 **81** PhillipMakin 3 88
(Kevin Ryan) *cl up: led over 2f out: sn rdn: hdd ins fnl f: r.o same pce* **8/1**

2000 **4** *4½* **High Office**[28] 5271 5-9-11 **89** JPO'Brien(3) 5 89
(Richard Fahey) *in tch: hdwy over 2f out: sn rdn: no ex ins fnl f* **11/2**[3]

0011 **5** *nse* **Sharp Relief (IRE)**[17] 5623 3-8-3 **73** SilvestreDeSousa 10 73+
(Hughie Morrison) *t.k.h: trckd ldrs: chal over 2f out: one pce whn n.m.r ins fnl f* **4/1**[1]

6-00 **6** *3¾* **Graceful Descent (FR)**[55] 4360 6-9-1 **76** FrannyNorton 2 70
(Jim Goldie) *in tch: rdn over 2f out: edgd lft and wknd over 1f out* **14/1**

6015 **7** *3¼* **Chookie Hamilton**[14] 5724 7-9-1 **76** EddieAhern 7 65
(Keith Dalgleish) *hld up: hdwy on outside over 5f out: rdn and wknd fr 2f out* **11/1**

0166 **8** *nse* **Bridle Belle**[14] 5700 3-9-1 **88** LeeTopliss(3) 8 77
(Richard Fahey) *hld up: effrt over 2f out: edgd lft and sn btn* **11/2**[3]

0445 **9** *nk* **Gogeo (IRE)**[22] 5435 4-9-0 **80** GarryWhillans(5) 9 69
(Alan Swinbank) *led to over 2f out: edgd lft and wknd wl over 1f out* **15/2**

002 **10** *8* **Spirit Of A Nation (IRE)**[22] 5440 6-9-1 **76**....................(p) PaddyAspell 1 53
(James Moffatt) *chsd ldrs: rdn along over 3f out: wknd over 2f out* **20/1**

3m 5.79s (11.79) **Going Correction** +0.475s/f (Yiel)
WFA 3 from 4yo+ 9lb **10** Ran SP% **122.6**
Speed ratings (Par 107): **82,81,80,78,78 75,73,73,73,68**
Tote Swingers:1&2:£8.60, 2&3:£15.10, 1&3:£7.60 CSF £42.21 CT £284.11 TOTE £6.70: £2.20, £1.60, £3.10; EX 51.50.
Owner Keith Denham & Tony Denham **Bred** Mrs Vanessa Hutch **Trained** Musley Bank, N Yorks

FOCUS
They didn't go much of a gallop early, but the first two came from off the pace. The winner built on his latest effort and may do a bit better.

NOTEBOOK
Lexington Bay(IRE) coped best of all with what turned out to be a bit of a sprint for home. He likes some cut in the ground and also acts on Fibresand, so there should be further opportunities for him this autumn. (op 6-1)
Bollin Greta, held up in last, kept on well in the closing stages to once again finish in the frame. She's versatile when it comes to ground conditions and has been steadily progressive throughout this season, but unfortunately this performance will result in another bump up the weights. (op 6-1)
King Kurt(IRE), whose winning form is on good to firm, showed he can handle a soft surface just as well. He was well placed in second when the sprint for home began. (op 12-1)
High Office travelled up well heading to the 2f marker, but the response under pressure wasn't that great. He's looked held ever since winning on his seasonal return and forced to race off marks around 90. (op 6-1)
Sharp Relief(IRE), a progressive sort since switched to handicaps, had to prove she could be as effective on this softer ground in a stronger race. Her defeat had less to do with the ground being testing than the fact that she raced keenly, and as a consequence had less in reserve for the finish. (op 5-1)
Graceful Descent(FR), a C&D winner last autumn, had shown little in her previous two starts this term and this was only slightly more promising.
Bridle Belle looked to be found out by the combination of a longer trip and softer ground. (op 5-1)
T/Jkpt: Not won. T/Plt: £425.00 to a £1 stake. Pool £165,413.72. 284.09 winning tickets. T/Qpdt: £26.90 to a £1 stake. Pool £11,017.95. 302.50 winning tickets. RY

5367 CATTERICK (L-H)
Saturday, September 17

OFFICIAL GOING: Good (good to soft in places; 7.3)
Wind: Fresh, against. Weather: Cloudy

6152 E B F "MONSIEUR BOND" MAIDEN STKS 5f 212y
2:05 (2:05) (Class 5) 2-Y-O **£3,234** (£962; £481; £240) **Stalls** Low

Form RPR
33 **1** **Indego Blues**[23] 5398 2-9-3 0.. PaulQuinn 3 80+
(David Nicholls) *trckd ldrs: hdwy to ld over 1f out: rdn clr fnl f* **5/4**[1]
6 **2** *2 ½* **Taffe**[16] 5646 2-9-3 0.. FrederikTylicki 10 72
(James Given) *w ldr: rdn over 2f out: kpt on* **18/1**
44 **3** *1 ½* **Dubious Escapade (IRE)**[17] 5618 2-8-12 0......................... PBBeggy 9 63
(Ann Duffield) *in tch: rdn over 2f out: kpt on: wnt 3rd fnl 100yds* **8/1**
03 **4** *2 ½* **Findhornbay**[17] 5618 2-8-12 0.. JoeFanning 4 55
(Mark Johnston) *led: rdn whn hdd over 1f out: wknd fnl f* **11/4**[2]
04 **5** *¾* **Holy Angel (IRE)**[14] 5726 2-9-3 0................................. DuranFentiman 2 58
(Tim Easterby) *dwlt: in midfield: rdn over 2f out: kpt on fnl f* **11/2**[3]
6 *5* **Whip It In (IRE)** 2-8-12 0.. RussKennemore 7 37
(Paul Midgley) *dwlt: hld up: hdwy into midfield over 3f out: rdn over 2f out: no imp* **28/1**
06 **7** *2* **Lady Romanza (IRE)**[10] 5819 2-8-8 0 ow1...............(b[1]) LanceBetts(5) 5 32
(Tim Easterby) *hld up: rdn over 2f out: nvr threatened* **66/1**
0 **8** *1 ¼* **Harbour Sands**[33] 5104 2-9-3 0.. DavidNolan 1 32
(James Given) *trckd ldrs: rdn over 2f out: wknd over 1f out* **40/1**
9 *14* **Script** 2-8-9 0.. PaulPickard(3) 11 —
(Alan Berry) *slowly away: a outpcd towards rr* **150/1**
4 **10** *¾* **Latenfast**[7] 5919 2-8-10 0.. DavidSimmonson(7) 6 —
(Michael Easterby) *s.i.s: a outpcd in rr* **50/1**

1m 10.00s (2.00) **Going Correction** +0.50s/f (Yiel) **10** Ran SP% **112.9**
Speed ratings (Par 95): **106,102,100,97,96 89,87,85,66,65**
Tote Swingers:1&2:£11.00, 2&3:£11.00, 1&3:£1.80 CSF £25.53 TOTE £2.20: £1.10, £5.70, £2.60; EX 38.20.
Owner Pinnacle Indesatchel Partnership **Bred** Bearstone Stud **Trained** Sessay, N Yorks

FOCUS
No more than a fair maiden and one that few got into despite the pace not looking particularly strong. The runners stayed far side. The winner built on his earlier form to score in good style.

NOTEBOOK
Indego Blues took another step forward to shed his maiden tag as his form suggested he had every right to, winning with something in hand after getting to the front readily. He still looks to have some filling out to do, so should have a fair bit more progress in him, and a return to a more galloping track kept to this trip should also see him in a better light. (op 11-8 tchd 6-4)
Taffe had clearly learned plenty from his Redcar debut when he was soon well adrift, always in the van on this occasion. He might be open to a shade more progress without being anything out of the ordinary. (op 20-1 tchd 16-1)
Dubious Escapade(IRE) continued her run of in-frame efforts without threatening to finish any closer. She can go into nurseries now where she might be an interesting runner at a low level given she clearly needs at least 7f.
Findhornbay couldn't confirm Carlisle placings with Dubious Escapade but she possibly wasn't completely at home on the track, looking something of a leggy sort. She's another with better claims of getting her head in front in a nursery than in a maiden. (op 3-1)
Holy Angel(IRE) again left the impression he's more one for nurseries, possibly over a longer trip given that he wasn't able to get competitive. (op 5-1 tchd 6-1 in a place)
Whip It In(IRE), a cheaply bought daughter of Whipper, was always about the same place and is entitled to improve given that she looked green. (op 25-1)
Latenfast Official explanation: jockey said gelding hung right-handed

6153 HAPPY RETIREMENT IRIS H'CAP 1m 5f 175y
2:35 (2:37) (Class 6) (0-65,64) 3-Y-O **£2,045** (£603; £302) **Stalls** Low

Form RPR
-546 **1** **Ad Value (IRE)**[10] 5832 3-8-7 **50** ow1.............................. PJMcDonald 2 60
(Alan Swinbank) *in rr: drvn over 3f out: hdwy over 2f out: swtchd outside over 1f out: styd on to ld jst ins fnl f: kpt on wl* **5/1**[2]
6234 **2** *2* **Royal Bonsai**[17] 5623 3-9-1 **58**.. PBBeggy 6 65
(John Quinn) *trckd ldrs: effrt 4f out: upsides 1f out: styd on same pce last 100yds* **6/1**[3]
0563 **3** *2* **Shirls Son Sam**[16] 5651 3-8-9 **52**.............................. KellyHarrison 11 56
(Chris Fairhurst) *s.i.s: t.k.h in rr: hdwy to trck ldrs 6f out: led over 2f out: edgd rt and hdd jst ins fnl f: kpt on one pce* **8/1**
231 **4** *nk* **Al Furat (USA)**[16] 5650 3-9-2 **64**.............................. ShaneBKelly(5) 4 68
(Ron Barr) *dwlt: t.k.h in midfield: hdwy over 3f out: rdn and hung lft over 1f out: kpt on at one pce* **6/4**[1]
4002 **5** *½* **Rapturous Applause**[17] 5623 3-8-10 **53**.............................. FrederikTylicki 8 56
(Micky Hammond) *hld up in rr: hdwy over 1f out: styng on at fin* **10/1**
010 **6** *5* **Downtown Boy (IRE)**[47] 4612 3-8-10 **53**.............................. JoeFanning 5 49
(Ray Craggs) *gave problems in stalls: trckd ldrs: t.k.h: chal over 2f out: wknd last 150yds: eased nr fin* **12/1**
-004 **7** *7* **Sister Sioux (IRE)**[10] 5822 3-8-2 **45**.............................. AdrianMcCarthy 13 31
(Robin Bastiman) *trckd ldrs: led over 3f out: hdd over 2f out: wknd over 1f out* **33/1**
006- **8** *2 ¼* **Imperial Waltzer**[28] 5020 3-8-7 **50**.............................. AndrewMullen 9 33
(George Moore) *w ldrs: drvn over 5f out: lost pl over 3f out: sn bhd* **40/1**
4441 **9** *20* **Brook Star (IRE)**[21] 5489 3-8-10 **53**.............................. DuranFentiman 7 —
(Michael Dods) *led: qcknd pce over 4f out: hdd over 3f out: sn lost pl and bhd: t.o* **10/1**
0-05 **10** *66* **Pope Potter**[85] 2785 3-8-2 **45**..................................(p) PatrickMathers 12 —
(Richard Guest) *in rr: drvn after 5f: bhd fnl 6f: t.o whn virtually p.u 3f out* **100/1**

3m 11.39s (7.79) **Going Correction** +0.50s/f (Yiel) **10** Ran SP% **114.3**
Speed ratings (Par 99): **97,95,94,94,94 91,87,86,74,36**
Tote Swingers:1&2:£10.10, 2&3:£8.70, 1&3:£9.50 CSF £33.98 CT £235.25 TOTE £6.60: £1.60, £1.70, £3.00; EX 45.40.
Owner Mrs V McGee **Bred** Michael Dalton **Trained** Melsonby, N Yorks

FOCUS
Weak fare but the principals have largely been running well, so it's likely that the right horses contested the finish, despite the pace being steady for a long way.
Imperial Waltzer Official explanation: trainer's rep said gelding was struck into behind

6154 LOUISE JOHNSON 26TH BIRTHDAY NURSERY 7f
3:10 (3:16) (Class 4) (0-85,79) 2-Y-O **£4,398** (£1,309; £654; £327) **Stalls** Low

Form RPR
033 **1** **Rusty Rocket (IRE)**[24] 5367 2-8-9 **67**.............................. PJMcDonald 4 73+
(Paul Green) *mde all: drvn over 1f out: kpt on* **11/1**
3310 **2** *1 ¾* **Repeater**[7] 5931 2-9-6 **78**.. StevieDonohoe 3 80+
(Sir Mark Prescott Bt) *dwlt: hld up: short of room over 3f out: sn pushed along: rdn and hdwy over 1f out: kpt on strly fnl f: wnt 2nd cl home* **5/4**[1]
5222 **3** *½* **Fayr Fall (IRE)**[13] 5755 2-9-1 **73**.............................. DuranFentiman 6 73
(Tim Easterby) *hld up: rdn and hdwy over 2f out: chsd wnr appr fnl f: kpt on at one pce: lost 2nd cl home* **5/1**[2]
1610 **4** *5* **See Clearly**[10] 5825 2-8-13 **76**.............................. LanceBetts(5) 1 63
(Tim Easterby) *hld up: rdn over 2f out: kpt on fnl f: nvr trbld ldrs* **12/1**
435 **5** *nk* **Thewinningmachine**[21] 5480 2-8-11 **69**.............................. PatrickMathers 7 55
(Richard Fahey) *chsd ldrs: rdn and outpcd over 3f out: kpt on at one pce fnl f* **17/2**
5024 **6** *4* **Alborz (IRE)**[19] 5550 2-8-7 **65**.. JoeFanning 8 41
(Mark Johnston) *w ldr: rdn over 2f out: wknd over 1f out* **10/1**
316 **7** *4* **Stormy Whatever (FR)**[36] 4984 2-9-5 **77**.............................. FrederikTylicki 9 42
(James Given) *prom on outer: rdn over 2f out: wknd over 1f out* **8/1**[3]
0300 **8** *nk* **Electrickery**[18] 5597 2-8-1 **59**.............................. AdrianMcCarthy 11 23
(Mark Johnston) *midfield: rdn and lost pl over 3f out: wknd 2f out* **22/1**
3006 **9** *20* **Dicky Mint**[13] 5755 2-8-4 **62**.. KellyHarrison 10 —
(Michael Easterby) *midfield on outer: pushed along and lost pl over 3f out: wknd over 2f out: eased* **20/1**

1m 29.98s (2.98) **Going Correction** +0.50s/f (Yiel) **9** Ran SP% **117.0**
Speed ratings (Par 97): **102,100,99,93,93 88,84,83,61**
Tote Swingers:1&2:£11.70, 2&3:£1.20, 1&3:£11.70 CSF £25.53 CT £82.56 TOTE £22.60: £4.80, £1.20, £1.20; EX 47.40.
Owner Seven Stars Racing **Bred** Mike Hyde **Trained** Lydiate, Merseyside

FOCUS
Just an ordinary nursery with the top weight officially rated 7lb below the ceiling for the grade. Three came clear turning for home and the well-backed favourite ended up with too much to do. Significant improvement from the winner.

NOTEBOOK
Rusty Rocket(IRE) had qualified for nurseries with three runs over 5f, but he had shown before he could handle this track and that was one thing that couldn't be said of the favourite. He looks a handy type, cornering well, and so might be best kept to sharp tracks and, given he readily saw off the pair that kept him company in front, will probably prove just as effective at 6f. (op 5-1)
Repeater was well backed in the face of a seemingly much-easier task than at Doncaster last time, but he was poorly placed even before he got hampered on the home turn and in the circumstances did well to even get second. That said, he didn't impress with his head carriage and looks one to tread slightly warily with. (op 9-4)
Fayr Fall(IRE) turned in another creditable effort off his highest mark yet. He was another that let the winner have a bit too much rope but he looks vulnerable now he's risen in the weights. (op 4-1)
See Clearly might have gone off the boil for now, taking an age to pick up considering she'd won at 6f here only last month. (tchd 10-1)
Alborz(IRE) fared least well of the trio that cut out the pace but he wasn't beaten far and might be of interest in a weaker event than this retuned to Fibresand. (tchd 11-1)
Stormy Whatever(FR) again wasn't able to dominate and didn't see his race out in the manner of one likely to prove as good at 7f as 6f for now. (op 13-2)

6155 PIN POINT RECRUITMENT SEPTEMBER STKS (H'CAP) 1m 3f 214y
3:45 (3:45) (Class 4) (0-80,80) 3-Y-O+ **£5,239** (£1,559; £779; £389) **Stalls** Low

Form RPR
/0-0 **1** **Ultimate**[21] 5465 5-9-2 **73**.............................. PaulPickard(3) 9 89
(Brian Ellison) *mde all: drvn clr wl over 1f out: kpt on: eased towards fin* **12/1**
643 **2** *7* **George Adamson (IRE)**[26] 5311 5-9-7 **75**.............................. PJMcDonald 14 80
(Alan Swinbank) *dwlt: hld up: rdn and hdwy over 2f out: wnt 2nd appr fnl f: kpt on: no ch w wnr* **7/1**[2]
4003 **3** *2* **Ethics Girl (IRE)**[14] 5729 5-9-11 **79**...........................(t) StevieDonohoe 5 81
(John Berry) *hld up in midfield: rdn over 3f out: swtchd rt and hdwy over 1f out: kpt on: wnt 3rd fnl 50yds* **12/1**
2015 **4** *1 ¼* **Ailsa Craig (IRE)**[18] 5593 5-9-5 **76**.............................. PatrickDonaghy(3) 13 76
(Edwin Tuer) *midfield: rdn over 3f out: styd on one pce* **7/1**[2]
2526 **5** *nk* **Amir Pasha (UAE)**[4] 6029 6-8-7 **66** ow1..............(p) ShaneBKelly(5) 7 65
(Micky Hammond) *midfield: rdn over 3f out: one pce* **7/1**[2]
4400 **6** *3 ½* **Saint Thomas (IRE)**[20] 5504 4-9-1 **69**.............................. StephenCraine 4 63
(John Mackie) *trckd ldr: rdn over 3f out: wknd over 1f out* **25/1**
2006 **7** *nk* **Mica Mika (IRE)**[51] 4473 3-9-4 **80**.............................. PatrickMathers 11 73
(Richard Fahey) *hld up in midfield: rdn over 3f out: no imp* **5/1**[1]
0126 **8** *½* **Plattsburgh (USA)**[44] 4697 3-9-3 **79**.............................. JoeFanning 3 71
(Mark Johnston) *trckd ldr: rdn over 3f out: wknd over 1f out* **15/2**[3]
6360 **9** *2 ¼* **Arizona John (IRE)**[72] 3758 6-9-5 **76**.............................. DeclanCannon(3) 2 65
(John Mackie) *in tch: rdn over 3f out: wknd over 1f out* **12/1**

2450 **10** *3* **Hidden Glory**[18] 5593 4-9-3 71 .... FrederikTylicki 12 55
(James Given) *hld up: hdwy to trck ldrs 6f out: rdn to chse wnr over 2f out: wknd over 1f out* **14/1**

4/ **11** *2 ½* **Gentleman Jeff (USA)**[178] 6341 7-9-2 70 .... DavidNolan 8 50
(Chris Grant) *hld up: a towards rr* **25/1**

-002 **12** *1* **Dzesmin (POL)**[12] 5791 9-8-9 66 oh3 .... (p) RobertLButler(3) 6 44
(Richard Guest) *trckd ldr: rdn over 3f out: wknd 2f out* **16/1**

216 **13** *½* **Iulus**[30] 5199 3-9-2 78 .... PBBeggy 1 56
(John Quinn) *midfield: rdn over 4f out: wknd over 2f out* **12/1**

0420 **14** *4 ½* **Tarantella Lady**[106] 2677 3-8-6 68 .... AndrewMullen 10 38
(George Moore) *midfield: lost pl over 4f out: wknd over 2f out* **22/1**

2m 42.98s (4.08) **Going Correction** +0.50s/f (Yiel)
WFA 3 from 4yo+ 8lb **14** Ran SP% **121.3**
Speed ratings (Par 105): **106,101,100,99,98 96,96,96,94,92 90,90,89,86**
Tote Swingers:1&2:£17.60, 2&3:£6.70, 1&3:£17.60 CSF £92.10 CT £1041.34 TOTE £13.90: £5.00, £2.90, £3.20; EX 489.30.
Owner Dan Gilbert **Bred** Avington Manor Stud **Trained** Norton, N Yorks

FOCUS
A fair handicap for the track but one run at no more than a medium pace and the winner was able to dictate.

6156 PROJECT MANAGEMENT SCOTLAND MAIDEN STKS 7f
4:20 (4:21) (Class 5) 3-4-Y-O **£2,264** (£673; £336; £168) **Stalls** Low

Form RPR

0332 **1** **Salik Tag (USA)**[17] 5619 3-9-3 63 .... (t) PaulQuinn 9 71
(David Nicholls) *trckd ldrs: rdn and swtchd rt to stands' side over 2f out: overall ldr over 1f out: kpt on* **7/2**[3]

32 **2** *1 ¼* **Strong Man**[24] 5368 3-8-10 0 .... DavidSimmonson(7) 2 68
(Michael Easterby) *trckd ldrs: led over 2f out: hdd over 1f out: kpt on* **9/4**[1]

2364 **3** *1 ¾* **Alensgrove (IRE)**[35] 5034 3-8-12 57 .... (b[1]) RussKennemore 6 58
(Paul Midgley) *midfield: rdn over 2f out: hdwy over 1f out: kpt on fnl f* **11/1**

3045 **4** *½* **American Lover (FR)**[16] 5649 4-9-1 56 .... DavidNolan 13 57
(John Wainwright) *hld up: rdn and hdwy over 2f out: chal over 1f out: one pce fnl f* **16/1**

6 **5** *3* **Maven**[19] 5556 3-8-12 0 .... DuranFentiman 5 49
(Tim Easterby) *midfield: pushed along over 3f out: hdwy to chse ldrs over 2f out: sn one pce* **25/1**

36 **6** *¾* **Lady By Red (IRE)**[35] 5030 3-8-12 0 .... PJMcDonald 3 47
(Michael Dods) *w ldr: led 4f out: hung bdly rt to stands' side and hdd over 2f out: wknd over 1f out* **20/1**

0000 **7** *3 ¼* **Ruler's Honour (IRE)**[36] 5008 4-9-6 50 .... (p) GregFairley 7 43
(Tim Etherington) *slowly away: sn pushed along towards rr: kpt on fnl f: nvr threatened* **100/1**

5503 **8** *5* **Wing N Prayer (IRE)**[3] 6049 4-8-11 36 ow3 .... JustinNewman(7) 10 27
(John Wainwright) *sn pushed along towards rr: nvr on terms* **22/1**

5 **9** *2 ¼* **Eqtiraab (IRE)**[22] 5443 3-9-3 0 .... StephenCraine 1 23
(Tony Coyle) *dwlt: sn in tch: rdn over 2f out: wknd over 1f out* **9/1**

10 *hd* **Pivotal Prospect** 3-8-12 0 .... PatrickMathers 4 18
(Tracy Waggott) *a outpcd in rr* **66/1**

-434 **11** *2 ½* **Daffydowndilly**[16] 5640 3-8-12 69 .... StevieDonohoe 12 11
(Hughie Morrison) *midfield: rdn over 2f out: wknd over 1f out* **3/1**[2]

00 **12** *9* **Peteron**[16] 5649 3-8-12 0 .... LanceBetts(5) 8 —
(Colin Teague) *sn led: hdd 4f out: carried rt to stands' side over 2f out: sn wknd* **200/1**

13 *29* **Nine Carrot Gold**[85] 4-9-6 0 .... PBBeggy 14 —
(George Charlton) *slowly away: a bhd: t.o* **100/1**

1m 30.6s (3.60) **Going Correction** +0.50s/f (Yiel)
WFA 3 from 4yo 3lb **13** Ran SP% **119.1**
Speed ratings (Par 103): **99,97,95,95,91 90,87,81,78,78 75,65,32**
Tote Swingers:1&2:£2.60, 2&3:£3.30, 1&3:£4.30 CSF £11.13 TOTE £5.20: £1.10, £1.70, £2.30; EX 9.20.
Owner Malih Lahej Al Basti **Bred** Lantern Hill Farm Llc **Trained** Sessay, N Yorks

FOCUS
A modest maiden in which the form horses with the exception of the favourite came to the fore. The winner was one of a trio that ended up on the stands' rail.
Lady By Red(IRE) Official explanation: jockey said filly hung right-handed
Eqtiraab(IRE) Official explanation: trainer said, on returning home, gelding was found to have burst a blood vessel
Daffydowndilly Official explanation: jockey said filly was unsuited by the good (good to soft places) ground

6157 NORTHALLERTON AND DALES BRANCH OF SAMARITANS H'CAP 1m 5f 175y
4:55 (4:55) (Class 6) (0-65,65) 4-Y-0+ **£2,045** (£603; £302) **Stalls** Low

Form RPR

0616 **1** **Miss Ferney**[12] 5791 7-8-9 56 .... DeclanCannon(3) 7 65
(Alan Kirtley) *dwlt: hld up in rr: hdwy and c stands' side over 2f out: chsd ldr over 1f out: led last 150yds: hld on towards fin* **14/1**

0013 **2** *nk* **Daytime Dreamer (IRE)**[31] 5166 7-8-13 57 .... PJMcDonald 11 66
(Martin Todhunter) *trckd ldrs: c stands' side and led over 1f out: hdd ins fnl f: no ex nr fin* **22/1**

4022 **3** *4 ½* **Danceintothelight**[24] 5369 4-9-5 63 .... KellyHarrison 5 66
(Micky Hammond) *trckd ldrs: pushed along over 5f out: c wd over 2f out: styd on same pce appr fnl f* **4/1**[2]

1211 **4** *½* **Eijaaz (IRE)**[46] 4637 10-9-5 63 .... (p) FrederikTylicki 15 65
(Geoffrey Harker) *mid-div: lost pl over 6f out: kpt on fnl 2f: styd on ins fnl f* **7/1**[3]

3440 **5** *hd* **Maslak (IRE)**[11] 5804 7-9-2 60 .... RussKennemore 12 62+
(Peter Hiatt) *led over 2f: chsd ldrs: drvn over 4f out: overall ldr centre 2f out: sn hdd: kpt on same pce fnl f* **25/1**

0434 **6** *2* **Tropical Bachelor (IRE)**[36] 4982 5-9-2 65 .... LanceBetts(5) 13 64
(Richard Ford) *trckd ldrs: effrt 3f out: chal over 1f out: fdd last 100yds* **12/1**

0-50 **7** *3 ¾* **Ananda Kanda (USA)**[14] 5723 4-9-4 65 .... PaulPickard(3) 2 59
(Brian Ellison) *hld up in rr: kpt on fnl 2f: nvr on terms* **20/1**

2254 **8** *½* **Simple Jim (FR)**[12] 5790 7-8-13 57 .... StephenCraine 3 50
(David O'Meara) *hld up in rr: effrt over 3f out: kpt on fnl 2f: nvr nr ldrs* **7/2**[1]

0405 **9** *1 ¼* **Dubara Reef (IRE)**[11] 5804 4-9-2 60 .... (p) StevieDonohoe 4 51
(Paul Green) *chsd ldrs: drvn over 7f out: outpcd over 3f out* **8/1**

005 **10** *1* **Visions Of Johanna (USA)**[20] 5520 6-8-13 57 .... (t) MarkLawson 8 47
(Richard Guest) *in rr div: sme hdwy over 3f out: wknd over 1f out* **40/1**

2410 **11** *2* **Lady Norlela**[12] 5791 5-8-11 60 .... ShaneBKelly(5) 1 47
(Brian Rothwell) *hld up in rr: nvr on terms* **8/1**

6400 **12** *2* **Donna Elvira**[12] 5791 4-8-10 54 .... PBBeggy 14 38
(Edwin Tuer) *chsd ldrs: wknd over 1f out* **16/1**

0U00 **13** *4* **Valdan (IRE)**[14] 5723 7-8-11 55 .... (p) PatrickMathers 9 34
(Ruth Carr) *t.k.h: trckd ldrs: led over 11f out: hdd 2f out: sn wknd: eased clsng stages* **20/1**

3m 11.0s (7.40) **Going Correction** +0.50s/f (Yiel) **13** Ran SP% **117.3**
Speed ratings (Par 101): **98,97,95,94,94 93,91,91,90,90 88,87,85**
Tote Swingers:1&2:£34.00, 2&3:£10.40, 1&3:£16.40 CSF £293.38 CT £1464.95 TOTE £19.10: £4.00, £4.70, £2.30; EX 166.10.
Owner Mrs P J Taylor-Garthwaite **Bred** K And P J Garthwaite **Trained** West Auckland, Co Durham
■ Stewards' Enquiry : Shane B Kelly caution: used whip when out of contention
Stevie Donohoe two-day ban: used whip with excessive frequency (Oct 1,3)

FOCUS
A modest handicap run at a sound pace that favoured those that were held up. The first three ended up closest to the stand rail.
Simple Jim(FR) Official explanation: jockey said gelding was unsuited by the good (good to soft places) ground

6158 RACINGUK.COM H'CAP (DIV I) 7f
5:30 (5:31) (Class 6) (0-65,67) 3-Y-0+ **£1,704** (£503; £251) **Stalls** Low

Form RPR

3640 **1** **No Quarter (IRE)**[22] 5455 4-9-2 60 .... PatrickMathers 14 69
(Tracy Waggott) *hld up in midfield: short of room 2f out and again over 1f out: hdwy appr fnl f: kpt on strly to ld nr fin* **9/1**

3002 **2** *½* **Hoppy's Flyer (FR)**[7] 5924 3-9-5 66 .... RussKennemore 7 73
(Paul Midgley) *trckd ldrs: rdn to ld over 1f out: kpt on: hdd towards fin* **4/1**[2]

6321 **3** *½* **Watts Up Son**[10] 5821 3-8-13 67 .... (bt) JasonHart(7) 6 72+
(Declan Carroll) *chsd ldrs: rdn and outpcd over 2f out: rallied over 1f out: kpt on fnl f* **85/40**[1]

6230 **4** *½* **Jaldarshaan (IRE)**[33] 5106 4-8-8 57 .... LanceBetts(5) 5 62
(Colin Teague) *hld up in midfield: rdn and hdwy over 2f out: chal over 1f out: kpt on* **10/1**

6260 **5** *nse* **Tombellini (IRE)**[36] 4987 4-8-12 56 .... AndrewMullen 2 61
(David Nicholls) *led: rdn whn hdd over 1f out: no ex fnl 50yds* **7/1**

4003 **6** *3* **Electioneer (USA)**[14] 5732 4-9-4 62 .... (v) DavidNolan 11 59
(Michael Easterby) *chsd ldrs: rdn over 2f out: sn one pce* **11/2**[3]

5630 **7** *1 ¾* **Needwood Park**[17] 5619 3-8-8 55 .... FrederikTylicki 8 46
(Ray Craggs) *prom: rdn over 2f out: wknd ins fnl f* **66/1**

0060 **8** *3 ¼* **Boga (IRE)**[20] 5502 4-8-7 51 oh3 .... PBBeggy 9 34
(Karen Tutty) *sn pushed along in midfield: wknd over 1f out* **22/1**

0500 **9** *2 ½* **Peppercorn Rent (IRE)**[16] 5652 3-8-4 51 oh6 .... PaulQuinn 4 26
(John Davies) *sn pushed along towards rr: nvr on terms* **33/1**

0000 **10** *2 ¾* **Mujahope**[52] 4443 6-8-7 51 oh6 .... (v) KellyHarrison 12 20
(Colin Teague) *racd keenly: sn trckd ldrs: lost pl whn short of room on rail 2f out: sn wknd* **66/1**

006 **11** *4* **Friday Night Lad (IRE)**[134] 1860 4-8-7 51 .... PJMcDonald 1 —
(Alan Swinbank) *midfield early: lost pl over 3f out: bhd over 2f out* **16/1**

1m 30.66s (3.66) **Going Correction** +0.50s/f (Yiel)
WFA 3 from 4yo+ 3lb **11** Ran SP% **115.1**
Speed ratings (Par 101): **99,98,97,97,97 93,91,88,85,82 77**
Tote Swingers:1&2:£11.50, 2&3:£1.90, 1&3:£1.50 CSF £42.90 CT £107.24 TOTE £12.90: £3.40, £1.20, £1.30; EX 53.50.
Owner Miss T Waggott **Bred** Mrs T V Ryan **Trained** Spennymoor, Co Durham

FOCUS
A modest if uncompetitive handicap with few if any down the bottom of the weights looking to hold much chance on recent form. The field headed for the stand rail in the straight.
Mujahope Official explanation: jockey said gelding suffered interference

6159 RACINGUK.COM H'CAP (DIV II) 7f
6:00 (6:01) (Class 6) (0-65,64) 3-Y-0+ **£1,704** (£503; £251) **Stalls** Low

Form RPR

130 **1** **Viking Warrior (IRE)**[54] 4379 4-9-2 59 .... PBBeggy 10 73
(Michael Dods) *prom: rdn to ld over 2f out: kpt on to go clr fnl f* **8/1**

3203 **2** *3 ¾* **Meandmyshadow**[17] 5619 3-8-10 59 .... PaulPickard(3) 8 62+
(Alan Brown) *sn outpcd in rr: gd hdwy over 1f out: kpt on fnl f: wnt 2nd post* **8/1**

6250 **3** *hd* **Lindoro**[22] 5455 6-8-13 63 .... JustinNewman(7) 2 66
(Kevin M Prendergast) *led narrowly: hdd 4f out: chsd wnr over 1f out: one pce fnl f: lost 2nd post* **4/1**[1]

3110 **4** *nk* **Whats For Pudding (IRE)**[12] 5789 3-8-2 55 .... JasonHart(7) 13 57
(Declan Carroll) *hld up: hdwy on outer 3f out: rdn to chse ldrs over 1f out: kpt on* **5/1**[2]

3043 **5** *1 ¼* **Monsieur Pontaven**[12] 5789 4-8-7 50 .... (b) AdrianMcCarthy 11 49
(Robin Bastiman) *midfield: rdn over 2f out: kpt on one pce* **9/1**

2334 **6** *1 ¾* **Emeralds Spirit (IRE)**[14] 5721 4-9-3 60 .... KellyHarrison 9 54
(John Weymes) *racd keenly: w ldr: led narrowly 4f out: hdd over 2f out: wknd ins fnl f* **7/1**[3]

4034 **7** *nk* **Foreign Rhythm (IRE)**[16] 5647 6-9-1 63 .... ShaneBKelly(5) 4 57+
(Ron Barr) *hld up: rdn over 2f out: hdwy to chse ldrs over 1f out: wknd ins fnl f* **8/1**

0050 **8** *1 ½* **Ghost (IRE)**[23] 5404 4-9-7 64 .... AndrewMullen 7 54
(David Nicholls) *in tch: rdn over 2f out: wknd over 1f out* **8/1**

0000 **9** *1 ¼* **Viking Dancer**[12] 5789 4-8-12 55 .... PJMcDonald 6 41
(Ruth Carr) *hld up in midfield: rdn over 2f out: sn no imp* **22/1**

0060 **10** *4* **Elegant Dancer (IRE)**[11] 5803 4-8-7 50 oh5 .... FrederikTylicki 1 25
(Paul Green) *trckd ldrs: rdn over 2f out: sn wknd* **50/1**

0000 **11** *2* **Crocodile Bay (IRE)**[12] 5789 8-8-7 50 oh5 .... (b) PatrickMathers 12 20
(Richard Guest) *hld up: rdn over 3f out: a towards rr* **50/1**

5420 **12** *18* **Wandering Lad**[24] 5394 3-8-11 57 .... RussKennemore 3 —
(Paul Midgley) *hld up in midfield: rdn over 2f out: wknd qckly* **16/1**

1m 30.9s (3.90) **Going Correction** +0.50s/f (Yiel)
WFA 3 from 4yo+ 3lb **12** Ran SP% **117.8**
Speed ratings (Par 101): **97,92,92,92,90 88,88,86,85,80 78,57**
Tote Swingers:1&2:£17.60, 2&3:£7.30, 1&3:£10.70 CSF £69.11 CT £299.59 TOTE £8.70: £2.50, £3.00, £2.20; EX 46.50.
Owner Transpennine Partnership **Bred** Darley **Trained** Denton, Co Durham

FOCUS
The second division of a modest handicap in which the runners once again headed for the stands' rail. As in the previous race, the advantage was again with those that raced prominently.
Wandering Lad Official explanation: jockey said gelding had no more to give
T/Plt: £162.80 to a £1 place. Pool of £43,370.01. 194.44 winning tickets. T/Qpdt: £11.50 to a £1 stake. Pool of £3,553.05. 227.38 winning tickets. AS

[6123]NEWBURY (L-H)

Saturday, September 17

OFFICIAL GOING: Good (good to soft in places; 6.9)

Wind: Moderate across Weather: Sunny showers

6160 WEDGEWOOD ESTATES E B F MAIDEN STKS (DIV I) 7f (S)

1:25 (1:27) (Class 4) 2-Y-O **£4,722** (£1,405; £702; £351) **Stalls** Centre

Form				RPR
	1		**Mighty Ambition (USA)** 2-9-3 0 .... FrankieDettori 10 (Mahmood Al Zarooni) *gd sort: scope: hld up in tch: stdy hdwy over 2f out: qckd to ld over 1f out: styd on strly* **9/2**[2]	81+
	2	¾	**Rewarded** 2-9-3 0 .... KirstyMilczarek 9 (James Toller) *leggy: attr: chsd ldrs: pushed along over 2f out: rallied appr fnl f: styd on wl to take 2nd cl home: no imp on wnr* **12/1**	79+
	3	nk	**Model Pupil** 2-9-3 0 .... IanMongan 6 (Charles Hills) *athletic: attr: in tch: drvn and styd on fr 2f out: kpt on wl in clsng stages to take 3rd: no imp on wnr* **16/1**	79+
2303	4	hd	**Firestarter**[14] 5697 2-9-3 78 .... (b[1]) DaneO'Neill 1 (David Elsworth) *hld up towards rr: hdwy over 2f out: chsd ldrs 1f out: sn no imp and one pce fnl 120yds* **7/2**[1]	78
	5	2 ¼	**Aazif (IRE)** 2-9-3 0 .... RichardHills 4 (John Dunlop) *str: on toes: chsd ldrs: drvn to ld over 2f out: hdd over 1f out: wknd ins fnl f* **14/1**	72
	6	1 ¼	**Sir Bedivere (IRE)** 2-9-3 0 .... MartinDwyer 13 (Brian Meehan) *w'like: scope: towards rr: hdwy over 2f out: drvn and green over 1f out: kpt on in clsng stages but nvr a threat* **6/1**[3]	69+
	7	nk	**Bohemian Rhapsody (IRE)** 2-9-3 0 .... NeilCallan 8 (J W Hills) *unf: in tch: drvn and styd on over 1f out: nvr rchd ldrs: kpt on same pce* **12/1**	69
	8	1 ¾	**Highland Duke (IRE)** 2-9-3 0 .... WilliamBuick 14 (Clive Cox) *w'like: cl cpld: hld up in mid-div: pushed along and hdwy fr 3f out: chsd ldrs 2f out: wknd ins fnl f* **16/1**	64
	9	nk	**Altona (IRE)** 2-8-12 0 .... ChrisCatlin 16 (Mick Channon) *w'like: in rr: pushed along and sme hdwy fr over 1f out* **100/1**	58
	10	½	**Varnish** 2-8-12 0 .... RichardHughes 5 (Richard Hannon) *leggy: sn led: rdn 3f out: hdd over 2f out: wknd over 1f out* **10/1**	57+
	11	¾	**Vexillum (IRE)** 2-9-3 0 .... SamHitchcott 15 (Mick Channon) *leggy: pressed ldrs: rdn and ev ch over 2f out: wknd ins fnl 2f* **33/1**	60
0	12	6	**Twenty One Choice (IRE)**[15] 5681 2-9-3 0 .... PatCosgrave 7 (Ed de Giles) *w'like: rangy: s.i.s: rdn over 2f out: a towards rr* **100/1**	45
	13	3 ¼	**Imperial Elegance** 2-8-5 0 .... CharlesBishop[(7)] 3 (Mick Channon) *leggy: rdn 3f out: a bhd* **100/1**	32
0	14	2 ¼	**Kai**[21] 5480 2-9-3 0 .... JimmyFortune 11 (Michael Bell) *w'like: pressed ldr: rdn over 2f out: wknd sn after* **66/1**	32
	15	1 ¼	**Teacher (IRE)** 2-9-3 0 .... KierenFallon 12 (William Haggas) *lengthy: in rr early: sme hdwy into mid-div 4f out: sn bhd* **9/1**	28

1m 29.43s (3.73) **Going Correction** +0.20s/f (Good) **15** Ran SP% **115.0**
Speed ratings (Par 97): **86,85,84,84,82 80,80,78,77,77 76,69,65,63,61**
toteswingers:1&2:£14.90, 2&3:£36.70, 1&3:£21.50 CSF £53.84 TOTE £4.40: £2.30, £4.10, £4.70; EX 71.60.

Owner Godolphin **Bred** Darley **Trained** Newmarket, Suffolk

FOCUS

The rail had not been moved since the previous day so all round course races were six metres longer than standard. There was rain around and the ground remained on the easy side. They raced up the middle of the track and the pace was modest, resulting in a time 1.87 seconds slower than the second leg. Unsurprisingly this maiden has produced some smart types, although no real top notchers in recent years. The winner could be good but the fourth and the time limit the form.

NOTEBOOK

Mighty Ambition(USA) ◆ made a striking impression on his racecourse debut. It will be a while before the true merit of this performance is established, although Firestarter, officially rated 78, helps give the form a solid enough look, and it was impossible not to be impressed with the winner. Despite being by Street Cry out of a 1m2f Group 3-winning sister to Islington, he travelled so easily over this 7f trip and could be called the winner from some way out. It's true he found only a brief burst of acceleration once asked, but it was enough. Had he quickened away in the manner that had looked likely it's no exaggeration to say he'd be prominent in the ante-post betting for the Derby. He wasn't even quoted immediately afterwards, but his lack of end-race speed shouldn't be held against him considering both his pedigree and sizeable physique mean he's not made for what turned into a dash. It's early days to be thinking about Epsom, but he looks like being pretty smart over further as an older horse and it might not be a bad idea to try and get him on-side. If looking for a negative it's possible to argue his head carriage was ever so slightly awkward on occasions and he had a sheepskin noseband fitted, but so do many runners from this stable. He has no big-race juvenile entries in Britain or Ireland, so it remains to be seen how much more we'll see of him this term. (tchd 5-1)

Rewarded represents a relatively small yard, but they have another smart juvenile (also runs in these colours) in the shape of Saigon, who ran third in the Mill Reef on this card. This one, a 28,000gns purchase, is a half-brother to some useful types and kept on well having been in a good position throughout. He looks decent. (op 9-1)

Model Pupil ◆, a half-brother to 7f-1m winner Intense, out of a 1m3f-1m6f (including Listed) winner, travelled nicely for some of the way and kept on. He's a nice prospect. (tchd 14-1)

Firestarter has useful form to his name, but he was 0-5 coming here and now tried in blinkers, so it was surprising to see him start favourite against some well-bred newcomers. He ran well to be best of those from behind, but he likely needs his sights lowered to get off the mark. (op 4-1 tchd 9-2 in places)

Aazif(IRE) ◆ holds an entry in the Racing Post Trophy, but he's a half-brother to, among others, Group-class stayer Akmal, and he's going to want further. This was a promising start as he travelled like an above-average colt.

Sir Bedivere(IRE) ◆, an 82,000gns first foal of a 7f (Listed) and 1m winner, is entered in the Royal Lodge and Racing Post Trophy. This was just the sort of performance he should improve significantly from, coming off the bridle and running green a fair way out before keeping on gradually. (op 5-1 tchd 13-2)

Bohemian Rhapsody(IRE), for whom there was money around at big prices, showed ability. (op 40-1)

Teacher(IRE), a 100,000euros purchase out of a stakes winner, was sent off at a single-figure price but failed to beat a rival. (op 10-1)

6161 DUBAI DUTY FREE ARC TRIAL (GROUP 3) 1m 3f 5y

2:00 (2:00) (Class 1) 3-Y-O+

£28,355 (£10,750; £5,380; £2,680; £1,345; £675) **Stalls** Low

Form				RPR
0101	1		**Green Destiny (IRE)**[29] 5252 4-9-6 117 .... KierenFallon 7 (William Haggas) *hld up in rr: nt clr run over 2f out: swtchd sharply rt sn after and racd towards middle of crse: hrd rdn and r.o gamely ins fnl f to chse wnr fnl 120yds: led u.p last strides* **2/1**[1]	121+
-212	2	½	**Al Kazeem**[31] 5182 3-8-10 107 .... SteveDrowne 1 (Roger Charlton) *trckd ldrs: drvn to ld over 2f out: styd on wl ins fnl f: ct last strides* **7/2**[2]	115
2421	3	2 ¾	**Sea Of Heartbreak (IRE)**[48] 4582 4-9-0 103 .... RichardHughes 6 (Roger Charlton) *hld up in rr: stdy hdwy on bit to trck ldrs over 2f out: sn pushed along to go 2nd: no imp over 1f out: lost 2nd fnl 120yds and eased cl whn readily hld* **11/1**	107
0363	4	4 ½	**Black Spirit (USA)**[10] 5829 4-9-3 106 .... (t) WilliamBuick 4 (Clive Cox) *t.k.h early: in rr tl hdwy fr 4f out to press ldrs 3f out: plugged on same pce u.p 2f out* **18/1**	102
-233	5	nk	**Sri Putra**[77] 3646 5-9-3 116 .... NeilCallan 3 (Roger Varian) *sn chsng ldrs: rdn and wl there 3f out: plugged on same pce u.p 2f out* **4/1**[3]	101
0505	6	8	**Halicarnassus (IRE)**[13] 5776 7-9-3 107 .... ChrisCatlin 8 (Mick Channon) *chsd ldrs: drvn to ld over 3f out: hdd over 2f out: sn btn* **50/1**	87
11-0	7	3 ½	**Dangerous Midge (USA)**[175] 1001 5-9-3 119 .... MartinDwyer 5 (Brian Meehan) *in rr: rdn and no prog fr 4f out: wknd wl over 2f out* **5/1**	81
/310	8	37	**Passion For Gold (USA)**[91] 3153 4-9-3 113 .... (v[1]) FrankieDettori 2 (Saeed Bin Suroor) *lw: sn led: hdd over 3f out: wknd qckly and sn eased* **14/1**	14

2m 21.83s (0.63) **Going Correction** +0.20s/f (Good)
WFA 3 from 4yo+ 7lb **8** Ran SP% **114.4**
Speed ratings (Par 113): **105,104,102,99,99 93,90,63**
toteswingers:1&2:£3.40, 2&3:£4.60, 1&3:£3.40 CSF £9.08 TOTE £2.80: £1.50, £1.50, £2.10; EX 12.40 Trifecta £93.40 Pool: £877.70 - 6.95 winning units..
Owner Saleh Al Homaizi & Imad Al Sagar **Bred** Mubkera Syndicate **Trained** Newmarket, Suffolk

FOCUS

Continuing to title this race an Arc Trial makes little sense. Last year, though, Dangerous Midge won en-route to taking the Breeders' Cup Turf. The pace looked ordinary. A decent race for the grade, the winner a bit better than the bare form. The second confirmed his Great Voltigeur improvement.

NOTEBOOK

Green Destiny(IRE) did really well to win. He was conceding weight all round owing to the penalty picked up for his success in the Group 3 Strensall Stakes last time and he had a poor trip, having to wait for a run before being switched extremely wide. It might be that the runner-up had got to the front too soon, but Kieren Fallon's mount had to be high class to make up the ground and he did so, despite flashing his tail. It was no real surprise to hear he'll probably take his chance in the Champion Stakes, but on his only previous start at Ascot he ran poorly in the Wolferton. (op 5-2 tchd 11-4 in places)

Al Kazeem came here after his heavy defeat by Sea Moon in a bizarre running of the Great Voltigeur. He looked the winner when going to the front in the straight, but probably got there a bit too soon and was worn down. Lightly raced, it's doubtful we've seen the best of him and he's a terrific 4-y-o prospect. (op 9-2)

Sea Of Heartbreak(IRE), a Listed winner against her own sex over 1m4f here 48 days earlier, travelled well under a patient ride and had her chance, but her bid flattened out late on. (tchd 9-1)

Black Spirit(USA) isn't quite up to this level but he ran well. (tchd 20-1)

Sri Putra had been given a break since twice getting within around 6l of So You Think, but he chucked in one of his mulish displays and this performance did little boost the form of the so-called superstar. (tchd 9-2)

Halicarnassus(IRE) was due to be retired to stud in Turkey after his fourth over there in the Bosphorus Cup, but that's been delayed owing to quarantine issues. He won this in 2007 and was having his fifth start in the race, but dropped away after showing in front halfway up the straight.

Dangerous Midge(USA) won this last year en-route to taking the Breeders' Cup Turf. He had been well beaten in the Dubai Sheema Classic on his only start since then and offered nothing on this return to the track, racing lazily from a long way out. Presumably headgear (wore blinkers at Churchill Downs) will go on next time, but he'll still look best avoided.

Passion For Gold(USA), who was returning from three months off and wearing a first-time visor, made the running but dropped away as though as he had a problem and was heavily eased. (op 8-1)

6162 DUBAI DUTY FREE MILL REEF STKS (GROUP 2) 6f 8y

2:30 (2:30) (Class 1) 2-Y-O

£34,026 (£12,900; £6,456; £3,216; £1,614; £810) **Stalls** Centre

Form				RPR
3231	1		**Caspar Netscher**[29] 5251 2-9-4 114 .... KierenFallon 3 (Alan McCabe) *t.k.h: hld up in rr: swtchd lft and hdwy 2f out: drvn to ld over 1f out: hung rt u.p ins fnl f: kpt on strly in clsng stages* **15/8**[1]	114+
1140	2	½	**Redact (IRE)**[19] 5558 2-9-1 97 .... RichardHughes 5 (Richard Hannon) *chsd ldrs: rdn and one pce 2f out: rallied u.p to take 2nd fnl 100yds but no imp on wnr* **9/1**	109
1153	3	nk	**Saigon**[14] 5715 2-9-1 104 .... KirstyMilczarek 2 (James Toller) *chsd ldrs: drvn to chal ins fnl 2f: chsd wnr over 1f out but no imp: one pce and lost 2nd fnl 100yds* **9/2**[2]	108
14	4	2	**Foxtrot Romeo (IRE)**[10] 5826 2-9-1 92 .... TomEaves 7 (Bryan Smart) *lw: sn led: rdn over 2f out: hdd over 1f out: wknd ins fnl f* **28/1**	102
3002	5	½	**Factory Time (IRE)**[9] 5849 2-9-1 93 .... ChrisCatlin 9 (Mick Channon) *in rr: rdn and hdwy fr 2f out: hung lft ins fnl f: kpt on cl home: nvr a threat* **25/1**	100
21	6	3 ¾	**Swiss Spirit**[98] 2936 2-9-1 85 .... NeilCallan 6 (David Elsworth) *lw: hld up in tch: travelling ok over 2f out: sn rdn: wknd ins fnl f* **9/2**[2]	89
3405	7	1 ¼	**Crown Dependency (IRE)**[14] 5715 2-9-1 100 .... JimmyFortune 4 (Richard Hannon) *in tch: drvn to press ldrs 2f out: wknd ins fnl f* **14/1**	85
6625	8	½	**B Fifty Two (IRE)**[29] 5251 2-9-1 107 .... FrankieDettori 8 (J W Hills) *pressed ldrs to 1/2-way: wknd 2f out* **8/1**[3]	84
621	9	18	**Otto The Great**[54] 4384 2-9-1 84 .... WilliamBuick 1 (Walter Swinburn) *on toes: stmbld s: sn rcvrd: racd wd and prom 3f out: wknd qckly over 2f out: eased* **16/1**	30

1m 13.49s (0.49) **Going Correction** +0.20s/f (Good) **9** Ran SP% **112.1**
Speed ratings (Par 107): **104,103,102,100,99 94,92,92,68**
toteswingers:1&2:£5.00, 2&3:£7.70, 1&3:£2.80 CSF £19.05 TOTE £2.80: £1.20, £1.90, £1.70; EX 15.50 Trifecta £44.00 Pool: £3524.49 - 59.24 winning units..
Owner Charles Wentworth **Bred** Meon Valley Stud **Trained** Averham Park, Notts

FOCUS
This race usually works out at the top level, with six of the last ten winners subsequently successful in Group 1 company, including four of the last five. The latest running looked sub-standard, they raced up the middle of the track and the pace seemed fair. Straightforward form, Caspar Netscher rated to his Gimcrack level.

NOTEBOOK
Caspar Netscher deserves credit for becoming the first winner to defy a penalty (for his Gimcrack success) since Firebreak (subsequent Group 1-winning miler) in 2001. He had a lot to spare over most of these at the weights judged on official figures (including 14lb over the runner-up) and it's doubtful he had to improve. However, he had more in hand than the margin suggests having again wandered and idled under pressure. This was his eighth start, but he evidently thrives on racing and his connections are absolutely right to crack on this year in search of further big prizes, with the Breeders' Cup Juvenile Turf being mentioned as a target. (op 9-4)
Redact(IRE) had been held in two starts in lesser company since winning his maiden, though he was going on at the finish in the Super Sprint over 5f, then had excuses in Listed company at Ripon (apparently didn't enjoy soft ground or the ridges, and missed the break). This looked his best performance so far. (op 17-2 tchd 8-1)
Saigon raced a bit freely without cover. He kept on, but it's quite possible he'd have fared even better if more was kept in reserve for the closing stages. (op 4-1)
Foxtrot Romeo(IRE) was up in class with a bit to prove, but his trainer has had plenty of smart juveniles and this one ran well. (op 20-1 tchd 33-1)
Factory Time(IRE), runner-up in a sales race on his previous start, ran okay without proving himself up to the class. (op 16-1)
Swiss Spirit, absent since winning a York maiden in June, travelled like a machine but he's a big horse and looked weak off the bridle, not being given a hard race late on. All speed, the stronger the pace the better he'll be and he could be a high-class sprinter when he strengthens up. (op 7-1)
B Fifty Two(IRE)'s trainer reported the colt was unsuited by the ground. Official explanation: trainer said colt was unsuited by the good (good to soft places) ground (op 17-2)
Otto The Great's rider reported the gelding stumbled leaving the stalls. Official explanation: jockey said gelding stumbled leaving stalls (op 12-1)

6163 DUBAI DUTY FREE H'CAP — 1m 2f 6y
3:05 (3:10) (Class 2) (0-105,101) 3-Y-O+

£46,687 (£13,980; £6,990; £3,495; £1,747; £877) **Stalls** Low

Form — RPR
0501 **1** **Taqleed (IRE)**[15] 5686 4-9-1 **92** 5ex — TadhgO'Shea 8 — 108
(John Gosden) *lw: hld up in last pair: swtchd to centre of trck 3f out: sn rdn and hdwy: chsd ldr ent fnl f: sn led: kpt on wl: drvn out* **12/1**
166 **2** *nk* **Naqshabban (USA)**[31] 5185 3-8-13 **96** — WilliamBuick 14 — 111
(Luca Cumani) *ponied to s: hld up towards rr of midfield: swtchd rt 3f out: hdwy sn after: rdn to ld ent fnl f: wandered sltly and hdd ins fnl f: responded to driving: kpt on* **11/1**
-600 **3** *3 ½* **Master Of Arts (USA)**[19] 5557 6-8-13 **90** — JamieSpencer 20 — 98
(Mark Johnston) *hld up in last: stdy prog fr 3f out: rdn 2f out: styd on to go 3rd ins fnl f but nt gng pce of ldng pair* **33/1**
1510 **4** *1 ¾* **First Post (IRE)**[15] 5686 4-8-7 **87** — HarryBentley(3) 12 — 92
(Derek Haydn Jones) *hld up towards rr: hdwy fr 3f out: rdn over 2f out: led wl over 1f out: sn edgd lft: hdd ent fnl f: no ex* **40/1**
1142 **5** *½* **Beaumont's Party (IRE)**[28] 5275 4-9-3 **94** — JimmyFortune 11 — 98
(Andrew Balding) *mid-div: hdwy over 3f out: sn rdn: styd on same pce ins fnl f* **10/1**
0004 **6** *nk* **Oceanway (USA)**[7] 5940 3-8-11 **94** — SteveDrowne 16 — 97+
(Mark Johnston) *chsd ldrs: rdn 3f out: styng on at same pce whn nt clr run briefly ins fnl f* **33/1**
0065 **7** *1 ¾* **Resurge (IRE)**[19] 5544 6-9-9 **100** — (v[1]) IanMongan 13 — 99
(Stuart Kittow) *s.i.s: towards rr: hdwy over 3f out: sn rdn: swtchd lft ent fnl f: styd on: nvr trbld ldrs* **40/1**
3231 **8** *1 ¾* **Our Joe Mac (IRE)**[31] 5185 4-9-10 **101** — (p) PatCosgrave 10 — 97
(Richard Fahey) *mid-div: hdwy over 3f out: sn rdn to chse ldrs: fdd ins fnl f* **16/1**
1252 **9** *½* **Kirthill (IRE)**[21] 5483 3-8-10 **93** — KierenFallon 6 — 88+
(Luca Cumani) *mid-div: rdn over 2f out: making stdy prog whn denied clr run jst over 1f out: no ch after* **4/1**[2]
3401 **10** *2* **Dhaamer (IRE)**[42] 4788 4-9-4 **95** — (v) RichardHills 4 — 86
(John Gosden) *mid-div: hdwy over 3f out: sn rdn to chse ldrs: wknd ins fnl f* **7/1**[3]
0600 **11** *3 ¾* **Ingleby Spirit**[31] 5185 4-8-10 **87** — ChrisCatlin 15 — 70
(Richard Fahey) *lw: trckd ldrs: rdn 3f out: wknd 2f out* **40/1**
0130 **12** *1 ¼* **Tinshu (IRE)**[42] 4788 5-8-8 **85** — WilliamCarson 1 — 66
(Derek Haydn Jones) *swtg: trckd ldrs: rdn and ev ch over 2f out: wknd ins fnl f* **40/1**
5264 **13** *2 ¾* **Ellemujie**[3] 6068 6-8-9 **86** — (p) MartinDwyer 7 — 61
(Dean Ivory) *rdn over 3f out: a towards rr* **40/1**
2003 **14** *nk* **Moriarty (IRE)**[43] 4764 3-8-11 **97** — SeanLevey(3) 5 — 72
(Richard Hannon) *led for 2f: trckd ldr: led 4f out: sn rdn: hdd wl over 1f out: wknd ins fnl f* **16/1**
4231 **15** *hd* **Labarinto**[51] 4467 3-9-0 **97** — RichardHughes 2 — 71
(Sir Michael Stoute) *trckd ldrs: rdn over 3f out: wknd 2f out* **7/2**[1]
1000 **16** *½* **Leviathan**[21] 5483 4-9-0 **91** — DaneO'Neill 3 — 64
(Tony Newcombe) *mid-div: rdn 3f out: wknd over 1f out* **16/1**
5000 **17** *3 ¾* **Merchant Of Dubai**[14] 5705 6-9-6 **97** — GrahamGibbons 9 — 63
(Jim Goldie) *on toes: mid-div: rdn 3f out: wknd over 1f out* **25/1**
4206 **18** *3 ¼* **Malthouse (GER)**[21] 5466 3-9-1 **98** — TomEaves 17 — 57
(Mark Johnston) *lw: led after 2f: rdn and hdd 4f out: wknd 2f out* **40/1**
0445 **19** *1* **Jutland**[9] 5853 4-9-7 **98** — NeilCallan 19 — 55
(Mark Johnston) *lw: mid-div: rdn over 3f out: wknd 2f out* **25/1**

2m 8.44s (-0.36) **Going Correction** +0.20s/f (Good)
WFA 3 from 4yo+ 6lb — **19** Ran SP% **125.7**
Speed ratings (Par 109): **109,108,105,104,104 103,102,101,100,99 96,95,92,92,92 92,89,86,85**
toteswingers:1&2:£23.00, 2&3:£64.60, 1&3:£119.80 CSF £127.39 CT £4162.83 TOTE £13.00: £3.50, £3.20, £7.50, £8.90; EX 149.60 TRIFECTA Not won..
Owner Hamdan Al Maktoum **Bred** Shadwell Estate Co Ltd **Trained** Newmarket, Suffolk
■ Stewards' Enquiry : Ian Mongan three-day ban: careless riding (Oct 1,3-4)
Harry Bentley two-day ban: careless riding (Oct 1,3)

FOCUS
This race has produced the Cambridgeshire winner four times in the last seven years, namely Tazeez (unplaced 2008), Formal Decree (third 2006), Blue Monday (second 2005) and Spanish Don (unplaced 2004). However, in those days the gap between the two races was a couple of weeks, and this time around there is only a week until the big Newmarket handicap. Whatever, this is usually a really good race in its own right, by far the most notable winner in recent times being Presvis, who later added a number of Group 1s. This time around the pace was overly strong, setting the race up for those waited with, and consequently a high draw was also helpful. Those who chased the pace want their performance upgrading. The shape of the race suited the first two, but both looked possible improvers coming into this.

NOTEBOOK
Taqleed(IRE) was still last when looking for an ambitious run towards the inside around halfway up the straight and had to switch out wide. He ran on strongly once in the clear, the result looking inevitable from a little way out, and was taking advantage of being 3lb well in under the penalty for his recent Haydock success over this trip. He had the run of the race in front on his previous start, and this time had the run of the race in contrasting circumstances, but he's long been considered quite smart and is evidently now fulfilling his potential. (op 10-1)
Naqshabban(USA) has twice refused to enter the stalls, but he ran well when consenting to go forward after an enforced break at York last time and, ponied to the start, he built on that here, despite seemingly being passed over by Kieren Fallon. He raced slightly closer to the pace than the winner, but was still helped by the run of the race. This was only his fifth run and he now seems to be going the right way mentally. (op 14-1 tchd 10-1)
Master Of Arts(USA) was 3lb wrong but he was in the right place early on considering the pace and would have been closer had he enjoyed a better run in the straight, being kept to the inside rather than going wide. He's been lightly raced and unreliable in recent times, but he will have obvious claims if able to run off his correct mark next time. (tchd 28-1)
First Post(IRE) was eased last time after hitting the rail and stumbling. He's not a straightforward horse, sometimes wandering around, and he did so again this time, but he still ran a big race to make up a lot of ground out wide until his exertions told, albeit he was helped by being held up early. A strongly run 1m probably suits best and he could be one for next year's Lincoln. He was reported to have hung left. Official explanation: jockey said gelding hung left (op 33-1)
Beaumont's Party(IRE) was 13lb higher than when last winning and was held. (op 9-1)
Oceanway(USA) ◆ fared best of those close to the pace and deserves credit, especially being a 3-y-o filly up against some tough campaigners. Steve Drowne reported the filly suffered interference. Official explanation: jockey said filly suffered interference in running (op 28-1)
Kirthill(IRE), representing the same owner and trainer as 2008 winner Presvis, was 1lb well in but he endured a terrible trip. Kieren Fallon was trying to repeat the tactics that saw him successful on the same stable's Forte Dei Marmi in this 12 months ago, going the shortest way and hoping for a run, although in fairness a relatively low draw didn't give him much choice (seven of the eight in front of him were drawn in double figures). The horse found all sorts of trouble and otherwise might have been in the shake-up. Official explanation: jockey said colt suffered interference in running (op 11-2)
Dhaamer(IRE), up 9lb for winning in a first-time visor at Haydock, was seemingly the choice of Richard Hills over the winner, but he was well held. A low draw probably didn't help, though. (op 8-1)
Labarinto, absent since off 4lb lower at Glorious Goodwood, dropped away after chasing the overly quick pace. (op 9-2)

6164 DUBAI INTERNATIONAL WORLD TROPHY (GROUP 3) — 5f 34y
3:40 (3:41) (Class 1) 3-Y-O+

£28,355 (£10,750; £5,380; £2,680; £1,345; £675) **Stalls** Centre

Form — RPR
2111 **1** **Deacon Blues**[41] 4836 4-9-3 120 — FrankieDettori 8 — 120+
(James Fanshawe) *lw: hld up in rr but in tch: hdwy on bit over 1f out: drvn and qcknd ins fnl f to ld fnl 120yds: in command in clsng stages* **5/4**[1]
1100 **2** *1* **Masamah (IRE)**[14] 5707 5-9-5 112 — JamieSpencer 4 — 118
(Kevin Ryan) *pressed ldrs: drvn to chal ins fnl f and stl upsides fnl 120yds: kpt on but nt gng pce of wnr* **14/1**
2132 **3** *¾* **Dinkum Diamond (IRE)**[10] 5827 3-8-13 106 — WilliamBuick 3 — 110
(Henry Candy) *lw: in rr but in tch: pushed along over 1f out: styd on wl u.p ins fnl f and fin wl to take 3rd in last strides: nt gng pce of ldng duo* **7/1**[3]
6424 **4** *½* **Beyond Desire**[51] 4468 4-8-11 101 — NeilCallan 5 — 106
(Roger Varian) *pressed ldr: drvn to take slt ld 1f out: hdd and outpcd fnl 120yds: lost 3rd last strides* **28/1**
1141 **5** *1* **Night Carnation**[77] 3644 3-8-13 109 — JimmyFortune 6 — 105
(Andrew Balding) *lw: pressed ldrs: rdn to chal appr fnl f: edgd lft u.p: wknd fnl 75yds* **11/2**[2]
-000 **6** *2* **Astrophysical Jet**[77] 3644 4-8-11 106 — GrahamGibbons 10 — 95
(Ed McMahon) *chsd ldrs: rdn 2f out: wknd appr fnl f* **10/1**
5350 **7** *nk* **Piccadilly Filly (IRE)**[29] 5253 4-8-11 95 — (t) MartinDwyer 1 — 94
(Edward Creighton) *narrow ld: hdd 2f out: wknd 1f out* **66/1**
1123 **8** *½* **Medicean Man**[10] 5827 5-9-0 109 — (p) PatCosgrave 2 — 95
(Jeremy Gask) *s.i.s: rdn 1/2-way and nvr gng pce to get into contention* **9/1**
-024 **9** *½* **Katla (IRE)**[59] 4219 3-8-10 105 — KierenFallon 9 — 90
(J F Grogan, Ire) *chsd ldrs: slt ld 2f out: hdd & wknd 1f out* **11/1**
-002 **10** *7* **Moorhouse Lad**[19] 5543 8-9-0 94 — TomEaves 7 — 68
(Bryan Smart) *spd to 1/2-way: wknd 2f out* **66/1**

60.49 secs (-0.91) **Going Correction** +0.20s/f (Good)
WFA 3 from 4yo+ 1lb — **10** Ran SP% **112.9**
Speed ratings (Par 113): **115,113,112,111,109 106,106,105,104,93**
CSF £20.15 TOTE £1.90: £1.20, £2.40, £1.90; EX 12.60 Trifecta £51.90 Pool: £7607.70 - 108.38 winning units..
Owner Jan & Peter Hopper & Michelle Morris **Bred** Mr & Mrs K W Grundy, Mr & Mrs P Hopper **Trained** Newmarket, Suffolk

FOCUS
They raced middle to near side and the pace was predictably frantic. This was mainly Group 3 standard sprinters competing against a probable Group 1 performer and it was far more one-sided than the official winning margin suggests. Deacon Blues has stong claims to be rate the best European sprinter now. The time was fast.

NOTEBOOK
Deacon Blues, despite carrying a 3lb penalty, came here on a four-timer after winning the Wokingham and twice at this level (the latest by 7l), had upwards of 8lb in hand on official ratings, and it showed. He missed the Haydock Sprint Cup with a dirty scope and had never previously raced over shorter than 5.5f (when third in last year's Portland), but he cruised along until asked to win the race a furlong out. Despite the lack of serious opposition this was still impressive, especially as his trainer remains convinced the horse is even better suited by an extra furlong. If he turns up at Ascot (where he already has one big win to his name) for the Champions Sprint in this sort of form it could take a big performance to turn him over. Victory there would have to see him enter the mix when it comes to deciding this year's champion sprinter and that could lead to controversy considering he hasn't even competed in a Group 1 yet (Ascot race a Group 2), let alone won at the top level. (op 11-8 tchd 11-10)
Masamah(IRE) had to concede weight all round owing to the penalty picked up for his success in the Group 2 King George Stakes at Glorious Goodwood. He had 10lb to find with the winner so this was a fine effort. (op 12-1)
Dinkum Diamond(IRE) took an age to get going but finished strongly. He looks ready for another try over 6f. (op 15-2)
Beyond Desire had something to find with the three who finished ahead of her, and she was well beaten in this last year, but she ran a fine race. (op 25-1)
Night Carnation, returning from 77 days off, had a Group 3 penalty to contend with and her connections hoped the ground had not dried out too much. She was always up there, but her head carriage was a bit awkward and she was one paced for pressure. She's entitled to come on for this. (op 5-1 tchd 6-1)
Astrophysical Jet escaped a penalty for last year's success in this, but she hasn't been in the same form in 2011 and was well held after 77 days off. (op 12-1)

Piccadilly Filly(IRE) came into this officially rated just 95, but she was good enough to finish third in last year's Nunthorpe and she ran better than of late with the visor left off. (op 80-1)
Medicean Man was never going after a slow start but finished closer than had looked likely for much of the way. His last three wins have been at Ascot. (op 7-1)

6165 WEDGEWOOD ESTATES E B F MAIDEN STKS (DIV II) 7f (S)
4:15 (4:16) (Class 4) 2-Y-O **£4,722** (£1,405; £702; £351) **Stalls** Centre

Form RPR
1 **Miblish** 2-9-3 0 .... PhilipRobinson 9 81+
(Clive Brittain) *gd sort: scope: rangy: lw: mid-div: hdwy over 2f out: chal sn after: led jst over 1f out: drifted lft: kpt on: rdn out* **2/1**[1]
2 *nk* **Kaafel (IRE)** 2-9-3 0 .... RichardHills 8 80+
(Charles Hills) *w'like: scope: lw: hld up towards rr: making hdwy whn swtchd rt wl over 1f out: sn rdn: drifted lft ins fnl f: styd on: clsng wl on wnr* **9/1**
3 *1* **Cathedral** 2-9-3 0 .... MartinDwyer 2 78+
(Brian Meehan) *w'like: athletic: scope: slowly away and hmpd s: towards rr: hdwy 2f out: pushed along and styd on wl ins fnl f: nrst fin* **16/1**
3 4 *1 1/2* **Buster Brown (IRE)**[89] 3229 2-9-3 0 .... KierenFallon 11 74
(James Given) *angular: led: rdn whn hrd pressed fr over 2f out: hdd jst over 1f out: no ex* **9/2**[3]
620 5 *3/4* **Breaking The Bank**[66] 3986 2-9-3 73 .... NeilCallan 13 72
(William Muir) *lw: stmbld leaving stalls: mid-div: rdn to chse ldrs 2f out: kpt on same pce ins fnl f* **12/1**
6 *1/2* **Princess Maya** 2-8-13 0 ow1 .... IanMongan 15 68+
(Jo Crowley) *w'like: trckd ldrs: rdn 2f out: disputing 2nd but hld whn squeezed out ins fnl f: nt rcvr* **80/1**
7 *1/2* **Jupiter Storm** 2-9-3 0 .... PatCosgrave 10 69+
(Gary Moore) *wlike: str: attr: s.i.s: sn prom: rdn and ev ch 2f out: sn one pce* **16/1**
8 *2* **Spanish Fork (IRE)** 2-9-3 0 .... ChrisCatlin 5 64
(Mick Channon) *str: lw: s.i.s: outpcd in rr: sme late prog: nvr a factor* **100/1**
9 *1 3/4* **Golden Jubilee (USA)** 2-9-3 0 .... RichardHughes 14 59
(Richard Hannon) *str: lw: mid-div: sn pushed along wknd 2f out* **10/1**
10 *1/2* **Moidore** 2-9-3 0 .... SteveDrowne 12 58
(Roger Charlton) *leggy: attr: chsd ldrs tl lost pl over 3f out: nvr gng pce to get bk on terms* **4/1**[2]
11 *1 1/4* **Imperial Stargazer** 2-9-3 0 .... SamHitchcott 6 55
(Mick Channon) *athletic: bit bkwd: sn outpcd: a towards rr* **100/1**
12 *1 1/4* **Gabrial's Bounty (IRE)** 2-9-3 0 .... JamieSpencer 1 52
(Mick Channon) *lengthy: trckd ldrs: rdn and ev ch over 2f out: wknd ent fnl f* **16/1**
13 *nk* **Malih** 2-9-3 0 .... GrahamGibbons 3 51
(Peter Makin) *str: mid-div: rdn over 2f out: sn wknd* **40/1**
14 *2* **Surrey Dream (IRE)** 2-9-3 0 .... DaneO'Neill 7 46
(Roger Teal) *w'like: scope: mid-div tl wknd 2f out* **18/1**
56 15 *21* **No More Shoes (IRE)**[98] 2902 2-9-3 0 .... KirstyMilczarek 4 —
(Brendan Powell) *chsd ldrs: rdn 3f out: wknd 2f out* **100/1**

1m 27.56s (1.86) **Going Correction** +0.20s/f (Good) **15** Ran SP% **127.9**
Speed ratings (Par 97): **97,96,95,93,92 92,91,89,87,86 85,84,83,81,57**
toteswingers:1&2:£8.20, 2&3:£32.90, 1&3:£13.40 CSF £22.63 TOTE £2.80: £1.30, £3.60, £5.20; EX 41.60.
Owner Saeed Manana **Bred** N E Poole And George Thornton **Trained** Newmarket, Suffolk

FOCUS
Plenty of big stables went unrepresented in this division, but the time was 1.87 seconds quicker than the modestly run first leg, and even more significantly it was also 0.14 seconds faster than the later Class 4 handicap for the 3-y-os. This maiden should produce some nice winners. The fifth helps with the level.

NOTEBOOK
Miblish's sales price decreased from 165,000gns as a foal to 100,000gns as a yearling, but he's his trainer's only entry in the Royal Lodge, Dewhurst and Racing Post Trophy, and the market spoke strongly in his favour. A further indication that he's well regarded came from the booking of stable jockey Philip Robinson on a day the yard won a sales race at Newmarket. Miblish was under pressure before the strong travelling runner-up but kept responding and is evidently pretty useful. This half-brother to useful Irish 6.7f winner Count John, out of a 5f juvenile scorer, will presumably now go up in grade. (op 5-2)
Kaafel(IRE) ◆, the first foal of an unraced dam, travelled strongly, looking the winner for much of the way, but he was not given a hard time. He should improve plenty and looks a decent prospect. (tchd 12-1)
Cathedral ◆, a half-brother to seven winners, including the very smart Vangelis (French 1m-1m2f winner), was short of room at the start and was really going on in the closing stages. He should do a lot better next time.
Buster Brown(IRE) had been absent since finishing third over 6f on his debut in June. Bred to appreciate the step up in trip, this was a pleasing return under a positive ride. (tchd 5-1)
Breaking The Bank, 73-rated, seemed to recover okay from a stumble at the start and ran respectably. (op 11-1 tchd 10-1)
Princess Maya, the only filly in the line-up, was held when short of room in the closing stages, but she would otherwise have finished closer and this was a promising debut. Official explanation: jockey said filly suffered interference inside final furlong
Jupiter Storm ◆, a 55,000gns half-brother to four winners, including high-class French/US 7f-1m1f (Grade 1) winner Gorella, has a Racing Post Trophy entry and that's particularly noteworthy coming from this stable. He was always held but it was eyecatching how strongly he galloped out, going well clear shortly after the line. (tchd 18-1)
Moidore is in the Racing Post Trophy, but this close relation to 1m4f winner Going For Gold was well held. (op 7-1)

6166 DUBAI DUTY FREE DOUBLE MILLIONAIRE NURSERY 6f 8y
4:50 (4:50) (Class 3) (0-95,87) 2-Y-O
£7,158 (£2,143; £1,071; £535; £267; £134) **Stalls** Centre

Form RPR
1 1 **Ortac Rock (IRE)**[14] 5697 2-8-13 82 .... SeanLevey(3) 2 87+
(Richard Hannon) *w'like: lw: chsd ldrs: rdn fr 2f out: chal between horses and n.m.r ins fnl f: styd on gamely to assert fnl 50yds* **5/2**[1]
214 2 *hd* **Key Ambition**[20] 5505 2-8-10 76 .... TomEaves 5 80
(Bryan Smart) *b.hind: hld up in rr but in tch: hdwy to chal 2f out: slt ld jst ins fnl f: hdd and no ex fnl 50yds* **12/1**
1621 3 *1/2* **Democretes**[14] 5708 2-9-5 85 .... RichardHughes 3 88
(Richard Hannon) *sn led: rdn and jnd fr 2f out: narrowly hdd jst ins fnl f: rallied and styd chalng tl outpcd fnl 120yds* **11/4**[2]
0035 4 *1 1/2* **Majestic Rose**[18] 5584 2-8-3 68 ow1 .... ChrisCatlin 6 67
(Mick Channon) *in rr: drvn and hdwy 2f out: styd on ins fnl f to take 4th in clsng stages* **28/1**
4541 5 *1/2* **Dressed In Lace**[9] 5840 2-7-11 66 .... HarryBentley(3) 1 63
(Andrew Balding) *chsd ldrs: rdn 2f out and styd on same pce fnl f: lost 4th in clsng stages* **9/1**
1640 6 *5* **Rooknrasbryripple**[9] 5840 2-7-11 64 oh2 ow2 .... SophieDoyle(3) 4 48
(Mick Channon) *chsd ldrs: drvn over 2f out: sn btn* **50/1**
3412 7 *3 1/2* **Shere Khan**[16] 5638 2-9-6 86 .... SteveDrowne 11 57
(Richard Hannon) *in rr: rdn and sme prog over 2f out: sn edgd lft: nvr nr ldrs and no ch ins fnl f* **10/1**
6210 8 *shd* **Avon Pearl**[49] 4536 2-8-12 78 .... DaneO'Neill 10 49
(Henry Candy) *in tch whn rdn over 2f out: sn outpcd* **7/1**[3]
1130 9 *6* **Mister Musicmaster**[19] 5558 2-9-7 87 .... JamesMillman 9 40
(Rod Millman) *broke wl: rdn and bhd fr 1/2-way* **12/1**
2112 10 *20* **Fanrouge (IRE)**[14] 5701 2-9-5 85 .... IanMongan 8 —
(Malcolm Saunders) *trckd ldrs tl rdn 2f out and wknd qckly: eased whn no ch fnl f* **10/1**

1m 15.57s (2.57) **Going Correction** +0.20s/f (Good) **10** Ran SP% **116.7**
Speed ratings (Par 99): **90,89,89,87,86 79,75,74,66,40**
toteswingers:1&2:£8.80, 2&3:£6.30, 1&3:£2.60 CSF £33.75 CT £88.80 TOTE £3.40: £1.60, £3.00, £1.70; EX 33.60.
Owner Coriolan Links Partnership Iii **Bred** Liam Queally **Trained** East Everleigh, Wilts

FOCUS
They gradually edged towards the nearside rail in this decent nursery. The winner progressed and the second confirmed his Beverley win didn't flatter him.

NOTEBOOK
Ortac Rock(IRE) ◆ made a winning debut over 7f at Ascot,at odds of 66-1, but there seemed no fluke about the success (runner-up looked pretty good when winning next time) and it was slightly surprising Hannon's go-to rider didn't take over this time, albeit the drop back to 6f was an unknown. Perhaps the horse isn't a flashy worker, but he was narrowly favoured in the market this time and was able to follow up. He still looked a bit green and had to be game to take a narrow gap, so all things considered there was much to like about the performance. It seems likely he can rate quite a bit higher, especially back over further. (op 3-1)
Key Ambition, up in trip, showed loads of speed out wide but was gradually worn down by a stronger stayer, one who could be a decent sort. (op 10-1)
Democretes Richard Hughes's chosen mount from the trainer's three runners, was found out by a 7lb rise for his recent Haydock success. This was still a creditable effort in defeat, though. (op 7-2)
Majestic Rose was going on at the finish and might be worth a try over further. (op 25-1)
Dressed In Lace was held off 4lb higher than when winning a lesser race at Chepstow on her previous start (op 8-1)

6167 HEATHERWOLD STUD H'CAP 7f (S)
5:25 (5:25) (Class 4) (0-80,80) 3-Y-O **£3,881** (£1,155; £577; £288) **Stalls** Centre

Form RPR
4411 1 **Ellie In The Pink (IRE)**[20] 5511 3-8-6 68 .... HarryBentley(3) 13 79+
(Alan Jarvis) *hld up in tch on rail: n.m.r over 2f out: qcknd sn after and drvn to ld jst ins fnl f: styd on wl clsng stages* **6/1**[1]
31-0 2 *1/2* **Little Curtsey**[87] 3283 3-9-2 75 .... SteveDrowne 12 85+
(Hughie Morrison) *t.k.h in rr: hdwy towards outside over 2f out: styd on u.p to take 2nd fnl 50yds but no imp on wnr* **12/1**
-060 3 *1/2* **Heezararity**[75] 3688 3-8-4 66 .... LouisBeuzelin(3) 4 75
(Stuart Kittow) *chsd ldrs: drvn and slt ld over 2f out: hdd jst ins fnl f: edgd lft u.p and lost 2nd fnl 50yds* **25/1**
0214 4 *1* **Snow Trooper**[57] 4281 3-8-11 70 .... MartinDwyer 6 76
(Dean Ivory) *towards rr early: hdwy towards outer 3f out: pressed ldrs fr 2f out: styd chalng ins fnl f tl n.m.r and wknd in clsng stages* **12/1**
3514 5 *1* **Silverware (USA)**[18] 5581 3-9-5 78 .... RichardHughes 9 81
(Richard Hannon) *pressed ldrs: rdn and ev ch over 2f out: wknd ins fnl f* **7/1**[2]
3661 6 *1/2* **Apollo D'Negro (IRE)**[31] 5171 3-9-1 74 .... (v) TadhgO'Shea 10 76
(Clive Cox) *chsd ldr: rdn over 2f out: styd on same pce ins fnl f* **11/1**
3640 7 *1* **Riverdale (IRE)**[13] 5760 3-9-1 74 .... (t) TomEaves 8 73
(Nigel Tinkler) *in tch: hdwy over 2f out: chsd ldrs over 1f out: styd on one pce* **33/1**
1000 8 *hd* **Bajan Bear**[11] 5811 3-9-1 74 .... DaneO'Neill 15 73
(Michael Blanshard) *b. hind: s.i.s: in rr: hdwy over 2f out but n.m.r: kpt on ins fnl f: nt rch ldrs* **33/1**
3342 9 *1 1/2* **Uppercut**[18] 5586 3-9-6 79 .... NeilCallan 16 74+
(Stuart Kittow) *chsd ldrs: rdn over 2f out: wknd ins fnl f* **8/1**[3]
0211 10 *1 3/4* **Mrs Greeley**[15] 5676 3-9-3 76 .... WilliamCarson 20 66
(Eve Johnson Houghton) *in rr: rdn over 2f out: sme hdwy ins fnl f* **10/1**
5140 11 *4 1/2* **Uncle Dermot (IRE)**[illegible] [illegible] [illegible] .... KirstyMilczarek 17 18
(Brendan Powell) *in tch: rdn 3f out: sme prog on ins: wknd wl over 1f out* **25/1**
0020 12 *3 1/2* **Sonning Rose (IRE)**[7] 5920 3-9-5 78 .... (v1) ChrisCatlin 2 46
(Mick Channon) *in rr: rdn and sme hdwy on outside over 2f out: nvr rchd ldrs and sn wknd* **14/1**
1063 13 *6* **Loving Thought**[18] 5581 3-8-8 67 .... JamieSpencer 1 19
(Sir Henry Cecil) *in tch towards outside and t.k.h: sme prog and pushed along 2f out: wknd qckly* **9/1**
2640 14 *nk* **Fieldgunner Kirkup (GER)**[14] 5730 3-9-6 79 .... GrahamGibbons 7 30
(David Barron) *s.i.s: in rr: rdn and sme prog 3f out: sn btn* **16/1**
0041 15 *1 3/4* **Colorado Gold**[23] 5412 3-9-7 80 .... PatCosgrave 3 27
(Ed de Giles) *chsd ldrs over 4f out* **40/1**
5256 16 *6* **Roy The Boy (USA)**[35] 5056 3-9-3 76 .... IvaMilickova 14 —
(Jane Chapple-Hyam) *pitched on leaving stalls: sn led on stands' rails: hdd over 2f out: sn wknd* **10/1**
0100 17 *2 3/4* **Da Ponte**[55] 4353 3-9-3 76 .... SamHitchcott 19 —
(Walter Swinburn) *outpcd most of way* **66/1**
0210 18 *2 1/4* **Orpen'Arry (IRE)**[24] 5392 3-9-3 76 .... IanMongan 5 —
(Andrew Haynes) *chsd ldrs 4f* **33/1**
-315 19 *3* **Lucky Meadows (IRE)**[15] 5676 3-8-9 71 .... SeanLevey(3) 18 —
(Richard Hannon) *s.i.s: outpcd most of way* **28/1**

1m 27.7s (2.00) **Going Correction** +0.20s/f (Good) **19** Ran SP% **126.2**
Speed ratings (Par 103): **96,95,94,93,92 92,90,90,88,86 81,77,70,70,68 61,58,56,52**
toteswingers:1&2:£23.10, 2&3:£138.80, 1&3:£46.30. CSF £71.30 CT £1760.16 TOTE £5.00: £1.70, £2.90, £8.40, £3.00; EX 66.60.
Owner Jakellie **Bred** J Jamgotchian **Trained** Twyford, Bucks

FOCUS
A race won in 2007 by subsequent Group-class performer Premio Loco. This was a competitive running, which was hardly surprising considering the number of runners, and they raced towards the near-side rail. Prominent runners fared best and he winner is progressing nicely.
Loving Thought Official explanation: jockey said filly was unsuited by the good (good to soft places) ground
Da Ponte Official explanation: jockey said gelding suffered interference in running
Orpen'Arry(IRE) Official explanation: jockey said gelding ran flat
T/Plt: £253.20 to a £1 stake. Pool of £94,587.92 - 272.64 winning tickets. T/Qpdt: £60.50 to a £1 stake. Pool of £6,552.42 - 80.10 winning tickets. ST

5478 NEWMARKET (R-H)

Saturday, September 17

OFFICIAL GOING: Good to firm (8.9)

Wind: fresh, half behind Weather: dry and breezy

6168 BRITISH STALLION STUDS SUPPORTING BRITISH RACING E B F MAIDEN FILLIES' STKS 1m

1:45 (1:47) (Class 4) 2-Y-O **£4,528** (£1,347; £673; £336) **Stalls** Centre

Form RPR

4 **1** **Gathering (USA)**[64] 4061 2-9-0 0 RobertHavlin 5 84+
(John Gosden) *w ldr tl led travelling wl over 2f out: rdn and qcknd clr wl over 1f out: tiring ins fnl f but a gng to hold on* **3/1**[2]

6 **2** *1 ¼* **Bana Wu**[22] 5445 2-9-0 0 DavidProbert 12 81
(Andrew Balding) *pushed lft s and slowly away: t.k.h: in tch: hdwy to press ldrs 5f out: outpcd over 2f out: rallied u.p to chse clr wnr 1f out: kpt on wl but nvr gng to rch wnr* **11/4**[1]

3 *2 ¼* **Epoque (USA)** 2-9-0 0 TomQueally 4 75+
(Sir Henry Cecil) *s.i.s: rn green: in tch in rr: pushed along and outpcd over 2f out: rallied and swtchd rt over 1f out: styd on steadily ins fnl f: snatched 3rd last strides* **4/1**[3]

00 **4** *hd* **Amelia May**[11] 5806 2-9-0 0 JimCrowley 1 75
(John Gosden) *w ldrs: chsd clr wnr and outpcd wl over 1f out: plugged on same pce ins fnl f* **33/1**

0 **5** *nse* **Seaside Escape (USA)**[22] 5444 2-9-0 0 LiamJones 10 75+
(Brian Meehan) *w ldrs: rdn and unable qck w wnr wl over 1f out: styd on same pce ins fnl f* **20/1**

02 **6** *1 ½* **Cresta Star**[25] 5337 2-9-0 0 PatDobbs 9 71
(Richard Hannon) *sn led and set stdy gallop: hdd over 2f out: rdn and nt gng pce of wnr wl over 1f out: btn and plugged on same pce fr over 1f out* **5/1**

7 *¾* **Cantal** 2-9-0 0 RichardMullen 2 70
(Sir Michael Stoute) *chsd ldrs: rdn and outpcd whn wnr qcknd wl over 1f out: wknd ins fnl f* **8/1**

8 *1 ½* **Mariposa (IRE)** 2-8-11 0 LouisBeuzelin(3) 7 66
(Sir Michael Stoute) *wnt rt at s: t.k.h and sn wl in tch in midfield: rdn and outpcd ent 2f out: wl hld fr over 1f out* **20/1**

0 **9** *4 ½* **Brundon**[19] 5537 2-9-0 0 FergusSweeney 8 56
(Henry Candy) *awkward s and s.i.s: hld up wl in tch in rr: rdn and struggling wl over 2f out: wknd 2f out* **40/1**

03 **10** *8* **Loved By All (IRE)**[31] 5170 2-9-0 0 ShaneKelly 6 41
(Brian Meehan) *in tch: reminders and struggling 3f out: wknd over 2f out: wl bhd and eased ins fnl f* **25/1**

11 *2 ¼* **Corn Maiden** 2-9-0 0 TomMcLaughlin 11 35
(Phil McEntee) *wnt bdly lft s: in tch in rr: rdn and struggling 3f out: sn wl btn: wl bhd and eased ins fnl f* **125/1**

1m 39.27s (0.67) **Going Correction** -0.175s/f (Firm) **11 Ran SP% 119.0**

Speed ratings (Par 94): **89,87,85,85,85 83,83,81,77,69 66**

toteswingers:1&2:£1.90, 2&3:£2.90, 1&3:£2.10 CSF £10.87 TOTE £3.80: £1.60, £1.80, £1.80; EX 14.40 Trifecta £26.40 Pool: £447.86 - 12.51 winning units..

Owner George Strawbridge **Bred** George Strawbridge Jr **Trained** Newmarket, Suffolk

FOCUS

Good to firm ground for the first meeting on the Rowley Mile this autumn. Not a bad-looking fillies' maiden but the pace was very steady early, which didn't help some in terms of settling. The winner can do a good bit better in time.

NOTEBOOK

Gathering(USA) ◆, who made a promising debut on the July course a couple of months ago, skipped clear going into the Dip and, although she got a bit tired late on, won pretty convincingly. She showed a good cruising speed before quickening well and looks a nice filly. Trip wise, this looks about right, both on run style and breeding. (op 7-2 tchd 4-1)

Bana Wu shaped with promise, staying on well in the closing stages from off the pace and she has a pedigree that suggests she'll be a much better filly next year. (op 3-1 tchd 10-3)

Epoque(USA) ◆, whose trainer had won this race in previous years with Midday and Light Shift, could be held in some regard on that evidence. She shaped with enough promise to think she'll be winning races before long. (op 3-1)

Amelia May hadn't shown too much in two previous runs but this was a marked step forward and she is now eligible for handicaps.

Seaside Escape(USA) shaped with promise on her debut but it doesn't look like she has improved on that here. (tchd 22-1)

Cresta Star, who helped set the standard on her previous effort, made the running but did not get home. (tchd 9-2)

Cantal, a half-sister to the Group 3 winner Evasive, showed ability on this debut before weakening. (op 12-1)

6169 £100,000 TATTERSALLS MILLIONS FILLIES' MEDIAN AUCTION STKS (FILLIES) 6f

2:20 (2:22) (Class 2) 2-Y-O

£54,100 (£24,590; £9,840; £4,910; £2,960; £1,970) **Stalls** Centre

Form RPR

45 **1** **Wahylah (IRE)**[42] 4803 2-8-11 0 TomMcLaughlin 10 80
(Clive Brittain) *stdd s: t.k.h: hld up in tch: effrt over 2f out: drvn and pressed ldrs over 1f out: ev ch ins fnl f: kpt on gamely to ld cl home* **10/1**

0446 **2** *nk* **Glee**[12] 5783 2-8-7 75 DavidProbert 2 75
(Richard Hannon) *w ldrs: rdn and ev ch over 1f out: led ent fnl f: kpt on wl u.p tl hdd and no ex cl home* **6/1**[2]

2626 **3** *nk* **Lemon Rock**[21] 5479 2-8-9 75 (p) BACurtis 11 76
(Noel Quinlan) *hld up in tch in rr: hdwy and nt clr run jst over 2f out: drvn and chsd ldrs ent fnl f: ev ch ins fnl f: styd on same pce fnl 50yds* **11/1**

402 **4** *1 ¾* **Symphony Time (IRE)**[23] 5418 2-8-9 53 ShaneKelly 8 71
(Brian Meehan) *led: rdn ent fnl 2f: edgd rt u.p over 1f out: hdd ent fnl f: no ex and btn ins fnl f* **66/1**

3323 **5** *shd* **Roedean (IRE)**[19] 5537 2-8-5 79 RichardMullen 5 67+
(Richard Hannon) *w ldrs: rdn over 2f out: unable qck u.p over 1f out: styd on same pce u.p ins fnl f* **6/1**[2]

4624 **6** *nk* **Tina's Spirit (IRE)**[19] 5562 2-8-13 73 PatDobbs 3 74
(Richard Hannon) *w ldrs: ev ch and rdn jst over 2f out: unable qck over 1f out: styd on same pce u.p ins fnl f* **9/1**[3]

60 **7** *½* **Soho Rocks**[21] 5479 2-8-7 0 RobertHavlin 13 66
(James Toller) *hld up in tch towards rr: hdwy over 2f out: edgd rt and kpt on u.p ins fnl f: nt gng pce to rch ldrs* **33/1**

00 **8** *2 ¼* **Symphony Star (IRE)**[21] 5479 2-8-7 0 CathyGannon 14 59
(Paul D'Arcy) *w ldrs: rdn jst over 2f out: unable qck over 1f out: wknd jst ins fnl f* **25/1**

4 **9** *2 ¾* **Silver Marizah (IRE)**[11] 5813 2-8-9 0 TomQueally 6 53
(Gary Moore) *wl in tch in midfield: rdn and unable qck over 2f out: sn wknd* **5/1**[1]

10 **10** *2* **Kyanight (IRE)**[36] 4999 2-8-7 77 LukeMorris 7 45
(Clive Cox) *in tch in midfield: effrt u.p over 2f out: drvn and no imp wl over 1f out: nvr trbld ldrs* **5/1**[1]

0 **11** *shd* **Moody Dancer**[16] 5655 2-8-9 0 JamesDoyle 12 47
(William Muir) *stdd s: hld up in tch in rr: rdn and struggling over 2f out: no threat to ldrs fr wl over 1f out* **80/1**

12 *3 ½* **Macchiara** 2-8-7 0 MartinLane 1 34
(Rae Guest) *s.i.s: rn green and racing awkwardly in rr: rdn and struggling 3f out: sn wknd* **100/1**

4550 **13** *7* **Busy Bimbo (IRE)**[21] 5479 2-8-5 61 JamesSullivan 4 11
(Alan Berry) *hld up wl in tch: rdn wl over 2f out: sn struggling: wknd qckly ent 2f out* **125/1**

23 **14** *2 ¾* **Gallery**[25] 5351 2-8-7 0 JimCrowley 9 5
(William Haggas) *stdd s: hld up in tch in rr: rdn and no rspnse over 2f out: sn wknd and wl bhd over 1f out* **5/1**[1]

1m 11.46s (-0.74) **Going Correction** -0.175s/f (Firm) **14 Ran SP% 117.3**

Speed ratings (Par 98): **97,96,96,93,93 93,92,89,86,83 83,78,69,65**

toteswingers:1&2:£14.50, 2&3:£13.80, 1&3:£22.10 CSF £65.44 TOTE £11.50: £3.90, £2.30, £3.70; EX 107.90 TRIFECTA Not won..

Owner Saeed Manana **Bred** Rabbah Bloodstock Limited **Trained** Newmarket, Suffolk

FOCUS

Not a strong race despite the big pot, with all bar two of these still maidens coming into the race. They finished compressed and it's hard to rate the form any higher, with the fourth rated only 53.

NOTEBOOK

Wahylah(IRE) refused to enter the stalls on the July course last month but she was much better behaved this time and stepped up on her first two runs to get off the mark. She was dropping back to 6f but the way she finished her race suggests she'll be a better filly over slightly further. She is in the Cheveley Park and Fillies' Mile, so connections are keeping their options open in terms of trip, but either way she will need to improve a good deal on this bare form to be a major player at that level. (op 11-1 tchd 12-1)

Glee, the most exposed runner in the field and rated 75, looked like she'd done enough down the middle of the track but was run out of it close home. She is clearly versatile trip-wise having gone close over 1m2f last time, but her rating of 75 highlights the modest nature of this form. (op 7-2)

Lemon Rock, also rated 75, was a bit keen in the early stages despite sporting cheekpieces for the first time and, while running creditably, she didn't build on previous efforts. (op 10-1 tchd 12-1)

Symphony Time(IRE), rated just 53, made the running but, even allowing for the fact she showed improved form, holds down the race level.

Roedean(IRE), for whom this trip looks a bit too sharp,was only narrowly beaten over 1m last time and she ran well once again but lacked the pace to land a serious blow in the closing stages. (op 13-2)

Silver Marizah(IRE) did not build on the promise of her Polytrack debut on this first try on turf. (op 11-2 tchd 6-1)

Kyanight(IRE) looked useful when winning her maiden on easy ground but has been well held in two subsequent starts on a sound surface. (tchd 11-2, 13-2 in a place)

6170 £200,000 TATTERSALLS MILLIONS MEDIAN AUCTION TROPHY 7f

2:55 (2:57) (Class 2) 2-Y-O

£108,200 (£49,180; £19,680; £9,820; £5,920; £3,940) **Stalls** Centre

Form RPR

0512 **1** **Tell Dad**[3] 6060 2-8-7 89 RichardMullen 4 99
(Richard Hannon) *chsd ldrs: rdn and effrt ent 2f out: drvn ahd over 1f out: styd on strly to forge clr ins fnl f: rdn out* **8/1**

2 *2 ¾* **Alkazim (IRE)**[26] 5333 2-8-7 0 WMLordan 8 92
(David Wachman, Ire) *hld up in tch in midfield: effrt jst over 2f out: rdn and chsd ldng trio over 1f out: kpt on u.p ins fnl f: wnt 2nd last strides: no threat to wnr* **12/1**

1310 **3** *shd* **Mehdi (IRE)**[9] 5849 2-8-13 96 (t) ShaneKelly 13 98
(Brian Meehan) *chsd ldrs: rdn and pressing wnr over 1f out: no ex and btn ins fnl f: lost 2nd last strides* **5/1**[2]

0103 **4** *hd* **Balty Boys (IRE)**[21] 5479 2-8-11 92 MichaelHills 11 95
(Charles Hills) *led: rdn wl over 1f out: drvn and hdd over 1f out: no ex and btn jst ins fnl f: styd on same pce after* **13/2**

2111 **5** *2 ¼* **Coupe De Ville (IRE)**[29] 5234 2-9-1 98 PatDobbs 2 93
(Richard Hannon) *hld up in midfield: rdn and effrt ent fnl 2f: no imp and drvn over 1f out: kpt on ins fnl f but nvr gng pce to chal ldrs* **4/1**[1]

11 **6** *¾* **Tidentime (USA)**[14] 5713 2-8-11 82 JimCrowley 3 87
(Mick Channon) *in tch: rdn and effrt ent fnl 2f: drvn and no imp over 1f out: styd on same pce ins fnl f* **14/1**

0 **7** *shd* **Gregorian (IRE)**[22] 5447 2-8-7 0 RobertHavlin 16 83
(John Gosden) *s.i.s: bhd: hdwy 3f out: rdn and wandering u.p over 1f out: styng on whn nt clr run jst ins fnl f: kpt on fnl 150yds: nvr able to chal* **33/1**

0121 **8** *hd* **Jubilance (IRE)**[16] 5638 2-8-5 87 JohnFahy 6 80
(Jeremy Noseda) *s.i.s: hld up in rr: stl plenty to do whn swtchd rt and rdn over 2f out: hdwy u.p over 1f out: styd on wl ins fnl f: nvr trbld ldrs* **6/1**[3]

6322 **9** *1 ½* **Perfect Delight**[11] 5807 2-8-0 75 LukeMorris 9 72
(Clive Cox) *chsd ldrs: rdn 1/2-way: struggling u.p ent fnl 2f: wknd jst over 1f out* **28/1**

02 **10** *¾* **Hazaz (IRE)**[79] 3552 2-8-13 0 TomQueally 12 83
(Clive Brittain) *chsd ldrs: rdn 2f out: unable qck and edgd lft u.p 1f out: wknd fnl 150yds* **12/1**

661 **11** *nse* **Daghash**[3] 6048 2-8-5 0 AhmedAjtebi 14 75
(Clive Brittain) *hld up towards rr: effrt and nt clr run 2f out: edgd rt and hdwy over 1f out: kpt on but nvr threatened ldrs* **18/1**

2655 **12** *1 ¼* **Orders From Rome (IRE)**[21] 5479 2-8-7 85 CathyGannon 1 73
(Eve Johnson Houghton) *hld up in midfield: rdn and effrt over 2f out: no imp and wknd over 1f out* **25/1**

624 **13** *nk* **Chapter Seven**[21] 5479 2-8-7 82 BarryMcHugh 5 72
(Richard Fahey) *in tch in midfield: rdn and struggling wl over 2f out: drvn and no imp fnl 2f* **14/1**

6 **14** *8* **Charley's Mount (IRE)**[36] 4996 2-8-13 0 LiamJones 10 58
(Brian Meehan) *chsd ldrs: rdn and lost pl qckly wl over 2f out: wl bhd over 1f out* **66/1**

15 *5* **Dance With Me (IRE)** 2-8-13 0 DavidProbert 15 45
(Andrew Balding) *s.i.s: rn green and in rr thrght: lost tch and hung bdly rt over 2f out* **20/1**

000 **16** *11* **Itsonlymakebelieve (IRE)**[21] 5479 2-8-2 40 (v) MartinLane 7 —
(Ian Wood) *a towards rr: rdn and toiling 1/2-way: sn lost tch: t.o ins fnl f* **200/1**

1m 22.97s (-2.43) **Going Correction** -0.175s/f (Firm) 2y crse rec **16 Ran SP% 126.4**

Speed ratings (Par 101): **106,102,102,102,99 99,98,98,97,96 96,94,94,85,79 66**

toteswingers:1&2:£27.40, 2&3:£14.40, 1&3:£9.90 CSF £98.14 TOTE £10.20: £2.80, £3.60, £2.10; EX 140.80 Trifecta £615.00 Part won. Pool: £831.19 - 0.10 winning units..

Owner Andrew Tinkler **Bred** Wallace Holmes & Partners **Trained** East Everleigh, Wilts

The Form Book, Raceform Ltd, Compton, RG20 6NL

FOCUS
A much stronger race than the fillies' event earlier, with the leading contenders rated in the high 90s and the winner on an upward curve. He is rated to his Ripon mark.

NOTEBOOK
Tell Dad had work to do on these terms and he had still to prove this trip was ideal coming into the race, but he won in convincing style and just looks a better horse since being gelded. He displayed an impressive turn of foot to quicken away from his rivals and is better than official rating on this evidence.

Alkazim(IRE), who had finished second in three Irish maidens, was stepping back in trip here and he lacked the gear change of the winner in the closing stages. That said, he looks sure to win races back up to a mile and further, especially next year. (tchd 11-1)

Mehdi(IRE), for whom things didn't go to plan at Doncaster, had were no excuses this time and he had every chance up the stands' rail. This was solid enough but the two in front of him are rated in the 80s, whereas he is rated 96, so it's likely he's a touch flattered by that mark. (tchd 9-2 and 11-2)

Balty Boys(IRE) was outpointed in the closing stages and the Group 1 entries he holds look a bit fanciful now. (op 9-1)

Coupe De Ville(IRE), a Racing Post Trophy entry, was abit disappointing but he was outpaced going into the Dip and maybe these conditions were a bit quick for him. (tchd 9-2)

Gregorian(IRE)'s rider reported that the colt lost his action in the Dip. Official explanation: jockey said colt lost its action in the dip

Jubilance(IRE), a dual winner at this trip, missed the break and only started to close down on the leaders up the hill. (op 13-2 tchd 7-1)

6171 BETFRED CESAREWITCH TRIAL (H'CAP) 2m 2f
3:30 (3:35) (Class 2) (0-105,95) 3-Y-O+ **£32,345** (£9,625; £4,810; £2,405) **Stalls** Centre

Form RPR

0651 **1** **Cosimo de Medici**[22] 5448 4-8-13 **84**............................(t) RobertHavlin 3 93
(Hughie Morrison) *stdd s: hld up in last quartet: hdwy to join ldrs travelling wl 3f out: led over 2f out: rdn and wnt clr w rival ent fnl 2f: styd on wl and forged ahd ins fnl f* **13/2**[2]

1002 **2** *1* **Dark Ranger**[46] 4635 5-7-13 **70**.. MartinLane 10 78
(Tim Pitt) *in tch: hdwy to chal over 3f out: ev ch and rdn clr w wnr ent 2f out: no ex ins fnl f: styng on same pce and btn whn rdr dropped reins fnl 100yds* **16/1**

0553 **3** *1 ½* **Gordonsville**[15] 5685 8-8-6 **80**.. JohnFahy(3) 6 86
(Jim Goldie) *hld up in last quartet: hdwy over 4f out: rdn over 2f out: chsd clr ldng pair over 1f out: kpt on dourly u.p ins fnl f: nt rch ldrs* **12/1**

/0-6 **4** *6* **Secret Tune**[36] 4998 7-8-6 **77**..(t) AhmedAjtebi 2 77
(Shaun Lycett) *chsd ldrs tl led over 4f out: rdn and hdd over 2f out: wknd u.p wl over 1f out* **25/1**

3122 **5** *1* **Mohanad (IRE)**[9] 5857 5-8-8 **79**.. JamesDoyle 18 78
(Sheena West) *in tch in midfield: hdwy 8f out: pressed ldrs and rdn 4f out: wknd ent fnl 2f* **17/2**

0111 **6** *hd* **French Hollow**[28] 5273 6-8-7 **78**.. JamesSullivan 14 76
(Tim Fitzgerald) *stdd s: t.k.h: hld up towards rr: hdwy into midfield 12f out: rdn and effrt 3f out: no prog and drvn ent fnl 2f: wl hld after* **7/1**[3]

0000 **7** *2 ¾* **L Frank Baum (IRE)**[13] 5759 4-8-7 **78**.. DavidProbert 17 73
(Gay Kelleway) *in tch: effrt u.p and chsd ldrs 4f out: wknd over 2f out* **16/1**

1004 **8** *1 ½* **My Arch**[22] 5448 9-9-3 **88**.. TomQueally 4 82
(Ollie Pears) *chsd ldr tl 4f out: sn lost pl u.p: no ch fr wl over 2f out* **9/1**

9 *1* **Big Occasion (IRE)**[342] 6787 4-9-10 **95**..........................(b) JimCrowley 9 88
(David Pipe) *t.k.h: chsd ldrs: ev ch over 4f out: rdn and wknd wl over 2f out* **6/1**[1]

0201 **10** *7* **Hollins**[52] 4423 7-8-5 **81**.. JamesRogers(5) 16 66
(Micky Hammond) *led tl hdd and rdn over 4f out: wknd 3f out* **12/1**

-004 **11** *½* **Palomar (USA)**[88] 3243 9-9-0 **85**.. JimmyQuinn 12 69
(Brian Ellison) *taken down early: stdd s: hld up in last quartet: rdn and struggling 4f out: wknd 3f out* **22/1**

4222 **12** *16* **Eshtyaaq**[28] 5273 4-8-7 **78**.. CathyGannon 13 45
(David Evans) *t.k.h: hld up towards rr: hdwy into midfield 12f out: rdn and dropped out qckly over 3f out: wl bhd 2f out: t.o* **10/1**

32-0 **13** *27* **Sea Change (IRE)**[30] 5221 4-8-5 **76** RichardMullen 1 13
(Jim Goldie) *in tch in midfield: struggling u.p 6f out: wknd over 4f out: t.o 2f out* **33/1**

2103 **14** *19* **Rosewin (IRE)**[28] 5273 5-8-12 **83**.. BarryMcHugh 8 —
(Ollie Pears) *taken down early: hld up in rr: lost tch over 4f out: sn t.o* **20/1**

3m 49.25s (-7.55) **Going Correction** -0.175s/f (Firm)
WFA 3 from 4yo+ 13lb **14** Ran SP% **112.8**
Speed ratings (Par 109): **109,108,107,105,104 104,103,102,102,99 99,91,79,71**
toteswingers:1&2:£10.20, 2&3:£74.30, 1&3:£17.00 CSF £84.87 CT £907.50 TOTE £7.70: £2.60, £5.20, £4.10; EX 125.30 Trifecta £515.60 Part won. Pool: £696.78 - 0.50 winning units..
Owner Bevan, Doyle & Lawrence **Bred** Shortgrove Manor Stud **Trained** East Ilsley, Berks
■ Montparnasse (17/2) was withdrawn. Deduct 10p in the £ under R4.

FOCUS
A competitive Cesarewitch trial but the front three finished clear.

NOTEBOOK
Cosimo de Medici ◆ looks to be an improving stayer, having won decisively on soft ground at the July course last month, and he proved those conditions aren't paramount by following up on a much quicker surface here. Whether the 4lb penalty he picks up for this will be enough to get him into the Cesarewitch remains to be seen but he's got a good cruising speed and he finds plenty for pressure, so he'll be winning more races no matter where he goes. If he does get into the Cesarewitch, he'll be a threat to all off a low weight. (op 8-1)

Dark Ranger ◆ ran a blinder off a light weight, travelling smoothly into contention and going down fighting. He looks appealingly handicapped on this evidence.

Gordonsville has been running well of late and this was another solid effort. He doesn't win much nowadays but he's clearly still got the ability to win off this sort of mark if he can hold this level of form.

Secret Tune is potentially well handicapped on the level given he is a 126-rated hurdler and there was enough encouragement in this effort to suggest he can win off this sort of mark, especially on slightly easier ground.

Mohanad(IRE) ran okay but the handicapper has him where he wants him. (op 12-1)

French Hollow has been most progressive this summer but this was easily his toughest assignement to date and he was beaten fair and square. (tchd 8-1)

Eshtyaaq's rider reported that the gelding ran too free. Official explanation: jockey said gelding ran too free (op 11-1)

Sea Change(IRE)'s rider reported that the gelding did not stay. Official explanation: jockey said gelding did not stay (op 40-1)

Rosewin(IRE)'s rider reported that the mare ran too free to post. Official explanation: jockey said mare ran too free to post (op 16-1)

6172 E B F "NOTNOWCATO" FILLIES' H'CAP 1m 4f
4:05 (4:10) (Class 3) (0-95,92) 3-Y-O+ **£8,409** (£2,502; £1,250; £625) **Stalls** Centre

Form RPR

3012 **1** **Qushchi**[21] 5482 3-9-3 **89**.. TomQueally 3 102
(William Jarvis) *chsd ldr: rdn over 2f out: ev ch over 1f out: led 1f out: forged ahd fnl 100yds: kpt on wl: rdn out* **5/1**[1]

2602 **2** *1 ¼* **Quiz Mistress**[14] 5714 3-8-1 **73**.. CathyGannon 12 84
(Gerard Butler) *stdd s: t.k.h: hld up towards rr early: hdwy to ld over 10f out: rdn wl over 2f out: battled on gamely and forged ahd w wnr wl over 1f out: hdd 1f out: kpt on trying tl no ex and btn fnl 100yds* **16/1**

1115 **3** *1 ½* **Twin Soul (IRE)**[37] 4971 3-8-1 **73** oh1.. DavidProbert 13 82
(Andrew Balding) *t.k.h: hld up wl in tch in midfield: rdn and effrt over 2f out: chsd ldng pair and hung rt over 1f out: kpt on* **8/1**

301 **4** *5* **Dubai Glory**[37] 4971 3-8-8 **80**.. JamesDoyle 2 81
(Sheena West) *led tl over 10f out: chsd ldrs after: rdn over 2f out: unable qck u.p 2f out: btn over 1f out: wknd ins fnl f* **8/1**

201 **5** *2* **Golden Waters**[15] 5666 4-8-10 **74**.. ShaneKelly 4 72
(Eve Johnson Houghton) *wl in tch in midfield: rdn and effrt over 2f out: no imp and flashing tail u.p over 1f out: sn edgd lft and wknd* **33/1**

1111 **6** *3 ¼* **Easy Terms**[87] 3277 4-9-8 **86**.. JamesSullivan 8 79
(Edwin Tuer) *hld up wl in tch: rdn and unable qck ent 2f out: btn over 1f out: wknd ins fnl f* **9/1**

10-0 **7** *hd* **Midnight Caller**[136] 1807 3-9-1 **87**.. RobertHavlin 9 79
(John Gosden) *hld up wl in tch and travelled wl: rdn and fnd little jst over 2f out: sn btn: wknd over 1f out* **14/1**

1042 **8** *13* **Creme Anglaise**[31] 5177 3-9-6 **92**.. RichardMullen 10 63
(Michael Bell) *hld up in tch in towards rr: rdn and effrt 3f out: fnd little and sn btn: wknd over 2f out: wl bhd and eased ins fnl f* **9/1**

2152 **9** *2 ¼* **Crassula**[35] 5057 3-8-11 **83**.. LukeMorris 5 51
(Terry Clement) *chsd ldrs: rdn 6f out: styd chsng ldrs tl lost pl u.p 3f out: wl bhd 2f out: eased wl ins fnl f* **7/1**[3]

0320 **10** *8* **Chilly Filly (IRE)**[8] 5878 5-9-3 **81**..........................(be[1]) JimmyQuinn 1 36
(Brian Ellison) *dwlt: in tch in rr: rdn and fnd nil wl over 2f out: sn wl bhd: eased ins fnl f: t.o* **6/1**[2]

1220 **11** *10* **Masaraat (FR)**[28] 5283 3-9-1 **87**.. MichaelHills 11 26
(John Dunlop) *hld up wl in tch: rdn and fnd nil over 2f out: sn lost tch: t.o and eased ins fnl f* **6/1**[2]

2m 27.07s (-4.93) **Going Correction** -0.175s/f (Firm)
WFA 3 from 4yo+ 8lb **11** Ran SP% **115.5**
Speed ratings (Par 104): **109,108,107,103,102 100,100,91,90,84 78**
toteswingers:1&2:£19.10, 2&3:£32.60, 1&3:£13.40 CSF £84.40 CT £630.43 TOTE £5.20: £1.90, £5.70, £2.10; EX 93.90 TRIFECTA Not won..
Owner Gillian, Lady Howard De Walden **Bred** Avington Manor Stud **Trained** Newmarket, Suffolk

FOCUS
Not a strong race for the level with top-weight rated 9lb below the race ceilinge.

NOTEBOOK
Qushchi had to work hard to get the better of the gallant Quiz Mistress but she has a great attitude of her own and she stayed on the better of the pair in the closing stages to win her second race of the season and third in all. She seems to handle most ground, can be ridden in different ways, and still seems to be improving, so must be a cracking filly to own. (op 6-1)

Quiz Mistress ◆ ran a cracker from the front despite racing a bit keenly early on. She is still to win on turf but the drop back to this trip appeared to suit and she looks well up to winning races off this sort of mark. (tchd 20-1)

Twin Soul(IRE) has been progressive on Polytrack this year but is clearly at least as good on turf on this evidence. She stayed on well, building on her Salisbury return last month, and remains on an upward curve. (op 7-1 tchd 6-1)

Dubai Glory, for whom a 6lb rise for her emphatic Salisbury success looked fair enough, couldn't run to the same level this time and probably needs to take another step forward. (op 7-1)

Golden Waters was up in trip and did not appear to get home on this very differnet track to her favourite Brighton.

Easy Terms was bidding for a five-timer on this return from a break but was 8lb higher and could not get involved. (op 7-1)

Midnight Caller was down in grade on this first start since May but might prefer easier ground. (op 11-1 tchd 10-1)

Masaraat(FR)'s trainer reported that the filly was unsuited by the good to firm ground. Official explanation: trainer said filly was unsuited by the good to firm ground (op 7-1)

6173 HQ HOSPITALITY H'CAP 1m
4:40 (4:43) (Class 3) (0-90,89) 3-Y-O+ **£8,409** (£2,502; £1,250; £625) **Stalls** Centre

Form RPR

1006 **1** **Indian Jack (IRE)**[14] 5712 3-9-2 **85**.. RichardMullen 3 95
(Alan Bailey) *hld up in rr: rdn and effrt 3f out: hdwy u.p over 1f out: ev ch ins fnl f: led fnl 75yds: kpt on wl u.p* **10/1**

4501 **2** *½* **Hacienda (IRE)**[7] 5920 4-9-4 **83**.. LukeMorris 8 92
(Mark Johnston) *led: rdn ent fnl 2f: battled on gamely u.p tl hdd and no ex fnl 75yds* **13/2**[3]

1411 **3** *1 ½* **Invincible Hero (IRE)**[10] 5828 4-8-8 **78**..........................(t) NeilFarley(5) 2 84
(Declan Carroll) *t.k.h: chsd ldrs: rdn and pressed ldr ent 2f out: ev ch 1f out: no ex and btn fnl 100yds: wknd towards fin* **10/3**[1]

3440 **4** *hd* **Arabian Spirit**[49] 4561 6-9-9 **88**.. BarryMcHugh 10 93
(Richard Fahey) *hld up in tch towards rr: hdwy over 2f out: chsd ldng trio ent fnl f: styd on same pce u.p ins fnl f* **8/1**

3123 **5** *1 ½* **Saskia's Dream**[22] 5450 3-8-8 **77**..........................(p) RobertHavlin 11 79+
(Jane Chapple-Hyam) *hld up in rr: c to r against stands' rail after 2f out: nt clr run over 2f out: swtchd rt 2f out: hdwy u.p over 1f out: kpt on ins fnl f: nvr gng pce to rch ldrs* **14/1**

5200 **6** *½* **Mcbirney (USA)**[21] 5482 4-8-11 **83**.......................... ChristopherGraham(7) 4 83
(Paul D'Arcy) *in tch in midfield: pushed along 3f out: kpt on same pce fr over 1f out* **14/1**

0013 **7** *shd* **Spa's Dancer (IRE)**[14] 5240 4-9-2 **81**.. MichaelHills 1 81
(J W Hills) *in tch: lost pl and dropped in rr over 2f out: pushed along and hdwy over 1f out: edgd lft and rdn 1f out: kpt on ins fnl f: unable to chal* **14/1**

3110 **8** *¾* **Master Mylo (IRE)**[14] 5718 4-9-5 **84**.. ShaneKelly 5 83
(Dean Ivory) *taken down early: hld up in rr: hdwy 3f out: drvn and no imp over 1f out: plugged on same pce and n.d ins fnl f* **18/1**

256 **9** *3 ¾* **Trojan Nights (USA)**[49] 4553 3-9-3 **89**.. JohnFahy(3) 12 79
(William Haggas) *rdn along leaving stalls and c to r against stands' rail thrght: chsd ldr: rdn 2f out: drvn and wknd over 1f out* **5/1**[2]

0020 **10** *2 ¼* **Camerooney**[8] 5888 8-9-1 **80**.. JamesSullivan 6 65
(Brian Ellison) *pressed ldrs: c to r against stands' rail after 2f: lost pl and rdn 3f out: bhd and wkng whn pushed rt and hmpd 2f out: sn bhd* **16/1**

60-0 **11** *shd* **King Of Windsor (IRE)**[29] 5240 4-9-4 **83**.......................... JimCrowley 9 68
(Ralph Beckett) *in tch in midfield: rdn and hdwy 3f out: wknd wl over 1f out* **8/1**

1m 35.46s (-3.14) **Going Correction** -0.175s/f (Firm)
WFA 3 from 4yo+ 4lb **11** Ran SP% **115.5**
Speed ratings (Par 107): **108,107,106,105,104 103,103,102,99,96 96**
CSF £72.32 CT £269.44 TOTE £11.40: £2.80, £2.10, £1.70; EX 72.90 Trifecta £167.10 Pool: £884.93 - 3.91 winning units..
Owner Forza Azzurri **Bred** Waterford Hall Stud **Trained** Newmarket, Suffolk
■ Stewards' Enquiry : Robert Havlin caution; careless riding.

NOTEBOOK
Indian Jack(IRE) ◆, whose trainer's horses are in really good form, emphasised that by building on a very encouraging return to action on the all-weather this month. Still lightly raced, he resumed his early-season progress here, staying on well down the middle of the track to land his first turf success. He looks a horse still on the up and he might prove better on easier ground than this, as his sire was a much better horse on soft. (op 8-1)
Hacienda(IRE) loves quick ground and he ran well from the front and kept on well in the closing stages. He will win more races off this sort of mark, especially when allowed to dominate. (op 5-1 tchd 9-2)
Invincible Hero(IRE), the legends' race winner, was up another 8lb, which is probably a bit harsh given the unreliable nature of that form, but he ran another solid race despite racing quite keenly early on. The handicapper is asking a serious question now though. (op 6-1 tchd 3-1)
Arabian Spirit is a reliable performer in the main and he bounced back from a forgettable effort in first-time blinkers last time. This was much more like it and he'll be getting his head back in front soon. (op 9-1)
Saskia's Dream ◆ is the one to take out of the race from the remainder, she was travelling well up the rail when short of room, and she stayed on well once in the clear but never had any chance given the way things panned out. (op 12-1)
Spa's Dancer(IRE)'s rider reported that the gelding hung left. Official explanation: jockey said gelding hung left (op 12-1 tchd 16-1)
King Of Windsor(IRE)'s rider reported that the gelding was unsuited by the good to firm ground. Official explanation: jockey said gelding was unsuited by the good to firm ground (op 7-1)

6174 SHOEBURYNESS CONSERVATIVE CLUB H'CAP 6f
5:15 (5:18) (Class 4) (0-85,85) 3-Y-0+ **£5,175** (£1,540; £769; £384) **Stalls** Centre

Form RPR
5-15 **1** **Murura (IRE)**[55] 4357 4-9-5 **83**........................(b) DavidProbert 10 93
(Kevin Ryan) *racd keenly: chsd ldrs: chsd ldr after 2f out: ev ch and rdn wl over 1f out: led narrowly over 1f out: kpt on wl: rdn out* **11/2**[2]

5036 **2** *½* **Jack My Boy (IRE)**[22] 5451 4-8-11 **75**....................(v) CathyGannon 14 83
(David Evans) *chsd ldrs: effrt u.p 2f out: ev ch 1f out: no ex and hld towards fin* **12/1**

0040 **3** *½* **Button Moon (IRE)**[14] 5703 3-9-3 **83**......................(p) MartinLane 2 90
(Ian Wood) *chsd ldr tl led over 4f out: rdn 2f out: hdd over 1f out: kpt on wl and stl ev ch tl no ex wl ins fnl f* **25/1**

2311 **4** *hd* **Cape Classic (IRE)**[46] 4643 3-8-12 **78**........................ LiamJones 15 84+
(William Haggas) *in tch: rdn and outpcd over 2f out: rallied u.p 1f out: styd on wl ins fnl f: nt quite rch ldrs* **6/1**[3]

4025 **5** *hd* **Silver Wind**[4] 6022 6-8-9 **73**..............................(b) ShaneKelly 12 79
(Alan McCabe) *dwlt: sn chsng ldrs: rdn and outpcd over 2f out: rallied u.p 1f out: kpt on wl ins fnl f* **25/1**

2441 **6** *hd* **Sluggsy Morant**[18] 5587 3-9-1 **81**........................ FergusSweeney 4 86
(Henry Candy) *in tch: rdn and outpcd 3f out: rallied and hdwy u.p ent fnl f: styd on wl fnl 100yds: could nt rch ldrs* **12/1**

2200 **7** *1* **Cornus**[6] 5972 9-9-0 **78**....................................(be) JamesDoyle 1 80+
(Alan McCabe) *in rr of main gp: hdwy u.p ent fnl f: styd on strly fnl 100yds: nt rch ldrs* **25/1**

/031 **8** *nse* **Fabreze**[15] 5683 6-9-7 **85**.. TomQueally 3 87+
(Peter Makin) *s.i.s: sn detached in last trio: rdn and struggling 1/2-way: hdwy over 1f out: edgd lft jst ins fnl f: r.o strly fnl 100yds: nt rch ldrs* **10/1**

4U20 **9** *hd* **Restless Bay (IRE)**[15] 5680 3-8-11 **77**.................(p) FrankieMcDonald 16 78
(Reg Hollinshead) *dwlt: sn in tch: rdn and outpcd over 2f out: rallied u.p jst over 1f out: kpt on ins fnl f* **40/1**

-006 **10** *nk* **Lenny Bee**[14] 5703 5-9-6 **84**.................................(t) RobertHavlin 19 84
(George Foster) *led tl over 4f out: chsd ldrs after tl rdn and outpcd wl over 1f out: btn 1f out and kpt on same pce after* **33/1**

5113 **11** *½* **Oneladyowner**[6] 5972 3-9-5 **85**............................ RichardMullen 17 83+
(David Brown) *s.i.s: bhd: hdwy into midfield and rdn 1/2-way: kpt on f but nvr gng pce to rch ldrs* **5/1**[1]

160 **12** *1* **Redvers (IRE)**[6] 5972 3-9-5 **85**.............................. JimCrowley 6 80+
(Ralph Beckett) *sn bhd in last trio: rdn and detached 1/2-way: hdwy over 1f out: styng on but stl plenty to do whn sltly hmpd ins fnl f: kpt on: nvr trbld ldrs* **20/1**

5040 **13** *1 ½* **One Way Or Another (AUS)**[59] 4215 8-8-4 **75**......... RaulDaSilva(7) 20 65
(Jeremy Gask) *chsd ldrs: stdd bk into midfield after 1f: effrt and rdn 2f out: hung rt and no prog over 1f out* **12/1**

1111 **14** *1* **Blues Jazz**[13] 5760 5-9-2 **80**.................................. BarryMcHugh 11 67
(Ian Semple) *s.i.s: sn outpcd and detached in last: styd on u.p fr over 1f out: nvr trbld ldrs* **9/1**

0126 **15** *¾* **Picabo (IRE)**[10] 5831 3-8-10 **76**.............................. LukeMorris 7 61
(Lucy Wadham) *dwlt: towards rr: hdwy into midfield and rdn 1/2-way: wknd jst over 1f out* **16/1**

1600 **16** *2 ¼* **Desert Strike**[10] 5831 5-8-5 **74**........................(p) RosieJessop(5) 18 52
(Alan McCabe) *dwlt: sn in tch: rdn and unable qck over 2f out: steadily lost pl fr over 1f out: wknd ins fnl f* **66/1**

1011 **17** *3 ¼* **George Baker (IRE)**[25] 5341 4-9-2 **80**........................ MichaelHills 9 47
(George Baker) *hld up in midfield: rdn and no hdwy 2f out: in rr and wkng whn hmpd and snatched up jst ins fnl f: eased after* **12/1**

1m 10.35s (-1.85) **Going Correction** -0.175s/f (Firm)
WFA 3 from 4yo+ 2lb **17** Ran SP% **125.3**
Speed ratings (Par 105): **105,104,103,103,103 102,101,101,101,100 100,98,96,95,94 91,87**
toteswingers:1&2:£25.60, 2&3:£56.20, 1&3:£25.60 CSF £65.89 CT £1612.26 TOTE £8.30: £2.10, £2.90, £5.40, £2.20; EX 111.60.
Owner Mrs R G Hillen **Bred** Corrin Stud **Trained** Hambleton, N Yorks

FOCUS
They looked to go quite hard here and a lot of these were struggling two out, but the pace held up as the principles were all close up throughout. There were a lot of horses covered by just a few lengths at the finish though, which casts doubt over the validity of the form.
T/Plt: £265.00 to a £1 stake. Pool of £69,958.08 - 192.71 winning tickets. T/Qpdt: £31.20 to a £1 stake. Pool of £4,191.05 - 99.38 winning tickets. SP

[6131]WOLVERHAMPTON (A.W) (L-H)
Saturday, September 17

OFFICIAL GOING: Standard
Wind: half behind Weather: sunny turning overcast

6175 GREAT OFFERS @ WOLVERHAMPTON-RACECOURSE.CO.UK H'CAP (DIV I) 5f 20y(P)
5:50 (5:50) (Class 6) (0-55,55) 3-Y-0+ **£1,363** (£402; £201) **Stalls** Low

Form RPR
0214 **1** **Griffin Point (IRE)**[6] 5965 4-9-3 **55**.............................. GeorgeBaker 7 68
(William Muir) *mde all: rdn and edgd rt over 1f out: hld on wl: all out* **11/4**[2]

0000 **2** *shd* **Canadian Danehill (IRE)**[79] 3556 9-8-9 **47**..................(p) JackMitchell 6 60
(Robert Cowell) *mounted outside paddock: rdn and carried hd high 2f out: drvn to chse ldng pair ins fnl f and edgd rt: fin wl: jst failed* **9/1**

3365 **3** *2 ¾* **Sharp Bullet (IRE)**[14] 5719 5-9-2 **54**........................(p) NeilChalmers 9 57
(Bruce Hellier) *chsd ldr: rdn 2f out: wknd and lost tch w ldng pair ins fnl f: jst hld on for 3rd* **6/1**

3043 **4** *nse* **Little Perisher**[7] 5917 4-8-6 **47**..........................(b) KierenFox(3) 1 50
(Karen George) *s.i.s: urged along and outpcd 3f out: styd on past btn horses ins fnl f: nrly snatched 3rd* **5/2**[1]

0600 **5** *¾* **Vhujon (IRE)**[74] 3714 6-8-13 **51**.......................... RobbieFitzpatrick 5 51
(Peter Grayson) *midfield: rdn over 2f out: wknd 1f out: one pce* **20/1**

4605 **6** *nk* **Lithaam (IRE)**[9] 5865 7-8-6 **47** oh1 ow1..................(tp) RyanClark(3) 8 46
(Milton Bradley) *prom: rdn 3f out: hrd drvn 2f out: wknd ins fnl f* **11/1**

6426 **7** *nk* **Best One**[5] 5996 7-8-11 **49**.................................(v) TomMcLaughlin 2 47
(Ronald Harris) *midfield: rdn and sn one pce 2f out: wknd ins fnl f* **11/2**[3]

6660 **8** *1* **Running Water**[24] 5388 3-8-7 **46** oh1..........................(p) MarcHalford 4 40
(Hugh McWilliams) *slowly away: a in rr: drvn and no imp fnl 2f* **66/1**

61.12 secs (-1.18) **Going Correction** -0.175s/f (Stan)
WFA 3 from 4yo+ 1lb **8** Ran SP% **109.5**
Speed ratings (Par 101): **102,101,97,97,96 95,95,93**
toteswingers:1&2:£4.90, 2&3:£6.60, 1&3:£3.70 CSF £25.02 CT £123.37 TOTE £3.30: £1.40, £2.60, £2.20; EX 25.50.
Owner F Hope **Bred** Vincent Dunne **Trained** Lambourn, Berks

FOCUS
There were plenty who liked to be held up and come late, but the race did not pan out as expected.

6176 GREAT OFFERS @ WOLVERHAMPTON-RACECOURSE.CO.UK H'CAP (DIV II) 5f 20y(P)
6:20 (6:20) (Class 6) (0-55,55) 3-Y-0+ **£1,363** (£402; £201) **Stalls** Low

Form RPR
4440 **1** **Howyadoingnotsobad (IRE)**[7] 5917 3-8-10 **52**............. KierenFox(3) 1 60
(Karen George) *pressed ldr: rdn and led over 1f out: r.o strly and sn in command* **7/2**[2]

/2-0 **2** *2* **Nordic Light (USA)**[7] 5917 7-8-3 **46** oh1................. JemmaMarshall(5) 5 47
(Mrs A Malzard, Jersey) *rdn and sn led: hdd over 1f out: sn no ch w wnr: kpt on* **16/1**

5041 **3** *½* **Rightcar**[9] 5865 4-9-0 **52**...................................... RobbieFitzpatrick 3 51
(Peter Grayson) *s.i.s: niggled along 3f out: nt clr run over 2f out: drvn along and styd on wl 1f out: fin wl* **10/3**[1]

300 **4** *2 ¼* **These Dreams**[30] 5215 3-8-9 **48**.................................. NeilChalmers 7 39
(Richard Guest) *in rr: rdn and short of room wl over 1f out: swtchd rt and kpt on past btn horses ins fnl f* **14/1**

0543 **5** *nk* **Instructress**[7] 5941 3-8-12 **51**.................................. JackMitchell 8 41
(Robert Cowell) *t.k.h: midfield: rdn 2f out: forced wd on home bnd: hung lft and kpt on one pce ins fnl f* **11/2**

0000 **6** *½* **Lovely Lynn (IRE)**[24] 5373 3-8-7 **46** oh1..................... SaleemGolam 4 34
(Declan Carroll) *midfield: urged along 3f out: rdn and effrt over 1f out: wknd ins fnl f* **33/1**

0-00 **7** *1* **Arakova (IRE)**[45] 4657 3-8-5 **47**..........................(p) RossAtkinson(3) 6 31
(Matthew Salaman) *s.i.s: in rr: rdn 3f out: no imp ins fnl f* **20/1**

5660 **8** *½* **Lady Rumba**[87] 3272 3-8-0 **46** oh1.............................. NoelGarbutt(7) 2 29
(John O'Shea) *in tch: bmpd and rdr lost iron (nvr rcvrd it) after 2f out: effrt over 1f out: one pce ins fnl f* **22/1**

0400 **9** *nk* **Lily Wood**[18] 5603 5-8-4 **47**................................(b[1]) MatthewCosham(5) 9 29
(James Unett) *midfield: forced wd over 2f out: rdn and bmpd over 1f out: sn wknd* **9/2**[3]

0000 **10** *3* **Sensational Love (IRE)**[17] 5620 3-9-2 **55**..............(v[1]) GeorgeBaker 10 26
(Keith Dalgleish) *taken down early: pressed ldng pair: rdn and wknd qckly over 1f out: eased cl home* **9/1**

61.64 secs (-0.66) **Going Correction** -0.175s/f (Stan)
WFA 3 from 4yo+ 1lb **10** Ran SP% **113.5**
Speed ratings (Par 101): **98,94,94,90,89 89,87,86,86,81**
CSF £53.98 CT £200.42 TOTE £4.10: £1.40, £4.60, £1.20; EX 59.30.
Owner Ten Four Fun **Bred** J G Reid **Trained** Higher Eastington, Devon

FOCUS
The gallop was decent for a weak sprint handicap which was full of exposed performers, bar one.
Sensational Love(IRE) Official explanation: jockey said filly hung right

6177 WILLIAM HILL - THE HOME OF BETTING H'CAP 5f 216y(P)
6:50 (6:51) (Class 5) (0-75,75) 3-Y-0+ **£2,264** (£673; £336; £168) **Stalls** Low

Form RPR
1551 **1** **Emiratesdotcom**[8] 5895 5-9-5 **73**.............................. RoystonFfrench 3 84
(Milton Bradley) *midfield: hdwy to chse ldrs over 1f out: pushed along and led 1f out: kpt on wl* **5/1**[3]

2 *½* **Good Authority (IRE)**[97] 2971 4-8-6 **67**.................... JulieCumine(7) 10 76+
(Karen George) *in rr: forced wd over 2f out: carried rt and hdwy wl over 1f out: styd on wl under hand and heels riding: jst failed* **12/1**

0126 **3** *¾* **Showboating (IRE)**[14] 5717 3-9-0 **73**....................(tp) MartinHarley(3) 12 80
(Alan McCabe) *in tch: rdn and hung rt 2f out: drvn and kpt on wl ins fnl f* **9/2**[2]

3602 **4** *¾* **Ishetoo**[8] 5895 7-9-2 **70**.. MichaelStainton 1 75
(Ollie Pears) *cl up: drvn 2f out: remained pressing ldrs tl hung lft and wknd 100yds out* **11/2**

-214 **5** *½* **Supercharged (IRE)**[23] 5419 3-9-2 **72**....................(p) GeorgeBaker 13 75
(Chris Wall) *swtchd lft to ins sn after s: in rr: rdn along 2f out: drvn 1f out: swtchd rt and one pce ins fnl f* **10/3**[1]

3303 **6** *½* **Athaakeel (IRE)**[15] 5677 5-8-11 **65**..........................(b) TomMcLaughlin 8 66
(Ronald Harris) *rdn and sn led: hdd after 1f: led again 2f out: drvn and hung rt over 1f out: hdd 1f out: wknd fnl 100yds* **20/1**

3405 **7** *shd* **Absa Lutte (IRE)**[42] 4780 8-9-2 **70** KierenFallon 6 71
(Michael Mullineaux) *taken to s early: t.k.h: cl up: rdn 2f out: one pce ins fnl f* **8/1**

0004 **8** *1* **Garstang**[22] 5457 8-9-3 **71** (b) SaleemGolam 7 72+
(Bruce Hellier) *midfield: urged along 2f out: drvn and kpt on one pce fnl f: hmpd 100yds out: nt rcvr* **40/1**

5500 **9** *2* **Shostakovich (IRE)**[8] 5890 3-9-5 **75** (p) TravisBlock 11 66
(Sylvester Kirk) *led after 1f tl hdd over 2f out: drvn and wknd 2f out: sn btn* **28/1**

0060 **10** *4* **Sarah's Art (IRE)**[35] 5053 8-9-7 **75** (t) RobbieFitzpatrick 5 54
(Derek Shaw) *stdd s: in rr: rdn and no imp fnl 2f* **25/1**

0000 **11** *22* **Befortyfour**[22] 5434 6-9-6 **74** TonyCulhane 9 —
(Richard Guest) *v keen to post: t.k.h: chsd ldr: drvn and wknd qckly over 2f out: eased ins fnl f* **17/2**

1m 13.72s (-1.28) **Going Correction** -0.175s/f (Stan)
WFA 3 from 4yo+ 2lb **11** Ran SP% **117.1**
Speed ratings (Par 103): **101,100,99,98,97 97,96,95,92,87 58**
toteswingers:1&2:£16.60, 2&3:£14.00, 1&3:£5.50 CSF £59.66 CT £295.21 TOTE £5.70: £2.00, £4.70, £2.40; EX 108.40.
Owner Ms S Howell **Bred** Newsells Park Stud **Trained** Sedbury, Gloucs
■ Stewards' Enquiry : Royston Ffrench three-day ban: careless riding (Oct 1,3-4)

FOCUS
A weak handicap lacking in depth and they were strung right across the track at the finish.

6178 THE BLACK COUNTRY'S ONLY RACECOURSE (S) STKS 5f 216y(P)
7:20 (7:21) (Class 6) 2-Y-O **£1,533** (£452; £226) **Stalls** Low

Form RPR

4505 **1** **Faraway**[17] 5625 2-8-12 66 (v) MatthewCosham(5) 8 64
(David Evans) *in rr and outpcd early: urged along 3f out: rdn and hdwy over 1f out: styd on wl to ld 100yds out* **20/1**

0004 **2** *1 3/4* **Liebeszie**l[8] 5896 2-8-8 60 (p) MartinHarley(3) 2 53
(Alan McCabe) *sn led: rdn 2f out: drifted rt over 1f out: hdd 100yds out* **10/1**

3562 **3** *nk* **Balm**[26] 5316 2-8-6 68 JimmyQuinn 4 47
(Richard Hannon) *cl up: swtchd rt 2f out and hdwy: drvn to chse ldng pair 1f out: kpt on* **5/2**[1]

3105 **4** *1* **Steady The Buffs**[98] 2902 2-8-9 71 (b[1]) RyanClark(3) 3 50
(Hugo Palmer) *s.i.s: sn rdn: hrd drvn and hdwy 2f out: kpt on past btn horses ins fnl f* **10/1**

0502 **5** *1/2* **Tyre Giant Dot Com**[42] 4808 2-8-11 67 JamesSullivan 9 47
(Geoffrey Oldroyd) *in rr: hdwy 3f out: swtchd rt and nt looking willing 2f out: kpt on one pce ins fnl f* **3/1**[3]

065 **6** *2 1/2* **Sonsie Lass**[36] 5017 2-8-6 53 JoeFanning 1 35
(Mark Johnston) *ponied to s and taken to post early: cl up: rdn and carried hd on one side 2f out: sn gave up* **16/1**

4303 **7** *1 1/4* **Spring Daisy (IRE)**[23] 5418 2-8-6 46 (v[1]) RoystonFfrench 5 31
(Tom Dascombe) *chsd ldr: drvn and wknd over 2f out: sn wl btn* **33/1**

8 *19* **Multi Blessing**[116] 2380 2-9-3 81 KierenFallon 10 —
(Alan Jarvis) *walked to post: t.k.h on outer: cl up: rdn and wknd rapidly 2f out: eased ins fnl f: t.o* **11/4**[2]

00 **9** *1 1/4* **Ashes Star**[19] 5564 2-8-8 0 RossAtkinson(3) 11 —
(Jonathan Portman) *in rr: drvn 3f out: sn lost tch: t.o* **80/1**

1m 15.15s (0.15) **Going Correction** -0.175s/f (Stan) **9** Ran SP% **113.2**
Speed ratings (Par 93): **92,89,89,87,87 83,82,56,55**
toteswingers:1&2:£30.00, 2&3:£7.70, 1&3:£7.80 CSF £197.54 TOTE £21.70: £5.70, £4.40, £1.10; EX 370.70.There was no bid for the winner.
Owner Nick Shutts **Bred** Stourbank Stud **Trained** Pandy, Monmouths

FOCUS
A weak contest, but the pace was strong. The form is viewed negatively and rated through the winner to his pre-race mark.

NOTEBOOK
Faraway had won in this grade for William Haggas at Haydock in June and subsequently looked out of his depth in nursery company. He fared better when dropped into a 6f seller at Folkestone when visored for the first time, but could not take advantage of racing in front from a promising draw there. Trying this surface for the first time, different tactics were applied and he came from off the pace to wear down the long-time leader. This would be a confidence-boosting win, but it is arguable he will follow up. (tchd 22-1)
Liebesziel had been slowly away here when dropped into this company last time following a three-month break. He broke smartly this time, but was very free. He is capable of picking up a similar event when settling better. (op 14-1 tchd 16-1)
Balm was trying 6f on this surface for the first time, having found the trip beyond her on a couple of occasions on turf. She again flattered, looming large on the outside of Leibesziel, but faded, suggesting she doesn't have the stamina for this trip. (op 11-4)
Steady The Buffs had shown little when upped in grade after winning a Brighton maiden in May. Dropping into this level for the first time and equipped with first-time blinkers, she didn't get a good start, jumping awkwardly leaving the stalls. She made a little late headway and may be worth another try at this trip. Official explanation: jockey said filly jumped awkwardly leaving stalls (op 11-1 tchd 12-1)
Tyre Giant Dot Com was well backed when flopping in this grade on his penultimate start at Ripon, and was subsequently touched off over 6f at that same track. Again well backed here, he spoiled his chance with a tardy start, rearing leaving the stalls, but he stayed on. He is still lightly-raced and should be able to pick up a race at this level before too long. Official explanation: jockey said gelding reared leaving stalls (op 7-2)
Sonsie Lass has a tendency to pull hard and is not one to trust until she learns to settle. (op 12-1)

6179 WILLIAMHILL.COM H'CAP 7f 32y(P)
7:50 (7:51) (Class 6) (0-65,65) 3-Y-O **£1,704** (£503; £251) **Stalls** High

Form RPR

3301 **1** **Justbookie Dot Com (IRE)**[9] 5864 3-9-6 **64** (v) GeorgeBaker 4 77
(David Evans) *in tch: hdwy to chse ldrs 2f out: rdn to ld 1f out: sn drew clr* **6/1**[3]

6533 **2** *4* **Elegant Muse**[14] 5736 3-9-2 **60** FergusSweeney 2 62
(Walter Swinburn) *cl up: rdn 3f out: hdwy to chse ldr 2f out: kpt on but no ch w wnr* **10/1**

0431 **3** *1/2* **Beautiful Lando (FR)**[8] 5902 3-9-7 **65** (b) KierenFallon 8 66
(Heather Main) *led: rdn 2f out: hdd 1f out: no ex and lost 3rd post* **5/2**[1]

4550 **4** *hd* **Amazing Win (IRE)**[12] 5793 3-8-12 **59** MartinHarley(3) 12 59
(Mick Channon) *t.k.h: in tch: rdn 3f out: kpt on ins fnl 2f: swtchd lft and one pce ins fnl f* **50/1**

4300 **5** *2 3/4* **Scoglio**[18] 5606 3-8-13 **57** (b) JamesDoyle 9 50
(Frank Sheridan) *s.i.s and reminders: in rr: brief effrt over 3f out: kpt on: no imp on ldrs* **20/1**

0030 **6** *2 1/2* **Crucis Abbey (IRE)**[14] 5736 3-9-7 **65** WilliamCarson 3 51
(James Unett) *midfield: short of room after 3f: rdn over 2f out: one pce 2f out* **28/1**

5565 **7** *3/4* **Midnight Trader (IRE)**[44] 4730 3-9-4 **62** (t) TonyCulhane 11 46
(David Flood) *in rr on outer: rdn and outpcd 3f out: sme late hdwy* **7/1**

2105 **8** *1/2* **Putin (IRE)**[8] 5902 3-8-9 **53** ShaneKelly 5 36
(Derek Haydn Jones) *cl up: drvn along 3f out: wknd 2f out* **12/1**

3220 **9** *1/2* **Bilko Pak (IRE)**[23] 5419 3-9-2 **65** MarkCoumbe(5) 10 46
(Derek Shaw) *in rr: drvn along 3f out: kpt on one pce 2f out* **14/1**

4422 **10** *1* **Cadmium Loch**[9] 5864 3-8-11 **62** JackDuern(7) 7 41
(Reg Hollinshead) *cl up: rdn 3f out: wknd 2f out* **5/1**[2]

0660 **11** *3/4* **Indian Emperor (IRE)**[14] 5735 3-9-7 **65** RoystonFfrench 1 41
(Peter Niven) *in rr: rdn and outpcd 5f out: drvn and no hdwy fnl 3f* **66/1**

5613 **12** *19* **One Of Twins**[29] 5248 3-8-9 **53** JamesSullivan 6 —
(Michael Easterby) *in rr: hmpd and dropped last 3f: sn lost tch* **15/2**

1m 27.82s (-1.78) **Going Correction** -0.175s/f (Stan) **12** Ran SP% **118.9**
Speed ratings (Par 99): **103,98,97,97,94 91,90,90,89,88 87,65**
toteswingers:1&2:£7.80, 2&3:£5.40, 1&3:£3.50 CSF £62.64 CT £193.76 TOTE £7.80: £2.90, £3.10, £1.80; EX 71.70.
Owner J A Wilcox **Bred** Haydock Park Stud **Trained** Pandy, Monmouths

FOCUS
A competitive handicap for the grade, contested by plenty of pace horses, and the gallop was consequently a generous one.
One Of Twins Official explanation: jockey said gelding ran flat

6180 BRITISH STALLION STUDS SUPPORTING BRITISH RACING E B F MAIDEN STKS 1m 141y(P)
8:20 (8:21) (Class 5) 2-Y-O **£3,234** (£962; £481; £240) **Stalls** Low

Form RPR

1 **Ambivalent (IRE)** 2-8-12 0 NeilCallan 1 72+
(Roger Varian) *t.k.h: midfield: rn green thrght: rdn over 2f out: swtchd rt and hdwy over 1f out: styd on strly to ld fnl 50yds* **5/2**[2]

4 **2** *3/4* **Ahzeemah (IRE)**[22] 5454 2-8-12 0 (p) AntiocoMurgia(5) 8 73
(Saeed Bin Suroor) *midfield: hdwy 4f out: chsd ldr 3f out: rdn to ld 2f out: hdd fnl 50yds: no ex* **7/1**

0 **3** *2 1/4* **His Royal Highness (CAN)**[14] 5697 2-9-3 0 GeorgeBaker 13 68
(Mikael Magnusson) *led: rdn and hdd 2f out: no ex cl home* **20/1**

0 **4** *4* **Roman Myst (IRE)**[25] 5337 2-9-3 0 JamesDoyle 6 60
(Sylvester Kirk) *cl up: rdn along 2f out: steadily wknd ins fnl f* **66/1**

0 **5** *1 1/4* **Seven Veils (IRE)**[24] 5384 2-8-12 0 StevieDonohoe 10 52+
(Sir Mark Prescott Bt) *in rr: hdwy 5f out: rdn 3f out: kpt on nicely past btn horses 2f out: possible improver* **16/1**

5 **6** *1/2* **Haymarket**[43] 4762 2-9-3 0 AhmedAjtebi 4 56
(Mahmood Al Zarooni) *midfield: rdn 3f out: fnd nthing and wknd 2f out* **15/8**[1]

0 **7** *1 3/4* **Pelican Rock (IRE)**[15] 5681 2-9-3 0 RichardKingscote 9 53
(Tom Dascombe) *prom: pushed along 3f out: grad wknd 2f out* **33/1**

8 *3 1/2* **Search And Rescue (USA)** 2-9-0 0 PatrickHills(3) 7 45
(J W Hills) *slowly away: in rr: rdn and no imp 4f out* **50/1**

0 **9** *2 1/2* **Fouracres**[20] 5514 2-8-12 0 RobbieFitzpatrick 2 35
(Michael Appleby) *midfield: lost pl 4f out: no further imp* **200/1**

10 *1/2* **Jericho (IRE)** 2-9-3 0 FergusSweeney 3 42
(Jamie Osborne) *in rr: brief effrt on outer 4f out: hung bdly rt and wknd 3f out: eased ins fnl f* **40/1**

0 **11** *5* **Aldgate (USA)**[36] 5013 2-9-3 0 KierenFallon 5 28
(Mahmood Al Zarooni) *in rr and rn v green: pushed along and no imp 4f out* **4/1**[3]

0 **12** *2 1/2* **Last Zak**[14] 5727 2-9-3 0 JamesSullivan 11 23
(Michael Easterby) *midfield: lost pl 4f out: sn btn* **100/1**

1m 50.62s (0.12) **Going Correction** -0.175s/f (Stan) **12** Ran SP% **116.8**
Speed ratings (Par 95): **92,91,89,85,84 84,82,79,77,76 72,70**
toteswingers:1&2:£4.10, 2&3:£14.00, 1&3:£17.00 CSF £19.19 TOTE £4.10: £1.70, £1.20, £2.50; EX 21.30.
Owner Ali Saeed **Bred** Darley **Trained** Newmarket, Suffolk

FOCUS
A modest maiden despite representation from some big yards, and the pace was decent. The winner can rate higher than the bare form.

NOTEBOOK
Ambivalent(IRE) hails from an in-form yard who have plenty of good juveniles among their ranks and this relatively cheap purchase (24,000gns) looked fitter than most. A compact and well-made daughter of Derby winner Authorized, she made a winning debut, showing a neat turn of foot after being angled out off the rail, despite pulling hard in the early stages. She has no lofty entries but clearly has plenty of ability and will be better over further. (op 15-8)
Ahzeemah(IRE), one of three Godolphin runners, had made a modest debut with a staying-on fourth to a 74-rated winner over 1m at Thirsk last month. Equipped with cheekpieces for the first time, this 60,000gns yearling showed he'd learned plenty for that debut and was simply beaten by a filly with a decent turn of foot. He needs further. (op 11-2)
His Royal Highness(CAN) was well beaten on his 7f Ascot debut last month, having raced alone in a better maiden. He seemed to appreciate this step up in trip, although his Dewhurst entry looks fanciful.
Roman Myst(IRE) clouds the worth of the form somewhat. To be fair, he lost a shoe during the race and this was a much better effort than he showed when well beaten at big odds in a Leicester maiden on his debut. He will benefit from going a bit further in due course. Official explanation: vet said gelding lost a shoe (op 100-1)
Seven Veils(IRE) cost 330,000gns as a yearling and is a sister to Italian Oaks winner Contredanse. Unfancied and well beaten on her 7f Kempton AW debut last month, she was up in trip here, but spoiled her chance by being very slowly into her stride. She still looks a bit weak and should be much better with another winter behind her. (tchd 20-1)
Haymarket attracted plenty of support after showing a little promise in a 7f Newmarket maiden last month. This 130,000gns buy would have found this track and trip plenty sharp enough, though. He will be better with time and experience. (op 5-2)
Aldgate(USA) was the other Godolphin runner and the Derby entrant also had plenty of support despite being well beaten on his 1m Newmarket debut. He cost 130,000gns but on this evidence it does not appear to be money well spent. His Derby entry looks a pipe dream. (op 6-1)

6181 WOLVERHAMPTON-RACECOURSE.CO.UK H'CAP 1m 141y(P)
8:50 (8:51) (Class 5) (0-70,70) 3-Y-O **£1,704** (£503; £251) **Stalls** Low

Form RPR

-246 **1** **Midas Moment**[24] 5391 3-9-7 **70** GeorgeBaker 1 77
(William Muir) *cl up: rdn and led over 1f out: all out* **6/1**[3]

5032 **2** *hd* **Duquesa (IRE)**[1] 6134 3-8-11 **65** (v) MatthewCosham(5) 5 72
(David Evans) *in rr: hrd drvn 3f out: hdwy over 2f out: styd on strly ins fnl f: jst failed* **4/1**[2]

5246 **3** *1 1/2* **Conducting**[10] 5828 3-9-3 **66** ShaneKelly 12 70
(Gay Kelleway) *in rr: forced wd on bnd 2f out: rdn and styd on wl over 1f out: fin strly to take 3rd wl ins fnl f* **12/1**

6060 **4** *nse* **Golden Taurus (IRE)**[9] 5858 3-8-13 **65** PatrickHills(3) 3 68
(J W Hills) *t.k.h: cl up: rdn and carried hd awkwardly over 2f out: nt qckn ins fnl f* **33/1**

1500 **5** *2* **Barnum (USA)**[12] 5791 3-8-11 **60** .... JamesSullivan 7 59
(Michael Easterby) *wore no hind shoes: keen: chsd ldr: rdn 3f out: outpcd and drvn 2f out: lost no further grnd ins fnl f* **16/1**
1240 **6** *¾* **Double Duchess**[17] 5630 3-9-2 **65** .... WilliamCarson 2 62
(Paul D'Arcy) *walked to post: led: rdn 2f out: hung rt and wknd ins fnl f* **14/1**
4000 **7** *1 ¼* **My Mate Jake (IRE)**[40] 4854 3-9-1 **64** .... NeilCallan 9 58
(James Given) *cl up: urged along 3f out: drvn and hung lft over 1f out: btn whn short of room ins fnl f* **9/1**
-000 **8** *2 ¾* **Fists And Stones**[22] 5449 3-9-1 **67** .... MartinHarley(3) 4 55
(Mick Channon) *midfield: rdn along 3f out: no imp 2f out* **10/1**
5002 **9** *shd* **Iron Green (FR)**[8] 5900 3-9-2 **65** .... (v[1]) KierenFallon 11 53
(Heather Main) *in rr: wd and effrt over 3f out: rdn 2f out: one pce* **3/1[1]**
3024 **10** *2* **Prince Of Passion (CAN)**[4] 6033 3-8-10 **59** .... JoeFanning 6 42
(Derek Shaw) *slowly away: nvr on terms: struggling 4f out* **6/1[3]**
4240 **11** *1 ½* **McCool Bannanas**[14] 5740 3-8-13 **62** .... LiamJones 10 42
(James Unett) *a in rr: drvn and no imp 3f out* **25/1**
260 **12** *3* **Silk Lingerie**[89] 3236 3-8-9 **58** .... JimmyQuinn 8 31
(Mandy Rowland) *nvr on terms: rdn and btn 5f out* **50/1**

1m 49.37s (-1.13) **Going Correction** -0.175s/f (Stan) **12** Ran SP% **121.7**
Speed ratings (Par 101): **98,97,96,96,94 94,92,90,90,88 87,84**
toteswingers:1&2:£4.40, 2&3:£9.00, 1&3:£18.40 CSF £30.60 CT £291.95 TOTE £7.40: £2.70, £2.10, £5.60; EX 35.20.
Owner Foursome Thoroughbreds **Bred** Foursome Thoroughbreds **Trained** Lambourn, Berks

FOCUS
A poor and open handicap with plenty of out-of-form, exposed types. The pace was fair.

6182 MOBET.WILLIAMHILL.COM H'CAP — 1m 4f 50y(P)
9:20 (9:21) (Class 6) (0-65,65) 3-Y-O+ — **£2,070** (£616; £307; £153) **Stalls** Low

Form RPR
3332 **1** **Boa**[18] 5609 6-9-12 **65** .... GeorgeBaker 3 74
(Reg Hollinshead) *cl up: rdn to ld 1f out: hrd drvn fnl 100yds: all out* **9/2[3]**
0024 **2** *½* **Singzak**[43] 4752 3-9-3 **64** .... JamesSullivan 12 72
(Michael Easterby) *led tl hdd 7f out: rdn to ld again 4f out: drvn and hdd ins fnl f: kpt on* **4/1[2]**
4400 **3** *¾* **Green Lightning (IRE)**[20] 5504 4-9-7 **60** .... (b) JoeFanning 2 67
(Mark Johnston) *cl up: rdn and carried hd high 2f out: kpt on wl u.str.p ins fnl f* **3/1[1]**
-610 **4** *1* **Joan D'Arc (IRE)**[12] 5790 4-9-3 **61** .... AntiocoMurgia(5) 6 66
(Noel Quinlan) *midfield: pushed along 3f out: swtchd rt and styd on fnl f: nvr threatened* **8/1**
0661 **5** *hd* **Dazakhee**[10] 5836 4-9-11 **64** .... TonyCulhane 5 69+
(David Flood) *t.k.h in rr: hdwy and gng wl 4f out: rdn along 2f out: n.m.r ins fnl f: kpt on* **8/1**
2006 **6** *1 ¼* **Carnac (IRE)**[40] 4870 5-8-12 **54** .... (p) MartinHarley(3) 10 57
(Alan McCabe) *chsd ldr tl led 7f out: hdd 4f out: drvn and grad wknd* **16/1**
2244 **7** *¾* **Munaawer (USA)**[28] 4148 4-9-9 **62** .... KierenFallon 7 64
(James Bethell) *midfield on outer: rdn and hdwy 3f out: one pce 2f out* **7/1**
2620 **8** *hd* **Barbirolli**[25] 5357 9-8-12 **51** oh4 .... WilliamCarson 9 53?
(William Stone) *in rr: drvn along 3f out: sn btn* **25/1**
0-00 **9** *2 ¾* **Aureate**[7] 5916 7-9-2 **55** .... NeilChalmers 8 52
(Brian Forsey) *midfield: rdn 3f out: no imp fnl 2f* **50/1**
1005 **10** *½* **Turjuman (USA)**[18] 5609 6-9-8 **61** .... StevieDonohoe 4 57
(Willie Musson) *hld up: rdn and no imp fnl 3f* **12/1**
0000 **11** *23* **Frosty Reception**[15] 5674 3-8-8 **55** .... RobbieFitzpatrick 11 15
(Michael Appleby) *in rr: rdn over 4f out: t.o fnl f* **66/1**

2m 38.55s (-2.55) **Going Correction** -0.175s/f (Stan)
WFA 3 from 4yo+ 8lb **11** Ran SP% **118.8**
Speed ratings (Par 101): **101,100,100,99,99 98,98,97,96,95 80**
toteswingers:1&2:£4.40, 2&3:£5.30, 1&3:£2.80 CSF £22.87 CT £63.20 TOTE £4.00: £2.20, £1.90, £1.10; EX 29.10.
Owner Geoff Lloyd **Bred** R Hollinshead **Trained** Upper Longdon, Staffs

FOCUS
A weak handicap contested by very few in-form horses, and the few that were fought out the finish. The pace was modest.
T/Plt: £120.50 to a £1 stake. Pool of £76,435.57 - 462.68 winning tickets. T/Qpdt: £25.70 to a £1 stake. Pool of £9,453.29 - 271.70 winning tickets. CS

3888 BELMONT PARK (L-H)
Saturday, September 17

OFFICIAL GOING: Turf: firm

6183a GARDEN CITY STKS (GRADE 1) (3YO FILLIES) (TURF) — 1m 1f (T)
10:18 (12:00) 3-Y-O
£96,153 (£32,051; £16,025; £8,012; £4,807; £1,068)

RPR
1 **Winter Memories (USA)**[27] 3-8-11 0 .... JJCastellano 4 115+
(James J Toner, U.S.A) **11/10[1]**
2 *nk* **Theyskens' Theory (USA)**[28] 5277 3-8-6 0 .... GKGomez 7 107
(Brian Meehan) **9/2[3]**
3 *1 ½* **More Than Real (USA)**[52] 3-8-8 0 .... CNakatani 1 106
(Todd Pletcher, U.S.A) **67/10**
4 *hd* **Hungry Island (USA)**[27] 3-8-8 0 .... ASolis 3 105
(Claude McGaughey III, U.S.A) **11/4[2]**
5 *hd* **Arch Support (USA)**[110] 3-8-5 0 ow1 .... DCohen 5 102
(Gary Contessa, U.S.A) **61/1**
6 *½* **Salary Drive (USA)**[50] 3-8-4 0 .... (b) JBravo 2 100
(Edward Plesa Jr, U.S.A) **73/1**
7 *nk* **Pinch Pie (USA)**[28] 3-8-4 0 .... JRose 8 99
(Anthony Dutrow, U.S.A) **189/10**
8 *hd* **Kathmanblu (USA)**[27] 3-8-6 0 .... JLezcano 6 101
(Kenneth McPeek, U.S.A) **123/10**

1m 51.06s (111.06) **8** Ran SP% **121.0**
PARI-MUTUEL (all including $2 stakes): WIN 4.20; PLACE (1-2) 2.60, 4.80; SHOW (1-2-3) 2.20, 3.50, 3.60; SF 24.80.
Owner Phillips Racing Partnership **Bred** Phillips Racing Partnership **Trained** USA

NOTEBOOK
Winter Memories(USA) swamped her rivals with a brilliant turn of foot.
Theyskens' Theory(USA) was produced three wide to charge to the lead inside the final furlong, only for the favourite to stride past for a comfortable victory. She will stay in the US now before another tilt at the Breeders' Cup.

5985 LONGCHAMP (R-H)
Saturday, September 17

OFFICIAL GOING: Turf: good

6184a PRIX DES CHENES (GROUP 3) (2YO COLTS & GELDINGS) (TURF) — 1m
1:30 (12:00) 2-Y-O — **£34,482** (£13,793; £10,344; £6,896; £3,448)

RPR
1 **Vizir Bere (FR)**[65] 4036 2-9-2 0 .... ChristopheSoumillon 1 107
(D Prod'Homme, France) *settled in 2nd bhd ldr: rdn 1 1/2f out: qcknd wl: led 1f out: r.o wl: comf* **36/5[3]**
2 *¾* **Saint Pellerin (GER)**[25] 5365 2-9-2 0 .... Christophe-PatriceLemaire 2 105
(J-C Rouget, France) *led: qcknd in front 2f out: hdd 1f out: r.o but no answer to wnr* **1/2[1]**
3 *3* **Kadyny**[14] 2-9-2 0 .... GeraldMosse 4 98
(T Lemer, France) *racd 4th initially but sn dropped bk to rr: rdn early in st: swtchd to outside and r.o wl fnl f: wnt 3rd on line* **23/1**
4 *nse* **Ostrea (FR)**[49] 2-9-2 0 .... DominiqueBoeuf 3 98
(Y Barberot, France) *s.i.s but rdn to go 4th bef st: rdn 2f out: r.o to go 3rd 1f out: lost 3rd on line* **44/5**
5 *2* **Demokles (FR)**[54] 2-9-2 0 .... OlivierPeslier 6 93
(J-M Beguigne, France) *racd 5th tl proging to 3rd bef st: rdn 2f out: r.o: nt qckn fnl f* **7/2[2]**
6 *1 ½* **Around The Moon (IRE)**[22] 2-9-2 0 .... SebastienMaillot 5 90
(Robert Collet, France) *racd 3rd: dropped bk to 5th bef st: sn rdn: no ex: styd on fnl f* **27/1**

1m 41.4s (3.00) **6** Ran SP% **119.0**
WIN (incl. 1 euro stake): 8.20. PLACES: 2.10, 1.20. SF: 19.30.
Owner Bryan Lynam **Bred** S N C Reigneur & San Gabriel Inv Inc **Trained** France

NOTEBOOK
Vizir Bere(FR), given a break since his last run, stayed on well to beat the favourite. He could go for the Criterium International at Saint-Cloud next.
Saint Pellerin(GER) made the running and there seemed no excuses, other than that he might have preferred softer ground.

6185a PRIX DU PRINCE D'ORANGE (GROUP 3) (3YO+) (TURF) — 1m 2f
2:40 (12:00) 3-Y-O — **£34,482** (£13,793; £10,344; £6,896; £3,448)

RPR
1 **Casamento (IRE)**[104] 2751 3-9-2 0 .... MickaelBarzalona 6 111+
(Mahmood Al Zarooni) *settled in rr: plld freely: rdn bef st: swtchd to wd outside: qcknd wl: ct ldrs wl ins fnl f: led 50yds out: comf* **93/10**
2 *1* **Barocci (JPN)**[55] 4376 3-9-2 0 .... ChristopheSoumillon 3 109
(E Lellouche, France) *racd 3rd: rdn over 1 1/2f out: led 110yds out: r.o wl: hdd 50yds out: jst hld 2nd on line* **9/1[3]**
3 *nse* **Desert Blanc**[48] 4595 3-9-2 0 .... StephanePasquier 5 109
(P Bary, France) *settled 5th on rail: rdn over 1 1/2f out: no room to chal: swtchd away fr rail: unable to find opening 1f out: swtchd bk towards rail: fnd split wl ins fnl f: r.o strly: unlucky* **2/1[1]**
4 *shd* **Bubble Chic (FR)**[65] 4038 3-9-2 0 .... GeraldMosse 4 109
(G Botti, Italy) *settled 4th: rdn 1 1/2f out: r.o wl fnl f: sltly impeded cl home* **2/1[1]**
5 *nse* **Staros (IRE)**[77] 3653 3-9-2 0 .... Pierre-CharlesBoudot 7 109
(E Lellouche, France) *settled towards rr: rdn over 1 1/2f out on outside: r.o wl fnl f* **39/1**
6 *1* **Slow Pace (USA)**[33] 5128 3-9-2 0 .... OlivierPeslier 2 107
(F Head, France) *sn led on rail: stl in front 1f out: rdn: hdd 110yds out: nt qckn: styd on* **7/2[2]**
7 *8* **Lindenthaler (GER)**[27] 5308 3-9-2 0 .... MaximeGuyon 8 91
(P Schiergen, Germany) *chsd ldr in 2nd: rdn bef st: r.o u.p: bmpd w eventual runner-up 1f out: sn wknd: eased fnl f* **10/1**

2m 6.70s (2.70) **7** Ran SP% **120.2**
WIN (incl. 1 euro stake): 10.30. PLACES: 2.70, 2.60, 1.60. DF: 30.00. SF: 71.40.
Owner Godolphin **Bred** D And J Cantillon & C & K Canning **Trained** Newmarket, Suffolk

NOTEBOOK
Casamento(IRE), absent since June, bounced back to form with a comfortable victory. Barzalona rode an intelligent race, dropping his partner out last early on and then bringing him with a sweeping late run up the centre of the track to take the lead with 50 yards left to run. The colt's options include the Qipco Champion Stakes and the Queen Elizabeth II Stakes at Ascot. Official explanation: , absent since June, bounced back to form with a comfortable victory. Barzalona rode an intelligent race, dropping his partner out last early on and then bringing him with a sweeping late run up the centre of the track to take the lead with 50 yards left to run. The colt's options include the Qipco Champion Stakes and the Queen Elizabeth II Stakes at Ascot.
Barocci(JPN), a consistent colt, just held second.
Desert Blanc looked unlucky. A gap for him did not open up until well inside the final furlong, from where he ran on well.
Bubble Chic(FR) failed to boost the form of Prix de l'Arc de Triomphe hope Reliable Man, who beat him in the Prix du Jockey Club in June. The ground might have been too fast for him. \n\x\x \n

5431 HAMILTON (R-H)
Sunday, September 18

OFFICIAL GOING: Soft (7.1)
Wind: Almost nil Weather: Cloudy

6186 TOTEPLACEPOT NURSERY — 6f 5y
2:10 (2:10) (Class 5) (0-75,72) 2-Y-O — **£2,587** (£770; £384; £192) **Stalls** High

Form RPR
5455 **1** **Pitt Rivers**[3] 6092 2-9-3 **71** .... MartinHarley(3) 7 74
(Mick Channon) *rrd and dwlt s: bhd: rdn over 3f out: edgd rt and hdwy over 1f out: led ins fnl f: kpt on wl* **13/2[3]**
034 **2** *1 ¼* **Wish Again (IRE)**[34] 5105 2-8-7 **58** .... AdrianNicholls 11 57
(David Nicholls) *t.k.h: led to over 2f out: sn rdn and rallied: chsd wnr and wnt both ways ins fnl f: kpt on* **11/1**
1353 **3** *½* **First Bid**[40] 4892 2-9-0 **68** .... AmyRyan(3) 10 66
(Kevin Ryan) *prom: effrt and rdn over 2f out: kpt on ins fnl f* **7/1**
0562 **4** *¾* **Celestial Dawn**[11] 5817 2-8-5 **56** .... DuranFentiman 6 51
(John Weymes) *w ldr: led over 2f out: drifted lft appr fnl f: r.o same pce* **4/1[1]**

011 **5** *3 1/4* **Sinai (IRE)**[23] 5431 2-9-7 **72**............ DanielTudhope 3 58
(Geoffrey Harker) *t.k.h: trckd ldrs: effrt over 2f out: one pce whn checked ins fnl f* **5/1**[2]
1 **6** *1* **Irrational**[65] 4040 2-9-4 **69**............ TomEaves 12 52
(Bryan Smart) *dwlt: bhd: hdwy over 2f out: edgd rt and no imp over 1f out* **15/2**
4012 **7** *1* **Whisky Bravo**[8] 5913 2-9-4 **69**............ PhillipMakin 5 49
(David Brown) *bhd: rdn over 3f out: hdwy 2f out: sn no imp* **13/2**[3]
5613 **8** *1* **Dansili Dutch (IRE)**[23] 5431 2-8-10 **61**............ LeeNewman 9 38
(David Barron) *dwlt: bhd and sn pushed along: shortlived effrt over 2f out: nvr able to chal* **17/2**
104 **9** *2 1/4* **Schmooze (IRE)**[46] 4667 2-8-3 **59**............(v[1]) JulieBurke(5) 8 29
(Linda Perratt) *t.k.h: trckd ldrs tl wknd fr 2f out* **33/1**
0305 **10** *6* **Never In (IRE)**[5] 6026 2-7-7 **49** oh2............ DanielleMcCreery(5) 1 —
(Alan Berry) *dwlt: bhd on outside: struggling over 2f out: sn btn* **125/1**

1m 16.9s (4.70) **Going Correction** +0.75s/f (Yiel) **10** Ran SP% **110.2**
Speed ratings (Par 95): **98,96,95,94,90 89,87,86,83,75**
toteswingers:1&2:£13.40, 1&3:£8.40, 2&3:£11.50 CSF £70.30 CT £483.31 TOTE £6.20: £2.10, £3.60, £2.60; EX 106.80 TRIFECTA Not won..
Owner Jon and Julia Aisbitt **Bred** Jnp Bloodstock Ltd **Trained** West Ilsley, Berks

FOCUS
There was 1.7mm of rain overnight and the ground was given as soft (GoingStick 6.7). All races beyond 6f were eight yards shorter than advertised due to the configuration of the rail on the loop, which was providing fresh ground. Just a modest nursery, and a tough test in the ground. The third set a solid level.

NOTEBOOK
Pitt Rivers had been as big as 14-1 in the morning and the support for him suggested there was confidence that he would show improved form for getting to race on soft ground for the first time. He was rearing as the stalls opened, so missed the break slightly, but he got plenty of cover in behind and, once switched to the stands' rail and brought with his run, stayed on strongly to score handily. There could be more to come from him on this sort of ground. (op 9-1 tchd 11-2)
Wish Again(IRE), running in a nursery for the first time, was in the front rank throughout and kept on while others tired. The longer trip was in his favour and he can win a similar race. (op 10-1)
First Bid didn't run badly but it's possible he needs quicker ground to be seen at his very best. (op 10-1 tchd 11-1)
Celestial Dawn showed good speed throughout but didn't quite see her race out. Given the testing ground, perhaps she went a shade too fast early. (tchd 3-1)
Sinai(IRE) was crossed by the runner-up half a furlong out and had to be snatched up slightly, but she wasn't really going anywhere at the time. (op 7-2)
Irrational, a winner on fast ground on her debut two months earlier, had contrasting conditions to deal with here. (op 6-1 tchd 11-2)

6187 BRITISH STALLION STUDS SUPPORTING BRITISH RACING EBF MAIDEN STKS 1m 65y
2:40 (2:40) (Class 5) 2-Y-O **£3,234** (£962; £481; £240) **Stalls** Low

Form RPR
1 **Gabrial's Star** 2-9-3 0............ TomEaves 6 81
(Bryan Smart) *missed break: hld up: effrt and rn green fr over 3f out: hdwy wl over 1f out: styd on wl to ld cl home* **20/1**
2302 **2** *hd* **Choisan (IRE)**[20] 5548 2-9-3 77............ DavidAllan 5 81
(Tim Easterby) *prom: effrt over 2f out: rdn to ld over 1f out: kpt on fnl f: hdd nr fin* **3/1**[3]
642 **3** *1 3/4* **Savanna Days (IRE)**[19] 5583 2-8-9 79............ MartinHarley(3) 8 72
(Mick Channon) *hld up: hdwy 3f out: rdn and ev ch ins fnl f: hld nr fin* **9/4**[1]
25 **4** *1/2* **Rocktherunway (IRE)**[23] 5454 2-9-3 0............ TonyHamilton 1 76
(Michael Dods) *dwlt: sn trcking ldrs: effrt over 2f out: kpt on same pce ins fnl f* **18/1**
0022 **5** *7* **Hyperlink (IRE)**[9] 5875 2-9-3 74............ JoeFanning 2 61
(Mark Johnston) *led: rdn over 2f out: hdd over 1f out: wknd ins fnl f* **5/2**[2]
66 **6** *7* **Altnaharra**[62] 4140 2-9-3 0............ DanielTudhope 7 45
(Jim Goldie) *s.i.s: bhd: struggling 1/2-way: sme late hdwy: nvr on terms* **66/1**
05 **7** *2* **Spirit Na Heireann (IRE)**[22] 5464 2-8-12 0............ PaulHanagan 4 36
(Richard Fahey) *chsd ldrs: drvn over 3f out: wknd over 1f out* **8/1**
3 **8** *6* **Greyhope**[31] 5202 2-9-3 0............ JamieGoldstein 9 28
(Lucinda Russell) *hld up: rdn and outpcd 4f out: rallied over 2f out: sn btn* **[illegible]/1**
5000 **9** *1* **Grippa**[11] 5818 2-9-3 52............ PhillipMakin 3 25
(David Brown) *in tch: pushed along after 3f: rdn and wknd 3f out* **100/1**

1m 53.24s (4.84) **Going Correction** +0.75s/f (Yiel) **9** Ran SP% **110.9**
Speed ratings (Par 95): **105,104,103,102,95 88,86,80,79**
toteswingers:1&2:£9.00, 1&3:£7.50, 2&3:£2.50 CSF £75.17 TOTE £21.80: £3.70, £1.60, £1.30; EX 56.30 Trifecta £339.90 Part won. Pool £549.36 - 0.30 winning units..
Owner Dr Marwan Koukash **Bred** Miss K Rausing **Trained** Hambleton, N Yorks
■ Stewards' Enquiry : David Allan one-day ban: used whip with excessive frequency (Oct 3)

FOCUS
This proved quite a test in the conditions and the leaders were paddling in the closing stages. A decent debut from the winner but the runner-up limits the form.

NOTEBOOK
Gabrial's Star, who's bred to stay 1m4f well next year, stayed on best of all to collect on his debut. Clearly not much was expected from him first time up - he was green beforehand and in the race itself, and has plenty of developing still to do - so it has to be hugely positive that he was able to win. He's a brother to a three-time winner over middle distances and could well develop into a useful handicapper next season. (op 25-1 tchd 18-1)
Choisan(IRE), despite being sprint-bred, ran well over 7f at Newcastle last time out and figured to appreciate this extra distance. He came to have every chance but, once he hit the front, just began to go up and down on the spot, and was done close home by the winner. He'll always have the option of trying the AW to get off the mark. (op 11-4)
Savanna Days(IRE) has plenty of stamina in her pedigree (dam was second in the German Oaks) but she too got tired in the closing stages in a race that proved quite a test. (op 5-2 tchd 11-4 in places)
Rocktherunway(IRE) had a bit to find with a few of these and ran about as well as could be expected. Handicaps are now an option for him. (op 22-1)
Hyperlink(IRE) simply found this too much of a slog. He's by Cape Cross and this probably just isn't his ground. (tchd 11-4)
Spirit Na Heireann(IRE) dropped right away from 2f out and the combination of a longer trip on softer ground seemed to find her out as well. (op 7-1)

6188 TOTEQUICKPICK CLAIMING STKS 1m 1f 36y
3:10 (3:10) (Class 6) 3-5-Y-O **£3,234** (£962; £481; £240) **Stalls** Low

Form RPR
5100 **1** **You've Been Mowed**[20] 5546 5-8-4 81............ MatthewLawson(5) 3 83
(Richard Price) *pressed ldr: led over 3f out: edgd rt and clr over 1f out: kpt on wl fnl f* **9/2**[2]
4-40 **2** *3 1/2* **Triple Eight (IRE)**[84] 3445 3-8-10 92............ PaulPickard(3) 1 84
(Philip Kirby) *hld up: rdn over 3f out: rallied 2f out: chsd wnr ins fnl f: r.o* **11/1**
0055 **3** *1/2* **Changing The Guard**[14] 5757 5-9-1 76............ PaulHanagan 7 80
(Richard Fahey) *t.k.h early: prom: outpcd over 3f out: rallied over 1f out: kpt on fnl f: no imp* **85/40**[1]
0200 **4** *1 1/4* **Osgood**[3] 6079 4-9-0 77............ MartinHarley(3) 5 79
(Mick Channon) *led: rdn and hdd over 3f out: hung rt over 1f out: lost two pls ins fnl f* **85/40**[1]
1022 **5** *6* **Golden Creek (USA)**[19] 5602 3-8-13 72............ DanielTudhope 6 67
(Mrs K Burke) *trckd ldrs tl rdn and wknd over 2f out* **6/1**[3]
3200 **6** *1/2* **Just Five (IRE)**[31] 5205 5-8-13 69............ PhillipMakin 2 61
(John Weymes) *hld up in tch: rdn over 3f out: edgd rt: wknd fr 2f out* **25/1**

2m 7.21s (7.51) **Going Correction** +0.75s/f (Yiel)
WFA 3 from 4yo+ 5lb **6** Ran SP% **108.6**
Speed ratings (Par 101): **96,92,92,91,86 85**
toteswingers:1&2:£3.70, 1&3:£2.90, 2&3:£4.40 CSF £45.08 TOTE £4.70: £2.50, £4.50; EX 20.30.
Owner Mrs K Oseman **Bred** T E Pocock **Trained** Ullingswick, H'fords

FOCUS
An average claimer.

6189 TOTEPOOL EBF FLOWER OF SCOTLAND FILLIES' H'CAP 6f 5y
3:40 (3:40) (Class 3) (0-95,89) 3-Y-O+ **£7,762** (£2,310; £1,154; £577) **Stalls** Centre

Form RPR
4632 **1** **Jeannie Galloway (IRE)**[2] 6113 4-9-5 **82**............ PaulHanagan 8 95
(Richard Fahey) *t.k.h: mde virtually all: rdn and edgd rt over 1f out: hld on wl* **1/1**[1]
2213 **2** *2* **Spinatrix**[20] 5554 3-9-1 **80**............ TomEaves 2 87
(Michael Dods) *w ldrs: effrt and drvn along 2f out: kpt on ins fnl f* **13/2**[3]
3110 **3** *1* **Lady Paris (IRE)**[30] 5255 3-9-1 **87**............ JustinNewman(7) 7 91
(Bryan Smart) *trckd ldrs: effrt and rdn over 1f out: edgd rt: kpt on same pce ins fnl f* **7/2**[2]
2130 **4** *1 1/4* **Red Roar (IRE)**[8] 5918 4-8-1 **69**............ JulieBurke(5) 6 69
(Alan Berry) *dwlt: bhd: outpcd over 3f out: kpt on fnl f: n.d* **18/1**
2500 **5** *hd* **Ursula (IRE)**[2] 6113 5-8-13 **79**............(p) MartinHarley(3) 3 78
(Mrs K Burke) *in tch: effrt and rdn over 2f out: no imp over 1f out* **14/1**
-005 **6** *11* **Amitola (IRE)**[16] 5684 4-9-9 **86**............ PhillipMakin 5 50
(David Barron) *w ldrs tl rdn and wknd fr 2f out* **9/1**

1m 15.86s (3.66) **Going Correction** +0.75s/f (Yiel)
WFA 3 from 4yo+ 2lb **6** Ran SP% **107.5**
Speed ratings (Par 104): **105,102,101,99,99 84**
toteswingers:1&2:£1.80, 1&3:£1.80, 2&3:£2.40 CSF £7.21 CT £13.11 TOTE £2.10: £1.30, £3.00; EX 7.00 Trifecta £14.70 Pool £465.97 - 23.35 winning units..
Owner David Renwick **Bred** G And J Bloodstock **Trained** Musley Bank, N Yorks

FOCUS
Not a bad fillies' sprint,

NOTEBOOK
Jeannie Galloway(IRE), who came within a short head of winning the Ayr Bronze Cup on Friday, gained compensation. Running off the same mark, she was a bit keen early but was still going best heading into the final 2f and had more than enough in reserve to comfortably see off her main rivals thereafter - she does after all have plenty of 7f form to her name. (op 5-4 tchd 11-8 in places)
Spinatrix had conditions to suit and ran a solid race behind a rival who was well in at the weights based on her effort a couple of days earlier. She's now 23lb higher than when she began winning in July, though, and perhaps her improvement has reached a plateau. (op 5-1)
Lady Paris(IRE), back over 6f, won on soft ground as a 2yo but her recent improvement has come on a quicker surface. Perhaps she's more at home on fast ground these days. (op 9-2)
Red Roar(IRE) could easily be excused her run at Chester last time as she was hampered, but bouncing back over 6f at a track which puts an emphasis on stamina (her best form is over the minimum distance) was always going to be difficult. (op 14-1)
Ursula(IRE), only 11th (fifth on her side) in the Bronze Cup, again finished some way behind Jeannie Galloway. She needs help from the handicapper. (tchd 12-1 and 16-1)
Amitola(IRE) has had a disappointing season and, while she hinted at a return to form at Haydock last time, she failed to build on it here. (op 11-2)

6100 TOTEEXACTA H'CAP 6f 5y
4:10 (4:10) (Class 5) (0-70,73) 3-Y-O **£2,587** (£770; £384; £192) **Stalls** Centre

Form RPR
51 **1** **Hills Of Dakota**[36] 5063 3-9-4 **67**............ GrahamGibbons 7 82+
(David Barron) *in tch: effrt 2f out: led ins fnl f: rdn and r.o wl* **11/4**[2]
5525 **2** *1* **Captain Kolo (IRE)**[11] 5821 3-9-2 **65**............ DavidAllan 3 75
(Tim Easterby) *hld up: effrt and swtchd rt appr fnl f: kpt on fnl f* **8/1**
4300 **3** *3 3/4* **Babich Bay (IRE)**[16] 5674 3-8-7 **56** oh1............(b) FrederikTylicki 1 54
(Jo Hughes) *led: rdn 2f out: hdd ins fnl f: kpt on same pce* **10/1**
6003 **4** *nk* **Unwrapit (USA)**[23] 5433 3-8-7 **56** oh1............(p) TomEaves 6 53
(Bryan Smart) *prom: effrt over 2f out: kpt on same pce appr fnl f* **18/1**
6040 **5** *5* **Saxonette**[3] 6076 3-9-1 **64**............ PJMcDonald 8 45
(Linda Perratt) *dwlt: hld up: rdn and hdwy over 1f out: nvr able to chal* **20/1**
0111 **6** *hd* **Deliberation (IRE)**[10] 5859 3-9-5 **73**............ JulieBurke(5) 4 53
(Kevin Ryan) *chsd ldrs: rdn over 2f out: one pce ins fnl f: eased last 100yds* **9/4**[1]
0501 **7** *11* **Brave Battle**[23] 5437 3-8-9 **63**............ ShaneBKelly(5) 5 —
(Ron Barr) *in tch: drvn and outpcd 1/2-way: sn struggling* **12/1**
2333 **8** *1 1/2* **I Got You Babe (IRE)**[10] 5859 3-8-12 **61**............ PaulHanagan 2 —
(Richard Guest) *hld up: shortlived effrt over 2f out: sn wknd* **11/2**[3]

1m 16.68s (4.48) **Going Correction** +0.75s/f (Yiel) **8** Ran SP% **110.7**
Speed ratings (Par 101): **100,98,93,93,86 86,71,69**
toteswingers:1&2:£3.00, 1&3:£7.40, 2&3:£13.80 CSF £23.24 CT £181.24 TOTE £3.10: £1.80, £2.00, £2.20; EX 22.10 Trifecta £348.80 Part won. Pool £471.41 - 0.10 winning units..
Owner J Cringan & D Pryde **Bred** Messinger Stud Ltd **Trained** Maunby, N Yorks

FOCUS
A modest handicap.
Deliberation(IRE) Official explanation: jockey said gelding lost its action

6191 TOTETRIFECTA H'CAP 1m 5f 9y
4:40 (4:41) (Class 4) (0-80,80) 3-Y-O+ **£4,722** (£1,405; £702; £351) **Stalls** Low

Form RPR
3216 **1** **Jeu De Vivre (IRE)**[21] 5504 3-8-12 **73**............ JoeFanning 4 87+
(Mark Johnston) *chsd clr ldrs: smooth hdwy to ld over 2f out: clr whn edgd rt fnl f: eased nr fin* **10/1**
1414 **2** *4* **Getabuzz**[15] 5710 3-9-3 **78**............ DavidAllan 7 84
(Tim Easterby) *hld up: hdwy to chse wnr 2f out: sn one pce* **4/1**[2]

0251 **3** *1 1/4* **Jonny Delta**[15] 5724 4-9-2 **71** .... GaryBartley(3) 9 75
(Jim Goldie) *hld up: stdy hdwy over 3f out: sn rdn: kpt on fr 2f out: no imp* **2/1**[1]

2250 **4** *nse* **Royal Swain (IRE)**[14] 5761 5-9-12 **78** .... PJMcDonald 3 82
(Alan Swinbank) *hld up in tch: effrt and rdn over 2f out: kpt on fnl f: no imp* **7/1**

4003 **5** *3/4* **Comedy Act**[14] 5761 4-9-7 **78** .... DarylByrne(5) 1 81
(Mark Johnston) *chsd ldr and clr of rest: led over 3f out to 2f out: one pce fnl f* **11/1**

1105 **6** *15* **Bradbury (IRE)**[21] 5504 3-8-7 **68** ow1 .... (p) GrahamGibbons 8 48
(James Bethell) *prom: rdn over 4f out: rallied: wknd 2f out: eased whn btn ins fnl f* **16/1**

1231 **7** *4 1/2* **Think Its All Over (USA)**[15] 5723 4-9-1 **67** .... FrederikTylicki 5 41
(Julie Camacho) *led to over 3f out: wknd over 2f out* **11/2**[3]

-404 **8** *6* **Goldenveil (IRE)**[22] 5466 3-9-5 **80** .... PaulHanagan 6 45
(Richard Fahey) *t.k.h: hld up: struggling over 2f outf: edgd rt and sn btn* **14/1**

50-0 **9** *31* **Lochiel**[15] 5729 7-9-7 **73** .... TomEaves 2 —
(Ian Semple) *hld up towards rr: struggling over 3f out: sn lost tch* **50/1**

3m 0.32s (6.42) **Going Correction** +0.75s/f (Yiel)
WFA 3 from 4yo+ 9lb 9 Ran SP% **113.2**
Speed ratings (Par 105): **110,107,106,106,106 97,94,90,71**
toteswingers:1&2:£6.70, 1&3:£5.20, 2&3:£1.90 CSF £48.77 CT £112.70 TOTE £10.20: £3.60, £1.30, £1.10; EX 42.40 Trifecta £68.30 Pool £766.41 - 8.30 winning units..
Owner Ms J Bianco **Bred** Rockhart Trading Ltd **Trained** Middleham Moor, N Yorks
■ Stewards' Enquiry : Gary Bartley one-day ban: careless riding (Oct 3)

FOCUS
There was a good gallop considering the testing ground, and this was quite a test in the conditions.
Bradbury(IRE) Official explanation: jockey said gelding was unsuited by the soft ground

6192 TOTESWINGER H'CAP — 1m 3f 16y
5:10 (5:10) (Class 5) (0-70,69) 3-Y-O — **£2,587** (£770; £384; £192) Stalls Low

Form RPR

4002 **1** **Damascus Symphony**[20] 5553 3-8-9 **57** .... AndrewElliott 2 65
(James Bethell) *hld up: hdwy over 2f out: styd on wl fnl f: led nr fin* **7/1**

0003 **2** *1/2* **Srimenanti**[18] 5623 3-8-7 **55** oh2 .... (p) FrederikTylicki 8 62
(Brian Rothwell) *led 2f: cl up: led again over 2f out: edgd rt and kpt on fnl f: hdd nr fin* **22/1**

0142 **3** *6* **Deep Applause**[11] 5823 3-9-1 **63** .... (p) TomEaves 1 59
(Michael Dods) *t.k.h: in tch: effrt and rdn over 2f out: edgd rt and sn outpcd: kpt on fnl f* **5/1**

4553 **4** *hd* **Nicola's Dream**[33] 5150 3-9-5 **67** .... PaulHanagan 6 63
(Richard Fahey) *prom: hdwy and ev ch over 2f out: edgd rt: no ex over 1f out* **11/4**[1]

3320 **5** *1/2* **Philharmonic Hall**[27] 5311 3-9-0 **62** .... (p) BarryMcHugh 3 57
(Richard Fahey) *in tch: effrt 3f out: hung rt 2f out: sn outpcd* **10/3**[2]

5033 **6** *nk* **Free Art**[20] 5560 3-9-7 **69** .... DanielTudhope 4 64
(Geoffrey Harker) *t.k.h: hld up: effrt over 2f out: sn no imp: btn fnl f* **9/2**[3]

501 **7** *19* **Caledonia Prince**[19] 5602 3-8-1 **56** oh1 ow1 .... (p) JoshBaudains(7) 7 16
(Jo Hughes) *led after 2f to over 2f out: sn rdn and struggling: t.o* **10/1**

2m 34.68s (9.08) **Going Correction** +0.75s/f (Yiel) 7 Ran SP% **110.5**
Speed ratings (Par 101): **96,95,91,91,90 90,76**
toteswingers:1&2:£15.00, 1&3:£5.10, 2&3:£16.00. totesuper7: WIN: Not won. PLACE: £1,468.90 CSF £122.42 CT £795.19 TOTE £10.50: £5.00, £6.60; EX 119.70 Trifecta £532.80 Part won. Pool £720.11 - 0.83 winning units..
Owner Clarendon Thoroughbred Racing **Bred** Jeremy Green And Sons And P Bickmore **Trained** Middleham Moor, N Yorks
■ Stewards' Enquiry : Andrew Elliott One-day ban: used whip with excessive frequency (Oct 3)

FOCUS
A modest contest featuring only two previous winners. They didn't go that quick early, but the winner still came from off the pace.
T/Jkpt: Not won. T/Plt: £198.90 to a £1 stake. Pool:£67,647.47 - 248.22 winning tickets T/Qpdt: £13.00 to a £1 stake. Pool:£4,943.98 - 280.20 winning tickets RY

6193 - 6195a (Foreign Racing) - See Raceform Interactive

3890 FAIRYHOUSE (R-H)
Sunday, September 18

OFFICIAL GOING: Yielding to soft

6196a TATTERSALLS IRELAND SUPER AUCTION SALE STKS — 7f
3:45 (3:59) 2-Y-O
£63,362 (£24,568; £15,948; £7,327; £3,017; £431)

RPR

1 **Seanie (IRE)**[31] 5227 2-8-13 .... CO'Donoghue 18 88+
(David Marnane, Ire) *hld up in rr: hdwy on outer to chse ldrs over 1f out: led ins fnl f: wandered a bit in clsng stages* **40/1**

2 *1 1/2* **Absolute Crackers (IRE)**[31] 5227 2-8-12 .... FMBerry 6 83
(Mrs John Harrington, Ire) *towards rr: rdn st: r.o strly ins fnl f: nt get to wnr* **14/1**

3 *1/2* **Azamata (IRE)**[8] 5956 2-9-1 .... DPMcDonogh 8 85
(Kevin Prendergast, Ire) *towards rr: kpt on wl wout threatening u.p ins fnl f* **9/2**[2]

4 *1/2* **Three Am Tour (IRE)**[10] 5861 2-8-12 .... RichardHughes 3 81
(Richard Hannon) *sn mid-div: impr to chse ldrs over 2f out: no imp and kpt on same pce ins fnl f* **11/2**[3]

5 *hd* **Tough As Nails (IRE)**[8] 5951 2-8-13 112 .... GFCarroll 17 81
(Michael Mulvany, Ire) *sn led: attempted to assert fr over 2f out: reduced ld and hdd ins fnl f: no ex* **4/1**[1]

6 *nk* **Beau Amadeus (IRE)**[20] 5571 2-8-13 82 .... (b) CDHayes 16 80
(Adrian McGuinness, Ire) *in rr of mid-div: kpt on wout threatening u.p fr 2f out* **25/1**

7 *1/2* **Quick Bite (IRE)**[20] 5550 2-8-10 .... LukeMorris 11 76
(Hugo Palmer) *chsd ldrs: 5th over 2f out: no imp u.p and kpt on same pce ins fnl f* **16/1**

8 *hd* **Evervescent (IRE)**[40] 4891 2-8-13 .... SeamieHeffernan 9 79
(J S Moore) *sn mid-div: kpt on same pce fr 2f out* **33/1**

9 *3* **Blue Mimosa (IRE)**[20] 5571 2-8-8 78 .... SHJames 1 66
(Kevin Prendergast, Ire) *sn mid-div: kpt on same pce fr 2f out* **14/1**

10 *hd* **Raphael Santi (IRE)**[104] 2776 2-9-5 92 .... (b[1]) JPO'Brien 5 77
(A P O'Brien, Ire) *towards rr: kpt on wout threatening u.p fr 2f out* **12/1**

11 *2 1/4* **City Dazzler (IRE)**[7] 5959 2-8-10 .... NGMcCullagh 13 62
(Richard Hannon) *prom: 2nd for much: no ex and kpt on same pce fnl f* **33/1**

12 *2* **Let Your Love Flow (IRE)**[19] 5605 2-8-8 .... DMGrant 15 55
(Sylvester Kirk) *sn mid-div: kpt on same pce fr 2f out* **33/1**

13 *3/4* **Battleroftheboyne (IRE)**[7] 5973 2-8-13 82 .... BACurtis 4 58
(Michael Mulvany, Ire) *sn mid-div: kpt on same pce fr 2f out* **16/1**

14 *1 3/4* **My Solitaire (IRE)**[39] 4913 2-8-12 .... (b[1]) JohnFahy 10 53
(Clive Cox) *sn mid-div: kpt on same pce fr 2f out* **50/1**

15 *nk* **Chandigarh (IRE)**[5] 6021 2-8-8 .... FrankieMcDonald 2 48
(Paul Fitzsimons) *chsd ldrs: no ex fr 2f out* **16/1**

16 *2* **Gatepost (IRE)**[28] 5305 2-9-1 107 .... PJSmullen 14 50
(Mick Channon) *trckd ldrs: no ex fr 2f out* **11/2**[3]

17 *6* **Tamam Namoose (IRE)**[21] 5521 2-8-13 .... WJSupple 7 33
(P D Deegan, Ire) *trckd ldrs: no ex fr 2f out* **25/1**

18 *9* **Rockview Diamond (IRE)**[79] 3601 2-8-13 82 .... ShaneFoley 12 10
(John C McConnell, Ire) *prom early: no ex fr 2f out* **25/1**

1m 33.07s (2.57) 18 Ran SP% **132.4**
CSF £531.79 TOTE £46.50: £9.40, £5.60, £2.60; DF 1326.10.
Owner Damian Lavelle **Bred** Mrs Teresa Thornton **Trained** Bansha, Co Tipperary

FOCUS
A typical sales race that changed dramatically in the final furlong and it produced a promising winner. This looked looked a decent race but the sixth helps limit the form. The first three all came from off the pace, but the front-runner seemed to go a sensible gallop and simply ran out of puff.

NOTEBOOK
Seanie(IRE) ◆ won like a smart horse. Last turning in, he produced a superb turn of foot to get to the front. When he got there, he showed marked signs of inexperience and gives the impression the best is yet to come. He looks a lovely prospect and the quality of horse his yard deserves to have. He would easily get a mile but has enough pace to drop back in trip too. Ultimately, he is considered a longer-term prospect.
Absolute Crackers(IRE) ◆, held up like the winner, absolutely flashed home. She had finished ahead of the winner last time and was ahead of him here not long after the line, which came too soon. She can be considered a smart filly. (op 16/1)
Azamata(IRE) was also finishing to fine effect and ran another good race. He made up considerable ground in the final couple of furlongs and would certainly not be out of place in Pattern company. He seems to handle this ground well. (op 9/2 tchd 5/1)
Three Am Tour(IRE) stepped up considerably on the form of her maiden success, giving best close home but running a solid race. She had no obvious excuses. (op 13/2)
Tough As Nails(IRE)'s possible lack of stamina was considered beforehand to be his weakness and in that regard the race went entirely to script. He was sent quickly to the front and was given a good front-running ride. However, he slowed dramatically in the final furlong, with the work he had to do to get to the lead from his draw belatedly telling. He looks best on deep ground at 5f. (op 4/1 tchd 7/2)
Beau Amadeus(IRE) ran a blinder, considering he had looked fairly exposed and is rated 82. He deserves to win a maiden. (op 28/1)
Quick Bite(IRE) had every chance and ran about as well as could be expected. (op 14/1)
Gatepost(IRE) weakened quite dramatically. Official explanation: jockey said colt travelled well but ran flat in the latter stages (op 5/1)

6197 - 6199a (Foreign Racing) - See Raceform Interactive

3334 DORTMUND (R-H)
Sunday, September 18

OFFICIAL GOING: Turf: soft

6200a DEUTSCHES ST LEGER (GROUP 3) (3YO+) (TURF) — 1m 6f
4:25 (12:00) 3-Y-O+
£27,586 (£9,482; £4,741; £2,586; £1,724; £1,293)

RPR

1 **Fox Hunt (IRE)**[29] 5285 4-9-6 0 .... SilvestreDeSousa 8 112
(Mark Johnston) *broke fast: settled in 2nd bhd ldr: rdn into fnl turn: r.o wl in st: hdd longtime ldr 1 1/2f out: battled for ld thrght fnl f: tk ld 50yds out* **1/1**[1]

2 *3/4* **Fair Boss (IRE)**[21] 3-8-10 0 .... APietsch 1 111
(W Hickst, Germany) *broke wl: settled 3rd: rdn ent st: jnd battle w eventual wnr 1 1/2f out: hdd 50yds out* **22/5**[2]

3 *2 1/2* **Dawn Twister (GER)**[35] 5092 4-9-6 0 .... ADeVries 4 107
(J Hirschberger, Germany) *broke fast: sn led: set mod pce: led into st: r.o wl: hdd 1 1/2f out: no ansswer to 1st 2* **63/10**

4 *2* **Earlsalsa (GER)**[79] 7-9-6 0 .... AHelfenbein 7 104
(C Von Der Recke, Germany) *bkmarker fr s: prog towards end of bk st: r.o wl in st: styd on fnl f* **183/10**

5 *3/4* **Aviator (GER)**[28] 5308 3-8-10 0 .... THellier 5 103
(T Mundry, Germany) *settled 6th: styd on in st wout threatening ldrs* **9/1**

6 *6* **Altano (GER)**[472] 5-9-6 0 .... EPedroza 3 95
(A Wohler, Germany) *settled 5th: rdn bef fnl turn: r.o early in st: wknd 1f out* **23/5**

7 *10* **Lacateno**[51] 4524 4-9-6 0 .... AStarke 2 81
(W Hickst, Germany) *settled 4th: r.o wl early in st: wknd u.p fnl 2f* **9/2**[3]

3m 10.26s (4.76)
WFA 3 from 4yo+ 10lb 7 Ran SP% **133.4**
WIN (incl. 10 euro stake): 20. PLACES: 10, 11, 14. SF: 111.
Owner Sheikh Hamdan Bin Mohammed Al Maktoum **Bred** Ballylinch Stud **Trained** Middleham Moor, N Yorks

NOTEBOOK
Fox Hunt(IRE) is the third British-trained horse to win a German Classic this term after Excelebration in the 2,000 Guineas and Dancing Rain in the Oaks. Sent for home two out, he kept on pulling out more for a battling win. This qualifies him for the Melbourne Cup, one of several options he has.

4599 MUNICH (L-H)
Sunday, September 18

OFFICIAL GOING: Turf: soft

6201a GROSSE EUROPA MEILE (GROUP 2) (3YO+) (TURF) — 1m
3:30 (12:00) 3-Y-O+
£34,482 (£13,362; £5,603; £2,801; £2,801; £1,293)

RPR

1 **Sommerabend**[14] 5772 4-9-2 0 .... GeraldMosse 8 108
(U Stoltefuss, Germany) *hld up bhd ldrs: shkn up on ins rail ent st: no immediate rspnse: qcknd wl 1/2-way in st: tk ld jst ins fnl f: had to battle w eventual runner-up but a fnd more to win convincingly* **17/10**[1]

2 ³/₄ **Silver Ocean (USA)**[112] 2541 3-8-11 0........................... NicolaPinna 10 105
(Riccardo Santini, Italy) *hld up towards rr: produced on outside in st: r.o wl to chal eventual wnr: a being hld* **25/1**
3 *nk* **Point Blank (GER)**[17] 5664 3-8-11 0........................... ASuborics 6 105
(Mario Hofer, Germany) *settled in midfield: r.o wl in st: threatened briefly ent fnl f: r.o wl to go 3rd on line* **135/10**
4 *shd* **Blue Panis (FR)**[17] 5664 4-9-2 0........................... KKerekes 11 105
(F Chappet, France) *led fr s w Gereon: r.o wl in st: styd on wl fnl f: lost 3rd on line* **23/5**[3]
4 *dht* **Usbeke (GER)**[21] 5530 5-9-2 0........................... FabriceVeron 2 105
(J-P Carvalho, Germany) *settled towards rr: rdn early in st: r.o wl to look threatening 2f out but unable qck fnl f* **227/10**
6 *nk* **Neatico (GER)**[17] 5664 4-9-2 0........................... JiriPalik 4 105
(P Schiergen, Germany) *prom fr s: r.o wl in st: ev ch tl 1 1/2f out then wknd* **81/10**
7 *3* **Indomito (GER)**[14] 5777 5-9-2 0........................... JBojko 1 98
(A Wohler, Germany) *settled in midfield: styd on one pce in st* **31/5**
8 *4* **Gereon (GER)**[28] 5308 3-8-11 0........................... FilipMinarik 7 88
(C Zschache, Germany) *shared ld w Blue Panis: ev ch 2 1/2f out: rdn 2f out: no rspnse: sn btn* **18/5**[2]
9 *2* **Le Big (GER)**[17] 5664 7-9-2 0........................... WPanov 5 84
(U Stoltefuss, Germany) *settled in midfield: mde no imp in st* **172/10**
10 *1 ¹/₂* **Setareh (GER)**[58] 6-9-2 0........................... EFrank 3 81
(P Olsanik, Germany) *settled in rr: no imp* **33/1**

1m 39.82s (99.82)
WFA 3 from 4yo+ 4lb **10** Ran SP% **124.9**
WIN (incl. 10 euro stake): 27. PLACES: 19, 41, 25. SF: 714.
Owner Stall Bedford Lodge **Bred** Gestut Schlenderhan **Trained** In Germany

NOTEBOOK
Sommerabend ran out a narrow but convincing winner. He loved the soft ground.

3449 SAN SIRO (R-H)
Sunday, September 18
OFFICIAL GOING: Turf: heavy

6202a PREMIO FEDERICO TESIO (GROUP 2) (3YO+) (TURF) 1m 3f
3:15 (12:00) 3-Y-0+ **£60,344** (£26,551; £14,482; £7,241)

RPR
1 **Sneak A Peek (ITY)**[112] 3-8-5 0........................... MircoDemuro 5 115
(S Botti, Italy) *trckd ldr on outside of Voila Ici: moved up to ld after 2f: hdd ins fnl 3f: disputing 2nd and pushed along over 2f out: styd on to join ldr ins fnl f: r.o gamely to assert fnl 50yds* **4/1**[3]
2 ³/₄ **Jakkalberry (IRE)**[98] 2982 5-8-11 0........................... FabioBranca 3 113
(E Botti, Italy) *broke wl and led: hdd after 2f and trckd ldr on ins: pressed ldr over 3f out and sn led: 2 l up and hrd rdn ins fnl 1 1/2f: jnd ins fnl f: r.o gamely but no ex fnl 50yds* **5/3**[2]
3 *2* **Voila Ici (IRE)**[98] 2982 6-9-2 0........................... UmbertoRispoli 4 114
(Vittorio Caruso, Italy) *trckd ldr on ins of Sneak A Peek: and after 2f on outside of Jakkalberry: outpcd and 3rd 3 1/2f out: bk on bridle and travelling wl in share of 2nd 2f out: rdn appr fnl f: styd on but nt pce to chal first two* **51/50**[1]
4 *7* **Keep Cool**[15] 4-8-11 0........................... MEsposito 2 96
(Andreas Lowe, Germany) *last: effrt towards ins 3f out: lft bhd by 1st 3 fr 2f out* **27/4**
5 *6* **Plushenko (IRE)**[58] 3-8-5 0...........................(b) CristianDemuro 1 87
(L Riccardi, Italy) *settled in 4th: rdn and wknd fnl 2f* **214/10**
6 *3 ¹/₂* **Cima De Pluie**[98] 2982 4-8-11 0........................... DarioVargiu 6 79
(B Grizzetti, Italy) *settled in 5th: rdn and no imp 2 1/2f out: wknd fnl 2f* **162/10**

2m 19.0s (0.40)
WFA 3 from 4yo+ 7lb **6** Ran SP% **130.2**
WIN (incl. 1 euro stake): 5.02. PLACES: 2.27, 1.92. DF: 18.82.
Owner Dioscuri Srl **Bred** Azienda Agricola Al Deni S R L **Trained** Italy

3208 WOODBINE (R-H)
Sunday, September 18
OFFICIAL GOING: Turf: firm

6203a NORTHERN DANCER TURF STKS PRESENTED BY VTECH S (GRADE 1) (3YO+) (TURF) 1m 4f (T)
9:34 (9:35) 3-Y-0+
£192,307 (£64,102; £32,051; £16,025; £6,410; £3,846)

RPR
1 **Wigmore Hall (IRE)**[36] 5074 4-8-11 0........................... JamieSpencer 4 114
(Michael Bell) *w.w towards rr: 7th on ins 2 1/2f out: hdwy on rail passing 2f pole: r.o to ld 150yds out: hld on wl u.p* **29/20**[1]
2 *nk* **Simmard (USA)**[44] 6-8-7 0...........................(b) PHusbands 5 110
(Roger L Attfield, Canada) *hld up: rapid hdwy on outside over 5f out to dispute ld: wnt on 4f out: 2l clr and u.p 1 1/2f fr home: hdd 150yds out: rallied gamely u.p* **54/10**
3 ¹/₂ **Al Khali (USA)**[36] 5076 5-8-9 0........................... AGarcia 8 111
(William Mott, U.S.A) *w.w in last: shkn up 2 1/2f out: last and swtchd outside 2f out: r.o u.p to chal on outside of front two ins fnl f: run flattened out fnl 60yds* **71/20**[3]
4 *1 ³/₄* **Laureate Conductor (USA)**[29] 5-8-7 0........................... JStein 7 106
(Michael P De Paulo, Canada) *w.w towards rr: hdwy u.p over 2f out: wnt 4th ins fnl f but nt pce to chal ldrs* **69/1**
5 *1 ³/₄* **Hailstone (USA)**[28] 4-8-7 0...........................(b) JRLeparoux 3 103
(Mark Casse, Canada) *racd in midfield: rdn and nt qckn 2 1/2f out: styd on again ins fnl f wout threatening ldrs* **11/1**
6 *1 ³/₄* **Hotep (CAN)**[36] 4-8-7 0........................... EmmaJayneWilson 1 101
(Mark Frostad, Canada) *trckd ldng gp: 4th and scrubbed along to hold pl over 2f out: nt qckn u.p fr 2f out: fdd ins fnl f* **238/10**
7 *2* **Seaside Retreat (USA)**[29] 8-8-7 0........................... LContreras 6 97
(Mark Casse, Canada) *racd keenly trcking ldr: 3rd and u.p on outside over 2f out: wknd u.p appr fnl f* **163/10**
8 ¹/₂ **Bourbon Bay (USA)**[21] 5-8-11 0...........................(b) JTalamo 2 101
(Neil Drysdale, U.S.A) *led: jnd ins fnl 5f: hdd 4f out: rdn and nt qckn 2f out: dropped out tamely* **13/4**[2]

2m 30.67s (1.07) **8** Ran SP% **121.5**
PARI-MUTUEL (all including $2 stakes): WIN 4.90; PLACE (1-2) 3.20, 5.50; SHOW (1-2-3) 2.80, 3.70, 3.50; SF 29.10.
Owner M B Hawtin **Bred** K And Mrs Cullen **Trained** Newmarket, Suffolk

FOCUS
A slow pace and not strong form for the grade.

NOTEBOOK
Wigmore Hall(IRE), reunited with usual partner Jamie Spencer, took a similar inside path as he had with Hayley Turner in the Arlington Million, saving ground throughout. The gelding was trapped in at one stage, but a hole eventually opened up on the rail and he willingly took advantage to forge ahead under a strong Spencer drive. He will run in the Champion Stakes at Ascot before a campaign in Dubai.

6204a RICOH WOODBINE MILE STKS (GRADE 1) (3YO+) (TURF) 1m (T)
10:42 (12:00) 3-Y-0+
£384,615 (£128,205; £64,102; £32,051; £12,820; £6,410)

RPR
1 **Turallure (USA)**[23] 4-8-9 0........................... JRLeparoux 8 118
(Charles Lopresti, U.S.A) **13/2**[2]
2 *nk* **Courageous Cat (USA)**[78] 3652 5-8-12 0........................... PValenzuela 4 120
(William Mott, U.S.A) **23/20**[1]
3 *nse* **Right One (FR)**[64] 5-8-7 0........................... GKGomez 5 115
(Christophe Clement, U.S.A) **94/10**
4 *1* **Side Glance**[38] 4972 4-8-7 0........................... JimmyFortune 9 113
(Andrew Balding) **74/10**[3]
5 *hd* **Riding The River (USA)**[21] 4-8-5 0...........................(b) RDosRamos 7 110
(David Cotey, U.S.A) **34/1**
6 *nk* **Dance And Dance (IRE)**[38] 4972 5-8-5 0........................... JamieSpencer 11 111+
(Edward Vaughan) **41/5**
7 *1 ¹/₄* **Court Vision (USA)**[91] 6-8-9 0...........................(b) RAlbarado 12 111
(Dale Romans, U.S.A) **157/10**
8 ¹/₂ **Hollinger (CAN)**[43] 4-8-6 0 ow1........................... TPizarro 1 106
(Roger L Attfield, Canada) **55/1**
9 *1 ¹/₄* **Grand Adventure (USA)**[21] 5-8-7 0........................... PHusbands 6 105
(Mark Frostad, Canada) **178/10**
10 ¹/₂ **Forte Dei Marmi**[20] 5544 5-8-5 0........................... JRVelazquez 2 101
(Roger L Attfield, Canada) **24/1**
11 *1 ³/₄* **Kara's Orientation (USA)**[28] 4-8-9 0........................... ERamsammy 10 101
(Steven Chircop, U.S.A) **147/10**
12 *4 ¹/₄* **Woodbourne (CAN)**[29] 7-8-5 0........................... EmmaJayneWilson 3 88
(Robert Tiller, Canada) **43/1**

1m 34.92s (94.92) **12** Ran SP% **120.8**
PARI-MUTUEL (all including $2 stakes): WIN 14.90; PLACE (1-2) 5.90, 3.10; SHOW (1-2-3) 4.10, 2.90, 4.90; SF 42.30.
Owner Donna C Arnold **Bred** 4-D Stables **Trained** USA

NOTEBOOK
Turallure(USA) flew down the stretch from the back of the field to land a last-gasp victory.
Side Glance, upped in grade, had every chance.
Dance And Dance(IRE) looked unlucky. The Royal Hunt Cup runner-up appeared to be full of running with nowhere to go in the final furlong under Jamie Spencer.

6183 BELMONT PARK (L-H)
Sunday, September 18
OFFICIAL GOING: Turf: firm

6205a MAIDEN SPECIAL WEIGHT (MAIDEN) (2YO FILLIES) (TURF) 1m 110y
7:36 (7:36) 2-Y-0 **£19,615** (£6,538; £3,269; £1,634; £980)

RPR
1 **Singin On Thames (USA)** 2-8-7 0 DCohen 1
(Gary Contessa, U.S.A) **69/20**[2]
2 ¹/₂ **Fashion's Flight (USA)**[23] 5445 2-8-7 0........................... JBravo 5 —
(Brian Meehan) *settled in 3rd on outside bhd v stdy pce: ct flat-footed whn pce qcknd fnl bnd: styd on last f but a hld by wnr* **9/20**[1]
3 *1 ¹/₂* **Richbelle (USA)** 2-8-7 0........................... CVelasquez 4 —
(George Weaver, U.S.A) **93/10**
4 *1 ¹/₄* **McCarren Park (USA)** 2-8-2 0........................... RCuratolo(5) 3 —
(Dominick A Schettino, U.S.A) **11/2**[3]
5 *12 ¹/₂* **Cluain Meala (USA)** 2-8-7 0...........................(b) FBoyce 2 —
(Susan Cooney, U.S.A) **27/1**

1m 45.44s (105.44) **5** Ran SP% **120.1**
PARI-MUTUEL (all including $2 stakes): WIN 8.90; PLACE (1-2) 3.20, 2.10; SHOW (1-2-3) 2.70, 2.10, 3.00; DF 6.80; SF 17.60.
Owner McConnell Racing Stable, Harold Lerner LLC Et Al **Bred** Town & Country Farms Corp **Trained** USA

NOTEBOOK
Fashion's Flight(USA) raced in third but could only stay on into second in the straight as the winner flew for home.

6206 - (Foreign Racing) - See Raceform Interactive

6186 HAMILTON (R-H)
Monday, September 19
OFFICIAL GOING: Soft (good to soft in places; 6.7)
Wind: Light, half behind Weather: Overcast

6207 BRITISH STALLION STUDS SUPPORTING BRITISH RACING E B F MAIDEN STKS 6f 5y
2:10 (2:10) (Class 5) 2-Y-0 **£3,234** (£962; £481) **Stalls** High

Form RPR
3654 1 **I'll Be Good**[14] 5786 2-9-0 74........................... GaryBartley(3) 3 72
(Robert Johnson) *t.k.h: trckd ldrs: effrt over 1f out: led ins fnl f: r.o* **11/2**[3]
24 2 *nk* **Personal Touch**[15] 5756 2-9-3 0........................... PaulHanagan 1 71
(Richard Fahey) *led: rdn over 1f out: hdd ins fnl f: kpt on u.p towards fin* **5/4**[2]

6402 **3** *2* **Represent (IRE)**[11] 5854 2-8-9 71 MartinHarley(3) 6 60
(Mick Channon) *t.k.h: sn trcking ldr: effrt and ev ch over 1f out: edgd rt: kpt on same pce ins fnl f* **11/10**[1]

1m 16.26s (4.06) **Going Correction** +0.575s/f (Yiel) **3** Ran SP% **107.4**
Speed ratings (Par 95): **95,94,91**
CSF £12.03 TOTE £5.20; EX 8.60 TRIFECTA Not won..
Owner Do Well Racing **Bred** Cobhall Court Stud **Trained** Newburn, Tyne & Wear

FOCUS
Half of those originally declared were non-runners, but this was still quite a tight little maiden, and it went to the outsider of three. Just ordinary form.

NOTEBOOK
I'll Be Good was winning at the ninth attempt. Already a dual runner-up, he'd shown himself effective in similar conditions when fourth off a mark of 72 at Newcastle last time, and can continue to give a good account returned to handicaps.
Personal Touch battled right the way to the line when challenged, but was always just being held. He should stay 7f and now has the option of handicaps. (op 6-5 tchd 11-8)
Represent(IRE) was a bit keen tracking the leader and, having initially picked up to draw level, she didn't get home in the conditions. She's ordinary, but good enough to win a small race on a faster surface. (op 5-4)

6208 TOTEPOOL H'CAP 6f 5y
2:40 (2:40) (Class 6) (0-65,65) 3-Y-0+ **£1,940** (£577; £288; £144) **Stalls** Centre

Form RPR

3003 **1** **Babich Bay (IRE)**[1] 6190 3-9-0 **55** (p) SilvestreDeSousa 11 72
(Jo Hughes) *chsd ldrs stands' side: led over 1f out: drew clr ins fnl f: readily* **8/1**

6254 **2** *7* **Cheyenne Red (IRE)**[14] 6787 5-8-8 **47** TomEaves 14 42
(Michael Dods) *cl up: effrt 2f out: chsd (clr) wnr wl ins fnl f: r.o* **8/1**

0605 **3** *nk* **Mark Anthony (IRE)**[10] 5881 4-9-4 **62** (p) LMcNiff(5) 13 56
(Shaun Harris) *led tl hdd over 1f out: kpt on same pce ins fnl f* **22/1**

3330 **4** *1 ½* **I Got You Babe (IRE)**[1] 6190 3-9-6 **61** FrederikTylicki 8 50
(Richard Guest) *midfield in centre: rdn and hung rt 1/2-way: nt clr run briefly 2f out: edgd rt and kpt on ins fnl f: nrst fin* **9/1**

-000 **5** *1 ½* **Hedgerow (IRE)**[25] 5402 4-8-3 **47** oh1 ow1 ShaneBKelly(5) 15 31
(Dianne Sayer) *in tch stands' side: rdn and hung rt over 1f out: sn no ex* **33/1**

60 **6** *hd* **King Bertolini (IRE)**[14] 5789 4-8-7 **49** oh1 ow3 (p) PaulPickard(3) 4 32
(Alan Berry) *sn bhd centre: struggling 1/2-way: edgd lft and styd on fnl f: nvr on terms: horse lost cheekpiece* **66/1**

3402 **7** *nse* **Ivestar (IRE)**[28] 5309 6-9-0 **58** (vt) JulieBurke(5) 10 41
(Ben Haslam) *dwlt bhd centre: rdn and hung rt over 1f out: styd on ins fnl f: nrst fin* **15/2**[3]

2005 **8** *¾* **Desert Auction (IRE)**[34] 5151 4-9-2 **62** (b) JustinNewman(7) 2 43
(Ian Semple) *hld up centre: rdn and effrt over 2f out: wknd over 1f out* **33/1**

5200 **9** *1* **Tahitian Princess (IRE)**[19] 5619 3-8-13 **54** (p) FrannyNorton 16 32
(Ann Duffield) *bhd stands' side: rdn along over 2f out: no imp over 1f out* **12/1**

2556 **10** *½* **Tadalavil**[4] 6076 6-9-12 **65** PaulHanagan 3 41
(Linda Perratt) *trckd centre ldrs tl rdn and wknd over 1f out* **7/1**[2]

4346 **11** *1* **Bonnie Prince Blue**[22] 5502 8-9-9 **65** (b) DaleSwift(3) 6 38
(Ian McInnes) *in tch in centre tl rdn and wknd fr 2f out* **20/1**

5112 **12** *nk* **Mission Impossible**[12] 5824 6-9-7 **60** PatrickMathers 12 32
(Tracy Waggott) *in tch stands' side: drvn along over 2f out: wknd over 1f out* **3/1**[1]

0054 **13** *nk* **Kalahari Desert (IRE)**[19] 5620 4-8-7 **46** oh1 (v) AndrewMullen 1 17
(Richard Whitaker) *dwlt: bhd centre: hdwy whn hmpd 2f out: n.d* **25/1**

0340 **14** *10* **Classlin**[4] 6076 4-8-7 **46** oh1 AndrewElliott 9 —
(Jim Goldie) *bhd centre: struggling after 2f out: nvr on terms* **40/1**

6004 **15** *8* **Fulford**[14] 5789 6-8-9 **46** oh1 ow2 GrahamGibbons 5 —
(Mel Brittain) *in tch centre: outpcd 1/2-way: wknd 2f out: t.o* **14/1**

505 **16** *10* **Miss Pronounce**[14] 5793 3-8-2 **46** oh1 DeclanCannon(3) 7 —
(Linda Perratt) *prom centre: rdn and outpcd whn hung both ways 2f out: sn wknd: t.o* **50/1**

1m 15.45s (3.25) **Going Correction** +0.575s/f (Yiel)
WFA 3 from 4yo+ 2lb **16** Ran SP% **120.6**
Speed ratings (Par 101): **101,91,91,89,87 87,86,85,84,83 82,82,81,68,57 44**
toteswingers:1&2:£16.30, 2&3:£54.70, 1&3:£36.60 CSF £63.43 CT £903.33 TOTE £8.50: £2.40, £2.00, £4.90, £2.50; EX 70.50.
Owner B Allen & J Hughes **Bred** Pat Beirne **Trained** Lambourn, Berks

FOCUS
Few got into this low-grade handicap, with there being an advantage towards those who raced both prominently and near the stands' rail. There is some doubt over Babich Bay's wide-margin win given the conditions, although this rates a clear personal best.
Babich Bay(IRE) Official explanation: trainer had no explanation for the apparent improvement in form
King Bertolini(IRE) Official explanation: jockey said colt hung right and lost a cheekpiece
Ivestar(IRE) Official explanation: jockey said gelding missed the break

6209 TOTEQUADPOT CONDITIONS STKS 6f 5y
3:10 (3:11) (Class 2) 3-Y-0+ **£9,960** (£2,982; £1,491; £745; £372) **Stalls** Centre

Form RPR

3004 **1** **Nasri**[51] 4534 5-8-9 97 MichaelO'Connell 4 104
(David Nicholls) *mde all: rdn over 1f out: edgd lft ins fnl f: kpt on wl* **15/8**[1]

5005 **2** *1 ½* **Atlantic Sport (USA)**[16] 5699 6-8-9 96 MatthewDavies 3 103+
(Mick Channon) *hld up in tch: n.m.r briefly over 1f out: hdwy and ev ch whn hmpd ins fnl f: kpt on same pce* **5/2**[3]

0030 **3** *3* **Kaldoun Kingdom (IRE)**[2] 6147 6-8-9 98 PaulHanagan 1 90
(Richard Fahey) *t.k.h: trckd ldrs: n.m.r briefly over 2f out: effrt over 1f out: edgd rt: kpt on same pce ins fnl f* **9/4**[2]

00 **4** *3 ¾* **Icelandic**[131] 2000 9-8-9 87 (t) SilvestreDeSousa 5 78
(Frank Sheridan) *sn trcking ldr: rdn over 2f out: edgd rt wknd ent fnl f* **10/1**

0020 **5** *5* **Captain Royale (IRE)**[87] 3359 6-8-9 72 (p) PatrickMathers 6 62
(Tracy Waggott) *t.k.h: cl up: rdn over 2f out: sn wknd* **50/1**

1m 14.46s (2.26) **Going Correction** +0.575s/f (Yiel) **5** Ran SP% **105.2**
Speed ratings (Par 109): **107,105,101,96,89**
CSF £6.19 TOTE £2.70: £1.40, £1.50; EX 5.20.
Owner Dab Hand Racing **Bred** Lady Hardy **Trained** Sessay, N Yorks
■ Stewards' Enquiry : Matthew Davies caution: entered wrong stall
Michael O'Connell two-day ban: careless riding (Oct 3-4)

FOCUS
A trappy little conditions race. The winner is rated to this year's handicap best. The second would have gone close with a clear run.

NOTEBOOK
Nasri gained compensation for missing the Ayr Silver Cup at the weekend. He'd been withdrawn on that occasion due to soft ground, so it was in his favour that there wasn't any further rain here, and he made all for a second victory this season. It may have been interesting between he and the runner-up had that one not been squeezed out when challenging strongly against the stands' rail, but it's possible he was idling in front, so hard to quibble with the result. (op 7-4 tchd 2-1)
Atlantic Sport(USA) hasn't won in three years, but he's been running well in some competitive handicaps this season and picked up nicely once switched to the stands' rail, only to run out of room as the winner edged across. He deserves to pick up a race. (op 9-4 tchd 2-1)
Kaldoun Kingdom(IRE), well held in the Ayr Gold Cup two days earlier, ended up having to challenge wide and was unable to quite match the front two. He's another on a bit of a losing stretch. (op 5-2 tchd 11-4)
Icelandic, back from a 131-day absence, looked a threat with 2f to run, but that lack of a recent outing told. He should be straighter next time. (op 17-2)
Captain Royale(IRE) had easily the lowest BHA mark of these and duly struggled. (tchd 66-1)

6210 TOTEQUICKPICK OPEN MAIDEN 1m 1f 36y
3:40 (3:46) (Class 5) 3-4-Y-0 **£2,587** (£770; £384; £192) **Stalls** Low

Form RPR

33 **1** **Ampleforth**[20] 5598 3-9-3 0 SilvestreDeSousa 6 79
(Mark Johnston) *cl up: rdn over 3f out: sn ev ch: led ins fnl f: drvn and styd on wl* **5/2**[2]

42 **2** *1* **Tadabeer**[14] 5792 3-9-3 0 PaulHanagan 7 77
(Ian Williams) *t.k.h early: trckd ldrs: led over 2f out: sn rdn: hdd ins fnl f: kpt on same pce towards fin* **11/10**[1]

00 **3** *5* **Afrikaans (IRE)**[49] 4611 3-9-3 0 FrannyNorton 8 66
(Mark Johnston) *led to over 2f out: sn drvn along: no ex fr over 1f out* **40/1**

2 **4** *4 ½* **Vinniespride (IRE)**[24] 5432 4-9-3 0 (t) LMcNiff(5) 4 56
(Mark Michael McNiff, Ire) *t.k.h: in tch: drvn over 3f out: edgd both ways over 2f out: sn outpcd* **14/1**[3]

5 *3* **Lady Gargoyle** 3-8-12 0 DanielTudhope 5 45
(Jim Goldie) *hld up: rdn over 2f out: sn no imp* **50/1**

6 **6** *6* **Carnelian (IRE)**[24] 5432 4-9-5 0 DaleSwift(3) 2 36
(Ian Semple) *hld up: drvn along 3f out: sn wknd* **125/1**

2m 5.97s (6.27) **Going Correction** +0.575s/f (Yiel)
WFA 3 from 4yo 5lb **6** Ran SP% **88.1**
Speed ratings (Par 103): **95,94,89,85,83 77**
CSF £3.20 TOTE £2.60: £1.40, £1.20; EX 3.30 Trifecta £12.20 Pool: £206.31 - 12.51 winning units..
Owner Sheikh Hamdan Bin Mohammed Al Maktoum **Bred** Plantation Stud **Trained** Middleham Moor, N Yorks

FOCUS
An ordinary maiden, with two of the runners, Appeal and Doynosaur, being withdrawn at the start. The time was relatively slow but the first pair finished clear.

6211 TOTEEXACTA H'CAP 1m 1f 36y
4:10 (4:11) (Class 5) (0-70,67) 3-Y-0+ **£2,587** (£770; £384; £192) **Stalls** Low

Form RPR

6034 **1** **Botham (USA)**[19] 5622 7-9-4 **61** DanielTudhope 5 74
(Jim Goldie) *hld up: hdwy over 2f out: led and hung rt ins fnl f: r.o wl towards fin* **9/1**

-200 **2** *1 ¾* **Brockfield**[101] 2887 5-9-4 **61** SilvestreDeSousa 9 70
(Mel Brittain) *led: rdn over 2f out: hdd ins fnl f: rallied: hld nr fin* **9/2**[2]

3 *4 ½* **Mighty Whitey (IRE)**[46] 3666 5-9-1 **63** (t[1]) LMcNiff(5) 7 62
(Noel C Kelly, Ire) *t.k.h early: cl up: effrt and ev ch over 2f out: no ex over 1f out* **25/1**

121 **4** *2 ¼* **Smart Violetta (IRE)**[12] 5822 3-8-12 **63** (t) DaleSwift(3) 6 57
(Ann Duffield) *t.k.h early: hld up towards rr: effrt over 2f out: sn rdn and edgd rt: no imp over 1f out* **4/1**[1]

0500 **5** *2 ¾* **Ejteyaaz**[15] 5759 4-9-9 **66** PaulHanagan 1 54
(Richard Fahey) *hld up towards rr: rdn and outpcd over 3f out: no imp fnl 2f* **4/1**[1]

4502 **6** *½* **Bright Applause**[12] 5822 3-9-0 **62** FrannyNorton 2 49
(Tracy Waggott) *s.i.s: bhd: rdn over 3f out: sme late hdwy: nvr on terms* **8/1**

021 **7** *1* **Master Of Dance (IRE)**[21] 5549 4-9-10 **67** (p) TomEaves 11 52
(Keith Dalgleish) *in tch: hdwy over 3f out: sn rdn: wknd over 1f out* **11/2**[3]

0620 **8** *5* **Petomic (IRE)**[16] 5728 6-9-5 **65** (p) RobertLButler(3) 4 39
(Richard Guest) *hld up: rdn along over 3f out: sn btn* **25/1**

0623 **9** *5* **Nolecce**[24] 5441 4-9-0 **64** (p) CharlesEddery(7) 3 27
(Richard Guest) *trckd ldrs tl edgd rt and wknd wl over 1f out* **20/1**

04-0 **10** *13* **Ella Woodcock (IRE)**[25] 5402 7-8-12 **62** JustinNewman(7) 8 —
(Eric Alston) *hld up: hdwy and prom 1/2-way: wknd over 2f out* **16/1**

2m 3.98s (4.28) **Going Correction** +0.575s/f (Yiel)
WFA 3 from 4yo+ 5lb **10** Ran SP% **113.0**
Speed ratings (Par 103): **103,101,97,95,93 92,91,87,82,71**
toteswingers:1&2:£8.40, 2&3:£24.60, 1&3:£14.60 CSF £46.38 CT £970.84 TOTE £8.40: £3.80, £2.20, £5.60; EX 61.50 TRIFECTA Not won..
Owner Caledonia Racing **Bred** France Weiner & Neal Hayias **Trained** Uplawmoor, E Renfrews

FOCUS
The front pair drew clear in what was a moderate handicap. The pace was good and the form is sound.
Bright Applause Official explanation: jockey said gelding had no more to give

6212 TOTETRIFECTA H'CAP 5f 4y
4:40 (4:44) (Class 4) (0-80,80) 3-Y-0+ **£4,528** (£1,347; £673; £336) **Stalls** Centre

Form RPR

6464 **1** **Captain Scooby**[5] 6044 5-8-5 **64** AmyRyan(3) 1 80
(Richard Whitaker) *bhd and sn pushed along: gd hdwy on outside to ld ent fnl f: r.o strly* **8/1**

0600 **2** *2 ¼* **Doc Hay (USA)**[16] 5720 4-9-10 **80** PaulHanagan 5 88
(Keith Dalgleish) *bhd and hung rt: rdn and hdwy over 1f out: chsd wnr ins fnl f: r.o* **8/1**

5350 **3** *1 ½* **The Nifty Fox**[3] 6112 7-9-7 **79** TomEaves 3 82
(Tim Easterby) *hld up in tch: rdn over 2f out: effrt over 1f out: kpt on ins fnl f* **15/2**[3]

00-2 **4** *½* **Trade Secret**[5] 6044 4-9-0 **70** SilvestreDeSousa 9 71
(Mel Brittain) *w ldrs: led appr to ent fnl f: kpt on same pce* **7/2**[1]

4260 **5** *2* **Bosun Breese**[16] 5720 6-9-0 **70** GrahamGibbons 11 64
(David Barron) *led tl hdd appr fnl f: kpt on same pce* **14/1**

4125 **6** *nk* **Wicked Wilma (IRE)**[9] 5923 7-8-12 **73** JulieBurke(5) 2 65
(Alan Berry) *prom on outside: effrt and ev ch over 1f out: no ex ins fnl f* **16/1**

5311 **7** *nse* **Ingleby Star (IRE)**[16] 5720 6-9-3 **80** (p) JustinNewman(7) 4 72
(Ian McInnes) *in tch: rdn over 2f out: outpcd ins fnl f* **12/1**

540 **8** ¾ **Cruise Tothelimit (IRE)**[9] 5918 3-8-11 **71**.................... LeeTopliss(3) 10 61
(Patrick Morris) *w ldrs: ev ch over 1f out: wknd ins fnl f* **20/1**
2600 **9** 4 **Carrie's Magic**[16] 5725 4-8-3 **64**.................(b) ShaneBKelly(5) 6 39
(Alistair Whillans) *bhd and sn drvn along: nvr on terms* **33/1**
5533 **10** hd **Rylee Mooch**[3] 6112 3-8-9 **73**...................................(e) CharlesEddery(7) 7 47
(Richard Guest) *midfield: rdn and hung rt over 2f out: no imp over 1f out* **8/1**
0065 **11** ½ **Tillys Tale**[9] 5918 4-9-1 **71**.. FrederikTylicki 8 44
(Paul Midgley) *cl up tl rdn and wknd over 1f out* **14/1**
506 **12** 1¾ **Walvis Bay (IRE)**[17] 5679 4-9-5 **75**................................ FrannyNorton 12 41
(Tom Tate) *chsd ldrs against stands' rail tl wknd over 1f out* **7/1**[2]

62.46 secs (2.46) **Going Correction** +0.575s/f (Yiel)
WFA 3 from 4yo+ 1lb **12** Ran SP% **114.4**
Speed ratings (Par 105): **103,99,97,96,93 92,92,91,84,84 83,80**
CSF £68.08 CT £499.92 TOTE £7.50: £3.40, £3.40, £2.80; EX 88.10 Trifecta £321.60 Pool: £478.07 - 1.10 winning units..
Owner Paul Davies (H'gte) **Bred** Hellwood Stud Farm & Paul Davies (h'Gate) **Trained** Scarcroft, W Yorks

FOCUS
A fairly modest sprint handicap. The winner rates similarly to when winning this last year. The earlier stands'-side bias was turned on its head here.

6213 TOTESWINGER H'CAP 5f 4y
5:10 (5:10) (Class 6) (0-65,65) 3-Y-0+ **£1,940** (£577; £288; £144) **Stalls** Centre

Form RPR
3142 **1** **Tongalooma**[4] 6076 5-9-2 **60**.. PJMcDonald 6 75
(James Moffatt) *prom: led 2f out: clr whn edgd lft ins fnl f: kpt on strly* **11/4**[1]
3653 **2** 6 **Sharp Bullet (IRE)**[2] 6175 5-8-10 **54**.........................(p) FrederikTylicki 3 47
(Bruce Hellier) *bhd tl hdwy over 1f out: chsd (clr) wnr ins fnl f: no imp* **6/1**[3]
-346 **3** hd **Cheeky Wee Red**[11] 5865 3-8-6 **51** oh1........................... PaulHanagan 2 44
(Richard Fahey) *bhd and outpcd: hdwy over 1f out: kpt on ins fnl f: nvr able to chal* **20/1**
2000 **4** 1¼ **Royal Blade (IRE)**[10] 5881 4-9-1 **64**.................................. JulieBurke(5) 4 52
(Alan Berry) *sn outpcd and drvn along: rallied over 1f out: nvr rchd ldrs* **12/1**
0000 **5** ½ **Tenancy (IRE)**[12] 5824 7-8-8 **52**..................................... FrannyNorton 5 38
(Shaun Harris) *w ldrs: ev ch tl no ex over 1f out* **33/1**
3001 **6** 1½ **Sparking**[24] 5436 4-9-6 **64**.. SilvestreDeSousa 12 45
(David Barron) *wnt lft s: in tch: rdn over 2f out: btn over 1f out* **4/1**[2]
060 **7** ½ **Milton Of Campsie**[39] 4942 6-9-4 **65**...........................(p) RyanClark(3) 7 44
(John Balding) *trckd ldrs: ev ch over 2f out to 1f out: drifted rt and wknd ins fnl f* **9/1**
0010 **8** 2 **Monte Mayor One**[4] 6076 4-8-13 **57**.............................. DanielTudhope 8 29
(Jim Goldie) *towards rr: drvn along 1/2-way: nvr able to chal* **8/1**
6-60 **9** 4 **Lujiana**[109] 2655 6-8-7 **51** oh6... TomEaves 9 —
(Mel Brittain) *in tch: drvn along over 2f out: sn wknd* **33/1**
2003 **10** 3 **Ballarina**[16] 5719 5-8-11 **62** ow2.................................. JustinNewman(7) 11 —
(Eric Alston) *slt ld to 2f out: sn rdn and wknd* **7/1**

62.46 secs (2.46) **Going Correction** +0.575s/f (Yiel)
WFA 3 from 4yo+ 1lb **10** Ran SP% **112.9**
Speed ratings (Par 101): **103,93,93,91,90 87,87,83,77,72**
toteswingers:1&2:£4.90, 2&3:£6.30, 1&3:£6.60 CSF £18.13 CT £266.19 TOTE £4.00: £1.70, £1.70, £2.90; EX 28.10 Trifecta £88.20 Pool: £454.55 - 3.81 winning units..
Owner Mrs Jennie Moffatt **Bred** Mrs J A Moffatt And Brian T Clark **Trained** Cartmel, Cumbria

FOCUS
Another open-looking sprint that was turned into a rout. The winner's effort is worth more at face value but there are doubts due to the testing ground.
Sparking Official explanation: jockey said filly hung right-handed
T/Plt: £232.70 to a £1 stake. Pool of £53,578.78 - 168.05 winning tickets. T/Qpdt: £16.60 to a £1 stake. Pool of £4,827.74 - 214.20 winning tickets. RY

6083 KEMPTON (A.W) (R-H)
Monday, September 19

OFFICIAL GOING: Standard
Wind: Moderate across Weather: Sunny spells

6214 32 FOR POKER MEDIAN AUCTION MAIDEN STKS 7f (P)
2:30 (2:32) (Class 5) 2-Y-0 **£2,264** (£673; £336; £168) **Stalls** Low

Form RPR
043 **1** **Venetian View (IRE)**[10] 5889 2-9-3 71............................. TomQueally 10 78+
(Gary Moore) *in tch: drvn and hdwy over 1f out: wnt 2nd ins fnl f: r.o strly to ld in clsng stages* **10/3**[2]
U43 **2** hd **Equity Card (FR)**[38] 4992 2-8-12 0................................ FrankieDettori 11 72
(Mahmood Al Zarooni) *pressed ldrs: chal 3f out tl led over 1f out: drvn and kpt on ins fnl f: ct in clsng stages* **5/2**[1]
4 **3** 3 **Jack Of Diamonds (IRE)**[26] 5382 2-9-3 0......................... JackMitchell 3 70+
(Roger Teal) *slowly in stride: in rr: drvn and hdwy over 1f out: str run ins fnl f: tk 3rd last strides but no ch w ldng duo* **6/1**[3]
030 **4** nk **Philipstown**[34] 5133 2-9-3 75.. RichardHughes 13 69
(Richard Hannon) *pressed ldrs: rdn along fr 3f out: one pce ins fnl f: lost 3rd last strides* **15/2**
03 **5** 1 **Young Prince (IRE)**[26] 5382 2-9-0 0................................ SeanLevey(3) 5 66
(Robert Mills) *led tl hdd over 1f out: wknd ins fnl f* **13/2**
0 **6** 1½ **Raffinn**[75] 3746 2-9-3 0.. JamesDoyle 14 62
(Sylvester Kirk) *s.i.s: sn plld hrd and chsd ldrs: rdn 2f out: wknd ins fnl f* **33/1**
0 **7** ½ **Calculated Risk**[25] 5411 2-9-3 0...................................... TomMcLaughlin 6 61+
(Willie Musson) *hld up in rr: styd on wl thrght fnl f: gng on cl home* **80/1**
04 **8** ½ **Malekat Jamal (IRE)**[35] 5097 2-8-12 0............................ JamieSpencer 4 55
(David Simcock) *chsd ldrs: rdn over 2f out: wknd ins fnl f* **8/1**
0 **9** ½ **Poetry Writer**[11] 5841 2-9-3 0.. NeilChalmers 9 59
(Michael Blanshard) *chsd ldrs: wknd and hung rt appr fnl f* **100/1**
0 **10** hd **Kelpie Blitz (IRE)**[91] 3229 2-9-3 0...................................... MarkLawson 7 58
(Seamus Durack) *chsd ldrs: rdn over 2f out: wknd over 1f out* **80/1**
0 **11** 5 **Fisher**[13] 5801 2-9-3 0... JimCrowley 8 45
(Richard Hannon) *in rr: drvn and brief effrt 2f out: sn wknd* **16/1**
12 7 **Fine Finale** 2-9-3 0.. RobertHavlin 12 27
(Jeremy Gask) *s.i.s: a towards rr* **80/1**
0 **13** 2½ **Oratrix (IRE)**[13] 5814 2-8-12 0.. TadhgO'Shea 2 15
(Denis Coakley) *green and a bhd* **100/1**
0 **14** 8 **Don't Tempt Me (IRE)**[105] 2767 2-8-12 0.......................... FergusSweeney 1 —
(Sylvester Kirk) *chsd ldrs: rdn over 2f out: sn btn* **50/1**

1m 26.3s (0.30) **Going Correction** -0.05s/f (Stan) **14** Ran SP% **118.6**
Speed ratings (Par 95): **96,95,92,92,90 89,88,88,87,87 81,73,70,61**
toteswingers:1&2:£1.70, 2&3:£2.10, 1&3:£2.10 CSF £11.67 TOTE £4.20: £1.80, £1.10, £2.80; EX 13.00.
Owner R A Green **Bred** J F Tuthill **Trained** Lower Beeding, W Sussex

FOCUS
An ordinary maiden run in a time 0.83 seconds quicker than the following fillies' event. Improved form from the winner with more to come. The runner-up ran to her pre-race mark.

NOTEBOOK
Venetian View(IRE) continued his progression, despite still looking green. He very much caught the eye under a less than inspired ride when dropped back to 5f at Sandown last time and the return to this longer distance suited. Once asked for his effort he took a while to get organised, and didn't help his rider, who was trying to switch him left, but it looked nothing more than inexperience. He should have learnt plenty and is expected to keep going the right way. (op 4-1 tchd 3-1)
Equity Card(FR), third over C&D last time, was always well placed but she didn't do a great deal for pressure, looking vulnerable before being caught. She might win a race, but isn't one to follow. (op 2-1)
Jack Of Diamonds(IRE), a well-held fourth over 1m here on his debut (one place behind Young Prince), ruined his chance with a slow start. He was going on at the finish and can do better. (op 5-1 tchd 13-2)
Philipstown probably didn't run up to his official mark of 75. (op 9-1 tchd 10-1)
Young Prince(IRE) had the benefit of experience when ahead of Jack Of Diamonds over 1m here last time. Dropped in trip, he was keen under a positive ride and didn't see his race out. (op 15-2)
Calculated Risk, up in trip on his second start, caught the eye running on nicely in the closing stages and is one to keep in mind, especially for when he's in handicaps over further. (op 100-1)

6215 NORMAN ANDERTON MEMORIAL E B F MAIDEN FILLIES' STKS 7f (P)
3:00 (3:01) (Class 5) 2-Y-0 **£3,299** (£981; £490; £245) **Stalls** Low

Form RPR
0 **1** **Napoleon's Muse (IRE)**[20] 5583 2-9-0 0............................ JimCrowley 9 75+
(Ralph Beckett) *chsd ldrs: rdn fr 2f out: str chal ins fnl f: led last strides* **14/1**
2 hd **Irishstone (IRE)** 2-9-0 0.. MartinDwyer 8 75+
(Gerard Butler) *in tch: drvn and qcknd fr 2f out: str chal ins fnl f: upsides fnl 50yds: no ex last strides* **25/1**
3 **3** nk **Berwin (IRE)**[13] 5813 2-9-0 0... JamesDoyle 2 74+
(Sylvester Kirk) *chsd ldrs: hrd rdn to ld appr fnl f: sn strly chal: kpt slt advantage u.p tl hdd last strides* **5/2**[1]
4 **4** 3½ **Traveller's Tales**[87] 3362 2-9-0 0................................... RichardHughes 14 65
(Richard Hannon) *sn led: rdn and hdd appr fnl f: wknd fnl 120yds* **11/4**[2]
5 1¼ **Royale Ransom** 2-8-11 0.. JohnFahy(3) 10 62
(Clive Cox) *chsd ldrs: rdn over 2f out: kpt on ins fnl f: nt rch ldrs* **16/1**
6 hd **Downton Abbey (IRE)** 2-8-11 0...................................... SeanLevey(3) 12 61+
(Richard Hannon) *in rr but in tch: pushed along over 2f out: styd on ins fnl f: nt rch ldrs* **16/1**
7 ½ **Honour** 2-9-0 0... KierenFallon 1 60
(Sir Michael Stoute) *in tch: pushed along over 2f out: styd on same pce ins fnl f* **7/1**[3]
6 **8** 4 **Perfect Day (IRE)**[136] 1870 2-9-0 0..................................(b[1]) JoeFanning 6 49
(Paul Cole) *chsd ldrs: rdn over 2f out: wknd sn after* **20/1**
9 3½ **Castalian Spring (IRE)** 2-9-0 0...................................... AdamKirby 11 40
(Walter Swinburn) *s.i.s: green and rdn 3f out: a towards rr* **40/1**
10 hd **Pre Catalan** 2-9-0 0... JamieSpencer 4 40
(Ed Dunlop) *s.i.s: in rr: rdn: green and no ch whn hung rt over 2f out* **14/1**
11 18 **Poncho** 2-9-0 0... SebSanders 5 —
(Sir Mark Prescott Bt) *sn rdn and green: a in rr* **20/1**
12 94 **Hoop** 2-9-0 0.. WilliamBuick 3 —
(John Gosden) *slowly away: sn wl bhd: virtually p.u 2f out* **8/1**

1m 27.13s (1.13) **Going Correction** -0.05s/f (Stan) **12** Ran SP% **119.8**
Speed ratings (Par 92): **91,90,90,86,85 84,84,79,75,75 54,—**
toteswingers:1&2:£59.40, 2&3:£36.70, 1&3:£8.80 CSF £329.08 TOTE £14.00: £6.70, £8.40, £1.10; EX 315.10.
Owner Mrs Emma Kennedy **Bred** W J Kennedy **Trained** Kimpton, Hants

FOCUS
A pretty ordinary event for fillies run at a steady pace and in a time 0.83 seconds slower than the earlier juvenile maiden. The third helps with the level.

NOTEBOOK
Napoleon's Muse(IRE) improved a good deal on the form she showed when beating only one rival on her debut over 1m at Goodwood. She was under pressure early in the straight, sooner than her main rivals as it turned out, but she kept responding. It's likely she'll have learnt more from this and she should stay further. (op 12-1)
Irishstone(IRE), a sister to 7f winners Charlotte Bronte and Storm Mountain, travelled nicely. She didn't find quite as much as had looked likely but was up against rivals with experience and kept on well. There should be more to come. (op 28-1)
Berwin(IRE) finished third behind a potentially decent type over this trip on Lingfield's Polytrack first-time up, but she didn't really boost the form, albeit she again showed enough to suggest she can win races. She travelled well in a good position but was one paced for pressure. (op 3-1 tchd 7-2)
Traveller's Tales, absent since finishing fourth in a hot maiden over 6f behind Discourse and Gamilati, had to use up energy to get to the front from the widest draw. She got tired in the straight and shaped as though in need of the run. (op 7-2, tchd 9-2 in a place)
Royale Ransom's sales price increased from 6,500gns as a yearling to £60,000 this year. A half-sister to useful 7f-1m2f performer Without A Prayer, she made a respectable start and should go on from this. (op 25-1)
Downton Abbey(IRE), a 48,000gns purchase, was keeping on at the finish and can do better.
Honour is a half-sister to six winners, including the high-class Virtual (7f-1m1f, notably Lockinge), and Coventry winner Iceman, but she showed little. (op 9-2)
Hoop Official explanation: vet said filly returned lame left-hind

6216 32 ONLINE CASINO E B F MAIDEN STKS 1m (P)
3:30 (3:30) (Class 5) 2-Y-0 **£3,299** (£981; £490; £245) **Stalls** Low

Form RPR
6 **1** **Trois Vallees (USA)**[24] 5447 2-9-3 0............................ FrankieDettori 11 84+
(Mahmood Al Zarooni) *trckd ldrs: pushed along to ld 2f out: drvn out ins fnl f* **4/1**[2]
63 **2** 1½ **Goldream**[24] 5447 2-9-3 0.. KierenFallon 9 81+
(Luca Cumani) *in tch: hdwy fr 2f out: r.o to chse wnr ins fnl f: kpt on in clsng stages but a hld* **7/4**[1]
3 3 **Prince Alzain (USA)** 2-9-3 0.. JamieSpencer 3 74+
(Gerard Butler) *sn chsng ldrs: rdn 2f out: styd on to take one pce 3rd ins fnl f* **9/2**[3]
620 **4** nk **Dynamic Duo (IRE)**[11] 5851 2-9-3 75.............................. RichardHughes 1 73
(Richard Hannon) *led: hdd 2f out: wknd ins fnl f* **9/2**[3]

5 3 3/4 **Willie Wag Tail (USA)** 2-9-3 0 J-PGuillambert 8 64+
(Ed Walker) *s.i.s: in rr: hdwy on outside fr 3f out: rdn fr 2f out: sme prog ins fnl f* **50/1**

0 6 2 1/4 **Compton Air (USA)**[40] 4906 2-9-3 0 (t) JamesDoyle 7 59
(Hans Adielsson) *mid-div: rdn and sme hdwy fr 2f out: nvr a threat* **66/1**

0 7 2 1/2 **Multilateral (USA)**[13] 5801 2-9-3 0 IanMongan 13 53
(Amanda Perrett) *s.i.s: sn rcvrd to chse ldrs: rdn over 2f out: sn wknd* **33/1**

054 8 1/2 **Samasana (IRE)**[7] 6001 2-8-9 52 (v) JohnFahy(3) 6 47
(Ian Wood) *in rr: rdn and sme hdwy into mid-div on ins over 2f out: nvr nr ldrs and sn wknd* **100/1**

0 9 1 3/4 **Grande Illusion**[17] 5672 2-9-3 0 MartinDwyer 2 48
(J W Hills) *t.k.h: chsd ldrs over 5f out* **40/1**

10 5 **Solar View (IRE)** 2-9-3 0 SebSanders 5 37+
(Sir Mark Prescott Bt) *slowly away: green: rdn and sn detached: sme prog u.p ins fnl f* **40/1**

11 2 3/4 **Fennell Bay (IRE)** 2-9-3 0 AhmedAjtebi 4 30
(Mahmood Al Zarooni) *nvr beyond mid-div: bhd 3f out* **9/1**

0 12 1 1/4 **The Ploughman**[40] 4912 2-9-3 0 NeilChalmers 12 28
(John Bridger) *a in rr* **100/1**

1m 39.41s (-0.39) **Going Correction** -0.05s/f (Stan) **12** Ran SP% **116.0**
Speed ratings (Par 95): **99,97,94,94,90 88,85,85,83,78 75,74**
toteswingers:1&2:£2.90, 2&3:£5.00, 1&3:£6.30 CSF £10.81 TOTE £4.60: £2.00, £1.20, £2.00; EX 12.40.
Owner Godolphin **Bred** Stone Farm **Trained** Newmarket, Suffolk

FOCUS
A fair maiden, but they didn't seem to go that quick and it paid to be handy. The first two stepped forward and the fourth helps with the level.

NOTEBOOK
Trois Vallees(USA) showed ability when green on his debut behind Goldream at the July course and improved on that with a straightforward success, finding plenty after being well placed. He looks just a handicapper for now. (op 7-2)

Goldream couldn't confirm form with Trois Vallees, but he wasn't helped by racing further back than that rival and this was still a respectable effort. He's now qualified for a handicap mark. (op 15-8 tchd 2-1)

Prince Alzain(USA) cost $200,000 as a foal, but only $60,000 last year. A half-brother to 6f and 7f (Listed) 2yo winner Echo River, out of a 6f (at two) to 1m2f (Listed) winner, was solid in the market and shaped well. He couldn't quicken off the steady pace but kept on to win the battle for third. (op 11-2)

Dynamic Duo(IRE) came into this with some fair form but he struggled against less-exposed rivals. (op 7-2)

Willie Wag Tail(USA), a 40,000gns purchase, is a half-brother to six winners (including jumpers), out of a US 1m winner. He was wide into the straight but showed ability and can improve. (op 66-1)

Multilateral(USA) started slowly but was soon handy and raced wide. It was no surprise he got tired and he can do better in time, probably when handicapped. (tchd 25-1)

6217 32 FOR BINGO H'CAP 6f (P)

4:00 (4:00) (Class 3) (0-95,90) 3-Y-O
£6,411 (£1,919; £959; £479; £239; £120) **Stalls** Low

Form RPR

401 1 **Fair Value (IRE)**[19] 5627 3-8-13 82 SebSanders 1 92
(Simon Dow) *mde all: rdn fr 2f out: fading cl home: jst hld on* **16/1**

6226 2 hd **Dimension**[11] 5852 3-9-7 90 KierenFallon 10 99
(James Fanshawe) *in rr: drvn and hdwy on outside appr fnl f: str run cl home to dispute 2nd: could nt quite rch fading wnr: fin 3rd: plcd 2nd* **11/4[1]**

613 3 3/4 **Ganas (IRE)**[17] 5683 3-9-2 85 AdamKirby 3 91
(Clive Cox) *chsd ldrs: wnt 2nd and rdn 2f out: no imp ins fnl f and lost 2 pls in clsng stages: fin 4th: plcd 3rd* **11/4[1]**

0210 4 2 3/4 **Diamond Charlie (IRE)**[21] 5543 3-9-1 84 RichardHughes 8 82
(Simon Dow) *stdd s: t.k.h in rr: rdn and hdwy on ins appr 2f out: styd on same pce ins fnl f: fin 5th: plcd 4th* **16/1**

1404 5 3/4 **Sand Owl**[96] 3048 3-8-10 79 JamieSpencer 7 74
(Peter Chapple-Hyam) *t.k.h: sn trcking ldrs: rdn to dispute 2nd over 1f out: hung rt and wknd sn after: fin sixth: plcd 5th* **10/1[3]**

-61U 6 3/4 **Monsieur Jamie**[181] 940 3-8-8 77 AdrianMcCarthy 9 70
(J R Jenkins) *wnt lft s: chsd ldrs: wknd over 1f out: fin seventh: plcd sixth* **33/1**

2002 7 1 1/2 **Sadafiya**[34] 5146 3-9-0 83 TadhgO'Shea 5 71
(Ed Dunlop) *sn chsng ldrs: rdn 2f out: wknd over 1f out: fin eight: plcd seventh* **16/1**

1400 8 10 **Quality Art (USA)**[30] 5288 3-9-5 88 GeorgeBaker 4 43
(Gary Moore) *chsd ldr to 2f out: eased whn no ch ins fnl f: fin ninth: plcd eighth* **14/1**

4545 9 nk **Barnet Fair**[11] 5852 3-9-4 90 KierenFox(3) 6 100+
(Richard Guest) *hld up in rr: rdn and hdwy fr over 1f out: str run u.p thrght fnl f: tk clsng 2nd in last strides: nt quite rch fading wnr: fin 2nd: disqualified and plcd last* **7/2[2]**

1m 11.95s (-1.15) **Going Correction** -0.05s/f (Stan) **9** Ran SP% **111.9**
Speed ratings (Par 105): **105,104,103,99,98 97,95,82,104**
toteswingers:1&2:£12.30, 2&3:£2.70, 1&3:£10.20 CSF £57.57 CT £161.10 TOTE £14.90: £3.20, £1.70, £1.40; EX 80.20.
Owner Edward Hyde **Bred** Edward Hyde **Trained** Epsom, Surrey

FOCUS
A fair race for the grade run at a reasonable pace although Fair Value made all. Barnet Fair was unlucky and has been rated the winner.

NOTEBOOK
Fair Value(IRE), drawn lowest of all, was allowed to dominate. She was defying a mark 10lb higher than when successful from the front over her regular trip of 5f at Folkestone last time, but everything went her way and she only just held on. A drop back to the minimum distance might help.

Dimension, just behind Barnet Fair when dropped to this trip last time (sole win gained at 1m), wasn't helped by the widest stall but kept on gradually. He might get away with this distance when the pace is contested and/or he's berthed more favourably, but in long term he may prove most effective back over further. (op 5-2 tchd 3-1)

Ganas(IRE) pulled hard early and that probably contributed to his lack of end-race speed. The ability is there, but he looks best watched for now. (op 3-1 tchd 9-4)

Diamond Charlie(IRE), the winner's stable companion, won from the front two starts ago but this time got going too late and was not given a hard ride in the closing stages. (op 12-1)

Barnet Fair, not for the first time lately, looked a bit unlucky, getting going too late after having to wait for a clear run. He remains in good enough form to win when things go his way. He was later disqualified from second position and placed last after Kieren Fox weighed in a pound and a half light. (op 4-1 tchd 9-2)

6218 32 FOR BLACKJACK H'CAP 1m 4f (P)

4:30 (4:31) (Class 4) (0-85,85) 3-Y-O **£4,075** (£1,212; £606; £303) **Stalls** Centre

Form RPR

-142 1 **Robin Hoods Bay**[70] 3919 3-8-12 76 JamieSpencer 4 87+
(Edward Vaughan) *hld up in rr: hdwy on bit to trck ldr over 1f out: shkn up and qcknd ins fnl f: led fnl 120yds: cosily* **9/4[1]**

5122 2 1/2 **Area Fifty One**[30] 5266 3-9-2 80 MartinDwyer 2 87
(William Muir) *led: rdn and kpt on u.p fr 2f out: hdd fnl 120yds: styd on but no ch w cosy wnr* **3/1[3]**

-026 3 2 1/2 **Ullswater (IRE)**[16] 5716 3-8-12 76 JoeFanning 5 79
(Mark Johnston) *chsd ldr to 7f out: styd disputing 3rd: rdn and effrt to dispute 2nd 2f out: outpcd by ldng duo ins fnl f* **17/2**

231 4 3/4 **Word Power**[43] 4826 3-9-2 80 TomQueally 6 82
(Sir Henry Cecil) *chsd ldrs: rdn to dispute 2nd over 2f out: wknd ins fnl f* **9/2**

1111 5 1 3/4 **Kepler's Law**[25] 5416 3-9-7 85 SebSanders 1 84
(Sir Mark Prescott Bt) *hld up in rr but in tch hdwy to chse ldr 7f out: drvn along over 4f out: rdn 3f out: wknd over 1f out* **11/4[2]**

2m 38.35s (3.85) **Going Correction** -0.05s/f (Stan) **5** Ran SP% **111.1**
Speed ratings (Par 103): **85,84,83,82,81**
CSF £9.36 TOTE £3.20: £1.10, £1.90; EX 12.00.
Owner A M Pickering **Bred** Palm Tree Thoroughbreds **Trained** Newmarket, Suffolk

FOCUS
A fair handicap but this wasn't a stamina test and the form is muddling. The winner is rated better than the bare result, with the runner-up the best guide.

6219 32 FOR SLOTS H'CAP (DIV I) 1m (P)

5:00 (5:00) (Class 4) (0-85,85) 3-Y-O+ **£4,075** (£1,212; £606; £303) **Stalls** Low

Form RPR

3200 1 **Loyalty**[16] 5712 4-9-6 81 (v) JoeFanning 1 90
(Derek Shaw) *mde all: qcknd fr 2f out: pushed along and r.o strly ins fnl f* **11/1**

0265 2 1 **Avon Lady**[16] 5702 4-9-3 78 KierenFallon 8 85
(James Fanshawe) *in tch: rdn and one pce over 2f out: styd on u.p ins fnl f: kpt on in clsng stages to take 2nd cl home: no imp on wnr* **7/2[1]**

1103 3 1/2 **Rustic Deacon**[42] 4860 4-9-0 75 RichardHughes 3 81
(Willie Musson) *chsd ldrs: rdn to chse wnr 2f out: no imp but styd on ins fnl f tl one pce into 3rd cl home* **9/1**

0010 4 hd **Red Somerset (USA)**[17] 5687 8-9-4 79 FergusSweeney 7 84
(Mike Murphy) *in rr: drvn and hdwy over 1f out: styd on wl ins fnl f: gng on in clsng stages: could nt trble wnr* **28/1**

5004 5 nk **Blue Moon**[24] 5455 4-9-5 80 JamieSpencer 11 84
(Kevin Ryan) *racd w 3f out: chsd ldrs: drvn to disp 2nd fr over 2f out: no imp on wnr: one pce ins fnl f* **12/1**

3040 6 1 3/4 **Suited And Booted (IRE)**[23] 5483 4-9-10 85 (p) TedDurcan 4 85
(Jane Chapple-Hyam) *in tch: rdn and sme hdwy on ins fr 2f out: nvr rchd ldrs and one pce ins fnl f* **11/2[2]**

1650 7 hd **Gobama**[18] 5657 4-9-8 83 SebSanders 9 83
(J W Hills) *racd wd 3f: chsd ldrs: riddn and one pce fr 2f out* **8/1**

0000 8 1 3/4 **Vitznau (IRE)**[8] 5969 7-9-1 76 (p) JimCrowley 5 72
(Robert Cowell) *s.i.s: in rr: rdn on outside over 2f out: nvr in contention* **33/1**

0400 9 1 **Merchant Of Medici**[16] 5712 4-9-7 82 MartinDwyer 2 76
(William Muir) *s.i.s: in rr: rdn on ins and no imp 2f out* **13/2[3]**

1241 10 1/2 **Daneside (IRE)**[10] 5894 4-8-11 72 MarkLawson 6 64
(Gary Harrison) *chsd ldrs: rdn over 2f out: wknd 2f out* **9/1**

000 11 5 **Freeforaday (USA)**[9] 5936 4-9-10 85 GeorgeBaker 10 66
(John Best) *s.i.s: racd on outside: rdn over 2f out: a in rr* **8/1**

1m 38.62s (-1.18) **Going Correction** -0.05s/f (Stan) **11** Ran SP% **115.6**
Speed ratings (Par 105): **103,102,101,101,101 99,99,97,96,95 90**
toteswingers:1&2:£10.20, 2&3:£8.90, 1&3:£21.80 CSF £48.48 CT £373.28 TOTE £15.00: £4.10, £2.30, £2.00; EX 62.30.
Owner Mrs Lyndsey Shaw **Bred** Ecoutila Partnership **Trained** Sproxton, Leics

FOCUS
A lack of pace was the key to this race and the time was 0.52 seconds slower than the second division. The winner was value for a length personal best.

6220 32 FOR SLOTS H'CAP (DIV II) 1m (P)

5:30 (5:30) (Class 4) (0-85,85) 3-Y-O+ **£4,075** (£1,212; £606; £303) **Stalls** Low

Form RPR

003 1 **Santefisio**[39] 4958 5-9-5 80 (p) TomQueally 5 91
(Peter Makin) *t.k.h: trckd ldrs: drvn to ld ins fnl f: kpt on wl* **7/1**

1061 2 1/2 **Trumpington Street (IRE)**[19] 5635 3-9-6 85 WilliamBuick 7 95
(John Gosden) *trckd ldr: led appr 2f out: rdn and hdd ins fnl f: styd on same pce* **13/8[1]**

0060 3 2 1/4 **Saint Pierre (USA)**[37] 5043 4-9-10 85 KierenFallon 8 90
(Luca Cumani) *in tch: hdwy fr 2f out: sn rdn: styd on for one pce 3rd ins fnl f* **7/2[2]**

0000 4 shd **Fremont (IRE)**[73] 3797 4-9-3 78 RichardHughes 4 82
(Richard Hannon) *led: hdd appr 2f out: wknd ins fnl f* **6/1[3]**

0100 5 3/4 **Willow Dancer (IRE)**[16] 5712 7-9-5 83 [1] SeanLevey(3) 6 86
(Walter Swinburn) *s.i.s: in rr: drvn and hdwy fr 2f out: kpt on ins fnl f: nt trble ldrs* **14/1**

6/06 6 3 1/2 **Doncosaque (IRE)**[26] 5383 5-8-12 73 (t) TedDurcan 10 68
(P J O'Gorman) *in rr but in tch: rdn and sme hdwy on outside fr 2f out: n.d* **14/1**

1555 7 2 1/4 **Tiradito (USA)**[16] 5717 4-9-6 81 (v) AdamKirby 2 70
(Michael Attwater) *chsd ldrs tl over 2f out: sn wknd* **12/1**

5040 8 7 **Hurricane Spirit (IRE)**[10] 5894 7-9-2 77 JimCrowley 1 50
(Terry Clement) *s.i.s: towards rr most of way* **16/1**

00-0 9 2 1/4 **Councellor (FR)**[38] 4993 9-9-9 84 (t) JoeFanning 9 52
(Derek Shaw) *s.i.s: t.k.h: rdn: hung rt and nt keen 3f out* **50/1**

1m 38.1s (-1.70) **Going Correction** -0.05s/f (Stan)
WFA 3 from 4yo+ 4lb **9** Ran SP% **116.0**
Speed ratings (Par 105): **106,105,103,103,102 98,96,89,87**
CSF £18.85 CT £47.53 TOTE £8.60: £2.00, £1.50, £1.70; EX 21.00.
Owner Weldspec Glasgow Limited **Bred** D Brocklehurst **Trained** Ogbourne Maisey, Wilts

FOCUS
The time was 0.52 seconds quicker than the modestly run first division. Sound form, with the winner on his lowest mark since his last win two years ago.
T/Jkpt: Not won. T/Plt: £26.60 to a £1 stake. Pool of £60,280.36 - 1,652.54 winning tickets. T/Qpdt: £12.80 to a £1 stake. Pool of £3,751.98 - 215.42 winning tickets. ST

The Form Book, Raceform Ltd, Compton, RG20 6NL

5801 LEICESTER (R-H)

Monday, September 19

OFFICIAL GOING: Good (good to soft in places; 7.0)

Wind: Fresh behind Weather: Cloudy with sunny spells

6221 BRITISH STALLION STUDS SUPPORTING BRITISH RACING E B F NOVICE STKS 5f 218y

2:20 (2:20) (Class 4) 2-Y-O **£4,334** (£1,289; £644; £322) **Stalls** High

Form RPR

10 **1** **Mezmaar**[97] 3012 2-9-3 95.. RichardHills 5 92+
(Charles Hills) *s.i.s: sn trcking ldrs: led over 2f out: hrd rdn ins fnl f: r.o* **2/5**[1]

1 **2** ½ **Samminder (IRE)**[132] 1988 2-9-3 91.................................. DaneO'Neill 4 90
(Peter Chapple-Hyam) *dwlt: hld up in tch: rdn and ev ch ins fnl f: unable qck nr fin* **3/1**[2]

1325 **3** ½ **Mr Majeika (IRE)**[20] 5592 2-9-0 87.............................. KieranO'Neill(3) 2 89
(Richard Hannon) *chsd ldr: rdn and ev ch over 1f out: styd on same pce wl ins fnl f* **16/1**[3]

3062 **4** 5 **Redair (IRE)**[24] 5427 2-8-12 76.. CathyGannon 1 68
(David Evans) *sn led: hdd over 4f out: rdn over 2f out: wknd ins fnl f* **20/1**

3000 **5** 11 **Pius Parker (IRE)**[99] 2953 2-8-12 65................................ MartinLane 3 33
(John Gallagher) *chsd ldrs: led over 4f out: rdn and hdd over 2f out: sn wknd* **100/1**

1m 11.24s (-1.76) **Going Correction** -0.175s/f (Firm) **5** Ran SP% **108.1**

Speed ratings (Par 97): **104,103,102,96,81**

CSF £1.75 TOTE £1.40: £1.10, £1.20; EX 1.80.

Owner Hamdan Al Maktoum **Bred** Denford Stud Ltd **Trained** Lambourn, Berks

FOCUS

Overnight rain eased the ground from Good, good to firm in places, to good, good to soft in places. Various levels of ability amongst the five runners in this novice stakes but a couple of potentially smart sorts returning from absences featured at the head of the market. They filled the first two places but that does not tell the whole story. Both look decent prospects.

NOTEBOOK

Mezmaar, an impressive winner on his debut but well held in the Coventry, had been absent since with minor problems. As at Ascot he was keen early here and came under pressure around 2f out, only to find extra when challenged by the runner-up. He should be better for the outing but whether he is up to making his mark in either the Middle Park or Dewhurst - his big-race entries - is open to doubt. (op 8-13)

Samminder(IRE) beat a subsequent dual winner on his debut at Yarmouth in May but his trainer reported he was likely to need this. He was keen under restraint early but moved up looking a serious threat to the winner entering the furlong before his effort flattened out. He is also in the Middle Park but might be better aimed at something like a Listed contest next. (op 9-4)

Mr Majeika(IRE) has been running reasonably well and was not beaten far by a couple with potential. He looks a fair yardstick for the form. (op 14-1)

Redair(IRE) has not won since her debut on Polytrack in March but still seems to be running fairly and might be worth a try in a nursery back on sand. (op 16-1 tchd 12-1)

6222 ASTON FLAMVILLE FILLIES' NURSERY 5f 218y

2:50 (2:52) (Class 5) (0-75,75) 2-Y-O **£2,264** (£673; £336; £168) **Stalls** High

Form RPR

26 **1** **Alice's Dancer (IRE)**[81] 3547 2-9-3 71........................... WilliamCarson 8 83
(William Muir) *mde all: clr 4f out: rdn and wandered over 2f out: unchal* **20/1**

052 **2** 3¾ **Gifted Dancer**[43] 4823 2-9-3 71.. DaneO'Neill 10 72+
(Henry Candy) *s.i.s: hdwy 4f out: rdn to go 2nd 1f out: no ch w wnr* **6/1**[2]

2032 **3** 1 **Middleton Flyer (IRE)**[11] 5840 2-9-4 75.................... RichardEvans(3) 9 73
(David Evans) *chsd wnr: rdn over 2f out: hung rt over 1f out: styd on same pce* **18/1**

000 **4** 1 **Small Steps (IRE)**[17] 5681 2-8-4 58 ow1.......................... MartinLane 13 53
(Ed McMahon) *s.i.s: outpcd: hdwy over 1f out: r.o: nvr nrr* **11/1**

040 **5** 1 **Damask (IRE)**[73] 3812 2-9-0 68.. PhillipMakin 14 60
(Kevin Ryan) *hld up: swtchd rt and hdwy u.p over 1f out: nvr trbld ldrs* **10/1**

3125 **6** nk **Molly Jones**[24] 5427 2-9-3 71.. ShaneKelly 12 62
(Derek Haydn Jones) *prom: rdn over 2f out: no ex ins fnl f* **16/1**

2101 **7** shd **Aquasulis (IRE)**[11] 5090 2-9-1 69.................................... CathyGannon 3 60
(David Evans) *mid-div: drvn along 1/2-way: hdwy over 2f out: no ex ins fnl f* **20/1**

12 **8** nk **Baltic Fizz (IRE)**[21] 5562 2-9-3 71.................................... LukeMorris 1 61
(Mrs K Burke) *sn outpcd: rdn over 2f out: r.o ins fnl f: nvr nrr* **15/2**[3]

2200 **9** 2 **Midas Medusa (FR)**[33] 5184 2-9-1 72......................(b1) KieranO'Neill(3) 6 56
(Richard Hannon) *s.i.s: sn pushed along in rr: nvr nrr* **25/1**

4155 **10** 1½ **Alabanda (IRE)**[11] 5847 2-9-7 75.................................... DavidAllan 4 54
(Tim Easterby) *mid-div: hdwy u.p 1/2-way: wknd over 1f out* **17/2**

6331 **11** 5 **Phoenix Clubs (IRE)**[25] 5399 2-8-11 65........................ BarryMcHugh 2 29
(Paul Midgley) *hld up in tch: lost pl whn swvd rt 2f out: no ch whn hung lft over 1f out* **16/1**

1 **12** 2½ **Three Sugars (AUS)**[20] 5596 2-9-0 68........................ DarryllHolland 16 25
(Jeremy Noseda) *sn outpcd* **3/1**[1]

3400 **13** 2½ **Elegant Flight**[17] 5690 2-8-3 60.................................... HarryBentley(3) 11 9
(Alan Jarvis) *mid-div: rdn and wknd over 2f out* **12/1**

664 **14** ¾ **Bella Ponte**[122] 2241 2-7-12 52 oh1................................ JimmyQuinn 5 —
(John Gallagher) *chsd ldrs tl wknd 2f out* **100/1**

430 **15** nk **Yearbook**[12] 5817 2-8-5 59.. JamesSullivan 7 5
(Tim Easterby) *prom: rdn 1/2-way: wknd over 2f out* **50/1**

1m 11.49s (-1.51) **Going Correction** -0.175s/f (Firm) **15** Ran SP% **120.0**

Speed ratings (Par 92): **103,98,96,95,94 93,93,93,90,88 81,78,75,74,73**

toteswingers:1&2:£26.90, 2&3:£19.50, 1&3:£56.30 CSF £129.18 CT £2232.49 TOTE £25.00: £10.00, £2.00, £5.70; EX 100.50.

Owner Perspicacious Punters Racing Club **Bred** Rathasker Stud **Trained** Lambourn, Berks

FOCUS

A fair and quite competitive fillies' nursery on paper, but it turned out to be a one-horse race and was a quarter of a second slower than the opening contest. There is no reason to think the winner is flattered but it was a bit of a strange race with runners all the way across the track.

NOTEBOOK

Alice's Dancer(IRE), making her handicap debut, had shown her best previous form on soft ground and made all here. She looked to have gone off too fast and was quite keen, but it was clear 2f out she was not stopping and she scored unchallenged. She will go up a fair amount for this and it remains to be seen if she can repeat the performance. (op 16-1)

Gifted Dancer ◆ ran pretty well on this handicap debut and first encounter with ground easier than good to firm. She travelled well and beat the rest comfortably enough, but never got in a blow at the runaway winner. She should be up to winning a similar contest. (tchd 5-1)

Middleton Flyer(IRE) is a consistent sort who acts on any ground and ran well up the stands' rail. He helps set the level here and deserves to pick up another race before long. (op 14-1)

Small Steps(IRE), making her handicap debut, was out the back with the disappointing favourite early on but stayed on steadily in the closing stages and might appreciate a little further in future. (op 12-1)

Damask(IRE) was making her handicap debut for a new trainer having not shown much in three starts for Richard Hannon and did not fare badly. (op 9-1 tchd 11-1)

Molly Jones appeared to run her race before fading late and might need a truly sound surface to get home over this distance. (op 14-1)

Aquasulis(IRE) had gained her wins in sellers and claimers and, although she ran reasonably here, is better off at that level. (op 22-1)

Baltic Fizz(IRE) was well beaten when second on her handicap debut last time and was unable to find extra under pressure down the centre of the track. (tchd 7-1 and 8-1)

Three Sugars(AUS) was made favourite for this on the basis of having won on her debut over this trip on Fibresand. However, she never got competitive on this first run on turf. Darryll Holland reported that the filly was never travelling and the Stewards ordered her to be routine tested. Official explanation: jockey said filly never travelled (op 7-2)

6223 GOLDEN HAND (S) STKS 7f 9y

3:20 (3:21) (Class 6) 3-Y-O **£1,617** (£481; £240; £120) **Stalls** High

Form RPR

505 **1** **Flying Phoenix**[5] 6067 3-8-11 61................................(b) RobertWinston 5 66
(Gay Kelleway) *trckd ldrs: led over 2f out: rdn over 1f out: styd on wl* **12/1**

0-03 **2** 3¼ **Poppet's Joy**[61] 4203 3-8-6 45.. ChrisCatlin 3 52
(Reg Hollinshead) *s.i.s: sn pushed along in rr: hdwy 1/2-way: rdn over 2f out: chsd wnr over 1f out: styd on same pce ins fnl f* **25/1**

0330 **3** 1 **Catalyze**[47] 4656 3-9-2 79..(t) LiamKeniry 12 60
(Andrew Balding) *trckd ldrs: rdn and hung rt fr over 1f out: styd on same pce ins fnl f* **10/11**[1]

5200 **4** 1 **Brio**[16] 5734 3-8-8 56..(v1) KieranO'Neill(3) 7 52
(Alan McCabe) *hld up: swtchd rt and hdwy over 1f out: nt rch ldrs* **22/1**

5220 **5** nse **Diamond Vine (IRE)**[21] 5542 3-9-2 69..........................(p) DavidProbert 9 57
(Ronald Harris) *mid-div: hdwy 1/2-way: rdn over 1f out: no ex ins fnl f* **11/2**[2]

4063 **6** 2¾ **Captain Dimitrios**[41] 4885 3-8-11 58..........................(v) StevieDonohoe 4 44
(David Evans) *chsd ldrs: rdn over 2f out: wknd ins fnl f* **22/1**

0650 **7** 2 **Penny's Pearl (IRE)**[21] 5561 3-8-11 66............................(p) CathyGannon 8 39
(David Evans) *hld up: hdwy u.p 2f out: wknd over 1f out* **9/1**[3]

5030 **8** shd **Magic Rhythm**[16] 5731 3-8-6 58.................................... LukeMorris 10 34
(Mrs K Burke) *chsd ldrs: rdn 1/2-way: wknd over 1f out* **10/1**

0200 **9** 56 **Roman Dancer (IRE)**[10] 5895 3-9-2 67..........................(b1) MartinLane 1 —
(John Gallagher) *led over 4f out: sn wknd and eased: t.o* **25/1**

05 **10** shd **Zoriana**[202] 717 3-8-6 0.. WilliamCarson 2 —
(Christine Dunnett) *chsd ldrs tl rdn and wknd 1/2-way: bhd whn hung rt over 2f out* **125/1**

1m 25.37s (-0.83) **Going Correction** -0.175s/f (Firm) **10** Ran SP% **111.7**

Speed ratings (Par 99): **97,93,92,91,90 87,85,85,21,21**

toteswingers:1&2:£12.80, 2&3:£6.40, 1&3:£4.30 CSF £264.50 TOTE £9.80: £3.00, £4.50, £1.10; EX 160.00.There was no bid for the winner. Catalyze was claimed by W McKay for £6000.

Owner M Whatley & G Kelleway **Bred** Winterbeck Manor Stud **Trained** Exning, Suffolk

FOCUS

Not a bad seller with the majority rated between 56 and 79, but there were doubts over plenty and the form is not rated too positively.

Catalyze Official explanation: jockey said colt hung right

6224 SIS LIVE H'CAP 5f 2y

3:50 (3:51) (Class 3) (0-95,93) 3-Y-O+ **£5,822** (£1,732; £865; £432) **Stalls** High

Form RPR

1141 **1** **Ajjaadd (USA)**[30] 5278 5-8-8 83.................................... KieranO'Neill(3) 7 96+
(Ted Powell) *s.i.s: outpcd: hdwy over 1f out: hung rt and r.o to ld wl ins fnl f* **11/2**[1]

5500 **2** 1¼ **Taurus Twins**[12] 5831 5-8-10 82................................(b) RobertWinston 8 90
(Richard Price) *chsd ldrs: led over 3f out: rdn and hdd over 1f out: styd on* **28/1**

6220 **3** ¾ **Hazelrigg (IRE)**[16] 5706 6-9-1 87..................................(be) DavidAllan 2 92
(Tim Easterby) *chsd ldrs: led and hung rt over 1f out: hdd and unable qck wl ins fnl f* **7/1**[2]

3602 **4** ½ **Sutton Veny (IRE)**[16] 5703 5-8-9 88............................ RaulDaSilva(7) 18 92+
(Jeremy Gask) *hld up: hung rt and r.o ins fnl f: nt rch ldrs* **11/1**

0300 **5** hd **R Woody**[66] 4340 4-9-4 90.. ShaneKelly 15 93+
(Dean Ivory) *dwlt: hld up: r.o ins fnl f: nt rch ldrs* **17/2**

5022 **6** ½ **Bathwick Bear (IRE)**[6] 6035 3-9-6 93............................ CathyGannon 3 94
(David Evans) *sn led: hdd over 3f out: rdn 1/2-way: styd on same pce ins fnl f* **11/1**

6050 **7** ¾ **Waking Warrior**[11] 5852 3-8-11 84.................................. StephenCraine 4 82
(Kevin Ryan) *broke out of stalls sltly early: prom: outpcd 1/2-way: rdn and swtchd rt over 1f out: r.o ins fnl f* **14/1**

0 **8** nse **West Coast Dream**[22] 5508 4-9-1 87.............................. WilliamCarson 17 85
(Roy Brotherton) *prom: rdn and hung rt fr over 1f out: no ex ins fnl f* **16/1**

400 **9** ¾ **Medici Time**[16] 5706 6-9-2 88......................................(v) RichardMullen 11 83
(Tim Easterby) *sn outpcd: r.o towards fin: nvr nrr* **14/1**

2005 **10** nse **Solemn**[16] 5703 6-9-0 86..(b) LiamKeniry 14 81
(Milton Bradley) *prom: rdn 1/2-way: sn outpcd* **28/1**

0513 **11** hd **Judge 'n Jury**[16] 5703 7-9-1 87.................................... LukeMorris 9 82
(Ronald Harris) *chsd ldrs: rdn over 1f out: no ex ins fnl f* **11/1**

1140 **12** nk **Living It Large (FR)**[16] 5703 4-8-11 86........................ HarryBentley(3) 16 79
(Ed de Giles) *chsd ldrs: rdn and nt clr run over 1f out: no ex* **18/1**

2063 **13** hd **Sohraab**[21] 5543 7-9-4 90.. SteveDrowne 1 83
(Hughie Morrison) *dwlt: outpcd: nvr on terms* **8/1**[3]

1001 **14** 1¼ **Le Toreador**[89] 3279 6-9-0 86..(tp) PhillipMakin 6 74
(Kevin Ryan) *chsd ldrs: rdn over 1f out: wknd ins fnl f* **20/1**

5264 **15** 1½ **La Fortunata**[21] 5543 4-8-11 83.................................... TonyCulhane 13 66
(Mike Murphy) *mid-div: rdn over 3f out: wknd over 1f out* **16/1**

58.86 secs (-1.14) **Going Correction** -0.175s/f (Firm)

WFA 3 from 4yo+ 1lb **15** Ran SP% **116.5**

Speed ratings (Par 107): **102,100,98,98,97 96,95,95,94,94 94,93,93,91,88**

toteswingers:1&2:£17.40, 2&3:£27.30, 1&3:£9.40 CSF £163.90 CT £1081.10 TOTE £5.60: £2.40, £3.00, £2.70; EX 211.50.

Owner Katy & Lol Pratt **Bred** Darley **Trained** Reigate, Surrey

FOCUS

A good, competitive sprint with 11lb covering the whole of this big field on official ratings. The field drifted towards the far rail in the closing stages. It was well run and the winner came from the rear, recording a clear personal best.

NOTEBOOK

Ajjaadd(USA) has been in terrific form this summer and is well suited by cut in the ground. He recorded his fourth win in his last five starts, finishing strongly having not picked up instantly when asked, but he still looks to be on the upgrade. (tchd 5-1)

Taurus Twins ◆, whose saddle slipped last time, went off in front but hit a flat spot around 2f out and looked sure to weaken out of it. However, he rallied well for pressure and chased the winner home. He is 5lb above his last winning mark but is one to bear in mind this autumn, especially back on a flat track.
Hazelrigg(IRE) gained his last two successes in September last year and has been in reasonable form recently. He went on around 2f out but drifted to the far rail and his effort petered out. He seems ideally suited by being held onto for longer, but he was rather left in front on this occasion. David Allan reported that the gelding hung right. Official explanation: jockey said gelding hung right (op 8-1)
Sutton Veny(IRE) has been running consistently but had gone up 5lb for being touched off last time. She handles cut but has the option of the return to Polytrack, the surface on which her last four successes were gained. (op 9-1)
R Woody has been a bit below par in recent runs but is suited by cut in the ground and finished well. He is only 1lb above his last winning mark now and similar conditions might see him back to winning ways. (op 12-1)
Bathwick Bear(IRE) has been running well in conditions stakes of late and she showed good pace under top weight here, but could not sustain it. (op 12-1 tchd 8-1)
Waking Warrior has been running over further but appeared to burst the stalls as they opened. He could not go the early pace though and only stayed on late. (op 16-1)
West Coast Dream's rider reported that the gelding hung badly right. Official explanation: jockey said gelding hung badly right (op 14-1 tchd 12-1)
Sohraab was unable to go the early pace and never got involved. Steve Drowne reported that the gelding was never travelling. Official explanation: jockey said gelding never travelled (op 15-2)
Le Toreador showed good early pace on this return from three months off and this should set him up nicely for an autumn/winter campaign. (op 18-1)

6225 HENRY ALKEN CLASSIFIED CLAIMING STKS — 1m 1f 218y
4:20 (4:20) (Class 6) 3-4-Y-O — **£1,617** (£481; £240; £120) **Stalls** Low

Form — RPR
5312 **1** **Royal Opera**[6] 6017 3-8-13 70 ... JamesMillman 2 — 72
(Rod Millman) *mde virtually all: rdn over 1f out: styd on* **7/4**[1]
6305 **2** 1 ¾ **Mighty Clarets (IRE)**[6] 6028 4-9-7 72 ... BarryMcHugh 7 — 71
(Richard Fahey) *a.p: chsd wnr 7f out: rdn and hung rt fr over 2f out: nt run on* **11/4**[2]
4055 **3** ½ **Frontline Phantom (IRE)**[37] 5036 4-9-2 68 ... MatthewLawson(5) 1 — 70
(Mrs K Burke) *chsd wnr 3f: remained handy: rdn over 2f out: no ex ins fnl f* **3/1**[3]
5660 **4** 2 **El Djebena (IRE)**[20] 5608 3-8-11 68 ... (b[1]) StevieDonohoe 3 — 62
(Sir Mark Prescott Bt) *s.s: hld up: hdwy and nt clr run over 2f out: sn rdn: no ex ins fnl f* **11/2**
3040 **5** 17 **Flaming Nora**[17] 5666 3-8-9 61 ... (v) EddieAhern 5 — 26
(James Fanshawe) *chsd ldrs: pushed along 4f out: rdn and wknd over 2f out* **20/1**

2m 10.1s (2.20) **Going Correction** -0.10s/f (Good)
WFA 3 from 4yo 6lb — 5 Ran SP% **108.2**
Speed ratings (Par 101): **87,85,85,83,70**
CSF £6.55 TOTE £2.10: £1.40, £1.50; EX 5.10.Royal Opera was claimed by D Gilbert for £10000.
Owner The Links Partnership **Bred** Redmyre Bloodstock & Newhall Farm Estate **Trained** Kentisbeare, Devon
■ Stewards' Enquiry : Barry McHugh one-day ban: used whip down shoulder in the forehand (Oct 4)

FOCUS
A fair claimer but the early pace was steady and the winner made all. He's the best guide to this form.

6226 HIGHFIELDS H'CAP (DIV I) — 1m 60y
4:50 (4:50) (Class 5) (0-75,75) 3-Y-0+ — **£1,940** (£577; £288; £144) **Stalls** Low

Form — RPR
1-01 **1** **Yensi**[43] 4829 4-9-7 **72** ... PatCosgrave 5 — 82+
(George Baker) *mde all: set stdy pce tl qcknd over 3f out: rdn clr over 1f out: styd on* **7/2**[1]
2664 **2** 1 ¼ **Sweet Secret**[13] 5808 4-8-6 **64** ... (p) RaulDaSilva(7) 6 — 71
(Jeremy Gask) *chsd wnr: rdn over 2f out: styd on* **14/1**
2051 **3** 1 ¼ **Jordaura**[26] 5390 5-9-7 **72** ... RobertWinston 1 — 76+
(Gay Kelleway) *hld up: rdn over 2f out: r.o ins fnl f: nt rch ldrs* **7/1**[3]
4053 **4** nk **Two Certainties**[7] 6005 4-8-11 **62** ... WilliamCarson 3 — 66
(Stuart Williams) *trckd ldrs: racd keenly: rdn over 2f out: styd on same pce ins fnl f* **13/2**[2]
006 **5** ½ **Rock Anthem (IRE)**[35] 5101 7-9-6 **71** ... TonyCulhane 12 — 73+
(Mike Murphy) *s.i.s: hld up: rdn over 2f out: r.o u.p ins fnl f: nt rch ldrs* **20/1**
4054 **6** ¾ **Effigy**[8] 5968 7-9-6 **71** ... FrankieMcDonald 8 — 72+
(Henry Candy) *dwlt: pushed along early in rr: hdwy u.p and n.m.r over 1f out: no imp ins fnl f* **13/2**[2]
1021 **7** nk **Wiseman's Diamond (USA)**[24] 5441 6-8-13 **64**..(b) RussKennemore 11 — 64
(Paul Midgley) *prom: rdn over 2f out: no ex ins fnl f* **16/1**
6303 **8** nk **Trend Line (IRE)**[23] 5496 3-9-4 **73** ... ChrisCatlin 2 — 72
(Peter Chapple-Hyam) *prom: rdn over 2f out: sn outpcd: rallied and nt clr run over 1f out: swtchd lft: one pce ins fnl f* **7/1**[3]
04 **9** 2 ¼ **Caldercruix (USA)**[26] 5383 4-9-10 **75** ... DaneO'Neill 13 — 69
(James Evans) *hld up in tch: rdn over 2f out: wknd over 1f out* **15/2**
4161 **10** 2 ½ **Gallego**[18] 5653 9-8-9 **67** ... RachealKneller(7) 7 — 55
(Richard Price) *s.s: hld up: a in rr* **20/1**
04 **11** 1 ¾ **Xpres Maite**[39] 4945 8-8-5 **61** oh2 ... (b) DavidKenny(5) 9 — 45
(Roy Bowring) *hld up: hdwy over 3f out: rdn over 2f out: sn wknd* **20/1**

1m 44.26s (-0.84) **Going Correction** -0.10s/f (Good)
WFA 3 from 4yo+ 4lb — 11 Ran SP% **112.5**
Speed ratings (Par 103): **100,98,97,97,96 95,95,95,93,90 88**
toteswingers:1&2:£8.10, 2&3:£16.00, 1&3:£8.90 CSF £50.78 CT £320.84 TOTE £4.30: £1.90, £4.90, £2.70; EX 48.30.
Owner Wayne Hennessey **Bred** Michael Ng **Trained** Whitsbury, Hants

FOCUS
The first division of this ordinary handicap was run at a modest pace as the first two held those positions throughout. It was the faster division and it wouldn't pay to be too negative about the winner.

6227 HIGHFIELDS H'CAP (DIV II) — 1m 60y
5:20 (5:20) (Class 5) (0-75,75) 3-Y-0+ — **£1,940** (£577; £288; £144) **Stalls** Low

Form — RPR
0516 **1** **West End Lad**[16] 5728 8-9-8 **73** ... (b) RussKennemore 5 — 80
(Roy Bowring) *mde all: rdn over 1f out: styd on* **11/1**
6055 **2** 1 ¾ **Compton Blue**[20] 5586 5-9-4 **72** ... (b) KieranO'Neill(3) 12 — 75+
(Richard Hannon) *hld up: rdn over 1f out: hung rt and r.o to go 2nd wl ins fnl f: nt rch wnr* **10/1**
0222 **3** ½ **Ferruccio (IRE)**[12] 5835 3-9-6 **75** ... EddieAhern 4 — 77
(James Fanshawe) *chsd ldrs: rdn over 1f out: styd on same pce ins fnl f* **11/4**[1]
0506 **4** nk **Hits Only Jude (IRE)**[4] 6098 8-8-3 **61** oh3 ... (v) MichaelKenny(7) 1 — 62
(Declan Carroll) *a.p: chsd wnr over 2f out: rdn over 1f out: styd on same pce* **16/1**
5145 **5** ½ **Oetzi**[12] 5835 3-8-8 **66** ... HarryBentley(3) 3 — 66+
(Alan Jarvis) *hld up: hdwy 3f out: nt clr run fr over 1f out: nvr able to chal* **9/2**[2]
0005 **6** nk **Miss Chicane**[19] 5614 3-8-13 **68** ... LiamKeniry 9 — 67
(Walter Swinburn) *chsd wnr 6f out: sn rdn: styd on* **33/1**
6404 **7** 1 ½ **Ra Junior (USA)**[34] 5151 5-8-11 **62** ... BarryMcHugh 6 — 58
(Paul Midgley) *hld up: rdn over 1f out: nvr trbld ldrs* **9/1**[3]
1022 **8** 1 ¾ **Cootehill Lass (IRE)**[5] 6051 3-9-6 **75** ... (p) CathyGannon 7 — 66
(David Evans) *dwlt: hld up: rdn over 2f out: n.d* **9/2**[2]
-502 **9** hd **Greek Islands (IRE)**[44] 4799 3-9-2 **71** ... PatCosgrave 10 — 62
(Ed de Giles) *s.i.s: hld up: rdn over 1f out: nvr on terms* **9/1**[3]
0603 **10** 34 **Tuxedo**[28] 5318 6-9-0 **65** ... (b) LukeMorris 11 — —
(Peter Hiatt) *chsd ldrs: pushed along 1/2-way: wknd 3f out: t.o* **20/1**

1m 44.68s (-0.42) **Going Correction** -0.10s/f (Good)
WFA 3 from 4yo+ 4lb — **10** Ran SP% **114.0**
Speed ratings (Par 103): **98,96,95,95,94 94,93,91,91,57**
toteswingers: 1&2 £11.60, 1&3 £6.10, 2&3 £6.60 CSF £113.10 CT £397.91 TOTE £13.20: £3.10, £3.20, £1.70; EX 87.60.
Owner K Nicholls **Bred** Keith Nicholls **Trained** Edwinstowe, Notts

FOCUS
The second leg of this handicap was run 0.42secs slower than the first, so the early pace was steady and again the winner made all. He very much had the run of things and the form is a bit suspect.

6228 RACING EXCELLENCE "HANDS AND HEELS" APPRENTICE SERIES H'CAP — 7f 9y
5:50 (5:50) (Class 5) (0-70,68) 3-Y-O+ — **£1,940** (£577; £288; £144) **Stalls** High

Form — RPR
2125 **1** **George Thisby**[21] 5539 5-9-4 **65** ... LukeRowe 2 — 71
(Rod Millman) *hld up: hdwy over 1f out: r.o to ld nr fin* **9/2**[2]
3400 **2** shd **Aviso (GER)**[6] 6033 7-8-10 **60** ... (p) KevinLundie(3) 11 — 66
(David Evans) *chsd ldrs: pushed along over 2f out: r.o* **16/1**
5524 **3** ½ **Links Drive Lady**[6] 6022 3-9-3 **67** ... NoelGarbutt 1 — 70
(Mark Rimmer) *s.i.s: hdwy 1/2-way: led over 2f out: shkn up over 1f out: hdd nr fin* **17/2**
1640 **4** nk **Muftarres (IRE)**[24] 5455 6-9-3 **67** ... (p) DavidSimmonson(3) 13 — 71
(Paul Midgley) *s.i.s: hdwy 1/2-way: shkn up over 1f out: hung rt: r.o* **8/1**
3024 **5** 1 ¾ **Sairaam (IRE)**[13] 5803 5-9-5 **66** ... RaulDaSilva 10 — 65
(Charles Smith) *hld up: swtchd rt over 2f out: hdwy over 1f out: styd on same pce ins fnl f* **13/2**[3]
4221 **6** shd **Catallout (IRE)**[16] 5725 3-8-13 **66** ... JasonHart(3) 8 — 64
(Declan Carroll) *hld up: hdwy over 1f out: gng wl ins fnl f: shkn up nr fin: nvr nr to chal* **3/1**[1]
6443 **7** ½ **Norcroft**[5] 6071 9-8-4 **54** oh9 ... (p) DanielHarris(3) 6 — 51?
(Christine Dunnett) *chsd ldrs: pushed along over 2f out: no ex ins fnl f* **25/1**
0-31 **8** ½ **Twinkled**[136] 1869 3-8-12 **65** ... IanBurns(3) 9 — 60
(Michael Bell) *led over 4f: no ex ins fnl f* **8/1**
6004 **9** 5 **Cape Melody**[17] 5676 5-9-7 **68** ... LucyKBarry 3 — 50
(George Baker) *chsd ldrs: pushed along over 2f out: wknd over 1f out* **14/1**
03-3 **10** 2 ½ **Laugh Or Cry**[228] 398 3-8-13 **68** ... PaulBooth(5) 12 — 43
(Dean Ivory) *prom tl wknd over 2f out* **25/1**
260- **11** ¾ **Lordship (IRE)**[298] 7402 7-8-7 **54** oh1 ... JakePayne 4 — 28
(Tony Carroll) *prom: pushed along 1/2-way: wknd over 2f out* **40/1**

1m 25.55s (-0.65) **Going Correction** -0.175s/f (Firm)
WFA 3 from 4yo+ 3lb — 11 Ran SP% **111.9**
Speed ratings (Par 103): **96,95,95,94,92 92,92,91,86,83 82**
toteswingers: 1&2 £16.80, 1&3 £9.50, 2&3 £23.00. Tote Super 7: Win: Not won. Place: Not won. CSF £68.17 CT £593.74 TOTE £5.20: £1.50, £5.00, £3.50; EX 97.70.
Owner Robert Thisby **Bred** Meon Valley Stud **Trained** Kentisbeare, Devon
■ Stewards' Enquiry : Jason Hart ten-day ban: failed to take all reasonable and permissable measures to obtain best possible placing (Oct 3-12)

FOCUS
A modest "hands and heels" apprentice handicap run 0.18secs slower than the earlier seller. There was a bunch finish and it's doubtful the winner improved.
Catallout(IRE) Official explanation: jockey said, regarding running and riding, this his orders were to drop the filly out, wait for a run and not produce it too soon, it missed the break and was denied a clear run 3f out, he then tried to make an effort closing stages; trainer's rep said he was not aware of the instructions given.
T/Plt: £49.00 to a £1 station. Pool of £65,840.00 - 979.75 winning tickets. T/Qpdt: £8.90 to a £1 stake. Pool of £5,177.55 - 426.95 winning tickets. CR

6043 BEVERLEY (R-H)
Tuesday, September 20

OFFICIAL GOING: Good to firm (8.1)
Wind: Virtually nil Weather: Overcast and raining

6229 SEASON FINALE (S) STKS — 1m 4f 16y
2:00 (2:00) (Class 5) 3-4-Y-O — **£2,264** (£673; £336; £168) **Stalls** Low

Form — RPR
2560 **1** **Cat O' Nine Tails**[5] 6095 4-8-11 73 ... SilvestreDeSousa 5 — 55
(Mark Johnston) *trckd ldrs: hdwy on outer 3f out: chal over 2f out: sn rdn to ld: edgd rt and clr over 1f out: styd on wl* **8/15**[1]
0104 **2** 6 **Valantino Oyster (IRE)**[49] 4633 4-9-7 62 ... (p) PatrickMathers 7 — 56
(Tracy Waggott) *hld up towards rr: hdwy to trck ldrs 1/2-way: rdn along over 3f out: hdwy 2f out: drvn to chse wnr ins fnl f: no imp* **10/1**[3]
5345 **3** 1 **Commander Veejay**[31] 4403 3-8-1 44 ... (b[1]) JasonHart(7) 3 — 49
(Brian Rothwell) *trckd ldrs on inner: effrt 3f out: rdn along over 2f out: plugging on whn n.m.r on inner over 1f out: swtchd lft and kpt on same pce* **40/1**
4253 **4** 9 **Goodmanyourself**[56] 4403 3-8-9 46 ow1 ... RussKennemore 1 — 36
(Paul Midgley) *led: rdn along 3f out: jnd over 2f out and sn hdd: drvn and wknd over 1f out* **14/1**
0330 **5** 2 ¼ **Indochina**[15] 5784 4-9-2 65 ... (v) TonyHamilton 4 — 31
(Ian Williams) *cl up: rdn along over 4f out: drvn wl over 2f out and sn wknd* **4/1**[2]

4655 **6** *41* **Sally Anne**[21] 5589 3-8-3 30 PaulQuinn 6 —
(John Harris) *a in rr: bhd 3f out* **100/1**

0 **7** *12* **Tunduce (IRE)**[14] 5816 3-8-3 0 PaulHanagan 8 —
(Noel Quinlan) *a in rr: bhd 3f out* **12/1**

2m 39.19s (-0.61) **Going Correction** +0.025s/f (Good)
WFA 3 from 4yo 8lb 7 Ran SP% **112.1**
Speed ratings (Par 103): **103,99,98,92,90 63,55**
toteswingers:1&2:£2.30, 2&3:£12.00, 1&3:£6.30 CSF £6.81 TOTE £1.50: £1.10, £3.20; EX 7.70 Trifecta £106.50 Pool: £607.39 - 4.22 winning units..The winner was sold to G Sparkes for £8,500.
Owner Stevie Richards & Nick Browne **Bred** The Duke Of Devonshire & Floors Farming **Trained** Middleham Moor, N Yorks

FOCUS
A weak seller and the winner did not need to be near her recent handicap form.
Tunduce(IRE) Official explanation: jockey said filly hung left throughout

6230 BRITISH STALLION STUDS SUPPORTING BRITISH RACING E B F MAIDEN STKS 7f 100y
2:30 (2:34) (Class 5) 2-Y-O £3,340 (£986; £493) Stalls Low

Form RPR

5 **1** **Nelson's Bay**[38] 5051 2-9-3 0 ShaneKelly 8 81+
(Brian Meehan) *mde all: rdn 2f out: clr over 1f out: styd on strly* **16/1**

233 **2** *3* **Surfer (USA)**[22] 5564 2-9-3 82 PaulHanagan 1 74
(Mahmood Al Zarooni) *t.k.h: trckd ldrs on inner: hdwy to chse wnr wl over 2f out: rdn wl over 1f out: drvn and no imp appr fnl f* **13/8**[1]

3 *1 3/4* **Rebel Song (IRE)** 2-9-3 0 AhmedAjtebi 9 70+
(Mahmood Al Zarooni) *wnt lft s and towards rr: hdwy on outer 3f out: rdn and rn green wl over 1f out: kpt on wl ins fnl f: nrst fin* **7/2**[3]

0 **4** *1 1/4* **Ellastina (IRE)**[24] 5486 2-8-12 0 TonyHamilton 2 62+
(Richard Fahey) *towards rr: hdwy on inner 1/2-way: chsd ldrs over 2f out: sn rdn and kpt on same pce* **28/1**

03 **5** *1 1/4* **Byron Blue (IRE)**[17] 5727 2-9-3 0 SaleemGolam 3 64
(Jamie Osborne) *t.k.h: trckd ldrs: hdwy 3f out: rdn along over 2f out: drvn and one pce fr over 1f out* **3/1**[2]

05 **6** *1/2* **Ardmay (IRE)**[15] 5786 2-9-3 0 PhillipMakin 4 63+
(Kevin Ryan) *hld up towards rr: effrt on inner 2f out: sn rdn and n.m.r whn swtchd lft ent fnl f: sn no imp* **16/1**

7 *5* **Ashwaat** 2-9-3 0 SilvestreDeSousa 7 51
(Mark Johnston) *chsd ldrs: pushed along 1/2-way: sn rdn and wknd* **7/1**

0 **8** *2 1/2* **Firefly**[22] 5548 2-9-3 0 JamesSullivan 6 45
(John Weymes) *t.k.h: chsd ldrs early: lost pl and towards rr 1/2-way: sn outpcd* **100/1**

0 **9** *12* **Bells Of Berlin**[12] 5851 2-9-3 0 (t) RobertWinston 5 17
(Alan McCabe) *sn chsng wnr: rdn along wl over 2f out: sn wknd* **28/1**

1m 34.5s (0.70) **Going Correction** +0.025s/f (Good) 9 Ran SP% **117.5**
Speed ratings (Par 95): **97,93,91,90,88 88,82,79,65**
toteswingers:1&2:£3.10, 2&3:£2.00, 1&3:£7.00 CSF £42.92 TOTE £18.30: £3.30, £1.40, £1.50; EX 37.90 Trifecta £141.00 Pool: £750.31 - 3.93 winning units..
Owner Raymond Tooth & Invictus **Bred** Raymond Clive Tooth **Trained** Manton, Wilts

FOCUS
Quite an interesting juvenile maiden, although the runner-up did not run to his official mark of 82. The winner got a great trip up front in a slowly run race.

NOTEBOOK
Nelson's Bay, fifth first time at Newmarket in a race that has worked out well, overcame his outside draw and was soon taking them along. He proved very willing in front and was firmly in command at the line. It all depends now on what mark he is given.
Surfer(USA), small and lacking scope, was warm beforehand. Taken gingerly to post, he took quite a tug and looked to be saving a bit for himself when asked to close down the winner. He has ability but is simply not progressing. (op Evens tchd 15-8 and 2-1 in a place)
Rebel Song(IRE), out of a daughter of the 1,000 Guineas winner Cape Verdi, is quite a big type. Very relaxed beforehand, he went left out of the stalls from his outside draw. He didn't handle the bend too well, but there was much to like about the way he knuckled down to claim third spot. This will have taught him plenty. (op 11-2)
Ellastina(IRE), on her second start, was very keen early on. She tired late in the day and will not be seen at her best until next year. (op 25-1 tchd 33-1)
Byron Blue(IRE), a good-bodied individual, did not run as well as he had done when third at Thirsk on his second start. He may appreciate a return to a more orthodox track. (op 4-1 tchd 11-4)
Ardmay(IRE), up in trip on his third start, appeared late on the scene after running very freely early on. He looks a likely type for modest handicaps at three. (op 14-1 tchd 12-1)

6231 GEORGE KILBURN MEMORIAL H'CAP 7f 100y
3:00 (3:01) (Class 5) (0-75,74) 3-Y-O+ £2,264 (£673; £336; £168) Stalls Low

Form RPR

00-0 **1** **Shotley Mac**[21] 5594 7-9-3 **70** (b) SilvestreDeSousa 7 81
(Neville Bycroft) *mde all: rdn wl over 1f out: clr appr fnl f: drvn out* **9/1**

3402 **2** *2 1/4* **Violent Velocity (IRE)**[17] 5728 8-8-11 **69** ShaneBKelly(5) 2 74
(John Quinn) *midfield: hdwy over 2f out: rdn to chse ldrs over 1f out: styd on ins fnl f* **8/1**

65-0 **3** *shd* **Makbullet**[25] 5441 4-8-10 **63** PaulHanagan 5 68+
(Michael Smith) *t.k.h: hld up towards rr: hdwy whn n.m.r and swtchd rt over 1f out: rdn and nt clr run jst ins fnl f: sn swtchd lft and fin strly* **20/1**

0556 **4** *1/2* **Whispered Times (USA)**[76] 3733 4-8-9 **62** (p) PatrickMathers 3 66
(Tracy Waggott) *in tch: hdwy to chse ldrs 3f out: rdn along 2f out: drvn over 1f out: kpt on u.p ins fnl f* **20/1**

36 **5** *1 1/2* **Summer Dancer (IRE)**[10] 5948 7-9-4 **71** PhillipMakin 6 71+
(Paul Midgley) *hld up towards rr: hdwy 2f out: n.m.r and swtchd rt ins fnl f: styng on whn nt clr run nr fin* **9/2**[1]

4100 **6** *hd* **Moral Issue**[16] 5760 3-8-10 **69** PatrickDonaghy(3) 8 68
(Jedd O'Keeffe) *chsd wnr: rdn along over 2f out: drvn over 1f out and grad wknd* **33/1**

3030 **7** *2* **Aspectus (IRE)**[18] 5669 8-9-3 **73** (b) SophieDoyle(3) 1 68
(Jamie Osborne) *t.k.h: chsd ldng pair: rdn along on inner 2f out: drvn and wknd ent fnl f* **14/1**

2600 **8** *1 1/2* **First Class Favour (IRE)**[12] 5862 3-8-11 **72** LanceBetts(5) 9 62
(Tim Easterby) *chsd ldrs: rdn along 2f out: drvn over 1f out and sn wknd* **25/1**

4200 **9** *nk* **Ours (IRE)**[21] 5594 8-9-5 **72** (p) BarryMcHugh 4 62+
(John Harris) *dwlt: a in rr* **10/1**

0000 **10** *1 1/4* **Steed**[10] 5920 4-9-4 **74** (p) RobertLButler(3) 11 61
(Richard Guest) *a towards rr* **20/1**

3-00 **11** *1/2* **Steel Stockholder**[16] 5760 5-8-11 **64** ow1 RobertWinston 10 50
(Mel Brittain) *chsd ldrs: rdn along 3f out: sn wknd* **6/1**[3]

321 **12** *3 1/4* **Green Howard**[27] 5368 3-9-2 **72** DanielTudhope 12 49+
(Robin Bastiman) *a in rr* **11/2**[2]

1401 **13** *1 1/2* **Thatcherite (IRE)**[17] 5731 3-9-1 **71** (t) StephenCraine 14 44+
(Tony Coyle) *dwlt: a in rr* **17/2**

1004 **14** *2 3/4* **Legal Legacy**[17] 5728 5-9-4 **71** TomEaves 13 38+
(Michael Dods) *s.i.s: a in rr* **14/1**

1m 32.4s (-1.40) **Going Correction** +0.025s/f (Good)
WFA 3 from 4yo+ 3lb 14 Ran SP% **123.0**
Speed ratings (Par 103): **109,106,106,105,104 103,101,99,99,98 97,93,92,88**
toteswingers:1&2:£12.40, 2&3:£21.40, 1&3:£51.40 CSF £74.50 CT £1428.30 TOTE £9.40: £4.20, £2.80, £5.80; EX 87.10 TRIFECTA Not won..
Owner J A Swinburne **Bred** N Bycroft **Trained** Brandsby, N Yorks

FOCUS
What beforehand looked a wide open 62-74 handicap was turned into a procession by the all-the-way winner who has a good record here and showed his best form this season. Few got involved.
Shotley Mac Official explanation: trainer said, regardinmg apparent improvement in form, that the gelding had been suited by making the running and had also improved in fitness.
Summer Dancer(IRE) Official explanation: jockey said gelding ran too free
Thatcherite(IRE) Official explanation: trainer had no explanation for the poor form shown

6232 THANKS FOR YOUR SUPPORT IN 2011 MAIDEN AUCTION STKS 5f
3:30 (3:31) (Class 4) 2-Y-O £3,428 (£1,020; £509; £254) Stalls Low

Form RPR

4455 **1** **Ashpan Sam**[22] 5562 2-8-9 62 SilvestreDeSousa 4 72
(John Spearing) *trckd ldrs: hdwy to chal 2f out: rdn to ld appr fnl f: styd on strly* **13/2**

3255 **2** *2 3/4* **Just Like Heaven (IRE)**[17] 5726 2-8-9 68 DavidAllan 8 62
(Tim Easterby) *cl up: led after 1f: rdn along and jnd 2f out: drvn and ev ch over 1f out: kpt on same pce ins fnl f* **5/1**[3]

3343 **3** *nk* **Half A Billion (IRE)**[17] 5726 2-9-0 73 PJMcDonald 2 66
(Michael Dods) *cl up on inner: effrt 1/2-way: rdn wl over 1f out and ev ch tl drvn: edgd lft and one pce wl ins fnl f* **7/4**[1]

4 *1 1/2* **Tarquin (IRE)** 2-9-0 0 TomEaves 3 61+
(Linda Stubbs) *towards rr: hdwy and in tch 1/2-way: effrt wl over 1f out: sn rdn and rn green: swtchd lft ent fnl f: kpt on wl towards fin* **11/4**[2]

3040 **5** *2 1/4* **Trust Fund Babe (IRE)**[5] 6092 2-8-5 59 DuranFentiman 9 44
(Tim Easterby) *chsd ldrs: rdn along 2f out: grad wknd* **14/1**

00 **6** *3 1/2* **Brunswick Vale (IRE)**[6] 6045 2-8-1 0 DeclanCannon(3) 5 30
(Paul Midgley) *in tch: effrt 1/2-way: sn rdn along and n.d* **100/1**

7 *3 1/4* **Al Dain (IRE)** 2-8-7 0 PaulHanagan 1 21
(Kevin Ryan) *s.i.s and a in rr* **9/1**

0530 **8** *nse* **Economic Crisis (IRE)**[13] 5817 2-8-5 55 (p) PatrickMathers 7 19
(Alan Berry) *a towards rr* **50/1**

3640 **9** *2 1/2* **Nellie Pickersgill**[119] 2387 2-8-8 57 ow1 GrahamGibbons 6 13
(Tim Easterby) *led 1f: chsd ldrs tl rdn along over 2f out and sn wknd* **40/1**

64.39 secs (0.89) **Going Correction** +0.05s/f (Good) 9 Ran SP% **115.1**
Speed ratings (Par 97): **94,89,89,86,83 77,72,72,68**
toteswingers:1&2:£5.20, 2&3:£2.40, 1&3:£3.40 CSF £38.53 TOTE £8.40: £1.90, £1.50, £1.20; EX 37.10 Trifecta £57.20 Pool: £623.51 - 8.05 winning units..
Owner Advantage Chemicals Holdings Ltd **Bred** Advantage Chemicals Holdings Ltd **Trained** Kinnersley, Worcs

FOCUS
A very modest maiden auction event. The winner is a surprise improver at face value and the form could rate higher.

NOTEBOOK
Ashpan Sam showed a willing attitude under substitute rider Silvestre de Sousa and ran out a decisive winner. (tchd 7-1)
Just Like Heaven(IRE), rated 68 and having his eighth start, was dropping back to 5f. He reversed Thirsk placings with Half A Billion but the pair found the winner much too strong late on. (op 4-1)
Half A Billion(IRE), third over 6f at Thirsk when Just Like Heaven was fifth, had a good draw but raced keenly and in truth didn't find much for final pressure. Rated 73, this was his seventh start and he is not progressing at all. (op 2-1)
Tarquin(IRE) was expected to score on his debut judging by the market support. He was fairly clueless when first called on for an effort, hanging right, but he picked up in encouraging fashion late on. He had presumably been showing a fair bit more at home. (op 10-3 tchd 5-2)
Trust Fund Babe(IRE), rated 59, was having her sixth start and looks to need a return to 6f. (op 10-1)
Brunswick Vale(IRE) showed a bit more than on her first two starts and may be more at home in claiming or selling company.

6233 VIOLET AND EDDIE SMITH MEMORIAL CONDITIONS STKS 5f
4:00 (4:01) (Class 3) 3-Y-O+ £6,411 (£1,919; £959; £479; £239) Stalls Low

Form RPR

6011 **1** **Internationaldebut (IRE)**[12] 5852 6-8-9 101 FrederikTylicki 1 107
(Paul Midgley) *in rr: hdwy over 2f out: rdn wl over 1f out: styd on strly ins fnl f to ld last 50yds* **13/8**[1]

0300 **2** *1 1/2* **Favourite Girl (IRE)**[10] 5927 5-8-4 92 (p) DuranFentiman 3 97
(Tim Easterby) *cl up: led after 1f: jnd and rdn 2f out: drvn over 1f out: hdd and no ex last 50yds* **8/1**[2]

5001 **3** *2 1/4* **Mister Manannan (IRE)**[14] 5805 4-9-3 97 AdrianNicholls 4 102
(David Nicholls) *dwlt: sn trcking ldrs on outer: swtchd wd and rdn 2f out: drvn over 1f out: kpt on to take 3rd nr fin* **9/1**[3]

344 **4** *nk* **Group Therapy**[13] 5827 6-8-9 105 GrahamGibbons 5 92
(David Barron) *sn cl up: chal 2f out: sn rdn and ev ch tl drvn and wknd ins fnl f: lost 3rd nr line* **13/8**[1]

0400 **5** *3* **Golden Destiny (IRE)**[24] 5467 5-8-4 96 (b) PaulHanagan 2 77
(Peter Makin) *led 1f: rdn along 1/2-way: sn outpcd* **8/1**[2]

62.57 secs (-0.93) **Going Correction** +0.05s/f (Good) 5 Ran SP% **108.4**
Speed ratings (Par 107): **109,106,103,102,97**
CSF £14.51 TOTE £2.20: £1.20, £3.10; EX 11.70.
Owner A Taylor Jnr **Bred** Ennistown Stud **Trained** Westow, N Yorks

FOCUS
A competitive conditions event. The winner has been better than ever of late and is rated close to his recent handicap form.

NOTEBOOK
Internationaldebut(IRE) ended a drought stretching back two and a half years when winning over 6f at York from a mark of 87. He followed up under a 6lb penalty over the same trip at Doncaster and went into this 5f event rated 101. His trainer, who has done such a brilliant job reviving him, reckons he works to a level a stone higher at home. Given the strong gallop he needs, he came from off the pace to score in decisive fashion in the end. Quick ground is important to him and he may struggle for another opportunity. (op 9-4)
Favourite Girl(IRE), who had 4lb to find with the winner, was tried in cheekpieces again. She showed all her old speed against the far side rail and this was probably her best effort this year. She sets the standard for the form. (tchd 7-1)
Mister Manannan(IRE), who had an 8lb penalty to cope with, had plenty to find on official ratings. After making virtually all when ending his drought in a class lower at Leicester, he was dropped in and eventually brought wide. At the weights this was a commendable effort. (op 8-1)
Group Therapy, withdrawn from the Ayr Gold Cup on account of the ground, had the best chance on official figures, but he is much better suited by bigger fields and was able to be covered up. After matching strides with Favourite Girl, he dropped away tamely. (op 11-8)

Golden Destiny(IRE) has just one decent effort to her credit this year when fourth in Listed company at York in July one place ahead of Group Therapy. Otherwise she has disappointed badly and it was the same here. (op 7-1)

6234 BEVERLEY ANNUAL BADGEHOLDERS H'CAP 1m 100y
4:30 (4:31) (Class 5) (0-75,75) 3-Y-O £2,264 (£673; £336; £168) Stalls Low

Form RPR

2624 **1** **Switchback**[20] 5635 3-9-4 **71** RichardMullen 4 83+
(Sir Michael Stoute) *trckd ldrs on inner: hdwy 2f out: rdn and nt clr run over 1f out and ent fnl f: drvn and styd on to ld last 75yds* **6/1**

2311 **2** *1* **Abidhabidubai**[26] 5401 3-9-5 **72** PBBeggy 1 79
(John Quinn) *trckd ldrs on inner: hdwy over 2f out: swtchd lft and rdn to ld over 1f out: drvn ins fnl f: hdd and no ex last 75yds* **9/2**[2]

6024 **3** *2 1/2* **St Oswald**[17] 5731 3-8-8 **61** SilvestreDeSousa 9 62
(David O'Meara) *a.p: hung lft bnd 4f out: rdn to chal over 2f out: drvn and ev ch over 1f out tl no ex ins fnl f* **5/1**[3]

2052 **4** *2* **Save The Bees**[17] 5731 3-8-12 **72** JasonHart(7) 6 69
(Declan Carroll) *trckd ldrs: effrt over 2f out: rdn over 1f out: kpt on same pce* **7/2**[1]

0060 **5** *3* **Iceblast**[16] 5760 3-8-10 **70** DavidSimmonson(7) 2 60
(Michael Easterby) *hld up in rr: hdwy wl over 2f out: rdn wl over 1f out: sn no imp* **20/1**

1430 **6** *1* **Ryedale Dancer (IRE)**[17] 5731 3-8-13 **66** DavidAllan 5 53
(Tim Easterby) *led: rdn along over 2f out: drvn wl over 1f out: hdd appr fnl f and sn wknd* **9/1**

000 **7** *2 1/2* **Oasis Storm**[55] 4432 3-9-6 **73** TomEaves 7 55
(Michael Dods) *prom: effrt on outer 3f out: rdn over 2f out and sn wknd* **20/1**

361 **8** *2 3/4* **Lady Sledmere (IRE)**[25] 5443 3-9-7 **74** PaulHanagan 8 49
(Paul Midgley) *hld up towards rr: effrt on outer 3f out: sn rdn and wknd* **9/2**[2]

5101 **9** *3 1/4* **Adorable Choice (IRE)**[5] 6098 3-9-8 **75** 6ex (v) StephenCraine 3 43
(Tom Dascombe) *a in rr* **14/1**

1m 46.73s (-0.87) **Going Correction** +0.025s/f (Good) **9** Ran SP% **115.7**
Speed ratings (Par 101): **105,104,101,99,96 95,93,90,87**
toteswingers:1&2:£3.30, 2&3:£6.00, 1&3:£4.20 CSF £33.23 CT £144.03 TOTE £7.50: £3.10, £2.10, £1.70; EX 26.70 Trifecta £203.10 Pool: £818.03 - 2.98 winning units..

Owner Cheveley Park Stud **Bred** Cheveley Park Stud Ltd **Trained** Newmarket, Suffolk

■ Stewards' Enquiry : Silvestre De Sousa one-day ban: used whip with excessive frequency down shoulder in the forehand (Oct 4)

FOCUS
Quite a messy 61-75 handicap and the winner would have been a very unlucky loser.

6235 BRIAN AND JASON MERRINGTON MEMORIAL AMATEUR RIDERS' H'CAP (DIV I) 1m 1f 207y
5:00 (5:02) (Class 6) (0-60,60) 3-Y-O+ £1,247 (£387; £193; £96) Stalls Low

Form RPR

0200 **1** **Dean Iarracht (IRE)**[20] 5622 5-10-3 **54** (p) MrGRSmith(5) 16 64
(Tracy Waggott) *hld up in rr: hdwy 3f out: rdn wl over 1f out: styd on strly appr fnl f: led last 100yds* **8/1**[3]

0050 **2** *2* **Hurricane Thomas (IRE)**[24] 5485 7-9-9 **46** oh1. MissPhillipaTutty(5) 11 52
(Karen Tutty) *trckd ldrs: hdwy over 2f out: swtchd lft and rdn to ld over 1f out: drvn and hdd last 100yds* **20/1**

4210 **3** *1/2* **Maybeme**[7] 6029 5-10-9 **60** MrSebSpencer(5) 7 67+
(Neville Bycroft) *hld up and bhd: hdwy over 2f out: sn rdn: styd on strly ins fnl f: nrst fin* **8/1**[3]

400 **4** *3/4* **Tropical Duke (IRE)**[24] 5485 5-9-10 **47** MissVBarr(5) 15 51
(Ron Barr) *hld up in rr: hdwy on wd outside over 2f out: rdn to chse ldrs over 1f out: kpt on same pce ins fnl f* **11/1**

0233 **5** *nse* **Laconicos (IRE)**[17] 5739 9-10-7 **60** (t) MissCScott(7) 9 63
(William Stone) *in tch: hdwy to chse ldrs 3f out: rdn over 2f out: drvn and kpt on appr fnl f* **8/1**[3]

4003 **6** *1* **Phoenix Flame**[13] 5823 3-10-2 **54** MrPCollington 12 55
(Alan McCabe) *in tch: hdwy to chse ldrs 3f out: rdn over 2f out: drvn and one pce appr fnl f* **14/1**

0600 **7** *nk* **Applaude**[24] 5485 6-9-12 **49** (b) MrMTStanley(5) 13 50
(Jason Ward) *hld up in rr: hdwy over 2f out: rdn: n.m.r and edgd rt over 1f out: drvn and hung rt ins fnl f: kpt on: nrst fin* **100/1**

0012 **8** *1* **Herrera (IRE)**[5] 6082 6-10-6 **59** (p) MrSAHuggan(7) 8 58+
(Richard Fahey) *hld up towards rr: effrt and sme hdwy over 2f out: sn rdn and n.d* **11/2**[1]

0302 **9** *1 3/4* **Kheskianto (IRE)**[6] 6050 5-10-0 **46** oh1 (b) MissSBrotherton 5 41
(Michael Chapman) *in tch: hdwy to trck ldrs 3f out: led 2f out: sn rdn and hdd over 1f out: sn wknd* **7/1**[2]

0030 **10** *1 1/4* **Magic Millie (IRE)**[41] 4902 4-10-4 **50** MissJCoward 1 43
(David O'Meara) *led 1f: trckd ldr: pushed along over 3f out: rdn over 2f out: n.m.r over 1f out: sn wknd* **11/1**

5-00 **11** *1 3/4* **Tayarat (IRE)**[31] 1881 6-9-11 **50** (p) MrAaronJames(7) 10 39
(Michael Chapman) *midfield: hdwy and in tch 3f out: sn rdn along and grad wknd 2f out* **40/1**

0030 **12** *1/2* **Yossi (IRE)**[19] 5642 7-10-0 **46** oh1 (b) MrSWalker 6 34
(Richard Guest) *cl up: led after 1f: rdn along 3f out: hdd 2f out and sn wknd* **12/1**

4003 **13** *2* **Island Chief**[13] 5822 5-10-7 **58** (b) MissFCumani(5) 4 42
(Michael Easterby) *trckd ldrs: n.m.r and hmpd bnd at 1/2-way: hdwy to chse ldrs over 2f out: sn rdn and wknd* **9/1**

6600 **14** *1 3/4* **Dabbers Ridge (IRE)**[26] 5414 9-11-0 **60** MrsCBartley 2 41
(Ian McInnes) *a bhd* **16/1**

00-0 **15** *2 3/4* **Bernix**[158] 1373 9-9-11 **50** MissLWilson(7) 3 25
(Mark Campion) *stmbld s: a towards rr* **25/1**

2m 7.86s (0.86) **Going Correction** +0.025s/f (Good)
WFA 3 from 4yo+ 6lb **15** Ran SP% **120.2**
Speed ratings (Par 101): **97,95,95,94,94 93,93,92,91,90 88,88,86,85,83**
toteswingers:1&2:£40.80, 2&3:£40.70, 1&3:£14.70 CSF £164.66 CT £1331.48 TOTE £8.20: £2.40, £8.20, £3.50; EX 170.80 TRIFECTA Not won..

Owner Michael Howarth **Bred** Ken Carroll **Trained** Spennymoor, Co Durham

■ Richard Smith's first Flat winner.

FOCUS
Division one of a rock bottom 46-60 amateur riders' handicap and the pace was very strong. The time was very similar to division II and the winner is rated basically to form.

6236 BRIAN AND JASON MERRINGTON MEMORIAL AMATEUR RIDERS' H'CAP (DIV II) 1m 1f 207y
5:30 (5:31) (Class 6) (0-60,60) 3-Y-O+ £1,247 (£387; £193; £96) Stalls Low

Form RPR

3050 **1** **Harare**[13] 5822 10-9-7 **46** (v) MissGTutty(7) 16 59
(Karen Tutty) *hld up in rr: gd hdwy over 3f out: chsd ldrs 2f out: swtchd lft and rdn to ld 1 1/2f out: sn clr: styd on wl* **40/1**

4030 **2** *8* **General Tufto**[81] 3574 6-10-9 **55** (b) MissEJJones 12 52
(Charles Smith) *hld up towards rr: gd hdwy over 3f out: chsd ldrs 2f out: rdn to chse wnr over 1f out: sn drvn and no imp* **12/1**

0250 **3** *2* **Rowan Lodge (IRE)**[40] 4946 9-10-9 **60** (b) MrJohnWilley(5) 7 53
(Ollie Pears) *midfield: hdwy over 2f out: rdn to chse ldng pair ent fnl f: kpt on* **16/1**

4-62 **4** *nk* **Rose Aurora**[15] 5785 4-9-9 **46** oh1 (v) MrJRWilliams(5) 5 38
(Marcus Tregoning) *s.i.s: sn into midfield: trckd ldrs after 3f: rdn along 3f out: drvn 2f out: kpt on u.p ins fnl f* **4/1**[1]

2210 **5** *4* **Obara D'Avril (FR)**[53] 4499 9-9-12 **49** (p) MissCarlyFrater(5) 8 33
(Simon West) *hld up in rr: hdwy over 2f out: rdn over 1f out: kpt on ins fnl f: nrst fin* **9/1**

0000 **6** *2 1/4* **Verluga (IRE)**[34] 5167 4-9-10 **47** MissRRichardson(5) 11 27
(Tim Easterby) *midfield: hdwy 3f out: rdn to chse ldrs over 2f out: sn drvn and wknd* **16/1**

5540 **7** *1/2* **Grethel (IRE)**[7] 6029 7-9-9 **48** MrMGrossett(7) 3 27
(Alan Berry) *towards rr: hdwy over 3f out: rdn along 2f out: n.d* **33/1**

0404 **8** *1/2* **Minortransgression (USA)**[13] 5832 4-9-9 **46** oh1 MissSallyRandell(5) 15 24
(Paul Rich) *chsd ldrs: rdn along 3f out: grad wknd* **16/1**

0006 **9** *1 1/4* **Call Of Duty (IRE)**[21] 5594 6-10-9 **58** MissECSayer(3) 9 33
(Dianne Sayer) *chsd ldrs: rdn along over 3f out: wknd over 2f out* **9/1**

5005 **10** *1 3/4* **Barnum (USA)**[3] 6181 3-9-13 **51** (b) MissSBrotherton 14 23
(Michael Easterby) *led: rdn clr 3f out: hdd and drvn 2f out: wknd over 1f out* **5/1**[2]

1030 **11** *hd* **Guga (IRE)**[28] 5349 5-10-6 **59** (b) MissABlakemore(7) 10 31
(John Mackie) *a towards rr* **20/1**

60-0 **12** *1/2* **Orpen Wide (IRE)**[68] 181 9-10-1 **52** (b) ThomasGarner(5) 17 23
(Michael Chapman) *a towards rr* **50/1**

306 **13** *6* **Dimashq**[26] 5405 9-10-0 **46** (p) MrSWalker 4 5
(Paul Midgley) *trckd ldrs: hdwy over 3f out: rdn to ld 2f out: sn drvn and hdd 1 1/2f out: sn wknd* **8/1**[3]

/000 **14** *1 1/2* **Lil Ella (IRE)**[29] 5311 4-10-9 **60** (b) MrsFreyaBrewer(5) 1 16
(Patrick Holmes) *sn led: hdd after 3f out and cl up: rdn along over 2f out: sn wknd* **12/1**

3344 **15** *46* **Light The City (IRE)**[15] 5791 4-10-1 **54** MrBHowe(7) 6 —
(Ruth Carr) *prom: wd st and sn rdn along: wknd qckly wl over 2f out: sn bhd and eased* **9/1**

2m 7.64s (0.64) **Going Correction** +0.025s/f (Good)
WFA 3 from 4yo+ 6lb **15** Ran SP% **122.9**
Speed ratings (Par 101): **98,91,90,89,86 84,84,83,82,81 81,81,76,75,38**
toteswingers:1&2:£106.90, 2&3:£33.10, 1&3:£51.70 Tote Super 7: Win: Not won. Place: Not won. CSF £462.49 CT £7809.01 TOTE £34.00: £7.70, £3.60, £3.40; EX 535.40 TRIFECTA Not won..

Owner N D Tutty **Bred** Limestone Stud **Trained** Osmotherley, N Yorks

■ Gemma Tutty's first winner under rules. Carlitos Spirit (14/1) was withdrawn (rdr inj in prelims). Deduct 5p in the £ under R4.

■ Stewards' Enquiry : Thomas Garner four-day ban: used whip with excessive frequency when out of contention (tbn)

FOCUS
A 51-60 affair and the overall time was a fraction quicker than part one. The winner benefited from the strong pace and this is not form to take too literally.

Light The City(IRE) Official explanation: trainer said gelding bled from the nose; jockey said saddle slipped

T/Plt: £39.30 to a £1 stake. Pool of £47,128.77 - 874.92 winning tickets. T/Qpdt: £17.60 to a £1 stake. Pool of £3,471.28 - 145.50 winning tickets. JR

6017 FOLKESTONE (R-H)
Tuesday, September 20

OFFICIAL GOING: Good (good to firm in places; 7.7)
Wind: fresh, half behind Weather: overcast

6237 LIPSCOMB.CO.UK NURSERY 5f
2:20 (2:21) (Class 5) (0-70,74) 2-Y-O £2,726 (£805; £402) Stalls High

Form RPR

3641 **1** **Billyrayvalentine (CAN)**[6] 6058 2-9-11 **74** 6ex (t) FrankieDettori 3 86+
(George Baker) *stdd and short of room sn after s: bhd: hdwy in centre 2f out: rdn and chsd clr ldr ent fnl f: qcknd and jnd ldr fnl 100yds: sn led and in command: eased cl home* **4/9**[1]

602 **2** *1/2* **Sister Guru**[62] 4212 2-8-12 **64** HarryBentley(3) 11 72
(Peter Hedger) *t.k.h: w ldr tl led 1/2-way: rdn clr over 1f out: hdd and nt gng pce of wnr wl ins fnl f:* **7/1**[2]

4305 **3** *6* **Invincible Dream (IRE)**[6] 6058 2-9-7 **70** (v[1]) KierenFallon 10 56
(Robert Mills) *in tch in midfield: pushed along 1/2-way: rdn and outpcd over 1f out: no ch w ldng pair but plugged on to go modest 3rd ins fnl f* **9/1**[3]

2300 **4** *1* **Masivo Man (IRE)**[6] 6043 2-8-1 **50** (b[1]) AndreaAtzeni 7 32
(Chris Dwyer) *led tl 1/2-way: rdn 2f out: outpcd u.p over 1f out and sn btn: lost 3rd ins fnl f* **66/1**

4164 **5** *1/2* **Triggerlo**[7] 6021 2-8-13 **62** TedDurcan 9 47
(Mick Channon) *stdd short of room sn after s: hld up bhd: rdn and hdwy 2f out: swtchd rt over 1f out: keeping on but no ch w ldrs whn nt clr run jst over 1f out: swtchd lft and kpt on ins fnl f: n.d* **14/1**

6232 **6** *1/2* **Stans Deelyte**[30] 5297 2-8-5 **54** LukeMorris 1 33
(Lisa Williamson) *wnt rt s: sn rcvrd and chsng ldrs: rdn over 2f out: outpcd over 1f out: no ch w ldrs ins fnl f* **25/1**

0060 **7** *3/4* **Royal Blush**[12] 5847 2-9-5 **68** (b[1]) ChrisCatlin 6 44
(Paul Cole) *sn pushed along: in tch: struggling u.p over 2f out: sn outpcd and no threat to ldrs 2f out* **11/1**

0303 **8** *2* **Picura**[30] 5297 2-8-3 **52** MartinLane 5 21
(William Muir) *a towards rr: rdn and no imp 1/2-way: n.d* **25/1**

2360 **9** *hd* **Sea Poet**[8] 5998 2-8-6 **58** SeanLevey(3) 4 26
(John Bridger) *chsd ldrs: rdn and struggling 1/2-way: sn wknd* **50/1**

0434 **10** *14* **Empressive**[47] 4702 2-8-5 **54**.. MartinDwyer 2 —
(William Muir) *taken down early: in tch: rdn and hung lft over 3f out: lost pl 1/2-way: wl bhd 2f out* **33/1**

59.21 secs (-0.79) **Going Correction** -0.425s/f (Firm) **10** Ran SP% **120.8**
Speed ratings (Par 95): **89,88,78,77,76 75,74,71,70,48**
toteswingers:1&2:£2.40, 2&3:£4.50, 1&3:£2.80 CSF £4.06 CT £16.32 TOTE £1.50: £1.10, £1.50, £2.40; EX 5.10.

Owner Russell, Wheeler, Vail Partnership **Bred** Windfields Farm **Trained** Whitsbury, Hants

FOCUS
A modest nursery, but a well-handicapped winner who had something to spare. As usual the stands' rail looked to provide a significant advantage. The first two were clear.

NOTEBOOK
Billyrayvalentine(CAN) deserves even more credit considering the track is rarely conducive to waiting tactics. He was 5lb well in following a taking success on his nursery debut at Sandown five days earlier, and although he made hard enough work of getting to the front, that's understandable, and he was eased late on. He was declared to run again quickly over 6f at Wolverhampton, and although he'd have a double penalty, his claims would be obvious with the extra furlong likely to suit. (op 8-13 tchd 4-6 in places)

Sister Guru, reappearing after a two-month break, showed good speed against the favoured fence and pulled well clear of all bar the winner. (op 11-2)

Invincible Dream(IRE) had a visor on for the first time, but he never really travelled, despite racing near the rail, and achieved little. (op 10-1)

Masivo Man(IRE) had blinkers on for the first time but didn't offer much.

Triggerlo was denied a clear run in closing stages and otherwise probably would have finished third. Official explanation: jockey said gelding was denied a clear run (op 16-1)

6238 EARLY BIRD H'CAP 5f
2:50 (2:50) (Class 6) (0-60,60) 3-Y-O+ **£2,045** (£603; £302) **Stalls** High

Form RPR

100 **1** **Lord Of The Reins (IRE)**[62] 4210 7-9-4 **60**.................. KieranO'Neill(3) 8 75
(P J O'Gorman) *trckd ldng pair: hanging rt but waiting for gap on stands' rail over 1f out: pushed along and qcknd to ld ins fnl f: sn clr: comf* **11/2**[2]

050 **2** *3* **The Strig**[94] 3179 4-9-3 **59**..(t) RyanClark(3) 7 63
(Stuart Williams) *bustled along leaving stalls: chsd ldr: rdn and effrt 2f out: pressed ldr over 1f out: nt gng pce of wnr and btn jst ins fnl f: wnt 2nd towards fin* **5/4**[1]

0503 **3** *1/2* **Cloth Ears**[8] 5997 5-8-7 **49**....................................(be) AdamBeschizza(3) 4 51
(Phil McEntee) *led and grad crossed to r against stands' rail: rdn and hrd pressed over 1f out: hdd jst ins fnl f: nt gng pce of wnr and sn btn: lost 2nd towards fin* **6/1**[3]

02 **4** *nk* **Avonvalley**[34] 5175 4-8-9 **48**....................................... RobbieFitzpatrick 5 49
(Peter Grayson) *awkward leaving stalls: racd in midfield: effrt u.p wl over 1f out: styd on fnl 100yds: no ch w wnr* **17/2**

3420 **5** *2 1/4* **Bateleur**[20] 5616 7-9-4 **57**.. ChrisCatlin 2 50
(Mick Channon) *hld up in rr: rdn and effrt 2f out: no imp u.p over 1f out: wl btn ins fnl f* **10/1**

65U **6** *3/4* **Chester Deelyte (IRE)**[27] 5388 3-8-10 **50**.......................(p) LukeMorris 1 41
(Lisa Williamson) *chsd ldrs: rdn 1/2-way: wknd qckly over 1f out* **14/1**

20-6 **7** *7* **Know No Fear**[260] 26 6-8-6 **52**.................................. KatiaScallan(7) 6 17
(Alastair Lidderdale) *racd in midfield: rdn and struggling jst over 2f out: wknd wl over 1f out: fdd ins fnl f* **13/2**

6000 **8** *9* **Bird Dog**[63] 4187 5-8-0 **46** oh1.....................................(v) DannyBrock(7) 3 —
(Phil McEntee) *sn outpcd and rdn in last: swtchd rt after 1f out: nvr on terms* **125/1**

58.65 secs (-1.35) **Going Correction** -0.425s/f (Firm) course record
WFA 3 from 4yo+ 1lb **8** Ran SP% **114.5**
Speed ratings (Par 101): **93,88,87,86,83 82,70,56**
toteswingers:1&2:£2.80, 2&3:£3.10, 1&3:£6.60 CSF £12.81 CT £42.72 TOTE £9.80: £2.80, £1.02, £3.20; EX 17.70.

Owner Racing To The Max **Bred** C Farrell **Trained** Newmarket, Suffolk
■ Stewards' Enquiry : Robbie Fitzpatrick caution: used whip with excessive frequency.

FOCUS
The ridiculous stands'-side rail bias was in evidence once again in what was a really moderate handicap. The time was only 0.47 seconds outside the track record. Tricky form to assess with the first two potentially well treated.

6239 KENT PHARMACEUTICALS H'CAP 7f (S)
3:20 (3:20) (Class 4) (0-85,85) 3-Y-O+ **£4,204** (£1,251; £625; £312) **Stalls** High

Form RPR

0232 **1** **Mingun Bell (USA)**[25] 5425 4-8-12 **76**............................. PatCosgrave 4 86
(Ed de Giles) *chsd ldrs: swtchd lft and effrt wl over 1f out: drvn to ld over 1f out: kpt on wl u.p ins fnl f* **11/2**

1224 **2** *3/4* **Romantic Wish**[19] 5657 3-9-1 **85**.................................... SeanLevey(3) 5 92+
(Robert Mills) *wnt lft s: hld up in tch: effrt and carried rt wl over 1f out: drvn: edgd rt and ev ch ins fnl f: styd on same pce fnl 100yds* **5/2**[2]

0164 **3** *2 1/4* **Watch Amigo (IRE)**[14] 5811 5-9-7 **85**............................. KierenFallon 2 87
(Walter Swinburn) *pressed ldr: reminder 1/2-way: edgd rt u.p over 1f out: one pce and hld ins fnl f* **4/1**[3]

2-10 **4** *3/4* **Cape Rambler**[29] 5322 3-8-12 **79**.. DaneO'Neill 7 78+
(Henry Candy) *stdd s: t.k.h: hld up in tch: rdn and unable qck wl over 1f out: kpt on same pce ins fnl f* **9/1**

31 **5** *9* **Emkanaat**[14] 5810 3-8-13 **80**... RichardHills 8 66
(Roger Varian) *led: hung rt fr over 2f out: rdn: continued to hang rt and hdd over 1f out: sn btn: eased ins fnl f* **2/1**[1]

0000 **6** *3 1/2* **King's Colour**[14] 5811 6-8-12 **76** ow1.................................. IanMongan 1 42
(Brett Johnson) *sn detached in last: rdn and no hdwy 1/2-way: nvr on terms* **33/1**

1200 **7** *hd* **Taqaat (USA)**[38] 5056 3-8-11 **78**.. TomQueally 9 43
(Tim McCarthy) *chsd ldrs tl lost pl and rdn 4f out: wl bhd 2f out* **33/1**

1m 24.95s (-2.35) **Going Correction** -0.425s/f (Firm)
WFA 3 from 4yo+ 3lb **7** Ran SP% **113.2**
Speed ratings (Par 105): **96,95,92,91,81 77,77**
CSF £19.24 CT £59.61 TOTE £6.70: £2.40, £2.30; EX 23.90.

Owner Blackham And Gould Partnership **Bred** Paula W Cline **Trained** Ledbury, Herefordshire

FOCUS
An uncompetitive handicap and not strong form for the level. The winner was up a length on this year's form but the favourite disappointed.

Emkanaat Official explanation: jockey said gelding held its breath

6240 KENT CRICKET H'CAP 1m 7f 92y
3:50 (3:51) (Class 6) (0-60,60) 3-Y-O+ **£2,045** (£603; £302) **Stalls** High

Form RPR

4025 **1** **Marcus Antonius**[57] 4396 4-10-0 **60**................................ PatCosgrave 7 71
(Jim Boyle) *chsd ldrs tl pressed ldr over 4f out: led on inner 3f out: rdn clr w runner-up 2f out: flashed tail u.p over 1f out: edgd lft but hld on ins fnl f* **10/1**

5040 **2** *shd* **Rose Of Sarratt (IRE)**[10] 5915 3-9-1 **58**........................... MartinLane 9 69
(Rae Guest) *chsd ldrs: rdn to chse wnr and wnt clr 2f out: ev ch fr over 1f out: kpt on but a jst hld ins fnl f* **12/1**

6501 **3** *4 1/2* **Dark And Dangerous (IRE)**[15] 5784 3-9-1 **58**............ CathyGannon 11 63
(Peter Winkworth) *chsd ldr tl over 4f out: rdn to chse ldng pair but unable qck ent 2f out: styd on same pce after* **11/2**[2]

0503 **4** *2 3/4* **Stormy Morning**[10] 5916 5-9-8 **59**........................(p) JamesRogers(5) 13 60
(Pat Eddery) *t.k.h: hld up in midfield: rdn and effrt ent 2f out: sn outpcd by ldrs: wnt modest 4th 1f out: kpt on* **8/1**[3]

0053 **5** *2 1/2* **Dhampas**[22] 5566 3-7-13 **47**..(b) NathanAlison(5) 8 45
(Jim Boyle) *t.k.h: hld up towards rr: hdwy on outer 3f out: rdn and no prog ent 2f out: hung lft and wl hld after* **17/2**

-311 **6** *1* **Red Current**[20] 5628 7-9-6 **57**.. DavidKenny(5) 10 54+
(Michael Scudamore) *hld up in rr: stuck bhd a wall of horses 3f out: rdn and effrt whn nt clr run ent 2f out: sme hdwy over 1f out: n.d* **10/1**

6066 **7** *7* **Royal Reason**[21] 5585 3-8-9 **55**.................................. HarryBentley(3) 14 43
(Joseph Tuite) *chsd ldrs: rdn and fnd little ent 2f out: sn wknd* **17/2**

5105 **8** *3/4* **Royal Premier (IRE)**[47] 4732 8-9-9 **55**..........................(p) SebSanders 6 42
(Tom Keddy) *pushed along early: sme hdwy whn hmpd on inner and dropped in rr 4f out: rdn and no prog over 2f out: sn wknd: nvr trbld ldrs* **20/1**

66-0 **9** *shd* **Sure Fire (GER)**[164] 1253 6-9-6 **52**.................................... TomQueally 4 39
(Barney Curley) *hld up in last trio: pushed along and no hdwy 3f out: wknd over 2f out* **14/1**

4064 **10** *14* **Divine Rule (IRE)**[96] 3089 3-9-3 **60**................................... IanMongan 5 28
(Laura Mongan) *hld up towards rr: rdn and no hdwy over 2f out: wknd 2f out: t.o* **8/1**[3]

060- **11** *5* **Goodison Park**[245] 7398 4-8-9 **46** oh1.............................. LauraPike(5) 1 —
(Tim McCarthy) *led tl 3f out: rdn and wknd qckly over 2f out: t.o* **100/1**

0214 **12** *7* **Thundering Home**[40] 4952 4-9-11 **57**............................(t) KierenFallon 12 55
(George Baker) *chsd ldrs tl rdn and outpcd ent 2f out: 4th and wl hld over 1f out: eased and virtually p.u ins fnl f: t.o* **4/1**[1]

3m 27.93s (-1.77) **Going Correction** -0.125s/f (Firm)
WFA 3 from 4yo+ 11lb **12** Ran SP% **117.0**
Speed ratings (Par 101): **99,98,96,95,93 93,89,89,89,81 78,75**
toteswingers:1&2:£23.90, 2&3:£18.30, 1&3:£23.90 CSF £122.63 CT £731.95 TOTE £11.40: £3.10, £4.80, £2.30; EX 172.40.

Owner The Grosvenor Club **Bred** Mrs J J Dye **Trained** Epsom, Surrey
■ Stewards' Enquiry : Pat Cosgrave one-day ban: careless riding (Oct 4)

FOCUS
A moderate staying handicap in which the principals were always prominent. A 4lb personal best from the winner.

Dhampas Official explanation: jockey said colt hung left

6241 CLAYDON HORSE EXERCISERS H'CAP 1m 1f 149y
4:20 (4:20) (Class 4) (0-80,80) 3-Y-O+ **£4,204** (£1,251; £625; £312) **Stalls** Centre

Form RPR

1054 **1** **Danderek**[51] 4577 5-9-7 **77**.. MartinDwyer 4 89+
(Brian Meehan) *t.k.h: hld up in midfield: hdwy to chse ldr over 2f out: pushed ahd over 1f out: sn clr and in command 1f out: eased towards fin* **5/1**[3]

1032 **2** *5* **Miss Aix**[9] 5962 3-9-4 **80**.. EddieAhern 10 80
(Michael Bell) *hld up off the pce in last pair: hdwy on inner 2f out: swtchd lft and pressing for 2nd 1f out: chsd clr wnr fnl 75yds: kpt on but no ch w wnr* **11/2**

4142 **3** *3/4* **Battle Of Britain**[22] 5568 3-9-2 **78**.................................(t) KierenFallon 5 76
(Giles Bravery) *sn niggled along and outpcd in last pair: hdwy and pressing for placings u.p over 1f out: kpt on but no ch w wnr* **11/4**[1]

1102 **4** *2* **Colinca's Lad (IRE)**[28] 5356 9-8-6 **67**............................ RosieJessop(5) 2 61
(Peter Charalambous) *led: clr 7f out: rdn ent fnl 2f: drvn and hdd over 1f out: sn outpcd and no ch w wnr 1f out: wknd fnl 100yds* **8/1**

5214 **5** *5* **Medaille D'Or**[30] 5303 3-9-0 **76**...................................... JackMitchell 6 59
(Roger Varian) *racd off the pce in last trio: rdn and effrt ent 2f out: wknd u.p over 1f out* **7/2**[2]

0020 **6** *6* **Understory (USA)**[11] 5893 4-9-6 **76**................................. TomQueally 9 47
(Tim McCarthy) *chsd ldng pair: rdn and c wd over 2f out: wknd 2f out* **18/1**

3214 **7** *14* **Lifetime (IRE)**[11] 5880 3-9-2 **78**.................................... JoeFanning 7 19
(Mark Johnston) *chsd ldr tl over 2f out: wknd qckly 2f out: virtually p.u ins fnl f: t.o* **5/1**[3]

2m 4.04s (-0.86) **Going Correction** -0.125s/f (Firm)
WFA 3 from 4yo+ 6lb **7** Ran SP% **114.0**
Speed ratings (Par 105): **98,94,93,91,87 83,71**
toteswingers:1&2:£6.80, 2&3:£4.60, 1&3:£3.30 CSF £31.92 CT £89.73 TOTE £6.60: £2.70, £2.30; EX 30.80.

Owner B Buckley D Rowlands & D Keenan **Bred** Mrs Maureen Buckley **Trained** Manton, Wilts

FOCUS
A fair handicap run at a strong pace. Improvement from the winner but he may have been flattered.

Battle Of Britain Official explanation: jockey said colt was slowly away

6242 GARDEN OF ENGLAND MAIDEN STKS 1m 1f 149y
4:50 (4:51) (Class 5) 3-Y-O+ **£2,385** (£704; £352) **Stalls** Centre

Form RPR

00 **1** **Novirak (IRE)**[21] 5607 3-9-3 0.. JackMitchell 3 79+
(James Fanshawe) *chsd ldrs: swtchd lft and n.m.r over 1f out: rdn and ev ch ins fnl f: hung lft fnl 75yds: r.o u.p to ld cl home* **100/1**

6426 **2** *hd* **Ela Gonda Mou**[36] 5113 4-9-4 69................................. KirstyMilczarek 1 74
(Peter Charalambous) *led: rdn 2f out: hung lft fnl f: hdd and no ex towards fin* **17/2**[3]

32 **3** *1* **Kahraba (USA)**[11] 5877 3-8-12 0.................................... FrankieDettori 12 73
(Saeed Bin Suroor) *t.k.h: chsd ldr: rdn and ev ch over 1f out: stl ev ch but nt qckning ins fnl f: pushed lft: hmpd and eased towards fin* **11/8**[1]

0 **4** *2 1/4* **Vasily**[10] 5911 3-9-3 0...(t) AndreaAtzeni 11 72
(Robert Eddery) *s.i.s: steadily rcvrd and chsd ldrs over 7f out: rdn and unable qck 2f out: styd on same pce u.p fr over 1f out* **12/1**

5-23 **5** *1/2* **Raahin (IRE)**39 4989 3-9-3 79 RichardHills 9 71
(Sir Michael Stoute) *t.k.h: in tch: rdn and unable qck wl over 1f out: styd on same pce and no imp fr over 1f out* **11/4**[2]
00- **6** *8* **Dust Cloud (IRE)**363 6279 3-9-3 0 LukeMorris 4 54
(Peter Winkworth) *taken down early: t.k.h: hld up in midfield: rdn ent fnl 2f: sn outpcd: wknd over 1f out* **66/1**
5 **7** *1 1/4* **Nakhutha (FR)**9 5960 3-9-3 0 KierenFallon 7 52+
(Mahmood Al Zarooni) *v.s.a: rn green and outpcd in last pair: n.d* **14/1**
04 **8** *4* **Illustration (IRE)**15 5792 3-9-3 0 JoeFanning 6 43
(Mark Johnston) *s.i.s: pushed along in midfield: rdn and struggling 3f: wknd over 2f out* **20/1**
9 *20* **Lord Golan** 3-9-0 0 MartinHarley(3) 2 —
(Des Donovan) *stdd s: hld up towards rr: lost tch over 2f out: t.o* **100/1**
000 **10** *7* **April Belle**126 2175 3-8-12 25 EddieAhern 8 —
(Tim McCarthy) *s.i.s: a in rr: lost tch qckly 3f out: t.o* **200/1**

2m 4.82s (-0.08) **Going Correction** -0.125s/f (Firm)
WFA 3 from 4yo+ 6lb **10** Ran SP% **102.4**
Speed ratings (Par 103): **95,94,94,92,91 85,84,81,65,59**
toteswingers:1&2:£37.00, 2&3:£3.00, 1&3:£21.70 CSF £637.36 TOTE £106.00: £16.50, £1.80, £1.50; EX 626.00.
Owner Norman Brunskill **Bred** Loughbrown Stud **Trained** Newmarket, Suffolk
■ Marhaba was withdrawn (7/1, ref to ent stalls). Deduct 10p in the £ under R4.
■ Stewards' Enquiry : Kirsty Milczarek two-day ban: careless riding (Oct 4-5)
Jack Mitchell two-day ban: careless riding (Oct 6-7)

FOCUS
They didn't seem to go that quick and the time was 0.78 seconds slower than the earlier Class 4 handicap. This is modest maiden form, with a shock winner and the second the best guide.
Ela Gonda Mou Official explanation: jockey said filly hung left
T/Jkpt: Not won. T/Plt: £114.80 to a £1 stake. Pool of £82,918.88 - 527.23 winning tickets.
T/Qpdt: £54.80 to £1. Pool of £4,725.93 - 63.80 w. tckts SP 6243a (Foreign Racing) - See RI

5966 GOODWOOD (R-H)
Wednesday, September 21

OFFICIAL GOING: Soft (6.5)
Wind: Brisk across Weather: Sunny spells

6244 BRITISH STALLION STUDS SUPPORTING BRITISH RACING E B F MAIDEN STKS 7f
2:00 (2:02) (Class 5) 2-Y-O **£3,234** (£962; £481; £240) **Stalls** Low

Form RPR
3 **1** **Genius Step (IRE)**116 2510 2-9-3 0 FrankieDettori 8 83+
(Mahmood Al Zarooni) *trckd ldr: led ins fnl 2f: shkn up and in n.d fnl f: easily* **6/4**[1]
2 *1 1/2* **Okimono** 2-9-3 0 AhmedAjtebi 6 77+
(Mahmood Al Zarooni) *towards rr but in tch: hdwy 3f out: hung rt and rdn ins fnl 2f: continued to hang and chsd wnr jst ins fnl f but nvr any ch* **8/1**
50 **3** *2 3/4* **Expense Claim (IRE)**53 4535 2-9-3 0 JimmyFortune 9 70
(Andrew Balding) *led: rdn and hdd ins fnl 2f: sn no ch w wnr: wknd and lost 2nd jst ins fnl f* **9/2**[3]
4 *6* **Sunley Pride** 2-9-3 0 TonyCulhane 3 55
(Mick Channon) *in rr but in tch: hdwy 3f out: chsd ldrs over 2f out: wknd wl over 1f out* **33/1**
5 *1 3/4* **Shredding (IRE)** 2-9-3 0 WilliamBuick 1 53+
(William Haggas) *s.i.s: in rr: pushed along 3f out: mod prog ins fnl f* **16/1**
2 **6** *4* **Shomberg**85 3483 2-9-3 0 KierenFallon 2 41
(Mark H Tompkins) *chsd ldrs: wkng whn hmpd ins fnl 2f* **8/1**
7 *9* **Impel (IRE)** 2-9-3 0 RichardHughes 4 18
(Richard Hannon) *chsd ldrs: pushed along 3f out: wknd over 2f out* **7/2**[2]

1m 33.75s (6.85) **Going Correction** +0.875s/f (Soft) **7** Ran SP% **111.4**
Speed ratings (Par 95): **95,93,90,83,81 76,66**
Tote Swingers: 1&2 £3.10, 1&3 £2.30, 2&3 £6.70 CSF £13.69 TOTE £2.10: £1.40, £3.40; EX 13.50 Trifecta £37.70 Pool: £764.89 - 14.98 winning units..
Owner Godolphin **Bred** Allevamento Pian Di Neve Srl **Trained** Newmarket, Suffolk

FOCUS
The lower bend was dolled out 6 yards increasing distances by about 8 yards on races using that bend. Jockeys in the first thought that the ground was bordering on heavy, certainly softer than the official description, and the time was 9.55sec slower than standard. This maiden is only in its third year but it went to Workforce in 2009 and last season was won by Dominant, a smart performer for the late Michael Jarvis. Gordon Stakes winner Namibian was sixth 12 months ago. This renewal looked no more than a fairly modest affair on paper, although the winner impressed. The pace was ordinary and the runners came up the middle of the track once into the straight. They finished stretched out in the testing conditions.

NOTEBOOK
Genius Step(IRE) had been a promising third on his debut at Newmarket in May, behind a couple of useful sorts, but had not been on the track since. Cruising up to the long-time leader, he came away for a very comfortable victory. Clearly well at home in this ground, he looks a useful colt but it should be stressed that the opposition was limited. (op 11-10 tchd 13-8)
Okimono, a stablemate of the winner, ran on quite well after edging to his right once first coming under pressure. He is flattered by his proximity to the winner, but this was still a promising debut. His dam was smart over 1m4f and he'll get further than this. (op 14-1)
Expense Claim(IRE) didn't shape badly in a maiden at the big meeting here when last seen. Getting across from the outside stall to make the running, he could only plug on at the same pace once headed. He can run in handicaps now and the return to better ground will suit him. (op 5-1)
Sunley Pride is a half-brother to several winners, including the formerly useful sprinter Resplendent Alpha. After improving from the rear he was no threat to the first three in the last quarter-mile. (op 25-1)
Shredding(IRE) ◆ is bred to come into his own at around 1m4f. He ran green when first asked to pick up but was running on from the back at the end, and connections will be fairly pleased with this introduction. There is better to come in time. (tchd 20-1)
Shomberg, runner-up on his debut at Hamilton in June in a race that has not been working out, had been sidelined by a bout of ringworm and a virus since. Carrying his head rather high, he dropped away very tamely. The ground was a likely excuse.
Impel(IRE) came in for support after Richard Hughes was switched from the withdrawn Juvenal to ride him, but after racing in touch on the outside the colt found nothing. (op 5-1)

6245 R H HALL E B F MAIDEN STKS 1m 1f
2:35 (2:36) (Class 4) 2-Y-O **£4,237** (£1,260; £630; £315) **Stalls** Low

Form RPR
2 **1** **Welcome Gift**26 5447 2-8-12 0 AntiocoMurgia(5) 8 83+
(Mahmood Al Zarooni) *trckd ldrs: led ins fnl 2f: pushed clr over 1f out: easily* **7/4**[1]
00 **2** *10* **Pinseeker (IRE)**42 4906 2-9-3 0 LukeMorris 6 60
(Peter Winkworth) *in rr: rdn after 2f: rdn again 4f out: hdwy fr 3 out: styd on u.p fr 2f out to take wl hld 2nd fnl 120yds* **66/1**
6 **3** *1* **Ctappers**11 5937 2-9-3 0 TonyCulhane 9 58
(Mick Channon) *in rr: drvn and hdwy over 2f out: styd on to take one-pced 3rd fnl 30yds* **66/1**
2 **4** *3/4* **Good Morning Star (IRE)**23 5537 2-8-12 0 SilvestreDeSousa 4 52
(Mark Johnston) *chsd ldrs: rdn and one pce 4f out: sn rallied and led over 2f out: hdd ins fnl 2f: sn no ch w wnr: wknd and lost 2 pls fnl 120yds* **3/1**[2]
5 *hd* **Samba King** 2-9-3 0 AhmedAjtebi 1 56+
(Mahmood Al Zarooni) *in rr: hrd rdn and green over 2f out: styd on to cl on wl-hld plcd horses fnl 120yds* **8/1**[3]
0054 **6** *8* **Next Cry (USA)**19 5668 2-9-3 69 RichardHughes 10 40
(Richard Hannon) *led tl hdd over 2f out: sn rdn and btn* **14/1**
0663 **7** *6* **Foster's Road**16 5783 2-9-0 70 MartinHarley(3) 11 28
(Mick Channon) *chsd ldrs: wnt 2nd briefly 4f out: rdn 3f out: wknd wl over 2f out* **14/1**
00 **8** *1/2* **Topanga Canyon**40 5013 2-9-3 0 JimmyFortune 2 27
(Andrew Balding) *s.i.s: towards rr: hdwy 4f out: rdn 3f out: wknd over 2f out* **10/1**
9 *22* **Gabrial The Prince (IRE)** 2-9-3 0 JamieSpencer 7 —
(David Simcock) *s.i.s: a in rr: t.o* **20/1**
0 **10** *13* **Kaiser Wilhelm (IRE)**13 5851 2-9-3 0 WilliamBuick 3 —
(Paul Cole) *in tch: pushed along and wknd fr 3f out: eased whn no ch fnl f: t.o* **8/1**[3]

2m 4.67s (8.37) **Going Correction** +0.875s/f (Soft) **10** Ran SP% **113.8**
Speed ratings (Par 97): **97,88,87,86,86 79,73,73,53,42**
Tote Swingers: 1&2 £31.70, 1&3 £16.40, 2&3 £42.30 CSF £148.77 TOTE £2.50: £1.40, £9.50, £11.30; EX 158.50 TRIFECTA Not won..
Owner Godolphin **Bred** Darley **Trained** Newmarket, Suffolk

FOCUS
A stiff stamina test for these juveniles, and not many gave their running. Once again the mid-track route was taken. The next four home finished in a heap behind the wide-margin winner, the second and third plugging on from the rear behind rivals who were weakening in the ground. The winner could be worth 10lb more but a cautious view has been taken.

NOTEBOOK
Welcome Gift made it a maiden double for the stable, trouncing his field to win easing down. His superiority was no doubt exaggerated by the conditions, but it's hard to quibble too much with a ten-length win - the victory paid a compliment to Most Improved, the Dewhurst and Racing Post Trophy entry who beat him at Newmarket. The winner, who has no big-race entries, did carry his head a little high, and it will be interesting to see his response when he is required to battle. He stays well and has yet to run on a sound surface. (op 15-8 tchd 2-1)
Pinseeker(IRE) was off the bridle very early and did well to finish where he did on this turf debut. He stays well and is now qualified for handicaps. (op 100-1)
Ctappers was in trouble going up the first hill, dropping to the rear of the field, but was another to stay on past toiling rivals. He should come into his own next year.
Good Morning Star(IRE) represented a yard with a good record in this maiden, taking it with Dordogne last year. Losing her pitch turning in, she rallied to lead briefly and was still in second with half a furlong left, albeit a long way behind the winner. Conditions were against her. (op 9-4)
Samba King, the winner's stablemate, is a half-brother to the high-class Godolphin pair Charnwood Forest and Medaaly. A big colt, he ran green and needed some sharp liveners, but was keeping on at the end and will have learnt from this debut. (op 10-1)
Next Cry(USA) didn't get home after making the running. (op 12-1)
Foster's Road, officially rated 70, was another found out by the heavy ground. (op 16-1)
Topanga Canyon was soundly beaten, but the ground is an excuse and his mark won't suffer for this. He looks an interesting middle-distance handicap prospect for next season. (op 12-1 tchd 9-1)
Gabrial The Prince(IRE) needed two handlers in the paddock. (op 16-1)
Kaiser Wilhelm(IRE) Official explanation: jockey said colt hung right

6246 3663 FIRST FOR FOOD SERVICE STKS (H'CAP) 6f
3:10 (3:10) (Class 4) (0-80,80) 3-Y-O+ **£4,204** (£1,251; £625; £312) **Stalls** High

Form RPR
6261 **1** **Silenzio**8 6022 3-8-13 **74** 6ex RichardHughes 5 83
(Richard Hannon) *trckd ldrs: drvn 2f out: styd on to chal fr 1f out: kpt on u.p to take slt ld fnl 30yds: all out* **7/2**[1]
0000 **2** *shd* **Rash Judgement**26 5434 6-9-1 **74** JamieSpencer 10 83
(Stuart Kittow) *stdd sed: swtchd rt to outside 1/2-way: hdwy 2f out: drvn to chal fr 1f out and stl upsides thrght fnl 120yds: no ex last strides* **9/1**
1132 **3** *1/2* **Night Trade (IRE)**10 5972 4-9-6 **79** LukeMorris 9 86
(Ronald Harris) *chsd ldrs: hrd rdn to ld appr fnl f: kpt slt advantage tl narrowly hdd fnl 30yds: no ex clsng stages* **15/2**
1212 **4** *2* **Interakt**19 5671 4-8-10 **72** HarryBentley(3) 13 73
(Joseph Tuite) *chsd ldrs: drvn to chal over 1f out: hung rt and wknd fnl 120yds* **8/1**
3611 **5** *1/2* **Stonecrabstomorrow (IRE)**13 5858 8-8-5 **66** oh1 ow3 MarkCoumbe(5) 12 68
(Michael Attwater) *in rr: stl last 2f out: hdwy on stands' rail over 1f out: kpt on wl clsng stages: nt rch ldrs* **20/1**
1263 **6** *2 1/2* **Jungle Bay**11 5924 4-9-1 **74** (p) WilliamBuick 2 65
(Jane Chapple-Hyam) *pressed ldrs in centre of crse: chal 2f out: slt ld wl over 1f out: hdd appr fnl f: wknd sn after* **9/2**[2]
1324 **7** *1/2* **Aye Aye Digby (IRE)**22 5587 6-9-7 **80** GeorgeBaker 8 70
(Patrick Chamings) *pressed ldrs: rdn over 2f out: wknd ins fnl f* **10/1**
01-0 **8** *1 1/2* **Mi Regalo**238 302 3-9-3 **78** DavidProbert 7 63
(Andrew Balding) *chsd ldrs: rdn over 2f out: wknd appr fnl f* **22/1**
0450 **9** *1 1/2* **Dream Catcher (FR)**11 5948 3-8-12 **78** JamesRogers(5) 3 58
(David Pinder) *narrow ldr tl hdd wl over 1f out: wknd sn after* **25/1**
-146 **10** *5* **Sharpened Edge**52 4583 5-9-4 **77** CathyGannon 6 41
(Christopher Mason) *blindfold removed marginally late: sn drvn along: outpcd most of way* **20/1**
5302 **11** *2* **Muffraaj**32 5268 3-9-2 **80** JohnFahy(3) 4 38
(David Simcock) *chsd ldrs over 3f* **6/1**[3]
1430 **12** *8* **Alpha Delta Whisky**32 5278 3-9-0 **75** TomQueally 11 7
(John Gallagher) *a outpcd* **25/1**

1m 17.36s (5.16) **Going Correction** +0.90s/f (Soft)
WFA 3 from 4yo+ 2lb **12** Ran SP% **118.2**
Speed ratings (Par 105): **101,100,100,97,96 93,92,90,88,82 79,68**
Tote Swingers: 1&2 £9.30, 1&3 £5.10, 2&3 £15.00 CSF £31.94 CT £223.85 TOTE £4.10: £1.70, £4.10, £2.50; EX 41.10 Trifecta £469.60 Part won. Pool: £634.70 - 0.82 winning units..
Owner White Beech Farm **Bred** Lady Whent **Trained** East Everleigh, Wilts

FOCUS
A fair handicap contested by some in-form sprinters, and it produced a tight finish. This form seems sound enough amongst the principals, with another step up from the winner.

Sharpened Edge Official explanation: jockey said blindfold got stuck in bridle and mare was slowly away

6247 TANQUERAY STKS (LISTED RACE) (REGISTERED AS THE FOUNDATION STAKES) 1m 1f 192y

3:45 (3:45) (Class 1) 3-Y-O+

£17,013 (£6,450; £3,228; £1,608; £807; £405) **Stalls** Low

Form RPR

0136 **1** **Hunter's Light (IRE)**[35] 5182 3-8-8 106 .... TedDurcan 6 116
(Saeed Bin Suroor) *hld up in rr: hdwy 3f out to ld over 2f out: drvn and styd on wl fr over 1f out* **10/1**

5514 **2** 2 1/4 **Fallen Idol**[14] 5829 4-9-0 108 .... WilliamBuick 1 112
(John Gosden) *sn in tch: drvn along over 4f out: rdn and hdwy fr 3f out to chse wnr appr fnl 2f: wandered rt and lft u.p and no imp fnl f* **3/1**[2]

5425 **3** 4 1/2 **Mirror Lake**[34] 5220 4-8-9 100 .... TomQueally 7 98
(Amanda Perrett) *in tch: drvn and styd on fr over 2f out to take 3rd over 1f out but nvr any ch w ldng duo* **9/1**

0106 **4** 2 **Distant Memories (IRE)**[25] 5494 5-9-0 107 .... JamieSpencer 9 99
(Tom Tate) *chsd ldr: rdn over 2f out: sn btn* **16/1**

6011 **5** shd **Prince Siegfried (FR)**[25] 5494 5-9-3 113 .... KierenFallon 4 101
(Saeed Bin Suroor) *chsd ldrs: rdn fr 3f out: wknd 2f out* **7/2**[3]

3214 **6** 1/2 **Opera Gal (IRE)**[11] 5934 4-8-9 101 .... JimmyFortune 2 92
(Andrew Balding) *led tl hdd over 2f out: wknd sn after* **10/1**

0041 **7** 1 **Debussy (IRE)**[11] 5921 5-9-0 110 .... FrankieDettori 8 95
(Mahmood Al Zarooni) *hld up in rr: shkn up and hdwy over 2f out to trck ldrs: sn rdn: fnd nthing and dropped away* **2/1**[1]

2m 12.51s (4.51) **Going Correction** +0.875s/f (Soft)
WFA 3 from 4yo+ 6lb **7** Ran SP% **114.6**
Speed ratings (Par 111): **116,114,110,109,108 108,107**
Tote Swingers: 1&2 £8.20, 1&3 £8.40, 2&3 £5.30 CSF £40.24 TOTE £11.30: £4.30, £2.10; EX 66.50 TRIFECTA Not won..

Owner Godolphin **Bred** Darley **Trained** Newmarket, Suffolk

FOCUS

Twice Over, successful in 2009, is the best recent winner of this Listed event. It was a tight race on adjusted official ratings, with just 5lb between the runners. Given the conditions this is not the strongest form for the grade, and the winning time emphasised how slow the ground was. Saeed Bin Suroor has an outstanding record in this race with six wins since 2003 now. Four of his previous five winners came with favourites, but he was on target with the stable second string here and the outsider of the three Godolphin runners. Hunter's Light posted a 7lb personal best, with the second setting the standard.

NOTEBOOK

Hunter's Light(IRE) won a Listed race at Hamilton before stepping up in grade, finishing third in the Gordon Stakes but disappointing in the Great Voltigeur. Like a number of others he didn't handle the dead going at York, but conditions here were not a problem to him. Held up, he made ground nicely to lead and probably hit the front soon enough, but kept going in good style. He is worth keeping to this trip and he could win again this autumn. (op 12-1)

Fallen Idol was the first of the field to come off the bridle but he stuck on to have his chance. He wandered a little under pressure and this is probably as far as he would want to go. He is likely to head to the sales now.

Mirror Lake, another to disappoint at the Ebor meeting, stuck on for a respectable third without causing the first pair much concern. She now has two wins and three places from five visits to Goodwood. (tchd 10-1)

Distant Memories(IRE) was beaten with 2f to run but kept going to shade fourth. He has winning form in heavy ground and was perhaps a little below par here. (op 12-1)

Prince Siegfried(FR), the better fancied of Bin Suroor's two, carried a 3lb penalty for his win in the Grade 3 Winter Hill Stakes. He disappointed here and could not confirm his Windsor superiority over Distant Memories, but can probably be forgiven this. (op 4-1)

Opera Gal(IRE) always makes the running these days and she held a healthy break on the field at one stage, but they reeled her in comfortably. She ran better in a Group 3 over C&D last time. (op 11-1)

Debussy(IRE), back over what is perhaps his optimum trip and in the first Godolphin colours, was ridden differently and failed to pick up, looking ill at ease in this very soft ground. Frankie Dettori reported that the horse ran flat, and the Stewards ordered Debussy to be routine tested. Official explanation: jockey said horse ran flat (op 5-4 tchd 13-8 and 7-4 in a place)

6248 PIPER CHAMPAGNE STKS (H'CAP) 1m 3f

4:20 (4:20) (Class 4) (0-85,85) 3-Y-O **£4,204** (£1,251; £625; £312) **Stalls** High

Form RPR

5-14 **1** **Sandusky**[131] 2076 3-9-3 81 .... AhmedAjtebi 7 96
(Mahmood Al Zarooni) *hld up towards rr: stdy hdwy fr 3f out to ld wl over 1f out: drvn out fnl f* **15/2**

-022 **2** 2 1/2 **Billy Buttons**[36] 5140 3-9-2 80 .... DavidProbert 1 90
(Andrew Balding) *t.k.h: trckd ldrs: led over 2f out: rdn and hdd wl over 1f out: styd on fnl f but no imp on wnr* **11/4**[1]

3-02 **3** 6 **Estourah (IRE)**[18] 5716 3-9-7 85 ....(vt[1]) FrankieDettori 6 84
(Saeed Bin Suroor) *in tch: hdwy to chse ldrs 1/2-way: fnd little u.p and tk wl hld 3rd fr over 1f out* **7/2**[2]

0414 **4** 2 **Pandorica**[67] 4083 3-8-7 74 .... JohnFahy(3) 4 70
(Clive Cox) *in rr: rdn over 3f out: hung rt u.p fr 2f out: tk mod 4th clsng stages* **5/1**

214 **5** 3/4 **Neumark (GER)**[40] 5020 3-9-2 80 .... TomQueally 2 74
(Sir Henry Cecil) *led: hdd over 2f out: sn hung rt and btn: lost mod 4th clsng stages* **9/2**[3]

1310 **6** 2 1/4 **Highlife Dancer**[12] 5880 3-8-11 78 .... MartinHarley(3) 9 68
(Mick Channon) *rdn over 3f out and sme progres in bhd ldrs: wknd over 2f out* **16/1**

5-04 **7** 8 **Mafeteng**[22] 5585 3-8-5 69 .... MartinLane 3 45
(John Dunlop) *chsd ldrs: rdn 3f out: wknd sn after* **14/1**

623 **8** 16 **Spyder**[24] 5518 3-8-10 74 ....(b) IvaMilickova 8 21
(Jane Chapple-Hyam) *t.k.h: chsd ldrs tl wknd wl over 2f out* **16/1**

2m 35.49s (8.99) **Going Correction** +0.875s/f (Soft) **8** Ran SP% **113.9**
Speed ratings (Par 103): **102,100,95,94,93 92,86,74**
Tote Swingers: 1&2 £5.40, 1&3 £4.00, 2&3 £2.50 CSF £28.26 CT £85.22 TOTE £7.60: £2.40, £1.50, £1.50; EX 37.50 Trifecta £74.30 Pool: £728.69 - 7.25 winning units..

Owner Godolphin **Bred** Genesis Green Stud Ltd **Trained** Newmarket, Suffolk

FOCUS

The field went a steady pace in this fair 3-y-o handicap but even so only the first pair really got home. They came up the middle again. The first two home could be rated 4-5lb higher at face value.This was the fourth winner on the card for Godolphin, spread among both trainers, four jockeys and three different coloured caps.

Neumark(GER) Official explanation: jockey said filly hung left

6249 DISCOVERY FOODS STKS (H'CAP) 1m 4f

4:55 (4:55) (Class 3) (0-90,89) 3-Y-O+ **£6,792** (£2,021; £1,010; £505) **Stalls** High

Form RPR

4-15 **1** **Samsons Son**[40] 4998 7-9-6 83 .... RichardHughes 13 93
(Alan King) *in rr rdn and hdwy fr 3f out: styd on u.p to chal ins fnl f: slt ld fnl 75yds: hld on all out* **16/1**

-166 **2** nk **Tahaamah**[48] 4723 3-8-10 81 ....(t) FrankieDettori 11 91
(Saeed Bin Suroor) *hld up towards rr: hdwy 3f out: led 2f out: rdn and jnd ins fnl f: narrowly hdd fnl 75yds: styd chalng: no ex last strides* **8/1**[3]

16-3 **3** 2 1/4 **Valid Reason**[12] 5888 4-9-3 80 .... ShaneKelly 8 86
(Dean Ivory) *chsd ldr: slt ld but hrd pressed fr 4f out tl hdd 2f out: styd chsng ldrs: kpt on u.p ins fnl f but nt trble ldng duo* **16/1**

6530 **4** 1 3/4 **Time To Work (IRE)**[10] 5966 3-9-0 85 ....(v) JimmyFortune 12 88
(Andrew Balding) *towards rr: hdwy fr 3f out: chsd ldrs over 2f out: styd on same pce u.p fnl f* **10/1**

0040 **5** 1 1/2 **Nave (USA)**[18] 5705 4-9-7 84 .... SilvestreDeSousa 6 85
(Mark Johnston) *chsd ldrs: chal fr 4f out but sn u.str.p: upsides w ldr 2f out: wknd over 1f out* **13/2**[2]

150 **6** 3 3/4 **La Estrella (USA)**[88] 3420 8-9-11 88 .... DaneO'Neill 1 83
(Don Cantillon) *hld up in rr: hdwy over 3f out: drvn and no imp on ldrs and no ch fnl 2f* **20/1**

0431 **7** hd **Yes Chef**[18] 5716 4-9-4 81 .... JamesMillman 14 75
(Rod Millman) *chsd ldrs: rdn 3f out: n.m.r on stands' rail 2f out: wknd sn after* **16/1**

0005 **8** 28 **Big Creek (IRE)**[137] 1883 4-9-12 89 .... WilliamBuick 2 39
(Jeremy Noseda) *in rr: mod prog over 3f out: in tch over 2f out: sn wknd: t.o* **16/1**

111/ **9** 7 **Blimey O'Riley (IRE)**[1089] 6279 6-9-2 79 .... TomQueally 5 17
(Mark H Tompkins) *in rr: mod prog fr 3f out: wknd over 2f out: t.o* **12/1**

6315 **10** 1/2 **Significant Move**[10] 5971 4-9-5 82 .... IanMongan 4 20
(Stuart Kittow) *in rr: hdwy fr 3f out and in tch: wl over 2f out: sn wknd: t.o* **16/1**

101 **11** 1 1/2 **Tameen**[10] 5971 3-8-12 83 6ex .... TadhgO'Shea 9 18
(John Dunlop) *chsd ldrs: wknd qckly over 2f out: t.o* **7/4**[1]

-100 **12** 12 **Dance Tempo**[74] 3867 4-9-6 83 .... GeorgeBaker 3 —
(Hughie Morrison) *in rr: sme hdwy 5f out: wknd over 2f out: t.o* **33/1**

-04 **13** 23 **Kristalette (IRE)**[19] 5693 4-9-5 82 .... AdamKirby 10 —
(Walter Swinburn) *led tl hdd 4f out: wknd fr 3f out: t.o* **16/1**

2m 46.56s (8.16) **Going Correction** +0.875s/f (Soft)
WFA 3 from 4yo+ 8lb **13** Ran SP% **120.6**
Speed ratings (Par 107): **107,106,105,104,103 100,100,81,77,76 75,67,52**
Tote Swingers: 1&2 £26.80, 1&3 £48.10, 2&3 £23.50 CSF £139.97 CT £2103.62 TOTE £18.20: £4.00, £3.00, £4.30; EX 205.60 Trifecta £367.90 Part won. Pool: £497.22 - 0.10 winning units..

Owner M Folan **Bred** John Best **Trained** Barbury Castle, Wilts

FOCUS

Just a reasonable handicap for the grade. After racing under the trees down the far side they came to the stands' side in the straight. The first two home came from the rear. The form seems sound enough amongst the principals.

NOTEBOOK

Samsons Son produced a sustained challenge which got him to the front close home. This was the lightly raced 7-y-o's second win in three starts this term, but following a lesser run last time at Newbury he had been due to be dropped a pound before this. He was found out by an extended 1m5f last time and this is his trip. (op 20-1)

Tahaamah so nearly made it five winners on the day for Godolphin. After taking up the running going best he edged to the rail and was caught near the line. He had been dropped 2lb since his last run and saw out this longer trip well enough. (tchd 17-2)

Valid Reason was unable to lead this time, but he raced prominently and stuck on quite well for third. This was only his second run of the campaign and the return to this trip suited. (tchd 14-1)

Time To Work(IRE) had been found out by 2m last time, but he stays this trip well and he was battling on at the finish here. (op 8-1)

Nave(USA), who became warm in the preliminaries, was another to run creditably after racing up with the pace. He seems to like it here. (op 8-1)

La Estrella(USA) was staying on from the back on this first appearance since June.

Yes Chef didn't stay in the ground.

Significant Move Official explanation: jockey said gelding hung left throughout

Tameen was 4lb well in under the penalty for her C&D win, which came in soft ground, but she seemed to want to hang this time and dropped right away before being eased. The Stewards ordered her to be routine tested.\n Official explanation: jockey said filly hung right (op 15-8 tchd 2-1)

Kristalette(IRE) Official explanation: trainer's rep said filly was unsuited by the soft going

6250 MERBURY CATERING CONSULTANTS APPRENTICE STKS (H'CAP) 5f

5:30 (5:30) (Class 5) (0-75,75) 3-Y-O+ **£2,587** (£770; £384; £192) **Stalls** High

Form RPR

1403 **1** **Mata Hari Blue**[12] 5890 5-8-8 67 ....(t) MatthewLawson(5) 4 76
(John Holt) *trckd ldrs: rdn to go 2nd appr fnl f: r.o wl to ld fnl 75yds: drvn out* **11/4**[1]

5231 **2** 3/4 **Seamus Shindig**[16] 5781 9-9-2 70 .... MartinHarley 6 76
(Henry Candy) *hld up in tch: hdwy over 1f out: styd on fnl f to take 2nd fnl 25yds: nt gng pce to rch wnr* **3/1**[2]

5300 **3** 3/4 **Boogie Waltzer**[12] 5890 4-9-2 70 ....(t) RyanClark 3 73
(Stuart Williams) *led in centre of crse: drvn along 1/2-way: hdd fnl 75yds: wknd into 3rd fnl 25yds* **4/1**[3]

4546 **4** 1 **Even Bolder**[5] 6119 8-9-1 69 .... KierenFox 1 69
(Eric Wheeler) *chsd ldrs: disp 2nd fr 2f out tl wknd 1f out* **11/2**

2132 **5** 12 **Go Nani Go**[21] 5627 5-9-7 75 .... JohnFahy 2 32
(Ed de Giles) *in tch: hdwy and rdn 2f out: wknd over 1f out* **4/1**[3]

0600 **6** 3 1/2 **Dolly Parton (IRE)**[10] 5972 3-8-5 65 ....(v[1]) CharlesBishop(5) 5 9
(John Bridger) *pressed ldrs: rdn 1/2-way: hung rt and wknd 2f out* **20/1**

62.78 secs (4.38) **Going Correction** +0.90s/f (Soft)
WFA 3 from 4yo+ 1lb **6** Ran SP% **111.8**
Speed ratings (Par 103): **100,98,97,96,76 71**
Tote Swingers: 1&2 £2.30, 1&3 £2.20, 2&3 £3.10 CSF £11.20 CT £30.57 TOTE £3.60: £2.10, £1.30; EX 11.90 Trifecta £34.80 Pool: £492.40 - 10.45 winning units..

Owner M J Golding **Bred** R T And Mrs Watson **Trained** Peckleton, Leics

FOCUS

A weak apprentice handicap, in which the field split even though only six ran. The form is rated around the first two.

T/Plt: £209.80 to a £1 stake. Pool of £68,605.00 - 238.70 winning tickets. T/Qpdt: £68.00 to a £1 stake. Pool of £4,137.00 - 45.00 winning tickets. ST

6214

KEMPTON (A.W) (R-H)

Wednesday, September 21

OFFICIAL GOING: Standard

Wind: medium, half against Weather: dry

6251 FREE ENTRY FOR BETDAQ MEMBERS MEDIAN AUCTION MAIDEN STKS 5f (P)

5:50 (5:55) (Class 6) 3-4-Y-0 **£1,617** (£481; £240; £120) **Stalls** Low

Form RPR

35 **1** **Sleep Dance**[8] 6020 3-8-12 0.. CathyGannon 5 59+
(Eve Johnson Houghton) *s.i.s: in rr of main gp: effrt and nt clr run over 1f out: gd hdwy between horses 1f out: led fnl 75yds: sn in command: r.o wl* **5/2**[1]

06 **2** *1 ½* **Glastonberry**[11] 5946 3-8-9 0.. SophieDoyle(3) 3 53
(Geoffrey Deacon) *sn chsng ldr: rdn to ld ent fnl f: drvn and hdd fnl 75yds: no ex* **5/1**[3]

0-5 **3** *nk* **Itum**[8] 6034 4-9-4 0.. SebSanders 9 57
(Christine Dunnett) *dwlt: sn in tch on outer: rdn and hdwy over 1f out: ev ch ins fnl f: styd on same pce fnl 75yds* **11/1**

5454 **4** *1 ¾* **Miakora**[16] 5780 3-8-12 52.. PatCosgrave 4 46
(Michael Quinn) *in tch: rdn and effrt over 1f out: kpt on same pce and no imp ins fnl f* **10/1**

U **5** *nk* **Arowana (IRE)**[109] 2720 3-8-12 56........................ FrankieMcDonald 7 45
(Zoe Davison) *chsd ldrs: rdn and edgd lft bnd jst over 2f out: unable qck u.p over 1f out: one pce and btn fnl f* **25/1**

5-36 **6** *2 ½* **Bint Alakaaber (IRE)**[77] 3747 3-8-12 58........................ NeilCallan 8 36
(J R Jenkins) *led and crossed to rail: rdn over 1f out: hdd ent fnl f: wknd ins fnl f* **3/1**[2]

006 **7** *1* **Grayfriars**[35] 5176 3-9-3 45.. FergusSweeney 2 37
(J R Jenkins) *t.k.h: hld up wl in tch: rdn and unable qck over 1f out: wknd ins fnl f* **20/1**

8 *2* **Dan Donnelly (IRE)** 3-9-3 0.. SteveDrowne 6 30
(Jeremy Gask) *s.i.s: a outpcd in rr: n.d* **11/2**

00 **9** *43* **Avon Rising**[42] 4923 4-9-1 0.. RossAtkinson(3) 1 —
(Derek Shaw) *sn struggling and dropped to last: lost tch 3f out: t.o fnl 2f* **66/1**

60.94 secs (0.44) **Going Correction** -0.075s/f (Stan)
WFA 3 from 4yo 1lb 9 Ran SP% **113.1**
Speed ratings (Par 101): **93,90,90,87,86 82,81,78,9**
Tote Swingers: 1&2 £3.70, 1&3 £4.40, 2&3 £11.20 CSF £14.61 TOTE £3.40: £1.30, £2.20, £3.80; EX 18.80 Trifecta £113.00.
Owner David Redvers **Bred** Redmyre Bloodstock And Stuart McPhee **Trained** Blewbury, Oxon

FOCUS

A typically weak sprint maiden for the time of year.

6252 BETDAQ MULTIPLES MAIDEN STKS 5f (P)

6:20 (6:22) (Class 5) 2-Y-0 **£2,264** (£673; £336; £168) **Stalls** Low

Form RPR

52 **1** **Planet I T (IRE)**[14] 5834 2-9-3 0.. NeilCallan 8 80+
(Mark Usher) *chsd ldng pair: swtchd lft over 1f out: rdn to chse ldr 1f out: qcknd to ld fnl 100yds: sn in command: readily* **10/3**[2]

232 **2** *2* **Lupo D'Oro (IRE)**[7] 6058 2-9-3 74.. SteveDrowne 10 72
(John Best) *chsd ldr tl pushed ahd jst over 1f out: rdn fnl f: hdd fnl 100yds: sn outpcd and no ch w wnr: kpt on for clr 2nd* **2/1**[1]

00 **3** *4 ½* **Kaylee**[26] 5424 2-8-12 0.. PatCosgrave 3 52+
(Gary Moore) *in tch: hmpd bnd 4f out: rdn and effrt wl over 1f out: outpcd by ldng pair ent fnl f: no ch but plugged on to go 3rd ins fnl f* **20/1**

6422 **4** *¾* **Meloneras**[14] 5833 2-8-12 70.. TomMcLaughlin 1 48
(Rod Millman) *sn bustled along to ld: rdn wl over 1f out: hdd jst over 1f out: sn outpcd: wknd ins fnl f* **7/2**[3]

6403 **5** *nk* **The Name Is Don (IRE)**[21] 5625 2-9-3 64................ FergusSweeney 9 52
(Mark Gillard) *taken down early: chsd ldrs: rdn and unable qck wl over 1f out: outpcd and wl btn 1f out: plugged on same pce fnl f* **10/1**

6 *2* **Invincible Beauty (IRE)** 2-8-12 0.. MarkLawson 7 40
(Seamus Durack) *s.i.s: a towards rr: sme modest late hdwy: n.d* **33/1**

0 **7** *3 ¼* **Electric Daydream (IRE)**[30] 5323 2-8-12 0........................ JamesDoyle 5 28
(J S Moore) *hld up in tch: hung lft bnd 4f out: struggling 1/2-way: sn wknd* **66/1**

8 *½* **Meet Joe Black (IRE)** 2-9-3 0.. CathyGannon 2 31
(David Evans) *s.i.s: a outpcd in rr* **14/1**

9 *7* **Athenian (IRE)** 2-8-12 0.. SebSanders 11 —
(Sir Mark Prescott Bt) *v.s.a: sn rdn and immediately outpcd in last: t.o 1/2-way: no ch but styd on ins fnl f* **8/1**

10 *6* **Clouds Of Glory** 2-8-9 0.. HarryBentley(3) 4 —
(Ron Hodges) *in tch: hung bdly lft and v wd bnd 3f out: sn dropped out and t.o fnl 2f* **100/1**

60.44 secs (-0.06) **Going Correction** -0.075s/f (Stan) 10 Ran SP% **115.7**
Speed ratings (Par 95): **97,93,86,85,84 81,76,75,64,54**
Tote Swingers: 1&2 £2.80, 1&3 £9.40, 2&3 £5.40 CSF £10.04 TOTE £4.70: £1.60, £1.10, £6.00; EX 14.70 Trifecta £197.70.
Owner High Five Racing **Bred** Miss Anne Ormsby **Trained** Upper Lambourn, Berks
■ Stewards' Enquiry : Neil Callan one-day ban: careless riding (Oct 5)

FOCUS

A moderate sprint maiden for juveniles. There was a solid pace on and the first pair dominated from the furlong marker. It was a quicker winning time than the preceding C&D maiden for older horses. The form could be rated up to 7lb better.

NOTEBOOK

Planet I T(IRE) got off the mark at the third attempt under a straightforward ride. He was never far away and allowed the two leaders to take each other on up front. Neil Callan asked him to win the race half a furlong out and he was comfortably on top at the finish. Racing prominently back down at this trip proved ideal for him and he's open to some more improvement, but the handicapper will probably introduce him into nurseries off a mark in the high 70s at least. (op 6-1 tchd 13-2)

Lupo D'Oro(IRE)'s second at Sandown a week earlier was boosted when the winner followed up earlier this week and he was the one to beat back in a maiden. Her pinged out to negate his poor draw and travelled kindly into the lead nearing the final furlong. His early exertions told once the winner hit top gear and, finishing a clear second-best, this wasn't a bad effort in the circumstances. A current mark of 74 is not going to make his life simple, though. (tchd 15-8 and 9-4)

Kaylee was doing her best work towards the finish and posted a career best. She can now enter nurseries and returning to 6f in that sphere should prove best. (op 16-1)

Meloneras, a runner-up the last twice, including over C&D last time out, had the plum draw and set out to make all. She was hassled by the runner-up, however, and disappointingly fell in a hole nearing the final furlong. (op 9-4 tchd 2-1)

The Name Is Don(IRE) had to race wide throughout and was undone by this drop back a furlong. (tchd 12-1)

Electric Daydream(IRE) Official explanation: jockey said filly hung left

Clouds Of Glory Official explanation: jockey said filly hung left

6253 BACK OR LAY AT BETDAQ.COM H'CAP 1m 2f (P)

6:50 (6:51) (Class 6) (0-60,60) 3-Y-0 **£1,617** (£481; £240; £120) **Stalls** Low

Form RPR

01U4 **1** **Librettela**[14] 5838 3-8-12 54.. HarryBentley(3) 9 62
(Alan Jarvis) *chsd ldrs: jnd ldr travelling wl over 2f out: led 2f out: rdn and fnd ex over 1f out: r.o wl fnl f* **6/1**[2]

3022 **2** *1* **Rowan Ridge**[7] 6052 3-9-4 57..(v) PatCosgrave 5 63
(Jim Boyle) *in tch in midfield: hdwy to chse wnr 2f out: sn rdn and ev ch: unable qck and styd on same pce ins fnl f* **9/2**[1]

6341 **3** *¾* **Appyjack**[14] 5832 3-9-1 54.. NeilCallan 6 59
(Tony Carroll) *chsd ldrs: shuffled bk and in midfield 1/2-way: rdn and hdwy over 2f out: chsd ldng pair u.p over 1f out: kpt on same pce ins fnl f* **9/2**[1]

401 **4** *¾* **Harry Lime**[7] 6067 3-9-6 59 6ex.. CathyGannon 3 62+
(Chris Dwyer) *bhd: hdwy 4f out: nt clr run and hmpd wl over 1f out: hdwy u.p over 1f out: styd on strly ins fnl f: nt rch ldrs* **8/1**

6450 **5** *nse* **Tamara Bay**[21] 5630 3-9-5 58.. JamieSpencer 14 61
(William Haggas) *led tl over 8f out: chsd ldr after tl over 2f out: drvn and styd on same pce fr over 1f out* **7/1**[3]

640 **6** *1 ¼* **Beckfield Dancer**[45] 4826 3-8-11 50.. SaleemGolam 11 50
(Stuart Williams) *in tch on outer: effrt and wd bnd 2f out: kpt on same pce u.p fr over 1f out* **66/1**

30-0 **7** *1* **Pursuing**[16] 5792 3-9-2 55.. SilvestreDeSousa 4 53
(Nigel Tinkler) *stdd s: t.k.h: hld up in rr: swtchd wd and hdwy over 1f out: kpt on but nvr able to chal* **10/1**

0440 **8** *½* **Sir Randolf (IRE)**[14] 5832 3-9-0 53..(t) JamesDoyle 8 50
(Sylvester Kirk) *stdd s: hld up in last trio: effrt whn hmpd and pushed rt wl over 1f out: kpt on ins fnl f: nvr able to chal* **18/1**

6600 **9** *7* **Charlie Fable (IRE)**[45] 4822 3-9-7 60.. SteveDrowne 1 43
(Hughie Morrison) *chsd ldrs: shuffled bk into midfield 3f out: effrt and rdn on inner wl over 1f out: wknd ent fnl f* **12/1**

0405 **10** *1 ¾* **Another Whisper (IRE)**[13] 5845 3-9-4 60........................ SeanLevey(3) 13 40
(Richard Hannon) *in tch: hdwy on outer to chse ldrs 4f out: rdn and struggling ent fnl 2f: wknd wl over 1f out* **15/2**

3410 **11** *3* **Lady On Top (IRE)**[106] 2792 3-9-0 53........................ FrankieMcDonald 2 27
(Nerys Dutfield) *towards rr: pushed along 1/2-way: rdn and wknd over 2f out* **40/1**

650 **12** *8* **Khaki (IRE)**[43] 4888 3-9-3 56.. KierenFallon 10 14
(David Evans) *t.k.h: chsd ldrs tl hdwy to ld over 5f out: hdd 2f out: wknd over 1f out: eased whn bhd wl ins fnl f* **25/1**

2m 7.95s (-0.05) **Going Correction** -0.075s/f (Stan) 12 Ran SP% **115.8**
Speed ratings (Par 99): **97,96,95,95,94 93,93,92,87,85 83,76**
Tote Swingers: 1&2 £6.10, 1&3 £5.30, 2&3 £3.50 CSF £31.88 CT £133.55 TOTE £7.40: £2.70, £1.60, £1.80; EX 37.40 Trifecta £170.60.
Owner Jarvis Associates **Bred** L Dettori **Trained** Twyford, Bucks

FOCUS

This ordinary 3yo handicap was run at an average pace and it proved hard to make up sufficient ground from off the pace.

Khaki(IRE) Official explanation: jockey said filly hung badly left

6254 BETDAQ MOBILE APPS H'CAP 1m 2f (P)

7:20 (7:21) (Class 5) (0-75,75) 3-Y-0+ **£2,264** (£673; £336; £168) **Stalls** Low

Form RPR

0541 **1** **Sit Tight**[21] 5630 3-9-3 74.. GeorgeBaker 3 83
(Chris Wall) *chsd ldrs: chsd ldr jst over 2f out: rdn clr w runner-up and ev ch ent fnl f: led fnl 50yds: styd on* **2/1**[1]

5404 **2** *hd* **Classically (IRE)**[9] 6005 5-9-7 72..(e) SteveDrowne 4 81
(Peter Hedger) *led after 1f: rdn and clr w wnr ent fnl f: battled on wl tl hdd and no ex fnl 50yds* **11/1**

1110 **3** *2* **Stand Guard**[17] 5757 7-9-8 73.. AdamKirby 10 78+
(Noel Quinlan) *hld up towards rr: effrt and nt clr run wl over 1f out: swtchd lft over 1f out: r.o strly ins fnl f: nt rch ldrs* **12/1**

120 **4** *hd* **Mauritino (GER)**[45] 4825 7-9-10 75.. JimCrowley 1 80
(Jonjo O'Neill) *hld up in tch: effrt to chse ldng pair wl over 1f out: drvn and unable qck over 1f out: styd on same pce ins fnl f* **12/1**

0060 **5** *1 ½* **Sohcahtoa (IRE)**[12] 5893 5-9-5 73.. SeanLevey(3) 5 75
(Robert Mills) *in tch: chsd ldrs 4f out: rdn and unable qck over 2f out: kpt on same pce u.p fr over 1f out* **20/1**

-005 **6** *1 ¾* **Botanist**[23] 5547 4-9-6 71..(t) StevieDonohoe 9 69
(Tobias B P Coles) *hld up in last trio: c wd and effrt wl over 1f out: styd on fnl f: nvr able to chal* **25/1**

-004 **7** *nk* **Tenessee**[18] 5716 4-9-10 75.. LukeMorris 7 73
(Peter Makin) *chsd ldrs: rdn and unable qck over 2f out: one pce and no threat to ldrs fr over 1f out* **4/1**[2]

-130 **8** *hd* **Futurism**[20] 5653 3-8-12 72.. KieranO'Neill(3) 14 69
(Richard Hannon) *in tch in midfield: pushed along 4f out: no imp u.p whn edgd rt ent fnl f: one pce after* **25/1**

1121 **9** *2* **Eagle Nebula**[13] 5866 7-9-9 74.. IanMongan 12 67+
(Brett Johnson) *sn detached in last and niggled along: hdwy on inner over 1f out: running on but stl plenty to do to catch up whn nt clr run and snatched up 1f out: nt rcvr and n.d after* **8/1**[3]

60-6 **10** *3 ¾* **Shalambar (IRE)**[142] 1775 5-9-0 65.. NeilCallan 13 51
(Tony Carroll) *hld up in last trio: n.d* **33/1**

5133 **11** *¾* **Point Du Jour (FR)**[14] 5835 3-8-13 70.. JamesDoyle 8 54
(Ian Wood) *chsd ldrs: rdn over 2f out: wknd u.p over 1f out: fdd fnl f* **8/1**[3]

1300 **12** *8* **Mountrath**[91] 3285 4-9-2 70..(v) PatCosgrave 6 35
(Gary Moore) *t.k.h: led for 1f: styd upsides ldr tl over 2f out: wknd u.p over 1f out* **25/1**

13 *9* **Maimonides**[360] 5-9-7 72.. JamieSpencer 2 22
(Ed Dunlop) *in tch in midfield: losing pl and towards rr whn pushed lft and hmpd over 1f out: no ch after and eased ins fnl f* **16/1**

2m 6.50s (-1.50) **Going Correction** -0.075s/f (Stan)
WFA 3 from 4yo+ 6lb 13 Ran SP% **124.4**
Speed ratings (Par 103): **103,102,101,101,99 98,98,98,96,93 92,86,79**
Tote Swingers: 1&2 £9.00, 1&3 £9.10, 2&3 £12.50 CSF £24.84 CT £227.65 TOTE £3.20: £1.30, £4.30, £5.00; EX 40.90 Trifecta £336.30.
Owner Des Thurlby **Bred** Mrs D O Joly **Trained** Newmarket, Suffolk

FOCUS

A tight handicap and not bad fare for the class. It was another race where it paid to race handy and the first pair went clear nearing the final furlong.

Stand Guard Official explanation: jockey said gelding hung right

Eagle Nebula Official explanation: jockey said gelding was denied a clear run

Point Du Jour(FR) Official explanation: jockey said gelding ran too free

6255 TFM NETWORKS H'CAP 1m 4f (P)
7:50 (7:52) (Class 5) (0-70,70) 3-Y-O **£2,264** (£673; £336; £168) **Stalls** Centre

Form RPR
2653 **1** **Battery Power**[42] 4932 3-9-2 **65**.................................. KierenFallon 8 77
(Mark H Tompkins) *t.k.h early: hld up in midfield: rdn and hdwy to ld jst over 1f out: sn clr and in command fnl f: rdn out* **8/1**
3055 **2** *6* **Warneford**[14] 5837 3-9-6 **69**...................................(b) MartinDwyer 4 71
(Brian Meehan) *rdn along early: chsd ldr after 1f tl led over 3f out: rdn jst over 2f out: hdd jst over 1f out: immediately btn: plugged on to hold 2nd fnl f* **13/2**
620 **3** *1* **Viva Diva**[21] 5629 3-9-7 **70**................................... TedDurcan 7 71
(David Lanigan) *in tch towards rr of main gp: clsd and nt clr run 3f out: effrt u.p on inner jst over 2f out: no ch w wnr and plugged on same pce fnl f* **5/1**[2]
4-32 **4** *3/4* **Waltzing Cat (USA)**[14] 5838 3-9-3 **66**........................ SebSanders 3 66
(Sir Mark Prescott Bt) *urged along leaving stalls: chsd ldr for 1f: rdn and qcknd jst over 2f out: outpcd by wnr and btn 1f out: one pce after* **15/8**[1]
6432 **5** *nk* **Convention**[10] 5964 3-9-7 **70**.............................. JamieSpencer 1 69
(Ed Dunlop) *in tch: rdn and effrt 3f out: outpcd by wnr and wl btn fr over 1f out* **6/1**[3]
12U5 **6** *4 1/2* **Peira**[16] 5782 3-9-3 **66**.. LukeMorris 5 58
(Jane Chapple-Hyam) *chsd ldrs: drvn and unable qck 3f out: wknd 2f out* **9/1**
0350 **7** *1 1/4* **Tagansky**[13] 5856 3-9-4 **67**............................ EddieCreighton 10 57
(Simon Dow) *stdd s: t.k.h: hld up in rr: rdn and wknd over 2f out: wl btn and hung rt 2f out* **40/1**
5-06 **8** *2 1/2* **Cyber Star**[20] 5639 3-8-11 **60**....................................[1] JackMitchell 9 46
(James Fanshawe) *chsd ldrs: rdn and dropped out rapidly 4f out: wl btn fnl 3f* **20/1**
03F0 **9** *1/2* **Steely**[15] 5816 3-9-2 **65**..................................... SteveDrowne 2 50
(Jim Best) *sn pushed along in rr: nvr on terms* **50/1**
1112 **10** *2 3/4* **Tegan (IRE)**[19] 5665 3-9-2 **68**.......................... KieranO'Neill(3) 6 49
(Richard Hannon) *led tl over 3f out: wknd u.p wl over 2f out* **10/1**

2m 32.23s (-2.27) **Going Correction** -0.075s/f (Stan) **10** Ran SP% **118.4**
Speed ratings (Par 101): **104,100,99,98,98 95,94,93,92,90**
Tote Swingers: 1&2 £7.00, 1&3 £16.80, 2&3 £5.80 CSF £59.03 CT £290.93 TOTE £8.40: £2.50, £1.40, £2.10; EX 76.40.
Owner H-Squared Electronics Ltd **Bred** Pollards Stables **Trained** Newmarket, Suffolk
FOCUS
An ordinary 3yo handicap, run at a fair enough pace.

6256 SKYSPORTS.COM RACING FILLIES' H'CAP 7f (P)
8:20 (8:21) (Class 4) (0-85,80) 3-Y-O+ **£4,075** (£1,212; £606; £303) **Stalls** Low

Form RPR
5421 **1** **Eclipseoftheheart**[21] 5633 3-8-13 **75**...................... KierenFallon 1 85+
(James Fanshawe) *in tch in main gp: rdn and hdwy to chse clr ldr jst over 2f out: clsd and swtchd lft 1f out: drvn and styd on to ld wl ins fnl f* **11/4**[2]
45-1 **2** *3/4* **Port Hollow**[49] 4663 3-9-1 **77**............................. MichaelHills 2 85
(Charles Hills) *racd freely: led and sn clr: rdn wl over 1f out: drvn ent fnl f: hdd and no ex wl ins fnl f* **9/4**[1]
3354 **3** *3/4* **Chevise (IRE)**[9] 6003 3-9-2 **78**.......................... MatthewDavies 5 84
(Steve Woodman) *racd in midfield in main gp: rdn and effrt to chse ldrs 2f out: clsd u.p and pressed ldrs ins fnl f: one pce fnl 100yds* **12/1**
6303 **4** *1 1/2* **Sakhee's Pearl**[28] 5383 5-9-3 **76**...............................(b) IanMongan 7 79
(Jo Crowley) *racd in midfield on outer: hdwy over 2f out: kpt on u.p ins fnl f: nt rch ldrs* **9/2**[3]
05 **5** *1/2* **Chaussini**[19] 5671 4-8-11 **70**............................... JamieSpencer 10 72
(James Toller) *stdd and dropped in bhd after s: swtchd to outer after 1f: rdn and hdwy ent fnl f: r.o: nvr able to chal* **25/1**
0252 **6** *2 1/4* **Barathea Dancer (IRE)**[9] 5999 3-9-0 **76**.........................(t) NeilCallan 9 71
(Roger Teal) *chsd clr ldr tl jst over 2f out: unable qck and no prog fr over 1f out* **16/1**
6315 **7** *3/4* **Requisite**[11] 5948 6-9-3 **76**.......................................(b) JamesDoyle 3 69
(Ian Wood) *restless in stalls: racd in midfield in main gp: effrt u.p jst over 2f out: kpt on but no imp fr over 1f out* **9/1**
1000- **8** *4 1/2* **My Best Bet**[335] 6430 5-9-5 78 AdamKirby 8 59
(Derek Shaw) *restless in stalls: stdd and dropped in bhd after s: hld up in rr: rdn and no prog 2f out: n.d* **33/1**
10-0 **9** *12* **Days Of Summer (IRE)**[124] 2255 3-9-1 **77**.................... JimCrowley 11 25
(Ralph Beckett) *prom in main gp: hemmed in and lost pl over 2f out: dropped to rr and no ch after: eased ins fnl f* **25/1**
300 **10** *21* **Primo Lady**[22] 5581 3-9-2 **78**...............................(e[1]) DavidProbert 4 —
(Gay Kelleway) *sn pushed along and nvr gng wl: dropped to rr after 2f: lost tch over 2f out: t.o* **20/1**

1m 25.05s (-0.95) **Going Correction** -0.075s/f (Stan)
WFA 3 from 4yo+ 3lb **10** Ran SP% **114.6**
Speed ratings (Par 102): **102,101,100,98,98 95,94,89,75,51**
Tote Swingers: 1&2 £1.90, 1&3 £8.90, 2&3 £9.70 CSF £8.62 CT £60.62 TOTE £5.60: £1.20, £1.50, £2.80; EX 9.20 Trifecta £189.00.
Owner Landseer Racing **Bred** B Smith & Miss I Williams **Trained** Newmarket, Suffolk
FOCUS
A fair handicap, run at a good pace and the form is sound.

6257 RACING@SKYSPORTS.COM H'CAP (DIV I) 6f (P)
8:50 (8:52) (Class 6) (0-65,65) 3-Y-O+ **£1,617** (£481; £240; £120) **Stalls** Low

Form RPR
0005 **1** **Micky P**[15] 5803 4-9-2 **60**......................................(v) SaleemGolam 7 69
(Stuart Williams) *hld up in tch: hdwy jst over 2f out: rdn and chal over 1f out: led jst ins fnl f: r.o wl* **11/4**[1]
-5R5 **2** *1* **Timeteam (IRE)**[11] 5924 5-9-7 **65**.............................. LukeMorris 8 71
(Alan Bailey) *s.i.s: bhd: rdn and hdwy on inner jst over 2f out: r.o u.p ins fnl f: snatched 2nd on post* **7/2**[2]
6544 **3** *nse* **Catalinas Diamond (IRE)**[13] 5846 3-8-13 **59**............... SteveDrowne 5 65
(Pat Murphy) *chsd ldrs: rdn and qcknd to ld 2f out: hrd pressed over 1f out: hdd jst ins fnl f: styd on same pce fnl 100yds: lost 2nd on post* **7/1**
1050 **4** *hd* **Silvee**[24] 5513 4-8-11 **55**... NeilChalmers 3 60
(John Bridger) *in tch in last trio: rdn and effrt to chse ldrs over 1f out: kpt on u.p fnl f* **10/1**
0054 **5** *1 1/2* **Brandywell Boy (IRE)**[7] 6056 8-9-4 **62**................. SilvestreDeSousa 6 62
(Dominic Ffrench Davis) *dwlt: in tch in last pair: rdn and effrt whn swtchd lft jst over 2f out: kpt on ins fnl f but nvr gng pce to rch ldrs* **5/1**[3]
2-03 **6** *3/4* **River Bounty**[39] 5037 6-8-4 **51** oh1........................... HarryBentley(3) 10 49
(Alan Jarvis) *chsd ldr: rdn and unable qck ent fnl 2f: styd on same pce fr over 1f out* **6/1**
53 **7** *7* **Acclamatory**[19] 5670 3-8-5 **51** oh3...................................(t) DavidProbert 1 27
(Stuart Williams) *led: rdn wl over 2f out: hdd and unable qck 2f out: wknd over 1f out: eased wl ins fnl f* **9/1**
565 **8** *1 1/4* **Demoiselle Bond**[9] 5995 3-8-5 **51** oh3..................(e[1]) RichardThomas 9 23
(Lydia Richards) *t.k.h: in tch in midfield on outer: rdn and struggling over 2f out: wknd wl over 1f out* **40/1**

1m 12.45s (-0.65) **Going Correction** -0.075s/f (Stan)
WFA 3 from 4yo+ 2lb **8** Ran SP% **113.9**
Speed ratings (Par 101): **101,99,99,99,97 96,87,85**
Tote Swingers: 1&2 £3.80, 1&3 £4.80, 2&3 £5.50 CSF £12.33 CT £58.99 TOTE £5.00: £1.30, £1.20, £1.70; EX 12.90 Trifecta £84.90.
Owner O Pointing **Bred** O Pointing **Trained** Newmarket, Suffolk
FOCUS
A weak sprint handicap, run at a fair pace.
Timeteam(IRE) Official explanation: jockey said blindfold became caught in bridle and gelding was slowly away

6258 RACING@SKYSPORTS.COM H'CAP (DIV II) 6f (P)
9:20 (9:20) (Class 6) (0-65,65) 3-Y-O+ **£1,617** (£481; £240; £120) **Stalls** Low

Form RPR
0030 **1** **One Cool Chick**[23] 5542 3-8-5 **51** oh2........................ NeilChalmers 8 60
(John Bridger) *dwlt: t.k.h: hld up in last trio: effrt on outer 2f out: rdn and hdwy over 1f out: led fnl 100yds: r.o wl* **14/1**
4010 **2** *1* **The Name Is Frank**[11] 5914 6-8-13 **57**....................(t) FergusSweeney 4 63
(Mark Gillard) *led: rdn ent fnl 2f: drvn over 1f out: hdd and one pce fnl 100yds* **11/4**[1]
2646 **3** *2 1/2* **Patch Patch**[22] 5600 4-9-2 **60**...(v) AdamKirby 2 58
(Derek Shaw) *t.k.h: chsd ldrs: rdn and unable qck over 2f out: rallied u.p and chsd ldr over 1f out: no ex and btn ins fnl f: wknd fnl 75yds* **6/1**
3040 **4** *nse* **Jemimaville (IRE)**[9] 5996 4-8-7 **51** oh6............................ LukeMorris 10 49
(Giles Bravery) *hld up in tch in last pair: rdn and effrt wl over 1f out: kpt on u.p ins fnl f: nt rch ldrs* **16/1**
0000 **5** *shd* **Fivefold (USA)**[14] 5836 4-9-4 **62**..............................(b[1]) J-PGuillambert 9 60
(John Akehurst) *chsd ldr: rdn and nt qckn jst over 2f out: styd on same pce u.p fr over 1f out* **4/1**[2]
-430 **6** *3/4* **Cara Carmela**[115] 2524 3-8-5 **51** oh3................................ SaleemGolam 5 46
(Stuart Williams) *chsd ldrs: rdn jst over 2f out: wknd ent fnl f* **10/1**
0034 **7** *1 3/4* **Premier League**[22] 5600 4-8-13 **57**............................(p) RoystonFfrench 3 47
(Julia Feilden) *in tch in last pair: effrt u.p 2f out: no imp over 1f out* **9/2**[3]
4050 **8** *nse* **Here To Eternity (USA)**[15] 5803 3-9-5 **65**...................... JackMitchell 1 54
(Peter Chapple-Hyam) *hld up in tch: effrt on inner and rdn jst over 2f out: chsd ldrs and drvn over 1f out: no prog 1f out: wknd ins fnl f* **6/1**

1m 12.73s (-0.37) **Going Correction** -0.075s/f (Stan)
WFA 3 from 4yo+ 2lb **8** Ran SP% **115.1**
Speed ratings (Par 101): **99,97,94,94,94 93,90,90**
Tote Swingers: 1&2 £2.30, 1&3 £14.40, 2&3 £7.10 CSF £52.96 CT £265.54 TOTE £22.00: £3.20, £1.10, £3.00; EX 42.80 Trifecta £169.10.
Owner Mr & Mrs K Finch **Bred** Ms Jon Horley And Bishopswood Bloodstock **Trained** Liphook, Hants
FOCUS
The second division of the weak 6f handicap. It was run at a sound pace and there was a bunched finish.
T/Plt: £86.70 to a £1 stake. Pool of £55,088.00 - 463.52 winning tickets. T/Qpdt: £41.20 to a £1 stake. Pool of £6,510.00 - 116.70 winning tickets. SP

5645 REDCAR (L-H)
Wednesday, September 21

OFFICIAL GOING: Good to firm (9.2)
Wind: Strong, half-behind Weather: fine but very windy, becoming overcast, rain race 4 onwards

6259 BRITISH STALLION STUDS SUPPORTING BRITISH RACING E B F MAIDEN STKS 7f
2:15 (2:15) (Class 5) 2-Y-O **£2,975** (£885; £442; £221) **Stalls** Centre

Form RPR
5 **1** **Lawn Jamil (USA)**[19] 5681 2-9-3 0................................ RichardHills 5 73+
(Charles Hills) *trckd ldrs: swtchd rt and hdwy over 2f out: led wl over 1f out: rdn and hung lft ins fnl f: jst hld on* **13/8**[1]
0 **2** *nse* **Silver Blaze**[23] 5548 2-9-3 0..................................... PJMcDonald 3 73+
(Alan Swinbank) *trckd ldrs: hdwy and cl up 3f out: rdn wl over 1f out: kpt on u.p fnl f: jst hld* **5/1**[3]
60 **3** *4 1/2* **Sabhan (IRE)**[16] 5786 2-9-3 0................................. RobertWinston 9 61
(Geoffrey Harker) *hld up towards rr: hdwy over 2f out: rdn to chse ldrs over 1f out: kpt on same pce fnl f* **10/1**
0 **4** *1 3/4* **Claretintheblood (IRE)**[27] 5398 2-9-3 0......................... DavidNolan 2 56
(Richard Fahey) *led: rdn along over 2f out: hdd wl over 1f out: grad wknd* **20/1**
5 *1 1/2* **Ukrainian (IRE)** 2-9-3 0.. JoeFanning 6 53
(Mark Johnston) *prom: pushed along 3f out: rdn over 2f out and grad wknd* **9/2**[2]
5 **6** *1/2* **Dance For Georgie**[62] 4232 2-8-12 0............................ PhillipMakin 1 46
(Ben Haslam) *hld up in rr: hdwy over 2f out: sn rdn and no imp fnl f* **16/1**
60 **7** *1/2* **Fine Altomis**[23] 5548 2-9-3 0.................................... TonyHamilton 8 50
(Michael Dods) *chsd ldrs: rdn along wl over 2f out: sn wknd* **20/1**
0 **8** *1* **Night Flash (GER)**[117] 2460 2-9-3 0............................ FrederikTylicki 10 47
(James Given) *a towards rr* **40/1**
9 *2* **Cone Donkey (IRE)** 2-8-12 0.. TomEaves 11 37
(Bryan Smart) *in tch on outer: chsd ldrs 1/2-way: sn rdn and wknd over 2f out* **12/1**
10 *27* **Master Chipper** 2-9-0 0.. LeeTopliss(3) 7 —
(Michael Dods) *sn outpcd and bhd: t.o fnl 3f* **28/1**

1m 23.25s (-1.25) **Going Correction** -0.325s/f (Firm) **10** Ran SP% **111.0**
Speed ratings (Par 95): **94,93,88,86,85 84,83,82,80,49**
Tote Swingers: 1&2 £1.90, 1&3 £4.20, 2&3 £8.70 CSF £8.31 TOTE £2.20: £1.10, £1.70, £2.60; EX 8.40.
Owner Hamdan Al Maktoum **Bred** Shadwell Farm LLC **Trained** Lambourn, Berks
■ Stewards' Enquiry : Tony Hamilton two-day ban: used whip with excessive frequency (Oct 5-6)
FOCUS
The front pair drew clear in what was no more than an ordinary maiden. They can improve on this fair form.

NOTEBOOK

Lawn Jamil(USA), given a gentle introduction having run green over 6f at Haydock earlier in the month, looked a certain improver with the experience behind him, especially over the extra furlong, but ultimately it was very hard work. He'd proven uneasy in the market beforehand and is clearly no star, but should have more to offer when sent handicapping, with 1m and more likely to suit on breeding. (op Evens tchd 7-4 in a place)

Silver Blaze, possibly unsuited by soft ground when only seventh on debut, showed much-improved form switched to a faster surface, staying on strongly to lose out in a head-bobber. Clear of the third, he ought to be suited by 1m and can win something similar. (op 15-2)

Sabhan(IRE) bounced back to form returned to this faster surface and looks an interesting sort for handicaps. (op 8-1 tchd 7-1)

Claretintheblood(IRE) improved markedly on his debut effort and should prove just as effective back at 6f for the time being. (op 33-1)

Ukrainian(IRE) cost 120,000gns as a yearling and looks to have the necessary scope to improve on this debut effort. (op 5-1)

6260 HOLD YOUR CHRISTMAS PARTY HERE NURSERY — 1m

2:50 (2:51) (Class 6) (0-65,71) 2-Y-O — **£1,617** (£481; £240; £120) **Stalls** Centre

Form — RPR

6451 **1** **Fiction Or Fact (IRE)**[5] 6132 2-9-8 **71** 6ex............(p) BrianToomey(5) 11 — 79
(Kevin Ryan) *mid-div: hdwy over 2f out: chsd ldr last 100yds: styd on wl to ld towards fin* **9/1**[3]

0050 **2** ½ **Bedlam**[32] 5287 2-9-4 **62**...........................(b¹) DavidAllan 4 — 69
(Tim Easterby) *led: edgd lft fnl f: hdd cl home* **10/1**

4550 **3** 1 ¾ **Spoken Words**[14] 5817 2-8-10 **54**............ FrederikTylicki 8 — 57
(Hugh McWilliams) *chsd ldrs: hung lft 2f out: sn wknd* **25/1**

664 **4** ¾ **Bathwick Street**[23] 5536 2-8-9 **58**............ MatthewCosham(5) 2 — 59
(David Evans) *chsd ldrs: kpt on same pce fnl 2f* **11/1**

0344 **5** 1 ¾ **Doctor Banner**[6] 6101 2-9-1 **59**.....................(v¹) ChrisCatlin 12 — 56
(Mick Channon) *mid-div: kpt on fnl 2f: nvr nr to chal* **12/1**

4U63 **6** 2 ¼ **Margo Channing**[51] 4606 2-8-9 **53**............ PJMcDonald 5 — 45
(Micky Hammond) *mid-div: kpt on fnl 2f: nvr nr ldrs* **20/1**

0050 **7** nk **Laurel Lad (IRE)**[22] 5577 2-9-7 **65**............ RichardHills 13 — 56
(Charles Hills) *in rr: hdwy over 2f out: kpt on fnl f* **12/1**

604 **8** 2 **Nayef Flyer**[46] 4781 2-9-1 **59**............ TonyHamilton 15 — 46
(Richard Fahey) *chsd ldrs: one pce fnl 2f* **14/1**

0030 **9** ½ **Angel Cake (IRE)**[15] 5809 2-8-13 **62**............ DarylByrne(5) 3 — 48
(Amy Weaver) *chsd ldrs: drvn over 2f out: wknd over 1f out* **28/1**

3002 **10** 2 ¼ **Priestley's Reward (IRE)**[49] 4667 2-9-7 **65**............ AndrewElliott 10 — 45
(Mrs K Burke) *swvd lft s: in rr: sme hdwy 2f out: nvr a factor* **14/1**

300 **11** 2 **Quiet Appeal (IRE)**[56] 4427 2-8-13 **57**............ JoeFanning 7 — 33
(Mark Johnston) *t.k.h: chsd ldrs: wknd 2f out* **14/1**

403 **12** shd **Karma Chameleon**[20] 5645 2-8-12 **56**............ RobertWinston 20 — 32
(Richard Guest) *in rr: sme hdwy over 2f out: nvr on terms* **7/1**[1]

0000 **13** 1 ¾ **Sir Elmo (IRE)**[14] 5817 2-8-5 **54**............ NeilFarley(5) 17 — 26
(Declan Carroll) *prom: effrt over 2f out: sn btn* **25/1**

6060 **14** 2 ¼ **Revitalise**[29] 5343 2-8-12 **56**............ PhillipMakin 14 — 22
(Kevin Ryan) *a towards rr* **25/1**

000 **15** shd **Divine Success (IRE)**[44] 4851 2-8-11 **58**............ LeeTopliss(3) 16 — 24
(Richard Fahey) *mid-div: sn drvn along: lost pl over 2f out* **12/1**

650 **16** 1 ½ **Astonished Harry (GER)**[28] 5393 2-8-13 **57**............ GrahamGibbons 1 — 20
(Reg Hollinshead) *prom: lost pl 3f out* **20/1**

0034 **17** ½ **Emley Moor**[22] 5597 2-9-1 **59**............ KellyHarrison 6 — 21
(Chris Fairhurst) *chsd ldrs: lost pl over 2f out* **28/1**

450 **18** 38 **Fine Kingdom**[44] 4853 2-9-2 **60**............ TomEaves 9 — —
(Michael Dods) *in rr: bhd whn hung lft over 2f out: virtually p.u: t.o* **17/2**[2]

1m 35.89s (-2.11) **Going Correction** -0.325s/f (Firm) 2y crse rec **18** Ran SP% **121.5**
Speed ratings (Par 93): **97,96,94,94,92 90,89,87,87,84 82,82,81,78,78 77,76,38**
Tote Swingers: 1&2 £16.20, 1&3 £49.80, 2&3 £54.10 CSF £84.46 CT £2232.92 TOTE £8.20: £2.70, £2.90, £7.20, £3.40; EX 81.50.
Owner Mrs Margaret Forsyth **Bred** Michael O'Mahony **Trained** Hambleton, N Yorks
■ Stewards' Enquiry : David Allan one-day ban: used whip with excessive frequency (Oct 5)
Matthew Cosham one-day ban: used whip with excessive frequency (Oct 5)

FOCUS

This didn't prove as competitive as it looked on paper, few getting into the race with there looking a bias towards those racing prominently. The winner, therefore, can have his effort upgraded, having come from furthest back of the first four. No more than a fair nursery.

NOTEBOOK

Fiction Or Fact(IRE) left his maiden form behind when staying on strongly to win on his nursery debut over 7f at Wolverhampton last time, clearly benefiting from having been gelded and also fitted with first-time cheekpieces. With all bar 1lb of the penalty being offset by his rider's claim, it was no surprise to see him follow up, appreciating the step up to 1m and doing well to win having found himself with plenty of ground to make up inside the final 2f. A tough and progressive sort, he can continue to give a good account, with 1m2f likely to be within range. (op 13-2 tchd 10-1)

Bedlam was soon on the speed in the first-time blinkers, and found plenty for pressure to fend off all bar the strong-finishing winner. (op 14-1)

Spoken Words travelled well up with the pace, only to spoil her chance by hanging. This was still an improvement. (op 40-1)

Bathwick Street kept on without ever looking the winner. His dam was related to a top 1m2f performer, and he may need that trip on this evidence. (op 14-1)

Doctor Banner was wearing a first-time visor, but could only keep on at the one pace. (op 11-1)

Laurel Lad(IRE) Official explanation: trainer's rep said colt was unsuited by the good to firm ground

Karma Chameleon disappointed off the same mark as when third here last time. Official explanation: jockey said gelding was unsuited by the good to firm ground (op 13-2 tchd 8-1)

Fine Kingdom was hanging badly and virtually pulled up. Official explanation: trainer had no explanation for the poor form shown (op 9-1 tchd 8-1)

6261 SUBSCRIBE TO RACING UK H'CAP (DIV I) — 6f

3:25 (3:26) (Class 6) (0-65,70) 3-Y-O+ — **£1,363** (£402; £201) **Stalls** Centre

Form — RPR

0016 **1** **Song Of Parkes**[29] 5338 4-9-7 **65**............................¹ DavidAllan 1 — 77
(Eric Alston) *mde most: rdn clr and hung lft 2f out: styd on strly* **13/2**[2]

4040 **2** 2 ¼ **Greek Secret**[35] 5175 8-8-11 **55**...........................(b) FrederikTylicki 3 — 60
(Paul Midgley) *in tch: hdwy to chse ldrs 1/2-way: swtchd rt and rdn to chse wnr over 1f out: kpt on* **16/1**

0345 **3** 1 ¾ **Lady Del Sol**[14] 5824 3-9-3 **63**...........................(p) DanielTudhope 10 — 62
(Marjorie Fife) *in tch: hdwy 2f out: rdn wl over 1f out: styd on fnl f: nrst fin* **9/1**

0450 **4** ½ **Dotty Darroch**[18] 5719 3-8-8 **54**............ LeeNewman 2 — 52
(Robin Bastiman) *chsd wnr: rdn along over 2f out: drvn wl over 1f out and kpt on same pce* **22/1**

0411 **5** ¾ **Darcey**[7] 6065 5-9-7 **70** 6ex............ DarylByrne(5) 11 — 65
(Amy Weaver) *racd towards stands' side: towards rr: pushed along 1/2-way: rdn and hdwy 2f out: styd on fnl f: nrst fin* **7/2**[1]

0036 **6** nk **Prince Of Vasa (IRE)**[35] 5162 4-9-4 **62**............ AdrianNicholls 7 — 56
(Michael Smith) *chsd ldrs: rdn along 2f out: sn drvn and kpt on same pce* **14/1**

5634 **7** hd **Belinsky (IRE)**[18] 5732 4-8-13 **60**...........................(p) DaleSwift(3) 15 — 54
(Mark Campion) *in tch: hdwy to chse ldrs 1/2-way: rdn along over 2f out: drvn and kpt on same pce fr wl over 1f out* **7/1**[3]

250- **8** 1 **Rowayton**[82] 3603 5-8-13 **57**...........................(t) RobertWinston 5 — 47
(Muredach Kelly, Ire) *chsd ldrs: rdn along wl over 2f out: drvn and one pce fr wl over 1f out* **15/2**

6252 **9** shd **Memphis Man**[12] 5881 8-8-10 **59**............ MatthewCosham(5) 13 — 49
(David Evans) *bhd and swtchd lft after 2f: rdn along wl over 2f out: sme late hdwy* **14/1**

4625 **10** hd **Rio's Girl**[26] 5457 4-8-13 **57**...........................(p) PhillipMakin 16 — 46
(Kevin Ryan) *racd towards stands' rail: chsd ldrs: rdn along over 2f out: sn drvn and grad wknd* **12/1**

0003 **11** 4 **Flying Applause**[39] 5034 6-9-6 **64**...........................(bt) RussKennemore 6 — 41
(Roy Bowring) *rrd s: a in rr* **12/1**

0000 **12** hd **Micky Mac (IRE)**[56] 4443 7-8-7 **51** oh3............ ChrisCatlin 8 — 27
(Colin Teague) *chsd ldrs on wd outside: rdn along 1/2-way: sn wknd* **20/1**

0600 **13** ½ **Morermaloke**[32] 5274 3-8-13 **62**............ PaulPickard(3) 9 — 36
(Ian McInnes) *chsd ldrs: rdn along 2f out: sn drvn and wknd* **50/1**

0255 **14** 2 ¾ **Isle Of Ellis (IRE)**[25] 5490 4-8-4 **53** oh6 ow2..........(v) ShaneBKelly(5) 12 — 19
(Ron Barr) *a in rr* **28/1**

5000 **15** 11 **Peppercorn Rent (IRE)**[4] 6158 3-8-5 **51** oh6............(be) KellyHarrison 4 — —
(John Davies) *a in rr* **33/1**

69.12 secs (-2.68) **Going Correction** -0.325s/f (Firm)
WFA 3 from 4yo+ 2lb **15** Ran SP% **121.9**
Speed ratings (Par 101): **104,101,98,98,97 96,96,95,94,94 89,89,88,84,70**
Tote Swingers: 1&2 £34.80, 1&3 £13.60, 2&3 £14.30 CSF £99.74 CT £970.36 TOTE £12.10: £4.50, £4.50, £4.10; EX 108.70.
Owner Joseph Heler **Bred** Joseph Heler **Trained** Longton, Lancs

FOCUS

The first division of a moderate sprint handicap. The runners were spread across the track.

Flying Applause Official explanation: jockey said gelding reared on leaving stalls

6262 FOLLOW REDCARRACING ON FACEBOOK & TWITTER (S) STKS — 1m

4:00 (4:00) (Class 5) 3-Y-O+ — **£2,264** (£673; £336; £168) **Stalls** Centre

Form — RPR

5564 **1** **Whispered Times (USA)**[1] 6231 4-9-0 62.............(p) PatrickMathers 19 — 63
(Tracy Waggott) *chsd ldrs: effrt and hung lft over 2f out: led over 1f out: hld on towards fin* **20/1**

0400 **2** ¾ **Orange Ace**[7] 6063 3-8-10 69...........................(t) ChrisCatlin 15 — 61
(Paul Cole) *in rr: sn drvn along: hdwy over 2f out: styd on wl to chse wnr last 75yds: clsng at line* **16/1**

3010 **3** 1 ¼ **Auto Mac**[28] 5370 3-9-1 72...........................(b) GrahamGibbons 18 — 63
(Neville Bycroft) *led: hdd over 1f out: kpt on same pce* **14/1**

-100 **4** 1 ½ **Freda's Rose (IRE)**[7] 6049 7-8-9 49............ LMcNiff(5) 12 — 55
(Owen Brennan) *in rr: hdwy over 2f out: kpt on wl fnl f* **50/1**

6030 **5** nk **Ginger Grey (IRE)**[14] 5828 4-9-0 67...........................(b) DanielTudhope 11 — 54
(David O'Meara) *hld up towards rr: effrt over 2f out: kpt on: nvr nr ldrs* **7/1**

4040 **6** 2 **Ra Junior (USA)**[2] 6227 5-9-5 62............ FrederikTylicki 8 — 55
(Paul Midgley) *mid-div: effrt over 2f out: kpt on fnl f* **6/1**[3]

3553 **7** shd **Fremen (USA)**[9] 6006 11-9-5 73............ AdrianNicholls 20 — 54
(David Nicholls) *chsd ldrs stands' side: edgd lft 2f out: one pce* **10/1**

-020 **8** 1 ¾ **Doctor Crane (USA)**[46] 4774 5-8-11 91............ MichaelO'Connell(3) 13 — 45
(David Nicholls) *mid-div: effrt over 2f out: sn rdn: hmpd appr fnl f: wknd* **5/2**[1]

4024 **9** 2 ½ **Billy Cadiz**[16] 5788 6-8-8 45 ow1............ JacobButterfield(7) 14 — 41
(Mark Campion) *mid-div: effrt over 2f out: nvr a factor* **40/1**

0030 **10** 8 **Riczar**[11] 5943 3-8-5 48............ RichardKingscote 4 — 16
(Tom Dascombe) *chsd ldrs: wknd over 2f out* **50/1**

050- **11** 10 **Musigny (USA)**[401] 5155 5-9-0 45............ DavidAllan 6 — —
(Sally Hall) *chsd ldrs: lost pl over 2f out* **100/1**

0040 **12** 2 ¾ **Tootie Flutie**[21] 5619 3-8-3 47 ow1............ AmyRyan(3) 7 — —
(Richard Whitaker) *a towards rr* **66/1**

-00 **13** 17 **Blonde Maite**[34] 5212 5-9-0 0...........................(b¹) RussKennemore 2 — —
(Roy Bowring) *swvd lft s: sn chsng ldrs: reminders 4f out: sn lost pl: bhd whn eased 2f out: t.o* **100/1**

0-23 **P** **Soccerjackpot (USA)**[20] 5648 7-9-0 74............ BarryMcHugh 16 — —
(Paul Midgley) *chsd ldrs: wknd over 2f out: bhd whn collapsed ins fnl f: fatally injured* **11/4**[2]

1m 34.99s (-3.01) **Going Correction** -0.325s/f (Firm)
WFA 3 from 4yo+ 4lb **14** Ran SP% **118.3**
Speed ratings (Par 103): **102,101,100,98,98 96,96,94,91,83 73,71,54,—**
Tote Swingers: 1&2 £32.10, 1&3 £14.00, 2&3 £17.90 CSF £295.36 TOTE £19.60: £4.70, £3.80, £3.50; EX 637.10.No bid for the winner.
Owner M Howarth & Miss T Waggott **Bred** Hetrich-McCarthy Livestock **Trained** Spennymoor, Co Durham

FOCUS

An open-looking seller.

6263 VOLTIGEUR RESTAURANT 2 COURSE SPECIAL FOR #10.95 H'CAP — 1m 2f

4:35 (4:35) (Class 5) (0-75,75) 3-Y-O+ — **£2,264** (£673; £336; £168) **Stalls** Low

Form — RPR

3361 **1** **Miss Blink**[27] 5406 4-9-5 **70**............ RobertWinston 6 — 79+
(Robin Bastiman) *hld up towards rr: hdwy on outer over 2f out: rdn to ld 1f out and sn hung lft: drvn and edgd rt wl ins fnl f: hld on wl* **15/2**[3]

6600 **2** ¾ **Tartan Gunna**[45] 4818 5-9-10 **75**...........................(b) JoeFanning 1 — 82
(Mark Johnston) *s.i.s and bhd: hdwy on outer wl over 2f out: rdn over 1f out: str run ent fnl f: nrst fin* **10/1**

3040 **3** nse **Amazing Blue Sky**[18] 5729 5-9-7 **72**............ JamesSullivan 14 — 79
(Ruth Carr) *chsd ldr: effrt 3f out: rdn over 2f out: drvn over 1f out: n.m.r and swtchd rt ins fnl f: kpt on* **22/1**

1005 **4** nk **Spes Nostra**[21] 5621 3-9-0 **71**............ LeeNewman 2 — 77
(David Barron) *hld up: hdwy on inner 3f out: rdn to chse ldr over 1f out: n.m.r and swtchd rt ins fnl f: kpt on* **11/1**

3421 **5** nk **Brouhaha**[8] 6028 7-9-10 **75**............ RichardKingscote 8 — 81
(Tom Dascombe) *hld up: hdwy over 3f out: rdn along wl over 2f out: drvn and styd on fnl f: n.m.r towards fin* **11/4**[1]

5140 **6** 2 ¼ **Gala Casino Star (IRE)**[25] 5465 6-9-7 **75**............ LeeTopliss(3) 5 — 76
(Richard Fahey) *hld up towards rr: hdwy on inner wl over 2f out: rdn and styd on ins fnl f: nrst fin* **12/1**

0010 **7** nk **Daaweitza**[40] 4982 8-9-5 **73**...........................(be) DaleSwift(3) 10 — 74
(Brian Ellison) *midfield: rdn along wl over 2f out: styd on appr fnl f: nrst fin* **16/1**

3000 **8** *nk* **Sirgarfieldsobers (IRE)**[8] 6028 5-9-9 **74**.................... DanielTudhope 3 74
(Declan Carroll) *chsd ldrs: rdn along 3f out: drvn 2f out and kpt on same pce* **11/1**

-626 **9** *1 1/4* **Smirfy's Silver**[29] 5356 7-9-4 **69**.................... TomEaves 9 67
(Deborah Sanderson) *led: rdn along over 2f out: drvn and hdd 1f out: wknd* **25/1**

1023 **10** *1/2* **Sartingo (IRE)**[25] 5485 4-9-4 **69**.................... PJMcDonald 11 66
(Alan Swinbank) *chsd ldrs: rdn along over 3f out: drvn over 2f out and grad wknd* **7/1[2]**

05-4 **11** *4 1/2* **Spey Song (IRE)**[12] 5877 3-9-1 **72**.................... PhilipRobinson 15 60
(James Bethell) *s.i.s: a in rr* **15/2[3]**

40-0 **12** *nk* **Snoqualmie Boy**[22] 5594 8-9-5 **70**.................... AdrianNicholls 7 57
(David Nicholls) *chsd ldng pair: rdn along 3f out: drvn over 2f out and sn wknd* **12/1**

2m 7.19s (0.09) **Going Correction** -0.20s/f (Firm)
WFA 3 from 4yo+ 6lb **12 Ran SP% 117.9**
Speed ratings (Par 103): **91,90,90,90,89 88,87,87,86,86 82,82**
Tote Swingers: 1&2 £10.30, 1&3 £18.80, 2&3 £23.60 CSF £79.98 CT £1581.84 TOTE £7.50: £2.70, £2.70, £5.10; EX 89.90.
Owner A Reed **Bred** Anthony Reed **Trained** Cowthorpe, N Yorks
■ Stewards' Enquiry : Robert Winston one-day ban: careless riding (Oct 5)

FOCUS
It started to rain heavily in the run up to this modest handicap.
Spey Song(IRE) Official explanation: jockey said filly was slowly away

6264 WEDDING RECEPTIONS AT REDCAR RACECOURSE (S) STKS 1m 2f
5:10 (5:12) (Class 6) 3-5-Y-O **£1,704** (£503; £251) **Stalls** Low

Form RPR
1652 **1** **Yorksters Prince (IRE)**[22] 5589 4-9-7 55....................(b) BarryMcHugh 7 66
(Tony Coyle) *led after 1f: drvn clr 4f out: kpt on: unchal* **15/2[3]**

0460 **2** *4* **Sinatramania**[14] 5823 4-9-7 54.................... PatrickMathers 13 58
(Tracy Waggott) *s.i.s: swtchd lft after s: gd hdwy on outer over 2f out: edgd lft and chsd wnr over 1f out: no imp* **14/1**

0160 **3** *3 1/4* **Escape Artist**[21] 5622 4-9-7 57....................(p) GrahamGibbons 11 52
(Tim Easterby) *chsd ldrs: hung rt and drvn bnd over 5f out: chsd wnr over 2f out: kpt on same pce* **10/1**

0303 **4** *3/4* **En Fuego**[22] 5589 4-9-1 57.................... RobertWinston 15 44
(Geoffrey Harker) *mid-div: hdwy over 2f out: kpt on fnl f* **9/1**

-150 **5** *3/4* **Dance For Julie (IRE)**[37] 5107 4-8-13 68.................... PatrickDonaghy(3) 6 44
(Ben Haslam) *awkward to load: s.i.s: drvn along early stages: in rr and reminders over 4f out: swtchd lft over 2f out: kpt on appr fnl f: nvr a factor* **9/4[1]**

0000 **6** *3/4* **Global**[18] 5722 5-8-12 62.................... PaulPickard(3) 2 41
(Brian Ellison) *s.i.s: sn drvn along in rr: hmpd 7f out: swtchd outside 3f out: kpt on: nvr a factor* **5/1[2]**

7 *3 3/4* **Eyeforglory**[52] 5-8-10 0.................... AndrewElliott 8 29
(Suzzanne France) *dwlt: in rr: swtchd outside and hdwy over 2f out: nvr nr ldrs* **100/1**

0500 **8** *3 3/4* **Charity Fair**[23] 5549 4-8-7 35....................(v) DaleSwift(3) 3 21
(Ron Barr) *mid-div: hdwy 4f out: wknd 2f out* **100/1**

0500 **9** *2 1/4* **Monkton Vale (IRE)**[18] 5721 4-9-1 56.................... DanielTudhope 4 22
(Noel Wilson) *trckd ldrs: chsd wnr 5f out: wknd over 1f out: sn eased* **9/1**

6305 **10** *6* **Star Addition**[13] 5860 5-8-10 46.................... DarylByrne(5) 9 10
(Eric Alston) *mid-div: effrt on wd outside over 4f out: wknd 3f out* **16/1**

6060 **11** *2 1/2* **Prime Circle**[11] 5944 5-9-1 48.................... TomEaves 1 —
(Alan Brown) *in tch: lost pl 3f out* **25/1**

1055 **12** *3/4* **Unex Goya (IRE)**[50] 4637 3-8-9 53.................... AdrianNicholls 14 —
(Michael Smith) *sn chsng ldrs: lost pl 3f out* **22/1**

4250 **13** *hd* **Lady Excel (IRE)**[21] 5622 5-8-10 49.................... FrederikTylicki 5 —
(Brian Rothwell) *chsd ldrs: drvn over 4f out: lost pl 3f out* **10/1**

0 **14** *87* **Diumara**[28] 5368 4-8-3 0.................... TerenceFury(7) 12 —
(Neville Bycroft) *t.k.h: led 1f: lost pl over 3f out: bhd and eased 2f out: virtually p.u: hopelessly t.o* **100/1**

2m 7.22s (0.12) **Going Correction** -0.20s/f (Firm)
WFA 3 from 4yo+ 6lb **14 Ran SP% 121.1**
Speed ratings (Par 101): **91,87,85,84,84 83,80,77,75,70 68,68,68,—**
Tote Swingers: 1&2 £22.00, 1&3 £6.50, 2&3 £14.80 CSF £105.15 TOTE £7.80: £2.10, £4.80, £3.50; EX 106.20.There was no bid for the winner. Dance For Julie claimed by Mr Lee Bolingbroke for £6,000.
Owner B Kerr, N Kench, T Coyle **Bred** Lady Legard & Sir Tatton Sykes **Trained** Norton, N Yorks

FOCUS
Few got into this seller.

6265 TWO YEAR OLD TROPHY COMES NEXT H'CAP 5f
5:40 (5:41) (Class 5) (0-70,70) 3-Y-O+ **£2,264** (£673; £336; £168) **Stalls** Centre

Form RPR
2043 **1** **Rhal (IRE)**[41] 4942 3-8-12 **69**.................... JustinNewman(7) 3 75
(Bryan Smart) *mde all: rdn and edgd lft wl over 1f out: drvn ins fnl f: hld on wl* **9/2[2]**

000 **2** *hd* **Cayman Fox**[18] 5719 6-8-8 **57** oh2 ow1.................... PJMcDonald 12 63
(Linda Perratt) *racd wd: prom: rdn along 2f out: drvn: edgd lft and ev ch ins fnl f: kpt on* **20/1**

100 **3** *hd* **Hypnosis**[18] 5720 8-9-5 **68**.................... RobertWinston 4 73
(Noel Wilson) *chsd ldrs: rdn wl over 1f out: drvn and ev ch ins fnl f: kpt on* **12/1**

242 **4** *1/2* **Dispol Grand (IRE)**[26] 5457 5-9-0 **63**.................... RussKennemore 6 66
(Paul Midgley) *chsd wnr: rdn along 2f out: drvn over 1f out: kpt on same pce* **5/1[3]**

0452 **5** *1 1/4* **Commanche Raider (IRE)**[18] 5732 4-9-7 **70**....................(p) PhillipMakin 2 69
(Michael Dods) *chsd ldrs: rdn along 2f out: drvn over 1f out: kpt on same pce* **11/4[1]**

0103 **6** *shd* **Sea Salt**[20] 5647 8-9-3 **69**.................... DaleSwift(3) 11 67
(Ron Barr) *towards rr: rdn along 1/2-way: edgd lft and styd on appr fnl f: nrst fin* **8/1**

3146 **7** *1/2* **Boundless Spirit**[32] 5274 3-9-2 **69**....................(t) MichaelO'Connell(3) 10 66
(David Nicholls) *t.k.h: chsd ldrs: rdn wl over 1f out: drvn and one pce ins fnl f* **10/1**

-103 **8** *3 1/4* **Lizzie (IRE)**[26] 5456 3-9-5 **69**....................(b) DavidAllan 7 54
(Tim Easterby) *sn outpcd and rdn along in rr: swtchd rt and drvn wl over 1f out: n.d* **6/1**

0102 **9** *5* **Green Warrior**[11] 5939 3-8-13 **66**.................... RobertLButler(3) 8 33
(Richard Guest) *t.k.h: in tch: rdn along 1/2-way: sn wknd* **9/1**

57.94 secs (-0.66) **Going Correction** -0.325s/f (Firm)
WFA 3 from 4yo+ 1lb **9 Ran SP% 118.5**
Speed ratings (Par 103): **92,91,91,90,88 88,87,82,74**
Tote Swingers: 1&2 £18.60, 1&3 £14.00, 2&3 £16.90 CSF £89.94 CT £1026.13 TOTE £4.60: £1.20, £9.10, £5.20; EX 132.10.
Owner Crossfields Racing **Bred** Epona Bloodstock Ltd **Trained** Hambleton, N Yorks

FOCUS
Another race on the straight track where it was an advantage to race on the pace.

6266 SUBSCRIBE TO RACING UK H'CAP (DIV II) 6f
6:10 (6:11) (Class 6) (0-65,65) 3-Y-O+ **£1,363** (£402; £201) **Stalls** Centre

Form RPR
0001 **1** **Secret City (IRE)**[25] 5490 5-9-0 **58**....................(b) RobertWinston 8 69
(Robin Bastiman) *sn chsng ldrs: styd on to ld jst ins fnl f: drvn out* **5/1[2]**

0000 **2** *3* **Prince James**[175] 1034 4-8-13 **57**....................(b[1]) GrahamGibbons 5 58
(Michael Easterby) *led tl last 150yds: kpt on same pce* **11/4[1]**

2600 **3** *nk* **Wolf Slayer**[18] 5736 3-9-3 **63**.................... RichardKingscote 3 63
(Tom Dascombe) *chsd ldrs: upsides appr fnl f: kpt on same pce* **16/1**

1000 **4** *2 1/4* **Choc'A'Moca (IRE)**[25] 5468 4-9-6 **64**....................(v) FrederikTylicki 6 57
(Paul Midgley) *chsd ldrs: kpt on same pce over 1f out* **15/2**

6020 **5** *3/4* **Distant Sun (USA)**[6] 6076 7-8-3 **52**....................(p) NeilFarley(5) 13 42
(Linda Perratt) *in rr: kpt on fnl 2f: nvr nr ldrs* **16/1**

6100 **6** *nk* **Ryedane (IRE)**[12] 5881 9-9-2 **65**....................(b) AdamCarter(5) 7 54
(Tim Easterby) *mid-div: hdwy 2f out: kpt on same pce fnl f* **16/1**

0000 **7** *1/2* **Divertimenti (IRE)**[38] 5083 7-9-2 **60**....................(b) RussKennemore 11 48
(Roy Bowring) *chsd ldrs: one pce over 1f out* **12/1**

340 **8** *1* **Uddy Mac**[6] 6091 4-8-5 **56**....................(p) TerenceFury(7) 4 41
(Neville Bycroft) *chsd ldrs: one pce fnl 2f* **12/1**

0340 **9** *nk* **Foreign Rhythm (IRE)**[4] 6159 6-9-2 **63**.................... DaleSwift(3) 12 47
(Ron Barr) *in rr: kpt on fnl 2f: nvr on terms* **13/2[3]**

4000 **10** *nk* **Spanish Acclaim**[32] 5262 4-9-7 **65**.................... PJMcDonald 14 48
(Ruth Carr) *hood removed v late: s.i.s: hdwy 2f out: nvr nr ldrs* **16/1**

0060 **11** *5* **Rio Sands**[28] 5373 6-8-4 **51** oh6.................... AmyRyan(3) 15 18
(Richard Whitaker) *in rr: nvr on terms* **40/1**

0210 **12** *hd* **Piccoluck**[21] 5624 3-9-2 **62**....................(b) ChrisCatlin 2 28
(Amy Weaver) *drvn to chse ldrs on outside: wknd over 1f out* **16/1**

4456 **13** *1 3/4* **Bachelor Knight (IRE)**[154] 1494 3-9-3 **63**.................... BarryMcHugh 9 23
(Suzzanne France) *a in rr* **28/1**

0060 **14** *2 3/4* **Hitches Dubai (BRZ)**[16] 5787 6-8-7 **51** oh3.................... JoeFanning 10 3
(Geoffrey Harker) *in rr: bhd fnl 2f* **40/1**

0600 **15** *4* **Colamandis**[46] 4813 4-8-7 **51** oh6....................(p) JamesSullivan 1 —
(Hugh McWilliams) *chsd ldrs: wknd 2f out* **33/1**

1m 10.59s (-1.21) **Going Correction** -0.325s/f (Firm)
WFA 3 from 4yo+ 2lb **15 Ran SP% 124.5**
Speed ratings (Par 101): **95,91,90,87,86 86,85,84,83,83 76,76,74,70,65**
Tote Swingers: 1&2 £5.10, 1&3 £9.20, 2&3 £17.00. ToteSuper7: Win: not won Place: not won CSF £18.97 CT £212.85 TOTE £7.10: £2.60, £1.60, £6.60; EX 23.30.
Owner Ms M Austerfield **Bred** Miss Karen Theobald **Trained** Cowthorpe, N Yorks

FOCUS
The second division of the sprint handicap was run at a good pace, and produced a comfortable winner.
T/Jkpt: Not won. T/Plt: £8,317.70 to a £1 stake. Pool of £68,935.00 - 6.05 winning tickets. T/Qpdt: £1,299.40 to a £1 stake. Pool of £4,039.00 - 2.30 winning tickets. WG

6168 NEWMARKET (R-H)
Thursday, September 22

OFFICIAL GOING: Good to firm (good in places; overall: 8.4; far side 8.6; stands' side 8.5; centre 8.3)
A new-look Cambridgeshire meeting, run a week earlier than in previous years.
Wind: Fresh, half behind Weather: Dry, breezy

6267 EBF "ZAMINDAR" MAIDEN STKS 1m
2:10 (2:15) (Class 4) 2-Y-O **£4,528** (£1,347; £673; £336) **Stalls** High

Form RPR
0 **1** **Dandy (GER)**[57] 4446 2-9-0 0.................... JimmyFortune 13 83
(Andrew Balding) *pressed ldrs: rdn to ld narrowly 2f out: kpt on wl and a jst holding rivals fnl f: rdn out* **16/1**

3 **2** *hd* **Almaas (USA)**[20] 5688 2-9-0 0.................... FrankieDettori 10 83
(Saeed Bin Suroor) *w'like: scope: tall: lw: led: narrowly hdd and rdn 2f out: ev ch after: edgd rt 1f out: kpt on wl u.p but a jst hld fnl f* **11/8[1]**

3 *hd* **Anomaly** 2-9-0 0.................... NeilCallan 11 82
(Mahmood Al Zarooni) *w'like: scope: str: bit bkwd: in tch in midfield: hdwy to chse ldrs over 2f out: rdn and pressing ldrs over 1f out: kpt on wl ins fnl f* **9/1**

4 *1 1/4* **Engrossing** 2-9-0 0.................... WilliamBuick 15 79+
(David Elsworth) *w'like: tall: lw: s.i.s: hld up in tch in rr: hdwy 1/2-way: jnd ldrs 3f out: ev ch and rdn wl over 1f out: unable qck and outpcd 1f out: styd on same pce fnl 150yds* **33/1**

5 *3/4* **Prince Of Orange (IRE)** 2-9-0 0.................... ChrisCatlin 14 77
(Mahmood Al Zarooni) *athletic: lw: in tch: rdn and hdwy over 2f out: chsd ldrs over 1f out: kpt on u.p ins fnl f: nt gng pce to rch ldrs* **7/1[3]**

6 *3/4* **Waafid (USA)** 2-9-0 0.................... RichardHills 2 76+
(Marcus Tregoning) *w'like: scope: bit bkwd: chsd ldrs: ev ch ent fnl 2f: rdn and unable qck over 1f out: struggling whn n.m.r ent fnl f: wknd fnl 150yds* **14/1**

00 **7** *5* **Imperial Order (IRE)**[14] 5851 2-9-0 0.................... RichardHughes 3 64
(Richard Hannon) *chsd ldrs: rdn over 2f out: wknd wl over 1f out: wl btn whn edgd rt over 1f out* **5/1[2]**

8 *3 1/4* **Weaam (IRE)** 2-9-0 0.................... MartinDwyer 9 57+
(Marcus Tregoning) *w'like: scope: bit bkwd: str: v.s.a: rn green in rr and sn pushed along: plugged on past btn horses ins fnl f: n.d* **22/1**

9 *1 1/2* **Moonship** 2-9-0 0.................... TomQueally 12 53+
(Sir Michael Stoute) *str: bit bkwd: s.i.s: sn in tch in rr: rdn and struggling 3f out: wknd over 2f out* **12/1**

10 *2 1/2* **Rye House (IRE)** 2-9-0 0.................... KierenFallon 5 48+
(Sir Michael Stoute) *w'like: v.s.a: rn green and sn pushed along in rr: hdwy and in tch 1/2-way: wknd qckly over 2f out* **14/1**

0 **11** *6* **Tigertoo (IRE)**[16] 5801 2-9-0 0.................... SaleemGolam 7 34
(Stuart Williams) *w'like: t.k.h: chsd ldr tl 3f out: wknd qckly wl over 2f out: wl bhd and eased ins fnl f* **125/1**

1m 37.41s (-1.19) **Going Correction** -0.225s/f (Firm) **11 Ran SP% 116.3**
Speed ratings (Par 97): **96,95,95,94,93 92,87,84,83,80 74**
toteswingers: 1&2 £7.00, 1&3 £18.80, 2&3 £3.00. CSF £37.50 TOTE £22.10: £4.90, £1.10, £2.60; EX 65.80 Trifecta £458.10 Pool: £736.68 - 1.19 winning units..
Owner Robert E Tillett **Bred** Gestut Rottgen **Trained** Kingsclere, Hants

FOCUS
There was a strong tailwind up the straight and that was a help to front-runners, especially on what was a quick surface. The winning time was 1.42 seconds quicker than the following nursery. Those drawn high dominated. A typically interesting course maiden for the time of year, largely made up of middle-distance horses with next season in mind. The race should produce more than its share of winners. The race averages and the time set the level of the form.
NOTEBOOK
Dandy(GER), only eighth on his debut at Sandown, narrowly prevailing. He'd clearly learnt plenty from that initial experience and certainly proved suited by the step up to 1m, seeing the race out well. He has scope to improve further and ought to make a useful handicapper at three. (op 22-1)
Almaas(USA) was soon in front, but for a horse who looked shy of pace on his debut, it was surprising Dettori didn't try to get them on the stretch, as all he did once headed was keep on at the one pace. He can win a maiden, with the step up to 1m2f likely to help. (op 13-8)
Anomaly ◆, outsider of the Godolphin trio, is a brother to the useful Iguazu Falls, as well as half-brother to Irish 1,000 Guineas runner-up Anna Salai. He made a promising start, picking up nicely to challenge, and for all that he never looked like winning, an ordinary maiden should come his way, especially faced with slower ground. (op 14-1)
Engrossing ◆, a half-brother to six different winners from 6f-1m6f, was one of the slowest away and fared much the best of those coming from off the pace, travelling up strongly and looking the likely winner only to become unbalanced in the dip. Runners from this yard often benefit from a run and he looks another ready-made winner. (op 25-1)
Prince Of Orange(IRE) ◆, related to numerous winners, ran green under pressure and was another who didn't look to handle the dip. He should improve markedly and can leave this form behind in time. (op 8-1 tchd 13-2)
Waafid(USA) ◆, one of the more speedily bred runners in the field, travelled like a good horse until tiring late on. Normal progress should see him winning, with a drop to 7f perhaps no bad thing for the time being. (op 12-1 tchd 11-1)
Imperial Order(IRE) now has the option of nurseries. He's likely to get a rating in the mid-70s and can show himself better than this. (op 13-2)
Weaam(IRE) ◆, half-brother to a useful 1m winner for the yard, was very green after a slow start and didn't get going until the race was all over. He should improve enormously and can win a maiden at a lesser track. (op 40-1 tchd 20-1)
Moonship, a half-brother to Workforce, offered little promise with the immediate future in mind. He looks more a long-term prospect. (op 15-2)
Rye House(IRE) was slowly away and also ran green. He did at least make a mid-race move before fading, though. (op 12-1)

6268 AVIVA COMMERCIAL FINANCE NURSERY 1m
2:45 (2:45) (Class 3) (0-95,91) 2-Y-O **£5,822** (£1,732; £865; £432) **Stalls** High

Form				RPR
1203	**1**		**That's Dangerous**[12] 5931 2-8-3 **76** HarryBentley(3) 9 (Roger Charlton) *stdd and dropped in bhd after s: t.k.h: hld up in tch in rr: rdn and effrt 2f out: hdwy to chse ldrs 1f out: led fnl 100yds: r.o wl: rdn out* **11/1**	81
61	**2**	½	**Chil The Kite**[26] 5475 2-8-13 **83** SteveDrowne 6 (Hughie Morrison) *lw: led and set stdy gallop: rdn and qcknd 2f out: hdd fnl 100yds: kpt on wl but a hld after* **4/1**[2]	87
3421	**3**	1¾	**Devdas (IRE)**[27] 5446 2-8-8 **81** JohnFahy(3) 5 (Clive Cox) *t.k.h: chsd ldr for 2f and again jst over 2f out: sn rdn: ev ch and drvn 1f out: no ex and btn fnl 75yds* **9/2**[3]	81
21	**4**	1¼	**Kid Suitor (IRE)**[24] 5536 2-8-7 **80** SeanLevey(3) 7 (Richard Hannon) *t.k.h: hld up in tch: rdn 2f out: chsd ldrs and unable qck ent fnl f: wknd fnl 100yds* **8/1**	77
0203	**5**	¾	**Magic City (IRE)**[15] 5825 2-9-4 **88** RichardHughes 3 (Richard Hannon) *stdd s: hld up in rr: clsd 1/2-way: hdwy to chse ldrs and rdn wl over 1f out: unable qck over 1f out: no imp and hld fr 1f out* **4/1**[2]	83
0236	**6**	1¼	**Benzanno (IRE)**[27] 5446 2-8-4 **74** DavidProbert 2 (Andrew Balding) *lw: t.k.h: hld up in tch: rdn and effrt 2f out: no imp u.p over 1f out: wknd 1f out* **11/1**	66
206	**7**	2½	**Roman Province (IRE)**[14] 5855 2-7-9 **68** oh1 KieranO'Neill(3) 8 (Roger Teal) *t.k.h: chsd ldrs: wnt 2nd after 2f tl jst over 2f out: wknd wl over 1f out* **33/1**	55
101	**8**	3	**Ghostwriting (USA)**[15] 5825 2-9-7 **91** WilliamBuick 4 (John Gosden) *lw: t.k.h: hld up in tch: wnt rt after 2f: rdn and struggling whn hmpd wl over 1f out: sn wknd* **7/2**[1]	71

1m 38.83s (0.23) **Going Correction** -0.225s/f (Firm) **8** Ran SP% **111.1**
Speed ratings (Par 99): **89,88,86,85,84 83,81,78**
toteswingers: 1&2 £7.90, 1&3 £7.70, 2&3 £4.20. CSF £51.51 CT £224.21 TOTE £11.40: £2.60, £1.80, £1.80; EX 58.60 Trifecta £376.80 Pool: £840.31 - 1.65 winning units..
Owner D Carter and P Inglett **Bred** Mrs G Sainty **Trained** Beckhampton, Wilts
FOCUS
A strong-looking nursery on paper, despite there being quite a bit of weight between those at top and bottom of the ratings. However, the early pace wasn't that strong. The first two are on the upgrade.
NOTEBOOK
That's Dangerous, whose only previous success came in a seller, was already 8lb higher than when starting off in nurseries so the fact that he was able to pick up quite a few runners inside the final furlong doesn't bode well for those he beat. (tchd 12-1)
Chil The Kite's jockey decided to make the running when nothing else wanted to lead. The horse ran on really well when rivals closed around him, showing a willing attitude in an attempt to give the winner 10lb. (op 9-2)
Devdas(IRE) was on his toes in the paddock and became a bit unbalanced in the dip when keeping on. It remains to be seen how much more progression he has in him. (op 5-1 tchd 4-1)
Kid Suitor(IRE) ◆ won his maiden (second start) at 4-7 in late August, but hadn't been out since. A horse with scope and size, he was one of many to pull too hard early and can be readily given another chance. (tchd 7-1)
Magic City(IRE) was given a patient ride and appeared not to get home after coming through to look dangerous. (op 3-1)
Ghostwriting(USA) was eased after finding trouble when staying on, albeit looking held. However, it may be worth bearing in mind that the same connections ran Buthelezi in this contest last year, and he ran poorly before proving himself to be a Listed performer at least. Official explanation: jockey said colt ran too keen (op 4-1)

6269 PRINCESS ROYAL RICHARD HAMBRO EBF STKS (LISTED RACE) (F&M) 1m 4f
3:20 (3:22) (Class 1) 3-Y-O+
£17,013 (£6,450; £3,228; £1,608; £807; £405) **Stalls** Centre

Form				RPR
-016	**1**		**Mohedian Lady (IRE)**[19] 5748 3-8-9 94 KierenFallon 2 (Luca Cumani) *hld up in tch: hdwy to ld 3f out: rdn clr and edgd rt wl over 1f out: pushed out fnl f: comf* **3/1**[1]	108+
3245	**2**	1¾	**Imperial Pippin (USA)**[43] 4915 3-8-9 93 WilliamBuick 1 (John Gosden) *t.k.h: hld up in midfield tl hdwy to chse ldrs 10f out: ev ch and rdn 3f out: nt qckn w wnr and swtchd lft over 1f out: kpt on but a hld fnl f* **8/1**	104
-303	**3**	7	**Cill Rialaig**[15] 5839 6-9-3 102 SteveDrowne 4 (Hughie Morrison) *stdd s: t.k.h: hld up in midfield: hdwy to chse ldrs 3f out: rdn and wknd 2f out* **3/1**[1]	93
4602	**4**	1½	**Roxy Flyer (IRE)**[21] 5659 4-9-3 96 JimmyQuinn 6 (Amanda Perrett) *in tch: rdn and effrt 3f out: sn outpcd and no threat to ldrs fnl 2f: edgd rt u.p over 1f out: plugged on fnl f* **13/2**[3]	90
-566	**5**	2¾	**Brushing**[19] 5711 5-9-3 102 TomQueally 3 (Mark H Tompkins) *hld up in last pair: rdn and effrt wl over 2f out: no imp and wl hld whn carried rt over 1f out* **8/1**	86
4210	**6**	6	**Parvana (IRE)**[56] 4473 3-8-9 81 JamieSpencer 8 (William Haggas) *stdd and dropped in bhd after s: hld up in rr: rdn and shortlived effrt 3f out: sn wknd and bhd* **25/1**	76
2046	**7**	4½	**Spin (IRE)**[14] 5850 3-8-9 101 CO'Donoghue 5 (A P O'Brien, Ire) *leggy: led tl 3f out: sn rdn and immediately dropped out: stmbld over 2f out and sn wl bhd* **9/2**[2]	69
3501	**8**	20	**Bramalea**[24] 5545 6-9-3 90 DarryllHolland 7 (Hughie Morrison) *t.k.h: chsd ldr tl over 3f out: sn bhd: eased fr wl over 1f out: t.o* **20/1**	37

2m 26.07s (-5.93) **Going Correction** -0.225s/f (Firm) course record
WFA 3 from 4yo+ 8lb **8** Ran SP% **112.3**
Speed ratings (Par 111): **110,108,104,103,101 97,94,81**
toteswingers: 1&2 £5.40, 1&3 £2.60, 2&3 £5.20. CSF £26.79 TOTE £3.10: £1.10, £2.90, £1.50; EX 23.10 Trifecta £52.70 Pool: £862.22 - 12.09 winning units..
Owner Mrs Olivia Hoare **Bred** Kildaragh Stud **Trained** Newmarket, Suffolk
■ This event has been transferred from Ascot.
FOCUS
Not the strongest race for the grade on pre-race fugures, but it was run at a good gallop. Aided by a tailwind, it was run in a course record time, taking exactly one second off the old one. A pair of improved 3yos finished clear.
NOTEBOOK
Mohedian Lady(IRE) ◆, who was aided by the tailwind, powered to victory in a course record time, knocking exactly a second off the old one. Successful from a mark of 86 at Nottingham in August, things didn't fall her way in a decent 1m4f handicap at Leopardstown last time, but she travelled really strongly in behind the leaders on this occasion and always looked in control once sent on. There was a lot to like about this performance and she is surely capable of winning at Group level, but we'll probably have to wait until next season to see her again. (op 7-2 tchd 11-4)
Imperial Pippin(USA) hasn't progressed as expected this season, often travelling well before not seeing it out, and she was allowed to take a forward role here having been keen early. She stuck on well to finish clear of the remainder, a performance that suggests she's up to winning at this level, and it would be no surprise to see her end up in the US, just like her dam.
Cill Rialaig was readily brushed aside by the 3yos and it's probably safe to assume she wasn't at her best. Official explanation: jockey said mare was unsuited by the track (op 10-3)
Roxy Flyer(IRE) remains without a win since last summer, though in fairness she has been chasing black type this season. This was a credible run, no more. (op 15-2)
Brushing travelled noticeably well, her rider taking a pull over 3f out, but once asked to pick up and chase the winner, she couldn't respond. (op 7-1)
Spin(IRE) probably overexerted herself through the early stages, hence she dropped right out. Official explanation: trainer's rep said filly finished lame (tchd 5-1)
Bramalea was keen and helped push the pace before weakening. Official explanation: trainer said mare was unsuited by the good to firm (good in places) ground (op 16-1)

6270 SOMERVILLE TATTERSALL STKS (GROUP 3) (C&G) 7f
3:55 (3:56) (Class 1) 2-Y-O
£19,281 (£7,310; £3,658; £1,822; £914; £459) **Stalls** High

Form				RPR
1122	**1**		**Crius (IRE)**[19] 5709 2-8-12 94 RichardHughes 7 (Richard Hannon) *racd against stands' rail: led for over 1f: chsd ldr after tl led again 2f out: rdn over 1f out: clr jst ins fnl f: styd on wl: pushed out fnl 100yds* **15/2**	109
211	**2**	2½	**Farraaj (IRE)**[8] 6060 2-8-12 88 FrankieDettori 8 (Roger Varian) *swtchd rt to r in centre gp sn after s: in midfield: rdn and effrt over 2f out: drvn over 1f out: kpt on ins fnl f to snatch 2nd last stride: nt gng pce to trble wnr* **11/8**[1]	102+
6	**3**	shd	**Zip Top (IRE)**[67] 4131 2-8-12 0 KJManning 9 (J S Bolger, Ire) *w'like: scope: str: lw: racd against stands' rail: midfield: rdn over 2f out: outpcd and looked wl hld over 1f out: rallied 1f out: styd on wl ins fnl f: wnt 3rd last strides: no threat to wnr* **14/1**	102
0	**4**	nk	**Crusade (USA)**[25] 5521 2-8-12 0 CO'Donoghue 3 (A P O'Brien, Ire) *str: lw: chsd ldrs: rdn over 2f out: drvn and chsd wnr jst over 1f out: kpt on same pce fnl f: lost 2 pls cl home* **5/1**[2]	101
2403	**5**	hd	**Letsgoroundagain (IRE)**[14] 5849 2-8-12 92 MichaelHills 1 (Charles Hills) *chsd ldrs but sn pushed along: lost pl and towards rr 1/2-way: hdwy u.p over 1f out: kpt on u.p ins fnl f: nt gng pce to threaten wnr* **20/1**	100
110	**6**	1	**Red Seventy**[57] 4424 2-8-12 92 JimmyFortune 5 (Richard Hannon) *chsd ldrs: rdn and outpcd over 2f out: kpt on same pce and no imp fr over 1f out* **25/1**	98
2211	**7**	1	**Storming Bernard (USA)**[7] 6077 2-8-12 88 DarryllHolland 6 (Alan Bailey) *taken down early: chsd ldr tl led over 5f out: sn clr: hdd and rdn 2f out: lost 2nd jst over 1f out: wknd ins fnl f* **8/1**	95
21	**8**	2¼	**Ghost Protocol (IRE)**[35] 5196 2-8-12 83 JamieSpencer 4 (David Simcock) *lw: hld up in rr: rdn and effrt over 2f out: no imp: nvr trbld ldrs* **33/1**	89
21	**9**	3¼	**Electrician**[8] 6064 2-8-12 0 WilliamBuick 2 (John Gosden) *hld up towards rr: hdwy 3f out: rdn and struggling jst over 2f out: sn wknd* **6/1**[3]	81

1m 22.88s (-2.52) **Going Correction** -0.225s/f (Firm) 2y crse rec **9** Ran SP% **114.1**
Speed ratings (Par 105): **105,102,102,101,101 100,99,96,92**
toteswingers: 1&2 £2.20, 1&3 £10.70, 2&3 £7.30. CSF £17.61 TOTE £5.60: £1.50, £1.10, £4.40; EX 19.90 Trifecta £112.50 Pool: £1,641.76 - 12.09 winning units..
Owner Titan Assets **Bred** Oak Lodge Bloodstock **Trained** East Everleigh, Wilts
FOCUS
A race with a mixed history, the most notable recent winners being subsequent Group 1 performers Aussie Rules (2005) and Milk It Mick (2003). The pace was sound and the form has been given a chance with the winner taking a big step forward. The first and third had the benefit of the stands' rail.
NOTEBOOK
Crius(IRE) finished second to Hong Kong-bound Caledonian Spring last time at Haydock in Listed company (1m), but upped that sort of level with a clear success against some smart types. It might be dangerous to underestimate this performance considering he probably should have won his first three starts, but one does get then impression that he'll need to find plenty more to handle himself at a higher level. Connections said afterwards that he may not race again this season and could reappear in the Greenham. (op 8-1 tchd 7-1)
Farraaj(IRE), whose last piece of form was boosted by Tell Dad recently in a big sales race, was chasing a hat-trick but got out paced towards the centre of the course before keeping on well. It was a slightly disappointing performance as he never really looked like winning, and one would imagine that'll he'll be given a break now. (op 6-5 tchd 6-4)

Zip Top(IRE) had been off since running disappointingly in the Group 3 Anglesey Stakes at the Curragh. He needed plenty of pushing when the tempo lifted but stayed on really well while following the winner's path. Evidently well regarded considering his debut victory at short odds, hopefully he can build on this. (tchd 12-1)

Crusade(USA) travelled really well down the middle of the track and seemed sure to get involved as the field started to sort itself out, but he didn't get home as well as a couple around him, and lost third only yards from the line. (tchd 9-2 and 11-2)

Letsgoroundagain(IRE) ran a cracker in the valuable sales race run at Doncaster towards the start of this month, and ran at least to that level again, although he never looked like taking this. (op 25-1 tchd 33-1)

Red Seventy, off the course since finishing last in the Group 2 Vintage Stakes, made some late ground after getting caught flat-footed and is entitled to be straighter next time. (tchd 20-1)

Storming Bernard(USA) wasn't beaten far after his early exertions, but the result needs treating with some caution as the winner raced on possibly favoured ground against the stands' rail. (op 10-1)

Electrician won a maiden eight days previously at Yarmouth but found this contest and all together proposition and couldn't get involved. (op 15-2)

6271 JOCKEY CLUB ROSE BOWL (LISTED RACE) 2m
4:30 (4:31) (Class 1) 3-Y-O+

£17,013 (£6,450; £3,228; £1,608; £807; £405) **Stalls** Centre

Form RPR

1123 **1** **Times Up**[40] 5045 5-9-6 109 EddieAhern 2 116+
(John Dunlop) *lw: hld up in last pair: cruised up to join ldr on bit over 2f out: led over 1f out: pushed along and qcknd ahd ins fnl f: easily* **9/4**[2]

1100 **2** *1 1/2* **Chiberta King**[33] 5284 5-9-6 107 (p) JimmyFortune 7 111
(Andrew Balding) *led: rdn 3f out: edgd rt u.p wl over 1f out: hdd jst over 1f out: readily brushed aside by wnr ins fnl f: hld on for 2nd fnl 75yds* **8/1**

0102 **3** *nk* **Nehaam**[19] 5705 5-9-3 105 RichardHills 1 108+
(John Gosden) *hld up in midfield: rdn and effrt on inner 2f out: kpt on u.p and pressing for 2nd fnl 75yds: no threat to wnr* **2/1**[1]

0316 **4** *1 3/4* **Fictional Account (IRE)**[12] 5952 6-9-1 103 FMBerry 3 104
(V C Ward, Ire) *hld up in rr: rdn and effrt wl over 2f out: hdwy u.p to chse ldrs over 1f out: plugged on same pce fnl f* **7/1**

2030 **5** *4 1/2* **Theology**[13] 5883 4-9-3 103 WilliamBuick 6 100
(Jeremy Noseda) *hld up in tch in midfield: hdwy to chse ldrs 4f out: stl pressing ldrs but unable qck whn hmpd and swtchd rt over 1f out: wknd fnl f* **6/1**[3]

0-00 **6** *hd* **Precision Break (USA)**[13] 5883 6-9-3 94 JamieSpencer 4 100
(David Simcock) *chsd ldng pair tl lost pl u.p over 3f out: no threat to ldrs fnl 2f* **16/1**

/0-0 **7** *3* **End Of The Affair (IRE)**[13] 5907 7-8-12 99 (b) KJManning 5 91
(V C Ward, Ire) *chsd ldr: clsd and pressed ldr 5f out: rdn and ev ch 3f out: wknd wl over 1f out* **16/1**

3m 18.64s (-11.86) **Going Correction** -0.225s/f (Firm) course record **7** Ran SP% **113.8**
Speed ratings (Par 111): **120,119,119,118,115 115,114**
toteswingers: 1&2 £3.40, 1&3 £1.80, 2&3 £3.50. CSF £20.18 TOTE £2.50: £1.40, £3.40; EX 21.80 Trifecta £49.80 Pool: £1,554.38 - 23.06 winning units..
Owner Mrs I H Stewart-Brown & M J Meacock **Bred** I Stewart-Brown And M Meacock **Trained** Arundel, W Sussex
■ A new title for a race previously run at Ascot as the Fenwolf Stakes.

FOCUS
They went a decent gallop for this staying event and the form looks solid, with the three highest-rated runners coming to the fore. The winner impressed but only needed to run to form.

NOTEBOOK
Times Up ◆, one of two penalised runners, has progressed into a smart middle-distance stayer this year, winning a 1m6f Listed contest at York earlier in the season, and twice running well in Group company subsequently. He's long looked worth a try at this distance, though, being a half-brother to Group-1 winning stayer Give Notice, and having travelled supremely well under a confident Eddie Ahern, just had to be nudged out to score an impressive victory. It'll be fascinating to see how he fares stepped back up in grade, with the Long Distance Cup at Ascot in three weeks' time looking a suitable target. (op 2-1 tchd 5-2 in places)

Chiberta King, carrying a penalty for his 2m Listed win at Sandown earlier in the year, returned to his best with the cheekpieces reapplied, ensuring the pace was honest and finding plenty for pressure to hold second. He too is entitled to take his chance in the Long Distance Cup. (tchd 9-1)

Nehaam has done well this season since returning from injury and he ran up to his best on this return to 2m. (op 3-1)

Fictional Account(IRE), winner of the race last year when it was run at Ascot, claimed the notable scalp of Fame And Glory last month, only to run a shocker in the Irish St Leger. Her retirement was deferred and this was more like her true form, even if she never looked like winning. (op 8-1)

Theology remains inconsistent and hasn't lived up to expectations since his close miss in last year's Queen's Vase. He's the right type to send hurdling. (op 5-1)

Precision Break(USA) isn't up to Listed level (op 14-1)

End Of The Affair(IRE) didn't look up to this grade. (op 20-1 tchd 25-1)

6272 EBF "OASIS DREAM" FILLIES' H'CAP 6f
5:05 (5:05) (Class 2) (0-100,98) 3-Y-O+

£9,960 (£2,982; £1,491; £745; £372; £187) **Stalls** High

Form RPR

2640 **1** **La Fortunata**[3] 6224 4-8-7 84 oh1 AndreaAtzeni 3 92
(Mike Murphy) *mde all and sn crossed to r against stands' rail: rdn wl over 1f out: kpt on wl ins fnl f* **11/1**

1010 **2** *1/2* **Swiss Dream**[12] 5927 3-9-5 98 NickyMackay 1 105
(David Elsworth) *sn chsng wnr: upsides wnr 2f out: sltly outpcd by wnr whn drvn over 1f out: rallied and chalng again ins fnl f: no ex towards fin* **4/1**[1]

5006 **3** *hd* **Cochabamba (IRE)**[26] 5481 3-9-1 94 JackMitchell 11 100+
(Roger Teal) *hld up off the pce in midfield: swtchd rt and effrt wl over 1f out: hdwy ent fnl f: drvn and kpt on wl fnl 100yds: nt rch ldrs* **10/1**

011 **4** *1 3/4* **Fair Value (IRE)**[3] 6217 3-8-9 88 6ex SebSanders 5 88
(Simon Dow) *t.k.h: chsd ldrs: rdn and unable qck wl over 1f out: kpt on same pce ins fnl f* **13/2**

0500 **5** *2* **Gouray Girl (IRE)**[19] 5702 4-8-11 88 (t) RichardHughes 4 82
(Walter Swinburn) *b: lw: racd off the pce in last pair: swtchd rt and effrt over 2f out: edgd lft u.p and styd on same pce fr over 1f out* **5/1**[3]

6114 **6** *1* **Manoori (IRE)**[37] 5146 3-8-5 84 MartinDwyer 2 75
(Chris Wall) *hld up in midfield: hdwy 1/2-way: rdn and chsng ldrs wl over 1f out: wknd jst ins fnl f* **9/2**[2]

0230 **7** *1/2* **Admirable Spirit**[11] 5972 3-8-2 84 oh3 KieranO'Neill(3) 8 73
(Richard Hannon) *lw: racd in midfield: rdn and unable qck over 2f out: no imp u.p fr over 1f out* **8/1**

000 **8** *12* **Dubai Media (CAN)**[39] 5080 4-8-13 90 (t) JamieSpencer 6 41
(Ed Dunlop) *hld up wl in rr: rdn and no imp jst over 2f out: wl btn and eased ins fnl f* **7/1**

000- **9** *1 3/4* **Elkmait**[355] 6563 3-8-5 84 oh4 ChrisCatlin 10 29
(Clive Brittain) *lw: sn pushed along and struggling to go pce towards rr: lost tch 2f out* **33/1**

69.87 secs (-2.33) **Going Correction** -0.225s/f (Firm) course record
WFA 3 from 4yo 2lb **9** Ran SP% **112.2**
Speed ratings (Par 96): **106,105,105,102,100 98,98,82,79**
toteswingers: 1&2 £9.30, 1&3 £19.60, 2&3 £8.10. CSF £52.70 CT £458.95 TOTE £12.50: £3.50, £1.70, £3.80; EX 57.20 TRIFECTA Pool: £995.52 - 3.38 winning units..
Owner James Patton **Bred** James Patton **Trained** Westoning, Beds

FOCUS
This result appeared to confirm an earlier impression that it was best to come up the stands' rail. The 1-2 were always the front pair and plenty can be excused this.

NOTEBOOK
La Fortunata, who finished last of 15 at Leicester the previous Monday, got across from her wide draw and made virtually every yard once bagging the fence. This success came off a career-high mark, so she'll need to find more improvement to follow up. Official explanation: trainer's rep said, regarding apparent improvement in form, that the filly was better suited by the good to firm (good in places) ground (op 10-1)

Swiss Dream won a Listed contest two starts previously, but didn't get involved in the Portland Handicap last time. She was another to come across from a low draw and just failed to give plenty of weight away to the winner. (tchd 9-2)

Cochabamba(IRE), who finished behind Swiss Dream last time, was having her first start in a handicap and ran well, especially as she had to come off the rail to deliver her effort. (tchd 14-1 in places)

Fair Value(IRE) was a making a swift return to the track in an attempt to claim a third successive win but pulled too hard. (op 6-1 tchd 11-2)

Gouray Girl(IRE) ◆ is on what looks a fair mark, but she had no chance of getting involved after sitting towards the rear and making her effort around horses. She looks ready to go much closer in the future when conditions are more even. (tchd 9-2)

Manoori(IRE) didn't give the impression that she stays 6f in this sort of company considering how quickly she stopped. (op 5-1 tchd 11-2)

6273 ARKLE FINANCE H'CAP 1m
5:40 (5:41) (Class 3) (0-95,94) 3-Y-O+

£6,847 (£2,050; £1,025; £512; £256; £128) **Stalls** High

Form RPR

-136 **1** **Boogie Shoes**[56] 4467 3-9-4 92 NeilCallan 11 100+
(Roger Varian) *t.k.h: chsd ldrs: led ent fnl 2f: drvn over 1f out: kpt on wl fnl f* **10/3**[1]

2056 **2** *hd* **Cruiser**[13] 5892 3-8-10 84 (b[1]) MartinDwyer 10 92
(William Muir) *in tch in midfield: rdn and effrt ent fnl 2f: chal and drvn ins fnl f: kpt on wl* **13/2**[3]

0005 **3** *1 1/4* **Chapter And Verse (IRE)**[19] 5712 5-8-13 83 RichardHughes 2 88+
(Mike Murphy) *stdd s: hld up in tch in last quartet: hdwy 2f out: chsd ldrs and nt clr run ent fnl f: swtchd lft 1f out: n.m.r ins fnl f and no ex fnl 75yds* **4/1**[2]

5250 **4** *1* **Duster**[12] 5940 4-9-4 88 DaneO'Neill 9 91
(Hughie Morrison) *chsd ldrs tl wnt 2nd after 2f: ev ch and rdn 2f out: unable qck and drvn ent fnl f:* **13/2**[3]

3000 **5** *2 3/4* **Dubai Dynamo**[24] 5557 6-9-7 91 JimmyFortune 5 88
(Ruth Carr) *hld up in tch in last quartet: rdn and effrt ent fnl 2f: kpt on same pce and no imp fnl f* **16/1**

0405 **6** *1/2* **Slim Shadey**[48] 4764 3-9-4 92 (b) JamieSpencer 7 87
(J S Moore) *chsd ldr for 2f: styd chsng ldrs: rdn and ev ch 2f out: wknd 1f out* **20/1**

-050 **7** *2 3/4* **Loving Spirit**[98] 3068 3-9-6 94 RobertHavlin 1 83
(James Toller) *stdd and dropped in bhd after s: hld up in tch in last quartet: rdn and effrt on far side 2f out: edgd lft and no prog over 1f out* **7/1**

560 **8** *nk* **Emma's Gift (IRE)**[40] 5053 3-8-10 84 ow1 DarryllHolland 8 72
(Julia Feilden) *in tch in midfield: rdn 3f out: struggling and losing pl over 2f out: wknd 2f out* **33/1**

6236 **9** *1 1/4* **Fantasy Gladiator**[8] 6069 5-8-11 81 (p) JimmyQuinn 6 66
(Robert Cowell) *taken down early: restless in stalls: hld up in tch in midfield: [illegible] pushed along jst over 2f out: no prog and wl hld whn swtchd rt 1f out* **20/1**

3101 **10** *1 1/2* **Polish World (USA)**[26] 5465 7-9-2 86 BarryMcHugh 3 68
(Paul Midgley) *led tl ent fnl 2f: sn lost pl u.p: wknd 2f out* **10/1**

0503 **11** *1* **Mahadee (IRE)**[11] 5969 6-8-10 83 (p) HarryBentley(3) 4 63
(Ed de Giles) *stdd s: hld up in rr: pushed along and no hdwy whn hmpd ent fnl 2f: n.d after* **20/1**

1m 35.84s (-2.76) **Going Correction** -0.225s/f (Firm)
WFA 3 from 4yo+ 4lb **11** Ran SP% **114.4**
Speed ratings (Par 107): **104,103,102,101,98 98,95,95,94,92 91**
toteswingers: 1&2 £5.90, 1&3 £4.00, 2&3 £6.00. CSF £22.68 CT £89.69 TOTE £3.60: £1.10, £2.70, £2.00; EX 22.00 Trifecta £83.40 Pool: £923.26 - 8.19 winning units..
Owner A D Spence **Bred** Haydock Park Stud **Trained** Newmarket, Suffolk

FOCUS
Just a fair handicap and the pace was ordinary. The winner didn't need to improve much but is likely to have more to offer.

NOTEBOOK
Boogie Shoes, who hadn't run since finishing sixth in a decent 1m2f handicap at Glorious Goodwood, tends to take a grip in his races, so the drop to 1m was no bad thing, and despite shunning the apparently favoured stands' rail, just did enough to hold on. He'd struggle to defy much of a rise, and doesn't look up to pattern level, so is probably best watched next time. (tchd 11-4 and 7-2)

Cruiser showed improved form in the first-time blinkers, getting a nice tow into the race and staying on well. He'd have got up in a few more strides, but it remains to be seen whether the headgear will work as well a second time. (op 8-1 tchd 6-1)

Chapter And Verse(IRE) tracked the winner through, apparently travelling well under Richard Hughes, but he doesn't win very often and was unable to pick up when asked. (op 9-2)

Duster had his chance on this drop in grade, but the handicapper seemingly remains in control. (op 15-2)

Dubai Dynamo is beginning to ease in the weights again and there was a bit more encouragement in this display. (op 14-1)

Loving Spirit, who was running in a handicap for the first time having been highly tried earlier in the season, never looked likely to be suited by the drop in trip. He travelled well, but raced away from the main action and then couldn't quicken. Withdrawn earlier in the season because of fast ground, there's definitely a race in this well-regarded sort when ground conditions ease and he's faced with a more suitable trip. (op 13-2 tchd 8-1)

T/Jkpt: Not won. T/Plt: £41.90 to a £1 stake. Pool of £136,922.08 - 2,380.33 winning tickets. T/Qpdt: £8.30 to a £1 stake. Pool of £5,798.81 - 513.00 winning tickets. SP

6091 PONTEFRACT (L-H)

Thursday, September 22

OFFICIAL GOING: Good to firm (8.1)

Wind: Fresh half behind Weather: Cloudy

6274 WILLIAMHILL.COM/BRITISH STALLION STUDS EBF MAIDEN STKS 6f

2:30 (2:31) (Class 4) 2-Y-O **£4,463** (£1,328; £663; £331) **Stalls** Low

Form RPR

42 **1** **Glamorous Angel (IRE)**[22] 5618 2-9-3 0........................ PJMcDonald 9 82
(Alan Swinbank) *trckd ldrs: hdwy to ld 2f out: rdn clr over 1f out: kpt on* **2/1**[1]

230 **2** *1 ¼* **Right Result (IRE)**[68] 4094 2-9-3 72........................ PBBeggy 2 78
(John Quinn) *trckd ldrs: hdwy wl over 1f out: rdn to chse wnr ins fnl f: kpt on wl towards fin* **10/3**[3]

3445 **3** *9* **Marching On (IRE)**[19] 5727 2-9-3 74........................ PhillipMakin 5 50+
(Kevin Ryan) *towards rr: hdwy over 2f out and sn rdn: styd on fnl f to take 3rd nr line* **11/4**[2]

0 **4** *nk* **Classic Falcon (IRE)**[25] 5514 2-8-12 0........................ PaulHanagan 4 44+
(William Haggas) *trckd ldrs: hdwy over 2f out: rdn to chse wnr wl over 1f out: drvn and wknd ins fnl f: lost 3rd nr line* **15/2**

0 **5** *1 ¾* **Crossley**[67] 4122 2-9-0 0........................ DaleSwift(3) 7 44+
(Geoffrey Oldroyd) *dwlt and in rr: hdwy 2f out: swtchd outside and rdn wl over 1f out: kpt on: nrst fin* **25/1**

00 **6** *2 ¼* **Only A Round (IRE)**[45] 4853 2-9-3 0........................ FrederikTylicki 8 37
(Micky Hammond) *midfield: rdn along over 2f out and sn outpcd* **150/1**

525 **7** *7* **Reve Du Jour (IRE)**[39] 5077 2-8-12 64........................(p) PaddyAspell 6 10
(Alan McCabe) *hung rt thrght: led: rdn along 1/2-way: sn hdd & wknd* **16/1**

6 **8** *17* **Pavers Star**[9] 6026 2-9-3 0........................ DuranFentiman 1 —
(Noel Wilson) *dwlt: a in rr* **100/1**

9 *8* **Beaumont Cooper** 2-9-3 0........................ RussKennemore 3 —
(Anabel K Murphy) *dwlt: a in rr* **33/1**

0050 **10** *18* **Sabusa (IRE)**[8] 6043 2-9-3 55........................(p) RobertWinston 10 —
(Alan McCabe) *wnt rt s: sn chsng ldr and hanging rt: lost pl bef 1/2-way: sn bhd and eased* **50/1**

1m 16.83s (-0.07) **Going Correction** -0.05s/f (Good) **10** Ran SP% **111.1**

Speed ratings (Par 97): **98,96,84,83,81 78,69,46,35,11**

toteswingers: 1&2 £1.90, 1&3 £1.80, 2&3 £2.30. CSF £8.08 TOTE £3.00: £1.50, £1.10, £1.50; EX 9.10.

Owner S P C Woods **Bred** Carlo Soria **Trained** Melsonby, N Yorks

■ Stewards' Enquiry : Duran Fentiman caution: used whip without giving gelding time to respond.

FOCUS

Not a maiden with a great deal of depth. It was all about the first two, who finished clear. The second helps govern the level of the form.

NOTEBOOK

Glamorous Angel(IRE) confirmed himself a useful sprinter in the making by going one better than Carlisle. He had to be ridden out pretty firmly in the end but that's because he'd gone hard in the middle of the race and there's highly likely more to come, a drop to 5f and/or an easier 6f likely to suit him even better at this stage given the speed he's showing. (op 15-8)

Right Result(IRE), who'd left Richard Hannon and been gelded since last seen in July, has had a few chances now (placed five times) but sprint maidens get weaker at this time of year and he won't always run into one with the winner's potential. He saw out the stiff 6f well, pulling clear of the rest. (op 4-1)

Marching On(IRE) had shown enough speed over 7f to suggest he'd cope with this shorter trip but he didn't go with much fluency from an early stage, plugging on without ever threatening and almost certainly below the form he'd shown previously. He's one of few juveniles from the yard who hasn't gone the right way this year. (op 3-1)

Classic Falcon(IRE) may be one for handicaps after her next run but there was certainly promise in this effort, simply paying in the end for trying to keep tabs on the winner. She's well bred and it'll be a surprise if there isn't a fair bit more to come at some stage. (op 13-2 tchd 8-1)

Crossley has now hinted at ability in maidens a couple of months apart but probably won't be of any real interest until he goes handicapping. (op 33-1)

Reve Du Jour(IRE) is starting to look exposed and weakened after going hard in front, also showing a tendency to hang right. Official explanation: jockey said filly hung right (op 12-1)

Sabusa(IRE) Official explanation: jockey said gelding hung right

6275 BEST HORSE RACING SKY CHANNEL 432 FILLIES' NURSERY 1m 4y

3:05 (3:06) (Class 4) (0-85,83) 2-Y-O **£3,428** (£1,020; £509; £254) **Stalls** Low

Form RPR

010 **1** **Royal Majestic**[26] 5478 2-8-6 68........................ FrannyNorton 2 72
(Mick Channon) *trckd ldrs: hdwy 2f out: rdn to chse ldr ent fnl f: sn drvn and styd on wl to ld on line* **9/2**[3]

454 **2** *shd* **Scarlet Whispers**[26] 5464 2-8-10 72........................ GrahamGibbons 6 76
(Pam Sly) *trckd ldrs: hdwy over 2f out: effrt to chal wl over 1f out: rdn to ld appr fnl f: drvn last 100yds: hdd on line* **3/1**[2]

4404 **3** *2 ½* **Daring Damsel (IRE)**[30] 5343 2-7-12 60........................(p) CathyGannon 3 58
(Paul Cole) *led 1f: chsd ldrs: rdn along over 2f out: drvn over 1f out: kpt on u.p towards fin* **20/1**

440 **4** *shd* **Dorry K (IRE)**[26] 5464 2-8-3 65........................ DuranFentiman 1 63
(David Barron) *in rr: hdwy on inner over 2f out: rdn over 1f out: kpt on fnl f: nrst fin* **16/1**

410 **5** *½* **Basantee**[34] 5234 2-9-7 83........................ RichardKingscote 8 80
(Tom Dascombe) *cl up: led after 1 1/2f: rdn along wl over 2f out: drvn and hdd over 1f out: grad wknd* **25/1**

21 **6** *2 ¼* **Rythmic**[40] 5029 2-9-6 82........................ AhmedAjtebi 10 73
(Mahmood Al Zarooni) *hld up in rr: effrt and sme hdwy 3f out: rdn along wl over 1f out and sn no imp* **2/1**[1]

10 **7** *½* **Zingana**[47] 4803 2-9-4 80........................ PhillipMakin 7 70
(Eve Johnson Houghton) *hld up in rr: hdwy 3f out: rdn along wl over 1f out: sn btn* **8/1**

040 **8** *3 ½* **Maliha (IRE)**[16] 5806 2-8-6 68........................ TomEaves 11 50
(Kevin Ryan) *chsd ldng pair: cl up 1/2-way: rdn along over 3f out: sn wknd* **33/1**

003 **9** *15* **Aliante**[16] 5806 2-8-10 72........................ SilvestreDeSousa 9 20+
(Mark Johnston) *chsd ldrs on outer: wandered and edgd lft 3f out: hung bdly rt and rn wd home turn: bhd after* **9/1**

1m 46.37s (0.47) **Going Correction** -0.05s/f (Good) **9** Ran SP% **115.1**

Speed ratings (Par 94): **95,94,92,92,91 89,89,85,70**

toteswingers: 1&2 £3.80, 1&3 £11.80, 2&3 £13.50. CSF £17.88 CT £242.80 TOTE £4.40: £1.10, £1.70, £4.60; EX 23.30.

Owner Jaber Abdullah **Bred** Mrs B Skinner **Trained** West Ilsley, Berks

FOCUS

A soundly run nursery. Limited, straightforward form.

NOTEBOOK

Royal Majestic's Newmarket seventh had come in what's looking like a strong race and she took full advantage of a 3lb drop in the weights, the step up to 1m another thing in her favour. She's steadily going the right way and there could be more to come. (op 7-1)

Scarlet Whispers had shown promise in maidens and ran another solid race switched to a nursery, caught only near the line. Her pedigree suggests she'll stay further still in due course and it'll be a surprise if we've seen the best of her. (op 9-2)

Daring Damsel(IRE) has now made the frame on both starts in nurseries but there's no obvious sign she's progressing, having no apparent excuses here. (op 18-1)

Dorry K(IRE) is one to bear in mind for a similar event next time, still looking in need of the experience for the first half of this nursery debut but finishing to good effect late on. The step up to 1m was clearly in her favour. (op 18-1 tchd 12-1)

Basantee wasn't discredited under top weight, though had no extra inside the last having cut out the running. A drop back to 7f may suit but she's always going to be vulnerable to less-exposed types off this mark.

Rythmic had runner-up here Scarlet Whispers behind her when winning her maiden at Doncaster last month and might have been expected to do a lot better, even though she was always caught a little wider/further back than ideal. She's probably worth another chance. Official explanation: trainer's rep said filly was unsuited by the track (op 13-8)

Zingana had a more realistic chance than in pattern company last time but never threatened a serious blow. The form of the maiden she won at Newbury hasn't really worked out overall. (op 7-1)

Aliante had caught the eye on her third start but just looked a hard ride here, hanging left initially then losing all chance by veering badly right at the top of the straight. It's clearly still early days but she'll have a bit to prove next time. Official explanation: jockey said filly hung both ways throughout (op 8-1)

6276 WILLIAM HILL - THE HOME OF BETTING H'CAP 5f

3:40 (3:40) (Class 5) (0-75,74) 3-Y-O+ **£2,264** (£673; £336; £168) **Stalls** Low

Form RPR

0300 **1** **Dancing Freddy (IRE)**[8] 6044 4-9-1 71........................(tp) RobertLButler(3) 2 85
(Richard Guest) *trckd ldrs on inner: smooth hdwy 2f out: led over 1f out: rdn and qcknd clr ins fnl f: kpt on strly* **16/1**

0052 **2** *2 ¾* **Silvanus (IRE)**[29] 5373 6-8-11 64........................(p) PaulHanagan 3 68
(Paul Midgley) *trckd ldrs on inner: hdwy 2f out: swtchd rt and rdn over 1f out: chsd wnr ins fnl f: sn drvn and no imp* **12/1**

0110 **3** *1 ¾* **Lady Kildare (IRE)**[8] 6044 3-8-11 68........................ PatrickDonaghy(3) 1 66
(Jedd O'Keeffe) *led: rdn along 2f out: drvn and hdd over 1f out: kpt on same pce* **11/1**

0661 **4** *1 ½* **Select Committee**[8] 6044 6-9-6 73 6ex........................(v) PBBeggy 10 65+
(John Quinn) *in tch: effrt and nt clr run 2f out: swtchd lft to inner over 1f out: sn rdn and styd on fnl f: nrst fin* **9/1**

0223 **5** *nk* **Tislaam (IRE)**[7] 6091 4-8-13 66........................(p) RobertWinston 9 57+
(Alan McCabe) *towards rr: swtchd rt and nt clr run 2f out: swtchd outside: sn rdn and hdwy whn edgd lft over 1f out: styd on wl fnl f: nrst fin* **6/1**[3]

-512 **6** *½* **Gooseberry Bush**[13] 5890 4-9-0 67........................ SilvestreDeSousa 5 56
(Peter Makin) *chsd ldrs: rdn along 2f out: drvn over 1f out and sn no imp* **4/1**[1]

2655 **7** *2* **Mr Wolf**[7] 6091 10-9-2 69........................(p) TonyHamilton 7 51
(John Quinn) *prom: rdn along 2f out: sn drvn and grad wknd* **12/1**

4541 **8** *nk* **Bond Fastrac**[15] 5824 4-9-1 71........................ DaleSwift(3) 6 52
(Geoffrey Oldroyd) *midfield: effrt over 2f out: sn rdn and n.d* **5/1**[2]

6000 **9** *½* **Desert Strike**[5] 6174 5-9-7 74........................(p) PaddyAspell 4 53
(Alan McCabe) *dwlt: a in rr* **20/1**

0000 **10** *¾* **Mey Blossom**[7] 6094 6-9-4 71........................(v[1]) MichaelStainton 11 48
(Richard Whitaker) *chsd ldrs: rdn along 1/2-way: sn drvn and wknd* **33/1**

0205 **11** *¾* **Captain Royale (IRE)**[3] 6209 6-9-5 72........................(p) PatrickMathers 8 46
(Tracy Waggott) *chsd ldrs: rdn 2f out: sn drvn and wknd over 1f out* **8/1**

1566 **12** *2* **Lucky Dan (IRE)**[12] 5923 5-9-6 73........................ FrannyNorton 12 40
(Paul Green) *a towards rr* **10/1**

62.43 secs (-0.87) **Going Correction** -0.05s/f (Good)

WFA 3 from 4yo+ 1lb **12** Ran SP% **118.5**

Speed ratings (Par 103): **104,99,96,94,93 93,89,89,88,87 86,83**

toteswingers: 1&2 £43.60, 1&3 £50.00, 2&3 £23.10. CSF £195.04 CT £1417.21 TOTE £19.60: £6.20, £4.70, £5.70; EX 198.50.

Owner Rakebackmypoker.com **Bred** Vincent Duignan **Trained** Stainforth, S Yorks

■ Stewards' Enquiry : Robert Winston one-day ban: used whip continuously down shoulder (Oct 17)

FOCUS

They went a sound gallop in this sprint but very few ever threatened to land a serious blow. There is some doubt over how literally to take this, with the winner apparently back to his old 2yo best. The first three came out of the three lowest stalls.

Dancing Freddy(IRE) Official explanation: trainer's rep had no explanation for the apparent improvement in form

6277 SIMON SCROPE DALBY SCREW-DRIVER H'CAP 1m 2f 6y

4:15 (4:16) (Class 2) (0-105,105) 3-Y-O+

£9,960 (£2,982; £1,491; £745; £372; £187) **Stalls** Low

Form RPR

0526 **1** **Art History (IRE)**[13] 5888 3-8-3 86 oh2........................ SilvestreDeSousa 4 95+
(Mark Johnston) *in tch: pushed along 1/2-way: rdn 3f out: hdwy 2f out: drvn ent fnl f: styd on wl to ld nr fin* **3/1**[1]

6120 **2** *hd* **Suits Me**[62] 4267 8-9-4 95........................ PaulHanagan 1 104
(David Barron) *led: pushed along and qcknd over 2f out: rdn over 1f out: drvn ins fnl f and kpt on gamely: hdd and no ex nr fin* **11/2**[3]

3 *nk* **Fattsota**[88] 3-8-5 93........................ AntiocoMurgia(5) 5 101
(Marco Botti) *trckd ldrs: hdwy 3f out: chsd ldr whn wandered and hung lft over 1f out: drvn and ev ch whn edgd lft ins fnl f: kpt on wl towards fin* **8/1**

0232 **4** *1* **Hong Kong Island (IRE)**[27] 5435 4-8-6 86........................ DaleSwift(3) 3 92
(Micky Hammond) *hld up in rr: gd hdwy on inner 3f out: rdn to chse ldrs wl over 1f out: sn swtchd rt and rdn: kpt on ins fnl f: nrst fin* **9/2**[2]

3401 **5** *14* **Demolition**[18] 5757 7-8-10 90........................ LeeTopliss(3) 6 68
(Richard Fahey) *hld up: hdwy over 3f out: rdn along over 2f out: n.d* **8/1**

3135 **6** *hd* **Udabaa (IRE)**[69] 4058 4-9-0 91........................(p) TadhgO'Shea 7 69
(Marcus Tregoning) *chsd ldrs: rdn along over 2f out: wkng whn hmpd over 1f out* **8/1**

-006 **7** *17* **Royal Revival**[196] 829 4-10-0 105........................ TedDurcan 8 49
(Saeed Bin Suroor) *hld up in rr: effrt and sme hdwy over 2f out: sn rdn and btn: eased wl over 1f out* **14/1**

15 **8** *30* **Classic Punch (IRE)**[19] 5711 8-9-8 99........................ PhillipMakin 2 —
(David Elsworth) *cl up: rdn along 3f out: drvn 2f out: wkng whn hmpd 1f out: sn bhd whn eased wl over 1f out* **6/1**

2m 10.05s (-3.65) **Going Correction** -0.125s/f (Firm)

WFA 3 from 4yo+ 6lb **8** Ran SP% **112.9**

Speed ratings (Par 109): **109,108,108,107,96 96,82,58**

toteswingers: 1&2 £3.10, 1&3 £6.40, 2&3 £7.60. CSF £19.02 CT £116.93 TOTE £4.40: £1.70, £2.20, £3.10; EX 19.60.

The Form Book, Raceform Ltd, Compton, RG20 6NL

Owner Sheikh Hamdan Bin Mohammed Al Maktoum **Bred** Kenilworth House Stud **Trained** Middleham Moor, N Yorks
■ Stewards' Enquiry : Dale Swift one-day ban: careless riding (Oct 6)

FOCUS
A useful contest. The pace looked a fair one once Suits Me had won the early battle for the lead. The first four all raced on the rail but the form seems solid.

NOTEBOOK
Art History(IRE) had never threatened in what is likely to turn out to be a strong conditions race at Doncaster last time but a return to a stiffer 1m2f saw him resume winning ways, staying on strongly to lead near the finish. He has had a fair bit of racing but it would be no surprise if he still had more to offer and he's got to be worth another try over 1m4f at some stage. (op 4-1 tchd 9-2)
Suits Me is consistent in the main and was back on track after a break since his Ascot flop in July, as usual giving it his all from the front. He's likely to continue to give a good account. (op 13-2)
Fattsota, a half-brother to Falbrav amongst others, certainly offered enough to suggest he has the ability to win races off this sort of mark over here (previously trained in Italy), travelling comfortably but not helping his cause by hanging to his left off the bridle under his claimer. He has the odd quirk but it would be no surprise if he kept a straighter line for stronger handling. (op 9-1 tchd 10-1)
Hong Kong Island(IRE) has been one of the most consistent handicappers around this season and this was another sound effort down in trip, but he has crept up the ratings without winning of late. (op 11-2)
Demolition had taken advantage of a drop in grade at York last time but might still have been expected to do better back in a handicap. (op 15-2 tchd 9-1 in a place)
Udabaa(IRE), who'd been gelded since last seen in July, didn't go with any encouragement back from his break. (tchd 7-1)
Classic Punch(IRE) Official explanation: trainer's rep had no explanation for the poor form shown

6278 VISIT WILLIAMHILL.COM ON YOUR MOBILE EBF MAIDEN STKS 1m 4y
4:50 (4:50) (Class 4) 2-Y-O **£4,463** (£1,328; £663; £331) **Stalls** Low

Form				RPR
43	**1**		**Sir Trevor (IRE)**[13] 5875 2-9-3 0................ RichardKingscote 6 (Tom Dascombe) *mde all: rdn clr over 1f out: drvn out* **10/3**[2]	79
	2	*2 ¾*	**El Lail (USA)** 2-8-12 0................ TadhgO'Shea 8 (Mark Johnston) *a trcking wnr: effrt over 2f out: sn rdn: green and sltly outpcd: drvn and styd on ins fnl f* **12/1**	68+
0	**3**	*3 ½*	**Blue Top**[27] 5454 2-9-3 0................ DuranFentiman 2 (Tim Walford) *a.p: rdn along 2f out: drvn over 1f out and kpt on same pce* **66/1**	65
03	**4**	*1*	**Really Lovely (IRE)**[26] 5464 2-8-12 0................ PhillipMakin 4 (Jeremy Noseda) *dwlt: t.k.h in rr: hdwy over 2f out: rdn wl over 1f out: kpt on ins fnl f: nvr rchd ldrs* **6/4**[1]	57+
60	**5**	*3 ¾*	**Cloud Cuckooland (IRE)**[15] 5819 2-8-12 0................ JamesSullivan 1 (James Given) *in rr: rdn along 1/2-way: sme late hdwy* **50/1**	49
	6	*6*	**No Dominion (IRE)** 2-9-3 0................ FrederikTylicki 5 (James Given) *a towards rr* **12/1**	40
	7	*hd*	**Jarrah** 2-9-3 0................ TedDurcan 3 (Saeed Bin Suroor) *hld up in tch: effrt 3f out: rdn along over 2f out: sn wknd* **7/2**[3]	39
	8	*31*	**Run Richard Run** 2-9-3 0................ TomEaves 7 (Bryan Smart) *chsd ldrs on outer: rdn along 4f out: sn wknd and bhd* **10/1**	—

1m 46.43s (0.53) **Going Correction** -0.05s/f (Good) **8** Ran SP% **113.2**
Speed ratings (Par 97): **95,92,88,87,84 78,77,46**
toteswingers: 1&2 £6.00, 1&3 £15.70, 2&3 £23.20. CSF £41.17 TOTE £4.00: £1.90, £2.00, £8.30; EX 45.30.
Owner D R Passant **Bred** Barry Noonan And Denis Noonan **Trained** Malpas, Cheshire

FOCUS
A maiden which lacked depth. The winner dictated a steady pace and the second put in a fair debut.

NOTEBOOK
Sir Trevor(IRE) has got better with each start and did this comfortably for all he had the advantage of dictating. There's no reason he won't continue to go the right way. (op 4-1 tchd 3-1)
El Lail(USA), a daughter of Haafhd, was no match for the winner but this was a promising start and she's achieved enough in pulling clear of the rest to suggest she'll pick up a race before long, particularly as improvement is likely. (op 9-1 tchd 14-1)
Blue Top had been well beaten on testing ground on his debut a month ago and the quicker conditions provide a ready explanation for the big improvement, though he never seriously threatened the leading pair. (op 80-1)
Really Lovely(IRE) didn't have things go her way and is better judged on her Beverley third, going well under restraint (again raced keenly) but not getting in the clear until it was too late. Official explanation: jockey said filly missed the break and ran too free (op 13-8 tchd 11-8)
Cloud Cuckooland(IRE) offered a little more than her first two starts and this opens up the handicap route for her. Longer trips are likely to suit if her pedigree is any guide. (op 40-1)
Jarrah was the obvious disappointment given he was prominent in the betting. (tchd 4-1)

6279 WILLIAM HILL - TRANSFORMING, INNOVATING, PERFORMING APPRENTICE H'CAP 1m 4f 8y
5:25 (5:25) (Class 5) (0-75,81) 3-Y-0+ **£2,264** (£673; £336; £168) **Stalls** Low

Form				RPR
0031	**1**		**The Bells O Peover**[8] 6046 3-9-11 **81** 6ex................(b) DarylByrne 8 (Mark Johnston) *cl up: led after 3f: rdn clr 2f out: styd on strly: unchal* **7/2**[2]	95
1010	**2**	*18*	**Brasingaman Eric**[23] 5595 4-8-8 **61** oh1................ JasonHart(5) 2 (George Moore) *hld up in tch: hdwy over 3f out: rdn to chse wnr over 1f out: kpt on but no ch w wnr* **6/1**	46
6146	**3**	*2 ¾*	**Mason Hindmarsh**[19] 5724 4-9-0 **67**................ DavidSimmonson(5) 5 (Karen McLintock) *led 3f: prom: rdn along over 2f out: sn drvn and plugged on one pce* **11/1**	48
43/0	**4**	*2 ½*	**Mr Crystal (FR)**[18] 5759 7-9-9 **74**................ GeorgeChaloner(3) 10 (Micky Hammond) *towards rr: hdwy 1/2-way: rdn along and outpcd over 4f out: styd on fr wl over 1f out: nvr nr ldrs* **14/1**	51
530	**5**	*5*	**Munaawib**[23] 5598 3-8-12 **68**................ CharlesBishop 1 (David C Griffiths) *chsd ldrs on inner: rdn along over 3f out: drvn over 2f out and sn wknd* **33/1**	37
2205	**6**	*1 ½*	**Rubi Dia**[27] 5440 4-9-2 **64**................(tp) JustinNewman 7 (Kevin M Prendergast) *hld up: hdwy 1/2-way: rdn to chse ldrs 4f out: drvn along 3f out: sn wknd* **16/1**	30
2010	**7**	*3*	**Lauberhorn**[16] 5804 4-9-0 **62**................(b) AntiocoMurgia 6 (Eve Johnson Houghton) *chsd ldrs: rdn along and lost pl 1/2-way: sn bhd* **11/1**	24
6432	**8**	*22*	**George Adamson (IRE)**[5] 6155 5-9-13 **75**................ GarryWhillans 3 (Alan Swinbank) *racd wd: in tch: effrt to chse ldrs 1/2-way rdn along over 4f out: sn wknd and bhd* **9/4**[1]	—
0151	**9**	*12*	**Kian's Delight**[29] 5372 3-8-5 **61**................ DavidKenny 4 (Jedd O'Keeffe) *towards rr: hdwy 1/2-way: rdn to chse ldrs 4f out: wknd over 3f out: sn bhd and eased* **11/2**[3]	—

2m 38.62s (-2.18) **Going Correction** -0.125s/f (Firm)
WFA 3 from 4yo+ 8lb **9** Ran SP% **114.8**
Speed ratings (Par 103): **102,90,88,86,83 82,80,65,57**
toteswingers: 1&2 £4.80, 1&3 £9.40, 2&3 £8.30. CSF £24.70 CT £207.76 TOTE £4.30: £1.80, £2.10, £3.10; EX 28.30.
Owner D & G Mercer **Bred** Belgrave Bloodstock Ltd **Trained** Middleham Moor, N Yorks
■ Stewards' Enquiry : Justin Newman one-day ban: used whip with excessive frequency (Oct 6)

FOCUS
A most one-sided handicap and it's hard to put a figure on the winner. It was a day that front-runners did well through the card and a number of the others were below par. The winner has been rated up 10lb.
George Adamson(IRE) Official explanation: trainer's rep had no explanation for the poor form shown
Kian's Delight Official explanation: jockey said gelding never travelled
T/Plt: £674.50 to a £1 stake. Pool of £51,651.34 - 55.90 winning tickets. T/Qpdt: £97.80 to a £1 stake. Pool of £3,211.58 - 24.30 winning tickets. JR

6175 WOLVERHAMPTON (A.W) (L-H)
Thursday, September 22

OFFICIAL GOING: Standard changing to standard to fast after race 3 (6.30).
STANDARD changing to STANDARD TO FAST after Race 3 (6.30).
Wind: Fresh behind Weather: Overcast

6280 DAY TIME, NIGHT TIME, GREAT TIME CLAIMING STKS 7f 32y(P)
5:30 (5:31) (Class 6) 2-Y-O **£1,704** (£503; £251) **Stalls** High

Form				RPR
5000	**1**		**Adranian (IRE)**[13] 5899 2-9-1 64................(v) JamesDoyle 4 (David Evans) *a.p: nt clr run wl over 1f out: sn rdn: r.o u.p to ld post* **14/1**	64
4351	**2**	*nk*	**King Kenobi (IRE)**[16] 5802 2-8-13 61................ LiamKeniry 1 (J S Moore) *chsd ldrs: rdn over 1f out: led nr fin: hdd post* **4/1**[2]	61
5403	**3**	*nk*	**Emerald Smile (IRE)**[21] 5637 2-8-2 55................ LukeMorris 5 (J S Moore) *led: rdn over 1f out: hdd nr fin* **14/1**	50
063	**4**	*1 ½*	**Zammy**[12] 5919 2-9-0 68................ MatthewLawson(5) 3 (Charles Hills) *hld up: hdwy over 2f out: rdn over 1f out: styd on: nt rch ldrs* **9/1**	63
46	**5**	*3*	**Bogey Hole (IRE)**[23] 5596 2-8-0 0................ CathyGannon 8 (Tom Dascombe) *s.i.s: hld up: nt clr run fr over 1f out tl swtchd lft ins fnl f: r.o: nvr rchd ldrs* **25/1**	41
2650	**6**	*½*	**Maccabees**[11] 5967 2-9-5 70................ JamesMillman 10 (Rod Millman) *hld up in tch: rdn over 1f out: no ex ins fnl f* **7/4**[1]	54
0020	**7**	*2 ¼*	**Mormoran**[10] 6002 2-8-3 50................(p) AdamBeschizza(3) 9 (Chris Dwyer) *hld up: rdn over 2f out: nvr trbld ldrs* **33/1**	36
5106	**8**	*1*	**Colourful Event (IRE)**[8] 6053 2-8-6 59................(v[1]) DavidAllan 7 (David Arbuthnot) *chsd ldrs: rdn over 2f out: wknd fnl f* **7/1**[3]	33
6	**9**	*6*	**Ned Causer**[34] 5246 2-9-1 0................ GrahamGibbons 6 (Reg Hollinshead) *chsd ldr tl rdn and wknd over 1f out* **8/1**	28
3563	**10**	*¾*	**Reina Sofia**[30] 5353 2-8-0 55................(p) FrankieMcDonald 11 (David Bridgwater) *in rr whn reminders over 5f out: bhd fnl 4f* **16/1**	11
0	**11**	*12*	**Cool Ice**[17] 5779 2-7-13 0................ IanBurns(7) 12 (Ron Hodges) *s.i.s: a in rr: bhd fnl 4f* **100/1**	—
00	**12**	*1 ¼*	**Goon Piper**[28] 5413 2-8-5 0................(b[1]) AndrewElliott 2 (Tom Dascombe) *a in rr: bhd fnl 4f* **100/1**	—

1m 30.14s (0.54) **Going Correction** -0.125s/f (Stan) **12** Ran SP% **118.0**
Speed ratings (Par 93): **91,90,90,88,85 84,82,80,74,73 59,58**
toteswingers: 1&2 £12.50, 1&3 £17.50, 2&3 £6.90. CSF £67.96 TOTE £29.20: £6.30, £1.80, £5.10; EX 94.00 TRIFECTA Not won..
Owner Cos We Can Partnership **Bred** Hugh O'Brien **Trained** Pandy, Monmouths

FOCUS
This was dominated by horses that race handily. Solid but limited form.

NOTEBOOK
Adranian(IRE) showed improved form in a maiden in his previous race, where he did not quite last 1m, and made the drop in class pay. However, he is higher in the weights now, so a return to handicaps is likely to be tough.
King Kenobi(IRE), switching from selling grade to a claimer, ran with credit and looks an honest performer in either grade. (op 7-2 tchd 10-3)
Emerald Smile(IRE), given a good front-running ride, was just run out of it late on. She is effective at this trip but only just gets it at present. (op 10-1)
Zammy, who has some respectable maiden form on turf, did best of the hold-up runners. He should find a race at a modest level.
Bogey Hole(IRE), who is more stamina than speed, appeared to stay the extra 1f well and could even get 1m on this evidence. (op 33-1)
Maccabees, stuck wide throughout from an unhelpful draw, is worth another chance at this level. (op 5-2 tchd 13-8)

6281 WILLIAM HILL - THE HOME OF BETTING MEDIAN AUCTION MAIDEN STKS 5f 216y(P)
6:00 (6:01) (Class 5) 2-Y-O **£2,264** (£673; £336; £168) **Stalls** Low

Form				RPR
	1		**For Shia And Lula (IRE)**[25] 5521 2-9-3 0................ ShaneKelly 6 (Daniel Mark Loughnane, Ire) *hld up: hdwy over 2f out: led over 1f out: rdn and hdd ins fnl f: rallied to ld post* **20/1**	75
533	**2**	*shd*	**Ashbina**[24] 5541 2-8-12 70................ LiamJones 7 (William Haggas) *chsd ldrs: rdn over 2f out: led ins fnl f: hdd post* **11/4**[2]	70+
	3	*3*	**Jake's Destiny (IRE)** 2-9-3 0................ PatCosgrave 9 (George Baker) *chsd ldrs: pushed along over 2f out: rdn and swtchd lft ent fnl f: styd on* **13/2**	66+
6202	**4**	*3 ¼*	**Chillie Billie**[14] 5863 2-9-3 74................ KierenFallon 1 (Phil McEntee) *led: rdn and hdd over 1f out: wknd ins fnl f* **5/4**[1]	56
55	**5**	*¾*	**Princess Palmer**[14] 5854 2-8-5 0................ LeonnaMayor(7) 3 (Hugo Palmer) *chsd ldr tl rdn wl over 1f out: nt clr run sn after: wknd ins fnl f* **18/1**	49+
0	**6**	*1 ½*	**La Sonadora**[30] 5347 2-8-12 0................ CathyGannon 8 (John Spearing) *plld hrd and prom: n.m.r and lost pl 5f out: n.d after* **50/1**	44+
02	**7**	*11*	**Arctic Stryker**[27] 5424 2-9-3 0................ LukeMorris 4 (John Best) *chsd ldrs: rdn over 2f out: wknd wl over 1f out* **5/1**[3]	15
	8	*15*	**The Quarterjack** 2-9-3 0................ DavidProbert 5 (Ron Hodges) *s.s: a in rr: lost tch fr wl over 2f out: t.o* **40/1**	—

1m 14.92s (-0.08) **Going Correction** -0.125s/f (Stan) **8** Ran SP% **115.5**
Speed ratings (Par 95): **95,94,90,86,85 83,68,48**
toteswingers: 1&2 £7.40, 1&3 £9.90, 2&3 £3.50. CSF £74.62 TOTE £17.60: £4.60, £1.10, £2.50; EX 87.00 Trifecta £630.20 Pool: £8,005.85 - 9.40 winning units..
Owner M V Kirby **Bred** A M F Persse **Trained** Trim, Co Meath

FOCUS
A routine maiden. Limited form set around the second and fourth, but an improved effort from the winner.

NOTEBOOK
For Shia And Lula(IRE) still looked a bit green in the finish but battled back to regain it on the line. Related to two winners on Polytrack, he would be at home on this surface during the winter but connections expect him to mature, so he will have just one more race this season in nursery company, and then wait for next year. (tchd 22-1)
Ashbina nearly made a winning AW debut, only to lose out in last two strides, but there will be similar opportunities. (tchd 5-2 and 3-1)
Jake's Destiny(IRE), a gelded debutant, is a half-brother to a 2yo winner at 7f and out of a 2yo winner at the same distance. He was off the bridle after 2f so, like them, he should be suited by an extra furlong. (tchd 11-2)
Chillie Billie showed plenty of speed but was easily passed. He got this trip well last time but is exposed in maiden company. (op 11-8 tchd 6-4, 7-4 in places)
Princess Palmer has shown some ability in turf and Polytrack maidens but looks more of a nursery type. Official explanation: vet said filly finished distressed (op 14-1)
La Sonadora is out of a winning sprinter, but what early pace she showed did not last long, and her main hope may stem from other winners in the family with more stamina. (op 66-1)
Arctic Stryker Official explanation: jockey said colt hung left

6282 WILLIAMHILL.COM H'CAP (DIV I) 5f 216y(P)
6:30 (6:32) (Class 5) (0-75,75) 3-Y-O+ **£1,940** (£577; £288; £144) **Stalls** Low

Form RPR
6663 **1** **Shifting Star (IRE)**[17] 5781 6-9-3 **74**....[1] SeanLevey(3) 1 84
(Walter Swinburn) *chsd ldrs: pushed along over 2f out: rdn to ld ins fnl f: hung lft: r.o* **10/3**[1]
2500 **2** *nk* **Roman Strait**[47] 4799 3-8-8 **64**.... LiamKeniry 6 73
(Michael Blanshard) *hld up: hdwy over 2f out: rdn over 1f out: r.o* **17/2**
5104 **3** *nk* **Dazeen**[15] 5835 4-9-3 **71**....(b) TonyCulhane 5 79+
(David Flood) *hld up: nt clr run over 2f out: hdwy u.p over 1f out: r.o* **13/2**[2]
020 **4** *4* **Sir Nod**[13] 5881 9-9-5 **73**.... DavidAllan 2 68
(Julie Camacho) *w ldr tl led over 3f out: rdn and hdd over 1f out: no ex ins fnl f* **8/1**[3]
5563 **5** *¾* **Interchoice Star**[13] 5881 6-8-10 **64**....(p) LukeMorris 9 57
(Ray Peacock) *prom: chsd ldr 1/2-way: rdn to ld over 1f out: hdd and no ex ins fnl f* **12/1**
04 **6** *4 ½* **Fantasy Fighter (IRE)**[13] 5895 6-8-4 **61**....(p) AdamBeschizza(3) 10 39
(John E Long) *s.s: hld up: rdn over 2f out: n.d* **14/1**
6043 **7** *nk* **Maverik**[29] 5370 3-9-5 **75**.... TonyHamilton 7 52
(Michael Dods) *prom: rdn over 2f out: wknd wl over 1f out* **10/3**[1]
5240 **8** *2 ¾* **Sherjawy (IRE)**[21] 5640 7-8-13 **67**.... KirstyMilczarek 8 36
(Zoe Davison) *led: hdd over 3f out: sn rdn: wknd wl over 1f out* **25/1**
3000 **9** *¾* **Zip Lock (IRE)**[12] 5948 5-9-2 **75**....(tp) LucyKBarry(5) 3 41
(Olivia Maylam) *prom: pushed along over 2f out: wknd over 1f out* **10/1**
6250 **10** *1 ½* **Ace Of Spies (IRE)**[13] 5895 6-8-10 **67**....(b) MartinHarley(3) 4 28
(Conor Dore) *chsd ldrs: rdn over 2f out: sn wknd* **33/1**

1m 13.47s (-1.53) **Going Correction** -0.125s/f (Stan)
WFA 3 from 4yo+ 2lb **10** Ran SP% **111.4**
Speed ratings (Par 103): **105,104,104,98,97 91,91,87,86,84**
toteswingers: 1&2 £10.80, 1&3 £3.80, 2&3 £9.50. CSF £30.74 CT £172.02 TOTE £3.60: £1.50, £2.80, £2.30; EX 31.60 Trifecta £252.30 Pool: £7,708.91 - 20.76 winning units..
Owner Night Shadow Syndicate **Bred** Hardys Of Kilkeel Ltd **Trained** Aldbury, Herts

FOCUS
A fairly run contest, with the winner always handy and the next two coming from the rear. It was the faster division and the form looks fair for the level. The winner will still be on a good mark after this.

6283 WILLIAMHILL.COM H'CAP (DIV II) 5f 216y(P)
7:00 (7:00) (Class 5) (0-75,75) 3-Y-O+ **£1,940** (£577; £288; £144) **Stalls** Low

Form RPR
1132 **1** **Little Jimmy Odsox (IRE)**[24] 5554 3-9-5 **75**.... DavidAllan 6 83+
(Tim Easterby) *chsd ldrs: rdn over 2f out: led and edgd lft ins fnl f: r.o* **11/4**[1]
5460 **2** *nk* **Scarlet Rocks (IRE)**[23] 5578 3-8-13 **69**.... JamesDoyle 8 76
(David Evans) *s.i.s: hld up: hdwy over 1f out: rdn and ev ch ins fnl f: r.o* **12/1**
2011 **3** *nse* **Mount Hollow**[7] 6091 6-8-10 **64**....(p) GrahamGibbons 5 71+
(Reg Hollinshead) *s.i.s: hld up: hdwy over 1f out: sn rdn: nt clr run ins fnl f: r.o wl* **11/4**[1]
4050 **4** *¾* **Absa Lutte (IRE)**[5] 6177 8-9-2 **70**.... KierenFallon 9 74
(Michael Mullineaux) *s.i.s: hld up: rdn over 1f out: r.o wl ins fnl f: nt quite rch ldrs* **12/1**
0204 **5** *2 ¼* **Tamareen (IRE)**[12] 5918 3-9-4 **74**.... TonyHamilton 3 71
(Richard Fahey) *led: rdn over 1f out: hdd and no ex ins fnl f* **5/1**[2]
3-06 **6** *½* **First In Command (IRE)**[19] 5736 6-8-5 **62**....(t) MartinHarley(3) 10 58
(Daniel Mark Loughnane, Ire) *hld up: rdn over 2f out: r.o ins fnl f: nvr nrr* **9/1**[3]
420 **7** *1 ½* **Caledonia Princess**[26] 5467 5-9-5 **73**.... J-PGuillambert 4 64
(Jo Hughes) *prom: chsd ldr 4f out: rdn over 1f out: no ex ins fnl f* **11/1**
0600 **8** *2* **Sarah's Art (IRE)**[5] 6177 8-9-7 **75**....(t) RobbieFitzpatrick 7 59
(Derek Shaw) *mid-div: rdn over 2f out: wknd over 1f out* **33/1**
0460 **9** *½* **Kyllachy Storm**[24] 5539 7-8-0 **61** oh1....(b) IanBurns(7) 1 44
(Ron Hodges) *chsd ldr 2f: rdn 1/2-way: wknd over 1f out* **28/1**
0000 **10** *7* **Insolenceofoffice (IRE)**[12] 5924 3-8-6 **65**....(p) BillyCray(3) 2 25
(Bruce Hellier) *chsd ldrs: rdn over 3f out: wknd wl over 1f out* **40/1**

1m 14.22s (-0.78) **Going Correction** -0.125s/f (Stan)
WFA 3 from 5yo+ 2lb **10** Ran SP% **112.5**
Speed ratings (Par 103): **100,99,99,98,95 94,92,90,89,80**
toteswingers: 1&2 £7.40, 1&3 £2.60, 2&3 £7.90. CSF £36.35 CT £96.89 TOTE £2.80: £1.10, £3.60, £1.50; EX 32.50 Trifecta £114.20 Pool: £4,995.00 - 32.35 winning units..
Owner Reality Partnerships III **Bred** Dr D Crone & P Lafarge & P Johnston **Trained** Great Habton, N Yorks
■ Stewards' Enquiry : James Doyle one-day ban: used whip with excessive frequency without giving filly time to respond (Oct 6)

FOCUS
This was modest but competitive, with a close three-way finish. It was slower than division I although the pace looked alright. A bunch finish, but sound enough form.

6284 BOOK NOW FOR CHRISTMAS NURSERY 5f 216y(P)
7:30 (7:30) (Class 5) (0-70,80) 2-Y-O **£1,908** (£563; £281) **Stalls** Low

Form RPR
1010 **1** **Aquasulis (IRE)**[3] 6222 2-9-7 **69**.... KierenFallon 5 71
(David Evans) *chsd ldrs: shkn up over 2f out: rdn to ld wl ins fnl f: r.o* **7/2**[1]
3433 **2** *¾* **Fast On (IRE)**[29] 5374 2-9-3 **65**....(v) GrahamGibbons 10 65
(Ed McMahon) *a.p: chsd ldr 4f out: led over 1f out: rdn and hdd wl ins fnl f* **4/1**[2]
006 **3** *nk* **Millibar (IRE)**[98] 3092 2-9-4 **66**.... TomMcLaughlin 6 65
(Nick Littmoden) *hld up in tch: racd keenly: rdn over 1f out: r.o* **10/1**
5051 **4** *¾* **Faraway**[5] 6178 2-9-5 **72** 6ex....(v) MatthewCosham(5) 8 69
(David Evans) *s.i.s: hld up: nt clr run over 2f out: hdwy over 1f out: r.o* **9/1**
040 **5** *½* **Love Tale**[16] 5801 2-8-12 **60**.... LukeMorris 7 55
(Mark Rimell) *chsd ldrs: rdn over 1f out: styd on* **16/1**
0213 **6** *1 ½* **Artists Corner**[34] 5246 2-9-1 **63**.... PaulHanagan 4 53
(Richard Fahey) *s.i.s: hld up: rdn over 1f out: edgd lft and styd on ins fnl f: nvr nrr* **9/2**[3]
5200 **7** *nse* **Key Addition (IRE)**[14] 5840 2-9-5 **67**....(b) SilvestreDeSousa 12 57
(William Muir) *sn led: rdn and hdd over 1f out: no ex ins fnl f* **14/1**
1305 **8** *1 ½* **Lady Nickandy (IRE)**[10] 5998 2-8-8 **59**.... MartinHarley(3) 2 44
(Alan McCabe) *hld up: rdn over 1f out: n.d* **33/1**
0160 **9** *1 ¼* **Selbaar**[10] 5998 2-8-8 **59**....(b[1]) AdamBeschizza(3) 11 41
(Chris Dwyer) *mid-div: rdn over 2f out: wknd over 1f out* **16/1**
5334 **P** **Sunley Valentine**[10] 6002 2-9-1 **63**.... TonyCulhane 1 —
(Mick Channon) *s.i.s: last whn wnt lame wl over 3f out: sn p.u* **8/1**

1m 14.74s (-0.26) **Going Correction** -0.125s/f (Stan) **10** Ran SP% **112.0**
Speed ratings (Par 95): **96,95,94,93,92 90,90,88,87,—**
toteswingers: 1&2 £4.30, 1&3 £8.20, 2&3 £14.60. CSF £16.51 CT £123.46 TOTE £4.20: £1.40, £1.80, £2.80; EX 17.50 Trifecta £78.00 Pool: £5,718.11 - 54.18 winning units..
Owner Bathwick Gold Partnership **Bred** Rathasker Stud **Trained** Pandy, Monmouths

FOCUS
A well contested nursery, run at a good pace. Modest but straightforward form.

NOTEBOOK
Aquasulis(IRE) made it three wins from five visits to Wolverhampton. However, this was her first win outside selling and claiming company, so she still seems to be improving at a modest level. (op 9-2)
Fast On(IRE) continues to run well in the visor, but yet again he wasn't quite good enough. He seems fine at this trip but ought to stay 7f.
Millibar(IRE) made an encouraging first appearance in handicap company and looks a likely future winner. This trip suits her better than 5f, and 7f should be within reach.
Faraway, whose two wins were in sellers, put in a solid effort under a big weight. (op 17-2)
Love Tale made a creditable handicap debut and should be competitive again. 7f seemed a fraction too far on turf but this run suggests she will stay that trip. (op 20-1)

6285 MOBET.WILLIAMHILL.COM FILLIES' H'CAP 1m 141y(P)
8:00 (8:01) (Class 5) (0-75,74) 3-Y-O+ **£2,264** (£673; £336; £168) **Stalls** Low

Form RPR
-F12 **1** **Mrs Dee Bee (IRE)**[26] 5496 3-9-5 **74**.... RobertWinston 7 85+
(Charles Hills) *led 7f out: rdn over 1f out: edgd lft ins fnl f: styd on* **6/4**[1]
6304 **2** *1 ½* **Indian Valley (USA)**[26] 5496 4-9-6 **70**....(b) LukeMorris 8 78
(Hugo Palmer) *hld up: hdwy 4f out: rdn over 1f out: r.o to go 2nd wl ins fnl f: nt rch wnr* **8/1**
5000 **3** *½* **Hill Tribe**[19] 5740 4-8-10 **60**.... KierenFallon 4 67
(Richard Guest) *chsd ldrs: rdn over 1f out: styd on same pce ins fnl f* **12/1**
5060 **4** *2* **Red Yarn**[34] 5231 4-9-3 **67**.... GeorgeBaker 6 69
(Gary Moore) *sn led: hdd 7f out: chsd wnr: rdn over 2f out: no ex fnl f* **16/1**
0304 **5** *2 ¼* **Symphonic Dancer (USA)**[13] 5900 4-8-12 **62**.... J-PGuillambert 1 59
(Brian Baugh) *hld up: hdwy u.p over 1f out: nt trble ldrs* **16/1**
40 **6** *¾* **Dan's Martha**[38] 5109 3-8-12 **70**....(t) PatrickDonaghy(3) 10 65
(Ben Haslam) *s.i.s: hld up: rdn over 1f out: nt trble ldrs* **33/1**
3562 **7** *2 ¾* **Carcinetto (IRE)**[6] 6138 9-8-13 **63**.... SilvestreDeSousa 9 52
(David Evans) *chsd ldrs: rdn over 2f out: wknd over 1f out* **5/1**[2]
1-53 **8** *3 ¼* **Swift Breeze**[20] 5676 3-9-0 **69**.... LiamJones 5 51
(William Haggas) *s.i.s: hld up: rdn over 2f out: n.d* **7/1**[3]
0606 **9** *2 ¾* **Forward Feline (IRE)**[14] 5845 5-9-3 **67**.... DavidProbert 3 42
(Bryn Palling) *hld up: hdwy 3f out: rdn and wknd wl over 1f out* **16/1**
0063 **P** **Satwa Sunrise (FR)**[49] 4713 4-8-10 **60** oh3.... PaulHanagan 2 —
(Ed Dunlop) *prom tl lost action and p.u over 6f out* **10/1**

1m 48.77s (-1.73) **Going Correction** -0.125s/f (Stan)
WFA 3 from 4yo+ 5lb **10** Ran SP% **117.6**
Speed ratings (Par 100): **102,100,100,98,96 95,93,90,88,—**
toteswingers: 1&2 £3.50, 1&3 £9.20, 2&3 £18.00. CSF £14.27 CT £109.15 TOTE £3.80: £1.40, £2.00, £2.30; EX 18.60 Trifecta £149.50 Pool: £388.14 - 1.92 winning units..
Owner South Bank Thoroughbred Racing **Bred** M Fahy **Trained** Lambourn, Berks

FOCUS
This went to one of the less exposed runners in the field. The winner looked better than the bare form in a muddling race.
Forward Feline(IRE) Official explanation: jockey said mare hung right-handed
Satwa Sunrise(FR) Official explanation: jockey said filly was struck into and lost its action

6286 WOLVERHAMPTON-RACECOURSE.CO.UK MAIDEN STKS 1m 4f 50y(P)
8:30 (8:32) (Class 5) 3-Y-O+ **£2,264** (£673; £336; £168) **Stalls** Low

Form RPR
3-5 **1** **Tonnerre (IRE)**[12] 5911 3-9-3 0.... KierenFallon 7 89+
(Sir Michael Stoute) *hld up: hdwy 1/2-way: shkn up to ld over 1f out: sn hung lft: styd on wl: readily* **10/3**[2]
23 **2** *3 ¼* **Asaid**[12] 5911 3-9-3 0....(v[1]) PaulHanagan 12 81
(Saeed Bin Suroor) *led: hung rt and reminder over 9f out: rdn over 2f out: hdd and hmpd over 1f out: no ex ins fnl f* **2/1**[1]
6 **3** *1 ½* **Agadir Summer**[46] 4826 3-8-12 0.... MartinLane 11 74
(David Simcock) *s.s: hld up: hdwy over 2f out: rdn over 1f out: styd on to go 3rd wl ins fnl f: nrst fin* **16/1**
4 *1 ¾* **Wolf Heart (IRE)** 3-9-3 0.... TedDurcan 1 76+
(Saeed Bin Suroor) *chsd ldr: rdn over 2f out: no ex fnl f* **2/1**[1]
02 **5** *5* **Midnight Waltz**[23] 5607 3-8-12 0.... SebSanders 8 63
(Sir Mark Prescott Bt) *hld up: hdwy u.p over 5f out: wknd over 1f out* **4/1**[3]
0 **6** *24* **Greeley House**[148] 1605 3-9-3 0.... GeorgeBaker 9 30
(Chris Wall) *chsd ldrs tl wknd over 2f out: t.o* **25/1**
0 **7** *1 ¾* **On Alert**[12] 5911 3-9-3 0.... TravisBlock 10 27
(Seamus Durack) *chsd ldrs: rdn over 5f out: wknd wl over 2f out: t.o* **100/1**
8 *nk* **Cogito Ergo Sum (ITY)**[19] 6-9-11 0.... JamesDoyle 5 27
(Frank Sheridan) *hld up: a in rr: t.o* **50/1**
0 **9** *½* **Chapatti (IRE)**[31] 5327 3-8-12 0.... SaleemGolam 6 21
(Stuart Williams) *chsd ldrs tl rdn and wknd over 2f out: t.o* **50/1**
10 *2 ½* **Harrys Yer Man**[131] 7-9-11 0.... TomMcLaughlin 3 22
(Mark Brisbourne) *s.s: rdn 7f out: a in rr: t.o* **100/1**

11 19 **Hopeand**[37] 6-9-1 0 NathanAlison(5) 4 —
(Mandy Rowland) *s.s: hld up: a in rr: bhd fnl 5f: t.o* **100/1**

2m 38.25s (-2.85) **Going Correction** -0.125s/f (Stan)
WFA 3 from 6yo+ 8lb **11 Ran SP% 126.4**
Speed ratings (Par 103): **104,101,100,99,96 80,79,78,78,76 64**
toteswingers: 1&2 £1.70, 1&3 £10.90, 2&3 £6.00. CSF £11.21 TOTE £4.80: £1.10, £1.90, £4.40; EX 11.90 Trifecta £74.70 Pool: £429.25 - 4.25 winning units..
Owner Ballymacoll Stud **Bred** Ballymacoll Stud Farm Ltd **Trained** Newmarket, Suffolk

FOCUS
A fair maiden featuring some lesser lights from top stables. It was sound run and the winner reversed Bath form with the runner-up, who set the pre-race standard.
Hopeand Official explanation: jockey said mare never travelled

6287 ENJOY THE PARTY PACK GROUP OFFER H'CAP 1m 4f 50y(P)
9:00 (9:00) (Class 6) (0-60,62) 3-Y-O+ **£1,704** (£503; £251) **Stalls** Low

Form RPR

-431 **1** **Shouda (IRE)**[114] 2600 5-9-7 **56** TomQueally 8 68+
(Barney Curley) *hld up: hdwy over 1f out: n.m.r ins fnl f: r.o to ld last strides* **7/2**[2]

2042 **2** ½ **Saloon (USA)**[19] 5739 7-9-5 **54** (p) IvaMilickova 2 61
(Jane Chapple-Hyam) *hld up: hdwy over 1f out: rdn to ld wl ins fnl f: hdd last strides* **17/2**

000- **3** ½ **Manshoor (IRE)**[237] 6055 6-9-11 **60** LukeMorris 4 66
(Lucy Wadham) *chsd ldrs: rdn over 2f out: led over 1f out: hdd wl ins fnl f* **12/1**

-000 **4** ½ **Aureate**[5] 6182 7-9-6 **55** DavidProbert 5 60
(Brian Forsey) *mid-div: hdwy to ld wl over 4f out: rdn and hdd over 1f out: styd on* **16/1**

4003 **5** nse **Green Lightning (IRE)**[5] 6182 4-9-11 **60** (b) SilvestreDeSousa 11 65
(Mark Johnston) *sn chsng ldr: led over 8f out: hdd wl over 4f out: chsd ldr: rdn over 1f out: styd on same pce ins fnl f* **9/4**[1]

604 **6** ¾ **Alternative Choice (USA)**[28] 5416 5-9-11 **60** KierenFallon 12 64
(Nick Littmoden) *hld up: hdwy over 1f out: r.o: nt rch ldrs* **8/1**

6161 **7** shd **Miss Ferney**[5] 6157 7-9-10 **62** 6ex PaulPickard(3) 10 66
(Alan Kirtley) *hld up: hdwy over 2f out: rdn over 1f out: styd on* **6/1**[3]

3632 **8** 1 ½ **Dream Of Fortune (IRE)**[16] 5815 7-9-5 **57** (bt) RichardEvans(3) 3 58
(David Evans) *led: hdd over 8f out: chsd ldrs: rdn over 1f out: styd on same pce fnl f* **8/1**

005- **9** 2 ¼ **Hammer**[497] 875 6-8-8 **50** JordanNason(7) 7 48
(Geoffrey Harker) *hld up in tch: plld hrd: jnd ldr over 6f out: wknd ins fnl f* **50/1**

10 1 ¾ **Priest Field (IRE)**[730] 6181 7-8-11 **51** MatthewCosham(5) 1 46
(Pam Ford) *rn wout declared tongue strap: prom: rdn over 3f out: wknd over 1f out* **50/1**

-250 **11** 4 ½ **Prickles**[9] 6029 6-9-0 **49** RobbieFitzpatrick 9 37
(Derek Shaw) *hld up: a in rr* **25/1**

2m 41.5s (0.40) **Going Correction** -0.125s/f (Stan) **11 Ran SP% 121.4**
Speed ratings (Par 101): **93,92,92,92,91 91,91,90,88,87 84**
toteswingers: 1&2 £5.80, 1&3 £20.20, 2&3 £26.80. CSF £34.28 CT £327.84 TOTE £7.70: £3.50, £3.30, £5.70; EX 57.70 Trifecta £166.40 Pool: £420.71 - 1.87 winning units..
Owner Curley Leisure **Bred** Gestut Schlenderhan **Trained** Newmarket, Suffolk

FOCUS
There was a modest pace, with many pulling for their heads, and things only began to speed up around the home turn. Muddling form. The winner is potentially a lot better than the bare figures, with the second and fifth the best guides.
T/Plt: £56.90 to a £1 stake. Pool of £72,045.12 - 923.37 winning tickets. T/Qpdt: £5.60 to a £1 stake Pool of £9,698.76 - 1,269.09 w. tckts CR 6288 - 6289a (Foreign Racing) - See RI

6024 HAYDOCK (L-H)
Friday, September 23

OFFICIAL GOING: Good to soft (soft in places on round course; 6.7)
Wind: Light, half-against Weather: Fine

6290 VALE UK H'CAP 1m
2:05 (2:06) (Class 3) (0-90,88) 3-Y-O+ **£7,439** (£2,213; £1,106; £553) **Stalls** Low

Form RPR

5400 **1** **Oriental Scot**[42] 5012 4-9-1 **79** TomEaves 3 90
(William Jarvis) *hld up: n.m.r on inner and hmpd after 2f: rdn and hdwy over 2f out: chsd ldrs ins fnl f: styd on wl to ld fnl stride* **12/1**

102 **2** hd **Robemaker**[13] 5940 3-9-5 **87** RobertHavlin 9 98+
(John Gosden) *dwlt: hld up: hdwy over 3f out: rdn to ld 1f out: styd on for press: hdd fnl stride* **9/1**

5012 **3** ½ **Hacienda (IRE)**[6] 6173 4-9-5 **83** SilvestreDeSousa 11 93
(Mark Johnston) *sn dropped to midfield: hdwy over 2f out: led wl over 1f out: hdd 1f out: continued to chal: hld fnl strides* **15/2**[2]

1500 **4** 6 **Moheebb (IRE)**[41] 5059 7-9-5 **83** (b) PJMcDonald 10 79
(Ruth Carr) *midfield: niggled along 5f out: rdn and hdwy 1f out: styd on ins fnl f: unable to trble front trio* **25/1**

0030 **5** ½ **African Cheetah**[12] 5968 5-8-13 **77** (v) StevieDonohoe 12 72
(Reg Hollinshead) *dwlt: in rr: rdn over 2f out: styd on ins fnl f: nt rch ldrs* **66/1**

11-0 **6** ¾ **Flipping**[93] 3276 4-9-1 **79** DavidAllan 5 72
(Eric Alston) *trckd ldrs: rdn and outpcd: over 3f out: kpt on fr over 1f out: one pce ins fnl f* **40/1**

110 **7** 2 **I'm Super Too (IRE)**[20] 5722 4-9-1 **84** GarryWhillans(5) 6 73
(Alan Swinbank) *prom: rdn over 2f out: wknd wl over 1f out* **16/1**

05 **8** nse **Rigolleto (IRE)**[16] 5830 3-9-5 **87** TonyCulhane 14 75
(Mick Channon) *prom: rdn 2f out: btn fnl f* **25/1**

1255 **9** nse **Powerful Presence (IRE)**[30] 5383 5-9-2 **80** PaulHanagan 8 68
(David O'Meara) *midfield: rdn over 2f out: no imp* **14/1**

3620 **10** ¾ **Amazing Star (IRE)**[36] 5205 6-8-9 **78** NeilFarley(5) 4 65
(Declan Carroll) *awkward s: hld up: rdn over 2f out: nvr a threat* **10/1**

1300 **11** 1 ¼ **Point North (IRE)**[63] 4267 4-9-8 **86** (t) EddieAhern 13 70
(Jeremy Noseda) *hld up: hdwy over 3f out: rdn over 2f out: unable to chal ldrs: wknd fnl f* **9/1**

5-1 **12** 3 ¾ **Alakhan (IRE)**[14] 5879 5-9-5 **86** RyanClark(3) 16 61
(Ian Williams) *slowly away: hld up in rr: rdn and hdwy over 2f out: sn edgd lft: no imp on ldrs: wknd fnl f* **8/1**[3]

3005 **13** 8 **Captain Bertie (IRE)**[13] 5936 3-9-6 **88** RobertWinston 7 45
(Charles Hills) *midfield: pushed along over 4f out: wknd wl over 1f out* **4/1**[1]

1000 **14** 7 **Vito Volterra (IRE)**[55] 4561 4-9-3 **81** AdrianNicholls 15 22
(Michael Smith) *led: rdn and hdd wl over 1f out: sn wknd* **28/1**

3025 **15** 6 **Venutius**[13] 5920 4-9-7 **85** GrahamGibbons 2 12
(Ed McMahon) *prom tl pushed along and wknd 2f out* **8/1**[3]

-136 **16** 1 ¼ **Aquarian Spirit**[112] 2674 4-8-11 **78** LeeTopliss(3) 1 —
(Richard Fahey) *midfield: rdn and lost pl 3f out: bhd after* **28/1**

1m 43.41s (0.51) **Going Correction** +0.05s/f (Good)
WFA 3 from 4yo+ 4lb **16 Ran SP% 121.8**
Speed ratings (Par 107): **99,98,98,92,91 91,89,89,88,88 86,83,75,68,62 60**
Tote Swingers: 1&2 £31.30, 1&3 £13.10, 2&3 £4.20 CSF £107.99 CT £917.88 TOTE £14.00: £3.30, £2.20, £1.50, £5.90; EX 185.90.
Owner Dr J Walker **Bred** Miss K Rausing **Trained** Newmarket, Suffolk

FOCUS
A total of 35mm of rain fell from last Friday to Tuesday but a dry spell since saw the going change overnight to good to soft, soft in places on the round course. The jockeys reported the ground was on the soft side but that the horses were getting through it. Mainly exposed sorts in a useful handicap. A sound pace suited those held up and field raced centre to stands' side in the straight.

NOTEBOOK
Oriental Scot's form has been patchy since his last win but he was suited by the good gallop back over this trip and showed a good attitude to prove he's fully effective in a soft surface. He's versatile ground-wise but it remains to be seen whether things pan out as well next time. (op 14-1)
Robemaker had conditions to suit and ran right up to his best, despite hanging late on, from this career-high mark after travelling like the best horse in the race for a long way. He should be able to win again when he gets his ground. (op 8-1)
Hacienda(IRE) is at the top of his game and ran another solid race to confirm his effectiveness in soft ground. He pulled clear of the rest and, although he'll be 3lb higher in future, he should continue to give a good account. (op 7-1)
Moheebb(IRE) was far from disgraced but he has only won once in just over two years and didn't really show enough to suggest he'd be one to go in head down for next time.
African Cheetah, with the visor back on to replace cheekpieces, ran his best race on turf for some time and will be 4lb lower in future, but his grass form is very uneven and he'll be of most interest returned to Wolverhampton, the scene of both his wins. (op 50-1)
Flipping can be rated a bit better than the bare form as he fared the best of those who raced up with the decent gallop. He goes well in testing ground and will be one to keep an eye on away from progressive or well-handicapped sorts. (op 33-1)
Captain Bertie(IRE) had shaped on his previous run as though though the return to this trip would suit but he proved a disappointment. He's lightly raced enough to be worth another chance. Official explanation: jockey said colt ran flat (op 5-1 tchd 11-2 in places)

6291 E B F VALE UK MAIDEN FILLIES' STKS 6f
2:35 (2:37) (Class 5) 2-Y-O **£3,234** (£962; £481; £240) **Stalls** Centre

Form RPR

1 **Cardigan (IRE)** 2-8-10 0 PaulHanagan 9 86+
(William Haggas) *racd keenly in midfield: hdwy over 2f out: led 1f out: edgd lft ins fnl f: r.o wl: in command towards fin* **11/2**[2]

2 **2** 2 ¼ **Riot Of Colour**[21] 5689 2-9-0 0 JimCrowley 7 81
(Ralph Beckett) *midfield: impr to chse ldrs over 2f out: chalng fr over 1f out: outpcd by wnr fnl 100yds* **10/11**[1]

3402 **3** 7 **Lady Jameela**[18] 5779 2-9-0 68 TonyCulhane 5 60
(Mick Channon) *prom: led 4f out: rdn and hdd 1f out: sn outpcd and no ch w front 2* **8/1**[3]

03 **4** 3 ¼ **Takealookatmenow (IRE)**[8] 6075 2-9-0 0 AdrianNicholls 8 50
(David Nicholls) *led: hdd 4f out: remained handy: rdn over 1f out: swtchd lft ins fnl f: one pce* **20/1**

40U **5** 1 ½ **Be Calm**[7] 6110 2-9-0 0 GrahamGibbons 6 46+
(Michael Easterby) *prom: lost pl bef 1/2-way: plugged on fnl f but n.d* **25/1**

5 **6** ½ **Wood Nymph (IRE)**[22] 5646 2-9-0 0 DavidAllan 2 44
(Tim Easterby) *midfield: rdn 1/2-way: no imp on ldrs* **28/1**

04 **7** 1 ¼ **Authora (IRE)**[7] 6127 2-8-11 0 KieranO'Neill(3) 12 41
(Richard Hannon) *hld up: effrt over 2f out: no imp: sn outpcd* **10/1**

8 ½ **Gentle Sands** 2-8-7 0 JohnFahy(3) 3 35
(Clive Cox) *hld up: u.p over 2f out: nvr on terms* **12/1**

0 **9** 5 **The Games Gone (IRE)**[32] 5323 2-8-7 0 KevinLundie(7) 10 24
(David Evans) *chsd ldrs: rdn over 3f out: wknd over 2f out* **100/1**

20 **10** 4 ½ **Miss Purity Pinker (IRE)**[46] 4864 2-9-0 0 SilvestreDeSousa 11 11
(David Evans) *hld up: rdn over 3f out: no imp on ldrs: eased whn wl btn ins fnl f* **14/1**

00 **11** 5 **Bolshoi Melody**[17] 5812 2-8-7 0 (t) RaulDaSilva(7) 1 —
(Jeremy Gask) *midfield: rdn over 2f out: wknd over 1f out* **40/1**

12 28 **Tijuca (IRE)** 2-8-10 0 TomEaves 4 —
(Ed de Giles) *rrd in paddock: s.i.s: hld up: outpcd over 2f out: nvr a threat* **100/1**

1m 16.07s (2.27) **Going Correction** +0.325s/f (Good) **12 Ran SP% 118.8**
Speed ratings (Par 92): **97,94,84,80,78 77,76,75,68,62 56,18**
Tote Swingers: 1&2 £3.70, 1&3 £7.30, 2&3 £3.40 CSF £10.26 TOTE £8.90: £2.10, £1.30, £2.10; EX 15.80.
Owner Raymond Tooth **Bred** Forenaghts Stud **Trained** Newmarket, Suffolk

FOCUS
Those with previous experience were no better than fair but the winner created a favourable impression on her racecourse debut and could be rated a few lengths better. The gallop was a reasonable one and the winner raced towards stands' side in the closing stages.

NOTEBOOK
Cardigan(IRE) ◆, the third foal of a 7f-1m winner, herself a half-sister to winners from 6f-1m4f, was nibbled at in the market and created a favourable impression on this racecourse debut. She'll have no problems with 7f and should be able to hold her own in stronger company in due course. (op 15-2)
Riot Of Colour was well supported on this turf debut after posting a fair effort first time out on Polytrack and she ran at least as well to pull clear of a 66-rated rival. She should have no problems going one better in this type of event. (op 6-5 tchd 5-4 in places)
Lady Jameela, having her first run in a soft surface, wasn't disgraced and looks a decent marker for the level of this form but again had her limitations exposed. She should be able to pick up a small race at some point.
Takealookatmenow(IRE) wasn't far off her best and she'll be seen to better effect in run-of-the-mill nursery company. (op 14-1)
Be Calm has still to match her debut Carlisle form but she wasn't knocked about over a trip that looks a bare minimum and she'll be of more interest returned to further in ordinary nurseries. (op 16-1)
Wood Nymph(IRE) showed ability at a moderate level on her debut and probably ran to a similar level in these softer conditions over this longer trip. Low-grade handicaps will be the way forward with her. (op 22-1)

6292 E B F VALE UK MAIDEN STKS (C&G) 6f
3:10 (3:11) (Class 5) 2-Y-O **£3,234** (£962; £481; £240) **Stalls** Centre

Form RPR

3042 **1** **Ballesteros**[14] 5889 2-9-0 78 EddieAhern 5 77
(Brian Meehan) *racd keenly: trckd ldrs: rdn to ld over 1f out: r.o ins fnl f: in control towards fin* **3/1**[3]

62 **2** *1* **Jay Bee Blue**^{10} 6025 2-9-0 0 RichardKingscote 2 74
(Tom Dascombe) *a.p: led 2f out: rdn and hdd over 1f out: kpt on: hld towards fin* **7/1**

524 **3** *¾* **Money Never Sleeps**^{15} 5855 2-9-0 80 RobertHavlin 3 72
(John Gosden) *hld up: effrt 2f out: chsd ldrs ins fnl f: styd on same pce fnl 75yds* **5/2**^{2}

043 **4** *3¼* **Police Force (USA)**^{27} 5480 2-9-0 79 PaulHanagan 8 62
(Mahmood Al Zarooni) *racd keenly: hld up: rdn over 1f out: no imp and one pce ins fnl f* **15/8**^{1}

0 **5** *1¾* **Gulf Storm (IRE)**^{20} 5726 2-9-0 0 TomEaves 4 57
(Bryan Smart) *led: pushed along and hdd 2f out: wknd over 1f out* **14/1**

0 **6** *hd* **Chicarito**^{23} 5613 2-9-0 0 JimCrowley 1 56
(John Gallagher) *prom: rdn to chal over 1f out: wknd ins fnl f* **33/1**

0 **7** *13* **Gone To Ground**^{15} 5863 2-8-7 0 RaulDaSilva(7) 7 17
(Jeremy Gask) *in rr: toiling fnl 2f: nvr a danger* **100/1**

1m 16.46s (2.66) **Going Correction** +0.325s/f (Good) 7 Ran SP% **111.5**
Speed ratings (Par 95): **95,93,92,88,86 85,68**
Tote Swingers: 1&2 £2.60, 1&3 £1.70, 2&3 £4.30 CSF £22.64 TOTE £3.20: £1.40, £2.50; EX 21.50.
Owner Mrs P Good **Bred** Exors Of The Late J R Good **Trained** Manton, Wilts

FOCUS
A fair maiden in which the gallop was an ordinary one. The field raced down the centre. Not form to get exicted about, the winner rated to his recent level.

NOTEBOOK
Ballesteros, back up in trip and on this first start in soft ground, probably didn't have to improve too much after racing with the choke out to get off the mark at the sixth attempt. He's a fair sort but, while life will be tougher from now on, he should continue to give a good account. (tchd 10-3 in a place)
Jay Bee Blue had shown improved form in easy ground at this course on his previous start and bettered that effort to chase home a fairly reliable yardstick. He should be able to pick up a small event in this grade or when stepping into nurseries. (op 6-1)
Money Never Sleeps was far from disgraced but was again below the form he showed at Newmarket in August and he's likely to remain vulnerable against the better types in this grade, and will have to improve to defy his current mark of 80 in nurseries. (tchd 11-4)
Police Force(USA) had shown steadily progressive form in good and easier ground but he failed to run up to his best in these softer conditions after wandering under pressure in the closing stages. He'll be worth another chance in less-testing ground. (op 5-2)
Gulf Storm(IRE) fared better than on his debt at Thirsk but he'll have to raise his game by some way if he's to win a race in this grade and his best chance of success is likely to be in ordinary nursery company. (op 12-1)

6293 GRIFFITHS & ARMOUR NURSERY 6f
3:45 (3:45) (Class 5) (0-75,74) 2-Y-O **£2,587** (£770; £384; £192) **Stalls** Centre

Form RPR

504 **1** **Al's Memory (IRE)**^{17} 5812 2-9-2 69 StevieDonohoe 14 75
(David Evans) *hld up: rdn over 2f out: hdwy over 1f out: r.o to ld fnl 75yds: pushed out whn in command towards fin* **16/1**

1065 **2** *1½* **Silvas Romana (IRE)**^{15} 5840 2-9-3 70 TomMcLaughlin 10 71
(Mark Brisbourne) *n.m.r and hmpd s: hld up: hdwy 1/2-way: led over 1f out: hdd fnl 75yds: hld cl home* **9/1**

6044 **3** *1¾* **Iced Opal**^{21} 5689 2-9-5 72 LiamKeniry 15 68
(Michael Blanshard) *trckd ldrs: rdn and ch over 1f out: styd on same pce fnl 75yds* **22/1**

4516 **4** *nk* **Beau Mistral (IRE)**^{13} 5922 2-9-6 73 CathyGannon 5 68
(Paul Green) *led: rdn and hdd over 1f out: ch ins fnl f: no ex fnl 75yds* **14/1**

0350 **5** *1¾* **Dazzlin Bluebell (IRE)**^{18} 5786 2-7-9 53 NeilFarley(5) 16 43
(Tim Easterby) *in tch: effrt over 2f out: hung lft whn chsng ldrs ins fnl f: styd on same pce fnl 100yds* **12/1**

2032 **6** *½* **Marcus Augustus (IRE)**^{10} 6018 2-9-2 72 KieranO'Neill(3) 17 60
(Richard Hannon) *prom: rdn over 2f out: nt qckn over 1f out: styd on same pce ins fnl f* **4/1**^{1}

065 **7** *2* **Larwood (IRE)**^{14} 5889 2-9-2 69 FergusSweeney 1 51
(Henry Candy) *in tch: effrt to chse ldrs 2f out: one pce ins fnl f* **13/2**^{2}

2260 **8** *2½* **Justine Time (IRE)**^{9} 6043 2-8-7 60 ow1 (b) GrahamGibbons 7 35
(David Barron) *hld up: rdn over 2f out: no imp* **18/1**

406 **9** *2½* **My Pearl (IRE)**^{21} 5681 2-8-6 59 PaulHanagan 6 26
(Kevin Ryan) *hld up: outpcd 1/2-way: nvr able to chal* **4/1**^{1}

0004 **10** *1* **La Taniere**^{49} 4749 2-8-2 55 JamesSullivan 11 19
(Michael Easterby) *in rr: pushed along and edgd rt over 3f out: nvr a danger* **14/1**

5000 **11** *6* **Bojangle (IRE)**^{31} 5343 2-7-5 51 oh2 KevinLundie(7) 2 —
(Dominic Ffrench Davis) *in tch: rdn over 2f out: wknd over 1f out: eased whn wl btn ins fnl f* **25/1**

6004 **12** *2¾* **Farzan (IRE)**^{8} 6092 2-8-1 57 (b) DeclanCannon(3) 12 —
(Tim Easterby) *a bhd* **16/1**

054 **13** *8* **Alnair (IRE)**^{90} 3398 2-9-0 67 DavidAllan 8 —
(Declan Carroll) *in tch: rdn and wknd over 2f out* **8/1**^{3}

5054 **14** *28* **Come To Mind**^{32} 5310 2-7-7 51 oh6 (p) DanielleMcCreery(5) 13 —
(Alan Berry) *in tch: wknd over 2f out: t.o* **100/1**

1m 16.73s (2.93) **Going Correction** +0.325s/f (Good) 14 Ran SP% **121.7**
Speed ratings (Par 95): **93,91,88,88,85 85,82,79,75,74 66,62,52,14**
Tote Swingers: 1&2 £20.80, 1&3 £27.80, 2&3 £38.30 CSF £152.56 CT £3183.07 TOTE £25.20: £6.20, £3.50, £6.20; EX 225.50.
Owner Will Dawson **Bred** Brian Miller **Trained** Pandy, Monmouths

FOCUS
A handful of unexposed sorts in an ordinary nursery. The gallop was and the action unfolded against the stands' rail. Routine form, rated around the third and fourth.

NOTEBOOK
Al's Memory(IRE) looked on a stiffish mark after three maiden runs but he turned in an improved effort to score on this nursery debut. He'll be at least as effective over 7f and he's lightly raced enough to be open to further progress. (op 18-1)
Silvas Romana(IRE) hadn't been at her best since her Chepstow win but she returned to form against the stands' rail. She is fairly exposed and it remains to be seen whether this will be reproduced next time. (op 15-2)
Iced Opal had shown improved form on Polytrack on her last two starts and she matched those efforts returned to turf. She's well worth another try over 7f. (tchd 20-1)
Beau Mistral(IRE) hadn't been at her best from a wide draw at Chester on her previous start but she fared better back at this more conventional course. She doesn't have much in hand of her mark but she's largely consistent. (tchd 16-1)
Dazzlin Bluebell(IRE) isn't fully exposed and she wasn't disgraced but she didn't look entirely straightforward under pressure. Her record to date has a very uneven look to it and she'll have to show a fair bit more before she's a reliable betting proposition.
Marcus Augustus(IRE), dropped in trip, wasn't disgraced on this nursery debut but, although consistent, he'll have to raise his game to win a similar event from his current mark. (op 5-1)
Larwood(IRE), who raced away from the main action on the wide outside of the field, looks better than the bare facts suggest. It's likely he'll be dropped in the weights for this and he's one to keep an eye on. (op 11-2)
My Pearl(IRE) was soundly beaten on this nursery debut after attracting support. He's probably worth another chance on a sounder surface. (op 13-2)

6294 FRANK FITZGERALD H'CAP 1m 6f
4:20 (4:20) (Class 4) (0-80,80) 3-Y-O **£4,528** (£1,347; £673; £336) **Stalls** Low

Form RPR

-311 **1** **Lordofthehouse (IRE)**^{25} 5553 3-8-13 72 PaulHanagan 8 83
(William Haggas) *slowly away: sn prom: rdn to ld over 1f out: hdd fnl 150yds: rallied to regain ld towards fin* **11/4**^{1}

6415 **2** *nk* **Wayward Glance**^{34} 5283 3-9-6 79 EddieAhern 7 89
(Michael Bell) *led: rdn over 2f out: hdd over 1f out: regained ld fnl 150yds: hdd towards fin* **5/1**^{3}

1212 **3** *3* **A Boy Named Suzi**^{8} 6103 3-9-7 80 LukeMorris 3 86
(James Eustace) *trckd ldrs: rdn to chal over 1f out: styd on same pce fnl 100yds* **4/1**^{2}

6422 **4** *1¾* **Kleitomachos (IRE)**^{35} 5235 3-9-1 74 FergusSweeney 4 77
(Stuart Kittow) *hld up: hdwy over 2f out: edgd lft over 1f out: one pce and no imp ins fnl f* **8/1**

5120 **5** *2* **Dark Dune (IRE)**^{34} 5273 3-8-12 71 DavidAllan 5 72
(Tim Easterby) *racd keenly: hld up in rr: carried sltly lft 2f out: no imp on ldrs u.p over 1f out: one pce fnl f* **20/1**

521 **6** *1* **My Heart's On Fire (IRE)**^{30} 5386 3-9-3 76 RichardKingscote 6 75
(Tom Dascombe) *trckd ldrs: effrt 3f out: wknd over 2f out* **12/1**

1-03 **7** *3¾* **Encore Une Annee**^{35} 5235 3-9-4 77 JimCrowley 1 71
(Ralph Beckett) *midfield: rdn over 2f out: no imp: bhd fnl f* **11/1**

0226 **8** *nk* **Man Of God (IRE)**^{35} 5236 3-9-2 75 RobertHavlin 2 68
(John Gosden) *hld up in rr: hdwy to chse ldrs over 2f out: wknd 1f out* **5/1**^{3}

3m 3.62s (2.42) **Going Correction** +0.05s/f (Good) 8 Ran SP% **111.9**
Speed ratings (Par 103): **95,94,93,92,90 90,88,88**
Tote Swingers: 1&2 £2.80, 1&3 £3.00, 2&3 £4.60 CSF £15.85 CT £52.36 TOTE £3.10: £2.20, £1.90, £1.10; EX 14.80.
Owner Lael Stable **Bred** Lael Stables **Trained** Newmarket, Suffolk

FOCUS
A fair handicap featuring several in-form sorts. The gallop was an ordinary one and the principals edged from the centre to the far side in the closing stages.

6295 BETDAQ THE BETTING EXCHANGE HAYDOCK PARK APPRENTICE TRAINING SERIES H'CAP 1m 2f 95y
4:55 (4:56) (Class 5) (0-70,70) 3-Y-O+ **£2,587** (£770; £384; £192) **Stalls** Centre

Form RPR

2210 **1** **Market Puzzle (IRE)**^{17} 5808 4-8-7 56 oh6 (p) RachealKneller(3) 13 65
(Mark Brisbourne) *a.p: upsides on bit 2f out: confidently rdn: led fnl 110yds: sn rdn: a doing enough cl home* **22/1**

2230 **2** *½* **Sharp Sovereign (USA)**^{20} 5724 5-9-6 66 LMcNiff 8 74
(David Barron) *led: rdn over 2f out: sn hrd pressed: hdd fnl 110yds: hld cl home* **5/1**^{3}

3632 **3** *nse* **Glyn Ceiriog**^{13} 5925 3-8-12 67 (p) DavidKenny(3) 10 75
(George Baker) *midfield: hdwy over 3f out: rdn over 2f out: hung lft over 1f out: swtchd rt ins fnl f: r.o towards fin* **9/2**^{2}

0420 **4** *¾* **Lakota Ghost (USA)**^{13} 5942 3-8-6 61 MatthewLawson(3) 2 67
(Seamus Durack) *in tch: pushed along 4f out: rdn to chal fr 2f out tl styd on same pce cl home* **20/1**

4231 **5** *1¼* **Kodicil (IRE)**^{26} 5507 3-8-11 63 JulieBurke 4 67
(Tim Walford) *a.p: rdn over 2f out: styd on u.p ins fnl f but nvr able to mount serious chal* **10/3**^{1}

6606 **6** *3* **Zaplamation (IRE)**^{23} 5622 6-9-2 62 ShaneBKelly 6 60
(John Quinn) *midfield: rdn over 2f out: kpt on ins fnl f: nvr able to chal* **15/2**

0016 **7** *shd* **Black Coffee**^{10} 6028 6-9-7 67 (b) JamesRogers 7 65
(Mark Brisbourne) *hld up in rr: rdn over 2f out: hdwy over 1f out: styd on ins fnl f: nt rch ldrs* **12/1**

4550 **8** *2¼* **Edgeworth (IRE)**^{22} 5653 5-9-3 68 JoshBaudains(5) 9 62
(David Bridgwater) *s.s: hld up: n.m.r on bnd briefly 6f out: rdn over 1f out: nvr able to trble ldrs* **20/1**

400 **9** *4½* **Orpen Bid (IRE)**^{43} 4951 6-8-5 56 oh11 (be^{1}) JackDuern(5) 12 41
(Michael Mullineaux) *hld up: effrt over 2f out: nvr able to trble ldrs* **66/1**

1064 **10** *1* **Reset To Fit**^{16} 5823 4-8-10 56 KieranO'Neill 5 39
(Eric Alston) *racd keenly: prom tl rdn and wknd over 2f out* **20/1**

4156 **11** *nse* **Circle Of Angels**^{74} 3904 3-9-4 70 RyanClark 3 53
(Ian Williams) *midfield: pushed along 4f out: no imp: wknd fnl f* **14/1**

6-50 **12** *5* **Taste The Victory (USA)**^{143} 1800 4-9-2 65 GarryWhillans(3) 15 39
(Alan Swinbank) *hld up: u.p 4f out: nvr on terms* **16/1**

600- **13** *17* **Marafong**^{276} 7958 4-8-7 56 oh11 RaulDaSilva(3) 11 —
(Brian Baugh) *cl up tl wknd 4f out* **50/1**

00-0 **14** *8* **Huntingfortreasure**^{22} 5648 4-9-9 69 ow2 BrianToomey 14 —
(Philip Kirby) *rrd a couple of times leaving stalls: hld up: u.p over 3f out: nvr on terms* **10/1**

2m 15.57s (-0.43) **Going Correction** +0.05s/f (Good)
WFA 3 from 4yo+ 6lb 14 Ran SP% **121.1**
Speed ratings (Par 103): **103,102,102,101,100 98,98,96,93,92 92,88,74,68**
Tote Swingers: 1&2 £20.30, 1&3 £15.10, 2&3 £5.70 CSF £121.32 CT £603.29 TOTE £32.00: £5.70, £2.20, £2.10; EX 190.10.
Owner Mark Brisbourne **Bred** Yeomanstown Stud **Trained** Great Ness, Shropshire

■ Stewards' Enquiry : L McNiff four-day ban: used whip with erxcessive frequency (Oct 7,9-11)

FOCUS
Mainly exposed sorts in a modest handicap. Although the gallop seemed reasonable, those held up were at a disadvantage. The action unfolded towards the far side and the first five finished clear.
Market Puzzle(IRE) Official explanation: trainer had no explanation for the apparent improvement in form
Edgeworth(IRE) Official explanation: jockey said regarding slow removal of blindfold that the gelding dropped its head causing him to miss blindfold handle at first attempt

T/Plt: £127.40 to a £1 stake. Pool of £59,763.00 - 973.56 winning tickets. T/Qpdt: £42.20 to a £1 stake. Pool of £3,953.00 - 133.60 winning tickets. DO

[6267]NEWMARKET (R-H)

Friday, September 23

OFFICIAL GOING: Good to firm (overall 8.4, stands' side:8.2, far side 8.4, centre 8.2)

Wind: medium, behind Weather: dry and fine

6296 SAKHEE OH SO SHARP STKS (GROUP 3) (FILLIES) 7f

1:15 (1:15) (Class 1) 2-Y-O

£19,281 (£7,310; £3,658; £1,822; £914; £459) **Stalls** Low

Form				RPR
1	**1**		**Alsindi (IRE)**[26] 5514 2-8-12 83 .... TomQueally 10 (Clive Brittain) *hld up in rr: hdwy over 2f out: rdn over 1f out: styd on strly ins fnl f to ld cl home* **5/1[1]**	103+
13	**2**	*nk*	**Questing**[27] 5472 2-8-12 0 .... WilliamBuick 1 (John Gosden) *led: rdn and qcknd wl over 1f out: drvn ent fnl f: kpt on wl tl hdd and no ex cl home* **5/1[1]**	100
0243	**3**	*½*	**Nayarra (IRE)**[13] 5933 2-8-12 95 .... RichardHughes 5 (Mick Channon) *chsd ldr: ev ch and rdn 2f out: unable qck u.p ins fnl f: hld whn short of room last strides* **14/1**	99
1	**4**	*1 ¼*	**Minidress**[48] 4804 2-8-12 0 .... AhmedAjtebi 8 (Mahmood Al Zarooni) *chsd ldrs: outpcd and rdn jst over 2f out: edgd rt u.p and trying to rally wl over 1f out: styd on steadily ins fnl f: nt gng pce to chal ldrs* **11/2[2]**	95+
14	**5**	*1 ½*	**Desert Gazelle (USA)**[48] 4803 2-8-12 90 .... KierenFallon 4 (Saeed Bin Suroor) *chsd ldrs: rdn and unable qck wl over 1f out: wknd fnl 100yds* **11/2[2]**	91
311	**6**	*1*	**Emirates Art**[41] 5039 2-8-12 82 .... MartinLane 3 (David Simcock) *hld up in tch in rr: rdn and no imp over 2f out: hdwy ent fnl f: styd on but nvr gng pce to chal ldrs* **22/1**	89+
41	**7**	*4 ½*	**Villeneuve**[29] 5418 2-8-12 80 .... MartinDwyer 6 (William Muir) *t.k.h: chsd ldrs tl 3f out: sn rdn and losing pl: wknd 2f out* **20/1**	76
2011	**8**	*2 ¼*	**Elusive Flame**[15] 5847 2-8-12 85 .... JamieSpencer 9 (David Elsworth) *hld up in tch in rr: rdn and no hdwy over 2f out: sn wknd* **8/1**	70
10	**9**	*6*	**Cockney Dancer**[15] 5849 2-8-12 83 .... MichaelHills 2 (Charles Hills) *t.k.h: hld up in tch in midfield: rdn and wknd over 2f out: wl bhd and eased ins fnl f* **12/1**	54
12	**P**		**Rakasa**[27] 5472 2-8-12 0 .... FrankieDettori 7 (Mahmood Al Zarooni) *s.i.s: rdr immediately looking down and nt striding out: sn detached in last and btn: lost tch after 2f: eventually p.u 2f out* **6/1[3]**	—

1m 24.46s (-0.94) **Going Correction** -0.125s/f (Firm) **10** Ran SP% **113.0**

Speed ratings (Par 102): **100,99,99,97,95 94,89,87,80,—**

Tote Swingers: 1&2 £5.80, 1&3 £14.90, 2&3 £16.60 CSF £28.64 TOTE £5.80: £1.90, £2.30, £3.80; EX 18.90 Trifecta £556.30 Part won. Pool: £751.85 - 0.94 winning units..

Owner Saeed Manana **Bred** D G Hardisty Bloodstock **Trained** Newmarket, Suffolk

FOCUS

An average event for the class, where it paid to race handily. The winner did well to overcome the pace bias on the card and the next two were close to their Prestige Stakes figures.

NOTEBOOK

Alsindi(IRE), whose trainer's juveniles have taken off in recent weeks, was well backed to follow up her Yarmouth maiden win last month. She had different ground to contend with here so is obviously adaptable on that front and won despite not looking in love with the track. There seems little reason not to strike while the iron is hot and her trainer said afterwards that she may turn out quickly for the Group 1 Prix Marcel Boussac at Longchamp. That's over an extra furlong and her pedigree strongly suggests staying beyond 7f would be an issue. Her running style gives hope she might be okay over that trip, though, and she could be the exception in the family (tchd 9-2 and 11-2 in places)

Questing, who got warm beforehand, made a bold bid to make all and was only nabbed at the death. She finished third in this class at Goodwood last time out and, again suited by racing positively, improved a touch on that form. She rates a solid enough benchmark. (tchd 9-2)

Nayarra(IRE), having her eighth outing, finished close up to [illegible] previous appearance and, also well positioned through the race this time, ran very close to that level so also gives the form a straightforward look. She's picked up some decent prize money, but surely deserves a confidence boost back in a maiden. (op 16-1)

Minidress arrived on the back of a debut success in a 7f maiden on the July track last month and came in for support. She did her best to get involved on the far rail nearing the furlong marker and fared best of the three from Godolphin, but lacked the required turn of foot. She's crying out for another furlong. (op 7-1)

Desert Gazelle(USA) was somewhat disappointing behind impressive Discourse (same ownership) in the Sweet Solera on the July course last month, but there was a chance returning to quicker ground would suit. She had her chance, but ultimately paid for running with the choke out and this trip looks to stretch her at present. (op 13-2)

Emirates Art, bidding for a hat-trick, faced a tough task on this debut in Pattern company and never figured, although she was given enough to do as the race panned out. (op 25-1 tchd 20-1)

Villeneuve Official explanation: jockey said filly lost its action

Rakasa was the choice of Frankie Dettori and had finished just ahead of Questing and Nayarra at Goodwood 27 days earlier, but she drifted right out in the market. It was clear shortly after a tardy start all was not well and she was pulled up lame around halfway. Official explanation: trainer said filly finished lame behind (op 9-2)

6297 MAWATHEEQ ROSEMARY STKS (LISTED RACE) (F&M) 1m

1:50 (1:51) (Class 1) 3-Y-O+

£17,013 (£6,450; £3,228; £1,608; £807; £405) **Stalls** Low

Form				RPR
-143	**1**		**Dark Promise**[20] 5704 4-9-0 102 .... NeilCallan 2 (Roger Varian) *t.k.h: mde all: rdn and qcknd 2f out: forged ahd u.p 1f out: styd on wl fnl f* **4/1[2]**	109
1035	**2**	*1*	**Seta**[15] 5848 4-9-0 107 .... KierenFallon 3 (Luca Cumani) *chsd ldrs: swtchd lft and effrt 2f out: rdn over 1f out: drvn and styd on to chse wnr ins fnl f: no imp fnl 50yds* **2/1[1]**	107
0-10	**3**	*2*	**The Shrew**[145] 1719 3-8-10 86 .... WilliamBuick 4 (John Gosden) *t.k.h: chsd wnr: rdn over 2f out: upsides wnr and drvn over 1f out: no ex 1f out: wknd fnl 75yds* **25/1**	102
3250	**4**	*1 ¼*	**Off Chance**[15] 5848 5-9-0 99 .... DuranFentiman 8 (Tim Easterby) *taken down early and ponied to s: stdd s: hld up in tch in last trio: swtchd lft: rdn and effrt over 2f out: no imp tl kpt on fnl f: nvr able to chal* **11/1**	99+
3022	**5**	*nk*	**Wake Up Call**[13] 5936 5-9-0 94 .... GeorgeBaker 7 (Chris Wall) *stdd s: hld up in midfield: rdn and outpcd over 2f out: kpt on ins fnl f but no threat to ldrs* **14/1**	99
121	**6**	*1*	**Electra Star**[20] 5702 3-8-10 93 .... AdamBeschizza 9 (William Haggas) *taken down early: stdd s: hld up in tch in rr: rdn and effrt jst over 2f out: no imp over 1f out: sme hdwy but no ch w ldrs whn nt clr run ins fnl f: n.d* **11/2[3]**	96+
3144	**7**	*shd*	**Sooraah**[13] 5929 4-9-0 98 .... RichardHughes 1 (William Haggas) *t.k.h: hld up in midfield: rdn and outpcd over 2f out: no imp tl styd on ins fnl f but no threat to ldrs* **7/1**	96
1000	**8**	*¾*	**Reem (AUS)**[34] 5277 4-9-0 103 .... PatCosgrave 5 (M F De Kock, South Africa) *chsd ldrs: rdn and struggling ent fnl 2f: carried hd high and outpcd wl over 1f out: wknd fnl f* **20/1**	94
40-0	**9**	*9*	**Ragsah (IRE)**[34] 5277 3-8-10 100 .... FrankieDettori 6 (Saeed Bin Suroor) *hld up in tch in last trio: rdn and wknd over 2f out: wl bhd and eased ins fnl f* **12/1**	74

1m 36.94s (-1.66) **Going Correction** -0.125s/f (Firm)

WFA 3 from 4yo+ 4lb **9** Ran SP% **112.5**

Speed ratings (Par 111): **103,102,100,98,98 97,97,96,87**

Tote Swingers: 1&2 £2.00, 1&3 £15.90, 2&3 £11.50 CSF £11.97 TOTE £4.50: £1.50, £1.40, £3.70; EX 10.60 Trifecta £137.90 Pool: £909.98 - 4.88 winning units..

Owner Lordship Stud **Bred** Lordship Stud **Trained** Newmarket, Suffolk

FOCUS

A Listed contest that was run as a handicap at Ascot last season but was one of the races switched as a result of the re-organisation of Champions Day next month. It looked an ordinary contest for the grade with less than half the field rated 100 or above and again racing handily was a must. The winenr confirmed her latest Haydock effort.

NOTEBOOK

Dark Promise was progressive over the winter and carried it on this year on turf, winning over 1m on the July course and finishing in the frame in two Listed races subsequently. She made the running here, her rider dictating a steady pace before kicking on at the bushes and staying on strongly up the hill. She looks to have more to offer and it will be interesting to see if connections opt to race her again next season. (tchd 7-2 and 9-2)

Seta, a three-time winner at Listed level who may have had excuses regarding the trip on her last two starts, was sent off favourite and came through to chase the winner home without ever looking as if she would quite catch her. (op 11-4 tchd 3-1 in places)

The Shrew had finished well beaten in the 1,000 Guineas and had not been seen since. She ran a terrific race on this comeback, only fading from the Dip, and the run should bring her on a fair amount. (op 22-1)

Off Chance found 7f in Group 3 company too much last time but is consistent at this trip in Listed class and did best of those held up, especially as she rather anticipated the start. She stayed on well, her effort can be upgraded and she really deserves to score again at this level. (op 12-1 tchd 10-1)

Wake Up Call, who was on her toes in the paddock, had not run over this trip since her debut and was held up. She ran on but without looking like getting seriously involved. (op 12-1)

Electra Star, a progressive filly who had won three of her previous four starts in a maiden and handicaps, adopted the same hold-up tactics on this rise in grade that have worked so well for her recently. However, as the race was run they did not pay off and she was not helped by being briefly short of room in the latter stages. She can be given another chance at this level. (op 5-1 tchd 13-2 in a place)

Sooraah, a Listed winner at this trip on soft, handles fast ground but after chasing the leaders failed to pick up under pressure. (op 6-1)

6298 NAYEF JOEL STKS (GROUP 2) 1m

2:25 (2:25) (Class 1) 3-Y-O+

£56,710 (£21,500; £10,760; £5,360; £2,690; £1,350) **Stalls** Low

Form				RPR
0525	**1**		**Ransom Note**[40] 5094 4-9-3 113 .... MichaelHills 1 (Charles Hills) *mde all: sn clr: rdn and wnt further clr ent fnl f: drvn and kpt on gamely ins fnl f: unchal* **4/1[2]**	118
0651	**2**	*2 ¼*	**Premio Loco (USA)**[13] 5930 7-9-3 114 .... GeorgeBaker 5 (Chris Wall) *hld up in midfield: rdn and effrt over 2f out: chsd clr wnr over 1f out: kpt on u.p ins fnl f: nvr able to chal* **13/2**	113
-200	**3**	*1*	**Poet's Voice**[27] 5473 4-9-3 119 .... (t) FrankieDettori 4 (Saeed Bin Suroor) *stdd s: hld up in rr: stl last over 2f out: hdwy and edging rt 2f out: disputing 2nd and drvn over 1f out: no ex and styd on same pce fnl 100yds* **5/1[3]**	111+
1542	**4**	*4*	**Tazahum (USA)**[35] 5252 3-8-13 114 .... RichardHills 7 (Sir Michael Stoute) *in tch: rdn and effrt to chse ldng pair wl over 2f out: drvn and no imp over 1f out: wknd ins fnl f* **5/2[1]**	101
1043	**5**	*¾*	**Emerald Commander (IRE)**[illegible] [illegible] [illegible] 110 .... (t) [illegible] 2 (Saeed Bin Suroor) *jostled leaving stalls: chsd wnr but racd away fr rivals: rdn and outpcd by wnr jst over 2f out: edgd lft and btn over 1f out: wknd ent fnl f* **6/1**	100
6-00	**6**	*2 ¾*	**Karam Albaari (IRE)**[13] 5934 3-8-13 100 .... KierenFallon 6 (J R Jenkins) *racd in last pair: pushed along 5f out: rdn and sme hdwy over 3f out: edgd rt and wknd wl over 1f out* **33/1**	93
4401	**7**	*10*	**Librann**[26] 5510 3-8-13 112 .... RichardHughes 3 (Richard Hannon) *taken down early: t.k.h: chsd ldrs: rdn and struggling ent fnl 2f: sn wknd: wl bhd and eased ins fnl f* **11/2**	70

1m 34.68s (-3.92) **Going Correction** -0.125s/f (Firm)

WFA 3 from 4yo+ 4lb **7** Ran SP% **111.2**

Speed ratings (Par 115): **114,111,110,106,106 103,93**

Tote Swingers: 1&2 £5.90, 1&3 £4.50, 2&3 £3.30 CSF £27.91 TOTE £5.10: £2.30, £3.20; EX 16.40.

Owner H R Mould **Bred** Rabbah Bloodstock Limited **Trained** Lambourn, Berks

FOCUS

Not a strong race for the class with doubts over the field. There was a solid early pace on, but it was a case of the winner being given too much rope out in front. He recorded a personal best, and the second helps set the level.

NOTEBOOK

Ransom Note was gifted too much rope out in front and this was the third consecutive race on the day where it proved a disadvantage racing from off the pace. He scored over an extra furlong on this course when returning to action back in April, but had been somewhat inconsistent since then. His stable is now in much better form, though, and he looked to have benefited for a recent 40-day break. The aggressive tactics proved right up his street back down in trip and the ground was perfect for him. It was his first win in this class and he's a hard horse to catch when in this current mood, but he did get very much the run of the race. His connections later reported he is now due to travel overseas in search of success at the top level. (op 5-1)

Premio Loco(USA) bounced back from some below-par efforts when scoring in this company over 7f at Doncaster 13 days earlier. He proved easy to back returned to 1m and was never going to catch the winner, but posted another respectable run in defeat and helps to set the standard. (op 5-1)

Poet's Voice, easy to back, quickened 2f out on the far side yet it was clear from the furlong marker he had too much to do. He flattened out up the rising finish, but is a little better than the bare form and this was a step back in the right direction. (op 7-2)

Tazahum(USA) was well backed to land a first race in Group company on this drop back from 1m2f. He looked a possible threat when making his move 3f out, but his effort proved short-lived and perhaps this track was not for him. His best form has also been on an easier surface. (op 11-4 tchd 3-1)

Emerald Commander(IRE) was more popular in the market than stablemate Poet's Voice, who he finished in front of at Goodwood two runs back, and he was nicely placed through the early stages. He petered out before the final furlong, though, and probably found the ground plenty quick enough. (op 8-1)
Karam Albaari(IRE) was never a threat, though this was a better effort again, and needs his sights lowered. (op 40-1)
Libranno, who has won on this course but reportedly looked edgy in the paddock, looked to be beaten by something other than stamina for this extra furlong and disappointed. Perhaps it was not being able to dominate as he seems to prefer, but it could also well be that he's had enough for the year. Official explanation: trainer said colt was unsuited by the good to firm ground (op 13-2)

6299 SHADWELL FILLIES' MILE (GROUP 1) — 1m
3:00 (3:01) (Class 1) 2-Y-O

£92,720 (£35,152; £17,592; £8,763; £4,398; £2,207) **Stalls** Low

Form			Horse	RPR
11	**1**		**Lyric Of Light**[14] 5885 2-8-12 111 ... FrankieDettori 7 (Mahmood Al Zarooni) *stdd s: hld up in tch in rr: hdwy travelling wl over 3f out: rdn and qcknd to chse ldr 1f out: sn hung rt and ev ch: drvn ins fnl f: led last strides* **2/1**[1]	112+
3123	**2**	*hd*	**Samitar**[14] 5885 2-8-12 105 ... JamieSpencer 3 (Mick Channon) *led: rdn 2f out: drvn and fnd ex over 1f out: jnd ins fnl f: battled on wl tl hdd and no ex last strides* **17/2**[3]	108
21	**3**	*4 1/2*	**Firdaws (USA)**[22] 5655 2-8-12 0 ... RichardHills 1 (Roger Varian) *chsd ldr: rdn and unable qck 2f out: edgd rt ent fnl f: wknd fnl 150yds* **3/1**[2]	97
3125	**4**	*hd*	**Salford Art (IRE)**[28] 5446 2-8-12 83 ... DaneO'Neill 4 (David Elsworth) *hld up in tch: lost pl and rdn 1/2-way: sn outpcd and bhd: swtchd lft over 1f out: rallied u.p and hdwy ent fnl f: swtchd lft again ins fnl f: styd on wl but no threat to ldrs* **20/1**	96+
12	**5**	*3/4*	**Fallen For You**[14] 5885 2-8-12 110 ... WilliamBuick 8 (John Gosden) *stdd s: t.k.h: hld up in tch: hdwy to chse ldrs 1/2-way: rdn and effrt wl over 1f out: unable qck ent fnl f: wknd fnl 150yds* **3/1**[2]	95+
4	**6**	*1 1/2*	**Devotion (IRE)**[12] 5974 2-8-12 0 ... CO'Donoghue 2 (A P O'Brien, Ire) *chsd ldrs: rdn and unable qck over 2f out: drvn and btn over 1f out: wknd fnl f* **25/1**	91
015	**7**	*1 3/4*	**Semayyel (IRE)**[14] 5885 2-8-12 90 ... KierenFallon 6 (Clive Brittain) *hld up in last trio: rdn and n.m.r over 2f out: swtchd rt and drvn 2f out: wknd over 1f out* **20/1**	87+
21	**8**	*1/2*	**Albamara**[24] 5579 2-8-12 77 ... SebSanders 5 (Sir Mark Prescott Bt) *chsd ldrs: rdn and struggling over 2f out: wknd wl over 1f out* **14/1**	86

1m 35.98s (-2.62) **Going Correction** -0.125s/f (Firm) 2y crse rec **8** Ran SP% **113.9**
Speed ratings (Par 106): **108,107,103,103,102 100,99,98**
Tote Swingers: 1&2 £3.50, 1&3 £2.40, 2&3 £4.40 CSF £19.21 TOTE £2.80: £1.10, £2.40, £1.30; EX 21.50 Trifecta £62.10 Pool: £2,580.09 - 30.72 winning units..
Owner Godolphin **Bred** Darley **Trained** Newmarket, Suffolk

FOCUS
The first running of the Fillies' Mile at its new home, although the 2005 edition was run here when Ascot was being developed. It looked a decent bunch this year and, run at a solid pace, the form looks decent with the first pair coming clear. The winner impressed but this may not have taken as much winning ratings-wise as the May Hill.

NOTEBOOK
Lyric Of Light ◆ took her career record to 3-3 with a last-gasp success and confirmed herself a filly out of the top drawer, extending the excellent record of May Hill winners in the race. She again raced under restraint, which wasn't the place to be according to earlier races on the card, and travelled supremely well into contention on the outside when Frankie Dettori asked her to close. She initially hit a flat spot when put under pressure, though, and despite responding at the furlong marker again hung right nearing the finish. However, her rider always looked confident of getting there at the business end and she is value for a good deal better than the bare margin. This was the quickest ground she had raced on thus far and she's evidently versatile, which will prove a notable advantage going forward in her career. Her tendency to hang under maximum pressure is probably still down to inexperience, though Dettori felt she wasn't in love with the surface, and she certainly has the scope to continue on an upwards curve. At 10-1 she looks the solid pick to hand Godolphin a second successive 1000 Guineas, as there is still very likely more to come as she matures. Somewhat surprisingly her trainer later didn't rule out a trip to the Breeder's Cup in November for the very valuable Juvenile Fillies Turf, and that dictates one should hold fire at present on any ante-post betting until plans become clearer. (op 15-8 tchd 9-4 in places)
Samitar appeared to have her work cut out reversing last-time-out Doncaster form with the winner, but connections got the tactics spot on switching to front-running considering the pace bias and she very nearly pulled it off. She was there to be shot at 2f out, but kept responding and proved most game. She got the run of things, but finished well clear of the remainder and evidently enjoyed this quicker surface. (op 12-1)
Firdaws(USA) ◆ should have won her Newbury debut yet made hard work of justifying prohibitive odds when off the mark at Salisbury next time. That was probably another decent maiden, though, and she proved popular on this big jump up in class, upped to a trip she seemed likely to relish. She sat just off the pace and held every chance, but lacked the speed of the first pair late on. She remains a top prospect for middle-distances next year and can be backed at 25-1 for the Oaks, the Classic her dam won in 2005. (op 4-1)
Salford Art(IRE) ◆, rated 83, wasn't seen near her best on easier ground in a nursery on the July course last time (well backed) and this was much more like her true colours. Again she did her best work late in the day, against the pace bias, and strongly appeals as one to follow up in trip next year. She may go for the Zetland Stakes over 1m2f here next month. (op 33-1)
Fallen For You was just touched off by the winner in the May Hill last time and looked to have solid claims of gaining revenge seeing as she wasn't done any favours by that rival there. However, she pulled her way into a prominent position from halfway and ultimately paid the price once meeting the rising finish. The fact she was still travelling as well as any nearing the final furlong shows what an engine she possesses and, while she may not quite be a filly for the top level next year, she is certainly not one to be writing off yet. (op 5-2)
Devotion(IRE) finished fourth in Listed company at the Curragh on her fourth start 12 days earlier. Her powerful connections will be satisfied with her proximity here, giving them a handle on the form, but no doubt this was a career-best back on suitably quicker ground. She could well have more to offer over a longer trip as a 3-y-o. (op 20-1)
Semayyel(IRE), whose stable won the opening Group 3 for juvenile fillies, was unsurprisingly ridden with more restraint than when trying to make all into a headwind behind the winner at Doncaster last time. She once again proved troublesome at the stalls, though, and never threatened in the race. (op 25-1)
Albamara was an easy winner on her second start at Epsom last month and looked up against it on form, but is bred to be smart. She was the first beaten, though, not looking happy on the track or quicker ground. She ought to leave this behind over a stiffer test next year. (op 9-1)

6300 HAAFHD E B F MAIDEN STKS — 7f
3:35 (3:36) (Class 4) 2-Y-O **£5,175** (£1,540; £769; £384) **Stalls** Low

Form			Horse	RPR
3	**1**		**Spiritual Star (IRE)**[106] 2837 2-9-3 0 ... JimmyFortune 5 (Andrew Balding) *sn led: mde rest: pushed along and readily wnt clr wl over 1f out: in n.d after: v easily* **7/2**[1]	95+
	2	*6*	**Ellaal** 2-9-3 0 ... RichardHills 11 (Charles Hills) *dwlt: sn in tch: chsd wnr 4f out: rdn and outpcd wl over 1f out: no ch w wnr after: kpt on for clr 2nd fnl f* **5/1**[3]	76+
20	**3**	*1 3/4*	**Snooky**[47] 4815 2-9-3 0 ... DaneO'Neill 9 (Henry Candy) *in tch: chsd ldng pair and drvn over 2f out: sn outpcd and no ch w wnr: plugged on same pce u.p after* **9/1**	71
0	**4**	*1 1/4*	**Mr Churchill (IRE)**[17] 5801 2-9-3 0 ... FrankieDettori 14 (Mahmood Al Zarooni) *hld up in rr of main gp: hdwy on outer 1/2-way: rdn and outpcd by wnr 2f out: plugged on same pce and wl hld after* **11/1**	68+
0	**5**	*1 1/4*	**Confirmed**[20] 5727 2-9-3 0 ... (t) AdamKirby 2 (Marco Botti) *t.k.h: hld up wl in tch: rdn and unable qck over 2f out: sn outpcd and no ch over 1f out* **9/2**[2]	64
	6	*hd*	**Bayan (IRE)** 2-9-3 0 ... MartinDwyer 6 (Brian Meehan) *hld up in tch: rdn and outpcd jst over 2f out: no ch whn swtchd lft over 1f out: plugged on fnl f* **8/1**	64+
	7	*2 1/2*	**Red Bay** 2-9-3 0 ... GeorgeBaker 4 (Jane Chapple-Hyam) *chsd ldr for 2f: styd chsng ldrs tl rdn and unable qck ent fnl 2f: sn wknd* **33/1**	57
0	**8**	*2 1/2*	**Thecornishcowboy**[9] 6064 2-9-3 0 ... KirstyMilczarek 1 (John Ryan) *hld up wl in tch in midfield: rdn and unable qck over 2f out: wknd 2f out* **100/1**	50+
	9	*hd*	**Cayuga** 2-9-3 0 ... TomQueally 8 (Sir Michael Stoute) *s.i.s: in tch in rr of main gp: rdn and wknd over 2f out: no ch whn rn green and edgd lft ent fnl f* **9/1**	50+
	10	*8*	**Aubrietia** 2-8-12 0 ... JamieSpencer 15 (Edward Vaughan) *wnt lft s and v.s.a: a wl detached in rr* **16/1**	23+
	11	*13*	**Clapped** 2-9-3 0 ... KierenFallon 7 (Edward Vaughan) *chsd ldrs tl wnt 2nd 6f out tl 4f out: wknd rapidly over 2f out: wl bhd and virtually p.u ins fnl f: t.o* **25/1**	—
	12	*26*	**Tarkoor** 2-9-3 0 ... WilliamBuick 12 (Peter Chapple-Hyam) *s.i.s: a outpcd and detached in rr: t.o fr 1/2-way* **11/1**	—

1m 24.53s (-0.87) **Going Correction** -0.125s/f (Firm) **12** Ran SP% **118.5**
Speed ratings (Par 97): **99,92,90,88,87 87,84,81,81,71 57,27**
Tote Swingers: 1&2 £4.60, 1&3 £4.90, 2&3 £10.10 CSF £20.23 TOTE £4.70: £1.80, £2.10, £2.60; EX 18.40 Trifecta £152.20 Pool: £1,053.22 - 5.12 winning units..
Owner Thurloe Thoroughbreds XXIX **Bred** John Quigley **Trained** Kingsclere, Hants

FOCUS
A fair maiden where once more it paid to race on the pace. The time was only fractionally slower than the opening fillies' Group 3. The winner was very impressive but had the big advantage of the rail, otherwise the performance could be worth a lot more.

NOTEBOOK
Spiritual Star(IRE) ◆ had made a promising debut at Newbury in June, a race that has thrown up three subsequent winners. Despite being not seen since, he was a strong favourite and, taking the lead over 4f out, gradually pulled clear to win as he liked with his rider hardly moving. It is difficult to know what he beat here but he looks potentially Group class. His low, fluent action suggests fast ground is ideal. (tchd 10-3 and 4-1)
Ellaal ◆, a 220,000gns brother to a 6f juvenile winner and half-brother to several other winners, was backed on this debut. He went after the winner from halfway but could make no impression, although he beat the rest well enough. He should have no problem winning a similar race. (op 17-2)
Snooky made a promising debut behind a subsequent winner at Salisbury but was well beaten next time. He ran much better here, having been held up early, and probably sets the standard on his debut effort.
Mr Churchill(IRE) made significant late ground after a very slow start on his debut over 7f at Leicester and improved on that here, although he faded late on. (op 8-1)
Confirmed raced keenly on his debut before staying on nicely in the straight while running green, and was again keen here. He did not fare badly considering and looks the sort to improve for the switch to handicaps after one more run. (op 5-1)
Bayan(IRE), a 210,000gns yearling out of a mare who stayed 2m and from a family who were mostly best in excess of a mile, was well supported but missed the break before running on late. He should come on a fair amount for the experience, and longer trips will suit in time. (op 15-2 tchd 7-1)
Cayuga, a Montjeu half-brother to Zacinto, was quite laid back in the preliminaries and ran green when asked to make headway from the rear. He is another who should benefit from the outing. (op 7-1)

6301 AQLAAM GODOLPHIN STKS (LISTED RACE) — 1m 4f
4:10 (4:12) (Class 1) 3-Y-O+ **£17,013** (£6,450; £3,228; £1,608; £807) **Stalls** Centre

Form			Horse	RPR
2335	**1**		**Mahbooba (AUS)**[27] 5494 4-8-11 103 ... PatCosgrave 7 (M F De Kock, South Africa) *t.k.h: chsd ldrs tl wnt 2nd 7f out: led 6f out: pushed clr 2f out: in n.d after: pushed along and edgd lft ins fnl f: easily* **3/1**[2]	108
0600	**2**	*6*	**Al Shemali**[25] 5544 7-9-4 104 ... AhmedAjtebi 1 (Mahmood Al Zarooni) *hld up in last pair: rdn and effrt 3f out: sn drvn and outpcd: swtchd lft over 1f out: styd on u.p to take 2nd ins fnl f: no ch w wnr* **9/2**	105
6/40	**3**	*2*	**All The Aces (IRE)**[41] 5045 6-9-4 103 ... NeilCallan 2 (Roger Varian) *t.k.h: chsd ldr tl 7f out: swtchd lft and pushed along over 4f out: drvn and nt qckn w wnr over 2f out: wl btn and plugged on same pce after* **4/1**[3]	102
0402	**4**	*shd*	**Sirvino**[27] 5493 6-9-4 100 ... TomQueally 3 (David Barron) *led tl 6f out: drvn and nt qckn w wnr over 2f out: wl btn and plugged on same pce fr over 1f out* **11/2**	102
2604	**5**	*7*	**Myplacelater**[20] 5711 4-8-13 107 ... WilliamBuick 6 (David Elsworth) *hld up in last pair: rdn and no prog 3f out: wl btn over 1f out: eased wl ins fnl f* **9/4**[1]	89

2m 28.56s (-3.44) **Going Correction** -0.125s/f (Firm) **5** Ran SP% **109.3**
Speed ratings (Par 111): **106,102,100,100,95**
CSF £15.92 TOTE £3.80: £1.10, £3.20; EX 18.80.
Owner Sheikh Mohammed Bin Khalifa Al Maktoum **Bred** Sheikh Mohammed Bin Khalifa Al Maktoum **Trained** South Africa

FOCUS
Multiple Group winner Mubtaker and Champion Stakes winner Storming Home are the best recent winners of this Listed contest. This was a weak race for the grade, and not a race to be positive about.

NOTEBOOK
Mahbooba(AUS), an Australian-bred filly, had a good winter in Meydan, being a Listed winner (UAE Guineas) on Tapeta and was placed in the UAE Oaks and Derby. She wore blinkers and was too keen on her return here last month and then was held on easy ground next time. Trying her longest trip to-date and racing on fast ground, she was keen under restraint early but settled better once in front and gradually pulled clear of her rivals from the bushes. (op 7-2 tchd 4-1 in places)
Al Shemali, who won the Dubai Duty Free in 2010 and was once rated 119, had shown only minor promise on his return from five months off last month at Epsom. He was held up early and, although no match for the winner, stayed on pretty well in the closing stages, passing two rivals up the hill (op 5-1)

All The Aces(IRE), a 1m4f Listed winner and once rated 115, missed 2010 and had not shown much since. He was the first under pressure and could merely plug on at the one pace. (op 7-2 tchd 10-3)
Sirvino, a Windsor handicap winner off 89 in June and runner-up in a Listed race on the same track last time, led early and had his chance but could not pick up. The Berkshire venue seems to bring out the best in him nowadays. (op 9-2 tchd 6-1 in a place)
Myplacelater was bidding to follow up last year's success in a contest that was weakened considerably by the withdrawal of Dangerous Midge. However, she was edgy beforehand and never got out of last position. The ground was much faster than ideal for her. Official explanation: trainer said filly was unsuited by the good to firm ground (op 11-4)

6302 STANDING FOR SUCCESS H'CAP SILVER CAMBRIDGESHIRE — 1m 1f
4:45 (4:45) (Class 2) 3-Y-O+
£18,675 (£5,592; £2,796; £1,398; £699; £351) **Stalls** Low

Form	Pos	Dist	Horse / details	RPR
6133	**1**		**Arabian Star (IRE)**[14] 5892 3-8-13 **80** ... SteveDrowne 1 (Andrew Balding) *mde all: rdn wl over 1f out: clr w runner-up over 1f out: battled on wl fnl f* **12/1**[3]	92
6643	**2**	*hd*	**Classic Colori (IRE)**[24] 5593 4-9-10 **86** ... DanielTudhope 10 (David O'Meara) *in tch: rdn and effrt to chse wnr 2f out: chal over 1f out: no ex wl ins fnl f* **16/1**	98
530	**3**	*6*	**Viva Vettori**[14] 5888 7-9-9 **85** ... NickyMackay 3 (David Elsworth) *hld up in rr: hdwy 3f out: rdn and styd on over 1f out: wnt 3rd 1f out: kpt on but no ch w ldng pair* **12/1**[3]	84+
1125	**4**	*3/4*	**Carragold**[19] 5761 5-8-4 **66** ... DuranFentiman 16 (Mel Brittain) *racd in centre tl merged w far side 6f out: in tch: rdn and unable qck 3f out: no threat to ldrs but rallied u.p 1f out: styd on fnl f* **33/1**	63
3410	**5**	*1/2*	**Shamdarley (IRE)**[41] 5049 3-8-13 **80** ... RoystonFfrench 22 (Michael Dods) *racd in centre tl merged w far side 6f out: hld up towards rr: pushed along and effrt 3f out: kpt on u.p fnl f: no ch w ldrs* **25/1**	76+
1600	**6**	*1/2*	**Layline (IRE)**[12] 5981 4-9-6 **82** ... AndreaAtzeni 11 (Gay Kelleway) *taken down early: towards rr: rdn and effrt wl over 2f out: styd on fnl f: nvr trbld ldrs* **33/1**	77
6500	**7**	*1 3/4*	**Jo'Burg (USA)**[27] 5488 7-8-13 **78** ... MichaelO'Connell(3) 18 (David O'Meara) *taken down early: racd in centre tl merged w far side 6f out: in tch: rdn and chsd ldng pair 2f out: sn outpcd and btn over 1f out: wknd ins fnl f* **33/1**	69
2303	**8**	*2*	**Licence To Till (USA)**[7] 6124 4-9-5 **81** ... JoeFanning 23 (Mark Johnston) *racd in centre tl merged w far side 6f out: chsd ldrs: rdn and effrt 3f out: struggling and outpcd ent fnl 2f: wknd over 1f out* **8/1**[2]	68
0200	**9**	*1/2*	**Camerooney**[6] 6173 8-9-8 **84** ... JackMitchell 19 (Brian Ellison) *racd in centre tl merged w far side 6f out: chsd ldrs: rdn to chse wnr 3f out tl 2f out: sn btn: wknd over 1f out* **40/1**	70
0010	**10**	*1*	**Emerald Wilderness (IRE)**[14] 5894 7-9-2 **78** ...(v[1]) FrankieDettori 13 (Robert Cowell) *racd in centre tl merged w far side 6f out: hld up towards rr: rdn and effrt 3f out: no imp2f out and n.d after: plugged on* **22/1**	61
4342	**11**	*hd*	**Dolphin Rock**[25] 5557 4-9-8 **84** ... LeeNewman 24 (David Barron) *racd solo against stands' rail: chsd ldrs: rdn 3f out: wknd u.p over 1f out* **12/1**[3]	67+
2155	**12**	*1/2*	**Paramour**[12] 5969 4-9-9 **85** ... DarryllHolland 7 (David O'Meara) *hld up in rr: pushed along and effrt 3f out: rdn and no imp over 2f out: n.d* **12/1**[3]	67
3344	**13**	*hd*	**Hawaana (IRE)**[9] 6069 6-9-3 **79** ... NeilCallan 15 (Gay Kelleway) *swtchd rt after s: in tch in midfield: rdn and no prog 4f out: wknd u.p 2f out* **25/1**	60
0040	**14**	*shd*	**Follow The Flag (IRE)**[32] 5328 7-8-9 **71** ...(v) MartinLane 6 (Alan McCabe) *a towards rr: rdn and no hdwy 4f out: sme modest late hdwy: n.d* **50/1**	52
1300	**15**	*1/2*	**Tinshu (IRE)**[6] 6163 5-9-9 **85** ... DaneO'Neill 21 (Derek Haydn Jones) *racd in centre tl merged w far side 6f out: in tch in midfield: rdn and effrt 3f out: no imp and wknd 2f out* **28/1**	65
2250	**16**	*1*	**Destiny Blue (IRE)**[24] 5593 4-9-7 **83** ... PatCosgrave 2 (Jamie Osborne) *chsd ldrs: rdn 3f out: drvn and struggling over 2f out: wknd 2f out* **16/1**	61
[illegible]	**17**	*1*	**Dhaular Dhar (IRE)**[14] 5888 [illegible] **84** ... GaryBartley(3) 9 (Jim Goldie) *hld up towards rr: effrt wl over 2f out: [illegible] clr run jst over 2f out: n.d after* **28/1**	60+
2500	**18**	*1/2*	**Night Lily (IRE)**[20] 5712 5-9-6 **82** ... KierenFallon 14 (Paul D'Arcy) *racd in centre tl merged w far side 6f out: racd in midfield: rdn and struggling over 3f out: wknd over 2f out* **14/1**	57
423	**19**	*1*	**Jewelled**[24] 5586 5-9-0 **76** ... RichardHughes 12 (Lady Herries) *stdd s: hld up in midfield: rdn and no imp wl over 2f out: wknd over 1f out* **14/1**	48
0514	**20**	*27*	**Capaill Liath (IRE)**[28] 5450 3-9-9 **90** ...(p) JamieSpencer 5 (Michael Bell) *chsd ldr tl 3f out: sn wknd u.p: wl bhd and virtually p.u fnl f: t.o* **12/1**[3]	—
02	**21**	*hd*	**Nelson's Bounty**[9] 6069 4-9-9 **85** ... WilliamBuick 8 (Paul D'Arcy) *hld up in tch: rdn 3f out: sn btn and wknd: wl bhd and eased ins fnl f: t.o* **18/1**	—
1231	**22**	*2 1/2*	**Galiando**[32] 5328 3-9-10 **91** ... JimmyFortune 4 (Jeremy Noseda) *taken down early: in tch in midfield: rdn and lost pl 3f out: sn wl bhd: t.o and virtually p.u fr over 1f out* **5/1**[1]	—

1m 48.53s (-3.17) **Going Correction** -0.125s/f (Firm)
WFA 3 from 4yo+ 5lb **22** Ran SP% **128.8**
Speed ratings (Par 109): **109,108,103,102,102 101,100,98,98,97 97,96,96,96,95 95,94,93,92,68 68,66**
Tote Swingers: 1&2 £98.50, 1&3 £39.40, 2&3 £106.40 CSF £174.44 CT £2417.38 TOTE £14.80: £4.40, £4.90, £4.40, £6.70; EX 267.10 Trifecta £1256.90 Part won. Pool: £1,698.60 - 0.60 winning units..
Owner Jackie & George Smith **Bred** G A E And J Smith Bloodstock Ltd **Trained** Kingsclere, Hants

FOCUS
The consolation race for those failing to make the cut for the Cambridgeshire. The draw played a big part with the far rail the place to be and it was the seventh straight race on the card where racing handily was a must. The first pair were clear in a good time.

NOTEBOOK
Arabian Star(IRE) has developed into a consistent handicapper this term and had previously scored over this trip. Drawn nearest to the far rail in stall one, he set out to make all and that proved a winning move. Considering it had proved a nightmare coming from out the back in previous races, it's surprising he wasn't hassled more for the lead. He looked vulnerable when the runner-up came at him, but dug deep and getting 11lb from that rival told near the finish. A likely rise will make his life a deal harder now, but his attitude will continue to hold him in good stead. (op 14-1)
Classic Colori(IRE) was drawn in stall ten but made his challenge nearer to the far rail than the winner. He travelled sweetly in a sensibly handy position and this rates a decent effort under joint-top weight. He fully deserves to open his account for the year. (op 14-1)
Viva Vettori has to rate somewhat unfortunate as none travelled better in the race, but he was never going to emerge on top racing from so far back due to the pace bias. He's become expensive to follow, but this is his ground and he's clearly on a decent mark. (op 14-1)
Carragold, a triple winner this year, came under pressure a long way out in mid-field but battled on most gamely to bag a share of the placings. He's a likeable sort and is not weighted out of winning again just yet.
Shamdarley(IRE), another 3-y-o, returned to the sort of form that saw him win at Ayr in July and looks well worth another chance over 1m2f on this sort of ground.
Layline(IRE), who got warm beforehand, stayed on well late in the day and this was better from him back on turf.
Jo'Burg(USA) ◆ arrived with plenty to prove, but it was his debut for David O'Meara, who also saddled the runner-up, and it was a more encouraging display. He's very well treated and one to keep on side from now on. (tchd 40-1 in a place)
Dolphin Rock went solo on the near side and, while well beaten, wasn't disgraced in the circumstances.
Paramour Official explanation: trainer said gelding was unsuited by the track
Dhaular Dhar(IRE) Official explanation: jockey said horse was denied a clear run
Night Lily(IRE) Official explanation: jockey said mare moved poorly
Capaill Liath(IRE) Official explanation: jockey said gelding was struck into
Galiando is an imposing son of Galileo who was 2-4 coming here and was well backed. He was up against it being held up again, but came under pressure from an early stage and ultimately was eased right off. Something clearly went amiss. Official explanation: trainer had no explanation for the poor form shown (op 11-2 tchd 9-2)

6303 NEWMARKET CHALLENGE WHIP (A H'CAP) — 1m 2f
5:20 (5:20) (Class 6) (0-85,77) 3-Y-O+ **£0 Stalls** Low

Form	Pos	Dist	Horse / details	RPR
2-42	**1**		**Vita Lika**[28] 5429 3-8-12 **74** ... FrankieDettori 10 (Brian Meehan) *broke wl: stdd and hld up in tch: rdn and qcknd to ld over 1f out: clr and edgd rt ins fnl f: pushed out last100yds* **11/4**[2]	83
0050	**2**	*2*	**Sand Skier**[85] 3533 4-9-1 **71** ... WilliamBuick 3 (Hans Adielsson) *chsd ldrs: rdn over 2f out: pressing ldrs and unable qck over 1f out: chsd wnr after: drvn and tried to rally ins fnl f: kpt on* **5/1**[3]	76
-103	**3**	*4 1/2*	**Fujin Dancer (FR)**[20] 4603 6-9-7 **77** ... RichardHughes 7 (Brian Ellison) *hld up in last pair: rdn and effrt wl over 1f out: chsng ldrs whn hmpd over 1f out: no imp and wl hld after: eased towards fin* **11/4**[2]	73
0300	**4**	*2 3/4*	**Cornish Beau (IRE)**[31] 5357 4-7-13 **62** ... CharlesEddery(7) 5 (Mark H Tompkins) *led: rdn over 2f out: hung rt and hdd over 1f out: sn wknd* **20/1**	53
0051	**5**	*3 1/4*	**Ambala**[16] 5838 3-8-5 **67** ... NickyMackay 6 (Chris Wall) *chsd ldr: rdn and unable qck over 2f out: wknd over 1f out* **5/2**[1]	51
4240	**6**	*14*	**Getcarter**[30] 5383 5-9-2 **72** ... GeorgeBaker 4 (John Best) *t.k.h: hld up in tch in rr: rdn and btn 2f out: lost tch over 1f out: wl bhd and eased ins fnl f* **8/1**	28

2m 5.65s (-0.15) **Going Correction** -0.125s/f (Firm)
WFA 3 from 4yo+ 6lb **6** Ran SP% **114.4**
Speed ratings (Par 101): **95,93,89,87,85 73**
Tote Swingers: 1&2 £3.40, 1&3 £1.70, 2&3 £2.60 CSF £17.11 CT £40.21 TOTE £3.40: £2.30, £2.90; EX 19.10 Trifecta £56.20 Pool: £572.06 - 7.53 winning units..
Owner P & F Stanley, J Marsh, P Vela, S Farr **Bred** Breeding Capital Plc **Trained** Manton, Wilts

FOCUS
What had looked like being the biggest field in many years for this historic contest was reduced considerably by withdrawals, and it became an ordinary race with most of the runners having questions to answer. A personal best from the winner.
Fujin Dancer(FR) Official explanation: trainer's rep said gelding was unsuited by the good to firm ground
Getcarter Official explanation: jockey said gelding had no more to give
T/Jkpt: £16,610.50 to a £1 stake. Pool of £2,921,589.00 - 124.88 winning tickets. T/Plt: £127.40 to a £1 stake. Pool of £169,964.00 - 973.56 winning tickets. T/Qpdt: £42.20 to a £1 stake. Pool of £7,630.00 - 133.60 winning tickets. SP

6280 WOLVERHAMPTON (A.W) (L-H)
Friday, September 23

OFFICIAL GOING: Standard to fast
Wind: Light, behind. Weather: Cloudy with sunny spells

6304 WILLIAM HILL - THE HOME OF BETTING H'CAP — 5f 216y(P)
5:15 (5:15) (Class 6) (0-55,55) 3-Y-O+ **£1,636** (£483; £241) **Stalls** Low

Form	Pos	Dist	Horse / details	RPR
5503	**1**		**Trojan Rocket (IRE)**[15] 5864 3-9-2 **55** ... SilvestreDeSousa 7 (George Prodromou) *sn pushed along in rr: hdwy over 2f out: rdn to ld ins fnl f: r.o* **9/2**[1]	67+
4020	**2**	*1*	**Ivestar (IRE)**[4] 6208 6-9-0 **51** ...(vt) PJMcDonald 6 (Ben Haslam) *s.s: bhd: hdwy over 1f out: r.o wl: no ch w wnr* **6/1**[2]	59
0300	**3**	*3/4*	**The Jailer**[12] 5965 8-8-13 **55** ...(p) LucyKBarry(5) 2 (John O'Shea) *led: rdn over 1f out: hdd and unable qck ins fnl f* **25/1**	60
4023	**4**	*1*	**Flaxen Lake**[11] 5996 4-8-13 **53** ... SeanLevey(3) 1 (Milton Bradley) *chsd ldrs: rdn over 2f out: styd on same pce ins fnl f* **15/2**[3]	55
6042	**5**	*shd*	**Desert Falls**[38] 5138 5-9-4 **55** ...(v) TonyCulhane 10 (Richard Whitaker) *chsd ldrs: rdn over 1f out: styd on same pce ins fnl f* **12/1**	57
0402	**6**	*shd*	**Greek Secret**[2] 6261 8-9-4 **55** ...(b) RussKennemore 9 (Paul Midgley) *chsd ldr: rdn and ev ch fr over 1f out tl no ex wl ins fnl f* **15/2**[3]	57
6605	**7**	*2 1/4*	**Lethal**[11] 5996 8-9-0 **51** ... ShaneKelly 3 (Richard Price) *chsd ldrs: rdn over 1f out: styd on same pce* **9/1**	45
0456	**8**	*shd*	**Dingaan (IRE)**[13] 5943 8-9-1 **52** ... RobbieFitzpatrick 12 (Peter Grayson) *s.s: sn pushed along in rr: nt clr run over 2f out: hdwy over 1f out: nvr trbld ldrs* **10/1**	46
3056	**9**	*shd*	**Charlie Delta**[25] 5540 8-8-13 **53** ...(b) AmyRyan(3) 5 (John O'Shea) *mid-div: lost pl 1/2-way: n.d after* **14/1**	47
0031	**10**	*1/2*	**Porthgwidden Beach (USA)**[13] 5941 3-9-2 **55** ...(t) JimmyQuinn 4 (Anthony Middleton) *chsd ldrs: rdn over 2f out: wknd fnl f* **12/1**	47
/16-	**11**	*7*	**San Jose City (IRE)**[84] 3603 6-9-3 **54** ...(p) RobertWinston 8 (Muredach Kelly, Ire) *prom: rdn over 3f out: wknd 2f out* **9/2**[1]	24

1m 14.88s (-0.12) **Going Correction** -0.10s/f (Stan)
WFA 3 from 4yo+ 2lb **11** Ran SP% **119.2**
Speed ratings (Par 101): **96,94,93,92,92 92,89,88,88,88 78**
Tote Swingers:1&2:£5.70, 2&3:£30.50, 1&3:£21.30 CSF £31.31 CT £627.00 TOTE £8.00: £2.50, £1.40, £7.50; EX 35.90.
Owner G D J Linder **Bred** J G F Fox **Trained** East Harling, Norfolk

FOCUS
A modest opener but the principals largely came here in good heart and the form looks reliable enough.
San Jose City(IRE) Official explanation: jockey said gelding never travelled

6305 ENJOY THE PARTY PACK GROUP OFFER (S) STKS 5f 216y(P)
5:45 (5:45) (Class 6) 3-4-Y-O **£1,567** (£462; £231) **Stalls** Low

Form RPR
510 **1** **Main Beach**[21] 5669 4-9-6 74.....(t) ShaneKelly 5 81+
(Tobias B P Coles) *s.s: hld up: hdwy over 2f out: led ins fnl f: shkn up and r.o wl* **11/4**[1]
0354 **2** 1¾ **Mottley Crewe**[7] 6133 4-9-3 70.....RobertLButler(3) 6 75
(Richard Guest) *chsd ldr 5f out: led over 3f out: rdn over 1f out: hdd and unable qck ins fnl f* **3/1**[2]
0165 **3** 6 **Paper Dreams (IRE)**[39] 5109 3-8-10 63.....(p) AmyRyan(3) 1 51
(Kevin Ryan) *chsd ldrs: nt clr run over 2f out: sn rdn: wknd over 1f out* **11/2**
0060 **4** 1 **Pippa's Gift**[30] 5387 3-8-12 65.....(p) SilvestreDeSousa 7 47
(William Muir) *chsd ldrs: rdn over 2f out: wknd over 1f out* **7/2**[3]
0240 **5** ½ **Diamond Johnny G (USA)**[47] 4828 4-9-0 62.....(t) JimmyQuinn 2 45
(Edward Creighton) *led: hdd over 3f out: sn rdn: wknd over 1f out* **11/1**
0636 **6** ½ **Captain Dimitrios**[4] 6223 3-8-9 58.....(v) SeanLevey(3) 8 44
(David Evans) *chsd ldrs: lost pl 4f out: rdn over 2f out: wknd wl over 1f out* **7/1**

1m 14.47s (-0.53) **Going Correction** -0.10s/f (Stan)
WFA 3 from 4yo 2lb 6 Ran SP% **110.1**
Speed ratings (Par 101): **99,96,88,87,86 86**
Tote Swingers:1&2:£2.60, 2&3:£2.10, 1&3:£2.80 CSF £10.80 TOTE £2.50: £1.30, £1.10; EX 14.60.The winner was bought in for 7,750gns. Paper Dreams was claimed by P. R. Hedger for £6,000.
Owner Mrs R Coles **Bred** Miss J Chaplin **Trained** Newmarket, Suffolk

FOCUS
Three non-runners made this an uncompetitive affair and it was fought out by the pair with the highest BHA ratings. The pace was steady and a couple raced keenly.

6306 WILLIAMHILL.COM H'CAP 1m 5f 194y(P)
6:15 (6:16) (Class 5) (0-75,81) 3-Y-O+ **£2,522** (£750; £375; £187) **Stalls** Low

Form RPR
1101 **1** **Fire Fighter (IRE)**[9] 6057 3-9-10 **81** 6ex..... RobertWinston 12 97+
(Sir Mark Prescott Bt) *hld up: hdwy 2f out: led 1f out: shkn up: edgd rt and styd on wl: comf* **11/8**[1]
-351 **2** 2¼ **Mazagee (FR)**[7] 6121 3-9-9 **80** 6ex..... TedDurcan 9 90
(David Lanigan) *hld up: hdwy over 2f out: rdn and ev ch 1f out: styd on same pce* **5/2**[2]
0006 **3** 3¼ **Suzi's A Class Act**[10] 6037 3-8-10 **67**.....(p) JimmyQuinn 2 72
(James Eustace) *s.i.s: hld up: hdwy over 6f out: rdn to chse ldr 2f out: no ex fnl f* **40/1**
043 **4** hd **Tarkeeba (IRE)**[86] 3519 3-9-1 **72**.....(p) TadhgO'Shea 10 77
(Roger Varian) *led 1f: chsd ldr tl led again over 8f out: hdd over 6f out: led 4f out: rdn and hdd 1f out: no ex* **7/1**[3]
0004 **5** 8 **Langley**[15] 5866 4-9-7 **68**..... StevieDonohoe 3 62
(Pat Murphy) *chsd ldrs: rdn over 2f out: wknd over 1f out* **33/1**
35-0 **6** hd **Grand Art (IRE)**[29] 3157 7-9-8 **69**..... RobbieFitzpatrick 4 63
(Frank Sheridan) *led 13f out: hdd over 8f out: led again over 6f out: hdd 4f out: rdn and wknd over 1f out* **66/1**
4202 **7** 2¼ **If I Were A Boy (IRE)**[11] 6005 4-9-9 **70**.....(p) JamesDoyle 11 61
(Dominic Ffrench Davis) *prom: rdn over 2f out: wknd over 1f out* **14/1**
2004 **8** shd **Accumulate**[30] 5389 8-9-4 **72**..... MatthewMcGhee(7) 1 62
(Bill Moore) *s.i.s: hld up: rdn over 3f out: nvr on terms* **33/1**
55 **9** ¾ **Penang Cinta**[24] 5580 8-8-12 **59**..... SilvestreDeSousa 5 48
(David Evans) *prom: rdn over 3f out: wknd over 2f out* **18/1**
0005 **10** 1 **Storm Hawk (IRE)**[13] 5947 4-8-13 **63**.....(p) SeanLevey(3) 6 51
(Pat Eddery) *chsd ldrs: rdn over 3f out: wknd wl over 1f out* **10/1**
150 **11** 30 **No Time For Tears (IRE)**[40] 5079 4-8-4 **56** oh4....(p) ChrisDCogan(5) 13 —
(Lucinda Featherstone) *hld up: a in rr: pushed along 7f out: wknd 4f out* **40/1**

3m 1.81s (-4.19) **Going Correction** -0.10s/f (Stan)
WFA 3 from 4yo+ 10lb 11 Ran SP% **116.5**
Speed ratings (Par 103): **107,105,103,103,99 99,97,97,97,96 79**
Tote Swingers:1&2:£1.40, 2&3:£18.10, 1&3:£12.90 CSF £4.42 CT £85.51 TOTE £2.50: £1.10, £1.60, £6.60; EX 5.80.
Owner J Fishpool - Osborne House **Bred** Airlie Stud And Sir Thomas Pilkington **Trained** Newmarket, Suffolk

FOCUS
A fair staying handicap dominated by the younger generation with their four representatives all making the frame. The gallop seemed reasonable enough and it looks strong form for the grade among the principals.
Suzi's A Class Act Official explanation: vet said filly lost a shoe

6307 RINGSIDE CONFERENCE SUITE MEDIAN AUCTION MAIDEN STKS 7f 32y(P)
6:45 (6:46) (Class 6) 3-5-Y-O **£1,908** (£563; £281) **Stalls** High

Form RPR
4332 **1** **Tanmawy (IRE)**[22] 5639 3-9-3 74..... TadhgO'Shea 11 76+
(Ed Dunlop) *mde all: rdn over 1f out: styd on* **2/1**[1]
0P23 **2** ½ **Chokidar (IRE)**[16] 5821 3-9-3 72.....(b) IanMongan 8 75
(David Nicholls) *chsd ldr to 1/2-way: sn rdn: hung lft ins fnl f: r.o* **5/1**[3]
2540 **3** shd **Brick Dust (IRE)**[21] 5687 3-9-3 70..... J-PGuillambert 1 74
(Luca Cumani) *chsd ldrs: rdn over 2f out: r.o* **7/2**[2]
20 **4** 3¼ **Tenavon**[25] 5567 3-8-12 0..... ShaneKelly 5 61
(William Knight) *prom: chsd wnr 1/2-way: rdn over 1f out: no ex fnl f* **8/1**
54 **5** 2½ **Harvest Mist (IRE)**[17] 5810 3-8-12 0..... LukeMorris 2 54
(Michael Blanshard) *mid-div: rdn over 2f out: no hdwy* **25/1**
6 ¾ **Hubood** 3-8-12 0..... ChrisCatlin 4 52
(Clive Brittain) *hld up: rdn over 2f out: nvr trbld ldrs* **22/1**
-2 **7** 2¾ **Hitman Hatton**[147] 1654 4-9-1 0.....(p) ChrisDCogan(5) 10 49
(Lucinda Featherstone) *prom tl rdn and wknd over 2f out* **14/1**
5 **8** ¾ **Fastnette (IRE)**[23] 5633 4-9-1 0..... JamesDoyle 9 42
(Ian Wood) *hld up: hdwy over 2f out: sn rdn and wknd* **50/1**
9 13 **Mr Mystere** 3-9-3 0..... TedDurcan 3 12
(Chris Wall) *hld up: a in rr* **5/1**[3]
10 68 **Poppy Socks** 3-8-12 0..... WilliamCarson 7 —
(Roy Brotherton) *s.s: hdwy over 4f out: sn wknd: t.o* **66/1**

1m 29.62s (0.02) **Going Correction** -0.10s/f (Stan)
WFA 3 from 4yo 3lb 10 Ran SP% **118.3**
Speed ratings (Par 101): **95,94,94,90,87 86,83,82,68,—**
Tote Swingers:1&2:£2.80, 2&3:£4.10, 1&3:£2.60 CSF £12.09 TOTE £2.60: £1.10, £2.10, £1.80; EX 9.90.
Owner Hamdan Al Maktoum **Bred** P D Savill **Trained** Newmarket, Suffolk

FOCUS
A modest maiden, as the official ratings of the first three suggest. It was run at just a fair gallop and little was good enough or able to get competitive from off the pace.

6308 BOOK NOW FOR CHRISTMAS MAIDEN STKS 7f 32y(P)
7:15 (7:16) (Class 5) 2-Y-O **£2,522** (£750; £375; £187) **Stalls** High

Form RPR
62 **1** **Samuel Pickwick (IRE)**[20] 5713 2-9-3 0..... DavidProbert 8 88+
(Sir Michael Stoute) *a.p: chsd ldr over 1f out: led ins fnl f: shkn up and r.o wl* **3/1**[2]
2 1½ **Van Rooney (USA)**[19] 5763 2-9-3 0..... ShaneKelly 6 82
(T Stack, Ire) *chsd ldrs: led 2f out: rdn over 1f out: hdd and unable qck ins fnl f* **10/11**[1]
243 **3** 3½ **Grizzle**[18] 5786 2-8-12 0..... AntiocoMurgia(5) 12 75+
(Mahmood Al Zarooni) *hld up: shkn up over 1f out: fin wl: too much to do* **10/3**[3]
00 **4** 1¾ **I'm Harry**[30] 5384 2-9-3 0..... RobertWinston 5 69
(Charles Hills) *prom: rdn over 2f out: hung lft and no ex fnl f* **25/1**
0 **5** 1¼ **Shamardeliah (IRE)**[98] 3132 2-8-12 0..... ChrisCatlin 11 61
(Ed Dunlop) *hld up: rdn over 2f out: styd on fr over 1f out: nvr trbld ldrs* **22/1**
00 **6** 5 **Calculated Risk**[4] 6214 2-9-3 0..... StevieDonohoe 9 54
(Willie Musson) *hld up: racd keenly: rdn over 1f out: nvr trbld ldrs* **33/1**
7 ½ **Capriska** 2-8-12 0..... JamieMackay 7 48
(Willie Musson) *hld up: nvr nrr* **100/1**
000 **8** 1 **Doctor Dalek (IRE)**[10] 6019 2-9-0 0..... AlanCreighton(3) 1 50
(Edward Creighton) *chsd ldr: rdn and ev ch 2f out: wknd fnl f* **100/1**
65 **9** 4 **Twelve Strings (IRE)**[15] 5863 2-9-3 0..... J-PGuillambert 10 40+
(Luca Cumani) *stdd s: hld up: shkn up 1/2-way: nvr nr to chal* **10/1**
0 **10** 1 **Solar View (IRE)**[4] 6216 2-8-12 0..... RosieJessop(5) 3 38+
(Sir Mark Prescott Bt) *mid-div: pushed along over 4f out: n.d* **50/1**
0 **11** 2½ **All Good News (IRE)**[29] 5398 2-9-3 0..... SilvestreDeSousa 4 32
(Lisa Williamson) *led: rdn and hdd 2f out: wknd over 1f out* **100/1**
00 **12** shd **Fouracres**[6] 6180 2-8-12 0..... RobbieFitzpatrick 2 27
(Michael Appleby) *chsd ldrs tl wknd over 2f out* **100/1**

1m 28.73s (-0.87) **Going Correction** -0.10s/f (Stan) 12 Ran SP% **126.6**
Speed ratings (Par 95): **100,98,94,92,90 85,84,83,78,77 74,74**
Tote Swingers:1&2:£1.90, 2&3:£2.10, 1&3:£2.40 CSF £6.33 TOTE £2.90: £1.10, £1.40, £1.60; EX 7.00.
Owner Sir Robert Ogden **Bred** Tony O'Dwyer **Trained** Newmarket, Suffolk

FOCUS
A fair maiden but a wide variety of abilities on show and not many that were fancied according to the betting. The field were soon strung out despite the pace being no more than fair. The winner impressed and the form is rated through the second.

NOTEBOOK
Samuel Pickwick(IRE) is progressing nicely and put his unfortunate Kempton run behind him with a clearcut win and that despite allowing the runner-up first run into the straight. He picked him well without his rider needing to go for everything and seems likely to make up into a useful prospect at around 1m. (op 5-2)
Van Rooney(USA) looked to set a tall standard on the evidence of his recent third in a minor event at Dundalk but he didn't look to have any excuses after getting first run on the winner. That said, he was unfortunate to bump into an above-average sort for the track but pulled clear of the rest and a similar race should be within his grasp. (op Evens tchd 11-8 and 6-4 in places)
Grizzle ◆ had shaped last time as if he would be suited by a step up to 7f and proved that right in no uncertain terms, staying on strongly from an unpromising position in rear stuck behind horses on the bend. This run doesn't do him justice and he'd be interesting in a nursery given more of a test next time. (tchd 7-2)
I'm Harry had the run of the race to a degree but turned in an improved effort and shapes as though he will prove just as effective at 1m now he is eligible for nurseries. (op 50-1)
Shamardeliah(IRE) ◆ looked a different filly to the one who had made her debut at 6f in June but she is still a fair bit better than this makes her look given that she made a lot of late progress from a very poor position on the turn. She will improve further at 1m. (op 20-1 tchd 18-1)
Calculated Risk ran as well as might have been expected kept to this trip and, being by Motivator, is likely to come into his own in modest handicaps further down the line. (tchd 25-1)
Capriska shaped well on her debut without being given a particularly hard time.
Twelve Strings(IRE) showed some promise despite his finishing position on his final run before qualifying for a mark. (tchd 9-1)

6309 ENJOY THE PARTY PACK GROUP OFFER H'CAP (DIV I) 1m 141y(P)
7:45 (7:45) (Class 6) (0-55,55) 3-Y-O+ **£1,363** (£402; £201) **Stalls** Low

Form RPR
-006 **1** **Monashee Rock (IRE)**[13] 5944 6-9-1 **51**..... ChrisCatlin 10 59
(Matthew Salaman) *stdd s: hld up: hdwy over 1f out: r.o to ld wl ins fnl f* **8/1**
000- **2** ¾ **Daniel Thomas (IRE)**[288] 7787 9-8-13 **52**.....(tp) RobertLButler(3) 6 58+
(Richard Guest) *s.i.s: hld up: hdwy over 1f out: edgd rt ins fnl f: r.o* **20/1**
5504 **3** shd **Hathaway (IRE)**[15] 5860 4-8-4 **47**..... RachealKneller(7) 13 53
(Mark Brisbourne) *hld up and bhd: hdwy on outer over 1f out: r.o wl: wnt 3rd nr fin* **7/1**
6050 **4** ½ **Tigerbill**[14] 5900 3-8-11 **52**..... LukeMorris 4 57
(Nicky Vaughan) *led 1f: chsd ldr tl rdn to ld over 1f out: hdd and unable qck wl ins fnl f* **13/2**[3]
-240 **5** 1¾ **Kristollini**[24] 5603 3-8-12 **53**..... SilvestreDeSousa 1 54
(William Muir) *plld hrd and prom: rdn over 2f out: styd on same pce fnl f* **12/1**
-050 **6** 5 **River Ardeche**[66] 4177 6-9-2 **55**.....(bt[1]) PatrickDonaghy(3) 8 44
(Ben Haslam) *s.i.s: rcvrd to ld over 7f out: clr over 6f out: hdd over 1f out: wknd ins fnl f* **11/1**
5000 **7** ½ **Cwmni**[15] 5843 5-8-13 **49**..... DavidProbert 9 37
(Bryn Palling) *mid-div: hdwy over 1f out: hung lft and wknd ins fnl f* **14/1**
5404 **8** 2½ **Smarty Sam (USA)**[7] 6135 4-9-3 **53**.....(b) RussKennemore 5 35
(Paul Midgley) *s.i.s: hld up: hdwy over 2f out: wknd over 1f out* **11/2**[2]
050 **9** 1¾ **Indefinite Hope (ITY)**[13] 5912 4-8-11 **47**.....(bt[1]) JamesDoyle 3 25
(Frank Sheridan) *chsd ldrs: rdn over 2f out: wknd over 1f out* **12/1**
/05- **10** 3¼ **Nicky Nutjob (GER)**[23] 355 5-9-0 **50**..... WilliamCarson 11 21
(John O'Shea) *hld up: bhd fnl 3f* **20/1**
0436 **11** 3¾ **Farmers Dream (IRE)**[21] 5674 4-8-12 **48**..... RobertWinston 2 10
(Richard Price) *hld up in tch: nt clr run over 2f out: rdn and wknd over 1f out* **9/2**[1]
6200 **12** hd **Beating Harmony**[15] 5843 3-8-13 **54**..... CathyGannon 7 16
(Tony Carroll) *prom tl rdn and wknd over 1f out* **16/1**

1m 49.75s (-0.75) **Going Correction** -0.10s/f (Stan)
WFA 3 from 4yo+ 5lb 12 Ran SP% **116.3**
Speed ratings (Par 101): **99,98,98,97,96 91,91,89,87,84 81,81**
Tote Swingers:1&2:£54.30, 2&3:£36.40, 1&3:£13.40 CSF £153.69 CT £1178.53 TOTE £7.80: £1.80, £8.00, £2.10; EX 212.50.

The Form Book, Raceform Ltd, Compton, RG20 6NL

Owner M Salaman **Bred** M J Lewin And D Grieve **Trained** Upper Lambourn, Berks

FOCUS

A weak handicap in which none of the runners had finished in the first three last time out. It was strongly run and the complexion changed very late on with the eventual fourth arguably the moral winner.

Smarty Sam(USA) Official explanation: jockey said gelding hit gates at start

Farmers Dream(IRE) Official explanation: jockey said filly ran too freely

6310 ENJOY THE PARTY PACK GROUP OFFER H'CAP (DIV II) 1m 141y(P)

8:15 (8:15) (Class 6) (0-55,55) 3-Y-O+ **£1,363** (£402; £201) **Stalls** Low

Form				RPR
0-3	**1**		**Ashgrove Nell (IRE)**[30] 5396 3-9-0 **54** EddieAhern 4 (Daniel Mark Loughnane, Ire) *trckd ldrs: racd keenly: rdn to ld and edgd lft ins fnl f: r.o* **20/1**	63
6304	**2**	*1*	**Rigid**[13] 5944 4-8-12 **47** JamesDoyle 6 (Tony Carroll) *hld up: hdwy on bit over 1f out: stl gng wl ins fnl f: shkn up fnl 50yds: r.o: nt rch wnr* **15/2**	54+
0500	**3**	*1 ½*	**Poppy Golightly**[16] 5822 4-8-12 **52** NeilFarley(5) 9 (Declan Carroll) *sn led: rdn over 2f out: hdd over 1f out: stl ev ch ins fnl f: styd on same pce* **10/1**	56
0051	**4**	*hd*	**Fairy Mist (IRE)**[9] 6050 4-8-5 **47** (p) JasonHart(7) 7 (Brian Rothwell) *plld hrd and prom: rdn to ld over 1f out: hdd ins fnl f: hmpd sn after: styd on same pce* **10/3**[1]	50
0050	**5**	*¾*	**Endaxi Mana Mou**[23] 5631 3-8-13 **53** (b[1]) KellyHarrison 1 (Noel Quinlan) *hld up: rdn and r.o wl ins fnl f: nvr nrr* **33/1**	54
4100	**6**	*hd*	**Excellent Vision**[8] 6083 4-8-13 **51** (t) RyanClark(5) 2 (Milton Bradley) *hld up: hdwy over 1f out: nt clr run wl ins fnl f: r.o: nvr able to chal* **9/2**[2]	58+
4555	**7**	*¾*	**Durgan**[25] 4445 5-9-2 **51** (v) IanMongan 11 (Linda Jewell) *hld up: rdn over 1f out: nvr trbld ldrs* **12/1**	50
0001	**8**	*2 ¼*	**Gee Major**[8] 6083 4-9-6 **55** 6ex LukeMorris 12 (Nicky Vaughan) *chsd ldrs: rdn over 3f out: wknd fnl f* **11/2**[3]	49
0620	**9**	*nk*	**All In A Paddy**[21] 5674 3-8-12 **52** (b) GrahamGibbons 5 (Ed McMahon) *mid-div: rdn over 2f out: styd on same pce* **8/1**	45
03	**10**	*shd*	**Indian Dumaani**[15] 5843 4-9-0 **49** RobbieFitzpatrick 8 (David Bridgwater) *chsd ldrs: rdn over 1f out: wknd fnl f* **16/1**	42
1000	**11**	*¾*	**Hi Spec (IRE)**[184] 950 8-8-13 **48** (tp) JimmyQuinn 13 (Mandy Rowland) *s.s: a in rr* **25/1**	39

1m 49.84s (-0.66) **Going Correction** -0.10s/f (Stan)
WFA 3 from 4yo+ 5lb **11** Ran SP% **113.7**
Speed ratings (Par 101): **98,97,95,95,94 94,94,92,91,91 91**
Tote Swingers:1&2:£31.70, 2&3:£17.30, 1&3:£94.50 CSF £154.75 CT £1628.82 TOTE £23.30: £5.40, £2.60, £5.00; EX 110.00.

Owner Phil Brown **Bred** Don Commins **Trained** Trim, Co Meath

FOCUS

More recent form was on show than in the first division but still not a race to get excited about. The gallop was only fair and the result has a misleading look to it.

Rigid Official explanation: jockey said, regarding running and riding, that his orders were to get the gelding covered up and wait as long as possible before making a challenge; trainer added that it is very difficult ride who stops when hitting the front and does not respond to the whip, all sorts of tactics have been tried without success.

Excellent Vision Official explanation: jockey said gelding was denied a clear run

Hi Spec(IRE) Official explanation: jockey said mare was slow into its stride

6311 MOBET.WILLIAMHILL.COM H'CAP 1m 1f 103y(P)

8:45 (8:46) (Class 5) (0-70,70) 3-Y-O **£2,522** (£750; £375; £187) **Stalls** Low

Form				RPR
0553	**1**		**Silver Alliance**[11] 5992 3-9-4 **67** JimmyQuinn 8 (Walter Swinburn) *hld up: hdwy and nt clr run over 1f out: rdn to ld ins fnl f: r.o* **11/2**[2]	78
623	**2**	*¾*	**Yourinthewill (USA)**[12] 5964 3-8-13 **62** CathyGannon 12 (Daniel Mark Loughnane, Ire) *hld up: hdwy and hmpd over 1f out: rdn and r.o wl ins fnl f: nt rch wnr* **11/1**	71
6502	**3**	*½*	**Fluvial (IRE)**[7] 6135 3-9-2 **65** SilvestreDeSousa 2 (Mark Johnston) *chsd ldrs: rdn to ld over 1f out: hung lft and hdd ins fnl f: styd on same pce* **7/2**[1]	73
0325	**4**	*nse*	**Miss Exhibitionist**[54] 4584 3-9-7 **70** LukeMorris 6 (James Eustace) *s.i.s: hld up: hdwy over 1f out: r.o* **8/1**	78
1650	**5**	*6*	**Piave (IRE)**[92] 3325 3-9-4 **67** JamesDoyle 7 (Peter Chapple-Hyam) *prom: rdn over 2f out: wknd fnl f* **14/1**	63
2512	**6**	*shd*	**Empress Charlotte**[21] 5666 3-9-6 **69** EddieAhern 4 (Michael Bell) *chsd ldrs: rdn over 1f out: wknd ins fnl f* **6/1**[3]	64
0554	**7**	*1 ¾*	**For What (USA)**[23] 5630 3-9-5 **68** (p) TedDurcan 5 (David Lanigan) *prom: chsd ldr over 2f out: rdn and ev ch whn hmpd over 1f out: wknd ins fnl f* **11/2**[2]	60
-400	**8**	*5*	**Guisho (IRE)**[72] 3988 3-9-7 **70** (b[1]) ShaneKelly 3 (Brian Meehan) *sn led: rdn: hung rt and hdd over 1f out: wknd fnl f* **8/1**	51
-045	**9**	*shd*	**Winged Valkyrie (IRE)**[94] 3259 3-9-4 **67** RobertWinston 1 (Charles Hills) *mid-div: rdn and lost pl over 4f out: bhd fnl 3f* **28/1**	48
4050	**10**	*3*	**Beyeh (IRE)**[42] 5020 3-9-0 **63** ChrisCatlin 11 (Clive Brittain) *s.i.s: a in rr: bhd fnl 3f* **25/1**	38
00-3	**11**	*2 ¼*	**Way Chief (FR)**[32] 5315 3-8-8 **60** ow1 LeeTopliss(3) 13 (Richard Fahey) *prom tl rdn and wknd over 2f out* **20/1**	30
0333	**12**	*16*	**Princesse Gaelle**[51] 4664 3-9-1 **69** AntiocoMurgia(5) 9 (Marco Botti) *chsd ldrs tl rdn and wknd over 2f out: t.o* **16/1**	—

1m 58.98s (-2.72) **Going Correction** -0.10s/f (Stan) **12** Ran SP% **122.4**
Speed ratings (Par 101): **108,107,106,106,101 101,99,95,95,92 90,76**
Tote Swingers:1&2:£10.00, 2&3:£11.70, 1&3:£5.30 CSF £65.28 CT £247.21 TOTE £7.70: £2.20, £3.10, £2.70.

Owner In It To Win Partnership **Bred** Peter Harris **Trained** Aldbury, Herts

FOCUS

A touch more quality to end proceedings but like the previous race there wasn't much more than a fair pace on.

T/Plt: £25.80 to a £1 stake. Pool £66,072.36. 1,868.52 winning tickets. T/Qpdt: £7.00 to a £1 stake. Pool £9,286.84. 968.40 winning tickets. CR

6317 - 6320a (Foreign Racing) - See Raceform Interactive

6243 MAISONS-LAFFITTE (R-H)

Friday, September 23

OFFICIAL GOING: Turf: good

6321a LA COUPE DE MAISONS-LAFFITTE (GROUP 3) (3YO+) (TURF) 1m 2f (S)

1:50 (12:00) 3-Y-O+ **£34,482** (£13,793; £10,344; £6,896; £3,448)

			RPR
1		**One Clever Cat (IRE)**[54] 4597 5-8-10 0 ChristopheSoumillon 3 (T Clout, France) *settled 5th on outside: qcknd wl to go 4th 2f out: r.o strly ent fnl f: sn led 150yds out: r.o wl: comf* **14/5**[2]	109
2	*1 ½*	**Agent Secret (IRE)**[26] 5531 5-9-0 0 Francois-XavierBertras 6 (F Rohaut, France) *settled 4th towards outside: wnt 3rd 2f out gng easily: chal for ld over 1 1/2f out: led briefly 1f out: hdd 150yds out: styd on wl* **5/2**[1]	110
3	*snk*	**Kya One (FR)**[21] 5694 3-8-5 0 StephanePasquier 9 (Y De Nicolay, France) *settled towards rr: rdn 2f out: qcknd wl ent fnl f: r.o strly on outside to go 3rd cl home* **12/1**	107
4	*nse*	**Lancelot (FR)**[40] 5094 4-9-0 0 OlivierPeslier 1 (F Head, France) *settled 3rd bhd ldr: gng wl 2 1/2f out: led over 2f out: sn chal and hdd over 1 1/2f out: styd on fnl f: lost 3rd cl home* **4/1**[3]	110
5	*6*	**Rock My Soul (IRE)**[21] 5696 5-8-10 0 Pierre-CharlesBoudot 4 (A Fabre, France) *settled towards rr: rdn over 2 1/2f out on outside: nt qckn: styd on fnl 1 1/2f* **6/1**	94
6	*2 ½*	**Great Event (FR)**[56] 4-9-0 0 DavidMichaux 5 (M Cheno, France) *settled bhd ldrs: rdn but no ex fr over 2f out: styd on fnl f* **11/1**	93
7	*4*	**Oekaki (FR)**[16] 5839 4-8-10 0 ThierryJarnet 7 (Y Barberot, France) *bkmarker fr s: rdn 2 1/2f out: no rspnse: mde no imp* **18/1**	81
8	*1*	**Lustre (FR)**[39] 5127 3-8-8 0 Christophe-PatriceLemaire 8 (Y De Nicolay, France) *settled 5th: rdn but no ex fr 2 1/2f out: fdd* **23/1**	83
9	*1*	**Shamardanse (IRE)**[46] 3-8-5 0 TheoBachelot 2 (S Wattel, France) *sn led: stl in front and u.p 2 1/2f out: sn wknd* **58/1**	78

2m 3.10s (0.70)
WFA 3 from 4yo+ 6lb **9** Ran SP% **116.3**
WIN (incl. 1 euro stake): 3.80. PLACES: 1.50, 1.50, 2.30. DF: 5.80. SF: 12.50.
Owner Patrick Hendrickx **Bred** G Mulligan **Trained** France

NOTEBOOK

One Clever Cat(IRE) earned her reward after a string of consistent performances, including having been beaten by the likes of Sarafina and Cirrus Des Aigles, getting on top in the final 100 yards. A return to the long straight of her favourite track did the trick, on what could be her swansong, although she could run in the Group 2 Prix Daniel Wildenstein at the Arc meeting if she comes out of this race well enough.

5918 CHESTER (L-H)

Saturday, September 24

OFFICIAL GOING: Good to soft (good in home straight; 6.9)

Wind: Moderate 1/2 behind Weather: overcast, light showers, becoming fine and sunny

6322 BEST ODDS GUARANTEED AT VICTORCHANDLER.COM MAIDEN FILLIES' STKS 7f 2y

2:30 (2:31) (Class 4) 2-Y-O **£4,528** (£1,347; £673; £336) **Stalls** Low

Form				RPR
3253	**1**		**Self Centred**[35] 5287 2-9-0 **81** MichaelHills 2 (Charles Hills) *led 1f: trckd ldr: led over 2f out: pushed clr over 1f out: eased towards fin* **1/3**[1]	84+
05	**2**	*4*	**The Giving Tree (IRE)**[18] 5807 2-9-0 0 JamesDoyle 3 (Sylvester Kirk) *chsd ldrs: wnt 3rd over 1f out: chsd wnr last 150yds: no imp* **10/1**[3]	67+
0	**3**	*4*	**Tinzapeas**[8] 6117 2-9-0 0 MatthewDavies 4 (Mick Channon) *dwlt: sn chsng ldrs: wnt 2nd 2f out: one pce* **18/1**	57
000	**4**	*5*	**She's Flawless (USA)**[12] 6000 2-9-0 **54** (b[1]) ShaneKelly 1 (Brian Meehan) *prom: outpcd over 2f out: hung bdly rt ins fnl f* **12/1**	44
	5	*5*	**Gabrial's Layla (IRE)** 2-9-0 0 FrannyNorton 5 (Mark Johnston) *led after 1f: hdd over 2f out: hung rt and wknd over 1f out* **9/2**[2]	32
	6	*4 ½*	**Silent Ambition** 2-9-0 0 RobbieFitzpatrick 7 (Mark Brisbourne) *dwlt and wnt rt s: a in rr* **33/1**	20
	7	*4*	**April Leyf (IRE)** 2-8-11 0 KierenFox(3) 8 (Mark Brisbourne) *dwlt and sltly hmpd s: sn bhd and drvn along* **25/1**	10

1m 30.74s (4.24) **Going Correction** +0.50s/f (Yiel) **7** Ran SP% **122.0**
Speed ratings (Par 94): **95,90,85,80,74 69,64**
Tote Swingers:1&2:£1.50, 2&3:£19.40, 1&3:£3.60 CSF £6.03 TOTE £1.30: £1.10, £3.60; EX 4.90.

Owner Mrs E Roberts **Bred** Bloomsbury Stud **Trained** Lambourn, Berks

FOCUS

An uncompetitive juvenile fillies' maiden.

NOTEBOOK

Self Centred tracked the early pace in second and was sent about her work approaching halfway, settling the race in a matter of strides before being eased down. This was an easy victory and she is capable of earning some black type. (op 8-15 tchd 4-7 and 8-13 in places)

The Giving Tree(IRE) improved from her debut when a fair fifth to Esentepe at Leicester last time. Back in trip here, she stayed on nicely and will be better with another winter on her back. (op 9-1 tchd 11-1)

Tinzapeas stepped up on her fast-ground Lingfield debut effort last week, tracking the winner through but not having the turn of foot to match that rival. She's related to winners and will be interesting in handicaps next season (op 14-1)

She's Flawless(USA) had been well held in fillies' maidens over 6f, 7f and 1m at big prices. Equipped with first-time blinkers and held up, she hung badly right up the straight. (tchd 11-1)

Gabrial's Layla(IRE) is closely related to useful 1m-9.5f winner General Elliott. She looked well in the parade ring, was solid in the market and set the pace before being picked off approaching the turn into the straight. Not given a hard time thereafter, she needs more experience and a longer trip. (op 4-1)

April Leyf(IRE) Official explanation: jockey said filly ran green

6323 PLAY CASINO AT VICTORCHANDLER.COM NURSERY 5f 110y
3:00 (3:00) (Class 2) 2-Y-O **£9,703** (£2,887; £1,443; £721) **Stalls** Low

Form RPR

0012 **1** **Free Zone**[14] 5922 2-8-8 **79** TomEaves 4 84
(Bryan Smart) *chsd ldr: styd on to ld last 100yds: hld on towards fin* **9/2**[1]

1130 **2** *nk* **Sea Odyssey (IRE)**[16] 5849 2-8-10 **81** MichaelHills 5 85
(Charles Hills) *restless in stalls: chsd ldrs: kpt on wl fnl f: no ex nr fin* **9/2**[1]

1105 **3** *1 ¼* **Fulbright**[69] 4131 2-9-7 **92** FrannyNorton 3 92
(Mark Johnston) *in rr: effrt on ins whn hmpd over 2f out: hdwy over 1f out: styd on wl to take 3rd nr fin* **9/2**[1]

0451 **4** *½* **Bubbly Ballerina**[14] 5922 2-8-13 **84** (p) DarryllHolland 9 82+
(Alan Bailey) *dwlt: hld up in rr: hmpd over 2f out: swtchd outside over 1f out: styng on wl at fin* **7/1**[3]

2412 **5** *nse* **Kimbali (IRE)**[15] 5876 2-8-7 **78** JimCrowley 8 77
(Richard Fahey) *in rr: hmpd over 2f out: hdwy: nt clr run and hmpd over 1f out: kpt on wl clsng stages* **7/1**[3]

3462 **6** *shd* **Sunrise Dance**[38] 5184 2-8-7 **78** MatthewDavies 2 76
(Alan Jarvis) *led: hdd ins fnl f: wknd nr fin* **11/2**[2]

0323 **7** *3 ¼* **Middleton Flyer (IRE)**[5] 6222 2-8-2 **78** ow3 MatthewCosham(5) 11 65
(David Evans) *chsd ldrs: sn drvn along: hung lft over 2f out: wknd appr fnl f* **16/1**

3420 **8** *3 ¼* **Musical Valley**[26] 5562 2-8-4 **75** (t) CathyGannon 1 61
(Tom Dascombe) *hld up in mid-div: hmpd over 2f out: hung rt nt clr run over 1f out: coasted home* **12/1**

4225 **9** *½* **Banksy**[81] 3707 2-7-13 **70** (t) JamieMackay 6 44
(Kevin Ryan) *prom: hung rt over 1f out: sn wknd* **25/1**

1200 **10** *15* **Nearly A Gift (IRE)**[21] 5708 2-8-11 **82** (b1) ShaneKelly 7 —
(Tim Easterby) *hld up in rr: effrt over 2f out: sn lost pl: eased fnl f: t.o* **20/1**

68.89 secs (2.69) **Going Correction** +0.50s/f (Yiel) **10** Ran SP% **117.1**
Speed ratings (Par 101): **102,101,99,99,99 99,94,90,89,69**
Tote Swingers:1&2:£32.80, 2&3:£3.10, 1&3:£4.00 CSF £24.47 CT £96.88 TOTE £6.10: £1.60, £2.00, £2.40; EX 34.80.

Owner Fromthestables.com Racing **Bred** R G Levin **Trained** Hambleton, N Yorks

FOCUS
A competitive nursery chock-full of in-form horses and, as always in sprints round this tight track, the draw played a significant part in the outcome. The three co-favourites filled the frame.

NOTEBOOK
Free Zone had put a couple of ordinary runs behind him when winning a Catterick maiden and ran well over C&D when overcoming a poor draw behind Bubbly Ballerina two weeks ago. Closely weighted with that rival again, the tables were turned thanks to a better draw. He broke well and had a target to aim at, staying on strongly four wide off the rail, to score nicely. He'll remain competitive and seems to appreciate juice in the ground. (op 5-1)

Sea Odyssey(IRE), who ran with credit despite facing a tough task in a valuable 7f sales race at Doncaster last time, was dropping back in trip. He seems to prefer front-running tactics, but was unable to get there, having to come through a gap between horses to challenge. He stayed on well and battled hard. He'll make a nice three-year-old. (op 11-2)

Fulbright had proven himself a very useful performer on a sound surface earlier in the season and had scored at Listed level at Epsom. Coming here off a 69-day break and shouldering top weight, he didn't enjoy the run of the race, but once the gaps arrived in the straight he stayed on really well up the far rail. There should be plenty more to come next season and he looks one to follow. (op 5-1)

Bubbly Ballerina found the winning groove here last time and, wearing cheekpieces for the first time, she was undone by the draw and missed the break, so to get as close as she did means she ran another cracker in the circumstances. Official explanation: jockey said filly missed the break (op 6-1)

Kimbali(IRE) had finished second here over 7f last time but was beaten over three lengths. Dropping in trip and outpaced early, he found this trip a little sharp for him, but was staying on with purpose from a poor draw. (op 13-2)

Sunrise Dance had five previous starts - all at 6f - without breaking his maiden. Dropping to a trip that looked sure to suit and ridden positively from his good draw, he still didn't appear to see it out. He has the ability to win a race or two, however. (op 5-1 tchd 9-2)

Middleton Flyer(IRE) Official explanation: jockey said filly hung left-handed

Musical Valley Official explanation: jockey said gelding hung right-handed

Banksy Official explanation: jockey said colt hung right-handed

6324 BET MOBILE AT VICTORCHANDLER.COM MAIDEN STKS 1m 2f 75y
3:35 (3:35) (Class 4) 3-Y-0+ **£5,175** (£1,540; £769; £384) **Stalls** High

Form RPR

32 **1** **Dick Doughtywylie**[25] 5585 3-9-3 0 MarcHalford 5 96+
(John Gosden) *led 2f: w ldr: led over 5f out: styd on fnl 2f: hld on nr fin* **5/6**[1]

32 **2** *nk* **Fruehling (IRE)**[44] 4956 3-9-3 0 ShaneKelly 8 95+
(Sir Michael Stoute) *trckd ldrs: wnt 2nd over 4f out: chal over 2f out: styd on towards fin: jst hld* **7/2**[2]

6-0 **3** *17* **Musical Flight**[166] 1271 3-9-3 0 MichaelHills 1 61
(Charles Hills) *trckd ldrs: wnt modest 3rd over 2f out: one pce* **9/1**[3]

324- **4** *4 ½* **Postscript (IRE)**[458] 3326 3-9-3 76 JimCrowley 4 52
(Ian Williams) *mid-div: effrt over 3f out: one pce* **9/1**[3]

0 **5** *1 ½* **Marshmallow**[33] 5327 3-8-12 0 JackMitchell 3 44
(Chris Wall) *hld up in mid-div: wnt poor 5th over 2f out: nvr nr ldrs* **16/1**

0 **6** *4* **Sailor's Chant (USA)**[29] 5449 3-9-3 0 FrannyNorton 9 41
(Mark Johnston) *s.s: bhd and drvn along: sme hdwy over 3f out: nvr on terms* **25/1**

50 **7** *12* **Eqtiraab (IRE)**[7] 6156 3-9-3 0 StephenCraine 7 17
(Tony Coyle) *s.s: in rr: bhd fnl 4f* **66/1**

8 *17* **Medal Of Valour (JPN)** 3-9-3 0 DarryllHolland 10 —
(Mark Johnston) *w ldrs: drvn over 5f out: wknd over 3f out* **14/1**

0 **9** *33* **Gorau Glas**[15] 5877 3-8-12 0 RobbieFitzpatrick 2 —
(Mark Brisbourne) *hld up in rr: rdn 4f out: sn bhd: t.o* **66/1**

600/ **10** *2* **Danesman**[938] 6868 6-9-6 52 RichardEvans(3) 6 —
(David Evans) *w ldr: narrow ld after 2f: hdd over 5f out: sn lost pl: bhd fnl 3f: t.o* **50/1**

2m 13.55s (2.35) **Going Correction** +0.50s/f (Yiel)
WFA 3 from 6yo 6lb **10** Ran SP% **118.1**
Speed ratings (Par 105): **110,109,96,92,91 88,78,64,38,36**
Tote Swingers:1&2:£1.20, 2&3:£6.30, 1&3:£3.10 CSF £3.75 TOTE £1.90: £1.10, £1.30, £2.30; EX 3.10.

Owner Ms Rachel D S Hood **Bred** Ms Rachel Hood **Trained** Newmarket, Suffolk

FOCUS
A modest and uncompetitive staying maiden with plenty of dead wood in behind the front two. Very few got into it and the two market leaders fought out an exciting finish, drawing a long way clear of the remainder.

6325 BEST FOOTBALL PRICES AT VICTORCHANDLER.COM H'CAP 1m 2f 75y
4:10 (4:11) (Class 2) (0-105,102) 3-Y-0
£18,675 (£5,592; £2,796; £1,398; £699; £351) **Stalls** High

Form RPR

5011 **1** **Belle Royale (IRE)**[21] 5730 3-9-4 **102** KierenFox(3) 2 112
(Mark Brisbourne) *mid-div: drvn over 3f out: swtchd outside over 1f out: r.o wl to ld last 100yds: readily* **6/1**

1422 **2** *2 ½* **Mashaaref**[15] 5888 3-8-5 **86** TadhgO'Shea 5 91
(Roger Varian) *mid-div: effrt over 3f out: led and edgd lft over 1f out: hdd and no ex ins fnl f* **9/4**[1]

1013 **3** *shd* **Weapon Of Choice (IRE)**[14] 5920 3-8-6 **87** SamHitchcott 1 92
(David Simcock) *trckd ldrs: effrt 3f out: edgd rt over 1f out: kpt on to take 3rd last 100yds* **5/1**[3]

3331 **4** *1* **Swift Alhaarth (IRE)**[14] 5932 3-8-12 **93** FrannyNorton 9 96
(Mark Johnston) *dwlt: sn trcking ldrs: led over 2f out: hdd and hung lft over 1f out: kpt on same pce* **10/3**[2]

4021 **5** *1 ¼* **Spanish Plume**[14] 5925 3-7-12 **79** oh6 JamieMackay 3 80
(Reg Hollinshead) *hld up in rr: drvn 3f out: hdwy over 1f out: kpt on fnl f* **20/1**

4210 **6** *3* **Ivan Vasilevich (IRE)**[38] 5177 3-8-9 **90** oh1 DarryllHolland 7 85
(Jane Chapple-Hyam) *led: hdd over 2f out: sn hmpd: wknd last 100yds* **11/1**

0501 **7** *4* **Blaise Chorus (IRE)**[33] 5317 3-8-9 **90** MichaelHills 6 77
(Charles Hills) *dwlt: hld up in rr: hdwy over 3f out: wknd and eased jst ins fnl f* **8/1**

1014 **8** *¾* **Groomed (IRE)**[10] 6063 3-8-1 **82** CathyGannon 8 67
(William Haggas) *trckd ldrs: drvn 3f out: hung rt and wknd over 1f out* **12/1**

2m 13.83s (2.63) **Going Correction** +0.50s/f (Yiel) **8** Ran SP% **116.7**
Speed ratings (Par 107): **109,107,106,106,105 102,99,98**
Tote Swingers:1&2:£4.80, 2&3:£1.30, 1&3:£4.30 CSF £20.39 CT £73.53 TOTE £5.70: £1.70, £1.50, £1.80; EX 26.30 Trifecta £106.20 Pool £419.37 - 2.92 winning units..

Owner Peter Mort **Bred** Dxb Bloodstock Ltd **Trained** Great Ness, Shropshire

FOCUS
A cracking handicap run at a searing pace and the form looks solid.

NOTEBOOK
Belle Royale(IRE) had caused a shock in a valuable handicap over 7.5f here last month, before following up over 1m in good style at Thirsk. Upped in trip again for her first try beyond a mile and carrying a 7lb penalty, there were plenty of questions left to answer, but this in-form filly completed her hat-trick in great style. Hemmed in near the rail with 3f to go and seemingly struggling, she picked up the bit after being angled out and flew up the middle of the track. This track clearly plays to her strengths. It was her fourth win from six starts here (she'd been placed as well) and she appears capable of winning at a higher level if this form can be translated to other tracks over this sort of trip. (op 11-2)

Mashaaref had shown improvement in his last two starts, when second in 1m2f handicaps at Ascot and Doncaster, and he probably stepped up on that form here. Raised 1lb for his latest run, he travelled well and moved into contention approaching the final turn, but had no chance once the winner kicked. He will be a nice horse next year and this was only his sixth run. (op 3-1)

Weapon Of Choice(IRE) had finished well over 1m here when third to Hacienda last time and, although his sole run over this trip was a disappointment, it was worth another try. Connections won't have been disappointed, either. He travelled well, had plenty of pace to aim at, and stayed on well, just failing to grab second spot. There are now plenty of options for him. (op 9-2)

Swift Alhaarth(IRE) is a consistent sort who had shown up well over 1m4f on his last three starts. Dropped back in trip here, he could not get the lead he likes. He still gives the impression he needs further and his rider reported that he hung left-handed. Official explanation: jockey said gelding hung left-handed (op 4-1)

Spanish Plume had come from off the pace to prevail in a blanket finish over C&D two weeks ago, but was running from 6lb out of the handicap in a much better race here. He didn't settle early but still had enough in reserve to stay on in good style late on. He is in good form and there's more to come on this evidence. (op 14-1)

Ivan Vasilevich(IRE) had won four times over 1m2f this season and finished a close second over C&D. His previous run at Nottingham was disappointing, however. His rider set a searching gallop, but he didn't appear to like being taken on and he emptied quickly when they turned in. (op 12-1 tchd 14-1)

Groomed(IRE) Official explanation: jockey said gelding hung right-handed

6326 INNOSPEC H'CAP 7f 2y
4:45 (4:45) (Class 3) (0-95,95) 3-Y-0+ **£12,938** (£3,850; £1,924; £962) **Stalls** Low

Form RPR

-001 **1** **Greensward**[21] 5717 5-8-13 **87** MichaelHills 10 95+
(Brian Meehan) *in rr: effrt over 2f out: r.o to ld last 75yds: hld on towards fin* **7/1**

0005 **2** *½* **Dubai Dynamo**[2] 6273 6-9-3 **91** CathyGannon 3 98
(Ruth Carr) *hld up in rr: effrt over 2f out: styd on wl fnl f: snatched 2nd nr fin* **7/1**

0 **3** *hd* **Naabegha**[22] 5684 4-9-0 **88** PatCosgrave 2 94
(Ed de Giles) *trckd ldrs: chal over 2f out: led over 1f out: hdd and no ex last 75yds* **11/1**

0302 **4** *nk* **Baby Strange**[15] 5879 7-9-1 **89** RobbieFitzpatrick 1 95
(Derek Shaw) *hld up in rr: effrt over 2f out: edgd rt over 1f out: styd on wl fnl f* **5/1**[2]

0000 **5** *1 ¾* **Kyllachy Star**[15] 5879 5-9-4 **92** JimCrowley 6 93
(Richard Fahey) *s.i.s: drvn and chsd ldrs over 3f out: one pce appr fnl f* **4/1**[1]

0000 **6** *1 ¼* **Kingscroft (IRE)**[14] 5936 3-8-12 **89** FrannyNorton 8 87
(Mark Johnston) *rr-div: hdwy over 4f out: sn chsng ldrs: kpt on same pce fnl f* **13/2**

6500 **7** *2 ½* **Kay Gee Be (IRE)**[14] 5920 7-8-8 **89** GeorgeChaloner(7) 12 80
(Richard Fahey) *in rr: sn drvn along: kpt on fnl f* **14/1**

2130 **8** *1* **One Scoop Or Two**[14] 5920 5-8-11 **85** (p) StephenCraine 5 73
(Reg Hollinshead) *led: hdd over 1f out: wknd fnl 150yds* **11/2**[3]

0300 **9** *5* **Dubai Hills**[123] 2390 5-9-5 **93** TomEaves 4 68
(Bryan Smart) *trckd ldrs: drvn and n.m.r over 3f out: lost pl and hmpd over 2f out* **14/1**

-020 **10** *9* **Clockmaker (IRE)**[54] 4609 5-9-2 **90** DarryllHolland 11 40
(Tim Easterby) *sn chsng ldrs: lost pl over 2f out: sn bhd* **11/1**

1m 29.54s (3.04) **Going Correction** +0.50s/f (Yiel)
WFA 3 from 4yo+ 3lb **10** Ran SP% **120.4**
Speed ratings (Par 107): **102,101,101,100,98 97,94,93,87,77**
Tote Swingers:1&2:£16.00, 2&3:£59.80, 1&3:£99.20 CSF £57.19 CT £557.81 TOTE £8.30: £2.40, £2.40, £3.80; EX 71.60.

Owner Smoke & Mirrors **Bred** Kincorth Investments Inc **Trained** Manton, Wilts

FOCUS
A decent handicap, again run at a generous gallop, with those coming off the pace faring best.

NOTEBOOK
Greensward was strongly fancied by connections, having been an impressive 7f winner on the Kempton Polytrack following a near four-month break. The handicapper had left his turf mark unchanged and with ground conditions in his favour, it was surprising he didn't have more market support. After being held up, he made stealthy headway down the back straight and came wide to deliver his challenge, wearing down the eventual third. He seems to like this tight track and looks ahead of the handicapper. (tchd 15-2 and 8-1 in places)
Dubai Dynamo has had a busy season but has been largely consistent, having draw excuses on his last couple of defeats. Though this trip looked on the sharp side for him, he looked well beaten turning in, but made significant late headway and would have collared the winner in another few strides. He has been given a chance by the handicapper and can make it pay if in this mood. (tchd 9-1)
Naabegha came here on the back of a pipe-opener at Haydock, having previously shown quite useful form on easy ground up to 7f at the Paris tracks. A proven front-runner, this imposing sort made most of the running and, despite flashing his tail under pressure, still showed plenty of guts once he was passed. He seems fairly treated at present. (op 8-1)
Baby Strange is another who has run well here in the past and he stayed on well over C&D last time, despite trying this trip for the first time in two years, having previously raced over shorter. He didn't have a lot of room 2f out, but stayed on really well from some way back. This was a solid effort from an awkward draw and he is one to keep on the right side. (op 7-2)
Kyllachy Star doesn't always get the run of the race round here because of his hold-up style, and that was the case again after he started slowly. This trip was plenty sharp enough for him in any case. (op 5-1)
Kingscroft(IRE) had not been in great form coming into this and, held up here, he made good progress but his run flattened out. (op 10-1)
One Scoop Or Two was having his fourth start in nine days and made a bold bid from the front, but there wasn't much left in the tank and he faded. (op 6-1 tchd 5-1)
Clockmaker(IRE) Official explanation: jockey said gelding stopped very quickly

6327 ADVANCED INSULATION PLC H'CAP — 6f 18y
5:20 (5:21) (Class 4) (0-85,85) 3-Y-O+ **£6,469** (£1,925; £962; £481) **Stalls** Low

Form | | | | RPR
0630 **1** **Courageous (IRE)**[8] 6112 5-9-2 **83**............(t) DarryllHolland 4 96
(Kevin Ryan) *led after 1f: drvn 3 l clr over 1f out: hld on nr fin* **9/2**[2]
0000 **2** ½ **Corporal Maddox**[15] 5879 4-9-3 **84**............ FrannyNorton 7 95
(Jamie Osborne) *rr-div: hdwy over 2f out: styd on to go 2nd 75yds out: kpt on wl* **6/1**[3]
3000 **3** 2 ¾ **King Of Eden (IRE)**[20] 5758 5-9-3 **84**............ ShaneKelly 1 86
(Eric Alston) *led 1f: chsd wnr: kpt on same pce fnl 2f* **10/1**
4510 **4** 1 ¼ **Bravo King (IRE)**[14] 5918 3-8-11 **83**............ RobertLButler(3) 2 81
(Richard Guest) *mid-div: hdwy and prom over 2f out: hung rt and one pce over 1f out* **10/1**
3131 **5** 1 ¾ **Pearl Blue (IRE)**[35] 5279 3-9-0 **83**............ JackMitchell 3 76
(Chris Wall) *chsd ldrs: effrt over 2f out: one pce* **9/4**[1]
6114 **6** 1 ¾ **Barons Spy (IRE)**[13] 5972 10-9-2 **83**............ JamesDoyle 10 70
(Richard Price) *restless in stalls: in rr: sme hdwy over 1f out: nvr a factor* **10/1**
0200 **7** 1 ¼ **Julius Geezer (IRE)**[21] 5706 3-9-2 **85**............ StephenCraine 6 68
(Tom Dascombe) *in rr: sme hdwy over 1f out: nvr a factor* **20/1**
0005 **8** hd **Rocket Rob (IRE)**[17] 5831 5-9-0 **81**............ JamieMackay 12 63
(Willie Musson) *s.s: sme hdwy on outer 2f out: nvr a factor* **16/1**
3020 **9** 1 ¼ **My Kingdom (IRE)**[35] 5272 5-9-2 **83**............(t) JimCrowley 5 61
(Patrick Morris) *mid-div: hdwy over 2f out: wknd fnl f* **7/1**
0140 **10** 3 ¾ **Last Sovereign**[15] 5879 7-9-0 **81**............ TomEaves 8 47
(Ollie Pears) *s.s: effrt on outer over 2f out: sn wknd* **18/1**
-26 **11** 1 ¼ **Conry (IRE)**[251] 186 5-9-1 **82**............ CathyGannon 9 44
(Patrick Morris) *chsd ldrs on outer: lost pl over 1f out* **25/1**

1m 17.04s (3.24) **Going Correction** +0.50s/f (Yiel)
WFA 3 from 4yo+ 2lb **11** Ran SP% **122.8**
Speed ratings (Par 105): **98,97,93,92,89 87,85,85,83,78 77**
Tote Swingers:1&2:£5.30, 2&3:£16.30, 1&3:£11.30 CSF £33.34 CT £269.30 TOTE £6.40: £2.20, £2.50, £3.30; EX 33.80.
Owner Dab Hand Racing **Bred** Yeomanstown Lodge Stud **Trained** Hambleton, N Yorks

FOCUS
A competitive 0-85 sprint handicap with just 4lb separating the runners.

6328 CHESHIRE JETS H'CAP — 1m 5f 89y
5:55 (5:55) (Class 4) (0-85,84) 3-Y-O **£6,469** (£1,925; £962; £481) **Stalls** Low

Form | | | | RPR
1515 **1** **Gottany O'S**[10] 6046 3-9-7 **84**............ SamHitchcott 1 92
(Mick Channon) *mid-div: hdwy on inner over 2f out: sn chsng ldr: styd on to ld last 100yds* **9/1**
213 **2** 1 ¼ **Quails Hollow (IRE)**[14] 5938 3-8-8 **71**............ CathyGannon 3 77
(William Haggas) *led: qcknd over 4f out: hdd and no ex ins fnl f* **7/2**[2]
0441 **3** ¾ **Palazzo Bianco**[22] 5685 3-9-5 **82**............ MarcHalford 5 87+
(John Gosden) *hld up in rr: effrt on outer over 4f out: outpcd over 2f out: hdwy over 1f out: edgd lft and styd on to take 3rd last 75yds: keeping on wl at fin* **10/3**[1]
6414 **4** 2 ½ **One Lucky Lady**[19] 5782 3-8-10 **73**............ MichaelHills 4 74
(Charles Hills) *dwlt: sn chsng ldrs: chal 3f out: sn rdn: one pce over 1f out* **9/1**
322 **5** ½ **Devoted (IRE)**[63] 4336 3-8-13 **76**............ JimCrowley 2 77
(Ralph Beckett) *hld up in rr: hdwy over 3f out: n.m.r over 2f out: swtchd rt over 1f out: one pce* **6/1**
12 **6** 1 ¼ **Mezyaad (USA)**[140] 1903 3-9-4 **81**............ JackMitchell 8 80
(Roger Varian) *t.k.h in rr: effrt on ins over 2f out: nvr rchd ldrs* **10/1**
1201 **7** 5 **Shalloon (IRE)**[10] 6063 3-9-6 **83**............ FrannyNorton 6 74
(Mark Johnston) *trckd ldrs: drvn 3f out: wknd appr fnl f* **5/1**[3]
1263 **8** hd **King Of The Celts (IRE)**[10] 6046 3-8-13 **76**............ TomEaves 7 67
(Tim Easterby) *chsd ldrs: drvn 4f out: hung lft and lost pl over 1f out* **11/1**

3m 1.88s (9.08) **Going Correction** +0.50s/f (Yiel) **8** Ran SP% **113.7**
Speed ratings (Par 103): **92,91,90,89,88 88,85,84**
Tote Swingers:1&2:£8.50, 2&3:£2.90, 1&3:£9.10 CSF £40.06 CT £127.39 TOTE £11.30: £3.30, £1.40, £1.80; EX 47.00.
Owner Dr Marwan Koukash **Bred** Phil Jen Racing **Trained** West Ilsley, Berks

FOCUS
The pace was nothing out of the ordinary for this wide-open handicap where all bar one of the runners had finished either first or second in their last two starts.
T/Plt: £29.40 to a £1 stake. Pool:£60,703.00 - 1,504.31 winning tickets T/Qpdt: £18.00 to a £1 stake. Pool:£2,923.55 - 119.80 winning tickets WG

6290 HAYDOCK (L-H)
Saturday, September 24

OFFICIAL GOING: Good to soft (soft in places on round course; 6.6)
Wind: Virtually nil Weather: Overcast

6329 EBF MH CONSTRUCTION MAIDEN FILLIES' STKS — 1m
1:40 (1:42) (Class 5) 2-Y-O **£3,234** (£962; £481; £240) **Stalls** Low

Form | | | | RPR
1 **Oojooba** 2-9-0 0............ FergusSweeney 3 87+
(Roger Varian) *hld up in midfield: stdy hdwy on inner over 3f out: chal 2f out: led over 1f out: rdn and kpt on wl fnl f* **11/1**
02 **2** 2 ½ **Balady (IRE)**[29] 5444 2-9-0 0............ TadhgO'Shea 2 81
(John Dunlop) *trckd ldrs: smooth hdwy over 3f out: rdn to ld 2f out: hdd over 1f out: sn drvn and kpt on same pce* **5/1**[3]
3 1 **Supreme Luxury (IRE)** 2-9-0 0............ PhillipMakin 5 79+
(Kevin Ryan) *hld up in tch: hdwy 3f out: swtchd lft and rdn to chse ldrs wl over 1f out: kpt on ins fnl f* **33/1**
4 3 ¼ **Minnie Diva (IRE)** 2-9-0 0............ StephenCraine 13 72
(Kevin Ryan) *towards rr: hdwy 3f out: swtchd lft to outer and rdn 2f out: styd on to chse ldrs appr fnl f: sn no imp* **80/1**
5 ¾ **Great Heavens** 2-9-0 0............ RobertHavlin 15 70+
(John Gosden) *hld up in midfield: hdwy on inner and in tch 3f out: pushed along 2f out: swtchd lft and rdn over 1f out: kpt on: nrst fin* **8/1**
3 **6** 1 **Corsetry (USA)**[18] 5807 2-9-0 0............ EddieAhern 10 68
(Sir Henry Cecil) *in tch: hdwy on inner 4f out: chsd ldrs over 2f out: sn rdn along and no imp fr over 1f out* **9/2**[2]
0 **7** ½ **Forgive**[23] 5655 2-9-0 0............ LiamKeniry 9 67
(Richard Hannon) *in tch: hdwy to chse ldrs 4f out: rdn along wl over 2f out: grad wknd fnl 2f* **12/1**
00 **8** nk **Saratoga Slew (IRE)**[26] 5565 2-9-0 0............ KierenFallon 6 66
(Charles Hills) *led: rdn along over 3f out: drvn and hdd 2f out: grad wknd* **20/1**
9 7 **Harmonie (IRE)** 2-9-0 0............ MartinLane 14 51
(Noel Quinlan) *dwlt: a towards rr* **100/1**
32 **10** ½ **Aleut**[17] 5819 2-9-0 0............ FrederikTylicki 8 50
(James Given) *prom: rdn along over 3f out: drvn and wknd over 2f out* **17/2**
5 **11** shd **Miss Cap Estel**[23] 5655 2-9-0 0............ JimmyFortune 11 49
(Andrew Balding) *t.k.h: chsd ldrs: rdn along 3f out: wknd 2f out* **5/2**[1]
50 **12** ½ **Good Clodora (IRE)**[120] 2467 2-9-0 0............ SilvestreDeSousa 4 48
(Brian Meehan) *chsd ldrs: cl up over 4f out: rdn over 3f out: drvn wl over 2f out and sn wknd* **25/1**
13 5 **Angelic Note (IRE)** 2-9-0 0............ EddieCreighton 7 37
(Brian Meehan) *dwlt: a in rr* **40/1**
14 shd **Amthal (IRE)** 2-9-0 0............ RoystonFfrench 12 37
(Clive Brittain) *a in rr* **66/1**
15 28 **Bovs Castle** 2-9-0 0............ TomMcLaughlin 1 —
(Lucinda Featherstone) *hmpd s: a in rr* **200/1**

1m 44.01s (1.11) **Going Correction** -0.05s/f (Good) **15** Ran SP% **119.3**
Speed ratings (Par 92): **92,89,88,85,84 83,83,82,75,75 75,74,69,69,41**
Tote Swingers:1&2:£13.50, 2&3:£35.00, 1&3:£39.60 CSF £61.07 TOTE £14.20: £3.80, £1.70, £10.40; EX 86.80.
Owner Sheikh Ahmed Al Maktoum **Bred** Darley **Trained** Newmarket, Suffolk

FOCUS
A fair fillies' maiden where the holding surface played its part. The second sets the level.

NOTEBOOK
Oojooba ◆ came home a decisive debut winner, looking right at home on the deteriorating ground. She was given time to find her feet by her substitute rider and easily got to the leaders after being asked to close from halfway. The race was soon in the bag after she went for everything in between the final two furlongs and this rates a promising display. She obviously stays well and it wouldn't surprise to see her try her hand in an Oaks trial early next season. (op 8-1 tchd 12-1 in a place)
Balady(IRE) set the standard on her Newmarket second last month and her trainer has an excellent record in this event. She travelled kindly throughout and was ideally placed 2f out, but tended to hang once challenged by the winner. That suggests this ground was a bit too much for her and she deserves another chance. (op 7-2 tchd 3-1)
Supreme Luxury(IRE) ◆ was doing all of her best work towards the finish and posted a pleasing debut effort. She left the impression she would learn a good deal for the experience and ought to be winning before the season's end.
Minnie Diva(IRE) is another debutante and a stablemate of the third (second string). She too evidently stays well and ought to relish another couple of furlongs next year
Great Heavens ◆, a sister to this year's top 3yo Nathaniel, proved easy to back ahead of this racecourse debut and ran accordingly but showed enough to think she has a fair future. (tchd 15-2)
Corsetry(USA) finished third in a modest maiden on her debut and looked to find this ground against her. (op 11-2)
Forgive also failed to act on this deeper surface that well but has ability. (op 11-1)
Miss Cap Estel, well backed, wasn't seen near her best due to being lit up early and pulling too hard. She also looked all at sea on the different ground. (op 7-2 tchd 4-1)

6330 EBF "SAGAMIX" "REPROCOLOR" FILLIES' H'CAP — 1m 2f 95y
2:15 (2:16) (Class 3) (0-90,88) 3-Y-O+ **£12,938** (£3,850; £1,924; £962) **Stalls** Centre

Form | | | | RPR
5100 **1** **Askaud (IRE)**[21] 5730 3-9-3 **87**............(p) FrederikTylicki 15 95
(David Nicholls) *towards rr: hdwy over 3f out and sn rdn along: drvn wl over 1f out: styd on u.p ent fnl f: led nr line* **25/1**
1124 **2** shd **Kenyan Cat**[15] 5888 4-8-11 **80**............ NeilFarley(5) 6 90+
(Ed McMahon) *in tch: hdwy 3f out: rdn to ld 1 1/2f out: drvn and edgd rt ins fnl f: hdd nr line* **5/1**[2]
0020 **3** ½ **Antigua Sunrise (IRE)**[29] 5435 5-8-10 **81**............ LauraBarry(7) 16 88
(Richard Fahey) *in tch: hdwy 3f out: rdn wl over 1f out and sn ev ch: drvn ins fnl f: no ex nr fin* **14/1**
00 **4** 2 ¼ **All Annalena (IRE)**[49] 4788 5-9-7 **85**............ RichardMullen 13 88
(Lucy Wadham) *chsd ldrs: rdn along 3f out: drvn and outpcd 2f out: styd on ins fnl f* **20/1**
2056 **5** 1 ½ **Ken's Girl**[13] 5968 7-9-1 **79**............ FergusSweeney 17 79
(Stuart Kittow) *cl up: effrt over 3f out: sn rdn and ev ch tl drvn and wknd ent fnl f* **11/1**
154- **6** shd **Hidden Fire**[378] 5972 4-8-10 **74**............ LiamKeniry 14 74
(David Elsworth) *midfield: hdwy over 3f out: chsd ldrs over 2f out: drvn to chal and ev ch over 1f out: wknd ent fnl f* **18/1**

0-61 **7** *2* **Qaraaba**[114] 2649 4-8-13 **77** KierenFallon 7 73
(Seamus Durack) *hld up in rr: hdwy 3f out: rdn along 2f out: styd on appr fnl f: nt rch ldrs* **8/1**

0000 **8** *½* **Snow Dancer (IRE)**[15] 5888 7-9-2 **80** PhillipMakin 10 75
(Hugh McWilliams) *dwlt and in rr: sme hdwy 2f out: sn rdn and n.d* **20/1**

-456 **9** *shd* **Umseyat (USA)**[43] 5020 3-8-11 **81** (p) TadhgO'Shea 12 76
(John Gosden) *led: rdn along 3f out: drvn 2f out: sn hdd and grad wknd appr fnl f* **6/1**[3]

2341 **10** *2 ½* **El Torbellino (IRE)**[43] 5020 3-9-2 **86** SilvestreDeSousa 9 76
(David O'Meara) *cl up: rdn along 3f out: drvn 2f out and grad wknd* **8/1**

621 **11** *shd* **Fashionable Gal (IRE)**[61] 4090 4-9-2 **80** EddieAhern 2 70
(Neil King) *prom: effrt 4f out: rdn along wl over 2f out: sn drvn and grad wknd* **10/1**

115 **12** *1 ½* **Making Eyes (IRE)**[14] 5940 3-9-2 **86** JimmyFortune 11 73
(Hugo Palmer) *towards rr: sme hdwy on wd outside 3f out: sn rdn along and nvr a factor* **4/1**[1]

2500 **13** *nk* **She's A Character**[9] 6078 4-8-11 **78** LeeTopliss(3) 5 64
(Richard Fahey) *a in rr* **20/1**

3410 **14** *23* **Miss Bootylishes**[13] 5962 6-8-8 **77** JamesRogers(5) 1 20
(Paul Burgoyne) *a in rr* **25/1**

340 **15** *4 ½* **Bella Noir**[21] 5702 4-8-11 **75** NeilCallan 4 —
(Mrs K Burke) *in tch on inner: rdn along 1/2-way: sn wknd* **20/1**

2m 13.95s (-2.05) **Going Correction** -0.05s/f (Good)
WFA 3 from 4yo+ 6lb **15** Ran SP% **129.3**
Speed ratings (Par 104): **106,105,105,103,102 102,100,100,100,98 98,97,96,78,74**
Tote Swingers:1&2: not won, 2&3:£17.30, 1&3: not won CSF £142.34 CT £1879.75 TOTE £32.30: £10.50, £2.00, £5.30; EX 288.10.

Owner Paul J Dixon **Bred** John P Jones **Trained** Sessay, N Yorks

FOCUS

A very competitive fillies' handicap. It was run at a fair pace and again the runners came more towards stands' side in the home straight.

NOTEBOOK

Askaud(IRE) hit top gear late in the day giving been set plenty to do and just did enough to reel in the placed horses where it mattered. She had stamina to prove hence she was held up out the back, but does act on soft ground and was right at the top of her game here as this was her highest winning mark to date. It opens up for few more options now connections know she stays. (op 33-1)

Kenyan Cat was well backed. She sweating up and took a keen hold in mid-field, but that didn't stop her throwing down a strong challenge and she was only nabbed on the line. She's had a cracking season since joining her present trainer and is evidently still on an upwards curve. (op 6-1 tchd 13-2 in places)

Antigua Sunrise(IRE) has become inconsistent this season, but finished third in this event last year and returned to her best with a game effort on ground that holds no fears. She wasn't beaten far and was in turn clear of the remainder.

All Annalena(IRE), last year's winner, came into this looking out of sorts after two poor efforts, but she had her ground. She failed to land a serious blow, but was staying on with some purpose late in the day and it was a step back in the right direction. She looks ready for another got over 1m4f. (op 16-1)

Ken's Girl wasn't able to lead, but does go well on this sort of ground and ran close enough to her mark, helping to set the standard. (op 12-1)

Hidden Fire ◆, who won her first two outings last year, was making her belated seasonal debut. She travelled kindly into contention on the near side in the home straight, but hit something of a flat spot after switching to the rail and was done with from the furlong marker. She could improve a good deal for this and it was a pleasing return. (op 14-1)

Making Eyes(IRE) proved popular back against her own sex, but was well beaten off and, despite being a winner on soft, this ground may have been too tacky for her. Official explanation: jockey said filly hung left (op 9-2 tchd 7-2)

Bella Noir Official explanation: jockey said filly never travelled

6331 SPORTS360 H'CAP 6f
2:45 (2:45) (Class 3) (0-90,89) 3-Y-O+ **£8,409** (£2,502; £1,250; £625) **Stalls** Centre

Form RPR

3100 **1** **Valery Borzov (IRE)**[7] 6145 7-9-1 **88** LeeTopliss(3) 6 98
(Richard Fahey) *in tch: smooth hdwy to join ldrs: led wl over 1f out: sn rdn and styd on wl* **12/1**

0065 **2** *½* **Mass Rally (IRE)**[7] 6145 4-9-4 **88** (v) LiamKeniry 5 96
(Michael Dods) *towards rr: hdwy 2f out: sn rdn and styd on wl fnl f* **15/2**[2]

0001 **3** *nk* **Tagula Night (IRE)**[13] 5972 5-9-1 **85** KierenFallon 9 92
(Walter Swinburn) *midfield: pushed along over 2f out: swtchd lft and rdn wl over 1f out: styd on wl fnl f* **7/1**[1]

-533 **4** *¾* **Gentle Lord**[25] 5578 3-9-0 **86** (t) RichardKingscote 12 91
(Tom Dascombe) *a.p: cl up 1/2-way: rdn wl over 1f out and ev ch tl drvn ent fnl f and kpt on same pce* **8/1**[3]

00 **5** *1* **West Coast Dream**[5] 6224 4-9-3 **87** PhillipMakin 1 88
(Roy Brotherton) *led: rdn along 2f out: edgd rt and hdd wl over 1f out: drvn and one pce ins fnl f* **12/1**

6020 **6** *shd* **We Have A Dream**[16] 5852 6-9-3 **87** NeilCallan 3 88
(William Muir) *prom: rdn along 2f out: drvn whn nt clr run over 1f out: one pce after* **20/1**

2013 **7** *½* **Esprit De Midas**[8] 6113 5-9-5 **89** AdrianNicholls 13 89
(David Nicholls) *dwlt and in rr: swtchd lft to outer 2f out: sn rdn and kpt on fnl f: nrst fin* **8/1**[3]

0001 **8** *hd* **Noverre To Go (IRE)**[32] 5345 5-9-3 **87** (t) LukeMorris 4 86
(Ronald Harris) *chsd ldrs: rdn along 2f out: sn drvn and grad wknd* **25/1**

0005 **9** *hd* **Ballista (IRE)**[21] 5706 3-9-0 **86** AndrewElliott 16 84+
(Tom Dascombe) *in rr: pushed along 1/2-way: swtchd wd and rdn wl over 1f out: kpt on ins fnl f: nrst fin* **20/1**

0-00 **10** *½* **Summerinthecity (IRE)**[16] 5852 4-9-4 **88** PatCosgrave 10 85
(Ed de Giles) *a towards rr* **12/1**

3200 **11** *½* **Whozthecat (IRE)**[20] 5758 4-8-10 **85** NeilFarley(5) 11 80
(Declan Carroll) *chsd ldrs: rdn along 2f out: grad wknd* **14/1**

0010 **12** *½* **Baldemar**[7] 6145 6-9-1 **85** FrederikTylicki 15 78
(Richard Fahey) *hld up: effrt towards stands' rail 2f out: sn n.m.r and no hdwy* **20/1**

4316 **13** *1 ½* **Layla's Hero (IRE)**[8] 6113 4-9-2 **86** StevieDonohoe 14 75
(John Quinn) *a towards rr* **7/1**[1]

2200 **14** *6* **Thirteen Shivers**[7] 6148 3-9-1 **87** PaddyAspell 7 56
(Michael Easterby) *in tch: rdn along 2f out: sn wknd* **20/1**

1120 **15** *4* **Tyfos**[21] 5703 6-9-3 **87** TomMcLaughlin 17 44
(Brian Baugh) *chsd ldrs: rdn along over 2f out: sn wknd* **20/1**

0126 **16** *5* **Quasi Congaree (GER)**[27] 5508 5-9-3 **87** (t) SilvestreDeSousa 2 28
(Ian Wood) *midfield: swtchd lft to outer and sme hdwy over 2f out: sn rdn and nvr a factor* **16/1**

1m 14.93s (1.13) **Going Correction** +0.35s/f (Good)
WFA 3 from 4yo+ 2lb **16** Ran SP% **122.3**
Speed ratings (Par 107): **106,105,104,103,102 102,101,101,101,100 99,99,97,89,83 77**
Tote Swingers:1&2: £28.30, 2&3:£11.20, 1&3: £11.80 CSF £87.39 CT £694.38 TOTE £15.40: £3.00, £2.90, £1.80, £1.90; EX 139.90.

Owner D R Kilburn/John Nicholls Trading **Bred** Vincent Harrington **Trained** Musley Bank, N Yorks

FOCUS

A fair sprint and typically competitive for the grade. Unsurprisingly they all wanted to be stands' side and those drawn nearest the rail were at an advantage.

NOTEBOOK

Valery Borzov(IRE) had flopped the last twice and the visor was abandoned. That move worked the oracle, as he ran out a game winner on ground he loves. It was actually the first time he had raced without the headgear since finishing sixth in this last year off a 3lb lower mark and he's very useful on such ground when the mood strikes him.

Mass Rally(IRE) ◆ posted his best effort for current connections when not beaten far in the Silver Cup at Ayr last week and, while unable to confirm that form with the winner, took another step forward in defeat here. His two wins came on Polytrack and he looks a surefire AW winner later on if unable to go one better before the turf season is out. (tchd 8-1)

Tagula Night(IRE), 3lb higher, was motoring down the centre inside the final furlong, but got going all too late in the day. He obviously remains in decent heart and helps to set the level. (op 6-1)

Gentle Lord gained his sole win in a C&D maiden on soft ground last year. He raced against the stands' rail and held every chance, but left the impression more aggressive tactics may be what he wants. (tchd 9-1)

West Coast Dream went with the winner until fading half a furlong out. He likes this ground and it was an improved run, but the handicapper probably has his measure. (op 11-1)

We Have A Dream bounced back to form and ran very close to his fifth in this event last term off the same mark. (op 16-1)

Ballista(IRE) Official explanation: jockey said, regarding running and riding, that his orders were to jump out, keep the gelding covered up as it is a 5f horse and to get the 6f trip.

Layla's Hero(IRE) was well beaten off, but this race didn't suit his run style and he needs all to fall right in his races. (tchd 13-2)

Thirteen Shivers Official explanation: vet said gelding bled from the nose

Quasi Congaree(GER) Official explanation: jockey said gelding stopped quickly

6332 SPORTS360.CO.UK LESTER PIGGOTT "START TO FINISH" H'CAP 5f
3:20 (3:20) (Class 2) (0-105,103) 3-Y-O+**£19,407** (£5,775; £2,886; £1,443) **Stalls** Centre

Form RPR

0362 **1** **Marine Commando**[16] 5852 3-8-8 **88** FrederikTylicki 8 97
(Richard Fahey) *trckd ldrs: effrt and n.m.r wl over 1f out: swtchd lft and rdn 1f out: qcknd to ld last 75yds* **10/1**

0202 **2** *nk* **Confessional**[14] 5927 4-9-4 **97** (be) SilvestreDeSousa 1 105
(Tim Easterby) *trckd ldr: gd hdwy 2f out: rdn to ld ent fnl f: sn drvn: hdd and nt qckn last 75yds* **8/1**

4062 **3** *hd* **Racy**[38] 5180 4-9-0 **93** PhillipMakin 15 100+
(Kevin Ryan) *in tch towards stands' rail: effrt and nt clr run over 1f out: swtchd rt and rdn ent fnl f: fin strly* **15/2**[3]

2203 **4** *1 ¼* **Hazelrigg (IRE)**[5] 6224 6-8-8 **87** (be) EddieAhern 5 90
(Tim Easterby) *trckd ldrs: effrt whn n.m.r appr fnl f: sn rdn and kpt on same pce* **11/1**

5130 **5** *hd* **Judge 'n Jury**[5] 6224 7-8-8 **87** LukeMorris 11 89
(Ronald Harris) *cl up: rdn and ev ch wl over 1f out tl drvn and one pce ent fnl f* **16/1**

1032 **6** *hd* **Master Rooney (IRE)**[21] 5706 5-8-9 **88** RoystonFfrench 12 89
(Bryan Smart) *racd towards stands' rail: led: rdn along 2f out: drvn over 1f out: hdd ent fnl f and one pce* **14/1**

1650 **7** *nse* **Secret Witness**[14] 5927 5-8-13 **92** (b) TomMcLaughlin 13 93
(Ronald Harris) *dwlt and towards rr: hdwy 2f out: sn rdn and kpt on fnl f: nrst fin* **16/1**

2100 **8** *½* **Strike Up The Band**[26] 5543 8-8-7 **86** AdrianNicholls 6 85
(David Nicholls) *towards rr: hdwy wl over 1f out: sn swtchd lft and rdn: styd on ins fnl f: nrst fin* **33/1**

5000 **9** *hd* **Waffle (IRE)**[7] 6147 5-9-10 **103** GrahamGibbons 10 102
(David Barron) *in rr: effrt and sme hdwy 2f out: sn rdn and n.d* **7/1**[2]

0041 **10** *¾* **Cheveton**[7] 6145 7-8-11 **93** DaleSwift(3) 2 89
(Richard Price) *dwlt and towards rr: hdwy on wd outside 2f out: rdn to chse ldrs over 1f out: drvn and one pce fnl f* **5/1**[1]

5503 **11** *½* **Addictive Dream (IRE)**[14] 5927 4-9-6 **99** KierenFallon 17 98+
(Walter Swinburn) *trckd ldrs: effrt wl over 1f out whn nt clr run ent fnl f: eased* **8/1**

2501 **12** *¾* **Foxy Music**[14] 5918 7-8-9 **88** RichardKingscote 7 79
(Eric Alston) *cl up: rdn along wl over 1f out: sn drvn and wknd* **22/1**

0000 **13** *½* **Rain Delayed (IRE)**[14] 5927 5-9-0 **93** LiamKeniry 14 83
(Michael Dods) *nvr bttr than midfield* **33/1**

2000 **14** *1 ¼* **Falasteen (IRE)**[21] 5706 4-8-13 **92** StevieDonohoe 16 77
(Kevin Ryan) *dwlt: a in rr* **50/1**

0110 **15** *1 ¾* **Steps (IRE)**[78] 3820 3-8-12 **92** NeilCallan 9 71
(Roger Varian) *chsd ldrs: rdn along wl over 2f out: drvn whn n.m.r over 1f out and wknd* **12/1**

4304 **16** *1 ¾* **Fathom Five (IRE)**[26] 5543 7-8-7 **86** RichardMullen 3 58
(David Nicholls) *cl up on outer: rdn along 2f out: sn wknd* **20/1**

61.40 secs (0.60) **Going Correction** +0.35s/f (Good)
WFA 3 from 4yo+ 1lb **16** Ran SP% **123.7**
Speed ratings (Par 109): **109,108,108,106,105 105,105,104,104,103 102,101,100,98,95 92**
Tote Swingers:1&2 £21.00, 2&3 £7.90, 1&3 £71.90 CSF £83.83 CT £676.09 TOTE £13.80: £3.20, £2.20, £2.10, £2.60; EX 150.10 Trifecta £678.40 Part won. Pool £916.81 - 0.10 winning units..

Owner M Wynne **Bred** L J Vaessen **Trained** Musley Bank, N Yorks

FOCUS

A decent sprint handicap. Again the stands' side was the preferred place to be and it saw plenty of chances, but there was ultimately a tight three-way finish.

NOTEBOOK

Marine Commando finally registered a first success since resuming at three and did the job readily. He's been in much better form again of late, finishing runner-up last time out off 1lb lower, and was still very well treated on his 2yo form. He got a lovely ride too from Freddie Tylicki, who was registering a double on the card, and was produced late to win cosily. It's hoped he'll now go on from this as this looks the way to ride him and appeals as one for something like the Ayr Gold Cup next year. (op 9-1)

Confessional, a close second in the Portland off 2lb lower last time out, travelled sweetly up with the pace and was only caught by the winner late on. He's hard to actually win with but remains in great form and really deserves a change of fortune.

Racy broke well against the stands' rail but was taken back and that probably cost him as he got a troubled passage when trying to make his challenge. He flew when in the clear and wasn't beaten at all far. He's become expensive to follow and this wasn't the first time he's run an eyecatching race this term, but there is surely one of these in him before the season's end. (op 9-1)

The Form Book, Raceform Ltd, Compton, RG20 6NL

Hazelrigg(IRE), who found himself in front too soon at Leicester last time out, again travelled kindly through his race and was produced with every chance. He found just the same pace when asked to win the race, though, and finished one place worse than his third in the race last season. (op 14-1)

Judge 'n Jury had his ground and ran a perfectly respectable race, just holding on for fifth, but has become hard to win with. (tchd 20-1 in places)

Master Rooney(IRE), 3lb higher, helped cut out the pace on the stands' rail and wasn't disgraced on ground a bit too soft for his liking. (op 12-1)

Secret Witness ◆ would have gone very close had he not blown the start as he endured a nightmare passage on the near side late on.

Waffle(IRE) didn't look happy through the first half of the race and was finishing off all too late down the centre. He's a tricky customer to get right. (op 10-1)

Cheveton won the Bronze Cup at Ayr last season before following up in this event. He's confirmed himself very much an autumn horse this month and won the Silver Cup last time out. A 5lb rise put him to only 1lb higher this time round and he looked sure to go close, but things didn't go to plan after he made a tardy start. Official explanation: vet said gelding bled from the nose (op 11-2)

Addictive Dream(IRE), the Portland third, had his chance off 2lb higher and looked held before being snatched up inside the closing stages.

Rain Delayed(IRE) Official explanation: jockey said gelding was denied a clear run

6333 STAINLESS WIRE H'CAP — 1m 6f

3:55 (3:55) (Class 2) (0-100,97) 3-Y-O+ **£19,407** (£5,775; £2,886; £1,443) **Stalls** Low

Form	Pos	Dist	Horse / details	Jockey	RPR
1451	**1**		**Lexington Bay (IRE)**[7] 6151 3-7-11 **81** (Richard Fahey) *hld up towards rr: gd hdwy on outer over 3f out: rdn to chse ldrs over 1f out: drvn and styd on ins fnl f to ld last 50yds* **12/1**	NeilFarley(5) 16	92
0035	**2**	*½*	**Royal Trooper (IRE)**[21] 5729 5-8-12 **81** (James Given) *hld up: hdwy over 3f out: rdn to chse ldrs 2f out: drvn and styd on wl fnl f* **40/1**	FrederikTylicki 17	91
5001	**3**	*hd*	**Status Symbol (IRE)**[28] 5482 6-9-5 **88** (Giles Bravery) *cl up: led after 3f: rdn along 3f out: drvn over 1f out: kpt on gamely ins fnl f tl hdd and no ex last 50yds* **16/1**	(t) JimmyFortune 7	98
2501	**4**	*nk*	**Motivado**[21] 5710 3-9-3 **96** (Sir Mark Prescott Bt) *hld up towards rr: gd hdwy on inner over 3f out: swtchd rt 2f out and rdn to chse ldrs: drvn and ev ch ins fnl f tl no ex last 50yds* **5/1**[3]	StevieDonohoe 2	105+
1200	**5**	*1*	**Ithoughtitwasover (IRE)**[21] 5700 3-8-11 **90** ow2 (Mark Johnston) *prom: effrt to chse ldr over 2f out and sn rdn: drvn over 1f out: hung rt fnl f: one pce* **12/1**	NeilCallan 10	98+
0605	**6**	*2 ¼*	**English Summer**[15] 5878 4-9-6 **89** (Mark Johnston) *hld up in rr: hdwy 4f out: rdn along over 3f out: drvn and kpt on fnl 2f: nrst fin* **20/1**	SilvestreDeSousa 12	94
6134	**7**	*hd*	**Ardlui (IRE)**[35] 5283 3-8-8 **87** (Henry Candy) *trckd ldrs: hdwy 6f out: chsd ldr 4f out: rdn along wl over 2f out: sn drvn and grad wknd* **9/2**[2]	FergusSweeney 14	91
425-	**8**	*nk*	**Alcalde**[141] 3456 5-8-13 **82** (John Berry) *in tch: hdwy to chse ldrs 6f out: rdn along 3f out: drvn over 1f out and kpt on same pce* **40/1**	RobertHavlin 15	86
0350	**9**	*1*	**Chock A Block (IRE)**[28] 5482 5-9-9 **92** (Saeed Bin Suroor) *in tch: rdn along 4f out: drvn wl over 2f out: kpt on one pce* **25/1**	RichardMullen 8	95
-156	**10**	*14*	**Lyric Street (IRE)**[35] 5283 3-9-4 **97** (Luca Cumani) *trckd ldrs on inner: hdwy over 4f out: rdn along 3f out: wkng whn hmpd 2f out: sn in rr* **7/2**[1]	KierenFallon 6	80
10B0	**11**	*1 ¾*	**Activate**[21] 5705 4-9-11 **94** (Michael Bell) *chsd ldrs: rdn along 5f out: wknd wl over 3f out* **20/1**	PhillipMakin 11	75
-312	**12**	*1 ¼*	**Protaras (USA)**[13] 5963 4-8-13 **82** (Sir Henry Cecil) *dwlt: hld up: a in rr* **9/1**	EddieAhern 1	61
0003	**13**	*1*	**La Vecchia Scuola (IRE)**[49] 4775 7-9-5 **91** (Jim Goldie) *a in rr* **16/1**	GaryBartley(3) 5	68
3430	**14**	*1 ½*	**Deauville Flyer**[21] 5705 5-9-8 **94** (Tim Easterby) *a towards rr: bhd fnl 3f* **12/1**	DaleSwift(3) 13	69
3150	**15**	*2 ¾*	**Itlaaq**[15] 5883 5-9-10 **93** (Michael Easterby) *trckd ldrs on inner: pushed along over 4f out: rdn along over 3f out: sn wknd* **25/1**	(t) GrahamGibbons 3	65
1366	**16**	*9*	**Stagecoach Danman (IRE)**[41] 5078 3-8-3 **82** (Mark Johnston) *led 3f: prom: rdn along 6f out: wknd 4f out* **20/1**	LukeMorris 9	41

3m 0.43s (-0.77) **Going Correction** -0.05s/f (Good)
WFA 3 from 4yo+ 10lb — **16** Ran SP% **128.8**
Speed ratings (Par 109): **100,99,99,99,98 97,97,97,96,88 87,87,86,85,84 78**
Tote Swingers:1&2: not won, 2&3:£42.70, 1&3:£14.60 CSF £445.70 CT £7502.93 TOTE £12.90: £2.40, £5.40, £3.70, £2.10; EX 587.80.

Owner Keith Denham & Tony Denham **Bred** Mrs Vanessa Hutch **Trained** Musley Bank, N Yorks

■ Stewards' Enquiry : Stevie Donohoe two-day ban: careless riding (Oct 9-10)

FOCUS

A strong staying handicap. There appeared to be a sound pace on, but not many got involved from off the pace and most were found out before 2f out. The first five finished in a heap.

NOTEBOOK

Lexington Bay(IRE) clearly relishes cut underfoot and, from the foot of the handicap, he most gamely followed up his Ayr success a week earlier off a 3lb higher mark. He still looked nicely handicapped on that form, but had to come from way back in the home straight. The further he went the stronger he got, however, and he showed a very willing attitude for pressure. This 3-y-o should only improve with another winter on his back and connections obviously have a nice stayer in the making.

Royal Trooper(IRE) came from a similar position as the winner and ran a massive race in defeat, just getting up for second place on the line. He goes on any ground and this fully proves his stamina. (op 33-1)

Status Symbol(IRE) showed vastly improved form when making all off 6lb lower over 1m4f at Newmarket 28 days earlier and set out to repeat the feat with a tongue tie reapplied. He so nearly led all the way, just running out of gas nearing the business end, and he's clearly a progressive 6-y-o with cut in the ground.

Motivado ◆ was upped 9lb for his romp over C&D 21 days previously, but looked well worthy of it and had to go close if adapting to the softer ground. He got going a bit too late in the day having sat in mid-field on the inside and left the impression he may well have gone in again under more positive tactics. (op 7-1)

Ithoughtitwasover(IRE), whose jockey put up 2lb overweight, travelled nicely and bounced back from two lacklustre efforts to post a career-best display over the longer trip.

Ardlui(IRE), fourth in the Melrose last time out, raced handily and had his chance but was done with before the final furlong. The ground most likely went against him. (op 11-2 tchd 6-1)

Lyric Street(IRE) was well backed to improve on his sixth in the Melrose at York last month and sat more handily this time. He didn't act on the softer ground once asked for an effort, though, and this run is best forgiven. (op 4-1)

6334 BRITISH STALLION STUDS SUPPORTING BRITISH RACING EBF MAIDEN STKS — 1m

4:30 (4:30) (Class 5) 2-Y-O **£3,234** (£962; £481; £240) **Stalls** Low

Form	Pos	Dist	Horse / details	Jockey	RPR
0	**1**		**Mazeydd**[29] 5454 2-9-0 0 (Roger Varian) *t.k.h: trckd ldng pair: cl up 3f out: rdn to ld 1 1/2f out: styd on wl* **14/1**	NeilCallan 16	80+
	2	*¾*	**Went The Day Well (USA)** 2-9-0 0 (Ed McMahon) *towards rr: hdwy 3f out: rdn along wl over 1f out: swtchd rt and styd on strly ins fnl f* **28/1**	GrahamGibbons 8	78+
52	**3**	*1*	**Strident Force**[22] 5668 2-9-0 0 (Sir Michael Stoute) *trckd ldr: cl up 1/2-way: led wl over 2f out: rdn and hdd 1 1/2f out: sn drvn and one pce fnl f* **7/4**[1]	KierenFallon 12	76
04	**4**	*1 ¾*	**Tallevu (IRE)**[25] 5579 2-9-0 0 (Tom Dascombe) *trckd ldrs: hdwy 3f out: rdn to chse ldrs wl over 1f out: sn drvn and one pce* **25/1**	RichardKingscote 15	72
	5	*2 ¼*	**Touch Gold (IRE)** 2-9-0 0 (Sir Henry Cecil) *in tch: hdwy on outer 3f out: effrt 2f out: sn rdn and kpt on same pce fr over 1f out* **7/1**[3]	EddieAhern 2	67
	6	*1*	**Theturnofthesun (IRE)** 2-9-0 0 (John Gosden) *in tch: hdwy 3f out: rdn along 2f out: drvn and wknd appr fnl f* **25/1**	RobertHavlin 3	65
	7	*3*	**Expert Fighter (USA)** 2-9-0 0 (Saeed Bin Suroor) *in rr: rdn along 1/2-way: sme late hdwy: n.d* **16/1**	RoystonFfrench 13	58
5	**8**	*nk*	**Stature (IRE)**[23] 5654 2-9-0 0 (Andrew Balding) *chsd ldrs: rdn along over 2f out: grad wknd* **7/1**[3]	JimmyFortune 1	58
	9	*nse*	**Mojave (IRE)** 2-8-9 0 (Mahmood Al Zarooni) *wnt lft s: in tch: rdn along 3f out and sn wknd* **15/2**	AntiocoMurgia(5) 9	58
4	**10**	*1 ½*	**Curzon Line**[16] 5851 2-9-0 0 (Mahmood Al Zarooni) *hld up: effrt and in tch 1/2-way: rdn along 3f out: sn wknd* **6/1**[2]	SilvestreDeSousa 10	54
00	**11**	*3 ½*	**Son Of May**[8] 6110 2-9-0 0 (Jo Hughes) *hld up: sme hdwy on outer over 3f out: sn rdn and wknd* **33/1**	(b) FergusSweeney 17	47
00	**12**	*1 ¾*	**Season Spirit**[15] 5891 2-9-0 0 (James Given) *hmpd s: a in rr* **50/1**	FrederikTylicki 5	43
	13	*hd*	**Kenmay (IRE)** 2-9-0 0 (Brian Meehan) *a towards rr* **40/1**	EddieCreighton 4	42
505	**14**	*nse*	**Paladin (IRE)**[22] 5688 2-9-0 72 (Mahmood Al Zarooni) *led: rdn along 4f out: hdd wl over 2f out: sn wknd* **11/1**	AhmedAjtebi 11	42

1m 45.21s (2.31) **Going Correction** -0.05s/f (Good) — **14** Ran SP% **126.8**
Speed ratings (Par 95): **86,85,84,82,80 79,76,75,75,74 70,69,68,68**
Tote Swingers:1&2:£26.20, 2&3:£32.20, 1&3:£9.10 CSF £376.16 TOTE £21.90: £4.80, £6.00, £1.60; EX 617.70.

Owner Sheikh Ahmed Al Maktoum **Bred** Darley **Trained** Newmarket, Suffolk

FOCUS

An average juvenile maiden, run at a sound enough pace and the form should work out.

NOTEBOOK

Mazeydd ◆ was never a factor on his Thirsk debut last month, but he raced an awful lot more professionally this time and got off the mark with more in hand than the bare margin indicates. He's nicely bred being half-brother to most notably stablemate Mijhaar and obviously goes well with some juice underfoot. Neil Callan was perfectly placed aboard him 2f out, but he still showed signs of inexperience when asked to get to the front. The penny dropped passing the furlong marker, though, and he was able to take it easy nearing the finish. It will be interesting to see how he's now campaigned, and he looks a decent middle-distance prospect for next year.

Went The Day Well(USA) ◆ ran a massive race on this belated debut. He came from well back in the home straight, but was eating into the winner's advantage when motoring home inside the final furlong. He's a colt with scope and it will be very surprising if she doesn't go one better before long. (op 25-1)

Strident Force proved popular to make it third time lucky, but he looked vulnerable to anything useful. He was always up there and took it up around 2f out. He lacked a change of gear, however, possibly down to the soft ground, and was held from the furlong pole. His future now lies with the handicapper and he sets the standard. (op 6-4)

Tallevu(IRE) put his previous experience to good use back down a furlong in trip and ran a nice race in defeat. He has some scope and nurseries are now an option.

Touch Gold(IRE), entered in the Group 1 Racing Post Trophy, shaped very much as though this debut outing was needed and it wouldn't surprise to see him step up significantly next time out. (op 11-2)

Theturnofthesun(IRE) was seemingly unfancied, but he raced professionally for a debutant and ran an encouraging race. There should be more to come from this 90,000gns purchase and perhaps dropping back a furlong would be ideal in the short term.

Stature(IRE) was somewhat disappointing after an encouraging debut at Salisbury 23 days earlier, but the ground was probably to blame. (tchd 10-1)

Mojave(IRE) (op 10-1 tchd 14-1 in a place)

6335 R. DRAPER LTD 65TH ANNIVERSARY H'CAP — 1m

5:05 (5:05) (Class 2) (0-105,98) 3-Y-O+ **£12,938** (£3,850; £1,924; £962) **Stalls** Low

Form	Pos	Dist	Horse / details	Jockey	RPR
3-12	**1**		**Skilful**[21] 5730 3-9-3 **93** (John Gosden) *mde all: qckned clr 2f out: easily* **2/1**[1]	RobertHavlin 6	112+
43-0	**2**	*3 ¾*	**Call To Reason (IRE)**[145] 1760 4-9-0 **86** (Jeremy Noseda) *midfield: hdwy over 3f out: rdn to chse wnr fr wl over 1f out: drvn and no imp fnl f* **10/1**	EddieAhern 7	92
6003	**3**	*hd*	**Master Of Arts (USA)**[7] 6163 6-9-4 **90** (Mark Johnston) *hld up in rr: hdwy on outer 3f out: rdn to chse ldrs wl over 1f out: drvn and edgd lft ins fnl f: kpt on same pce* **11/2**[3]	SilvestreDeSousa 10	96
2362	**4**	*3 ½*	**Extraterrestrial**[7] 6150 7-9-2 **88** (Richard Fahey) *hld up: hdwy 3f out: rdn to chse ldrs wl over 1f out: sn drvn and kpt on same pce* **15/2**	FrederikTylicki 8	85
2202	**5**	*2 ¾*	**My Freedom (IRE)**[29] 5450 3-9-2 **92** (Saeed Bin Suroor) *stdd and swtchd lft s: hdwy into midfield 1/2-way: rdn along to chse ldrs over 2f out: drvn wl over 1f out and sn btn* **7/2**[2]	(p) KierenFallon 9	83
0003	**6**	*1 ¼*	**Bawaardi (IRE)**[22] 5684 5-8-11 **86** (Richard Fahey) *chsd ldrs: rdn along wl over 2f out: drvn wl over 1f out and sn wknd* **20/1**	LeeTopliss(3) 12	74
2100	**7**	*1 ¾*	**Sinfonico (IRE)**[21] 5712 3-8-13 **89** (Richard Hannon) *prom: rdn along over 3f out: drvn wl over 2f out and sn wknd* **20/1**	JimmyFortune 4	73
050-	**8**	*2*	**Mull Of Killough (IRE)**[465] 3069 5-9-8 **94** (Richard Fahey) *hld up: hdwy on inner: over 3f out: rdn along wl over 2f out: sn btn* **16/1**	PaddyAspell 1	74

0046 **9** *4* **Wannabe King**[26] 5557 5-9-10 **96**....................(b) NeilCallan 11 66
(David Lanigan) *hld up: a towards rr* **12/1**
6-0 **10** *2 3/4* **Memory Cloth**[7] 6150 4-9-3 **92**.................... DaleSwift(3) 3 56
(Brian Ellison) *chsd wnr: rdn along over 3f out: drvn wl over 1f out: wknd qckly appr fnl f* **25/1**
0000 **11** *hd* **Light From Mars**[7] 6147 6-9-12 **98**.................... StevieDonohoe 2 62
(John Quinn) *chsd ldrs: rdn along over 3f out: sn wknd* **25/1**

1m 42.7s (-0.20) **Going Correction** -0.05s/f (Good)
WFA 3 from 4yo+ 4lb **11** Ran SP% **122.6**
Speed ratings (Par 109): **99,95,95,91,88 87,85,83,79,77 76**
Tote Swingers:1&2:£10.00, 2&3:£13.00, 1&3:£5.10 CSF £23.25 CT £99.13 TOTE £2.80: £1.30, £3.00, £2.40; EX 31.10.
Owner Mark Dixon & J L Rowsell **Bred** Ashbrittle Stud & M H Dixon **Trained** Newmarket, Suffolk

FOCUS
A good handicap, but the lightly raced winner proved a class apart. Decent form.

NOTEBOOK
Skilful ◆ had all of his rivals in trouble 2f out and ultimately made all as he pleased. He was ridden patiently when second at Thirsk last time, but connections got it just right with him here and he made it 2-4 with a taking effort, easing down near the business end. This lightly raced son of Selkirk could well be Pattern class in time and, despite being allowed plenty of rope in this, he did pull his way into a clear lead so was no doubt by far the best horse in attendance. It will be interesting to see what the handicapper makes of him. (op 5-2 tchd 3-1 in places)
Call To Reason(IRE) ◆ is a year older than the winner, but this was only her fifth appearance to date. She has won fresh in the past, and handles cut, but it was clear shortly after she made an effort nearing 2f out she wasn't going to get near that rival. This should bring her on and she'll probably compliment Skillful by resuming winning ways next time out. (op 8-1)
Master Of Arts(USA) ◆ returned to something like his best when finishing fast for third place at Newbury a week earlier. He again did his best work late on here, but would have probably finished a clear second-best had he not been handed so much to do from out the back. Compensation likely awaits him. (tchd 6-1)
Extraterrestrial performed up to his mark at Ayr when a runner-up a week previously and he ran his race again here, giving the form a decent look about it. (op 7-1 tchd 8-1, 9-1 in a place)
My Freedom(IRE) is proven on this sort of ground, but he was done with as soon as the winner kicked for home and now has a bit to prove. (op 5-1)
T/Plt: £353.30 to a £1 stake. Pool: £75,832.26 - 156.68 winning tickets T/Qpdt: £25.50 to a £1 stake. Pool:£4,026.34 - 116.42 winning tickets JR

6296 NEWMARKET (R-H)
Saturday, September 24

OFFICIAL GOING: Good to firm (overall 8.3, far side 8.2, stands' side 8.2, centre 8.1)
Wind: modest, half aginst Weather: dry, sunny spells

6336 JUDDMONTE ROYAL LODGE STKS (GROUP 2) (C&G) 1m
2:05 (2:05) (Class 1) 2-Y-O

£56,710 (£21,500; £10,760; £5,360; £2,690; £1,350) **Stalls** Low

Form RPR
4 **1** **Daddy Long Legs (USA)**[14] 5926 2-8-12 0.................... CO'Donoghue 2 112+
(A P O'Brien, Ire) *mde all: rdn 3f out: drvn and forged clr 2f out: styd on wl and in command after* **11/4**[2]
33 **2** *3 1/4* **Tenth Star (IRE)**[65] 4257 2-8-12 0.................... WilliamBuick 4 104
(A P O'Brien, Ire) *in tch: rdn 3f out: outpcd u.p ent fnl 2f: rallied and carried rt ent fnl f: styd on wl to go 2nd wl ins fnl f: no threat to wnr* **6/1**
3 *1/2* **Wrote (IRE)**[26] 5571 2-8-12 0.................... JamieSpencer 3 103
(A P O'Brien, Ire) *stdd s: hld up in tch in rr: edgding rt over 2f out: swtchd lft and effrt 2f out: drvn and pressing for 2nd whn edgd rt ent fnl f: wnt 2nd fnl 100yds: kpt on same pce: lost 2nd wl ins fnl f* **9/2**[3]
1215 **4** *1 1/2* **Rockinante (FR)**[32] 5365 2-8-12 105.................... RichardHughes 1 100
(Richard Hannon) *t.k.h: hld up in bhd ldrs: rdn and effrt 2f out: drvn and unable qck over 1f out: wknd ins fnl f* **9/2**[3]
211 **5** *3/4* **Farhaan (USA)**[23] 5654 2-8-12 94.................... RichardHills 5 98
(John Dunlop) *chsd wnr: upsides wnr over 2f out: rdn and unable qck 2f out: no imp on wnr and btn jst over 1f out: lost 2nd fnl 100yds: wknd* **5/2**[1]
134 **6** *19* **Shamrocked (IRE)**[9] 6077 2-8-12 84.................... TedDurcan 7 54
(Mick Channon) *t.k.h: hld up in tch: rdn and btn 2f out: wl bhd and eased fnl f* **33/1**

1m 37.77s (-0.83) **Going Correction** +0.05s/f (Good) **6** Ran SP% **108.8**
Speed ratings (Par 107): **106,102,102,100,100 81**
Tote Swingers: 1&2 £3.40, 1&3 £2.30, 2&3 £3.70 CSF £17.84 TOTE £3.90: £2.00, £2.40; EX 22.50.
Owner M Tabor, D Smith & Mrs John Magnier **Bred** Woodford Thoroughbreds LLC **Trained** Ballydoyle, Co Tipperary

FOCUS
There was 3mm of water applied to the final 1m1f after racing on Friday, but it was a bright and breezy day and the ground remained quick. This prestigious juvenile contest is named after a royal residence in Windsor Great Park and was traditionally staged at nearby Ascot. Following a controversial restructuring of the fixture list the race has been moved to Newmarket, although this isn't the first time it's been staged here - the track also played host in 2005 when Ascot was under reconstruction. It's a race that has predictably produced plenty of high-class types over the years, and although not long ago it went through a period of being unfashionable, it's hard to argue with the quality of the last three editions. The 2008 running went to Jukebox Jury (dead-heated in this year's Irish St Leger) with smart miler Cityscape in second, in 2009 Joshua Tree (Canadian International) had Vale Of York (Breeders' Cup Juvenile) back in third, and last term Frankel had Treasure Beach (Irish Derby, Secretariat Stakes) behind. This season's race, though, looked weak. Again staged on the same weekend as the Beresford Stakes (1m juvenile Group 2 in Ireland), Aidan O'Brien was set to have three runners in both events, and despite this trio coming here with inferior RPRs to a couple of his runners in the Irish contest, the Ballydoyle trainer had the 1-2-3. The action unfolded in much the same way as had been the theme the previous day, with a prominent ride towards the far rail proving advantageous. The time was only 0.17 seconds slower than the Sun Chariot, although that looked modestly run.

NOTEBOOK
Daddy Long Legs(USA) gave Aidan O'Brien a fifth win in this race, stepping up on the form he showed when only fourth of five in what had looked an ordinary running of the Champagne Stakes, despite having got a bit warm on his neck. He had Farhaan for company for much of the way, but was still able to dictate a pace to suit and stayed on powerfully, relishing the step up in trip. Clearly he had the run of the race and it remains to be seen whether he's close to the best of his generation at his powerful yard (O'Brien rarely runs his top-notchers in this, though Treasure Beach was third last year), but he impressed physically as having more scope than his two stablemates. His attitude is likeable as well and there should be more to come as he strengthens up. Bookmakers were unimpressed, though, with both Ladbrokes and William Hill leaving him at 33-1 for the Guineas. In the shorter term, considering his US pedigree, it wouldn't surprise to see him go to the Breeders' Cup. (op 7-2)

Tenth Star(IRE) won a 7f Listed race on his third start but had been absent since being well held in the Group 3 Tyros Stakes over the same trip in July. Upped to 1m for the first time, he was a bit rusty on this return, needing to be ridden along to get going early and then taking a while to respond when under more serious pressure in the closing stages. (op 5-1)
Wrote(IRE) landed a 1m maiden at Cork on his second start before dropping back to 7f to follow up off 89 in a nursery, the same race Treasure Beach had won off 84 the previous year ahead his third in this. Set a bit to do and not asked for everything until late, he didn't look comfortable on the track and hung right late on. (op 3-1)
Rockinante(FR) was free to post and far too keen in the race itself. (op 5-1 tchd 11-2 in places)
Farhaan(USA) is well regarded and looks the part physically, but having won his maiden well he didn't look a Group horse when scraping home in a muddling novice event at Salisbury last time, albeit Cityscape won the same race in 2008 before finishing runner-up in this. He moved scratchily to post this time, though Richard Hills didn't use the ground as an excuse afterwards, instead pointing out that some of John Dunlop's runners have performed poorly and scoped dirty lately. Whatever, he has the size to make a better older horse. (op 3-1)
Shamrocked(IRE) raced a bit freely without cover and was well beaten. He was out of his depth, but is a big horse and should do better in time. (op 28-1 tchd 40-1)

6337 JAGUAR CARS CHEVELEY PARK STKS (GROUP 1) (FILLIES) 6f
2:35 (2:35) (Class 1) 2-Y-O

£92,720 (£35,152; £17,592; £8,763; £4,398; £2,207) **Stalls** Low

Form RPR
31 **1** **Lightening Pearl (IRE)**[27] 5522 2-8-12 0.................... JMurtagh 1 110+
(G M Lyons, Ire) *chsd ldr tl rdn and qcknd to ld ent fnl 2f: clr over 1f out: edgd lft but kpt on fnl f: a gng to hold on* **3/1**[2]
410 **2** *1/2* **Sunday Times**[37] 5217 2-8-12 89.................... WilliamBuick 6 109+
(Peter Chapple-Hyam) *hld up in tch in last trio: swtchd lft and effrt wl over 1f out: str run u.p ins fnl f: wnt 2nd fnl 100yds: pressing wnr and clsng nr fin: nvr quite getting to wnr* **33/1**
1100 **3** *1 1/4* **Angels Will Fall (IRE)**[15] 5882 2-8-12 104.................... RobertWinston 9 105
(Charles Hills) *t.k.h: hld up in bhd ldrs: rdn and effrt ent fnl 2f: lft chsng clr wnr over 1f out: styd on same pce fnl f* **16/1**
0022 **4** *1 1/4* **Miss Work Of Art**[7] 6146 2-8-12 98.................... PaulHanagan 2 101
(Richard Fahey) *sn bustled along: chsd ldrs: rdn 1/2-way: hdwy u.p and lft chsng ldng pair over 1f out: styd on same pce and no imp after* **20/1**
1111 **5** *1 3/4* **Best Terms**[37] 5217 2-8-12 115.................... RichardHughes 8 96
(Richard Hannon) *racd keenly: chsd ldrs: rdn and struggling jst over 2f out: btn and losing pl whn sltly hmpd and swtchd lft over 1f out: styd on same pce and no threat to ldrs after* **11/8**[1]
513 **6** *3/4* **Hello Glory**[37] 5217 2-8-12 99.................... JamieSpencer 3 94
(David Simcock) *stdd s: hld up in rr: clsd 2f out: swtchd rt and effrt u.p over 1f out: no imp 1f out: wknd ins fnl f* **12/1**
210 **7** *1 1/2* **Lady Gorgeous**[37] 5217 2-8-12 85.................... TedDurcan 7 89
(Mick Channon) *in tch towards rr: rdn over 2f out: keeping on same pce whn hmpd and swtchd lft over 1f out: no imp after* **25/1**
2301 **8** *2* **Shumoos (USA)**[21] 5715 2-8-12 105.................... MartinDwyer 4 83
(Brian Meehan) *in tch: rdn and unable qck jst over 2f out: wknd over 1f out* **13/2**[3]
1051 **P** **Sajwah (IRE)**[23] 5656 2-8-12 101.................... RichardHills 5 —
(Charles Hills) *led tl rdn and hdd ent fnl 2f: sn edgd rt and outpcd by wnr: lost action and eased over 1f out: p.u and dismntd ins fnl f: fatally injured* **11/1**

1m 11.23s (-0.97) **Going Correction** +0.05s/f (Good) **9** Ran SP% **113.9**
Speed ratings (Par 106): **108,107,105,104,101 100,98,96,—**
Tote Swingers: 1&2 £15.70, 1&3 £11.00, 2&3 £23.50 CSF £98.76 TOTE £4.70: £1.60, £8.60, £5.00; EX 166.50 Trifecta £1364.50 Pool £2,286.56 - 1.24 winning units.
Owner Pearl Bloodstock Ltd **Bred** Castlemartin Stud And Skymarc Farm **Trained** Dunsany, Co. Meath
■ The first Group 1 winner for both Ger Lyons and owner Sheikh Fahad Al Thani of Pearl Bloodstock.

FOCUS
The Cheveley Park was this year run a week earlier than usual, being staged in September for the first time since 2006. It's a race that often fully justifies its top-notch status and has produced the 1,000 Guineas winner three times in the last decade, namely Russian Rhythm (runner-up 2002), Natagora (won 2007) and Special Duty (won 2009). Last season Margot Did, who won this year's Nunthorpe, finished fifth. It's hard to know exactly what to make of this year's race, but fourth-placed Miss Work Of Art, who's tough and has run close to 100 on RPRs a few times, helps give the form a solid enough look, and the winner is a high-class juvenile. Soon after the runners left the stalls there briefly looked set to be a split, with Best Terms leading Angels Will Fall more towards the centre of the course than the others, but the field were as one before long, racing far side. Like the previous day's racing and this card's opener, a forward ride near the far rail was helpful and that was the route taken by the winner.

NOTEBOOK
Lightening Pearl(IRE) raced closer to the fence than most. Supplemented at a cost of £15,000 and a first Group 1 winner for Ger Lyons, she paid a compliment of sorts to Maybe, having finished third behind Aidan O'Brien's unbeaten filly in the Group 2 Debutante Stakes over 7f two starts ago, although this one improved when dropped back to 6f for a wide-margin Group 3 success next time. She's bred to get 1m (her dam won a Listed race at the trip) and it might be somewhat coincidental that the her improvement has coincided with a drop in distance, but clearly 6f suits her well and she was a decisive scorer after being well placed. Her low, fluent action suggests the quick ground was also favourable. Her connections have every right to point her towards the Guineas and, while she has to prove she can mix it at this level over further, that's built into her odds for the first fillies' Classic with 20-1 being generally available. Her ability to handle this track, especially on quick ground, is an obvious plus. There is apparently an outside chance she will run in the Marcel Boussac which Pearl Bloodstock sponsor. (op 10-3 tchd 7-2)
Sunday Times ◆ was well beaten in the Lowther, but prior to that she'd impressed when winning her maiden at Goodwood, so her performance here perhaps wasn't quite the surprise her odds suggest. She was going on strongly at the finish and deserves extra credit considering the track had been favouring pace. It's possible she'll now go for the Bosra Sham Stakes, a C&D fillies' Listed event in which Peter Chapple-Hyam sent out this one's sister, Question Times, to finish runner-up last season.
Angels Will Fall(IRE) had struggled since creating a good impression in the Princess Margaret at Ascot (subsequent Prestige Stakes winner Regal Realm runner-up), but this was more like it. Her performance needs upgrading a touch as she was keen without a great deal of cover for a lot of the way, probably not helped by being draw high and racing wide of the majority of the others early on.
Miss Work Of Art has been busy, most recently finishing a well beaten second in what looked an ordinary running of the Group 3 Firth of Clyde on soft going. Faced with contrasting conditions here, she was under pressure a fair way out but raced close to the helpful far rail and kept on admirably. (op 16-1)
Best Terms came into this unbeaten in four starts, including the Queen Mary and Lowther (defied 3lb penalty), but she had the run of the race from the front in the latter. Lacking the scope of some of these, she was much too keen from the start and it was soon apparent she wouldn't be extending her winning sequence. She was kept apart from the main bunch early, but wouldn't settle and gradually faded out of it after facing pace pressure. We've probably seen the best of this likeable type. (tchd 6-4 in places)

Hello Glory, who was on her toes in the paddock, impressed when winning an Ascot maiden before finishing third in the Lowther, but she struggled on this further rise in class.

Lady Gorgeous was well beaten in the Lowther and doesn't look up to this level even allowing for her finding a bit of trouble late on. (op 33-1)

Shumoos(USA), who was on her toes in the paddock, lacks size, and, though she somewhat belatedly added to her impressive maiden win when taking a Polytrack Group 3 latest, she was well beaten on her return to turf. (op 7-1)

Sajwah(IRE), who was on her toes in the paddock, responded well to a positive ride to win a Salisbury Listed contest (race won in 2008 by Serious Attitude, who followed up here) on her previous start, and she was again ridden forwardly, but she went lame. It was reported that she broke her pelvis and later she sadly had to be put down. (op 14-1 tchd 10-1)

6338 KINGDOM OF BAHRAIN SUN CHARIOT STKS (GROUP 1) (F&M) 1m

3:10 (3:10) (Class 1) 3-Y-O+

£98,902 (£37,496; £18,765; £9,347; £4,691; £2,354) **Stalls** Low

Form — RPR

1223 **1** **Sahpresa (USA)**[40] 5129 6-9-3 119............ Christophe-PatriceLemaire 7 119+
(Rod Collet, France) *hld up wl in tch in midfield: pushed along and qcknd to ld over 1f out: in command and r.o wl fnl f: rdn out fnl 100yds* **13/8**[1]

1213 **2** *1* **Chachamaidee (IRE)**[16] 5848 4-9-3 113.............. IanMongan 8 116
(Sir Henry Cecil) *stdd s: t.k.h: hld up in tch in last trio: rdn and effrt over 1f out: hdwy and edgd rt jst over 1f out: styd on wl to go 2nd wl ins fnl f: no threat to wnr* **9/1**

-500 **3** *¾* **Strawberrydaiquiri**[35] 5277 5-9-3 112............................ MartinDwyer 4 114
(Brian Meehan) *taken down early and ponied to s: led at stdy gallop: rdn and qcknd wl over 1f out: hdd and nt gng pce of wnr over 1f out: kpt on gamely but one pce fnl f: lost 2nd wl ins fnl f* **20/1**

-156 **4** *1 ¾* **I'm A Dreamer (IRE)**[78] 3822 4-9-3 110......................... WilliamBuick 5 110
(David Simcock) *stdd s: hld up in tch in rr: effrt over 1f out: nt clr run and swtchd lft 1f out: styd on wl fnl 100yds: unable to chal* **14/1**

4404 **5** *nse* **Music Show (IRE)**[21] 5753 4-9-3 107......................(v[1]) RichardHughes 6 110
(Mick Channon) *chsd ldr: rdn 3f out: outpcd and lost pl u.p over 1f out: rallied and kpt on fnl 150yds: no threat to wnr* **16/1**

11 **6** *½* **Alanza (IRE)**[16] 5848 3-8-13 109... JMurtagh 1 109
(John M Oxx, Ire) *hld up in tch in last trio: swtchd rt and effrt wl over 1f out: kpt on same pce and no imp u.p fnl f* **4/1**[2]

2252 **7** *nk* **Together (IRE)**[21] 5745 3-8-13 112................................ CO'Donoghue 2 108
(A P O'Brien, Ire) *chsd ldrs: rdn over 2f out: drvn and unable qck over 1f out: no ex and btn jst ins fnl f* **8/1**

1132 **8** *1 ¾* **Timepiece**[34] 5306 4-9-3 114... TomQueally 3 104
(Sir Henry Cecil) *chsd ldrs: rdn ent fnl 2f: drvn and unable qck over 1f out: wknd jst ins fnl f* **6/1**[3]

1m 37.6s (-1.00) **Going Correction** +0.05s/f (Good)
WFA 3 from 4yo+ 4lb 8 Ran SP% **110.8**
Speed ratings (Par 117): **107,106,105,103,103 102,102,100**
Tote Swingers: 1&2 £3.70, 1&3 £6.90, 2&3 £13.60 CSF £16.09 TOTE £2.00: £1.10, £3.60, £5.20; EX 18.90 Trifecta £177.50 Pool £14,298.70 - 59.59 winning units..

Owner Teruya Yoshida **Bred** Douglas McIntyre **Trained** France

FOCUS

A reasonable renewal of this event, which was elevated to Group 1 status in 2004. Three of the field already had a top-level win against their name, while two more had been second in Group 1 company. Three of last year's first four were here again, but recent Matron Stakes winner Emulous was a notable absentee. Sahpresa has run to the same mark in each of her three wins in this race, not needing to match her best. The early pace was fairly slow, although it picked up after halfway and the race turned into something of a sprint. While the winner produced a dominant performance, her three closest market rivals were below par. Unlike the first two races, this time is seeemed disadvantageous to race near the far rail.

NOTEBOOK

Sahpresa(USA) became the first mare to win this race three times. She's also the only horse aged older than four to win it. Everything had gone wrong for her on her trip to the July course for the Falmouth Stakes in which she finished second to Timepiece after sitting too far off the slow pace, but she had shown her mettle with a pair of solid runs in France since. Christophe Lemaire had her closer to the front this time and she was never in any danger once quickening up smartly to lead. She is a genuine Group 1 performer although, unlike Immortal Verse and Goldikova, who beat her in the Prix Jacques le Marois last time, she hasn't beaten the colts at the top level. Her owner is Japanese and she is likely to head to to Kyoto next month for the Grade 1 Mile Championship, in which she was fourth last year and third in 2009. She acts on most types of ground these days. (op 2-1)

Chachamaidee(IRE) has taken her form to a new level since being fitted with a hood, impressing at Goodwood prior to a sound third behind Alanza at Doncaster on her latest start. Ostensibly Sir Henry Cecil's second string, she was tackling Group 1 company for only the second time. She proved well up to it, held up as usual and taking a bit of a tug before running on nicely, although the French mare was always in control. She is equally effective at 7f and is likely to go for the Challenge Stakes over that trip here in a fortnight. (op 17-2)

Strawberrydaiquiri was fourth in this in 2009 and runner-up last year, when trained by Sir Michael Stoute. She had run a pleasing race on her debut for Brian Meehan at Sandown and built on that here, setting a steady initial pace and sticking on for third. This likeable mare is still looking for her first Group 1 win after six tries, one of them in the Dubai Duty Free at Meydan earlier this year, which is the only time she has taken on male opposition. (op 25-1)

I'm A Dreamer(IRE) has been freshened up since her never-dangerous sixth to Timepiece in the Falmouth. Racing in touch, but still towards the back in a slowly run race, she was staying on well in the final furlong. She deserves the chance she can show what she can do over 1m2f.

Alanza(IRE) came here on a four-timer, having beaten Chachamaidee in the Group 3 Sceptre Stakes at Doncaster last time. Supplemented for this, she was held up in last place, perhaps not the place to be, and although she picked up her forward move flattened out as she ended up on the slower ground nearest the fence. She was the least experienced member of this field and it may pay to forgive her this. (op 7-2 tchd 9-2 in places)

Together(IRE), who along with Alanza raced nearest to the inside rail, where the ground was more worn, had every chance but was unable to quicken up. She has finished second in four Group 1s, most recently to Emulous at Leopardstown, but has yet to win in seven tries in the top grade. Her stamina only just lasts 1m and she holds a couple of forthcoming entries over shorter trips.

Timepiece pinched the Falmouth Stakes when racing close to a near farcically slow pace, and had run near to that level when placed in a pair of French Group 1s since, albeit unable to confirm the form with Sahpresa in the first of them. She was well enough positioned tracking the leaders, but dropped away disappointingly once the pace lifted. This ground was perhaps a shade quick for her. (op 11-2)

6339 BETFRED CAMBRIDGESHIRE (HERITAGE H'CAP) 1m 1f

3:50 (3:51) (Class 2) 3-Y-O+

£99,600 (£29,824; £14,912; £7,456; £3,728; £1,872) **Stalls** Low

Form — RPR

254 **1** **Prince Of Johanne (IRE)**[16] 5853 5-8-9 91................(p) JohnFahy[(3)] 31 101
(Tom Tate) *racd in centre tl merged w stands' side trio over 4f out: in tch: hdwy to chse ldr over 4f out: led and rdn wl over 2f out: edgd lft u.p 1f out: styd on wl fnl f* **40/1**

-011 **2** *1 ¾* **Stevie Thunder**[26] 5557 6-8-10 92 4ex............................ RyanClark[(3)] 5 98+
(Ian Williams) *chsd ldrs: grad crossed over and merged w stands' side trio over 2f out: drvn wl over 1f out: chsd wnr ins fnl f: kpt on but no imp fnl 100yds* **25/1**

4202 **3** *nse* **Proponent (IRE)**[57] 4494 7-9-7 100................................. TedDurcan 24 106
(Roger Charlton) *racd tl centre tl merged w stands' side trio over 4f out: in tch: swtchd rt and hdwy u.p ent fnl f: styd on wl fnl 100yds* **14/1**

1002 **4** *nse* **Nanton (USA)**[15] 5883 9-9-9 102................................ DanielTudhope 27 108
(Jim Goldie) *racd in centre tl merged w stands' side trio over 4f out: bhd: effrt on stands' rail and nt clr run 2f out: hdwy u.p over 1f out: styd on wl fnl 150yds* **33/1**

4315 **5** *1* **Markazzi**[37] 5218 4-8-13 92... RichardHills 26 96
(Sir Michael Stoute) *racd in centre tl merged w stands' side trio over 4f out: chsd ldrs: rdn to chse wnr 2f out: styd on same pce u.p: lost 3 pls ins fnl f* **16/1**

0261 **6** *shd* **Circumvent**[14] 5940 4-9-6 99 4ex...........(p) Christophe-PatriceLemaire 10 102
(Paul Cole) *racd in centre tl merged w stands' side trio over 4f out: hld up in rr: rdn and hdwy u.p over 1f out: kpt on same pce fnl 75yds* **16/1**

1630 **7** *½* **Shavansky**[14] 5940 7-9-1 94... JamesMillman 28 96
(Rod Millman) *racd in centre tl merged w stands' side trio over 4f out: t.k.h: hld up in tch: rdn and effrt 2f out: drvn and edgd rt over 1f out: kpt on same pce fnl 100yds* **33/1**

2204 **8** *shd* **Maali (IRE)**[43] 5021 3-8-8 92...............................(bt[1]) KirstyMilczarek 20 94
(Clive Brittain) *racd in centre tl merged w stands; side trio over 4f out: s.i.s: bhd: rdn 4f out: hdwy and nt clr run 2f out: swtchd rt and hdwy over 1f out: kpt on u.p fnl f: nt rch ldrs* **40/1**

53/4 **9** *½* **Ideology**[21] 5-9-3 96... TomQueally 6 97+
(Mario Hofer, Germany) *racd in centre tl merged w stands' side trio over 4f out: hld up bhd: edging rt and hdwy over 1f out: styd on u.p fnl f but nvr gng to rch wnr* **28/1**

050 **10** *1* **Nice Style (IRE)**[56] 4553 6-8-2 88..........................(t) RaulDaSilva[(7)] 17 87
(Jeremy Gask) *racd in centre tl merged w stands' side trio over 4f out: bhd: hdwy and edging rt over 1f out: swtchd rt 1f out: no imp fnl 75yds* **33/1**

0033 **11** *1 ¼* **Pintura**[37] 5218 4-9-6 99.. AdamKirby 12 95+
(David Simcock) *racd in centre tl merged w stands' side trio over 4f out: hld up in rr: hdwy u.p on far side of field over 1f out: edgd lft and styd on same pce fnl 150yds* **25/1**

0004 **12** *½* **Harrison George (IRE)**[7] 6150 6-9-4 97........................ PaulHanagan 30 92
(Richard Fahey) *racd in centre tl merged w stands' side trio over 4f out: t.k.h: chsd ldrs: rdn 2f out: unable qck and edgd lft over 1f out: wknd ins fnl f* **33/1**

0406 **13** *nse* **Brick Red**[14] 5940 4-8-11 90..(p) DavidProbert 34 85
(Andrew Balding) *racd against stands' rail thrght: hld up towards rr overall: nt clr run and swtchd rt 2f out: drvn over 1f out: kpt on ins fnl f: nvr gng pce to rch ldrs* **33/1**

5302 **14** *¾* **Questioning (IRE)**[21] 5704 3-9-1 99..........................(v[1]) WilliamBuick 13 92+
(John Gosden) *racd in centre tl merged w stands' side trio over 4f out: hld up in rr: looking for run and bdly hmpd 2f out: swtchd rt and denied a run tl ins fnl f: pushed along and past btn horses fnl 150yds: nvr a threat* **9/1**[2]

0000 **15** *½* **Crown Counsel (IRE)**[14] 5929 3-8-10 94.................... CO'Donoghue 29 86
(Mark Johnston) *racd in centre tl merged w stands: side trio over 4f out: chsd ldr tl led over 4f out: rdn and hdd wl over 2f out: drvn and unable qck 2f out: wknd ent fnl f* **50/1**

-053 **16** *nk* **Pires**[27] 5526 7-8-10 89..(p) JohnEgan 25 80
(A J Martin, Ire) *racd in centre tl merged w stands' side trio over 4f out: in tch in midfield: rdn and effrt ent fnl 2f: drvn and no imp whn edgd lft over 1f out: one pce and no threat to ldrs after* **40/1**

611 **17** *nk* **Albaqaa**[56] 4537 6-8-11 93.. KieranO'Neill[(3)] 3 84
(P J O'Gorman) *racd in centre tl merged w stands' side trio over 4f out: t.k.h: hld up towards rr: swtchd rt and hdwy over 2f out: drvn and no imp over 1f out: edgd lft and wknd ins fnl f* **14/1**

23/3 **18** *shd* **Combat Zone (IRE)**[21] 5-9-6 99.. THellier 32 90
(Mario Hofer, Germany) *racd aginst stands' rail thrght: in tch overall: rdn and unable qck 2f out: no imp after and btn 1f out: wknd ins fnl f* **50/1**

0661 **19** *hd* **Man Of Action (USA)**[14] 5929 4-9-6 99 4ex.............(v) FrankieDettori 14 89+
(Saeed Bin Suroor) *racd in centre tl merged w stands' side trio over 4f out: hld up bhd: continually denied and clr run fr 2f out: pushed lft and hmpd over 1f out: stl nt clr run and nt pushed ins fnl f: nvr able to chal* **8/1**[1]

3012 **20** *1 ¾* **Arlequin**[38] 5185 4-9-10 103.. PhilipRobinson 7 89
(James Bethell) *racd in centre tl merged w stands' side trio over 4f out: t.k.h: hmpd after 2f out: hld up in midfield: rdn and effrt on far side of field 2f out: no imp over 1f out: wknd ent fnl f* **33/1**

0121 **21** *1* **Red Gulch**[21] 5712 4-9-7 100 4ex................................... J-PGuillambert 4 90+
(Ed Walker) *racd in centre tl merged w stands' side trio over 4f out: hld up in tch: rdn and effrt over 1f out: no imp and btn whn short of room ins fnl f: eased towards fin* **16/1**

4450 **22** *nse* **Jutland**[7] 6163 4-9-0 98... DarylByrne[(5)] 23 82
(Mark Johnston) *racd in centre tl merged w stands' side trio over 4f out: in tch in midfield: rdn and struggling 2f out: btn over 1f out* **66/1**

04 **23** *¾* **Roayh (USA)**[50] 4764 3-8-12 96................................ MartinDwyer 16 78+
(Saeed Bin Suroor) *racd in centre tl merged w stands' side trio over 4f out: hld up bhd: stl in rr and pushed lft 2f out: sn rdn: stuck bhd wall of horses and no ch after* **40/1**

1510 **24** *½* **Cry Fury**[14] 5929 3-8-13 97... RichardHughes 18 78
(Roger Charlton) *racd in centre tl merged w stands' side trio over 4f out: t.k.h: chsd ldrs: rdn over 2f out: wknd over 1f out: no ch whn hmpd and swtchd rt towards fin* **10/1**[3]

5104 **25** *hd* **First Post (IRE)**[7] 6163 4-8-8 **87** .... WilliamCarson 9 68
(Derek Haydn Jones) *racd in centre tl merged w stands' side trio over 4f out: in tch in midfield: rdn and struggling ent fnl 2f: btn over 1f out: wknd fnl f* **40/1**

41-0 **26** *hd* **Credit Swap**[14] 5940 6-9-1 **94** .... IanMongan 1 74
(Venetia Williams) *in tch: rdn and struggling 4f out: sn drvn and no imp: no ch fr over 1f out* **33/1**

0040 **27** *½* **Desert Romance (IRE)**[26] 5557 5-8-10 **89** .... DaneO'Neill 35 68
(David O'Meara) *racd against stands' rail thrght: overall ldr tl over 4f out: rdn and struggling over 2f out: wkng and towards rr whn hmpd 2f out: no ch and eased ins fnl f* **33/1**

0006 **28** *½* **Riggins (IRE)**[28] 5473 7-9-5 **98** .... GeorgeBaker 22 76+
(Ed Walker) *racd in centre tl merged w stands' side trio over 4f out: midfield: rdn and lost pl 3f out: towards rr whn hmpd and swtchd rt over 1f out: keeping on but no ch whn nt clr run ins fnl f* **25/1**

2100 **29** *1 ½* **Constant Contact**[60] 4410 4-8-12 **94** .... (p) AdamBeschizza(3) 15 69
(Andrew Balding) *racd in centre tl merged w stands' side trio over 4f out: in tch in midfield: rdn and struggling over 3f out: bhd 2f out* **40/1**

2221 **30** *½* **Maqaraat (IRE)**[98] 3167 3-9-1 **99** .... RobertWinston 2 73
(Charles Hills) *racd in centre tl merged w stands' side trio over 4f out: in tch: rdn and struggling over 2f out: wknd over 1f out: wl btn whn short of room and eased ins fnl f* **25/1**

6440 **31** *shd* **Pendragon (USA)**[37] 5218 8-8-11 **90** .... JimmyQuinn 19 64
(Brian Ellison) *racd in centre tl merged w stands' side trio over 4f out: rdn and struggling over 2f out: wkng and towards rr whn hmpd over 1f out: wl btn and eased ins fnl f* **33/1**

2110 **32** *5* **Sagramor**[57] 4494 3-9-1 **99** .... NickyMackay 11 62
(Hughie Morrison) *racd in centre tl merged w stands' side trio over 4f out: rdn and losing pl over 3f out: bhd fnl 2f* **14/1**

1m 49.14s (-2.56) **Going Correction** +0.05s/f (Good)
WFA 3 from 4yo+ 5lb **32** Ran SP% **133.2**
Speed ratings (Par 109): **113,111,111,111,110 110,109,109,109,108 107,106,106,106,105 105,105,105,105,103 102,102,101,10**
Tote Swingers: 1&2 £379.90, 1&3 £189.90, 2&3 £77.50 CSF £831.57 CT £13785.88 TOTE £67.60: £12.10, £5.50, £4.10, £5.80; EX 2571.10 TRIFECTA Not won..
Owner David Storey **Bred** T J Rooney And Corduff Stud **Trained** Tadcaster, N Yorks

FOCUS
Like the Cheveley Park, a reshuffling of the fixture list saw the Cambridgeshire run a week earlier than usual this season. It was typically competitive, but none of the 3yos (fancied Dare To Dance withdrawn owing to quick ground) came to the fore and it was dominated by exposed types. There were three groups through the first furlong or so, but the majority of runners soon merged up the middle before gradually edging towards the stands' side rail. Three of these stayed towards that side throughout, namely Brick Red, Combat Zone and Desert Romance. Considering how the race unfolded clearly a high draw was favourable.

NOTEBOOK
Prince Of Johanne(IRE), well drawn, soon joined the main group towards the middle, but he was well enough placed to grab the fence when the field edged left in the closing stages and there looked to be an advantage. This isn't form to get carried away with, but he has a good strike-rate (now 7-22) and has a steadily progressive profile on quick ground, with this undoubtedly a career best. Prior to this, when getting good to firm ground to race, he'd won three of his last four starts, with the sole defeat coming when runner-up to Nanton in the Zetland Gold Cup, and he reversed form with the grey despite being only 1lb better off.

Stevie Thunder ◆, the only runner from a single-figure stall to finish in the first eight, deserves enormous credit. Bidding for a hat-trick after two wins at 1m (latest off 4lb lower), he was given a prominent ride and gradually made his way towards the near side, though unlike the winner he never got to the rail. Despite that, he stuck on gamely. This was better than when he finished sixth off 3lb lower in the 2009 running, and although his trainer was hoping for a bit of rain, the horse handled the quick ground well.

Proponent(IRE), only ninth in this on soft ground last year but 3-6 at the course, had been absent since finishing second in the totesport Mile off 3lb lower at Goodwood in July. This was a smart performance in defeat. (op 16-1)

Nanton(USA), runner-up in this in 2008 and third in 2009, ran another fine race to fare best of those held up, helped by having the stands' rail to race against from some way out. He could go to Dubai.

Markazzi ◆ was always handy and had his chance, but he didn't quite see it out as well as some. It will be interesting to see if connections persevere with this lightly raced gelding (only his 11th start) and he could be one for next year's Lincoln.

Circumvent, 1lb well in under the penalty picked up for his recent Goodwood win on easy ground, wasn't helped by stall 10 but kept on quite well. This was a lot better than when he was only 16th in this last year off 8lb higher. (op 20-1)

Shavansky, 7lb higher than when fifth in the 2009 running, was always in a reasonable position from a handy draw and ran well without being up to the task.

Maali(IRE) is a maiden and had been going the wrong way, but his trainer has struck form lately and this was a promising effort, with the combination of blinkers and a tongue-tie for the first time seeming to help. He can find easier opportunities and could build on this. (op 50-1)

Ideology, a German-trained runner whose most recent win came in a Deauville handicap, ran a good race from an unhelpful stall. Held up, he had to wait a while for a run and it was only late on that his jockey went for everything, but the horse's finishing effort looked to be levelling out near the line. (tchd 33-1 in places)

Nice Style(IRE) kept on from some way back after a 56-day break.

Brick Red ◆, one of three to race on the stands' side, kept on to post a creditable effort on ground was faster than ideal.

Questioning(IRE) hasn't convinced that he's straightforward and, with a visor on instead of cheekpieces, was ridden for luck, being held up well off the pace. His position in relation to the leaders wasn't a problem (Nanton showed closers could get involved), but he continually found trouble in running and was unlucky not to finish a good deal closer. Things will probably be tougher from now on seeing as he was 10lb well in and is unlikely to be eased much, if at all, but he looks the type to win a race or two in Dubai. Official explanation: jockey said colt was denied a clear run (op 10-1)

Man Of Action(USA) ◆, who was 2lb well in under the penalty picked up for his 1m Doncaster win, was unlucky. He got no run at all, hardly coming off the bridle at any stage, and otherwise would surely have gone close to winning. Official explanation: jockey said gelding was denied a clear run (tchd 9-1 in a place)

Arlequin Official explanation: jockey said colt suffered interference halfway.

Roayh(USA) would have been closer with a better trip but didn't look unlucky.

Cry Fury was totally unsuited by this speed test and is easily excused. He's out of a 2m winner and is more of a middle-distance/staying type.

Credit Swap, 7lb higher than when winning this for a different stable last year, had the worst draw of all and the ground was probably quicker than ideal.

Riggins(IRE) was another who endured a terrible run in the closing stages and is a lot better than he showed. Official explanation: jockey said gelding was denied a clear run

Maqaraat(IRE) Official explanation: trainer said colt unsuited by the good to firm ground

6340 E B F "DANSILI" JERSEY LILY FILLIES' NURSERY 7f
4:25 (4:25) (Class 2) 2-Y-O

£12,450 (£3,728; £1,864; £932; £466; £234) **Stalls** Low

Form RPR

1213 **1** **Pimpernel (IRE)**[23] 5656 2-9-7 **96** .... FrankieDettori 3 107+
(Mahmood Al Zarooni) *stdd s: in last pair: swtchd to centre and smooth prog fr over 3f out: led travelling strly 2f out: sn pushed clr: readily* **11/4**[1]

11 **2** *1 ½* **Nemushka**[23] 5645 2-8-1 **76** .... PaulHanagan 10 83+
(Richard Fahey) *fly-leapt and wnt lft leaving stalls: bhd: sn nudged along: rdn whn swtchd to centre and hdwy 2f out: chsd wnr ent fnl f: kpt on to draw clr of remainder but a being hld by wnr* **4/1**[2]

5133 **3** *5* **Nimiety**[21] 5708 2-7-12 **73** .... JimmyQuinn 7 67
(Mark Johnston) *led: rdn over 2f out: hdd over 1f out: kpt on but nt gng pce of ldrs ent fnl f* **11/2**

2531 **4** *¾* **Dare To Dream**[55] 4581 2-8-0 **78** .... KieranO'Neill(3) 9 70
(Richard Hannon) *trckd ldrs: rdn over 3f out: kpt on but nt pce to chal* **9/1**

1253 **5** *1* **Responsive**[16] 5847 2-9-0 **89** .... RichardHughes 1 78
(Hughie Morrison) *trckd ldrs: rdn over 3f out: styd on same pce fnl 2f* **9/2**[3]

021 **6** *1 ½* **Emmuska**[15] 5891 2-7-12 **73** .... FrankieMcDonald 2 59
(Richard Hannon) *in tch tl drvn along 4f out: nvr gng pce to get bk on terms* **9/1**

212 **7** *1 ¾* **Ziefhd**[22] 5691 2-8-4 **84** .... MatthewLawson(5) 6 65
(Paul Cole) *w ldr: rdn and ev ch 2f out: wknd ent fnl f* **8/1**

051 **8** *8* **Travelling**[31] 5393 2-7-12 **73** .... NickyMackay 5 33
(J W Hills) *trckd ldrs: rdn over 3f out: wknd over 1f out* **20/1**

1m 24.28s (-1.12) **Going Correction** +0.05s/f (Good) **8** Ran SP% **116.1**
Speed ratings (Par 98): **108,106,100,99,98 96,94,85**
Tote Swingers: 1&2 £4.50, 1&3 £3.80, 2&3 £3.10 CSF £14.04 CT £56.38 TOTE £2.70: £1.70, £1.30, £1.90; EX 14.40 Trifecta £58.30 Pool £683.38 - 8.67 winning units..
Owner Godolphin **Bred** Peter Harris **Trained** Newmarket, Suffolk

FOCUS
A good fillies' nursery, although it was weakened by non-runners. They went a fair lick up front and the first two both came from off the pace, finishing clear of the remainder.

NOTEBOOK
Pimpernel(IRE) travelled well towards the rear before cruising up to lead and clearing away. The return to 7f was a plus and this was a smart performance off 96, a mark 6lb higher than when winning on the July course last month. Third in a Listed race at Salisbury since, she is well up to another crack at something better and has a choice next month of the Rockfel Stakes back here or the Radley Stakes at Newbury. (op 3-1 tchd 5-2 and 7-2 in places)

Nemushka relinquished her unbeaten record but loses little in defeat. After another slow start, she stayed on well down the outside despite not looking entirely straightforward, just as she had when winning a nursery at Redcar. A flatter track than this might suit her. (op 5-1)

Nimiety's performance probably merits marking up, as she set a strong gallop and raced close to the rail, but still stuck on for third. Back up in trip, she was 4lb better off with Pimpernel on their meeting on the July course two runs back but finished further behind that filly here. (op 5-1 tchd 9-2 and 6-1 in places)

Dare To Dream ran respectably off a 3lb higher higher mark than when winning a lesser nursery at Newbury. This was the fastest ground she has raced on. (op 10-1)

Responsive, third in a warm fillies' nursery at Doncaster earlier this month, was racing off 5lb higher here. She looked set to drop away at one stage, but was keeping on at the end and may be worth another try at this trip. (op 6-1)

Emmuska was one of the first off the bridle but was running on when it was all over. Her maiden win came over 1m and she'll benefit from a return to that distance. (op 8-1 tchd 15-2)

Ziefhd paid for forcing too strong a gallop and angling to the rail on this nursery debut. (op 7-1)

Travelling dropped away after racing a shade keenly.

6341 BETFRED THE BONUS KING H'CAP 7f
5:00 (5:00) (Class 2) (0-100,98) 3-Y-O+

£12,450 (£3,728; £1,864; £932; £466; £234) **Stalls** Low

Form RPR

4000 **1** **Golden Desert (IRE)**[14] 5936 7-8-13 **90** .... MartinDwyer 11 100
(Robert Mills) *in tch: pushed along over 2f out: rdn for str run ent fnl f: edgd sltly rt: led fnl 75yds: readily* **16/1**

2060 **2** *1 ½* **Mia's Boy**[14] 5929 7-9-2 **96** .... RyanClark(3) 10 102
(Chris Dwyer) *mid-div: rdn and no imp over 2f out: r.o wl ins fnl f: snatched 2nd nr fin* **18/1**

1116 **3** *nk* **White Frost (IRE)**[17] 5830 3-8-12 **92** .... WilliamCarson 1 97
(Charles Hills) *disp ld: rdn into narrow advantage wl over 1f out: sn drifted lft: hdd fnl 75yds: kpt on but no ex* **6/1**[2]

0000 **4** *nk* **Striking Spirit**[20] 5758 6-8-12 **89** .... TedDurcan 16 93
(Tim Easterby) *sn prom: rdn over 2f out: nt clr run whn swtchd rt ent fnl f: ev ch ins fnl f: styd on but no ex nr fin* **16/1**

1261 **5** *½* **Golden Delicious**[23] 5657 3-8-3 **86** .... KieranO'Neill(3) 4 89
(Hughie Morrison) *disp ld: rdn and narrowly hdd over 1f out: drifted lft: nk down and styng on whn squeezed out fnl 100yds: nt rcvr* **15/2**

0005 **6** *hd* **Citrus Star (USA)**[15] 5887 4-9-2 **93** .... GeorgeBaker 7 95
(Chris Wall) *trckd ldrs: rdn over 2f out: nt quite pce to chal: styd on ins fnl f* **11/2**[1]

4214 **7** *¾* **Woodcote Place**[14] 5936 8-8-11 **88** .... NickyMackay 2 88
(Patrick Chamings) *trckd ldrs: rdn over 2f out: ev ch ent fnl f: kpt on but no ex nring fin* **20/1**

1030 **8** *nk* **Space Station**[14] 5936 5-8-5 **87** .... (b) DavidKenny(5) 14 87
(Simon Dow) *mid-div: rdn over 2f out: no imp tl styd on ins fnl f* **25/1**

0000 **9** *1 ¼* **Gallagher**[7] 6145 5-8-8 **85** .... (t) PaulHanagan 9 81
(Ruth Carr) *hld up towards rr: rdn and sme prog 2f out: no further imp fnl f* **16/1**

1261 **10** *1 ½* **Bonnie Brae**[63] 4332 4-8-13 **90** .... DaneO'Neill 12 82
(David Elsworth) *rdn over 2f out: a towards rr* **9/1**

/2-4 **11** *nk* **Asraab (IRE)**[151] 1594 4-9-1 **92** .... (t) FrankieDettori 15 83
(Saeed Bin Suroor) *s.i.s: bhd: rdn in centre over 2f out: nvr any imp on ldrs* **7/1**[3]

2202 **12** *2 ¼* **Lutine Bell**[15] 5887 4-9-3 **94** .... RichardHughes 8 79
(Mike Murphy) *s.i.s: towards rr: hdwy on rails into midfield over 3f out: rdn over 2f out: wknd ins fnl f* **8/1**

0301 **13** *nse* **Elna Bright**[21] 5703 6-8-10 **87** .... JimmyQuinn 13 72
(Brett Johnson) *hld up towards rr: rdn over 2f out: nvr any imp* **20/1**

0306 **14** *20* **Mr David (USA)**[21] 5699 4-9-3 **94** .... JamieSpencer 5 79
(Jamie Osborne) *mid-div: rdn over 2f out: btn whn eased over 1f out: virtually p.u* **10/1**

1m 24.02s (-1.38) **Going Correction** +0.05s/f (Good)
WFA 3 from 4yo+ 3lb **14** Ran SP% **120.4**
Speed ratings (Par 109): **109,107,106,106,106 105,104,104,103,101 101,98,98,75**
Tote Swingers: 1&2 £25.40, 1&3 £22.30, 2&3 £17.80 CSF £269.48 CT £1979.97 TOTE £23.90: £7.90, £7.70, £2.70; EX 244.40 TRIFECTA Not won..

Owner S Parker **Bred** Mervyn Stewkesbury **Trained** Headley, Surrey
FOCUS
An open handicap, if not a particularly strong race for the grade. The pace was reasonable but not many were able to become involved. They finished in a heap behind the winner.
NOTEBOOK
Golden Desert(IRE), who had raced keenly, burst through to lead late on and won going away. He had run well in a classified stakes at Glorious Goodwood, but had failed to trouble the judge otherwise this season and this was his first win for two years. This is his ground. (op 14-1)
Mia's Boy, another coming here on a lengthy losing sequence, had a lot in front of him entering the final furlong, but finished fast. He is currently on his last winning mark. (op 16-1)
White Frost(IRE), one of two 3yos in the field, made the running against the rail but edged to his left when the pressure was on, something he has done before. Only caught for second on the line, he is probably capable of winning off this mark. (op 8-1)
Striking Spirit seemed to appreciate this return to 7f and stuck on well after switching right. His last win came back in July 2009, when 4lb higher than he is now. (op 20-1)
Golden Delicious was raised 3lb for winning at Salisbury. Always up with the pace, she hung to her left in company with the third and was still in there fighting, but under pressure, when she was squeezed out between him and the winner late on. (tchd 7-1 and 8-1)
Citrus Star(USA) ran creditably without stepping up on his Doncaster effort. He is 6lb below his last winning mark. (op 13-2 tchd 7-1 in places)
Woodcote Place is consistent and there is no reason to think he didn't run his race. (op 22-1)
Space Station was running on when it was too late.
Asraab(IRE), racing for only the fourth time and tried in a tongue-strap, failed to pick up from the rear. (op 6-1)
Lutine Bell, again without the blinkers, was dropped in like at Doncaster but was off the bridle much sooner this time and could never make an impact. He raced on the possibly slower ground against the rail. (op 7-1)

6342 TURFTV H'CAP — 1m 4f
5:35 (5:36) (Class 3) (0-95,92) 3-Y-O — **£8,409** (£2,502; £1,250; £625) **Stalls** Centre

Form — RPR
0211 **1** — **Anatolian**[42] 5049 3-9-7 **92** .... FrankieDettori 1 — 103+
(Mahmood Al Zarooni) *w ldr: rdn to ld over 1f out: edgd lft but r.o wl fnl f: readily* **11/10**[1]
-231 **2** *1 ½* **Tmaam (USA)**[14] 5911 3-9-5 **90** .... PaulHanagan 4 — 99+
(Mark Johnston) *led and set stdy gallop: hdd ent fnl 3f: rdn and outpcd 2f out: drvn and rallied to chse wnr ins fnl f: no imp* **7/4**[2]
2010 **3** *3 ½* **Haylaman (IRE)**[22] 5693 3-9-3 **88** .... JamieSpencer 3 — 91
(Ed Dunlop) *hld up in tch in last tl hdwy to ld and qcknd 3f out: rdn over 2f out: hdd over 1f out: wknd ins fnl f* **7/1**[3]
3240 **4** *5* **Borug (USA)**[99] 3108 3-9-5 **90** ....(p) WilliamBuick 6 — 85
(Saeed Bin Suroor) *chsd ldrs: rdn and outpcd over 2f out: wknd ent fnl f* **8/1**

2m 33.85s (1.85) **Going Correction** +0.05s/f (Good) — 4 Ran SP% **107.6**
Speed ratings (Par 105): **95,94,91,88**
CSF £3.26 TOTE £1.70; EX 2.70.
Owner Godolphin **Bred** Darley **Trained** Newmarket, Suffolk
FOCUS
A disappointing turnout for this new event. As expected it was somewhat tactical and the pace was pretty steady with the four runners racing in pairs down the middle of the track.
NOTEBOOK
Anatolian ◆ completed his hat-trick, picking up nicely to lead and running on strongly. Defying a 10lb rise for his win at Newbury, he saw out the longer trip well in this slowly run event and got away with the quick ground without relishing it. He is progressive and connections can start thinking about stepping him up to Listed company. (op Evens tchd 10-11)
Tmaam(USA) set a steady pace and was caught out when the third suddenly quickened it up. He took time to gather full stride, but was staying on well inside the final furlong and remains one to keep on side. A stiffer test should definitely suit him. (op 11-4 tchd 13-8)
Haylaman(IRE)'s rider was the first to commit, switching his mount to his right and quickening to lead with three furlongs to run, but the gelding was soon collared. It does look as if he might be happier back at 1m2f. (op 13-2 tchd 6-1)
Borug(USA), the Godolphin second string, had been off since Royal Ascot, where he contested the Queen's Vase over 2m. He looked less than straightforward, not really settling and carrying his head high, and he failed to pick up when the race developed. (op 6-1)
T/Jkpt: Not won. T/Plt: £2,548.00 to a £1 stake. Pool:£166,772.02 - 47.78 winning tickets T/Qpdt: £114.50 to a £1 stake. Pool:£10,942.01 - 70.66 winning tickets SP

5589 RIPON (R-H)
Saturday, September 24
OFFICIAL GOING: Good (8.1)
Wind: light behind Weather: Cloudy

6343 RIPON-RACES.CO.UK APPRENTICE (S) STKS — 6f
2:10 (2:12) (Class 6) 3-4-Y-O — **£2,385** (£704; £352) **Stalls** High

Form — RPR
2032 **1** — **Meandmyshadow**[7] 6159 3-9-5 59 .... PaulPickard 8 — 63
(Alan Brown) *chsd ldrs: rdn to ld over 1f out: kpt on* **11/2**[2]
0300 **2** *2* **Magic Rhythm**[5] 6223 3-9-0 58 ....(b[1]) MartinHarley 11 — 52
(Mrs K Burke) *trckd ldrs: swtchd rt over 1f out: rdn to chse wnr jst ins fnl f: kpt on* **12/1**
6053 **3** *½* **Mark Anthony (IRE)**[5] 6208 4-9-4 62 ....(p) LMcNiff(3) 10 — 55
(Shaun Harris) *prom: rdn over 2f out: kpt on* **6/1**[3]
0004 **4** *nk* **Royal Blade (IRE)**[5] 6213 4-9-9 64 .... JulieBurke(3) 7 — 59+
(Alan Berry) *midfield towards outer: rdn over 2f out: hdwy over 1f out: kpt on fnl f* **9/1**
0540 **5** *3* **Kalahari Desert (IRE)**[5] 6208 4-9-7 42 ....(v) AmyRyan 15 — 44
(Richard Whitaker) *dwlt: sn chsd ldrs: rdn over 2f out: no ex fnl 100yds* **25/1**
0600 **6** *1 ¼* **Blue Rum (IRE)**[73] 3972 4-9-1 40 ow1 .... GerardGalligan(7) 12 — 41
(Alan Kirtley) *w ldr: lost pl 1/2-way: sn rdn: no imp* **80/1**
45 **7** *1 ¼* **Lady Lube Rye (IRE)**[43] 5009 4-8-9 43 .... ShirleyTeasdale(7) 6 — 31
(Noel Wilson) *hld up: rdn over 2f out: kpt on fnl f: nvr trbld ldrs* **40/1**
0050 **8** *1* **Stamp Duty (IRE)**[47] 4854 3-9-5 60 ....(p) JamesSullivan 1 — 33
(Ollie Pears) *sn reminders in rr: swtchd lft to rail 4f out: hdwy whn short of room over 1f out: kpt on fnl f: nvr trbld ldrs* **12/1**
6366 **9** *hd* **Captain Dimitrios**[1] 6305 3-9-5 58 ....(v) SeanLevey 5 — 33
(David Evans) *midfield: rdn over 3f out: no imp* **12/1**
333 **10** *1 ½* **Eeny Mac (IRE)**[10] 6050 4-9-0 51 .... TerenceFury(7) 9 — 28
(Neville Bycroft) *hld up: pushed along over 3f out: n.d* **8/1**
0300 **11** *1 ¾* **Bay Of Fires (IRE)**[26] 5559 3-9-0 69 ....(v[1]) DeclanCannon 13 — 17
(David O'Meara) *led narrowly: rdn whn hdd over 1f out: wknd qckly* **9/2**[1]
5010 **12** *3 ¼* **Brave Battle**[6] 6190 3-9-3 63 .... DavidSimmonson(7) 2 — 17
(Ron Barr) *hld up towards outer: pushed along 4f out: nvr threatened* **25/1**
- **13** *14* **Noimead Draiochta (IRE)**[86] 3564 3-9-10 74 ....(t) MichaelO'Connell 4 — —
(David Nicholls) *hld up: rdn over 2f out: a towards rr* **9/2**[1]
306R **14** *10* **Tinzo (IRE)**[24] 5619 3-9-0 44 .... JustinNewman(5) 3 — —
(Alan Berry) *slowly away: swtchd lft s: hld up: a towards rr* **100/1**
0 **15** *43* **Exceeded**[19] 5793 3-8-11 0 .... ShaneBKelly(3) 14 — —
(Robert Johnson) *dwlt: sn pushed along in rr: t.o fnl 2f* **100/1**

1m 13.16s (0.16) **Going Correction** -0.20s/f (Firm)
WFA 3 from 4yo 2lb — 15 Ran SP% **123.6**
Speed ratings (Par 101): **90,87,86,86,82 80,78,77,77,75 73,68,50,36,—**
Tote Swingers: 1&2 £2.20, 1&3 £5.70, 2&3 £4.30 CSF £68.53 TOTE £7.20: £2.30, £3.90, £3.00; EX 126.00.The winner was bought in for £6,500.
Owner G Morrill **Bred** M J Dawson **Trained** Yedingham, N Yorks
■ Stewards' Enquiry : Shirley Teasdale three-day ban: careless riding (Oct 9-11)
Gerard Galligan two-day ban: weighed in 2lb heavy (Oct 9-10)
FOCUS
Exposed performers in a modest seller. The gallop was sound but those that attempted to come from off the pace were at a disadvantage. The field raced towards the stands' side and the riders agreed the ground was as the official.
Captain Dimitrios Official explanation: jockey said he lost an iron leaving stalls
Noimead Draiochta(IRE) Official explanation: jockey said colt never travelled

6344 AT THE RACES SKY 415 MAIDEN STKS — 6f
2:40 (2:41) (Class 5) 2-Y-O — **£2,911** (£866; £432; £216) **Stalls** High

Form — RPR
00 **1** — **Border Revia (IRE)**[19] 5786 2-9-3 0 .... TonyHamilton 10 — 75+
(Richard Fahey) *in tch: pushed along over 2f out: hdwy to chse ldr over 1f out: kpt on: led fnl 50yds* **15/2**[3]
04 **2** *1 ½* **Dark Don (IRE)**[18] 5801 2-9-3 0 .... SebSanders 7 — 70
(Charles Hills) *sn led: rdn over 1f out: hdd fnl 50yds: no ex* **8/11**[1]
66 **3** *6* **Endless Applause**[25] 5592 2-8-12 0 .... MichaelStainton 6 — 47
(Richard Whitaker) *chsd ldrs: rdn over 2f out: one pce: no match ldng pair fnl f* **12/1**
00 **4** *3 ¼* **Emily Hall**[10] 6045 2-8-12 0 .... JoeFanning 1 — 37
(Bryan Smart) *prom: rdn over 2f out: wknd fnl f* **20/1**
06 **5** *1 ½* **Ashkan**[56] 4525 2-9-3 0 .... LiamJones 8 — 38
(William Haggas) *dwlt: hld up: sn pushed along: kpt on fnl f: n.d* **7/1**[2]
0 **6** *shd* **Lizzie Drippin**[17] 5819 2-8-12 0 .... JamesSullivan 9 — 32
(Michael Easterby) *in tch: pushed along over 3f out: wknd over 1f out* **20/1**
0 **7** *nk* **Duchesse Satin (IRE)**[10] 6048 2-8-12 0 .... DuranFentiman 5 — 32
(Tim Easterby) *hld up: sn pushed along: nvr threatened* **25/1**
8 *¾* **Brave One (IRE)** 2-8-9 0 .... MichaelO'Connell(3) 3 — 29
(David Nicholls) *v.s.a: sn pushed along: a in rr* **7/1**[2]

1m 13.67s (0.67) **Going Correction** -0.20s/f (Firm) — 8 Ran SP% **115.7**
Speed ratings (Par 95): **87,85,77,72,70 70,70,69**
Tote Swingers: 1&2 £2.20, 1&3 £5.70, 2&3 £4.30 CSF £13.26 TOTE £9.60: £1.80, £1.10, £3.00; EX 22.20.
Owner James Gaffney **Bred** River Downs Stud **Trained** Musley Bank, N Yorks
FOCUS
A modest and uncompetitive maiden in which the gallop was fair and the first two pulled clear.
NOTEBOOK
Border Revia(IRE), who hadn't shown much in soft-ground maidens, turned in easily his best effort on this first run on a sounder surface. He'll have no problems with 7f, he looks to have a decent attitude, has a bit of size and scope and, given he can't be rated too highly for this, he should be able to win in handicap company. (op 11-2)
Dark Don(IRE) had the run of the race and matched his improved Leicester effort on his first run over this trip. He's a modest sort so is likely to remain vulnerable against the better types in this grade but should be able to pick up a handicap. (op 5-4)
Endless Applause bettered her two previous (very moderate) efforts over this longer trip. She is another that will appreciate the step into low-grade handicaps. (op 8-1)
Emily Hall ran her best race to date but she will have to show a fair bit more before she rates a solid betting proposition. (op 11-1)
Ashkan is now qualified for a mark and may do better in handicaps granted a stiffer test. (op 5-1 tchd 9-2)
Lizzie Drippin will be of more interest in low-grade handicaps in due course. (op 16-1 tchd 12-1)

6345 ERIN AND RICHARD HAPPILY EVER AFTER NURSERY — 1m
3:15 (3:16) (Class 4) (0-85,80) 2-Y-O — **£5,040** (£1,508; £754; £377; £188) **Stalls** Low

Form — RPR
3102 **1** — **Repeater**[7] 6154 2-9-7 **80** .... SebSanders 5 — 89+
(Sir Mark Prescott Bt) *hld up in midfield and keen: pushed along to chse ldrs over 1f out: squeezed through gap ins fnl f: r.o strly to ld post* **9/4**[1]
0011 **2** *hd* **Spirit Of The Law (IRE)**[10] 6053 2-8-8 **67** .... ChrisCatlin 2 — 74
(Ed Dunlop) *trckd ldrs: rdn to ld appr fnl f: kpt on: hdd post* **7/2**[2]
0401 **3** *2 ¾* **Jimmy The Lollipop (IRE)**[30] 5413 2-8-9 **68** ....(b) BarryMcHugh 3 — 68
(Kevin Ryan) *led: rdn over 2f out: hdd appr fnl f: one pce* **16/1**
6451 **4** *½* **Stateos (IRE)**[26] 5541 2-8-11 **77** .... CharlesEddery(7) 1 — 76
(Sir Henry Cecil) *dwlt: sn midfield on inner: pushed along over 3f out: hdwy and ev ch over 1f out: one pce ins fnl f* **9/2**[3]
0055 **5** *½* **Voodoo Rhythm (USA)**[15] 5899 2-8-12 **74** .... LouisBeuzelin(3) 11 — 72
(Brian Meehan) *trckd ldrs: rdn over 2f out: hdwy and ev ch appr fnl f: no ex fnl 100yds* **20/1**
4321 **6** *1 ½* **Mcvicar**[15] 5875 2-9-2 **75** .... TonyCulhane 6 — 69
(Mick Channon) *trckd ldrs: pushed along over 3f out: sn lost pl: kpt on again fnl f* **7/1**
4015 **7** *½* **Balti's Sister (IRE)**[43] 4984 2-8-1 **60** .... JamesSullivan 9 — 53
(Michael Easterby) *rrd s: slowly away: hld up: pushed along over 2f out: kpt on fnl f: n.d* **16/1**
0503 **8** *shd* **Docs Legacy (IRE)**[44] 4943 2-8-1 **60** .... PatrickMathers 12 — 53
(Richard Fahey) *hld up: pushed along on outer over 4f out: drvn over 2f out: one pce* **14/1**
1600 **9** *nse* **Comical**[11] 6031 2-9-4 **77** .... JoeFanning 4 — 70
(Mark Johnston) *prom: rdn over 3f out: wknd fnl f* **16/1**
1640 **10** *1* **Ortea**[37] 5216 2-9-3 **79** .... SeanLevey(3) 8 — 70
(David Evans) *midfield: pushed along over 3f out: wknd over 1f out* **20/1**
000 **11** *37* **Isolde's Return**[97] 3200 2-7-12 **57** oh12 .... AndrewMullen 10 — —
(George Moore) *hld up and t.k.h: rdn over 3f out: sn wknd* **100/1**

1m 40.94s (-0.46) **Going Correction** -0.10s/f (Good) — 11 Ran SP% **118.5**
Speed ratings (Par 97): **98,97,95,94,94 92,92,91,91,90 53**
Tote Swingers: 1&2 £2.90, 1&3 £8.50, 2&3 £12.80 CSF £9.66 CT £101.73 TOTE £3.10: £1.10, £2.60, £5.00; EX 10.90.
Owner Cheveley Park Stud **Bred** W & R Barnett Ltd & Balmerino B'Stock **Trained** Newmarket, Suffolk
■ Stewards' Enquiry : Seb Sanders caution: used whip without giving colt time to respond.
FOCUS
A fair and competitive handicap featuring several in-form types. The gallop was only fair but the first two finished a few lengths clear and this race should throw up winners.

NOTEBOOK

Repeater ◆ is a progressive sort who turned in his best effort returned to this longer trip to justify the market confidence, in the process shaping as though he was better than the bare facts suggest after faring easily the best of those held up and after waiting to get a gap. He'll be suited by 1m2f and a more galloping track and is the sort to win more races. (op 11-4 tchd 2-1)

Spirit Of The Law(IRE) ◆ a progressive sort, narrowly failed in the hat-trick bid but turned in his best effort back on turf (got first run) from this 10lb higher mark. He was unfortunate to bump into a similarly progressive sort but he finished clear of the rest and appeals as the sort to win again. (op 4-1 tchd 9-2)

Jimmy The Lollipop(IRE), a claiming winner on his all-weather debut on his previous start, had the run of the race and ran as well as he ever has done against two progressive sorts returned to turf. However, things went his way and his record suggests he wouldn't be certain to build on this next time. (op 14-1)

Stateos(IRE), who scrambled home in maiden company on his previous start, was far from disgraced in this competitive handicap returned to this trip. He shaped as though a stiffer overall test of stamina would have suited. (op 5-1)

Voodoo Rhythm(USA) ◆ had shown ability at a modest level in maidens and ran creditably against a couple of improving types on this handicap debut. He's equally effective on Polytrack and there is a race to be won with him. (tchd 18-1)

Mcvicar did well to win over 7f at Chester on his previous trip given that 1m at this course looked an insufficient test of his stamina. He should have no problems with further and is capable of picking up another race granted a suitable test. (op 6-1)

Balti's Sister(IRE) Official explanation: jockey said filly reared as stalls opened

Docs Legacy(IRE) failed to build on the form shown on his handicap debut in this stronger event after racing on the outside but he's not fully exposed, is in good hands and will almost certainly be capable of better in due course. (op 12-1)

6346 RIPON LAND ROVER H'CAP — 1m 1f 170y

3:45 (3:45) (Class 4) (0-85,84) 3-Y-0+ **£5,040** (£1,508; £754; £377; £188) **Stalls** Low

Form — RPR

4035 **1** **Jonny Lesters Hair (IRE)**[9] 6093 6-9-3 **77** .... DavidAllan 8 — 88
(Tim Easterby) *sn led: clr over 5f out: rdn 2f out: kpt on: eased fnl 50yds: comf* — **8/1**[2]

0040 **2** *5* **Pass Muster**[15] 5888 4-9-6 **83** .... MichaelO'Connell(3) 6 — 87+
(Ollie Pears) *hld up: hdwy on inner fr over 3f out: short of room and swtchd lft wl over 1f out: kpt on wl: wnt 2nd ins fnl f: kpt on: no ch w wnr* — **17/2**[3]

0510 **3** *1 1/4* **Lucky Windmill**[29] 5440 4-9-4 **78** .... PJMcDonald 5 — 76
(Alan Swinbank) *midfield: rdn and hdwy over 3f out: kpt on fnl f: wnt 3rd fnl 75yds* — **20/1**

2133 **4** *nk* **Rio's Rosanna (IRE)**[54] 4608 4-9-1 **75** .... RussKennemore 10 — 73
(Richard Whitaker) *midfield: rdn and hdwy to chse clr ldr over 2f out: kpt on* — **8/1**[2]

4144 **5** *1/2* **El Muqbil (IRE)**[42] 5049 3-9-2 **82** ....(tp) LiamJones 2 — 79
(Brian Meehan) *in tch: rdn over 3f out: hdwy to go 2nd appr fnl f: wknd fnl 100yds* — **13/2**[1]

2100 **6** *3/4* **Euston Square**[9] 6079 5-9-1 **80** .... GarryWhillans(5) 16 — 75
(Alistair Whillans) *swtchd rt s: hld up in rr: hdwy on inner over 2f out: kpt on fnl f: nrst fin* — **12/1**

0030 **7** *nk* **Ginger Jack**[25] 5593 4-9-8 **82** .... JamesSullivan 12 — 76
(Geoffrey Harker) *hld up: rdn over 3f out: kpt on: n.d* — **18/1**

4226 **8** *hd* **Veiled Applause**[9] 6078 8-8-9 **74** .... ShaneBKelly(5) 7 — 68
(John Quinn) *hld up: rdn over 2f out: kpt on one pce* — **9/1**

0050 **9** *1 1/2* **Tartan Gigha (IRE)**[37] 5205 6-9-4 **78** .... JoeFanning 13 — 69
(Mark Johnston) *hld up in midfield: rdn over 3f out: sn no imp* — **16/1**

6042 **10** *3/4* **Solar Spirit (IRE)**[9] 6093 6-9-0 **74** .... PatrickMathers 1 — 63
(Tracy Waggott) *racd keenly: in tch: hdwy to chse clr ldr 3f out: wknd appr fnl f* — **12/1**

2301 **11** *5* **Satwa Dream (IRE)**[18] 5816 4-9-6 **80** .... ChrisCatlin 3 — 59
(Ed Dunlop) *trckd ldr: rdn 3f out: wknd over 1f out* — **14/1**

0033 **12** *4 1/2* **Good Boy Jackson**[9] 6079 3-9-3 **83** .... DavidNolan 15 — 53
(Kevin Ryan) *midfield: rdn over 3f out: sn no imp* — **8/1**[2]

6200 **13** *5* **Fastnet Storm (IRE)**[25] 5593 5-9-10 **84** .... LeeNewman 4 — 44
(David Barron) *trckd ldr: rdn over 3f out: wknd over 1f out* — **11/1**

0402 **14** *1 1/2* **Fazza**[21] 5733 4-9-1 **75** .... TonyHamilton 11 — 32
(Edwin Tuer) *trckd ldr: rdn over 3f out: sn wknd* — **14/1**

0100 **15** *10* **Doctor Zhivago**[20] 5757 4-9-3 **77** .... BarryMcHugh 9 — 13
(Ian McInnes) *hld up: a in rr* — **33/1**

2m 2.97s (-2.43) **Going Correction** -0.10s/f (Good)
WFA 3 from 4yo+ 6lb — **15** Ran SP% **123.1**
Speed ratings (Par 105): **105,101,100,99,99 98,98,98,97,96 92,88,84,83,75**
Tote Swingers: 1&2 £16.40, 1&3 £53.90, 2&3 £42.70 CSF £75.61 CT £1337.59 TOTE £7.60: £1.80, £4.10, £6.60; EX 88.10.
Owner Reality Partnerships II **Bred** Gary O'Reilly **Trained** Great Habton, N Yorks

FOCUS

Not too many progressive types in a useful handicap but, although the gallop wasn't overly strong, this race only ever concerned the enterprisingly ridden winner.

Good Boy Jackson Official explanation: jockey said gelding hung left throughout

6347 RIPON CATHEDRAL CITY OF THE DALES H'CAP — 6f

4:15 (4:16) (Class 2) (0-105,103) 3-Y-0+
£12,450 (£3,728; £1,864; £932; £466; £234) **Stalls** High

Form — RPR

0403 **1** **Advanced**[7] 6145 8-8-8 **90** .... AmyRyan(3) 13 — 100
(Kevin Ryan) *prom stands' side: rdn over 2f out: kpt on: led post* — **5/1**[3]

5000 **2** *hd* **Singeur (IRE)**[20] 5758 4-8-13 **92** .... LeeNewman 11 — 101
(Robin Bastiman) *racd stands' side: overall ldr: rdn 2f out: kpt on: hdd post: 2nd of 10 in gp* — **12/1**

-500 **3** *1 1/2* **Bohemian Melody**[21] 5699 4-8-12 **91** .... SebSanders 1 — 95
(Marco Botti) *hld up last of 3 far side: rdn and hdwy 2f out: led gp 1f out: kpt on: 1st of 3 in gp* — **12/1**

2000 **4** *1/2* **Tajneed (IRE)**[7] 6147 8-9-6 **102** .... MichaelO'Connell(3) 10 — 105
(David Nicholls) *in tch stands' side: rdn over 2f out: kpt on fnl f: 3rd of 10 in gp* — **9/2**[2]

4300 **5** *hd* **Star Rover (IRE)**[27] 5508 4-8-8 **90** ....(v) SeanLevey(3) 9 — 92
(David Evans) *prom stands' side: rdn over 2f out: no ex ins fnl f: 4th of 10 in gp* — **16/1**

1000 **6** *hd* **Capone (IRE)**[7] 6145 6-8-8 **90** .... DominicFox(3) 7 — 91
(David Nicholls) *in tch stands' side: rdn over 2f out: edgd rt ins fnl f: kpt on: 5th of 10 in gp* — **18/1**

2600 **7** *1 1/2* **Cocktail Charlie**[20] 5758 3-8-11 **92** ....(p) DavidAllan 3 — 89
(Tim Easterby) *led narrowly far side: rdn over 2f out: hdd on side 1f out: no ex: 2nd of 3 in gp* — **8/1**

0050 **8** *3/4* **Arctic Feeling (IRE)**[7] 6145 3-8-8 **89** ow1 .... TonyHamilton 8 — 83
(Richard Fahey) *dwlt: hld up stands's side: rdn 1/2-way: kpt on fnl f: 6th of 10 in gp* — **22/1**

1556 **9** *shd* **Kanaf (IRE)**[15] 5887 4-9-4 **97** .... ChrisCatlin 6 — 91+
(Ed Dunlop) *hld up stands' side: rdn over 2f out: kpt on ins fnl f: nvr trbld ldrs: 7th of 10 in gp* — **11/2**

1110 **10** *2 1/2* **Pepper Lane**[7] 6147 4-9-10 **103** .... DavidNolan 2 — 89
(David O'Meara) *w ldr far side: rdn over 2f out: wknd fnl f: last of 3 in gp* — **4/1**[1]

0000 **11** *1 1/2* **Orpsie Boy (IRE)**[15] 5879 8-8-6 **85** .... JamesSullivan 5 — 66
(Ruth Carr) *hld up stands' side: a towards rr: 8th of 10 in gp* — **16/1**

0000 **12** *1* **Discanti (IRE)**[16] 5852 6-8-5 **84** oh1 ....(t) DuranFentiman 12 — 62
(Tim Easterby) *in tch stands' side: rdn over 2f out: wknd over 1f out: 9th of 10 in gp* — **14/1**

623 **U** **Murbeh (IRE)**[78] 3820 3-9-2 **97** .... LiamJones 4 — —
(Brian Meehan) *chsd ldrs stands' side: ev ch whn sddle slipped and uns rdr appr fnl f* — **5/1**[3]

1m 11.55s (-1.45) **Going Correction** -0.20s/f (Firm)
WFA 3 from 4yo+ 2lb — **13** Ran SP% **141.4**
Speed ratings (Par 109): **101,100,98,98,97 97,95,94,94,91 89,87,—**
Tote Swingers: 1&2 £11.70, 1&3 £16.70, 2&3 £22.30 CSF £76.91 CT £755.58 TOTE £7.10: £2.00, £3.70, £5.60; EX 73.70.
Owner Mrs J Ryan **Bred** Gestut Gorlsdorf **Trained** Hambleton, N Yorks
■ Stewards' Enquiry : Amy Ryan caution: used whip down shoulder in the forehand.

FOCUS

Not too many bang in-form types but a good quality handicap in which the larger stands' side group held the edge over the trio that raced far side. The gallop was sound throughout.

NOTEBOOK

Advanced, a fine third after racing alone in the Ayr Silver Cup, had the run of the race from his favourable draw and showed a good attitude to break a losing run that stretched back two years. He's clearly very useful and tough and is fully effective over 7f, but he wouldn't be an obvious one to follow up after reassessment. (op 7-1)

Singeur(IRE) hadn't been at his best on his last three starts but he returned to something like his best to confirm he's a very useful sprinter. He's equally effective over 5f and, although he'll remain vulnerable against the more progressive sorts after reassessment, he is the type to win again. (op 16-1)

Bohemian Melody ◆ fared the best of the trio that raced on the far side on this return to sprinting. He is not fully exposed on turf, is a dual winner on Polytrack and he can win again either over this trip or over 7f.

Tajneed(IRE) is a smart sprinter who goes particularly well at this course and he bettered his last three efforts returned to this track. He has little margin for error from this mark and hasn't won for over a year but should be able to pick up a conditions event at some point. (op 6-1 tchd 13-2)

Star Rover(IRE) isn't a regular winner (due to the fact he's had little respite from the handicapper owing to his consistency) but, although he was far from disgraced in the larger stands' side group, he is likely to remain vulnerable against the better handicapped sorts in this type of event. (op 25-1)

Capone(IRE) wasn't disgraced and bettered his three previous runs but, although he's worth another try over 7f, he's going to have to raise his game to win a competitive handicap from this sort of mark. (op 25-1)

Kanaf(IRE) Official explanation: trainer's rep said, regarding running, that the gelding was unsuited by the track

Pepper Lane, even allowing for the fact she raced in the smaller far-side group, proved disappointing for the second time in succession. It's possible she may well have had enough for the time being. (op 9-2 tchd 7-2)

Murbeh(IRE) was in the process of running creditably and was still in with a chance when unshipping his rider due to a slipping saddle. He isn't fully exposed and is worth another chance. Official explanation: jockey said saddle slipped (op 9-2)

6348 SIS LIVE H'CAP (DIV I) — 5f

4:50 (4:50) (Class 4) (0-85,87) 3-Y-0+ **£5,040** (£1,508; £754; £377; £188) **Stalls** High

Form — RPR

4315 **1** **Another Wise Kid (IRE)**[84] 3613 3-9-2 **81** .... RussKennemore 11 — 91
(Paul Midgley) *hld up towards inner and t.k.h: pushed along and gd hdwy over 1f out: rdn and r.o wl fnl f: led post* — **7/1**

1300 **2** *nk* **Berberana (IRE)**[17] 5831 3-9-0 **79** ....(t) DavidAllan 6 — 88
(Tim Easterby) *led narrowly: rdn 2f out: kpt on: hdd post* — **16/1**

1256 **3** *3/4* **Wicked Wilma (IRE)**[5] 6212 7-8-4 **73** .... JulieBurke(5) 4 — 79
(Alan Berry) *wth ldr: rdn over 2f out: no ex towards fin* — **16/1**

6614 **4** *1 1/4* **Select Committee**[2] 6276 6-8-9 **73** ....(v) PBBeggy 10 — 75
(John Quinn) *midfield: pushed along over 2f out: kpt on fnl f: wnt 4th towards fin* — **9/1**

4-00 **5** *nk* **Drift And Dream**[17] 5831 4-9-0 **78** .... ChrisCatlin 9 — 79
(Chris Wall) *trckd ldrs: rdn 2f out: kpt on one pce* — **5/1**[3]

4215 **6** *1/2* **Haajes**[8] 6112 7-9-4 **82** .... BarryMcHugh 3 — 81+
(Paul Midgley) *hld up in tch towards outer: rdn over 2f out: kpt on one pce* — **4/1**[1]

461 **7** *nse* **Secret Millionaire (IRE)**[11] 6036 4-9-6 **87** .... LouisBeuzelin(3) 7 — 86
(Patrick Morris) *trckd ldrs: rdn over 2f out: no ex ins fnl f* — **9/2**[2]

0040 **8** *1 3/4* **Indian Trail**[8] 6112 11-9-5 **83** ....(b) PaulQuinn 2 — 75
(David Nicholls) *dwlt: hld up: rdn over 2f out: n.d* — **12/1**

0032 **9** *2 1/4* **Soap Wars**[11] 6036 6-9-7 **85** .... SebSanders 1 — 69
(Hugo Palmer) *hld up: rdn over 2f out: nvr threatened* — **9/2**[2]

112- **10** *6* **Jameela Girl**[389] 5639 3-8-13 **81** .... SeanLevey(3) 5 — 44
(Robert Cowell) *in tch: rdn over 2f out: wknd over 1f out* — **10/1**

-300 **11** *3 1/2* **Major Muscari (IRE)**[17] 5831 3-8-12 **77** .... PatrickMathers 8 — 27
(Geoffrey Oldroyd) *sn pushed along in midfield: wknd over 1f out* — **20/1**

59.02 secs (-1.68) **Going Correction** -0.20s/f (Firm)
WFA 3 from 4yo+ 1lb — **11** Ran SP% **128.8**
Speed ratings (Par 105): **105,104,103,101,100 100,99,97,93,83 78**
Tote Swingers: 1&2 £33.20, 1&3 £30.40, 2&3 £25.90 CSF £123.84 CT £1799.68 TOTE £9.70: £3.00, £4.60, £5.40; EX 189.10.
Owner Michael Ng **Bred** Paul Kavanagh **Trained** Westow, N Yorks
■ Stewards' Enquiry : Russ Kennemore caution: used whip without giving gelding time to respond

FOCUS

A decent gallop to this useful sprint and one in which the whole field raced stands' side this time.

Soap Wars Official explanation: trainer's rep said gelding was unsuited by the track

6349 TOTEPOOL FLEXI BETTING MAIDEN STKS — 1m 4f 10y

5:25 (5:26) (Class 5) 3-Y-0+ **£2,911** (£866; £432; £216) **Stalls** Low

Form — RPR

253 **1** **Eagle Rock (IRE)**[43] 5007 3-9-3 74 .... AndrewMullen 10 — 82
(Tom Tate) *mde all: rdn over 2f out: strly pressed ins fnl f: hld on towards fin* — **9/2**[3]

43 **2** *nk* **Yasir (USA)**[24] 5629 3-9-3 0 .... SebSanders 1 — 81
(Saeed Bin Suroor) *dwlt: hld up in tch: hdwy to trck ldrs 4f out: rdn to chse wnr over 1f out: hrd drvn and upsides ins fnl f: hld nr fin* — **10/11**[1]

3 *4* **Eyedoro (USA)** 3-9-3 0 .... JoeFanning 2 — 75+
(Mark Johnston) *midfield: hdwy to trck wnr 4f out: rdn over 2f out: kpt on one pce* — **8/1**

3 **4** *1 3/4* **Tricksofthetrade (IRE)**[133] 2114 5-9-11 0........................ PJMcDonald 7 72
(Alan Swinbank) *trckd wnr: rdn over 3f out: no ex ins fnl f* **7/2**[2]
0 **5** *14* **Eila Wheeler**[19] 5792 4-9-1 0........................ ShaneBKelly(5) 6 45
(Robert Johnson) *hld up: rdn over 3f out: n.d* **100/1**
00 **6** *4 1/2* **Labroc (IRE)**[9] 6097 3-9-3 0........................ LiamJones 5 42
(William Haggas) *prom: rdn over 4f out: wknd over 3f out* **25/1**
7 *1* **Ornithologist (USA)** 3-9-3 0........................ DavidNolan 9 41
(David O'Meara) *hld up: n.d* **33/1**
0 **8** *1 3/4* **Minnie Mambo (USA)**[64] 4279 3-8-12 0........................ MartinLane 4 33
(Michael Bell) *hld up: a towards rr* **16/1**
60 **9** *2 1/2* **Stillington**[9] 6096 5-9-11 0........................ DavidAllan 8 34
(Mel Brittain) *dwlt: trckd ldrs on outer and keen: rdn over 3f out: sn wknd* **80/1**
0-6 **10** *8* **Fantastic Times**[9] 6097 5-9-4 0........................ JohnCavanagh(7) 3 21
(Mel Brittain) *in tch and keen: lost pl over 5f out: wknd over 3f out* **80/1**

2m 37.7s (1.00) **Going Correction** -0.10s/f (Good)
WFA 3 from 4yo+ 8lb **10** Ran SP% **120.0**
Speed ratings (Par 103): **92,91,89,87,78 75,74,73,72,66**
Tote Swingers: 1&2 £1.20, 1&3 £6.20, 2&3 £2.40 CSF £9.13 TOTE £5.90: £1.60, £1.50, £2.10; EX 11.40.
Owner The Ivy Syndicate **Bred** Silk Fan Syndicate **Trained** Tadcaster, N Yorks

FOCUS
A fair maiden run at just an ordinary gallop and one in which the four at the head of the market pulled clear in the straight.

6350 SIS LIVE H'CAP (DIV II) 5f
6:00 (6:00) (Class 4) (0-85,85) 3-Y-0+ **£5,040** (£1,508; £754; £377; £188) **Stalls** High

Form RPR
13 **1** **Beauty Pageant (IRE)**[22] 5679 4-8-13 **80**........................ SeanLevey(3) 9 87
(Ed McMahon) *w ldr: rdn to ld narrowly over 1f out: hdd ins fnl f: rallied u.str.p to ld again nr fin* **7/2**[1]
5062 **2** *nse* **Legal Eagle (IRE)**[14] 5918 6-9-0 **78**........................(p) JamesSullivan 10 85
(Paul Green) *chsd ldrs: rdn over 2f out: kpt on strly ins fnl f: jst failed* **9/1**[3]
5002 **3** *nk* **Taurus Twins**[5] 6224 5-9-4 **82**........................(b) MartinLane 3 88+
(Richard Price) *w ldr: rdn 2f out: led narrowly ins fnl f: edgd rt fnl 75yds: hdd nr fin* **13/2**[2]
0400 **4** *3 1/4* **Arry's Orse**[29] 5434 4-9-0 **78**........................(t) JoeFanning 4 72
(Bryan Smart) *hld up: rdn 2f out: kpt on fnl f: wnt 4th towards fin: no threat ldng trio* **13/2**[2]
5-46 **5** *3/4* **Crimea (IRE)**[26] 5543 5-9-7 **85**........................ AdrianNicholls 5 77
(David Nicholls) *hld up in tch: rdn 2f out: kpt on fnl f: nvr threatened ldrs* **7/2**[1]
2110 **6** *1* **Lady Royale**[35] 5288 3-9-5 **84**........................(b) PBBeggy 6 72
(Geoffrey Oldroyd) *sn pushed along towards rr: kpt on fnl f: nvr threatened* **10/1**
1000 **7** *3/4* **Cadeaux Pearl**[16] 5852 3-9-3 **85**........................(b) BillyCray(3) 8 70
(David Nicholls) *led narrowly: rdn whn hdd over 1f out: wknd fnl f* **9/1**[3]
2300 **8** *1 1/4* **Nomoreblondes**[10] 6044 7-8-6 **73**........................(p) DeclanCannon(3) 1 54
(Paul Midgley) *chsd ldrs on outer: wknd over 1f out* **20/1**
0460 **9** *2 1/4* **On The High Tops (IRE)**[14] 5923 3-8-11 **76**........................ BarryMcHugh 7 49
(Ruth Carr) *racd keenly: chsd ldrs: rdn over 2f out: wknd over 1f out* **25/1**
6400 **10** *3* **Gottcher**[8] 6112 3-8-9 **74**........................ LeeNewman 2 36
(David Barron) *chsd ldrs: sn pushed along: lost pl over 2f out: wknd over 1f out* **11/1**

59.71 secs (-0.99) **Going Correction** -0.20s/f (Firm)
WFA 3 from 4yo+ 1lb **10** Ran SP% **117.1**
Speed ratings (Par 105): **99,98,98,93,92 90,89,87,83,78**
Tote Swingers: 1&2 £3.20, 1&3 £9.80, 2&3 £4.20 CSF £36.39 CT £203.07 TOTE £5.40: £2.10, £2.60, £1.80; EX 26.10.
Owner J C Fretwell **Bred** Mesnil, Mount Coote, New England Stud **Trained** Lichfield, Staffs
■ Stewards' Enquiry : Sean Levey two-day ban: used whip with excessive frequency (Oct 9-10)

FOCUS
Another useful handicap and one run at a decent gallop throughout. The first three finished clear and those held up weren't seen to best effect.
T/Plt: £1,148.50 to a £1 stake. Pool:£47,831.76 - 30.40 winning tickets T/Qpdt: £341.80 to a £1 stake. Pool:£2,817.79 - 6.10 winning tickets AS

6304 WOLVERHAMPTON (A.W) (L-H)
Saturday, September 24

OFFICIAL GOING: Standard to fast
Wind: Fresh behind Weather: Overcast

6351 WOLVERHAMPTON HOLIDAY INN CLAIMING STKS 5f 20y(P)
5:50 (5:50) (Class 6) 3-Y-0+ **£1,704** (£503; £251) **Stalls** Low

Form RPR
2110 **1** **Deerslayer (USA)**[17] 5831 5-8-7 80........................(p) MartinHarley(3) 5 84
(Richard Guest) *chsd ldr: rdn to ld ins fnl f: jst hld on* **3/1**[1]
040/ **2** *hd* **Master Of Disguise**[735] 6089 5-7-13 86........................(t) NicoleNordblad(7) 3 79
(Hans Adielsson) *chsd ldrs: swtchd lft ins fnl f: r.o wl: jst failed* **8/1**
0140 **3** *hd* **Drawnfromthepast (IRE)**[42] 5033 6-9-0 94.......... MichaelJMurphy(7) 7 94
(Ed Walker) *chsd ldrs: rdn and ev ch ins fnl f: styd on* **4/1**[2]
0520 **4** *1/2* **Lucky Art (USA)**[22] 5679 5-8-8 70........................ KellyHarrison 8 79
(Ruth Carr) *led: rdn and hdd ins fnl f: unable qck towards fin* **20/1**
40 **5** *3 1/2* **Estonia**[14] 5914 4-8-7 68........................ LukeMorris 11 65
(Michael Squance) *hld up: hmpd 1/2-way: rdn over 1f out: r.o ins fnl f: nvr nrr* **28/1**
0550 **6** *1* **Look Who's Kool**[24] 5615 3-8-9 71........................(b) RichardMullen 6 65
(Ed McMahon) *hld up: rdn over 1f out: nvr trbld ldrs* **25/1**
0010 **7** *nk* **Le Toreador**[5] 6224 6-9-1 88........................(tp) PhillipMakin 13 68
(Kevin Ryan) *chsd ldrs: shkn up over 1f out: wknd ins fnl f* **5/1**[3]
0002 **8** *1/2* **Tombi (USA)**[38] 5162 7-9-4 80........................ LiamKeniry 1 70
(Ollie Pears) *sn pushed along and a in rr* **8/1**
0300 **9** *1/2* **Frognal (IRE)**[10] 6056 5-8-1 70........................(b) ChrisDCogan(5) 9 56
(Conor Dore) *dwlt: outpcd* **28/1**
-600 **10** *3 3/4* **Skylla**[118] 2525 4-9-2 79........................ RossAtkinson(3) 2 55
(Derek Shaw) *mid-div: rdn 1/2-way: wknd over 1f out* **25/1**
30- **P** **Rebel Duke (IRE)**[499] 2054 7-9-1 88........................ AndrewElliott 12 —
(Ollie Pears) *mid-div tl p.u 1/2-way: lame* **8/1**

60.75 secs (-1.55) **Going Correction** -0.225s/f (Stan)
WFA 3 from 4yo+ 1lb **11** Ran SP% **114.4**
Speed ratings (Par 101): **103,102,102,101,95 94,93,93,92,86** —
Tote Swingers:1&2:£12.10, 2&3:£6.10, 1&3:£3.60 CSF £24.26 TOTE £4.20: £1.50, £4.40, £1.60; EX 77.20 Trifecta £430.00 Pool £3,457.65 - 5.95 winning units.Deerslayer was claimed by Miss A. Weaver for £10,000. Frognal was claimed by S. Arnold for £6,000. Master of Disguise was claimed by P. D. Evans for £6,000.
Owner Rakebackmypoker.com **Bred** Bjorn Nielsen **Trained** Stainforth, S Yorks
■ Stewards' Enquiry : Martin Harley two-day ban: used whip with excessive frequency down shoulder in the forehand (Oct 9-10)

FOCUS
An above average claimer with the front three carrying official ratings of 80, 86 and 94 respectively, and the strongest time performance of the night per furlong, so this looks useful form for the grade.

6352 WILLIAM HILL - THE HOME OF BETTING MEDIAN AUCTION MAIDEN STKS 5f 20y(P)
6:20 (6:20) (Class 6) 2-Y-O **£2,070** (£616; £307; £153) **Stalls** Low

Form RPR
52 **1** **Confucius Elite**[30] 5410 2-9-3 0........................ PatCosgrave 6 84+
(Jim Boyle) *chsd ldrs: led over 1f out: shkn up and r.o wl* **8/13**[1]
423 **2** *6* **Samba Night (IRE)**[32] 5347 2-9-3 72........................ RichardMullen 3 62
(Ed McMahon) *led: rdn and hdd over 1f out: outpcd fnl f* **10/3**[2]
2 **3** *1/2* **Regal Lady**[21] 5737 2-8-12 0........................ PhillipMakin 8 56
(David Brown) *chsd ldr: rdn 1/2-way: styd on same pce fr over 1f out* **11/2**[3]
50 **4** *4 1/2* **Majestic Breeze (IRE)**[25] 5590 2-8-9 0........................ PaulPickard(3) 1 39+
(Brian Ellison) *hld up: r.o ins fnl f: nvr nr to chal* **14/1**
0 **5** *4 1/2* **Sandbanks**[33] 5323 2-8-12 0........................ LiamKeniry 7 23
(Sylvester Kirk) *s.i.s: hdwy 1/2-way: wknd wl over 1f out* **50/1**
03 **6** *2 3/4* **Brilliant Crystal**[51] 4702 2-8-12 0........................ AndrewElliott 2 13
(Mrs K Burke) *mid-div: sn pushed along: wknd 1/2-way* **28/1**
0 **7** *5* **Brian's Best**[72] 4012 2-9-0 0........................ MartinHarley(3) 5 —
(Bruce Hellier) *s.i.s: sn pushed along and a in rr: bhd whn rdn and hung rt over 1f out* **100/1**
8 *46* **Midnight Diva** 2-8-12 0........................ TomMcLaughlin 4 —
(Christopher Kellett) *s.s: outpcd: t.o* **100/1**

61.21 secs (-1.09) **Going Correction** -0.225s/f (Stan) **8** Ran SP% **114.4**
Speed ratings (Par 93): **99,89,88,81,74 69,61,—**
Tote Swingers:1&2:£1.30, 2&3:£2.50, 1&3:£1.90 CSF £2.88 TOTE £1.80: £1.10, £1.30, £1.50; EX 4.40 Trifecta £6.30 Pool £13,998.81 - 1,631.98 winning units.
Owner Albert Kwok **Bred** Genesis Green & Deerpark Stud **Trained** Epsom, Surrey

FOCUS
Not much depth to this maiden.

NOTEBOOK
Confucius Elite proved different class, powering clear in the straight having always been close to the pace. Whether the winner has had to improve on his second at Lingfield last month is debatable but he showed here that he has the speed for this shorter trip and the way he galloped clear in the final furlong suggests he'll be at least as effective back up to 6f in the future. He has routed a 72-rated runner-up, so is likely to get a mark somewhere around 80. (op 8-11)
Samba Night(IRE) disappointed at Warwick on his third start and although this was a little more encouraging, he is not going forward and this performance emphasised his vulnerability in maiden company. (tchd 7-2)
Regal Lady backed up the promise of her debut run without really building on it to any great extent. She looks worth a try at 6f. (op 5-1)
Majestic Breeze(IRE) ◆ has had her three qualifying runs now and looks one to be interested in when upped in trip in nurseries. (op 12-1)

6353 EILEEN ROSE GREEN 90TH BIRTHDAY CELEBRATION MAIDEN STKS 5f 216y(P)
6:50 (6:50) (Class 5) 3-Y-O **£2,070** (£616; £307; £153) **Stalls** Low

Form RPR
2-42 **1** **Question Times**[11] 6034 3-8-12 90........................ RobertHavlin 3 78+
(Peter Chapple-Hyam) *chsd ldr: led on bit over 1f out: shkn up: edgd rt and c clr fnl f: easily* **7/4**[1]
4202 **2** *4 1/2* **Arrivaderci**[52] 4680 3-8-12 65........................ MichaelStainton 8 64
(Richard Whitaker) *hld up: hdwy over 2f out: rdn to chse wnr ins fnl f: no imp* **5/1**
2 **3** *nk* **Cool Rhythm**[19] 5793 3-9-3 0........................ SilvestreDeSousa 6 68
(David O'Meara) *chsd ldrs: rdn over 3f out: styd on same pce fr over 1f out* **85/40**[2]
5- **4** *1 1/2* **State Senator (USA)**[348] 6811 3-9-3 0........................ StevieDonohoe 2 63
(Sir Mark Prescott Bt) *s.i.s: sn prom: rdn over 2f out: sn outpcd* **4/1**[3]
00- **5** *2* **Blueberry Fizz (IRE)**[318] 7385 3-8-12 0........................ KirstyMilczarek 7 52?
(John Ryan) *s.i.s: hdwy over 2f out: rdn and wknd over 1f out* **80/1**
00 **6** *nk* **Oosisit**[19] 5793 3-8-12 0........................ FrederikTylicki 1 51?
(Ruth Carr) *led over 4f: wknd fnl f* **50/1**

1m 13.86s (-1.14) **Going Correction** -0.225s/f (Stan) **6** Ran SP% **108.2**
Speed ratings (Par 101): **98,92,91,89,86 86**
Tote Swingers:1&2:£1.70, 2&3:£1.70, 1&3:£1.10 CSF £10.12 TOTE £2.70: £1.20, £2.90; EX 9.70 Trifecta £19.70 Pool £10,523.80 - 394.60 winning units.
Owner Allan Belshaw **Bred** Times Of Wigan Ltd **Trained** Newmarket, Suffolk

FOCUS
Again no depth to this maiden.
Oosisit Official explanation: jockey said filly hung right-handed

6354 GEOFF SAWARD RETIREMENT H'CAP 7f 32y(P)
7:20 (7:22) (Class 5) (0-70,73) 3-Y-0+ **£2,264** (£673; £336; £168) **Stalls** High

Form RPR
0420 **1** **Khajaaly (IRE)**[29] 5422 4-9-4 **70**........................ JimmyQuinn 5 79
(Julia Feilden) *hld up in tch: shkn up to ld wl ins fnl f: r.o* **8/1**[3]
0340 **2** *1/2* **Ishiadancer**[16] 5862 6-9-4 **70**........................ PatCosgrave 11 78
(Eric Alston) *chsd ldr tl led over 1f out: rdn: edgd lft and hdd wl ins fnl f* **9/1**
3011 **3** *nk* **Justbookie Dot Com (IRE)**[7] 6179 3-9-4 **73**........................(v) KierenFallon 7 80
(David Evans) *hld up: hdwy over 2f out: rdn over 1f out: r.o* **2/1**[1]
0260 **4** *nse* **Saharia (IRE)**[10] 6051 4-9-1 **67**........................(v) ShaneKelly 9 74
(Michael Attwater) *s.i.s: hld up: hdwy over 2f out: hung lft over 1f out: r.o ins fnl f: nt rch ldrs* **16/1**
520- **5** *2* **L'Astre De Choisir (IRE)**[345] 6870 3-8-12 **70**........................ JohnFahy(3) 1 71+
(Walter Swinburn) *hld up: plld hrd: shkn up over 1f out: r.o strly ins fnl f: nrst fin* **12/1**
1200 **6** *3/4* **Dhhamaan (IRE)**[20] 5760 6-9-3 **69**........................(b) PhillipMakin 12 68
(Ruth Carr) *led: rdn and hdd over 1f out: no ex fnl f* **22/1**
5115 **7** *3 1/4* **Glenridding**[15] 5879 7-9-4 **70**........................ FrederikTylicki 8 61
(James Given) *chsd ldrs: rdn over 2f out: wknd ins fnl f* **9/2**[2]
3050 **8** *2* **Copperwood**[17] 5835 6-9-4 **70**........................ LiamKeniry 3 55
(Michael Blanshard) *dwlt: hld up: rdn over 2f out: n.d* **12/1**
0001 **9** *nk* **Needwood Ridge**[47] 4866 4-9-3 **69**........................(bt) RobbieFitzpatrick 2 53
(Frank Sheridan) *hld up: rdn over 1f out: nvr on terms* **12/1**
6616 **10** *1/2* **Downhill Skier (IRE)**[15] 5881 7-8-11 **70**........................ JackDuern(7) 6 53
(Mark Brisbourne) *hld up: rdn 1/2-way: a in rr* **20/1**

0231 **11** *3 1/4* **Polemica (IRE)**[15] 5901 5-9-2 **68**........................(bt) JamesDoyle 4 42
(Frank Sheridan) *chsd ldrs tl wknd over 1f out: eased ins fnl f* **11/1**

1m 28.05s (-1.55) **Going Correction** -0.225s/f (Stan)
WFA 3 from 4yo+ 3lb **11** Ran SP% **119.0**
Speed ratings (Par 103): **99,98,98,98,95 94,91,88,88,87 84**
Tote Swingers:1&2:£7.30, 2&3:£7.00, 1&3:£3.90 CSF £79.01 CT £205.46 TOTE £11.10: £2.80, £3.50, £1.10; EX 110.20 Trifecta £338.80 Pool £3,548.60 - 7.75 winning units.
Owner Geegeez.co.uk **Bred** Barry Noonan And Denis Noonan **Trained** Exning, Suffolk

FOCUS
The pace looked reasonable for a fair handicap.
Copperwood Official explanation: jockey said gelding anticipated the start

6355 WILLIAMHILL.COM H'CAP 1m 141y(P)
7:50 (7:52) (Class 5) (0-75,78) 3-Y-0+ **£2,911** (£866; £432; £216) **Stalls** Low

Form RPR
5450 **1** **Count Bertoni (IRE)**[31] 5383 4-9-3 **68**....................(b) SilvestreDeSousa 10 77
(David O'Meara) *mde all: rdn over 1f out: hung rt ins fnl f: jst hld on* **5/1**[3]
1053 **2** *nk* **Key Breeze**[24] 5622 4-9-0 **65**....................(t) PhillipMakin 7 73+
(Kevin Ryan) *dwlt: hld up: hdwy u.p over 1f out: r.o wl: jst failed* **9/2**[2]
5620 **3** *1 1/4* **Carcinetto (IRE)**[2] 6285 9-9-0 **65**.................... KierenFallon 6 70
(David Evans) *sn chsng wnr: rdn over 1f out: styd on* **9/1**
0504 **4** *1* **Who's Shirl**[16] 5862 5-9-9 **74**.................... KellyHarrison 11 77
(Chris Fairhurst) *hld up: hdwy over 2f out: rdn over 1f out: styd on* **14/1**
063 **5** *1* **Eastern Gift**[8] 6138 6-8-11 **62**.................... RobertWinston 5 63
(Gay Kelleway) *hld up: hdwy over 1f out: r.o: nt rch ldrs* **9/1**
0000 **6** *3/4* **L'Hirondelle (IRE)**[36] 5240 7-9-10 **75**.................... ShaneKelly 4 74
(Michael Attwater) *prom: rdn over 2f out: styd on same pce ins fnl f* **16/1**
011 **7** *2 1/2* **Yensi**[5] 6226 4-9-13 **78** 6ex.................... PatCosgrave 3 71
(George Baker) *chsd ldrs: rdn to go 2nd 2f out: wknd ins fnl f* **9/4**[1]
0334 **8** *3/4* **Ilie Nastase (FR)**[82] 3677 7-8-11 **62**....................(b) KirstyMilczarek 12 53
(Conor Dore) *hld up: rdn over 2f out: n.d* **20/1**
6244 **9** *1/2* **Midnight Strider (IRE)**[168] 1250 5-8-13 **64**.................... MatthewDavies 1 54
(Joseph Tuite) *prom: rdn 1/2-way: wknd over 2f out* **33/1**
2554 **10** *7* **Gemma's Delight (IRE)**[14] 5924 4-8-12 **63**.................... WilliamCarson 8 37
(James Unett) *trckd ldrs: plld hrd: rdn and wknd over 2f out* **14/1**
3030 **11** *7* **Batgirl**[27] 5516 4-9-9 **74**.................... TomMcLaughlin 9 32
(John Berry) *s.s: a in rr* **33/1**

1m 47.87s (-2.63) **Going Correction** -0.225s/f (Stan) **11** Ran SP% **115.5**
Speed ratings (Par 103): **102,101,100,99,98 98,95,95,94,88 82**
Tote Swingers:1&2:£5.80, 2&3:£7.20, 1&3:£22.40 CSF £26.59 CT £193.94 TOTE £7.30: £2.60, £2.20, £1.20; EX 53.50 Trifecta £678.00 Pool £2,418.98 - 2.64 winning units.
Owner Equality Racing **Bred** Le Thenney S A **Trained** Nawton, N Yorks

FOCUS
A modest handicap.

6356 COOPER COATED COIL H'CAP 2m 119y(P)
8:20 (8:20) (Class 6) (0-65,65) 3-Y-0+ **£1,704** (£503; £251) **Stalls** Low

Form RPR
1-60 **1** **Resplendent Ace (IRE)**[36] 5249 7-9-9 **60**.................... JimmyQuinn 2 71
(Karen Tutty) *a.p: led 1f out: styd on wl* **20/1**
0461 **2** *4 1/2* **Ministry**[9] 6087 3-9-2 **65**.................... LukeMorris 9 71
(John Best) *hld up in tch: led over 4f out: rdn and hdd 1f out: styd on same pce* **11/8**[1]
2500 **3** *2* **Prickles**[2] 6287 6-8-8 **48**.................... RossAtkinson(3) 4 51
(Derek Shaw) *hld up: hdwy to chse ldr 3f out: rdn and hung lft fr over 1f out: styd on same pce* **20/1**
2540 **4** *1/2* **Simple Jim (FR)**[7] 6157 7-9-5 **56**.................... SilvestreDeSousa 1 59
(David O'Meara) *hld up: hdwy 1/2-way: outpcd over 2f out: styd on fr over 1f out* **7/2**[2]
4304 **5** *5* **Mountain Myst**[10] 6057 3-8-0 **49**.................... CathyGannon 6 46
(William Muir) *chsd ldrs: rdr dropped whip 7f out: chal 4f out: wknd wl over 1f out* **13/2**[3]
4000 **6** *1/2* **William's Way**[14] 5947 9-9-4 **60**....................(t) AntiocoMurgia(5) 5 56
(Ian Wood) *hld up: rdn over 2f out: nvr on terms* **22/1**
6200 **7** *hd* **Barbirolli**[7] 6182 9-8-10 **47**.................... WilliamCarson 7 43
(William Stone) *hld up: hdwy u.p over 2f out: wknd wl over 1f out* **14/1**
0400 **8** *19* **Himalayan Moon**[14] 5947 4-8-11 **48**.................... JamesDoyle 3 21
(Ian Wood) *chsd ldr tl led over 5f out: hdd over 4f out: wknd over 3f out: t.o* **25/1**
0003 **9** *24* **Dan Buoy (FR)**[9] 6095 8-8-13 **53**....................(b) RobertLButler(3) 8 —
(Richard Guest) *set stdy pce tl hdd over 5f out: wknd 4f out: t.o* **15/2**

3m 39.44s (-2.36) **Going Correction** -0.225s/f (Stan)
WFA 3 from 4yo+ 12lb **9** Ran SP% **113.8**
Speed ratings (Par 101): **96,93,92,92,90 90,90,81,69**
Tote Swingers:1&2:£7.90, 2&3:£12.30, 1&3:£55.50 CSF £45.40 CT £589.21 TOTE £18.20: £3.80, £1.20, £7.50; EX 53.30 Trifecta £211.30 Part won. Pool £285.65 - 0.75 winning units..
Owner N D Tutty **Bred** Newlands House Stud **Trained** Osmotherley, N Yorks

FOCUS
Just a steady gallop to this staying event and, furlong per furlong, the slowest time of the evening.
Mountain Myst Official explanation: jockey said she dropped whip passing winning post second circuit
Himalayan Moon Official explanation: vet said filly lost left-fore shoe

6357 MOBET.WILLIAMHILL.COM H'CAP (DIV I) 1m 1f 103y(P)
8:50 (8:50) (Class 6) (0-60,62) 3-Y-0+ **£1,363** (£402; £201) **Stalls** Low

Form RPR
0043 **1** **Painted Tail (IRE)**[15] 5900 4-9-10 **60**.................... PJMcDonald 6 72+
(Alan Swinbank) *a.p: chsd ldr over 2f out: led wl over 1f out: rdn out* **2/1**[1]
6320 **2** *1 1/2* **Dream Of Fortune (IRE)**[2] 6287 7-9-7 **57**....................(bt) KierenFallon 9 66
(David Evans) *hld up: hdwy over 2f out: chsd wnr over 1f out: rdn ins fnl f: styd on* **5/1**[3]
6041 **3** *shd* **Knowe Head (NZ)**[8] 6134 4-9-12 **62**.................... PatCosgrave 7 72+
(James Unett) *hld up: hdwy over 1f out: hung rt and r.o ins fnl f: nrst fin* **5/2**[2]
4503 **4** *1/2* **Warden Bond**[11] 6032 3-8-5 **46** oh1....................(p) CathyGannon 1 54
(William Stone) *chsd ldrs: rdn over 1f out: styd on same pce ins fnl f* **33/1**
3040 **5** *1 1/2* **Valley Tiger**[27] 5507 3-8-11 **57**.................... JamesRogers(5) 5 62
(William Muir) *s.i.s: hld up: nt clr run over 2f out: hdwy over 1f out: nt rch ldrs* **20/1**
154 **6** *4 1/2* **Cane Cat (IRE)**[32] 5356 4-9-10 **60**....................(t) LukeMorris 3 55
(Tony Carroll) *prom: rdn over 1f out: wknd ins fnl f* **14/1**
605 **7** *1 1/2* **Lunar River (FR)**[8] 6135 8-9-1 **51**....................(t) JamesDoyle 8 43
(David Pinder) *hld up: rdn over 3f out: wknd fnl f* **16/1**
0000 **8** *7* **Zartina (IRE)**[32] 5352 3-8-5 **46** oh1.................... SilvestreDeSousa 11 23
(Sylvester Kirk) *hld up: pushed along 4f out: n.d* **50/1**
6/0 **9** *2* **Le Reveur**[21] 5739 9-8-10 **46** oh1.................... KellyHarrison 2 19
(Richard Guest) *chsd ldr tl rdn over 2f out: wknd over 1f out* **100/1**
34 **10** *shd* **Arctic Cat (IRE)**[46] 4878 3-9-4 **59**.................... RobertWinston 4 32
(Mrs K Burke) *led: hdd wl over 1f out: wkng whn hmpd sn after* **10/1**
3442 **11** *3* **King Columbo (IRE)**[12] 5994 6-9-3 **56**....................(p) AdamBeschizza(3) 12 23
(Julia Feilden) *mid-div: hdwy over 3f out: sn rdn: wknd and eased over 1f out* **16/1**
0000 **12** *12* **King Of Connacht**[137] 1987 8-8-10 **46** oh1....................(b) LiamKeniry 10 —
(Mark Wellings) *s.i.s: hld up: a in rr: wknd over 2f out* **40/1**

1m 59.68s (-2.02) **Going Correction** -0.225s/f (Stan)
WFA 3 from 4yo+ 5lb **12** Ran SP% **119.2**
Speed ratings (Par 101): **99,97,97,97,95 91,90,84,82,82 79,69**
Tote Swingers:1&2:£2.90, 2&3:£2.30, 1&3:£2.20 CSF £11.85 CT £26.34 TOTE £4.20: £2.00, £1.80, £1.10; EX 12.10 Trifecta £53.60 Pool £228.26 - 3.15 winning units.
Owner Matthew Green **Bred** Rabbah Bloodstock Limited **Trained** Melsonby, N Yorks

FOCUS
A modest heat.
Knowe Head(NZ) Official explanation: jockey said saddle slipped on run to line
Arctic Cat(IRE) Official explanation: jockey said gelding had a breathing problem
King Columbo(IRE) Official explanation: jockey said gelding hung right throughout

6358 MOBET.WILLIAMHILL.COM H'CAP (DIV II) 1m 1f 103y(P)
9:20 (9:21) (Class 6) (0-60,61) 3-Y-0+ **£1,363** (£402; £201) **Stalls** Low

Form RPR
0003 **1** **Hill Tribe**[2] 6285 4-9-10 **60**.................... KierenFallon 4 72
(Richard Guest) *chsd ldr tl led over 2f out: rdn out* **4/1**[2]
03 **2** *3/4* **Wings Of Apollo (IRE)**[40] 5116 3-8-6 **50**.................... MartinHarley(3) 5 60
(Mrs K Burke) *trckd ldrs: racd keenly: rdn to chse wnr over 1f out: r.o* **9/2**[3]
4006 **3** *7* **So Is She (IRE)**[24] 5631 3-8-12 **56**....................(b) DominicFox(3) 10 52
(Alan Bailey) *s.s: hld up: hdwy over 3f out: rdn over 2f out: styd on same pce: wnt 3rd nr fin* **11/1**
2304 **4** *3/4* **Jaldarshaan (IRE)**[7] 6158 4-9-2 **57**.................... LanceBetts(5) 11 51
(Colin Teague) *led: clr 6f out: rdn and hdd over 2f out: wknd fnl f: lost 3rd nr fin* **8/1**
0644 **5** *2 3/4* **Prince Of Thebes (IRE)**[23] 5643 10-8-13 **54**.................... MarkCoumbe(5) 12 42
(Michael Attwater) *s.s: hld up: rdn over 3f out: n.d* **16/1**
3320 **6** *3 1/2* **Syncopated Lady (IRE)**[17] 5822 3-8-12 **53**..........(e) SilvestreDeSousa 3 34
(David O'Meara) *plld hrd and prom: rdn over 3f out: wknd over 2f out* **13/2**
066 **7** *3/4* **Broughtons Fawn**[236] 368 3-8-5 **46** oh1.................... JamieMackay 6 25
(Willie Musson) *hld up: rdn over 1f out: n.d* **18/1**
00 **8** *3/4* **Money Note**[10] 6071 3-9-2 **57**.................... StevieDonohoe 9 35
(Tobias B P Coles) *hld up: rdn over 3f out: n.d* **18/1**
2342 **9** *3 3/4* **Indian Violet (IRE)**[22] 5667 5-9-11 **61**.................... JamieGoldstein 7 31
(Ralph Smith) *hld up in tch: rdn over 2f out: wknd over 1f out* **7/2**[1]
0002 **10** *47* **Look For Love**[10] 6049 3-8-0 **48**.................... JackDuern(7) 2 —
(Reg Hollinshead) *plld hrd and prom: sddle slipped sn after s: lost pl over 5f out: sn t.o* **14/1**

1m 59.41s (-2.29) **Going Correction** -0.225s/f (Stan)
WFA 3 from 4yo+ 5lb **10** Ran SP% **116.3**
Speed ratings (Par 101): **101,100,94,93,91 87,87,86,83,41**
Tote Swingers:1&2:£4.80, 2&3:£4.30, 1&3:£26.90 CSF £22.34 CT £183.38 TOTE £3.50: £1.20, £2.10, £3.50; EX 24.60 Trifecta £204.10 Part won. Pool £275.90 - 0.80 winning units..
Owner EERC & Alison Ibbotson **Bred** The Kingwood Partnership **Trained** Stainforth, S Yorks

FOCUS
They went a good gallop.
Look For Love Official explanation: jockey said saddle slipped
T/Plt: £33.60 to a £1 stake. Pool £62,981.45 - 1,368.03 winning tickets T/Qpdt: £37.40 to a £1 stake. Pool £6,000.31 - 118.70 winning tickets CR

6359 - 6361a (Foreign Racing) - See Raceform Interactive

4933 GOWRAN PARK (R-H)
Saturday, September 24

OFFICIAL GOING: Good (good to firm in places)

6362a DENNY CORDELL LAVARACK & LANWADES STUD FILLIES STKS (GROUP 3) 1m 1f 100y
3:30 (3:32) 3-Y-0+ **£39,224** (£11,465; £5,431; £1,810)

RPR
1 **Flowers Of Spring (IRE)**[13] 5976 4-9-3 97....................(b[1]) CDHayes 7 105
(Andrew Oliver, Ire) *sn towards rr: wd and hdwy st: rdn to ld under 2f out: styd on wl fnl f: reduced ld nr fin* **11/2**[2]
2 *3/4* **Zaminast**[139] 1928 3-8-12 .... PJSmullen 8 103+
(D K Weld, Ire) *sn towards rr: wd and hdwy st: rdn into 3rd 1f out: styd on wl fnl f: nt quite get to wnr* **13/2**[3]
3 *2* **Hurricane Havoc (IRE)**[21] 5748 3-8-12 100....................(bt) KJManning 5 99
(J S Bolger, Ire) *sn led: rdn over 2f out: hdd under 2f out: remained cl up: kpt on same pce and dropped to 3rd clsng stages* **14/1**
4 *2* **Look At Me (IRE)**[13] 5976 3-8-12 105.................... SeamieHeffernan 2 95
(A P O'Brien, Ire) *sn trckd ldrs: 3rd fr over 2f out: no imp and kpt on same pce fr over 1f out* **9/4**[1]
5 *1 3/4* **Malayan Mist (IRE)**[21] 5743 3-8-12 92....................(b) PShanahan 10 91
(D K Weld, Ire) *mid-div: 6th bef 1/2-way: struggling fr under 2f out: sn no imp and kpt on same pce fr over 1f out* **16/1**
6 *3 1/2* **Handassa**[125] 2334 3-8-12 102....................(b) DPMcDonogh 9 84
(Kevin Prendergast, Ire) *sn mid-div: 8th bef 1/2-way: stuggling fr under 2f out: sn no imp and kpt on same pce* **15/2**
7 *2* **Babycakes (IRE)**[42] 5075 4-9-3 .... JPO'Brien 11 80
(Michael Bell) *sn prom: pushed along in 2nd appr st: no imp fr under 2f out* **7/1**
8 *1/2* **Enchanted Evening (IRE)**[13] 5978 5-9-3 88....................(b) LFRoche 3 79
(D K Weld, Ire) *chsd ldrs: 5th bef 1/2-way: no imp fr under 2f out* **33/1**
9 *1* **Blaze Brightly (IRE)**[27] 5523 4-9-3 101.................... FMBerry 1 77
(Mrs John Harrington, Ire) *sn mid-div: 7th bef 1/2-way: no imp fr under 2f out* **12/1**
10 *1 1/2* **Negotiate**[45] 4936 3-8-12 99....................(b[1]) BACurtis 4 74
(Andrew Oliver, Ire) *prom: pushed along bef st: sn no imp* **16/1**
11 *4 3/4* **Puttore (IRE)**[29] 5459 3-8-12 94.................... WJSupple 6 64
(Kevin Prendergast, Ire) *towards rr for most: no imp fr 2f out* **10/1**
12 *5* **Sapphire Pendant (IRE)**[32] 5361 3-8-12 96....................(b) WMLordan 12 54
(David Wachman, Ire) *mid-div best: no imp st* **16/1**

1m 58.93s (-8.07)
WFA 3 from 4yo+ 5lb **12** Ran SP% **127.8**
CSF £44.74 TOTE £8.20: £2.40, £2.00, £6.60; DF 50.70.
Owner Peter Jones **Bred** Peter Jones and GG Jones **Trained** Caledon, Co Tyrone

The Form Book, Raceform Ltd, Compton, RG20 6NL

FOCUS
The front-running third has been rated to her C&D mark.
NOTEBOOK
Flowers Of Spring(IRE), winner of three handicaps and a conditions race, had finished fourth in the Group 2 Blandford Stakes 13 days previously on her first venture into Pattern company. With first-time blinkers replacing cheekpieces here, she showed her adaptability in terms of ground - this was the fastest on which she has won - to win well. Held up in rear, she made rapid headway turning for home where she swung wide and, after hitting the front 2f out, she was always doing enough for pressure, despite idling, to prevail. (op 10/1)
Zaminast ◆, winner of a maiden which her trainer always targets with a smart filly at last year's Galway festival on her only juvenile start, had not run since finishing fifth in a Group 3 event at Leopardstown early in the season. Like the winner, she was held up at the back of the field before beginning her effort on the outside into the straight. She sustained her run all the way to the line but the winner had first run on her. The ground was probably plenty quick enough for her and an opportunity should be found for this half-sister to multiple Pattern winner Famous Name before the end of the season. (op 5/1)
Hurricane Havoc(IRE) had run poorly in a 1m4f handicap on her previous start but back to a more suitable trip she reached the first three in a Group race for the first time. Soon in front, she was headed 2f out but kept to her task quite well. (op 14/1 tchd 16/1)
Look At Me(IRE) had finished four and a half lengths in front of Flowers Of Spring when third in the Blandford Stakes and led the market on the strength of that effort and a couple of placed efforts at this level of competition. Soon close up on the inside, she tracked the leaders into the straight but was unable to raise her game sufficiently to mount a serious challenge. It was difficult to see any obvious excuse for her. (op 11/4 tchd 3/1)
Malayan Mist(IRE), whose two wins include a maiden over this course and trip, was contesting her first Group race. She performed creditably without being able to get into serious contention. (op 16/1 tchd 20/1)

6363 - 6368a & 6371a (Foreign Racing) - See Raceform Interactive

6202 SAN SIRO (R-H)
Saturday, September 24

OFFICIAL GOING: Turf: good

6369a PREMIO VITTORIO DI CAPUA (GROUP 1) (3YO+) (TURF) 1m
3:15 (12:00) 3-Y-0+ £116,379 (£51,206; £27,931; £13,965)

RPR
1 **Dick Turpin (IRE)**[40] 5129 4-9-2 0........................ ChristopheSoumillon 2 122
(Richard Hannon) *w.w in 5th: shkn up ent fnl 2f: 4th and hrd rdn on outside over 1f out: r.o strly ins fnl f to ld fnl strides* **13/20**[1]
2 *shd* **Cityscape**[13] 5977 5-9-2 0........................ SteveDrowne 6 122
(Roger Charlton) *trckd ldr in share of 2nd w Vanjura: shkn up and qcknd to ld ins fnl 2f: 2 l clr ent fnl f: r.o u.p: ct fnl strides* **67/20**[2]
3 *1 3/4* **Vanjura (GER)**[21] 5753 4-8-13 0........................ APietsch 5 115
(R Dzubasz, Germany) *trckd ldr in share of 2nd: rdn and nt qckn appr fnl f: kpt on at one pce* **109/20**
4 *snk* **Fanunalter**[44] 4972 5-9-2 0........................ MircoDemuro 1 118
(Marco Botti) *dwlt and racd in rr: tk clsr order on rail over 3f out: no gap and swtchd outside over 1 1/2f out: styd on u.p fnl f: jst failed to grab 2nd* **15/4**[3]
5 *4* **Shamalgan (FR)**[23] 5664 4-9-2 0........................ FilipMinarik 7 108
(A Savujev, Czech Republic) *led: hdd ins fnl 2f: rdn and wknd fnl f* **195/10**
6 *4* **Silver Ocean (USA)**[6] 6201 3-8-11 0........................ NicolaPinna 3 98
(Riccardo Santini, Italy) *a bhd: rdn and wknd fnl 2f* **57/1**
7 *12* **Ransom Hope**[118] 2541 6-9-2 0........................ CristianDemuro 4 72
(L Riccardi, Italy) *racd 4th on outside: rdn and nt qckn over 2f out: grad wknd fnl 1 1/2f* **33/1**

1m 33.2s (-8.90)
WFA 3 from 4yo+ 4lb 7 Ran SP% **129.7**
WIN (incl. 1 euro stake): 1.64. PLACES: 1.16, 1.18. DF: 2.64.
Owner John Manley **Bred** John McEnery **Trained** East Everleigh, Wilts
FOCUS
The form is rated around the third.
NOTEBOOK
Dick Turpin(IRE) produced a strong late charge to snatch victory from his fellow British raider in the final stride. Soumillon was happy to wait in the middle of the pack before producing a late surge. He's still in the QEII but much depends on how he comes out of this race, and ground conditions will also determine his next target.
Cityscape settled in the leader's slipstream before being asked to quicken with just over 2f to run. He still had two lengths to spare over his nearest pursuer at the furlong marker but was run down late by his compatriot. He can gain compensation given ease in the ground.
Vanjura(GER) was never far away and kept on well to just hold on to third.
Fanunalter was held up after a tardy start and might have finished third had he enjoyed a clear run when he was looking to challenge approaching the final furlong.

6370a PREMIO SERGIO CUMANI (GROUP 3) (3YO+ FILLIES & MARES) (TURF) 1m
3:50 (12:00) 3-Y-0+ £34,482 (£15,172; £8,275; £4,137)

RPR
1 **Khor Sheed**[57] 4497 3-8-9 0........................ MircoDemuro 2 108+
(Luca Cumani) *settled in 4th: smooth prog to join ldrs over 2f: qcknd to ld ins fnl 2f: pushed clr last f: eased fnl 30yds: impressive* **7/10**[1]
2 *2 1/2* **Malagenia (IRE)**[97] 3213 3-8-9 0........................ CristianDemuro 5 101
(L Riccardi, Italy) *racd keenly towards rr: 6th and outpcd 2f out: r.o u.p fnl f: wnt 2nd cl home: no ch w wnr* **125/10**
3 *nse* **Adamantina**[118] 2539 3-8-9 0........................ UmbertoRispoli 3 101
(Vittorio Caruso, Italy) *chsd ldrs: 4th and ev ch appr fnl 1 1/2f: sn rdn and nt qckn* **26/5**[3]
4 *snk* **Crystal Gal (IRE)**[49] 4790 4-9-0 0........................ SteveDrowne 8 102
(Lucy Wadham) *trckd ldr: 2nd and shkn up 2f out: nt qckn w wnr: kpt on at one pce fnl f* **57/20**[2]
5 *1/2* **Prakasa (FR)**[34] 4-9-0 0........................ FilipMinarik 7 101
(Markus Klug, Germany) *racd in midfield: hdwy on ins to jnd ldrs over 2f out: sn rdn: one pce fnl f: fdd fnl 50yds* **217/10**
6 *2 1/2* **Omkara**[90] 3449 3-8-9 0........................ NicolaPinna 6 94
(E Borromeo, Italy) *a towards rr: outpcd over 2 1/2f out: sme hdwy u.p 1 1/2f out: rdn and nt qckn fnl f* **144/10**
7 *2 1/2* **Amazing Beauty (GER)**[21] 4-9-0 0........................ EFrank 1 89
(M Figge, Germany) *broke wl: sn settled towards rr: last and rdn over 2f out: no imp* **10/1**
8 *1/2* **Quissisana (IRE)**[314] 4-9-0 0........................ NMurru 4 88
(S Ribarszki, Hungary) *led: hdd ins fnl 2f: sn wknd: eased fnl 100yds* **191/10**

1m 35.3s (-6.80)
WFA 3 from 4yo 4lb 8 Ran SP% **133.3**
WIN (incl. 1 euro stake): 1.69. PLACES: 1.17, 2.30, 1.80. DF: 7.22.
Owner Sheikh Mohammed Obaid Al Maktoum **Bred** Card Bloodstock **Trained** Newmarket, Suffolk
NOTEBOOK
Khor Sheed outclassed her seven opponents to give her trainer a win in the race run in memory of his father Sergio, who was champion trainer in Italy on ten occasions. Settled in the middle of the small field, once her rider decided to send the filly to the front inside the final quarter-mile, there was only going to be one result. She was nudged clear in the last furlong and was allowed to coast home in the closing stages.

5854 EPSOM (L-H)
Sunday, September 25

OFFICIAL GOING: Good (8.2)
Wind: fresh, across Weather: dry, breezy

6372 ABBOT ALE NURSERY 7f
2:00 (2:01) (Class 4) (0-85,85) 2-Y-0 £5,175 (£1,540; £769; £384) Stalls Low

Form RPR
611 1 **Producer**[26] 5577 2-9-4 82........................ RichardHughes 4 88+
(Richard Hannon) *led for 1f: pressed ldr after tl shkn up to ld over 1f out: in command and pushed out fnl f: comf* **1/1**[1]
3301 2 *1 1/4* **Tidy Affair (IRE)**[17] 5855 2-9-3 81........................ NeilCallan 3 83
(Richard Hannon) *chsd ldrs: rdn and effrt ent fnl 2f: edgd lft u.p over 1f out: chsd wnr ent fnl f: styd on same pce fnl f* **15/2**[3]
5116 3 *nk* **Pride And Joy (IRE)**[15] 5931 2-9-7 85........................ FergusSweeney 7 86
(Jamie Osborne) *hld up in tch: hdwy and swtchd rt 3f out: chsd ldng pair 1f out: kpt on but no imp on wnr fnl f* **5/1**[2]
0316 4 *2* **Maroosh**[29] 5478 2-8-11 75........................ ShaneKelly 8 71
(Brian Meehan) *hld up in tch: effrt on outer 3f out: hdwy and edging lft over 1f out: kpt on steadily fnl f: nvr gng pce to threaten ldrs* **10/1**
010 5 *3 1/4* **Golden Valley**[50] 4803 2-8-6 70........................ AndreaAtzeni 1 57
(Rod Millman) *led after 1f: rdn ent fnl 2f: hdd over 1f out: wknd fnl f* **14/1**
0663 6 *1 3/4* **Tigers Tale (IRE)**[14] 5967 2-7-9 62 oh3........................(v) KieranO'Neill[(3)] 9 45
(Roger Teal) *sn outpcd in last: modest hdwy past btn horses over 1f out: n.d* **16/1**
650 7 *7* **Always Eager**[22] 5697 2-8-4 68........................ SilvestreDeSousa 5 33
(Mark Johnston) *chsd ldrs: rdn and struggling over 2f out: wknd 2f out: wl btn and eased wl ins fnl f* **25/1**
365 8 *2* **Esprit Danseur**[19] 5814 2-8-4 68........................ NickyMackay 6 27
(Jim Boyle) *chsd ldrs: pushed along over 4f out: wknd over 2f out: wl bhd and eased ins fnl f* **40/1**
4604 9 *1 1/4* **Whinging Willie (IRE)**[38] 5197 2-8-10 74........................(v) JamesDoyle 2 30
(Gary Moore) *chsd ldrs: rdn and struggling over 3f out: wknd and bhd 2f out: no ch and eased wl ins fnl f* **12/1**

1m 23.82s (0.52) **Going Correction** +0.075s/f (Good) 9 Ran SP% **114.0**
Speed ratings (Par 97): **100,98,98,95,92 90,82,79,78**
Tote Swingers: 1&2 £2.60, 1&3 £2.20, 2&3 £3.90 CSF £8.90 CT £26.48 TOTE £2.00: £1.10, £2.20, £1.50; EX 6.40 Trifecta £22.50 Pool: £858.31 - 28.11 winning units..
Owner J Palmer-Brown **Bred** Cheveley Park Stud Ltd **Trained** East Everleigh, Wilts
FOCUS
Good ground and a stiff, drying breeze. A reasonable nursery run at an ordinary gallop. It proved difficult to get involved from the rear.
NOTEBOOK
Producer was completing an Epsom hat-trick. The son of leading first-season sire Dutch Art was raised 10lb for his latest win in a Class 5 nursery, but that was insufficient to stop him and, never out of the first two, he did the job fairly comfortably. All three victories have come over 7f on ground officially described as good. (op 5-6 tchd 11-10)
Tidy Affair(IRE) closed into second but wandered on the camber and never quite proved able to challenge his stablemate. There had been market support for him ahead of this nursery debut. (op 9-1 tchd 13-2)
Pride And Joy(IRE) improved from the rear down the outside but appeared to be hanging in under pressure. He just looks held by the handicapper at present.
Maroosh was eased 2lb after his run at Newmarket. Racing keenly again near the back, he made late progress without threatening the placed horses.
Golden Valley was in a more suitable class after finishing last in a Newmarket Group 3. This cheap buy made the running, but could not fend off the winner and weakened out of the frame in the final furlong. (op 10-1)
Tigers Tale(IRE) was never involved from 3lb out of the weights, but finished clear of the remainder. (op 20-1)

6373 GREENE KING IPA CONDITIONS STKS 1m 114y
2:30 (2:30) (Class 3) 2-Y-0 £6,225 (£1,864; £932; £466) Stalls Low

Form RPR
1342 1 **Mister Music**[24] 5654 2-8-11 92........................ RichardHughes 4 83+
(Richard Hannon) *stdd after s: t.k.h: dropped in bhd after 1f: gd hdwy to chse ldr 3f out: carried lft and swtchd rt over 2f out: rdn and hdwy to ld 1f out: sn clr: kpt on wl* **10/11**[1]
03 2 *2 1/4* **Hint Of Mint**[32] 5375 2-8-11 0........................ LiamKeniry 3 78
(Andrew Balding) *chsd ldr tl 3f out: sn outpcd and dropped to last: styd on fnl f to go 2nd fnl 75ds: no threat to wnr* **16/1**
43 3 *1 1/4* **Surrey Storm**[9] 6117 2-8-3 0........................ KieranO'Neill[(3)] 1 71
(Roger Teal) *chsd ldrs: rdn and unable qck 3f out: outpcd 2f out: plugged on same pce after* **6/1**[3]
661 4 *1 3/4* **Gabrial's Gift (IRE)**[32] 5382 2-8-11 84........................ JamieSpencer 5 72
(David Simcock) *led: edgd lft 3f out: clr 2f out: sn hung rt and rdn: hdd 1f out: immediately btn: fdd ins fnl f* **15/8**[2]

1m 46.65s (0.55) **Going Correction** +0.075s/f (Good) 4 Ran SP% **107.3**
Speed ratings (Par 99): **100,98,96,95**
CSF £12.87 TOTE £1.70; EX 8.90.
Owner Longview Stud & Bloodstock Ltd **Bred** Longview Stud & Bloodstock Ltd **Trained** East Everleigh, Wilts
FOCUS
A decent standard for this conditions race, and even though there were only four runners that is twice as many as there were last year. They didn't go a great pace. None of the field looked comfortable on the track's cambers, especially as they were being buffeted by a gusty wind.
NOTEBOOK
Mister Music, runner-up at Salisbury to beaten Royal Lodge favourite Farhaan, is officially rated 92 and was 8lb clear on these terms. Held up last of the four, he burst through into second entering the straight but had to be switched off the rail before a clear passage opened up for him. Despite not looking at home on the track he came clear to win very comfortably, value for further. He may step up to 1m2f for Newmarket's Zetland Stakes next month. (op Evens)
Hint Of Mint, third to the very useful Cavaleiro on his second start, did not appear entirely at ease on the track's undulations but was staying on at the end. He is flattered to have finished as close as he did to the winner. (op 11-1)
Surrey Storm is only small but, like her dam, is a tough filly. The first of these off the bridle, she stuck to her guns and was rewarded with third as the pacesetter fell away. (op 8-1 tchd 11-2)

Gabrial's Gift(IRE), an easy Kempton winner, made the running, his rider steadying the pace at halfway. The colt edged away from the camber under pressure, and finished so weakly that he ended up last. He has yet to really prove himself on turf. Jamie Spencer reported his mount hung right, and the stewards ordered the colt to be routine tested. Official explanation: jockey said colt hung right (op 6-4 tchd 2-1)

6374 TOTEEXACTA H'CAP — 1m 114y

3:00 (3:01) (Class 3) (0-90,88) 3-Y-O — £7,762 (£2,310; £1,154; £577) Stalls Low

Form — RPR

4021 **1** **Sure Route**[16] 5892 3-9-7 **88** .... RichardHughes 4 — 97+
(Richard Hannon) *stdd after s and t.k.h early: hld up in tch: trckd ldrs 3f out: squeezed between horses and ld over 1f out: styd on wl fnl f: rdn out* **7/2**[2]

0501 **2** ¾ **Yojimbo (IRE)**[17] 5856 3-8-9 **76** .... MatthewDavies 7 — 83
(Mick Channon) *sn pressed ldr: rdn and ev ch 2f out: edgd lft and led wl over 1f out: sn hdd: styd on one pce u.p fnl f* **7/1**[3]

0103 **3** 1 ¼ **Our Gal**[22] 5702 3-8-10 **77** .... MartinLane 3 — 81
(Noel Quinlan) *stdd s: hld up in last pair: clsd over 3f out: rdn and chsd ldng pair over 1f out: kpt on same pce and no imp fnl f* **16/1**

1 **4** 1 ¼ **Dubawi Sound**[162] 1409 3-9-7 **88** .... NeilCallan 2 — 94+
(Roger Varian) *stdd s: t.k.h and hld up in last: gng for run up inner in st: nt clr run and swtchd rt 2f out: stl nt clr run tl jst over 1f out: chsd ldrs and edgd lft ins fnl f: eased towards fin* **11/10**[1]

5510 **5** 1 ¾ **Orientalist**[16] 5892 3-8-9 **76** .... SilvestreDeSousa 5 — 73
(Eve Johnson Houghton) *in tch in last trio but sn niggled along: outpcd u.p 3f out: plugged on fnl f but no threat to ldrs* **8/1**

5246 **6** ½ **Tasfeya**[87] 3538 3-8-12 **79** .... KierenFallon 6 — 75
(John Akehurst) *t.k.h: hld up in tch: rdn and effrt over 2f out: outpcd wl over 1f out: styd on same pce and no threat to ldrs after* **20/1**

1000 **7** 1 **Norse Blues**[15] 5936 3-9-5 **86** .... JamesDoyle 1 — 80
(Sylvester Kirk) *led: rdn ent fnl 2f: hdd wl over 1f out: sn short of room and hmpd: wknd ent fnl f* **11/1**

1m 45.44s (-0.66) **Going Correction** +0.075s/f (Good) — **7** Ran SP% **112.4**
Speed ratings (Par 105): **105,104,103,102,100 100,99**
Tote Swingers: 1&2 £3.20, 1&3 £5.70, 2&3 £8.40 CSF £26.71 CT £338.97 TOTE £4.40: £2.10, £2.70; EX 17.50 Trifecta £82.10 Pool: £760.31 - 6.85 winning units..
Owner Malih Lahej Al Basti **Bred** Malih L Al Basti **Trained** East Everleigh, Wilts

FOCUS
A fair handicap but a messy race.

NOTEBOOK
Sure Route's Sandown win was given a boost when third home Arabian Star won the Silver Cambridgeshire at Newmarket on Friday, and a 6lb rise looked lenient. This progressive filly squeezed through between the two leaders to take it up and was never in much danger thereafter. She may still have further improvement in her. (op 3-1)
Yojimbo(IRE) was always towards the fore and briefly edged in front, but could not repel the winner inside the last. This was a solid run off 5lb higher than when winning over C&D earlier in the month. (op 8-1)
Our Gal has not proved entirely consistent but this was a sound run to follow a creditable effort at Ascot last time. She gets the mile well enough. (op 14-1)
Dubawi Sound won a decent Newbury maiden on his sole previous start back in April. Sidelined by a setback since, he has also changed ownership. Held up, he attempted to improve up the inner in the straight but lost momentum when the gap was shut and had to switch. He lacked the pace to get to the leaders from there, the course's gradients not helping, but is well worth another chance. However he had moved to post keenly and was reluctant to go in the stalls, so he may not be entirely straightforward. (tchd 6-5)
Orientalist, a winner at this venue two runs back, was behind Sure Route at Sandown last time and it was a similar story here after he came under pressure early in the straight. (op 9-1 tchd 10-1)
Tasfeya, sold out of Mark Johnston's yard for 30,000gns since his last appearance in June, made late progress after losing his pitch. This is not his track and he may do better with the run under his belt. (tchd 16-1)
Norse Blues has struggled since a wide-margin win here on Oaks day. Going off in front again, he had just been headed when he was hampered against the fence. He has yet to prove he stays a mile. (op 16-1)

6375 TOTESWINGER H'CAP — 1m 2f 18y

3:35 (3:37) (Class 3) (0-95,94) 3-Y-O+

£9,337 (£2,796; £1,398; £699; £349; £175) Stalls Low

Form — RPR

22-0 **1** **Con Artist (IRE)**[134] 2105 4-9-9 **93** .... KierenFallon 3 — 103
(Saeed Bin Suroor) *led: pushed along and qcknd 3f out: drvn 2f out: hdd narrowly 1f out: kpt on wl to ld again fnl 75yds: outbattled runner-up* **11/2**[3]

2103 **2** ½ **Romeo Montague**[14] 5971 3-8-4 **80** ....(v) SilvestreDeSousa 4 — 89
(Ed Dunlop) *s.i.s: hld up in tch in last pair: pushed along and hdwy over 3f out: chal over 1f out: led 1f out: hung lft u.p ins fnl f: hdd and nt qckn fnl 75yds* **9/1**

510 **3** 4 ½ **Silver Grey (IRE)**[46] 4915 4-8-11 **84** ....(p) JohnFahy(3) 7 — 84
(Roger Ingram) *t.k.h: chsd ldr for 1f: chsd ldrs after: drvn and effrt over 2f out: chsd wnr 2f out tl over 1f out: wknd ins fnl f: eased towards fin* **12/1**

2431 **4** 2 **Ramona Chase**[14] 5968 6-8-10 **85** ....(t) MarkCoumbe(5) 6 — 81
(Michael Attwater) *s.i.s: hld up in last pair: rdn and outpcd over 2f out: sme hdwy u.p over 1f out: wnt modest 4th ins fnl f: nvr threatened ldrs* **13/2**

1-64 **5** 2 ¾ **Roman Eagle (IRE)**[52] 4718 3-9-2 **92** .... NeilCallan 5 — 83
(Roger Varian) *t.k.h: chsd ldr after 1f tl 2f out: drvn and wknd over 1f out* **7/2**[1]

0061 **6** 3 ½ **Colour Scheme (IRE)**[11] 6068 4-9-3 **87** ....(t) ShaneKelly 2 — 71
(Brian Meehan) *t.k.h: hld up in tch in midfield: rdn and outpcd 3f out: wknd 2f out* **7/2**[1]

2400 **7** 4 **Right Step**[37] 5250 4-9-10 **94** .... JamieSpencer 8 — 70
(Alan Jarvis) *hld up in tch in last trio: rdn and outpcd 3f out: wl btn after* **9/2**[2]

6/0 **8** 23 **Lastofthemohicans (FR)**[45] 4962 4-9-0 **84** .... RichardHughes 1 — 14
(Paul Webber) *chsd ldrs: rdn over 3f out: sn struggling: wknd over 2f out: wl bhd and virtually p.u fnl f: t.o* **28/1**

2m 9.57s (-0.13) **Going Correction** +0.075s/f (Good)
WFA 3 from 4yo+ 6lb — **8** Ran SP% **112.5**
Speed ratings (Par 107): **103,102,99,97,95 92,89,70**
Tote Swingers: 1&2 £5.80, 1&3 £7.90, 2&3 £12.20 CSF £51.44 CT £563.55 TOTE £4.50: £2.00, £2.20, £3.70; EX 40.60 Trifecta £576.10 Pool: £1,004.33 - 1.29 winning units..
Owner Godolphin **Bred** Airlie Stud **Trained** Newmarket, Suffolk

FOCUS
A decent handicap in which the winner set his own pace.

NOTEBOOK
Con Artist(IRE) had not run since finishing tailed off on his reappearance back in May. He was a little keen early, but soon settled for Fallon and dictated the gallop. He was briefly headed by the runner-up, but fought his way back past a less than doughty opponent. There are no concrete plans, but he is a likeable performer with more in his locker. (op 5-1)
Romeo Montague improved up the inside and the race looked his for the taking, but he hung into the rail and just would not go past. He is well capable of adding to his tally but things will have to fall exactly right for him. A decent gallop at this shorter trip may suit. (op 11-1)
Silver Grey(IRE) had her chance but was 6lb higher than when winning at Sandown and would probably prefer a bit of ease in the ground. (op 10-1)
Ramona Chase was having his eighth run of the season at Epsom and has proved commendably consistent, but the 5lb rise for his last-gasp Goodwood win took him to his highest mark for more than two years. He could only make late progress for a well-held fourth. (op 11-2)
Roman Eagle(IRE) won a two-runner race in heavy ground at the equivalent meeting a year ago. He had looked worth a try over this longer trip, but in the event it appeared as if he didn't stay. Roger Varian reported to the stewards that he didn't get home. Official explanation: trainer said colt failed to stay (op 4-1 tchd 10-3)
Colour Scheme(IRE) won well at Yarmouth and a 5lb rise looked fair, but he is a big colt and he was not seen to best effect on this track. He is well regarded and should not be written off. Shane Kelly reported his mount was never travelling. Official explanation: jockey said colt never travelled (tchd 10-3 and 4-1)
Right Step was 3lb lower than when second here at the Derby meeting, but always trailed. (op 6-1)
Lastofthemohicans(FR) Official explanation: jockey said gelding lost its action

6376 MAY FAMILY APPRENTICES' DERBY H'CAP — 1m 4f 10y

4:10 (4:13) (Class 4) (0-80,87) 3-Y-O+ — £5,175 (£1,540; £769; £384) Stalls Centre

Form — RPR

0215 **1** **Gunslinger (FR)**[37] 4719 6-9-4 **77** .... DavidKenny(5) 6 — 88
(Michael Scudamore) *s.i.s: hld up in last pair: gd hdwy on outer 3f out: hanging lft and chsd ldr over 1f out: led 1f out: kpt on wl fnl 100yds* **25/1**

0111 **2** 1 ¾ **Shesha Bear**[17] 5857 6-9-5 **73** ....(p) HarryBentley 13 — 81
(Jonathan Portman) *hld up in last trio: hdwy over 4f out: chsd ldrs and rdn 3f out: pushed lft jst over 2f out: chsd ldr 2f out tl swtchd rt over 1f out: ev ch 1f out: no ex and one pce fnl 100yds* **4/1**[2]

0311 **3** 2 ¾ **The Bells O Peover**[3] 6279 3-9-6 **87** 6ex........(b) DarylByrne(5) 10 — 91+
(Mark Johnston) *in tch: hdwy to chse ldr over 7f out: led 5f out and sn clr: rdn over 1f out: hdd 1f out: looked btn whn pushed lft and hit rail jst ins fnl f: wknd fnl 100yds* **7/4**[1]

426 **4** 1 ¾ **Super Duplex**[38] 5200 4-8-12 **66** .... KierenFox 15 — 67
(Pat Phelan) *stdd s: hld up in last trio: hdwy on outer 4f out: chsd ldr and hung lft over 2f out tl 2f out: outpcd and btn over 1f out: styd on same pce after* **20/1**

4113 **5** 1 ½ **Memory Lane**[60] 4449 3-8-13 **78** .... RosieJessop(3) 3 — 76+
(Sir Mark Prescott Bt) *chsd ldrs: in tch: rdn and lost pl over 3f out: bhd and no ch w ldrs 2f out: switching rt after: rallied and styd on strly fnl f* **8/1**[3]

6103 **6** hd **Soundbyte**[23] 5692 6-8-13 **67** .... JohnFahy 11 — 65
(John Gallagher) *sn bustled along to chse ldr tl over 9f out: in tch after tl lost pl 4f out: wl btn and switching rt 2f out: rallied and r.o wl fnl f: no ch w ldrs* **28/1**

224 **7** 5 **Epsom Salts**[17] 5857 6-8-11 **68** ....(p) MatthewCosham(3) 5 — 58
(Pat Phelan) *in tch in midfield: pushed along and lost pl 8f out: bhd and swtchd rt 3f out: sme hdwy but no ch w ldrs 2f out: no prog after* **8/1**[3]

8 ½ **Winning Spark (USA)**[115] 4-9-7 **75** .... RossAtkinson 2 — 64
(Gary Moore) *t.k.h: hld up towards rr: effrt on inner but no imp on ldrs wl over 2f out: wl btn over 1f out* **50/1**

1255 **9** 3 ¼ **Choral Festival**[14] 5968 5-9-2 **70** .... MatthewDavies 4 — 54
(John Bridger) *in tch in midfield: rdn and no imp 3f out: no ch fnl 2f* **25/1**

6520 **10** 1 **Beat Route**[26] 5580 4-8-12 **66** oh2........ RyanClark 8 — 48
(Michael Attwater) *in tch: rdn and nt qckning whn short of room and hmpd ent fnl 3f: sn wknd* **22/1**

14 **11** 6 **Dubai Glory**[8] 6172 3-8-11 **80** .... MartinLeonard(7) 7 — 53
(Sheena West) *chsd ldrs: wnt 2nd over 9f out tl over 7f out: chsd clr ldr again 4f out tl over 2f out: sn wknd* **17/2**

0-00 **12** 24 **Missionaire (USA)**[158] 1477 4-9-7 **80** .... GeorgeDowning(5) 12 — 14
(Tony Carroll) *led tl 5f out: dropped out qckly over out: wl bhd fnl 2f: t.o* **66/1**

2m 40.28s (1.38) **Going Correction** +0.075s/f (Good)
WFA 3 from 4yo+ 8lb — **12** Ran SP% **112.8**
Speed ratings (Par 105): **98,96,95,93,92 92,89,89,86,86 82,66**
Tote Swingers: 1&2 £17.70, 1&3 £13.50, 2&3 £2.00 CSF £110.56 CT £272.13 TOTE £25.20: £6.40, £1.50, £1.30; EX 246.30 Trifecta £591.80 Part won. Pool: £799.84 - 0.10 winning units..
Owner S M Smith & Keith Hunter **Bred** Dayton Investments Ltd **Trained** Bromsash, Herefordshire

FOCUS
A competitive handicap on paper, although in the event a group of four pulled clear. They went a respectable gallop and the form seems sound enough.
Epsom Salts Official explanation: jockey said gelding was slowly away
Beat Route Official explanation: jockey said gelding suffered interference in running

6377 OLD SPECKLED HEN MAIDEN STKS — 1m 2f 18y

4:45 (4:50) (Class 5) 3-Y-O — £2,587 (£770; £384; £192) Stalls Low

Form — RPR

3 **1** **Sandbanks Sizzler (IRE)**[121] 2469 3-9-3 0........ JimCrowley 1 — 93+
(Ralph Beckett) *dwlt: hld up in tch: pushed along and hdwy over 3f out: led over 2f out: rdn clr 2f out: wl clr and in n.d over 1f out: easily* **15/8**[1]

2 14 **Astragal** 3-8-12 0........ JimmyFortune 4 — 60
(Andrew Balding) *chsd ldrs: effrt on inner and ev ch over 2f out: outpcd by wnr 2f out and wl btn after* **12/1**

42-5 **3** 1 **The Mongoose**[34] 5327 3-9-3 73........ NeilCallan 2 — 63
(Sir Michael Stoute) *chsd ldrs: rdn and effrt to chal 3f out: led over 2f out: sn hdd and outpcd by wnr: wl btn after* **10/3**[2]

04 **4** 4 ½ **Perilously (USA)**[34] 5317 3-8-12 0........ RichardHughes 6 — 49+
(Jeremy Noseda) *chsd ldrs after: stdd bk into midfield but wl in tch after 2f: rdn 4f out: outpcd and wl btn over 2f out* **8/1**[3]

00 **5** 2 ½ **Fascinating (IRE)**[95] 3267 3-9-3 0........ SilvestreDeSousa 5 — 49
(Mark Johnston) *hld up in last pair: outpcd over 3f out: no ch but plugged on past btn horses over 1f out: n.d* **28/1**

0 **6** 8 **Russian Storm**[10] 6085 3-8-12 0........ IanMongan 9 — 28
(Pat Phelan) *t.k.h: hdwy to chse ldr over 7f out: rdn and ev ch 3f out: wknd qckly ent fnl 2f: wl bhd whn hung lft over 1f out: eased ins fnl f* **100/1**

4406 **7** 1 ¾ **High Samana**[20] 5784 3-9-3 67........(b) GeorgeBaker 7 — 30
(Ralph Beckett) *dwlt: sn in tch on outer: rdn and struggling over 3f out: wknd qckly over 2f out: wl bhd and eased ins fnl f: t.o* **16/1**

52 **8** *11* **Grand Theft Equine**[19] 5816 3-9-3 0......................... MatthewDavies 10 —
(Jim Boyle) *led tl over 2f out: sn wknd and hung lft: wl bhd and eased ins fnl f: t.o* **10/1**

6 **9** *39* **Just Gillian**[37] 5247 3-8-12 0.......................... WilliamCarson 8 —
(Peter Hiatt) *s.i.s: in tch in last pair: rdn and struggling over 5f out: lost tch over 3f out: t.o and virtually p.u fnl 2f* **200/1**

2m 9.83s (0.13) **Going Correction** +0.075s/f (Good) 9 Ran SP% **96.6**
Speed ratings (Par 101): **102,90,90,86,84 78,76,67,36**
Tote Swingers: 1&2 £4.50, 1&3 £1.40, 2&3 £6.70 CSF £17.43 TOTE £2.90: £1.20, £3.10, £1.50; EX 16.30 Trifecta £53.80 Pool: £509.57 - 7.00 winning units..
Owner I J Heseltine **Bred** Norelands Bloodstock **Trained** Kimpton, Hants

FOCUS
Just a fair maiden on paper, weakened by the withdrawal at the start of Montefeltro, but it produced a wide-margin winner. They went a decent pace and the time was creditable.\n
Perilously(USA) Official explanation: jockey said filly hung right

6378 TOTEPOOL EPSOM TRAINERS CHAMPIONSHIP FINALE H'CAP 7f
5:15 (5:17) (Class 4) (0-85,83) 3-Y-0+ **£5,175** (£1,540; £769; £384) **Stalls** Low

Form RPR

2422 **1** **Valencha**[14] 5970 4-9-6 **82**.. RichardHughes 7 92+
(Hughie Morrison) *t.k.h: hld up in tch: hdwy to trck ldrs and nt clr run 2f out: pushed along to chal 1f out: led and rdn ins fnl f: r.o wl* **15/8**[1]

6603 **2** *1/2* **My Learned Friend (IRE)**[57] 4546 7-8-10 **72**................. DavidProbert 2 80
(Andrew Balding) *pressed ldrs: rdn and ev ch 2f out: drvn to ld 1f out: hdd ins fnl f: r.o but a hld after* **22/1**

3162 **3** *1 1/4* **Rondeau (GR)**[34] 5322 6-9-7 **83**....................................... GeorgeBaker 12 87
(Patrick Chamings) *hld up towards rr: rdn and effrt on outer over 2f out: hdwy over 1f out: kpt on wl to go 3rd wl ins fnl f* **12/1**

0422 **4** *1/2* **Flameoftheforest (IRE)**[12] 6022 4-8-13 **75**...............(p) PatCosgrave 15 78
(Ed de Giles) *hld up in last quartet: rdn and hdwy ent fnl 2f: styng on whn nt clr run and swtchd rt jst over 1f out: r.o wl ins fnl f: nt rch ldrs* **11/1**

2535 **5** *nk* **Russian Rave**[24] 5657 5-9-4 **80**.. StephenCraine 1 82
(Jonathan Portman) *w ldr: rdn to ld 3f out: hrd pressed and drvn 2f out: hdd 1f out: no ex btn ins fnl f: wknd towards fin* **12/1**

3154 **6** *1/2* **Frozen Over**[79] 3801 3-8-2 **70**.. JohnFahy(3) 6 71+
(Stuart Kittow) *s.i.s: wl bhd and detached in last: rdn and stl plenty to do whn hung rt u.p over 1f out: r.o v strly fnl f: nt rch ldrs* **20/1**

2030 **7** *1 1/4* **Major Conquest (IRE)**[56] 4574 3-9-1 **80**................. SilvestreDeSousa 4 77
(J W Hills) *chsd ldrs: rdn and hdwy over 3f out: drvn and ev ch 2f out: no ex and btn ins fnl f: wknd fnl 100yds* **16/1**

5455 **8** *hd* **Rough Rock (IRE)**[11] 6069 6-8-9 **74**................................. RyanClark(3) 14 71
(Chris Dwyer) *towards rr: rdn and effrt on outer over 3f out: kpt on ins fnl f: nvr gng pce to rch ldrs* **20/1**

10-0 **9** *1 3/4* **Avertis**[45] 4958 6-8-12 **77**...(tp) HarryBentley(3) 10 69
(Alastair Lidderdale) *led tl 3f out: wknd u.p over 1f out* **25/1**

2024 **10** *2 1/2* **Another Try (IRE)**[26] 5578 6-9-6 **82**................................... KierenFallon 5 67
(Alan Jarvis) *t.k.h: in tch in midfield: rdn and effrt over 1f out: drvn and no prog 2f out: wknd fnl f* **9/1**[2]

5516 **11** *1 1/2* **Layla Jamil (IRE)**[10] 6094 3-8-12 **77**............................ MatthewDavies 9 58
(Mick Channon) *in tch in midfield: rdn and effrt over 2f out: hanging lft and no imp over 1f out: wknd fnl f* **20/1**

2304 **12** *3 1/4* **Dukes Art**[22] 5718 5-9-4 **80**.. NeilCallan 8 53
(James Toller) *towards rr: rdn and hdwy on inner 3f out: no prog 2f out: wknd fnl f* **12/1**

5003 **13** *4* **Salient**[16] 5894 7-8-6 **73**.. MarkCoumbe(5) 13 35
(Michael Attwater) *a outpcd in last quartet: rdn and no prog over 2f out: n.d* **16/1**

0023 **14** *2 1/2* **Big Noise**[58] 4509 7-9-7 **83**..(v) TedDurcan 11 38
(Dr Jon Scargill) *s.i.s: a bhd: no ch whn hung lft and swtchd rt wl over 1f out* **10/1**[3]

401 **15** *6* **Kakapuka**[15] 5948 4-9-5 **81**.. IanMongan 3 20
(Anabel K Murphy) *chsd ldrs tl over 3f out: sn struggling and wknd 2f out: eased ins fnl f* **18/1**

1m 24.03s (0.73) **Going Correction** +0.075s/f (Good)
WFA 3 from 4yo+ 3lb 15 Ran SP% **124.8**
Speed ratings (Par 105): **98,97,96,95,95 94,93,92,90,88 86,82,78,75,68**
Tote Swingers: 1&2 £17.50, 1&3 £6.40, 2&3 £51.40 CSF £56.60 CT £434.58 TOTE £2.60: £1.30, £6.50, £3.10; EX 68.10 Trifecta £623.10 Pool: £926.25 - 1.10 winning units..
Owner Pangfield Partners **Bred** T J Billington **Trained** East Ilsley, Berks

FOCUS
A competitive handicap run at a strong gallop, and the form should prove sound.
T/Plt: £30.40 to a £1 stake. Pool: £83,009.00 - 1,988.76 winning tickets. T/Qpdt: £15.30 to a £1 stake. Pool: £5,629.00 - 271.85 winning tickets. SP

6006 MUSSELBURGH (R-H)
Sunday, September 25

OFFICIAL GOING: Straight course - good (good to firm in places; 6.5); round course - good to firm (good in places; 6.9)
Wind: Fresh across Weather: Bright and sunny

6379 RACING UK CLASSIFIED (S) STKS 1m 4f 100y
2:15 (2:15) (Class 6) 3-Y-0+ **£1,811** (£539; £269; £134) **Stalls** Low

Form RPR

0022 **1** **Record Breaker (IRE)**[9] 6121 7-9-10 67.........................(b) JoeFanning 7 71
(Mark Johnston) *midfield: rdn and hdwy over 2f out: rdn to ld over 1f out: kpt on to go clr ins fnl f* **7/2**[2]

0-20 **2** *4* **Croix Rouge (USA)**[23] 5692 9-9-4 57............................. PaulHanagan 2 59
(Ralph Smith) *trckd ldrs: rdn to chal over 2f out: kpt on one pce: no ch w wnr ins fnl f* **7/1**

1042 **3** *1/2* **Valantino Oyster (IRE)**[5] 6229 4-9-10 62..................(p) PatrickMathers 8 64
(Tracy Waggott) *w ldr on outer: reminders over 9f out: led over 6f out: strly pressed over 2f out: hdd over 1f out: kpt on one pce* **9/1**

6435 **4** *4* **Ajdaad (USA)**[12] 6017 4-9-4 65.. RobertWinston 6 52
(Alan McCabe) *awkwardly away: hld up: hdwy to chse ldrs 2f out: sn drvn and one pce: no ex ins fnl f* **9/2**[3]

0553 **5** *2 3/4* **Frontline Phantom (IRE)**[6] 6225 4-9-7 68................... MartinHarley(3) 4 54
(Mrs K Burke) *midfield: hdwy to chse ldrs over 2f out: wknd over 1f out* **10/3**[1]

0520 **6** *7* **Stags Leap (IRE)**[3] 5723 4-8-13 63..........................(v) GarryWhillans(5) 3 37
(Alistair Whillans) *trckd ldrs: chal over 2f out: sn rdn and wknd* **10/3**[1]

-500 **7** *8* **Mystified (IRE)**[118] 1473 8-8-11 49..............................(t) JustinNewman(7) 1 25
(Alan Berry) *led narrowly: hdd over 6f out: rdn over 3f out: sn wknd* **100/1**

060 **8** *15* **Dimashq**[5] 6236 9-9-10 46..(p) RussKennemore 5 —
(Paul Midgley) *s.i.s: hld up: a towards rr* **40/1**

2m 39.66s (-2.34) **Going Correction** -0.125s/f (Firm) 8 Ran SP% **112.5**
Speed ratings (Par 101): **102,99,99,96,94 89,84,74**
Tote Swingers: 1&2 £4.80, 1&3 £3.80, 2&3 £7.20 CSF £27.08 TOTE £3.80: £1.20, £3.00, £2.40; EX 23.50.No bid for the winner.
Owner Triplin Racing **Bred** Sir E J Loder **Trained** Middleham Moor, N Yorks

FOCUS
This seller was run at a routine sort of pace.

6380 EUROPEAN BREEDERS' FUND / FERRULE MAIDEN STKS 7f 30y
2:45 (2:45) (Class 5) 2-Y-O **£2,911** (£866; £432; £216) **Stalls** Low

Form RPR

40 **1** **Ptolemaic**[79] 3826 2-9-3 0..(v[1]) TomEaves 1 80
(Bryan Smart) *led: drvn whn hdd over 1f out: rallied to ld again jst ins fnl f: kpt on wl* **11/1**

3333 **2** *2 1/4* **Serene Oasis (IRE)**[9] 6110 2-8-12 71.............................. FrannyNorton 3 69
(Mick Channon) *racd keenly in 3rd: rdn over 2f out: kpt on: wnt 2nd towards fin* **9/4**[3]

42 **3** *1 3/4* **Idler (IRE)**[10] 6099 2-9-3 0.. JoeFanning 5 69
(Mark Johnston) *trckd ldr in 2nd: rdn over 2f out: led narrowly over 1f out: hdd jst ins fnl f: wknd: lost 2nd towards fin* **2/1**[2]

20 **4** *28* **Shevington**[17] 5849 2-9-3 0.. PaulHanagan 4 —
(Richard Fahey) *s.i.s: hld up: rdn over 3f out: sn btn: eased ins fnl f* **15/8**[1]

1m 28.52s (-0.48) **Going Correction** -0.125s/f (Firm) 4 Ran SP% **107.2**
Speed ratings (Par 95): **97,94,92,60**
CSF £33.85 TOTE £14.60; EX 34.90.
Owner Mrs F Denniff **Bred** Mrs Fiona Denniff **Trained** Hambleton, N Yorks

FOCUS
A modest maiden.

NOTEBOOK
Ptolemaic was equipped with a first-time visor and made it third-time lucky with a gutsy effort on this return from a 79-day absence. He flopped when last seen at York, but had run promisingly on his debut before that and, while looking quirky, clearly has a fair engine. He will get another furlong no bother, but much depends on the headgear continuing to have the desired effect and also what mark the handicapper now hands him. (op 9-1 tchd 12-1)
Serene Oasis(IRE) came into this having finished third on her four previous outings and it looked likely for a lot of the home straight as though she was booked for that position once more. She did her best work late on - looking ready for a return to 1m - and sets the standard. (op 2-1 tchd 5-2)
Idler(IRE) showed much-improved form when second over 6f at Yarmouth ten days earlier and it appeared 2f out as though he was going to go one better. It looked a case of stamina deserting him over this extra furlong, something his breeding would back up, but there's a chance also the race came soon enough. Nurseries are now an option. (tchd 9-4)
Shevington, up again in trip, never looked happy off the pace and found nil once asked to close at the top of the home straight. He now has it to prove. Official explanation: trainer's rep said colt was unsuited by the good to firm (good in places) ground (op 9-4 tchd 7-4)

6381 JAMES BIRTLEY RETIREMENT H'CAP (DIV I) 7f 30y
3:20 (3:20) (Class 4) (0-80,79) 3-Y-0+ **£4,204** (£1,251; £625; £312) **Stalls** Low

Form RPR

0562 **1** **Fishforcompliments**[10] 6081 7-9-1 73.........................(p) PaulHanagan 2 83
(Richard Fahey) *hld up: pushed along over 4f out: gd hdwy on inner over 1f out: led ins fnl f: kpt on* **7/2**[1]

3211 **2** *1/2* **Kingswinford (IRE)**[79] 3805 5-9-4 79............................. PaulPickard(3) 3 88
(Brian Ellison) *trckd ldr: rdn to chal over 1f out: kpt on: hld towards fin* **5/1**[2]

2250 **3** *1 1/4* **Music Festival (USA)**[10] 6098 4-8-7 65............................ LeeNewman 1 70
(Jim Goldie) *midfield: rdn and hdwy 2f out: led over 1f out: hdd ins fnl f: no ex* **8/1**

610 **4** *1 3/4* **Chookie Royale**[34] 5314 3-8-13 74....................................... JoeFanning 4 75
(Keith Dalgleish) *midfield: rdn over 3f out: kpt on fnl f: wnt 4th fnl 100yds* **22/1**

0600 **5** *2* **Cara's Request (AUS)**[9] 6113 6-9-3 75......................... AdrianNicholls 5 70
(David Nicholls) *led: rdn over 2f out: edgd lft 2f out: hdd over 1f out: wknd ins fnl f* **13/2**

365 **6** *hd* **Summer Dancer (IRE)**[5] 6231 7-8-13 71.................. RussKennemore 9 66
(Paul Midgley) *racd keenly: trckd ldr: rdn to chal over 2f out: wknd ins fnl f* **11/2**[3]

2222 **7** *1 1/4* **Vizean (IRE)**[46] 4925 3-8-3 69.. JulieBurke(5) 7 60
(John Mackie) *midfield: rdn over 2f out: no imp* **8/1**

0640 **8** *1/2* **Malcheek (IRE)**[88] 3506 9-9-5 77.. DavidAllan 10 67
(Tim Easterby) *trckd ldrs on outer: rdn over 2f out: wknd over 1f out* **8/1**

0200 **9** *shd* **Mujaadel (USA)**[23] 5684 6-9-4 76..................................(p) AndrewMullen 6 66
(David Nicholls) *hld up: rdn over 2f out: nvr threatend* **20/1**

6401 **10** *1/2* **No Quarter (IRE)**[8] 6158 4-8-7 65 oh2............................. PatrickMathers 8 53
(Tracy Waggott) *hld up: a towards rr* **14/1**

1m 27.8s (-1.20) **Going Correction** -0.125s/f (Firm)
WFA 3 from 4yo+ 3lb 10 Ran SP% **116.7**
Speed ratings (Par 105): **101,100,99,97,94 94,93,92,92,91**
Tote Swingers: 1&2 £2.40, 1&3 £3.40, 2&3 £8.80 CSF £20.62 CT £119.33 TOTE £3.10: £1.70, £1.70, £2.60; EX 16.70.
Owner R A Fahey **Bred** Dunchurch Lodge Stud Co **Trained** Musley Bank, N Yorks

FOCUS
A modest handicap with a competitive look about it. There was a sound pace on and plenty were in with chances in the final 2f. The form looks fair.

6382 JAMES BIRTLEY RETIREMENT H'CAP (DIV II) 7f 30y
3:55 (3:56) (Class 4) (0-80,79) 3-Y-0+ **£4,204** (£1,251; £625; £312) **Stalls** Low

Form RPR

0412 **1** **Imperator Augustus (IRE)**[22] 5722 3-8-13 74........... DanielTudhope 1 93+
(Patrick Holmes) *in tch: smooth hdwy to ld over 2f out: pushed clr: eased towards fin: comf* **11/4**[1]

1316 **2** *5* **Boy The Bell**[11] 6044 4-8-10 71.. DaleSwift(3) 2 73
(Brian Ellison) *trckd ldr: rdn to chal over 2f out: kpt on but no ch w wnr fr over 1f out* **5/1**[3]

2000 **3** *1/2* **Cornus**[8] 6174 9-9-2 77..(be) MartinHarley(3) 3 78
(Alan McCabe) *trckd ldr: rdn over 2f out: kpt on* **12/1**

3126 **4** *3* **Rutterkin (USA)**[17] 5859 3-8-4 65 oh1............................. PaulHanagan 6 58
(Alan Berry) *midfield: rdn over 2f out: kpt on one pce* **18/1**

1461 **5** *1/2* **Toby Tyler**[24] 5647 5-9-3 75...(v) PJMcDonald 7 66
(Paul Midgley) *hld up: rdn over 2f out: kpt on one pce: nvr trbld ldrs* **8/1**

0000 **6** *1 3/4* **Adaria**[22] 5735 3-8-7 66..(p) TomEaves 9 54
(David C Griffiths) *prom on outer: rdn over 2f out: wknd over 1f out* **25/1**

2200 **7** *4* **North Central (USA)**[10] 6081 4-8-6 69.....................(p) ShaneBKelly(5) 4 45
(Jim Goldie) *midfield: rdn over 2f out: sn wknd* **18/1**

5263 **8** *3 ½* **Nufoudh (IRE)**[58] 4503 7-8-9 **67** .... PatrickMathers 8 33
(Tracy Waggott) *restless in stall: led: rdn whn hdd over 2f out: sn wknd* **9/2**[2]

6130 **9** *1 ¾* **Jarrow (IRE)**[23] 5683 4-9-4 **79** .... MichaelO'Connell(3) 10 41
(David Nicholls) *hld up: rdn over 3f out: a towards rr* **15/2**

6400 **10** *8* **Fieldgunner Kirkup (GER)**[8] 6167 3-9-2 **77** ....(b[1]) LeeNewman 5 17
(David Barron) *s.i.s: sn pushed along in rr: wnt rt and hit rail twice over 2f out: eased after* **11/1**

1m 27.68s (-1.32) **Going Correction** -0.125s/f (Firm)
WFA 3 from 4yo+ 3lb **10** Ran SP% **114.8**
Speed ratings (Par 105): **102,96,95,92,91 89,85,81,79,70**
Tote Swingers: 1&2 £14.30, 2&3 £7.00 CSF £15.86 CT £128.43 TOTE £2.70: £1.10, £1.70, £3.90; EX 20.70.
Owner Foulrice Park Racing Limited **Bred** Western Bloodstock **Trained** Brandsby, N. Yorks

FOCUS
The second division of the 7f handicap was another open-looking affair.
Jarrow(IRE) Official explanation: jockey said gelding ran flat
Fieldgunner Kirkup(GER) Official explanation: jockey said gelding hung badly right in straight

6383 BRITISH STALLION STUDS SUPPORTING BRITISH RACING E B F FILLIES' H'CAP 1m

4:30 (4:32) (Class 3) (0-90,86) 3-Y-O+
£7,470 (£2,236; £1,118; £559; £279; £140) **Stalls** Low

Form RPR

3003 **1** **Metropolitain Miss (IRE)**[11] 6062 3-9-6 **84** .... FrannyNorton 2 92+
(Mick Channon) *racd keenly: trckd ldr: rdn to chal over 2f out: kpt on: led fnl 75yds* **4/1**[1]

510 **2** *½* **Neutrafa (IRE)**[11] 6062 3-8-6 **75** .... JulieBurke(5) 1 82
(John Mackie) *hld up in midfield: rdn and hdwy over 1f out: kpt on strly ins fnl f: wnt 2nd nr fin* **16/1**

0045 **3** *½* **Blue Moon**[6] 6219 4-9-0 **77** .... AmyRyan(3) 11 83
(Kevin Ryan) *led: rdn over 2f out: hdd fnl 75yds: no ex: lost 2nd cl home* **12/1**

2504 **4** *½* **No Poppy (IRE)**[18] 5820 3-9-2 **80** .... DavidAllan 10 84+
(Tim Easterby) *hld up: rdn and hdwy on outer over 2f out: chsd ldrs over 1f out: kpt on fnl f* **18/1**

1220 **5** *3 ¼* **Epernay**[26] 5593 4-8-8 **71** ....(vt) MichaelO'Connell(3) 9 68
(Ian Williams) *trckd ldr: rdn to chal over 2f out: wknd ins fnl f* **7/1**[3]

1 **6** *5* **Dubai Bay (FR)**[9] 6137 3-8-9 **73** .... RussKennemore 8 58
(Paul Midgley) *racd keenly: midfield on outer: rdn over 2f out: sn no imp* **12/1**

3561 **7** *1 ¾* **Imaginary World (IRE)**[10] 6093 3-9-0 **78** ....(be) RobertWinston 3 59
(Alan McCabe) *s.i.s: hld up: pushed along over 3f out: nvr threatened* **9/2**[2]

4230 **8** *2 ¼* **Cairncross (IRE)**[17] 5856 3-8-8 **72** .... JoeFanning 6 48
(Mark Johnston) *midfield: rdn over 2f out: wknd over 1f out* **9/1**

1230 **9** *½* **Izzy The Ozzy (IRE)**[22] 5730 3-9-1 **79** .... LeeNewman 4 54
(David Barron) *in tch: pushed along over 3f out: wknd over 1f out* **10/1**

120 **10** *nk* **Climaxfortackle (IRE)**[10] 6093 3-8-4 **68** ....(v) PatrickMathers 7 42
(Derek Shaw) *dwlt: hld up: pushed along over 3f out: a towards rr* **33/1**

103 **11** *13* **Deity**[106] 2926 3-9-8 **86** .... PaulHanagan 5 30
(Jeremy Noseda) *midfield: pushed along over 3f out: sn lost pl and wknd: eased* **4/1**[1]

1m 38.65s (-2.55) **Going Correction** -0.125s/f (Firm) course record
WFA 3 from 4yo 4lb **11** Ran SP% **119.2**
Speed ratings (Par 104): **107,106,106,105,102 97,95,93,92,92 79**
Tote Swingers: 1&2 £14.30, 1&3 £13.70, 2&3 £34.10 CSF £70.36 CT £730.10 TOTE £4.50: £1.40, £5.00, £5.20; EX 51.60.
Owner Saeed Misleh **Bred** Rabbah Bloodstock Limited **Trained** West Ilsley, Berks

FOCUS
A fair fillies' handicap in which all bar two of the runners were 3yos. There was no hanging about in the early part of the race and the first four finished in a heap.

NOTEBOOK
Metropolitain Miss(IRE) gained reward for some largely consistent efforts on turf since winning on her debut at Kempton in April. She met trouble at Sandown when third last time out and, 2lb higher here, this was a deserved win. Another rise will make things tougher, but she could well improve further as a 4yo next year. (op 11-2 tchd 6-1 in a place)
Neutrafa(IRE) ◆ fared best of the hold-up horses and finished an awful lot closer to the winner than had been the case at Sandown last time out. It was just her fourth career outing and her turn looks to be nearing again. (op 20-1)
Blue Moon did plenty in getting across to lead from her wide draw and set a brisk pace. She kept on surprisingly well for third and this was a solid effort six days after finishing fifth at Kempton. (op 11-1 tchd 10-1)
No Poppy(IRE) came under the pump a fair way out, but kept responding and wasn't beaten far. This proves her stamina for the trip, indeed she looked to need every yard of it, but she does find winning hard. (op 14-1)
Epernay bounced back from her Ripon flop last month and will be suited by getting more cut underfoot again. (op 10-1)
Dubai Bay(FR) Official explanation: jockey said filly hung left in straight
Deity put in a lifeless effort, and something was clearly amiss with her on this first run since June. Official explanation: trainer's rep had no explanation for the poor form shown (op 9-2)

6384 ROYAL SCOTS NURSERY 5f

5:00 (5:00) (Class 6) (0-65,65) 2-Y-O **£1,811** (£539; £269; £134) **Stalls** High

Form RPR

0036 **1** **Wake Up Sioux (IRE)**[22] 5737 2-8-11 **55** .... AdrianNicholls 10 57
(David C Griffiths) *racd keenly: trckd ldrs: rdn 2f out: short of room over 1f out: sn swtchd rt: kpt on: led post* **16/1**

5500 **2** *nse* **Busy Bimbo (IRE)**[8] 6169 2-8-9 **58** .... JulieBurke(5) 4 60
(Alan Berry) *w ldr: rdn to ld over 1f out: kpt on: hdd post* **8/1**

0064 **3** *hd* **Headstight (IRE)**[11] 6043 2-8-3 **50** .... DeclanCannon(3) 11 51
(Paul Midgley) *trckd ldrs: rdn over 1f out: kpt on ins fnl f: jst failed* **6/1**[2]

3310 **4** *¾* **Phoenix Clubs (IRE)**[6] 6222 2-9-7 **65** .... BarryMcHugh 6 66
(Paul Midgley) *hld up: pushed along over 2f out: hdwy over 1f out: kpt on fnl f: nrst fin* **7/1**

4055 **5** *½* **Valley Of Hope**[11] 6043 2-9-2 **60** .... PaulHanagan 5 57
(Richard Fahey) *midfield on outer: rdn and hdwy 2f out: ev ch appr fnl f: no ex fnl 100yds* **3/1**[1]

1645 **6** *3 ¾* **Triggerlo**[5] 6237 2-9-2 **60** .... FrannyNorton 2 44
(Mick Channon) *chsd ldrs on outer: rdn 2f out: bmpd appr fnl f: nt rcvr* **13/2**[3]

300 **7** *½* **Yearbook**[6] 6222 2-9-1 **59** .... DavidAllan 7 40
(Tim Easterby) *led narrowly: rdn whn hdd over 1f out: wknd ins fnl f* **14/1**

0042 **8** *nk* **Liebesziel**[8] 6178 2-9-3 **64** ....(p) MartinHarley(3) 12 44
(Alan McCabe) *w ldr: rdn over 2f out: wknd ins fnl f* **9/1**

6004 **9** *1 ¾* **Rhianna Brianna (IRE)**[45] 4940 2-8-11 **55** ....(t) JamesSullivan 9 29
(Michael Easterby) *midfield: rdn over 2f out: wknd over 1f out* **40/1**

0040 **10** *4* **Doyouknowwhoiam**[39] 5161 2-9-0 **58** ....(p) TomEaves 8 18
(Bryan Smart) *hld up: rdn 3f out: a towards rr* **7/1**

0054 **11** *½* **Burnwynd Spirit (IRE)**[30] 5431 2-8-9 **55** ow1 .... DaleSwift(3) 3 14
(Ian Semple) *slowly away: early reminder and veered bdly rt: sn wl bhd: swvd rt again over 1f out: mod late hdwy* **25/1**

59.77 secs (-0.63) **Going Correction** -0.225s/f (Firm) **11** Ran SP% **117.6**
Speed ratings (Par 93): **96,95,95,94,93 87,86,86,83,77 76**
CSF £138.30 CT £882.00 TOTE £19.30: £3.50, £3.30, £2.30; EX 216.00.
Owner D Clarke, R P B Michaelson, D Griffiths **Bred** Floors Farming **Trained** Bawtry, S Yorks
■ Stewards' Enquiry : Adrian Nicholls three-day ban: careless riding (Oct 9-11)

FOCUS
A moderate nursery. The first five were closely covered and finished clear.

NOTEBOOK
Wake Up Sioux(IRE) overcame trouble in running and got on top right on the line to shed her maiden tag at the sixth time of asking. She got no run around the furlong marker, but barged her way out (hampered two rivals) and was forced in front where it mattered. She's progressive, but this looks her sort of level. (op 14-1 tchd 12-1)
Busy Bimbo(IRE) ◆ had not shown all that much previously, but this was a drop in class and she met support. She looked to have done enough near the finish, but was nabbed at the death. There is surely one of these within her compass. (op 10-1)
Headstight(IRE) had a much better draw this time and posted his best effort to date under a positive ride. (op 13-2)
Phoenix Clubs(IRE) didn't get the best of runs and is a bit better than the bare form. This proved his Leicester flop over 6f last week to be all wrong.
Valley Of Hope had her chance and ran close to her last-time-out form with the third, but wasn't helped by having to race widest of all. (op 4-1)
Rhianna Brianna(IRE) Official explanation: trainer's rep said filly bled from the nose

6385 ROYAL SCOTS CLUB H'CAP 1m 6f

5:30 (5:30) (Class 4) (0-80,79) 3-Y-O+ **£4,528** (£1,347; £673; £336) **Stalls** Low

Form RPR

1610 **1** **Miss Ferney**[3] 6287 7-8-10 **61** .... PaulPickard(3) 4 69
(Alan Kirtley) *hld up in tch: smooth hdwy over 2f out: led wl over 1f out: sn rdn: edgd rt ins fnl f: hld on all out* **11/2**

2161 **2** *shd* **Jeu De Vivre (IRE)**[7] 6191 3-9-7 **79** 6ex .... JoeFanning 5 87+
(Mark Johnston) *trckd ldr: rdn to chal 2f out: kpt on fnl f: jst failed* **5/4**[1]

0150 **3** *3 ¼* **Chookie Hamilton**[8] 6151 7-10-0 **76** .... PaulHanagan 1 79
(Keith Dalgleish) *trckd ldr: rdn over 2f out: kpt on one pce* **11/4**[2]

0660 **4** *3* **Grand Diamond (IRE)**[22] 5723 7-8-12 **60** .... DanielTudhope 2 59
(Jim Goldie) *hld up in tch: rdn over 2f out: sn no imp* **14/1**

11-5 **5** *1 ½* **Lady Bluesky**[136] 2034 8-9-0 **67** .... GarryWhillans(5) 3 64
(Alistair Whillans) *led: rdn whn hdd wl over 1f out: wknd fnl f* **9/2**[3]

3m 2.45s (-2.85) **Going Correction** -0.125s/f (Firm)
WFA 3 from 7yo+ 10lb **5** Ran SP% **111.3**
Speed ratings (Par 105): **103,102,101,99,98**
CSF £13.13 TOTE £5.60: £1.90, £1.10; EX 14.70.
Owner Mrs P J Taylor-Garthwaite **Bred** K And P J Garthwaite **Trained** West Auckland, Co Durham

FOCUS
An ordinary little staying handicap in which the first two pulled clear.

6386 ROYAL REGIMENT OF SCOTLAND H'CAP 5f

6:00 (6:03) (Class 6) (0-60,58) 3-Y-O+ **£1,811** (£539; £269; £134) **Stalls** High

Form RPR

0205 **1** **Distant Sun (USA)**[4] 6266 7-8-9 **51** ....(p) ShaneBKelly(5) 9 62
(Linda Perratt) *midfield: pushed along over 2f out: hdwy over 1f out: kpt on: led towards fin* **10/1**

002 **2** *1* **Cayman Fox**[4] 6265 6-9-3 **54** .... PJMcDonald 6 61
(Linda Perratt) *led: rdn over 1f out: kpt on: hdd towards fin* **4/1**[2]

0502 **3** *2 ½* **Missile Attack (IRE)**[46] 4924 3-9-1 **56** .... DaleSwift(3) 14 54+
(Ian Semple) *t.k.h in midfield: rdn 2f out: kpt on strly ins fnl f: wnt 3rd post* **5/1**[3]

2000 **4** *hd* **Dower Glen**[40] 5148 4-9-3 **54** ....(v) JoeFanning 4 51+
(Keith Dalgleish) *chsd ldrs on outer: rdn over 2f out: kpt on one pce* **16/1**

5012 **5** *hd* **Spirit Of Coniston**[26] 5600 8-9-7 **58** .... PaulHanagan 10 55
(Paul Midgley) *chsd ldrs: rdn 2f out: kpt on one pce* **3/1**[1]

460 **6** *hd* **Lees Anthem**[39] 5175 4-8-13 **55** .... LanceBetts(5) 8 51
(Colin Teague) *chsd ldr: rdn over 2f out: kpt on one pce* **12/1**

0000 **7** *½* **Future Gem**[44] 4986 5-8-8 **45** ....(p) AndrewElliott 13 39
(David Thompson) *hld up: rdn 2f out: kpt on ins fnl f: nrst fin* **80/1**

00-0 **8** *1 ¼* **Drumpellier (IRE)**[18] 5824 4-8-11 **51** .... PaulPickard(3) 3 41
(Simon West) *prom on outer: rdn over 2f out: wknd ins fnl f* **20/1**

4006 **9** *shd* **Ya Boy Sir (IRE)**[22] 5725 4-8-8 **45** ....(b) DuranFentiman 11 34
(Ian Semple) *dwlt: hld up: rdn 2f out: nvr threatened* **20/1**

3463 **10** *½* **Cheeky Wee Red**[6] 6213 3-8-12 **50** .... BarryMcHugh 5 37
(Richard Fahey) *hld up: rdn over 2f out: n.d* **9/1**

00-4 **11** *1 ½* **Monte Cassino (IRE)**[20] 5793 6-8-13 **50** .... TomEaves 2 32
(Bryan Smart) *dwlt: hld up on outer: nvr threatened* **16/1**

1500 **12** *¾* **My Love Fajer (IRE)**[15] 5941 3-9-2 **54** .... RobertWinston 7 33
(Alan McCabe) *hld up: pushed along over 2f out: nvr threatened* **25/1**

0100 **13** *¾* **Monte Mayor One**[6] 6213 4-9-5 **56** .... LeeNewman 1 33
(Jim Goldie) *hld up: rdn over 2f out: a towards rr* **8/1**

00-0 **14** *3* **Clanachy**[20] 5793 5-8-3 **45** ....(p) JulieBurke(5) 12 11
(George Foster) *midfield: rdn over 2f out: wknd over 1f out* **50/1**

59.13 secs (-1.27) **Going Correction** -0.225s/f (Firm)
WFA 3 from 4yo+ 1lb **14** Ran SP% **127.9**
Speed ratings (Par 101): **101,99,95,95,94 94,93,91,91,90 88,87,85,81**
Tote Swingers: 1&2 £12.80, 1&3 £16.00, 2&3 £6.60. ToteSuper7: Win: not won Place: £1,296.40. CSF £50.29 CT £242.52 TOTE £13.00: £4.10, £1.80, £2.50; EX 65.60.
Owner Jackton Racing Club **Bred** Forging Oaks Llc **Trained** East Kilbride, S Lanarks

FOCUS
An ordinary sprint handicap, run at a decent pace and again those drawn high were at an advantage. Few landed a blow.
Distant Sun(USA) Official explanation: trainer had no explanation for ther apparent improvement in form

T/Jkpt: Not won. T/Plt: £4,307.70 to a £1 stake. Pool: £75,239.00 - 12.75 winning tickets. T/Qpdt: £96.90 to a £1 stake. Pool: £8,030.00 - 61.30 winning tickets. AS

6387 - (Foreign Racing) - See Raceform Interactive

[5973]CURRAGH (R-H)

Sunday, September 25

OFFICIAL GOING: Soft changing to heavy after race 1 (2.10)

6388a IRISH STALLION FARMS JOE MCGRATH EUROPEAN BREEDERS FUND H'CAP (PREMIER HANDICAP) 6f

2:40 (2:45) 3-Y-0+ **£25,215** (£7,370; £3,491; £1,163)

RPR

1 **Maarek**[8] [6145] 4-9-0 89 WMLordan 17 99
(David Peter Nagle, Ire) *mid-div: pushed along and hdwy fr 2f out: wnt 3rd 1f out: led u.p 100yds out and kpt on wl* **15/2**[2]

2 *1* **Murura (IRE)**[8] [6174] 4-8-13 88 (b) PhillipMakin 18 95
(Kevin Ryan) *a.p: 2nd 2f out: led wl over 1f out: strly pressed and hdd 100yds out: kpt on same pce* **7/1**[1]

3 *4* **Eur Elusive (IRE)**[17] [5872] 4-7-11 79 oh3 RossCoakley(7) 22 73
(J C Hayden, Ire) *a.p on stands' side: led bef 1/2-way: hdd wl over 1f out: 3rd and no imp fr early fnl f* **20/1**

4 *3/4* **Jedward (IRE)**[93] [3372] 4-7-11 79 oh3 MMMonaghan(7) 21 71
(Charles O'Brien, Ire) *trckd ldrs on stands' side: 5th 1/2-way: 3rd 2f out: no imp fr 1f out: kpt on one pce* **10/1**

5 *1/2* **Lake George (IRE)**[11] [6073] 3-8-5 82 RPCleary 25 72
(James M Barrett, Ire) *prom on stands' side: 3rd 1/2-way: 5th 2f out: no imp fr over 1f out* **10/1**

6 *2 3/4* **Simla Sunset (IRE)**[22] [5746] 5-9-5 94 (p) CDHayes 23 75
(P J Prendergast, Ire) *chsd ldrs: sme hdwy to go 5th over 1f out: no imp ins fnl f* **16/1**

7 *3/4* **Toufan Express**[11] [6073] 9-8-10 85 DPMcDonogh 10 64
(Adrian McGuinness, Ire) *in rr of mid-div: hdwy into 10th 1f out: kpt on wout threatening* **14/1**

8 *1* **Snaefell (IRE)**[45] [4976] 7-9-6 95 (b) JMurtagh 19 71
(M Halford, Ire) *mid-div: no imp fr 1 1/2f out: kpt on one pce* **20/1**

9 *nse* **Queenie Keen (IRE)**[49] [4835] 4-8-5 85 CPHoban(5) 20 60
(M Halford, Ire) *prom and disp early: 2nd 1/2-way: no ex fr wl over 1f out* **16/1**

10 *3 3/4* **Just For Mary**[15] [5955] 7-8-0 82 oh4 ow3 (b) RADoyle(7) 15 45
(Daniel Mark Loughnane, Ire) *in rr: nvr a factor: kpt on fr over 1f out* **20/1**

11 *7* **Quinmaster (USA)**[21] [5762] 9-8-12 87 ShaneFoley 12 28
(M Halford, Ire) *chsd ldrs in mid-div: 12th 1/2-way: no ex fr wl over 1f out* **50/1**

12 *1 1/4* **Luisant**[22] [5746] 8-9-6 102 RDawson(7) 5 39+
(J A Nash, Ire) *chsd ldrs on far side: nvr a factor: kpt on one pce* **12/1**

13 *3 1/4* **Blue Dahlia (IRE)**[15] [5955] 4-9-3 99 SAGray(7) 13 26
(T Stack, Ire) *chsd ldrs: 6th 1/2-way: no imp in 8th over 1f out: no ex fnl f* **16/1**

14 *1/2* **Peahen**[22] [5746] 3-9-3 101 DJBenson(7) 14 26
(G M Lyons, Ire) *in rr of mid-div: nvr a factor: kpt on one pce* **16/1**

15 *1* **Yellow Dandy (IRE)**[30] [5430] 3-7-13 81 oh2 LFRoche(5) 26 3
(Liam McAteer, Ire) *chsd ldrs on stands' side: 7th 1/2-way: no ex fr 1 1/2f out* **16/1**

16 *1* **Thats A Fret (IRE)**[9] [6112] 5-8-4 79 oh3 (b) MCHussey 3 —+
(Liam McAteer, Ire) *prom on far side: no threat overall fr 1 1/2f out* **25/1**

17 *1/2* **Three Way Stretch (IRE)**[11] [6073] 5-8-6 81 ow1 (t) WJSupple 16 —
(J T Gorman, Ire) *towards rr: nvr a factor* **40/1**

18 *1 1/2* **Cheviot (USA)**[70] [4135] 5-9-9 98 (p) NGMcCullagh 7 10+
(Reginald Roberts, Ire) *chsd ldrs on far side: n.d overall fr 1 1/2f out* **8/1**[3]

19 *1/2* **One Of Three (IRE)**[12] [6041] 5-7-8 79 oh8 GJPhillips(10) 4 —+
(Michael Mulvany, Ire) *chsd ldrs on far side: no threat overall fr 1 1/2f out* **33/1**

20 *hd* **Tornadodancer (IRE)**[21] [5762] 8-8-4 79 oh2 (b) BACurtis 9 —+
(T G McCourt, Ire) *chsd ldrs on far side: no threat overall fr 1 1/2f out* **25/1**

21 *2 1/4* **Arctic (IRE)**[14] [5979] 4-9-9 103 (tp) RPWhelan(5) 8 6+
(Tracey Collins, Ire) *chsd ldrs on far side: no [illegible]* **14/1**

22 *1 3/4* **Foot Perfect (IRE)**[49] [4835] 3-8-7 84 (b) CO'Donoghue 11 —+
(David Marnane, Ire) *chsd ldrs in centre: 8th 1/2-way: no ex fr 2f out* **14/1**

23 *13* **Flic Flac (IRE)**[52] [4734] 3-8-11 88 PJSmullen 2 —+
(D K Weld, Ire) *towards rr on far side: nvr a factor* **12/1**

24 *nk* **Calm Bay (IRE)**[15] [5955] 5-9-1 90 (bt) KJManning 6 —+
(H Rogers, Ire) *towards rr on far side: nvr a factor* **25/1**

25 *9* **Bonnie Acclamation (IRE)**[9] [6139] 3-8-4 81 oh2 DMGrant 1 —+
(Patrick J Flynn, Ire) *prom on far side: no threat overall fr 1 1/2f out: wknd* **16/1**

1m 18.53s (3.53) **Going Correction** +0.625s/f (Yiel)
WFA 3 from 4yo+ 2lb **25** Ran SP% **157.4**
Speed ratings: **101,99,94,93,92 89,88,86,86,81 72,70,66,65,64 62,62,60,59,59 56,54,36,36,24**
CSF £64.87 CT £1109.62 TOTE £8.30: £2.90, £2.80, £6.70, £3.40; DF 39.40.

Owner Lisbunny Syndicate **Bred** New England Stud & P J & P M Vela **Trained** Fethard, Co Tipperary

FOCUS
A good Listed race in which they split into two groups, the bulk of them on the stands' side. The latter batch came home a long way in front. Those drawn low can be forgiven this. The first and second have been rated to fair personal bests.

NOTEBOOK
Maarek had his ideal challenge - 6f on heavy ground - and duly delivered. Confidently ridden, he looked the likely winner throughout and found plenty when he needed to in the final furlong. Winning here off 89, the success shows how much this cheap purchase has progressed since scoring earlier in the season. He really needs soft ground to be at his best but, if he gets it, a Listed race - which is his next aim - is far from a flight of fancy. (op 7/1)

Murura(IRE) went down gamely and probably would have won on better ground. A progressive type, he coped with conditions surprisingly well and continues to improve. He should have no problem winning again and will have plenty of options on visits here.

Eur Elusive(IRE) made this a genuine test and ran a fine race on just her ninth start. A winner here previously on slightly easy ground, she only gave way late on and it was encouraging how she coped with conditions.

Jedward(IRE) never really threatened but ran a decent race and remains on a reasonable mark. (op 12/1)

Lake George(IRE) is probably in the grip of the handicapper now. He loves this place and ran his usual honest race. (op 20/1)

Simla Sunset(IRE) handles ease but would probably not be in love with it this deep. (op 20/1)

6389a C.L. WELD PARK STKS (GROUP 3) (FILLIES) 7f

3:10 (3:12) 2-Y-0 **£30,818** (£9,008; £4,267; £1,422)

RPR

1 **Coral Wave (IRE)**[14] [5974] 2-8-12 105 DPMcDonogh 3 105
(P J Prendergast, Ire) *trckd ldrs: 2nd bef 1/2-way: led narrowly 2f out: strly pressed ins fnl f: kpt on best u.p* **4/1**[2]

2 *nk* **Homecoming Queen (IRE)**[7] [6195] 2-8-12 86 SeamieHeffernan 1 104
(A P O'Brien, Ire) *led: narrowly hdd 2f out: kpt on u.p fr over 1f out: ev ch ins fnl f: nt quite match wnr* **25/1**

3 *nk* **Princess Sinead (IRE)**[28] [5525] 2-8-12 105 FMBerry 9 104
(Mrs John Harrington, Ire) *hld up: hdwy into 4th 1/2-way: 3rd 2f out: rdn to chal ins fnl f: kpt on u.p but no imp clsng stages* **4/1**[2]

4 *1 3/4* **Lady Wingshot (IRE)**[14] [5974] 2-8-12 98 KJManning 8 99
(J S Bolger, Ire) *chsd ldrs: 7th 1/2-way: wnt 4th over 2f out: no imp fr over 1f out: kpt on one pce* **12/1**

5 *1 1/4* **Remember Alexander**[49] [4833] 2-9-1 106 JMurtagh 7 99
(Mrs John Harrington, Ire) *hld up towards rr: 8th 1/2-way: rdn and sme hdwy into 6th under 2f out: kpt on same pce fnl f wout troubling ldrs* **7/2**[1]

6 *1 3/4* **After (IRE)**[38] [5217] 2-8-12 100 CO'Donoghue 4 92
(A P O'Brien, Ire) *towards rr: 9th 1/2-way: sme hdwy into 6th over 2f out: rdn and no imp in 5th over 1f out* **10/1**

7 *4 3/4* **Kinetica**[17] [5873] 2-8-12 CDHayes 10 80
(Sir Mark Prescott Bt) *trckd ldrs: 3rd 1/2-way: rdn in 5th over 2f out: no ex over 1f out* **11/2**[3]

8 *2 1/2* **Madhmoonah (IRE)**[15] [5949] 2-8-12 95 PJSmullen 6 74
(D K Weld, Ire) *trckd ldrs: 5th 1/2-way: rdn and no imp fr 2f out: eased whn btn ins fnl f* **11/2**[3]

9 *5 1/2* **Strike Action**[13] [6014] 2-8-12 WMLordan 5 60
(David Wachman, Ire) *a towards rr: rdn 3f out: no imp fr 2f out* **33/1**

10 *2 1/4* **Angel Bright (IRE)**[12] [6038] 2-8-12 LFRoche 2 54
(D K Weld, Ire) *prom early: 6th 1/2-way: no threat fr 2f out: wknd* **40/1**

1m 32.9s (2.10) **Going Correction** +0.475s/f (Yiel) **10** Ran SP% **119.0**
Speed ratings: **107,106,106,104,102 100,95,92,86,83**
CSF £101.87 TOTE £4.10: £1.70, £5.70, £1.30; DF 119.60.

Owner Richard Barnes **Bred** Grangecon Stud **Trained** Melitta Lodge, Co Kildare

■ Stewards' Enquiry : Seamie Heffernan three-day ban: used whip with excessive frequency and failed to give his mount time to respond (Oct 9, 14-15)

FOCUS
A smart Group 3, although questionable how many of these fully coped with what was really testing ground.

NOTEBOOK
Coral Wave(IRE) toughed it out and probably won easier than the visual impression implies. Always tanking and sitting just off the speed, she went for home a fair way out and had to battle, with a filly challenging her either side. Given her versatility regarding ground, the manner of how she goes about her business and how little racing she has had, Coral Wave's connections can dream about a fine season as a three-year-old. Her trainer is talking of her as an Oaks filly but it has to be a slight concern about a half-sister to Astrophysical Jet by Rock Of Gibraltar getting 1m4f. A soft-ground mile on heavy ground or over 1m2f might prove her optimum. Either way, she is really likeable and her trainer says she has to fill out plenty yet. (op 7/2 tchd 9/2)

Homecoming Queen(IRE) ran a blinder and she is completely unrecognisable from the filly who looked below the standard required just to win a maiden a month ago. She obviously went on the ground and the three-parts sister to Dylan Thomas has improved dramatically in recent weeks, front-running seemingly a key component in that progress. She was ultra-tough under an aggressive ride and has vital Group 3 placing now. (op 25/1 tchd 28/1)

Princess Sinead(IRE) was also game in defeat. A winner here earlier in the year on yielding to soft, is possibly a better filly on faster ground than this and raw courage got her close to the winner. She has probably done enough for the year and is an admirable filly. (op 4/1 tchd 9/2)

Lady Wingshot(IRE), second to Coral Wave here two weeks ago, ran a similar race. She is holding her form well and ought to be able to obtain Group placing at some stage, perhaps on better ground.

Remember Alexander's ability to go on this ground was far from assured and one must remember that her win at Leopardstown was due in no small way to the passage her jockey chose. She was beaten a long way out here and is worth another chance on more suitable terrain. (op 4/1 tchd 3/1)

After(IRE) has been kept going and, while she has her limitations, she seemed to cope reasonably well with conditions. (op 12/1)

Kinetica, a soft-ground winner, was beating a retreat a long way from home. (op 5/1 tchd 9/2)

Madhmoonah(IRE), a recent winner of a hot course maiden, is another who is definitely worth another chance as she might easily have hated the ground. (op 5/1)

6391a JUDDMONTE BERESFORD STKS (GROUP 2) 1m

4:20 (4:20) 2-Y-0 **£53,232** (£15,560; £7,370; £2,456)

RPR

1 **David Livingston (IRE)**[15] [5951] 2-9-1 114 SeamieHeffernan 2 115
(A P O'Brien, Ire) *mde all: 3 l ld early st: kpt on wl u.p fr over 1f out: reduced advantage clsng stages: hld on* **7/2**[2]

2 *1/2* **Akeed Mofeed**[22] [5742] 2-9-1 JMurtagh 7 114+
(John M Oxx, Ire) *trckd ldrs: 4th 1/2-way: niggled along to go 2nd early st: no imp on wnr 1f out: styd on u.p wl ins fnl f: nt rch wnr* **5/6**[1]

3 *9 1/2* **Athens (IRE)**[12] [6039] 2-9-1 98 CO'Donoghue 6 93
(A P O'Brien, Ire) *trckd ldr in 2nd: pushed along in 3rd early st: no imp on wnr over 1f out: no ex fnl f* **11/2**

4 *nse* **Furner's Green (IRE)**[15] [5951] 2-9-1 113 JPO'Brien 1 93
(A P O'Brien, Ire) *trckd ldrs: 3rd 1/2-way: rdn along in 4th 2f out: sn no imp and no ex fnl f* **4/1**[3]

5 *nk* **Blue White Fire (IRE)**[57] [4565] 2-9-1 98 (b[1]) PJSmullen 3 92
(D K Weld, Ire) *towards rr: rdn early st: no imp fr over 1f out: no ex fnl f* **16/1**

1m 46.23s (0.23) **Going Correction** +0.20s/f (Good) **5** Ran SP% **118.0**
Speed ratings: **107,106,97,96,96**
CSF £7.49 TOTE £4.10: £1.50, £1.20; DF 9.30.

Owner Derrick Smith **Bred** Rhinestone Bloodstock & Lynch-Bages Ltd **Trained** Ballydoyle, Co Tipperary

FOCUS
A Group 2 that John Oxx has won with such horses as Alamshar, Azamour and Sea The Stars. In that context, much was expected of Akeed Mofeed here but he had to settle for second.

NOTEBOOK

David Livingston(IRE) lacked the hype that surrounded the favourite but his claims were solid. After all, he came here as a progressive horse with placed Group 1 form and a proven ability to go on easy terrain. The question was whether he would have the raw ability to hold on as he again made the speed. Aware of the tough nature of his horse, Seamus Heffernan was happy to make the pace and had every faith in the son of Galileo lasting out the trip. He had them all in trouble a long way out and, although tiring close home, one could not conclude other than he was the best horse on the day on the ground. Quite how good he can become is hard to say but he is a likeable and tough horse who should make a three-year-old. A mile at that stage would probably be short enough for him, but he deserves Classic consideration and has a fair chance of getting the Derby distance.

Akeed Mofeed came up short on this step up to Group 2 level. He was tardy enough at the start, then a little free early, and turning into the straight one could sense that Johnny Murtagh was not entirely happy and that he had a lot of ground to make up on the winner. Driven to close, he did so without ever looking as though he would get there and he wandered a little at the end on the gruelling ground. Murtagh was not too hard on him close home but the battle was lost. He remains a colt of considerable potential and one would expect him to emerge as the best horse of these longer term. (op 4/5 tchd 1/1)

Athens(IRE), well beaten behind the runner-up for the second time in their short careers, is surely worth another chance given the nature of the ground and the likelihood that he struggled as a consequence of it. He was beaten before they turned in and his honesty ensured he finished third. (op 8/1 tchd 5/1)

Furner's Green(IRE) is likely to do better on decent ground. The market suggested he would run better but he was never travelling as though he would get involved. (op 4/1 tchd 9/2)

Blue White Fire(IRE) did not run too badly considering the step up in class, but whether he handles deep ground adequately remains to be seen. (op 14/1)

6390a & 6392 - 6393a (Foreign Racing) - See Raceform Interactive

5092 COLOGNE (R-H)

Sunday, September 25

OFFICIAL GOING: Turf: soft

6394a ILSE UND HEINZ RAMM-ERINNERUNGSRENNEN (LISTED RACE) (3YO+ FILLIES & MARES) (TURF) 1m

2:15 (2:18) 3-Y-0+ **£11,206** (£3,448; £1,724; £862)

RPR

1 **Clinical**[46] 4915 3-9-0 0 .... SebSanders 6 105+
(Sir Mark Prescott Bt) *hld up towards rr: travelling smoothly: mde easy prog arnd fnl turn: swtchd to outside: qcknd wl fr 1 1/2f out: fin strly ins fnl f to take ld cl home* **2/1**[1]

2 ½ **Julie's Love**[14] 5980 3-9-0 0 .... MircoDemuro 7 104
(Manfred Hofer, Germany) **15/2**

3 1 ¾ **Jardina (GER)**[21] 3-8-11 0 .... AStarke 10 97
(P Schiergen, Germany) **48/10**[2]

4 hd **Conciliatory**[42] 5096 4-9-2 0 .... THellier 5 98
(Rae Guest) *settled 4th: r.o wl in st wout threatening ldrs ins fnl f* **17/2**

5 ½ **Semina (GER)**[21] 4-9-2 0 .... DPorcu 3 96
(S Smrczek, Germany) **53/10**[3]

6 1 ¼ **Reine Heureuse (GER)**[115] 2657 4-9-2 0 .... KClijmans 2 93
(Uwe Ostmann, Germany) **115/10**

7 2 ½ **Dariya (GER)**[21] 3-8-11 0 .... FilipMinarik 9 87
(S Smrczek, Germany) **30/1**

8 2 ½ **Tech Exceed (GER)**[22] 5749 4-9-2 0 .... EPedroza 4 82
(A Wohler, Germany) **94/10**

9 2 ½ **Zaphira (GER)**[693] 4-9-2 0 .... ASuborics 5 76
(S Smrczek, Germany) **83/10**

10 hd **Quesada (IRE)**[35] 3-9-0 0 .... APietsch 8 78
(W Hickst, Germany) **175/10**

11 nse **Savannah Blue (GER)**[21] 3-8-11 0 .... MSuerland 11 75
(Markus Klug, Germany) **218/10**

1m 36.17s (-2.22)
WFA 3 from 4yo 4lb **11** Ran SP% **130.1**
WIN (incl. 10 euro stake): 30. PLACES: 16, 19, 16. SF: 216.
Owner Cheveley Park Stud **Bred** Cheveley Park Stud Ltd **Trained** Newmarket, Suffolk

NOTEBOOK

Clinical, on softer ground than she had previously faced, failed to handle the bends but picked up really well in the final furlong and got up close home.

Conciliatory, with the headgear left off this time, ran on well to take fourth, just missing out on a place.

6395a KOLNER HERBST-STUTENPREIS (GROUP 3) (3YO+ FILLIES & MARES) (TURF) 1m 3f

2:45 (2:50) 3-Y-0+

£27,586 (£9,482; £4,741; £2,586; £1,724; £1,293)

RPR

1 **Kapitale (GER)**[49] 4839 3-8-11 0 .... MircoDemuro 5 109
(A Wohler, Germany) *broke wl: sn led: settled in 2nd bhd Ovambo Queen in bk st: rdn early in st: chal for ld: battled all the way to fin: edgd ahd jst bef line* **102/10**

2 hd **Ovambo Queen (GER)**[49] 4842 4-9-5 0 .... ASuborics 11 109
(Dr A Bolte, Germany) *broke fast: settled bhd ldr then led down bk st: r.o wl in st whn chal by eventual wnr: battled all the way to fin: hdd jst bef line* **13/10**[1]

3 3 ½ **Lagalp (GER)**[22] 5749 4-9-5 0 .... AStarke 8 103
(P Schiergen, Germany) *settled midfield: r.o wl in st: chsd ldrs home: no threat* **77/10**

4 1 **Nicea (GER)**[22] 5749 4-9-5 0 .... FilipMinarik 6 101
(P Schiergen, Germany) *bkmarker fr s: r.o wl in st but no threat to ldrs* **109/10**

5 1 ½ **Nautika Danon (GER)** 3-8-11 0 .... APietsch 2 98
(W Hickst, Germany) *broke wl to r 3rd: styd on one pce in st* **93/10**

6 nk **Temida (IRE)**[41] 3-8-11 0 .... THellier 9 97
(M G Mintchev, Germany) *settled towards rr: dropped bk to last 1/2-way down bk st: r.o in st but only passed btn horses* **47/10**[2]

7 10 **Albaraka**[73] 4015 3-8-11 0 .... SebSanders 10 79
(Sir Mark Prescott Bt) *towards rr fr s: proged down bk st: r.o wl early in st: sn no ex: fdd* **7/1**[3]

8 5 **Aigrette Garzette (IRE)**[22] 5749 3-8-11 0 .... MrDennisSchiergen 3 70
(P Schiergen, Germany) *settled 3rd or 4th: rdn and r.o early in st but sn wknd* **118/10**

9 2 **Mombasa (GER)**[28] 4-9-5 0 .... KClijmans 4 67
(P Schiergen, Germany) *hld up in 5th: briefly threatened turning for home but sn wknd* **32/1**

10 nk **Guiana (GER)**[43] 5075 4-9-5 0 .... MCadeddu 7 67
(J Hirschberger, Germany) *settled in midfield: nvr a threat* **105/10**

2m 16.22s (-4.58)
WFA 3 from 4yo 7lb **10** Ran SP% **131.6**
WIN (incl. 10 euro stake): 112. PLACES: 33, 14, 21. SF: 435.
Owner Gestut Karlshof **Bred** Gestut Karlshof **Trained** Germany

NOTEBOOK

Albaraka tackling soft ground for the first time, appeared not to get home on it.

6396a PREIS VON EUROPA (GROUP 1) (3YO+) (TURF) 1m 4f

3:55 (4:01) 3-Y-0+ **£86,206** (£25,862; £12,931; £6,034; £2,586)

RPR

1 **Campanologist (USA)**[21] 5776 6-9-6 0 .... FrankieDettori 4 114
(Saeed Bin Suroor) *hld up towards rr: mde smooth prog arnd fnl turn: swtchd to outside: r.o strly: led 1 1/2f out: rdn out hands and heels: comf* **23/10**[2]

2 1 ¼ **Ibicenco (GER)**[21] 5771 3-8-13 0 .... FilipMinarik 6 113
(J Hirschberger, Germany) *a.p bhd ldr: first to chal in st: r.o gamely: led over 2f out: hdd 1 1/2f out: nt qckn: styd on* **47/10**

3 1 ¾ **Earl Of Tinsdal (GER)**[42] 5092 3-8-13 0 .... EPedroza 3 110
(A Wohler, Germany) *sent to ld: set str pce: r.o wl in st but hdd over 2f out: styd on one pce fr 1 1/2f out* **9/10**[1]

4 nk **Saltas (GER)**[42] 5092 3-8-13 0 .... AStarke 5 110
(P Schiergen, Germany) *settled in midfield: sn rdn in st: styd on fnl 2f* **41/10**[3]

5 11 **Flamingo Fantasy (GER)**[14] 5990 6-9-6 0 .... ASuborics 1 91
(S Smrczek, Germany) *bkmarker fr s: rdn early in st: no ex: sn wknd* **199/10**

6 7 **Seismos (IRE)**[29] 5498 3-8-13 0 .... MircoDemuro 2 81
(A Wohler, Germany) *settled in midfield then dropped bk towards rr: rdn early in st: sn btn* **125/10**

2m 28.66s (-4.24)
WFA 3 from 6yo 8lb **6** Ran SP% **132.3**
WIN (incl. 10 euro stake): 33. PLACES: 29, 32. SF: 142.
Owner Godolphin **Bred** Darley **Trained** Newmarket, Suffolk

NOTEBOOK

Campanologist(USA) landed his third Group 1 win in Germany with an easy success under a confident ride from Frankie Dettori, who waited in fifth place as the placed horses made the running at a steady pace. Pulled to the outside early in the straight he quickened up like a class act, putting the race to bed in a matter of strides. He bounced back from a narrow defeat in the International Bosphorus Cup at Veliefendi last time out to win the sixth Group race of his career. It was the third success in this contest for Godolphin since 2001 and he will go for another Group 1, possibly in Milan next month.

Ibicenco(GER) was never far away and, although no match for the winner, stayed on strongly for second.

Earl Of Tinsdal(GER), was sent off favourite and made the running but would have preferred softer ground. His trainer thought the colt was over the top and said he would be put away for next season.

6397 - (Foreign Racing) - See Raceform Interactive

5911 BATH (L-H)

Monday, September 26

OFFICIAL GOING: Good to soft (soft in places)

Wind: Virtually nil Weather: Sunny periods

6398 BEST ODDS @ ODDSCHECKER.COM H'CAP 5f 11y

2:30 (2:31) (Class 6) (0-60,60) 3-Y-0+ **£1,617** (£481; £240; £120) **Stalls** Centre

Form RPR

1205 **1** **Jolly Ranch**[40] 5175 5-9-4 57 .... FergusSweeney 12 69
(Tony Newcombe) *racd wd in centre of crse: chsd ldrs: edgd lft to far side over 1f out and led ins fnl f: readily* **7/1**

1612 **2** 2 ½ **My Meteor**[16] 5917 4-9-2 60 .... DavidKenny(5) 7 63
(Tony Newcombe) *chsd ldrs: slt ld fr 2f out: rdn over 1f out: hdd ins fnl f: styd on same pce* **2/1**[1]

3246 **3** ¾ **Madam Isshe**[24] 5678 4-9-1 54 .... TomMcLaughlin 10 54
(Malcolm Saunders) *racd towards centre of crse: rdn and edgd lft to far side over 1f out: styd on for one pce 3rd ins fnl f* **5/1**[2]

4260 **4** 1 **Best One**[9] 6175 7-8-8 47 ....(b) JamesDoyle 6 44
(Ronald Harris) *chsd ldrs: rdn and styd on same pce fnl f* **10/1**

0506 **5** 1 ½ **Greyemkay**[15] 5965 3-8-3 50 .... RachealKneller(7) 5 41
(Richard Price) *s.i.s: in rr: rdn: hdwy and hung rt over 1f out: kpt on fnl f but nvr a threat* **16/1**

5355 **6** 1 ¾ **Spic 'n Span**[24] 5678 6-9-0 53 ....(v) LukeMorris 9 38
(Ronald Harris) *led briefly early: chsd ldrs: rdn over 2f out: wknd fnl f* **8/1**

4600 **7** 2 ¾ **Kyllachy Storm**[4] 6283 7-9-7 60 .... GeorgeBaker 8 35
(Ron Hodges) *sn led: hdd 2f out: wknd over 1f out* **6/1**[3]

5400 **8** 1 ¼ **My Best Man**[234] 421 5-8-7 46 oh1 .... FrannyNorton 4 17
(Tony Carroll) *rdn 1/2-way: outpcd most of way* **16/1**

6554 **9** 3 ¼ **Cliffords Reprieve**[54] 4684 3-8-10 50 .... EddieCreighton 1 —
(Eric Wheeler) *in tch to halafway: sn bhd* **25/1**

64.06 secs (1.56) **Going Correction** +0.35s/f (Good)
WFA 3 from 4yo+ 1lb **9** Ran SP% **112.6**
Speed ratings (Par 101): **101,97,95,94,91 89,84,82,76**
toteswingers:1&2:£4.40, 1&3:£7.60, 2&3:£2.90 CSF £20.73 CT £76.55 TOTE £6.40: £2.10, £1.20, £2.20; EX 22.80.
Owner Joli Racing **Bred** C G Reid **Trained** Yarnscombe, Devon

FOCUS

Following 5mm of rain overnight the ground was given as good to soft, soft in places. An ordinary handicap and, despite the ground being very different to that which they encountered here on two occasions in July, stablemates Jolly Ranch and My Meteor again finished first and second. The winner posted a personal best and may have been helped by racing wide.

6399 COMPARE ODDS - WIN MORE.ODDSCHECKER.COM NURSERY 1m 2f 46y

3:00 (3:00) (Class 5) (0-75,75) 2-Y-O **£2,264** (£673; £336; £168) **Stalls** Low

Form RPR

2523 **1** **Sheila's Buddy**[14] 5991 2-8-13 **67** .... LiamKeniry 6 71
(J S Moore) *in tch: hdwy 3f out: ev ch fr 2f out and c rt towards stands' side: led over 1f out: drvn out* **12/1**

0000 **2** nk **Cato Minor**[12] 6053 2-8-1 **55** ow3 ....(b) DavidProbert 10 58
(Amanda Perrett) *chsd ldrs: rdn and c to stands' side over 2f out and ev ch styd on u.p fnl f but nt pce of wnr clsng stages* **20/1**

3606 **3** *1 1/4* **Tudor Empire (IRE)**[13] 6031 2-9-0 **68**............................ NickyMackay 9 69
(John Gosden) *rrd stalls: chsd ldrs: rdn 3f out: slt ld and c towards stands' side 2f out: hdd over 1f out: one pce ins fnl f* **7/1**

2015 **4** *1 1/4* **Snowed In (IRE)**[21] 5783 2-9-3 **71**...................................... LukeMorris 1 70
(J S Moore) *sn in tch: drvn in centre of crse to chse ldrs over 2f out: one pce fnl f* **12/1**

002 **5** *4 1/2* **Dont Take Me Alive**[33] 5375 2-9-2 **70**.............................. AdamKirby 11 61
(Clive Cox) *chsd ldrs: rdn to chal towards centre of crse appr fnl 2f: wknd over 1f out* **6/1**[3]

0061 **6** *3 1/4* **Enjoying (IRE)**[21] 5783 2-8-6 **63**................................(b) KieranO'Neill(3) 5 48
(Richard Hannon) *mid-div: rdn: sme hdwy and styd towards far side over 2f out: wknd u.p sn after* **5/1**[2]

6522 **7** *1/2* **Always Ends Well (IRE)**[18] 5844 2-8-9 **63**.................... FrannyNorton 2 47
(Mark Johnston) *sn led: racd towards centre of crse and hdd u.p 2f out: sn wknd* **4/1**[1]

0604 **8** *1* **Welsh Nayber**[21] 5783 2-8-7 **61**.. EddieAhern 4 43
(Amanda Perrett) *hld up towards rr: sme hdwy and moving towards centre crse over 2f out: hung lft to far side and wknd sn after* **6/1**[3]

053 **9** *1 1/4* **Shivsingh**[16] 5937 2-9-1 **69**.. ChrisCatlin 8 49
(Mick Channon) *hld up in rr: rdn 3f out and nvr beyond mid-div: styd towards far side and no ch fnl 2f* **9/1**

5360 **10** *14* **Choisirez (IRE)**[18] 5844 2-8-2 **61** ow1.................... MatthewCosham(5) 7 16
(David Evans) *chsd ldrs: styd towards far side and wknd over 2f out* **33/1**

6213 **11** *3 1/2* **Compton Target (IRE)**[16] 5913 2-9-7 **75**......................... JamesDoyle 3 24
(Hans Adielsson) *hld up in rr: rdn and lost tch fnl 3f* **16/1**

2m 16.57s (5.57) **Going Correction** +0.425s/f (Yiel) **11** Ran SP% **116.7**
Speed ratings (Par 95): **94,93,92,91,88 85,85,84,83,72 69**
toteswingers:1&2:£37.60, 1&3:£25.20, 2&3:£23.00 CSF £225.97 CT £1807.24 TOTE £15.30: £3.10, £6.70, £2.80; EX 356.80.
Owner Ray Styles **Bred** Mrs Anita R Dodd **Trained** Upper Lambourn, Berks
■ Stewards' Enquiry : David Probert two-day ban: used whip with excessive frequency (Oct 10-11)

FOCUS
A modest nursery in which the principals came centre to stands' side in the straight. Relatively straightforward form, the winner back to his pre-race best.

NOTEBOOK
Sheila's Buddy looked pretty exposed going into the race, but this was his first try over 1m2f and the step up in trip suited him. He's a half-brother to Sheila's Bond, a dual winner on the Polytrack, and should pay his way on that surface over the winter. (op 14-1)
Cato Minor didn't achieve a great deal on his handicap debut at Kempton last time, but back on turf and upped 2f in distance he posted his best effort to date. This opens up more options. (tchd 18-1)
Tudor Empire(IRE) is a half-brother to a German 1m3f/1m4f winner and also appreciated this longer distance. (op 8-1)
Snowed In(IRE) reversed recent C&D form with Enjoying on 4lb better terms, perhaps due to the easier ground. (op 9-1)
Dont Take Me Alive didn't seem to quite get home over this longer trip, although he did race up the centre while the main action developed towards the stands'-side rail. (op 11-2)
Enjoying(IRE) could not follow up his C&D win over this easier ground. (op 11-2)
Always Ends Well(IRE) dropped out having made the early running and looked a non-stayer. (op 11-2)

6400 BRITISH STALLION STUDS E.B.F./ JOHN SISK & SONS MAIDEN STKS — 1m 2f 46y
3:30 (3:40) (Class 5) 2-Y-O — £3,234 (£962; £481; £240) Stalls Low

Form — RPR

63 **1** **Winner's Wish**[14] 6000 2-8-12 0...................................... JimmyFortune 12 71
(Jeremy Noseda) *led 2f: styd chsng ldrs: rdn and chal over 1f out and persistently flashed tail: kpt on to take slt ld ins fnl f: drvn out* **13/2**[3]

42 **2** *1 1/4* **Amoralist**[33] 5382 2-9-3 0.. JamieSpencer 4 74
(Ed Dunlop) *sn chsng ldrs: led 7f out: travelling wl 2f out: jnd and rdn over 1f out: sn carried hd high: edgd lft and hdd ins fnl f: wknd clsng tages* **6/4**[1]

0 **3** *3 1/2* **No Time To Lose**[38] 5239 2-9-3 0................................ FergusSweeney 2 68
(Jamie Osborne) *chsd ldrs: pushed along over 2f out: outpcd by ldng duo ins fnl f* **40/1**

4 *nk* **Sir Graham Wade (IRE)** 2-9-3 0.................................. FrannyNorton 1 67+
(Mark Johnston) *in rr: drvn along 3f out: hdwy over 2f out: styd on to take 4th ins fnl f and clsng for 3rd but no ch w ldng duo* **20/1**

02 **5** *1 3/4* **Ballyheigue (IRE)**[17] 5899 2-9-3 0.................................. ShaneKelly 11 64
(Brian Meehan) *led after 2f: hdd 7f out: drvn to chal over 2f out: wknd appr fnl f* **9/1**

06 **6** *2 3/4* **Annaluna (IRE)**[18] 5841 2-8-7 0........................... MatthewCosham(5) 10 54
(David Evans) *uns rdr and loose bef s: sn pushed along in rr: rdn and styd on fr over 1f out: nvr a threat* **100/1**

7 *3/4* **My Destination (IRE)** 2-9-3 0.. AhmedAjtebi 3 58
(Mahmood Al Zarooni) *in rr: pushed along over 3f out: mod hdwy fr 2f out* **11/2**[2]

50 **8** *2 3/4* **Tushuk Tash (USA)**[17] 5891 2-9-3 0..................................... ChrisCatlin 8 53
(Mick Channon) *in rr: hdwy over 5f out: rdn over 3f out and nvr rchd ldrs: wknd 2f out* **28/1**

9 *2* **Wreaths Of Empire (IRE)** 2-9-3 0.................................. JimCrowley 13 49
(Richard Hannon) *chsd ldrs: rdn 3f out: sn btn* **12/1**

60 **10** *3* **Compton Bell**[17] 5899 2-9-3 0.. JamesDoyle 5 44
(Hans Adielsson) *chsd ldrs 6f* **100/1**

6 **11** *1/2* **Inqadh (USA)**[17] 5899 2-9-3 0.. EddieAhern 6 43
(Saeed Bin Suroor) *chsd ldrs to 3f out: wknd qckly over 2f out* **8/1**

00 **12** *3/4* **Hartside (GER)**[11] 6100 2-9-3 0.......................................(v1) TomQueally 7 42
(Sir Michael Stoute) *s.i.s: bhd most of way* **20/1**

05 **13** *3 1/2* **Seven Veils (IRE)**[9] 6180 2-8-12 0.................................... SebSanders 9 30
(Sir Mark Prescott Bt) *mid-div and rdn 4f out: wknd 3f out* **25/1**

2m 16.51s (5.51) **Going Correction** +0.425s/f (Yiel) **13** Ran SP% **118.8**
Speed ratings (Par 95): **94,93,90,89,88 86,85,83,81,79 79,78,75**
toteswingers:1&2:£3.70, 1&3:£37.10, 2&3:£20.10 CSF £15.35 TOTE £5.70: £1.60, £1.60, £9.30; EX 19.40.
Owner Abdulla Al Mansoori **Bred** Ashbrittle Stud **Trained** Newmarket, Suffolk

FOCUS
Straightforward form, no more than fair with the close two close to pre-race marks.

NOTEBOOK
Winner's Wish kept battling away despite flashing her tail when hit, and saw the longer distance out well. She simply showed the greater resolution than the smooth-travelling Amoralist in the finish. She could build on this in handicap company as she promises to stay even further - dam is out of Park Hill winner Anna Of Saxony. (op 11-2)
Amoralist stuck his head in the air and hung left once pressure was applied. He looks one to be wary of in future. (op 15-8 tchd 5-4, 2-1 in a place)
No Time To Lose was on the heels of the leaders 2f out and, although he slowly dropped out of contention, he wasn't given a hard time and looks likely to improve again for this outing. He needs one more run for a mark and it'll probably be in handicaps that he shines. (op 33-1)
Sir Graham Wade(IRE) ♦ was slowly away and clueless through the early part of the race. Out the back entering the straight, he made eyecatching headway once in line for home and this half-brother to Group 3 winner Yasoodd and Listed winner Gript looks sure to improve plenty for this debut effort. (tchd 25-1)
Ballyheigue(IRE) was up there most of the way but didn't see his race out. Handicaps will provide him with better opportunities. (op 10-1)
Annaluna(IRE) kept on late from off the pace to take sixth place, improving for the longer trip. She'd run loose beforehand so might be deserving of extra credit.
My Destination(IRE) is a brother to high-class Racing Post Trophy winner Ibn Khaldun, but the fact that he was showing up here for his debut suggested he wasn't anything special. Very green, he can improve for the outing but he'll not live up to his pedigree. (op 8-1)

6401 ODDSCHECKER.MOBI "BE HOPEFUL" H'CAP (DIV I) — 1m 2f 46y
4:00 (4:06) (Class 5) (0-75,75) 3-Y-0+ — £2,264 (£673; £336; £168) Stalls Low

Form — RPR

0513 **1** **Jordaura**[7] 6226 5-9-7 **72**... RobertWinston 8 85
(Gay Kelleway) *hld up in rr: hdwy and hung lft 2f out: styd on wl u.p fnl f to ld fnl 50yds: sn in command* **3/1**[1]

6050 **2** *1* **Discovery Bay**[27] 5598 3-9-1 **72**..................................... JimmyFortune 6 83
(Roger Charlton) *trckd ldr fr 7f out: chal fr over 3f out tl hrd rdn to take slt ld and hd high appr fnl f: kpt slt advantasge tl hdd and outpcd fnl 50yds* **4/1**[3]

4612 **3** *1 1/4* **Minsky Mine (IRE)**[20] 5808 4-9-2 **67**......................... RobbieFitzpatrick 2 76
(Michael Appleby) *led after 2f: jnd over 3f out and kpt slt ld tl hdd appr fnl f: styd chalng tl wknd fnl 75yds* **7/2**[2]

4044 **4** *8* **Oriental Girl**[16] 5915 6-9-1 **66**..(v) LiamKeniry 11 59
(Jonathan Geake) *hld up in tch: chsd ldrs and rdn 3f out: wknd qckly 2f out* **17/2**

5430 **5** *4 1/2* **Spring Secret**[20] 5804 5-9-3 **68**... LukeMorris 3 52
(Bryn Palling) *chsd ldrs: rdn 4f out: wknd over 2f out* **7/1**

2550 **6** *4* **Baqaat (USA)**[18] 5856 3-9-4 **75**...................................... JamieSpencer 5 51
(Ed Dunlop) *stdd s: hld up towards rr: rdn and sme hdwy 3f out: nvr in contention and sn wknd* **8/1**

-620 **7** *16* **Sottovoce**[159] 1481 3-8-11 **66** ow2.................................. SebSanders 7 12
(Simon Dow) *led 2f: styd chsng ldrs: rdn and wknd 3f out* **25/1**

0440 **8** *1 1/4* **Wisecraic**[19] 5828 4-9-0 **65**..(p) ShaneKelly 4 —
(J S Moore) *chsd ldrs: rdn and wknd 3f out* **12/1**

2m 14.3s (3.30) **Going Correction** +0.425s/f (Yiel)
WFA 3 from 4yo+ 6lb **8** Ran SP% **112.9**
Speed ratings (Par 103): **103,102,101,94,91 88,75,74**
toteswingers:1&2:£3.40, 1&3:£2.40, 2&3:£4.40 CSF £14.74 CT £42.14 TOTE £5.20: £1.60, £1.40, £1.90; EX 18.40.
Owner Whispering Winds **Bred** Pendley Farm **Trained** Exning, Suffolk

FOCUS
A duel developed from early in the straight between Minsky Mine and Discovery Bay and the pair somewhat set things up for the winner. It was the clear pick of five C&D times and looks good form for the grade, with the first three clear.

6402 ODDSCHECKER.MOBI "BE HOPEFUL" H'CAP (DIV II) — 1m 2f 46y
4:30 (4:31) (Class 5) (0-75,74) 3-Y-0+ — £2,264 (£673; £336; £168) Stalls Low

Form — RPR

4-00 **1** **Gale Green**[86] 3632 4-9-2 **66**.. FergusSweeney 12 74
(Henry Candy) *chsd ldrs: drvn to chal over 2f out: stl upsides ins fnl f: styd on u.p on stands' rail to ld last strides* **20/1**

320 **2** *hd* **Pivot Bridge**[28] 5560 3-8-11 **67**..................................... RobertWinston 7 75
(Charles Hills) *in rr and hmpd bnd 4f out: gd hdwy over 2f out and chal between horses sn after: tk slt ld 50yds out: hd last strides* **15/2**[3]

1604 **3** *1 1/4* **Misty Isles**[15] 5962 3-9-2 **72**.. EddieAhern 8 77
(Heather Main) *chsd ldrs: drvn to ld over 2f out: jnd sn after and narrowly hdd fnl 150yds: wknd clsng stages* **8/1**

-031 **4** *2* **Bowsers Brave (USA)**[20] 5808 5-9-9 **73**......................(t) GeorgeBaker 3 74+
(Marcus Tregoning) *s.i.s: in rr whn hmpd bnd 4f out: hdwy over 2f out: styd on fnl f: nt rch ldrs* **10/3**[1]

4520 **5** *5* **With Hindsight (IRE)**[38] 5242 3-9-4 **74**.............................. AdamKirby 2 65
(Clive Cox) *chsd ldrs: rdn and ev ch 2f out: wknd over 1f out* **8/1**

230 **6** *7* **Blue Spartan (IRE)**[17] 5893 6-9-3 **70**...................... LouisBeuzelin(3) 11 47
(Brian Meehan) *led 2f: styd chsng ldr tl rdn 3f out: wknd 2f out* **15/2**[3]

6000 **7** *[illegible]* **Fenchesco (IRE)**[17] 6030 3-9-0 **64**................................(b) TomQueally 10 34
(Amanda Perrett) *led after 2f: hdd over 2f out: sn btn* **16/1**

4-40 **8** *1/2* **Nothing To Hide (IRE)**[14] 6005 3-8-10 **66**......................... JamesDoyle 1 35
(Dominic Ffrench Davis) *a towards rr* **25/1**

3220 **9** *3/4* **Bold Cross (IRE)**[16] 5942 8-8-13 **66**.................................. KierenFox(3) 4 33
(Edward Bevan) *chsd ldrs: rdn 3f out: wknd sn after* **18/1**

5-51 **10** *25* **History Repeating**[26] 5614 3-8-4 **60** oh1......................... DavidProbert 5 —
(Mark Usher) *hmpd bnd 4f out: a in rr* **9/1**

64 **11** *22* **Amistress**[34] 5340 3-9-3 **73**... SebSanders 6 —
(Eve Johnson Houghton) *stmbld bnd 4f out: sn wknd: virtually p.u fnl 2f* **11/2**[2]

2m 16.29s (5.29) **Going Correction** +0.425s/f (Yiel)
WFA 3 from 4yo+ 6lb **11** Ran SP% **114.0**
Speed ratings (Par 103): **95,94,93,92,88 82,79,79,78,58 41**
toteswingers:1&2:£30.80, 1&3:£33.00, 2&3:£10.90 CSF £158.00 CT £1308.71 TOTE £29.90: £5.60, £2.60, £2.00; EX 234.70.
Owner Major M G Wyatt **Bred** Dunchurch Lodge Stud Co **Trained** Kingston Warren, Oxon

FOCUS
The slower of the two divisions by 1.99sec.
Bowsers Brave(USA) Official explanation: jockey said gelding suffered interference in running
Blue Spartan(IRE) Official explanation: jockey said gelding slipped on bend

6403 DIGIBET.COM "HANDS AND HEELS" APPRENTICE SERIES H'CAP (PART OF THE RACING EXCELLENCE INITIATIVE) — 5f 161y
5:00 (5:00) (Class 5) (0-70,70) 3-Y-0 — £2,264 (£673; £336; £168) Stalls Centre

Form — RPR

3416 **1** **Minety Lass**[27] 5587 3-9-6 **69**.. LucyKBarry 5 84
(Adrian Chamberlain) *trckd ldrs in 3rd: drvn to ld wl over 1f out: pushed clr fnl f: easily* **11/2**[2]

2205 **2** *4 1/2* **Diamond Vine (IRE)**[7] 6223 3-9-6 **69**.........................(p) CharlesBishop 4 69
(Ronald Harris) *in rr: hdwy and rdn over 2f out: chsd wnr 1f out but nvr any ch* **7/1**[3]

1203 **3** *4 1/2* **Delira (IRE)**[24] 5671 3-9-5 **68**... NoelGarbutt 3 53
(Jonathan Portman) *in rr: drvn and styd on fr 2f out: tk one pce 3rd ins fnl f* **10/1**

0550 **4** *1 1/4* **Forty Proof (IRE)**[46] 4960 3-9-7 **70**........................... MichaelJMurphy 1 51
(William Knight) *in rr: drvn and sme hdwy 2f out: nvr rchd ldrs* **9/1**

4321 **5** *3* **Ginzan**[16] 5917 3-8-13 **62**.. JakePayne 8 33+
(Malcolm Saunders) *slt ld tl hdd & wknd wl over 1f out* **13/8**[1]

5001 **6** ¾ **Too Many Questions (IRE)**[11] 6105 3-9-1 **64**.........(p) RachealKneller 2 33+
(David Evans) *w ldr tl over 2f out: sn wknd* **11/2**[2]

5435 **7** 2 ¼ **Festival Dance**[16] 5917 3-8-10 **62**....................................... IanBurns(3) 6 23
(Ron Hodges) *s.i.s: c to r on stands' rail wl over 2f out: a bhd* **10/1**

1m 13.02s (1.82) **Going Correction** +0.35s/f (Good) 7 Ran SP% **109.5**
Speed ratings (Par 101): **101,95,89,87,83 82,79**
toteswingers:1&2:£6.60, 1&3:£4.40, 2&3:£9.90 CSF £39.01 CT £342.52 TOTE £5.60: £2.00, £3.40; EX 38.60.

Owner Colin Rogers **Bred** Longdon Stud Ltd **Trained** Ashton Keynes, Wilts

FOCUS
There was a disputed lead between Ginzan and Too Many Questions here and the race panned out nicely for the winner, who was unexposed. The form is taken at face value.

6404 BRITISH STALLION STUDS E.B.F./SEDDON CONSTRUCTION MAIDEN FILLIES' STKS 1m 2f 46y
5:30 (5:34) (Class 5) 3-Y-O+ **£3,557** (£1,058; £529; £264) **Stalls** Low

Form RPR

-463 **1** **Always The Lady**[27] 5585 3-8-12 81.................................... AdamKirby 4 81+
(Clive Cox) *chsd ldrs: led over 3f out: rdn and chal whn hung rt over 1f out: styd on u.p fnl f: in command clsng stages* **2/1**[2]

065 **2** ¾ **Balandra**[17] 5877 3-8-12 0.. JimmyFortune 7 79+
(Luca Cumani) *chsd ldr then chsd wnr fr 3f out: drvn to chal 2f out: hung lft and sn green: stl hanging lft whn ev ch ins fnl f: no ex clsng stages* **16/1**

30 **3** 4 ½ **Tetbury Lass**[14] 5999 3-8-5 0.................................... RachealKneller(7) 11 70
(Adrian Chamberlain) *reluctant to load: sn chsng ldrs: rdn and outpcd over 3f out: styd on again fnl f to take wl-hld 3rd last strides* **80/1**

22 **4** ½ **Paoletta (USA)**[120] 2528 3-8-12 0.................................. JamieSpencer 3 69
(Mahmood Al Zarooni) *chsd ldrs: wnt 3rd over 2f out but no imp on ldng duo: wknd and ct for 3rd last strides* **1/1**[1]

5 **5** 11 **Appeal (IRE)**[14] 5999 3-8-12 0.. SebSanders 10 47
(Sir Mark Prescott Bt) *in rr: drvn along 6f out sme hdwy over 3f out: nvr rchd ldrs and wknd over 2f out* **7/1**[3]

6 shd **Sky Crystal (GER)** 3-8-12 0... NickyMackay 9 47+
(John Gosden) *in rr: rdn and rn green over 5f out: mod prog u.p fnl 2f* **16/1**

-000 **7** 24 **No Refraction (IRE)**[118] 2586 3-8-12 40.............................. LiamKeniry 2 —
(Mark Usher) *led tl hdd & wknd over 3f out: t.o* **100/1**

0 **8** 11 **Brunston Keys**[50] 4826 3-8-12 0.. JamesDoyle 6 —
(Tony Carroll) *reluctant to load: t.k.h: chsd ldrs tl wknd qckly over 3f out* **100/1**

6 **9** 15 **Hairpin (USA)**[14] 5999 3-8-12 0...................................... AhmedAjtebi 5 —
(Mahmood Al Zarooni) *a in rr: t.o: virtually p.u fnl f* **20/1**

40 **10** 79 **Reluctant Heroine (USA)**[17] 5877 3-8-12 0.................. FrannyNorton 1 —
(Mark Johnston) *in tch early: dropped out fnl 4f: t.o: virtually p.u fnl 2f* **50/1**

2m 17.28s (6.28) **Going Correction** +0.425s/f (Yiel) **10** Ran SP% **117.5**
Speed ratings (Par 100): **91,90,86,86,77 77,58,49,37,—**
toteswingers:1&2:£5.30, 1&3:£17.00, 2&3:£56.80 CSF £32.04 TOTE £3.50: £1.40, £3.30, £8.60; EX 24.60.

Owner A D Spence **Bred** R Ahamad And P Scott **Trained** Lambourn, Berks

FOCUS
No more than a fair maiden, run in a slow time. Few got involved. The winner is rated close to her best with the second and improver.

6405 ODDSCHECKER.COM H'CAP 2m 1f 34y
6:00 (6:01) (Class 5) (0-75,75) 3-Y-O+ **£2,264** (£673; £336; £168) **Stalls** Centre

Form RPR

0000 **1** **L Frank Baum (IRE)**[9] 6171 4-10-0 **75**........................ RobertWinston 10 84
(Gay Kelleway) *trckd ldrs: chsd ldr 3f out: slt ld fr 2f out: styd on wl u.p: asserted fnl 75yds* **6/1**[3]

2 1 ½ **Pateese (FR)**[172] 6-9-12 **73**... JamieSpencer 3 80
(Philip Hobbs) *in rr: hdwy fr 3f out: drvn to chse ldrs fr 2f out: chal 1f out: styd on for 2nd fnl 50yds but no ch w wnr* **2/1**[1]

1063 **3** ¾ **Warne's Way (IRE)**[94] 3352 8-9-11 **72**........................... TomQueally 7 78
(Brendan Powell) *chsd ldr tl led 3f out: narrowly hdd 2f out: styd chalng and ev ch 1f out: one pce into 3rd fnl 50yds* **14/1**

5254 **4** 1 ¼ **Salontyre (GER)**[37] 4941 5-9-5 **66**..........................(p) JimmyFortune 13 71
(Bernard Llewellyn) *in rr: hdwy over 4f out: drvn to chse ldrs over 2f out: one pce ins fnl f* **8/1**

6500 **5** 7 **Gaselee (USA)**[82] 3738 5-9-5 **69**........................... AdamBeschizza(3) 6 65
(Rae Guest) *led tl hdd 3f out: styd chssing ldrs tl wknd ins fnl 2f* **20/1**

6015 **6** 3 ½ **Raktiman (IRE)**[18] 5866 4-9-8 **69**......................(p) RichardKingscote 8 61
(Tom Dascombe) *towards rr: hdwy 7f out: drvn to chse ldrs 3f out: stl wl there u.p 2f out: wknd sn after* **25/1**

2222 **7** 19 **Oneiric**[42] 5098 3-9-0 **73**.. JimCrowley 4 42
(Ralph Beckett) *chsd ldrs and disp 2nd 6f out: rdn over 3f out: wknd qckly wl over 2f out* **13/2**

0543 **8** ½ **Sula Two**[33] 5389 4-9-6 **67**.. GeorgeBaker 5 36
(Ron Hodges) *sn bhd: hdwy to cl on ldrs over 3f out: sn rdn: wknd qckly wl over 2f out* **5/1**[2]

-050 **9** 19 **Uncle Keef (IRE)**[43] 5079 5-8-9 **56** oh2...................... RussKennemore 1 —
(Brendan Powell) *a towards rr: t.o* **33/1**

5031 **10** 8 **Where's Susie**[24] 5692 6-9-9 **70**.. ChrisCatlin 12 —
(Michael Madgwick) *in rr: rdn and brief effrt 4f out: nvr nr ldrs and wknd qckly fr 3f out: t.o* **16/1**

0420 **11** 93 **Bute Street**[189] 622 6-8-13 **60**.. JamesDoyle 9 —
(Ron Hodges) *in tch tl wknd rapidly 5f out: sn eased and t.o* **40/1**

3m 59.99s (8.09) **Going Correction** +0.425s/f (Yiel)
WFA 3 from 4yo+ 12lb 11 Ran SP% **115.3**
Speed ratings (Par 103): **97,96,95,95,92 90,81,81,72,68 24**
toteswingers:1&2:£3.20, 1&3:£13.60, 2&3:£7.60 CSF £17.18 CT £161.88 TOTE £7.10: £2.50, £1.30, £4.70; EX 20.70.

Owner Aussie Connection **Bred** Ballymacoll Stud Farm Ltd **Trained** Exning, Suffolk

FOCUS
The top three on the racecard came home in weight order here. The first four were clear and the form seems sound enough.

T/Jkpt: Not won. T/Plt: £766.00 to a £1 stake. Pool:£81,372.17 - 77.54 winning tickets T/Qpdt: £37.40 to a £1 stake. Pool:£7,074.45 - 139.94 winning tickets ST

5959 FFOS LAS (L-H)
Monday, September 26

OFFICIAL GOING: Soft (good to soft in places; 7.3)
Wind: Light, against Weather: Overcast

6406 BRITISH STALLION STUDS SUPPORTING BRITISH RACING E B F MAIDEN STKS 5f
2:20 (2:21) (Class 5) 2-Y-O **£3,234** (£962; £481; £240) **Stalls** High

Form RPR

50 **1** **Beach Candy (IRE)**[17] 5889 2-8-12 0.............................. MartinDwyer 9 74
(Richard Hannon) *prom: led 4f out: mde rest: rdn over 1f out: r.o wl and in command fnl 75yds* **11/2**[3]

2 **2** 2 **Sheer Vanity (USA)**[13] 6026 2-8-12 0........................(t) RichardMullen 8 67
(Ed McMahon) *dwlt: hld up in midfield: rdn and hdwy to chse ldrs over 1f out: wnt 2nd towards fin: no imp on wnr* **7/2**[2]

0 **3** ½ **Million Faces**[17] 5889 2-8-12 0.. SteveDrowne 10 65
(Rae Guest) *racd keenly and travelled wl: a.p: rdn to chal over 1f out: no ex fnl 75yds* **7/4**[1]

5220 **4** nk **Night Angel (IRE)**[18] 5840 2-8-12 65............................ JamesMillman 7 64
(Rod Millman) *led for 1f: trckd ldrs after: rdn and nt qckn over 1f out: styd on same pce ins fnl f* **12/1**

0 **5** 5 **Gabrial's Bounty (IRE)**[9] 6165 2-9-3 0............................. KierenFallon 3 51
(Mick Channon) *midfield: u.p fr 3f out: nvr able to trble ldrs* **7/2**[2]

0 **6** ½ **Diamond Rainbow (IRE)**[151] 1639 2-9-3 0................ RoystonFfrench 5 49
(Rodger Sweeney, Ire) *prom: rdn over 1f out: wknd ent fnl f* **50/1**

04 **7** nk **Trusting (IRE)**[21] 5779 2-8-9 0.................................... JohnFahy(3) 1 43
(Eve Johnson Houghton) *hld up: rdn wl over 1f out: no imp on ldrs: wl btn ins fnl f* **40/1**

0 **8** ½ **Speedy Yaki (IRE)**[68] 4217 2-9-0 0.......................... MartinHarley(3) 2 46
(Daniel Mark Loughnane, Ire) *in rr: outpcd 2f out: nvr able to get on terms* **66/1**

9 ½ **Desert Spree** 2-8-5 0.. RaulDaSilva(7) 4 40
(Jeremy Gask) *in rr: outpcd 2f out: nvr on terms* **33/1**

10 12 **Jeremy Sue** 2-8-12 0.. FrankieMcDonald 6 —
(Derek Haydn Jones) *missed break: a outpcd and wl bhd* **66/1**

60.82 secs (2.52) **Going Correction** +0.40s/f (Good) **10** Ran SP% **114.2**
Speed ratings (Par 95): **95,91,91,90,82 81,81,80,79,60**
toteswingers:1&2:£5.10, 1&3:£2.80, 2&3:£2.50 CSF £23.93 TOTE £7.50: £1.60, £1.30, £1.10; EX 30.90.

Owner S Mahal, R Morecombe & D Anderson **Bred** Lynn Lodge Stud **Trained** East Everleigh, Wilts

FOCUS
This looked just a modest sprint maiden. They raced towards the stands' side. The winner built on his previous promise with the runner-up to his mark.

NOTEBOOK
Beach Candy(IRE) had shown ability on her first two starts, including when not getting the clearest of runs dropped to this trip last time, and she produced an improved performance to get off the mark. There might be more to come and she shouldn't get too stiff a mark for nurseries/handicaps. (op 5-1 tchd 7-1)
Sheer Vanity(USA) ◆, beaten just a short-head over this trip on easy ground at Haydock first time out, took too long to pick up. She has a US pedigree and her dam won her only race on Polytrack, so there might be better to come when she switches to a sound surface. (op 3-1 tchd 4-1)
Million Faces was only a head behind Beach Candy despite finding trouble on her debut over 5f at Sandown, and it looked a performance she'd go forward from (not given hard time), but she failed to progress as expected. This ground may have been too testing, though, and she can be given another chance. (op 2-1, tchd 9-4 in a place)
Night Angel(IRE), officially rated 65, plugged on at the one pace without looking likely to win. She's now 0-12. (op 9-1)
Gabrial's Bounty(IRE), well held on his debut over 7f at Newbury, made some late headway and should find his level when he can switch to handicaps. (op 9-2 tchd 3-1)
Jeremy Sue Official explanation: jockey said filly missed the break

6407 SELWOOD PUMP AND PLANT HIRE MEDIAN AUCTION MAIDEN STKS 6f
2:50 (2:52) (Class 6) 3-5-Y-O **£1,681** (£500; £250; £125) **Stalls** High

Form RPR

6030 **1** **Choose The Moment**[12] 6070 3-8-12 54...................(b[1]) RichardMullen 1 63
(Eve Johnson Houghton) *a.p: rdn over 2f out: chalng over 1f out: led fnl 120yds: styd on and in control towards fin* **11/1**

3332 **2** 1 **Cheherazad (IRE)**[18] 5842 3-8-12 65.................................. IanMongan 4 60
(Paul Cole) *led: rdn whn pressed over 1f out: hdd fnl 120yds: hld towards fin* **5/1**[3]

3 2 ¾ **Swedish Rhapsody (IRE)**[79] 3885 3-8-9 0......................... JohnFahy(3) 3 51
(John Joseph Murphy, Ire) *trckd ldrs for 2f: sn stdd and hld up: hdwy 2f out: rdn to chse ldrs over 1f out: one pce fnl 100yds* **9/1**

204 **4** 3 ¼ **Tenavon**[3] 6307 3-8-12 0.. JoeFanning 2 41
(William Knight) *hld up: hdwy to chal over 2f out: rdn over 1f out: wknd fnl 110yds* **15/8**[2]

4344 **5** 8 **Tiberius Claudius (IRE)**[13] 6034 3-9-3 72....................... KierenFallon 5 20
(George Margarson) *racd keenly: handy: rdn over 2f out: sn wknd: wl bhd fnl f* **6/4**[1]

1m 13.88s (3.88) **Going Correction** +0.65s/f (Yiel) **5** Ran SP% **109.8**
Speed ratings (Par 101): **100,98,95,90,80**
CSF £59.72 TOTE £14.30: £4.20, £2.80; EX 51.30.

Owner Eden Racing Club **Bred** Michael Nelmes-Crocker **Trained** Blewbury, Oxon

FOCUS
A weak sprint maiden in which the market leaders ran poorly and the first two had been regressive. They raced up the centre of the track.
Tiberius Claudius(IRE) Official explanation: jockey said saddle slipped

6408 STRADEY PARK H'CAP 6f
3:20 (3:22) (Class 5) (0-70,70) 3-Y-O+ **£2,264** (£673; £336; £168) **Stalls** High

Form RPR

0300 **1** **Supreme Spirit (IRE)**[12] 6065 4-9-7 **70**..........................(b[1]) IanMongan 4 78
(George Margarson) *dwlt: racd keenly: hld up: swtchd lft over 2f out: hdwy under 2f out: r.o ins fnl f: led fnl stride* **9/1**

3560 **2** shd **Madame Kintyre**[10] 6119 3-8-10 **61**........................(b[1]) JamesMillman 2 69
(Rod Millman) *led: rdn over 1f out: pressed thrght fnl f: hdd fnl stride* **8/1**

0025 **3** ½ **Pose (IRE)**[38] 5238 4-8-6 **60**..................................(t) MatthewLawson(5) 1 66
(Roger Ingram) *a.p: rdn over 1f out: chalng ins fnl f: hld fnl strides* **25/1**

0460 **4** 1 ¾ **Gracie's Games**[16] 5917 5-8-6 **58**.............................. SophieDoyle(3) 6 58+
(Richard Price) *hld up in rr: swtchd rt 2f out: hdwy and edgd lft overt 1f out: styd on towards fin: nt quite get to ldrs* **9/2**[2]

0-00 **5** *7* **Johnstown Lad (IRE)**[26] 5616 7-9-5 **68**........................(t) KierenFallon 3 46
(Daniel Mark Loughnane, Ire) *chsd ldrs: bmpd under 2f out: sn u.p: btn and no imp fnl f* **9/2**[2]

0601 **6** *1* **Bathwick Xaara**[29] 5513 4-8-10 **62**............................ RossAtkinson(3) 5 37+
(Jonathan Portman) *in tch: rdn and bmpd under 2f out: wknd over 1f out* **10/3**[1]

-000 **7** *3/4* **Superior Edge**[26] 5616 4-9-2 **70**..................................(p) RyanPowell(5) 8 42
(Christopher Mason) *chsd ldr to 3f out: rdn and hung lft over 2f out: wknd fnl f* **20/1**

0004 **8** *1* **Dream Number (IRE)**[36] 5301 4-8-10 **59**........................ MartinDwyer 9 28
(William Muir) *hld up: rdn whn n.m.r and hmpd over 1f out: n.d after* **13/2**

0554 **9** *nk* **Jeeran**[73] 4067 3-8-1 **59**.. KatiaScallan(7) 7 27
(Alastair Lidderdale) *midfield: pushed along 1/2-way: rdn and wknd 2f out: sn edgd lft whn n.d* **11/2**[3]

1m 13.38s (3.38) **Going Correction** +0.65s/f (Yiel)
WFA 3 from 4yo+ 2lb **9** Ran SP% **117.9**
Speed ratings (Par 103): **103,102,102,99,90 89,88,86,86**
toteswingers:1&2:£14.30, 1&3:£23.20, 2&3:£22.30 CSF £80.10 CT £1743.72 TOTE £10.20: £2.10, £1.80, £8.70; EX 112.00.
Owner Mrs C C Regalado-Gonzalez **Bred** Jill Finnegan And Noel Cogan **Trained** Newmarket, Suffolk
■ Stewards' Enquiry : Ryan Powell caution: careless riding.

FOCUS
A modest but reasonably competitive handicap and the pace was quick for the conditions. They were spread out across the track in the closing stages. The form is not necessarily the most solid.

6409 AMEC ENVIRONMENT AND INFRASTRUCTURE H'CAP 1m 2f (R)
3:50 (3:51) (Class 4) (0-85,83) 3-Y-O **£4,075** (£1,212; £606; £303) **Stalls** Low

Form RPR

3006 **1** **Pivotman**[15] 5971 3-9-7 **83**..(t) IanMongan 8 101+
(Amanda Perrett) *mde all: styd on strly to draw clr over 1f out: wl in command after: eased down fnl 75yds* **8/1**

0030 **2** *8* **Stentorian (IRE)**[17] 5893 3-8-13 **75**.............................(b) JoeFanning 5 74
(Mark Johnston) *hld up: hdwy whn nt clr run briefly over 3f out: rdn whn wnt 2nd 2f out: no ch w wnr but chalng for pls after: kpt on* **22/1**

316 **3** *1/2* **Gobool**[17] 5880 3-9-6 **82**... KierenFallon 2 80
(William Haggas) *in tch: pusherd along over 3f out: rdn whn chalng for pls over 1f out: no ch w wnr: kpt on: hld for 2nd cl home* **7/1**

0321 **4** *1 3/4* **West Brit (IRE)**[45] 5007 3-9-6 **82**...................................... SteveDrowne 9 77
(Ed Dunlop) *hld up: rdn and edgd lft whn hdwy over 2f out: chalng for pls over 1f out: nvr any ch w wnr: kpt on same pce fnl 100yds* **9/2**[3]

6321 **5** *9* **Icebuster**[17] 5893 3-9-7 **83**.. JamesMillman 7 60
(Rod Millman) *hld up in rr: pushed along over 4f out: swtchd lft 1f out: plugged on for press wout troubling ldrs* **2/1**[1]

4535 **6** *nk* **Captain Loui (IRE)**[167] 1295 3-7-11 **64**.......................... RyanPowell(5) 3 40
(Dai Burchell) *hld up: u.p over 3f out: nvr able to trble ldrs* **80/1**

0416 **7** *3 3/4* **Red Inca**[16] 5925 3-8-11 **73**.. MartinDwyer 4 41
(Brian Meehan) *racd keenly: trckd ldrs: u.p over 4f out: rdn and wknd over 2f out* **4/1**[2]

4421 **8** *3 1/4* **Swift Bird (IRE)**[31] 5429 3-8-12 **74**.............................(b) RichardMullen 1 36
(Noel Quinlan) *chsd wnr tl rdn over 2f out: sn wknd* **10/1**

3106 **9** *1/2* **Highlife Dancer**[5] 6248 3-8-13 **78**................................. MartinHarley(3) 6 39
(Mick Channon) *prom: rdn 3f out: wknd over 2f out: eased whn wl btn over 1f out* **16/1**

2m 17.69s (8.29) **Going Correction** +0.80s/f (Soft) **9** Ran SP% **115.7**
Speed ratings (Par 103): **98,91,91,89,82 82,79,76,76**
toteswingers:1&2:£22.90, 1&3:£11.80, 2&3:£12.90 CSF £162.80 CT £1289.57 TOTE £7.30: £1.80, £6.30, £3.00; EX 168.20.
Owner John Connolly **Bred** Cheveley Park Stud Ltd **Trained** Pulborough, W Sussex

FOCUS
They raced up the centre of the track in the straight. Often superiority can be exaggerated on testing ground and there were some wide-margin winners on the round course, so it's hard to know exactly what Pivotman achieved. He's worth more at face value but there are doubts whether anything else showed their form.
Swift Bird(IRE) Official explanation: jockey said filly was unsuited by the soft (good to soft places) ground

0410 LINCWEAN II'OAP 1m 6f (R)
4:20 (4:20) (Class 3) (0-90,87) 3-Y-O+ **£6,663** (£1,982; £990; £495) **Stalls** Low

Form RPR

0601 **1** **Becausewecan (USA)**[19] 5837 5-9-13 **86**.......................... JoeFanning 1 97
(Mark Johnston) *mde all: rdn 2f out: styd on wl thrght fnl f and a in command* **9/1**

/14- **2** *3* **Oldrik (GER)**[331] 6957 8-9-2 **75**.................................(p) RichardMullen 3 84+
(Philip Hobbs) *hld up in rr: hdwy over 3f out: nt clr run over 2f out: swtchd lft shortly after: wnt 2nd over 1f out: styd on ins fnl f: no imp on wnr* **10/1**

5312 **3** *3 1/2* **Qahriman**[25] 5641 3-9-4 **87**.. KierenFallon 7 89
(Luca Cumani) *in tch: impr over 4f out: in contention whn hung lft over 2f out: one pce fnl f* **3/1**[3]

410- **4** *2 1/2* **Just Rob**[452] 3588 6-9-9 **82**.. RoystonFfrench 9 80
(Ian Williams) *hld up: rdn over 2f out: kpt on modly fnl f: no imp* **20/1**

0211 **5** *2 1/4* **Rastaban**[46] 4957 3-9-1 **84**.. MartinDwyer 2 79+
(William Haggas) *in tch: effrt over 3f out: rdn to chse wnr over 2f out tl over 1f out: wknd ins fnl f* **11/4**[2]

4214 **6** *20* **Slight Advantage (IRE)**[17] 5878 3-8-11 **83**...................... JohnFahy(3) 8 50
(Clive Cox) *chsd ldrs: chsd wnr over 5f out tl rdn over 2f out: sn n.m.r and hmpd: wknd over 1f out: eased whn wl btn ins fnl f* **2/1**[1]

0160 **7** *9* **Lady of Burgundy**[15] 5962 5-8-9 **72** ow1...................... LeeNewnes(5) 4 28
(Mark Usher) *hld up in rr: sddle slipped after 2f: nvr able to threaten and allowed to coast home in st* **33/1**

0030 **8** *20* **Parhelion**[60] 4464 4-9-2 **75**.. SteveDrowne 5 —
(Derek Haydn Jones) *chsd wnr to over 5f out: wknd wl over 3f out: eased whn wl btn over 2f out: t.o* **40/1**

6560 **9** *3 1/4* **Nibani (IRE)**[19] 5837 4-9-3 **76**.. IanMongan 6 —
(Alastair Lidderdale) *hld up: u.p over 4f out: bhd fnl 3f: t.o* **25/1**

3m 17.16s (13.36) **Going Correction** +0.80s/f (Soft)
WFA 3 from 4yo+ 10lb **9** Ran SP% **118.1**
Speed ratings (Par 107): **93,91,89,87,86 75,70,58,56**
toteswingers:1&2:£8.10, 1&3:£4.50, 2&3:£5.60 CSF £89.66 CT £337.20 TOTE £10.70: £2.90, £2.60, £1.20; EX 62.30.
Owner Douglas Livingston **Bred** Tony Holmes & Walter Zent **Trained** Middleham Moor, N Yorks

FOCUS
Again the action was up the middle of the track in the straight. Fair form, but plenty didn't show their form in the ground. The winner was rated to his turf best.

NOTEBOOK
Becausewecan(USA), just like when successful at Kempton on his previous start off 4lb lower over 1m4f on Polytrack, was allowed an uncontested lead. He had to go off fast enough to get the lead, but then slowed the pace noticeably before the straight and had his ears pricked, clearly saving plenty. He won't make great appeal next time unless it's clear he'll again get the run of the race. (op 11-1 tchd 12-1)
Oldrik(GER), returning from the best part of a year off, seemed to travel okay but his rider took a while to get serious and he also had to be switched, so this was a creditable effort behind the front-running winner. (op 12-1)
Qahriman, up in trip and faced with testing conditions for the first time, was well enough placed but didn't convince that he was handing the ground when under pressure. He can be given another chance. (op 11-4)
Just Rob, returning from a 452-day absence, travelled well to a point and retains ability.
Rastaban was up in trip after two wins at 1m4f on better ground, the latest off 4lb lower. Evidently these conditions didn't suit. (tchd 9-4)
Slight Advantage(IRE) has winning from on soft ground but she ran poorly. She found trouble in the straight, but was beaten at the time. Official explanation: jockey said filly was unsuited by the soft (good to soft places) ground (op 5-2 tchd 11-4)
Lady of Burgundy Official explanation: jockey said saddle slipped
Nibani(IRE) Official explanation: jockey said gelding was unsuited by the soft (good to soft places) ground

6411 SPIFFING CRABBIE'S ALCOHOLIC GINGER BEER H'CAP 1m (R)
4:50 (4:52) (Class 6) (0-60,57) 3-Y-O+ **£1,772** (£523; £261) **Stalls** Low

Form RPR

2353 **1** **Fitz**[46] 4948 5-9-3 **55**.. LeeNewnes(5) 14 65
(Matthew Salaman) *hld up: hdwy 3f out: rdn to chse ldrs: styd on to ld wl ins fnl f: on top fnl strides* **6/1**[2]

226- **2** *1/2* **Harting Hill**[313] 7483 6-9-2 **56**.. KatiaScallan(7) 15 65
(Marcus Tregoning) *midfield: hdwy 3f out: rdn to chal over 1f out: sn led: hdd wl ins fnl f: hld cl home* **13/2**[3]

3-03 **3** *1* **Qaraqum (USA)**[16] 5944 4-9-8 **55**.................................. KierenFallon 13 62
(Denis Coakley) *midfield: hdwy 4f out: wnt 2nd over 3f out: led over 1f out: sn hdd: stl ch ins fnl f: styd on same pce fnl 75yds* **4/1**[1]

0002 **4** *1 3/4* **Croeso Mawr**[13] 6033 5-9-4 **51**.................................... SteveDrowne 7 54
(John Spearing) *midfield: rdn and hdwy 3f out: chsd ldrs over 1f out: styd on same pce fnl 150yds* **7/1**

10 **5** *2 1/4* **Caledonia Prince**[8] 6192 3-9-3 **54**..............................(p) JoeFanning 2 52
(Jo Hughes) *led: rdn over 2f out: hdd over 1f out: stl wl there ent fnl f: wknd fnl 100yds* **20/1**

6 *7* **Gothen Niece (IRE)**[76] 3965 7-8-12 **45**.............................. IanMongan 8 27
(C P Donoghue, Ire) *midfield: pushed along 3f out: kpt on modly fnl f: nvr able to trble ldrs* **10/1**

004 **7** *1* **Lightning Spirit**[31] 5423 3-8-12 **52**........................(p) MartinHarley(3) 11 31
(Gary Moore) *hld up: rdn and hdwy into midfield over 2f out: nvr able to trble ldrs* **9/1**

6551 **8** *2 1/4* **Mister Fantastic**[11] 6084 5-9-0 **52**............................ AntiocoMurgia(5) 5 26
(Dai Burchell) *handy: rdn over 2f out: wknd over 1f out* **7/1**

060 **9** *7* **Pagan Warrior (IRE)**[87] 3594 3-9-3 **57**.........................(t) JohnFahy(3) 10 15
(Clive Cox) *prom tl rdn and wknd 3f out* **12/1**

10 *1 1/2* **Draoicht (IRE)**[14] 6015 3-8-8 **45**.................................. FrankieMcDonald 9 —
(John Joseph Murphy, Ire) *s.i.s: in tch: rdn 3f out: wknd over 2f out* **16/1**

/060 **11** *3/4* **Spring Buck (IRE)**[11] 6090 6-9-4 **56**............................ RyanPowell(5) 6 —
(Paul Cole) *pushed along ealry: impoved into midfield after 2f: effrt and hdwy over 3f out: wknd over 1f out* **40/1**

000 **12** *1 1/2* **Prana (USA)**[26] 5633 3-8-8 **45**...................................... MartinDwyer 1 —
(Jeremy Gask) *trckd ldrs: rdn over 3f out: wknd over 1f out* **40/1**

0600 **13** *11* **Tuscan King**[14] 5994 4-9-1 **48**................................(bt) RoystonFfrench 4 —
(Bernard Llewellyn) *pushed along thrght: a bhd* **28/1**

0004 **14** *3 1/4* **Lennoxwood (IRE)**[11] 6083 3-8-11 **48**......................(b) RichardMullen 12 —
(Mark Usher) *hld up in rr: u.p over 2f out: nvr on terms: eased whn wl btn over 1f out* **20/1**

0-00 **15** *14* **Lucky Tricks**[41] 5137 3-8-1 **45**.................................(v[1]) RaulDaSilva(7) 3 —
(Jeremy Gask) *prom tl rdn and wknd over 3f out: t.o* **50/1**

1m 47.13s (6.13) **Going Correction** +0.80s/f (Soft)
WFA 3 from 4yo+ 4lb **15** Ran SP% **125.1**
Speed ratings (Par 101): **101,100,99,97,95 88,87,85,78,76 76,74,63,60,46**
toteswingers:1&2:£6.50, 1&3:£6.50, 2&3:£6.80 CSF £42.78 CT £158.64 TOTE £4.60: £1.70, £2.40, £2.10; EX 47.60.
Owner Mrs Victoria Keen **Bred** Bearstone Stud **Trained** Upper Lambourn, Berks

FOCUS
They raced middle to far side. A moderate but quite competitive handicap and unlike some results on the card this makes sense. A turf best from the winner.

6412 DIGIBET.COM APPRENTICE H'CAP 1m 4f (R)
5:20 (5:20) (Class 5) (0-75,74) 3-Y-O **£2,264** (£673; £336; £168) **Stalls** Low

Form RPR

1263 **1** **Lemon Drop Red (USA)**[10] 6121 3-9-5 **72**...................... RyanPowell 3 85
(Ed Dunlop) *chsd ldrs: wnt 2nd over 3f out: rdn to ld over 2f out: drew clr over 1f out: unchal after: in command whn edgd rt ins fnl f: styd on wl* **7/2**[2]

1333 **2** *10* **Chatterer (IRE)**[20] 5804 3-8-12 **70**............................... KatiaScallan(5) 5 67
(Marcus Tregoning) *hld up in rr: effrt over 2f out: chsd clr wnr over 1f out: no ch* **6/4**[1]

4632 **3** *3 3/4* **Ecossaise**[16] 5915 3-9-4 **74**.. DarylByrne(3) 2 65
(Mark Johnston) *led: rdn and hdd over 2f out: lost 2nd over 1f out: wl btn fnl f* **6/4**[1]

6320 **4** *20* **Enriching (USA)**[19] 5836 3-8-6 **62** oh3 ow2............(t) AntiocoMurgia(3) 4 21
(Noel Quinlan) *chsd ldr tl pushed along over 3f out: bhd fnl 2f* **12/1**[3]

2m 50.82s (13.42) **Going Correction** +0.80s/f (Soft) **4** Ran SP% **109.9**
Speed ratings (Par 101): **87,80,77,64**
CSF £9.28 TOTE £3.30; EX 9.60.
Owner R J Arculli **Bred** Nancy M Leonard Living Trust **Trained** Newmarket, Suffolk

FOCUS
The action was up the middle of the track. There's a doubt over how literally to take the winner's effort but this was a clear personal best.

T/Plt: £866.20 to a £1 stake. Pool:£61,444.63 - 51.78 winning tickets T/Qpdt: £248.50 to a £1 stake. Pool:£5,811.77 - 17.30 winning tickets DO

6207 HAMILTON (R-H)

Monday, September 26

OFFICIAL GOING: Soft (heavy in places; 6.6)

Wind: Fairly strong, across Weather: Cloudy, bright

6413 SCOTTISH RACING AUCTION NURSERY 6f 5y

2:10 (2:10) (Class 5) 2-Y-O **£2,587** (£770; £384; £192) **Stalls** High

Form RPR

4125 **1** **Kimbali (IRE)**[2] 6323 2-9-7 **78** .... PaulHanagan 4 83
(Richard Fahey) *trckd ldrs: effrt over 1f out: rdn and led ins fnl f: hld on gamely* **11/4**[3]

0120 **2** *nk* **Blue Shoes (IRE)**[18] 5847 2-8-6 **63** .... DuranFentiman 3 67
(Tim Easterby) *w ldr: rdn and led over 1f out: hdd ins fnl f: rallied: hld towards fin* **11/1**

6635 **3** *6* **Jay Kay**[32] 5399 2-7-10 **58** .... NeilFarley(5) 5 44
(Robert Wylie) *t.k.h: sn prom: nt clr run over 2f and over 1f out: outpcd by ldng pair fnl f* **25/1**

10 **4** *1 1/4* **Sardanapalus**[38] 5251 2-9-5 **76** .... PhillipMakin 2 58
(Kevin Ryan) *dwlt: sn trcking ldrs: effrt over 1f out: wknd ins fnl f* **15/8**[1]

61 **5** *7* **Alice's Dancer (IRE)**[7] 6222 2-9-6 **77** 6ex .... WilliamCarson 1 38
(William Muir) *plld hrd: led to over 1f out: sn wknd* **2/1**[2]

0030 **6** *19* **Landaho**[19] 5819 2-7-12 **55** oh4 .... JamesSullivan 6 —
(Hugh McWilliams) *sn outpcd and hung rt: no ch fr 1/2-way* **100/1**

1m 16.16s (3.96) **Going Correction** +0.55s/f (Yiel) **6** Ran SP% **108.0**

Speed ratings (Par 95): **95,94,86,84,75 50**

toteswingers:1&2:£2.60, 1&3:£4.30, 2&3:£8.30 CSF £28.09 TOTE £4.00: £1.80, £3.50; EX 21.70.

Owner Dr Marwan Koukash **Bred** P Kelly **Trained** Musley Bank, N Yorks

■ Stewards' Enquiry : Duran Fentiman one-day ban: used whip with excessive frequency (Oct 10)

FOCUS

Further rain before racing led to the ground being changed to soft, heavy in places. All races beyond 6f were run over 8yds shorter than advertised due to rail configuration. The front pair drew clear in what was a modest nursery. The form is rated around them.

NOTEBOOK

Kimbali(IRE), winner of a C&D claimer last month, picked up well when switched and just prevailed under a strong ride from Hanagan. This was compensation for when receiving a shocking run at Chester last time. (tchd 5-2)

Blue Shoes(IRE) didn't get home in a more competitive race than this over 7f at Doncaster last time (wore cheekpieces), but was seen to better effect here, racing on the pace against the rail in a smaller field, and she duly pulled clear of the third.

Jay Kay was keen on this step up to 6f and will need to settle if he's to be winning. (op 33-1)

Sardanapalus, out of his depth in a Group 2 last time, was disappointing on this drop into handicap company and may need better ground. (op 7-4 tchd 2-1 and 9-4 in places)

Alice's Dancer(IRE) pulled hard under a penalty and stopped quickly. This clearly wasn't her form. (op 9-4 tchd 15-8)

6414 OVERTON FARM SHOP CLASSIFIED CLAIMING STKS 6f 5y

2:40 (2:40) (Class 6) 3-Y-O+ **£2,045** (£603; £302) **Stalls** High

Form RPR

513 **1** **Desert Icon (IRE)**[12] 6056 5-8-8 **68** .... MartinLane 8 70
(David Simcock) *dwlt: sn bhd and hung rt thrght: gd hdwy to ld over 1f out: kpt on wl* **5/2**[1]

3460 **2** *1/2* **Bonnie Prince Blue**[7] 6208 8-8-5 **65** ....(v) PaulHanagan 1 65
(Ian McInnes) *bhd: struggling over 3f out: hdwy over 1f out: chsd wnr ins fnl f: r.o* **10/1**

3144 **3** *4 1/2* **Northern Bolt**[28] 5554 6-8-13 **69** .... PatrickMathers 7 59
(Ian McInnes) *sn pushed along bhd ldrs: effrt wl over 1f out: no ex fnl f* **11/4**[2]

0005 **4** *1 3/4* **Sonny Red (IRE)**[11] 6076 7-8-7 **65** .... ShirleyTeasdale(7) 9 54
(David Nicholls) *w ldrs: led over 2f tl over 1f out: wknd ins fnl f* **11/2**

606 **5** *3 1/4* **King Bertolini (IRE)**[7] 6208 4-8-6 **42** ....(p) SilvestreDeSousa 4 36
(Alan Berry) *dwlt: bhd and sn struggling: kpt on fnl f: nvr on terms* **66/1**

6000 **6** *1* **Carrie's Magic**[7] 6212 4-8-9 **64** ....(b) GarryWhillans(5) 5 41
(Alistair Whillans) *prom tl rdn and wknd fr 2f out* **16/1**

0064 **7** *shd* **Honest And True (IRE)**[12] 6049 4-8-8 **47** ....(b) TomEaves 2 34
(Ian Semple) *w ldrs tl wknd fr 2f out* **25/1**

-034 **8** *5* **Logans Legend (IRE)**[95] 3320 3-8-11 **68** .... LanceBetts(5) 3 28
(Lawrence Mullaney) *led to over 2f out: sn rdn and wknd* **16/1**

0044 **9** *3 1/4* **Royal Blade (IRE)**[2] 6343 4-8-11 **64** .... JulieBurke(5) 6 16
(Alan Berry) *in tch: drvn over 2f out: sn wknd* **5/1**[3]

1m 16.99s (4.79) **Going Correction** +0.775s/f (Yiel)

WFA 3 from 4yo+ 2lb **9** Ran SP% **113.5**

Speed ratings (Par 101): **99,98,92,90,85 84,84,77,73**

toteswingers:1&2:£5.60, 1&3:£2.10, 2&3:£7.00 CSF £27.82 TOTE £3.70: £1.60, £3.00, £2.00; EX 30.40 Trifecta £107.60 Pool: £485.99 - 3.34 winning units..

Owner Tick Tock Partnership **Bred** Lynch Bages Ltd & Samac Ltd **Trained** Newmarket, Suffolk

FOCUS

As in the opening contest, the first two home pulled a little way clear of the remainder. The form is rated around the first two but is not the most convincing.

Royal Blade(IRE) Official explanation: trainer said gelding returned lame

6415 NEILSLAND AND EARNOCK H'CAP 1m 65y

3:10 (3:10) (Class 6) (0-65,60) 3-Y-O **£2,045** (£603; £302) **Stalls** Low

Form RPR

0510 **1** **Smart Step**[10] 6122 3-9-0 **53** .... SilvestreDeSousa 4 66
(Mark Johnston) *pressed ldr: led over 2f out: sn rdn: styd on wl fnl f* **11/4**[1]

-006 **2** *1/2* **Uncle Bryn**[26] 5619 3-9-4 **57** .... PBBeggy 6 69
(John Quinn) *prom: pushed along 3f out: hdwy to chse wnr over 1f out: kpt on fnl f but a hld* **7/2**[2]

0036 **3** *7* **Phoenix Flame**[6] 6235 3-9-1 **54** ....(v[1]) PaulHanagan 1 50
(Alan McCabe) *led to over 2f out: sn drvn and no ex fr over 1f out* **9/2**[3]

4254 **4** *6* **Purkab**[35] 5315 3-8-13 **52** ....(p) DanielTudhope 3 34
(Jim Goldie) *hld up in tch: drvn and outpcd over 3f out: rallied over 1f out: nvr able to chal* **9/1**

1104 **5** *1 1/4* **Whats For Pudding (IRE)**[9] 6159 3-8-11 **55** .... NeilFarley(5) 2 34
(Declan Carroll) *trckd ldrs: rdn 3f out: wknd wl over 1f out* **9/2**[3]

6050 **6** *5* **Abernethy (IRE)**[23] 5725 3-8-2 **46** oh1 .... JulieBurke(5) 7 14
(Linda Perratt) *dwlt: hld up: rdn and outpcd over 3f out: shortlived effrt on outside 2f out: edgd rt and sn btn* **20/1**

-300 **7** *8* **Indian Giver**[19] 5821 3-9-7 **60** ....(p) PhillipMakin 8 —
(Hugh McWilliams) *hld up: rdn and struggling over 3f out: nvr on terms* **14/1**

8 **8** *1 1/2* **Skystream (IRE)**[362] 6481 3-9-7 **60** .... TomEaves 5 —
(Ian Semple) *hld up: rdn 4f out: sn struggling* **20/1**

1m 55.36s (6.96) **Going Correction** +0.85s/f (Soft) **8** Ran SP% **111.4**

Speed ratings (Par 99): **99,98,91,85,84 79,71,69**

toteswingers:1&2:£3.30, 1&3:£3.60, 2&3:£4.20 CSF £11.75 CT £39.37 TOTE £4.20: £1.60, £1.70, £1.80; EX 15.50 Trifecta £253.80 Pool: £404.74 - 1.18 winning units.

Owner S R Counsell **Bred** Hascombe And Valiant Studs **Trained** Middleham Moor, N Yorks

FOCUS

A moderate handicap. The first pair were clear but there are doubts over what they achieved.

6416 E B F "PROCLAMATION" CONDITIONS STKS 1m 65y

3:40 (3:40) (Class 3) 3-Y-O+ **£7,115** (£2,117; £1,058) **Stalls** Low

Form RPR

3553 **1** **Penitent**[10] 6125 5-9-4 **108** ....(p) PaulHanagan 5 109
(William Haggas) *mde all at stdy pce: rdn 2f out: sn hung rt: hld on wl u.p fnl f* **13/8**[2]

-104 **2** *nk* **Secrecy**[46] 4972 5-9-7 **109** .... TedDurcan 2 111
(Saeed Bin Suroor) *trckd wnr: effrt and ev ch over 1f out: hrd rdn and carried rt ins the fnl f: jst hld* **10/11**[1]

4003 **3** *6* **Field Of Dream**[13] 6027 4-9-4 **102** .... J-PGuillambert 4 95
(Luca Cumani) *trckd ldrs: niggled 1/2-way: effrt and drvn over 2f out: wknd appr fnl f* **9/2**[3]

1m 54.05s (5.65) **Going Correction** +0.85s/f (Soft) **3** Ran SP% **108.7**

Speed ratings (Par 107): **105,104,98**

CSF £3.55 TOTE £3.00; EX 2.90.

Owner Cheveley Park Stud **Bred** Cheveley Park Stud Ltd **Trained** Newmarket, Suffolk

■ Stewards' Enquiry : Paul Hanagan caution: careless riding.

Ted Durcan seven-day ban: used whip with excessive frequency without giving gelding time to respond (Oct 10-16)

FOCUS

It was hard to rule any of these out in an open race, despite there being two non-runners. Decent conditions form but it has not been rated too positively.

NOTEBOOK

Penitent enjoyed the run of the race under Paul Hanagan, and the pair just prevailed in a prolonged battle with Secrecy. Behind very smart sorts each of the last twice, this was a great opportunity for a horse who's been hard to place this season. It remains to be see whether he can add to it, though, back up in grade. (op 11-8 tchd 5-4)

Secrecy's last-time-out Salisbury fourth had received a boost, but the winner would have appreciated the testing ground more than he did, and he just couldn't stay on as well. He emerges the best horse at the weights. (op 11-10 tchd 6-5)

Field Of Dream picked up well to challenge, but he was beaten from over 1f out and the ground perhaps wouldn't have been in his favour. (op 5-1)

6417 HAMILTON PARK APPRENTICE SERIES FINAL H'CAP 1m 1f 36y

4:10 (4:10) (Class 6) (0-65,67) 3-Y-O+ **£1,940** (£577; £288; £144) **Stalls** Low

Form RPR

0341 **1** **Botham (USA)**[7] 6211 7-9-7 **67** 6ex .... JasonHart(5) 7 75
(Jim Goldie) *dwlt: bhd: drvn along over 3f out: rallied to ld 2f out: edgd rt and hld on wl fnl f* **9/4**[1]

-202 **2** *3* **Croix Rouge (USA)**[1] 6379 9-9-2 **57** .... JustinNewman 3 58
(Ralph Smith) *chsd ldr: rdn and outpcd over 2f out: rallied and regained 2nd ins fnl f: r.o: nt pce of wnr* **5/1**[3]

4460 **3** *1* **Spread Boy (IRE)**[12] 6050 4-8-10 **51** oh6 .... GarryWhillans 8 50?
(Alan Berry) *hld up towards rr: hdwy over 3f out: rdn over 2f out: sn outpcd: kpt on fnl f: no imp* **66/1**

3 **4** *hd* **Mighty Whitey (IRE)**[7] 6211 5-9-8 **63** ....(t) LMcNiff 2 62
(Noel C Kelly, Ire) *t.k.h: in tch: rdn over 2f out: kpt on fnl f: nvr able to chal* **7/1**

322 **5** *1 1/2* **Strong Man**[9] 6156 3-9-0 **65** .... DavidSimmonson(5) 6 60
(Michael Easterby) *in tch: outpcd and lost pl over 3f out: rallied over 1f out: edgd rt and no imp fnl f* **11/2**

0005 **6** *2* **Baby Driver**[28] 5560 3-9-0 **60** .... HarryBentley 1 51
(Tom Dascombe) *led to 2f out: hung rt and sn wknd* **4/1**[2]

2455 **7** *2 3/4* **Nicholas Pocock (IRE)**[10] 6134 5-9-3 **58** .... ShaneBKelly 4 43
(Ian McInnes) *t.k.h: trckd ldrs: rdn over 2f out: sn wknd* **14/1**

0400 **8** *1 3/4* **Royal Straight**[11] 6082 6-9-2 **57** ....(t) JulieBurke 5 38
(Linda Perratt) *missed break: hld up: hdwy to chse ldrs over 3f out: wknd over 2f out* **14/1**

2m 9.04s (9.34) **Going Correction** +0.85s/f (Soft)

WFA 3 from 4yo+ 5lb **8** Ran SP% **110.1**

Speed ratings (Par 101): **92,89,88,88,86 85,82,81**

toteswingers:1&2:£4.20, 1&3:£14.50, 2&3:£26.30 CSF £12.57 CT £509.06 TOTE £3.40: £1.50, £1.80, £8.50; EX 18.60 TRIFECTA Not won..

Owner Caledonia Racing **Bred** France Weiner & Neal Hayias **Trained** Uplawmoor, E Renfrews

■ Stewards' Enquiry : Justin Newman five-day ban: used whip with excessive frequency (Oct 10-14)

Shane B Kelly two-day ban: careless riding (Oct 10-11)

FOCUS

A low-grade handicap and they struggled home in the bad ground. The third is a big doubt over the form.

6418 HOWARD AND NANCY MCDOWALL MEMORIAL H'CAP 5f 4y

4:40 (4:40) (Class 5) (0-75,75) 3-Y-O+ **£2,587** (£770; £384; £192) **Stalls** High

Form RPR

4641 **1** **Captain Scooby**[7] 6212 5-9-2 **70** 6ex .... AmyRyan(3) 6 85
(Richard Whitaker) *prom: pushed along after 2f: effrt over 1f out: led ins fnl f: rdn and r.o wl* **10/3**[3]

0031 **2** *nk* **Babich Bay (IRE)**[7] 6208 3-8-9 **61** 6ex ....(p) SilvestreDeSousa 1 75
(Jo Hughes) *pressed ldr: led over 1f out to ins fnl f: kpt on u.p towards fin* **2/1**[1]

2602 **3** *2* **Ballinargh Girl (IRE)**[24] 5683 3-9-9 **75** .... JamesSullivan 8 82
(Robert Wylie) *trckd ldrs: drvn along over 2f out: edgd lft and kpt on ins fnl f* **8/1**

1421 **4** *1* **Tongalooma**[7] 6213 5-9-6 **71** 6ex .... PJMcDonald 7 74
(James Moffatt) *led tl rdn and hdd over 1f out: no ex ins fnl f* **9/4**[2]

6661 **5** *12* **Hinton Admiral**[11] 6076 7-9-10 **75** .... PaulHanagan 4 35
(Keith Dalgleish) *in tch: sn pushed along: struggling 1/2-way: sn lost tch* **7/1**

63.24 secs (3.24) **Going Correction** +0.775s/f (Yiel)

WFA 3 from 5yo+ 1lb **5** Ran SP% **110.8**

Speed ratings (Par 103): **105,104,101,99,80**

CSF £10.49 TOTE £3.00: £1.70, £2.00; EX 10.50 Trifecta £51.00 Pool: £450.88 - 6.54 winning units.

Owner Paul Davies (H'gte) **Bred** Hellwood Stud Farm & Paul Davies (h'Gate) **Trained** Scarcroft, W Yorks

FOCUS
Four of the five remaining runners in this sprint handicap were last-time-out winners. The form looks solid with the winner better than ever.
Hinton Admiral Official explanation: jockey said gelding anticipated the start, hitting the gates and missed the break

6419 JOIN US ON FACEBOOK H'CAP — 1m 4f 17y
5:10 (5:11) (Class 5) (0-70,70) 3-Y-0+ — **£2,587** (£770; £384; £192) **Stalls** Low

Form			Horse		RPR
001P	**1**		**Epic (IRE)**[13] 6037 4-9-13 **69** .... SilvestreDeSousa 4		81+
			(Mark Johnston) *mde all: rdn over 2f out: styd on strly fnl f*	**7/1**	
2030	**2**	*3*	**Pokfulham (IRE)**[10] 6115 5-9-8 **64** .... (v) LeeNewman 2		71
			(Jim Goldie) *pressed wnr: effrt and ev ch over 2f out: kpt on same pce fnl f*	**4/1**[3]	
0-11	**3**	*2*	**La Bacouetteuse (FR)**[32] 5405 6-9-5 **61** .... (p) PaulHanagan 8		65
			(Iain Jardine) *hld up: rdn and edgd rt over 2f out: hdwy u.p to chse clr ldrs over 1f out: no imp*	**5/2**[1]	
6330	**4**	*8*	**Bavarian Nordic (USA)**[21] 5791 6-9-4 **60** .... TonyHamilton 9		51
			(Richard Whitaker) *hld up: drvn along over 3f out: plugged on fnl f: nvr able to chal*	**17/2**	
0400	**5**	*14*	**Ritsi**[40] 5166 8-8-4 **51** oh5 .... JulieBurke(5) 7		20
			(Marjorie Fife) *missed break: bhd: drvn over 3f out: nvr on terms*	**14/1**	
	6	*3/4*	**Cyrus (IRE)**[165] 1350 4-8-9 **51** .... (p) PBBeggy 6		18
			(John C McConnell, Ire) *in tch tl rdn and wknd over 2f out*	**28/1**	
0006	**7**	*7*	**Tayacoba (CAN)**[25] 5650 4-8-13 **55** .... (p) TomEaves 1		11
			(Martin Todhunter) *trckd ldrs: rdn over 3f out: wknd over 2f out*	**14/1**	
1-04	**8**	*nk*	**Mahab El Shamaal**[23] 5714 3-9-6 **70** .... (b1) MartinLane 3		26
			(David Simcock) *t.k.h: trckd ldrs: drvn and wandered over 3f out: wknd wl over 2f out*	**3/1**[2]	

2m 49.89s (11.29) **Going Correction** +0.85s/f (Soft)
WFA 3 from 4yo+ 8lb — **8** Ran SP% **113.4**
Speed ratings (Par 103): **96,94,92,87,78 77,72,72**
toteswingers:1&2:£6.20, 1&3:£3.50, 2&3:£2.80. Totesuper 7: Win: Not won, Place: Not won. CSF £34.46 CT £88.84 TOTE £6.60: £2.50, £1.40, £1.30; EX 26.70 Trifecta £53.00 Pool: £726.93 - 10.14 winning units.
Owner Racegoers Club Owners Group **Bred** P D Savill **Trained** Middleham Moor, N Yorks
FOCUS
A good test in the conditions and the runners finished well strung out. The winenr was well in on his old form and got closer to it.
T/Plt: £57.90 to a £1 stake. Pool:£56,115.74 - 706.97 winning tickets T/Qpdt: £16.80 to a £1 stake Pool:£3,576.41 - 157.29 w. tckts RY

6420 - 6423a (Foreign Racing) - See RI

6144 AYR (L-H)
Tuesday, September 27
OFFICIAL GOING: Soft (heavy in places; 7.9)
Wind: Fresh, half against Weather: Cloudy

6424 BET LIVE AT VICTORCHANDLER.COM NURSERY — 7f 50y
2:10 (2:10) (Class 6) (0-65,62) 2-Y-0 — **£1,704** (£503; £251) **Stalls** High

Form			Horse		RPR
4406	**1**		**Red Tyke (IRE)**[46] 5005 2-8-6 **47** .... TomEaves 7		51
			(John Quinn) *t.k.h early: w ldr: led over 1f out: hld on wl ins fnl f*	**14/1**	
0601	**2**	*nk*	**Regal Acclaim (IRE)**[20] 5817 2-8-8 **49** .... DuranFentiman 3		52
			(Tim Easterby) *t.k.h early: led to over 1f out: rallied and ev ch ins fnl f: hld nr fin*	**7/4**[1]	
443	**3**	*3/4*	**Dubious Escapade (IRE)**[10] 6152 2-9-7 **62** .... PBBeggy 5		63
			(Ann Duffield) *trckd ldrs: rdn over 2f out: kpt on u.p ins fnl f*	**3/1**[2]	
0000	**4**	*nk*	**Street Angel (IRE)**[67] 4277 2-8-1 **45** .... (v1) DominicFox(3) 6		45
			(Alan Bailey) *hld up: hdwy on outside to chse ldrs 1f out: kpt on same pce last 100yds*	**22/1**	
4030	**5**	*2*	**Karma Chameleon**[6] 6260 2-9-1 **56** .... FrederikTylicki 2		52
			(Richard Guest) *trckd ldrs: rdn over 2f out: no ex over 1f out*	**4/1**[3]	
050	**6**	*2 1/2*	**Siberian Belle (IRE)**[25] 5681 2-9-1 **56** .... PaulHanagan 4		46
			(Richard Fahey) *trckd ldrs tl rdn and wknd over 1f out*	**5/1**	
0400	**7**	*hd*	**After Timer (IRE)**[28] 5597 2-8-4 **45** .... PatrickMathers 1		34
			(Julie Camacho) *plld hrd: hld up: rdn over 2f out: hung lft and wknd over 1f out*	**66/1**	

1m 40.33s (6.93) **Going Correction** +0.75s/f (Yiel) — **7** Ran SP% **110.5**
Speed ratings (Par 93): **90,89,88,88,86 83,83**
torewingers:1&2:£2.80, 2&3:£1.50, 1&3:£5.10 CSF £36.48 TOTE £6.00: £3.90, £1.60; EX 54.40.
Owner T G S Wood **Bred** Tally-Ho Stud **Trained** Settrington, N Yorks
FOCUS
The rail had been moved out 8 metres in the home straight and 6 metres elsewhere, adding approximately 18 yards to race distances between 7f and 1m2f. The ground was officially described as soft, heavy in places, despite a GoingStick reading of 7.9. The winning rider in the opener described the ground as "soft" and the time was 10.83 seconds slower than standard. This was a moderate nursery, run at a modest pace, and the front pair dominated throughout. There was a compressed finish and the form is rated around those in the frame behind the winner.
NOTEBOOK
Red Tyke(IRE) was racing beyond 5f for the first time, but his dam was a 2m6f hurdle winner so the longer trip in testing ground was likely to suit, and he also benefited from racing handily in a steadily run race. It took him a long time to get on top of the runner-up following a protracted battle and although still unexposed at the trip, he will need to improve again in order to follow up. Official explanation: trainer's rep said, regarding apparent improvement in form, that the gelding was better suited by the step up in trip.
Regal Acclaim(IRE) handled the easy conditions well enough when making a successful nursery debut at Catterick (first start since being gelded) and was up a furlong off a 4lb higher mark here. He made a bold bid to make all and went down fighting, but was helped by the way the race was run. (op 2-1)
Dubious Escapade(IRE), making her nursery debut after making the frame in three 6f maidens, is bred to appreciate this extra furlong but she didn't find her stride until it was too late and would probably have preferred a stronger gallop. (op 11-4)
Street Angel(IRE), who had only beaten a total of two rivals in four previous outings, had a visor on for the first time and showed improved form, especially as she had to make her effort widest. She is not without hope if the headgear works again. (tchd 20-1)
Karma Chameleon was on very different ground to when a disappointing favourite over 1m at Redcar six days earlier, but again he didn't get home. (tchd 7-2)
Siberian Belle(IRE) had shown some ability in three maidens, but an effort just after halfway here came to little. (tchd 13-2)
After Timer(IRE)'s rider reported that the filly ran too free. Official explanation: jockey said filly ran too free

6425 VICTORCHANDLER.COM MAIDEN AUCTION STKS — 6f
2:40 (2:44) (Class 5) 2-Y-0 — **£2,328** (£693; £346; £173) **Stalls** Low

Form			Horse		RPR
U332	**1**		**Mistress Of Rome**[12] 6075 2-8-6 **68** .... TomEaves 6		60+
			(Michael Dods) *sn drvn along and reminders in rr: gd hdwy to chal over 2f out: edgd lft and led appr fnl f: kpt on strly*	**4/7**[1]	
4040	**2**	*2 1/2*	**Johnson's Cat (IRE)**[28] 5597 2-8-9 **51** .... FrederikTylicki 4		56
			(Richard Guest) *slt ld appr fnl f: kpt on same pce last 150yds*	**25/1**	
	3	*4 1/2*	**Ballroom Blitz** 2-8-4 **0** .... JamesSullivan 5		37
			(Richard Guest) *dwlt: bhd: edgd lft and hdwy over 2f out: rdn and ev ch wl over 1f out: no ex ins fnl f*	**33/1**	
0	**4**	*1/2*	**Gone By Sunrise**[162] 1434 2-8-13 **0** .... PaulHanagan 7		45+
			(Richard Fahey) *trckd ldrs: drvn and outpcd wl over 1f out: rallied ins fnl f: nvr able to chal*	**7/1**[3]	
3050	**5**	*3/4*	**Never In (IRE)**[9] 6186 2-8-2 **47** ow3 .... JulieBurke(5) 3		36
			(Alan Berry) *disp ld tl rdn and wknd over 1f out*	**100/1**	
6	**6**	*2 3/4*	**Gibraltar Road**[24] 5726 2-8-11 **0** .... PBBeggy 1		32
			(John Quinn) *trckd ldrs: drvn and outpcd over 2f out: btn over 1f out*	**5/1**[2]	

1m 18.01s (5.61) **Going Correction** +0.75s/f (Yiel) — **6** Ran SP% **100.6**
Speed ratings (Par 95): **92,88,82,82,81 77**
toteswingers:1&2:£2.40, 2&3:£11.30, 1&3:£3.00 CSF £13.75 TOTE £1.40: £1.10, £5.20; EX 7.90.
Owner Kevin Kirkup **Bred** Dr A Gillespie **Trained** Denton, Co Durham
FOCUS
A very weak maiden auction rated around the second and fourth. The winner could be rated a shade better.
NOTEBOOK
Mistress Of Rome had the best form in this field having been placed in all three previous completed starts and had already shown that she could handle soft ground, but this was hard work as she was being given reminders early on and had to be hard ridden to hit the front a furlong out before forging clear. A return to 7f will show her in a better light. (op 4-6)
Johnson's Cat(IRE) helped force the pace for a long way, but he is basically exposed with a rating of 51 and would be better off back in modest nurseries. (op 20-1)
Ballroom Blitz, a £2,000 half-sister to four winners at up to 1m, was very slowly away and finished tired, but she did show some ability in between and may do better on quicker ground with the experience under her belt.
Gone By Sunrise hadn't been seen since finishing well beaten on his Redcar debut back in April and was on very different ground here. He plugged on again after getting outpaced mid-race, but still didn't show much. (op 8-1)

6426 KENNY LUCAS 30YRS AT AYR RACECOURSE H'CAP — 6f
3:10 (3:11) (Class 5) (0-70,69) 3-Y-0+ — **£2,328** (£693; £346; £173) **Stalls** Low

Form			Horse		RPR
2220	**1**		**Beckermet (IRE)**[12] 6081 9-9-5 **67** .... PJMcDonald 4		76
			(Ruth Carr) *trckd ldrs: rdn over 2f out: led ins fnl f: hld on wl*	**6/1**[2]	
0362	**2**	*3/4*	**Ingleby Arch (USA)**[26] 5647 8-9-5 **67** .... PhillipMakin 5		74
			(David Barron) *w ldrs: led 2f out to ins fnl f: kpt on: hld towards fin*	**13/2**[3]	
1443	**3**	*1 1/2*	**Northern Bolt**[1] 6414 6-9-7 **69** .... PatrickMathers 7		71
			(Ian McInnes) *in tch: drvn along and outpcd over 3f out: edgd lft and rallied over 1f out: kpt on ins fnl f*	**10/1**	
0000	**4**	*3/4*	**Gracie's Gift (IRE)**[28] 5601 9-8-4 **55** oh3 .... (v) KierenFox(3) 12		55
			(Richard Guest) *w ldrs: edgd lft 2f out: kpt on same pce ins fnl f*	**20/1**	
0000	**5**	*1*	**Berbice (IRE)**[12] 6081 6-8-9 **62** .... ShaneBKelly(5) 6		59
			(Linda Perratt) *t.k.h: hld up: smooth hdwy over 2f out: shkn up over 1f out: no ex ins fnl f*	**9/1**	
4602	**6**	*3/4*	**Bonnie Prince Blue**[1] 6414 8-9-0 **65** .... (v) DaleSwift(3) 1		59
			(Ian McInnes) *bhd and sn outpcd: hdwy over 1f out: kpt on ins fnl f: nrst fin*	**20/1**	
0312	**7**	*1/2*	**Babich Bay (IRE)**[1] 6418 3-8-11 **61** 6ex .... (b) FrederikTylicki 8		54
			(Jo Hughes) *trckd ldrs gng wl: rdn wl over 1f out: sn btn*	**15/8**[1]	
0000	**8**	*3 1/4*	**Durham Express (IRE)**[29] 5554 4-8-11 **59** .... (p) TonyHamilton 9		41
			(Michael Dods) *led: hdd whn checked 2f out: sn rdn and btn*	**16/1**	
0440	**9**	*nk*	**Monel**[11] 6116 3-8-8 **58** .... LeeNewman 11		39
			(Jim Goldie) *dwlt: sn in tch: rdn and wknd fr 2f out*	**8/1**	
2500	**10**	*10*	**Blown It (USA)**[12] 6076 5-9-4 **66** .... PaulHanagan 2		15
			(Keith Dalgleish) *in tch: rdn over 2f out: wknd over 1f out*	**14/1**	

1m 16.34s (3.94) **Going Correction** +0.75s/f (Yiel)
WFA 3 from 4yo+ 2lb — **10** Ran SP% **114.7**
Speed ratings (Par 103): **103,102,100,99,97 96,96,91,91,77**
toteswingers:1&2:£5.20, 2&3:£6.40, 1&3:£9.50 CSF £43.96 CT £379.05 TOTE £4.90: £1.20, £2.00, £2.80; EX 27.70.
Owner Shopping, Shoes & Champers Partnership **Bred** Fritz Von Ball Moss **Trained** Huby, N Yorks
FOCUS
A fair sprint handicap, but the well-in favourite disappointed and this is basically ordinary form.

6427 BET WITH YOUR MOBILE AT VICTORCHANDLER.COM H'CAP — 5f
3:40 (3:40) (Class 6) (0-65,76) 3-Y-0+ — **£1,704** (£503; £251) **Stalls** Low

Form			Horse		RPR
6411	**1**		**Captain Scooby**[1] 6418 5-10-1 **76** 12ex .... AmyRyan(3) 6		86
			(Richard Whitaker) *in tch: pushed along 1/2-way: hdwy wl over 1f out: led ins fnl f: kpt on strly*	**15/8**[1]	
6425	**2**	*nk*	**Sharp Shoes**[29] 5552 4-9-7 **65** .... (p) DavidNolan 7		74
			(Ann Duffield) *led: rdn 2f out: hdd ins fnl f: rallied u.p: jst hld*	**11/2**[2]	
424	**3**	*2 1/4*	**Dispol Grand (IRE)**[6] 6265 5-9-5 **63** .... PaulHanagan 2		64
			(Paul Midgley) *cl up: rdn over 2f out: kpt on same pce ins fnl f*	**15/8**[1]	
0-00	**4**	*2 3/4*	**Pavement Games**[117] 2655 4-8-4 **51** oh5 .... KierenFox(3) 3		42
			(Richard Guest) *rrd s: bhd and pushed along: styd on ins fnl f: nvr rchd ldrs*	**20/1**	
6450	**5**	*1/2*	**Bygones For Coins (IRE)**[22] 5793 3-8-2 **52** oh6 ow1 .... JulieBurke(5) 4		41
			(Alan Berry) *in tch: rdn and edgd lft 1/2-way: no imp over 1f out*	**50/1**	
0000	**6**	*4 1/2*	**Chosen One (IRE)**[12] 6076 6-9-4 **62** .... (p) JamesSullivan 5		35
			(Ruth Carr) *cl up tl rdn and wknd wl over 1f out*	**13/2**[3]	
060	**7**	*1*	**Lambrini Lace (IRE)**[25] 5678 6-8-7 **51** oh6 .... (b) TomEaves 1		20
			(Lisa Williamson) *chsd ldrs to 2f out: sn rdn and wknd*	**33/1**	

63.81 secs (4.41) **Going Correction** +0.75s/f (Yiel)
WFA 3 from 4yo+ 1lb — **7** Ran SP% **107.9**
Speed ratings (Par 101): **94,93,89,85,84 77,75**
toteswingers:1&2:£1.80, 2&3:£2.30, 1&3:£1.70 CSF £11.29 TOTE £2.80: £1.50, £2.20; EX 11.20.
Owner Paul Davies (H'gte) **Bred** Hellwood Stud Farm & Paul Davies (h'Gate) **Trained** Scarcroft, W Yorks
FOCUS
A weak sprint handicap with three of the seven runners out of the weights. Ordinary form, the winner confirming his personal best from the previous day.

Pavement Games Official explanation: jockey said filly reared as stalls opened

6428 BEST ODDS GUARANTEED AT VICTORCHANDLER.COM H'CAP 7f 50y
4:10 (4:11) (Class 6) (0-60,60) 3-Y-O+ **£1,704** (£503; £251) **Stalls** High

Form RPR

1400 **1** **Benny The Bear**[24] 5721 4-9-4 **57**.................(p) PhillipMakin 3 65
(Linda Perratt) *t.k.h: cl up: led 2f out to over 1f out: rdn: edgd lft and regained ld ins fnl f: hld on wl* **5/1**[2]

6631 **2** ½ **Chookie Avon**[22] 5789 4-9-7 **60**.................(p) TomEaves 8 67+
(Keith Dalgleish) *hld up in tch: smooth hdwy over 2f out: led and rdn over 1f out: hdd ins fnl f: hld towards fin* **13/8**[1]

-056 **3** 2¾ **Little Book**[93] 3431 3-8-11 **53**................. DanielTudhope 4 53
(Jim Goldie) *in tch: rdn over 2f out: kpt on ins fnl f: nt gng pce of first two* **8/1**[3]

0030 **4** 3½ **Spin A Wish**[46] 4987 3-8-5 **50**.................(v[1]) AmyRyan(3) 2 41
(Richard Whitaker) *led to over 2f out: rdn and sn rallied: outpcd ins fnl f* **40/1**

5420 **5** 3 **Eilean Eeve**[22] 5789 5-9-2 **55**.................(p) JamesSullivan 11 38
(George Foster) *s.i.s: hld up: rdn over 2f out: sme late hdwy: nvr on terms* **20/1**

400 **6** 1½ **See The Storm**[13] 6050 3-8-8 **50**................. BarryMcHugh 10 29
(Patrick Morris) *hld up: effrt on ins over 2f out: no imp fr over 1f out* **9/1**

0330 **7** 3¼ **Broughtons Silk**[22] 5788 6-8-8 **47** oh1 ow1..........(b[1]) PJMcDonald 12 18
(Alistair Whillans) *s.i.s: bhd on outside: rdn over 2f out: sn n.d* **12/1**

0005 **8** 2¾ **Shunkawakhan (IRE)**[24] 5725 8-8-8 **47**.................(tp) JoeFanning 6 10
(Linda Perratt) *trckd ldrs tl rdn and wknd over 2f out* **14/1**

665 **9** 2½ **Refusetosurrender (IRE)**[221] 593 3-8-8 **50**................. PaulHanagan 1 7
(Richard Fahey) *trckd ldrs: drvn over 2f out: sn btn* **5/1**[2]

06R0 **10** 39 **Tinzo (IRE)**[3] 6343 3-8-2 **49** oh1 ow3................. JulieBurke(5) 9 —
(Alan Berry) *s.s: sn t.o: nvr on terms* **80/1**

1m 38.45s (5.05) **Going Correction** +0.75s/f (Yiel)
WFA 3 from 4yo+ 3lb **10** Ran SP% **115.3**
Speed ratings (Par 101): **101,100,97,93,89 88,84,81,78,33**
toteswingers:1&2:£3.20, 2&3:£4.20, 1&3:£7.00 CSF £13.13 CT £63.68 TOTE £6.40: £2.00, £1.50, £1.20; EX 16.60.
Owner R R Whitton **Bred** R R Whitton **Trained** East Kilbride, S Lanarks

FOCUS
A moderate handicap and another race where it paid to race handily. The winner is rated to last month's C&D form.
Benny The Bear Official explanation: trainer said, regarding apparent improvement in form, that the gelding was better suited by first-time cheekpieces.
Tinzo(IRE) Official explanation: jockey said gelding was slow away

6429 DAILY RECORD H'CAP 1m 2f
4:40 (4:41) (Class 3) (0-95,93) 3-Y-O+ **£6,145** (£1,828; £913; £456) **Stalls** Low

Form RPR

11 **1** **Dare To Dance (IRE)**[31] 5483 3-9-4 **93**................. PaulHanagan 5 111+
(Jeremy Noseda) *sn chsng ldr: niggled along 1/2-way: pushed along and led over 2f out: edgd lft and clr over 1f out: kpt on wl: eased nr fin* **8/15**[1]

0203 **2** 3 **Mirrored**[12] 6080 5-9-4 **87**................. DuranFentiman 7 94
(Tim Easterby) *hld up: hdwy on outside over 2f out: chsd (clr) wnr wl ins fnl f: no imp* **12/1**

5415 **3** ½ **Tres Coronas (IRE)**[25] 5686 4-9-3 **86**................. LeeNewman 8 92
(David Barron) *hld up in tch: effrt over 2f out: kpt on same pce wl ins fnl f* **7/1**[2]

2102 **4** hd **Calaf**[18] 5880 3-8-5 **80**................. BarryMcHugh 3 86
(Richard Fahey) *cl up: chsd wnr over 2f out to wl ins fnl f: no ex* **7/1**[2]

02-0 **5** 10 **Full Toss**[12] 6079 5-8-10 **79**................. DanielTudhope 2 65
(Jim Goldie) *prom: drvn along over 2f out: sn wknd* **50/1**

400 **6** 11 **Nazreef**[11] 6124 4-8-12 **81**.................(t) JoeFanning 1 45
(Hughie Morrison) *led to over 2f out: sn struggling: t.o* **10/1**[3]

2m 19.38s (7.38) **Going Correction** +0.75s/f (Yiel)
WFA 3 from 4yo+ 6lb **6** Ran SP% **109.0**
Speed ratings (Par 107): **100,97,97,97,89 80**
CSF £7.52 CT £19.50 TOTE £1.30: £1.10, £5.00; EX 4.40.
Owner R A Pegum **Bred** Round Hill Stud **Trained** Newmarket, Suffolk

FOCUS
An interesting contest.
NOTEBOOK
Dare To Dance(IRE), who was favourite for Saturday's Cambridgeshire, but was a late withdrawal due to the quickening ground, came here in search of more favourable underfoot conditions. It wasn't all plain sailing as Hanagan was having to nudge him along at various stages, but once in front over 2f from home he proved different gear to these rivals. This was only his fourth start and although he can expect a hefty rise after this, he is probably a Listed-class performer waiting to happen in any case. (op 1-2 tchd 4-9)
Mirrored, 1lb higher than when narrowly beaten over C&D last time, came from last place to just win the separate race for second and was unfortunate to come up against such a nice prospect in a race like this. (tchd 14-1)
Tres Coronas(IRE), up 1lb to a new career-high mark after an encouraging return from a ten-week absence at Haydock earlier in the month, ran with credit and with his liking for soft ground there should be other opportunities before the season ends.
Full Toss, well beaten on his debut for the yard here 12 days earlier when returning from 524 days off, never figured but is getting fitter all the time. (op 40-1)
Nazreef set the pace, but was easily picked off over 2f from home and dropped right out. He is now 0-11 on turf, but is. 5-5 on the all-weather so it will be interesting to see how he would cope back on artificial surfaces. (op 14-1 tchd 16-1)

6430 BETFAIR RACING EXCELLENCE APPRENTICE TRAINING SERIES H'CAP 1m
5:10 (5:12) (Class 6) (60-92,58) 3-Y-O+ **£1,704** (£503; £251) **Stalls** Low

Form RPR

3346 **1** **Emeralds Spirit (IRE)**[10] 6159 4-9-9 **58**................. JustinNewman 1 66
(John Weymes) *trckd ldrs: led wl over 1f out: sn hrd pressed: hld on wl u.p ins fnl f* **4/1**[2]

-000 **2** ½ **Funky Munky**[5] 5822 6-8-6 **46** ow1................. DavidSimmonson(5) 12 53
(Alistair Whillans) *trckd ldr: effrt and ev ch over 1f out: kpt on ins fnl f: hld nr fin* **16/1**

4550 **3** 1¼ **Nicholas Pocock (IRE)**[1] 6417 5-9-9 **58**................. ShaneBKelly 4 62
(Ian McInnes) *trckd ldrs: effrt and rdn over 2f out: kpt on ins fnl f* **7/1**

4 ½ **Pacey Outswinger (IRE)**[41] 5189 4-8-7 **45**................. JakePayne(3) 6 48
(John C McConnell, Ire) *hld up in midfield: hdwy over 2f out: rdn and kpt on ins fnl f* **16/1**

2325 **5** 2 **Goninodaethat**[11] 6116 3-8-11 **55**................. JasonHart(5) 3 53
(Jim Goldie) *t.k.h: led to wl over 1f out: kpt on same pce* **3/1**[1]

0-21 **6** 2½ **Piper's Song (IRE)**[38] 5208 8-8-12 **52**................. RossSmith(5) 2 45+
(Linda Perratt) *s.i.s: bhd tl hdwy 2f out: no imp ins fnl f* **8/1**

7 1¼ **Sultana Belle (IRE)**[41] 5187 3-8-3 **47**................. ShirleyTeasdale(5) 11 37
(Lee Smyth, Ire) *hld up in tch: rdn over 2f out: edgd lft and btn over 1f out* **66/1**

5000 **8** 2¼ **Blue Charm**[70] 4179 7-9-0 **52**................. GeorgeChaloner(3) 7 37
(Ian McInnes) *missed break: bhd tl hdwy over 2f out: no imp over 1f out* **20/1**

5064 **9** 7 **Hits Only Jude (IRE)**[8] 6227 8-9-0 **56**.................(v) MichaelKenny(7) 9 24
(Declan Carroll) *trckd ldrs on outside tl rdn and wknd over 2f out* **6/1**[3]

0040 **10** 2½ **Captain Peachey**[27] 5622 5-8-10 **45**................. GarryWhillans 8 —
(Alistair Whillans) *hld up towards rr: rdn along over 3f out: wknd over 2f out* **14/1**

500 **11** 7 **Schoolboy Champ**[18] 5881 4-9-3 **57**.................(v) LauraBarry(5) 5 —
(Patrick Morris) *trckd ldrs tl rdn and wknd over 2f out* **22/1**

3030 **12** 3 **Buzz Bird**[146] 1814 4-8-10 **45**................. DarylByrne 10 —
(David Barron) *hld up towards rr: struggling over 3f out: hung lft and sn btn* **9/1**

1m 49.94s (6.14) **Going Correction** +0.75s/f (Yiel)
WFA 3 from 4yo+ 4lb **12** Ran SP% **121.9**
Speed ratings (Par 101): **99,98,97,96,94 92,91,88,81,79 72,69**
toteswingers:1&2:£13.20, 2&3:£29.90, 1&3:£6.50 CSF £67.02 CT £451.44 TOTE £4.40: £1.30, £6.80, £3.10; EX 67.80.
Owner T A Scothern **Bred** Epona Bloodstock Ltd **Trained** Middleham Moor, N Yorks
■ Stewards' Enquiry : David Simmonson caution: used whip with excessive frequency.
Justin Newman one-day ban: used whip with excessive frequency (Oct 16)

FOCUS
A moderate apprentice handicap and the front pair were up with the pace throughout. The winner is probably the best guide to the form.
Blue Charm Official explanation: jockey said gelding missed the break; trainer said gelding was unsuited by the soft (heavy in places) ground
Hits Only Jude(IRE) Official explanation: trainer had no explanation for the poor form shown
T/Plt: £14.20 to a £1 stake. Pool of £51,094.61 - 2,613.53 winning tickets. T/Qpdt: £6.40 to a £1 stake. Pool of £3,855.44 - 441.80 winning tickets. RY

5840 CHEPSTOW (L-H)
Tuesday, September 27

OFFICIAL GOING: Soft (5.6)
Wind: Virtually nil Weather: Sunny intervalls

6431 WESTERN DAILY PRESS NURSERY 6f 16y
2:00 (2:00) (Class 4) (0-85,80) 2-Y-O **£3,105** (£924; £461; £230) **Stalls** Centre

Form RPR

2412 **1** **Karuga**[14] 6021 2-8-8 **70**................. KieranO'Neill(3) 1 77
(Richard Hannon) *stdd into 4th but wl in tch: hdwy between horses to join a four way chal appr fnl f: sn led and in command: drvn clr fnl 150yds: comf* **10/3**[3]

4100 **2** 4½ **Moustache (IRE)**[24] 5701 2-9-7 **80**................. RichardHughes 6 74
(Richard Hannon) *sn slt ld but hrd pressed tl narrowly hdd over 2f out: pushed along and jnd four way chal appr fnl f: sn no ch w wnr but kpt on wl for 2nd* **15/8**[1]

61 **3** ½ **Full Support (IRE)**[59] 4557 2-9-5 **78**................. RichardMullen 4 70
(David Brown) *chsd ldrs in 3rd: drvn along 3f out: qcknd to join four-way chal appr fnl f: sn no ch w wnr and styd on same pce for 3rd* **2/1**[2]

0624 **4** ¾ **Redair (IRE)**[8] 6221 2-9-3 **76**.................(v[1]) KierenFallon 5 66
(David Evans) *sn pressing ldr and slt advantage over 2f out: jnd in 4-way chal appr fnl f and sn hdd: sn oner pce into 4th* **6/1**

1m 16.09s (4.09) **Going Correction** +0.575s/f (Yiel) **4** Ran SP% **105.5**
Speed ratings (Par 97): **95,89,88,87**
CSF £9.40 TOTE £5.80; EX 7.70.
Owner Fairway Racing **Bred** David J Brown, Slatch Farm Stud & J Berry **Trained** East Everleigh, Wilts

FOCUS
Following the opener, describing conditions, Richard Mullen said it was "soft and very soft in places", while Kieran O'Neill said it was "soft to heavy." They raced up the middle of the track. Despite three non-runners leaving a field of four, this looked an interesting little nursery. The form's difficult to gauge and as the winner was perhaps the only one to handle conditions the race has been rated negatively.
NOTEBOOK
Karuga was the only one who appreciated the ground. Consequently this isn't a performance to get carried away with, but she was better than the bare form at Folkestone on her previous start (raced off favoured stands' rail) and is going the right way. (op 7-2 tchd 4-1)
Moustache(IRE) hasn't gone on as expected since winning a Glorious Goodwood maiden, although he was totally unsuited by a drop to 5f last time and travelled much better on this occasion, although he ultimately floundered in the ground when under pressure. He was seemingly the choice of Richard Hughes over the winner and this sort of mark may not prove beyond him back on a sound surface. (op 2-1)
Full Support(IRE) had been absent since winning a 5f Thirsk maiden on a sound surface two months earlier and he ran in snatches on his return. The ground may have been softer than ideal and he is likely to be a lot sharper next time, so he's probably worth another chance.
Redair(IRE), visored for the first time, didn't seem to handle the ground. She won a maiden on her only previous start on Polytrack and will surely be worth another try on that surface. (op 9-2 tchd 4-1)

6432 EVENING POST MAIDEN STKS 7f 16y
2:30 (2:31) (Class 4) 2-Y-O **£3,105** (£924; £461; £230) **Stalls** Centre

Form RPR

1 **Electrelane** 2-8-12 0................. JimCrowley 4 74+
(Ralph Beckett) *trckd ldrs tl wnt 2nd 4f out: pushed along and led over 1f out: drvn to assert ins fnl f: wnt clr fnl 120yds: easily* **11/4**[2]

0230 **2** 3¾ **Forest Edge (IRE)**[17] 5922 2-9-3 78................. KierenFallon 8 73
(David Evans) *narrow ldr tl def advantage after 2f: rdn over 2f out: hdd over 1f out: sn outpcd by wnr but styd on for 2nd* **13/8**[1]

3 1 **La Pampita (IRE)** 2-8-9 0................. HarryBentley(3) 1 62+
(William Knight) *trcking ldrs whn j. path after 2f and t.k.h: chsd ldng duo 2f out: sn pushed along and one pce: kpt on again in clsng stages but nvr any ch w wnr* **9/1**

4 1¼ **Dutch Master** 2-9-3 0................. JimmyFortune 5 64+
(Andrew Balding) *w ldr 2f: styd trcking ldrs: pushed along and one pce appr fnl 2f: kpt on again in clsng stages: nvr any ch w wnr* **10/3**[3]

00 **5** 4½ **My Boy Ginger**[19] 5841 2-9-3 0................. JamesMillman 7 53
(Rod Millman) *chsd ldrs: rdn in 3rd 3f out: wknd qckly 2f out* **20/1**

1m 29.53s (6.33) **Going Correction** +0.575s/f (Yiel) **5** Ran SP% **102.6**
Speed ratings (Par 97): **86,81,80,79,74**
CSF £6.54 TOTE £2.50: £1.10, £2.40; EX 7.40 Trifecta £26.50 Pool: £379.57- 10.59 winning units..
Owner Clipper Logistics **Bred** Bigwigs Bloodstock **Trained** Kimpton, Hants

The Form Book, Raceform Ltd, Compton, RG20 6NL

FOCUS
They ended up towards the far-side rail in what was an uncompetitive maiden, and the time was the slowest of three 7f races, although the other two were for older horses. The runner-up is the key to the level.

NOTEBOOK
Electrelane had little to beat with the favourite not staying, but she travelled like a filly with at least a fair amount of ability and did what was required when under pressure. A 35,000gns purchase, she is half-sister to 5f winner (Listed placed over 6f) Imperialistic Diva and fair dual 1m scorer Quite Sparky, out of a useful multiple 6f-1m winner. She might struggle next time if the handicapper takes the form literally (runner-up rated 78), but otherwise she should do alright. (op 9-4)
Forest Edge(IRE), the outstanding form choice, looked a doubtful stayer beforehand, especially on testing ground, and he ran as though the trip stretched him after being a bit keen early. (op 2-1)
La Pampita(IRE) fetched 30,000gns as a foal but was unsold at 15,000gns last year. The first foal of a winner over 7f on good to soft, she's from a yard that rarely has winning newcomers but hinted at ability.\n
Dutch Master was solid in the market but he cost only £5,000 and has already been gelded. He was well held.

6433 DIGIBET.COM CLASSIFIED CLAIMING STKS 7f 16y
3:00 (3:00) (Class 6) 3-Y-0+ **£1,617** (£481; £240; £120) **Stalls** Centre

Form RPR
1562 **1** **Opus Maximus (IRE)**[12] 6098 6-8-6 66....................(p) SophieDoyle(3) 2 72
(Jennie Candlish) *t.k.h: hld up in rr: hdwy fr 2f out: chsd ldr over 1f out: drvn to chal ins fnl f: styd on to ld fnl 50yds and edgd rt: all out* **4/1**[3]
1324 **2** *hd* **Barista (IRE)**[11] 6120 3-8-7 70.................... MartinHarley(3) 1 75
(Mick Channon) *chsd ldrs: drvn to ld over 1f out: strly chal ins fnl f: hdd and bmpd fnl 50yds: no ex in clsng stages* **7/4**[1]
0220 **3** *2 ¾* **Cootehill Lass (IRE)**[8] 6227 3-8-10 75....................(p) RichardHughes 5 68
(David Evans) *chsd ldrs tl rdn and outpcd over 2f out: sn rdn: rallied appr fnl f and styd on to take 3rd cl to home: no ch w ldng duo* **9/4**[2]
0050 **4** *hd* **Mcconnell (USA)**[14] 6017 6-8-11 70....................(v[1]) FergusSweeney 4 66
(Gary Moore) *hd high and awkward leaving stalls: t.k.h: and chsd ldrs: wnt 2nd 3f out: slt ld over 2f out tl hdd over 1f out: wknd fnl 120yds and lost 3rd cl home* **16/1**
0-00 **5** *7* **Arachnophobia (IRE)**[132] 2206 5-8-9 67.......................... LukeMorris 3 46
(Martin Bosley) *led 1f: chsd ldrs: rdn over 3f out: styd wl there u.p tl wknd wl over 1f out* **16/1**
0144 **6** *2 ¾* **Dark Lane**[28] 5604 5-8-11 74..(v) NeilCallan 10 40
(Tony Carroll) *s.i.s: in rr but in tch: rdn and hdwy to chse ldrs 3f out: wknd fr 2f out* **10/1**
4030 **7** *2* **Dimaire**[68] 4224 4-8-11 55 ow1.. DaneO'Neill 7 35
(Derek Haydn Jones) *led after 1f: rdn and hdd over 2f out: wknd over 1f out* **33/1**

1m 28.3s (5.10) **Going Correction** +0.575s/f (Yiel)
WFA 3 from 4yo+ 3lb **7** Ran SP% **110.9**
Speed ratings (Par 101): **93,92,89,89,81 78,75**
toteswingers:1&2:£2.50, 2&3:£1.70, 1&3:£2.50 CSF £10.72 TOTE £4.60: £2.40, £1.90; EX 8.90 Trifecta £44.60 Pool: £630.12 - 10.44 winning units..
Owner Alan Baxter **Bred** Mrs Anne Marie Burns **Trained** Basford Green, Staffs

FOCUS
A modest claimer in which they didn't seem to go that quick early, and the time was 1.52 seconds slower than the following Class 6 handicap. They raced towards the stands' side, but the front two were well away from the rail in the closing stages. Both ran close to their respective official marks.

6434 PROFAB WINDOWS (SW) H'CAP 7f 16y
3:30 (3:30) (Class 6) (0-65,65) 3-Y-0+ **£1,617** (£481; £240; £120) **Stalls** Centre

Form RPR
6004 **1** **Myboyalfie (USA)**[19] 5845 4-9-3 61..............................(v) IanMongan 15 72
(J R Jenkins) *racd on stands' side: sn chsng ldr: led ins fnl 2f: rdn clr fnl 120yds* **7/1**[3]
0622 **2** *2 ¾* **Leelu**[43] 5100 5-8-13 57.. CathyGannon 16 61
(David Arbuthnot) *racd stands' side and led: rdn and hdd ins fnl 2f: styd on but no ch w wnr fnl 120yds* **5/1**[2]
1230 **3** *3 ½* **Sarangoo**[47] 4973 3-9-4 65.. NeilCallan 5 60+
(Malcolm Saunders) *racd towards centre of crse and towards rr tl hdwy wl over 2f out: styd on to go 3rd over 1f out: no imp on ldng duo* **11/1**
0105 **4** *1 ¼* **Fleetwoodsands (IRE)**[29] 5538 4-9-6 64.....................(t) DaneO'Neill 17 56
(Milton Bradley) *racd on stands' side and chsd ldrs: rdn and styd on to take one pce 4th ins fnl f* **16/1**
0051 **5** *1 ¼* **Cape Kimberley**[29] 5539 4-9-6 64.................................... RobertHavlin 6 52+
(Tony Newcombe) *chsd ldrs in centre of crse: rdn over 2f out: wknd ins fnl f* **7/2**[1]
2560 **6** *nk* **Arctic Mirage**[16] 5970 3-9-4 65.. LiamKeniry 13 52
(Michael Blanshard) *chsd ldrs towards centre of crse: rdn and lost pl over 2f out: swtchd rt to stands' side over 1f out and kpt on again in clsng stages* **25/1**
6060 **7** *3 ¼* **Forward Feline (IRE)**[5] 6285 5-8-11 55.............................. DavidProbert 1 34
(Bryn Palling) *pressed ldrs in centre of crse: rdn over 2f out: wknd wl over 1f out* **14/1**
0021 **8** *¾* **Spinning Ridge (IRE)**[19] 5843 6-9-4 62..................(v) TomMcLaughlin 9 39
(Ronald Harris) *s.i.s: in rr and racd in centre of crse: rdn and hdwy 3f out: pressed ldrs 2f out: wknd ins fnl f* **10/1**
010 **9** *½* **Abacist (IRE)**[29] 5539 3-9-1 62..(p) JimCrowley 8 38
(Ralph Beckett) *pressed ldrs in centre of crse: rdn 3f out: wknd wl over 1f out* **10/1**
5200 **10** *5* **Beneath**[11] 6135 4-9-2 60.. AdamKirby 11 23
(Neil Mulholland) *racd in centre of crse: sn in rr and n.d* **16/1**
004 **11** *3 ½* **Miss Dutee**[25] 5669 3-8-12 59.................................(b[1]) RichardHughes 14 13
(Richard Hannon) *pressed ldrs in centre of crse: wknd qckly ins fnl 2f* **16/1**
4000 **12** *7* **Slumbering Sioux**[25] 5673 3-8-11 58.........................(b[1]) LukeMorris 10 —
(Harry Dunlop) *chsd ldrs in centre crse 4f out* **33/1**
0-00 **13** *7* **Mirabile Visu**[16] 5972 3-8-12 59..(b) EddieAhern 3 —
(Heather Main) *racd towards centre of crse: bhd most of way* **16/1**

1m 26.78s (3.58) **Going Correction** +0.575s/f (Yiel)
WFA 3 from 4yo+ 3lb **13** Ran SP% **114.9**
Speed ratings (Par 101): **102,98,94,93,92 91,87,87,86,80 76,68,60**
toteswingers:1&2:£6.10, 2&3:£9.60, 1&3:£14.00 CSF £40.12 CT £394.02 TOTE £8.00: £2.60, £2.00, £3.40; EX 39.50 Trifecta £365.70 Part won. Pool: £494.29 - 0.64 winning units..
Owner D Badham **Bred** Robert Pierz & Robert Brooks **Trained** Royston, Herts
■ Stewards' Enquiry : David Probert two-day ban: careless riding (Oct 12-13)

FOCUS
There seemed a notable track bias with the three runners who raced towards the stands' side throughout, well away from the majority of the others up the middle, all finishing in the first four.
Miss Dutee Official explanation: jockey said filly ran flat

6435 BRISTOL OBSERVER H'CAP 1m 14y
4:00 (4:02) (Class 5) (0-75,75) 3-Y-0+ **£2,264** (£673; £336; £168) **Stalls** Centre

Form RPR
601 **1** **Ancient Greece**[15] 5992 4-9-7 72..................................(t) DaneO'Neill 5 80
(George Baker) *hld up in rr: hdwy fr 3f out: led appr fnl f: drvn and styd on wl ins fnl f: rdn out* **8/1**
3536 **2** *hd* **Bidable**[21] 5808 7-9-1 66.. CathyGannon 11 74
(Bryn Palling) *towards rr: swtchd lft to outside over 2f out: str run u.p appr fnl f: rn wl to chse wnr fnl 100yds: gaining cl home: a jst hld* **22/1**
4032 **3** *1 ¼* **Encore Un Fois**[15] 5992 3-9-1 70.................................... KierenFallon 9 75
(Luca Cumani) *dismntd and reluctant to go bhd stalls: trckd ldrs: chal fr 4f out tl led ins fnl 3f: hdd appr fnl f: kpt on same pce* **15/8**[1]
14-0 **4** *¾* **Menadati (USA)**[119] 2582 3-9-6 75.................................. ChrisCatlin 7 78
(Peter Hiatt) *s.i.s: hld up in rr: gd hdwy on outside over 2f out: chsd ldrs over 1f out: nt qckn ins fnl f* **66/1**
0322 **5** *1 ¼* **Duquesa (IRE)**[10] 6181 3-8-13 68............................(v) RichardHughes 12 69+
(David Evans) *chsd ldrs tl rdn and outpcd 3f out: styd on again u.p fr over 1f out: one pce and eased in clsng stages* **9/2**[2]
5011 **6** *2 ½* **Mr Udagawa**[19] 5845 5-9-2 67..(p) MartinLane 1 62
(Bernard Llewellyn) *w ldr tl slt ld fr over 4f out: hdd ins fnl 3f: wknd appr fnl f* **14/1**
2004 **7** *3* **Osgood**[9] 6188 4-9-7 75... MartinHarley(3) 3 63
(Mick Channon) *sn slt ld but jnd after 1f: hdd over 4f out: wknd over 2f out* **17/2**
5203 **8** *2* **Gallant Eagle (IRE)**[17] 5948 4-9-4 72............................ JohnFahy(3) 14 55
(Ed de Giles) *bhd most of way* **6/1**[3]
4530 **9** *6* **Final Verse**[15] 5992 8-9-2 67... AdamKirby 4 36
(Matthew Salaman) *chsd ldrs tl wknd over 2f out* **28/1**
0-24 **10** *14* **Russian Affair**[29] 5567 3-9-5 74.. NeilCallan 10 11
(Roger Varian) *t.k.h: chsd ldr: rdn 3f out: wknd and eased appr fnl 2f* **8/1**

1m 40.1s (3.90) **Going Correction** +0.575s/f (Yiel)
WFA 3 from 4yo+ 4lb **10** Ran SP% **116.0**
Speed ratings (Par 103): **103,102,101,100,99 97,94,92,86,72**
toteswingers:1&2:£27.00, 2&3:£13.20, 1&3:£5.10 CSF £165.87 CT £465.65 TOTE £14.90: £3.10, £4.60, £1.80; EX 199.00 Trifecta £459.70 Part won. Pool: £621.28 - 0.20 winning units..
Owner Inkin, Inkin, Byng, Baker & Partners **Bred** Darley **Trained** Whitsbury, Hants

FOCUS
A modest handicap. It wasn't a surprise they all raced stands' side given the evidence of the previous race, but the rail wasn't important.\
Duquesa(IRE) Official explanation: jockey said filly ran out of room closing stages
Final Verse Official explanation: jockey said gelding stopped quickly
Russian Affair Official explanation: jockey said colt never travelled

6436 MOTORS.CO.UK H'CAP 5f 16y
4:30 (4:30) (Class 5) (0-75,73) 3-Y-0+ **£2,264** (£673; £336; £168) **Stalls** Centre

Form RPR
5506 **1** **Equuleus Pictor**[18] 5890 7-9-7 73................................(p) CathyGannon 7 81
(John Spearing) *trckd ldrs: drvn to take narrow advantage appr fnl f but styd hrd pressed u.p tl asserted in clsng stages: all out* **9/2**[3]
2200 **2** *nk* **Triple Dream**[18] 5890 6-9-4 70..................................(tp) KierenFallon 3 77
(Milton Bradley) *led but hrd pressed: narrowly hdd appr fnl f: styd upsides u.p and remained pressing wnr tl no ex in clsng stakes* **13/2**
0026 **3** *½* **Cape Royal**[15] 5997 11-8-13 65...............................(tp) RoystonFfrench 8 70
(Milton Bradley) *pressed ldrs and stl upsides and rdn 1f out: stl chalng tl no ex fnl 50yds* **11/1**
6411 **4** *2 ¼* **Two Turtle Doves (IRE)**[19] 5846 5-8-9 64.................... HarryBentley(3) 1 61
(Michael Mullineaux) *chsd ldrs: rdn and no imp over 1f out: wknd ins fnl f* **9/4**[1]
3121 **5** *½* **Royal Box**[18] 5881 4-8-10 62..(p) KellyHarrison 5 57
(Dai Burchell) *chsd ldrs: rdn 2f out: nvr gng pce to chal and wknd ins fnl f* **11/4**[2]
0000 **6** *¾* **Superior Edge**[1] 6408 4-9-4 70..................................(p) DavidProbert 9 63
(Christopher Mason) *hld up in rr but in tch: rdn and no imp on ldrs 2f out: no ch ins fnl f* **25/1**
0160 **7** *3 ¼* **Sulis Minerva (IRE)**[18] 5890 4-8-11 70....................(t) RaulDaSilva(7) 6 51
(Jeremy Gask) *rdn 1/2-way: a outpcd* **14/1**
5-00 **8** *1 ¾* **Namir (IRE)**[228] 512 9-8-13 65.....................................(vt) JimCrowley 4 40
(James Evans) *rdn 1/2-way: a outpcd* **22/1**

62.23 secs (2.93) **Going Correction** +0.575s/f (Yiel) **8** Ran SP% **112.1**
Speed ratings (Par 103): **99,98,97,94,93 92,86,84**
toteswingers:1&2:£5.20, 2&3:£7.00, 1&3:£7.40 CSF £32.23 CT £300.51 TOTE £3.60: £1.10, £2.60, £2.40; EX 25.20 Trifecta £336.00 Part won. Pool of £454.17 - 0.50 winning units..
Owner Masonaires **Bred** A J And Mrs L Brazier **Trained** Kinnersley, Worcs

FOCUS
A modest sprint handicap. Again they raced stands' side, although once more the rail was not a particular advantage.

6437 LINDLEY CATERING H'CAP (DIV I) 1m 2f 36y
5:00 (5:03) (Class 6) (0-65,64) 3-Y-0+ **£1,617** (£481; £240; £120) **Stalls** Low

Form RPR
-500 **1** **Grandad Mac**[29] 5539 3-8-10 56.. RichardHughes 4 64+
(Jane Chapple-Hyam) *trckd ldrs: led appr fnl 2f: drvn and styd on ins fnl f: rdn out* **15/8**[1]
3640 **2** *¾* **Carinya (IRE)**[27] 5630 3-9-3 63.. KierenFallon 8 71+
(Amy Weaver) *v.s.a and lost 10 l s: rcvrd and in tch after 3f: hdwy on ins whn nt clr run and hung lft over 2f out: swtchd rt to outside: 6th appr fnl f: fin strly: nt rcvr: unlucky* **11/2**[3]
044R **3** *1* **Command Marshal (FR)**[15] 5994 8-9-4 61........................ JohnFahy(3) 1 65
(Ed de Giles) *led 2f: styd chsng ldr and led ins fnl 3f tl hdd appr fnl f: styd chsng wnr but no imp: lost 2nd fnl 75yds* **20/1**
0434 **4** *3* **Fastada (IRE)**[30] 5512 3-8-4 50 oh2.................................(v) LukeMorris 3 48
(Jonathan Portman) *chsd ldrs: nt clr run and hanging lft on ins fr 2f out and stl hanging whn no imp and wknd fnl 120yds* **5/1**[2]
653 **5** *1 ¾* **Kavachi (IRE)**[15] 5994 8-9-8 62.. GeorgeBaker 2 57
(Gary Moore) *hld up in rr but in tch: hdwy over 2f out and chsd ldrs over 1f out: no imp: wknd fnl 120yds* **8/1**
4014 **6** *5* **Resplendent Light**[29] 5545 6-9-10 64.............................(t) MartinLane 11 49
(Bernard Llewellyn) *chsd ldrs: rdn and effrt to chal 2f out: wknd ins fnl f* **17/2**
0-00 **7** *18* **Callie's Angel**[29] 5538 3-8-7 53.. DavidProbert 6 —
(Bryn Palling) *a towards rr: rdn 4f out: lost tch fnl 3f* **25/1**

2350 **8** *13* **Pennfield Pirate**[27] 5611 4-9-6 **60** .... JimCrowley 10 —
(Hughie Morrison) *led after 2f: hdd ins fnl 3f: wknd qckly* **5/1**[2]
2m 17.5s (6.90) **Going Correction** +0.575s/f (Yiel)
WFA 3 from 4yo+ 6lb **8** Ran SP% **113.7**
Speed ratings (Par 101): **95,94,93,91,89 85,71,61**
toteswingers:1&2:£3.20, 2&3:£10.10, 1&3:£8.00 CSF £12.26 CT £152.21 TOTE £3.10: £1.70, £1.60, £4.00; EX 13.00 Trifecta £577.80 Part won. Pool: £780.84 - 0.97 winning units..
Owner Mrs Jane Chapple-Hyam **Bred** Aiden Murphy **Trained** Dalham, Suffolk

FOCUS
A weak handicap run at a modest pace. The time was 1.24 seconds slower than the second leg.
Grandad Mac Official explanation: trainer said, regarding apparent improvement in form, that the colt was suited by the longer trip

6438 LINDLEY CATERING H'CAP (DIV II) 1m 2f 36y
5:30 (5:30) (Class 6) (0-65,63) 3-Y-0+ **£1,617** (£481; £240; £120) **Stalls** Low

Form RPR
-352 **1** **Sweet World**[22] 4952 7-9-6 **59** .... MartinLane 6 69
(Bernard Llewellyn) *in rr: hdwy 4f out: led 3f out: rdn 2f out: styd on strly ins fnl f* **5/1**[3]
0150 **2** *2 ¾* **Shy**[14] 6023 6-9-10 **63** .... (b) JamesMillman 2 66
(Rod Millman) *chsd ldrs: rdn and lost pl fr over 3f out: drvn: swtchd rt to outside and hdwy appr fnl f: styd on to take 2nd fnl 75yds: no ch w wnr* **9/2**[2]
-254 **3** *2 ¼* **Cuckoo Rock (IRE)**[27] 5611 4-9-8 **61** .... StephenCraine 4 62+
(Jonathan Portman) *chsd ldrs: led ins fnl 4f: hdd 3f out: styd chsng wnr to 2f out: n.m.r sn after and lost position: rallied to go 2nd again ins fnl f: no imp: dropped to 3rd fnl 75yds* **5/1**[3]
4046 **4** *½* **My Sister**[17] 5912 4-8-10 **49** oh3 .... LukeMorris 9 47
(Mark Usher) *chsd ldrs: rdn to dispute 2nd 2f out and hung lft u.p: no imp on wnr and styd on one pce ins fnl f* **15/2**
6324 **5** *1 ½* **Chik's Dream**[16] 5964 4-9-2 **55** .... DaneO'Neill 3 50
(Derek Haydn Jones) *chsd ldrs: rdn 4f out: styd on same pce fr 2f out: wknd ins fnl f* **12/1**
060- **6** *hd* **Plug In Baby**[327] 7311 3-8-4 **52** ow1 .... JohnFahy(3) 8 46
(Nick Mitchell) *in rr: drvn along and losing tch 4f out: hrd rdn 3f out: styd on fr over 1f out: kpt on wl in clsng stages but nvr any threat* **33/1**
0653 **7** *9* **Levantera (IRE)**[27] 5614 3-9-3 **62** .... AdamKirby 10 38
(Clive Cox) *led after 1f: hdd ins fnl 4f: one pce whn hmpd on rails jst ins fnl 2f: wknd ins fnl f* **5/2**[1]
5100 **8** *8* **Miskin Diamond (IRE)**[26] 5642 3-8-4 **49** oh1 .... CathyGannon 5 9
(Bryn Palling) *led 1f: styd chsng ldrs tl rdn and wknd over 3f out* **16/1**
0026 **9** *60* **Barodine**[180] 808 8-9-6 **59** .... GeorgeBaker 7 —
(Ron Hodges) *hld up in rr: shkn up and no imp over 3f out: sn bhd* **25/1**
2m 16.26s (5.66) **Going Correction** +0.575s/f (Yiel)
WFA 3 from 4yo+ 6lb **9** Ran SP% **112.2**
Speed ratings (Par 101): **100,97,96,95,94 94,87,80,32**
toteswingers: 1&2 £5.80, 2&3 £5.20 1&3 not won.Tote Super 7: Win: Not won. Place: £531.60. CSF £26.71 CT £116.19 TOTE £5.10: £1.60, £1.30, £2.50; EX 28.00 Trifecta £149.00 Pool: £569.92 - 2.83 winning units..
Owner B J Llewellyn **Bred** Natton House Thoroughbreds **Trained** Fochriw, Caerphilly

FOCUS
The time was 1.24 seconds quicker than the first division.
Barodine Official explanation: jockey said gelding stopped quickly
T/Jkpt: £19,499.90 to a £1 stake. Pool of £27,464.78 - 1.00 winning tickets. T/Plt: £165.20 to a £1 stake. Pool of £77,376.43 - 341.84 winning tickets. T/Qpdt: £40.10 to a £1 stake. Pool of £4,981.59 - 91.90 winning tickets. ST

6251 KEMPTON (A.W) (R-H)
Wednesday, September 28

OFFICIAL GOING: Standard
Wind: Behind, moderate becoming light after race 2 Weather: Cloudless, warm!

6439 FREE ENTRY FOR BETDAQ MEMBERS H'CAP 1m 2f (P)
5:40 (5:40) (Class 4) (0-85,85) 3-Y-0+ **£4,075** (£1,212; £606; £303) **Stalls** Low

Form RPR
6025 **1** **Mutajare (IRE)**[19] 5892 3-8-12 **79** .... RichardHills 12 89+
(Mark Johnston) *trckd ldng pair: shkn up to ld 2f out: rdn over 1f out: styd on fnl f* **14/1**
1662 **2** *1* **Tahaamah**[7] 6249 3-9-0 **81** .... (t) TedDurcan 1 89
(Saeed Bin Suroor) *hld up in midfield: progover 2f out: rdn over 1f out and hanging: styd on to chse wnr ins fnl f: nvr able to chal* **3/1**[1]
-610 **3** *shd* **Complexion**[53] 4807 3-8-12 **79** .... ShaneKelly 6 87
(Sir Michael Stoute) *hld up in last trio: prog on inner over 2f out: drvn and r.o to dispute 2nd ins fnl f: unable to chal* **13/2**
3102 **4** *1* **Destiny Of A Diva**[63] 4432 4-9-8 **83** .... IanMongan 7 89
(Reg Hollinshead) *settled midfield: pushed along and prog fr 3f out: rdn to chse wnr over 1f out: no imp: lost 2nd and one pce ins fnl f* **16/1**
-000 **5** *2* **Aktia (IRE)**[74] 4109 4-8-12 **80** .... HayleyBurton(7) 4 82+
(Luca Cumani) *hld up in midfield: lost pl as r unfolded 2f out: nudged along and styd on wl fnl f: nrst fin* **28/1**
0 **6** *1 ¼* **Tindaro (FR)**[138] 2066 4-9-10 **85** .... StevieDonohoe 11 85
(Paul Webber) *hmpd s: hld up in last trio: rdn on outer over 2f out: styd on fr over 1f out: nt pce to threaten* **28/1**
0004 **7** *1 ¼* **Fremont (IRE)**[9] 6220 4-9-3 **78** .... JimmyQuinn 5 75
(Richard Hannon) *trckd ldrs: niot qckn and wl outpcd fr 2f out: kpt on same pce fnl f* **11/1**
0614 **8** *8* **Uncle Fred**[29] 5586 6-9-4 **79** .... SebSanders 9 60
(Patrick Chamings) *wnt lft s: a towards rr: pushed along on outer 3f out: no prog: bhd over 1f out* **25/1**
354- **9** *2 ¾* **Reverend Green (IRE)**[261] 7756 5-9-0 **75** .... FrannyNorton 8 51
(Chris Down) *t.k.h: pressed ldr: led briefly over 2f out: wknd rapidly fnl f* **66/1**
31-5 **10** *2 ½* **Dubai Bounty**[154] 1622 4-9-7 **82** .... (p) SteveDrowne 3 53
(Gerard Butler) *prom on inner: rdn 3f out: wknd qckly 2f out* **11/1**
2020 **11** *2 ¾* **Time Square (FR)**[12] 6130 4-8-12 **73** .... (t) DavidProbert 14 38
(Tony Carroll) *heavily restrained s and dropped in fr wd draw: hld up in last pair: no prog over 2f out: bhd over 1f out* **40/1**
3011 **12** *1 ¾* **Kyllachy Spirit**[18] 5942 3-9-3 **84** .... LiamJones 2 46
(William Knight) *led to over 2f out: wknd qckly* **9/2**[2]
-412 **13** *1* **Dean Swift**[19] 5893 3-8-13 **80** .... MichaelHills 13 40
(Brian Meehan) *forced to r wd thrght: nvr bttr than midfield: wknd over 2f out: eased* **5/1**[3]
2m 4.47s (-3.53) **Going Correction** -0.225s/f (Stan)
WFA 3 from 4yo+ 6lb **13** Ran SP% **117.1**
Speed ratings (Par 105): **105,104,104,103,101 100,99,93,91,89 86,85,84**
Tote Swingers: 1&2 £3.70, 1&3 £4.30, 2&3 £9.60 CSF £52.28 CT £309.24 TOTE £25.80: £6.90, £2.50, £2.30; EX 104.40 Trifecta £158.50 Pool: £2,163.47 - 10.10 winning units..
Owner Hamdan Al Maktoum **Bred** Epona Bloodstock Ltd **Trained** Middleham Moor, N Yorks

FOCUS
Quite a competitive handicap rated around those in the frame behind the winner, who recored a personal best.
Dubai Bounty Official explanation: jockey said filly had a breathing problem

6440 BETDAQ MULTIPLES MAIDEN FILLIES' STKS (DIV I) 7f (P)
6:10 (6:12) (Class 5) 2-Y-0 **£2,264** (£673; £336; £168) **Stalls** Low

Form RPR
620 **1** **Whimsical (IRE)**[20] 5849 2-9-0 83 .... RichardHughes 14 85+
(Richard Hannon) *trckd ldng pair: pushed up to ld over 1f out: shkn up and readily asserted fnl f* **9/2**[2]
2 *2 ½* **Yanabeeaa (USA)** 2-9-0 0 .... RichardHills 6 79+
(Sir Michael Stoute) *trckd ldrs: swtchd to outer over 2f out: cl 4th whn edgd rt wl over 1f out: styd on to take 2nd nr fin: fair debut* **12/1**
3 *nk* **No Compromise** 2-9-0 0 .... SteveDrowne 12 78
(Hughie Morrison) *trckd ldr: chal 2f out: upsides over 1f out: outpcd fnl f: lost 2nd nr fin* **50/1**
25 **4** *3 ¾* **Amber Silk (IRE)**[29] 5583 2-9-0 0 .... MichaelHills 4 68
(Charles Hills) *led: rdn and hdd over 1f out: wknd fnl f* **11/4**[1]
5 **5** *½* **Jellicle (IRE)**[15] 6030 2-9-0 0 .... NickyMackay 13 67
(John Gosden) *chsd ldrs: rdn and outpcd over 2f out: kpt on fnl f: n.d* **11/2**[3]
46 **6** *¾* **Proud Pearl (USA)**[96] 3362 2-9-0 0 .... ShaneKelly 8 65
(Brian Meehan) *chsd ldrs: rdn over 2f out: sn outpcd: kpt on one pce fnl f* **6/1**
7 *2 ¼* **Aiaam Al Wafa (IRE)** 2-9-0 0 .... IanMongan 2 59+
(David Lanigan) *late into paddock: in tch in midfield: outpcd and shkn up over 2f out: nvr on terms after* **20/1**
8 *¾* **Beauchamp Orange** 2-8-7 0 .... NicoleNordblad(7) 7 57+
(Hans Adielsson) *s.i.s: wl in rr: shuffled along over 2f out: sme late prog* **80/1**
9 *hd* **Operettist** 2-9-0 0 .... JimmyQuinn 1 56+
(Richard Hannon) *slowly away: wl in rr: shkn up over 2f out: sme late prog* **28/1**
10 *nk* **Joy To The World (IRE)** 2-9-0 0 .... StevieDonohoe 9 56+
(Paul Cole) *s.i.s: rn green and wl detached in last: nvr a factor but sme late prog* **50/1**
0 **11** *nk* **Pre Catalan**[9] 6215 2-9-0 0 .... TomMcLaughlin 10 55
(Ed Dunlop) *a towards rr: rdn and no prog over 2f out: wl btn after* **100/1**
12 *2* **Furzanah** 2-9-0 0 .... DavidProbert 11 50
(Luca Cumani) *a wl in rr and rn green: shkn up and no prog 3f out: no ch after* **14/1**
13 *1* **Garzoni** 2-9-0 0 .... SebSanders 5 47
(Sir Mark Prescott Bt) *rn green and sn shoved along: a in rr: wknd over 1f out* **33/1**
1m 25.49s (-0.51) **Going Correction** -0.075s/f (Stan) **13** Ran SP% **106.2**
Speed ratings (Par 92): **99,96,95,91,90 90,87,86,86,86 85,83,82**
Tote Swingers: 1&2 £6.30, 1&3 £23.00, 2&3 £65.70 CSF £42.46 TOTE £4.60: £1.90, £1.80, £14.10; EX 27.60 TRIFECTA Not won..
Owner Miss Yvonne Jacques **Bred** Churchtown House Stud **Trained** East Everleigh, Wilts
■ Ihtifal was withdrawn (8/1, ref to ent stalls). Deduct 10p in the £ under R4.

FOCUS
A fair maiden.

NOTEBOOK
Whimsical(IRE), despite being drawn out wide, was able to get out and cross over fairly comfortably and, prominent throughout, picked up well in the straight without her rider having to go for absolutely everything. She came home a cosy winner, which was no more than she was entitled to as an 83-rated filly in this field. (op 4-1)
Yanabeeaa(USA), a $400,000 Street Cry filly, travelled well through the race and looked threatening early in the straight, but she hung right once switched to challenge and her rider was far from hard on her while running on for second. She'll come on a bundle for this and will take some beating in similar company next time. (op 10-1 tchd 9-1)
No Compromise, half-sister to 7f winner Fungible, showed good pace from stall 12 to chase the leader into the first bend and hung in there well with a more experienced rival until seen off inside the last. She clearly has ability and should be capable of winning on the AW this autumn.
Amber Silk(IRE) probably went too fast in front but she's now eligible for nurseries, which opens up another avenue. (op 4-1)
Jellicle(IRE), who was on her toes beforehand, tracked the winner through but was outpaced by her early in the straight. She was of some interest switched to this surface given her pedigree but she could only plug on in the closing stages. (op 5-1)
Proud Pearl(USA), not seen since finishing sixth in the Newmarket maiden won by Discourse back in June, was disappointing, finding little for pressure in the straight. She's another for whom handicaps now become an option. (op 7-1)
Operettist Official explanation: jockey said filly was slowly away

6441 BETDAQ MULTIPLES MAIDEN FILLIES' STKS (DIV II) 7f (P)
6:40 (6:40) (Class 5) 2-Y-0 **£2,264** (£673; £336; £168) **Stalls** Low

Form RPR
026 **1** **Cresta Star**[11] 6168 2-9-0 70 .... RichardHughes 5 72+
(Richard Hannon) *mde virtually all and waited in front: kicked on 2f out: rdn whn hrd pressed fnl f: fnd enough: cosily* **9/4**[1]
6 **2** *¾* **Fine Painting (IRE)**[28] 5632 2-9-0 0 .... FergusSweeney 14 70+
(Gary Moore) *t.k.h: hld up fr wd draw: last of main gp over 2f out: gd prog on outer over 1f out: chal ins fnl f: nt qckn last 100yds* **9/2**[2]
3 *¾* **Yours Ever** 2-9-0 0 .... SebSanders 12 68+
(Sir Mark Prescott Bt) *dwlt: hld up in rr: gd prog 2f out to chse wnr over 1f out: lost 2nd jst ins fnl f: styd on* **11/1**
00 **4** *hd* **Chatterati (USA)**[33] 5444 2-9-0 0 .... AhmedAjtebi 2 68+
(Mahmood Al Zarooni) *hld up towards rr: prog 2f out to chse ldrs over 1f out: styd on but unable to chal* **6/1**[3]
5 *2 ¾* **Twin Shadow (IRE)** 2-9-0 0 .... StevieDonohoe 9 60+
(James Fanshawe) *trckd ldrs: effrt over 2f out: disp 2nd wl over 1f out: sn outpcd* **7/1**
6 *2 ¼* **Cambridge Duchess** 2-8-11 0 .... RyanClark(3) 7 55
(Stuart Williams) *dwlt: hld up in midfield on inner: effrt over 2f out: cl enough wl over 1f out: sn outpcd* **28/1**

60 **7** *hd* **Perfect Day (IRE)**[9] 6215 2-9-0 0........................ TedDurcan 10 54
(Paul Cole) *prom: rdn and cl enough wl over 1f out: sn wl outpcd* **33/1**

8 *3/4* **Lily Potts** 2-9-0 0........................ SteveDrowne 4 52+
(Chris Down) *late into paddock: dwlt: detached in last pair after 2f: same situation and pushed along over 2f out: styd on stoutly fnl f* **80/1**

00 **9** *1 1/2* **Refreshestheparts (USA)**[20] 5863 2-9-0 0........................ TonyCulhane 8 48
(George Baker) *dwlt: tk fierced hold and hld up in midfield: racd wd in st: nudged along and grad fdd* **20/1**

0 **10** *1/2* **Perchance**[37] 5323 2-9-0 0........................ IanMongan 13 47
(Sir Henry Cecil) *chsd ldrs: rdn over 2f out: wknd over 1f out* **12/1**

11 *1 1/4* **Compton Rainbow** 2-9-0 0........................ JamesDoyle 11 44
(Hans Adielsson) *prog to press wnr after 2f: rdn and upsides 2f out: hanging and wknd qckly over 1f out* **40/1**

12 *nse* **End Of Dreams (USA)** 2-9-0 0........................ FrannyNorton 1 44
(Kevin Ryan) *prom: rdn to dispute 2nd wl over 1f out: sn wknd qckly* **12/1**

13 *15* **Hip Hop** 2-9-0 0........................ EddieCreighton 6 5
(Brett Johnson) *sn struggling in last pair: t.o* **150/1**

1m 27.46s (1.46) **Going Correction** -0.075s/f (Stan) **13** Ran SP% **114.9**
Speed ratings (Par 92): **88,87,86,86,82 80,80,79,77,76 75,75,58**
Tote Swingers: 1&2 £3.70, 1&3 £4.30, 2&3 £9.60 CSF £10.38 TOTE £3.10: £1.50, £1.90, £4.60; EX 14.80 Trifecta £137.90 Pool: £1,509.72 - 8.10 winning units..
Owner P T Tellwright **Bred** P T Tellwright **Trained** East Everleigh, Wilts

FOCUS
This didn't look as strong a maiden as the first division and there was a lack of early pace, too, resulting in a winning time 1.97sec slower.

NOTEBOOK
Cresta Star broke well and was able to dictate a pace to suit herself. The runner-up came with what looked a winning run down the outside but Cresta Star had a bit left in the locker to repel her challenge and was comfortably holding her at bay at the line. She came into the race rated just 70 and it'll be a surprise if she goes up much for winning.
Fine Painting(IRE) didn't settle at all through the early stages and so the fact she was able to produce a terrific burst of speed to come from the back of the field 2f out to challenge the winner inside the last was highly creditable. She hit 1.01 in running and, while unable to get past, she showed more than enough to suggest she'll be winning races in due course. (op 7-2)
Yours Ever, a 180,000gns purchase out of a mare who won a Group 3 over 1m4f, wasn't best away and ended up being held up towards the rear of the main pack. She was given a lot to do allowing for the steady gallop up front, but she picked up well to get involved and looks to have a future. She'll get further next year. (op 10-1)
Chatterati(USA), one of Godolphin's lesser lights judged on her previous two efforts, didn't pick up well enough to make the frame, but she's now eligible for a handicap rating and she might be able to get off the mark in that sphere. (op 7-1)
Twin Shadow(IRE), a half-sister to 6f 2-y-o winner Rahya Cass, didn't run badly on her debut. (op 10-1)
Cambridge Duchess was green and is bred to appreciate a longer trip in time.
Compton Rainbow Official explanation: jockey said filly ran too free

6442 BACK OR LAY AT BETDAQ.COM H'CAP 6f (P)
7:10 (7:13) (Class 5) (0-75,75) 3-Y-O £2,264 (£673; £336; £168) Stalls Low

Form RPR

4130 **1** **Numeral (IRE)**[20] 5856 3-9-2 70........................ RichardHughes 3 79
(Richard Hannon) *towards rr: rdn and prog fr 2f out: chal on inner fnl f: r.o wl to ld last strides* **11/2**[3]

451 **2** *nse* **Libys Dream (IRE)**[18] 5946 3-8-9 63........................ JimmyQuinn 8 72
(Michael Mullineaux) *patiently rdn in rr: gd prog on outer over 1f out: led 150yds out but hrd pressed: r.o: hdd last strides* **7/1**

5012 **3** *1* **Crew Cut (IRE)**[18] 5914 3-8-10 71........................ RaulDaSilva[(7)] 6 77
(Jeremy Gask) *trckd ldng pair: rdn to ld narrowly 1f out: sn hdd: styd on same pce* **9/2**[2]

1455 **4** *1 1/4* **Millyluvstobouggie**[32] 5476 3-9-4 75........................ JohnFahy[(3)] 1 77
(Clive Cox) *sn restrained into last trio: prog on inner over 2f out: tried to cl on ldrs 1f out: one pce* **6/1**

31 **5** *3/4* **Grandmas Dream**[14] 6056 3-9-2 73........................(p) RobertLButler[(3)] 4 73
(Richard Guest) *prom: rdn to chal 2f out: upsides 1f out: nt qckn and sn btn* **16/1**

4314 **6** *2 1/2* **Midnight Rider (IRE)**[15] 6036 3-9-7 75........................(p) TedDurcan 5 67
(Chris Wall) *chsd ldrs: rdn 2f out: fdd fr over 1f out* **8/1**

201 **7** *1 1/4* **Blink Of An Eye**[47] 4991 3-9-7 75........................ AdamKirby 11 63
(Michael Bell) *led at str pce: rdn and hanging 2f out: hdd 1f out: wknd qckly* **4/1**[1]

5006 **8** *hd* **Charles Fosterkane**[12] 6120 3-9-2 70........................(b[1]) SteveDrowne 7 57
(John Best) *t.k.h: hld up in last trio: nt qckn 2f out: one pce after: no threat* **28/1**

4500 **9** *3/4* **Dream Catcher (FR)**[7] 6246 3-9-1 74........................ JamesRogers[(5)] 10 59
(David Pinder) *chsd ldr to 2f out: sn wknd* **33/1**

2022 **10** *2* **Blue Deer (IRE)**[20] 5859 3-9-2 70........................ StevieDonohoe 9 48
(John Akehurst) *sn bhd: detached in last fr 1/2-way: kpt on fnl f* **16/1**

1m 11.81s (-1.29) **Going Correction** -0.075s/f (Stan) **10** Ran SP% **109.6**
Speed ratings (Par 101): **105,104,103,101,100 97,95,95,94,92**
Tote Swingers: 1&2 £8.00, 1&3 £6.80, 2&3 £7.60 CSF £39.14 CT £164.64 TOTE £6.30: £2.20, £3.80, £1.50; EX 53.20 Trifecta £551.80 Pool: £2,088.12 - 2.80 winning units..
Owner Highclere Thoroughbred Racing-Flying Fox **Bred** Tinnakill Bloodstock & Forenaghts Stud **Trained** East Everleigh, Wilts
■ Lady Bayside was withdrawn (12/1, ref to ent stalls). Deduct 5p in the £ under R4.

FOCUS
An open-looking handicap run at a good gallop thanks to a disputed lead, and there was a tight finish. The form looks sound enough rated around the first three.

6443 BETDAQ MOBILE APPS NURSERY 1m (P)
7:40 (7:40) (Class 6) (0-65,65) 2-Y-O £1,617 (£481; £240; £120) Stalls Low

Form RPR

042 **1** **Anginola (IRE)**[16] 6001 2-9-3 61........................ GeorgeBaker 12 69
(Joseph Tuite) *trckd ldng pair: wnt 2nd 2f out: rdn to cl over 1f out: led last 150yds: sn asserted: readily* **16/1**

6052 **2** *2* **Spunky**[28] 5634 2-9-2 60........................ KierenFallon 4 63
(Luca Cumani) *dwlt: sn pushed up into midfield: rdn and effrt over 2f out: edgd lft over 1f out: styd on to take 2nd last stride* **13/8**[1]

4600 **3** *shd* **Siouxperhero (IRE)**[12] 6132 2-9-2 65........................(b) JamesRogers[(5)] 14 68
(William Muir) *led at gd pce: kicked on over 2f out: hdd and one pce last 150yds: lost 2nd post* **40/1**

603 **4** *3/4* **Orwellian**[36] 5337 2-9-7 65........................ LiamJones 8 66
(Brian Meehan) *towards rr: pushed along and effrt on outer over 3f out: drvn and outpcd 2f out: styd on fr over 1f out: nrst fin* **15/2**[2]

0246 **5** *1 1/2* **Alborz (IRE)**[11] 6154 2-9-6 64........................(b[1]) FrannyNorton 1 62
(Mark Johnston) *trckd ldrs: rdn over 2f out: nt qckn wl over 1f out: fdd ins fnl f* **12/1**

650 **6** *1 3/4* **Ironically (IRE)**[19] 5899 2-9-7 65........................ TedDurcan 11 59
(David Lanigan) *sn in last pair: rdn and hanging over 2f out: prog wl over 1f out: kpt on: n.d* **33/1**

0004 **7** *nk* **Valiant Runner**[14] 6053 2-9-4 62........................ ShaneKelly 6 55
(Jeremy Noseda) *chsd ldrs: hanging u.p and outpcd 2f out: no ch after: kpt on* **16/1**

040 **8** *4 1/2* **Percythepinto (IRE)**[100] 3229 2-9-4 62........................(t) TonyCulhane 3 45
(George Baker) *sn hld up in last: rowed along over 2f out: passed wkng rivals over 1f out: nvr involved* **11/1**

000 **9** *2* **Methaen (USA)**[30] 5564 2-9-5 63........................ RichardHills 10 41
(Ed Dunlop) *mostly chsd ldr to 2f out: sn wknd* **14/1**

056 **10** *nk* **Northern Territory (IRE)**[30] 5541 2-9-2 60........................ TomQueally 9 38
(Jim Boyle) *a in rr: rdn and no prog over 2f out* **12/1**

0060 **11** *1/2* **Always A Sinner (USA)**[28] 5634 2-9-5 63........................(v[1]) JimCrowley 2 39
(William Knight) *wl in rr: effrt on inner over 2f out: no hdwy wl over 1f out: sn wknd* **16/1**

006 **12** *1/2* **Big Time Charlie (IRE)**[20] 5861 2-9-0 58........................ RichardHughes 13 33
(Richard Hannon) *racd wd in rr: rdn and no prog on outer wl over 2f out* **8/1**[3]

060 **13** *1* **Vergrigio (IRE)**[60] 4545 2-9-2 60........................ SebSanders 5 33
(Brian Meehan) *chsd ldrs: u.p sn after 1/2-way: wknd 3f out* **16/1**

1m 39.26s (-0.54) **Going Correction** -0.075s/f (Stan) **13** Ran SP% **120.3**
Speed ratings (Par 93): **99,97,96,96,94 92,92,88,86,85 85,84,83**
Tote Swingers: 1&2 £3.90, 1&3 £48.20, 2&3 £19.30 CSF £42.32 CT £1133.28 TOTE £18.10: £4.30, £1.30, £8.50; EX 33.50 TRIFECTA Not won..
Owner E C Everall **Bred** T C Clarke **Trained** Great Shefford, Berkshire

FOCUS
A modest nursery.

NOTEBOOK
Anginola(IRE), who narrowly failed to score over 7f here on her handicap debut when backed into favouritism, was relatively ignored in the market this time, despite being only 2lb higher. Drawn wide, she travelled well to the outer of the leaders and picked up when asked. She drifted right a little under pressure but was comfortably on top at the finish, and there could be more improvement in her. (op 20-1)
Spunky, sent off favourite again, finished second again. He tracked the winner through and had every chance, but lacked the pace to pick her up. The stronger the gallop the better he'll be. (op 6-4)
Siouxperhero(IRE) managed to cross over from stall 14 to make the running and got first run on his rivals entering the straight. He couldn't quite hold them all off but he got the longer trip well and is now on a competitive mark.
Orwellian, running in a handicap for the first time, got outpaced on the turn in and stayed on all too late. A stronger all-round pace would have been to his advantage. (op 8-1)
Alborz(IRE), blinkered for the first time, was well placed on the turn in but couldn't pick up once in line for home. He'd be of more interest back at Southwell. (op 11-1)
Ironically(IRE) was at the back of the field and had a lot to do turning in. She made some headway but looks on a stiff enough mark for what she's achieved.

6444 BUYING BUSINESS TRAVEL H'CAP 6f (P)
8:10 (8:12) (Class 6) (0-60,60) 3-Y-O+ £1,617 (£481; £240; £120) Stalls Low

Form RPR

001 **1** **Swansea Jack**[14] 6070 4-9-2 59........................(vt) RyanClark[(3)] 2 70+
(Stuart Williams) *dwlt and reminder sn after s: chsd ldrs after 1f: effrt to go 2nd 2f out but hanging and plld wd: clsd to ld last 100yds: idled but hld on* **6/4**[1]

1321 **2** *hd* **Golden Compass**[27] 5644 3-9-4 60........................ WilliamCarson 11 70
(Giles Bravery) *trckd ldr: led over 2f out: rdn over 1f out: hdd last 100yds: styd on but jst hld* **9/2**[2]

0504 **3** *1 1/2* **Silvee**[7] 6257 4-8-12 55........................ KieranO'Neill[(3)] 3 61
(John Bridger) *chsd ldrs: rdn over 2f out: prog over 1f out: tk 3rd ins fnl f but nt quite pce to chal* **10/1**

2334 **4** *1 1/2* **Till Dawn (IRE)**[13] 6105 3-9-0 56........................ DavidProbert 1 57
(Tony Carroll) *hld up in midfield: prog to chse ldng pair over 1f out: nt qckn and lost 3rd ins fnl f* **12/1**

5350 **5** *1/2* **Dualagi**[30] 5561 7-9-6 60........................ GeorgeBaker 8 59+
(Martin Bosley) *hld up in last quartet and wl off the pce: shuffled along fnl 2f: nvr remotely nr ldrs but fin w a flourish* **25/1**

1223 **6** *1* **Running Mate (IRE)**[76] 3999 4-9-1 55........................(t) IanMongan 13 51
(Jo Crowley) *wl in rr: effrt on inner over 2f out: plugged on but no imp on ldrs fnl f* **7/1**[3]

0102 **7** *nk* **The Name Is Frank**[7] 6258 6-9-3 57........................(t) FergusSweeney 9 52
(Mark Gillard) *chsd ldng pair to 2f out: wknd fnl f* **8/1**

0-00 **8** *1 1/4* **Cut The Cackle (IRE)**[23] 5788 5-8-12 55........................(t) RobertLButler[(3)] 5 46
(Richard Guest) *chsd ldrs: taken wd in st: reminder over 1f out: nvr on terms after* **33/1**

6463 **9** *1/2* **Patch Patch**[7] 6258 4-9-6 60........................(e[1]) AdamKirby 10 49
(Derek Shaw) *blindfold off late and dwlt: a wl in rr: rdn and no prog over 2f out* **16/1**

6600 **10** *7* **Zee Zee Dan (IRE)**[52] 4819 3-9-1 57........................(p) TomQueally 7 24
(Noel Quinlan) *nvr bttr than midfield: wknd u.p over 2f out* **33/1**

6600 **11** *2 1/2* **Super Frank (IRE)**[13] 6090 8-9-5 59........................(b) SamHitchcott 4 18
(Zoe Davison) *led to over 2f out: wknd rapidly* **50/1**

1m 12.44s (-0.66) **Going Correction** -0.075s/f (Stan)
WFA 3 from 4yo+ 2lb **11** Ran SP% **116.1**
Speed ratings (Par 101): **101,100,98,96,96 94,94,92,92,82 79**
Tote Swingers: 1&2 £2.30, 1&3 £4.30, 2&3 £4.10 CSF £7.42 CT £50.20 TOTE £2.40: £1.10, £1.70, £2.50; EX 10.50 Trifecta £66.20 Pool: £735.60 - 8.22 winning units..
Owner K J Mercer **Bred** Usk Valley Stud **Trained** Newmarket, Suffolk
■ Stewards' Enquiry : Ryan Clark one-day ban; excessive use of whip (12th Oct)

FOCUS
Just an ordinary handicap best rated around the third and fourth.

6445 RACING@SKYSPORTS.COM CLAIMING STKS 1m 4f (P)
8:40 (8:40) (Class 6) 3-Y-O+ £1,617 (£481; £240; £120) Stalls Centre

Form RPR

2-05 **1** **Raucous Behaviour (USA)**[125] 2435 3-8-12 80........................ KierenFallon 9 75
(George Prodromou) *stmbld bdly s: sn trckd ldrs: wound up to cl and led wl over 1f out: hrd pressed after: jst prevailed* **8/1**

0/00 **2** *nse* **First Avenue**[69] 4253 6-9-6 74........................ IanMongan 1 75
(Laura Mongan) *hld up in midfield: effrt 2f out: chsd wnr fnl f: upsides last strides: jst pipped* **40/1**

504 **3** *1 1/2* **Porgy**[24] 5757 6-9-11 83........................ TedDurcan 4 78
(David Simcock) *hld up in last: clsd over 2f out: carried hd high and n.g.t w effrt over 1f out: styd on to take 3rd nr fin* **5/2**[1]

4545 **4** *1/2* **Foxhaven**[12] 6130 9-9-10 77........................(v) JimCrowley 2 78+
(Patrick Chamings) *trckd ldrs: brought to chal 2f out: nt qckn over 1f out: disputing 3rd and hld whn bmpd wl ins fnl f* **3/1**[2]

0 **5** ½ **Uphold**[33] 5435 4-9-11 86 (be) GeorgeBaker 5 79+
(Gay Kelleway) *led after 1f: sn stdd pce: tried to kick on 2f out but field clsng and sn hdd: kpt pressing tl hld in 3rd whn bmpd wl ins fnl f* **9/2**

4 **6** 1¾ **Ashammar (FR)**[15] 6017 6-9-4 0 (t) StevieDonohoe 6 66
(Paul Webber) *hld up towards rr: nt qckn whn pce qcknd fr 2f out: one pce after* **20/1**

3305 **7** ½ **Scamperdale**[26] 5693 9-9-8 89 KierenFox(3) 7 72
(Brian Baugh) *hld up in last pair: nt qckn whn sprint sed 2f out: one pce after* **7/2**[3]

364R **8** 1 **Negotiation (IRE)**[36] 5356 5-9-4 63 FrannyNorton 3 64
(Michael Quinn) *t.k.h: led 1f: chsd ldr to 2f out: sn lost pl in dash for the fin* **28/1**

1332 **9** nse **What About Now**[16] 6004 3-8-1 62 (b) KieranO'Neill(3) 8 58
(J W Hills) *t.k.h: trckd ldng pair: sn lost pl whn pce qcknd 2f out* **16/1**

2m 34.98s (0.48) **Going Correction** -0.075s/f (Stan)
WFA 3 from 4yo+ 8lb **9** Ran SP% **121.6**
Speed ratings (Par 101): **95,94,93,93,93 92,91,91,91**
Tote Swingers: 1&2 £47.00, 1&3 £4.10, 2&3 £101.60 CSF £289.43 TOTE £12.50: £7.40, £9.20, £2.00; EX 141.30 TRIFECTA Not won..Porgy was claimed by Mr T. J. Pitt for £15,000.
Owner Matt Bartram **Bred** Stonerside Stable **Trained** East Harling, Norfolk
■ Stewards' Enquiry : Kieren Fallon two-day ban; careless riding (12th-13th Oct)

FOCUS
A messy race pace-wise and it developed into something of a sprint from early in the straight. As a result the form looks muddling, with the sixth possibly the best guide.

6446 TFM NETWORKS CLASSIFIED STKS 1m 3f (P)
9:10 (9:10) (Class 6) 3-Y-0+ **£1,617** (£360; £360; £120) **Stalls** Low

Form RPR

0003 **1** **Fifty Cents**[21] 5832 7-9-7 52 (p) KierenFallon 4 62+
(Brendan Powell) *led 1f: trckd ldr: led over 2f out and dashed 2 l clr: drvn and kpt on: a holding on* **7/2**[1]

0004 **2** 1 **Alhaque (USA)**[56] 4654 5-9-7 52 (bt) TonyCulhane 6 58
(David Flood) *hld up in rr: gd prog on outer fr 2f out to chse wnr over 1f out: kpt on but a hld* **20/1**

0024 **2** dht **Reggie Perrin**[12] 6122 3-9-0 54 IanMongan 12 60+
(Pat Phelan) *dwlt: hld up in last quartet: effrt and nt clrest of passages fr over 2f out: gd run fnl f: clsng at fin* **7/2**[1]

-362 **4** 1 **Zelos Diktator**[10] 5643 5-9-7 55 (p) GeorgeBaker 13 56
(Gary Moore) *settled towards rr: stdy prog fr 1/2-way: cl up over 2f out but sn outpcd by wnr: kpt on* **11/2**[2]

4400 **5** nk **Sir Randolf (IRE)**[7] 6253 3-9-0 53 (t) JamesDoyle 1 55
(Sylvester Kirk) *hld up towards rr: prog on inner over 2f out: pressed for a pl over 1f out: one pce* **16/1**

3540 **6** ½ **Raghdaan**[18] 5912 4-9-7 46 ChrisCatlin 3 55
(Peter Hiatt) *prom: rdn to chse wnr 2f out but outpcd: lost 2nd over 1f out: one pce* **20/1**

0-30 **7** 4 **Savaronola (USA)**[34] 5406 6-9-7 55 TomQueally 8 47
(Barney Curley) *pushed along early in rr: effrt on outer over 2f out: sn outpcd: nt on terms after* **8/1**[3]

0005 **8** nk **Azurinta (IRE)**[19] 5898 3-8-7 54 IanBurns(7) 9 47
(Michael Bell) *wl in tch on inner: n.m.r briefly over 2f out: bmpd along and fdd* **12/1**

0000 **9** ½ **Iztaccihuatl**[21] 5832 3-9-0 39 JamieGoldstein 10 46
(Michael Scudamore) *prom: chsd ldng pair 8f out to 2f out: wknd over 1f out* **50/1**

4-04 **10** 1 **Melancholy Hill (IRE)**[24] 3744 3-9-0 53 FergusSweeney 14 44
(Alan King) *hld up last: no real prog over 2f out: nvr on terms* **16/1**

0350 **11** shd **Fair Dinkum (IRE)**[21] 5832 3-8-11 51 SophieDoyle(3) 2 44
(Jamie Osborne) *w ldrs tl wknd 2f out* **40/1**

040 **12** 1¼ **The Right Time**[30] 5567 3-9-0 53 DavidProbert 7 42
(Tony Carroll) *hld up towards rr: effrt over 2f out and nt clr run briefly: sn no prog and btn* **12/1**

60 **13** 22 **Wodian (IRE)**[27] 5643 3-9-0 48 (t) TedDurcan 11 —
(David Lanigan) *racd wd in midfield: wknd over 2f out: t.o and eased* **20/1**

0604 **14** 12 **Danceyourselfdizzy (IRE)**[14] 6067 3-8-7 51 LeonnaMayor(7) 5 —
(Phil McEntee) *led after 1f to over 2f out: wknd rapidly: t.o and eased* **33/1**

2m 21.37s (-0.53) **Going Correction** -0.075s/f (Stan)
WFA 3 from 4yo+ 7lb **14** Ran SP% **119.7**
Speed ratings (Par 101): **98,97,97,96,96 95,93,92,92,91 91,90,74,66**
Place: Alhaque £7.10, Reggie Perrin £1.70. Ex: FC,A £31.30, FC,RP £9.30 CSF: FC,A £41.43 FC,RP £6.46. Tote Swingers: FC&A £6.00, FC&RP £6.10, A&RP £30.50 TOTE £3.90: £1.30 TRIFECTA Not won..
Owner Miss Chris Elks **Bred** Belgrave Bloodstock **Trained** Upper Lambourn, Berks

FOCUS
A poor contest restricted to horses who had not won more than one race. The winner looked better than the bare result while the second ran his best race of the year on his debut for a new yard.
T/Plt: £26.30 to a £1 stake. Pool of £54,067.00 - 1,498.70 winning tickets. T/Qpdt: £7.50 to a £1 stake. Pool of £6,733.00 - 657.14 winning tickets. JN

5786 NEWCASTLE (L-H)
Wednesday, September 28

OFFICIAL GOING: Good (good to firm in places; 7.3)
Wind: Breezy, half behind Weather: Warm, sunny

6447 BRITISH STALLION STUDS SUPPORTING BRITISH RACING E B F MAIDEN STKS 1m 3y(S)
2:10 (2:10) (Class 4) 2-Y-0 **£4,398** (£1,309; £654; £327) **Stalls** Low

Form RPR

6 **1** **Deia Sunrise (IRE)**[20] 5851 2-9-3 0 WilliamBuick 3 77+
(John Gosden) *in tch: hdwy to ld over 1f out: sn pushed along: styd on wl ins fnl f* **4/1**[3]

3022 **2** 1¼ **Choisan (IRE)**[10] 6187 2-9-3 78 DavidAllan 5 74
(Tim Easterby) *chsd ldr: rdn over 2f out: effrt and ev ch ins fnl f: kpt on: hld nr fin* **7/2**[2]

3 2 **Ibtahaj** 2-9-3 0 TomEaves 2 70+
(Saeed Bin Suroor) *trckd ldrs: effrt and ev ch 2f out: kpt on same pce ins fnl f* **20/1**

2433 **4** 1 **Dark Ambition (IRE)**[22] 5809 2-9-0 67 AdamBeschizza(3) 1 68
(William Haggas) *led: rdn and hdd over 1f out: kpt on same pce ins fnl f* **20/1**

5 3 **Gabrial The Great (IRE)** 2-9-3 0 PaulHanagan 7 61+
(Michael Bell) *cotly and green in paddock: hld up in last: rdn and rn green over 2f out: hdwy over 1f out: no imp ins fnl f: bttr for r* **5/2**[1]

6 1½ **Guardi (IRE)** 2-9-3 0 RoystonFfrench 6 58
(Mahmood Al Zarooni) *hld up: rdn and outpcd over 3f out: n.d after* **16/1**

5 **7** 6 **Brailsford (IRE)**[20] 5851 2-9-3 0 PhillipMakin 4 45
(Mahmood Al Zarooni) *in tch: rdn over 2f out: sn btn* **5/1**

0 **8** 5 **Youcouldbelucky (USA)**[68] 4264 2-9-3 0 JoeFanning 9 34
(Mark Johnston) *trckd ldrs tl rdn and wknd qckly over 2f out* **16/1**

1m 39.3s (-4.10) **Going Correction** -0.40s/f (Firm) **8** Ran SP% **108.7**
Speed ratings (Par 97): **104,102,100,99,96 95,89,84**
toteswingers:1&2:£3.60, 2&3:£10.70, 1&3:£13.70 CSF £16.51 TOTE £5.90: £2.60, £1.10, £5.20; EX 19.60.
Owner M Kerr-Dineen M Hughes Ms R Hood **Bred** John O'Connor **Trained** Newmarket, Suffolk

FOCUS
An ordinary maiden and experience counted with the front pair having raced before. The winner and third are the best guide.

NOTEBOOK
Deia Sunrise(IRE) had shown ability when sixth of 15 on his Doncaster debut and looked much more professional here, especially in the way he pulled out more when pressed by the runner-up inside the last furlong. Already a gelding, he should improve again. (op 5-1)
Choisan(IRE), in the frame in five of his first six starts, set the standard with a mark of 78 but again had to give best to a more progressive rival. He may be worth switching to nurseries now. (tchd 3-1)
Ibtahaj, a 200,000gns son of a Group 3 winner, did best of the newcomers and impressed with the way he travelled, but he did appear to run green under pressure in the last furlong. He is likely to prove the best of these in the longer term.
Dark Ambition(IRE) was another with plenty of experience under his belt and made much of the running until before the furlong pole. Rated 11lb inferior to the runner-up, he again ran his race but looks exposed.
Gabrial The Great(IRE), a 120,000euros brother to a Listed winner and half-brother to two useful winners in France, arrived here with a big reputation but he was full of himself in the paddock and going down and made no impression from off the pace in the race itself. It was noticeable, however, that he was never hit with the whip so is surely capable of much better. He is bred to come into his own over middle distances in due course. (op 13-8 tchd 6-4 in places)
Brailsford(IRE) finished in front of the winner on his Doncaster debut, so this was bitterly disappointing. (op 6-1 tchd 7-1)

6448 E.B.F./T.S.G. MAIDEN STKS 7f
2:40 (2:42) (Class 4) 2-Y-0 **£4,398** (£1,309; £654; £327) **Stalls** Low

Form RPR

1 **Al Saham** 2-9-3 0 WilliamBuick 2 88+
(Saeed Bin Suroor) *prom: rdn to ld over 1f out: kpt on u.p ins fnl f: hld on wl towards fin* **12/1**

24 **2** ½ **Sholaan (IRE)**[19] 5875 2-9-3 0 PaulHanagan 10 87+
(William Haggas) *prom: led 3f out: hdd wl over 1f out: remained w ev ch: edgd lft and rt u.p ins fnl f: hld nr fin* **11/4**[2]

32 **3** 8 **Talk Of The North**[12] 6117 2-8-12 0 LukeMorris 13 62
(Hugo Palmer) *hld up: hdwy to trck ldrs over 3f out: sn rdn: kpt on one pce: wnt 3rd fnl 75yds: no threat on ldng pair* **9/4**[1]

4 ½ **Clon Brulee (IRE)** 2-9-3 0 LeeNewman 9 66+
(David Barron) *midfield: pushed along and outpcd over 3f out: kpt on wl fr over 1f out: wnt 4th fnl 50yds* **14/1**

5 1¾ **Peter Anders** 2-9-3 0 JoeFanning 5 61
(Mark Johnston) *w ldr: rdn over 2f out: wknd and lost 2 pls ins fnl f* **5/1**[3]

6 4½ **Seattle Sounder (IRE)** 2-9-3 0 DavidNolan 7 50
(Ann Duffield) *led narrowly: rdn whn hdd 3f out: sn btn* **80/1**

0 **7** ¾ **Captivity**[97] 3314 2-9-3 0 RoystonFfrench 1 48
(Mahmood Al Zarooni) *hld up: rdn 3f out: nvr threatened* **14/1**

0 **8** shd **Kung Hei Fat Choy (USA)**[20] 5851 2-9-3 0 JamesSullivan 4 48
(James Given) *trckd ldrs: pushed along 3f out: wknd over 1f out* **14/1**

06 **9** ½ **Roll Of Thunder**[28] 5618 2-9-3 0 PBBeggy 15 47
(John Quinn) *racd keenly: trckd ldrs: rdn over 2f out: sn wknd* **50/1**

65 **10** 3½ **More Bottle (IRE)**[21] 5818 2-8-12 0 AndrewMullen 11 33
(Tom Tate) *hld up in tch: pushed along over 3f out: sn btn* **40/1**

11 4 **Turned To Gold (IRE)** 2-9-0 0 HarryBentley(3) 12 28
(Alan Jarvis) *hld up: pushed along over 2f out: nvr threatened* **40/1**

12 1¼ **Luctor Emergo (IRE)** 2-9-3 0 TomEaves 3 25
(Keith Dalgleish) *s.i.s: sn pushed along in rr: a bhd* **40/1**

13 4½ **Lady Kashaan (IRE)** 2-8-12 0 PJMcDonald 8 8
(Alan Swinbank) *trckd ldrs: rdn over 3f out: sn wknd* **20/1**

0 **14** ¾ **Ottavino (IRE)**[25] 5726 2-9-0 0 DeclanCannon(3) 16 12
(Nigel Tinkler) *hld up: a towards rr* **200/1**

1m 25.5s (-2.30) **Going Correction** -0.40s/f (Firm) **14** Ran SP% **117.6**
Speed ratings (Par 97): **97,96,87,86,84 79,78,78,78,74 69,68,62,62**
toteswingers:1&2:£4.50, 2&3:£2.40, 1&3:£6.80 CSF £42.37 TOTE £9.10: £2.20, £1.90, £1.10; EX 34.90.
Owner Godolphin **Bred** Darley **Trained** Newmarket, Suffolk
■ Stewards' Enquiry : Declan CannonD caution; entered wrong stall

FOCUS
Another ordinary maiden overall, but the first two pulled a long way clear and showed strong form.

NOTEBOOK
Al Saham has a nice pedigree, being by Authorized out of a winning sister to the high-class Crimplene, and this successful debut bodes well for his future too. He and the runner-up had the race to themselves in the latter stages, but despite conceding experience to his rival he looked the more professional of the pair where it mattered. He should go on to better things. (op 10-1)
Sholaan(IRE) may not have been suited by Chester when a disappointing favourite last time following an eye-catching debut, but he had no excuses here. In front at halfway, he was still just about in front half a furlong from home, with the winner as his only conceivable danger, when he hung dramatically all over the place and threw the race away. Perhaps the quick ground wasn't suitable, but he has a question to answer now. (op 3-1)
Talk Of The North was never too far away, but seemed to get outpaced passing the 2f pole at which stage the front pair got away from her. A return to further will help and she now gets a mark. (op 2-1 tchd 5-2 in places)
Clon Brulee(IRE) was noted doing some solid late work and this son of a dual winner over 1m4f should improve, especially when faced with more of a test. (op 25-1)
Peter Anders, retained for 30,000gns as a 2yo, is a half-brother to three winners at up to 1m2f and ran well for a long way on this debut before lack of race-fitness told.
Seattle Sounder(IRE), a £15,000 half-brother to two winners at up to 1m2f, showed ability on this debut and should find easier assignments than this.

6449 E.B.F./NORTH SEA LOGISTICS MAIDEN FILLIES' STKS 6f
3:10 (3:12) (Class 4) 2-Y-0 **£4,398** (£1,309; £654; £327) **Stalls** Low

Form RPR

3223 **1** **Van Der Art**[26] 5681 2-8-11 78 HarryBentley(3) 10 80+
(Alan Jarvis) *trckd ldrs: hdwy to ld 1f out: kpt on strly to go clr last 100yds* **2/1**[1]

The Form Book, Raceform Ltd, Compton, RG20 6NL

33 **2** *3 3/4* **Khaleejiya (IRE)**[44] 5117 2-9-0 0 .... LukeMorris 6 69
(James Toller) *trckd ldrs: rdn and edgd rt over 1f out: kpt on fnl f to take 2nd nr fin: no ch w wnr* **11/2**[3]

4 **3** *1/2* **Kyleakin Lass**[98] 3287 2-9-0 0 .... JoeFanning 4 67
(Ian Wood) *led: rdn 2f out: hdd 1f out: kpt on same pce: lost 2nd nr fin* **12/1**

33 **4** *2* **Persidha**[15] 6030 2-9-0 0 .... PaulHanagan 7 61
(Gay Kelleway) *t.k.h: trckd ldrs: effrt 2f out: kpt on same pce ins fnl f* **11/2**[3]

524 **5** *nk* **Tahnee Mara (IRE)**[60] 4557 2-9-0 73 .... PhillipMakin 8 60
(Kevin Ryan) *t.k.h: cl up tl rdn and nt qckn over 1f out* **4/1**[2]

36 **6** *1/2* **Trioomph**[13] 6092 2-9-0 0 .... JamesSullivan 3 59
(James Given) *hld up bhd ldng gp: pushed along over 2f out: no imp over 1f out* **28/1**

0 **7** *2 1/4* **Indivisible**[14] 6045 2-9-0 0 .... DavidAllan 5 52
(Tim Easterby) *s.i.s: hld up bhd main gp: rdn and outpcd 2f out: no imp after* **50/1**

0 **8** *3 1/2* **Watanee**[27] 5655 2-9-0 0 .... RoystonFfrench 11 42
(Clive Brittain) *hld up: rdn and hung lft over 2f out: sn btn* **33/1**

9 *9* **Bright Eyed Girl (IRE)** 2-8-11 0 .... MichaelO'Connell(3) 12 15
(Kate Walton) *bhd: struggling over 3f out: nvr on terms* **125/1**

606 **10** *1 1/2* **Perfect Paradise**[29] 5583 2-9-0 70 .... WilliamBuick 1 10
(John Gosden) *prom tl edgd lft and wknd fr 2f out* **13/2**

11 *4* **Last Supper** 2-9-0 0 .... AndrewElliott 2 —
(James Bethell) *missed break: bhd: drvn over 3f out: sn btn* **100/1**

000 **12** *3/4* **Cherchedi (IRE)**[21] 5819 2-9-0 33 .... BarryMcHugh 9 —
(Alan Berry) *bhd: struggling after 3f: sn btn: eased 2f out* **200/1**

1m 12.5s (-2.10) **Going Correction** -0.40s/f (Firm) 2y crse rec **12** Ran SP% **115.8**
Speed ratings (Par 94): **98,93,92,89,89 88,85,80,68,66 61,60**
toteswingers:1&2:£3.60, 2&3:£8.50, 1&3:£7.00 CSF £12.56 TOTE £3.70: £1.60, £1.70, £3.60; EX 16.90.
Owner Market Avenue Racing Club Ltd **Bred** Natton House Thoroughbreds & Mark Woodall **Trained** Twyford, Bucks

FOCUS
Another ordinary maiden, though the majority had already shown some ability. The pace wasn't that strong and it paid to be up there with the first five home prominent throughout. The winner looks the best guide.

NOTEBOOK
Van Der Art was rated 78 having been placed in her first four starts, but the form of her third at Haydock earlier this month could hardly have worked out better with the second, fourth and fifth all successful since. She won this going away after leading a furlong out and there is no reason why she shouldn't make her mark in nurseries. (op 7-4 tchd 9-4)
Khaleejiya(IRE) was held by Van Der Art on the previous month's Yarmouth running, but she ran on again to take second after getting outpaced passing the 2f pole. She isn't progressing in maidens, but now gets a mark and may have more success in nurseries. (op 7-1 tchd 5-1)
Kyleakin Lass hadn't been seen since showing promise on her Salisbury debut in June (winners have come out of that race) but she travelled well at the head of affairs until the winner collared her a furlong out. This was a good effort and she can certainly win a race. (op 10-1)
Persidha is bred to need much further than this, so it was little surprise that she was being niggled along to stay in touch from some way out. She now qualifies for nurseries and is well worth watching out for when stepped up in trip. (op 6-1 tchd 13-2)
Tahnee Mara(IRE), rated 73, again ran as though this trip is beyond her. (op 5-1)
Trioomph may fare better in low-grade nurseries. (op 33-1)
Perfect Paradise Official explanation: jockey said filly stopped quickly

6450 DIGIBET.COM H'CAP — 7f
3:45 (3:46) (Class 5) (0-70,70) 3-Y-O+ **£2,264** (£673; £336; £168) **Stalls** Low

Form RPR

2133 **1** **Viking Rose (IRE)**[13] 6098 3-8-9 61 .... LukeMorris 10 69
(James Eustace) *trckd ldrs: led and rdn 2f out: hrd pressed ins fnl f: jst hld on* **11/2**[1]

0041 **2** *nse* **Just The Tonic**[25] 5721 4-8-13 65 .... PaulPickard(3) 14 73
(Marjorie Fife) *midfield: drvn and hdwy over 1f out: ev ch ins fnl f: kpt on wl: jst failed* **11/1**

6-10 **3** *1/2* **Shayla**[13] 6098 4-9-4 67 .... PJMcDonald 15 74
(Alan Swinbank) *s.i.s: hld up: hdwy 1/2-way: effrt over 2f out: kpt on ins fnl f* **14/1**

3645 **4** *1 3/4* **Breezolini**[13] 6094 3-9-1 70 .... (v) AmyRyan(3) 12 72
(Richard Whitaker) *dwlt: sn prom: drvn 2f out: kpt on same pce ins fnl f* **10/1**

1214 **5** *nse* **Ellies Image**[12] 6138 4-9-0 63 .... DuranFentiman 13 65
(Brian Baugh) *hld up: rdn over 2f out: hdwy over 1f out: nrst fin* **7/1**[3]

2216 **6** *1* **Catallout (IRE)**[9] 6228 3-8-7 66 .... JasonHart(7) 4 65+
(Declan Carroll) *hld up: drvn over 2f out: no imp tl styd on wl last 150yds: nrst fin* **6/1**[2]

1050 **7** *1/2* **Alluring Star**[25] 5731 3-9-2 68 .... JamesSullivan 8 66
(Michael Easterby) *led to 2f out: rallied: kpt on same pce ins fnl f* **40/1**

3643 **8** *3/4* **Alensgrove (IRE)**[11] 6156 3-8-4 56 .... PaulHanagan 9 52
(Paul Midgley) *hld up: drvn and outpcd over 2f out: kpt on wl ins fnl f: n.d* **12/1**

4306 **9** *1* **Ryedale Dancer (IRE)**[8] 6234 3-9-0 66 .... DavidAllan 6 59
(Tim Easterby) *disp ld to 2f out: sn drvn: outpcd fnl f* **9/1**

066 **10** *1 1/4* **Cardrona**[47] 5001 3-8-11 63 .... WilliamBuick 3 53
(John Gosden) *dwlt: hld up: effrt on outside over 2f out: edgd lft: no imp over 1f out* **8/1**

4643 **11** *3/4* **Red Scintilla**[27] 5652 4-8-7 56 .... TomEaves 1 44
(Nigel Tinkler) *in tch: effrt and drvn over 2f out: btn ins fnl f* **16/1**

5235 **12** *1 1/4* **Ffajir (IRE)**[36] 5356 3-8-13 65 .... (b[1]) RoystonFfrench 5 49
(Clive Brittain) *trckd ldrs: drvn over 2f out: wknd over 1f out* **25/1**

1434 **13** *4 1/2* **Fenella Fudge**[13] 6089 3-9-1 67 .... (b) PhillipMakin 2 39
(James Given) *cl up: drvn over 2f out: wknd wl over 1f out* **11/1**

1m 25.71s (-2.09) **Going Correction** -0.40s/f (Firm)
WFA 3 from 4yo+ 3lb **13** Ran SP% **115.6**
Speed ratings (Par 103): **95,94,94,92,92 91,90,89,88,87 86,84,79**
toteswingers:1&2:£7.00, 2&3:£31.40, 1&3:£14.70 CSF £63.00 CT £574.94 TOTE £7.00: £1.90, £4.20, £5.00; EX 48.30.
Owner J C Smith **Bred** Littleton Stud **Trained** Newmarket, Suffolk
■ Stewards' Enquiry : Paul Pickard one-day ban; excessive use of whip (12th Oct)

FOCUS
A modest handicap, but a competitive affair. The form is ordinary, the winner rated to her penultimate level.

6451 MGM PRECISION ENGINEERING LTD H'CAP — 2m 19y
4:20 (4:20) (Class 5) (0-75,75) 3-Y-O+ **£2,264** (£673; £336; £168) **Stalls** Low

Form RPR

652/ **1** **Hunting Tower**[19] 5909 7-9-6 67 .... (t) CDHayes 6 76+
(J J Lambe, Ire) *hld up: rdn and hdwy over 2f out: kpt on strly ins fnl f: led nr fin* **17/2**

4523 **2** *1/2* **First Rock (IRE)**[147] 1817 5-8-12 59 .... PJMcDonald 2 66
(Alan Swinbank) *midfield: hdwy to trck ldr over 3f out: led narrowly over 2f out: sn rdn: kpt on: hdd nr fin* **10/1**

2014 **3** *nk* **Jeu De Roseau (IRE)**[22] 5079 7-9-7 68 .... WilliamBuick 8 75
(Chris Grant) *trckd ldrs: rdn over 2f out: kpt on ins fnl f* **5/1**[3]

11P0 **4** *nk* **Birdwatcher (IRE)**[12] 6136 3-8-9 68 .... JoeFanning 3 74
(Mark Johnston) *led narrowly: rdn whn hdd over 2f out: remained w ev ch tl no ex cl home* **25/1**

5001 **5** *1 3/4* **The Oil Magnate**[13] 6082 6-9-11 72 .... TonyHamilton 5 76
(Michael Dods) *hld up in tch: hdwy to chse ldrs over 2f out: sn rdn: no ex ins fnl f* **25/1**

5111 **6** *1/2* **Mina's Boy**[30] 5566 3-8-6 65 .... RoystonFfrench 12 69
(Ed Dunlop) *midfield: rdn over 2f out: kpt on one pce: nvr threatened ldrs* **4/1**[2]

6413 **7** *1 1/4* **Mohawk Ridge**[12] 6115 5-9-10 71 .... TomEaves 11 73
(Michael Dods) *trckd ldrs: swtchd to outer to press ldr 5f out: rdn over 3f out: wknd ins fnl f* **9/1**

2135 **8** *5* **Harvey's Hope**[26] 5685 5-10-0 75 .... PaulHanagan 9 71
(Keith Reveley) *hld up in tch: pushed along and brief hdwy over 2f out: wknd over 1f out* **11/4**[1]

-120 **9** *1 1/4* **Blackmore**[139] 2034 4-9-11 75 .... AdamBeschizza(3) 10 70
(Julia Feilden) *hld up: a towards rr* **10/1**

4264 **10** *17* **Miereveld**[29] 5599 4-8-10 57 oh3 .... KellyHarrison 7 31
(Shaun Harris) *prom: rdn over 3f out: wknd over 2f out: eased ins fnl f* **66/1**

3m 41.87s (2.47) **Going Correction** -0.40s/f (Firm)
WFA 3 from 4yo+ 12lb **10** Ran SP% **111.2**
Speed ratings (Par 103): **77,76,76,76,75 75,74,72,71,63**
toteswingers:1&2:£11.20, 2&3:£7.20, 1&3:£7.90 CSF £83.87 CT £457.13 TOTE £12.70: £3.60, £3.10, £1.10; EX 87.80.
Owner Mighty Macs Syndicate **Bred** The Queen **Trained** Dungannon, Co. Tyrone
■ Stewards' Enquiry : Joe Fanning caution; excessive use of whip

FOCUS
They didn't go much of a pace in this staying handicap with the result that a few took a grip and there wasn't much covering the first seven at the line. The winner could do better on his jumps/old Flat form.
Harvey's Hope Official explanation: jockey said gelding boiled over in the preliminaries and hung both ways throughout.

6452 POSTRACING.NET SITE FOR WINNERS H'CAP (DIV I) — 1m 3y(S)
4:50 (4:51) (Class 5) (0-70,76) 3-Y-O+ **£2,264** (£673; £336; £168) **Stalls** Low

Form RPR

0210 **1** **Master Of Dance (IRE)**[9] 6211 4-9-7 67 .... (p) JoeFanning 6 76
(Keith Dalgleish) *hld up: smooth hdwy over 2f out: led appr fnl f: kpt on wl fnl f* **9/2**[1]

2600 **2** *1* **Seldom (IRE)**[13] 6098 5-9-2 62 .... DavidAllan 11 68
(Mel Brittain) *trckd ldrs: hdwy to ld briefly over 1f out: kpt on ins fnl f: hld towards fin* **10/1**

040 **3** *1/2* **Xpres Maite**[9] 6226 8-8-13 59 .... (b) PhillipMakin 3 64
(Roy Bowring) *dwlt: bhd: hdwy and rdn 2f out: kpt on fnl f: nrst fin* **20/1**

6056 **4** *2* **Isheforreal (IRE)**[25] 5721 4-8-10 56 .... PBBeggy 1 56
(Brian Ellison) *hld up: rdn over 2f out: hdwy over 1f out: kpt on: nvr able to chal* **16/1**

6423 **5** *1/2* **Scottish Lake**[12] 6116 3-8-12 65 .... PatrickDonaghy(3) 10 64
(Jedd O'Keeffe) *prom: rdn and outpcd over 2f out: rallied over 1f out: one pce fnl f* **9/1**

40-0 **6** *2 1/2* **Ten To The Dozen**[27] 5652 8-8-10 56 oh11 .... AndrewElliott 2 50
(David Thompson) *taken early to post: hld up: rdn over 2f out: hdwy over 1f out: nvr able to chal* **200/1**

5110 **7** *nk* **Broctune Papa Gio**[23] 5788 4-9-0 63 .... DeclanCannon(3) 14 56
(Keith Reveley) *prom: rdn over 2f out: no ex over 1f out* **6/1**[2]

3110 **8** *nse* **Talent Scout (IRE)**[21] 5828 5-9-9 69 .... DuranFentiman 13 62
(Tim Walford) *led to over 3f out: wknd appr fnl f* **11/1**

3233 **9** *2* **Jupiter Fidius**[15] 6028 4-8-10 61 .... (p) ShaneBKelly(5) 7 49
(Kate Walton) *s.i.s: sn midfield: drvn over 2f out: sn no ex* **7/1**[3]

0-01 **10** *3/4* **Shotley Mac**[8] 6231 7-10-2 76 6ex .... (b) BarryMcHugh 12 62
(Neville Bycroft) *cl up: led 3f to over 1f out: sn wknd* **8/1**

0210 **11** *hd* **Wiseman's Diamond (USA)**[9] 6226 6-9-4 64 .... (b) PaulHanagan 15 50
(Paul Midgley) *prom: drvn over 2f out: sn btn* **8/1**

6160 **12** *hd* **Tanforan**[26] 5673 9-8-11 57 .... KellyHarrison 8 42
(Brian Baugh) *hld up towards rr: rdn over 2f out: btn over 1f out* **40/1**

00-0 **13** *2 3/4* **Transmit (IRE)**[156] 1558 4-9-0 65 .... AdamCarter(5) 9 44
(Tim Easterby) *midfield: hdwy over 3f out: rdn and wknd fr 2f out* **25/1**

0060 **14** *1/2* **Thrust Control (IRE)**[13] 6098 4-8-9 62 .... JacobButterfield(7) 5 40
(Tracy Waggott) *taken early to post: trckd ldrs tl rdn and wknd over 2f out* **33/1**

10-0 **15** *12* **Newport Arch**[25] 5731 3-9-0 64 .... TomEaves 4 14
(John Quinn) *hld up: struggling over 3f out: sn btn* **33/1**

1m 39.53s (-3.87) **Going Correction** -0.40s/f (Firm)
WFA 3 from 4yo+ 4lb **15** Ran SP% **117.9**
Speed ratings (Par 103): **103,102,101,99,99 96,96,96,94,93 93,93,90,89,77**
toteswingers:1&2:£9.40, 2&3:£25.30, 1&3:£21.60 CSF £44.64 CT £841.63 TOTE £6.40: £1.60, £3.00, £7.60; EX 55.20.
Owner Gordon McDowall **Bred** Mick McGinn **Trained** Carluke, South Lanarkshire

FOCUS
Another modest, if competitive handicap, run slightly more slowly than division II. The form looks sound enough.

6453 POSTRACING.NET SITE FOR WINNERS H'CAP (DIV II) — 1m 3y(S)
5:20 (5:22) (Class 5) (0-70,69) 3-Y-O+ **£2,264** (£673; £336; £168) **Stalls** Low

Form RPR

00 **1** **Captain Macarry (IRE)**[44] 5106 6-9-3 62 .... (v) JoeFanning 14 76
(Stuart Williams) *trckd ldrs: led over 2f out: pushed clr ins fnl f* **16/1**

5641 **2** *3 1/2* **Whispered Times (USA)**[7] 6262 4-9-9 68 6ex .... (p) PatrickMathers 12 74
(Tracy Waggott) *trckd ldrs: effrt over 2f out: wnt 2nd ins fnl f: kpt on: nt gng pce of wnr* **15/2**

6001 **3** 1 1/4 **Horatio Carter**[25] 5733 6-9-10 **69** .... DanielTudhope 8 72
(David O'Meara) *cl up: rdn and ev ch over 2f out: sn chsng wnr: lost 2nd ins fnl f: one pce* **7/2**[1]

0514 **4** 3 **Edas**[32] 5485 9-9-2 **61** .... KellyHarrison 3 57
(Thomas Cuthbert) *hld up: rdn and hdwy 3f out: kpt on ins fnl f: no imp* **20/1**

2002 **5** 1 **Brockfield**[9] 6211 5-9-2 **61** .... PhillipMakin 15 55
(Mel Brittain) *led to over 2f out: rdn and nt qckn over 1f out* **4/1**[2]

4556 **6** 1/2 **Fibs And Flannel**[25] 5722 4-9-5 **64** .... DavidAllan 4 57
(Tim Easterby) *trckd ldrs: chal gng wl over 2f out: sn rdn: wknd ins fnl f* **9/2**[3]

50 **7** 4 1/2 **Thoroughly Red (IRE)**[13] 6081 6-9-7 **66** .... TonyHamilton 11 48
(Linda Stubbs) *chsd ldrs tl wknd fr 2f out* **22/1**

3015 **8** 3 1/4 **Silly Gilly (IRE)**[25] 5733 7-8-13 **63** .... ShaneBKelly(5) 10 38
(Ron Barr) *trckd ldrs: drvn over 2f out: sn wknd* **20/1**

0504 **9** 3/4 **Classic Descent**[13] 6098 6-8-12 **57** ....(bt) JamesSullivan 13 30
(Ruth Carr) *slowly away: bhd: drvn over 3f out: btn fnl 2f* **16/1**

0443 **10** 8 **Madrasa (IRE)**[30] 5553 3-8-13 **62** ....(t) TomEaves 2 17
(Keith Reveley) *s.i.s: bhd: struggling 1/2-way: nvr on terms* **16/1**

0003 **11** 2 **Social Rhythm**[25] 5721 7-8-9 **59** .... GarryWhillans(5) 7 9
(Alistair Whillans) *missed break: bhd and pushed along after 3f: nvr on terms* **10/1**

000- **12** 6 **North Shadow**[336] 5361 4-8-10 **55** oh8........ AndrewMullen 1 —
(Alan Brown) *cl up on outside tl wknd fr 2f out* **100/1**

0600 **13** 4 1/2 **Idealism**[15] 6028 4-8-10 **55** oh10........ BarryMcHugh 9 —
(Micky Hammond) *bhd: drvn along 1/2-way: wknd over 2f out* **50/1**

10-0 **14** 18 **Striking Priorite**[12] 6133 3-9-2 **65** .... PaulHanagan 5 —
(Tim Fitzgerald) *midfield: struggling wl over 2f out: sn wknd: t.o* **40/1**

1m 38.96s (-4.44) **Going Correction** -0.40s/f (Firm)
WFA 3 from 4yo+ 4lb **14** Ran SP% **118.2**
Speed ratings (Par 103): **106,102,101,98,97 96,92,89,88,80 78,72,67,49**
toteswingers:1&2:£19.60, 2&3:£7.20, 1&3:£13.20 CSF £119.69 CT £538.53 TOTE £23.10: £5.90, £3.20, £2.10; EX 80.60.
Owner GJSS **Bred** Humphrey Okeke **Trained** Newmarket, Suffolk

FOCUS
The winning time was 0.57 seconds faster than the first division. Few were involved. The winner was back to form out of the blue.

6454 BRITISH HEART FOUNDATION MENDING BROKEN HEARTS APPEAL H'CAP 5f
5:50 (5:50) (Class 6) (0-60,58) 3-Y-O+ **£1,617** (£481; £240; £120) **Stalls** Low

Form RPR

2213 **1** **Cool In The Shade**[13] 6076 3-9-6 **58** ....(b) TonyHamilton 6 73+
(Paul Midgley) *t.k.h: w ldr: led after 2f: edgd to far rail wl over 1f out: sn clr* **2/1**[1]

6532 **2** 4 1/2 **Sharp Bullet (IRE)**[9] 6213 5-9-2 **53** ....(p) JoeFanning 3 50
(Bruce Hellier) *prom: effrt 2f out: chsd (clr) wnr ins fnl f: no imp* **4/1**[2]

0-40 **3** 1 **Hygrove Gal**[103] 3143 3-9-5 **57** .... TomEaves 4 50
(Bryan Smart) *trckd ldrs: rdn and edgd lft 2f out: kpt on same pce ins fnl f* **16/1**

022 **4** nk **Cayman Fox**[3] 6386 6-9-3 **54** .... PJMcDonald 5 46
(Linda Perratt) *led 2f: cl up: pushed along over 1f out: one pce and lost two pls ins fnl f* **2/1**[1]

0000 **5** 1 1/4 **Future Gem**[3] 6386 5-8-8 **45** ....(p) AndrewElliott 2 33
(David Thompson) *bhd and outpcd: styd on fnl f: nvr able to chal* **25/1**

-600 **6** 1 **Lujiana**[9] 6213 6-8-8 **45** .... DuranFentiman 9 29
(Mel Brittain) *trckd ldrs tl rdn and wknd over 2f out* **16/1**

0005 **7** 1 1/4 **Hedgerow (IRE)**[9] 6208 4-8-4 **46** ow1........ ShaneBKelly(5) 1 26
(Dianne Sayer) *sn outpcd and drvn along: nvr on terms* **8/1**[3]

59.06 secs (-2.04) **Going Correction** -0.40s/f (Firm)
WFA 3 from 4yo+ 1lb **7** Ran SP% **113.4**
Speed ratings (Par 101): **100,92,91,90,88 87,85**
toteswingers:1&2:£1.40, 2&3:£5.90, 1&3:£6.40. Tote Super 7: Win: Not won. Place: Not won. CSF £10.20 CT £95.33 TOTE £2.90: £1.90, £1.10; EX 10.10.
Owner The Rumpole Partnership **Bred** R W Gittins **Trained** Westow, N Yorks

FOCUS
This moderate sprint looked relatively uncompetitive with the market suggesting only three were fancied. That trio all figured early but in the end it was a runaway success for the topweight. The winner apparently improved, but there are doubts over the form.
T/Jkpt: Not won. T/Plt: £180.90 to a £1 stake. Pool of £67,058.21 - 270.52 winning tickets. T/Qpdt: £104.70 to a £1 stake. Pool of £5,350.68 - 37.80 winning tickets. RY

5174 NOTTINGHAM (L-H)
Wednesday, September 28

OFFICIAL GOING: Good to firm (7.3)
Wind: light 1/2 against Weather: fine and sunny, very warm

6455 BRITISH STALLION STUDS SUPPORTING BRITISH RACING E B F MAIDEN STKS 6f 15y
2:20 (2:21) (Class 5) 2-Y-O **£3,234** (£962; £481; £240) **Stalls** Centre

Form RPR

62 **1** **Taffe**[11] 6152 2-9-3 0........ FrederikTylicki 3 79+
(James Given) *mde all: drvn and styd on wl to forge clr ins fnl f* **6/1**[2]

3 **2** 3 **Rhagori**[27] 5655 2-8-12 0........ RichardKingscote 5 65
(Ralph Beckett) *trckd ldrs: t.k.h: drvn to chse wnr 1f out: no imp* **4/5**[1]

0 **3** 3 1/4 **Vexillum (IRE)**[11] 6160 2-9-3 0........ MatthewDavies 6 60
(Mick Channon) *chsd ldrs: kpt on same pce appr fnl f* **13/2**[3]

4 4 1/2 **Glen Ellyn** 2-9-3 0........ SilvestreDeSousa 2 47
(Mark Johnston) *chsd ldrs: wknd ins fnl f* **9/1**

0 **5** 3 1/2 **Meet Joe Black (IRE)**[7] 6252 2-9-3 0........ CathyGannon 8 36
(David Evans) *s.i.s: sn drvn along: nvr nr ldrs* **66/1**

005 **6** 3/4 **Merv (IRE)**[48] 4954 2-9-3 63........ FergusSweeney 7 34
(Henry Candy) *hld up: effrt and swtchd rt over 2f out: hung bdly lft over 1f out: sn wknd* **14/1**

0 **7** 3/4 **Coup De Grace (IRE)**[12] 6127 2-9-3 0........ TomQueally 1 32
(Amanda Perrett) *s.s and wnt lft s: a outpcd in rr* **20/1**

00 **8** 4 **Regal Gold**[30] 5541 2-9-3 0........ KierenFallon 9 20
(Richard Hannon) *s.i.s: drvn along in rr: hung lft thrght: sme hdwy 2f out: sn wknd* **14/1**

9 1 1/4 **Madame Feu** 2-8-12 0........ FrankieMcDonald 4 11
(Henry Candy) *dwlt: sn chsng ldrs: wkng whn sltly hmpd over 1f out* **100/1**

1m 13.48s (-1.42) **Going Correction** -0.175s/f (Firm) **9** Ran SP% **113.8**
Speed ratings (Par 95): **102,98,93,87,83 82,81,75,74**
toteswingers:1&2:£2.30, 2&3:£2.20, 1&3:£6.70 CSF £10.88 TOTE £5.70: £1.50, £1.10, £2.00; EX 13.90 Trifecta £186.40 Pool: £516.61 - 2.05 winning units..
Owner Ingram Racing **Bred** Graham Wilson **Trained** Willoughton, Lincs
■ Stewards' Enquiry : Fergus Sweeney caution; used whip down shoulder

FOCUS
A modest maiden that was run at an average pace and the form looks straightforward.

NOTEBOOK
Taffe, second at Catterick 11 days earlier, came right away inside the final furlong and made it third time lucky. He was visibly sweating and did the donkey work out in front, but found plenty when asked for everything. He's evidently progressive and his future now lies with the handicapper. (op 9-2 tchd 4-1)
Rhagori faded when third on her debut behind the smart Firdaws and was back down a furlong here. She hit a flat spot nearing 2f out and, while attempting to rally, her effort flattened out from the furlong marker. This was quicker ground, but it was probably more a case of failing to settle over this sharper test finding her out. (op 6-5 tchd 5-4)
Vexillum(IRE) dropped out late on his debut over 7f at Newbury last time and didn't go unbacked on this drop in trip. He ran with greater encouragement, but will surely be going back up in trip after this. (op 17-2 tchd 6-1)
Glen Ellyn, one of two newcomers, knew his job from the gates but ran distinctly green in the second half of the contest. He looks set to enjoy a stiffer test now this initial experience is behind him and he can improve a deal. (op 17-2 tchd 8-1)
Merv(IRE) Official explanation: jockey said gelding hung left
Coup De Grace(IRE) Official explanation: jockey said colt was slowly away

6456 RED BOX RECORDERS MOBILE PHONE RECORDING H'CAP 5f 13y
2:50 (2:50) (Class 5) (0-75,75) 3-Y-O **£2,264** (£673; £336; £168) **Stalls** Centre

Form RPR

2315 **1** **Best Be Careful (IRE)**[18] 5914 3-8-6 **67**........ RachealKneller(7) 1 75
(Mark Usher) *hld up: swtchd lft and hdwy far side 2f out: led appr fnl f: hld on wl* **7/1**[3]

1256 **2** 3/4 **Irish Boy (IRE)**[25] 5719 3-8-11 **65**........ RussKennemore 10 70
(Paul Midgley) *chsd ldrs: edgd lft and styd on fnl f: no ex in clsng stages* **15/2**

0-25 **3** 1/2 **Poppy**[28] 5624 3-8-4 **61** oh3........ KieranO'Neill(3) 6 64
(Richard Hannon) *hmpd s: sn chsng ldrs: styd on same pce last 100yds* **20/1**

0231 **4** shd **Surely This Time (IRE)**[23] 5793 3-8-8 **62**........(tp) CathyGannon 5 65
(Kevin Ryan) *wnt rt after s: sn chsng ldrs: hmpd over 3f out: hung lft and kpt on same pce last 150yds* **11/1**

3141 **5** 3/4 **Whitecrest**[12] 6119 3-9-4 **72**........ SilvestreDeSousa 8 72
(John Spearing) *hmpd s: swtchd rt after 1f: sn chsng ldrs: kpt on same pce ins fnl f* **7/2**[1]

4010 **6** 1 **Stilettoesinthemud (IRE)**[20] 5864 3-8-7 **64**........ DaleSwift(3) 7 61
(James Given) *hmpd s: mid-div: sn drvn along: kpt on fnl 2f: nvr trbld ldrs* **20/1**

4030 **7** nk **Royal Bajan (USA)**[18] 5939 3-9-0 **68**........ FrederikTylicki 4 63
(James Given) *chsd ldrs: one pce over 1f out* **10/1**

2335 **8** nk **Yasmeena (USA)**[39] 5279 3-9-0 **68**........ TadhgO'Shea 9 62
(Charles Hills) *sn outpcd and in rr: hdwy 2f out: no imp whn hmpd 100yds out* **8/1**

4200 **9** 1 1/4 **Ice Trooper**[14] 6044 3-9-6 **74**........(p) KierenFallon 2 64
(Linda Stubbs) *w ldrs: wknd jst ins fnl f* **16/1**

6165 **10** 2 1/2 **Mazovian (USA)**[52] 4819 3-8-6 **67**........ NoelGarbutt(7) 12 48
(Michael Chapman) *led one other stands' side: hung lft 3f out: sn outpcd* **33/1**

U200 **11** nse **Restless Bay (IRE)**[11] 6174 3-9-7 **75**........(p) FrankieMcDonald 11 56
(Reg Hollinshead) *s.i.s: racd w one other stands' side: a bhd* **13/2**[2]

2105 **12** 1 **Nine Before Ten (IRE)**[27] 5647 3-9-6 **74**........(t) NeilCallan 3 51
(John Balding) *led: edgd rt over 3f out: hdd appr fnl f: wknd and heavily eased last 100yds* **9/1**

59.71 secs (-1.29) **Going Correction** -0.175s/f (Firm) **12** Ran SP% **116.7**
Speed ratings (Par 101): **103,101,101,100,99 98,97,97,95,91 91,89**
CSF £56.12 CT £1019.56 TOTE £10.90: £4.30, £3.40, £5.60; EX 78.30 TRIFECTA Not won..
Owner Mrs Jill Pellett **Bred** M Phelan **Trained** Upper Lambourn, Berks
■ Stewards' Enquiry : Russ Kennemore two-day ban; careless riding (12th-13th Oct)

FOCUS
A moderate 3yo sprint handicap. It was run at a solid pace and the main action was down the centre of the track, but the winner raced nearest to the far side. The form is rated around the placed horses but limited by the fourth and sixth.
Surely This Time(IRE) Official explanation: jockey said gelding hung left
Yasmeena(USA) Official explanation: jockey said filly suffered interference in running
Mazovian(USA) Official explanation: jockey said gelding hung left

6457 NOTTINGHAM RACECOURSE H'CAP 1m 75y
3:20 (3:22) (Class 4) (0-85,84) 3-Y-O **£4,075** (£1,212; £606; £303) **Stalls** Centre

Form RPR

1243 **1** **Chokurei (IRE)**[27] 5657 3-9-2 **82**........ JohnFahy(3) 14 91
(Clive Cox) *hld up on outside: dropped bk bnd after 3f: hdwy over 3f out: chal appr fnl f: r.o ins fnl f: led towards fin* **8/1**[3]

2006 **2** 1/2 **Majestic Dream (IRE)**[16] 6003 3-9-6 **83**........(v) NeilCallan 5 91+
(Walter Swinburn) *trckd ldrs: led over 1f out: hdd and no ex nr fin* **20/1**

10 **3** shd **Tanaami (USA)**[14] 6062 3-9-1 **78**........ TadhgO'Shea 13 86+
(Saeed Bin Suroor) *s.i.s: hdwy and swtchd outside over 2f out: styd on ins fnl f: fin strly* **12/1**

1-56 **4** 1 1/4 **Spanish Pride (IRE)**[86] 3676 3-8-7 **70** oh3........ CathyGannon 15 75+
(John Dunlop) *hld up towards rr: styd on fnl 2f: nt rch ldrs* **25/1**

5432 **5** nk **Birdolini**[16] 6003 3-8-10 **73**........ FergusSweeney 16 77
(Alan King) *in rr: hdwy on outside over 2f out: styd on same pce fnl f* **11/1**

0231 **6** 1 1/4 **Semmsu (IRE)**[15] 6020 3-9-3 **80**........ KierenFallon 6 81
(Luca Cumani) *t.k.h in mid-div: hdwy 3f out: chal 100yds out: nt run on: eased nr fin* **11/2**[2]

5120 **7** 2 1/4 **Early Applause**[55] 4718 3-9-4 **81**........ WilliamCarson 7 77
(Charles Hills) *trckd ldrs: effrt over 3f out: fdd fnl f* **28/1**

0312 **8** nse **El Wasmi**[82] 3797 3-9-7 **84**........(b) TomQueally 4 80
(Clive Brittain) *mid-div: nt clr run over 2f out: edgd rt over 1f out: kpt on* **9/1**

3312 **9** nk **Totheendoftheearth (IRE)**[63] 4429 3-9-3 **80**........ SilvestreDeSousa 1 75+
(Sylvester Kirk) *sn chsng ldrs: drvn over 3f out: wknd fnl f* **9/2**[1]

4022 **10** 1 1/4 **Come Here Yew (IRE)**[13] 6079 3-9-1 **78**........ FrederikTylicki 10 70
(Declan Carroll) *in rr: kpt on fnl 2f: nvr a factor* **10/1**

1235 **11** 1/2 **Saskia's Dream**[11] 6173 3-9-0 **77**..............(p) RobertHavlin 11 68
(Jane Chapple-Hyam) *hld up in mid-div: hdwy over 2f out: chsng ldrs over 1f out: sn wknd* **11/1**

0603 **12** 1 1/2 **General Synod**[15] 6020 3-8-9 **75**..............(b) KieranO'Neill(3) 3 63
(Richard Hannon) *t.k.h: led 1f: chsd ldr: wknd appr fnl f* **22/1**

1021 **13** 2 **Quadrant (IRE)**[17] 5960 3-9-4 **81**..............(b) MartinDwyer 2 64
(Brian Meehan) *t.k.h: led after 1f: hdd over 1f out: sn lost pl: eased in clsng stages* **8/1**[3]

0000 **14** 13 **May's Boy**[16] 6003 3-8-3 **73**..............(p) RachealKneller(7) 8 26
(Mark Usher) *in rr: drvn over 4f out: lost pl over 1f out: eased towards fin* **80/1**

1m 44.39s (-1.21) **Going Correction** -0.075s/f (Good) **14** Ran SP% **116.9**
Speed ratings (Par 103): **103,102,102,101,100 99,97,97,97,95 95,93,91,78**
toteswingers:1&2:£40.10, 2&3:£59.30, 1&3:£30.90 CSF £163.13 CT £1952.01 TOTE £9.40: £2.30, £6.90, £5.30; EX 155.90 TRIFECTA Not won..
Owner H E Sheikh Sultan Bin Khalifa Al Nahyan **Bred** Sheikh Sultan Bin Khalifa Al Nayhan **Trained** Lambourn, Berks

FOCUS
An interesting 3yo handicap for the class. There was a strong pace on and the first five came clear, finishing in something of a heap.

6458 BRITISH STALLION STUDS SUPPORTING BRITISH RACING E B F MAIDEN FILLIES' STKS 1m 75y

3:55 (3:58) (Class 5) 2-Y-O **£3,234** (£962; £481; £240) **Stalls** Centre

Form RPR

1 **Tactfully (IRE)** 2-9-0 0.............. NeilCallan 8 85+
(Mahmood Al Zarooni) *in rr: hdwy on outside over 3f out: led wl over 1f out: wnt clr: eased nr fin* **7/1**[3]

2 4 **Shirocco Star** 2-9-0 0.............. RobertHavlin 17 74+
(Hughie Morrison) *hld up in rr: smooth hdwy over 3f out: chsd wnr ins fnl f: no imp* **33/1**

3 4 **Inffiraaj (IRE)** 2-8-11 0.............. JohnFahy(3) 14 65+
(Mick Channon) *hld up detached in last pair: hdwy over 2f out: kpt on fnl f* **20/1**

0 **4** nk **Running Deer (IRE)**[14] 6048 2-9-0 0.............. TomQueally 5 64
(Sir Henry Cecil) *s.i.s: t.k.h: sn mid-div: n.m.r 3f out: kpt on same pce over 1f out* **12/1**

04 **5** nk **Farleaze**[60] 4552 2-9-0 0.............. MartinDwyer 15 63
(Brian Meehan) *chsd ldrs: kpt on one pce over 1f out* **5/1**[2]

03 **6** hd **Baileys Over Ice**[14] 6047 2-9-0 0.............. FrederikTylicki 6 63
(James Given) *chsd ldrs: edgd lft over 1f out: one pce* **14/1**

0 **7** 1 1/2 **Jamhara**[15] 6030 2-9-0 0.............. RussellPrice 7 59
(Clive Brittain) *t.k.h in mid-div: effrt over 2f out: one pce* **14/1**

8 2 1/2 **Layali Dubai (USA)** 2-9-0 0.............. KierenFallon 4 54
(Saeed Bin Suroor) *in rr div: effrt on outside over 2f out: wknd appr fnl f* **7/2**[1]

000 **9** 2 1/2 **Cool Light**[35] 5382 2-9-0 50.............. MatthewDavies 13 48
(Alan Jarvis) *led 1f: w ldrs: led over 2f out: hdd wl over 1f out: sn wknd* **200/1**

10 1 3/4 **Key Gold** 2-9-0 0.............. SilvestreDeSousa 1 44
(Mark Johnston) *mid-div: hdwy over 3f out: wknd over 1f out* **9/1**

4 **11** shd **Sally Pepper (USA)**[50] 4875 2-8-11 0.............. DaleSwift(3) 10 44
(James Given) *chsd ldrs: wknd over 1f out* **28/1**

0 **12** 1 1/4 **Velvet Star (IRE)**[22] 5807 2-9-0 0.............. RichardKingscote 3 41
(Paul Cole) *in rr: hdwy over 3f out: lost pl over 1f out* **33/1**

35 **13** 2 3/4 **Livia's Dream (IRE)**[38] 5299 2-9-0 0.............. AndreaAtzeni 2 34
(Ed Walker) *s.i.s: in rr: drvn over 3f out: nvr on terms* **5/1**[2]

06 **14** 9 **Minne Wa Wa**[66] 4365 2-9-0 0.............. TadhgO'Shea 9 14
(David Brown) *w ldr: led after 1f: hdd over 2f out: wkng whn hmpd over 1f out: bhd whn eased last 100yds* **50/1**

0 **15** 2 3/4 **Astroscarlet**[15] 6018 2-8-7 0.............. CharlesEddery(7) 12 7
(Mark H Tompkins) *in rr div: rn wd bnd over 4f out: sn bhd* **150/1**

1m 45.23s (-0.37) **Going Correction** -0.075s/f (Good) 2y crse rec **15** Ran SP% **116.3**
Speed ratings (Par 92): **98,94,90,89,89 89,87,85,82,80 80,79,76,67,65**
toteswingers:1&2:£42.20, 2&3:£42.20, 1&3:£42.20 CSF £224.33 TOTE £11.10: £3.70, £13.10, £8.10; EX 332.20 TRIFECTA Not won..
Owner Godolphin **Bred** Darley **Trained** Newmarket, Suffolk

FOCUS
The betting suggested this fillies' maiden was wide open, but the debut winner proved a class apart. It was the quickest winning time by a 2-y-o over the trip since the track was realigned in 2008.

NOTEBOOK
Tactfully(IRE) ◆ stormed clear from the furlong marker and thrashed her rivals, posting a cracking winning time. She hails from a trainer in cracking form, but despite shortening in the betting proved relatively easy to back ahead of this racecourse debut. She took time to settle and showed her inexperience early, but the penny dropped from 2f out. She had the race won from the furlong marker and rates a promising middle-distance performer for next year. (op 9-1 tchd 10-1)
Shirocco Star ◆'s yard has done well with 2yos so far this season. Drawn widest of all, she got a tricky early passage, but none was travelling better around 3f out. She was caught out when the winner kicked, but finished a clear second-best and looks useful. She ought to prove hard to beat next time. (op 25-1)
Inffiraaj(IRE) ◆ emerges with credit. She was seemingly unfancied for this debut and also had a tricky draw, which resulted in her being last turning for home. She kept on nicely despite not getting the best passage from 2f out and is a deal better than the bare form. (op 25-1)
Running Deer(IRE), disappointing on her debut a fortnight earlier, didn't look the most straightforward but this was better. She clearly stays well and needs one more run to qualify for a mark. (op 8-1)
Farleaze finished fourth behind Fallen For You at Newmarket when last seen 60 days earlier. She raced prominently and had her chance, but was found out by this extra distance. (op 9-2 tchd 4-1)
Layali Dubai(USA), representing a trainer with a decent 2yo strike-rate here, flattened out disappointingly on the outside from 2f out. She probably got further back than she wanted early, though, and ought to improve for the outing. (op 9-2 tchd 5-1)
Livia's Dream(IRE) never looked like taking advantage of her low draw and now has something to prove. Official explanation: jockey said filly had no more to give having ran freely in the early stages (op 11-2 tchd 9-2)

6459 RED BOX RECORDERS TELEPHONE RECORDING SOLUTIONS MAIDEN STKS 1m 75y

4:30 (4:31) (Class 5) 3-Y-O+ **£2,264** (£673; £336; £168) **Stalls** Centre

Form RPR

0 **1** **Sadeek's Song (USA)**[13] 6085 3-9-3 0.............. KierenFallon 10 90+
(Mahmood Al Zarooni) *in rr: drvn over 4f out: hdwy over 2f out: swtchd rt over 1f out: str run to ld last 100yds: wnt clr* **9/2**[2]

345 **2** 5 **Hayaku (USA)**[17] 5962 3-8-12 71..............(bt[1]) RichardKingscote 9 73
(Ralph Beckett) *led after 1f: clr over 3f out: jnd over 1f out: hdd and no ex ins fnl f* **9/2**[2]

3353 **3** nk **Shuhra (IRE)**[19] 5877 3-8-12 74.............. TadhgO'Shea 1 72
(William Haggas) *led 1f: chsd ldr: wnt 2nd 3f out: chal 1f out: kpt on same pce last 150yds* **9/2**[2]

6255 **4** 3 **Muqtarrib (IRE)**[19] 5894 3-9-3 73..............(b) MartinDwyer 13 70
(Brian Meehan) *slowly into st: sn bhd and drvn along: gd hdwy and n.m.r 2f out: kpt on one pce ins fnl f* **4/1**[1]

00 **5** 2 3/4 **Shopping Oasis**[90] 3543 3-9-3 0.............. SilvestreDeSousa 4 64
(Mark Johnston) *chsd ldrs: edgd rt over 1f out: wandered: one pce* **18/1**

43 **6** 6 **Love Your Looks**[27] 5639 3-8-12 0.............. AndreaAtzeni 8 45
(Mike Murphy) *chsd ldrs: wknd over 1f out* **25/1**

604 **7** 7 **Rasteau (IRE)**[49] 4932 3-8-12 35.............. DavidKenny(5) 5 34
(Tom Keddy) *in rr div: sme hdwy over 2f out: nvr on terms* **250/1**

8 nk **Martine's Spirit (IRE)** 3-8-12 0..............[1] CathyGannon 7 28
(William Haggas) *s.s: bhd tl kpt on fnl 2f* **40/1**

04 **9** 3/4 **Korithi**[13] 6096 3-8-12 0.............. TomQueally 2 27+
(Roger Charlton) *mid-div: hdwy on ins over 2f out: wknd over 1f out* **11/1**

0-00 **10** 2 1/2 **Supreme Seductress (IRE)**[138] 2065 3-8-12 65.......... WilliamCarson 3 21
(Charles Hills) *prom early: effrt 3f out: sn wknd* **50/1**

0-3 **11** 5 **Huwayit (IRE)**[16] 5999 3-8-12 0.............. NeilCallan 12 —
(Clive Brittain) *chsd ldrs: drvn over 3f out: wknd over 1f out: eased last 100yds* **11/2**[3]

12 4 **Dicey Vows (USA)** 3-9-3 0.............. MatthewDavies 14 —
(Alan Jarvis) *w ldrs on wd outside: hung rt: lost pl over 3f out: sn bhd* **25/1**

0 **13** 2 **Morgana**[134] 2175 3-8-12 0.............. RobertHavlin 11 —
(Brendan Powell) *a in rr* **200/1**

00 **14** 59 **Femme D'Espere**[19] 5900 5-9-2 0.............. FrankieMcDonald 6 —
(Christopher Kellett) *chsd ldrs: lost pl 4f out: sn bhd: virtually p.u: hopelessly t.o* **250/1**

1m 43.73s (-1.87) **Going Correction** -0.075s/f (Good)
WFA 3 from 5yo 4lb **14** Ran SP% **116.9**
Speed ratings (Par 103): **106,101,100,97,94 88,81,81,80,78 73,69,67,8**
toteswingers:1&2:£5.60, 2&3:£7.60, 1&3:£6.40 CSF £23.51 TOTE £5.10: £2.80, £2.90, £2.80; EX 24.00 Trifecta £84.10 Pool: £477.55 - 4.20 winning units..
Owner Godolphin **Bred** Darley **Trained** Newmarket, Suffolk

FOCUS
A weak affair and another wide-open race. Most were in trouble shortly after straightening for home and the form should work out. The third looks the best guide to the level.
Love Your Looks Official explanation: jockey said filly lost front shoe
Dicey Vows(USA) Official explanation: jockey said colt hung left
Femme D'Espere Official explanation: jockey said mare lost her action turning for home

6460 NOTTINGHAM RACECOURSE HOSPITALITY NURSERY 1m 2f 50y

5:00 (5:02) (Class 5) (0-75,70) 2-Y-O **£2,264** (£673; £336; £168) **Stalls** Low

Form RPR

0003 **1** **Better Be Mine (IRE)**[18] 5945 2-7-13 **48**.............. CathyGannon 4 52+
(John Dunlop) *hld up: effrt and nt clr run 3f out: styd on to ld last 50yds* **7/2**[2]

060 **2** 1/2 **Tiger Cub**[22] 5806 2-8-11 **60**..............(t) RichardKingscote 5 63
(Roger Charlton) *trckd ldrs: nt clr run over 3f out: wnt 2nd over 1f out: sn led: edgd lft ins fnl f: hdd and no ex in clsng stages* **5/1**[3]

305 **3** 2 3/4 **Hurricane Emerald (IRE)**[70] 4201 2-9-5 **68**.......... SilvestreDeSousa 2 66
(Mark Johnston) *sn led: drvn over 4f out: hdd 1f out: one pce whn hmpd and snatched up last 50yds* **6/4**[1]

6644 **4** 3 **Bathwick Street**[7] 6260 2-8-9 **58**.............. RobertHavlin 8 50
(David Evans) *led early: trckd ldr: wknd over 1f out* **11/2**

6630 **5** 1 3/4 **Foster's Road**[7] 6245 2-9-7 **70**.............. MatthewDavies 6 59
(Mick Channon) *hld up in rr: hdwy over 6f out: wknd 2f out* **15/2**

060 **6** 1/2 **Le Cagnard**[15] 6018 2-9-4 **67**.............. MartinDwyer 7 55
(Michael Bell) *s.i.s: hld up in last: effrt over 3f out: nt clr run 2f out and over 1f out: sn wknd* **16/1**

2m 14.57s (2.87) **Going Correction** -0.075s/f (Good) **6** Ran SP% **111.9**
Speed ratings (Par 95): **85,84,82,80,78 78**
CSF £20.72 CT £35.22 TOTE £4.00: £3.40, £2.70; EX 24.80 Trifecta £41.00 Pool: £543.81 - 9.81 winning units..
Owner Windflower Overseas Holdings Inc **Bred** Windflower Overseas **Trained** Arundel, W Sussex
■ Stewards' Enquiry : Richard Kingscote two-day ban; careless riding (12th-13th Oct)

FOCUS
A moderate staying nursery, run at a fair pace.

NOTEBOOK
Better Be Mine(IRE) was the one runner more obviously bred to enjoy this sort of staying test, but she proved uneasy in the market. She got behind turning for home, but her superior stamina came into play from 2f out and she was nicely on top at the finish. She won this off just a mark of 48, so shouldn't be discounted after a likely rise. (op 10-3 tchd 9-2)
Tiger Cub was tried in a first-time tongue tie and ran a bit freely early on. None were going better 3f out and she held every chance, but was ultimately outstayed by the winner. She's evidently found her level and sort of trip. (op 9-2 tchd 4-1)
Hurricane Emerald(IRE) was up from 7f on this return from a 70-day break and, on his nursery debut, got very well backed. He was ridden as though stamina wasn't an issue, but didn't help his rider from an early stage and he would have likely collected had he put it all in down the home straight. He was held before being hampered by the second and may need more time, but evidently has his own ideas. (op 3-1)
Bathwick Street looked to find this stiffer test too much. (op 4-1)

6461 AJA INSURE THEIR MEMBERS H'CAP (FOR GENTLEMAN AMATEUR RIDERS) 1m 2f 50y

5:30 (5:30) (Class 5) (0-70,70) 3-Y-O+ **£2,183** (£677; £338; £169) **Stalls** Low

Form RPR

0031 **1** **Desert Vision**[28] 5622 7-11-3 **66**..............(vt) MrOGreenall 5 80
(Michael Easterby) *led: clr over 3f out: drvn over 2f out: unchal* **3/1**[2]

425 **2** 3 **Petsas Pleasure**[13] 6098 5-10-12 **61**.............. MrSWalker 3 69
(Ollie Pears) *hld up towards rr: swtchd wd 4f out: wnt 5 l 2nd 2f out: sn rdn: no real imp* **11/4**[1]

2440 **3** 8 **Potentiale (IRE)**[29] 5582 7-11-0 **70**.............. MrFTett(7) 4 63
(J W Hills) *hld up in mid-div: effrt over 3f out: kpt on to take modest 3rd nr fin* **10/1**

0320 **4** 3/4 **Mustajed**[15] 6029 10-10-6 **60**..............(b) MrPMillman(5) 9 52
(Rod Millman) *trckd ldrs: wnt 2nd over 3f out: one pce fnl 2f* **12/1**

6411 **5** nk **James Pollard (IRE)**[33] 5428 6-11-2 **70**..............(t) MrRJWilliams(5) 8 61
(Bernard Llewellyn) *hld up in mid-div: effrt over 3f out: one pce fnl 2f* **8/1**

1610 **6** 3/4 **Gallego**[9] 6226 9-11-1 **67**.............. MrMPrice(3) 10 57
(Richard Price) *stdd and swtchd lft s: hld up detached in last: hdwy and swtchd rt over 2f out: kpt on: nvr a factor* **16/1**

0006 **7** 3 1/4 **Verluga (IRE)**[8] 6236 4-10-2 **56** oh9.............. MrWEasterby(5) 6 40
(Tim Easterby) *chsd ldrs: one pce fnl 3f* **25/1**

6500 **8** *7* **Wordiness**[28] [5630] 3-10-7 **65**.. JamesBest(3) 2 35
(Barry Brennan) *chsd ldrs: wknd 2f out* **15/2**[3]

0-00 **9** *½* **Red Mercury (IRE)**[80] [2368] 3-10-8 **63**........................ MrRGHenderson 1 32
(Alan King) *trckd ldrs: effrt over 3f out: lost pl 2f out* **12/1**

4000 **10** *5* **Ahlawy (IRE)**[21] [5828] 8-10-9 **65**..(t) MrDSatalia(7) 7 25
(Frank Sheridan) *s.s and reminders: racd wd: hdwy 7f out: wd and lost pl bnd over 4f out: bhd whn edgd lft 2f out* **50/1**

2m 11.47s (-0.23) **Going Correction** -0.075s/f (Good)
WFA 3 from 4yo+ 6lb **10** Ran SP% **110.7**
Speed ratings (Par 103): **97,94,88,87,87 86,84,78,78,74**
toteswingers:1&2:£1.10, 2&3:£5.40, 1&3:£6.70 CSF £10.87 CT £65.78 TOTE £4.00: £2.10, £1.30, £3.00; EX 12.40 Trifecta £89.50 Pool: £304.95 - 2.52 winning units..
Owner A Black,R Edmonds,J Holdroyd,J Quickfall **Bred** Gainsborough Stud Management Ltd **Trained** Sheriff Hutton, N Yorks

FOCUS
An ordinary handicap for gentleman amateur riders. Few landed a blow and the first pair came well clear. The time was quick and the form is rated around the first two.
T/Plt: £3,522.10 to a £1 stake. Pool of £50,420.48 - 10.45 winning tickets. T/Qpdt: £241.00 to a £1 stake. Pool of £3,419.81 - 10.50 winning tickets. WG

5653 SALISBURY (R-H)

Wednesday, September 28

OFFICIAL GOING: Good to soft changing to soft after race 1 (1.30)
Wind: fresh half behind Weather: sunny and warm

6462 BRITISH STALLION STUDS E B F MOLSON COORS MAIDEN STKS (DIV I) 1m

1:30 (1:32) (Class 4) 2-Y-O **£4,690** (£1,395; £697; £348) **Stalls** Low

Form RPR

1 **Oxford Charley (USA)** 2-9-3 0.. GeorgeBaker 12 83+
(Mikael Magnusson) *athletic: lw: hld up towards rr: pushed along fr over 3f out: styd on to weave through horses fr 2f out: str run ins fnl f: led fnl strides* **12/1**

002 **2** *nk* **Journalistic (USA)**[17] [5959] 2-9-3 78............................. RichardMullen 3 79
(Marcus Tregoning) *lw: led: rdn 2f out: 3 l clr ent fnl f: ct fnl strides* **7/2**[2]

3 *½* **Circus Mondao (USA)** 2-9-3 0.............................. AhmedAjtebi 4 78+
(Mahmood Al Zarooni) *str: attractive: mid-div: swtchd lft over 3f out: hdwy over 2f out: swtchd rt over 1f out: running on wl whn nt clr run and swtchd lft fnl 75yds: kpt on but nt time to rcvr* **8/1**

0 **4** *hd* **Eshaab (USA)**[19] [5891] 2-9-3 0.. RichardHills 5 77
(Ed Dunlop) *str: lw: hld up towards rr: hdwy on rails over 3f out: swtchd lft over 2f out: sn rdn: styd on ins fnl f* **5/1**[3]

5 *nk* **Estrela** 2-8-12 0.. JamesDoyle 13 72+
(Roger Charlton) *str: trckd ldrs: effrt 3f out: wnt 2nd over 1f out: nt gng pce to chal: kpt on towards fin* **14/1**

0 **6** *½* **Pilgrims Rest (IRE)**[14] [6059] 2-9-3 0......................... RichardHughes 11 76
(Richard Hannon) *athletic: lw: prom: rdn jst over 2f out lost 2nd over 1f out: kpt on same pce* **3/1**[1]

0 **7** *10* **Imperial Stargazer**[11] [6165] 2-9-3 0............................ SamHitchcott 10 54
(Mick Channon) *towards rr: sme prog u.p 2f out: wknd ins fnl f* **66/1**

8 *2¾* **Burnham** 2-9-3 0.. SteveDrowne 14 48+
(Hughie Morrison) *w'like: scope: bit bkwd: slowly away fr outside draw: a struggling towards rr* **33/1**

9 *nk* **Rock Band** 2-9-3 0.. DaneO'Neill 6 47
(Richard Hannon) *w'like: leggy: bit bkwd: mid-div: effrt 2f out: wknd ent fnl f* **14/1**

10 *5* **Lady Sylvia** 2-8-12 0.. LiamKeniry 8 31
(Joseph Tuite) *leggy: racd keenly: trckd ldrs: rdn over 2f out: sn wknd* **125/1**

11 *2¼* **Lean On Pete (IRE)** 2-9-3 0.. TedDurcan 1 31
(David Lanigan) *w'like: str: bit bkwd: trckd ldrs: rdn over 2f out: wknd over 1f out* **8/1**

0 **12** *3½* **Tokyo Brown (USA)**[20] [5861] 2-9-3 0........................(b[1]) EddieCreighton 9 23
(Heather Main) *cmpt: s.i.s: sn mid-div on outer: effrt 3f out: wknd over 2f out* **100/1**

13 *1¼* **Fine Resolve** 2-9-3 0.. JimmyFortune 7 21
(Andrew Balding) *w'like: bit bkwd: mid-div tl over 3f out: sn struggling in rr* **16/1**

00 **14** *17* **The Ploughman**[9] [6216] 2-9-3 0.. AdamKirby 2 —
(John Bridger) *mid-div tl wknd over 3f out: t.o* **200/1**

1m 46.41s (2.91) **Going Correction** +0.20s/f (Good) **14** Ran SP% **119.7**
Speed ratings (Par 97): **93,92,92,92,91 91,81,78,78,73 70,67,66,49**
toteswingers:1&2:£9.30, 2&3:£8.30, 1&3:£18.10 CSF £53.39 TOTE £12.90: £4.30, £1.20, £3.80; EX 85.30.
Owner Eastwind Racing Ltd And Martha Trussell **Bred** Robert Estill Courtney Jr **Trained** Upper Lambourn, Berks

FOCUS
The riders in the first were of the opinion that the ground was soft, and the official going description was duly amended after this race. Oaks winner Look Here took this maiden in 2007, and last year Census and Carlton House finished runner-up in the two divisions. They went a fairly steady initial pace, increasing it from halfway. The time was over six seconds outside the standard, confirming that the ground was riding slow. The first half-dozen finished in a heap, a long way clear of the rest. The bare form is only fairly useful, but there were several promising performances and it's worth being positive about the race.

NOTEBOOK
Oxford Charley(USA) still had five horses in front of him with half a furlong left to run, but he flew home to grab the race near the line. He had travelled well in rear and been forced to switch at least twice as his rider searched for a clear passage. A $140,000 yearling, he is a half-brother to July Cup winner Les Arcs, amongst others, and he should step up on this bare form as he was not knocked about yet was still good enough to go in first time.
Journalistic(USA), who set the standard with a BHA rating of 78, would probably have won at Ffos Las on his latest start had he received stronger handling. With Richard Mullen replacing the apprentice who rode him there, he made much of the running and looked to have seen off all the challengers, only to be nabbed late on. His chance should come.
Circus Mondao(USA) ◆ made signficant headway for pressure to get in the mix but had to be switched left close home, which cost him impetus. This was a promising debut from the $150,000 colt, who is out of an unraced half-sister to One Cool Cat. (tchd 9-1)
Eshaab(USA) duly stepped up on what he showed on his debut at Sandown, where he wasn't given a hard time, and there is a maiden to be won with him. He looked held at one point but was running on near the rail late on. (op 11-2)
Estrela momentarily got loose in the paddock and was slightly keen in the race, but she showed prominently all the way and just missed a place in the frame after edging to her left late on. This half-sister to six winners can win a maiden confined to her own sex. (op 12-1)
Pilgrims Rest(IRE) was up with the pace all the way but could not produce any extra late on. He may find 1m stretching him at this stage of his career. (op 11-4 tchd 7-2)
Imperial Stargazer stayed on for a well beaten seventh. (op 100-1)
Burnham ◆ was slowly away and green in rear before coming home quite well. Out of his connections' smart middle-distance mare Salim Toto, he should step up considerably on this. (op 25-1)

6463 BRITISH STALLION STUDS E B F MOLSON COORS MAIDEN STKS (DIV II) 1m

2:00 (2:04) (Class 4) 2-Y-O **£4,690** (£1,395; £697; £348) **Stalls** Low

Form RPR

1 **Bonfire** 2-9-3 0.. DavidProbert 5 85+
(Andrew Balding) *str: lw: ponied to s early: mid-div: stdy prog but nvr best of runs fr 3f out: swtchd lft over 1f out: led jst ins fnl f: sn pushed clr: readily* **7/2**[1]

2 *2* **Cubanita** 2-8-12 0.. JimCrowley 4 76+
(Ralph Beckett) *w'like: scope: s.i.s and hmpd s: towards rr: nt clrest of runs but stdy prog fr 3f out: styd on strly ins fnl f: wnt 2nd towards fin: no ch w wnr* **16/1**

633 **3** *1¾* **Juvenal (IRE)**[25] [5713] 2-9-3 74.. JimmyFortune 6 75
(Richard Hannon) *lw: trckd ldrs: led over 2f out: sn rdn and hrd pressed: hdd jst ins fnl f: no ex whn lost 2nd towards fin* **9/1**

03 **4** *2¼* **Uprise**[22] [5801] 2-9-3 0.. RichardMullen 1 70
(Sir Michael Stoute) *trckd ldrs: chal over 2f out: rdn and ev ch over 1f out: no ex ins fnl f* **9/2**[2]

05 **5** *1¾* **Winter Dress**[16] [6000] 2-8-12 0.................................... GrahamGibbons 9 61
(Roger Teal) *lw: led tl rdn over 2f out: chsd ldrs tl fdd ins fnl f* **50/1**

6 *1½* **Halling's Quest** 2-9-3 0.. GeorgeBaker 8 63
(Hughie Morrison) *athletic: s.i.s: bhd: rdn whn swtchd lft and rt 3f out: styd on fr 2f out: nvr gng pce to trble ldrs* **28/1**

7 *2* **Dedication** 2-8-12 0.. SteveDrowne 10 53
(Roger Charlton) *unf: scope: s.i.s: mid-div on outer: rdn over 2f out: nt gng pce to get involved* **14/1**

0 **8** *nk* **Golden Jubilee (USA)**[11] [6165] 2-9-3 0.......................... RichardHughes 2 58
(Richard Hannon) *wnt lft s: mid-div: effrt over 2f out: wknd over 1f out* **9/2**[2]

9 *2¼* **Edraaq** 2-9-3 0.. RichardHills 11 53
(Brian Meehan) *lengthy: hld up towards rr: hdwy into midfield 3f out: sn rdn: no further imp* **20/1**

00 **10** *nk* **Mayo Lad (IRE)**[20] [5855] 2-9-3 0.. EddieAhern 14 58+
(Richard Hannon) *t.k.h: mid-div: trckd ldrs 6f out: rdn 2f out: sn hung rt: hmpd whn btn sn after* **16/1**

11 *6* **Top Frock (IRE)** 2-8-12 0.. AdamKirby 12 34
(Clive Cox) *w'like: lengthy: bit bkwd: trckd ldrs tl wknd over 2f out* **16/1**

12 *16* **Mr Opulence** 2-9-3 0.. DaneO'Neill 7 4
(Henry Candy) *w'like: s.i.s: sn chsng ldrs: rdn over 3f out: wknd over 2f out* **33/1**

0 **13** *hd* **Seraphiel**[12] [6123] 2-9-3 0.. LiamKeniry 13 3
(Chris Down) *prom tl over 2f out* **125/1**

14 *23* **Dubawi Island (FR)** 2-9-3 0.. AhmedAjtebi 3 —
(Mahmood Al Zarooni) *w'like: str: carried lft s: hld up towards rr: struggling 1/2-way: sn wknd* **6/1**[3]

1m 45.26s (1.76) **Going Correction** +0.20s/f (Good) **14** Ran SP% **121.1**
Speed ratings (Par 97): **99,97,95,93,91 89,87,87,85,84 78,62,62,39**
toteswingers:1&2:£20.40, 2&3:£40.50, 1&3:£10.90 CSF £60.24 TOTE £5.20: £2.00, £7.90, £2.90; EX 80.90.
Owner Highclere Thoroughbred Racing-Pocahontas **Bred** Highclere Stud And Floors Farming **Trained** Kingsclere, Hants

FOCUS
The quicker division by just over a second. The third helps with the averages and the winner was quite impressive.

NOTEBOOK
Bonfire, a half-brother to this year's Musidora winner Joviality, came in for considerable support and was representing a trainer whose 2yos are in fine form. The colt improved from mid-pack and ran green when first issuing his challenge, before pulling away to score very comfortably. A son of Manduro, he will get further next year and looks a nice prospect. He has his quirks and was ponied early to the start. (op 10-3 tchd 4-1)
Cubanita ◆, representing the stable on the mark in this race with Look Here, was slowly away and green early on but came home in fine style for second. She is bred for middle-distances next season and looks very much one to follow. (op 20-1)
Juvenal(IRE) came here with an official rating of 74 but was the Hannon second string on jockey bookings. He ran a solid race but didn't convince he fully saw out the extra furlong in the soft ground. (tchd 17-2)
Uprise had every chance against the rail but could not build on his Leicester third, which came on fast ground. He did not quite get home over this extra furlong. (op 5-1 tchd 11-2 in places)
Winter Dress showed up well on this turf debut and stuck on for a creditable fifth. She's qualified for handicaps now. (op 33-1)
Halling's Quest was staying on when it was all over and will have learnt a lot from this. His owners have had a good deal of success with the family and he should pay his way next year. Official explanation: jockey said colt was slowly away (op 25-1)
Dedication shaped with promise and will benefit from a step up in trip. She comes from the family of Commander In Chief, Warning and Deploy, and will be a valuable commodity if she can win a race. (op 16-1)
Golden Jubilee(USA), the Hannon first string, was in trouble a good way out and may not have handled the ground. (op 5-1)
Mayo Lad(IRE) was again rather keen but did not shape badly with handicaps in mind, probably over shorter. (op 20-1)
Dubawi Island(FR) was markedly green and always at the back of the field, stumbling slightly when trying to improve on the inside at halfway. He is a half-brother to Group winners Bushman and Grand Vent and is not one to give up on yet. Official explanation: jockey said colt ran flat (op 8-1)

6464 E B F "HAAFHD" BATHWICK TYRES NOVICE STKS 6f 212y

2:30 (2:32) (Class 4) 2-Y-O **£5,175** (£1,540; £769; £384) **Stalls** Low

Form RPR

31 **1** **Frog Hollow**[48] [4969] 2-9-0 85.. JimCrowley 6 88+
(Ralph Beckett) *trckd ldrs: rdn wl over 1f out: chal ent fnl f: kpt on to ld nring fin: drvn out* **11/10**[1]

2324 **2** *hd* **Lord Ofthe Shadows (IRE)**[27] [5654] 2-9-3 96........... RichardHughes 5 90
(Richard Hannon) *trckd ldr: led ent fnl f: sn rdn and hrd pressed: kpt on: narrowly hdd nring fin* **15/8**[2]

0 **3** *¾* **Emperor Vespasian**[25] [5697] 2-8-12 0........................ JimmyFortune 3 83
(Andrew Balding) *lw: led: rdn whn chal over 1f out: hdd ent fnl f: kpt on and ev ch tl no ex fnl 75yds* **20/1**

020 **4** *1* **Norse Gold**[39] [5280] 2-9-0 79.. TedDurcan 1 82
(David Elsworth) *trckd ldrs: nt clr run on rails fr 2f out tl swtchd lft ent fnl f: kpt on* **20/1**

3 **5** *3 ¾* **Cape Rainbow**[19] 5891 2-8-12 0 .... DaneO'Neill 7 71
(Mark Usher) *little slowly away: trckd ldrs: rdn over 3f out: kpt on same pce* **9/1**[3]

143 **6** *3 ¼* **Waseem Faris (IRE)**[19] 5886 2-9-3 85 .... ChrisCatlin 4 67
(Mick Channon) *swtg: hld up bhd ldrs: rdn 2f out: nt pce to get involved* **14/1**

1m 30.73s (2.13) **Going Correction** +0.20s/f (Good) **6** Ran SP% **108.6**
Speed ratings (Par 97): **95,94,93,92,88 84**
toteswingers:1&2:£1.10, 2&3:£4.30, 1&3:£6.20 CSF £3.06 TOTE £2.60: £1.70, £1.10; EX 3.00.

Owner R A Pegum **Bred** Reid & Shriver **Trained** Kimpton, Hants

FOCUS
A decent novice event. The winner is going the right way and the runner-up was not quite back to his best.

NOTEBOOK
Frog Hollow ◆, as he had when winning his maiden here, took time to engage top gear, but he did enough to get up in the last few strides. This likeable gelding handled the different surface and there is a good prospect that he will stay a mile. He should make a nice handicapper next season. (op 6-4 tchd Evens, 7-4 in a place)

Lord Ofthe Shadows(IRE), rated 96, was 8lb clear on adjusted official ratings but had been below par on his latest run at this venue. Always close up and let down to lead a furlong out, he did very little wrong but was just caught by a progressive opponent. He gets a mile and was well at home in the ground. (tchd 2-1 in places)

Emperor Vespasian was another Andrew Balding juvenile to run well, leading for 6f and sticking on for third. This was a big improvement on his debut effort at Ascot, where he had been slowly away. (tchd 33-1)

Norse Gold had to switch away from the rail, which cost him ground, but was clawing back the leaders late on. This run appears to confirm that he acts on turf. (op 16-1)

Cape Rainbow became warm beforehand and was the first in trouble. This drop in trip was against him. (tchd 17-2 and 10-1)

Waseem Faris(IRE) was rather edgy in the preliminaries and raced a little keenly. Always towards the rear, he ran below his official mark of 85. (op 15-2)

6465 FRANCIS CLARK CHARTERED ACCOUNTANTS CLAIMING STKS 1m 1f 198y
3:00 (3:00) (Class 5) 3-4-Y-O **£2,425** (£721; £360; £180) **Stalls** Low

Form RPR

3021 **1** **Avon River**[15] 6017 4-9-2 78 .... RichardHughes 2 78+
(Richard Hannon) *led for 1f: trckd ldr: led 3f out: shkn up to assert whn chal ins fnl f: readily on top at fin* **2/1**[1]

5600 **2** *½* **Persian Herald**[17] 5968 3-8-10 67 .... JimCrowley 1 75
(William Muir) *in tch tl lost pl over 4f out: hdwy over 2f out: swtchd rt over 1f out: rdn to chal ins fnl f: kpt on but readily hld towards fin hld* **16/1**

4465 **3** *3* **Kingarrick**[19] 5893 3-8-12 71 .... EddieAhern 5 71
(Eve Johnson Houghton) *cl up: effrt 2f out: kpt on same pce ins fnl f* **4/1**[3]

6140 **4** *shd* **Rock The Stars (IRE)**[39] 5275 4-9-8 77 .... DaneO'Neill 7 75
(J W Hills) *trckd ldrs: effrt 2f out: kpt on same pce ins fnl f* **10/3**[2]

555 **5** *5* **Rosairlie (IRE)**[17] 5964 3-8-3 65 ....(v[1]) DavidProbert 6 52
(Harry Dunlop) *led after 1f: rdn and hdd 3f out: sn hung lft: wknd jst over 1f out* **12/1**

4002 **6** *shd* **Orange Ace**[7] 6262 3-8-9 65 ....(t) ChrisCatlin 3 58
(Paul Cole) *hld up in last: pushed along over 5f out: rdn over 4f out: nvr gng pce to threaten: wknd over 1f out* **8/1**

0060 **7** *3 ½* **Signor Verdi**[48] 4962 4-9-4 76 .... JadeMuggeridge[(7)] 8 61
(Brian Meehan) *trckd ldrs: ev ch 3f out: sn rdn: wknd over 1f out* **8/1**

-643 **8** *3* **Lord Of The Storm**[14] 6067 3-8-4 57 ....(t) KierenFox[(3)] 4 43
(Bill Turner) *hld up in last pair: rdn and hdwy over 3f out: wknd 2f out* **40/1**

2m 11.96s (2.06) **Going Correction** +0.20s/f (Good)
WFA 3 from 4yo 6lb **8** Ran SP% **114.6**
Speed ratings (Par 103): **99,98,96,96,92 92,89,86**
toteswingers:1&2:£5.30, 2&3:£17.90, 1&3:£3.60 CSF £36.76 TOTE £3.10: £1.60, £5.50, £1.30; EX 48.90.

Owner Jim Horgan **Bred** Poulton Stud **Trained** East Everleigh, Wilts

FOCUS
Not a bad claimer, but the winner is rated 10lb [illegible] off this year's best.

6466 VERONICA STEWART MEMORIAL CONDITIONS STKS 6f
3:35 (3:36) (Class 2) 2-Y-O **£7,762** (£2,310; £1,154; £577) **Stalls** Low

Form RPR

153 **1** **Artistic Jewel (IRE)**[21] 5826 2-8-10 91 .... GrahamGibbons 5 91+
(Ed McMahon) *trckd ldr: shkn up to ld over 1f out: r.o wl: rdn out* **15/8**[1]

2 **2** *1* **Arnold Lane (IRE)**[39] 5263 2-9-1 90 .... SamHitchcott 3 93
(Mick Channon) *trckd ldng trio: rdn over 1f out: r.o to go 2nd ins fnl f: a being hld* **15/2**

1 **3** *1* **Ihsas (USA)**[22] 5813 2-8-10 0 .... TedDurcan 4 85+
(Saeed Bin Suroor) *athletic: lw: sn led: rdn and hdd over 1f out: kpt on same pce* **2/1**[2]

3146 **4** *1 ¼* **Gusto**[30] 5558 2-9-1 95 .... RichardHughes 2 86+
(Richard Hannon) *trckd ldr: pushed along to mount chal whn nt clr run on rails over 1f out: swtchd lft: keeping on whn nt clr run again ins fnl f: no ch after* **5/2**[3]

1m 17.64s (2.84) **Going Correction** +0.20s/f (Good) **4** Ran SP% **108.5**
Speed ratings (Par 101): **89,87,86,84**
CSF £13.64 TOTE £2.50; EX 11.10.

Owner R L Bedding **Bred** Jim McDonald **Trained** Lichfield, Staffs

FOCUS
A good little conditions race, the best recent winner of which was smart miler Ouqba in 2008. It was a tight contest on official figures and there was not a great deal between the four at the line. It will be no surprise if this proves a better race than the bare form.

NOTEBOOK
Artistic Jewel(IRE) won decisively enough. The filly carried her head a little high and gave the impression that the ground was softer than she really cared for, but she has an engine and is worth another try in Listed company. (op 2-1)

Arnold Lane(IRE)'s trainer has won this race three times in the past decade, including with Galtymore Lad in a two-horse renewal 12 months ago. Racing keenly at the back of a closely bunched field, the colt ran on well for second without troubling the winner too much. This was his first run on soft ground. (op 6-1)

Ihsas(USA) made the running but could not counter when headed a furlong out. The sister to stable stalwart Rio De La Plata had made a winning debut on the Polytrack at Lingfield over 7f, and she shaped as if this drop in trip was against her. A big filly, she was not given a hard time when held and is capable of better. (op 9-4)

Gusto, down in grade after contesting a couple of Listed races, had to be switched when a gap against the rail closed, and he lacked the pace to get back into the race. Things did not go his way here but he is not going to be easy to place successfully. (op 11-4 tchd 3-1)

6467 CATHEDRAL HOTEL H'CAP 6f
4:10 (4:10) (Class 4) (0-85,85) 3-Y-O+ **£4,204** (£1,251; £625; £312) **Stalls** Low

Form RPR

0363 **1** **Camache Queen (IRE)**[22] 5811 3-8-9 75 .... EddieAhern 1 86
(Denis Coakley) *chsd ldrs: rdn to ld 2f out: r.o wl ins fnl f* **8/1**[3]

1061 **2** *1* **Maze (IRE)**[18] 5914 6-9-0 83 .... LucyKBarry[(5)] 13 91
(Tony Carroll) *hld up bhd: swtchd to nrr stands' side rails over 2f out: sn rdn: hdwy over 1f out: r.o wl fnl f: wnt 2nd towards fin* **14/1**

0362 **3** *½* **Jack My Boy (IRE)**[11] 6174 4-8-13 77 ....(v) GrahamGibbons 14 83
(David Evans) *lw: mid-div: rdn over 2f out: hdwy over 1f out: styd on ins fnl f* **10/1**

4052 **4** *shd* **Oil Strike**[22] 5811 4-9-2 85 .... JamesRogers[(5)] 2 91
(Peter Winkworth) *prom: rdn over 2f out: drifted sltly lft: kpt on ins fnl f: eased nring fin: lost 3rd line* **6/1**[2]

50/ **5** *hd* **Indian Art (IRE)**[716] 6731 5-9-1 79 .... GeorgeBaker 6 84
(Richard Hannon) *mid-div: rdn over 2f out: styd on fnl f: wnt 5th nring fin* **28/1**

2262 **6** *nk* **Perfect Pastime**[29] 5587 3-9-1 81 ....[1] JimmyFortune 9 85
(Walter Swinburn) *hld up towards rr: hdwy over 2f out: sn rdn: chsd ldrs over 1f out: no ex ins fnl f* **12/1**

5440 **7** *1 ¼* **Galatian**[17] 5970 4-9-0 78 ....(b) JamesMillman 16 78
(Rod Millman) *s.i.s: sn chsng ldrs: led over 3f out tl drifted lft and hdd 2f out: fdd ins fnl f* **14/1**

1- **8** *nse* **Iron Range (IRE)**[363] 6488 3-9-5 85 .... RichardMullen 17 88+
(Ed McMahon) *unf: scope: lw: taken down early: mid-div in centre: rdn over 2f out: styng on at same pce whn nt clr run ins fnl f: no further imp* **9/4**[1]

4523 **9** *hd* **Macdillon**[18] 5914 5-9-0 78 ....(b) LiamKeniry 18 78
(Stuart Kittow) *hld up bhd: rdn and hdwy over 1f out: nt best of runs whn swtchd lft ins fnl f: no further imp* **14/1**

1100 **10** *nk* **Kings 'n Dreams**[18] 5948 4-8-10 74 ow1 ....(b) JimCrowley 11 73
(Dean Ivory) *rdn over 2f out: nvr bttr than mid-div* **28/1**

1000 **11** *4 ½* **Ivory Silk**[20] 5852 6-8-12 83 ....(b) RaulDaSilva[(7)] 3 67
(Jeremy Gask) *trckd ldrs: rdn over 2f out: wknd on far side rails ins fnl f* **16/1**

6060 **12** *½* **Avonmore Star**[17] 5972 3-9-2 82 .... RichardHughes 5 65
(Richard Hannon) *trckd ldrs: rdn over 2f out: wknd ent fnl f* **16/1**

10-0 **13** *hd* **Signore Momento (IRE)**[24] 5760 5-8-11 75 ....(tp) EddieCreighton 4 57
(Amy Weaver) *s.i.s: a towards rr* **50/1**

1560 **14** *nk* **Munaaseb**[16] 6003 3-8-13 79 .... ChrisCatlin 15 60
(Ed Dunlop) *a towards rr* **25/1**

0612 **15** *2 ½* **Dasho**[25] 5735 3-8-13 79 .... AdamKirby 7 52
(Olivia Maylam) *swtg: taken down early: led tl hdd over 3f out: rdn over 2f out: wknd over 1f out* **14/1**

1035 **16** *1 ¼* **Spanish Bounty**[36] 5339 6-8-13 80 .... RossAtkinson[(3)] 8 49
(Jonathan Portman) *chsd ldrs tl wknd 2f out* **66/1**

1m 15.43s (0.63) **Going Correction** +0.20s/f (Good)
WFA 3 from 4yo+ 2lb **16** Ran SP% **125.6**
Speed ratings (Par 105): **103,101,101,100,100 100,98,98,98,97 91,91,90,90,87 85**
toteswingers:1&2:£18.60, 2&3:£18.90, 1&3:£9.10 CSF £113.48 CT £1195.76 TOTE £11.60: £2.00, £2.90, £2.40, £1.90; EX 210.20.

Owner Keeper's 12 **Bred** Yeomanstown Stud **Trained** West Ilsley, Berks

■ Stewards' Enquiry : James Rogers 21 day ban; dropped hands before line (12th-22nd Oct/24th-29th Oct/31st Oct-3rd Nov)

FOCUS
A competitive sprint handicap in which the field spread out across the track after the intersection. Pretty solid form despite the surprise personal best from the winner.

6468 BET WITH YOUR MOBILE AT VICTORCHANDLER.COM H'CAP 1m
4:40 (4:46) (Class 6) (0-65,65) 3-Y-O+ **£1,940** (£577; £288; £144) **Stalls** Low

Form RPR

1455 **1** **Push Me (IRE)**[31] 5511 4-8-12 60 .... KierenFox[(3)] 14 79
(Jamie Poulton) *mid-div: [illegible] 2f out: [illegible] comf* **9/1**

2302 **2** *3 ½* **Zafeen's Pearl**[14] 6070 4-8-13 63 .... RyanPowell[(5)] 2 73
(Dean Ivory) *trckd ldrs: rdn to ld over 2f out: hdd sn after: kpt on but sn hld by comfortable wnr* **5/1**[1]

0000 **3** *1* **May Be Some Time**[18] 5942 3-9-0 63 .... LiamKeniry 15 71
(Stuart Kittow) *swtchd rt sn after s: towards rr: crept clsr fr over 3f out: rdn to chse ldrs 2f out: styd on ins fnl f wout ever threatening* **22/1**

5-60 **4** *2 ¼* **Spirit Of Gondree (IRE)**[19] 5893 3-9-2 65 .... EddieAhern 12 68
(John Dunlop) *uns rdr leaving paddock: sn ct: reluctant to go bhd stalls: mid-div: hdwy over 2f out: sn rdn to chse ldrs: one pce ins fnl f* **11/2**[2]

0020 **5** *1 ¼* **Rojo Boy**[35] 5381 3-8-7 63 ....(b) CharlesBishop[(7)] 11 63
(David Elsworth) *s.i.s: mid-div: rdn over 2f out: styd on fnl f: nvr trbld ldrs* **11/1**

2360 **6** *2 ¼* **Cahala Dancer (IRE)**[19] 5894 3-9-0 63 .... JamesDoyle 8 58
(Roger Teal) *towards rr: stdy prog fr over 5f out: rdn 3f out: styd on same pce fnl 2f* **25/1**

6642 **7** *nk* **Sweet Secret**[9] 6226 4-8-12 64 ....(p) RaulDaSilva[(7)] 6 58
(Jeremy Gask) *trckd ldrs: rdn over 2f out: drifted sltly lft and fdd over 1f out* **8/1**[3]

5342 **8** *nk* **Jodawes (USA)**[15] 6032 4-9-1 60 .... AdamKirby 1 54
(John Best) *led tl rdn and hdd over 2f out: wknd over 1f out* **10/1**

6201 **9** *3 ¼* **Bennelong**[16] 5994 5-8-11 63 .... LukeRowe[(7)] 5 49
(Richard Rowe) *trckd ldr tl rdn over 3f out: wknd over 1f out* **14/1**

6644 **10** *1 ¼* **Woolston Ferry (IRE)**[18] 5942 5-9-1 60 .... JimmyFortune 7 43
(David Pinder) *mid-div: hdwy 3f out: ev ch jst over 2f out: sn rdn: wknd over 1f out* **16/1**

6053 **11** *½* **Folly Drove**[55] 4707 3-9-1 64 .... JimCrowley 10 46
(Jonathan Portman) *a towards rr* **14/1**

3006 **12** *16* **Commerce**[18] 5942 4-9-1 60 .... GeorgeBaker 13 —
(Gary Moore) *in tch: rdn over 3f out: wknd wl over 1f out* **20/1**

1251 **13** *¾* **George Thisby**[9] 6228 5-9-6 65 .... JamesMillman 9 —
(Rod Millman) *nvr travelling in rr* **11/2**[2]

0-00 **14** *10* **Honourable Knight (IRE)**[99] 3259 3-9-2 65 .... ChrisCatlin 4 —
(Mark Usher) *sn struggling: a in rr* **16/1**

1m 43.63s (0.13) **Going Correction** +0.20s/f (Good)
WFA 3 from 4yo+ 4lb **14** Ran SP% **124.0**
Speed ratings (Par 101): **107,103,102,100,99 96,96,96,92,91 91,75,74,64**
toteswingers:1&2:£11.30, 2&3:£41.00, 1&3:£50.30 CSF £53.71 CT £1015.14 TOTE £13.00: £3.70, £1.20, £10.30; EX 73.90.

Owner Alex and Janet Card **Bred** Mrs Dolores Gleeson **Trained** Telscombe, E Sussex

FOCUS
A moderate handicap but it was well run and was probably a fair race for the grade. The winner produced a clear personal best.
George Thisby Official explanation: jockey said gelding was never travelling

6469 BOOKER WHOLESALE H'CAP — 1m 6f 21y
5:10 (5:13) (Class 5) (0-75,74) 3-Y-0+ £2,425 (£721; £360; £180)

Form RPR
3640 **1** **Hawridge King**[17] 5966 9-9-3 **67**............(v) LiamKeniry 8 77
(Stuart Kittow) *mid-div in chsng gp: hdwy fr 4f out: rdn for str chal fr over 2f out: led ins fnl f: styd on: drvn out* **13/2**
4205 **2** *nk* **Penangdouble O One**[26] 5692 4-9-1 **65**............(tp) JimCrowley 13 75
(Ralph Beckett) *chsd clr ldrs: clsd on ldrs to ld over 2f out: sn hrd pressed and rdn: styd on gamely but no ex whn hdd ins fnl f* **5/1**[3]
0-00 **3** *10* **Isobar (GER)**[45] 5078 5-9-7 **71**............J-PGuillambert 9 67+
(Luca Cumani) *hld up towards rr: hdwy fr over 5f out: rdn 3f out: chsd ldng pair 2f out: nvr any ch* **14/1**
4042 **4** *2 1/2* **Wily Fox**[15] 6023 4-9-1 **68**............KieranFox(3) 6 60
(James Eustace) *led for 2f: chsd ldrs: rdn 3f out: wknd 1f out* **7/2**[1]
06-0 **5** *2 1/4* **Numide (FR)**[17] 5971 8-9-7 **71**............JamesMillman 4 60
(Rod Millman) *mid-div in chsng gp: rdn over 4f out: chal for 4th fr wl over 2f out: nvr trbld ldrs: wknd ins fnl f* **8/1**
0066 **6** *3 1/2* **Issabella Gem (IRE)**[67] 4341 4-9-0 **69**............LucyKBarry(5) 11 53
(Clive Cox) *pushed along early: led briefly after 2f: chsd ldr: led over 6f out: rdn on far side rails alone over 3f out: hdd over 2f out: grad fdd* **4/1**[2]
0560 **7** *7* **Kiss A Prince**[21] 5837 5-9-1 **65**............JimmyFortune 7 39
(Dean Ivory) *struggling over 4f out: a towards rr* **16/1**
1320 **8** *3 1/4* **Gems**[15] 6023 4-9-3 **67**............ChrisCatlin 5 37
(Peter Hiatt) *chsd clr ldrs: rdn over 3f out: wknd over 2f out* **9/1**
62-5 **9** *21* **Lombok**[46] 2562 5-9-3 **67**............(v) GeorgeBaker 10 —
(Gary Moore) *wknd over 3f out: a towards rr* **14/1**
2454 **10** *40* **Samarinda (USA)**[21] 804 8-9-9 **73**............(b) AdamKirby 1 —
(P J O'Gorman) *led after 2f: hdd over 6f out: rdn over 5f out: dropped out tamely: t.o fnl 3f* **25/1**

3m 8.43s (1.03) **Going Correction** +0.20s/f (Good)
WFA 3 from 4yo+ 10lb — 10 Ran SP% **116.4**
Speed ratings (Par 103): **105,104,99,97,96 94,90,88,76,53**
toteswingers:1&2:£7.20, 2&3:£12.60, 1&3:£16.10 CSF £38.95 CT £442.85 TOTE £8.90: £2.40, £2.90, £3.40; EX 44.20.
Owner Eric Gadsden **Bred** Old Mill Stud **Trained** Blackborough, Devon
■ Stewards' Enquiry : Liam Keniry two-day ban; excessive use of whip (12th-13th Oct)

FOCUS
An ordinary staying handicap and something of a messy race, with three of the runners racing clear of the others for the first part of the contest and the field fanning out in the home straight. The first two fought out the finish near the stands' side, coming home clear of the others. Probably not form to take too literally, and it has been rated on the cautious side.
T/Plt: £68.10 to a £1 stake. Pool of £48,917.31 - 523.84 winning tickets. T/Qpdt: £13.10 to a £1 stake. Pool of £3,745.29 - 210.84 winning tickets. TM

TOULOUSE
Wednesday, September 28
OFFICIAL GOING: Turf: good to soft

6470a PRIX PANACEE (LISTED RACE) (3YO+ FILLIES & MARES) (TURF) — 1m 4f
5:25 (12:00) 3-Y-0+ £22,413 (£8,965; £6,724; £4,482; £2,241)

RPR
1 **Gradara**[21] 5839 4-9-1 0............TheoBachelot 3 102
(S Wattel, France) **105/10**
2 *nk* **Loonora (FR)**[45] 5093 5-9-1 0............Francois-XavierBertras 9 102
(D De Watrigant, France) **9/1**
3 *1 1/2* **Santa Biatra (FR)**[45] 5093 5-9-1 0............AdrienFouassier 7 100
(A Couetil, France) **2/1**[1]
4 *1 1/2* **Vertana (IRE)**[25] 5749 4-9-1 0............(p) FabriceVeron 4 97
(H-A Pantall, France) **10/1**
5 *1* **Sinndarina (FR)**[21] 5839 4-9-1 0............(b) PhilippeSogorb 10 96
(P Demercastel, France) **59/1**
6 *1/2* **Ma Coeur (FR)**[80] 4-9-1 0............DavidMichaux 6 95
(M Delzangles, France) **26/1**
7 *2* **Makadane** 4-9-1 0............Jean-BernardEyquem 2 92
(J-C Rouget, France) **63/10**[3]
8 *3 1/2* **Love Over Gold (FR)**[38] 5303 4-9-1 0............MartinLane 11 86
(Ralph Beckett) *settled in 2nd: rdn bef fnlng st: u.str.p and fnd no ex: fdd* **78/1**
9 *2 1/2* **First Blush (IRE)**[116] 4-9-1 0............EmilienRevolte 1 82
(H-A Pantall, France) **58/1**
10 *1* **Never Forget (FR)**[21] 4-9-1 0............AnthonyCrastus 5 80
(E Lellouche, France) **5/2**[2]
11 *2* **Zennor**[18] 5921 4-9-1 0............StephenCraine 8 77
(Tom Dascombe) *sn led: stl in front ent fnlng st: hdd 1 1/2f out: wandered off st line: hrd rdn: sn wknd* **12/1**

2m 28.27s (-4.03) — 11 Ran SP% **119.4**
WIN (incl. 1 euro stake): 11.50. PLACES: 2.80, 2.50, 1.70. DF: 36.60. SF: 110.20.
Owner Haras De La Perelle **Bred** Haras De La Perelle **Trained** France

6439 KEMPTON (A.W) (R-H)
Thursday, September 29
OFFICIAL GOING: Standard
Wind: virtually nil Weather: warm and dry

6471 32REDPOKER.COM CLAIMING STKS — 1m (P)
5:40 (5:40) (Class 6) 2-Y-0 £1,617 (£481; £240; £120) Stalls Low

Form RPR
0154 **1** **Snowed In (IRE)**[3] 6399 2-9-4 71............LukeMorris 10 67+
(J S Moore) *hld up in rr of main gp: effrt over 2f out: drvn and hdwy over 1f out: led and edgd rt 1f out: styd on wl and in command ins fnl f* **9/4**[1]
0000 **2** *1 1/4* **Astraios (IRE)**[29] 5634 2-9-7 62............(b) ShaneKelly 3 66+
(Brian Meehan) *hld up in tch towards rr: rdn and hdwy ent fnl 2f: racd awkwardly and no imp over 1f out: swtchd lft jst over 1f out: styd in wl ins fnl f to go 2nd fnl 50yds: nvr gng to rch wnr* **20/1**
0514 **3** *1* **Faraway**[7] 6284 2-8-13 74............(v) KierenFallon 7 55
(David Evans) *dwlt: t.k.h: hld up towards rr: hmpd after 2f: hdwy into midfield 1/2-way: rdn and effrt ent fnl 2f: led over 1f out: hdd 1f out: no ex: lost 2nd fnl 50yds* **3/1**[2]
040 **4** *3/4* **Dutchman's Field**[21] 5851 2-8-8 59............(p) MichaelO'Connell(3) 8 51
(David Nicholls) *chsd ldrs: pushed lft 5f out: rdn ent fnl 2f: drvn and ev ch over 1f out: one pce and btn whn short of room and swtchd lft fnl 100yds* **16/1**
3512 **5** *nk* **King Kenobi (IRE)**[7] 6280 2-8-13 60............LiamKeniry 2 52
(J S Moore) *in tch: hmpd over 5f out: rdn and struggling 4f out: rallied u.p over 1f out: styd on fnl f: no threat to wnr* **6/1**
00 **6** *3* **Scarlet Prince**[49] 4968 2-9-7 0............EddieAhern 9 54
(Gary Moore) *dwlt: sn outpcd in last pair: styd on past btn horses fr over 1f out: nvr trbld ldrs* **100/1**
0506 **7** *nk* **Milwr**[17] 6001 2-8-12 43............(e[1]) AndreaAtzeni 5 44
(Chris Dwyer) *sn led: rdn 2f out: hdd over 1f out: wknd ins fnl f* **66/1**
006 **8** *nk* **Three Tenors**[23] 5802 2-8-7 46............JohnFahy(3) 4 41
(J S Moore) *chsd ldrs: swtchd lft over 4f out: rdn and struggling over 2f out: short of room 2f out: one pce and n.d after* **100/1**
4133 **9** *3 3/4* **Yammos (IRE)**[15] 6053 2-9-0 63............TonyCulhane 11 37
(Mick Channon) *chsd ldrs: swtchd lft over 4f out: chsd ldr 3f out tl 2f out: sn wknd* **7/2**[3]
10 *hd* **Plead The Fifth (USA)** 2-9-2 0............(b[1]) MartinDwyer 6 38
(Brian Meehan) *s.i.s: outpcd and detached in last: wd bnd 3f out: n.d* **25/1**
44 **11** *9* **Beacon Lady**[38] 5325 2-8-1 0............KieranO'Neill(3) 1 —
(Bill Turner) *racd freely: chsd ldr: swtchd lft over 5f out: hung lft bnd over 3f out: lost 2nd 3f out: wknd qckly ent fnl 2f: wl bhd and eased fnl 100yds* **16/1**

1m 40.47s (0.67) **Going Correction** -0.025s/f (Stan) — 11 Ran SP% **116.1**
Speed ratings (Par 93): **95,93,92,92,91 88,88,88,84,84 75**
toteswingers:1&2:£9.60, 2&3:£8.20, 1&3:£3.50 CSF £53.55 TOTE £4.70: £2.10, £6.20, £1.10; EX 61.30.Beacon Lady was claimed by W. J. Knight for £3000.
Owner Norton Common Farm Racing **Bred** T Cahalan & D Cahalan **Trained** Upper Lambourn, Berks

FOCUS
A modest claimer but one run at a good pace set up for those ridden from behind.

NOTEBOOK
Snowed In(IRE) had the second highest official rating of these and the recent form in the book to figure prominently, and the good pace back in trip suited him ideally. He looks nothing but a galloper and ought to be well suited by at least 1m2f on this surface. He'll win another claimer or two this winter. (op 11-4)
Astraios(IRE) left his previous form behind on the back of a four-week break but it's easy to see why blinkers have been tried so quickly, taking an age to pick up but seeing his race out well when he did. He'll go back up in the weights for this but might be best campaigned in claimers. (op 16-1)
Faraway wasn't discredited back in third despite being the highest rated officially of these, as he was given a more aggressive ride early in the race than the pair that beat him, despite missing the break. He saw the trip out well, for all that 7f might turn out to suit for now. (op 11-4)
Dutchman's Field shaped with more promise in first-time cheekpieces in the face of a more realistic task, and probably wants his effort upgrading a bit considering he chased the good pace and was still disputing second when squeezed inside the last.
King Kenobi(IRE) was nearest at the finish after seeming to stumble on the bend when poorly placed, but he showed enough to think he'll be persevered with at this trip from now on. (op 13-2 tchd 11-2)
Scarlet Prince clearly has some ability for all he was favoured by the leaders coming back to him and this looks more his level. He looks to have inherited some stamina from his sire Sir Percy and may well be capable of better given a stiffer test of stamina in nurseries.
Milwr left his previous form behind tried in first-time eyeshields and needs his effort upgrading seeing as he lasted longest of the front runners. (tchd 50-1)
Yammos(IRE) seemed to pay for being close to the strong pace and didn't see his race out. (op 9-2)

6472 £32 FREE BET AT 32RED.COM CLASSIFIED CLAIMING STKS — 1m (P)
6:10 (6:10) (Class 6) 3-4-Y-0 £1,617 (£481; £240; £120) Stalls Low

Form RPR
-521 **1** **Larkrise Star**[16] 6032 4-9-8 65............ShaneKelly 5 72
(Dean Ivory) *stdd s: hld up in tch in last trio: hdwy 2f out: rdn to ld 1f out: drvn and r.o wl ins fnl f* **7/2**[1]
0023 **2** *1* **Burning Stone (USA)**[13] 6133 4-9-9 65............DeclanCannon(3) 2 73
(Gay Kelleway) *in tch in midfield: hdwy on inner ent fnl 2f: chsd wnr jst ins fnl f: styd on same pce u.p fnl 150yds* **11/2**[2]
1036 **3** *1/2* **Lutine Charlie (IRE)**[22] 5836 4-9-2 64............LukeMorris 11 62
(Ronald Harris) *hld up in tch on outer: nt clr run and swtchd lft over 2f out: rdn and hdwy to chse ldrs over 1f out: hung rt and kpt on same pce ins fnl f* **10/1**
5153 **4** *2 3/4* **Out Of The Storm**[27] 5666 3-8-13 61............JimCrowley 7 56
(Simon Dow) *w ldr tl rdn to ld over 2f out: drvn and hdd 1f out: wknd ins fnl f* **10/1**
3455 **5** *hd* **Jackie Love (IRE)**[13] 6120 3-8-4 49............(v) KellyHarrison 6 47
(Olivia Maylam) *stdd s: hld up in tch in last trio: hmpd and swtchd lft over 1f out: rdn and effrt wl over 1f out: kpt on fnl f: nvr gng pce to chal ldrs* **40/1**
000 **6** *4 1/2* **Bell's Ocean (USA)**[14] 6084 3-8-8 47............EddieAhern 9 36
(John Ryan) *hld up in tch in last trio: rdn and effrt ent fnl 2f: no imp over 1f out: wknd fnl f* **40/1**
0000 **7** *1/2* **A B Celebration**[14] 6084 3-8-5 40............(p) KieranO'Neill(3) 4 39
(John Bridger) *chsd ldrs: rdn over 1f out: wknd u.p over 1f out* **100/1**
0050 **8** *1 3/4* **Hackett (IRE)**[15] 6070 3-8-6 55............AndreaAtzeni 8 33
(Michael Quinn) *chsd ldrs: rdn and unable qck over 2f out: wknd u.p wl over 1f out* **40/1**
0642 **9** *5* **Beach Babe**[21] 5860 3-8-13 61............NickyMackay 12 29
(Jonathan Portman) *dwlt: sn pushed along and rcvrd to chse ldrs: rdn and struggling over 3f out: wknd over 2f out* **11/1**
6400 **10** *2 1/2* **Kalahaag (IRE)**[22] 5828 3-8-11 62............(b) MichaelO'Connell(3) 3 24
(David Nicholls) *racd freely: led tl over 2f out: wknd and hung rt ent 2f out* **8/1**[3]

1m 39.33s (-0.47) **Going Correction** -0.025s/f (Stan)
WFA 3 from 4yo 4lb — 10 Ran SP% **83.5**
Speed ratings (Par 101): **101,100,99,96,96 92,91,89,84,82**
toteswingers:1&2:£3.50, 2&3:£4.40, 1&3:£3.40 CSF £10.83 TOTE £3.70: £1.30, £1.10, £2.40; EX 13.70.
Owner Radlett Racing **Bred** D K Ivory **Trained** Radlett, Herts

FOCUS
Another modest claimer rated through the runner-up to the best of his British form. The runners were well bunched to the home turn yet the winning time was 1.14 secs faster than the opener.

6473 32RED.COM MAIDEN STKS 7f (P)
6:40 (6:41) (Class 5) 3-4-Y-O £2,264 (£673; £336; £168) Stalls Low

Form RPR
1 **Intercept (IRE)** 3-9-3 0 WilliamBuick 13 79+
(John Gosden) *in tch: pushed along and effrt to join press ldrs 2f out: led 1f out: rn green ins fnl f: a gng to hold on* **8/1**
0- 2 *nk* **Fakhuur**[461] 3411 3-8-12 0 MartinDwyer 12 73+
(Clive Brittain) *s.i.s: pushed along early: hdwy into midfield but stuck wd after 2f out: rdn ent fnl 2f: 6th and looked wl hld over 1f out: str run ins fnl f: pressing wnr cl home* **33/1**
645 3 *3/4* **George Guru**[14] 6085 4-9-1 71 MarkCoumbe(5) 3 76
(Michael Attwater) *chsd ldrs: rdn and effrt ent fnl 2f: styd on wl u.p ins fnl f* **16/1**
24 4 *3/4* **Wadha (IRE)**[17] 5999 3-8-12 0 KierenFallon 14 69
(Saeed Bin Suroor) *t.k.h: chsd ldr: rdn and led 2f out: hdd ent fnl f: no ex and styd on same pce ins fnl f* **15/2[3]**
56 5 *nk* **En Hiver**[31] 5567 3-8-12 0 JimCrowley 7 68+
(Ralph Beckett) *bmpd s: sn rcvrd and chsd ldrs: rdn and ev ch 2f out: unable qck ent fnl f: styd on same pce fnl 150yds* **20/1**
62 6 *1 3/4* **Press Office (USA)**[14] 6085 3-9-3 0 FrankieDettori 6 68
(Mahmood Al Zarooni) *wnt lft s: led: narrowly hdd 2f out: rdn and unable qck over 1f out: wknd ins fnl f* **1/1[1]**
3 7 *2 1/4* **Darsan (IRE)**[29] 5633 3-8-12 0 LukeMorris 8 57+
(Chris Wall) *hld up towards rr of main gp: rdn and effrt 2f out: edgd rt and no imp over 1f out* **11/2[2]**
8 *2 1/4* **Splice (USA)** 3-9-3 0 RichardHughes 10 56+
(Jeremy Noseda) *chsd ldrs: rdn and unable qck over 2f out: wknd over 1f out* **16/1**
6 9 *2 1/4* **Shannons Brook**[39] 5300 3-8-12 0 IanMongan 5 45
(Brett Johnson) *in rr of main gp: rdn and outpcd over 2f out: n.d and styd on same pce after* **80/1**
10 *1/2* **Barachiel** 3-9-3 0 DavidProbert 11 49
(Andrew Balding) *s.i.s: sn rdn along: clsd 1/2-way: rdn and outpcd again over 2f out: wknd 2f out* **25/1**
0 11 *5* **Heavenly Games**[29] 5633 4-9-1 0 EddieCreighton 9 30
(Jeremy Gask) *s.i.s: in rr of main gp: rdn and wknd over 2f out* **80/1**
12 *6* **Amaroni** 3-9-3 0 RichardThomas 2 19
(John E Long) *s.i.s and short of room s: a detached in last: n.d* **80/1**
0 13 *3* **Glens Wobbly**[14] 6085 3-9-3 0 RobertHavlin 1 11
(Jonathan Geake) *wnt lft s: chsd ldrs: wnt lft s: rdn and struggling 3f out: wknd qckly jst over 2f out* **80/1**

1m 25.93s (-0.07) **Going Correction** -0.025s/f (Stan)
WFA 3 from 4yo 3lb **13** Ran SP% **116.5**
Speed ratings (Par 103): **99,98,97,96,96 94,92,89,86,86 80,73,70**
toteswingers:1&2:£53.40, 2&3:£73.40, 1&3:£13.10 CSF £245.72 TOTE £7.00: £2.00, £7.80, £5.30; EX 207.60.
Owner H R H Princess Haya Of Jordan **Bred** Swordlestown Stud **Trained** Newmarket, Suffolk

FOCUS
Just a fair maiden as the proximity of the third with a BHA rating of 71 would suggest. The pace wasn't strong and the result might prove a bit misleading. The bare form looks ordinary, although the first two may be able to do a bit better.
Splice(USA) Official explanation: jockey said colt ran green
Heavenly Games Official explanation: trainer said filly bled

6474 32RED CASINO MAIDEN AUCTION STKS 7f (P)
7:10 (7:11) (Class 5) 2-Y-O £2,264 (£673; £336; £168) Stalls Low

Form RPR
26 1 **Halling Dancer**[77] 4007 2-8-10 0 NeilCallan 7 78+
(John Akehurst) *t.k.h: hld up in tch in midfield: nt clr run and swtchd lft 2f out: rdn and qcknd to ld 1f out: r.o strly and sn clr: readily* **7/2[2]**
64 2 *4 1/2* **Jasie Jac (IRE)**[16] 6018 2-8-13 0 EddieAhern 14 70
(Robert Mills) *in tch: rdn and effrt 2f out: led ent fnl f: sn hdd and outpcd by wnr ins fnl f: r.o for clr 2nd* **7/1[3]**
0 3 *1 1/4* **It's A Privilege**[33] 5475 2-9-0 0 JimCrowley 2 69+
(Ralph Beckett) *chsd ldrs: rdn and effrt over 1f out: short of room and hmpd jst ins fnl f: no ch w wnr and styd on same pce after* **11/1**
4 *shd* **Maistro (IRE)** 2-9-1 0 KierenFallon 6 71+
(Luca Cumani) *s.i.s: in rr: swtchd rt and effrt on inner ent fnl 2f: gd hdwy over 1f out: chsng ldrs and styng on 1f out: hmpd and hit rail jst ins fnl f: styd on same pce and no ch w wnr after* **10/1**
0 5 *1 1/4* **Hesperides**[23] 5812 2-8-1 0 JohnFahy(3) 10 55
(Harry Dunlop) *sn pushed along to ld and grad crossed to rail: rdn over 2f out: hdd ent fnl f: sn outpcd: wknd ins fnl f* **100/1**
6 6 *1/2* **Arabic**[15] 6064 2-8-11 0 ShaneKelly 4 64+
(James Fanshawe) *in tch towards rr: pushed along and effrt on inner 2f out: sme hdwy whn squeezed for room and hmpd ent fnl f: n.d after but kpt on fnl 100yds* **15/2**
4 7 *1* **Flaming Ferrari (IRE)**[32] 5514 2-8-4 0 SilvestreDeSousa 1 51
(Peter Chapple-Hyam) *t.k.h: chsd ldrs: rdn and effrt on inner ent fnl 2f: nt qckn and outpcd ent fnl f: sn edgd rt and bmpd rival: wknd qckly ins fnl f* **2/1[1]**
00 8 *1* **Oratrix (IRE)**[10] 6214 2-8-7 0 TadhgO'Shea 5 51
(Denis Coakley) *s.i.s: sn outpcd and detached in last: clsd 1/2-way: styd on past btn horses fr over 1f out: n.d* **100/1**
04 9 *2* **Roman Myst (IRE)**[12] 6180 2-8-12 0 LiamKeniry 8 52
(Sylvester Kirk) *t.k.h: chsd ldrs: rdn and unable qck over 2f out: wknd wl over 1f out* **25/1**
0 10 *1 1/4* **Awesome Rock (IRE)**[22] 5834 2-8-12 0 IanMongan 11 49
(Louise Best) *dwlt: in tch towards rr: pushed along over 3f out: rdn and unable qck over 2f out: sn wknd* **80/1**
04 11 *nk* **Hollywood All Star (IRE)**[17] 5991 2-8-10 0 MartinDwyer 13 46
(William Muir) *t.k.h: in tch in midfield: rdn over 3f out: wknd u.p over 2f out* **50/1**
0 12 *nse* **Pacific Trader**[26] 5726 2-8-9 0 WilliamBuick 12 46
(William Haggas) *chsd ldrs: rdn and struggling whn sltly hmpd jst over 2f out: sn wknd* **16/1**
0 13 *2 1/2* **Enthrall (IRE)**[13] 6117 2-8-6 0 CathyGannon 9 36
(Denis Coakley) *hld up towards rr: rdn and hung rt over 2f out: sn struggling and wknd jst over 2f out* **25/1**

1m 26.21s (0.21) **Going Correction** -0.025s/f (Stan) **13** Ran SP% **116.0**
Speed ratings (Par 95): **97,91,90,90,88 88,87,86,83,82 81,81,79**
toteswingers:1&2:£4.20, 2&3:£14.40, 1&3:£6.70 CSF £26.15 TOTE £4.20: £1.40, £2.00, £3.40; EX 25.10.
Owner Tattenham Corner Racing IV **Bred** Meon Valley Stud **Trained** Epsom, Surrey

FOCUS
Quite an interesting maiden auction but one dominated as things panned out by a couple with more experience than most.

NOTEBOOK
Halling Dancer might not have been right last time given his absence since but it's equally likely more patient tactics here helped produce an improved performance characterised by a smart turn of foot once in the clear. This win won't have done his nursery mark much good, but given his pedigree there's every chance he'll improve again at 1m. (op 4-1)
Jasie Jac(IRE) looks to be making steady progress and though no match for the winner, can improve again stepped up to 1m when going into nurseries. (op 8-1 tchd 13-2)
It's A Privilege is another that looks as if he'll be suited by further in time although, looking at his running style, an end-to-end gallop might turn out to be equally important. (tchd 12-1)
Maistro(IRE) ◆ the only newcomer, was the eye-catcher of the race. Poorly positioned turning for home, he made swift progress on reaching the cutaway and might well have been second had he had an uninterrupted run along the inside rail. By Excellent Art out of a French 11f winner, this trip is likely to prove a minimum for now and he should improve enough to win a similar event. (op 9-1 tchd 12-1)
Hesperides is rather flattered by her proximity to a couple of these given she had the run of the race more than most, but this was still an improvement on her first run and she's bred for middle distances next year.
Arabic was the chief sufferer in the interference passing the furlong marker, just as he was starting to hit full stride, and he's worth rating upsides the third at least. He'll be an interesting runner in a similar event next time. (op 10-1)
Flaming Ferrari(IRE) suffered some minor trouble in running but was already beaten at the time anyway. Her debut Yarmouth form on softish ground has been working out well, so she might be worth another chance. (op 13-8 tchd 9-4)

6475 32REDBET.COM MEDIAN AUCTION MAIDEN STKS 1m 4f (P)
7:40 (7:41) (Class 5) 3-5-Y-O £2,264 (£673; £336; £168) Stalls Centre

Form RPR
5363 1 **Evergreen Forest (IRE)**[24] 5784 3-9-3 67 (b[1]) RichardHughes 8 66+
(Alastair Lidderdale) *hld up in tch in midfield: hdwy to chse ldrs 6f out: led wl over 2f out: rdn clr over 2f out: in n.d fnl 2f: pushed out ins fnl f* **5/2[2]**
5 2 *3* **Ultimate Best**[14] 6086 3-8-12 0 JimmyQuinn 1 53
(Michael Mullineaux) *in tch in midfield: outpcd u.p wl over 1f out: styd on to chse clr wnr 1f out: kpt on but no threat to wnr* **15/2**
50 3 *3 1/4* **Cardi King**[14] 6086 3-9-3 0 SilvestreDeSousa 6 53
(Ian Wood) *hld up in tch in last trio: rdn and outpcd over 2f out: no ch w wnr but plugged on u.p to go modest 3rd ins fnl f* **16/1**
50 4 *4 1/2* **Maloof**[63] 4478 3-9-3 0 (b[1]) TadhgO'Shea 3 46
(Roger Varian) *chsd ldr over 8f out: ld over 3f out: rdn and hdd wl over 2f out: fnd little u.p and btn 2f out: fdd 1f out* **2/1[1]**
00 5 *1 1/2* **Lucky Dime**[38] 5317 3-8-12 0 IanMongan 7 38
(Noel Quinlan) *t.k.h: hld up in tch: rdn and outpcd wl over 2f out: swtchd lft ent fnl 2f: wl btn after* **100/1**
00 6 *shd* **Suffolini**[16] 6034 3-8-12 0 CathyGannon 4 38
(William Stone) *stdd s: hld up in detached last: rdn 6f out: wknd 3f out: no ch but plugged on past btn horses ins fnl f* **80/1**
7 *1/2* **Four Steps Back** 4-9-11 0 LiamKeniry 9 42
(Mark Usher) *stdd s: in tch in last trio: rdn 4f out: sn struggling: wknd wl over 2f out* **50/1**
0 8 *8* **Broken Eagle (USA)**[23] 5816 3-9-3 0 (bt) GeorgeBaker 5 29
(Mikael Magnusson) *t.k.h: led after 1f out tl over 3f out: sn wknd* **25/1**
0-64 9 *1 1/4* **Samanda (IRE)**[14] 6086 3-9-3 67 (v) KierenFallon 2 27
(Luca Cumani) *t.k.h: led for 1f: chsd ldrs after tl wknd 3f out: sn bhd* **3/1[3]**

2m 35.57s (1.07) **Going Correction** -0.025s/f (Stan)
WFA 3 from 4yo 8lb **9** Ran SP% **112.6**
Speed ratings (Par 103): **95,93,90,87,86 86,86,81,80**
toteswingers:1&2:£3.50, 2&3:£7.90, 1&3:£5.60 CSF £20.36 TOTE £3.50: £1.10, £2.50, £5.00; EX 22.20.
Owner C S J Beek **Bred** Shadwell Estate Company Limited **Trained** Eastbury, Berks

FOCUS
An uncompetitive maiden run at a modest pace and best rated through the placed horses to recent C&D form.

6476 32REDBINGO.COM H'CAP 2m (P)
8:10 (8:13) (Class 6) (0-65,63) 4-Y-0+ £1,617 (£481; £240; £120) Stalls Low

Form RPR
-104 1 **Steady Gaze**[17] 5993 6-8-1 **50** ow2 LukeRowe(7) 10 61
(Richard Rowe) *mde all: rdn and qcknd ent fnl 2f: clr over 1f out: styd on wl* **20/1**
404 2 *3 3/4* **Squad**[29] 5612 5-9-3 **59** (v) EddieAhern 9 65
(Simon Dow) *hld up in tch in last quartet: rdn and gd hdwy on inner jst over 2f out: chsd clr wnr over 1f out: r.o but no imp* **11/1**
5411 3 *3 1/2* **Maydream**[19] 5916 4-9-0 **59** KieranO'Neill(3) 2 61+
(Jimmy Fox) *s.i.s: hld up in rr: hdwy on outer 4f out: midfield and stl plenty to do whn bmpd wl over 1f out: swtchd lft over 1f out: r.o to go 3rd fnl 100yds: no ch w wnr* **5/1[2]**
624 4 *2 1/2* **Rose Aurora**[9] 6236 4-8-3 **45** (v) SilvestreDeSousa 8 44
(Marcus Tregoning) *hld up in tch: hdwy to chse ldrs 1/2-way: rdn and unable qck over 2f out: styd on same pce and wl hld after* **7/1[3]**
0513 5 *shd* **Katies Tuitor**[14] 6087 8-9-7 **63** (p) LiamKeniry 14 62
(J S Moore) *in tch: hdwy to chse wnr 10f out: rdn and unable qck over 2f out: sn outpcd by wnr and wl btn over 1f out* **5/1[2]**
6440 6 *3/4* **Now What**[41] 5236 4-9-6 **62** JimCrowley 1 60
(Jonathan Portman) *chsd ldrs: wnt 3rd over 4f out: rdn and unable qck over 2f out: sn outpcd and btn 2f out: wknd over 1f out* **12/1**
7 *nk* **Frosted Grape (IRE)**[9] 5737 5-9-4 **60** (vt) NeilCallan 6 57
(David Pipe) *rn in snatches: in tch in midfield: drvn and no rspnse over 3f out: wknd u.p over 2f out* **9/2[1]**
5442 8 *4* **Delorain (IRE)**[14] 6087 8-8-4 **51** (v) LauraPike(5) 5 44
(William Stone) *t.k.h: hld up in tch: rdn and struggling over 2f out: wkng whn hung rt and bmpd rival wl over 1f out: sn fdd* **11/1**
0445 9 *shd* **Colliers Castle (IRE)**[13] 6121 5-9-1 **57** ShaneKelly 11 50
(Lisa Williamson) *stdd s: hld up in tch in last quartet: pushed along and sme hdwy over 3f out: wknd over 2f out* **40/1**
-411 10 *1/2* **Spinning Waters**[111] 2873 5-8-10 **52** KellyHarrison 13 44
(Dai Burchell) *chsd wnr tl 10f out: rdn over 3f out: wknd over 2f out* **14/1**
1050 11 *8* **Royal Premier (IRE)**[9] 6240 8-8-13 **55** (e[1]) SebSanders 3 37
(Tom Keddy) *a towards rr: rdn and struggling whn nt clr run over 3f out: sn wl btn* **33/1**
1-06 12 *25* **Jennerous Blue**[14] 6087 4-8-7 **49** (p) PaulQuinn 12 —
(Dean Ivory) *in tch in midfield on outer: pushed along and hdwy over 4f out: wknd over 2f out: wl bhd and eased ins fnl f: t.o* **10/1**

563- **13** 2 **Colonel Flay**[391] 5722 7-9-3 **59**.................................. RichardHughes 7 —
(Nerys Dutfield) *in tch in midfield: rdn over 2f out: sn btn and wknd: wl bhd and eased ins fnl f: t.o* **10/1**

3m 29.19s (-0.91) **Going Correction** -0.025s/f (Stan) **13** Ran SP% **123.4**
Speed ratings (Par 101): **101,99,97,96,96 95,95,93,93,93 89,76,75**
toteswingers:1&2:£67.80, 2&3:£9.80, 1&3:£26.50 CSF £228.65 CT £1291.48 TOTE £81.70: £11.60, £4.90, £1.90; EX 354.20.
Owner Miss Victoria Baalham **Bred** Juddmonte Farms Ltd **Trained** Sullington, W Sussex

FOCUS
A modest handicap lacking progressive sorts given that it was open only to four-year-olds and upwards. It was also a muddling contest on account of a sedate pace. The runner-up sets the level, rated to his recent best.
Jennerous Blue Official explanation: trainer said cheek pieces possibly came loose when filly left stalls

6477 32RED H'CAP (DIV I) 7f (P)
8:40 (8:44) (Class 4) (0-85,85) 3-Y-0+ **£4,075** (£1,212; £606; £303) **Stalls** Low

Form RPR
0006 **1** **Rulesn'regulations**[20] 5879 5-9-7 **85**.....................(b) SilvestreDeSousa 9 94
(Matthew Salaman) *s.i.s: hdwy to ld over 5f out: mde rest: clr and drvn over 1f out: kpt on wl fnl 100yds: all out* **13/2**[3]
1-02 **2** 1 **Little Curtsey**[12] 6167 3-8-11 **78**.................................... SteveDrowne 11 84
(Hughie Morrison) *hld up in tch in midfield: rdn and effrt 2f out: chsd wnr jst ins fnl f: r.o but hld fnl 50yds* **5/1**[2]
6160 **3** shd **Dominium (USA)**[23] 5811 4-8-12 **76**..............................(b[1]) NeilCallan 10 82
(Jeremy Gask) *t.k.h: hld up towards rr on outer: swtchd lft and effrt 2f out: hdwy u.p over 1f out: r.o u.p ins fnl f: no imp fnl 50yds* **9/1**
600 **4** ½ **Flowing Cape (IRE)**[27] 5682 6-9-5 **83**............................. GeorgeBaker 4 88
(Reg Hollinshead) *hld up in tch in midfield: effrt and nt clr run 2f out: swtchd rt and hdwy to chse ldrs 1f out: no imp u.p fnl 100yds* **14/1**
600 **5** 1¼ **Redvers (IRE)**[12] 6174 3-9-2 **83**...................................... JimCrowley 5 84
(Ralph Beckett) *in rr of main gp: rdn and outpcd over 3f out: hdwy u.p over 1f out: styd on wl ins fnl f: nvr gng pce to rch ldrs* **8/1**
105- **6** ¾ **Regeneration (IRE)**[316] 7488 5-9-1 **79**........................... EddieAhern 3 78
(Michael Bell) *chsd ldr: rdn and no imp 2f out: lost 2nd jst ins fnl f: styd on same pce after* **7/1**
0020 **7** 2 **Whitechapel**[22] 5828 4-8-7 **71** oh4.................................... DavidProbert 6 65
(Andrew Balding) *chsd ldrs: rdn and unable qck ent fnl 2f: one pce and struggling whn edgd rt over 1f out: wknd ins fnl f* **16/1**
1-20 **8** ½ **If You Whisper (IRE)**[29] 5635 3-8-10 **77**......................... TonyCulhane 7 70
(Mike Murphy) *bhd: detached last after 2f out: rdn and effrt wl over 1f out: sme hdwy ins fnl f: n.d* **20/1**
510 **9** 4 **Soweto Star (IRE)**[146] 1843 3-8-13 **80**............................ LukeMorris 1 62
(John Best) *led for over 1f out: chsd ldrs after tl wknd u.p over 1f out* **10/1**
00-0 **10** ¾ **Elkmait**[7] 6272 3-8-13 **80**... SebSanders 2 60
(Clive Brittain) *in tch in midfield: rdn and unable qck ent fnl 2f: wknd over 1f out* **66/1**
0142 **P** **Great Acclaim**[26] 5718 3-9-0 **81**... KierenFallon 8 —
(James Fanshawe) *hld up in tch towards rr: lost action and eased over 3f out: p.u and dismntd over 2f out: fatally injured* **3/1**[1]

1m 24.74s (-1.26) **Going Correction** -0.025s/f (Stan)
WFA 3 from 4yo+ 3lb **11** Ran SP% **116.5**
Speed ratings (Par 105): **106,104,104,104,102 101,99,99,94,93** —
toteswingers:1&2:£7.30, 2&3:£14.80, 1&3:£13.10 CSF £38.62 CT £241.17 TOTE £10.20: £3.40, £2.10, £2.80; EX 42.70.
Owner M Salaman & J H Widdows **Bred** Marshalla Salaman **Trained** Upper Lambourn, Berks

FOCUS
Ordinary fare for the grade with the race going to one dropping to this level for the first time. The pace, dictated by the winner, was only fair. The form looks pretty solid rated around the first two.

6478 32RED H'CAP (DIV II) 7f (P)
9:10 (9:17) (Class 4) (0-85,85) 3-Y-0+ **£4,075** (£909; £909; £303) **Stalls** Low

Form RPR
0000 **1** **Celtic Sultan (IRE)**[20] 5879 7-9-1 **79**............................... FrannyNorton 7 88
(Tom Tate) *chsd ldr: rdn and ev ch over 1f out: led fnl 100yds: kpt on wl u.p: all out* **9/1**
6262 **2** ¾ **Ree's Rascal (IRE)**[52] 4860 3-8-13 **80**............................ PatCosgrave 6 86
(Jim Boyle) *in tch: pushed along 1/2-way: effrt u.p 2f out: kpt on wl u.p ins fnl f* **10/1**
3562 **2** dht **Regal Approval**[26] 5717 3-8-10 **77**.................................... JimCrowley 2 83
(Hughie Morrison) *taken down early: chsd ldrs: rdn and led 2f out: hrd pressed and drvn jst over 1f out: hdd and no ex fnl 100yds* **11/2**[1]
0312 **4** nk **Ongoodform (IRE)**[19] 5948 4-9-0 **78**...............................(v) EddieAhern 3 84
(Paul D'Arcy) *hld up towards rr: rdn and effrt towards inner 2f out: chsd ldrs 1f out: kpt on same pce u.p fnl 100yds* **11/2**[1]
1040 **5** hd **New Leyf (IRE)**[52] 4859 5-9-7 **85**...................................(b) SteveDrowne 9 91+
(Jeremy Gask) *taken down early: stdd s: t.k.h: hld up in rr: rdn and hdwy over 1f out: kpt on u.p ins fnl f: nt rch ldrs* **11/2**[1]
6031 **6** 3¼ **Mishrif (USA)**[15] 6051 5-8-12 **76**...............................(b) RichardHughes 4 73
(J R Jenkins) *in tch in midfield: hmpd bnd 4f out: rdn and effrt over 2f out: no imp over 1f out: wknd ins fnl f* **6/1**[2]
1600 **7** ¾ **Divine Call**[34] 5451 4-9-2 **83**..................................(t) AdamBeschizza[(3)] 11 78
(William Haggas) *s.i.s: bhd: hdwy into midfield 1/2-way: drvn and no prog jst over 2f out: wknd ent fnl f* **15/2**[3]
1625 **8** ½ **Midnight Feast**[43] 5171 3-8-12 **79**.................................... LukeMorris 1 72
(Peter Winkworth) *in tch: rdn and effrt on inner ent fnl 2f: no imp over 1f out: wknd ins fnl f* **6/1**[2]
6456 **9** ¾ **Nezami (IRE)**[15] 6056 6-8-7 **71** oh3.................................. DavidProbert 5 62
(John Akehurst) *led tl 2f out: wknd u.p over 1f out* **33/1**
5550 **10** ¾ **Tiradito (USA)**[10] 6220 4-8-12 **81**............................(v) MarkCoumbe[(5)] 8 70
(Michael Attwater) *bhd: rdn and effrt on inner ent 2f out: no imp u.p over 1f out* **20/1**
0410 **11** 9 **Colorado Gold**[12] 6167 3-8-10 **80**.................................... JohnFahy[(3)] 10 44
(Ed de Giles) *chsd ldrs: rdn and struggling over 2f out: wknd qckly u.p wl over 1f out* **33/1**

1m 24.92s (-1.08) **Going Correction** -0.025s/f (Stan)
WFA 3 from 4yo+ 3lb **11** Ran SP% **116.2**
Speed ratings (Par 105): **105,104,104,103,103 99,99,98,97,96 86**PL: Ree's Rascal £2.70 Regal Approve £2.00 EX: Celtic Sultan/RR £11.60 CS/RA £40.80 CSF; CS/RR £46.11, CS/RA £27.99 TRI: CD/RR/RA £274.56, CS/RA/RR £256.25. toteswingers:1&RR:£14.10, 1&RA £14.70, RA&RR:£6.10 CSF £27.99 CT £256.25 TOTE £17.50: £4.00; EX 40.80.

FOCUS
A tight finale with little between the runners for much of the straight at the end of a well-run race. The form looks sound enough with the placed horses rated to their marks.
T/Plt: £1,062.50 to a £1 stake. Pool of £61,018.48 - 41.92 winning tickets. T/Qpdt: £250.60 to a £1 stake. Pool of £5,995.92 - 17.70 winning tickets. SP

5561 WARWICK (L-H)
Thursday, September 29

OFFICIAL GOING: Good to firm
Wind: Nil Weather: Sunny

6479 CHRISTMAS SNOWBALL 17TH DECEMBER BOOK NOW H'CAP 6f
2:10 (2:10) (Class 6) (0-65,65) 3-Y-0+ **£1,940** (£577; £288; £144) **Stalls** Low

Form RPR
0000 **1** **Divertimenti (IRE)**[8] 6266 7-9-2 **60**.........................(b) RussKennemore 13 69
(Roy Bowring) *chsd ldrs: led ins fnl 2f: drvn out* **33/1**
0234 **2** ¾ **Flaxen Lake**[6] 6304 4-8-10 **54**.. LukeMorris 3 61
(Milton Bradley) *in rr: hdwy and rdn over 2f out: styd on to chse wnr fnl 120yds: no ex in clsng stages* **10/1**
0030 **3** ¾ **Flying Applause**[8] 6261 6-9-6 **64**...............................(bt) JimmyQuinn 12 69+
(Roy Bowring) *in rr: rdn and hdwy fr 2f out: styd on wl fnl f to take 3rd in clsng stages: nt rch ldrs* **25/1**
6525 **4** hd **Dancing Welcome**[21] 5843 5-8-8 **55**.............................(b) RyanClark[(3)] 9 59
(Milton Bradley) *hdwy 1/2-way and sn chsng ldrs: styd on to dispute 3rd fnl 120yds: one pce in clsng stages* **7/1**[1]
0305 **5** hd **Leadenhall Lass (IRE)**[20] 5890 5-9-4 **62**......................... IanMongan 10 65
(Pat Phelan) *chsd ldrs: rdn over 2f out: styd on fnl f but nvr gng pce to chal* **15/2**[2]
-600 **6** 1¼ **Mambo Spirit (IRE)**[14] 6090 7-9-5 **63**.............................. DaneO'Neill 2 62+
(Tony Newcombe) *slowly away: in rr: rdn over 2f out: hdwy appr fnl f: kpt on wl in clsng stages: nt rch ldrs* **16/1**
4220 **7** ¾ **Cadmium Loch**[12] 6179 3-9-2 **62**..............................(p) JamieSpencer 16 59
(Reg Hollinshead) *w ldr tl led over 3f out: hdd ins fnl 2f: wknd ins fnl f: eased whn hld* **8/1**[3]
0545 **8** hd **Brandywell Boy (IRE)**[8] 6257 8-9-0 **65**..................... HarryPoulton[(7)] 5 61
(Dominic Ffrench Davis) *in rr: hdwy and nt clr run wl over 1f out: r.o in clsng stages* **20/1**
2536 **9** ¾ **Steel City Boy (IRE)**[16] 6035 8-8-13 **57**.................... TomMcLaughlin 14 51
(Garry Woodward) *chsd ldrs: rdn over 2f out: wknd ins fnl f* **12/1**
6120 **10** nk **Full Shilling (IRE)**[27] 5677 3-8-6 **57**.................. MatthewLawson[(5)] 7 50+
(John Spearing) *in rr: hdwy whn hmpd over 1f out: styd on ins fnl f* **9/1**
2430 **11** nk **Hand Painted**[16] 6022 5-9-2 **63**......................................(p) JohnFahy[(3)] 17 55
(Anthony Middleton) *outpcd: hdwy and n.m.r on ins fr over 1f out: kpt on in clsng stages* **20/1**
4045 **12** hd **Danzoe (IRE)**[13] 6119 4-9-6 **64**.. SebSanders 15 55
(Christine Dunnett) *in rr: sme hdwy whn nt clr run appr fnl f: no ch after* **11/1**
2502 **13** 3½ **Adaeze (IRE)**[37] 5346 3-8-9 **55**.............................. RichardKingscote 11 35
(Jonathan Portman) *chsd ldrs over 4f* **16/1**
5300 **14** 3¾ **Watch Chain (IRE)**[26] 5736 4-9-3 **61**...........................(p) TomQueally 6 29
(Alan McCabe) *in tch and rdn over 2f out: no imp on ldrs and no ch fnl f* **20/1**
4110 **15** 9 **Crimson Queen**[38] 5326 4-9-6 **64**....................................... JamesDoyle 1 3
(Roy Brotherton) *chsd ldrs: rdn 2f out: wknd ins fnl f* **8/1**[3]
0-00 **16** 4 **Chris's Ridge**[19] 5924 4-9-6 **64**...................................... JimmyFortune 4 —
(Eric Alston) *slt ld tl hdd over 3f out: wknd qckly over 2f out* **25/1**

1m 12.44s (0.64) **Going Correction** +0.075s/f (Good)
WFA 3 from 4yo+ 2lb **16** Ran SP% **118.3**
Speed ratings (Par 101): **98,97,96,95,95 93,92,92,91,91 90,90,85,80,68 63**
toteswingers:1&2:£45.50, 2&3:£48.10, 1&3:£167.40 CSF £300.54 CT £8507.23 TOTE £36.30: £6.30, £1.80, £6.60, £1.80; EX 366.40 TRIFECTA Not won..
Owner K Nicholls **Bred** Airlie Stud **Trained** Edwinstowe, Notts

FOCUS
A dry night and more unseasonably hot weather saw the ground quicken up to good to firm, good in places. Jockeys reported the ground was "good" and "on the fast side of good". A modest but open handicap in which the gallop was sound. The field raced centre-to-stands' side in the straight. The runner-up to his recent best is the guide to the form.
Divertimenti(IRE) Official explanation: trainer said, regarding apparent improvement in form, that the gelding broke well and was able to dominate.
Mambo Spirit(IRE) Official explanation: jockey said gelding missed the break
Full Shilling(IRE) Official explanation: jockey said filly missed the break and was denied a clear run
Adaeze(IRE) Official explanation: jockey said filly was unsuited by the good to firm (good in places) ground
Crimson Queen Official explanation: trainer had no explanation for ther poor form shown

6480 E B F "ALFLORA" MAIDEN FILLIES' STKS 7f 26y
2:40 (2:43) (Class 5) 2-Y-0 **£3,476** (£1,026; £513) **Stalls** Low

Form RPR
66 **1** **Pretty Pebble (IRE)**[16] 6030 2-9-0 0................................ MartinDwyer 5 72
(Brian Meehan) *mde virtually all but a clly attended by runner-up: strly chal fr over 1f tl asserted in clsng stages* **9/2**[1]
2 shd **Mirror Ball** 2-9-0 0.. JimmyFortune 6 72+
(Peter Chapple-Hyam) *pressed wnr thrght: rdn and str chal fnl f: no ex in clsng stages* **15/2**[3]
3 2½ **Frosty Secret** 2-9-0 0.. LukeMorris 1 66+
(Jane Chapple-Hyam) *chsd ldrs: rdn and green 1/2-way and outpcd ins fnl 3f: stl green but styd on to take 3rd ins fnl f: no imp on ldng duo* **25/1**
0 **4** 2¼ **Altona (IRE)**[12] 6160 2-9-0 0....................................... MatthewDavies 14 60+
(Mick Channon) *slowly away: sn bhd and outpcd: rdn and green 3f out: stl green but kpt on wl thrght fnl f: nvr gng pce to rch ldrs* **6/1**[2]
0 **5** ¾ **Cincinnati Kit**[22] 5834 2-9-0 0.......................................(t) NeilCallan 10 58
(Stuart Williams) *chsd ldrs: rdn over 2f out: wknd ins fnl f* **20/1**
4336 **6** ½ **Kyllasie**[35] 5409 2-9-0 67.. SteveDrowne 11 57
(Richard Hannon) *chsd ldrs early: rdn and outpcd over 3f out: mod prog ins fnl f* **15/2**[3]
7 3 **Kylin** 2-9-0 0... DaneO'Neill 3 50
(Richard Hannon) *chsd ldrs: rdn along 3f out: wknd fr 2f out* **9/2**[1]
8 3½ **Chambles** 2-9-0 0.. SilvestreDeSousa 13 41
(Andrew Reid) *in tch early: bhd fnl 3f* **20/1**
04 **9** 1½ **Al Doha**[33] 5486 2-9-0 .... PhillipMakin 7 37
(Kevin Ryan) *chsd ldrs and rdn 3f out: wknd qckly over 2f out* **12/1**
10 24 **Ladram Bay (IRE)** 2-9-0 0.. RichardKingscote 12 —
(Jonathan Portman) *slowly away: a struggling in rr* **66/1**

1m 27.32s (2.72) **Going Correction** +0.075s/f (Good) **10** Ran SP% **96.7**
Speed ratings (Par 92): **91,90,88,85,84 84,80,76,74,47**
toteswingers:1&2:£5.30, 2&3:£17.50, 1&3:£16.20 CSF £25.00 TOTE £4.40: £1.40, £2.20, £5.70; EX 24.20 Trifecta £190.30 Part won. Pool: £257.22 - 0.43 winning units..
Owner Bayardo **Bred** J Hanly, Advancing B/Stock & T Cahallan **Trained** Manton, Wilts

The Form Book, Raceform Ltd, Compton, RG20 6NL

FOCUS
Little strength in depth to this ordinary fillies' maiden. The gallop was an ordinary one and the first two pulled clear in the closing stages. The field again made for the stands' side in the straight.

NOTEBOOK
Pretty Pebble(IRE) had shown ability at a modest level on her two previous starts and turned in an improved effort after being allowed a fairly easy lead. She should stay 1m and may do better still in ordinary nursery company. (tchd 4-1)

Mirror Ball, a 15,000GBP half-sister to a juvenile sprint winner, was relatively easy in the market but showed form bordering on fair on this racecourse debut. This wasn't much of a race and she was well placed given the way things unfolded but she is capable of picking up a small race with this behind her. (op 11-1)

Frosty Secret, who is out of a 1m2f winner, was green in the preliminaries and in the race itself but she showed ability at a modest level. She'll be at least as good over 1m and is open to improvement. (op 20-1 tchd 18-1)

Altona(IRE) wasn't disgraced after a tardy start but the best of her is unlikely to be seen until she steps into handicaps. (op 8-1)

Cincinnati Kit, fitted with a tongue-tie, offered more than on her debut which was on Polytrack. She is another that will be seen to best effect in handicaps when the market speaks in her favour. (tchd 22-1)

Kyllasie wasn't at her best returned to turf and she's going to remain vulnerable in this grade. (op 7-1 tchd 8-1)

Kylin has winners in her pedigree and ran well, despite her inexperience, for a long way. (tchd 5-1)

Ladram Bay(IRE) Official explanation: jockey said filly plunged leaving stalls

6481 E B F "BLACK SAM BELLAMY" MAIDEN STKS (DIV I) 7f 26y
3:10 (3:13) (Class 5) 2-Y-O **£2,911** (£866; £432; £216) **Stalls** Low

Form RPR

63 **1** **Asifa (IRE)**[16] 6018 2-9-0 0 ....(p) JimmyFortune 1 75
(Saeed Bin Suroor) *mde virtually all: rdn and jnd 2f out: asserted u.p ins fnl f: in command in clsng stages* **5/2**[2]

2 *1 ½* **Intuition** 2-9-0 0 .... DaneO'Neill 8 71+
(Richard Hannon) *chsd ldrs: rdn to chse wnr ins fnl f and edgd rt: kpt on but nt gng pce of wnr in clsng stages* **14/1**

3 *½* **Isthmus** 2-9-0 0 .... TomQueally 10 70+
(Amanda Perrett) *towards rr but in tch: drvn and hdwy over 1f out: styd on to take 3rd in clsng stages: no imp on wnr* **9/1**[3]

4 *½* **Qannaas (USA)** 2-9-0 0 .... RichardHills 6 69+
(Charles Hills) *s.i.s: t.k.h in rr: hdwy over 1f out: styd on ins fnl f to briefly take 3rd: no imp on wnr and outpcd into 4th in clsng stages* **7/4**[1]

0 **5** *shd* **Spanish Fork (IRE)**[12] 6165 2-9-0 0 .... MatthewDavies 9 69+
(Mick Channon) *chsd ldrs: rdn over 3f out: styng on whn n.m.r ins fnl f: one pce in clsng stages* **9/1**[3]

0 **6** *2 ¾* **Happy Sun Percy**[13] 6110 2-9-0 0 .... NeilCallan 7 62
(Jo Hughes) *t.k.h: pressed wnr: rdn and upsides fr 2f out tl 1f out: wknd ins fnl f* **28/1**

7 *3 ¼* **Grain Of Sand** 2-9-0 0 .... LiamKeniry 3 54+
(Andrew Balding) *in tch: pushed along and bhd fnl 3f* **18/1**

0 **8** *7* **Teacher (IRE)**[12] 6160 2-9-0 0 .... MichaelHills 2 36+
(William Haggas) *s.i.s: a outpcd* **11/1**

9 *5* **Frederickthegreat** 2-9-0 0 ....(t) SteveDrowne 4 24
(Hughie Morrison) *s.i.s: a outpcd* **25/1**

1m 27.47s (2.87) **Going Correction** +0.075s/f (Good) **9** Ran SP% **112.5**
Speed ratings (Par 95): **86,84,83,83,83 79,76,68,62**
toteswingers:1&2:£4.70, 2&3:£11.80, 1&3:£5.40 CSF £35.96 TOTE £3.90: £1.10, £3.20, £2.90; EX 17.10 Trifecta £79.70 Pool: £959.26 - 8.90 winning units..
Owner Godolphin **Bred** Tullpark Ltd **Trained** Newmarket, Suffolk

FOCUS
An interesting maiden on paper featuring a handful of well-bred newcomers but the gallop was an ordinary one and this bare form looks no better than fair. The field again came to the stands' side in the straight.

NOTEBOOK
Asifa(IRE) had the run of the race in the first-time cheekpieces and, after settling better than the majority of his (less experienced) rivals, turned in his best effort to get off the mark at the third attempt. Things were in his favour and he wouldn't be an obvious one to follow up. (op 9-4 tchd 3-1)

Intuition, who cost 70,000GBP and who is out of a Listed-placed 6f winner, was easy in the market but showed more than enough against a more experienced winner on this racecourse debut to suggest a similar event can be found. (op 12-1)

Isthmus has several winners in his pedigree and showed ability at an ordinary level on this racecourse debut. He should stay 1m and is entitled to improve for this experience. (op 10-1 tchd 11-1)

Qannaas(USA) ◆ attracted plenty of support but was found out by his inexperience (missed break and pulled too hard) on this racecourse debut. Nevertheless, he showed ability without being knocked about and is well worth another chance. (op 2-1 tchd 9-4)

Spanish Fork(IRE) failed to build on the form of his debut but he may do better granted a stiffer overall test of stamina once qualified for a handicap mark. (op 17-2 tchd 8-1)

Happy Sun Percy stepped up on the form shown on his debut and will be seen to best effect once qualified for a handicap mark. He may do better in due course. (tchd 33-1)

Grain Of Sand, a half-brother to a smart 1m winner in Chile, looked in need of this experience and should improve. (op 16-1)

6482 WARWICK (S) STKS 1m 6f 213y
3:40 (3:40) (Class 5) 3-Y-O **£2,385** (£704; £352) **Stalls** Low

Form RPR

3300 **1** **Imperial Fong**[13] 6122 3-8-9 49 .... RyanClark(3) 1 54
(Chris Dwyer) *in rr: rdn and hdwy fr 6f out: styd on to chse 6 l ldr ins fnl 3f: kpt on u.p to cl appr fnl f: led fnl 75yds: all out* **18/1**

0330 **2** *½* **Reillys Daughter**[24] 5784 3-8-12 62 .... LukeMorris 6 53+
(J S Moore) *chsd ldrs: wnt 2nd over 5f out: led 4f out: drvn 6 l clr ins fnl 3f: rdn over 2f out: wknd appr fnl f: hdd and no ex fnl 75yds* **9/4**[2]

3050 **3** *19* **Pizzetti (IRE)**[29] 5628 3-9-3 53 ....(b[1]) SebSanders 2 36
(Sir Mark Prescott Bt) *reminder fr stalls: led 11f out: rdn 5f out: hdd 4f out: sn wknd: lost 2nd ins fnl 3f* **15/2**

0634 **4** *16* **Hawridge Knight**[28] 4491 3-9-3 49 ....(t) JamesMillman 3 16
(Rod Millman) *in tch tl rdn 7f out: sn lost tch* **9/2**[3]

5444 **5** *79* **Green Future (USA)**[14] 6087 3-9-3 57 ....(b) NeilCallan 5 —
(Amanda Perrett) *sn led: hdd 11f out: wknd qckly 5f out* **6/4**[1]

3m 22.69s (3.69) **Going Correction** +0.075s/f (Good) **5** Ran SP% **106.0**
Speed ratings (Par 101): **93,92,82,74,31**
CSF £53.76 TOTE £7.70: £1.90, £1.80; EX 61.30.There was no bid for the winner.
Owner Mrs Shelley Dwyer **Bred** Newsells Park Stud **Trained** Burrough Green, Cambs
■ Stewards' Enquiry : Ryan Clark six-day ban: used whip with excessive frequency (Oct 13-18)

FOCUS
A low-grade seller run at at fair gallop and one that didn't take as much winning as seemed likely with the market leader disappointing. The field again raced towards the stands' side in the straight and the winner is rated to her best, although the form is shaky.

6483 E B F "BLACK SAM BELLAMY" MAIDEN STKS (DIV II) 7f 26y
4:10 (4:11) (Class 5) 2-Y-O **£2,911** (£866; £432; £216) **Stalls** Low

Form RPR

5 **1** **Famous Poet (IRE)**[21] 5855 2-9-0 0 .... RichardHills 8 78+
(Saeed Bin Suroor) *disp 2nd tl chsd ldr appr fnl 2f: led wl over 1f out: pushed clr ins fnl f: easily* **9/4**[1]

2 *2 ¾* **Born To Surprise** 2-9-0 0 .... JamieSpencer 4 71+
(Michael Bell) *s.i.s: in rr: hdwy over 2f out: styd on to chse wnr ins fnl f: kpt on but no ch w wnr* **7/2**[2]

3 *2 ½* **Whipcrackaway (IRE)** 2-8-9 0 .... DavidKenny(5) 10 65+
(Peter Hedger) *slowly away: in rr: stl bhd whn pushed along and hdwy over 1f out: styd on wl to take 3rd in clsng stages* **50/1**

4 **4** *1 ½* **Light Burst (USA)**[133] 2221 2-9-0 0 .... AhmedAjtebi 2 61
(Mahmood Al Zarooni) *t.k.h: disp 2nd tl 2f out: sn rdn: green over 1f out: sn btn* **7/2**[2]

0 **5** *1* **Aleksandar**[23] 5801 2-9-0 0 .... NeilCallan 3 61+
(Luca Cumani) *in tch: pushed along over 2f out: styng on same pce whn pushed rt 1f out* **17/2**

00 **6** *1* **Bountiful Catch**[31] 5565 2-9-0 0 .... JimmyQuinn 7 56
(Pam Sly) *led: rdn 3f out: hdd wl over 1f out: btn whn edgd rt ins fnl f* **80/1**

00 **7** *2 ½* **Never Satisfied**[31] 5564 2-9-0 0 .... MichaelHills 5 50
(Charles Hills) *pushed along over 2f out: outpcd most of way* **4/1**[3]

0 **8** *4* **Red Shimmer (IRE)**[14] 6075 2-9-0 0 .... SilvestreDeSousa 6 40
(Jo Hughes) *chsd ldrs 4f* **33/1**

1m 26.38s (1.78) **Going Correction** +0.075s/f (Good) **8** Ran SP% **111.9**
Speed ratings (Par 95): **92,88,86,84,83 82,79,74**
toteswingers:1&2:£2.50, 2&3:£12.30, 1&3:£10.60 CSF £9.82 TOTE £3.60: £1.90, £1.60, £5.20; EX 11.60 Trifecta £96.20 Pool: £971.32 - 7.47 winning units..
Owner Godolphin **Bred** Hadi Al Tajir **Trained** Newmarket, Suffolk

FOCUS
Not the most competitive of maidens and just modest form behind the first two. The gallop was a moderate one and the field again came centre-to-stands' side in the straight.

NOTEBOOK
Famous Poet(IRE), tackling much quicker ground, duly stepped up on his encouraging debut effort to take an uncompetitive event in decisive fashion. He now has the option of handicaps and may do better but it'll be a surprise if he confirms placings with the runner-up should the pair meet again. (op 15-8)

Born To Surprise ◆ was easy to back and shaped with plenty of promise without being knocked about on this racecourse debut. This 50,000gns yearling and half-brother to very useful pair Sand Skier and Star Surprise has plenty of size and scope, should have no problems with 1m and is sure to pick up a similar event at least. (op 3-1 tchd 9-2)

Whipcrackaway(IRE), a half-brother to a winning hurdler, was easy to back for a yard not noted for debut winners in this grade but he showed clear signs of ability at an ordinary level. He'll be suited by a step up to 1m but the best of him may not be seen until he goes into handicaps. (op 33-1)

Light Burst(USA), who showed ability despite his greenness on his debut in May, attracted support but was too keen to do himself justice on this first run since. However, he should be better for this run and will be worth another chance as he learns to settle. (tchd 3-1 and 4-1)

Aleksandar bettered his debut form after being nibbled at in the market and is the type to fare better, but he's another whose medium-term future lies in ordinary handicap company over a bit further. (op 9-1 tchd 8-1)

6484 IAN BELL TESTIMONIAL NURSERY 7f 26y
4:40 (4:41) (Class 5) (0-75,77) 2-Y-O **£2,587** (£770; £384; £192) **Stalls** Low

Form RPR

561 **1** **Amadeus Wolfe Tone (IRE)**[21] 5841 2-9-4 72 .... NeilCallan 6 79
(Jamie Osborne) *trckd ldrs: wnt 2nd ins fnl 3f: led 2f out: sn drvn: styd on strly fnl 120yds* **7/2**[1]

0431 **2** *¾* **Venetian View (IRE)**[10] 6214 2-9-9 77 6ex .... GeorgeBaker 13 82+
(Gary Moore) *in tch early: drvn and outpcd over 2f out: styd on over 1f out and fin strly to take 2nd fnl 50yds: no imp on wnr* **7/1**[3]

3432 **3** *3* **Khazium (IRE)**[27] 5690 2-9-2 70 .... AdamKirby 7 68
(Pat Eddery) *in tch: rdn along 4f out: hdwy to chse ldrs 2f out: chsd wnr appr fnl f but no imp: wknd and lost 2nd fnl 50yds* **7/1**[3]

0416 **4** *1 ¾* **Dishy Guru**[19] 5913 2-9-7 75 .... DaneO'Neill 10 69
(Michael Blanshard) *chsd ldrs: rdn to disp 2nd over 1f out but no imp on wnr: wknd fnl 150yds* **33/1**

2556 **5** *1* **Brimstone Hill (IRE)**[40] 5280 2-8-13 72 .... MatthewLawson(5) 8 63
(Charles Hills) *chsd ldrs tl led over 4f out: hdd 2f out: wknd ins fnl f* **16/1**

2045 **6** *1 ½* **Correct**[19] 5945 2-8-9 68 .... DarylByrne(5) 3 55
(Michael Bell) *chsd ldrs: rdn 2f out: wknd over 1f out* **28/1**

10 **7** *¾* **Brickfielder (IRE)**[26] 5708 2-9-3 71 .... SteveDrowne 2 57
(Roger Charlton) *chsd ldrs: rdn over 2f out: sn btn* **13/2**[2]

045 **8** *hd* **Abshir Zain (IRE)**[20] 5886 2-9-2 70 ....(bt[1]) TomQueally 1 55
(Clive Brittain) *sn pushed along in rr: styd on fr 2f out: nvr gng pce to rch ldrs* **33/1**

2U15 **9** *1 ½* **Uncle Roger (IRE)**[19] 5913 2-9-6 74 .... CathyGannon 12 55
(Eve Johnson Houghton) *rdn over 3f out and in rr: mod prog ins fnl f* **28/1**

3605 **10** *nse* **Ivor's Princess**[30] 5577 2-9-2 70 .... TomMcLaughlin 14 51
(Rod Millman) *s.i.s: in rr and sn drvn along: mod prog ins fnl f* **40/1**

01 **11** *10* **Wyndham Wave**[37] 5337 2-9-2 70 .... JamesMillman 5 27
(Rod Millman) *in tch tl wknd 3f out* **7/2**[1]

2300 **12** *8* **Wolf Spirit (IRE)**[27] 5690 2-9-2 70 ....(b[1]) PhillipMakin 4 7
(Kevin Ryan) *sn led: hdd over 4f out: wknd fr 3f out* **33/1**

0430 **13** *4* **Gold Coin**[16] 6021 2-9-2 70 .... SebSanders 9 —
(J W Hills) *sn bhd* **25/1**

1m 25.79s (1.19) **Going Correction** +0.075s/f (Good) **13** Ran SP% **110.7**
Speed ratings (Par 95): **96,95,91,89,88 86,86,85,84,84 72,63,58**
toteswingers:1&2:£4.10, 2&3:£8.40, 1&3:£6.60 CSF £22.38 CT £144.22 TOTE £4.50: £2.00, £2.20, £1.60; EX 26.50 Trifecta £97.00 Pool: £477.27 - 3.64 winning units..
Owner Dr Brendan McDonald & John Duddy **Bred** Brian Williamson **Trained** Upper Lambourn, Berks

FOCUS
A fair nursery featuring several unexposed sorts. The gallop was a reasonable one and the winner grabbed the stands' rail early in the straight.

NOTEBOOK
Amadeus Wolfe Tone(IRE) is a progressive sort who turned in his best effort back on a sound surface, despite racing with the choke out in the first half of the race. There may well be a bit more to come and he should continue to give a good account. (op 3-1)

Venetian View(IRE) didn't get the run of the race to the same degree as the winner but he ran well under his penalty from his wide draw returned to turf. He fared best of those to come from off the pace, finished a few lengths clear of the rest and appeals as the type to win again. (op 15-2 tchd 13-2)
Khazium(IRE) has yet to win but he's a consistent sort who ran creditably against a couple of progressive sorts returned to turf and to this longer trip. There will be easier opportunities than this one. (op 17-2)
Dishy Guru looks on a stiffish mark but he bettered the form of his nursery debut back on a sound surface, at the same time leaving the impression that he wouldn't be inconvenienced by the return to 6f. (op 40-1)
Brimstone Hill(IRE) had the run of the race and wasn't disgraced returned to a sound surface after his short break but he's going to have to raise his game to win a similar event from this sort of mark.
Brickfielder(IRE) was again below the form of his easy ground 7f debut win but is probably worth another chance at some point. (op 15-2)
Wyndham Wave's Leicester win had been franked by the runner-up earlier in the week and he is probably worth another chance. (op 9-2 tchd 10-3)

6485 IGNITE INCENTIVES H'CAP — 1m 6f 213y
5:10 (5:10) (Class 4) (0-85,85) 3-Y-0+ — **£5,498** (£1,636; £817; £408) **Stalls** Low

Form — RPR

4220 **1** **Seaside Sizzler**[42] 5221 4-10-0 **85**......(bt) StevieDonohoe 11 — 94
(Ralph Beckett) *in tch whn rdn 1/2-way: drvn and hdwy over 2f out: styd on u.p to take slt ld 1f out: sn jnd and hrd pressed thrght fnl f: won on the nod* **8/1**

5060 **2** *nse* **Halifax (IRE)**[40] 5283 3-9-3 **85**...... SilvestreDeSousa 8 — 94+
(Mark Johnston) *hld up in rr: gd hdwy over 2f out and styd on to chal 1f out: upsides u.p thrght fnl f: btn on the nod* **3/1**[1]

322 **3** *4* **Wild Desert (FR)**[74] 3095 6-9-8 **79**...... CathyGannon 5 — 83
(Charlie Longsdon) *chsd ldrs: wnt 2nd 3f out: drvn to chal appr 1f out: outpcd by ldng duo ins fnl f* **7/1**[3]

0033 **4** *1* **Ethics Girl (IRE)**[12] 6155 5-9-7 **78**......(t) TomQueally 4 — 84+
(John Berry) *in rr tl hdwy fr 3f out: chsd ldrs u.p appr fnl f whn nt clr run: kpt on same pce* **12/1**

111 **5** *1* **Final Liberation (FR)**[35] 5417 3-8-13 **81**...... SebSanders 10 — 82
(Sir Mark Prescott Bt) *led after 2f: hrd drvn fr 3f out and kpt narrow ld tl hdd 1f out: sn btn* **9/2**[2]

0602 **6** *1 ¾* **High On A Hill (IRE)**[47] 5050 4-9-6 **77**...... DaneO'Neill 3 — 76
(Sylvester Kirk) *chsd ldrs: rdn over 2f out: drvn to chal and hung rt over 1f out: wknd ins fnl f* **10/1**

0452 **7** *7* **Double Handful (GER)**[14] 6104 5-9-0 **71** ow1...... AdamKirby 2 — 61
(Venetia Williams) *chsd ldrs: rdn and effrt over 2f out: wknd fnl 2f* **16/1**

3100 **8** *3* **Mister Angry (IRE)**[25] 5759 4-9-11 **82**...... PhillipMakin 6 — 68
(Mark Johnston) *rdn over 4f out: a towards rr* **20/1**

15/6 **9** *1* **Mobaasher (USA)**[18] 5966 8-9-9 **80**...... JamesMillman 9 — 65
(Rod Millman) *rdn 6f out: a towards rr* **12/1**

4034 **10** *2 ½* **Rajeh (IRE)**[51] 4890 8-9-12 **83**...... LiamJones 1 — 64
(John Spearing) *led 2f: styd chsng ldr to 3f out: wknd qckly* **15/2**

3m 18.24s (-0.76) **Going Correction** +0.075s/f (Good)
WFA 3 from 4yo+ 11lb — **10** Ran SP% **113.7**
Speed ratings (Par 105): **105,104,102,102,101 100,97,95,94,93**
toteswingers:1&2:£6.20, 2&3:£4.90, 1&3:£8.60 CSF £31.37 CT £177.20 TOTE £7.60: £2.30, £1.40, £2.50; EX 42.20 Trifecta £211.00 Pool: £621.62 - 2.18 winning units..
Owner I J Heseltine **Bred** Redmyre Bloodstock And S Hillen **Trained** Kimpton, Hants
■ Stewards' Enquiry : Dane O'Neill two-day ban: careless riding (Oct 13-14)

FOCUS
A useful handicap in which a reasonable gallop suited those coming from off the pace. As had been the trend, the field came centre-to-stands' side in the straight. The third is the best guide to the form, backed up by the runner-up.

6486 LEAMINGTON AMATEUR RIDERS' H'CAP — 1m 2f 188y
5:45 (5:45) (Class 6) (0-60,59) 3-Y-0+ — **£1,646** (£506; £253) **Stalls** Low

Form — RPR

0030 **1** **Taste The Wine (IRE)**[30] 5588 5-10-7 **57**...... MrRJWilliams(5) 17 — 68
(Bernard Llewellyn) *chsd ldrs: rdn to ld ins fnl 2f: drvn out ins fnl f* **20/1**

6005 **2** *3 ¾* **Sail Home**[30] 5588 4-11-0 **59**...... MrRBirkett 14 — 64
(Julia Feilden) *in tch: hdwy 3f out: styd on appr fnl f to chse wnr fnl 150yds but no ch* **10/1**

0010 **3** *2 ¼* **Fair Breeze**[19] 5912 4-10-0 **50**...... MrJSherwood(5) 15 — 51
(Richard Phillips) *t.k.h: chsd ldrs: styd on to chse wnr over 1f out but no imp: wknd into 3rd fnl 150yds* **20/1**

050 **4** *¾* **Visions Of Johanna (USA)**[12] 6157 6-10-9 **54**.....(p) MissSBrotherton 7 — 54
(Richard Guest) *chsd ldrs: rdn along 3f out: styd on same pce fr over 1f out* **9/1**

050 **5** *2* **Lunar River (FR)**[5] 6357 8-10-3 **51**......(t) MrCMartin(3) 5 — 47
(David Pinder) *in rr: hdwy on outside over 3f out: styd on fnl 2f: nt gng pce to rch ldrs* **20/1**

466 **6** *2* **Supa Seeker (USA)**[13] 6135 5-10-8 **58**...... MrCCarroll(5) 11 — 51
(Tony Carroll) *led: rdn 3f out: hdd fnl 2f: wknd over 1f out* **10/1**

0501 **7** *nk* **Harare**[9] 6236 10-10-2 **52** 6ex......(v) MissGTutty(5) 6 — 44
(Karen Tutty) *chsd ldrs: rdn over 3f out: wknd fnl 2f* **7/1**[2]

0302 **8** *1* **General Tufto**[9] 6236 6-10-10 **55**......(b) MissEJJones 3 — 46
(Charles Smith) *in tch: drvn along and hdwy on ins fr 3f out: sn rdn and nvr gng pce to rch ldrs* **16/1**

3523 **9** *7* **Ermyntrude**[30] 5582 4-10-7 **57**...... MrFMitchell(5) 2 — 36
(Pat Phelan) *in tch: rdn and outpcd 5f out: rdn and sme hdwy 3f out: nvr rchd ldrs and no imp: wknd 2f out* **5/1**[1]

3503 **10** *hd* **Wrecking Crew (IRE)**[30] 5609 7-10-7 **57**...... MrsDBamonte(5) 4 — 35
(Rod Millman) *a towards rr* **9/1**

32/5 **11** *1 ¼* **Bring It On Home**[42] 5209 7-10-3 **55**......(b) MissSKerswell(7) 9 — 31
(Sophie Leech) *nvr bttr tha mid-div* **50/1**

-460 **12** *1* **Alqaahir (USA)**[22] 5836 9-10-3 **53**......(p) MissMBryant(5) 8 — 27
(Paddy Butler) *in tch: hdwy 4f out: chsd ldrs fnl 3f: wknd fr 2f out* **80/1**

230- **13** *1 ¾* **Honoured (IRE)**[31] 6747 4-10-3 **55**...... MissCHenderson(7) 12 — 26
(Nicky Henderson) *sn chsng ldrs: wknd qckly fnl 3f* **7/1**[2]

0-66 **14** *7* **Poor Prince**[42] 2922 4-10-13 **58**......(t) MrSWalker 13 — 18
(Chris Gordon) *chsd ldrs 7f out* **40/1**

4225 **U** **Into The Wind**[24] 5785 4-10-6 **56**...... MrPMillman(5) 10 — —
(Rod Millman) *in rr whn clipped heels: stmbld and uns rdr over 7f out* **15/2**[3]

2m 23.03s (1.93) **Going Correction** +0.075s/f (Good) — **15** Ran SP% **117.4**
Speed ratings (Par 101): **95,92,90,90,88 87,86,86,81,81 80,79,78,73,—**
toteswingers:1&2:£44.40, 2&3:£28.80, 1&3:£44.40. Totesuper 7: Win: Not won. Place: Not won. CSF £190.63 CT £4023.55 TOTE £20.90: £4.40, £2.90, £6.40; EX 209.70 TRIFECTA Not won..
Owner Alan J Williams **Bred** Trevor Reilly **Trained** Fochriw, Caerphilly

FOCUS
A moderate handicap in which a few of the market leaders disappointed. The gallop was a reasonable one and the field came down the centre in the straight. The winner is rated to last year's form while the third ran close to her previous C&D mark.
T/Jkpt: Not won. T/Plt: £252.40 to a £1 stake. Pool of £55,178.65 - 159.57 winning tickets. T/Qpdt: £13.70 to a £1 stake. Pool of £3,734.85 - 201.41 winning tickets. ST

6351 WOLVERHAMPTON (A.W) (L-H)
Thursday, September 29

OFFICIAL GOING: Standard
Wind: Light behind Weather: Fine and sunny

6487 WOLVERHAMPTON-RACECOURSE.CO.UK NURSERY (DIV I) — 7f 32y(P)
2:00 (2:00) (Class 6) (0-65,70) 2-Y-0 — **£1,704** (£503; £251) **Stalls** High

Form — RPR

056 **1** **Amoure Medici**[60] 4571 2-9-6 **64**...... MartinLane 5 — 73+
(Noel Quinlan) *s.i.s: hld up: hdwy over 2f out: nt clr run and swtchd lft over 1f out: rdn to ld ins fnl f: r.o wl* **7/2**[1]

5653 **2** *3 ½* **Galilee Chapel (IRE)**[16] 6021 2-9-5 **63**...... NickyMackay 1 — 62
(David Elsworth) *chsd ldrs: rdn over 2f out: styd on same pce ins fnl f* **6/1**[3]

4604 **3** *1 ½* **Lady Victory (IRE)**[23] 5809 2-9-7 **65**......(v) SamHitchcott 9 — 61
(Mick Channon) *mid-div: hdwy over 2f out: rdn to ld over 1f out: sn hung lft: hdd and no ex ins fnl f* **28/1**

0001 **4** *nk* **Adranian (IRE)**[7] 6280 2-9-7 **70** 6ex......(v) MatthewCosham(5) 4 — 65
(David Evans) *a.p: rdn over 1f out: nt clr run and swtchd lft ins fnl f: one pce* **11/1**

0264 **5** *¾* **Vociferous (USA)**[18] 5967 2-9-2 **60**...... JoeFanning 3 — 53
(Mark Johnston) *led: rdn and hdd over 1f out: no ex ins fnl f* **11/2**[2]

0406 **6** *hd* **Cheviot Quest (IRE)**[14] 6102 2-9-3 **61**...... TedDurcan 11 — 54
(William Jarvis) *s.i.s: hld up: rdn over 1f out: r.o wl ins fnl f: nvr nrr* **12/1**

050 **7** *1 ¾* **Allegri (IRE)**[15] 6048 2-9-5 **63**...... DavidNolan 6 — 52
(Ann Duffield) *chsd ldr: rdn and ev ch over 1f out: hmpd and wknd ins fnl f* **22/1**

400 **8** *1 ¼* **Rapid Heat Lad (IRE)**[27] 5681 2-9-2 **63**...... PaulPickard(3) 2 — 48
(Reg Hollinshead) *mid-div: rdn over 2f out: nvr on terms* **15/2**

606 **9** *1* **Camrock Star (IRE)**[27] 5690 2-8-12 **59**...... HarryBentley(3) 8 — 42
(William Knight) *chsd ldrs: rdn over 2f out: wknd over 1f out* **14/1**

0001 **10** *5* **Inniscastle Boy**[17] 6001 2-9-5 **63**...... PaulHanagan 10 — 34
(William Muir) *hld up: rdn 1/2-way: sn lost tch* **6/1**[3]

0502 **11** *7* **No More Games**[15] 6043 2-8-11 **58**......(p) AmyRyan(3) 7 — 11
(Kevin Ryan) *prom: rdn over 2f out: sn wknd* **16/1**

1m 30.31s (0.71) **Going Correction** 0.0s/f (Stan) — **11** Ran SP% **114.3**
Speed ratings (Par 93): **95,91,89,88,88 87,85,84,83,77 69**
toteswingers:1&2:£5.30, 2&3:£30.90, 1&3:£23.70 CSF £23.06 CT £509.02 TOTE £3.70: £3.90, £2.00, £5.50; EX 29.10.
Owner Mrs D Jeromson **Bred** Breeding Capital Plc **Trained** Newmarket, Suffolk
■ Stewards' Enquiry : Sam Hitchcott two-day ban: careless riding (Oct 13-14)

FOCUS
A modest nursery and the pace was strong enough to set this up for a closer.

NOTEBOOK
Amoure Medici had shown gradual improvement in turf maidens and continued to go the right way on this switch to nursery company after a two-month break, helped by a ground-saving run into the straight. He was described beforehand by his trainer as "temperamental" but clearly he's capable of fair form when getting a good trip. Official explanation: trainer said, regarding apparent improvement in form, that it had been gelded since its last run and benefited from the drop in class. (op 9-2 tchd 5-1)
Galilee Chapel(IRE), on his second start for this yard, was up in trip and trying Polytrack for the first time, but he still came off the bridle before the straight and lacked the end-race speed of the winner. Some headgear might sharpen him up. (op 9-2)
Lady Victory(IRE), making her Polytrack debut, had a wide trip, notably into the straight, but kept on. She's been given a chance by the handicapper and her performance wants upgrading slightly.
Adranian(IRE) was 2lb wrong under the penalty picked up for his recent C&D claiming success and he wasn't good enough. (op 9-1)
Vociferous(USA) was able to dominate but never convinced. Now 0-7, she offered little. (op 9-2)
Cheviot Quest(IRE) is by Sir Percy out of a 1m4f-winning daughter of Montjeu. He was keeping on having lacked the pace and is in need of a lot further.
Inniscastle Boy, up 3lb for winning over this trip on Kempton's Polytrack, ran poorly. Maybe he needs to go right-handed. Official explanation: trainer had no explanation for the poor form shown (op 11-2 tchd 13-2)

6488 WIN A CAR EVERY DAY - WILLIAMHILLBINGO H'CAP — 7f 32y(P)
2:30 (2:30) (Class 6) (0-60,60) 3-Y-0+ — **£1,704** (£503; £251) **Stalls** High

Form — RPR

3405 **1** **Pytheas (USA)**[15] 6071 4-8-9 **55**......(p) MarkCoumbe(5) 3 — 64
(Michael Attwater) *chsd ldrs: led wl over 2f out: rdn clr over 1f out: styd on* **12/1**

2254 **2** *1 ½* **Annes Rocket (IRE)**[15] 6051 6-9-2 **60**......(p) KieranO'Neill(3) 12 — 65+
(Jimmy Fox) *s.i.s: hld up: hdwy and nt clr run over 1f out: r.o: nt rch wnr* **9/2**[2]

0-60 **3** *nk* **Know No Fear**[9] 6238 6-9-4 **59**......(p) PaulHanagan 1 — 63
(Alastair Lidderdale) *a.p: rdn over 2f out: styd on* **14/1**

050 **4** *3 ¾* **July Days (IRE)**[26] 5740 5-9-1 **56**...... FrederikTylicki 2 — 50
(Brian Baugh) *prom: nt clr run and lost pl over 2f out: hdwy over 1f out: rdn and no ex ins fnl f* **14/1**

1301 **5** *nk* **Diamond Run**[15] 6071 3-9-2 **60**...... StevieDonohoe 11 — 53
(J W Hills) *chsd ldrs: led over 5f out: hdd wl over 2f out: no ex ins fnl f* **7/2**[1]

1050 **6** *¾* **Drive Home (USA)**[19] 5924 4-9-4 **59**......(p) DuranFentiman 8 — 50
(Noel Wilson) *mid-div: lost pl 4f out: rdn over 1f out: styd on ins fnl f: nvr trbld ldrs* **9/1**

0425 **7** *1 ½* **Karate (IRE)**[13] 6122 3-8-8 **59**...... NicoleNordblad(7) 7 — 46+
(Hans Adielsson) *s.i.s: hld up: swtchd rt over 1f out: r.o nr fin: nvr nrr* **13/2**[3]

0000 **8** *1* **Perlachy**[20] 5895 7-9-5 **60**......(v) KellyHarrison 10 — 44
(Ronald Harris) *hld up: hdwy 1/2-way: rdn over 1f out: wknd ins fnl f* **40/1**

0502 **9** *½* **Peter Tchaikovsky**[36] 5394 5-8-12 **56**...... PaulPickard(3) 6 — 39
(Ian McInnes) *hld up: rdn 1/2-way: hdwy over 2f out: wknd over 1f out* **7/1**

3401 **10** *1 ¼* **Jonnie Skull (IRE)**[13] 6138 5-9-4 **59**......(vt) ChrisCatlin 9 — 39
(Phil McEntee) *led: hdd over 5f out: rdn over 2f out: sn wknd* **8/1**

The Form Book, Raceform Ltd, Compton, RG20 6NL

0000 **11** 1 ¾ **Seneschal**[15] 6051 10-9-0 **60** .... LucyKBarry(5) 4 35
(Adrian Chamberlain) *chsd ldrs: rdn over 2f out: wknd over 1f out* **20/1**

1m 29.65s (0.05) **Going Correction** 0.0s/f (Stan)
WFA 3 from 4yo+ 3lb **11** Ran SP% **115.6**
Speed ratings (Par 101): **99,97,96,92,92 91,89,88,88,86 84**
toteswingers:1&2:£12.10, 2&3:£11.90, 1&3:£22.40 CSF £64.17 CT £788.91 TOTE £12.40: £4.80, £2.00, £2.50; EX 68.40.
Owner Bagden Wood Building Services Limited **Bred** Darley **Trained** Epsom, Surrey

FOCUS
A moderate handicap run at a good pace. The form looks sound enough rated around the first three.

6489 WOLVERHAMPTON-RACECOURSE.CO.UK NURSERY (DIV II) 7f 32y(P)
3:00 (3:00) (Class 6) (0-65,65) 2-Y-O **£1,704** (£503; £251) **Stalls** High

Form RPR
5005 **1** **Come On Blue Chip (IRE)**[13] 6132 2-9-6 **64** ....(b) PaulHanagan 7 75+
(Paul D'Arcy) *hld up: hdwy over 1f out: shkn up to ld ins fnl f: sn clr: comf* **15/8**[1]

040 **2** 5 **Welsh Royale**[29] 5632 2-9-2 **60** .... WilliamCarson 9 59
(William Muir) *a.p: chsd ldr 1/2-way: led over 2f out: rdn over 1f out: hdd and unable qck ins fnl f* **16/1**

2140 **3** nse **Stellar Express (IRE)**[20] 5876 2-9-7 **65** .... RobbieFitzpatrick 10 64
(Michael Appleby) *hld up in tch: rdn over 1f out: styd on same pce ins fnl f* **16/1**

0001 **4** 1 ½ **Outlaw Torn (IRE)**[17] 6002 2-9-0 **58** .... GrahamGibbons 8 54
(Alan McCabe) *s.i.s: hld up: hdwy over 2f out: rdn over 1f out: styd on same pce* **5/1**[2]

525 **5** hd **Courtesy Call (IRE)**[54] 4781 2-9-4 **62** .... JoeFanning 11 56
(Mark Johnston) *hld up: pushed along 1/2-way: hung lft and r.o ins fnl f: nvr nrr* **6/1**[3]

4320 **6** hd **Hearts And Minds (IRE)**[30] 5597 2-9-2 **63** ....(b) SophieDoyle(3) 4 59
(Jamie Osborne) *hld up: hdwy and nt clr run over 1f out: swtchd lft ins fnl f: nvr trbld ldrs* **16/1**

0004 **7** nk **Saint Irene**[13] 6132 2-9-5 **63** .... TedDurcan 6 56
(Michael Blanshard) *hld up: r.o towards fin: nvr nrr* **15/2**

0060 **8** 1 ¼ **Dicky Mint**[12] 6154 2-9-0 **58** ....(bt[1]) PaddyAspell 3 48
(Michael Easterby) *chsd ldr tl led over 5f out: rdn and hdd over 2f out: wknd ins fnl f* **33/1**

4260 **9** 4 ½ **Bajan Hero**[23] 5802 2-9-6 **64** .... StevieDonohoe 5 43
(David Evans) *chsd ldrs: rdn 1/2-way: wknd over 1f out* **40/1**

6406 **10** 2 ½ **Rooknrasbryripple**[12] 6166 2-9-2 **60** .... SamHitchcott 2 33
(Mick Channon) *mid-div: rdn over 2f out: wknd over 1f out* **25/1**

0664 **11** ½ **The Wicked Lord**[17] 5998 2-9-3 **61** .... ChrisCatlin 1 33
(Stuart Kittow) *led: hdd over 5f out: chsd ldr to 1/2-way: wknd 2f out* **12/1**

500 **12** 25 **Dana's Present**[35] 5410 2-9-5 **63** .... TonyCulhane 12 —
(George Baker) *s.i.s: hld up: a in rr: bhd fr 1/2-way: t.o* **33/1**

1m 30.53s (0.93) **Going Correction** 0.0s/f (Stan) **12** Ran SP% **115.0**
Speed ratings (Par 93): **94,88,88,86,86 86,85,84,79,76 75,47**
toteswingers:1&2:£7.90, 2&3:£20.70, 1&3:£7.60 CSF £33.41 CT £374.17 TOTE £2.40: £1.10, £4.40, £3.70; EX 45.60.
Owner Blue Chip Feed Ltd **Bred** Gerry Flannery Developments **Trained** Newmarket, Suffolk

FOCUS
A moderate nursery run at a good pace. The time was almost identical to the first division and, like that race, it set up for a closer.

NOTEBOOK
Come On Blue Chip(IRE) found trouble when one place behind Saint Irene in first-time blinkers over C&D on his previous start, but he stepped up on that form to readily reverse placings, despite again having to wait for a run. He was well handicapped on the form of his debut in May and, although it's taken him a while, he was belatedly confirming that promise so there might be more to come. (op 2-1 tchd 7-4)
Welsh Royale, up in trip on his nursery debut, plugged on having been handy throughout but he didn't shape as being particularly well weighted. (op 14-1)
Stellar Express(IRE) just missed second and the winner was simply better handicapped. (op 12-1)
Outlaw Torn(IRE), raised 6lb for winning over this trip at Kempton on his previous start, didn't get the best of trips but was essentially well held. (op 6-1)
Courtesy Call(IRE) ◆ was caught really wide on the first bend and was never going the pace. He's not the finished article yet and can win races, probably over further. (tchd 5-1)
Hearts And Minds(IRE) ◆ can be excused a poor run on Fibresand last time and he's better than he showed here as well, losing all chance when short of room on the final bend before staying on. (tchd 18-1)
Dana's Present Official explanation: jockey said gelding had no more to give

6490 NAME A TO ENHANCE YOUR BRAND (S) STKS 1m 141y(P)
3:30 (3:30) (Class 6) 3-5-Y-O **£1,533** (£452; £226) **Stalls** Low

Form RPR
4354 **1** **Ajdaad (USA)**[4] 6379 4-9-3 65 .... GrahamGibbons 13 71
(Alan McCabe) *hld up: hdwy over 1f out: r.o u.p to ld nr fin* **13/2**[3]

1526 **2** ¾ **Whispering Spirit (IRE)**[13] 6133 5-9-4 67 ....(v) PaulHanagan 9 70
(Ann Duffield) *a.p: led over 1f out: sn rdn: hung lft ins fnl f: hdd nr fin* **9/2**[2]

0050 **3** 3 ½ **Desert Auction (IRE)**[10] 6208 4-9-3 65 ....(b) TomEaves 3 61
(Ian Semple) *chsd ldrs: rdn over 1f out: styd on same pce* **16/1**

2122 **4** 1 ¼ **Sky Diamond (IRE)**[13] 6120 3-9-4 69 ....(b) FrederikTylicki 6 64
(James Given) *chsd ldrs: led over 2f out: rdn and hdd over 1f out: no ex ins fnl f* **9/4**[1]

5140 **5** 2 **Empress Leizu (IRE)**[26] 5740 4-9-1 56 .... HarryBentley(3) 2 54
(Tony Carroll) *chsd ldr over 5f: wknd ins fnl f* **12/1**

0333 **6** ¾ **Sienna Blue**[27] 5674 3-8-13 64 .... SamHitchcott 1 53
(Malcolm Saunders) *mid-div: hmpd and lost pl 7f out: hld up: rdn over 1f out: nvr trbld ldrs* **10/1**

051 **7** shd **Flying Phoenix**[10] 6223 3-8-13 58 ....(b) ChrisCatlin 10 53
(Gay Kelleway) *hld up: rdn over 1f out: nvr on terms* **9/1**

0000 **8** 1 ½ **Born To Be Achamp (BRZ)**[35] 5404 5-9-3 62 ....(b[1]) FrannyNorton 4 48
(Geoffrey Harker) *led: clr over 6f out: rdn and hdd over 2f out: wknd ins fnl f* **16/1**

6604 **9** 18 **El Djebena (IRE)**[10] 6225 3-9-4 68 ....(b) StevieDonohoe 7 13
(Sir Mark Prescott Bt) *s.s: hld up: hdwy over 2f out: sn rdn and wknd* **13/2**[3]

0 **10** 26 **Loganberry**[15] 6067 3-8-7 0 ....(p) AndrewElliott 11 —
(Robert Cowell) *in rr: sme hdwy over 5f out: rdn and wknd wl over 3f out: t.o* **100/1**

1m 51.36s (0.86) **Going Correction** 0.0s/f (Stan)
WFA 3 from 4yo+ 5lb **10** Ran SP% **115.2**
Speed ratings (Par 101): **96,95,92,91,89 88,88,87,71,48**
toteswingers:1&2:£5.20, 2&3:£14.60, 1&3:£16.90 CSF £35.38 TOTE £10.80: £2.30, £2.00, £4.30; EX 39.40.There was no bid for the winner.
Owner Mrs Z Wentworth **Bred** Pontchartain **Trained** Averham Park, Notts

FOCUS
A standard seller run at a good pace courtesy of Born To Be Achamp. The time, though, was 0.81 seconds slower than the later Class 6 handicap. The winner is rated close to this year's turf best with the runner-up running to her best of the past year.
Born To Be Achamp(BRZ) Official explanation: jockey said gelding ran too free

6491 WILLIAM HILL BINGO H'CAP 5f 216y(P)
4:00 (4:01) (Class 5) (0-75,75) 3-Y-O+ **£1,908** (£563; £281) **Stalls** Low

Form RPR
1036 **1** **Titus Gent**[24] 5781 6-8-11 **72** .... RaulDaSilva(7) 6 86
(Jeremy Gask) *chsd ldrs: rdn over 2f out: led ins fnl f: r.o* **12/1**

0113 **2** 1 **Mount Hollow**[7] 6283 6-8-6 **67** ....(p) JackDuern(7) 3 78+
(Reg Hollinshead) *s.i.s: hld up: pushed along over 2f out: hdwy over 1f out: r.o ins fnl f: nt rch wnr* **7/2**[1]

1263 **3** ½ **Showboating (IRE)**[12] 6177 3-9-4 **74** ....(p) GrahamGibbons 5 83
(Alan McCabe) *led over 5f out: rdn and hdd ins fnl f: styd on same pce* **7/2**[1]

1450 **4** 3 ¼ **Anjomarba (IRE)**[15] 6044 4-8-11 **68** .... HarryBentley(3) 8 67
(Conor Dore) *led early: remained handy: chsd ldr over 3f out: rdn over 1f out: styd on same pce fnl f* **22/1**

0040 **5** hd **Garstang**[12] 6177 8-9-1 **69** ....(p) SaleemGolam 2 67
(Bruce Hellier) *chsd ldrs: rdn over 1f out: styd on same pce* **25/1**

4602 **6** nk **Scarlet Rocks (IRE)**[7] 6283 3-8-13 **69** .... JamesDoyle 4 66+
(David Evans) *hld up: effrt and nt clr run over 1f out: swtchd rt ins fnl f: r.o towards fin: nvr able to chal* **7/1**[2]

0042 **7** ½ **Co Dependent (USA)**[15] 6056 5-8-10 **67** .... SophieDoyle(3) 1 63+
(Jamie Osborne) *s.i.s: hld up: r.o ins fnl f: nvr trbld ldrs* **10/1**

2000 **8** ½ **Restless Bay (IRE)**[1] 6456 3-9-2 **75** ....(p) PaulPickard(3) 13 69
(Reg Hollinshead) *s.i.s: hld up: rdn over 2f out: r.o towards fin: nvr nrr* **7/1**[2]

6024 **9** 1 **Ishetoo**[12] 6177 7-9-2 **70** .... MichaelStainton 9 61
(Ollie Pears) *w ldrs tl stdd to trck the pce after 1f: rdn over 2f out: styd on same pce* **15/2**[3]

300 **10** 5 **Cloud's End**[14] 6094 4-9-7 **75** .... PaulHanagan 11 50
(Robert Cowell) *chsd ldrs: rdn over 2f out: wknd over 1f out* **17/2**

0000 **11** 3 ¼ **Punching**[26] 5732 7-8-13 **72** .... LucyKBarry(5) 12 36
(Conor Dore) *hld up: wknd 2f out* **40/1**

1m 15.03s (0.03) **Going Correction** 0.0s/f (Stan)
WFA 3 from 4yo+ 2lb **11** Ran SP% **119.2**
Speed ratings (Par 103): **99,97,97,92,92 92,91,90,89,82 78**
toteswingers:1&2:£10.60, 2&3:£3.50, 1&3:£10.80 CSF £53.50 CT £184.32 TOTE £6.20: £1.90, £1.30, £1.70; EX 94.90.
Owner Tony Bloom **Bred** Heather Raw **Trained** Sutton Veny, Wilts

FOCUS
A modest sprint handicap run at a good pace and the form appears sound, rated around the winner and third.
Co Dependent(USA) Official explanation: jockey said gelding suffered interference in runing

6492 WOLVERHAMPTON HOLIDAY INN MAIDEN STKS 5f 20y(P)
4:30 (4:30) (Class 5) 2-Y-O **£2,264** (£673; £336; £168) **Stalls** Low

Form RPR
6 **1** **Little China**[66] 4386 2-8-12 0 .... WilliamCarson 5 71+
(William Muir) *chsd ldr tl led 2f out: clr ins fnl f: comf* **16/1**

23 **2** 4 **Regal Lady**[5] 6352 2-8-12 0 .... FrederikTylicki 3 57
(David Brown) *led 3f: sn rdn: styd on same pce ins fnl f* **13/2**

3 1 ¼ **Compton Ashdown** 2-8-10 0 .... NicoleNordblad(7) 8 57
(Hans Adielsson) *hld up: hdwy over 1f out: r.o to go 3rd wl ins fnl f: nt trble ldrs* **66/1**

04 **4** 1 ¼ **Elite**[20] 5889 2-8-12 0 .... RichardMullen 4 48
(Sir Michael Stoute) *chsd ldrs: rdn over 1f out: no ex whn rdr dropped reins ins fnl f* **5/4**[1]

0003 **5** ½ **Jawim**[31] 5535 2-8-12 43 .... SamHitchcott 2 46
(Malcolm Saunders) *hld up: rdn over 1f out: styd on ins fnl f: nvr nrr* **50/1**

5 **6** nk **Yeeoow (IRE)**[42] 5202 2-9-3 0 .... AndrewElliott 9 52+
(Mrs K Burke) *prom: lost pl wl over 3f out: rdn and hung lft over 1f out: hung rt ins fnl f: nvr trbld ldrs* **10/1**

2024 **7** 2 ¼ **Chillie Billie**[7] 6281 2-9-3 74 ....(be[1]) ChrisCatlin 1 42
(Phil McEntee) *trckd ldrs: plld hrd: rdn over 1f out: sn wknd* **10/3**[2]

24 **8** 10 **Fantastic Smartie**[21] 5863 2-8-12 0 .... JamesDoyle 6 —
(David Evans) *prom: rdn and hung rt 1/2-way: wknd wl over 1f out* **6/1**[3]

62.30 secs **Going Correction** 0.0s/f (Stan) **8** Ran SP% **113.6**
Speed ratings (Par 95): **100,93,91,89,88 88,84,68**
toteswingers:1&2:£8.80, 2&3:£13.40, 1&3:£23.70 CSF £113.30 TOTE £30.20: £3.30, £1.40, £10.20; EX 138.90.
Owner S Lamb **Bred** Stephen Lamb **Trained** Lambourn, Berks

FOCUS
A modest juvenile maiden, the proximity of the 43-rated Jawim doing little for the form until she shows more.

NOTEBOOK
Little China didn't show much on her debut over this trip at Windsor in July, although her trainer had yet to get off the mark with his 2-y-os then and they are in good form now. This was a much-improved performance from the filly on her return and she looks of at least fair ability. (op 20-1)
Regal Lady was given a positive ride but was one-paced and isn't progressing. (op 7-1 tchd 15-2)
Compton Ashdown, a 7,000gns half-brother to triple 6f winner China Cherub, out of a 7f winner, has already been gelded. He ran to only a modest level but shaped okay and should have learnt something.
Elite shaped okay when dropped to this trip at Sandown on her second start (race working out okay), but she found nothing for pressure this time. Her trainer continues to have a disappointing year by his standards and started the day only 9-73 with his juveniles in 2011. (op 13-8)
Chillie Billie finished weakly over 6f here on his previous start. This time headgear was tried over a shorter trip, and he wasn't ridden as forcefully, but the colt didn't respond to any of the changes. (tchd 3-1 and 7-2)
Fantastic Smartie Official explanation: jockey said filly hung right

6493 FREE BINGO EVERY DAY AT WILLIAMHILLBINGO.COM H'CAP 1m 4f 50y(P)
5:00 (5:02) (Class 6) (0-65,71) 3-Y-O+ **£1,704** (£503; £251) **Stalls** Low

Form RPR
5224 **1** **Lady Barastar (IRE)**[24] 5784 3-8-12 **62** .... AdamBeschizza(3) 3 72
(Walter Swinburn) *mid-div: hdwy over 5f out: led over 2f out: sn rdn: styd on wl* **8/1**[3]

0333 **2** 2 ¼ **Hygrove Welshlady (IRE)**[16] 6037 3-9-3 **64** .... JoeFanning 5 70
(J W Hills) *hld up: hdwy over 2f out: rdn to chse wnr over 1f out: styd on same pce ins fnl f* **10/1**

2350 **3** *3 ¼* **Mrs Neat (IRE)**[15] 6052 3-9-2 **63**....................(p) JamesDoyle 11 64+
(Sylvester Kirk) *hld up: rdn over 1f out: edgd lft and r.o ins fnl f: nvr nrr* **12/1**

1226 **4** *1 ¼* **White Deer (USA)**[30] 5595 7-9-2 **55**....................(p) FrannyNorton 4 54
(Geoffrey Harker) *hld up: hdwy and nt clr run over 2f out: sn rdn: styd on: nt trble ldrs* **12/1**

0060 **5** *nse* **Blue Cossack (IRE)**[15] 6052 3-8-4 **54**....................(v[1]) HarryBentley(3) 8 53
(Mark Usher) *prom: rdn over 1f out: sn hung lft and no ex* **14/1**

5053 **6** *1 ¾* **Twisted**[21] 5860 5-9-8 **61**....................(b) JamesSullivan 7 57
(Michael Easterby) *trckd ldrs: plld hrd: wnt 2nd over 3f out: rdn over 1f out: sn wknd* **9/1**

0422 **7** *2 ½* **Saloon (USA)**[7] 6287 7-9-1 **54**....................(p) IvaMilickova 1 46
(Jane Chapple-Hyam) *chsd ldrs: rdn over 2f out: wknd over 1f out* **8/1[3]**

56 **8** *1* **Mahfal (FR)**[20] 5900 3-8-11 **61**.................... PaulPickard(3) 10 52
(Brian Ellison) *chsd ldr tl rdn over 3f out: wknd over 1f out* **5/2[1]**

0006 **9** *2* **Vanilla Rum**[13] 6134 4-8-13 **52**....................(p) GrahamGibbons 12 39
(John Mackie) *hld up: rdn over 2f out: a in rr* **12/1**

0040 **10** *2 ¾* **Beauchamp Xiara**[21] 5860 5-8-7 **53**.................... NicoleNordblad(7) 9 36
(Hans Adielsson) *hld up: a in rr* **33/1**

0631 **11** *11* **Herminella**[17] 6004 3-8-10 **57**.................... WilliamCarson 6 22
(William Muir) *led: rdn and hdd over 2f out: wknd wl over 1f out* **13/2[2]**

2m 40.76s (-0.34) **Going Correction** 0.0s/f (Stan)
WFA 3 from 4yo+ 8lb 11 Ran SP% **115.9**
Speed ratings (Par 101): **101,99,97,96,96 95,93,92,91,89 82**
toteswingers:1&2:£10.50, 2&3:£15.70, 1&3:£19.60 CSF £84.13 CT £956.75 TOTE £10.70: £3.00, £2.70, £5.30; EX 65.80.
Owner Starry Eye Partnership **Bred** Dr M Klay **Trained** Aldbury, Herts

FOCUS
The first two in the betting underperformed and consequently this looks weak form, with the first pair closely matched on last month's form.
Mahfal(FR) Official explanation: jockey said gelding hung right
Herminella Official explanation: jockey said filly stopped quickly

6494 BOOK NOW FOR CHRISTMAS APPRENTICE H'CAP 1m 141y(P)
5:30 (5:30) (Class 6) (0-55,55) 3-Y-O+ **£1,533** (£452; £226) **Stalls** Low

Form RPR

0600 **1** **Prime Circle**[8] 6264 5-8-7 **48**....................(p) JacobButterfield(5) 8 58
(Alan Brown) *a.p: chsd ldr over 1f out: led ins fnl f: pushed out* **14/1**

0606 **2** *1 ¼* **Arkaim**[16] 6032 3-9-0 **55** ow3....................(v[1]) MichaelJMurphy 1 62
(Ed Walker) *led: rdn over 1f out: hdd and unable qck ins fnl f* **7/1**

5046 **3** *3 ¼* **Burnwynd Boy**[24] 5788 6-9-5 **55**.................... GeorgeChaloner 12 55+
(Ian Semple) *hld up: hdwy over 2f out: rdn over 1f out: no ex ins fnl f* **10/1**

640 **4** *2 ½* **Baltimore Jack (IRE)**[73] 4148 7-8-13 **54**.................... DavidSimmonson(5) 9 48
(G P Kelly) *chsd ldr: rdn over 3f out: wknd ins fnl f* **3/1[1]**

4006 **5** *2 ¼* **Ad Vitam (IRE)**[30] 5602 3-8-4 **52**....................(p) JulieCumine(7) 11 41
(David C Griffiths) *prom: rdn over 2f out: wknd over 1f out* **8/1**

3042 **6** *1 ¼* **Rigid**[6] 6310 4-8-11 **47**.................... GeorgeDowning 6 33
(Tony Carroll) *hld up: sme hdwy over 2f out: n.d* **7/2[2]**

5043 **7** *4* **Hathaway (IRE)**[6] 6309 4-8-11 **47**.................... KatiaScallan 13 24
(Mark Brisbourne) *hld up: effrt on outer over 2f out: wknd over 1f out* **9/2[3]**

0000 **8** *nse* **Meydan Style (USA)**[13] 6138 5-8-13 **49**.................... JakePayne 2 25
(Bruce Hellier) *hld up: n.d* **20/1**

5030 **9** *2 ¼* **Wing N Prayer (IRE)**[12] 6156 4-8-11 **47**.................... NatashaEaton 10 18
(John Wainwright) *s.s: a in rr* **33/1**

06/0 **10** *nk* **Circus Polka (USA)**[13] 6135 7-8-3 **46**.................... RichardOld(7) 4 17
(Owen Brennan) *s.i.s: a in rr* **33/1**

4000 **11** *2* **Charlietoo**[62] 4487 5-8-12 **48**.................... NoelGarbutt 7 14
(Pam Ford) *hld up: hdwy over 2f out: sn wknd* **28/1**

5-00 **12** *1 ¼* **By Implication**[52] 4863 3-8-4 **50**.................... DannyBrock(5) 5 13
(Patrick Morris) *hld up: rdn over 2f out: sn wknd* **66/1**

0500 **13** *21* **Anathena**[19] 5917 3-8-11 **52**.................... JackDuern 3 —
(Reg Hollinshead) *chsd ldrs tl rdn and wknd over 3f out: t.o* **16/1**

1m 50.55s (0.05) **Going Correction** 0.0s/f (Stan)
WFA 3 from 4yo+ 5lb 13 Ran SP% **126.2**
Speed ratings (Par 101): **99,97,95,92,90 89,86,86,84,83 82,80,62**
toteswingers:1&2:£15.10, 2&3:£17.30, 1&3:£25.70 CSF £109.61 CT £1087.88 TOTE £17.90: £6.40, £2.00, £6.10; EX 130.20.
Owner S Pedersen **Bred** Gainsborough Stud Management Ltd **Trained** Yedingham, N Yorks

FOCUS
A moderate apprentices' handicap rated through the winner with the third the only one to get involved from the rear and worth a little more.
Prime Circle Official explanation: trainer said, regarding apparent improvement in form, that the gelding was suited by the shorter trip, the all-weather surface and refitting of cheek pieces.
Ad Vitam(IRE) Official explanation: jockey said gelding lost a shoe
Charlietoo Official explanation: jockey said gelding lost a shoe
T/Plt: £2,169.80 to a £1 stake. Pool of £56,177.40 - 18.90 winning tickets. T/Qpdt: £245.90 to a £1 stake. Pool of £4,686.01 - 14.10 winning tickets. CR

5697 ASCOT (R-H)
Friday, September 30

OFFICIAL GOING: Good (good to firm in places) changing to good after race 1 (2.20)
Wind: Light, across Weather: Sunny, very warm

6495 PWC H'CAP 7f
2:20 (2:20) (Class 3) (0-95,93) 3-Y-O **£8,409** (£2,502; £1,250; £625) **Stalls** High

Form RPR

2263 **1** **Dimension**[11] 6217 3-9-4 **90**.................... KierenFallon 4 102
(James Fanshawe) *mde all and sn racd against rail: rdn over 1f out: styd on wl: readily* **3/1[1]**

3114 **2** *1 ¾* **Cape Classic (IRE)**[13] 6174 3-8-7 **79**.................... LiamJones 6 87
(William Haggas) *trckd wnr 2f: wnt 2nd again 3f out: rdn 2f out: styd on but readily hld ins fnl f* **9/2[2]**

0114 **3** *1 ¾* **Azameera (IRE)**[27] 5702 3-9-3 **89**.................... AdamKirby 9 92
(Clive Cox) *stdd s: hld up in rr: prog to chse ldng pair over 2f out: one pce and no imp over 1f out* **11/2[3]**

4036 **4** *3* **Tuscania**[35] 5450 3-9-3 **89**.................... RyanMoore 1 84+
(Sir Michael Stoute) *hld up in last: shkn up over 2f out: kpt on to take 4th fnl f: nt gng pce to threaten* **8/1**

6531 **5** *1 ½* **Yair Hill (IRE)**[24] 5811 3-8-9 **81**.................... TedDurcan 2 72
(John Dunlop) *hld up towards outer: rdn wl over 2f out: no prog and btn wl over 1f out* **7/1**

0061 **6** *hd* **Indian Jack (IRE)**[13] 6173 3-9-3 **89**.................... RichardMullen 5 79
(Alan Bailey) *dwlt: racd on outer: in tch: rdn 3f out: struggling and hanging 2f out: sn btn* **8/1**

0314 **7** *¾* **Close To The Edge (IRE)**[15] 6094 3-8-7 **82**.................... MartinHarley(3) 8 70
(Alan McCabe) *cl up bhd ldrs against rail: rdn over 2f out: wknd wl over 1f out* **22/1**

3412 **8** *1 ½* **Golden Tempest (IRE)**[16] 6062 3-9-1 **87**.................... RichardHughes 7 71
(Walter Swinburn) *t.k.h: chsd wnr after 2f to 3f out: sn wknd: eased fnl f* **8/1**

0200 **9** *2 ½* **Sonning Rose (IRE)**[13] 6167 3-8-7 **79** oh3.................... ChrisCatlin 3 56
(Mick Channon) *racd wd: a towards rr: rdn 3f out: sn wknd* **33/1**

1m 28.54s (1.34) **Going Correction** +0.075s/f (Good) 9 Ran SP% **111.7**
Speed ratings (Par 105): **95,93,91,87,85 85,84,83,80**
toteswingers:1&2:£4.00, 2&3:£4.20, 1&3:£4.10 CSF £15.44 CT £68.07 TOTE £4.20: £1.30, £1.60, £1.70; EX 21.20 Trifecta £82.40 Pool: £935.46 - 8.40 winning units..
Owner Cheveley Park Stud **Bred** Cheveley Park Stud Ltd **Trained** Newmarket, Suffolk

FOCUS
The ground was changed to good all over following the first race. The round course rail was positioned approximately four meters inside for the whole circuit. The stands'-side rail was positioned approximately eight meters inside the normal position. Distances were increased by approximately: 2m (20 yards), 1m6f (18 yards) and 1m4f (16 yards). This is form to treat with caution as the race was not strongly run and hence is muddling.

NOTEBOOK
Dimension soon grabbed the rail and set a modest pace in an uncontested lead, resulting in several of these racing freely and/or being left with too much to do. The winner appreciated the step back up in trip after two runs over 6f but he's unlikely to appeal as one to back to follow up. (op 7-2 tchd 4-1)
Cape Classic(IRE) was better placed than most, but the colt was sweating and raced a bit freely, and he could make no impression on the winner. He is a half-brother to Group 1 winner King's Apostle, who improved with age, and he can do better off a stronger pace, maybe back over 6f.
Azameera(IRE) gained her latest win over a stiff 1m, so a steadily run race over this shorter trip was no use and she could only plug on all too late having been keen early. (op 9-2)
Tuscania, Ryan Moore's first ride back after a lengthy injury absence, was poorly positioned throughout, being held up last off the slow pace. Her rider reasoned he had to get her settled from the outside stall, but the filly had little hope. She ran on reasonably well until her bid understandably flattened out near the line. (tchd 9-1)
Yair Hill(IRE) was another waited with in an unpromising position and had little chance. Whatever, he's probably flattered by his win off 4lb lower on soft ground last time. (op 17-2)
Indian Jack(IRE), up 4lb for winning over 1m at Newmarket, had little cover and found this an insufficient test. (op 7-1)

6496 E B F "FIREBREAK" RATCLIFFES SYNDICATION CLASSIFIED STKS 1m (S)
2:55 (2:56) (Class 3) 3-Y-O+
£9,337 (£2,796; £1,398; £699; £349; £175) **Stalls** High

Form RPR

211 **1** **Mundana (IRE)**[38] 5354 3-8-9 87.................... KierenFallon 4 95+
(Luca Cumani) *t.k.h: prog against rail to ld after 2f: edgd rt fr 3f out: last one on bridle until rdn over 1f out: continued to edge rt fnl f: drvn out* **3/1[2]**

4014 **2** *1 ¼* **Primaeval**[27] 5712 5-9-2 86....................(v) StevieDonohoe 3 95
(James Fanshawe) *in tch: rdn to chse wnr over 2f out: tried to chal fr over 1f out: keeping on but hld whn carried rt ins fnl f* **9/2[3]**

0066 **3** *¾* **Vainglory (USA)**[20] 5929 7-9-2 88.................... MartinLane 1 93
(David Simcock) *settled in rr: rdn 3f out: hanging but prog 2f out: tried to cl on ldrs 1f out: styd on same pce* **8/1**

2500 **4** *3* **Benandonner (USA)**[20] 5940 8-9-2 89.................... RichardMullen 5 86
(Mike Murphy) *blindfold off late and dwlt: sn in tch: rdn 3f out and struggling after: edgd rt but kpt on ins fnl f* **16/1**

6432 **5** *nk* **Classic Colori (IRE)**[7] 6302 4-9-2 85.................... DavidProbert 8 86
(David O'Meara) *mostly chsd ldr to over 2f out: nt qckn u.p: fdd over 1f out* **2/1[1]**

1330 **6** *9* **Truism**[20] 5936 5-9-2 90.................... JimCrowley 2 65
(Amanda Perrett) *in tch: rdn 3f out: wknd 2f out* **8/1**

0000 **7** *7* **Invincible Soul (IRE)**[20] 5940 4-9-2 90....................(b[1]) RichardHughes 6 49
(Richard Hannon) *led 2f: taken to centre of crse 1/2-way: rdn over 2f out: wknd rapidly over 1f out: eased* **14/1**

1m 42.39s (1.79) **Going Correction** +0.075s/f (Good)
WFA 3 from 4yo+ 4lb 7 Ran SP% **111.3**
Speed ratings (Par 107): **94,92,92,89,88 79,72**
toteswingers:1&2:£3.30, 2&3:£4.20, 1&3:£3.60 CSF £15.89 TOTE £3.00: £2.10, £2.40; EX 17.20 Trifecta £68.10 Pool: £1488.28 - 16.15 winning units..
Owner Sheikh Mohammed Obaid Al Maktoum **Bred** Scuderia Archi Romani **Trained** Newmarket, Suffolk

FOCUS
The field started off stands' side but bizarrely all of them ended up towards the far side. That's despite the winner of the first racing tight against the near rail. Perhaps some riders felt they had to follow Richard Hughes, who switched Invincible Soul right when delivering his challenge, presumably in an attempt to race away from the others. This was not a particularly competitive classified event and the early pace seemed modest. The form is rated around the placed horses.

NOTEBOOK
Mundana(IRE), racing beyond 7f for the first time, improved her career record to 3-4 by defying a 7lb rise for her Yarmouth victory. Kieren Fallon was shrewd in letting the filly stride into the lead with the early pace not strong and she was always doing enough when asked, despite continually going right. She may go on improving and her connections will presumably want to try and add some black type to her profile. (tchd 7-2 in a place)
Primaeval would have been 4lb better off with the winner in a handicap and was always held. He's proven himself better on Polytrack lately, but this was still a useful performance.
Vainglory(USA) didn't help his chance by hanging right and is winless since May 2010. (op 15-2)
Benandonner(USA) was below his official mark of 89 after a tardy start.
Classic Colori(IRE) might have found the race coming too soon after his second-place finish in the Silver Cambridgeshire seven days earlier. He was too keen early. (op 9-4 tchd 5-2)

6497 BOLLINGER H'CAP 1m 4f
3:30 (3:30) (Class 2) (0-100,93) 3-Y-O **£11,644** (£3,465; £1,731; £865) **Stalls** Low

Form RPR

1141 **1** **Caravan Rolls On**[14] 6136 3-8-8 **80**.................... JamieSpencer 8 93+
(Peter Chapple-Hyam) *shoved along early in last pair and nt gng wl: travelling bttr after 4f: stl in last pair over 2f out: weaved through after: wnt 2nd ins fnl f: qcknd smartly to reel in ldr last 50yds: won gng away* **14/1**

2005 **2** *1 ½* **Ithoughtitwasover (IRE)**[6] 6333 3-9-2 **88**.................... JoeFanning 4 99+
(Mark Johnston) *trckd ldng pair: clsd to ld over 2f out: rdn clr over 1f out: 3 l up ins fnl f: mown down last 50yds* **11/2[2]**

1210 **3** *2 ½* **Kinyras (IRE)**[41] 5283 3-9-2 **88**.................... RyanMoore 5 95
(Sir Michael Stoute) *settled in midfield disputing 6th: rdn 3f out: prog to chse clr ldr over 1f out: no imp: lost 2nd ins fnl f: one pce* **7/1[3]**

2416 **4** *shd* **Almagest**[16] 6068 3-9-1 **87**.......... WilliamBuick 6 94
(John Gosden) *hld up in last quartet: rdn over 3f out: effrt on outer u.p over 2f out: styd on fr over 1f out: nrly snatched 3rd* **14/1**

0162 **5** *1* **Midnight Oil**[20] 5932 3-9-7 **93**.......... KierenFallon 7 98
(Luca Cumani) *dropped in fr wd draw and hld up in last quartet: effrt on outer over 2f out: prog and edgd rt wl over 1f out: kpt on one pce ins fnl f* **4/1**[1]

3500 **6** *¾* **Well Sharp**[27] 5700 3-9-4 **90**.......... PhillipMakin 2 94
(Michael Dods) *trckd ldrs disputing 4th: rdn over 2f out: eased off rail wl over 1f out and sn disputing 2nd: fdd ins fnl f* **7/1**[3]

122 **7** *3 ¾* **Dubawi Dancer**[16] 6046 3-8-6 **78**.......... CathyGannon 9 76
(William Haggas) *stdd s: t.k.h: hld up in last pair: effrt 2f out: one pce and nvr a threat* **11/1**

3113 **8** *nk* **The Bells O Peover**[5] 6376 3-8-9 **81**..........(b) SilvestreDeSousa 11 79
(Mark Johnston) *led: clr after 4f: hdd over 2f out: wknd rapidly over 1f out* **4/1**[1]

3110 **9** *12* **Watered Silk**[27] 5710 3-8-9 **81**..........(b) RichardMullen 10 59
(Marcus Tregoning) *trckd ldng trio: rdn 3f out: wkng whn squeezed out wl over 1f out: eased* **25/1**

2106 **10** *3 ½* **Ivan Vasilevich (IRE)**[6] 6325 3-9-3 **89**..........(p) MartinDwyer 3 62
(Jane Chapple-Hyam) *chsd ldr: clsd and upsides wl over 2f out: wknd qckly wl over 1f out: eased* **25/1**

0513 **11** *7* **Junoob**[16] 6068 3-9-0 **86**.......... RichardHills 1 48
(John Dunlop) *hld up in midfield disputing 6th: rdn and wknd over 2f out: eased* **16/1**

2m 31.03s (-1.47) **Going Correction** +0.075s/f (Good) **11** Ran SP% **115.6**
Speed ratings (Par 107): **107,106,104,104,103 103,100,100,92,90 85**

CSF £87.73 CT £587.80 TOTE £16.70: £3.50, £2.30, £2.20; EX 121.90 Trifecta £188.80 Pool: £1352.77 - 5.30 winning units..

Owner Paul Hancock **Bred** Miss K Rausing **Trained** Newmarket, Suffolk

FOCUS
A good handicap and run at a decent gallop and solid form.

NOTEBOOK
Caravan Rolls On ◆ wasn't travelling through the opening stages, but that left him well placed considering how the race unfolded. He found trouble early in the straight, but having his run delayed was no bad thing and he stayed on strongly to defy a 6lb rise for his recent Wolverhampton success, making it four wins from his last five starts. This was only his seventh outing in total and it seems likely there's plenty more to come, making him a very useful prospect, especially as he seems likely to get further.

Ithoughtitwasover(IRE) looked the winner when taking over, quickening to hold a clear lead for much of the straight (touched 1.02 on Betfair), but he faded late on and had probably got there too soon considering the strong pace. (op 6-1)

Kinyras(IRE) had no obvious excuse and might be worth another try over a staying trip. (op 8-1)

Almagest was reported to have moved poorly when a beaten favourite at Yarmouth 16 days earlier. This was better and he did enough to justify another try at 1m4f. (tchd 12-1 and 16-1)

Midnight Oil stayed on in the straight, but not as well as some. He has plenty of talent but isn't straightforward. (op 7-2)

Dubawi Dancer had the race run to suit but failed to pick up. She had been in fine form but may now have had enough for the time being. (op 14-1 tchd 10-1)

The Bells O Peover was much too free and soon clear. He's struggled in more competitive company since winning by 18l at Pontefract two starts ago and was failing to take advantage of being 11lb well in here. It seems the blinkers are lighting him up too much now. (op 9-2)

6498 KELTBRAY NOEL MURLESS STKS (LISTED RACE) 1m 6f
4:05 (4:07) (Class 1) 3-Y-O

£19,848 (£7,525; £3,766; £1,876; £941; £472) **Stalls** Low

Form RPR

2511 **1** **Barbican**[27] 5700 3-9-0 104.......... DarryllHolland 3 111
(Alan Bailey) *t.k.h: trckd ldr 2f then restrained into 3rd: effrt over 2f out: led briefly wl over 1f out: r.o wl u.p fnl f to ld post* **7/2**[2]

1501 **2** *shd* **Highland Castle**[29] 5659 3-9-0 106.......... JamieSpencer 1 111
(David Elsworth) *stdd s: t.k.h and hld up in last: prog over 2f out: rdn to ld over 1f out: jinked sltly lft 75yds out: hdd post* **15/8**[1]

2126 **3** *1 ¼* **Solar Sky**[85] [illegible] 3-9-0 100.......... TomQueally 5 104
(Sir Henry Cecil) *trckd ldr after 2f to wl over 1f out: sn outpcd: one pce after* **4/1**[3]

5020 **4** *1 ¼* **Eternal Heart (IRE)**[21] 5883 3-9-0 100.......... JoeFanning 4 102
(Mark Johnston) *led and dictated mod pce: tried to kick on over 3f out: hdd wl over 1f out: fdd* **10/1**

1153 **5** *1 ¾* **Twin Soul (IRE)**[13] 6172 3-8-9 75.......... DavidProbert 6 95
(Andrew Balding) *hld up disputing 4th: rdn over 2f out: no prog over 1f out: fdd* **33/1**

3340 **6** *3 ¼* **Buthelezi (USA)**[20] 5928 3-9-0 105.......... WilliamBuick 2 95
(John Gosden) *hld up disputing 4th: urged along 3f out: rdn and fnd nil over 2f out: sn dropped to last and btn* **4/1**[3]

3m 4.11s (184.11) **6** Ran SP% **109.0**
toteswingers:1&2:£1.80, 2&3:£2.20, 1&3:£3.10 CSF £9.87 TOTE £4.80: £1.90, £1.60; EX 7.00.

Owner John Stocker **Bred** Hascombe And Valiant Studs **Trained** Newmarket, Suffolk

FOCUS
The first race over 1m6f at Ascot in living memory. An ordinary early gallop probably explains why Twin Soul, officially rated only 75, wasn't beaten that form. She can obviously be used to limit the form, albeit she could have improved for her first try at this trip, but it's probably worth being relatively positive about the front two, who finished clear, while the third sets the standard.

NOTEBOOK
Barbican was on a hat-trick after a conditions race win over 1m2f at the July course and a handicap win off 100 going 1m4f, and proved extremely game. It might be that his stamina wasn't severely tested and the form can't be rated too highly, but he was strong at the line and there's much to like about his profile. There could be more to come next year seeing as this was just the eighth start of his career.

Highland Castle returned to form to win a conditions race at Salisbury last time and was the best off at the weights here (would have been 2lb worse off with the winner in a handicap). Given his usual patient ride, perhaps a stronger gallop would have been more beneficial, but he still looked set to tough out a narrow victory until near the line when he changed his legs and edged left. He remains a smart prospect for next year so long as a hard 3-y-o campaign doesn't leave its mark. (op 2-1)

Solar Sky had been absent for 85 days and couldn't go with the front two, despite being well placed. (tchd 9-2 in places)

Eternal Heart(IRE) had a bit to find but better could have been expected considering he was allowed to dominate. (op 11-1)

Buthelezi(USA) defeated today's winner earlier in the season and contested the St Leger last time, but this was a dismal display. He was much too keen.

6499 TABAC GORDON CARTER STKS (H'CAP) 2m
4:40 (4:40) (Class 3) (0-95,94) 3-Y-O+ **£7,439** (£2,213; £1,106; £553) **Stalls** Low

Form RPR

2100 **1** **Thimaar (USA)**[27] 5700 3-8-11 **89**.......... RichardHills 4 99
(John Gosden) *trckd ldr: chal 6f out and pce lifted: led 4f out and sn at least 2 l clr: drvn 2f out: kpt on wl* **6/1**[3]

3101 **2** *1 ½* **Cunning Act**[19] 5966 3-9-0 **92**.......... JimCrowley 6 100
(Jonathan Portman) *hld up in 7th: in tch whn pce lifted 6f out: rdn and prog over 2f out: chsd wnr wl over 1f out: threatened to cl fnl f: no ex* **9/4**[1]

0124 **3** *2 ¾* **Spice Fair**[19] 5971 4-8-13 **79**.......... RichardHughes 8 84+
(Mark Usher) *stdd s: hld up in last pair: lft w plenty to do whn pce lifted 6f out: prog 3f out: styd on to take 3rd 1f out: no imp after: eased fnl 50yds* **9/1**

6P1 **4** *1 ¾* **Colloquial**[84] 3794 10-10-0 **94**..........(v) DaneO'Neill 5 97
(Henry Candy) *trckd ldng pair: rdn to chse wnr 3f out to wl over 1f out: fdd* **9/1**

140 **5** *½* **Roberto Pegasus (USA)**[55] 4806 5-8-12 **78** ow1.......... IanMongan 3 80
(Pat Phelan) *trckd ldrs in 5th: nt qckn u.p 3f out and sn outpcd: kpt on again over 1f out* **25/1**

4103 **6** *3 ½* **Elrasheed**[27] 5710 3-7-12 **76** oh1.......... SilvestreDeSousa 1 74
(John Dunlop) *t.k.h: trckd ldng pair: nt qckn and n.m.r 3f out: no prog 2f out: wknd ins fnl f* **7/2**[2]

2461 **7** *nk* **Bow To No One (IRE)**[26] 5759 5-9-1 **81**.......... MartinLane 9 79+
(Alan Jarvis) *hld up in last: lft w plenty to do whn pce lifted 6f out: drvn 3f out: plugged on fnl 2f: no ch* **7/1**

0100 **8** *9* **Dr Livingstone (IRE)**[14] 6130 6-9-4 **84**.......... SteveDrowne 10 71
(Charles Egerton) *hld up in last trio: lft w plenty to do whn pce lifted 6f out: drvn wl over 2f out: no prog wl over 1f out: wknd fnl f* **25/1**

1230 **9** *27* **Red Kestrel (USA)**[35] 5448 6-9-4 **84**.......... PhillipMakin 7 38
(Kevin Ryan) *led: pressed and kicked on 6f out: hdd 4f out: wknd qckly 3f out: t.o* **16/1**

200 **10** *dist* **Sunwise (USA)**[84] 3794 5-9-8 **88**.......... KierenFallon 2 —
(William Haggas) *settled in 6th: lost pl 1/2-way: dropped to last over 6f out: virtually p.u 4f out* **20/1**

3m 31.4s (2.40) **Going Correction** +0.075s/f (Good)
WFA 3 from 4yo+ 12lb **10** Ran SP% **118.1**
Speed ratings (Par 107): **97,96,94,94,93 92,91,87,73,—**
toteswingers:1&2:£4.80, 2&3:£6.20, 1&3:£10.50 CSF £19.63 CT £120.53 TOTE £6.30: £2.30, £1.30, £2.90; EX 25.40 Trifecta £274.20 Pool: £1405.62 - 3.79 winning units..

Owner Hamdan Al Maktoum **Bred** Shadwell Farm LLC **Trained** Newmarket, Suffolk

FOCUS
The pace seemed muddling and consequently a forward ride was advantageous. The race is rated at face value through the fourth.

NOTEBOOK
Thimaar(USA) was well placed throughout by Richard Hills and got first run on his main dangers. He hadn't gone on since winning his maiden, including finishing well behind Barbican last time, but he was thought good enough to contest the Great Voltigeur and evidently this step up to a staying trip has helped him fulfil his potential. That said, he might be a touch flattered. (op 15-2)

Cunning Act, up 9lb for winning over this trip on soft ground at Goodwood, travelled well but gave the classy winner too much of a start. This was a very useful performance in defeat. (op 7-2)

Spice Fair tends to need the leaders to come back, which wasn't the case this time, so he deserves credit. He's still improving. (op 8-1 tchd 15-2)

Colloquial had been absent since scraping home over C&D in July. Up 5lb, he was one paced despite being handily enough placed. (op 15-2)

Roberto Pegasus(USA), carrying 1lb overweight, has yet to prove his stamina for this trip.

Elrasheed, 1lb out of the weights, was too keen early and failed to pick up. (op 9-2)

Bow To No One(IRE) was only 2lb higher than when winning at York last time, but she had no chance of following up having been held up last. (op 6-1)

Red Kestrel(USA) Official explanation: jockey said gelding hung right throughout

6500 BERKSHIRE MEDIA GROUP H'CAP 6f
5:15 (5:16) (Class 2) (0-105,104) 3-Y-O

£11,205 (£3,355; £1,677; £838; £419; £210) **Stalls** High

Form RPR

2101 **1** **Sirius Prospect (USA)**[21] 5887 3-8-11 **94**.......... ShaneKelly 2 110
(Dean Ivory) *rrd s and slowly away: hld up last: stalked eventual runner-up through fr over 2f out: produced ins fnl f: r.o wl to ld last 100yds* **9/2**[3]

2441 **2** *1* **Elusivity (IRE)**[35] 5451 3-8-6 **89**.......... JamieSpencer 5 102
(Brian Meehan) *stdd s: hld up in rr: smooth prog over 2f out: waited tl rdn to ld jst over 1f out: sn hung lft: hdd and outpcd last 100yds* **3/1**[2]

1132 **3** *1 ¼* **Louis The Pious**[23] 5830 3-8-11 **94**.......... PhillipMakin 7 103
(Kevin Ryan) *trckd ldrs: rdn and nt qckn over 1f out: styd on wl ins fnl f: unable to chal* **5/2**[1]

1520 **4** *6* **King Ferdinand**[48] 5054 3-8-6 **89**..........(v[1]) DavidProbert 3 79
(Andrew Balding) *prom: trckd ldr 1/2-way gng strly: chal and upsides 2f out: wknd qckly 1f out* **10/1**

111 **5** *½* **Swendab (IRE)**[37] 5378 3-7-11 **85** oh6..........(v) RyanPowell(5) 4 73
(John O'Shea) *led: rdn over 2f out and wandered: hdd & wknd qckly jst over 1f out* **25/1**

6210 **6** *1* **Elusive Prince**[13] 6145 3-8-10 **93**..........(v) LeeNewman 1 78
(David Barron) *towards rr and pushed along bef 1/2-way: lost tch 2f out: no ch after* **12/1**

0203 **7** *2 ½* **Pabusar**[24] 5805 3-9-7 **104**.......... JimCrowley 8 81
(Ralph Beckett) *wl in tch towards nr side: rdn and cl enough over 1f out: sn wknd qckly* **11/1**

1130 **8** *1 ¼* **Oneladyowner**[13] 6174 3-8-3 **86**.......... SilvestreDeSousa 9 59
(David Brown) *in tch towards nr side: pushed along fr 1/2-way: cl enough wl over 1f out: sn wknd qckly* **15/2**

0000 **9** *nk* **Norse Blues**[5] 6374 3-8-3 **86**.......... NickyMackay 6 58
(Sylvester Kirk) *chsd ldr to 1/2-way: sn lost pl and bhd* **20/1**

1m 13.57s (-0.83) **Going Correction** +0.075s/f (Good) **9** Ran SP% **117.2**
Speed ratings (Par 107): **108,106,105,97,96 95,91,90,89**
toteswingers:1&2:£3.90, 2&3:£2.60, 1&3:£3.20 CSF £18.73 CT £41.30 TOTE £5.30: £2.00, £1.40, £1.50; EX 22.40 Trifecta £26.80 Pool: £1572.86 - 43.35 winning units..

Owner Miss N Yarrow **Bred** Brookdale And Dr Ted Folkerth **Trained** Radlett, Herts

FOCUS
A good sprint handicap run at a quick pace, and the front two appeal as worth following. They raced middle to stands' side, but not against the rail. The winner is still improving and the form could rate a bit higher.

NOTEBOOK

Sirius Prospect(USA) ◆, up 6lb for his win over 7f at Doncaster when returning from a short break earlier in the month, was last to deliver his challenge and had to be smart to pick up Elusivity, who had himself quickened to lead. He was awkward away from the stalls, continuing his habit of missing the break, but that's not such a bad thing when the pace is strong and he has the natural ability to make the jump up to pattern company in due course. (op 11-2)

Elusivity(IRE) ◆, whose rider was at pains to deliver him late, produced only a brief burst of acceleration, being picked off by a rival who challenged even later, although in fairness he kept on okay for second. He's spent much of his career over 7f, but was a winner over this trip (off 4lb lower) at the July course last time and very much shapes as though he'll progress again if dropped to the minimum distance. Indeed, his pedigree is not short of speed. (tchd 11-4)

Louis The Pious couldn't reverse Newmarket form from August 13 with Elusivity, but stuck on to finish well clear of the remainder. (op 10-3 tchd 7-2)

King Ferdinand didn't improve for a first-time visor after 48 days off. (op 9-1 tchd 8-1)

Swendab(IRE) ran well from 6lb out of the weights, only gradually fading after setting a quick pace. He was on a four-timer after wins in lesser company and was 10lb higher than when having only a short-head to spare last time. (tchd 28-1 in a place)

T/Jkpt: Not won. T/Plt: £48.90 to a £1 stake. Pool of £146,195.23 - 2,181.15 winning tickets. T/Qpdt: £16.40 to a £1 stake. Pool of £7,648.40 - 345.01 winning tickets. JN

6487 WOLVERHAMPTON (A.W) (L-H)

Friday, September 30

OFFICIAL GOING: Standard

Wind: Light behind Weather: Fine and sunny

6501 BOOK NOW FOR CHRISTMAS H'CAP — 5f 20y(P)

5:45 (5:47) (Class 6) (0-60,60) 3-Y-O+ — **£1,567** (£462; £231) **Stalls** Low

Form				RPR
056	**1**		**Riflessione**[22] 5846 5-9-2 **55**...(v) JamesDoyle 6	66+
			(Ronald Harris) *hld up in tch: pushed along 1/2-way: nt clr run and swtchd rt ins fnl f: rdn to ld nr fin* **4/1**[1]	
0650	**2**	*1*	**Kinlochrannoch**[23] 5824 3-9-6 **60**...(p) PaulHanagan 9	67
			(Ben Haslam) *led: rdn over 1f out: hdd nr fin* **11/1**	
0002	**3**	*nk*	**Canadian Danehill (IRE)**[13] 6175 9-8-13 **52**...(p) RobertWinston 11	58+
			(Robert Cowell) *s.i.s: sn pushed along in rr: hdwy over 1f out: nt clr run ins fnl f: r.o wl* **9/1**	
3350	**4**	*½*	**Star Twilight**[14] 6119 4-9-5 **58**...(v) AdamKirby 7	62
			(Derek Shaw) *hld up in tch: rdn over 1f out: styd on same pce ins fnl f* **9/2**[2]	
3105	**5**	*¾*	**Nafa (IRE)**[20] 5941 3-9-2 **56**... JimmyQuinn 2	57
			(Michael Mullineaux) *a.p: chsd wnr over 1f out: sn rdn: edgd rt and no ex ins fnl f* **15/2**[3]	
0430	**6**	*3*	**Commander Wish**[47] 5083 8-8-4 **46**...(p) KieranO'Neill(3) 8	37
			(Lucinda Featherstone) *sn outpcd: r.o ins fnl f: nrst fin* **8/1**	
4400	**7**	*½*	**Fear Nothing**[114] 2798 4-9-7 **60**...(b) PJMcDonald 4	49
			(Ian McInnes) *chsd ldrs: rdn 1/2-way: wknd ins fnl f* **8/1**	
0600	**8**	*nk*	**Rio Sands**[9] 6266 6-8-7 **46** oh1... MichaelStainton 5	34
			(Richard Whitaker) *s.s: outpcd: styd on ins fnl f: nvr nrr* **20/1**	
4650	**9**	*1 ¾*	**Kassaab**[35] 5436 3-9-1 **55**...(b) TomEaves 12	36
			(Ian Semple) *prom: rdn over 1f out: hung lft and wknd fnl f* **25/1**	
0614	**10**	*3 ½*	**Wotatomboy**[45] 5139 5-8-7 **49**...(v) AmyRyan(3) 10	18
			(Richard Whitaker) *chsd ldrs: rdn over 1f out: wknd fnl f* **12/1**	
2-02	**11**	*¾*	**Nordic Light (USA)**[13] 6176 7-8-2 **46**... JemmaMarshall(5) 13	12
			(Mrs A Malzard, Jersey) *prom: lost pl wl over 3f out: n.d after* **20/1**	
5435	**12**	*5*	**Instructress**[13] 6176 3-8-11 **51**...(p) GrahamGibbons 3	—
			(Robert Cowell) *chsd ldrs: rdn over 1f out: sn wknd* **20/1**	

61.99 secs (-0.31) **Going Correction** -0.15s/f (Stan)

WFA 3 from 4yo+ 1lb — **12** Ran SP% **116.3**

Speed ratings (Par 101): **96,94,93,93,91 87,86,85,83,77 76,68**

toteswingers:1&2:£12.70, 2&3:£9.30, 1&3:£6.00 CSF £44.02 CT £381.66 TOTE £5.60: £1.90, £4.30, £3.10; EX 69.20.

Owner Mrs Jan Adams **Bred** Tom & Evelyn Yates **Trained** Earlswood, Monmouths

FOCUS

The going was standard. A gamble was landed in this low-grade sprint handicap, in which the first five pulled clear. The winner posted his best effort since the spring while the third sets the level.

Rio Sands Official explanation: jockey said gelding missed the break

6502 RINGSIDE CONFERENCE SUITE - 700 THEATRE STYLE CLAIMING STKS — 5f 216y(P)

6:15 (6:16) (Class 6) 3-Y-O+ — **£1,533** (£452; £226) **Stalls** Low

Form				RPR
6500	**1**		**Penny's Pearl (IRE)**[11] 6223 3-8-1 66... AndreaAtzeni 3	67
			(David Evans) *a.p: rdn over 1f out: edgd lft ins fnl f: r.o to ld nr fin* **25/1**	
6234	**2**	*nk*	**Piddie's Power**[30] 5616 4-9-1 73... GrahamGibbons 6	78
			(Ed McMahon) *chsd ldrs: rdn to ld ins fnl f: edgd lft: hdd nr fin* **11/4**[1]	
3021	**3**	*shd*	**Magic Cross**[15] 6090 3-8-4 69... AdamBeschizza(3) 10	72+
			(Philip McBride) *s.i.s: sn pushed along in rr: hdwy over 2f out: rdn over 1f out: r.o* **9/2**[2]	
0322	**4**	*1 ½*	**Brynfa Boy**[14] 6133 5-8-11 69...(t) SeanLevey(3) 12	72+
			(Patrick Morris) *stdd s: hld up: hdwy and nt clr run fnl f: r.o: nvr able to chal* **13/2**[3]	
1000	**5**	*¾*	**Red Cape (FR)**[28] 5683 8-9-0 77... PJMcDonald 8	69
			(Ruth Carr) *led: rdn over 1f out: hdd and unable qck ins fnl f* **15/2**	
3440	**6**	*½*	**Tro Nesa (IRE)**[28] 5682 3-8-9 71...(p) PaulHanagan 7	65
			(Ann Duffield) *hld up: pushed along 1/2-way: r.o ins fnl f: nrst fin* **14/1**	
1200	**7**	*½*	**Rainy Night**[21] 5895 5-8-5 66...(v) KieranO'Neill(3) 11	60
			(Reg Hollinshead) *chsd ldr: rdn and hung lft over 1f out: styd on same pce ins fnl f* **11/1**	
6000	**8**	*shd*	**Sarah's Art (IRE)**[8] 6283 8-8-12 73...(t) RobbieFitzpatrick 13	64
			(Derek Shaw) *broke wl: sn lost pl: rdn over 1f out: r.o: nvr trbld ldrs* **33/1**	
2210	**9**	*½*	**Cavitie**[14] 6133 5-8-12 69...(tp) JamesDoyle 4	62
			(Frank Sheridan) *prom: rdn over 2f out: styd on same pce fnl f* **13/2**[3]	
6605	**10**	*3*	**Steelcut**[16] 6056 7-9-0 70...(p) PatCosgrave 1	55
			(David Evans) *chsd ldrs: rdn over 1f out: looked hld whn hmpd and wknd ins fnl f* **14/1**	

1m 14.22s (-0.78) **Going Correction** -0.15s/f (Stan)

WFA 3 from 4yo+ 2lb — **10** Ran SP% **111.7**

Speed ratings (Par 101): **99,98,98,96,95 94,94,94,93,89**

toteswingers:1&2:£16.70, 2&3:£3.10, 1&3:£20.80 CSF £89.44 TOTE £38.40: £6.30, £1.30, £2.50; EX 114.20.Penny's Pearl was the subject of a friendly claim.

Owner Malcolm Brown & Mrs Penny Brown **Bred** Liam O'Neill **Trained** Pandy, Monmouths

■ Stewards' Enquiry : Andrea Atzeni caution: used whip down shoulder in the forehand.

FOCUS

A competitive claimer, seven of the runners were officially rated between 69 and 77. The pace wasn't very strong and there was a tight three-way finish. The runner-up looks the best guide with the third close to his latest mark.

6503 WIN A CAR A DAY - WILLIAMHILLBINGO.COM H'CAP — 1m 5f 194y(P)

6:45 (6:45) (Class 6) (0-65,65) 3-Y-O+ — **£1,908** (£563; £281) **Stalls** Low

Form				RPR
0035	**1**		**Green Lightning (IRE)**[8] 6287 4-9-9 **60**...(b) FrannyNorton 4	76
			(Mark Johnston) *hld up: hdwy over 3f out: led 2f out: shkn up and styd on wl: hung lft nr fin* **9/2**[2]	
0242	**2**	*2*	**Singzak**[13] 6182 3-9-4 **65**... PaddyAspell 10	78
			(Michael Easterby) *a.p: chsd ldr over 3f out: rdn and ev ch 2f out: styd on same pce ins fnl f* **4/1**[1]	
0050	**3**	*9*	**Turjuman (USA)**[13] 6182 6-9-8 **59**... StevieDonohoe 11	60
			(Willie Musson) *hld up: hdwy over 2f out: rdn over 1f out: nt trble ldrs* **14/1**	
0-00	**4**	*½*	**Venir Rouge**[12] 5050 7-9-10 **61**... AdamKirby 5	61
			(Matthew Salaman) *hld up: hdwy u.p over 1f out: nvr nrr* **16/1**	
0050	**5**	*3*	**Storm Hawk (IRE)**[7] 6306 4-9-9 **63**...(p) SeanLevey(3) 9	59
			(Pat Eddery) *s.s: hld up: hdwy over 5f out: rdn over 2f out: wknd over 1f out* **17/2**	
6143	**6**	*1 ½*	**Ferney Boy**[25] 5791 5-9-0 **51**... RobertWinston 7	45
			(Chris Fairhurst) *hld up: rdn over 3f out: nvr nrr* **13/2**[3]	
0622	**7**	*7*	**Dove Cottage (IRE)**[20] 5916 9-9-7 **58**...(v) ChrisCatlin 13	42
			(Stuart Kittow) *chsd ldr tl led over 12f out: sn clr: rdn and hdd over 3f out: wknd over 2f out* **9/1**	
5020	**8**	*nk*	**Drawn Gold**[17] 6029 7-9-12 **63**...(p) GrahamGibbons 2	46
			(Reg Hollinshead) *prom: chsd ldr over 6f out tl led over 3f out: rdn and hdd 2f out: wknd over 1f out* **11/1**	
000-	**9**	*1 ¾*	**Layla's Boy**[191] 6895 4-9-6 **57**...(t) TomEaves 8	38
			(John Mackie) *hld up: bhd 4f out: n.d* **50/1**	
5436	**10**	*3 ½*	**Operateur (IRE)**[24] 4904 3-9-1 **62**...(t) PaulHanagan 3	38
			(Ben Haslam) *led: hdd over 12f out: chsd ldr tl over 6f out: rdn and wknd 3f out* **16/1**	
0-45	**11**	*6*	**Bariolo (FR)**[193] 392 7-9-13 **64**... SamHitchcott 1	32
			(Noel Chance) *mid-div: hdwy over 5f out: rdn and wknd wl over 3f out: t.o* **16/1**	
1500	**12**	*18*	**No Time For Tears (IRE)**[7] 6306 4-8-12 **52**...(v[1]) KieranO'Neill(3) 6	—
			(Lucinda Featherstone) *sn pushed along in rr: drvn along 6f out: bhd fnl 4f: t.o* **33/1**	
6104	**13**	*28*	**Joan D'Arc (IRE)**[13] 6182 4-9-5 **61**... AntiocoMurgia(5) 12	—
			(Noel Quinlan) *chsd ldrs: rdn over 3f out: wknd over 2f out: eased: t.o* **9/1**	

3m 2.80s (-3.20) **Going Correction** -0.15s/f (Stan)

WFA 3 from 4yo+ 10lb — **13** Ran SP% **119.6**

Speed ratings (Par 101): **103,101,96,96,94 93,89,89,88,86 83,72,56**

toteswingers:1&2 £13.60, 2&3 £16.80, 1&3 £4.30 CSF £22.82 CT £237.90 TOTE £5.80: £1.90, £2.20, £4.70; EX 31.80.

Owner The Green Dot Partnership **Bred** Western Bloodstock **Trained** Middleham Moor, N Yorks

FOCUS

A minor staying handicap run at a good pace. A well handicapped runner and a progressive type pulled clear and the form looks solid, being rated slightly positively.

Operateur(IRE) Official explanation: jockey said gelding hung both ways

6504 ENJOY THE PARTY PACK GROUP OFFER MAIDEN STKS — 1m 5f 194y(P)

7:15 (7:18) (Class 5) 3-Y-O+ — **£2,328** (£693; £346; £173) **Stalls** Low

Form				RPR
0/2-	**1**		**Harry Hunt**[198] 7306 4-9-13 63... AdamKirby 1	83
			(Graeme McPherson) *chsd ldrs: led over 1f out: drvn out* **20/1**	
5	**2**	*1*	**Light Well (IRE)**[110] 2956 3-9-3 0... WilliamBuick 7	82
			(John Gosden) *chsd ldr tl led over 11f out: hdd 7f out: chsd ldr tl led again over 3f out: rdn over 2f out: hdd over 1f out: styd on same pce* **1/2**[1]	
2302	**3**	*12*	**Maher (USA)**[21] 5897 3-9-3 70... PaulHanagan 6	65
			(David Simcock) *hld up: plld hrd: hdwy 4f out: wnt 3rd over 2f out: sn rdn and no imp* **6/1**[3]	
-022	**4**	*20*	**Rien Ne Vas Plus (IRE)**[16] 6057 3-8-9 73... LouisBeuzelin(3) 2	32
			(Sir Michael Stoute) *led: hdd over 11f out: chsd ldr tl 7f out: remained handy tl rdn and wknd over 2f out: t.o* **7/2**[2]	
00/	**5**	*1 ½*	**Rory Boy (USA)**[131] 5951 6-9-13 0... MichaelStainton 8	35
			(Graeme McPherson) *hood rem late: s.s: bhd and rdn 6f out: nvr nrr: t.o* **40/1**	
00	**6**	*12*	**On Alert**[8] 6286 3-9-3 0... TravisBlock 11	18
			(Seamus Durack) *prom: racd keenly: lost pl 7f out: sn pushed along: hdwy over 4f out: wknd over 3f out: t.o* **125/1**	
66	**7**	*19*	**Carnelian (IRE)**[11] 6210 4-9-13 0... TomEaves 3	—
			(Ian Semple) *hld up: hdwy over 5f out: n.m.r and wknd 3f out: t.o* **100/1**	
	8	*4 ½*	**Muzey's Princess**[103] 5-9-8 0... JimmyQuinn 5	—
			(Michael Mullineaux) *chsd ldrs tl wknd 5f out: t.o* **150/1**	
	9	*9*	**Mikeys Sister**[497] 6-9-8 0... FrannyNorton 4	—
			(Tony Carroll) *hld up: plld hrd: hdwy to ld 7f out: hdd & wknd over 3f out: t.o* **100/1**	

3m 4.91s (-1.09) **Going Correction** -0.15s/f (Stan)

WFA 3 from 4yo+ 10lb — **9** Ran SP% **113.8**

Speed ratings (Par 103): **97,96,89,78,77 70,59,57,51**

toteswingers:1&2:£2.70, 2&3:£2.60, 1&3:£5.50 CSF £30.84 TOTE £17.50: £3.70, £1.02, £1.70; EX 40.70.

Owner Arion Racing **Bred** Darley **Trained** Upper Oddington, Gloucs

FOCUS

The hot favourite was outgunned in the closing stages of this steadily run maiden. The first two finished a long way clear with the second rated to form, but not much depth behind.

Rory Boy(USA) Official explanation: jockey said blindfold was tightly tucked into bridle and took two attempts to remove, gelding was slowly away

Mikeys Sister Official explanation: jockey said mare ran too freely

6505 WOLVERHAMPTON-RACECOURSE.CO.UK H'CAP — 7f 32y(P)

7:45 (7:46) (Class 5) (0-75,75) 3-Y-O — **£2,045** (£603; £302) **Stalls** High

Form				RPR
0430	**1**		**Maverik**[8] 6282 3-9-7 **75**... TomEaves 5	81
			(Michael Dods) *plld hrd: trckd ldrs: rdn to ld ins fnl f: r.o* **7/1**	
0-11	**2**	*nk*	**Amelia's Surprise**[157] 1579 3-9-6 **74**... AdamKirby 9	79
			(Michael Bell) *hld up: hdwy over 1f out: rdn and edgd lft ins fnl f: r.o* **6/1**[3]	
035-	**3**	*shd*	**Spin Cast**[329] 7335 3-8-13 **70**... SeanLevey(3) 6	75
			(Walter Swinburn) *hld up: pushed along 1/2-way: hdwy over 1f out: hmpd ins fnl f: r.o* **15/2**	
0113	**4**	*shd*	**Justbookie Dot Com (IRE)**[6] 6354 3-9-2 **73**...(v) RichardEvans(3) 7	78
			(David Evans) *chsd ldrs: rdn over 1f out: r.o* **11/4**[1]	

4010 **5** 3/4 **Thatcherite (IRE)**[10] 6231 3-9-3 **71**..............................(t) BarryMcHugh 8 74
(Tony Coyle) *s.i.s: hld up: hdwy over 1f out: rdn and ev ch ins fnl f: styd on* **15/2**
5000 **6** 3/4 **Shostakovich (IRE)**[13] 6177 3-9-4 **72**........................(tp) PaulHanagan 2 73
(Sylvester Kirk) *sn led: rdn over 1f out: hdd and edgd rt ins fnl f: no ex* **16/1**
1330 **7** *nk* **Point Du Jour (FR)**[9] 6254 3-9-2 **70**.................................. JamesDoyle 3 70
(Ian Wood) *chsd ldrs: rdn over 1f out: no ex towards fin* **4/1**[2]
0060 **8** *12* **Gentleman Is Back (USA)**[16] 6051 3-8-10 **64**............. PatCosgrave 11 31
(Ed de Giles) *chsd ldr over 5f out tl rdn and wknd over 1f out* **33/1**
2200 **9** 1/2 **Bilko Pak (IRE)**[13] 6179 3-8-8 **62**........................... RobbieFitzpatrick 4 28
(Derek Shaw) *hld up: rdn and wknd over 2f out* **14/1**
1m 28.26s (-1.34) **Going Correction** -0.15s/f (Stan) **9** Ran SP% **112.5**
Speed ratings (Par 101): **101,100,100,100,99 98,98,84,84**
toteswingers:1&2:£5.50, 2&3:£5.50, 1&3:£8.60 CSF £46.96 CT £324.50 TOTE £8.50: £2.50, £2.10, £3.70; EX 24.80.
Owner Andrew Tinkler **Bred** J G Davis & Star Pointe Ltd **Trained** Denton, Co Durham
FOCUS
A reasonable handicap but the form is ordinary. The pace was decent and there was an exciting bunch finish.

6506 WILLIAM HILL BINGO MAIDEN AUCTION STKS 1m 141y(P)
8:15 (8:16) (Class 5) 2-Y-0 **£2,070** (£616; £307; £153) **Stalls** Low

Form RPR
22 **1** **Presburg (IRE)**[22] 5855 2-8-7 0.............................. MartinHarley(3) 8 76+
(Joseph Tuite) *chsd ldr tl led on bit over 1f out: sn rdn: r.o* **15/8**[1]
0 **2** 1 1/4 **Quizzed**[35] 5445 2-8-8 0.. WilliamBuick 9 71
(Edward Vaughan) *a.p: chsd wnr over 1f out: sn rdn and edgd lft: r.o* **15/8**[1]
20 **3** 1 3/4 **Let Your Love Flow (IRE)**[12] 6196 2-8-7 0.................. PaulHanagan 3 67+
(Sylvester Kirk) *hld up: shkn up over 2f out: hdwy over 1f out: rdn and edgd lft ins fnl f: r.o* **4/1**[2]
0 **4** 1 1/2 **La Romantique (IRE)**[14] 6117 2-8-5 0.......................... AndreaAtzeni 7 62
(Marco Botti) *chsd ldrs: rdn over 1f out: no ex ins fnl f* **7/1**[3]
5 2 1/2 **Holly Martins** 2-8-3 0...(t) NicoleNordblad(7) 6 61
(Hans Adielsson) *s.i.s: hld up: r.o ins fnl f: nvr nrr* **50/1**
5 **6** *1* **Porcini**[28] 5691 2-8-2 0...................................... AdamBeschizza(3) 13 54
(Philip McBride) *prom: rdn over 2f out: wknd fnl f* **14/1**
0 **7** 3/4 **Search And Rescue (USA)**[13] 6180 2-8-11 0............. SebSanders 11 59
(J W Hills) *prom: rdn over 2f out: wknd fnl f* **40/1**
0 **8** *4* **Cool Fantasy (IRE)**[104] 3171 2-8-9 0.......................(b[1]) FrannyNorton 5 48
(Paul D'Arcy) *led: rdn and hdd over 1f out: sn hung lft and wknd* **33/1**
00 **9** 3/4 **No Plan B (IRE)**[21] 5899 2-8-6 0.................................... ChrisCatlin 1 44
(Noel Quinlan) *a in rr: rdn over 3f out: wknd over 2f out* **40/1**
00 **10** *6* **Inch Or Two**[15] 6100 2-8-9 0.................................... GrahamGibbons 2 34
(Des Donovan) *sn pushed along towards rr: wknd over 2f out* **100/1**
11 *35* **Mountainofstrength** 2-8-9 0.................................... BarryMcHugh 12 —
(Tony Coyle) *dwlt: outpcd: t.o* **80/1**
1m 50.04s (-0.46) **Going Correction** -0.15s/f (Stan) **11** Ran SP% **120.7**
Speed ratings (Par 95): **96,94,93,92,89 88,88,84,84,78 47**
toteswingers:1&2:£1.10, 2&3:£2.90, 1&3:£3.60 CSF £5.26 TOTE £3.50: £1.10, £1.10, £1.90; EX 6.20.
Owner Ise Language **Bred** Limestone And Tara Studs **Trained** Great Shefford, Berkshire
FOCUS
The leading form contender delivered in good style in this maiden auction. His main market rival chased him home and the next two in the betting finished in the frame. The winner can rate higher but the time was modest.
NOTEBOOK
Presburg(IRE) set the standard on his 100-1 second at Salisbury on debut and another runner-up effort at Epsom last time. A solid favourite, he travelled well near the pace and showed a turn of foot to open up a gap and score with something in hand stepped up in trip and switched to Polytrack. He seems to have exceeded expectations this season, but is related to seven winners at 5f-2m4f and has plenty of scope for further progress. (tchd 2-1)
Quizzed shaped with promise when just over 4l eighth behind subsequent May Hill and Fillies' Mile winner Lyric Of Light in a 7f Newmarket maiden on debut last month. Strong in the market on the switch to AW, this half-sister to 1m AW/1m2f Listed winner Primevere gave it a good try but never really looked like getting to grips with the winner. (op 2-1 tchd 9-4)
Let Your Love Flow(IRE) had a stiff assignment in sales race at Fairyhouse earlier this month, but she was runner-up in a small-field 7f maiden on her on debut and confirmed the promise with a decent effort stepped up in trip. (op 13-2)
La Romantique(IRE) showed promise when a staying-on seventh in a 1m Lingfield maiden on recent debut and got a few lengths closer to the target in another encouraging run. (op 5-1)
Holly Martins ran green but showed some ability staying on out wide from a long way back with a tongue tie applied on this debut. Official explanation: jockey said, regarding running and riding, that her orders were to get a good position and to achieve the best possible placing, the gelding was slowly away and she decided to settle in and then as it was running free kept it balanced around the final bend and asked for an effort in the straight.

6507 FREE BINGO EVERYDAY AT WILLIAMHILLBINGO.COM H'CAP 1m 1f 103y(P)
8:45 (8:45) (Class 5) (0-75,74) 3-Y-0+ **£2,522** (£750; £375; £187) **Stalls** Low

Form RPR
5100 **1** **Amoya (GER)**[16] 6069 4-9-5 **72**.............................(t) AdamBeschizza(3) 13 83
(Philip McBride) *hld up: hdwy over 2f out: rdn to ld over 1f out: jst hld on* **20/1**
0640 **2** *shd* **Vimiero (USA)**[21] 5893 4-9-7 **74**....................................... SeanLevey(3) 6 85+
(Walter Swinburn) *hmpd s: hld up: hdwy: nt clr run and swtchd lft over 1f out: sn rdn: r.o wl* **4/1**[1]
46-0 **3** 3/4 **Brigadoon**[167] 1398 4-9-1 **65**.. PaulHanagan 7 74
(William Jarvis) *hld up: hdwy over 1f out: rdn and hung lft ins fnl f: r.o* **8/1**[3]
0502 **4** *2* **Sand Skier**[7] 6303 4-9-0 **71**... NicoleNordblad(7) 4 76
(Hans Adielsson) *went lft st: chsd ldr 7f out: led over 2f out: hdd over 1f out: styd on same pce ins fnl f* **10/1**
5403 **5** 1 1/4 **Tapis Libre**[20] 5925 3-8-11 **66**..................................... GrahamGibbons 10 68
(Michael Easterby) *chsd ldrs: rdn over 3f out: no ex ins fnl f* **10/1**
556 **6** *nk* **Cape Princess**[16] 6054 3-9-2 **71**...................................(t) TomEaves 9 73
(Michael Bell) *hld up: hdwy over 5f out: rdn over 2f out: styd on same pce fnl f* **9/1**
00 **7** *nk* **Strike Force**[65] 4444 7-9-5 **69**................................(t) JamesDoyle 12 70
(Clifford Lines) *hld up: hdwy over 1f out: hung lft ins fnl f: nt rch ldrs* **16/1**
0004 **8** 2 1/4 **King Zeal (IRE)**[17] 6028 7-9-7 **71**.............................(t) RobertWinston 8 67
(Barry Leavy) *hld up: hdwy over 2f out: rdn and hmpd over 1f out: no ex* **10/1**
4042 **9** 3 3/4 **Classically (IRE)**[9] 6254 5-9-7 **71**.............................(e) SteveDrowne 11 62
(Peter Hedger) *chsd ldrs: rdn and ev ch over 2f out: wknd and eased ins fnl f* **5/1**[2]

0050 **10** 1 1/2 **Hydrant**[48] 5036 5-9-5 **69**... AndrewElliott 3 54
(Peter Salmon) *led: rdn and hdd over 2f out: wknd over 1f out* **20/1**
500 **11** 3 1/4 **Regal Kiss**[20] 5925 3-9-0 **69**... FrannyNorton 5 48
(Mark Johnston) *hmpd s: sn prom: nt clr run over 2f out: n.d after* **16/1**
0140 **12** 3/4 **Ugo (USA)**[51] 4905 3-9-2 **71**......................................(v[1]) AdamKirby 1 48
(Heather Main) *chsd ldrs: rdn over 2f out: wknd over 1f out* **20/1**
-201 **13** *3* **Secret Era**[21] 5900 4-8-7 **62**.................................... JamesRogers(5) 2 33
(William Muir) *hld up: bhd fnl 4f* **8/1**[3]
1m 59.16s (-2.54) **Going Correction** -0.15s/f (Stan)
WFA 3 from 4yo+ 5lb **13** Ran SP% **122.2**
Speed ratings (Par 103): **105,104,104,102,101 101,100,98,95,94 91,90,87**
toteswingers:1&2:£36.90, 2&3:£5.30, 1&3:£73.80 CSF £98.05 CT £704.28 TOTE £43.80: £9.90, £1.90, £2.80; EX 165.80.
Owner Black Star Racing **Bred** Gestut Ebbesloh **Trained** Newmarket, Suffolk
FOCUS
There was a lively market and a hard-luck story in this handicap. The runner-up is rated to his best but the fourth limits the form.
Regal Kiss Official explanation: jockey said filly suffered interference at start
T/Plt: £22.10 to a £1 stake. Pool £76,218.91 - 2,512.81 winning tickets. T/Qpdt: £5.90 to a £1 stake. Pool £8,750.20 - 1,079.80 winning tickets. CR

6508 - 6510a (Foreign Racing) - See Raceform Interactive

6312 DUNDALK (A.W) (L-H)
Friday, September 30

OFFICIAL GOING: Standard

6511a BOOKINGS@DUNDALKSTADIUM.COM H'CAP (DIV II) 1m (P)
7:30 (7:33) (50-70,70) 3-Y-0+ **£3,310** (£751; £317; £172)

RPR
1 **Just On Fire (IRE)**[21] 5906 3-9-6 66..................................(tp) BACurtis 3 75
(Andrew Oliver, Ire) *chsd ldrs: 5th 1/2-way: hdwy to chal 2f out: kpt on wl u.p in centre to ld 100yds out* **8/1**[2]
2 3/4 **Fleeting Moment (IRE)**[22] 5870 6-9-1 62.................(p) APThornton(5) 4 69
(Patrick Martin, Ire) *mid-div: 7th on inner 1/2-way: hdwy to ld 1 1/2f out: kpt on u.p: hdd 100yds out and no ex* **25/1**
3 3 1/4 **Saint By Day (IRE)**[47] 5088 5-10-0 70............................ ShaneFoley 11 70
(M Halford, Ire) *in rr: hdwy early st: wnt 3rd 1f out: no imp and kpt on one pce fnl f* **10/1**
4 3/4 **Hot Sand (IRE)**[22] 5868 4-10-0 70.................................... PShanahan 9 68
(Gerard O'Leary, Ire) *chsd ldrs: 6th 1/2-way: rdn 2f out: no imp in 5th 1f out: kpt on one pce* **14/1**
5 1 1/4 **El Toreros (USA)**[45] 5159 3-9-6 66.................................(b) PJSmullen 2 61
(D K Weld, Ire) *mid-div: rdn early st: wnt 4th over 1f out: no ex ins fnl f* **10/1**
6 1/2 **Gagnant (IRE)**[25] 5796 5-10-0 70.................................... DPMcDonogh 13 64
(Mrs Prunella Dobbs, Ire) *towards rr: sme hdwy on outer early st: kpt on fnl f wout troubling ldrs* **16/1**
7 1 3/4 **Sionan (IRE)**[25] 5797 3-9-9 69... JPO'Brien 8 59
(A P O'Brien, Ire) *towards rr on inner: sme hdwy early st: 8th 1f out: kpt on one pce* **12/1**
8 1/2 **Alpha And Omega (IRE)**[57] 4735 3-9-5 65.................(p) DMGrant 1 54
(Patrick J Flynn, Ire) *disp early: 3rd on inner 1/2-way: rdn early st: no ex fr over 1f out: wknd* **9/1**[3]
9 *nk* **Secret Hero**[22] 5869 5-9-6 62.......................................(b) JMurtagh 5 50
(Adrian McGuinness, Ire) *prom and led after 2f: jnd early st: hdd under 2f out and sn no ex: wknd* **9/1**[3]
10 *nk* **Sports Casual**[47] 5089 8-9-4 65.................................(b) LFRoche(5) 14 52
(Mrs Y Dunleavy, Ire) *in rr of mid-div: hdwy and chal briefly on outer 2f out: sn no ex* **8/1**[2]
11 4 1/4 **Funatfuntasia**[47] 5089 7-9-8 64.. WMLordan 10 41
(Michael J Browne, Ire) *prom: 4th 1/2-way: disp briefly early st: no ex under 2f out: wknd* **8/1**[2]
12 1 1/4 **Calle Aneto (IRE)**[29] 5662 5-9-12 68..........................(t) CO'Donoghue 6 43
(Michael John Phillips, Ire) *prom early: rdn and lost pl appr st: sn in rr* **20/1**
13 2 3/4 **Atlas Peak (IRE)**[38] 5362 6-9-4 65...........................(b) CPHoban(5) 12 33
(John G Carr, Ire) *nvr a factor: no threat in st* **25/1**
14 3/4 **Fluvial (IRE)**[7] 6311 3-9-8 68... FMBerry 7 35
(Mark Johnston) *prom: 2nd 1/2-way: rdn early st and sn no ex: wknd (reportedly struck into in running and lost a shoe)* **9/2**[1]
1m 37.25s (97.25)
WFA 3 from 4yo+ 4lb **14** Ran SP% **122.4**
CSF £200.87 CT £2070.64 TOTE £8.80: £2.60, £8.30, £3.70; DF 566.10.
Owner R A Pegum **Bred** Patrick Roche **Trained** Caledon, Co Tyrone
FOCUS
The time of this contest was good and the winner put up a personal best.
NOTEBOOK
Just On Fire(IRE) was able to tuck in behind the pacesetters and he was produced with his challenge 2f out. The only worry was the trip as his Down Royal win came over 7f, but the extra yardage if anything was to his liking as he galloped to the line to win more decisively than the winning margin suggests. (op 8/1 tchd 7/1)
Fleeting Moment(IRE) was swallowed up by the winner inside the final furlong after edging to the front 2f out. (op 33/1)
Saint By Day(IRE) was only one to make late progress as he stayed on well in the home straight, leaving the impression that a step up to 1m2f would be more to his liking. (op 10/1 tchd 9/1)
Hot Sand(IRE) had yet to win from 21 starts going into this contest, but his latest effort on the beach at Laytown suggests that an overdue success might be on the cards sooner rather than later. After chasing the leaders here, he came under strong pressure 2f out and just plugged on at the one pace without landing a telling blow. (op 12/1)
El Toreros(USA) never looked likely to shed his maiden tag despite running on quite well in the closing stages. (op 8/1)
Gagnant(IRE) did his best work late.
Fluvial(IRE) ran a shocker, but was examined afterwards and found to have been struck into, to have lost a shoe, and was also sore post-race. Official explanation: vet said filly was struck into in running, lost a shoe and was found to be sore post-race (op 4/1 tchd 5/1)

6513a WWW.DUNDALKSTADIUM.COM H'CAP 1m 2f 150y(P)
8:30 (8:32) (70-100,100) 3-Y-0+ **£11,206** (£3,275; £1,551; £517)

RPR
1 **Licence To Till (USA)**[7] 6302 4-9-3 89................................ WJSupple 14 97
(Mark Johnston) *a.p: led after 3f: rdn early st and strly pressed fr over 1f out: kpt on best u.p ins fnl f* **4/1**[2]

2 1 1/4 **Back Burner (IRE)**[27] 5743 3-8-11 89 FMBerry 8 95
(Mrs John Harrington, Ire) *trckd ldrs: 4th 1/2-way: hdwy into 2nd early st and chal over 1f out: no imp on wnr ins fnl f* **8/1**[3]

3 2 1/4 **Prince Chaparral (IRE)**[134] 7261 5-9-5 91 DMGrant 3 92
(Patrick J Flynn, Ire) *in rr of mid-div: rdn and sme hdwy on far rail over 1f out: 5th ins fnl f and kpt on u.p* **20/1**

4 3/4 **Elusive Ridge (IRE)**[27] 5743 5-9-4 90 (p) PJSmullen 13 90
(H Rogers, Ire) *led: hdd after 3f: rdn and dropped to 3rd early st: no ex ins fnl f* **9/1**

5 nse **Fighting Brave (USA)**[106] 3100 4-9-13 99 (b[1]) WMLordan 6 98
(David Wachman, Ire) *mid-div: 8th 1/2-way: drvn along in 6th early st: no imp over 1f out: kpt on one pce* **25/1**

6 shd **Waydownsouth (IRE)**[20] 5952 4-9-7 100 (p) DJBenson(7) 1 99
(Patrick J Flynn, Ire) *mid-div on inner: 7th 1/2-way: pushed along early st: no imp fr over 1f out* **16/1**

7 hd **Dawariya (IRE)**[27] 5743 3-9-3 95 (t) JMurtagh 4 95
(John M Oxx, Ire) *settled in rr of mid-div on inner: 10th 1/2-way: sme hdwy 1 1/2f out: no imp u.p fnl f* **5/2**[1]

8 shd **Super Say (IRE)**[78] 4034 5-9-12 98 BACurtis 10 97
(Andrew Oliver, Ire) *towards rr: stdy hdwy on outer to go 5th bef 1/2-way: 4th ent st and sn rdn: no ex fr over 1f out* **14/1**

9 2 3/4 **Syann (IRE)**[27] 5748 4-9-1 92 SHJames(5) 5 85
(David Marnane, Ire) *in rr and reminders early: nvr a factor: kpt on one pce in st* **16/1**

10 nk **Cornakill (USA)**[6] 6364 4-9-1 87 (b) DPMcDonogh 11 80
(Kevin Prendergast, Ire) *mid-div: 9th 1/2-way: no threat fr under 2f out* **14/1**

11 hd **Napa Starr (FR)**[19] 5978 7-9-6 92 CO'Donoghue 9 84
(C Byrnes, Ire) *towards rr: sme hdwy on outer 1/2-way: no ex fr early st* **14/1**

12 4 1/4 **Billyford (IRE)**[1199] 3119 6-9-4 90 SeamieHeffernan 2 74
(Liam Roche, Ire) *in rr of mid-div: nvr a factor* **28/1**

13 1/2 **Sinntani (IRE)**[82] 3894 3-8-10 88 NGMcCullagh 7 72
(John M Oxx, Ire) *trckd ldrs and t.k.h: 3rd 1/2-way: rdn and no ex early st: sn wknd* **12/1**

14 nk **Do The Bosanova (IRE)**[6] 6361 3-8-10 88 KJManning 12 71
(J S Bolger, Ire) *trckd ldrs: 6th 1/2-way: no imp fr 2f out: eased whn btn* **14/1**

2m 13.11s (133.11)
WFA 3 from 4yo+ 7lb 14 Ran SP% **127.9**
CSF £37.83 CT £601.55 TOTE £4.40: £2.10, £3.30, £6.30; DF 28.70.
Owner The Vine Accord **Bred** John Hettinger **Trained** Middleham Moor, N Yorks

FOCUS
This can be rated around the third and fourth.

NOTEBOOK
Licence To Till(USA) registered his third all-weather success and did so with plenty of authority. Drawn widest of all, his rider managed to secure a prominent early position and assumed pace-setting duties after 3f. He was pestered for the remainder of the journey, but kept on galloping in the home straight and was going away again at the finish. Another rise in the weights is guaranteed, but he probably isn't too far short of Listed level when in this sort of mood. (op 6/1)
Back Burner(IRE) was given a 13lb penalty for winning a Tipperary maiden by 5l back in June and hasn't coped too well with the burden since. This was a much improved performance, however, and he challenged the winner inside the final furlong without looking likely to win the argument. (op 7/1)
Prince Chaparral(IRE) returned to something near his best form. After a couple of disappointing spins over hurdles, the son of High Chaparral stayed on well to grab third after being ridden patiently. (op 20/1 tchd 25/1)
Elusive Ridge(IRE) stayed on well enough to finish fourth having been taken on for the lead by the winner after 3f. (op 7/1)
Fighting Brave(USA) stuck to his task well after coming under pressure early in the home straight.
Dawariya(IRE) was ridden patiently and looked to be moving menacingly 3f out, but his effort was short-lived and he made no impression inside the final furlong. The blinkers seemed to bring about no improvement. (op 7/2)

6514a DIAMOND STKS (GROUP 3) 1m 2f 150y(P)
9:00 (9:00) 3-Y-O+ **£32,219** (£9,418; £4,461; £1,487)

RPR

1 **Freedom (IRE)**[16] 6074 3-9-0 102 SeamieHeffernan 10 105+
(A P O'Brien, Ire) *trckd ldrs: 3rd 1/2-way: chal early st and led 1 1/2f out: pressed ins fnl f: kpt on u.p* **13/2**[2]

2 nk **High Ruler (USA)**[132] 2324 3-9-0 105 CO'Donoghue 9 104
(A P O'Brien, Ire) *trckd ldrs: 5th 1/2-way: rdn appr st: wnt 2nd over 1f out: kpt on u.p: nt quite match wnr* **16/1**

3 1/2 **Zanughan (IRE)**[32] 5573 3-9-0 107 (t) JMurtagh 8 103
(John M Oxx, Ire) *towards rr: hdwy early st: wnt 3rd 1f out: kpt on ins fnl f wout rching ldrs* **2/1**[1]

4 1/2 **Mid Mon Lady (IRE)**[19] 5976 6-9-3 100 (b) CDHayes 2 98
(H Rogers, Ire) *dwlt and in rr: rdn and hdwy early st: forced way between horses and wnt 4th 1f out: no imp and kpt on one pce fnl f* **28/1**

5 4 1/2 **Clare Glen (IRE)**[16] 6074 5-9-3 96 BACurtis 3 89
(Sarah Dawson, Ire) *chsd ldrs on inner: 4th 1/2-way: rdn appr st: no ex fr 1f out* **16/1**

6 1 1/4 **Confidence (USA)**[7] 6319 4-9-6 75 (bt) GFCarroll 6 90?
(Luke Comer, Ire) *chsd ldrs: 7th 1/2-way: no imp fr 1 1/2f out: kpt on one pce* **100/1**

7 2 1/2 **Northgate (IRE)**[21] 5907 6-9-6 103 PJSmullen 7 85
(Joseph G Murphy, Ire) *chsd ldrs: 6th 1/2-way: rdn ent st: no ex fr 2f out* **7/1**[3]

8 1 **Bob Le Beau (IRE)**[57] 4737 4-9-6 109 FMBerry 4 83
(Mrs John Harrington, Ire) *led or disp ld: strly pressed and hdd 1 1/2f out: sn no ex: eased whn btn ins fnl f* **2/1**[1]

9 21 **Dubawi Star**[51] 4937 3-9-0 105 (p) NGMcCullagh 1 43
(John M Oxx, Ire) *disp ld: hdd ent st and sn no ex: wknd* **12/1**

2m 10.92s (130.92)
WFA 3 from 4yo+ 7lb 9 Ran SP% **116.4**
CSF £103.48 TOTE £7.60: £2.10, £4.10, £1.02; DF 59.60.
Owner Michael Tabor **Bred** Jane Hogan **Trained** Ballydoyle, Co Tipperary
■ Stewards' Enquiry : C D Hayes two-day ban: careless riding (Oct 14-15)

FOCUS
A Group 3 in name but the fact that a 75-rated performer was only beaten 7l leaves question marks hanging over the quality of the contest.

NOTEBOOK
Freedom(IRE) hasn't progressed as quickly as anticipated since landing a Curragh maiden in June, but did run well at Listowel on his previous start. Stepping back down in trip, the beautifully-bred son of Hurricane Run tracked the pace-setters before making his move early in the home straight. His rider needed to be at his strongest in the closing stages to ensure success, but he had a willing partner and they held on to gain some black type. (op 11/2)
High Ruler(USA) was returning from a 132-day absence. That run came in the Irish 2,000 Guineas when fourth behind Roderic O'Connor and he showed that he retains plenty of ability here. Despite being one of the first to come under pressure, he galloped on well in the home straight and was gaining on the winner at the finish. He looks tailor-made for 1m4f.
Zanughan(IRE) was an impressive winner of a Listed contest over 2f further at Galway last time, but the drop in trip proved his undoing here as he could never quite get on terms after being held up in rear early. (op 9/4 tchd 5/2)
Mid Mon Lady(IRE) missed the kick and was ridden patiently as a consequence. She was still close enough if good 2f out, but couldn't quicken when it mattered most.
Clare Glen(IRE) never featured last time at Listowel, but stepped up on that effort here without looking a serious threat.
Confidence(USA) was rated 27lb inferior to the winner, but ran better than his starting price suggested he should.
Northgate(IRE) was a revelation last time at Down Royal, but failed to show the same zest here and was one of the first horses beaten. (op 9/2)
Bob Le Beau(IRE) was relieved of his pace-setting duties 2f out and folded tamely. Official explanation: jockey said gelding ran flat (op 11/4)

6512a, 6515 - 6517a - (Foreign Racing) - See Raceform Interactive

6495 ASCOT (R-H)
Saturday, October 1

OFFICIAL GOING: Good
Wind: Almost nil Weather: Sunny, very warm

6518 JAGUAR XJ CORNWALLIS STKS (GROUP 3) 5f
2:05 (2:05) (Class 1) 2-Y-O
£19,848 (£7,525; £3,766; £1,876; £941; £472) Stalls High

Form RPR

0616 1 **Ponty Acclaim (IRE)**[15] 6114 2-8-11 94 TedDurcan 12 104
(Tim Easterby) *pressed ldr: rdn to ld over 1f out: drvn out and styd on wl* **20/1**

1405 2 1 **Miss Lahar**[14] 6146 2-8-11 93 MartinHarley 4 100
(Mick Channon) *pressed ldr: rdn to chal and upsides over 1f out: chsd wnr after: styd on but a hld* **28/1**

3431 3 1 1/2 **Caledonia Lady**[15] 6114 2-8-11 105 NeilCallan 3 95
(Jo Hughes) *dwlt: hld up wl in rr: prog towards far side 2f out: edgd rt fr over 1f out: styd on to take 3rd wl ins fnl f* **4/1**[1]

1210 4 1/2 **Stonefield Flyer**[67] 4413 2-9-0 103 JimCrowley 16 96
(Keith Dalgleish) *taken down early and led to s: racd along against nr side rail: on terms w overall ldr: stl upsides over 1f out: edgd rt and one pce* **4/1**[1]

2120 5 nk **Rex Imperator**[23] 5849 2-9-0 93 GeorgeBaker 7 95+
(Roger Charlton) *rrd s and slowly away: hld up in last and detached fr rest: gd prog over 1f out: styd on wl fnl f: nrst fin* **17/2**

5101 6 3/4 **Chunky Diamond (IRE)**[28] 5701 2-9-0 85 JimmyFortune 11 92
(Peter Chapple-Hyam) *hld up wl in rr: pushed along and prog 2f out: styd on fnl f: nt gng pce to threaten* **16/1**

4010 7 1 1/4 **Forevertheoptimist (IRE)**[42] 5286 2-9-0 97 KierenFallon 1 88
(Linda Stubbs) *in tch towards far side but sn pushed along: effrt 2f out: kpt on one pce: n.d* **20/1**

4330 8 1 **Signifer (IRE)**[15] 6114 2-9-0 87 TonyCulhane 14 84
(Mick Channon) *hld up wl in rr: prog 2f out: kpt on one pce and no further hdwy fnl f* **50/1**

1000 9 hd **Church Music (IRE)**[42] 5286 2-9-0 93 DarryllHolland 13 84
(Michael Scudamore) *prom to 1/2-way: sn lost pl and struggling: plugged on again fnl f* **50/1**

010 10 3/4 **My Propeller (IRE)**[22] 5882 2-8-11 99 WilliamBuick 2 78
(Peter Chapple-Hyam) *prom towards far side: wknd over 1f out* **6/1**[2]

1120 11 1 **Fanrouge (IRE)**[14] 6166 2-8-11 85 RobertWinston 10 74
(Malcolm Saunders) *in tch: rdn bef 1/2-way and struggling to go the pce: n.d over 1f out* **40/1**

0 11 dht **Hestian (IRE)**[8] 6312 2-9-0 0 WMLordan 15 77
(T Stack, Ire) *chsd ldrs: outpcd sn after 1/2-way: nvr on terms after* **13/2**[3]

6411 13 1 3/4 **Royal Award**[20] 5961 2-8-11 81 MartinDwyer 5 68
(Ian Wood) *led main gp in centre of crse: hdd & wknd rapidly over 1f out* **25/1**

0400 14 4 1/2 **Betty Fontaine (IRE)**[23] 5849 2-8-11 90 FrannyNorton 6 52
(Mick Channon) *chsd ldrs 3f: sn wknd* **66/1**

3000 15 2 3/4 **Pyman's Theory (IRE)**[18] 6042 2-8-11 94 SebSanders 8 42
(Tom Dascombe) *chsd ldrs towards far side: hanging and wknd rapidly over 1f out: eased* **25/1**

402 16 2 1/4 **Hexagonal (IRE)**[15] 6114 2-9-0 0 CDHayes 9 37
(Lee Smyth, Ire) *a in rr: struggling sn after 1/2-way: bhd over 1f out* **25/1**

60.54 secs (-0.66) **Going Correction** +0.075s/f (Good) 16 Ran SP% **116.4**
Speed ratings (Par 105): **108,106,104,103,102 101,99,97,97,96 94,94,92,84,80 76**
toteswingers: 1&2 £114.90, 1&3 £21.10, 2&3 £32.70. CSF £452.51 TOTE £19.50: £5.00, £7.80, £2.20; EX 612.50 TRIFECTA Not won..
Owner Rapcalone **Bred** T Darcy & Vincent McCarthy **Trained** Great Habton, N Yorks

FOCUS
The Cornwallis has been won by some classy sprinters in the past ten years including Majestic Missile, Captain Gerrard and Amour Propre, whilst the recent Ayr Gold Cup-winner Our Jonathan took it two years ago. The field used almost the full width of the track, though those that raced closest to the far rail seemed at a disadvantage. Previous experience proved the key with the winner and second both having already raced eight times each and the third horse seven. The form is ordinary for the race, and best rated around the runner-up, sixth and eighth.

NOTEBOOK
Ponty Acclaim(IRE) had finished adrift of a couple of these at Ayr last month and looked exposed, but perhaps this better ground suited her better and she saw her race out well after taking over in front over a furlong from home. She has lots of pace and this will have added plenty of value to her. (op 16-1)
Miss Lahar's form looked to have flattened out, but she ran well in her only previous visit here when third in the Princess Margaret and this return to the minimum trip seemed to suit her. She was always prominent in the centre of the track, had every chance, and never stopped trying. (op 33-1)
Caledonia Lady was best in on official ratings having made the frame in the Queen Mary, Lowther and Flying Childers, and she made no mistake when justifying favouritism in an Ayr Listed contest last month. She may not have been on the ideal part of the track closer to the far rail than most here, however, and although she stayed on well from over a furlong out, she was never getting there. (op 9-2 tchd 5-1)
Stonefield Flyer was disappointing when last seen in the Molecomb, but his second to Frederick Engels over C&D in the Windsor Castle was among the best form on show. He raced alone against the stands' rail for much of the way, but hung right towards his rivals from over a furlong out and there was no more to come. (op 5-1)

Rex Imperator ◆, dropping to the minimum trip for the first time, can be rated much closer than his finishing position. He was all over the place exiting the stalls, giving away plenty of ground, and found himself in last place, but he finished with quite a rattle and he is one to keep an eye on. His rider reported that the gelding missed the break. Official explanation: jockey said gelding missed the break (op 9-1 tchd 8-1)
Chunky Diamond(IRE) was another to stay on late from off the pace and this was a fair effort as he had a good deal more on his plate than when winning a C&D nursery off 79 early last month.
My Propeller(IRE) lost her chance at the start in the Flying Childers, but her previous win in a York Listed event showed her to be a speedy filly. However, although she showed up for a long way she may have been up against it in racing closer to the far rail than the principals. (op 11-2)

6519 GROSVENOR CASINOS CUMBERLAND LODGE STKS (GROUP 3) 1m 4f
2:40 (2:40) (Class 1) 3-Y-0+

£31,190 (£11,825; £5,918; £2,948; £1,479; £742) **Stalls** Low

Form RPR
1 **1** **Quest For Peace (IRE)**[89] 3695 3-8-7 108 .... KierenFallon 7 116+
(Luca Cumani) *t.k.h: trckd ldr to 1/2-way and again 3f out: rdn to ld 2f out: drvn and steadily asserted fr over 1f out* **3/1**[2]
231- **2** *2* **Arctic Cosmos (USA)**[385] 5945 4-9-0 120 ....(b) WilliamBuick 3 113
(John Gosden) *led: hdd 6f out but sn pushed bk up to ld 5f out: rdn and hdd 2f out: styd on wl but readily hld fnl f* **9/4**[1]
0024 **3** *4 1/2* **Nanton (USA)**[7] 6339 9-9-0 105 .... DanielTudhope 4 106
(Jim Goldie) *hld up last: lft w plenty to do whn pce lifted sn after 1/2-way: drvn and prog over 2f out: chsd clr ldng pair over 1f out: no imp* **16/1**
2320 **4** *nk* **Lost In The Moment (IRE)**[42] 5285 4-9-0 111 ....(p) TedDurcan 2 106+
(Saeed Bin Suroor) *hld up in tch: lft w plenty to do whn pce qcknd sn after 1/2-way: pushed along and struggling over 4f out: last over 2f out: styd on fr over 1f out* **3/1**[2]
3640 **5** *3 1/4* **Yaseer (IRE)**[49] 5045 3-8-7 104 ....(v) TadhgO'Shea 6 100
(Marcus Tregoning) *stdd s: tk fierce hold and sn prom: plld way through to ld 1/2-way: hdd 5f out: lost 2nd 3f out: sn btn* **16/1**
404 **6** *1* **Ted Spread**[34] 5531 4-9-0 105 .... GeorgeBaker 5 99
(Mark H Tompkins) *hld up in tch: lft w plenty to do whn pce lifted sn after 1/2-way: sme prog over 2f out: ch of a pl over 1f out: wknd* **14/1**
10 **7** *11* **City Leader (IRE)**[48] 5094 6-9-0 112 ....(b) NeilCallan 1 81
(Brian Meehan) *trckd ldrs: in tch 4f out: wknd qckly over 2f out* **13/2**[3]

2m 33.36s (0.86) **Going Correction** +0.075s/f (Good)
WFA 3 from 4yo+ 7lb **7** Ran SP% **112.5**
Speed ratings (Par 113): **100,98,95,95,93 92,85**
toteswingers: 1&2 £1.90, 1&3 £6.30, 2&3 £5.10. CSF £9.85 TOTE £3.40: £1.70, £1.90; EX 8.00.
Owner O T I Racing **Bred** Macquarie **Trained** Newmarket, Suffolk

FOCUS
The early pace was very steady in this Group 3, causing a few to pull much too hard. The winner recorded a personal best but the form is limited somewhat by the proximity of the third.

NOTEBOOK
Quest For Peace(IRE) ◆, a dual winner for Aidan O'Brien, was making his debut for the Luca Cumani yard after three months off and was one of those to take a strong grip behind the leader in the early stages, but despite that he maintained his challenge to hit the front over a furlong from home and ran on gamely. He has done nothing but improve as he has gone up in trip and his new Australian owners must have been delighted with this effort, with the possibility of a future tilt at the Melbourne Cup in mind. (op 10-3 tchd 7-2)
Arctic Cosmos(USA) hadn't been seen since winning last year's St Leger in first-time blinkers and he had upwards of 8lb in hand of these rivals, but despite a recent racecourse gallop at Newbury he was fully entitled to need the outing. Although soon bowling along in front, the pace he set was ordinary, causing some of his rivals to pull, and it wouldn't necessarily have been ideal for a horse like him with proven stamina either. Pressed around 5f from home, he stuck to his task well, even after being headed by the winner over a furlong out, and the outing can only have done him good with big autumn targets in mind. (op 2-1 tchd 5-2)
Nanton(USA) seems better than ever at the age of nine and finished in the frame in the Cambridgeshire for the third time when fourth in the big Newmarket handicap seven days earlier. Held up last, the way the race was run was never going to bring out the very best in him, but he plugged on into third and that was probably the best that could have been hoped for. (op 11-1)
Lost In The Moment(IRE) hadn't enjoyed much luck on a few occasions since returning from Meydan and the way things panned out here weren't ideal either, as he became outpaced when the tempo quickened around 5f from home and there was no way back. He now goes for the Melbourne Cup. (op 7-2)
Yaseer(IRE)'s trainer had won this the race five times between 2001 and 2009, but this colt has looked an awkward ride this year and he compromised any chance he had here by taking a furious grip at various stages of the contest and sapping his energy. (tchd 20-1)
Ted Spread hadn't been at his best in his last two starts and this was another modest effort. His best form has been when fresh. (tchd 12-1)
City Leader(IRE) has now run two very poor races since winning at Goodwood. (op 8-1)

6520 JOHN GUEST BENGOUGH STKS (GROUP 3) 6f
3:15 (3:15) (Class 1) 3-Y-0+

£39,697 (£15,050; £7,532; £3,752; £1,883; £945) **Stalls** High

Form RPR
0031 **1** **Royal Rock**[18] 6035 7-9-1 100 .... TedDurcan 5 112
(Chris Wall) *taken down early: hld up in last trio: prog wl over 1f out: rdn and r.o wl to ld last 75yds* **16/1**
0360 **2** *3/4* **Rose Bonheur**[20] 5979 3-8-11 107 .... DPMcDonogh 3 107
(Kevin Prendergast, Ire) *hld up in last pair: prog and squeezed through jst over 1f out: r.o wl to take 2nd nr fin: jst outpcd* **20/1**
2132 **3** *3/4* **Desert Poppy (IRE)**[21] 5935 4-8-12 99 .... JimmyFortune 7 105
(Walter Swinburn) *taken down early: trckd ldr: led over 2f out: rdn and r.o fnl f: hdd and outpcd last 75yds* **9/1**
1405 **4** *nk* **Elzaam (AUS)**[28] 5707 3-9-0 112 .... TadhgO'Shea 1 107
(Roger Varian) *trckd ldrs: rdn 2f out: nt qckn over 1f out: styd on same pce fnl f* **10/3**[2]
1644 **5** *1/2* **Genki (IRE)**[28] 5707 7-9-5 116 ....(v) GeorgeBaker 6 109
(Roger Charlton) *stdd s: hld up in last pair: coaxed along and effrt over 1f out: styd on but w hd to one side fnl f: nvr able to chal* **11/4**[1]
2500 **6** *3/4* **War Artist (AUS)**[20] 5985 8-9-1 115 .... MartinHarley 8 103
(Markus Klug, Germany) *trckd ldrs: poised to chal 2f out: rdn and nt qckn over 1f out: styd on same pce after* **15/2**
-524 **7** *shd* **Gramercy (IRE)**[18] 6035 4-9-1 101 .... KierenFallon 4 103
(Michael Bell) *chsd ldrs: pushed along bef 1/2-way: disp 2nd over 1f out: stl cl up but wl hld whn squeezed out fnl 75yds* **10/1**
1600 **8** *nk* **Perfect Tribute**[49] 5046 3-9-1 105 ....[1] JamesDoyle 10 102
(Clive Cox) *taken down early: trckd ldrs: rdn 2f out: nt qckn over 1f out: one pce after* **14/1**
1323 **9** *3 1/2* **Dinkum Diamond (IRE)**[14] 6164 3-9-0 106 .... WilliamBuick 2 90
(Henry Candy) *restrained s: tk fierce hold early: in tch: rdn and effrt 2f out: losing pl whn sltly impeded jst over 1f out* **5/1**[3]
1043 **10** *11* **Dazeen**[9] 6282 4-9-1 78 ....(b) TonyCulhane 9 55
(David Flood) *led to over 2f out: wknd rapidly* **100/1**

1m 13.51s (-0.89) **Going Correction** +0.075s/f (Good)
WFA 3 from 4yo+ 1lb **10** Ran SP% **115.6**
Speed ratings (Par 113): **108,107,106,105,104 103,103,103,98,84**
toteswingers: 1&2 £29.20, 1&3 £11.30, 2&3 £24.90. CSF £291.41 TOTE £22.50: £4.80, £5.00, £2.10; EX 355.10 TRIFECTA Not won..
Owner Ms Aida Fustoq **Bred** Deerfield Farm **Trained** Newmarket, Suffolk

FOCUS
Strangely for a race of its type, the pace was not at all strong and several still had a chance a furlong out. The runners started off racing down the centre, but hung away to the far side in the closing stages. The placed horses are the best guides to the level.

NOTEBOOK
Royal Rock, winner of this race in 2009 but last of 17 in 2010, returned to winning form in a Yarmouth conditions event last time, but despite that he was noticeably weak in the market. Held up off the pace early, he needed the gaps to appear at the right time, but fortunately one did and he maintained his effort to hit the front around 50 yards from the line. (op 12-1 tchd 20-1)
Rose Bonheur, a dual Listed winner in Ireland this year, hadn't been at her best in her latest two starts, but this was a lot better and she did well to finish so close having been held up out the back in a race run at an ordinary early pace. (op 16-1)
Desert Poppy(IRE) was having her first try in a Group race and, having gained the advantage over a furlong from home, was only run out of it inside the last 50 yards. She has become very consistent.
Elzaam(AUS), in front of Genki in the Golden Jubilee, but behind him in the July Cup and Betfred Sprint Cup, had every chance a furlong from home, but he was racing closest to the far rail and that may not have been to his advantage. (op 7-2 tchd 3-1)
Genki(IRE), runner-up in this last year, has been acquitting himself well at the highest level recently, but his 4lb penalty made this a little more difficult. Even so, a bigger problem turned out to be a tardy start and the lack of a decent pace to aim at, so he can probably be forgiven this. (op 7-2)
War Artist(AUS) may not be as good as he was, but he was still the one to beat on official ratings. However, despite travelling better than anything behind the leaders, once asked for an effort the response was very limited. (op 8-1)
Dinkum Diamond(IRE), having only his third try at the trip, pulled like a train early on. He put in an effort over a furlong from home, but looked to have run his race and was held when hampered soon afterwards.

6521 TOTESCOOP6 CHALLENGE CUP (HERITAGE H'CAP) 7f
3:50 (3:51) (Class 2) 3-Y-0+

£93,375 (£27,960; £13,980; £6,990; £3,495; £1,755) **Stalls** High

Form RPR
6645 **1** **Pastoral Player**[14] 6147 4-9-1 **101** .... DarryllHolland 13 114
(Hughie Morrison) *taken down early: slowly away: hld up in rr nr side gp: prog wl over 1f out: drifted rt towards far side but led 1f out: r.o wl and sn clr* **17/2**[3]
0321 **2** *2 1/2* **Smarty Socks (IRE)**[28] 5699 7-9-1 **101** .... DanielTudhope 10 108
(David O'Meara) *hld up last of far side gp: prog fr 2f out: styd on wl to take 2nd ins fnl f: no ch w wnr* **11/2**[1]
4643 **3** *1* **The Cheka (IRE)**[21] 5930 5-9-8 **108** ....(p) GeorgeBaker 16 112
(Eve Johnson Houghton) *trckd nr side ldrs: led gp 2f out: edgd rt towards far side over 1f out and ch: styd on same pce fnl f* **12/1**
4100 **4** *1* **Hawkeyethenoo (IRE)**[14] 6147 5-9-4 **104** .... KierenFallon 8 105
(Jim Goldie) *trckd ldrs nr side: prog 2f out: drvn to try to chal jst over 1f out: styd on same pce* **15/2**[2]
1203 **5** *nse* **Joe Packet**[15] 6129 4-8-10 **96** .... LiamKeniry 2 97
(Jonathan Portman) *prom far side: led gp 2f out and overall ldr: hdd and one pce 1f out* **12/1**
0041 **6** *3 1/4* **Nasri**[12] 6209 5-9-0 **103** 6ex.................................. MichaelO'Connell[(3)] 18 95
(David Nicholls) *prom nr side: on terms w ldr 2f out: fdd jst over 1f out* **12/1**
5053 **7** *nk* **Imperial Guest**[18] 6035 5-8-11 **97** .... SebSanders 9 89
(George Margarson) *trckd ldrs far side: cl enough 2f out: wknd fnl f* **16/1**
0052 **8** *1/2* **Atlantic Sport (USA)**[12] 6209 6-8-10 **96** .... TonyCulhane 12 86
(Mick Channon) *in tch nr side: rdn and outpcd fr over 2f out: rdn out all the way to the fin* **14/1**
3420 **9** *1/2* **Parisian Pyramid (IRE)**[14] 6145 5-8-10 **96** .... FrannyNorton 14 85
(Kevin Ryan) *nrly burst through stalls s: led nr side gp of 9: hdd & wknd 2f out* **16/1**
2212 **10** *1 1/2* **Webbow (IRE)**[35] 5474 9-8-11 **97** .... ShaneFoley 6 82
(Mark Campion) *taken down early and free to post: t.k.h: prom far side 4f: sn btn* **12/1**
4051 **11** *1 1/2* **Decent Fella (IRE)**[21] 5936 5-8-10 **96** ....(vt) JimmyFortune 3 77
(Andrew Balding) *led far side gp of 7 and overall ldr to 2f out: wknd sn after* **9/1**
0050 **12** *1/2* **Al Khaleej (IRE)**[21] 5936 7-8-9 **95** .... MartinLane 15 74
(David Simcock) *taken down early: dwlt: racd nr side: in tch tl wknd 2f out* **20/1**
3504 **13** *3 1/2* **Dream Eater (IRE)**[27] 5777 6-9-3 **110** ....(t) ThomasBrown[(7)] 11 80
(Andrew Balding) *hld up in nr side gp: shkn up 2f out: sn wknd and eased* **16/1**
3100 **14** *15* **Below Zero (IRE)**[14] 6147 4-9-5 **105** .... FMBerry 17 34
(Mark Johnston) *prom nr side tl wknd rapidly jst over 2f out: eased: t.o* **33/1**
2103 **15** *6* **Casual Glimpse**[21] 5929 3-9-1 **103** .... WilliamBuick 7 16
(Richard Hannon) *hld up far side: struggling fr 1/2-way: sn bhd and eased: t.o* **16/1**
0001 **16** *2 1/4* **Golden Desert (IRE)**[7] 6341 7-8-10 **96** 6ex.......................... MartinDwyer 4 —
(Robert Mills) *hld up far side: wknd 2f out: eased: t.o* **14/1**

1m 26.31s (-0.89) **Going Correction** +0.075s/f (Good)
WFA 3 from 4yo+ 2lb **16** Ran SP% **123.0**
Speed ratings (Par 109): **108,105,104,102,102 99,98,98,97,95 94,93,89,72,65 63**
toteswingers: 1&2 £10.60, 1&3 £23.80, 2&3 £13.20. CSF £54.93 CT £577.94 TOTE £9.40: £2.10, £1.80, £4.30, £2.10; EX 54.40 Trifecta £1027.20 Pool: £117,302.53 - 84.50 winning units..
Owner The Pursuits Partnership **Bred** Whitsbury Manor Stud & Pigeon House Stud **Trained** East Ilsley, Berks

FOCUS
The rail movement in order to provide fresh ground for Qipco British Champions Day in two weeks' time had a major impact on this contest. For the previous two runnings, 28 runners had gone to post, but this time the field size was limited to 18 with only 16 taking part following two withdrawals. The field split into two early groups, with seven racing closer to the far rail while nine came nearside, but the two groups eventually came together and, as in the previous contest, the principals all hung towards the far side. The placed horses, backed up by the fifth, set the level.

NOTEBOOK
Pastoral Player had run well behind Smarty Socks over C&D last month, but his very best form up until now had come at 6f. However, he was given a well-judged hold-up ride in the nearside group and produced a potent turn of foot after being switched right over a furlong from home, scything through a narrowing gap and winning going away. With his stamina now proven, he should be up to winning more decent prizes. (tchd 8-1 and 9-1)
Smarty Socks(IRE), still improving at the age of seven, was 6lb higher than when winning another hot handicap over C&D early last month. Held up in the far-side group, he put in a strong finish but his old rival was finishing even more strongly and he had to settle for second. This was arguably his best effort yet off a mark 41lb higher than for his first success in this country three years ago. (op 6-1)
The Cheka(IRE), a Group 3 winner in the spring contesting his very first handicap at the age of five, like the winner was held up in the nearside group and ran on well from over a furlong out to snatch third. This was a good effort off a mark of 108 and he should continue to pay his back in Pattern company. (op 14-1)
Hawkeyethenoo(IRE), twice well beaten since winning the Victoria Cup over C&D off 8lb lower in May, stayed on in the latter stages but never really looked like winning and this sort of mark looks beyond him. (op 7-1 tchd 8-1)
Joe Packet would have had 8lb more to carry had his recent third in a Newbury Listed contest been taken into account, but his stamina wasn't totally guaranteed. He travelled smoothly into the lead in the far side group over a furlong out and held the overall advantage, but he was run out of it inside the last furlong and again this trip looked a shade too far. Things will get even more difficult once his new mark kicks in. (op 11-1)
Nasri, third in the Victoria Cup and fourth in the Stewards' Cup, showed up prominently in the nearside group for a long way, but his 6lb penalty for a win in a Hamilton conditions event 12 days earlier did him few favours. (op 14-1)
Imperial Guest's narrow defeat of Deacon Blues over 6f here in May looks outstanding form now and even his recent third to Royal Rock at Yarmouth was franked in the previous contest, but he could never land a blow in the far-side group and looks held off this mark.
Atlantic Sport(USA) usually times his finishing effort too late and it was a similar story here. He is now on a losing run of 22. (op 16-1)
Casual Glimpse Official explanation: jockey said colt never travelled

6522 MACQUARIE GROUP ROUS STKS (LISTED RACE) 5f
4:25 (4:27) (Class 1) 3-Y-0+

£19,848 (£7,525; £3,766; £1,876; £941; £472) **Stalls** High

Form | | | | RPR
3324 **1** **Move In Time**[34] 5524 3-8-12 102 RobertWinston 2 106
(Bryan Smart) *mde all: hrd rdn over 1f out and over a l in front: hld on nr fin* **10/1**
5030 **2** *shd* **Addictive Dream (IRE)**[7] 6332 4-8-12 99 DarryllHolland 14 106+
(Walter Swinburn) *t.k.h: hld up bhd ldrs: plld out and effrt over 1f out: r.o wl fnl f: jst failed* **12/1**
6-30 **3** *nk* **Mayson**[14] 6147 3-8-12 98 FMBerry 7 105
(Richard Fahey) *taken down early: pressed ldrs: rdn over 1f out: tried to chal fnl f: styd on but lost 2nd nr fin* **11/1**
2022 **4** *½* **Confessional**[7] 6332 4-8-12 99 (be) FrannyNorton 4 103
(Tim Easterby) *pressed ldrs: rdn over 1f out: tried to chal fnl f: nt qckn last 100yds* **9/1**
10 **5** *¾* **Zero Money (IRE)**[21] 5927 5-8-12 102 (b) WilliamBuick 15 100
(Roger Charlton) *mostly chsd wnr: wandered and nt qckn u.p over 1f out: one pce after* **5/1**[1]
6500 **6** *1 ½* **Secret Witness**[7] 6332 5-8-12 92 (b) JamesDoyle 3 95
(Ronald Harris) *dwlt: chsd ldrs but nvr really on terms: rdn over 1f out: styd on ins fnl f* **33/1**
1411 **7** *½* **Ajjaadd (USA)**[12] 6224 5-8-12 89 SebSanders 6 93
(Ted Powell) *pressed ldrs: rdn and nt qckn over 1f out: fdd ins fnl f* **20/1**
142 **8** *1 ¾* **Albany Rose (IRE)**[64] 4498 3-8-7 87 TedDurcan 10 82
(Rae Guest) *hld up wl in rr: sme prog over 1f out: kpt on but nvr on terms* **25/1**
0306 **9** *¾* **Jimmy Styles**[21] 5927 7-9-1 106 (p) KierenFallon 12 87
(Clive Cox) *hld up in rr: rdn over 1f out: kpt on fnl f: nvr a danger* **15/2**
4216 **10** *1 ¼* **Desert Law (IRE)**[21] 5935 3-8-12 100 JimmyFortune 5 80
(Andrew Balding) *hld up wl in rr: effrt and sme prog over 1f out: no hdwy fnl f* **6/1**[3]
0304 **11** *2 ½* **Monsieur Joe (IRE)**[25] 5805 4-8-12 102 (v) NeilCallan 11 71
(Walter Swinburn) *v awkward s and v.s.a: nvr able to rcvr: plugged on u.p fnl f* **16/1**
500 **12** *½* **Rowe Park**[33] 5543 8-8-12 90 (v) LiamKeniry 16 69
(Linda Jewell) *nvr beyond midfield: outpcd and btn wl over 1f out* **80/1**
0006 **13** *1* **Astrophysical Jet**[14] 6164 4-8-7 104 GrahamGibbons 9 60
(Ed McMahon) *dwlt: a in rr: struggling fnl 2f* **11/2**[2]
5420 **14** *hd* **Darajaat (USA)**[14] 6147 3-8-7 100 TadhgO'Shea 1 60
(Marcus Tregoning) *taken down early: pressed ldrs 3f: sn wknd* **20/1**
001 **15** *8* **Lord Of The Reins (IRE)**[11] 6238 7-9-1 68 ow3 MichaelJMurphy 8 39
(P J O'Gorman) *chsd ldrs to 1/2-way: bmpd along and wknd qckly fnl 2f* **100/1**
4005 **16** *33* **Golden Destiny (IRE)**[11] 6233 5-8-7 92 (p) MartinDwyer 13 —
(Peter Makin) *restless in stalls: completely missed break and rel to r: t.o thrght* **66/1**

59.82 secs (-1.38) **Going Correction** +0.075s/f (Good) **16** Ran SP% **119.1**
Speed ratings (Par 111): **114,113,113,112,111 108,108,105,104,102 98,97,95,95,82 29**
toteswingers: 1&2 £29.40, 1&3 £23.90, 2&3 £38.70. CSF £113.95 TOTE £11.80: £4.00, £4.70, £3.80; EX 159.20 Trifecta £1981.00 Part won. Pool: £2,677.13 - 0.64 winning units..
Owner A Turton, J Blackburn & R Bond **Bred** Bond Thoroughbred Corporation **Trained** Hambleton, N Yorks

FOCUS
The first running of this Listed sprint since it was moved from Newmarket, but despite the change of venue a familiar result with Bryan Smart winning it for the third year in a row. The form is ordinary for the grade and the runner-up and fourth set the standard.

NOTEBOOK
Move In Time ◆ has been running well in Group 3/Listed company since winning a three-runner conditions event at Beverley and he was runner-up in the Cornwallis last year, so obviously likes it here. Soon in front, he proved particularly game when challenged and held on to win with nothing to spare. He is very consistent and there seems to reason why cannot win again at this level, or perhaps something even better with time on his side.
Addictive Dream(IRE) may be better over 6f these days, so perhaps it wasn't surprising that his finishing burst fell a couple of strides short, but this was still a fine effort and he has the ability to win a race like this back over an extra furlong. (op 16-1)
Mayson ◆ was disappointing on soft ground in the Ayr Gold Cup after his excellent return from a long layoff in the Great St Wilfrid, but returned to form here. Despite fly-jumping leaving the stalls, he was able to hold a handy position and kept at it all the way to the line. The best of him may be yet to be seen and he looks one for next year. (op 12-1)
Confessional has run some cracking races this season and this staying-on performance was another creditable effort, but he has gone over a year without a win. (op 11-1 tchd 17-2)
Zero Money(IRE) found himself racing on the 'wrong' side when bidding for a hat-trick in the Portland, but having been up there from the off he had every chance here until finding no extra in the last half-furlong. (tchd 9-2)
Secret Witness ran on late without ever looking like figuring and a record of 2-30 on turf isn't good enough for a race like this in any case. (op 40-1)
Ajjaadd(USA) has been in cracking form in handicaps lately, winning four of his previous five starts, but this was something different so he probably ran as well as could be expected. (op 16-1)
Desert Law(IRE) Official explanation: trainer said colt would prefer faster ground
Monsieur Joe(IRE) Official explanation: jockey said gelding was reluctant to race
Astrophysical Jet Official explanation: jockey said filly anticipated start and hit stalls
Golden Destiny(IRE) Official explanation: jockey said mare reared as stalls opened

6523 MILES & MORRISON E B F OCTOBER STKS (LISTED RACE) 7f
5:00 (5:02) (Class 1) 3-Y-0+

£19,848 (£7,525; £3,766; £1,876; £941; £472) **Stalls** High

Form | | | | RPR
0100 **1** **Crying Lightening (IRE)**[23] 5848 3-8-11 100 MartinDwyer 6 102
(Peter Chapple-Hyam) *mde all: drvn over 1f out: styd on u.p fnl f* **16/1**
0400 **2** *¾* **Elshabakiya (IRE)**[21] 5935 3-8-11 92 NeilCallan 11 100+
(Clive Brittain) *stdd s: hld up in last: stl there tl plld out over 1f out: hrd rdn and rapid prog fnl f: tk 2nd last 75yds: too much to do* **16/1**
-464 **3** *½* **Marvada (IRE)**[23] 5848 3-8-11 103 ShaneFoley 2 99
(K J Condon, Ire) *trckd ldrs: rdn to chse wnr over 1f out: styd on but a hld: lost 2nd last 75yds* **5/1**
5000 **4** *2 ¼* **Sharnberry**[48] 5080 3-8-11 102 FMBerry 8 93
(Ed Dunlop) *hld up bhd ldrs: rdn and nt qckn 2f out: kpt on one pce after* **14/1**
3366 **5** *1 ½* **Perfect Silence**[30] 5657 6-8-13 88 JamesDoyle 5 89
(Clive Cox) *chsd wnr to 3f out: nt qckn u.p 2f out: wl hld in midfield after* **16/1**
3-64 **6** *1 ½* **Rainfall (IRE)**[28] 5704 4-8-13 110 (t) WilliamBuick 10 84
(Saeed Bin Suroor) *dwlt: hld up in rr: rdn and sme prog 2f out: nt qckn over 1f out: sn wknd* **10/3**[2]
0/10 **7** *nk* **Theladyinquestion**[30] 5657 4-8-13 79 JimmyFortune 3 84
(Andrew Balding) *stdd s: wl in tch: effrt to chse ldrs wl over 1f out: wknd fnl f* **33/1**
1206 **8** *½* **Flambeau**[23] 5848 4-9-2 105 DaneO'Neill 9 85
(Henry Candy) *hld up in tch: shkn up and nt qckn over 2f out: wknd over 1f out* **7/2**[3]
2242 **9** *nse* **Dubai Queen (USA)**[30] 5657 3-8-11 96 KierenFallon 1 82
(Luca Cumani) *prom: chsd wnr 3f out to over 1f out: sn wknd* **3/1**[1]

1m 27.61s (0.41) **Going Correction** +0.075s/f (Good)
WFA 3 from 4yo+ 2lb **9** Ran SP% **114.2**
Speed ratings (Par 111): **100,99,98,96,94 92,92,91,91**
toteswingers: 1&2 £17.50, 1&3 £10.70, 2&3 £10.70. CSF £238.50 TOTE £17.80: £4.00, £4.30, £1.90; EX 170.00 Trifecta £1658.50 Part won. Pool: £2,241.23 - 0.90 winning units..
Owner J Barton & C Pizarro **Bred** Paulyn Limited **Trained** Newmarket, Suffolk

FOCUS
A race that has been totally dominated by the Classic generation in recent years, with 3yos taking the previous 11 runnings, and they filled the first four places here. Despite the smallish field and the stalls against the stands' rail, the runners made straight for the middle of the track and ended up against the far rail late on. The winner is rated back to her best with the third just below her latest mark.

NOTEBOOK
Crying Lightening(IRE) had finished well held in both starts since returning from Meydan in the spring, including when behind a couple of these rivals at Doncaster last month, but she was returning from an absence of 148 days there so the race must have brought her on. Again sent straight to the front, being that much fitter meant she had enough in reserve this time to keep all her rivals at bay, though she was being run down near the finish. (op 14-1)
Elshabakiya(IRE), 0-8 coming into this, has faced some impossible tasks but had made the frame in a couple of Listed races including when beaten a head by Dubawi Gold on Polytrack in March. Held up well off the pace early, she suddenly took off inside the last furlong and was closing in fast on the winner near the line. She has the ability to win a nice race and will no doubt be given a few more chances to do so. (op 12-1)
Marvada(IRE) had the winner behind her when a running-on fourth in the Sceptre Stakes at Doncaster last month, but despite holding every chance she could never quite get to her old rival. (op 13-2)
Sharnberry has been disappointing since finishing fifth in the French 1000 Guineas and, although this was a bit better back over a more suitable trip, she never looked like getting there. (op 11-1)
Perfect Silence was close enough if good enough towards the far side of the field and to be fair, being rated 88 gave her plenty to find in this company. (op 20-1)
Rainfall(IRE), 2-2 over C&D having taken the Jersey Stakes and this race last year, had upwards of 7lb in hand of these rivals but she made little impact from off the pace and the fact that this was only her third start of the campaign suggests that all has not been well. Her rider reported that the filly hung right. Official explanation: jockey said filly hung right (op 3-1 tchd 7-2)
Dubai Queen(USA) had a bit to find at the weights, but unlike many of her rivals she came into this with a consistent profile so this was disappointing. (op 10-3 tchd 11-4 and 7-2 in a place)

6524 BRIGHTWELLS ASCOT SALES (CONDITIONS STKS) 6f
5:35 (5:36) (Class 2) 2-Y-0 **£16,172** (£4,812; £2,405; £1,202) **Stalls** High

Form | | | | RPR
5033 **1** **Our Cool Cat (IRE)**[17] 6058 2-9-3 61 (b) GeorgeBaker 1 80
(Gary Moore) *racd against far rail: hld up in tch: prog over 1f out: r.o to ld last 150yds: hld on wl* **25/1**
0010 **2** *nk* **Toffee Tart**[23] 5847 2-8-12 73 SebSanders 2 74
(J W Hills) *racd against far rail: hld up: prog over 1f out: drvn and r.o to chal ins fnl f: a jst hld* **12/1**
2302 **3** *2 ¼* **Forest Edge (IRE)**[4] 6432 2-9-3 78 RichardEvans 17 72+
(David Evans) *racd on outer: in tch: rdn and prog over 2f out: chsd ldr over 1f out: drvn to chal fnl f: one pce last 100yds* **20/1**
6231 **4** *½* **Marygold**[21] 5913 2-8-12 83 DarryllHolland 5 66
(John Akehurst) *led and racd against far rail: edgd lft 2f out: hdd & wknd last 150yds* **13/2**[3]
2300 **5** *nk* **Dream Whisperer**[63] 4557 2-8-12 69 (b[1]) DaneO'Neill 8 65
(Dominic Ffrench Davis) *hld up in tch: gng strly 2f out: plld out and prog over 1f out: brought w dangerous looking chal fnl f: wknd last 100yds* **50/1**
43 **6** *shd* **Jack Of Diamonds (IRE)**[12] 6214 2-9-3 0 WilliamBuick 18 70
(Roger Teal) *wl in rr on outer: pushed along bef 1/2-way: prog u.p 2f out: kpt on fnl f: nt rch ldrs* **5/1**[2]
1016 **7** *5* **Sans Loi (IRE)**[86] 3773 2-9-13 85 RobertWinston 16 65+
(Alan McCabe) *hld up wl in rr: trapped bhd wall of horses over 2f out to over 1f out: styd on fnl f: no ch* **13/2**[3]

6541 **8** *nk* **I'll Be Good**[12] 6207 2-9-6 74 .... GaryBartley 4 57+
(Robert Johnson) *hld up in midfield: gng wl enough but nvr much room whn trying to make prog fr over 2f out to over 1f out: one pce whn in the clr fnl f* **18/1**

124 **9** *1* **Hot Sugar (USA)**[22] 5886 2-9-6 84 .... NeilCallan 3 54
(Kevin Ryan) *chsd ldr: hrd rdn and lost 2nd over 1f out: wknd and eased fnl f* **4/1**[1]

05 **10** *2 1/4* **Our Phylli Vera (IRE)**[23] 5841 2-8-12 0 .... MartinLane 9 39
(Harry Dunlop) *wl in rr: struggling over 2f out: modest late prog against far rail* **100/1**

040 **11** *1/2* **Kings Decree**[16] 6099 2-9-3 68 .... DanielTudhope 6 42
(Rod Millman) *taken down early: disp 2nd pl to 2f out: stl prom jst over 1f out: wknd* **40/1**

0105 **12** *nk* **Golden Valley**[6] 6372 2-8-12 70 .... JamesMillman 7 37
(Rod Millman) *prom to 2f out: sn lost pl and btn* **14/1**

403 **13** *1 1/2* **Purley Queen (IRE)**[23] 5863 2-8-12 66 .... JimmyFortune 14 32
(Sylvester Kirk) *a wl in rr: no ch over 2f out* **33/1**

5231 **14** *1 1/4* **Sheila's Buddy**[5] 6399 2-9-3 67 .... LiamKeniry 12 33
(J S Moore) *n.m.r s: nvr bttr than midfield towards outer: struggling 2f out* **14/1**

5451 **15** *1 1/2* **Courtland Avenue (IRE)**[26] 5779 2-9-3 69 .... TedDurcan 15 29
(Jonathan Portman) *racd on outer: hmpd after 2f: struggling in rr 2f out* **28/1**

4 **16** *3/4* **Little Rainbow**[49] 5048 2-8-12 0 .... JamesDoyle 13 22
(Clive Cox) *nvr on terms w ldrs towards outer: struggling in rr 2f out* **8/1**

250 **17** *3* **Miss Conduct**[40] 5324 2-8-12 64 ....(b[1]) FrannyNorton 10 13
(John Spearing) *prom over 3f: sn wknd* **33/1**

5060 **18** *32* **Queen Of The Hop**[23] 5844 2-8-12 51 ....(b[1]) MartinDwyer 11 —
(J S Moore) *reminders after 1f: sn dropped out: t.o* **100/1**

1m 14.97s (0.57) **Going Correction** +0.075s/f (Good) 18 Ran SP% **125.1**
Speed ratings (Par 101): **99,98,95,94,94 94,87,87,86,83 82,81,79,78,76 75,71,28**
toteswingers: 1&2 £31.00, 1&3 £46.40, 2&3 £50.40. CSF £287.49 TOTE £24.10: £4.60, £3.90, £6.40; EX 314.10 TRIFECTA Not won..
Owner Five Star Racing Group & Partners **Bred** Grangemore Stud **Trained** Lower Beeding, W Sussex

FOCUS
Despite the size of the field, this was nothing like as competitive as the numbers would suggest. The runners again made straight for the far rail, though that meant those that raced tight against it soon had to negotiate the false rail inside the last 4f. The sixth looks a good guide to the level.

NOTEBOOK
Our Cool Cat(IRE), third in a Bath maiden and a Sandown nursery in his last two starts, had finished well over 5f in the latter contest and appreciated this return to 6f, staying on well towards the far rail to lead inside the last furlong. He is rated just 61, however, which speaks volumes about the overall quality of this contest, not that such an issue will bother his connections after pocketing over £16,000. (op 33-1)
Toffee Tart, half a length in front of Marygold at Windsor in August but 5lb worse off, came from further back than the winner and followed him through against the far rail, but despite running on well she could never quite get there.
Forest Edge(IRE), a beaten favourite over 7f on soft ground last time, appreciated the return to this trip on a less demanding surface and having been up there from the start, had every chance under strong pressure. (op 16-1)
Marygold, best in at the weights, had made all for her two wins and attempted the same tactics, but she hung away from the far rail over a furlong from home and the front pair made full use of the gap she left. (tchd 6-1)
Dream Whisperer, tried in blinkers after appearing to be going the wrong way, travelled better than anything behind the leaders and looked the most likely winner when pulled out for her effort, but she didn't appear to quite go through with it and it may be she didn't quite get home on this first attempt at 6f. (op 40-1)
Jack Of Diamonds(IRE), in the frame in two Polytrack maidens over further, was drawn highest so was in theory inconvenienced most by the runners making for the far rail, but he ran on well down the outside in the closing stages and may prove better than those who beat him here in due course. (op 13-2 tchd 7-1)
Hot Sugar(USA) may not have stayed when stepped up to 7f last time, but despite holding a prominent position early from his low draw, again appeared not to get home. His rider reported that the colt would prefer faster ground. Official explanation: jockey said colt would prefer fast ground (op 5-1)
T/Jkpt: Not won. T/Plt: £6,491.40 to a £1 stake. Pool of £165,842.70 - 18.65 winning tickets. T/Qpdt: £560.90 to a £1 stake. Pool of £10,005.71 - 13.20 winning tickets. JN

6336 NEWMARKET (R-H)
Saturday, October 1

OFFICIAL GOING: Good to firm (watered; 8.2)
GOOD TO FIRM (Watered; 8.2)
Wind: Virtually nil Weather: Very warm

6525 E B F FEDERATION OF BLOODSTOCK AGENTS MAIDEN STKS 6f
1:50 (1:52) (Class 4) 2-Y-O £5,175 (£1,540; £769; £384) **Stalls** High

Form RPR

1360 **1** **Campanology**[23] 5849 2-9-3 90 .... RichardHughes 8 84
(Richard Hannon) *w ldr: travelling best whn short of room and jostled over 1f out: led 1f out: pushed ahd ins fnl f: sn in command: eased cl home* **11/10**[1]

0 **2** *1* **Sheikh The Reins (IRE)**[35] 5480 2-9-3 0 .... SteveDrowne 6 79+
(John Best) *racd in midfield: outpcd and pushed along 1/2-way: swtchd rt and chsd clr ldng pair wl over 1f out: no imp tl r.o strly ins fnl f: wnt 2nd wl ins fnl f* **16/1**

62 **3** *3/4* **Mizwaaj (IRE)**[22] 5886 2-9-3 0 .... RichardMullen 5 76
(Saeed Bin Suroor) *led narrowly: rdn and edgd lft over 1f out: hdd 1f out: wknd fnl 100yds* **11/8**[2]

06 **4** *4* **Conowen**[16] 6099 2-9-3 0 .... TomQueally 7 64
(William Jarvis) *a towards rr: rdn and struggling 1/2-way: sn outpcd and wl hld whn swtchd rt over 1f out* **100/1**

5 *4 1/2* **Al Wajba (USA)** 2-8-12 0 .... JMurtagh 2 44
(William Haggas) *s.i.s: sn niggled in rr: rdn and struggling over 3f out: lost tch over 2f out: no ch whn swtchd rt ins fnl f* **12/1**[3]

6 *14* **Switzerland (IRE)** 2-9-3 0 .... JoeFanning 1 4
(Mark Johnston) *s.i.s: a towards rr: rdn and wknd qckly over 2f out: wl bhd over 1f out* **14/1**

6 **7** *4 1/2* **Papal Power (IRE)**[103] 3221 2-9-3 0 .... RichardHills 4 —
(J W Hills) *dwlt: sn rcvrd to chse ldng pair: wkng whn stmbld wl over 1f out: rdr looking down and sn lost pl: wl bhd and eased fnl f: t.o* **100/1**

1m 12.57s (0.37) **Going Correction** 0.0s/f (Good) 7 Ran SP% **111.9**
Speed ratings (Par 97): **97,95,94,89,83 64,58**
toteswingers: 1&2 £2.60, 1&3 £1.10, 2&3 £3.50. CSF £19.51 TOTE £2.30: £1.30, £5.00; EX 16.20.
Owner Andrew Tinkler **Bred** A H Bennett **Trained** East Everleigh, Wilts

FOCUS
This looked a decent maiden but the market concerned only two and they dominated for much of the race. The winner is value for more than the official margin but rated below his best.

NOTEBOOK
Campanology set the standard off a mark of 90 and finally got off the mark. Not beaten far in recent starts having been disqualified after scoring at Haydock in July; the visor he wore last time was left off here. Always close up, he was nursed along by Richard Hughes and then found enough to draw away from his market rival up the hill. He could improve over the winter but will need to in order to win handicaps off his current rating. (op 6-5 tchd 5-4)
Sheikh The Reins(IRE) had missed the break and been hampered when well held in a 6f maiden on the July course in August, but ran much better than that here. He struggled to go the early pace and was being chased along before halfway, but picked up well on meeting the rising ground and finished strongly to hunt up the winner. He should be able to go on again from this. (op 14-1)
Mizwaaj(IRE) improved from an encouraging debut in the Convivial at York to finish second in a conditions event at Doncaster with previous winners in first, third and fourth. Dropping in trip, he made the running but never got any peace with the winner close up on his inside, and gave best on the climb to the line. He will probably be better off on a flatter track. (op 13-8)
Conowen had finished well beaten in previously but showed a little more this time. He now qualifies for a handicap mark. (tchd 80-1)
Al Wajba(USA), a US bred half-sister to a Group 3 winner from a family of Group and Listed performers, looked in need of this and only displayed minor promise, but should benefit from the experience. (op 11-1 tchd 14-1)
Papal Power(IRE)'s rider reported that the colt stumbled. The representative of the trainer reported that the colt lost a shoe. Official explanation: jockey said colt stumbled; trainer's rep said colt lost a shoe

6526 £300,000 TATTERSALLS MILLIONS 2YO FILLIES' TROPHY 7f
2:25 (2:26) (Class 2) 2-Y-O
£162,330 (£66,420; £29,550; £14,730; £7,380; £2,940) **Stalls** High

Form RPR

1232 **1** **Samitar**[8] 6299 2-9-0 110 .... SamHitchcott 2 87+
(Mick Channon) *chsd ldrs: wnt 2nd 3f out: rdn to ld over 1f out: drvn and styd on wl ins fnl f* **5/4**[1]

31 **2** *1 1/4* **Hazel Lavery (IRE)**[15] 6128 2-9-0 95 .... MichaelHills 11 84
(Charles Hills) *in tch in midfield: n.m.r and swtchd rt over 5f out: rdn and effrt 2f out: chsd ldng pair over 1f out: kpt on u.p to chse wnr ins fnl f: no imp fnl 100yds* **7/2**[2]

4462 **3** *1* **Glee**[14] 6169 2-9-0 77 .... DaneO'Neill 15 81
(Richard Hannon) *chsd ldr tl led 5f out: hdd over 1f out: kpt on same pce u.p fnl f* **20/1**

6246 **4** *1 1/4* **Tina's Spirit (IRE)**[14] 6169 2-9-0 77 ....(b[1]) ShaneKelly 1 78
(Richard Hannon) *hld up in tch in midfield: rdn and outpcd ent fnl 2f: drvn and rallied ent fnl f: styd on u.p: nt gng pce to threaten ldrs* **40/1**

4120 **5** *1* **Arsaadi (IRE)**[42] 5296 2-9-0 93 .... TomMcLaughlin 16 75
(Ed Dunlop) *chsd ldrs: rdn and edgd rt 2f out: kpt on same pce u.p and no imp fr over 1f out* **20/1**

0 **6** *1/2* **Aniseed (IRE)**[63] 4552 2-9-0 0 .... JMurtagh 9 74+
(William Haggas) *hld up in rr: sme hdwy whn nt clr run and hmpd wl over 1f out: swtchd rt over 1f out: r.o wl ins fnl f: nvr able to chal* **16/1**

451 **7** *3/4* **Wahylah (IRE)**[14] 6169 2-9-0 82 .... TomQueally 5 72
(Clive Brittain) *hld up in tch: n.m.r jst over 2f out: rdn and effrt to chse ldrs wl over 1f out: unable qck over 1f out: wknd ins fnl f* **12/1**

3220 **8** *3/4* **Perfect Delight**[14] 6170 2-9-0 75 .... KirstyMilczarek 18 70
(Clive Cox) *led tl 5f out: chsd ldr tl 3f out: unable qck u.p 2f out: wknd over 1f out* **50/1**

3235 **9** *1 1/4* **Roedean (IRE)**[14] 6169 2-9-0 77 .... RichardMullen 17 67
(Richard Hannon) *in tch in midfield: rdn 3f out: no imp u.p 2f out and no threat to ldrs after* **50/1**

06 **10** *1 1/2* **Princess Caetani (IRE)**[25] 5807 2-9-0 0 .... RichardHills 10 63
(Mark Johnston) *s.i.s: in tch towards rr: rdn and no imp whn nt clr run and hmpd 2f out: kpt on same pce and no threat to ldrs after* **100/1**

3 **11** *1 1/2* **Coplow**[15] 6128 2-9-0 0 .... RichardHughes 14 59
(Richard Hannon) *chsd ldrs: rdn 3f out: wkng whn hmpd and snatched up wl over 1f out: n.d after: eased fnl f* **8/1**[3]

600 **12** *shd* **Soho Rocks**[14] 6169 2-9-0 69 .... RobertHavlin 4 59
(James Toller) *in tch in midfield: rdn and unable qck over 2f out: sn outpcd and no threat to ldrs fnl 2f* **100/1**

35 **13** *nk* **Buzkashi (IRE)**[25] 5806 2-9-0 0 .... SteveDrowne 3 58
(Roger Varian) *in tch: chsd ldrs and rdn 2f out: sn unable qck and wknd over 1f out: wl btn and eased ins fnl f* **16/1**

6263 **14** *2 3/4* **Lemon Rock**[14] 6169 2-9-0 78 ....(p) BACurtis 13 51
(Noel Quinlan) *hld up in tch in midfield: rdn and unable qck over 2f out: sn outpcd and btn* **33/1**

000 **15** *3/4* **Symphony Star (IRE)**[14] 6169 2-9-0 63 .... WilliamCarson 6 49
(Paul D'Arcy) *a towards rr: rdn and struggling 3f out: n.d fnl 2f* **100/1**

0000 **16** *8* **Itsonlymakebelieve (IRE)**[14] 6170 2-9-0 40 .... TonyHamilton 12 28
(Ian Wood) *s.i.s: a towards rr: rdn and struggling 1/2-way: sn bhd* **200/1**

17 *7* **Lost Highway (IRE)** 2-9-0 0 .... JoeFanning 7 10
(Mark Johnston) *s.i.s and flashing tail early: a in rr: rdn and struggling 1/2-way: no ch fnl 2f: eased ins fnl f* **66/1**

05 **18** *32* **Party Line**[33] 5548 2-9-0 0 .... J-PGuillambert 8 —
(Mark Johnston) *a bhd: lost tch over 4f out: t.o* **100/1**

1m 24.55s (-0.85) **Going Correction** 0.0s/f (Good) 18 Ran SP% **122.0**
Speed ratings (Par 98): **104,102,101,100,98 98,97,96,95,93 91,91,91,88,87 78,70,33**
toteswingers: 1&2 £1.70, 1&3 £8.30, 2&3 £17.00. CSF £4.46 TOTE £2.20: £1.10, £1.90, £5.70; EX 7.30 Trifecta £106.00 Pool: £832.90 - 5.81 winning units..
Owner Nick & Olga Dhandsa & John & Zoe Webster **Bred** Norman Court Stud **Trained** West Ilsley, Berks

FOCUS
A very valuable sales race for fillies whose best previous winner was the subsequent dual Group 1 winner Lillie Langtry. That filly had already won at Group level and been placed in a Group 1 before taking this, and the winner this time had a similar profile. Samitar ran well below her best in success with the third and fourth the best guides to the level.

NOTEBOOK
Samitar was 15lb clear on the official ratings, having been the winner of the Group 3 Albany Stakes at Royal Ascot, touched off in a sales race on the July Course by a colt next time, and only just beaten in the Group 1 Fillies' mile here the previous week. None the worse for those exertions, she was always close to the pace and asserted up the hill. She didn't need to run to her official mark here to score but this big prize takes her earnings to over a quarter of a million pounds, a big return on the original 39,000gns she cost at the sales. She is likely to be aimed at the 1000 Guineas next season. (tchd 11-10 tchd 11-8 in a place)
Hazel Lavery(IRE) made a promising debut before taking a Newbury maiden next time, both of those runs on easy ground. She came from off the pace having been drawn in the centre of the track and, despite staying on, never looked like troubling the winner. (op 4-1)

Glee, a 6f maiden winner in May had finished second in a sales race over 6f here two weeks previously and brought home another sizeable chunk of prize-money, which has more than covered the cost of her original purchase. (op 22-1)
Tina's Spirit(IRE) placed in nurseries before finishing sixth in a sales race here two weeks ago, had a bit to find on that but, aided by first-time blinkers, finished well, having had to race on the outside of the pack throughout. (op 66-1)
Arsaadi(IRE), a winner over this trip at Newbury, then finished runner-up in a Listed race next time before running last in a Group 3 at Deauville. She was always in the leading group but could only stay on at the one speed up the hill. (op 16-1)
Aniseed(IRE) ◆, a 60,000gns yearling who ran with promise on her debut in a 7f maiden on the July Course two months previously, was held up out the back and was making ground when getting stuck behind the weakening Coplow over a furlong out. She finished well once in the clear and can be rated better than the official margin suggests. She should be winning races before too long.
Wahylah(IRE), fifth in a Group 3 before beating a number of these in a sales race here two weeks previously, travelled well for a long way but was unable to pick up when asked. (op 11-1)
Coplow had made a promising debut in a 7f maiden on easy ground at Newbury, and raced handily until dropping away quickly as if something was amiss. The rider reported that the filly hung badly left throughout. Official explanation: jockey said filly hung badly left throughout (op 9-1 tchd 10-1)

6527 £500,000 TATTERSALLS MILLIONS 2YO TROPHY — 7f
3:00 (3:01) (Class 2) 2-Y-O

£270,550 (£110,700; £49,250; £24,550; £12,300; £4,900) **Stalls** High

Form				RPR
1115	**1**		**Coupe De Ville (IRE)**[14] 6170 2-9-3 97 .... RichardHughes 6 (Richard Hannon) *hld up towards rr: bdly hmpd and snatched up 3f out: plenty to do but making hdwy and edging rt over 2f out: drvn and chsd ldrs 1f out: chal and hung lft ins fnl f: led fnl 75yds: sn in command* **8/1**	104+
5121	**2**	1	**Tell Dad**[14] 6170 2-9-3 97 .... RichardMullen 14 (Richard Hannon) *in tch: swtchd rt and drvn to chse ldrs 1f out: pressed ldr ins fnl f: nt pce of wnr but kpt on fnl 75yds* **7/1**	99
3103	**3**	½	**Mehdi (IRE)**[14] 6170 2-9-3 97 ....(t) ShaneKelly 12 (Brian Meehan) *led: rdn 2f out: hrd pressed ent fnl f: hdd and no ex fnl 75yds* **17/2**	98
2	**4**	1 ½	**Alkazim (IRE)**[14] 6170 2-9-3 0 .... CO'Donoghue 9 (David Wachman, Ire) *chsd ldr: rdn 2f out: drvn and pressing ldr but unable qck ent fnl f: wknd fnl 100yds* **18/1**	94
113	**5**	hd	**Entifaadha**[21] 5926 2-9-3 105 .... RichardHills 5 (William Haggas) *in tch: rdn 1/2-way: hdwy and drvn to chse ldrs over 1f out: pressed ldrs ent fnl f: no ex and btn ins fnl f: one pce* **9/4**[1]	94+
0210	**6**	2 ¼	**Charitable Act (FR)**[35] 5479 2-9-3 79 .... SteveDrowne 15 (William Muir) *stdd s: hld up in rr: nt clr run over 2f out: swtchd rt wl over 1f out: kpt on wl fnl f: nvr trbld ldrs* **100/1**	88
1110	**7**	nse	**Talwar (IRE)**[21] 5951 2-9-3 109 .... JMurtagh 8 (Jeremy Noseda) *chsd ldrs: rdn and pressed ldrs wl over 1f out: unable qck and drvn over 1f out: wknd ins fnl f* **9/2**[2]	88
020	**8**	¾	**Hazaz (IRE)**[14] 6170 2-9-3 86 .... TomMcLaughlin 16 (Clive Brittain) *in tch in midfield: rdn and edgd rt over 2f out: styd on same pce and no imp over 1f out* **33/1**	86
6610	**9**	4 ½	**Daghash**[14] 6170 2-9-3 79 .... J-PGuillambert 13 (Clive Brittain) *hld up towards rr: n.m.r 1/2-way: sn rdn and plenty to do: plugged on same pce and no threat to ldrs fr over 1f out* **100/1**	74
0	**10**	¾	**Dance With Me (IRE)**[14] 6170 2-9-3 0 .... NeilChalmers 7 (Andrew Balding) *s.i.s: hld up towards rr: nt clr run 3f out: sme hdwy and carried rt over 2f out: no hdwy over 1f out: sn wknd* **100/1**	72
0114	**11**	¾	**Sovereign Debt (IRE)**[70] 4334 2-9-3 87 .... PatCosgrave 3 (Michael Bell) *in tch in midfield: rdn and unable qck whn edgd lft 3f out: wknd wl over 1f out* **20/1**	70
1	**12**	2 ¾	**Miblish**[14] 6165 2-9-3 0 .... TomQueally 1 (Clive Brittain) *in tch in midfield on outer: rdn and effrt over 2f out: wknd u.p over 1f out* **13/2**[3]	63
0	**13**	2	**Jupiter Storm**[14] 6165 2-9-3 0 .... MichaelHills 4 (Gary Moore) *a towards rr: rdn and struggling 3f out: n.d after* **33/1**	58
3162	**14**	2	**Noor Zabeel (USA)**[17] 6055 2-9-3 90 ....(v[1]) SamHitchcott 2 (Mick Channon) *in tch: drvn and unable qck over 2f out: wknd wl over 1f out* **40/1**	53
210	**15**	4	**Rock Supreme (IRE)**[45] 5181 2-9-3 82 .... TonyHamilton 11 (Michael Dods) *in tch: rdn and struggling 3f out: wknd over 2f out* **80/1**	42
5	**16**	½	**Ukrainian (IRE)**[10] 6259 2-9-3 0 .... JoeFanning 10 (Mark Johnston) *chsd ldrs: rdn and losing pl qckly over 3f out: bhd fnl 2f* **100/1**	41

1m 24.34s (-1.06) **Going Correction** 0.0s/f (Good) **16** Ran SP% **120.0**
Speed ratings (Par 101): **106,104,104,102,102 99,99,98,93,92 92,88,86,84,79 79**
toteswingers: 1&2 £4.70, 1&3 £15.40, 2&3 £11.80. CSF £58.87 TOTE £9.10: £2.10, £2.20, £3.40; EX 33.80 Trifecta £491.80 Pool: £1,395.79 - 2.10 winning units..
Owner Coupe de Ville Partnership **Bred** Flor Ryan **Trained** East Everleigh, Wilts

FOCUS
This race for colts was more valuable than the fillies' race that preceded it and the time was 0.21secs faster. The best previous winner of this was Donativum, who went on to score at the Breeders' Cup next time and there were a number high-class colts in this year's line-up. The form is rated around the placed horses who ran close to their respective bests.

NOTEBOOK
Coupe De Ville(IRE), a three-time winner before finishing fifth behind today's runner-up here last time, put that below-par effort behind him. Held up early towards the outside, he had a fair amount of ground to make up 2f out but he swept through as the leaders began to tire, despite drifting left in the closing stages, and eventually scored a little comfortably. This ground was probably faster than ideal but he is a useful type and might have more to offer.
Tell Dad got off the mark in a nursery but put up an improved effort to win a sales race here a fortnight previously with several of today's field behind. He ran his race again though, confirming that form with all bar the winner, his stablemate. He has proven to be a real money-spinner, earning more than three times his purchase price this season. (op 15-2)
Mehdi(IRE) narrowly beat the earlier winner Samitar in a sales race on the July Course in August and had since finished third behind Tell Dad here two weeks ago. He improved on that and is another who has proved a bargain, winning almost three times what he cost at the sales in prize-money. (op 10-1)
Alkazim(IRE), runner-up in all four starts at 7f-1m on a sound surface, including a sales race here two weeks previously behind Tell Dad, was never far away and ran pretty close to that form with his old rival. (op 20-1 tchd 22-1)
Entifaadha won the Group 3 Acomb Stakes before finishing third in the Champagne Stakes at Doncaster with the subsequent Royal Lodge winner in fourth. Sent off favourite here, he was being urged along from around halfway but could only stay on at the one pace. Perhaps he found this ground too fast for him. (op 5-2 tchd 11-4)
Charitable Act(FR) ◆, a good second in a decent maiden on his second start before scoring over 7f on Polytrack, was out the back before staying on strongly in the closing stages to grab some prize-money. He should be winning before long on this evidence.
Talwar(IRE) completed a hat-trick when bolting up in the Group 3 Solario Stakes but had finished well beaten in a Group 1 last time. All his wins had been on good and easy ground and, having raced close to the pace, he dropped away on this faster surface. (op 5-1)
Miblish, a well-backed favourite when making a winning debut at Newbury two weeks previously, was up in grade here and, having raced towards the outside of his field throughout, faded out of contention in the last quarter-mile. This possibly came too early in his career. (op 5-1 tchd 7-1)

6528 32RED H'CAP — 1m 4f
3:35 (3:36) (Class 2) (0-105,100) 3-Y-O+

£12,450 (£3,728; £1,864; £932; £466; £234) **Stalls** Centre

Form				RPR
5261	**1**		**Art History (IRE)**[9] 6277 3-8-9 88 .... JoeFanning 9 (Mark Johnston) *chsd ldr: pressed ldr and rdn 3f out: carried lft but stl pressing ldr ins fnl f: kpt on wl fnl 50yds to ld last stride* **9/2**[2]	97+
2150	**2**	shd	**Warlu Way**[43] 5250 4-9-4 90 .... RichardHughes 5 (John Dunlop) *led and set stdy gallop 3f out: drvn and edgd lft ins fnl f: kpt on wl tl hdd last stride* **5/1**[3]	99
4220	**3**	1 ¼	**Butler (IRE)**[36] 5435 4-8-13 85 .... J-PGuillambert 3 (Luca Cumani) *wnt rt s: chsd ldng pair: rdn 3f out: edgd lft 2f out: kpt on same pce u.p ins fnl f* **6/1**	92
1500	**4**	1	**Itlaaq**[7] 6333 5-9-6 92 ....(t) PaddyAspell 6 (Michael Easterby) *stdd s: t.k.h: hld up towards rr: hdwy into midfield 1/2-way: rdn 3f out: chsd ldrs and edgd rt over 1f out: kpt on same pce ins fnl f* **20/1**	97
5252	**5**	½	**Incendo**[24] 5837 5-8-13 85 ....(t) JMurtagh 1 (James Fanshawe) *hld up in tch in midfield: rdn and effrt jst over 2f out: drvn and chsd ldrs over 1f out: styd on same pce and no imp ins fnl f* **7/1**	90
563	**6**	3 ½	**Greylami (IRE)**[29] 5693 6-9-3 89 .... MichaelHills 8 (Robert Mills) *stdd s: hld up in rr: rdn and outpcd over 2f out: swtchd lft 2f out: kpt on but no threat to ldrs fnl f* **11/1**	88
3-21	**7**	½	**Jameel (USA)**[16] 6096 3-8-7 86 .... RichardHills 10 (Saeed Bin Suroor) *chsd ldng trio: rdn 3f out: no imp and struggling 2f out: wknd over 1f out* **3/1**[1]	84
0050	**8**	shd	**Big Creek (IRE)**[10] 6249 4-8-13 85 .... ShaneKelly 2 (Jeremy Noseda) *bmpd s: t.k.h: hld up in midfield: rdn 3f out: no imp whn edgd rt over 1f out: wknd ins fnl f* **33/1**	83
1400	**9**	3	**The Betchworth Kid**[84] 3875 6-9-11 100 .... AdamBeschizza[(3)] 7 (Alan King) *stdd s: hld up in last trio: pushed along 5f out: rdn and outpcd 3f out: wl btn 2f out* **18/1**	93
410-	**10**	½	**Topolski (IRE)**[176] 6565 5-9-4 90 .... TomQueally 11 (David Arbuthnot) *t.k.h: hld up towards rr: rdn and outpcd 3f out: wl btn 2f out* **11/1**	82

2m 31.38s (-0.62) **Going Correction** 0.0s/f (Good)
WFA 3 from 4yo+ 7lb **10** Ran SP% **116.3**
Speed ratings (Par 109): **102,101,101,100,100 97,97,97,95,95**
toteswingers: 1&2 £5.10, 1&3 £3.20, 2&3 £8.20. CSF £27.24 CT £136.40 TOTE £5.30: £1.80, £2.10, £2.50; EX 20.60 Trifecta £119.40 Pool: £1,376.46 - 8.53 winning units..
Owner Sheikh Hamdan Bin Mohammed Al Maktoum **Bred** Kenilworth House Stud **Trained** Middleham Moor, N Yorks

FOCUS
A high-class handicap that often falls to an improver and this time there were two 3yos that fitted the description taking on older rivals, and one of those proved just the best. The early pace was steady, the first two held those positions throughout and it proved difficult to come from off the pace. The form is a bit muddling but best rated through the third with slight personal bests for the first two.

NOTEBOOK
Art History(IRE) had not won beyond 1m2f but acts on fast ground and had previously won on this track. Only raised 2lb for his recent win, he was always keeping the leader company and they had a good tussle over the last 3f. He looked held in the Dip but his rider had saved a bit for the climb and he was able to force his mount to the front on the line. (op 5-1)
Warlu Way, a three-time winner on fast ground at 1m2f-1m4f was 6lb above last winning mark but was given a fine waiting-in-front ride. He looked to have taken the winner's measure in the Dip but, despite running on, was caught near the line. He is probably ideally suited by a flat track but deserves compensation for this narrow defeat. (op 7-1)
Butler(IRE), a progressive performer at up to this trip this season until well beaten on easy ground last time, tracked the pace throughout and had his chance, but could not close the gap up the hill. He is 10lb above his last winning mark and the handicapper may be in charge now. (tchd 13-2)
Itlaaq, a 2m handicap winner in July off 88 but held off higher marks since, was dropped to 92 here. He tracked the pace and moved on to the heels of the leaders in the Dip, looking a big threat, but could not sustain his run up the hill. (op 16-1)
Incendo, well suited by this trip and fast ground, is another who is 10lb above his last winning mark and, although never that far off the lead, could not produce a change of gear in the closing stages. (op 8-1)
Jameel(USA) got off the mark in a maiden on fast ground last time, but was up in trip for this handicap debut and, having been close enough for most of the way, faded as if he did not stay. (op 7-2)

6529 BRITISH STALLION STUDS SUPPORTING BRITISH RACING E B F MAIDEN STKS — 1m
4:10 (4:13) (Class 4) 2-Y-O **£5,175** (£1,540; £769; £384) **Stalls** High

Form				RPR
2	**1**		**Encke (USA)**[23] 5851 2-9-3 0 .... RichardHughes 11 (Mahmood Al Zarooni) *stdd s: hld up in midfield: travelling wl but nt clr run over 2f out: swtchd rt and chsd ldrs wl over 1f out: gap opened and readily qcknd to ld over 1f out: clr and pushed out fnl f: easily* **8/13**[1]	89+
4	**2**	4 ½	**Sunley Pride**[10] 6244 2-9-3 0 .... SamHitchcott 10 (Mick Channon) *hld up in tch towards rr: rdn and hdwy ent fnl 2f: hdwy over 1f out: chsd clr wnr 1f out: kpt on but no ch w wnr* **66/1**	76
0	**3**	2 ¾	**Venegazzu (IRE)**[23] 5851 2-9-3 0 .... RobertHavlin 6 (Peter Chapple-Hyam) *in tch: rdn and effrt 2f out: nt pce of wnr over 1f out: no ch w wnr and plugged on same pce fnl f* **8/1**[3]	70
	4	¾	**Commitment** 2-9-3 0 .... J-PGuillambert 9 (Luca Cumani) *dwlt: sn nudged along and rn green in last trio: hdwy and nt clr run over 1f out: swtchd lft ent fnl f: no ch w wnr but styd on ins fnl f* **16/1**	69+
24	**5**	hd	**Good Morning Star (IRE)**[10] 6245 2-8-12 0 .... JoeFanning 7 (Mark Johnston) *chsd ldrs: rdn jst over 2f out: drvn and nt pce of wnr over 1f out: wl btn and plugged on same pce fnl f* **9/1**	62
0	**6**	1	**Renegotiate**[38] 5382 2-9-3 0 .... PatCosgrave 2 (Andrew Balding) *chsd ldr tl led 3f out: rdn 2f out: hdd over 1f out and immediately outpcd by wnr over 1f out: wknd fnl f* **33/1**	65
	7	hd	**Valiant Girl** 2-8-12 0 .... SteveDrowne 4 (Roger Charlton) *s.i.s: rn green and pushed along in rr: sme hdwy and n.m.r over 1f out: keeping on but no ch w wnr whn nt clr run wl ins fnl f* **16/1**	64+

The Form Book, Raceform Ltd, Compton, RG20 6NL

0 **8** 1 ¼ **Harry Buckle**[50] 5011 2-9-0 0 AdamBeschizza(3) 1 62
(Philip McBride) *s.i.s: hld up in tch towards rr: rdn and unable qck over 2f out: sn wknd* **66/1**

9 1 **Leitrim King (IRE)** 2-9-3 0 JMurtagh 5 60
(William Haggas) *hld up in tch in midfield: rdn and struggling over 2f out: wknd 2f out* **25/1**

10 ¾ **Attraction Ticket** 2-9-3 0 ShaneKelly 8 58
(David Simcock) *s.i.s: a last trio: rdn and stuggling over 2f out: sn wknd* **66/1**

11 1 **Sadma** 2-9-3 0 RichardHills 12 56
(Saeed Bin Suroor) *led tl 3f out: pushed along and outpcd 2f out: wknd over 1f out: fdd fnl f* **13/2**[2]

6 **12** 8 **Lazeez (USA)**[25] 5813 2-8-12 0 TomQueally 3 32
(Clive Brittain) *in tch: rdn and unable qck over 2f out: wknd 2f out: wl bhd fnl f* **33/1**

1m 38.48s (-0.12) **Going Correction** 0.0s/f (Good) **12** Ran SP% **122.3**
Speed ratings (Par 97): **100,95,92,92,91 90,90,89,88,87 86,78**
toteswingers: 1&2 £26.50, 1&3 £4.30, 2&3 £68.00. CSF £92.43 TOTE £1.60: £1.10, £11.80, £2.10; EX 43.00.
Owner Godolphin **Bred** Darley **Trained** Newmarket, Suffolk

FOCUS
A typically interesting backend maiden with several major yards represented but an easy win for the odds-on favourite. The winner looks capable of better while a couple of those behind made promising debuts.

NOTEBOOK
Encke(USA) ◆, a brother to Genius Beast, made an encouraging debut over 1m at Doncaster on good ground and was a well-backed favourite to build on that. He tracked the pace from the start and, once asked to take a gap running into the Dip, picked up well and quickly put the race to bed. He drew away under a hand-ride and this Derby entry looks a smart prospect for next season. (tchd 8-15 and 4-6)

Sunley Pride, a half-brother to several winners, including the formerly useful sprinter Resplendent Alpha, built on his debut effort, coming through in the wake of the winner and chasing him at a respectful distance up the hill. He looks capable of winning maiden on this evidence, especially with his yard going so well at present.

Venegazzu(IRE), out of Irish Oaks winner Vintage Tipple, had made late headway on his debut behind today's winner on their respective debuts, had every chance and, although unable to pick up under pressure, finished a bit closer this time. (op 10-1)

Commitment ◆, an 85,000gns half-brother to six winners at 7f-1m4f, including Fury, Secret Liason and Tryst, made a promising debut, staying on well from the back of the field. He has a Derby entry, so is clearly well regarded, and can be expected to come on a fair amount with this under his belt. (tchd 20-1 in a place)

Good Morning Star(IRE), narrowly beaten on her debut over 1m on easy ground, but well held on soft next time, was tackling fast ground for the first time and ran reasonably. She looks the sort who can make her mark in handicaps now she qualifies for a mark. (op 8-1)

Renegotiate, well beaten on his debut in a 1m Polytrack maiden in August, put up a much better effort on this turf debut under a positive ride. (tchd 40-1 and 66-1 in a place)

Valiant Girl ◆, a sister to Group 2 winner Bronze Cannon, was difficult to load on this debut and missed the break slightly. However, she was still going well when short of room on the downhill run under 2f out, and stayed on despite not getting the clearest of passages on the climb to the line. She looks one to put in the notebook with middle-distance races next season in mind.

6530 TRM SEVERALS STKS (LISTED RACE) (F&M) 1m 2f
4:45 (4:45) (Class 1) 3-Y-O+
£17,013 (£6,450; £3,228; £1,608; £807; £405) **Stalls** High

Form RPR

1301 **1** **Principal Role (USA)**[17] 6066 4-9-5 114 TomQueally 7 108+
(Sir Henry Cecil) *trckd ldrs: travelling wl but nt clr run over 2f out: swtchd rt and cruised into ld over 1f out: rdn ins fnl f: a doing enough* **4/6**[1]

5463 **2** ¾ **Poplin**[22] 5880 3-8-11 91 KirstyMilczarek 5 103
(Luca Cumani) *stdd s: t.k.h: hld up in last pair: swtchd rt and effrt wl over 1f out: chsd wnr ins fnl f: kpt on but no imp fnl 100yds* **9/1**[3]

5603 **3** 2 ¼ **Bea Remembered**[20] 5982 4-9-2 95 ShaneKelly 6 99
(Brian Meehan) *stdd s: hld up in tch in last: pushed along and effrt 2f out: edgd rt and chse ldrs 1f out: styd on same pce ins fnl f* **16/1**

-260 **4** 1 ¾ **Charleston Lady**[52] 4915 3-8-11 96 JimCrowley 4 95
(Ralph Beckett) *chsd ldrs: rdn 4f out: chsd ldr u.p over 2f out tl over 1f out: wknd ins fnl f* **10/1**

1413 **5** ¾ **Thistle Bird**[21] 5940 3-8-11 95 SteveDrowne 3 94
(Roger Charlton) *taken down early: w ldr tl led 3f out: rdn and hdd over 1f out: wknd jst ins fnl f* **7/2**[2]

4262 **6** 16 **Ela Gonda Mou**[11] 6242 4-9-2 72 AdamBeschizza 2 62
(Peter Charalambous) *led tl 3f: sn rdn: dropped out qckly over 2f out: wl bhd fnl f* **100/1**

7 1 ¾ **Ghar Shoop (IRE)** 3-8-11 0 TomMcLaughlin 1 58
(Clive Brittain) *in tch: rdn over 4f out: dropped to last and struggling over 3f out: lost tch over 2f out* **66/1**

2m 3.77s (-2.03) **Going Correction** 0.0s/f (Good)
WFA 3 from 4yo 5lb **7** Ran SP% **109.7**
Speed ratings (Par 111): **108,107,105,104,103 90,89**
toteswingers: 1&2 £2.00, 1&3 £3.00, 2&3 £8.40. CSF £7.02 TOTE £1.60: £1.10, £3.80; EX 5.20.
Owner K Abdulla **Bred** Juddmonte Farms Inc **Trained** Newmarket, Suffolk

FOCUS
Varying levels of ability in this fillies' Listed race. The winner did not have to run to her best and there are doubts over the form of those in the frame behind her.

NOTEBOOK
Principal Role(USA) stood out on official ratings and won this in the fashion that the figures suggested she would. She was a little keen early, but cruised through a gap inside the last quarter-mile to take the lead and ran out a comfortable winner, always holding the runner-up without her rider having to do more than push her out. (tchd 8-13)

Poplin beaten by a stablemate of the winner in a handicap on her previous start, was keen early but came with a good run to challenge the winner. Although she was always being held, she stayed on steadily and secured black type that will enhance her value as a broodmare. (op 8-1 tchd 10-1)

Bea Remembered had been unable to really build on her handicap success in June in four subsequent tries at this level, but she stayed on steadily from the back to secure the minor placing. Her best form is on fast ground so her options might prove limited in the short-term. (op 14-1 tchd 20-1)

Charleston Lady has not built on her good second in the Pretty Polly Stakes over C&D in the spring and, after having every chance, she could not produce an extra gear in the last 2f. (op 9-1)

Thistle Bird made the running alongside Ela Gonda Mou but, as soon as she had shaken that filly off she was challenged by the fourth and the winner and had nothing in reserve to fight them off. She is worth another try at this level. (op 4-1 tchd 3-1)

6531 E B F BAHAMIAN BOUNTY BOADICEA FILLIES' STKS (LISTED RACE) 6f
5:20 (5:20) (Class 1) 3-Y-O+
£17,013 (£6,450; £3,228; £1,608; £807; £405) **Stalls** High

Form RPR

1013 **1** **Blanche Dubawi (IRE)**[21] 5935 3-8-12 97 RichardHughes 8 106+
(Noel Quinlan) *stdd s: hld up in last pair: nt clr run: hmpd and stmbld wl over 1f out: swtchd rt and stl plenty to do over 1f out: str run fnl f to ld last stride* **2/1**[1]

6500 **2** shd **Anne Of Kiev (IRE)**[14] 6147 6-9-2 98 (t) PatCosgrave 11 106
(Jeremy Gask) *hld up in tch: swtchd rt and effrt over 1f out: rdn and qcknd to ld jst ins fnl f: hdd last stride* **9/1**

3214 **3** 1 **Rose Blossom**[34] 5528 4-9-2 103 TonyHamilton 6 103
(Richard Fahey) *led and crossed to r against stands' rail: rdn 2f out: drvn and hdd jst ins fnl f: styd on same pce fnl 100yds* **3/1**[2]

1 **4** 1 ½ **Sandslash (IRE)**[78] 3-9-3 105 JMurtagh 2 100
(Marco Botti) *stdd s: hld up in rr: rdn 2f out: hdwy on outer 1f out: r.o wl ins fnl f: nvr gng pce to rch ldrs* **15/2**

2020 **5** ¾ **Aneedah (IRE)**[24] 5827 3-8-12 97 (p) RobertHavlin 7 96+
(John Gosden) *t.k.h: hld up in tch: stl travelling wl whn nt clr run and snatched up over 1f out: nt clr run again sn after: swtchd rt and styd on same pce ins fnl f* **8/1**

431 **6** ½ **Ziraun**[18] 6034 3-8-12 72 TomQueally 1 91
(Clive Brittain) *t.k.h: hld up in tch towards rr: rdn and hdwy over 2f out: drvn and chsng ldrs whn edgd lft over 1f out: wknd ins fnl f* **40/1**

0403 **7** 3 ½ **Button Moon (IRE)**[14] 6174 3-8-12 84 (p) TomMcLaughlin 3 80
(Ian Wood) *pressed ldrs: rdn and edgd lft 2f out: wknd ent fnl f* **33/1**

0056 **8** nk **Amitola (IRE)**[13] 6189 4-8-13 83 LeeNewman 5 79
(David Barron) *chsd ldrs: rdn 1/2-way: wknd wl over 1f out* **33/1**

0063 **9** shd **Cochabamba (IRE)**[9] 6272 3-8-12 94 JoeFanning 4 79
(Roger Teal) *w ldr tl over 2f out: sn struggling and lost pl: wl btn over 1f out* **6/1**[3]

0041 **10** 1 ¼ **Misplaced Fortune**[16] 6094 6-8-13 86 (v) LouisBeuzelin 10 75
(Nigel Tinkler) *in tch: losing pl u.p over 2f out: bhd over 1f out* **16/1**

1m 11.07s (-1.13) **Going Correction** 0.0s/f (Good)
WFA 3 from 4yo+ 1lb **10** Ran SP% **119.7**
Speed ratings (Par 108): **107,106,105,103,102 101,97,96,96,95**
toteswingers: 1&2 £5.20, 1&3 £2.30, 2&3 £7.60. CSF £21.70 TOTE £3.20: £1.30, £3.60, £1.50; EX 21.00.
Owner Burns Farm Racing **Bred** Burns Farm Stud **Trained** Newmarket, Suffolk

FOCUS
Not the strongest line-up for this Listed fillies' sprint and it was something of a rough race, but the time was the best of the day. The form appears sound enough rated around the placed horses.

NOTEBOOK
Blanche Dubawi(IRE) had progressed really well this season and her third on her first try at this level last time was another step forward. Held up early, she was denied a run when the field closed up in the Dip and had to be switched to the outside. Once in the clear though, she picked up well and, under an inspired Richard Hughes (riding his fourth winner of the day), got up on the line. Considering she would have been an unlucky loser, she should be capable of building further on this. (op 5-2 tchd 13-8)

Anne Of Kiev(IRE) has not really be able to go on from her Listed race win in May, despite a couple of sound efforts. However, she had run well on her only previous visit here and, after getting a gap when others didn't, she got to the front and established what looked to be a winning lead, only to have the prize snatched away on the line. She deserves compensation but really needs fast ground to produce her best, although she does go on Polytrack. (op 8-1)

Rose Blossom set off in front as usual and got over to the rail. She made the best of her way home but was collared by the runner-up coming out of the Dip and could not respond. (tchd 11-4 and 7-2)

Sandslash(IRE) ◆ making her debut in this country for a new trainer, was carrying a 5lb penalty for her Group 3 success in Italy. She was held up at the back and, although she had a clear run down the outside and avoided the trouble, was noted making good late headway to reach the frame. She looks sure to improve on this. (op 8-1)

Aneedah(IRE), wearing cheekpieces for the first time, tracked the leaders but was short of room running into the Dip more than once before recovering to stay on up the hill. She should have finished closer.

Ziraun, who was rated just 72 after winning her maiden, was taking a big step up in grade. She looked up on the outside around 2f but could not go on and weakened up the hill.

Cochabamba(IRE) raced up with the pace early but paid for those efforts in the closing stages. (op 7-1 tchd 8-1)

Misplaced Fortune's rider reported that the mare stumbled. Official explanation: jockey said mare stumbled (tchd 18-1)

T/Plt: £21.40 to a £1 stake. Pool of £71,922.80 - 2,442.54 winning tickets. T/Qpdt: £9.60 to a £1 stake. Pool of £3,955.75 - 302.54 winning tickets. SP

6259 REDCAR (L-H)
Saturday, October 1

OFFICIAL GOING: Good to firm (firm in places; watered; 9.0)
Wind: Light half behind Weather: Warm and sunny

6532 BRITISH STALLION STUDS SUPPORTING BRITISH RACING E B F MAIDEN STKS 7f
2:15 (2:19) (Class 5) 2-Y-O **£2,975** (£885; £442; £221) **Stalls** High

Form RPR

50 **1** **Right Divine (IRE)**[73] 4213 2-9-3 0 EddieCreighton 3 83+
(Brian Meehan) *hld up: pushed along and gd hdwy over 2f out: chsd ldr over 1f out: led ins fnl f: kpt on: eased towards fin* **33/1**

422 **2** 1 ¼ **Fa'lz (IRE)**[23] 5861 2-9-3 82 ChrisCatlin 4 79
(Saeed Bin Suroor) *w ldr: led over 3f out: rdn over 1f out: edgd lft jst ins fnl f: sn hdd: no ex* **2/1**[1]

34 **3** 2 ½ **Buster Brown (IRE)**[14] 6165 2-9-3 0 FrederikTylicki 7 72
(James Given) *midfield: hdwy to chse ldr over 3f out: rdn over 2f out: kpt on* **5/2**[2]

4 4 **Springheel Jake** 2-9-3 0 DavidNolan 8 62
(Ann Duffield) *hld up in tch: hdwy to chse ldr over 2f out: kpt on one pce* **16/1**

5 1 **Kathleensluckylad (IRE)** 2-9-3 0 PhillipMakin 5 59
(Kevin Ryan) *dwlt: hld up: hdwy to chse ldrs over 3f out: kpt on one pce* **20/1**

6 ½ **Le King Beau (USA)** 2-9-3 0 BarryMcHugh 14 58+
(Tony Coyle) *s.i.s: hld up: hdwy into midfield over 3f out: sn rdn: kpt on one pce* **25/1**

00 **7** *shd* **Firefly**[11] 6230 2-9-3 0 JamesSullivan 2 58
(John Weymes) *hld up: rdn over 3f out: kpt on fnl f: nvr trbld ldrs* **100/1**

03 **8** *shd* **Blue Top**[9] 6278 2-9-3 0 DuranFentiman 11 57
(Tim Walford) *led narrowly: hdd over 3f out: wknd over 1f out* **40/1**

9 *2 ¼* **Vite (IRE)** 2-9-3 0 TomEaves 13 52
(Bryan Smart) *trckd ldrs: rdn over 3f out: sn wknd* **20/1**

2 **10** *5* **Invasor Girl (USA)**[25] 5814 2-8-12 0 PaulHanagan 1 34
(William Haggas) *w ldr: rdn over 3f out: sn wknd* **7/2**[3]

3040 **11** *3 ½* **Angel Kiss (IRE)**[33] 5555 2-8-7 47 AshleyMorgan(5) 12 24
(David O'Meara) *midfield: rdn over 3f out: sn wknd* **150/1**

12 *2 ¼* **Avonbridge Lad** 2-9-0 0 PaulPickard(3) 10 24+
(Alan Brown) *v.s.a: a in rr* **100/1**

13 *3 ¾* **Henry George** 2-9-3 0 SilvestreDeSousa 6 14
(Mark Johnston) *hld up in tch: pushed along over 3f out: sn wknd* **14/1**

00 **14** *10* **Demolition Blue (IRE)**[17] 6047 2-8-12 0 PJMcDonald 9 —
(Ben Haslam) *chsd ldrs: wknd over 3f out* **200/1**

1m 23.9s (-0.60) **Going Correction** -0.25s/f (Firm) **14** Ran SP% **118.6**
Speed ratings (Par 95): **93,91,88,84,83 82,82,82,79,73 69,67,63,51**
toteswingers:1&2:£15.70, 1&3:£19.80, 2&3:£2.30 CSF £93.76 TOTE £45.30: £8.70, £1.20, £1.40; EX 168.10.
Owner Right Tack Partnership **Bred** Mrs Mary Coonan **Trained** Manton, Wilts

FOCUS
A total of 16mm of water had been put down over the previous two days but with the hot spell continuing and the temperature nudging 25C the ground was described as fast. Traditionally quite a strong maiden, but this year's race could prove the exception. The winner was an improver and the placed horses set the level.

NOTEBOOK
Right Divine(IRE), a respectable fifth on his debut, flopped in soft ground next time. Soon in the rear and driven along, he made his effort on the wide outside and won going away. A mile nursery presumably now beckons. Official explanation: trainer's rep said, regarding apparent improvement in form, that the gelding was better suited by the firmer ground. (op 40-1)
Fa'lz(IRE), runner-up on his second and third starts, is already rated 82. After taking charge he was readily put in his place. He lacks scope and is looking fully exposed. (op 9-4 tchd 5-2 in a place)
Buster Brown(IRE), stepping up in trip, ran near to the level of his two previous efforts when in the frame at Windsor and Newbury. He is the type to do better over 1m2f plus at three. (tchd 11-4)
Springheel Jake showed ability on his debut but is another who will not reach his peak until next year. (op 12-1)
Kathleensluckylad(IRE), a relatively cheap buy, is a half-brother to two winners. He showed plenty of toe on his debut until tiring late on. He is another who will not be seen at his best until next year. (op 14-1)
Le King Beau(USA) ◆, by a top US turf horse out of a mare who has produced three winners in France, was backed at long odds. After blowing the start he made significant late ground and is worth bearing in mind. (op 66-1)
Firefly, who showed nothing on his first two starts, shaped much better but this will have blown a lowly nursery mark out of the water.
Invasor Girl(USA), runner-up first time on the all-weather at Lingfield, looked very fit, if a shade lean. She again wore a hood but after showing good speed dropped away. (op 4-1)

6533 JOHN SMITH'S REDCAR STRAIGHT-MILE CHAMPIONSHIP FINAL (H'CAP) 1m
2:50 (2:51) (Class 3) 3-Y-0+
£12,450 (£3,728; £1,864; £932; £466; £234) **Stalls** High

Form RPR

6020 **1** **Kiwi Bay**[16] 6079 6-9-4 **84** TomEaves 2 95+
(Michael Dods) *midfield: smooth hdwy over 2f out: led over 1f out: sn drvn: kpt on: jst hld on* **15/2**[3]

5000 **2** *hd* **Jo'Burg (USA)**[8] 6302 7-8-9 **75** SilvestreDeSousa 8 86+
(David O'Meara) *s.i.s: hld up: pushed along over 3f out: drvn and gd hdwy over 1f out: r.o strly fnl f: jst failed* **8/1**

2000 **3** *2* **Just Bond (IRE)**[21] 5929 9-9-2 **85** DaleSwift(3) 1 91
(Geoffrey Oldroyd) *hld up: rdn and hdwy over 2f out: chsd ldrs over 1f out: kpt on fnl f* **20/1**

0300 **4** *1* **Ginger Jack**[7] 6346 4-9-0 **80** DuranFentiman 3 84
(Geoffrey Harker) *midfield: rdn over 2f out: kpt on fnl f: wnt 4th towards fin* **10/1**

4252 **5** *hd* **Staff Sergeant**[14] 6148 4-8-11 **77** PhillipMakin 4 80
(Jim Goldie) *trckd ldr: rdn over 2f out: one pce fnl f* **11/2**[1]

6206 **6** *½* **Sir George (IRE)**[16] 6093 6-8-9 **75** (p) BarryMcHugh 16 77+
(Ollie Pears) *hld up: pushed along and hdwy over 2f out: chsd ldrs over 1f out: one pce fnl f* **16/1**

0351 **7** *2* **Jonny Lesters Hair (IRE)**[7] 6346 6-9-6 **86** DavidAllan 7 83
(Tim Easterby) *led: rdn whn hdd over 1f out: wknd ins fnl f* **6/1**[2]

2000 **8** *2* **Mujaadel (USA)**[6] 6381 6-8-10 **76** (p) AndrewMullen 6 69
(David Nicholls) *trckd ldrs: rdn over 2f out: wknd fnl f* **33/1**

3000 **9** *3 ½* **Cono Zur (FR)**[16] 6093 4-8-4 **70** (b) JamesSullivan 14 55
(Ruth Carr) *w ldr: rdn over 2f out: wknd over 1f out* **28/1**

2250 **10** *2 ¼* **File And Paint (IRE)**[43] 5255 3-8-3 **75** DeclanCannon(3) 12 55
(Lawrence Mullaney) *midfield: rdn over 2f out: sn no imp* **40/1**

0034 **11** *1 ½* **Northern Fling**[50] 5006 7-8-9 **75** FrederikTylicki 11 51
(Jim Goldie) *hld up: nvr threatened* **25/1**

2440 **12** *½* **Law To Himself (IRE)**[31] 5622 4-7-12 **64** oh1 JimmyQuinn 10 39
(Alan Swinbank) *in tch: rdn over 2f out: sn wknd* **16/1**

2-10 **13** *2 ¼* **Mullins Way (USA)**[14] 6148 3-9-3 **86** FergusSweeney 5 56
(Jo Hughes) *midfield: rdn over 3f out: wknd over 2f out* **14/1**

0412 **14** *nk* **Just The Tonic**[3] 6450 4-7-13 **65** CathyGannon 9 34
(Marjorie Fife) *hld up in midfield: rdn over 2f out: wknd over 1f out* **11/1**

1360 **15** *shd* **Aquarian Spirit**[8] 6290 4-8-10 **76** PaulHanagan 15 45
(Richard Fahey) *in tch: rdn over 2f out: sn wknd* **14/1**

0314 **16** *5* **Charlie Cool**[19] 6006 8-9-10 **90** (b) PJMcDonald 13 47
(Ruth Carr) *dwlt: hld up: rdn over 3f out: a in rr* **12/1**

1m 34.54s (-3.46) **Going Correction** -0.25s/f (Firm)
WFA 3 from 4yo+ 3lb **16** Ran SP% **120.2**
Speed ratings (Par 107): **107,106,104,103,103 103,101,99,95,93 91,91,89,88,88 83**
toteswingers:1&2:£6.90, 1&3:£37.70, 2&3:£42.60 CSF £61.02 CT £1215.76 TOTE £9.20: £2.10, £2.60, £4.80, £3.10; EX 43.70.
Owner Kiwi Racing **Bred** Templeton Stud **Trained** Denton, Co Durham

FOCUS
A wide-open renewal of this Straight-Mile Final. The form is not that strong for the grade with it being something of a draw race, and the third is probably the best guide to the level.

NOTEBOOK
Kiwi Bay had taken this 12 months ago from a 5lb higher mark. He loves coming between horses and this was his fourth course win. He travelled strongly towards the outer but in the end the post came just in time. (op 7-1 tchd 13-2)
Jo'Burg(USA) ◆, a multiple winner at up to 1m2f, came into this on the back of a year's drought. As a result he has slipped down the ratings and this was just his second start for this yard. Last away, he made up a deal of ground on the wide outside and needed just one more stride. He looks sure to go one better soon. (tchd 17-2)
Just Bond(IRE), 4lb higher than his win at Beverley in May, came into this on the back of three moderate efforts. He loves fast ground though. (op 25-1)
Ginger Jack, a winner four times last year for another yard, is now 7lb below his last success and this was much his best effort this year. He can find a race this backend. (op 9-1)
Staff Sergeant, winner of just one of his previous 12 starts, continues in good form but that second career success is proving elusive. (op 8-1)
Sir George(IRE), who won four times last year and is now 7lb below his last winning mark, wore cheekpieces for the second time and this was one of his better efforts. He is struggling to string two sound efforts together this time. (op 14-1)
Jonny Lesters Hair(IRE), hoisted 9lb after his win from the front over 1m2f at Ripon, took them along but over this trip on this fast ground was readily out-speeded in the end. (tchd 11-2)

6534 GUISBOROUGH STKS (LISTED RACE) 7f
3:25 (3:25) (Class 1) 3-Y-0+ **£17,013** (£6,450; £3,228; £1,608; £807) **Stalls** High

Form RPR

1401 **1** **Chilworth Lad**[15] 6129 3-9-1 108 MatthewDavies 2 114
(Mick Channon) *hld up: hdwy 3f out: led over 2f out: strly pressed fnl f: kpt on: hld on towards fin* **5/1**[2]

1020 **2** *nk* **Majestic Myles (IRE)**[14] 6147 3-9-1 111 PaulHanagan 1 113
(Richard Fahey) *led for 1f: remained prom: rdn over 2f out: chal strly fnl f: kpt on: jst hld* **9/4**[1]

1030 **3** *3* **High Standing (USA)**[14] 6147 6-9-0 103 (p) PJMcDonald 4 102
(William Haggas) *led after 1f: hdd over 2f out: sn rdn: one pce fnl f* **7/1**[3]

5160 **4** *hd* **Doncaster Rover (USA)**[28] 5707 5-9-3 107 SilvestreDeSousa 5 104
(David Brown) *hld up: pushed along over 3f out: one pce* **5/1**[2]

3412 **5** *12* **Colonial (IRE)**[15] 6129 4-9-0 108 PhillipMakin 3 69
(Saeed Bin Suroor) *prom: rdn over 2f out: wknd over 1f out* **9/4**[1]

1m 22.14s (-2.36) **Going Correction** -0.25s/f (Firm)
WFA 3 from 4yo+ 2lb **5** Ran SP% **107.4**
Speed ratings (Par 111): **103,102,99,99,85**
CSF £15.71 TOTE £6.80: £2.20, £1.60; EX 19.10.
Owner 7Rus **Bred** Phil Jen Racing **Trained** West Ilsley, Berks

FOCUS
A tight Listed race. Just 5lb between the field on official ratings but in the end the two 3-y-os pulled clear. the form is not the most solid and the first two look the best guides.

NOTEBOOK
Chilworth Lad is as tough as old boots and has made noticeable improvement during the course of the season. After taking a handicap at Salisbury in May from a mark of 95 he has followed up twice at Newbury, the latest a Listed event on easy ground. After a head-to-head and a bumping match he came out just on top. He will have a big sales price on his head now, looking ideal material for rich prizes abroad. (op 9-2)
Majestic Myles(IRE), fifth home on the far side in the Ayr Gold Cup, is another 3-y-o to have made marked progress during the season, having taken a handicap Newmarket in May from a mark of 93. Beaten a head by Doncaster Rover at York in August, he met that rival on 2lb better terms. After a barging match he came off just second-best. (op 5-2 tchd 11-4 in a place)
High Standing(USA), one place ahead of Majestic Myles on the far side at Ayr, elected to race virtually alone down the stands' side but persisted in hanging left and gave his rider little assistance. (op 15-2 tchd 8-1)
Doncaster Rover(USA), the first to come under pressure, proved gallant in defeat, though well held in the end. (op 9-2 tchd 4-1)
Colonial(IRE), beaten three-quarters of a length by Chilworth Lad at Newbury, had a 4lb pull in the weights but dropped out in a matter of strides. He may be the type who needs to have his own way in front, which was not the case here. Official explanation: trainer's rep said colt was unsuited by the good to firm (firm in places) ground (tchd 5-2)

6535 TOTEPOOL TWO-YEAR-OLD TROPHY (LISTED RACE) 6f
4:00 (4:03) (Class 1) 2-Y-0
£117,786 (£44,655; £22,348; £11,132; £5,587; £2,803) **Stalls** High

Form RPR

1016 **1** **Bogart**[23] 5849 2-8-12 103 PhillipMakin 3 107
(Kevin Ryan) *trckd ldr: rdn over 1f out: sn edgd rt: led 1f out: kpt on wl* **11/2**[2]

1123 **2** *1 ½* **Excelette (IRE)**[42] 5286 2-8-9 95 DavidAllan 6 99
(Bryan Smart) *led: rdn 2f out: edgd rt appr fnl f: sn hdd: kpt on but no ch w wnr* **10/1**[3]

2342 **3** *hd* **Silverheels (IRE)**[42] 5276 2-8-12 103 PaulHanagan 12 101
(Paul Cole) *chsd ldrs: rdn over 2f out: kpt on fnl f* **11/1**

0020 **4** *2 ¼* **Evervescent (IRE)**[13] 6196 2-8-3 83 (p) AndreaAtzeni 10 85
(J S Moore) *hld up: pushed along 3f out: hdwy over 1f out: kpt on fnl f* **50/1**

4012 **5** *nse* **Imelda Mayhem**[28] 5708 2-7-12 82 (p) JimmyQuinn 14 80
(J S Moore) *hld up: rdn over 2f out: hdwy over 1f out: kpt on fnl f* **33/1**

1122 **6** *1 ½* **Gold City (IRE)**[24] 5826 2-9-2 98 ChrisCatlin 11 93
(Saeed Bin Suroor) *prom: rdn over 2f out: wknd ins fnl f* **14/1**

21 **7** *½* **Place In My Heart**[39] 5351 2-8-4 86 NickyMackay 13 80
(George Baker) *prom: rdn to chal 2f out: wknd ins fnl f* **12/1**

0345 **8** *¾* **Jack Who's He (IRE)**[22] 5876 2-8-9 87 PJMcDonald 17 82
(David Evans) *sn pushed along towards rr: kpt on fnl f: nvr trbld ldrs* **66/1**

5200 **9** *nk* **Es Que Love (IRE)**[24] 5825 2-8-12 85 AdrianNicholls 15 84
(Mark Johnston) *chsd ldrs: rdn over 2f out: wknd fnl f* **50/1**

3122 **10** *¾* **Vital Gold**[35] 5487 2-8-9 89 LiamJones 8 79
(William Haggas) *prom: rdn and lost pl over 1f out: wkng whn short of room ins fnl f* **20/1**

1053 **11** *½* **Fulbright**[7] 6323 2-9-3 92 FrederikTylicki 9 85
(Mark Johnston) *chsd ldrs: rdn over 2f out: wknd over 1f out* **20/1**

0153 **12** *2 ¼* **Bling King**[22] 5876 2-8-9 93 (b[1]) FergusSweeney 16 70
(Eve Johnson Houghton) *midfield: rdn over 2f out: no imp* **40/1**

2632 **13** *1* **Bannock (IRE)**[64] 4495 2-8-6 108 SilvestreDeSousa 22 64
(Mark Johnston) *chsd ldrs towards stands' side: rdn over 2f out: sn btn* **2/1**[1]

1330 **14** *¾* **Hidden Passion (USA)**[30] 5656 2-8-11 85 (t) EddieCreighton 5 66
(Brian Meehan) *s.i.s: hld up: rdn over 2f out: nvr threatened* **100/1**

0121 **15** *nk* **Free Zone**[7] 6323 2-9-0 83 JamesSullivan 19 68
(Bryan Smart) *chsd ldrs: wknd over 1f out* **50/1**

4206 **16** *shd* **Monnoyer**[70] 4334 2-8-12 82 AndrewMullen 7 66
(David Nicholls) *midfield: rdn 3f out: sn no imp* **200/1**

1044 **17** *¾* **The Penny Horse (IRE)**[72] 4228 2-8-3 83 (t) RyanPowell 1 55
(J S Moore) *s.i.s: hld up: nvr threatened* **100/1**

1100 **18** *1 ¼* **Cockney Fire**[30] 5656 2-8-4 85 CathyGannon 20 52
(David Evans) *chsd ldrs towards stands' side: rdn over 2f out: wknd over 1f out* **66/1**

6011 **19** *nse* **Bop It**^{63} 4538 2-8-12 84 .... TomEaves 4 60
(Bryan Smart) *hld up: rdn over 2f out: sn no imp* **16/1**
4440 **20** *shd* **North Star Boy (IRE)**^{23} 5849 2-9-2 97 .... (b) SeanLevey 18 63
(Richard Hannon) *hld up: nvr threatened* **25/1**
4026 **21** *1* **Bear Behind (IRE)**^{24} 5827 2-8-9 99 .... RichardKingscote 21 53
(Tom Dascombe) *hld up towards stands' side: a towards rr* **20/1**
2324 **22** *5* **Kool Henry (IRE)**^{15} 6114 2-8-3 87 .... DuranFentiman 23 31
(David O'Meara) *in tch stands' side: wknd qckly over 2f out* **40/1**

69.21 secs (-2.59) **Going Correction** -0.25s/f (Firm) 2y crse rec **22** Ran SP% **123.7**
Speed ratings (Par 103): **107,105,104,101,101 99,99,98,97,96 95,92,91,90,90 90,89,87,87,87 85,79**
toteswingers:1&2:£10.60, 1&3:£9.10, 2&3:£58.10 CSF £49.91 TOTE £7.40: £2.80, £3.40, £3.10; EX 80.00 Trifecta £385.20 Pool: £1,431.72 - 2.75 winning units..
Owner Mrs Angie Bailey **Bred** Toby Barker **Trained** Hambleton, N Yorks

FOCUS
A strong renewal of this valuable Listed race, the weights carried depending on the median price of the sire's stock at the public auction yearling sales in 2010. Not many got into it and those drawn towards the stands' side seemed to be at a disadvantage. The third and fourth help to set the standard in a straightforward contest.

NOTEBOOK
Bogart, who had taken the valuable sales race on easy ground at York in August, did not get home after racing with the choke out over an extra half-furlong in a similar event at Doncaster. This time happy to accept a lead, he went to the front travelling strongly. This 23,000gns purchase brought his prize-money total to £269,491 and will now be aimed at a Group race in France. (op 6-1)
Excelette(IRE), placed in Listed races at Newbury and York, had 5lb to find with the winner on official ratings. Stepping up to 6f, she dominated the field racing middle to far side but the colt saw it out much the better. (op 14-1)
Silverheels(IRE), who had the same chance as the winner on ratings, was dropping back in trip after finishing runner-up in a Listed race over 7f at Sandown. He is looking exposed and will appreciate a return to 7f. (op 9-1)
Evervescent(IRE), runner-up in the Woodcote Stakes at Epsom's Derby meeting, has struggled since. In first-time cheekpieces, he was putting in all his best work at the finish and he, too, needs a return to 7f.
Imelda Mayhem, in good form in nurseries, was receiving weight from all her rivals. Another sporting first-time cheekpieces, she appeared very late on the scene and will be suited by a return to 7f.
Gold City(IRE), who made mincemeat of Evervescent at Nottingham in August, has since finished runner-up at Ripon and Doncaster and this is as good as he is. (tchd 12-1)
Place In My Heart, a Yarmouth maiden winner on her second start and the least exposed in the field, showed plenty of speed but at this stage 5f may play more to her strengths. (op 9-1)
Jack Who's He(IRE), eighth in the Coventry, ran much his best race since. (tchd 50-1)
Es Que Love(IRE) was another to run above his official mark on the back of two poor efforts. (op 66-1)
Bannock(IRE), 11lb clear on official ratings, had been placed behind top youngsters in Group 2 races at Newmarket and Goodwood. Absent for two months, he was reported to have suffered a minor set-back and missed a bit of work. Racing towards the unfavoured stands' side, he was flat out and going nowhere at halfway. Expect him to bounce back. Official explanation: jockey said colt had no more to give (op 9-4)
Monnoyer Official explanation: jockey said gelding had a breathing problem

6536 MARKET CROSS JEWELLERS (S) STKS 1m 2f
4:35 (4:35) (Class 5) 3-5-Y-O **£1,940** (£577; £288; £144) **Stalls** Low

Form RPR
6521 **1** **Yorksters Prince (IRE)**^{10} 6264 4-9-6 63 .... (b) BarryMcHugh 7 67
(Tony Coyle) *mde all: qcknd clr 4f out: kpt on wl fnl 2f: unchal* **7/4**^{1}
4602 **2** *3 1/4* **Sinatramania**^{10} 6264 4-9-6 56 .... PatrickMathers 5 60
(Tracy Waggott) *hld up: hdwy to chse (clr) wnr over 2f out: edgd lft: kpt on fnl f: no imp* **6/1**^{3}
0-00 **3** *1/2* **Pursuing**^{10} 6253 3-8-4 54 .... PaulHanagan 1 48
(Nigel Tinkler) *t.k.h: prom: outpcd over 4f out: rallied over 2f out: kpt on fnl f: no imp* **13/2**
3034 **4** *5* **En Fuego**^{10} 6264 4-9-0 54 .... SilvestreDeSousa 6 43
(Geoffrey Harker) *hld up: rdn over 3f out: hdwy over 1f out: nvr able to chal* **5/1**^{2}
0300 **5** *3 1/4* **Magic Millie (IRE)**^{11} 6235 4-8-4 48 .... AshleyMorgan$^{(5)}$ 3 32
(David O'Meara) *s.i.s: t.k.h and sn chsng ldrs: rdn and outpcd over 2f out: sn btn* **10/1**
2534 **6** *nk* **Goodmanyourself**^{11} 6229 3-8-9 46 .... RussKennemore 8 36
(Paul Midgley) *t.k.h: sn pressing wnr: rdn and edgd lft 4f out: lost 2nd and wknd over 2f out* **20/1**
6560 **7** *1 1/4* **Valentine's Gift**^{31} 5619 3-8-9 54 .... AndrewElliott 9 33
(Neville Bycroft) *t.k.h: in tch on outside: rdn and outpcd over 4f out: n.d after* **25/1**
0-00 **8** *1/2* **Huntingfortreasure**^{8} 6295 4-9-0 63 .... PhillipMakin 2 32
(Philip Kirby) *t.k.h: hld up in tch: drvn and edgd lft over 3f out: wknd over 2f out* **8/1**
300/ **9** *1 1/4* **Bridge Valley**^{693} 7290 4-9-0 68 .... MichaelStainton 4 30
(Jason Ward) *hld up: drvn along over 3f out: sn wknd* **33/1**

2m 6.67s (-0.43) **Going Correction** -0.25s/f (Firm)
WFA 3 from 4yo 5lb **9** Ran SP% **111.0**
Speed ratings (Par 103): **91,88,88,84,81 81,80,79,78**
toteswingers:1&2:£3.10, 1&3:£3.40, 2&3:£6.20 CSF £11.35 TOTE £2.50: £1.60, £1.90, £2.50; EX 7.00.The winner was bought in for 7,000gns.
Owner B Kerr, N Kench, WPS Johnson **Bred** Lady Legard & Sir Tatton Sykes **Trained** Norton, N Yorks

FOCUS
A one-horse seller but the form looks sound with the winner, second and fourth close to the previous month's course form.

6537 WIN A VIP DAY OUT @ REDCARRACING.CO.UK H'CAP 5f
5:10 (5:12) (Class 5) (0-75,72) 3-Y-0+ **£1,940** (£577; £288; £144) **Stalls** High

Form RPR
6105 **1** **Forever's Girl**^{17} 6044 5-9-2 67 .... SilvestreDeSousa 2 79
(Geoffrey Oldroyd) *dwlt: midfield: rdn and hdwy over 1f out: led ins fnl f: kpt on* **7/2**^{1}
-004 **2** *3/4* **Igoyougo**^{28} 5720 5-9-1 66 .... PaulQuinn 4 76
(Noel Wilson) *w ldr: rdn over 2f out: kpt on fnl f* **8/1**
650 **3** *1 1/4* **Style And Panache (IRE)**^{24} 5831 3-9-5 70 .... CathyGannon 5 75
(David Evans) *prom: rdn over 2f out: kpt on* **22/1**
6144 **4** *nse* **Select Committee**^{7} 6348 6-9-7 72 .... (v) PhillipMakin 6 77
(John Quinn) *midfield: rdn over 2f out: kpt on ins fnl f* **9/2**^{2}
3000 **5** *nk* **Nomoreblondes**^{7} 6350 7-9-5 70 .... (v) PJMcDonald 11 74
(Paul Midgley) *chsd ldrs: rdn over 2f out: kpt on ins fnl f* **12/1**
1003 **6** *nk* **Hypnosis**^{10} 6265 8-9-0 70 .... NeilFarley$^{(5)}$ 1 73
(Noel Wilson) *led narrowly: rdn over 2f out: hdd ins fnl f: wknd* **20/1**
1460 **7** *1 1/4* **Boundless Spirit**^{10} 6265 3-9-2 67 .... (p) AdrianNicholls 7 65
(David Nicholls) *dwlt: hld up: rdn 2f out: kpt on one pce fnl f: nvr trbld ldrs* **20/1**
200 **8** *shd* **Caledonia Princess**^{9} 6283 5-9-7 72 .... (b) FrederikTylicki 3 70
(Jo Hughes) *prom: rdn over 2f out: wknd ins fnl f* **14/1**
0000 **9** *1/2* **Mey Blossom**^{9} 6276 6-9-2 67 .... MichaelStainton 8 63
(Richard Whitaker) *hld up in rr: sn pushed along: nvr threatened* **33/1**
0522 **10** *nk* **Silvanus (IRE)**^{9} 6276 6-8-13 64 .... (p) PaulHanagan 10 59
(Paul Midgley) *hld up: rdn over 2f out: no imp* **7/1**^{3}
0040 **11** *3/4* **Nadeen (IRE)**^{33} 5554 4-9-6 71 .... TomEaves 9 63
(Michael Smith) *midfield: rdn over 2f out: wknd ins fnl f* **12/1**
0431 **12** *1* **Rhal (IRE)**^{10} 6265 3-9-0 72 .... JustinNewman$^{(7)}$ 12 61
(Bryan Smart) *hld up: rdn over 2f out: a towards rr* **8/1**
0064 **13** *49* **Senate Majority**^{16} 6076 4-9-1 66 .... (b) DavidNolan 13 —
(Tim Easterby) *continuously bucked and virtually p.u after 1f* **9/1**

57.51 secs (-1.09) **Going Correction** -0.25s/f (Firm) **13** Ran SP% **121.6**
Speed ratings (Par 103): **98,96,94,94,94 93,91,91,90,90 89,87,9**
toteswingers:1&2:£9.10, 1&3:£19.40, 2&3:£39.30 CSF £30.24 CT £433.10 TOTE £5.10: £2.00, £4.70, £5.20; EX 49.30.
Owner R C Bond **Bred** R C Bond **Trained** Brawby, N Yorks

FOCUS
A low-grade dash with just 8lb between top and bottom weight but the form is straightforward rated around the placed horses.
Senate Majority Official explanation: jockey said gelding bucked for the first furlong

6538 FOLLOW REDCARRACING ON FACEBOOK & TWITTER H'CAP 1m 2f
5:45 (5:45) (Class 5) (0-75,73) 3-Y-0+ **£1,940** (£577; £288; £144) **Stalls** Low

Form RPR
050 **1** **Phluke**^{23} 5845 10-9-0 63 .... FergusSweeney 7 71
(Eve Johnson Houghton) *led: rdn whn hdd over 1f out: rallied to ld again fnl 100yds* **28/1**
4500 **2** *1 1/4* **Hidden Glory**^{14} 6155 4-9-6 69 .... FrederikTylicki 5 75
(James Given) *hld up: pushed along and gd hdwy on outer over 2f out: led over 1f out: hdd fnl 100yds* **9/2**^{2}
0103 **3** *1 1/4* **Auto Mac**^{10} 6262 3-9-2 70 .... (b) SilvestreDeSousa 1 73
(Neville Bycroft) *racd keenly: hld up in tch on inner: rdn and hdwy over 1f out: kpt on fnl f* **8/1**
0321 **4** *nk* **Sciampin**^{52} 4916 3-9-4 72 .... AndreaAtzeni 3 74
(Marco Botti) *in tch: rdn over 2f out: kpt on one pce* **15/8**^{1}
152 **5** *nk* **Military Call**^{28} 5721 4-8-12 61 .... PaulHanagan 8 63
(Alistair Whillans) *hld up: pushed along over 3f out: hdwy on outer over 1f out: one pce fnl f* **15/2**
0100 **6** *1 1/4* **Daaweitza**^{10} 6263 8-9-8 71 .... (be) PhillipMakin 2 70
(Brian Ellison) *trckd ldr: rdn over 2f out: wknd ins fnl f* **13/2**^{3}
001 **7** *2 1/4* **Dean Iarracht (IRE)**^{11} 6235 5-8-10 59 oh1 .... (p) PatrickMathers 6 54
(Tracy Waggott) *dwlt: midfield: rdn over 2f out: lost pl over 1f out: no imp fnl f* **10/1**
0403 **8** *4* **Amazing Blue Sky**^{10} 6263 5-9-10 73 .... JamesSullivan 9 60
(Ruth Carr) *trckd ldr: rdn over 2f out: wknd over 1f out* **9/1**

2m 6.57s (-0.53) **Going Correction** -0.25s/f (Firm)
WFA 3 from 4yo+ 5lb **8** Ran SP% **111.7**
Speed ratings (Par 103): **92,91,90,89,89 88,86,83**
toteswingers:1&2:£10.80, 1&3:£9.90, 2&3:£6.00 CSF £142.46 CT £1108.33 TOTE £21.10: £4.40, £1.50, £2.50; EX 246.00.
Owner Mrs R F Johnson Houghton **Bred** Mrs R F Johnson Houghton **Trained** Blewbury, Oxon

FOCUS
A modest handicap run at a very steady pace, and the form is messy and no better than modest.
T/Plt: £96.60 to a £1 stake. Pool:£61,180.99 - 462.00 winning tickets T/Qpdt: £33.90 to a £1 stake. Pool:£2,943.05 - 64.10 winning tickets AS

6501 WOLVERHAMPTON (A.W) (L-H)
Saturday, October 1

OFFICIAL GOING: Standard
Wind: Fresh behind Weather: Fine and sunny

6539 WOLVERHAMPTON-RACECOURSE.CO.UK MEDIAN AUCTION MAIDEN STKS 5f 216y(P)
5:50 (5:50) (Class 6) 2-Y-O **£2,070** (£616; £307; £153) **Stalls** Low

Form RPR
302 **1** **Right Result (IRE)**^{9} 6274 2-9-3 77 .... PBBeggy 11 80+
(John Quinn) *chsd ldrs: led over 1f out: rdn clr* **5/2**^{2}
2 **2** *6* **Gabriel's Lad (IRE)**^{25} 5812 2-9-0 0 .... MartinHarley$^{(3)}$ 8 62
(Denis Coakley) *sn led: rdn and hdd over 1f out: no ex ins fnl f* **6/4**^{1}
53 **3** *1 1/2* **Archers Prize (IRE)**^{16} 6092 2-9-3 0 .... RichardMullen 12 58
(Ed McMahon) *mid-div: pushed along 1/2-way: hdwy over 2f out: sn rdn: styd on same pce fr over 1f out: wnt 3rd ins fnl f: nt trble ldrs* **7/1**^{3}
4 *1* **Tiablo (IRE)** 2-8-7 0 .... LauraPike$^{(5)}$ 6 50+
(David Simcock) *s.s: sn pushed along in rr: hdwy over 1f out: r.o to go 4th ins fnl f: nvr nrr* **18/1**
06 **5** *5* **Raffinn**^{12} 6214 2-9-0 0 .... KieranO'Neill$^{(3)}$ 9 40
(Sylvester Kirk) *chsd ldr: rdn over 2f out: wknd over 1f out* **7/1**^{3}
035 **6** *1 1/4* **Monumental Man**^{133} 2283 2-9-0 70 .... AmyRyan$^{(3)}$ 3 36
(James Unett) *chsd ldrs: rdn over 2f out: wknd over 1f out* **16/1**
0250 **7** *3/4* **Monty Fay (IRE)**^{15} 6132 2-9-3 63 .... WilliamCarson 7 34
(Derek Haydn Jones) *prom: rdn 1/2-way: wknd over 2f out* **22/1**
0 **8** *1 1/2* **Knoydart (USA)**^{18} 6019 2-9-3 0 .... (b^{1}) FrankieMcDonald 1 29
(Amanda Perrett) *sn pushed along in rr: nvr nrr* **33/1**
06 **9** *3 1/2* **Lizzie Drippin**^{7} 6344 2-8-5 0 .... DavidSimmonson$^{(7)}$ 2 14
(Michael Easterby) *broke wl: sn lost pl: bhd fr 1/2-way* **80/1**
0 **10** *1 1/2* **Peters Pleasure**^{18} 6030 2-8-9 0 .... RyanClark$^{(3)}$ 4 9
(Robert Cowell) *mid-div: sn pushed along: bhd fr 1/2-way* **100/1**
11 *3 1/2* **Blackamoor Zara** 2-8-12 0 .... SaleemGolam 5 —
(Bruce Hellier) *s.s: outpcd* **125/1**
00 **12** *shd* **All Good News (IRE)**^{8} 6308 2-9-0 0 .... LeeTopliss$^{(3)}$ 13 —
(Lisa Williamson) *chsd ldrs: rdn over 3f out: wknd over 2f out* **150/1**

1m 13.76s (-1.24) **Going Correction** -0.15s/f (Stan) **12** Ran SP% **115.7**
Speed ratings (Par 93): **102,94,92,90,84 82,81,79,74,72 68,67**
toteswingers:1&2:£1.50, 1&3:£4.70, 2&3:£3.20 CSF £6.21 TOTE £4.20: £1.70, £1.10, £2.20; EX 6.00.
Owner Right Tack Partnership **Bred** Rathbarry Stud **Trained** Settrington, N Yorks

FOCUS
No more than a fair maiden and one in which only concerned the two market leaders in the straight. The gallop reasonable was and the winner edged towards the far rail in the closing stages. The rating could underestimate the winner who could have been assessed considerably higher.

NOTEBOOK

Right Result(IRE), the most experienced of these, ran as well as he ever has done on this all-weather debut when beating the market leader with plenty in hand. He looks worth a try at 7f and, although life will be tougher in nurseries, he'll be interesting back at this track in an ordinary event. (op 9-4 tchd 11-4)

Gabriel's Lad(IRE) had shaped well in soft ground on his debut but failed to build on that after racing with the choke out in the first half of this all-weather debut. Nevertheless he again showed enough to suggest he should be able to win an ordinary event at some point. (op 7-4)

Archers Prize(IRE) wasn't disgraced on this all-weather debut returned to this more suitable trip. Run-of-the-mill nurseries will be the way forward with him. (op 9-1)

Tiablo(IRE) ◆ shaped with promise without being knocked about after a tardy start on this racecourse debut. This half-sister to 1m firm-ground winner Grade 3 winner Fearless Flyer as well as to a couple of other winners is sure to improve for this experience and should win a race. (op 14-1)

Raffinn should benefit from the switch to handicaps and is likely to do better in due course. Official explanation: jockey said gelding hung left-handed (op 8-1 tchd 13-2)

Monumental Man again underlined his vulnerability in this type of event. (tchd 14-1)

6540 HOTEL & CONFERENCING AT WOLVERHAMPTON (S) STKS 5f 20y(P)

6:20 (6:20) (Class 6) 2-Y-O £1,533 (£452; £226) Stalls Low

Form RPR

5623 **1** **Balm**[14] 6178 2-8-3 67 KieranO'Neill(3) 1 64
(Richard Hannon) *led: hdd over 3f out: rdn to ld over 1f out: r.o* **9/4**[1]

4200 **2** *1 ¼* **Musical Valley**[7] 6323 2-8-13 74 (t) RossAtkinson(3) 2 70
(Tom Dascombe) *hld up: hdwy and swtchd rt over 1f out: sn rdn: r.o wl* **11/2**[3]

2132 **3** *1* **Pint Size**[22] 5896 2-8-11 84 (b[1]) AntiocoMurgia(5) 12 66
(Gay Kelleway) *chsd ldr tl led over 3f out: hdd over 1f out: styd on same pce ins fnl f* **10/3**[2]

050 **4** *½* **Bitter Lemon**[16] 6092 2-8-3 49 AmyRyan(3) 5 54
(Kevin Ryan) *mid-div: pushed along 3f out: hdwy over 1f out: nt clr run ent fnl f: r.o u.p* **25/1**

0420 **5** *½* **Liebesziel**[6] 6384 2-8-8 64 (b[1]) MartinHarley(3) 11 57
(Alan McCabe) *chsd ldrs: hung lft and no ex ins fnl f* **11/1**

505 **6** *½* **Vitalicious**[37] 5418 2-8-6 50 RichardMullen 3 51
(Ed McMahon) *prom: pushed along 3f out: outpcd 1/2-way: styd on ins fnl f* **16/1**

362 **7** *¾* **Courtland King (IRE)**[31] 5625 2-9-2 76 PBBeggy 6 58
(David Evans) *sn pushed along in rr: r.o ins fnl f: nvr nrr* **6/1**

3004 **8** *¾* **Masivo Man (IRE)**[11] 6237 2-8-11 46 (b) WilliamCarson 7 50
(Chris Dwyer) *prom: rdn 1/2-way: styd on same pce appr fnl f* **66/1**

0640 **9** *7* **Maria Medecis (IRE)**[17] 6043 2-8-6 49 (v) MarcHalford 13 20
(Ann Duffield) *s.i.s: a in rr* **100/1**

0000 **10** *hd* **Our Boy Billy**[18] 6021 2-8-8 45 RyanClark(3) 9 24
(Robert Cowell) *s.i.s: a in rr* **40/1**

2000 **11** *nk* **Key Addition (IRE)**[9] 6284 2-8-6 65 (b) JamesRogers(5) 4 23
(William Muir) *sn outpcd* **12/1**

00 **12** *1 ½* **Brian's Best**[7] 6352 2-8-4 0 JakePayne(7) 8 18
(Bruce Hellier) *sn outpcd* **200/1**

4600 **13** *8* **Imperial Weapon (IRE)**[24] 5833 2-8-6 40 SaleemGolam 10 —
(John Spearing) *hld up: rdn 3f out: sn lost tch* **125/1**

61.84 secs (-0.46) **Going Correction** -0.15s/f (Stan) **13** Ran SP% **115.5**

Speed ratings (Par 93): **97,95,93,92,91 91,89,88,77,77 76,74,61**

toteswingers:1&2:£3.50, 1&3:£2.10, 2&3:£4.50 CSF £13.88 TOTE £4.30: £1.60, £2.30, £1.60; EX 18.20.The winner was sold to Pat Morris for 3,000gns.

Owner Rockcliffe Stud **Bred** Rockcliffe Stud **Trained** East Everleigh, Wilts

FOCUS

A wide range of ability in this ordinary seller but the proximity of the 49-rated fourth holds the form down. The gallop was sound and the winner raced close to the inside rail throughout. A decent race of its type, with the fourth the key to the form.

NOTEBOOK

Balm had disappointed over 6f at this course on his previous outing but had a decent chance at the weights and fared better back in trip after getting a good tow. She was sold for 3,000gns (to Pat Morris) but she can win again in this grade. (op 3-1)

Musical Valley had a good chance at the weights but, although running creditably in terms of form down in grade against a rival that enjoyed the run of the race on this all-weather debut, he didn't look the easiest of rides and he may be worth a try in some form of headgear. (tchd 5-1)

Pint Size, a triple claiming winner, had a good chance at the weights but, although not beaten far after setting a solid gallop, wasn't at his very best returned to this trip in the first-time blinkers. He doesn't look anywhere near as good as his official rating of 84 suggests. (op 5-2)

Bitter Lemon seemed to run very well in the face of a stiff task on this first run in this grade. She'll be suited by 6f but her short-term future lies with the handicapper after this run. (op 22-1)

Liebesziel finished in front of the winner on his last visit to the track but failed to confirm those placings after racing with the choke out over this shorter trip in the first-time headgear. He has ability but doesn't look one for maximum faith at this stage. (tchd 12-1)

Key Addition(IRE) Official explanation: jockey said colt missed the break

6541 SPONSOR A RACE BY CALLING 01902 390000 CLAIMING STKS (DIV I) 7f 32y(P)

6:50 (6:50) (Class 6) 3-Y-O+ £1,363 (£402; £201) Stalls High

Form RPR

4523 **1** **Dialogue**[24] 5828 5-8-13 85 MichaelO'Connell(3) 6 89
(Ollie Pears) *s.i.s: hld up: hdwy over 2f out: r.o to ld wl ins fnl f: comf* **7/2**[2]

1150 **2** *2 ¼* **Zomerlust**[15] 6113 9-9-2 82 (v) PBBeggy 1 83
(John Quinn) *led: rdn over 1f out: hdd and unable qck wl ins fnl f* **16/1**

2112 **3** *hd* **Kingswinford (IRE)**[6] 6381 5-8-9 79 PaulPickard(3) 7 78
(Brian Ellison) *hld up: hdwy over 3f out: rdn to chse ldr over 1f out: edgd lft ins fnl f: styd on same pce* **7/2**[2]

5004 **4** *3* **Benandonner (USA)**[1] 6496 8-9-5 89 KierenFallon 8 77
(Mike Murphy) *chsd ldrs: rdn over 1f out: no ex ins fnl f* **9/4**[1]

0-00 **5** *¾* **Bavarian Princess (USA)**[16] 6098 3-8-7 60 ow3 MartinHarley(3) 11 68
(Mrs K Burke) *s.i.s: hld up: hdwy u.p over 1f out: nt rch ldrs* **66/1**

4212 **6** *3 ¾* **Unlimited**[28] 5734 9-8-5 80 GeorgeDowning(7) 9 58
(Tony Carroll) *s.i.s: hld up: r.o ins fnl f: nvr nr to chal* **10/1**

0-00 **7** *¾* **Councellor (FR)**[12] 6220 9-8-11 80 (t) RossAtkinson(3) 2 58
(Derek Shaw) *hld up: rdn over 2f out: n.d* **66/1**

0000 **8** *4 ½* **Brave Prospector**[14] 6147 6-9-7 93 (t) LeeTopliss(3) 5 56
(Richard Fahey) *chsd ldrs: rdn over 2f out: wknd fnl f* **5/1**[3]

50 **9** *6* **Lady Lube Rye (IRE)**[7] 6343 4-8-5 43 SaleemGolam 3 21
(Noel Wilson) *chsd ldrs: hmpd 1/2-way: sn wknd* **100/1**

0000 **10** *5* **Crocodile Bay (IRE)**[14] 6159 8-8-8 43 (b) RobbieFitzpatrick 4 —
(Richard Guest) *plld hrd and prom: hmpd over 3f out: sn rdn: wknd over 2f out* **80/1**

1m 27.9s (-1.70) **Going Correction** -0.15s/f (Stan)

WFA 3 from 4yo+ 2lb **10** Ran SP% **112.1**

Speed ratings (Par 101): **103,100,100,96,95 91,90,85,78,73**

toteswingers:1&2:£9.70, 1&3:£4.50, 2&3:£14.80 CSF £53.61 TOTE £5.30: £1.70, £5.20, £2.00; EX 67.50.

Owner Ollie Pears **Bred** Darley **Trained** Norton, N Yorks

FOCUS

A useful claimer in which the gallop was an ordinary one. The winner raced towards the centre in the straight and the form is a bit muddling, with the fifth holding things down.

6542 SPONSOR A RACE BY CALLING 01902 390000 CLAIMING STKS (DIV II) 7f 32y(P)

7:20 (7:20) (Class 6) 3-Y-O+ £1,363 (£402; £201) Stalls High

Form RPR

004 **1** **Flowing Cape (IRE)**[2] 6477 6-9-0 83 KierenFallon 5 70
(Reg Hollinshead) *chsd ldrs: rdn ins fnl f: r.o to ld post* **7/4**[1]

1040 **2** *hd* **Pravda Street**[23] 5852 6-9-5 87 DaleSwift(3) 6 77
(Brian Ellison) *chsd ldr: rdn and ev ch ins fnl f: r.o* **11/4**[2]

0425 **3** *shd* **Desert Falls**[8] 6304 5-8-5 55 RyanClark(3) 1 63
(Richard Whitaker) *led: rdn over 1f out: hdd wl ins fnl f: rallied to ld nr fin: hdd post* **18/1**

0000 **4** *¾* **Lovelace**[14] 6148 7-9-3 89 LeeTopliss(3) 4 73
(Richard Fahey) *hood removed sltly late and s.i.s: sn prom: rdn to ld wl ins fnl f: hdd and unable qck towards fin* **4/1**[3]

6/00 **5** *3 ¼* **Le Reveur**[7] 6357 9-8-9 38 KellyHarrison 7 53?
(Richard Guest) *hld up: rdn over 1f out: r.o: edgd lft ins fnl f: nvr trbld ldrs* **66/1**

0000 **6** *¾* **Everymanforhimself (IRE)**[21] 5920 7-9-2 80 (p) AmyRyan(3) 2 61
(Kevin Ryan) *chsd ldrs: rdn over 1f out: wknd ins fnl f* **5/1**

5-00 **7** *2 ¼* **Northern Genes (AUS)**[29] 5674 5-8-8 42 (p) RobbieFitzpatrick 10 44
(Michael Appleby) *s.i.s: hld up: rdn over 2f out: n.d* **50/1**

8 *22* **Henry's Hero**[409] 5-9-3 0 (b[1]) JoshCrane(7) 8 —
(Chris Dwyer) *s.i.s: hld up: rdn over 2f out: sn wknd* **66/1**

1m 28.62s (-0.98) **Going Correction** -0.15s/f (Stan) **8** Ran SP% **109.9**

Speed ratings (Par 101): **99,98,98,97,94 93,90,65**

toteswingers:1&2:£1.10, 1&3:£4.40, 2&3:£6.70 CSF £6.10 TOTE £3.20: £1.10, £1.70, £2.30; EX 6.60.

Owner John L Marriott **Bred** David Maher **Trained** Upper Longdon, Staffs

■ Stewards' Enquiry : Ryan Clark six-day ban: weighed in 2lb heavy, 2nd offence in 12 mths (Oct 19-22,24,25); one-day ban: used whip with excessive frequency (Oct 26)

FOCUS

A handful of useful sorts just an ordinary gallop and the form is held down by the proximity of the 55-rated third and the 38-rated fifth. The winner came down the centre in the straight. The form horses are rated well below their marks with the fifth and seventh limiting.

6543 BOOK NOW FOR CHRISTMAS H'CAP (DIV I) 1m 141y(P)

7:50 (7:50) (Class 5) (0-75,75) 3-Y-O+ £2,587 (£770; £384; £192) Stalls Low

Form RPR

3563 **1** **Elijah Pepper (USA)**[28] 5733 6-9-9 **74** GrahamGibbons 12 81
(David Barron) *a.p: chsd ldr over 2f out: rdn to ld and edgd rt over 1f out: styd on* **10/3**[1]

3202 **2** *nk* **Dream Of Fortune (IRE)**[7] 6357 7-8-10 **61** oh3 (bt) ShaneKelly 9 68
(David Evans) *s.i.s: hld up: hdwy over 1f out: sn rdn: r.o wl* **8/1**

1650 **3** *¾* **Jibaal (IRE)**[28] 5735 3-8-13 **73** AntiocoMurgia(5) 2 78+
(Marco Botti) *chsd ldrs: nt clr run and lost pl over 2f out: hdwy over 1f out: r.o* **7/1**

3042 **4** *1* **Indian Valley (USA)**[9] 6285 4-9-4 **72** (b) MartinHarley(3) 7 75+
(Hugo Palmer) *prom: lost pl over 3f out: hdwy over 1f out: r.o wl* **5/1**[3]

0320 **5** *nk* **Bloodsweatandtears**[43] 5240 3-9-4 **73** KierenFallon 10 75
(William Knight) *hld up: hdwy over 2f out: rdn over 1f out: edgd lft: styd on same pce ins fnl f* **9/2**[2]

5100 **6** *shd* **Justcallmehandsome**[28] 5740 9-8-3 **61** (v) RachealKneller(7) 1 63
(Dominic Ffrench Davis) *hld up: hdwy over 1f out: r.o: nt rch ldrs* **25/1**

0040 **7** *½* **Osgood**[4] 6435 4-9-10 **75** (v) TonyCulhane 11 76
(Mick Channon) *sn led: hdd 7f out: chsd ldr tl led again over 3f out: rdn and hdd over 1f out: no ex ins fnl f* **12/1**

0054 **8** *¾* **Paphos**[16] 6090 4-8-11 **65** (v) RyanClark(3) 6 64
(Stuart Williams) *hld up: hdwy over 1f out: nt clr run ins fnl f: nvr able to chal* **14/1**

0031 **9** *3 ½* **Hill Tribe**[7] 6358 4-8-11 **65** RobertLButler(3) 5 56
(Richard Guest) *led 7f out: hdd over 3f out: sn rdn: wknd fnl f* **9/1**

0000 **10** *5* **Bertie Blu Boy**[21] 5924 3-8-12 **70** LeeTopliss(3) 8 49
(Paul Green) *trckd ldrs: racd keenly: rdn over 2f out: wknd over 1f out* **28/1**

1m 49.03s (-1.47) **Going Correction** -0.15s/f (Stan)

WFA 3 from 4yo+ 4lb **10** Ran SP% **113.2**

Speed ratings (Par 103): **100,99,99,98,97 97,97,96,93,89**

toteswingers:1&2:£5.90, 1&3:£6.90, 2&3:£10.60 CSF £29.38 CT £177.18 TOTE £5.20: £1.70, £1.70, £2.60; EX 31.70.

Owner Wensleydale Bacon Limited **Bred** Liberation Farm & Oratis Thoroughbreds **Trained** Maunby, N Yorks

FOCUS

Mainly exposed sorts in a fair handicap. The gallop was an ordinary one and the winner came down the centre in the straight. The winner is rated to form with the second running his best race since last winter.

6544 BOOK NOW FOR CHRISTMAS H'CAP (DIV II) 1m 141y(P)

8:20 (8:20) (Class 5) (0-75,75) 3-Y-O+ £2,587 (£770; £384; £192) Stalls Low

Form RPR

0220 **1** **Aussie Blue (IRE)**[16] 6098 7-8-7 **61** oh2 (v) AmyRyan(3) 7 68
(Richard Whitaker) *a.p: chsd ldr over 2f out: rdn to ld ins fnl f: styd on* **8/1**

4525 **2** *½* **Lockantanks**[24] 5828 4-9-8 **73** RobbieFitzpatrick 5 79
(Michael Appleby) *hld up: hdwy over 1f out: sn rdn: r.o wl: nt quite get up* **11/1**

3030 **3** *1* **Mr Chocolate Drop (IRE)**[22] 5902 7-8-13 **64** (t) JimmyQuinn 10 68
(Mandy Rowland) *hld up: hdwy over 3f out: rdn over 1f out: r.o* **12/1**

040 **4** *½* **Caldercruix (USA)**[12] 6226 4-9-4 **72** (v[1]) PaulPickard(3) 1 75
(James Evans) *led: clr 7f out: rdn over 1f out: hdd and no ex ins fnl f* **9/2**[1]

5004 **5** *nk* **Moheebb (IRE)**[8] 6290 7-9-2 **70** (b) DaleSwift(3) 11 72
(Ruth Carr) *hld up: hdwy over 3f out: rdn over 1f out: r.o* **5/1**[2]

0400 **6** *shd* **Hip Hip Hooray**[22] 5894 5-9-2 **67** WilliamCarson 6 69
(Luke Dace) *hld up: rdn over 3f out: r.o ins fnl f: nrst fin* **25/1**

3242 **7** *2 1/2* **Barista (IRE)**[4] 6433 3-8-12 **70**...................................... MartinHarley(3) 2 66
(Mick Channon) *sn chsng clr ldr: rdn over 2f out: styd on same pce appr fnl f* **11/2**[3]

1211 **8** *4 1/2* **Istiqdaam**[37] 5404 6-9-10 **75**...(b) PaddyAspell 4 61
(Michael Easterby) *prom: rdn over 2f out: sn wknd* **5/1**[2]

1m 49.81s (-0.69) **Going Correction** -0.15s/f (Stan)
WFA 3 from 4yo+ 4lb **8** Ran SP% **97.9**
Speed ratings (Par 103): **97,96,95,95,94 94,92,88**
toteswingers:1&2:£15.10, 1&3:£4.80, 2&3:£15.30 CSF £65.30 CT £651.85 TOTE £9.00: £2.60, £3.40, £2.80; EX 46.70.
Owner G F Pemberton **Bred** T L Adams & G F Pemberton **Trained** Scarcroft, W Yorks

FOCUS
Exposed performers in a run-of-the-mill handicap. The gallop was soon sound and the winner raced centre-to-far side in the straight. The form looks reasonable with the first three close to their marks.
Istiqdaam Official explanation: jockey said gelding moved poorly

6545 ENJOY THE RINGSIDE ENTERTAINMENT AFTER RACING H'CAP 1m 1f 103y(P)
8:50 (8:50) (Class 6) (0-55,55) 3-Y-O **£2,070** (£616; £307; £153) **Stalls** Low

Form RPR

4345 **1** **Cathcart Castle**[31] 5619 3-9-0 **53**.................................. TonyCulhane 12 60
(Mick Channon) *hld up and bhd: hdwy over 1f out: shkn up to ld and edgd rt* **9/1**

6130 **2** *3/4* **One Of Twins**[14] 6179 3-9-0 **53**.. KierenFallon 10 58
(Michael Easterby) *hld up: hdwy over 2f out: rdn over 1f out: r.o* **5/1**[2]

3605 **3** *1/2* **Lord Emerson**[17] 6049 3-8-10 **52**................................ LeeTopliss(3) 5 56
(Richard Fahey) *chsd ldrs: led over 2f out: rdn over 1f out: hdd wl ins fnl f* **10/1**

0466 **4** *nk* **Princess Gail**[22] 5898 3-8-10 **49**.. ShaneKelly 9 53
(Mark Brisbourne) *s.i.s: hld up: hdwy over 4f out: chsd ldr over 1f out: sn rdn and ev ch: unable qck towards fin* **16/1**

0020 **5** *1/2* **Look For Love**[7] 6358 3-8-9 **48**.................................. GrahamGibbons 7 51
(Reg Hollinshead) *a.p: rdn and ev ch ins fnl f: no ex nr fin* **20/1**

550 **6** *3/4* **Nuba (IRE)**[18] 6032 3-9-0 **53**... WilliamCarson 4 54
(Luke Dace) *hld up: rdn over 3f out: hdwy u.p over 1f out: r.o: nt rch ldrs* **25/1**

050 **7** *1/2* **Full Stretch (USA)**[25] 5816 3-9-1 **54**............................... TadhgO'Shea 6 54
(Pat Eddery) *hld up: hdwy u.p over 2f out: styd on* **10/1**

4134 **8** *12* **Ippi N Tombi (IRE)**[18] 6033 3-8-10 **49**............................... ChrisCatlin 2 24
(Phil McEntee) *sn led: hdd 8f out: chsd ldr tl rdn over 2f out: wknd over 1f out* **8/1**[3]

2000 **9** *hd* **Beating Harmony**[8] 6309 3-8-11 **50**................................. JamesDoyle 8 24
(Tony Carroll) *hld up: rdn over 1f out: nvr on terms* **20/1**

4633 **10** *3* **Like A Boy**[53] 4888 3-9-2 **55**... RichardMullen 3 23
(Peter Makin) *mid-div: rdn over 3f out: wknd over 2f out* **7/2**[1]

0505 **11** *3/4* **Endaxi Mana Mou**[8] 6310 3-8-9 **51**..........................(b) MartinHarley(3) 13 18
(Noel Quinlan) *chsd ldrs: rdn over 2f out: wknd over 1f out* **14/1**

0030 **12** *shd* **Formidable Girl (USA)**[75] 4149 3-8-7 **49**....................(p) AmyRyan(3) 11 15
(Kevin Ryan) *led 8f out: rdn and hdd over 2f out: wknd over 1f out* **16/1**

41 **13** *9* **Diamond Sunrise (IRE)**[17] 6049 3-8-13 **52**...................... DuranFentiman 1 —
(Noel Wilson) *prom: rdn over 3f out: wknd over 2f out* **11/1**

2m 0.17s (-1.53) **Going Correction** -0.15s/f (Stan) **13** Ran SP% **118.3**
Speed ratings (Par 99): **100,99,98,98,98 97,97,86,86,83 82,82,74**
toteswingers:1&2:£9.00, 1&3:£29.60, 2&3:£18.70 CSF £51.42 CT £467.13 TOTE £11.80: £3.70, £1.70, £4.80; EX 38.50.
Owner A Brazil **Bred** A Brazil **Trained** West Ilsley, Berks

FOCUS
A moderate handicap run at a reasonable gallop. The winner made his ground towards the far rail in the straight. The placed horses set the level.
Lord Emerson Official explanation: jockey said gelding hung right-handed

6546 DINE IN THE HORIZONS RESTAURANT H'CAP 1m 4f 50y(P)
9:20 (9:20) (Class 5) (0-70,70) 3-Y-O+ **£2,045** (£603; £302) **Stalls** Low

Form RPR

3002 **1** **Pertemps Networks**[60] 3715 7-9-11 **69**..................... GrahamGibbons 5 81+
(Michael Easterby) *mde all: rdn clr over 1f out: eased nr fin* **13/8**[1]

0006 **2** *1* **Global**[10] 6264 5-8-11 **58**... DaleSwift(3) 11 66+
(Brian Ellison) *hld up: hdwy over 1f out: r.o to go 2nd ins fnl f: no ch w wnr* **20/1**

6123 **3** *5* **Minsky Mine (IRE)**[5] 6401 4-9-11 **69**.......................... RobbieFitzpatrick 3 69
(Michael Appleby) *chsd ldr to 1/2-way: rdn to go 2nd again over 2f out: no ex fnl f* **7/1**[3]

4630 **4** *1* **Kames Park (IRE)**[25] 5804 9-9-7 **68**........................... RobertLButler(3) 1 66
(Richard Guest) *hld up: r.o ins fnl f: nvr nrr* **20/1**

0-31 **5** *3/4* **Passion Play**[16] 6086 3-9-2 **67**... KierenFallon 2 64
(William Knight) *chsd ldrs: rdn over 2f out: edgd lft over 1f out: styd on same pce* **3/1**[2]

1400 **6** *1* **Irish Jugger (USA)**[23] 5866 4-9-9 **67**............................. JamesMillman 9 63
(Rod Millman) *s.i.s: hld up: effrt over 1f out: n.d* **14/1**

3045 **7** *shd* **Symphonic Dancer (USA)**[9] 6285 4-9-2 **60**............. J-PGuillambert 10 55
(Brian Baugh) *hld up: racd keenly: hdwy over 3f out: sn rdn: wknd ins fnl f* **12/1**

00-3 **8** *3/4* **Manshoor (IRE)**[9] 6287 6-9-3 **61**.. ChrisCatlin 6 55
(Lucy Wadham) *prom: pushed along over 4f out: rdn over 2f out: wknd fnl f* **17/2**

-500 **9** *16* **Ananda Kanda (USA)**[14] 6157 4-8-13 **60**...................... PaulPickard(3) 8 29
(Brian Ellison) *prom: chsd wnr 1/2-way tl rdn over 2f out: wknd over 1f out* **20/1**

2m 38.75s (-2.35) **Going Correction** -0.15s/f (Stan)
WFA 3 from 4yo+ 7lb **9** Ran SP% **114.8**
Speed ratings (Par 103): **101,100,97,96,95 95,95,94,83**
toteswingers:1&2:£29.40, 1&3:£1.50, 2&3:£26.30 CSF £40.56 CT £179.56 TOTE £2.50: £1.10, £5.20, £2.70; EX 56.30.
Owner E A Brook **Bred** H G Llewellyn **Trained** Sheriff Hutton, N Yorks

FOCUS
A modest handicap in which the steady gallop means this bare form isn't entirely reliable. However the first two, who raced towards the centre in the straight, did well to pull clear in the closing stages. The winner is rated back to hos best.
T/Plt: £43.10 to a £1 stake. Pool:£71,591.77 - 1,210.36 winning tickets T/Qpdt: £28.80 to a £1 stake. Pool:£7,077.63 - 181.60 winning tickets CR

6205 BELMONT PARK (L-H)
Saturday, October 1
OFFICIAL GOING: Dirt: muddy; turf: yielding

6548a JOE HIRSCH TURF CLASSIC INTERNATIONAL STKS (GRADE 1) (3YO+) (TURF) 1m 4f
8:22 (12:00) 3-Y-O+
£192,307 (£64,102; £32,051; £16,025; £9,615; £6,410)

RPR

1 **Cape Blanco (IRE)**[49] 5074 4-9-0 0................................ JamieSpencer 1 119
(A P O'Brien, Ire) *broke wl on rail but immediately angled outside to sit 2nd on ldr's quarters: shkn up and qcknd to ld over 3f out: hrd rdn and 2 l up ins fnl 2f: styd on u.str.p fnl f: hld on bravely: all out: front* **3/5**[1]

2 *nse* **Dean's Kitten (USA)**[49] 5074 4-9-0 0.........................(b) RADominguez 3 119
(Michael J Maker, U.S.A) *setled cl up in 3rd: wnt 2nd on outside 1 1/2f out: 1 1/2 l down but styng on u.p ent fnl f: inched bk ldr's advantage thrght fnl 100yds: jst failed* **143/10**

3 *8 3/4* **Grassy (USA)**[21] 5-9-0 0... JRVelazquez 6 105
(Christophe Clement, U.S.A) *racd 4th and in tch: rdn and no imp fnl 1 1/2f* **84/10**[3]

4 *4 1/4* **Mission Approved (USA)**[49] 5074 7-9-0 0........................... RMaragh 4 98
(Naipaul Chatterpaul, U.S.A) *led: set stead pce: hdd over 3f out: rdn and wknd fr over 1 1/2f out* **121/10**

5 *6 1/4* **Winchester (USA)**[49] 5076 6-9-0 0.................................(b) CVelasquez 5 88
(Christophe Clement, U.S.A) *hld up last but in tch: rdn and outpcd ins fnl 3f: sn wl adrift* **41/20**[2]

2m 36.61s (8.03) **5** Ran SP% **120.1**
PARI-MUTUEL (all including $2 stakes): WIN 3.20; PLACE (1-2) 2.40, 5.80; SHOW (1-2-3) 2.10, 3.30, 3.20; SF 17.20.
Owner Mrs F Hay,D Smith,Mrs J Magnier,M Tabor **Bred** Jack Ronan And Des Vere Hunt Farm Co **Trained** Ballydoyle, Co Tipperary

NOTEBOOK
Cape Blanco(IRE) looks almost certain to be named America's champion turf performer after completing a Grade 1 hat-trick - but it was oh-so-close for the Ballydoyle 4yo, who scored by a nose. Despite his having won last year's Irish Derby over 1m4f, Cape Blanco seemed to be at the very end of his stamina on this soft ground and Jamie Spencer needed to be at his strongest to get him home. As soon as he could, Spencer shrewdly took Cape Blanco off the rail from his inside draw, the inner line on the Belmont turf track being notoriously slow after it has rained. With the track looking much softer than the official description of yielding, Cape Blanco willingly moved up to collar Mission Approved 3f out but was never able to establish clear water as he paddled through the closing stages with Dean's Kitten virtually on top of him. There could be no faulting the winner's determination, however, as he held on by the shortest margin. Unfortunately, the colt sustained an injury during the race and he was immediately retired.

6547a, 6549 - 6554a (Foreign Racing) - See Raceform Interactive

6184 LONGCHAMP (R-H)
Saturday, October 1
OFFICIAL GOING: Turf: good

6555a QATAR PRIX CHAUDENAY (GROUP 2) (3YO) (TURF) 1m 7f
2:40 (12:00) 3-Y-O **£63,879** (£24,655; £11,767; £7,844; £3,922)

RPR

1 **Shankardeh (IRE)**[65] 4470 3-8-13 0........... Christophe-PatriceLemaire 3 110
(M Delzangles, France) *led: hdd after 3f and trckd ldr: rdn and chal on outside of ldr appr fnl 1 1/2f: led nring fnl f: r.o u.p* **3/1**[3]

2 *hd* **Miss Lago (IRE)**[27] 5771 3-8-13 0................................ AnthonyCrastus 5 110
(E Lellouche, France) *dwlt: sn settled 3rd on rail: hemmed in fr 2f out: nt get run outside eventual wnr tl ins fnl f: styd on wl u.p last 100yds: unlucky* **10/1**

3 *1* **Pacifique (IRE)**[27] 5771 3-8-10 0...................................... GeraldMosse 2 109
(A De Royer-Dupre, France) *hld up in rr: hdwy on outside under 2f out: styd on u.p last 150yds: nt pce to chal first two* **5/2**[2]

4 *1/2* **Bernieres (IRE)**[24] 5839 3-8-13 0................................. GregoryBenoist 1 108
(Mme Pia Brandt, France) *trckd ldng trio: scrubbed along to hold pl 2 1/2f out: kpt on wout being able to qckn* **14/1**

5 *1* **Gaily Game**[47] 5131 3-9-2 0... OlivierPeslier 4 110
(J-C Rouget, France) *racd keenly trcking ldr in share of 2nd: led after 3f: pushed along and qcknd over 2f out: sn rdn: hdd nring fnl f: unable qck u.p* **13/8**[1]

3m 24.59s (8.59) **Going Correction** +0.15s/f (Good) **5** Ran SP% **107.4**
Speed ratings: **83,82,82,82,81**
WIN (incl. 1 euro stake): 4.60. PLACES: 2.10, 3.80. SF: 30.70.
Owner H H Aga Khan **Bred** His Highness The Aga Khan's Studs S C **Trained** France

FOCUS
With temperatures high there'd been plenty of watering, and although the ground was officially good, they were kicking the top off. Only one of these (Pacifique) had won above Listed level, but three of the five runners came into the race having only had four previous starts, and were open to improvement. The pace was steady early until Gaily Game picked up front-running duties.

NOTEBOOK
Shankardeh(IRE) wasn't beaten at all far in the Group 2 Prix de Malleret two starts back and chased home Meeznah at Goodwood last time, when perhaps not entirely comfortable on the track/fast ground. Racing in second for most of the race, she eventually took the leader's measure heading into the final furlong and saw the trip out well, although she was fortunate that the line came when it did as the runner-up, who had traffic problems, was flying at the death and would have got up in another couple of strides. Having not raced at two, she should have more to offer at four, and it'll be interesting to see if she's kept in training. Before that decision is made, though, she could well turn up at Ascot for the Qipco British Champions Fillies' And Mares' Stakes, or more likely return here for the Prix Royal-Oak.
Miss Lago(IRE) was 2lb worse off with Pacifique despite finishing behind her last time, and also had 3l to find with Gaily Game on their meeting at Deauville in August, but the ground was quicker here than on both those occasions, and she relished conditions, quickening up well once eventually in the clear and reversing form with those two. Her problem was that, having got stuck in a pocket and been denied a run until well inside the last, she had too much ground to make up on the winner in the time left available. She has more to offer.
Pacifique(IRE), who was given a waiting ride, enjoyed an uninterrupted run down the outside in the straight but still couldn't confirm recent C&D form with Miss Lago. The better ground didn't look to be in her favour.
Bernieres(IRE) looked to have plenty on her plate despite being a Listed winner last time, and she was quite comfortably held, albeit not beaten far.

Gaily Game, the only colt in the field, was a bit keen tracking Shankardeh early, so his rider let him stride on heading into the back straight. Asked to quicken in the straight, he just wasn't able to shake off his rivals, and he was swamped with half a furlong to run. He had shown a nice turn of foot to win from off the pace in his previous two starts and it looked like the change in tactics backfired.

6556a QATAR PRIX DANIEL WILDENSTEIN (GROUP 2) (3YO+) (TURF) 1m

3:15 (12:00) 3-Y-O+ **£63,879** (£24,655; £11,767; £7,844; £3,922)

RPR

1 **Rajsaman (FR)**[20] 5988 4-9-3 0 ....(b) ThierryJarnet 2 120
(F Head, France) *broke wl and prom early: sn settled bhd ldrs: 5th and angled to outside over 1 1/2f out: rdn and r.o ins fnl f: led fnl strides* **9/2**[2]

2 *snk* **Rio De La Plata (USA)**[20] 5988 6-9-1 0 .... FrankieDettori 9 118
(Saeed Bin Suroor) *midfield: 4th on outside of eventual wnr 2 1/2f out: prog to chal ldr 1 1/2f out: led appr fnl f: r.o u.p: hdd fnl strides: no ex* **5/2**[1]

3 *1* **Best Dating (IRE)**[27] 5772 4-9-1 0 .... GregoryBenoist 1 116
(S Wattel, France) *settled in midfield: 6th and trcking eventual wnr 2 1/2f out: short of room fr jst over 1 1/2f out: swtchd ins and r.o u.p fnl f: nt able to chal first two* **8/1**

4 *1 1/4* **One Clever Cat (IRE)**[8] 6321 5-8-11 0 .... GeraldMosse 5 109
(T Clout, France) *racd in 7th: effrt on outside 2f out: 6th and styng on 1 1/2f out: nt qckn u.p fnl f* **14/1**

5 *shd* **Zinabaa (FR)**[34] 5530 6-9-1 0 .... YannickLetondeur 8 113
(M Mace, France) *settled towards rr: 8th and pushed along 2f out: styd on u.p fr 1f out: run flattened out tl r.o fnl 50yds* **14/1**

6 *1* **Royal Bench (IRE)**[20] 5988 4-9-1 0 .... IoritzMendizabal 10 110
(Robert Collet, France) *w.w towards rr: sltly hmpd whn One Clever Cat drifted outside 4f out: prog on outside 2f out: sn rdn and no imp ins fnl 1 1/2f* **6/1**[3]

7 *3/4* **Sandagiyr (FR)**[77] 4120 3-8-11 0 .... Christophe-PatriceLemaire 7 108
(A De Royer-Dupre, France) *a.p: racing freely: cl 3rd 3f out: qcknd to ld ent fnl 2f: hdd appr fnl f: no ex* **16/1**

8 *1 3/4* **Evaporation (FR)**[27] 5772 4-8-11 0 .... OlivierPeslier 11 101
(C Laffon-Parias, France) *hld up in last: shortlived effrt on outside 2f out: no imp fnl f* **10/1**

9 *2* **Set The Trend**[35] 5473 5-9-1 0 .... DavidProbert 4 100
(Andrew Balding) *racd keenly in share of the ld: led 4f out: hdd ent fnl 2f: dropped away fnl f* **8/1**

10 *1 1/2* **Private Jet (FR)**[21] 5957 3-8-11 0 ....(p) MaximeGuyon 3 95
(H-A Pantall, France) *shared ld on ins of Set The Trend: hdd 4f out: grad wknd fnl 1 1/2f* **33/1**

11 *1 1/4* **Kings Canyon (FR)**[48] 4-9-1 0 ....(b) HiroyasuTanaka 6 94
(S Kobayashi, France) *nvr in contention* **100/1**

1m 38.23s (-0.17) **Going Correction** +0.15s/f (Good)
WFA 3 from 4yo+ 3lb 11 Ran SP% **115.5**
Speed ratings: **106,105,104,103,103 102,101,100,98,96 95**
WIN (incl. 1 euro stake): 6.70. PLACES: 1.50, 1.20, 1.80. DF: 4.60. SF: 10.40.
Owner Saeed Nasser Al Romaithi **Bred** Hh The Aga Khan Studs Sc **Trained** France

FOCUS
This looked a solid Group 2 race on paper. Neither the winner nor second is quite good enough to beat the likes of Frankel, Goldikova or Excelebration in Group 1 company, but this is their level and they finally had their deserved day in the sun. The winner and fourth are rated to their marks.

NOTEBOOK
Rajsaman(FR) came into this race having only once been beaten in his five previous starts over a mile when running below Group 1 level and, despite being burdened with a 2lb penalty and letting Rio De La Plata get first run on him, having been kept in by that rival until 300m out, he found the necessary change of gear to close him down and edge past near the line. They don't get much more reliable than him at this sort of level, but he'll once again have to go up in grade now, and the Hong Kong Mile is apparently the plan - he was fourth in it last year.
Rio De La Plata(USA) had finished one place in front of Rajsaman in his two previous starts and was 2lb better off at the weights with his old rival this time. He was also given a cute ride by Frankie Dettori, who kept Rajsaman in on the rail early in the straight, and very much got the jump on him. In the circumstances he can have no excuses. Saeed Bin Suroor mentioned the possibility of going back to Italy with him.
Best Dating(IRE) shaped quite well as he didn't get the clearest of runs and yet this still represented another career-best. He's an improving 4-y-o and could have even more to offer next year.
One Clever Cat(IRE) has never won over a trip this short but she was coming here on the back of a win in Group 3 company eight days earlier, appreciates a decent surface and the strong pace was also in her favour.
Zinabaa(FR) was staying on at the finish but on this sort of ground it looks like he needs further.
Royal Bench(IRE), who won this race last year in soft ground, could make no impression in the straight and threw in another below-par effort.
Sandagiyr(FR), who was disappointing when upped to Group company earlier in the summer, chased the leaders and was the first to be committed in the straight. He didn't see it out, though, and will now be off to the sales.
Set The Trend was taken on in front by Private Jet, which didn't help his cause, but the pair of them ensured it was a truly run race.

6557a QATAR PRIX DE ROYALLIEU (GROUP 2) (3YO+ FILLIES & MARES) (TURF) 1m 4f 110y

3:50 (12:00) 3-Y-O+ **£63,879** (£24,655; £11,767; £7,844; £3,922)

RPR

1 **Sea Of Heartbreak (IRE)**[14] 6161 4-9-1 0 .... OlivierPeslier 4 109+
(Roger Charlton) *racd keenly in 3rd: cl 3rd whn shkn up and r.o ins fnl f: led cl home* **3/1**[3]

2 *1/2* **Miss Crissy (IRE)**[27] 5771 3-8-7 0 .... GregoryBenoist 2 108
(M Delzangles, France) *trckd ldr: chal on outside over 1 1/2f out: led briefly appr fnl f: sn hdd narrowly: led again over 100yds out: r.o u.p: ct cl home* **4/1**

3 *shd* **Modeyra**[17] 6066 4-9-1 0 .... FrankieDettori 1 108
(Saeed Bin Suroor) *led: set a stdy gallop: qcknd 2f out: jnd 1 1/2f out: hdd briefly appr fnl f: sn led again: hdd over 100yds out: no ex* **5/2**[2]

4 *1 1/2* **Shamanova (IRE)**[20] 5990 4-9-1 0 .... Christophe-PatriceLemaire 3 105+
(A De Royer-Dupre, France) *slowly away and settled in last: 4th and scrubbed along 1 1/2f out: nt qckn fnl f* **2/1**[1]

2m 53.9s (14.00) **Going Correction** +0.15s/f (Good)
WFA 3 from 4yo 7lb 4 Ran SP% **106.9**
Speed ratings: **62,61,61,60**
WIN (incl. 1 euro stake): 4.90. PLACES: 3.20, 2.40. SF: 14.40.
Owner D G Hardisty Bloodstock **Bred** D G Hardisty Bloodstock **Trained** Beckhampton, Wilts

FOCUS
A desperate fillies and mares Group 2, featuring only four runners, none of whom has scored above Listed grade despite 12 attempts between them. They went a steady gallop before sprinting in the straight, and this should be rated like an ordinary Group 3 race at best, with the second and third the best guides.

NOTEBOOK
Sea Of Heartbreak(IRE) is an improving filly and her turn of foot is a valuable asset in these tactical, small-field Group races. The good ground was perhaps also more to her advantage than her rivals, but either way, connections have done well to pick up such a weak Group 2. She could well be given her chance in Grade 1 company in the E.P Taylor Stakes in Canada later this month.
Miss Crissy(IRE), the only 3-y-o in the field, sat in second and was the first to attack the leader on turning in, but no sooner had she mastered her than the winner flew by. She didn't get home over 1m7f last time and looked much more effective back in distance on better ground.
Modeyra had the run of the race out in front. Dettori was able to set fractions to suit himself and the filly had no excuse apart from the obvious conclusion that she didn't stay the trip. She had never before run beyond 1m2f and on this evidence she lacks the stamina for this distance.
Shamanova(IRE), a hold-up performer who stays further than this, was always going to require a decent pace to run off, and she just didn't get that here. It wasn't a surprise to see her struggle to pick up when the sprint for home began.

6558a QATAR PRIX DOLLAR (GROUP 2) (3YO+) (TURF) 1m 1f 165y

4:25 (12:00) 3-Y-O+ **£63,879** (£24,655; £11,767; £7,844; £3,922)

RPR

1 **Byword**[111] 2980 5-9-0 0 .... MaximeGuyon 4 121+
(A Fabre, France) *racd in 5th: shoirt of room over 2f out: in clr over 1f out: sn rdn and qcknd: r.o u.p fnl f to ld cl home* **9/2**[2]

2 *snk* **Cirrus Des Aigles (FR)**[34] 5531 5-9-4 0 .... FranckBlondel 5 125
(Mme C Barande-Barbe, France) *racd in 4th: swtchd outside and qcknd to ld ins fnl 2f: r.o wl u.p: hdd cl home* **11/8**[1]

3 *1 1/4* **Shimraan (FR)**[27] 4-9-0 0 .... Christophe-PatriceLemaire 3 118+
(A De Royer-Dupre, France) *settled in fnl 3rd of field: tk clsr order on ins over 2f out: r.o u.p to go 3rd ins fnl f: nt able to chal first two* **16/1**

4 *2 1/2* **Famous Name**[28] 5747 6-9-0 0 .... PJSmullen 7 113
(D K Weld, Ire) *racd in midfield: 6th and trcking eventual wnr over 2 1/2f out: r.o u.p to dispute 3rd 1 1/2f out: nt qckn fnl f* **8/1**

5 *nse* **Saga Dream (FR)**[29] 5696 5-9-0 0 .... ThierryJarnet 10 113
(F Lemercier, France) *hld up towards rr: last 3f out: styd on u.p fr 1 1/2f out: nt pce to rch ldrs* **28/1**

6 *2* **Theo Danon (GER)**[41] 5308 3-8-9 0 .... ASuborics 2 109
(P Schiergen, Germany) *w.w towards rr: next to last ins fnl 3f: sme hdwy over 1 1/2f out: one pce ins fnl f* **33/1**

7 *3/4* **Vagabond Shoes (IRE)**[27] 5777 4-9-0 0 .... OlivierPeslier 1 108
(Y Durepaire, Spain) *a.p: cl 3rd on rail 1 1/2f out: sn rdn and nt qckn: wknd fnl f* **25/1**

8 *2 1/2* **Desert Blanc**[14] 6185 3-8-9 0 .... StephanePasquier 11 102
(P Bary, France) *w.w towards rr: rdn and no imp fnl 2f* **9/1**

9 *1 3/4* **French Navy**[21] 5934 3-8-9 0 .... AhmedAjtebi 9 99
(Mahmood Al Zarooni) *last: effrt on outside 3f out: in midfield whn hrd rdn and no imp fnl 1 1/2f* **6/1**[3]

10 *2* **Nakayama Knight (JPN)**[20] 5987 3-8-9 0 .... YoshitomiShibata 8 95
(Yoshitaka Ninomiya, Japan) *trckd ldr: rdn and nt qckn ins fnl 2f: fdd fr 1 1/2f out* **25/1**

11 *6* **Durban Thunder (GER)**[62] 4599 5-9-6 0 .... THellier 6 88
(T Mundry, Germany) *led: hdd ins fnl 2f: wknd qckly u.p* **14/1**

2m 0.41s (-2.49) **Going Correction** +0.15s/f (Good)
WFA 3 from 4yo+ 5lb 11 Ran SP% **122.3**
Speed ratings: **115,114,113,111,111 110,109,107,106,104 99**
WIN (incl. 1 euro stake): 4.70 (Byword coupled with Famous Name). PLACES: 1.90, 1.20, 4.40. DF: 5.00. SF: 16.20.
Owner K Abdulla **Bred** Juddmonte Farms Ltd **Trained** Chantilly, France

FOCUS
A good race, well up to its Group 2 status and sound enough rated around those immediately behind the first two.

NOTEBOOK
Byword ◆ had been off the track since taking a Group 3 at Chantilly in June but he's run well fresh before. Tracking the favourite through, he had to work hard to get by him, but ground conditions were more in his favour than the runner-up's, and the 4lb he received from him also made a difference in the end. The Hong Kong Cup is likely to be on his agenda now, and he should be a big player in that race.
Cirrus Des Aigles(FR), last year's winner, comes out of the race as the best horse, as he was giving 4lb to Byword. While clearly versatile, soft ground suits him particularly well and he wasn't quite good enough to hold off former Group 1 winner Byword without the help of cut underfoot. The Champion Stakes remains on his schedule, although the bookmakers reacted to this defeat by pushing him out a touch, with Coral going biggest at 7-1.
Shimraan(FR) let the first two get first run on him but he stayed on well to take third, nicely clear of the rest. Fifth in this race last year, this was confirmation of a return to form following a confidence-boosting win in lesser company over the C&D last time.
Famous Name, who has yet to win in higher grade than Group 3 company, probably wasn't far off his best in finishing fourth.
Saga Dream(FR) came here on the back of a career-best win in Listed grade over this C&D, and that followed on from finishing third to Cirrus Des Aigles in Vichy. He was outpaced by the principals when it mattered but this was still a sound effort.
Theo Danon(GER) had more on his plate than when taking a Group 3 in Hanover last time, and performed respectably in the circumstances.
Vagabond Shoes(IRE) put up a more encouraging performance, especially as he did plenty of racing early, chasing the leaders Durban Thunder and Nakayama Knight.
Desert Blanc, lightly raced and improving, had more on his plate in this grade. A shade keen early, he had some traffic problems early in the straight but didn't really pick up once he had room. Nevertheless, having only had six starts, there's surely better to come from him.
French Navy, held up out the back, came with his run round the wide outside and his effort flattened out with a furlong and a half to go. He'd looked good winning a Group 3 at Goodwood last time and, while this proved too much for him, he's another who's not had much racing and remains open to further improvement.
Durban Thunder(GER), who took a Group 1 in Munich last time out, beating Famous Name into second, had plenty of use made of him again, but he stopped quickly in the straight and, along with his fellow pacesetter Nakayama Knight, dropped right out.

6559 - 6560a (Foreign Racing) - See Raceform Interactive

[5223] TIPPERARY (L-H)

Sunday, October 2

OFFICIAL GOING: Flat course - heavy; jumps courses - soft

6561a COOLMORE STUD HOME OF CHAMPIONS CONCORDE STKS (GROUP 3) 7f 100y

3:05 (3:09) 3-Y-O+ **£36,422** (£10,646; £5,043; £1,681)

RPR

1 **Anam Allta (IRE)**[45] 5228 3-8-12 103 .... DPMcDonogh 4 115
(D K Weld, Ire) *trckd ldrs: chal fr 2f out and sn on terms: led 1 1/2f out and rdn clr fr over 1f out: styd on wl: easily* **5/2**[1]

2 *6* **Bay Knight (IRE)**[7] 6390 5-9-3 108 ShaneFoley 7 104
(K J Condon, Ire) *sn led: pressed fr 2f out and sn jnd: hdd 1 1/2f out: no imp and kpt on same pce fr over 1f out* **3/1**[2]

3 *3 1/2* **Across The Rhine (USA)**[21] 5977 5-9-6 109 PShanahan 11 98
(Tracey Collins, Ire) *trckd ldr: no imp u.p fr under 2f out: mod 4th and kpt on same pce fr over 1f out* **13/2**[3]

4 *1/2* **Dawn Eclipse (IRE)**[7] 6390 6-9-0 101 (p) BACurtis 1 91+
(T G McCourt, Ire) *in rr: rdn into mod 3rd over 1f out: sn no imp and kpt on same pce* **12/1**

5 *1 1/4* **Look At Me (IRE)**[8] 6362 3-8-12 105 WJSupple 6 87
(A P O'Brien, Ire) *trckd ldrs: niggled along bef st: dropped to mod 5th and no imp fr over 1f out* **5/2**[1]

6 *2 1/2* **Luisant**[7] 6388 8-9-3 100 (b) FMBerry 3 85+
(J A Nash, Ire) *chsd ldrs: pushed along in 5th appr st: dropped to mod 6th and no imp fr over 1f out* **20/1**

7 *7* **Puttore (IRE)**[8] 6362 3-8-12 92 CDHayes 9 63+
(Kevin Prendergast, Ire) *towards rr: pushed along in 6th appr st: sn no imp* **12/1**

1m 42.14s (102.14)
WFA 3 from 5yo+ 2lb **7** Ran SP% **115.6**
CSF £10.55 TOTE £2.30: £1.02, £3.10; DF 7.80.
Owner Ballylinch Stud **Bred** Ballylinch Stud **Trained** The Curragh, Co Kildare

FOCUS
Four withdrawals due to the ground made things that bit easier for Anam Alta, but this progressive filly, having only the sixth start of her career, won with an authority that suggests she would have been hard to beat even if all her scheduled opponents had turned up. The front-running runner-up and fourth have been rated to their marks.

NOTEBOOK
Anam Allta(IRE) has improved with each of her three outings since finishing third to the subsequent Group 3 winner Future Generation on her seasonal debut in a handicap over 7f at the Curragh in June. From the stable that won this race a year ago with subsequent Group 1 winner Emulous, she should continue to be a force at Pattern level if given the go-ahead to continue in training at four. (op 11/4)
Bay Knight(IRE) won a conditions event over the course and trip in August. He is holding his form well, with three more placings to his credit since then, but he was comprehensively beaten here.
Across The Rhine(USA) handles easy ground well enough, but this was probably too testing for him. (op 6/1)
Dawn Eclipse(IRE) has been running well, but was aiming high here. (op 12/1 tchd 14/1)
Look At Me(IRE) was in trouble before the straight. The shorter trip probably contributed to her failure. (op 11/4)
Luisant has been struggling to recapture last year's best form since a couple of good runs in the early part of the season.

6555 LONGCHAMP (R-H)
Sunday, October 2

OFFICIAL GOING: Turf: good

6562a QATAR PRIX DU CADRAN (GROUP 1) (4YO+) (TURF) 2m 4f
12:10 (12:10) 4-Y-0+ **£123,146** (£49,267; £15,387; £15,387; £6,163)

RPR

1 **Kasbah Bliss (FR)**[42] 5304 9-9-2 0 GeraldMosse 4 114
(F Doumen, France) *hld up: stl last over 2f out: rdn and hdwy over 1f out: r.o strly fnl f to ld towards fin* **7/2**[1]

2 *1 1/4* **Tres Rock Danon (FR)**[42] 5304 5-9-2 0 ASuborics 10 113
(W Hickst, Germany) *led at stdy pce: hdd 9f out: remained prom: rdn 2f out: led again jst ins fnl f: kpt on: hdd towards fin* **25/1**

3 *snk* **Brigantin (USA)**[21] 5990 4-9-2 0 Pierre-CharlesBoudot 1 113
(A Fabre, France) *midfield: rdn and hdwy 2f out: ev ch appr fnl f: kpt on* **4/1**[2]

3 *dht* **Ley Hunter (USA)**[21] 5990 4-9-2 0 MickaelBarzalona 3 113
(A Fabre, France) *hld up: rdn and hdwy on outer over 1f out: kpt on strly: wnt 3rd post* **7/2**[1]

5 *hd* **Silver Valny (FR)**[21] 5990 5-9-2 0 ThomasMessina 7 113
(Mlle M L Mortier, France) *midfield: rdn and hdwy 2f out: ev ch appr fnl f: kpt on* **20/1**

6 *snk* **Gentoo (FR)**[42] 5304 7-9-2 0 (p) Christophe-PatriceLemaire 5 113
(A Lyon, France) *trckd ldrs: rdn to ld narrowly over 1f out: hdd jst ins fnl f: no ex fnl 100yds* **15/2**[3]

7 *1 3/4* **Maria Royal (IRE)**[28] 5773 4-8-13 0 GregoryBenoist 2 108
(A De Royer-Dupre, France) *hld up in tch: rdn and hdwy to chse ldrs appr fnl f: one pce ins fnl f* **10/1**

8 *3/4* **Terre Du Vent (FR)**[25] 5839 5-8-13 0 StephanePasquier 6 107
(Y De Nicolay, France) *hld up: rdn over 2f out: sme hdwy over 1f out: one pce ins fnl f* **20/1**

9 *12* **Celtic Celeb (IRE)**[21] 5990 4-9-2 0 MaximeGuyon 8 98
(F Doumen, France) *trckd ldrs: rdn over 2f out: sn wknd: fin 10th: plcd 9th* **10/1**

D *6* **Elyaadi**[29] 5748 7-8-13 0 KierenFallon 9 89
(John Queally, Ire) *racd keenly: prom: led over 9f out: rdn whn hdd over 1f out: sn wknd: fin 9th: disqualified:* **25/1**

4m 30.52s (12.52) **Going Correction** +0.075s/f (Good) **10** Ran SP% **111.6**
Speed ratings: **77,76,76,76,76 76,75,75,68,72**
WIN (incl. 1 euro stake): 2.60 (Kasbah Bliss coupled with Celtic Celeb). PLACES: 1.10, 3.20, 1.20 (Ley Hunter), 1.10 (Brigantin). DF: 54.50. SF: 96.60.
Owner Henri De Pracomtal **Bred** Haras D'Ecouves Et H De Pracomtal **Trained** Bouce, France

FOCUS
Typically for this Group 1 event, the early pace was a steady one, though it did increase from past halfway after Elyaadi was allowed to stride on. Those with a finishing kick came to the fore in the straight.

NOTEBOOK
Kasbah Bliss(FR), who'd finished second, third, and fourth in previous years, raced to a much-deserved win. A triple Grade 2-winning hurdler in his time who's often been undone by tactics and/or bad luck in running in the top French staying races, the ground had come in his favour and he displayed smart acceleration to cut down his rivals, winning with a fair bit in hand. This marathon distance suits him well and Gerald Mosse, riding him for only the second time, deserves credit for a well-judged ride. The Hong Kong Vase was mentioned as a possible target.
Tres Rock Danon(FR), behind the winner in the Prix Kergolay, had the run of the race, leading early and then taking a tow into the final 1m or so. Nonetheless it still has to go down as a career-best effort.
Ley Hunter(USA) quickened best when winning the steadily-run Prix Gladiateur over 1m7f here last time (very soft ground), and he confirmed himself to be an up-and-coming stayer with this sound effort in defeat. He'd have preferred it softer and couldn't quite match the winner on this surface. The Royal-Oak is presumably where he'll head.
Brigantin(USA), third in the Ascot Gold Cup in the summer, was behind Ley Hunter in the Gladiateur, but had the drier surface and longer trip in his favour and couldn't be separated from his stablemate at the line.
Silver Valny(FR) showed his last-time-out Kergolay fourth to be no fluke.
Gentoo(FR), last year's winner, ran well on ground much faster than ideal.
Maria Royal(IRE) didn't have masses of room in which to operate, but the ground looked too fast anyway.
Terre Du Vent(FR) couldn't quicken, having travelled nicely into the race.
Celtic Celeb(IRE) dropped right out. He hasn't gone on as expected, the only hope now being that a return to hold-up tactics sparks him back to life.

6563a QATAR PRIX DE L'ABBAYE DE LONGCHAMP (GROUP 1) (2YO+) (TURF) 5f (S)
12:45 (12:00) 2-Y-0+ **£147,775** (£59,120; £29,560; £14,767; £7,396)

RPR

1 **Tangerine Trees**[36] 5467 6-9-11 0 (b) TomEaves 9 116
(Bryan Smart) *mde all: rdn 2f out: drvn fnl f: hld on all out* **14/1**

2 *snk* **Secret Asset (IRE)**[46] 5180 6-9-11 0 GeorgeBaker 8 115
(Jane Chapple-Hyam) *in tch: rdn to chse ldrs over 1f out: kpt on fnl f: wnt 2nd towards fin: nt quite rch wnr* **40/1**

3 *nse* **Sole Power**[29] 5707 4-9-11 0 KLatham 2 115+
(Edward Lynam, Ire) *hld up on inner: nt clr run and swtchd rt over 1f out: gd hdwy and r.o strly ins fnl f: unlucky* **8/1**[3]

4 *1* **Mar Adentro (FR)**[21] 5985 5-9-11 0 (p) ThierryJarnet 15 112
(R Chotard, France) *chsd ldng pair towards outer: 2nd and ev ch over 1f out: no ex and lost 2 pls fnl 50yds* **20/1**

5 *shd* **Wizz Kid (IRE)**[44] 5253 3-9-7 0 IoritzMendizabal 4 108
(Robert Collet, France) *midfield: rdn and hdwy over 1f out: kpt on fnl f* **11/2**[2]

6 *1 1/4* **Requinto (IRE)**[23] 5882 2-8-7 0 WMLordan 11 102
(David Wachman, Ire) *midfield: pushed along 1/2-way: sme hdwy over 1f out: one pce fnl f* **12/1**

7 *nk* **Prohibit**[21] 5985 6-9-11 0 (p) JimCrowley 1 106
(Robert Cowell) *in tch on inner: pushed along whn sltly short of room and lost pl 1/2-way: kpt on fnl f: nvr trbld ldrs* **4/1**[1]

8 *1 1/4* **Captain Dunne (IRE)**[25] 5827 6-9-11 0 (p) DavidAllan 5 101
(Tim Easterby) *w ldr: rdn 2f out: wknd ins fnl f* **14/1**

9 *nk* **Spectacle Du Mars (FR)**[21] 5985 4-9-11 0 GregoryBenoist 3 100
(X Nakkachdji, France) *hld up: rdn over 2f out: kpt on fnl f: nvr threatened ldrs* **14/1**

10 *nk* **Masamah (IRE)**[15] 6164 5-9-11 0 (p) PhillipMakin 10 99
(Kevin Ryan) *restless in stall: s.i.s: sn pushed along in rr: sme late hdwy: n.d* **10/1**

11 *3/4* **Bluster (FR)**[21] 5985 5-9-11 0 GeraldMosse 13 96
(Robert Collet, France) *chsd ldrs on outer: wknd over 1f out* **66/1**

12 *3/4* **Iver Bridge Lad**[110] 3010 4-9-11 0 (b) MichaelO'Connell 12 94
(John Ryan) *dwlt: sn pushed along in midfield: wknd ins fnl f* **40/1**

13 *2* **Alcohuaz (CHI)**[21] 6-9-11 0 MaximeGuyon 14 86
(Lennart Reuterskiold Jr, Sweden) *hld up towards outer: sn pushed along: nvr threatened* **66/1**

14 *nk* **Beyond Desire**[15] 6164 4-9-7 0 NeilCallan 6 81
(Roger Varian) *dwlt: hld up: nvr threatened* **25/1**

15 *5* **Margot Did (IRE)**[44] 5253 3-9-7 0 JamieSpencer 7 64
(Michael Bell) *chsd ldng pair: lost pl qckly 1/2-way: wknd and eased* **11/2**[2]

55.53 secs (-0.77) **Going Correction** +0.175s/f (Good) **15** Ran SP% **115.1**
Speed ratings: **113,112,112,111,110 108,108,106,105,105 104,103,99,99,91**
WIN (incl. 1 euro stake): 20.80. PLACES: 7.50, 10.90, 6.20. DF: 240.20. SF: 778.90.
Owner Tangerine Trees Partnership **Bred** Mrs B A Matthews **Trained** Hambleton, N Yorks

FOCUS
A prize that is usually marked for export, mainly to Britain, with the French only successful five times since the race was upgraded to Group 1 status in 1976. The draw played its part this year, with the first three home all berthed in single-digit stalls, and a few met trouble in running. The fourth looks the best guide to the form.

NOTEBOOK
Tangerine Trees, on the face of it, had plenty to find with a few of these on his running in the Temple Stakes and King's Stand, but quite apart from not showing his true form in either contest, he can be a very hard horse to catch when able to get to the front early, just as he showed when winning at Beverley last time. It didn't seem likely that he would be able to dominate in this field, but he broke very smartly from the stalls and was soon bowling along in front down the middle of the track and, despite facing a number of stern challenges in the closing stages, kept on to win with little to spare. The yard is in blinding form with its sprinters just now and this success is another testament to his trainer's skill with speedballs.
Secret Asset(IRE) had a lot to do in this line-up with a BHA rating of 100, but he is talented on his day and George Baker has been aboard for his last three wins. He was travelling as well as anything just behind the leaders for most of the way and ran on well when finally put under pressure, but the post was always going to beat him. He can probably wave goodbye to handicaps after this.
Sole Power ◆, although not the most consistent, his wins in last year's Nunthorpe and this season's Temple Stakes show him to be a top-class sprinter on his day and he looked a most unlucky loser. However, despite his decent draw, being held up well off the pace here meant that he was always going to require luck and the last thing he needed was to be trapped in behind rivals 2f out, just as the race was taking shape. Switched right soon after, he took off as though the turbo had just kicked in and finished so fast that he would have been in front in another couple of strides. This was one that got away.
Mar Adentro(FR), beaten a head by Prohibit here last month and 7lb worse off, was unlucky with the draw when third in this last year, and found himself drawn on the wide outside again here. He travelled well in a prominent position on the outside and had every chance, but was run out of the placings in the last few yards. This was another fine effort under the circumstances and he deserves to win at Group level.
Wizz Kid(IRE) reversed Nunthorpe form with Margot Did and Prohibit, where she didn't enjoy the clearest of runs, but on this occasion her finishing effort was too late. She may have preferred easier ground and remains open to further improvement.
Requinto(IRE), bidding to become the first 2-y-o to win this since Sigy in 1978, ran no sort of race in the Nunthorpe where he may not have handled the ground, but he had been impressive recently otherwise. Despite coming off the bridle just after halfway, he stayed on well to finish a highly creditable sixth and should take high rank as a sprinter next season.
Prohibit looked the one to beat, especially after landing the rails draw, but he didn't really make full use of it and didn't look happy behind the pacesetters. He wasn't done many favours by the weakening Margot Did when already being ridden along 2f out, but did run on again in the closing stages, if never having a prayer of making the frame.
Captain Dunne(IRE) showed his usual early speed against the stands' rail, but had run his race by the furlong pole.
Spectacle Du Mars(FR) was given plenty to do and didn't enjoy the clearest of runs over 1f out. He ran on late, but faced a hopeless task.
Masamah(IRE) became restless in the stalls and missed the break which would have been curtains for his chances here, though he did make up some late ground.

Beyond Desire missed the break and then took a grip, but although she was badly hampered passing the furlong pole she had no chance by that stage.
Margot Did(IRE) was handy early, but dropped away so quickly after halfway that something must have been amiss.

6564a TOTAL PRIX MARCEL BOUSSAC - CRITERIUM DES POULICHES (GROUP 1) (2YO FILLIES) (TURF) 1m

1:20 (12:00) 2-Y-O **£147,775** (£59,120; £29,560; £14,767; £7,396)

RPR

1 **Elusive Kate (USA)**43 5296 2-8-11 0 .... WilliamBuick 3 115
(John Gosden) *led: hung lft fr 2f out: pressed by Zantenda on ins rail ent fnl f: continued gng lft across Fire Lily: stened up and r.o wl fnl 125yds: in command fnl 50yds* **4/1**2

2 3 **Fire Lily (IRE)**35 5525 2-8-11 0 .... WMLordan 1 108
(David Wachman, Ire) *trckd ldr: carried lft by ldr fr 2f out: crossed by wnr ent fnl f but jockey kpt riding: styd on u.p: nt pce to chal wnr* **6/1**

3 1 1/4 **Zantenda**24 5873 2-8-11 0 .... OlivierPeslier 4 105+
(F Head, France) *racd freely in 4th: 5th and gng wl 3f out: effrt on ins rail to dispute 2nd over 1 1/2f out: r.o u.p to press ldr ins fnl f: nt qckn u.p: fdd fnl 75yds* **5/4**1

4 1 3/4 **Yellow Rosebud (IRE)**56 4833 2-8-11 0 .... PJSmullen 6 101
(D K Weld, Ire) *racd 3rd: shkn up ins fnl 2f: hrd rdn 1 1/2f out: no imp* **9/2**3

5 1/2 **Falls Of Lora (IRE)**29 5698 2-8-11 0 .... KierenFallon 5 99
(Mahmood Al Zarooni) *rrd as stalls opened but qckly in tch at bk of field: moved up to share 3rd appr 1/2-way: rdn and nt qckn fr 1 1/2f out* **7/1**

1m 38.1s (-0.30) **Going Correction** +0.075s/f (Good) 5 Ran SP% **109.4**
Speed ratings: **104,101,99,98,97**
WIN (incl. 1 euro stake): 4.90. PLACES: 2.50, 2.50. SF: 17.00.
Owner Magnolia Racing LLC & Ms Rachel Hood **Bred** Clovelly Farms **Trained** Newmarket, Suffolk

FOCUS
An unsatisfactory edition of this Group 1 fillies' contest, the pace being steady and the runners finishing scattered across the course. Most notable recent winners include Divine Proportions, the great Zarkava, and Misty For Me, but only the beaten favourite Zantenda has any hope of going on to make it as a top-level filly. The winner is progressing and the second is rated to her Irish form.

NOTEBOOK
Elusive Kate(USA), giving her trainer a third victory in the race, had won 7f Listed/Group 3 races at Deauville, and William Buick rode her intelligently to maximise her superior pace and quicken off the front. Despite drifting left under pressure, leading to all bar the favourite following her, she always looked to be doing enough, the slight interference she caused to the runner-up not affecting the result. Things very much went her way this time, so there's some doubt as to whether she can establish herself as a legitimate top-flight filly next season. A return trip here for the Pouliches will presumably be on the cards.
Fire Lily(IRE), another unraced beyond 7f prior to this and representing the Maybe form, was always well positioned, but couldn't accelerate as quickly as the winner, and would have finished second even without the slight interference.
Zantenda ◆ came into this unbeaten in two starts, displaying a fine change of acceleration under a confident ride the time before, but was free to post, keen in the race, and then looked uncomfortable on the faster surface having been switched inside to race on the rail. She can rate better than the bare result and is still likely to be a major player for next season's Pouliches.
Yellow Rosebud(IRE), runner-up to Maybe in a Group 2 at the Curragh last time, failed to improve for the step up to 1m.
Falls Of Lora(IRE), winner of a conditions race over this trip at Ascot, was simply not good enough.

6565a QATAR PRIX JEAN-LUC LAGARDERE (GROUP 1) (2YO COLTS & FILLIES) (TURF) 7f

1:55 (12:00) 2-Y-O **£172,405** (£68,974; £34,487; £17,228; £8,629)

RPR

1 **Dabirsim (FR)**42 5305 2-9-0 0 .... FrankieDettori 2 115+
(C Ferland, France) *settled in rr: last appr fnl f: shkn up and qcknd wl on ins rail: r.o strly fnl 150yds to ld 30yds out* **4/7**1

2 3/4 **Sofast (FR)**28 5770 2-9-0 0 .... OlivierPeslier 3 113
(F Head, France) *disp 4th: short of room ent fnl f: sn shkn up and r.o wl: nrest at fin* **9/2**2

3 shd **Salure**14 2-9-0 0 .... DarioVargiu 4 113
(B Grizzetti, Italy) *led and sn 8 l clr: 5 l clr and pushed along 1 1/2f out: hrd rdn but sing to fade ins fnl f: hdd fnl 30yds* **40/1**

4 nse **Veneto (FR)**24 2-9-0 0 .... ThierryJarnet 5 113
(B De Montzey, France) *racd 3rd: pushed along under 1 1/2f out: kpt on wl u.p fnl 150yds* **100/1**

5 3/4 **American Devil (FR)**28 5770 2-9-0 0 .... MaximeGuyon 1 111
(J Van Handenhove, France) *chsd clr ldr: 2nd and hrd rdn 1 1/2f out: styd on u.p fnl 110yds: nt pce to chal* **8/1**3

6 1 1/4 **Mac Row (IRE)**28 5770 2-9-0 0 .... Christophe-PatriceLemaire 6 107
(J-C Rouget, France) *racd keenly towards rr: shkn up over 2f out: last and kpt on u.p ins fnl f: nvr able to chal* **12/1**

7 nk **Fort Bastion (IRE)**46 5181 2-9-0 0 .... RichardHughes 7 106
(Richard Hannon) *disp 4th: rdn and nt qckn over 2f out: kpt on at same pce fnl f* **12/1**

1m 19.85s (-0.85) **Going Correction** +0.075s/f (Good) 7 Ran SP% **111.8**
Speed ratings: **107,106,106,105,105 103,103**
WIN (incl. 1 euro stake): 1.50. PLACES: 1.20, 1.60. SF: 2.90.
Owner Simon Springer **Bred** Mme L Monfort **Trained** France

FOCUS
Hard to evaluate the form, with outsider Salure trying to slip the field, and the runners finished in a bit of a heap, but there's no doubt we saw a quality performance from Morny winner Dabirsim. The form looks limited for the level.

NOTEBOOK
Dabirsim(FR) ◆, not the best away and soon in rear, he had a ton of running to do in the straight, but produced a prolonged burst of acceleration under Frankie Dettori, who took the brave man's route up the inner on the way to registering his 500th Group success. This was an impressive performance from a horse who his rider described as a "superstar" in his post-race interview, and it looks inevitable he'll be seen sporting the Godolphin silks next season. He'll presumably head to the 2000 Guineas at Newmarket, and despite possessing a ton of speed, there's enough stamina on the dam's side of the pedigree to suggest he'll have no trouble with 1m.
Sofast(FR), slowly away and probably not at his best when over 4l behind Dabirsim in the Morny, returned to winning ways in soft ground last time and took another step forward with a career-best effort in defeat. He wasn't unlucky, but very briefly got checked in his stride when starting his run, and had to begin again, by which time the winner had already gone past.
Salure, beaten in a 1m heavy ground Listed race at San Siro last time, attempted to get away from them on this drop in trip and it briefly looked as though he was going to do so, but with this race being run on the longer straight, he couldn't quite hold on. He should take high rank returned to Italy next season.
Veneto(FR) held little obvious chance and was clearly flattered.
American Devil(FR) led the main group and ran well to a point. He'll be ready for further next season.
Fort Bastion(IRE) deserves a chance to get his head in front returned to maiden-company.

6566a QATAR PRIX DE LA FORET (GROUP 1) (3YO+) (TURF) 7f

2:30 (12:00) 3-Y-O+ **£147,775** (£59,120; £29,560; £14,767; £7,396)

RPR

1 **Dream Ahead (USA)**29 5707 3-9-0 0 .... WilliamBuick 6 129+
(David Simcock) *a travelling wl in 4th (jst bhd Goldikova on her outside): swtchd outside Worthadd 1 1/2f out: pushed along and qcknd to ld fnl f: r.o wl u.p: hung lft for a few strides 100yds out: sn stened* **7/2**2

2 hd **Goldikova (IRE)**48 5129 6-8-13 0 .... OlivierPeslier 2 125+
(F Head, France) *settled cl up in 3rd on rail: led whn pcemaker moved off rail over 2f out: rdn 1 1/2f out: hdd fnl f: r.o wl u.p* **4/7**1

3 6 **Surfrider (IRE)**140 2139 3-9-0 0 .... Christophe-PatriceLemaire 7 112
(E Libaud, France) *racd in 6th: gd prog 2f out: r.o wl ins fnl 1 1/2f to go 3rd: kpt on u.p fnl f but nt pce of first two* **40/1**

4 1 3/4 **Bewitched (IRE)**21 5979 4-8-13 0 .... JMurtagh 4 104
(Charles O'Brien, Ire) *hld up towards rr: effrt on ins 2f out: 4th and scrubbed along over 1f out: nt qckn fnl f* **14/1**

5 2 **Worthadd (IRE)**48 5129 4-9-2 0 .... FrankieDettori 5 102
(Vittorio Caruso, Italy) *led for less than a f: trckd pcemaker on Goldikova's outside: stl 2nd over 1 1/2f out: sn rdn and nt qckn: wknd fnl f* **10/1**3

6 1/2 **Marchand D'Or (FR)**35 5532 8-9-2 0 .... DavyBonilla 8 100
(M Delzangles, France) *w.w in rr: rdn and no imp fnl 1 1/2f* **20/1**

7 9 **Flash Dance (IRE)**48 5129 5-8-13 0 .... MickaelBarzalona 1 73
(F Head, France) *hrd rdn to ld bef they had gone a f: led tl eased off rail over 2f out to let Goldikova through: sn wknd and eased fnl f* **200/1**

P **Dever Dream**24 5848 4-8-13 0 .... RichardHughes 3 —
(William Haggas) *trckd Goldikova in 5th on ins of Dream Ahd: faltered over 2 1/2f out and p.u* **33/1**

1m 18.1s (-2.60) **Going Correction** +0.075s/f (Good)
WFA 3 from 4yo+ 2lb 8 Ran SP% **112.3**
Speed ratings: **117,116,109,107,105 105,94,—**
WIN (incl. 1 euro stake): 5.70. PLACES: 1.20, 1.10, 1.70. DF: 3.60. SF: 16.60.
Owner Khalifa Dasmal **Bred** Darley **Trained** Newmarket, Suffolk

FOCUS
British stables had taken seven of the previous 13 runnings of the Foret, and that statistic was improved on following a thrilling finish between two prolific Group 1 winners. They went an even pace, even though Goldikova's pacemaker Flash Dance had to be hard ridden to gain the early advantage, and she did her job until pulled off the rail and allowed to coast home inside the last 2f. The winner is rated to his best.

NOTEBOOK
Dream Ahead(USA) was already a four-time Group 1 winner, including in France as a 2-y-o, but there remained a niggling doubt about him over the trip, having yet to win beyond 6f, and his flop in the Maurice de Gheest on ground that should have suited was still fresh in the mind, despite his successes on quicker ground in the July Cup and Betfred Sprint Cup either side. Content to sit just behind the leaders, he was switched to the outside for his effort 2f out and looked destined for a clear-cut success when ranging alongside Goldikova a furlong later but, not for the first time, he started to think about it and hung away to his left, giving the mare another chance, but after a thrilling duel he just had his nose in front where it mattered. This may have been his last race, but he is in such great form just now that there remains the possibility he could go for the Breeders' Cup or Hong Kong.
Goldikova(IRE), making her last appearance in Europe, finished third in this race two years ago but won it last year. She appeared to travel smoothly enough behind the leaders and the race was hers for the taking when her pacemaker accommodatingly pulled out to leave her a gap against the inside rail 2f from home. However, although she quickened once in front (pulling right away from the third), she wasn't able to establish enough of an advantage against a rival with such a potent turn of foot as the winner and, despite giving her all, was nosed out right on the line. Defeat in this race in 2009 didn't preclude a success in that year's Breeders' Cup Mile and there seems no reason why it should be any different this time.
Surfrider(IRE) was having his first start since finishing 11th in the French 2000 Guineas and ran on from off the pace inside the last 2f to finish a remote, if clear third. He has only had six starts and it will be interesting to see if he returns next year, because the best of him has probably still to be seen.
Bewitched(IRE), having her 19th start, is tough as old boots and ran on against the inside rail over the last 2f, but she is really an established Group 3 filly.
Worthadd(IRE), an eight-time winner in Italy, could be given a bit of a chance on his second to Canford Cliffs in the Lockinge, but after mixing it with Goldikova and her pacemaker for much of the way he folded completely from over 1f out. This ground was probably faster than ideal.

6567a QATAR PRIX DE L'ARC DE TRIOMPHE (GROUP 1) (3YO+ COLTS, FILLIES & MARES) (TURF) 1m 4f

3:15 (12:00) 3-Y-O-**£1,970,344** (£788,275; £394,137; £196,896; £98,620)

RPR

1 **Danedream (GER)**28 5773 3-8-8 0 .... AStarke 2 128+
(P Schiergen, Germany) *midfield: rdn and hdwy 2f out: led appr fnl f: sn qcknd clr: comf* **20/1**

2 5 **Shareta (IRE)**21 5989 3-8-8 0 .... ThierryJarnet 9 120
(A De Royer-Dupre, France) *trckd ldr: chal over 3f out: rdn over 2f out: kpt on but no ch w wnr fnl f* **66/1**

3 nk **Snow Fairy (IRE)**29 5747 4-9-2 0 .... FrankieDettori 11 121+
(Ed Dunlop) *hld up in midfield: pushed along over 3f out: rdn and hdwy over 1f out: kpt on fnl f: wnt 3rd towards fin* **14/1**

4 1/2 **So You Think (NZ)**29 5747 5-9-5 0 .... SeamieHeffernan 14 125+
(A P O'Brien, Ire) *hld up: pushed along and hdwy 2f out: kpt on wl fnl f: wnt 4th post: nvr nrr* **9/2**2

5 snk **St Nicholas Abbey (IRE)**21 5986 4-9-5 0 .... JPO'Brien 6 123
(A P O'Brien, Ire) *trckd ldrs: led narrowly over 3f out: drvn whn hdd appr fnl f: wknd fnl 100yds* **33/1**

6 snk **Meandre (FR)**21 5987 3-8-11 0 .... MaximeGuyon 10 122+
(A Fabre, France) *midfield: rdn over 2f out: hdwy over 1f out: kpt on fnl f* **12/1**

7 snk **Sarafina (FR)**21 5986 4-9-2 0 .... Christophe-PatriceLemaire 13 121+
(A De Royer-Dupre, France) *t.k.h early: hld up on outer: rdn and gd hdwy 2f out: one pce fnl f* **4/1**1

8 3/4 **Silver Pond (FR)**35 5531 4-9-5 0 .... ThierryThulliez 15 121+
(C Laffon-Parias, France) *hld up: stl last 3f out: gd hdwy 2f out: kpt on fnl f* **100/1**

9 4 **Galikova (FR)**21 5989 3-8-8 0 .... OlivierPeslier 4 111
(F Head, France) *midfield on inner: rdn 3f out: one pce* **7/1**3

10 3/4 **Hiruno D'Amour (JPN)**21 5986 4-9-5 0 .... ShinjiFujita 1 113
(Mitsugu Kon, Japan) *in tch: chsd ldrs over 2f out: wknd appr fnl f* **10/1**

11 2 1/2 **Nakayama Festa (JPN)**21 5986 5-9-5 0 .... MasayoshiEbina 16 109
(Yoshitaka Ninomiya, Japan) *hld up: rdn over 2f out: nvr threatened* **28/1**

12 nk **Workforce**71 4315 4-9-5 0 .... RyanMoore 8 109
(Sir Michael Stoute) *hld up in midfield: sltly short of room and shuffled bk a bit 6f out: rdn 3f out: sn no imp* **10/1**

13 *1* **Testosterone (IRE)**[21] 5989 3-8-8 0 StephanePasquier 3 103
(P Bary, France) *trckd ldrs: rdn over 2f out: wknd over 1f out* **66/1**

14 *2 1/2* **Treasure Beach**[50] 5072 3-8-11 0 CO'Donoghue 12 102
(A P O'Brien, Ire) *led: hdd over 3f out: sn rdn: wknd 2f out* **28/1**

15 *6* **Reliable Man**[21] 5987 3-8-11 0 GeraldMosse 7 93
(A De Royer-Dupre, France) *hld up in midfield: rdn over 2f out: sn btn* **12/1**

16 *2* **Masked Marvel**[22] 5928 3-8-11 0 WilliamBuick 5 90
(John Gosden) *in tch: rdn over 3f out: wknd 2f out* **14/1**

2m 24.49s (-5.91) **Going Correction** +0.075s/f (Good)
WFA 3 from 4yo+ 7lb **16** Ran SP% **116.2**
Speed ratings: **122,118,118,118,118 117,117,117,114,114 112,112,111,109,105 104**
WIN (incl. 1 euro stake): 27.80. places: 7.80, 13.00, 5.40. DF: 591.20. SF: 1,191.70.
Owner Gestut Burg Eberstein & T Yoshida **Bred** Gestut Brummerhof **Trained** Germany

FOCUS

The pace was an ordinary one, Ballydoyle's Irish Derby winner Treasure Beach being largely ignored in a clear lead, and though some will question the form with 66-1 shot Shareta holding on for second, she did have an easy enough time of it on the front. The result took the record of 3yos in the race to 15 wins in the last 18 years. With the ground the fastest it's been for a while in the Arc, the record winning time for the race, previously held by Peintre Celebre (1997), had 0.11 seconds shaved off it by hugely impressive winner Danedream. The filly is rated below the best recent winners of this race with several appearing to run below par.

NOTEBOOK

Danedream(GER), who'd been supplemented into the race just a couple of days earlier at a cost of 100,000 euros, became only the second 3-y-o filly to win, along with the great Zarkava, since Akiyda in 1982. She was always nicely positioned from a low draw under Andrasch Starke and was noted travelling extremely well as they started the turn into the home straight. Weaving her way through, victory was never in doubt for the daughter of Lomitas once switched left to come with her challenge, and the acceleration shown to go clear was that of a truly top-class filly, her 5l winning margin being one of the biggest ever in the race. The first German-trained winner since Star Appeal in 1975, she'd only cost 9,000 euros and started out this season with defeat in a 1m Listed race in Italy. Her rise to fame has been quite astonishing, winning the Italian Oaks with ease and twice romping to victory in 1m4f Group 1s in her homeland, on each occasion beating established older performers, including colts, with her latest win coming in the same race Marienbard used as a prep in 2002 before coming on to victory here. Whether we see her again in Europe remains to be seen, with the Breeders' Cup Turf or Japan Cup looking her next, and perhaps final, port of call.

Shareta(IRE), acting as a pacemaker for favourite Sarafina, made it a one-two for the 3-y-o fillies, defying her huge odds and showing a really likeable attitude to keep going for second on ground that clearly suited her well. This was a huge step up on previous efforts, having finished behind both Galikova and Testosterone in the Vermeille last time, and there's little doubt she was flattered to an extent, having enjoyed the run of things on the front of the main pack. It is unlikely she will ever run up to this level again.

Snow Fairy(IRE) has worked her way back to top form and was widely fancied to run a huge race here with ground conditions in her favour. Held up a little worse than midfield, she was only a length or two down on the winner when things really started to heat up, and simply lacked that rival's acceleration, despite keeping on well. She had no excuses and will head back to Japan to try and repeat last year's win in the QEII Commemorative Cup (or possibly the Japan Cup) before heading on to defend her Hong Kong Cup crown.

So You Think(NZ) had ground conditions were in his favour and he'd quite possibly have been second with a kinder draw, as he was unable to obtain a decent early position. He covered plenty of ground in the straight and, while not the superstar he was billed to be, he's still a tough, top-class performer who ought to take the beating if heading to Ascot in two weeks' time for the Champion Stakes. The Breeders' Cup Classic may also be on the agenda, a race in which he could easily run a big race in.

St Nicholas Abbey(IRE) hadn't been seen to best advantage since winning the Coronation Cup, being unsuited by the lack of pace in both the King George and Prix Foy. He travelled well in behind the pace, and moved to the front seemingly with plenty left in the tank around 3f out, but his lack of tactical speed was again exposed when it mattered. He can win next year's Ascot Gold Cup if connections opt to go that route.

Meandre(FR) unsurprisingly reversed Niel form with Reliable Man on this faster surface. Winner of the Grand Prix de Paris over C&D in July, he travelled kindly enough into the straight, but there was no change of pace when asked to get himself seriously involved. This is as good as he is.

Sarafina(FR), an unlucky third in last year's race, having nearly been brought down turning in, she'd enjoyed a perfect prep this time round, narrowly winning the Foy with a fair bit in hand last time, and was widely fancied to gain compensation. However, there were slight reservations over her on this surface and, having been wide from stall 13 and seen plenty of daylight, the finishing burst she's produced so often in the past just wasn't there. She wasn't at her best, but her best wouldn't have been good enough this year anyway.

Silver Pond(FR) did well considering he came from well of the pace. He's often looked all about stamina and it'll be interesting to see whether he goes up in trip next season, as he could really make an impact in the staying division.

Galikova(FR) carried plenty of confidence, with her trainer expecting the faster ground to be no problem, but this was easily the biggest field she's faced and, having been slightly short of room tight against the inside rail, was unable to recover the lost ground. She'd finished ahead of the runner-up on all three previous occasions they'd met, so connections were no doubt left scratching their heads as to why she was so comfortably beaten.

Hiruno D'Amour(JPN) was possibly the best backed horse in the race and he was certainly well positioned turning for home. However, there was a limited response once asked to quicken, and he ultimately dropped right out. This wasn't his true form.

Nakayama Festa(JPN) never looked like coming with a run and hasn't been the same horse since getting injured in the Japan Cup.

Workforce was a touch fortunate when winning last year, and he once again hadn't been seen since a disappointing outcome in the King George. In a stronger race this time round, with a trainer still quiet and jockey just back from injury, it was no surprise he failed to make an impact, for all that an awkward start and then suffering interference in running in the early stages and at the top of the hill didn't help.

Testosterone(IRE) failed to reproduce the form that saw her finish second in the Vermeille.

Reliable Man reversed earlier form with Meandre when winning the Niel, clearly appreciating the slow surface, but he'd been a drifter all week with the prospect of fast ground against him, and he was in trouble turning for home. This wasn't his true form.

Masked Marvel was supplemented into this as a last-minute replacement for Nathaniel, but the race came only 22 days after his huge effort at Doncaster, and he was always unlikely to be able to reproduce his best.

6568a QATAR PRIX DE L'OPERA (GROUP1) (3YO+ FILLIES & MARES) (TURF) 1m 2f

4:45 (12:00) 3-Y-0+ **£172,405** (£68,974; £34,487; £17,228; £8,629)

RPR

1 **Nahrain**[92] 3648 3-8-11 0 FrankieDettori 1 116+
(Roger Varian) *trckd ldrs: gng wl whn short of room on inner over 2f out tl over 1f out: qcknd to ld ins fnl f: sn strly pressed: jst hld on* **10/3**[2]

2 *nse* **Announce**[42] 5306 4-9-2 0 MaximeGuyon 5 115
(A Fabre, France) *in tch: rdn and ev ch over 1f out: kpt on: upsides fnl 50yds: jst failed* **11/4**[1]

3 *1 1/2* **Banimpire (IRE)**[45] 5219 3-8-11 0 KJManning 8 112
(J S Bolger, Ire) *trckd ldr: rdn to ld wl over 1f out: hdd ins fnl f: kpt on* **9/2**[3]

4 *1* **Sandy's Charm (FR)**[35] 5530 3-8-11 0 OlivierPeslier 9 110
(F Rohaut, France) *midfield: rdn over 2f out: kpt on ins fnl f: no threat to ldng trio* **13/2**

5 *snk* **Djumama (IRE)**[29] 5749 3-8-11 0 AHelfenbein 6 110
(Andreas Lowe, Germany) *hld up in tch: rdn over 2f out: hdwy over 1f out: kpt on ins fnl f: nvr threatened ldrs* **16/1**

6 *snk* **Epic Love (IRE)**[40] 5366 3-8-11 0 StephanePasquier 7 109
(P Bary, France) *hld up: stl last over 2f out: rdn and gd hdwy on outer over 1f out: kpt on fnl f* **15/2**

7 *snk* **Haya Landa (FR)**[40] 5366 3-8-11 0 FranckBlondel 11 109
(Mme L Audon, France) *hld up in tch: rdn 2f out: one pce* **25/1**

8 *2 1/2* **Julie's Love**[7] 6394 3-8-11 0 MickaelBarzalona 3 104
(Manfred Hofer, Germany) *midfield on inner: briefly short of room over 2f out: rdn over 1f out: sn no imp* **33/1**

9 *1/2* **Glorious Sight (IRE)**[64] 4570 3-8-11 0 GeraldMosse 10 103
(Robert Collet, France) *racd keenly: in tch: rdn and ev ch over 1f out: wknd appr fnl f* **12/1**

10 *1 3/4* **Shamardanse (IRE)**[9] 6321 3-8-11 0 Francois-XavierBertras 4 100
(S Wattel, France) *led: hdd wl over 1f out: wknd* **150/1**

2m 2.74s (-1.26) **Going Correction** +0.075s/f (Good)
WFA 3 from 4yo 5lb **10** Ran SP% **114.0**
Speed ratings: **108,107,106,105,105 105,105,103,103,101**
WIN (incl. 1 euro stake): 5.60. PLACES: 2.40, 1.50, 2.60. DF: 11.20. SF: 14.00.
Owner Sheikh Ahmed Al Maktoum **Bred** Darley **Trained** Newmarket, Suffolk

FOCUS

A Group 1 contest since 2000 at which stage the distance was increased to 1m2f. British and Irish yards had taken eight of the previous 20 runnings of the Prix de l'Opera and this was another statistic to be enhanced. The early gallop was very modest, resulting in a few taking a keen hold. The form is rated around the second, fifth and seventh.

NOTEBOOK

Nahrain came into this unbeaten, having won three times over 1m earlier in the season, but this was a big step up in class from Listed company, even though being out of the Musidora/Ribblesdale-winner Bahr meant the longer trip should have suited. Given a well-judged ride by Frankie Dettori, who had her in a good position just behind the leaders in a steadily run race, she was trapped behind horses passing the 2f pole and the runner-up tried to hold her in, but she managed to edge her way out far enough in order to see daylight and hit the front over 1f out. It did appear to the naked eye as though the second had caught her right on the line, but she had her head down passing the post and got the verdict in the photo. She then had to survive a stewards' inquiry, but was allowed to keep the race and give her young trainer his first Group 1 success. It will be interesting to see where she goes next as she has the scope for even more improvement.

Announce had already been successful at this level following her narrow defeat of Timepiece in the Prix Jean Romanet at Deauville in August, and her earlier defeats had been at the hands of the likes of Cirrus Des Aigles and Sarafina. Held up further off the pace than the winner, she tried to hold her rival in when making headway 2f out and, although the pair came close together soon afterwards, she had sufficient time to get back up had she been good enough. She ran on strongly and it looked as though she had done so, but the photo proved otherwise.

Banimpire(IRE) was having her 11th start of the season, which is a lot for a high-class performer, and her modest effort in the Yorkshire Oaks can be forgiven as she never looked happy on the ground there. Always handy, she was sent to the front 2f out, but was then found out for finishing pace and, for a filly that stays 1m4f well, the way the race was run was probably not ideal.

Sandy's Charm(FR) was racing beyond 1m for the first time and was out of a mare who was successful over further than this. Unfortunately, her pacemaker (in the same ownership) made a pig's ear of her front-running role, resulting in Sandy's Charm pulling too hard early as well and, despite making a promising effort on the outside 2f out, her run soon petered out as her earlier exertions took their toll.

Djumama(IRE), runner-up to Dancing Rain in the German Oaks and a winner over 1m3f, was another unsuited by the way the race was run, being held up at the back of the field in a steadily run race, and her finishing effort was always going to fall short.

Epic Love(IRE)'s style of running means she needs a strong pace to run at and she didn't get that here.

Haya Landa(FR) was another poorly positioned in a slowly run race.

Julie's Love didn't have much room to play with after turning for home, but didn't find much for pressure in any case.

Glorious Sight(IRE) was another to pull her chance away.

6367 SAN SIRO (R-H)

Sunday, October 2

OFFICIAL GOING: Turf: good

6569a PREMIO DUCA D'AOSTA (LISTED RACE) (3YO+) (TURF) 1m 6f

3:45 (3:45) 3-Y-0+ **£24,137** (£10,620; £5,793; £2,896)

RPR

1 **Figli Fanesi (IRE)**[105] 3-8-8 0 UmbertoRispoli 3 107
(Vittorio Caruso, Italy) **97/20**[3]

2 *2* **Caudillo (GER)**[126] 2540 8-9-0 0 LManiezzi 4 101
(Dr A Bolte, Germany) **53/20**[2]

3 *1 1/4* **Orsino (GER)**[65] 4-9-0 0 MEsposito 9 99
(R Rohne, Germany) **25/4**

4 *1/2* **Bourne**[23] 5883 5-9-0 0 MircoDemuro 1 98
(Luca Cumani) *settled in midfield: lost pl 4f out: rdn and styd on fnl 2 1/2f: nt pce to chal ldrs* **26/25**[1]

5 *3/4* **Wheredreamsare**[36] 5497 4-9-0 0 (b) DPorcu 5 97
(Frau J Mayer, Germany) **194/10**

6 *dist* **Boz**[686] 7-9-0 0 MKolmarkaj 2 —
(M Gasparini, Italy) **26/25**[1]

7 *1* **Crusch (IRE)**[72] 5-9-0 0 CristianDemuro 7 —
(S Botti, Italy) **112/10**

8 *dist* **Reventon**[168] 3-8-5 0 FabioBranca 8 —
(B Grizzetti, Italy) **17/1**

9 *nk* **Ryan (IRE)**[322] 8-9-3 0 (b) PierantonioConvertino 6 —
(J Hanacek, Slovakia) **125/10**

2m 53.6s (173.60)
WFA 3 from 4yo+ 9lb **9** Ran SP% **182.4**
PARI-MUTUEL (all including 1 euro stakes): WIN 5.84; PLACE 2.00, 1.73, 2.31; DF 11.45.
Owner Incolinx **Bred** Azienda Agricola Luciani Loreto **Trained** Italy

NOTEBOOK

Bourne could finish only fourth on his step up from handicap company. He raced in the middle of the field before being caught flat-footed approaching the last 4f, and although he stayed on, never looked like getting there.

6570 - 6571a (Foreign Racing) - See Raceform Interactive

6274 PONTEFRACT (L-H)

Monday, October 3

OFFICIAL GOING: Good to firm (8.0)

Wind: moderate 1/2 behind Weather: fine but becoming overcast and quite breezy

6572 E B F "FRANKLINS GARDENS" MAIDEN STKS 1m 2f 6y

2:10 (2:11) (Class 4) 2-Y-O £4,463 (£1,328; £663; £331) Stalls Low

Form RPR

32 **1** **Cherry Street**[23] 5937 2-9-3 0 DavidProbert 6 88+
(Andrew Balding) *trckd ldr: led over 1f out: styd on wl: eased nr fin* **7/2**[3]

4 **2** 3 ¼ **Sir Graham Wade (IRE)**[7] 6400 2-9-3 0 SilvestreDeSousa 4 82+
(Mark Johnston) *chsd ldrs: drvn over 3f out: styd on to take 2nd fnl 100yds: no imp* **3/1**[2]

443 **3** 2 ½ **Humungosaur**[41] 5365 2-9-3 0 PaulHanagan 2 77
(Paul Cole) *led: drvn over 2f out: hdd over 1f out: wknd fnl 100yds* **1/1**[1]

00 **4** 14 **Quixote**[35] 5565 2-9-3 0 MartinDwyer 11 50
(Clive Brittain) *mid-div: wnt modest 4th over 2f out: nvr nr ldrs* **40/1**

04 **5** 7 **Catramis**[26] 5818 2-9-0 0 DaleSwift(3) 12 37
(Geoffrey Oldroyd) *in rr: sme hdwy over 4f out: nvr nr ldrs* **66/1**

00 **6** ½ **Last Zak**[16] 6180 2-8-10 0 DavidSimmonson(7) 8 36
(Michael Easterby) *chsd ldrs: wknd over 2f out* **66/1**

04 **7** 4 ½ **Hareby (IRE)**[19] 6048 2-9-3 0 DuranFentiman 7 27
(Tim Easterby) *mid-div: drvn over 5f out: wknd over 2f out* **14/1**

500 **8** 18 **Tushuk Tash (USA)**[7] 6400 2-9-3 0 FrannyNorton 9 —
(Mick Channon) *in rr: bhd fnl 3f* **25/1**

00 **9** 21 **Bells Of Berlin**[13] 6230 2-9-3 0 (t) PaddyAspell 10 —
(Alan McCabe) *dwlt: in rr: drvn over 5f out: sn bhd: t.o 2f out* **50/1**

05 **10** 30 **Endangered Species**[52] 5003 2-9-3 0 TomEaves 1 —
(John Weymes) *dwlt: sn drvn along detached in last: reminders over 7f out: sn bhd: t.o 3f out* **66/1**

2m 12.42s (-1.28) **Going Correction** -0.10s/f (Good) **10** Ran SP% **116.6**

Speed ratings (Par 97): **101,98,96,85,79 79,75,61,44,20**

toteswingers: 1&2 £2.30, 2&3 £1.80, 1&3 £2.00 CSF £13.94 TOTE £4.90: £1.20, £1.20, £1.10; EX 13.10.

Owner James/Michaelson/Greenwood 1 **Bred** Andrew Sime & Co Ltd & Susanna Ballinger **Trained** Kingsclere, Hants

FOCUS

A decent test of stamina for these juveniles on this stiff track and a trio dominated both the market and the race. The first two are improvers but the third was below his foreign, soft-ground form.

NOTEBOOK

Cherry Street ◆ had already proved himself over this trip when second at Goodwood last time and took another step forward. Always travelling well behind the leader, he picked up the favourite with the minimum of fuss over a furlong out and won going away. The Zetland Stakes over this trip at Newmarket at the end of the month would seem the obvious target and he should develop into a nice stayer next year. (tchd 4-1 in places)

Sir Graham Wade(IRE) ◆ ran green when fourth of 13 over this trip on his Bath debut and still didn't look the finished article here, needing to be niggled along half a mile from home but plugging on all the way to the line to snatch second. Whatever, he achieves this year, he looks a 3-y-o through and through. (op 7-2)

Humungosaur, taking another step up in trip for the fourth race in a row, set the standard after finishing third in a Deauville Listed contest last time and was considered one of the yard's "nicest 2-y-os". He very much had the run of the race out in front, but proved a sitting duck for the winner and finished weakly. He ran like a non-stayer and the quicker ground may also have been an issue, but either way he has an awful lot to prove now. (tchd 10-11 and 11-10)

Quixote did pull clear of the others from the home bend and now gets a mark. (op 50-1)

6573 TOTESPORT DAY ON MONDAY 17TH OCTOBER NURSERY 6f

2:40 (2:47) (Class 4) (0-85,85) 2-Y-O £3,428 (£1,020; £509; £254) Stalls Low

Form RPR

01 **1** **Mince**[17] 6123 2-8-6 70 SteveDrowne 1 89+
(Roger Charlton) *t.k.h in midfield: smooth hdwy over 2f out: led over 1f out: qcknd clr jst ins fnl f: eased fnl 50yds* **2/1**[1]

6104 **2** 5 **See Clearly**[16] 6154 2-8-11 75 (b[1]) DuranFentiman 2 75
(Tim Easterby) *broke fast and led early: sn settled midfield: hdwy over 1f out: styd on wl to take 2nd fnl 100yds: no ch w wnr* **25/1**

0120 **3** 2 **Whisky Bravo**[15] 6186 2-8-5 69 FrannyNorton 5 63
(David Brown) *s.s: detached in last: hdwy on wd outside over 1f out: hung lft: styd on to take 3rd fnl 75yds* **25/1**

3153 **4** 1 ½ **Satanic Beat (IRE)**[29] 5755 2-9-2 80 PJMcDonald 8 69
(Jedd O'Keeffe) *in rr on outer: hdwy 2f out: kpt on same pce fnl f* **4/1**[2]

632 **5** 1 ¼ **Royal Trix**[18] 6092 2-8-8 72 MartinDwyer 3 57
(Marcus Tregoning) *chsd ldrs: one pce over 1f out* **9/1**

5314 **6** 4 ½ **Darnathean**[24] 5876 2-8-8 72 (b) PaulHanagan 10 43
(Paul D'Arcy) *led after 1f: swtchd lft to rail over 3f out: hdd over 1f out: wknd fnl 100yds* **11/1**

1425 **7** 3 **Mahkama (USA)**[23] 5922 2-9-2 85 AntiocoMurgia(5) 9 46
(Saeed Bin Suroor) *sn trcking ldrs: wnt 2nd over 2f out: wknd over 1f out* **16/1**

16 **8** 2 ¼ **Irrational**[15] 6186 2-8-3 67 JamesSullivan 4 21+
(Bryan Smart) *s.i.s: in rr: hmpd over 1f out: sme late hdwy* **20/1**

1204 **9** ¾ **West Leake Hare (IRE)**[26] 5825 2-8-13 77 RobertWinston 11 29
(Charles Hills) *chsd ldrs on outer: drvn over 2f out: hung rt: lost pl over 1f out* **5/1**[3]

1053 **10** 4 **Lolita Lebron (IRE)**[17] 6132 2-8-1 68 DeclanCannon(3) 7 7
(Lawrence Mullaney) *sn led: hdd after 1f: chsd ldrs: lost pl over 1f out: eased whn bhd clsng stages* **25/1**

034 **11** 2 ½ **Findhornbay**[16] 6152 2-8-0 64 SilvestreDeSousa 6 —
(Mark Johnston) *w wknd over 1f out: eased whn bhd clsng stages* **16/1**

1m 16.23s (-0.67) **Going Correction** -0.10s/f (Good) **11** Ran SP% **116.4**

Speed ratings (Par 97): **100,93,90,88,87 81,77,74,73,67 64**

toteswingers: 1&2 £12.70, 2&3 £55.70, 1&3 £13.20 CSF £64.88 CT £952.62 TOTE £3.60: £1.60, £5.70, £7.00; EX 34.90.

Owner Lady Rothschild **Bred** The Rt Hon Lord Rothschild **Trained** Beckhampton, Wilts

FOCUS

This competitive-looking nursery became a very one-sided event. The winner should have more to offer but the form of those behind is ordinary.

NOTEBOOK

Mince ◆ was still an unknown quantity, despite winning at Newbury on her second start, as she still looked green there, but she has certainly come to herself now. Given a bit to do, she scythed her way through the field on the home bend before leading over a furlong out, and then quickened clear of her rivals in effortless fashion. Her opening mark of 70 was obviously extremely lenient and she can look forward to a substantial rise, but she is likely to carry on improving. (tchd 15-8 and 5-2)

See Clearly, having her 11th start and back down to 6f, had blinkers on for the first time. She didn't see much daylight on the home turn and ran on well when switched, but the winner was in a completely different league. She may prefer easier ground. (tchd 22-1)

Whisky Bravo ◆ may have found the ground too testing at Hamilton last time, but ruined his chance here by breaking very slowly and giving his rivals a significant start. He was still in a detached last at halfway, but to his credit he took off down the wide outside in the straight to snatch third. He has won on Fibresand and could be one for a winter campaign on the sand.

Satanic Beat(IRE) ran on again after getting outpaced at halfway and on this evidence a return to 7f may be in order. (op 9-2)

Royal Trix, making her nursery debut after showing progressive form in three maidens, moved up to hold every chance turning for home but then proved one-paced under pressure. (op 8-1)

Darnathean, back down to probably his best trip, had to do a lot of early running in order to get across to the inside rail in front and had little left when challenged over a furlong from home. (tchd 10-1)

Irrational Official explanation: jockey said filly was denied a clear run

6574 DAVID BROTHERTON STEWARDING H'CAP 1m 4y

3:10 (3:11) (Class 3) (0-95,93) 3-Y-O £6,411 (£1,919; £959; £479; £239; £120) Stalls Low

Form RPR

0111 **1** **Diverting**[19] 6062 3-8-9 81 LeeNewman 3 92
(William Jarvis) *s.i.s: sn drvn along: hdwy after 2f: chsng ldrs whn n.m.r over 1f out: styd on to ld fnl 75yds* **11/4**[1]

2020 **2** nk **Tullius (IRE)**[30] 5730 3-9-3 89 DavidProbert 2 99
(Peter Winkworth) *chsd ldrs: hmpd and edgd rt over 1f out: led 100yds out: sn hdd and no ex* **5/1**[2]

3050 **3** 2 ¼ **Crown Counsel (IRE)**[9] 6339 3-9-7 93 SilvestreDeSousa 5 98
(Mark Johnston) *chsd ldrs: led over 1f out: hdd ins fnl f: kpt on same pce* **11/2**[3]

1300 **4** nk **Barney Rebel (IRE)**[67] 4467 3-9-0 86 RobertWinston 7 90
(Charles Hills) *hld up in rr: effrt over 2f out: chsng ldrs over 1f out: hung bdly lft: one pce* **7/1**

6304 **5** 10 **Muntasib (USA)**[24] 5892 3-8-9 81 (p) TadhgO'Shea 8 62
(Marcus Tregoning) *rr-div: hdwy over 4f out: chsng ldrs whn hmpd over 1f out: wknd fnl 150yds* **8/1**

6000 **6** 2 **Zenella**[18] 6080 3-8-9 81 (b[1]) PaulHanagan 4 58
(Ann Duffield) *led: hdd over 1f out: sn wknd* **10/1**

0562 **7** 30 **Cruiser**[11] 6273 3-9-0 86 (b) MartinDwyer 6 —
(William Muir) *t.k.h: hmpd and lost pl bnd after 2f: effrt on outside over 3f out: wknd over 2f out: sn bhd: eased over 1f out: virtually p.u: t.o* **5/1**[2]

1m 43.97s (-1.93) **Going Correction** -0.10s/f (Good) **7** Ran SP% **108.1**

Speed ratings (Par 105): **105,104,102,102,92 90,60**

toteswingers: 1&2 £3.50, 2&3 £3.30, 1&3 £2.60 CSF £14.57 CT £59.31 TOTE £3.30: £1.60, £2.80; EX 16.80.

Owner A Reed **Bred** Anthony Reed **Trained** Newmarket, Suffolk

FOCUS

A decent 3-y-o handicap, but quite a rough race. The winner recorded another personal best, while the third and fourth to their marks set the standard.

NOTEBOOK

Diverting was up another 6lb in her bid for a four-timer on this quicker surface, but she is a filly in blinding form and showed her toughness here as much as anything else. She didn't have much room to play with on the home bend and again didn't see much daylight coming to the last furlong. She also took a few bumps when things got tight at that stage, but despite that she sustained her effort to come out on top in a driving finish. She will go up again, but she couldn't be written off in her bid for a five-timer. (tchd 5-2)

Tullius(IRE), who did too much too soon at Thirsk last time, was another to become short of room as he tried to get closer coming to the last furlong and took a few bumps, but battled all the way to the line when in the clear. He is 12lb higher than for his last win, but is capable off this sort of mark. (op 11-2 tchd 9-2)

Crown Counsel(IRE), having his 17th start despite only making his debut in February, hit the front over a furlong out but didn't last there long and the front pair had the legs of him inside the last furlong. He remains 8lb higher than when winning at Haydock in June. (tchd 5-1 and 6-1)

Barney Rebel(IRE) didn't find things panning out for him when well beaten over 1m2f at Goodwood last time and should have appreciated the return to this trip, but he was forced to make his effort widest and, though in with every chance a furlong out, started to hang as though finding this ground too quick. (op 9-1)

Muntasib(USA)'s fourth at Sandown last time has worked out well with the winner, third and fifth all winning since. Known to hang, he was tried in cheekpieces and came through to hold every chance over a furlong out, but seemed to have run his race when then running out of room. (op 7-1)

Zenella, winner of a C&D Listed event on her final start at two, was tried in blinkers having run particularly poorly in her last three starts, but despite enjoying the run of the race out in front she was swamped over a furlong from home. (op 9-1 tchd 17-2)

Cruiser, 1-15 coming into this, was put up 2lb for his narrow defeat at Newmarket last month but he seemed to get into all sorts of trouble on the first bend and never figured afterwards. His rider reported that the colt failed to handle the first bend. Official explanation: jockey said colt failed to handle the first bend

6575 PHIL BULL TROPHY CONDITIONS STKS 2m 1f 216y

3:40 (3:40) (Class 3) 3-Y-O+ £6,411 (£1,919; £959; £479; £239) Stalls Low

Form RPR

2405 **1** **Colour Vision (FR)**[23] 5921 3-8-5 98 SilvestreDeSousa 1 87+
(Mark Johnston) *hld up: jnd ldrs over 5f out: led over 3f out: drvn over 1f out and styd on strly: readily* **11/8**[2]

1011 **2** 2 ¾ **Fire Fighter (IRE)**[10] 6306 3-8-5 89 DavidProbert 3 84+
(Sir Mark Prescott Bt) *hld up in rr: hdwy to trck ldrs 5f out: effrt and chsd wnr 2f out: sn rdn: no imp* **8/11**[1]

3020 **3** 22 **Spruzzo**[18] 6095 5-9-3 57 TomEaves 2 60
(Chris Fairhurst) *trckd ldrs: drvn over 3f out: wknd over 1f out* **40/1**

0030 **4** 10 **Dan Buoy (FR)**[9] 6356 8-9-0 63 (b) BillyCray(3) 4 49
(Richard Guest) *drvn to ld: clr tl 9f out: hdd over 3f out: lost pl over 2f out: sn bhd* **25/1**[3]

00-0 **5** dist **The Mighty Mod (USA)**[146] 1973 4-8-12 35 ChrisDCogan(5) 5 —
(Michael Chapman) *hld up towards rr: jnd ldrs 9f out: drvn 6f out: lost pl 4f out: sn t.o: virtually p.u over 1f out: walked to line* **250/1**

3m 59.68s (3.48) **Going Correction** -0.10s/f (Good)

WFA 3 from 4yo+ 12lb **5** Ran SP% **106.7**

Speed ratings (Par 107): **88,86,77,72,—**

CSF £2.50 TOTE £2.70: £1.10, £1.10; EX 2.90.

Owner Sheikh Hamdan Bin Mohammed Al Maktoum **Bred** Capricorn Stud **Trained** Middleham Moor, N Yorks

FOCUS

Five runners, but in truth a match between the 3-y-os and a fascinating tactical battle. Neither of the first two are rated at their best in a muddling contest.

NOTEBOOK

Colour Vision(FR) hadn't been at his best in his last two starts, but his smart form in midsummer meant he had 9lb in hand of his only serious rival and he won this due to a well-judged tactical ride from his jockey, who sent him for home on the outside over 3f from home and ran the finish out of the favourite. (tchd 5-4)

Fire Fighter(IRE), winner of four of his previous five starts, had 9lb to find with Colour Vision but, unlike his rival, came into this on the up. He seemed to be travelling better than the winner on the turn for home, but when the gun was put to his head he started to hang and couldn't make much impression. (op 4-5)

Dan Buoy(FR) has plenty of form around here and went tearing off in front before steadying things as halfway, but he was easily picked off inside the last half-mile and had no chance on these terms against the youngsters. (op 22-1)

6576 FAREWELL IRIS CLAIMING STKS — 1m 4y

4:10 (4:10) (Class 5) 3-Y-O — **£2,264** (£673; £336; £168) **Stalls** Low

Form — RPR

0114 **1** — **Poyle Judy**[25] 5856 3-8-2 73 .... SilvestreDeSousa 2 — 59
(Ralph Beckett) *t.k.h in rr: effrt over 2f out: styd on over 1f out: led fnl 75yds: hld on* **7/4**[1]

005 **2** *½* **Eastward Ho**[109] 3077 3-8-7 34 .... FrederikTylicki 1 — 63
(Jason Ward) *led early: trckd ldrs: effrt over 2f out: upsides on inner 100yds out: kpt on same pce to take 2nd post* **200/1**

1033 **3** *nse* **Auto Mac**[2] 6538 3-8-7 70 .... (b) MartinDwyer 3 — 63
(Neville Bycroft) *sn led: hdd ins fnl f: no ex* **13/2**[3]

5044 **4** *4* **No Poppy (IRE)**[8] 6383 3-8-4 80 .... DuranFentiman 5 — 51
(Tim Easterby) *hld up in rr: jnd ldrs over 4f out: drvn to chse ldr over 2f out: hung lft over 1f out: wknd jst ins fnl f* **7/4**[1]

5105 **5** *5* **Orientalist**[8] 6374 3-8-10 76 .... (b[1]) PaulHanagan 4 — 45
(Eve Johnson Houghton) *trckd ldr: effrt over 2f out: wknd over 1f out* **4/1**[2]

1m 44.25s (-1.65) **Going Correction** -0.10s/f (Good) — **5** Ran SP% **106.6**
Speed ratings (Par 101): **104,103,103,99,94**
CSF £72.03 TOTE £2.60: £1.80, £6.80; EX 68.00.
Owner Cecil And Miss Alison Wiggins **Bred** Cecil And Miss Alison Wiggins **Trained** Kimpton, Hants

FOCUS

A messy claimer and dubious form, due to the proximity of the lowly rated runner-up. The third is the best guide to the form.

6577 DEM WINDOW SOLUTIONS H'CAP — 1m 4f 8y

4:40 (4:42) (Class 5) (0-70,70) 3-Y-O — **£2,264** (£673; £336; £168) **Stalls** Low

Form — RPR

1P04 **1** — **Birdwatcher (IRE)**[5] 6451 3-9-5 **68** .... SilvestreDeSousa 1 — 79+
(Mark Johnston) *chsd ldrs: wnt 2nd over 2f out: led jst ins fnl f: hld on towards fin* **7/2**[1]

4202 **2** *nk* **Body Language (IRE)**[32] 5650 3-9-2 **65** .... (p) DavidNolan 10 — 76
(Ann Duffield) *led: drvn over 2f out: hdd 1f out: no ex clsng stages* **9/1**

2315 **3** *6* **Kodicil (IRE)**[10] 6295 3-9-0 **63** .... GrahamGibbons 6 — 64
(Tim Walford) *chsd ldrs: drvn 5f out: hung lft over 1f out: kpt on one pce* **4/1**[2]

6423 **4** *2* **Bouggatti**[23] 5942 3-9-5 **68** .... LeeNewman 7 — 66
(William Jarvis) *sn chsng ldrs: sn drvn along: outpcd over 3f out: one pce fnl 2f* **4/1**[2]

0025 **5** *5* **Rapturous Applause**[16] 6153 3-8-7 **56** oh3 .... FrederikTylicki 2 — 46
(Micky Hammond) *in rr: outpcd over 2f out: kpt on fnl f: nvr a factor* **12/1**

2630 **6** *14* **Tiny Temper (IRE)**[27] 5804 3-9-6 **69** .... PaulHanagan 8 — 37
(Richard Fahey) *hld up in rr: hdwy 6f out: chsng ldrs over 1f out: sn wknd* **9/1**

5440 **7** *1 ¾* **Bollin Mandy**[28] 5790 3-8-10 **59** .... FrannyNorton 5 — 24
(Tim Easterby) *s.i.s: t.k.h in rr: effrt and n.m.r over 2f out: sn wknd and bhd* **20/1**

1040 **8** *2 ¾* **Lady Gabrielle (IRE)**[36] 5518 3-9-7 **70** .... TomEaves 9 — 31
(David Elsworth) *hld up in rr: hdwy 4f out: lost pl over 2f out: sn bhd* **6/1**[3]

1400 **9** *½* **Szabo's Destiny**[9] 3989 3-9-3 **69** .... (b) DaleSwift[(3)] 3 — 29
(James Given) *trckd ldr: t.k.h: lost pl over 2f out: sn bhd* **12/1**

2m 38.66s (-2.14) **Going Correction** -0.10s/f (Good) — **9** Ran SP% **116.7**
Speed ratings (Par 101): **103,102,98,97,94 84,83,81,81**
toteswingers: 1&2 £6.00, 2&3 £9.20, 1&3 £3.50 CSF £35.93 CT £131.77 TOTE £4.80: £1.80, £2.90, £2.50; EX 22.90.
Owner Sheikh Hamdan Bin Mohammed Al Maktoum **Bred** Jeremy Gompertz **Trained** Middleham Moor, N Yorks

FOCUS

An ordinary handicap and they didn't go much of a pace. The runner-up looks the key to the form.

6578 BUY YOUR 2012 ANNUAL BADGE TODAY MAIDEN STKS — 1m 4y

5:10 (5:10) (Class 5) 3-Y-O — **£2,264** (£673; £336; £168) **Stalls** Low

Form — RPR

0 **1** — **Medal Of Valour (JPN)**[9] 6324 3-9-3 0 .... SilvestreDeSousa 6 — 72+
(Mark Johnston) *trckd ldr: led over 6f out: drvn over 2f out: styd on wl: forged clr fnl 150yds: eased nr fin* **18/1**[3]

2-3 **2** *3 ¼* **Moonscape**[18] 6085 3-9-3 0 .... RichardMullen 2 — 64+
(Sir Michael Stoute) *trckd ldrs: chal over 3f out: drvn over 2f out: kpt on to take 2nd fnl 100yds: no imp* **1/2**[1]

6526 **3** *1 ¼* **Anrheg**[34] 5601 3-8-12 54 .... FrederikTylicki 1 — 56
(David Brown) *trckd ldrs: t.k.h: effrt over 2f out: kpt on same pce to take 3rd fnl 100yds* **20/1**

0000 **4** *1 ¼* **Fists And Stones**[16] 6181 3-9-3 62 .... FrannyNorton 4 — 58?
(Mick Channon) *led tl over 6f out: chal over 3f out: one pce fnl f* **28/1**

35- **5** *½* **Starstuded (IRE)**[317] 7530 3-8-12 0 .... PaulHanagan 3 — 52
(William Haggas) *hld up in rr: hdwy to trck ldrs over 3f out: drvn over 2f out: one pce appr fnl f* **5/2**[2]

46-0 **6** *10* **Benidorm**[179] 1203 3-9-3 63 .... PaddyAspell 5 — 33
(John Wainwright) *hld up in rr: drvn 3f out: outpcd over 2f out: lost pl over 1f out: sn eased* **40/1**

1m 46.04s (0.14) **Going Correction** -0.10s/f (Good) — **6** Ran SP% **111.2**
Speed ratings (Par 101): **95,91,90,89,88 78**
toteswingers: 1&2 £2.70, 2&3 £2.30, 1&3 £5.00 CSF £28.04 TOTE £13.10: £4.30, £1.10; EX 22.80.
Owner Sheikh Hamdan Bin Mohammed Al Maktoum **Bred** Runnymeade Farm, Inc & Peter Callahan **Trained** Middleham Moor, N Yorks

FOCUS

An uncompetitive 3-y-o maiden, run in the slowest time of the three races over the trip at the meeting, and something of a turn-up. The bare form is muddling and limited by the third and fourth to some degree.

T/Plt: £20.30 to a £1 stake. Pool of £49,021.73 - 1,759.52 winning tickets. T/Qpdt: £9.60 to a £1 stake. Pool of £3,255.26 - 248.82 winning tickets. WG

6479 WARWICK (L-H)

Monday, October 3

OFFICIAL GOING: Good to firm (good in places; 7.9)

Wind: Brisk behind Weather: Sunny

6579 BRITISH STALLION STUDS SUPPORTING BRITISH RACING E B F MAIDEN STKS — 6f

2:20 (2:20) (Class 5) 2-Y-O — **£3,622** (£1,078; £538; £269) **Stalls** Low

Form — RPR

0 **1** — **Jinker Noble**[56] 4857 2-9-3 0 .... WilliamBuick 4 — 80
(Clive Cox) *slt ld tl hdd 3f out: styd chalng and slt advantage again jst ins fnl 2f: drvn over 1f out: styd on wl u.p ins fnl f* **8/1**[3]

222 **2** *1* **Glen Moss (IRE)**[17] 6127 2-9-3 83 .... MichaelHills 7 — 77
(Charles Hills) *pressed ldr tl slt advantage 3f out: narrowly hdd ins fnl 2f: one pce ins fnl f* **4/6**[1]

3 *1* **Desert Philosopher** 2-9-3 0 .... PhillipMakin 1 — 74
(Kevin Ryan) *chsd ldrs: wnt 3rd and rdn over 2f out: chal for 2nd appr fnl f: nvr rchd wnr and outpcd into 3rd fnl 150yds* **3/1**[2]

5 **4** *3 ¾* **Yes It's The Boy (USA)**[25] 5861 2-9-3 0 .... (t) J-PGuillambert 5 — 64+
(Ed Walker) *chsd ldrs: pushed along over 2f out: no imp: eased whn hld in clsng stages* **16/1**

06 **5** *5* **Chicarito**[10] 6292 2-9-3 0 .... NeilCallan 8 — 46
(John Gallagher) *chsd ldrs: rdn over 2f out: wknd qckly appr fnl f* **25/1**

00 **6** *¾* **Artful Lady (IRE)**[20] 6030 2-8-12 0 .... TomQueally 3 — 38
(George Margarson) *sn rdn and green: a towards rr* **66/1**

7 *7* **Moataz (USA)** 2-9-3 0 .... JoeFanning 2 — 21
(Mark Johnston) *in tch early: rdn and bhd fr 1/2-way* **12/1**

500 **8** *53* **Brown Eyed Lass**[40] 5375 2-8-7 0 .... JamesRogers[(5)] 6 — —
(Laura Young) *veered bdly rt s and lost all ch: sn t.o* **150/1**

1m 11.46s (-0.34) **Going Correction** -0.05s/f (Good) 2y crse rec — **8** Ran SP% **115.7**
Speed ratings (Par 95): **100,98,97,92,85 84,75,4**
toteswingers:1&2:£1.90, 2&3:£1.30, 1&3:£2.20 CSF £13.97 TOTE £9.30: £2.10, £1.02, £1.40; EX 15.50.
Owner Gwyn Powell and Peter Ridgers **Bred** A S Reid **Trained** Lambourn, Berks

FOCUS

Rail from 1m to 4f moved out 2yds for fresh ground. Runners came centre-to-stands' side for this opening juvenile maiden. The runner-up is the best guide to the level.

NOTEBOOK

Jinker Noble, slowly away and green en-route to finishing last on his Windsor debut, had been given 56 days off and knew his job this time. This was a major improvement and he remains capable of better when the ground is lively. (op 8-1 after early 12-1 in places)

Glen Moss(IRE) again did little wrong on the fastest ground he's tackled to date, so shouldn't be judged harshly despite now having four seconds next to his name. (op 4-5)

Desert Philosopher appeared to know his job, but didn't have the pace to make a winning debut. He may find a weak race up north. (op 5-2)

Yes It's The Boy(USA) improved on his initial effort, being helped by a tongue-tie, and he'll be of interest in low-grade handicaps over further following another outing. (tchd 14-1)

Chicarito Official explanation: jockey said gelding hung right

Moataz(USA), who cost £35,000 at the breeze-ups, quickly got left behind. One would hope he'll improve on this. (op 14-1)

6580 WARWICKRACECOURSE.CO.UK H'CAP — 5f

2:50 (2:51) (Class 6) (0-65,65) 3-Y-O+ — **£1,840** (£543; £271) **Stalls** Low

Form — RPR

3016 **1** — **Straboe (USA)**[32] 5658 5-8-13 **57** .... (v) JamesDoyle 4 — 65
(Stuart Williams) *pressed ldrs: slt ld over 2f out: sn hrd pressed but kpt narrow ld: edgd rt in clsng stages: all out* **16/1**

205 **2** *shd* **Bateleur**[13] 6238 7-8-12 **56** .... TonyCulhane 9 — 64
(Mick Channon) *towards rr: rdn and hdwy fr 2f out: styd on wl thrght fnl f: could nt quite get up* **20/1**

2141 **3** *½* **Griffin Point (IRE)**[16] 6175 4-8-12 **61** .... JamesRogers[(5)] 12 — 67+
(William Muir) *pressed ldrs tl sltly hmpd and lost position bnd over 2f out: rallied and r.o strly thrght fnl f: gng on cl home* **10/1**

0-23 **4** *hd* **Shadow Of The Sun**[23] 5946 3-9-3 **61** .... GeorgeBaker 14 — 66+
(Joseph Tuite) *outpcd and towards rr: gd hdwy on stands' rail over 1f out: r.o wl ins fnl f: gng on cl home* **7/1**[3]

0263 **5** *nk* **Cape Royal**[6] 6436 11-9-7 **65** .... (tp) RichardKingscote 1 — 69
(Milton Bradley) *slt ld tl narrowly hdd over 2f out: styd pressing wnr and stl ev ch fnl 50yds: nt qckn in clsng stages* **12/1**

502 **6** *¾* **The Strig**[13] 6238 4-9-1 **59** .... (v) NeilCallan 8 — 61
(Stuart Williams) *pressed ldrs: edgd rt bnd over 2f out: styd pressing ldrs: stl whn there whn hmpd and snatched up in clsng stages* **9/2**[1]

1314 **7** *shd* **Imaginary Diva**[17] 6119 5-9-1 **64** .... RyanPowell[(5)] 7 — 65
(George Margarson) *chsd ldrs: stl wl there whn bdly hmpd in clsng stages* **9/1**

2305 **8** *½* **Kinigi (IRE)**[38] 5426 5-8-12 **63** .... (b) RaulDaSilva[(7)] 3 — 63
(Ronald Harris) *chsd ldrs: drvn along 3f out: hld and one pce whn hmpd last strides* **12/1**

5360 **9** *¾* **Steel City Boy (IRE)**[4] 6479 8-8-13 **57** .... TomMcLaughlin 2 — 53
(Garry Woodward) *sn drvn to chse ldrs: rdn over 2f out: outpcd over 1f out* **15/2**

6250 **10** *4* **Rio's Girl**[12] 6261 4-8-9 **56** .... (b) AmyRyan[(3)] 10 — 38+
(Kevin Ryan) *pressing ldrs whe bmpd and stmbld bnd over 2f out: no ch after* **6/1**[2]

0550 **11** *2* **Make My Dream**[33] 5616 8-9-4 **62** .... TomQueally 6 — 37
(John Gallagher) *s.i.s: outpcd most of way* **16/1**

110/ **12** *2* **Mister Thatcher (IRE)**[470] 7-8-9 **53** .... (t) CathyGannon 5 — 21
(Mrs Annette McMahon-Reidy, France) *sn outpcd* **16/1**

00-0 **13** *1 ¼* **Sabys Gem (IRE)**[49] 5115 3-8-12 **56** .... DarryllHolland 13 — 19
(Michael Wigham) *sn outpcd* **28/1**

59.45 secs (-0.15) **Going Correction** -0.05s/f (Good) — **13** Ran SP% **117.1**
Speed ratings (Par 101): **99,98,98,97,97 96,95,95,93,87 84,81,79**
toteswingers:1&2:£29.00, 2&3:£34.60, 1&3:£64.90 CSF £296.57 CT £3450.20 TOTE £19.60: £5.60, £3.30, £3.80; EX 272.00.
Owner Brigid & Damian Hennessy-Bourke **Bred** Darley **Trained** Newmarket, Suffolk

FOCUS

Fast and furious stuff in this sprint handicap, with several taking each other on for the lead, and not many got into it. The form is straightforward with the runner-up and the fifth fair guides.

Imaginary Diva Official explanation: jockey said mare was denied a clear run

Make My Dream Official explanation: jockey said gelding was slowly away

6581 WARWICK CHRISTMAS PARTY NIGHTS MAIDEN AUCTION STKS — 7f 26y
3:20 (3:22) (Class 5) 2-Y-O — £2,264 (£673; £336; £168) Stalls Low

Form / RPR

06 **1** **Wordismybond**[17] 6127 2-8-11 0 .... TomQueally 7 — 68+
(Peter Makin) *chsd ldrs: rdn fr 2f out: styd on u.p to ld fnl 150yds: all out* — **4/1**[2]

44 **2** *hd* **Enery (IRE)**[34] 5605 2-8-11 0 .... WilliamBuick 4 — 67
(Mahmood Al Zarooni) *led 1f: styd chsng ldr tl rdn and one pce over 2f out: rallied u.p fnl f: styd on to press wnr cl home: nt quite get up* — **3/1**[1]

00 **3** *nse* **Emman Bee (IRE)**[21] 6000 2-8-6 0 .... FrankieMcDonald 3 — 62
(John Gallagher) *led after 1f: flashed tail bnd fr 3f out: rdn 2f out: hdd fnl 150yds: kpt on: lost 2nd last strides* — **50/1**

400 **4** *3 ¼* **Denton Dancer**[27] 5812 2-8-13 58 .... (p) LukeMorris 8 — 61
(James Eustace) *chsd ldrs: outpcd over 2f out: kpt on again in clsng stages but nvr nr ldrs* — **20/1**

644 **5** *7* **Chrissycross (IRE)**[26] 5834 2-8-1 65 .... KieranO'Neill(3) 5 — 34
(Roger Teal) *in tch: rdn and wknd fr 2f out* — **4/1**[2]

00 **6** *1 ½* **Emirates Jack (IRE)**[26] 5834 2-8-11 0 .... TonyCulhane 6 — 37
(George Baker) *reluctant to enter stalls: in tch tl wknd 2f out* — **8/1**

7 *½* **Run Of The Day** 2-8-4 0 .... CathyGannon 9 — 29
(Eve Johnson Houghton) *outpcd most of way* — **14/1**

0 **8** *¾* **Dangerous To Know**[33] 5613 2-8-4 0 .... ChrisCatlin 1 — 27
(Hughie Morrison) *outpcd most of way* — **9/2**[3]

9 *1* **Grand Liaison** 2-8-6 0 .... AdrianMcCarthy 2 — 26
(John Berry) *slowly away: a in rr* — **20/1**

1m 26.15s (1.55) **Going Correction** -0.05s/f (Good) — **9** Ran SP% **112.4**
Speed ratings (Par 95): **89,88,88,85,77 75,74,73,72**
toteswingers:1&2:£3.20, 2&3:£14.60, 1&3:£18.90 CSF £15.50 TOTE £3.20: £1.50, £1.20, £8.80; EX 15.20.
Owner T W Wellard **Bred** Henry And Mrs Rosemary Moszkowicz **Trained** Ogbourne Maisey, Wilts

FOCUS
A modest juvenile maiden with the winner finding a little bit to get off the mark, while the fourth looks the best guide to the level.

NOTEBOOK
Wordismybond, although proving weak in the market, just did enough despite not looking in love with the fast ground. He'd shown enough at Newbury the time before and could make a fair handicapper next season. (op 11-4)
Enery(IRE) lacks pace, but this was a definite improvement on previous efforts. He's crying out for 1m and can win a small race at the right level. (op 7-2 tchd 11-4)
Emman Bee(IRE) showed much improved form on this third attempt, despite again flashing her tail. She's got a bit of ability and can win at a moderate level. (tchd 40-1)
Denton Dancer fared a bit better with first-time cheekpieces applied, but is clearly limited. (op 28-1)
Chrissycross(IRE) was below par on this step up to 7f, although it's doubtful whether she was beaten purely by the distance. Her trainer remains winless since May. Official explanation: jockey said filly never travelled (op 3-1)
Emirates Jack(IRE) Official explanation: jockey said gelding hung right throughout

6582 WARWICK CLAIMING STKS — 1m 4f 134y
3:50 (3:50) (Class 6) 3-4-Y-O — £1,840 (£543; £271) Stalls Low

Form / RPR

0035 **1** **Comedy Act**[15] 6191 4-9-6 77 .... (p) JoeFanning 4 — 72
(Mark Johnston) *mde all: hrd pressed bnd ins fnl 3f: styd on to go clr ins fnl f* — **5/6**[1]

0100 **2** *3* **Lauberhorn**[11] 6279 4-9-1 61 ow1 .... (b) NeilCallan 1 — 62
(Eve Johnson Houghton) *t.k.h: sn chsng wnr: rdn and effrt bnd ins fnl 3f: hung lft appr fnl f and sn btn* — **8/1**

3302 **3** *¾* **Reillys Daughter**[4] 6482 3-7-12 62 .... (p) CathyGannon 5 — 52
(J S Moore) *reminders after s: sn t.k.h in rr but wl in tch: hdwy 4f out: chsd ldrs over 2f out: styd on same pce* — **7/2**[2]

-402 **4** *9* **Triple Eight (IRE)**[15] 6188 3-9-1 88 .... PaulPickard(3) 2 — 58
(Philip Kirby) *chsd ldrs: rdn 3f out: wknd and hung lft fr 2f out* — **9/2**[3]

650- **5** *22* **Highland Cadett**[319] 4991 4-8-4 46 .... RachealKneller(7) 3 — —
(Pam Ford) *a in last: lost tch fnl 4f* — **100/1**

2m 45.43s (0.83) **Going Correction** -0.05s/f (Good)
WFA 3 from 4yo 8lb — **5** Ran SP% **107.1**
Speed ratings (Par 101): **95,93,92,87,73**
CSF £7.66 TOTE £1.70: £1.40, £2.60; EX 5.10.
Owner Middleham Park racing XXII **Bred** Floors Farming & The Duke Of Devonshire **Trained** Middleham Moor, N Yorks

FOCUS
This claimer was never going to take much winning and the form looks worth treating negatively.

6583 WARWICK FOR WEDDINGS H'CAP — 1m 22y
4:20 (4:20) (Class 5) (0-75,74) 3-Y-O+ — £2,385 (£704; £352) Stalls Low

Form / RPR

0 **1** **Dr Wintringham (IRE)**[26] 5836 5-9-3 70 .... TomMcLaughlin 10 — 81
(Karen George) *s.i.s: sn pushed along in rr: hdwy over 3f out: str run on stands' rail appr fnl f: led fnl 120yds: readily* — **14/1**

2065 **2** *1 ¾* **Tewin Wood**[18] 6079 4-9-7 74 .... LiamJones 7 — 81
(Alan Bailey) *trckd ldr: chal over 4f out tl led over 3f out: sn drvn: kpt slt advantage tl hdd and no ex fnl 120yds* — **9/1**

6404 **3** *2* **Muftarres (IRE)**[14] 6228 6-9-0 67 .... (p) RussKennemore 11 — 69
(Paul Midgley) *chsd ldrs: drvn to chal over 1f out: wknd into 3rd fnl 75yds* — **10/1**

0203 **4** *2* **Full Bloom**[25] 5856 3-9-1 71 .... (p) CathyGannon 8 — 69
(Gerard Butler) *in rr: hrd rdn over 2f out: styd on u.p fnl f: nt rch ldrs* — **15/2**[3]

0400 **5** *2* **Follow The Flag (IRE)**[10] 6302 7-9-1 68 .... (p) JamesDoyle 1 — 61
(Alan McCabe) *in rr: rdn and plenty to do over 2f out: styd on fnl f: nt rch ldrs* — **12/1**

0556 **6** *¾* **Alhaban (IRE)**[22] 5970 5-9-5 72 .... LukeMorris 3 — 63
(Ronald Harris) *in rr: drvn and styd on u.p fnl 2f: nvr a threat* — **16/1**

0603 **7** *½* **Heezararity**[16] 6167 3-8-9 68 .... LouisBeuzelin(3) 5 — 58
(Stuart Kittow) *in tch early: rdn in mid-div over 2f out and styd on one pce* — **6/1**[2]

2200 **8** *hd* **Bold Cross (IRE)**[7] 6402 8-8-10 66 .... KieranO'Neill(3) 12 — 56
(Edward Bevan) *in rr: rdn and sme hdwy fr 2f out: nvr in contention* — **20/1**

2221 **9** *1* **Dare To Bare (IRE)**[18] 6089 3-9-4 74 .... (v) DarryllHolland 13 — 62
(Amanda Perrett) *racd wd and led: jnd 4f out: hdd over 3f out: hung rt u.p over 1f out: sn wknd* — **9/2**[1]

210- **10** *¾* **Effervesce (IRE)**[373] 6361 4-9-6 73 .... NeilCallan 9 — 59
(David Pipe) *s.i.s: in rr: sme hdwy u.p fr 3f out: nvr rchd ldrs* — **10/1**

2500 **11** *16* **Sir Mozart (IRE)**[19] 6069 8-9-3 70 .... TomQueally 2 — 19
(Barney Curley) *s.i.s: sn chsng ldrs: wknd over 2f out* — **25/1**

2461 **12** *2 ½* **Midas Moment**[16] 6181 3-9-4 74 .... GeorgeBaker 6 — 17
(William Muir) *chsd ldrs tl wknd qckly and eased over 1f out: dismntd after line* — **15/2**[3]

0500 **13** *¾* **Not My Choice (IRE)**[18] 6093 6-9-7 74 .... MichaelStainton 4 — 16
(David C Griffiths) *t.k.h: chsd ldrs: rdn 3f out: sn btn* — **50/1**

1m 39.93s (-1.07) **Going Correction** -0.05s/f (Good)
WFA 3 from 4yo+ 3lb — **13** Ran SP% **115.0**
Speed ratings (Par 103): **103,101,99,97,95 94,94,93,92,92 76,73,72**
toteswingers:1&2:£25.00, 2&3:£13.80, 1&3:£20.60 CSF £126.82 CT £1321.22 TOTE £15.20: £5.20, £3.20, £3.90; EX 139.50.
Owner Eastington Racing Syndicate 1 **Bred** Peter Molony **Trained** Higher Eastington, Devon

FOCUS
An open class 5 handicap in which the pace was sound and the form has been rated at face value.
Dare To Bare(IRE) Official explanation: vet said gelding lost right-fore shoe
Midas Moment Official explanation: jockey said filly lost its action

6584 JUMP SEASON IS NEXT H'CAP — 1m 6f 213y
4:50 (4:51) (Class 5) (0-75,73) 3-Y-O — £2,385 (£704; £352) Stalls Low

Form / RPR

2546 **1** **Light Blow (USA)**[19] 6046 3-9-6 72 .... TomQueally 6 — 81
(Sir Henry Cecil) *hld up in rr: hdwy 1/2-way: chsd ldr 6f out: hmpd and swtchd lft whn trying for stands' rail over 2f out: sn str chal: slt ld fnl 120yds: drvn out* — **9/2**

0216 **2** *nk* **Native Colony**[34] 5599 3-9-5 71 .... NeilCallan 3 — 80
(Roger Varian) *led: rdn and wnt rt to stands' rail over 2f out: sn hrd pressed: kpt slt advantage tl hdd and no ex fnl 120yds* — **10/3**[2]

2524 **3** *5* **Handles For Forks (IRE)**[18] 6095 3-9-4 70 .... TonyCulhane 2 — 72
(Mick Channon) *chsd ldrs: rdn 3f out: styd on same pce for 3rd ins fnl f* — **4/1**[3]

5333 **4** *1* **Bow River Arch (USA)**[82] 3978 3-9-7 73 .... (p) WilliamBuick 5 — 74
(Jeremy Noseda) *hld up in rr: rdn over 2f out and little rspnse: kpt on past btn horses ins fnl f* — **9/4**[1]

44 **5** *nk* **C P Joe (IRE)**[67] 4476 3-8-8 60 .... ChrisCatlin 1 — 60
(Paul Green) *in rr: rdn 3f out: sme prog and in tch u.p 2f out: wknd over 1f out* — **10/1**

0010 **6** *1* **Strewth (IRE)**[72] 4316 3-9-2 68 .... LukeMorris 7 — 67
(John Best) *chsd ldr to 7f out: styd front rnk: hrd drvn 2f out: wknd over 1f out* — **9/1**

3m 28.28s (9.28) **Going Correction** -0.05s/f (Good) — **6** Ran SP% **111.1**
Speed ratings (Par 101): **73,72,70,69,69 68**
toteswingers:1&2:£2.60, 2&3:£2.70, 1&3:£3.60 CSF £19.28 TOTE £5.70: £2.40, £2.10; EX 20.80.
Owner Niarchos Family **Bred** Flaxman Holdings Limited **Trained** Newmarket, Suffolk

FOCUS
The pace was a steady one for this staying handicap. The front pair drew clear and could be worth a bit more than they are rated here.

6585 WARWICK APPRENTICE H'CAP — 1m 4f 134y
5:20 (5:20) (Class 6) (0-60,60) 3-Y-O — £1,704 (£503; £251) Stalls Low

Form / RPR

3332 **1** **Hygrove Welshlady (IRE)**[4] 6493 3-9-2 60 .... BrendanPowell(5) 5 — 73
(J W Hills) *trckd ldrs and a gng wl: led 2f out: c clr ins fnl f: easily* — **11/10**[1]

0050 **2** *7* **Laffraaj (IRE)**[24] 5898 3-8-0 46 oh1 .... DavidWarren(7) 10 — 48
(Pat Eddery) *trckd ldr: led 1m out: narrowly hdd 4f out: one pce 2f out: kpt on again to chse wnr fnl f: nvr any ch* — **16/1**

6320 **3** *2 ¾* **Easydoesit (IRE)**[42] 5321 3-8-7 46 oh1 .... (p) NoraLooby 3 — 44
(Tony Carroll) *chsd ldrs: drvn to chse wnr ins fnl 2f but no imp: wknd into 3rd ins fnl f* — **13/2**[2]

0003 **4** *½* **Lechlade Lass**[18] 6084 3-8-9 53 .... DannyBrock(5) 8 — 50
(Adrian Chamberlain) *in tch: rdn 4f out: chsd ldrs 3f out: lost position 2f out: mod prog again in clsng stages* — **14/1**

0053 **5** *1 ¾* **Black Iceman**[24] 5898 3-8-11 50 .... SophieSilvester 9 — 44
(Lydia Pearce) *in rr: sme hdwy over 1f out: styd on same pce in clsng stages* — **15/2**

6040 **6** *3 ¼* **Noble Defender**[23] 5916 3-9-3 56 .... JakePayne 6 — 45
(Stuart Kittow) *towards rr most of way* — **9/1**

0660 **7** *½* **Royal Reason**[13] 6240 3-9-0 53 .... KatiaScallan 4 — 41
(Joseph Tuite) *sn led: hdd 1m out: led again 4f out: hdd & wknd 2f out* — **7/1**[3]

006 **8** *5* **Adaero Star**[31] 5675 3-8-0 46 oh1 .... JulieCumine(7) 1 — 27
(Karen George) *in rr: no ch whn hung lft fr 2f out* — **33/1**

2m 47.48s (2.88) **Going Correction** -0.05s/f (Good) — **8** Ran SP% **110.7**
Speed ratings (Par 99): **89,84,83,82,81 79,79,76**
toteswingers:1&2:£6.30, 2&3:£12.30, 1&3:£2.80 CSF £19.71 CT £76.13 TOTE £2.00: £1.40, £3.30, £1.60; EX 21.10.
Owner D H Francis **Bred** Marston & Dean Fleming Thoroughbreds **Trained** Upper Lambourn, Berks
■ Stewards' Enquiry : Danny Brock one-day ban: used whip down shoulder in the forehand (Oct 17)

FOCUS
An uncompetitive apprentice handicap and the form is weak, with the winner the only solid one.
T/Plt: £173.50 to a £1 stake. Pool of £41,717.87 - 175.52 winning tickets. T/Qpdt: £59.70 to a £1 stake. Pool of £3,889.52 - 48.20 winning tickets. ST

5491 WINDSOR (R-H)
Monday, October 3

OFFICIAL GOING: Good to firm
Wind: Fresh, half behind Weather: Sunny, warm

6586 CHEVRON MALTA HOLIDAYS H'CAP (DIV I) — 1m 67y
2:30 (2:30) (Class 5) (0-70,70) 3-Y-O+ — £1,940 (£577; £288; £144) Stalls Low

Form / RPR

4110 **1** **Catchanova (IRE)**[26] 5835 4-9-5 68 .... SebSanders 5 — 76
(Eve Johnson Houghton) *chsd ldrs in 5th: rdn and prog over 2f out to go 2nd over 1f out: drvn ahd ins fnl f: jst hld on* — **8/1**

1656 **2** *hd* **Sasheen**[28] 5782 4-9-3 66 .... FergusSweeney 11 — 74
(Jeremy Gask) *led: drvn 2f out: hdd ins fnl f: rallied wl: jst failed* — **16/1**

044 **3** *1 ¾* **Rosedale**[21] 5992 4-9-3 66 .... JimmyFortune 12 — 70+
(James Toller) *t.k.h early: hld up in last quartet: plenty to do 1/2-way: rdn and gd prog over 2f out: styd on to take 3rd ins fnl f: unable to chal* — **5/1**[1]

3554 **4** *1 ½* **Crystal Etoile**[34] 5598 3-9-4 70 .... RyanMoore 9 — 71
(Sir Michael Stoute) *chsd ldr after 2f to over 1f out: one pce u.p* — **13/2**[3]

5445 **5** *1* **Recalcitrant**[39] 5406 8-8-9 61 .... AdamBeschizza(3) 7 — 59
(Simon Dow) *chsd ldr 2f: prom after: rdn 3f out: nt qckn 2f out: one pce* — **14/1**

264 **6** *nk* **Green Earth (IRE)**^{25} 5858 4-8-11 **65**...................... JemmaMarshall(5) 3 63
(Pat Phelan) *wl in tch in 7th: rdn over 2f out: one pce and no prog* **16/1**

3332 **7** *1* **Could It Be Magic**^{31} 5675 4-8-10 **66**............................(b) JakePayne(7) 6 61
(Bill Turner) *chsd ldng trio: rdn over 2f out: sn lost pl and btn: one pce after* **20/1**

1400 **8** *3* **Uncle Dermot (IRE)**^{16} 6167 3-9-1 **67**.............................. JimCrowley 2 55
(Brendan Powell) *s.i.s: in tch in 9th: shkn up against nr side rail 2f out: no prog over 1f out* **12/1**

0462 **9** *½* **Skyfire**^{26} 5828 4-9-7 **70**.. PatCosgrave 14 57
(Ed de Giles) *chsd ldrs in 6th: rdn over 2f out and no prog: wknd over 1f out* **13/2**^{3}

4420 **10** *2 ¼* **Custom House (IRE)**^{47} 5171 3-9-0 **66**........................... DaneO'Neill 13 48
(John E Long) *in tch in 8th: rdn over 2f out: sn struggling and btn* **20/1**

0361 **11** *15* **Desert Chieftain**^{20} 6033 3-8-10 **62**..................................(b) KierenFallon 8 10
(Luca Cumani) *dwlt: settled in 10th: rdn wl over 2f out and no prog: wknd over 1f out: eased: t.o* **11/2**^{2}

4103 **12** *1 ½* **Ocean Countess (IRE)**^{38} 5422 5-8-8 **57**....................(v) JimmyQuinn 1 —
(Tony Carroll) *s.v.s: nvr able to rcvr: t.o* **25/1**

040 **13** *½* **Rafella (IRE)**^{34} 5581 3-8-8 **65**...................................... DavidKenny(5) 10 8
(Michael Scudamore) *s.s: a in last quartet: wknd over 2f out: t.o* **66/1**

4000 **14** *83* **My Vindication (USA)**^{33} 5630 3-9-0 **66**..................... RichardHughes 4 —
(Richard Hannon) *sn dropped in rr: lost tch 3f out: t.o and virtually p.u over 1f out* **9/1**

1m 41.49s (-3.21) **Going Correction** -0.325s/f (Firm)
WFA 3 from 4yo+ 3lb **14** Ran SP% **120.8**
Speed ratings (Par 103): **103,102,101,99,98 98,97,94,93,91 76,75,74,—**
toteswingers:1&2:£12.60, 2&3:£12.60, 1&3:£9.00 CSF £123.75 CT £733.08 TOTE £10.30: £3.00, £5.50, £1.80; EX 167.50 TRIFECTA Not won..
Owner Andrew Wyer Darrell Blake Hugh Arthur **Bred** G J King **Trained** Blewbury, Oxon

FOCUS
Stands' rail dolled out 4yds at 6f and 1y at Winning Post. Top bend at normal configuration. A moderate handicap that looked wide open. It was run at a fair gallop, but few landed a blow from off the pace. The runner-up sets the level having run a narrow personal best.
Ocean Countess(IRE) Official explanation: jockey said mare missed the break

6587 CHEVRON MALTA HOLIDAYS H'CAP (DIV II) 1m 67y
3:00 (3:00) (Class 5) (0-70,69) 3-Y-0+ **£1,940** (£577; £288; £144) **Stalls** Low

Form RPR

20-5 **1** **L'Astre De Choisir (IRE)**^{9} 6354 3-9-4 **69**......................... JimCrowley 2 78+
(Walter Swinburn) *chsd ldng trio: rdn over 2f out: clsd to take narrow ld over 1f out: drvn ins fnl f: hld on* **13/2**^{3}

2440 **2** *nk* **Tap Dance Way (IRE)**^{40} 5376 4-9-5 **67**............................. LiamKeniry 5 75
(Patrick Chamings) *chsd ldr: clsd to chal 2f out: upsides over 1f out: pressed wnr after: nt qckn last 75yds* **9/1**

0455 **3** *hd* **Young Dottie**^{49} 5113 5-8-11 **64**.............................. JemmaMarshall(5) 13 72
(Pat Phelan) *taken down early: hld up in 8th: prog on outer 3f out: rdn over 2f out: chal and upsides over 1f out: nt qckn ins fnl f* **7/1**

0635 **4** *4* **Eastern Gift**^{9} 6355 6-9-0 **62**... ShaneKelly 1 60
(Gay Kelleway) *chsd ldrs in 5th: shkn up and nt qckn 2f out: no imp on ldrs after* **6/1**^{2}

4002 **5** *shd* **Aviso (GER)**^{14} 6228 7-8-13 **61**.......................................(p) KierenFallon 6 59
(David Evans) *led at decent pce and racd freely: drvn over 2f out: hdd over 1f out: fdd* **5/1**^{1}

1300 **6** *1* **Come On Safari (IRE)**^{52} 5002 4-9-2 **67**.................... MartinHarley(3) 10 63
(Joseph Tuite) *hld up in last pair: gng wl enough over 3f out: rdn and no prog over 2f out: n.d after* **7/1**

03 **7** *1* **Polar Auroras**^{72} 4321 3-8-8 **59**... MartinLane 4 53
(Tony Carroll) *chsd ldng pair: rdn 3f out: lost pl and btn 2f out* **16/1**

0110 **8** *3* **Dannios**^{32} 5653 5-9-0 **69**.......................................(t) MichaelJMurphy(7) 8 56
(Ed Walker) *settled in last: pushed along and detached 1/2-way: no ch after: plugged on* **10/1**

1665 **9** *nk* **Fault**^{43} 5300 5-9-3 **65**...(t) DaneO'Neill 9 51
(Tony Newcombe) *hld up in 7th: shkn up and no prog 2f out: no ch after* **8/1**

3150 **10** *2* **Lucky Meadows (IRE)**^{16} 6167 3-9-4 **69**.................. RichardHughes 14 50
(Richard Hannon) *hld up in 6th: jst pushed along fr over 2f out and steadily lost pl* **12/1**

1m 40.81s (-3.89) **Going Correction** -0.325s/f (Firm)
WFA 3 from 4yo+ 3lb **10** Ran SP% **113.1**
Speed ratings (Par 103): **106,105,105,101,101 100,99,96,96,94**
toteswingers:1&2:£13.60, 2&3:£11.00, 1&3:£5.90 CSF £61.58 CT £429.63 TOTE £8.30: £2.50, £2.90, £2.00; EX 59.40 TRIFECTA Not won..
Owner The Selectors **Bred** Lynn Lodge Stud **Trained** Aldbury, Herts

FOCUS
The second division of the extended 1m handicap and another open heat. There was a solid pace on and a very tight three-way finish. The form is probably weaker than the other leg, but the winner could be capable of better.

6588 BRITISH STALLION STUDS SUPPORTING BRITISH RACING E B F MAIDEN STKS 1m 67y
3:30 (3:30) (Class 5) 2-Y-0 **£3,299** (£981; £490; £245) **Stalls** Low

Form RPR

04 **1** **Eurystheus (IRE)**^{30} 5697 2-9-3 0................................. RichardHughes 3 76
(Richard Hannon) *trckd ldng trio: pushed along over 3f out: looked hld u.p over 1f out: rallied fnl f to ld last 50yds* **3/1**^{2}

3 **2** *½* **Yaa Salam**^{18} 6100 2-9-3 0... FrankieDettori 11 75
(Mahmood Al Zarooni) *led: hanging lft bnd over 5f out: pressed over 2f out: hd quite high but battled on: hdd and outpcd last 50yds* **5/2**^{1}

0 **3** *nk* **Bank Bonus**^{38} 5447 2-9-3 0... JimmyFortune 4 76+
(Andrew Balding) *trckd ldng trio: pushed along over 3f out: nt qckn 2f out: styd on wl ins fnl f: gaining at fin despite little room* **11/2**^{3}

3 **4** *hd* **Prince Alzain (USA)**^{14} 6216 2-9-3 0.............................. SebSanders 10 74
(Gerard Butler) *trckd ldr: chal and upsides over 2f out: nt qckn and hld ins fnl f: lost 2nd pls after* **6/1**

6 **5** *5* **Counsel (IRE)**^{27} 5801 2-9-3 0.. RyanMoore 2 65+
(Sir Michael Stoute) *hld up in midfield: in tch over 3f out: outpcd 2f out: hld together after and fdd* **7/1**

6 **6** *2* **Downton Abbey (IRE)**^{14} 6215 2-8-12 0.............................. DaneO'Neill 1 53
(Richard Hannon) *in tch to 3f out: shkn up and wknd* **33/1**

0 **7** *3 ¾* **Silver Samba**^{38} 5444 2-8-12 0... LiamKeniry 7 44
(Andrew Balding) *n.m.r s: hld up in last pair: lost tch by 1/2-way: no ch after: modest late prog* **33/1**

00 **8** *2 ¼* **Norfolk Sky**^{35} 5564 2-8-12 0... TedDurcan 5 39
(Chris Wall) *hld up in rr: lost tch w ldng gp in 7th over 3f out: no ch after* **100/1**

0 **9** *3 ½* **Echo Of Dream**^{24} 5899 2-9-3 0.. AhmedAjtebi 8 36
(Mahmood Al Zarooni) *in tch to 1/2-way: wl bhd after* **33/1**

00 **10** *4* **My Scat Daddy (USA)**^{79} 4087 2-8-10 0................ AccursioRomeo(7) 9 27
(Brett Johnson) *awkward s and hld up last: lost tch bef 1/2-way: no ch after* **100/1**

64 **R** **Kiwayu**^{25} 5861 2-9-3 0.. KierenFallon 6 —
(Luca Cumani) *in tch tl hung lft and rn out off the crse bnd over 5f out* **14/1**

1m 43.05s (-1.65) **Going Correction** -0.325s/f (Firm) 2y crse rec **11** Ran SP% **113.2**
Speed ratings (Par 95): **95,94,94,94,89 87,83,81,77,73 —**
toteswingers:1&2:£1.50, 2&3:£3.60, 1&3:£4.30 CSF £10.10 TOTE £4.80: £1.50, £1.10, £2.20; EX 10.10 Trifecta £36.50 Pool: £651.59 - 13.20 winning units..
Owner AFerguson, GMason, SHassiakos, PNicholls **Bred** Calley House Uk **Trained** East Everleigh, Wilts

FOCUS
This looked a fairly interesting maiden. It was run at a fair enough pace and, despite the first four finishing in a heap, the race should throw up future winners. The winner, second and fourth help set the level.

NOTEBOOK
Eurystheus(IRE), who was a morning gamble, made it third time lucky thanks to a fine ride by Richard Hughes. He took time to settle and things didn't look great for him as he began to feel the pinch around 3f out, but Hughes got stuck into him and he hit top gear just as the leaders were coming to a halt. He ultimately won a little cosily and, despite having plenty of speed in his pedigree, clearly stays very well. His future lies with the handicapper, though. (op 9-4 tchd 2-1 and 10-3 in a place)
Yaa Salam ◆ confirmed the promise of his debut third at Yarmouth 18 days earlier and nearly made all, but such tactics over this slightly stiffer test just found him out. He shouldn't be long in going one better. (op 3-1)
Bank Bonus ◆ was doing his best work late over 7f on soft ground at Newmarket first time out last month. He didn't seem to be helping Jimmy Fortune much from 2f out, who looked to pretty much accept the situation when the winner went past, but despite the rider easing off he still stayed on to grab third at the line. Indeed, he was in front not long after the line and one has to think he would have gone closer under more vigorous handling. (op 6-1 tchd 7-1 and 5-1)
Prince Alzain(USA) advertised his stamina when a close-up third over 1m on his debut at Kempton a fortnight earlier and attracted support on this switch to turf. He put it up to the second in the home straight and ran a bold race, but was done with half a furlong out. He deserves to find a race. (op 8-1)
Counsel(IRE) again wasn't best away and ran green. He briefly threatened to play a part, but flattened out before the final furlong and looks to need more time. (op 15-2 tchd 8-1)
Downton Abbey(IRE), the Hannon second-string, again shaped with ability on this turf debut and needs one more run for a mark.

6589 ROYAL WINDSOR RACING CLUB CLAIMING STKS 1m 2f 7y
4:00 (4:00) (Class 6) 3-4-Y-0 **£1,617** (£481; £240; £120) **Stalls** Centre

Form RPR

5535 **1** **Frontline Phantom (IRE)**^{8} 6379 4-9-1 68...............(p) MartinHarley(3) 5 68
(Mrs K Burke) *pressed ldr: led over 2f out: sn rdn: kpt on fr over 1f out: jst hld on* **4/1**^{2}

0211 **2** *shd* **Avon River**^{5} 6465 4-9-4 78.. RichardHughes 9 68
(Richard Hannon) *hld up bhd ldrs: wnt 4th over 3f out but pushed along: drvn into 2nd over 1f out: clsd ins fnl f: jst failed* **2/5**^{1}

00 **3** *2 ½* **Royal Alcor (IRE)**^{18} 6086 4-8-10 0.........................(b^{1}) FergusSweeney 3 55?
(Alastair Lidderdale) *slowly away: hld up in last: prog on outer fr 3f out: rdn and styd on to take 3rd ins fnl f* **50/1**

0000 **4** *1* **Beggers Belief**^{17} 6122 3-8-6 43...............................(b^{1}) EddieCreighton 4 54
(Eric Wheeler) *trckd ldng pair: rdn wl over 2f out: cl enough over 1f out: no ex* **50/1**

5000 **5** *1 ¼* **Malanos (IRE)**^{21} 5992 3-9-2 67...................................(b^{1}) NickyMackay 1 62
(David Elsworth) *led: rdn and hdd over 2f out: lost 2nd and wknd over 1f out* **13/2**^{3}

4000 **6** *2 ¾* **Rainsborough**^{35} 4666 4-8-12 45... JimCrowley 7 47?
(Peter Hedger) *hld up in 8th: effrt over 3f out: rdn and no imp on ldrs 2f out: fdd* **40/1**

0500 **7** *12* **Rather Cool**^{33} 5630 3-7-13 52.....................................(t) RosieJessop(5) 2 20
(John Bridger) *chsd ldng pair tl wknd qckly over 3f out* **14/1**

8 *5* **Cant Sell (IRE)** 3-9-2 0.. AndreaAtzeni 6 22
(David Evans) *in tch tl dropped in rr and struggling 4f out: sn bhd* **20/1**

040 **9** *nse* **Conesuala**^{21} 5999 4-8-11 47... MatthewDavies 8 —
(Alan Jarvis) *in tch tl wknd 4f out: sn bhd* **28/1**

2m 6.37s (-2.33) **Going Correction** -0.325s/f (Firm)
WFA 3 from 4yo 5lb **9** Ran SP% **126.0**
Speed ratings (Par 101): **96,95,93,93,92 89,80,76,76**
toteswingers:1&2:£1.30, 2&3:£12.20, 1&3:£24.10 CSF £6.37 TOTE £3.90: £1.40, £1.02, £12.60; EX 9.90 Trifecta £583.90 Pool: £978.46 - 1.24 winning units..
Owner Frontline Bathrooms **Bred** Joe Rogers **Trained** Middleham Moor, North Yorks

FOCUS
The two market leaders dominated this claimer inside the final furlong but the form looks shaky with the first two some way off their best.

6590 CSP NURSERY 5f 10y
4:30 (4:30) (Class 4) (0-85,82) 2-Y-0 **£3,428** (£1,020; £509; £254) **Stalls** Low

Form RPR

0421 **1** **Ballesteros**^{10} 6292 2-9-7 **82**... RyanMoore 11 87
(Brian Meehan) *hld up off the pce in last quartet: prog on outer 2f out: chsd ldr fnl f: r.o to ld last strides* **3/1**^{1}

2052 **2** *shd* **Blanc De Chine (IRE)**^{47} 5174 2-8-7 **68**..................... FergusSweeney 1 73
(Peter Makin) *led against nr side rail: rdn 2f out: kpt on wl but hdd last strides* **12/1**

6124 **3** *2* **Sonko (IRE)**^{23} 5922 2-8-8 **69**.. MartinLane 9 67
(Tim Pitt) *pushed along in 6th early: prog to chse ldr 1/2-way: hld by ldr 1f out: sn lost 2nd: kpt on* **18/1**

1 **4** *2* **Relentless Harry (IRE)**^{30} 5737 2-9-1 **76**.................(t) FrankieDettori 10 67
(George Baker) *hld up off the pce in last quartet: tried to make prog fr 2f out: styd on to take 4th ins fnl f* **3/1**^{1}

105 **5** *1 ¾* **Charlotte Rosina**^{45} 5237 2-9-4 **79**..................................^{1} SebSanders 7 63
(Roger Teal) *prom: rdn over 2f out: fdd over 1f out* **28/1**

2021 **6** *¾* **Rougini (IRE)**^{32} 5646 2-8-5 **69** ow3...........................(v) MartinHarley(3) 4 51
(Mrs K Burke) *chsd ldrs against rail: rdn 1/2-way: wknd over 1f out* **16/1**

6022 **7** *3* **Sister Guru**^{13} 6237 2-8-7 **68**.. LiamKeniry 6 39
(Peter Hedger) *t.k.h: mostly chsd ldr to 1/2-way: sn lost pl and btn* **9/1**^{3}

035 **8** *¾* **Princess Alessia**^{65} 4548 2-8-5 **66**.............................. KirstyMilczarek 5 34
(Terry Clement) *prom to 1/2-way: sn lost pl and btn* **33/1**

1140 **9** *4 ½* **Amis Reunis**^{25} 5847 2-9-0 **75**.. RichardHughes 2 27
(Richard Hannon) *hld up off the pce in last quartet: pushed along and no prog 1/2-way* **7/2**^{2}

0101 **10** *8* **Aquasulis (IRE)**[11] 6284 2-8-12 **73**.................................. KierenFallon 8 —
(David Evans) *anticpated s and missed break: outpcd in last and a bhd* **12/1**

58.71 secs (-1.59) **Going Correction** -0.325s/f (Firm) 2y crse rec **10** Ran SP% **115.1**
Speed ratings (Par 97): **99,98,95,92,89 88,83,82,75,62**
toteswingers:1&2:£7.60, 2&3:£17.10, 1&3:£11.40 CSF £39.86 CT £563.56 TOTE £4.10: £1.80, £3.70, £5.20; EX 44.30 Trifecta £539.80 Part won. Pool of £729.56 - 0.62 winning units..
Owner Mrs P Good **Bred** Exors Of The Late J R Good **Trained** Manton, Wilts

FOCUS
A modest nursery, run at a strong pace and the winning time was fractionally outside the juvenile course record set by Charles The Great earlier in the year. The form looks straightforward rated around the placed horses.

NOTEBOOK
Ballesteros just did enough to follow up his deserved maiden win at Haydock ten days earlier on this switch into nursery company, handing Ryan Moore a first winner back from his injury. This drop back to the minimum on much quicker ground looked to be finding him out entering the home straight, but to his credit he kept finding for pressure down the centre and just reeled in the runner-up. Returning to a stiffer test should only suit this likeable sort and therefore he shouldn't be taken lightly when bidding for the hat-trick. (op 4-1, tchd 9-2 in a place)
Blanc De Chine(IRE) ◆ was 4lb lower and so nearly made all to open her account. She's now found one too strong in three of her five career outings, but fully deserves to go one better now. (op 10-1 tchd 9-1)
Sonko(IRE), back down in trip with the cheekpieces abandoned, looks exposed, so he rates a fair benchmark for the form. (op 12-1)
Relentless Harry(IRE) ◆ won readily on his debut over this trip at Wolverhampton last month and had Frankie Dettori, who was previously 5-8 for the yard, on for this switch to turf. He found things happening all too quickly for him and also looked to find the ground quick enough. It wouldn't be surprising to see him go in again over a stiffer test, considering the experience should be of benefit. (op 11-4)
Amis Reunis was well backed but was another taken off her feet early on and ran no sort of race. Official explanation: jockey said filly stumbled leaving stalls (op 5-1)
Aquasulis(IRE) Official explanation: jockey said filly hit its head on gate

6591 JOE WARD HILL MEMORIAL MAIDEN STKS 6f
5:00 (5:01) (Class 5) 3-Y-O+ **£2,264** (£673; £336; £168) **Stalls** Low

Form RPR
55 **1** **Triple Charm**[24] 5900 3-8-12 0.. JimmyFortune 6 76+
(Jeremy Noseda) *hld up in tch: prog 1/2-way: chsd ldr 2f out: drvn to ld jst over 1f out: styd on wl* **11/4**[2]
420 **2** *2 ½* **Obiter Dicta**[35] 5539 3-8-12 65.. DaneO'Neill 11 68
(Henry Candy) *pressed ldrs: led 1/2-way: hrd rdn and hdd jst over 1f out: one pce* **5/2**[1]
4340 **3** *3 ½* **Daffydowndilly**[16] 6156 3-8-12 65............................(t) RichardHughes 3 57
(Hughie Morrison) *chsd ldrs: effrt over 2f out: wnt 3rd over 1f out: drew clr of rest but no imp on ldng pair* **7/2**[3]
0 **4** *5* **Dan Donnelly (IRE)**[12] 6251 3-9-3 0................................ RobertHavlin 5 46
(Jeremy Gask) *led to 1/2-way: lost pl qckly 2f out: hung lft over 1f out: won battle for modest 4th* **40/1**
05 **5** *1* **Bunkered Again**[27] 5810 4-8-13 0................................ PatCosgrave 8 38
(Jeremy Gask) *anticipated s and missed break: sn prom: pressed ldr 1/2-way to 2f out: wknd* **50/1**
00- **6** *1 ¼* **Cairanne**[353] 6882 3-8-12 0.. JimmyQuinn 2 39+
(Tom Keddy) *hld up in last pair: nudged along and no ch fr 1/2-way: hmpd over 1f out: kpt on: nt disgracd* **100/1**
46 **7** *nk* **Dolly Bay**[33] 5626 3-8-9 0...................................... AdamBeschizza(3) 7 33
(Julia Feilden) *dwlt: nvr on terms w ldrs: effrt on outer over 2f out: sn wknd* **33/1**
8 *2* **First Class** 3-9-3 0.. MartinLane 10 31
(Rae Guest) *dwlt: chsd ldrs but pushed along bef 1/2-way: lost pl over 2f out: wl btn after* **7/1**
0 **9** *4* **Mr Mystere**[10] 6307 3-9-3 0.. TedDurcan 4 18
(Chris Wall) *a wl in rr: struggling bef 1/2-way* **12/1**
10 *nk* **Evening Pinot** 3-8-12 0.. SebSanders 9 12
(Simon Dow) *rn green and a in rr: wknd 2f out* **16/1**

1m 11.62s (-1.38) **Going Correction** -0.325s/f (Firm)
WFA 3 from 4yo 1lb **10** Ran SP% **111.9**
Speed ratings (Par 103): **96,92,88,81,80 78,77,75,69,69**
toteswingers:1&2:£2.10, 2&3:£2.20, 1&3:£2.60 CSF £9.37 TOTE £3.30: £1.30, £1.60, £1.50; EX 7.60 Trifecta £16.30 Pool: £1140.04 - 51.56 winning units..
Owner Bluehills Racing Limited **Bred** Hesmonds Stud Ltd **Trained** Newmarket, Suffolk
■ Stewards' Enquiry : Robert Havlin one-day ban: careless riding (Oct 17)

FOCUS
An ordinary sprint maiden and straightforward form. The runner-up sets the level.
Dan Donnelly(IRE) Official explanation: jockey said gelding hung left

6592 70'S CHRISTMAS PARTIES HERE 01753 498440 H'CAP 1m 3f 135y
5:30 (5:32) (Class 5) (0-75,75) 3-Y-O+ **£2,264** (£673; £336; £168) **Stalls** Centre

Form RPR
3503 **1** **Countess Comet (IRE)**[23] 5915 4-9-7 **71**.....................(p) JimCrowley 8 80
(Ralph Beckett) *chsd ldrs in 5th: prog to go 2nd over 2f out: drvn to cl fnl f: led last 50yds* **15/2**[3]
5216 **2** *nk* **Flying Power**[20] 6023 3-9-2 **73**..(p) TedDurcan 16 81
(David Lanigan) *led at gd pce: breather bnd over 6f out to over 4f out: kicked on again 3f out: looked like holding on tl worn down last 50yds* **6/1**[2]
4000 **3** *¾* **Mons Calpe (IRE)**[70] 4389 5-9-4 **68**..............................(p) ShaneKelly 10 75+
(Paul Cole) *dwlt and hmpd s: hld up in last quartet: gng strly over 3f out but stl plenty to do over 2f out: drvn and prog after: styd on wl to take 3rd nr fin* **25/1**
2550 **4** *1* **Choral Festival**[8] 6376 5-9-6 **70**.. NeilChalmers 1 75
(John Bridger) *hld up in midfield: gng strly over 3f out: prog over 2f out: chsd ldng pair over 1f out: styd on: nvr quite able to chal and lost 3rd nr fin* **14/1**
2015 **5** *1 ½* **Golden Waters**[16] 6172 4-9-10 **74**...................................... SebSanders 2 77
(Eve Johnson Houghton) *t.k.h: hld up towards rr: rdn and effrt over 3f out: kpt on fnl 2f: nvr rchd ldrs* **9/1**
0546 **6** *hd* **Effigy**[14] 6226 7-9-0 **69**.. AmyScott(5) 7 71
(Henry Candy) *hld up in last and sn detached: taken to wd outside and prog wl over 2f out: kpt on fnl 2f: nvr rchd ldrs* **12/1**
4264 **7** *1 ½* **Super Duplex**[8] 6376 4-8-13 **66**...................................... KierenFox(3) 3 66
(Pat Phelan) *hld up in last quartet: gng wl enough but no prog over 3f out: rdn 2f out: styd on: no ch of being involved* **17/2**
2660 **8** *6* **Hurakan (IRE)**[20] 6023 5-9-4 **68**................................(vt) KierenFallon 15 58
(George Baker) *pressed ldng pair: wnt 2nd 5f out to over 2f out: wknd* **9/1**
2006 **9** *nse* **On The Feather**[27] 5804 5-9-4 **68**.................................. JamesMillman 4 58
(Rod Millman) *chsd ldrs: in 6th: rdn 3f out: wknd 2f out* **28/1**
6330 **10** *1 ¾* **Chain Of Events**[37] 5482 4-9-2 **73**........................ MichaelJMurphy(7) 11 60
(Neil King) *fractious bef gng in stalls: rrd and wnt lft s: mostly in midfield: effrt on outer over 3f out: wknd 2f out* **12/1**
0060 **11** *3* **Beaubrav**[15] 5693 5-9-0 **64**.......................................(t) FrankieMcDonald 12 46
(Michael Madgwick) *mostly in midfield: drvn on outer and effrt over 3f out: wknd 2f out* **20/1**
0056 **12** *1 ¼* **Botanist**[12] 6254 4-9-5 **69**..(t) MartinLane 6 48
(Tobias B P Coles) *rousted along leaving stalls to go prom: rdn and wknd over 2f out* **20/1**
61 **13** *5* **Songburst**[18] 6085 3-9-4 **75**.. RichardHughes 9 46+
(Richard Hannon) *stmbld bdly s: nvr bttr than midfield: rdn 5f out: effrt on outer over 3f out: sn wknd* **5/1**[1]
5010 **14** *11* **Loyaliste (FR)**[22] 5968 4-9-6 **70**.. DaneO'Neill 13 22
(Richard Hannon) *s.v.s: a wl in rr: brief effrt 4f out: sn wknd: eased and t.o* **20/1**
0040 **15** *7* **Tenessee**[12] 6254 4-9-10 **74**.. FergusSweeney 5 14
(Peter Makin) *mostly chsd ldr to 5f out: sn wknd: t.o and eased over 1f out* **20/1**

2m 25.32s (-4.18) **Going Correction** -0.325s/f (Firm)
WFA 3 from 4yo+ 7lb **15** Ran SP% **121.6**
Speed ratings (Par 103): **100,99,99,98,97 97,96,92,92,91 89,88,85,77,73**
toteswingers:1&2:£6.90, 2&3:£44.60, 1&3:£59.10. Totesuper 7: Win: Not won. Place: £342.80. CSF £46.01 CT £1092.60 TOTE £10.30: £3.70, £2.30, £12.10; EX 42.60 Trifecta £561.90 Part won. Pool of £759.39 - 0.30 winning units..
Owner Lady Cobham & Giles Irwin **Bred** Lady Cobham **Trained** Kimpton, Hants

FOCUS
Another wide-open handicap and another race run at something of an uneven pace. The third and fourth look the best guides to the level.
Mons Calpe(IRE) Official explanation: jockey said gelding suffered interference at start
Songburst Official explanation: jockey said colt suffered interference at start
T/Jkpt: £30,489.30 to a £1 stake. Pool of £450,898.78 - 10.50 winning tickets. T/Plt: £47.80 to a £1 stake. Pool of £90,530.97 - 1,381.68 winning tickets. T/Qpdt: £3.40 to a £1 stake. Pool of £7,811.82 - 1,653.98 winning tickets. JN

6321 MAISONS-LAFFITTE (R-H)
Monday, October 3

OFFICIAL GOING: Turf: good

6593a PRIX L'EXPRESS (CLAIMER) (4YO+) (TURF) 4f
1:35 (12:00) 4-Y-O+ **£9,482** (£3,793; £2,844; £1,896; £948)

RPR
1 **Skyteam (FR)**[31] 7-9-1 0........................(b) Christophe-PatriceLemaire 19 87
(M Boutin, France) **57/10**[2]
2 *1 ½* **Moscow Eight (IRE)**[31] 5-9-2 0.................................. ThierryThulliez 15 82
(E J O'Neill, France) **9/2**[1]
3 *1 ½* **Pax Soprana (IRE)**[31] 5-8-7 0.............................. BenjaminBoutin(6) 11 73
(Braem Horse Racing Sprl, Belgium) **40/1**
4 *snk* **Kolokol (IRE)**[31] 4-9-1 0..(b) OlivierPeslier 9 74
(D Prod'Homme, France) **13/2**[3]
5 *1 ¾* **Heaven King (FR)**[22] 4-8-11 0...................................... FranckBlondel 18 63
(M Pimbonnet, France) **19/1**
6 *½* **Fasilight**[517] 4-8-13 0..(b) GlenBraem 14 63
(Braem Horse Racing Sprl, Belgium) **64/1**
7 *½* **Wise Boy (GER)**[44] 4-8-11 0.. DavyBonilla 12 59
(W Baltromei, Germany) **24/1**
8 *1 ½* **Out The Ordinary**[1075] 8-9-1 0............................(b) SoufyaneMoulin(5) 7 62
(Stal Pink Panther, Belgium) **9/1**
9 *hd* **Lisselan Gardens (USA)**[31] 8-8-11 0.............................. JohanVictoire 17 53
(Mme J Bidgood, France) **11/1**
10 *nk* **Orpen's Art (IRE)**[31] 6-9-2 0...................................... MickaelBarzalona 3 56
(R Houthoofd, Belgium) **10/1**
0 **Brown Colt (IRE)**[104] 6-8-11 0.. VincentVion 10 —
(Mme I T Oakes-Cottin, France) **31/1**
0 **Kidibul (BEL)**[693] 5-8-6 0..(b) FlavienMasse(5) 13 —
(J-C Blandiot, Belgium) **117/1**
0 **Rogalt (IRE)**[31] 5-8-11 0...(b) AnthonyDeau 16 —
(R Houthoofd, Belgium) **60/1**
0 **Rock Of Nassau (FR)**[12] 5-9-1 0.............................(p) GregoryBenoist 2 —
(X Nakkachdji, France) **13/2**[3]
0 **Lady Royal Oak (IRE)**[93] 3640 4-8-8 0................................ LauraPike 5 —
(Olivia Maylam) *broke wl: disp ld after first f: remained w ldrs tl rdn and nt qckn 1 1/2f out: wknd fnl f* **50/1**
0 **Bugsy (FR)**[339] 4-8-5 0.................................(b) AlexandreChampenois(3) 4 —
(Mme J Bidgood, France) **52/1**
0 **Pisa No Varon (JPN)**[57] 5-8-11 0...................................... ThierryJarnet 6 —
(S Kobayashi, France) **32/1**
0 **Transmission (USA)**[21] 4-8-11 0..................................(b) CyrilleStefan 1 —
(C Plisson, France) **65/1**
0 **Dido Park (FR)** 4-8-11 0.. AnthonyCrastus 8 —
(B Legros, France) **66/1**

46.90 secs (46.90) **19** Ran SP% **115.7**
WIN (incl 1 euro stake): 6.70. PLACES: 2.40, 2.00, 8.00. DF: 13.20. SF: 35.60..
Owner Jean-Pierre Vanden Heede **Bred** Brookdale Thoroughbred **Trained** France

6394 COLOGNE (R-H)
Monday, October 3

OFFICIAL GOING: Turf: good

6594a WETTEN XXL-SPRINT-PREIS PREMIUM-DREIERWETTE (LISTED RACE) (3YO+) (TURF) 5f
4:00 (12:00) 3-Y-O+ **£11,206** (£3,448; £1,724; £862)

RPR
1 **Birthday Lion (GER)**[12] 6-9-0 0.. AHelfenbein 2 100
(U Stoltefuss, Germany) **187/10**
2 *hd* **Exciting Life (IRE)**[22] 5985 3-9-3 0...................................... MSrnec 8 102
(Adam Wyrzyk, Poland) **53/10**
3 *nse* **Walero (GER)**[15] 5-9-6 0.. KClijmans 3 105
(Uwe Ostmann, Germany) **53/10**

4 nk **Calrissian (GER)**[22] 7-9-3 0 RafaelSchistl 10 101
(Fredrik Reuterskiold, Sweden) 4/1[2]

5 nk **Dreamacha**[109] 3078 4-8-10 0 WilliamCarson 4 93
(Stuart Williams) *broke wl: racd keenly in 4th: tk ld 2f out: rdn and hdd 1f out: wknd* 27/10[1]

6 1 1/4 **Golden Eagle**[15] 5-9-0 0 EFrank 1 92
(A Savujev, Czech Republic) 49/10[3]

7 1 **Anna (GER)** 5-8-10 0 (b) SHellyn 7 85
(Peggy Bastiaens-Van Cauwenbergh, Belgium) 109/10

8 1 3/4 **Sumaro (GER)** 4-9-0 0 THellier 9 82
(W Hickst, Germany) 63/10

9 nse **Saldenaera (GER)**[113] 4-8-10 0 JiriPalik 6 78
(Werner Glanz, Germany) 33/1

10 2 1/2 **Fairhope (GER)**[1621] 9-9-0 0 AndreBest 5 73
(Barbara Sofsky, Germany) 213/10

54.42 secs (-2.51) **10** Ran SP% **130.3**
WIN (incl. 10 euro stake): 197. PLACES: 42, 28, 25. SF: 1,069.
Owner Stall Tondose **Bred** Mme M Haller **Trained** In Germany

4373 HOPPEGARTEN (R-H)

Monday, October 3

OFFICIAL GOING: Turf: good

6595a WESTMINSTER PREIS DER DEUTSCHEN EINHEIT (GROUP 3) (3YO+) (TURF) 1m 2f

3:15 (12:00) 3-Y-0+

£36,206 (£14,224; £6,034; £3,879; £2,586; £1,724)

RPR

1 **Russian Tango (GER)**[64] 4599 4-9-4 0 EPedroza 1 110
(A Wohler, Germany) *broke fast: sn led: set str pce: r.o wl in st: fought off all chals to win comf* 7/2[3]

2 1 1/4 **Auvano (GER)**[1461] 5929 7-9-4 0 APietsch 3 108
(R Dzubasz, Germany) *hld up in 4th on rail: chal for ld ent st: r.o wl to hold rest of pack but no ch w wnr* 10/1

3 hd **Lindenthaler (GER)**[16] 6185 3-9-0 0 AStarke 4 108
(P Schiergen, Germany) *settled in 5th: r.o wl in st: moved up to 3rd: hrd rdn and had to settle for 3rd fnl f* 32/5

4 hd **Wiener Walzer (GER)**[120] 2753 5-9-4 0 (b) ADeVries 5 107
(J Hirschberger, Germany) *racd bhd ldr: rdn to chal early in st: ev ch but no ex fnl f* 21/10[2]

5 hd **Empire Storm (GER)**[37] 5497 4-9-4 0 JBojko 6 106
(A Wohler, Germany) *settled in 3rd bhd ldr: r.o u.p in st: kpt on fnl f* 105/10

6 1/2 **Zazou (GER)**[37] 5497 4-9-4 0 ASuborics 2 105
(W Hickst, Germany) *broke slowly: settled in rr: ev ch ent st: kpt on u.p fnl f but no ex* 2/1[1]

7 34 **Sunshine Lemon (USA)**[807] 4369 7-9-4 0 FilipMinarik 8 37
(A Lyakhov, Russia) *broke slowly: a bhd: unable to go pce: nvr figured* 89/10

2m 5.50s (-1.20)
WFA 3 from 4yo+ 5lb **7** Ran SP% **129.2**
WIN (incl. 10 euro stake): 45. PLACES: 14, 22, 17. SF: 616.
Owner Rennstall Darboven **Bred** Gestut Idee **Trained** Germany

6596a - See Raceform Int

6152 CATTERICK (L-H)

Tuesday, October 4

OFFICIAL GOING: Good to firm (8.3)

Wind: strong half against Weather: Cloudy

6597 YORKSHIRE-OUTDOOR.CO.UK ADVENTURE ACTIVITIES NURSERY 5f

2:30 (2:30) (Class 6) (0-65,65) 2-Y-0 **£1,704** (£503; £251) **Stalls** Low

Form RPR

6656 1 **Uncle Timmy**[20] 6043 2-8-6 **50** JoeFanning 1 53
(John Quinn) *chsd ldr: short of room against rail over 1f out: squeezed through narrow gap ins fnl f: led towards fin* 6/1

5021 2 nk **Look Here's Lady**[20] 6043 2-8-13 **57** GrahamGibbons 6 59
(Ed McMahon) *chsd ldr: rdn over 2f out: chal over 1f out: kpt on jst hld* 7/2[1]

364 3 nk **Dark Ages (IRE)**[20] 6058 2-9-7 **65** (b) PaulHanagan 2 66
(Noel Quinlan) *led: rdn over 1f out: kpt on: hdd towards fin* 5/1[3]

0410 4 hd **Elusive Bonus (IRE)**[20] 6043 2-8-13 **57** DanielTudhope 7 57
(David O'Meara) *in tch: rdn over 2f out: kpt on ins fnl f* 14/1

0004 5 hd **M J Woodward**[53] 5005 2-8-6 **50** JamesSullivan 10 49+
(Paul Green) *hld up: rdn over 2f out: hdwy on outer over 1f out: kpt on ins fnl f: nrst fin* 25/1

000 6 2 **Our Monica (IRE)**[46] 5245 2-8-1 **45** DuranFentiman 9 37+
(Ann Duffield) *dwlt: outpcd in rr tl kpt on ins fnl f: nvr nrr* 100/1

2250 7 1/2 **Banksy**[10] 6323 2-9-7 **65** (t) PhillipMakin 12 55
(Kevin Ryan) *midfield: rdn over 2f out: one pce* 7/1

2600 8 3/4 **Justine Time (IRE)**[11] 6293 2-8-10 **54** (b) LeeNewman 11 42
(David Barron) *s.i.s: hld up: sme hdwy over 1f out: nvr threatened* 14/1

0040 9 1 1/2 **Farzan (IRE)**[11] 6293 2-9-4 **62** (b) DavidAllan 13 44
(Tim Easterby) *midfield on outer: drvn over 2f out: wknd over 1f out* 22/1

2450 10 nk **Slenningford**[18] 6132 2-9-7 **65** PJMcDonald 3 46
(Ollie Pears) *hld up: rdn over 2f out: nvr threatened* 9/2[2]

064 11 hd **Dolly Danca**[123] 2665 2-8-13 **57** BarryMcHugh 8 38
(Paul Midgley) *midfield: rdn over 2f out: wknd over 1f out* 18/1

0540 12 9 **Burnwynd Spirit (IRE)**[9] 6384 2-8-11 **55** (p) FrederikTylicki 5 3
(Ian Semple) *sn pushed along in rr: bhd after 2f: t.o* 66/1

61.69 secs (1.89) **Going Correction** +0.225s/f (Good) **12** Ran SP% **113.1**
Speed ratings (Par 93): **93,92,92,91,91 88,87,86,83,83 83,68**
toteswingers:1&2:£5.20, 2&3:£4.20, 1&3:£6.10 CSF £25.12 CT £111.81 TOTE £6.70: £2.40, £1.60, £2.40; EX 29.60 Trifecta £77.10 Pool: £352.40 - 3.38 winning units..
Owner Mrs Alurie O'Sullivan **Bred** Mrs A M O'Sullivan **Trained** Settrington, N Yorks

FOCUS

The weather was dry and there was a strong crosswind. A modest nursery but fairly competitive, as evidenced by the fact that the first five were separated by just under a length. The runner-up and fourth help set the level in a messy contest.

NOTEBOOK

Uncle Timmy was 8lb better off with the favourite for 4l compared with their Beverley running, but he had a wide draw that day and was able to reverse the form. He was on the tail of the leader throughout and had to be brave to take a narrow opening between that rival and the rail, but forced his head through to lead well inside the last furlong and then just hold the late run of the favourite. Official explanation: trainer's rep said, regarding apparent improvement in form, that the gelding had been hampered on its last run and was only beaten 3 3/4lths. (op 11-2)

Look Here's Lady, bought in after winning a selling nursery last time, was a well-backed favourite. She chased the two leaders and gradually closed them down, but could not quite get to the winner. She probably needs a stiffer test at this distance. (op 5-1)

Dark Ages(IRE), back on fast ground for the first time since winning his maiden in May, went off in front but possibly a little too quickly and was collared in the last 100yds. (op 11-2 tchd 6-1)

Elusive Bonus(IRE), whose win was gained on easy ground, chased the leading trio throughout and gradually reeled them in but could not quite get there. (op 12-1)

M J Woodward ◆, whose best effort was when dropped to this trip on heavy ground last time, had to race wide and came from well back to finish right on the heels of the leaders. His turn does not look far away. (op 18-1)

Slenningford, whose best previous effort was over C&D on his debut, has been running over further of late and could never go the pace back at this trip. (op 4-1)

6598 BRITISH STALLION STUDS SUPPORTING BRITISH RACING E B F MAIDEN STKS 5f

3:00 (3:00) (Class 5) 2-Y-0 **£3,299** (£981; £490; £245) **Stalls** Low

Form RPR

43 1 **Annie Beach (IRE)**[21] 6026 2-8-12 0 GrahamGibbons 9 69
(David Barron) *trckd ldr: rdn to ld over 1f out: kpt on* 7/2[3]

63 2 2 3/4 **Untold Melody**[20] 6045 2-8-12 0 PhillipMakin 5 59
(Kevin Ryan) *midfield: pushed along and hdwy over 1f out: kpt on ins fnl f: wnt 2nd fnl 75yds: no ch w wnr* 5/1

0002 3 3 1/4 **Come On Dave (IRE)**[41] 5367 2-9-3 **75** AdrianNicholls 8 52
(David Nicholls) *led: rdn whn hdd over 1f out: wknd and lost 2nd fnl 100yds* 5/2[2]

0 4 3/4 **Gran Canaria Queen**[34] 5618 2-8-12 0 BarryMcHugh 6 45
(Ian Semple) *s.i.s: hld up: pushed along 3f out: hdwy over 1f out: kpt on ins fnl f: wnt 4th post* 150/1

3433 5 nk **Half A Billion (IRE)**[14] 6232 2-9-3 **71** PaulHanagan 4 49
(Michael Dods) *in tch: rdn over 2f out: sn one pce: lost 4th post* 15/8[1]

0 6 4 **Brave One (IRE)**[10] 6344 2-8-5 0 ShirleyTeasdale[(7)] 10 29
(David Nicholls) *hld up: sn pushed along: sme late hdwy: nvr threatened* 100/1

25 7 shd **Verus Delicia (IRE)**[29] 5779 2-8-9 0 KieranO'Neill[(3)] 3 29
(Patrick Morris) *chsd ldrs: rdn over 2f out: wknd appr fnl f* 25/1

06 8 1 1/4 **Kieron's Rock (IRE)**[20] 6048 2-9-0 0 PatrickDonaghy[(3)] 7 29
(Jedd O'Keeffe) *dwlt: sn pushed along towards rr: nvr threatened* 14/1

0 9 9 **Script**[17] 6152 2-8-7 0 JulieBurke[(5)] 1 —
(Alan Berry) *a in rr* 200/1

60.83 secs (1.03) **Going Correction** +0.225s/f (Good) **9** Ran SP% **114.9**
Speed ratings (Par 95): **100,95,90,89,88 82,82,80,65**
CSF £21.04 TOTE £4.30: £1.50, £1.90, £1.50; EX 20.10 Trifecta £129.50 Pool: £580.75 - 3.31 winning units..
Owner Mrs Christine Barron **Bred** D And Mrs D Veitch **Trained** Maunby, N Yorks
■ Stewards' Enquiry : Phillip Makin three-day ban: weighed in without girth (Oct 18-20)

FOCUS

A modest maiden and fairly uncompetitive, with the betting featuring just four. The time was 0.86secs faster than the opening nursery, though, and the form looks reasonably solid.

NOTEBOOK

Annie Beach(IRE) was just beaten on easy ground at Haydock last time when racing into a headwind and gained compensation on this faster surface, keeping the leader company before asserting decisively in the last furlong. Already a bargain at just 800euros, she looks capable of winning again, but much depends on what the handicapper does with her. (op 9-2)

Untold Melody ran on from well back and was closing in on the winner all the way to the line, but never looked like catching her. She had looked in her previous runs to need longer trips and, now qualified for handicaps, will be of interest over 6f plus. (tchd 11-2)

Come On Dave(IRE), who was reluctant to load, went left out of the gates but was soon in front and did his best to make all. However, he could not shake off the winner and faded quite quickly once headed. (op 2-1 tchd 7-4)

Gran Canaria Queen ◆ was squeezed out at the start and had to come from well back to reach her final position. This was a big improvement on her debut effort and she looks one to be interested in once qualified for handicaps. (op 200-1)

Half A Billion(IRE) had finished in the frame on his seven previous starts but the most recent of those were on a stiffer track, on softer ground or over further. He chased the leaders from the start, but could make no impression in the second half of the race. (op 11-4 tchd 3-1 in a place)

6599 RACINGUK.COM NURSERY 7f

3:30 (3:30) (Class 4) (0-85,78) 2-Y-0 **£3,557** (£1,058; £529; £264) **Stalls** Low

Form RPR

0025 1 **Indepub**[27] 5825 2-9-1 **75** AmyRyan[(3)] 6 80
(Kevin Ryan) *hld up: swtchd to outer over 1f out and sn gd hdwy: kpt on ins fnl f: led fnl 50yds* 11/2[3]

01 2 3/4 **Annie Walker (IRE)**[53] 4983 2-8-8 **65** AdrianNicholls 1 68
(David Nicholls) *prom: rdn to ld over 2f out: kpt on: hdd fnl 50yds* 10/1

3451 3 1 1/2 **Always Et Toujours**[19] 6102 2-9-4 **75** JoeFanning 10 74
(Mark Johnston) *prom on outer: rdn over 2f out: hung lft over 1f out: kpt on one pce ins fnl f* 4/1[1]

4450 4 nk **Baltic Bomber (IRE)**[20] 6045 2-8-5 **62** BarryMcHugh 9 61
(John Quinn) *hld up: hdwy on inner over 2f out: chsd ldr over 1f out: briefly short of room ins fnl f: kpt on* 22/1

5041 5 hd **Al's Memory (IRE)**[11] 6293 2-9-7 **78** GrahamGibbons 8 76
(David Evans) *hld up: in rr whn reminders over 3f out: hdwy on outer over 1f out: kpt on: nvr trbld ldrs* 10/1

6330 6 1/2 **Art Law (IRE)**[39] 5446 2-8-10 **67** (b[1]) ShaneKelly 3 64
(Brian Meehan) *trckd ldrs: rdn over 2f out: one pce ins fnl f* 11/2[3]

1550 7 2 1/4 **Alabanda (IRE)**[15] 6222 2-9-2 **73** DavidAllan 4 65
(Tim Easterby) *in tch: rdn whn short of room over 1f out: one pce after* 8/1

0114 8 3 1/4 **Bu Naaji (IRE)**[19] 6102 2-9-5 **76** AndreaAtzeni 7 59
(Roger Varian) *hld up in tch: rdn over 2f out: sltly short of room over 1f out and again ins fnl f: nvr on terms* 5/1[2]

2520 9 2 3/4 **Koalition (IRE)**[36] 5555 2-8-3 **60** PaulHanagan 5 35
(David O'Meara) *led narrowly: hdd 4f out: wknd over 1f out* 11/1

000 10 4 1/2 **Pontius Pilate (IRE)**[31] 5727 2-7-12 **55** oh5 (p) JamesSullivan 2 18
(Bryan Smart) *w ldr: led 4f out: rdn whn hdd over 2f out: wkng whn hmpd over 1f out* 20/1

0340 **11** *15* **Emley Moor**[13] 6260 2-7-9 **55**........................ KieranO'Neill(3) 11 —
(Chris Fairhurst) *sn detached in rr: a bhd* **100/1**

1m 27.26s (0.26) **Going Correction** -0.025s/f (Good) **11** Ran SP% **115.2**
Speed ratings (Par 97): **97,96,94,94,93 93,90,87,83,78 61**
toteswingers:1&2:£8.90, 2&3:£4.90, 1&3:£5.60 CSF £56.76 CT £248.52 TOTE £4.70: £1.40, £3.40, £2.50; EX 39.70 Trifecta £243.40 Pool: £542.92 - 1.65 winning units..
Owner D W Barker **Bred** Mrs Deborah O'Brien **Trained** Hambleton, N Yorks

FOCUS
A fair nursery with some unexposed types on show but something of a rough race. The form looks straightforward and could rate a little higher.

NOTEBOOK
Indepub has been running pretty well and this faster ground suited, as he came from the rear and managed to avoid the trouble on his inside, pulling away nicely once in front. (op 7-1)
Annie Walker(IRE), the winner of a C&D seller on easy ground last time, went on around 2f out in this better race and battled well but could not hold off the winner. (op 7-1)
Always Et Toujours, a winner on his previous start, tracked the pace and ran on after being slightly affected by the scrimmaging over a furlong out. He looks a galloper who might not have been ideally suited by the track. (tchd 9-2)
Baltic Bomber(IRE) was held up early and found a gap up the rail which got him to the heels of the runner-up but a narrow opening then closed, leaving him slightly short of room and unable to pick up again.
Al's Memory(IRE) ◆, whose win came on easy ground over 6f, could not go the early pace on this faster surface but stayed on well in the closing stages. He will be happier back on a more galloping track. (op 12-1)
Art Law(IRE), dropping in trip and blinkered for the first time, tracked the pace throughout but was under pressure early in the straight and failed to pick up. (op 6-1)
Bu Naaji(IRE) was unable to go the early pace and was then short of room when trying to make headway in the straight. He can be given another chance. (op 9-2)

6600 SKYRAM H'CAP — 1m 7f 177y
4:00 (4:00) (Class 6) (0-60,60) 3-Y-0+ — **£2,726** (£805; £402) **Stalls** Low

Form — RPR
563 **1** **Strikemaster (IRE)**[35] 5595 5-9-3 **49**..........................(t) DuranFentiman 9 59
(Lee James) *hld up: rdn and hdwy over 2f out: sn chsng ldrs: styd on ins fnl f: led post* **11/1**
0000 **2** *hd* **Hi Dancer**[57] 4856 8-9-3 **49**........................ PaulHanagan 6 59
(Ben Haslam) *trckd ldr: led wl over 3f out: rdn over 2f out: kpt on: ct post* **11/1**
6464 **3** *3 ¾* **Dane Cottage**[31] 5723 4-9-8 **54**........................ GrahamGibbons 10 59
(Brian Ellison) *in tch: hdwy 3f out: rdn to chse ldr over 2f out: no ex ins fnl f* **6/1**[2]
2342 **4** *4 ½* **Royal Bonsai**[17] 6153 3-9-3 **60**........................ PBBeggy 7 60
(John Quinn) *midfield: rdn to chse ldrs over 2f out: one pce over 1f out* **13/2**[3]
0033 **5** *1 ¾* **They All Laughed**[33] 5650 8-9-2 **48**..........................(p) PhillipMakin 2 46
(Marjorie Fife) *hld up: rdn over 3f out: nvr threatened* **6/1**[2]
5461 **6** *2 ¼* **Ad Value (IRE)**[17] 6153 3-8-13 **56**........................ PJMcDonald 12 51
(Alan Swinbank) *midfield: rdn and hdwy over 3f out: chsd ldrs over 2f out: wknd over 1f out* **10/3**[1]
23-3 **7** *20* **Sheila's Castle**[128] 1994 7-9-9 **60**........................ DavidKenny(5) 4 31
(Sean Regan) *trckd ldr: wknd over 2f out* **20/1**
2600 **8** *1* **Bright Sparky (GER)**[110] 3086 8-9-1 **47**..................(vt) JamesSullivan 8 17
(Michael Easterby) *midfield: rdn over 3f out: sn btn* **33/1**
4000 **9** *16* **Morning Air (IRE)**[20] 6050 3-8-3 **49** ow1........................ AmyRyan(3) 13 —
(Ann Duffield) *dwlt: a towards rr* **25/1**
-302 **10** *2 ¼* **Haka Dancer (USA)**[31] 4814 8-9-0 **46**..........................(p) JimmyQuinn 5 —
(Philip Kirby) *s.i.s: hld up: a towards rr* **14/1**
2620 **11** *dist* **Miss Whippy**[37] 5519 4-9-3 **49**........................ ShaneKelly 11 —
(Michael Squance) *led: rdn 7f out: hdd wl over 3f out: sn wknd: eased over 2f out: t.o* **11/1**
0044 **P** **Milton Hill**[61] 4703 4-8-13 **48**........................ KieranO'Neill(3) 3 —
(Dominic Ffrench Davis) *in tch: lost action over 2f out and eased: p.u ins fnl f* **12/1**

3m 33.9s (1.90) **Going Correction** +0.175s/f (Good)
WFA 3 from 4yo+ 11lb **12** Ran SP% **115.9**
Speed ratings (Par 101): **102,101,100,97,96 95,85,85,77,76 —,—**
toteswingers:1&2:£21.50, 2&3:£14.00, 1&3:£18.50 CSF £120.34 CT £798.26 TOTE £14.20: £5.60, £2.90, £3.00; EX 187.70 Trifecta £247.30 Part won. Pool: £334.20 - 0.65 winning units..
Owner Mrs Carol Lloyd-James **Bred** Dr Peter Harms **Trained** Norton, N Yorks

FOCUS
A very moderate staying handicap and they finished well strung out. The form is ordinary rated around the placed horses to recent marks.
Miss Whippy Official explanation: jockey said filly lost its action turning in

6601 GO RACING IN YORKSHIRE H'CAP — 1m 3f 214y
4:30 (4:30) (Class 5) (0-75,75) 3-Y-0+ — **£4,010** (£1,193; £596; £298) **Stalls** Low

Form — RPR
2422 **1** **Singzak**[4] 6503 3-8-9 **65**........................ JamesSullivan 3 76
(Michael Easterby) *mde all: rdn over 2f out: kpt on wl* **3/1**[1]
0431 **2** *2* **Painted Tail (IRE)**[10] 6357 4-9-2 **65**........................ PJMcDonald 7 73+
(Alan Swinbank) *dwlt: hld up in midfield: pushed along over 3f out: rdn and hdwy on outer over 1f out: kpt on to go 2nd fnl 100yds* **3/1**[1]
1100 **3** *1* **Jewelled Dagger (IRE)**[31] 5724 7-9-11 **74**........................ PaulHanagan 2 80
(Keith Dalgleish) *trckd ldrs: rdn over 2f out: kpt on* **14/1**
1344 **4** *½* **Miracle Play (IRE)**[18] 6136 3-8-2 **61** oh1........................ KieranO'Neill(3) 6 66
(David Evans) *midfield: rdn over 2f out: hdwy over 1f out: kpt on ins fnl f* **16/1**
2114 **5** *1 ¾* **Eijaaz (IRE)**[17] 6157 10-9-0 **63**..........................(p) FrederikTylicki 8 66
(Geoffrey Harker) *hld up: rdn over 2f out: kpt on ins fnl f: nvr nrr* **11/1**[3]
0302 **6** *1* **Stentorian (IRE)**[8] 6409 3-9-5 **75**..........................(b) JoeFanning 12 76
(Mark Johnston) *t.k.h early: trckd ldrs: rdn over 2f out: wknd ins fnl f* **15/2**[2]
3121 **7** *¾* **Royal Opera**[15] 6225 3-9-1 **71**........................ GrahamGibbons 9 71
(Brian Ellison) *racd keenly: prom: rdn over 2f out: wknd ins fnl f* **15/2**[2]
3140 **8** *2* **Christmas Light**[38] 5485 4-9-7 **70**........................ DanielTudhope 1 67
(David O'Meara) *hld up: rdn over 2f out: nvr on terms* **16/1**
0-00 **9** *1* **Snoqualmie Boy**[13] 6263 8-9-3 **66**........................ AdrianNicholls 5 61
(David Nicholls) *hld up in midfield: rdn over 2f out: sn no imp* **40/1**
4006 **10** *1 ½* **Saint Thomas (IRE)**[17] 6155 4-9-3 **66**........................ DavidNolan 10 59
(John Mackie) *midfield: rdn over 2f out: wknd over 1f out* **14/1**
0423 **11** *11* **Valantino Oyster (IRE)**[9] 6379 4-8-12 **61** oh1........(p) PatrickMathers 11 36
(Tracy Waggott) *midfield: dropped in rr 4f out: sn btn* **14/1**

2m 40.05s (1.15) **Going Correction** +0.175s/f (Good)
WFA 3 from 4yo+ 7lb **11** Ran SP% **116.1**
Speed ratings (Par 103): **103,101,101,100,99 98,98,97,96,95 88**
toteswingers:1&2:£4.30, 2&3:£8.60, 1&3:£9.00 CSF £10.33 CT £107.15 TOTE £3.00: £1.10, £2.30, £4.80; EX 17.70 Trifecta £407.00 Part won. Pool of £550.12 - 0.85 winning units..

Owner Clark Industrial Services Partnership **Bred** Clark Industrial Services Partnership **Trained** Sheriff Hutton, N Yorks

FOCUS
A modest handicap but the third, fourth and fifth set a sound-looking standard.
Royal Opera Official explanation: jockey said gelding was unsuited by the track

6602 CATTERICKBRIDGE.CO.UK AMATEUR RIDERS' H'CAP — 5f
5:00 (5:00) (Class 6) (0-55,55) 3-Y-0+ — **£1,646** (£506; £253) **Stalls** Low

Form — RPR
5322 **1** **Sharp Bullet (IRE)**[6] 6454 5-10-5 **53**..........................(p) MissNStead(7) 15 62
(Bruce Hellier) *chsd ldrs: rdn over 2f out: kpt on ins fnl f: led post* **7/1**[2]
6450 **2** *hd* **Triskaidekaphobia**[34] 5620 8-9-12 **46** oh1............(t) MissSMDoolan(7) 7 54
(Wilf Storey) *led: rdn over 1f out: kpt on: hdd post* **25/1**
4035 **3** *1 ¾* **See Vermont**[34] 5620 3-10-6 **52**........................ MrFMitchell(5) 1 54
(Robin Bastiman) *chsd ldrs: rdn over 2f out: kpt on* **7/1**[2]
400 **4** *nk* **Uddy Mac**[13] 6266 4-10-9 **55**..........................(b) MissVBarr(5) 14 56
(Neville Bycroft) *hld up: rdn and hdwy on outer over 2f out: kpt on ins fnl f* **14/1**
5-4 **5** *½* **Danum Dancer**[36] 5552 7-10-9 **55**..........................(b) MrSebSpencer(5) 8 54
(Neville Bycroft) *prom towards centre: rdn over 2f out: one pce fnl f: eased fnl 50yds* **11/2**[1]
006 **6** *nk* **Kyllachykov (IRE)**[29] 5793 3-10-2 **46** oh1........................ MrMEnnis(3) 13 44
(Robin Bastiman) *hld up: rdn over 2f out: kpt on ins fnl f: nvr nrr* **33/1**
0004 **7** *½* **Dower Glen**[9] 6386 4-10-13 **54**..........................(v) MrSWalker 6 50
(Keith Dalgleish) *in tch: rdn over 2f out: one pce* **11/2**[1]
1433 **8** *nk* **Francis Albert**[26] 5865 5-10-11 **55**........................ MissMMullineaux(3) 11 50+
(Michael Mullineaux) *rrd s and v.s.a: bhd tl kpt on ins fnl f: nrst fin* **7/1**[2]
6006 **9** *¾* **Blue Rum (IRE)**[10] 6343 4-10-5 **46** oh1........................ MissLHorner 10 38
(Alan Kirtley) *chsd ldrs: wknd over 1f out* **14/1**
2550 **10** *1 ¼* **Isle Of Ellis (IRE)**[13] 6261 4-10-0 **46** oh1..........................(v) MissGTutty(5) 5 34
(Ron Barr) *in tch: rdn over 2f out: wknd ins fnl f* **16/1**
0010 **11** *¾* **Almaty Express**[25] 5895 9-10-4 **52**........................ MrEKingsley(7) 3 37
(John Weymes) *in tch: lost pl 1/2-way: no threat after* **11/1**
0600 **12** *2 ¼* **Boga (IRE)**[17] 6158 4-10-2 **48**........................ MissPhillipaTutty(5) 2 25
(Karen Tutty) *chsd ldrs: rdn over 2f out: wknd over 1f out* **10/1**[3]
065 **13** *½* **King Bertolini (IRE)**[8] 6414 4-10-1 **49** oh1 ow3........................ MrRHogg(7) 9 24
(Alan Berry) *a in rr* **25/1**
4505 **14** *6* **Bygones For Coins (IRE)**[7] 6427 3-9-12 **46** oh1........ MrMGrossett(7) 4 —
(Alan Berry) *dwlt: hld up: a bhd* **40/1**

62.64 secs (2.84) **Going Correction** +0.225s/f (Good) **14** Ran SP% **118.0**
Speed ratings (Par 101): **86,85,82,82,81 81,80,79,78,76 75,71,52,43**
toteswingers:1&2:£31.40, 2&3:£32.00, 1&3:£11.10 CSF £176.55 CT £1308.50 TOTE £6.40: £1.80, £4.90, £3.40; EX 238.30 TRIFECTA Not won..
Owner The Haydock Club **Bred** Gerrardstown House Stud **Trained** Garstang, Lancs
■ Stewards' Enquiry : Mr Seb Spencer four-day ban: failed to ride out for 4th (Oct 24,26,Nov 16,22)

FOCUS
A moderate amateur riders' sprint and they were spread across the track. The time was slower than the two earlier juvenile races but the form looks straightforward, with the third and fourth close to their marks.
T/Jkpt: Not won. T/Plt: £128.60 to a £1 stake. Pool of £79,869.16 - 453.30 winning tickets. T/Qpdt: £31.50 to a £1 stake. Pool of £4,984.48 - 117.00 winning tickets. AS

6221 LEICESTER (R-H)
Tuesday, October 4

OFFICIAL GOING: Good to firm (7.5)
Wind: Fresh behind Weather: Overcast

6603 BRITISH STALLION STUDS SUPPORTING BRITISH RACING E B F MAIDEN FILLIES' STKS — 7f 9y
2:10 (2:11) (Class 4) 2-Y-0 — **£4,334** (£1,289; £644; £322) **Stalls** High

Form — RPR
1 **Abishena (IRE)** 2-9-0 0........................ FrannyNorton 16 81+
(Mark Johnston) *dwlt: in rr: rdn and stmbld wl over 2f out: hdwy over 1f out: r.o u.p to ld post* **16/1**
2 *nse* **Fulney** 2-9-0 0........................ CathyGannon 10 81
(James Eustace) *a.p: rdn to ld ins fnl f: r.o: hdd post* **100/1**
3 *1 ¾* **Eluding** 2-9-0 0........................ AhmedAjtebi 15 76
(Mahmood Al Zarooni) *chsd ldrs: led over 2f out: sn rdn: hdd and unable qck ins fnl f* **9/1**
4 *1 ½* **Available (IRE)** 2-9-0 0........................ DaneO'Neill 9 72
(Richard Hannon) *chsd ldrs: led 1/2-way: hdd over 2f out: rdn and ev ch over 1f out: styd on same pce ins fnl f* **50/1**
5 *2 ¼* **Strathnaver** 2-9-0 0........................ KierenFallon 1 67+
(Ed Dunlop) *sn pushed along in rr: hdwy over 2f out: rdn over 1f out: styd on same pce* **12/1**
6 *½* **Shabora (IRE)** 2-9-0 0........................ NeilCallan 8 65
(Roger Varian) *prom: rdn over 2f out: no ex ins fnl f* **8/1**[3]
00 **7** *3 ¾* **Dalacara**[35] 5583 2-9-0 0........................ LukeMorris 6 56
(Clive Cox) *prom: rdn over 2f out: wknd ins fnl f* **14/1**
2 **8** *1 ½* **Irishstone (IRE)**[15] 6215 2-9-0 0........................ SebSanders 18 52
(Gerard Butler) *chsd ldrs: rdn over 2f out: edgd rt over 1f out: wknd fnl f* **9/2**[2]
9 *nk* **Kogershin (USA)** 2-9-0 0........................ JimmyFortune 2 51
(Jeremy Noseda) *chsd ldrs: rdn over 2f out: wknd fnl f* **11/1**
10 *¾* **Estiqbaal** 2-9-0 0........................ FrankieDettori 17 49
(Saeed Bin Suroor) *chsd ldrs: rdn over 2f out: hung rt and wknd over 1f out* **7/2**[1]
11 *nk* **Authoritarian** 2-8-13 0 ow2........................ SeanLevey(3) 7 50
(Richard Hannon) *s.i.s: a towards rr* **66/1**
12 *nk* **Salaaheb (IRE)** 2-9-0 0........................ RichardHills 13 47
(Mark Johnston) *prom: rdn over 2f out: wknd over 1f out* **20/1**
0 **13** *2* **Manbaa (USA)**[81] 4052 2-9-0 0........................ MichaelHills 3 42
(John Dunlop) *s.i.s: a in rr: wknd over 2f out* **22/1**
14 *1 ½* **Excellent News (IRE)** 2-9-0 0........................ DarryllHolland 5 38+
(J W Hills) *s.i.s: outpcd* **80/1**
15 *2* **Throne** 2-9-0 0........................ RichardHughes 4 33
(Richard Hannon) *sn prom: rdn over 2f out: wknd over 1f out* **8/1**[3]
16 *8* **Balaton** 2-9-0 0........................ MartinDwyer 14 12
(Brian Meehan) *outpcd* **50/1**

0 **17** *7* **Bovs Castle**[10] 6329 2-9-0 0 .... JamesDoyle 12 —
(Lucinda Featherstone) *led to 1/2-way: wknd over 2f out* **250/1**
1m 24.26s (-1.94) **Going Correction** -0.175s/f (Firm) **17** Ran SP% **118.3**
Speed ratings (Par 94): **104,103,101,100,97 97,92,91,90,89 89,89,86,85,82 73,65**
toteswingers:1&2:£135.00, 2&3:£174.30, 1&3:£28.40 CSF £1131.62 TOTE £37.10: £8.00, £16.80, £3.10; EX 860.00.
Owner Sheikh Hamdan Bin Mohammed Al Maktoum **Bred** Darley **Trained** Middleham Moor, N Yorks

FOCUS
False rail from round course bend to the Winning Post positioned 10yds from inside rail and increasing distances on Round course by about 10yds. The ground had dried to good to firm on the morning of racing. There was a false rail from the round course bend all the way to the winning line, increasing race distances by ten yards. A typically interesting juvenile maiden for the course and time of year, full of well-bred newcomers from the top yards.

NOTEBOOK
Abishena(IRE), a daughter of Pivotal who is related to a couple of winners, came out on top in a tight finish. She did very well to win, not being the best away and then appearing to stumble when making ground, but she really picked up well once switched on to the rail. She looks to have some physical scope and should have more to offer over 1m. It'll be interesting to see where she goes next. (op 20-1 tchd 14-1)
Fulney ◆, first foal of a mare who won up to 1m2f, was dismissed in the betting, but having raced prominently throughout she found plenty for pressure, only to be cruelly denied. This was a promising start.
Eluding, the apparent Godolphin second string, is out of a Group-placed stayer so she can be expected to need further next year. She travelled well before being unable to quicken and should benefit from an extra furlong. (op 12-1)
Available(IRE) has speed in her pedigree, being out of a 5f winner, and she went well for a long way before others proved stronger in the final furlong. A drop to 6f may suit for the time being and she can win a maiden. (op 40-1)
Strathnaver ◆, a 230,000gns half-sister to UAE 1000 Guineas winner Siyaadah, was green early on but stayed on most encouragingly under an educational ride and should relish 1m. She's another likely maiden winner. (op 14-1)
Shabora(IRE), a daughter of Cape Cross closely related to three winners, showed ability before fading and can improve.
Dalacara is now qualified for a mark and can find a handicap at the right level, with a step back up in trip likely to suit. (op 16-1)
Irishstone(IRE), making her turf debut, was unable to build on last month's Kempton second and may prefer an easier surface. (op 7-2)
Estiqbaal, the choice of Frankie Dettori, apparently looked a bit weak in the preliminaries and didn't get home having showed up well for a long way. She can improve and may prove as effective at 6f for the time being. (op 4-1 tchd 3-1)
Throne, a half-sister to Kyllachy, offered little immediate promise, but was clearly thought capable of more and may fare better with this run under her belt dropped to 6f.

6604 GRETA & TERRY STRAY 50TH WEDDING ANNIVERSARY FILLIES' H'CAP — 5f 218y
2:40 (2:41) (Class 5) (0-70,70) 3-Y-O+ **£2,264** (£673; £336; £168) **Stalls** High

Form RPR
0321 **1** **Meandmyshadow**[10] 6343 3-8-13 **63** .... DarrylHolland 5 72
(Alan Brown) *led 2f: chsd ldr: rdn over 1f out: r.o to ld wl ins fnl f* **6/1**[2]
5602 **2** *3/4* **Madame Kintyre**[8] 6408 3-8-11 **61** ....(b) JamesMillman 3 68
(Rod Millman) *chsd ldr tl led 4f out: rdn over 1f out: hdd wl ins fnl f* **7/1**[3]
5243 **3** *1* **Links Drive Lady**[15] 6228 3-9-0 **67** ....(p) LouisBeuzelin(3) 4 71
(Mark Rimmer) *mid-div and sn pushed along: hdwy over 2f out: rdn over 1f out: styd on same pce ins fnl f* **5/1**[1]
4504 **4** *shd* **Anjomarba (IRE)**[5] 6491 4-9-5 **68** .... JamesDoyle 1 71
(Conor Dore) *prom: rdn 1/2-way: styd on u.p* **15/2**
-560 **5** *1 3/4* **Methayel (IRE)**[76] 4199 3-8-10 **60** .... TomQueally 9 58
(Clive Brittain) *s.i.s: outpcd: swtchd rt and hdwy over 1f out: nt rch ldrs* **16/1**
5000 **6** *1* **Winniepeg**[106] 3230 3-8-3 **56** oh2 .... JohnFahy(3) 2 51
(Clive Cox) *mid-div: rdn over 2f out: no ex ins fnl f* **50/1**
1030 **7** *3* **Lizzie (IRE)**[13] 6265 3-9-4 **68** ....(b) TedDurcan 11 53
(Tim Easterby) *sn outpcd: styd on ins fnl f: nvr nrr* **10/1**
0106 **8** *nk* **Stilettoesinthemud (IRE)**[6] 6456 3-8-11 **64** .... LeeTopliss(3) 10 48
(James Given) *outpcd: styd on ins fnl f: nrst fin* **14/1**
00 **9** *1* **Milton Of Campsie**[15] 6213 6-9-0 **63** ....(e[1]) TonyCulhane 12 44
(Richard Guest) *prom: rdn over 2f out: wknd over 1f out* **12/1**
1006 **10** *2 1/4* **My Own Way Home**[33] 5640 3-9-1 **65** .... NeilCallan 6 39
(Dee Donovan) *chsd ldrs: rdn 1/2-way: wknd ins fnl f* **16/1**
0056 **11** *3 1/4* **Flashbang**[59] 4799 3-9-6 **70** .... ChrisCatlin 8 33
(Paul Cole) *s.i.s: outpcd* **9/1**
0444 **12** *21* **Diapason (IRE)**[29] 5781 5-9-3 **66** ....(t) RichardKingscote 13 —
(Tom Dascombe) *sn outpcd* **15/2**
1m 11.52s (-1.48) **Going Correction** -0.175s/f (Firm)
WFA 3 from 4yo+ 1lb **12** Ran SP% **114.2**
Speed ratings (Par 100): **102,101,99,99,97 95,91,91,90,87 82,54**
CSF £45.79 CT £224.80 TOTE £5.60: £2.20, £1.70, £1.90; EX 29.70.
Owner G Morrill **Bred** M J Dawson **Trained** Yedingham, N Yorks

FOCUS
Few got into this moderate sprint handicap but it looks solid form for the grade, rated around the placed horses.
Milton Of Campsie Official explanation: jockey said mare hung right
Diapason(IRE) Official explanation: jockey said mare ran too free to post

6605 STOAT (S) STKS — 1m 1f 218y
3:10 (3:10) (Class 6) 3-Y-O **£1,617** (£481; £240; £120) **Stalls** Low

Form RPR
3120 **1** **Jack's Revenge (IRE)**[33] 3118 3-9-2 73 ....(vt[1]) KierenFallon 4 64
(George Baker) *a.p: chsd ldr 1/2-way: led over 3f out: rdn: hung lft and idled fr over 1f out: styd on* **8/13**[1]
0026 **2** *1/2* **Orange Ace**[6] 6465 3-8-11 62 ....(t) ChrisCatlin 5 58
(Paul Cole) *hld up: pushed along 7f out: hdwy 1/2-way: rdn over 2f out: chsd wnr ins fnl f: styd on* **5/1**[3]
0 **3** *1 1/4* **Aqua Lad**[51] 5082 3-8-11 0 .... FrannyNorton 2 56
(Mark Johnston) *chsd ldrs: lost pl 1/2-way: bhd and rdn 3f out: hdwy over 1f out: r.o* **25/1**
4000 **4** *7* **Guisho (IRE)**[11] 6311 3-8-11 67 ....(b) MartinDwyer 3 42
(Brian Meehan) *sn led: rdn and hdd over 3f out: wknd ins fnl f* **7/2**[2]
0205 **5** *3 1/2* **Look For Love**[3] 6545 3-8-11 48 .... TomQueally 6 35
(Reg Hollinshead) *hld up: rdn: hung lft and wknd over 3f out* **14/1**
05 **6** *15* **Ellephil (IRE)**[26] 5842 3-8-6 0 .... DavidProbert 1 —
(Bryn Palling) *chsd ldr to 1/2-way: rdn: hung lft and wknd 2f out* **125/1**
2m 8.52s (0.62) **Going Correction** +0.125s/f (Good) **6** Ran SP% **112.1**
Speed ratings (Par 99): **102,101,100,95,92 80**
.There was no bid for the winner. Orange Ace was claimed by D Barlow for £7000.\n\x\x

Owner PJL Racing **Bred** Con Marnane **Trained** Whitsbury, Hants

FOCUS
An uncompetitive seller and probably weaker than the figures suggest, with the runner-up to his recent best the guide.

6606 SQUIRREL CONDITIONS STKS — 1m 1f 218y
3:40 (3:40) (Class 3) 2-Y-O **£5,822** (£1,732; £865) **Stalls** Low

Form RPR
15 **1** **Rougemont (IRE)**[52] 5044 2-8-13 80 .... RichardHughes 3 86+
(Richard Hannon) *chsd ldr tl led over 8f out: shkn up ins fnl f: a doing enough* **13/8**[2]
1021 **2** *hd* **Repeater**[10] 6345 2-8-13 86 .... SebSanders 1 86+
(Sir Mark Prescott Bt) *hld up: plld hrd: tk cl order over 3f out: rdn to chse wnr ins fnl f: r.o* **1/1**[1]
3421 **3** *1 1/4* **Tidal Way (IRE)**[39] 5454 2-8-13 78 .... SamHitchcott 2 81
(Mick Channon) *led: hdd over 8f out: chsd ldr tl chal 1/2-way: rdn over 1f out: styd on same pce ins fnl f* **5/1**[3]
2m 11.37s (3.47) **Going Correction** +0.125s/f (Good) **3** Ran SP% **104.8**
Speed ratings (Par 99): **91,90,89**
CSF £3.52 TOTE £2.30; EX 3.40.
Owner Mrs J Wood **Bred** Mrs Clodagh McStay **Trained** East Everleigh, Wilts

FOCUS
An intriguing three-runner conditions race. the first two can do better but the form here is limited by the proximity of the third.

NOTEBOOK
Rougemont(IRE), disappointing behind a smart sort in a 7f Listed race at Newbury last time, having been hailed as a the yard's best 2-y-o after a 25-1 winning debut at Newmarket, is clearly no star but could make up into a very useful handicapper/Listed performer next season, his rider feeling he's still rather weak. (op 7-4 tchd 15-8)
Repeater, winner of a 1m handicap of 80 at Ripon last time, has raced keenly in the past and he refused to settle in this small field racing over this trip for the first time. Sanders was keen to delay his challenge as long as possible, having him tucked in behind his two rivals, but it's hard to argue that he misjudged it, not switching until 1f out and failing to get up in time. The son of Montjeu remains capable of better if he can settle. (op 10-11 tchd 5-6)
Tidal Way(IRE), off the mark at the sixth attempt in a 1m soft-ground maiden at Thirsk last time, handles this faster surface and was expected to be suited by the additional 2f. He ran well, drawing alongside the winner early in the straight, only to be outpaced near the finish. He's another potentially useful handicap prospect. (tchd 9-2 and 6-1)

6607 QUORN H'CAP — 1m 3f 183y
4:10 (4:10) (Class 4) (0-85,80) 3-Y-O **£4,075** (£1,212; £606; £303) **Stalls** Low

Form RPR
1132 **1** **Franciscan**[24] 5938 3-9-6 **80** .... KierenFallon 1 94+
(Luca Cumani) *chsd ldrs: stdd and lost pl over 10f out: pushed along over 3f out: hdwy to chse ldr over 2f out: led over 1f out: sn rdn: r.o: eased nr fin: readily* **11/4**[3]
1051 **2** *1/2* **Hot Spice**[28] 5804 3-9-2 **76** .... TedDurcan 4 88+
(John Dunlop) *chsd ldrs: rdn over 2f out: chsd wnr ins fnl f: r.o* **85/40**[1]
6022 **3** *6* **Quiz Mistress**[17] 6172 3-9-3 **77** ....(p) CathyGannon 2 80
(Gerard Butler) *s.i.s: plld hrd: hdwy to ld over 10f out: clr 1/2-way: rdn and hdd over 1f out: no ex* **4/1**
-451 **4** *6* **Armoise**[21] 6037 3-9-0 **74** ....(t) TomQueally 3 67
(Marco Botti) *led: hdd over 10f out: chsd ldr tl rdn over 2f out: wknd over 1f out* **5/2**[2]
2m 34.4s (0.50) **Going Correction** +0.125s/f (Good) **4** Ran SP% **107.2**
Speed ratings (Par 103): **103,102,98,94**
CSF £8.69 TOTE £2.00; EX 7.30.
Owner Fittocks Stud For Camilla Millbank **Bred** Fittocks Stud **Trained** Newmarket, Suffolk

FOCUS
It was hard to rule out any of these in what looked a competitive handicap. The winner is rated a little better than the bare form.

6608 DORMOUSE MAIDEN STKS — 7f 9y
4:40 (4:40) (Class 5) 3-Y-O **£2,264** (£673; £336; £168) **Stalls** High

Form RPR
22 **1** **Upcountry**[21] 6020 3-9-3 0 .... MichaelHills 6 88+
(Charles Hills) *mde all: pushed clr and hung rt fr over 2f out: easily* **4/9**[1]
5-4 **2** *4* **State Senator (USA)**[10] [illegible] 3-9-3 0 .... SebSanders 2 73+
(Sir Mark Prescott Bt) *sn chsng wnr: rdn over 2f out: styd on same pce* **8/1**[3]
3 *1* **Haamaat (IRE)** 3-8-12 0 .... RichardHills 7 65+
(William Haggas) *dwlt: hld up: plld hrd: hdwy over 2f out: sn rdn and no imp* **11/2**[2]
05 **4** *7* **Days In May (IRE)**[18] 6137 3-8-7 0 .... AntiocoMurgia(5) 8 46
(Edward Vaughan) *chsd ldrs: rdn over 2f out: wknd wl over 1f out* **20/1**
0 **5** *1 3/4* **Najraan**[109] 3135 3-8-12 0 .... TomQueally 4 42
(Clive Brittain) *chsd ldrs: rdn 1/2-way: wknd 2f out* **12/1**
0- **6** *3 1/4* **Calico Bay (IRE)**[375] 6333 3-9-3 0 .... DavidProbert 9 38
(Alan McCabe) *hld up: rdn 1/2-way: sn wknd* **66/1**
0 **7** *nk* **Mufasa Rules (USA)**[21] 6020 3-9-3 0 ....(t) JamesDoyle 5 37
(Sylvester Kirk) *hld up: rdn 1/2-way: sn wknd* **66/1**
4 **8** *nk* **Master Jack**[21] 6020 3-9-3 0 .... MartinDwyer 10 36
(Bill Turner) *chsd ldrs: rdn 1/2-way: wknd over 2f out* **20/1**
00 **9** *1* **Moonlark**[22] 5999 3-8-12 0 .... ChrisCatlin 3 29
(John Holt) *prom: rdn over 2f out: sn wknd* **100/1**
050 **10** *17* **Zoriana**[15] 6223 3-8-12 0 .... AdrianMcCarthy 1 —
(Christine Dunnett) *hld up: hdwy 1/2-way: wknd over 2f out* **150/1**
1m 24.21s (-1.99) **Going Correction** -0.175s/f (Firm) **10** Ran SP% **117.6**
Speed ratings (Par 101): **104,99,98,90,88 84,84,83,82,63**
toteswingers:1&2:£2.20, 2&3:£2.30, 1&3:£1.60 CSF £4.45 TOTE £1.40: £1.02, £1.90, £1.80; EX 4.90.
Owner K Abdulla **Bred** Juddmonte Farms Ltd **Trained** Lambourn, Berks

FOCUS
A race easily won by the favourite and the form is worth regarding fairly positively.

6609 LEVERET APPRENTICE H'CAP (DIV I) — 7f 9y
5:10 (5:10) (Class 6) (0-60,65) 3-Y-O+ **£1,293** (£385; £192; £96) **Stalls** High

Form RPR
0240 **1** **Prince Of Passion (CAN)**[17] 6181 3-9-3 **58** .... MatthewCosham 2 66
(Derek Shaw) *hld up: hdwy over 2f out: r.o to ld wl ins fnl f* **16/1**
-000 **2** *3/4* **Forks**[25] 5894 4-9-1 **57** .... AntiocoMurgia(3) 6 63
(Jane Chapple-Hyam) *chsd ldrs: rdn to ld 1f out: hdd wl ins fnl f* **9/1**
-603 **3** *shd* **Know No Fear**[5] 6488 6-8-6 **50** ....(p) KatiaScallan(5) 11 56
(Alastair Lidderdale) *led 6f out: rdn and hdd over 2f out: sn hung rt: styd on* **8/1**[3]

0001 **4** 1 3/4 **Divertimenti (IRE)**[5] 6479 7-9-9 **65** 6ex........................(b) LucyKBarry(3) 9 66
(Roy Bowring) *s.i.s: hdwy over 4f out: rdn: nt clr run and swtchd lft over 1f out: styd on* **7/2**[1]
0604 **5** 2 1/4 **Titan Diamond (IRE)**[25] 5902 3-8-6 **50**.................... RachealKneller(3) 8 45
(Mark Usher) *prom: lost pl 4f out: r.o wl ins fnl f* **10/1**
6340 **6** 3/4 **Belinsky (IRE)**[13] 6261 4-9-1 **59**.........................(p) JacobButterfield(5) 10 52
(Mark Campion) *led 1f: chsd ldr: led again over 2f out: rdn and hdd 1f out: no ex* **7/1**[2]
4020 **7** 3/4 **Trade Centre**[32] 5674 6-8-13 **52**.. JamesRogers 5 43
(Milton Bradley) *chsd ldrs: rdn over 1f out: no ex ins fnl f* **17/2**
3560 **8** 2 1/4 **Ghost Dancer**[32] 5677 7-8-8 **47**..(p) RyanPowell 3 32
(Milton Bradley) *s.s: outpcd: styd on u.p fr over 1f out: nvr nrr* **16/1**
065 **9** hd **Munaa's Dream**[41] 5368 3-8-2 **46** oh1........................... RaulDaSilva(3) 1 31
(Mrs K Burke) *prom: rdn over 1f out: wknd ins fnl f* **28/1**
0600 **10** 1 1/4 **Elegant Dancer (IRE)**[17] 6159 4-8-2 **46** oh1...........(p) NatashaEaton(5) 4 27
(Paul Green) *hld up: rdn over 2f out: a in rr* **100/1**
340 **11** 3/4 **Chambers (IRE)**[51] 5083 5-8-12 **54**........................... NathanAlison(3) 15 33
(Eric Alston) *chsd ldrs: rdn over 2f out: hung rt and wknd* **16/1**
0-0 **12** 5 **Bigern**[138] 2219 4-8-2 **46** oh1... NoelGarbutt(5) 13 12
(Michael Mullineaux) *mid-div: bhd fr 1/2-way* **80/1**
0204 **13** 5 **Kenswick**[26] 5843 4-8-9 **55**..(v) DavidWarren(7) 12 —
(Pat Eddery) *s.i.s: a in rr* **16/1**
03 **14** 6 **Mister Ben Vereen**[32] 5675 3-9-5 **60**...............................(b) AmyScott 14 —
(Eve Johnson Houghton) *chsd ldrs tl wknd over 2f out* **12/1**
0000 **15** 2 3/4 **Cwmni**[11] 6309 5-8-3 **47**.. ThomasBrown(5) 7 —
(Bryn Palling) *sn pushed along in rr: bhd fr 1/2-way* **20/1**

1m 25.01s (-1.19) **Going Correction** -0.175s/f (Firm)
WFA 3 from 4yo+ 2lb **15** Ran SP% **117.1**
Speed ratings (Par 101): **99,98,98,96,93 92,91,89,88,87 86,80,75,68,65**
toteswingers:1&2:£28.70, 2&3:£16.10, 1&3:£17.30 CSF £144.55 CT £1279.73 TOTE £15.90: £4.90, £3.10, £2.20; EX 250.60.
Owner Chris Hamilton **Bred** Majestic Thoroughbred Investments Inc **Trained** Sproxton, Leics

FOCUS
The first division of a low-grade apprentice handicap. The time was 0.35 seconds slower than the second division but the form appears sound enough for the grade.
Chambers(IRE) Official explanation: jockey said gelding hung right

6610 LEVERET APPRENTICE H'CAP (DIV II) 7f 9y
5:40 (5:40) (Class 6) (0-60,61) 3-Y-0+ **£1,293** (£385; £192; £96) **Stalls** High

Form RPR
0-00 **1** **Michael's Nook**[73] 4337 4-8-11 **50**... LMcNiff 5 64+
(David Barron) *w ldrs tl led 5f out: rdn over 1f out: styd on wl* **11/1**
-060 **2** 3 1/4 **Chicamia**[20] 6049 7-8-2 **46**... NoelGarbutt(5) 11 51+
(Michael Mullineaux) *s.i.s: outpcd and bhd: r.o wl ins fnl f: wnt 2nd nr fin: nt rch wnr* **25/1**
6035 **3** 1/2 **Strike A Deal (IRE)**[37] 5515 4-9-0 **58**........................... DannyBrock(5) 9 62
(Chris Wall) *sn outpcd: hdwy over 1f out: rdn to chse wnr ins fnl f tl towards fin: r.o* **6/1**[2]
0052 **4** 1 3/4 **Half A Crown (IRE)**[19] 6091 6-9-0 **58**......................... HannahNunn(5) 8 57
(Peter Salmon) *a.p: rdn to chse wnr over 1f out: tl no ex ins fnl f* **28/1**
5254 **5** 3/4 **Dancing Welcome**[5] 6479 5-8-13 **55**.....................(b) NathanAlison(3) 15 52+
(Milton Bradley) *sn outpcd: hung rt and r.o ins fnl f: nrst fin* **9/2**[1]
0054 **6** 1/2 **El Dececy (USA)**[39] 5436 7-9-0 **53**.........................(p) MatthewCosham 10 49
(Richard Guest) *chsd ldrs: hung rt almost thrght: rdn over 2f out: no ex ins fnl f* **9/2**[1]
6000 **7** 1 3/4 **Osgoodisgood**[19] 6105 3-8-2 **46** oh1...........................(t) RaulDaSilva(3) 7 37
(Stuart Williams) *prom: rdn over 2f out: wknd ins fnl f* **28/1**
434 **8** 1 **Avec Moi**[20] 6070 4-8-2 **46** oh1..................................... DanielHarris(5) 13 34
(Christine Dunnett) *mid-div: sn pushed along: hdwy over 1f out: nvr on terms* **20/1**
0600 **9** 1 1/4 **Spring Buck (IRE)**[8] 6411 6-9-3 **56**.................................. RyanPowell 1 41
(Paul Cole) *sn outpcd: rdn over 2f out: n.d* **33/1**
6340 **10** nk **Whitstable Native**[24] 5917 3-9-2 **57**............................ TobyAtkinson 2 41
(John Best) *led 2f: chsd ldrs: rdn 1/2-way: wknd over 1f out* **25/1**
0061 **11** 1/2 **Monashee Rock (IRE)**[11] 6309 6-9-8 **61** ow1............... BrianToomey 6 44
(Matthew Salaman) *sn pushed along in rr: wknd over 2f out* **13/2**[3]
03 **12** 1 1/4 **Wheatfield (IRE)**[34] 5617 7-8-3 **47**..........................(t) ThomasBrown(5) 4 26
(Thomas McGivern, Ire) *prom: rdn over 2f out: wknd over 1f out* **14/1**
4000 **13** 1 **My Best Man**[8] 6398 5-8-7 **46** oh1....................................... AdamCarter 14 23
(Tony Carroll) *bhd fr 1/2-way* **50/1**
2560 **14** 3/4 **Lough Corrib (USA)**[25] 5901 3-8-10 **51**.....................(p) AmyScott 12 26
(Alastair Lidderdale) *s.i.s: outpcd* **40/1**
0501 **15** shd **Avon Light**[22] 5996 3-8-9 **50**....................................(p) JamesRogers 3 24
(Milton Bradley) *chsd ldrs: rdn 1/2-way: wknd ins fnl f* **14/1**

1m 24.66s (-1.54) **Going Correction** -0.175s/f (Firm)
WFA 3 from 4yo+ 2lb **15** Ran SP% **116.6**
Speed ratings (Par 101): **101,97,96,94,93 93,91,90,88,88 87,86,85,84,84**
CSF £260.68 CT £1845.27 TOTE £10.60: £4.40, £8.60, £2.60; EX 398.90.
Owner Reg Gifford **Bred** D R Tucker **Trained** Maunby, N Yorks

FOCUS
The winning time was 0.35 seconds faster than the first division. The third to this year's form looks the best guide.
Chicamia Official explanation: jockey said mare was slowly away
Dancing Welcome Official explanation: jockey said mare was slowly away
El Dececy(USA) Official explanation: jockey said gelding hung right throughout
Spring Buck(IRE) Official explanation: jockey said gelding was denied a clear run
Wheatfield(IRE) Official explanation: jockey said mare was denied a clear run
Avon Light Official explanation: jockey said gelding hung right
T/Plt: £283.50 to a £1 stake. Pool of £59,122.76 - 152.19 winning tickets. T/Qpdt: £12.20 to a £1 stake. Pool of £4,802.56 - 290.04 winning tickets. CR

5596 SOUTHWELL (L-H)
Tuesday, October 4

OFFICIAL GOING: Standard
Wind: moderate 1/2 behind Weather: overcast

6611 20 YEARS AGO, I WON HERE NURSERY 1m (F)
2:20 (2:22) (Class 6) (0-60,60) 2-Y-0 **£1,704** (£503; £251) **Stalls** Low

Form RPR
2645 **1** **Vociferous (USA)**[5] 6487 2-9-7 **60**.......................... SilvestreDeSousa 3 78+
(Mark Johnston) *mde all: wnt clr 3f out: heavily eased fnl 100yds* **4/1**[1]
0460 **2** 10 **Man Of My Word**[27] 5825 2-9-4 **60**.................................. BillyCray(3) 13 49
(David Nicholls) *chsd ldrs: wnt 2nd over 4f out: kpt on same pce* **11/1**
000 **3** shd **Bada Bing**[38] 5464 2-8-12 **51**...................................... MartinLane 2 40
(David Nicholls) *prom: wnt 3rd over 2f out: kpt on same pce* **18/1**
600 **4** 3 **Disco Sensation**[20] 6048 2-9-4 **57**................................. PatCosgrave 12 39
(David Nicholls) *s.i.s: in rr: hdwy on outer over 2f out: kpt on: nvr nr ldrs* **10/1**
000 **5** 3 3/4 **Singspiel Spirit**[19] 6100 2-8-13 **52**........................... TomMcLaughlin 10 25
(Clive Brittain) *s.i.s: sme hdwy on ins over 2f out: nvr nr ldrs* **16/1**
5443 **6** hd **Manderston**[19] 6101 2-8-10 **54**..................................... DarylByrne(5) 5 27
(Mark Johnston) *mid-div: drvn over 3f out: one pce* **9/1**[3]
066 **7** 2 1/2 **Absolute Fun (IRE)**[20] 6047 2-9-7 **60**.......................... RobertWinston 9 27
(Tim Easterby) *chsd ldrs: wknd appr fnl f* **11/2**[2]
3030 **8** 5 **Rosie's Lady (IRE)**[54] 4943 2-9-0 **53**............................ StephenCraine 8 9
(David O'Meara) *chsd ldrs: drvn over 3f out: wknd 2f out* **12/1**
000 **9** 4 1/2 **Blue Ridges (IRE)**[78] 4140 2-8-13 **52**................................... TomEaves 1 —
(Geoffrey Harker) *chsd ldrs: lost pl 3f out* **10/1**
0000 **10** 3/4 **Indyend**[20] 6043 2-8-8 **47**..(b) PaddyAspell 6 —
(Tim Easterby) *mid-div: lost pl over 3f out* **40/1**
6660 **11** 1 **Ingleby Angel (IRE)**[27] 5817 2-9-0 **58**......................... AshleyMorgan(5) 4 —
(David O'Meara) *chsd ldrs: drvn over 3f out: wknd over 2f out* **10/1**
0600 **12** 1/2 **Vergrigio (IRE)**[6] 6443 2-9-7 **60**.................................(b[1]) EddieCreighton 11 —
(Brian Meehan) *s.i.s: in rr: reminders after 1f: sn bhd* **16/1**
000 **13** 19 **King Fong**[25] 5891 2-8-12 **51** ow1.................................... StevieDonohoe 14 —
(John Ryan) *in rr: bhd over 4f out: t.o over 2f out* **22/1**
025 **14** 28 **Champagne Valley**[27] 5819 2-9-1 **54**............................. TonyHamilton 7 —
(Sharon Watt) *sn bhd: t.o over 2f out: virtually p.u* **18/1**

1m 47.2s (3.50) **Going Correction** +0.40s/f (Slow) **14** Ran SP% **117.8**
Speed ratings (Par 93): **98,88,87,84,81 80,78,73,68,68 67,66,47,19**
toteswingers:1&2:£10.00, 2&3:£8.60, 1&3:£17.40 CSF £46.71 CT £734.56 TOTE £4.80: £1.40, £3.20, £5.10; EX 44.20.
Owner Sheikh Hamdan Bin Mohammed Al Maktoum **Bred** Darley **Trained** Middleham Moor, N Yorks

FOCUS
A moderate nursery in which the winner produced much-improved form. He could be worth more and looks one to be with on this surface.

NOTEBOOK
Vociferous(USA) offered little over 7f on Polytrack the week before, taking her record to 0-7, but progressed significantly for this step up in trip and switch back to Fibresand for the first time since her 6f debut - this took her sire's record to 10-40 on the surface. She was heavily eased late on, looking value for more than 15l, but had been allowed to dominate moderate rivals on a surface that clearly very much suited and she won't appeal as one to back elsewhere, particularly when reassessed, until proving herself more versatile. Still, she's smartly bred - out of Albany and Cherry Hinton winner Sander Camillo - and this will have increased her paddock value. (tchd 7-2)
Man Of My Word, up in trip, hadn't shown much on two previous starts here and it's questionable what he achieved this time. (op 12-1)
Bada Bing hadn't shown much in three turf maidens over 6f-7f. This was a bit more encouraging and she might do better on Polytrack considering she's related to a few winners on that surface. (tchd 20-1)
Disco Sensation is a half-sister to dual Fibresand winner Je Suis Unrockstar, by a sire with a good record on the surface. She was out the back after a sluggish start but made late headway and can probably do better as she gains experience. (op 12-1)
Singspiel Spirit was another who was doing his best work at the finish after starting slowly and not travelling early. (op 22-1)

6612 BRITISH STALLION STUDS SUPPORTING BRITISH RACING E B F MAIDEN FILLIES' STKS 6f (F)
2:50 (2:51) (Class 5) 2-Y-0 **£3,408** (£1,006; £503) **Stalls** Low

Form RPR
0236 **1** **Scrooby Doo**[26] 5847 2-8-11 60.. BillyCray(3) 5 67
(David Nicholls) *chsd ldr: chal over 1f out: led jst ins fnl f: all out* **7/2**[2]
2 nk **Subtle Knife** 2-9-0 0.. WilliamCarson 1 66
(Giles Bravery) *led: qcknd 3f out: hdd jst ins fnl f: kpt on nr fin* **9/2**[3]
0 **3** 5 **Athenian (IRE)**[13] 6252 2-9-0 0...................................... StevieDonohoe 2 51
(Sir Mark Prescott Bt) *sn chsng ldrs: kpt on one pce fnl 2f* **28/1**
34 **4** 1 **By Invitation (USA)**[69] 4430 2-9-0 0................................. JimCrowley 3 48
(Ralph Beckett) *dwlt: sn drvn along: kpt on fnl f: nvr a threat* **11/8**[1]
5 1/2 **Hurriya** 2-9-0 0.. WilliamBuick 8 47
(Saeed Bin Suroor) *trckd ldrs: edgd lft over 2f out: kpt on one pce: eased nr fin* **9/2**[3]
6040 **6** 7 **Angel Of Hope (IRE)**[40] 5399 2-9-0 56..........................(p) TomEaves 6 26
(Bryan Smart) *chsd ldrs: reminders and lost pl over 3f out* **20/1**
30 **7** 3 1/4 **Medam**[29] 5786 2-9-0 0... RobbieFitzpatrick 7 16
(Shaun Harris) *swtchd lft after s: in rr: sme hdwy over 2f out: wknd over 1f out* **80/1**
8 hd **Sweetnessandlight** 2-9-0 0.. MichaelStainton 4 15
(Jason Ward) *s.s: bucked repeatedly immediately after s: eased and sn t.o: kpt on fnl 2f: nvr on terms* **100/1**

1m 19.34s (2.84) **Going Correction** +0.40s/f (Slow) **8** Ran SP% **111.1**
Speed ratings (Par 92): **97,96,89,88,87 78,74,74**
CSF £18.02 TOTE £2.70: £1.20, £1.80, £8.70; EX 22.00.
Owner P J Dixon & The Nulli Secundus Friends **Bred** Mrs Yvette Dixon **Trained** Sessay, N Yorks

FOCUS
A modest maiden - the winner came into this officially rated just 60. She sets the level with the first two clear.

NOTEBOOK
Scrooby Doo again flashed her tail continually under pressure but proved game enough to record her first success on her seventh start. She won't appeal as one to back to follow up (op 3-1 tchd 5-2)
Subtle Knife, a half-sister to a dual 6f winner, was the subject of a significant gamble having been 16-1 in a place in the morning. She has certainly been well educated as it's rare to see a newcomer so professional through the early stages here, showing good pace to lead, and she kept on strongly in the straight, including coming back at the winner near the line. It's tempting to say there won't be much improvement to come, but she has some size about her. (op 5-1 tchd 11-2)
Athenian(IRE), well beaten on her debut over 5f at Kempton, showed more this time. This wasn't much of a race, though, and she probably remains best watched until handicapping. (op 25-1)
By Invitation(USA), absent since being beaten at odds on at Leicester in July, did not look happy at any stage on her return. She didn't face the kickback but will still have a bit to prove next time. (op 7-4)
Hurriya, the first foal of a 1m2f winner in France, was weak in the market considering her trainer's record at the track (6-11 with juveniles last five years prior to this) and offered nothing. Saeed Bin Suroor said beforehand the filly "doesn't show much in the mornings". (op 7-2)
Medam Official explanation: trainer said filly had a breathing problem

Sweetnessandlight Official explanation: jockey said filly bucked leaving stalls

6613 32RED H'CAP 1m 4f (F)
3:20 (3:20) (Class 6) (0-55,55) 3-Y-0+ £1,704 (£503; £251) Stalls Low

Form RPR

2230 **1** **Master Of Song**[20] 6049 4-9-3 **51**..........................(p) RussKennemore 14 66+
(Roy Bowring) *t.k.h: swtchd lft after s: w ldr: led 5f out: clr over 2f out: eased fnl 75yds* **11/2**[2]

0605 **2** *4½* **Blue Cossack (IRE)**[5] 6493 3-8-13 **54**.........................(be[1]) LiamKeniry 2 57
(Mark Usher) *chsd ldrs: wnt 2nd over 4f out: kpt on same pce fnl 3f* **16/1**

0004 **3** *1½* **Aureate**[12] 6287 7-9-7 **55**.. NeilChalmers 1 55
(Brian Forsey) *chsd ldrs: wnt 3rd 3f out: kpt on same pce* **12/1**

000- **4** *5* **Slip**[43] 4980 6-9-7 **55**.. FergusSweeney 3 47
(Tim Vaughan) *in rr and sn drvn along: hdwy 3f out: kpt on: nvr nr ldrs* **18/1**

040 **5** *1¾* **Illustration (IRE)**[14] 6242 3-9-0 **55**............................ SilvestreDeSousa 7 45
(Mark Johnston) *sn in rr and drvn along: hmpd bnd after 2f: reminders over 5f out: hdwy 3f out: kpt on: nvr on terms* **3/1**[1]

0060 **6** *1¼* **Dunaskin (IRE)**[33] 5643 11-8-9 **46**..........................(b) RobertLButler(3) 4 34
(Richard Guest) *led tl 5f out: one pce fnl 3f* **66/1**

0-44 **7** *6* **Astrolibra**[37] 5519 7-9-5 **53**.. WilliamBuick 8 31
(Mark H Tompkins) *in tch: reminders after 3f: outpcd over 3f out: no threat after* **6/1**[3]

05-0 **8** *3¾* **Hammer**[12] 6287 6-8-7 **48**.. JordanNason(7) 13 20
(Geoffrey Harker) *mid-div: effrt 5f out: lost pl 3f out* **33/1**

4226 **9** *1½* **Politbureau**[31] 5739 4-9-6 **54**.. PaddyAspell 5 24
(Michael Easterby) *chsd ldrs: wknd over 2f out* **7/1**

2105 **10** *¾* **Obara D'Avril (FR)**[14] 6236 9-8-10 **47**............................ PaulPickard(3) 6 15
(Simon West) *s.i.s: in rr and sn drvn along: nvr on terms* **25/1**

/664 **11** *1¼* **Graycliffe (IRE)**[138] 2237 5-9-0 **48**................................ StephenCraine 10 14
(Jennie Candlish) *hld up in mid-div: lost pl 4f out* **20/1**

-410 **12** *55* **Jackie Kiely**[224] 645 10-9-6 **54**................................(tp) WilliamCarson 9 —
(Roy Brotherton) *mid-div: sn drvn along: bhd fnl 3f: virtually p.u: wl t.o* **18/1**

/F3- **13** *12* **Altos Reales**[418] 1207 7-9-3 **51**.................................... JamieGoldstein 12 —
(Michael Scudamore) *sn in rr: lost tch over 5f out: virtually p.u and sn t.o* **40/1**

-600 **14** *nse* **Baoli**[40] 5406 4-9-3 **51**.. JimCrowley 11 —
(Noel Chance) *hld up in rr: reminders 6f out: sn bhd: t.o 3f out: eased* **33/1**

2m 46.59s (5.59) **Going Correction** +0.40s/f (Slow)
WFA 3 from 4yo+ 7lb **14** Ran SP% **117.4**
Speed ratings (Par 101): **97,94,93,89,88 87,83,81,80,79 78,42,34,34**
toteswingers:1&2:£19.20, 2&3:£26.40, 1&3:£29.00 CSF £83.50 CT £1017.63 TOTE £8.50: £2.20, £4.70, £4.40; EX 96.60.
Owner S R Bowring **Bred** S R Bowring **Trained** Edwinstowe, Notts
■ Stewards' Enquiry : Jordan Nason two-day ban: careless riding (Oct 18-19)

FOCUS
A moderate handicap with the favourite disappointing and, as usual for this sort of distance at Southwell, they finished strung out. The time was 2.5 seconds slower than the following maiden, a useful contest. The form looks reasonable rated through the runner-up to his recent mark.

6614 DAVE MORGAN MEMORIAL MAIDEN STKS 1m 4f (F)
3:50 (3:50) (Class 5) 3-Y-0+ £2,264 (£673; £336; £168) Stalls Low

Form RPR

0224 **1** **Deraasa (USA)**[20] 6054 3-8-12 77.................................... TadhgO'Shea 3 88+
(Saeed Bin Suroor) *trckd ldrs: drvn to ld 3f out: rdn clr over 1f out: heavily eased last 100yds* **3/1**[2]

3 **2** *10* **Eyedoro (USA)**[10] 6349 3-9-3 0................................ SilvestreDeSousa 2 75
(Mark Johnston) *w ldr: chal over 4f out: drvn 3f out: one pce* **2/1**[1]

22 **3** *2¾* **Sweet Lavender (IRE)**[20] 6054 3-8-12 0............................ WilliamBuick 1 66
(Saeed Bin Suroor) *led: qcknd pce over 4f out: hdd 3f out: wl hld 3rd whn eased last 75yds* **2/1**[1]

34 **4** *8* **Tricksofthetrade (IRE)**[10] 6349 5-9-10 0.......................... RobertWinston 4 58
(Alan Swinbank) *dwlt: sn drvn along in last: hdwy to trck ldrs over 8f out: drvn and outpcd over 4f out: sn lost pl* **5/1**[3]

2m 44.09s (3.09) **Going Correction** +0.40s/f (Slow)
WFA 3 from 5yo 7lb **4** Ran SP% **108.3**
Speed ratings (Par 103): **105,98,96,91**
CSF £9.22 TOTE £4.20; EX 10.80.
Owner Godolphin **Bred** Shadwell Farm LLC **Trained** Newmarket, Suffolk

FOCUS
An uncompetitive maiden, but all four runners had shown at least fair form. The time was 2.5 seconds quicker than the earlier Class 6 handicap. The form looks sound with the runner-up to his debut form.

6615 £32 FREE AT 32RED.COM (S) STKS 5f (F)
4:20 (4:20) (Class 6) 3-4-Y-0 £1,704 (£503; £251) Stalls High

Form RPR

06 **1** **Bond Blade**[39] 5443 3-8-9 0.. DaleSwift(3) 3 68
(Geoffrey Oldroyd) *s.i.s: hdwy over 2f out: led jst ins fnl f: drvn out* **20/1**

2 *1* **Coastal Passage** 3-8-9 0.. DominicFox(3) 5 64
(Alan Bailey) *s.i.s: hdwy and edgd rt over 1f out: kpt on wl* **13/2**[3]

0150 **3** *½* **Suddenly Susan (IRE)**[27] 5824 3-8-6 60................(b) LeonnaMayor(7) 9 63
(David Nicholls) *trckd ldrs on inner: led over 3f out: hdd jst ins fnl f: edgd lft and kpt on same pce* **13/2**[3]

5000 **4** *1½* **Je Suis Unrockstar**[35] 5600 3-8-9 59.............................(p) BillyCray(3) 1 57
(David Nicholls) *racd wd: chsd ldrs: kpt on same pce ins fnl f* **16/1**

0420 **5** *shd* **Winning Draw (IRE)**[29] 5787 3-8-4 55....................(b) DeclanCannon(3) 2 52
(Paul Midgley) *chsd ldrs: sn drvn along: one pce fnl 2f* **9/2**[2]

030- **6** *3¼* **Good Timin'**[402] 5523 3-8-12 60..............................(b[1]) SilvestreDeSousa 8 45
(David Brown) *chsd ldrs: rdn over 2f out: wknd ins fnl f* **15/2**

1050 **7** *6* **Nine Before Ten (IRE)**[6] 6456 3-8-10 74......................(t) RyanClark(3) 7 24
(John Balding) *chsd ldrs: rdn over 2f out: wknd over 1f out: eased towards fin* **6/4**[1]

0600 **8** *10* **Hereselle (IRE)**[64] 4607 3-8-2 54.................................... ChrisDCogan(5) 6 —
(Michael Chapman) *led tl over 3f out: hung rt and lost pl 2f out: sn bhd and eased* **66/1**

60.41 secs (0.71) **Going Correction** +0.175s/f (Slow) **8** Ran SP% **108.7**
Speed ratings (Par 101): **101,99,98,96,96 90,81,65**
CSF £129.43 TOTE £30.80: £4.90, £2.40, £2.50; EX 152.90.There was no bid for the winner. Coastal Passage was claimed by W McKay for £5000.
Owner R C Bond **Bred** Bond Thoroughbred Corporation **Trained** Brawby, N Yorks

FOCUS
A moderate seller rated through the third to her recent best.

6616 32REDBINGO.COM H'CAP (DIV I) 7f (F)
4:50 (4:51) (Class 5) (0-75,75) 3-Y-0+ £2,264 (£673; £336; £168) Stalls Low

Form RPR

500 **1** **Il Battista**[18] 6133 3-8-8 **67**....................................(be[1]) DeclanCannon(3) 5 78+
(Alan McCabe) *chsd ldrs: drvn over 4f out: led 2f out: styd on wl: eased towards fin* **7/2**[2]

0005 **2** *1½* **J R Hartley**[39] 5439 3-8-12 **75**................................(p) JustinNewman(7) 11 81
(Bryan Smart) *s.i.s: sn w ldrs on outer: rdn and edgd lft over 2f out: kpt on same pce ins fnl f* **14/1**

0300 **3** *1¾* **Totally Trusted**[35] 5598 3-8-2 **61** oh3.................................. BillyCray(3) 2 62
(David Nicholls) *chsd ldrs: kpt on same pce fnl 2f* **40/1**

3000 **4** *½* **Watch Chain (IRE)**[5] 6479 4-8-0 **61**.................................(p) RyanTate(7) 4 61
(Alan McCabe) *in rr: hdwy to chse ldrs over 3f out: n.m.r and swtchd rt over 2f out: kpt on same pce over 1f out* **14/1**

0050 **5** *¾* **Striker Torres (IRE)**[38] 5488 5-8-11 **68**............................ DaleSwift(3) 3 66
(Geoffrey Oldroyd) *in rr: sn drvn along: gd hdwy over 1f out: hung lft: styng on at fin* **5/1**[3]

5120 **6** *1* **Zarius**[98] 3495 4-8-7 **61**.. SilvestreDeSousa 1 56+
(Chris Wall) *n.m.r on inner and dropped in rr after 1f: hdwy and swtchd outside over 1f out: gng on at fin* **11/2**

1065 **7** *1* **April Fool**[23] 5970 7-9-2 **70**.................................(b) LukeMorris 10 63
(Ronald Harris) *swtchd lft after s: led: hdd 2f out: wknd ins fnl f* **3/1**[1]

4560 **8** *8* **Bookiesindex Boy**[26] 5846 7-8-12 **66**............................ TonyCulhane 6 37
(J R Jenkins) *trckd ldrs: hmpd over 2f out: wknd over 1f out* **33/1**

3000 **9** *3* **Frognal (IRE)**[10] 6351 5-8-10 **67**..............................(t[1]) RobertLButler(3) 8 30
(Richard Guest) *hld up in rr: effrt over 2f out: sn wknd* **22/1**

6433 **10** *5* **Rubenstar (IRE)**[139] 2206 8-9-3 **71**.............................. StephenCraine 9 20
(Patrick Morris) *dwlt: hld up in rr: effrt 3f out: sn wknd* **16/1**

2006 **11** *7* **Just Five (IRE)**[16] 6188 5-9-4 **72**.................................... TomEaves 7 —
(John Weymes) *in rr on outer and sn drvn along: bhd fnl 3f* **16/1**

1m 33.18s (2.88) **Going Correction** +0.40s/f (Slow)
WFA 3 from 4yo+ 2lb **11** Ran SP% **114.1**
Speed ratings (Par 103): **99,97,95,94,93 92,91,82,79,73 65**
toteswingers:1&2:£10.20, 2&3:£26.60, 1&3:£35.10 CSF £48.82 CT £1682.38 TOTE £7.00: £2.20, £3.70, £9.80; EX 54.70.
Owner Alotincommon Partnership **Bred** Cheveley Park Stud Ltd **Trained** Averham Park, Notts

FOCUS
A modest handicap in which the pace was contested. The time was 0.42 seconds slower than the second division and the placed horses ran close to their marks, while this was the winner's best effort since last winter.

6617 32REDBINGO.COM H'CAP (DIV II) 7f (F)
5:20 (5:24) (Class 5) (0-75,72) 3-Y-0+ £2,264 (£673; £336; £163) Stalls Low

Form RPR

5310 **1** **Eastern Hills**[55] 4900 6-9-3 **71**....................................(p) MartinHarley(3) 8 82
(Alan McCabe) *w ldrs on outer: led 2f out: edgd lft ins fnl f: hld on wl* **14/1**

3162 **2** *½* **Boy The Bell**[9] 6382 4-9-6 **71**.................................... SilvestreDeSousa 5 81
(Brian Ellison) *w ldrs: chal over 2f out: crowded 100yds out: kpt on: no ex in clsng stages* **11/4**[2]

2223 **3** *1* **Elusive Warrior (USA)**[35] 5600 8-8-0 **58**.....................(p) NoraLooby(7) 4 65
(Alan McCabe) *led early: chsd ldrs: effrt on ins over 2f out: kpt on same pce ins fnl f* **10/1**

0201 **4** *2¼* **Beechcraft Baron (IRE)**[47] 5212 3-9-0 **70**................. GilmarPereira(3) 2 71
(William Haggas) *sn led: rdn over 2f out: sn hdd: wknd last 100yds* **13/8**[1]

260 **5** *1* **Conry (IRE)**[10] 6327 5-9-7 **72**.. StephenCraine 3 70
(Patrick Morris) *dwlt: in rr: effrt over 3f out: kpt on down wd outside fnl f: nvr nr ldrs* **20/1**

561 **6** *1½* **National Hope (IRE)**[34] 5624 3-9-3 **70**...........................(t) TonyCulhane 6 64
(George Baker) *chsd ldrs: drvn over 4f out: sn outpcd: kpt on ins fnl f* **14/1**

4263 **7** *16* **Red Marling (IRE)**[61] 4706 3-8-9 **67**......................... MatthewLawson(5) 7 18
(Charles Hills) *s.i.s: hdwy on outer to chse ldrs over 3f out: sn lost pl: eased ins fnl f* **12/1**

0302 **8** *24* **Llewellyn**[33] 5649 3-9-2 **69**.. StevieDonohoe 9 —
(James Fanshawe) *s.i.s: in rr on outer: drvn over 3f out: bhd whn eased over 2f out: t.o* [illegible]

0050 **9** *31* **Style Margi (IRE)**[22] 5995 3-9-0 **67**................................ PatCosgrave 1 —
(Ed de Giles) *rrd s: drvn to chse ldrs on ins: lost pl over 3f out: bhd and eased over 2f out: sn t.o* **66/1**

1m 32.76s (2.46) **Going Correction** +0.40s/f (Slow)
WFA 3 from 4yo+ 2lb **9** Ran SP% **112.2**
Speed ratings (Par 103): **101,100,99,96,95 93,75,48,12**
toteswingers:1&2:£8.00, 2&3:£3.80, 1&3:£9.20 CSF £50.76 CT £411.35 TOTE £17.40: £3.80, £1.10, £2.80; EX 46.60.
Owner Charles Wentworth **Bred** Azienda Agricola Patrizia **Trained** Averham Park, Notts

FOCUS
The time was 0.42 seconds quicker than the first division, yet nothing got involved from off the pace. The third setrs the standard.
Llewellyn Official explanation: jockey said gelding never travelled

6618 32REDBET.COM H'CAP 6f (F)
5:50 (5:54) (Class 6) (0-55,61) 3-Y-0+ £1,704 (£503; £251) Stalls Low

Form RPR

0561 **1** **Riflessione**[4] 6501 5-9-8 **61** 6ex.......................................(v) LukeMorris 6 74+
(Ronald Harris) *mid-div: n.m.r bnd over 4f out: hdwy on inner to chal over 1f out: sn led: edgd rt and styd on wl: readily* **11/4**[1]

6050 **2** *2¼* **Lethal**[11] 6304 8-8-8 **50**..(p) DaleSwift(3) 1 56
(Richard Price) *chsd ldrs: chal over 1f out: styd on same pce last 150yds* **10/1**

0005 **3** *1¼* **Tenancy (IRE)**[15] 6213 7-8-11 **50**............................ RobbieFitzpatrick 5 52
(Shaun Harris) *led: hdd 1f out: kpt on same pce* **25/1**

440 **4** *½* **Stylistickhill (IRE)**[74] 4282 3-9-1 **55**..........................(tp) MartinLane 9 55+
(David Nicholls) *in rr: n.m.r after 100yds: hdwy on ins over 2f out: kpt on ins fnl f* **9/1**[3]

0240 **5** *3¼* **Fluctuation (IRE)**[28] 5803 3-8-11 **54**........................(b[1]) RyanClark(3) 7 44
(Ian Williams) *dwlt: sn chsng ldrs: upsides over 1f out: wknd last 150yds* **7/2**[2]

4026 **6** *¾* **Greek Secret**[11] 6304 8-9-2 **55**................................(b) RussKennemore 2 43
(Paul Midgley) *trckd ldrs: wknd ins fnl f* **10/1**

4504 **7** *3¾* **Dotty Darroch**[13] 6261 3-9-0 **54**.................................... LeeNewman 14 30
(Robin Bastiman) *in rr: hdwy over 3f out: one pce whn eased last 100yds* **14/1**

-000 **8** *1¼* **Cut The Cackle (IRE)**[6] 6444 5-8-13 **55**................(t) RobertLButler(3) 13 27
(Richard Guest) *s.i.s: detached 3f out: kpt on fnl 2f* **28/1**

004 **9** 2 3/4 **Gala Spirit (IRE)**[24] 5943 4-8-12 **51**................................ TonyHamilton 4 14
(Peter Niven) *mid-div: effrt over 2f out: wknd over 1f out* **10/1**

6300 **10** 3/4 **Needwood Park**[17] 6158 3-8-12 **52**................................(p) TomEaves 3 12
(Ray Craggs) *sn bhd: detached 3f out: sme late hdwy* **25/1**

0310 **11** 1 1/4 **Porthgwidden Beach (USA)**[11] 6304 3-9-1 **55**..............(t) LiamKeniry 8 11
(Anthony Middleton) *chsd ldrs: wknd 2f out: eased in clsng stages* **20/1**

6043 **12** 1 1/2 **Sophie's Beau (USA)**[42] 5339 4-8-11 **50**............... SilvestreDeSousa 10 —
(Michael Chapman) *s.i.s: sn chsng ldrs: outpcd and lost pl over 3f out: sme hdwy on outside over 2f out: sn wknd: bhd whn eased ins fnl f* **16/1**

0-00 **13** 1/2 **Drumpellier (IRE)**[9] 6386 4-8-9 **51**.............................. PaulPickard(3) 12 —
(Simon West) *chsd ldrs on outer: lost pl over 3f out: bhd whn eased ins fnl f* **25/1**

1m 18.92s (2.42) **Going Correction** +0.40s/f (Slow)
WFA 3 from 4yo+ 1lb **13** Ran SP% **118.5**
Speed ratings (Par 101): **99,96,94,93,89 88,83,81,78,77 75,73,72**
toteswingers:1&2:£8.90, 2&3:£46.80, 1&3:£26.10. Totesuper 7: Win: Not won. Place: Not won. CSF £27.96 CT £578.88 TOTE £3.40: £1.80, £5.40, £10.60; EX 24.30.
Owner Mrs Jan Adams **Bred** Tom & Evelyn Yates **Trained** Earlswood, Monmouths

FOCUS
A moderate sprint handicap best rated around the placed horses.
T/Plt: £912.20 to a £1 stake. Pool of £62,855.34 - 50.30 winning tickets. T/Qpdt: £195.00 to a £1 stake. Pool of £4,217.26 - 16.00 winning tickets. WG

6471 KEMPTON (A.W) (R-H)
Wednesday, October 5

OFFICIAL GOING: Standard
Wind: Strong, half behind Weather: Fine becoming cloudy with occasional drizzle

6619 FREE ENTRY FOR BETDAQ MEMBERS H'CAP 5f (P)
5:40 (5:40) (Class 7) (0-50,50) 3-Y-O+ **£1,455** (£433; £216; £108) **Stalls** Low

Form RPR

6005 **1** **Vhujon (IRE)**[18] 6175 6-8-13 **49**..............................(t) RobbieFitzpatrick 6 62
(Peter Grayson) *sn outpcd in last pair and pushed along: prog wl over 1f out: r.o fnl f to ld last stride* **8/1**

5540 **2** *hd* **Cliffords Reprieve**[9] 6398 3-9-0 **50**............................ EddieCreighton 8 62+
(Eric Wheeler) *chsd clr ldr: clsd to ld jst over 1f out: hanging but sn 3 l clr: idled and hdd post* **16/1**

0050 **3** 2 3/4 **Clerical (USA)**[20] 6105 5-8-11 **47**.....................................(p) ShaneKelly 9 49
(Robert Cowell) *sn outpcd in last gp: hanging fr over 1f out: styd on fnl f to take 3rd post* **5/1**[3]

5002 **4** *shd* **Wreningham**[56] 4930 6-9-0 **50**..................................... WilliamCarson 11 52
(Stuart Williams) *chsd clr ldng pair: rdn 2f out: kpt on to take 2nd briefly ins fnl f: sn wknd: lost 3rd post* **4/1**[2]

5033 **5** 2 1/2 **Cloth Ears**[15] 6238 5-8-7 **50**.......................................(be) DannyBrock(7) 7 43
(Phil McEntee) *led and spreadeagled field: hdd & wknd jst over 1f out* **7/1**

6536 **6** 3/4 **Radiator Rooney (IRE)**[121] 2755 8-8-11 **50**................ KieranO'Neill(3) 3 40
(Patrick Morris) *s.s: outpcd in last gp: nvr on terms* **6/1**

0404 **7** 1 **Jemimaville (IRE)**[14] 6258 4-8-11 **47**................................ LukeMorris 2 34
(Giles Bravery) *chsd clr ldng trio: rdn 2f out: keeping on and ch of a pl whn hmpd 100yds out: eased* **7/2**[1]

5604 **8** 3 1/4 **Mi Sun Donk**[27] 5865 3-8-8 **47**.. BillyCray(3) 5 22
(Brett Johnson) *hld up: sn bdly outpcd: a bhd* **9/1**

60.49 secs (-0.01) **Going Correction** -0.075s/f (Stan) **8** Ran SP% **112.7**
Speed ratings (Par 97): **97,96,92,92,88 86,85,80**
toteswingers: 1&2 £9.40, 2&3 £8.90, 1&3 £10.90 CSF £118.47 CT £700.72 TOTE £6.30: £1.90, £5.20, £2.10; EX 50.50 Trifecta £423.20 Pool: £8,637.11 - 15.10 winning units..
Owner Richard Teatum **Bred** Robert Berns **Trained** Formby, Lancs

FOCUS
A low-grade handicap run at a strong gallop. The winner raced centre to far side in the straight.
Jemimaville(IRE) Official explanation: jockey said filly was denied a clear run

6620 BETDAQ MULTIPLES BRITISH STALLIONS STUDS E B F MAIDEN STKS 5f (P)
6:10 (6:10) (Class 5) 2-Y-O **£3,234** (£962; £481; £240) **Stalls** Low

Form RPR

0635 **1** **Bookiesindexdotnet**[43] 5351 2-8-12 58...................... RichardHughes 6 63
(J R Jenkins) *disp ld thrght: kpt on gamely fnl f: jst hld on* **7/1**[3]

4626 **2** *shd* **Sunrise Dance**[11] 6323 2-8-9 78................................. HarryBentley(3) 11 63
(Alan Jarvis) *w wnr thrght: cajoled along fnl f: nt qckn last strides* **4/6**[1]

05 **3** 2 3/4 **Gabrial's Bounty (IRE)**[9] 6406 2-9-3 0......................... SamHitchcott 8 58+
(Mick Channon) *dwlt: poorly plcd in rr: prog 2f out: pushed along and styd on to take 3rd fnl f: clsng at fin* **5/1**[2]

0 **4** 1 **Compton Rainbow**[7] 6441 2-8-12 0...........................(t[1]) SteveDrowne 2 49+
(Hans Adielsson) *taken down early: chsd ldrs: outpcd over 2f out: kpt on fr over 1f out: n.d* **16/1**

5045 **5** 2 3/4 **Mr Hendrix**[44] 5316 2-9-3 52... WilliamCarson 1 44
(Brett Johnson) *t.k.h: chsd ldng pair: outpcd over 2f out: wknd over 1f out* **16/1**

00 **6** 2 3/4 **Electric Daydream (IRE)**[14] 6252 2-8-12 0...................... LiamKeniry 3 29
(J S Moore) *chsd ldng pair tl wknd over 1f out* **33/1**

0440 **7** 3/4 **Nude (IRE)**[20] 6101 2-8-9 50.......................................(b) KieranO'Neill(3) 5 27
(Sylvester Kirk) *sn pushed along in midfield: outpcd and struggling fr 1/2-way* **25/1**

0 **8** *nse* **My Name Is Sam**[35] 5613 2-9-3 0....................................... LukeMorris 7 31
(Ronald Harris) *dwlt: racd wd in rr bnd over 3f out: nvr on terms after* **25/1**

05 **9** 8 **Sandbanks**[11] 6352 2-8-12 0.. JamesDoyle 10 —
(Sylvester Kirk) *a struggling in rr: wl bhd fnl f* **50/1**

60 **10** *hd* **Surrey Spirit**[26] 5889 2-8-9 0.. JohnFahy(3) 9 —
(Harry Dunlop) *racd wd bnd over 3f out: a wl in rr* **33/1**

11 34 **Azamara Star** 2-8-12 0.. RobbieFitzpatrick 12 —
(Derek Shaw) *sn t.o* **66/1**

60.22 secs (-0.28) **Going Correction** -0.075s/f (Stan) **11** Ran SP% **117.9**
Speed ratings (Par 95): **99,98,94,92,88 84,82,82,69,69 15**
toteswingers: 1&2 £1.80, 2&3 £4.80, 1&3 £1.80 CSF £11.49 TOTE £4.90: £1.50, £1.10, £2.10; EX 15.70 Trifecta £43.30 Pool: £9,931.43 - 169.54 winning units..
Owner Bookmakers Index Ltd **Bred** D R Tucker **Trained** Royston, Herts

FOCUS
A modest and uncompetitive event in which the gallop was reasonable and the first two, who raced close to the inside rail, pulled a few lengths clear. The form is weak and probably not a race to be with until proven otherwise.

NOTEBOOK
Bookiesindexdotnet had the run of the race and showed improved form and a good attitude to thwart a (below-par) rival who would have been conceding 20lb had this been a handicap. She should stay 6f and it will be interesting to see what the handicapper makes of this. (op 6-1)
Sunrise Dance looked to have strong claims, despite her wide draw, in an uncompetitive event on her all-weather debut but, although just touched off, she looked some way below her best against a rival officially rated 20lb her inferior. She pulled clear of the rest and is capable of picking up a weak event but she doesn't look one for skinny odds. (op 4-5)
Gabrial's Bounty(IRE) has improved steadily with every outing and posted her best effort over an inadequate trip on this all-weather debut. The return to 6f plus and the step into handicaps will suit and she should be able to pick up a small event. (op 6-1)
Compton Rainbow, who wore a first-time tongue-tie and hood, should be seen in a more favourable light in ordinary handicaps. She bettered her debut effort by some way, she will be suited by further (half-sister to a Queen's Vase winner) and may do better.
Mr Hendrix had the run of the race but again underlined his vulnerability in this type of event. (op 14-1)
Azamara Star Official explanation: jockey said filly was slowly away

6621 BACK OR LAY AT BETDAQ.COM H'CAP (DIV I) 1m 4f (P)
6:40 (6:41) (Class 6) (0-65,66) 3-Y-O+ **£1,617** (£481; £240; £120) **Stalls** Centre

Form RPR

-340 **1** **Deceptive**[117] 2874 3-9-1 **61**... SteveDrowne 12 77+
(Roger Charlton) *trckd ldrs: smooth prog to ld 2f out: shkn up and drew rt away: eased last 50yds* **12/1**

5400 **2** 7 **Bin End**[37] 3546 5-9-3 **61**... LeeNewnes(5) 5 64
(Barry Brennan) *hld up in midfield disputing 7th: rdn over 2f out: prog over 1f out: styd on to take 2nd last 130yds: no ch w wnr* **25/1**

3420 **3** 3/4 **Jodawes (USA)**[7] 6468 4-9-7 **60**....................................... JimCrowley 10 62
(John Best) *hld up in last trio: drvn wl over 2f out: prog over 1f out: styd on to take 3rd nr fin* **12/1**

4000 **4** 1 **Suhailah**[50] 5141 5-8-12 **51** oh1... ShaneKelly 13 51
(Michael Attwater) *trckd ldr: led 3f out to 2f out: no ch w wnr after: lost 2 pls ins fnl f* **50/1**

0351 **5** 1/2 **Green Lightning (IRE)**[5] 6503 4-9-13 **66** 6ex.............(b) FrannyNorton 1 65
(Mark Johnston) *trckd ldrs in 6th: rdn over 2f out: sn wl outpcd: kpt on fr over 1f out* **5/2**[1]

0520 **6** 1 **Free Tussy (ARG)**[101] 3426 7-9-12 **65**.........................(bt) GeorgeBaker 7 63
(Gary Moore) *hld up in last trio: gng easily whn nt clr run jst over 2f out: shkn up and limited rspnse over 1f out: kpt on* **20/1**

4420 **7** *hd* **Mediterranean Sea (IRE)**[25] 5947 5-9-9 **62**............. RichardHughes 14 59
(J R Jenkins) *hld up in last trio: prog on inner wl over 2f out: no imp on ldrs over 1f out: wknd fnl f* **8/1**

043 **8** 4 **Fairest Isle (IRE)**[20] 6086 3-9-4 **64**.........................(t) StevieDonohoe 11 55
(James Fanshawe) *settled in midfield disputing 7th: rdn and struggling 3f out: sn n.d* **15/2**[3]

1515 **9** *hd* **Newby Lodge (IRE)**[3] 5642 3-9-1 **61**............................ DarryllHolland 3 52
(Alan Bailey) *prom: rdn over 2f out: sn wknd* **14/1**

3533 **10** 1/2 **Drumadoon (IRE)**[23] 5993 3-8-11 **57**..................................(p) TedDurcan 6 47
(John Dunlop) *stdd s: hld up towards rr: looking for room on inner over 2f out: sn no prog and btn* **8/1**

2022 **11** 1 1/2 **Croix Rouge (USA)**[9] 6417 9-8-13 **57**..................... MatthewLawson(5) 8 45
(Ralph Smith) *prom on outer: chal over 3f out: drvn and wknd over 2f out* **20/1**

0246 **12** 5 **Rosy Dawn**[23] 5993 6-8-12 **51** oh5.................................... WilliamCarson 4 31
(Mark Hoad) *led to 3f out: wknd qckly* **40/1**

6615 **13** 6 **Dazakhee**[18] 6182 4-9-11 **64**... TonyCulhane 9 34
(David Flood) *hld up in rr: prog into midfield 6f out: rdn over 3f out: sn wknd* **6/1**[2]

2m 33.95s (-0.55) **Going Correction** -0.075s/f (Stan)
WFA 3 from 4yo+ 7lb **13** Ran SP% **116.7**
Speed ratings (Par 101): **98,93,92,92,91 91,91,88,88,87 86,83,79**
toteswingers: 1&2 £60.80, 2&3 £24.00, 1&3 £54.10 CSF £285.52 CT £3632.90 TOTE £15.90: £5.10, £13.30, £4.60; EX 659.20 Trifecta £1551.00 Pool: £2,724.87 - 1.30 winning units..
Owner The Queen **Bred** The Queen **Trained** Beckhampton, Wilts

FOCUS
A modest handicap but an ordinary gallop and a wide-margin winner, who came down the centre in the straight.
Dazakhee Official explanation: jockey said filly ran too free

6622 BACK OR LAY AT BETDAQ.COM H'CAP (DIV II) 1m 4f (P)
7:10 (7:10) (Class 6) (0-65,65) 3-Y-O+ **£1,617** (£481; £240; £120) **Stalls** Centre

Form RPR

0222 **1** **Rowan Ridge**[14] 6253 3-9-0 **60**...................................(v) PatCosgrave 6 69+
(Jim Boyle) *patiently rdn in midfield: prog jst over 2f out: r.o to ld jst over 1f out: sn in command: readily* **9/2**[2]

/000 **2** 1 1/2 **Phonic (IRE)**[103] 3366 4-9-9 **62**... EddieAhern 7 68
(John Dunlop) *hld up in last trio: gng strly over 3f out: rdn over 2f out: styd on fr over 1f out to take 2nd last 75yds: no ch to chal* **8/1**

0001 **3** 1 **Ulla**[27] 5860 3-9-1 **61**.. TedDurcan 11 65
(Chris Wall) *trckd ldr: led wl over 2f out: sn jnd: hdd u.p jst over 1f out: one pce* **8/1**

5023 **4** 1/2 **Corvette**[21] 6052 3-9-3 **63**.......................................(v) RichardHughes 9 66
(J R Jenkins) *hld up in midfield: pushed along over 2f out and in tch: nt qckn over 1f out: styd on again ins fnl f* **4/1**[1]

6013 **5** 3/4 **Prince Blue**[34] 5642 4-9-0 **53**.. SamHitchcott 12 55
(John E Long) *trckd ldng trio: prog to chal and upsides over 2f out: looking arnd and n.g.t w effrt: wknd fnl f* **14/1**

2306 **6** 1/2 **Bubbly Braveheart (IRE)**[36] 5580 4-9-10 **63**.................. IanMongan 3 64
(Pat Phelan) *hld up in last trio: pushed along over 2f out: hanging but kpt on one pce fr over 1f out: n.d* **13/2**[3]

3031 **7** 3 **Abigails Angel**[40] 5421 4-9-6 **59**...................................... GeorgeBaker 4 55
(Brett Johnson) *trckd ldng pair: tried to chal on inner and cl enough 2f out: sn wknd* **8/1**

0-01 **8** 5 **Mister Bit (IRE)**[167] 1508 4-9-12 **65**...............................(b) LukeMorris 10 53
(John Best) *trckd ldrs in 5th: rdn over 2f out: wknd qckly over 1f out* **10/1**

6406 **9** 6 **Beckfield Dancer**[14] 6253 3-8-5 **51** oh2...................... WilliamCarson 13 30
(Stuart Williams) *wl in tch: drvn over 2f out: wknd rapidly wl over 1f out* **16/1**

3364 **10** 22 **Carlton Scroop (FR)**[29] 5815 8-9-8 **64**.......................... RobertLButler(3) 1 —
(Paddy Butler) *led to wl over 2f out: wknd rapidly: t.o* **11/1**

0006 **11** 45 **Burnbrake**[34] 5643 6-8-12 **51** oh1.................................(v) DarryllHolland 8 —
(Les Hall) *hld up in rr: rdn 4f out: sn wknd: wl t.o* **33/1**

2m 34.35s (-0.15) **Going Correction** -0.075s/f (Stan)
WFA 3 from 4yo+ 7lb **11** Ran SP% **117.8**
Speed ratings (Par 101): **97,96,95,95,94 94,92,88,84,70 40**
toteswingers: 1&2 £9.70, 2&3 £4.50, 1&3 £10.70 CSF £40.57 CT £282.70 TOTE £5.80: £2.30, £2.80, £2.90; EX 56.70 Trifecta £663.20 Pool: £1,434.12 - 1.60 winning units..
Owner Rowan Stud Partnership 1 **Bred** Rowan Farm Stud **Trained** Epsom, Surrey

FOCUS
The second division of a modest handicap. The gallop was an ordinary one and the winner came down the centre in the straight.

Bubbly Braveheart(IRE) Official explanation: jockey said gelding hung right
Burnbrake Official explanation: vet said gelding had an irregular heartbeat

6623 BETDAQ MOBILE APPS NURSERY 1m (P)
7:40 (7:41) (Class 4) (0-85,84) 2-Y-O **£3,428** (£1,020; £509; £254) **Stalls** Low

Form RPR

1 **1** **Misdemeanour (IRE)**[23] 6000 2-9-3 **80**........................ RichardHughes 5 87+
(Richard Hannon) *nt wl away but sn in midfield: pushed along fr 1/2-way: prog and swtchd lft wl over 1f out: r.o to ld last 150yds: a holding on after* **3/1**[2]

016 **2** ½ **Position**[37] 5550 2-9-5 **82**........................ SebSanders 11 86
(Sir Mark Prescott Bt) *tried to dispute ld but unable to do fr 1/2-way despite reminders: dropped to 3rd over 1f out u.p: rallied fnl f to press wnr: a jst hld* **12/1**

0001 **3** ½ **Mr Knightley (IRE)**[34] 5637 2-8-12 **78**........................(b) KieranO'Neill(3) 8 81
(Richard Hannon) *led at decent pce: kicked on fr 1/2-way: 2 l clr over 1f out: hdd and no ex last 150yds* **12/1**

2301 **4** *shd* **Costa Del Fortune (IRE)**[48] 5197 2-9-1 **78**........................ JamesDoyle 9 80
(Richard Hannon) *settled in midfield: drvn over 2f out: nt qckn over 1f out: styd on fnl f: nvr quite able to chal* **20/1**

3164 **5** 1 ¼ **Maroosh**[10] 6372 2-8-12 **75**........................ MartinDwyer 4 75
(Brian Meehan) *trckd ldrs: prog to chse ldr over 1f out: no imp: wknd ins fnl f* **16/1**

0555 **6** ½ **Voodoo Rhythm (USA)**[11] 6345 2-8-11 **74** ow1...........(b[1]) ShaneKelly 1 72
(Brian Meehan) *hld up in last pair: effrt over 2f out: sme prog u.p over 1f out: nt pce to threaten* **16/1**

4164 **7** 4 **Shamaal Nibras (USA)**[22] 6031 2-9-7 **84**........................ JamieSpencer 6 80+
(Ed Dunlop) *t.k.h: hld up in last pair: hrd rdn 3f out: prog over 1f out: nt rch ldrs ins fnl f and heavily eased last 100yds* **12/1**

1 **8** 1 ¾ **Ambivalent (IRE)**[18] 6180 2-8-12 **75**........................ NeilCallan 2 60
(Roger Varian) *prom on inner: rdn to dispute 2nd 2f out: wknd over 1f out* **5/2**[1]

4514 **9** 1 ¾ **Stateos (IRE)**[11] 6345 2-9-0 **77**........................ IanMongan 7 58
(Sir Henry Cecil) *sn pressed ldng pair: drvn 3f out: wknd fr 2f out* **16/1**

216 **10** 2 ¾ **Rythmic**[13] 6275 2-8-12 **80**........................ AntiocoMurgia(5) 3 55
(Mahmood Al Zarooni) *a towards rr: pushed along 1/2-way: wknd u.p wl over 1f out* **8/1**

4502 **11** 10 **Bewilder**[21] 6053 2-8-5 **68**........................ NickyMackay 10 20
(John Gosden) *a towards rr: struggling fr 3f out: t.o* **6/1**[3]

1m 39.26s (-0.54) **Going Correction** -0.075s/f (Stan) **11** Ran SP% **124.5**
Speed ratings (Par 97): **99,98,98,97,96 96,92,90,88,85 75**
toteswingers: 1&2 £14.30, 2&3 £10.50, 1&3 £30.00 CSF £42.01 CT £404.47 TOTE £5.40: £1.70, £3.40, £4.30; EX 37.80 Trifecta £290.30 Pool: £392.31 - 0.50 winning units..
Owner Thurloe Thoroughbreds XXIX **Bred** Ceka Ireland Limited **Trained** East Everleigh, Wilts
■ Stewards' Enquiry : Antioco Murgia three-day ban: used whip when out of contention (Oct 19-21)

FOCUS
Several winners in a useful handicap. An ordinary gallop picked up turning for home. The third, fourth and fifth help set the level.

NOTEBOOK
Misdemeanour(IRE) created a favourable impression when taking her maiden over C&D on her debut and she bettered that form after overcoming early scrimmaging in this much stronger event on this handicap debut. She isn't the most robust of individuals but is in good hands and may well be capable of better. (op 11-4 tchd 7-2 and 4-1 in places)
Position ◆ got bogged down in testing ground on his nursery debut but showed that to be all wrong on only this second Polytrack start. He's a strong sort with plenty of scope who should be even better suited by 1m2f and he appeals strongly as the type to win another race. (op 10-1)
Mr Knightley(IRE) bettered his recent claiming race form under another positive ride back up in trip. He doesn't have much in hand of his mark but should continue to run well on this surface when he can dominate. (op 16-1)
Costa Del Fortune(IRE) ran creditably returned to Polytrack on her first run over this trip, leaving the impression that a stronger end-to-end gallop would have suited better. She should continue to give a good account. (op 25-1)
Maroosh had the run of the race from his low draw and wasn't disgraced on this all-weather debut and first run over 1m. He won't be inconvenienced by the return to 7f but will have to raise his game to win a competitive handicap from this mark. (tchd 20-1)
Voodoo Rhythm(USA) wasn't disgraced back on Polytrack in the first-time headgear in a race in which those dropped out weren't seen to best advantage. He's yet to win a race but remains capable of picking up an ordinary event. (tchd 20-1)
Ambivalent(IRE) failed to confirm the pleasing impression she made at Wolverhampton on this handicap debut. However, she's only lightly raced, is in very good hands and will be worth another chance at some point. (op 11-4 tchd 3-1)
Rythmic Official explanation: jockey said filly suffered interference in running

6624 TURFTV H'CAP 1m (P)
8:10 (8:10) (Class 6) (0-60,65) 3-Y-O+ **£1,617** (£481; £240; £120) **Stalls** Low

Form RPR

5003 **1** **Dichoh**[28] 5836 8-9-1 **57**........................(p) ChrisCatlin 8 66
(Michael Madgwick) *wl in tch: rdn and prog to chal over 2f out: pressed ldr after: drvn ahd last 75yds* **20/1**

4010 **2** *nk* **Jonnie Skull (IRE)**[6] 6488 5-9-3 **59**........................(vt) KierenFallon 9 67
(Phil McEntee) *sn pressed ldr: led 3f out: drvn and hrd pressed fnl 2f: hdd last 75yds* **11/1**

4/04 **3** *nk* **Nina Rose**[25] 5912 4-8-12 **57**........................ JohnFahy(3) 13 64
(Clive Cox) *wl in tch in midfield on outer: rdn over 2f out: prog to go 3rd jst over 1f out: styd on but nvr quite able to chal* **8/1**

0600 **4** 1 ¾ **Ninfea (IRE)**[27] 5845 3-9-1 **60**........................(p) JamesDoyle 3 63
(Sylvester Kirk) *pressed ldng pair to over 2f out: styd chsng: kpt on same pce fr over 1f out* **15/2**[3]

6000 **5** ½ **Gallantry**[63] 4666 9-9-2 **58**........................ ShaneKelly 2 60
(Michael Squance) *hld up last: rdn and prog on inner over 2f out: nt qckn over 1f out: one pce after* **33/1**

3340 **5** *dht* **Ilie Nastase (FR)**[11] 6355 7-9-4 **60**........................(b) RichardHughes 7 62
(Conor Dore) *hld up but wl in tch in midfield: asked for effrt over 2f out but fnd nil: tried to cl again over 1f out: one pce* **8/1**

3004 **7** 1 ½ **Wishformore (IRE)**[28] 5836 4-9-3 **59**........................(p) LiamKeniry 5 58
(J S Moore) *pressed ldrs: chal between rivals and nrly upsides over 2f out: sn nt qckn: wknd fnl f* **11/1**

011 **8** ½ **Swansea Jack**[7] 6444 4-9-6 **65** 6ex........................(vt) HarryBentley(3) 14 63
(Stuart Williams) *hld up in last trio: effrt on wd outside over 2f out: nt qckn wl over 1f out: no imp after* **9/4**[1]

5332 **9** 2 **Elegant Muse**[18] 6179 3-8-12 **60**........................[1] SeanLevey(3) 6 53
(Walter Swinburn) *hld up towards rr on inner: hmpd by wkng rival over 2f out: nt rcvr* **13/2**[2]

5532 **10** 3 ½ **Kai Mook**[116] 2922 4-8-11 **60**........................(bt) HarryPoulton(7) 11 45
(Roger Ingram) *a in last trio: struggling and no prog 2f out* **16/1**

4000 **11** ¾ **Querido (GER)**[28] 5836 7-8-12 **57**........................(tp) RobertLButler(3) 1 40
(Paddy Butler) *nvr bttr than midfield on inner: wknd over 1f out* **40/1**

5540 **12** 33 **Jeeran**[9] 6408 3-9-0 **59**........................(bt) JamieSpencer 4 —
(Alastair Lidderdale) *led to 3f out: wknd rapidly: t.o* **10/1**

1m 39.73s (-0.07) **Going Correction** -0.075s/f (Stan)
WFA 3 from 4yo+ 3lb **12** Ran SP% **119.9**
Speed ratings (Par 101): **97,96,96,94,94 94,92,92,90,86 85,52**
toteswingers: 1&2 £29.30, 2&3 £22.80, 1&3 £17.40 CSF £223.58 CT £1922.14 TOTE £21.90: £5.30, £2.90, £2.80; EX 124.40 TRIFECTA Not won..
Owner M Madgwick **Bred** Red House Stud **Trained** Denmead, Hants

FOCUS
Exposed performers in a modest handicap and one in which the market leader disappointed. The gallop was a fair one and the principals came down the centre in the straight.
Kai Mook Official explanation: trainer said filly bled from the nose

6625 GBI SPONSORS LEADING IN RACING NOVICE STKS 6f (P)
8:40 (8:40) (Class 5) 2-Y-O **£2,264** (£673; £336; £168) **Stalls** Low

Form RPR

1464 **1** **Gusto**[7] 6466 2-9-5 95........................ RichardHughes 6 96+
(Richard Hannon) *mde all: qcknd clr jst over 2f out: shkn up and in n.d over 1f out: eased last 75yds* **6/4**[1]

134 **2** 2 ½ **Quite A Thing**[36] 5592 2-9-2 87........................ SebSanders 1 83
(Sir Mark Prescott Bt) *n.m.r after 100yds and sn dropped to last pair: prog on inner 2f out: styd on to take 2nd last 75yds: no ch w wnr* **15/2**

4120 **3** *shd* **Shere Khan**[18] 6166 2-9-2 86........................ KieranO'Neill(3) 3 85
(Richard Hannon) *hld up in last pair: prog on outer over 2f out: chsd clr wnr over 1f out but hanging rt: no imp and lost 2nd last 75yds* **7/1**[3]

21 **4** 3 **Heyward Girl (IRE)**[28] 5834 2-8-11 82........................ AndreaAtzeni 2 68
(Robert Eddery) *trckd wnr 1f: styd cl up: effrt to go 2nd briefly wl over 1f out but already outpcd: fdd* **9/4**[2]

021 **5** 7 **Indian Tinker**[26] 5889 2-9-5 82........................ ShaneKelly 4 55
(Robert Cowell) *in tch: wl outpcd over 2f out: nvr on terms after* **10/1**

6053 **6** 3 ¼ **Piranha (IRE)**[24] 5961 2-9-2 82........................(b[1]) KierenFallon 5 42
(Ed Dunlop) *t.k.h: pressed wnr after 1f to over 2f out: wkng whn checked wl over 1f out* **9/1**

300 **7** 11 **Joe M**[58] 4848 2-9-0 45........................ EddieAhern 8 —
(Simon Dow) *prom tl wknd rapidly over 2f out: eased* **66/1**

1m 12.5s (-0.60) **Going Correction** -0.075s/f (Stan) **7** Ran SP% **115.6**
Speed ratings (Par 95): **101,97,97,93,84 79,65**
toteswingers: 1&2 £3.10, 2&3 £1.70, 1&3 £5.30 CSF £14.09 TOTE £2.90: £2.00, £4.60; EX 9.60 Trifecta £22.90 Pool: £338.72 - 10.90 winning units..
Owner Highclere Thoroughbred Racing-Rock Sand **Bred** New England, Mount Coote & P Barrett **Trained** East Everleigh, Wilts
■ Stewards' Enquiry : Andrea Atzeni two-day ban: careless riding (Oct 19-20)

FOCUS
Several winners in a decent novice event but a very useful performance from the winner. The gallop was an ordinary one and the winner raced towards the far rail in the straight. The form looks straightforward and solid, rated around the placed horses.

NOTEBOOK
Gusto ◆, the pick of the weights, went with the choke out on this all-weather debut but showed a fine turn of foot to quickly settle the issue passing the intersection to win with a fair bit more in hand than the winning margin suggested. He has scope for improvement, has bags of foot and is worth another chance in Listed company when the emphasis will be on speed. (op 7-4)
Quite A Thing hadn't been at her best in easy ground on her previous start but fared better back on synthetics and on her first run over this trip to chase home a potentially smart sort. She's clearly useful but she is lacking in physical scope and may not be the easiest to place successfully next season. (op 8-1 tchd 7-1)
Shere Khan also proved suited by the return to this surface and wasn't far off his best. He would be better suited by a stronger gallop over this trip or the return to 7f and he should continue to run well on this surface. (op 10-1)
Heyward Girl(IRE) looked interesting in receipt of weight from all her rivals after her maiden C&D form had been franked by the runner-up, but she was found out in this much stronger event. However, she isn't fully exposed and will be worth another chance when switched to handicap company. (op 2-1 tchd 5-2)
Indian Tinker's Sandown win had been franked several times but he had a bit to find at the weights on this all-weather debut and didn't get home after racing with the choke out returned to this longer trip. He'll be worth another chance back on turf. (op 12-1)
Piranha(IRE) had won her two previous Polytrack starts and had been a consistent sort but, although she had a bit to find at the weights, she wasn't anywhere near her best after pulling hard in the first-time blinkers. Presumably the headgear will be left off next time. (op 8-1)

6626 GBI WELCOME LEADERS IN RACING H'CAP 7f (P)
9:10 (9:10) (Class 6) (0-55,55) 3-Y-O+ **£1,617** (£481; £240; £120) **Stalls** Low

Form RPR

0430 **1** **Fedora (IRE)**[20] 6105 5-9-0 **52**........................(t) CathyGannon 4 62
(Olivia Maylam) *settled in midfield: prog on inner over 2f out: squeezed through to ld jst ins fnl f: styd on wl* **8/1**

5043 **2** 1 ¼ **Silvee**[7] 6444 4-9-0 **55**........................ KieranO'Neill(3) 3 62
(John Bridger) *prom: rdn over 2f out: clsd to chal over 1f out: nudged by wnr jst ins fnl f: one pce after* **8/1**

0245 **3** ¾ **Sairaam (IRE)**[16] 6228 5-8-12 **53**........................ JohnFahy(3) 1 58
(Charles Smith) *led 1f: chsd clr ldr after: clsd to ld over 1f out: hdd and outpcd jst ins fnl f* **9/2**[2]

2261 **4** ¾ **Love Nest**[25] 5944 3-9-1 **55**........................ EddieAhern 7 58
(John Dunlop) *in tch in midfield: effrt on inner over 2f out: kpt on fr over 1f out: nvr able to chal* **3/1**[1]

2342 **5** 1 **Flaxen Lake**[6] 6479 4-9-2 **54**........................ LukeMorris 6 54
(Milton Bradley) *chsd ldrs: drvn and nt qckn over 2f out: nt on terms after: kpt on fnl f* **8/1**

2425 **6** *nk* **Deslaya (IRE)**[20] 6105 3-9-1 **55**........................ NickyMackay 8 54+
(Chris Wall) *racd on outer towards rr: drvn over 2f out: kpt on fr over 1f out: n.d* **5/1**[3]

660 **7** 3 ½ **Shaws Diamond (USA)**[108] 3202 5-9-1 **53**...........(v) RobbieFitzpatrick 5 43
(Derek Shaw) *pushed up to ld after 1f and sn clr: edgd lft: hdd & wknd qckly over 1f out* **14/1**

0200 **8** 2 ¼ **Tymismoni (IRE)**[107] 3223 3-8-9 **54**........................(p) MarkCoumbe(5) 14 38
(Michael Attwater) *hld up in last trio: swtchd ins and modest prog over 2f out: no hdwy over 1f out* **16/1**

00-5 **9** 4 **Blueberry Fizz (IRE)**[11] 6353 3-9-1 **55**........................ ShaneKelly 10 28
(John Ryan) *awkward s: hld up last: modest prog over 2f out but stl bhd: shkn up over 1f out: no hdwy after* **33/1**

0100 **10** 4 ½ **Rileys Crane**[21] 6071 4-9-0 **52**........................(v) SaleemGolam 11 13
(Christine Dunnett) *sn prom: hrd rdn and wknd over 2f out* **33/1**

0-60 **11** 1 ¼ **Teazel**[55] 4948 3-9-0 **54**........................ JamesDoyle 2 12
(Dominic Ffrench Davis) *hld up in last trio: snatched up over 2f out: no ch after* **20/1**

60-0 **12** 4 ½ **Lordship (IRE)**16 6228 7-8-7 **52**.................................... JakePayne(7) 12 —
(Tony Carroll) *prom tl wknd qckly wl over 2f out* **50/1**

1m 26.48s (0.48) **Going Correction** -0.075s/f (Stan)
WFA 3 from 4yo+ 2lb **12** Ran SP% **118.3**
Speed ratings (Par 101): **94,92,91,90,89 89,85,82,78,73 71,66**
toteswingers: 1&2 £12.20, 2&3 £7.90, 1&3 £2.60 CSF £67.82 CT £267.13 TOTE £9.60: £3.00, £2.40, £1.90; EX 69.80 Trifecta £259.00 Pool: £350.12 - 1.00 winning units..
Owner Mrs V A Ward **Bred** Forenaghts Stud And Dermot Cantillon **Trained** Epsom, Surrey
■ Stewards' Enquiry : Mark Coumbe two-day ban: careless riding (Oct 19-20)

FOCUS
A moderate handicap run at a reasonable gallop. The winner raced close to the inside rail in the straight.
Love Nest Official explanation: jockey said colt was denied a clear run
Teazel Official explanation: jockey said filly suffered interference in running
T/Plt: £2,099.60 to a £1 stake. Pool: £78,953.51. 27.45 winning tickets. T/Qpdt: £1,115.80 to a £1 stake. Pool: £10,705.77. 7.10 winning tickets. JN

6455 NOTTINGHAM (L-H)
Wednesday, October 5

OFFICIAL GOING: Good to firm (7.1)
Wind: strong 1/2 against, brief shower race 6 Weather: overcast, very windy

6627 ANN WHELBOURNE 20TH ANNIVERSARY CELEBRATION NURSERY (DIV I) 6f 15y
2:00 (2:01) (Class 6) (0-60,60) 2-Y-O **£1,681** (£500; £250; £125) **Stalls** Centre

Form RPR
4456 **1** **Guava**35 5625 2-9-4 **60**.................................... SeanLevey(3) 7 65
(Richard Hannon) *trckd ldrs: led jst ins fnl f: styd on wl* **10/1**
0060 **2** 1 ¼ **Mount McLeod (IRE)**23 5998 2-8-12 **51**.................. FergusSweeney 17 54+
(Jamie Osborne) *hld up in rr: hdwy 2f out: nt clr run and swtchd lft and styd on ins fnl f* **10/1**
663 **3** *hd* **Endless Applause**11 6344 2-9-0 **56**.............................. AmyRyan(3) 4 57
(Richard Whitaker) *mid-div: hdwy 2f out: hmpd and swtchd lft appr fnl f: styd on* **16/1**
0342 **4** ½ **Wish Again (IRE)**17 6186 2-9-5 **58**............................ AdrianNicholls 9 57
(David Nicholls) *led: hdd jst ins fnl f: no ex* **15/2**3
5513 **5** 1 ½ **First Rebellion**28 5833 2-8-10 **49**.................................... NeilCallan 11 44
(Tony Carroll) *chsd ldrs: one pce over 1f out* **9/1**
4000 **6** 1 ½ **Elegant Flight**16 6222 2-9-1 **57**..............................(v1) HarryBentley(3) 16 47
(Alan Jarvis) *chsd ldrs: edgd lft over 1f out: kpt on same pce* **16/1**
4416 **7** *shd* **Sweet Ovation**27 5840 2-8-10 **56**.......................... RachealKneller(7) 2 46
(Mark Usher) *dwlt: hld up towards rr: hdwy over 2f out: one pce ins fnl f* **9/1**
565 **8** 1 ¾ **Chorister Girl**83 4012 2-9-0 **53**.................................... TomQueally 15 38
(William Jarvis) *hld up towards rr: kpt on fnl 2f: nvr nr ldrs* **13/2**1
4060 **9** *nk* **Rooknrasbryripple**6 6489 2-9-7 **60**............................. TonyCulhane 10 44
(Mick Channon) *in rr s: hdwy over 2f out: sn chsng ldrs: wknd over 1f out* **22/1**
4450 **10** 2 **Flosse**23 5998 2-9-1 **54**..(v1) J-PGuillambert 14 32
(Ed Walker) *s.i.s: sn drvn along in midfield: swtchd lft over 1f out: nvr a factor* **20/1**
6353 **11** *nk* **Jay Kay**9 6413 2-9-0 **58**.................................... NeilFarley(5) 13 35
(Robert Wylie) *chsd ldrs: wknd over 1f out* **12/1**
0503 **12** *nse* **Dylan's Dream (IRE)**37 5555 2-8-9 **48**.............................. DavidAllan 1 25
(Tim Easterby) *chsd ldrs far side: wknd over 1f out* **16/1**
0403 **13** ½ **Lady Gadfly**54 4983 2-8-13 **52**.............................. FrederikTylicki 3 27
(Micky Hammond) *in rr: nvr a factor* **50/1**
000 **14** 4 ½ **Ferdy (IRE)**33 5681 2-8-11 **50**.............................. JamesSullivan 6 12
(Paul Green) *chsd ldrs: wknd over 2f out* **40/1**
566 **15** ½ **Villa Reigns**64 4632 2-8-11 **50**.. TomEaves 5 10
(John Weymes) *chsd ldrs: lost pl over 2f out* **100/1**
0560 **16** ½ **Kathryn Perry (IRE)**37 5535 2-8-13 **52**.......................... CathyGannon 12 11
(David Evans) *hld up in rr: bhd fnl 2f* **25/1**
504 **17** 5 **I'm A Doughnut**21 6045 2-9-6 **59**.............................. KierenFallon 8 3
(Tom Dascombe) *s.i.s: in rr: hung rt over 2f out and racd alone stands' side: bhd whn eased in clsng stages* **7/1**2

1m 16.63s (1.73) **Going Correction** +0.025s/f (Good) **17** Ran SP% **119.5**
Speed ratings (Par 93): **89,87,87,86,84 82,82,79,79,76 76,76,75,69,69 68,61**
toteswingers:1&2:£30.00, 2&3:£63.30, 1&3:£54.40 CSF £96.15 CT £1655.46 TOTE £9.20: £2.10, £1.80, £4.90, £2.20; EX 196.40 TRIFECTA Not won..
Owner Middleham Park Racing Vi **Bred** B R Marsden **Trained** East Everleigh, Wilts
■ Stewards' Enquiry : Harry Bentley two-day ban: careless riding (Oct 19-20)

FOCUS
Outer track used and rail at normal configuration with distances as advertised. The action unfolded up the middle of the track. A modest but competitive nursery and the pace was quick (time 0.15 seconds faster than second division). Straightforward form with the winner back to her best.

NOTEBOOK
Guava came into this 0-6, but she would have gone close to winning a Folkestone seller on her previous start had she not been denied a clear run, and she made the most of a better trip this time. Her chance may have been helped by the runner-up finding trouble, but it wouldn't surprise if she defied a rise. (op 12-1)
Mount McLeod(IRE) would have gone close to winning had she not been denied a run when beginning to pick up, forcing her to switch. This was by far her best effort so far. (op 14-1 tchd 9-1)
Endless Applause had shown ability in maidens and has found her level now handicapping.
Wish Again(IRE) raced in a clear lead. He kept on surprisingly well and his natural speed should see him win a race. (op 5-1 tchd 8-1)
First Rebellion didn't really improve for the step back up in trip. (op 11-1)
Sweet Ovation kept on but was never doing enough and very much looked the type who needs stronger handling. Her sole win so far came under a non-claiming jockey. Racheal Kneller reported the filly was slowly away. Official explanation: jockey said filly was slowly away (op 10-1)
Chorister Girl, debuting for a new stable after 83 days off, seemed to be hanging under pressure. On two of her three previous starts she had been reported to have hung left handed. (op 17-2)
I'm A Doughnut Official explanation: jockey said, regarding running, that the gelding lost its action

6628 ANN WHELBOURNE 20TH ANNIVERSARY CELEBRATION NURSERY (DIV II) 6f 15y
2:30 (2:32) (Class 6) (0-60,60) 2-Y-O **£1,681** (£500; £250; £125) **Stalls** Centre

Form RPR
0304 **1** **Fifteentwo**41 5399 2-9-6 **59**.................................... AdrianNicholls 5 71+
(David Nicholls) *hld up: hdwy over 2f out: led last 150yds: forged clr* **6/1**2
1530 **2** 3 ¼ **Class Monitor**26 5896 2-9-4 **60**.............................. MartinHarley(3) 11 63
(Mrs K Burke) *chsd ldrs: led over 1f out: hdd and no ex ins fnl f* **10/3**1
000 **3** 1 ½ **Aussie Guest (IRE)**19 6123 2-9-5 **58**.......................... MatthewDavies 12 56
(Mick Channon) *mid-div: hdwy over 2f out: kpt on fnl f: tk 3rd nr fin* **9/1**
000 **4** ¾ **Echo Of Dubai (IRE)**26 5899 2-8-11 **50**......................(b1) ChrisCatlin 14 46
(Clive Brittain) *chsd ldrs: led over 2f out: hdd over 1f out: one pce* **22/1**
654 **5** 2 ½ **New Romantic**36 5596 2-9-3 **56**.............................. BarryMcHugh 15 44
(Julie Camacho) *s.i.s: hld up in rr: hdwy over 2f out: kpt on fnl f* **14/1**
0602 **6** 5 **Inya House**23 5998 2-9-2 **55**.. SebSanders 16 28
(Nigel Tinkler) *hld up: effrt over 2f out: wknd over 1f out: hung lft and eased ins fnl f* **7/1**3
5020 **7** ¾ **Cataract**37 5562 2-8-13 **52**..(b) JamesSullivan 8 23
(John Weymes) *rr-div: hdwy to chse ldrs over 2f out: wknd over 1f out* **10/1**
000 **8** 2 ¾ **First Of February (IRE)**27 5854 2-8-8 **47**...................... NickyMackay 4 10
(Jim Boyle) *mid-div on outer: som hdwy over 2f out: sn wknd* **16/1**
0006 **9** ¾ **Cat Queen**23 5998 2-9-5 **58**.. DavidProbert 2 19
(Gay Kelleway) *sn in rr: drvn over 3f out: nvr on terms* **10/1**
0046 **10** 2 ½ **Deduction (IRE)**21 6058 2-9-4 **57**.............................. WilliamCarson 7 10
(Charles Hills) *hld up towards rr: drvn over 2f out: nvr a factor* **8/1**
3350 **11** 1 ¼ **Ave Sofia**32 5727 2-9-0 **53**..(v1) JoeFanning 1 2
(John Holt) *sn in rr: sme hdwy over 2f out: sn lost pl* **16/1**
0500 **12** 1 **Sabusa (IRE)**13 6274 2-8-5 **51**..................................(be) NoraLooby(7) 17 —
(Alan McCabe) *swvd lft s: sn chsng ldrs: led over 3f out: hdd over 2f out: edgd lft and sn wknd* **20/1**
3030 **13** 2 ¾ **Picura**15 6237 2-8-13 **52**.. MartinDwyer 13 —
(William Muir) *led over 2f: wknd over 2f out* **16/1**

1m 16.78s (1.88) **Going Correction** +0.025s/f (Good) **13** Ran SP% **122.6**
Speed ratings (Par 93): **88,83,81,80,77 70,69,66,65,61 60,58,55**
toteswingers:1&2:£6.90, 2&3:£9.00, 1&3:£13.30 CSF £26.91 CT £186.17 TOTE £9.20: £1.80, £1.90, £3.40; EX 41.40 Trifecta £257.90 Part won. Pool: £348.61 - 0.95 winning units..
Owner C A Mills,A Fallon,G Purchase **Bred** J Khan & P Wilson **Trained** Sessay, N Yorks
■ Stewards' Enquiry : Adrian Nicholls four-day ban: used whip with excessive frequency without giving colt time to respond (Oct 19-21,24)

FOCUS
The time was 0.15 seconds slower than the rapidly run first leg. Again they raced up the middle of the track. The winner scored easily and the third and fourth offer perspective.

NOTEBOOK
Fifteentwo, returning from 41 days off, improved for the return to 6f with his first success on his fifth start, building on an eyecatching display at Carlisle last time. There was plenty to like about this performance (travelled best, found plenty) and he can win again. (op 13-2 tchd 7-1 and 8-1 in places)
Class Monitor had been given a real chance by the handicapper and was well backed. The winner was simply on a better mark, but she showed enough to suggest she can add to her debut claiming win. (tchd 7-2 and 4-1 in places)
Aussie Guest(IRE) hadn't shown much in maidens at Ascot and Newbury, but this represented a significant class drop. He showed sufficient ability to believe he can win a similar event. (op 10-1 tchd 8-1)
Echo Of Dubai(IRE), dropped in trip, was noticeably sharpened up by first-time blinkers but still finished well held. (op 20-1 tchd 16-1)
New Romantic kept on steadily and needs more of a stamina test, as her breeding suggests. She was too keen on her only previous try at 7f, but will have a chance if settling better when next tried at that trip or beyond. (tchd 12-1)
Inya House hung left and that cost him his chance. Official explanation: jockey said gelding hung left (op 15-2 tchd 8-1)

6629 BRITISH STALLION STUDS SUPPORTING BRITISH RACING EBF MAIDEN STKS 6f 15y
3:00 (3:00) (Class 5) 2-Y-O **£3,234** (£962; £481; £240) **Stalls** Centre

Form RPR
3 **1** **Lucky Henry**19 6123 2-9-0 0.. JohnFahy(3) 3 80
(Clive Cox) *trckd ldrs: chsd wnr over 2f out: 3 l down 1f out: styd on to ld towards fin* **7/4**1
423 **2** 1 ½ **Idler (IRE)**10 6380 2-9-3 0.............................. SilvestreDeSousa 7 76
(Mark Johnston) *led: qcknd clr over 2f out: edgd lft appr fnl f: hdd nr fin* **3/1**2
3 8 **Lady Mandy** 2-8-12 0.. PaulHanagan 2 50+
(Richard Fahey) *s.i.s: drvn in rr 3f out: kpt on to take modest 3rd 1f out* **17/2**
0 **4** 9 **Ailanthus**29 5812 2-8-12 0.. DaneO'Neill 6 20
(Henry Candy) *trckd ldrs: wknd over 2f out* **28/1**
3 **5** ½ **Excellent Jem**21 6064 2-9-3 0.. TomQueally 1 23
(George Margarson) *s.i.s: drvn 3f out: sn wl outpcd* **9/2**3
6 ¾ **Tioman Pearl** 2-9-3 0.. NeilCallan 8 21
(Roger Varian) *chsd ldrs: wknd over 2f out* **9/2**3

1m 15.3s (0.40) **Going Correction** +0.025s/f (Good) **6** Ran SP% **111.7**
Speed ratings (Par 95): **98,96,85,73,72 71**
toteswingers:1&2:£2.00, 2&3:£2.90, 1&3:£4.10 CSF £7.14 TOTE £2.00: £1.10, £1.80; EX 6.00 Trifecta £16.00 Pool: £609.29 - 28.01 winning units..
Owner Tim Bostwick **Bred** Tim Bostwick **Trained** Lambourn, Berks

FOCUS
A few of these ran below expectations, but it might be worth being positive about the front two considering they pulled a long way clear in a time much quicker than both divisions of the Class 6 nursery.

NOTEBOOK
Lucky Henry finished third on his debut over this trip at Newbury, a race that's already working out well. Indeed, the winner bolted up next time, albeit off a surprisingly lenient opening mark of 70, and the well-beaten tenth was third in the second division of the nursery on this card. Like last time, he shaped as though he'll improve when upped in trip. (op 11-8 tchd 5-4 and 2-1 in a place)
Idler(IRE) ran to a fair level when runner-up over this trip two starts ago before being unsuited by 7f. He raced in a clear lead and looked the winner for much of the way (touched 1.03 on Betfair), but hung left when getting tired late on. Even so, this still looked a career best and, bred for speed, he may do even better over the minimum trip. (op 5-2 tchd 10-3)
Lady Mandy, a 36,000gns half-sister to a few winners, out of a 1m2f scorer, was a bit free to post. This trip seemed inadequate but she made late headway and can do a lot better. (op 14-1 tchd 8-1)
Ailanthus didn't offer much. (tchd 25-1)
Excellent Jem was nowhere near the form he showed when third on his debut over 7f. (tchd 5-1)
Tioman Pearl, a 40,000gns purchase, travelled well to halfway but found disappointingly little. Perhaps the run was badly needed. (op 15-2)

6630 EUROPEAN BREEDERS' FUND MAIDEN STKS 1m 75y
3:30 (3:30) (Class 5) 2-Y-O **£3,234** (£962; £481; £240) **Stalls** Centre

Form RPR
0 **1** **Fennell Bay (IRE)**16 6216 2-9-3 0.............................. FrankieDettori 7 72
(Mahmood Al Zarooni) *led 2f: trckd ldrs: rdn over 1f out: styd on to ld towards fin* **5/1**3

2 ½ **Teide Peak (IRE)** 2-9-3 0 .... SilvestreDeSousa 4 71
(Mark Johnston) *s.i.s: chsd ldrs after 2f: rdn to ld over 2f out: edgd lft ins fnl f: no ex and hdd nr fin* **13/2**

0045 **3** 2 ¼ **Onebytheknows**[41] 5409 2-9-0 67 .... SeanLevey(3) 6 66
(Richard Hannon) *trckd ldrs: effrt over 2f out: kpt on ins fnl f: tk 3rd post* **14/1**

05 **4** nse **Free House**[21] 6059 2-9-3 0 .... (b1) MartinDwyer 2 69+
(Brian Meehan) *chsd ldrs: drvn over 3f out: clr in 3rd whn hmpd ins fnl f: lost 3rd at post* **3/1**[2]

5 2 **Grey Mirage** 2-9-3 0 .... WilliamBuick 3 61
(Marco Botti) *s.s: wd bnd after 1f: sn trcking ldrs: wknd over 1f out* **11/4**[1]

6 1 ¼ **Poetic Power (IRE)** 2-9-3 0 .... PaulHanagan 1 58+
(David Elsworth) *walked to post: trckd ldr: led after 2f: hdd over 2f out: wknd over 1f out* **5/1**[3]

63 **7** 10 **Ctappers**[14] 6245 2-9-3 0 .... MatthewDavies 5 35
(Mick Channon) *in rr: drvn to chse ldrs 3f out: lost pl 2f out* **14/1**

05 **8** 23 **Meet Joe Black (IRE)**[7] 6455 2-9-3 0 .... CathyGannon 9 —
(David Evans) *prom early: lost pl after 2f: drvn over 3f out: sn wl bhd: t.o* **66/1**

9 7 **Misty Eyes** 2-8-12 0 .... GrahamGibbons 8 —
(Geoffrey Harker) *s.i.s: bhd and drvn over 5f out: t.o whn eased over 1f out* **50/1**

1m 48.68s (3.08) **Going Correction** +0.025s/f (Good) 9 Ran SP% **115.1**
Speed ratings (Par 95): **85,84,82,82,80 78,68,45,38**
toteswingers:1&2:£6.80, 2&3:£9.30, 1&3:£14.10 CSF £37.28 TOTE £5.90: £1.40, £1.30, £5.00; EX 40.70 Trifecta £604.90 Part won. Pool of £817.44 - 0.50 winning units..
Owner Godolphin **Bred** J R Wills **Trained** Newmarket, Suffolk
■ Stewards' Enquiry : Silvestre De Sousa four-day ban: careless riding (Oct 19-21,24)

FOCUS
The proximity of the 67-rated third suggests the form is no more than fair. The pace was steady.

NOTEBOOK
Fennell Bay(IRE) was beaten 23l on his recent Polytrack debut but he stepped up a good deal on that performance, helped by being well placed and his experience was crucial in getting past the runner-up, a newcomer. This was no better than a fair performance, but considering the rate of improvement from his debut, another significant step forward cannot be ruled out. (op 9-1)
Teide Peak(IRE), a half-sister to useful sprinter Albany Rose, out of a 1m1f winner, cost 100,000gns. He looked green from some way out, went left under pressure and was just worried out of it. There should be improvement to come. His rider picked up a four-day ban for careless riding. (op 5-1)
Onebytheknows improved a little for the step up in trip after 41 days off. (op 22-1 tchd 12-1)
Free House, blinkered for the first time, was keeping on when squeezed up against the rail by the runner-up late on. He was possibly held at the time, but still wouldn't have been far away and it undoubtedly cost him third. (op 7-2 tchd 5-2)
Grey Mirage ◆, a brother to a successful miler, out of a 1m2f Group 2 winner in Italy, had a cross noseband fitted. Having lost several lengths with a slow start, he then raced a bit keenly without cover. He can leave this form behind. (op 5-2 tchd 7-2)
Poetic Power(IRE) had to be withdrawn ahead of his recent intended debut at Newmarket after bolting beyond the start. Fitted with a cross noseband, this 70,000gns purchase checked out tamely after setting an ordinary pace, but the run was probably needed. (op 9-2 tchd 4-1)

6631 KEOGHS IRISH BAR NOTTINGHAM H'CAP (DIV I) 1m 2f 50y
4:00 (4:00) (Class 4) (0-85,84) 3-Y-O+ **£4,075** (£1,212; £606; £303) **Stalls** Low

Form RPR

0553 **1** **Changing The Guard**[17] 6188 5-9-2 76 .... PaulHanagan 6 84
(Richard Fahey) *trckd ldrs: led over 1f out: hld on wl* **12/1**

5463 **2** ½ **Wiggy Smith**[26] 5893 12-8-13 73 .... DaneO'Neill 2 80
(Henry Candy) *hld up towards rr: hdwy over 3f out: chal 1f out: no ex nr fin* **8/1**

331 **3** 2 **Ampleforth**[16] 6210 3-8-11 76 .... SilvestreDeSousa 3 79+
(Mark Johnston) *mid-div: effrt and rdn 3f out: n.m.r on inner over 1f out: styd on to take 3rd post* **4/1**[1]

-023 **4** nse **Estourah (IRE)**[14] 6248 3-9-5 84 .... (tp) FrankieDettori 5 87
(Saeed Bin Suroor) *trckd ldrs: t.k.h: drvn 3f out: nt clr run over 1f out: kpt on same pce* **9/2**[2]

3440 **5** 2 ¾ **Hawaana (IRE)**[12] 6302 6-9-4 78 .... DavidProbert 9 76
(Gay Kelleway) *hld up in mid-div: effrt on outer over 3f out: kpt on fnl f: nvr a factor* **10/1**

05 **6** ½ **Audemar (IRE)**[26] 5888 5-9-10 84 .... AndreaAtzeni 10 81
(Edward Vaughan) *led: hdd over 2f out: wknd over 1f out* **8/1**

0003 **7** 2 **Oratory (IRE)**[39] 5465 5-9-8 82 .... DuranFentiman 4 75
(Geoffrey Harker) *hld up in rr: effrt over 3f out: nvr a factor* **14/1**

1125 **8** nse **Street Secret (USA)**[32] 5716 3-9-3 82 .... NeilCallan 7 75
(Roger Varian) *trckd ldrs: t.k.h: led over 2f out: hdd over 1f out: sn wknd* **13/2**[3]

1024 **9** 1 ¾ **Destiny Of A Diva**[7] 6439 4-9-9 83 .... KierenFallon 1 72
(Reg Hollinshead) *dwlt: hld up in rr: drvn on outer 3f out: nvr a factor* **9/2**[2]

2m 12.44s (0.74) **Going Correction** +0.025s/f (Good)
WFA 3 from 4yo+ 5lb 9 Ran SP% **115.4**
Speed ratings (Par 105): **98,97,96,95,93 93,91,91,90**
CSF £103.57 CT £456.21 TOTE £21.00: £4.40, £3.30, £2.30; EX 183.40 Trifecta £595.70 Part won. Pool of £805.08 - 0.50 winning units..
Owner I L Davies **Bred** R A Bonnycastle And Marston Stud **Trained** Musley Bank, N Yorks
■ Stewards' Enquiry : Andrea Atzeni caution: used whip down shoulder in the forehand.

FOCUS
An ordinary handicap for the class and they didn't seem to go that quick.

6632 KEOGHS IRISH BAR NOTTINGHAM H'CAP (DIV II) 1m 2f 50y
4:30 (4:31) (Class 4) (0-85,84) 3-Y-O+ **£4,075** (£1,212; £606; £303) **Stalls** Low

Form RPR

1222 **1** **Area Fifty One**[16] 6218 3-9-1 80 .... MartinDwyer 10 92
(William Muir) *led early: trckd ldrs: wnt 2nd over 2f out: led over 1f out: drew clr ins fnl f* **6/1**

113 **2** 3 ½ **Hunter Forward (AUS)**[40] 5440 5-9-2 76 .... KierenFallon 6 81
(Luca Cumani) *ponied to post: t.k.h: sn trcking ldrs: drvn 4f out: styd on same pce appr fnl f* **2/1**[1]

0-40 **3** ½ **Sea Of Galilee**[102] 3411 4-9-10 84 .... DaneO'Neill 9 88
(Henry Candy) *hld up in mid-div: effrt over 3f out: kpt on fnl f* **12/1**

5161 **4** nk **West End Lad**[16] 6227 8-9-4 78 .... RussKennemore 3 81
(Roy Bowring) *trckd ldr: chal 4f out: outpcd over 2f out: rallied and edgd lft over 1f out: kpt on same pce* **25/1**

1400 **5** shd **Star In Flight**[33] 5693 4-9-5 79 .... SebSanders 5 82
(Brian Meehan) *s.i.s: hld up in rr: drvn and outpcd over 3f out: kpt on fnl f* **14/1**

2006 **6** 2 ½ **Mcbirney (USA)**[18] 6173 4-9-8 82 .... PaulHanagan 8 80
(Paul D'Arcy) *hld up in rr: hdwy to chse ldrs over 2f out: fdd fnl f* **11/2**[3]

251 **7** nk **Landaman (IRE)**[20] 6097 3-9-4 83 .... SilvestreDeSousa 1 81
(Mark Johnston) *sn led: hdd over 1f out: wknd last 150yds* **7/2**[2]

40 **8** 1 ¼ **Amistress**[9] 6402 3-8-8 73 .... CathyGannon 2 68
(Eve Johnson Houghton) *in rr: drvn over 4f out: hdwy over 2f out: n.m.r over 1f out: wknd and eased ins fnl f* **10/1**

600 **9** 5 **Emma's Gift (IRE)**[13] 6273 3-9-1 80 .... JimmyQuinn 7 66
(Julia Feilden) *in rr: sme hdwy over 3f out: wknd 2f out* **33/1**

2m 12.18s (0.48) **Going Correction** +0.025s/f (Good)
WFA 3 from 4yo+ 5lb 9 Ran SP% **115.5**
Speed ratings (Par 105): **99,96,95,95,95 93,93,92,88**
toteswingers:1&2:£3.20, 2&3:£5.90, 1&3:£12.60 CSF £18.38 CT £140.50 TOTE £5.40: £1.30, £1.50, £3.30; EX 20.90 Trifecta £161.90 Pool of £886.59 - 4.05 winning units..
Owner Martin P Graham **Bred** Carmel Stud **Trained** Lambourn, Berks

FOCUS
The visual impression was of a modest early gallop that increased prematurely and most of these were under pressure early in the straight. The time was 0.26 seconds faster than the first division.

6633 NOTTINGHAM RACECOURSE RATING RELATED MAIDEN STKS 1m 2f 50y
5:00 (5:00) (Class 5) 3-Y-O+ **£2,264** (£673; £336; £168) **Stalls** Low

Form RPR

4262 **1** **Figaro**[20] 6096 3-9-0 80 .... PaulHanagan 1 88
(William Haggas) *mde all: pushed along and styd on wl fnl 3f: readily* **6/5**[1]

4430 **2** 3 ¼ **Monopolize**[25] 5911 3-9-0 77 .... TomQueally 2 81
(Sir Henry Cecil) *chsd ldrs: dropped bk last and drvn after 3f: chsd wnr 3f out: hung lft: no imp* **3/1**[3]

0232 **3** 22 **Sunday Bess (JPN)**[19] 6136 3-8-11 77 .... (b1) KierenFallon 3 35
(Tom Dascombe) *s.s: sn trcking ldrs: drvn over 5f out: lost pl over 2f out: sn bhd* **2/1**[2]

5305 **4** 25 **Munaawib**[13] 6279 3-9-0 65 .... (p) SilvestreDeSousa 4 —
(David C Griffiths) *chsd wnr: drvn over 4f out: wknd 3f out: bhd whn eased over 1f out: t.o* **33/1**

2m 10.6s (-1.10) **Going Correction** +0.025s/f (Good) 4 Ran SP% **106.7**
Speed ratings (Par 103): **105,102,84,64**
CSF £4.96 TOTE £1.90; EX 6.50.
Owner A Duke & R Smith **Bred** Cheveley Park Stud Ltd **Trained** Newmarket, Suffolk

FOCUS
An uncompetitive maiden, though the time was faster than both divisions of the handicap.

6634 RACINGUK.COM APPRENTICE H'CAP 6f 15y
5:30 (5:30) (Class 5) (0-70,68) 3-Y-O+ **£2,264** (£673; £336; £168) **Stalls** Centre

Form RPR

3114 **1** **Paradise Spectre**[20] 6091 4-9-7 68 .... MartinHarley 14 81
(Mrs K Burke) *racd stands' side: in rr: hdwy to chse ldrs 3f out: styd on to ld last 100yds* **15/2**

3140 **2** 1 ¾ **Brave Dream**[43] 5338 3-9-0 65 .... JulieBurke(3) 13 72
(Kevin Ryan) *racd stands' side: chsd ldrs: overall ldr over 1f out: hdd and no ex ins fnl f* **12/1**

2235 **3** 1 **Tislaam (IRE)**[13] 6276 4-9-0 68 .... (e1) RyanTate(7) 16 72
(Alan McCabe) *racd stands' side: mid-div: hdwy 2f out: styd on ins fnl f* **7/1**[3]

2022 **4** 2 ¾ **Arrivaderci**[11] 6353 3-9-3 65 .... (p) AmyRyan 15 60
(Richard Whitaker) *racd stands' side: in rr: kpt on fnl 2f: nvr trbld ldrs* **12/1**

2004 **5** hd **Bermondsey Bob (IRE)**[37] 5561 5-9-6 67 .... JamesSullivan 10 62
(John Spearing) *s.i.s: racd stands' side: hdwy to chse ldrs over 2f out: kpt on same pce ins fnl f* **12/1**

1065 **6** shd **Volito**[36] 5587 5-9-5 66 .... MichaelO'Connell 7 60
(Anabel K Murphy) *hld up towards rr: hdwy 2f out: kpt on fnl f: nvr rchd ldrs* **16/1**

2000 **7** ½ **Rainy Night**[5] 6502 5-9-5 66 .... (v) PaulPickard 5 59
(Reg Hollinshead) *racd far side: chsd ldrs: overall ldr 2f out: sn hdd and fdd* **16/1**

001 **8** 1 ¾ **Captain Macarry (IRE)**[7] 6453 6-9-7 68 6ex .... (v) RyanClark 2 55
(Stuart Williams) *racd far side: mid-div: kpt on fnl 2f: nvr nr to chal* **7/2**[1]

2136 **9** 1 ½ **Starbound (IRE)**[32] 5731 3-9-4 66 .... AdamBeschizza 4 48
(William Haggas) *racd far side: chsd ldrs: wknd appr fnl f* **11/2**[2]

6003 **10** 1 ½ **Wolf Slayer**[14] 6266 3-9-1 63 .... (t) RossAtkinson 3 40
(Tom Dascombe) *s.i.s: racd far side: nvr a factor* **25/1**

1006 **11** nk **Moral Issue**[15] 6231 3-9-6 68 .... DeclanCannon 1 44
(Jedd O'Keeffe) *racd far side: chsd ldrs: lost pl over 1f out* **18/1**

0400 **12** 5 **Dubai Celebration**[25] 5925 3-9-3 65 .... (b1) PatrickDonaghy 17 25
(Jedd O'Keeffe) *racd stands' side: chsd ldrs: lost pl 2f out* **16/1**

5140 **13** 4 ½ **South African Gold (USA)**[19] 6119 4-9-1 62 .... (p) MatthewDavies 11 —
(James Eustace) *racd far side: chsd ldrs: wknd 2f out* **22/1**

0500 **14** 3 ½ **Besty**[32] 5732 4-8-6 60 .... (v) ShirleyTeasdale(7) 9 —
(David Nicholls) *racd far side: w ldr: wknd 2f out* **20/1**

0016 **15** 5 **Too Many Questions (IRE)**[9] 6403 3-9-2 64 .... (p) SophieDoyle 8 —
(David Evans) *racd far side: led tl hdd & wknd 2f out* **40/1**

1m 15.64s (0.74) **Going Correction** +0.025s/f (Good)
WFA 3 from 4yo+ 1lb 15 Ran SP% **123.3**
Speed ratings (Par 103): **96,93,92,88,88 88,87,85,83,81 80,74,68,63,56**
toteswingers:1&2:£13.60, 2&3:£22.40, 1&3:£10.10. Tote Super 7: Win: Not won. Place: £110.00 CSF £91.58 CT £483.07 TOTE £7.40: £3.30, £5.20, £2.60; EX 73.20 Trifecta £72.30 Pool: £654.99 - 6.70 winning units..
Owner The Paradise Partnership **Bred** Bearstone Stud **Trained** Middleham Moor, North Yorks

FOCUS
The field split into two groups after a couple of furlongs or so and those stands' side were at an advantage over the far-side bunch, with the first five finishers drawn in double figures.
T/Jkpt: Not won. T/Plt: £68.90 to a £1 stake. Pool of £73,052.35 - 773.98 winning tickets. T/Qpdt: £26.40 to a £1 stake. Pool of £4,527.27 - 126.50 winning tickets. WG

6635 - 6643a (Foreign Racing) - See Raceform Interactive

6424 AYR (L-H)
Thursday, October 6

OFFICIAL GOING: Heavy (abandoned after race 3 in the interests of safety due to deteriorating weather conditions)
Wind: Strong, half against Weather: Overcast, showers

6644 SERIC SYSTEMS STKS BRITISH STALLION STUDS E B F MAIDEN STAKES 1m
2:10 (2:13) (Class 4) 2-Y-O **£4,463** (£1,328; £663; £331) **Stalls** High

Form RPR

4 **1** **Never Perfect (IRE)**[38] 5548 2-9-3 0 .... JamieSpencer 1 74+
(Tom Tate) *prom: sn pushed along: rdn over 3f out: hdwy to ld 2f out: pushed out hands and heels fnl f* **4/9**[1]

0 **2** *1 ¼* **Hunting Gonk**[22] 6048 2-9-3 0 .... FrederikTylicki 4 69
(James Given) *led 1f: trckd ldr: rdn and ev ch 2f out: sn rdn: kpt on fnl f: nt rch wnr* **20/1**

0443 **3** *3 ½* **Joshua The First**[19] 6144 2-9-3 70 .... JoeFanning 5 61
(Keith Dalgleish) *trckd ldrs: pushed along whn n.m.r over 2f out: edgd lft over 1f out: one pce* **7/2**[2]

00 **4** *4* **Night Flash (GER)**[15] 6259 2-9-3 0 .... JamesSullivan 6 52
(James Given) *bhd and sn outpcd: rdn to improve over 3f out: outpcd and struggling over 2f out: nvr on terms* **66/1**

0 **5** *1 ¼* **Ashwaat**[16] 6230 2-9-3 0 .... SilvestreDeSousa 3 49
(Mark Johnston) *led after 1f: rdn and hdd 2f out: sn wknd* **9/1**[3]

1m 56.62s (12.82) **Going Correction** +1.55s/f (Heav) **5** Ran SP% **107.7**
Speed ratings (Par 97): **97,95,92,88,87**
CSF £10.48 TOTE £1.50: £1.10, £5.60; EX 13.00.
Owner Mrs Fitri Hay **Bred** Dr K Schulte **Trained** Tadcaster, N Yorks

FOCUS
Home straight moved out 6m from innermost line. After 9mm of rain overnight and plenty more in the lead up to racing, the ground was testing in the extreme and conditions were made worse by a strong, swirling wind. The form has been rated negatively through the fourth.

NOTEBOOK
Never Perfect(IRE), a son of Galileo, had shaped with promise after a slow start when fourth first time at Newcastle. A grand type, he still has plenty to learn, but definitely has a future, probably over middle distances at three. Not the best away, he needed plenty of driving and seemed to idle in front. His handicap mark surely cannot exceed 80 and he will be much more the finished article mentally and physically next year. (op 2-5 tchd 1-2)
Hunting Gonk, who showed little on his debut, deserves credit for the way he stuck to his task in pursuit of the winner. He finished clear of the 70-rated third, so he cannot expect a lenient handicap mark after one more outing. (op 25-1)
Joshua The First, placed seven times in 11 previous starts, seemed to struggle in the conditions and it is very doubtful if he ran to his official mark of 70. (tchd 3-1)
Night Flash(GER), having his third run, had shown little and was soon struggling to keep up. (op 50-1 tchd 40-1)
Ashwaat, soon taking them along on his second start, tired badly and, eased, lost fourth place near the line. A well-made son of Authorised, he can surely do better at three. (op 8-1)

6645 BUD AND JOE PIERONI MEMORIAL NURSERY 6f
2:40 (2:45) (Class 5) (0-75,75) 2-Y-O **£2,264** (£673; £336; £168) **Stalls** Low

Form RPR

260 **1** **First Phase**[22] 6045 2-8-5 **59** .... DuranFentiman 4 63
(Mel Brittain) *chsd ldng gp: rdn and outpcd over 2f out: hdwy over 1f out: hrd rdn and led ins fnl f: kpt on wl* **25/1**

1264 **2** *1 ½* **Act Your Shoe Size**[20] 6111 2-9-7 **75** .... JoeFanning 9 75
(Keith Dalgleish) *trckd ldrs: pushed along 2f out: effrt and chsd wnr ins fnl f: no ex nr fin* **6/1**[2]

3160 **3** *3 ½* **Stormy Whatever (FR)**[19] 6154 2-9-6 **74** ....(t) FrederikTylicki 1 63
(James Given) *cl up: led over 2f out: rdn and hdd ins fnl f: wknd towards fin* **6/1**[2]

0402 **4** *hd* **Johnson's Cat (IRE)**[9] 6425 2-7-12 **52** oh1 .... JamesSullivan 6 40
(Richard Guest) *in tch: rdn and outpcd over 2f out: rallied appr fnl f: kpt on fin: nvr able to chal* **9/1**[3]

0652 **5** *½* **Silvas Romana (IRE)**[13] 6293 2-9-6 **74** .... TomMcLaughlin 8 61
(Mark Brisbourne) *cl up: ev ch over 2f out: sn rdn: n.m.r and wknd ins fnl f* **10/1**

0115 **6** *6* **Sinai (IRE)**[18] 6186 2-9-4 **72** .... RobertWinston 2 41
(Geoffrey Harker) *hld up: hdwy over 2f out: sn cl up: wknd ent fnl f* **11/1**

4332 **7** *2 ¼* **Fast On (IRE)**[14] 6284 2-8-8 **67** ....(v) ShaneBKelly(5) 3 29
(Ed McMahon) *w ldrs: rdn over 2f out: wknd over 1f out* **6/1**[2]

0540 **8** *6* **Alnair (IRE)**[13] 6293 2-8-11 **65** .... DanielTudhope 10 9
(Declan Carroll) *in tch: effrt over 2f out: wknd over 1f out* **16/1**

3000 **9** *22* **Quiet Appeal (IRE)**[15] 6260 2-7-12 **52** .... SilvestreDeSousa 5 —
(Mark Johnston) *dwlt: bhd and sn pushed along: lost tch fr 1/2-way: t.o* **11/1**

1202 **10** *1 ¾* **Blue Shoes (IRE)**[10] 6413 2-8-9 **63** .... PaulHanagan 7 —
(Tim Easterby) *led to over 2f out: sn rdn and wknd: eased whn no ch fr over 1f out* **3/1**[1]

1m 26.15s (13.75) **Going Correction** +2.275s/f (Heav) **10** Ran SP% **113.3**
Speed ratings (Par 95): **99,97,92,92,91 83,80,72,43,40**
Toteswingers:1&2:£39.40, 1&3:£32.70, 2&3:£6.30 CSF £163.91 CT £1052.15 TOTE £33.80: £8.80, £2.20, £2.20; EX 265.90 Trifecta £481.70 Part won. Pool: £651.03 - 0.65 winning units..
Owner Mel Brittain **Bred** Mel Brittain **Trained** Warthill, N Yorks
■ Stewards' Enquiry : Tom McLaughlin two-day ban: failed to ride out for 4th (Oct 20-21)

FOCUS
A modest nursery, run in a time almost 16 seconds slower than the RP standard. It has been rated around the first two.

NOTEBOOK
First Phase, runner-up in a soft ground maiden at Beverley on her debut, had failed to reproduce that effort in two subsequent starts on much quicker ground. Making her nursery debut from a mark of 59, she was off the pace and under pressure with just one behind her at halfway. Making ground down the wide outside, in the end her stamina carried her to the front near the line. Whether she can reproduce this effort on anything but almost unraceable ground remains to be seen. (op 20-1)
Act Your Shoe Size, who took a 7f Catterick soft-ground nursery from a 4lb lower mark, worked hard to get her head in front only to be mugged by the winner near the line. She is tough and consistent. (op 5-1 tchd 7-1)
Stormy Whatever(FR), whose four previous starts were all at Catterick, readily accounted for Blue Shoes in a soft-ground maiden on his second start. After a couple of moderate efforts he bounced back in a first-time tongue tie. (op 15-2)
Johnson's Cat(IRE), who gave problems at the start, seemed to show much improved form on his sixth start when runner-up in a non-handicap here a week earlier. Due to race from a 9lb higher mark in future, he stayed on when it was all over. (op 10-1 tchd 11-1)
Silvas Romana(IRE), raised 4lb after finishing runner-up from a favourable draw at Haydock, travelled strongly but didn't seem to get home in the conditions. (op 11-1)
Blue Shoes(IRE), due to go up 3lb after her hard-fought and narrow defeat in the mud at Hamilton 10 days earlier, dropped right out soon after halfway and came home in her own time. This was probably too soon in the conditions after her hard race there. Official explanation: trainer had no explanation for the poor form shown (op 5-2)

6646 INTECHNOLOGY SERVICES H'CAP 6f
3:10 (3:22) (Class 6) (0-65,63) 3-Y-O+ **£1,704** (£503; £251) **Stalls** Low

Form RPR

2542 **1** **Cheyenne Red (IRE)**[17] 6208 5-8-7 **49** oh2 .... PJMcDonald 9 56
(Michael Dods) *cl up: rdn to ld over 1f out: kpt on wl u.p fnl f* **6/1**[2]

0533 **2** *¾* **Mark Anthony (IRE)**[12] 6343 4-9-5 **61** ....(p) FrannyNorton 1 66
(Shaun Harris) *led to over 1f out: sn drvn: rallied to chse wnr ins fnl f: kpt on* **14/1**

5560 **3** *1 ¼* **Tadalavil**[17] 6208 6-9-4 **63** .... DaleSwift(3) 4 64
(Linda Perratt) *trckd ldrs: drvn and edgd lft over 1f out: kpt on ins fnl f* **7/1**

0004 **4** *nk* **Gracie's Gift (IRE)**[9] 6426 9-8-10 **52** ....(v) SilvestreDeSousa 11 52
(Richard Guest) *hld up in midfield: hdwy and ev ch over 1f out: no ex ins fnl f* **13/2**[3]

3542 **5** *1* **Mottley Crewe**[13] 6305 4-9-4 **63** .... MartinHarley(3) 6 60
(Richard Guest) *hld up: smooth hdwy over 2f out: chsd ldrs 1f out: wknd ins fnl f* **10/1**

1000 **6** *½* **Monte Mayor One**[11] 6386 4-8-13 **55** .... LeeNewman 7 51
(Jim Goldie) *in tch: drvn and outpcd over 2f out: kpt on fnl f: no imp* **28/1**

4630 **7** *6* **Cheeky Wee Red**[11] 6386 3-8-7 **50** .... PaulHanagan 5 28
(Richard Fahey) *in tch: drvn and outpcd over 2f out: sn btn* **14/1**

0004 **8** *2 ¾* **Choc'A'Moca (IRE)**[15] 6266 4-9-7 **63** ....(v) FrederikTylicki 3 33
(Paul Midgley) *hld up in tch: shortlived effrt over 2f out: sn btn* **10/1**

0000 **9** *4 ½* **Durham Express (IRE)**[9] 6426 4-9-0 **59** ....(b) LeeTopliss(3) 2 15
(Michael Dods) *taken early to post: cl up tl rdn and wknd wl over 1f out* **14/1**

6312 **10** *1 ¾* **Chookie Avon**[9] 6428 4-9-4 **60** ....(p) JoeFanning 10 11
(Keith Dalgleish) *hld up: struggling over 2f out: sn btn* **7/4**[1]

1m 25.55s (13.15) **Going Correction** +2.275s/f (Heav)
WFA 3 from 4yo+ 1lb **10** Ran SP% **118.1**
Speed ratings (Par 101): **103,102,100,99,98 97,89,86,80,77**
Toteswingers:1&2:£9.40, 1&3:£8.40, 2&3:£15.10 CSF £87.29 CT £617.92 TOTE £5.90: £2.00, £3.30, £2.80; EX 82.40 Trifecta £403.20 Part won. Pool: £544.94 - 0.43 winning units..
Owner Crown Lanark And The Beverley Boys **Bred** Crandon Park Stud **Trained** Denton, Co Durham

FOCUS
A low-grade sprint handicap, no better than a seller. The race was delayed while the jockeys were consulted about the safety of the ground. Winning jockey P J McDonald, a former jump rider who won a Scottish National here, reckoned it was the worst ground he has ever ridden on on the Flat. Weak and unreliable form.
Chookie Avon Official explanation: jockey said gelding lost its action closing stages

6647 BEAZLEY MARINE INSURANCE H'CAP 5f
() (Class 5) (0-70,) 3-Y-O £

6648 LASER LIFE H'CAP 1m 2f
() (Class 4) (0-80,) 3-Y-O+ £

6649 GILES INSURANCE H'CAP (DIV I) 1m 1f 20y
() (Class 5) (0-70,) 3-Y-O+ £

6650 GILES INSURANCE AYR H'CAP (DIV II) 1m 1f 20y
() (Class 5) (0-70,) 3-Y-O+ £

6651 GILES INSURANCE CORPORATE H'CAP 7f 50y
() (Class 5) (0-75,) 3-Y-O+ £

T/Plt: £14.90 to a £1 stake. Pool:£73,416.77 - 3,595.86 winning tickets T/Qpdt: £3.30 to a £1 stake. Pool:£4,887.56 - 1,073.16 winning tickets RY

6539 WOLVERHAMPTON (A.W) (L-H)
Thursday, October 6

OFFICIAL GOING: Standard
Wind: Strong behind Weather: Cloudy

6652 BETDSL.COM (S) STKS 7f 32y(P)
5:20 (5:20) (Class 6) 2-Y-O **£1,704** (£503; £251) **Stalls** High

Form RPR

5014 **1** **Latte**[30] 5802 2-9-2 70 ....(p) KierenFallon 5 67
(Linda Stubbs) *chsd ldrs: rdn to ld ins fnl f: r.o* **5/1**[2]

2 *nse* **Hilali (IRE)** 2-8-11 0 .... LiamKeniry 8 62
(Gary Brown) *chsd ldrs: rdn: edgd lft and ev ch ins fnl f: r.o* **20/1**

0634 **3** *1 ½* **Zammy**[14] 6280 2-8-11 68 .... DarryllHolland 3 58+
(Charles Hills) *a.p: nt clr run fr over 1f out tl swtchd rt wl ins fnl f: r.o to go 3rd nr finnish: nt rch ldrs* **7/2**[1]

2420 **4** *nk* **Flying Pickets (IRE)**[22] 6053 2-9-2 62 .... NeilCallan 2 64
(Alan McCabe) *prom: hmpd and lost pl over 6f out: hdwy 2f out: rdn and ev ch ins fnl f: no ex nr fin* **8/1**

2136 **5** *1 ¼* **Artists Corner**[14] 6284 2-8-11 62 .... BarryMcHugh 6 54
(Richard Fahey) *hld up: hdwy over 1f out: rdn and n.m.r ins fnl f: styd on same pce* **6/1**[3]

4013 **6** *1* **Jimmy The Lollipop (IRE)**[12] 6345 2-9-2 67 ....(b) PhillipMakin 12 57
(Kevin Ryan) *led: rdn over 1f out: hdd and no ex ins fnl f* **7/2**[1]

0030 **7** *¾* **Garrarufa (IRE)**[21] 6101 2-8-11 59 ....(b[1]) JamesMillman 7 50
(Rod Millman) *hld up: rdn 1/2-way: hdwy 2f out: no ex fnl f* **14/1**

525 **8** *hd* **Marie's Fantasy**[139] 2248 2-8-3 60 .... DeclanCannon(3) 4 44
(Gay Kelleway) *hld up: hdwy over 2f out: sn rdn and no ex fnl f* **22/1**

5025 **9** *2 ¾* **Tyre Giant Dot Com**[19] 6178 2-8-11 66 ....(p) TomEaves 9 43
(Geoffrey Oldroyd) *chsd ldr: rdn over 2f out: wknd fnl f* **10/1**

5 **10** *4* **Factor Three**[98] 3554 2-8-11 0 ....(p) RobbieFitzpatrick 10 33
(Michael Appleby) *s.i.s: a in rr* **40/1**

60 **11** *19* **Ned Causer**[14] 6280 2-8-11 0 .... TonyCulhane 11 —
(Reg Hollinshead) *hld up: a in rr: wknd over 2f out* **50/1**

1m 31.63s (2.03) **Going Correction** +0.05s/f (Slow) **11** Ran SP% **115.8**
Speed ratings (Par 93): **90,89,88,87,86 85,84,84,81,76 54**
.There was no bid for the winner. Hilali was subject to a freindly claim. Jimmy The Lollipop was claimed by Neil Mulholland for £6,000. Zammy was claimed by D. Hassan for £6,000.\n\x\x
Owner Tyme Partnership **Bred** Edmond And Richard Kent **Trained** Norton, N Yorks
■ Stewards' Enquiry : Phillip Makin three-day ban: careless riding (Oct 21,24-25)

FOCUS
The going was standard on a windy and rainy evening. A modest seller for 2yos. There was tight finish in a strongly run race and the well-backed third didn't get much luck.

NOTEBOOK
Latte benefited from the application of cheekpieces when slamming his rivals in a Yarmouth seller. He was unable to dominate in the same grade last time, but a switch to more patient tactics worked and he found a determined run to register a second win. A current mark of 70 may overrate him a bit, but he has done well since cheekpieces have been applied and should continue to be formidable in this grade. (tchd 9-2)
Hilali(IRE), a Shadwell cast-off who changed hands for just £2,200 in June, finished well out wide but was just denied at a big price on debut. (op 66-1)
Zammy did best of those ridden from off the pace when fourth behind a 64-rated rival in a C&D claimer last time. One of the least exposed runners in the line-up, he was strong in the market but ran into some traffic problems before staying on well. He rates better than his finishing position and seems to be quietly progressing. (op 9-2)

Flying Pickets(IRE) seemed to have stamina issues over 1m at Kempton last time, but he had claims on his previous trailblazing second off 58 at Southwell and did well to work his way into fourth after getting hampered at an early stage. Official explanation: jockey said gelding suffered interference shortly after start (op 7-1)
Artists Corner was niggled along early on, but she battled well to finish near the leading bunch. (op 9-2)
Jimmy The Lollipop(IRE) set a decent pace, but couldn't fight off closers on both sides. He may have paid the price for using up energy to grab the lead from a wide draw. (tchd 10-3)

6653 BIDS 5 SCREEN SYSTEM FROM MRG MEDIAN AUCTION MAIDEN STKS 7f 32y(P)
5:50 (5:50) (Class 5) 3-4-Y-O £2,264 (£673; £336; £168) Stalls High

Form RPR
5032 **1** **Ducal**[21] 6089 3-9-3 71 .... SebSanders 10 79
(Sir Mark Prescott Bt) *prom: chsd ldr over 2f out: led over 1f out: rdn out* **1/1**[1]
2 **2** 1/2 **Good Authority (IRE)**[19] 6177 4-9-5 70 .... DarryllHolland 5 78
(Karen George) *hld up: hdwy over 1f out: r.o to go 2nd towards fin: nt rch wnr* **11/4**[2]
P232 **3** 1 3/4 **Chokidar (IRE)**[13] 6307 3-9-3 72 ....(b) IanMongan 2 73
(David Nicholls) *led: rdn and hdd wl over 1f out: styd on same pce ins fnl f* **7/2**[3]
0406 **4** 6 **Faith And Hope (IRE)**[30] 5803 3-8-12 64 ....(vt[1]) KierenFallon 7 52
(James Fanshawe) *hld up in tch: rdn over 1f out: wknd fnl f* **10/1**
50 **5** 1 1/2 **Goldstorm**[26] 5946 3-8-12 0 .... J-PGuillambert 8 48
(Brian Baugh) *sn pushed along in rr: styd on ins fnl f: nvr nrr* **66/1**
3-30 **6** 1 3/4 **Laugh Or Cry**[17] 6228 3-9-3 65 .... ShaneKelly 3 48
(Dean Ivory) *chsd ldrs: rdn over 1f out: sn wknd* **16/1**
0 **7** 2 1/4 **Skystream (IRE)**[10] 6415 3-8-12 60 .... TomEaves 6 37
(Ian Semple) *chsd ldrs tl rdn and wknd over 2f out* **25/1**
5000 **8** 2 **Gessabelle**[22] 6071 4-8-7 30 ....(tp) LauraSimpson(7) 9 32
(Phil McEntee) *prom: jnd ldr over 5f out tl rdn 1/2-way: wknd over 2f out* **200/1**
5000 **9** 3/4 **Anathena**[7] 6494 3-8-12 52 .... TonyCulhane 1 30
(Reg Hollinshead) *hld up: nt clr run over 2f out: nt rcvr* **50/1**
4000 **10** 2 1/2 **Dark Pegasus**[35] 5644 3-9-0 45 .... KierenFox(3) 4 28
(Karen George) *sn pushed along in rr: bhd fr 1/2-way* **100/1**

1m 29.72s (0.12) **Going Correction** +0.05s/f (Slow)
WFA 3 from 4yo 2lb 10 Ran SP% 122.6
Speed ratings (Par 103): **101,100,98,91,89 87,85,83,82,79**
toteswingers:1&2:£2.10, 1&3:£2.20, 2&3:£2.40 CSF £4.18 TOTE £2.90: £1.10, £1.10, £1.10; EX 5.50.
Owner Cheveley Park Stud **Bred** Cheveley Park Stud Ltd **Trained** Newmarket, Suffolk
FOCUS
The three market leaders, who were rated between 70 and 72, pulled clear in this modest maiden.

6654 SIS LIVE MEDIAN AUCTION MAIDEN STKS 5f 216y(P)
6:20 (6:21) (Class 6) 2-Y-0 £1,704 (£503; £251) Stalls Low

Form RPR
5 **1** **Purple 'n Gold (IRE)**[20] 6118 2-9-3 0 .... PatCosgrave 4 76+
(George Baker) *hld up in tch: rdn to ld ins fnl f: r.o wl* **3/1**[1]
04 **2** 2 1/4 **Remix (IRE)**[20] 6131 2-8-12 0 .... SebSanders 5 64
(J W Hills) *chsd ldr: rdn to ld over 1f out: hdd and unable qck ins fnl f* **7/1**[3]
55 **3** 3/4 **Art Show**[34] 5689 2-8-12 0 .... KierenFallon 7 62
(Ed Dunlop) *s.i.s: hdwy over 2f out: sn rdn: styd on* **4/1**[2]
56 **4** 1 **Stepharlie**[21] 6075 2-8-12 0 .... TomEaves 1 59
(Bryan Smart) *sn led: rdn and hdd over 2f out: no ex ins fnl f* **14/1**
5 2 3/4 **Decision By One** 2-9-3 0 .... RichardKingscote 12 56+
(Tom Dascombe) *hld up: r.o ins fnl f: nvr nrr* **20/1**
6 1 1/4 **Chaud Lapin** 2-9-3 0 .... WilliamCarson 3 55+
(Giles Bravery) *chsd ldrs: led over 2f out: rdn and hdd over 1f out: wknd ins fnl f* **4/1**[2]
7 nk **Princess Kaiulani (IRE)** 2-8-12 0 .... MartinDwyer 9 46
(William Muir) *hld up: hdwy over 1f out: nvr on terms* **16/1**
0356 **8** hd **Monumental Man**[5] 6539 2-9-3 70 ....(p) LiamJones 8 51
(James Unett) *hld up in tch: rdn over 1f out: sn wknd* **14/1**
40 **9** 2 1/4 **Whatyououghttodo (IRE)**[71] 4080 2-9-3 0 .... ChrisCatlin 10 43
(David Lanigan) *prom: rdn over 2f out: wknd over 1f out* **10/1**
04 **10** 3/4 **Claretintheblood (IRE)**[15] 6259 2-9-3 0 .... BarryMcHugh 6 41
(Richard Fahey) *chsd ldrs tl rdn and wknd over 2f out* **14/1**
11 3/4 **Lana Mae** 2-8-12 0 .... LukeMorris 11 34
(Jeremy Gask) *sn pushed along in rr: n.d* **33/1**
0 **12** hd **You Got The Love**[52] 5111 2-8-9 0 .... KierenFox(3) 13 33
(Jeremy Gask) *s.i.s: a in rr* **66/1**
0 **13** 1 1/2 **Jeremy Sue**[10] 6406 2-8-12 0 .... FrankieMcDonald 2 28
(Derek Haydn Jones) *s.i.s: outpcd* **200/1**

1m 15.97s (0.97) **Going Correction** +0.05s/f (Slow) 13 Ran SP% 122.2
Speed ratings (Par 93): **95,92,91,89,86 84,83,83,80,79 78,78,76**
toteswingers:1&2:£6.60, 1&3:£3.60, 2&3:£2.40 CSF £24.39 TOTE £4.10: £1.40, £2.80, £1.80; EX 29.80.
Owner M Khan X2 **Bred** Stonethorn Stud Farms Ltd **Trained** Whitsbury, Hants
■ Stewards' Enquiry : Pat Cosgrave caution: used whip with excessive frequency.
FOCUS
An ordinary maiden run at a decent pace and little depth in behind the winner.
NOTEBOOK
Purple 'n Gold(IRE) looked too green to do himself justice when 11-2 for a Lingfield maiden on debut, but he looked more streetwise this time and stayed on strongly out wide to win going away stepped up to 6f. The form is not very strong, but there was quite a bit to like about the style of victory and he has plenty of scope for further improvement at this trip and beyond. (op 4-1)
Remix(IRE), a staying-on fourth to a 63-rated rival in a C&D maiden on her recent return from a break, ran a decent race switched to more prominent tactics. She seems to be quietly progressing after three runs and should be suited by stepping up to 7f. (op 6-1 tchd 11-2)
Art Show had decent form claims and made a promising move early in the straight, but her effort flattened out. She still needs to learn to settle and break a bit better, but is a Dutch Art half-sister to tough multiple 5f winner Six Wives and should have scope for improvement as a sprinter. (op 7-2 tchd 3-1)
Stepharlie failed to build on her debut form last time, but she gave it a decent try switched to Polytrack, particularly as she set a strong pace. (tchd 16-1)
Decision By One, a speedily bred £50,000 half-brother to outside useful sprinter Taurus Twins, ran green from a wide draw but showed promise in staying on well from a long way back on debut. Official explanation: jockey said colt hung right-handed throughout (op 14-1)
Chaud Lapin was strongly supported and showed up well for a long way before fading on debut. He was retained for just 1,500gns at the breeze-ups, but is out of a quite useful 2yo winner and seems to have inherited quite a bit of speed. (op 5-1 tchd 11-2)
Jeremy Sue Official explanation: jockey said filly ran green

6655 ELITE DIGITAL SYSTEMS LAUNCHING SYSTEMBEE 01925232882 H'CAP 5f 20y(P)
6:50 (6:51) (Class 6) (0-65,65) 3-Y-0+ £1,704 (£503; £251) Stalls Low

Form RPR
2163 **1** **Colourbearer (IRE)**[28] 5846 4-9-7 65 ....(t) KierenFallon 6 80
(Milton Bradley) *hld up: plld hrd: hdwy over 1f out: rdn to ld wl ins fnl f: sn clr* **7/2**[1]
0400 **2** 2 1/4 **Tabaret**[22] 6044 8-9-7 65 .... TonyCulhane 2 72
(Richard Whitaker) *a.p: pushed along 1/2-way: rdn to ld ins fnl f: sn hdd and unable qck* **22/1**
6000 **3** nk **Morermaloke**[15] 6261 3-8-12 59 ....(p) PaulPickard(3) 1 66
(Ian McInnes) *hld up: hdwy over 1f out: r.o wl* **25/1**
4000 **4** 1/2 **Fear Nothing**[6] 6501 4-9-2 60 ....(b) TomEaves 5 64
(Ian McInnes) *led: hdd over 3f out: rdn and ev ch ins fnl f: one pce* **16/1**
4401 **5** shd **Howyadoingnotsobad (IRE)**[19] 6176 3-8-11 58 .... KierenFox(3) 7 63
(Karen George) *chsd ldrs: rdn over 1f out: nt clr run ins fnl f: kpt on* **6/1**[3]
4225 **6** 1/2 **Adventure Story**[28] 5846 4-9-7 65 .... FergusSweeney 3 67
(Peter Makin) *hld up: nt clr run 2f out: swtchd rt and hdwy over 1f out: nt rch ldrs* **10/1**
4252 **7** 1 3/4 **Sharp Shoes**[9] 6427 4-9-7 65 ....(p) DavidNolan 4 61
(Ann Duffield) *chsd ldr: led over 3f out: rdn over 1f out: hdd and no ex ins fnl f* **9/2**[2]
5400 **8** 1/2 **Defector (IRE)**[20] 6133 5-9-7 65 .... MarkLawson 10 59
(Seamus Durack) *s.i.s: hld up: nt clr run over 1f out: r.o ins fnl f: nrst fin* **9/1**
5363 **9** 2 1/4 **Towy Boy (IRE)**[27] 5895 6-9-5 63 ....(bt) MartinLane 13 49
(Ian Wood) *dwlt: a in rr* **12/1**
5606 **10** 2 **Ignatieff (IRE)**[38] 5552 4-9-4 62 .... DarryllHolland 11 40
(Linda Stubbs) *hld up: nvr on terms* **18/1**
3000 **11** 2 1/4 **Grand Stitch (USA)**[55] 4986 5-9-1 64 ....(v) NeilFarley(5) 12 34
(Declan Carroll) *s.i.s: sn pushed along and a in rr* **22/1**
1020 **12** 1 1/4 **Eshoog (IRE)**[22] 6065 3-8-12 63 ....(bt) LeonnaMayor(7) 9 30
(Phil McEntee) *chsd ldrs: rdn 1/2-way: sn wknd* **11/1**
4260 **13** 2 3/4 **Black Baccara**[22] 6065 4-8-11 62 .... DannyBrock(7) 8 18
(Phil McEntee) *mid-div: rdn and wknd 1/2-way* **33/1**

61.88 secs (-0.42) **Going Correction** +0.05s/f (Slow) 13 Ran SP% 116.4
Speed ratings (Par 101): **105,101,100,100,99 99,96,95,91,88 85,83,78**
toteswingers:1&2:£12.80, 1&3:£33.60, 2&3:£76.20 CSF £87.62 CT £1668.47 TOTE £4.90: £2.10, £7.50, £11.70; EX 96.00.
Owner E A Hayward **Bred** Corduff Stud & J Corcorcan **Trained** Sedbury, Gloucs
■ Stewards' Enquiry : Paul Pickard two-day ban: used whip with excessive frequency (Oct 20-21)
FOCUS
A modest handicap. The pace was strong and the favourite scored in good style.
Adventure Story Official explanation: jockey said filly missed the break

6656 MANNY BERNSTEIN CLAIMING STKS 1m 4f 50y(P)
7:20 (7:20) (Class 6) 3-Y-0+ £1,704 (£503; £251) Stalls Low

Form RPR
05 **1** **Uphold**[8] 6445 4-9-12 86 ....(v[1]) NeilCallan 12 85+
(Gay Kelleway) *mde all: set stdy pce tl qcknd over 3f out: sn clr* **6/4**[1]
1300 **2** 9 **Ravi River (IRE)**[33] 5722 7-9-11 78 .... TomEaves 5 70+
(Brian Ellison) *hld up: plld hrd: hdwy over 1f out: nvr nr to chal* **11/4**[2]
0000 **3** shd **Ahlawy (IRE)**[8] 6461 8-8-13 79 ....(t) LiviaMachalikova(7) 9 65
(Frank Sheridan) *s.i.s: sn mid-div: hdwy to go 3rd over 2f out: nvr nrr* **33/1**
5-06 **4** 1 **Grand Art (IRE)**[13] 6306 7-8-13 65 ....(t) PatrickDonaghy(3) 3 59
(Frank Sheridan) *prom tl rdn and wknd over 2f out* **9/1**[3]
3204 **5** 1/2 **Mustajed**[8] 6461 10-9-5 63 ....(b) JamesMillman 4 61
(Rod Millman) *hld up: hdwy over 1f out: nvr on terms* **12/1**
5040 **6** hd **Kingsdale Orion (IRE)**[6] 5723 7-8-13 56 ....(t) PaulPickard(3) 2 58
(Brian Ellison) *hld up: nvr on terms* **10/1**
0465 **7** 1/2 **Peaceful Means (IRE)**[29] 5739 8-8-13 50 ....(t) NeilChalmers 10 54
(Michael Appleby) *mid-div: wknd over 2f out* **22/1**
5200 **8** 1 **Cloudy Bay (USA)**[43] 5389 4-9-6 61 ....(p) CathyGannon 8 59
(John Flint) *chsd wnr 2f: remained handy: wnt 2nd again 3f out: sn rdn and wknd over 1f out* **12/1**
4000 **9** 13 **Himalayan Moon**[12] 6356 4-9-3 46 .... MartinLane 11 36
(Ian Wood) *plld hrd: trckd wnr 10f out tl rdn 3f out: sn wknd* **80/1**
0 **10** hd **Harrys Yer Man**[14] 6286 7-9-8 0 .... ShaneKelly 1 40
(Mark Brisbourne) *hld up: bhd fnl 3f* **100/1**
0003 **11** 8 **Bold Indian (IRE)**[40] 5470 7-9-2 42 .... BarryMcHugh 7 22
(Mike Sowersby) *prom: wkng whn hmpd over 2f out* **66/1**
05-0 **12** 68 **Mouchez**[272] 86 4-9-0 46 .... PaulBooth(7) 6 —
(Dean Ivory) *s.s: sn pushed along in rr: bhd fr 1/2-way: t.o* **40/1**

2m 40.79s (-0.31) **Going Correction** +0.05s/f (Slow) 12 Ran SP% 114.6
Speed ratings (Par 101): **103,97,96,96,95 95,95,94,86,86 80,35**
toteswingers:1&2:£2.30, 1&3:£11.80, 2&3:£12.70 CSF £4.85 TOTE £2.30: £1.60, £1.30, £8.90; EX 6.60.Grand Art was claimed by D. B. Roberts for £2,000.
Owner Whispering Winds **Bred** Juddmonte Farms Ltd **Trained** Exning, Suffolk
■ Stewards' Enquiry : Patrick Donaghy two-day ban: careless riding (Oct 20-21)
FOCUS
The 86-rated favourite hammered his rivals in this claimer.

6657 CHRIS O'KEEFFE MEMORIAL H'CAP (DIV I) 1m 141y(P)
7:50 (7:51) (Class 6) (0-55,59) 3-Y-0+ £1,363 (£402; £201) Stalls Low

Form RPR
4664 **1** **Princess Gail**[5] 6545 3-8-10 49 .... ShaneKelly 12 61
(Mark Brisbourne) *hld up: hdwy over 3f out: chsd ldr over 2f out: led ins fnl f: rdn out* **5/1**[2]
0065 **2** 2 1/2 **Ad Vitam (IRE)**[7] 6494 3-8-13 52 ....(vt[1]) MichaelStainton 6 58
(David C Griffiths) *trckd ldrs: plld hrd: led on bit over 2f out: rdn over 1f out: hdd and no ex ins fnl f* **6/1**[3]
3451 **3** 4 **Cathcart Castle**[5] 6545 3-9-6 59 6ex .... TonyCulhane 8 56
(Mick Channon) *hld up: rdn and swtchd rt over 1f out: r.o ins fnl f: nrst fin* **3/1**[1]
0400 **4** 1 1/2 **Beauchamp Xiara**[7] 6493 5-8-11 53 .... NicoleNordblad(7) 3 46
(Hans Adielsson) *prom: lost pl over 3f out: n.d after* **18/1**
0000 **5** 1/2 **Hi Spec (IRE)**[13] 6310 8-8-13 48 ....(tp) JimmyQuinn 4 39
(Mandy Rowland) *hld up: hdwy over 2f out: rdn over 1f out: one pce* **28/1**
1006 **6** 4 **Excellent Vision**[13] 6310 4-8-13 51 ....(t) RyanClark(3) 9 33
(Milton Bradley) *s.s: in rr: rdn over 2f out: nvr on terms* **7/1**
0010 **7** 2 **Gee Major**[13] 6310 4-9-3 52 ....(t) LukeMorris 5 30
(Nicky Vaughan) *led: hdd over 6f out: chsd ldrs tl rdn and wknd over 2f out* **7/1**

0640 **8** *nk* **Honest And True (IRE)**[10] 6414 4-8-12 **47**..................(v[1]) TomEaves 13 24
(Ian Semple) *prom: rdn over 2f out: sn wknd* **9/1**

1000 **9** *½* **Century Dancer**[108] 3223 3-8-7 **51**.................................. RyanPowell(5) 7 28
(Tor Sturgis) *chsd ldrs tl wknd over 2f out* **33/1**

2305 **10** *1 ¾* **Derby Desire (IRE)**[24] 5994 7-8-11 **46**.......................(t) CathyGannon 10 18
(Des Donovan) *chsd ldrs: led over 6f out: rdn and hdd over 2f out: wknd over 1f out* **12/1**

0046 **11** *2 ¼* **Pearly Wey**[21] 6105 8-9-0 **52**.. PaulPickard(3) 11 19
(Ian McInnes) *hld up: rdn and wknd over 2f out* **20/1**

1m 50.22s (-0.28) **Going Correction** +0.05s/f (Slow)
WFA 3 from 4yo+ 4lb 11 Ran SP% **115.1**
Speed ratings (Par 101): **103,100,97,95,95 91,90,89,89,87 85**
toteswingers:1&2:£5.70, 1&3:£4.10, 2&3:£6.20 CSF £33.41 CT £107.06 TOTE £3.70: £1.40, £2.60, £1.60; EX 27.90.
Owner R Rickett **Bred** Ash Tree Farm Ltd **Trained** Great Ness, Shropshire

FOCUS
A low-grade handicap. The pace was fair and the first two finished clear of the rest.

6658 BIDS 5 STUDIO SOFTWARE FROM MRG H'CAP 1m 141y(P)
8:20 (8:20) (Class 4) (0-80,80) 3-Y-O+ **£3,234** (£962; £481; £240) **Stalls** Low

Form RPR

0453 **1** **Blue Moon**[11] 6383 4-9-7 **80**.. PhillipMakin 11 89
(Kevin Ryan) *hld up: hdwy over 2f out: rdn to ld ins fnl f: edgd lft: jst hld on* **8/1**

5252 **2** *shd* **Lockantanks**[5] 6544 4-9-0 **73**.............................. RobbieFitzpatrick 1 82
(Michael Appleby) *hld up: hdwy over 2f out: sn rdn: rdr dropped whip ins fnl f: r.o wl* **10/1**

4000 **3** *1* **Merchant Of Medici**[17] 6219 4-9-7 **80**.......................... MartinDwyer 4 87
(William Muir) *chsd ldrs: rdn over 2f out: r.o u.p* **16/1**

1031 **4** *1 ¾* **Sound Amigo (IRE)**[33] 5735 3-9-1 **78**......................... BarryMcHugh 2 82
(Ollie Pears) *led 7f out: rdn over 1f out: hdd and unable qck ins fnl f* **3/1**[1]

643 **5** *hd* **Standpoint**[21] 6093 5-9-1 **77**......................................(p) PaulPickard(3) 13 79
(Reg Hollinshead) *led: hdd 7f out: chsd ldrs: rdn over 1f out: styd on same pce ins fnl f* **9/1**

1500 **6** *hd* **Laughing Jack**[20] 6124 3-9-0 **77**..................................(e[1]) KierenFallon 5 80
(Ed Dunlop) *hld up: rdn over 1f out: r.o ins fnl f: nrst fin* **7/1**[3]

54-6 **7** *¾* **Hidden Fire**[12] 6330 4-9-0 **73**.. NeilCallan 3 73
(David Elsworth) *hld up in tch: plld hrd: hmpd 7f out: rdn over 1f out: styd on same pce* **6/1**[2]

-600 **8** *1 ½* **Chosen Forever**[145] 2115 6-9-7 **80**.................................... TomEaves 8 77
(Geoffrey Oldroyd) *hld up: r.o ins fnl f: nvr nrr* **50/1**

1423 **9** *2 ¾* **Battle Of Britain**[16] 6241 3-9-0 **77**.............................(t) WilliamCarson 6 68
(Giles Bravery) *chsd ldrs: rdn over 1f out: wknd ins fnl f* **12/1**

5600 **10** *nk* **Nibani (IRE)**[10] 6410 4-8-10 **76**...............................(b[1]) KatiaScallan(7) 12 66
(Alastair Lidderdale) *s.i.s: hld up: a in rr* **50/1**

30-4 **11** *3* **Peponi**[27] 5894 5-9-3 **76**... SteveDrowne 9 59
(Peter Makin) *trckd ldrs: racd keenly: wknd 2f out* **7/1**[3]

6200 **12** *2 ¼* **Amazing Star (IRE)**[13] 6290 6-9-3 **76**............................. SebSanders 10 53
(Declan Carroll) *hld up: wknd over 2f out* **20/1**

1m 50.22s (-0.28) **Going Correction** +0.05s/f (Slow)
WFA 3 from 4yo+ 4lb 12 Ran SP% **116.7**
Speed ratings (Par 105): **103,102,102,100,100 100,99,98,95,95 92,90**
toteswingers:1&2:£6.30, 1&3:£32.70, 2&3:£16.70 CSF £82.78 CT £1261.92 TOTE £10.60: £3.20, £2.80, £5.00; EX 43.40.
Owner Guy Reed **Bred** Theakston Stud **Trained** Hambleton, N Yorks

FOCUS
A decent handicap. It was run at a stop-start gallop and there was tight finish.
Peponi Official explanation: jockey said horse hung left-handed

6659 CHRIS O'KEEFFE MEMORIAL H'CAP (DIV II) 1m 141y(P)
8:50 (8:51) (Class 6) (0-55,55) 3-Y-O+ **£1,363** (£402; £201) **Stalls** Low

Form RPR

3413 **1** **Appyjack**[15] 6253 3-9-1 **55**... NeilCallan 7 66
(Tony Carroll) *midfield: hdwy 1/2-way: rdn to ld and hung rt ins fnl f: styd on* **4/1**[2]

6001 **2** *¾* **Prime Circle**[7] 6494 5-8-4 **47** ow1........................(p) JacobButterfield(7) 8 56+
(Alan Brown) *s.i.s: in rr: hdwy over 1f out: r.o* **13/8**[1]

5003 **3** *2 ½* **Poppy Golightly**[13] 6310 4-8-11 **52**............................... NeilFarley(5) 13 55
(Declan Carroll) *chsd ldr: led 3f out: rdn and hdd ins fnl f: no ex* **9/1**

052- **4** *2* **Hilbre Court (USA)**[346] 7128 6-9-4 **54**.......................... J-PGuillambert 6 52
(Brian Baugh) *a.p: rdn to chse ldr over 2f out: ev ch ins fnl f: wknd towards fin* **11/1**

6040 **5** *1 ½* **Danceyourselfdizzy (IRE)**[8] 6446 3-8-4 **51**........... LeonnaMayor(7) 10 47
(Phil McEntee) *chsd ldrs: rdn over 2f out: no ex fnl f* **50/1**

3005 **6** *1 ½* **Scoglio**[19] 6179 3-8-12 **55**................................... PatrickDonaghy(3) 4 48
(Frank Sheridan) *s.i.s: hld up: r.o ins fnl f: nrst fin* **12/1**

6 **7** *2* **Pagan Steps (IRE)**[20] 6139 4-8-11 **47**.........................(p) CathyGannon 9 34
(Stephen Michael Cox, Ire) *hld up: plld hrd: rdn and hung lft over 1f out: n.d* **20/1**

8 *2 ¼* **Mujady Star (IRE)**[62] 4772 3-8-7 **50** ow3....................(t) PaulPickard(3) 5 33
(Kevin M Prendergast) *s.i.s: hld up: a in rr* **25/1**

-000 **9** *nk* **Polly McGinty**[20] 6137 3-8-9 **49**.....................................(t) LukeMorris 3 31
(Nicky Vaughan) *chsd ldrs: rdn over 3f out: wknd over 1f out* **22/1**

00-0 **10** *6* **Stay On Track (IRE)**[37] 5601 4-8-12 **48**.................... FergusSweeney 2 15
(Garry Woodward) *led: hdd 3f out: wknd over 1f out* **66/1**

0500 **11** *14* **Royal Acclamation (IRE)**[20] 6138 6-8-11 **52**............ DavidKenny(5) 1 —
(Michael Scudamore) *hld up: a in rr: wknd and eased over 1f out* **50/1**

3050 **F** **Star Addition**[15] 6264 5-9-0 **50**....................................... PatCosgrave 11 —
(Eric Alston) *hld up: hdwy whn n.m.r and fell wl over 1f out* **8/1**[3]

1m 51.34s (0.84) **Going Correction** +0.05s/f (Slow)
WFA 3 from 4yo+ 4lb 12 Ran SP% **113.6**
Speed ratings (Par 101): **98,97,95,93,92 90,88,86,86,81 68,—**
toteswingers:1&2:£2.80, 1&3:£2.50, 2&3:£4.70 CSF £9.51 CT £53.87 TOTE £5.10: £2.00, £1.10, £2.30; EX 12.20.
Owner Mayden Stud **Bred** Mayden Stud, J A And D S Dewhurst **Trained** Cropthorne, Worcs

FOCUS
The second division of a low-grade handicap. It was run at a good pace and there was another close finish.
Royal Acclamation(IRE) Official explanation: jockey said gelding was hampered by faller
T/Jkpt: £4,487.00 to a £1 stake. Pool:£338,105.47 - 53.50 winning tickets T/Plt: £18.80 to a £1 stake. Pool:£108,624.98 - 4,204.73 winning tickets T/Qpdt: £6.70 to a £1 stake. Pool:£11,524.32 - 1,260.06 winning tickets CR

6517 SAINT-CLOUD (L-H)
Thursday, October 6

OFFICIAL GOING: Turf: good to soft

6660a PRIX THOMAS BRYON (GROUP 3) (2YO) (TURF) 1m
2:55 (12:00) 2-Y-O **£34,482** (£13,793; £10,344; £6,896; £3,448)

RPR

1 **Abtaal (USA)**[22] 2-8-11 0.. MaximeGuyon 5 109+
(J-C Rouget, France) *qckly into stride: sn led: qcknd wl 2 1/2f out: sn clr: r.o wl: easily* **8/5**[1]

2 *3* **French Fifteen (FR)**[31] 5799 2-8-11 0........................... ThierryThulliez 2 102
(N Clement, France) *settled 3rd: dropped bk to 4th ent st: shkn up ent fnl 1 1/2f: r.o wl fnl 100yds: wnt 2nd fnl strides* **3/1**[2]

3 *snk* **Ice Cool (FR)**[20] 6143 2-8-11 0............................... MickaelBarzalona 3 102
(W Hefter, Germany) *settled 3rd on outer: wnt 2nd bef st: rdn and r.o fr 2 1/2f out: hdd for 2nd fnl strides* **12/1**

4 *½* **Maradini (FR)**[19] 2-8-11 0........................... Christophe-PatriceLemaire 1 101
(A De Royer-Dupre, France) *broke slowly: sn mde up grnd to r 4th: rdn early in st: nt qckn: rallied ent fnl f: r.o* **3/1**[2]

5 *shd* **Tifongo (FR)**[80] 2-8-11 0... FabriceVeron 7 100
(H-A Pantall, France) *racd in rr: rdn 2f out: r.o fnl f: nrest at fin* **25/1**

6 *hd* **Regina Ejina (FR)**[32] 5770 2-8-8 0............................... GregoryBenoist 4 97
(M Delzangles, France) *settled 4th on outer: rdn and r.o wl fr 2f out: no ex fnl 100yds* **11/1**

7 *1 ¾* **Kadyny**[19] 6184 2-8-11 0... OlivierPeslier 6 96
(T Lemer, France) *settled 6th: wnt 5th early in st: rdn and r.o but no ex fr 1 1/2f out: fdd* **44/5**[3]

1m 49.8s (2.30) 7 Ran SP% **118.5**
WIN (incl. 1 euro stake): 2.60. PLACES: 1.50, 1.90. SF: 6.70.
Owner Hamdan Al Maktoum **Bred** Lothenbach Stables Inc **Trained** Pau, France

NOTEBOOK
Abtaal(USA) set a steady pace and quickened nicely to win easily. This is often seen as a trial for the Group 1 Criterium de Saint-Cloud and Criterium International, but his trainer suggested that he might just put him away for the year.

6661a PRIX SCARAMOUCHE (LISTED RACE) (3YO+) (TURF) 1m 6f
3:25 (12:00) 3-Y-O+ **£22,413** (£8,965; £6,724; £4,482; £2,241)

RPR

1 **Be Fabulous (GER)**[99] 4-8-13 0...................................... MaximeGuyon 4 105
(A Fabre, France) **17/5**[2]

2 *¾* **Pouvoir Absolu**[16] 6-9-2 0.......................................(b) AnthonyCrastus 7 107
(E Lellouche, France) **13/2**

3 *1 ¼* **Balaythous (FR)**[134] 2408 5-9-4 0.. FlavienPrat 3 107
(Mlle B Renk, France) **53/10**[3]

4 *nk* **Tac De Boistron (FR)**[25] 5990 4-9-2 0....... Christophe-PatriceLemaire 5 105
(A Lyon, France) **2/1**[1]

5 *hd* **Lacateno**[18] 6200 4-9-4 0.. JohanVictoire 2 106
(W Hickst, Germany) **9/1**

6 *1 ¼* **Electrolyser (IRE)**[70] 4469 6-9-2 0............................... StephanePasquier 8 103
(Clive Cox) *sn amongst ldrs: rdn and r.o in st: no ex fnl f* **7/1**

7 *6* **Ile De Re (FR)**[33] 5705 5-9-2 0.. JimCrowley 1 94
(Ian Williams) *towards rr: no imp in st* **19/1**

8 *6 ½* **Irish Song (FR)**[143] 4-8-13 0...................................... AdrienFouassier 6 82
(A Couetil, France) **31/1**

3m 21.1s (8.90) 8 Ran SP% **115.9**
WIN (incl. 1 euro stake): 4.40. PLACES: 2.00, 2.20, 2.20. DF: 13.70. SF: 27.20.
Owner Godolphin SNC **Bred** Gestut Karlshof **Trained** Chantilly, France

6652 WOLVERHAMPTON (A.W) (L-H)
Friday, October 7

OFFICIAL GOING: Standard
Wind: Fresh across Weather: Cloudy

6662 32REDPOKER.COM MEDIAN AUCTION MAIDEN STKS (DIV I) 7f 32y(P)
5:40 (5:40) (Class 6) 2-Y-O **£1,567** (£462; £231) **Stalls** High

Form RPR

6532 **1** **Galilee Chapel (IRE)**[8] 6487 2-9-3 63............................ NickyMackay 3 66
(David Elsworth) *led early: chsd ldr tl over 4f out: remained handy: rdn to ld over 1f out: r.o* **3/1**[2]

00 **2** *½* **Rocky Reef**[21] 6127 2-9-3 0.. LiamKeniry 6 65
(Andrew Balding) *dwlt: hld up: hdwy over 1f out: r.o wl* **7/2**[3]

3 **3** *¾* **Yeomanoftheguard**[107] 3274 2-9-3 0.......................... PaulHanagan 1 63
(Richard Fahey) *s.s: sn prom: outpcd 1/2-way: hdwy u.p over 1f out: r.o* **10/11**[1]

00 **4** *¾* **Stag Hill (IRE)**[92] 3761 2-9-3 0.. JamesDoyle 4 61
(Sylvester Kirk) *prom: rdn 1/2-way: edgd lft ins fnl f: no ex nr fin* **100/1**

005 **5** *4* **Arrow Lake (FR)**[21] 6117 2-8-12 65.............................. ChrisCatlin 10 46
(Noel Quinlan) *sn led: rdn and hdd over 1f out: wknd ins fnl f* **16/1**

00 **6** *hd* **Miss Granger**[29] 5841 2-8-12 0...................................... LukeMorris 5 46
(Ronald Harris) *hld up: rdn over 2f out: nvr on terms* **150/1**

0063 **7** *4* **Great Mystery (IRE)**[25] 6002 2-9-3 54.......................... SebSanders 9 41
(J W Hills) *prom: chsd ldr over 4f out tl rdn over 1f out: wknd ins fnl f* **33/1**

1m 29.79s (0.19) **Going Correction** -0.15s/f (Stan) 7 Ran SP% **110.1**
Speed ratings (Par 93): **92,91,90,89,85 84,80**
toteswingers:1&2:£1.50, 2&3:£1.80, 1&3:£1.60 CSF £12.73 TOTE £2.80: £1.40, £1.20; EX 17.20.
Owner Mrs S Johnson **Bred** Tally-Ho Stud **Trained** Newmarket, Suffolk

FOCUS
An ordinary juvenile maiden, run at an average pace and straightforward enough form.

NOTEBOOK
Galilee Chapel(IRE) put his previous experience to great use and, getting first run on his main rivals, shed his maiden tag at the sixth time of asking. He finished a onepaced second over C&D in a nursery off 63 on his AW debut last week and this rates a slight step forward, but it was his professionalism that won him the day. (op 11-4)
Rocky Reef ◆ was free under restraint on this return to 7f on Polytrack and ultimately hit top gear too late in the day. He ought to find a small race before long and nurseries are now an option. (op 11-2)

Yeomanoftheguard headed the betting on his return from a 107-day break as he ran a race of promise on his debut at Carlisle. He stumbled out of the gates and raced most lazily until Paul Hanagan got stuck into him turning for home. He showed an engine to make up his ground, but didn't look to be putting it all in and it's hoped that was still down to greenness. (op 4-5 tchd Evens)

Stag Hill(IRE) showed up a lot more encouragingly for this switch to Polytrack and didn't get the best of runs late on. He ought to come on nicely and is another now qualified for nurseries.

6663 32REDPOKER.COM MEDIAN AUCTION MAIDEN STKS (DIV II) 7f 32y(P)

6:10 (6:10) (Class 6) 2-Y-O **£1,567** (£462; £231) **Stalls** High

Form RPR
522 **1** **Chelsea Mick**[27] 5919 2-9-0 76 .... DaleSwift(3) 9 62+
(Ed McMahon) *chsd ldrs: rdn over 2f out: hung lft fr over 1f out: styd on to ld wl ins fnl f* **8/11**[1]
00 **2** *nk* **Thecornishcowboy**[14] 6300 2-9-3 0 .... KirstyMilczarek 1 61
(John Ryan) *led tl over 4f out: led again 3f out: rdn over 1f out: hdd wl ins fnl f* **22/1**
50 **3** *3/4* **Path Finder (FR)**[79] 4201 2-9-3 0 .... GeorgeBaker 10 60
(Reg Hollinshead) *hld up: hdwy over 1f out: sn rdn: r.o* **14/1**
4 *1 1/4* **Elmora** 2-8-12 0 .... JamesDoyle 8 51
(Sylvester Kirk) *hld up in tch: rdn and swtchd rt over 1f out: r.o* **14/1**
000 **5** *1* **King's Future**[21] 6118 2-9-3 47 .... LukeMorris 2 54
(John Akehurst) *w ldr tl led over 4f out: hdd 3f out: rdn over 1f out: no ex ins fnl f* **40/1**
0430 **6** *1 1/4* **Hi There (IRE)**[41] 5478 2-9-3 66 .... SebSanders 6 51
(J W Hills) *trckd ldrs: plld hrd: rdn over 1f out: no ex fnl f* **3/1**[2]
0 **U** **Statementofintent (IRE)**[24] 6019 2-9-3 0 .... (b[1]) ShaneKelly 3 —
(Brian Meehan) *pitched and uns rdr leaving stalls* **9/1**[3]

1m 30.14s (0.54) **Going Correction** -0.15s/f (Stan) 7 Ran SP% **113.0**
Speed ratings (Par 93): **90,89,88,87,86 84,—**
toteswingers:1&2:£4.70, 2&3:£16.90, 1&3:£3.30 CSF £20.21 TOTE £1.50: £1.10, £10.80; EX 15.00.
Owner Tony Ashley **Bred** Barry Walters **Trained** Lichfield, Staffs

FOCUS
This second division of the 7f maiden was also run at an average pace and there was a tight finish.

NOTEBOOK
Chelsea Mick deservedly got off the mark at the fourth attempt, but made hard work of landing the odds. He was always well placed and settled nicely, but took an age to find top gear after straightening for home. His rider always looked confident of just getting there at the business end, though, and he may well enjoy reverting to 1m now. It could also be he's happiest from the front. (tchd 4-6)
Thecornishcowboy hadn't shown much in two previous outings on turf at big odds. He raced much more aggressively on this switch to the AW from the inside draw, and was only picked off near the finish. He's evidently improving, but this won't have helped his prospective nursery mark, though. (op 25-1 tchd 28-1)
Path Finder(FR) shaped a lot more respectably on this return from a 79-day break and return to C&D. He can now enter nurseries, but is another whose prospective mark will not have been helped by this career-best effort. (op 12-1 tchd 16-1)
Elmora shaped very much as though he'd come on for the initial experience. (op 12-1)
Hi There(IRE) proved far too keen early on. (tchd 11-4 and 10-3)
Statementofintent(IRE), equipped with first-time blinkers, propped on leaving the gates and the rider stood little chance of staying aboard. (op 12-1)

6664 32REDBET.COM H'CAP 7f 32y(P)

6:40 (6:40) (Class 6) (0-65,71) 3-Y-O+ **£1,908** (£563; £281) **Stalls** High

Form RPR
6005 **1** **Global Village (IRE)**[21] 6138 6-9-2 63 .... SilvestreDeSousa 6 72
(Brian Ellison) *led 1f: chsd ldr tl led again over 2f out: sn rdn: jst hld on* **6/4**[1]
-310 **2** *hd* **Twinkled**[18] 6228 3-8-9 65 .... IanBurns(7) 7 73
(Michael Bell) *a.p: rdn to chse wnr over 1f out: r.o* **14/1**
0210 **3** *1* **Spinning Ridge (IRE)**[10] 6434 6-9-1 62 .... (v) PaulHanagan 1 67
(Ronald Harris) *prom: rdn over 1f out: r.o* **11/1**
2101 **4** *hd* **Master Of Dance (IRE)**[9] 6452 4-9-10 71 6ex .... (p) JoeFanning 12 76
(Keith Dalgleish) *chsd ldrs: rdn over 1f out: edgd lft ins fnl f: styd on* **15/2**[2]
2303 **5** *shd* **Sarangoo**[10] 6434 3-9-2 65 .... LukeMorris 3 69
(Malcolm Saunders) *s.i.s: hld up: rdn 1/2-way: hdwy over 1f out: r.o* **11/1**
3305 **6** *1/2* **Eager To Bow (IRE)**[69] 4546 5-9-4 65 .... GeorgeBaker 9 68
(Patrick Chamings) *a.p: rdn over 1f out: r.o* **17/2**[3]
5540 **7** *1 1/4* **Gemma's Delight (IRE)**[13] 6355 4-9-1 62 .... (p) LiamJones 4 62
(James Unett) *hld up: racd keenly: r.o ins fnl f: nt rch ldrs* **20/1**
5R52 **8** *2 1/4* **Timeteam (IRE)**[16] 6257 5-9-4 65 .... RichardMullen 5 59
(Alan Bailey) *s.s and rel to r: bhd tl r.o ins fnl f: nrst fin* **11/1**
0604 **9** *hd* **Golden Taurus (IRE)**[20] 6181 3-9-2 65 .... SebSanders 10 61
(J W Hills) *hld up: hdwy over 1f out: hmpd ins fnl f: nt rcvr* **11/1**
653 **10** *2 1/4* **All Honesty**[28] 5902 3-9-1 64 .... JimCrowley 8 51
(William Knight) *led 6f out tl rdn and hdd over 2f out: edgd rt and wknd ins fnl f* **16/1**
5244 **11** *12* **Army Of Stars (IRE)**[28] 5901 5-9-0 61 .... ChrisCatlin 11 16
(Michael Blake) *hld up: rdn 1/2-way: wknd 2f out* **12/1**

1m 29.76s (0.16) **Going Correction** -0.15s/f (Stan)
WFA 3 from 4yo+ 2lb 11 Ran SP% **119.0**
Speed ratings (Par 101): **93,92,91,91,91 90,89,86,86,83 70**
toteswingers:1&2:£7.40, 2&3:£18.50, 1&3:£3.50 CSF £25.28 CT £185.35 TOTE £2.30: £1.20, £3.80, £3.80; EX 26.60.
Owner Jack Racing Melksham **Bred** Kilfrush Stud **Trained** Norton, N Yorks

FOCUS
A moderate handicap, run at a fair pace and few landed a blow from out the back.

6665 32RED.COM H'CAP 5f 216y(P)

7:15 (7:16) (Class 5) (0-75,78) 3-Y-O+ **£2,522** (£750; £375; £187) **Stalls** Low

Form RPR
0361 **1** **Titus Gent**[8] 6491 6-9-1 78 6ex .... RaulDaSilva(7) 1 86
(Jeremy Gask) *chsd ldrs: led 1f out: rdn out* **8/1**
4434 **2** *3/4* **Wooden King (IRE)**[27] 5914 6-9-3 73 .... CathyGannon 9 79
(Malcolm Saunders) *led over 5f out: rdn and hdd 1f out: styd on* **7/1**[3]
040 **3** *nk* **Mawjoodah**[22] 6094 3-9-0 71 .... SilvestreDeSousa 3 76+
(Brian Ellison) *hld up: hdwy over 1f out: sn rdn: r.o* **7/1**[3]
5410 **4** *hd* **Bond Fastrac**[15] 6276 4-8-12 71 .... DaleSwift(3) 5 75
(Geoffrey Oldroyd) *sn pushed along in rr: hdwy over 1f out: r.o wl* **10/1**
2145 **5** *1* **Supercharged (IRE)**[20] 6177 3-9-1 72 .... (p) TedDurcan 2 73
(Chris Wall) *s.i.s: sn prom: rdn over 1f out: styd on* **9/2**[1]
010 **6** *2* **Aldermoor (USA)**[23] 6051 5-9-1 71 .... WilliamCarson 7 66+
(Stuart Williams) *sn pushed along in rr: r.o ins fnl f: nrst fin* **9/2**[1]
5112 **7** *3/4* **Six Wives**[118] 2913 4-9-1 74 .... BillyCray(3) 8 66
(David Nicholls) *s.i.s: hdwy over 4f out: chsd ldr over 2f out tl rdn over 1f out: no ex ins fnl f: eased nr fin* **14/1**
1260 **8** *1/2* **Picabo (IRE)**[20] 6174 3-9-4 75 .... IanMongan 6 66
(Lucy Wadham) *prom: rdn over 1f out: edgd lft and no ex ins fnl f* **13/2**[2]
0000 **9** *3/4* **Punching**[8] 6491 7-9-2 72 .... KirstyMilczarek 4 60
(Conor Dore) *mid-div: rdn over 1f out: no imp* **66/1**
0033 **10** *1/2* **Methaaly (IRE)**[128] 2610 8-9-2 72 .... (be) KierenFallon 12 59
(Michael Mullineaux) *s.i.s: hdwy on outer over 2f out: rdn over 1f out: no ex* **16/1**
204 **11** *nk* **Sir Nod**[15] 6282 9-9-2 72 .... PaulHanagan 10 58
(Julie Camacho) *trckd ldrs: plld hrd: n.m.r and lost pl over 5f out: n.d after* **14/1**
-110 **12** *7* **Questionnaire (IRE)**[74] 4378 3-9-1 72 .... LukeMorris 11 35
(Nicky Vaughan) *trckd ldr: plld hrd: rdn and wknd over 1f out* **22/1**

1m 13.51s (-1.49) **Going Correction** -0.15s/f (Stan)
WFA 3 from 4yo+ 1lb 12 Ran SP% **120.0**
Speed ratings (Par 103): **103,102,101,101,100 97,96,95,94,94 93,84**
toteswingers:1&2:£11.10, 2&3:£12.50, 1&3:£16.60 CSF £63.87 CT £425.18 TOTE £11.20: £3.70, £4.00, £1.40; EX 57.10.
Owner Tony Bloom **Bred** Heather Raw **Trained** Sutton Veny, Wilts

FOCUS
A wide-open sprint handicap and those drawn wide were at a real disadvantage.

6666 32RED CASINO H'CAP 1m 5f 194y(P)

7:45 (7:47) (Class 5) (0-75,75) 3-Y-O+ **£2,425** (£721; £360; £180) **Stalls** Low

Form RPR
110- **1** **Jasmeno**[362] 6774 4-9-6 67 .... (t) SteveDrowne 4 76
(Hughie Morrison) *hld up: hdwy over 2f out: sn rdn: styd on to ld wl ins fnl f* **12/1**
0214 **2** *1/2* **Zamina (IRE)**[27] 5938 3-9-3 73 .... JamesDoyle 2 81
(Sylvester Kirk) *a.p: rdn over 2f out: ev ch ins fnl f: styd on* **9/1**
6000 **3** *1 1/4* **Fantino**[36] 5650 5-8-13 60 .... (t) DavidProbert 1 66
(John Mackie) *a.p: led over 1f out: rdn and hdd wl ins fnl f* **9/1**
-601 **4** *1* **Resplendent Ace (IRE)**[13] 6356 7-9-5 66 .... JimmyQuinn 10 71
(Karen Tutty) *s.i.s: hld up: hdwy over 2f out: rdn over 1f out: r.o* **20/1**
3321 **5** *nk* **Boa**[20] 6182 6-9-6 67 .... GeorgeBaker 9 71
(Reg Hollinshead) *set stdy pce tl hdd 6f out: remained handy: rdn over 1f out: no ex nr fin* **8/1**
6203 **6** *1 1/4* **Viva Diva**[16] 6255 3-9-0 70 .... TedDurcan 11 73
(David Lanigan) *chsd ldrs: led over 2f out: rdn and hdd over 1f out: styd on same pce* **9/2**[2]
4512 **7** *2* **Corr Point (IRE)**[60] 4870 4-9-10 71 .... (t) KierenFallon 6 71
(Jamie Osborne) *hld up in tch: rdn over 1f out: styd on same pce* **15/2**[3]
6101 **8** *nk* **Miss Ferney**[12] 6385 7-9-3 67 6ex .... PaulPickard(3) 7 66
(Alan Kirtley) *hld up: rdn over 2f out: nvr trbld ldrs* **20/1**
00-0 **9** *shd* **Layla's Boy**[7] 6503 4-8-10 57 .... (t) SilvestreDeSousa 3 56
(John Mackie) *prom: nt clr run over 2f out: sn rdn: no ex ins fnl f* **33/1**
1103 **10** *1 3/4* **Stand Guard**[16] 6254 7-9-13 74 .... StevieDonohoe 8 71
(Noel Quinlan) *hld up: rdn over 3f out: nvr on terms* **11/1**
4210 **11** *6* **Calculating (IRE)**[113] 3095 7-9-5 71 .... LeeNewnes(5) 13 59
(Mark Usher) *s.i.s: hld up: hdwy over 4f out: wknd over 2f out* **33/1**
2631 **12** *11* **Lemon Drop Red (USA)**[11] 6412 3-9-2 72 .... PaulHanagan 12 45
(Ed Dunlop) *chsd ldrs: led 6f out: rdn and hdd over 2f out: wknd over 1f out* **3/1**[1]

3m 2.50s (-3.50) **Going Correction** -0.15s/f (Stan)
WFA 3 from 4yo+ 9lb 12 Ran SP% **117.5**
Speed ratings (Par 103): **104,103,103,102,102 101,100,100,100,99 95,89**
toteswingers:1&2:£18.60, 2&3:£23.70, 1&3:£36.80 CSF £108.93 CT £1020.85 TOTE £19.20: £6.00, £4.10, £3.30; EX 208.60.
Owner Melksham Craic **Bred** Melksham Craic **Trained** East Ilsley, Berks

FOCUS
This staying handicap was another open event and there was a sound enough pace on.
Resplendent Ace(IRE) Official explanation: jockey said that the gelding was unruly in the stalls
Stand Guard Official explanation: jockey said that the gelding hung right-handed
Lemon Drop Red(USA) Official explanation: jockey said that the gelding hung right-handed

6667 32RED NURSERY 1m 141y(P)

8:15 (8:16) (Class 6) (0-65,70) 2-Y-O **£1,908** (£563; £281) **Stalls** Low

Form RPR
0051 **1** **Come On Blue Chip (IRE)**[8] 6489 2-9-12 70 6ex .... (b) PaulHanagan 4 82+
(Paul D'Arcy) *hld up: nt clr run over 2f out: hdwy sn after: led 1f out: sn clr* **10/11**[1]
5255 **2** *5* **Courtesy Call (IRE)**[8] 6489 2-9-4 62 .... JoeFanning 2 64
(Mark Johnston) *chsd ldr: led over 2f out: rdn and hdd 1f out: no ex* **7/1**[2]
40U5 **3** *1 1/4* **Be Calm**[14] 6291 2-8-13 57 .... JamesSullivan 3 56
(Michael Easterby) *prom: rdn over 2f out: chsd ldr wl over 1f out tl no ex fnl f* **33/1**
0155 **4** *3 1/4* **Meanwhile (IRE)**[49] 5233 2-9-0 58 .... JimCrowley 8 50
(William Knight) *hmpd s: hld up: hdwy over 1f out: nt rch ldrs* **10/1**[3]
3445 **5** *2* **Doctor Banner**[16] 6260 2-8-13 57 .... MartinHarley 5 45
(Mick Channon) *hld up: hdwy over 2f out: wknd over 1f out* **12/1**
0345 **6** *6* **Curtain Patch (USA)**[23] 6047 2-8-11 62 .... (v[1]) JustinNewman(7) 13 37
(Bryan Smart) *pushed along in rr: n.d* **33/1**
000 **7** *shd* **Up Ten Down Two (IRE)**[42] 5454 2-8-13 57 ow1 .... (t) PaddyAspell 7 32
(Michael Easterby) *sn pushed along in rr: bhd 6f out: nvr nrr* **100/1**
6034 **8** *shd* **Orwellian**[9] 6443 2-9-7 65 .... ShaneKelly 9 40
(Brian Meehan) *prom: rdn over 2f out: wknd over 1f out* **7/1**[2]
065 **9** *hd* **Ashkan**[13] 6344 2-8-13 57 .... KierenFallon 12 31
(William Haggas) *hld up: rdn over 1f out: nvr on terms* **11/1**
510 **10** *6* **Flurry Of Hands (IRE)**[39] 5550 2-9-2 60 .... (p) SilvestreDeSousa 1 22
(Ann Duffield) *led tl hdd over 2f out: wknd over 1f out* **33/1**
0300 **11** *14* **Garrarufa (IRE)**[1] 6652 2-9-1 59 .... (b) JamesMillman 6 —
(Rod Millman) *sn pushed along in rr: wknd over 2f out: t.o* **33/1**
0500 **12** *44* **Laurel Lad (IRE)**[16] 6260 2-9-4 62 .... RobertWinston 11 —
(Charles Hills) *chsd ldrs: rdn over 3f out: sn wknd and eased: virtually p.u and t.o* **25/1**

1m 49.07s (-1.43) **Going Correction** -0.15s/f (Stan) 12 Ran SP% **119.1**
Speed ratings (Par 93): **100,95,94,91,89 84,84,84,84,78 66,27**
toteswingers:1&2:£3.50, 2&3:£32.90, 1&3:£15.20 CSF £6.91 CT £132.38 TOTE £1.90: £1.50, £3.60, £11.40; EX 10.80.
Owner Blue Chip Feed Ltd **Bred** Gerry Flannery Developments **Trained** Newmarket, Suffolk

FOCUS
An ordinary nursery, run at a sound pace and the form should work out.

NOTEBOOK

Come On Blue Chip(IRE) easily followed up his recent C&D success under a penalty. He was made to sweat turning into the home straight, but once getting himself organised after being angled out, there was only going to be one winner. Transformed since fitted with blinkers, he was already due to race off 6lb higher in future and the handicapper will very probably up him again for this. (tchd Evens)
Courtesy Call(IRE), six lengths behind the winner last time out, was able to race more handily this time and ran a lot better as a result. This was more like it and he looks to be crying out for a stiffer test. (op 15-2)
Be Calm was making his AW and nursery debut. He looked suited by the return to 7f and it was his most encouraging effort to date.
Meanwhile(IRE), back on Polytrack, was messed about at the start and is a bit better than the bare form. Official explanation: jockey said that the filly suffered interference at the start (op 9-1 tchd 11-1)
Doctor Banner moved well in midfield and was upsides the winner straightening for home, but was left for dead once that rival asserted. (op 10-1)
Up Ten Down Two(IRE) Official explanation: trainer said that the gelding had a breathing problem
Ashkan Official explanation: jockey said that the colt lost its action in the home straight

6668 £32 FREE AT 32RED.COM MEDIAN AUCTION MAIDEN STKS 1m 141y(P)
8:45 (8:46) (Class 6) 3-5-Y-O £1,704 (£503; £251) Stalls Low

Form RPR
646 1 **Lieutenant Kojak**[23] 6061 3-9-2 74 RobertWinston 5 67
(Peter Charalambous) *a.p: rdn to ld ins fnl f: r.o* 10/11[1]
6 2 ¾ **Mad Ginger Alice**[39] 5778 3-8-11 0 KirstyMilczarek 2 60
(Olivia Maylam) *hld up: hdwy over 2f out: rdn over 1f out: sn ev ch: r.o* 33/1
0 3 hd **Collaborate (IRE)**[56] 4991 3-9-2 0 LiamKeniry 8 65
(Andrew Balding) *led: hdd over 6f out: chsd ldr tl led again over 2f out: rdn and hdd ins fnl f: kpt on* 7/2[2]
2- 4 5 **Fonnie (IRE)**[368] 6628 3-8-11 0 MartinLane 7 48
(Rae Guest) *s.i.s: sn pushed along in rr: styd on ins fnl f: nvr nrr* 7/1
5 ½ **Debbie Doo** 3-8-11 0 WilliamCarson 9 47
(Giles Bravery) *prom: rdn over 2f out: wknd ins fnl f* 18/1
6 14 **Automotive**[107] 3-9-2 62 JimmyQuinn 6 20
(Julia Feilden) *prom: racd keenly: rdn over 2f out: wknd over 1f out* 6/1[3]
0 7 17 **Henry's Hero**[6] 6542 5-8-13 0 (b) JoshCrane(7) 10 —
(Chris Dwyer) *plld hrd and prom: led over 6f out: clr 4f out: hdd & wknd over 2f out: t.o* 100/1

1m 51.08s (0.58) **Going Correction** -0.15s/f (Stan)
WFA 3 from 4yo+ 4lb 7 Ran SP% **110.6**
Speed ratings (Par 101): **91,90,90,85,85 72,57**
toteswingers:1&2:£3.60, 2&3:£12.90, 1&3:£1.60 CSF £33.77 TOTE £2.30: £1.40, £10.30; EX 25.10.
Owner P Charalambous **Bred** Cheveley Park Stud Ltd **Trained** Newmarket, Suffolk

FOCUS
A modest maiden and a slow time.

6669 32REDBINGO.COM H'CAP 1m 1f 103y(P)
9:15 (9:15) (Class 5) (0-70,70) 3-Y-O+ £2,522 (£750; £375; £187) Stalls Low

Form RPR
0060 1 **Gritstone**[24] 6028 4-9-7 70 LeeTopliss(3) 2 83
(Richard Fahey) *chsd ldrs: led over 1f out: rdn out* 7/1[3]
00 2 1¼ **Strike Force**[7] 6507 7-9-9 69 (t) JamesDoyle 9 79
(Clifford Lines) *hld up: hdwy over 2f out: rdn to chse wnr over 1f out: r.o* 14/1
0532 3 nk **Key Breeze**[13] 6355 4-9-7 67 (t) PaulHanagan 10 76
(Kevin Ryan) *s.i.s: hld up: hdwy over 2f out: rdn over 1f out: r.o* 7/2[1]
2022 4 4½ **Dream Of Fortune (IRE)**[6] 6543 7-8-12 58 (bt) SilvestreDeSousa 3 58
(David Evans) *hld up in tch: rdn over 1f out: no ex ins fnl f* 11/2[2]
4502 5 1 **Mill Mick**[24] 6028 4-9-6 66 StephenCraine 1 64
(John Mackie) *chsd ldrs: rdn over 1f out: no ex fnl f* 14/1
1361 6 2½ **Monster Munchie (JPN)**[21] 6135 3-9-4 68 JimCrowley 11 61
(William Knight) *hld up: hdwy over 2f out: styd on same pce fr over 1f out* 7/1[3]
0050 7 3¼ **Barnum (USA)**[17] 6236 3-8-6 56 JamesSullivan 8 42
(Michael Easterby) *chsd ldr tl led over 2f out: rdn and hdd over 1f out: wknd fnl f* 28/1
5640 8 2¼ **Marie Rose**[49] 5243 3-8-11 61 (b) ShaneKelly 12 42
(Brian Meehan) *prom: lost pl over 7f out: n.d after* 28/1
0105 9 1½ **Maybe I Wont**[31] 5808 6-9-2 65 KieranO'Neill(3) 6 43
(Lucinda Featherstone) *chsd ldrs tl rdn and wknd over 2f out* 25/1
0310 10 2¾ **Hill Tribe**[6] 6543 4-9-2 65 RobertLButler(3) 5 37
(Richard Guest) *led 7f: wknd over 1f out* 20/1
1200 11 2¼ **Addikt (IRE)**[25] 6005 6-9-5 70 DavidKenny(5) 13 37
(Michael Scudamore) *hld up: a in rr* 50/1
423 12 44 **Cookieshake**[31] 5810 3-9-4 68 KierenFallon 4 —
(Luca Cumani) *s.i.s: sn pushed along: bhd fnl 3f: t.o* 7/2[1]

1m 58.29s (-3.41) **Going Correction** -0.15s/f (Stan)
WFA 3 from 4yo+ 4lb 12 Ran SP% **115.6**
Speed ratings (Par 103): **109,107,107,103,102 100,97,95,94,91 89,50**
toteswingers:1&2:£14.80, 2&3:£14.00, 1&3:£5.00 CSF £90.09 CT £401.19 TOTE £6.10: £1.90, £7.90, £1.10; EX 108.60.
Owner The Living Legend Racing Partnership **Bred** D W Armstrong **Trained** Musley Bank, N Yorks

FOCUS
A moderate handicap and yet another open event on the card. The first three dominated off the home turn.
T/Plt: £313.60 to a £1 stake. Pool of £88,378.60 - 205.71 winning tickets. T/Qpdt: £103.30 to a £1 stake. Pool of £9,202.28 - 65.90 winning tickets. CR

5755 YORK (L-H)
Friday, October 7

OFFICIAL GOING: Good (7.4)
Wind: fresh 1/2 against Weather: fine, very breezy

6670 TSG STKS (NURSERY) 6f
2:00 (2:04) (Class 3) (0-95,90) 2-Y-O £6,469 (£1,925; £962; £481) Stalls Centre

Form RPR
561 1 **Red Quartet (IRE)**[42] 5424 2-8-3 72 AndreaAtzeni 17 79+
(Robert Eddery) *in rr: hdwy over 2f out: nt clr run over 1f out: r.o to ld nr fin* 28/1
1 2 1 **Radio Gaga**[35] 5681 2-8-13 82 GrahamGibbons 10 86
(Ed McMahon) *trckd ldrs: effrt over 1f out: led last 75yds: edgd lft and hdd nr fin* 5/2[1]
211 3 hd **Deepsand (IRE)**[21] 6111 2-8-9 78 DavidAllan 9 81
(Tim Easterby) *chsd ldrs: upsides 1f out: keeping on same pce whn carried lft last 50yds* 8/1[2]
116 4 nk **Jessie's Spirit (IRE)**[30] 5825 2-8-13 82 DavidNolan 6 85
(Ann Duffield) *mid-div: sn drvn along: hdwy over 1f out: styd on towards fin* 16/1
1100 5 ½ **Parc De Launay**[50] 5216 2-9-7 90 JamieSpencer 7 91
(Tom Tate) *hld up in rr: hdwy and swtchd lft over 1f out: kpt on wl last 100yds: n.m.r nr fin* 16/1
4410 6 nse **Our Boy Jack (IRE)**[51] 5184 2-7-13 68 PatrickMathers 16 69
(Richard Fahey) *in rr: hdwy over 1f out: kpt on wl towards fin* 40/1
0041 7 1½ **Dutch Heritage**[60] 4851 2-8-2 71 CathyGannon 1 67
(Richard Fahey) *chsd ldrs: led 1f out: hdd last 75yds: wl hld whn hmpd nr fin* 20/1
1565 8 ½ **Springinmystep (IRE)**[34] 5701 2-8-12 81 (t) TomQueally 8 76
(Michael Dods) *hld up in rr: hdwy and swtchd lft over 1f out: nvr nr ldrs* 14/1
2125 9 1¼ **Tip Top Gorgeous (IRE)**[26] 5967 2-8-10 79 SilvestreDeSousa 20 70
(David O'Meara) *mid-div: hdwy over 2f out: kpt on fnl f* 20/1
2142 10 ½ **Key Ambition**[20] 6166 2-8-10 79 TomEaves 2 69
(Bryan Smart) *stdd s: hld up: hdwy over 2f out: led over 1f out: sn hdd: wknd last 100yds* 11/1
0202 11 2 **Nameitwhatyoulike**[21] 6111 2-8-6 75 JamesSullivan 4 59
(Michael Easterby) *led tl over 1f out: sn wknd* 20/1
21 12 1 **Passionada**[22] 6092 2-8-4 73 PaulHanagan 19 54
(Ollie Pears) *chsd ldrs: drvn 3f out: wknd over 1f out* 10/1[3]
0161 13 1¼ **Gung Ho Jack**[38] 5584 2-9-1 84 AdamKirby 11 61
(John Best) *chsd ldrs: wknd over 1f out* 12/1
5344 14 1 **On The Hoof**[33] 5755 2-8-1 73 ow1 DeclanCannon(3) 12 47
(Michael Easterby) *chsd ldrs: wknd 2f out* 20/1
2000 15 shd **Nearly A Gift (IRE)**[13] 6323 2-8-11 80 PJMcDonald 3 54
(Tim Easterby) *chsd ldrs: drvn over 2f out: sn wknd* 100/1
5600 16 ½ **On The Dark Side (IRE)**[28] 5882 2-9-7 90 PhillipMakin 13 62
(Kevin Ryan) *chsd ldrs: drvn 3f out: wknd over 1f out* 33/1
4120 17 nk **Guru Girl**[34] 5701 2-8-8 77 MartinHarley 5 48
(Mrs K Burke) *chsd ldrs: wknd 2f out* 33/1
4106 18 ½ **Mabroor (USA)**[34] 5708 2-9-4 87 RichardHills 15 57
(Mark Johnston) *a towards rr: nvr on terms* 33/1
2135 19 2 **Verbeeck**[55] 5061 2-9-3 86 (v[1]) KierenFallon 18 50
(Alan McCabe) *mid-div: drvn 2f out: sn wknd* 33/1
3311 20 4½ **Rent Free**[40] 5505 2-9-2 85 J-PGuillambert 14 35
(Nigel Tinkler) *in rr: sn drvn along: bhd whn eased clsng stages* 16/1

1m 13.58s (1.68) **Going Correction** +0.275s/f (Good) 20 Ran SP% **126.8**
Speed ratings (Par 99): **99,97,97,97,96 96,94,93,91,91 88,87,85,84,84 83,83,82,79,73**
Toteswingers:1&2:£40.20, 1&3:£46.50, 2&3:£4.40 CSF £87.52 CT £676.82 TOTE £36.90: £7.90, £1.70, £2.10, £4.50; EX 200.90 Trifecta £452.50 Part won. Pool of £611.58 - 0.10 winning units..
Owner Anderson, Donaldson, Keane & Rayment **Bred** Mrs Brid Cosgrove **Trained** Newmarket, Suffolk
■ Stewards' Enquiry : Graham Gibbons two-day ban: careless riding (21 and 24th Oct)

FOCUS
The rail was moved in from 1m1f until the entrance to the home straight to provide fresh ground, and consequently distances were reduced in races over 1m-plus by 27 yards. A good, competitive nursery. The runners were spread across the track, but the action unfolded towards far side late on.

NOTEBOOK
Red Quartet(IRE), off the mark on soft ground at Brighton on his third start, looked in tremendous order beforehand and showed himself on a good mark with a sustained challenge from off the pace. He can cope with a rise. (tchd 33-1)
Radio Gaga's debut win over this trip at Haydock has worked out exceptionally well with the runner-up, third, fourth (twice) and fifth all successful since. Although she came up just short, this was still a useful performance off 82 and represents improvement. She edged left under pressure, perhaps intimidated by the winner who also went that way and she leaned on Deepsand, but she was allowed to keep second after a stewards' enquiry. The impression is she'll come on again. (op 11-4 tchd 3-1)
Deepsand(IRE) was bidding for a hat-trick and ran well off 3lb higher than when taking a lesser race at Ayr on his most recent start. He might have got second with a clear run.
Jessie's Spirit(IRE) kept on well, shaping as though she might be worth another try over further. (op 20-1)
Parc De Launay ran well under joint-top weight after a break of 50 days. (op 20-1)
Our Boy Jack(IRE) kept on under a strong ride to fare best of those who finished middle-to-near side.
Passionada made all in a Pontefract maiden last time and was the mount of title-chasing Paul Hanagan, who presumably could have ridden one of the Fahey runners. The filly basically seemed to find this tougher going. (op 8-1)
Rent Free, the winner of his last two starts over 5f, was up a further 7lb. He didn't seem to travel early but was continually blocked in the closing stages so there's little way of knowing how well he could have run on. (op 18-1)

6671 GARBUTT & ELLIOTT CONDITIONS STKS 1m 2f 88y
2:30 (2:31) (Class 3) 3-Y-O+ £7,762 (£2,310; £1,154; £577) Stalls Low

Form RPR
1202 1 **Jet Away**[21] 6125 4-9-4 109 TomQueally 1 116
(Sir Henry Cecil) *hld up in rr: t.k.h: smooth hdwy 3f out: chsd wnr 2f out: shkn up to ld appr fnl f: wnt wl clr: v easily* 9/4[1]
-060 2 9 **Rasmy**[30] 5829 4-9-2 105 RichardHills 7 97
(Marcus Tregoning) *led: qcknd over 3f out: hdd appr fnl f: no ch w wnr* 12/1
0-43 3 1¼ **Treasury Devil (USA)**[160] 1689 3-8-11 100 WilliamBuick 6 95
(John Gosden) *sn trcking ldr: hung lft and kpt on same pce fnl 2f* 11/4[2]
3346 4 6 **Le Drakkar (AUS)**[195] 997 6-9-2 112 (t) FrankieDettori 2 83
(Saeed Bin Suroor) *t.k.h in rr: hdwy over 3f out: hung rt and wknd over 1f out* 11/2
2033 5 1¼ **Enak (ARG)**[22] 6088 5-9-2 102 (t) KierenFallon 4 81
(Saeed Bin Suroor) *chsd ldrs: effrt over 3f out: wknd 2f out* 14/1
1-00 6 6 **Dangerous Midge (USA)**[20] 6161 5-9-2 117 (b) MartinDwyer 3 69
(Brian Meehan) *chsd ldrs: drvn over 4f out: lost pl over 1f out: eased nr fin* 10/3[3]

2m 8.50s (-4.00) **Going Correction** -0.125s/f (Firm)
WFA 3 from 4yo+ 5lb 6 Ran SP% **110.3**
Speed ratings (Par 107): **111,103,102,98,97 92**
Toteswingers:1&2:£6.30, 1&3:£2.20, 2&3:£7.60 CSF £27.22 TOTE £2.90: £1.50, £5.70; EX 33.40.
Owner K Abdulla **Bred** Juddmonte Farms Ltd **Trained** Newmarket, Suffolk

The Form Book, Raceform Ltd, Compton, RG20 6NL

FOCUS
Both conditions race form and York form are often best treated with some caution, so the two combined hardly screams reliability, but Jet Away has long looked something of an underachiever with Group-race potential. While it's hard to know exactly how seriously to take this 9l demolition (good deal more in hand), a time 1.76 seconds faster than the later Class 4 handicap adds substance to the visual impression.

NOTEBOOK
Jet Away ◆'s conditions race win on the Lingfield turf in May suggested he was sitting on this kind of performance (runner-up Sri Putra third in Group 1s next two goes, third-placed Passion For Gold won Listed race), and on his latest start he was second to the so-far unbeaten and potentially high-class Dubai Prince when trying to concede 12lb (third won next time). He has proved a bit of a let-down in the past (only sixth in this last year), but this was only his tenth start and it's got to be worth seeing if he can repeat this level in Group company - he's wasted in this class at his best. (tchd 2-1)
Rasmy would only have been 2lb better off with the winner in a handicap, but 5lb worse off with the third. He was allowed an uncontested lead and kept on, but was no match at all for Jet Away. It's hard to know what he achieved, and he's been unconvincing this season, but he was too good for the rest. (tchd 14-1)
Treasury Devil(USA) was well placed, but had been off for 160 days and might have needed the run. (op 3-1 tchd 10-3)
Le Drakkar(AUS) ran nowhere near his official mark of 112 on his debut for Saeed Bin Suroor after a 195-day absence. (op 9-2)
Enak(ARG) offered nothing. (op 11-1 tchd 10-1)
Dangerous Midge(USA) had blinkers re-fitted and was presumably on trial for the Breeders' Cup Turf, a race he won last year. On this evidence a return trip to Churchill Downs would be a waste of time, although he would have the option of Lasix. (op 9-2 tchd 5-1)

6672 ACORN WEB OFFSET STKS (H'CAP) 1m
3:05 (3:08) (Class 2) (0-100,100) 3-Y-0+ **£11,644** (£3,465; £1,731; £865) **Stalls** Low

Form				RPR
0663	**1**		**Vainglory (USA)**[7] 6496 7-8-4 **88** ... LauraPike(5) 3 (David Simcock) *hld up in mid-div: swtchd outside over 1f out: styd on wl to ld nr fin* **9/1**[3]	98+
3624	**2**	*nk*	**Extraterrestrial**[13] 6335 7-8-9 **88** ... FrederikTylicki 12 (Richard Fahey) *hld up towards rr: hdwy on outer over 2f out: led last 50yds: hdd nr fin* **14/1**	96
110	**3**	*1 3/4*	**Hot Rod Mamma (IRE)**[22] 6080 4-8-8 **92** ... ShaneBKelly(5) 17 (Dianne Sayer) *in tch: effrt over 2f out: led 75yds out: sn hdd: edgd lft and kpt on same pce* **20/1**	96
2616	**4**	*1/2*	**Circumvent**[13] 6339 4-9-7 **100** ... (p) SilvestreDeSousa 2 (Paul Cole) *trckd ldrs: led 1f out: hdd 100yds out: no ex* **9/2**[1]	103
4404	**5**	*nk*	**Arabian Spirit**[20] 6173 6-8-9 **88** ... TonyHamilton 13 (Richard Fahey) *chsd ldrs: kpt on same pce appr fnl f* **16/1**	90
0052	**6**	*hd*	**Dubai Dynamo**[13] 6326 6-8-13 **92** ... CathyGannon 8 (Ruth Carr) *s.i.s: in rr: hdwy over 2f out: n.m.r: swtchd ins and styd on last 50yds* **16/1**	94
0140	**7**	*1 1/2*	**Osteopathic Remedy (IRE)**[20] 6150 7-8-13 **92** ... PhillipMakin 16 (Michael Dods) *sn bhd: hdwy over 2f out: nt clr run over 1f out: kpt on wl last 100yds* **20/1**	90
0060	**8**	*3/4*	**Riggins (IRE)**[13] 6339 7-9-4 **97** ... J-PGuillambert 7 (Ed Walker) *mid-div: effrt over 2f out: kpt on fnl f* **10/1**	94
0420	**9**	*nk*	**Prime Exhibit**[20] 6145 6-8-9 **91** ... LeeTopliss(3) 19 (Richard Fahey) *racd wd first 2f: w ldrs: led 2f out: edgd rt and hdd 1f out: wknd* **14/1**	87
0300	**10**	*1 1/2*	**Docofthebay (IRE)**[28] 5887 7-9-0 **93** ... IanMongan 14 (David Nicholls) *dwlt: hld up towards rr: hdwy over 2f out: sn chsng ldrs: wknd fnl f* **14/1**	85
0040	**11**	*1 3/4*	**Harrison George (IRE)**[13] 6339 6-9-2 **95** ... DavidNolan 4 (Richard Fahey) *chsd ldrs: fdd fnl f* **10/1**	83
3143	**12**	*1 1/4*	**Barren Brook**[35] 5686 4-8-11 **90** ... PaddyAspell 9 (Michael Easterby) *s.s: hdwy over 2f out: swtchd ins over 1f out: nvr nr ldrs* **8/1**[2]	75
0310	**13**	*nk*	**City Of The Kings (IRE)**[39] 5557 6-8-8 **90** ow2.. MichaelO'Connell(3) 15 (Ollie Pears) *a towards rr* **33/1**	75
3000	**14**	*6*	**Dubai Hills**[13] 6326 5-8-11 **90** ... TomEaves 11 (Bryan Smart) *hld up in mid-div: hdwy on outer 3f out: wknd over 1f out* **66/1**	61
0200	**15**	*2 1/2*	**Clockmaker (IRE)**[13] 6326 5-8-10 **89** ... DuranFentiman 18 (Tim Easterby) *t.k.h: racd wd 2f: trckd ldrs: wknd 2f out* **50/1**	54
5000	**16**	*3 1/4*	**Snow Bay**[20] 6150 5-8-11 **90** ... AdrianNicholls 5 (David Nicholls) *led: hdd 2f out: sn wknd* **10/1**	48
3024	**17**	*8*	**Baby Strange**[13] 6326 7-8-10 **89** ... RobbieFitzpatrick 6 (Derek Shaw) *hld up in rr: effrt 3f out: sn wknd: eased towards fin* **25/1**	28
02-4	**18**	*6*	**Togiak (IRE)**[21] 6125 4-8-13 **92** ... JamieSpencer 10 (David Pipe) *sn bhd: detached last 6f* **16/1**	18

1m 37.76s (-1.04) **Going Correction** -0.125s/f (Firm)
WFA 3 from 4yo+ 3lb **18** Ran SP% **124.0**
Speed ratings (Par 109): **100,99,97,97,97 96,95,94,94,92 91,89,89,83,81 77,69,63**
Toteswingers:1&2:£24.20, 1&3:£28.20, 2&3:£41.00 CSF £119.67 CT £2539.94 TOTE £11.10: £2.80, £3.60, £3.10, £1.80; EX 147.20 Trifecta £1335.00 Part won. Pool of £1804.17 - 0.02 winning units..
Owner D M I Simcock **Bred** Darley **Trained** Newmarket, Suffolk
■ Stewards' Enquiry : Shane B Kelly three-day ban: careless riding (21 and 24 Oct)

FOCUS
A decent, predictably competitive handicap and they went a fair pace.

NOTEBOOK
Vainglory(USA) took a long time to pick up, as is usually the case, but he got there in enough time to gain his first success since a win off 1lb lower at Newmarket in May 2010. He's never followed up and this race set up well for him, so he won't make obvious appeal off a higher rating next time. (op 11-1)
Extraterrestrial was 1lb lower than when only seventh in this last year. Clearly there was enough give underfoot to allow him to give his running.
Hot Rod Mamma(IRE)'s remarkable winning run came to an end at Ayr last time, but she was reported to have clipped heels. This was more like it, although she didn't find as much as had looked likely having travelled easily until about halfway up the straight. (op 16-1)
Circumvent produced his fourth smart performance from his last five starts, this following on from a sixth-place finish in the Cambridgeshire. He looks the type to be suited by racing in Dubai. (op 13-2)
Arabian Spirit remains weighted up to his best.
Dubai Dynamo, only 17th in this last year, might have been a bit closer with a better trip. (op 14-1)
Osteopathic Remedy(IRE), from the same mark as when third in this last term, also kept on well despite not getting a clear run through.
Barren Brook missed the break and didn't get the best of runs towards the inside in the straight. Although not unlucky, he's better than he showed. (op 7-1 tchd 9-1)

City Of The Kings(IRE) Official explanation: jockey said that the gelding was never travelling

6673 PIPER-HEIDSIECK NATIONAL RACECOURSE CATERING AWARDS E B F MAIDEN STKS 5f 89y
3:40 (3:42) (Class 3) 2-Y-0 **£6,469** (£1,925; £962; £481) **Stalls** Centre

Form				RPR
	1		**Pearl Secret** 2-9-3 0 ... JamieSpencer 3 (David Barron) *t.k.h in rr: smooth hdwy over 2f out: nt clr run over 1f out and swtchd lft: led last 150yds: pushed out: readily* **9/2**[1]	86+
322	**2**	*1 1/2*	**Lupo D'Oro (IRE)**[16] 6252 2-9-3 76 ... SteveDrowne 1 (John Best) *trckd ldrs: led 2f out: hdd and no ex ins fnl f* **6/1**[3]	77
56	**3**	*1*	**Yeeoow (IRE)**[8] 6492 2-9-3 0 ... MartinHarley 10 (Mrs K Burke) *swvd lft s: trckd ldrs: effrt 2f out: kpt on same pce* **22/1**	74
2	**4**	*1 3/4*	**Lisiere (IRE)**[33] 5756 2-8-12 0 ... TonyHamilton 6 (Richard Fahey) *chsd ldrs: sn pushed along: outpcd over 2f out: kpt on fnl f* **5/1**[2]	62
420	**5**	*2*	**Byronic Hero**[50] 5216 2-9-3 85 ... PJMcDonald 8 (Jedd O'Keeffe) *hmpd s: rr-div: sn pushed along: hung lft over 1f out: kpt on: nvr a factor* **7/1**	60
02	**6**	*1 1/4*	**Master Bond**[41] 5486 2-9-3 0 ... TomEaves 7 (Bryan Smart) *n.m.r s: t.k.h in rr: hdwy over 1f out: nvr nr ldrs* **9/2**[1]	59+
3	**7**	*2*	**Anton Chigurh**[24] 6025 2-9-3 0 ... StephenCraine 13 (Tom Dascombe) *swtchd lft after s: hld up towards rr: effrt 2f out: nvr nr to chal* **10/1**	49
5002	**8**	*1/2*	**Busy Bimbo (IRE)**[12] 6384 2-8-7 58 ... (p) JulieBurke(5) 4 (Alan Berry) *w ldrs: wknd over 1f out* **50/1**	42
	9	*1*	**Forget Me Not Lane (IRE)** 2-9-3 0 ... PhillipMakin 5 (Kevin Ryan) *dwlt and swvd lft s: hdwy on outside over 2f out: wknd over 1f out* **10/1**	44
6	**10**	*1/2*	**Whip It In (IRE)**[20] 6152 2-8-12 0 ... RussKennemore 12 (Paul Midgley) *a towards rr* **66/1**	37
00	**11**	*1*	**Weood (IRE)**[104] 3402 2-8-12 0 ... TomQueally 9 (Clive Brittain) *n.m.r s: sn chsng ldrs: wknd 2f out* **50/1**	34
0525	**12**	*3/4*	**Bengaline**[23] 6045 2-9-3 65 ... IanMongan 2 (David Nicholls) *led: hdd 2f out: sn wknd* **28/1**	36

65.30 secs (1.20) **Going Correction** +0.275s/f (Good) **12** Ran SP% **111.2**
Speed ratings (Par 99): **101,98,97,94,91 89,85,85,83,82 81,79**
Toteswingers:1&2:£6.10, 1&3:£20.90, 2&3:£23.50 CSF £25.50 TOTE £4.80: £1.50, £2.60, £6.50; EX 29.00 Trifecta £510.90 Part won. Pool of £690.52 - 0.20 winning units..
Owner Pearl Bloodstock Ltd **Bred** Whitsbury Manor Stud & Pigeon House Stud **Trained** Maunby, N Yorks

FOCUS
They raced up the middle of the track. The 77-rated Lupo d'Oro, finishing runner-up for the fourth successive race, looks a fair guide to the level of the form.

NOTEBOOK
Pearl Secret ◆, whose sales price increased from 20,000gns to £90,000, is out of a 5f winner (including selling and Listed company). He travelled through the race like an above-average type, moving powerfully and only having to be shaken up late on. Considered more of a 3yo prospect, he could be smart in time. (op 11-2 tchd 6-1)
Lupo D'Oro(IRE) had his chance, but ran into a potentially decent type. (op 8-1 tchd 9-1 in places)
Yeeoow(IRE) improved on his debut performance on his second start and this represented further progression. He's bred to get a bit further and now has the option of nurseries/handicaps. (op 25-1 tchd 20-1)
Lisiere(IRE) didn't build on the form she showed when runner-up over C&D on her debut, shaping as though in need of another furlong. (op 4-1 tchd 6-1)
Byronic Hero didn't run anywhere near his official mark of 85. He was a bit short of room soon after the start, but that was no real excuse. (tchd 11-2)
Master Bond was another who was hampered at the start and he got too far behind. He was runner-up over 6f on soft ground on his previous start and faced different conditions this time. (op 11-2)

6674 PARSONAGE HOTEL SPA OPENING SPRING 2012 STKS (H'CAP) 1m 2f 88y
4:15 (4:15) (Class 4) (0-80,80) 3-Y-0 **£5,239** (£1,559; £779; £389) **Stalls** Low

Form				RPR
4105	**1**		**Shamdarley (IRE)**[14] 6302 3-9-6 **79** ... PhillipMakin 16 (Michael Dods) *hld up in rr: hdwy on outer 3f out: hmpd over 1f out: r.o to ld nr fin* **11/1**	90
5560	**2**	*1/2*	**Musnad (USA)**[22] 6098 3-8-4 **66** ... PaulPickard(3) 5 (Brian Ellison) *s.i.s: smooth hdwy on outside over 3f out: hung lft and led over 1f out: hdd nr fin* **14/1**	76
106	**3**	*1 1/2*	**Look Left**[23] 6063 3-9-6 **79** ... WilliamBuick 3 (John Gosden) *s.i.s: hdwy on outer over 3f out: styd on to take 3rd last 50yds* **14/1**	87
3515	**4**	*nk*	**She's Got The Luck (IRE)**[27] 5925 3-8-10 **69** ... BarryMcHugh 10 (Richard Fahey) *chsd ldrs: styd on same pce fnl f* **20/1**	76
0230	**5**	*nk*	**Dysios (IRE)**[49] 5240 3-9-3 **76** ... KierenFallon 13 (Luca Cumani) *trckd ldrs: upsides over 3f out: led over 2f out: hdd and n.m.r over 1f out: one pce* **13/2**[2]	82+
1401	**6**	*2*	**Shadow Catcher**[56] 5004 3-9-7 **80** ... TomEaves 18 (Michael Dods) *hld up in rr: hdwy over 3f out: chsng ldrs over 2f out: hmpd over 1f out: kpt on same pce* **16/1**	83
1060	**7**	*1 3/4*	**Highlife Dancer**[11] 6409 3-8-10 **76** ... CharlesBishop(7) 8 (Mick Channon) *in rr: hdwy 3f out: kpt on fnl f* **33/1**	75
00-3	**8**	*shd*	**Cottam Donny**[22] 6097 3-8-7 **66** oh2 ... DavidAllan 14 (Mel Brittain) *chsd ldrs: led over 3f out: hdd over 2f out: one pce* **50/1**	65
0220	**9**	*1 1/2*	**Come Here Yew (IRE)**[9] 6457 3-9-5 **78** ... DanielTudhope 9 (Declan Carroll) *mid-div: effrt 3f out: nvr nr ldrs* **16/1**	74
-421	**10**	*nk*	**Vita Lika**[14] 6303 3-9-5 **78** ... FrankieDettori 4 (Brian Meehan) *trckd ldrs: keeping on same pce whn hmpd 1f out: eased last 100yds* **9/2**[1]	79+
0215	**11**	*2 1/2*	**Spanish Plume**[13] 6325 3-9-2 **75** ... RobertWinston 19 (Reg Hollinshead) *swtchd lft after s: hld up towards rr: sme hdwy on ins 3f out: nvr a factor* **16/1**	66
1314	**12**	*1 1/2*	**Sangar**[27] 5925 3-8-9 **68** ... GrahamGibbons 7 (Ollie Pears) *chsd ldrs: wknd fnl f* **8/1**[3]	56
0524	**13**	*1*	**Save The Bees**[17] 6234 3-8-8 **72** ... NeilFarley(5) 11 (Declan Carroll) *prom: drvn over 3f out: wknd 2f out* **20/1**	58
0054	**14**	*hd*	**Spes Nostra**[16] 6263 3-8-12 **71** ... LeeNewman 1 (David Barron) *hld up: hdwy into mid-div 7f out: effrt over 2f out: sn wknd* **14/1**	57
2630	**15**	*3/4*	**King Of The Celts (IRE)**[13] 6328 3-9-2 **75** ... PJMcDonald 15 (Tim Easterby) *rr-div: hdwy to chse ldrs over 2f out: sn wknd* **16/1**	59
0326	**16**	*2 1/4*	**Buzz Law (IRE)**[54] 5081 3-9-4 **77** ... MartinHarley 6 (Mrs K Burke) *hld up in mid-div: hdwy on ins 4f out: wknd 2f out* **25/1**	57
2140	**17**	*6*	**Lifetime (IRE)**[17] 6241 3-9-3 **76** ... SilvestreDeSousa 2 (Mark Johnston) *sn chsng ldrs: t.k.h: lost pl 2f out* **20/1**	45

0652 **18** *5* **Hernando Torres**[44] 5372 3-8-7 **66** oh3 .... JamesSullivan 17 25
(Michael Easterby) *chsd ldrs: lost pl 3f out* **33/1**
1055 **19** *18* **Abdicate (IRE)**[28] 5880 3-9-2 **75** .... TonyHamilton 12 —
(Richard Fahey) *t.k.h: led tl over 3f out: sn lost pl: bhd whn eased ins fnl f* **33/1**

2m 10.26s (-2.24) **Going Correction** -0.125s/f (Firm) **19** Ran SP% **123.4**
Speed ratings (Par 103): **103,102,101,101,100 99,97,97,96,96 94,93,92,92,91 89,85,81,66**
Toteswingers:1&2:£52.70, 1&3:£39.20, 2&3:£56.80 CSF £138.40 CT £2187.04 TOTE £11.50: £2.90, £3.70, £4.90, £4.40; EX 187.40 TRIFECTA Not won..
Owner Andrew Tinkler **Bred** D Veitch & R O'Brien **Trained** Denton, Co Durham
■ Stewards' Enquiry : Paul Pickard three-day ban: careless riding (24-26 Oct)

FOCUS
Another competitive handicap and fair form, although considering the early positions of the front three it seems the pace was overly strong.

6675 BACK A WINNER BY TRAIN 25TH ANNIVERSARY STKS (MEDIAN AUCTION MAIDEN) 1m

4:50 (4:50) (Class 4) 2-Y-O **£5,239** (£1,559; £779; £389) **Stalls** Low

Form RPR
2 **1** **El Lail (USA)**[15] 6278 2-8-12 0 .... RichardHills 7 85+
(Mark Johnston) *w ldr: led over 6f out: drvn clr over 1f out: eased nr fin* **5/1**[3]
0 **2** *5* **Scrupul (IRE)**[34] 5697 2-9-3 0 .... KierenFallon 6 79+
(Luca Cumani) *trckd ldrs: t.k.h: drvn to chse wnr over 1f out: no imp* **9/1**
22 **3** *1 1/4* **Blades Lad**[23] 6048 2-9-3 0 .... TonyHamilton 1 76
(Richard Fahey) *trckd ldrs: kpt on same pce fnl 2f* **9/2**[2]
5 **4** *4* **Linkable**[21] 6126 2-9-3 0 .... MichaelHills 4 66
(Charles Hills) *dwlt: hdwy to trck ldrs after 2f: drvn over 2f out: sn wknd* **11/8**[1]
5 *2* **Serjeant Buzfuz** 2-9-3 0 .... DavidNolan 3 62+
(Richard Fahey) *s.i.s: drvn and sme hdwy over 3f out: nvr a factor* **25/1**
56 **6** *3/4* **Haymarket**[20] 6180 2-9-3 0 .... FrankieDettori 8 60
(Mahmood Al Zarooni) *racd wd and led over 1f: rdn over 2f out: sn wknd: eased nr fin* **9/2**[2]
40 **7** *6* **Latenfast**[20] 6152 2-9-3 0 .... PaddyAspell 5 46
(Michael Easterby) *in rr: bhd fnl 3f* **100/1**
060 **8** *1/2* **Lizzie Drippin**[6] 6539 2-8-12 0 .... JamesSullivan 2 40
(Michael Easterby) *sn in rr: bhd fnl 3f* **66/1**

1m 39.95s (1.15) **Going Correction** -0.125s/f (Firm) **8** Ran SP% **111.5**
Speed ratings (Par 97): **89,84,82,78,76 76,70,69**
Toteswingers:1&2:£5.30, 1&3:£2.60, 2&3:£6.50 CSF £45.10 TOTE £5.20: £2.40, £3.20, £1.80; EX 56.40 Trifecta £202.80 Pool: £1493.95 - 5.45 winning units..
Owner Hamdan Al Maktoum **Bred** Shadwell Farm LLC **Trained** Middleham Moor, N Yorks
■ Stewards' Enquiry : Paddy Aspell two-day ban: used whip when out of contention (21 & 24 Oct)

FOCUS
They raced middle to near side in the straight. Plenty of powerful connections were represented, but the form doesn't look much better than fair.

NOTEBOOK
El Lail(USA), one of only two fillies in the line-up, didn't have to over-exert herself to take the field along and kept on strongly to build on her debut second at Pontefract. Presumably securing black type is the main aim. (op 4-1)
Scrupul(IRE) was tailed off on his debut at Ascot, but an SP of 6-1 suggested a lot better was expected that day and he duly improved significantly. He was keen early before travelling well when settling, and, although unable to seriously challenge the winner, he kept on. There should be more to come. (op 17-2 tchd 8-1)
Blades Lad finished runner-up at lesser tracks on his first two starts and this was tougher. He's now eligible for a handicap mark. (op 11-2)
Linkable didn't improve as might have been expected from his Newbury debut, but he raced closer to the stands' rail than his main rivals and may have been at a disadvantage. (op 5-4)
Serjeant Buzfuz was sent off at a much bigger price than his stablemate and needed this first experience. (tchd 33-1)
Haymarket hasn't progressed from a promising debut. (op 6-1)

6676 FUTURE CLEANING SERVICES "HANDS AND HEELS" APPRENTICE SERIES STKS (H'CAP) 1m 4f

5:20 (5:20) (Class 4) (0-85,85) 4-Y-O+ **£5,239** (£1,559; £779; £389) **Stalls** Centre

Form RPR
2554 **1** **Trip The Light**[24] 6024 6-9-3 **81** ....(v) GeorgeChaloner 11 89
(Richard Fahey) *mid-div: hdwy on inner 3f out: kpt on to ld towards fin* **9/1**
0314 **2** *nk* **Bowsers Brave (USA)**[11] 6402 5-8-9 **73** ....(t) KatiaScallan 10 80
(Marcus Tregoning) *hld up in rr: hdwy on wd outside over 2f out: led last 50yds: hdd nr fin* **8/1**[2]
2101 **3** *nk* **Dancing Primo**[24] 6029 5-8-7 **71** oh1 .... JackDuern 8 78
(Mark Brisbourne) *dwlt: drvn over 4f out: hdwy over 2f out: led last 150yds: hdd and no ex last 50yds* **12/1**
0021 **4** *nk* **Pertemps Networks**[6] 6546 7-8-11 **75** 6ex .... NoelGarbutt 13 81
(Michael Easterby) *trckd ldr: led over 3f out: hdd over 1f out: kpt on same pce* **5/1**[1]
06-2 **5** *1* **Red Jade**[33] 5761 6-9-4 **85** .... LauraBarry(3) 14 90
(Richard Fahey) *hld up towards rr: hdwy over 4f out: chsng ldrs over 2f out: one pce* **5/1**[1]
5005 **6** *1* **Ejteyaaz**[18] 6211 4-8-4 **71** oh8 .... ShirleyTeasdale(3) 3 74
(Richard Fahey) *prom: one pce fnl 2f* **22/1**
01P1 **7** *1 3/4* **Epic (IRE)**[11] 6419 4-8-11 **75** 6ex .... CharlesBishop 12 75
(Mark Johnston) *sn chsng ldrs: led over 1f out: hdd last 150yds: fdd* **10/1**
2260 **8** *2* **Veiled Applause**[13] 6346 8-8-9 **73** .... NatashaEaton 9 70
(John Quinn) *swtchd rt after s: in rr: kpt on fnl 2f: nvr a factor* **20/1**
-003 **9** *2 1/4* **Kings Troop**[29] 5857 5-9-3 **81** .... LucyKBarry 1 74
(Alan King) *trckd ldrs: drvn over 3f out: hung rt and lost pl over 1f out* **12/1**
2103 **10** *2 1/4* **Maybeme**[17] 6235 5-8-4 **71** oh11 .... TerenceFury(3) 2 61
(Neville Bycroft) *dwlt: in rr: styd far side and sme hdwy over 4f out: edgd rt over 2f out: nvr a factor* **40/1**
3600 **11** *16* **Arizona John (IRE)**[20] 6155 6-8-8 **72** .... GeorgeDowning 7 36
(John Mackie) *mid-div: styd far side over 4f out: sn chsng ldrs: lost pl 3f out: sn bhd* **16/1**
0-10 **12** *1 1/4* **Alsahil (USA)**[24] 6024 5-8-12 **76** .... LukeRowe 4 38
(Micky Hammond) *led: hdd over 3f out: lost pl 2f out* **17/2**[3]
0311 **13** *3 1/2* **Desert Vision**[9] 6461 7-8-5 **72** 6ex ....(vt) DavidSimmonson(3) 5 29
(Michael Easterby) *chsd ldrs: lost pl over 2f out* **10/1**
5266 **14** *2 1/2* **Overrule (USA)**[31] 5757 7-8-8 **75** .... JacobButterfield(3) 6 28
(Brian Ellison) *rr-div: drvn over 3f out: sn lost pl and bhd* **20/1**

2m 31.72s (-1.48) **Going Correction** -0.125s/f (Firm) **14** Ran SP% **120.7**
Speed ratings (Par 105): **99,98,98,98,97 97,95,94,93,91 80,80,77,76**
Toteswingers:1&2:£13.60, 1&3:£21.60, 2&3:£15.80 CSF £75.37 CT £881.86 TOTE £10.10: £3.00, £3.00, £4.30; EX 72.80 Trifecta £737.40 Part won. Pool of £996.62 - 0.63 winning units..
Owner The Matthewman One Partnership **Bred** Darley **Trained** Musley Bank, N Yorks

FOCUS
They raced towards the middle of the track in the closing stages. This was another race in which the leaders went off plenty fast enough and set it up for the closers. These apprentices were not allowed to use their whips.
T/Jkpt: Not won. T/Plt: £779.90 to a £1 stake. Pool of £130,427.82 - 122.08 winning tickets. T/Qpdt: £147.60 to a £1 stake. Pool of £7,763.42 - 38.90 winning tickets. WG

6677a, 6680 - 6685a (Foreign Racing) - See Raceform Interactive

LYON PARILLY (R-H)

Friday, October 7

OFFICIAL GOING: Turf: soft

6686a PRIX ANDRE BABOIN (GRAND PRIX DES PROVINCES) (GROUP 3) (3YO+) (TURF) 1m 2f

1:35 (12:00) 3-Y-O+ **£34,482** (£13,793; £10,344; £6,896; £3,448)

RPR
1 **Akarlina (FR)**[19] 6206 5-8-9 0 .... ThierryThulliez 1 105
(N Clement, France) *sn led: then settled in 2nd: regained ld bef end of bk st: qckmd wl to go clr over 1 1/2f out: r.o wl: chal fnl 50yds: jst hung on* **4/1**[2]
2 *nse* **Agent Secret (IRE)**[14] 6321 5-9-2 0 .... OlivierPeslier 7 112
(F Rohaut, France) *settled 3rd: wnt 2nd early in st: rdn but nt qckn 1 1/2f out: railled ent fnl f: r.o strly fnl 100yds: chal for ld 50yds out: jst failed* **9/5**[1]
3 *1* **Skallet (FR)**[27] 5958 3-8-8 0 ....(b) StephanePasquier 11 107
(S Wattel, France) *at rr fr s then sent forward to ld on outer after 1 1/2f: hdd bef end of bk st: u.p 1 1/2f out: r.o fnl f* **73/10**
4 *nk* **Staros (IRE)**[20] 6185 3-8-8 0 .... Christophe-PatriceLemaire 10 106
(E Lellouche, France) *settled midfield: wnt 4th bef st: r.o wl on outer fnl f wout threatening ldrs* **17/1**
5 *1* **Tagar Bere (FR)**[35] 5696 4-8-13 0 .... FranckBlondel 9 104
(M Pimbonnet, France) *towards rr: hmpd ent st on wd outside: hrd rdn and r.o fnl 1 1/2f: no threat to ldrs ins fnl f* **22/1**
6 *snk* **Polarena (FR)**[28] 5910 3-8-5 0 .... TonyPiccone 6 101
(X Betron, France) *settled 3rd: dropped bk towards rr bef end of bk st: rdn ent st: r.o fnl 1 1/f out wout threatening ldrs* **43/1**
7 *nse* **Dalarua (IRE)**[45] 5366 3-8-11 0 .... TheoBachelot 8 107
(S Wattel, France) *racd towards rr: rdn ent st: r.o one pce u.p fnl 1 1/2f: nvr threatened* **18/1**
8 *2 1/2* **Skarabeus (USA)**[26] 4-8-13 0 ....(b) JohanVictoire 3 99
(G Wroblewski, Czech Republic) *racd in midfield: wnt 5th early in st: sn u.p: fnd no ex: wknd bef fnl f* **15/1**
9 *2* **Fleur Enchantee (FR)**[33] 7-8-9 0 ....(p) GregoryBenoist 4 91
(P Van De Poele, France) *settled in midfield on inner: rdn early in st but failed to qckn: wknd fnl f* **9/1**
10 *3* **Don't Hurry Me (IRE)**[103] 3449 3-8-11 0 .... Jean-BernardEyquem 5 92
(J-C Rouget, France) *bkmarker tl ent st: swtchd to outside: lost action and dropped bk to rr: eased fnl 1 1/2f* **11/2**[3]

2m 12.01s (132.01)
WFA 3 from 4yo+ 5lb **10** Ran SP% **116.8**
WIN (incl. 1 euro stake): 5.00. PLACES: 1.50, 1.30, 1.80. DF: 7.30. SF: 16.30.
Owner Ecurie Mister Ess A S **Bred** Haras De La Faisanderie **Trained** Chantilly, France

6525 NEWMARKET (R-H)

Saturday, October 8

OFFICIAL GOING: Good (overall 7.8, stands' side 7.8, centre 7.6, far side 7.7)
Wind: fresh, behind Weather: chilly, light rain

6687 BURJ KHALIFA CHALLENGE STKS (GROUP 2) 7f

2:05 (2:07) (Class 1) 3-Y-O+
£45,368 (£17,200; £8,608; £4,288; £2,152; £1,080) **Stalls** High

Form RPR
6131 **1** **Strong Suit (USA)**[74] 4412 3-9-5 118 .... RichardHughes 4 126
(Richard Hannon) *a travelling wl: trckd ldng pair tl wnt 2nd 1/2-way: led on bit wl over 1f out: rdn and qckmd clr 1f out: r.o wl and in n.d after: eased cl home* **13/8**[1]
2132 **2** *4 1/2* **Chachamaidee (IRE)**[14] 6338 4-9-0 113 .... TomQueally 6 107
(Sir Henry Cecil) *hld up in tch: switching rt fr 1/2-way: rdn and effrt wl over 1f out: outpcd by wnr ent fnl f: no ch w wnr after but kpt on to snatch 2nd on post* **7/4**[2]
3005 **3** *nse* **Maqaasid**[71] 4497 3-8-12 108 .... RichardHills 1 107
(John Gosden) *hld up in tch: effrt over 2f out: rdn and press wnr wl over 1f out: outpcd and readily brushed aside 1f out: styd on same pce after and lost 2nd on post* **6/1**[3]
0400 **4** *2 1/4* **Rimth**[30] 5848 3-8-12 107 .... WilliamBuick 2 101
(Paul Cole) *stdd s: hld up in tch: hdwy 1/2-way: rdn and chsd ldrs 2f out: outpcd over 1f out and btn ent fnl f: wknd ins fnl f* **14/1**
4002 **5** *2 1/2* **Elshabakiya (IRE)**[7] 6523 3-8-12 102 .... NeilCallan 3 94
(Clive Brittain) *in tch: rdn and unable qck ent fnl 2f: wknd over 1f out* **25/1**
1633 **6** *2 1/4* **Across The Rhine (USA)**[6] 6561 5-9-3 109 .... PShanahan 5 91
(Tracey Collins, Ire) *led: rdn jst over 2f out: hdd wl over 1f out: sn wknd* **20/1**
1 **7** *1/2* **Giant Sandman (IRE)**[27] 4-9-3 106 ....(t) FJohansson 7 89
(Rune Haugen, Norway) *stdd s: t.k.h: hld up in tch in rr: rdn and struggling over 2f out: sn wknd* **20/1**
-603 **8** *7* **Lechevalier Choisi (IRE)**[49] 5282 3-9-1 103 ....(v) PJSmullen 8 71
(James Bernard McCabe, Ire) *chsd ldr tl 4f out: rdn and wknd ent fnl 2f* **25/1**

1m 22.74s (-2.66) **Going Correction** 0.0s/f (Good)
WFA 3 from 4yo+ 2lb **8** Ran SP% **112.6**
Speed ratings (Par 115): **115,109,109,107,104 101,101,93**
toteswingers:1&2:£1.20, 2&3:£1.90, 1&3:£2.60 CSF £4.28 TOTE £2.10: £1.02, £1.20, £2.10; EX 3.20 Trifecta £6.30 Pool: £7863.62 - 910.19 winning units..
Owner Qatar Bloodstock Ltd **Bred** Mcdowell Farm, Gainsborough Farm Et Al **Trained** East Everleigh, Wilts

FOCUS
Stands' side track of Rowley Mile used with stalls on stands' side with the exception of the Cesarewitch: Far side. Repositioning of bend into home straight increased distance of the Cesarewitch by 12m. The runners were racing on a 20-metre wide strip (stands' side) that had not been used since May, providing fresh ground for a prestigious day's racing. The wind came from behind the horses, which helped to give this contest a creditable winning time on the going. A fairly even split of 3yos and older horses had taken this contest over the previous seasons, but this year's renewal was dominated by a Classic generation colt. The third and fourth have not been at their best since early in the season and the race has been rated cautiously, although the winner is still entitled to be rated among the leading 3yos behind Frankel and Dream Ahead.

NOTEBOOK
Strong Suit(USA) ◆, who beat last year's winner of this contest Red Jazz on his previous outing at Goodwood in the Lennox Stakes, was the highest rated of these on official figures and duly won with plenty in hand after being given a prominent ride. Replated before leaving the paddock to go to the start, forcing a small delay, he was a class above his rivals despite carrying a 4lb penalty and will head to the Breeders' Cup Mile with every chance of dethroning the mighty Goldikova around a course that ought to suit him, despite the distance. Bookmakers reacted by making him between a 3-1 and 5-1 shot for the Churchill Downs event. (op 11-8, tchd 7-4 in places)
Chachamaidee(IRE) had been in terrific form during the summer and chased home Sahpresa in the Sun Chariot (Group 1) on her previous outing. This is said to be her ideal distance, but she raced a bit freely in rear and wasn't able to get on terms with the winner. It wasn't surprising to hear afterwards that Tom Queally felt they'd "bumped into one" and connections hinted that she may race on as a 5yo. (op 9-4 tchd 13-8 and 5-2 in a place)
Maqaasid, off the track since late July, had almost 6l to make up on Chachamaidee on their Oak Tree Stakes clash but had been reported to have worked well in the lead up to this contest. She appeared to run a lot better, reversing form with Rimth from that Goodwood run, but may be heading for the paddocks now. (op 7-1)
Rimth, who had the cheekpieces she wore last time removed, had pieces of good form to her name (trainer Paul Cole felt she'd had a few excuses this season as well) but hadn't managed to finish in front of Chachamaidee previously and that didn't change here. She ran okay, wide of the field, but never looked like winning.
Elshabakiya(IRE) couldn't have been given a realistic chance of gaining a first career victory against this calibre of rival, and so it proved.
Across The Rhine(USA), third of seven the previous Sunday in the Group 3 Concorde Stakes at Tipperary, is a multiple winner in Ireland (he also won a Meydan handicap in the spring) but dropped out after leading early. (op 28-1, tchd 33-1 in place)
Giant Sandman(IRE), who races in Norway where they have no whips and had ear plugs in before the race to keep him calm, sat in rear and made no impression.

6688 EMAAR MIDDLE PARK STKS (GROUP 1) (ENTIRE COLTS) 6f
2:35 (2:38) (Class 1) 2-Y-O

£92,720 (£35,152; £17,592; £8,763; £4,398; £2,207) **Stalls** High

Form				RPR
04	**1**		**Crusade (USA)**[16] 6270 2-8-12 0 ... SeamieHeffernan 8 (A P O'Brien, Ire) *in tch: rdn and effrt ent fnl 2f: drvn and led ins fnl f: styd on wl: drvn out* **25/1**	114
1424	**2**	¾	**Lilbourne Lad (IRE)**[29] 5882 2-8-12 111 ... RichardHughes 11 (Richard Hannon) *chsd ldrs: rdn ent fnl 2f: ev ch over 1f out: kpt on same pce u.p ins fnl f* **8/1**[3]	112
1561	**3**	hd	**Reply (IRE)**[30] 5849 2-8-12 109 ... RyanMoore 13 (A P O'Brien, Ire) *chsd ldrs: rdn to chse ldr 2f out: sn ev ch tl led jst over 1f out: hdd jst ins fnl f: styd on same pce after* **9/1**	111
1034	**4**	hd	**Balty Boys (IRE)**[21] 6170 2-8-12 96 ... MichaelHills 1 (Charles Hills) *racd alone on far side: a.p: ev ch u.p over 1f out: styd on same pce ins fnl f* **40/1**	110
2311	**5**	hd	**Caspar Netscher**[21] 6162 2-8-12 114 ... RobertWinston 7 (Alan McCabe) *taken down early: s.i.s: bhd: swtchd lft 2f out: stl plenty to do and racing against stands' rail whn hdwy 1f out: clsng on ldrs whn nt clr run and swtchd rt fnl 75yds: fin wl: nt rch ldrs* **5/1**[1]	113+
1533	**6**	shd	**Saigon**[21] 6162 2-8-12 106 ... JMurtagh 5 (James Toller) *in tch: rdn and unable qck ent fnl 2f: outpcd over 1f out: rallied u.p fnl 150yds: styd on wl u.p fnl 100yds* **10/1**	109
1100	**7**	1	**West Leake Diman (IRE)**[30] 5849 2-8-12 87 ... FrankieDettori 10 (Charles Hills) *chsd ldr tl 2f out: unable qck u.p over 1f out: styd on same pce ins fnl f* **66/1**	106
6250	**8**	1	**B Fifty Two (IRE)**[21] 6162 2-8-12 105 ... SebSanders 15 (J W Hills) *led: rdn ent fnl 2f: hdd jst over 1f out: no ex jst ins fnl f: styd on same pce after* **40/1**	103
2355	**9**	nk	**Tough As Nails (IRE)**[20] 6196 2-8-12 0 ... GFCarroll 6 (Michael Mulvany, Ire) *in tch: rdn and effrt ent fnl 2f: unable qck u.p over 1f out: styd on same pce after* **25/1**	102
112	**10**	½	**Family One (FR)**[48] 5305 2-8-12 0 ... OlivierPeslier 12 (Y Barberot, France) *t.k.h: hld up in tch in midfield: rdn and outpcd ent fnl 2f: plugged on but no threat to ldrs ins fnl f* **5/1**[1]	100
2142	**11**	hd	**Justineo**[28] 5933 2-8-12 106 ... KierenFallon 14 (William Haggas) *in tch in midfield: rdn and unable qck ent fnl f: kpt on same pce u.p and no threat to ldrs fr over 1f out* **25/1**	100
12	**12**	1 ¾	**Samminder (IRE)**[19] 6221 2-8-12 91 ... WilliamBuick 9 (Peter Chapple-Hyam) *hld up in tch towards rr: hdwy 1/2-way: effrt u.p ent fnl 2f: no imp fr over 1f out* **20/1**	94
101	**13**	2 ¼	**Rebellious Guest**[61] 4858 2-8-12 99 ... TomQueally 4 (George Margarson) *hld up in tch in midfield: rdn and nt qckn ent fnl 2f: wknd u.p over 1f out* **8/1**[3]	87
22	**14**	nk	**Arnold Lane (IRE)**[10] 6466 2-8-12 94 ... SamHitchcott 3 (Mick Channon) *hld up in tch in rr: effrt and swtchd rt ent fnl 2f: no imp and nvr threatened ldrs* **80/1**	86
2232	**15**	hd	**Burwaaz**[29] 5882 2-8-12 109 ... RichardHills 2 (Ed Dunlop) *in tch in midfield: rdn ent fnl 2f: wknd over 1f out* **12/1**	85
11	**16**	18	**Bapak Chinta (USA)**[114] 3064 2-8-12 109 ... PhillipMakin 16 (Kevin Ryan) *in tch tl 1/2-way: sn lost pl: lost tch wl over 1f out: t.o and eased ins fnl f* **11/2**[2]	28

1m 10.75s (-1.45) **Going Correction** 0.0s/f (Good) **16** Ran SP% **121.6**
Speed ratings (Par 109): **109,108,107,107,107 107,105,104,104,103 103,100,97,97,97 73**
toteswingers:1&2:£72.50, 2&3:£13.60, 1&3:£93.40 CSF £201.69 TOTE £43.80: £11.70, £3.20, £3.90; EX 443.90 Trifecta £3025.30 Part won. Pool: £4088.32 - 0.20 winning units..
Owner M Tabor, D Smith & Mrs John Magnier **Bred** La Traviata Syndicate **Trained** Ballydoyle, Co Tipperary

FOCUS
A clash of the Middle Park (week later than usual) and Dewhurst (week earlier than usual) is unsatisfactory. The last horse to complete the double was Diesis in 1982, but since the turn of the millennium 12 horses have contested both races and there were some big names among them, notably Dream Ahead (won this, fifth in Dewhurst). Over the past decade the winner's RPR has ranged from 114 to 125, but none of this lot had previously run above 112 and a bunch finish seems to confirm the pre-race impression that this is sub-standard form. The majority were positioned middle to stands' side, but Balty Boys raced alone against the far rail. The runner-up is among those that help set a pretty solid standard.

NOTEBOOK
Crusade(USA) didn't stay 7f when fourth in the Somerville Tattersall Stakes and the return to the trip of his maiden win saw a greatly improved performance, albeit his chance was helped by the fifth meeting trouble. His SP suggested victory was a surprise, but he's bred to make a pretty smart type at around this distance considering his sire was runner-up in a Breeders' Cup Sprint and his dam won a Grade 3 over 6f on dirt for Coolmore. It makes sense for him to go to the Breeders' Cup, and while he might not have the stamina for the Juvenile or the Juvenile Turf (both around 1m), the Juvenile Sprint, a new race over 6f on the main track could be worth a shot.
Lilbourne Lad(IRE), who was back up in trip after his fourth in the Flying Childers, ran a similar race to when second in the Gimcrack, showing pace before hitting a flat spot and then keeping on. He is due to retire to Rathbarry Stud to help ease the demand on his increasingly popular sire, Acclamation, but may go the Breeders' Cup beforehand.
Reply(IRE), who won a Doncaster sales race over slightly further last time, simply wasn't good enough but hung on to a place after showing speed. (op 11-1)
Balty Boys(IRE) going far side was an understandable tactic considering he was drawn one and the track was narrower than usual, although Michael Hills said the colt could have done with some company. It's hard to know if he was at an advantage, but a fair showing wasn't a total surprise considering he's a decent looker and had been keeping good company in sales races. That's probably it for the season and the Free Handicap was mentioned as a possible 2012 target. (op 50-1)
Caspar Netscher, the Gimcrack and Mill Reef winner, probably would have got the hat-trick up with a clear run, but he was continually blocked. His finishing effort was rapid when belatedly in the open, and it was all the more impressive considering he came from last in a race in which pace horses dominated. The Breeders' Cup is apparently still the plan and he must not be underestimated if taking the turf option.
Saigon got going too late after failing to handle the dip as well as some. The impression is this colt remains capable of better and his trainer, with the benefit of hindsight, was apparently wishing he'd run him in the Dewhurst. (op 14-1)
West Leake Diman(IRE) had plenty to find, but he was suited by racing handily. (op 100-1)
Family One(FR) didn't pick up after racing keenly. He looks flattered by his earlier profile as he won a weak Robert Papin and was then thrashed in the Prix Morny by Dabirsim, who although winning the Lagardere next time, recorded a lower RPR in doing so. (op 11-2 tchd 6-1)
Rebellious Guest again failed to cope with Group company. Maybe he needs soft ground. (tchd 9-1 in places)
Burwaaz was too keen without cover. He has the scope to make a high-class older sprinter.
Bapak Chinta(USA) ran as though something was amiss on his belated return. Absent since winning the Norfolk, he had missed the Nunthorpe after he struck into himself (apparently had cut on inside of his hock). Official explanation: trainer could not offer any explanation for the poor performance shown (op 5-1)

6689 DUBAI DEWHURST STKS (GROUP 1) (ENTIRE COLTS & FILLIES) 7f
3:10 (3:10) (Class 1) 2-Y-O

£179,770 (£68,155; £34,109; £16,991; £8,527; £4,279) **Stalls** High

Form				RPR
202	**1**		**Parish Hall (IRE)**[49] 5293 2-9-1 0 ... KJManning 3 (J S Bolger, Ire) *chsd ldr: ev ch 2f out: rdn to ld over 1f out: drvn and styd on wl u.p ins fnl f* **20/1**	118
1121	**2**	½	**Power**[28] 5951 2-9-1 117 ... RyanMoore 9 (A P O'Brien, Ire) *in tch: rdn and effrt ent fnl 2f: chsd ldrs and edging rt u.p jst ins fnl f: kpt on wl u.p fnl 100yds to go 2nd last strides* **15/8**[1]	117
21	**3**	hd	**Most Improved (IRE)**[43] 5447 2-9-1 0 ... FrankieDettori 6 (Brian Meehan) *t.k.h early: hld up in tch: hdwy 1/2-way: rdn and chsd ldrs 2f out: ev ch jst over 1f out: styd on same pce u.p fnl 100yds* **6/1**[3]	116
11	**4**	½	**Bronterre**[28] 5933 2-9-1 109 ... RichardHughes 1 (Richard Hannon) *racd alone towards centre tl jnd rivals after 2f: chsd ldrs: rdn and ev ch whn hung rt over 1f out: stl pressing ldrs and wnt rt again jst ins fnl f: wknd cl home* **10/3**[2]	115
2141	**5**	nk	**Trumpet Major (IRE)**[28] 5926 2-9-1 110 ... JMurtagh 5 (Richard Hannon) *hld up in tch: squeezed for room and lost pl 4f out: plenty to do and swtchd rt 2f out: hdwy u.p over 1f out: kpt on wl ins fnl f: nt rch ldrs* **10/1**	114
0025	**6**	2 ½	**Factory Time (IRE)**[21] 6162 2-9-1 100 ... ChrisCatlin 8 (Mick Channon) *hld up in tch in last pair: switching rt and effrt 2f out: styd on same pce and no imp fr over 1f out* **66/1**	107
31	**7**	nk	**Spiritual Star (IRE)**[15] 6300 2-9-1 95 ... JimmyFortune 4 (Andrew Balding) *awkward leaving stalls: sn led: rdn ent fnl 2f: hdd over 1f out: wknd jst ins fnl f* **14/1**	106
1132	**8**	nse	**Red Duke (USA)**[28] 5926 2-9-1 110 ... TomEaves 2 (John Quinn) *in tch in midfield: effrt and rdn 2f out: no prog and btn whn edgd lft u.p jst ins fnl f* **10/1**	106
11	**9**	4 ½	**Ektihaam (IRE)**[29] 5886 2-9-1 95 ... RichardHills 7 (Roger Varian) *stdd and sltly hmpd s: t.k.h and sn in tch: rdn and unable qck wl over 1f out: btn whn short of room jst ins fnl f: eased after* **8/1**	97+

1m 23.81s (-1.59) **Going Correction** 0.0s/f (Good) **9** Ran SP% **114.4**
Speed ratings (Par 109): **109,108,108,107,107 104,104,104,98**
toteswingers:1&2:£9.60, 2&3:£3.20, 1&3:£17.60 CSF £57.35 TOTE £29.20: £5.50, £1.10, £2.30; EX 77.20 Trifecta £1220.00 Pool: £7254.27 - 4.40 winning units..
Owner Mrs J S Bolger **Bred** J S Bolger **Trained** Coolcullen, Co Carlow

FOCUS
As well as now clashing with the Middle Park, the Dewhurst (run a week earlier than usual) followed only six days after the Prix Jean-Luc Lagardere. Since 2000 a total of 17 horses ran in this after contesting the French race, and Rock Of Gibraltar did the double, while six others who took in both either won here (four) or had won the Lagardere (two). This time no horses came here from Longchamp and the absence of Dabirsim was particularly noteworthy considering he started the day as the highest-rated juvenile in Europe on RPRs. Harbour Watch was another big name missing. All bar Bronterre, who was positioned up the middle for the first 3f, raced stands' side throughout. The first five were covered by just over a length and the form looks ordinary at best by the race's usual standard. That's a view supported by the clock with the time 1.07sec off the Challenge Stakes and 0.06sec slower than the Rockfel. Solid form rated around the runner-up, fourth and fifth.

NOTEBOOK
Parish Hall(IRE), whose trainer won this three times in a row from 2006, may have been at a slight advantage in having the stands' rail to race against in the closing stages. He hardly had the profile of a Teofilo or New Approach (first-named his sire and both previous Bolger Dewhurst winners) as he'd been held in Group company since his maiden win. However, he's a big, strong colt with plenty of scope and has clearly benefited from a 49-day break. He should make further progress, but this isn't Guineas-winning form and his trainer sees him more of a Derby horse, but while he probably won't have the speed for the Newmarket Classic, it would be dangerous to rule him out with there being no standout candidate. (op 16-1)
Power's rider wasn't able to go for everything until inside the final furlong, having had to switch his mount away from the rail, and the way the colt finished suggests he might have been the best horse on the day. That's far from certain, though, as it was notable he didn't pass Parish Hall after the line. This does not represent improvement on his National Stakes-winning form and he doesn't strike as a Newmarket Guineas winner in the making. He's out to 14-1 in a few places. (op 11-4, tchd 3-1 in places)

Most Improved(IRE) deserves credit considering he lacked the experience of the front two. He only had two maiden starts to his name (wide-margin winner second time) and there should be more to come. It wouldn't surprise if Godolphin were after him. (op 7-1)
Bronterre came here 2-2, the latest a Goodwood Listed race by 5l, but he never looked totally happy and wandered a bit under pressure. He's capable of better. (op 3-1 tchd 11-4)
Trumpet Major(IRE) was passed over by Richard Hughes, despite having won the Champagne Stakes last time. Having lost his place at around halfway he was left with an awful lot to do before finishing strongly out widest. Official explanation: jockey said that the colt suffered interference in running (op 12-1, tchd 14-1 in a place)
Factory Time(IRE) didn't look up to this class, but he ran better than might have been expected and the step up in trip evidently suited.
Spiritual Star(IRE) was supplemented after impressing with a 6l maiden win over C&D, but he wasn't up to it. (op 9-1)
Red Duke(USA) has had excuses since his success in the Superlative Stakes. This time he wasn't helped by racing wide without cover, so it wasn't a surprise he faded. (tchd 12-1 in a place)
Ektihaam(IRE) came here after winning a conditions event at Doncaster (race won last year by Frankel), but the rise in class found him out. He was too keen and found a bit of trouble when not picking up, and at no stage did Richard Hills give him a hard time. (op 7-1, tchd 13-2 in a place)

6690 BETFRED CESAREWITCH (HERITAGE H'CAP) 2m 2f
3:50 (3:56) (Class 2) 3-Y-O+

£99,600 (£29,824; £14,912; £7,456; £3,728; £1,872) **Stalls** Low

Form RPR

121 **1** **Never Can Tell (IRE)**[29] 5878 4-8-11 **89** 4ex................ FrankieDettori 36 98
(Jamie Osborne) *mde all: c centre st: rdn over 2f out: hrd pressed over 1f out: battled on gamely and forged ahd ins fnl f* **25/1**

-224 **2** 1 ½ **Ermyn Lodge**[63] 4775 5-8-12 **90**..(v) IanMongan 2 98
(Pat Phelan) *a.p: chsd wnr 10f out: rdn ent fnl 3f: lost 2nd over 1f out: swtchd rt and kpt on to go 2nd again wl ins fnl f* **16/1**

4051 **3** ½ **Colour Vision (FR)**[5] 6575 3-9-1 **105** 4ex............................. NeilCallan 6 112
(Mark Johnston) *hld up in tch: rdn and effrt to chse ldrs 3f out: ev ch over 1f out: hung rt 1f out: no ex and btn ins fnl f: wknd cl home* **20/1**

4440 **4** 3 ¼ **Mount Athos (IRE)**[49] 5285 4-9-10 **102**......................... JimmyFortune 9 105
(David Wachman, Ire) *in tch in midfield: rdn and effrt to chse ldrs 3f out: no imp and styd on same pce fr over 1f out* **14/1**

5 3 **Rainforest Magic (IRE)**[71] 4417 4-8-9 **87**......................(b) PJSmullen 29 87
(D K Weld, Ire) *hld up towards rr: hdwy 7f out: rdn and chsd ldrs 3f out: 5th and no imp u.p whn edgd rt over 1f out* **16/1**

-060 **6** 4 **Sentry Duty (FR)**[70] 4532 9-9-5 **97**.. JMurtagh 1 93
(Nicky Henderson) *hld up wl in tch: rdn and unable qck 3f out: 6th and wl hld over 1f out: plugged on* **14/1**

11-1 **7** ¾ **Beyond (IRE)**[99] 3593 4-8-6 **84**.. WilliamBuick 3 79
(David Pipe) *chsd wnr tl 10f out: styd prom tl rdn and unable qck ent fnl 3f: wknd u.p 2f out* **10/1**[2]

5333 **8** shd **Regal Park (IRE)**[43] 5448 4-8-5 **86**............................. HarryBentley(3) 23 81
(Marco Botti) *uns rdr and loose bef s: hld up towards rr: hdwy 5f out: 8th and no imp whn edgd rt wl over 1f out* **33/1**

-506 **9** nse **Ashbrittle**[35] 5705 4-8-12 **90**...(v) JimCrowley 26 85
(Ralph Beckett) *in tch in midfield: hdwy to chse ldrs and rdn 3f out: sn outpcd and struggling: btn whn edgd rt u.p wl over 1f out* **25/1**

0-11 **10** 10 **Veiled**[116] 3013 5-9-3 **95**... EddieAhern 22 79
(Nicky Henderson) *in tch in midfield: rdn and struggling over 4f out: wknd over 3f out: no ch fnl 2f* **12/1**[3]

6011 **11** 1 ¼ **Becausewecan (USA)**[12] 6410 5-8-11 **89** 7ex.................. JoeFanning 7 71
(Mark Johnston) *chsd ldrs: rdn and struggling 4f out: wknd over 3f out: wl btn fnl 2f* **33/1**

- **12** ½ **Buy Back Bob (IRE)**[14] 6364 4-8-12 **90**........................... WMLordan 10 72
(A J Martin, Ire) *hld up towards rr: hdwy 6f out: rdn and no prog over 3f out: wknd and no ch fnl 2f* **25/1**

-400 **13** ¾ **Abergavenny**[36] 5685 4-8-4 **85** ow2............................ PaulPickard(3) 21 66
(Brian Ellison) *stdd s: hld up in rr: rdn over 4f out: swtchd lft over 3f out: no ch but plugged on past btn horses fnl 2f: n.d* **16/1**

0040 **14** 4 **My Arch**[21] 6171 9-8-10 **88**.. TomQueally 13 65
(Ollie Pears) *a towards rr: rdn and struggling over 4f out: no ch but plugged on past btn horses fnl 2f: n.d* **40/1**

4610 **15** ¾ **Bow To No One (IRE)**[8] 6499 5-8-5 **83** 4ex...................... MartinLane 4 59
(Alan Jarvis) *racd in tch in midfield: rdn and no prog over 4f out: wknd wl over 3f out: wl btn fnl 2f* **40/1**

6511 **16** 3 **Cosimo de Medici**[21] 6171 4-8-10 **88** 4ex...................(t) RobertHavlin 33 60
(Hughie Morrison) *stdd s: hld up in rr: sme hdwy 7f out: rdn and struggling over 4f out: sn wknd* **16/1**

5031 **17** nk **Bowdler's Magic**[23] 6103 4-8-10 **88** 4ex......................... PhillipMakin 25 60
(Mark Johnston) *in tch: rdn and struggling wl over 4f out: wknd over 3f out: wl bhd fnl 2f* **33/1**

4211 **18** 3 **Keys (IRE)**[78] 4266 4-9-2 **94**....................................(b) RichardHughes 24 76+
(Roger Charlton) *hld up in midfield: hdwy 6f out: rdn and shortlived effrt ent fnl 3f: sn wknd and btn: eased fr over 1f out* **6/1**[1]

0201 **19** 3 **Gifted Leader (USA)**[119] 2931 6-8-5 **86**.....................(v) RyanClark(3) 30 52
(Ian Williams) *hld up towards rr: rdn and no rspnse 5f out: sn wknd and wl btn fnl 3f* **40/1**

0 **20** 2 ½ **Red Anthem**[29] 5888 4-8-6 **84**...(p) LiamJones 5 47
(Gerard Butler) *t.k.h: chsd ldrs tl struggling u.p 5f out: wknd 4f out: wl bhd fnl 3f: t.o* **50/1**

0001 **21** 1 ¾ **L Frank Baum (IRE)**[12] 6405 4-8-3 **84** 4ex............. DeclanCannon(3) 20 45
(Gay Kelleway) *dwlt and bustled along leaving stalls: towards rr: rdn and no hdwy over 5f out: wknd over 4f out: t.o* **66/1**

010- **22** 1 **Bernie The Bolt (IRE)**[416] 5220 5-9-3 **95**......................... DavidProbert 8 55
(Andrew Balding) *chsd ldrs: rdn and struggling u.p 4f out: sn wknd: t.o* **16/1**

2001 **23** ½ **Dazinski**[51] 5221 5-8-13 **91**.. JimmyQuinn 18 50
(Mark H Tompkins) *in tch in midfield: rdn and struggling over 4f out: wknd 4f out: t.o* **50/1**

0306 **24** 2 **Phoenix Flight (IRE)**[63] 4775 6-8-10 **88**.......................... ChrisCatlin 31 45
(James Evans) *t.k.h: hld up in rr: rdn and no prog over 4f out: sn wknd: t.o* **50/1**

0 **25** ¾ **Big Occasion (IRE)**[21] 6171 4-9-3 **95**.................................(b) JPO'Brien 34 51
(David Pipe) *in tch: rdn and struggling 5f out: wknd u.p over 4f out: t.o* **33/1**

506 **26** 2 ¼ **La Estrella (USA)**[17] 6249 8-8-10 **88**............................... DaneO'Neill 14 42
(Don Cantillon) *hld up towards rr: rdn and no progs 5f out: sn wknd and bhd: t.o* **40/1**

0040 **27** 5 **Palomar (USA)**[21] 6171 9-8-7 **85**...................................... TomEaves 11 33
(Brian Ellison) *taken down early: hld up towards rr: no prog u.p 5f out: wknd over 4f out: t.o* **33/1**

134/ **28** 2 ¾ **Tasheba**[7] 3143 6-8-1 **82**...(b) KieranO'Neill(3) 19 27
(David Pipe) *in tch in midfield tl lost pl u.p over 4f out: wknd 4f out: t.o* **50/1**

1-U3 **29** 2 ¾ **Tuscan Gold**[27] 5966 4-8-8 **86**.. SebSanders 17 28
(Sir Mark Prescott Bt) *t.k.h: hld up towards rr: plld way up to chse ldr 12f out: rdn and lost pl qckly 5f out: wl btn fnl 3f: t.o* **20/1**

0 **30** 11 **Dayia (IRE)**[78] 4266 7-9-1 **93**... OlivierPeslier 32 23
(Lydia Pearce) *hld up towards rr: hdwy on outer 7f out: wkng whn hmpd over 4f out: sn bhd: t.o and eased fnl f* **50/1**

050 **31** 2 ¾ **Mystery Star (IRE)**[37] 5659 6-9-4 **96**.............................. MartinDwyer 12 23
(Mark H Tompkins) *hld up in rr: rdn and no prog over 4f out: wl bhd over 3f out: t.o* **33/1**

3-00 **32** 3 **Braveheart Move (IRE)**[51] 5221 5-8-9 **87**.................. RobertWinston 28 11
(Geoffrey Harker) *t.k.h: hld up in tch towards rr: swtchd lft 6f out: rdn and struggling: over 4f out: sn wknd and bhd: t.o* **40/1**

0122 **33** dist **Kazbow (IRE)**[29] 5878 5-9-0 **92**... KierenFallon 35 —
(Luca Cumani) *chsd ldrs tl lost pl qckly over 4f out: virtually p.u and eased fnl 3f: wl t.o* **25/1**

3m 48.04s (-8.76) **Going Correction** -0.25s/f (Firm)
WFA 3 from 4yo+ 12lb **33** Ran SP% **139.9**
Speed ratings (Par 109): **109,108,108,106,105 103,103,103,103,98 98,97,97,95,95 94,94,92,91,90 89,89,88,87,87 86,84,83,**
toteswingers:1&2:£93.10, 2&3:£156.40, 1&3:£257.60 CSF £327.78 CT £7978.79 TOTE £30.70: £6.30, £5.70, £4.10, £5.20; EX 948.40 Trifecta £20662.70 Part won. Pool: £27922.63 - 0.50 winning units..
Owner Dr Marwan Koukash **Bred** Shaanara Syndicate **Trained** Upper Lambourn, Berks

FOCUS

Every year the draw is always considered a significant pointer to success in the Cesarewitch and with good reason, even though the race distance would suggest there shouldn't be an advantage. However, as if anyone needed reminding, Frankie Dettori, whose mount was drawn widest, produced yet another world-class ride to secure success in one of the season's most famous handicaps. The third ran a big race under his penalty and the fourth has been rated close to his best handicap form.

NOTEBOOK

Never Can Tell(IRE) rarely runs badly and caught the eye on jockey bookings, but it wasn't easy to envisage the Montjeu filly taking this considering her stalls position, despite sound staying form. Her jockey got her away smartly and the pair soon got to the lead in the early stages. On turning in, Dettori made a conscious effort to take his mount towards the centre of the track down the long home straight, away from her rivals initially, a manoeuvre that quite probably proved to be the winning one. She showed determination in the final stages to claim another memorable handicap success for her owner.
Ermyn Lodge attracted some market support the previous day and rewarded those who went in each-way after being given a positive ride. He is a credit to all concerned with him and was given the right sort of ride from what looked a decent draw. Lightly raced for his age, it wouldn't be a surprise to see him back next year for another crack at this, and connections also revealed that there is a chance he could go hurdling after a break as he's already schooled well.
Colour Vision(FR) ◆, the only 3yo, won the previous Monday, for which he was carrying a 4lb penalty. He had beaten the winner when they met at Chester in July and looked to have a good chance when he made a positive surge over 3f out. However, hard though he tried, he didn't get home as strongly as the winner. Clearly a grand staying type at his best, one would imagine he'll be campaigned as a Cup horse next year. (tchd 22-1 in a place)
Mount Athos(IRE), the owner's first string on cap colours, travelled strongly in midfield for much of the contest and plugged on for an honourable fourth after getting into a leading position still going well. Undoubtedly his burden proved just too much when it counted. (op 16-1)
Rainforest Magic(IRE), off since winning a handicap hurdle at Galway in July, is a half-brother to a horse who twice ran poorly in this race so did much better than his relation with a keeping-on effort.
Sentry Duty(FR), beaten a little over 4l in this last year off a 5lb higher mark, had his chance but couldn't make up the ground to the leading bunch in the final stages. (op 12-1)
Beyond(IRE) looked a candidate for this race when winning on his Flat turf debut on his first outing for David Pipe in early July, and had a handy looking draw. He broke quite well and raced handily, but lost his position before running on again. (op 11-1 tchd 12-1)
Regal Park(IRE), who lost his jockey on the way to the start, was given a very patient ride and made respectable late headway from the rear.
Ashbrittle had the visor back on, but he tended to run about when placed under maximum pressure.
Veiled, racing of a 15lb higher mark than when making her Flat debut for Nicky Henderson, settled towards the midfield but couldn't get involved. One would imagine she is a lot better than she showed.
Buy Back Bob(IRE) had never raced over further than 1m4f on the Flat (sole try over hurdles saw him finish 3rd, beaten 5l, over 2m) so it was pure guesswork as to whether he'd stay the distance. Representing a trainer with a decent record in this contest, he looked to be going well 4f out but failed to make the progress that look likely.
Cosimo de Medici won the Cesarewitch Trial here back in September, a second victory in a row, but never threatened.
Keys(IRE) came into this unbeaten in handicaps (raced off a 16lb higher mark here than when bolting up at Newbury in July) and was well supported in the minutes leading up to the off. Settled towards midfield, he moved well under Richard Hughes but offered little when push came to shove and the jockey didn't give his mount a hard time from over 1f out. Official explanation: jockey said that the gelding had no more to give (op 8-1 tchd 11-2 after 14-1 in a place and 12-1 in places)
Tuscan Gold was less exposed than some and obviously represented connections to be feared on the big day, but he was under the pump a long way out and dropped out. (op 16-1)

6691 VISION.AE ROCKFEL STKS (GROUP 2) (FILLIES) 7f
4:25 (4:30) (Class 1) 2-Y-O

£34,026 (£12,900; £6,456; £3,216; £1,614; £810) **Stalls** High

Form RPR

1 **Wading (IRE)**[15] 6314 2-8-12 0... RyanMoore 5 115+
(A P O'Brien, Ire) *trckd ldrs: shkn up to ld over 1f out: kpt on strly and in command fnl f: quite impressive* **11/4**[2]

2131 **2** 2 **Pimpernel (IRE)**[14] 6340 2-8-12 105........................... FrankieDettori 2 110
(Mahmood Al Zarooni) *t.k.h early: hld up in last pair: swtchd out and hdwy 2f out: sn rdn: kpt on to go 2nd fnl 75yds: nvr rching wnr* **5/2**[1]

1 **3** nk **Gray Pearl**[56] 5048 2-8-12 85... MichaelHills 3 109
(Charles Hills) *led: rdn and hdd over 1f out: kpt chsng wnr but sn hld: no ex whn lost 2nd fnl 75yds* **20/1**

62 **4** 1 ½ **Bana Wu**[21] 6168 2-8-12 0... DavidProbert 9 105
(Andrew Balding) *prom: rdn over 2f out: sn outpcd by ldrs: kpt on same pce fnl f* **40/1**

4102 **5** shd **Sunday Times**[14] 6337 2-8-12 109.................................. WilliamBuick 6 104
(Peter Chapple-Hyam) *in tch: rdn over 2f out: kpt on same pce fnl f* **5/1**[3]

6 1 **Janey Muddles (IRE)**[140] 2321 2-8-12 0........................ KJManning 8 102
(J S Bolger, Ire) *little keen early: trckd ldrs: rdn 2f out: nt gng pce to chal* **11/1**

1363 **7** *1* **Mary Fildes (IRE)**[21] 6146 2-8-12 93.................................... LiamKeniry 7 99
(J S Moore) *hld up in last trio: rdn over 2f out: nvr gng pce to make imp* **40/1**

1214 **8** *½* **Regal Realm**[29] 5885 2-8-12 103.................................... JimmyFortune 1 98
(Jeremy Noseda) *hld up in last pair: pushed along half way: rdn over 2f out: nvr gng pce to get involved* **9/1**

11 **9** *1¼* **Alsindi (IRE)**[15] 6296 2-8-12 102.................................... TomQueally 4 94
(Clive Brittain) *in tch: effrt 2f out: sn short of room: fdd ins fnl f* **6/1**

1m 23.75s (-1.65) **Going Correction** 0.0s/f (Good) **9** Ran SP% **114.2**
Speed ratings (Par 104): **109,106,106,104,104 103,102,101,100**
toteswingers:1&2:£2.10, 2&3:£8.00, 1&3:£7.50 CSF £9.71 TOTE £3.60: £1.80, £1.10, £3.20; EX 10.70 Trifecta £101.80 Pool: £2021.08 - 14.68 winning units..
Owner Mrs John Magnier, M Tabor & D Smith **Bred** Roncon & Chelston **Trained** Ballydoyle, Co Tipperary

FOCUS
The Rockfel produced consecutive 1,000 Guineas winners in 2005 and 2006, Speciosa and Finsceal Beo doubling up. Since then it hasn't had much bearing on the first fillies' Classic, although the 2009 winner Music Show was undone by a draw bias in the Guineas, and the race has still produced top-level performers. They raced up the middle of the track. The bare form doesn't look anything special, but the time was 0.06sec quicker than the Dewhurst and the winner is a really smart prospect. The winner is one of the best 2yo fillies we've seen this year, with the third, fourth and seventh the long-term key to the level of the form.

NOTEBOOK
Wading(IRE) ◆ readily confirmed the impression she made when earning an RPR of 100 in a Polytrack maiden on her second start. Her head-carriage was a touch high, but that's the case with many of her sire's progeny and she showed a good attitude for a straightforward success. She displayed a lovely, long and fluent stride. Further improvement is needed if she's to make a Guineas filly - the runner-up's stable have at least a couple better - but that's entirely possible and her course form is an obvious plus. The general 10-1 is fair, but more interesting is the 12-1 for the Oaks considering her dam is closely related to Sea The Stars and a half-sister to Galileo. (op 5-2 tchd 2-1 and 3-1 in places)
Pimpernel(IRE) impressed when winning a C&D nursery off 96 last time, but this asked more. The result should please her connections considering they have at least two better fillies in the shape of Discourse and Lyric Of Light. (op 3-1, tchd 10-3 in a place)
Gray Pearl hadn't been seen since winning an ordinary 6f maiden at Newbury on her debut back in August, but she's a big filly and has made good progress. There should be more to come. (op 25-1)
Bana Wu does little for the form having run to just a fair level in two maidens, but presumably she wouldn't have run unless Andrew Balding believed her to be close to this class. (op 50-1)
Sunday Times, the Cheveley Park runner-up, was the first to test that form but she did nothing for it. (op 7-2 tchd 11-2)
Janey Muddles(IRE) had been off since winning a 6f Curragh maiden on her debut in May. This was a satisfactory return. (op 9-1 tchd 12-1)
Regal Realm hasn't gone on since winning a weak and muddling Prestige Stakes. (op 12-1)
Alsindi(IRE) overcame a pace bias to win the Group 3 Oh So Sharp over C&D, but something was presumably amiss this time. (op 13-2 tchd 7-1)

6692 AUTUMN STKS (GROUP 3) 1m
5:00 (5:00) (Class 1) 2-Y-O

£19,281 (£7,310; £3,658; £1,822; £914; £459) **Stalls** High

Form RPR

2154 **1** **Rockinante (FR)**[14] 6336 2-9-0 105.................................... RichardHughes 6 105
(Richard Hannon) *racd on stands' side rails: mde all: rdn 2f out: kpt on gamely* **8/1**

1 **2** *1¾* **Perennial**[30] 5851 2-9-0 90.................................... MichaelHills 10 101
(Charles Hills) *racd away fr stands' side rails: hld up: tk clsr order 3f out: rdn 2f out: styd on ins fnl f: wnt 2nd nring fin* **5/1**[3]

3 **3** *½* **Astrology (IRE)**[49] 5293 2-9-0 0.................................... JPO'Brien 3 100
(A P O'Brien, Ire) *racd away fr stands' side rails: trckd ldrs: rdn to chal over 2f out: wandered u.p over 1f out: styd on same pce: lost 2nd nring fin* **11/8**[1]

20 **4** *1* **Whip Rule (IRE)**[28] 5951 2-9-0 0.................................... KJManning 7 98
(J S Bolger, Ire) *racd away fr stands' side rails: in tch: rdn over 2f out: styd on ins fnl f: nvr quite gng pce to chal* **25/1**

21 **5** *3¾* **Validus**[36] 5688 2-9-0 95.................................... KierenFallon 9 89
(Luca Cumani) *racd away fr stands' side rails: trckd ldr: effrt 2f out: one pce ins fnl f* **3/1**[2]

331 **6** *4½* **Swing Alone (IRE)**[29] 5899 2-9-0 81.................................... RobertWinston 8 79
(Gay Kelleway) *reluctant to go to post: racd away fr stands' side rails: hld up: effrt and hung rt 2f out: wknd ins fnl f* **50/1**

104 **7** *1¼* **Moon Pearl (USA)**[30] 5849 2-9-0 98.................................... JimCrowley 4 76
(Ralph Beckett) *hld up on stands' side rails: rdn over 3f out: nvr any imp: wknd wl over 1f out* **12/1**

2014 **8** *3¼* **Red Aggressor (IRE)**[28] 5933 2-9-0 90.................................... TomQueally 5 68
(Clive Brittain) *racd away fr stands' side rails: led gp: rdn over 2f out: chsng ldrs whn bdly hmpd over 1f out: wknd* **33/1**

1m 37.71s (-0.89) **Going Correction** 0.0s/f (Good) **8** Ran SP% **111.3**
Speed ratings (Par 105): **104,102,101,100,97 92,91,88**
toteswingers:1&2:£6.20, 2&3:£2.40, 1&3:£3.20 CSF £44.52 TOTE £8.30: £1.80, £2.30, £1.20; EX 38.60 Trifecta £124.40 Pool: £1637.54 - 9.73 winning units..
Owner Coriolan Links Partnership Iii **Bred** Azienda Agricola Il Tiglio **Trained** East Everleigh, Wilts

FOCUS
This produced some quality horses when run at Ascot, with names including Nashwan, Dr Fong and Nayef immediately springing to mind. More recent winners include Ibn Kaldoun, who added the Racing Post Trophy in 2007, and Kite Wood, who proved good enough to finish runner-up in the St Leger. It's also worth mentioning that this year's Doncaster Classic winner Masked Marvel was a disappointing sixth of eight in the final running at the Berkshire venue. Hopefully with the move to a new course, the race may become reinvigorated but this year's result looked a touch ordinary, especially as there is a chance the winner came up a favoured path. The second has more to offer and the third looks the type to run his biggest fugures in defeat.

NOTEBOOK
Rockinante(FR) wasn't beaten too far over C&D in the Royal Lodge despite racing a bit freely, and he boosted Daddy Long Legs' credentials with what looked to be a fluent success after dominating up the stands' rail. However, it would be surprising if he developed into a Group 1 performer at three considering he has been exposed at one level below that this season.
Perennial ◆ beat the hugely promising Encke on their debuts at Doncaster and is bred to be an above-average performer in the long term. He gave the impression that he was still learning in this contest, which could have been expected, and might be the one to take from the race. (op 4-1, tchd 11-2 in a place)
Astrology(IRE) seemed a surprise winner on his debut over 1m and then ran really well on his next outing when third to Dragon Pulse in the Group 2 Futurity Stakes at the Curragh (7f). On that occasion he was one place in front of stablemate and subsequent Beresford Stakes winner David Livingston, and just behind Dewhurst winner Parish Hall. Back up to 1m, he raced prominently in the bunch that came towards the middle, but edged left at least twice when given a reminder. This course may have been a bit too undulating for him and he'll be better judged on a flatter track. (op 7-4, tchd 15-8 in a place)
Whip Rule(IRE), well beaten behind Power in the National Stakes last time when tried in cheekpieces, made his bid wide of the field and didn't look entirely straightforward under maximum pressure. (op 22-1)
Validus finished third in what has turned out to be a hot maiden on the July course in August before winning by 6l at Kempton (horse beaten almost 9l into fourth that night has won since). He had every chance, but found disappointingly little. That said, this was a big step up in grade so he can easily be given another opportunity. (tchd 11-4 and 10-3 and 7-2 in places)
Swing Alone(IRE) had plenty to do on official figures despite a Wolverhampton success last time.
Moon Pearl(USA) kept on really well in the Doncaster sales race won by Reply, who finished third in the Group 1 Middle Park earlier in the card, but shaped as though something was amiss here after chasing the winner early. (op 9-1)

6693 DARLEY STKS (GROUP 3) 1m 1f
5:35 (5:35) (Class 1) 3-Y-O+

£28,355 (£10,750; £5,380; £2,680; £1,345; £675) **Stalls** High

Form RPR

2254 **1** **Bubble Chic (FR)**[21] 6185 3-8-13 119.................................... OlivierPeslier 4 109+
(G Botti, Italy) *mde all: rdn and qcknd 2f out: edgd rt but r.o strly ins fnl f* **9/2**[2]

3132 **2** *1¼* **Dux Scholar**[42] 5494 3-8-13 112.................................... RyanMoore 7 106
(Sir Michael Stoute) *t.k.h: hld up in tch: rdn and effrt 2f out: drvn to press wnr ent fnl f: edgd rt and no imp fnl 100yds* **15/8**[1]

3020 **3** *1¼* **Questioning (IRE)**[14] 6339 3-8-13 109..........................(v) WilliamBuick 8 104+
(John Gosden) *stdd s: hld up wl in tch in rr: swtchd lft and effrt wl over 1f out: drvn and hdwy to chse ldrs 1f out: no imp fnl 100yds* **11/2**[3]

6110 **4** *nk* **Albaqaa**[14] 6339 6-9-3 92.................................... KieranO'Neill 10 103?
(P J O'Gorman) *stdd s: t.k.h: hld up in tch in rr: hdwy and hung rt over 1f out: chsd ldrs and styd on same pce ins fnl f* **50/1**

5 *shd* **Retrieve (AUS)**[168] 4-9-3 115..........................(t) FrankieDettori 1 103
(Saeed Bin Suroor) *stdd s: hld up wl in tch in rr: rdn and effrt 2f out: chsd ldrs ent fnl f: one pce and no imp ins fnl f* **10/1**

6106 **6** *1¾* **Navajo Chief**[22] 6129 4-9-3 107.................................... HarryBentley 2 99
(Alan Jarvis) *pressed wnr tl wl over 1f out: sn unable qck and rdn: wknd jst ins fnl f* **33/1**

6512 **7** *1¼* **Premio Loco (USA)**[15] 6298 7-9-9 114.................................... GeorgeBaker 3 102
(Chris Wall) *stdd s: sn trcking ldrs: rdn and unable qck over 1f out: wknd ins fnl f* **16/1**

2040 **8** *nse* **Maali (IRE)**[14] 6339 3-8-13 92..........................(bt) TomQueally 6 96?
(Clive Brittain) *wl in tch in rr: pushed along 3f out: rdn and outpcd ent fnl 2f: no imp and no threat to ldrs fr over 1f out* **50/1**

2335 **9** *½* **Sri Putra**[21] 6161 5-9-3 116.................................... NeilCallan 5 95
(Roger Varian) *dwlt: sn rcvrd and chsng ldrs: rdn 3f out: hrd drvn and unable qck over 2f out: wknd over 1f out* **6/1**

-410 **10** *2¾* **King Torus (IRE)**[24] 6061 3-8-13 110.................................... RichardHughes 9 89
(Richard Hannon) *trckd ldrs: rdn and effrt to press ldr 2f out tl outpcd over 1f out: btn ins fnl f: fdd fnl 150yds* **10/1**

1m 50.85s (-0.85) **Going Correction** 0.0s/f (Good)
WFA 3 from 4yo+ 4lb **10** Ran SP% **113.6**
Speed ratings (Par 113): **103,101,100,100,100 98,97,97,97,94**
toteswingers:1&2:£2.60, 2&3:£4.30, 1&3:£5.20 CSF £12.79 TOTE £4.50: £1.60, £1.10, £2.40; EX 13.40 Trifecta £70.90 Pool: £2967.71 - 30.96 winning units..
Owner F Tabone **Bred** Suc. Z Hakam **Trained** Italy

FOCUS
This looked well up to the standard you'd hope to see for a race of this nature, but the early fractions didn't look that quick so it wasn't surprising to see a class horse steal it from the front. The fourth and eighth finished too close to take the form literally.

NOTEBOOK
Bubble Chic(FR) was a fascinating contender on his very best form and was given a perfect ride considering the way the race unfolded. He hadn't run badly on his return from a break in France last time, and that had obviously put him right for this. Connections indicated that he may go to Capannelle for the Premio Roma next before looking to run in Hong Kong. (op 4-1, tchd 11-2 in places)
Dux Scholar had maintained a good level of ability during the season and kept up that momentum with another sound performance. One got the impression he was one of many who would have preferred a better gallop to chase. (op 9-4 tchd 7-4 and 5-2 in places)
Questioning(IRE) got no sort of run in the Cambridgeshire after being towards the rear for that race, and went some way to proving he'd have gone fairly close there - when 10lb well in - granted a clear passage, with a good effort here. (op 15-2)
Albaqaa had never run in a Group race previously and had plenty to find on official figures, despite a run of good form. He ran a blinder here considering the ratings but was more-or-less upsides Questioning in the Cambridgeshire, so that performance was repeated, albeit on much better terms here. (op 40-1)
Retrieve(AUS), who was third in the Victoria Derby in late October last year (winner Lion Tamer currently leading fancy for Melbourne Cup), had six runs in Australia between February and April, and although he didn't win, he ran horses like exciting New Zealand-trained star Jimmy Choux to half a length off level weights over a similar trip. Without any of the headgear he wore when trained by Peter Snowden for Sheikh Mohammed, he made a satisfactory if unspectacular start to his European career and it would be amazing if he didn't have a lot more to come. (op 8-1 tchd 11-1)
Navajo Chief didn't look the easiest to fancy for this despite the odd really solid performance, so ran well in the circumstances.
Premio Loco(USA) has proved to be a really consistent Group performer over the years, and this was a slight ease in grade. Conceding weight all round, he rarely posed a serious threat. (op 11-1)
Maali(IRE) keeps facing stiff tasks, running well in the main, and got completely outpaced about 2f out before running on strongly. (op 66-1)
Sri Putra was disappointing at Newbury last time and again here. The only excuse one could offer is that he has been reported in the past to be best on much quicker ground. (op 11-2)
King Torus(IRE) ran a shocker at Sandown (jockey reported that his mount stopped quickly) after beating Questioning at Haydock, and again dropped out tamely when the tempo lifted, the track not appearing to suit. He was looked after once beaten. (op 11-1 tchd 12-1)
T/Plt: £119.90 to a £1 stake. Pool of £179,163.59 - 1,090.07 winning tickets. T/Qpdt: £35.40 to a £1 stake. Pool of £10,573.35 - 220.53 winning tickets. SP

6662 WOLVERHAMPTON (A.W) (L-H)
Saturday, October 8

OFFICIAL GOING: Standard

6694 32REDPOKER.COM H'CAP (DIV I) 5f 216y(P)
5:30 (5:30) (Class 6) (0-60,65) 3-Y-O+ **£1,746** (£519; £259; £129) **Stalls** Low

Form RPR

0255 **1** **Silver Wind**[21] 6174 6-9-4 57..........................(b) JamesDoyle 6 65
(Alan McCabe) *a.p: pushed along 1/2-way: rdn to ld over 1f out: edgd lft: jst hld on* **7/4**[1]

6450 **2** *nk* **Caramelita**[61] 4850 4-9-6 **59**......(v) AdamKirby 7 66
(J R Jenkins) *mid-div: hdwy over 1f out: rdn and r.o wl ins fnl f* **20/1**
4026 **3** *½* **Meia Noite**[81] 4187 4-9-7 **60**...... LukeMorris 5 65
(Chris Wall) *chsd ldrs: rdn over 1f out: r.o* **8/1**
2520 **4** *¾* **Memphis Man**[17] 6261 8-8-10 **54**...... MatthewCosham(5) 3 57
(David Evans) *hld up: hdwy over 1f out: r.o* **14/1**
0000 **5** *¾* **Perlachy**[9] 6488 7-9-4 **57**......(v) KellyHarrison 2 58
(Ronald Harris) *hld up: hdwy over 1f out: r.o* **22/1**
0304 **6** *½* **Spin A Wish**[11] 6428 3-8-8 **48**......(v) MichaelStainton 12 47
(Richard Whitaker) *chsd ldr tl rdn over 2f out: styd on same pce fnl f* **28/1**
4330 **7** *½* **Francis Albert**[4] 6602 5-8-9 **55**...... JackDuern(7) 10 52
(Michael Mullineaux) *s.i.s: hld up: plld hrd: hdwy over 1f out: nt rch ldrs* **6/1**[2]
1040 **8** *2* **Avoncreek**[29] 5881 7-8-10 **49**......(v) WilliamCarson 4 40
(Brian Baugh) *chsd ldrs: rdn over 2f out: edgd rt and no ex fnl f* **20/1**
0440 **9** *2* **Hootys Agogo**[30] 5864 3-8-2 **47**......(p) NeilFarley(5) 1 32
(Declan Carroll) *s.i.s: hld up: nvr on terms* **28/1**
2051 **10** *¾* **Distant Sun (USA)**[13] 6386 7-9-7 **65**......(p) ShaneBKelly(5) 8 47
(Linda Perratt) *hld up: plld hrd: hdwy 1/2-way: sn rdn: wknd fnl f* **10/1**
600 **11** *1* **Yungaburra (IRE)**[22] 6138 7-9-2 **55**......(tp) JamesMillman 11 34
(David C Griffiths) *sn led: rdn and hdd over 1f out: wknd ins fnl f* **40/1**
4306 **12** *1* **Cara Carmela**[17] 6258 3-8-8 **48**...... SaleemGolam 13 24
(Stuart Williams) *chsd ldrs: rdn over 1f out: wknd fnl f* **25/1**
3222 **13** *47* **Mucky Molly**[26] 5996 3-9-2 **56**...... KirstyMilczarek 9 —
(Olivia Maylam) *s.i.s: sn outpcd: t.o* **7/1**[3]

1m 14.21s (-0.79) **Going Correction** -0.20s/f (Stan)
WFA 3 from 4yo+ 1lb **13** Ran SP% **117.1**
Speed ratings (Par 101): **97,96,95,94,93 93,92,89,87,86 84,83,20**
Tote Swingers: 1&2 £14.10, 1&3 £3.20, 2&3 £31.40 CSF £44.64 CT £232.27 TOTE £2.50: £1.30, £7.10, £3.10; EX 45.80.
Owner Derek Buckley **Bred** W H R John And Partners **Trained** Averham Park, Notts

FOCUS
A competitive race of its type, with just over three lengths covering the first seven. Ordinary form rated around the runner-up to his best form since last winter, with the third and fourth close to their marks.
Distant Sun(USA) Official explanation: jockey said that the gelding hung right-handed throughout
Mucky Molly Official explanation: vet said the filly finished lame having received a bump leaving the stalls

6695 32RED NURSERY — 5f 216y(P)
6:00 (6:00) (Class 6) (0-65,65) 2-Y-O — **£1,704** (£503; £251) **Stalls** Low

Form RPR
U200 **1** **Berlusca (IRE)**[30] 5840 2-9-4 **62**...... WilliamCarson 13 65
(William Jarvis) *hld up: hdwy u.p over 1f out: r.o to ld nr fin* **8/1**[3]
0050 **2** *nk* **Ionwy**[30] 5840 2-8-10 **54**...... FrankieMcDonald 3 56
(Derek Haydn Jones) *chsd ldr 5f out: rdn to ld 1f out: hdd nr fin* **66/1**
6424 **3** *½* **Thorpe Bay**[31] 5833 2-9-3 **61**...... SteveDrowne 12 62
(Mark Rimmer) *mid-div: hdwy over 2f out: rdn and ev ch ins fnl f: r.o* **11/1**
4040 **4** *1* **Princess Banu**[24] 6058 2-9-3 **61**...... MatthewDavies 7 59
(Mick Channon) *led 1f: chsd ldrs: rdn over 2f out: r.o* **25/1**
0500 **5** *½* **Allegri (IRE)**[9] 6487 2-9-4 **62**...... DavidNolan 11 58
(Ann Duffield) *hld up: r.o ins fnl f: nrst fin* **16/1**
6000 **6** *½* **Justine Time (IRE)**[4] 6597 2-8-10 **54**......(b) MartinHarley 8 49
(David Barron) *prom: rdn over 2f out: r.o* **12/1**
000 **7** *1¼* **Songbird Blues**[45] 5384 2-8-12 **56**...... LukeMorris 10 51+
(Mark Usher) *hld up: nt clr run over 1f out: r.o ins fnl f: nvr trbld ldrs* **11/1**
635 **8** *nk* **Baltic Flyer (IRE)**[46] 5337 2-9-7 **65**...... AndreaAtzeni 1 55
(Robert Eddery) *led 5f out: rdn and hdd over 1f out: no ex ins fnl f* **11/4**[1]
200 **9** *nk* **Miss Purity Pinker (IRE)**[15] 6291 2-9-4 **62**......(v[1]) CathyGannon 9 51
(David Evans) *prom: rdn over 2f out: styd on same pce fnl f* **20/1**
6000 **10** *nk* **Armiger**[26] 5998 2-8-7 **56**...... JamesRogers(5) 2 44
(William Muir) *chsd ldrs: rdn over 2f out: no ex ins fnl f* **33/1**
2204 **11** *1* **Night Angel (IRE)**[12] 6406 2-9-7 **65**...... JamesMillman 6 50
(Rod Millman) *s.i.s: hld up: hdwy over 1f out: nt rch ldrs* **13/2**[2]
4035 **12** *1¼* **The Name Is Don (IRE)**[17] 6252 2-9-5 **63**...... AdamKirby 4 50+
(Mark Gillard) *sn prom: hmpd and lost pl over 3f out: nt clr run over 2f out: nvr able to chal* **10/1**
0264 **13** *7* **Essexvale (IRE)**[28] 5945 2-9-5 **63**...... JamesDoyle 5 23
(Richard Hannon) *sn pushed along in rr: bhd fr 1/2-way* **8/1**[3]

1m 15.53s (0.53) **Going Correction** -0.20s/f (Stan) **13** Ran SP% **114.6**
Speed ratings (Par 93): **88,87,86,85,84 84,82,82,81,81 80,78,69**
Tote Swingers: 1&2 £93.90, 1&3 £15.90, 2&3 £54.50 CSF £462.71 CT £5845.02 TOTE £4.90: £1.10, £22.20, £3.10; EX 411.00.
Owner The Berlusca Partnership **Bred** Value Bloodstock **Trained** Newmarket, Suffolk

FOCUS
An ordinary nursery, but the winner is unexposed on Polytrack and can do better. The principals have been rated close to their marks.

NOTEBOOK
Berlusca(IRE), who unseated his rider on his only previous AW outing, showed himself to be capable on the surface. This was a good effort from the worst stall, so he looks capable of improving a few pounds. (op 10-1)
Ionwy ran by far her best race to date and looks to be on a decent mark if she tries Polytrack again next time. (op 100-1)
Thorpe Bay ran a creditable race from a wide stall. Though on a higher mark now, he is running well enough to make him one to consider next time. (op 12-1)
Princess Banu's handicap mark is slipping, but that reflects her lower level of form compared with earlier in the season and she wasn't quite good enough to take advantage. (op 28-1)
Allegri(IRE) has arrived in handicaps on a testing mark, but he is showing enough to suggest he can become more competitive if dropped a few pounds. (tchd 20-1)
Justine Time(IRE) did reasonably well on this AW debut without suggesting she can win off this mark. (op 14-1)
Songbird Blues did better than may appear on this nursery debut, because she met serious traffic problems which prevented her getting into the race. Expect a better show next time because this opening handicap mark looks fair. (tchd 12-1)
Baltic Flyer(IRE) looked likely to be suited by the drop back to 6f, but the forcing tactics did not pay off. (op 5-2 tchd 3-1)
The Name Is Don(IRE) had not had the run of the race in his previous two outings and this time he had little room for much of the journey. He is a bit better than he has looked since switching to Polytrack. (tchd 11-1)

6696 32REDPOKER.COM H'CAP (DIV II) — 5f 216y(P)
6:30 (6:30) (Class 6) (0-60,64) 3-Y-O+ — **£1,746** (£519; £259; £129) **Stalls** Low

Form RPR
1200 **1** **Full Shilling (IRE)**[9] 6479 3-9-2 **56**...... AdamKirby 2 66
(John Spearing) *s.i.s: hld up: hdwy 2f out: r.o u.p to ld post* **7/1**
0434 **2** *nse* **Little Perisher**[21] 6175 4-8-8 **47**......(b) TadhgO'Shea 8 57
(Karen George) *a.p: rdn to ld ins fnl f: hdd post* **9/1**
3212 **3** *1½* **Golden Compass**[10] 6444 3-9-10 **64**...... WilliamCarson 6 69
(Giles Bravery) *chsd ldrs: rdn to ld and edgd rt over 1f out: hdd and unable qck ins fnl f* **5/2**[1]
5460 **4** *2* **Argentine (IRE)**[24] 6044 7-9-1 **54**......(b) TomEaves 10 53
(Ian Semple) *s.i.s: hld up: plld hrd: hdwy over 1f out: styd on u.p* **14/1**
0014 **5** *½* **Circuitous**[30] 5864 3-9-3 **57**......(b) JoeFanning 9 54
(Keith Dalgleish) *sn led: rdn and hdd over 1f out: styd on same pce* **6/1**[3]
4051 **6** *nk* **Pytheas (USA)**[9] 6488 4-9-1 **59**......(p) MarkCoumbe(5) 11 55
(Michael Attwater) *prom: rdn over 1f out: hung lft and no ex ins fnl f* **4/1**[2]
0563 **7** *2½* **Main Opinion (IRE)**[30] 5842 3-8-6 **46**...... CathyGannon 12 34
(Mick Channon) *chsd ldr: rdn and ev ch over 1f out: hung lft and wknd ins fnl f* **33/1**
0006 **8** *1* **Maharanee (USA)**[30] 5864 3-8-10 **50**......(p) LukeMorris 4 35
(Ann Duffield) *hld up: rdn over 2f out: n.d* **25/1**
-006 **9** *1¾* **Future Impact (IRE)**[28] 5941 3-9-2 **56**...... JamesDoyle 5 35
(Ed de Giles) *sn pushed along in rr: nvr on terms* **16/1**
4000 **10** *2¼* **Lily Wood**[21] 6176 5-8-7 **46**......(p) AndreaAtzeni 3 18
(James Unett) *mid-div: pushed along 1/2-way: wknd over 1f out* **16/1**
1060 **11** *2¾* **Gothic Chick**[98] 3630 3-8-12 **52**......(p) MartinHarley 1 15
(Alan McCabe) *chsd ldrs: rdn over 2f out: wknd over 1f out* **50/1**

1m 14.21s (-0.79) **Going Correction** -0.20s/f (Stan)
WFA 3 from 4yo+ 1lb **11** Ran SP% **112.5**
Speed ratings (Par 101): **97,96,94,92,91 91,87,86,84,81 77**
Tote Swingers: 1&2 £6.50, 1&3 £4.60, 2&3 £3.90 CSF £64.18 CT £203.26 TOTE £5.70: £1.50, £1.20, £2.10; EX 80.10.
Owner Not The Full Shilling Syndicate **Bred** Michael Dalton **Trained** Kinnersley, Worcs

FOCUS
They went a good gallop, which suited the winner. The runner-up has been rated to this year's best and the third a length off her Kempton effort.
Golden Compass Official explanation: vet said filly lost its off-hind shoe
Main Opinion(IRE) Official explanation: jockey said that the filly hung right-handed in the straight

6697 32RED CASINO MEDIAN AUCTION MAIDEN STKS — 1m 141y(P)
7:00 (7:00) (Class 6) 2-Y-O — **£2,070** (£616; £307; £153) **Stalls** Low

Form RPR
4 **1** **Coquet**[26] 6000 2-8-12 0...... RobertHavlin 11 78+
(Hughie Morrison) *a.p: chsd ldr over 2f out: shkn up to ld ins fnl f: r.o wl: readily* **6/4**[1]
00 **2** *2¼* **Captivity**[10] 6448 2-9-3 0...... JoeFanning 8 76
(Mahmood Al Zarooni) *led: shkn up over 1f out: hdd and unable qck ins fnl f* **15/2**[3]
3 *5* **Ehkam (USA)** 2-9-3 0...... TadhgO'Shea 2 66
(Saeed Bin Suroor) *chsd ldrs: rdn over 2f out: edgd rt over 1f out: wknd fnl f* **7/1**[2]
4 *2¼* **Mr Fong** 2-9-3 0...... MartinLane 7 61+
(David Simcock) *hld up: shkn up over 1f out: r.o ins fnl f: nvr nr to chal* **14/1**
5 *½* **Mutual Regard (IRE)** 2-9-3 0...... SebSanders 1 60
(Sir Mark Prescott Bt) *prom: sn pushed along: rdn and wknd over 1f out* **9/1**
00 **6** *½* **Tigertoo (IRE)**[16] 6267 2-9-3 0...... SaleemGolam 9 59+
(Stuart Williams) *prom: pushed along over 2f out: wkng whn hmpd over 1f out* **100/1**
7 *1½* **Knave Of Clubs (IRE)** 2-9-3 0...... SteveDrowne 4 56
(Peter Makin) *dwlt: hld up in rr: nvr on terms* **20/1**
8 *¾* **Flashman** 2-9-3 0...... DavidNolan 5 54
(Richard Fahey) *s.s: hdwy over 6f out: rdn and wknd 2f out* **22/1**
9 *nk* **Lithograph (USA)** 2-8-12 0...... AhmedAjtebi 6 49
(Mahmood Al Zarooni) *nvr on terms* **9/1**
10 *¾* **Rei D'Oro (USA)** 2-9-3 0...... AndreaAtzeni 10 52
(David Simcock) *s.s: hld up: a in rr* **10/1**
0 **11** *2¼* **Clapped**[15] 6300 2-9-3 0...... CathyGannon 3 47
(Edward Vaughan) *t.k.h: trckd ldr tl rdn and wknd over 1f out* **33/1**
0 **12** *4* **April Leyf (IRE)**[14] 6322 2-8-12 0...... LukeMorris 13 34
(Mark Brisbourne) *hld up: pushed along 6f out: lost tch over 2f out* **100/1**

1m 50.53s (0.03) **Going Correction** -0.20s/f (Stan) **12** Ran SP% **114.1**
Speed ratings (Par 93): **91,89,84,82,82 81,80,79,79,78 76,73**
Tote Swingers: 1&2 £2.50, 1&3 £2.70, 2&3 £4.80 CSF £11.36 TOTE £3.00: £1.50, £1.20, £2.50; EX 14.00.
Owner Hon Mary Morrison & Partners **Bred** Meon Valley Stud **Trained** East Ilsley, Berks

FOCUS
Many late-developing and unexposed juveniles contested this. They went a disappointing pace, but the first two finished clear. The level of the form is questionable.

NOTEBOOK
Coquet ◆ put up a taking performance in victory, quickening well to score with a bit in hand. Though not the most robust at present, this well-bred filly looks above average for the surface and should go on from here. (tchd 13-8)
Captivity had control of a modest gallop but still looked green in the home straight and was comfortably outpaced by the useful winner. With the third some way back, he is capable of winning an AW maiden but handicaps now look a viable alternative. (op 10-1)
Ehkam(USA), a Derby entry out of a well-related 1m4f winner, made a satisfactory debut. Though no danger to the first two, he should come on for the run and a maiden is within reach, with longer trips likely to suit as he matures. (op 13-2 tchd 6-1)
Mr Fong ◆, a 23,000gns Dr Fong colt out of a 7f winner, arrived late in mid-track from a long way back despite running green. A good-looker, he looks certain to improve and is one to note next time. (op 12-1)
Mutual Regard(IRE), whose dam was a winning juvenile sprinter, is not as precocious but showed enough to be worth monitoring. (tchd 17-2)
Tigertoo(IRE), though beaten some way in the end, ran his best race yet and will be interesting if switched to handicaps next time.
Flashman, a well grown Doyen colt, should improve for this debut and is one to monitor. (op 16-1)

6698 32REDBET.COM H'CAP — 1m 1f 103y(P)
7:30 (7:31) (Class 6) (0-55,57) 3-Y-O+ — **£1,704** (£503; £251) **Stalls** Low

Form RPR
6062 **1** **Arkaim**[9] 6494 3-9-3 **57**......(v) KierenFallon 9 67
(Ed Walker) *mde all: rdn over 1f out: styd on gamely* **10/3**[1]
0060 **2** *1¼* **Vanilla Rum**[9] 6493 4-9-0 **50**......(b[1]) JamesDoyle 11 57
(John Mackie) *hld up in tch: rdn over 1f out: r.o to go 2nd nr fin* **10/1**
0504 **3** *¾* **Tigerbill**[15] 6309 3-9-0 **54**......(t) LukeMorris 3 60
(Nicky Vaughan) *chsd ldrs: rdn over 1f out: styd on same pce ins fnl f* **10/1**
33 **4** *hd* **Yellow Printer**[23] 6083 5-9-5 **55**......(b) AdamKirby 13 60
(Mark Gillard) *chsd wnr: rdn over 1f out: styd on same pce ins fnl f* **14/1**

4513 **5** *1 1/4* **Cathcart Castle**[2] 6657 3-9-3 **57**.................................... TonyCulhane 12 60+
(Mick Channon) *hld up and bhd: rdn over 2f out: hdwy over 1f out: swtchd rt ins fnl f: nt rch ldrs* **7/2**[2]

00-2 **6** *7* **Daniel Thomas (IRE)**[15] 6309 9-9-2 **55**................(tp) RobertLButler(3) 10 43
(Richard Guest) *s.s: bhd: hdwy over 3f out: hung rt and wknd over 1f out* **10/1**

4603 **7** *1 1/4* **Dandarrell**[22] 6134 4-9-3 **53**..(p) PaulHanagan 8 38
(Julie Camacho) *prom: rdn over 3f out: wknd over 1f out* **8/1**[3]

0050 **8** *2 1/2* **Shunkawakhan (IRE)**[11] 6428 8-9-0 **50**.........................(tp) JoeFanning 2 30
(Linda Perratt) *hld up: rdn over 2f out: n.d* **33/1**

0063 **9** *2 1/2* **So Is She (IRE)**[6] 6358 3-8-12 **55**...............................(b) DominicFox(3) 4 30
(Alan Bailey) *s.s: outpcd* **12/1**

6040 **10** *2 3/4* **Highland Love**[14] 4902 6-9-5 **55**.. TomEaves 7 24
(Jedd O'Keeffe) *hld up: rdn over 5f out: wknd over 2f out* **20/1**

0-04 **11** *1/2* **Lunar Limelight**[70] 4549 6-9-1 **51**.................................... SteveDrowne 6 19
(Peter Makin) *prom: lost pl 4f out: rdn and wknd over 1f out* **14/1**

060- **12** *11* **Sunshine Buddy**[466] 2619 4-9-0 **50**.................................. JamesMillman 1 —
(Rod Millman) *prom: rdn over 5f out: wknd over 3f out* **50/1**

1m 59.48s (-2.22) **Going Correction** -0.20s/f (Stan)
WFA 3 from 4yo+ 4lb **12** Ran SP% **114.4**
Speed ratings (Par 101): **101,99,99,99,97 91,90,88,86,83 83,73**
Tote Swingers: 1&2 £20.70, 1&3 £6.00, 2&3 £25.50 CSF £34.77 CT £300.49 TOTE £5.00: £2.10, £4.50, £3.80; EX 84.40.
Owner Alpine Racing **Bred** Harton Limited **Trained** Newmarket, Suffolk
■ Stewards' Enquiry : James Doyle two-day ban: careless riding (24-25 Oct)

FOCUS
The winner dictated it at a routine tempo which began to wind up 4f out. It's hard to be positive about the form given the overall records of these.

6699 ALISON & TONY JOHNSON WEDDING ANNIVERSARY NURSERY 7f 32y(P)
8:00 (8:01) (Class 5) (0-75,75) 2-Y-O **£2,911** (£866; £432; £216) **Stalls** High

Form RPR
004 **1** **Chalk And Cheese (USA)**[23] 6099 2-9-1 **69**...............(p) RobertHavlin 2 74
(John Gosden) *prom: chsd ldr 5f out: led over 1f out: rdn and hung rt ins fnl f: styd on* **13/2**[3]

0561 **2** *3/4* **Amoure Medici**[9] 6487 2-9-4 **72**.. MartinLane 12 75
(Noel Quinlan) *s.s: hld up: hdwy over 1f out: rdn and r.o: wnt 2nd towards fin: nt rch wnr* **5/1**[2]

331 **3** *1/2* **Red Alpha (IRE)**[93] 3779 2-9-7 **75**.................................. PaulHanagan 9 77
(Jeremy Noseda) *hld up in tch: rdn to chse wnr fnl f: styd on: lost 2nd towards fin* **7/1**

10 **4** *1 3/4* **Oscan (USA)**[22] 6126 2-9-7 **75**.. AhmedAjtebi 11 74+
(Mahmood Al Zarooni) *hld up: r.o ins fnl f: nrst fin* **8/1**

001 **5** *1/2* **Holiday Reading (USA)**[25] 6018 2-9-7 **75**.................... MartinDwyer 6 71
(Brian Meehan) *mid-div: rdn over 2f out: hdwy over 1f out: nt rch ldrs* **7/2**[1]

2223 **6** *nse* **Fayr Fall (IRE)**[21] 6154 2-9-6 **74**.................................... DuranFentiman 4 70
(Tim Easterby) *prom: rdn and hung lft over 1f out: styd on same pce* **10/1**

5143 **7** *3/4* **Faraway**[9] 6471 2-9-3 **71**..(v) KierenFallon 3 65
(David Evans) *prom: rdn over 2f out: styd on same pce fnl f* **20/1**

0014 **8** *1* **Adranian (IRE)**[9] 6487 2-8-9 **68**...........................(v) MatthewCosham(5) 8 60
(David Evans) *hld up: rdn over 2f out: nvr on terms* **40/1**

4012 **9** *2* **Crowning Star (IRE)**[79] 4226 2-9-6 **74**.......................... JamesDoyle 5 61
(J S Moore) *mid-div: rdn over 2f out: wknd over 1f out* **10/1**

006 **10** *hd* **Calculated Risk**[15] 6308 2-8-12 **66**............................ StevieDonohoe 7 52
(Willie Musson) *hld up: bhd and rdn 1/2-way: nvr nrr* **28/1**

120 **11** *1 1/4* **Baltic Fizz (IRE)**[19] 6222 2-9-3 **71**................................ MartinHarley 1 54
(Mrs K Burke) *chsd ldr 2f: remained handy: rdn over 2f out: wknd fnl f* **18/1**

0331 **12** *nse* **Rusty Rocket (IRE)**[21] 6154 2-9-5 **73**........................ JamesSullivan 10 56
(Paul Green) *led: rdn and hdd over 1f out: wknd fnl f* **14/1**

1m 28.47s (-1.13) **Going Correction** -0.20s/f (Stan) **12** Ran SP% **116.6**
Speed ratings (Par 95): **98,97,96,94,94 93,93,91,89,89 88,87**
Tote Swingers: 1&2 £10.60, 1&3 £9.00, 2&3 £9.40 CSF £37.44 CT £239.79 TOTE £5.20: £1.70, £3.10, £1.20; EX 45.20.
Owner H R H Princess Haya Of Jordan **Bred** Darley **Trained** Newmarket, Suffolk

FOCUS
A competitive nursery run at a good gallop which should produce several future winners. The third and sixth suggest this opening level is sensible.

NOTEBOOK
Chalk And Cheese(USA), making a winning handicap debut, had a few pounds in hand. The handicapper is likely to correct that, but this lightly-raced gelding for whom the cheekpieces are a help, can do even better if his concentration improves further. (tchd 8-1)
Amoure Medici dropped in behind and travelled well from the widest stall, eventually finishing nicely on the inside rail. Given a better draw, he looks capable of following up his recent win even from this much higher mark. (op 6-1 tchd 13-2 and 9-2)
Red Alpha(IRE)'s only win was on turf when last seen three months earlier. Though not quite reaching that level on Polytrack to date, he acts well on it and should find a suitable race. (op 13-2)
Oscan(USA) ◆ made a creditable AW debut over a trip that looked likely to suit better than the 1m in his previous race. In the event he ran as if an extra 1f would be appreciated after all, and he did well enough to keep an eye on. (op 11-1)
Holiday Reading(USA) did not match his turf form on this AW debut, but he was going on at the finish and deserves another chance. (op 3-1 tchd 11-4 and 4-1)
Fayr Fall(IRE) ran his race as usual, but was forced out of the places by some less-exposed types. (op 9-1)
Faraway, yet to win outside selling grade, ran with credit in this decent nursery. Official explanation: vet said colt moved poorly immediately following the race but was subsequently sound

6700 £32 FREE AT 32RED.COM MAIDEN STKS 5f 20y(P)
8:30 (8:31) (Class 5) 3-Y-O+ **£2,264** (£673; £336; £168) **Stalls** Low

Form RPR
33 **1** **Queen Grace (IRE)**[27] 5965 4-8-12 63............................ PaulHanagan 6 73
(Michael J Browne, Ire) *mde all: rdn clr fnl f* **3/1**[2]

-253 **2** *4* **Poppy**[10] 6456 3-8-9 61.. KieranO'Neill(3) 2 59
(Richard Hannon) *prom: chsd wnr over 3f out: rdn over 1f out: no ex fnl f* **3/1**[2]

-234 **3** *3 3/4* **Shadow Of The Sun**[5] 6580 3-8-12 61............................ SteveDrowne 7 46
(Joseph Tuite) *hld up in tch: wnt 3rd wl over 1f out: sn rdn and outpcd* **9/4**[1]

044 **4** *5* **Galloping Minister (IRE)**[51] 5206 3-9-3 63........... RichardKingscote 10 33
(Tom Dascombe) *prom: rdn 1/2-way: wknd wl over 1f out* **8/1**

5023 **5** *1 3/4* **Missile Attack (IRE)**[13] 6386 3-9-3 56............................ TomEaves 9 26
(Ian Semple) *chsd ldrs tl rdn and wknd over 1f out* **6/1**[3]

6 *1* **Career Quest** 3-8-5 0.. MatthewMcGhee(7) 5 18
(Bill Moore) *s.i.s: outpcd* **100/1**

00 **7** *2 1/4* **Peace Seeker**[40] 5567 3-9-3 0.. WilliamCarson 8 15
(Giles Bravery) *s.i.s: sn in tch: rdn 1/2-way: sn hung rt and wknd* **28/1**

0006 **8** *1 1/4* **Lovely Lynn (IRE)**[21] 6176 3-8-7 39.............................. NeilFarley(5) 4 —
(Declan Carroll) *chsd wnr tl pushed along over 3f out: rdn 1/2-way: wknd wl over 1f out* **50/1**

000- **9** *4* **Primo Muscovado**[358] 6894 3-8-10 35............................ JackDuern(7) 1 —
(Michael Mullineaux) *sn outpcd* **80/1**

60.46 secs (-1.84) **Going Correction** -0.20s/f (Stan) **9** Ran SP% **113.8**
Speed ratings (Par 103): **106,99,93,85,82 81,77,75,69**
Tote Swingers: 1&2 £2.00, 1&3 £1.90, 2&3 £2.60 CSF £12.08 TOTE £7.20: £2.30, £2.10, £1.02; EX 11.80.
Owner Michael J Browne **Bred** Michael J Woodlock **Trained** Cashel, Co. Tipperary

FOCUS
A fair maiden featuring several runners with placed form on turf. The winner has been rated as running a personal best, although the runner-up and third are hardly bombproof.
Peace Seeker Official explanation: vet said gelding lost a front shoe
Primo Muscovado Official explanation: jockey said that the colt hung left-handed

6701 32RED.COM H'CAP 1m 4f 50y(P)
9:00 (9:00) (Class 6) (0-60,60) 3-Y-O **£1,704** (£503; £251) **Stalls** Low

Form RPR
-501 **1** **Castlemorris King**[29] 5898 3-9-2 **60**............................ MarkCoumbe(5) 5 75+
(Michael Attwater) *prom: chsd ldr over 6f out: led 3f out: rdn out* **9/4**[1]

2200 **2** *4* **Golestan Palace (IRE)**[37] 5651 3-9-3 **56**...............(v[1]) J-PGuillambert 11 62
(Ed Walker) *hld up: hdwy over 1f out: r.o to go 2nd post: no ch w wnr* **13/2**[3]

5330 **3** *nk* **Cadgers Brig**[33] 5790 3-9-3 **56**......................................(v[1]) JoeFanning 12 62
(Keith Dalgleish) *chsd ldr: led over 11f out: hdd 3f out: no ex fnl f* **9/1**

3444 **4** *1 1/2* **Miracle Play (IRE)**[4] 6601 3-9-7 **60**...............................(p) KierenFallon 10 63
(David Evans) *hld up in tch: rdn over 2f out: styd on same pce fnl f* **4/1**[2]

5535 **5** *3 1/2* **Disturbia (IRE)**[36] 5665 3-8-7 **46**.. MartinDwyer 2 44
(J W Hills) *hld up: hung lft and styd on ins fnl f: nvr nrr* **16/1**

634 **6** *5* **Mayan Flight (IRE)**[29] 5898 3-8-9 **48**........................(b) MichaelStainton 6 38
(Richard Whitaker) *hld up: hdwy over 2f out: rdn and wknd over 1f out* **14/1**

0405 **7** *2 1/2* **Valley Tiger**[14] 6357 3-8-11 **55**.. JamesRogers(5) 1 41
(William Muir) *s.i.s: hdwy over 6f out: rdn and wknd over 1f out* **12/1**

0005 **8** *1 3/4* **Hertford Street**[23] 6084 3-8-4 **46** oh1.........................(p) KieranO'Neill(3) 8 29
(Peter Makin) *led: hdd over 11f out: chsd ldrs: rdn over 5f out: wknd over 2f out* **33/1**

000 **9** *36* **Money Note**[14] 6358 3-8-13 **52**......................................(bt) StevieDonohoe 9 —
(Tobias B P Coles) *chsd ldrs tl rdn and wknd over 3f out* **40/1**

000- **10** *6* **Old Boy Ted**[344] 7202 3-9-2 **55**.. PaulHanagan 4 —
(Mark H Tompkins) *hld up: rdn over 4f out: sn wknd* **7/1**

2m 38.2s (-2.90) **Going Correction** -0.20s/f (Stan) **10** Ran SP% **112.2**
Speed ratings (Par 99): **101,98,98,97,94 91,89,88,64,60**
CSF £16.23 CT £107.36 TOTE £2.50: £1.10, £3.30, £1.50; EX 19.00.
Owner C O'Connell **Bred** Peter Storey **Trained** Epsom, Surrey
■ Stewards' Enquiry : Michael Stainton two-day ban: careless riding (24-25 Oct)

FOCUS
A race containing a number of runners short on pace, with the exception of the progressive winner. The runner-up has been rated back to his best, along with the third.
Cadgers Brig Official explanation: jockeu said that his saddle slipped
Valley Tiger Official explanation: jockey said that the colt ran too freely
T/Plt: £116.40 to a £1 stake. Pool of £82,695.00 - 518.56 winning tickets. T/Qpdt: £8.60 to a £1 stake. Pool of £10,424.00 - 896.60 winning tickets.

6670 YORK (L-H)
Saturday, October 8

OFFICIAL GOING: Good (7.4)
Wind: almost nil Weather: overcast, persistent light rain

6702 BET ON YOUR MOBILE WITH CORAL E B F "SAKHEE" MAIDEN STKS 7f
1:50 (1:51) (Class 3) 2-Y-O **£7,439** (£2,213; £1,106; £553) **Stalls** Low

Form RPR
30 **1** **Mickdaam (IRE)**[70] 4535 2-9-3 0.................................... PaulHanagan 10 85
(Richard Fahey) *chsd ldrs: drvn and outpcd over 3f out: hdwy and hung lft 2f out: styd on to ld nr fin* **9/4**[1]

0222 **2** *1 1/2* **Choisan (IRE)**[10] 6447 2-9-3 77.. DavidAllan 7 81
(Tim Easterby) *w ldr: led over 1f out: hdd and no ex in clsng stages* **5/2**[2]

3 *3 1/4* **Three Darlings (IRE)** 2-8-12 0.................................... AdrianNicholls 6 68
(David Nicholls) *dwlt: in rr: hdwy on ins over 4f out: sn chsng ldrs: led 2f out: sn hdd: kpt on same pce* **20/1**

4 *nk* **Brockwell** 2-9-3 0.. RichardKingscote 3 72+
(Tom Dascombe) *s.i.s: in rr: hdwy 2f out: fin wl* **15/2**

06 **5** *4* **Happy Sun Percy**[9] 6481 2-9-3 0.............................. SilvestreDeSousa 8 61
(Jo Hughes) *t.k.h: trckd ldrs: wknd fnl f* **11/1**

4453 **6** *3/4* **Marching On (IRE)**[16] 6274 2-9-3 72............................ StephenCraine 4 59
(Kevin Ryan) *chsd ldrs: edgd lft over 1f out: sn wknd* **13/2**[3]

05 **7** *4 1/2* **Lord Franklin**[25] 6025 2-9-3 0.. WJSupple 1 48
(Eric Alston) *led tl 2f out: sn wknd* **50/1**

04 **8** *3 1/2* **Northern Jewel (IRE)**[24] 6047 2-8-12 0............................ TonyHamilton 11 34
(Richard Fahey) *wnt rt s: chsd ldrs: rn wd bnd over 4f out: lost pl over 2f out* **16/1**

9 *9* **Maybeagrey** 2-8-12 0.. DuranFentiman 2 10
(Tim Easterby) *in rr: sn drvn along: bhd fnl 2f* **25/1**

0 **10** *8* **Confused Sphere (IRE)**[25] 6025 2-9-3 0.......................... BarryMcHugh 9 —
(Noel Wilson) *t.k.h: trckd ldrs: lost pl 3f out* **100/1**

60 **11** *17* **Pavers Star**[16] 6274 2-9-3 0.. DanielTudhope 5 —
(Noel Wilson) *w ldrs: lost pl 3f out: sn bhd* **100/1**

1m 26.12s (0.82) **Going Correction** -0.05s/f (Good) **11** Ran SP% **111.2**
Speed ratings (Par 99): **93,91,87,87,82 81,76,72,62,53 33**
toteswingers:1&2:£1.90, 2&3:£8.90, 1&3:£7.20 CSF £7.04 TOTE £2.90: £1.20, £1.60, £3.20; EX 7.40.
Owner Sheikh Mohammed Bin Khalifa Al Maktoum **Bred** Victor Stud Bloodstock Ltd **Trained** Musley Bank, N Yorks

FOCUS
Rail moved from 9f to entrance to home straight reducing race distances of one mile and beyond by 27yds. A fair maiden, won by the subsequent dual Group 3 winner Namibian last year, but it's debatable whether any of these will match his exploits. Quite straightforward form to rate.

NOTEBOOK

Mickdaam(IRE) had been bitterly disappointing at Goodwood last time following his promising debut effort at Newmarket, but this was more like it. He made hard work of it, hanging when brought to challenge over a furlong out and looking as though he might not go through with it, but was persuaded by his rider to do so. He is bred to get further and, while a Derby entry looks fanciful, he should be able to add to this success. (op 5-2 tchd 11-4 in a place)

Choisan(IRE), rated 77 and runner-up in four of his seven previous starts, stays further than this and was ridden positively. Again he had every chance until a less exposed rival cut him down. He deserves to win a race but will remain vulnerable to an improver in contests like this. (tchd 11-4 in places)

Three Darlings(IRE), an 8,500euros filly out of a dual 1m4f winner, made a promising debut, coming through to hold every chance over 2f from home until fading inside the last furlong. She should find a race. (op 16-1)

Brockwell ◆, 70,000gns colt out of a 1m4f winner, was green early, starting slowly and racing in last place, but ran on strongly from over a furlong out and only just failed to get up for third. He was expected to need the experience and should go on from here. (op 8-1 tchd 7-1)

Happy Sun Percy attracted market support despite having been unplaced in his first two starts. He did himself no favours by racing keenly early and that eventually told. He seems to have some ability if he settles better, and he now gets a mark. (op 12-1 tchd 17-2)

Marching On(IRE), rated 72, has shown some ability but faded after showing up early and isn't progressing. (op 6-1 tchd 7-1)

6703 CORAL.CO.UK STKS (H'CAP) 5f

2:20 (2:21) (Class 4) (0-85,85) 3-Y-0+ **£6,469** (£1,925; £962; £481) **Stalls** Centre

Form RPR

1400 **1** **Living It Large (FR)**[19] 6224 4-9-0 **85**........ JohnFahy(3) 10 95
(Ed de Giles) *w ldr: rdn over 2f out: led wl ins fnl f: kpt on* **20/1**

0100 **2** *nk* **Le Toreador**[14] 6351 6-9-3 **85**........(tp) DPMcDonogh 6 94
(Kevin Ryan) *led narrowly: rdn over 2f out: hdd wl ins fnl f: kpt on* **33/1**

0000 **3** *½* **Barney McGrew (IRE)**[30] 5852 8-9-2 **84**........ DanielTudhope 3 91+
(Michael Dods) *hld up: rdn and hdwy over 1f out: r.o strly ins fnl f: wnt 3rd cl home* **16/1**

-240 **4** *½* **Flash City (ITY)**[28] 5918 3-8-8 **83**........(v) JustinNewman(7) 9 88
(Bryan Smart) *chsd ldrs: rdn over 2f out: ev ch ins fnl f: no ex cl home* **14/1**

2000 **5** *¾* **Whozthecat (IRE)**[14] 6331 4-8-10 **83**........(v) NeilFarley(5) 12 86
(Declan Carroll) *in tch: pushed along 3f out: kpt on ins fnl f* **9/1**

3040 **6** *2¾* **Rasaman (IRE)**[22] 6113 7-8-12 **83** ow1........ GaryBartley(3) 17 76+
(Jim Goldie) *midfield: rdn over 2f out: kpt on ins fnl f* **20/1**

0400 **7** *1* **Indian Trail**[14] 6348 11-9-0 **82**........(v) PaulQuinn 5 71
(David Nicholls) *hld up: rdn 2f out: kpt on wl ins fnl f: nrst fin* **25/1**

0050 **8** *nk* **Solemn**[19] 6224 6-9-2 **84**........(b) RichardKingscote 11 72
(Milton Bradley) *in tch: rdn over 2f out: one pce* **20/1**

3635 **9** *nse* **Lujeanie**[25] 6036 5-9-1 **83**........(p) AdamKirby 4 71
(Dean Ivory) *sn pushed along towards rr: kpt on fnl f: nvr trbld ldrs* **14/1**

1106 **10** *shd* **Lady Royale**[14] 6350 3-8-12 **83**........(b) DaleSwift(3) 7 71
(Geoffrey Oldroyd) *dwlt: hld up: kpt on fnl f: n.d* **20/1**

0023 **11** *1* **Taurus Twins**[14] 6350 5-9-2 **84**........(b) SilvestreDeSousa 18 68
(Richard Price) *w ldrs: wknd over 1f out* **8/1**[3]

3200 **12** *¾* **Noodles Blue Boy**[56] 5033 5-9-1 **83**........ TonyHamilton 13 64
(Ollie Pears) *chsd ldrs: rdn over 2f out: wknd ins fnl f* **16/1**

0000 **13** *hd* **Cadeaux Pearl**[14] 6350 3-8-7 **82**........(b) LeonnaMayor(7) 2 62
(David Nicholls) *isolated towards far side: in tch: rdn over 2f out: wknd ins fnl f* **33/1**

1000 **14** *¾* **Strike Up The Band**[14] 6332 8-9-3 **85**........ AdrianNicholls 15 63
(David Nicholls) *chsd ldrs: rdn over 2f out: wknd over 1f out* **16/1**

2262 **15** *¾* **Eland Ally**[31] 5831 3-9-0 **82**........ SteveDrowne 14 57
(Tom Tate) *dwlt: sn midfield: rdn over 2f out: sn no imp* **15/2**[2]

2156 **16** *½* **Haajes**[14] 6348 7-9-0 **82**........ FrederikTylicki 19 55
(Paul Midgley) *sn pushed towards rr: nvr threatened* **7/1**[1]

0502 **17** *¾* **Dorback**[46] 5339 4-9-1 **83**........ PaulHanagan 16 54
(Noel Wilson) *midfield towards stands' side: rdn 2f out: sn btn* **14/1**

0100 **18** *2¾* **Baldemar**[14] 6331 6-8-13 **84**........ LeeTopliss(3) 8 45
(Richard Fahey) *midfield: rdn over 2f out: wknd over 1f out* **20/1**

0000 **19** *8* **Gallagher**[14] 6341 5-9-1 **83**........(bt[1]) PJMcDonald 1 15
(Ruth Carr) *slowly away: a in rr* **12/1**

6243 **20** *1* **Bronze Beau**[25] 6036 4-9-2 **84**........(t) JamesSullivan 20 12
(Linda Stubbs) *prom towards stands' side: wknd over 2f out* **25/1**

58.40 secs (-0.90) **Going Correction** -0.05s/f (Good) **20** Ran SP% **128.1**

Speed ratings (Par 105): **105,104,103,102,101 97,95,95,95,95 93,92,91,90,89 88,87,83,70,68**

CSF £546.65 CT £10525.11 TOTE £28.70: £6.00, £12.40, £4.40, £3.70; EX 1376.70 Trifecta £971.60 Pool: £1312.98 - 0.50 winning units..

Owner T Gould **Bred** Sunny Days Limited **Trained** Ledbury, Herefordshire

■ Stewards' Enquiry : D P McDonogh caution: used whip down the shoulder in the forehand position

FOCUS

A hot sprint handicap with only 3lb covering the 20 runners, but it proved almost impossible to make up ground from off the pace and the front pair dominated throughout. All bar Cadeaux Pearl (who raced alone towards the far rail) raced centre-to-stands-side. The runner-up has been rated close to the best of last winter's AW form.

6704 GREEN TICK FOR BETTER ODDS AT CORAL.CO.UK STKS (H'CAP) 1m 208y

2:50 (2:52) (Class 2) (0-100,96) 3-Y-0 **£12,938** (£3,850; £1,924; £962) **Stalls** Low

Form RPR

0046 **1** **Oceanway (USA)**[21] 6163 3-9-4 **93**........ SilvestreDeSousa 4 101
(Mark Johnston) *chsd ldrs: rdn and sltly outpcd over 2f out: kpt on wl ins fnl f: led nr fin* **7/2**[2]

0133 **2** *¾* **Weapon Of Choice (IRE)**[14] 6325 3-8-12 **87**........ SteveDrowne 5 93
(David Simcock) *trckd ldrs: led over 1f out: hdd and no ex towards fin* **5/1**[3]

01 **3** *hd* **Sadeek's Song (USA)**[10] 6459 3-9-1 **90**........ AhmedAjtebi 9 96+
(Mahmood Al Zarooni) *hld up in rr: hdwy on outside 4f out: edgd rt over 1f out: styd on fnl 100yds* **7/1**

0340 **4** *¾* **Sergeant Ablett (IRE)**[29] 5880 3-8-12 **87**........ FrederikTylicki 1 91
(James Given) *led: qckn over 3f out: hdd over 1f out: one pce* **10/1**

1216 **5** *½* **Electra Star**[15] 6297 3-9-1 **93**........ AdamBeschizza(3) 6 96+
(William Haggas) *s.s: hdwy over 3f out: styd on to chal last 150yds: no ex* **10/3**[1]

4506 **6** *1* **Janood (IRE)**[30] 5853 3-9-7 **96**........(p) RichardMullen 2 97
(Saeed Bin Suroor) *trckd ldrs: stdy hdwy on inner over 2f out: fdd ins fnl f* **14/1**

40 **7** *1* **Roayh (USA)**[14] 6339 3-9-6 **95**........ TedDurcan 8 94
(Saeed Bin Suroor) *mid-div: effrt over 2f out: sn chsng ldrs: wknd fnl f* **17/2**

6204 **8** *3½* **Robert The Painter (IRE)**[23] 6093 3-8-7 **82** oh2........ PaulHanagan 7 73
(Richard Fahey) *hld up in midfield: effrt over 2f out: wknd over 1f out* **10/1**

1m 51.8s (-0.20) **Going Correction** -0.05s/f (Good) **8** Ran SP% **109.8**

Speed ratings (Par 107): **98,97,97,96,96 95,94,91**

toteswingers:1&2:£4.40, 2&3:£4.10, 1&3:£4.40 CSF £19.56 CT £106.08 TOTE £4.40: £1.40, £1.70, £2.00; EX 22.70 Trifecta £160.80 Pool: £1263.18 - 5.81 winning units..

Owner Sheikh Hamdan Bin Mohammed Al Maktoum **Bred** Darley **Trained** Middleham Moor, N Yorks

FOCUS

A decent handicap, but the early pace was modest. The runners made for the centre of the track on reaching the straight. The form is a bit muddling, with the winner rated back to her best and the runner-up to form. The third has been rated as improving, with the fourth possibly flattered.

NOTEBOOK

Oceanway(USA) was still 8lb above her last winning mark, but ran very well to finish sixth of 19 against older horses in a red-hot handicap at Newbury last month despite meeting interference. Never far away here, she came off the bridle a fair way out but she kept on digging deep and forged her way to the front in the last few strides. She looks a tough sort who may do even better as a 4yo. (op 9-2)

Weapon Of Choice(IRE) came into this in good form and, with the ground coming in his favour, recorded another fine effort. He was in front passing the 2f pole and was only just run out of it. He should continue to do his best with conditions likely to stay in his favour. (op 9-2)

Sadeek's Song(USA) didn't look obviously well handicapped off 90, having beaten three rivals rated in the low 70s in a Nottingham maiden last time, but he won that race easily and this was only his third start. He was given more to do than the pair that beat him and was finishing best of all. The Godolphin colt has more scope for improvement than his rivals. (op 13-2)

Sergeant Ablett(IRE) enjoyed the run of the race out in front and plugged on after being headed, but has now been beaten 11 times since a successful racecourse debut. (op 11-1 tchd 9-1)

Electra Star, a consistent and progressive filly this season, didn't find the race panning out her way when stepped up to Listed class last time and gave her rivals a start here with a slow break. The modest pace enabled her to catch up quickly and she had a chance a furlong out, but the start still wasn't ideal and she can be given some extra credit. (op 7-2)

Roayh(USA) has become disappointing. Official explanation: trainer's representative said that the filly was unsuited by the good going (op 15-2 tchd 9-1)

6705 CORAL.CO.UK ROCKINGHAM STKS (LISTED RACE) 6f

3:25 (3:26) (Class 1) 2-Y-0

£22,684 (£8,600; £4,304; £2,144; £1,076; £540) **Stalls** Centre

Form RPR

6320 **1** **Bannock (IRE)**[7] 6535 2-9-0 **108**........ SilvestreDeSousa 2 108
(Mark Johnston) *w ldr: drvn over 2f out: led over 1f out: styd on strly* **5/2**[1]

4052 **2** *2* **Miss Lahar**[7] 6518 2-8-9 **102**........ MartinHarley 6 96
(Mick Channon) *hld up: eased outside over 1f out: chsd wnr fnl f: edgd lft: no real imp* **11/2**[3]

216 **3** *3* **Swiss Spirit**[21] 6162 2-9-0 **91**........ PaulHanagan 4 92
(David Elsworth) *hld up: t.k.h: effrt 2f out: kpt on to take 3rd in clsng stages* **7/2**[2]

2440 **4** *½* **Luv U Forever**[21] 6146 2-8-9 **96**........ CathyGannon 3 86
(Jo Hughes) *led: hdd over 1f out: kpt on same pce* **16/1**

0441 **5** *5* **Roger Sez (IRE)**[21] 6146 2-9-0 **104**........(b) DavidAllan 1 76
(Tim Easterby) *chsd ldrs: drvn over 2f out: wknd over 1f out* **7/2**[2]

0150 **6** *3* **Semayyel (IRE)**[15] 6299 2-8-9 **90**........ TomMcLaughlin 7 62
(Clive Brittain) *trckd ldrs: effrt over 2f out: wknd over 1f out* **16/1**

145 **7** *10* **Desert Gazelle (USA)**[15] 6296 2-8-9 **94**........ TedDurcan 5 32
(Saeed Bin Suroor) *trckd ldrs: effrt over 2f out: lost pl over 1f out: heavily eased towards fin* **13/2**

1m 11.57s (-0.33) **Going Correction** -0.05s/f (Good) **7** Ran SP% **113.5**

Speed ratings (Par 103): **100,97,93,92,86 82,68**

CSF £16.42 TOTE £3.60: £1.80, £3.40; EX 18.00.

Owner Sheikh Hamdan Bin Mohammed Al Maktoum **Bred** Darley **Trained** Middleham Moor, N Yorks

FOCUS

This race has been won by some decent types in the past ten years, with both Avonbridge and Balthazaar's Gift going on to become high-class sprinters. The third helps pin down the form, while the fifth never looked likely to replicate her Ayr form that came in a bog.

NOTEBOOK

Bannock(IRE) should have done much better in the previous weekend's Redcar Two-Year-Old Trophy following his placed efforts in the July Stakes and Richmond, but he may have had excuses as he had suffered a setback since his previous start and was drawn on the wrong side. By contrast, everything went right for him here and, having raced prominently throughout, he was never going to be caught after leading a furlong out. He is fairly exposed, but horses from this yard are always liable to find a bit more improvement. (op 11-4 tchd 3-1 and 10-3 in a place)

Miss Lahar, nearly 8l behind Roger Sez in the Firth Of Clyde, had since run much better to finish runner-up in the Cornwallis. Not best away, she looked a real danger when produced with her effort towards the nearside over a furlong from home, but she hung away to her left in behind the winner and was never doing enough. For a filly of her ability, a record of 1-10 is modest. (op 6-1)

Swiss Spirit proved a disappointing second favourite in the Mill Reef when returning from three months off and was allowed to take his chance here only after enough rain fell. Another to miss the break, he took a grip at the back of the field early and when asked for his effort he didn't find as much as had seemed likely. He is such a big colt that it may be he hasn't grown into his frame yet and may make a better 3yo. (op 9-2)

Luv U Forever finished more than 17l behind Roger Sez in the Firth Of Clyde and, having made much of the running, turned that form around on this less testing ground, but with this being her tenth start she has little in the way of scope. (op 12-1)

Roger Sez(IRE) proved a revelation in the Firth Of Clyde when bolting up in first-time blinkers, but they didn't work a second time and she was struggling just after halfway.

Semayyel(IRE), well beaten in the May Hill and Fillies' Mile since winning her maiden over 7f, didn't improve for the return to this trip. (op 14-1)

Desert Gazelle(USA) didn't look as effective over 7f in the Sweet Solera and Oh So Sharp after a successful debut over this trip. She dropped out so tamely that something must have been amiss. Official explanation: trainer's representative said that the filly was unsuited by the good going (op 6-1 tchd 7-1)

6706 CORAL SPRINT TROPHY (H'CAP) 6f

4:05 (4:07) (Class 2) (0-105,105) 3-Y-0+

£46,687 (£13,980; £6,990; £3,495; £1,312; £1,312) **Stalls** Centre

Form RPR

1011 **1** **Sirius Prospect (USA)**[8] 6500 3-9-5 **101**........ ShaneKelly 19 115+
(Dean Ivory) *hld up in rr stands' side: effrt and n.m.r over 1f out: str run to ld last 50yds: won gng rt away* **13/2**[1]

0303 **2** *2¼* **Kaldoun Kingdom (IRE)**[19] 6209 6-9-0 **95**........ PaulHanagan 6 101
(Richard Fahey) *trckd ldrs: styd on to ld last 50yds: sn hdd and no ex* **14/1**

0623 **3** *1* **Racy**[14] 6332 4-8-9 **95**........................ JulieBurke(5) 10 98
(Kevin Ryan) *gave problems in stalls: trckd ldrs: led and hung lft over 1f out: hdd last 50yds* **10/1**

6620 **4** *nse* **Sioux Rising (IRE)**[21] 6145 5-8-12 **96**........................ LeeTopliss(3) 18 99
(Richard Fahey) *in rr: gd hdwy over 1f out: chsng ldrs jst ins fnl f: edgd lft and styng on at fin* **33/1**

4200 **5** *½* **Parisian Pyramid (IRE)**[7] 6521 5-9-0 **95**..................(p) StephenCraine 11 96
(Kevin Ryan) *chsd ldrs: kpt on same pce last 100yds* **16/1**

001 **5** *dht* **Nocturnal Affair (SAF)**[28] 5927 5-9-10 **105**........................ ShaneFoley 7 106
(David Marnane, Ire) *mid-div: hdwy 2f out: kpt on same pce ins fnl f* **8/1**[2]

0111 **7** *½* **Internationaldebut (IRE)**[18] 6233 6-9-8 **103**................ FrederikTylicki 3 104+
(Paul Midgley) *mid-div: hdwy over 1f out: styng on whn nt clr run towards fin* **9/1**[3]

2020 **8** *1 ¼* **Lutine Bell**[14] 6341 4-8-13 **94**........................ StevieDonohoe 16 90
(Mike Murphy) *restless in stalls: s.i.s: in rr: styd on fnl 2f: nt rch ldrs* **25/1**

0002 **9** *½* **Singeur (IRE)**[14] 6347 4-9-0 **95**........................ DanielTudhope 20 89
(Robin Bastiman) *in rr stands' side: hdwy 2f out: keeping on at fin* **20/1**

0004 **10** *¾* **Tajneed (IRE)**[14] 6347 8-9-6 **101**........................ AdrianNicholls 15 93
(David Nicholls) *chsd ldrs: one pce appr fnl f* **18/1**

-030 **11** *1* **Bajan Tryst (USA)**[28] 5927 5-9-2 **97**........................(b[1]) DPMcDonogh 13 86
(Kevin Ryan) *in rr centrre: swtchd rt to stands' side over 1f out: kpt on* **33/1**

1253 **12** *nk* **Son Of The Cat (USA)**[21] 6147 5-9-5 **100**...........(t) SilvestreDeSousa 17 88
(Brian Gubby) *in rr stands' side: kpt on fnl 2f: nvr on terms* **8/1**[2]

0500 **13** *1* **Breathless Kiss (USA)**[21] 6147 4-8-10 **94**..................(b) AmyRyan(3) 8 78
(Kevin Ryan) *hood removed v late: in rr: hdwy and edgd lft over 1f out: kpt on: nvr nr ldrs* **33/1**

0640 **14** *¾* **Ancient Cross**[21] 6147 7-9-6 **101**........................(t) GrahamGibbons 14 83
(Michael Easterby) *towards rr: nvr a factor* **16/1**

0302 **15** *shd* **Addictive Dream (IRE)**[7] 6522 4-9-3 **101**........................ SeanLevey(3) 4 83
(Walter Swinburn) *chsd ldr: led over 2f out: hdd over 1f out: sn wknd* **10/1**

2460 **16** *½* **Lexi's Hero (IRE)**[28] 5927 3-9-6 **102**........................(b) DavidAllan 1 82
(Kevin Ryan) *led tl over 2f out: wknd 1f out* **16/1**

0614 **17** *1 ½* **Colonel Mak**[21] 6147 4-9-4 **99**........................ LeeNewman 9 74
(David Barron) *mid-div: effrt over 2f out: nvr a factor* **16/1**

4000 **18** *2* **Doctor Parkes**[28] 5927 5-8-13 **94**........................ WJSupple 5 63
(Eric Alston) *chsd ldrs far side: wknd over 1f out* **40/1**

2035 **19** *nk* **Joe Packet**[7] 6521 4-9-6 **104**........................ JohnFahy(3) 2 72
(Jonathan Portman) *chsd ldrs far side: wknd over 1f out* **16/1**

0040 **20** *2 ½* **Castles In The Air**[21] 6147 6-8-13 **94**........................ TonyHamilton 12 54
(Richard Fahey) *mid-div: lost pl 2f out* **33/1**

1m 11.14s (-0.76) **Going Correction** -0.05s/f (Good)
WFA 3 from 4yo+ 1lb **20** Ran SP% **127.9**
Speed ratings (Par 109): **103,100,98,98,97 97,97,95,94,93 92,92,90,89,89 89,87,84,84,80**
toteswingers:1&2:£28.10, 2&3:£26.10, 1&3:£14.30 CSF £90.35 CT £948.05 TOTE £8.80: £2.50, £2.40, £3.20, £9.90; EX 151.50 TRIFECTA Not won..
Owner Miss N Yarrow **Bred** Brookdale And Dr Ted Folkerth **Trained** Radlett, Herts

FOCUS
A red-hot handicap won by some classy sprinters in the past ten years, including The Tatling (before his heyday) and Borderlescott. There is every reason to believe that this year's renewal may have produced a smart performer too. There were plenty in good form coming into the race and the form looks sound rated around the winner, who has Group-race potential, and fourth.

NOTEBOOK
Sirius Prospect(USA) ◆ was up 7lb for this hat-trick bid, but had more in hand than the margin would suggest when winning at Ascot last time. He can start slowly and gave himself a bit to do here, with only one horse behind him 2f out, but he then took off, hit the front well inside the last furlong and won going away. This effort can even be upgraded as the way the course was riding suggested that front-runners were favoured and his main rivals were fighting it out on the other side of the track. A hefty rise can be expected, but he looks a Pattern-class sprinter and is a most interesting prospect. (op 8-1)
Kaldoun Kingdom(IRE), 2lb higher than when winning this race two years ago, was ridden closer to the pace and came with a well-timed challenge to pick up the leader on the far side well inside the final furlong, but the winner on the opposite side of the track was in a different league. He is without a success since March of last year but has the ability when things fall right.
Racy hasn't enjoyed much luck this season, including at Haydock last time, and is without a win since his second start at two, but this was a fine effort. Having got upset in the stalls and dumped his rider on the ground, he did best of those who helped force the pace and wasn't worn down until very late. (op 11-1)
Sioux Rising(IRE) probably found the ground too soft when well beaten in the Ayr Silver Cup and the rain during racing here was probably not ideal, but she flew home from off the pace and this was a good effort in the circumstances
Parisian Pyramid(IRE) was a stone better off with Internationaldebut for a half-length defeat over C&D last month when ridden less prominently than usual, but while his old rival had improved plenty in the meantime Parisian Pyramid had twice disappointed. Another to be in the firing line from the off, he put in a more solid effort but is now on a losing run of 15. (tchd 9-1)
Nocturnal Affair(SAF), raised 4lb for his success in the Portland, looked a danger when moving up to challenge over a furlong out but couldn't land an effective blow. He won on soft ground in South Africa, so the rain shouldn't have bothered him, and perhaps this mark was just beyond him. (tchd 9-1)
Internationaldebut(IRE), who was bidding for a four-timer, made a move from midfield over a furlong out but, although short of room well inside the last furlong, didn't look unlucky. He was 10lb higher than when winning a Doncaster handicap two starts back and the handicapper may have him now, while the rain may not have been ideal. (op 15-2 tchd 7-1)
Lutine Bell, 13lb better off with Sirius Prospect for a beating of just under 2l at Doncaster last month (allowing for weight-for-age), did well considering he missed the break but this effort demonstrates just how much the winner has improved.
Son Of The Cat(USA) reportedly ran flat. Official explanation: jockey said that the gelding ran flat (op 9-1)

6707 CORAL.CO.UK GREEN TICK WIN MORE EVERY RACE STKS (H'CAP) 2m 2f
4:40 (4:41) (Class 4) (0-85,81) 3-Y-0+ **£6,469** (£1,925; £962; £481) **Stalls** Low

Form RPR

20/3 **1** **Orsippus (USA)**[135] 2433 5-8-10 **63** oh1........................ SilvestreDeSousa 12 73+
(Michael Smith) *midfield: pushed along and hdwy to chse ldr over 3f out: led wl over 1f out: styd on wl* **20/1**

6-33 **2** *2 ¼* **Valid Reason**[17] 6249 4-10-0 **81**........................ ShaneKelly 8 87
(Dean Ivory) *led: rdn over 3f out: hdd wl over 1f out: styd on: no ch w wnr ins fnl f* **11/1**

1116 **3** *¾* **French Hollow**[21] 6171 6-9-10 **77**........................ FrederikTylicki 6 82
(Tim Fitzgerald) *hld up: hdwy 6f out: pushed along to chse ldr over 3f out: rdn over 2f out: kpt on* **8/1**

1123 **4** *2 ½* **Beat The Shower**[34] 5759 5-9-9 **76**........................ DavidAllan 2 78
(Peter Niven) *midfield: rdn over 3f out: styd on* **9/1**

1203 **5** *nk* **Los Nadis (GER)**[17] 5724 7-9-5 **72**........................ LeeNewman 11 74
(Jim Goldie) *s.i.s: hld up: rdn and hdwy over 3f out: kpt on* **12/1**

221 **6** *1 ¾* **Astromagick**[23] 6104 3-8-7 **72**........................ PaulHanagan 3 72
(Mark H Tompkins) *hld up: rdn and hdwy over 3f out: disputing 4th jst ins fnl f: wknd fnl 100yds* **3/1**[1]

1404 **7** *5* **Forrest Flyer (IRE)**[23] 6082 7-9-2 **69**........................ WJSupple 4 64
(Jim Goldie) *in tch: rdn 5f out: sn lost pl: n.d after* **33/1**

4656 **8** *4 ½* **Spiekeroog**[36] 5685 5-9-3 **70**........................ DanielTudhope 1 60
(David O'Meara) *trckd ldr: rdn over 3f out: wknd ins fnl f* **5/1**[2]

2410 **9** *6* **Petella**[23] 6095 5-9-1 **68**........................ PJMcDonald 9 51
(George Moore) *hld up in midfield: rdn over 4f out: sn btn* **16/1**

1135 **10** *1 ¼* **Memory Lane**[13] 6376 3-8-12 **77**........................ StevieDonohoe 10 59
(Sir Mark Prescott Bt) *trckd ldr: rdn over 3f out: sn wknd* **7/1**[3]

5601 **11** *1* **Cat O' Nine Tails**[18] 6229 4-9-2 **69**........................ BarryMcHugh 5 50
(Brian Rothwell) *hld up in tch: rdn over 3f out: sn wknd* **20/1**

2101 **12** *75* **May Contain Nuts**[23] 6095 3-8-11 **76**........................ FergusSweeney 7 —
(Brendan Powell) *in tch: rdn over 3f out: sn wknd: heavily eased over 1f out* **17/2**

3m 56.44s (-1.76) **Going Correction** -0.05s/f (Good)
WFA 3 from 4yo+ 12lb **12** Ran SP% **120.2**
Speed ratings (Par 105): **101,100,99,98,98 97,95,93,90,90 89,56**
toteswingers:1&2:£29.10, 2&3:£15.80, 1&3:£25.70 CSF £222.78 CT £1922.88 TOTE £22.90: £6.20, £4.10, £3.40; EX 307.10.
Owner Mrs Sandra Smith **Bred** Stephen H Batchelder & Gainesway Farm **Trained** Kirkheaton, Northumberland

FOCUS
With the rain still falling, they went a steady early pace in this marathon handicap but it was still too much for a few. The runners made for the stands' rail on reaching the home straight. The winner was well in on his jumps form/early Flat form and saw the trip out well, while the runner-up and third give the form a pretty solid look.
May Contain Nuts Official explanation: trainer's representative said that the gelding was unsuited by the good going

6708 COLDSTREAM GUARDS ASSOCIATION CUP (HANDICAP STKS) 1m 2f 88y
5:15 (5:16) (Class 4) (0-85,85) 3-Y-0+ **£6,469** (£1,925; £962; £481) **Stalls** Low

Form RPR

0301 **1** **Licence To Till (USA)**[8] 6513 4-9-6 **82**........................ SilvestreDeSousa 9 91
(Mark Johnston) *chsd ldrs: drvn over 3f out: led 2f out: hld on gamely towards fin* **5/1**[2]

0002 **2** *hd* **Jo'Burg (USA)**[7] 6533 7-9-4 **80**........................ DanielTudhope 4 89+
(David O'Meara) *in rr: stdy hdwy over 3f out: chsng ldrs over 1f out: styd on to take cl 2nd nr fin* **9/2**[1]

303 **3** *nk* **Viva Vettori**[15] 6302 7-9-9 **85**........................ NickyMackay 5 93
(David Elsworth) *s.i.s: hdwy over 3f out: chsng ldrs over 1f out: almost upsides last 75yds: no ex last 50yds* **14/1**

0330 **4** *1 ½* **Good Boy Jackson**[14] 6346 3-8-12 **82**........................ AmyRyan(3) 10 87
(Kevin Ryan) *chsd ldrs: chal over 2f out: kpt on same pce ins fnl f* **14/1**

0020 **5** *1* **Space War**[23] 6080 4-9-2 **85**........................ DavidSimmonson(7) 15 90+
(Michael Easterby) *in tch: nt clr run stands' side over 2f out tl swtchd lft over 1f out: kpt on wl ins fnl f* **33/1**

1006 **6** *½* **Euston Square**[14] 6346 5-9-0 **79**........................ DaleSwift(3) 19 81
(Alistair Whillans) *in rr: hdwy towards centre over 3f out: one pce over 1f out* **25/1**

0402 **7** *nk* **Pass Muster**[14] 6346 4-9-4 **83**........................ MichaelO'Connell(3) 2 85
(Ollie Pears) *in rr div: hdwy over 3f out: sn chsng ldrs: styd on same pce fnl f* **13/2**[3]

0203 **8** *3 ¾* **Antigua Sunrise (IRE)**[14] 6330 5-8-12 **81**........................ LauraBarry(7) 6 75
(Richard Fahey) *in tch: pushed along over 6f out: one pce fnl 3f* **8/1**

0000 **9** *3* **Dhaular Dhar (IRE)**[15] 6302 9-9-3 **82**........................ GaryBartley(3) 1 71
(Jim Goldie) *in rr: hdwy and styd alone far side over 4f out: chsd ldrs: wknd appr fnl f* **25/1**

2000 **10** *9* **Fastnet Storm (IRE)**[14] 6346 5-9-5 **81**........................ GrahamGibbons 8 53
(David Barron) *led: hdd 2f out: sn wknd* **20/1**

2550 **11** *1 ¾* **Powerful Presence (IRE)**[15] 6290 5-8-12 **79**........ AshleyMorgan(5) 13 47
(David O'Meara) *chsd ldrs: wknd 2f out* **33/1**

1-22 **12** *5* **On Her Way**[36] 5686 4-9-8 **84**........................ J-PGuillambert 11 43
(Luca Cumani) *trckd ldrs: t.k.h: wknd over 2f out: eased over 1f out* **13/2**[3]

0154 **13** *1 ¼* **Ailsa Craig (IRE)**[21] 6155 5-9-0 **76**........................ TonyHamilton 20 32
(Edwin Tuer) *chsd ldrs: wknd over 2f out* **20/1**

0105 **14** *8* **Munsarim (IRE)**[37] 5648 4-9-4 **80**........................ DavidAllan 17 21
(Keith Dalgleish) *mid-div: drvn over 4f out: lost pl over 2f out: eased over 1f out* **33/1**

0001 **15** *24* **Totally Ours**[39] 5608 4-9-8 **84**........................ RichardMullen 14 —
(William Muir) *chsd ldrs: drvn over 4f out: lost pl over 3f out: virtually p.u over 1f out* **20/1**

3120 **16** *6* **El Wasmi**[10] 6457 3-9-3 **84**........................(b) TomMcLaughlin 18 —
(Clive Brittain) *chsd ldrs: drvn 4f out: wknd over 2f out: bhd whn eased over 1f out* **25/1**

2m 10.55s (-1.95) **Going Correction** -0.05s/f (Good)
WFA 3 from 4yo+ 5lb **16** Ran SP% **120.6**
Speed ratings (Par 105): **105,104,104,103,102 102,101,98,96,89 87,83,82,76,57 52**
toteswingers:1&2:£5.30, 2&3:£17.10, 1&3:£12.00 CSF £22.89 CT £294.26 TOTE £5.10: £1.50, £1.90, £3.40, £3.80; EX 31.50.
Owner The Vine Accord **Bred** John Hettinger **Trained** Middleham Moor, N Yorks

FOCUS
A competitive handicap, run at a reasonable pace. Again the runners came stands' side in the straight, except for Dhaular Dhar, who stayed far side. The winner is better on the AW, the third helps set the standard and this was another good effort from the fourth.
Totally Ours Official explanation: trainer's representative said that the filly was unsuited by the good going
T/Jkpt: Not won. T/Plt: £1,047.20 to a £1 stake. Pool of £145,736.66 - 101.59 winning tickets.
T/Qpdt: £63.40 to £1 Pool of £9,095.64 - 106.13 w. tckts WG 6709a (Foreign Racing) - See RI

5773 BADEN-BADEN (L-H)
Saturday, October 8

OFFICIAL GOING: Turf: soft

6710a BADEN-WURTTEMBERG-TROPHY (GROUP 3) (3YO+) (TURF) 1m 4f
3:35 (12:00) 3-Y-0+
£27,586 (£9,482; £4,741; £2,586; £1,724; £1,293)

RPR

1 **Silvaner (GER)**[34] 5773 3-8-8 0........................ FilipMinarik 1 103
(P Schiergen, Germany) *hld up in midfield on rail: travelling wl: proged through field arnd fnl turn: rdn early in st: r.o wl fr 1 1/2f out: chal for ld 100yds out: led fnl 50yds* **44/5**

2 nk **Seismos (IRE)**[13] 6396 3-8-8 0 EPedroza 4 103
(A Wohler, Germany) *a.p bhd ldr: racing keenly: rdn to chal early in st: r.o wl: led over 1 1/2f out: chal ent fnl f: hdd fnl 50yds* **36/5**[3]
3 hd **Saltas (GER)**[13] 6396 3-8-8 0 AStarke 3 102
(P Schiergen, Germany) *settled 3rd: travelling wl: rdn coming out of fnl turn: r.o but failed to qckn initially: looked threatening ent fnl f: nt qckn again fnl 50yds* **1/2**[1]
4 3 **Hot Six (BRZ)**[27] 5984 6-9-2 0 ValmirDeAzeredo 2 98
(Fabricio Borges, Sweden) *settled at rr of field: proged through field down bk st: r.o wl in st: looked threatening over 1 1/2f out: no ex fnl f* **9/1**
5 1 1/4 **Keep Cool**[20] 6202 4-9-0 0 AHelfenbein 5 94
(Andreas Lowe, Germany) *settled 4th: r.o in st but no threat to ldrs* **139/10**
6 3 **Dawn Twister (GER)**[20] 6200 4-9-0 0 ADeVries 6 90
(J Hirschberger, Germany) *sent to ld fr s: set solid pce: led into st: rdn but sn hdd over 1 1/2f out: wknd* **42/10**[2]
7 11 **Lyssio (GER)**[35] 4-9-2 0 THellier 7 74
(P Schiergen, Germany) *settled towards rr: slipped bk to rr 1/2-way down bk st: rdn but no prog ent st: sn btn* **163/10**

2m 37.53s (4.07)
WFA 3 from 4yo+ 7lb 7 Ran SP% **130.8**
WIN (incl. 10 euro stake): 98. PLACES: 10, 10, 10. SF: 505.
Owner Frau M Herbert **Bred** Stiftung Gestut Fahrhof **Trained** Germany

CAULFIELD (R-H)
Saturday, October 8
OFFICIAL GOING: Turf: good to soft

6711a SPORTINGBET HERBERT POWER STKS (GROUP 2) (3YO+) (TURF) 1m 4f
2:45 (12:00) 3-Y-0+
£79,084 (£23,529; £11,764; £5,882; £3,267; £2,614)

RPR
1 **Shewan (AUS)** 5-8-8 0 ChrisSymons 4 106
(Robert Smerdon, Australia) *trckd ldrs gng wl on rail: 6th 4f out: rdn along 2f out to hold pl: swtchd outside 1 1/2f out: sn hrd rdn: 3rd and r.o ins fnl f: led fnl 30yds: all out* **5/2**[1]
2 snk **Tanby (AUS)** 5-8-8 0 (t) NicholasHall 7 106
(Robert Hickmott, Australia) *trckd ldrs on outside of eventual wnr: 5th and nudged along 3f out: clsd on outside fnl bnd: led appr fnl f: r.o u.p: hdd fnl 30yds: no ex* **4/1**[2]
3 1 **Moyenne Corniche**[49] 5285 6-9-0 0 MarkZahra 5 110+
(Brian Ellison) *hld up at rr of midfield on ins: swtchd towards outside and tk clsr order ins fnl 2f: briefly short of room over 1f out: r.o fnl 150yds and tk 3rd cl home* **25/1**
4 3/4 **Midnight Martini (AUS)**[28] 4-8-8 0 GlynSchofield 6 105
(Mark Kavanagh, Australia) *sn trcking ldrs: disp ld on outside of two rivals fr 2f out: wnt on over 1 1/2f out: rdn and hdd appr fnl f: wknd cl home and lost 3rd* **12/1**
5 3/4 **Anudjawun (NZ)**[42] 6-8-8 0 (b) CoreyBrown 2 102
(Shaun Dwyer, Australia) *racd in midfield: effrt towards outside 2f out: c wd fnl bnd: kpt on at one pce fnl f: nvr threatened ldrs* **12/1**
6 nk **Bauer (IRE)**[35] 5705 8-9-0 0 DamienOliver 11 108+
(Luca Cumani) *settled towards rr: pushed along 3 1/2f out: sme hdwy on outside: 11th and styd on appr fnl f: r.o ins fnl 100yds: nrest at fin* **9/1**
7 3/4 **Macedonian (NZ)**[168] 6-8-8 0 (b) LukeNolen 10 100
(Peter G Moody, Australia) *settled towards rr: pushed along and prog over 2f out: styd on wl ins fnl f: nvr rchd ldrs* **10/1**
8 hd **Saptapadi (IRE)**[49] 5285 5-9-0 0 KerrinMcEvoy 16 106
(Brian Ellison) *racd in midfield abt 8 l off pce: hdwy on outside 2 1/2f out: c wd fnl turn: 9th 1 1/2f out: rdn and nt qckn fnl f* **18/1**
9 shd **Lucky Eighty Eight (AUS)**[21] 6-8-9 0 (t) MichellePayne 14 100
(Mathew Ellerton & Simon Zahra, Australia) *chsd ldrs: 5th ins fnl 2f: sn rdn and nt qckn: wknd ins fnl 150yds* **13/2**[3]
10 1 **Prussian Officer (AUS)** 6-8-8 0 StevenKing 1 98
(Steve Richards, Australia) *racd in midfield: rdn and no imp 1 1/2f out: wknd ins fnl f* **150/1**
11 2 1/4 **Lopov (NZ)** 4-8-8 0 DwayneDunn 8 96
(Danny O'Brien, Australia) *trckd ldr: in middle of three ldrs fnl turn: sn rdn: wknd appr fnl f* **20/1**
12 3/4 **My Scotsgrey (NZ)**[951] 6-8-8 0 (b) LisaCropp 9 93
(Shaune Ritchie, New Zealand) *dwlt and rdn to go early pce: sn settled towards rr: rdn and no imp fnl 1 1/2f* **13/1**
13 1/2 **Two For Tea (NZ)**[14] 5-8-8 0 (t) CraigNewitt 13 92
(Gai Waterhouse, Australia) *broke wl fr outside draw and swtchd ins to ld on rail: ins of three ldrs fnl turn: sn rdn: hdd & wknd* **25/1**
14 2 1/4 **Exceptionally (NZ)**[21] 5-8-8 0 (t) DannyNikolic 15 89
(Terry & Karina O'Sullivan, Australia) *hld up towards rr: rdn and bhd fnl 1 1/2f* **60/1**
15 2 1/4 **Master O'Reilly (NZ)**[21] 9-8-11 0 StephenBaster 12 88
(Judy Mawer, Australia) *a bhd* **100/1**

2m 30.75s (150.75) 15 Ran SP% **124.5**
PARI-MUTUEL (NSW TAB - all including au$1 stakes): WIN 4.10 PLACE 1.90, 2.20, 6.90; DF 8.20; SF 19.50.
Owner Clay Hero Pty Ltd & W R Phillpot **Bred** Clay Hero Breeding Venture **Trained** Australia

NOTEBOOK
Shewan(AUS) took a long time to get on top but slowly got to the front. He took this on his first try in Group company and holds entries in the Caulfield and Melbourne Cup.
Tanby(AUS), a three-time winner this year, had every chance but couldn't quite last out.
Moyenne Corniche put up a hugely encouraging start to his spell in Australia with a staying-on performance. Always well placed, he ran a perfectly satisfactory trial for Flemington and will head for the Melbourne Cup if getting in. He looks more than capable of going close if ridden in a similar fashion.
Bauer(IRE) was hardly given the best of rides (held up and sent wide round runners on turning in) but ran on in pleasing style inside the final furlong. Connections hinted that he could head for the Geelong Cup now, a race he won in 2008.
Saptapadi(IRE) wasn't completely disgraced and one got the impression he wasn't asked for everything when it became clear he couldn't win. He may run in the Caulfield Cup.

6713a NEW ZEALAND BLOODSTOCK CAULFIELD STKS (GROUP 1) (3YO+) (TURF) 1m 2f
4:00 (12:00) 3-Y-0+
£158,169 (£47,058; £23,529; £11,764; £6,535; £5,228)

RPR
1 **Descarado (NZ)**[14] 5-9-4 0 NashRawiller 10 123
(Gai Waterhouse, Australia) **12/1**
2 3/4 **Avienus (AUS)**[28] 6-9-0 0 (b) BradRawiller 4 117+
(Mark C Webb, Australia) **50/1**
3 1 1/2 **Lights Of Heaven (NZ)**[21] 4-8-11 0 (p) LukeNolen 11 111
(Peter G Moody, Australia) **10/1**
4 1 3/4 **Mighty High (FR)**[132] 5-9-4 0 DarrenBeadman 8 115
(J Moore, Hong Kong) **15/2**
5 shd **Sincero (AUS)**[7] 4-9-2 0 ChrisO'Brien 7 112+
(Stephen Farley, Australia) **5/1**[2]
6 shd **Playing God (AUS)**[6] 4-9-2 0 StevenParnham 9 112
(Neville Parnham, Australia) **9/1**
7 2 3/4 **Sahara Sun (CHI)**[31] 5829 4-9-2 0 (t) StevenArnold 1 107+
(Luca Cumani) *racd keenly under restraint in 7th on rail: dropped to last over 3f out: last and rdn ins fnl 2f: styd on ins fnl f: n.d* **40/1**
8 1 1/4 **Lion Tamer (NZ)**[21] 4-9-2 0 (t) MichaelRodd 6 104+
(Murray & Bjorn Baker, New Zealand) **8/5**[1]
9 3 1/4 **Alcopop (AUS)**[28] 7-9-4 0 DominicTourneur 3 100+
(Jake Stephens, Australia) **7/1**[3]

2m 2.50s (122.50) 9 Ran SP% **110.6**
PARI-MUTUEL (NSW TAB - all including au$1 stakes): WIN 12.90 PLACE 3.10, 9.70, 3.00; DF 216.20; SF 441.10.
Owner D A & Mrs R J Henderson Et Al **Bred** W S McQuoid **Trained** Australia

FOCUS
The race was run a dwadle and the winner stole it from the front.

NOTEBOOK
Descarado(NZ) is undoubtedly a top-class horse, as his 2010 Caulfield Cup victory shows, but he completely stole this from the front while allowed an easy lead.
Avienus(AUS) sat reasonably close but, like most, got caught flat footed before staying on.
Lights Of Heaven(NZ), the winner of the Schweppes Oaks in March, is a decent filly and ran on well at the end.
Mighty High(FR) got caught in trouble on the inside when the race started to get serious and needed to be brought wide to make a challenge. He's better than the bare result.
Sahara Sun(CHI) sat in rear and predictably got outpaced. Nothing could have been learnt from his run.
Lion Tamer(NZ) ran terribly after sitting out the back. Trainer Murray Baker said afterwards "It was a poor effort. It was like he wasn't interested. I'll put blinkers on him in the Cox. That was a shocker."

6712a, 6714 - 6715a, 6717 - 6718a, 6720a (Foreign Racing) - See Raceform Interactive

6547 BELMONT PARK (L-H)
Saturday, October 8
OFFICIAL GOING: Turf: firm; dirt: fast

6716a JAMAICA H'CAP (GRADE 1) (3YO) (TURF) 1m 1f (T)
9:13 (12:00) 3-Y-0
£96,153 (£32,051; £16,025; £8,012; £4,807; £1,602)

RPR
1 **Western Aristocrat (USA)**[23] 6088 3-8-7 0 ow3 CNakatani 4 114
(Jeremy Noseda) *mde all: set v stdy pce: qckd over 2 1/2f out: pushed along and r.o wl fnl 1 1/2f: a holding runner-up* **7/1**[3]
2 1 **Brilliant Speed (USA)**[34] 3-8-9 0 JRVelazquez 5 114
(Thomas Albertrani, U.S.A) *racd on ldr's outside: pressed ldr over 2 1/2f out: r.o fnl 1 1/2f: a hld by wnr* **11/10**[1]
3 3/4 **Wilkinson (USA)**[22] 3-8-4 0 AGarcia 2 107
(Neil J Howard, U.S.A) *chsd ldrs: pushed along to hold position over 2f out: nt qckn u.p 1 1/2f out: styd on u.p fnl 150yds* **224/10**
4 2 1/2 **Top Surprize (USA)**[22] 3-8-5 0 ow1 (b) RMaragh 6 103
(Naipaul Chatterpaul, U.S.A) *broke wl and trckd ldrs on outside of wilkinson: rdn and nt qckn over 2f out: kpt on at one pce fnl f* **14/1**
5 3/4 **Sky Blazer (USA)**[34] 3-8-6 0 ow2 CVelasquez 7 103
(Barclay Tagg, U.S.A) *hld up: effrt on outside to press 3rd and 4th pls over 2f out: run sn flattened out and no ex fnl f* **36/5**
6 hd **Casino Host (USA)**[56] 5072 3-8-5 0 ow1 ASolis 1 101
(Chad C Brown, U.S.A) *hld up in rr: scrubbed along 2 1/2f out: hdwy on ins: 4th 1 1/2f out: nt qckn fnl f* **5/2**[2]
7 1/2 **Seal Cove (USA)**[34] 3-8-5 0 JJCastellano 3 100
(Claude McGaughey III, U.S.A) *a w bkmarkers: rdn and no imp over 2f out* **109/10**

1m 50.34s (110.34) 7 Ran SP% **120.2**
PARI-MUTUEL (all including $2 stakes): WIN 16.00; PLACE (1-2) 6.90, 3.00; SHOW (1-2-3) 4.30, 2.20, 6.40; SF 45.80.
Owner Vinery Stables **Bred** Grapestock Llc **Trained** Newmarket, Suffolk

NOTEBOOK
Western Aristocrat(USA), who took nearly a second off the track record on the Kempton Polytrack last time, was allowed the run of the race at a steady pace and this isn't form to get carried away with. He could stay in the US, possibly for the Breeders' Cup Mile, and there was also talk of next year's Godolphin Mile in Dubai.

6685 KEENELAND (L-H)
Saturday, October 8
OFFICIAL GOING: Turf: firm; polytrack: fast

6719a FIRST LADY STKS (GRADE 1) (3YO+ FILLIES & MARES) (TURF) 1m
9:37 (12:00) 3-Y-0+
£134,615 (£44,871; £22,435; £11,217; £6,730; £641)

RPR
1 **Never Retreat (USA)**[20] 6-8-12 0 JRLeparoux 12 117
(Chris Block, U.S.A) **4/1**[2]

The Form Book, Raceform Ltd, Compton, RG20 6NL

2 1 ½ **Together (IRE)**[14] 6338 3-8-9 0 CO'Donoghue 6 114
(A P O'Brien, Ire) **9/2**[3]
3 nse **Daveron (GER)**[42] 6-8-12 0 ECastro 3 114+
(H Graham Motion, U.S.A) **18/5**[1]
4 ½ **Wasted Tears (USA)**[54] 6-8-12 0 JRosario 8 113
(Bart B Evans, U.S.A) **7/1**
5 ½ **Bay To Bay (USA)**[20] 4-8-12 0 RAlbarado 1 112
(Brian A Lynch, Canada) **102/10**
6 ¾ **Gypsy's Warning (SAF)**[119] 2948 6-8-12 0 RADominguez 10 110
(H Graham Motion, U.S.A) **119/10**
7 1 ½ **C. S. Silk (USA)**[69] 5-8-12 0 KDesormeaux 7 106
(Dale Romans, U.S.A) **101/10**
8 2 ½ **Cherokee Queen (USA)**[69] 6-8-12 0 JKCourt 2 101
(Martin D Wolfson, U.S.A) **45/1**
9 ½ **Eclair De Lune (GER)**[56] 5073 5-8-12 0 JamesGraham 11 100
(Ronald McAnally, U.S.A) **50/1**
10 2 **Absinthe Minded (USA)**[35] 4-8-12 0 TJThompson 5 95
(D Wayne Lukas, U.S.A) **53/1**
11 ¾ **Theyskens' Theory (USA)**[21] 6183 3-8-9 0 GKGomez 9 93
(Claude McGaughey III, U.S.A) **59/10**
12 ¾ **Category Seven (USA)**[28] 6-8-12 0 (b) SSellers 4 91
(Kenneth L Hargrave, U.S.A) **73/1**

1m 34.08s (94.08)
WFA 3 from 4yo+ 3lb **12** Ran SP% **119.9**
PARI-MUTUEL (all including $2 stakes): WIN 10.00; PLACE (1-2) 5.20, 6.00; SHOW (1-2-3) 3.60, 3.40, 3.20; SF 61.20.
Owner Team Block **Bred** Gerald O'Meara & Stanley Inman **Trained** USA

NOTEBOOK
Together(IRE) ran a solid race on her return to the US, but while this was a competitive race, the form is not strong by Grade 1 standards. She could be set for another Keeneland outing soon.

6721a SHADWELL TURF MILE STKS (GRADE 1) (3YO+) (TURF) 1m
10:45 (12:00) 3-Y-O+
£230,769 (£76,923; £38,461; £19,230; £11,538; £2,564)

RPR
1 **Gio Ponti (USA)**[56] 5074 6-9-0 0 RADominguez 5 121
(Christophe Clement, U.S.A) **19/10**[1]
2 ½ **Get Stormy (USA)**[43] 5-9-0 0 GKGomez 8 120
(Thomas Bush, U.S.A) **138/10**
3 1 **Sidney's Candy (USA)**[35] 5751 4-9-0 0 JRosario 2 118
(Todd Pletcher, U.S.A) **56/10**
4 nk **Wise Dan (USA)**[28] 4-9-0 0 JKCourt 7 117
(Charles Lopresti, U.S.A) **11/2**[3]
5 2 ¾ **Dance And Dance (IRE)**[20] 6204 5-9-0 0 JamieSpencer 3 111
(Edward Vaughan) **31/5**
6 1 ½ **Tajaaweed (USA)**[56] 5074 6-9-0 0 JamesGraham 1 107
(Daniel Peitz, U.S.A) **45/1**
7 nse **Society's Chairman (CAN)**[33] 8-9-0 0 JRLeparoux 6 107
(Roger L Attfield, Canada) **193/10**
8 6 ¾ **Zoffany (IRE)**[62] 4838 3-8-11 0 CO'Donoghue 4 92
(A P O'Brien, Ire) **13/5**[2]

1m 34.17s (94.17)
WFA 3 from 4yo+ 3lb **8** Ran SP% **120.5**
PARI-MUTUEL (all including $2 stakes): WIN 5.80; PLACE (1-2) 3.20, 9.40; SHOW (1-2-3) 2.40, 5.20, 4.60; SF 52.40.
Owner Castleton Lyons **Bred** Kilboy Estate Inc **Trained** USA

NOTEBOOK
Gio Ponti(USA) found the pace just strong enough for him to quicken up and record back-to-back wins in this Grade 1. The Breeders' Cup Mile, a race he was second in last year, will be tougher.
Zoffany(IRE) ran poorly with no obvious excuse.

6244 GOODWOOD (R-H)
Sunday, October 9

OFFICIAL GOING: Good (good to firm in places on round course; 7.9)
Wind: Moderate, against Weather: Fine

6722 FORNELLS ALDERBROOK STKS (H'CAP) (FOR NATIONAL HUNT JOCKEYS) 2m
2:00 (2:00) (Class 5) (0-70,69) 4-Y-O+ **£2,587** (£770; £384; £192) **Stalls** Low

Form RPR
2240 **1** **Epsom Salts**[14] 6376 6-11-10 **67** ColinBolger 8 76
(Pat Phelan) *sn cl up: trckd ldng pair 5f out: led gng strly over 2f out and sn rdn clr: tired fnl f but in n.d* **13/2**[2]
0605 **2** 1 ¾ **Sohcahtoa (IRE)**[7] 6254 5-11-10 **67** AlanO'Keeffe 12 74
(Robert Mills) *hld up last: stl in last pair 4f out: prog over 3f out: drvn and styd on to go 2nd last 150yds: clsd on wnr but no ch* **7/1**[3]
-205 **3** 3 **Ned Ludd (IRE)**[59] 4951 8-10-12 **55** (p) HaddenFrost 4 58
(Jonathan Portman) *prom: rdn and nt qckn over 3f out: sn outpcd: styd on to take 3rd wl ins fnl f* **14/1**
4520 **4** 1 ¾ **Double Handful (GER)**[10] 6485 5-11-12 **69** AidanColeman 13 70
(Venetia Williams) *pressed ldr: led over 3f out to over 2f out: chsd wnr after but outpcd: wknd ins fnl f* **12/1**
14- **5** 3 ½ **Oscar Close (IRE)**[157] 1446 6-11-10 **67** GerardTumelty 11 64
(George Baker) *sn prom: on terms but rdn over 3f out: wknd fr 2f out* **14/1**
3446 **6** ½ **Sancho Panza**[41] 5545 4-11-8 **65** LiamTreadwell 3 62
(Julia Feilden) *towards rr but wl in tch: rdn 4f out: sme prog 3f out: outpcd sn after* **15/2**
0066 **7** shd **Carnac (IRE)**[22] 6182 5-10-10 **53** (b) JoeTizzard 7 49
(Alan McCabe) *hld up towards rr but wl in tch: prog 4f out: drvn to chse ldng trio 3f out: no imp 2f out: wknd fnl f* **22/1**
4342 **8** 1 ½ **Rosewood Lad**[45] 5417 4-11-10 **67** AndrewThornton 9 62
(J S Moore) *towards rr but wl in tch: rdn and outpcd fr 4f out: no real prog after* **17/2**
3/13 **9** ½ **Whenever**[29] 5947 7-11-8 **65** DenisO'Regan 10 59
(Richard Phillips) *prom: pushed along and lost pl 6f out: struggling in rr over 4f out: n.d after* **4/1**[1]
1/5- **10** 2 ½ **No Rules**[396] 4983 6-11-10 **67** MattieBatchelor 6 58
(Mark H Tompkins) *mde most at stdy pce to over 3f out: wknd over 2f out* **20/1**
4566 **11** 4 **Musashi (IRE)**[21] 5667 6-10-12 **55** (b) HarrySkelton 5 41
(Laura Mongan) *hld up in last pair: sme prog over 3f out: no hdwy over 2f out: sn wknd* **50/1**
1-06 **12** 31 **Perception (IRE)**[37] 5692 5-11-11 **68** RobertThornton 2 17
(Alan King) *prom tl wknd over 3f out: t.o* **9/1**
3622 **13** 3 ¼ **Vertueux (FR)**[43] 4697 6-11-1 **58** WayneHutchinson 1 —
(Tony Carroll) *prom tl wknd wl over 3f out: t.o* **12/1**

3m 36.25s (7.25) **Going Correction** +0.175s/f (Good) **13** Ran SP% **117.9**
Speed ratings (Par 103): **88,87,85,84,83 82,82,81,81,80 78,62,61**
toteswinger: 1&2 £14.50, 1&3 £14.80, 2&3 £27.00 CSF £49.63 CT £621.69 TOTE £7.20: £2.50, £2.80, £5.10; EX 60.80 Trifecta £391.70 Pool: £529.34 - 1.00 winning units..
Owner The Epsom Racegoers **Bred** Heatherwold Stud **Trained** Epsom, Surrey

FOCUS
The top bend was dolled out three yards, increasing distances by six yards for races on that course. The lower bend was dolled out three yards, increasing distances by five yards for races run on that course. A modest staying handicap. The winner was down in grade and probably only needed to match this year's form to score.

6723 GOODWOOD AERO CLUB STKS (H'CAP) 6f
2:35 (2:36) (Class 3) (0-95,93) 3-Y-O+ **£7,439** (£2,213; £1,106; £553) **Stalls** High

Form RPR
5334 **1** **Gentle Lord**[15] 6331 3-8-13 **86** (t) RichardKingscote 5 95
(Tom Dascombe) *w ldrs in centre: drvn into narrow ld over 1f out: hld on wl nr fin* **11/1**
1000 **2** shd **Seal Rock**[59] 4965 3-9-6 **93** DaneO'Neill 11 102+
(Henry Candy) *wl in rr in centre: prog and drifted lft 2f out: drvn and r.o fnl f: jst failed* **13/2**[1]
3005 **3** hd **Star Rover (IRE)**[15] 6347 4-9-3 **89** (v) CathyGannon 2 97
(David Evans) *prom in centre gp: rdn to chal over 1f out: nrly upsides ins fnl f: jst hld* **20/1**
0020 **4** ½ **Mac Gille Eoin**[29] 5935 7-9-1 **87** IanMongan 4 94
(John Gallagher) *chsd ldrs in centre: prog and hung lft over 1f out: tried to chal fnl f: nt qckn fnl 100yds* **16/1**
5005 **5** ¾ **Gouray Girl (IRE)**[17] 6272 4-9-0 **86** (t) JimCrowley 6 90
(Walter Swinburn) *hld up in centre: stdy prog over 2f out: rdn to chal and almost against far side rail 1f out: fdd fnl 100yds* **16/1**
3010 **6** ½ **Elna Bright**[15] 6341 6-9-1 **87** JimmyQuinn 14 90
(Brett Johnson) *trckd ldng pair nr side: clsd to ld gp over 1f out: styd on but nvr quite on terms* **22/1**
1260 **7** 2 ¼ **Quasi Congaree (GER)**[15] 6331 5-8-13 **85** (t) JamesDoyle 20 81
(Ian Wood) *towards rr nr side: rdn over 2f out: styd on same pce against nr side rail fnl f* **33/1**
-102 **8** nk **Dickie's Lad (IRE)**[50] 5288 3-9-1 **88** (t) DarryllHolland 1 83
(Kevin Ryan) *overall ldr in centre to over 1f out: steadily wknd* **15/2**[2]
6024 **9** nk **Sutton Veny (IRE)**[20] 6224 5-8-9 **88** RaulDaSilva(7) 3 82
(Jeremy Gask) *pressed ldrs in centre 4f: steadily wknd* **14/1**
0300 **10** 1 ½ **Novellen Lad (IRE)**[31] 5852 6-9-2 **88** RichardHughes 9 77
(Willie Musson) *hld up last of centre gp: prog 2f out: kpt on same pce fnl f: n.d* **20/1**
0002 **11** ½ **Corporal Maddox**[15] 6327 4-9-1 **87** FergusSweeney 7 74
(Jamie Osborne) *racd in centre: nvr beyond midfield: one pce fr over 1f out and no prog* **10/1**
0013 **12** hd **Tagula Night (IRE)**[15] 6331 5-9-1 **87** KierenFallon 19 74+
(Walter Swinburn) *towards rr nr side: effrt but plenty to do whn bmpd 2f out: no ch after* **8/1**[3]
050 **13** ¾ **Kuanyao (IRE)**[30] 5887 5-9-2 **88** SteveDrowne 13 72
(Peter Makin) *nvr beyond midfield in centre: effrt whn bmpd 2f out: no ch after* **25/1**
0050 **14** nk **Ballista (IRE)**[15] 6331 3-8-13 **86** StephenCraine 18 69
(Tom Dascombe) *led nr side gp to over 1f out: wknd* **25/1**
6401 **15** nk **La Fortunata**[17] 6272 4-9-1 **87** TonyCulhane 8 69
(Mike Murphy) *pressed ldrs in centre 4f: wknd* **14/1**
1100 **16** nk **Steps (IRE)**[15] 6332 3-9-4 **91** NeilCallan 15 72
(Roger Varian) *racd towards nr side early: a wl in rr: no ch over 1f out* **25/1**
0206 **17** 1 ½ **We Have A Dream**[15] 6331 6-8-8 **85** JamesRogers(5) 16 62
(William Muir) *chsd nr side ldr to wl over 1f out: wknd* **16/1**
0010 **18** 5 **Noverre To Go (IRE)**[15] 6331 5-8-13 **85** (t) LukeMorris 10 46
(Ronald Harris) *v awkward s: wl in rr in centre: effrt but stl plenty to do whn bmpd 2f out: bhd after* **25/1**
250 **19** 3 ½ **Piscean (USA)**[36] 5706 6-9-2 **88** TomQueally 17 37
(Tom Keddy) *racd towards nr side early: a wl in rr: no ch whn sltly impeded wl over 1f out* **16/1**

1m 12.93s (0.73) **Going Correction** +0.30s/f (Good)
WFA 3 from 4yo+ 1lb **19** Ran SP% **122.7**
Speed ratings (Par 107): **107,106,106,105,104 104,101,100,100,98 97,97,96,96,95 95,93,86,82**
toteswinger: 1&2 £15.80, 1&3 £43.70, 2&3 £29.80 CSF £69.18 CT £1473.53 TOTE £10.50: £3.10, £2.30, £4.60, £5.10; EX 94.90 Trifecta £553.00 Part won. Pool of £747.29 - 0.20 winning units..
Owner K P Trowbridge **Bred** R Phillips And Tweenhills Farm And Stud **Trained** Malpas, Cheshire

FOCUS
They were spread out across the track and the main action took place centre-field. This was a good, really competitive heat. The third and fourth help set the standard.

NOTEBOOK
Gentle Lord stepped up just a notch of some recent creditable efforts to record his second win. He's only had eight starts, so there's no telling how far he'll progress. (op 12-1)
Seal Rock was in the clear with about 2f to run, but it proved to be just a stride too late. This was a very useful performance under top weight and he's had one fewer run than the winner. He could progress into a Group horse. (op 11-1)
Star Rover(IRE) is much more exposed than the front two, but he's tough. This was another decent performance.
Mac Gille Eoin often goes well at Goodwood and he did so again.
Gouray Girl(IRE) challenged closest to the far rail, but others finished stronger.
Elna Bright ran well considering he was positioned away form the main bunch. (op 20-1)
Quasi Congaree(GER) raced against the stands' rail and kept on reasonably at a track that's probably sharp enough for him these days.
Dickie's Lad(IRE) faded a bit disappointingly after taking them along, although he had been off for 50 days. He'll be worth another try at 5f.
Tagula Night(IRE), ahead of today's winner last time, would have been a bit closer had he not been short of room in the last third. (tchd 9-1 in a place)
Kuanyao(IRE) might be one to keep in mind. He was bumped when beginning his run and wasn't given anything like a hard ride. (op 22-1)
Steps(IRE) was denied a clear run but didn't look unlucky.

Noverre To Go(IRE) lost all chance when bumped inside the final 2f.

6724 EUROPEAN BREEDERS' FUND NURSERY 7f
3:10 (3:10) (Class 4) (0-85,80) 2-Y-O **£4,528** (£1,347; £673; £336) **Stalls** Low

Form	Pos	Btn	Horse	RPR
6301	1		**Poetic Lord**[33] 5809 2-9-5 **78** .... RichardHughes 1 (Richard Hannon) *mde virtually all: nudged along and lened away jst over 2f out: 4 l up and in n.d over 1f out: eased fnl 100yds* **11/4**[1]	85+
4412	2	2	**Dixie's Dream (IRE)**[61] 4892 2-9-2 **75** .... DaneO'Neill 3 (Richard Hannon) *hld up in tch: rdn and prog 2f out: styd on to take 2nd ins fnl f: no ch w wnr* **12/1**	74
01	3	¾	**Point Made (IRE)**[26] 6025 2-9-6 **79** .... RichardMullen 2 (Ed McMahon) *trckd ldrs: rdn on inner 2f out and outpcd by wnr: disp 2nd 1f out: one pce after* **20/1**	76
0304	4	1	**Philipstown**[20] 6214 2-8-12 **74** .... KieranO'Neill(3) 8 (Richard Hannon) *prom: chsd wnr 3f out: lft bhd 2f out: wknd ins fnl f* **16/1**	69
044	5	1 ¾	**Lovage**[31] 5854 2-8-6 **68** .... HarryBentley(3) 9 (Roger Charlton) *racd wd in rr: struggling u.p over 2f out: kpt on fr over 1f out: no ch* **6/1**	58
31	6	1 ¾	**Royal Reyah**[39] 5613 2-8-8 **67** .... FergusSweeney 4 (Stuart Kittow) *plld hrd: hld up in tch: nt clr run over 2f out: wknd over 1f out* **9/2**[2]	53
01	7	½	**Biba Diva (IRE)**[24] 6099 2-9-2 **75** .... JimmyFortune 6 (Jeremy Noseda) *t.k.h: hld up in midfield: rdn over 2f out: wknd over 1f out* **9/2**[2]	64+
1252	8	1 ¾	**The Blue Banana (IRE)**[32] 5825 2-9-7 **80** ....(b) ShaneKelly 7 (Brian Meehan) *s.s: hanging bdly and looked reluctant in last: nvr on terms: plugged on fnl f* **5/1**[3]	60
0020	9	2 ½	**Dine Out**[26] 6021 2-8-6 **65** .... JimmyQuinn 5 (Mark H Tompkins) *a in rr: rdn 3f out: no prog and wl btn 2f out* **50/1**	39
3600	10	7	**Sea Poet**[19] 6237 2-7-12 **57** oh3 .... CathyGannon 10 (John Bridger) *chsd wnr to 3f out: wknd qckly* **80/1**	14

1m 28.85s (1.95) **Going Correction** +0.175s/f (Good) **10** Ran SP% **115.5**
Speed ratings (Par 97): **95,92,91,90,88 86,86,84,81,73**
toteswinger: 1&2 £5.90, 1&3 £20.90, 2&3 £55.30 CSF £37.32 CT £448.30 TOTE £3.90: £2.10, £3.60, £2.90; EX 19.50 Trifecta £693.30 Part won. Pool of £936.91 - 0.53 winning units..
Owner Mrs John Lee **Bred** Howard Barton Stud **Trained** East Everleigh, Wilts

FOCUS
No one is riding better than Richard Hughes and he schooled his colleagues, setting a steady pace in an uncontested lead. It was a ride reminiscent of the jockey's effort on Chandlery over the same C&D in the Vintage Stakes. Clearly, this form needs treating with some caution, though Poetic Lord was value for around 5l having been eased near the line and, given he's considered more of a 3yo prospect, there was much to like. The runner-up and fourth help set a reliable level.

NOTEBOOK
Poetic Lord was up 6lb for a win on the Lingfield turf (overcame track bias) and followed up despite not appearing totally at ease in the closing stages, possibly not handling the track and/or still being on the weak side. He also seemed to have his heels clipped around 2f out. (op 10-3)
Dixie's Dream(IRE), another of Richard Hannon's three runners, made it a one-two for the stable. Up in trip after two months off, he stayed on well once switched out for a run. His stamina wasn't severely tested, but he should win a similar race. (op 11-1 tchd 10-1)
Point Made(IRE) was up in trip after winning a 6f Haydock maiden. Like so many, the steady pace didn't help him. (op 16-1)
Philipstown was better placed than most, but didn't see it out. There's loads of speed on the dam's side of his pedigree and he looks a sprinter. (tchd 20-1)
Lovage ◆ can be excused this as she had a wide trip. There's better to come. (op 7-1 tchd 15-2)
Royal Reyah, up in trip after a Bath maiden win, got warm and was too keen. (op 11-2)
Biba Diva(IRE) was disappointing on this step up in trip, making no impression. (tchd 4-1)
The Blue Banana(IRE) threw away a winning chance at Doncaster last time and looked thoroughly awkward here, starting slowly and never travelling with any enthusiasm. Official explanation: jockey said that the gelding was never travelling (op 4-1)

6725 GREENE KING IPA MEDIAN AUCTION MAIDEN STKS 6f
3:40 (3:41) (Class 5) 2-Y-O **£2,587** (£770; £384; £192) **Stalls** High

Form	Pos	Btn	Horse	RPR
	1		**Fillionaire** 2-8-12 0 .... SamHitchcott 6 (Mick Channon) *chsd ldrs in centre: rdn and prog over 2f out: led over 1f out: r.o wl and sn clr* **40/1**	80+
	2	2 ¼	**Opera Flute (IRE)** 2-9-3 0 .... DaneO'Neill 16 (Richard Hannon) *racd nr side and last of trio: pushed along over 2f out: prog to ld gp jst ins fnl f and sn chsng wnr: no ch but styd on wl* **22/1**	78
0	3	2 ½	**Impel (IRE)**[18] 6244 2-9-3 0 .... RichardHughes 14 (Richard Hannon) *chsd ldrs in centre: effrt 2f out: prog to dispute 2nd 1f out: no ch w wnr: nudged along and jst hld on for 3rd* **5/1**[2]	72+
0	4	shd	**Rock Song**[58] 4996 2-9-3 0 .... JimCrowley 17 (Amanda Perrett) *chsd nr side ldr: effrt 2f out: rdn and styd on fnl f: nvr able to chal* **22/1**	70+
2	5	nse	**Cristal Gem**[141] 2302 2-8-12 0 .... JimmyFortune 8 (Richard Hannon) *sn last of centre gp: pushed along and prog 1/2-way: styd on steadily fnl 2f: nrst fin* **15/2**[3]	65
05	6	1 ½	**Generalyse**[23] 6123 2-9-3 0 .... RobertHavlin 5 (Ben De Haan) *trckd ldrs in centre gng wl: shkn up and cl enough wl over 1f out: fdd* **12/1**	66
622	7	½	**Jay Bee Blue**[16] 6292 2-9-3 79 ....(v[1]) RichardKingscote 18 (Tom Dascombe) *led nr side trio and wl on terms: hdd and fdd jst ins fnl f* **8/1**	64
	8	hd	**Fabled City (USA)** 2-9-3 0 ....[1] AdamKirby 12 (Clive Cox) *dwlt: wl in rr centre: pushed along and kpt on steadily fnl 2f: nt disgracd* **33/1**	63
	9	¾	**Cynthia Calhoun** 2-8-9 0 .... JohnFahy(3) 11 (Clive Cox) *towards rr in centre: effrt 1/2-way: hanging rt fnl 2f but kpt on* **12/1**	56
02	10	1 ¼	**Diamond Belle**[36] 5726 2-8-12 0 .... TomQueally 9 (Noel Quinlan) *disp ld in centre to over 1f out: wknd qckly* **5/1**[2]	52
05	11	¾	**Swift Cat**[41] 5541 2-9-0 0 .... KierenFox(3) 1 (John Best) *nvr beyond midfield in centre: struggling 2f out* **25/1**	55
0	12	¾	**Bareback (IRE)**[95] 3746 2-9-3 0 .... LukeMorris 10 (John Best) *sn lost prom position in centre: rdn in rr 1/2-way: nvr on terms after* **33/1**	53
00	13	2 ½	**All Nighter (IRE)**[134] 2510 2-9-3 0 .... ShaneKelly 7 (Brian Meehan) *disp ld in centre to wl over 1f out: wknd qckly* **12/1**	45
00	14	12	**Knoydart (USA)**[8] 6539 2-9-3 0 ....(b) NeilCallan 4 (Amanda Perrett) *racd freely: disp ld in centre to 2f out: hanging and wknd rapidly: t.o* **100/1**	9
	15	nk	**Santadelacruze** 2-9-3 0 .... SteveDrowne 15 (Gary Moore) *a wl in rr in centre: t.o* **100/1**	9
	16	12	**I B A Gee Gee** 2-9-3 0 .... FergusSweeney 2 (Tony Newcombe) *dwlt: spd in centre to 1/2-way: wknd rapidly: wl t.o* **100/1**	—
3023	17	3 ¾	**Forest Edge (IRE)**[8] 6524 2-9-3 77 .... KierenFallon 3 (David Evans) *nvr gng wl in centre and a in rr: struggling whn snatched up over 2f out: eased: wl t.o* **9/2**[1]	—

1m 13.96s (1.76) **Going Correction** +0.30s/f (Good) **17** Ran SP% **121.3**
Speed ratings (Par 95): **100,97,93,93,93 91,90,90,89,87 86,85,82,66,66 50,45**
toteswinger: 1&2 £85.50, 1&3 £50.30, 2&3 £36.60 CSF £735.36 TOTE £36.50: £7.20, £5.10, £2.40; EX 1105.80 TRIFECTA Not won..
Owner Mrs Ann C Black **Bred** Mr & Mrs Kevan Watts **Trained** West Ilsley, Berks

FOCUS
A fair maiden that should produce a few winners. The majority of these raced up the middle, but three runners (Opera Flute, Rock Song and Jay Bee Blue) raced stands' side throughout.

NOTEBOOK
Fillionaire ◆, a 55,000gns purchase, is a half-sister to a couple of winners, notably the very useful Pabusar, a C&D winner, and the dam was decent over 5f-6f. She showed a likeable attitude, taking this in a professional manner, and considering it reportedly took her connections by surprise, it's reasonable to think there's plenty more to come. In time she could be very useful.
Opera Flute(IRE), a 78,000gns buy, is a half-brother to 1m Group 3 winner Ballybacka Lady. He was passed over by Richard Hughes, but saw his race out well and can build on this. (op 25-1)
Impel(IRE) showed nothing on his debut over 7f on soft ground here, but he was just 7-2 that day and Hughes kept the faith, choosing him over the other two Hannon runners. This was a lot better and he should come on again. (op 13-2)
Rock Song was well beaten in a good maiden on his debut, but he'd been given 58 days off. This was more encouraging. (op 25-1 tchd 20-1)
Cristal Gem had been off since being beaten as 6-4 favourite on her debut in May. She wasn't the yard's first string on jockey bookings, but this was a satisfactory comeback. (op 8-1)
Generalyse showed ability in a fair Newbury maiden on his second start and did so again. He's now eligible for a handicap mark and should find his level.
Jay Bee Blue disappointed in a first-time visor, finishing last of the trio who raced stands' side from the start. (op 7-1)
Diamond Belle checked out tamely after showing speed, not building on her second-place finish at Thirsk. (op 11-2 tchd 9-2 and 6-1 in a place)
Forest Edge(IRE) was having his fourth run in the space of a month and ran flat, never travelling at any stage. Official explanation: jockey said that the colt missed the break, was never travelling and suffered interference in running (op 5-1)

6726 BRITISH STALLION STUDS SUPPORTING BRITISH RACING E B F MAIDEN STKS 1m 1f
4:10 (4:12) (Class 4) 2-Y-O **£4,528** (£1,347; £673; £336) **Stalls** Low

Form	Pos	Btn	Horse	RPR
5	1		**Aazif (IRE)**[22] 6160 2-9-3 0 .... RichardHills 5 (John Dunlop) *led after 100yds: mde rest: skipped clr 2f out: wl in command after: readily* **11/4**[1]	82+
6	2	1 ¼	**Theturnofthesun (IRE)**[15] 6334 2-9-3 0 .... RobertHavlin 10 (John Gosden) *hld up bhd ldrs: plld out and effrt over 2f out: styd on fr over 1f out: wnt 2nd ins fnl f and briefly threatened to cl: wl hld nr fin* **9/1**	79+
04	3	3 ½	**Mr Churchill (IRE)**[16] 6300 2-9-3 0 .... AhmedAjtebi 4 (Mahmood Al Zarooni) *hld up in last trio: taken wd over 3f out: reminder and prog over 2f out: styd on steadily fr over 1f out to take 3rd nr fin* **9/1**	72
06	4	½	**Pilgrims Rest (IRE)**[11] 6462 2-9-3 0 .... RichardHughes 2 (Richard Hannon) *restrained bhd ldrs: effrt over 2f out: rdn to chse wnr over 1f out: no imp: lost pl and pushed along fnl f* **7/2**[2]	71
0	5	¾	**Bohemian Rhapsody (IRE)**[22] 6160 2-9-3 0 .... SebSanders 3 (J W Hills) *hld up towards rr: shuffled along over 2f out: n.m.r over 1f out: kpt on steadily: possible improver* **8/1**	71+
05	6	nk	**Spanish Fork (IRE)**[10] 6481 2-9-3 0 .... MatthewDavies 8 (Mick Channon) *towards rr: pushed along 3f out: no prog 2f out: rdn and kpt on same pce after* **14/1**	69
00	7	½	**Imperial Stargazer**[11] 6462 2-9-3 0 .... SamHitchcott 9 (Mick Channon) *stdd s and hld up in last: sme prog on inner 3f out: shkn up 2f out: one pce but kpt on* **66/1**	68
433	8	½	**Surrey Storm**[14] 6373 2-8-12 70 .... KierenFallon 7 (Roger Teal) *led 100yds: w wnr to over 2f out: sn outpcd: lost 2nd over 1f out: wkng whn snatched up jst ins fnl f* **8/1**	62
0	9	1 ¾	**Burnham**[11] 6462 2-9-3 0 .... SteveDrowne 11 (Hughie Morrison) *pushed up to press ldng pair: rdn over 2f out: wknd wl over 1f out* **40/1**	63
0	10	1 ¼	**Kaylena**[38] 5655 2-8-12 0 .... JimmyFortune 6 (Jeremy Noseda) *trckd ldrs: pushed along and lost pl 2f out: fdd* **15/2**[3]	56
	11	16	**Sea Fret** 2-8-12 0 .... DarryllHolland 1 (Hughie Morrison) *s.i.s and rn green: a in last trio: wknd 3f out: t.o* **25/1**	24

1m 59.23s (2.93) **Going Correction** +0.175s/f (Good) **11** Ran SP% **117.3**
Speed ratings (Par 97): **93,91,88,88,87 87,86,86,84,83 69**
toteswinger: 1&2 £6.60, 1&3 £6.60, 2&3 £13.60 CSF £27.90 TOTE £3.00: £1.30, £4.00, £2.50; EX 31.80 Trifecta £206.30 Pool: £900.77 - 3.23 winning units..
Owner Hamdan Al Maktoum **Bred** Shadwell Estate Company Limited **Trained** Arundel, W Sussex
■ Stewards' Enquiry : Robert Havlin caution: careless riding

FOCUS
The form looks just fair and the winner was allowed the run of the race, but he still looks decent.

NOTEBOOK
Aazif(IRE) might have run behind a really good one in the shape of Mighty Ambition on his debut, finishing an encouraging fifth in a steadily run maiden over 7f. This more demanding test suited and he was helped by being allowed the lead on a day when front-runners did well. A scopey type, he's a smart long-term staying prospect. (op 2-1 tchd 3-1 in places)
Theturnofthesun(IRE) travelled well, but took a while to pick up and is not surprisingly still learning. He shaped well on his debut at Haydock and should continue to go the right way. (op 14-1)
Mr Churchill(IRE), up a couple of furlongs in trip, was poorly placed turning into the straight but kept on. Nurseries are now an option. (tchd 8-1)
Pilgrims Rest(IRE) was below the form of his first two starts and failed to prove his stamina. (op 4-1)
Bohemian Rhapsody(IRE) was only two places behind today's winner on his debut, but he didn't progress. (tchd 17-2)
Kaylena didn't go on as expected from a promising debut over 7f at Salisbury. Seemingly, she was unsuited by the stamina test. (op 12-1)

6727 GOODWOOD RACEHORSE OWNERS GROUP STKS (H'CAP) (DIV I) 1m
4:45 (4:45) (Class 4) (0-85,85) 3-Y-O+ **£4,204** (£1,251; £625; £312) **Stalls** Low

Form	Pos	Btn	Horse	RPR
4006	1		**Nazreef**[12] 6429 4-9-1 79 ....(bt[1]) DarryllHolland 5 (Hughie Morrison) *blindfold off sltly late and dwlt: sn pushed up and prom: urged along to ld over 5f out: mde rest: drvn and styd on wl fnl 2f* **8/1**[3]	88

0552 **2** *1 3/4* **Compton Blue**[20] 6227 5-8-9 **73**....................(b) DaneO'Neill 14 78
(Richard Hannon) *hld up in midfield and wl in tch: rdn on outer 2f out: styd on fr over 1f out: tk 2nd wl ins fnl f: unable to chal* **12/1**

5030 **3** *nse* **Mahadee (IRE)**[17] 6273 6-9-1 **82**....................(p) HarryBentley(3) 3 88+
(Ed de Giles) *trckd ldrs: prog on inner 2f out to chse wnr wl over 1f out: trying to chal against rail whn no room and checked 150yds out: lost 2nd but kpt on* **16/1**

4204 **4** *1/2* **Satwa Laird**[28] 5969 5-8-10 **74**.................... NeilCallan 12 78
(Ed Dunlop) *hld up in midfield: prog over 2f out: rdn and pressing for 2nd over 1f out: styd on same pce after* **9/1**

4400 **5** *nk* **Moynahan (USA)**[48] 5328 6-9-4 **82**....................(p) ChrisCatlin 1 85+
(Paul Cole) *hld up wl in rr: looking for room over 2f out: stl in last pair whn swtchd lft over 1f out: r.o fnl f: nrst fin* **8/1[3]**

1643 **6** *shd* **Watch Amigo (IRE)**[19] 6239 5-9-6 **84**....................(p) JimCrowley 11 87
(Walter Swinburn) *t.k.h: hld up towards rr: effrt on outer over 2f out: prog over 1f out: sn nt qckn: one pce fnl f* **7/1[2]**

0550 **7** *1/2* **Chosen Character (IRE)**[29] 5920 3-8-11 **78**..........(vt) StephenCraine 9 80
(Tom Dascombe) *s.s: hld up in last: kpt covered up and swtchd ins 2f out: shkn up and styd on fr over 1f out: nvr rchd ldrs* **14/1**

065 **8** *nk* **Rock Anthem (IRE)**[20] 6226 7-8-4 **71** oh2.................... KieranO'Neill(3) 10 72
(Mike Murphy) *dropped in fr wd draw and hld up wl in rr: prog on inner over 2f out: chsd ldrs over 1f out: one pce after* **8/1[3]**

4005 **9** *1 3/4* **Follow The Flag (IRE)**[6] 6583 7-8-4 **71** oh3....................(p) JohnFahy(3) 8 69
(Alan McCabe) *trckd ldrs: rdn to dispute 2nd wl over 1f out: nt qckn sn after: losing pl whn hmpd and snatched up 50yds out* **18/1**

4-04 **10** *4* **Menadati (USA)**[12] 6435 3-8-8 **75**.................... WilliamCarson 2 66
(Peter Hiatt) *dwlt: hld up wl in rr: effrt over 2f out: sme prog over 1f out: styng on but no ch whn short of room ins fnl f: eased* **12/1**

4100 **11** *2 1/4* **Miss Bootylishes**[15] 6330 6-8-8 **77**.................... DavidKenny(5) 7 60
(Paul Burgoyne) *prom: lost pl over 2f out: wknd over 1f out* **28/1**

5145 **12** *6* **Silverware (USA)**[22] 6167 3-8-11 **78**.................... RichardHughes 4 47
(Richard Hannon) *led to over 5f out: chsd wnr to wl over 1f out: losing pl whn n.m.r after: eased* **7/2[1]**

100 **13** *28* **Soweto Star (IRE)**[10] 6477 3-8-13 **80**.................... LukeMorris 6 —
(John Best) *prom: disp 2nd 3f out: wknd rapidly over 2f out: virtually p.u fnl f* **14/1**

1m 40.94s (1.04) **Going Correction** +0.175s/f (Good)
WFA 3 from 4yo+ 3lb **13** Ran SP% **121.4**
Speed ratings (Par 105): **101,99,99,98,98 98,97,97,95,91 89,83,55**
toteswinger: 1&2 £20.10, 1&3 £19.80, 2&3 £40.20 CSF £102.16 CT £1557.65 TOTE £8.90: £3.20, £3.00, £5.70; EX 141.20 Trifecta £453.10 Part won. Pool of £612.32 - 0.64 winning units..

Owner Deborah Collett & M J Watson **Bred** M J Watson **Trained** East Ilsley, Berks

FOCUS
The time was 0.73 seconds slower than the second leg. They didn't go that quick and there was another front-running winner, although it wasn't straightforward for Nazreef. The runner-up has been rated as running his best race since his reappearance, while the third has been rated as likely to have run to form had he had a clear run.
Mahadee(IRE) Official explanation: jockey said that the gelding was denied a clear run
Menadati(USA) ◆ Official explanation: jock said that the gelding was denied a clear run

6728 GOODWOOD RACEHORSE OWNERS GROUP STKS (H'CAP) (DIV II) 1m

5:15 (5:15) (Class 4) (0-85,85) 3-Y-0+ **£4,204** (£1,251; £625; £312) **Stalls** Low

Form RPR

3000 **1** **Byrony (IRE)**[25] 6062 3-8-10 **80**.................... KieranO'Neill(3) 3 91
(Richard Hannon) *trckd ldng pair: prog to ld over 2f out: sn rdn clr: in n.d over 1f out* **16/1**

5012 **2** *3 1/2* **Yojimbo (IRE)**[14] 6374 3-8-12 **79**.................... MatthewDavies 2 82
(Mick Channon) *hld up in 6th: effrt on outer over 2f out: no ch w wnr but styd on to take 2nd nr fin* **4/1[1]**

0004 **3** *1/2* **Marajaa (IRE)**[37] 5687 9-9-0 **78**.................... KierenFallon 10 80
(Willie Musson) *hld up in last quartet and wl off the pce: prog and squeezed through over 2f out: chsd clr wnr wl over 1f out: no imp: lost 2nd last strides* **13/2[3]**

1050 **4** *shd* **My Son Max**[36] 5717 3-8-11 **78**.................... RichardHughes 5 80+
(Richard Hannon) *stdd s: hld up in last quartet: trying to make prog on inner whn hmpd over 2f out and dropped to last: plld out and hrd rdn over 1f out: r.o fnl f: gaining at fin* **8/1**

1005 **5** *nk* **Willow Dancer (IRE)**[20] 6220 7-9-4 **82**....................(p) AdamKirby 11 83+
(Walter Swinburn) *hld up in last and wl off the pce: plld out wd and rdn 2f out: styd on after: nrst fin* **14/1**

0053 **6** *1/2* **Chapter And Verse (IRE)**[17] 6273 5-9-5 **83**.................... TonyCulhane 6 83
(Mike Murphy) *hld up in 9th and wl off the pce: trying to make prog whn hmpd over 2f out: effrt again over 1f out: kpt on same pce fnl f* **9/2[2]**

2210 **7** *hd* **Dare To Bare (IRE)**[6] 6583 3-8-8 **75** ow1....................(b[1]) JimCrowley 9 74
(Amanda Perrett) *chsd ldng trio: drvn and nt qckn over 2f out: disp pls fnl 2f tl wknd last 100yds* **8/1**

0130 **8** *3/4* **Spa's Dancer (IRE)**[22] 6173 4-9-3 **81**.................... SebSanders 8 79
(J W Hills) *hld up in last trio: swtchd to r alone against nr side rail in st and wl bhd: kpt on fr over 1f out* **10/1**

-104 **9** *2 3/4* **Cape Rambler**[19] 6239 3-8-10 **77**.................... DaneO'Neill 7 68
(Henry Candy) *chsd ldr's str pce to 3f out: sn wknd* **12/1**

0030 **10** *shd* **Salient**[14] 6378 7-8-8 **72**.................... KirstyMilczarek 1 63
(Michael Attwater) *pushed along to chse ldng quartet: lost pl over 2f out: sn btn* **20/1**

0060 **11** *1/2* **Judd Street**[99] 3627 9-9-7 **85**....................(t) TomQueally 12 75
(Eve Johnson Houghton) *hld up in 7th and off a str pce: effrt on outer over 2f out: sn no prog: wknd over 1f out* **25/1**

3543 **12** *5* **Chevise (IRE)**[18] 6256 3-8-10 **77**.................... CathyGannon 13 55
(Steve Woodman) *hld up off the pce in 8th: rdn over 3f out: drifted rt over 2f out then n.m.r: sn wknd* **16/1**

3000 **13** *4* **Mountrath**[18] 6254 4-8-4 **71** oh2....................(v) HarryBentley(3) 4 40
(Gary Moore) *won battle for ld and set str pce: hdd over 2f out: wknd rapidly wl over 1f out* **25/1**

1m 40.21s (0.31) **Going Correction** +0.175s/f (Good)
WFA 3 from 4yo+ 3lb **13** Ran SP% **121.4**
Speed ratings (Par 105): **105,101,101,100,100 100,99,99,96,96 95,90,86**
toteswinger: 1&2 £21.20, 1&3 £37.20, 2&3 £7.80 CSF £78.33 CT £487.13 TOTE £28.10: £8.20, £1.60, £2.70; EX 165.50 Trifecta £357.70 Part won. Pool of £483.38 - 0.10 winning units..
Owner Axom XXIII **Bred** Mr & Mrs C Booth **Trained** East Everleigh, Wilts

FOCUS
The time was 0.73 seconds faster than the modestly run first division. The runner-up has been rated close to his best, while the third is forgiven having got no run, along with the fifth, who was wide throughout.

Byrony(IRE) Official explanation: trainer was unable to offer any explanation for the apparent imrprovement of form

6729 GOODWOOD HOTEL STKS (H'CAP) 1m 4f

5:50 (5:50) (Class 5) (0-75,75) 3-Y-0 **£2,587** (£770; £384; £192) **Stalls** High

Form RPR

-356 **1** **Knightly Escapade**[33] 5816 3-9-5 **73**.................... IanMongan 5 82+
(John Dunlop) *trckd ldrs: rdn and prog to go 2nd whn hung rt 2f out: clsd on ldr and drvn to ld last 150yds* **14/1**

-424 **2** *1/2* **Reem Star**[60] 4905 3-9-7 **75**.................... GeorgeBaker 1 83
(Ed Dunlop) *trckd ldrs: looking for room over 2f out: prog to go 3rd wl over 1f out: drvn and styd on: wnt 2nd last strides: nt quite rch wnr* **8/1**

3332 **3** *1/2* **Chatterer (IRE)**[13] 6412 3-9-2 **70**.................... RichardMullen 7 77
(Marcus Tregoning) *led after 1f and set mod pce: kicked on over 3f out: drvn and hdd last 150yds: lost 2nd fnl strides* **7/1**

2260 **4** *4* **Man Of God (IRE)**[16] 6294 3-9-6 **74**.................... RobertHavlin 2 75+
(John Gosden) *dwlt: hld up in last: gng bttr than most 3f out: rdn and prog to take 4th over 1f out: one pce and no imp after* **9/2[2]**

0115 **5** *3/4* **Sharp Relief (IRE)**[22] 6151 3-9-5 **73**.................... DarryllHolland 6 72
(Hughie Morrison) *trckd ldrs: prog to chse ldr 3f out: carried rt and lost 2nd 2f out: sn outpcd* **4/1[1]**

0624 **6** *1/2* **The Calling Curlew**[26] 6023 3-9-2 **70**.................... DaneO'Neill 11 69
(Henry Candy) *hld up in rr: effrt whn nt clr run wl over 2f out: no prog after tl styd on fnl f* **10/1**

4144 **7** *3/4* **Pandorica**[18] 6248 3-9-6 **74**.................... AdamKirby 4 71
(Clive Cox) *chsd ldng pair to 3f out: nt qckn: steadily fdd fnl 2f* **15/2**

531 **8** *2 3/4* **Battery Power**[18] 6255 3-9-6 **74**.................... KierenFallon 9 67
(Mark H Tompkins) *mostly settled towards rr: rdn and effrt on outer 3f out: no prog 2f out: wknd over 1f out* **6/1[3]**

2013 **9** *16* **Around The Clock (USA)**[30] 5897 3-8-11 **65**.................... NeilCallan 10 32
(Amanda Perrett) *led 1f: chsd ldr to 3f out: sn wknd: bhd fnl f* **14/1**

00-6 **10** *17* **Mujarah (IRE)**[114] 3118 3-8-7 **61** oh2.................... TadhgO'Shea 3 —
(John Dunlop) *hld up in last pair: rdn and struggling 4f out: sn wknd: t.o* **16/1**

2m 41.37s (2.97) **Going Correction** +0.175s/f (Good) **10** Ran SP% **116.1**
Speed ratings (Par 101): **97,96,96,93,93 92,92,90,79,68**
toteswinger: 1&2 £18.20, 1&3 £16.80, 2&3 £9.90 CSF £120.68 CT £859.02 TOTE £15.20: £3.40, £2.60, £2.70; EX 134.70 TRIFECTA Not won..
Owner Mrs I H Stewart-Brown & M J Meacock **Bred** M Meacock & The Late I Stewart-Brown **Trained** Arundel, W Sussex

FOCUS
A modest handicap run at a steady pace. The runner-up is generally progressive, while the third has been rated a shade off her best for more positive tactics.
Sharp Relief(IRE) Official explanation: jockey said that the filly hung left
T/Jkpt: Not won. T/Plt: £2,327.20 to a £1 stake. Pool of £106,447.77 - 33.39 winning tickets. T/Qpdt: £124.30 to a £1 stake. Pool of £9,227.29 - 54.90 winning tickets. JN

6730 - 6732a (Foreign Racing) - See Raceform Interactive

6387 CURRAGH (R-H)
Sunday, October 9

OFFICIAL GOING: Straight course - soft; round course - yielding to soft

6733a GO RACING IN KILDARE WATERFORD TESTIMONIAL STKS (LISTED RACE) 6f

3:45 (3:45) 3-Y-0+ **£22,413** (£6,551; £3,103; £1,034)

RPR

1 **Eton Rifles (IRE)**[22] 6147 6-9-4 .... JMurtagh 11 109
(David Elsworth) *trckd ldrs: 3rd 1/2-way: hdwy to ld 2f out: kpt on wl whn chal ins fnl f* **5/4[1]**

2 *3/4* **Seeharn (IRE)**[59] 4976 3-9-0 104.................... DPMcDonogh 12 104
(Kevin Prendergast, Ire) *trckd ldrs: 7th 1/2-way: hdwy between horses to chal early fnl f: kpt on same pce wout making any real imp on wnr* **10/1**

3 *1 1/4* **Cheviot (USA)**[14] 6388 5-9-4 98....................(b) GFCarroll 15 103
(Reginald Roberts, Ire) *prom: led bef 1/2-way: hdd 2f out: 3rd early fnl f: no imp and kpt on one pce* **16/1**

4 *1* **Northern Rocked (IRE)**[36] 5746 5-9-4 100....................(b) PShanahan 16 100
(D K Weld, Ire) *chsd ldrs on stands' side: pushed along in 6th 2f out: 4th 1f out and kpt on same pce* **20/1**

5 *1 1/4* **Gossamer Seed (IRE)**[47] 5361 3-9-0 94....................(t) DMGrant 9 93
(John Joseph Murphy, Ire) *chsd ldrs: 8th 1/2-way: kpt on same pce fnl f wout troubling ldrs* **22/1**

6 *2 1/4* **Batchelors Star (IRE)**[48] 5329 3-9-3 75.................... WJSupple 13 89
(W McCreery, Ire) *settled towards rr: sme hdwy under 2f out: kpt on fnl f wout troubling ldrs* **50/1**

7 *3/4* **Croisultan (IRE)**[22] 6147 5-9-4 106.................... NGMcCullagh 7 86
(Liam McAteer, Ire) *prom: 2nd 1/2-way: 3rd 2f out: no ex fr over 1f out* **8/1[3]**

8 *3 1/4* **Knock Stars (IRE)**[28] 5979 3-9-0 93....................(t) BACurtis 3 73
(Patrick Martin, Ire) *chsd ldrs: no imp in 9th over 1f out: kpt on one pce* **25/1**

9 *1 1/4* **Morache Music**[42] 5532 3-9-3 .... FMBerry 6 72
(Peter Makin) *chsd ldrs: no ex fr wl over 1f out* **9/2[2]**

10 *1 1/2* **Bay Knight (IRE)**[7] 6561 5-9-4 108.................... ShaneFoley 5 67
(K J Condon, Ire) *led early: hdd bef 1/2-way: 4th 2f out: sn no ex* **9/1**

11 *2 1/4* **Blue Dahlia (IRE)**[14] 6388 4-9-1 98.................... WMLordan 2 57
(T Stack, Ire) *chsd ldrs on outer: 6th 1/2-way: no ex fr over 1f out* **20/1**

12 *nk* **Luisant**[7] 6561 8-9-4 99....................(b) KJManning 8 59
(J A Nash, Ire) *chsd ldrs: no ex fr 2f out: eased whn btn fnl f* **25/1**

13 *2* **Simla Sunset (IRE)**[14] 6388 5-9-1 93....................(p) CDHayes 4 49
(P J Prendergast, Ire) *nvr a factor* **33/1**

14 *36* **Katla (IRE)**[22] 6164 3-9-3 105.................... PJSmullen 1 —
(J F Grogan, Ire) *settled in rr: nvr a factor: eased whn btn over 1f out* **8/1[3]**

1m 15.5s (0.50) **Going Correction** +0.375s/f (Good)
WFA 3 from 4yo+ 1lb **14** Ran SP% **136.3**
Speed ratings: **111,110,108,107,105 102,101,97,95,93 90,89,87,39**
CSF £16.32 TOTE £1.70: £1.02, £3.30, £4.80; DF 14.30.
Owner Transcend Bloodstock LLP **Bred** Grangecon Stud **Trained** Newmarket, Suffolk

FOCUS
The winner was the form choice and the placed horses confirm the level.

NOTEBOOK
Eton Rifles(IRE), who had been performing consistently well in handicaps, achieved a first Listed success here with ground conditions to his liking. He raced close to the leaders before edging ahead a furlong and a half out and once in front he was always doing enough to prevail. (op 7/4)

Seeharn(IRE), twice a winner over this trip, was back down in distance having scored her third win at Leopardstown (7f) last month. All her wins were achieved on better ground than she encountered here and, having chased the leaders, she began her effort under 2f out and kept on for pressure throughout the final furlong without quite getting to the winner. (op 9/1)
Cheviot(USA), a dual winner and a consistent performer this season bar on her previous start here when unfavourably drawn, was well drawn and, with blinkers replacing cheekpieces this year, he led and disputed the lead until headed by the winner. He appeared to falter briefly but kept on. (op 20/1)
Northern Rocked(IRE), twice a winner over 7f early this season, was down in trip and acquitted himself well, chasing the leaders and staying on inside the final furlong.
Gossamer Seed(IRE), twice a winner but with plenty on her plate in this company, ran a good race, chasing the leaders and sticking to her task through the final furlong. (op 20/1)

6736a GO RACING IN KILDARE FINALE STKS (LISTED RACE) 1m 4f
5:20 (5:25) 3-Y-0+ **£22,413** (£6,551; £3,103; £1,034)

RPR
1 **Sapphire (IRE)**[28] 5976 3-8-11 107 PJSmullen 11 113+
(D K Weld, Ire) *trckd ldrs: 4th 1/2-way: led 2f out: sn asserted and clr 1f out: kpt on wl: v easily* **5/2**[1]
2 4 3/4 **Kissable (IRE)**[25] 6074 3-8-11 100 CDHayes 5 104
(Kevin Prendergast, Ire) *in rr of mid-div: 9th 1/2-way: sme hdwy into 5th 2f out: wnt mod 2nd 1f out: kpt on same pce but no ch w easy wnr* **11/1**
3 4 1/4 **Amazing Beauty (IRE)**[16] 6319 3-8-11 97 ShaneFoley 3 99
(A P O'Brien, Ire) *mid-div: 8th 1/2-way: hdwy appr st and wnt 3rd 2f out: no ch w easy wnr fr over 1f out: kpt on one pce* **16/1**
4 2 3/4 **Celtic Soprano (IRE)**[21] 6199 6-9-4 99 WJSupple 1 93
(P D Deegan, Ire) *chsd ldrs: 5th 1/2-way: rdn and no imp in 7th early st: kpt on same pce fr over 1f out wout threatening* **16/1**
5 nse **Aoife Alainn (IRE)**[42] 5523 4-9-4 105 DPMcDonogh 10 93
(Tracey Collins, Ire) *hld up in rr: rapid hdwy on inner ent st to join issue: no ch w easy wnr and dropped to 4th 1f out: no ex* **20/1**
6 5 1/2 **What A Charm (IRE)**[25] 6074 4-9-7 105 (p) JMurtagh 6 87
(John M Oxx, Ire) *led and sn clr: reduced advantage 1/2-way: hdd u.p appr st: no imp in 8th 2f out: kpt on one pce* **5/2**[1]
7 8 **Pink Symphony**[70] 4589 4-9-9 103 WMLordan 4 76
(David Wachman, Ire) *chsd ldrs: 6th 1/2-way: sme hdwy to go 4th briefly early st: no ex fr over 1f out* **12/1**
8 3 1/4 **Cape Of Good Grace (IRE)**[25] 6074 3-8-11 95 NGMcCullagh 2 66
(John M Oxx, Ire) *chsd clr ldr: clsr in 3rd 1/2-way: led appr st: hdd u.p 2f out: sn no ex and wknd* **13/2**[2]
9 1 1/2 **Make My Heart Sing (IRE)**[21] 6199 3-8-11 82 GFCarroll 12 64
(A P O'Brien, Ire) *towards rr: nvr a factor: kpt on one pce in st* **50/1**
10 7 1/2 **Swampfire (IRE)**[25] 6074 3-9-0 99 (b) BACurtis 13 55
(John M Oxx, Ire) *chsd ldrs: 8th 1/2-way: no ex early st: wknd* **10/1**[3]
11 4 3/4 **Bancnuanaheireann (IRE)**[14] 6390 4-9-7 99 KJManning 9 47
(J S Bolger, Ire) *a towards rr: nvr a factor* **25/1**
12 5 1/2 **Western Pearl**[70] 4582 4-9-4 FMBerry 8 35
(William Knight) *chsd clr ldr: clsr in 2nd 1/2-way: drvn along and no ex ent st: wknd* **16/1**
13 1 3/4 **Noble Prince (GER)**[168] 6497 7-9-7 JPO'Brien 7 35
(Paul Nolan, Ire) *a bhd: nvr a factor* **14/1**

2m 42.4s (3.90) **Going Correction** +0.525s/f (Yiel)
WFA 3 from 4yo+ 7lb 13 Ran SP% **130.5**
Speed ratings: **108,104,102,100,100 96,91,88,87,82 79,76,74**
Daily Double: Not won. Pick Six: Not won. CSF £36.35 TOTE £2.90: £1.50, £2.80, £6.10; DF 31.00.
Owner Moyglare Stud Farm **Bred** Moyglare Stud Farm Ltd **Trained** The Curragh, Co Kildare

FOCUS
The second, third and fourth all have standout efforts that would see this rated higher, but the race has been rated in line with the rest of their form.

NOTEBOOK
Sapphire(IRE), minus the blinkers she has worn all season for this first attempt over 1m4f, won in good style. Winner of a 1m maiden on the opening day of the Curragh season in March, she has proved consistent and posted her best effort when second in the Group 2 Blandford Stakes over 1m2f here last month. Always handy, she went to the front 2f out and had the race in safe keeping once she went clear approaching the final furlong. She won easily and is to be kept in training next year. All three of her wins have been on ground with plenty of ease. (op 9/4 tchd 2/1)
Kissable(IRE), third in the Group 1 Moyglare Stud Stakes last season, has had a light campaign and, although no match for the winner here, she is worth keeping in mind if she runs again before the end of season. Held up, she began to close into the straight and kept on steadily, going second entering the final furlong, without ever troubling the winner. (op 10/1)
Amazing Beauty(IRE) had been twiced placed in a couple of Group 3 events over the trip this season. She ran a solid race on ground softer than ideal, improving from mid-division before the straight and having every chance 2f out before failing to make much impression from over 1f out.
Celtic Soprano(IRE), well beaten in a handicap since finishing second in a Listed event over 1m4f at Listowel last month, chased the leaders and was staying on from over 1f out having lost his place approaching the straight. (op 14/1)
Aoife Alainn(IRE), a Group 1 winner over 1m2f in Italy last year, had the ground in her favour but was trying a new trip. Held up in rear, she got a clear run through on the inside to dispute the lead early in the straight before appearing not to stay the distance.
T/Jkpt: @375.00. Pool of @5,000.00 - 10 winning units. T/Plt: @51.40. Pool of @27,698.82 - 403.72 winning units. II

6734 - 6735a & 6738a (Foreign Racing) - See Raceform Interactive

6710 BADEN-BADEN (L-H)
Sunday, October 9

OFFICIAL GOING: Turf: soft

6737a PREIS DER WINTERKONIGIN (GROUP 3) (2YO FILLIES) (TURF) 1m
3:20 (12:00) 2-Y-0
£51,724 (£19,827; £9,482; £5,172; £2,586; £1,724)

RPR
1 **Monami (GER)** 2-9-2 0 JBojko 3 100
(A Wohler, Germany) *broke fast: then settled in 3rd trcking ldr: a travelling wl: rdn to ld under 2f out: r.o wl: qcknd clr ins fnl f: comf* **132/10**
2 2 1/2 **Dessau (GER)** 2-9-2 0 APietsch 9 95
(W Hickst, Germany) *settled in 2nd: rdn and r.o wl in st: chsd ldr wout threatening ins fnl f* **211/10**
3 1 3/4 **Paraisa**[38] 2-9-2 0 EPedroza 12 91
(A Wohler, Germany) *settled in midfield travelling wl: shkn up early in st: r.o wl on outer ins fnl f: nrest at fin* **22/5**[2]
4 2 1/2 **Nevada (GER)** 2-9-2 0 AStarke 1 86
(P Schiergen, Germany) *settled towards rr: unable qck early in st: rallied and r.o wl ins fnl f* **23/10**[1]
5 6 **Caitania (IRE)**[40] 5610 2-9-2 0 MaximeGuyon 10 72
(H-W Hiller, Germany) *broke slowly and settled in rr: prog 1/2-way: styd on in st* **6/1**
6 1 **Lights On Me**[36] 2-9-2 0 AHelfenbein 8 70
(H-W Hiller, Germany) *settled in 6th: u.p early in st: no ex* **8/1**
7 4 **Miss Coral (GER)**[43] 2-9-2 0 ADeVries 7 61
(H-W Hiller, Germany) *bkmarker fr s: styd on one pce in st* **89/10**
8 2 1/2 **Flying Star (GER)**[29] 2-9-2 0 DPorcu 13 56
(R Rohne, Germany) *broke wl: racd promly pulling hrd: threatened briefly early in st: sn wknd* **45/1**
9 hd **All For You (GER)** 2-9-2 0 OlivierPeslier 2 55
(T Mundry, Germany) *broke wl: settled in 5th: rdn and sn btn in st* **23/5**[3]
10 6 **Dalida (GER)**[56] 2-9-2 0 FilipMinarik 5 42
(Markus Klug, Germany) *broke fast: sent to ld after 1f: set gd pce: hdd and sn btn under 2f out* **229/10**
U **Reine Liberte (GER)** 2-9-2 0 ASuborics 11 —
(Uwe Ostmann, Germany) *uns rdr at s* **87/10**

1m 40.99s (1.88) 11 Ran SP% **130.4**
WIN (incl. 10 euro stake): 142. PLACES: 39, 64, 25. SF: 6,461.
Owner Gestut Etzean **Bred** Gestut Etzean **Trained** Germany

6569 SAN SIRO (R-H)
Sunday, October 9

OFFICIAL GOING: Turf: good

6739a PREMIO VERZIERE-MEMORIAL ALDO CIRLA (GROUP 3) (3YO+ FILLIES & MARES) (TURF) 1m 2f
3:05 (3:05) 3-Y-0+ **£34,482** (£15,172; £8,275; £4,137)

RPR
1 **Temida (IRE)**[14] 6395 3-8-9 0 MEsposito 2 106
(M G Mintchev, Germany) *settled in 3rd: rdn and styd on 1 1/2f out: grad wore down ldr ins fnl f: led ent fnl 50yds: all out* **19/2**
2 1/2 **Toi Et Moi (IRE)**[32] 5839 4-9-0 0 MircoDemuro 1 105
(P Bary, France) *sn led: 2 l clr ins fnl 2f: sn hrd rdn: hdd ins fnl 50yds: no ex* **47/20**[2]
3 1 1/4 **Not For Sale (GER)**[36] 5749 4-9-0 0 EFrank 4 103
(T Mundry, Germany) *settled in midfield: hdwy u.p over 2f out: r.o fnl f to go 3rd 100yds out: nt rch ldrs* **109/10**
4 1 **She Is Great (IRE)**[105] 4-9-0 0 MRossini 8 101
(B Grizzetti, Italy) *settled in midfield: 6th and pushed along 3f out: kpt on fnl f: nt pce to chal* **84/1**
5 1/2 **Irini (GER)**[55] 5-9-0 0 LManiezzi 10 100
(H J Groschel, Germany) *hld up towards rr: r.o fr 2f out: styd on wl fnl f: nrest at fin* **77/20**[3]
6 nk **Amare**[49] 4-9-0 0 PierantonioConvertino 11 99
(T Mundry, Germany) *trckd ldr: rdn appr 2f out: nt qckn: wknd u.p fnl 1 1/2f* **45/1**
7 1 1/4 **Shamal Sally (USA)**[55] 4-9-0 0 MSrnec 5 96
(Zuzana Kubovicova, Salvador) *w.w towards rr: tk clsr order 3f out: kpt on at one pce fnl f: nvr threatened ldrs* **215/10**
8 shd **Navarra Queen**[49] 5308 3-8-11 0 CristianDemuro 7 98
(P Schiergen, Germany) *chsd ldrs: rdn and nt qckn 2f out: wknd u.p fnl f* **1/1**[1]
9 2 1/4 **Oeuvre D'Art (IRE)**[105] 3449 3-8-9 0 DarioVargiu 6 92
(B Grizzetti, Italy) *w.w in midfield: rdn and no imp fnl 2f* **103/10**
10 1 **Salona (GER)**[58] 5028 3-8-9 0 UmbertoRispoli 3 90
(J-P Carvalho, Germany) *chsd ldrs: lost pl over 2f out: sn btn* **35/1**
11 5 **Lisa's Strong (IRE)**[337] 4-9-0 0 FabioBranca 9 80
(L Polito, Italy) *hld up towards rr: no imp whn rdn over 2f out: eased whn btn fnl f* **31/1**

2m 2.20s (-4.50)
WFA 3 from 4yo+ 5lb 11 Ran SP% **140.9**
WIN (incl. 1 euro stake): 10.49. PLACES: 2.63, 1.95, 3.66. DF: 7.18.
Owner Litex Commerce Ad **Bred** Anne & Gerard Corry **Trained** Germany

6740a PREMIO GRAN CRITERIUM (GROUP 1) (2YO COLTS & FILLIES) (TURF) 1m
3:40 (3:40) 2-Y-0 **£116,379** (£51,206; £27,931; £13,965)

RPR
1 **Nayarra (IRE)**[16] 6296 2-8-8 0 MartinDwyer 1 108
(Mick Channon) *broke wl: chsd clr ldr: shkn up and cut bk ldr over 2f out: led appr fnl f: r.o wl* **207/100**[3]
2 1/2 **Rosa Eglanteria**[15] 6368 2-8-8 0 MircoDemuro 2 107
(B Grizzetti, Italy) *trckd eventual wnr in 3rd: rdn and followed wnr 2f out: r.o fnl f: a hld by wnr* **97/100**[1]
3 nk **Vedelago (IRE)**[112] 3212 2-8-11 0 MEsposito 5 109
(L Polito, Italy) *hld up in rr: hdwy over 2f out: wnt 3rd ins fnl f: kpt on wout qckning* **6/4**[2]
4 2 3/4 **Vola E Va**[98] 2-8-11 0 FabioBranca 3 103
(B Grizzetti, Italy) *w.w: chsd ldrs over 2f out: kpt on at one pce fnl f* **97/100**[1]
5 3 **Lui E La Luna**[14] 2-8-11 0 DarioVargiu 7 96
(B Grizzetti, Italy) *hld up: 5th and effrt appr fnl f: one pce* **97/100**[1]
6 8 **Lo Zoccolo Duro (IRE)**[21] 2-8-11 0 UmbertoRispoli 4 78
(B Grizzetti, Italy) *rdn into clr ld fr the off: 12 l clr over 3f out: rdn and wknd ins fnl 1 1/2f: hdd appr fnl f* **32/1**
7 6 **Royal Approval (ITY)**[21] 2-8-11 0 LManiezzi 6 64
(R Menichetti, Italy) *racd in 4th: rdn and wknd ins fnl 2f* **29/1**

1m 35.7s (-6.40) 7 Ran SP% **231.2**
WIN (incl. 1 euro stake): 3.06. PLACES: 2.06, 2.44. DF: 10.29.
Owner Prince A A Faisal **Bred** Nawara Stud Co Ltd **Trained** West Ilsley, Berks

NOTEBOOK
Nayarra(IRE), third in the Group 3 Oh So Sharp Stakes last time out, broke her maiden on this supposed rise in class. The fifth successive British-trained winner of this Group 1, she led approaching the final furlong and saw out the longer trip well. It's unlikely she'll run again this season.

5981 TABY (R-H)

Sunday, October 9

OFFICIAL GOING: Turf: heavy; dirt: standard

6741a LANWADES STUD STKS (LISTED RACE) (3-5YO FILLIES & MARES) (TURF) 1m

2:27 (12:00) 3-5-Y-O **£19,157** (£9,578; £4,597; £3,065; £1,915)

RPR

1 **La Zona (IRE)**[14] 5-9-3 0 .... FJohansson 2 101
(Wido Neuroth, Norway) **68/10[2]**

2 *2* **Entangle**[14] 5-9-3 0 .... JacobJohansen 4 96
(Arnfinn Lund, Norway) **1/100[1]**

3 *4 1/2* **Match Point (FR)**[56] 5096 5-9-3 0 .... Per-AndersGraberg 1 86
(Niels Petersen, Norway) **238/10**

4 *5* **Gobama**[20] 6219 4-9-3 0 .... EspenSki 3 74
(J W Hills) *broke wl: sn restrained in rr: moved up 3rd after 2f: lost pl over 3f out: sn rdn and btn appr 2f out* **78/10[3]**

5 *shd* **Ede Sensation (SWE)** 3-9-0 0 .... CarlosLopez 5 74
(Patrick Wahl, Sweden) **199/10**

1m 38.4s (98.40)
WFA 3 from 4yo+ 3lb **5 Ran SP% 132.0**
PARI-MUTUEL (all including 1sek stake): WIN 7.84; PLACE 1.45, 1.10; DF 14.85.
Owner Stall Perlen **Bred** Century Farms **Trained** Norway

6462 SALISBURY (R-H)

Monday, October 10

OFFICIAL GOING: Good (good to firm in places; 8.8)

Wind: quite strong against Weather: cloudy with sunny periods

6742 BATHWICK TYRES MAIDEN AUCTION STKS (DIV I) 6f 212y

1:50 (1:52) (Class 5) 2-Y-O **£2,264** (£673; £336; £168) **Stalls** Centre

Form RPR

0 **1** **Keepax**[24] 6123 2-8-10 0 .... ChrisCatlin 10 73+
(Chris Wall) *mid-div: hdwy 2f out: sn rdn: nt clr run whn swtchd lft jst over 1f out: r.o wl to ld fnl 30yds* **14/1**

4 **2** *nk* **Dutch Master**[13] 6432 2-8-10 0 .... JimmyFortune 9 72
(Andrew Balding) *prom: rdn to ld over 2f out: edgd lft and narrowly hdd jst ins fnl f: kpt on* **10/3[2]**

0063 **3** *nse* **Millibar (IRE)**[18] 6284 2-8-7 67 .... RobertHavlin 6 69
(Nick Littmoden) *trckd ldrs: chal 2f out: sn rdn: led narrowly jst ins fnl f: no ex whn hdd fnl 30yds: lost 2nd fnl stride* **12/1**

0522 **4** *1* **Gifted Dancer**[21] 6222 2-8-0 71 .... AmyScott(5) 7 66
(Henry Candy) *mid-div: rdn to chse ldrs 2f out: nt clr run over 1f out: kpt on but nt pce to chal* **6/4[1]**

03 **5** *2* **Tinzapeas**[16] 6322 2-7-13 0 .... RyanPowell(5) 11 59
(Mick Channon) *trckd ldrs: rdn 2f out: sltly hmpd jst over 1f out: kpt on same pce* **14/1**

6 *3/4* **Feisty Champion (IRE)** 2-8-12 0 .... DaneO'Neill 2 64
(J W Hills) *s.i.s: towards rr: rdn over 2f out: no imp* **33/1**

7 *2* **Indian Blossom** 2-8-3 0 .... JohnFahy(3) 4 53
(Harry Dunlop) *squeezed out sn after s: towards rr: pushed along over 2f out: sme late prog: nvr trbld ldrs* **40/1**

06 **8** *1* **La Sonadora**[18] 6281 2-8-4 0 .... NickyMackay 8 48
(John Spearing) *s.i.s: rdn 3f out: nvr threatened: a towards rr* **100/1**

0 **9** *1* **Run Of The Day**[7] 6581 2-8-1 0 .... HarryBentley(3) 5 46
(Eve Johnson Houghton) *mid-div: pushed along 3f out: wknd jst over 1f out* **50/1**

064 **10** *1 1/2* **Elbow Beach**[24] 6117 2-8-7 70 .... SteveDrowne 3 45
(Dr Jon Scargill) *led: rdn and hdd over 2f out: wknd ent fnl f* **7/1[3]**

11 *2 1/4* **Hardy Plume** 2-8-11 0 .... TadhgO'Shea 1 43
(Denis Coakley) *trckd ldrs: rdn over 2f out: sn wknd* **11/1**

1m 32.34s (3.74) **Going Correction** +0.15s/f (Good) **11 Ran SP% 110.0**
Speed ratings (Par 95): **84,83,83,82,80 79,77,75,74,73 70**
Tote Swingers: 1&2 £17.80, 1&3 £23.10, 2&3 £11.40 CSF £57.40 TOTE £16.90: £4.30, £1.70, £3.70; EX 80.30.
Owner Follow The Flag Partnership **Bred** Follow The Flag Partnership **Trained** Newmarket, Suffolk

FOCUS

The rail was up 16ft off the permanent far-side rail up to the last 6.5f. This looked just a modest juvenile maiden and the time was slow, being 2.23 seconds off the second division.

NOTEBOOK

Keepax hinted at ability in a good 6f Newbury maiden on his debut and stepped up plenty on that form on this rise in trip, helped by a strong ride from Chris Catlin, who only went for the stick three times. He didn't get into the clear until late, but finished well and gave the impression he'll come on again for this, especially when stepped up in trip. (op 18-1)

Dutch Master, who was fourth in a weak race over this trip on soft ground on his debut, might have stepped up a little but this was another ordinary maiden. (op 4-1 tchd 9-2)

Millibar(IRE) did well to finish so close considering she was keen on this step up in trip. Officially rated 67, she looks a reasonable guide to the form. (op 9-1)

Gifted Dancer didn't improve for the step up in trip. Admittedly she didn't get a particularly smooth trip, finding trouble at a crucial stage, but she was one paced when in the clear. (tchd 11-8 and 7-4 in places)

Tinzapeas now has the option of nurseries (op 12-1)

Feisty Champion(IRE), a 15,000euros purchase, is bred to stay well on the dam's side. He was conceding weight all round and showed ability.

6743 BATHWICK TYRES MAIDEN AUCTION STKS (DIV II) 6f 212y

2:20 (2:23) (Class 5) 2-Y-O **£2,264** (£673; £336; £168) **Stalls** Centre

Form RPR

454 **1** **Medieval Bishop (IRE)**[87] 4073 2-8-10 58 .... NickyMackay 4 77
(David Elsworth) *trckd ldrs: rdn whn swtchd to centre wl over 2f out: kpt on to ld briefly ins fnl f: rallied to regain ld on nod line* **16/1**

3 **2** *nse* **No Compromise**[12] 6440 2-8-6 0 .... SteveDrowne 5 73
(Hughie Morrison) *mid-div: pushed along over 4f out: hdwy fr 2f out: led narrowly fnl 120yds: edgd rt: hdd on nod line* **2/1[1]**

65 **3** *1 3/4* **Haafhd Handsome**[33] 5834 2-8-11 0 .... RichardHughes 2 73+
(Richard Hannon) *chsd ldrs tl outpcd 2f out: styd on again ins fnl f* **10/1**

6 **4** *hd* **Pawprints (IRE)**[32] 5854 2-8-7 0 .... ChrisCatlin 1 69
(William Haggas) *towards rr pushed along 4f out: hdwy fr 2f out: styd on fnl f* **16/1**

3332 **5** *1/2* **Serene Oasis (IRE)**[15] 6380 2-8-8 71 .... TonyCulhane 8 69
(Mick Channon) *sn led: rdn whn chal 2f out: hdd fnl 120yds: no ex* **5/1[3]**

0 **6** *2 1/4* **Malih**[23] 6165 2-8-9 0 .... JimCrowley 9 64
(Peter Makin) *hld up towards rr: rdn over 2f out: styd on fr over 1f out: nvr trbld ldrs* **20/1**

7 *2* **Intransigent** 2-8-9 0 .... JimmyFortune 10 58
(Andrew Balding) *little slowly away: sn trcking ldrs: chal over 2f out: sn rdn: fdd ent fnl f* **9/2[2]**

205 **8** *2* **Rafaella**[52] 5232 2-8-3 65 .... JohnFahy(3) 7 50
(Harry Dunlop) *prom for 3f: chsd ldrs: rdn over 2f out: wknd ent fnl f* **18/1**

43 **9** *31* **Theresnoneedfordat (IRE)**[45] 5424 2-8-11 0 .... KierenFallon 3 —
(Lydia Pearce) *led early: prom tl wknd over 2f out: t.o* **5/1[3]**

0 **10** *nk* **Ladram Bay (IRE)**[11] 6480 2-8-6 0 .... TadhgO'Shea 6 —
(Jonathan Portman) *struggling 1/2-way: a towards rr* **100/1**

1m 30.11s (1.51) **Going Correction** +0.15s/f (Good) **10 Ran SP% 116.7**
Speed ratings (Par 95): **97,96,94,94,94 91,89,87,51,51**
Tote Swingers: 1&2 £7.90, 1&3 £15.40, 2&3 £6.40 CSF £48.31 TOTE £16.10: £3.20, £1.40, £1.90; EX 61.70.
Owner Mrs S Johnson **Bred** Keatly Overseas Ltd **Trained** Newmarket, Suffolk

FOCUS

The time was 2.23 seconds faster than the first leg, and it was the second quickest of the six races at this trip.

NOTEBOOK

Medieval Bishop(IRE), up in trip, improved on his first three efforts on his debut for a new trainer after 87 days off. He should make a fair handicapper. (op 20-1)

No Compromise seemed to run below the form she showed when third on Polytrack first time out. She looked the winner when edging ahead late on - touching 1.01 on Betfair - but she was worried out of it, quite possibly not helped by a lack of whip action. (op 3-1 tchd 10-3)

Haafhd Handsome was up in trip, but still lacked the pace to hold his position and was going a stride quicker than he wanted to throughout. He was given a persistent ride, though, and finished well. There's a good deal of stamina on the dam's side and he can win a nursery/handicap when upped in trip. (op 9-1 tchd 8-1)

Pawprints(IRE) ran green on her debut at Epsom and needed this further experience. She was under pressure a fair way out, but kept on gradually. (tchd 14-1)

Serene Oasis(IRE) had finished in the top three in her first five starts, but she didn't see her race out this time. (op 6-1 tchd 9-2)

Malih still looked green, but made late progress and has ability. (op 18-1 tchd 16-1)

Intransigent has already been gelded and he was well held, although his SP suggests better was expected. (op 7-2 tchd 11-2)

Theresnoneedfordat(IRE) Official explanation: jockey said that the colt moved poorly throughout

6744 BATHWICK TYRES MAIDEN FILLIES' STKS (DIV I) 6f 212y

2:50 (2:53) (Class 5) 2-Y-O **£2,264** (£673; £336; £168) **Stalls** Centre

Form RPR

0 **1** **Afnoon (USA)**[39] 5655 2-9-0 0 .... TadhgO'Shea 14 72
(John Dunlop) *hld up towards rr: hdwy fr 3f out: shkn up to ld ent fnl f: styd on wl: rdn out* **33/1**

2 *1 1/4* **Scarlet Belle** 2-8-7 0 .... KatiaScallan(7) 11 69
(Marcus Tregoning) *trckd ldr: pushed into ld over 1f out: hdd ent fnl f: kpt on but sn hld by wnr* **25/1**

3 *1* **Sweet Ophelia** 2-9-0 0 .... FrankieDettori 5 67+
(George Baker) *hld up towards rr: swtchd to centre whn rdn and hdwy fr 2f out: styd on to go 3rd ins fnl f: nrst fin* **15/2**

0 **4** *1* **Aiaam Al Wafa (IRE)**[12] 6440 2-9-0 0 .... RichardMullen 1 64
(David Lanigan) *mid-div: rdn 2f out: little imp tl styd on fnl f* **16/1**

5 **5** *3/4* **Wye Valley**[34] 5813 2-9-0 0 .... JimCrowley 9 62
(Amanda Perrett) *trckd ldr: chal 2f out: sn rdn: kpt on same pce fnl f* **11/2[3]**

6 *1 1/4* **Dreams Of Fire (USA)** 2-9-0 0 .... RyanMoore 3 64+
(Sir Michael Stoute) *trckd ldrs: trying to mount chal whn nt clr run wl over 1f out: nt clr run again ent fnl f: no ch after* **7/2[2]**

7 *1/2* **Blonde (IRE)** 2-9-0 0 .... RichardHughes 12 58+
(Richard Hannon) *mid-div: hdwy over 3f out: rdn to chal 2f out: fdd ent fnl f* **10/3[1]**

8 *nk* **Bramshill Lass** 2-9-0 0 .... PatCosgrave 10 57
(Amanda Perrett) *rdn over 2f out: short of room over 1f out: nvr bttr than mid-div* **66/1**

9 *hd* **Mabel's Song** 2-9-0 0 .... DaneO'Neill 6 56
(Henry Candy) *in tch tl outpcd 2f out: styd on fnl f but nvr any danger* **16/1**

10 *1/2* **Glaze** 2-9-0 0 .... SteveDrowne 2 55
(Hughie Morrison) *s.i.s: towards rr: sme hdwy over 2f out: no further imp fr over 1f out* **20/1**

11 *1 1/4* **Wicked Wench** 2-9-0 0 .... MarkLawson 7 52
(Jo Hughes) *in tch: rdn 3f out: wknd over 1f out* **50/1**

12 *1/2* **White Flight** 2-9-0 0 .... StephenCraine 13 50
(Jonathan Portman) *s.i.s: towards rr: hdwy over 3f out: sn rdn: wknd over 1f out* **80/1**

5 **13** *shd* **Royale Ransom**[21] 6215 2-8-11 0 .... JohnFahy(3) 8 50
(Clive Cox) *led: rdn 2f out: sn hdd: wknd fnl f* **15/2**

0 **14** *1* **Castalian Spring (IRE)**[21] 6215 2-9-0 0 .... KierenFallon 4 47
(Walter Swinburn) *swtchd to centre whn rdn over 2f out: a towards rr* **20/1**

1m 32.17s (3.57) **Going Correction** +0.15s/f (Good) **14 Ran SP% 117.0**
Speed ratings (Par 92): **85,83,82,81,80 79,78,78,77,77 75,75,75,74**
Tote Swingers: 1&2 £38.80, 1&3 £38.80, 2&3 £12.90 CSF £650.87 TOTE £36.00: £10.30, £7.10, £3.10; EX 1197.10.
Owner Hamdan Al Maktoum **Bred** Shadwell Farm LLC **Trained** Arundel, W Sussex

FOCUS

The time was comparatively modest, suggesting they didn't go that quick. The bare form looks pretty ordinary.

NOTEBOOK

Afnoon(USA) beat only one rival in a 17-runner maiden over C&D on her debut and this represented significant improvement. Considering the rate of progression from her first start, it's possible there's a lot more to come and she should make a nice 3yo. (op 28-1)

Scarlet Belle, a 50,000gns half-sister to five winners, including some pattern performers, had a 7lb claimer up for her debut and was dismissed in the market, but she showed plenty of ability. (tchd 22-1)

Sweet Ophelia, whose sales price increased to 24,000gns, is a half-sister to five winners, including Tiger Reigns (useful 6f-1m), and she stayed on from well off the pace. She should improve enough to win a similar race. (op 11-2)

Aiaam Al Wafa(IRE) stepped up on her Kempton debut and should find her level once handicapped, probably over further. (op 14-1)

Wye Valley didn't progress as expected from a promising debut on the Lingfield Polytrack and that race is not working out. Maybe she's one for handicaps. (op 5-1 tchd 6-1)

Dreams Of Fire(USA) ♦, who is closely related to the stable's Derby winner Kris Kin, is a lot better than she was able to show as he was continually short of room when having something to offer in the closing stages. She can leave this form behind. (op 9-2 tchd 5-1)

Blonde(IRE) ◆, a 60,000gns yearling, has some size but needed the run. She wasn't given anything close to a hard ride and significant improvement is expected. Her trainer's juveniles are winning at a strike-rate of around 22% second time out this season. (op 5-1)
Mabel's Song was keeping on quite nicely in the closing stages without getting a hard ride and can improve plenty. (op 14-1)

6745 BATHWICK TYRES MAIDEN FILLIES' STKS (DIV II) 6f 212y
3:25 (3:27) (Class 5) 2-Y-0 **£2,264** (£673; £336; £168) **Stalls** Centre

Form RPR

0 **1** **Operettist**[12] 6440 2-9-0 0 RichardHughes 9 74+
(Richard Hannon) *mid-div: hdwy 2f out: chal jst over 1f out: tk narrow advantage fnl 120yds: nudged out* **3/1**[1]

44 **2** *hd* **Traveller's Tales**[21] 6215 2-9-0 0 RyanMoore 7 73+
(Richard Hannon) *trckd ldrs: led 2f out: sn rdn whn hrd pressed: narrowly hdd fnl 120yds: kpt on* **9/2**[2]

04 **3** *2 1/4* **Altona (IRE)**[11] 6480 2-9-0 0 TonyCulhane 12 67+
(Mick Channon) *hld up towards rr: pushed along and hdwy fr 2f out: rdn and styd on fnl f but nvr rching front pair* **12/1**

4 *4* **Present Day** 2-9-0 0 RichardMullen 14 57+
(Clive Cox) *in tch: effrt 2f out: styd on same pce fnl f* **18/1**

5 *1/2* **Easter Diva (IRE)** 2-9-0 0 PatCosgrave 1 59+
(Amanda Perrett) *slowly away: sn mid-div: nt clr run on rails wl over 1f out: styd on fnl f* **66/1**

6 *1/2* **Brief Chat (USA)** 2-9-0 0 JimCrowley 6 54
(Amanda Perrett) *trckd ldrs: effrt over 2f out: sn one pce* **16/1**

6 **7** *1 1/4* **Princess Maya**[23] 6165 2-9-0 0 ChrisCatlin 5 51
(Jo Crowley) *led for 1f: trckd ldr: rdn and ev ch briefly 2f out: fdd fnl f* **9/2**[2]

8 *shd* **Amy Dorrit** 2-9-0 0 RobertHavlin 13 59+
(John Gosden) *s.i.s: sn swtchd to far side rails fr wd draw: towards rr: hdwy over 2f out: styng on whn nt clr run 2f out: hmpd on rails jst over 1f out: nt rcvr: improve* **7/1**[3]

9 *shd* **Supaheart** 2-9-0 0 SteveDrowne 11 50
(Hughie Morrison) *sn nudged along towards rr: nvr any real imp on ldrs* **20/1**

10 *3/4* **Thawabel (IRE)** 2-9-0 0 TadhgO'Shea 4 49+
(Marcus Tregoning) *hld up towards rr: sme hdwy whn nt clr run over 2f out tl swtchd lft wl over 1f out: sn rdn: no further imp* **16/1**

11 *3 1/4* **Adelindus** 2-9-0 0 KierenFallon 2 42
(Walter Swinburn) *wnt lft leaving stalls: trckd ldrs: rdn 2f out: styng on at same pce and hld whn squeezed out jst ins fnl f* **14/1**

12 *17* **Time For A Tiger** 2-9-0 0 DaneO'Neill 3 —
(Henry Candy) *a towards rr* **16/1**

0 **13** *3 1/2* **Gentle Sands**[17] 6291 2-8-11 0 JohnFahy(3) 10 —
(Clive Cox) *plld hrd: sn led: rdn and hdd jst over 2f out: sn wknd* **28/1**

1m 31.13s (2.53) **Going Correction** +0.15s/f (Good) **13** Ran SP% **120.8**
Speed ratings (Par 92): **91,90,88,83,83 82,81,80,80,79 76,56,52**
Tote Swingers: 1&2 £2.50, 1&3 £10.00, 2&3 £7.20 CSF £15.50 TOTE £5.40: £1.40, £1.20, £5.30; EX 10.70.
Owner Longview Stud & Bloodstock Ltd **Bred** Longview Stud & Bloodstock Ltd **Trained** East Everleigh, Wilts

FOCUS
An ordinary fillies' maiden.

NOTEBOOK
Operettist hinted at ability on her Polytrack debut and improved a good deal with Richard Hughes taking over, justifying strong market support in the process. She wasn't given a hard time after travelling best and can step forward again, with further set to suit in time. (op 4-1)
Traveller's Tales, a stablemate of the winner, stepped up a little on her first two performances. She's now eligible for a handicap mark. (op 6-1 tchd 4-1)
Altona(IRE) stayed on from off the pace without matching the front pair. She's going the right way and should find her level in handicaps, maybe over 1m. (op 14-1)
Present Day, a 40,000gns purchase who is closely related to very useful 7f-1m2f performer Auld Burns and smart 7f-1m1f winner Pickle, fared best of the newcomers. She should improve enough to win a similar race. (op 16-1)
Easter Diva(IRE) ◆ didn't have much room in the closing stages and was unlucky not to go quite a bit closer. She has plenty of size and a lot better is expected next time.
Brief Chat(USA), who went off a shorter price than her stable-companion who finished just ahead of her, should come on for the run.
Princess Maya didn't build on the form she showed on her debut at Newbury. This was a bit disappointing. (tchd 4-1 and 5-1)
Amy Dorrit, a 50,000gns purchase, missed the break and was then continually blocked against the far rail in the closing stages, otherwise she would have finished quite a bit closer. (tchd 8-1)
Thawabel(IRE) Official explanation: jockey said that the filly was denied a clear run

6746 BATHWICK TYRES BOURNEMOUTH H'CAP 6f 212y
4:00 (4:01) (Class 6) (0-60,60) 3-Y-0+ **£1,940** (£577; £288; £144) **Stalls** Centre

Form RPR

0402 **1** **Caldermud (IRE)**[26] 6071 4-9-7 60 (t) SteveDrowne 11 72
(Olivia Maylam) *mid-div: hdwy over 2f out: rdn to ld over 1f out: kpt on wl to assert towards fin* **8/1**

2542 **2** *2 1/4* **Annes Rocket (IRE)**[11] 6488 6-9-7 60 (p) RichardHughes 3 68+
(Jimmy Fox) *bmpd leaving stalls: patiently rdn in rr: smooth hdwy fr 2f out: trckd wnr ent fnl f: sn shkn up for effrt: flattered briefly: no ex towards fin* **4/1**[1]

0605 **3** *6* **Rio Royale (IRE)**[25] 6090 5-9-0 53 (v) JimCrowley 14 43
(Amanda Perrett) *racd alone in centre most of way: roughly mid-div: rdn over 2f out: edgd rt: styd on same pce: wnt 3rd towards fin* **12/1**

5263 **4** *1/2* **Anrheg**[7] 6578 3-8-13 54 DaneO'Neill 5 42
(David Brown) *chsd ldrs: pushed along fr 1/2-way: rdn over 2f out: styd on same pce* **15/2**

0301 **5** *1 1/4* **One Cool Chick**[19] 6258 3-9-2 57 NeilChalmers 9 42
(John Bridger) *mid-div: rdn over 2f out: styd on same pce* **20/1**

0253 **6** *3/4* **Pose (IRE)**[14] 6408 4-9-2 60 (t) MatthewLawson(5) 10 43
(Roger Ingram) *prom: led over 2f out: sn rdn: edgd lft and hdd over 1f out: fdd ins fnl f* **16/1**

0505 **7** *1* **Silly Billy (IRE)**[31] 5901 3-9-0 55 StephenCraine 4 35
(Sylvester Kirk) *hld up towards rr: sme prog u.p over 2f out: nvr trbld ldrs* **25/1**

0301 **8** *1 3/4* **Choose The Moment**[14] 6407 3-9-5 60 (b) RichardMullen 12 36
(Eve Johnson Houghton) *mid-div: rdn over 2f out: wknd ent fnl f* **16/1**

-033 **9** *nk* **Qaraqum (USA)**[14] 6411 4-8-13 55 JohnFahy(3) 7 30
(Denis Coakley) *hmpd leaving stalls: towards rr: struggling 3f out: nvr a factor* **9/2**[2]

6332 **10** *1/2* **Doctor Hilary**[32] 5843 9-9-2 55 (v) ChrisCatlin 1 28
(Mark Hoad) *led tl rdn over 2f out: wknd fnl f* **10/1**

6000 **11** *2 1/2* **Spring Buck (IRE)**[6] 6610 6-8-9 53 RyanPowell(5) 6 20
(Paul Cole) *mid-div: rdn over 2f out: wknd ent fnl f* **28/1**

6006 **12** *3/4* **Dolly Parton (IRE)**[19] 6250 3-9-2 60 (v) HarryBentley(3) 2 25
(John Bridger) *chsd ldrs: rdn over 2f out: wknd over 1f out* **50/1**

0666 **13** *nk* **Whoateallthepius (IRE)**[30] 5939 3-8-12 60 PaulBooth(7) 8 24
(Dean Ivory) *fly-jmpd leaving stalls: trckd ldrs: rdn over 2f out: sn wknd* **28/1**

4313 **14** *10* **Beautiful Lando (FR)**[23] 6179 3-9-5 60 (b) KierenFallon 13 —
(Heather Main) *trckd ldrs: effrt over 2f out: wknd over 1f out* **6/1**[3]

1m 30.6s (2.00) **Going Correction** +0.15s/f (Good)
WFA 3 from 4yo+ 2lb **14** Ran SP% **121.4**
Speed ratings (Par 101): **94,91,84,84,82 81,80,78,78,77 74,73,73,62**
Tote Swingers: 1&2 £20.00, 1&3 £63.90, 2&3 £24.20 CSF £37.81 CT £404.09 TOTE £12.10: £3.30, £2.20, £5.70; EX 34.90.
Owner Miss Olivia Maylam **Bred** P J B O Callaghan **Trained** Epsom, Surrey

FOCUS
A moderate handicap. The winner found a bit more on recent form.

6747 BATHWICK TYRES FREE ADMISSION RACEDAY CONDITIONS STKS 6f 212y
4:30 (4:31) (Class 3) 3-Y-0+ **£6,663** (£1,982; £990; £495) **Stalls** Centre

Form RPR

212- **1** **Ecliptic (USA)**[458] 3868 3-9-0 105 FrankieDettori 4 111+
(Mahmood Al Zarooni) *wnt to post early: sweating: settled in last: swtchd lft and hdwy fr 2f out: shkn up over 1f out: qcknd up wl to ld ins fnl f: comf* **5/4**[1]

2050 **2** *3 1/4* **Mon Cadeaux**[42] 5563 4-9-2 97 JimmyFortune 7 102
(Andrew Balding) *awkward leaving stalls: hld up: hdwy over 2f out: rdn to ld briefly ins fnl f: kpt on but nt pce of wnr* **15/2**

000 **3** *2* **Atlantis Star**[37] 5704 4-8-11 95 AntiocoMurgia(5) 9 97
(Mahmood Al Zarooni) *mid-div: hdwy 3f out: rdn to dispute ld over 2f out tl hdd and no ex ins fnl f* **25/1**

0000 **4** *1 3/4* **Oasis Dancer**[128] 2706 4-9-2 95 JimCrowley 3 92
(Ralph Beckett) *trckd ldrs: rdn to dispute ld fr over 2f out tl hdd and no ex ins fnl f* **20/1**

-060 **5** *nse* **Mabait**[235] 586 5-9-7 110 KierenFallon 10 97
(Luca Cumani) *slowly away: sn mid-div: hdwy over 2f out: rdn for str chal fr 2f out tl no ex ins fnl f* **9/2**[2]

0405 **6** *1* **Inler (IRE)**[42] 5563 4-9-2 103 (b[1]) RichardHughes 6 89
(Brian Meehan) *mid-div: rdn over 2f out: nt pce to get involved* **11/2**[3]

-034 **7** *6* **Lord Zenith**[74] 4456 4-9-7 100 SteveDrowne 2 78
(Andrew Balding) *wnt to post early: prom for over 3f: chsd ldrs: rdn over 2f out: wknd jst over 1f out* **14/1**

-232 **8** *6* **Al Aasifh (IRE)**[27] 6027 3-9-5 99 (p) RichardMullen 1 62
(Saeed Bin Suroor) *chsd ldrs: rdn over 2f out: wknd over 1f out* **14/1**

6101 **9** *13* **Polar Annie**[67] 4707 6-8-11 80 DaneO'Neill 5 17
(Malcolm Saunders) *sn led: rdn and hdd over 2f out: wknd over 1f out* **28/1**

6560 **10** *7* **Simpulse**[64] 4828 3-8-9 48 ChrisCatlin 8 —
(Norma Twomey) *trckd ldrs: rdn over 2f out: sn wknd* **200/1**

1m 28.06s (-0.54) **Going Correction** +0.15s/f (Good)
WFA 3 from 4yo+ 2lb **10** Ran SP% **115.7**
Speed ratings (Par 107): **109,105,103,101,100 99,92,86,71,63**
Tote Swingers: 1&2 £3.60, 1&3 £11.60, 2&3 £47.40 CSF £10.67 TOTE £2.40: £1.30, £3.00, £6.50; EX 12.20.
Owner Godolphin **Bred** Darley **Trained** Newmarket, Suffolk

FOCUS
A good conditions race. The time was easily the quickest of the six 7f races, which was no surprise. With dounts over most of these, the race has been rated loosely around the runner-up.

NOTEBOOK
Ecliptic(USA), absent since finishing a close second in the Group 2 Superlative Stakes last July, won like a class act on his return. He was ridden with a lot of confidence by Frankie Dettori and quickened well when asked. There are plenty of opportunities for him at around 1m in Dubai next year. (op 6-4 tchd 7-4 in places and 15-8 in a place)
Mon Cadeaux would have been 8lb better off with the winner in a handicap. He simply ran into a Group horse. (op 8-1 tchd 9-1)
Atlantis Star, the owner's third string on colours, had a bit to find in this company (officially rated just 95), but he performed with credit. (op 40-1)
Oasis Dancer, without the blinkers, had a tough task on these terms and had been off for 128 days.
Mabait didn't run anywhere near his official mark of 110 on his return from 235 days away. (op 7-2)
Inler(IRE) was a bit free in first-time blinkers and certainly didn't improve for the headgear. (op 5-1 tchd 6-1)
Lord Zenith Official explanation: jockey said that the gelding hung right

6748 BATHWICK TYRES SALISBURY H'CAP 1m 1f 198y
5:00 (5:03) (Class 5) (0-70,70) 3-Y-0 **£2,264** (£673; £336; £168) **Stalls** Low

Form RPR

3430 **1** **Orthodox Lad**[30] 5938 3-9-4 70 KierenFox(3) 13 77
(John Best) *trckd ldr: led over 3f out: rdn over 2f out: hdd ent fnl f: rallied u.p to regain ld fnl 120yds: hld on: all out* **15/2**

1455 **2** *shd* **Oetzi**[21] 6227 3-9-0 66 HarryBentley(3) 3 73
(Alan Jarvis) *trckd ldrs: ev ch whn rdn 2f out: disputing 2nd ent fnl f: styd on towards fin: jst failed* **6/1**[2]

0246 **3** *3/4* **Swift Blade (IRE)**[32] 5856 3-9-5 68 RichardHughes 8 74
(Lady Herries) *in tch: hdwy 3f out to trck ldrs: rdn for str chal ent fnl f: tended to lean rt: no ex nring fin* **13/2**[3]

0056 **4** *1* **Miss Chicane**[21] 6227 3-9-1 67 JohnFahy(3) 4 71
(Walter Swinburn) *mid-div: hdwy 3f out: pushed along to ld ent fnl f: wandered: swished tail and hdd fnl 120yds: no ex* **20/1**

-033 **5** *2 3/4* **Rocky Rebel**[34] 5816 3-9-6 69 (p) JimCrowley 5 67
(Ralph Beckett) *led for 1f: trckd ldr: rdn over 2f out: styd on same pce* **9/1**

545 **6** *3 1/4* **Madam Tessa (IRE)**[45] 5429 3-8-13 62 NeilChalmers 6 54
(Bryn Palling) *mid-div: rdn 3f out: styd on same pce* **66/1**

4430 **7** *1 3/4* **Spade**[80] 4275 3-9-0 63 (b) NickyMackay 7 51
(David Elsworth) *wnt to post early: hld up towards rr: hdwy 3f out: rdn 2f out: wknd fnl f* **25/1**

-564 **8** *14* **Spanish Pride (IRE)**[12] 6457 3-9-6 69 JimmyFortune 9 29
(John Dunlop) *hld up towards rr: rdn 3f out: nvr threatened: eased whn btn fnl f* **3/1**[1]

2043 **9** *6* **Mini's Destination**[52] 5231 3-8-11 65 MatthewLawson(5) 14 13
(John Holt) *mid-div: effrt 3f out: wknd 2f out* **16/1**

504 **10** *34* **Maloof**[11] 6475 3-9-4 67 (b) TadhgO'Shea 12 —
(Roger Varian) *s.i.s: sn swtchd out and pushed along for hdwy: led after 1f: rdn and hdd over 3f out: sn btn* **20/1**

5060 **11** *40* **Rockerfellow**[61] 4908 3-9-3 **66**............................ DaneO'Neill 11 —
(J W Hills) *a bhd: t.o fnl 3f* **50/1**

2m 10.39s (0.49) **Going Correction** -0.125s/f (Firm) **11** Ran SP% **97.1**
Speed ratings (Par 101): **93,92,92,91,89 86,85,74,69,42 10**
Tote Swingers: 1&2 £7.10, 1&3 £7.50, 2&3 £6.10 CSF £33.56 CT £186.03 TOTE £9.50: £3.70, £1.20, £2.70; EX 53.50.
Owner SN Racing II **Bred** S Nunn **Trained** Hucking, Kent
■ The first jockeys were penalised under strict new whip rules, Kieren Fox picking up a 15-day ban and Richard Hughes 5 days.
■ Stewards' Enquiry : Richard Hughes 5-day ban: excessive use of whip (Oct 24-28)
Kieren Fox 15-day ban: excessive use of whip (Oct 24-29, 31, Nov 1-5, 9-11)

FOCUS
Modest form though the winner recorded a personal best.

6749 BATHWICK TYRES "SEASON FINALE" H'CAP — 1m 6f 21y
5:30 (5:33) (Class 4) (0-85,83) 3-Y-O+ **£4,075** (£1,212; £606; £303) **Stalls** Far side

Form — RPR

6026 **1** **High On A Hill (IRE)**[11] 6485 4-9-7 **76**........................ StephenCraine 1 84
(Sylvester Kirk) *trckd ldrs: rdn 3f out: led over 2f out: hrd pressed ins fnl f: hld on gamely: all out* **28/1**

3512 **2** *1/2* **Mazagee (FR)**[17] 6306 3-9-4 **82**............................ RichardMullen 13 89
(David Lanigan) *mid-div: hdwy over 2f out: sn rdn: chsd ldrs over 1f out: str run ent fnl f: hld nring fin* **9/1**

1243 **3** *hd* **Spice Fair**[10] 6499 4-9-10 **79**............................ RichardHughes 12 86
(Mark Usher) *hld up towards rr: hdwy fr 3f out: rdn to chse ldrs 2f out: swtchd rt and ch ins fnl f: styd on* **15/2**[2]

421 **4** *shd* **Miss Topsy Turvy (IRE)**[73] 4515 3-8-10 **74**.................. SteveDrowne 7 81
(John Dunlop) *mid-div: hdwy 3f out: rdn to chse ldrs over 2f out: styd on to chal fnl f: no ex nring fin* **9/1**

0334 **5** *2 1/4* **Ethics Girl (IRE)**[11] 6485 5-9-8 **77**............................ RobertHavlin 2 80
(John Berry) *in tch: rdn over 2f out: disputing cl 2nd jst over 1f out: no ex fnl 100yds* **16/1**

2125 **6** *2 3/4* **Number Theory**[42] 5568 3-8-8 **77**.................... MatthewLawson(5) 11 77
(John Holt) *hld up towards rr: hdwy fr over 3f out: rdn over 2f out: styd on same pce fnl f* **16/1**

0320 **7** *2 3/4* **Huff And Puff**[25] 6103 4-9-11 **80**............................(v) PatCosgrave 6 76
(Amanda Perrett) *trckd ldr: led 6f out: rdn and hdd over 2f out: wknd fnl f* **14/1**

0410 **8** *1/2* **Sherman McCoy**[45] 5448 5-10-0 **83**............................ JamesMillman 4 78
(Rod Millman) *led tl 6f out: upsides ldr: rdn wl over 2f out: sn hld: grad fdd fr over 1f out* **16/1**

5206 **9** *1 3/4* **Sunny Future (IRE)**[60] 4974 5-8-9 **67**............................ JohnFahy(3) 10 60
(Malcolm Saunders) *a towards rr* **25/1**

0015 **10** *4* **Boston Blue**[32] 5857 4-9-4 **76**............................ HarryBentley(3) 9 63
(Tony Carroll) *hld up towards rr: rdn 3f out: no imp* **16/1**

0040 **11** *5* **Kitty Wells**[38] 5685 4-9-12 **81**............................ KierenFallon 3 61
(Luca Cumani) *slowly away: a towards rr* **14/1**

1002 **12** *1 1/4* **Galivant (IRE)**[29] 5966 3-9-0 **78**............................ DaneO'Neill 14 56
(J W Hills) *in tch: rdn 3f out: wknd wl over 1f out* **12/1**

225 **13** *2 1/4* **Devoted (IRE)**[16] 6328 3-8-12 **76**............................ JimCrowley 5 51
(Ralph Beckett) *mid-div: rdn over 4f out: wknd over 2f out* **17/2**[3]

0222 **14** *3/4* **Billy Buttons**[19] 6248 3-9-4 **82**............................ JimmyFortune 8 56
(Andrew Balding) *trckd ldrs: effrt over 2f out: wknd wl over 1f out: eased whn btn* **3/1**[1]

3m 3.89s (-3.51) **Going Correction** -0.125s/f (Firm)
WFA 3 from 4yo+ 9lb **14** Ran SP% **119.1**
Speed ratings (Par 105): **105,104,104,104,103 101,100,99,98,96 93,92,91,91**
Tote Swingers: 1&2 £0.00, 1&3 £52.60, 2&3 £8.60 CSF £260.76 CT £2102.50 TOTE £33.80: £11.30, £3.60, £1.80; EX 457.60.
Owner Seahorse Five & Tim Pearson **Bred** Dominic Fagan **Trained** Upper Lambourn, Berks

FOCUS
A fair staying handicap and the form looks sound for a late-season handicap.
Billy Buttons Official explanation: jockey said that the gelding ran too free
T/Plt: £569.00 to a £1 stake. Pool of £48,796.19 - 62.60 winning tickets. T/Qpdt: £100.20 to a £1 stake. Pool of £4,716.77 - 34.80 winning tickets. TM

6586 WINDSOR (R-H)
Monday, October 10

OFFICIAL GOING: Good to firm (9.4)
Wind: Strong, half behind Weather: Fine becoming cloudy

6750 AEGIS TRUST HAGELOU EVENT MAIDEN STKS (DIV I) — 1m 67y
2:00 (2:01) (Class 5) 3-Y-O+ **£1,940** (£577; £288; £144) **Stalls** Low

Form — RPR

452 **1** **Hayaku (USA)**[12] 6459 3-8-12 73............................(bt) RichardKingscote 1 78
(Ralph Beckett) *mde all: shkn up and drew clr 2f out: wl clr fnl f* **11/8**[1]

240 **2** *8* **Russian Affair**[13] 6435 3-9-3 74............................ AndreaAtzeni 2 65
(Roger Varian) *chsd wnr: rdn over 2f out: lft wl bhd sn after: jst hld on for 2nd* **6/1**[3]

3 *shd* **Floating Mountain** 3-8-12 0............................ LukeMorris 8 59+
(William Jarvis) *sn off the pce in rr: rdn over 2f out: hanging lft over 1f out but styd on and nrly snatched 2nd* **18/1**

63 **4** *1 1/2* **Drakes Drum**[29] 5960 3-9-3 0............................ AdamKirby 4 61
(Clive Cox) *t.k.h: trckd ldng pair: shkn up and nt qckn over 2f out: hanging and wl btn over 1f out: lost 3rd ins fnl f* **7/4**[2]

\- **5** *12* **Archelao (IRE)** 3-9-3 0............................ SebSanders 9 33
(Marcus Tregoning) *s.i.s: sn bhd in last: brief effrt 3f out: wknd over 2f out* **12/1**

0 **6** *17* **Cant Sell (IRE)**[7] 6589 3-8-12 0............................ MatthewCosham(5) 11 —
(David Evans) *t.k.h for 1f: pushed along in 4th after: wknd 3f out: t.o* **66/1**

00- **P** **Jan Smuts (IRE)**[402] 5718 3-9-3 0............................ JamieSpencer 6 —
(Brian Meehan) *in rr whn rel to r bnd over 5f out and p.u* **20/1**

1m 42.46s (-2.24) **Going Correction** -0.25s/f (Firm) **7** Ran SP% **112.0**
Speed ratings (Par 103): **101,93,92,91,79 62,—**
Tote Swingers: 1&2 £2.10, 1&3 £5.20, 2&3 £11.30 CSF £9.90 TOTE £2.50: £1.30, £1.40; EX 10.70 Trifecta £71.20 Pool: £555.69 - 5.77 winning units..
Owner G B Partnership **Bred** George Strawbridge & London Thoroughbred Services **Trained** Kimpton, Hants

FOCUS
Stands' rail dolled out 4yds at 6f and 1y at Winning Post. Top bend at normal configuration. The first division of a modest 3yo maiden. The winner has been rated to her best with nothing else running its race.
Drakes Drum Official explanation: jockey said that the gelding hung right from three furlongs out
Cant Sell(IRE) Official explanation: jockey said that the gelding had a breathing problem
Jan Smuts(IRE) Official explanation: jockey said that the gelding was unsteerable

6751 E B F "REFUSE TO BEND" MAIDEN STKS — 6f
2:30 (2:31) (Class 5) 2-Y-O **£3,299** (£981; £490; £245) **Stalls** Low

Form — RPR

5243 **1** **Money Never Sleeps**[17] 6292 2-9-3 78............................ WilliamBuick 9 82+
(John Gosden) *trckd ldng trio: prog to ld over 1f out: sn rdn clr* **5/4**[1]

2 *4* **Madgenta (IRE)** 2-8-12 0............................ TomQueally 12 64+
(Richard Hannon) *s.i.s: sn in midfield on outer: shkn up and prog 2f out: styd on to take 2nd ins fnl f: no ch w wnr* **14/1**

0 **3** *1 3/4* **Kylin**[11] 6480 2-8-12 0............................ JamieSpencer 11 59
(Richard Hannon) *led to over 1f out: outpcd by wnr: lost 2nd ins fnl f* **8/1**

33 **4** *3/4* **Mister Mackenzie**[24] 6118 2-9-3 0............................ LukeMorris 4 61
(John Best) *chsd ldr to 2f out: outpcd after* **17/2**

5 *1 1/2* **Flexible Flyer** 2-9-3 0............................ GeorgeBaker 8 56+
(Hughie Morrison) *s.i.s: t.k.h in midfield: outpcd over 2f out: pushed along and kpt on fr over 1f out* **15/2**[3]

6 *1* **Mandianna (IRE)** 2-8-12 0............................ FergusSweeney 7 48
(Jo Crowley) *cl up bhd ldrs tl steadily wknd fr 2f out* **28/1**

7 *1 3/4* **Priceless Jewel** 2-8-12 0............................ JamesDoyle 10 43
(Roger Charlton) *in tch in midfield: pushed along on outer over 2f out: wknd over 1f out* **7/1**[2]

8 *1 1/4* **Tartiflette** 2-8-12 0............................ GrahamGibbons 6 39
(Ed McMahon) *slowest away: wl in rr: outpcd and struggling over 2f out: kpt on fnl f* **12/1**

00 **9** *2* **The Games Gone (IRE)**[17] 6291 2-8-7 0............ MatthewCosham(5) 2 32
(David Evans) *sn dropped to rr: struggling fr 1/2-way: no ch fnl 2f* **100/1**

0 **10** *2* **Surrey Dream (IRE)**[23] 6165 2-9-3 0............................ LiamKeniry 5 31
(Roger Teal) *chsd ldrs 2f: sn dropped to rr and struggling: no ch fnl 2f* **22/1**

60 **11** *35* **Papal Power (IRE)**[9] 6525 2-9-3 0............................ SebSanders 3 —
(J W Hills) *s.i.s: a in rr: no ch over 1f out: eased after and t.o* **66/1**

1m 11.01s (-1.99) **Going Correction** -0.40s/f (Firm) **11** Ran SP% **115.0**
Speed ratings (Par 95): **97,91,89,88,86 85,82,81,78,75 29**
Tote Swingers: 1&2 £6.20, 1&3 £3.70, 2&3 £12.80 CSF £19.86 TOTE £2.20: £1.10, £5.10, £2.80; EX 23.20 Trifecta £110.70 Pool: £610.61 - 4.08 winning units..
Owner Normandie Stud Ltd **Bred** Normandie Stud Ltd **Trained** Newmarket, Suffolk

FOCUS
A modest juvenile maiden.

NOTEBOOK
Money Never Sleeps was faced with fast ground for the first time and seemed to enjoy it. She had the form in the book to win a minor race such as this, but her current rating of 78 means she'll need to improve once switched to handicaps. (op 13-8 tchd 7-4)
Madgenta(IRE), a 50,000gns half-sister to five winners, wasn't best away but travelled up kindly on the outer and should learn plenty from the experience. A similar contest should come her way, with 7f likely to suit.
Kylin improved on her debut effort under a positive ride and is the type to fare better in ordinary handicaps next season. (op 12-1)
Mister Mackenzie clearly has limitations, but shapes as though a stiffer test will suit and he has a future in modest handicaps. (op 13-2)
Flexible Flyer, a 16,000gns half-brother to a 6f winner, wasn't best away and displayed signs of greenness before keeping on late. He ought to improve. (op 6-1)
The Games Gone(IRE) Official explanation: jockey said that the filly lost her action half way

6752 LADBROKES MOBILE H'CAP — 6f
3:05 (3:05) (Class 5) (0-70,70) 3-Y-O+ **£2,264** (£673; £336; £168) **Stalls** Low

Form — RPR

0123 **1** **Oh So Spicy**[26] 6065 4-9-4 **67**............................ GeorgeBaker 16 78
(Chris Wall) *racd wdst of all: trckd ldrs: prog over 2f out: rdn to ld over 1f out: hld on fnl f* **7/2**[1]

0000 **2** *nk* **Seneschal**[11] 6488 10-8-9 **65**............................ RachealKneller(7) 12 75
(Adrian Chamberlain) *cl up on outer: prog to chal over 1f out: pressed wnr fnl f: jst hld* **33/1**

5504 **3** [illegible] **Forty Proof (IRE)**[14] 6403 3-9-4 **68**............................ JamieSpencer 15 7[illegible]
(William Knight) *wl off the pce in last trio: prog on outer over 2f out: styd on wl to take 3rd nr fin* **16/1**

5611 **4** *hd* **Riflessione**[6] 6618 5-9-2 **65** 6ex............................(v) LukeMorris 7 68
(Ronald Harris) *chsd ldrs: rdn over 2f out against nr side rail: prog to chse ldng pair fnl f: nvr able to chal: lost 3rd last strides* **15/2**[3]

0045 **5** *2 1/2* **Bermondsey Bob (IRE)**[5] 6634 5-9-4 **67**.................. SilvestreDeSousa 5 62
(John Spearing) *led to 1/2-way: rdn and struggling to hold pl over 2f out: steadily outpcd* **9/2**[2]

2033 **6** *hd* **Delira (IRE)**[14] 6403 3-9-2 **66**............................ RichardKingscote 2 60
(Jonathan Portman) *w ldr: led 1/2-way to over 1f out: fdd* **16/1**

2300 **7** *hd* **Matavia Bay (IRE)**[61] 4908 3-8-12 **62**............................ FergusSweeney 13 56+
(Alan Jarvis) *wl off the pce in last trio: rdn and stl last 2f out: styd on fnl f: nrst fin* **14/1**

0003 **8** *1/2* **Dvinsky (USA)**[39] 5640 10-8-12 **61**............................(b) WilliamBuick 14 53
(Michael Squance) *prom on outer: rdn over 2f out: fdd over 1f out* **25/1**

2052 **9** *nk* **Diamond Vine (IRE)**[14] 6403 3-9-3 **67**............................(p) JamesDoyle 3 58
(Ronald Harris) *w ldrs: disp ld 1/2-way: rdn over 2f out: wknd over 1f out* **11/1**

5204 **10** *shd* **Memphis Man**[2] 6694 8-8-5 **59**............................ MatthewCosham(5) 10 56+
(David Evans) *s.i.s: wl off the pce in last trio: rdn 2f out: keeping on but no ch whn nt clr run into trble ins fnl f and eased* **10/1**

503 **11** *3 1/2* **Style And Panache (IRE)**[9] 6537 3-9-6 **70**............................ CathyGannon 8 50
(David Evans) *hld up off the pce in 10th: pushed along bef 1/2-way: rdn and no prog 2f out* **16/1**

665- **12** *8* **Mack's Sister**[313] 7655 4-8-11 **60**............................ SamHitchcott 4 14
(Dean Ivory) *lost prom pl after 2f: struggling in rr after: wknd and eased fnl f* **10/1**

0060 **13** *1* **Charles Fosterkane**[12] 6442 3-8-11 **61**............................(b) LiamKeniry 6 12
(John Best) *pushed along to stay in tch: struggling fr 1/2-way: wknd and eased over 1f out* **20/1**

1m 10.08s (-2.92) **Going Correction** -0.40s/f (Firm) course record
WFA 3 from 4yo+ 1lb **13** Ran SP% **114.5**
Speed ratings (Par 103): **103,102,99,99,96 96,95,95,94,94 89,79,77**
Tote Swingers: 1&2 £34.40, 1&3 £11.50, 2&3 £74.50 CSF £129.01 CT £1173.15 TOTE £4.80: £1.40, £18.90, £5.70; EX 163.10 TRIFECTA Not won..
Owner The Eight Of Diamonds **Bred** Mrs C J Walker **Trained** Newmarket, Suffolk

FOCUS
A competitive sprint handicap. The form looks solid with the winner still improving, despite the presence of a 33-1 shot in second.

6753 LADBROKES GAME ON! NURSERY (DIV I) 1m 67y
3:35 (3:35) (Class 5) (0-75,75) 2-Y-O **£1,940** (£577; £288; £144) **Stalls** Low

Form RPR

0602 **1** **Tiger Cub**[12] 6460 2-8-9 **63**........................ RichardKingscote 12 75+
(Roger Charlton) *sn trckd ldr: led over 2f out: rdn clr over 1f out: styd on wl* **6/1**[3]

0005 **2** *3 1/4* **Joyful Spirit (IRE)**[34] 5809 2-8-6 **60**........................ SilvestreDeSousa 5 64
(John Dunlop) *t.k.h: hld up bhd ldrs: prog over 2f out: chsd wnr over 1f out: no imp: jst hld on for 2nd* **13/2**

034 **3** *shd* **Really Lovely (IRE)**[18] 6278 2-9-4 **72**........................ JamieSpencer 6 75
(Jeremy Noseda) *sn pushed up to ld: jinked lft bnd 5f out: hanging lft over 3f out: hdd and nt qckn over 2f out: lost 2nd over 1f out: styd on fnl f* **7/2**[1]

0510 **4** *1 1/4* **Travelling**[16] 6340 2-9-3 **71**........................ SebSanders 9 71
(J W Hills) *trckd ldrs: effrt 3f out: tried to cl over 1f out: one pce after* **16/1**

004 **5** *hd* **I'm Harry**[17] 6308 2-9-4 **72**........................ MichaelHills 3 72
(Charles Hills) *trckd ldng pair: rdn and nt qckn over 2f out: one pce after* **17/2**

3216 **6** *1 1/4* **Mcvicar**[16] 6345 2-9-6 **74**........................ SamHitchcott 7 71
(Mick Channon) *wl in rr: urged along and no prog 1/2-way: rdn and sme hdwy 2f out: no imp fnl f* **8/1**

0200 **7** *1 1/2* **Accustomed**[35] 5783 2-8-11 **65**........................ JamesDoyle 10 59
(Sylvester Kirk) *hld up last: gng bttr than sme but stl last over 2f out: reminders and modest prog after: nvr nr ldrs* **10/1**

0051 **8** *hd* **Plym**[52] 5233 2-9-0 **68**........................ FrankieMcDonald 2 61
(Richard Hannon) *nvr gng wl and a in rr: struggling bdly fr 1/2-way: kpt on fnl f* **4/1**[2]

0600 **9** *3 1/2* **Superinjunction**[26] 6053 2-8-8 **62**........................(b[1]) MartinDwyer 8 47
(Brian Meehan) *pushed along in midfield 1/2-way: no prog and wl btn over 2f out* **66/1**

030 **10** *6* **Derfenna Art (IRE)**[37] 5697 2-9-2 **70**........................ MickyFenton 1 41
(Seamus Durack) *pushed along in midfield bef 1/2-way: dropped to rr and struggling 3f out: sn bhd* **12/1**

1m 42.46s (-2.24) **Going Correction** -0.25s/f (Firm) 2y crse rec **10** Ran SP% **115.6**
Speed ratings (Par 95): **101,97,97,96,96 94,93,93,89,83**
Tote Swingers: 1&2 £5.40, 1&3 £5.50, 2&3 £4.80 CSF £44.36 CT £161.66 TOTE £6.80: £2.10, £1.10, £3.00; EX 57.10 Trifecta £303.80 Pool: £525.53 - 1.28 winning units..
Owner Lady Rothschild **Bred** Carwell Equities Ltd **Trained** Beckhampton, Wilts

FOCUS
The first division of an ordinary handicap. Few got into it.

NOTEBOOK
Tiger Cub kicked for home early in the straight and ran on strongly. She hadn't quite got home over 1m2f at Nottingham the time before, having looked the likely winner 1f out, and is clearly better at this distance. There may be more to come. (op 7-1 tchd 8-1)
Joyful Spirit(IRE) has plenty of stamina in her pedigree and duly improved for the step up to 1m, keeping on well having briefly been denied a clear run and forced to switch. She can win something similar over 1m2f. (tchd 6-1 and 15-2)
Really Lovely(IRE) did herself few favours in maidens by failing to settle, and she again looked less than straightforward under a positive ride. She has ability and perhaps connections will reach for the blinkers. (op 4-1)
Travelling, well beaten on her handicap debut at Newmarket, returned to the sort of form that saw her win a 7f Wolverhampton maiden previously. She has a future off this sort of mark. (op 18-1 tchd 20-1)
I'm Harry didn't convince with his stamina for the trip. (op 10-1 tchd 11-1)
Accustomed Official explanation: jockey said that the filly hung right
Plym was the undoubted disappointment of the race. Having made a winning nursery debut on easy ground at Salisbury, she simply looked unable to act on the much faster surface here. (tchd 7-2)

6754 AEGIS TRUST HAGELOU EVENT MAIDEN STKS (DIV II) 1m 67y
4:10 (4:10) (Class 5) 3-Y-O+ **£1,940** (£577; £288; £144) **Stalls** Low

Form RPR

5030 **1** **Indian Mist (IRE)**[41] 5598 3-8-12 67........................(p) TomQueally 10 73
(Roger Varian) *trckd ldng pair: lft 2nd bnd 5f out: led over 4f out: drew clr 2f out: hanging lft but wnt further clr fnl f* **10/3**[3]

04 **2** *8* **Beauchamp Zorro**[29] 5960 3-9-3 0........................ FergusSweeney 9 60
(Henry Candy) *hld up in last pair: effrt 3f out: shkn up to go 2nd jst over 1f out: no ch w wnr* **3/1**[2]

06 **3** *1* **Greeley House**[18] 6286 3-9-3 0........................ GeorgeBaker 1 57+
(Chris Wall) *in tch: chsd wnr gng strly over 3f out: shkn up and no imp 2f out: lost 2nd jst over 1f out: one pce* **16/1**

0 **4** *hd* **Barachiel**[11] 6473 3-9-3 0........................ LiamKeniry 4 57
(Andrew Balding) *in rr whn awkward bnd after 2f: effrt 4f out: rdn over 2f out: one pce and no threat* **11/2**

06 **5** *9* **Treasure Act**[25] 6085 3-8-12 0........................ LukeMorris 6 31
(Patrick Chamings) *racd freely: led: hanging lft bnd 5f out: sn hdd: wknd over 2f out* **10/1**

6 *21* **Salford Prince (IRE)** 3-9-3 0........................ JamieSpencer 5 —
(David Elsworth) *s.i.s: a wl bhd in last: t.o 3f out* **11/4**[1]

06 **R** **Russian Storm**[15] 6377 3-8-7 0........................ JemmaMarshall[(5)] 2 —
(Pat Phelan) *t.k.h: chsd ldr tl rn out off the crse bnd 5f out* **22/1**

1m 41.76s (-2.94) **Going Correction** -0.25s/f (Firm) **7** Ran SP% **109.5**
Speed ratings (Par 103): **104,96,95,94,85 64,—**
Tote Swingers: 1&2 £2.60, 1&3 £6.80, 2&3 £5.70 CSF £12.51 TOTE £2.80: £1.30, £2.80; EX 11.40 Trifecta £39.70 Pool: £766.83 - 14.29 winnint units..
Owner Thurloe Thoroughbred XXVII **Bred** Joseph Stewart Investments **Trained** Newmarket, Suffolk

FOCUS
The pace was a good one and, like the first division, this didn't take much winning with the winner not needing to improve. The time was 0.7 seconds faster.

6755 LADBROKES ODDS ON! H'CAP 1m 2f 7y
4:40 (4:40) (Class 4) (0-85,84) 3-Y-O **£4,075** (£1,212; £606; £303) **Stalls** Centre

Form RPR

2210 **1** **Lucky Legs (IRE)**[47] 5392 3-9-1 **78**........................ MichaelHills 9 85
(Charles Hills) *hld up in 7th: stdy prog on outer fr wl over 2f out: rdn to ld over 1f out: styd on wl* **17/2**

2466 **2** *1/2* **Tasfeya**[15] 6374 3-9-0 **77**........................ AdamKirby 1 83
(John Akehurst) *trckd ldng pair: led wl over 2f out to over 1f out: pressed wnr after: jst hld* **10/1**

1263 **3** *1 3/4* **Arabian Heights**[44] 5466 3-9-7 **84**........................ SebSanders 5 88+
(Sir Mark Prescott Bt) *t.k.h: hld up in midfield: effrt whn nt clr run 2f out: styd on fr over 1f out to take 3rd nr fin* **9/2**[2]

-150 **4** *1/2* **Shooting Line (IRE)**[26] 6063 3-9-2 **82**........................(v[1]) AdamBeschizza[(3)] 3 84
(Walter Swinburn) *t.k.h early: trckd ldrs: effrt over 2f out: cl enough in 3rd over 1f out: nt qckn and wl hld after* **5/1**[3]

52-0 **5** *1/2* **Barwick**[152] 2008 3-8-13 **76**........................ TomQueally 6 77
(Mark H Tompkins) *hld up last and off the pce: sme prog on outer fr 2f out: one pce fnl f* **8/1**

2-53 **6** *6* **The Mongoose**[15] 6377 3-8-9 **72**........................ WilliamBuick 8 61
(Sir Michael Stoute) *led 3f: pressed ldr after: upsides wl over 2f out: edgd lft and fnd nil sn after: wknd over 1f out* **4/1**[1]

6043 **7** *1/2* **Misty Isles**[14] 6402 3-8-9 **72**........................ LukeMorris 4 60
(Heather Main) *led after 3f to wl over 2f out: wknd wl over 1f out* **11/2**

0221 **8** *8* **Whodathought (IRE)**[52] 5231 3-8-7 **73**........................(b) KieranO'Neill[(3)] 2 45
(Richard Hannon) *in tch: urged along wl over 3f out: sn dropped to rr and btn* **8/1**

2m 5.34s (-3.36) **Going Correction** -0.25s/f (Firm) **8** Ran SP% **112.1**
Speed ratings (Par 103): **103,102,101,100,100 95,95,88**
Tote Swingers: 1&2 £12.70, 1&3 £6.00, 2&3 £7.30 CSF £84.70 CT £428.93 TOTE £5.60: £1.50, £4.40, £1.20; EX 127.90 TRIFECTA Not won..
Owner J Acheson **Bred** Lynch Bages Ltd **Trained** Lambourn, Berks

FOCUS
An ordinary handicap with the winner improving to best maiden form.

6756 BET IN PLAY WITH LADBROKES H'CAP 1m 3f 135y
5:10 (5:11) (Class 5) (0-70,70) 3-Y-O **£2,264** (£673; £336; £168) **Stalls** Centre

Form RPR

3225 **1** **Duquesa (IRE)**[13] 6435 3-9-0 **68**........................ MatthewCosham[(5)] 11 78
(David Evans) *hld up towards rr: prog on outer fr 3f out: rdn and clsd to ld jst over 1f out: styd on wl* **15/2**[3]

5211 **2** *2 1/2* **Peachez**[73] 4491 3-9-2 **70**........................(p) AmyScott[(5)] 9 76
(Alastair Lidderdale) *stdd s: hld up last: prog on outer over 2f out: styd on to take 2nd last strides: nvr on terms w wnr* **5/1**[1]

2241 **3** *nk* **Lady Barastar (IRE)**[11] 6493 3-9-1 **67**........................ AdamBeschizza[(3)] 10 72
(Walter Swinburn) *hld up in midfield: prog over 3f out: rdn to ld towards nr side wl over 2f out: hdd jst over 1f out: one pce* **11/2**[2]

5-40 **4** *hd* **Spey Song (IRE)**[19] 6263 3-9-7 **70**........................(p) TomQueally 13 75
(James Bethell) *dwlt: sn trckd ldrs in 6th: prog over 3f out: chsd ldr over 2f out to over 1f out: styd on same pce* **9/1**

14P3 **5** *7* **Little Jazz**[24] 6136 3-9-5 **68**........................ CathyGannon 5 61
(Paul D'Arcy) *hld up in midfield: effrt over 3f out: no imp on ldrs 2f out: wknd over 1f out* **11/1**

005 **6** *6* **Fascinating (IRE)**[15] 6377 3-8-9 **58**........................ SilvestreDeSousa 7 41
(Mark Johnston) *chsd ldng trio: urged along 5f out: effrt over 3f out: wknd 2f out* **5/1**[1]

1560 **7** *5* **Circle Of Angels**[17] 6295 3-9-1 **67**........................ RyanClark[(3)] 6 41
(Ian Williams) *hld up wl in rr: urged along over 4f out: no prog and struggling over 3f out: wknd* **14/1**

4224 **8** *1/2* **Echos Of Motivator**[140] 2360 3-9-6 **69**........................ LukeMorris 12 42
(Ronald Harris) *hld up in rr: rdn and no prog over 3f out: wknd 2f out* **8/1**

-400 **9** *hd* **Nothing To Hide (IRE)**[14] 6402 3-8-12 **61**........................ JamesDoyle 2 34
(Dominic Ffrench Davis) *trckd ldrs: no prog nr side 3f out: wknd rapidly 2f out* **20/1**

3F00 **10** *3 1/4* **Steely**[19] 6255 3-8-11 **60**........................(b[1]) MickyFenton 8 27
(Jim Best) *trckd ldr to 3f out: racd awkwardly and wknd rapidly* **66/1**

0016 **11** *1 3/4* **Fairling**[24] 6136 3-9-3 **66**........................ SebSanders 3 30
(Hughie Morrison) *led to wl over 2f out: wknd rapidly* **10/1**

1400 **12** *40* **Ugo (USA)**[10] 6507 3-9-7 **70**........................(b[1]) WilliamBuick 1 —
(Heather Main) *pressed ldng pair: rdn wl over 3f out: sn wknd rapidly: virtually p.u over 1f out* **16/1**

2m 26.66s (-2.84) **Going Correction** -0.25s/f (Firm) **12** Ran SP% **117.8**
Speed ratings (Par 101): **99,97,97,97,92 88,85,84,84,82 81,54**
Tote Swingers: 1&2 £7.20, 1&3 £8.30, 2&3 £3.70 CSF £44.52 CT £226.20 TOTE £5.70: £2.40, £2.30, £1.30; EX 45.70 TRIFECTA Not won..
Owner Raymond N R Auld **Bred** R N Auld **Trained** Pandy, Monmouths

FOCUS
There was an advantage towards the hold-up runners in this class 5 handicap. Despite the first four finishing clear, this isn't a race to be positive about ratings-wise.
Ugo(USA) Official explanation: jockey said that the colt stopped quickly

6757 LADBROKES GAME ON! NURSERY (DIV II) 1m 67y
5:40 (5:40) (Class 5) (0-75,75) 2-Y-O **£1,940** (£577; £288; £144) **Stalls** Low

Form RPR

5122 **1** **Fire Ship**[52] 5233 2-9-3 **71**........................ LukeMorris 7 78+
(Peter Winkworth) *dwlt: rousted along to go prom: wnt 2nd 3f out: led jst over 2f out: edgd rt over 1f out: rdn clr* **7/2**[1]

6005 **2** *3* **Finley Connolly (IRE)**[40] 5634 2-8-6 **60**........................ AndreaAtzeni 9 60
(Brian Meehan) *settled towards rr: effrt on outer 3f out: rdn and styd on fr over 2f out: wnt 2nd last strides* **12/1**

0546 **3** *nk* **Next Cry (USA)**[19] 6245 2-8-9 **66**........................ KieranO'Neill[(3)] 8 65
(Richard Hannon) *led: rdn and hdd jst over 2f out: tried to rally but hld over 1f out: lost 2nd last strides* **14/1**

3405 **4** *3/4* **Flying Trader (USA)**[25] 6102 2-9-1 **69**........................ AdamKirby 6 68
(Jane Chapple-Hyam) *in tch on outer: effrt 3f out: rdn and styd on same pce fnl 2f: nvr able to chal* **15/2**[3]

1 **5** *2 3/4* **Four Better**[24] 6117 2-9-7 **75**........................ FergusSweeney 3 66
(Jamie Osborne) *hld up in midfield: looking for room 3f out: shkn up and one pce fnl 2f* **13/2**[2]

5045 **6** *2 1/4* **Loxton Lad (IRE)**[26] 6053 2-8-7 **61**........................ JamesDoyle 10 47
(Roger Charlton) *prom: rdn 3f out: steadily wknd fnl 2f* **7/2**[1]

0000 **7** *3 3/4* **Highly Likely (IRE)**[26] 6053 2-8-1 **55**........................ CathyGannon 4 32
(John Dunlop) *t.k.h early: hld up bhd ldrs: rdn over 2f out: lost pl and btn sn after* **20/1**

004 **8** *3 3/4* **Amelia May**[23] 6168 2-9-5 **73**........................ WilliamBuick 11 42
(John Gosden) *dwlt: rcvrd to press ldr: lost 2nd 3f out: sn wknd* **17/2**

5556 **9** *2 1/4* **Voodoo Rhythm (USA)**[5] 6623 2-9-4 **72**........................(b) MartinDwyer 5 36
(Brian Meehan) *hld up in rr: effrt on outer 3f out: no prog 2f out: sn wknd* **9/1**

5565 **P** **Brimstone Hill (IRE)**[11] 6484 2-9-2 **70**........................ MichaelHills 1 —
(Charles Hills) *hld up last: lost tch bef 1/2-way: t.o whn p.u and dismntd 1f out: sdlle slipped* **10/1**

1m 43.07s (-1.63) **Going Correction** -0.25s/f (Firm) 2y crse rec **10** Ran SP% **118.3**
Speed ratings (Par 95): **98,95,94,93,91 88,85,81,79,—**
Tote Swingers: 1&2 £10.80, 1&3 £10.70, 2&3 £26.70 CSF £49.07 CT £531.25 TOTE £3.40: £1.30, £7.90, £7.50; EX 67.60 Trifecta £335.30 Won won..
Owner IGP Partnership & Partner **Bred** Yorton Farm **Trained** Chiddingfold, Surrey
■ Stewards' Enquiry : Kieran O'Neill two-day ban: 24-25 October (careless riding)

FOCUS
As in the earlier division of this nursery, there was a clear-cut winner.

NOTEBOOK

Fire Ship posted an improved display for the return to faster ground. Although there's plenty of speed in the pedigree, he certainly stays 1m well and, although a sharp rise will follow, one couldn't rule out further progress. (tchd 9-2)

Finley Connolly(IRE), as was the case on his nursery debut at Kempton the time before, came strong in the final furlong and he looks a ready-made winner once upped to 1m2f. (tchd 10-1)

Next Cry(USA) proved well suited by the drop to 1m on fast ground, conditions he'd not previously encountered. He's clearly moderate, but is capable of wining something small. (tchd 16-1)

Flying Trader(USA) is quite well exposed. (op 9-1)

Four Better, although briefly short of room, simply didn't look up to it from an opening mark of 75. (op 6-1 tchd 9-2)

Loxton Lad(IRE) has now disappointed on both starts since handicapping and looks moderate. (op 11-2)

Amelia May had shown promise in maidens, so it was disappointing to see her fold so tamely on this nursery debut. (op 11-2)

Brimstone Hill(IRE) Official explanation: jockey said that the saddle slipped

T/Plt: £70.50 to a £1 stake. Pool of £61,120.80 - 632.86 winning tickets. T/Qpdt: £32.30 to a £1 stake. Pool of £60,69.25 - 139.00 winning tickets. JN

6099 YARMOUTH (L-H)

Monday, October 10

OFFICIAL GOING: Good (7.5)

Wind: strong across Weather: bright and breezy

6758 BRITISH STALLION STUDS SUPPORTING BRITISH RACING E B F MAIDEN FILLIES' STKS 6f 3y

1:40 (1:41) (Class 5) 2-Y-O **£3,234** (£962; £481; £240) **Stalls** Centre

Form RPR

1 **Ihtiraam (IRE)** 2-9-0 0 IanMongan 1 78+
(Saeed Bin Suroor) *in tch: rdn and effrt 2f out: chsd ldrs and carried lft jst over 1f out: chal ins fnl f: kpt on wl to ld fnl 50yds* **10/1**3

2 2 nk **Shaleek**27 6030 2-9-0 0 NeilCallan 12 77
(Roger Varian) *pressed ldr: ev ch and rdn 2f out: led ins fnl f: kpt on wl tl hdd and no ex fnl 50yds* **4/7**1

0 3 1 1/2 **Intense Pink**24 6128 2-9-0 0 PaulHanagan 8 73+
(Chris Wall) *hld up in tch in midfield: hdwy to chse ldng quartet ent fnl 2f: kpt on wl ins fnl f: nt gng pce to rch ldng pair* **12/1**

4 4 1 3/4 **Fanoos**164 1657 2-9-0 0 RichardHills 11 67+
(John Gosden) *taken down v early: led: rdn over 1f out: hdd jst ins fnl f: no ex and wknd fnl 75yds* **9/2**2

0 5 1/2 **Crazy Too (IRE)**27 6030 2-9-0 0 JoeFanning 9 65
(David Simcock) *t.k.h: chsd ldrs: rdn and pressing ldrs over 1f out: unable qck and outpcd 1f out: wknd ins fnl f* **20/1**

6 6 **Jwala** 2-9-0 0 ShaneKelly 13 46
(Robert Cowell) *hld up in midfield: rdn and struggling ent fnl 2f: 6th and wl btn 1f out* **14/1**

0 7 5 **Aubrietia**17 6300 2-9-0 0 JimmyQuinn 2 30
(Edward Vaughan) *dwlt: towards rr: pushed along and struggling 3f out: sn wknd and no ch fnl 2f* **100/1**

8 1/2 **Connishka** 2-8-11 0 DominicFox(3) 3 29
(Alan Bailey) *s.i.s: pushed along and rn green in rr: lost tch over 2f out* **150/1**

9 3 **Grey Seal (IRE)** 2-9-0 0 MartinLane 6 19
(James Fanshawe) *s.i.s: hld up towards rr: swtchd rt 3f out: sn struggling and outpcd: wl bhd fnl 2f* **66/1**

10 2 1/2 **Sarah Berry** 2-9-0 0 LiamJones 10 11
(Chris Dwyer) *a towards rr: rdn and struggling 1/2-way: lost tch wl over 2f out* **200/1**

0 11 1 1/4 **Poncho**21 6215 2-8-9 0 RosieJessop(5) 7 —
(Sir Mark Prescott Bt) *dwlt: a towards rr: rdn and struggling 1/2-way: lost tch wl over 2f out* **200/1**

0 12 3/4 **Skyblue**27 6030 2-9-0 0 (t) TomMcLaughlin 4 —
(Tobias B P Coles) *pressed ldng pair tl rdn and struggling over 2f out: sn wknd: t.o fr over 1f out* **300/1**

1m 14.57s (0.17) **Going Correction** -0.15s/f (Firm) 12 Ran SP% 114.5

Speed ratings (Par 92): **92,91,89,87,86 78,71,71,67,63 62,61**

toteswingers:1&2:£3.00, 2&3:£3.30, 1&3:£10.40 CSF £15.60 TOTE £10.30: £3.90, £1.02, £4.50; EX 24.30.

Owner Godolphin **Bred** Lodge Park Stud **Trained** Newmarket, Suffolk

FOCUS

Outside of back straight dolled out. This modest juvenile maiden for fillies signalled the beginning of a new era for British racing, being the first race run under the new whip rules, with riders restricted to using it no more than seven times in any Flat race. That was further complicated by a blustery day with a fierce cross wind in the home straight.

NOTEBOOK

Ihtiraam(IRE) made a belated winning debut and rates value for further. She knew her job and travelled kindly just off the pace. Her rider didn't have to get too serious with her to master the runner-up nearing the business end and she's clearly a useful prospect. Another furlong should be within her range in due course (op 17-2)

Shaleek was just held over C&D on her debut 27 days earlier and was heavily backed to gain compensation. She nearly went one better, but looked to race somewhat lazily late in the day and was a sitting duck for the winner. Her turn shouldn't be too far off. (op 8-13 tchd 4-6)

Intense Pink ◆ stepped up plenty on her debut level last month, but looks to be crying out for a return to a stiffer test. She's one to take from the race. (op 16-1)

Fanoos was having her first outing since failing to land a gamble on her debut at Leicester in April. She was more convincing this time, despite proving easier to back, but was outstayed by the principals over this extra furlong. Perhaps the run will bring her on. (tchd 4-1)

Crazy Too(IRE) showed the benefit of her debut experience over C&D last month and finished closer to the runner-up this time. Another furlong is likely to prove ideal now. (op 22-1 tchd 18-1)

6759 LORD NELSON MUSEUM H'CAP 7f 3y

2:10 (2:12) (Class 5) (0-75,76) 3-Y-O+ **£2,264** (£673; £336; £168) **Stalls** Centre

Form RPR

0000 1 **Frognal (IRE)**6 6616 5-9-6 75 (bt) RobertWinston 2 83
(Richard Guest) *wnt rt s: racd towards outside: strly rdn and hdwy 2f out: led fnl 100yds: kpt on wl* **40/1**

00-3 2 1/2 **Quarrel (USA)**58 5053 4-9-3 72 LiamJones 13 78
(William Haggas) *led: rdn and jnd 2f out: wnt lft briefly ins fnl f: hdd 100yds out: nt qckn* **6/1**2

2636 3 3/4 **Jungle Bay**19 6246 4-9-2 74 (p) LouisBeuzelin(3) 7 78
(Jane Chapple-Hyam) *prom: jnd ldr 2f out: rdn and ev ch 1f out: one pce after* **7/1**3

4550 4 nk **Rough Rock (IRE)**15 6378 6-9-0 76 ow3 MichaelJMurphy(7) 10 79
(Chris Dwyer) *midfield: effrt on outside 2f out: drvn and tried to chal ins fnl f: no ex last 100yds* **11/1**

3321 5 1/2 **Tanmawy (IRE)**17 6307 3-9-3 74 RichardHills 15 76
(Ed Dunlop) *towards rr: rdn and looked labouring over 3f out: drftd rt and hmpd rival 300yds out: kpt on wl ins fnl f: unable to chal* **5/1**1

0-00 6 nk **Avertis**15 6378 6-9-1 75 (tp) LucyKBarry(5) 16 76
(Alastair Lidderdale) *chsd ldrs: sn pushed along: nt qckn over 1f out* **14/1**

0010 7 3/4 **Captain Macarry (IRE)**5 6634 6-9-1 70 (v) WilliamCarson 6 69
(Stuart Williams) *prom: rdn 3f out: nt qckn over 1f out* **8/1**

4166 8 1 1/2 **Aleqa**26 6051 4-8-11 73 DannyBrock(7) 8 68
(Chris Wall) *midfield: rdn and no imp fr over 1f out* **16/1**

0000 9 1 3/4 **Bajan Bear**23 6167 3-9-2 73 ShaneKelly 4 63
(Michael Blanshard) *sn toiling in rr: hrd drvn and plugging on whn hmpd 300yds out, nt rcvr* **12/1**

4115 10 1/2 **Darcey**19 6261 5-9-2 71 KellyHarrison 3 60
(Amy Weaver) *chsd ldrs over 5f: sn lost pl* **11/1**

0000 11 3/4 **Steed**20 6231 4-8-13 71 (p) RobertLButler(3) 14 58
(Richard Guest) *sn drvn along: nvr looked keen: struggling 1/2-way* **14/1**

5000 12 1 1/4 **Not My Choice (IRE)**7 6583 6-9-5 74 (t) MichaelStainton 11 58
(David C Griffiths) *pressed ldr: rdn 3f out: wknd over 2f out* **80/1**

-616 13 hd **Celestyna**67 4727 3-8-8 72 CharlesEddery(7) 12 55
(Sir Henry Cecil) *taken down early: in last pair and nvr gng wl: detached last over 2f out* **20/1**

5160 14 2 1/4 **Layla Jamil (IRE)**15 6378 3-9-4 75 PaulHanagan 1 52
(Mick Channon) *racd towards outside: rdn over 3f out: n.d after: eased ins fnl f* **10/1**

1m 26.35s (-0.25) **Going Correction** -0.15s/f (Firm)

WFA 3 from 4yo+ 2lb 14 Ran SP% 115.7

Speed ratings (Par 103): **95,94,93,93,92 92,91,89,87,87 86,84,84,82**

toteswingers:1&2:£29.00, 2&3:£10.70, 1&3:£49.10 CSF £255.05 CT £1954.43 TOTE £30.90: £10.00, £1.90, £2.40; EX 338.60.

Owner Rakebackmypoker.com **Bred** Bryan Ryan **Trained** Stainforth, S Yorks

FOCUS

A wide-open handicap. The field raced towards the stands' side, but the principals were away from the rail and the winner made his challenge widest of all.

6760 GREAT YARMOUTH RACECOURSE NURSERY 1m 2f 21y

2:40 (2:41) (Class 6) (0-60,66) 2-Y-O **£1,617** (£481; £240; £120) **Stalls** Low

Form RPR

6040 1 **Welsh Nayber**14 6399 2-9-7 60 NeilCallan 8 64
(Amanda Perrett) *chsd ldrs: rdn to ld jst over 2f out: pushed lft by str wind lft 2f out: clr and styng on wl whn blown into rail fnl 100yds: rcvrd and rdn out* **15/2**3

000 2 1 1/2 **Istan Star (USA)**33 5818 2-8-13 52 BarryMcHugh 5 53
(Julie Camacho) *t.k.h early: stdd after s and hld up in tch: swtchd rt and effrt over 2f out: chsd wnr jst over 1f out: kpt on same pce ins fnl f* **20/1**

4455 3 3/4 **Doctor Banner**3 6667 2-9-4 57 (v) IanMongan 9 57
(Mick Channon) *hld up off the pce in last quartet: swtchd rt and hdwy u.p over 2f out: chsd ldrs over 1f out: styd on same pce ins fnl f* **8/1**

2655 4 1 **Jaci Uzzi (IRE)**25 6101 2-8-12 51 MartinLane 2 49
(David Evans) *hld up in midfield: hdwy over 3f out: chsd ldrs and unable qck u.p over 1f out: styd on same pce ins fnl f* **28/1**

0001 5 nse **Remember Rocky**32 5844 2-9-6 59 LiamJones 6 57
(Steve Gollings) *chsd ldrs: rdn 4f out: drvn and styd on same pce fr over 1f out* **15/2**3

1330 6 2 **Yammos (IRE)**11 6471 2-9-7 60 MatthewDavies 3 54
(Mick Channon) *hld up towards rr: hdwy on outer over 3f out: chsd ldrs u.p and nt qckn over 1f out: wknd ins fnl f* **7/1**2

003 7 8 **Strictly Mine**38 5672 2-9-2 55 LeeNewman 7 35
(Jonathan Portman) *sn bustled along to chse ldr: rdn and struggling to qckn whn pushed lft 2f out: wknd qckly over 1f out* **16/1**

000 8 15 **Oratrix (IRE)**11 6474 2-9-3 56 JimmyQuinn 10 9
(Denis Coakley) *a in rr: lost tch over 2f out* **50/1**

006 9 hd **Scarlet Prince**11 6471 2-9-3 56 JamesSullivan 4 9
(Gary Moore) *nvr gng wl and a wl off the pce in last quartet: lost tch wl over 2f out* **16/1**

6451 10 12 **Vociferous (USA)**6 6611 2-9-13 66 6ex JoeFanning 1 —
(Mark Johnston) *led: rdn and hdd jst over 2f out: bdly hmpd and pushed into rail 2f out: sn eased and wl btn after: t.o* **9/4**1

4043 11 1 **Daring Damsel (IRE)**18 6275 2-9-6 59 (p) PaulHanagan 11 —
(Paul Cole) *racd in midfield: rdn over 5f out: wknd 3f out: sn lost tch: t.o* **11/1**

000 12 11 **Flight Connection**38 5688 2-8-12 51 (t) KirstyMilczarek 12 —
(Clive Brittain) *v.s.a: nvr gng wl and a last: lost tch 3f: t.o* **14/1**

2m 11.77s (1.27) **Going Correction** -0.15s/f (Firm) 12 Ran SP% 114.8

Speed ratings (Par 93): **88,86,86,85,85 83,77,65,65,55 54,46**

toteswingers:1&2:£32.00, 2&3:£32.70, 1&3:£10.70 CSF £146.63 CT £1227.82 TOTE £11.20: £3.90, £5.00, £2.50; EX 273.60.

Owner Coombelands Racing Syndicate **Bred** Usk Valley Stud **Trained** Pulborough, W Sussex

FOCUS

A moderate staying nursery, run at an average pace and the cross wind played its part in the home straight.

NOTEBOOK

Welsh Nayber opened his account at the sixth attempt despite proving hard to steer. He raced on the outer, close to the pace, and Neil Callan kicked him on around 3f out. That proved a winning move, but he struggled with the wind from 2f out and lost momentum more than once. He is value for a bit further, this is obviously his ground, and he appeals as the type to rate higher over longer trips next year. (op 13-2 tchd 8-1)

Istan Star(USA) ◆ showed his first worthwhile form on this nursery debut and is an improving juvenile. He clearly stays well and can be found an opportunity to go one better shortly (op 22-1)

Doctor Banner fared best of those coming from off the pace and had his chance on this quick reappearance. He can be ridden more positively now connections know he stays. (op 12-1)

Jaci Uzzi(IRE) ran well and had every chance, but her proximity sums up the strength of this event. (op 33-1)

Oratrix(IRE) Official explanation: jockey said that the filly moved poorly

Vociferous(USA) hosed up on Fibresand last week and was chucked in on that form under her penalty. This was a totally contrasting test up in trip, however, and she was beaten before being badly hampered on the rail 2f out. Official explanation: jockey said that the filly was never travelling (op 2-1 tchd 15-8)

Flight Connection Official explanation: jockey said that the colt was never travelling

6761 GREAT YARMOUTH CHRISTMAS PARTY H'CAP (DIV I) 6f 3y
3:15 (3:16) (Class 4) (0-85,85) 3-Y-O+ **£4,075** (£1,212; £606; £303) **Stalls** Centre

Form RPR

6631 **1** **Shifting Star (IRE)**^{18} 6282 6-9-0 **78**.................................. IanMongan 3 89
(Walter Swinburn) *trckd ldrs towards outside: rdn to ld over 1f out: kpt up to work and a maintaining advantage ins fnl f* **8/1**

0320 **2** *1 ½* **Soap Wars**^{16} 6348 6-9-7 **85**.. PaulHanagan 1 91
(Hugo Palmer) *t.k.h: 2nd towards outer tl led wl over 1f out: hdd over 1f out: rdn and a hld after* **8/1**

-005 **3** *1 ¼* **Drift And Dream**^{16} 6348 4-8-12 **76**...................................... NeilCallan 8 78
(Chris Wall) *prom and plld hrd: rdn 2f out: nt qckn fr over 1f out* **11/2**^{1}

3623 **4** *¾* **Jack My Boy (IRE)**^{12} 6467 4-8-13 **77**............................(v) MartinLane 11 77+
(David Evans) *chsd ldrs: sn pushed along: rdn and sltly outpcd 2f out: kpt on ins fnl f: no threat* **6/1**^{2}

5000 **5** *nk* **Dickie Le Davoir**^{85} 4126 7-9-1 **82**........................(b) RobertLButler$^{(3)}$ 10 81
(Richard Guest) *midfield towards outer: rdn over 2f out: no imp fnl f* **33/1**

0000 **6** *1* **Orpsie Boy (IRE)**^{16} 6347 8-9-3 **84**....................................... DaleSwift$^{(3)}$ 4 79
(Ruth Carr) *midfield: rdn and outpcd 1/2-way: sme prog ins fnl f: no ch* **18/1**

1000 **7** *nk* **Levitate**^{24} 6113 3-9-3 **82**...(p) RobertWinston 9 76
(Alan McCabe) *dwlt: sn chsng ldrs: drvn over 3f out: btn over 1f out* **7/1**^{3}

0050 **8** *hd* **Rocket Rob (IRE)**^{16} 6327 5-9-2 **80**............................ TomMcLaughlin 7 74
(Willie Musson) *t.k.h early: nvr bttr than midfield: rdn and btn 2f out* **11/1**

1101 **9** *1* **Deerslayer (USA)**^{16} 6351 5-9-1 **79**..............................(p) JoeFanning 2 70
(Amy Weaver) *racd freely: led tl rdn and hdd wl over 1f out: steadily lost pl* **10/1**

500 **10** *½* **Seek The Fair Land**^{59} 5012 5-8-12 **76**........................ MatthewDavies 5 65
(Jim Boyle) *s.s: a bhd* **9/1**

0000 **11** *2* **Ivory Silk**^{12} 6467 6-8-10 **81**..(b) RaulDaSilva$^{(7)}$ 13 64
(Jeremy Gask) *in rr and nvr gng wl: last of pair towards stands' side: struggling 1/2-way* **16/1**

0300 **12** *1 ¾* **Major Conquest (IRE)**^{15} 6378 3-9-0 **79**.......................... LiamJones 14 56
(J W Hills) *led pair towards stands' side: midfield: rdn and wknd 2f out* **16/1**

3100 **13** *2 ¼* **Waabel**^{199} 961 4-9-0 **78**... WilliamCarson 12 48
(Richard Guest) *sn bhd: outpcd 1/2-way: eased ins fnl f* **22/1**

1m 12.7s (-1.70) **Going Correction** -0.15s/f (Firm)
WFA 3 from 4yo+ 1lb **13** Ran SP% **116.1**
Speed ratings (Par 105): **105,103,101,100,99 98,98,97,96,95 93,90,87**
toteswingers:1&2:£6.50, 2&3:£8.90, 1&3:£6.90 CSF £68.60 CT £398.01 TOTE £10.60: £3.30, £2.80, £2.80; EX 70.90.
Owner Night Shadow Syndicate **Bred** Hardys Of Kilkeel Ltd **Trained** Aldbury, Herts

FOCUS
A typically open sprint handicap for the class. Those racing towards the stands' side failed to land a blow and the first pair dominated inside the final furlong.

6762 GREAT YARMOUTH CHRISTMAS PARTY H'CAP (DIV II) 6f 3y
3:45 (3:47) (Class 4) (0-85,84) 3-Y-O+ **£4,075** (£1,212; £606; £303) **Stalls** Centre

Form RPR

6000 **1** **Loki's Revenge**^{24} 6113 3-9-1 **79**....................................(b^{1}) JoeFanning 4 88
(William Jarvis) *dwlt and short of room s: towards rr: hdwy into midfield 1/2-way: 7th and stl plenty to do ent fnl f: str run fnl 100yds to ld last stride* **9/2**^{1}

1165 **2** *shd* **Mosaicist (IRE)**^{55} 5146 3-9-4 **82**...................................... MartinLane 5 90
(James Fanshawe) *handy in main gp: effrt wl over 1f out: rdn to chse ldr and clsng jst over 1f out: led ins fnl f: kpt on tl hdd last stride* **8/1**^{2}

0213 **3** *1* **Celtic Sixpence (IRE)**^{30} 5939 3-9-1 **79**............................ IanMongan 3 84
(Noel Quinlan) *chsd ldr for 1f: led main gp: rdn and clsd on ldrs over 1f out: kpt on ins fnl f* **8/1**^{2}

0350 **4** *nk* **Cardinal**^{31} 5890 6-8-9 **72**.. LiamJones 2 76
(Robert Cowell) *prom in main gp: rdn and effrt over 1f out: kpt on u.p ins fnl f* **16/1**

0060 **5** *¾* **Lenny Bee**^{23} 6174 5-9-5 **82**...(t) LeeNewman 14 84
(George Foster) *sn led and clr: stl clr and rdn over 1f out: hdd ins fnl f: no ex and btn fnl 75yds* **9/1**^{3}

0602 **6** *2 ¼* **Boundaries**^{42} 5559 3-9-0 **78**.. NeilCallan 7 72
(Tim Easterby) *t.k.h: hld up in midfield: rdn 1/2-way: no imp u.p over 1f out: plugged on ins fnl f* **16/1**

3001 **7** *nse* **Dancing Freddy (IRE)**^{18} 6276 4-8-13 **79**...........(tp) RobertLButler$^{(3)}$ 10 73
(Richard Guest) *t.k.h: chsd clr ldr after 1f: rdn wl over 1f out: lost 2nd jst over 1f out: wknd ins fnl f* **16/1**

0003 **8** *1 ¾* **Cornus**^{15} 6382 9-8-13 **76**...(be) RobertWinston 6 65
(Alan McCabe) *racd off the pce in midfield: rdn and lost pl over 2f out: plugged on but no threat to ldrs fr over 1f out* **10/1**

0612 **9** *shd* **Maze (IRE)**^{12} 6467 6-9-2 **84**... LucyKBarry$^{(5)}$ 9 72
(Tony Carroll) *t.k.h: hld up off the pce in midfield: rdn and fnd little wl over 1f out: sn wknd and n.d after* **8/1**^{2}

5101 **10** *¾* **Main Beach**^{17} 6305 4-9-1 **78**...(t) ShaneKelly 12 64
(Tobias B P Coles) *s.i.s: a bhd: swtchd rt 2f out: nvr trbld ldrs* **8/1**^{2}

0000 **11** *3 ¼* **Bassett Road (IRE)**^{45} 5451 3-9-0 **78**............................ TomMcLaughlin 8 54
(Willie Musson) *t.k.h: broke kay but grad stdd bk in rr: rdn and no rspnse over 2f out: bhd fnl 2f* **22/1**

1603 **12** *¾* **Dominium (USA)**^{11} 6477 4-9-0 **77**..........................(b) EddieCreighton 13 50
(Jeremy Gask) *a in rr: rdn and no prog over 2f out and wl bhd over 1f out* **11/1**

0200 **13** *1* **My Kingdom (IRE)**^{16} 6327 5-9-5 **82**..........................(t) PaulHanagan 11 52
(Patrick Morris) *racd off the pce in midfield: rdn and struggling over 2f out: wl bhd fnl f* **16/1**

1m 12.86s (-1.54) **Going Correction** -0.15s/f (Firm)
WFA 3 from 4yo+ 1lb **13** Ran SP% **117.9**
Speed ratings (Par 105): **104,103,102,102,101 98,98,95,95,94 90,89,87**
toteswingers:1&2:£5.80, 2&3:£7.40, 1&3:£6.10 CSF £38.20 CT £229.68 TOTE £5.90: £2.10, £1.90, £2.70; EX 45.80.
Owner Dr J Walker **Bred** The Athenians **Trained** Newmarket, Suffolk

FOCUS
The second division of the 6f handicap and it was another wide-open heat.

6763 WATERAID CHARITY CLAIMING STKS 1m 3y
4:20 (4:21) (Class 6) 2-Y-O **£1,617** (£481; £240; £120) **Stalls** Centre

Form RPR

060 **1** **Camrock Star (IRE)**^{11} 6487 2-8-2 57.............................. JimmyQuinn 9 57
(William Knight) *towards rr: rdn and hdwy towards far side to go 2nd 2f out: led 1f out: drvn out* **6/1**^{3}

0 **2** *1 ¼* **Barn Dance (FR)**^{24} 6123 2-9-5 0.................................... LeeNewman 4 71
(Jonathan Portman) *cl up: pushed along over 3f out: wnt 2nd 1f out: two reminders ins fnl f and a hld* **11/4**^{2}

0002 **3** *3 ¾* **Astraios (IRE)**^{11} 6471 2-8-13 70......................................(b) ShaneKelly 2 57
(Brian Meehan) *led: 2 l clr 2f out: drvn and threw in the towel as sn as hdd 1f out* **5/2**^{1}

465 **4** *1 ¾* **Bogey Hole (IRE)**^{18} 6280 2-8-1 50................................. PaulHanagan 1 41
(Tom Dascombe) *taken down early: last away: pushed along early: sn t.k.h and prom but a racing awkwardly: 4th and rdn and btn wl over 1f out* **6/1**^{3}

4436 **5** *8* **Manderston**^{6} 6611 2-8-7 54.. JoeFanning 6 30
(Mark Johnston) *pressed ldr tl 2f out: rdn and lost pl bdly: poor 5th over 1f out* **7/1**

5060 **6** *13* **Milwr**^{11} 6471 2-8-5 45..^{1} LouisBeuzelin$^{(3)}$ 8 —
(Chris Dwyer) *towards rr: drvn 1/2-way and fnd nil: labouring bdly after: t.o fnl 2f* **20/1**

0 **7** *20* **Plead The Fifth (USA)**^{11} 6471 2-8-8 0..................(bt) EddieCreighton 5 —
(Brian Meehan) *sn drvn along: a bdly outpcd: t.o fnl 3f: v reluctant* **14/1**

0200 **8** *7* **Mormoran**^{18} 6280 2-8-3 44 ow1..(p) MartinLane 7 —
(Chris Dwyer) *towards rr: rdn over 4f out and fnd nil: nvr travelling after: eased and t.o over 2f out* **33/1**

1m 41.12s (0.52) **Going Correction** -0.15s/f (Firm) **8** Ran SP% **110.7**
Speed ratings (Par 93): **91,89,86,84,76 63,43,36**
toteswingers:1&2:£4.00, 2&3:£2.20, 1&3:£4.30 CSF £21.37 TOTE £7.30: £1.60, £2.00, £1.60; EX 23.10.Bogey Hole was claimed by N Evans for £3000. Camrock Star was claimed by P. D. Evans for £4000.
Owner The Old Brokers **Bred** N Ormiston **Trained** Patching, W Sussex

FOCUS
This weak juvenile claimer was run at an ordinary pace and the first pair fought it out from the furlong marker.

NOTEBOOK
Camrock Star(IRE) allayed any stamina fears on this first run over 1m and shed her maiden tag at the sixth attempt. The drop in grade made all the difference and she was nicely on top at the finish. (op 13-2 tchd 11-2)

Barn Dance(FR), subject of a gamble, hinted at ability in a 6f Newbury maiden on his debut last month. He got warm beforehand and, although going close, still proved too green to do himself full justice. He's evidently now found his level and correct sort of trip. (op 5-1)

Astraios(IRE) travelled best, but appeared to down tools shortly after going to the front and obviously has a few quirks. He's flattered by his mark at present, but helps to set the level. (op 2-1 tchd 11-4)

Bogey Hole(IRE), up in trip, was having her first outing on turf and looked a tricky ride. (op 9-2)

6764 DIGIBET.COM H'CAP 1m 3y
4:50 (4:52) (Class 6) (0-65,65) 3-Y-O+ **£1,617** (£481; £240; £120) **Stalls** Centre

Form RPR

5650 **1** **Glass Mountain (IRE)**^{47} 5381 3-9-2 **63**.......................... MartinLane 11 71
(James Fanshawe) *in tch: hdwy over 2f out: rdn to ld over 1f out: hdd ins fnl 100yds: kpt on to ld again last stride* **16/1**

6045 **2** *shd* **Yakama (IRE)**^{27} 6032 6-8-7 **51** oh6..........................(p) AdrianMcCarthy 9 59
(Christine Dunnett) *towards rr: pushed along over 2f out: hdwy over 1f out: rdn to ld ins fnl f: pushed along fnl 50yds: hdd last stride* **50/1**

4252 **3** *1* **Petsas Pleasure**^{12} 6461 5-9-5 **63**.................................. PaulHanagan 3 69
(Ollie Pears) *stdd s: hld up towards rr: hdwy on far side over 2f out: ev ch over 1f out: no ex and btn fnl 100yds* **11/4**^{1}

403 **4** *nse* **Xpres Maite**^{12} 6452 8-9-1 **59**.................................(b) RussKennemore 12 65
(Roy Bowring) *chsd ldr: rdn 2f out: kpt on same pce ins fnl f* **9/1**^{3}

0006 **5** *1* **Adaria**^{15} 6382 3-9-4 **65**.. IanMongan 10 68
(David C Griffiths) *towards rr: rdn over 2f out: hanging lft and stl plenty to do over 1f out: styd on wl ins fnl f: nt rch ldrs* **22/1**

1331 **6** *½* **Viking Rose (IRE)**^{12} 6450 3-9-4 **65**.............................. LeeNewman 16 67
(James Eustace) *chsd ldrs: rdn 2f out: styd on same pce fr over 1f out* **9/2**^{2}

0040 **7** *½* **Lightning Spirit**^{14} 6411 3-8-1 **51**.........................(p) LouisBeuzelin$^{(3)}$ 15 52
(Gary Moore) *bhd: rdn over 2f out: hdwy and n.m.r ent fnl f: drvn ins fnl f: kpt on same pce fnl 100yds: nvr trbld ldrs* **33/1**

3610 **8** *2* **Desert Chieftain**^{7} 6586 3-9-1 **62**...............................(b) KirstyMilczarek 6 58
(Luca Cumani) *in tch: rdn 2f out: unable qck u.p over 1f out: one pce and hld ins fnl f* **9/1**^{3}

0025 **9** *3 ¾* **Aviso (GER)**^{7} 6587 7-8-10 **61**.....................................(p) KevinLundie$^{(7)}$ 5 49
(David Evans) *t.k.h: led tl rdn and hdd over 1f out: wknd fnl f* **16/1**

6200 **10** *1 ¼* **Petomic (IRE)**^{21} 6211 6-9-3 **64**.............................(p) RobertLButler$^{(3)}$ 4 49
(Richard Guest) *chsd ldrs: rdn and unable qck wl over 1f out: wknd ins fnl f* **25/1**

5605 **11** *2* **Diplomasi**^{25} 6089 3-9-1 **62**.. NeilCallan 2 42
(Clive Brittain) *chsd ldrs: rdn and pressing ldrs wl over 1f out: btn ent fnl f: wknd* **14/1**

0000 **12** *nk* **Emerald Girl (IRE)**^{30} 5944 4-9-1 **59**............................ WilliamCarson 7 39
(Richard Guest) *rring in stalls: in tch: rdn and unable qck ent fnl 2f: wknd jst over 1f out* **50/1**

002 **13** *¾* **Gay Gallivanter**^{48} 5352 3-8-8 **54** ow1.............................. ShaneKelly 14 33
(Michael Quinn) *stdd and dropped in bhd after s: hld up in rr: rdn and no rspnse 3f out: n.d* **14/1**

000 **14** *½* **Milton Of Campsie**^{6} 6604 6-9-5 **63**.............................(e) RobertWinston 1 40
(Richard Guest) *hld up towards rr: hdwy on far side over 2f out: rdn and no prog over 1f out: wknd ent fnl f* **20/1**

0004 **15** *¾* **Fists And Stones**^{7} 6578 3-9-1 **62**............................ MatthewDavies 8 37
(Mick Channon) *in tch in midfield: rdn 1/2-way: wknd wl over 1f out: bhd fnl f* **25/1**

3020 **16** *14* **General Tufto**^{11} 6486 6-8-2 **53**...................................(b) RaulDaSilva$^{(7)}$ 13 —
(Charles Smith) *a in rr: rdn and no rspnse over 3f out: eased fr wl over 1f out: t.o* **22/1**

1m 39.42s (-1.18) **Going Correction** -0.15s/f (Firm)
WFA 3 from 4yo+ 3lb **16** Ran SP% **118.0**
Speed ratings (Par 101): **99,98,97,97,96 96,95,93,90,88 86,86,85,85,84 70**
toteswingers:1&2:£97.30, 2&3:£34.30, 1&3:£6.10 CSF £659.45 CT £2944.14 TOTE £19.70: £5.00, £8.00, £1.10, £2.90; EX 1545.50.
Owner Simon Gibson **Bred** C McEvoy **Trained** Newmarket, Suffolk

FOCUS
A weak handicap and yet another wide-open race on the card. It was run at a routine sort of pace.

Milton Of Campsie Official explanation: jockey said that the mare hung right

6765 MERRIVALE MODEL VILLAGE H'CAP 5f 43y

5:20 (5:21) (Class 6) (0-60,60) 3-Y-0+ **£1,617** (£481; £240; £120) **Stalls** Centre

Form RPR

5026 **1** **The Strig**[7] 6580 4-9-6 **59**....(v) WilliamCarson 11 69
(Stuart Williams) *isolated fr rest and mde all on stands' rails: drvn and a maintaining advantage through fnl f* **4/1**[2]

052 **2** *1 1/4* **Bateleur**[7] 6580 7-8-10 **56**.... CharlesBishop(7) 9 62
(Mick Channon) *towards rr: shkn up 1/2-way: gd prog in 5th over 1f out: wnt 2nd wl ins fnl f: fin willingly but too much to do* **4/1**[2]

-453 **3** *3 1/4* **Mr Skipiton (IRE)**[25] 6105 6-9-2 **55**.... TomMcLaughlin 4 49
(Brian McMath) *prom: led centre bunch 1/2-way w wnr alone on rails: rdn and wknd ins fnl f: lost 2nd cl home* **9/2**[3]

0023 **4** *3/4* **Canadian Danehill (IRE)**[10] 6501 9-8-13 **52**....(p) RobertWinston 3 43
(Robert Cowell) *racd freely: led main bunch down centre tl 1/2-way: cl up tl over 1f out: rdn w little rspnse* **13/2**

3504 **5** *1 1/2* **Star Twilight**[10] 6501 4-9-7 **60**....(v) PaulHanagan 1 46
(Derek Shaw) *broke wl but sn struggling in rr: racd awkwardly and nvr on terms after 2f: sme hdwy ins fnl f* **3/1**[1]

4544 **6** *hd* **Miakora**[19] 6251 3-8-11 **50**.... ShaneKelly 8 35
(Michael Quinn) *midfield: drvn 1/2-way: racing awkwardly and sn wl btn* **20/1**

-004 **7** *2 1/4* **Pavement Games**[13] 6427 4-8-0 **46**.... RaulDaSilva(7) 7 23
(Richard Guest) *midfield: drvn 1/2-way: struggling after* **16/1**

0-00 **8** *nk* **Bombay Mist**[69] 4650 4-8-7 **46** oh1....(e) AdrianMcCarthy 5 22
(Richard Guest) *last away: rcvrd to chse ldrs on outside after 2f: sn hrd drvn: wknd bdly jst over 1f out* **50/1**

006 **9** *1 1/2* **Oosisit**[16] 6353 3-9-1 **54**.... JamesSullivan 6 24
(Ruth Carr) *cl up: rdn 1/2-way: sn dropped out* **25/1**

62.59 secs (-0.11) **Going Correction** -0.15s/f (Firm) 9 Ran SP% **113.0**
Speed ratings (Par 101): **94,92,86,85,83 82,79,78,76**
toteswingers:1&2:£3.70, 2&3:£4.80, 1&3:£5.00 CSF £19.41 CT £73.26 TOTE £3.80: £3.50, £1.50, £1.50; EX 21.70.
Owner Brian Piper & David Cobill **Bred** Old Mill Stud **Trained** Newmarket, Suffolk

FOCUS

An ordinary sprint where few landed a serious blow.

Star Twilight Official explanation: jockey said that the filly lost her action

T/Jkpt: Not won. T/Plt: £288.30 to a £1 stake. Pool of £68,583.98 - 173.64 winning tickets. T/Qpdt: £58.20 to a £1 stake. Pool of £6,061.11 - 77.05 winning tickets. SP

6603 LEICESTER (R-H)

Tuesday, October 11

OFFICIAL GOING: Good (good to soft in places; 7.0)

Wind: Fresh, behind Weather: Cloudy

6766 WYMESWOLD CONDITIONS STKS 7f 9y

2:10 (2:11) (Class 4) 2-Y-0 **£4,851** (£1,443; £721; £360) **Stalls** High

Form RPR

2031 **1** **Cravat**[32] 5876 2-8-13 91.... SilvestreDeSousa 4 91
(Mark Johnston) *prom: pushed along 1/2-way: rdn to ld over 1f out: r.o wl* **11/4**[2]

4114 **2** *2* **Amazing Storm (IRE)**[31] 5931 2-9-2 87.... RichardHughes 3 89
(Richard Hannon) *racd keenly: led and sn clr: rdn and hdd over 1f out: styd on same pce: wnt 2nd nr fin* **11/4**[2]

31 **3** *nk* **Mabaany**[31] 5919 2-9-2 94.... RichardHills 5 88
(William Haggas) *hld up: hdwy over 2f out: rdn and ev ch over 1f out: styd on same pce ins fnl f* **5/2**[1]

6210 **4** *1/2* **Otto The Great**[24] 6162 2-9-2 84.... ShaneKelly 2 87
(Walter Swinburn) *chsd ldr: rdn and ev ch over 1f out: styd on same pce ins fnl f* **20/1**

1100 **5** *6* **Wise Venture (IRE)**[53] 5251 2-9-2 88.... HarryBentley(3) 1 77
(Alan Jarvis) *chsd ldrs: rdn 2f out: wknd fnl f* **16/1**

1 **6** *8* **Newnton Lodge**[53] 5239 2-9-2 85.... JamesDoyle 6 50
(Roger Charlton) *dwlt: sn pushed along in rr: wknd 2f out* **9/2**[3]

1m 25.31s (-0.89) **Going Correction** -0.15s/f (Firm) 6 Ran SP% **110.7**
Speed ratings (Par 97): **99,96,96,95,88 79**
toteswingers:1&2:£1.90, 2&3:£2.20, 1&3:£1.10 CSF £10.41 TOTE £3.40: £1.10, £2.30; EX 8.70.

Owner Sheikh Hamdan Bin Mohammed Al Maktoum **Bred** Darley **Trained** Middleham Moor, N Yorks

FOCUS

False rail from round course bend to the Winning Post positioned 10yds from inside rail and increasing distances on Round course by about 10yds. A tight little conditions race with all six being previous winners. The winner and second raced closest to the stands' rail, which may have been significant.

NOTEBOOK

Cravat was by far the most exposed in the field - this was his 11th start of the campaign - but he was the only runner not carrying a penalty. He was one of the first to come off the bridle, but responded and scythed his way up the stands' rail to lead inside the distance. He wouldn't appear to have much scope for improvement, but with horses from this yard you never know. (tchd 5-2 and 3-1)

Amazing Storm(IRE), just behind a subsequent winner when foiled in his hat-trick bid in a Doncaster nursery over a furlong further, tried to make his stamina count under a positive ride. He looked like finishing fourth at best when the winner headed him a furlong out, but fought back to regain second near the line. A return to 1m may help. (op 3-1 tchd 10-3)

Mabaany's 10l romp at Chester on his second start received a boost when the runner-up went in next time and he looked a danger when produced with his effort widest 2f from home, but weakened towards the finish. He may not have been racing on the best part of the track as things turned out, so is worth another chance. (op 9-4 tchd 11-4)

Otto The Great, tailed off in the Mill Reef after stumbling at the start, had every chance passing the furlong pole but finished weakly and may not have seen out the extra furlong. (tchd 16-1 and 25-1)

Wise Venture(IRE) had twice been found out in Pattern company since winning his first two starts in May and was again left behind despite the drop in class.

Newnton Lodge was fitted with a hood despite not appearing to do much wrong when making a successful debut at Sandown in August (couple of subsequent winners behind), but on this occasion he ran a stinker and this was far too bad to be true. (op 11-2 tchd 4-1)

6767 WHISSENDINE (S) STKS 7f 9y

2:40 (2:41) (Class 6) 3-4-Y-0 **£1,617** (£481; £240; £120) **Stalls** High

Form RPR

2004 **1** **Brio**[22] 6223 3-8-10 56....(v) MartinHarley 14 64
(Alan McCabe) *mde all: rdn over 1f out: r.o* **12/1**

0300 **2** *3 1/2* **Dimaire**[14] 6433 4-8-7 55.... FrankieMcDonald 1 50
(Derek Haydn Jones) *racd alone far-side: up w the pce: rdn over 1f out: styd on same pce ins fnl f* **25/1**

0510 **3** *1 1/2* **Flying Phoenix**[12] 6490 3-8-10 65....(b) ShaneKelly 4 51
(Gay Kelleway) *chsd ldrs: rdn over 1f out: no ex* **5/2**[2]

0305 **4** *3/4* **Ginger Grey (IRE)**[20] 6262 4-8-12 65....(b) RichardHughes 2 48
(David O'Meara) *swtchd lft sn after s: hld up and bhd: hdwy u.p over 1f out: nt rch ldrs* **2/1**[1]

5655 **5** *2* **Piccarello**[59] 5041 3-8-10 55.... JimmyQuinn 3 43
(Mark H Tompkins) *in rr: hdwy u.p over 1f out: nvr on terms* **25/1**

0300 **6** *nk* **Riczar**[20] 6262 3-8-5 44.... RichardKingscote 13 37
(Tom Dascombe) *prom: rdn over 2f out: wknd over 1f out* **33/1**

0123 **7** *1* **My Lord**[180] 1334 3-8-12 74.... KierenFox(3) 8 45
(Bill Turner) *chsd ldr tl rdn over 2f out: wknd over 1f out:* **11/2**[3]

0646 **8** *4 1/2* **Talkative Guest (IRE)**[27] 6071 3-8-5 49.... AdrianMcCarthy 9 22
(George Margarson) *in rr: rdn over 2f out: nvr on terms* **25/1**

0-6 **9** *3 1/2* **Calico Bay (IRE)**[7] 6608 3-8-10 0.... GrahamGibbons 11 18
(Alan McCabe) *s.i.s: hdwy over 5f out: rdn 1/2-way: wknd over 2f out:* **40/1**

-032 **10** *nk* **Poppet's Joy**[22] 6223 3-8-5 53.... ChrisCatlin 12 12
(Reg Hollinshead) *prom: sn pushed along: wknd 1/2-way* **10/1**

0400 **11** *20* **Conesuala**[8] 6589 4-8-4 47.... HarryBentley(3) 6 —
(Alan Jarvis) *mid-div: pushed along 1/2-way: sn wknd* **40/1**

00- **12** *3 1/2* **Great Show**[341] 7310 4-8-7 0.... MartinLane 7 —
(Bernard Llewellyn) *prom: rdn and wknd 3f out: t.o* **100/1**

5000 **13** *9* **Farmer's Wife**[52] 4953 3-8-2 47.... JohnFahy(3) 5 —
(Bernard Llewellyn) *s.s: outpcd: t.o* **100/1**

1m 25.72s (-0.48) **Going Correction** -0.15s/f (Firm)
WFA 3 from 4yo 2lb **13** Ran SP% **115.4**
Speed ratings (Par 101): **96,92,90,89,87 86,85,80,76,76 53,49,39**
toteswingers:1&2:£45.60, 2&3:£14.40, 1&3:£5.80 CSF £271.57 TOTE £12.40: £2.90, £7.20, £1.40; EX 251.00.There was no bid for the winner. My Lord was claimed by Mark Benton for £6,000.
Owner Sale Of The Century **Bred** Ashbrittle Stud **Trained** Averham Park, Notts

FOCUS

A poor seller and nothing got into it from off the pace. As in the first race, bagging the stands' rail proved the key. The winner ran a personal best, but there are doubts over the rest.

6768 BRITISH STALLION STUDS E B F REFERENCE POINT MAIDEN STKS (C&G) 7f 9y

3:10 (3:11) (Class 4) 2-Y-0 **£4,334** (£1,289; £644; £322) **Stalls** High

Form RPR

0 **1** **Afaal (USA)**[46] 5447 2-9-0 0.... TadhgO'Shea 4 79
(William Haggas) *s.i.s: hld up: hdwy over 2f out: led over 1f out: shkn up and r.o* **14/1**

6 **2** *2* **Fourth Of June (IRE)**[25] 6123 2-9-0 0.... TomMcLaughlin 8 74
(Ed Dunlop) *s.i.s: hld up: hdwy over 1f out: rdn to go 2nd ins fnl f: no ch w wnr* **17/2**[3]

3 *1 1/4* **Flaxen Flare (IRE)** 2-9-0 0.... JimmyFortune 7 72+
(Andrew Balding) *hld up: hdwy over 1f out: swtchd lft ins fnl f: r.o: wnt 3rd post* **40/1**

5 **4** *shd* **Peak Storm**[123] 2868 2-9-0 0.... MartinLane 2 70
(John Gallagher) *mid-div: hdwy 1/2-way: sn pushed along: styd on same pce ins fnl f* **150/1**

5 *1/2* **Mokbil (IRE)** 2-9-0 0.... AndreaAtzeni 1 69
(Roger Varian) *chsd ldrs: pushed along 2f out: one pce fnl f* **20/1**

2 **6** *1 3/4* **Kaafel (IRE)**[24] 6165 2-9-0 0.... RichardHills 14 64
(Charles Hills) *hld up: hdwy over 2f out: rdn over 1f out: no ex ins fnl f* **4/5**[1]

5 **7** *nk* **Aim Higher**[103] 3552 2-9-0 0.... NickyMackay 3 64
(John Gosden) *led: racd keenly: pushed along and hung rt fr over 2f out: hdd over 1f out: no ex ins fnl f* **15/2**[2]

640 **8** *1 1/2* **Kiwayu**[8] 6588 2-9-0 0.... KirstyMilczarek 12 60
(Luca Cumani) *hld up: hdwy over 1f out: nt rch ldrs* **40/1**

9 *3* **Dakota Canyon (IRE)** 2-9-0 0.... DavidNolan 13 52
(Richard Fahey) *mid-div: pushed along 1/2-way: n.d* **25/1**

44 **10** *1 3/4* **Light Burst (USA)**[12] 6483 2-9-0 0.... RichardHughes 11 47
(Mahmood Al Zarooni) *hld up: plld hrd: hdwy over 2f out: wknd over 1f out* **9/1**

0 **11** *3* **Moataz (USA)**[8] 6579 2-9-0 0.... SilvestreDeSousa 9 40
(Mark Johnston) *chsd ldr: pushed along over 2f out: wknd over 1f out* **40/1**

00 **12** *11* **Awesome Rock (IRE)**[12] 6474 2-9-0 0.... FrankieMcDonald 15 11
(Louise Best) *prom to 1/2-way* **200/1**

00 **13** *3* **Gone To Ground**[18] 6292 2-9-0 0.... SteveDrowne 10 —
(Jeremy Gask) *bhd fnl 4f* **200/1**

60 **14** *2* **Charley's Mount (IRE)**[24] 6170 2-9-0 0.... ShaneKelly 6 —
(Brian Meehan) *chsd ldrs tl wknd over 2f out* **33/1**

15 *7* **Combat Rock (IRE)** 2-9-0 0.... FergusSweeney 5 —
(Jo Hughes) *plld hrd and prom: wknd 1/2-way: t.o* **150/1**

1m 25.71s (-0.49) **Going Correction** -0.15s/f (Firm) **15** Ran SP% **115.7**
Speed ratings (Par 97): **96,93,92,92,91 89,89,87,84,82 78,66,62,60,52**
CSF £115.28 TOTE £10.40: £3.80, £2.90, £12.60; EX 114.10.
Owner Hamdan Al Maktoum **Bred** Shadwell Farm LLC **Trained** Newmarket, Suffolk

FOCUS

This looked a fair maiden and the winning time was 0.4 seconds slower than the conditions race, but fractionally faster than the older horses in the seller.

NOTEBOOK

Afaal(USA) was 100-1 when well beaten on his Newmarket debut in August, but was a completely different proposition here. Held up early, he quickened up nicely when asked and was in little danger after hitting the front over a furlong from home. Out of an unraced sister to the 1,000 Guineas winner Shadayid, there is probably more to come. (op 12-1)

Fourth Of June(IRE) was running on late over 6f on his Newbury debut which suggested this extra furlong would suit and the form of that maiden has worked out well. Despite the longer trip, he was doing all his best work late again here and it shouldn't be long before he goes one better. (op 13-2 tchd 9-1)

Flaxen Flare(IRE) ◆, a 20,000gns half-brother to four winners at a variety of trips all over Europe, did best of the newcomers and was the real eye-catcher, coming from a long way back and running on strongly to grab third on the line. This was a promising start and he should win races. (op 50-1)

Peak Storm, not seen since finishing a well-beaten fifth of six on his debut in a Chepstow novice event in June, did well to finish where he did as he was one of the first off the bridle, but kept on trying. He has ability and will qualify for a mark after one more run.

Mokbil(IRE), a half-brother to a winning hurdler and in the same ownership as the winner, showed up for a long way and kept on going to the line. There was enough promise here to build on. (op 18-1 tchd 33-1)

Kaafel(IRE) was beaten just a neck on his Newbury debut last month and was the choice of Richard Hills over the winner and fifth, but a brief effort over 2f from home came to nothing. The form of the Newbury race hasn't worked out (14 subsequent runs have yielded just two placings). The trainer's representative reported that the colt was unsuited by the ground. Official explanation: trainer's rep said colt was unsuited by the good (good to soft places) ground (op 8-11)
Aim Higher, not seen since running green when fifth of nine on his Yarmouth debut in June, set the pace until veering away to his right over 2f from and soon losing the advantage. He still seems to be learning. (op 10-1 tchd 12-1)

6769 FOSSE WAY CLASSIFIED CLAIMING STKS 1m 3f 183y
3:40 (3:40) (Class 6) 3-5-Y-O **£1,617** (£481; £240; £120) **Stalls** Low

Form RPR
0552 **1** **Warneford**[20] 6255 3-9-3 70 (v[1]) ShaneKelly 6 77
(Brian Meehan) *trckd ldrs: led over 1f out: rdn clr* **11/4**[1]
6430 **2** *9* **Lord Of The Storm**[13] 6465 3-8-4 53 (t) KierenFox(3) 8 53
(Bill Turner) *hld up: hdwy over 2f out: rdn over 1f out: styd on same pce* **28/1**
3541 **3** *shd* **Royal Defence (IRE)**[29] 5993 5-8-12 61 SeanLevey(3) 9 53
(Michael Quinn) *chsd ldr: led 9f out: rdn and hdd over 1f out: no ex* **11/2**
0450 **4** *6* **Cloudy Start**[28] 6023 5-9-5 70 FergusSweeney 1 48
(Jamie Osborne) *hld up bhd: kpt on fr over 1f out: nvr nrr* **7/2**[2]
4406 **5** *1* **Now What**[12] 6476 4-9-3 60 JimCrowley 5 44
(Jonathan Portman) *prom: chsd ldr 5f out: rdn and ev ch wl over 1f out: sn wknd* **6/1**
6 *2* **Zulu Principle**[7] 4832 4-8-13 64 (b) MartinHarley 2 37
(John Joseph Hanlon, Ire) *prom: rdn over 2f out: sn wknd* **16/1**
3005 **7** *1 ¾* **Magic Millie (IRE)**[10] 6536 4-8-7 45 AshleyMorgan(5) 4 33
(David O'Meara) *led over 3f: remained handy: rdn over 2f out: wknd wl over 1f out* **40/1**
0000 **8** *24* **Himalayan Moon**[5] 6656 4-9-3 51 SilvestreDeSousa 3 —
(Ian Wood) *hld up: bhd fnl 3f: t.o* **22/1**
3320 **9** *30* **What About Now**[13] 6445 3-8-10 62 ow1 (b) RichardHughes 7 —
(J W Hills) *hld up: hdwy 5f out: sn pushed along: wknd and eased 3f out: t.o* **5/1**[3]

2m 33.44s (-0.46) **Going Correction** +0.125s/f (Good)
WFA 3 from 4yo+ 7lb **9** Ran SP% **111.3**
Speed ratings (Par 101): **106,100,99,95,95 93,92,76,56**
toteswingers:1&2:£9.40, 2&3:£18.00, 1&3:£4.50 CSF £82.09 TOTE £3.90: £1.90, £4.20, £1.80; EX 56.10.Warneford was claimed by Mustafa Khan for £15,000.
Owner Brimacombe,McNally,Vinciguerra,Sangster **Bred** Five Horses Ltd **Trained** Manton, Wilts

FOCUS
A very one-sided claimer and with doubts over many of these not form to take too literally.
Himalayan Moon Official explanation: jockey said filly lost its action
What About Now Official explanation: jockey said filly moved poorly throughout; trainer's rep said filly was unsuited by the good (good to soft places) ground

6770 WREAKE FILLIES' CONDITIONS STKS 1m 60y
4:10 (4:10) (Class 3) 3-Y-O+ **£6,490** (£1,942; £971; £486; £242) **Stalls** Low

Form RPR
2652 **1** **Avon Lady**[22] 6219 4-8-12 79 EddieAhern 7 96
(James Fanshawe) *chsd ldr: rdn to ld over 1f out: r.o* **12/1**
11-0 **2** *½* **Zoowraa**[149] 2137 3-8-9 103 SilvestreDeSousa 6 95
(Mahmood Al Zarooni) *trckd ldrs: racd keenly: rdn over 2f out: ev ch ins fnl f: r.o* **4/6**[1]
6406 **3** *3* **Musharakaat (IRE)**[76] 4429 3-8-9 90 RichardHills 2 88
(Ed Dunlop) *led: rdn and hdd over 1f out: no ex ins fnl f* **10/1**[3]
0 **4** *1* **Fugnina**[28] 6027 3-8-12 92 AdamKirby 3 89
(Marco Botti) *prom: rdn over 2f out: one pce fnl f* **33/1**
0031 **5** *1* **Metropolitain Miss (IRE)**[16] 6383 3-8-9 86 MartinHarley 4 83
(Mick Channon) *hld up: rdn over 2f out: edgd rt: nvr trbld ldrs* **4/1**[2]
0-00 **6** *3* **Ragsah (IRE)**[18] 6297 3-8-9 94 RichardMullen 1 76
(Saeed Bin Suroor) *hld up in tch: rdn over 1f out: wknd ins fnl f* **12/1**

1m 45.3s (0.20) **Going Correction** +0.125s/f (Good)
WFA 3 from 4yo 3lb **6** Ran SP% **107.4**
Speed ratings (Par 104): **104,103,100,99,98 95**
toteswingers:1&2:£1.70, 2&3:£2.30, 1&3:£1.80 CSF £19.06 TOTE £7.20: £3.10, £1.10; EX 19.60.
Owner Helena Springfield Ltd **Bred** Meon Valley Stud **Trained** Newmarket, Suffolk

FOCUS
An interesting conditions race in more ways than one, but as is often the case in races like this the form looks dubious.

NOTEBOOK
Avon Lady appeared to face a stiff task against the 3yos on these terms, having upwards of 7lb to find, but she was given a good ride. Always in a decent position, she proved game after leading over a furlong from home, but this performance won't do much for her handicap mark. (op 14-1)
Zoowraa hadn't been seen since finishing last in the French 1,000 Guineas in May when making her debut for Godolphin, but this looked a good opportunity for her as she was 24lb well in with the winner. She was keen enough early and was being niggled along over 2f from home, but she responded to the pressure and looked to be gaining on her rival inside the last furlong, but her rider then put his whip down and she could make no further impression in the last few yards. Her jockey had given her just four cracks with the whip, with only one inside the last furlong, and if he believed he was close to surpassing his quota, when he actually wasn't, then he was put in an impossible position which punters will have to get used to. (op 8-13 tchd 4-7)
Musharakaat(IRE) has faced some stiff tasks since a successful racecourse debut, but she had the run of the race out in front here with no apparent excuse. (tchd 11-1)
Fugnina, a dual winner in Italy, was well beaten on her British debut at Haydock last month though the 7f was probably inadequate. She couldn't make much impression here despite the longer trip and may need a more strongly run race. (op 25-1 tchd 40-1)
Metropolitain Miss(IRE)'s success in a Musselburgh fillies' handicap last month has been boosted since, but after pulling hard early she could make little impression once off the bridle at halfway. (op 7-2)
Ragsah(IRE), whose stable had won the last two runnings of this, was a very useful juvenile (fourth in the Cheveley Park), but two heavy defeats in Listed company since returning from a lengthy absence in August left her with major questions marks against her. This effort confirms that she has gone badly the wrong way. (op 16-1 tchd 18-1)

6771 BRITISH STALLION STUDS SUPPORTING BRITISH RACING E B F SOAR MAIDEN STKS (DIV I) 1m 60y
4:40 (4:41) (Class 4) 2-Y-O **£4,010** (£1,193; £596; £298) **Stalls** Low

Form RPR
0 **1** **Thomas Chippendale (IRE)**[53] 5254 2-9-3 0 TomQueally 6 86+
(Sir Henry Cecil) *hld up: hdwy on bit over 2f out: shkn up ins fnl f: r.o to ld nr fin* **9/4**[1]
2 **2** *nk* **Went The Day Well (USA)**[17] 6334 2-9-3 0 GrahamGibbons 8 83+
(Ed McMahon) *led: rdn and edgd lft ins fnl f: hdd nr fin* **4/1**[2]
3 **3** *3* **Zaeem**[33] 5855 2-9-3 0 RichardHughes 1 76
(Mahmood Al Zarooni) *chsd ldr to 1/2-way: rdn over 1f out: styd on same pce fnl f* **9/2**[3]
4 **4** *shd* **Mysterious Man (IRE)**[25] 6126 2-9-3 0 JimmyFortune 3 76
(Andrew Balding) *prom: chsd ldr 1/2-way: pushed along over 2f out: no ex ins fnl f* **9/4**[1]
0 **5** *1 ¾* **Key Gold**[13] 6458 2-8-12 0 SilvestreDeSousa 4 67+
(Mark Johnston) *chsd ldrs: pushed along over 3f out: rdn over 1f out: styd on same pce* **25/1**
6 *1 ¾* **Hallmark Star** 2-9-3 0 NickyMackay 10 68
(Gerard Butler) *s.s: pushed along 1/2-way: styd on ins fnl f: nvr nrr* **40/1**
05 **7** *2 ¼* **Rogue Reporter (IRE)**[28] 6019 2-9-3 0 KirstyMilczarek 11 63+
(Luca Cumani) *hld up: hdwy over 2f out: rdn and edgd rt over 1f out: sn wknd* **50/1**
8 *½* **Villa Royale** 2-8-12 0 DaneO'Neill 7 56
(Harry Dunlop) *hld up: pushed along 1/2-way: n.d* **80/1**
9 *¾* **Storm King** 2-9-3 0 AdrianMcCarthy 9 60
(George Margarson) *hld up: hdwy over 3f out: rdn and wknd over 1f out* **100/1**
0 **10** *hd* **Jericho (IRE)**[24] 6180 2-9-3 0 FergusSweeney 2 59
(Jamie Osborne) *prom: nt clr run over 2f out: wknd over 1f out* **150/1**
6 **11** *¾* **Emperors Waltz (IRE)**[28] 6018 2-8-12 0 MartinLane 5 53
(Rae Guest) *hld up: pushed along over 2f out: n.d* **125/1**

1m 46.6s (1.50) **Going Correction** +0.125s/f (Good) **11** Ran SP% **111.6**
Speed ratings (Par 97): **97,96,93,93,91 90,87,87,86,86 85**
toteswingers:1&2:£2.70, 2&3:£3.20, 1&3:£2.90 CSF £10.75 TOTE £3.90: £1.90, £2.00, £1.10; EX 12.60.
Owner Sir Robert Ogden **Bred** Premier Bloodstock **Trained** Newmarket, Suffolk

FOCUS
This maiden can go to a useful sort, with the high-class stayer Opinion Poll winning it three years ago, and this year's winner looks a nice type.

NOTEBOOK
Thomas Chippendale(IRE) ◆ showed a bit more on his debut than his finishing position of 13th of 17 would suggest in the Convivial Maiden at the Ebor Meeting, and that form is working out well. Ridden with plenty of confidence at the back of the field early, he moved smoothly into a challenging position and although he had to work harder to get the better of the runner-up than had seemed likely, his rider never went for his whip. He should make up into a very nice 3yo. (op 15-8 tchd 5-2)
Went The Day Well(USA) ◆ showed plenty of ability when runner-up on his Haydock debut and this was another good effort. Admittedly he did have the run of the race out in front, but proved a tough nut to crack and was only just caught by a nice prospect. He will surely get off the mark before too long. (tchd 7-2)
Zaeem, surrounded by subsequent winners when third of nine on last month's Epsom debut, plugged on against the inside rail from over a furlong out, but it's debatable whether he stepped up that much from his first effort. (op 4-1 tchd 7-2)
Mysterious Man(IRE) faced a stiff task on his debut when fourth of seven in the Haynes, Hanson & Clark. Always close to the pace, he lacked a turn of foot but that's not surprising for a colt who's bred to stay all day and the best of him will be seen next season. (op 11-4)
Key Gold, well beaten on last month's Nottingham debut, kept on fairly well considering she was off the bridle over 3f out and she looks one for the longer term. (tchd 22-1)
Hallmark Star ◆, an already-gelded 20,000gns half-brother to seven winners including the Listed-winner Inglenook, made some late progress from off the pace down the wide outside and will do better in due course. (op 66-1)
Rogue Reporter(IRE) now qualifies for a mark and looks one for handicaps next season. (tchd 66-1)

6772 BRITISH STALLION STUDS SUPPORTING BRITISH RACING E B F SOAR MAIDEN STKS (DIV II) 1m 60y
5:10 (5:12) (Class 4) 2-Y-O **£4,010** (£1,193; £596; £298) **Stalls** Low

Form RPR
0 **1** **Mojave (IRE)**[17] 6334 2-9-3 0 RichardHughes 6 87+
(Mahmood Al Zarooni) *led 7f out: pushed clr over 1f out: easily* **11/2**[3]
6 **2** *6* **Ruscello (IRE)**[59] 5051 2-9-3 0 RichardMullen 8 72
(Sir Michael Stoute) *chsd ldrs: rdn over 2f out: edgd rt and wnt 2nd over 1f out: no ch w wnr* **13/2**
0 **3** *nk* **Moidore**[24] 6165 2-9-3 0 SteveDrowne 11 73+
(Roger Charlton) *hld up: hmpd 6f out: pushed along over 3f out: styd on fr over 1f out: nrst fin* **3/1**[1]
4 *shd* **Star Date (IRE)** 2-9-3 0 NickyMackay 9 71+
(Gerard Butler) *s.s: hld up: hdwy over 1f out: r.o: nrst fin* **20/1**
5 *½* **Headline News (IRE)** 2-8-12 0 MartinLane 3 65+
(Rae Guest) *s.i.s: hld up: r.o ins fnl f: nvr nrr* **28/1**
0 **6** *1 ½* **Lost Highway (IRE)**[10] 6526 2-8-12 0 SilvestreDeSousa 4 62+
(Mark Johnston) *hmpd s: hld up: plld hrd: swtchd rt and hdwy 2f out: no ex ins fnl f* **16/1**
0 **7** *hd* **Watheeq (USA)**[53] 5239 2-9-3 0 RichardHills 10 66
(Roger Varian) *hld up: edgd lft 6f out: hdwy over 2f out: wknd fnl f* **13/2**
03 **8** *4 ½* **Vexillum (IRE)**[13] 6455 2-9-3 0 MatthewDavies 1 56
(Mick Channon) *led 1f: chsd wnr: rdn over 2f out: wknd over 1f out* **10/1**
9 *9* **Andrea Bellevica (IRE)**[73] 4567 2-8-12 0 MartinHarley 5 30
(John Joseph Hanlon, Ire) *hld up in tch: rdn and wknd over 2f out* **12/1**
03 **10** *19* **Wayne Manor (IRE)**[43] 5536 2-9-3 0 JimCrowley 2 —
(Ralph Beckett) *hld up: bhd fnl 3f: t.o* **5/1**[2]
0 **11** *8* **Fine Finale**[22] 6214 2-9-3 0 LukeMorris 7 —
(Jeremy Gask) *chsd ldrs: rdn over 3f out: wknd over 2f out: t.o* **150/1**

1m 45.82s (0.72) **Going Correction** +0.125s/f (Good) **11** Ran SP% **115.3**
Speed ratings (Par 97): **101,95,94,94,94 92,92,87,78,59 51**
toteswingers:1&2:£8.80, 2&3:£4.90, 1&3:£4.70 CSF £39.56 TOTE £5.90: £2.30, £2.90, £1.40; EX 46.10.
Owner Godolphin **Bred** Mrs Eithne Hamilton **Trained** Newmarket, Suffolk

FOCUS
This was more one-sided than the first division and the winning time was 0.78 seconds quicker. Despite the places still being up for grabs inside the last furlong, use of the whip by the riders was conspicuous by its absence.

NOTEBOOK
Mojave(IRE) ◆ didn't show much on last month's Haydock debut, but the contrast here could hardly have been greater. Soon in front, he ground his rivals into submission over the last 2f and this 200,000gns half-brother to six winners, including the high-class Dubai Prince, should go on from here. (op 6-1 tchd 13-2 and 5-1)
Ruscello(IRE) beat only one home on his Yarmouth debut in august, but would have found that 6f inadequate on breeding. This extra 2f suited him much better and he had every chance, but although beaten pointless by the winner he still looked green so may not come into his own until next year. (op 5-1 tchd 4-1)
Moidore ◆ showed little when well beaten on last month's Newbury debut, but having been given plenty to do here, especially after being hampered on the bend, he made up plenty of late ground down the wide outside and looks capable of even better. (op 4-1)

Star Date(IRE) ◆, already gelded and retained for 40,000gns as a yearling, is a half-brother to the recent Cumberland Lodge winner Quest For Peace. Another to be given a lot to do, he stayed on well down the outside to fare best of the two newcomers and better can be expected with this experience under his belt. (tchd 25-1)
Headline News(IRE) ◆, a 62,000euros foal but only a 12,000gns yearling, caught the eye in staying on well to finish on the heels of the placed horses and considering she is from a yard whose juveniles are rarely wound up first time, this was an encouraging start. (op 20-1)
Lost Highway(IRE) faced a stiff task on her debut when beating just one home in a valuable fillies' sales race at Newmarket earlier this month and showed a bit more here. (op 25-1)

6773 STEWARDS H'CAP — 1m 1f 218y
5:40 (5:40) (Class 5) (0-75,75) 3-Y-0+ **£2,264** (£673; £336; £168) **Stalls** Low

Form RPR
0500 **1** **Tartan Gigha (IRE)**[17] 6346 6-9-10 **75**.................... SilvestreDeSousa 3 86+
(Mark Johnston) *mid-div: hdwy over 4f out: sn pushed along: rdn and qckndd to ld wl ins fnl f: r.o* **7/1**[2]
-330 **2** *1 ½* **Looking On**[32] 5892 3-9-4 **74**.................... DaneO'Neill 14 82
(Henry Candy) *mid-div: outpcd over 3f out: hdwy over 1f out: edgd rt ins fnl f: r.o* **9/1**
5002 **3** *hd* **Hidden Glory**[10] 6538 4-9-4 **69**.................... FrederikTylicki 1 76
(James Given) *hld up: hdwy over 2f out: rdn to ld ins fnl f: sn hdd and unable qck* **12/1**
440 **4** *nk* **Obsession (IRE)**[141] 2368 3-9-4 **74**....................(v) JimmyFortune 16 81
(Jeremy Noseda) *racd wd for 2f: chsd ldrs: pushed along 4f out: rdn and ev ch whn hung lft ins fnl f: one pce* **12/1**
4305 **5** *1 ¾* **Spring Secret**[15] 6401 5-9-1 **66**....................(p) LukeMorris 15 69
(Bryn Palling) *chsd ldr 8f out tl over 4f out: rdn and ev ch ins fnl f: no ex* **33/1**
6260 **6** *3* **Smirfy's Silver**[20] 6263 7-9-2 **67**.................... LiamKeniry 12 64
(Deborah Sanderson) *led: rdn over 1f out: hdd and no ex ins fnl f* **33/1**
6060 **7** *nk* **Bilidn**[26] 6093 3-9-3 **73**.................... TomQueally 6 69
(Clive Brittain) *prom: rdn and outpcd over 2f out: styd on ins fnl f* **40/1**
2413 **8** *¾* **Shabak Hom (IRE)**[44] 5509 4-9-10 **75**.................... MartinLane 17 70
(David Simcock) *s.i.s: hld up: hdwy over 2f out: sn rdn: nt trble ldrs* **14/1**
5531 **9** *1* **Silver Alliance**[18] 6311 3-9-2 **72**.................... JimmyQuinn 4 65
(Walter Swinburn) *hld up: hdwy 2f out: sn rdn and hung rt: no ex fnl f* **8/1**[3]
0305 **10** *1 ¼* **African Cheetah**[18] 6290 5-9-8 **73**....................(v) AdamKirby 10 63
(Reg Hollinshead) *hld up: nt clr run over 1f out: n.d* **20/1**
1343 **11** *nk* **Transfer**[28] 6029 6-8-11 **65**.................... RyanClark(3) 2 55
(Richard Price) *hld up: rdn over 1f out: nvr on terms* **11/2**[1]
1033 **12** *hd* **Rustic Deacon**[22] 6219 4-9-10 **75**.................... RichardHughes 9 64
(Willie Musson) *chsd ldr 2f: remained handy: rdn and ev ch ins fnl f: sn wknd and eased* **7/1**[2]
4-06 **13** *¾* **Lyric Poet (USA)**[76] 4432 4-9-6 **71**....................(t) WilliamCarson 8 59
(Giles Bravery) *hld up: a in rr* **16/1**
6106 **14** *1 ½* **Gallego**[13] 6461 9-8-7 **65**.................... RachealKneller(7) 7 50
(Richard Price) *hld up: hdwy 6f out: chsd ldr over 4f out tl rdn over 1f out: wknd fnl f* **33/1**
F600 **15** *1* **Embsay Crag**[28] 6024 5-9-7 **72**.................... JimCrowley 5 55
(Kate Walton) *s.i.s: a in rr* **8/1**[3]

2m 8.31s (0.41) **Going Correction** +0.125s/f (Good)
WFA 3 from 4yo+ 5lb **15** Ran SP% **116.6**
Speed ratings (Par 103): **103,101,101,101,100 97,97,96,95,94 94,94,93,92,91**
toteswingers:1&2:£12.90, 2&3:£19.40, 1&3:£7.20 CSF £61.94 CT £746.84 TOTE £6.50: £2.00, £3.40, £4.20; EX 97.10.
Owner Exors of the Late Mrs I Bird **Bred** Gainsborough Stud Management Ltd **Trained** Middleham Moor, N Yorks

FOCUS
A competitive, if modest handicap and several still held a chance entering the last furlong.
Silver Alliance Official explanation: jockey said gelding stumbled
African Cheetah Official explanation: jockey said horse had no more to give
Rustic Deacon Official explanation: jockey said gelding stumbled
T/Plt: £275.90 to a £1 stake. Pool of £60,627.98 - 160.37 winning tickets. T/Qpdt: £48.90 to a £1 stake. Pool of £5,003.15 - 75.70 winning tickets. CR

6447 NEWCASTLE (L-H)
Tuesday, October 11

OFFICIAL GOING: Soft (good to soft in places; 5.8)
Wind: Fresh, half against Weather: Cloudy, bright

6774 BRITISH STALLION STUDS SUPPORTING BRITISH RACING E B F MAIDEN STKS (C&G) — 1m 3y(S)
2:00 (2:01) (Class 5) 2-Y-0 **£3,234** (£962; £481; £240) **Stalls** Centre

Form RPR
1 **Thought Worthy (USA)** 2-9-0 0.................... WilliamBuick 4 77+
(John Gosden) *s.i.s: hdwy over 2f out: led 1f out: hld on wl towards fin* **6/1**[3]
02 **2** *¾* **Silver Blaze**[20] 6259 2-9-0 0.................... PJMcDonald 2 75+
(Alan Swinbank) *in rr: hdwy over 3f out: chsd wnr 1f out: no ex towards fin* **5/1**[2]
3 *4 ½* **Future Security (IRE)** 2-9-0 0.................... RobertHavlin 6 65+
(Saeed Bin Suroor) *mid-div: hdwy over 2f out: kpt on to take 3rd last 50yds* **11/1**
4 *1 ½* **Handsome Man (IRE)** 2-9-0 0.................... PaulHanagan 5 62+
(Saeed Bin Suroor) *trckd ldrs: wnt 2nd over 3f out: wknd last 100yds* **7/1**
5 *½* **Sirious Oss** 2-9-0 0.................... JamesSullivan 8 61+
(Michael Easterby) *dwlt: in rr: hdwy over 2f out: styd on to take 5th last 50yds* **100/1**
632 **6** *3 ¾* **Goldream**[22] 6216 2-9-0 79.................... KierenFallon 13 52+
(Luca Cumani) *led: sn wl clr: edgd rt and wknd over 1f out: sn hdd* **13/8**[1]
7 *6* **Queen's Estate (GER)** 2-9-0 0.................... JoeFanning 12 39
(Mark Johnston) *mid-div: sme hdwy over 2f out: nvr factor* **16/1**
4500 **8** *2* **Fine Kingdom**[20] 6260 2-9-0 60.................... TomEaves 9 35
(Michael Dods) *chsd ldrs: drvn over 4f out: wknd 2f out* **66/1**
9 *¾* **Vamoose** 2-9-0 0.................... PhillipMakin 15 33
(Kevin Ryan) *s.i.s: a towards rr* **25/1**
10 *5* **Kian's Joy** 2-9-0 0.................... TonyHamilton 14 22
(Jedd O'Keeffe) *s.s: nvr on terms* **200/1**
11 *5* **Awesome Pearl (USA)** 2-9-0 0.................... SebSanders 7 11
(Sir Mark Prescott Bt) *s.s: a in rr* **33/1**
0 **12** *28* **Double Bass (USA)**[87] 4080 2-9-0 0.................... AhmedAjtebi 1 —
(Mahmood Al Zarooni) *chsd ldrs on outside: drvn over 4f out: sn lost pl: eased over 1f out: t.o* **16/1**
0 **13** *59* **Avonbridge Lad**[10] 6532 2-9-0 0.................... AndrewMullen 10 —
(Alan Brown) *chsd ldr: wknd over 3f out: sn wl bhd: virtually p.u: hopelessly t.o* **150/1**

1m 47.28s (3.88) **Going Correction** +0.475s/f (Yiel) **13** Ran SP% **112.1**
Speed ratings (Par 95): **99,98,93,92,91 88,82,80,79,74 69,41,—**
toteswingers: 1&2 £4.50, 1&3 £12.50, 2&3 £9.00 CSF £32.83 TOTE £7.30: £2.20, £1.80, £3.40; EX 31.40 Trifecta £246.50 Pool: £499.71 - 1.50 winning units..
Owner George Strawbridge **Bred** George Strawbridge Jr **Trained** Newmarket, Suffolk

FOCUS
Times suggest the ground was heavy, and the winning rider of this race William Buick described the going as "very soft".

NOTEBOOK
Thought Worthy(USA) is a brother to the owner and trainer's St Leger winner Lucarno. Having looked set to win tidily when picking up well, he was strongly challenged by a horse with the benefit of experience, but showed a fine attitude to pull out extra. He's probably a smart prospect. (op 9-2 tchd 7-1)
Silver Blaze, nicely backed when close second over this trip at Redcar on his second start, was again solid in the market. He overcame being bumped around 2f out, but was just held by a potentially above-average rival. Now qualified for a handicap mark, he looks useful. (op 11-2)
Future Security(IRE) is a 160,000gns half-brother to a few winners, notably 6f-7f Group 3 winner Confuchias, out of a 1m4f winner. He sported the owner's third colours, but showed ability, travelling well for a long way. (op 12-1 tchd 10-1)
Handsome Man(IRE), a 140,000gns half-brother to a 1m1f Listed winner, out of a 7f (Listed) and 1m (Group 2) scorer, ran a bit green under pressure, going left at one stage, and should come on this. (tchd 13-2)
Sirious Oss has already been gelded, but this was a pleasing introduction, producing a sustained challenge from well off the pace. His pedigree is a mix of speed and stamina, but whatever, there should be better to come.
Goldream was the clear form pick and went off a short-priced favourite. A mile on ground this testing was always going to take plenty of getting (time over eight seconds above standard), but Luca Cumani's colt set off at a rapid pace for the conditions, going upwards of 8l clear by around halfway. He was matched at 1.16 in running on Betfair, but it soon became apparent that he'd gone much too fast and he was slowing dramatically by the 2f pole, ultimately finishing really tired. Unless the horse simply bolted, which didn't appear the case, Fallon had a shocker. (tchd 6-4)

6775 NORTH SEA LOGISTICS H'CAP — 1m 4f 93y
2:30 (2:30) (Class 6) (0-65,64) 3-Y-0+ **£1,617** (£481; £240; £120) **Stalls** Low

Form RPR
0021 **1** **Damascus Symphony**[23] 6192 3-9-0 **60**.................... KierenFallon 7 70
(James Bethell) *hld up: stdy hdwy over 2f out: shkn up to ld ins fnl f: edgd lft: kpt on strly* **13/2**[3]
232 **2** *2 ¼* **Mighty Mambo**[68] 4700 4-9-9 **62**.................... SebSanders 13 69
(George Margarson) *led at ordinary gallop: rdn over 2f out: hdd ins fnl f: kpt on: nt pce of wnr* **10/1**
3321 **3** *nk* **Hygrove Welshlady (IRE)**[8] 6585 3-8-8 **61**.................... BrendanPowell(7) 1 68
(J W Hills) *hld up in midfield on ins: stdy hdwy over 2f out: shkn up and chsd wnr briefly over 1f out: one pce ins fnl f* **10/3**[1]
5423 **4** *4* **Hurlingham**[9] 4902 7-9-1 **54**....................(b) PaddyAspell 5 55
(Michael Easterby) *in tch: shkn up over 2f out: kpt on fnl f: no imp* **12/1**
0020 **5** *1 ¾* **Dzesmin (POL)**[24] 6155 9-9-7 **63**....................(p) RobertLButler(3) 10 61
(Richard Guest) *trckd ldr: rdn over 2f out: wknd wl over 1f out* **14/1**
401- **6** *hd* **Gosforth Park**[426] 4946 5-9-1 **54**.................... RobertWinston 2 52
(Mel Brittain) *plld hrd: hld up: hdwy to chse ldrs 1/2-way: rdn and wknd fr 2f out* **12/1**
5026 **7** *1 ½* **Bright Applause**[22] 6211 3-9-1 **61**.................... PatrickMathers 3 56
(Tracy Waggott) *hld up: rdn along 3f out: hdwy over 1f out: nvr able to chal* **14/1**
4100 **8** *¾* **Lady Norlela**[24] 6157 5-9-6 **59**.................... BarryMcHugh 6 53
(Brian Rothwell) *bhd tl hdwy over 1f out: kpt on: nvr on terms* **12/1**
4430 **9** *2 ¼* **Madrasa (IRE)**[13] 6453 3-9-0 **60**....................(t) TomEaves 14 51
(Keith Reveley) *hld up: pushed along 3f out: nvr able to chal* **28/1**
4342 **10** *¾* **Chapter Five**[80] 4329 4-9-7 **60**.................... PaulHanagan 12 50
(Keith Reveley) *hld up: rdn and outpcd 3f out: n.d after* **6/1**[2]
2640 **11** *2* **Miereveld**[13] 6451 4-9-0 **53**....................(tp) RobbieFitzpatrick 11 40
(Shaun Harris) *midfield on outside: drvn and outpcd 3f out: sn n.d* **100/1**
6053 **12** *shd* **Lord Emerson**[10] 6545 3-8-7 **53**.................... JamesSullivan 9 40
(Richard Fahey) *t.k.h: trckd ldrs tl rdn and wknd over 2f out* **14/1**
[illegible] **13** [illegible] **[illegible]**[13] [illegible] [illegible].................... [illegible] 4 40
(Jedd O'Keeffe) *trckd ldrs: rdn and outpcd over 2f out: no imp whn hmpd over 1f out: wknd* **12/1**

2m 56.21s (10.61) **Going Correction** +0.60s/f (Yiel)
WFA 3 from 4yo+ 7lb **13** Ran SP% **115.0**
Speed ratings (Par 101): **88,86,86,83,82 82,81,80,79,78 77,77,75**
toteswingers: 1&2 £7.00, 1&3 £4.20, 2&3 £4.80 CSF £67.33 CT £254.19 TOTE £7.80: £2.60, £2.90, £1.60; EX 77.50 Trifecta £132.90 Pool: £371.84 - 2.07 winning units..
Owner Clarendon Thoroughbred Racing **Bred** Jeremy Green And Sons And P Bickmore **Trained** Middleham Moor, N Yorks

FOCUS
A moderate handicap run a slow pace and the time was over 17 seconds above standard.
Gosforth Park Official explanation: jockey said gelding ran too free
Chapter Five Official explanation: jockey said filly never travelled

6776 BRITISH STALLION STUDS SUPPORTING BRITISH RACING E B F MAIDEN FILLIES' STKS — 1m 3y(S)
3:00 (3:01) (Class 5) 2-Y-0 **£3,234** (£962; £481; £240) **Stalls** Centre

Form RPR
4 **1** **Saytara (IRE)**[35] 5806 2-9-0 0.................... PaulHanagan 3 79+
(Saeed Bin Suroor) *trckd ldrs: effrt over 2f out: led appr fnl f: edgd lft: hld on wl* **3/1**[2]
4 **2** *1* **Dulkashe (IRE)**[40] 5655 2-9-0 0.................... KierenFallon 13 77
(Luca Cumani) *hdwy to trck ldrs 4f out: led over 2f out: hdd appr fnl f: kpt on same pce last 100yds* **9/4**[1]
3 **3** *1 ½* **Yours Ever**[13] 6441 2-9-0 0.................... SebSanders 9 74
(Sir Mark Prescott Bt) *hld up: hdwy over 2f out: upsides over 1f out: kpt on same pce last 150yds* **12/1**
0 **4** *4 ½* **See Emily Play (IRE)**[46] 5445 2-9-0 0.................... RobertHavlin 12 64+
(John Gosden) *in rr: hdwy 2f out: styd on to take 4th last 100yds: will improve* **18/1**
5 *1 ¼* **Millymonkin** 2-9-0 0.................... PaddyAspell 8 61
(Michael Easterby) *chsd ldrs: outpcd over 3f out: kpt on fnl f* **80/1**
6 *½* **Derivatives (IRE)** 2-9-0 0.................... WilliamBuick 6 60
(John Gosden) *s.s: chsng ldrs after 2f: outpcd over 2f out: kpt on fnl f* **8/1**
7 *1 ¾* **Oops Caroline (IRE)** 2-9-0 0.................... DanielTudhope 4 56
(David O'Meara) *in rr: swtchd far side over 1f out: kpt on: nvr nr ldrs* **100/1**
00 **8** *½* **Chocolat Chaud (IRE)**[59] 5029 2-9-0 0.................... StevieDonohoe 5 55
(J W Hills) *s.s: chsng ldrs after 2f: wknd over 2f out* **66/1**

3 **9** *hd* **Supreme Luxury (IRE)**[17] 6329 2-9-0 0 ... PhillipMakin 1 54
(Kevin Ryan) *w ldrs: hung rt and wknd over 1f out* **9/2**[3]

54 **10** *2* **Specific (IRE)**[42] 5583 2-9-0 0 ... AhmedAjtebi 7 50
(Mahmood Al Zarooni) *led tl over 2f out: wknd over 1f out* **8/1**

0000 **11** *18* **Bea Persuasive**[42] 5597 2-9-0 36 ... RobbieFitzpatrick 10 10
(Shaun Harris) *chsd ldrs: lost pl 3f out: sn bhd: t.o* **200/1**

0 **12** *shd* **Art Of Gold**[39] 5688 2-9-0 0 ... TomEaves 11 10
(Amy Weaver) *in rr: bhd fnl 3f: t.o* **200/1**

1m 47.71s (4.31) **Going Correction** +0.475s/f (Yiel) **12** Ran SP% **113.8**
Speed ratings (Par 92): **97,96,94,90,88 88,86,86,85,83 65,65**
toteswingers: 1&2 £2.70, 1&3 £7.80, 2&3 £7.20 CSF £9.74 TOTE £4.30: £1.60, £1.40, £2.20; EX 12.20 Trifecta £125.20 Pool: £653.15 - 3.86 winning units..
Owner Godolphin **Bred** Peter Savill **Trained** Newmarket, Suffolk

FOCUS
A fair fillies' maiden and the pace was sensibly modest. The time was only 0.43 seconds slower than the earlier maiden for colts and geldings.

NOTEBOOK
Saytara(IRE), fourth on her debut over this trip on quick ground at Leicester, handled these vastly different conditions really well and showed a good attitude. Her rider talked her up afterwards and her pedigree suggests she'll improve with time and distance. (op 4-1)
Dulkashe(IRE), a promising fourth in a fair Salisbury maiden on her debut, had her chance but found the winner was too strong. This still represents improvement and she should continue to go the right way. (op 3-1)
Yours Ever, third on her debut over 7f on Polytrack, stepped up on that form, showing a knee action that suggests the ground was okay. (op 25-1 tchd 11-1)
See Emily Play(IRE), well held on her debut behind Lyric Of Light, was the apparent John Gosden second string, but she kept on nicely without being given a hard time. She should continue to make good progress with time and distance. (op 25-1 tchd 16-1)
Millymonkin, a half-sister to a bumper winner, out of a 1m winner, stayed on gradually and should do better in time. (op 66-1)
Derivatives(IRE), a half-sister to a 1m3f winner, out of Nassau winner Favourable Terms, missed the break and was never a threat. Surely she'll be capable of better. (tchd 7-1)
Supreme Luxury(IRE)'s rider reported the filly hung right-handed in the final 2f. She was nowhere near the form of her debut third on easy ground at Haydock. Official explanation: jockey said filly hung right-handed final 2f (op 3-1)
Specific(IRE) was unsuited by the ground. Official explanation: trainer's rep said filly was unsuited by the soft (good to soft places) ground (op 4-1)

6777 SPIFFING CRABBIE'S ALCOHOLIC GINGER BEER H'CAP 7f
3:30 (3:30) (Class 6) (0-65,65) 3-Y-0+ **£1,617** (£481; £240; £120) **Stalls** Centre

Form RPR

-602 **1** **Moonlight Mystery**[36] 5788 3-9-4 **64** ... WilliamBuick 11 73
(Chris Wall) *cl up in centre gp: led whn gps merged over 2f out: hrd pressed ins fnl f: drvn and hld on wl* **5/2**[1]

0303 **2** *hd* **Flying Applause**[12] 6479 6-9-6 **64** ...(bt) RussKennemore 13 72
(Roy Bowring) *cl up centre gp: effrt over 2f out: ev ch ins fnl f: kpt on: hld nr fin* **16/1**

0060 **3** *2 1/2* **Aerodynamic (IRE)**[57] 5106 4-9-2 **60** ... PaddyAspell 7 62
(Clive Mulhall) *hld up centre gp: stdy hdwy over 2f out: rdn over 1f out: kpt on same pce ins fnl f* **17/2**

0243 **4** *1 1/2* **St Oswald**[21] 6234 3-9-0 **60** ...(v[1]) DanielTudhope 5 58
(David O'Meara) *cl up far side: effrt and ev ch over 2f out: rdn and one pce fnl f* **9/2**[2]

0-00 **5** *1/2* **Transmit (IRE)**[13] 6452 4-9-4 **62** ... DavidAllan 12 58
(Tim Easterby) *stmbld s: racd alone stands' rail: rdn 1/2-way: edgd lft and styd on fnl f: nrst fin* **25/1**

4001 **6** *1 1/4* **Benny The Bear**[14] 6428 4-9-2 **60** ...(p) PhillipMakin 16 53
(Linda Perratt) *led centre gp to over 2f out: sn drvn: outpcd fnl f* **8/1**[3]

1100 **7** *nk* **Broctune Papa Gio**[13] 6452 4-9-2 **63** ... DeclanCannon(3) 1 55
(Keith Reveley) *hld up far side: rdn 1/2-way: hdwy over 1f out: no imp* **16/1**

/045 **8** *1/2* **Monthly Medal**[29] 6006 8-9-4 **62** ...(t) JamesSullivan 9 53
(Wilf Storey) *hld up centre gp: effrt over 2f out: sn rdn: btn ins fnl f* **33/1**

0164 **9** *2 1/4* **Edgware Road**[34] 5821 3-9-3 **63** ...(v[1]) JoeFanning 10 48
(Keith Dalgleish) *dwlt: sn in tch centre: rdn over 2f out: wknd over 1f out* **10/1**

6026 **10** *15* **Bonnie Prince Blue**[14] 6426 8-9-5 **63** ...(v) PaulHanagan 6 —
(Ian McInnes) *bhd far side: drvn after 2f: nvr on terms: eased whn no ch fnl 2f* **16/1**

1510 **11** *1 3/4* **Sofias Number One (USA)**[133] 2581 3-9-5 **65** ...(p) StevieDonohoe 4 —
(Roy Bowring) *in tch far side: struggling over 3f out: sn btn* **40/1**

430 **12** *5* **Naafetha (IRE)**[36] 5792 3-9-1 **61** ... LeeNewman 15 —
(George Foster) *missed break: bhd centre: drvn over 3f out: sn btn: eased fnl 2f* **50/1**

-000 **13** *13* **Steel Stockholder**[21] 6231 5-9-5 **63** ... RobertWinston 3 —
(Mel Brittain) *led far side to over 2f out: sn wknd: eased fr wl over 1f out* **10/1**

1m 31.46s (3.66) **Going Correction** +0.475s/f (Yiel)
WFA 3 from 4yo+ 2lb **13** Ran SP% **115.4**
Speed ratings (Par 101): **98,97,94,93,92 91,90,90,87,70 68,62,48**
toteswingers: 1&2 £9.10, 1&3 £6.70, 2&3 £34.40 CSF £42.92 CT £298.02 TOTE £2.80: £1.10, £4.40, £3.60; EX 53.00 Trifecta £415.20 Part won. Pool: £561.12 - 0.72 winning units..
Owner Peter R Pritchard **Bred** Tarworth Bloodstock Investments Ltd **Trained** Newmarket, Suffolk

FOCUS
A moderate handicap, but the form looks sound considering the ground.
Transmit(IRE) Official explanation: jockey said gelding stumbled leaving stalls
Steel Stockholder Official explanation: jockey said gelding hung right-handed

6778 ODDSCHECKER.COM H'CAP (DIV I) 6f
4:00 (4:01) (Class 5) (0-75,75) 3-Y-0+ **£2,264** (£673; £336; £168) **Stalls** Centre

Form RPR

4615 **1** **Toby Tyler**[16] 6382 5-9-7 **75** ...(v) MickyFenton 1 85
(Paul Midgley) *dwlt: effrt 3f out: gd hdwy over 1f out: styd on to ld last 50yds* **14/1**

6104 **2** *1/2* **Chookie Royale**[16] 6381 3-9-4 **73** ... JoeFanning 2 81
(Keith Dalgleish) *dwlt: hdwy far side rail to chse ldrs over 2f out: overall ldr over 1f out: edgd rt: hdd and no ex clsng stages* **12/1**

1130 **3** *3/4* **Cross Of Lorraine (IRE)**[34] 5824 8-8-10 **64** ...(b) TonyHamilton 3 70
(Chris Grant) *w ldrs: led over 2f out: hdd over 1f out: sn crowded: kpt on same pce last 100yds* **33/1**

5603 **4** *1/2* **Tadalavil**[5] 6646 6-8-9 **63** ... BarryMcHugh 5 67
(Linda Perratt) *mid-div: hdwy to chse ldrs over 2f out: styd on same pce fnl f* **10/1**[3]

3622 **5** *nk* **Ingleby Arch (USA)**[14] 6426 8-8-9 **68** ... LMcNiff(5) 6 71
(David Barron) *overall ldr far side: hdd over 2f out: kpt on same pce appr fnl f* **8/1**[2]

1120 **6** *nse* **Mission Impossible**[22] 6208 6-8-7 **61** oh1 ... PatrickMathers 7 64
(Tracy Waggott) *t.k.h: hdwy to chse ldrs 3f out: kpt on same pce appr fnl f* **12/1**

0243 **7** *nk* **Youhavecontrol (IRE)**[41] 5621 3-9-5 **74** ... PaulHanagan 13 76
(Michael Dods) *s.i.s: hld up stands' side: hdwy to ld other 3 over 1f out: no ch w main body of field* **10/1**[3]

4433 **8** *1 3/4* **Northern Bolt**[14] 6426 6-8-12 **69** ...(b) DaleSwift(3) 9 65
(Ian McInnes) *in rr: kpt on fnl 2f: nvr nr ldrs* **11/1**

2201 **9** *1 1/2* **Beckermet (IRE)**[14] 6426 9-9-2 **70** ... PJMcDonald 14 62
(Ruth Carr) *led stands' side gp: hdd & wknd over 1f out* **11/2**[1]

6023 **10** *nk* **Ballinargh Girl (IRE)**[15] 6418 3-9-6 **75** ... JamesSullivan 8 66
(Robert Wylie) *chsd ldrs: wknd over 1f out* **14/1**

3400 **11** *2 3/4* **Foreign Rhythm (IRE)**[20] 6266 6-8-3 **62** ... NeilFarley(5) 10 44
(Ron Barr) *chsd ldrs: lost pl wl over 1f out* **25/1**

-663 **12** *6* **Dancing Maite**[122] 2938 6-9-3 **71** ... RussKennemore 15 34
(Roy Bowring) *trckd ldr stands' side: wknd over 1f out: eased clsng stages* **11/2**[1]

5252 **13** *2* **Captain Kolo (IRE)**[23] 6190 3-9-0 **69** ... DavidAllan 16 25
(Tim Easterby) *chsd ldr stands' side: wknd over 1f out: eased towards fin* **12/1**

0-00 **14** *32* **Signore Momento (IRE)**[13] 6467 5-9-5 **73** ...(tp) WilliamBuick 4 —
(Amy Weaver) *s.i.s: in rr: bhd fnl 2f: virtually p.u: t.o* **18/1**

1m 17.24s (2.64) **Going Correction** +0.475s/f (Yiel)
WFA 3 from 4yo+ 1lb **14** Ran SP% **116.9**
Speed ratings (Par 103): **101,100,99,98,98 98,97,95,93,93 89,81,78,36**
toteswingers: 1&2 £17.00, 1&3 £71.30, 2&3 £72.90 CSF £167.52 CT £3104.18 TOTE £21.90: £3.80, £3.50, £10.40; EX 154.20 Trifecta £416.60 Part won. Pool: £562.98 - 0.10 winning units..
Owner Anthony D Copley **Bred** Whitsbury Manor Stud **Trained** Westow, N Yorks

FOCUS
A moderate, wide-open handicap and the time was 0.26 seconds slower than the second division. It was run at a sound pace and the main action developed nearer the far side.
Signore Momento(IRE) Official explanation: jockey said gelding lost its action

6779 ODDSCHECKER.COM H'CAP (DIV II) 6f
4:30 (4:32) (Class 5) (0-75,75) 3-Y-0+ **£2,264** (£673; £336; £168) **Stalls** Centre

Form RPR

4224 **1** **Flameoftheforest (IRE)**[16] 6378 4-9-7 **75** ...(p) KierenFallon 14 86
(Ed de Giles) *hld up: stdy hdwy 2f out: shkn up to ld ins fnl f: pushed out* **9/2**[1]

4104 **2** *3/4* **Bond Fastrac**[4] 6665 4-9-3 **71** ... WilliamBuick 12 79
(Geoffrey Oldroyd) *in tch: rdn along over 2f out: hdwy to chse wnr wl ins fnl f: r.o* **6/1**[2]

4031 **3** *1 1/4* **Mata Hari Blue**[20] 6250 5-9-3 **71** ...(t) PhillipMakin 5 75
(John Holt) *hld up in midfield: hdwy to ld over 1f out: hdd ins fnl f: kpt on same pce* **14/1**

1000 **4** *nk* **Frequency**[26] 6081 4-9-3 **71** ...(b) JoeFanning 11 74
(Keith Dalgleish) *dwlt: hld up: smooth hdwy and ev ch over 1f out: shkn up and fnd little ins fnl f* **25/1**

0005 **5** *1 1/4* **Berbice (IRE)**[14] 6426 6-8-7 **61** oh1 ...(p) BarryMcHugh 9 60
(Linda Perratt) *dwlt: hld up: smooth hdwy to trck ldrs over 1f out: sn pushed along: one pce fnl f* **16/1**

1304 **6** *1/2* **Red Roar (IRE)**[23] 6189 4-8-9 **68** ... JulieBurke(5) 2 65
(Alan Berry) *midfield: rdn over 2f out: rallied over 1f out: no imp fnl f* **12/1**

2050 **7** *1 1/4* **Captain Royale (IRE)**[19] 6276 6-8-13 **70** ...(p) MichaelO'Connell(3) 10 63
(Tracy Waggott) *led: rdn and edgd rt over 2f out: hdd over 1f out: sn outpcd* **12/1**

1036 **8** *nse* **Sea Salt**[20] 6265 8-8-12 **69** ... DaleSwift(3) 8 62
(Ron Barr) *w ldrs tl rdn: edgd lft and no ex over 1f out* **20/1**

4525 **9** *3/4* **Commanche Raider (IRE)**[20] 6265 4-9-1 **69** ...(p) PaulHanagan 3 60
(Michael Dods) *in tch: rdn over 2f out: btn fnl f* **14/1**

3001 **10** *1 3/4* **Supreme Spirit (IRE)**[15] 6408 4-9-5 **73** ...(b) SebSanders 1 58
(George Margarson) *hld up: rdn over 2f out: nvr able to chal* **10/1**

0036 **11** *hd* **Electioneer (USA)**[24] 6158 4-8-7 **61** oh1 ... JamesSullivan 4 45
(Michael Easterby) *bhd: rdn over 2f out: nvr on terms* **16/1**

2135 **12** *1 3/4* **Needy McCredie**[81] 4288 5-8-8 **62** ... PaddyAspell 15 41
(James Turner) *hld up: stdy hdwy over 2f out: rdn and wknd over 1f out* **14/1**

1-05 **13** *1/2* **Henry Morgan**[163] 1712 4-8-9 **63** ... TomEaves 7 40
(Bryan Smart) *w ldrs tl edgd lft and wknd appr fnl f* **9/1**[3]

0011 **14** *6* **Secret City (IRE)**[20] 6266 5-8-11 **65** ...(b) RobertWinston 13 23
(Robin Bastiman) *midfield on nr side of gp: struggling over 2f out: sn btn* **12/1**

1m 16.98s (2.38) **Going Correction** +0.475s/f (Yiel) **14** Ran SP% **115.0**
Speed ratings (Par 103): **103,102,100,99,98 97,95,95,94,92 92,89,89,81**
toteswingers: 1&2 £7.50, 1&3 £13.50, 2&3 £16.80 CSF £27.89 CT £357.28 TOTE £5.10: £2.00, £2.10, £3.40; EX 28.50 Trifecta £338.60 Part won. Pool: £457.67 - 0.72 winning units..
Owner Mrs Hugh McAlister **Bred** Western Bloodstock **Trained** Ledbury, Herefordshire

FOCUS
The time was 0.26 seconds faster than the first leg and the form looks sound.
Secret City(IRE) Official explanation: jockey said gelding never travelled

6780 ODDSCHECKER.MOBI H'CAP 2m 19y
5:00 (5:01) (Class 5) (0-75,72) 3-Y-0+ **£2,264** (£673; £336; £168) **Stalls** Low

Form RPR

6046 **1** **River Dragon (IRE)**[36] 5790 6-9-2 **60** ... BarryMcHugh 12 69
(Tony Coyle) *trckd ldr: led after 3f: 4 l clr over 3f out: rdn out* **9/1**

516 **2** *1 3/4* **Puy D'Arnac (FR)**[25] 6115 8-9-6 **69** ... JulieBurke(5) 9 76
(George Moore) *hld up towards rr: hdwy 6f out: chsd wnr 1f out: no real imp* **10/1**

1-55 **3** *2 1/2* **Lady Bluesky**[16] 6385 8-9-1 **64** ... GarryWhillans(5) 2 68
(Alistair Whillans) *mid-div: hdwy over4f out: chsd wnr over 1f out: kpt on one pce* **13/2**[2]

-212 **4** *2* **Spice Bar**[17] 5790 7-8-9 **58** ... NeilFarley(5) 11 60
(Declan Carroll) *chsd ldrs: one pce fnl 2f* **13/2**[2]

5005 **5** *2 1/4* **Gaselee (USA)**[15] 6405 5-9-9 **67** ... WilliamBuick 10 66
(Rae Guest) *led 3f: chsd ldrs: wknd 2f out* **8/1**

5232 **6** *2 1/2* **First Rock (IRE)**[13] 6451 5-9-4 **62** ... PJMcDonald 5 58
(Alan Swinbank) *trckd ldrs: t.k.h: chsd wnr over 2f out: wknd over 1f out* **5/1**[1]

4122 **7** *nk* **Dr Finley (IRE)**[26] 6095 4-9-12 **70** ... KierenFallon 8 66
(Lydia Pearce) *mid-div: hdwy to trck ldrs after 6f: drvn and outpcd over 4f out: one pce fnl 3f* **9/1**

0015 **8** *3/4* **The Oil Magnate**[13] 6451 6-10-0 **72** ... TonyHamilton 4 67
(Michael Dods) *hld up in rr: hdwy over 3f out: drvn 2f out: nvr nr ldrs* **14/1**

5254 **9** *23* **Riptide**[37] 5759 5-9-12 **70**...(p) JamieGoldstein 1 37
(Michael Scudamore) *mid-div: drvn and lost pl 9f out: nt run on: bhd fnl 5f* **7/1**[3]
0-50 **10** *3/4* **Willow's Wish**[245] 456 3-7-13 **54** oh8 ow1... AndrewMullen 6 20
(George Moore) *chsd ldrs: drvn over 4f out: lost pl 3f out* **100/1**
622/ **11** *1* **Dice (IRE)**[509] 6543 5-9-11 **69**... TomEaves 3 34
(Chris Grant) *hld up in tch: effrt over 4f out: sn lost pl and bhd* **66/1**
0120 **12** *11* **Herrera (IRE)**[21] 6235 6-9-4 **62**...(p) PaulHanagan 7 14
(Richard Fahey) *in rr: sme hdwy 6f out: rdn and lost pl over 2f out: bhd whn eased clsng stages* **14/1**
4000 **13** *2 1/4* **Maid Of Meft**[38] 5723 4-9-2 **60**... PhillipMakin 13 —
(Linda Perratt) *s.s: in rr: bhd fnl 3f: eased clsng stages* **22/1**

3m 47.59s (8.19) **Going Correction** +0.60s/f (Yiel)
WFA 3 from 4yo+ 11lb **13** Ran SP% **116.2**
Speed ratings (Par 103): **103,102,100,99,98 97,97,96,85,85 84,79,77**
toteswingers: 1&2 £16.50, 1&3 £19.70, 2&3 £15.70 CSF £92.32 CT £628.46 TOTE £9.70: £3.60, £3.20, £3.20; EX 133.20 Trifecta £157.90 Pool: £896.19 - 4.20 winning units..
Owner Brian Kerr & Tony Coyle **Bred** Barronstown Stud And Cobra Bloodstock **Trained** Norton, N Yorks

FOCUS
A modest staying handicap and probably not form to be too positive about.
Riptide Official explanation: jockey said gelding sulked after being unable to gain a prominent position

6781 BEST ODDS @ ODDSCHECKER.COM MEDIAN AUCTION MAIDEN STKS 1m 4f 93y
5:30 (5:31) (Class 6) 3-4-Y-0 **£1,617** (£481; £240; £120) **Stalls** Low

Form RPR
0 **1** **Sky High Diver (IRE)**[26] 6097 3-8-12 0... PJMcDonald 8 54
(Alan Swinbank) *hld up: pushed along over 4f out: hdwy on outside over 2f out: rdn to ld appr fnl f: edgd lft: kpt on wl* **11/1**
2 *1 1/4* **Miss Mysterious (FR)**[136] 3-8-12 0... JoeFanning 1 52
(Kate Walton) *t.k.h early: cl up: led over 3f out to over 2f out: rallied and ev ch over 1f out: kpt on fnl f* **8/1**[3]
5355 **3** *1 1/4* **Disturbia (IRE)**[3] 6701 3-8-12 46... SebSanders 7 50
(J W Hills) *hld up in midfield: smooth hdwy to ld over 2f out: rdn and hdd appr fnl f: rallied: one pce fnl 150yds* **3/1**[2]
4 *2 3/4* **Max My Boy (IRE)**[72] 4-9-7 0... MichaelO'Connell(3) 9 51
(Ollie Pears) *in tch on ins: hdwy 3f out: rdn and outpcd 2f out: r.o fnl f: no imp* **9/1**
0 **5** *1 1/4* **Thackeray**[26] 6097 4-9-5 0... LMcNiff(5) 10 49+
(Chris Fairhurst) *hld up: pushed along over 2f out: styd on steadily fnl 2f: nvr nrr* **16/1**
0/5- **6** *3/4* **Sory**[422] 5122 4-9-10 0... JamesSullivan 6 48
(Tina Jackson) *hld up: hdwy and in tch over 2f out: rdn and wknd over 1f out* **9/1**
7 *1* **Ivan The Terrible (IRE)** 3-9-0 0... RobertLButler(3) 11 46
(Richard Guest) *missed break: hld up: hdwy 3f out: rdn and wknd over 1f out* **16/1**
05 **8** *13* **Eila Wheeler**[17] 6349 4-9-0 0... GarryWhillans(5) 5 22
(Robert Johnson) *t.k.h: cl up: ev ch over 3f out: rdn and wknd 2f out* **25/1**
00-0 **9** *4* **Nella Sofia**[26] 6097 3-8-9 42... DaleSwift(3) 4 16
(James Given) *in tch on outside: drvn over 4f out: wknd fr 3f out* **33/1**
050- **10** *38* **Sandy Lonnen**[360] 6919 3-9-3 55... TomEaves 3 —
(Colin Teague) *t.k.h: led at stdy pce: rdn and hdd over 3f out: wknd over 2f out* **25/1**
-640 **11** *1 1/4* **Samanda (IRE)**[12] 6475 3-9-3 65...(b[1]) KierenFallon 2 —
(Luca Cumani) *t.k.h: prom: rdn over 3f out: wknd over 2f out* **11/4**[1]

2m 59.43s (13.83) **Going Correction** +0.60s/f (Yiel)
WFA 3 from 4yo 7lb **11** Ran SP% **113.5**
Speed ratings (Par 101): **77,76,75,73,72 72,71,62,60,34 34**
toteswingers: 1&2 £13.20, 1&3 £8.10, 2&3 £5.60 CSF £90.59 TOTE £13.70: £4.10, £2.10, £1.80; EX 85.80 Trifecta £214.10 Pool: £569.98 - 1.97 winning units..
Owner Mrs M C Keogh **Bred** Michael Downey & Roalso Ltd **Trained** Melsonby, N Yorks

FOCUS
A woeful maiden and the time was 3.22 seconds slower than the earlier Class 6 handicap.
T/Jkpt: £55,053.00 to a £1 stake. Pool: £193,848.78 - 2.50 winning tickets. T/Plt: £852.60 to a £1 stake. Pool of £97,242.07 - 83.25 winning tickets. T/Qpdt: £88.50 to a £1 stake. Pool of £7,144.73 - 59.70 winning tickets. RY

6782a (Foreign Racing) - see Raceform Interactive

6562 LONGCHAMP (R-H)
Tuesday, October 11
OFFICIAL GOING: Turf: good to soft

6783a PRIX DU RANELAGH (LISTED RACE) (3YO+) (TURF) 1m
2:55 (12:00) 3-Y-0+ **£22,413** (£8,965; £6,724; £4,482; £2,241)

RPR
1 **Red Gulch**[17] 6339 4-9-3 0... J-PGuillambert 3 104
(Ed Walker) *broke wl on ins: settled in midfield: moved forward to 5th bef end of bk st: swtchd away fr rail over 1 1/2f out: qcknd to chal 1f out: r.o wl: grabbed ld 50yds out* **165/10**
2 *nk* **Ball Prince (IRE)**[87] 4-9-3 0... FlavienPrat 10 103
(T Clout, France) **9/1**
3 *1 1/2* **Primera Vista**[38] 5-9-3 0...(b) StefanieHofer 8 100
(Mario Hofer, Germany) **10/1**
4 *nk* **Sulle Orme (FR)**[31] 5957 3-9-3 0... PhilippeSogorb 1 102
(C Ferland, France) **11/2**[2]
5 *3/4* **Gotlandia (FR)**[17] 6397 4-9-0 0... Christophe-PatriceLemaire 9 94
(M Delzangles, France) **19/1**
6 *1/2* **Stand My Ground (IRE)**[17] 6397 4-9-3 0... MickaelBarzalona 5 96
(Mme Pia Brandt, France) **35/1**
7 *1 1/2* **Kameruka**[17] 6397 5-9-0 0... RonanThomas 11 90
(R Pritchard-Gordon, France) **32/1**
8 *3/4* **Konig Concorde (GER)**[23] 6-9-6 0... GaetanMasure 14 94
(C Sprengel, Germany) **14/1**
9 *3/4* **Faithful One (IRE)**[17] 6397 4-9-0 0... ThomasHuet 7 86
(F Doumen, France) **26/1**
10 *snk* **Simba (FR)**[31] 5957 3-9-0 0... TonyPiccone 6 89
(C Lerner, France) **68/10**[3]
0 **Konig Bernard (FR)**[23] 5-9-3 0... ThierryThulliez 15 —
(W Baltromei, Germany) **13/1**
0 **Glad Sky**[17] 6397 5-9-6 0... AnthonyCrastus 4 —
(J-L Pelletan, France) **26/1**
0 **Letty**[18] 4-9-0 0... JohanVictoire 13 —
(A Klimscha Jr, Hungary) **68/1**
0 **Nobel Winner (FR)**[101] 3653 3-9-3 0... OlivierPeslier 2 —
(J-M Beguigne, France) **7/1**
0 **Pas Perdus**[46] 3-9-0 0... GregoryBenoist 12 —
(M Delzangles, France) **48/10**[1]

1m 38.48s (0.08)
WFA 3 from 4yo+ 3lb **15** Ran SP% **116.2**
WIN (incl. 1 euro stake): 17.50. PLACES: 5.80, 3.30, 4.10. DF: 82.40. SF: 116.00.
Owner S Al Ansari **Bred** Cheveley Park Stud Ltd **Trained** Newmarket, Suffolk

NOTEBOOK
Red Gulch handled the easy ground well and gained a Listed win at the first attempt.

6619 KEMPTON (A.W) (R-H)
Wednesday, October 12
OFFICIAL GOING: Standard
Wind: Light, across Weather: Cloudy, mild

6784 FREE ENTRY FOR BETDAQ MEMBERS H'CAP 7f (P)
5:40 (5:40) (Class 6) (0-58,63) 3-Y-0+ **£1,617** (£481; £240; £120) **Stalls** Low

Form RPR
0051 **1** **Vhujon (IRE)**[7] 6619 6-9-1 **55** 6ex... RobbieFitzpatrick 11 62
(Peter Grayson) *settled in midfield: prog fr 2f out: rdn and r.o fnl f: led post* **16/1**
0150 **2** *shd* **Gazboolou**[26] 6138 7-8-13 **56**... KierenFox(3) 9 63
(David Pinder) *led: rdn and narrowly hdd over 1f out: fought bk to ld again ins fnl f: hdd post* **10/1**
43 **3** *hd* **Hierarch (IRE)**[40] 5667 4-8-11 **56**... LauraPike(5) 10 62
(David Simcock) *patiently rdn in rr: prog over 1f out: r.o fnl f: squeezed through rivals nr fin: jst too much to do* **7/2**[1]
30 **4** *nk* **Tudor Prince (IRE)**[28] 6071 7-9-0 **54**... RichardHughes 1 60
(Tony Carroll) *pressed ldr: shkn up and narrowly led over 1f out: hdd ins fnl f: nt qckn nr fin* **9/2**[2]
402 **5** *3/4* **Blue Noodles**[27] 6084 5-9-1 **55**...(p) PaddyAspell 7 59
(John Wainwright) *a pressing ldrs: rdn over 1f out: nt qckn and a hld but kpt on* **12/1**
0031 **6** *2 1/2* **Dichoh**[7] 6624 8-9-9 **63** 6ex...(p) ChrisCatlin 8 60
(Michael Madgwick) *settled in midfield: rdn and no prog 2f out: kpt on fr over 1f out: no threat to ldrs* **8/1**[3]
0651 **7** *3/4* **Genes Of A Dancer (AUS)**[32] 5943 5-8-12 **57**...(p) LucyKBarry(5) 12 52
(Adrian Chamberlain) *spd fr wd draw and racd in ldng trio to wl over 1f out: wknd* **9/2**[2]
0242 **8** *2* **Atia**[37] 5780 3-9-1 **57**... StephenCraine 14 46
(Jonathan Portman) *dwlt: mostly in last pair: rdn and no prog over 2f out: kpt on fnl f* **25/1**
032 **9** *1* **Princess Willow**[36] 5810 3-9-1 **57**... RichardThomas 13 44
(John E Long) *awkward s: racd wd towards rr: rdn and no prog 2f out* **14/1**
0040 **10** *1* **Cut And Thrust (IRE)**[147] 2201 5-9-4 **58**... KirstyMilczarek 4 42
(Mark Wellings) *prom: rdn 2f out: sn wknd* **16/1**
500 **11** *2 1/2* **Red Zeus (IRE)**[55] 3688 3-8-11 **58**...(b[1]) RyanPowell(5) 2 35
(Jo Davis) *hit rail after 2f and dropped to rr: struggling fr 3f out* **40/1**
2000 **12** *shd* **Beneath**[15] 6434 4-9-4 **58**... FrankieMcDonald 3 35
(Neil Mulholland) *urged along sn after s in last: nvr gng: a bhd* **25/1**

1m 26.68s (0.68) **Going Correction** -0.10s/f (Stan)
WFA 3 from 4yo+ 2lb **12** Ran SP% **115.0**
Speed ratings (Par 101): **92,91,91,91,90 87,86,84,83,82 79,79**
toteswinger: 1&2 £16.60, 1&3 £11.10, 2&3 £8.10 CSF £159.05 CT £692.68 TOTE £24.80: £5.80, £2.70, £1.40; EX 372.40.
Owner Richard Teatum **Bred** Robert Berns **Trained** Formby, Lancs

FOCUS
This produced a blanket finish, with barely half a length covering the first four

6785 BETDAQ MULTIPLES CLAIMING STKS 1m 3f (P)
6:10 (6:10) (Class 6) 3-4-Y-0 **£1,617** (£481; £240; £120) **Stalls** Low

Form RPR
2112 **1** **Avon River**[9] 6589 4-9-6 78... RichardHughes 2 70+
(Richard Hannon) *sn settled in 3rd: nudged up to chal 2f out: led over 1f out: maintained narrow advantage after: cheekily* **4/5**[1]
0045 **2** *nk* **Langley**[19] 6306 4-9-2 65... PaddyAspell 5 65
(Pat Murphy) *trckd ldrs: moved up to chal 2f out: pressed wnr fnl f: a safely hld* **7/1**[3]
6000 **3** *1/2* **Nibani (IRE)**[6] 6658 4-9-7 72... AmyScott(5) 3 75
(Alastair Lidderdale) *stdd s: hld up in last: prog on inner over 1f out: wnt 3rd fnl f: styd on but readily hld* **20/1**
0600 **4** *1* **Signor Verdi**[14] 6465 4-9-7 73... JadeMuggeridge(7) 1 75
(Brian Meehan) *cl up: n.m.r 2f out as pce qcknd: one pce fr over 1f out: no real threat* **14/1**
6230 **5** *shd* **Nolecce**[23] 6211 4-8-13 70...(p) RobertLButler(3) 4 63
(Richard Guest) *hld up and sn in last pair: effrt and hanging over 2f out: kpt on same pce fr over 1f out* **10/1**
0420 **6** *1 1/2* **Kishanda**[79] 4389 3-8-4 63... HarryBentley(3) 7 57
(Hughie Morrison) *mde most and set stdy pce: tried to kick on over 2f out: hdd and lost pl over 1f out* **4/1**[2]
-513 **7** *3* **Fine Style (IRE)**[18] 1858 3-8-12 63...(v) ChrisCatlin 6 56
(Neil King) *mostly trckd ldr to over 2f out: sn lost pl and btn* **20/1**

2m 22.16s (0.26) **Going Correction** -0.10s/f (Stan)
WFA 3 from 4yo 6lb **7** Ran SP% **113.3**
Speed ratings (Par 101): **95,94,94,93,93 92,90**
toteswinger: 1&2 £1.80, 1&3 £5.90, 2&3 £9.30 CSF £6.99 TOTE £1.90: £1.60, £3.90; EX 7.80.Langley was claimed by T Vaughan for £8,000
Owner Jim Horgan **Bred** Poulton Stud **Trained** East Everleigh, Wilts

FOCUS
There was a muddling pace, but the best horse won with plenty to spare.

6786 BACK OR LAY AT BETDAQ.COM CLAIMING STKS 6f (P)
6:40 (6:45) (Class 6) 2-Y-0 **£1,617** (£481; £240; £120) **Stalls** Low

Form RPR
0013 **1** **Mr Knightley (IRE)**[7] 6623 2-9-1 78...(b) RichardHughes 8 81+
(Richard Hannon) *w ldr: narrow advantage over 2f out but sn jnd: rdn to assert narrowly fnl f: a holding on* **1/1**[1]

6244 **2** ¾ **Redair (IRE)**15 6431 2-8-8 80 .... JamesDoyle 9 70
(David Evans) *trckd ldng trio: moved up to chal over 2f out: pressed wnr hrd tl jst hld ins fnl f* **4/1[2]**

6135 **3** 1 **The Dancing Lord**98 3728 2-8-4 73 .... JakePayne(7) 5 70
(Bill Turner) *led or disp to over 2f out: one pce fr over 1f out* **40/1**

1054 **4** nk **Steady The Buffs**25 6178 2-8-3 68 .... (b) LukeMorris 4 61
(Hugo Palmer) *trckd ldng trio: drvn over 1f out: kpt on same pce: nvr able to chal* **25/1**

3222 **5** 1 ½ **Tidal's Baby**30 5991 2-9-1 75 .... (p) RobbieFitzpatrick 1 69
(Noel Quinlan) *trckd ldng trio: clsd on inner 2f out: nt qckn over 1f out: fdd ins fnl f* **7/1**

1323 **6** 3 ½ **Pint Size**11 6540 2-8-3 80 .... (b) AntiocoMurgia(5) 7 51
(Gay Kelleway) *prog to join ldng pair on outer after 2f: veered wd bnd 3f out and lost grnd: bmpd along and wknd over 1f out* **5/1[3]**

600 **7** 1 ¼ **Captain Baldwin**34 5861 2-8-2 44 .... SophieDoyle(3) 2 44
(David Evans) *sltly checked over 4f out: struggling in rr bef 1/2-way: nvr on terms after* **80/1**

0 **8** 7 **Multi Blessing**25 6178 2-8-4 77 .... JacobMoore(7) 3 29
(Alan Jarvis) *walked to post after others had already arrived: hung lft bnd over 4f out and ended on outer: v wd bnd 3f out: wl bhd after* **33/1**

9 1 ¾ **One Cool Breeze (IRE)** 2-8-2 0 .... MartinLane 6 15
(Ralph Beckett) *dwlt: a struggling in last pair: wl bhd fnl 2f* **16/1**

1m 13.19s (0.09) **Going Correction** -0.10s/f (Stan) **9** Ran SP% **115.5**
Speed ratings (Par 93): **95,94,92,92,90 85,83,74,72**
toteswinger: 1&2 £1.40, 1&3 £9.70, 2&3 £10.80 CSF £4.97 TOTE £2.20: £1.20, £1.70, £7.10; EX 6.10.
Owner P A Deal **Bred** Miss Deirdre Cogan **Trained** East Everleigh, Wilts

FOCUS
A decent claimer, with most of the contestants having solid recent form on turf or sand.

NOTEBOOK
Mr Knightley(IRE), for whom blinkers and Polytrack have been the key in recent races, was admirably game, holding off challengers on both sides. He has now proved adept at 6f, 7f and 1m in his last three outings. (op 11-10 tchd 5-4)
Redair(IRE), joint best-in on official ratings, looked ready to pick off the winner but was never able to get past. She has not won since her debut and looks the sort who needs a strong gallop. (op 9-2)
The Dancing Lord ran a solid race on these terms. This was his Polytrack debut and he looks at home on it.
Steady The Buffs's only win was in a sprint, but she looks as if she would stay 7f on this surface.
Tidal's Baby, repeatedly placed in turf maidens, showed he acts on Polytrack on this AW debut, but wasn't good enough at these weights. He might be worth another go in maiden company, this time on sand. (op 13-2 tchd 6-1)
Pint Size, joint top-rated on his official handicap mark, was disappointing. He was better without the blinkers. (op 11-2 tchd 9-2)
Captain Baldwin Official explanation: jockey said gelding was hampered on the bend
Multi Blessing Official explanation: jockey said colt hung left

6787 PACAIR/BRITISH STALLION STUDS E B F MAIDEN STKS 6f (P)
7:10 (7:10) (Class 5) 2-Y-O **£3,234** (£962; £481; £240) **Stalls** Low

Form RPR

5 **1** **Dissent (IRE)**158 1886 2-9-3 0 .... SebSanders 3 78+
(Gerard Butler) *s.i.s: hld up in last: smooth prog to ld over 1f out: sn pushed wl clr: quite impressive* **11/4[2]**

0005 **2** 6 **King's Future**5 6663 2-9-3 47 .... (p) LukeMorris 1 59
(John Akehurst) *chsd ldng pair: rdn to chal 2f out: wnr shot past over 1f out: jst won battle for modest 2nd* **25/1**

20 **3** ½ **Poseidon Grey (IRE)**33 5889 2-9-3 0 .... AdamKirby 4 57
(Walter Swinburn) *racd freely: led: hdd and easily outpcd over 1f out: lost modest 2nd nr fin* **4/1**

4 **4** hd **Available (IRE)**8 6603 2-8-12 0 .... RichardHughes 5 52
(Richard Hannon) *pressed ldr: shkn up over 2f out: outpcd over 1f out: one pce after* **15/8[1]**

5 5 **Khubala (IRE)** 2-9-3 0 .... WilliamBuick 2 41
(Ed Dunlop) *in tch in 4th: shkn up over 2f out: rn green and sn wknd* **3/1[3]**

1m 12.73s (-0.37) **Going Correction** -0.10s/f (Stan) **5** Ran SP% **110.3**
Speed ratings (Par 95): **98,90,89,89,82**
CSF £46.65 TOTE £3.40: £1.40, £5.90; EX 49.50.
Owner C McFadden **Bred** Corduff Stud Ltd & J Corcoran **Trained** Newmarket, Suffolk

FOCUS
There was little depth in this maiden, with the runner-up rated just 47 after four previous races.

NOTEBOOK
Dissent(IRE), who quickened past his rivals as if they were standing still, may not have beaten much but it would be unfair to knock him for that reason alone. Off since his debut at Ascot in May, he may yet prove useful, particularly on this surface. (op 4-1)
King's Future had looked barely up to selling grade in previous races, so this was better than could have been expected. However, he would have to do improve again to win a maiden (op 40-1)
Poseidon Grey(IRE) does not find much at the finish and had no response when the winner sailed past. He is now qualified for handicaps, but does not look like a winner waiting to happen. (op 9-2)
Available(IRE), an encouraging fourth on turf in her only previous race, did not appear to run up to that form on this switch to Polytrack. (op 9-4)
Khubala(IRE), a 100,000gns Acclamation half-brother to several winners from 5f to 1m4f, and out of a speedy winning juvenile, was green on this debut and has some way to go to live up to his price-tag and pedigree. (op 7-4)

6788 BETDAQ MOBILE APPS CONDITIONS STKS 1m (P)
7:40 (7:40) (Class 4) 2-Y-O **£3,428** (£1,020; £509; £254) **Stalls** Low

Form RPR

133 **1** **Kinglet (USA)**28 6060 2-9-0 91 .... SilvestreDeSousa 1 99
(Mahmood Al Zarooni) *trckd ldr: clsd to ld jst over 2f out: rdn clr over 1f out: styd on* **4/1[2]**

6141 **2** 2 ¼ **Graphic (IRE)**28 6055 2-9-0 98 .... RichardHughes 6 94
(Richard Hannon) *trckd ldrs: pushed along over 3f out: struggling sn after: effrt and drvn over 2f out: styd on to take 2nd jst ins fnl f: eased whn no ch of catching wnr last 50yds* **1/1[1]**

621 **3** 2 ¾ **Samuel Pickwick (IRE)**19 6308 2-9-0 86 .... RyanMoore 4 87
(Sir Michael Stoute) *s.i.s: wl in tch: effrt to chse ldng pair over 3f out: kpt on to dispute 2nd 1f out: one pce after* **7/1**

1010 **4** nk **Ghostwriting (USA)**20 6268 2-9-0 91 .... WilliamBuick 5 86
(John Gosden) *t.k.h: hld up and sn last: effrt on inner over 2f out: one pce fr over 1f out and nvr threatened ldrs* **7/1**

2110 **5** 1 ½ **Storming Bernard (USA)**20 6270 2-9-0 95 .... IanMongan 2 83
(Alan Bailey) *led at decent pce: hdd jst over 2f out: wknd fnl f* **9/2[3]**

1060 **6** 12 **Queens Sandridge (IRE)**26 6111 2-8-11 78 .... DominicFox(3) 3 55
(Alan Bailey) *t.k.h: cl up tl wknd 3f out: t.o* **40/1**

1m 38.16s (-1.64) **Going Correction** -0.10s/f (Stan) **6** Ran SP% **115.6**
Speed ratings (Par 97): **104,101,99,98,97 85**
toteswinger: 1&2 £1.80, 1&3 £3.20, 2&3 £1.10 CSF £8.81 TOTE £4.70: £1.60, £1.40; EX 10.80.
Owner Godolphin **Bred** Darley **Trained** Newmarket, Suffolk
■ Stewards' Enquiry : William Buick five-day ban: excessive use of whip (Oct 26-29,31)

FOCUS
An interesting race of some quality with some lightly raced juveniles on display.

NOTEBOOK
Kinglet(USA) made a winning AW debut, seizing the initiative 2f from home while the runner-up was struggling. Always in control after that, he can be a bit keen but he is learning well from his races and continues to progress. (op 5-1)
Graphic(IRE), a winner over 7f here last time, took a disappointingly long time to get going over this extra 1f, and then it was too late. He can do much better. (op 5-4)
Samuel Pickwick(IRE) appeared to run his race, just being outpaced by two better horses at these weights. He looks like developing into a strong contender in good handicaps, but there won't be many opportunities on this surface. (op 8-1)
Ghostwriting(USA), already a winner on Polytrack, has yet to prove he stays 1m. (op 13-2 tchd 15-2)
Storming Bernard(USA) had the turf form to mix it with these relatively unexposed rivals but, after adopting his familiar front-running role, he was comfortably left behind on this AW debut. (op 4-1)

6789 SKYSPORTS.COM RACING H'CAP (DIV I) 1m 3f (P)
8:10 (8:11) (Class 5) (0-70,70) 3-Y-O+ **£2,264** (£673; £336; £168) **Stalls** Low

Form RPR

3364 **1** **Green Wadi**57 5135 6-9-8 68 .... (p) GeorgeBaker 9 77
(Gary Moore) *racd on outer in midfield: cajoled along and prog fr 2f out: clsd to ld last 150yds: sn clr* **12/1[3]**

4403 **2** 1 ¼ **Potentiale (IRE)**14 6461 7-9-9 69 .... (b¹) SebSanders 8 76
(J W Hills) *hld up wl in rr: prog jst over 2f out: styd on wl to take 2nd last 50yds: no ch to chal* **20/1**

2314 **3** nk **Waahej**29 6029 5-9-6 66 .... ChrisCatlin 5 72
(Peter Hiatt) *settled in midfield: prog fr 2f out: drvn to chse ldrs over 1f out: kpt on fnl f to take 3rd nr fin* **20/1**

3401 **4** 1 ¼ **Deceptive**7 6621 3-9-1 67 6ex .... SteveDrowne 1 71
(Roger Charlton) *led at decent pce: gng strly over 2f out: rdn over 1f out: wknd and hdd last 150yds: lost 2 more pls nr fin* **4/5[1]**

3631 **5** ¾ **Evergreen Forest (IRE)**13 6475 3-9-4 70 .... (b) RichardHughes 7 73
(Alastair Lidderdale) *chsd ldr to over 2f out: shkn up and nt qckn: lost pl over 1f out: styd on again fnl f* **13/2[2]**

5254 **6** 1 ½ **Rodrigo De Freitas (IRE)**76 4454 4-9-1 61 .... (v) PatCosgrave 2 61
(Jim Boyle) *trckd ldng pair: wnt 2nd over 2f out: nt qckn over 1f out: wknd fnl f* **40/1**

023 **7** 1 ¾ **Maher (USA)**12 6504 3-9-1 70 .... AdamBeschizza(3) 4 67
(David Simcock) *dwlt: worked way through to chse ldng quartet bef 1/2-way: drvn on inner over 1f out: wknd fnl f* **14/1**

5200 **8** 2 **Beat Route**17 6376 4-9-1 66 .... JemmaMarshall(5) 11 59
(Michael Attwater) *mostly in midfield: outpcd and dropped to rr over 2f out: plugged on again over 1f out* **14/1**

05-4 **9** 1 ¼ **Barnmore**207 909 3-9-3 69 .... AdamKirby 12 60
(Peter Hedger) *dwlt: mostly towards rr but in tch: effrt over 2f out and sme prog: no hdwy over 1f out: fdd* **20/1**

5600 **10** 7 **Adoyen Spice**60 5042 4-9-0 60 .... MartinLane 6 39
(Mike Murphy) *s.v.s: mostly in last pair: rdn and struggling over 3f out: bhd after* **25/1**

-000 **11** hd **Missionaire (USA)**17 6376 4-9-8 68 .... JamesDoyle 13 46
(Tony Carroll) *mostly in last pair: rdn and struggling over 3f out: bhd after* **50/1**

4203 **12** nk **Jodawes (USA)**7 6621 4-9-0 60 .... JimCrowley 10 38
(John Best) *dwlt: a towards rr: rdn and struggling 3f out* **12/1[3]**

1300 **13** 2 ½ **Buddy Holly**44 4578 6-9-7 67 .... AndreaAtzeni 3 40
(Robert Eddery) *chsd ldng trio: shkn up over 4f out: wknd 3f out* **33/1**

2m 18.82s (-3.08) **Going Correction** -0.10s/f (Stan)
WFA 3 from 4yo+ 6lb **13** Ran SP% **123.1**
Speed ratings (Par 103): **107,106,105,104,104 103,102,100,99,94 94,94,92**
toteswinger: 1&2 £44.40, 1&3 £26.30, 2&3 £36.80 CSF £233.16 CT £4710.39 TOTE £15.60: £3.10, £4.60, £3.10; EX 97.80.
Owner Andrew Bradmore **Bred** Mrs P A Clark **Trained** Lower Beeding, W Sussex

FOCUS
The odds-on favourite was able to dictate the gallop, with the field strung out behind, but she failed to take advantage.
Evergreen Forest(IRE) Official explanation: jockey said gelding hung left

6790 SKYSPORTS.COM RACING H'CAP (DIV II) 1m 3f (P)
8:40 (8:41) (Class 5) (0-70,69) 3-Y-O+ **£2,264** (£673; £336; £168) **Stalls** Low

Form RPR

0003 **1** **Mons Calpe (IRE)**9 6592 5-9-9 68 .... (p) ShaneKelly 3 77+
(Paul Cole) *patiently rdn in midfield: stdy prog over 2f out: wnt 3rd jst ins fnl f: drvn and r.o wl to ld last 75yds* **13/2[3]**

4065 **2** ½ **Rosco Flyer (IRE)**32 5942 5-9-4 63 .... (b) AdamKirby 9 71
(Roger Teal) *rousted along to ld after 150yds: rdn and hdd jst over 2f out: rallied over 1f out: upsides 100yds out: jst outpcd* **12/1**

0031 **3** ¾ **Fifty Cents**14 6446 7-8-11 56 .... (p) SilvestreDeSousa 6 63
(Brendan Powell) *led 150yds: trckd ldr: led again jst over 2f out: hdd and no ex last 75yds* **6/1[2]**

044 **4** 2 **Perilously (USA)**17 6377 3-9-2 67 .... RichardHughes 12 70
(Jeremy Noseda) *trckd ldng trio: wnt 3rd over 3f out: rdn and nt qckn over 2f out: tried to rally over 1f out: one pce fnl f and eased nr fin* **9/2[1]**

6304 **5** ¾ **Kames Park (IRE)**11 6546 9-9-5 67 .... RobertLButler(3) 5 69
(Richard Guest) *stdd s: hld up last: taken wd in st and shkn up: styd on fr over 1f out: nt rch ldrs* **16/1**

2221 **6** ½ **Rowan Ridge**7 6622 3-9-1 66 6ex .... (v) PatCosgrave 11 67
(Jim Boyle) *wl in tch in midfield: effrt to chse ldrs 2f out: no imp over 1f out: one pce* **9/2[1]**

2000 **7** 2 **Lisahane Bog**32 5942 4-9-6 68 .... (b) JohnFahy(3) 8 65
(Peter Hedger) *hld up in midfield on outer: effrt over 2f out: nt qckn wl over 1f out: fdd* **25/1**

4201 **8** 2 **Kayaan**73 3311 4-9-6 65 .... MickyFenton 10 59
(Pam Sly) *stdd s: hld up in last trio: light reminders 2f out: nvr nr ldrs* **10/1**

1434 **9** ½ **Broughtons Swinger**33 5893 4-9-5 67 .... AdamBeschizza(3) 4 60
(Willie Musson) *wl in tch in midfield tl outpcd and btn over 2f out* **8/1**

0-60 **10** 1 **Shalambar (IRE)**21 6254 5-9-1 60 .... JamesDoyle 2 51
(Tony Carroll) *a in rr: rdn and no prog over 2f out* **40/1**

11 7 **Green To Gold (IRE)**56 5192 6-9-7 66 .... EddieCreighton 13 44
(Don Cantillon) *a towards rr: struggling 3f out: wknd* **20/1**

1300 12 15 **Futurism**[21] 6254 3-9-4 69 SteveDrowne 7 20
(Richard Hannon) *chsd ldng trio to over 3f out: wknd qckly: t.o* **20/1**

2m 20.67s (-1.23) **Going Correction** -0.10s/f (Stan)
WFA 3 from 4yo+ 6lb **12** Ran SP% **113.6**
Speed ratings (Par 103): **100,99,99,97,97 96,95,93,93,92 87,76**
toteswinger: 1&2 £9.00, 1&3 £10.80, 2&3 £15.50 CSF £73.67 CT £489.91 TOTE £10.00: £3.50, £3.20, £3.70; EX 98.50.
Owner H R H Sultan Ahmad Shah **Bred** Swettenham Stud **Trained** Whatcombe, Oxon

FOCUS
A good early gallop steadied to just a medium one after 2f before picking up again 3f out.

6791 RACING@SKYSPORTS.COM H'CAP 6f (P)
9:10 (9:14) (Class 6) (0-52,58) 3-Y-O+ £1,617 (£481; £240; £120) **Stalls** Low

Form RPR

062 1 **Glastonberry**[21] 6251 3-8-10 52 SophieDoyle(3) 1 65
(Geoffrey Deacon) *hld up in midfield gng wl: prog and taken to outer 2f out: shkn up to ld 1f out: styd on wl* **15/2**[3]

4560 2 1 **Dingaan (IRE)**[19] 6304 8-8-12 50 SilvestreDeSousa 5 59
(Peter Grayson) *settled in rr: prog over 2f out: rdn to chal jst over 1f out: edgd lft and nt qckn: kpt on* **7/2**[1]

0000 3 ½ **Cut The Cackle (IRE)**[8] 6618 5-8-11 52 (t) RobertLButler(3) 10 59
(Richard Guest) *settled in rr: effrt on outer 2f out: styd on fr over 1f out to take 3rd wl ins fnl f* **16/1**

3221 4 2 **Sharp Bullet (IRE)**[8] 6602 5-9-6 58 6ex (p) FrederikTylicki 4 59
(Bruce Hellier) *sn towards rr: prog against rail 2f out: drvn to chse ldrs over 1f out: fdd ins fnl f* **9/2**[2]

000 5 1 ¼ **Replicator**[43] 5603 6-8-10 51 (e) AdamBeschizza(3) 9 48
(Patrick Gilligan) *pressed ldr: led 2f out: hdd & wknd 1f out* **16/1**

5366 6 3 ¼ **Radiator Rooney (IRE)**[7] 6619 8-8-12 50 RichardHughes 11 37
(Patrick Morris) *stdd s: hld up in last: pushed along over 2f out: kpt on steadily fr over 1f out: nvr nr ldrs* **14/1**

0053 7 ½ **Tenancy (IRE)**[8] 6618 7-8-12 50 KellyHarrison 3 35
(Shaun Harris) *led to 2f out: sn wknd* **8/1**

0-05 8 5 **Thalia Grace**[103] 3597 4-8-12 50 LukeMorris 6 19
(Les Hall) *prom on inner: rdn over 2f out: no prog over 1f out: sn wknd qckly* **12/1**

45-0 9 nk **Fayre Bella**[271] 165 4-8-9 50 JohnFahy(3) 8 18
(John Gallagher) *chsd ldrs after 1f to over 2f out: wknd qckly* **11/1**

1000 10 ½ **Rileys Crane**[7] 6626 4-9-0 52 (b[1]) SebSanders 7 18
(Christine Dunnett) *pressed ldrs tl wknd qckly over 2f out* **16/1**

-036 11 1 ½ **River Bounty**[21] 6257 6-8-4 49 JordanUys(7) 2 —
(Alan Jarvis) *nvr bttr than midfield: bmpd along furiously and wknd 2f out* **10/1**

1m 12.81s (-0.29) **Going Correction** -0.10s/f (Stan)
WFA 3 from 4yo+ 1lb **11** Ran SP% **112.7**
Speed ratings (Par 101): **97,95,95,92,90 86,85,79,78,77 75**
toteswinger: 1&2 £6.40, 1&3 £32.70, 2&3 £15.80 CSF £31.07 CT £362.64 TOTE £9.30: £2.60, £1.10, £6.20; EX 27.70.
Owner Jim Kelly **Bred** Geoffrey Deacon **Trained** Reading, Berks

FOCUS
A decent tempo gave a chance to those racing off the pace, though the winner came from midfield.
T/Plt: £636.60 to a £1 stake. Pool of £56,367.38 - 64.63 winning units. T/Qpdt: £100.30 to a £1 stake. Pool of £7,658.91 - 56.50 winning units. JN

6117 LINGFIELD (L-H)
Wednesday, October 12

OFFICIAL GOING: Standard
Wind: Virtually nil Weather: Overcast

6792 DAILY MAIL MAIDEN AUCTION STKS 1m (P)
2:00 (2:04) (Class 6) 2-Y-O £1,704 (£503; £251) **Stalls** High

Form RPR

1 **Koko Loca (IRE)** 2-8-5 0 ow2 AntiocoMurgia(5) 2 71+
(Marco Botti) *chsd ldrs: led over 2f out: rdn 1f out: pushed out ins fnl f* **12/1**

442 2 ¾ **Enery (IRE)**[9] 6581 2-8-12 0 WilliamBuick 7 72
(Mahmood Al Zarooni) *uns rdr and loose bef s: hdwy to chse ldrs on outside fr 3f out: hung lft wl over 1f out: rdn and styd on fnl f: tk 2nd fnl strides: no imp on wnr* **4/1**[3]

5 3 nk **Holly Martins**[12] 6506 2-8-4 0 (t[1]) NicoleNordblad(7) 5 70
(Hans Adielsson) *pressed ldr: led over 4f out: hdd over 2f out: pushed along and one pce fnl f: lost 2nd fnl strides* **16/1**

00 4 2 ½ **Kelpie Blitz (IRE)**[23] 6214 2-8-11 0 MarkLawson 8 64
(Seamus Durack) *towards rr but in tch: drvn along towards outside 3f out: chsd ldrs over 1f out: outpcd ins fnl f* **14/1**

66 5 ¾ **Arabic**[13] 6474 2-8-12 0 ShaneKelly 3 64
(James Fanshawe) *in tch: chsd ldrs 1/2-way: drvn 3f out: outpcd fnl 2f* **5/2**[2]

6 1 ½ **Supreme Rock** 2-8-10 0 PatCosgrave 6 58
(Jim Boyle) *s.i.s: in rr but in tch: chsd ldrs 1/2-way: wknd 1f out* **25/1**

245 7 2 ¾ **Good Morning Star (IRE)**[11] 6529 2-8-6 72 SilvestreDeSousa 1 48
(Mark Johnston) *led tl hdd over 4f out: drvn over 2f out: wknd appr fnl f* **2/1**[1]

2060 8 3 ½ **Roman Province (IRE)**[20] 6268 2-8-7 64 LukeMorris 4 41
(Roger Teal) *chsd ldrs: rdn 3f out: wknd over 2f out* **11/1**

1m 38.16s (-0.04) **Going Correction** -0.075s/f (Stan) **8** Ran SP% **114.3**
Speed ratings (Par 93): **97,96,95,93,92 91,88,84**
toteswingers: 1&2 £4.70, 2&3 £11.20, 1&3 £5.10 CSF £59.41 TOTE £11.90: £5.40, £1.20, £5.90; EX 79.00.
Owner Mrs L Botti **Bred** Rory O'Brien **Trained** Newmarket, Suffolk

FOCUS
A modest maiden auction event, but they went a decent early pace with a disputed lead.

NOTEBOOK
Koko Loca(IRE), carrying 2lb overweight, travelled well just behind the leaders before cruising to the front over 2f from home, and then showed a decent attitude when challenged in the straight. A 14,000euros half-sister to the winning sprinter Lucky Numbers, she is entitled to improve but will probably need to as this doesn't look strong form. (op 14-1 tchd 16-1)
Enery(IRE) had been shaping as though this extra furlong would suit, but he dumped his rider going to post, ran loose, and then got warm. Wide throughout, he was never quite getting there and it's hard to know how much his earlier antics cost him. He doesn't have much room for improvement, however. (op 11-4)
Holly Martins showed ability over slightly further on his Wolverhampton debut and had a first-time hood added to the tongue-tie. Having attracted some market support, he disputed the lead from the off and, with his rider sitting quietly, wasn't seen off until very late. (op 25-1 tchd 28-1 and 14-1)
Kelpie Blitz(IRE), well held in his first two starts, ran a bit better and now has the option of nurseries. (op 20-1)
Arabic, up a furlong from his first two starts, was sent off well backed but never looked happy at any stage. (op 3-1 tchd 9-4)
Good Morning Star(IRE), rated 72, had shown ability in three turf maidens but she folded very tamely after showing up early. (op 15-8 tchd 7-4 and 9-4)
Roman Province(IRE), a springer in the market, was the first beaten and hasn't built on a promising debut. (op 16-1)

6793 NEWS INTERNATIONAL CLASSIFIED CLAIMING STKS (DIV I) 7f (P)
2:30 (2:31) (Class 6) 3-Y-O+ £1,704 (£503; £251) **Stalls** Low

Form RPR

066 1 **Doncosaque (IRE)**[23] 6220 5-7-12 70 (t) HarryBentley(3) 10 68
(P J O'Gorman) *chsd ldrs: chal 1f out: slt ld ins fnl f: hld on all out* **5/1**[2]

0006 2 nk **Shostakovich (IRE)**[12] 6505 3-8-5 70 (tp) ChrisCatlin 5 73
(Sylvester Kirk) *chsd ldrs: drvn to chal 1f out: rdn and styd on fnl f: nt quite get up* **16/1**

6403 3 shd **Speak The Truth (IRE)**[34] 5858 5-7-12 62 NathanAlison(5) 1 69
(Jim Boyle) *chsd ldrs: drvn and slt ld 1f out: hdd ins fnl f: stl ev ch clsng stages: no ex cl home* **20/1**

3400 4 2 ¼ **Whiskey Junction**[26] 6119 7-8-1 67 SilvestreDeSousa 14 61
(Michael Quinn) *led: drvn wl over 1f out: hdd ins fnl f: wknd fnl 120yds* **11/1**

0232 5 hd **Burning Stone (USA)**[13] 6472 4-8-11 68 (v[1]) RobertWinston 4 70
(Gay Kelleway) *chsd ldrs: drvn wl over 1f out: kpt on same pce ins fnl f* **9/2**[1]

0363 6 ¾ **Lutine Charlie (IRE)**[13] 6472 4-8-5 63 (p) LukeMorris 13 62
(Ronald Harris) *in rr: drvn and hdwy appr fnl f: r.o wl clsng stages* **16/1**

055 7 ¾ **Chaussini**[21] 6256 4-8-8 69 SteveDrowne 11 63
(James Toller) *chsd ldrs towards outside: drvn ins fnl 2f: wknd fnl f* **14/1**

0420 8 ¾ **Co Dependent (USA)**[13] 6491 5-7-12 67 SophieDoyle(3) 3 54
(Jamie Osborne) *s.i.s: t.k.h in rr: hdwy fnl f: kpt on wl clsng stages* **16/1**

3224 9 1 **Brynfa Boy**[12] 6502 5-8-1 69 (t) RyanPowell(5) 2 56
(Patrick Morris) *chsd ldrs: drvn 2f out: wknd over 1f out* **7/1**[3]

5425 10 ½ **Mottley Crewe**[6] 6646 4-8-2 68 JohnFahy(3) 12 54
(Richard Guest) *tood t.k.h: towards rr: mod prog towards outside over 1f out: nt rch ldrs* **12/1**

2304 11 nk **Florio Vincitore (IRE)**[114] 3235 4-8-11 64 EddieCreighton 8 59
(Edward Creighton) *s.i.s: in rr: sme hdwy on ins fr 2f out: nvr a threat* **25/1**

-330 12 1 ¾ **Lend A Grand (IRE)**[81] 4322 7-8-13 65 ow1 IanMongan 6 56
(Jo Crowley) *nvr bttr than mid-div* **20/1**

1500 13 5 **Lucky Meadows (IRE)**[9] 6587 3-8-13 69 RichardHughes 7 45
(Richard Hannon) *in rr: hdwy into mid-div over 3f out: wknd ins fnl 2f: no ch whn hung rt and eased fnl f* **12/1**

R520 R **Timeteam (IRE)**[5] 6664 5-8-0 65 KieranO'Neill(3) 9 —
(Alan Bailey) *ref to r* **10/1**

1m 23.84s (-0.96) **Going Correction** -0.075s/f (Stan)
WFA 3 from 4yo+ 2lb **14** Ran SP% **117.8**
Speed ratings (Par 101): **102,101,101,98,98 97,97,96,95,94 94,92,86,—**
toteswingers: 1&2 £35.20, 2&3 £37.50, 1&3 £36.30 CSF £78.26 TOTE £6.30: £2.10, £4.40, £6.30; EX 93.30.The winner was subject to a friendly claim.
Owner Racing To The Max **Bred** Ammerland Verwaltung Gmbh **Trained** Newmarket, Suffolk

FOCUS
A moderate classified claimer. At most meetings here the inside rail isn't the place to be, but this result confirmed the impression of the opening race that it was no disadvantage at all on this card. The time was 0.69 seconds faster than the second division.

6794 NEWS INTERNATIONAL CLASSIFIED CLAIMING STKS (DIV II) 7f (P)
3:00 (3:01) (Class 6) 3-Y-O+ £1,704 (£503; £251) **Stalls** Low

Form RPR

3454 1 **Tourist**[40] 5674 6-8-6 67 RyanPowell(5) 12 71+
(Ian Williams) *s.i.s: hdwy on outside over 1f out but stl plenty to do: str run fnl 120yds to ld fnl strides* **11/1**

-034 2 nk **For Life (IRE)**[60] 5038 9-8-0 65 NataliaGemelova(3) 9 62
(John E Long) *led: two l clr over 1f out: hrd rdn fnl f: hdd fnl strides* **33/1**

0651 3 1 **Hugely Exciting**[26] 6120 3-8-13 70 (b) LukeMorris 2 71
(J S Moore) *chsd ldrs: rdn drvn and kpt on ins fnl f: no ex clsng stages* **9/1**

0000 4 ¾ **Sarah's Art (IRE)**[12] 6502 8-8-1 69 (t) NickyMackay 7 55
(Derek Shaw) *t.k.h towards rr: hdwy on ins over 1f out: disp 2nd ins fnl f: wknd clsng stages* **12/1**

0001 5 nk **Frognal (IRE)**[2] 6759 5-8-5 67 (bt) JohnFahy(3) 5 61
(Richard Guest) *in tch: hdwy to chse ldrs over 1f out: disp 2nd ins fnl f: wknd clsng stages* **13/2**[3]

131 5 dht **Desert Icon (IRE)**[16] 6414 5-8-1 68 MartinLane 14 54
(David Simcock) *s.i.s: in rr: stl plenty to do wl over 1f out: r.o wl fnl f: kpt on cl home* **5/1**[2]

1224 7 ¾ **Sky Diamond (IRE)**[13] 6490 3-8-5 69 (b) SilvestreDeSousa 11 58
(James Given) *chsd ldrs: rdn over 1f out: n.m.r ins fnl f: wknd clsng stages* **4/1**[1]

5450 8 hd **Brandywell Boy (IRE)**[13] 6479 8-8-4 62 ow1 ChrisCatlin 13 55
(Dominic Ffrench Davis) *mid-div: drvn to chse ldrs appr fnl f: wknd fnl 50yds* **33/1**

4230 9 ¾ **Cristaliyev**[124] 2869 3-8-2 61 (p) DanielCremin(7) 3 60
(Jim Boyle) *chsd ldrs: drvn 1f out: wknd ins fnl f* **40/1**

3066 10 ½ **Bubbly Braveheart (IRE)**[7] 6622 4-8-0 63 JemmaMarshall(5) 10 52
(Pat Phelan) *in rr: sme hdwy on ins appr fnl f: sn rdn and no further prog* **16/1**

2100 11 1 **Piccoluck**[21] 6266 3-7-10 60 ow2 (be) RosieJessop(5) 1 48
(Amy Weaver) *chsd ldr tl appr fnl f: sn wknd* **40/1**

36 12 hd **Exchange**[35] 5835 3-8-5 70 TadhgO'Shea 6 51
(Andrew Haynes) *in rr: racd towards outside: a towards rr* **7/1**

4600 13 2 ¾ **Lastkingofscotland (IRE)**[51] 5318 5-8-4 70 (b) HarryBentley(3) 8 44
(Conor Dore) *racd towards outside: a towards rr* **8/1**

1m 24.53s (-0.27) **Going Correction** -0.075s/f (Stan)
WFA 3 from 4yo+ 2lb **13** Ran SP% **116.3**
Speed ratings (Par 101): **98,97,96,95,95 95,94,94,93,92 91,91,88**
toteswingers: 1&2 £41.10, 2&3 £46.00, 1&3 £13.20 CSF £334.36 TOTE £13.20: £4.30, £9.00, £1.80; EX 160.50.Desert Icon was claimed by Mr D. J. Flood for £5,000.
Owner Stratford Bards Racing No 2 **Bred** Juddmonte Farms Ltd **Trained** Portway, Worcs
■ Stewards' Enquiry : Natalia Gemelova seven-day ban: used whip with excessive frequency (Oct 26-29, Oct 31, Nov 1,2)

FOCUS
The winning time was 0.69 seconds slower than the first division. Muddling form.

Sky Diamond(IRE) Official explanation: jockey said gelding was denied a clear run

6795 MENZIES DISTRIBUTION BRITISH STALLION STUDS E B F MAIDEN STKS 7f (P)

3:35 (3:35) (Class 5) 2-Y-O **£3,234** (£962; £481; £240) **Stalls** Low

Form RPR

42 **1** **Ahzeemah (IRE)**[25] 6180 2-9-3 0................................(p) WilliamBuick 13 78
(Saeed Bin Suroor) *sn trcking ldr: chal 3f out: drvn 2f out: rdn and styd on to ld fnl 75yds: hld on all out* **9/4**[1]

40 **2** *nk* **Curzon Line**[18] 6334 2-9-3 0.. RichardHughes 5 77
(Mahmood Al Zarooni) *trckd ldrs: drvn and qcknd ins fnl f: pushed along and styd on strly to chse wnr fnl 50yds: fin wl: nt quite get up* **3/1**[2]

52 **3** *1* **Obliteright (IRE)**[63] 4906 2-9-3 0.. JimCrowley 10 74
(William Knight) *led: jnd 3f out: rdn and def advantage over 1f out: hdd and no ex fnl 75yds: sn one pce into 3rd* **9/1**

4 *2 1/2* **Instrumentalist (IRE)** 2-9-3 0.. LukeMorris 11 68+
(John Best) *chsd ldrs: drvn and one pce over 2f out: styd on again ins fnl f* **20/1**

03 **5** *1* **His Royal Highness (CAN)**[25] 6180 2-9-3 0............(v[1]) GeorgeBaker 8 65
(Mikael Magnusson) *chsd ldrs: drvn along 2f out: outpcd appr fnl f* **9/1**

6 **6** *4* **Saucy Cat (IRE)**[58] 5117 2-8-12 0.. ShaneKelly 9 50
(Murty McGrath) *chsd ldrs: drvn over 2f out: wknd over 1f out* **66/1**

0 **7** *nse* **Titus Bolt (IRE)**[29] 6019 2-9-3 0.. StephenCraine 4 55
(Jim Boyle) *in rr: hdwy and nt clr run ins fnl f: kpt on wl clsng stages* **80/1**

40 **8** *1/2* **Silver Marizah (IRE)**[25] 6169 2-8-12 0........................ FergusSweeney 2 48
(Gary Moore) *t.k.h early: chsd ldrs tl wknd over 1f out* **10/1**

9 *1/2* **Dubai Sunshine (IRE)** 2-9-3 0.. RichardMullen 6 52
(David Lanigan) *s.i.s: in rr: hdwy over 1f out: nvr a threat* **25/1**

00 **10** *2 1/4* **Astroscarlet**[14] 6458 2-8-12 0.. NickyMackay 7 41
(Mark H Tompkins) *chsd ldrs tl wknd ins fnl 2f* **80/1**

11 *1 1/4* **Arch Villain (IRE)** 2-9-3 0.. EddieAhern 14 43
(Amanda Perrett) *s.i.s: in rr: mod prog fnl f* **16/1**

12 *nk* **Tazweed (IRE)** 2-9-3 0.. NeilCallan 3 42
(Roger Varian) *green and a bhd* **8/1**[3]

13 *1* **Green Legacy (USA)** 2-9-3 0.. SteveDrowne 1 40
(Amanda Perrett) *slowly away: a bhd* **20/1**

1m 25.08s (0.28) **Going Correction** -0.075s/f (Stan) 13 Ran SP% **119.2**
Speed ratings (Par 95): **95,94,93,90,89 84,84,84,83,81 79,79,78**
toteswingers: 1&2 £2.30, 2&3 £9.00, 1&3 £5.70 CSF £8.00 TOTE £3.10: £1.10, £1.30, £1.50; EX 10.00.
Owner Godolphin **Bred** G O'Brien **Trained** Newmarket, Suffolk

FOCUS
Probably a fair maiden and it paid to be handy. Not only did it result in a 1-2 for Godolphin (albeit different trainers) but it was also a 1-2 for the sire Dubawi.

NOTEBOOK
Ahzeemah(IRE) showed he could handle Polytrack when runner-up over further at Wolverhampton last time, but this drop in trip may not have been totally in his favour so his effort can be upgraded. Always handy, he looked held by the third horse after turning in but his stamina then came into play and he got up in the last 50 yards. A return to further will help him. (op 3-1)
Curzon Line had looked a hard ride in two turf maidens and was hanging starting up the home straight here before staying on. He now gets a mark and can win a race, but he isn't one to take a short price about. (op 10-3 tchd 7-2)
Obliteright(IRE) ran well when runner-up at Kempton on his second start, but the race hasn't really worked out since (0-17). Given a positive ride, it seemed that he had done enough when edging clear off the final bend, but the Godolphin pair cut him down. He can now be handicapped. (op 8-1)
Instrumentalist(IRE) ◆ ran on well from the middle of the field to fare best of the newcomers. A £27,000 half-brother to four winners at up to 1m4f, he should get further and is worth keeping an eye on. (op 16-1 tchd 25-1 in a place)
His Royal Highness(CAN) had over 2l to find with Ahzeemah on Wolverhampton running and was tried in a visor, but having been handy early he hung away to the far rail over a furlong out and had little left. He is another who now gets a mark. (op 7-1 tchd 13-2)

6796 CITIPOST DIRECT DISTRIBUTION H'CAP (DIV I) 1m (P)

4:05 (4:05) (Class 5) (0-75,75) 3-Y-O+ **£2,385** (£704; £352) **Stalls** High

Form RPR

6453 **1** **George Guru**[13] 6473 4-9-0 **73**.. MarkCoumbe(5) 7 83+
(Michael Attwater) *s.i.s: in rr: stl plenty to do whn edgd lft bnd ent st: drvn and str run run thrght fnl f: edgd lft and led fnl 30yds* **11/1**

12 **2** *1/2* **Focail Eile**[33] 5894 6-9-7 **75**.. FrederikTylicki 12 84
(John Ryan) *in rr: hdwy on outside fr 2f out: drvn and styd on to ld fnl 120yds: edgd rt and hdd fnl 30yds: no ex* **5/1**[3]

1340 **3** *3 3/4* **Isingy Red (FR)**[56] 5171 3-8-13 **70**.. MatthewDavies 8 70
(Jim Boyle) *chsd ldrs: drvn and one pce 2f out: kpt on again fnl f to take one pce 3rd fnl 120yds* **20/1**

5020 **4** *1 1/4* **Greek Islands (IRE)**[23] 6227 3-9-0 **71**.. PatCosgrave 2 69
(Ed de Giles) *chsd ldrs tl pushed along and lost position 2f out: styd on again fnl f: kpt on clsng stages* **14/1**

0-30 **5** *nk* **Huwayit (IRE)**[14] 6459 3-9-2 **73**.. SebSanders 3 70
(Clive Brittain) *chsd ldrs: drvn along 2f out: wknd ins fnl f* **16/1**

2030 **6** *hd* **Danehill Dante (IRE)**[32] 5938 3-9-2 **73**.. RichardHughes 11 69
(Richard Hannon) *chsd ldrs: led over 1f out: hdd & wknd fnl 120yds* **9/2**[2]

0300 **7** *1 1/4* **Aspectus (IRE)**[22] 6231 8-9-1 **72**................................(b) SophieDoyle(3) 9 65
(Jamie Osborne) *led after 2f: pushed along over 2f out: hdd over 1f out: sn wknd* **12/1**

1406 **8** *1 3/4* **Alfresco**[31] 5972 7-9-6 **74**................................(b) GeorgeBaker 10 63
(John Best) *t.k.h towards rr: hdwy 1/2-way: rdn over 2f out: sn btn* **16/1**

2466 **9** *1* **Al Aqabah (IRE)**[128] 2771 6-9-4 **72**.. SilvestreDeSousa 5 59
(Brian Gubby) *sn slt ld hdd after 2f: wknd qckly over 1f out* **12/1**

2223 **10** *4* **Ferruccio (IRE)**[23] 6227 3-9-4 **75**................................(v[1]) EddieAhern 1 53
(James Fanshawe) *towards rr but in tch: drvn over 2f out and sn dropped away* **7/2**[1]

2-24 **11** *5* **Always Like This (IRE)**[32] 5946 3-8-13 **70**.. WilliamBuick 4 36
(Marco Botti) *pressed ldr 2f: lost pl and drvn 1/2-way: lost tch fnl 3f* **10/1**

1300 **12** *28* **Rezwaan**[32] 5948 4-9-7 **75**.. ShaneKelly 6 —
(Murty McGrath) *slowly away: sn drvn: lost tch fr 1/2-way* **20/1**

1m 36.7s (-1.50) **Going Correction** -0.075s/f (Stan)
WFA 3 from 4yo+ 3lb 12 Ran SP% **117.8**
Speed ratings (Par 103): **104,103,99,98,98 98,96,95,94,90 85,57**
toteswingers: 1&2 £12.90, 2&3 £25.40, 1&3 £42.30 CSF £64.78 CT £1098.32 TOTE £13.60: £3.10, £2.30, £7.80; EX 71.10.
Owner T M Jones **Bred** T M Jones **Trained** Epsom, Surrey

FOCUS
An ordinary handicap, but the front pair came clear and the form looks sound. The time was a second faster than the second division.

Alfresco Official explanation: jockey said gelding hung left under pressure

6797 CITIPOST DIRECT DISTRIBUTION H'CAP (DIV II) 1m (P)

4:40 (4:41) (Class 5) (0-75,75) 3-Y-O+ **£2,385** (£704; £352) **Stalls** High

Form RPR

-315 **1** **Tarooq (USA)**[43] 5608 5-9-3 **74**.. LeeTopliss(3) 3 87+
(Richard Fahey) *trckd ldrs: qcknd on ins to ld wl over 1f out: sn drvn clr: comf* **4/1**[2]

610 **2** *2 1/4* **Songburst**[9] 6592 3-9-1 **75**.. KieranO'Neill(3) 9 82
(Richard Hannon) *chsd ldrs: drvn to chse wnr fnl f but nvr any ch* **7/2**[1]

0-51 **3** *1/2* **L'Astre De Choisir (IRE)**[9] 6587 3-9-4 **75** 6ex................ JimCrowley 12 81
(Walter Swinburn) *chsd ldrs: drvn and styd on fr over 1f out to take 3rd ins fnl f: kpt on clsng stages* **5/1**

3446 **4** *nk* **Great Shot**[26] 6124 3-9-3 **74**.. JamesDoyle 10 79+
(Sylvester Kirk) *in rr: racd on outside and hdwy 2f out: drvn and styd on fnl f: kpt on clsng stages* **9/2**[3]

0006 **5** *1/2* **L'Hirondelle (IRE)**[18] 6355 7-9-4 **72**.. ShaneKelly 7 76
(Michael Attwater) *in tch: drvn and hdwy ins fnl 2f: kpt on ins fnl f: nt pce to rch ldrs* **10/1**

0400 **6** *3/4* **Hurricane Spirit (IRE)**[23] 6220 7-9-6 **74**..................(b[1]) RobertWinston 2 76
(Terry Clement) *s.i.s: in rr: hdwy on ins and drvn wl over 1f out and hd high: styd on again clsng stages* **25/1**

000 **7** *nse* **Rasheed**[110] 3361 3-9-1 **72**.. TadhgO'Shea 8 74
(John Gosden) *chsd ldrs: drvn along 3f out: one pce fr over 1f out* **12/1**

5500 **8** *3/4* **Montegonian (USA)**[75] 4489 3-9-2 **73**.. RichardMullen 1 73
(Marcus Tregoning) *in tch: drvn along over 2f out: chsd ldrs on ins over 1f out: wknd ins fnl f* **12/1**

-000 **9** *1/2* **Councellor (FR)**[11] 6541 9-9-4 **75**................................(t) RossAtkinson(3) 5 74
(Derek Shaw) *s.i.s: t.k.h: drvn over 2f out: no imp and one pce fnl f* **66/1**

0000 **10** *shd* **Beauchamp Yorker**[63] 4910 4-8-6 **67**................................(t) NicoleNordblad(7) 4 66
(Hans Adielsson) *led tl hdd wl over 1f out: wknd ins fnl f* **50/1**

0220 **11** *3/4* **Blue Deer (IRE)**[14] 6442 3-8-13 **70**.. NeilCallan 11 67
(John Akehurst) *a towards rr* **25/1**

6000 **12** *nk* **The Which Doctor**[27] 6093 6-8-11 **68**................................(e) JohnFahy(3) 6 64
(Richard Guest) *s.i.s: a towards rr* **25/1**

1m 37.7s (-0.50) **Going Correction** -0.075s/f (Stan)
WFA 3 from 4yo+ 3lb 12 Ran SP% **116.5**
Speed ratings (Par 103): **99,96,96,95,95 94,94,93,93,93 92,92**
toteswingers: 1&2 £3.10, 2&3 £4.70, 1&3 £3.80 CSF £17.04 CT £72.08 TOTE £5.50: £2.40, £2.00, £2.40; EX 20.60.
Owner Y Nasib **Bred** Kirsten Rausing **Trained** Musley Bank, N Yorks

FOCUS
The winning time was exactly a second slower than division one.
Great Shot ◆ Official explanation: jockey said gelding hung right

6798 SMITHS NEWS H'CAP 2m (P)

5:10 (5:11) (Class 6) (0-65,65) 3-Y-O+ **£1,704** (£503; £251) **Stalls** Low

Form RPR

-330 **1** **Henry Holmes**[27] 6087 8-8-9 **46** oh1.. SteveDrowne 9 53
(Lydia Richards) *chsd ldrs: drvn and one pce over 2f out: kpt on again over 1f out: styd wl fnl f to ld fnl stride* **28/1**

0251 **2** *shd* **Marcus Antonius**[22] 6240 4-10-0 **65**.. PatCosgrave 5 72
(Jim Boyle) *t.k.h: hld up in rr: stdy hdwy fr 4f out: chsd ldr 3f out: rdn and hung lft over 1f out: styd on fnl f to ld fnl 75yds: edgd rt clsng stages: hdd fnl stride* **8/1**

/14- **3** *1* **Albacocca**[440] 4519 4-9-4 **55**.. SebSanders 10 61
(Sir Mark Prescott Bt) *s.i.s: sn rcvrd and led after 2f: rdn fnl f: hdd and nt qckn fnl 75yds* **11/2**

4042 **4** *12* **Squad**[13] 6476 5-9-10 **61**................................(v) EddieAhern 6 52
(Simon Dow) *s.i.s: in rr: styd on fr over 2f out: tk mod 4th wl over 1f out* **6/1**

4322 **5** *2* **Jinto**[32] 5947 4-9-7 **58**................................(p) NickyMackay 11 47
(David Elsworth) *sn chsng ldrs: wknd appr fnl 2f* **4/1**[2]

0-50 **6** *2* **Tafaneen (USA)**[28] 6054 3-9-3 **65**.. TadhgO'Shea 3 52
(Roger Varian) *led 2f: styd chsng ldrs: drvn over 3f out: wknd ins fnl 2f* **5/1**[3]

2423 **7** *5* **Veloce (IRE)**[46] 5477 3-9-1 **63**................................(p) JimCrowley 2 44
(Ralph Beckett) *in rr: rdn along fr 1/2-way: nvr travelling after and a bhd* **11/4**[1]

5265 **8** *5* **Astrovenus**[42] 5628 4-8-12 **49**.. WilliamBuick 4 24
(Mark H Tompkins) *in rr: hdwy 1/2-way: drvn along 7f out: in tch over 3f out: wknd over 2f out: eased whn no ch fnl f* **25/1**

000/ **9** *18* **Dolores Ortiz (IRE)**[183] 4719 5-8-7 **49**.................. MatthewCosham(5) 1 —
(Dr Jeremy Naylor) *a bhd: lost tch fr 1/2-way* **100/1**

3m 23.34s (-2.36) **Going Correction** -0.075s/f (Stan)
WFA 3 from 4yo+ 11lb 9 Ran SP% **112.4**
Speed ratings (Par 101): **102,101,101,95,94 93,90,88,79**
toteswingers: 1&2 £9.90, 2&3 £6.00, 1&3 £18.00 CSF £226.80 CT £1423.04 TOTE £22.90: £6.50, £1.40, £2.10; EX 107.00.
Owner Mrs Judy Seal **Bred** Mrs Lydia Richards **Trained** Funtington, W Sussex
■ Stewards' Enquiry : Pat Cosgrave five-day ban: used whip with excessive frequency (Oct 26-29, 31)

FOCUS
A moderate staying handicap, but unusually for races over 2m here the pace seemed fair.
Jinto Official explanation: jockey said gelding hung left
Astrovenus Official explanation: jockey said filly was unsuited by the kickback

6799 SCA RECYCLING UK LTD H'CAP 1m 2f (P)

5:45 (5:46) (Class 5) (0-70,70) 3-Y-O **£2,385** (£704; £352) **Stalls** Low

Form RPR

2530 **1** **Focail Maith**[33] 5892 3-9-5 **68**.. FrederikTylicki 9 78
(John Ryan) *in tch: hdwy over 3f out: drvn and qcknd appr fnl f: led fnl 120yds: readily* **8/1**

5031 **2** *1 1/2* **Goodwood Treasure**[26] 6122 3-9-0 **63**.. JimCrowley 3 70
(John Dunlop) *chsd ldrs: drvn 2f out: styd on fnl f to take 2nd clsng stages but no imp on wnr* **7/2**[1]

-500 **3** *1* **The Holyman (IRE)**[35] 5835 3-9-7 **70**.. IanMongan 10 75
(Jo Crowley) *racd wd early: chsd ldrs: led 6f out: drvn 2f out: hdd fnl 120yds: one pce into 3rd clsng stages* **10/1**

3140 **4** *1* **Ice Nelly (IRE)**[47] 5428 3-9-2 **65**.. SteveDrowne 12 68+
(Hughie Morrison) *in rr: drvn and hdwy on outside wl over 1f out: styd on wl clsng stages: nt rch ldrs* **10/1**

2463 **5** *hd* **Conducting**[25] 6181 3-9-3 **66**.. ShaneKelly 14 69
(Gay Kelleway) *towards rr: drvn and hdwy wl over 1f out: styd on clsng stages: nt rch ldrs* **7/1**[3]

060 **6** *nk* **Graceful Act**[27] 6086 3-8-9 **58** .... TadhgO'Shea 7 60
(James Toller) *chsd ldrs: drvn over 2f out: wknd fnl f* **22/1**
4653 **7** *1 1/2* **Kingarrick**[14] 6465 3-9-7 **70** .... EddieAhern 6 69
(Eve Johnson Houghton) *in rr but in tch: kpt on fr over 1f out: nt rch ldrs* **13/2**[2]
000 **8** *2* **Regal Kiss**[12] 6507 3-9-3 **66** .... SilvestreDeSousa 4 61
(Mark Johnston) *led tl hdd 6f out: wknd qckly ins fnl f* **12/1**
5534 **9** *1 1/2* **Nicola's Dream**[24] 6192 3-8-13 **65** ....(p) LeeTopliss(3) 2 57
(Richard Fahey) *t.k.h: chsd ldrs: drvn 2f out: sn wknd* **10/1**
014 **10** *4 1/2* **Harry Lime**[21] 6253 3-8-10 **59** .... RobertWinston 5 42
(Chris Dwyer) *drvn along 3f out: bhd most of way* **8/1**
4000 **11** *4 1/2* **Uncle Dermot (IRE)**[9] 6586 3-9-4 **67** .... FergusSweeney 13 41
(Brendan Powell) *t.k.h: towards rr most of way* **14/1**
650 **12** *9* **Silent Ninja**[28] 6054 3-9-1 **64** .... NeilCallan 11 20
(Hughie Morrison) *racd wd: chsd ldrs towards outside early: wknd over 2f out* **16/1**

2m 6.07s (-0.53) **Going Correction** -0.075s/f (Stan) **12 Ran SP% 122.1**
Speed ratings (Par 101): **99,97,97,96,96 95,94,93,91,88 84,77**
toteswingers: 1&2 £6.70, 2&3 £9.10, 1&3 £24.00 CSF £37.20 CT £294.11 TOTE £12.00: £3.00, £1.90, £3.80; EX 46.80.
Owner Cathal Fegan **Bred** D Robb **Trained** Newmarket, Suffolk

FOCUS
An ordinary handicap, but soundly run.
T/Plt: £612.20 to a £1 stake. Pool £65,340.20. 77.91 winning tickets. T/Qpdt: £41.10 to a £1 stake. Pool £5,958.44. 107.20 winning tickets. ST

6627 NOTTINGHAM (L-H)
Wednesday, October 12

OFFICIAL GOING: Good (good to soft in places; 6.6) changing to good to soft after race 4 (3.15)
Wind: Fresh, against Weather: Cloudy

6800 WINNING FORECAST DG TAXIS 0115 9500 500 MAIDEN AUCTION STKS — 5f 13y
1:40 (1:59) (Class 5) 2-Y-O — £2,264 (£673; £336; £168) Stalls High

Form — RPR
1 **Dancheur (IRE)** 2-8-8 0 .... MartinHarley 6 68+
(Mrs K Burke) *hld up: hdwy and swtchd lft 1f out: r.o to ld wl ins fnl f* **3/1**[1]
6 **2** *nk* **Code Six (IRE)**[28] 6045 2-8-6 0 .... TomEaves 9 61
(Bryan Smart) *led: rdn and hdd wl ins fnl f* **12/1**
0640 **3** *1/2* **Dolly Danca**[8] 6597 2-8-4 57 .... JimmyQuinn 10 57
(Paul Midgley) *a.p: rdn to chse ldr over 1f out: sn ev ch: unable qck nr fin* **25/1**
0 **4** *1 1/4* **Smacker (IRE)**[26] 6127 2-8-12 0 .... JimmyFortune 4 61
(Hughie Morrison) *hld up in tch: shkn up over 1f out: styd on* **11/2**
3025 **5** *hd* **One Kool Dude**[27] 6075 2-8-10 70 ....(p) PaulHanagan 2 58
(Richard Fahey) *chsd ldrs: pushed along 1/2-way: no ex fnl f* **7/2**[2]
0 **6** *9* **Shamakat**[33] 5889 2-8-7 0 .... WilliamCarson 7 22
(Rae Guest) *chsd ldr tl pushed along over 1f out: sn wknd* **9/2**[3]
7 *9* **Chart** 2-8-10 0 .... MartinDwyer 1 —
(William Jarvis) *dwlt: outpcd* **9/2**[3]

63.29 secs (2.29) **Going Correction** +0.275s/f (Good) **7 Ran SP% 110.5**
Speed ratings (Par 95): **92,91,90,88,88 74,59**
toteswingers: 1&2 £6.50, 2&3 £14.40, 1&3 £10.20 CSF £35.75 TOTE £4.60: £2.40, £4.20; EX 42.90 Trifecta £323.10 Pool: £628.86 - 1.44 winning tickets..
Owner Mark James & Mrs Elaine Burke **Bred** A F O'Callaghan **Trained** Middleham Moor, North Yorks

FOCUS
Outer track used and rail on bottom bend moved out 3m increasing distance son Round course by 10yds. There was a significant delay to this opening juvenile maiden after Cathy Gannon was unseated by Forever Janey going to post and had to be taken to hospital. The remainder of the races were run around 30 minutes later than advertised. A modest maiden.

NOTEBOOK
Dancheur(IRE) picked up nicely once switched, squeezing between the placed runners and just doing enough. She's bred to stay further, so this was a most encouraging start, and it's probable she'll have more to offer in nurseries. (op 7-2)
Code Six(IRE) left her debut form behind, showing good early pace and bagging the rail. She did respond when challenged and headed by the winner, but just missed out. She has a future in ordinary company. (op 9-1)
Dolly Danca had previously finished well held in maidens, so this improved showing was unexpected. She's lowly rated and can find a small race. (tchd 22-1)
Smacker(IRE) made some promising late headway and will be of interest once qualified for handicaps. (op 9-2)
One Kool Dude raced away from the rail and was comfortably held. He's now 0-11. (op 11-4 tchd 4-1)

6801 RELIABLE CHOICE DG TAXIS 0115 9500 500 H'CAP — 5f 13y
2:10 (2:42) (Class 5) (0-75,75) 3-Y-O — £2,264 (£673; £336; £168) Stalls High

Form — RPR
2131 **1** **Cool In The Shade**[14] 6454 3-9-0 **68** ....(b) TonyHamilton 6 76+
(Paul Midgley) *mde all: swtchd to stands' side rail 3f out: rdn out* **13/2**[2]
3630 **2** *1/2* **Black Annis Bower**[27] 6076 3-9-1 **69** .... JamesSullivan 7 75
(Michael Easterby) *a.p: rdn over 1f out: r.o* **14/1**
5001 **3** *hd* **Rafaaf (IRE)**[33] 5890 3-9-4 **72** .... AndreaAtzeni 1 77+
(Robert Eddery) *hld up: hdwy 1/2-way: rdr dropped whip over 1f out: r.o* **15/2**[3]
1415 **4** *nk* **Whitecrest**[14] 6456 3-9-4 **72** .... DaneO'Neill 10 76
(John Spearing) *hld up: hdwy over 1f out: rdn and r.o ins fnl f* **8/1**
5030 **5** *1* **Style And Panache (IRE)**[2] 6752 3-9-2 **70** .... GrahamGibbons 2 71
(David Evans) *chsd ldrs: rdn over 1f out: styd on* **20/1**
0040 **6** *shd* **Above The Stars**[26] 6112 3-9-3 **71** .... PaulHanagan 9 71
(Richard Fahey) *hld up: rdn over 1f out: swtchd rt and r.o ins fnl f: nt rch ldrs* **8/1**
2633 **7** *1/2* **Showboating (IRE)**[13] 6491 3-9-6 **74** ....(tp) MartinHarley 4 72+
(Alan McCabe) *hld up: swtchd lft and hdwy 2f out: rdn over 1f out: styd on same pce fnl f* **17/2**
6022 **8** *1 1/4* **Madame Kintyre**[8] 6604 3-8-10 **64** ow1 ....(v[1]) JamesMillman 5 58
(Rod Millman) *chsd wnr: rdn over 1f out: no ex ins fnl f* **8/1**
3151 **9** *3/4* **Best Be Careful (IRE)**[14] 6456 3-8-10 **71** .... RachealKneller(7) 12 62
(Mark Usher) *hld up: nt clr run fr over 1f out: nvr able to chal* **6/1**[1]
2005 **10** *7* **Tom Sawyer**[81] 4324 3-9-7 **75** .... BarryMcHugh 8 41
(Julie Camacho) *s.i.s: a in rr* **20/1**
1020 **11** *2* **Green Warrior**[21] 6265 3-8-9 **66** ....(p) RobertLButler(3) 3 25
(Richard Guest) *unruly in stalls: s.i.s and hmpd sn after s: hld up: wknd over 1f out* **50/1**
4000 **12** *1 1/4* **Gottcher**[18] 6350 3-9-3 **71** .... LeeNewman 11 25
(David Barron) *chsd ldrs over 3f* **16/1**
4600 **13** *4 1/2* **Boundless Spirit**[11] 6537 3-8-12 **66** ....(tp) AdrianNicholls 14 4
(David Nicholls) *prom: rdn and hung lft 3f out: wknd wl over 1f out* **14/1**
0450 **P** **Jack Smudge**[32] 5939 3-9-1 **69** .... TomQueally 13 —
(James Given) *prom: lost pl 1/2-way: p.u and dismntd over 1f out* **25/1**

62.06 secs (1.06) **Going Correction** +0.275s/f (Good) **14 Ran SP% 117.8**
Speed ratings (Par 101): **102,101,100,100,98 98,97,95,94,83 80,78,71,—**
toteswingers: 1&2 £18.20, 2&3 £25.00, 1&3 £10.80 CSF £87.36 CT £720.35 TOTE £6.20: £1.80, £5.60, £3.00; EX 113.10 TRIFECTA Not won..
Owner The Rumpole Partnership **Bred** R W Gittins **Trained** Westow, N Yorks

FOCUS
An open sprint handicap and a good time compared to other races at the trip.
Boundless Spirit Official explanation: jockey said gelding hung left
Jack Smudge Official explanation: vet said gelding pulled up lame

6802 CONTINENTAL COMMERCIAL TYRES H'CAP — 5f 13y
2:40 (3:12) (Class 6) (0-65,65) 3-Y-O+ — £1,617 (£481; £240; £120) Stalls High

Form — RPR
2635 **1** **Cape Royal**[9] 6580 11-9-4 **65** ....(tp) SeanLevey(3) 8 74
(Milton Bradley) *mde all and overall ldr far side: rdn 2f out: kpt on wl fnl f: jst hld on: 1st of 9 in gp* **12/1**
0125 **2** *nse* **Spirit Of Coniston**[17] 6386 8-9-0 **58** .... MickyFenton 12 67
(Paul Midgley) *trckd far side ldrs: effrt and edgd lft over 1f out: kpt on wl fnl f: jst hld: 2nd of 9 in gp* **22/1**
002 **3** *nk* **Bouncy Bouncy (IRE)**[30] 5997 4-9-6 **64** ....(t) JamieSpencer 1 72+
(Michael Bell) *hld up far side: gd hdwy over 1f out: kpt on wl fnl f: jst hld: 3rd of 9 in gp* **12/1**
3600 **4** *3* **Steel City Boy (IRE)**[9] 6580 8-8-12 **56** .... TomMcLaughlin 17 53
(Garry Woodward) *hld up stands' side: hdwy and edgd lft wl over 1f out: led that gp ins fnl f: nt pce of far side ldrs: 1st of 8 in gp* **20/1**
1413 **5** *shd* **Griffin Point (IRE)**[9] 6580 4-9-3 **61** .... MartinDwyer 11 58+
(William Muir) *in tch far side: drvn and hung lft over 2f out: kpt on same pce fnl f: 4th of 9 in gp* **9/1**[3]
5500 **6** *shd* **Make My Dream**[9] 6580 8-9-4 **62** .... JoeFanning 9 58
(John Gallagher) *hld up stands' side: hdwy over 1f out: ev ch that gp ins fnl f: kpt on: no imp: 2nd of 8 in gp* **20/1**
3215 **7** *1/2* **Ginzan**[16] 6403 3-9-1 **62** .... LouisBeuzelin(3) 15 57
(Malcolm Saunders) *chsd stands' side ldrs: effrt and drvn over 1f out: edgd lft: nt qckn ins fnl f: 3rd of 8 in gp* **15/2**[2]
0000 **8** *nk* **Grand Stitch (USA)**[6] 6655 5-8-8 **57** ....(v) NeilFarley(5) 13 51
(Declan Carroll) *awkward s but led stands' side: rdn and hdd that gp ins fnl f: no ex: 4th of 8 in gp* **28/1**
0300 **9** *1 1/4* **Greenhead High**[39] 5731 3-9-2 **60** .... AdrianNicholls 2 49
(David Nicholls) *in tch far side: rdn and hung lft 2f out: kpt on same pce fnl f: 5th of 9 in gp* **33/1**
0014 **10** *nk* **Divertimenti (IRE)**[8] 6609 7-9-6 **64** ....(b) JimmyQuinn 16 52
(Roy Bowring) *hld up in tch stands' side: drvn over 2f out: no imp fr over 1f out: 5th of 8 in gp* **9/2**[1]
6500 **11** *nk* **Avertuoso**[39] 5732 7-9-2 **60** ....(v) TomEaves 4 47
(Bryan Smart) *chsd wnr far side: rdn 2f out: wknd ins fnl f: 6th of 9 in gp* **25/1**
0000 **12** *3/4* **Rainy Night**[7] 6634 5-9-0 **65** ....(v) JackDuern(7) 5 49
(Reg Hollinshead) *in tch on outside of stands' side gp: effrt and rdn 2f out: wknd ins fnl f: 6th of 8 in gp* **16/1**
6122 **13** *1/2* **My Meteor**[16] 6398 4-9-2 **60** .... DaneO'Neill 14 42
(Tony Newcombe) *cl up stands' side: effrt and rdn 2f out: wknd fnl f: 7th of 8 in gp* **9/2**[1]
0450 **14** *1/2* **Danzoe (IRE)**[13] 6479 4-9-5 **63** .... PaulHanagan 7 44
(Christine Dunnett) *bhd and drvn along far side: sme hdwy fnl f: nvr rchd ldrs: 7th of 9 in gp* **14/1**
0006 **15** *1 1/2* **Chosen One (IRE)**[15] 6427 6-9-2 **60** ....(v) JamesSullivan 3 35
(Ruth Carr) *chsd far side ldrs tl rdn and wknd over 1f out: 8th of 9 in gp* **20/1**
0000 **16** *3* **Incomparable**[39] 5732 6-9-7 **65** ....(bt) TomQueally 10 29
(David Nicholls) *dwlt: sn drvn along in rr stands' side: struggling fr 1/2-way: nvr on terms: last of 8 in gp* **25/1**
4630 **17** *4 1/2* **Patch Patch**[14] 6444 4-8-13 **57** ....(v) AdamKirby 6 —
(Derek Shaw) *dwlt: bhd and drvn far side: no ch fr 1/2-way: last of 9 in gp* **25/1**

62.88 secs (1.88) **Going Correction** +0.275s/f (Good) **17 Ran SP% 121.3**
Speed ratings (Par 101): **95,94,94,89,89 89,88,88,86,85 85,83,83,82,79 75,67**
toteswingers: 1&2 £69.70, 2&3 £29.80, 1&3 £18.00 CSF £255.29 CT £3328.25 TOTE £13.20: £4.30, £5.60, £1.90, £5.40; EX 486.30 TRIFECTA Not won..
Owner E A Hayward **Bred** D R Brotherton **Trained** Sedbury, Gloucs
■ Stewards' Enquiry : Micky Fenton two-day ban: careless riding (Oct 26-27)
Martin Dwyer two-day ban: failed to ride out for 4th (Oct 26-27)

FOCUS
The field split in this low-grade sprint, with those who raced far side coming out on top.
Spirit Of Coniston Official explanation: jockey said gelding hung left
Griffin Point(IRE) Official explanation: jockey said filly suffered interference in running

6803 DENMAN - BUILDING FOR YOU - H'CAP — 1m 2f 50y
3:15 (3:46) (Class 3) (0-95,95) 3-Y-O+ — £6,663 (£1,982; £990; £495) Stalls Low

Form — RPR
4015 **1** **Demolition**[20] 6277 7-8-12 **87** .... GaryBartley(3) 10 99
(Noel Wilson) *chsd ldrs: led over 2f out: rdn over 1f out: styd on wl* **25/1**
0322 **2** *3 1/2* **Absinthe (IRE)**[62] 4959 5-9-3 **89** .... DaneO'Neill 3 94
(Walter Swinburn) *a.p: swtchd rt and chsd wnr over 1f out: sn rdn: styd on same pce ins fnl f* **8/1**[3]
0205 **3** *2* **Northside Prince (IRE)**[27] 6080 5-8-13 **90** .... GarryWhillans(5) 2 92+
(Alan Swinbank) *prom: lost pl 6f out: rdn over 2f out: r.o ins fnl f* **14/1**
6300 **4** *nse* **Shavansky**[18] 6339 7-9-8 **94** .... JamesMillman 8 95
(Rod Millman) *hld up: hdwy over 2f out: styd on* **12/1**
2032 **5** *shd* **Mirrored**[15] 6429 5-9-2 **88** .... DuranFentiman 9 89
(Tim Easterby) *hld up: plld hrd: nt clr run over 2f out: hdwy over 1f out: nt rch ldrs* **14/1**
130 **6** *3/4* **Line Of Duty (IRE)**[39] 5705 4-9-1 **87** .... PJMcDonald 14 87
(Alan Swinbank) *hld up: hdwy over 4f out: rdn over 1f out: styd on same pce* **20/1**
4010 **7** *1 1/4* **Dhaamer (IRE)**[25] 6163 4-9-9 **95** ....(v) RichardHills 4 92
(John Gosden) *hld up: hdwy over 3f out: rdn over 1f out: wknd ins fnl f* **8/1**[3]

0400 **8** ½ **Desert Romance (IRE)**[18] 6339 5-9-0 **86**.................(p) DanielTudhope 6 83
(David O'Meara) *led over 7f: wknd fnl f* **25/1**

2405 **9** 2 **Waldvogel (IRE)**[32] 5932 7-9-4 **90**.. TomEaves 5 83
(Nicky Richards) *hld up: rdn over 2f out: n.d* **22/1**

5000 **10** 1½ **Kay Gee Be (IRE)**[18] 6326 7-9-1 **87**.............................. PaulHanagan 11 77
(Richard Fahey) *hld up: hdwy over 3f out: rdn over 2f out: sn wknd* **40/1**

101 **11** 3 **Midsummer Sun**[33] 5880 3-9-3 **94**.. TomQueally 1 78
(Sir Henry Cecil) *chsd ldr tl rdn over 2f out: wknd over 1f out* **5/2**[1]

4153 **12** nk **Tres Coronas (IRE)**[15] 6429 4-9-0 **86**............................ LeeNewman 12 70
(David Barron) *hood removed late and s.s: a in rr* **14/1**

3 **13** 1½ **Fattsota**[20] 6277 3-9-3 **94**.. AdamKirby 13 75
(Marco Botti) *prom: rdn over 2f out: wknd over 1f out* **11/2**[2]

2525 **14** 66 **Guest Book (IRE)**[74] 4537 4-8-11 **88**........................... DavidKenny(5) 16 —
(Michael Scudamore) *hld up: a in rr: bhd fr 1/2-way: t.o* **20/1**

2m 12.68s (0.98) **Going Correction** +0.275s/f (Good) **14** Ran SP% **117.9**
WFA 3 from 4yo+ 5lb
Speed ratings (Par 107): **107,104,102,102,102 101,100,100,98,97 95,95,93,41**
toteswingers: 1&2 £34.70, 2&3 £12.50, 1&3 £57.30 CSF £194.31 CT £2922.91 TOTE £34.50: £9.00, £3.50, £4.70; EX 267.10 TRIFECTA Not won..
Owner M Wormald **Bred** P D And Mrs Player **Trained** Sandhutton, N Yorks

FOCUS
A fair handicap. The first three were well positioned throughout.

NOTEBOOK
Demolition, back with his old yard having left Richard Fahey, was nicely treated on the pick of his efforts and won this with quite a bit in hand. Although well held the time before, conditions were more to his liking here and he'll presumably go back up in grade now.
Absinthe(IRE) travelled well and ran another solid race in defeat, but he can expect another small nudge up the weights and winning a decent handicap isn't going to become any easier.
Northside Prince(IRE) remains 12lb higher than when last winning and, although running well once more, is likely to remain vulnerable off his current rating. (op 12-1)
Shavansky, a creditable seventh in the Cambridgeshire, did best of those held up. (op 14-1)
Mirrored, another in rear early, would have probably challenged for a place had he not been short of room at a crucial stage. (tchd 16-1)
Midsummer Sun did well to win despite not settling at Chester the time before and looked feasibly treated off 6lb higher. However, there was no response when Queally asked him to pick up and he soon folded. This was disappointing, but it's quite possible he'll make a better 4yo. (tchd 11-4)
Tres Coronas(IRE) Official explanation: jockey said gelding reared up as gates opened resulting in blindfold being difficult to remove and gelding being slowly away
Fattsota had made a promising British debut at Pontefract, but was unable to build on it here on a slower surface. (tchd 5-1 and 6-1)

6804 NOTTINGHAM'S PREMIER COMPANY DG TAXIS 0115 9500 500 MAIDEN STKS 1m 2f 50y
3:45 (4:16) (Class 5) 3-Y-O **£2,264** (£673; £336; £168) **Stalls** Low

Form RPR

5 **1** **Eshtibaak (IRE)**[179] 1408 3-9-3 0.. RichardHills 6 90+
(John Gosden) *s.i.s: sn midfield on outside: smooth hdwy over 2f out: led and edgd lft over 1f out: sn rdn and qcknd clr: kpt on wl: readily* **1/1**[1]

3 **2** 2¼ **Montefeltro**[27] 6097 3-9-3 0.. AhmedAjtebi 2 81
(Mahmood Al Zarooni) *prom: rdn and rn green over 2f out: rallied over 1f out: chsd (clr) wnr wl ins fnl f: r.o* **14/1**

0 **3** nk **Martine's Spirit (IRE)**[14] 6459 3-8-12 0........................... LiamJones 14 75
(William Haggas) *hld up: hdwy over 2f out: edgd lft and chsd wnr over 1f out to wl ins fnl f: r.o* **66/1**

0-3 **4** 6 **Moon Over Water (IRE)**[26] 6137 3-8-12 0...................... AndreaAtzeni 3 64
(Roger Varian) *t.k.h: led: rdn over 2f out: hdd over 1f out: sn outpcd* **18/1**

0 **5** ½ **Ornithologist (USA)**[18] 6349 3-9-3 0.......................... DanielTudhope 13 68
(David O'Meara) *hld up: stdy hdwy on ins and in tch 3f out: rdn and outpcd fnl 2f* **100/1**

55 **6** ½ **Appeal (IRE)**[16] 6404 3-8-12 0.. StevieDonohoe 4 62+
(Sir Mark Prescott Bt) *s.i.s: sn midfield: drvn and outpcd over 3f out: rallied fnl f: nrst fin* **40/1**

02 **7** 2 **Covert Desire**[130] 2735 3-9-3 0.. FrankieDettori 5 63
(Mahmood Al Zarooni) *prom on outside: hdwy to chse ldr over 4f out: rdn over 2f out: lost 2nd and wknd over 1f out* **15/8**[2]

8 nse **Silver Blossom (IRE)** 3-8-12 0.. JimmyFortune 1 58
(Andrew Balding) *missed break: bhd: hdwy into midfield 1/2-way: rdn and wknd over 2f out* **33/1**

4- **9** ¾ **Baraaya (IRE)**[438] 4595 3-8-12 0.. PaulHanagan 8 57
(William Haggas) *t.k.h: chsd ldr to over 4f out: wknd fr 2f out* **9/1**[3]

64 **10** 5 **Millennium Star (IRE)**[36] 5816 3-8-12 0............................ TomQueally 9 47
(Sir Henry Cecil) *hld up in tch: stdy hdwy over 3f out: wknd fr 2f out* **20/1**

0 **11** 9 **Ascensive**[96] 3824 3-8-12 0.. MartinDwyer 12 30
(Ralph Beckett) *trckd ldrs tl rdn and wknd over 2f out* **50/1**

0 **12** 1¼ **Grand Sort**[27] 6085 3-9-3 0.. DaneO'Neill 15 33
(Tony Newcombe) *t.k.h: hld up: struggling 3f out: nvr on terms* **200/1**

0 **13** 12 **Red Marksman**[27] 6085 3-9-3 0.. RobertHavlin 16 10
(James Evans) *s.i.s: bhd: struggling over 3f out: sn btn* **150/1**

06 **14** 9 **Cant Sell (IRE)**[2] 6750 3-9-3 0.. GrahamGibbons 11 —
(David Evans) *s.i.s: bhd: struggling over 3f out: sn wknd* **200/1**

6 **15** 1¾ **Cherry Tree Hill (IRE)**[134] 2591 3-9-3 0............................ PJMcDonald 10 —
(Alan Swinbank) *hld up: rdn along and effrt over 3f out: wknd over 2f out* **100/1**

2m 15.53s (3.83) **Going Correction** +0.275s/f (Good) **15** Ran SP% **123.9**
Speed ratings (Par 101): **95,93,92,88,87 87,85,85,85,81 73,72,63,56,54**
toteswingers: 1&2 £6.90, 2&3 £69.10, 1&3 £21.90 CSF £18.61 TOTE £2.00: £1.10, £4.00, £13.40; EX 23.90 TRIFECTA Not won..
Owner Hamdan Al Maktoum **Bred** P D Savill **Trained** Newmarket, Suffolk

FOCUS
Probably not a bad maiden of its type despite mixed messages from the form.

6805 BRITISH STALLION STUDS SUPPORTING BRITISH RACING E B F MAIDEN STKS 1m 75y
4:20 (4:52) (Class 5) 2-Y-O **£3,234** (£962; £481; £240) **Stalls** Centre

Form RPR

0 **1** **Wrotham Heath**[68] 4762 2-9-3 0.. TomQueally 9 92+
(Sir Henry Cecil) *hld up in tch: led on bit over 1f out: shkn up and r.o strly: impressive* **15/8**[1]

3 **2** 6 **Rebel Song (IRE)**[22] 6230 2-9-3 0................................ FrankieDettori 7 78+
(Mahmood Al Zarooni) *led tl hdd over 1f out: sn outpcd* **15/8**[1]

0 **3** 2½ **Monopoli**[41] 5655 2-8-12 0.. StevieDonohoe 5 66+
(Ralph Beckett) *chsd ldr: rdn and wandered over 1f out: no ex* **25/1**

4 1½ **Kahruman (USA)** 2-9-3 0.. RichardHills 4 68+
(William Haggas) *s.s: hld up: hdwy over 1f out: nt trbld ldrs* **16/1**

6 **5** 3¾ **No Dominion (IRE)**[20] 6278 2-9-3 0................................ JamesSullivan 2 59
(James Given) *chsd ldrs: rdn over 2f out: wknd over 1f out* **80/1**

50 **6** 2 **Brailsford (IRE)**[14] 6447 2-9-3 0.. AhmedAjtebi 13 55
(Mahmood Al Zarooni) *hld up: hdwy over 2f out: wknd over 1f out* **8/1**[2]

7 1 **Tadmir (USA)** 2-9-3 0.. PaulHanagan 10 53
(Saeed Bin Suroor) *hld up: nvr nrr* **11/1**[3]

8 1½ **Thane Of Cawdor (IRE)** 2-9-3 0.. JamieSpencer 8 50
(Tom Tate) *s.s: hld up: effrt over 2f out: wknd* **12/1**

9 4½ **Ben Croy** 2-9-3 0.. MartinDwyer 6 40+
(Brian Meehan) *trckd ldrs: plld hrd: hmpd 6f out: wknd over 1f out* **50/1**

0000 **10** 2¼ **Fox's Ambers (FR)**[34] 5844 2-8-9 35................................ SeanLevey(3) 12 30
(Richard Hannon) *chsd ldrs: rdn 1/2-way: wknd over 3f out* **100/1**

0 **11** 3 **Lean On Pete (IRE)**[14] 6462 2-9-3 0................................ DaneO'Neill 11 28
(David Lanigan) *mid-div: rdn and wknd over 2f out* **22/1**

12 22 **Tiger Would** 2-9-3 0.. JimmyFortune 3 —
(David Elsworth) *s.s: a bhd: t.o* **50/1**

1m 49.54s (3.94) **Going Correction** +0.275s/f (Good) **12** Ran SP% **116.9**
Speed ratings (Par 95): **91,85,82,81,77 75,74,72,68,66 63,41**
toteswingers: 1&2 £1.90, 2&3 £11.90, 1&3 £11.40 CSF £4.51 TOTE £4.10: £1.40, £1.10, £5.70; EX 7.60 Trifecta £155.60 Pool: £616.35 - 2.93 winning tickets..
Owner K Abdulla **Bred** Juddmonte Farms Ltd **Trained** Newmarket, Suffolk

FOCUS
Not a particularly competitive maiden, but another impressive winner.

NOTEBOOK
Wrotham Heath ◆ had been well touted prior to disappointing on his Newmarket debut, won in the style of a classy sort. The form of his 7f debut had been mixed, but he clearly didn't deliver what was expected of him that day and, back from a 68-day break, he looked a completely different horse, travelling powerfully before readily asserting once asked to go and win his race. Whilst beating little of note, he's clearly got an engine and it'll be fascinating to see where he turns up next, the one proviso perhaps being that he needs some cut in he ground, having displayed rather a high knee action here. (op 2-1)
Rebel Song(IRE) ◆, third at Beverley on debut, had the run of things out in front and yet still got well and truly buried by the winner. He's clearly got limitations, but has shown enough to suggest he will win races. (op 9-4 tchd 7-4)
Monopoli improved markedly on her debut effort, appreciating the ease in the ground, and she'll be capable of winning a small maiden back at 7f. (op 22-1)
Kahruman(USA), first foal of a 1m winner, was noted making late headway, having not been best away, and should improve. Official explanation: jockey said colt was unruly in stalls and was slowly away (op 12-1)
No Dominion(IRE) showed a bit more than on debut and looks a likely sort for modest handicaps. (op 100-1)
Tadmir(USA), who cost $200,000, looked very green and never threatened to get involved. He ought to improve for the experience and a faster surface. (op 17-2 tchd 8-1)
Thane Of Cawdor(IRE) cost 280,000gns and should leave this debut form behind in time, Spencer being far from hard on him in the final 2f. (op 16-1)

6806 DG TAXIS GETTING YOU HOME SAFELY NURSERY (DIV I) 1m 75y
4:50 (5:21) (Class 5) (0-70,70) 2-Y-O **£2,264** (£673; £336; £168) **Stalls** Centre

Form RPR

1403 **1** **Stellar Express (IRE)**[13] 6489 2-9-6 **69**............................ NeilChalmers 5 81
(Michael Appleby) *mde all: qcknd clr 3f out: kpt on strly: unchal* **20/1**

0522 **2** 4½ **Spunky**[14] 6443 2-8-12 **61**.. J-PGuillambert 7 63
(Luca Cumani) *t.k.h: chsd ldrs: effrt and chsd (clr) wnr over 2f out: edgd lft over 1f out: sn no imp* **11/2**[1]

21 **3** 1¾ **Anginola (IRE)**[14] 6443 2-9-3 **66**.. TomQueally 12 64
(Joseph Tuite) *hld up: pushed along over 3f out: edgd lft and styd on fnl 2f: nvr able to chal* **6/1**[2]

036 **4** 4 **Baileys Over Ice**[14] 6458 2-9-4 **67**................................ PaulHanagan 9 55
(James Given) *dwlt: bhd: rdn and hdwy 2f out: nvr able to chal* **12/1**

3321 **5** 3 **Mistress Of Rome**[15] 6425 2-9-2 **65**................................ TomEaves 13 47
(Michael Dods) *midfield on outside: drvn and outpcd 1/2-way: styd on fnl f: nvr on terms* **7/1**[3]

4003 **6** hd **Raspberry Fizz**[34] 5844 2-8-0 **52**................................ LouisBeuzelin(3) 15 33
(Eve Johnson Houghton) *hld up: stdy hdwy over 3f out: rdn and no imp fr 2f out* **20/1**

0000 **7** 1¼ **Mick Slates (IRE)**[49] 5367 2-7-7 **47** oh2............................ NeilFarley(5) 1 25
(Declan Carroll) *chsd ldrs tl rdn and wknd fr 2f out* **10/1**

6305 **8** 1¼ **Foster's Road**[14] 6460 2-9-5 **68**.. TonyCulhane 3 43
(Mick Channon) *hld up: pushed along over 3f out: sme late hdwy: nvr on terms* **28/1**

6063 **9** 2 **Tudor Empire (IRE)**[16] 6399 2-9-6 **69**............................(b) RobertHavlin 2 40
(John Gosden) *plld hrd in rr: hmpd after 1f: rdn and effrt on ins over 2f out: wknd over 1f out* **10/1**

0315 **10** 3 **New Decade**[44] 5550 2-9-7 **70**.. JoeFanning 17 34
(Mark Johnston) *prom on outside: struggling 2f out: edgd lft and sn btn* **12/1**

6050 **11** 2¾ **Ivor's Princess**[13] 6484 2-9-5 **68**.. JamesMillman 8 25
(Rod Millman) *hld up: rdn along over 3f out: nvr on terms* **22/1**

0616 **12** 2¼ **Enjoying (IRE)**[16] 6399 2-8-10 **62**............................(b) SeanLevey(3) 11 14
(Richard Hannon) *missed break: bhd and sn pushed along: nvr on terms* **16/1**

4602 **13** 2 **Man Of My Word**[8] 6611 2-8-8 **60**.. BillyCray(3) 14 —
(David Nicholls) *midfield: rdn and outpcd over 3f out: sn btn* **25/1**

443 **14** 2¾ **Landown Littlerock**[28] 6048 2-9-3 **66**............................ GrahamGibbons 10 —
(Reg Hollinshead) *chsd wnr to over 2f out: sn rdn and wknd* **16/1**

3200 **15** 5 **Dickens Rules (IRE)**[26] 6132 2-9-3 **66**............................ JimmyFortune 4 —
(Sylvester Kirk) *midfield: drvn along over 3f out: edgd lft and wknd over 2f out* **10/1**

0150 **16** 3½ **Balti's Sister (IRE)**[18] 6345 2-8-8 **57**............................ JamesSullivan 6 —
(Michael Easterby) *dwlt: sn midfield: rdn along over 3f out: wknd wl over 2f out* **14/1**

1m 48.63s (3.03) **Going Correction** +0.275s/f (Good) **16** Ran SP% **124.4**
Speed ratings (Par 95): **95,90,88,84,81 81,80,79,77,74 71,69,67,64,59 55**
toteswingers: 1&2 £25.10, 2&3 £4.50, 1&3 £28.80 CSF £121.14 CT £797.37 TOTE £44.40: £8.60, £1.02, £2.10, £4.10; EX 157.20 TRIFECTA Not won..
Owner Mr & Mrs James Sumsion **Bred** Adrian Purvis **Trained** Danethorpe, Notts

FOCUS
There was plenty of pace on for the first division of a modest nursery and the time was 1.2 seconds faster than division two.

NOTEBOOK
Stellar Express(IRE) came home much the best, galloping on relentlessly and clearly appreciating the step up to 1m. Despite her pedigree suggesting otherwise, she seemed quite at home with some give underfoot, and connections will no doubt be keen to get her out under a penalty, as she's sure to be hammered by the handicapper.
Spunky has now finished runner-up on each of the last three occasions and looks ready for 1m2f. (tchd 5-1 and 6-1 in a place)
Anginola(IRE) was unable to confirm last-time-out form with the runner-up, but did get further back than ideal and can probably have her run upgraded. (op 7-1 tchd 15-2)
Baileys Over Ice duly improved for the switch to handicaps. (op 11-1)

Mistress Of Rome, winner of a weak 6f maiden last time, was surprisingly found wanting for speed over the longest trip she's tackled to date. (op 9-1)

6807 DG TAXIS GETTING YOU HOME SAFELY NURSERY (DIV II) 1m 75y

5:20 (5:52) (Class 5) (0-70,70) 2-Y-O **£2,264** (£673; £336; £168) **Stalls** Centre

Form				RPR
052	**1**		**The Giving Tree (IRE)**[18] 6322 2-9-3 **66**.................... JimmyFortune 14 (Sylvester Kirk) *hld up: hdwy 1/2-way: led wl over 1f out: drvn out* **11/1**	74
3342	**2**	1 1/4	**Takeitfromalady (IRE)**[50] 5342 2-9-6 **69**.................... StevieDonohoe 12 (Ralph Beckett) *hld up: hdwy over 2f out: rdn over 1f out: r.o to go 2nd nr fin: nt rch wnr* **7/1**[3]	74
530	**3**	1/2	**Finbar**[53] 5269 2-9-4 **67**.................... TomQueally 13 (James Given) *hld up: hdwy over 2f out: chsd wnr over 1f out: sn rdn: styd on same pce ins fnl f: lost 2nd nr fin* **15/2**	71
2465	**4**	1	**Alborz (IRE)**[14] 6443 2-8-13 **62**....................(b) JoeFanning 9 (Mark Johnston) *led 2f: chsd ldrs: rdn and ev ch over 1f out: styd on same pce ins fnl f* **8/1**	64
040	**5**	3/4	**Sugarpine (IRE)**[26] 6110 2-8-11 **60**.................... PaulHanagan 3 (Richard Fahey) *hld up in tch: rdn and ev ch over 1f out: one pce fnl f* **8/1**	60
0020	**6**	1/2	**Priestley's Reward (IRE)**[21] 6260 2-9-2 **65**.................... MartinHarley 15 (Mrs K Burke) *sn outpcd: rdn over 2f out: swtchd rt and r.o ins fnl f: nrst fin* **28/1**	64
4404	**7**	hd	**Dorry K (IRE)**[20] 6275 2-9-2 **65**.................... GrahamGibbons 10 (David Barron) *chsd ldrs: rdn over 2f out: one pce fnl f* **6/1**[2]	63
6551	**8**	1/2	**Bitaphon (IRE)**[43] 5597 2-9-3 **66**.................... DanielTudhope 7 (Deborah Sanderson) *chsd ldrs: rdn over 2f out: no ex fnl f* **10/1**	63
035	**9**	2 1/4	**Byron Blue (IRE)**[22] 6230 2-9-7 **70**.................... PhillipMakin 16 (Jamie Osborne) *s.s: nvr nrr* **5/1**[1]	62+
5605	**10**	nse	**High Five Prince (IRE)**[29] 6021 2-7-5 **47**.................... NoelGarbutt(7) 2 (Mark Usher) *trckd ldr: plld hrd: led 6f out: rdn and hdd wl over 1f out: wknd ins fnl f* **50/1**	39
0453	**11**	1	**Onebytheknows**[7] 6630 2-9-1 **67**.................... SeanLevey(3) 11 (Richard Hannon) *hld up: hdwy over 3f out: sn rdn: wknd fnl f* **8/1**	57
1060	**12**	1/2	**Colourful Event (IRE)**[20] 6280 2-8-7 **56**....................(v) MartinDwyer 6 (David Arbuthnot) *mid-div: rdn over 2f out: wknd over 1f out* **28/1**	44
0404	**13**	19	**Dutchman's Field**[13] 6471 2-8-8 **57**....................(p) AdrianNicholls 1 (David Nicholls) *mid-div: pushed along over 5f out: wknd over 2f out* **20/1**	—

1m 49.83s (4.23) **Going Correction** +0.275s/f (Good) **13** Ran SP% **119.6**
Speed ratings (Par 95): **89,87,87,86,85 85,84,84,82,82 81,80,61**
toteswingers: 1&2 £7.40, 2&3 £12.00, 1&3 £23.70 CSF £82.77 CT £460.73 TOTE £15.30: £5.10, £1.40, £2.50; EX 56.20 Trifecta £157.60 Pool: £234.39 - 1.10 winning tickets..
Owner Knockainey Stud **Bred** Knockainey Stud & Storway Ltd **Trained** Upper Lambourn, Berks

FOCUS
Not as much pace on as in division one and the time was 1.2 seconds slower as a result.

NOTEBOOK
The Giving Tree(IRE), making her handicap debut, looked on a feasible mark and, having made good headway, battled hard for a first success. Her dam won over 1m4f, so she should get further, and it's likely she has more to offer. (op 10-1)
Takeitfromalady(IRE), up 5lb having finished second on his handicap debut at Leicester, took a while to pick up and found the winner had gone by the time he reached top gear. He could improve for 1m2f. (op 11-2)
Finbar ran his best race in maidens when encountering an easy surface at Doncaster in June, and he looked to be coming to win his race over 1f out, but his effort somewhat flattened out late on. He remains capable of better and it's possible he'll be helped by a drop to 7f. (op 17-2)
Alborz(IRE) lacks pace, but kept grinding away and is worth a try at 1m2f. (op 11-1)
Sugarpine(IRE) didn't improve as expected for the step up to 1m. (op 10-1 tchd 11-1)
Byron Blue(IRE) was soon in trouble following a slow start. His mark looked high enough anyway, so there'll probably be other days for him. (op 15-2 tchd 9-2)
Dutchman's Field Official explanation: jockey said gelding had no more to give
T/Jkpt: Not won. T/Plt: £313.80 to a £1 stake. Pool: £63,137.94. 146.85 winning tickets. T/Qpdt: £39.20 to a £1 stake. Pool: £5,234.76. 98.70 winning tickets. CR

6709 MAISONS-LAFFITTE (R-H)

Wednesday, October 12

OFFICIAL GOING: Turf: soft

6808a PRIX ECLIPSE (GROUP 3) (2YO) (TURF) 6f (S)

1:50 (12:00) 2-Y-O **£34,482** (£13,793; £10,344; £6,896; £3,448)

			RPR
1		**Kendam (FR)**[29] 6042 2-8-8 0.................... MaximeGuyon 8 (H-A Pantall, France) *settled in 2nd bhd her pcemaker racing down centre of trck: rdn ent fnl 1 1/2f: wandered off st line whn taking ld 1f out: r.o wl whn stened to hold off chal of runner-up fnl 50yds* **41/10**[2]	103
2	1/2	**Chica Loca (FR)**[41] 2-8-9 0 ow1.................... ChristopheSoumillon 6 (M Figge, Germany) *led s: sn settled in 3rd racing bhd ldrs: rdn ent fnl f: r.o wl to chal for ld but a being hld* **13/10**[1]	102
3	1 1/4	**Hi Molly (FR)**[29] 6042 2-8-11 0.................... ThierryJarnet 3 (D Guillemin, France) *racd alone in 4th on stands' rail: styd on wl to go 3rd ent fnl f: no threat to first two* **22/1**	100
4	5	**Dont Teutch (FR)**[29] 6042 2-8-8 0.................... Christophe-PatriceLemaire 7 (D Smaga, France) *racd in 5th fr s: nt qckn fr 1 1/2f out: styd on fnl f* **17/2**	82
5	1 1/4	**Foreign Tune**[28] 2-8-8 0.................... MickaelBarzalona 2 (C Laffon-Parias, France) *settled towards rr: rdn over 1 1/2f out: nt qckn: styd on fnl f* **5/1**[3]	79
6	1 1/4	**Calahorra (FR)**[29] 6042 2-8-8 0.................... StephanePasquier 1 (C Baillet, France) *broke slowly and racd towards rr: rdn but nt qckn ent fnl 1 1/2f: styd on fnl f* **5/1**[3]	75
7	shd	**Louve Rouge (FR)**[9] 2-8-8 0.................... JohanVictoire 5 (C Boutin, France) *a towards rr: rdn but no ex fr over 1 1/2f out: styd on fnl f* **33/1**	74
8	4	**Misedargent (FR)**[23] 2-8-8 0.................... Pierre-CharlesBoudot 4 (C Boutin, France) *sn led: set pce for eventual wnr: rdn 1 1/2f out: hdd 1f out: sn wknd: eased ins fnl f* **36/1**	62

1m 14.7s (1.30) **8** Ran SP% **116.9**
WIN (incl. 1 euro stake): 5.10 (Kendam coupled with Misedargent). PLACES: 1.70, 1.30, 3.40. DF: 4.70. SF: 12.40.
Owner Guy Pariente **Bred** G Pariente **Trained** France

6809a PRIX DE SAINT-CYR (LISTED RACE) (3YO FILLIES) (TURF) 7f (S)

2:20 (12:00) 3-Y-O **£23,706** (£9,482; £7,112; £4,741; £2,370)

			RPR
1		**Faustina (FR)**[50] 3-8-9 0.................... ChristopheSoumillon 1 (J E Hammond, France) **11/2**[3]	109
2	1 1/4	**Procrastination**[25] 3-8-9 0.................... MickaelBarzalona 10 (A Fabre, France) **11/1**	106
3	1	**Nova Hawk**[73] 4597 3-9-2 0.................... GregoryBenoist 4 (Rod Collet, France) **6/4**[1]	110
4	nk	**Blue Blue Sea**[40] 5695 3-8-9 0.................... Pierre-CharlesBoudot 2 (Y De Nicolay, France) **33/1**	102
5	1	**Lady Meydan (FR)**[47] 3-8-9 0.................... Christophe-PatriceLemaire 6 (F Rohaut, France) **15/1**	99
6	shd	**Sweetie Time**[96] 3819 3-8-9 0.................... OlivierPeslier 9 (Michael Bell) *broke wl to r cl 3rd on outer: stl prom whn rdn 1 1/2f out: nt qckn ent fnl f: styd on one pce* **23/1**	99
7	2	**Helleborine**[150] 2137 3-8-13 0.................... StephanePasquier 5 (Mme C Head-Maarek, France) **53/10**[2]	98
8	1 1/4	**Newcastle (FR)**[29] 3-8-9 0.................... FranckBlondel 7 (C Baillet, France) **34/1**	90
9	1 3/4	**Finding Neverland (FR)**[20] 6288 3-8-9 0.................... ThierryThulliez 3 (N Clement, France) **53/10**[2]	86
10	1 1/2	**Angel Of Harlem (FR)**[52] 3-8-9 0.................... MaximeGuyon 8 (H-A Pantall, France) **24/1**	82

1m 28.1s (-0.20) **10** Ran SP% **115.7**
WIN (incl. 1 euro stake): 6.50. PLACES: 1.70, 2.60, 1.40. DF: 29.50. SF: 73.70.
Owner OTI Management Pty Ltd **Bred** H Honore, Sc De Moubray & M L P Consulting Ltd **Trained** France

5991 BRIGHTON (L-H)

Thursday, October 13

OFFICIAL GOING: Good to firm (7.3)
Wind: Light, across Weather: Overcast

6810 BRITISH STALLION STUDS SUPPORTING BRITISH RACING E B F MAIDEN STKS 1m 3f 196y

2:30 (2:30) (Class 5) 3-Y-O+ **£3,234** (£962; £481; £240) **Stalls** High

Form				RPR
04	**1**		**Vasily**[23] 6242 3-9-3 0....................(t) AndreaAtzeni 3 (Robert Eddery) *led for 1f: chsd ldrs tl led again 6f out: mde rest: rdn and clr over 1f out: rdn out hands and heels and styd on wl fnl f* **20/1**	83
232	**2**	2 3/4	**Asaid**[21] 6286 3-9-3 80....................(v) RichardHughes 1 (Saeed Bin Suroor) *stdd s: hld up in tch in rr: hdwy to press ldr over 5f out: rdn and unable qck 2f out: one pce and btn whn edgd lft ins fnl f: eased towards fin* **5/2**[2]	79
32	**3**	2	**Eyedoro (USA)**[9] 6614 3-9-3 0.................... SilvestreDeSousa 5 (Mark Johnston) *chsd ldr after 2f tl 6f out: rdn to chse ldng pair over 2f out: drvn and disputing 2nd over 1f out: unable qck and btn 1f out: wknd ins fnl f* **7/1**[3]	76
52	**4**	9	**Light Well (IRE)**[13] 6504 3-9-3 0.................... WilliamBuick 6 (John Gosden) *dwlt and pushed along early: in tch: rdn over 4f out: u.p and struggling wl over 2f out: wknd 2f out* **5/4**[1]	61
60	**5**	2	**Riviera Stars**[33] 5911 3-9-3 0.................... TomQueally 7 (Michael Bell) *s.i.s: bustled along early: in tch in rr: rdn and struggling over 3f out: wknd 2f out* **25/1**	58
0-3	**6**	7	**Mount Crystal (IRE)**[72] 4641 3-8-12 0.................... RobertWinston 2 (Charles Hills) *t.k.h: hld up in tch: rdn and wknd qckly wl over 2f out: no ch fnl 2f: eased ins fnl f* **16/1**	47
0	**7**	11	**Astragal**[18] 6377 3-8-12 0.................... JimmyFortune 4 (Andrew Balding) *led after 1f: hdd 6f out: lost pl 4f out: rdn and wknd wl over 2f out: wl bhd and eased ins fnl f* **10/1**	32

2m 30.04s (-2.66) **Going Correction** -0.15s/f (Firm) **7** Ran SP% **109.1**
Speed ratings (Par 103): **102,100,98,92,91 86,79**
toteswingers: 1&2 £6.50, 2&3 £2.50, 1&3 £4.60 CSF £63.63 TOTE £21.70: £9.00, £1.60; EX 91.50 Trifecta £444.70 Pool: £649.12 - 1.08 winning units..
Owner Owen O'Brien & David Bannon **Bred** Cheveley Park Stud Ltd **Trained** Newmarket, Suffolk

FOCUS
All races on innermost line and distances ad advertised. A better than average 3yo maiden for the time of year. Several of the runners had shown enough to suggest they could win an event of this type, but more than one ran below expectations. A personal best from the winner with the next two close to their marks.
Mount Crystal(IRE) Official explanation: trainer's rep said filly was unsuited by the track

6811 FROSTS FUN AT THE FIREWORKS - 4TH NOVEMBER H'CAP 1m 1f 209y

3:00 (3:00) (Class 6) (0-60,60) 3-Y-O+ **£1,617** (£481; £240; £120) **Stalls** High

Form				RPR
550	**1**		**Penang Cinta**[20] 6306 8-9-4 **57**.................... RichardEvans(3) 7 (David Evans) *w ldr tl led 7f out: mde rest: rdn over 2f out: kpt on wl to repel chalrs ins fnl f* **10/1**	63
6004	**2**	hd	**Ninfea (IRE)**[8] 6624 3-9-5 **60**....................(p) JamesDoyle 13 (Sylvester Kirk) *in tch in midfield: rdn 4f out: outpcd over 2f out and looked wl btn over 1f out: rallied and styd on strly ins fnl f: wnt 2nd cl home* **15/2**[3]	65
6445	**3**	1/2	**Prince Of Thebes (IRE)**[19] 6358 10-8-5 **46**.................... MarkCoumbe(5) 14 (Michael Attwater) *in tch in midfield: rdn and outpcd over 2f out: looked wl btn over 1f out: rallied ent fnl f: styd on wl fnl f to go 3rd cl home* **20/1**	50
6402	**4**	hd	**Advertise**[35] 5845 5-9-5 **58**.................... HarryBentley(3) 15 (Joseph Tuite) *t.k.h: hld up in tch towards rr: hdwy over 2f out: rdn to press ldr 1f out: unable qck ins fnl f: lost 2 pls cl home* **11/2**[1]	62
5500	**5**	hd	**Regal Rave (USA)**[28] 6083 4-8-11 **50**....................(v[1]) JohnFahy(3) 1 (Peter Hedger) *s.i.s: bhd: rdn and stl plenty to do 2f out: hdwy and switching rt jst over 1f out: styd on wl ins fnl f: nt rch ldrs* **20/1**	54
5135	**6**	nk	**Cathcart Castle**[5] 6698 3-9-2 **57**.................... TonyCulhane 6 (Mick Channon) *t.k.h: hld up in last trio: rdn along over 3f out: hdwy on inner over 2f out: rdn to chse ldrs and swtchd rt over 1f out: drvn and styd on same pce ins fnl f* **11/2**[1]	60
0103	**7**	1 3/4	**Fair Breeze**[14] 6486 4-8-13 **49**.................... RobertHavlin 8 (Richard Phillips) *chsd ldr: rdn and effrt over 2f out: pressed wnr u.p over 1f out: wknd fnl 100yds* **11/1**	49

0546 **8** *1* **El Dececy (USA)**[9] 6610 7-9-3 **53**.....(t) RichardHughes 11 51
(Richard Guest) *chsd wnr jst over 2f out: rdn and edgd rt over 1f out: unable qck ent fnl f: wknd fnl 150yds* **8/1**

6053 **9** *3 1/4* **Makheelah**[30] 6033 3-9-3 **58**..... SilvestreDeSousa 3 49
(Clive Brittain) *led for 2f: pressed ldrs after tl wknd over 1f out* **17/2**

4004 **10** *shd* **Agapanthus (GER)**[30] 6037 6-9-6 **56**..... TomQueally 4 47
(Barney Curley) *hld up in rr: rdn and struggling over 3f out: plugged on but no threat to ldrs fnl 2f* **7/1**[2]

2030 **11** *hd* **Inquisitress**[28] 6083 7-8-12 **51**..... KieranO'Neill(3) 5 41
(John Bridger) *hld up in tch towards rr: swtchd rt and effrt over 2f out: wknd ent fnl f* **12/1**

4205 **12** *3* **Vinces**[31] 5993 7-9-3 **53**.....(p) MartinDwyer 10 37
(Tim McCarthy) *w ldrs tl over 2f out: sn wknd* **20/1**

-600 **13** *1* **Teazel**[8] 6626 3-8-13 **54**..... ChrisCatlin 2 36
(Dominic Ffrench Davis) *chsd ldrs tl lost pl and rdn over 4f out: bhd wl over 2f out* **50/1**

2m 2.23s (-1.37) **Going Correction** -0.15s/f (Firm)
WFA 3 from 4yo+ 5lb **13** Ran **SP% 118.0**
Speed ratings (Par 101): **99,98,98,98,98 97,96,95,93,93 92,90,89**
toteswingers: 1&2 £17.10, 2&3 £40.40, 1&3 £44.00 CSF £77.76 CT £1481.84 TOTE £11.00: £3.00, £3.80, £6.00; EX 112.10 TRIFECTA Not won..
Owner Trevor Gallienne **Bred** Mrs A K H Ooi **Trained** Pandy, Monmouths

FOCUS
A modest handicap, with the top weight rated 59, but it was wide open and resulted in a bunch finish. Regulation form.

6812 BRITISH STALLION STUDS SUPPORTING BRITISH RACING E B F MEDIAN AUCTION MAIDEN STKS 7f 214y
3:30 (3:30) (Class 5) 2-Y-O **£3,234** (£962; £481; £240) **Stalls** Low

Form RPR

0 **1** **Expert Fighter (USA)**[19] 6334 2-9-3 0..... WilliamBuick 4 79+
(Saeed Bin Suroor) *chsd ldr: rdn over 2f out: clsd on ldr and chal over 1f out: drvn ahd 1f out: styd on wl and clr ins fnl f: readily* **9/4**[2]

6003 **2** *4* **Siouxperhero (IRE)**[15] 6443 2-9-3 66.....(b) MartinDwyer 3 70
(William Muir) *led: looked to be gng best 2f out: pressed and hdd over 1f out: hdd 1f out: sn btn but plugged on to hold 2nd* **14/1**

3034 **3** *nk* **Firestarter**[26] 6160 2-9-3 78.....(b) SilvestreDeSousa 9 69
(David Elsworth) *hld up in midfield: hdwy to chse ldrs 4f out: wnt 3rd over 2f out: rdn: hung lft and nt qckn over 1f out: no threat to wnr and wl hld fnl f* **15/8**[1]

06 **4** *2 3/4* **Renegotiate**[12] 6529 2-9-3 0..... JimmyFortune 2 63
(Andrew Balding) *chsd ldrs: rdn and struggling over 2f out: sn outpcd: 4th and wl hld over 1f out* **11/1**

540 **5** *3 3/4* **Samasana (IRE)**[24] 6216 2-8-12 52..... JamesDoyle 11 49
(Ian Wood) *t.k.h hld up in midfield: rdn and effrt wl over 2f out: struggling and wknd 2f out* **100/1**

6000 **6** *3* **Vergrigio (IRE)**[9] 6611 2-9-3 57.....(b) LiamJones 1 47
(Brian Meehan) *s.i.s: bhd: rdn and btn over 3f out: no ch but plugged on past btn horses fr over 1f out* **100/1**

00 **7** *1 1/2* **Golden Jubilee (USA)**[15] 6463 2-9-3 0..... RichardHughes 10 44
(Richard Hannon) *in tch: effrt in centre and rdn 3f out: wknd 2f out* **9/2**[3]

056 **8** *16* **Spanish Fork (IRE)**[4] 6726 2-9-3 0.....(v1) TonyCulhane 8 7
(Mick Channon) *dwlt: rdn along in rr thrght: lost tch over 2f out: wl bhd and eased ins fnl f* **12/1**

0 **9** *2 1/4* **Here Comes Jeanie**[27] 6118 2-8-12 0..... JamieGoldstein 5 —
(Michael Madgwick) *chsd ldrs: lost pl 4f out: wknd over 2f out: wl bhd and eased ins fnl f* **200/1**

5560 **10** *9* **Voodoo Rhythm (USA)**[3] 6757 2-9-3 72.....(b) EddieCreighton 6 —
(Brian Meehan) *dwlt: rdn along thrght: in tch in midfield: wknd wl over 2f out: wl bhd and eased ins fnl f* **33/1**

1m 33.67s (-2.33) **Going Correction** -0.15s/f (Firm) **10** Ran **SP% 111.8**
Speed ratings (Par 95): **105,101,100,97,94 91,89,73,71,62**
toteswingers: 1&2 £5.60, 2&3 £4.10, 1&3 £2.00 CSF £31.51 TOTE £3.50: £1.20, £4.10, £1.10; EX 41.50 Trifecta £124.60 Pool: £736.01 - 4.37 winning units..
Owner Godolphin **Bred** Darley **Trained** Newmarket, Suffolk

FOCUS
Just an ordinary juvenile maiden and half the field appeared exposed as moderate.

NOTEBOOK
Expert Fighter(USA) had shown a hint of ability when seventh on his only previous start and stepped up markedly on that performance. He seems to have a healthy attitude and should win more races. His pedigree suggests he will stay middle-distances next season. (op 7-2)
Siouxperhero(IRE), having his ninth run and officially rated 66, puts the standard achieved by the winner into perspective. Another prominent from the start, he stayed on gamely enough, but was comfortably out-pointed in the closing stages. (op 16-1 tchd 12-1)
Firestarter had had six previous chances and, while his official mark of 78 seemed fair on his best form, he does not look especially progressive. He was fractious on the way to post, throwing his head around, and hung badly under pressure in the last couple of furlongs. He clearly has the ability to win one of these, but his application may not match his talent. Official explanation: jockey said colt hung left (op 6-4)
Renegotiate, sixth in a decent Newmarket maiden 12 days earlier, probably ran to much the same level again. He may fare better in handicaps, for which he now qualifies. (tchd 12-1)
Samasana(IRE), now without a first-three placing in nine starts, ran as well as could be expected given that record. She too will have more obvious chances in handicaps.
Vergrigio(IRE) was badly outpaced in the first half of the race, but picked off a few tiring rivals in the closing stages. Perhaps a longer trip will help.

6813 PIPE CENTER H'CAP 7f 214y
4:00 (4:00) (Class 6) (0-60,60) 3-Y-O **£1,617** (£481; £240; £120) **Stalls** Low

Form RPR

5605 **1** **Methayel (IRE)**[9] 6604 3-9-7 **60**..... TomQueally 12 69
(Clive Brittain) *in tch and travelling wl: jnd ldrs on bit over 2f out: shkn up to ld over 1f out: in command and nudged along fnl f: comf* **6/1**[3]

5540 **2** *3/4* **Bedibyes**[97] 3803 3-8-11 **53**..... RobertLButler(3) 1 59
(Richard Mitchell) *stdd s: hld up in rr: stl plenty to do but stl on bridle over 2f out: hdwy on inner over 1f out: styd on wl to chse wnr wl ins fnl f: kpt on but no threat to wnr* **40/1**

006 **3** *1 1/4* **Tawseef (IRE)**[66] 4861 3-9-3 **56**..... WilliamCarson 5 59
(Roy Brotherton) *chsd ldrs: rdn over 2f out: nt clr run 2f out: swtchd rt wl over 1f out: kpt on u.p ins fnl f: wnt 3rd nr fin* **9/1**

0652 **4** *nk* **Ad Vitam (IRE)**[7] 6657 3-8-11 **50**.....(vt) MichaelStainton 4 52
(David C Griffiths) *chsd ldrs: rdn over 2f out: ev ch 2f out: nt pce of wnr over 1f out: wnt 2nd and no imp 1f out: lost 2 pls wl ins fnl f* **4/1**[2]

0005 **5** *hd* **Warbond**[28] 6083 3-8-10 **49**.....(v) FrankieMcDonald 7 51
(Michael Madgwick) *in tch in midfield: no prog and rdn over 2f out: rallied and styd on u.p ins fnl f: no threat to wnr* **20/1**

020 **6** *1 1/2* **Gay Gallivanter**[3] 6764 3-9-1 **54**..... MartinLane 9 53
(Michael Quinn) *bhd: struggling and rdn over 3f out: hdwy over 1f out: styd on ins fnl f: no threat to wnr* **8/1**

6006 **7** *1 1/2* **Piccolete**[29] 6070 3-8-4 **46**..... KieranO'Neill(3) 2 41
(Richard Hannon) *w ldr tl led wl over 2f out: hdd wl over 1f out: wknd fnl f* **11/1**

0521 **8** *1 1/4* **Pearl Opera**[50] 5381 3-9-5 **58**..... RichardHughes 8 50
(Denis Coakley) *taken down early: chsd ldrs: ev ch ent fnl 2f: rdn and unable qck over 1f out: btn 1f out: eased ins fnl f* **11/4**[1]

2000 **9** *7* **Tymismoni (IRE)**[8] 6626 3-8-10 **54**.....(v) MarkCoumbe(5) 13 30
(Michael Attwater) *a towards rr: rdn 5f out: wknd wl over 2f out: wl bhd fnl f* **25/1**

5600 **10** *2 1/2* **Lough Corrib (USA)**[9] 6610 3-8-7 **51**.....(p) JemmaMarshall(5) 10 21
(Alastair Lidderdale) *taken down early: stdd s: a in rr: rdn and btn 3f out: wl bhd fnl f* **33/1**

5330 **11** *8* **Trust Me Boy**[46] 5515 3-8-7 **46** oh1.....(v) KirstyMilczarek 11 —
(John E Long) *a in rr: rdn along over 5f out: lost tch over 2f out: wl bhd over 1f out* **18/1**

4565 **12** *11* **Prophet In A Dream**[48] 5423 3-9-3 **56**.....(p) RobertWinston 6 —
(Paddy Butler) *led tl wl over 2f: sn wknd: t.o and virtually p.u ins fnl f* **20/1**

6200 **13** *41* **Sottovoce**[17] 6401 3-9-7 **60**..... GeorgeBaker 3 —
(Simon Dow) *in tch in midfield tl wknd over 2f out: wl bhd and virtually p.u fr wl over 1f out: t.o* **14/1**

1m 34.7s (-1.30) **Going Correction** -0.15s/f (Firm) **13** Ran **SP% 121.1**
Speed ratings (Par 99): **100,99,98,97,97 96,94,93,86,83 75,64,23**
toteswingers: 1&2 £43.60, 2&3 £44.60, 1&3 £9.50 CSF £240.78 CT £2232.53 TOTE £5.00: £1.40, £14.20, £3.40; EX 448.10 TRIFECTA Not won..
Owner Saeed Manana **Bred** Lynchbages Edgeridge Ltd & Glenvale Stud **Trained** Newmarket, Suffolk

FOCUS
A modest handicap, in which the winning top weight came into this rated 60. The winner is rated back to her early maiden best.
Trust Me Boy Official explanation: trainer said gelding failed to act on the track
Sottovoce Official explanation: trainer's rep said filly has a breathing problem

6814 RICKY HATTON HERE 9TH NOVEMBER H'CAP 6f 209y
4:30 (4:30) (Class 5) (0-70,70) 3-Y-O+ **£2,264** (£673; £336; £168) **Stalls** Low

Form RPR

350 **1** **Cheylesmore (IRE)**[31] 5992 3-9-2 **67**..... WilliamCarson 10 78
(Stuart Williams) *mde virtually all: rdn 2f out: drvn and forged clr jst ins fnl f: styd on wl* **9/1**[3]

0250 **2** *1 3/4* **Aviso (GER)**[3] 6764 7-8-12 **61**.....(p) PatCosgrave 1 67
(David Evans) *chsd ldrs: rdn and effrt over 2f out: unable qck ent fnl f: kpt on same pce fnl f: wnt 2nd cl home* **7/1**[2]

6115 **3** *nk* **Stonecrabstomorrow (IRE)**[22] 6246 8-8-11 **65**..... MarkCoumbe(5) 7 70+
(Michael Attwater) *stdd s: bhd: effrt on outer 3f out: hdwy on outer over 1f out: chsd wnr and edgd lft ent fnl f: no ex fnl 100yds: lost 2nd cl home* **12/1**

5044 **4** *2 1/2* **Anjomarba (IRE)**[9] 6604 4-9-4 **67**..... KirstyMilczarek 9 65
(Conor Dore) *in tch in midfield: rdn over 2f out: edging lft and hdwy over 1f out: kpt on ins fnl f: no threat to wnr* **12/1**

3022 **5** *1* **Timpanist (USA)**[31] 5995 4-8-10 **62**.....(b) AdamBeschizza(3) 5 58
(Simon Dow) *t.k.h: hld up in midfield: hdwy over 2f out: chsd ldrs and unable qck whn rdn over 1f out: wknd ins fnl f* **12/1**

510 **6** *nk* **Mandhooma**[28] 6091 5-9-7 **70**..... ChrisCatlin 3 65
(Peter Hiatt) *bhd: swtchd rt and hdwy u.p over 1f out: styd on wl ins fnl f: nvr gng pce to rch ldrs* **11/1**

0014 **7** *shd* **Spirit Of Oakdale (IRE)**[43] 5624 3-8-7 **61**.....(v) LouisBeuzelin(3) 16 56
(Walter Swinburn) *chsd ldrs: rdn over 2f out: lost pl and edgd lft over 1f out: btn 1f out and styd on same pce after: swtchd rt wl ins fnl f* **14/1**

0211 **8** *1 1/4* **Olney Lass**[31] 5995 4-8-5 **61**..... SophieSilvester(7) 11 52+
(Lydia Pearce) *dwlt: bhd: pushed along 3f out: stl last and rdn 2f out: styd on past btn horses fnl f: nvr trbld ldrs* **5/1**[1]

4200 **9** *3/4* **Custom House (IRE)**[10] 6586 3-9-1 **66**..... RichardThomas 14 55
(John E Long) *in tch: rdn and effrt to chse ldrs over 2f out: wknd over 1f out* **20/1**

6650 **10** *3/4* **Fault**[10] 6587 5-8-11 **65**.....(t) AmyScott(5) 13 52
(Alastair Lidderdale) *hld up in tch towards rr: rdn and no prog over 2f out: no threat to ldrs fnl 2f* **16/1**

202 **11** *3/4* **Obiter Dicta**[10] 6591 3-9-0 **65**..... FergusSweeney 6 50
(Henry Candy) *chsd ldrs: swtchd rt and rdn over 2f out: wknd wl over 1f out* **7/1**[2]

3420 **12** *2* **Indian Violet (IRE)**[19] 6358 5-8-12 **61**..... JamieGoldstein 15 41
(Ralph Smith) *chsd ldrs: rdn and unable qck over 2f out: wknd over 1f out* **9/1**[3]

0005 **13** *7* **Buxton**[41] 5669 7-9-7 **70**.....(t) MartinLane 8 31
(Roger Ingram) *stdd s: hld up in last trio: rdn and no rspnse over 3f: wl btn fnl 2f* **16/1**

2460 **14** *26* **Noverton**[51] 5354 3-9-3 **68**..... StevieDonohoe 2 —
(James Eustace) *in tch in midfield: rdn and lost pl wl over 2f out: bhd and eased fr wl over 1f out: t.o* **25/1**

1m 21.47s (-1.63) **Going Correction** -0.15s/f (Firm)
WFA 3 from 4yo+ 2lb **14** Ran **SP% 120.1**
Speed ratings (Par 103): **103,101,100,97,96 96,96,94,93,93 92,89,81,52**
toteswingers: 1&2 £14.10, 2&3 £18.90, 1&3 £12.30 CSF £70.54 CT £791.25 TOTE £13.40: £3.60, £3.10, £3.00; EX 97.30 Trifecta £460.10 Part won. Pool: £621.85 - 0.60 winning units..
Owner Keith & Meta Pryce **Bred** John Cullinan **Trained** Newmarket, Suffolk

FOCUS
A competitive handicap. A clear personal best from the winner, who has a good record here.
Anjomarba(IRE) Official explanation: jockey said filly hung left
Noverton Official explanation: trainer's rep said filly was unsuited by the track

6815 CHRISTMAS PARTIES - 9TH, 16TH & 17TH DECEMBER H'CAP 5f 59y
5:00 (5:08) (Class 5) (0-75,75) 3-Y-O+ **£2,264** (£673; £336; £168) **Stalls** Low

Form RPR

15 **1** **Grandmas Dream**[15] 6442 3-9-2 **73**.....(b) RobertLButler(3) 4 81
(Richard Guest) *sn pushed along: chsd clr ldng trio: clsd u.p over 1f out: led ins fnl f: kpt on wl: rdn out* **11/1**

100 **2** *1* **Stratton Banker (IRE)**[59] 5108 4-9-2 **70**..... WilliamCarson 8 75
(Stuart Williams) *awkward leaving stalls and slowly away: bhd: c centre 3f out: hdwy over 1f out: chsd wnr ins fnl f: styd on same pce and no imp fnl 50yds* **15/2**

3542 **3** *1/2* **Billy Red**[27] 6119 7-9-2 **70**.....(b) FergusSweeney 10 73
(J R Jenkins) *broke fast: led and crossed to rail: rdn over 2f out: hdd jst ins fnl f: no ex and styd on same pce after* **6/1**[3]

4534 **4** ¾ **Magical Speedfit (IRE)**[43] 5627 6-9-0 **73**...................... RyanPowell(5) 5 73
(George Margarson) *bhd: c centre 3f out: hdwy over 1f out: styd on wl ins fnl f: nvr able to chal* **12/1**

5464 **5** ¾ **Even Bolder**[22] 6250 8-8-10 **67**... KierenFox(3) 1 65
(Eric Wheeler) *racd off the pce in midfield: clsd on inner over 1f out: chsng ldrs and styng on whn nt clr run and swtchd rt fnl 100yds: no imp after* **8/1**

2110 **6** ½ **Commandingpresence (USA)**[27] 6119 5-8-12 **69**..... KieranO'Neill(3) 7 65
(John Bridger) *racd off the pce in midfield: rdn and effrt 2f out: edgd rt ent fnl f: kpt on same pce and nvr threatened ldrs* **8/1**

420 **7** 1 ¾ **Clear Ice (IRE)**[30] 6036 4-9-7 **75**..................................(b) RobertWinston 3 65
(Gay Kelleway) *w ldrs and clr of field: c centre 3f out: rdn and unable qck 2f out: wknd ins fnl f* **5/1**[1]

1-00 **8** *nk* **Mi Regalo**[22] 6246 3-9-7 **75**.. MartinDwyer 6 64
(Andrew Balding) *sn outpcd in last trio and rdn along: keeping on same pce and no threat to ldrs whn hmpd ent fnl f: edgd lft after* **6/1**[3]

363 **9** ¾ **Athwaab**[42] 5658 4-8-13 **67**.. ChrisCatlin 2 53
(Noel Chance) *taken down early: chsd ldr and clr of field: ev ch and rdn 2f out: no ex ent fnl f: wknd fnl 150yds* **11/2**[2]

61.59 secs (-0.71) **Going Correction** -0.15s/f (Firm) **9** Ran SP% **110.6**
Speed ratings (Par 103): **99,97,96,95,94 93,90,90,88**
toteswingers: 1&2 £20.80, 2&3 £8.20, 1&3 £10.40 CSF £82.55 CT £472.83 TOTE £14.90: £4.00, £3.00, £2.10; EX 107.80 Trifecta £320.40 Pool: £1,056.70 - 2.44 winning units..
Owner Rakebackmypoker.com **Bred** Mrs Mary Taylor **Trained** Stainforth, S Yorks
■ Picansort was withdrawn (14/1, broke out of stalls). R4 applies, deduct 5p in the £.

FOCUS
A seemingly trappy finale, with wide-open betting, and few could be confidently discounted. They went a good pace and the winner is rated back to his early summer form.
Mi Regalo Official explanation: trainer's rep said gelding was unsuited by the track
T/Jkpt: Not won. T/Plt: £1,022.20 to a £1 stake. Pool of £78,532.84 - 56.08 winning units.
T/Qpdt: £55.10 to a £1 stake. Pool of £7,105.21 - 95.28 winning units. SP

6784 KEMPTON (A.W) (R-H)
Thursday, October 13

OFFICIAL GOING: Standard
Wind: Moderate behind Weather: Overcast, getting dark

6816 BLUESQ.COM CLASSIFIED STKS 1m (P)
5:20 (5:20) (Class 6) 3-Y-O+ **£1,617** (£481; £240; £120) **Stalls** Low

Form RPR

0524 **1** **Makyaal (IRE)**[30] 6032 3-9-0 54....................................(b¹) RichardHills 3 62+
(John Dunlop) *s.i.s: hld up in rr: stdy hdwy on ins over 2f out: qckd to ld appr fnl f: pushed out* **4/1**[1]

436 **2** 1 ¾ **Love Your Looks**[15] 6459 3-9-0 55................................. TonyCulhane 12 58+
(Mike Murphy) *towards rr but in tch: hdwy on outside over 2f out: drvn and styd on fnl f: tk 2nd clsng stages: no ch w wnr* **6/1**[2]

00-6 **3** ¾ **Dust Cloud (IRE)**[23] 6242 3-9-0 55..................................... IanMongan 1 56
(Peter Winkworth) *chsd ldrs: drvn and ev ch over 1f out: chsd wnr fnl f but no imp: lost 2nd clsng stages* **8/1**

00 **4** 1 ½ **Khaki (IRE)**[22] 6253 3-9-0 54....................................... SilvestreDeSousa 7 53
(David Evans) *in tch: chsd ldrs: drvn 2f out: outpcd ins fnl f* **16/1**

5025 **5** ¾ **Byrd In Hand (IRE)**[42] 5653 4-9-0 55............................ SeanLevey(3) 10 51
(John Bridger) *led: drvn 2f out: hdd appr fnl f: sn btn* **4/1**[1]

0454 **6** 1 **American Lover (FR)**[26] 6156 4-9-3 55............................ DavidNolan 6 49
(John Wainwright) *towards rr: hdwy towards outside over 3f out: kpt on fnl 2f: one pce fnl f* **10/1**

1050 **7** 7 **Putin (IRE)**[26] 6179 3-9-0 53.. ShaneKelly 9 32
(Derek Haydn Jones) *chsd ldr tl over 2f out: sn btn* **15/2**[3]

105 **8** 3 ½ **Caledonia Prince**[17] 6411 3-9-0 54.............................(p) J-PGuillambert 8 24
(Jo Hughes) *chsd ldrs: wknd 2f out* **8/1**

0450 **9** 10 **Saktoon (USA)**[44] 5606 3-9-0 54...................................... SebSanders 13 —
(Clive Brittain) *in rr and rdn towards outside 1/2-way: hdwy over 3f out: sn wknd* **20/1**

5306 **10** 1 ¼ **Waterbury Girl**[97] 3803 3-9-0 52.. JimCrowley 4 —
(Bryn Palling) *plld hrd: in rr: lost tch 4f out* **40/1**

0050 **11** ½ **Aaranyow (IRE)**[70] 4705 3-9-0 53..................................... TadhgO'Shea 11 —
(Bryn Palling) *a in rr* **50/1**

00/0 **12** *nk* **Bawdsey Bank**[53] 4706 5-9-0 46.................................. HarryBentley(3) 5 —
(Ron Hodges) *s.i.s: a in rr* **80/1**

3300 **13** 13 **Miss Firefox**[64] 4927 3-9-0 55...(t) LukeMorris 14 —
(Nicky Vaughan) *in tch 1/2-way: sn wknd* **14/1**

1m 39.37s (-0.43) **Going Correction** -0.075s/f (Stan)
WFA 3 from 4yo+ 3lb **13** Ran SP% **120.3**
Speed ratings (Par 101): **99,97,96,95,94 93,86,82,72,71 71,70,57**
toteswingers: 1&2 £4.30, 1&3 £10.60, 2&3 £14.50. CSF £26.81 TOTE £4.90: £1.90, £1.70, £3.30; EX 38.30.
Owner Hamdan Al Maktoum **Bred** Lord Harrington **Trained** Arundel, W Sussex

FOCUS
A low-grade but tightly knit classified event in which the reasonable gallop saw the hold-up horses come to the fore in the closing stages. The winner made his ground towards the inside rail passing the intersection before edging left late on. There are grounds to think the first two may do a bit better.
Waterbury Girl Official explanation: jockey said filly ran too free
Miss Firefox Official explanation: jockey said filly had no more to give

6817 WIN THOUSANDS OF SPORTS TICKETS AT BLUESQ.COM NURSERY 7f (P)
5:50 (5:50) (Class 6) (0-60,60) 2-Y-O **£1,617** (£481; £240; £120) **Stalls** Low

Form RPR

000 **1** **Regal Gold**[15] 6455 2-9-0 **56**.. RichardHughes 5 61
(Richard Hannon) *in rr and rdn along 4f out: hdwy on outside 3f out: styd on fr 2f out: str run to ld fnl 120yds: hung rt clsng stages: hld on wl* **11/2**[1]

040 **2** ½ **Trusting (IRE)**[17] 6406 2-9-0 **56**................................. SilvestreDeSousa 10 60
(Eve Johnson Houghton) *chsd ldrs: drvn to chse wnr fnl 120yds: no imp but hld on wl for 2nd last strides* **14/1**

6636 **3** *nse* **Tigers Tale (IRE)**[18] 6372 2-9-3 **59**................................(v) JamesDoyle 12 63
(Roger Teal) *wnt lft s: in rr: hdwy on ins over 2f out: drvn and styd on fnl f to press for 2nd last strides* **8/1**

0005 **4** 1 ¼ **Pius Parker (IRE)**[24] 6221 2-9-4 **60**.................................... NeilCallan 1 60
(John Gallagher) *chsd ldrs: led over 1f out: hdd and no ex fnl 120yds* **14/1**

0523 **5** ½ **Ermyn Flyer**[44] 5577 2-9-2 **58**... IanMongan 9 57
(Pat Phelan) *in rr: hdwy on outside over 2f out: kpt on fnl f: nt rch ldrs* **6/1**[2]

630 **6** ½ **Moment In The Sun**[35] 5844 2-9-0 **56**............................... JimCrowley 8 54
(William Muir) *towards rr: hdwy over 1f out: styd on ins fnl f: nt rch ldrs* **20/1**

5020 **7** ½ **No More Games**[14] 6487 2-9-2 **58**..................................(p) PhillipMakin 4 54
(Kevin Ryan) *led tl hdd over 1f out: wknd ins fnl f* **25/1**

006 **8** ¾ **Chater Garden (IRE)**[50] 5385 2-8-11 **56**.................... HarryBentley(3) 13 50
(Alan Jarvis) *hmpd s and in rr: hdwy on outside over 1f out: kpt on clsng stages* **33/1**

0014 **9** 2 **Outlaw Torn (IRE)**[14] 6489 2-9-2 **58**.............................. MartinHarley 2 47
(Alan McCabe) *t.k.h: in tch: nt clr run on ins over 4f out: drvn to chse ldrs over 2f out: wknd ins fnl f* **11/2**[1]

506 **10** 5 **House Limit (IRE)**[82] 4319 2-8-11 **56**............................... JohnFahy(3) 6 32
(Harry Dunlop) *crossed s: a towards rr* **14/1**

003 **11** ½ **Wrapped Up**[34] 5896 2-9-0 **56**.. EddieAhern 7 31
(Heather Main) *chsd ldrs: drvn over 2f out: wknd over 1f out* **16/1**

654 **12** ¾ **Trending (IRE)**[30] 6025 2-9-0 **56**....................................... SteveDrowne 14 29
(Jeremy Gask) *w ldr after 2f tl wknd over 2f out* **16/1**

4006 **13** 7 **Morning Muse (IRE)**[31] 6002 2-9-1 **57**..........................(p) LukeMorris 11 12
(Peter Winkworth) *a in rr* **33/1**

0003 **14** 8 **Aussie Guest (IRE)**[8] 6628 2-9-2 **58**............................ MatthewDavies 3 —
(Mick Channon) *chsd ldrs 4f* **7/1**[3]

1m 26.77s (0.77) **Going Correction** -0.075s/f (Stan) **14** Ran SP% **114.9**
Speed ratings (Par 93): **92,91,91,89,89 88,88,87,85,79 78,77,69,60**
toteswingers: 1&2 £26.50, 1&3 £6.70, 2&3 £27.60. CSF £74.22 CT £622.24 TOTE £5.40: £2.60, £4.40, £1.90; EX 97.60.
Owner N S Yong **Bred** Minehart Developments Ltd **Trained** East Everleigh, Wilts
■ Stewards' Enquiry : James Doyle five-day ban: used whip with excessive frequency (Oct 27-29,31,Nov 1)

FOCUS
A moderate but open nursery in which the gallop was soon reasonable. The winner came down the centre in the straight.

NOTEBOOK
Regal Gold had only hinted at ability in turf maidens but overcame greenness to post an improved effort on this all-weather and nursery debut. He should prove equally effective over 1m and should be able to progress further. Official explanation: trainer's rep said, regarding apparent improvement in form, that this was the colt's first run on the all-weather and had benefited from a drop in class. (op 5-1)
Trusting(IRE) was one of the first off the bridle on this nursery and all-weather debut but she kept responding in a manner that suggested she would prove better suited by 1m (backed up by pedigree). She should be able to pick up a similar event. (op 16-1 tchd 20-1)
Tigers Tale(IRE) has had a few chances and didn't look entirely straightforward but ran up to his best returned to Polytrack. He is unlikely to be inconvenienced by the return to 1m but his record suggests he wouldn't be certain to build on this next time. (op 11-1)
Pius Parker(IRE) wasn't disgraced on this all-weather debut and first run over 7f after racing with the choke out. The drop back to 6f may suit better but he has little margin for error from this mark. (op 16-1)
Ermyn Flyer wasn't disgraced back on Polytrack and, although she doesn't look very progressive at this stage, she again left the impression that she'd be suited by a try over 1m. (op 9-2 tchd 13-2)
Chater Garden(IRE) lost ground and was checked at the start but made up a fair bit of ground in the closing stages on this first run over 7f. He's worth a try over 1m and is one to keep an eye on at a similar level. (tchd 25-1)

6818 BLUE SQUARE MAIDEN AUCTION FILLIES' STKS (DIV I) 7f (P)
6:20 (6:20) (Class 5) 2-Y-O **£2,264** (£673; £336; £168) **Stalls** Low

Form RPR

0 **1** **Graser (IRE)**[30] 6030 2-8-12 0.................................... SilvestreDeSousa 6 76+
(Marco Botti) *chsd ldrs: chal 4f out: led ins fnl 2f: drvn out fnl f* **7/2**[2]

4024 **2** 1 ½ **Symphony Time (IRE)**[26] 6169 2-8-12 73............................. ShaneKelly 10 72
(Brian Meehan) *sn led: jnd 4f out: narrowly hdd ins fnl 2f: styd pressing wnr tl outpcd fnl 120yds but wl clr of 3rd* **4/1**[3]

3 5 **Bursting Bubbles (IRE)** 2-8-7 0.............................. TomMcLaughlin 3 54+
(Ed Dunlop) *t.k.h towards rr: drvn and hdwy fr 2f out: styd on to take wl hld 3rd clsng stages* **20/1**

4 ½ **Whatsofunny (IRE)** 2-8-11 0.. NeilCallan 9 57+
(Roger Varian) *rring in stalls: s.i.s: sn drvn to chse ldrs: travelling ok ins fnl 3f: drvn 2f out: sn green: wknd fnl f: lost wl hld 3rd clsng stages* **5/4**[1]

5 1 ¼ **Cockney Rhyme** 2-8-8 0... FrankieMcDonald 2 50+
(Heather Main) *s.i.s: t.k.h towards rr: hdwy and hanging rt over 2f out: kpt on clsng stages* **33/1**

0 **6** 2 ¾ **Capriska**[20] 6308 2-8-8 0... JamieMackay 8 43
(Willie Musson) *in rr: rn green and wd into st 3f out: green and hung rt sn after* **50/1**

43 **7** 1 ¼ **Lady Percy (IRE)**[35] 5841 2-8-9 0 ow1........................... RichardHughes 4 41
(Mark Usher) *t.k.h: trckd ldrs: wknd 2f out* **13/2**

050 **8** 3 ¾ **Sandbanks**[8] 6620 2-8-4 0.. SophieDoyle(3) 1 29
(Sylvester Kirk) *chsd ldrs tl wknd appr fnl 2f* **80/1**

9 16 **Isobella** 2-8-10 0.. JimCrowley 7 —
(Hughie Morrison) *slowly away: a in rr* **14/1**

1m 27.04s (1.04) **Going Correction** -0.075s/f (Stan) **9** Ran SP% **117.6**
Speed ratings (Par 92): **91,89,83,83,81 78,77,72,54**
toteswingers: 1&2 £2.60, 1&3 £7.00, 2&3 £8.90. CSF £17.75 TOTE £3.80: £2.00, £1.10, £4.20; EX 16.50.
Owner Augusto Cati **Bred** Alberto Panetta **Trained** Newmarket, Suffolk

FOCUS
A couple of interesting newcomers in a fair fillies' maiden in which the first two pulled clear in the closing stages. A modest early gallop resulted in a time nearly two and a half seconds outside Racing Post Standard.

NOTEBOOK
Graser(IRE) ◆ shaped with a modicum of promise over an inadequate 6f on her debut but stepped up a fair bit on that level to beat a 73-rated rival over this longer trip on this all-weather debut. She is bred to relish middle distances in due course and she appeals as the sort to win more races. (op 3-1)
Symphony Time(IRE) is a steadily progressive individual who had the run of the race and ran as well as she ever has done. She pulled a long way clear of the remainder and she's capable of winning an uncompetitive event in this grade. (tchd 7-2 and 9-2 in a place)
Bursting Bubbles(IRE), who has several winners in her pedigree from 7f-2m but who was a cheap yearling, showed ability at a modest level on this racecourse debut. She should be better for this experience, will be suited by further and will be interesting once qualified for a mark. (tchd 16-1)
Whatsofunny(IRE), the third foal of a Listed winner, herself is a sister to 1m4f Italian Group 1 winner Rainbow Peak, proved disappointing on the face of it after being well backed on this racecourse debut. However she is better than the bare facts suggest after missing the break, pulling hard and running green and is well worth another chance. (op 7-4 tchd 2-1 in a place and 15-8 in places)
Cockney Rhyme, a 3,500gns first foal of a 1m2f, was far from disgraced after running green on her racecourse debut. She should be all the better for this run, will be better suited by 1m and should be able to leave these bare facts behind at some point. (op 40-1)

Capriska never figured again but she left the impression she should be able to step up on what she has achieved so far once she switches to low-grade handicap company.

6819 BLUE SQUARE MAIDEN AUCTION FILLIES' STKS (DIV II) 7f (P)

6:50 (6:51) (Class 5) 2-Y-O **£2,264** (£673; £336; £168) **Stalls** Low

Form RPR

0 **1** **Amthal (IRE)**[19] 6329 2-8-10 0 .... MartinDwyer 4 66
(Clive Brittain) *s.i.s: in rr: plenty to do 2f out: str run towards outside fnl f: fin strly: edgd rt clsng stages: led last strides* **9/1**

4 **2** *hd* **Tiablo (IRE)**[12] 6539 2-8-7 0 .... LauraPike(5) 6 68
(David Simcock) *trckd ldrs: pushed along and qcknd to ld jst ins fnl f: hdd last strides* **4/1**[2]

05 **3** *hd* **Hesperides**[14] 6474 2-8-5 0 .... JohnFahy(3) 10 63
(Harry Dunlop) *led 1f: styd chsng ldrs: wnt 2nd on ins over 2f out: chsd wnr ins fnl f and str chal fnl 120yds: no ex clsng stages* **12/1**

606 **4** *1 ¼* **Ishiamiracle**[27] 6118 2-8-8 62 .... KirstyMilczarek 1 60
(Andrew Balding) *t.k.h: chsd ldrs: styng on whn n.m.r jst ins fnl f: drvn and r.o wl fnl 120yds: kpt on cl home* **15/2**

5 *shd* **Cha Ching (IRE)** 2-8-11 0 .... SebSanders 5 62
(J W Hills) *in rr tl hdwy on outer fr 2f out: chsd ldrs fnl f: one pce whn carried rt clsng stages* **20/1**

6 **6** *1 ¼* **Sweetscot (IRE)**[27] 6117 2-8-9 0 ow1 .... FergusSweeney 8 57
(Amy Weaver) *in rr but in tch: hdwy fr 2f out: pushed along and styd on fnl f: nt rch ldrs* **11/2**[3]

06 **7** *1* **Liquid Sunshine**[94] 3921 2-8-7 0 .... SilvestreDeSousa 9 53
(Sylvester Kirk) *led after 1f: drvn along 2f out: edgd rt whn rdn and hdd over 1f out: wknd ins fnl f* **14/1**

0 **8** *½* **Synfonica**[27] 6117 2-8-4 0 .... KieranO'Neill(3) 7 51
(Richard Hannon) *s.i.s: sn in tch: chsd ldrs 1/2-way: drvn along 2f out: wknd 1f out* **10/1**

2026 **9** *2 ½* **Rockme Cockney**[50] 5393 2-8-11 73 .... SteveDrowne 3 49
(Jeremy Gask) *t.k.h: chsd ldrs: wknd over 1f out* **3/1**[1]

10 *nk* **Aloysia** 2-8-7 0 .... ChrisCatlin 2 44
(Sylvester Kirk) *slowly away: a in rr but mod prog fnl f* **33/1**

1m 27.3s (1.30) **Going Correction** -0.075s/f (Stan) **10** Ran SP% **113.3**
Speed ratings (Par 92): **89,88,88,87,87 85,84,83,81,80**
toteswingers: 1&2 £9.70, 1&3 £17.20, 2&3 £9.70. CSF £43.61 TOTE £14.30: £3.40, £1.10, £1.90; EX 51.70.
Owner A M A Al Shorafa **Bred** Shadwell Estate Company Limited **Trained** Newmarket, Suffolk
■ Stewards' Enquiry : Martin Dwyer one-day ban: careless riding (Oct 28)

FOCUS
The second division of an ordinary maiden in which several finished in a heap. The gallop was another modest one (a quarter of a second slower than the first division) and the winner came down the centre in the straight.

NOTEBOOK
Amthal(IRE) ◆ was well supported and duly turned in a much-improved effort after having plenty to do turning for home in a moderately run race on this all-weather debut. She shaped as though the return to 1m will suit and she's capable of even better. (op 20-1)
Tiablo(IRE), easy in the market, despite catching the eye on her debut, posted a much-improved effort over this longer trip. There was enough promise in this run to think she should be able to pick up a minor event. (op 5-2)
Hesperides was nibbled at in the market and, after enjoying the run of the race (soon tacked to inside rail from wide draw), she turned in her best effort on this third run. She'll be suited by middle distances next year and she's capable of winning a race. (op 14-1)
Ishiamiracle's proximity holds the bare bones of this form down but there's a fair chance she improved for the switch to this longer trip and switch to Polytrack. She'll do better in ordinary handicap company. (op 8-1)
Cha Ching(IRE), a 16,000euro half-sister to several winners, including useful multiple turf and all-weather winner (up to 1m) Saddlers Bend, was easy in the market but showed ability at a modest level on this racecourse debut. She's entitled to improve for this experience. (op 25-1)
Rockme Cockney was again below the pick of her form on Polytrack. She will have to raise her game to win a race of this nature or a competitive handicap from her current mark. Official explanation: jockey said filly never travelled (op 7-2)

6820 PLAY RAINBOW RICHES AT BLUESQ.COM MAIDEN FILLIES' STKS 6f (P)

7:20 (7:21) (Class 5) 2-Y-O **£2,264** (£673; £336; £168) **Stalls** Low

Form RPR

1 **Lexington Pearl (USA)** 2-9-0 0 .... JimCrowley 10 79+
(Ralph Beckett) *led after 1f: strly chal thrght fnl f: hld on all out* **14/1**

2 *nk* **More Than Words (IRE)** 2-9-0 0 .... RichardHughes 7 78+
(Richard Hannon) *trckd ldrs: rdn and one pce whn swtchd rt 1f out: qcknd u.p fnl f and gaining on wnr clsng stages: nt quite get up* **6/5**[1]

62 **3** *1 ¾* **Fine Painting (IRE)**[15] 6441 2-9-0 0 .... RyanMoore 3 72
(Gary Moore) *led 1f: styd chsng wnr: chal over 1f out and ins fnl f: wknd clsng stages* **15/8**[2]

4 *2 ½* **Delft** 2-9-0 0 .... WilliamBuick 1 64+
(Jeremy Noseda) *in tch: chsd ldrs on ins 3f out: styd on same pce fnl f* **10/1**

04 **5** *nk* **Fareedha (IRE)**[30] 6030 2-9-0 0 .... RichardHills 11 63
(John Dunlop) *sn trcking ldrs: pushed along 2f out: wknd ins fnl f* **5/1**[3]

000 **6** *4* **Willow Beauty**[30] 6030 2-9-0 55 .... EddieAhern 2 51
(J R Jenkins) *towards rr but in tch: sme hdwy over 1f out: styd on one pce* **66/1**

7 *2* **It's A Girl Thing (IRE)** 2-9-0 0 .... JamieSpencer 9 44+
(George Baker) *s.i.s: sn drvn along in rr: hdwy over 2f out: kpt on fnl f but nvr any ch* **25/1**

0 **8** *1 ¼* **Naturalmente (IRE)**[29] 6047 2-9-0 0 .... PhillipMakin 6 40
(Kevin Ryan) *in rr: hmpd on bnd 3f out: no ch after* **33/1**

0 **9** *hd* **Desert Spree**[17] 6406 2-9-0 0 .... SteveDrowne 8 40
(Jeremy Gask) *chsd ldrs over 3f* **66/1**

0 **10** *3 ½* **Silent Mistress**[37] 5812 2-9-0 0 .... AdrianMcCarthy 5 28
(J R Jenkins) *outpcd most of the way* **80/1**

00 **11** *1 ¾* **Poncho**[3] 6758 2-9-0 0 .... SebSanders 4 23
(Sir Mark Prescott Bt) *a outpcd* **66/1**

1m 12.85s (-0.25) **Going Correction** -0.075s/f (Stan) **11** Ran SP% **125.2**
Speed ratings (Par 92): **98,97,95,91,91 86,83,81,81,76 74**
toteswingers: 1&2 £3.60, 1&3 £5.40, 2&3 £2.10. CSF £33.03 TOTE £20.40: £4.40, £1.10, £1.50; EX 48.60.
Owner Pearl Bloodstock Ltd **Bred** Mt Brilliant Farm LLC **Trained** Kimpton, Hants
■ Hughes picked up a second whip ban (10 days) under the new rules and promptly relinquished his licence in frustration.
■ Stewards' Enquiry : Richard Hughes ten-day ban: excessive use of whip (Oct 29,31,Nov 1-5,9-11)

FOCUS
Fair form from the first two, who look potentially useful sorts. The gallop was no more than fair and the winner came down the centre in the straight.

NOTEBOOK
Lexington Pearl(USA) ◆, who cost $100,000 as a yearling and who is a half-sister to a winner in the US, was nibbled at in the market and created a favourable impression after enjoying the run of the race on this racecourse debut. She's the type physically to make further progress, she will have no problems with 7f and it'll be a surprise if she doesn't win again. (op 16-1)
More Than Words(IRE) ◆, a 145,000euro yearling who is out of a Queen Mary winner, attracted support throughout the day and ran well, despite her inexperience, on this racecourse debut. She pulled a few lengths clear of a fair yardstick and is more than capable of making amends in similar company. Richard Hughes, however, used his whip six times inside the final furlong and under new rules was banned a further 10 days (double basic tariff, having already been found guilty of similar offence at Salisbury earlier in week). (op 15-8 tchd 2-1 in places)
Fine Painting(IRE) was well supported and probably ran to a similar level as she did over 7f on her previous start, depsite racing with the choke out in the first half of the race. She is in good hands and can be placed to best advantage in due course. (op 2-1)
Delft, the first foal of a 7f winner, herself a half-sister to several winners including smart pair Wunders Dream (sprinter) and Grecian Dancer (up to 1m), was fairly easy in the market but showed ability without being knocked about on this racecourse debut. She should leave this bare form behind at some point. (op 8-1)
Fareedha(IRE) had shown form bordering on fair on turf on her previous start but, although not disgraced from her wide draw, failed to build on that on this all-weather debut. She is likely to remain vulnerable against the better types in this grade. (op 9-2)
Willow Beauty's proximity holds this form down to a degree but she's probably flattered in a race run at less than a true gallop. Her best chance of success lies in moderate handicaps but she'll have to show something more solid before she's worth a bet.

6821 DOWNLOAD THE BLUE SQUARE APP NURSERY 6f (P)

7:50 (7:52) (Class 6) (0-60,66) 2-Y-O **£1,617** (£481; £240; £120) **Stalls** Low

Form RPR

0006 **1** **Elegant Flight**[8] 6627 2-8-12 57 .... (v) HarryBentley(3) 9 62
(Alan Jarvis) *chsd ldrs: drvn and styd on wl fnl f: led fnl 100yds: pushed out* **16/1**

4561 **2** *½* **Guava**[8] 6627 2-9-7 66 6ex .... SeanLevey(3) 3 69
(Richard Hannon) *in rr: rdn and hdwy 2f out: drvn and styd on wl fnl f: tk 2nd last strides: nt rch wnr* **9/2**[2]

0600 **3** *nk* **Rooknrasbryripple**[8] 6627 2-9-0 56 .... MartinHarley 1 58
(Mick Channon) *w ldr: slt ld over 2f out: kpt slt advantage tl hdd fnl 100yds: lost 2nd last strides* **14/1**

5056 **4** *1* **Vitalicious**[12] 6540 2-9-1 57 .... RichardMullen 2 56
(Ed McMahon) *slt ld tl hdd over 2f out: wknd fnl 120yds* **14/1**

600 **5** *2* **Perfect Day (IRE)**[15] 6441 2-9-3 59 .... SilvestreDeSousa 10 52
(Paul Cole) *t.k.h: in rr: hdwy 2f out: styd on fnl f: nt rch ldrs* **10/1**

3041 **6** *nk* **Littlecote Lady**[31] 5998 2-9-1 57 .... LukeMorris 6 49
(Mark Usher) *in tch: rdn 2f out: styd on same pce fnl f* **8/1**

3050 **7** *nse* **Lady Nickandy (IRE)**[21] 6284 2-9-0 56 .... (p) JamesDoyle 5 48
(Alan McCabe) *t.k.h: chsd ldrs: wknd fnl f* **25/1**

003 **8** *½* **Kaylee**[22] 6252 2-9-0 56 .... RyanMoore 11 47
(Gary Moore) *hld up in rr: t.k.h: drvn and hdwy on outside fr 2f out: nt rch ldrs and one pce fnl f* **4/1**[1]

0504 **9** *1 ¾* **Bitter Lemon**[12] 6540 2-9-3 59 .... PhillipMakin 12 44
(Kevin Ryan) *chsd ldrs: rdn over 2f out: wknd appr fnl f* **16/1**

006 **10** *hd* **Bountiful Catch**[14] 6483 2-9-1 57 .... MickyFenton 7 42
(Pam Sly) *hmpered after s: drvn along over 2f out: styd on fnl f: nvr a threat* **9/1**

000 **11** *2 ¾* **Bolshoi Melody**[20] 6291 2-9-0 56 .... SteveDrowne 4 32
(Jeremy Gask) *chsd ldrs over 3f* **25/1**

0003 **12** *3* **Romany Spirit (IRE)**[31] 5998 2-9-4 60 .... PatCosgrave 8 27
(Jim Boyle) *nvr bttr than mid-div* **11/2**[3]

1m 13.54s (0.44) **Going Correction** -0.075s/f (Stan) **12** Ran SP% **116.6**
Speed ratings (Par 93): **94,93,92,91,88 88,88,87,85,85 81,77**
toteswingers: 1&2 £19.30, 1&3 £45.80, 2&3 £12.90. CSF £85.17 CT £1055.68 TOTE £18.80: £6.90, £2.20, £5.20; EX 142.90.
Owner Grant & Bowman Limited **Bred** Mrs Ann Jarvis **Trained** Twyford, Bucks

FOCUS
A moderate nursery which comprised one colt taking on eleven fillies. The gallop was an ordinary one and the winner came down the centre in the straight.

NOTEBOOK
Elegant Flight, with the visor again fitted, turned in her best effort to reverse recent Nottingham placings with Guava. This was only her eighth race but her record suggests she wouldn't be certain to reproduce this next time.
Guava is a reliable type who failed to confirm recent placings with the winner but she ran creditably under her penalty returned to Polytrack to fare the best of those held up. She is worth a try over a bit further (dam a 1m2f winner) and she should continue to go well. (op 10-3)
Rooknrasbryripple had the run of the race and ran creditably from her favourable draw returned to Polytrack. However her record isn't one of consistency and she wouldn't be one to go in head down for next time.
Vitalicious had the run of the race and wasn't disgraced returned to 6f but she's going to have to step up a bit on what she's achieved to date if she is to win a competitive handicap from this mark. (op 12-1)
Perfect Day(IRE) ◆ turned in her best effort on this nursery debut over what looked a thoroughly inadequate trip. As her pedigree suggests (dam Irish 1000 Guineas winner and Oaks runner-up), she will be much better suited by the step up to 1m and she is one to keep an eye on granted a suitable test. (op 11-1 tchd 12-1)
Kaylee never figured from her wide draw on this nursery debut but is worth another chance. (tchd 9-2)
Bountiful Catch didn't get the run of the race but will have to settle better before he is a solid betting proposition. Official explanation: jockey said colt was denied a clear run (op 14-1)

6822 BET AT BLUESQ.COM ON YOUR MOBILE H'CAP 1m 4f (P)

8:20 (8:21) (Class 4) (0-85,85) 3-Y-O **£4,075** (£1,212; £606; £303) **Stalls** Centre

Form RPR

432 **1** **Yasir (USA)**[19] 6349 3-9-1 79 .... (v[1]) IanMongan 1 93
(Saeed Bin Suroor) *chsd ldrs: wnt 2nd and drvn over 1f out: styd on to ld fnl 120yds: hld on wl* **8/1**

1421 **2** *1 ¼* **Robin Hoods Bay**[24] 6218 3-9-3 81 .... JamieSpencer 11 93+
(Edward Vaughan) *s.i.s: in rr: lost footing on bnd towards outside 4f out: drvn and rapid hdwy wl over 1f out: styd on wl fnl f to take 2nd last strides: nt rch wnr* **5/1**[2]

-310 **3** *nse* **Samarkand (IRE)**[119] 3084 3-9-4 82 .... SebSanders 2 94+
(Sir Mark Prescott Bt) *chsd ldrs: led over 2f out: hdd and nt qckn fnl 120yds: lost 2nd last stride* **9/2**[1]

4331 **4** *2 ½* **Alshazah**[31] 6005 3-8-11 75 .... JamesMillman 6 83
(Rod Millman) *in tch: hdwy over 2f out: sn chsng ldrs: styd on same pce fnl f* **8/1**

1026 **5** *½* **Anton Dolin (IRE)**[55] 5235 3-9-3 81 .... EddieAhern 13 88
(John Dunlop) *in rr: stdy hdwy over 2f out: drvn and styd on same pce fnl f* **16/1**

011 **6** *1 1/4* **Dragonera**[101] 3681 3-9-5 **83**........ NeilCallan 12 88
(Ed Dunlop) *in rr: hdwy over 2f out: styd on fnl f: nt rch ldrs* **20/1**
3344 **7** *1/2* **Unex Renoir**[27] 6130 3-9-3 **81**........(b[1]) WilliamBuick 10 85
(John Gosden) *in rr: rdn: hd high and hung rt ins fnl 3f: sme late hdwy* **6/1**[3]
1260 **8** *nse* **Plattsburgh (USA)**[26] 6155 3-9-0 **78**........ SilvestreDeSousa 7 82
(Mark Johnston) *in rr: hdwy over 2f out: styd on fnl f: nt rch ldrs* **20/1**
2241 **9** *3/4* **Deraasa (USA)**[9] 6614 3-9-5 **83** 6ex........ TadhgO'Shea 5 86
(Saeed Bin Suroor) *led: hdd appr fnl 2f: wknd fnl f* **11/1**
100 **10** *4* **L'Hermitage (IRE)**[82] 4336 3-8-10 **74**........(p) MartinDwyer 9 71
(Brian Meehan) *chsd ldrs: rdn 3f out: wknd fr 2f out* **25/1**
160 **11** *3 1/4* **Val O'Hara (IRE)**[42] 5641 3-8-13 **77**........ JimCrowley 8 69
(Peter Winkworth) *chsd ldrs: wknd ins fnl 2f* **33/1**
5202 **12** *6* **Fanny May**[45] 5546 3-9-7 **85**........ PatCosgrave 4 67
(Denis Coakley) *in tch: rdn and wknd wl over 2f out* **10/1**
0410 **13** *5* **Height Of Summer (IRE)**[33] 5938 3-8-12 **76**........ LukeMorris 3 50
(Chris Wall) *chsd ldrs: wknd wl over 2f out* **33/1**
140 **14** *nk* **Dubai Glory**[18] 6376 3-9-1 **79**........ JamesDoyle 14 52
(Sheena West) *bhd most of way* **25/1**

2m 31.06s (-3.44) **Going Correction** -0.075s/f (Stan) **14** Ran SP% **117.8**
Speed ratings (Par 103): **108,107,107,105,105 104,103,103,103,100 98,94,91,91**
toteswingers: 1&2 £11.50, 1&3 £10.50, 2&3 £4.80. CSF £41.91 CT £203.22 TOTE £10.10: £2.90, £2.20, £1.80; EX 52.90.
Owner Godolphin **Bred** Shadwell Farm LLC **Trained** Newmarket, Suffolk

FOCUS
A useful handicap in which the gallop was a muddling one, but this race should throw up winners and the form has been viewed positively. The winner raced in the centre in the last furlong and produced a clear personal best.

6823 BLUE SQUARE H'CAP 2m (P)
8:50 (8:51) (Class 6) (0-60,60) 3-Y-O **£1,617** (£481; £240; £120) Stalls Low

Form RPR
6052 **1** **Blue Cossack (IRE)**[9] 6613 3-8-13 **52**........(be) IanMongan 2 58
(Mark Usher) *in rr: rapid hdwy 4f out: drvn and hdwy over 2f out: styd on to chal 1f out: narrow ld ins fnl f: all out* **9/2**[1]
0055 **2** *3/4* **Decana**[36] 5838 3-9-0 **53**........ TadhgO'Shea 7 58
(Hughie Morrison) *mid-div: hdwy on outside: 3f out: styd on to ld 1f out: hdd ins fnl f: styd on same pce* **6/1**[2]
0503 **3** *1 1/2* **Pizzetti (IRE)**[14] 6482 3-9-2 **55**........(t) SebSanders 5 58
(Sir Mark Prescott Bt) *in rr: drvn and hdwy fr 2f out: str run fnl f: fin wl to take 3rd clsng stages: nt rch ldrs* **12/1**
0535 **4** *3 1/4* **Dhampas**[23] 6240 3-8-7 **46**........(b) NickyMackay 4 45
(Jim Boyle) *led: wnt 10 l clr 1/2-way: drvn and wknd fr 2f out: hdd 1f out: sn btn* **7/1**[3]
4344 **5** *4 1/2* **Fastada (IRE)**[16] 6437 3-8-9 **48**........(v) JimCrowley 9 42
(Jonathan Portman) *chsd ldrs: drvn and wknd fr 2f out* **14/1**
3045 **6** *7* **Mountain Myst**[19] 6356 3-8-9 **48**........ WilliamCarson 1 34
(William Muir) *in tch: wknd over 2f out* **10/1**
6001 **7** *2* **Thank You Joy**[50] 5380 3-9-7 **60**........ SilvestreDeSousa 8 43
(J R Jenkins) *in rr: mod prog fnl 2f* **12/1**
3001 **8** *1 1/4* **Imperial Fong**[14] 6482 3-9-2 **55**........ AndreaAtzeni 6 37
(Chris Dwyer) *prom 12f* **16/1**
-060 **9** *3 1/4* **Cyber Star**[22] 6255 3-9-3 **56**........ EddieAhern 10 34
(James Fanshawe) *towards rr most of the way* **7/1**[3]
4445 **10** *17* **Green Future (USA)**[14] 6482 3-9-3 **56**........ PatCosgrave 3 13
(Amanda Perrett) *chsd ldrs tl wknd qckly ins fnl 3f* **6/1**[2]
5000 **11** *19* **Rather Cool**[10] 6589 3-8-10 **52**........(t) KieranO'Neill(3) 11 —
(John Bridger) *towards rr most of the way* **40/1**
606 **12** *4 1/2* **Ballina Blue**[13] 6086 3-9-7 **60**........ JamesDoyle 12 —
(Sheena West) *chsd ldr to 1/2-way* **16/1**

3m 29.41s (-0.69) **Going Correction** -0.075s/f (Stan) **12** Ran SP% **117.1**
Speed ratings (Par 99): **98,97,96,95,93 89,88,87,86,77 68,66**
toteswingers: 1&2 £6.00, 1&3 £6.80, 2&3 £22.20. CSF £29.99 CT £305.20 TOTE £5.60: £2.40, £2.60, £4.00; EX 28.40.
Owner Reg Brookes & Richard Jurd **Bred** Morgan Ferris **Trained** Upper Lambourn, Berks

FOCUS
A very moderate handicap in which several were trying the trip for the first time. The gallop was soon sound and the winner came down the in the straight. The winner did not need to improve much on recent efforts.
T/Plt: £233.00 to a £1 stake. Pool of £55,940.90 - 175.20 winning units. T/Qpdt: £27.60 to a £1 stake. Pool of £9,877.05 - 264.70 winning units. ST

6329 HAYDOCK (L-H)
Friday, October 14
OFFICIAL GOING: Heavy (soft in places; 6.3)
Wind: Light, behind Weather: Cloudy

6825 TRC MAIDEN STKS 1m 2f 95y
1:55 (1:56) (Class 5) 2-Y-O **£2,587** (£770; £384; £192) Stalls Centre

Form RPR
33 **1** **Beyond Conceit (IRE)**[71] 4714 2-9-3 0........ RobertWinston 10 82
(Tom Tate) *mde all: rdn whn pressed 2f out: kpt on wl ins fnl f* **10/11**[1]
0 **2** *1 1/4* **My Destination (IRE)**[18] 6400 2-8-12 0........ AntiocoMurgia(5) 9 80
(Mahmood Al Zarooni) *in tch: rdn and hung lft whn chsng ldrs over 2f out: styd on to take 2nd wl ins fnl f: nt rch wnr* **8/1**
5 **3** *3/4* **Samba King**[23] 6245 2-9-3 0........ FrankieDettori 8 78
(Mahmood Al Zarooni) *a.p: chalng upsides over 2f out: nt qckn 1f out: styd on same pce fnl 100yds* **11/2**[3]
4263 **4** *2 1/2* **Juno The Muffinman (IRE)**[35] 5899 2-9-3 75........ SebSanders 2 73
(Tom Dascombe) *in rr: u.p over 4f out: hdwy over 3f out: styd on fnl 2f but unable to rch ldrs* **10/1**
03 **5** *5* **No Time To Lose**[18] 6400 2-9-3 0........ FergusSweeney 7 64
(Jamie Osborne) *trckd ldrs: u.p over 3f out: sn no imp: wl btn fnl f* **5/1**[2]
000 **6** *5* **Season Spirit**[20] 6334 2-9-3 52........ JamesSullivan 3 54
(James Given) *s.i.s: in rr: pushed along 6f out: kpt on modly fnl 2f: nvr on terms w ldrs* **50/1**
7 *16* **Blue Pencil** 2-9-3 0........ FrankieMcDonald 5 24
(Paul Fitzsimons) *sn handy: rdn and wknd 4f out* **100/1**
066 **8** *3 3/4* **Annaluna (IRE)**[18] 6400 2-8-12 62........ GrahamGibbons 4 12
(David Evans) *midfield: pushed along 6f out: wknd over 4f out* **25/1**
9 *9* **Willy McBay** 2-9-3 0........ AndrewMullen 1 —
(George Moore) *s.i.s: hld up: pushed along over 4f out: t.o* **100/1**

2m 17.76s (1.76) **Going Correction** +0.075s/f (Good) **9** Ran SP% **112.4**
Speed ratings (Par 95): **95,94,93,91,87 83,70,67,60**
toteswingers: 1&2 £2.90, 2&3 £4.80, 1&3 £2.30 CSF £8.54 TOTE £2.00: £1.10, £1.80, £1.80; EX 8.30 Trifecta £30.20 Pool: £524.23 - 12.84 winning units..
Owner Mrs Fitri Hay **Bred** Barronstown Stud **Trained** Tadcaster, N Yorks
■ Stewards' Enquiry : Antioco Murgia five-day ban: excessive use of whip (Oct 28-29,31,Nov 1-2)

FOCUS
All races on Inner home straight and distance son Round course increased by 13yds. After riding in the opener, Frankie Dettori said: "It is heavy ground" and Robert Winston said: "It is soft, not heavy." The actual race distance was 1m2f 108yds. An extreme stamina test for juveniles and it proved hard to make up significant amounts of ground.

NOTEBOOK
Beyond Conceit(IRE) didn't go on as expected from a promising debut over 7f at Redcar when a beaten favourite upped to 1m here in August, but clearly he benefited from a 71-day break, as well as the greatly increased stamina test. A big, scopey colt who really takes the eye, he should make a smart older stayer. (op 11-10)
My Destination(IRE) improved on the form he showed when behind No Time To Lose on his debut over this trip at Bath, showing enough to suggest he can win a similar race. His rider was banned for five days under the harsh new whip rules for excessive frequency. (op 9-1 tchd 10-1)
Samba King ran better than when beaten a long way over 1m1f on soft ground at Goodwood first time up. (op 9-2)
Juno The Muffinman(IRE), a half-brother to a couple of winning jumpers, was never seen with a chance but was the only runner to make up ground from off the pace. (op 9-1)
No Time To Lose couldn't match the form of his recent third at Bath and was presumably unsuited by the conditions. (tchd 9-2)
Blue Pencil Official explanation: jockey said gelding lost its action

6826 BETFAIR SUPPORTS THE THOROUGHBRED REHABILITATION CENTRE CONDITIONS STKS 7f
2:25 (2:25) (Class 4) 2-Y-O **£3,881** (£1,155; £577) Stalls Low

Form RPR
4105 **1** **Basantee**[22] 6275 2-8-9 81........ RichardKingscote 4 81
(Tom Dascombe) *mde all: rdn over 2f out: hrd pressed 1f out: plld out more fnl 100yds: kpt on* **7/2**[3]
214 **2** *1 1/4* **Kid Suitor (IRE)**[22] 6268 2-9-0 78........ FrankieDettori 3 83
(Richard Hannon) *hld up in last pl: effrt to go cl 2nd 2f out: chalng upsides 1f out: no ex fnl 75yds* **7/4**[2]
311 **3** *1 3/4* **Lady Layla**[40] 5755 2-8-9 79........ TomEaves 1 73
(Bryan Smart) *trckd wnr tl rdn and dropped to last pl 2f out: one pce after: wl hld fnl f* **11/10**[1]

1m 33.58s (2.68) **Going Correction** +0.35s/f (Good) **3** Ran SP% **106.2**
Speed ratings (Par 97): **98,96,94**
CSF £8.95 TOTE £4.40; EX 5.90.
Owner The MHS 8X8 Partnership **Bred** R Phillips And Tweenhills Farm And Stud **Trained** Malpas, Cheshire

FOCUS
The actual race distance was 7f 13yds.

NOTEBOOK
Basantee was allowed an uncontested lead, so form to treat with caution. The winner's latest success was also gained against two rivals over this C&D and she struggles in more competitive races. (tchd 10-3)
Kid Suitor(IRE) looked the winner when looming up in the straight, but clearly the leader had saved enough. He would have been 8lb better off with Basantee in a handicap, so this was a useful performance, and his sizable physique suggests he'll progress well in time. (op 6-4)
Lady Layla was on a hat-trick after victories in a maiden and nursery, but seemingly didn't handle the ground - the softest she'd raced on - as well as the front two. (op 11-8)

6827 VECPRINT NURSERY 5f
3:00 (3:01) (Class 3) 2-Y-O **£6,469** (£1,925; £962; £481) Stalls Centre

Form RPR
4211 **1** **Ballesteros**[11] 6590 2-9-8 **88** 6ex........ JamieSpencer 2 93+
(Brian Meehan) *wnt rt s: hld up: swtchd lft and hdwy over 1f out: r.o to ld wl ins fnl f: jst doing enough fnl strides* **6/1**[3]
011 **2** *nse* **Mince**[11] 6573 2-8-10 **76** 6ex........ SteveDrowne 6 81+
(Roger Charlton) *dwlt: hld up in midfield: swtchd lft and hdwy over 1f out: str chal fnl 75yds: r.o* **1/1**[1]
521 **3** *nk* **Planet I T (IRE)**[23] 6252 2-9-1 **81**........ LiamKeniry 3 83
(Mark Usher) *n.m.r and hmpd s: towards rr: hdwy over 1f out: led ins fnl f: sn hdd and edgd rt: hld fnl strides* **25/1**
1420 **4** *1 1/4* **Key Ambition**[7] 6670 2-8-13 **79**........ TomEaves 5 77
(Bryan Smart) *led: rdn over 1f out: hdd ins fnl f: no ex towards fin* **9/1**
1343 **5** *3/4* **Chooseday (IRE)**[28] 6111 2-9-0 **80**........ PhillipMakin 8 75
(Kevin Ryan) *hld up: effrt ent fnl f to chse ldrs: styd on same pce fnl 75yds* **5/1**[2]
210 **6** *3/4* **Impassive**[90] 4094 2-8-4 **77**........ GeorgeChaloner(7) 1 69
(Ed McMahon) *chsd ldrs: rdn to chal over 1f out: stl ch ins fnl f: one pce fnl 75yds* **20/1**
3230 **7** *nse* **Middleton Flyer (IRE)**[20] 6323 2-8-7 **73**........ AndrewMullen 4 65
(David Evans) *w ldr: rdn and chalng fr over 1f out: one pce fnl 75yds* **22/1**
3300 **8** *1/2* **Signifer (IRE)**[13] 6518 2-9-7 **87**........ TonyCulhane 9 77
(Mick Channon) *hld up in rr: rdn over 1f out: no imp on ldrs* **20/1**
2552 **9** *3 3/4* **Just Like Heaven (IRE)**[24] 6232 2-8-0 **66**........ SilvestreDeSousa 7 43
(Tim Easterby) *hld up in midfield: pushed along 2f out: wknd ins fnl f* **18/1**

62.54 secs (1.74) **Going Correction** +0.35s/f (Good) **9** Ran SP% **113.9**
Speed ratings (Par 99): **100,99,99,97,96 95,94,94,88**
toteswingers: 1&2 £2.50, 2&3 £9.20, 1&3 £9.10 CSF £11.54 CT £140.01 TOTE £5.50: £1.90, £1.30, £4.60; EX 14.90 Trifecta £75.00 Pool: £1,189.96 - 11.74 winning units..
Owner Mrs P Good **Bred** Exors Of The Late J R Good **Trained** Manton, Wilts

FOCUS
The ground probably didn't suit all of these, but this is still strong nursery form.

NOTEBOOK
Ballesteros ◆ was 2lb wrong under the penalty for his success on quick ground at Windsor, but he usually travels like a smart type and that was the case again. He was completing a hat-trick having started his winning sequence in a 6f maiden here and it's no surprise the testing ground helped him progress again considering he's a son of Tomba, who did so well for this owner/trainer combination in the mud. It's possible to argue he was helped by Mince meeting trouble, but the winner was going every bit as well as that rival when the pair of them were denied a clear run, and they both switched into the clear at the same time. He could do with settling a bit better, but his cruising speed is his chief asset and there should be more to come. (tchd 11-2 and 15-2)
Mince ◆ failed to take advantage of being 11lb well in under the penalty for her nursery success over 6f on a fast surface, but there was still plenty to like. She just failed against a potentially smart type, and that's despite these conditions possibly not being ideal. This is no reason to give up on her and she remains a filly with pattern-class potential. (op 11-10 tchd 5-4 in places)

Planet I T(IRE) ◆ had progressed with each run prior to coming here and this was another step forward. He impressed when winning a Polytrack maiden last time and showed himself fully effective on turf, recovering from being hampered at the start and then only being worn down after seeing more daylight than the first two finishers. There's plenty more to come and he looks a very useful prospect. (op 22-1)
Key Ambition ran into three well-handicapped types. (op 11-1)
Chooseday(IRE) again travelled well before not finishing as strongly as some. (op 4-1)

6828 PROFESSIONAL FOOTBALLERS' ASSOCIATION MAIDEN STKS 1m
3:35 (3:38) (Class 5) 2-Y-O £2,587 (£770; £384; £192) Stalls Low

Form RPR

1 **Gold Rally (USA)** 2-9-3 0 FrankieDettori 8 78+
(Mahmood Al Zarooni) *midfield: c over to stands' rail over 3f out: hdwy over 2f out: hung lft after: led over 1f out: styd on: in control cl home* **3/1**[1]

2 ½ **Lelaps (USA)** 2-9-3 0 AdamKirby 5 77+
(Marco Botti) *dwlt: midfield: hdwy over 3f out: rdn over 2f out: chalng fr over 1f out: carried lft ins fnl f: hld fnl strides* **12/1**

3 1¾ **Key Appointment** 2-9-3 0 JamieSpencer 6 76+
(Tom Tate) *trckd ldrs: led over 3f out: hdd over 1f out: stl ev ch for press whn carried lft ins fnl f: hld and eased fnl 50yds* **11/2**[3]

0 4 7 **Mawaqeet (USA)**[35] 5891 2-9-3 0 TadhgO'Shea 10 58+
(Sir Michael Stoute) *trckd ldrs: rdn over 2f out: sn no imp: no ch fnl f* **5/1**[2]

2 5 5 **Intuition**[15] 6481 2-9-3 0 KierenFallon 9 47+
(Richard Hannon) *w ldr tl rdn over 2f out: wknd over 1f out* **3/1**[1]

6 nk **Tantamount** 2-9-3 0 SteveDrowne 2 46
(Roger Charlton) *dwlt: racd keenly in midfield: rdn 2f out: wknd over 1f out* **11/1**

0 7 1¼ **Eastlands Lad (IRE)**[91] 4073 2-9-3 0 FrederikTylicki 4 43
(Micky Hammond) *led: hdd over 3f out: rdn over 2f out: wknd over 1f out* **150/1**

8 4½ **Penang Pegasus** 2-9-3 0 RobertWinston 7 33
(David O'Meara) *dwlt: towards rr: pushed along and hdwy over 2f out: nvr able to chal: wl btn fnl f* **8/1**

00 9 10 **Solar View (IRE)**[21] 6308 2-9-3 0 SebSanders 1 11+
(Sir Mark Prescott Bt) *pushed along thrght: a bhd* **40/1**

00 10 2¾ **Red Shimmer (IRE)**[15] 6483 2-9-3 0 TonyCulhane 11 5
(Jo Hughes) *plld hrd: in tch: stdd after 2f: in rr: struggling over 3f out: wl bhd after* **50/1**

1m 46.73s (3.83) **Going Correction** +0.35s/f (Good) **10 Ran SP% 114.3**
Speed ratings (Par 95): **94,93,91,84,79 79,78,73,63,60**
toteswingers: 1&2 £7.50, 2&3 £10.30, 1&3 £4.30 CSF £40.85 TOTE £3.40: £1.50, £2.80, £2.50; EX 43.10 Trifecta £157.90 Pool: £1,086.62 - 5.09 winning units..
Owner Godolphin **Bred** Southern Equine Stables LLC **Trained** Newmarket, Suffolk

FOCUS
The actual race distance was 1m 13yds. Some interesting types lined up and this looked at least a fair maiden.

NOTEBOOK
Gold Rally(USA), a $450,000 half-brother to a US 6.5f Grade 2 winner, out of a triple winner in the US, was no sure thing to handle this ground but he went over it just fine and won despite hanging left after initially grabbing the stands' rail in the straight. A lovely looker with plenty of scope, there should be a good deal more to come. (op 10-3 tchd 11-4)
Lelaps(USA) was a bit unruly beforehand but showed plenty of ability, just being held having been carried left by the winner. A half-brother to Becrux, a Grade 1 winner in Canada over 1m, he could be quite decent in time. (op 17-2 tchd 8-1)
Key Appointment, a 150,000gns half-brother to six winners, out of a US 1m stakes winner, has plenty of size. He was clear of the others and looks a nice long-term prospect. (op 5-1)
Mawaqeet(USA) was well backed to improve significantly on a moderate Sandown debut. He failed to justify the support, being beaten a fair way, but the front three are all potentially decent and he can do better, probably on quicker ground. (op 8-1)
Intuition was nowhere near the form he showed when runner-up over 7f on quick ground on his debut, these conditions presumably not suiting. (op 5-2)
Red Shimmer(IRE) Official explanation: jockey said gelding hung right throughout

6829 PROFESSIONAL JOCKEYS SUPPORTING THE TRC NURSERY 1m
4:10 (4:11) (Class 4) (0-85,85) 2-Y-O £3,881 (£1,155; £577; £288) Stalls Low

Form RPR

41 1 **Mr Spiggott (IRE)**[39] 5786 2-9-0 78 TonyCulhane 6 83+
(Mick Channon) *in rr: hdwy over 2f out: led narrowly over 1f out: hung lft: styd on: in control cl home* **17/2**

2433 2 ½ **Grizzle**[21] 6308 2-9-0 78 FrankieDettori 4 82
(Mahmood Al Zarooni) *midfield: hdwy gng wl over 2f out: led briefly over 1f out: stl ev ch ins fnl f: hld cl home* **5/1**[3]

01 3 2¼ **Daneking**[34] 5937 2-8-13 77 WilliamBuick 3 76+
(John Gosden) *racd keenly: trckd ldrs: rdn over 1f out: styd on ins fnl f: no imp on front pair* **2/1**[1]

5611 4 1¾ **Amadeus Wolfe Tone (IRE)**[15] 6484 2-9-1 79 FergusSweeney 5 74
(Jamie Osborne) *midfield: hdwy over 3f out: rdn over 2f out: no imp on ldr: one pce ins fnl f* **6/1**

6500 5 nk **Always Eager**[19] 6372 2-7-12 62 SilvestreDeSousa 8 56
(Mark Johnston) *led: rdn over 2f out: hdd over 1f out: no ex fnl f* **22/1**

0415 6 1 **Al's Memory (IRE)**[10] 6599 2-9-0 78 StevieDonohoe 11 70
(David Evans) *in rr: rdn over 2f out: kpt on over 1f out: no imp on ldrs* **16/1**

3014 7 nse **Costa Del Fortune (IRE)**[9] 6623 2-9-0 78 JamesDoyle 7 70
(Richard Hannon) *towards rr: rdn over 2f out: midfield wl over 1f out: nvr able to chal* **16/1**

3611 8 15 **Zakreet**[27] 6144 2-9-7 85 PhillipMakin 9 44
(Kevin Ryan) *prom tl rdn and wknd 2f out* **9/2**[2]

0054 9 1¼ **Barolo Top (IRE)**[30] 6060 2-9-1 79 SebSanders 2 35
(Tom Dascombe) *trckd ldrs tl rdn and wknd over 2f out* **20/1**

3215 10 nk **Grand Gold**[105] 3595 2-8-12 76 MartinHarley 10 32
(Seamus Durack) *prom tl wknd over 3f out* **50/1**

1m 46.19s (3.29) **Going Correction** +0.35s/f (Good) **10 Ran SP% 115.8**
Speed ratings (Par 97): **97,96,94,92,92 91,91,76,74,74**
toteswingers: 1&2 £7.20, 2&3 £3.40, 1&3 £5.20 CSF £49.17 CT £118.92 TOTE £12.40: £3.20, £2.70, £1.40; EX 66.80 Trifecta £161.40 Pool: £933.94 - 4.28 winning units..
Owner M Channon **Bred** Martin Francis Ltd **Trained** West Ilsley, Berks

FOCUS
The actual race distance was 1m 13yds. The time was the quickest of four races at the trip, including both divisions of the older-horse Class 5 handicap.

NOTEBOOK
Mr Spiggott(IRE) had Grizzle behind in third when winning a 6f maiden on soft ground at Newcastle and was able to confirm form and follow up, despite hanging left. He intimidated his old rival when hanging towards the far rail, but basically proved the more resolute of the pair. (op 8-1 tchd 9-1)
Grizzle is 0-5 now, having also been beaten on Polytrack since that Newcastle event, but was clear of the others. (op 11-2 tchd 9-2)
Daneking, dropped in trip after winning a 1m2f maiden at Goodwood, ruined his chance by racing keenly and actually did well to finish so close. Official explanation: jockey said colt ran too free (op 11-4)
Amadeus Wolfe Tone(IRE) was on a hat-trick after a couple of 7f wins, the first in a maiden on soft and then a nursery (off 7lb lower) on good to firm, but he failed to prove his effectiveness in these conditions. (op 9-2)
Always Eager sweated up and couldn't sustain his effort having led. (tchd 25-1)
Zakreet came here after two soft-ground wins, the latest over this trip off 6lb lower, but he ran poorly. He showed up to a point but dropped away in the straight as though something was amiss. Official explanation: vet said colt was struck into (tchd 4-1)

6830 BETFRED H'CAP (DIV I) 1m
4:45 (4:46) (Class 5) (0-75,75) 3-Y-O+ £2,587 (£770; £384; £192) Stalls Low

Form RPR

5101 1 **Smart Step**[18] 6415 3-8-4 61 oh1 SilvestreDeSousa 12 71
(Mark Johnston) *in tch: rdn over 2f out: led ins fnl f: styd on: on top cl home* **5/1**[2]

2116 2 ½ **Icy Blue**[44] 5621 3-9-0 71 SebSanders 10 80
(Richard Whitaker) *midfield: hdwy over 3f out: led 2f out: hdd ins fnl f: stl ev ch after: hld fnl strides* **12/1**

200 3 3¼ **Climaxfortackle (IRE)**[19] 6383 3-8-9 66 (v) NickyMackay 2 67+
(Derek Shaw) *midfield: hdwy over 2f out: chsd ldrs ins fnl f: styd on: no imp fnl 100yds* **28/1**

2522 4 1½ **Lockantanks**[8] 6658 4-8-13 67 RobbieFitzpatrick 13 65+
(Michael Appleby) *hld up: hdwy over 2f out: kpt on ins fnl f: no imp on ldrs* **17/2**

122 5 1¼ **Focail Eile**[2] 6796 6-9-7 75 FrederikTylicki 1 70
(John Ryan) *midfield: hdwy to chse ldrs over 2f out: no ex ins fnl f* **4/1**[1]

4001 6 ½ **Keys Of Cyprus**[29] 6081 9-8-12 73 ShirleyTeasdale(7) 11 67
(David Nicholls) *led early: remained handy: lost pl and outpcd over 3f out: kpt on same pce ins fnl f: no imp on ldrs* **14/1**

1134 7 ½ **Justbookie Dot Com (IRE)**[14] 6505 3-9-2 73 (v) GrahamGibbons 9 66
(David Evans) *trckd ldrs: rdn 2f out: one pce fr over 1f out* **20/1**

2410 8 4 **Daneside (IRE)**[25] 6219 4-8-13 72 MatthewLawson(5) 7 56
(Gary Harrison) *hld up: u.p over 3f out: nvr able to trble ldrs* **11/1**

233- 9 2½ **Highkingofireland**[459] 3950 5-8-7 61 oh2 MartinHarley 6 39
(Mrs K Burke) *bhd: nvr on terms* **7/1**[3]

4060 10 1¼ **Luv U Too**[29] 6078 3-9-3 74 TonyCulhane 5 49
(Jo Hughes) *sn led: rdn and hdd 2f out: wknd over 1f out* **20/1**

1100 11 1½ **Talent Scout (IRE)**[16] 6452 5-9-1 69 TomEaves 3 40
(Tim Walford) *racd keenly: a bhd* **16/1**

2005 12 11 **Burns Night**[41] 5728 5-9-5 73 RobertWinston 8 19
(Geoffrey Harker) *prom: rdn over 2f out: sn wknd* **25/1**

24-4 13 10 **Postscript (IRE)**[20] 6324 3-9-1 72 JamieSpencer 4 —
(Ian Williams) *a bhd* **7/1**[3]

1m 46.6s (3.70) **Going Correction** +0.35s/f (Good)
WFA 3 from 4yo+ 3lb **13 Ran SP% 117.6**
Speed ratings (Par 103): **95,94,91,89,88 88,87,83,81,79 78,67,57**
toteswingers: 1&2 £11.50, 2&3 £64.90, 1&3 £28.20 CSF £58.89 CT £1576.76 TOTE £4.50: £2.40, £3.90, £9.50; EX 73.80 TRIFECTA Not won..
Owner S R Counsell **Bred** Hascombe And Valiant Studs **Trained** Middleham Moor, N Yorks

FOCUS
The actual race distance was 1m 13yds. Given the bad ground it's hard to know how literally this form can be taken, but the winner is on the upgrade.
Justbookie Dot Com(IRE) Official explanation: jockey said gelding ran too free
Luv U Too Official explanation: jockey said filly had no more to give
Postscript(IRE) Official explanation: jockey said gelding had no more to give

6831 BETFRED H'CAP (DIV II) 1m
5:20 (5:22) (Class 5) (0-75,75) 3-Y-O+ £2,587 (£770; £384; £192) Stalls Low

Form RPR

2602 1 **The Osteopath (IRE)**[46] 5549 8-9-4 72 (p) PhillipMakin 9 83
(Michael Dods) *midfield: nt clr run and hdwy over 2f out: led 1f out: styd on to assert fnl 100yds* **10/1**

6304 2 1¾ **Maz**[28] 6116 3-8-1 61 DominicFox(3) 4 68
(Alan Bailey) *midfield: hmpd on inner 6f out: hdwy over 3f out: led wl over 1f out: hdd 1f out: kpt on same pce and hld fnl 110yds* **14/1**

4020 3 nk **Fazza**[20] 6346 4-9-2 75 GarryWhillans(5) 8 81
(Edwin Tuer) *trckd ldrs: effrt over 1f out: nt qckn ins fnl f: styd on towards fin: nt quite pce of first 2* **8/1**

5621 4 ¾ **Opus Maximus (IRE)**[17] 6433 6-8-10 67 (p) SophieDoyle(3) 3 71+
(Jennie Candlish) *s.s: bhd: hdwy 3f out: chsd ldrs over 1f out: kpt on ins fnl f: nt quite pce of ldrs* **9/2**[1]

3204 5 1¼ **Lion Court (IRE)**[45] 5602 3-8-11 68 SebSanders 1 69
(Sir Mark Prescott Bt) *sn led: rdn and hdd wl over 1f out: one pce fnl 120yds* **7/1**[3]

5540 6 6 **Spavento (IRE)**[41] 5721 5-8-7 61 (p) AndrewMullen 6 49
(Eric Alston) *in tch: rdn over 2f out: no ch fnl f* **14/1**

2000 7 9 **Ours (IRE)**[24] 6231 8-9-2 70 (p) StevieDonohoe 2 37
(John Harris) *hld up: rdn over 2f out: no imp* **20/1**

4350 8 1¼ **Maggie Mey (IRE)**[29] 6093 3-9-1 72 TomEaves 5 36
(Paul Midgley) *prom tl rdn and wknd 2f out* **16/1**

6150 9 2½ **Dazakhee**[9] 6621 4-8-10 64 TonyCulhane 12 22
(David Flood) *in rr: rdn 3f out: hung lft over 1f out: nvr on terms* **18/1**

0506 10 11 **Avonrose**[137] 2566 4-9-4 72 AdamKirby 10 —
(Derek Shaw) *midfield: wknd 2f out* **33/1**

0013 11 14 **Horatio Carter**[16] 6453 6-9-1 69 RobertWinston 11 —
(David O'Meara) *midfield: hdwy over 3f out: wl there over 2f out: hung lft and wknd over 1f out* **5/1**[2]

0620 12 1¾ **Georgebernardshaw (IRE)**[34] 5924 6-9-2 70 JamieSpencer 7 —
(John Quinn) *trckd ldrs tl wknd over 3f out* **8/1**

3500 13 ¾ **Frontline Girl (IRE)**[29] 6081 5-9-5 73 MartinHarley 13 —
(Mrs K Burke) *stmbld s: hld up: rdn over 3f out: nvr on terms w ldrs* **10/1**

1m 46.67s (3.77) **Going Correction** +0.35s/f (Good)
WFA 3 from 4yo+ 3lb **13 Ran SP% 119.9**
Speed ratings (Par 103): **95,93,92,92,90 84,75,74,72,61 47,45,44**
toteswingers: 1&2 £22.30, 2&3 £23.90, 1&3 £14.50 CSF £143.06 CT £1186.54 TOTE £13.00: £4.40, £4.50, £3.40; EX 104.40 TRIFECTA Not won..
Owner Kevin Kirkup **Bred** Joe Rogers **Trained** Denton, Co Durham
■ Stewards' Enquiry : Sophie Doyle 11-day ban: used whip with excessive frequency (Oct 28,29,31, Nov 1-5,9-11)

FOCUS
The actual race distance was 1m 13yds. This was just an ordinary handicap, run in a similar time to division I. The thirs sets the standard.
Horatio Carter Official explanation: jockey said gelding had no more to give
Georgebernardshaw(IRE) Official explanation: jockey said gelding had no more to give

Frontline Girl(IRE) Official explanation: jockey said mare lost its action

6832 THETRC.CO.UK H'CAP — 2m 45y
5:55 (5:57) (Class 4) (0-85,85) 3-Y-0+ — **£4,528** (£1,347; £673; £336) **Stalls** Low

Form — RPR

3111 **1** — **All My Heart**[35] 5897 3-9-3 **85** ... SebSanders 2 — 95
(Sir Mark Prescott Bt) *prom: rdn to chal over 2f out: led 1f out: styd on: in control fnl strides* **7/1**[3]

11 **2** ¾ **Taikoo**[28] 6115 6-9-11 **82** ... NickyMackay 5 — 91
(Hughie Morrison) *led: clr fr 12f out to 10f out: rdn and hdd 1f out: ev ch ins fnl f: kpt on: hld fnl strides* **9/1**

2513 **3** 2 ¼ **Jonny Delta**[26] 6191 4-8-11 **71** ... GaryBartley(3) 4 — 77
(Jim Goldie) *midfield: hdwy over 3f out: rdn to chse ldrs 2f out: chalng over 1f out: styd on same pce fnl 75yds* **7/1**[3]

4413 **4** 2 **Palazzo Bianco**[20] 6328 3-9-1 **83** ... WilliamBuick 9 — 87
(John Gosden) *handy: racd wd for 2f: chalng wl over 2f out: one pce fr over 1f out: edgd lft whn hld ins fnl f* **6/4**[1]

220 **5** 1 ½ **Defence Of Duress (IRE)**[98] 3828 3-8-12 **80** ... JamieSpencer 1 — 82
(Tom Tate) *midfield: rdn over 2f out: kpt on ins fnl f: no imp on ldrs* **5/1**[2]

0420 **6** ½ **Kayef (GER)**[118] 3157 4-9-8 **84** ... DavidKenny(5) 10 — 86
(Michael Scudamore) *s.s: hld up: pushed along over 3f out: kpt on ins fnl f: no imp* **25/1**

000- **7** hd **Nezhenka**[318] 7648 4-10-0 **85** ... SilvestreDeSousa 11 — 86
(Mark Johnston) *ponied to s: hld up: hdwy over 3f out: chsd ldrs over 2f out: one pce over 1f out: no imp fnl f* **33/1**

4146 **8** 34 **Red Fama**[31] 6024 7-9-6 **77** ... SteveDrowne 7 — 37
(Neville Bycroft) *hld up: rdn 3f out: nvr on terms w ldrs* **22/1**

0010 **9** 25 **L Frank Baum (IRE)**[6] 6690 4-9-7 **78** ... RobertWinston 6 — —
(Gay Kelleway) *midfield: hdwy to go cl up 1/2-way: rdn over 4f out: wknd 3f out: t.o* **10/1**

10 4 **Moghaayer**[176] 6-9-2 **73** ... (p) PhillipMakin 3 — —
(James Moffatt) *prom: lost pl 9f out: bhd over 5f out: eased whn wl btn over 1f out: t.o* **100/1**

1-30 **11** 4 **Ocean Transit (IRE)**[126] 2888 6-9-8 **79** ow2 ... JamesDoyle 12 — —
(Richard Price) *hld up: struggling 5f out: eased whn wl btn over 2f out: t.o* **18/1**

3m 39.36s (3.36) **Going Correction** +0.35s/f (Good)
WFA 3 from 4yo+ 11lb — **11** Ran SP% **118.1**
Speed ratings (Par 105): **105,104,103,102,101 101,101,84,71,69 67**
toteswingers: 1&2 £2.70, 2&3 £8.20, 1&3 £8.20 CSF £66.08 CT £462.41 TOTE £6.80: £2.50, £2.20, £2.30; EX 41.10 Trifecta £87.30 Pool: £620.59 - 5.26 winning units..
Owner Miss K Rausing **Bred** Miss K Rausing And Shellin Blk **Trained** Newmarket, Suffolk
■ Stewards' Enquiry : Gary Bartley three-day ban: weighed in 2lb heavy (Oct 28,29,31)

FOCUS
The actual race distance was 2m 58yds. The form looks good for the level, the winner stepping up on her AW wins. It was a real test on the ground.
Red Fama Official explanation: jockey said gelding had no more to give
Ocean Transit(IRE) Official explanation: vet said mare finished lame
T/Plt: £73.00 to a £1 stake. Pool of £56,403.56 - 563.63 winning tickets. T/Qpdt: £14.70 to a £1 stake. Pool of £4,361.31 - 218.60 winning tickets. DO

6532 REDCAR (L-H)
Friday, October 14

OFFICIAL GOING: Straight course - good to soft (soft in places); round course - soft (good to soft in places)
Wind: Light half behind Weather: Overcast

6833 FOLLOW REDCARRACING ON FACEBOOK & TWITTER LADIES' H'CAP (FOR LADY AMATEUR RIDERS) — 1m 2f
1:30 (1:34) (Class 6) (0-60,60) 3-Y-0+ — **£1,646** (£506; £253) **Stalls** Low

Form — RPR

0000 **1** — **My Mate Jake (IRE)**[27] 6181 3-9-11 **60** ... MissAZetterholm(5) 12 — 71
(James Given) *trckd ldrs: hdwy 3f out: chal wl over 1f out and sn ev ch: rdn to ld ins fnl f: kpt on* **10/1**

0060 **2** 1 **Call Of Duty (IRE)**[24] 6236 6-9-13 **55** ... MissECSayer(3) 10 — 64
(Dianne Sayer) *[illegible] out: rdn to ld 1f out: hdd and no ex ins fnl f* **11/1**

2101 **3** 2 ¾ **Market Puzzle (IRE)**[21] 6295 4-10-1 **59** ... (p) MissBeckyBrisbourne(5) 6 — 63
(Mark Brisbourne) *a.p: effrt and cl up over 2f out: rdn: sltly outpcd and swtchd rt over 1f out: kpt on ins fnl f* **4/1**[1]

010 **4** 1 **Dean Iarracht (IRE)**[13] 6538 5-10-0 **58** ... (p) MissAngelaBarnes(5) 3 — 63+
(Tracy Waggott) *dwlt and hld up in rr: hdwy on inner whn n.m.r and hmpd 3f out: swtchd rt over 2f out: effrt on outer wl over 1f out: sn rdn and styd on wl fnl f: nrst fin* **9/1**

6000 **5** nk **Cool Baranca (GER)**[48] 5107 5-9-5 **51** ... MissRobynGray(7) 13 — 52
(Dianne Sayer) *cl up: led after 2f: rdn along 3f out: drvn over 1f out: sn hdd and grad wknd* **18/1**

5144 **6** ½ **Edas**[16] 6453 9-10-4 **60** ... MissHCuthbert(3) 9 — 60
(Thomas Cuthbert) *in tch: hdwy to trck ldrs over 4f out: effrt over 2f out: rdn to chal wl over 1f out and ev ch tl one pce appr fnl f* **5/1**[2]

4603 **7** 1 ¼ **Spread Boy (IRE)**[18] 6417 4-9-5 **49** ... MissPhillipaTutty(5) 5 — 46
(Alan Berry) *prom: rdn along over 3f out: grad wknd* **25/1**

5010 **8** 2 ½ **Harare**[15] 6486 10-9-9 **53** ... (v) MissGTutty(5) 8 — 45
(Karen Tutty) *in tch: rdn along over 3f out: grad wknd fnl 2f* **10/1**

4530 **9** 2 ¼ **Media Stars**[14] 5822 6-9-12 **56** ... MissCWalton(5) 7 — 44
(Robert Johnson) *prom: rdn along 3f out: sn wknd* **22/1**

504 **10** ¾ **Visions Of Johanna (USA)**[15] 6486 6-9-13 **52** ..(tp) MissSBrotherton 15 — 38
(Richard Guest) *nvr bttr than midfield* **7/1**[3]

004 **11** 1 ½ **Tropical Duke (IRE)**[24] 6235 5-9-2 **46** ... MissVBarr(5) 2 — 29
(Ron Barr) *hld up towards rr: sme hdwy over 2f out: sn rdn and nvr a factor* **12/1**

50-0 **12** 10 **Sandy Lonnen**[3] 6781 3-9-6 **55** ... MissCarlyFrater(5) 1 — 18
(Colin Teague) *plld hrd in midfield: rdn along and hung lft 3f out: sn wknd* **40/1**

300- **13** 19 **Moonbalej**[12] 7690 4-9-12 **58** ow3 ... MissSMDoolan(7) 14 — —
(Wilf Storey) *led 2f: cl up tl rdn along over 3f out and sn wknd* **22/1**

0-06 **14** 31 **Ten To The Dozen**[16] 6452 8-9-8 **47** ... MissLHorner 4 — —
(David Thompson) *a in rr: bhd fnl 3f* **25/1**

2m 12.9s (5.80) **Going Correction** +0.175s/f (Good)
WFA 3 from 4yo+ 5lb — **14** Ran SP% **116.1**
Speed ratings (Par 101): **83,82,80,79,78 78,77,75,73,73 71,63,48,23**
toteswingers: 1&2 £56.60, 2&3 £14.00, 1&3 £12.40 CSF £103.82 CT £515.93 TOTE £14.40: £3.30, £4.40, £2.10; EX 193.00.
Owner Alex Owen **Bred** Crandon Park Stud **Trained** Willoughton, Lincs
■ Amanda Zetterholm's first winner in Britain.

FOCUS
A rock bottom lady amateur riders' handicap run at a strong pace in the conditions. The winner's best form this year, close to his 2yo best.
Tropical Duke(IRE) Official explanation: jockey said gelding never travelled

6834 RACING UK ON SKY 432 MAIDEN STKS (DIV I) — 6f
2:00 (2:03) (Class 5) 3-Y-0+ — **£3,493** (£1,039; £519; £259) **Stalls** Centre

Form — RPR

1 — **Dream The Blues (IRE)** 3-8-12 0 ... PaulHanagan 3 — 70+
(Kevin Ryan) *dwlt: sn prom: cl up 1/2-way: pushed along and green over 2f out: rdn to ld wl over 1f out and sn edgd rt: kpt on fnl f* **1/1**[1]

2220 **2** 1 **Vizean (IRE)**[19] 6381 3-8-9 67 ... DaleSwift(3) 5 — 66
(John Mackie) *led: rdn along over 2f out: hdd wl over 1f out: kpt on u.p fnl f* **3/1**[2]

23 **3** 1 ¾ **Cool Rhythm**[20] 6353 3-9-3 0 ... DanielTudhope 10 — 66
(David O'Meara) *cl up: rdn along and ch 2f out: sn hung lft and one pce fnl f* **6/1**[3]

500 **4** 1 ½ **Eqtiraab (IRE)**[20] 6324 3-9-3 55 ... BarryMcHugh 1 — 61
(Tony Coyle) *in tch: rdn along wl over 2f out: kpt on u.p fnl f* **20/1**

65 **5** hd **Maven**[27] 6156 3-8-12 0 ... DuranFentiman 4 — 55
(Tim Easterby) *in tch: hdwy to chse ldrs over 2f out: sn rdn and kpt on same pce appr fnl f* **33/1**

4004 **6** 2 ¾ **Uddy Mac**[10] 6602 4-8-6 55 ... (b) TerenceFury(7) 8 — 47
(Neville Bycroft) *trckd ldrs: rdn along over 2f out: sn one pce* **50/1**

03 **7** 8 **Violet's Gift (IRE)**[43] 5649 3-8-12 0 ... EddieAhern 11 — 21
(James Fanshawe) *in tch on outer: rdn along 1/2-way: sn wknd* **9/1**

0-3 **8** ½ **Avoncharm**[39] 5793 3-8-12 0 ... DavidAllan 2 — 19
(Mel Brittain) *cl up: rdn along over 2f out: drvn wl over 1f out and sn wknd* **25/1**

0650 **9** shd **King Bertolini (IRE)**[10] 6602 4-9-4 42 ... PatrickMathers 7 — 24
(Alan Berry) *s.i.s: a bhd* **150/1**

10 14 **Mustafeed (USA)** 3-9-3 0 ... JoeFanning 6 — —
(Keith Dalgleish) *s.i.s: a bhd* **20/1**

1m 11.81s (0.01) **Going Correction** +0.175s/f (Good)
WFA 3 from 4yo 1lb — **10** Ran SP% **118.2**
Speed ratings (Par 103): **106,104,102,100,100 96,85,85,84,66**
toteswingers: 1&2 £1.70, 2&3 £3.40, 1&3 £3.30 CSF £3.69 TOTE £2.40: £1.40, £1.10, £1.50; EX 6.10.
Owner John Halley **Bred** Mrs Helen Keaveney **Trained** Hambleton, N Yorks

FOCUS
A weak sprint maiden but a winning newcomer of some potential. The second was rated to her recent efforts.
Violet's Gift(IRE) Official explanation: jockey said filly hung right

6835 MARKET CROSS JEWELLERS CLAIMING STKS — 7f
2:35 (2:35) (Class 6) 2-Y-0 — **£1,704** (£503; £251) **Stalls** Centre

Form — RPR

0200 **1** — **Daddy Warbucks (IRE)**[28] 6110 2-8-7 64 ... AdrianNicholls 1 — 68
(David Nicholls) *cl up: effrt wl over 1f out: rdn to ld ins fnl f: styd on* **2/1**[2]

1365 **2** 1 ¾ **Artists Corner**[8] 6652 2-7-12 62 ... (b1) PaulHanagan 4 — 54
(Richard Fahey) *s.i.s and in rr: hdwy after 2f out: chsd ldrs 3f out: rdn along 2f out: styd on to ld jst over 1f out: drvn and hdd ins fnl f: no ex* **15/8**[1]

5030 **3** 2 ¼ **Dylan's Dream (IRE)**[9] 6627 2-8-2 48 ... DuranFentiman 5 — 53
(Tim Easterby) *led: rdn along 2f out: drvn and hdd appr fnl f: kpt on same pce* **18/1**

0141 **4** 1 ¾ **Latte**[8] 6652 2-8-13 70 ... (p) DarryllHolland 9 — 59
(Linda Stubbs) *prom: rdn along over 2f out: drvn wl over 1f out and sn one pce* **4/1**[3]

0040 **5** 3 **Arrowroot**[43] 5645 2-8-5 49 ... (b1) KellyHarrison 10 — 43
(Tim Easterby) *chsd ldrs: rdn along wl over 2f out: grad wknd* **16/1**

400 **6** 1 ¾ **Latenfast**[7] 6675 2-8-0 0 ... (b1) DeclanCannon(3) 2 — 37
(Michael Easterby) *in tch: rdn along 1/2-way: outpcd fr wl over 2f out* **25/1**

0600 **7** 1 **Lizzie Drippin**[7] 6675 2-7-7 37 ... NeilFarley(5) 6 — 29
(Michael Easterby) *a towards rr* **20/1**

8 ¾ **Covington (IRE)** 2-8-9 0 ... TonyHamilton 8 — 38
(Ann Duffield) *a in rr* **16/1**

4000 **9** 1 ¼ [illegible] (IRE)[17] [illegible] ... [illegible] — [illegible]
(Julie Camacho) *chsd ldrs: rdn along 1/2-way: sn wknd* **66/1**

1m 25.73s (1.23) **Going Correction** +0.175s/f (Good) — **9** Ran SP% **115.2**
Speed ratings (Par 93): **99,97,94,92,89 87,85,85,83**
toteswingers: 1&2 £1.80, 2&3 £3.70, 1&3 £9.10 CSF £5.97 TOTE £3.80: £1.10, £1.10, £4.70; EX 7.30.
Owner Martin Love **Bred** Edmond Kent **Trained** Sessay, N Yorks

FOCUS
A late-season claimer with the first four places filled by relatively exposed horses, the winner the least so.

NOTEBOOK
Daddy Warbucks(IRE), runner-up in a maiden over this trip at Musselburgh on his second start, had taken his chance in two better races since. Quite keen upsides, in the end he saw it out better than the runner-up who would have been 5lb better off with him in a handicap. (op 11-4)
Artists Corner, having her ninth start and with Paul Hanagan down to his bare minimum, wore blinkers for the first time. After a tardy start she raced upsides over a furlong out, but in the end had to settle for second spot. This is as good as she is now. (tchd 2-1)
Dylan's Dream(IRE), who had 11lb to find with the winner, ran her best race so far on her seventh start. On this she would win a seller. (op 20-1)
Latte, winner of two sellers since cheekpieces were fitted, is unproven on soft ground and looked uncomfortable on it. (op 3-1)
Latenfast Official explanation: jockey said gelding hung right

6836 BRITISH STALLION STUDS SUPPORTING BRITISH RACING E B F MAIDEN STKS — 6f
3:10 (3:11) (Class 5) 2-Y-0 — **£2,975** (£885; £442; £221) **Stalls** Centre

Form — RPR

026 **1** — **Master Bond**[7] 6673 2-9-3 0 ... JoeFanning 4 — 72+
(Bryan Smart) *chsd ldrs: hdwy over 2f out: rdn to chal jst over 1f out: styd on to ld last 100yds: jst hld on* **7/5**[1]

034 **2** shd **Takealookatmenow (IRE)**[21] 6291 2-8-12 58 ... AdrianNicholls 10 — 67
(David Nicholls) *cl up: led after 2f: rdn along 2f out: drvn over 1f out: hdd last 100yds: rallied wl nr fin: jst failed* **14/1**

4 **3** 3 ½ **Springheel Jake**[13] 6532 2-9-3 0 ... DavidNolan 11 — 61
(Ann Duffield) *trckd ldrs: cl up 1/2-way: rdn and ev ch whn edgd lft 2f out: kpt on same pce fnl f* **15/2**[3]

0643 **4** 2 **Headstight (IRE)**[19] 6384 2-8-12 50 ... MickyFenton 1 — 50
(Paul Midgley) *prom on outer: effrt and ev ch 2f out: sn rdn and one pce appr fnl f* **20/1**

00 **5** *nse* **Phoenician Blaze**[62] 5029 2-8-9 0 .... MichaelO'Connell(3) 8 50
(Tim Etherington) *led 2f: prom: rdn along over 2f out: sn one pce* **200/1**

6 *nk* **Hawks Reef** 2-9-3 0 .... PaulHanagan 7 54
(Richard Fahey) *s.i.s: hdwy to trck ldrs after 1 1/2f: chsd ldrs whn n.m.r and swtchd rt 2f out: sn rdn and no imp* **4/1**[2]

0200 **7** *3/4* **Premier Choice**[44] 5618 2-9-3 69 .... DavidAllan 6 52
(Tim Easterby) *prom: rdn along over 2f out: grad wknd* **15/2**[3]

0 **8** *1/2* **Malvesi**[82] 4365 2-9-3 0 .... DarryllHolland 5 50
(Ann Duffield) *towards rr: rdn along 1/2-way: n.d* **100/1**

6 **9** *1 1/2* **Seattle Sounder (IRE)**[16] 6448 2-9-0 0 .... DaleSwift(3) 3 46
(Ann Duffield) *cl up: rdn along 1/2-way: sn wknd* **16/1**

10 *7* **Dark Ruler (IRE)** 2-9-3 0 .... PJMcDonald 2 25
(Alan Swinbank) *s.i.s: a in rr* **20/1**

11 *nk* **Homework** 2-9-3 0 .... TonyHamilton 9 24
(Richard Fahey) *s.i.s: a bhd* **20/1**

1m 12.6s (0.80) **Going Correction** +0.175s/f (Good) **11** Ran SP% **113.5**
Speed ratings (Par 95): **101,100,96,93,93 93,92,91,89,80 79**
toteswingers: 1&2 £4.80, 2&3 £7.20, 1&3 £3.10 CSF £21.06 TOTE £2.30: £1.20, £1.60, £2.00; EX 20.60.
Owner Bonded Twentyten Partnership **Bred** Bond Thoroughbred Corporation **Trained** Hambleton, N Yorks

FOCUS
An ordinary juvenile maiden with the first two pulling clear.

NOTEBOOK
Master Bond, runner-up to a now 79-rated winner here, had pulled much too hard after taking a bump at the start at York a week earlier. He settled better but in the end it was a very close run thing. He should make a better sprint handicapper at three. (op 6-4 tchd 11-8)
Takealookatmenow(IRE) is all speed. To her credit she fought hard all the way to the line. Rated just 58 going into this, her nursery mark will go up by about 10lb. (op 10-1)
Springheel Jake, fourth over 7f here on his debut two weeks earlier, improved on that effort, but is the type to do better over a mile plus at three. (op 8-1)
Headstight(IRE), having her sixth start, showed plenty of toe. Rated just 50, low-grade nurseries would surely be a better option, but she will struggle to find opportunities.
Phoenician Blaze, 200-1 and ahead of just one horse in two previous tries over further, stayed on in dour fashion after getting tapped for toe at halfway. This was much more encouraging and qualifies her for a handicap mark.
Hawks Reef, a half-brother to two winners, missed the break. Left alone towards the stands' side, he was picking up in encouraging fashion at the line. (op 9-2)

6837 HOLD YOUR CHRISTMAS PARTY @ REDCAR RACECOURSE MEDIAN AUCTION MAIDEN STKS 1m
3:45 (3:45) (Class 6) 2-Y-O **£1,704** (£503; £251) **Stalls** Centre

Form RPR

5 **1** **Willie Wag Tail (USA)**[25] 6216 2-9-3 0 .... J-PGuillambert 2 80+
(Ed Walker) *dwlt and hld up in rr: stdy hdwy over 3f out: chsd ldr 2f out: rdn to ld ent fnl f: styd on strly* **3/1**[3]

433 **2** *3 1/4* **Final Delivery**[35] 5899 2-9-3 74 .... AndreaAtzeni 5 71
(Marco Botti) *cl up: led 2f out: rdn over 1f out: hdd ent fnl f: kpt on same pce* **5/2**[1]

05 **3** *2* **Crossley**[22] 6274 2-9-0 0 .... DaleSwift(3) 1 66
(Geoffrey Oldroyd) *chsd ldrs on outer: rdn along wl over 1f out: kpt on same pce fnl f* **7/1**

6 **4** *4 1/2* **Le King Beau (USA)**[13] 6532 2-9-3 0 .... BarryMcHugh 4 56
(Tony Coyle) *led: rdn along over 2f out: sn hdd and grad wknd* **11/4**[2]

5 *3* **No Time To Cry** 2-8-12 0 .... TonyHamilton 7 44
(Ann Duffield) *trckd ldrs: pushed along over 3f out: rdn wl over 2f out: sn wknd* **14/1**

6 *nk* **Going Grey (IRE)** 2-9-3 0 .... PaulHanagan 8 48
(Richard Fahey) *dwlt: chsd ldrs: pushed along wl over 2f out: sn wknd* **7/1**

0 **7** *8* **Blackamoor Zara**[13] 6539 2-8-12 0 .... JoeFanning 3 25
(Bruce Hellier) *prom: chsd ldng pair over 3f out: sn rdn and wknd* **100/1**

1m 39.42s (1.42) **Going Correction** +0.175s/f (Good) **7** Ran SP% **112.9**
Speed ratings (Par 93): **99,95,93,89,86 85,77**
toteswingers: 1&2 £3.80, 2&3 £2.80, 1&3 £3.40 CSF £10.65 TOTE £4.30: £2.30, £1.60; EX 10.60.
Owner One Carat Partnership **Bred** Derry Meeting Farm & London Thoroughbred Services **Trained** Newmarket, Suffolk

FOCUS
They came home well strung out and the winner looks set to build on this clear-cut victory.

NOTEBOOK
Willie Wag Tail(USA), a promising fifth when sent off at 50-1 on his Polytrack debut at Kempton, was anchored in the rear. He swept to the front and shot clear. His handicap mark should be in the low 80s and this quite big type looks sure to make a decent handicapper at three. (op 11-4 tchd 5-2)
Final Delivery, rated 74 after finishing third in two all-weather maidens, does nothing wrong and deserves to break his duck. (op 9-4 tchd 10-3)
Crossley, up in trip, came in for support after showing ability when forced to race wide on his second start at Pontefract. He found himself rather isolated towards the far side but in the end came up well short. (op 14-1)
Le King Beau(USA), who showed ability on his debut here, took them along travelling strongly but rather fell in a heap in the end. The ground may well have been against him at this early stage of his development. (tchd 2-1 and 3-1)
No Time To Cry made a satisfactory debut and will do better given more time. (op 16-1 tchd 12-1)
Going Grey(IRE), bred for speed rather than stamina, made his debut over a mile. He was very inexperienced and looked some way off the finished article. He will surely show in a better light at three. (op 8-1)

6838 SAM HALL MEMORIAL H'CAP 1m 6f 19y
4:20 (4:20) (Class 5) (0-75,75) 3-Y-O+ **£2,264** (£673; £336; £168) **Stalls** Low

Form RPR

5134 **1** **Countrywide Flame**[46] 5064 3-8-13 72 .... DaleSwift(3) 8 87
(John Quinn) *mde all: pushed along 3f out: rdn and qcknd wl over 1f out: styd on wl fnl f* **9/4**[1]

/06- **2** *1 3/4* **Categorical**[174] 7145 8-8-6 56 oh2 .... DeclanCannon(3) 2 68
(Keith Reveley) *trckd ldrs: hdwy 3f out: chsd wnr wl over 1f out: sn rdn and kpt on fnl f* **20/1**

0102 **3** *6* **Brasingaman Eric**[22] 6279 4-8-13 60 .... PJMcDonald 1 64
(George Moore) *trckd ldrs: hdwy 4f out: chsd ldng pair wl over 1f out: sn rdn and kpt on same pce* **13/2**[2]

1503 **4** *3 3/4* **Chookie Hamilton**[19] 6385 7-10-0 75 .... JoeFanning 5 74
(Keith Dalgleish) *a chsng wnr: hdwy and cl up 3f out: rdn and ev ch 2f out: sn drvn and grad wknd* **8/1**

1205 **5** *1 1/4* **Dark Dune (IRE)**[21] 6294 3-9-0 70 .... DavidAllan 10 67
(Tim Easterby) *hld up towards rr: hdwy over 3f out: rdn to chse ldrs 2f out: sn edgd lft and no imp* **13/2**[2]

314 **6** *3/4* **Al Furat (USA)**[27] 6153 3-8-8 64 .... BarryMcHugh 4 60
(Ron Barr) *hld up towards rr: hdwy 4f out: chsd ldrs over 2f out: sn rdn and no imp* **7/1**[3]

5404 **7** *nk* **Simple Jim (FR)**[20] 6356 7-8-4 56 oh1 .... AshleyMorgan(5) 7 52
(David O'Meara) *hld up in rr: sme hdwy wl over 2f out: sn rdn and nvr a factor* **12/1**

1030 **8** *4 1/2* **Maybeme**[7] 6676 5-8-6 60 .... TerenceFury(7) 6 49
(Neville Bycroft) *hld up: a in rr* **14/1**

0430 **9** *9* **Fairest Isle (IRE)**[9] 6621 3-8-7 63 ow1 .... (t) EddieAhern 3 40
(James Fanshawe) *chsd ldrs: rdn along 4f out: wknd 3f out* **12/1**

0132 **10** *13* **Daytime Dreamer (IRE)**[17] 6157 7-8-10 60 .... LeeTopliss(3) 9 18
(Martin Todhunter) *in tch: rdn along over 4f out: sn wknd* **16/1**

3m 7.73s (3.03) **Going Correction** +0.175s/f (Good)
WFA 3 from 4yo+ 9lb **10** Ran SP% **113.7**
Speed ratings (Par 103): **98,97,93,91,90 90,90,87,82,74**
toteswingers: 1&2 £14.20, 2&3 £26.80, 1&3 £4.20 CSF £52.11 CT £256.55 TOTE £3.10: £1.10, £5.50, £2.70; EX 81.80.
Owner Estio Pinnacle Racing **Bred** Michael Clarke **Trained** Settrington, N Yorks
■ Stewards' Enquiry : Declan Cannon five-day ban: excessive use of whip (Oct 29,31,Nov 1-3)

FOCUS
A competitive stayers' handicap and a fine front-running ride by Dale Swift. The winner improved but this was not strong form for the grade.

6839 RACING UK ON SKY 432 MAIDEN STKS (DIV II) 6f
4:55 (4:55) (Class 5) 3-Y-O+ **£3,493** (£1,039; £519; £259) **Stalls** Centre

Form RPR

1 **Magic Secret** 3-9-3 0 .... MickyFenton 9 83+
(Jeremy Gask) *dwlt: hdwy and in tch after 2f: chal on bit 2f out: led 1 1/2f out: sn clr* **9/1**[3]

4045 **2** *11* **Bailadeira**[97] 3860 3-8-9 56 .... MichaelO'Connell(3) 3 45
(Tim Etherington) *led: rdn along and jnd 2f out: hdd 1/2f out: sn one pce* **6/1**[2]

244 **3** *2* **Wadha (IRE)**[15] 6473 3-8-12 72 .... (p) DarryllHolland 6 39
(Saeed Bin Suroor) *sn pushed along towards rr: rdn along 1/2-way: kpt on fr over 1f out to take remote 3rd nr fin* **4/9**[1]

400- **4** *1/2* **Cerejeira (IRE)**[328] 7528 3-8-12 46 .... DavidAllan 5 38
(Eric Alston) *a.p: effrt and cl up over 2f out: sn rdn and wknd over 1f out* **20/1**

00-5 **5** *nk* **Northgate Lodge (USA)**[30] 6050 6-8-11 44 .... JohnCavanagh(7) 2 42
(Mel Brittain) *prom: chsd ldr 1/2-way: rdn along over 2f out and sn wknd* **10/1**

000 **6** *2* **Stella Marris**[49] 5443 4-8-13 47 .... (p) PaddyAspell 7 31
(Christopher Wilson) *chsd ldrs: rdn along over 2f out: sn wknd* **28/1**

3006 **7** *3/4* **Chardonnay Star (IRE)**[43] 5649 4-8-10 45 .... (v) DaleSwift(3) 1 28
(Colin Teague) *sn pushed along towards rr: rdn 1/2-way: sn outpcd and bhd* **25/1**

8 *23* **Irish Law** 3-9-0 0 .... RobertLButler(3) 10 —
(John Balding) *a towards rr: rdn along 1/2-way: sn outpcd and bhd* **20/1**

060 **9** *11* **Indigo Sands (IRE)**[51] 5368 3-9-3 36 .... PatrickMathers 4 —
(Alan Berry) *towards rr: rdn along 1/2-way: sn outpcd and bhd* **100/1**

1m 13.09s (1.29) **Going Correction** +0.175s/f (Good)
WFA 3 from 4yo+ 1lb **9** Ran SP% **120.4**
Speed ratings (Par 103): **98,83,80,80,79 76,75,45,30**
toteswingers: 1&2 £2.90, 2&3 £1.80, 1&3 £2.40 CSF £58.64 TOTE £8.50: £1.90, £1.60, £1.02; EX 72.90.
Owner Carmel Stud **Bred** Carmel Stud **Trained** Sutton Veny, Wilts

FOCUS
Part two of the sprint maiden, and the slower of the pair although the ground seemed to worsen. Another weak affair and another newcomer winner of real potential. It is hard to know what he achieved.

6840 GO RACING AT CATTERICK TOMORROW H'CAP 7f
5:30 (5:30) (Class 5) (0-70,70) 3-Y-O **£1,940** (£577; £288; £144) **Stalls** Centre

Form RPR

3210 **1** **Green Howard**[24] 6231 3-9-7 70 .... DanielTudhope 4 83
(Robin Bastiman) *a.p: hdwy 2f out: rdn to ld ent fnl f: sn edgd rt and kpt on* **8/1**[3]

6563 **2** *1/2* **Le Chat D'Or**[50] 5403 3-8-10 59 .... PJMcDonald 3 70
(Michael Dods) *trckd ldrs: hdwy 3f out: swtchd rt and rdn over 1f out: styd on wl fnl f* **13/2**[2]

5U40 **3** *1/2* **Beautiful Day**[35] 5895 3-8-7 56 oh1 .... BarryMcHugh 17 66
(Kevin Ryan) *trckd ldrs: hdwy to ld 2f out: rdn over 1f out: hdd ent fnl f: no ex last 100yds* **20/1**

0 **4** *2 1/4* **Qubuh (IRE)**[28] 6116 3-9-2 65 .... DarryllHolland 5 69
(Linda Stubbs) *led: rdn along and hdd 2f out: one pce appr fnl f* **20/1**

2420 **5** *2 1/2* **Barista (IRE)**[13] 6544 3-9-4 70 .... MichaelO'Connell(3) 6 68
(Mick Channon) *in tch: hdwy to chse ldrs 3f out: rdn over 2f out: kpt on same pce appr fnl f* **8/1**[3]

0564 **6** *1/2* **Izzet**[30] 6050 3-8-7 56 oh2 .... PatrickMathers 10 52
(Ron Barr) *chsd ldrs: rdn along over 2f out: kpt on same pce* **25/1**

0000 **7** *1/2* **Insolenceofoffice (IRE)**[22] 6283 3-8-11 60 .... (p) JoeFanning 12 55
(Bruce Hellier) *hld up towards rr: hdwy over 2f out: rdn wl over 1f out: sn no imp* **40/1**

1260 **8** *6* **Rowan Spirit (IRE)**[41] 5735 3-9-5 68 .... EddieAhern 13 47
(Mark Brisbourne) *towards rr: hdwy after 2f: pushed along to chse ldrs 2f out: sn rdn and wknd* **14/1**

1100 **9** *nk* **Last Destination (IRE)**[28] 6116 3-8-12 68 .... DanielleMooney(7) 2 47
(Nigel Tinkler) *in rr tl sme late hdwy* **33/1**

0062 **10** *1/2* **Uncle Bryn**[18] 6415 3-9-0 63 .... PBBeggy 7 40
(John Quinn) *dwlt and sn pushed along into midfield: effrt and in tch over 2f out: sn rdn and btn* **7/2**[1]

6454 **11** *1/2* **Breezolini**[16] 6450 3-9-4 70 .... AmyRyan(3) 9 46
(Richard Whitaker) *dwlt and towards rr: pushed along and sme hdwy 3f out: sn rdn and nvr a factor* **9/1**

0200 **12** *2* **Cottam Stella**[65] 4902 3-8-8 57 oh7 ow1 .... DavidAllan 8 28
(Mel Brittain) *a towards rr* **40/1**

0022 **13** *2 3/4* **Hoppy's Flyer (FR)**[27] 6158 3-9-4 67 .... MickyFenton 14 31
(Paul Midgley) *a towards rr* **10/1**

0220 **14** *nk* **The Buska (IRE)**[41] 5731 3-8-11 67 .... JasonHart(7) 15 30
(Declan Carroll) *midfield: pushed along 1/2-way: sn rdn and n.d* **14/1**

3453 **15** *1 1/4* **Lady Del Sol**[23] 6261 3-8-11 63 .... (p) RobertLButler(3) 16 23
(Marjorie Fife) *a in rr* **14/1**

021 **16** *4* **Ingenti**[44] 5620 3-8-7 **56** oh1 .... PaddyAspell 11 5
(Christopher Wilson) *t.k.h: cl up: rdn along over 2f out: sn wknd* **20/1**

1m 26.9s (2.40) **Going Correction** +0.175s/f (Good) **16** Ran SP% **122.8**
Speed ratings (Par 101): **93,92,91,89,86 85,85,78,78,77 76,74,71,71,69 65**
toteswingers: 1&2 £11.10, 2&3 £30.70, 1&3 £44.30 CSF £54.12 CT £1057.52 TOTE £11.40: £2.60, £2.50, £6.40, £4.90; EX 74.30.
Owner Ms M Austerfield **Bred** Miss A J Rawding & P M Crane **Trained** Cowthorpe, N Yorks

FOCUS
A modest 50-70 finale and little to choose between the first three. The winner is rated in line with his maiden best.
Uncle Bryn Official explanation: jockey said gelding never travelled
T/Plt: £12.60 to a £1 stake. Pool of £49,038.40 - 2,832.27 winning tickets. T/Qpdt: £6.50 to a £1 stake. Pool of £3,739.17 - 423.65 winning tickets. JR

6694 WOLVERHAMPTON (A.W) (L-H)

Friday, October 14

OFFICIAL GOING: Standard
Wind: Almost nil Weather: Fine and sunny

6841 RINGSIDE CONFERENCE VENUE APPRENTICE H'CAP 5f 216y(P)
5:50 (5:51) (Class 6) (0-65,65) 3-Y-O+ **£1,908** (£563; £281) **Stalls** Low

Form RPR
3000 **1** **Haadeeth**[29] 6076 4-8-12 **63** .... (b) GeorgeChaloner(5) 5 74
(Richard Fahey) *chsd ldrs: led over 1f out: edgd lft ins fnl f: pushed out* **11/1**
5031 **2** *1 3/4* **Trojan Rocket (IRE)**[21] 6304 3-9-0 **61** .... RyanPowell 4 66+
(George Prodromou) *sn pushed along in rr: r.o wl fnl f: wnt 2nd post: nt rch wnr* **13/2**[3]
4000 **3** *shd* **Defector (IRE)**[8] 6655 5-9-0 **65** .... BrendanPowell(5) 12 70+
(Seamus Durack) *hld up: hdwy over 1f out: sn rdn: r.o* **8/1**
5635 **4** *shd* **Interchoice Star**[22] 6282 6-9-0 **63** .... (p) CharlesBishop(3) 6 68
(Ray Peacock) *hld up: hdwy 1/2-way: rdn to chse wnr fnl f: styd on same pce: lost 2 pls nr fin* **15/2**
5001 **5** *1 3/4* **Penny's Pearl (IRE)**[14] 6502 3-9-3 **64** .... MatthewCosham 8 63
(David Evans) *chsd ldrs: rdn over 1f out: no ex ins fnl f* **9/1**
2551 **6** *nse* **Silver Wind**[6] 6694 6-9-3 **63** 6ex .... (b) ShaneBKelly 7 62
(Alan McCabe) *sn pushed along in rr: rdn over 1f out: styd on ins fnl f: nt trble ldrs* **9/2**[1]
3050 **7** *1/2* **Kinigi (IRE)**[11] 6580 5-9-0 **63** .... (b) RaulDaSilva(3) 2 60
(Ronald Harris) *led 1f: chsd ldrs: hmpd and lost pl over 3f out: hdwy over 1f out: styd on same pce ins fnl f* **18/1**
0006 **8** *1/2* **Takajan (IRE)**[35] 5895 4-8-13 **62** .... RachealKneller(3) 1 58
(Mark Brisbourne) *s.i.s: sn mid-div: hdwy over 2f out: rdn over 1f out: no ex ins fnl f* **25/1**
1264 **9** *1 1/4* **Rutterkin (USA)**[19] 6382 3-9-3 **64** .... JulieBurke 13 56
(Alan Berry) *hld up: pushed along 1/2-way: nvr nrr* **12/1**
0100 **10** *2* **Almaty Express**[10] 6602 9-9-1 **61** .... LMcNiff 3 46
(John Weymes) *chsd ldrs: pushed along whn nt clr run over 2f out: wknd over 1f out* **22/1**
150 **11** *2 1/2* **Kipchak (IRE)**[35] 5901 6-9-1 **64** .... (b) LucyKBarry(3) 10 41
(Conor Dore) *chsd ldrs tl wknd wl over 1f out* **25/1**
0200 **12** *2 1/2* **Eshoog (IRE)**[8] 6655 3-8-13 **63** .... (bt) LeonnaMayor(3) 9 32
(Phil McEntee) *led 5f out: pushed along over 2f out: hdd & wknd over 1f out* **22/1**
02 **P** **Torres Del Paine**[29] 6090 4-8-13 **64** .... LukeRowe(5) 11 —
(Jimmy Fox) *mid-div: wknd over 2f out: bhd whn p.u ins fnl f* **6/1**[2]

1m 14.95s (-0.05) **Going Correction** -0.025s/f (Stan)
WFA 3 from 4yo+ 1lb **13** Ran SP% **116.4**
Speed ratings (Par 101): **99,96,96,96,94 94,93,92,91,88 85,81,—**
Tote Swingers: 1&2 £16.30, 1&3 £21.40, 2&3 £12.30 CSF £74.51 CT £626.05 TOTE £13.20: £5.20, £3.00, £3.40; EX 116.70.
Owner James Gaffney **Bred** Bolton Grange **Trained** Musley Bank, N Yorks

FOCUS
They went a fair pace in this modest apprentice handicap. The winner was on a good mark based on his best effort this year.
Silver Wind Official explanation: jockey said gelding never travelled
Torres Del Paine Official explanation: vet said colt bled from the nose and pulled up slightly lame left-fore

6842 HORIZONS RESTAURANT MEDIAN AUCTION MAIDEN STKS 5f 216y(P)
6:20 (6:21) (Class 6) 2-Y-O **£1,908** (£563; £281) **Stalls** Low

Form RPR
3 **1** **Jake's Destiny (IRE)**[22] 6281 2-9-3 0 .... KierenFallon 1 78+
(George Baker) *chsd ldrs: shkn up to ld 1f out: r.o strly* **11/8**[1]
503 **2** *3 3/4* **Tenbridge**[28] 6131 2-8-9 64 .... (p) HarryBentley(3) 3 60
(Derek Haydn Jones) *hld up: hdwy over 2f out: hung lft and nt clr run over 1f out: styd on same pce ins fnl f* **8/1**
3 *3/4* **Multi Bene** 2-9-0 0 .... RossAtkinson(3) 2 62+
(Tom Dascombe) *s.s: outpcd: hdwy over 1f out: nt clr run and swtchd rt ins fnl f: r.o to go 3rd post: nt rch ldrs* **14/1**
204 **4** *nse* **Shevington**[19] 6380 2-9-3 76 .... PaulHanagan 7 63
(Richard Fahey) *hld up: in rr and pushed along 1/2-way: hdwy and hung lft fr over 1f out: nt clr run ins fnl f: styd on same pce* **7/2**[2]
5 *1 1/4* **Jkt Prince (IRE)**[35] 5905 2-9-3 0 .... ShaneKelly 11 58
(Daniel Mark Loughnane, Ire) *hld up: hdwy and nt clr run over 2f out: rdn over 1f out: no ex ins fnl f* **10/1**
5400 **6** *3* **Burnwynd Spirit (IRE)**[10] 6597 2-9-3 51 .... JamesSullivan 6 49
(Ian Semple) *led 1f: chsd ldr: rdn and ev ch over 1f out: wknd ins fnl f* **100/1**
04 **7** *3/4* **Ellastina (IRE)**[24] 6230 2-8-12 0 .... FrederikTylicki 8 42
(Richard Fahey) *chsd ldrs: rdn and ev ch over 1f out: wknd ins fnl f* **7/1**[3]
0 **8** *2 1/4* **Valiant Blue (IRE)**[31] 6025 2-9-3 0 .... (vt[1]) RussKennemore 10 40
(Nicky Vaughan) *racd keenly: led 5f out: rdn: hdd & wknd 1f out* **40/1**
9 *6* **Minty Jones** 2-9-3 0 .... JimmyQuinn 5 21
(Michael Mullineaux) *s.s: outpcd* **40/1**
555 **10** *2 3/4* **Princess Palmer**[22] 6281 2-8-12 0 .... LukeMorris 9 —
(Hugo Palmer) *prom: rdn over 2f out: wknd over 1f out* **12/1**

1m 15.27s (0.27) **Going Correction** -0.025s/f (Stan) **10** Ran SP% **117.3**
Speed ratings (Par 93): **97,92,91,90,89 85,84,81,73,69**
Tote Swingers: 1&2 £3.30, 1&3 £5.80, 2&3 £11.70 CSF £13.42 TOTE £2.20: £1.10, £1.60, £4.60; EX 12.40.
Owner Delancey **Bred** Canice M Farrell Jnr **Trained** Whitsbury, Hants

FOCUS
The well-backed favourite surged clear from a 64-rated rival in this ordinary maiden.

NOTEBOOK
Jake's Destiny(IRE), a promising 13-2 third in a C&D maiden on debut, was always well positioned tucked away against the rail and powered clear to justify strong support. A gelded half-brother to a 7f 2yo winner and out of a 7f juvenile winner, he is quite a scopey type who should continue to progress as he goes up in distance. (op 6-5 tchd 11-10 and 6-4 in places)
Tenbridge looked a difficult character on her first two runs but she took a big step forward when third in a C&D maiden last time and confirmed that promise with a fair effort behind the runaway winner. She is a half-sister to a minor dual 9.4 winner and could find further progress over a stiffer test in handicaps. (tchd 10-1)
Multi Bene, a gelded second foal of an unraced half-sister to 1m 3yo winner The Galloping Shoe, ran green before doing some late work on debut. (tchd 12-1)
Shevington shaped like a future winner when a strong-finishing second in a 5f Newcastle maiden back in April. He had a tough task in a valuable sales race at Doncaster on return last month but flopped at 15-8 back in a maiden at Musselburgh last time and took a long while to get going before working his way into the chasing bunch on AW debut. He has ability and should be suited by going back up in trip but he looks on tough mark of 76 and could be difficult to place. (op 4-1)
Jkt Prince(IRE), beaten just over 4l off 66 in a 7f nursery at Down Royal last month, travelled well for a long way but his effort flattened out with something to find back in a maiden. (op 11-1 tchd 12-1)
Minty Jones Official explanation: jockey said colt missed the break

6843 WOLVERHAMPTON HOLIDAY INN NURSERY 5f 20y(P)
6:50 (6:50) (Class 4) (0-80,79) 2-Y-O **£3,557** (£1,058; £529; £264) **Stalls** High

Form RPR
2100 **1** **Worth**[30] 6058 2-8-12 **70** .... (b) ShaneKelly 4 75
(Brian Meehan) *hld up: hdwy over 1f out: rdn to ld nr fin* **10/1**
5531 **2** *nk* **Blodwen Abbey**[28] 6131 2-8-12 **70** .... LiamJones 2 74
(James Unett) *chsd ldrs: rdn to ld ins fnl f: hdd nr fin* **7/2**[1]
232 **3** *1 1/4* **Regal Lady**[15] 6492 2-8-5 **63** .... PaulHanagan 1 62
(David Brown) *led: rdn over 1f out: hdd and unable qck ins fnl f* **6/1**[3]
3401 **4** *1* **The Rising (IRE)**[30] 6045 2-9-1 **73** .... (v) GrahamGibbons 9 69
(Ed McMahon) *chsd ldr: rdn and edgd rt over 1f out: styd on same pce ins fnl f* **5/1**[2]
621 **5** *3/4* **Taffe**[16] 6455 2-9-7 **79** .... FrederikTylicki 11 72
(James Given) *prom: rdn and edgd lft over 1f out: styd on same pce fnl f* **7/2**[1]
1256 **6** *1/2* **Molly Jones**[25] 6222 2-8-9 **70** .... HarryBentley(3) 3 61
(Derek Haydn Jones) *hld up in tch: pushed along 1/2-way: rdn over 1f out: no ex ins fnl f* **8/1**
620 **7** *2* **Courtland King (IRE)**[13] 6540 2-8-10 **73** .... MatthewCosham(5) 10 57
(David Evans) *hld up: hdwy over 2f out: rdn over 1f out: sn wknd* **16/1**
3110 **8** *6* **Roy's Legacy**[30] 6058 2-8-8 **66** .... (t) RobbieFitzpatrick 6 29
(Shaun Harris) *hld up: pushed along 1/2-way: wknd over 1f out* **14/1**
6231 **9** *5* **Balm**[13] 6540 2-8-9 **67** .... LiamKeniry 7 12
(Patrick Morris) *hld up: pushed along 1/2-way: wknd wl over 1f out* **14/1**

62.23 secs (-0.07) **Going Correction** -0.025s/f (Stan) **9** Ran SP% **114.8**
Speed ratings (Par 97): **99,98,96,94,93 92,89,80,72**
CSF £44.74 CT £231.86 TOTE £13.80: £3.40, £1.60, £2.20; EX 69.80.
Owner Miss Penny Zygmant **Bred** Miss P A Zygmant **Trained** Manton, Wilts

FOCUS
A nursery involving four last-time-out winners. The pace was fair and there was a tight finish.

NOTEBOOK
Worth has a bit of an erratic profile, but she was a game front-running winner off 2lb lower in a 6f Kempton nursery in August and found a surging run to just prevail switched back to Polytrack. It is hard to know whether she will hit the same level next time, but this has to rate as a personal best on her ninth start and she is now 2-2 in nurseries on this surface. (tchd 9-1 and 11-1)
Blodwen Abbey found a change of gear when winning a 6f maiden here last month. She had a drop in trip and tricky mark to deal with on nursery debut but put in a commendable effort and was just overhauled. Her three best runs have been at this track and she should have scope for further improvement on Polytrack. (tchd 3-1)
Regal Lady showed plenty of speed when placed in three C&D maidens last month and there was similar scenario in a creditable run on nursery debut. (op 9-2 tchd 7-1)
The Rising(IRE) was a clear-cut winner of an ordinary 5f Beverley maiden last time, but his mark went up 6lb after that success and he was held back in a nursery on AW debut. (op 11-2)
Taffe made all when beating an odds-on rival in decisive style in a 6f Nottingham maiden last time. He couldn't make an impact on nursery debut but there were mitigating circumstances because he couldn't adopt a front-running role from an outside draw and was forced wide most of the way. (op 9-2 tchd 5-1)

6844 WOLVERHAMPTON-RACECOURSE.CO.UK (S) STKS 1m 141y(P)
7:20 (7:20) (Class 6) 3-5-Y-O **£1,533** (£452; £226) **Stalls** Low

Form RPR
2604 **1** **Saharia (IRE)**[20] 6354 4-9-0 67 .... (v) ShaneKelly 5 62+
(Michael Attwater) *s.i.s: hld up and bhd: hdwy on bit over 1f out: led towards fin: cosily* **5/2**[1]
5566 **2** *1/2* **Alhaban (IRE)**[11] 6583 5-9-0 72 .... (p) LukeMorris 10 61
(Ronald Harris) *a.p: rdn and hung lft over 1f out: styd on* **7/2**[2]
1405 **3** *3/4* **Empress Leizu (IRE)**[15] 6490 4-9-1 55 .... DavidProbert 9 60
(Tony Carroll) *led after 1f: pushed clr 3f out: sn rdn: hdd nr fin* **8/1**[3]
3541 **4** *1 1/2* **Ajdaad (USA)**[15] 6490 4-9-6 65 .... GrahamGibbons 4 62+
(Alan McCabe) *hld up: hdwy over 2f out: shkn up ins fnl f: styd on same pce* **5/2**[1]
-400 **5** *3* **My Mate Les (IRE)**[37] 5832 3-8-10 47 .... FrederikTylicki 3 49
(John Best) *prom: rdn over 1f out: wknd ins fnl f* **20/1**
614- **6** *1/2* **Hold The Bucks (USA)**[46] 5-9-0 45 .... (b) NeilChalmers 7 48?
(Adrian Chamberlain) *led 1f: chsd ldrs: rdn over 1f out: wknd ins fnl f* **10/1**
00/0 **7** *3/4* **Bridge Valley**[13] 6536 4-9-0 58 .... MichaelStainton 8 46?
(Jason Ward) *prom: chsd ldr over 6f out: rdn over 1f out: wknd fnl f* **28/1**
-000 **8** *13* **Northern Genes (AUS)**[13] 6542 5-9-0 42 .... (p) RobbieFitzpatrick 1 16
(Michael Appleby) *hld up: rdn and wknd over 2f out* **25/1**

1m 50.81s (0.31) **Going Correction** -0.025s/f (Stan)
WFA 3 from 4yo+ 4lb **8** Ran SP% **111.6**
Speed ratings (Par 101): **97,96,95,94,91 91,90,79**
Tote Swingers: 1&2 £2.30, 1&3 £5.70, 2&3 £7.40 CSF £10.73 TOTE £3.90: £1.30, £1.10, £2.30; EX 11.90.There was no bid for the winner.
Owner Brooklands Racing **Bred** Woodcote Stud Ltd **Trained** Epsom, Surrey

FOCUS
The winner did the job in very smooth style in this seller and was value for much more than the winning margin suggests. Muddling form, with the winner better than the bare result.

6845 CELEBRATE CHRISTMAS AT WOLVERHAMPTON RACECOURSE CLASSIFIED STKS 1m 1f 103y(P)
7:50 (7:50) (Class 6) 3-Y-O+ **£1,772** (£523; £261) **Stalls** Low

Form RPR
000 **1** **El Libertador (USA)**[34] 5912 5-9-2 54 .... (b) LiamKeniry 10 59
(Eric Wheeler) *trckd ldrs: rdn to ld wl ins fnl f: styd on* **9/1**

-003 **2** ½ **Pursuing**[13] 6536 3-8-12 52 .... SilvestreDeSousa 4 58
(Nigel Tinkler) *hld up: hdwy over 2f out: rdn and r.o to go 2nd post: nt rch wnr* **6/1**[3]
0052 **3** *hd* **Eastward Ho**[11] 6576 3-8-12 34 .... FrederikTylicki 8 58
(Jason Ward) *w ldrs tl led over 7f out: rdn over 1f out: hdd wl ins fnl f* **7/1**
4050 **4** 1 ½ **Valley Tiger**[6] 6701 3-8-12 55 .... WilliamCarson 13 54
(William Muir) *hld up: hdwy over 2f out: rdn and edgd lft ins fnl f: styd on same pce* **6/1**[3]
-600 **5** 2 ¾ **Illustrious Forest**[34] 5912 3-8-12 52 .... PaulHanagan 11 49
(John Mackie) *prom: chsd ldr over 6f out tl pushed along wl over 2f out: rdn to go 2nd again over 1f out tl no ex fnl f* **11/2**[2]
3050 **6** 3 **Mister Frosty (IRE)**[112] 3353 5-9-2 55 .... KierenFallon 6 42
(George Prodromou) *hld up in tch: chsd ldr wl over 2f out: tl rdn wl over 1f out: wknd ins fnl f* **5/1**[1]
0500 **7** 4 **Habsburg**[52] 5349 3-8-12 52 .... (p) FrankieMcDonald 5 34
(Paul Fitzsimons) *prom tl rdn and wknd over 2f out* **20/1**
0030 **8** 2 ½ **Subramaniam**[12] 4560 3-8-12 52 .... (t) JamesSullivan 1 29
(James Given) *prom: lost pl over 6f out: wknd over 3f out* **7/1**
0400 **9** 1 ¾ **The Right Time**[16] 6446 3-8-12 51 .... DavidProbert 2 25
(Tony Carroll) *led 2f: chsd ldrs: rdn over 3f out: wknd over 1f out* **11/1**
2600 **10** 18 **Silk Lingerie**[27] 6181 3-8-12 53 .... JimmyQuinn 12 —
(Mandy Rowland) *hld up: hdwy over 2f out: sn wknd: t.o* **25/1**
000 **11** 14 **Pronounce**[35] 5900 3-8-12 40 .... RobbieFitzpatrick 9 —
(Michael Appleby) *s.s: a in rr: bhd fr 1/2-way: t.o* **20/1**

2m 1.90s (0.20) **Going Correction** -0.025s/f (Stan)
WFA 3 from 5yo 4lb **11** Ran SP% **117.3**
Speed ratings (Par 101): **98,97,97,96,93 90,87,85,83,67 55**
Tote Swingers: 1&2 £11.00, 1&3 £11.80, 2&3 £4.90 CSF £60.19 TOTE £7.30: £2.50, £2.20, £2.90; EX 71.80.
Owner J L Day **Bred** Kingswood Farm **Trained** Whitchurch-on-Thames, Oxon

FOCUS
A 0-55 classified event run at a reasonable pace. Sound of limited form.
Silk Lingerie Official explanation: jockey said filly moved poorly

6846 SPONSOR A RACE BY CALLING - 01902 390000 NURSERY 7f 32y(P)
8:20 (8:21) (Class 6) (0-65,63) 2-Y-O £1,908 (£563; £281) **Stalls** High

Form RPR
3206 **1** **Hearts And Minds (IRE)**[15] 6489 2-9-6 62 .... (b) KierenFallon 4 69
(Jamie Osborne) *mde virtually all: clr 1/2-way: rdn ins fnl f: styd on* **9/2**[1]
660 **2** 1 ½ **Blackburn**[35] 5889 2-9-4 63 .... JohnFahy(3) 5 66
(Clive Cox) *led early: chsd wnr: rdn over 1f out: edgd lft ins fnl f: styd on* **6/1**[3]
0004 **3** 2 ¾ **She's Flawless (USA)**[20] 6322 2-8-12 54 .... (b) ShaneKelly 3 51
(Brian Meehan) *s.i.s: sn mid-div: pushed along 4f out: hdwy and hung rt fr over 2f out: sn rdn: styd on to go 3rd nr fin: nvr nrr* **22/1**
6545 **4** *nk* **New Romantic**[9] 6628 2-9-0 56 .... FrederikTylicki 7 52
(Julie Camacho) *prom: rdn to go 3rd over 2f out: edgd lft ins fnl f: styd on: lost 3rd nr fin* **25/1**
6545 **5** 2 **Topcoat (IRE)**[121] 3035 2-9-7 63 .... SilvestreDeSousa 2 54
(Mark Johnston) *prom: rdn over 2f out: styd on same pce appr fnl f* **6/1**[3]
000 **6** 1 **Methaen (USA)**[16] 6443 2-9-6 62 .... TadhgO'Shea 12 51
(Ed Dunlop) *dwlt: hld up: styd on fr over 1f out: nvr nrr* **14/1**
0000 **7** ¾ **Songbird Blues**[6] 6695 2-9-0 56 .... LukeMorris 9 43
(Mark Usher) *hld up: hdwy u.p over 1f out: nvr on terms* **8/1**
4243 **8** 2 **Thorpe Bay**[6] 6695 2-9-5 61 .... (p) TomMcLaughlin 11 43
(Mark Rimmer) *hld up: hdwy over 2f out: wknd over 1f out* **9/1**
4204 **9** 3 ½ **Flying Pickets (IRE)**[8] 6652 2-9-6 62 .... MartinHarley 1 35
(Alan McCabe) *s.i.s: a in rr* **15/2**
465 **10** 7 **Double Cee**[28] 6110 2-9-6 62 .... (b[1]) PaulHanagan 8 18
(Richard Fahey) *hld up: rdn over 2f out: sn wknd* **5/1**[2]
3456 **11** 1 ¼ **Curtain Patch (USA)**[7] 6667 2-9-6 62 .... (v) TomEaves 6 15
(Bryan Smart) *chsd ldrs tl rdn and wknd over 2f out* **33/1**

1m 29.49s (-0.11) **Going Correction** -0.025s/f (Stan) **11** Ran SP% **114.1**
Speed ratings (Par 93): **99,97,94,93,91 90,89,87,83,75 73**
Tote Swingers: 1&2 £5.90, 1&3 £22.70, 2&3 £34.20 CSF £29.44 CT £531.48 TOTE £5.60: £2.30, £1.90, £8.80; EX 40.40.
Owner G Gill **Bred** Stephanie Hanly **Trained** Upper Lambourn, Berks

FOCUS
There was an emphatic front-running winner in this low-grade nursery.

NOTEBOOK
Hearts And Minds(IRE) had a patchy six-race profile before this but he ran better than his finishing position in a C&D handicap last time and showed plenty of speed before running his rivals into submission switched back to forcing tactics here. Still relatively lightly raced, he is related to two decent winners and could win more races.
Blackburn showed some promise in three sprint maidens and kept battling to finish a clear second on nursery debut. She is out of a triple 5f winner but she stayed this trip well and has scope for further improvement.
She's Flawless(USA) looked a bit tricky in four maidens and she got outpaced here, but she did manage to stay on steadily from some way back in second-time blinkers. Official explanation: jockey said filly hung right-handed (op 25-1)
New Romantic made an underwhelming start to life in nurseries at Nottingham last week but this Singspiel filly who is out of a half-sister to Soviet Song, did better stepped up in trip and could go on from this. (op 28-1)
Topcoat(IRE) is a half-brother to numerous winners, notably high-class 6f-1m performer Lend A Hand, but he didn't do much in maidens and was well held up in trip on his first try in a nursery. (op 11-2 tchd 13-2)
Double Cee failed to build on his Haydock debut fourth in two subsequent maiden runs and was very laboured with blinkers applied on nursery debut. (op 6-1)

6847 ENJOY THE PARTY PACK GROUP OFFER H'CAP (DIV I) 7f 32y(P)
8:50 (8:50) (Class 6) (0-60,60) 3-Y-O+ £1,567 (£462; £231) **Stalls** High

Form RPR
-001 **1** **Michael's Nook**[10] 6610 4-8-6 50 .... LMcNiff(5) 5 65+
(David Barron) *hld up: hdwy over 1f out: led ins fnl f: r.o: readily* **13/8**[1]
6033 **2** 1 ¼ **Know No Fear**[10] 6609 6-9-6 59 .... (p) PaulHanagan 11 71
(Alastair Lidderdale) *hld up: hdwy over 1f out: rdn to ld and hung lft ins fnl f: sn hdd: r.o* **15/2**
1045 **3** 4 **Whats For Pudding (IRE)**[18] 6415 3-8-8 54 .... NeilFarley(5) 10 55
(Declan Carroll) *sn pushed along in rr: r.o ins fnl f: nvr nrr* **28/1**
2401 **4** *nk* **Prince Of Passion (CAN)**[10] 6609 3-8-12 58 .... MatthewCosham(5) 7 58
(Derek Shaw) *hld up: hdwy over 2f out: rdn over 1f out: styd on under same pce* **13/2**[3]
4250 **5** ¾ **Karate (IRE)**[15] 6488 3-8-11 59 .... NicoleNordblad(7) 2 57
(Hans Adielsson) *chsd ldrs: rdn over 1f out: sgtayed on same pce* **12/1**
0463 **6** ¾ **Burnwynd Boy**[15] 6494 6-8-9 53 .... GarryWhillans(5) 3 49
(Ian Semple) *chsd ldrs: led over 5f out tl over 2f out: wknd ins fnl f* **6/1**[2]
1060 **7** 2 ¼ **Stilettoesinthemud (IRE)**[10] 6604 3-9-5 60 .... FrederikTylicki 9 50
(James Given) *prom: rdn over 1f out: wknd fnl f* **22/1**
0000 **8** *hd* **Milton Of Campsie**[4] 6764 6-9-6 59 .... (t[1]) TonyCulhane 4 49
(Richard Guest) *hld up: rdn over 1f out: nvr on terms* **14/1**
230 **9** 1 ¾ **Northern Flyer (GER)**[28] 6133 5-9-7 60 .... (v) TomEaves 8 45
(John Quinn) *hld up in tch: rdn and ev ch over 1f out: wknd ins fnl f* **17/2**
00 **10** 10 **Johannesgray (IRE)**[35] 5881 4-8-13 52 .... MartinHarley 12 —
(Noel Wilson) *prom: chsd ldr over 5f out tl led over 3f out: hdd over 2f out: wknd over 1f out* **40/1**
5000 **11** 21 **Sonny G (IRE)**[76] 4544 4-8-9 48 .... LukeMorris 1 —
(John Best) *led: hdd over 5f out: rdn and wknd over 2f out: t.o* **33/1**

1m 29.37s (-0.23) **Going Correction** -0.025s/f (Stan)
WFA 3 from 4yo+ 2lb **11** Ran SP% **115.5**
Speed ratings (Par 101): **100,98,94,93,92 91,89,89,87,75 51**
Tote Swingers: 1&2 £2.80, 1&3 £14.20, 2&3 £33.50 CSF £13.05 CT £253.00 TOTE £3.20: £1.10, £1.20, £8.20; EX 18.90.
Owner Reg Gifford **Bred** D R Tucker **Trained** Maunby, N Yorks

FOCUS
The well handicapped favourite delivered in good style in this modest handicap and the first two pulled clear off a good pace. The winner may have more to offer.
Milton Of Campsie Official explanation: jockey said mare moved poorly and hung right

6848 ENJOY THE PARTY PACK GROUP OFFER H'CAP (DIV II) 7f 32y(P)
9:20 (9:21) (Class 6) (0-60,60) 3-Y-O+ £1,567 (£462; £231) **Stalls** High

Form RPR
2405 **1** **Kristollini**[21] 6309 3-8-11 52 .... SilvestreDeSousa 8 59
(William Muir) *a.p: rdn to ld over 1f out: r.o* **10/1**
600 **2** ½ **Shaws Diamond (USA)**[9] 6626 5-9-0 53 .... (v) RobbieFitzpatrick 1 59
(Derek Shaw) *chsd ldrs: rdn over 1f out: r.o u.p* **16/1**
0640 **3** ½ **Ereka (IRE)**[60] 5120 3-8-8 49 .... LukeMorris 10 54
(John Best) *hld up: hdwy over 1f out: sn rdn: r.o* **20/1**
0516 **4** *hd* **Pytheas (USA)**[6] 6696 4-9-1 59 .... (p) MarkCoumbe(5) 3 63
(Michael Attwater) *chsd ldr 1f: remained handy: rdn and ev ch over 1f out: styd on* **5/1**[3]
6000 **5** ½ **Yungaburra (IRE)**[6] 6694 7-9-2 55 .... (t) JamesSullivan 12 58
(David C Griffiths) *hld up: hdwy over 1f out: rdn ins fnl f: r.o* **50/1**
3363 **6** ½ **Valeo Si Vales (IRE)**[29] 6090 3-9-5 60 .... (b) FergusSweeney 5 61
(Jamie Osborne) *hld up: hdwy over 2f out: rdn and no ex ins fnl f* **6/1**
5422 **7** ½ **Annes Rocket (IRE)**[4] 6746 6-9-4 60 .... (p) KieranO'Neill(3) 6 60
(Jimmy Fox) *s.i.s: hld up: hdwy over 1f out: sn rdn: no ex ins fnl f* **9/4**[1]
0102 **8** 2 ½ **Jonnie Skull (IRE)**[9] 6624 5-9-6 59 .... (vt) KierenFallon 2 52
(Phil McEntee) *led: pushed along and hdd 3f out: rdn and ev ch over 1f out: wknd ins fnl f* **5/2**[2]
5020 **9** ½ **Peter Tchaikovsky**[15] 6488 5-9-0 56 .... PaulPickard(3) 7 48
(Ian McInnes) *chsd ldr 6f out: led 3f out: rdn and hdd over 1f out: wknd fnl f* **14/1**
0-00 **10** 13 **Spirit Of Dixie**[273] 167 4-8-13 52 .... PaulQuinn 11 —
(Noel Wilson) *s.i.s: hld up: hdwy 1/2-way: wknd wl over 1f out* **40/1**

1m 29.73s (0.13) **Going Correction** -0.025s/f (Stan)
WFA 3 from 4yo+ 2lb **10** Ran SP% **121.1**
Speed ratings (Par 101): **98,97,96,96,96 95,94,92,91,76**
Tote Swingers: 1&2 £21.90, 1&3 £10.00, 2&3 £66.00 CSF £158.09 CT £3213.25 TOTE £13.40: £2.60, £5.50, £5.60; EX 78.80.
Owner North Farm Stud **Bred** North Farm Stud **Trained** Lambourn, Berks
■ Stewards' Enquiry : Robbie Fitzpatrick 5-day ban: excessive use of whip (Oct 28,29,31, Nov 1-2)

FOCUS
They went a good pace in this second division of an ordinary handicap, but the time was slower than division I. Weak form, the winner back to her 2yo level.
T/Jkpt: Part won. £299,047.99 to a £1 stake. Pool: £421,194.00 - 0.50 winning tickets. T/Plt: £182.10 to a £1 stake. Pool of £98,398.00 - 394.41 winning tickets. T/Qpdt: £32.50 to a £1 stake. Pool of £9,468.00 - 215.40 winning tickets. CR

6849 - 6853a, 6855 - 6856a - (Foreign Racing) - See Raceform Interactive

6677 DUNDALK (A.W) (L-H)
Friday, October 14

OFFICIAL GOING: Standard

6854a IRISH STALLION FARMS EUROPEAN BREEDERS FUND FILLIES H'CAP 7f (P)
8:30 (8:45) (60-100,98) 3-Y-O+ £14,008 (£4,094; £1,939; £646)

RPR
1 **Blue Moon**[8] 6658 4-9-1 85 .... DPMcDonogh 7 97
(Kevin Ryan) *mid-div: gd hdwy early st: led wl over 1f out: sn asserted and kpt on wl fnl f* **13/2**
2 3 **Sioux Rising (IRE)**[6] 6706 5-9-8 97 .... RPWhelan(5) 1 101
(Richard Fahey) *trckd ldrs on inner: 3rd 1/2-way: rdn in 4th over 1f out: kpt on u.p ins fnl f: no ch w wnr* **5/1**[1]
3 ¾ **Flic Flac (IRE)**[19] 6388 3-9-1 87 .... PJSmullen 13 89
(D K Weld, Ire) *in rr of mid-div: hdwy ent st: 3rd over 1f out: no imp on wnr and kpt on one pce* **11/1**
4 1 ¼ **Queenie Keen (IRE)**[19] 6388 4-8-9 84 .... CPHoban(5) 3 83
(M Halford, Ire) *trckd ldrs: 4th 1/2-way: 2nd early st: no imp on wnr fr 1f out: no ex* **12/1**
5 *nse* **Foot Perfect (IRE)**[19] 6388 3-8-12 84 .... GFCarroll 14 82
(David Marnane, Ire) *in rr of mid-div: sme hdwy over 1f out: kpt on wout troubling ldrs* **16/1**
6 ½ **Act Of Love (IRE)**[26] 6197 3-8-7 79 .... (b) ShaneFoley 4 76
(David Marnane, Ire) *in rr of mid-div: hdwy early st: wnt 6th 1f out: no imp and kpt on one pce* **20/1**
7 *nk* **No Trimmings (IRE)**[26] 6197 5-8-6 76 .... (tp) BACurtis 9 72
(Gerard Keane, Ire) *mid-div best: no threat fr over 1f out: kpt on one pce* **12/1**
8 1 ½ **Brazilian Breeze (IRE)**[18] 6421 3-8-1 78 .... SHJames(5) 10 70
(Kevin Prendergast, Ire) *chsd ldrs: 7th 1/2-way: sme hdwy early st: 5th over 1f out: no ex ins fnl f* **15/2**
9 1 ¾ **Miranda's Girl (IRE)**[18] 6421 6-8-12 82 .... (b) RPCleary 5 70
(Thomas Cleary, Ire) *chsd ldrs: 5th 1/2-way: no ex under 2f out* **22/1**
10 1 ¼ **Coolminx (IRE)**[28] 6113 4-9-7 91 .... JPO'Brien 2 75
(Richard Fahey) *led: strly pressed early st: hdd under 2f out and sn no ex* **6/1**[3]
11 6 ½ **Allegra Tak (ITY)**[68] 4835 5-8-13 83 .... DMGrant 8 50
(H Rogers, Ire) *prom: 2nd 1/2-way: no ex fr early st* **20/1**

The Form Book, Raceform Ltd, Compton, RG20 6NL

12 4 1/4 **Posh Cracker (USA)**[152] 2131 3-8-11 83........................(bt[1]) JMurtagh 12 38
(G M Lyons, Ire) *chsd ldrs on outer: 6th 1/2-way: no ex fr early st* **20/1**
13 3/4 **Princess Severus (IRE)**[30] 6073 3-9-0 86............................ FMBerry 6 39
(Mrs John Harrington, Ire) *a towards rr* **16/1**
U **Lady Fashion**[121] 3057 3-9-12 98.. WJSupple 11 —
(P D Deegan, Ire) *towards rr: swtchd rt whn stmbld and uns rdr 2f out* **11/2**[2]

1m 23.0s (83.00)
WFA 3 from 4yo+ 2lb **14** Ran SP% **125.6**
CSF £38.28 CT £375.41 TOTE £5.00: £2.00, £1.70, £3.70; DF 23.70.
Owner Guy Reed **Bred** Theakston Stud **Trained** Hambleton, N Yorks

FOCUS
A one-two for cross-channel raiders in a competitive handicap.

NOTEBOOK
Blue Moon was held up towards the rear and it did take her some time to pick up, but when she did she really sustained her effort on the outside over the last furlong and a half to draw away in good style. She has a very likeable way of going about her business and was just too good. (op 6/1)
Sioux Rising(IRE) had a good position on the inner and ended up staying on again inside the final furlong after her chance seemed to be gone. It's hard to imagine her being good enough to have challenged the winner under any circumstances but she saw it out well. (op 11/2)
Flic Flac(IRE) looked to have come with a very well-timed challenge to throw her hat in the ring a furlong or so from the finish, but she has shown in the past that he's a filly that comes with just one run and doesn't really sustain her efforts. That was the case here to a smaller degree, but it was probably as well as she has done all season.
Queenie Keen(IRE) is probably more effective over shorter and did show plenty of early pace in this contest. She was unable to sustain it, although she did keep on reasonably well at one pace. (op 10/1)
Foot Perfect(IRE) was never really involved but kept on well inside the final furlong.
Lady Fashion clip heels with Posh Cracker, who was going backwards and drifted into her path. Willie Supple was unseated but came back in one piece. (op 8/1)

6518 ASCOT (R-H)
Saturday, October 15

OFFICIAL GOING: Good (gs: str: stands' side 9.7, centre 9.9, far side 9.6; rnd 9.8)
The first Qipco British Champions Day, which took the best races from Ascot's late September fixture and Champions Day at Newmarket.
Wind: Sunny Weather: Almost Nil

6857 QIPCO BRITISH CHAMPIONS LONG DISTANCE CUP (GROUP 3) 2m
1:50 (1:50) (Class 1) 3-Y-O+

£113,420 (£43,000; £21,520; £10,720; £5,380; £2,700) **Stalls** Low

Form RPR
1124 **1** **Fame And Glory**[35] 5952 5-9-0 120................................ JamieSpencer 2 115+
(A P O'Brien, Ire) *lw: trckd ldr after 1f: led after 4f and increased the pce: gng strly over 3f out: drew 3 l clr over 2f out: rdn and kpt on wl* **3/1**[2]
2112 **2** 1 1/4 **Opinion Poll (IRE)**[36] 5884 5-9-0 116........................ FrankieDettori 10 113+
(Mahmood Al Zarooni) *hld up in midfield: prog over 2f out: rdn to chse clr wnr over 1f out: kpt on but nvr able to chal: jst hld on for 2nd* **12/5**[1]
0513 **3** *nse* **Colour Vision (FR)**[7] 6690 3-8-3 109........................ SilvestreDeSousa 4 113+
(Mark Johnston) *hld up in last trio: prog on inner over 2f out: swtchd lft over 1f out: r.o wl fnl f: nrly snatched 2nd* **10/1**
1023 **4** *shd* **Nehaam**[23] 6271 5-9-0 105.. RichardHills 8 113
(John Gosden) *hld up in midfield: prog on inner 3f out: wnt 3rd over 2f out: rdn and tried to cl fr over 1f out: jst lost out in battle for 2nd* **12/1**
1231 **5** 2 1/4 **Times Up**[23] 6271 5-9-0 111.. EddieAhern 1 111
(John Dunlop) *lw: prom: chsd wnr over 3f out: rdn and no imp over 2f out: lost 2nd and fdd over 1f out* **10/3**[3]
0204 **6** 3 3/4 **Eternal Heart (IRE)**[15] 6498 3-8-3 99................................ JoeFanning 6 106
(Mark Johnston) *prom: rdn over 4f out: steadily wknd fr over 2f out* **50/1**
5433 **7** 1 1/4 **Polly's Mark (IRE)**[37] 5850 5-8-11 105.......................... GeraldMosse 9 102
(Clive Cox) *t.k.h: hld up in last trio: rdn 3f out: no prog and nvr on terms* **28/1**
62-0 **8** *shd* **Darley Sun (IRE)**[164] 1808 5-9-0 100.......................... WilliamBuick 5 104
(Saeed Bin Suroor) *dwlt: hld up in last: rdn and effrt on outer over 2f out: sn no prog and wl btn* **28/1**
0313 **9** 8 **Motrice**[36] 5884 4-8-11 107.. SebSanders 7 92
(Sir Mark Prescott Bt) *prom: rdn to chse wnr over 4f out to over 3f out: wknd rapidly* **12/1**
1002 **10** 22 **Chiberta King**[23] 6271 5-9-0 108................................(p) JimmyFortune 3 68
(Andrew Balding) *led after 1f at modest pce: hdd after 4f: chsd wnr to over 4f out: wknd rapidly: t.o* **33/1**

3m 26.5s (-2.50) **Going Correction** +0.075s/f (Good)
WFA 3 from 4yo+ 11lb **10** Ran SP% **113.8**
Speed ratings (Par 113): **109,108,108,108,107 105,104,104,100,89**
toteswingers:1&2:£2.00, 2&3:£4.40, 1&3:£5.20 CSF £9.93 CT £60.89 TOTE £3.30: £1.70, £1.20, £2.20; EX 8.10 Trifecta £90.40 Pool: £3,924.93 - 32.12 winning units..
Owner Mrs F Hay,D Smith,Mrs J Magnier,M Tabor **Bred** Ptarmigan Bloodstock And Miss K Rausing **Trained** Ballydoyle, Co Tipperary

FOCUS
A sunny, drying day and there was a decent chance the ground would ride somewhat quicker than the official description of good all over, but the riders later claimed it was indeed good ground. Formerly known as the Jockey Club Cup when staged at Newmarket, this Group 3 staying prize attracted a strong field for the first running at its new home and saw a repeat finish of the Gold Cup back in June. However it was something of a muddling race and is not really championship form. Fame And Glory did not need to match his best to hold off Opinion Poll, who was also below his best.

NOTEBOOK
Fame And Glory had flopped on his two outings since winning the big one at the royal meeting and was easy to back. He was very confidently ridden by Jamie Spencer, however, and was able to dictate his own pace from a long way out. Spencer sent him for home off the home bend and he responded willingly, never really looking like getting caught inside the final furlong. He's now 2-2 at Ascot and this rates a great training performance to get him back to his best after a long season. No doubt he'll take the beating when defending his crown in next year's Gold Cup. Official explanation: trainer said, regarding apparent improvement in form, that the horse had taken time to return to form after the Gold Cup and appreciated the even pace. (op 7-2 tchd 4-1 in a place)
Opinion Poll(IRE) probably got there too soon when losing out in his bid for a hat-trick in the Doncaster Cup last month and it was no surprise to see him restrained here. He made his move rounding the home turn, but allowed the winner first run and was all out to hold on to second place at the finish. The ground was that bit quicker than he ideally prefers, but this was still another solid effort and he gives the form a decent look. He's reportedly now to be aimed at a new 2m race on World Cup night at Meydan in Dubai next March. (op 5-2 tchd 9-4)
Colour Vision(FR) has had a decent season and advertised his durability when third in the Cesarewitch last weekend. He motored home from way back in the home straight and posted another personal-best effort. There's every chance he will improve again as a 4yo and will no doubt be campaigned as a Cup horse next term, very probably in the colours of Godolphin. (op 12-1)
Nehaam is a previous course winner and he ran the race of his life, reversing last-time-out form with Times Up. Interestingly his rider later said he felt he would have been second had he been able to be harder on him with the whip late on. He doesn't have many miles on the clock and deserves another winning turn. (op 14-1 tchd 11-1)
Times Up was so impressive when winning easily on his first venture over this trip at Newmarket last month and, well backed ante-post, again had his ground. He gave his all in defeat, but really raced closer to the pace than ideal, probably on account of taking a keen hold tracking the winner. He's better when patiently ridden and, given he's been on the go since April, still remains a live Gold Cup contender for next year. (op 3-1)
Eternal Heart(IRE) had the lowest official mark of these. He found it too hot, but did some decent late work and is another who could rate higher at four.

6858 QIPCO BRITISH CHAMPIONS SPRINT STKS (GROUP 2) 6f
2:25 (2:26) (Class 1) 3-Y-O+

£141,775 (£53,750; £26,900; £13,400; £6,725; £3,375) **Stalls** High

Form RPR
1111 **1** **Deacon Blues**[28] 6164 4-9-0 120.. JMurtagh 14 123+
(James Fanshawe) *trckd ldrs against nr side rail: smooth prog to ld over 1f out: rdn and a wl in command fnl f* **5/2**[1]
0155 **2** 1 1/2 **Wizz Kid (IRE)**[13] 6563 3-8-10 109.............................. GeraldMosse 8 115
(Robert Collet, France) *settled in midfield: shkn up and prog over 1f out: styd on to take 2nd last 75yds: nvr able to chal* **8/1**
4010 **3** *nk* **Libranno**[22] 6298 3-8-13 112.. KierenFallon 12 117
(Richard Hannon) *wl plcd: prog to chse wnr over 1f out: no imp: styd on but lost 2nd last 75yds* **25/1**
0311 **4** *nse* **Royal Rock**[14] 6520 7-9-0 108... NeilCallan 7 117
(Chris Wall) *hld up towards rr: effrt and hanging sltly fr 2f out: r.o fnl f: nrst fin* **25/1**
0211 **5** 2 **Moonlight Cloud**[69] 4838 3-8-10 118.............................. ThierryJarnet 9 113+
(F Head, France) *hld up in midfield towards nr side rail: effrt whn nt clr run over 1f out: r.o fnl f: nvr nrr* **10/3**[2]
1415 **6** *nk* **Night Carnation**[28] 6164 3-8-10 109............................ JimmyFortune 13 106
(Andrew Balding) *chsd ldrs and racd towards nr side: rdn over 1f out: nt qckn and readily hld after* **25/1**
0515 **7** 1 1/2 **Prime Defender**[56] 5264 7-9-0 109................................... RyanMoore 11 105
(Charles Hills) *lw: chsd ldr to wl over 1f out: fdd* **66/1**
6445 **8** 1 **Genki (IRE)**[14] 6520 7-9-0 116.......................................(v) GeorgeBaker 15 101
(Roger Charlton) *stdd s: hld up last: coaxed along 2f out: styd on fr over 1f out: nvr gng pce to threaten* **14/1**
6000 **9** 1 1/2 **Perfect Tribute**[14] 6520 3-8-10 102...................................... LukeMorris 3 94
(Clive Cox) *s.i.s: hld up in last trio: urged along over 2f out: styd on fr over 1f out: n.d* **66/1**
3060 **10** 1 1/4 **Jimmy Styles**[14] 6522 7-9-0 105...........................(p) AdamKirby 10 93
(Clive Cox) *prom: rdn 2f out: stl chsng ldrs over 1f out: fdd* **66/1**
1004 **11** 1/2 **Hooray**[48] 5510 3-8-10 109.. SebSanders 16 88
(Sir Mark Prescott Bt) *led against nr side rail: hdd & wknd over 1f out* **25/1**
2126 **12** 1 1/4 **Society Rock (IRE)**[42] 5707 4-9-0 117............................ PatCosgrave 2 87+
(James Fanshawe) *nvr bttr than midfield: rdn and no real prog 2f out: wl btn over 1f out* **7/1**[3]
1230 **13** 1 1/2 **Medicean Man**[28] 6164 5-9-0 109..................................(p) FrankieDettori 6 82+
(Jeremy Gask) *hld up towards rr on outer: gng wl enough but v limited prog over 1f out: nvr in it* **16/1**
0431 **14** 2 **Ladies Are Forever**[99] 3827 3-8-10 109................ SilvestreDeSousa 4 73
(Geoffrey Oldroyd) *racd on outer: nvr bttr than midfield: rdn and struggling wl over 1f out* **20/1**
2-52 **15** *nse* **Dafeef**[35] 5930 4-9-0 109... RichardHills 5 76
(William Haggas) *lw: hld up in rr and racd on wd outside: effrt 2f out: sn no prog and wknd* **25/1**
3031 **16** 1 1/2 **Silverside (USA)**[48] 5528 5-9-0 113............................. JulienGrosjean 1 71
(F Sanchez, France) *prom to 1/2-way on outer: sn wknd* **66/1**

1m 12.55s (-1.85) **Going Correction** +0.075s/f (Good)
WFA 3 from 4yo+ 1lb **16** Ran SP% **117.8**
Speed ratings (Par 115): **115,113,112,112,109 109,107,106,104,102 101,100,98,95,95 93**
toteswingers:1&2:£7.10, 2&3:£42.30, 1&3:£20.70 CSF £19.04 CT £397.38 TOTE £3.60: £1.60, £2.50, £8.40; EX 23.00 Trifecta £1012.80 Pool: £92,606.11 - 67.65 winning units..
Owner Jan & Peter Hopper & Michelle Morris **Bred** Mr & Mrs K W Grundy, Mr & Mrs P Hopper **Trained** Newmarket, Suffolk

FOCUS
A rebranded Diadem Stakes. Only three previous Group 1 winners lined up, but this was still a decent sprint. The race developed alongside the stands' rail, where Hooray took them along at a decent enough clip, and the winner got an ideal tow throughout. The winning time seemed to confirm that the ground was riding good on the straight course. Deacon Blues rates the top European sprinter on RPRs, although he's yet to contest a Group 1 contest. Small personal bests from the next two.

NOTEBOOK
Deacon Blues, while effective on a fast surface, is known to prefer some cut, but it wasn't anywhere near as quick as it could have been and the race couldn't have worked out any better for him. Tracking Hooray going well, he was switched to challenge 2f out and, with most of the opposition already under the pump, he put daylight between himself and the pack with a turn of foot that put the race to bed. Highly progressive since taking the Wokingham here at the royal meeting, he's now firmly established as one of the top sprinters around, despite lacking a Group 1 success. He promises to be even better next year, though, and will surely put that right soon enough, possibly in the Golden Jubilee back here in June. (op 11-4 tchd 3-1 in places)
Wizz Kid(IRE) finished well in both the Nunthorpe and Abbaye, and the return to 6f promised to be in her favour, but quicker ground wasn't so sure to suit. Her trainer had said he thought she was in the best form he'd ever had her, though, and she didn't let him down, staying on determinedly at the finish. Her profile suggests she should improve again for a winter on her back. (op 9-1)
Libranno found the ground too fast at Newmarket last time and this surface was much more to his liking. Always prominent three off the rail, he returned to the sort of form that saw him finish fourth in the July Cup. It's not been decided yet whether he stays in training next year.
Royal Rock, twice a C&D winner in the past, has been in fine form of late. Mounted on the track, he came from off the pace to stay on for fourth. This is about as much as could have been expected of him in a fair race, although a burn-up up front would have played to his strengths even more.
Moonlight Cloud ◆, held up a little further back in the pack than ideal given the way the race panned out, just as Deacon Blues was beginning to strike for home she found herself stuck behind the weakening Hooray and she then got hampered by Night Carnation, who edged left into her. Forced to drop back and switch, she finished better than anything to take fifth, and while it might be stretching things to suggest she might have won with a clear passage, she was no worse than the second best horse in this race. (tchd 3-1 and 7-2 in places)

Night Carnation, who did her owner's Moonlight Cloud no favours inside the final 2f, probably wasn't far off her best, although Deacon Blues increased his advantage over her from Newbury by a length. (op 20-1)

Prime Defender, who had a minor setback after his last run, doesn't look quite up to this level any more.

Genki(IRE) is usually fairly reliable in these events. He's at his best when the ground's quick and there's a strong pace on, though, and a disputed lead would have suited his style of running much better.

Jimmy Styles was a little out of his depth.

Hooray, who sweated up beforehand, dropped out quite quickly after making the running to 2f out.

Society Rock(IRE), who took the Golden Jubilee earlier this year, loves this place and seems to go on any ground. His draw in stall two was no help, though, with the action developing stands side, and he didn't get the clearest of runs either. That said, he was still a long below his best. Apparently a trip to Hong Kong is on the cards for him, but it's possible he's had enough for the year. (op 13-2 tchd 8-1 in a place)

Medicean Man, another with good course form, never threatened from off the pace and looks more effective over the minimum trip. (op 20-1)

Ladies Are Forever had been off the track for three months since taking a Group 3 at York and much more was demanded of her here. She wasn't alone in struggling from a low draw, but she's a sister to Hoof It, who has improved as a 4yo, and it wouldn't be a surprise if she too came back an improved filly next year.

6859 QIPCO BRITISH CHAMPIONS FILLIES' AND MARES' STKS (GROUP 2) 1m 4f

3:00 (3:05) (Class 1) 3-Y-O+

£141,775 (£53,750; £26,900; £13,400; £6,725; £3,375) **Stalls** Low

Form				RPR
2151	**1**		**Dancing Rain (IRE)**[69] 4839 3-8-10 116 JMurtagh 11 (William Haggas) *mde all: gd pce to 1/2-way and breather: stretched on again wl over 2f out: rdn and styd on wl fr over 1f out* **6/1**[3]	118
3-10	**2**	*2*	**Bible Belt (IRE)**[34] 5976 3-8-10 111 FMBerry 8 (Mrs John Harrington, Ire) *w'like: hld up in 7th: prog jst over 2f out: chsd wnr over 1f out and briefly looked dangerous: no imp fnl f* **14/1**	114
0-11	**3**	*2 1/4*	**Gertrude Bell**[105] 3624 4-9-3 110 WilliamBuick 2 (John Gosden) *lw: chsd wnr: rdn and outpcd over 2f out: lost 2nd over 1f out: clung on for 3rd at fin* **16/1**	111
4144	**4**	*hd*	**Crystal Capella**[58] 5219 6-9-3 117 RyanMoore 1 (Sir Michael Stoute) *hld up in last pair: rdn over 2f out and outpcd: styd on fr over 1f out: nrly snatched 3rd* **6/1**[3]	110
2101	**5**	*nk*	**Meeznah (USA)**[37] 5850 4-9-3 114 FrankieDettori 4 (David Lanigan) *trckd ldng trio: rdn and nt qckn over 2f out: sn lost pl: kpt on again fnl f* **6/1**[3]	110
3033	**6**	*1*	**Cill Rialaig**[23] 6269 6-9-3 99 SteveDrowne 6 (Hughie Morrison) *dwlt: hld up last: plenty to do whn rn into trble 2f out: stl only 9th 1f out: r.o wl: hopeless task* **33/1**	108
2153	**7**	*hd*	**Banimpire (IRE)**[13] 6568 3-8-10 114 KJManning 7 (J S Bolger, Ire) *hld up disputing 5th: rdn and nt qckn over 2f out: one pce and n.d fr over 1f out* **15/2**	108
5665	**8**	*1 1/4*	**Brushing**[23] 6269 5-9-3 102 KierenFallon 9 (Mark H Tompkins) *hld up in last trio: rdn over 2f out and outpcd: kpt on over 1f out: no ch and wknd last 100yds* **80/1**	106
1222	**9**	*1 1/2*	**Vita Nova (IRE)**[58] 5219 4-9-3 116 TomQueally 5 (Sir Henry Cecil) *swtg: chsd ldng pair: rdn and outpcd over 2f out: wknd over 1f out* **7/2**[1]	104
12-1	**10**	*dist*	**Ferdoos**[140] 2501 4-9-3 110 NeilCallan 10 (Roger Varian) *lw: hld up in midfield disputing 5th: rdn 4f out: wknd rapidly 3f out: t.o whn all but p.u fnl f: b.b.v* **4/1**[2]	—

2m 27.29s (-5.21) **Going Correction** +0.075s/f (Good)

WFA 3 from 4yo+ 7lb **10** Ran SP% **113.6**

Speed ratings (Par 112): **120,118,117,117,116 116,116,115,114,—**

toteswingers:1&2:£13.80, 2&3:£24.80, 1&3:£10.60 CSF £83.78 CT £1265.59 TOTE £6.50: £2.40, £4.50, £2.80; EX 94.40 Trifecta £1867.90 Pool: £13,277.40 - 5.26 winning units..

Owner M J & L A Taylor **Bred** Swettenham Stud **Trained** Newmarket, Suffolk

FOCUS

A cracking prize for this fillies' and mares' stakes, which was previously registered as the Pride Stakes when run at Newmarket, and it was a highly competitive-looking Group 2. The winner dictated and it was no fluke, but the form trio were not at their best. The winner is up 4lb on her dual Oaks form, with improvement from the next pair too.

NOTEBOOK

Dancing Rain(IRE) made all in typically gutsy fashion. She was the only previous Group 1 winner in the race and had proved her win in the Oaks no fluke when leading all the way in the German version at Dusseldorf when last seen in August. She looked tremendous in the preliminaries and the quicker ground was no bother to her. She was drawn on the outside but managed to get to the front without hassle and Johnny Murtagh, who was completing a quick-fire double, always looked happy. It seemed as though she might be in trouble when the runner-up came at her nearing the furlong marker, but she found extra when challenged and was well on top at the finish. She has been expertly handled by William Haggas this season and this was just the seventh race of her life, so there is every chance she can improve even further as she matures. Her trainer later said the plan is now to head to the Queen Elizabeth II Commemorative Cup in Japan next month and couldn't hide his excitement at seeing her race as a 4yo next year. (op 5-1 tchd 9-2)

Bible Belt(IRE) ♦'s winning sequence came to an abrupt end on her debut in this class at the Curragh last month. However, she bounced right back on this suitably quicker ground and turned in her best effort to date. She looked a big threat when easily getting to the leaders 2f out, but had no answer when the winner found more inside the final furlong and this was her first outing beyond 1m2f. She ought to win one of these next term. (op 16-1)

Gertrude Bell was having her first outing since a fortunate success in the Group 2 Lancashire Oaks in July, after which she reportedly had a poor blood count. She raced closest to the winner and appeared to blow up a little in the home straight before rallying to get back up for third. She now heads off to the paddocks. (op 14-1)

Crystal Capella has made this race her own in the last three years, winning it either side of a second place in 2009, and had won her only previous race over this C&D. She found herself with a near impossible task when straightening for home, however, and could never land a serious blow. (op 15-2 tchd 8-1)

Meeznah(USA) came here in preference to the opening Long Distance Cup and met support. She left the impression a stronger pace would have helped her finish closer on this drop back in trip. (op 8-1)

Cill Rialaig hasn't won since scoring over C&D at the royal meeting in 2010 and wasn't at her best last time, but this was a lot more encouraging considering she had plenty to find at the weights. She's better than the bare form and surely capable of finding another opening. (op 50-1 tchd 25-1)

Banimpire(IRE) bounced back to near her best when third in the Prix de l'Opera at Longchamp 13 days earlier and had won the Ribblesdale on her only previous visit her back in June. This looked a case of going to the well once too often, though, as she ran flat. (op 8-1 tchd 13-2)

Vita Nova(IRE) had been laid out for this after her second in the Yorkshire Oaks in August. She had reportedly suffered an interrupted preparation, though, and didn't help her chances by sweating up badly beforehand. She folded tamely in the home straight and obviously failed to give her true running. (tchd 4-1 in places)

Ferdoos has clearly had her problems but showed her class when winning on her sole start this term at Haydock in July, when she finished in front of three of today's rivals. She came under pressure around 5f out and was later reported by her trainer to have bled from the nose. Official explanation: trainer said filly bled from the nose (op 7-2)

6860 QUEEN ELIZABETH II STKS SPONSORED BY QIPCO (BRITISH CHAMPIONS MILE) (GROUP 1) 1m (S)

3:35 (3:42) (Class 1) 3-Y-O+

£567,100 (£215,000; £107,600; £53,600; £26,900; £13,500) **Stalls** High

Form				RPR
1111	**1**		**Frankel**[80] 4425 3-9-0 135 TomQueally 2 (Sir Henry Cecil) *lw: t.k.h early: hld up tl moved through to go 2nd 1/2-way: clsd to ld wl over 1f out and sn clr: reminders ins fnl f: r.o powerfully* **4/11**[1]	139+
1311	**2**	*4*	**Excelebration (IRE)**[34] 5988 3-9-0 126 JamieSpencer 7 (Marco Botti) *sweating: hld up: prog fr 1/2-way: rdn to take 2nd over 1f out: r.o wl but vain pursuit of wnr* **6/1**[2]	129
0111	**3**	*3 1/2*	**Immortal Verse (IRE)**[61] 5129 3-8-11 121 GeraldMosse 6 (Robert Collet, France) *s.i.s: hld up in last: prog 2f out to chse ldng pair over 1f out: no imp: jst hld on for 3rd* **7/1**[3]	118
6414	**4**	*nk*	**Dubawi Gold**[34] 5988 3-9-0 117 JMurtagh 3 (Richard Hannon) *racd in 3rd to 1/2-way: outpcd and struggling 3f out: n.d after: styd on fnl f* **28/1**	120
0101	**5**	*3/4*	**Dick Turpin (IRE)**[21] 6369 4-9-3 122 ChristopheSoumillon 5 (Richard Hannon) *racd in 2nd to 1/2-way but ignored pcemaker: taken alone to nr side rail and struggling 3f out: no ch fnl 2f: kpt on nr fin* **14/1**	118
2003	**6**	*1/2*	**Poet's Voice**[22] 6298 4-9-3 114 (t) FrankieDettori 1 (Saeed Bin Suroor) *hld up in rr: prog whn inclined hd towards Excelebration at 1/2-way: rdn over 2f out: sn btn* **33/1**	117
1314	**7**	*hd*	**Side Glance**[27] 6204 4-9-3 115 JimmyFortune 8 (Andrew Balding) *plld hrd early: hld up in rr: rdn and struggling in last over 2f out: no ch after* **50/1**	116
55-0	**8**	*2 3/4*	**Bullet Train**[184] 1342 4-9-3 106 IanMongan 4 (Sir Henry Cecil) *lw: led: drew 10 l clr after 2f: hdd & wknd wl over 1f out* **150/1**	110

1m 39.45s (-1.15) **Going Correction** +0.075s/f (Good)

WFA 3 from 4yo 3lb **8** Ran SP% **115.8**

Speed ratings (Par 117): **108,104,100,100,99 98,98,96**

toteswingers:1&2:£1.80, 2&3:£2.00, 1&3:£1.70 CSF £3.06 CT £6.86 TOTE £1.40: £1.02, £1.80, £1.50; EX 3.90 Trifecta £7.00 Pool: £49,011.44 - 5,121.28 winning units..

Owner K Abdulla **Bred** Juddmonte Farms Ltd **Trained** Newmarket, Suffolk

■ Stewards' Enquiry : Jamie Spencer four-day ban: careless riding (Oct 29,31, Nov 1-2)

FOCUS

A later date for this race, which took place over the straight mile for the first time. Five individual Group 1 winners lined up for this much-anticipated Group 1, including three of the four best milers in Europe. Frankel's pacemaker Bullet Train was largely ignored and they went an even pace. Top-class form which rates Frankel's best effort to date. Excelebration's form was good enough to have won all but two of the last ten runnings. Immortal Verse was 5lb off her French best.

NOTEBOOK

Frankel was bidding to extend his unbeaten record to nine races. Despite the quality of the opposition, he looked to have nothing to fear from them on the book - officially rated 9lb clear of his nearest rival - and the only real concern was whether he'd retained his form since the Sussex Stakes, having been on the go since April. He was keen early without cover but was allowed to stride on heading to the halfway mark and closed in on his pacemaker between 3f and 2f out (his quickest furlong), before stretching clear inside the last furlong and a half. He beat the runner-up Excelebration just as far here as he did when they met for the first time in the Greenham, but he seems an easier ride these days and getting him to settle better has been important, not least with a view to next year, when he's likely to be asked to challenge for top honours over 1m2f. There had been an outside chance that he'd go to the Breeders' Cup this year and, in what is a weak year for 3yos in the US, he'd surely have been a big player in the Classic as his style of running suggests the dirt should suit, but Sir Henry Cecil ruled it out and he'll now be given a winter's break. He'll end this year rated the best horse in the world and there's plenty to look forward to next season. (tchd 2-5 and 1-2 in places)

Excelebration(IRE)'s only defeats since his debut have been in races won by Frankel. Winner of the Moulin last time out, he's a top-class miler, effective on all ground, and as his trainer has quite rightly suggested, would probably be considered a champion in any other year. He quickened up well to go clear of the rest and, while once again outclassed by the winner, may yet have another big race in him if his connections, who now include the Coolmore team, decide to send him to the Breeders' Cup Mile or Hong Kong. (op 7-1)

Immortal Verse(IRE) showcased her terrific turn of foot when successful here at the royal meeting and again when seeing off Goldikova in the Jacques le Marois, but had to miss the Moulin on account of an overreach. Her trainer was confident she was over that setback, but she'd missed work (11 days) so her preparation for taking on such a formidable rival as Frankel had hardly been ideal. Held up at the back of the field, she couldn't live with the big two inside the final furlong but she didn't run badly in the circumstances. She won't go to the Breeders' Cup but stays in training as a 4-y-o, and with Goldikova not as good as she was and Frankel likely to be racing over further next year, she should have plenty of opportunities to add more Group 1 wins to her name. (op 8-1)

Dubawi Gold had probably seen enough of the backsides of Frankel and Excelebration, having twice been beaten by the former and three times by the latter already this season, but once again he had to watch them disappear over the horizon. A stronger gallop might have helped him finish closer as he was keen early. He could go for the Hong Kong Mile next, although he's been on the go since April and it might be one race too many, while his connections are keen on running him in Dubai early next year and he'll apparently be entered for three races on World Cup night, including the feature event. (op 40-1)

Dick Turpin(IRE) has tended to be found out against the very best in this division and it was the same story again. He would be better off returning to pot-hunting for weak Group 1s abroad. (op 20-1)

Poet's Voice has been lightly raced since taking part in the Dubai World Cup this season. Tracking the winner through, he was left behind from 2f out and just isn't in the same form as when taking this race last year. (op 40-1)

Side Glance looked outclassed in this field and his refusal to settle early on only made his task harder.

6861 QIPCO CHAMPION STKS (BRITISH CHAMPIONS MIDDLE DISTANCE) (GROUP 1) 1m 2f

4:10 (4:21) (Class 1) 3-Y-O+

£737,230 (£279,500; £139,880; £69,680; £34,970; £17,550) **Stalls** Low

Form				RPR
1112	**1**		**Cirrus Des Aigles (FR)**[14] 6558 5-9-3 125 ChristopheSoumillon 1 (Mme C Barande-Barbe, France) *racd keenly: mostly trckd ldng trio: moved up strly to chal over 1f out: drvn to ld ins fnl f: r.o wl to assert nr fin* **12/1**	130
2114	**2**	*3/4*	**So You Think (NZ)**[13] 6567 5-9-3 126 RyanMoore 9 (A P O'Brien, Ire) *trckd ldng pair: wnt 2nd over 2f out gng strly: led over 1f out but sn pressed: hdd ins fnl f: r.o but hld nr fin* **7/4**[1]	128

4223 **3** *1/2* **Snow Fairy (IRE)**[13] 6567 4-9-0 121 .... OlivierPeslier 2 125+
(Ed Dunlop) *trckd ldrs: effrt 3f out: cl up bhd ldng pair over 1f out but forced to wait: plld out fnl f: r.o but nvr able to deliver chal* **8/1**[3]

2212 **4** *2* **Midday**[59] 5183 5-9-0 120 .... TomQueally 3 120
(Sir Henry Cecil) *lw: t.k.h early and sn restrained to rr: drvn on outer over 2f out: styd on fnl 2f to take 4th last stride* **8/1**[3]

1211 **5** *shd* **Nathaniel (IRE)**[84] 4315 3-8-12 128 .... WilliamBuick 10 123
(John Gosden) *swtg: duelled for ld tl gained advantage over 3f out: kicked on wl over 2f out: hdd and one pce over 1f out* **5/1**[2]

1011 **6** *1 1/2* **Green Destiny (IRE)**[28] 6161 4-9-3 117 .... KierenFallon 11 120
(William Haggas) *lw: hld up last: effrt over 2f out: rdn and styd on fnl 2f: nvr any ch of rching ldrs* **14/1**

3350 **7** *2 1/4* **Sri Putra**[7] 6693 5-9-3 115 .... NeilCallan 5 116
(Roger Varian) *hld up in midfield: effrt 3f out: no prog whn edgd rt over 1f out: wl btn after* **100/1**

5251 **8** *2 1/4* **Ransom Note**[22] 6298 4-9-3 117 .... MichaelHills 7 111
(Charles Hills) *disp ld to over 3f out: wknd over 1f out* **40/1**

0041 **9** *shd* **Wigmore Hall (IRE)**[27] 6203 4-9-3 117 .... JamieSpencer 4 117+
(Michael Bell) *hld up in rr: sme prog on inner 2f out: no ch whn nt clr run over 1f out* **28/1**

6511 **10** *3/4* **Twice Over**[59] 5183 6-9-3 125 .... IanMongan 8 109
(Sir Henry Cecil) *settled in midfield: effrt over 4f out: drvn to chse ldrs 3f out: wknd wl over 1f out* **12/1**

-001 **11** *3 1/2* **Casamento (IRE)**[28] 6185 3-8-12 117 .... MickaelBarzalona 6 102
(Mahmood Al Zarooni) *a towards rr: struggling over 3f out: sn no ch* **25/1**

1-1 **12** *69* **Dubai Prince (IRE)**[29] 6125 3-8-12 113 .... FrankieDettori 12 —
(Mahmood Al Zarooni) *trckd ldrs on outer: wknd over 2f out: virtually p.u fnl f* **8/1**[3]

2m 2.52s (-4.48) **Going Correction** +0.075s/f (Good) course record
WFA 3 from 4yo+ 5lb **12** Ran SP% **119.1**
Speed ratings (Par 117): **120,119,119,117,117 116,114,112,112,111 109,53**
toteswingers:1&2:£4.20, 2&3:£4.40, 1&3:£11.10 CSF £32.66 CT £189.56 TOTE £5.50: £1.30, £1.40, £2.30; EX 25.40 Trifecta £126.10 Pool: £28,543.65 - 167.42 winning units..
Owner Jean-Claude-Alain Dupouy **Bred** Y Lelimouzin And B Deschamps **Trained** France
■ High controversy as Christophe Soumillon fell foul of the new whip rules, losing over £52,000 in prize money.
■ Stewards' Enquiry : Christophe Soumillon five-day ban: used whip with excessive frequency (Oct 29,31,Nov 1-3)

FOCUS
The inaugural running at Ascot of the Champion Stakes, now Britain's richest race, and for the first time it was run around a bend. It was a race with fantastic strength in depth boasting seven previous Group 1 winners who had amassed 24 successes at the top level between them. It was run at a solid pace and resulted in a course-record time, but it was a race in which it paid to race prominently and the principals dominated from 2f out. Cirrus Des Aigles confirmed he is still improving with a top-class effort to beat a basically to form second and third. The seventh offers perspective.

NOTEBOOK
Cirrus Des Aigles(FR), not allowed to contest the Arc due to him being a gelding, was just touched off by Byword in the Group 2 Prix Dollar on Arc weekend at Longchamp a fortnight earlier, but that was still up with his previous best efforts and he would have likely conceded weight all round and gained back-to-back wins in that race granted a stronger pace. He was a market drifter here, possibly on account of the ground as he does enjoy cut, but he got the strong pace he needs and clearly the surface posed him no problems. He was always well positioned and went for everything passing the furlong marker, but had to dig very deep to master the runner-up. This trip is a minimum for him, though, and his superior stamina kicked in nearing the business end. It was the 5yo's first success at the top level at the seventh time of asking and it was fully deserved. He's improved plenty since resuming this year and now looks set to have another crack at the Hong Kong Cup in December, in which he finished ninth last year behind Snow Fairy. He should go close in that. (op 8-1)
So You Think(NZ) got too far back to land a blow in the Arc when upped to 1m4f 13 days earlier and, a strong horse who takes his racing well, was heavily backed to land his ninth success at the top level. He unsurprisingly raced closer to the pace back down in trip and Ryan Moore got him in a good rhythm. He looked the one to be on nearing 2f out as he was still on the bridle, but despite quickening he couldn't shake off the winner and was held inside the final half-furlong. This was another sterling effort in defeat, but perhaps his exertions in the Arc just took a toll late on. It remains to be seen if he is now put away for the year or goes to the well once more by travelling to the Breeder's Cup next month. (tchd 13-8 and 2-1 in places)
Snow Fairy(IRE) ◆, one place ahead of old rival So You Think in the Arc last time, had Olivier Peslier replacing Frankie Dettori in the saddle and was sensibly allowed to get closer to the leaders from around halfway. She travelled sweetly into the home straight but had to wait for her effort as things got tight nearing the last furlong and that may well have cost her second place. She still ran another cracking race in defeat and it seems incredible that she has gone without success this term. That will probably be put right when she returns to the Far East next month. (op 9-1 tchd 10-1 in places)
Midday fared best of those coming from well off the pace and rates a little better than the bare form. This six-time Group 1 winner has still to win away from racing against her own sex, though. She may go to the Breeders' Cup. (op 10-1)
Nathaniel(IRE) loves this venue and was having his first outing since landing the highly eventful King George over 1m4f here in July. Officially the highest rated in the race, the 3-y-o was hampered by being drawn widest of all and ultimately paid for doing too much early on this drop back in trip. This confirms him somewhat flattered by a mark of 128, but it was a good run in the circumstances and there is likely better to come from him back up in distance. (op 6-1 tchd 13-2 in a place)
Green Destiny(IRE) made it 2-2 in Group 3 company at Newbury last time out, but had a lot to find on this debut at the top level and had flopped on his only previous run here at the royal meeting in June. He posted another career-best in defeat and is another whose run needs upgrading as he was last turning for home and met a little trouble around 2f out. (op 20-1)
Sri Putra was always held, but ran right up to his mark in defeat.
Ransom Note never got his own way out in front, but was ultimately outclassed. (op 66-1)
Wigmore Hall(IRE) was well held back down in trip on this return to Britain. Official explanation: jockey said gelding was denied a clear run
Twice Over proved very easy to back in his quest to win the race for a third successive time and was not a serious threat. He's never looked at his best at this course. (op 14-1)
Casamento(IRE) turned in a laboured effort and disappointed.
Dubai Prince(IRE) came into this a totally unknown quantity, but was later found to have a breathing problem and it's hoped he's not due another spell on the sidelines. Official explanation: jockey said colt had a breathing problem (tchd 15-2)

6862 QIPCO FUTURE STARS APPRENTICE H'CAP 7f
4:45 (4:56) (Class 2) (0-100,98) 3-Y-O+ **£16,172** (£4,812; £2,405; £1,202) **Stalls** High

Form RPR

1000 **1** **Edinburgh Knight (IRE)**[28] 6145 4-9-6 93 .... MatthewDavies 23 102
(Paul D'Arcy) *dwlt: racd nr side: hld up and sn in tch: prog 3f out: rdn to ld overall over 1f out: hld on u.p* **18/1**

0142 **2** *3/4* **Primaeval**[15] 6496 5-9-2 89 ....(v) LouisBeuzelin 24 96
(James Fanshawe) *trckd nr side ldrs: prog to chal over 1f out: styd on but hld last 75yds* **10/1**[2]

0400 **3** *nse* **Castles In The Air**[7] 6706 6-9-5 92 .... LeeTopliss 11 99
(Richard Fahey) *hld up in midfield far side: rdn and prog over 2f out: led gp jst over 1f out: styd on: nt quite on terms: 1st of 13 in gp* **12/1**

0206 **4** *nk* **Axiom**[35] 5936 7-9-6 98 .... MichaelJMurphy(5) 5 104
(Ed Walker) *dwlt: wl in rr on far side: gd prog against rail fr over 2f out: chal fnl f: jst hld: 2nd of 13 in gp* **40/1**

3665 **5** *3/4* **Perfect Silence**[14] 6523 6-8-10 88 .... LucyKBarry(5) 10 92
(Clive Cox) *lw: led far side gp to jst over 1f out: kpt on same pce fnl f: 3rd of 13 in gp: gd effrt* **25/1**

0530 **6** *1/2* **Imperial Guest**[14] 6521 5-9-6 96 .... RyanPowell(3) 13 99
(George Margarson) *hld up in rr far side: prog 2f out: styd on fnl f: nrst fin: 4th of 13 in gp* **25/1**

0602 **7** *hd* **Mia's Boy**[21] 6341 7-9-3 97 .... JoshCrane(7) 12 99
(Chris Dwyer) *hld up in rr far side: prog 2f out: styd on fnl f: nvr quite able to chal: 5th of 13 in gp* **28/1**

1163 **8** *nk* **White Frost (IRE)**[21] 6341 3-8-12 92 .... MatthewLawson(5) 26 93
(Charles Hills) *led nr side gp to over 1f out: one pce* **11/1**[3]

5611 **9** *nk* **Directorship**[63] 5043 5-9-0 90 .... MatthewCosham(3) 21 91
(Patrick Chamings) *hld up in rr nr side: effrt and rdn over 2f out: kpt on fr over 1f out: nvr able to chal* **12/1**

0046 **10** *hd* **Pleasant Day (IRE)**[30] 6080 4-8-7 87 ....(b) LauraBarry(7) 1 87
(Richard Fahey) *chsd far side ldr to over 1f out: one pce after: 6th of 13 in gp* **33/1**

3023 **11** *3/4* **The Confessor**[35] 5936 4-9-3 90 .... MartinHarley 25 88
(Henry Candy) *led nr side gp 2f: chsd ldr to 2f out: steadily fdd* **8/1**[1]

0004 **12** *1 1/4* **Striking Spirit**[21] 6341 6-9-2 89 .... SophieDoyle 18 84
(Tim Easterby) *pressed nr side ldrs: rdn over 2f out: fdd jst over 1f out* **20/1**

3060 **13** *3/4* **Mr David (USA)**[21] 6341 4-8-12 92 ....(p) BrendanPowell(7) 29 85
(Jamie Osborne) *hld up bhd ldrs nr side: gng wl 3f out: rdn and nt qckn over 2f out: fdd* **33/1**

03 **14** *2 1/4* **Naabegha**[21] 6326 4-9-2 89 .... JohnFahy 27 75
(Ed de Giles) *dwlt: hld up in rr nr side: effrt over 2f out: nvr on terms w ldrs* **20/1**

21- **14** *dht* **Pearl Ice**[366] 6869 3-8-11 89 .... RosieJessop(3) 8 75
(Sir Mark Prescott Bt) *prom far side tl wknd over 1f out: 7th of 13 in gp* **10/1**[2]

0010 **16** *nk* **Golden Desert (IRE)**[14] 6521 7-9-2 94 .... RaulDaSilva(5) 15 80
(Robert Mills) *racd in centre trio: chsd ldr 1/2-way: no imp as gps merged over 2f out: wl hld after* **33/1**

0201 **17** *1 1/4* **Kiwi Bay**[14] 6533 6-9-3 90 .... KierenFox 3 72
(Michael Dods) *prom in far side gp tl wknd over 1f out: 8th of 13 in gp* **20/1**

0130 **18** *shd* **Noble Citizen (USA)**[36] 5887 6-9-3 93 ....(b) AmyScott(3) 4 75
(David Simcock) *lw: dwlt: hld up in midfield far side: gng strly over 2f out: wknd qckly wl over 1f out: 9th of 13 in gp* **14/1**

0240 **19** *nk* **Baby Strange**[8] 6672 7-9-1 88 .... RossAtkinson 7 69
(Derek Shaw) *b: nvr bttr than midfield far side: rdn 3f out: n.d fnl 2f: 10th of 13 in gp* **50/1**

0526 **20** *1* **Dubai Dynamo**[8] 6672 6-9-5 92 .... JamesSullivan 9 71
(Ruth Carr) *dwlt: a wl in rr far side: 11th of 13 in gp* **33/1**

0200 **21** *1 1/2* **Lutine Bell**[7] 6706 4-9-1 93 .... DavidKenny(5) 14 67
(Mike Murphy) *dwlt: racd far side: a in rr: rdn and no prog over 2f out: 12th of 13 in gp* **33/1**

3000 **22** *3/4* **Docofthebay (IRE)**[8] 6672 7-9-0 90 ....(b) NeilFarley(3) 6 62
(David Nicholls) *rdn in midfield of far side gp by 1/2-way: sn btn: last of 13 in gp* **16/1**

1000 **23** *nk* **Thunderball**[36] 5887 5-8-13 91 ....(b) LeonnaMayor(5) 17 63
(David Nicholls) *b: racd in centre trio: probably overall ldr to over 1f out: wknd qckly* **50/1**

4221 **24** *3 1/2* **Valencha**[20] 6378 4-9-0 87 .... HarryBentley 19 49
(Hughie Morrison) *prom nr side over 2f: sn lost pl: struggling in rr over 2f out* **11/1**[3]

2504 **25** *1 1/2* **Duster**[23] 6273 4-8-9 87 .... CharlesBishop(5) 22 45
(Hughie Morrison) *[illegible] nr side 3f: sn lost pl and struggling* **16/1**

-000 **26** *1/2* **Kalk Bay (IRE)**[35] 5936 4-9-1 88 ....(vt[1]) AdamBeschizza 2 45
(William Haggas) *dwlt: racd freely: prom nr side tl wknd rapidly over 2f out* **25/1**

0061 **27** *10* **Rulesn'regulations**[16] 6477 5-9-1 88 ....(b) SeanLevey 16 18
(Matthew Salaman) *dropped to last of centre trio 1/2-way: sn wknd: t.o* **40/1**

2140 **28** *4* **Woodcote Place**[21] 6341 8-8-9 87 .... AntiocoMurgia(5) 20 —
(Patrick Chamings) *s.v.s: racd nr side and a bhd: t.o* **40/1**

0503 **29** *8* **Crown Counsel (IRE)**[12] 6574 3-9-3 92 .... MichaelO'Connell 28 —
(Mark Johnston) *lw: nvr gng wl: sn struggling u.p nr side: t.o* **25/1**

1m 27.44s (0.24) **Going Correction** +0.075s/f (Good)
WFA 3 from 4yo+ 2lb **29** Ran SP% **144.1**
Speed ratings (Par 109): **101,100,100,99,98 98,98,97,97,97 96,94,94,91,91 91,89,89,89,88 86,85,85,81,79 78,67,62,53**
toteswingers:1&2:£29.20, 2&3:£9.10, 1&3:£21.20 CSF £165.53 CT £2332.38 TOTE £32.90: £6.80, £3.10, £3.00, £13.50; EX 411.90 Trifecta £4417.60 Part won. Pool: £5,969.74 - 0.10 winning units..
Owner Knights Racing **Bred** New England Stud Myriad Norelands **Trained** Newmarket, Suffolk

FOCUS
It was a bit of a shame that such a cracking card featuring so many top-class horses should conclude with a humdrum handicap for apprentices and hopefully next year the meeting will end with, at the very least, a good-quality heritage handicap. Just 11lb covered the entire field and the betting reflected the fact that it looked a wide-open affair, confined to apprentice riders. They split into two groups but there looked to be no draw advantage. Sound form with a small personal best from the winner.

NOTEBOOK
Edinburgh Knight(IRE) has had a few goes in these sorts of events and posted one of his better efforts over 6f here in May when third in a race in which Deacon Blues was an unlucky second. He travelled well in the stands-side group before kicking on approaching the final furlong and held on all out. The surface here clearly suits him well and perhaps it's no coincidence that he also has a fine record on Polytrack. (op 16-1 tchd 20-1)
Primaeval, another who has a good record on Polytrack (rated 10lb higher on AW than on turf), ran well in defeat over 1m here last time. Equally effective over this distance, he pushed the winner all the way to the line and is one to keep in mind for similar races here in the future. (op 14-1)
Castles In The Air, seventh in a heritage handicap over this C&D in July, got to race off 6lb lower here and left behind a couple of down-the-field efforts with a return to form at his favourite track. He was first home from the group that raced on the far side.
Axiom could have done with softer ground but he still ran a good race off top weight, finishing strongly up the far rail to grab a place close home. (op 33-1)

Perfect Silence, outclassed in Listed company last time, ran a better race back in the right grade. Prominent throughout on the far side, she ran up to her recent best in defeat, but her current mark doesn't make things easy (tchd 33-1 in a place)
Imperial Guest had the winner behind when successful over 6f here in May but, despite being 2lb better off with him, couldn't confirm the form over this longer trip. He's 5-17 over 6f but 0-16 over further.
Mia's Boy kept on late from off the pace on the far side and posted another solid effort in defeat, but one win from his last 32 starts is no great return.
White Frost(IRE), one of the less-exposed runners and one of only three 3-y-os in the line-up, showed up well on the stands' side throughout. Progressive during the second half of this season, there has to be the potential of better to come if she's kept in training next year. (op 16-1)
Directorship, chasing a hat-trick on his return from a two-month break, did win over 7f last time but a mile seems to suit him best and he was staying on all too late on this occasion. It was still a good effort off 4lb higher, though. (op 14-1)
Pleasant Day(IRE) was back down to a mark 1lb lower than when successful at Ripon in June, but that victory came over 1m1f and he was unsurprisingly outpaced here inside the final furlong and a half.
The Confessor showed speed on the stands' side but making all the running in this type of event is always difficult and he didn't see his race out. He remains on a mark he should be able to win off when things fall more kindly, though. (op 9-1 tchd 10-1 in a place)
Pearl Ice was the most interesting horse in the race, but he was a major market drifter and finished well held on his handicap debut. He's clearly had his problems, though, so this was a perfectly satisfactory return to action and, given his proven form on Polytrack, it wouldn't be a surprise to see him back on that surface in the coming weeks. (tchd 12-1)
Noble Citizen(USA) invariably runs well in these types of events at this track but, having travelled well to 2f out, he dropped out tamely, suggesting perhaps that all was not well with him this time. (op 16-1)
Crown Counsel(IRE) Official explanation: jockey said colt never travelled
T/Jkpt: £36,959.70 to a £1 stake. Pool:£442,475.69 - 8.50 winning tickets T/Plt: £156.60 to a £1 stake. Pool:£253,611.75 - 1,181.66 winning tickets T/Qpdt: £48.30 to a £1 stake. Pool:£12,760.96 - 195.36 winning tickets JN

6597 CATTERICK (L-H)

Saturday, October 15

OFFICIAL GOING: Soft (good to soft in places; 6.8)
Wind: Virtually nil Weather: Fine and dry

6863 TOTEPLACEPOT NOVICE STKS — 5f
1:45 (1:45) (Class 5) 2-Y-O **£2,911** (£866; £432; £216) **Stalls** Low

Form — RPR
5410 **1** **I'll Be Good**[14] 6524 2-9-2 74 GaryBartley(3) 5 — 80
(Robert Johnson) *trckd ldrs: hdwy over 2f out: led wl over 1f out: clr ent fnl f: sn rdn and kpt on* **9/1**
1342 **2** *1* **Quite A Thing**[10] 6625 2-9-2 86 StevieDonohoe 2 — 73
(Sir Mark Prescott Bt) *s.i.s and sn rdn along in rr: hdwy wl over 1f out: rdn to chse wnr ins fnl f: kpt on wl towards fin* **11/4**[2]
32 **3** *2 ¾* **Red Shadow**[46] 5590 2-8-9 57 AndrewMullen 1 — 57
(Alan Brown) *cl up on inner: rdn along wl over 1f out: one pce appr fnl f* **25/1**
2442 **4** *3 ½* **Redair (IRE)**[3] 6786 2-9-0 74 (b[1]) PaulHanagan 6 — 49
(David Evans) *wnt rt s: sn cl up on outer: effrt 2f out and ev ch tl rdn appr fnl f and sn wknd* **13/2**[3]
421 **5** *7* **Glamorous Angel (IRE)**[23] 6274 2-9-5 83 PJMcDonald 4 — 29
(Alan Swinbank) *slt ld: pushed along 1/2-way: rdn 2f out: sn hdd & wknd* **5/6**[1]

62.26 secs (2.46) **Going Correction** +0.325s/f (Good) **5** Ran SP% **108.4**
Speed ratings (Par 95): **93,91,87,81,70**
toteswingers: 1&2 £14.60 CSF £32.25 TOTE £12.20: £4.60, £1.70; EX 36.20.
Owner Do Well Racing **Bred** Cobhall Court Stud **Trained** Newburn, Tyne & Wear

FOCUS
On a bright, sunny day the ground was described as soft. Four previous winners in this event but the form book went out of the window.

NOTEBOOK
I'll Be Good, winner of just one of his ten starts, is rated just 74 and had plenty to find. He travelled strongly and there was no fluke about it. He clearly relished give underfoot. (op 10-1)
Quite A Thing, who had 15lb in hand of the winner on official ratings, won two of her first three starts but has not really progressed since. She missed the break and left herself with too much to do. (op 2-1)
Red Shadow, the only maiden, is rated just 57 after nine previous attempts. It is hard to believe she has improved. (op 33-1)
Redair(IRE), runner-up in a claimer on the all-weather at Kempton three days earlier, is another who has not gone on after a bright start. She went right at the start and was always tending to edge left racing isolated towards the middle of the track. (tchd 6-1)
Glamorous Angel(IRE), a Pontefract 6f maiden winner, was a major disappointment, dropping right out after being in the firing line to halfway. This was simply too bad to be true and his rider reported 'he never went a yard on the soft ground'. Official explanation: trainer said, regarding running, that the colt was unsuited by the soft (good to soft places) ground (op 11-10)

6864 TOTEPOOL FILLIES' NURSERY — 7f
2:20 (2:20) (Class 4) (0-85,83) 2-Y-O **£4,528** (£1,347; £673; £336) **Stalls** Low

Form — RPR
103 **1** **Free Verse**[46] 5584 2-9-4 83 KieranO'Neill(3) 3 — 86
(Richard Hannon) *in rr: pushed along 3f out: hdwy on inner wl over 1f out: rdn to chse ldrs ent fnl f: styd on wl to ld last 50yds* **8/1**
1042 **2** *½* **See Clearly**[12] 6573 2-9-0 76 (b) DuranFentiman 8 — 78
(Tim Easterby) *led: pushed clr and c wd home bnd to stands' rail: rdn over 1f out: hdd and no ex last 50yds* **11/1**
5500 **3** *1 ¾* **Alabanda (IRE)**[11] 6599 2-8-7 69 DavidAllan 1 — 66
(Tim Easterby) *in tch: hdwy over 2f out: rdn to chse ldr jst over 1f out: kpt on same pce fnl f* **10/1**
1335 **4** *4* **Ladykin (IRE)**[41] 5755 2-8-7 76 GeorgeChaloner(7) 11 — 63
(Richard Fahey) *hld up: hdwy over 2f out: rdn to chse ldrs over 1f out: kpt on same pce fnl f* **10/1**
012 **5** *1 ¾* **Annie Walker (IRE)**[11] 6599 2-8-6 68 AdrianNicholls 10 — 51
(David Nicholls) *prom: chsd ldr wl over 2f out: rdn wl over 1f out: wknd appr fnl f* **7/1**[3]
2642 **6** *1 ¼* **Act Your Shoe Size**[9] 6645 2-9-1 77 DarryllHolland 7 — 57
(Keith Dalgleish) *chsd ldrs: rdn along over 2f out: grad wknd* **6/1**[2]
366 **7** *¾* **Trioomph**[17] 6449 2-8-0 65 ow1 DeclanCannon(3) 2 — 43
(James Given) *prom: rdn along wl over 2f out: grad wknd* **25/1**
41 **8** *1* **Feelthedifference**[31] 6047 2-8-10 72 PaulHanagan 12 — 48
(Sir Henry Cecil) *in rr and rdn along 1/2-way: nvr a factor* **3/1**[1]
0000 **9** *15* **Nearly A Gift (IRE)**[8] 6670 2-9-1 77 GrahamGibbons 6 — 15
(Tim Easterby) *chsd ldrs to 1/2-way: sn wknd* **33/1**
101 **10** *1 ¾* **Royal Majestic**[23] 6275 2-8-10 72 SamHitchcott 13 — 6
(Mick Channon) *dwlt: a in rr* **12/1**
5220 **11** *1 ¼* **Always Ends Well (IRE)**[19] 6399 2-8-1 63 JimmyQuinn 5 — —
(Mark Johnston) *dwlt: a towards rr* **10/1**
1010 **12** *17* **Aquasulis (IRE)**[12] 6590 2-8-10 72 StevieDonohoe 4 — —
(David Evans) *chsd ldrs: rdn along bef 1/2-way: sn wknd* **33/1**

1m 30.82s (3.82) **Going Correction** +0.525s/f (Yiel) **12** Ran SP% **115.9**
Speed ratings (Par 94): **99,98,96,91,89 88,87,86,69,67 65,46**
toteswingers:1&2:£9.50, 2&3:£9.20, 1&3:£7.40 CSF £88.91 CT £895.19 TOTE £7.10: £2.30, £3.00, £3.90; EX 118.60 TRIFECTA Not won..
Owner The Queen **Bred** The Queen **Trained** East Everleigh, Wilts

FOCUS
A competitive nursery run at a sound pace and in the end they all migrated towards the stands' side rail in the home straight.

NOTEBOOK
Free Verse, absent for six weeks and stepping up to 7f for the first time, looked a most unlikely winner in the first half of the race. Towards the rear and pushed along, she was last to make the diversion to the stands' side. Racing widest of all she finished strongly to lead in the closing stages. On this evidence she might be even better suited by 1m.
See Clearly, runner-up at Pontefract from a 1lb lower mark when blinkered for the first time, took them along and was the first to cross over. She held a useful lead over a furlong out only to be scythed down near the line. She is very tough and loves give. (op 10-1)
Alabanda(IRE) started life in handicap company from a harsh mark. She has slipped 8lb since and this was a much more encouraging effort. (op 12-1)
Ladykin(IRE) bounced back after a moderate effort but she has previously been placed third twice in nurseries and is looking exposed. (op 11-1)
Annie Walker(IRE), 3lb higher than when runner-up here last time, kept tabs on the leader and paid the price. (tchd 15-2)
Feelthedifference looked potentially leniently treated on 72 but she had an outside draw and dropped to the rear leaving the back straight. Paul Hanagan reported she was never travelling and it was possible she didn't handle the ground. Official explanation: jockey said filly never travelled (op 11-4)

6865 TOTESCOOP6 CATTERICK DASH (HANDICAP STKS) — 5f
2:55 (2:55) (Class 3) (0-95,95) 3-Y-O+ **£9,056** (£2,695; £1,346; £673) **Stalls** Low

Form — RPR
0130 **1** **Verinco**[35] 5927 5-8-13 94 (v) JustinNewman(7) 1 — 103
(Bryan Smart) *racd far side: mde all: rdn over 1f out: kpt on wl: 1st of 5 in gp* **3/1**[1]
3002 **2** *¾* **Favourite Girl (IRE)**[25] 6233 5-9-4 92 (p) DuranFentiman 4 — 98
(Tim Easterby) *prom far side: rdn to chal ent fnl f: kpt on: 2nd of 5 in gp* **9/1**
0020 **3** *½* **Singeur (IRE)**[7] 6706 4-9-7 95 (b) LeeNewman 7 — 100
(Robin Bastiman) *trckd ldrs stands' side: hdwy 2f out: rdn over 1f out: kpt on wl fnl f: 1st of 7 in gp* **13/2**[2]
6000 **4** *¾* **Cocktail Charlie**[21] 6347 3-9-2 90 (b[1]) DavidAllan 11 — 92
(Tim Easterby) *chsd ldrs stands' side: hdwy to ld that gp over 1f out and sn ev ch: rdn and one pce ins fnl f: 2nd of 7 in gp* **11/1**
5262 **5** *1 ½* **Lucky Numbers (IRE)**[35] 5923 5-8-11 85 PJMcDonald 6 — 81
(Paul Green) *chsd ldrs far side: rdn along wl over 1f out: no imp fnl f: 3rd of 5 in gp* **9/1**
0226 **6** *nk* **Bathwick Bear (IRE)**[26] 6224 3-9-3 94 ow1 RichardEvans(3) 14 — 89
(David Evans) *chsd ldrs stands' side: rdn wl over 1f out: kpt on same pce: 3rd of 7 in gp* **18/1**
0230 **7** *1 ¾* **Taurus Twins**[7] 6703 5-8-9 83 (b) RobertWinston 12 — 72
(Richard Price) *chsd ldrs stands' side: rdn along 2f out: sn one pce: 4th of 7 in gp* **12/1**
0326 **8** *nse* **Master Rooney (IRE)**[21] 6332 5-9-0 88 TomEaves 10 — 77
(Bryan Smart) *led stands' side: gp: rdn along 2f out: hdd & wknd over 1f out: 5th of 7 in gp* **10/1**
2421 **9** *nk* **Pelmanism**[43] 5680 4-8-7 81 BarryMcHugh 8 — 69
(Brian Ellison) *dwlt: a in rr stands' side: 6th of 7 in gp* **8/1**[3]
0406 **10** *1 ¼* **Rasaman (IRE)**[7] 6703 7-8-7 81 (v) FrederikTylicki 2 — 64
(Jim Goldie) *a in rr far side: 4th of 5 in gp* **14/1**
6301 **11** *hd* **Courageous (IRE)**[21] 6327 5-9-0 88 (t) PhillipMakin 13 — 71
(Kevin Ryan) *prom stands' side: rdn along 2f out: sn wknd: last of 7 in gp* **10/1**
3040 **12** *9* **Fathom Five (IRE)**[21] 6332 7-8-11 85 AdrianNicholls 3 — 35
(David Nicholls) *prom far side: rdn along 1/2-way: sn wknd and bhd whn eased fnl f: last of 5 in gp* **20/1**

60.37 secs (0.57) **Going Correction** +0.325s/f (Good) **12** Ran SP% **120.3**
Speed ratings (Par 107): **108,106,106,104,102 101,99,99,98,96 96,81**
toteswingers:1&2:£10.20, 2&3:£21.80, 1&3:£9.30 CSF £30.49 CT £170.80 TOTE £3.20: £1.50, £2.40, £2.70; EX 39.30 Trifecta £128.10 Pool: £429.63 - 2.48 winning units..
Owner B Smart **Bred** Mrs M Gutkin **Trained** Hambleton, N Yorks

FOCUS
Quite a valuable prize for this highly competitive 81-95 Dash. They raced in two distinct groups, five sticking to the far side headed by the first two home.

NOTEBOOK
Verinco is all speed and came into this in very good form. Better suited by stiffer tracks, the soft ground compensated and he made all from stall one. He is just the tough type of sprinter his trainer excels with. (op 4-1)
Favourite Girl(IRE), beaten a head from a 2lb lower mark a year ago, again had to settle for second spot. Her last win was from a 4lb lower mark over a year ago and she has returned to top form in cheekpieces. (tchd 8-1)
Singeur(IRE), back over his best trip and with blinkers reapplied, bounced back to his very best, leading the charge home on the stands' side. (op 8-1)
Cocktail Charlie, beaten on all ten starts since making a winning debut, wore blinkers instead of cheekpieces. He confirmed he is on the way back after a lean season, finishing second best on the stands' side. (op 8-1)
Lucky Numbers(IRE), unlucky not to score at Chester on his previous start, has a good record here. This was his first start for five weeks, unusual for a sprinter having his 44th career start, and he may well have needed it to sharpen him up. (tchd 17-2)
Courageous(IRE) Official explanation: jockey said gelding hung right

6866 TOTESWINGER MEDIAN AUCTION MAIDEN STKS — 7f
3:30 (3:30) (Class 5) 2-Y-O **£3,067** (£905; £453) **Stalls** Low

Form — RPR
3325 **1** **Serene Oasis (IRE)**[5] 6743 2-8-12 71 SamHitchcott 7 — 72
(Mick Channon) *trckd ldrs: hdwy to chse ldng pair over 2f out: effrt to chse ldr and n.m.r on inner over 1f out: swtchd rt and rdn ent fnl f: kpt on wl to ld last 50yds* **3/1**[1]
2 *hd* **Kinloch Castle** 2-9-3 0 PhillipMakin 4 — 77+
(Mark Johnston) *cl up: led over 2f out: rdn and edgd lft over 1f out: hdd and no ex last 50yds* **11/2**

00 **3** *6* **Dora's Sister (IRE)**[29] 6131 2-8-12 0 .... PBBeggy 11 57
(John Quinn) *hld up in rr: hdwy over 2f out: rdn over 1f out: kpt on fnl f: nrst fin* **25/1**

320 **4** *2* **Aleut**[21] 6329 2-8-12 71 .... PaulHanagan 5 52
(James Given) *led: rdn along 3f out: hdd over 2f out: wkng whn n.m.r over 1f out* **7/2**[2]

6220 **5** *½* **Not Bad For A Boy (IRE)**[65] 4969 2-9-0 71 .... KieranO'Neill(3) 10 55
(Richard Hannon) *towards rr tl sme late hdwy* **3/1**[1]

024 **6** *1 ¾* **Zain Point (IRE)**[51] 5411 2-9-3 69 ....(t) TomEaves 2 51
(Gerard Butler) *chsd ldrs: rdn along over 2f out: grad wknd* **5/1**[3]

7 *3 ½* **Ypres** 2-9-3 0 .... MichaelStainton 9 42
(Jason Ward) *dwlt: a in rr* **66/1**

5660 **8** *nk* **Villa Reigns**[10] 6627 2-8-11 45 ow1 .... JustinNewman(7) 3 42
(John Weymes) *chsd ldrs: rdn along wl over 2f out: sn wknd* **150/1**

9 *6* **Silken Satinwood (IRE)** 2-8-12 0 .... FrederikTylicki 1 21
(Ann Duffield) *chsd ldrs on inner for 2f: sn lost pl and bhd fnl 3f* **20/1**

0 **10** *7* **Bright Eyed Girl (IRE)**[17] 6449 2-8-12 0 .... PJMcDonald 8 4
(Kate Walton) *chsd ldrs: rdn along and lost pl bef 1/2-way: sn bhd* **66/1**

1m 31.18s (4.18) **Going Correction** +0.525s/f (Yiel) **10** Ran SP% **116.5**
Speed ratings (Par 95): **97,96,89,87,87 85,81,80,73,65**
toteswingers:1&2:£4.10, 2&3:£8.40, 1&3:£17.10 CSF £19.25 TOTE £5.00: £1.50, £2.00, £5.00; EX 24.60.
Owner Doric Racing **Bred** Round Hill Stud **Trained** West Ilsley, Berks

FOCUS
A modest backend maiden and the first two finished clear.

NOTEBOOK
Serene Oasis(IRE), rated 71, had finished placed in her first five starts. Last time she was ridden from the front at Salisbury, and here she was happy to take a lead and dug deep to get the better of a newcomer. Pulling up, she dived right on the paddock bend, lost her rider and ran loose. (op 11-4 tchd 100-30)
Kinloch Castle, bidding to give his trainer his fourth success in this race in ten years, certainly knew his job. He had the leader covered and kicked on early in the home straight. He had to play second fiddle in the end but can soon go one better. (op 5-1 tchd 6-1)
Dora's Sister(IRE), whose second start came five months after her debut in April, stayed on nicely and is now qualified for a handicap mark. (op 22-1 tchd 20-1)
Aleut, rated 71, came into this on the back of a poor effort at Haydock. After making the running she dropped away tamely. (op 9-2)
Not Bad For A Boy(IRE), restrained towards the rear on his first start for two months, is proven on soft ground. When pulled out for his effort the response was strictly limited. His rider reported that he was unsuited by the track. Official explanation: jockey said colt was unsuited by the track (op 100-30, tchd 7-2 in places)
Zain Point(IRE), who missed the break, hung badly left and looked reluctant to put his best foot forward.

6867 TOTETRIFECTA H'CAP (DIV I) 7f
4:00 (4:00) (Class 5) (0-75,75) 3-Y-0+ **£2,911** (£866; £432; £216) **Stalls** Low

Form RPR

5-03 **1** **Makbullet**[25] 6231 4-8-9 63 .... PaulHanagan 10 72
(Michael Smith) *midfield: hdwy wl over 2f out: rdn to chse ldr over 1f out: styd on to ld ins fnl f: kpt on strly* **7/1**

301 **2** *2 ½* **Viking Warrior (IRE)**[28] 6159 4-8-12 66 .... TomEaves 12 68
(Michael Dods) *prom: chsd ldr after 3f: led 2f out: rdn over 1f out: hdd ins fnl f: kpt on same pce* **14/1**

4106 **3** *nk* **Piceno (IRE)**[42] 5730 3-9-0 73 ....(b) BillyCray(3) 1 74
(David Nicholls) *in tch: hdwy to chse ldng pair wl over 2f out: rdn wl over 1f out: kpt on same pce fnl f* **8/1**

14 **4** *3 ¼* **Ted's Brother (IRE)**[30] 6079 3-9-3 73 .... J-PGuillambert 2 66
(Richard Guest) *hld up: hdwy wl over 2f out: rdn wl over 1f out: kpt on same pce fnl f* **7/2**[1]

3213 **5** *¾* **Watts Up Son**[28] 6158 3-8-4 67 ....(bt) JasonHart(7) 6 58
(Declan Carroll) *chsd ldrs: rdn along over 2f out: sn one pce* **11/2**[3]

6400 **6** *2 ¾* **Malcheek (IRE)**[20] 6381 9-9-7 75 .... DavidAllan 7 58
(Tim Easterby) *in tch: effrt over 2f out: sn rdn and no imp* **10/1**

6005 **7** *3 ½* **Cara's Request (AUS)**[20] 6381 6-9-5 73 .... AdrianNicholls 13 47
(David Nicholls) *led: rdn along 3f out: hdd 2f out and grad wknd* **4/1**[2]

0000 **8** *9 ¼* **Alluring Star**[17] 6450 3-8-11 67 .... TonyHamilton 11 31
(Michael Easterby) *a towards rr* **25/1**

-103 **9** *4 ½* **Shayla**[17] 6450 4-9-1 69 .... PJMcDonald 9 21
(Alan Swinbank) *a towards rr* **14/1**

0060 **10** *1* **Moral Issue**[10] 6634 3-8-7 66 .... PatrickDonaghy(3) 8 15
(Jedd O'Keeffe) *a towards rr* **28/1**

2006 **11** *17* **Dhhamaan (IRE)**[21] 6354 6-9-0 68 ....(b) PhillipMakin 3 —
(Ruth Carr) *cl up on inner: rdn along 1/2-way: sn wknd* **20/1**

1m 30.51s (3.51) **Going Correction** +0.525s/f (Yiel)
WFA 3 from 4yo+ 2lb **11** Ran SP% **115.7**
Speed ratings (Par 103): **100,97,96,93,92 89,85,81,75,74 55**
toteswingers:1&2:£12.40, 2&3:£21.00, 1&3:£12.20 CSF £95.63 CT £812.78 TOTE £8.70: £2.60, £2.90, £3.20; EX 97.80 TRIFECTA Not won..
Owner David Armstrong **Bred** Longdon Stud Ltd **Trained** Kirkheaton, Northumberland
■ Stewards' Enquiry : Adrian Nicholls three-day ban: careless riding (Oct 29,31,Nov 1)

FOCUS
A competitive 7f handicap with at least three attempting to make the running, and they stayed in one group on the far side.

6868 TOTEEXACTA CLAIMING STKS 1m 3f 214y
4:40 (4:40) (Class 6) 3-Y-0+ **£2,045** (£603; £302) **Stalls** Low

Form RPR

5541 **1** **Trip The Light**[8] 6676 6-9-12 84 ....(v) PaulHanagan 8 88
(Richard Fahey) *trckd ldrs: hdwy 4f out: rdn to chal 2f out: led appr fnl f: kpt on wl* **11/8**[1]

0351 **2** *2* **Comedy Act**[12] 6582 4-9-3 77 ....(p) DarylByrne(5) 10 81
(Mark Johnston) *trckd ldrs: cl up 1/2-way: led over 2f out: sn jnd and rdn: hdd appr fnl f: one pce* **5/2**[2]

001/ **3** *6* **Muskatsturm (GER)**[36] 5909 12-9-6 76 .... FrederikTylicki 12 69
(Shaun Harley, Ire) *in tch: rdn along and outpcd 3f out: kpt on u.p fnl 2f: tk 3rd nr fin* **33/1**

3002 **4** *1* **Ravi River (IRE)**[9] 6656 7-9-4 77 .... BarryMcHugh 5 66
(Brian Ellison) *in tch: hdwy 4f out: rdn along to chse ldrs wl over 2f out: sn one pce* **6/1**[3]

1145 **5** *hd* **Eijaaz (IRE)**[11] 6601 10-9-1 62 ....(p) RobertWinston 9 62
(Geoffrey Harker) *hld up in rr: hdwy 1/2-way: chsd ldrs over 3f out: rdn over 2f out and sn one pce* **14/1**

1003 **6** *15* **Jewelled Dagger (IRE)**[11] 6601 7-9-6 75 .... TomEaves 4 43
(Keith Dalgleish) *led: rdn along over 3f out: hdd wl over 2f out and sn wknd* **10/1**

-010 **7** *25* **Shotley Mac**[17] 6452 7-9-8 76 .... JimmyQuinn 7 —
(Neville Bycroft) *prom: rdn along 4f out: wknd 3f out* **16/1**

0055 **8** *nk* **Joe Rocco (IRE)**[45] 5623 3-8-13 46 .... PJMcDonald 6 —
(Alan Swinbank) *a towards rr: bhd fnl 3f* **66/1**

03 **9** *2* **Aqua Lad**[11] 6605 3-8-11 0 .... PhillipMakin 11 —
(Mark Johnston) *prom: rdn along 1/2-way: sn lost pl and bhd fnl 3f* **22/1**

00-0 **10** *1* **North Shadow**[17] 6453 4-9-6 47 .... AndrewMullen 2 —
(Alan Brown) *a in rr* **80/1**

2m 44.99s (6.09) **Going Correction** +0.525s/f (Yiel)
WFA 3 from 4yo+ 7lb **10** Ran SP% **116.6**
Speed ratings (Par 101): **100,98,94,94,93 83,67,67,65,65**
toteswingers:1&2:£1.60, 2&3:£11.90, 1&3:£9.20 CSF £4.63 TOTE £1.80: £1.02, £1.70, £6.10; EX 6.40.Trip The Light was claimed by P. W. Middleton for £16,000.
Owner The Matthewman One Partnership **Bred** Darley **Trained** Musley Bank, N Yorks

FOCUS
A fair claimer. The winner did not need to improve on his recent form.
Shotley Mac Official explanation: jockey said gelding lost its action
Aqua Lad Official explanation: jockey said gelding hung left

6869 TOTETRIFECTA H'CAP (DIV II) 7f
5:15 (5:15) (Class 5) (0-75,74) 3-Y-0+ **£2,911** (£866; £432; £216) **Stalls** Low

Form RPR

2010 **1** **Beckermet (IRE)**[4] 6778 9-9-3 70 .... PJMcDonald 6 84
(Ruth Carr) *trckd ldng pair: swtchd ins and hdwy 2f out: led 1 1/2f out: sn rdn clr: styd on* **6/1**[2]

1042 **2** *1 ¾* **Chookie Royale**[4] 6778 3-9-4 73 ....(p) DavidAllan 8 82+
(Keith Dalgleish) *dwlt and in rr: swtchd rt to outer and hdwy 2f out: rdn over 1f out: styd on ins fnl f: nt rch wnr* **5/1**[1]

3225 **3** *1 ¼* **Strong Man**[19] 6417 3-8-8 63 .... TonyHamilton 2 69+
(Michael Easterby) *towards rr: hdwy 2f out: n.m.r and rdn over 1f out: kpt on ins fnl f* **8/1**

050 **4** *6* **Clumber Place**[34] 5970 5-8-13 69 .... RobertLButler(3) 11 59
(Richard Guest) *chsd ldrs: rdn along 2f out: one pce appr fnl f* **25/1**

3211 **5** *½* **Meandmyshadow**[11] 6604 3-8-13 68 .... DarrylHolland 13 56
(Alan Brown) *cl up: led over 2f out: rdn and hdd 1 1/2f out: grad wknd* **9/1**

6000 **6** *1 ¼* **First Class Favour (IRE)**[25] 6231 3-8-10 70 .... AdamCarter(5) 3 55
(Tim Easterby) *chsd ldrs on inner: rdn along 2f out: sn no imp* **9/1**

5332 **7** *hd* **Mark Anthony (IRE)**[9] 6646 4-8-10 63 ....(p) AndrewMullen 10 47
(Shaun Harris) *led: rdn along and hdd over 2f out: sn wknd* **16/1**

2503 **8** *nk* **Music Festival (USA)**[20] 6381 4-8-12 65 .... PaulHanagan 9 49
(Jim Goldie) *a towards rr* **13/2**[3]

600 **9** *1 ½* **Thrust Control (IRE)**[17] 6452 4-8-7 60 oh3 .... PatrickMathers 1 40
(Tracy Waggott) *a towards rr* **33/1**

0400 **10** *2 ¾* **Osgood**[14] 6543 4-9-6 73 ....(v) SamHitchcott 4 45
(Mick Channon) *midfield: effrt over 2f out: rdn whn n.m.r wl over 1f out: sn wknd* **14/1**

3023 **11** *2* **Rio Cobolo (IRE)**[30] 6081 5-9-7 74 .... AdrianNicholls 7 41
(David Nicholls) *a towards rr* **9/1**

2166 **12** *1 ¾* **Catallout (IRE)**[17] 6450 3-8-11 66 .... DanielTudhope 5 28
(Declan Carroll) *a towards rr* **9/1**

4120 **U** **Just The Tonic**[14] 6533 4-8-10 68 .... ShaneBKelly(5) 12 —
(Marjorie Fife) *dwlt: in rr whn uns rdr shortly after s* **18/1**

1m 31.33s (4.33) **Going Correction** +0.525s/f (Yiel)
WFA 3 from 4yo+ 2lb **13** Ran SP% **120.0**
Speed ratings (Par 103): **96,94,92,85,85 83,83,83,81,78 76,74,—**
toteswingers:1&2:£8.20, 2&3:£9.80, 1&3:£14.00 CSF £36.19 CT £255.64 TOTE £9.30: £2.30, £2.40, £2.70; EX 43.80 Trifecta £346.80 Pool: £984.28 - 2.10 winning units..
Owner Shopping, Shoes & Champers Partnership **Bred** Fritz Von Ball Moss **Trained** Huby, N Yorks

FOCUS
Part two of the divided 7f handicap and again the pace was very strong, but it was the slowest of the three C&D times. The first three came clear to give the form a bit of substance.
Meandmyshadow Official explanation: jockey said filly was unsuited by the soft (good to soft places) ground
Catallout(IRE) Official explanation: jockey said filly was unsuited by the soft (good to soft places) ground

6870 TOTEQUICKPICK APPRENTICE H'CAP 1m 5f 175y
5:50 (5:50) (Class 6) (0-60,59) 3-Y-0+ **£2,045** (£603; £302) **Stalls** Low

Form RPR

0006 **1** **Vittachi**[30] 6082 4-8-9 45 .... DannyBrock(5) 12 63
(Alistair Whillans) *prom: cl up 1/2-way: led over 4f out: rdn clr 3f out: styd on strly* **25/1**

5034 **2** *11* **Stormy Morning**[25] 6240 5-9-10 58 ....(p) JustinNewman(3) 9 61
(Pat Eddery) *trckd ldrs on inner: hdwy to chse wnr over 4f out: rdn along over 2f out: no imp appr fnl f* **4/1**[1]

0002 **3** *¾* **Hi Dancer**[11] 6600 8-9-5 53 .... DarylByrne(3) 1 55
(Ben Haslam) *trckd ldrs: hdwy 4f out: rdn along 3f out: plugged on same pce fnl 2f* **6/1**[2]

4405 **4** *6* **Maslak (IRE)**[28] 6157 7-9-9 59 .... ThomasGarner(5) 2 53
(Peter Hiatt) *chsd ldrs: rdn along wl over 2f out: kpt on same pce* **16/1**

5633 **5** *1 ¼* **Shirls Son Sam**[28] 6153 3-8-12 52 .... LMcNiff 13 44
(Chris Fairhurst) *hld up towards rr: hdwy 6f out: in tch over 3f out: sn rdn and plugged on same pce fnl 2f* **13/2**[3]

5-00 **6** *4 ½* **Hammer**[11] 6613 6-8-8 46 .... JordanNason(7) 15 32
(Geoffrey Harker) *hld up in rr: sme hdwy 4f out: rdn along wl over 2f out: nvr nr ldrs* **33/1**

0032 **7** *hd* **Srimenanti**[27] 6192 3-8-12 57 ....(p) JasonHart(5) 8 42
(Brian Rothwell) *in tch on inner: effrt over 4f out: sn rdn along and outpcd fnl 3f* **8/1**

2033 **8** *shd* **Drawback (IRE)**[45] 5612 8-9-0 50 ....(p) JakePayne(5) 10 35
(Barry Brennan) *nvr bttr than midfield* **22/1**

0060 **9** *7* **Follow The Sun (IRE)**[49] 4856 7-8-9 45 ....(p) GeorgeChaloner(5) 14 20
(Peter Niven) *a towards rr* **22/1**

4330 **10** *1 ¾* **Short Supply (USA)**[13] 5790 5-9-10 55 .... BrianToomey 4 28
(Tim Walford) *in tch: pushed along 5f out: rdn 4f out and n.d* **14/1**

4050 **11** *19* **Dubara Reef (IRE)**[28] 6157 4-9-12 57 ....(p) AshleyMorgan 6 —
(Paul Green) *hld up: a towards rr* **7/1**

0665 **12** *2 ¼* **Kingaroo (IRE)**[67] 4889 5-9-9 54 .... AdamCarter 7 —
(Garry Woodward) *led: rdn along and hdd over 4f out: sn wknd* **33/1**

3303 **13** *7* **Cadgers Brig**[7] 6701 3-9-2 56 ....(v) ShaneBKelly 11 —
(Keith Dalgleish) *a towards rr* **9/1**

0060 **14** *56* **Friday Night Lad (IRE)**[28] 6158 4-9-0 48 .... GarryWhillans(3) 3 —
(Alan Swinbank) *midfield: lost pl 1/2-way: bhd and heavily eased fnl 2f* **28/1**

0502 **15** *3 ½* **Hurricane Thomas (IRE)**[25] 6235 7-8-10 **46**....... DavidSimmonson(5) 5 —
(Karen Tutty) *chsd ldrs tl lost pl over 5f out: sn bhd and heavily eased fnl 2f* **18/1**

3m 14.29s (10.69) **Going Correction** +0.525s/f (Yiel)
WFA 3 from 4yo+ 9lb **15** Ran SP% **120.9**
Speed ratings (Par 101): **90,83,83,79,79 76,76,76,72,71 60,59,55,23,21**
toteswingers:1&2:£25.90, 2&3:£8.00, 1&3:£53.50 CSF £114.76 CT £700.43 TOTE £30.20: £5.40, £2.50, £2.70; EX 256.40.
Owner Sutherland Five **Bred** London Thoroughbred Services Ltd **Trained** Newmill-On-Slitrig, Borders

FOCUS
A rock-bottom finale. The pace was very steady and the wide-margin winner seemed to steal a march. He was on a good mark on his 3yo form.
T/Plt: £440.40 to £1 stake. Pool:£45,221.84 - 74.95 winning tickets. T/Qpdt: £51.20 to a £1 stake. Pool:£3,663.29 - 52.90 winning tickets. JR

6841 WOLVERHAMPTON (A.W) (L-H)
Saturday, October 15

OFFICIAL GOING: Standard
Wind: Light behind Weather: Fine

6871 SATURDAY NIGHT IS PARTY NIGHT H'CAP (DIV I) 1m 1f 103y(P)
5:25 (5:25) (Class 6) (0-65,65) 3-Y-O+ **£2,070** (£616; £307; £153) **Stalls** Low

Form RPR
2010 **1** **Bennelong**[17] 6468 5-9-1 **63**.............................. LukeRowe(7) 8 68
(Richard Rowe) *a.p: chsd ldr over 1f out: led ins fnl f: sn rdn: jst hld on* **7/1**
0200 **2** *nse* **Celtic Step**[38] 5823 7-8-13 **57**.............................. DaleSwift(3) 3 61
(Peter Niven) *hld up: nt clr run over 2f out: hdwy over 1f out: nt clr run and swtchd lft ins fnl f: r.o wl* **16/1**
0536 **3** *hd* **Twisted**[16] 6493 5-9-5 **60**..............................(b) PaddyAspell 9 64
(Michael Easterby) *reminders sn after s: chsd ldr after 1f: led over 6f out: rdn over 1f out: edgd rt and hdd ins fnl f: styd on* **3/1**[1]
2000 **4** *1 ¼* **Petomic (IRE)**[5] 6764 6-9-3 **58**..............................(p) WilliamCarson 11 59
(Richard Guest) *plld hrd: set stdy pce tl hdd over 6f out: rdn over 3f out: swtchd rt ins fnl f: styd on* **4/1**[2]
3405 **5** *1 ½* **Ilie Nastase (FR)**[10] 6624 7-9-3 **58**..............................(b) KirstyMilczarek 4 56
(Conor Dore) *hld up: hdwy over 1f out: sn rdn: styd on* **3/1**[1]
6/00 **6** *nk* **Circus Polka (USA)**[16] 6494 7-8-5 **51** oh6.............................. JulieBurke(5) 7 49?
(Owen Brennan) *prom: chsd ldr over 5f out tl rdn over 1f out: no ex ins fnl f* **20/1**
-000 **7** *2 ½* **Honourable Knight (IRE)**[17] 6468 3-8-13 **58**..............................(v1) LiamKeniry 1 50
(Mark Usher) *sn pushed along in rr: bhd 3f out: r.o ins fnl f* **11/2**[3]
6000 **8** *3 ¾* **Cabal**[31] 6049 4-8-10 **51** oh1..............................(p) ShaneKelly 6 35
(Andrew Crook) *prom: rdn over 1f out: wknd fnl f* **9/1**

2m 2.26s (0.56) **Going Correction** -0.10s/f (Stan)
WFA 3 from 4yo+ 4lb **8** Ran SP% **118.5**
Speed ratings (Par 101): **93,92,92,91,90 90,87,84**
toteswingers:1&2:£6.90, 2&3:£7.60, 1&3:£4.00 CSF £111.21 CT £410.53 TOTE £10.20: £2.20, £3.60, £1.50; EX 109.70.
Owner Miss Victoria Baalham **Bred** The National Stud **Trained** Sullington, W Sussex
■ Stewards' Enquiry : William Carson one-day ban: careless riding (Oct 29)

FOCUS
They went a very slow early pace for division one of this poor handicap which produced a tight finish. The time was slow and the form is rated negatively.

6872 SATURDAY NIGHT IS PARTY NIGHT H'CAP (DIV II) 1m 1f 103y(P)
6:00 (6:00) (Class 6) (0-65,65) 3-Y-O+ **£2,070** (£616; £307; £153) **Stalls** Low

Form RPR
0000 **1** **True To Form (IRE)**[53] 5340 4-9-10 **65**..............................(p) TonyCulhane 4 79
(George Baker) *hld up in tch: shkn up to ld over 1f out: styd on* **6/5**[1]
6420 **2** *1 ½* **Beach Babe**[16] 6472 3-9-1 **60**.............................. NickyMackay 5 71
(Jonathan Portman) *hld up: hdwy over 1f out: rdn to chse wnr fnl f: kpt on* **16/1**
063P **3** *8* **Satwa Sunrise (FR)**[23] 6285 4-9-2 **57**.............................. TomMcLaughlin 1 51
(Ed Dunlop) *chsd ldrs: pushed along over 2f out: wknd ins fnl f* **25/1**
0660 **4** *1 ¼* **Broughtons Fawn**[21] 6358 3-8-6 **51** oh6.............................. JamieMackay 8 43
(Willie Musson) *hld up: hdwy u.p and hung lft fr over 1f out: nvr nrr* **40/1**
2305 **5** *1* **Loyal N Trusted**[52] 5381 3-9-3 **62**.............................. AndreaAtzeni 7 51
(Michael Wigham) *led: rdn and hdd over 1f out: wknd ins fnl f* **15/2**
005- **6** *2 ¾* **Number One Guy**[303] 7898 4-9-5 **63**.............................. PaulPickard(3) 2 47
(Philip Kirby) *prom: rdn over 2f out: wknd over 1f out* **50/1**
6232 **7** *½* **Yourinthewill (USA)**[22] 6311 3-9-6 **65**.............................. EddieAhern 9 48
(Daniel Mark Loughnane, Ire) *prom: chsd ldr over 6f out: rdn over 2f out: sn edgd lft and wknd* **9/2**[2]
00 **8** *1 ¼* **Saviour Sand (IRE)**[166] 1756 7-9-4 **59**..............................(t) KirstyMilczarek 3 39
(Olivia Maylam) *racd keenly: trckd ldr 3f: remained handy tl wknd over 2f out* **20/1**
525 **9** *2 ¾* **Military Call**[14] 6538 4-9-2 **60**..............................(p) DaleSwift(3) 10 34
(Alistair Whillans) *hld up in tch: pushed along over 3f out: wknd over 2f out* **9/1**
0405 **10** *6* **Illustration (IRE)**[11] 6613 3-8-10 **55**.............................. SilvestreDeSousa 11 17
(Mark Johnston) *s.s: a in rr: bhd fnl 4f* **7/1**[3]

1m 59.86s (-1.84) **Going Correction** -0.10s/f (Stan)
WFA 3 from 4yo+ 4lb **10** Ran SP% **116.8**
Speed ratings (Par 101): **104,102,95,94,93 91,90,89,87,81**
toteswingers:1&2:£7.40, 2&3:£21.10, 1&3:£11.50 CSF £22.71 CT £332.53 TOTE £2.20: £1.60, £3.10, £6.10; EX 26.70.
Owner Iraj Parvizi **Bred** Sir E J Loder **Trained** Whitsbury, Hants

FOCUS
Division two of this weak handicap was run at a much more even pace and a gamble was landed. The winner rates back to something like his 3yo form.
True To Form(IRE) Official explanation: trainer said, regarding apparent improvement in form, that the gelding has had recent foot problems and appeared better suited by the more forgiving Polytrack surface.
Illustration(IRE) Official explanation: jockey said colt reared at start

6873 STAY AT THE WOLVERHAMPTON HOLIDAY INN H'CAP 1m 4f 50y(P)
6:30 (6:30) (Class 6) (0-60,60) 3-Y-O+ **£2,070** (£616; £307; £153) **Stalls** Low

Form RPR
0056 **1** **Fascinating (IRE)**[5] 6756 3-9-0 **58**.............................. SilvestreDeSousa 5 72
(Mark Johnston) *a.p: chsd ldr 10f out: pushed along over 4f out: rdn to ld over 2f out: styd on: eased nr fin* **4/1**[1]
0060 **2** *1 ½* **Mick's Dancer**[33] 6005 6-9-9 **60**.............................. RobertHavlin 6 71
(Richard Phillips) *hld up: hdwy 3f out: chsd wnr over 1f out: rdn and ev ch ins fnl f: styd on same pce* **7/1**[3]
632 **3** *3 ¼* **Locum**[48] 5520 6-9-5 **56**.............................. GeorgeBaker 7 62+
(Mark H Tompkins) *hld up: hdwy over 1f out: edgd lft ins fnl f: nt rch ldrs* **6/1**[2]
516- **4** *3 ½* **Kickahead (USA)**[454] 1980 9-9-1 **52**..............................(t) MartinLane 4 52
(Ian Williams) *hld up: hdwy over 2f out: rdn and wknd over 1f out* **12/1**
U000 **5** *4 ½* **Valdan (IRE)**[28] 6157 7-9-1 **52**..............................(be) ShaneKelly 3 45
(Ruth Carr) *hld up: hdwy over 2f out: wknd over 1f out* **20/1**
0043 **6** *½* **Aureate**[11] 6613 7-9-4 **55**.............................. NeilChalmers 10 47
(Brian Forsey) *led after 1f: rdn and hdd over 2f out: wknd over 1f out* **16/1**
2335 **7** *1 ¼* **Laconicos (IRE)**[25] 6235 9-9-1 **57**..............................(t) LauraPike(5) 9 47
(William Stone) *prom: pushed along over 3f out: wknd over 2f out* **7/1**[3]
6000 **8** *2* **Bright Sparky (GER)**[11] 6600 8-9-1 **52**..............................(vt) PaddyAspell 1 39
(Michael Easterby) *prom: nt clr run and wknd over 3f out* **28/1**
6046 **9** *hd* **Alternative Choice (USA)**[23] 6287 5-9-8 **59**........... TomMcLaughlin 12 46
(Nick Littmoden) *hld up: hdwy over 2f out: sn rdn and wknd* **9/1**
0042 **10** *1* **Alhaque (USA)**[17] 6446 5-9-3 **54**..............................(bt) TonyCulhane 8 39
(David Flood) *prom: rdn over 2f out: wknd over 1f out* **8/1**
4643 **11** *2 ¼* **Dane Cottage**[11] 6600 4-9-1 **55**.............................. DaleSwift(3) 11 37
(Brian Ellison) *s.s: hld up and a in rr* **8/1**
12 *1 ½* **Galileo Figaro (AUS)**[57] 7-8-11 **51**.............................. PaulPickard(3) 2 30
(Philip Kirby) *led 1f: chsd ldrs: rdn over 4f out: wknd over 3f out* **25/1**

2m 38.58s (-2.52) **Going Correction** -0.10s/f (Stan)
WFA 3 from 4yo+ 7lb **12** Ran SP% **117.1**
Speed ratings (Par 101): **104,103,100,98,95 95,94,93,92,92 90,89**
toteswingers:1&2:£5.20, 2&3:£8.90, 1&3:£3.00 CSF £30.02 CT £167.67 TOTE £4.60: £2.40, £1.40, £2.10; EX 37.90.
Owner Nabil Mourad **Bred** Trebles Holford Farm Thoroughbreds **Trained** Middleham Moor, N Yorks

FOCUS
A moderate handicap run at an an ordinary pace. They finished strung out and the form looks straightforward enough. The winner was unexposed.
Fascinating(IRE) Official explanation: trainer's rep said, regarding apparent improvement in form, that the colt had possibly benefited from its first run on a Polytrack surface and the drop in class.

6874 LORNA IRVINE ALL THE FOURS 44 MAIDEN STKS 5f 20y(P)
7:00 (7:00) (Class 5) 3-Y-O+ **£1,940** (£577; £288; £144) **Stalls** Low

Form RPR
1 **Work Shy** 3-8-12 0.............................. RichardKingscote 8 63+
(Tom Dascombe) *s.s: bhd: hdwy over 1f out: led ins fnl f: r.o wl: readily* **9/2**[3]
2 **2** *2 ¼* **Coastal Passage**[11] 6615 3-9-3 0.............................. SilvestreDeSousa 6 60
(John Balding) *chsd ldrs: rdn over 1f out: styd on* **5/4**[1]
0235 **3** *nse* **Missile Attack (IRE)**[7] 6700 3-9-0 55.............................. DaleSwift(3) 7 60
(Ian Semple) *chsd ldr tl led over 3f out: rdn and hdd ins fnl f: styd on same pce* **3/1**[2]
00- **4** *3* **Lucky Royale**[369] 6796 3-8-12 0.............................. PatCosgrave 9 44
(Jeremy Gask) *chsd ldrs: rdn over 1f out: no ex fnl f* **20/1**
0000 **5** *1 ¾* **Gessabelle**[9] 6653 4-8-12 36..............................(t) KirstyMilczarek 11 38
(Phil McEntee) *mid-div: sn pushed along: kpt on ins fnl f: nvr trbld ldrs* **50/1**
600 **6** *¾* **Georgian Silver**[104] 3661 3-8-12 44..............................(b1) LeeNewman 2 35
(George Foster) *led tl over 3f out: chsd ldrs: rdn 1/2-way: wknd fnl f* **33/1**
4236 **7** *1* **Myjestic Melody (IRE)**[48] 5506 3-8-12 51.............................. DuranFentiman 10 32
(Noel Wilson) *hld up: rdn 1/2-way: n.d* **9/1**
0400 **8** *1 ½* **Lady Ellice**[35] 5946 3-8-12 48..............................(p) TomMcLaughlin 3 26
(Phil McEntee) *chsd ldrs: rdn 1/2-way: wknd over 1f out* **25/1**
6 **9** *½* **Career Quest**[7] 6700 3-8-5 0.............................. MatthewMcGhee(7) 1 24
(Bill Moore) *bhd fr 1/2-way* **66/1**
10 *2* **Bint Elnadim (IRE)** 3-8-12 0.............................. RobbieFitzpatrick 5 17
(Derek Shaw) *s.s: outpcd* **16/1**

61.77 secs (-0.53) **Going Correction** -0.10s/f (Stan) **10** Ran SP% **118.5**
Speed ratings (Par 103): **100,96,96,91,88 87,85,83,82,79**
toteswingers:1&2:£2.60, 2&3:£1.60, 1&3:£3.50 CSF £10.24 TOTE £5.70: £1.90, £1.20, £1.60; EX 12.20.
Owner Manor House Stables LLP **Bred** Peter Webb **Trained** Malpas, Cheshire

FOCUS
An interesting sprint maiden which did not take a lot of winning and the three market leaders fought it out. A nice start for the winner but the bare form is pretty limited.
Career Quest Official explanation: five-day ban: used whip when out of contention (Oct 29,31, Nov 1-3)

6875 CELEBRATE CHRISTMAS AT WOLVERHAMPTON RACECOURSE CLAIMING STKS 5f 20y(P)
7:30 (7:30) (Class 6) 3-Y-O+ **£1,704** (£503; £251) **Stalls** Low

Form RPR
40/2 **1** **Master Of Disguise**[21] 6351 5-8-5 86..............................(t) SilvestreDeSousa 3 81
(David Evans) *chsd ldrs: rdn to ld wl ins fnl f: r.o* **9/4**[2]
5204 **2** *¾* **Lucky Art (USA)**[21] 6351 5-8-7 78.............................. DuranFentiman 8 80
(Ruth Carr) *chsd ldr tl led 1f out: rdn and hdd wl ins fnl f* **12/1**
6615 **3** *½* **Hinton Admiral**[19] 6418 7-8-13 77.............................. JoeFanning 9 84
(Keith Dalgleish) *mid-div: hdwy 3f out: rdn over 1f out: edgd lft ins fnl f: styd on* **16/1**
0006 **4** *½* **Evens And Odds (IRE)**[28] 6147 7-9-0 93..............................(t) JulieBurke(5) 7 88
(Kevin Ryan) *dwlt: outpcd: r.o wl ins fnl f: nrst fin* **6/4**[1]
1403 **5** *1* **Drawnfromthepast (IRE)**[21] 6351 6-9-0 94 ow2... MichaelJMurphy(7) 1 87
(Ed Walker) *prom: lost pl after 1f: hdwy and nt clr run over 1f out: r.o: nt trble ldrs* **4/1**[3]
1540 **6** *3* **Ridley Didley (IRE)**[30] 6076 6-8-7 67.............................. WilliamCarson 2 62
(Noel Wilson) *sn led: rdn and hdd 1f out: wknd ins fnl f* **25/1**
5506 **7** *2 ¾* **Look Who's Kool**[21] 6351 3-8-8 69 ow1..............................(b) GrahamGibbons 4 53
(Ed McMahon) *chsd ldrs: rdn over 1f out: wknd ins fnl f* **28/1**
0005 **8** *3* **Egyptian Lord**[74] 4650 8-8-8 37 ow1..............................(b) RobbieFitzpatrick 10 42?
(Peter Grayson) *hld up: pushed along 1/2-way: sn wknd* **125/1**
0320 **9** *½* **Lesley's Choice**[137] 2585 5-9-5 82.............................. JamesDoyle 6 52
(Paul Rich) *sn pushed along in rr: wknd 1/2-way* **20/1**

61.25 secs (-1.05) **Going Correction** -0.10s/f (Stan) **9** Ran SP% **117.2**
Speed ratings (Par 101): **104,102,102,101,99 94,90,85,84**
toteswingers:1&2:£3.60, 2&3:£8.80, 1&3:£7.80 CSF £27.85 TOTE £3.80: £1.10, £6.70, £3.00; EX 22.70.Lucky Art was claimed by C. R. Dore for £6,000. Master of Disguise was claimed by B. Baugh for £5,000.
Owner J Babb **Bred** T R Lock **Trained** Pandy, Monmouths

FOCUS
A fair claimer on paoer but the time wasn't good. The winner only needed to match his reappearance form.

6876 RINGSIDE CONFERENCE SUITE - 700 THEATRE STYLE H'CAP 2m 119y(P)
8:00 (8:01) (Class 6) (0-60,57) 3-Y-O+ **£1,704** (£503; £251) **Stalls** Low

Form RPR
4020 **1** **Tigerino (IRE)**[40] [5790] 3-8-5 **45**.................................. DuranFentiman 10 55
(Chris Fairhurst) *hld up: hdwy 5f out: led over 2f out: drvn out* **7/1**
3116 **2** *3¾* **Red Current**[25] [6240] 7-9-9 **57**.. DavidKenny(5) 5 62
(Michael Scudamore) *s.s: hld up: hdwy 2f out: chsd wnr over 1f out: sn rdn: no imp ins fnl f* **11/1**
4420 **3** *hd* **Delorain (IRE)**[16] [6476] 8-9-2 **50**..................................(v) LauraPike(5) 13 55
(William Stone) *sn prom: pushed along over 2f out: styd on* **8/1**
200- **4** *½* **Hassadin**[436] [4765] 5-9-2 **45**... RobertHavlin 3 49
(Michael Blake) *chsd ldrs: wnt 2nd over 1f out: sn rdn: no ex ins fnl f* **13/2**[3]
5003 **5** *1* **Prickles**[21] [6356] 6-9-1 **47**... RossAtkinson(3) 1 50
(Derek Shaw) *hld up: hdwy over 1f out: nvr trbld ldrs* **12/1**
1041 **6** *1½* **Steady Gaze**[16] [6476] 6-9-6 **56**... LukeRowe(7) 12 57+
(Richard Rowe) *hld up: hung lft and styd on ins fnl f: nvr any ch* **4/1**[1]
0440 **7** *4½* **Ballade De La Mer**[44] [5650] 5-9-2 **45**..............................(v) LeeNewman 9 41
(George Foster) *mid-div: rdn over 3f out: wknd over 1f out* **25/1**
5/0- **8** *3½* **Skye But N Ben**[27] [7330] 7-9-2 **45**...................................(tp) MartinHarley 8 37
(Alan McCabe) *led 1f: chsd ldr tl rdn over 3f out: wknd over 1f out* **40/1**
4650 **9** *hd* **Peaceful Means (IRE)**[9] [6656] 8-9-7 **50**..................(t) RobbieFitzpatrick 6 41
(Michael Appleby) *mid-div: hmpd and wknd over 2f out* **16/1**
0406 **10** *1* **Kingsdale Orion (IRE)**[9] [6656] 7-9-10 **56**......................(t) DaleSwift(3) 11 46
(Brian Ellison) *hld up: rdn over 2f out: a in rr* **8/1**
0/0 **11** *5* **Crafty George (IRE)**[278] [114] 6-9-2 **45**............................. ShaneKelly 7 29
(Daniel Mark Loughnane, Ire) *chsd ldrs: rdn over 2f out: wknd wl over 1f out* **20/1**
244 **12** *18* **Rose Aurora**[16] [6476] 4-9-2 **45**.................................(v) SilvestreDeSousa 4 —
(Marcus Tregoning) *led after 1f: rdn and hdd over 2f out: sn wknd: eased over 1f out: t.o* **5/1**[2]

3m 40.36s (-1.44) **Going Correction** -0.10s/f (Stan)
WFA 3 from 4yo+ 11lb **12** Ran SP% **117.7**
Speed ratings (Par 101): **99,97,97,96,96 95,93,91,91,91 89,80**
toteswingers:1&2:£22.80, 2&3:£21.70, 1&3:£6.90 CSF £79.07 CT £633.78 TOTE £9.40: £3.20, £4.80, £1.70; EX 86.60.
Owner 980 Racing **Bred** Max Morris **Trained** Middleham Moor, N Yorks

FOCUS
Moderate stuff. A clear personal best from the winner with the second to his recent best.

6877 ENJOY THE RINGSIDE ENTERTAINMENT H'CAP (DIV I) 1m 141y(P)
8:30 (8:33) (Class 6) (0-65,65) 3-Y-O+ **£2,070** (£616; £307; £153) **Stalls** Low

Form RPR
3022 **1** **Zafeen's Pearl**[17] [6468] 4-9-10 **65**...................................... ShaneKelly 5 77+
(Dean Ivory) *hld up: hdwy over 3f out: led over 1f out: rdn out* **11/4**[2]
6440 **2** *1¾* **Woolston Ferry (IRE)**[17] [6468] 5-9-8 **63**........................ WilliamCarson 3 68
(David Pinder) *hld up: hdwy 2f out: rdn over 1f out: styd on* **12/1**
6203 **3** *1* **Carcinetto (IRE)**[21] [6355] 9-9-7 **65**.............................. RichardEvans(3) 2 68
(David Evans) *prom: pushed along over 4f out: outpcd over 3f out: hdwy over 1f out: r.o* **11/1**
0332 **4** *1¼* **Know No Fear**[1] [6847] 6-9-4 **59**..............................(p) SilvestreDeSousa 1 59
(Alastair Lidderdale) *prom: chsd ldr 6f out tl led over 2f out: rdn and hdd over 1f out: no ex ins fnl f* **13/2**[3]
3521 **5** *¾* **So Wise (USA)**[42] [5740] 3-9-6 **65**... PatCosgrave 8 63
(Keith Dalgleish) *prom: pushed along over 3f out: rdn over 1f out: no ex ins fnl f* **9/4**[1]
4502 **6** *5* **Holiday Snap**[36] [5901] 5-9-7 **62**.. GeorgeBaker 4 49
(Mary Hambro) *led: clr 6f out: hdd over 2f out: wknd fnl f* **13/2**[3]
000/ **7** *1¼* **Bertie Boo**[893] [1777] 6-8-10 **51** oh6.................................. NeilChalmers 7 35
(Michael Appleby) *hld up: rdn over 2f out: nvr on terms* **100/1**
0-31 **8** *4* **Ashgrove Nell (IRE)**[22] [6310] 3-8-13 **58**............................ EddieAhern 9 33
(Daniel Mark Loughnane, Ire) *chsd ldrs tl wknd over 1f out* **16/1**
500 **9** *1¼* **Thoroughly Red (IRE)**[17] [6453] 6-9-9 **64**.......................... JamesSullivan 11 36
(Linda Stubbs) *chsd ldr over 2f: remained handy tl rdn and wknd over 2f out* **25/1**
/005 **10** *44* **Le Reveur**[10] [6542] 9-8-10 **51** oh6...................................... KellyHarrison 6 —
(Richard Guest) *hld up: a in rr: lost tch over 3f out: eased: t.o* **66/1**

1m 48.82s (-1.68) **Going Correction** -0.10s/f (Stan)
WFA 3 from 4yo+ 4lb **10** Ran SP% **112.3**
Speed ratings (Par 101): **103,101,100,99,98 94,93,89,88,49**
toteswingers:1&2:£4.80, 2&3:£15.10, 1&3:£3.60 CSF £33.75 CT £309.35 TOTE £3.30: £1.40, £4.00, £2.50; EX 34.40.
Owner Heather Yarrow & Lesley Ivory **Bred** Mr And Mrs L Baker **Trained** Radlett, Herts

FOCUS
Division one of a modest handicap, though the pace was solid. They fanned out across the track up the straight. The form looks sound.
Le Reveur Official explanation: jockey said gelding moved poorly throughout

6878 ENJOY THE RINGSIDE ENTERTAINMENT H'CAP (DIV II) 1m 141y(P)
9:00 (9:01) (Class 6) (0-65,65) 3-Y-O+ **£2,070** (£616; £307; £153) **Stalls** Low

Form RPR
5600 **1** **Shelovestobouggie**[89] [4163] 3-9-0 **59**..............................(t) AndreaAtzeni 7 68
(Marco Botti) *a.p: chsd ldr over 3f out: led over 1f out: r.o* **4/1**[2]
1500 **2** *2* **Dazakhee**[1] [6831] 4-9-9 **64**... TonyCulhane 5 68
(David Flood) *s.s: hld up: hdwy over 1f out: r.o u.p* **13/2**
0030 **3** *hd* **Social Rhythm**[17] [6453] 7-9-0 **58**...................................... DaleSwift(3) 4 62
(Alistair Whillans) *hld up: rdn over 1f out: r.o ins fnl f: nt rch ldrs* **16/1**
1001 **4** *¾* **You've Been Mowed**[27] [6188] 5-9-2 **62**.......................... MatthewLawson(5) 6 64
(Richard Price) *led: rdn and hdd over 1f out: styd on same pce ins fnl f* **7/2**[1]
0000 **5** *1¼* **Qeethaara (USA)**[44] [5653] 7-9-10 **65**................................... ShaneKelly 10 64
(Mark Brisbourne) *prom: rdn over 1f out: no ex ins fnl f* **16/1**
1006 **6** *1* **Justcallmehandsome**[14] [6543] 9-8-12 **60**.............(v) RachealKneller(7) 8 57
(Dominic Ffrench Davis) *hld up: hdwy over 2f out: no ex fnl f* **8/1**
6500 **7** *1½* **Fault**[2] [6814] 5-9-8 **63**...(t) JamesDoyle 1 57
(Alastair Lidderdale) *prom: rdn over 1f out: wknd ins fnl f* **8/1**
6036 **8** *1¼* **Royal Premium**[40] [5789] 5-8-7 **51** oh6..............................(v) BillyCray(3) 3 42
(Bruce Hellier) *hld up: rdn and hung lft over 1f out: n.d* **40/1**
2201 **9** *2* **Aussie Blue (IRE)**[14] [6544] 7-9-6 **64**................................(v) AmyRyan(3) 9 50
(Richard Whitaker) *hld up: hdwy over 2f out: wknd fnl f* **9/2**[3]
0030 **10** *1¼* **Island Chief**[25] [6235] 5-8-11 **52**....................................... PaddyAspell 2 35
(Michael Easterby) *chsd ldr tl rdn 3f out: wknd over 1f out* **10/1**

1m 50.33s (-0.17) **Going Correction** -0.10s/f (Stan)
WFA 3 from 4yo+ 4lb **10** Ran SP% **119.3**
Speed ratings (Par 101): **96,94,94,93,92 91,90,88,87,86**
toteswingers:1&2:£8.40, 2&3:£13.50, 1&3:£14.00 CSF £31.09 CT £381.70 TOTE £4.40: £1.10, £2.70, £4.80; EX 48.40.
Owner The Sticky Wicket Syndicate IV **Bred** Mallalieu Bloodstock Ltd **Trained** Newmarket, Suffolk

FOCUS
The pace was fair for division two of a modest handicap, but it was the slower division. The winner was back to something like her debut form.
Royal Premium Official explanation: jockey said horse ran too freely
T/Plt: £198.40 to a £1 stake. Pool £74,135.43 - 272.77 winning tickets. T/Qpdt: £38.80 to a £1 stake. Pool £10,446.33 - 198.90 winning tickets CR

6879 - 6885a (Foreign Racing) - See Raceform Interactive

6711 CAULFIELD (R-H)
Saturday, October 15
OFFICIAL GOING: Turf: good to soft changing to good

6886a BMW CAULFIELD CUP (GROUP 1 H'CAP) (3YO+) (TURF) 1m 4f
6:05 (12:00) 3-Y-O+
£1,078,431 (£245,098; £130,718; £71,895; £58,823; £49,019)

RPR
1 **Southern Speed (AUS)**[13] 4-8-4 **0**............................(b) CraigAWilliams 4 115+
(Leon Macdonald & Andrew Gluyas, Australia) *chsd ldrs: pushed along ins fnl 2f: rdn appr fnl f: led 150yds out: r.o wl* **9/1**[3]
2 *1½* **Green Moon (IRE)**[30] 4-8-5 **0**.. NicholasHall 17 114
(Robert Hickmott, Australia) *settled towards front of middle 3rd: hdwy on outside 4f out: rdn and led appr 1 1/2f out: hdd 150yds out: kpt on u.p: no ex fnl 75yds* **10/1**
3 *½* **Tullamore (NZ)**[14] 5-8-8 **0**... CraigNewitt 15 114+
(Gai Waterhouse, Australia) *settled in midfield: pushed along ins fnl 4f: rdn 2f out and clsd on ldrs: 4th and u.p 1 1/2f out: styd on fnl f: nt pce to chal* **19/1**
4 *1* **Manighar (FR)**[55] [5304] 5-8-13 **0**... DamienOliver 5 117
(Luca Cumani) *w.w in midfield on rail: 9th and gng wl 4f out: pushed along and hdwy 3f out: 5th and scrubbed along 1 1/2f out: kpt on u.p tl run flattened out fnl 75yds* **12/1**
5 *shd* **Lucas Cranach (GER)**[83] [4374] 4-8-11 **0**........................(p) CoreyBrown 3 117+
(Anthony Freedman, Australia) *hld up towards rr: hdwy on outside 3f out: c wd fnl bnd: styd on fnl f: nt pce to trble ldrs* **14/1**
6 *½* **Unusual Suspect (USA)**[35] 7-8-13 **0**............................(v) NashRawiller 7 116+
(Michael Kent, Australia) *hld up towards rr: one fr last ins fnl 2f: styd on u.p 1 1/2f out: forced to switch outside runners 1f out: kpt on fnl f* **60/1**
7 *¾* **Drunken Sailor (IRE)**[49] [5471] 6-8-13 **0**......................(b) DwayneDunn 18 114
(Luca Cumani) *qckly swtchd ins fr wd draw: w.w towards rr: hdwy on ins bef 1/2-way to r in midfield: 12th and nudged along 4f out: squeezed out nring fnl 2 1/2f: sn chsng ldng gp: nt qckn u.p fnl f* **25/1**
8 *nk* **Macedonian (NZ)**[7] [6711] 6-8-5 **0**...................................(b) LukeNolen 10 106+
(Peter G Moody, Australia) *hld up: effrt on outside over 2 1/2f out: c wd fnl bnd: styd on fnl f: nvr nrr* **50/1**
9 *½* **Shootoff (NZ)**[14] 4-8-9 **0**..(b) KerrinMcEvoy 16 111
(Graeme Rogerson, Australia) *chsd ldng gp: lost pl over 2 1/2f out: rdn and no imp fnl 1 1/2f* **30/1**
10 *1* **Precedence (NZ)**[13] 6-8-11 **0**.. StevenArnold 20 110
(Bart Cummings, Australia) *w.w in midfield: chsd ldrs fr 4f out: rdn and no ex fnl 1 1/2f* **25/1**
11 *shd* **Absolutely (AUS)**[13] 4-8-7 **0**.. BradRawiller 22 107
(Michael Kent, Australia) *hld up towards rr: effrt on ins 2f out: no imp u.p fr 1 1/2f out* **20/1**
12 *hd* **Niwot (AUS)**[28] 7-8-6 **0**... DeanYendall 21 104
(Michael, Wayne & John Hawkes, Australia) *trckd ldr: led 3f out: rdn 2f out: hdd appr fnl 1 1/2f: grad wknd u.p* **40/1**
13 *1¼* **Hawk Island (IRE)**[14] 6-8-10 **0**..................................(t) GlynSchofield 14 106
(Chris Waller, Australia) *hld up towards rr: shortlived effrt on outside 2f out: n.d* **20/1**
14 *¾* **Saptapadi (IRE)**[7] [6711] 5-8-8 **0**... MarkZahra 6 103
(Brian Ellison) *w.w towards rr: 13th 3 1/2f out: hdwy on outside to dispute 8th ins fnl 2f: sn rdn: no ex fnl f* **20/1**
15 *2¼* **Dream Pedlar (AUS)**[15] 7-8-6 **0**.................................(b) ChrisSymons 19 97
(Troy Blacker, Australia) *chsd ldrs: 3rd and rdn 3f out: grad fdd u.p* **90/1**
16 *5½* **Domesky (AUS)**[15] 4-8-5 **0**.. BrentonAvdulla 9 89
(Michael Kent, Australia) *a bhd: nvr a factor* **150/1**
17 *6* **Mighty High (FR)**[7] [6713] 5-9-0 **0**.................................. DarrenBeadman 1 87
(J Moore, Hong Kong) *broke wl and led: scrubbed along and hdd 3f out: wknd u.p appr 2f out* **7/1**[2]
18 *2¾* **December Draw (IRE)**[13] 5-8-8 **0**.................................... MichaelRodd 11 76
(Mark Kavanagh, Australia) *racd in midfield: pushed along and lost pl 2 1/2f out: last and btn whn eased 1 1/2f out* **23/10**[1]

2m 28.44s (148.44) **18** Ran SP% **114.3**
PARI-MUTUEL (NSW TAB - all including au$1 stakes): WIN 10.60 PLACE 3.20, 3.40, 5.10; DF 49.10; SF 112.30.
Owner B H Perks, Ms A M Clough Et Al **Bred** Toorak Park Stud Pty Ltd **Trained** Australia

6738 KEENELAND (L-H)
Saturday, October 15
OFFICIAL GOING: Turf: firm; polytrack: fast

6887a QUEEN ELIZABETH II CHALLENGE CUP STKS (GRADE 1) (3YO FILLIES) (TURF) 1m 1f (T)
10:45 (10:50) 3-Y-O
£153,846 (£51,282; £25,641; £12,820; £7,692; £1,709)

RPR
1 **Together (IRE)**[7] [6719] 3-8-9 **0**.. CO'Donoghue 2 114
(A P O'Brien, Ire) **23/5**[3]
2 *1¼* **Marketing Mix (CAN)**[28] 3-8-9 **0**... GKGomez 4 111
(Thomas F Proctor, U.S.A) **109/10**

3 3 1/2 **Nereid (USA)**55 3-8-9 0 ...... JTalamo 5 104
(John Shirreffs, U.S.A) 19/2
4 3/4 **Winter Memories (USA)**28 6183 3-8-9 0 ...... JJCastellano 3 102
(James J Toner, U.S.A) 7/5[1]
5 3 3/4 **Summer Soiree (USA)**55 3-8-9 0 ...... RADominguez 8 95
(H Graham Motion, U.S.A) 27/10[2]
6 1/2 **Star Billing (USA)**55 3-8-9 0 ...... VEspinoza 1 94
(John Shirreffs, U.S.A) 11/1
7 1 1/2 **More Than Real (USA)**28 6183 3-8-9 0 ...... CNakatani 6 90
(Todd Pletcher, U.S.A) 203/10
8 10 3/4 **Kathmanblu (USA)**28 6183 3-8-9 0 ...... JRLeparoux 7 68
(Kenneth McPeek, U.S.A) 27/1
1m 48.83s (-0.97) 8 Ran SP% **121.1**
PARI-MUTUEL (all including $2 stakes): WIN 11.20; PLACE (1-2) 5.80, 8.60; SHOW (1-2-3) 4.00, 5.20, 5.40; SF 87.40.
Owner D Smith, Mrs J Magnier, M Tabor **Bred** Lynch Bages And Samac **Trained** Ballydoyle, Co Tipperary

NOTEBOOK
Together(IRE), the dual Guineas runner-up, was produced three wide in the stretch and edged clear of Marketing Mix in determined fashion. She deserved this after finishing second five times at the top level.

6398 BATH (L-H)

Sunday, October 16

OFFICIAL GOING: Good (good to soft in places; 7.9)
Wind: Moderate, half-across Weather: cloudy with sunny periods

6888 TOTETRIFECTA FILLIES' H'CAP (DIV I) 1m 2f 46y
1:30 (1:30) (Class 5) (0-70,70) 3-Y-O+ **£2,587** (£770; £384; £192) **Stalls** Low

Form RPR
6402 1 **Carinya (IRE)**19 6437 3-9-2 **67** ...... GeorgeBaker 9 75
(Amy Weaver) *stdd s: smooth prog fr 3f out: r.o wl to ld ins fnl f: rdn out* 4/1[1]
2140 2 1 1/2 **Blue Maisey**34 5992 3-9-3 **68** ...... SebSanders 3 73
(Peter Makin) *led: rdn over 2f out: hdd ins fnl f: no ex* 10/1
6030 3 3/4 **Corrib (IRE)**36 5912 8-8-10 **56** oh5 ......(p) RichardKingscote 6 60
(Bryn Palling) *hld up towards rr: rdn over 1f out: hdwy over 1f out: styd on fnl f* 33/1
3503 4 1 1/4 **Mrs Neat (IRE)**17 6493 3-8-11 **62** ......(p) JamesDoyle 1 63
(Sylvester Kirk) *mid-div: rdn 2f out: kpt on fnl f* 11/1
2205 5 1/2 **Epernay**21 6383 4-9-7 **70** ......(vt) MichaelO'Connell(3) 4 70
(Ian Williams) *chsd ldrs: rdn over 2f out: kpt on same pce fnl f* 6/1[3]
210 6 3/4 **Ashkalara**35 5962 4-9-2 **62** ...... JimCrowley 7 61
(Stuart Howe) *hld up towards rr: rdn and stdy hdwy fr over 2f out: kpt on same pce fnl f* 12/1
2U56 7 1 1/4 **Peira**25 6255 3-9-0 **65** ...... LukeMorris 5 61
(Jane Chapple-Hyam) *mid-div: rdn over 2f out: no imp* 14/1
0040 8 16 **Very Well Red**31 6098 8-9-5 **65** ...... WilliamCarson 11 29
(Peter Hiatt) *towards rr: rdn and hdwy over 2f out: wknd over 1f out* 20/1
6562 9 3 1/4 **Sasheen**13 6586 4-9-9 **69** ......(p) FergusSweeney 8 27
(Jeremy Gask) *prom: rdn over 2f out: wknd over 1f out* 9/1
2300 10 1/2 **Cairncross (IRE)**21 6383 3-9-5 **70** ...... SilvestreDeSousa 10 27
(Mark Johnston) *mid-div: rdn over 4f out: wknd over 1f out* 4/1[1]
6323 11 2 1/2 **Glyn Ceiriog**23 6295 3-9-3 **68** ......(v[1]) TonyCulhane 2 20
(George Baker) *trckd ldrs: wnt prom after 3f: rdn over 2f out: sn btn* 11/2[2]
2m 11.9s (0.90) **Going Correction** +0.125s/f (Good)
WFA 3 from 4yo+ 5lb 11 Ran SP% **119.2**
Speed ratings (Par 100): **101,99,99,98,97 97,96,83,80,80 78**
toteswingers:1&2:£12.30, 2&3:£35.00, 1&3:£38.20 CSF £45.71 CT £1170.22 TOTE £6.70: £2.20, £3.70, £9.80; EX 71.00 TRIFECTA Not won..
Owner Robert Boyd **Bred** E O'Gorman **Trained** Newmarket, Suffolk
FOCUS
Bottom bend dolled out increasing distances by 12.5yds. The ground was officially given as good, good to soft in places, and clerk of the course Katie Stephens reported that the good to soft parts were in the back straight. The jockeys reported it to be just on the easy side of good. The first division of a modest fillies' handicap, and while they didn't go a mad dash in front the winner came from the rear. The form looks ordinary rated around the third and fifth.

6889 TOTEPLACEPOT H'CAP 5f 161y
2:00 (2:05) (Class 6) (0-58,58) 3-Y-O+ **£1,876** (£558; £278; £139) **Stalls** Centre

Form RPR
5460 1 **El Dececy (USA)**3 6811 7-8-13 **52** ......(t) SilvestreDeSousa 8 64
(Richard Guest) *a.p: led over 2f out: r.o strly fnl f: comf* 9/2[1]
0522 2 2 3/4 **Bateleur**6 6765 7-8-12 **58** ...... CharlesBishop(7) 9 63
(Mick Channon) *chsd ldrs: rdn 2f out: wnt 2nd ent fnl f: kpt on but nt pce of wnr* 7/1[2]
5600 3 1/2 **Ghost Dancer**12 6609 7-8-9 **48** ow2 ......(p) EddieCreighton 6 51
(Milton Bradley) *s.i.s: in rr whn snatched up on bnd after 1f: rdn and hdwy over 1f out: r.o fnl f* 20/1
5010 4 1 1/4 **Avon Light**12 6610 3-8-10 **50** ......(p) RichardKingscote 17 49
(Milton Bradley) *trckd ldrs: rdn over 2f out: kpt on same pce fnl f* 11/1
3036 5 1/2 **Athaakeel (IRE)**29 6177 5-9-5 **58** ......(b) LukeMorris 7 55
(Ronald Harris) *towards rr: drvn along 3f out: hdwy over 1f out: styd on ins fnl f* 12/1
2420 6 1/2 **Atia**4 6784 3-9-0 **57** ......(p) RossAtkinson(3) 14 53
(Jonathan Portman) *in tch on outer: rdn over 2f out: styd on same pce fnl f* 14/1
403 7 hd **Hygrove Gal**18 6454 3-9-1 **55** ...... TomEaves 12 50
(Bryan Smart) *prom: rdn over 2f out: one pce fr over 1f out* 16/1
545 8 nk **Harvest Mist (IRE)**23 6307 3-9-1 **55** ...... LiamKeniry 13 49
(Michael Blanshard) *s.i.s: towards rr: styd on fr over 1f out: nvr any danger* 16/1
-000 9 1/2 **Welsh Dancer**61 5141 3-8-7 **47** ...... WilliamCarson 3 39
(Ronald Harris) *towards rr: sme late prog: nvr a factor* 50/1
2463 10 1 1/4 **Madam Isshe**20 6398 4-9-0 **53** ...... DaneO'Neill 5 41
(Malcolm Saunders) *led tl rdn over 2f out: sn hld: fdd fnl f* 8/1[3]
0010 11 nk **Welcome Approach**43 5736 8-8-12 **58** ...... JustinNewman(7) 2 45
(John Weymes) *pushed along over 3f out: nvr bttr than mid-div* 10/1
604 12 nse **Gracie's Games**20 6408 5-9-1 **57** ...... SophieDoyle(3) 16 44
(Richard Price) *towards rr: effrt to cl on outer over 2f out: nvr threatened ldrs* 16/1
0060 13 nk **Dream Express (IRE)**65 5008 6-8-0 **46** oh1 ...... JakePayne(7) 4 32
(Bill Turner) *trckd ldrs: rdn over 3f out: wknd over 1f out* 80/1
3344 14 nk **Till Dawn (IRE)**18 6444 3-9-1 **55** ...... DavidProbert 11 40
(Tony Carroll) *prom: rdn to chse wnr 2f out tl wknd qckly ent fnl f* 9/1
5355 15 1/2 **Lady Excellentia (IRE)**41 5780 3-7-13 **46** oh1 ...... RaulDaSilva(7) 1 29
(Ronald Harris) *s.i.s: a towards rr* 50/1
5065 16 1 1/2 **Greyemkay**20 6398 3-8-3 **48** ...... DavidKenny(5) 10 26
(Richard Price) *slowly away: sn prom: drvn over 3f out: sn lost pl: wknd over 1f out* 20/1
0016 17 2 **Mary's Pet**36 5917 4-9-5 **58** ......(p) NeilCallan 15 30
(John Akehurst) *s.i.s: towards rr: hdwy whn nt clr run and snatched up ent fnl f: no ch after* 10/1
1m 11.81s (0.61) **Going Correction** +0.075s/f (Good)
WFA 3 from 4yo+ 1lb 17 Ran SP% **125.0**
Speed ratings (Par 101): **98,95,94,92,92 91,91,90,90,88 87,87,87,87,86 84,81**
toteswingers:1&2:£6.00, 2&3:£32.80, 1&3:£26.30 CSF £32.60 CT £594.19 TOTE £5.20: £1.60, £1.80, £6.70, £2.90; EX 32.20 TRIFECTA Not won..
Owner Willie McKay **Bred** Shadwell Farm LLC **Trained** Stainforth, S Yorks
■ Stewards' Enquiry : Eddie Creighton 1st incident, one-day ban: careless riding (Oct 31), 2nd one-day ban: careless riding (Nov 1)
FOCUS
A gamble was landed in this moderate sprint with the form rated around the placed horses.

6890 TOTEQUICKPICK & EBF MEDIAN AUCTION MAIDEN STKS 5f 161y
2:30 (2:33) (Class 5) 2-Y-O **£2,716** (£808; £404; £202) **Stalls** Centre

Form RPR
0650 1 **Larwood (IRE)**23 6293 2-9-3 69 ...... DaneO'Neill 9 64+
(Henry Candy) *hld up towards rr: hdwy on outer fr jst over 2f out: shkn up ent fnl f: led fnl 100yds: r.o* 4/1[2]
6640 2 1/2 **The Wicked Lord**17 6489 2-9-3 61 ...... FergusSweeney 11 61
(Stuart Kittow) *disp ld: outrt ldr over 3f out: chal wl over 1f out: rdn ins fnl f: hdd fnl 100yds: kpt on* 16/1
0 3 1 1/4 **Red Bay**23 6300 2-9-3 0 ...... GeorgeBaker 4 58
(Jane Chapple-Hyam) *s.i.s: hdwy on inner to trck ldrs after 1f: rdn 2f out: keeping on in 3rd but hld whn short of room nring fin* 11/4[1]
4 1 1/4 **Safari Sunseeker (IRE)** 2-9-3 0 ...... LukeMorris 7 53+
(Peter Winkworth) *s.i.s: sn running green and pushed along in rr: hdwy 2f out: nt best of runs jst over 1f out: kpt on* 9/2[3]
0035 5 nk **Jawim**17 6492 2-8-12 50 ...... SilvestreDeSousa 8 47
(Malcolm Saunders) *chsd ldrs: rdn to chal wl over 1f out: fdd ins fnl f* 20/1
3 6 3 1/4 **Rode Two Destiny (IRE)**41 5779 2-8-12 0 ...... SteveDrowne 10 36
(Peter Makin) *mid-div: rdn over 2f out: nvr gng pce to get involved* 9/2[3]
0 7 nk **Shining Grace**80 4462 2-8-12 0 ...... DavidProbert 3 35
(Bryn Palling) *mid-div: rdn over 2f out: no imp* 50/1
8 2 1/4 **Breeze On Bye** 2-9-3 0 ...... EddieCreighton 6 33
(Brian Meehan) *hld towards rr: rdn over 2f out: little imp* 25/1
0350 9 nse **The Name Is Don (IRE)**8 6695 2-9-3 62 ...... IanMongan 5 32
(Mark Gillard) *towards rr: nt clr run over 2f out: sn rdn: nvr any imp* 14/1
00 10 3 **Musical Strike**140 2523 2-9-0 0 ...... MichaelO'Connell(3) 2 23
(Shaun Harris) *trckd ldrs: rdn over 2f out: wknd over 1f out* 100/1
4434 11 nk **King's Ciel**73 4704 2-8-12 66 ...... DavidKenny(5) 1 22
(George Baker) *disp ld tl rdn over 3f out: sn chsng ldrs: wknd fnl f* 10/1
1m 12.79s (1.59) **Going Correction** +0.075s/f (Good) 11 Ran SP% **116.2**
Speed ratings (Par 95): **92,91,89,88,87 83,82,79,79,75 75**
toteswingers:1&2:£12.70, 2&3:£11.30, 1&3:£3.80 CSF £62.04 TOTE £4.10: £1.10, £6.80, £2.00; EX 81.60 Trifecta £411.10 Part won. Pool £555.62 - 0.62 winning units..
Owner Six Too Many **Bred** Celbridge Estates Ltd **Trained** Kingston Warren, Oxon
FOCUS
Using the runner-up as a guide this form looks no more than modest. The form looks straightforward but weak, rated around the runner-up and fifth.
NOTEBOOK
Larwood(IRE), who is officially rated 8lb higher than the second, won with a bit more in hand than the margin suggests. Held up behind, he was brought with his challenge down the outside, edging ahead only well inside the last. He has a style of running that could see him thrive next year in sprint handicaps. (op 5-2)
The Wicked Lord broke well from the stalls and disputed the lead early. He gave the winner a race and clearly the drop back in trip was in his favour. (op 12-1)
Red Bay got a nice pitch, saving ground on the inside, but things got a bit tight inside the final furlong as the runner-up squeezed him up against the rail, and he came up a little short. He might be able to find a little race before the season is out. (op 4-1)
Safari Sunseeker(IRE), who came in for some support, was green early but showed some ability, and should come on for this debut effort. (op 13-2 tchd 7-1)
Jawim, who showed early pace before weakening, is no more than a plater on current evidence. Official explanation: jockey said filly hung right (op 12-1)
Rode Two Destiny(IRE) was well backed before finishing third here on her debut, but in contrast she was weak in the betting this time, and duly failed to build on that effort. (op 11-2)

6891 TOTEQUADPOT H'CAP 2m 1f 34y
3:05 (3:05) (Class 5) (0-75,74) 3-Y-O **£2,587** (£770; £384; £192) **Stalls** Centre

Form RPR
2045 1 **Hidden Valley**36 5938 3-9-1 **68** ......(v) DavidProbert 4 77
(Andrew Balding) *little slowly away: in last pair: hdwy over 2f out: led ent fnl f: styd on: pushed out* 8/1
0425 2 1 1/2 **Schism**35 5966 3-9-6 **73** ...... DaneO'Neill 2 80
(Henry Candy) *in tch: hdwy 4f out: rdn to ld jst over 2f out: hdd ent fnl f: no ex* 9/2[3]
2162 3 8 **Native Colony**13 6584 3-9-7 **74** ...... NeilCallan 5 72
(Roger Varian) *trckd ldrs: led 3f out: sn hdd: hdd and hung rt jst over 2f out: no ex fnl f* 6/1
5013 4 5 **Dark And Dangerous (IRE)**26 6240 3-8-5 **58** ...... LukeMorris 6 50
(Peter Winkworth) *trckd ldrs: rdn wl over 2f out: sn one pce* 7/2[1]
0234 5 7 **Corvette**11 6622 3-8-10 **63** ...... FergusSweeney 8 47
(J R Jenkins) *hld up in last pair: rdn 3f out: nvr any imp* 20/1
0025 6 7 **Compassion**32 6057 3-9-1 **68** ...... EddieAhern 1 44
(Michael Bell) *led tl rdn 3f out: wknd 2f out* 16/1
4224 7 40 **Kleitomachos (IRE)**23 6294 3-9-7 **74** ...... IanMongan 3 —
(Stuart Kittow) *in tch: slt promly 8f out: rdn over 2f out: wknd wl over 2f out: virtually p.u fr over 1f out* 9/2[3]
P041 8 5 **Birdwatcher (IRE)**13 6577 3-9-6 **73** ...... SilvestreDeSousa 7 —
(Mark Johnston) *prom: pushed along to hold pl fr 8f out: wknd whn rdn over 4f out: virtually p.u fnl 2f* 4/1[2]
3m 52.93s (1.03) **Going Correction** +0.125s/f (Good) 8 Ran SP% **114.6**
Speed ratings (Par 101): **102,101,97,95,91 88,69,67**
toteswingers:1&2:£9.10, 2&3:£5.30, 1&3:£8.10 CSF £43.88 CT £232.76 TOTE £12.10: £3.00, £2.00, £2.10; EX 55.40 Trifecta £535.20 Pool £817.38 - 1.13 winning units..
Owner Kingsclere Racing CLub **Bred** Kingsclere Stud **Trained** Kingsclere, Hants

7 *5* **Sapphire (FR)**[56] 4-9-0 0.. MEsposito 2 55
(Mario Hofer, Germany) *hung rt thrght: chsd ldr tl 1/2-way: sn wknd: wl btn and eased fr over 1f out* **126/10**

8 *8* **Above Limits (IRE)**[75] 4644 4-8-10 0...........................(b) PatCosgrave 5 22
(David Simcock) *in tch but sn pushed along: lost pl and towards rr whn pushed rt 1/2-way: sn lost tch* **19/1**

58.70 secs (-0.50) **8** Ran SP% **133.6**
PARI-MUTUEL (all including 1 euro stakes): WIN 3.86; PLACE 1.68, 2.42, 1.83; DF 15.74.
Owner Effevi **Bred** Razza Del Velino **Trained** Italy

NOTEBOOK
Dagda Mor(ITY) sealed his position as Italy's top sprinter with a decisive success.
Humidor(IRE) missed the break and was soon behind. He stayed on inside the final 300 yards but was never able to get on terms with the leaders.

6907a GRAN PREMIO JOCKEY CLUB ITALIANO (GROUP 1) (3YO+) (TURF) 1m 4f
4:25 (12:00) 3-Y-O+ **£116,379** (£51,206; £27,931; £13,965)

RPR

1 **Campanologist (USA)**[21] 6396 6-9-4 0........................... FrankieDettori 3 114
(Saeed Bin Suroor) *hld up off the pce in 4th: clsd on ldrs 4f out: chsd ldr 2f out: rdn to ld 1f out: r.o wl and in command fnl 150yds* **1/2**[1]

2 *1 ¼* **Arrigo (GER)**[105] 3672 3-8-13 0.. THellier 2 114
(J Hirschberger, Germany) *hld up off the pce in last pair: clsd on ldrs 4f out: rdn and effrt on outer jst over 2f out: no imp over 1f out: styd on ins fnl f to go 2nd fnl 50yds: nt threaten wnr* **47/10**[3]

3 *nk* **Lord Chaparral (IRE)**[15] 4-9-4 0.................................... MircoDemuro 1 112
(R Brogi, Italy) *led and styd cl to inner: rdn over 3f out: kpt on gamely tl hdd and unable qck 1f out: styd on same pce after: lost 2nd fnl 50yds* **885/100**

4 *1* **Voila Ici (IRE)**[28] 6202 6-9-4 0....................................... CristianDemuro 4 110
(Vittorio Caruso, Italy) *chsd ldng pair: rdn and chsd ldr 3f out: unable qck over 1f out: styd on same pce fnl f* **15/4**[2]

5 *3* **Figli Fanesi (IRE)**[14] 6569 3-8-13 0.............................. UmbertoRispoli 5 108
(Vittorio Caruso, Italy) *stdd s: hld up off the pce in last: clsd on ldrs 4f out: effrt and rdn to press ldrs on inner 2f out: no ex over 1f out: btn 1f out: eased ins fnl f* **15/4**[2]

6 *2 ½* **Sneak A Peek (ITY)**[28] 6202 3-8-13 0.............................. DarioVargiu 6 104
(S Botti, Italy) *chsd ldr tl 3f out: sn rdn: wknd over 1f out* **58/10**

2m 27.4s (-4.10)
WFA 3 from 4yo+ 7lb **6** Ran SP% **151.2**
PARI-MUTUEL (all including 1 euro stakes): WIN 1.50; PLACE 1.29, 2.06; DF 4.09.
Owner Godolphin **Bred** Darley **Trained** Newmarket, Suffolk

NOTEBOOK
Campanologist(USA) landed the fourth top-level success of his career, and the first outside Germany. He was always traveling well and stayed on too strongly for the runner-up once in front.

6203 WOODBINE (R-H)
Sunday, October 16
OFFICIAL GOING: Turf: yielding

6908a NEARCTIC STKS (GRADE 1) (3YO+) (TURF) 6f
7:59 (7:59) 3-Y-O+ **£192,307** (£64,102; £38,461; £16,025; £6,410; £3,205)

RPR

1 **Regally Ready (USA)**[41] 4-8-7 0.......................................(b) CNakatani 9 120
(Steven Asmussen, U.S.A) *mde all at ordinary gallop nr ins rail: pushed along and qcknd over 1f out: rdn and hld on wl fnl f* **98/10**

2 *nk* **Bated Breath**[43] 5707 4-8-5 0.. GKGomez 10 117+
(Roger Charlton) *in tch on outside: rdn and hdwy wl over 1f out: drvn and chsd wnr ins fnl f: kpt on but a being hld* **2/1**[1]

3 *hd* **Gypsy Ring (CAN)**[17] [illegible]..(b) [illegible] 7 110
(Paul M Buttigieg, Canada) *trckd ldrs: hdwy to chse wnr 1/2-way to ins fnl f: rdn and kpt on: hld cl home* **187/10**

4 *2* **Grand Adventure (USA)**[28] 6204 5-8-7 0........................... PHusbands 2 112
(Mark Frostad, Canada) *prom: effrt and shkn up whn n.m.r and swtchd rt ins fnl f: rdn and r.o fin* **125/10**

5 *1 ½* **Fiddlers Patriot (USA)**[112] 5-8-5 0................................. JRVelazquez 1 105
(George Weaver, U.S.A) *trckd wnr on ins to 1/2-way: cl up: rdn over 1f out: kpt on same pce fnl f* **122/10**

6 *nse* **Hitchens (IRE)**[43] 5707 6-8-7 0....................................... JamieSpencer 11 107
(David Barron) *s.i.s: hld up off ordinary gallop: drvn and hdwy over 1f out: kpt on fnl f: nvr able to chal* **178/10**

7 *1 ¼* **Bewitched (IRE)**[14] 6566 4-8-4 0.. JRosario 3 100
(Charles O'Brien, Ire) *s.i.s: sat last off ordinary gallop: outpcd 1/2-way: styd on wl last 100yds: nvr nr ldrs* **50/10**[3]

8 *1 ¼* **Right One (FR)**[28] 6204 5-8-7 0... JRLeparoux 6 99
(Christophe Clement, U.S.A) *sn bhd off ordinary gallop: rdn along 2f out: sme late hdwy: nvr on terms* **17/4**[2]

9 *½* **Riding The River (USA)**[28] 6204 4-8-5 0......................(b) RDosRamos 5 95
(David Cotey, U.S.A) *trckd ldrs: rdn along over 2f out: edgd lft and wknd appr fnl f* **148/10**

10 *2 ½* **Fatal Bullet (USA)**[49] 6-8-5 0.............................(b) EmmaJayneWilson 4 87
(Reade Baker, Canada) *prom: rdn and outpcd wl over 1f out: btn fnl f* **145/10**

11 *10* **Jenny's So Great (CAN)**[36] 4-8-5 0 ow1................. JesseMCampbell 8 55
(Gregory De Gannes, Canada) *hld up off ordinary gallop: rdn over 1f out: hung lft and sn btn* **23/1**

12 *¾* **Yield Bogey (USA)**[41] 7-8-7 0 ow2....................................... TPizarro 12 55
(Patrick J Kelly, U.S.A) *hld up midfield on outside: drvn and struggling wl over 1f out: edgd lft and sn btn* **55/1**

1m 11.35s (71.35) **12** Ran SP% **120.9**
PARI-MUTUEL (all including $2 stakes): WIN 21.60; PLACE (1-2) 9.10, 4.10; SHOW (1-2-3) 5.90, 3.50, 9.50; SF 79.00.
Owner Vinery Stables **Bred** Grapestock Llc **Trained** USA

NOTEBOOK
Regally Ready(USA), who made all, now goes for the Breeders' Cup Turf Sprint.
Bated Breath was again just denied a first victory at the highest level. He came four horses wide off the home turn with a powerful run, but although he was bearing down on the winner inside the final half-furlong he just never looked likely to get there in time. The ground was against him.
Hitchens(IRE) could never land a blow.
Bewitched(IRE), who missed the break, trailed for much of the race until a late rally propelled her into seventh.

6909a E P TAYLOR STKS - PRESENTED BY FLY EMIRATES (GRADE 1) (3YO+ FILLIES & MARES) (TURF) 1m 2f (T)
9:35 (9:35) 3-Y-O+ **£384,615** (£128,205; £64,102; £32,051; £12,820; £6,410)

RPR

1 **Miss Keller (IRE)**[28] 5-8-12 0.. JRVelazquez 11 114
(Roger L Attfield, Canada) **117/10**

2 *hd* **I'm A Dreamer (IRE)**[22] 6338 4-8-12 0.............................. WilliamBuick 3 114
(David Simcock) **89/10**

3 *nse* **Dream Peace (IRE)**[54] 5366 3-8-7 0................................ GeraldMosse 9 114
(Robert Collet, France) **2/1**[1]

4 *1* **Adventure Seeker (FR)**[44] 5694 3-8-7 0........... ChristopheSoumillon 7 112
(A De Royer-Dupre, France) **127/20**[3]

5 *nk* **Sea Of Heartbreak (IRE)**[15] 6557 4-8-12 0....................... GKGomez 10 111
(Roger Charlton) **84/10**

6 *2 ½* **Mahbooba (AUS)**[23] 6301 4-8-12 0................................ JamieSpencer 2 106
(M F De Kock, South Africa) **21/4**[2]

7 *2* **Laughing (IRE)**[129] 2865 3-8-7 0... JRosario 6 102
(Charles O'Brien, Ire) **13/1**

8 *hd* **Dyna Waltz**[78] 4-8-12 0.. JRLeparoux 8 102
(Jonathan E Sheppard, U.S.A) **146/10**

9 *nk* **Mekong Melody (IRE)**[28] 6-8-12 0.................................... PHusbands 5 101
(Roger L Attfield, Canada) **211/10**

10 *3 ¼* **Strawberrydaiquiri**[22] 6338 5-8-12 0................................ MartinDwyer 4 95
(Brian Meehan) **885/100**

11 *21* **Kinky Afro (IRE)**[103] 3703 4-8-12 0..................................... MichaelHills 1 95
(J S Moore) **76/1**

2m 6.98s (2.96)
WFA 3 from 4yo+ 5lb **11** Ran SP% **121.1**
PARI-MUTUEL (all including $2 stakes): WIN 25.30; PLACE (1-2) 10.90, 10.20; SHOW (1-2-3) 6.40, 4.50, 3.30; SF 265.30.
Owner Three Chimneys Racing Llc, Lordship Stud & Clodagh **Bred** Hascombe & Valiant Studs **Trained** Canada

NOTEBOOK
Miss Keller(IRE), who started her career in Ireland with John Oxx, had finished second to France's Reggane in the 2010 running of this $1 million event. She just got up for a home victory in a three-way photo finish.
I'm A Dreamer(IRE) had been pushed up to chase the leader Mahbooba at halfway before being driven for home just before the furlong pole. She kept on in determined fashion under pressure but just couldn't hold Miss Keller.
Dream Peace(IRE), held up, had to be switched from behind horses by Gerald Mosse before throwing down a sustained bid on the outer that failed only narrowly.
Sea Of Heartbreak(IRE) stayed on from the back without ever threatening to take a hand.
Strawberrydaiquiri faded badly.
Kinky Afro(IRE) dropped away to finish last.

6910a PATTISON CANADIAN INTERNATIONAL (GRADE 1) (3YO+) (TURF) 1m 4f (T)
10:42 (12:00) 3-Y-O+ **£576,923** (£192,307; £96,153; £48,076; £19,230; £9,615)

RPR

1 **Sarah Lynx (IRE)**[35] 5989 4-8-11 0...................(b) ChristopheSoumillon 1 120
(J E Hammond, France) **225/10**

2 *4* **Joshua Tree (IRE)**[42] 5773 4-9-0 0...................................... AdamKirby 7 117
(Marco Botti) **115/10**

3 *2* **Treasure Beach**[14] 6567 3-8-7 0.................................... CO'Donoghue 13 114
(A P O'Brien, Ire) **18/5**[1]

4 *¾* **Arctic Cosmos (USA)**[15] 6519 4-9-0 0..........................(b) WilliamBuick 2 113
(John Gosden) **56/10**[3]

5 *¾* **Quest For Peace (IRE)**[15] 6519 3-8-7 0............................ KierenFallon 5 111
(Luca Cumani) **39/10**[2]

6 *2 ¾* **Musketier (GER)**[56] 9-9-0 0... JRVelazquez 3 107
(Roger L Attfield, Canada) **171/10**

7 *1 ½* **Redwood**[79] 4492 5-9-0 0... MichaelHills 10 105
(Charles Hills) **56/10**[3]

8 *¾* **Mores Wells**[35] 5984 7-9-0 0.....................................(b) SebastienMaillot 6 103
(M Delzangles, France) **187/10**

9 *1 ¾* **Laureate Conductor (USA)**[28] 6203 5-9-0 0.................. LContreras 11 101
(Michael P De Paulo, Canada) **62/1**

10 *1 ¼* **Celtic Conviction (CAN)**[42] 3-8-7 0............................... ERamsammy 8 99
(Michael J Doyle, Canada) **58/1**

11 *3 ¼* **Kara's Orientation (USA)**[28] 6204 4-9-0 0........................... JRosario 14 93
(Steven Chircop, U.S.A) **249/10**

12 *¾* **Rahystrada (USA)**[36] 7-9-0 0.. JRLeparoux 9 92
(Byron G Hughes, U.S.A) **101/10**

13 *1* **Simmard (USA)**[28] 6203 6-9-0 0..(b) PHusbands 4 91
(Roger L Attfield, Canada) **197/10**

14 *2 ¾* **Mikhail Glinka (IRE)**[32] 6061 4-9-0 0.................... BernardFaydHerbe 12 86
(H J Brown, South Africa) **93/1**

15 *4 ¾* **Miami Deco (CAN)**[36] 4-9-0 0...(b) CNakatani 16 79
(Brian A Lynch, Canada) **75/1**

16 *17 ¾* **Bronze Cannon (USA)**[43] 5711 6-9-0 0............................ TomQueally 15 50
(H J Brown, South Africa) **57/1**

2m 34.9s (5.30)
WFA 3 from 4yo+ 7lb **16** Ran SP% **120.4**
PARI-MUTUEL (all including $2 stakes): WIN 46.90; PLACE (1-2) 21.40, 12.30; SHOW (1-2-3) 13.80, 8.40, 4.10; SF 659.50.
Owner Mrs Robert G Ehrnrooth **Bred** Grangecon Stud **Trained** France

NOTEBOOK
Sarah Lynx(IRE) sprinted away from a top-class international field to score emphatically. A huge gap opened up on the rail and she shot through under a fine ride from Soumillon.
Joshua Tree(IRE), last year's winner, missed the break. He quickened up well when in the clear but the winner was too strong.
Treasure Beach travelled well and was produced with what looked like a winning run until Sarah Lynx burst through on the inner. The ground was probably too soft for him.
Arctic Cosmos(USA) closed outside horses from the rear for fourth but could stay on at only one pace.
Quest For Peace(IRE), who beat Arctic Cosmos at Ascot, could not get a run.
Redwood, a C&D winner, raced wide.

6572 PONTEFRACT (L-H)

Monday, October 17

OFFICIAL GOING: Good (7.1)

Wind: Light across Weather: Cloudy

6911 TOTEPLACEPOT NURSERY — 1m 4y

2:10 (2:10) (Class 5) (0-75,74) 2-Y-O — **£2,264** (£673; £336; £168) Stalls Low

Form — RPR

650 **1** **Twelve Strings (IRE)**[24] 6308 2-8-12 **65** KirstyMilczarek 6 72+
(Luca Cumani) *midfield: hdwy on inner and n.m.r 2f out: chsd ldrs wl over 1f out: sn swtchd rt and rdn: styd on to chal ins fnl f: edgd lft and kpt on to ld last 75yds* **12/1**

4433 **2** ½ **Dubious Escapade (IRE)**[20] 6424 2-8-9 **62** JoeFanning 1 68
(Ann Duffield) *trckd ldr: hdwy to ld 2f out: rdn over 1f out: drvn ins fnl f: hdd and no ex last 75yds* **7/1**[3]

U636 **3** ¾ **Margo Channing**[26] 6260 2-8-0 **53** KellyHarrison 2 57
(Micky Hammond) *a.p: rdn and edgd lft 2f out: kpt on u.p fnl f* **25/1**

0305 **4** 4 **Dr Irv**[50] 5503 2-8-9 **65** MichaelO'Connell(3) 13 61
(Kate Walton) *in rr and sn pushed along: hdwy 3f out: chsd ldrs whn n.m.r over 1f out: rdn and kpt on fnl f* **100/1**

054 **5** 1 ½ **Free House**[12] 6630 2-9-7 **74** (b) JamieSpencer 10 68+
(Brian Meehan) *sn pushed along in rr: hdwy 2f out: rdn and kpt on appr fnl f: nrst fin* **6/1**[2]

254 **6** ¾ **Rocktherunway (IRE)**[29] 6187 2-9-7 **74** TomEaves 4 65
(Michael Dods) *prom: rdn along over 2f out: sn one pce* **6/1**[2]

6251 **7** 4 **Ventura Spirit**[40] 5818 2-9-4 **71** PaulHanagan 5 53
(Richard Fahey) *chsd ldrs: rdn along over 2f out: sn btn* **9/2**[1]

0405 **8** 1 **Damask (IRE)**[28] 6222 2-9-0 **67** PhillipMakin 7 47+
(Kevin Ryan) *in tch: hdwy 3f out: rdn along wl over 1f out: n.d* **10/1**

605 **9** 6 **Cloud Cuckooland (IRE)**[25] 6278 2-7-12 **51** oh3 JamesSullivan 16 17
(James Given) *s.i.s: a towards rr* **40/1**

030 **10** 2 **Blue Top**[16] 6532 2-8-10 **63** DuranFentiman 12 25
(Tim Walford) *chsd ldrs: rdn along 3f out: sn wknd* **16/1**

0502 **11** 2 **Bedlam**[26] 6260 2-8-12 **65** (b) DavidAllan 17 23
(Tim Easterby) *sn led: rdn along and hdd 2f out: sn wknd* **9/1**

000 **12** 9 **Iberian Rock**[33] 6047 2-8-5 **58** (p) LukeMorris 15 —
(Ann Duffield) *midfield: rdn along over 3f out: sn wknd* **40/1**

5000 **13** 3 ¾ **Tushuk Tash (USA)**[14] 6572 2-8-9 **62** ChrisCatlin 11 —
(Mick Channon) *midfield: rdn along over 3f out: nvr a factor* **33/1**

3053 **14** 20 **Hurricane Emerald (IRE)**[19] 6460 2-9-1 **68** (b[1]) SilvestreDeSousa 14 —
(Mark Johnston) *midfield: hdwy on outer to chse ldrs after 3f: rdn along 3f out: sn wknd: bhd and eased wl over 1f out* **15/2**

1m 48.19s (2.29) **Going Correction** +0.325s/f (Good) **14** Ran SP% **116.3**

Speed ratings (Par 95): **101,100,99,95,94 93,89,88,82,80 78,69,65,45**

toteswingers:1&2:£23.60, 1&3:£73.50, 2&3:£25.20 CSF £87.17 CT £1338.55 TOTE £11.60: £3.30, £2.30, £8.40; EX 69.30.

Owner S Stuckey **Bred** John & Anne-Marie O'Connor **Trained** Newmarket, Suffolk

■ Stewards' Enquiry : Joe Fanning five-day ban: used whip with excessive frequency (Oct 31,Nov 1-4)

FOCUS

After 29mm of rain since the previous meeting two weeks earlier the ground was described as tacky. A wide-open nursery run at a sound pace. Straightforward form rated on the postive side, with the first three clear.

NOTEBOOK

Twelve Strings(IRE), whose mandatory three previous outings were over shorter on AW, made his handicap bow from a mark of 65. After missing a beat at the start, he had to be pushed along at halfway and was momentarily short of room turning in, but when pulled outside the leader he stayed on willingly. He should be even better over 1m2f-plus at three. Official explanation: trainer's rep said, regarding apparent improvement in form, that this was the gelding's first run on Turf and appeared to be suited by the step up in trip (op 16-1)

Dubious Escapade(IRE), third at Ayr in testing conditions from the same mark, went down fighting. (op 6-1 tchd 15-2)

Margo Channing, well beaten on her nursery debut from the same mark, ran her best race so far, clearly suited by the stiff 1m. (tchd 28-1)

Dr Irv, absent seven weeks and gelded, put two poor efforts behind him.

Free House, sporting blinkers for the second time on his nursery debut, missed the break and looked reluctant. Pulled wide, he consented to stay on in the final furlong but is not one to trust. (op 13-2 tchd 7-1)

Rocktherunway(IRE), in the firing line from the off, looked to have been given a stiff mark for his handicap bow. (op 11-2)

Ventura Spirit, who broke his duck in soft ground at Carlisle, gave a problem or two in the stalls and was left behind once in line for home. (tchd 4-1)

6912 TOTEQUICKPICK MAIDEN AUCTION STKS — 6f

2:40 (2:42) (Class 5) 2-Y-O — **£2,264** (£673; £336; £168) Stalls Low

Form — RPR

4205 **1** **Byronic Hero**[10] 6673 2-8-10 79 TonyHamilton 9 77
(Jedd O'Keeffe) *mde virtually all: rdn 2f out: hld on gamely fnl f* **7/2**[2]

3 **2** 2 **Desert Philosopher**[14] 6579 2-9-0 0 JamieSpencer 7 75
(Kevin Ryan) *trckd ldrs: effrt and wnt 2nd over 2f out: rdn over 1f out: edgd rt ins fnl f: r.o same pce* **7/4**[1]

3 5 **Midnight Tryst** 2-8-6 0 PaulHanagan 11 54+
(Ann Duffield) *in tch on outside: pushed along and rn green over 2f out: hdwy to chse clr ldng pair over 1f out: no imp* **6/1**[3]

4 4 ½ **Grey Danube (IRE)**[10] 6678 2-8-9 0 BACurtis 5 42
(D J Bunyan, Ire) *prom: rdn over 2f out: outpcd fr wl over 1f out* **15/2**

5200 **5** ½ **Koalition (IRE)**[13] 6599 2-8-7 58 ow2 AshleyMorgan(5) 8 43
(David O'Meara) *w wnr: rdn and lost 2nd over 2f out: flashed tail and wknd over 1f out* **28/1**

4 **6** 4 ½ **Glen Ellyn**[19] 6455 2-9-0 0 SilvestreDeSousa 4 32
(Mark Johnston) *in tch: drvn and outpcd over 3f out: rallied appr 2f out: sn edgd lft and no imp: btn over 1f out* **8/1**

60 **7** nk **George Fenton**[54] 5367 2-8-11 0 RobbieFitzpatrick 10 28
(Richard Guest) *hld up: drvn along over 2f out: sn no imp: btn over 1f out* **100/1**

8 ¾ **Duke Liam (IRE)** 2-8-9 0 MichaelO'Connell(3) 1 26
(David Nicholls) *dwlt: bhd and rn green: sme late hdwy: nvr on terms* **33/1**

060 **9** ½ **Simpson Millar**[65] 5058 2-8-11 52 (p) BarryMcHugh 6 24
(Noel Wilson) *in tch: drvn along over 2f out: sn btn* **100/1**

0 **10** ½ **Kian's Joy**[6] 6774 2-8-7 0 PatrickDonaghy(3) 3 21
(Jedd O'Keeffe) *s.i.s: bhd and outpcd: nvr on terms* **100/1**

050 **11** 1 ¼ **Point At Issue (IRE)**[44] 5726 2-8-13 59 PaulQuinn 12 21
(David Nicholls) *bhd and sn drvn along: no ch fr 1/2-way* **80/1**

564 **12** 1 ¼ **Stepharlie**[11] 6654 2-8-8 63 TomEaves 13 12
(Bryan Smart) *prom on outside tl rdn and wknd wl over 1f out* **20/1**

13 ½ **Release The Funds (IRE)** 2-8-13 0 AdrianNicholls 14 15
(David Nicholls) *s.i.s: bhd and outpcd: nvr on terms* **28/1**

00 **14** 3 ½ **Pelican Rock (IRE)**[30] 6180 2-9-0 0 (t) StephenCraine 2 6
(Tom Dascombe) *towards rr: drvn along 1/2-way: sn struggling* **33/1**

1m 19.48s (2.58) **Going Correction** +0.325s/f (Good) **14** Ran SP% **117.5**

Speed ratings (Par 95): **95,92,85,79,79 73,72,71,70,70 68,66,66,61**

toteswingers:1&2:£2.60, 1&3:£4.90, 2&3:£3.50 CSF £8.93 TOTE £4.80: £1.80, £1.30, £2.00; EX 9.60.

Owner Highbeck Racing **Bred** Kevin Daniel Crabb **Trained** Middleham Moor, N Yorks

FOCUS

A maiden auction race lacking any strength in depth and the first three pulled clear. Straightforward, sound form.

NOTEBOOK

Byronic Hero, gelded after his third start, has an official rating of 79. He had an outside draw but was soon at the head of affairs and stuck on in willing fashion. He will get a bit further at three and should add to this in handicap company next year. (op 3-1)

Desert Philosopher, the pick of the paddock, had finished a pleasing third first time at Warwick two weeks earlier. He moved to the tail of the winner turning in but tended to edge right under pressure. (op 9-4)

Midnight Tryst has reportedly had an issue with the stalls at home. She had a wide draw and, taking third once in line for home, stayed on nicely under a sympathetic ride. This will have taught her plenty. (op 15-2 tchd 8-1)

Grey Danube(IRE), an Irish raider who was fourth at Dundalk, could never take a hand. Official explanation: jockey said gelding hung left (op 6-1)

Koalition(IRE), having his ninth start and runner-up in selling company, is rated just 58 yet still finished clear of the remainder. (op 25-1 tchd 20-1)

6913 TOTEQUADPOT H'CAP (DIV I) — 5f

3:10 (3:11) (Class 4) (0-85,85) 3-Y-O+ — **£4,075** (£1,212; £606; £303) Stalls Low

Form — RPR

6002 **1** **Doc Hay (USA)**[28] 6212 4-9-2 **80** JoeFanning 12 89
(Keith Dalgleish) *s.i.s and towards rr: hdwy on wd outside wl over 1f out: rdn and styd on strly ent fnl f to ld last 100yds* **9/1**

1560 **2** 1 ½ **Haajes**[9] 6703 7-9-3 **81** MickyFenton 13 85
(Paul Midgley) *towards rr: hdwy wl over 1f out: sn rdn and kpt on ins fnl f* **14/1**

1500 **3** hd **Hotham**[31] 6112 8-9-0 **78** BarryMcHugh 9 81
(Noel Wilson) *hld up: hdwy wl over 1f out: rdn ent fnl f: kpt on* **12/1**

4046 **4** ½ **Sand Owl**[28] 6217 3-9-0 **78** (p) JamieSpencer 1 79
(Peter Chapple-Hyam) *hld up towards rr: hdwy 2f out: swtchd rt towards outer and rdn over 1f out: kpt on ins fnl f: nrst fin* **7/1**[2]

2430 **5** nk **Bronze Beau**[9] 6703 4-9-4 **82** (tp) JamesSullivan 16 82
(Linda Stubbs) *cl up: led 2f out: rdn over 1f out: hdd and one pce fnl 100yds* **50/1**

150 **6** ½ **Italian Tom (IRE)**[36] 5972 4-8-13 **77** LukeMorris 15 75
(Ronald Harris) *towards rr: hdwy wl over 1f out: rdn and n.m.r ent fnl f: kpt on: nrst fin* **20/1**

3110 **7** 1 ¾ **Ingleby Star (IRE)**[28] 6212 6-8-12 **79** (p) PaulPickard(3) 8 71
(Ian McInnes) *cl up: rdn along 2f out: wknd ent fnl f* **20/1**

1202 **8** nse **Fol Hollow (IRE)**[31] 6112 6-9-3 **81** AdrianNicholls 17 73
(David Nicholls) *racd wd: led: rdn along and hdd 2f out: drvn ent fnl f: grad wknd* **14/1**

6500 **9** 1 **Bold Bidder**[37] 5923 3-9-1 **82** AmyRyan(3) 11 70
(Kevin Ryan) *prom: rdn wl over 1f out: wknd ent fnl f* **25/1**

2625 **10** ½ **Lucky Numbers (IRE)**[2] 6865 5-9-7 **85** SilvestreDeSousa 10 71
(Paul Green) *chsd ldrs: rdn along wl over 1f out: sn no imp* **6/1**[1]

2132 **11** ½ **Spinatrix**[29] 6189 3-9-2 **80** TomEaves 7 65
(Michael Dods) *dwlt: sn prom: rdn along on inner 2f out: wknd ent fnl f* **15/2**[3]

3002 **12** nk **Berberana (IRE)**[23] 6348 3-9-3 **81** (t) DavidAllan 4 64
(Tim Easterby) *nvr bttr than midfield* **17/2**

0104 **13** ½ **Green Park (IRE)**[37] 5923 8-8-11 **80** (b) NeilFarley(5) 6 62
(Declan Carroll) *in tch: rdn along wl over 1f out: sn one pce* **25/1**

0005 **14** ¾ **Dickie Le Davoir**[7] 6761 7-9-1 **82** (b) RobertLButler(3) 14 61
(Richard Guest) *s.i.s: a in rr* **18/1**

0000 **15** nse **Discanti (IRE)**[23] 6347 6-9-2 **80** (tp) DuranFentiman 5 59
(Tim Easterby) *hld up on inner: effrt and sme hdwy 2f out: sn rdn and btn* **20/1**

3110 **16** ½ **Comptonspirit**[37] 5914 7-8-13 **77** PaulHanagan 3 54
(Brian Baugh) *a towards rr* **14/1**

2000 **17** 1 ½ **Julius Geezer (IRE)**[23] 6327 3-9-4 **82** StephenCraine 2 54
(Tom Dascombe) *a in rr* **16/1**

64.71 secs (1.41) **Going Correction** +0.325s/f (Good) **17** Ran SP% **121.9**

Speed ratings (Par 105): **101,98,98,97,97 96,93,93,91,90 90,89,88,87,87 86,84**

toteswingers:1&2:£36.70, 1&3:£29.50, 2&3:£30.00 CSF £114.81 CT £1533.59 TOTE £14.30: £2.70, £3.60, £3.20, £2.50; EX 165.40.

Owner S Laffan **Bred** Colts Neck Stables Llc **Trained** Carluke, South Lanarkshire

■ Stewards' Enquiry : Micky Fenton seven-day ban: used whip with excessive frequency (Oct 31, Nov 1-5,9)

FOCUS

A fiercely competitive sprint handicap run at a furious pace and they fanned right across the course once in line for home. The winner is rated back to his best.

6914 TOTEPOOL SILVER TANKARD STKS (LISTED RACE) — 1m 4y

3:40 (3:40) (Class 1) 2-Y-O

£12,192 (£4,622; £2,313; £1,152; £578; £290) Stalls Low

Form — RPR

4035 **1** **Letsgoroundagain (IRE)**[25] 6270 2-9-2 100 WilliamCarson 1 100
(Charles Hills) *hld up in tch: hdwy over 2f out: rdn over 1f out: led ins fnl f: styd on strly to go clr* **15/2**

401 **2** 3 ¼ **Ptolemaic**[22] 6380 2-9-2 80 (v) TomEaves 7 93
(Bryan Smart) *racd keenly: led at ordinary gallop: over 3 l clr 1/2-way: rdn and hung lft over 1f out: hdd ins fnl f: kpt on same pce* **50/1**

14 **3** ¾ **Stipulate**[44] 5709 2-9-2 91 TomQueally 8 91
(Sir Henry Cecil) *t.k.h: hld up in tch: stdy hdwy over 2f out: rdn and edgd lft over 1f out: kpt on fnl f: nt pce to chal* **9/2**[3]

5 **4** hd **Toptempo**[52] 5445 2-8-11 0 TedDurcan 5 85
(Mark H Tompkins) *hld up on ins: rdn and hdwy 2f out: kpt of fnl f: nvr able to chal* **22/1**

1254 **5** 13 **Salford Art (IRE)**[24] 6299 2-8-11 100 PaulHanagan 2 55
(David Elsworth) *hld up in tch on outside: drvn and outpcd wl over 2f out: edgd lft and btn over 1f out* **4/1**[2]

1 **6** *1¼* **Al Saham**[19] 6448 2-9-2 **88** WilliamBuick 3 58
(Saeed Bin Suroor) *rrd in stalls: t.k.h: chsd ldr: rdn over 2f out: sn lost 2nd: wknd wl over 1f out* **7/2[1]**

0311 **7** *7* **Cravat**[6] 6766 2-9-2 **91** SilvestreDeSousa 6 41
(Mark Johnston) *prom: drvn and outpcd wl over 2f out: btn ent st* **4/1[2]**

3421 **8** *8* **Mister Music**[22] 6373 2-9-2 **92** JamieSpencer 4 23
(Richard Hannon) *n.m.r sn after s: bhd: rdn over 2f out: fnd little and sn btn: eased whn no ch fnl f* **7/1**

1m 47.42s (1.52) **Going Correction** +0.325s/f (Good) **8** Ran SP% **111.0**
Speed ratings (Par 103): **105,101,101,100,87 86,79,71**
toteswingers:1&2:£20.60, 1&3:£5.60, 2&3:£24.40 CSF £254.31 TOTE £8.70: £2.40, £8.70, £1.80; EX 322.60.
Owner AEGIS Partnership **Bred** Lynn Lodge Stud **Trained** Lambourn, Berks

FOCUS
Not a strong running of this Listed contest and a shock winner looked on the cards for much of the race. The race fell apart somewhat and the third helps set the level.

NOTEBOOK
Letsgoroundagain(IRE), who broke his duck when awarded a maiden at Haydock on his fourth start, has made great strides since. Stepping up to 1m and in no hurry to join issue, he was firmly in command at the line. (op 9-1 tchd 7-1)
Ptolemaic, visored for the first time when taking a 7f maiden race at Musselburgh, had 20lb to find with the winner on official ratings. He seemed to really enjoy himself bowling along in front and the winner had to dig deep to wear him down. However, this will have ruined his handicap mark. (op 40-1)
Stipulate, a Leicester maiden winner on his debut, had been too keen for his own good when fourth in Listed company at Haydock next time. He settled better and stuck on all the way to the line, but he lacks size and scope. (op 4-1)
Toptempo, fifth in a good maiden on her debut at Newmarket, stepped up on that effort with a highly creditable effort in fourth, clear of the remainder. She looks far from the finished article and looks sure to make her mark at three. (op 20-1)
Salford Art(IRE), raised 17lb to a mark of 100 after finishing fourth in the Group 1 Fillies' Mile, was warm beforehand on a cool, breezy day. She was under pressure at halfway and dropped right away. Whether she was highly flattered at Newmarket staying on past beaten horses remains to be seen. (op 7-2)
Al Saham anticipated the start and seemed to bang his head on the super-structure. He raced with the choke out and was another to drop away tamely. Connections will be hoping he shows this to be all wrong. (op 4-1)
Cravat, much improved of late and seeking a hat-trick, was stepping up to a mile. He was on the retreat before stamina became an issue. (op 9-2 tchd 7-2)
Mister Music never went a yard and Jamie Spencer threw in the towel in the end. (op 8-1)

6915 TOTEEXACTA BLUFF COVE H'CAP 2m 1f 216y
4:10 (4:12) (Class 5) (0-75,72) 3-Y-0+ **£2,264** (£673; £336; £168) **Stalls** Low

Form RPR

3400 **1** **Descaro (USA)**[5] 6095 5-9-9 **67** (v) SilvestreDeSousa 1 77
(David O'Meara) *hld up in midfield: stdy hdwy 5f out: swtchd ins and effrt to ld 2f out: rdn over 1f out: edgd rt ins fnl f: drvn out* **7/1[3]**

2540 **2** *½* **Riptide**[6] 6780 5-9-12 **70** (v) JamieGoldstein 5 79
(Michael Scudamore) *a.p: led over 7f out: pushed along 3f out: hdd 2f out and sn rdn: drvn and rallied fnl f: kpt on gamely* **17/2**

1220 **3** *27* **Dr Finley (IRE)**[6] 6780 4-9-12 **70** ChrisCatlin 3 50
(Lydia Pearce) *hld up: hdwy 6f out: rdn to chse ldrs over 2f out: plugged on same pce fr wl over 1f out* **17/2**

1266 **4** *¾* **Inside Knowledge (USA)**[207] 955 5-9-1 **59** KellyHarrison 4 38
(Garry Woodward) *dwlt and in rr: stdy hdwy 5f out: rdn along 3f out: plugged on same pce fnl 2f* **33/1**

0461 **5** *7* **River Dragon (IRE)**[6] 6780 6-9-8 **66** 6ex BarryMcHugh 9 37
(Tony Coyle) *trckd ldr: led after 6f: pushed along and hdd over 7f out: cl up tl rdn along 3f out and grad wknd* **9/2[1]**

4100 **6** *6* **Petella**[9] 6707 5-9-9 **67** PJMcDonald 11 32
(George Moore) *hld up in rr: hdwy 3f out: plugged on fnl 2f: nvr nr ldrs* **8/1**

3/04 **7** *½* **Mr Crystal (FR)**[25] 6279 7-9-7 **72** JasonHart(7) 12 36
(Micky Hammond) *trckd ldrs: hdwy and cl up 7f out: chal 4f out: rdn along 3f out and sn wknd* **11/2[2]**

350- **8** *14* **Divinatore**[336] 7465 5-8-9 **53** oh3 (p) PaddyAspell 8 —
(James Moffatt) *a in rr* **22/1**

0203 **9** *8* **Spruzzo**[14] 6575 5-8-13 **57** TomEaves 2 —
(Chris Fairhurst) *chsd ldrs: rdn along 3f out: sn outpcd* **17/2**

5340 **10** *36* **Spiders Star**[32] 6095 8-9-2 **63** PaulPickard(3) 6 —
(Simon West) *a in rr: bhd fnl 3f* **14/1**

0304 **11** *3* **Dan Buoy (FR)**[14] 6575 8-9-1 **62** (b) BillyCray(3) 10 —
(Richard Guest) *led: rdn along and hdd after 6f: lost pl over 7f out: bhd fnl 4f* **16/1**

1200 **12** *8* **Blackmore**[19] 6451 4-10-0 **72** (p) PaulHanagan 7 —
(Julia Feilden) *trckd ldrs: rdn along 6f out: sn wknd* **10/1**

4m 3.95s (7.75) **Going Correction** +0.45s/f (Yiel) **12** Ran SP% **117.7**
Speed ratings (Par 103): **100,99,87,87,84 81,81,75,71,55 54,50**
toteswingers:1&2:£11.60, 1&3:£7.30, 2&3:£16.00 CSF £64.88 CT £517.92 TOTE £6.10: £2.00, £3.20, £2.50; EX 74.80.
Owner R Fell & K Everitt **Bred** Langley House Stud **Trained** Nawton, N Yorks

FOCUS
A modest handicap, the final round of this season's Pontefract stayers' championship which carries a first prize of £3,000. The first two finished a long way clear but nothing else ran their race. The winner is the best guide to the form.

6916 TOTESWINGER H'CAP (DIV I) 1m 2f 6y
4:40 (4:43) (Class 5) (0-75,75) 3-Y-0+ **£2,264** (£673; £336; £168) **Stalls** Low

Form RPR

3153 **1** **Kodicil (IRE)**[14] 6577 3-8-6 **62** DuranFentiman 3 71+
(Tim Walford) *a.p: effrt 2f out: rdn to chal over 1f out: styd on to ld jst ins fnl f: r.o wl* **6/1[2]**

4030 **2** *1* **Amazing Blue Sky**[16] 6538 5-9-8 **73** JamesSullivan 1 80
(Ruth Carr) *led: rdn over 1f out: hdd ins fnl f: kpt on same pce* **18/1**

0025 **3** *3½* **Brockfield**[19] 6453 5-8-13 **64** DavidAllan 10 64
(Mel Brittain) *hld up: hdwy over 3f out: rdn wl over 1f out: kpt on fnl f* **12/1**

0600 **4** *½* **Highlife Dancer**[10] 6674 3-9-5 **75** MartinHarley 9 74
(Mick Channon) *trckd ldrs: effrt on inner 2f out: sn rdn and kpt on same pce appr fnl f* **12/1**

0600 **5** *2* **Solicitor**[39] 5857 4-9-9 **74** (b) SilvestreDeSousa 12 74+
(Mark Johnston) *hld up: hdwy to chse ldrs over 3f out: rdn over 2f out: no imp* **17/2**

00-1 **6** *1¾* **Cheddar George**[66] 5015 5-9-2 **67** JamieSpencer 7 59
(Peter Chapple-Hyam) *s.i.s and in rr: hdwy over 3f out: rdn along 2f out: sn no imp* **7/2[1]**

6010 **7** *26* **Cat O' Nine Tails**[9] 6707 4-9-2 **67** BarryMcHugh 6 7
(Brian Rothwell) *s.i.s: a in rr* **20/1**

2554 **8** *1* **Muqtarrib (IRE)**[19] 6459 3-9-2 **72** (b) TedDurcan 8 28
(Brian Meehan) *dwlt and towards rr: hdwy 6f out: rdn along to chse ldrs 3f out: sn wknd* **13/2[3]**

04-6 **9** *1* **Ergo (FR)**[241] 596 7-8-10 **61** oh1 (p) PaddyAspell 2 —
(James Moffatt) *in tch: pushed along and lost pl 1/2-way: sn in rr* **50/1**

1550 **10** *15* **Emperor Of Rome (IRE)**[65] 5064 3-8-12 **68** TomEaves 13 —
(Michael Dods) *chsd ldrs on outer: rdn along over 3f out: sn wknd* **22/1**

3052 **11** *2½* **Mighty Clarets (IRE)**[28] 6225 4-9-4 **69** PaulHanagan 11 19
(Richard Fahey) *chsd ldrs: rdn along 3f out: sn wknd* **11/1**

2020 **12** *1¼* **White Diamond**[114] 3386 4-9-7 **72** TonyHamilton 4 —
(Malcolm Jefferson) *prom: rdn along over 4f out: sn wknd* **11/1**

0000 **13** *54* **Sirgarfieldsobers (IRE)**[26] 6263 5-8-12 **70** (b[1]) JasonHart(7) 5 —
(Declan Carroll) *t.k.h: cl up on outer: lost pl bef 1/2-way: sn bhd: t.o fnl 3f* **16/1**

2m 17.44s (3.74) **Going Correction** +0.45s/f (Yiel)
WFA 3 from 4yo+ 5lb **13** Ran SP% **114.6**
Speed ratings (Par 103): **103,102,99,99,97 96,75,74,73,61 59,58,15**
toteswingers:1&2:£13.30, 1&3:£10.90, 2&3:£38.30 CSF £101.65 CT £1248.58 TOTE £7.10: £2.70, £3.60, £3.60; EX 110.40.
Owner D & S Woodall **Bred** Tally-Ho Stud **Trained** Sheriff Hutton, N Yorks

FOCUS
A strong gallop and they came home strung out, the first six well clear. The second had an uncontested lead and the winner can do better than the bare form.
Mighty Clarets(IRE) Official explanation: jockey said gelding ran flat

6917 TOTEQUADPOT H'CAP (DIV II) 5f
5:10 (5:11) (Class 4) (0-85,84) 3-Y-0+ **£4,075** (£1,212; £606; £303) **Stalls** Low

Form RPR

0020 **1** **Amenable (IRE)**[31] 6113 4-9-5 **82** AdrianNicholls 11 90
(David Nicholls) *racd wd thrght: mde virtually all: rdn and edgd lft over 1f out: hld on wl u.p fnl f* **16/1**

0010 **2** *shd* **Dancing Freddy (IRE)**[7] 6762 4-8-13 **79** (tp) RobertLButler(3) 1 86
(Richard Guest) *hld up: hdwy against far rail over 1f out: kpt on wl fnl f: jst hld* **20/1**

-030 **3** *nk* **Bonnie Charlie**[85] 4369 5-9-0 **80** MichaelO'Connell(3) 15 86+
(David Nicholls) *stdd and swtchd to far rail sn after s: hld up: hdwy over 1f out: kpt on strly under hands and heels riding fnl f: nrst fin* **25/1**

2626 **4** *1* **Perfect Pastime**[19] 6467 3-9-4 **81** ChrisCatlin 13 84
(Walter Swinburn) *prom: effrt and rdn 2f out: kpt on ins fnl f* **20/1**

6026 **5** *½* **Boundaries**[7] 6762 3-9-1 **78** (v) PaulHanagan 17 79
(Tim Easterby) *hld up on outside: hdwy over 1f out: edgd lft and kpt on fnl f: nvr able to chal* **25/1**

3151 **6** *nk* **Another Wise Kid (IRE)**[23] 6348 3-9-7 **84** MickyFenton 12 84
(Paul Midgley) *racd wd: prom: effrt and rdn over 1f out: kpt on same pce ins fnl f* **11/1[3]**

1125 **7** *hd* **Time Medicean**[36] 5972 5-8-8 **78** RaulDaSilva(7) 2 77
(Tony Carroll) *in tch against far rail: checked over 2f out: rdn and kpt on same pce fnl f* **15/2[2]**

0605 **8** *2* **Lenny Bee**[7] 6762 5-9-5 **82** (t) LeeNewman 10 74
(George Foster) *disp ld: rdn over 1f out: outpcd ins fnl f* **11/1[3]**

3503 **9** *hd* **The Nifty Fox**[28] 6212 7-9-0 **77** DavidAllan 16 68
(Tim Easterby) *t.k.h: hld up: hdwy over 1f out: kpt on: nvr able to chal* **14/1**

4615 **10** *1¾* **Invincible Force (IRE)**[45] 5682 7-9-3 **80** (b) JamesSullivan 7 65
(Paul Green) *trckd ldrs: edgd lft over 2f out: rdn and wknd over 1f out* **25/1**

0500 **11** *hd* **Waking Warrior**[28] 6224 3-8-13 **81** JulieBurke(5) 14 65
(Kevin Ryan) *midfield: rdn and effrt over 2f out: one pce over 1f out* **11/1[3]**

2000 **12** *1¾* **Noodles Blue Boy**[9] 6703 5-9-4 **81** TonyHamilton 6 59
(Ollie Pears) *towards rr: rdn and outpcd over 2f out: n.d after* **14/1**

2500 **13** *1¼* **Oldjoesaid**[31] 6112 7-9-3 **80** (b) PhillipMakin 8 53
(Kevin Ryan) *t.k.h: hld up: rdn 2f out: nvr able to chal* **16/1**

0622 **14** *½* **Legal Eagle (IRE)**[23] 6350 6-9-3 **80** (p) SilvestreDeSousa 9 52
(Paul Green) *prom tl rdn and wknd wl over 1f out* **12/1**

0005 **15** *¾* **Whozthecat (IRE)**[9] 6703 4-9-0 **82** (v) NeilFarley(5) 3 51
(Declan Carroll) *dwlt: bhd and sn pushed along: nvr on terms* **7/2[1]**

4251 **16** *hd* **Sugar Beet**[37] 6030 [illegible] DavidProbert 4 50
(Ronald Harris) *towards rr: rdn whn n.m.r briefly over 2f out: sn btn* **20/1**

4004 **17** *2* **Arry's Orse**[23] 6350 4-8-13 **76** (t) TomEaves 5 37
(Bryan Smart) *t.k.h: hld up towards rr: rdn over 2f out: sn btn* **12/1**

64.91 secs (1.61) **Going Correction** +0.325s/f (Good) **17** Ran SP% **125.3**
Speed ratings (Par 105): **100,99,99,97,96 96,96,92,92,89 89,86,84,83,82 82,79**
toteswingers:1&2:£78.10, 1&3:£57.80, 2&3:£119.50 CSF £316.11 CT £7937.99 TOTE £23.60: £4.80, £3.80, £8.10, £6.90; EX 516.20.
Owner Turton Brown Williams Lindley **Bred** Michael Downey & Roalso Ltd **Trained** Sessay, N Yorks
■ Stewards' Enquiry : Adrian Nicholls five-day ban: used whip with excessive frequency (Nov 2-5,9)

FOCUS
Part two of the 5f handicap. A blanket finish with less than three lengths covering the first seven home. Similar form to the first division and the winner was another to show that racing wide was no disadvantage on this card.
Invincible Force(IRE) Official explanation: jockey said gelding was denied a clear run
Sugar Beet Official explanation: jockey said filly knocked itself leaving stalls but returned sound

6918 TOTESWINGER H'CAP (DIV II) 1m 2f 6y
5:40 (5:42) (Class 5) (0-75,75) 3-Y-0+ **£2,264** (£673; £336; £168) **Stalls** Low

Form RPR

6-03 **1** **Brigadoon**[17] 6507 4-9-2 **67** LeeNewman 11 79
(William Jarvis) *trckd ldrs: hdwy 3f out: chsd ldr wl over 1f out: rdn and styd on to ld ins fnl f: kpt on* **12/1**

4400 **2** *¾* **Law To Himself (IRE)**[16] 6533 4-8-11 **62** PJMcDonald 13 72
(Alan Swinbank) *prom: cl up 1/2-way: led over 4f out: rdn over 1f out: hdd ins fnl f: no ex* **20/1**

1334 **3** *2¼* **Rio's Rosanna (IRE)**[23] 6346 4-9-9 **74** RussKennemore 2 80
(Richard Whitaker) *trckd ldrs: hdwy 3f out: rdn wl over 1f out: kpt on same pce fnl f* **9/4[1]**

2600 **4** *3* **Veiled Applause**[10] 6676 8-9-1 **71** ShaneBKelly(5) 1 71
(John Quinn) *s.i.s and bhd: hdwy on inner over 2f out: sn rdn and styd on fnl f: nrst fin* **10/1**

3143 **5** *1¾* **Waahej**[5] 6789 5-9-1 **66** ChrisCatlin 5 62
(Peter Hiatt) *in tch: effrt 3f out and sn cl up: rdn to chse ldr 2f out: wknd appr fnl f* **10/1**

0-30 **6** *5* **Cottam Donny**[10] 6674 3-8-8 **63** ow1 (t) DavidAllan 3 50
(Mel Brittain) *hld up: hdwy 4f out: chsd ldrs over 2f out: sn rdn and btn* **8/1**

1400 **7** *shd* **Christmas Light**[13] 6601 4-9-3 **68** DanielTudhope 8 54
(David O'Meara) *hld up: hdwy 3f out: rdn over 2f out: n.d* **25/1**

2302 **8** *½* **Sharp Sovereign (USA)**[24] 6295 5-8-11 **67** LMcNiff(5) 4 52+
(David Barron) *chsd ldrs: rdn along 2f out: sn wknd* **13/2**[3]

0263 **9** *18* **Ullswater (IRE)**[28] 6218 3-9-5 **75** SilvestreDeSousa 9 24
(Mark Johnston) *in tch: rdn along over 2f out: sn wknd* **6/1**[2]

4200 **10** *10* **Thunderstruck**[55] 5036 6-9-4 **72** (p) BillyCray(3) 6 —
(David Nicholls) *in rr and sn pushed along: hdwy over 3f out: rdn over 2f out: n.d* **40/1**

3536 **11** *7* **Cobo Bay**[68] 4920 6-9-2 **74** (v) KristinStubbs(7) 12 —
(Linda Stubbs) *dwlt: hdwy on outer to chse ldrs 1/2-way: rdn along over 3f out: sn wknd* **66/1**

5420 **12** *15* **Cadore (IRE)**[37] 5925 3-9-4 **74** JamieSpencer 7 —
(Peter Chapple-Hyam) *prom: cl up 4f out: rdn along 3f out: sn wknd and bhd whn eased wl over 1f out* **10/1**

1050 **13** *31* **Maybe I Wont**[10] 6669 6-8-13 **64** (v[1]) PaulHanagan 10 —
(Lucinda Featherstone) *led: hdd over 4f out: sn wknd and bhd fnl 2f* **33/1**

2m 16.25s (2.55) **Going Correction** +0.45s/f (Yiel)
WFA 3 from 4yo+ 5lb **13** Ran SP% **119.9**
Speed ratings (Par 103): **107,106,104,102,100 96,96,96,81,73 68,56,31**
toteswingers:1&2:£38.50, 1&3:£10.10, 2&3:£14.00 CSF £236.95 CT £742.01 TOTE £17.10: £4.10, £3.50, £1.60; EX 156.10.
Owner James Bowditch **Bred** Biddestone Stud **Trained** Newmarket, Suffolk

FOCUS
Part two of the 1m2f handicap, and the pace was very strong with the early leader eventually tailed off. The form is rated around the second.
T/Jkpt: Not won. T/Plt: £646.40 to a £1 stake. Pool:£65,750.62 - 74.25 winning tickets T/Qpdt: £87.60 to a £1 stake. Pool:£4,503.15 - 38.00 winning tickets JR

6750 WINDSOR (R-H)

Monday, October 17

OFFICIAL GOING: Good to firm (watered; 8.8)
Stands' rail dolled out 12yds at 6f and 6y at winning post. Top bend dolled out 5yds from normal configuration adding 22yds to races of 1m and over.
Wind: Moderate, half-behind Weather: Fine but cloudy

6919 CSP LTD MEDIAN AUCTION MAIDEN STKS 5f 10y
2:30 (2:30) (Class 5) 2-Y-O **£2,264** (£673; £336; £168) **Stalls** Low

Form RPR

06 **1** **Sandfrankskipsgo**[38] 5889 2-9-3 0 IanMongan 9 80
(Brett Johnson) *pressed ldr: rdn and clr of rest over 1f out: styd on to ld last 100yds: in command at fin* **7/1**

0522 **2** *¾* **Blanc De Chine (IRE)**[14] 6590 2-8-12 71 FergusSweeney 5 72
(Peter Makin) *led against rail: shkn up and pressed over 1f out: hdd last 100yds: styd on but a hld* **5/4**[1]

553 **3** *5* **Art Show**[11] 6654 2-8-12 67 KierenFallon 8 54
(Ed Dunlop) *racd wd: in tch: effrt 2f out: kpt on same pce to take modest 3rd jst over 1f out* **9/2**[2]

0545 **4** *1 ¾* **Get The Trip**[31] 6131 2-8-9 53 KieranO'Neill(3) 10 48
(James Toller) *in tch towards outer: rdn to dispute 3rd over 1f out but wl outpcd: one pce after* **40/1**

4232 **5** *½* **Samba Night (IRE)**[23] 6352 2-9-3 68 RichardMullen 1 51
(Ed McMahon) *chsd ldng pair: urged along 1/2-way: outpcd and lost 3rd over 1f out: one pce after* **7/1**

3005 **6** *1 ¾* **Dream Whisperer**[16] 6524 2-8-12 69 (b) DaneO'Neill 2 40
(Dominic Ffrench Davis) *trckd ldrs: rdn and nt qckn wl over 1f out: sn wknd* **5/1**[3]

0000 **7** *3 ¾* **Key Addition (IRE)**[16] 6540 2-9-3 62 (b) GeorgeBaker 3 31
(William Muir) *in tch to 1/2-way: sn shkn up and wknd* **50/1**

8 *1* **Naughtical** 2-8-12 0 SebSanders 7 23
(J W Hills) *dwlt: a in last pair: nvr a real factor* **25/1**

9 *12* **Strategic Action (IRE)** 2-9-3 0 LiamKeniry 6 —
(Linda Jewell) *s.i.s: a in last pair: wknd 2f out: t.o* **80/1**

59.02 secs (-1.28) **Going Correction** -0.30s/f (Firm) **9** Ran SP% **113.8**
Speed ratings (Par 95): **98,96,88,86,85 82,76,74,55**
toteswingers:1&2:£3.50, 1&3:£5.50, 2&3:£1.80 CSF £15.71 TOTE £10.50: £2.00, £1.30, £1.60; EX 19.50 Trifecta £44.00 Pool £357.37 - 6.00 winning units..
Owner Peter Crate **Bred** Peter Crate **Trained** Ashtead, Surrey

FOCUS
A routine maiden, run at a good pace, with the first two drawing clear. Straightforward, sound form.

NOTEBOOK
Sandfrankskipsgo had shown ability in two decent maidens, and this was easier. He looks the type to go on from here at a realistic level, and he should grow into a fair sort next year. (op 9-1)
Blanc De Chine(IRE) has enough speed to win a maiden at this trip but yet again she found one to beat her. There is nothing wrong with her attitude, and her luck should change. (tchd 6-5 and 6-4)
Art Show, who had shown promise at 6f, handled the drop in trip. Though beaten a fair way, she should find a suitable opportunity, and her ability to act on Polytrack will stand her in good stead if she is kept going during the winter. (op 11-2)
Get The Trip, rated 53, would struggle to win most maidens, and she ought to have a better chance in low-grade handicaps. (op 66-1)
Samba Night(IRE) has done reasonably well in maidens, and ought to be capable of winning one, but that is looking increasingly unlikely on turf this season. Handicaps are another option, but he is rated 68 so he would start on a testing mark. (op 6-1)
Dream Whisperer has had plenty of chances in maidens but handicaps wouldn't be easy off her current mark of 69. (op 4-1)

6920 WINDSOR VEHICLE LEASING CLAIMING STKS 6f
3:00 (3:00) (Class 6) 3-Y-O+ **£1,617** (£481; £240; £120) **Stalls** Low

Form RPR

6026 **1** **Scarlet Rocks (IRE)**[18] 6491 3-8-2 71 (p) AndreaAtzeni 12 76
(David Evans) *pressed ldrs: shkn up to ld wl over 1f out: r.o wl and in n.d fnl f* **11/1**

3240 **2** *2 ¾* **Aye Aye Digby (IRE)**[26] 6246 6-9-3 79 GeorgeBaker 10 81
(Patrick Chamings) *led 1f: styd w ldrs: rdn and one pce over 1f out* **10/1**

1500 **3** *¾* **Retainer (IRE)**[37] 5935 3-8-9 97 KieranO'Neill(3) 9 75
(Richard Hannon) *led after 1f: rdn and hdd wl over 1f out: one pce and no ch w wnr fnl f* **10/3**[1]

3500 **4** *nk* **Remotelinx (IRE)**[35] 6003 3-9-6 83 SebSanders 14 82
(J W Hills) *towards rr on outer: prog 2f out: chsd ldrs over 1f out but nt on terms: kpt on* **28/1**

6530 **5** *1* **Sunrise Safari (IRE)**[31] 6113 8-8-9 77 (v) FrederikTylicki 11 67
(Richard Fahey) *taken down early: settled wl in rr on outer: sme prog over 1f out: styd on fnl f: nrst fin* **5/1**[3]

2040 **6** *½* **Memphis Man**[7] 6752 8-8-3 59 ow1 MatthewCosham(5) 13 64
(David Evans) *taken down early: chsd ldrs: rdn and nt qckn 2f out: one pce after* **33/1**

051 **7** *1 ½* **Stevie Gee (IRE)**[31] 6133 7-8-11 73 KierenFallon 5 62
(Ian Williams) *t.k.h: hld up bhd ldrs: rdn and nt qckn 2f out: no prog after* **8/1**

6120 **8** *1 ¼* **Maze (IRE)**[7] 6762 6-8-10 84 HarryBentley(3) 1 60
(Tony Carroll) *towards rr: pushed along and no prog 1/2-way: nvr on terms after* **7/2**[2]

1146 **9** *1* **Barons Spy (IRE)**[23] 6327 10-8-11 83 JamesDoyle 6 55
(Richard Price) *chsd ldrs: lost pl and pushed along 1/2-way: no prog 2f out* **7/1**

3040 **10** *½* **Florio Vincitore (IRE)**[5] 6793 4-8-11 59 (b) EddieCreighton 4 53
(Edward Creighton) *s.s: a in rr and struggling to make any prog* **50/1**

43-2 **11** *3* **Majestical (IRE)**[49] 9-8-1 37 JemmaMarshall(5) 2 39
(Peter Hedger) *pressed ldrs to 1/2-way: wknd qckly 2f out* **100/1**

00 **12** *1 ¼* **Henry's Hero**[10] 6668 5-9-0 0 [1] JoshCrane(7) 8 50
(Chris Dwyer) *a in rr: shkn up and no prog 2f out: no ch after* **100/1**

1446 **13** *2* **Dark Lane**[20] 6433 5-8-4 72 KierenFox(3) 3 29
(Tony Carroll) *sn wl in rr and nt gng wl: bhd fnl 2f* **40/1**

1m 10.9s (-2.10) **Going Correction** -0.30s/f (Firm)
WFA 3 from 4yo+ 1lb **13** Ran SP% **115.8**
Speed ratings (Par 101): **102,98,97,96,95 94,92,91,89,89 85,83,80**
toteswingers:1&2:£13.60, 1&3:£8.90, 2&3:£7.00 CSF £107.78 TOTE £14.50: £3.70, £3.30, £1.90; EX 165.40 Trifecta £52.30 Pool £212.39 - 3.00 winning units..Scarlet Rocks was claimed by Mustafa Khan for £7,000.
Owner Nick Shutts **Bred** Mountarmstrong Stud **Trained** Pandy, Monmouths

FOCUS
A good claimer on paoer, but there were plenty of doubts over these. The winner and sixth are the most likely guides. Few got into this, with the race dominated by runners that had been prominent throughout.

6921 TOTEQUADPOT NURSERY 6f
3:30 (3:31) (Class 5) (0-75,75) 2-Y-O **£2,264** (£673; £336; £168) **Stalls** Low

Form RPR

501 **1** **Beach Candy (IRE)**[21] 6406 2-9-2 **73** SeanLevey(3) 7 77
(Richard Hannon) *cl up bhd ldrs: hrd rdn over 1f out: styd on to ld last 75yds: jst hld on* **8/1**

5415 **2** *shd* **Dressed In Lace**[30] 6166 2-8-10 **64** LiamKeniry 10 68
(Andrew Balding) *mde most: styd on whn rdn over 1f out: hdd last 75yds: kpt on wl nr fin* **11/1**

0433 **3** *¾* **Poker Hospital**[32] 6099 2-9-6 **74** (p) KierenFallon 15 76
(George Baker) *pressed ldr after 1f: drvn over 1f out: jst hld and lost 2nd ins fnl f: n.m.r nr fin* **15/2**[3]

4355 **4** *1* **Thewinningmachine**[30] 6154 2-8-10 **64** ow2 RobertWinston 12 63
(Richard Fahey) *chsd ldrs: rdn 2f out: styd on same pce fr over 1f out: nvr able to chal* **7/1**[2]

1203 **5** *1 ½* **Whisky Bravo**[14] 6573 2-9-0 **68** SteveDrowne 6 62+
(David Brown) *dwlt: mostly in last: shkn up and prog wl over 1f out: styd on fnl f: nrst fin* **14/1**

1000 **6** *2* **My Solitaire (IRE)**[29] 6196 2-8-11 **68** (v[1]) JohnFahy(3) 16 56
(Clive Cox) *prom on outer: drvn over 1f out: wknd ins fnl f* **16/1**

1346 **7** *hd* **Safari Storm (USA)**[48] 5584 2-9-7 **75** (t) ShaneKelly 8 63
(Brian Meehan) *hld up in last pair early: prog over 2f out: chsd ldrs over 1f out: shkn up and wknd* **14/1**

0030 **8** *1 ½* **Il Pazzo**[44] 5697 2-9-1 **69** AndreaAtzeni 11 52
(Mike Murphy) *t.k.h: hld up towards rr: rdn and nt qckn 2f out: limited prog over 1f out: fdd fnl f* **14/1**

5332 **9** *hd* **Ashbina**[25] 6281 2-8-13 **70** AdamBeschizza(3) 5 53
(William Haggas) *sn rousted along in midfield: nvr able to make any prog* **9/1**

2130 **10** *2 ½* **Compton Target (IRE)**[21] 6399 2-9-4 **72** JamesDoyle 4 47
(Hans Adielsson) *w ldrs to 1/2-way: sn lost pl and struggling* **40/1**

4164 **11** *4 ½* **Dishy Guru**[18] 6484 2-9-3 **71** DaneO'Neill 3 33
(Michael Blanshard) *hld up towards rr: shkn up and no prog 2f out: wknd over 1f out* **8/1**

4522 **12** *1 ½* **Continuity (IRE)**[62] 5144 2-8-13 **67** JimCrowley 13 24
(Ralph Beckett) *wl in rr early: sme prog on outer 1/2-way: nt on terms over 1f out: wknd qckly* **14/1**

1060 **13** *3* **Pen Bal Crag (IRE)**[31] 6111 2-8-13 **67** FrederikTylicki 1 15
(Richard Fahey) *w ldrs over 1f: lost pl qckly and sn struggling in rr* **14/1**

3634 **14** *19* **Eightfold**[45] 5690 2-9-0 **68** JimmyFortune 2 —+
(Richard Hannon) *w ldrs over 2f: sn lost pl: wknd over 2f out: eased: t.o* **13/2**[1]

1m 11.59s (-1.41) **Going Correction** -0.30s/f (Firm) **14** Ran SP% **119.8**
Speed ratings (Par 95): **97,96,95,94,92 89,89,87,87,84 78,76,72,46**
toteswingers:1&2:£13.60, 1&3:£8.90, 2&3:£7.00 CSF £92.76 CT £713.04 TOTE £7.90: £3.50, £5.00, £2.70; EX 134.80 Trifecta £279.70 Part won. Pool £378.04 - 0.30 winning units..
Owner S Mahal, R Morecombe & D Anderson **Bred** Lynn Lodge Stud **Trained** East Everleigh, Wilts
■ Stewards' Enquiry : Robert Winston seven-day ban: weighed in 2lb heavy (Oct 31,Nov 1-5,9)

FOCUS
A competitive nursery, won by one of the least-exposed runners. Routine form.

NOTEBOOK
Beach Candy(IRE) is progressing well with racing, following her soft-ground maiden win with a battling victory on her first venture into nursery company. There was little to spare but she should improve again. (op 13-2 tchd 6-1)
Dressed In Lace, racing against the stands' rail, only failed by a whisker. She has done well since switching to nurseries, so her mark looks about right. (op 9-1)
Poker Hospital, with cheekpieces fitted for this nursery debut, ran with credit, just as she had done in all her maidens. She has arrived in handicaps on a testing mark but looks capable of winning one. (op 9-1)
Thewinningmachine looks more at home over 6f than 7f at present, though that trip should be within reach in due course. Dropped 7lb since her nursery debut, she is not far above a winning mark now. (op 10-1)
Whisky Bravo did well to finish so close considering he lost several lengths at the start. He has now missed the break in his last two races, but if it isn't developing into a problem he will be worth keeping an eye on. (tchd 16-1)
My Solitaire(IRE) put in a better show in a first-time visor, but she was always going to be up against it from the widest stall. (op 14-1)
Safari Storm(USA) did not run badly, but he has gone slightly off the boil in his last two races. (op 11-1)

Eightfold ran poorly from a favourable draw, with Jimmy Fortune reporting that he had run flat. However, he was found to be coughing after the race. Official explanation: jockey said colt ran flat; vet said colt was found to be coughing (op 6-1 tchd 7-1)

6922 TOTEEXACTA H'CAP — 1m 2f 7y

4:00 (4:02) (Class 4) (0-85,85) 3-Y-0+ **£4,075** (£1,212; £606; £303) **Stalls** Centre

Form — RPR

1400 **1** **Discoteca**[102] 3774 3-9-5 **85** .... JimmyFortune 9 — 93+
(Andrew Balding) *prom: pushed along 3f out: rdn to take narrow ld over 1f out: jnd fnl f: jst prevailed* **9/2**[1]

6402 **2** *shd* **Vimiero (USA)**[17] 6507 4-9-2 **77** .... JimCrowley 6 — 85
(Walter Swinburn) *hld up towards rr: prog on outer 3f out: hrd rdn to chal 1f out: w wnr nr fin: jst pipped* **15/2**[3]

3126 **3** *nk* **Broughtons Paradis (IRE)**[43] 5761 5-8-11 **72** .... StevieDonohoe 8 — 79
(Willie Musson) *hld up in last trio: plenty to do whn prog over 2f out: shkn up over 1f out: clsd to chal last 75yds: jst hld* **10/1**

1200 **4** *1* **Early Applause**[19] 6457 3-8-13 **79** .... RobertWinston 1 — 84
(Charles Hills) *t.k.h: cl up bhd ldrs: rdn to chal 2f out: upsides over 1f out: one pce fnl f* **11/1**

0100 **5** *1/2* **Emerald Wilderness (IRE)**[24] 6302 7-9-1 **76** .... (p) PatCosgrave 4 — 80
(Robert Cowell) *wl plcd bhd ldrs: rdn over 2f out: tried to cl over 1f out: one pce fnl f* **18/1**

4632 **6** *3/4* **Wiggy Smith**[12] 6631 12-9-0 **75** .... DaneO'Neill 2 — 78
(Henry Candy) *hld up in last trio: sme prog 2f out: shkn up over 1f out: kpt on but nvr rchd ldrs* **11/1**

3000 **7** *1/2* **Tinshu (IRE)**[24] 6302 5-9-5 **83** .... JohnFahy(3) 5 — 85
(Derek Haydn Jones) *hld up in midfield: rdn and nt qckn over 2f out: tried to cl on ldrs over 1f out: one pce fnl f* **7/1**[2]

4215 **8** *1* **Brouhaha**[26] 6263 7-9-7 **82** .... RichardKingscote 12 — 82
(Tom Dascombe) *pushed up to ld: mde most tl hdd over 1f out: wknd fnl f* **16/1**

4310 **9** *1/2* **Yes Chef**[26] 6249 4-9-2 **77** .... JamesMillman 11 — 76
(Rod Millman) *prom: wnt 2nd 1/2-way: stl chalng over 1f out: wknd* **8/1**

10-0 **10** *4* **Effervesce (IRE)**[14] 6583 4-8-10 **71** oh1 .... SteveDrowne 7 — 62
(David Pipe) *s.s: hld up in last: pushed along and no prog 3f out: nvr on terms* **25/1**

103 **11** *nk* **Silver Grey (IRE)**[22] 6375 4-9-8 **83** .... (p) KierenFallon 3 — 73
(Roger Ingram) *walked to post and mounted at s: settled towards rr: rdn and no prog over 2f out: wknd over 1f out* **8/1**

4120 **12** *16* **Dean Swift**[19] 6439 3-8-13 **79** .... ShaneKelly 10 — 37
(Brian Meehan) *mostly chsd ldr to 1/2-way: wknd over 3f out: eased and t.o* **7/1**[2]

2m 6.02s (-2.68) **Going Correction** -0.30s/f (Firm)
WFA 3 from 4yo+ 5lb **12** Ran SP% **117.9**
Speed ratings (Par 105): **98,97,97,96,96 95,95,94,94,91 90,78**
toteswingers:1&2:£7.10, 1&3:£10.20, 2&3:£14.50 CSF £37.00 CT £324.08 TOTE £5.20: £2.20, £2.60, £3.20; EX 43.50 Trifecta £466.50 Part won. Pool £630.46 - 0.87 winning units..
Owner David Brownlow **Bred** Usk Valley Stud **Trained** Kingsclere, Hants

FOCUS
There was just a medium pace, but it was a fair one, with the winner racing handily and the next two coming from the rear. the winner is rated back to his early level, with the runner-up to form.
Silver Grey(IRE) Official explanation: jockey said filly hung left

6923 TOTEPOOL H'CAP — 1m 2f 7y

4:30 (4:40) (Class 6) (0-65,65) 3-Y-O **£1,617** (£481; £240; £120) **Stalls** Centre

Form — RPR

1U41 **1** **Librettela**[26] 6253 3-8-13 **60** .... HarryBentley(3) 7 — 71
(Alan Jarvis) *chsd ldr: clsd to dispute ld jst over 2f out: duelled w runner-up after: jst prevailed nr fin* **17/2**

0004 **2** *hd* **Beggers Belief**[14] 6589 3-8-7 **51** oh1 .... (b) EddieCreighton 9 — 62
(Eric Wheeler) *trckd ldrs: rdn 3f out: clsd to chal over 2f out: disp w wnr after: jst pipped* **40/1**

6014 **3** *3 3/4* **Woop Woop (IRE)**[38] 5897 3-8-11 **60** .... RyanPowell(5) 4 — 63
(Ian Williams) *hld up in midfield: effrt over 3f out: outpcd 2f out: styd on to take 3rd 1f out* **20/1**

0R11 **4** *1 1/4* **Arctic Maiden**[55] 5352 3-9-7 **65** .... [illegible] — [illegible]
(Willie Musson) *s.i.s: wl in rr: lost tch 5f out: sme prog over 3f out: hanging 2f out: kpt on: nrst fin* **5/1**[2]

0056 **5** *1* **Baby Driver**[21] 6417 3-8-13 **57** ....[1] RichardKingscote 14 — 56
(Tom Dascombe) *fast away: led at decent pce: hanging 3f out: hdd jst over 2f out: nt run on* **12/1**

0-00 **6** *7* **Star Rebel**[127] 2956 3-9-7 **65** .... AdrianMcCarthy 10 — 50
(George Margarson) *hld up in last: lost tch 5f out: nvr on terms after: kpt on fr over 2f out: reminder 1f out: nvr nrr* **22/1**

6505 **7** *nse* **Piave (IRE)**[24] 6311 3-9-6 **64** .... JimmyFortune 8 — 48
(Peter Chapple-Hyam) *trckd ldrs: rdn 3f out: sn wknd* **6/1**[3]

2564 **8** *2 1/2* **Swaninstockwell (IRE)**[84] 4389 3-9-2 **60** .... IanMongan 1 — 39
(Pat Phelan) *prom: rdn 3f out: sn wknd* **7/2**[1]

140 **9** *6* **Harry Lime**[5] 6799 3-9-1 **59** .... AndreaAtzeni 3 — 26
(Chris Dwyer) *settled in rr: last of those w ch over 4f out: wknd over 3f out* **9/1**

4131 **10** *10* **Appyjack**[11] 6659 3-9-4 **62** .... LiamJones 2 — —
(Tony Carroll) *rousted along early: a in rr: lost tch 5f out: eased and t.o* **12/1**

1534 **11** *3* **Out Of The Storm**[18] 6472 3-9-3 **61** .... KierenFallon 13 — —
(Simon Dow) *a in rr: lost tch 5f out: eased and t.o* **6/1**[3]

066- **12** *26* **Van Doesburg (IRE)**[439] 4691 3-8-11 **55** .... JimCrowley 11 — —
(Jonathan Portman) *fractious preliminaries: a in rr: lost tch 5f out: wl t.o* **28/1**

2m 7.26s (-1.44) **Going Correction** -0.30s/f (Firm) **12** Ran SP% **118.4**
Speed ratings (Par 99): **93,92,89,88,88 82,82,80,75,67 65,44**
toteswingers:1&2:£42.40, 1&3:£33.70, 2&3:£76.90 CSF £318.38 CT £6421.43 TOTE £10.30: £3.50, £13.00, £4.40; EX 346.10 TRIFECTA Not won..
Owner Jarvis Associates **Bred** L Dettori **Trained** Twyford, Bucks

FOCUS
They went a decent gallop, but none of the placed horses came from far back. Reasonable form for the grade, the winner progressing again.

6924 BEN WOOLLACOTT H'CAP — 1m 67y

5:00 (5:07) (Class 5) (0-70,70) 3-Y-0+ **£2,264** (£673; £336; £168) **Stalls** Low

Form — RPR

661 **1** **Doncosaque (IRE)**[5] 6793 5-8-13 **65** 6ex .... (t) HarryBentley(3) 9 — 77
(P J O'Gorman) *trckd ldng pair after 2f: rdn to ld wl over 1f out: sn pressed: styd on wl to assert ins fnl f* **16/1**

4551 **2** *1 1/2* **Push Me (IRE)**[19] 6468 4-9-2 **68** .... KierenFox(3) 11 — 77+
(Jamie Poulton) *hld up wl in rr: gd prog on wd outside fr 3f out: rdn to chal over 1f out: kpt on but readily hld ins fnl f* **17/2**[3]

650 **3** *1 3/4* **Rock Anthem (IRE)**[8] 6727 7-9-6 **69** .... KierenFallon 10 — 74
(Mike Murphy) *trckd ldrs: rdn 2f out: tried to chal over 1f out: one pce fnl f* **11/1**

0326 **4** *2 1/2* **Billion Dollar Kid**[15] 6022 6-9-7 **70** .... (t) JamesDoyle 5 — 69
(Jo Davis) *trckd ldrs: outpcd 2f out: hrd rdn and one pce over 1f out* **25/1**

0323 **5** *1/2* **Encore Un Fois**[20] 6435 3-9-4 **70** .... J-PGuillambert 14 — 68
(Luca Cumani) *trckd ldrs: rdn over 2f out: outpcd wl over 1f out: no imp after* **11/2**[1]

5211 **6** *nk* **Larkrise Star**[18] 6472 4-9-4 **67** .... ShaneKelly 6 — 64
(Dean Ivory) *settled towards rr: rdn over 2f out: kpt on fr over 1f out: nt pce to threaten* **17/2**[3]

1546 **7** *1 3/4* **Frozen Over**[22] 6378 3-9-3 **69** .... FergusSweeney 2 — 62
(Stuart Kittow) *s.i.s: hld up in last pair: stl there and shkn up 2f out: kpt on fnl f: no ch* **9/1**

443 **8** *1* **Rosedale**[14] 6586 4-9-3 **66** .... JimmyFortune 1 — 57
(James Toller) *hld up in rr: rdn over 2f out: no prog and btn over 1f out* **11/2**[1]

2463 **9** *1 1/2* **Swift Blade (IRE)**[7] 6748 3-9-2 **68** .... (b[1]) SebSanders 8 — 55
(Lady Herries) *hld up in mdfield: rdn and effrt 3f out: no prog 2f out: wknd* **10/1**

4402 **10** *2 1/2* **Tap Dance Way (IRE)**[14] 6587 4-9-5 **68** .... LiamKeniry 12 — 49
(Patrick Chamings) *pressed ldr: led over 4f out: hdd wl over 1f out: wandered and wknd qckly* **10/1**

5-26 **11** *2* **Ebony Song (USA)**[32] 6089 3-9-2 **68** .... DaneO'Neill 7 — 45
(Jo Crowley) *nvr bttr than midfield: wknd 2f out* **16/1**

2030 **12** *1/2* **Gallant Eagle (IRE)**[20] 6435 4-9-7 **70** .... PatCosgrave 3 — 46
(Ed de Giles) *led to over 4f out: w ldr to 2f out: wknd rapidly* **8/1**[2]

4006 **13** *3/4* **Hip Hip Hooray**[16] 6544 5-9-0 **63** .... IanMongan 13 — 45
(Luke Dace) *s.s: a in last pair: shkn up and no prog 2f out* **20/1**

1m 42.05s (-2.65) **Going Correction** -0.30s/f (Firm)
WFA 3 from 4yo+ 3lb **13** Ran SP% **119.8**
Speed ratings (Par 103): **101,99,97,95,94 94,92,91,90,87 85,85,84**
toteswingers:1&2:£28.90, 1&3:£30.20, 2&3:£15.20 CSF £146.39 CT £1578.56 TOTE £26.40: £7.20, £3.20, £3.70; EX 160.50 Trifecta £354.60 Part won. Pool £479.28 - 0.50 winning units..
Owner Racing To The Max **Bred** Ammerland Verwaltung Gmbh **Trained** Newmarket, Suffolk
■ Stewards' Enquiry : Kieren Fox ten-day ban: used whip with excessive frequency (Nov 12,14-24)

FOCUS
A good gallop helped the hold-up horses but it still went to one that raced handily. The form looks solid and the winner was still on a good mark despite his penalty.
T/Plt: £812.70 to a £1 stake. Pool:£76,279.31 - 68.51 winning tickets T/Qpdt: £342.30 to a £1 stake. Pool:£4,719.13 - 10.20 winning tickets JN

5075 CLAIREFONTAINE (R-H)

Monday, October 17

OFFICIAL GOING: Turf: very soft

6925a PRIX DILIGENCE PRESSE (CLAIMER) (2YO FILLIES) (TURF) — 1m 1f

1:05 (12:00) 2-Y-0 **£6,896** (£2,758; £2,068; £1,379; £689)

RPR

1 **Lady Jourdain (IRE)**[35] 6001 2-9-4 0 .... IoritzMendizabal 17 — 66
(Mrs K Burke) *broke wl fr wd outside draw: rdn to join ldrs after 4f: clr 2nd ent st: shkn up 2f out: chal and tk ld over 1f out: r.o wl: sn clr: hung on wl fnl 50yds* **[illegible]**

2 *1* **Bouncing Lily (FR)**[31] 2-9-0 0 .... ChristopheSoumillon 7 — 60
(C Boutin, France) **53/10**[2]

3 *1/2* **Dragon Ball (FR)**[50] 2-9-0 0 .... Christophe-PatriceLemaire 16 — 59
(Mme Pia Brandt, France) **14/5**[1]

4 *hd* **Rashflower (FR)** 2-8-8 0 .... EnzoCorallo(6) 9 — 59
(M Roussel, France) **22/1**

5 *hd* **Inches Away (FR)** 2-8-4 0 .... (b[1]) TheoBachelot(5) 1 — 53
(S Wattel, France) **22/1**

6 *hd* **Victoria Lagrange (FR)**[31] 2-8-9 0 .... TonyPiccone 2 — 53
(C Lerner, France) **9/1**

7 *nk* **Charlize (FR)** 2-8-4 0 .... (b[1]) MathieuTavaresDaSilva(5) 13 — 52
(F Doumen, France) **78/1**

8 *2* **Yalumba (FR)** 2-8-9 0 .... FabienLefebvre 5 — 48
(Mme Pia Brandt, France) **67/1**

9 *5* **Acina**[16] 2-9-0 0 .... AlexisBadel 14 — 43
(F-X De Chevigny, France) **12/1**

10 *8* **My Tendresse (FR)** 2-8-4 0 .... FlavienMasse(5) 6 — 22
(P Demercastel, France) **50/1**

0 **Clara De Lune (FR)**[31] 2-8-10 0 .... FrankieLeroy(4) 10 — —
(C Boutin, France) **129/1**

0 **Ahinga (FR)**[27] 2-8-9 0 .... (p) SylvainRuis 8 — —
(X Nakkachdji, France) **44/1**

0 **Majestic Chap (IRE)**[55] 2-9-0 0 .... DavidBreux 12 — —
(F Sanchez, France) **67/1**

0 **Baraamej (IRE)** 2-9-0 0 .... MaximeGuyon 11 — —
(F Rohaut, France) **53/10**[2]

0 **Miss Sabiango (FR)** 2-9-0 0 .... MorganDelalande 3 — —
(J-Y Artu, France) **102/1**

0 **Touch The Sky (FR)** 2-9-0 0 .... ThomasMessina 15 — —
(M Nigge, France) **34/1**

0 **Muskat Princesse (FR)** 2-8-9 0 .... MickaelBarzalona 4 — —
(Mario Hofer, Germany) **13/1**

1m 53.5s (113.50) **17** Ran SP% **117.2**
WIN (incl. 1 euro stake): 7.90. PLACES: 3.00, 2.30, 1.70. DF: 22.70. SF: 47.00.
Owner Mrs Elaine M Burke **Bred** Tally-Ho Stud **Trained** Middleham Moor, North Yorks

FOCUS
A compressed finish but the winner is rated to a positive view of her British form.

NOTEBOOK
Lady Jourdain(IRE) handled the soft ground and longer trip to add to her two British successes in July, picking up some decent prizemoney for the level.

6792 LINGFIELD (L-H)

Tuesday, October 18

OFFICIAL GOING: Standard

Wind: Fresh, across Weather: Fine

6926 FELBRIDGE APPRENTICE H'CAP — 1m 4f (P)

2:30 (2:30) (Class 6) (0-60,60) 3-Y-0+ — **£1,704** (£503; £251) **Stalls** Low

Form — RPR

03 **1** **Pinotage**[60] 5243 3-9-0 **58** JustinNewman(3) 11 — 67
(Richard Whitaker) *prom tl stdd bk in tch after 4f: rdn 4f out: hdwy over 2f out: led ins fnl f: flashed tail: drvn out* **7/1**[3]

0 **2** ½ **Fellisha (IRE)**[25] 6315 3-8-11 **55** RaulDaSilva(3) 6 — 63
(Andrew Heffernan, Ire) *plld hrd in rr: hdwy on ins and rdn 2f out: led ent st: hdd ins fnl f: kpt on u.p* **9/1**

4356 **3** 3 **Nutshell**[32] 6122 3-9-0 **58** MatthewLawson(3) 15 — 61
(Harry Dunlop) *led after 2f tl 5f out: w ldrs after and led again briefly over 2f out: one pce appr fnl f* **8/1**

0505 **4** 1½ **Lunar River (FR)**[19] 6486 8-8-11 **48** (t) DavidKenny(3) 4 — 49
(David Pinder) *towards rr: hdwy and in tch over 2f out: styd on same pce* **14/1**

0242 **5** nk **Reggie Perrin**[20] 6446 3-8-10 **54** DarylByrne(3) 16 — 55+
(Pat Phelan) *chsd ldrs: rdn 4f out: hung lft in st: no imp* **3/1**[1]

0650 **6** 1¼ **Sunset Boulevard (IRE)**[42] 5815 8-9-9 **57** (b) RyanPowell 12 — 56
(Paddy Butler) *hld up in rr: sme hdwy on outer over 3f out: wd and no significant prog fnl 2f* **66/1**

4204 **7** 1½ **Lakota Ghost (USA)**[25] 6295 3-9-0 **60** BrendanPowell(5) 5 — 56
(Seamus Durack) *in tch: outpcd over 2f out: sn btn* **4/1**[2]

1603 **8** ½ **Hi Note**[24] 5636 3-8-5 **53** MartinLeonard(7) 8 — 48
(Sheena West) *mid-div on outer: hdwy 7f out: led 5f out tl over 2f out: sn wknd* **11/1**

0004 **9** 1 **Suhailah**[13] 6621 5-8-9 **50** AaronChave(7) 7 — 44
(Michael Attwater) *mid-div: hdwy on outer and prom 5f out: wknd wl over 1f out* **16/1**

6335 **10** 2¾ **Miss Bounty**[82] 4454 6-9-4 **55** (v) NathanAlison(3) 3 — 44
(Jim Boyle) *broke wl: stdd bk in tch on rail: wkng whn n.m.r over 3f out* **11/1**

050 **11** 7 **In The Long Grass (IRE)**[42] 5816 3-8-3 **51** DanielCremin(7) 10 — 29
(Jim Boyle) *led for 2f: prom tl wknd over 4f out* **12/1**

2m 33.67s (0.67) **Going Correction** -0.025s/f (Stan)
WFA 3 from 5yo+ 7lb — **11** Ran **SP% 117.0**
Speed ratings (Par 101): **96,95,93,92,92 91,90,90,89,87 83**
toteswingers:1&2:£9.50, 2&3:£12.40, 1&3:£14.60 CSF £68.22 CT £518.30 TOTE £5.20: £2.10, £3.20, £3.30; EX 67.50.

Owner Nice Day Out Partnership **Bred** Hellwood Stud Farm **Trained** Scarcroft, W Yorks

FOCUS
Mainly inexperienced apprentices riding in this modest handicap. The pace was steady and the first four were all questionable stayers, so this looks pretty suspect form. The winner took another step forward.

Miss Bounty Official explanation: jockey said that the mare was denied a clear run

6927 LINGFIELD PARK OWNERS CLUB MAIDEN AUCTION STKS — 7f (P)

3:00 (3:07) (Class 6) 2-Y-0 — **£1,704** (£503; £251) **Stalls** Low

Form — RPR

25 **1** **Cristal Gem**[9] 6725 2-8-7 0 KieranO'Neill(3) 8 — 75
(Richard Hannon) *pressed ldr: led 3f out: rn green: drvn out* **2/1**[1]

04 **2** 2½ **La Romantique (IRE)**[18] 6506 2-8-4 0 KirstyMilczarek 1 — 62
(Marco Botti) *prom: rdn to chse wnr 1f out: nt qckn* **7/2**[2]

042 **3** nse **Remix (IRE)**[12] 6654 2-8-6 67 ChrisCatlin 9 — 64
(J W Hills) *a.p: kpt on u.p fnl 2f* **9/2**[3]

0 **4** 3 **Lady Arabella (IRE)**[42] 5812 2-8-7 0 ow1 JamesDoyle 4 — 57
(Alastair Lidderdale) *led 4f: pressed wnr after tl wknd 1f out* **10/1**

00 **5** 1 **Pacific Trader**[19] 6474 2-8-9 0 (b[1]) LiamKeniry 5 — 57
(William Haggas) *chsd ldrs: rdn and no hdwy fnl 2f* **16/1**

0002 **6** 1¾ **Doc Hill**[36] 6002 2-8-11 46 JimmyQuinn 7 — 54
(Michael Blanshard) *towards rr: drvn along over 3f out: nvr rchd ldrs* **50/1**

7 ¾ **Retromania (IRE)** 2-8-13 0 LukeMorris 3 — 54
(John Best) *mid-div: rdn 4f out: outpcd fnl 3f* **20/1**

3 **8** ½ **Whipcrackaway (IRE)**[19] 6483 2-8-6 0 JohnFahy(3) 6 — 49
(Peter Hedger) *a towards rr* **11/2**

9 13 **My Lady Picolla** 2-8-4 0 AdrianMcCarthy 10 — 10
(Dr Jon Scargill) *s.s: a wl bhd* **100/1**

0 **10** 4½ **Dare I Ask**[32] 6131 2-7-11 0 RaulDaSilva(7) 2 — —
(Bill Turner) *reluctant to go to s: mid-div: wknd over 3f out: sn bhd* **66/1**

1m 25.12s (0.32) **Going Correction** -0.025s/f (Stan) — **10** Ran **SP% 113.3**
Speed ratings (Par 93): **97,94,94,90,89 87,86,86,71,66**
toteswingers:1&2:£2.40, 2&3:£3.60, 1&3:£2.50 CSF £8.39 TOTE £2.90: £1.40, £1.10, £2.00; EX 10.40.

Owner R Gander **Bred** South Hatch Racing **Trained** East Everleigh, Wilts

FOCUS
Just a modest juvenile maiden, the form best viewed around the second and third. The winner improved.

NOTEBOOK
Cristal Gem won despite still looking green. She had been off for nearly four months after her debut second over 6f on turf, but showed ability on her return in a more competitive race than this at Goodwood (again 6f on the grass) and proved suited by the step up in trip on a different surface. Things are likely to be tougher next time, however. (tchd 15-8 and 9-4)

La Romantique(IRE), fourth over an extended 1m at Wolverhampton on her second start, was one-paced on this drop in trip. She's now eligible for a handicap mark, but looks limited. (op 4-1 tchd 9-2)

Remix(IRE) had progressed with each run, including over 6f at Wolverhampton the last twice, but she didn't prove her stamina this time. It was reported she'll be off to the sales in the near future. (tchd 4-1 and 5-1)

Lady Arabella(IRE) was backed in the morning but drifted out again on course. She showed speed, improving a good deal on the form of her 6f debut here, and has ability. (tchd 9-1 and 12-1)

Pacific Trader showed a bit more in first-time blinkers, but still only ran to a moderate level. Handicaps are now an option. (op 20-1)

Whipcrackaway(IRE) was nowhere near the level he showed in an uncompetitive turf maiden first time up. Official explanation: jockey said that the gelding would not face the kickback (tchd 9-2)

6928 BRITISH STALLION STUDS SUPPORTING BRITISH RACING E B F MEDIAN AUCTION MAIDEN STKS — 1m (P)

3:30 (3:31) (Class 5) 2-Y-0 — **£3,340** (£986; £493) **Stalls** High

Form — RPR

U432 **1** **Equity Card (FR)**[29] 6214 2-8-12 75 AhmedAjtebi 3 — 72
(Mahmood Al Zarooni) *trckd ldrs gng wl: shkn up over 1f out: qcknd to ld fnl 75yds* **2/1**[1]

2 ½ **Grandiloquent** 2-9-3 RyanMoore 12 — 75+
(Sir Michael Stoute) *prom: rdn to chal over 1f out: nt qckn fnl 75yds* **11/4**[2]

03 **3** ½ **It's A Privilege**[19] 6474 2-9-3 JimCrowley 4 — 74
(Ralph Beckett) *sn led: rdn and hdd fnl 75yds: nt gng pce of wnr* **11/2**[3]

0 **4** 3¾ **Good Luck Charm**[40] 5855 2-9-3 JamesDoyle 10 — 65
(Gary Moore) *in tch: effrt and disp 3rd 2f out: one pce* **40/1**

0 **5** 2¾ **Grain Of Sand**[19] 6481 2-9-3 LiamKeniry 7 — 59
(Andrew Balding) *towards rr: sme hdwy over 2f out: no imp* **20/1**

6 ¾ **Muhamee (IRE)** 2-9-0 LouisBeuzelin(3) 8 — 57+
(Saeed Bin Suroor) *mid-div on rail: lost pl 5f out: n.d fnl 3f: styng on at fin* **6/1**

66 **7** 1½ **Downton Abbey (IRE)**[15] 6588 2-8-9 SeanLevey(3) 1 — 49
(Richard Hannon) *sn prom: outpcd and btn 2f out* **14/1**

0 **8** hd **Fine Resolve**[20] 6462 2-9-3 (t) DavidProbert 9 — 53
(Andrew Balding) *bhd: pushed along 5f out: nvr a factor* **25/1**

9 nk **Lutfen Yavas (IRE)**[44] 5764 2-9-3 LukeMorris 2 — 53
(Bernard Anthony Heffernan, Ire) *t.k.h: chsd ldrs tl wknd 2f out* **33/1**

0 **10** 1¾ **Melodrama (IRE)**[73] 4804 2-8-12 RichardMullen 5 — 44
(David Lanigan) *rrd s: a bhd* **40/1**

11 2 **Swift Winged** 2-8-12 DarryllHolland 11 — 39
(Hughie Morrison) *s.s: mid-div after 3f: rdn 4f out: wknd 3f out* **25/1**

1m 38.78s (0.58) **Going Correction** -0.025s/f (Stan) — **11** Ran **SP% 116.6**
Speed ratings (Par 95): **96,95,95,91,88 87,86,86,85,84 82**
toteswingers:1&2:£2.60, 2&3:£4.40, 1&3:£3.00 CSF £6.65 TOTE £3.10: £1.20, £1.60, £1.60; EX 8.60.

Owner Godolphin **Bred** Darley Stud Management Co Ltd **Trained** Newmarket, Suffolk

■ Stewards' Enquiry : Louis Beuzelin two-day ban: careless riding (1-2 Nov)

FOCUS
An ordinary juvenile maiden run in a modest time. The winner was probably just below her mark.

NOTEBOOK
Equity Card(FR) improved up on the form she showed when placed over 7f on the Kempton Polytrack the last twice, helped by the step up in trip to gain her first win on her fifth start. She's out of a close relation to Lammtarra and this success will have boosted her paddock value, but she needs a lot more progress to make it at pattern level. (op 7-4 tchd 9-4)

Grandiloquent was solid enough in the market despite his stable not having a good season with their juveniles (started the day 4-45 with 2yo newcomers this year). He managed to get a handy position from the widest stall, but displayed an unorthodox action in the straight and lacked sufficient pace. A half-brother to three middle-distance winners, out of a 1m-1m4f (at up to Group 2 level) winner, he can do better over further next year, but this was not a debut to get carried away with. (op 4-1 tchd 9-2 in a place)

It's A Privilege lacked the pace of the front two and is still learning. He should find his level in handicaps, with further likely to suit in due course. (tchd 6-1)

Good Luck Charm showed more than on his debut at Epsom. He's probably a handicap prospect. (op 66-1)

Grain Of Sand improved on a moderate introduction and needs one more run for a mark. (op 25-1)

Muhamee(IRE), $70,000 half-brother to a 1m4f Polytrack winner, out of a 6f Listed winner, was hopelessly placed when the race got serious and looked green. He can do better. Official explanation: jockey said that the colt was never travelling (op 11-2 tchd 9-2)

6929 OXTED (S) STKS — 6f (P)

4:00 (4:01) (Class 6) 3-Y-0 — **£1,704** (£503; £251) **Stalls** Low

Form — RPR

2000 **1** **Ice Trooper**[20] 6456 3-9-0 72 (p) DarryllHolland 6 — 69
(Linda Stubbs) *mde all: rdn clr over 1f out: r.o wl: readily* **6/1**

0000 **2** 2 **Dusty Bluebells (IRE)**[46] 5674 3-8-9 52 (b) LiamKeniry 5 — 58
(J S Moore) *prom: wnt cl 2nd over 4f out: kpt on u.p but nt pce of wnr fr over 1f out: hld fnl f* **14/1**

3000 **3** ½ **Major Conquest (IRE)**[8] 6761 3-9-0 79 ChrisCatlin 1 — 61
(J W Hills) *mid-div: drvn to chse ldng pair over 1f out: one pce* **11/4**[1]

0600 **4** 2½ **Charles Fosterkane**[8] 6752 3-9-0 67 LukeMorris 11 — 53
(John Best) *stdd s: bhd: rdn and hdwy over 1f out: styd on* **16/1**

5050 **5** 1½ **Squires Gate (IRE)**[55] 5370 3-9-0 69 MichaelHills 7 — 48
(Charles Hills) *pushed along in midfield: hdwy into 3rd 2f out: no ex over 1f out* **8/1**

0224 **6** 1 **Arrivaderci**[13] 6634 3-8-6 65 (v[1]) AmyRyan(3) 12 — 40
(Richard Whitaker) *bhd: drvn along 3f out: nvr rchd ldrs* **4/1**[2]

5020 **7** 1½ **Bambika**[36] 5996 3-8-9 55 FergusSweeney 10 — 35
(Jo Crowley) *in tch abt 5th: outpcd fnl 2f* **20/1**

060 **8** hd **Russian Storm**[8] 6754 3-8-9 [1] FrankieMcDonald 2 — 35
(Pat Phelan) *stdd s: restrained in rr: hung lft and hld together whn n.d in st* **50/1**

U5 **9** ½ **Arowana (IRE)**[27] 6251 3-8-9 52 JamieGoldstein 3 — 33
(Zoe Davison) *chsd wnr over 1f: pushed along over 3f out: wknd over 2f out* **100/1**

042 **10** 1¾ **Silver Turn**[78] 4618 3-8-7 70 RaulDaSilva(7) 8 — 32
(Jeremy Gask) *racd wd: a towards rr* **9/2**[3]

5650 **11** 5 **Prophet In A Dream**[5] 6813 3-8-11 60 RobertLButler(3) 4 — 16
(Paddy Butler) *chsd ldrs tl wknd 2f out* **25/1**

1m 11.57s (-0.33) **Going Correction** -0.025s/f (Stan) — **11** Ran **SP% 114.4**
Speed ratings (Par 99): **101,98,97,94,92 91,89,88,88,85 79**
toteswingers:1&2:£12.70, 2&3:£9.20, 1&3:£4.70 CSF £80.10 TOTE £7.70: £2.10, £4.00, £1.50; EX 81.30.The winner was bought in for 5,200gns.

Owner J P Hames **Bred** Low Ground Stud **Trained** Norton, N Yorks

FOCUS
Plenty of grade droppers, but the form is limited by a few moderate types and this was an ordinary seller. The result might need treating with a bit of caution as Ice Trooper was allowed an uncontested lead. He is better than this grade on summer form.

Russian Storm Official explanation: jockey said that the filly hung left

6930 MITSUI SUMITOMO INSURANCE H'CAP (DIV I) — 6f (P)

4:30 (4:30) (Class 5) (0-70,70) 3-Y-0+ — **£2,045** (£603; £302) **Stalls** Low

Form — RPR

0062 **1** **Shostakovich (IRE)**[6] 6793 3-9-6 **70** (p) JamesDoyle 7 — 78
(Sylvester Kirk) *chsd ldrs: rdn 2f out: led 1f out: hld on wl u.p* **7/2**[2]

5002 **2** ½ **Roman Strait**[26] 6282 3-9-3 **67** LiamKeniry 10 73+
(Michael Blanshard) *bhd: rapid hdwy in centre to press wnr ins fnl f: jst hld* **10/3**[1]
0656 **3** 3 **Volito**[13] 6634 5-9-2 **65** LukeMorris 2 62
(Anabel K Murphy) *towards rr: hdwy into 4th over 1f out: kpt on u.p ins fnl f* **7/1**
046 **4** hd **Fantasy Fighter (IRE)**[26] 6282 6-8-10 **59** (p) JimmyQuinn 8 55
(John E Long) *bhd: rdn and styd on fnl 2f: nrst fin* **12/1**
3630 **5** hd **Towy Boy (IRE)**[12] 6655 6-8-13 **62** (bt) JimCrowley 4 58
(Ian Wood) *towards rr: rdn and hdwy 2f out: no imp fnl f* **10/1**
0000 **6** 2 **Punching**[11] 6665 7-9-0 **70** JustinNewman(7) 11 59
(Conor Dore) *chsd ldr: led over 2f out tl wknd 1f out* **33/1**
4253 **7** nk **Desert Falls**[17] 6542 5-8-6 **58** (v) AmyRyan(3) 5 46
(Richard Whitaker) *led tl over 2f out: wknd jst over 1f out* **13/2**
-000 **8** 1½ **Mirabile Visu**[21] 6434 3-8-6 **56** oh1 (b) FrankieMcDonald 3 39
(Heather Main) *prom tl wknd 2f out* **25/1**
1060 **9** 2¼ **Dead Cool**[50] 5561 3-9-4 **68** (t) DarryllHolland 1 44+
(Hughie Morrison) *in tch: lost pl 3f out: sme hdwy on rail 2f out: eased over 1f out: sddle slipped* **4/1**[3]

1m 11.25s (-0.65) **Going Correction** -0.025s/f (Stan)
WFA 3 from 5yo+ 1lb **9** Ran SP% **114.7**
Speed ratings (Par 103): **103,102,98,98,97 95,94,92,89**
toteswingers:1&2:£3.40, 2&3:£5.60, 1&3:£5.70 CSF £15.49 CT £76.60 TOTE £4.20: £2.00, £1.20, £2.10; EX 18.10.
Owner F J Stephens **Bred** Marchwood Aggregates **Trained** Upper Lambourn, Berks

FOCUS
A modest sprint handicap, but the time was the quickest of three races at the trip. The winner's best form on this surface.
Mirabile Visu Official explanation: jockey said that the filly hung right on the home turn
Dead Cool Official explanation: jockey said that the filly was slowly away and that his saddle slipped

6931 MITSUI SUMITOMO INSURANCE H'CAP (DIV II) 6f (P)
5:00 (5:00) (Class 5) (0-70,70) 3-Y-0+ **£2,045** (£603; £302) **Stalls** Low

Form RPR
0002 **1** **Seneschal**[8] 6752 10-8-0 **56** oh1 RachealKneller(7) 7 64
(Adrian Chamberlain) *w ldr gng wl: led wl over 1f out: hld on gamely ins fnl f* **8/1**
2600 **2** ½ **Black Baccara**[12] 6655 4-8-11 **60** (be) LukeMorris 6 66
(Phil McEntee) *chsd ldrs: rdn to press wnr ins fnl f: r.o: jst hld* **33/1**
5443 **3** nk **Catalinas Diamond (IRE)**[27] 6257 3-8-9 **59** (t) RobertHavlin 10 64
(Pat Murphy) *a.p: rdn and kpt on fr over 1f out* **10/1**
4512 **4** ½ **Libys Dream (IRE)**[20] 6442 3-9-2 **66** JimmyQuinn 4 69+
(Michael Mullineaux) *s.i.s: towards rr: rdn and r.o wl fr over 1f out: nrst fin* **5/2**[1]
4500 **5** 1½ **Brandywell Boy (IRE)**[6] 6794 8-8-13 **62** ChrisCatlin 9 61
(Dominic Ffrench Davis) *t.k.h: chsd ldrs: styd on same pce fnl 2f* **20/1**
0030 **6** hd **Dvinsky (USA)**[8] 6752 10-9-3 **66** (b) DarryllHolland 2 64
(Michael Squance) *led tl wl over 1f out: no ex ins fnl f* **20/1**
1112 **7** ¾ **Efistorm**[53] 5452 10-9-4 **67** KirstyMilczarek 3 63
(Conor Dore) *towards rr: rdn and hdwy on rail 1f out: nvr able to chal* **6/1**[3]
6140 **8** ¾ **Wotatomboy**[18] 6501 5-8-4 **56** oh8 (b) AmyRyan(3) 5 49
(Richard Whitaker) *dwlt: sn in midfield: effrt over 2f out: sn rdn and btn* **40/1**
1153 **9** nk **Stonecrabstomorrow (IRE)**[5] 6814 8-8-11 **65** MarkCoumbe(5) 8 57+
(Michael Attwater) *mid-div: outpcd 3f out: n.d after* **6/1**[3]
5006 **10** 1¼ **Loyal Royal (IRE)**[129] 2920 8-9-5 **68** (bt) RichardKingscote 1 56
(Milton Bradley) *in tch on rail: effrt 2f out: wknd over 1f out* **16/1**
646 **11** 1¾ **Green Earth (IRE)**[15] 6586 4-9-7 **70** IanMongan 11 53
(Pat Phelan) *sn bhd* **9/2**[2]

1m 11.66s (-0.24) **Going Correction** -0.025s/f (Stan)
WFA 3 from 4yo+ 1lb **11** Ran SP% **116.3**
Speed ratings (Par 103): **100,99,98,98,96 96,95,94,93,91 89**
toteswingers:1&2:£54.30, 2&3:£40.20, 1&3:£13.80 CSF £249.13 CT £2643.68 TOTE £12.00: £4.10, £7.30, £2.10; EX 216.40.
Owner Colin Rogers **Bred** Michael E Broughton **Trained** Ashton Keynes, Wilts

FOCUS
They didn't go that quick and the time was marginally the slowest of the three 6f races. The runner-up sets the standard.
Libys Dream(IRE) ◆ Official explanation: jockey said that the filly missed the break

6932 DORMANSLAND H'CAP 5f (P)
5:30 (5:31) (Class 5) (0-75,75) 3-Y-0+ **£2,385** (£704; £352) **Stalls** High

Form RPR
0504 **1** **Absa Lutte (IRE)**[26] 6283 8-9-2 **70** JimmyQuinn 2 76
(Michael Mullineaux) *s.i.s: sn in midfield on rail: hdwy wl over 1f out: str run to ld fnl strides* **9/1**
3003 **2** nk **Boogie Waltzer**[27] 6250 4-9-2 **70** (t) JamesDoyle 6 75
(Stuart Williams) *in tch: outpcd 2f out: rallied and str run fnl f: fin wl* **6/1**[2]
1325 **3** nse **Go Nani Go**[27] 6250 5-9-3 **74** JohnFahy(3) 4 82+
(Ed de Giles) *s.i.s: patiently rdn fr detached last: effrt and nt clr run ins fnl f: rapid hdwy whn clr: clsng fast at fin* **17/2**
4645 **4** nk **Even Bolder**[5] 6815 8-8-13 **67** (b[1]) LiamKeniry 1 71
(Eric Wheeler) *disp ld: led over 2f out: rdn 3 l clr over 1f out: wknd fnl 100yds: ct fnl strides* **15/2**[3]
112 **5** nk **Rebecca Romero**[47] 5658 4-9-0 **68** TadhgO'Shea 8 71
(Denis Coakley) *in tch: rdn and rn wd bnd 2f out: rallied and r.o ins fnl f* **9/2**[1]
010 **6** ¾ **Lord Of The Reins (IRE)**[17] 6522 7-9-1 **72** KieranO'Neill(3) 3 72
(P J O'Gorman) *t.k.h: chsd ldrs: wnt 3 l 2nd over 1f out: kpt on same pce* **9/2**[1]
405 **7** hd **Estonia**[24] 6351 4-8-13 **67** LukeMorris 7 66
(Michael Squance) *mid-div: rdn 2f out: kpt on ins fnl f* **15/2**[3]
1453 **8** 1¾ **Chjimes (IRE)**[213] 904 7-9-2 **70** (b) KirstyMilczarek 9 63
(Conor Dore) *s.i.s: bhd: mod effrt over 1f out: nvr trbld ldrs* **11/1**
630 **9** 3¼ **Athwaab**[5] 6815 4-8-13 **67** JimCrowley 10 48
(Noel Chance) *prom tl wknd over 1f out* **16/1**
6000 **10** nk **Skylla**[24] 6351 4-9-4 **75** RossAtkinson(3) 5 55
(Derek Shaw) *disp ld tl over 2f out: wknd over 1f out* **33/1**

58.68 secs (-0.12) **Going Correction** -0.025s/f (Stan) **10** Ran SP% **111.9**
Speed ratings (Par 103): **99,98,98,97,97 96,95,93,87,87**
toteswingers:1&2:£9.60, 2&3:£11.90, 1&3:£8.90 CSF £59.51 CT £471.47 TOTE £10.60: £3.00, £2.10, £3.60; EX 79.50.
Owner D & D Coatings Ltd **Bred** Ian Amond **Trained** Alpraham, Cheshire

FOCUS
The pace seemed ordinary yet this still set up for the closers. There was a bunch finish and the bare form was probably pretty ordinary. The third was unlucky.

T/Jkpt: £33,333.30 to a £1 stake. Pool of £140845.08 - 3.00 winning tickets. T/Plt: £98.40 to a £1 stake. Pool of £95,205.06 - 706.07 winning tickets. T/Qpdt: £29.10 to a £1 stake. Pool of £6,071.25 - 154.08 winning tickets. LM

6758 YARMOUTH (L-H)
Tuesday, October 18

OFFICIAL GOING: Good (good to soft in places; 7.3)
Wind: strong across Weather: bright and breezy

6933 BRITISH STALLION STUDS SUPPORTING BRITISH RACING E B F MAIDEN FILLIES' STKS (DIV I) 1m 3y
1:50 (1:52) (Class 5) 2-Y-0 **£3,150** (£943; £471; £236; £117) **Stalls** Centre

Form RPR
1 **Kailani** 2-9-0 0 FrankieDettori 6 77+
(Mahmood Al Zarooni) *chsd ldr tl over 3f out: nt clr run and swtchd rt over 1f out: rdn and hdwy to ld jst ins fnl f: r.o wl* **9/2**[2]
2 ½ **Shestheman** 2-9-0 0 TedDurcan 9 76+
(David Lanigan) *in tch: effrt to chse ldrs and rdn over 1f out: pressed wnr ins fnl f: r.o wl but a jst hld* **50/1**
562 **3** 2¾ **Protect**[42] 5806 2-9-0 75 KierenFallon 10 70
(Sir Michael Stoute) *led: rdn over 2f out: hdd jst ins fnl f: nt gng pce of ldng pair fnl 150yds* **7/1**
06 **4** 1 **Aniseed (IRE)**[17] 6526 2-9-0 0 PaulHanagan 13 68
(William Haggas) *in tch in midfield: n.m.r over 2f out: rdn and no imp over 1f out: swtchd rt 1f out and styd on ins fnl f: nt gng pce to chal* **5/4**[1]
0 **5** nk **Moment In Time (IRE)**[42] 5807 2-9-0 0 MartinLane 5 67
(David Simcock) *dwlt: in tch in rr: pushed along and hdwy jst over 2f out: kpt on ins fnl f: nvr trbld ldrs* **33/1**
6 ½ **Salacia (IRE)** 2-8-9 0 AntiocoMurgia(5) 3 66+
(Mahmood Al Zarooni) *in tch: chsd ldr over 3f out: ev ch and travelling wl 2f out: rdn and unable qck over 1f out: wknd ins fnl f* **20/1**
7 nk **Still I'm A Star (IRE)** 2-9-0 0 JamieSpencer 8 65+
(Ed Dunlop) *in tch: rdn and unable qck 2f out: kpt on but no threat to ldrs fnl f* **33/1**
0 **8** 1¼ **Panettone (IRE)**[57] 5320 2-9-0 0 NeilCallan 2 62+
(Roger Varian) *in tch: rdn and unable qck over 2f out: wknd over 1f out* **33/1**
0 **9** ½ **Furzanah**[20] 6440 2-8-7 0 HayleyBurton(7) 11 61+
(Luca Cumani) *chsd ldrs tl rdn and unable qck over 2f out: wknd wl over 1f out* **100/1**
6 **10** 2¼ **Mixora (USA)**[42] 5814 2-9-0 0 TomQueally 7 56
(Sir Henry Cecil) *s.i.s: hld up in tch towards rr: hung lft and wknd 2f out* **13/2**[3]
11 hd **Tempest Fugit (IRE)** 2-9-0 0 WilliamBuick 14 56
(John Gosden) *in tch towards rr: rdn and no hdwy over 2f out: wknd wl over 1f out* **10/1**
12 4½ **Langham Lily (USA)** 2-9-0 0 SebSanders 1 45
(Chris Wall) *a in rr: wknd over 2f out: wl bhd fnl f* **100/1**
0 **13** ½ **Connishka**[8] 6758 2-8-11 0 DominicFox(3) 12 44
(Alan Bailey) *t.k.h: hld up in tch towards rr: rdn and wknd over 2f out: wl bhd ins fnl f* **200/1**

1m 41.12s (0.52) **Going Correction** -0.075s/f (Good) **13** Ran SP% **115.6**
Speed ratings (Par 92): **94,93,90,89,89 88,88,87,86,84 84,79,79**
toteswingers:1&2:£46.90, 2&3:£37.40, 1&3:£4.00 CSF £215.26 TOTE £3.30: £1.30, £22.10, £1.90; EX 399.50 Trifecta £247.50 Pool: £505.04 - 1.51 winning units..
Owner Godolphin **Bred** Darley **Trained** Newmarket, Suffolk

FOCUS
After 3mm of rain in the morning the going was described as good, good to soft in places. A decent maiden run in quite a strong crosswind. The pace was not particularly fast but the first two pulled clear. There were lots of interesting types on show but the compressed finish holds down the form.

NOTEBOOK
Kailani, a half-sister to 1m-1m4f (Group 1) winner Eastern Anthem out of 1000 Guineas/Oaks winner Kazzia, was prominent in the market and found a strong run switched towards the near rail to win with a bit in hand on debut. She looks a nice prospect and this Monsun filly should stay quite a bit further than this in time. (op 4-1 tchd 7-2)
Shestheman ◆ ran a highly promising race on debut, particularly as she was a big price and is bred to come into her own over middle-distances next season.
Protect had solid form claims on her front-running second behind a 93-rated rival in a Leicester fillies' maiden last month. Ridden positively, she stuck to her task well but couldn't match the finishing speed of the first two. A half-sister to 1m-1m6f Flat/2m4f hurdle winner Worth A King's, she looks a staying type and should find her niche in middle-distance handicaps next year. (tchd 9-1)
Aniseed(IRE) improved on her debut run when staying on well for sixth after finding some trouble in a very valuable sales race at Newmarket early this month. She had fair claims on that form and was a strong favourite, but she still looked inexperienced when things got serious before staying on when it was all over. Official explanation: jockey said that the filly jumped the path and hung both ways thereafter (op 11-8)
Moment In Time(IRE) did some good late work on her second start. A half-sister to quite useful 7f-1m winner Fontley, she should continue to progress and is clearly well regarded having held a Fillies' Mile entry at one point. (op 28-1)
Salacia(IRE), a half-sister to decent winners at 6f-1m4f out of a French 1m-10.5f winner, shaped with promise on debut and should improve next time. (op 18-1)
Still I'm A Star(IRE), a 32,000gns half-sister to ten winners, notably Group 3 Irish 1m winner Swift Gulliver, was unfancied but showed some promise on debut.
Mixora(USA) showed promise on debut it Lingfield but it was disappointing that she couldn't build on that switched to turf.. (op 17-2)

6934 BRITISH STALLION STUDS SUPPORTING BRITISH RACING E B F MAIDEN FILLIES' STKS (DIV II) 1m 3y
2:20 (2:26) (Class 5) 2-Y-0 **£3,150** (£943; £471; £236; £117) **Stalls** Centre

Form RPR
00 **1** **Forgive**[24] 6329 2-9-0 0 DaneO'Neill 7 72
(Richard Hannon) *racd stands' side: towards rr: effrt and rdn and hung lft over 1f out: styd on to ld 120yds out: edgd clr cl home* **17/2**[3]
0 **2** 1 **Baheeja**[47] 5655 2-9-0 0 NeilCallan 3 70
(Roger Varian) *plld hrd: led: rdn and edgd lft over 1f out: hdd 120yds out and nt qckn ins fnl f* **4/1**[2]
3 1¼ **Morrow** 2-9-0 0 FrankieDettori 5 67+
(Mahmood Al Zarooni) *prom and gng wl: pushed along outpcd by ldng pair ins fnl f: kpt on steadily: promising* **11/4**[1]
5 **4** 1¼ **News Show**[38] 5937 2-9-0 0 MartinLane 4 64
(David Simcock) *pressed ldrs: rdn 2f out: nt qckn ins fnl f* **16/1**

0 **5** 3/4 **Wild Silk**[58] 5299 2-9-0 0 .... KierenFallon 1 62
(Sir Michael Stoute) *prom: ev ch 2f out: rdn and wknd ins fnl f* **10/1**
3 **6** *nse* **Darling Grace**[51] 5514 2-9-0 0 .... LiamJones 8 62
(William Haggas) *chsd ldrs: rdn 3f out: one pce and btn 2f out* **4/1**[2]
7 *hd* **Bassara (IRE)** 2-9-0 0 .... TedDurcan 12 62+
(Chris Wall) *bhd and sn rdn: kpt on fr over 1f out: unable to chal* **22/1**
8 3/4 **Cape Safari (IRE)** 2-9-0 0 .... TomMcLaughlin 14 60+
(Ed Dunlop) *towards rr: pushed along after 1/2-way: kpt on steadily but nt rch ldrs: rn green* **100/1**
9 2 **Anabedweyah (IRE)** 2-9-0 0 .... SebSanders 9 55
(Clive Brittain) *midfield: n.m.r 3f out: rdn and wknd wl over 1f out* **22/1**
10 4 1/2 **Hikma (USA)** 2-9-0 0 .... WilliamBuick 11 45+
(Saeed Bin Suroor) *chsd ldrs: pushed along 3f out: btn over 2f out* **10/1**
11 3/4 **Green Mountain (IRE)** 2-8-11 0 ....(t) AdamBeschizza(3) 13 43
(Philip McBride) *dwlt: nvr bttr than midfield: rdn 2f out: sn btn* **100/1**
12 32 **Karistar (IRE)** 2-9-0 0 .... SteveDrowne 2 —
(Tom Keddy) *s.s and bucking and plunging in last: sn t.o* **80/1**

1m 41.36s (0.76) **Going Correction** -0.075s/f (Good) **12** Ran SP% **113.2**
Speed ratings (Par 92): **93,92,90,89,88 88,88,87,85,81 80,48**
toteswingers:1&2:£6.50, 2&3:£3.30, 1&3:£5.80 CSF £39.10 TOTE £11.60: £2.60, £1.80, £1.60; EX 41.80 Trifecta £141.60 Pool: £597.22 - 3.12 winning units..
Owner Highclere Thoroughbred Racing-Spearmint **Bred** The Athenians And Cheveley Park Stud Ltd **Trained** East Everleigh, Wilts

FOCUS
This didn't look quite as strong as the first division, but the winner showed a good turn of speed to overhaul two of the market leaders. The form could rate a few lengths higher if working out.

NOTEBOOK
Forgive showed ability when in midfield in fillies maidens at Salisbury and Haydock, but she finished strongly this time to strike on a much improved third attempt. She has plenty of useful speedy winners in her pedigree but this daughter of Pivotal seems to have a fair amount of stamina at this early stage of her career and should be able to go on from this. (op 8-1)
Baheeja, an encouraging 33-1 seventh behind smart stable-companion Firdaws in a 7f Salisbury fillies maiden on debut last month, raced freely near the pace but did really well to hang in there. A scopey type, she has plenty of potential for improvement as she learns to settle better. (op 7-2 tchd 9-2)
Morrow was sent off favourite and kept battling in a promising debut run. She should improve for the experience, and is a powerfully built filly who is out of a speedy and smart French 2yo winner whose four winners are headed by US 7f-1m1f Grade 1 winner Flashing. (tchd 5-2, 3-1 in places)
News Show got a bit caught out when the pace increased before staying on steadily out wide. She has looked all about stamina in two 1m/1m2f maidens and could be an interesting staying handicap prospect for next season. (op 25-1)
Wild Silk ran green and didn't show much on 7f debut at Folkestone but there was quite a bit to like about this second effort from a 165,000gns first foal of an unraced half-sister to Racing Post Trophy winner Ibn Khaldun. (tchd 8-1)
Darling Grace was a stable second-string when a 25-1 keeping-on third behind subsequent Group 3 winner Alsindi in a 6f maiden here in August. The step up in trip looked likely to suit this Nayef filly but she was under pressure some way out and could only plug on. (op 9-2)

6935 BRITISH STALLION STUDS SUPPORTING BRITISH RACING E B F MAIDEN STKS 6f 3y
2:50 (2:53) (Class 5) 2-Y-O **£3,150** (£943; £471; £236; £117) **Stalls** Centre

Form RPR
1 **Aljamaaheer (IRE)** 2-9-3 0 .... RichardHills 2 84+
(Roger Varian) *s.i.s: t.k.h and sn rcvrd to chse ldrs: wnt 2nd 2f out: pushed into ld over 1f out: r.o strly ins fnl f: pushed out* **5/4**[1]
2 1 3/4 **Mezzotint (IRE)** 2-9-3 0 .... SAJackson(7) 1 77+
(Luca Cumani) *in tch in midfield: pushed along and effrt over 1f out: chsd wnr ins fnl f: kpt on wl for clr 2nd but nt gng pce to chal* **100/1**
3 2 1/2 **Cappielow Park** 2-9-3 0 .... SteveDrowne 5 69
(William Jarvis) *in tch in midfield: rdn and outpcd over 2f out: rallied 1f out: styd on wl ins fnl f: wnt 3rd towards fin: no ch w ldng pair* **25/1**
0 **4** 1/2 **Foot Tapper**[32] 6127 2-9-3 0 .... GeorgeBaker 4 68
(Chris Wall) *led tl rdn and hdd over 1f out: no ex 1f out: hung lft and outpcd ins fnl f* **12/1**
5 1/2 **Lady Macduff (IRE)** 2-8-12 0 .... SilvestreDeSousa 11 61
(Mark Johnston) *in tch in midfield: rdn and effrt 2f out: unable qck and btn over 1f out: kpt on same pce and no threat to ldrs ins fnl f* **5/1**[2]
6 1 1/2 **Shatter (IRE)** 2-8-12 0 .... PaulHanagan 6 57+
(William Haggas) *in tch: rdn and rn green jst over 2f out: outpcd and btn wl over 1f out: no threat to ldrs but kpt on ins fnl f* **8/1**
5 **7** 2 1/2 **Twin Shadow (IRE)**[20] 6441 2-8-12 0 .... NeilCallan 7 48
(James Fanshawe) *hld up in tch in midfield: rdn and effrt 2f out: unable qck and btn over 1f out: wknd ins fnl f* **13/2**[3]
4023 **8** 1/2 **Represent (IRE)**[29] 6207 2-8-12 69 .... TonyCulhane 10 47
(Mick Channon) *hld up in tch towards rr: rdn and short-lived effrt ent fnl 2f: wknd over 1f out* **7/1**
300 **9** 1 3/4 **Medam**[14] 6612 2-8-12 50 ....(t) RobbieFitzpatrick 3 41
(Shaun Harris) *chsd ldr tl jst over 2f out: sn rdn: wknd over 1f out: fdd ins fnl f* **150/1**
00 **10** 4 1/2 **Skyblue**[8] 6758 2-8-12 0 ....(t) StevieDonohoe 12 27
(Tobias B P Coles) *s.i.s: green and bucking leaving stalls: a towards rr: rdn and wknd over 2f out* **250/1**
11 4 1/2 **Petrol** 2-8-10 0 .... TalibHussain(7) 9 17+
(Luca Cumani) *v.s.a: a in rr: rdn and wknd over 2f out: bhd over 1f out* **28/1**
12 5 **Hearduthefirsttime (IRE)** 2-9-3 0 .... TomQueally 8 —
(Barney Curley) *chsd ldrs tl 1/2-way: sn lost pl: wl bhd over 1f out* **100/1**

1m 14.31s (-0.09) **Going Correction** -0.075s/f (Good) **12** Ran SP% **116.1**
Speed ratings (Par 95): **97,94,91,90,90 88,84,84,81,75 69,63**
toteswingers:1&2:£9.40, 2&3:£97.50, 1&3:£9.40 CSF £220.40 TOTE £2.10: £1.20, £15.10, £5.70; EX 100.40 TRIFECTA Not won..
Owner Hamdan Al Maktoum **Bred** Corrin Stud **Trained** Newmarket, Suffolk

FOCUS
The runners with experience didn't set a very high standard but there was an impressive win from a very well-bred Roger Varian-trained newcomer. The second showed a lot of promise too.

NOTEBOOK
Aljamaaheer(IRE) was a bit keen marooned out wide in the early stages but he gradually settled and travelled smoothly into contention before unleashing a good turn of foot to win in style on debut. A Derby entry, he cost 100,000gns as a foal and is a half-brother to useful 7f-1m winner Tinkertown, out of a 8.4f-1m2f winning half-sister to US Listed winner Cold Cold Woman. He looks a potentially smart prospect and should have bright future. (op 11-8 tchd 6-4)
Mezzotint(IRE), a £31,000 half-brother to useful 6f-7f winner Kaptain Kirkup, battled on well for a clear second at 100-1 on a very promising debut run.
Cappielow Park, an Exceed And Excel half-brother to ten winners including US 1m3f Listed winner Mabadi, showed promise staying on well from some way back on debut and should improve for the experience. (op 33-1)
Foot Tapper finished last of eleven at 33-1 on debut at Newbury, but this 35,000gns son of Invincible Spirit was a springer in the market and showed much improved form under front-running tactics on his second start. (op 22-1)
Lady Macduff(IRE) kept battling in an encouraging first run. She is out of a 7f winning half-sister to high-class sprinters Godfrey Street and Gilt Edge Girl, and her price rocketed to 200,000gns at the breeze-ups in April. (tchd 9-2)
Shatter(IRE), a 10,000euros yearling who is related to useful Irish 7f 2yo winner Cocozza, ran green and found a bit of trouble before staying on late on debut. (tchd 17-2)
Represent(IRE) is an exposed 69-rated filly who was never dangerous on her seventh start. (op 11-2 tchd 15-2)

6936 YARMOUTH STADIUM (S) STKS 1m 3f 101y
3:20 (3:20) (Class 6) 3-Y-O **£1,617** (£481; £240; £120) **Stalls** Low

Form RPR
460 **1** **Mazij**[32] 6122 3-8-7 57 .... WilliamCarson 2 58
(Peter Hiatt) *chsd ldr who sn wnt clr: clsd 5f out: led over 3f out: clr over 1f out: rdn out and inclined to wave tail* **8/1**
3200 **2** 5 **What About Now**[7] 6769 3-9-0 62 ....(b) SebSanders 6 57
(J W Hills) *trckd ldrs and t.k.h: rdn to chse wnr over 2f out: reluctant and nvr able to rch her and all out to hold mod 2nd* **11/1**
223 **3** *nk* **If What And Maybe**[16] 6122 3-8-12 58 ....(b) StevieDonohoe 1 54
(John Ryan) *sn pushed along: led and sn clr: 10 l ahd after 4f: hdd over 3f out: lost 2nd over 2f out: plugged on* **6/1**[3]
5130 **4** 5 **Fine Style (IRE)**[6] 6785 3-9-5 63 ....(v) EddieAhern 4 53
(Neil King) *pressed ldrs: rdn over 4f out: chal for 2nd over 3f out tl over 2f out: rdn and v one pce after: poor 4th 1f out* **14/1**
5103 **5** 12 **Flying Phoenix**[7] 6767 3-9-0 65 ....(b) RobertWinston 7 27
(Gay Kelleway) *stdd s: t.k.h in last: lost tch v tamely 4f out: stmbld wl over 2f out: t.o* **11/2**[2]
6555 **6** *nse* **Piccarello**[7] 6767 3-8-12 55 .... TedDurcan 5 25
(Mark H Tompkins) *last trio: rdn and struggling 4f out: t.o* **20/1**
1201 **7** 3 1/2 **Jack's Revenge (IRE)**[14] 6605 3-9-5 72 ....(vt) KierenFallon 3 26
(George Baker) *last trio: pushed along in 5th w no rspnse bef st: racing awkwardly and gng bdly after: sn wl bhd: t.o* **1/1**[1]

2m 30.22s (1.52) **Going Correction** -0.075s/f (Good) **7** Ran SP% **110.5**
Speed ratings (Par 99): **91,87,87,83,74 74,72**
toteswingers:1&2:£6.90, 2&3:£4.30, 1&3:£5.00 CSF £81.66 TOTE £11.80: £3.60, £6.20; EX 93.80.The winner was bought in for 6,200gns.
Owner P W Hiatt **Bred** The Hill Stud **Trained** Hook Norton, Oxon

FOCUS
The hot favourite was very disappointing in this seller which was won in decisive style by a 57-rated maiden. A weak race that has been rated negatively.
Jack's Revenge(IRE) Official explanation: jockey said that the gelding was never travelling

6937 CHRISTINE SHAW BIRTHDAY NURSERY 1m 3y
3:50 (3:52) (Class 6) (0-60,62) 2-Y-O **£1,617** (£481; £240; £120) **Stalls** Centre

Form RPR
0001 **1** **Regal Gold**[5] 6817 2-9-9 62 6ex ....(b1) KierenFallon 1 66
(Richard Hannon) *towards rr: rdn along over 5f out: hdwy and chsd ldrs u.p over 1f out: ev ch ins fnl f: styd on wl to ld towards fin* **8/1**[3]
0550 **2** *hd* **Artistic Thread (IRE)**[56] 5342 2-9-3 56 .... SebSanders 12 60
(Sir Mark Prescott Bt) *led: rdn wl over 1f out: hrd pressed 1f out: edgd lft u.p ins fnl f: hdd and no ex towards fin* **8/1**[3]
603 **3** *hd* **Sabhan (IRE)**[27] 6259 2-9-7 60 .... RobertWinston 8 63+
(Geoffrey Harker) *hld up in tch: rdn and effrt wl over 1f out: pressed wnr u.p 1f out: ev ch fnl f: no ex cl home* **9/2**[1]
1554 **4** 2 **Meanwhile (IRE)**[11] 6667 2-9-5 58 .... LiamJones 2 56
(William Knight) *in tch: rdn to chse ldrs jst over 2f out: drvn and unable qck 1f out: styd on same pce ins fnl f* **9/2**[1]
0560 **5** 1/2 **Northern Territory (IRE)**[20] 6443 2-9-7 60 .... PatCosgrave 13 57
(Jim Boyle) *t.k.h: hld up wl in tch: rdn and chsd ldrs over 1f out: no ex ins fnl f: wknd fnl 75yds* **25/1**
0000 **6** 1/2 **Carolingian (IRE)**[69] 4907 2-9-3 59 ....(p1) HarryBentley(3) 11 55
(William Knight) *chsd ldr: rdn over 1f out: unable qck ent fnl f: keeping on same pce and hld whn n.m.r ins fnl f: wknd fnl 75yds* **16/1**
550 **7** 5 **Atlantis Crossing (IRE)**[42] 5812 2-9-0 53 .... TomQueally 14 38
(Jim Boyle) *hld up in rr: pushed along over 3f out: switched rt and effrt jst over 2f out: no imp over 1f out: hung lft and wl hld fnl f* **25/1**
0600 **8** *hd* **Always A Sinner (USA)**[20] 6443 2-9-6 59 .... ShaneKelly 5 43
(William Knight) *hld up in rr: rdn and effrt on far side of field over 2f out: no imp over 1f out: plugged on but no threat to ldrs fnl f* **18/1**
6001 **9** 1 3/4 **Coach Montana (IRE)**[33] 6101 2-9-5 58 .... IvaMilickova 7 38
(Jane Chapple-Hyam) *s.i.s: in rr: rdn and edging lft ent fnl 2f: no prog and plugged on same pce fr over 1f out: nvr trbld ldrs* **16/1**
0630 **10** 1 **Great Mystery (IRE)**[11] 6662 2-9-0 53 .... SilvestreDeSousa 9 31
(J W Hills) *hld up in tch towards rr: rdn and edgd rt over 2f out: sn struggling: no ch w ldrs over 1f out* **28/1**
0400 **11** 5 **Percythepinto (IRE)**[20] 6443 2-9-7 60 ....(t) TonyCulhane 4 26
(George Baker) *t.k.h: chsd ldrs tl lost pl qckly over 2f out: wl btn over 1f out* **16/1**
4553 **12** 2 **Doctor Banner**[8] 6760 2-9-2 55 .... TedDurcan 16 17
(Mick Channon) *hld up in tch: rdn and effrt over 2f out: hung lft and wknd over 1f out: wl btn and eased towards fin* **13/2**[2]
0000 **13** 3/4 **Hawkino (IRE)**[56] 5343 2-9-0 53 ....(v1) RobbieFitzpatrick 3 13
(Derek Shaw) *chsd ldrs: lost pl 3f out: wknd over 2f out: wl bhd over 1f out* **28/1**
0650 **14** 2 **Ashkan**[11] 6667 2-9-4 57 .... PaulHanagan 10 12
(William Haggas) *in tch towards rr: rdn and no rspnse over 2f out: sn btn and bhd* **16/1**
0030 **15** 16 **Aussie Guest (IRE)**[5] 6817 2-9-5 58 .... MatthewDavies 15 —
(Mick Channon) *chsd ldrs tl lost pl over 3f out: wl bhd over 1f out: t.o and eased ins fnl f* **33/1**

1m 40.78s (0.18) **Going Correction** -0.075s/f (Good) **15** Ran SP% **118.2**
Speed ratings (Par 93): **96,95,95,93,93 92,87,87,85,84 79,77,76,74,58**
toteswingers:1&2:£8.50, 2&3:£10.40, 1&3:£4.90 CSF £64.27 CT £334.25 TOTE £6.00: £1.80, £4.30, £2.50; EX 72.70 Trifecta £137.10 Pool: £583.85 - 3.15 winning units..
Owner N S Yong **Bred** Minehart Developments Ltd **Trained** East Everleigh, Wilts

FOCUS
A low-grade nursery. It was hard work for the winner but he showed a good attitude to seize the initiative in the closing stages. Straightforward form, rated around the principals.

NOTEBOOK
Regal Gold showed marked improvement when winning on nursery debut at Kempton last week. His prospects of following up looked slim when he was under pressure some way out but he showed plenty of grit in blinkers and swooped late out wide to defy a penalty. He needs to learn to travel a bit more fluently but has potential for further progress after just five runs and should give it a good shot in a hat-trick bid. (op 7-1)

Artistic Thread(IRE) was well held as favourite in two previous nursery runs, but the switch back to slower ground and the fact that he had been gelded were a couple of positive angles on return from eight weeks off, and he ran a big race and was just reeled in. (op 17-2 tchd 9-1)
Sabhan(IRE) was well backed and stayed on strongly in a close call up in trip on nursery debut. A generally progressive 60,000gns son of Marju who is out of a 1m2f winner, he could be closing in on a first win and could appreciate another step up in trip. (tchd 4-1)
Meanwhile(IRE) didn't cut much ice on her first three nursery runs after a Wolverhampton maiden win, but she was a market mover and ran well here. She has stacks of useful 1m2f-1m6f winners on her dam's side and should be suited by middle-distances next season. (op 13-2)
Northern Territory(IRE) was always out the back on nursery debut last time but he showed more verve switched to a straight turf track.
Carolingian(IRE) faded on his 7f nursery debut at Kempton, but he has plenty of stamina on his dam's side and stuck to his task quite well stepped up in trip with two different types of headgear applied.

6938 SPIFFING CRABBIE'S ALCOHOLIC GINGER BEER H'CAP — 1m 3y
4:20 (4:22) (Class 6) (0-60,66) 3-Y-O+ **£1,617** (£481; £240; £120) **Stalls** Centre

Form — RPR

0024 **1** **Croeso Mawr**[22] 6411 5-8-11 **50**.............................. SteveDrowne 12 — 61
(John Spearing) *taken down v early: trckd ldrs: rdn 3f out: 3rd 1f out: sustained effrt to ld 100yds out: kpt on gamely* **12/1**

3500 **2** ¾ **Exopuntia**[51] 5515 5-8-13 **52**.............................. TonyCulhane 13 — 61
(Julia Feilden) *led: drvn 1f out: hdd 100yds out: unable qck* **22/1**

4003 **3** nk **Signora Frasi (IRE)**[38] 5912 6-9-3 **56**.............................. DaneO'Neill 10 — 64
(Tony Newcombe) *chsd ldrs: rdn and effrt 2f out: ev ch 1f out: no ex fnl 100yds* **12/1**

26-2 **4** 3¾ **Harting Hill**[22] 6411 6-9-5 **58**.............................. GeorgeBaker 15 — 58
(Marcus Tregoning) *chsd ldrs: rdn and effrt 2f out: wl hld by ldrs over 1f out* **5/1**[2]

5100 **5** 1½ **Zaheeb**[35] 6032 3-9-2 **58**..............................(p) TomQueally 6 — 54
(Dave Morris) *midfield: plugged on ins fnl f: nvr nr to chal* **28/1**

0303 **6** hd **Mr Chocolate Drop (IRE)**[17] 6544 7-9-4 **57**..........(t) SilvestreDeSousa 9 — 53
(Mandy Rowland) *midfield: rdn 1/2-way: sn outpcd: plugged on ins fnl f* **12/1**

000 **7** ¾ **Sumbe (USA)**[72] 4828 5-9-5 **58**..............................(p) AndreaAtzeni 2 — 52+
(Michael Wigham) *nvr bttr than midfield: rdn and btn wl over 1f out* **18/1**

4021 **8** shd **Caldermud (IRE)**[8] 6746 4-9-8 **66** 6ex..........................(t) LucyKBarry(5) 1 — 60
(Olivia Maylam) *taken down early: swtchd rt sn after s to r up centre of crse: prom over 5f: rdn and grad lost pl* **6/1**[3]

3320 **9** 2½ **Elegant Muse**[13] 6624 3-9-4 **60**.............................. AdamKirby 7 — 48
(Walter Swinburn) *t.k.h briefly: rdn after 3f: nvr on terms after* **14/1**

0036 **10** ¾ **Cornish Quest**[63] 5137 3-9-3 **59**.............................. TedDurcan 11 — 45
(Mark H Tompkins) *s.i.s: a bhd* **25/1**

000- **11** 1½ **Hurricane Hymnbook (USA)**[335] 7483 6-9-7 **60**.......... StevieDonohoe 3 — 43
(Willie Musson) *taken down early: swtchd rt sn after s and brought to r on stands' rails: nvr wnt a yard: detached in last and struggling bdly 1/2-way* **7/2**[1]

4064 **12** nk **Faith And Hope (IRE)**[12] 6653 3-9-4 **60**.....................(vt) KierenFallon 14 — 46
(James Fanshawe) *pressed ldr for 6f: sn lost pl: eased ins fnl f* **16/1**

0200 **13** ½ **General Tufto**[8] 6764 6-9-0 **53**..............................(b) PaulHanagan 5 — 34
(Charles Smith) *sn rdn and wl bhd* **40/1**

02 **14** ¾ **Avon Supreme**[74] 4745 3-8-11 **53**.............................. RobertWinston 4 — 32
(Gay Kelleway) *s.i.s: rdn and sme prog towards outside over 3f out: wknd wl over 1f out* **14/1**

0000 **15** 2¼ **Lord Theo**[48] 5611 7-9-0 **60**.............................. RichardOld(7) 16 — 34
(Nick Littmoden) *struggling fr 1/2-way* **50/1**

400- **16** 4½ **Parisian Dream**[380] 6335 7-8-11 **50**.............................. MartinLane 8 — 14
(Tim Pitt) *plld hrd briefly: midfield: rdn 1/2-way: sn gave up* **28/1**

1m 39.67s (-0.93) **Going Correction** -0.075s/f (Good)
WFA 3 from 4yo+ 3lb **16** Ran SP% **120.2**
Speed ratings (Par 101): **101,100,99,96,94 94,93,93,91,90 88,88,88,87,85 80**
toteswingers:1&2:£50.30, 2&3:£45.60, 1&3:£20.00 CSF £262.96 CT £3220.93 TOTE £18.50: £3.50, £5.70, £3.30, £1.20; EX 394.40 TRIFECTA Not won..
Owner Mrs Richard Evans **Bred** Richard Evans Bloodstock **Trained** Kinnersley, Worcs

FOCUS
An ordinary handicap. The first three pulled clear and the field converged towards the stands' side. The form is rated around the second
Faith And Hope(IRE) Official explanation: jockey said that the filly moved poorly

6939 DIGIBET.COM H'CAP — 7f 3y
4:50 (4:53) (Class 6) (0-65,65) 3-Y-O+ **£1,617** (£481; £240; £120) **Stalls** Centre

Form — RPR

2403 **1** **Cativo Cavallino**[34] 6051 8-9-4 **65**.............................. NataliaGemelova(3) 9 — 74
(John E Long) *chsd ldrs: rdn to ld 3f out: hrd pressed over 1f out: hld on wl ins fnl f* **11/1**

0002 **2** nse **Forks**[14] 6609 4-8-10 **59**.............................. AntiocoMurgia(5) 2 — 68
(Jane Chapple-Hyam) *chsd ldrs: chsd wnr over 2f out: rdn and ev ch fr over 1f out: r.o: jst hld* **9/2**[1]

-000 **3** 8 **Elusive Hawk (IRE)**[96] 4020 7-9-7 **65**.............................. TomQueally 3 — 52
(Barney Curley) *hld up in tch in rr: hdwy on far side of field 3f out: chsd ldng pair and rdn over 1f out: no ex and sn btn: wknd ins fnl f* **16/1**

0/0- **4** nk **Parc Aux Boules**[37] 5975 10-9-3 **61**..............................(t) MartinHarley 1 — 48
(John C McConnell, Ire) *in tch: rdn and chsd ldrs 2f out: btn over 1f out: plugged on but no ch w ldng pair ins fnl f* **18/1**

3320 **5** 2 **Mark Anthony (IRE)**[3] 6869 4-9-5 **63**.....................(p) RobbieFitzpatrick 8 — 44
(Shaun Harris) *led tl 3f out: rdn ent fnl 2f: 4th and btn over 1f out: wl hld but plugged on ins fnl f* **10/1**

4430 **6** 1½ **Norcroft**[29] 6228 9-8-1 **52** oh6 ow1..............................(p) DanielHarris(7) 16 — 29
(Christine Dunnett) *bhd: swtchd lft and effrt over 2f out: no ch but plugged on ins fnl f: n.d* **33/1**

0-50 **7** ½ **Blueberry Fizz (IRE)**[13] 6626 3-7-13 **52**.................... NatashaEaton(7) 5 — 28
(John Ryan) *chsd ldrs: rdn and struggling ent fnl 2f: wknd over 1f out: wl btn 1f out* **66/1**

110 **8** hd **Swansea Jack**[13] 6624 4-9-6 **64**..............................(vt) WilliamCarson 12 — 39
(Stuart Williams) *sn niggled along in rr and nvr travelling wl: reminders 1/2-way: no ch but plugged on past btn horses fnl f: n.d* **6/1**[2]

4502 **9** 7 **Caramelita**[10] 6694 4-9-3 **61**.............................. KierenFallon 13 — 17
(J R Jenkins) *hld up in tch in midfield: rdn and no reponse ent fnl 2f: wknd and wl btn over 1f out* **15/2**[3]

145 **10** 5 **Ellies Image**[20] 6450 4-9-5 **63**.............................. DuranFentiman 7 — —
(Brian Baugh) *in tch towards rr: rdn and struggling 1/2-way: no ch w ldrs fnl 2f* **8/1**

4300 **11** 2 **Spade**[8] 6748 3-9-3 **63**..............................(b) NickyMackay 11 — —
(David Elsworth) *stdd s: hld up in rr: shkn up and no rspnse wl over 2f out: wl btn fnl 2f* **6/1**[2]

0600 **12** shd **Jibouti (IRE)**[34] 6071 3-8-6 **52**.............................. SilvestreDeSousa 14 — —
(Clive Brittain) *in tch in midfield: rdn and struggling wl over 2f out: sn wknd and wl bhd over 1f out* **20/1**

3000 **13** nse **Double Carpet (IRE)**[138] 2653 8-9-7 **65**.................... TomMcLaughlin 15 — 2
(Garry Woodward) *in tch in midfield: rdn 3f out: no imp and wl btn over 1f out: wknd* **33/1**

5360 **14** 10 **Foxley (IRE)**[80] 4560 3-9-4 **64**.............................. LeeNewman 10 — —
(Robin Bastiman) *chsd ldrs tl lost pl 1/2-way: bhd and eased fr over 1f out: t.o* **28/1**

0500 **P** **Imjin River (IRE)**[47] 5640 4-8-13 **57**..............................(b) TedDurcan 6 — —
(Mark H Tompkins) *in tch towards rr: lost tch qckly over 2f out: wl bhd whn p.u and dismntd ins fnl f: burst blood vessel* **25/1**

1m 26.22s (-0.38) **Going Correction** -0.075s/f (Good)
WFA 3 from 4yo+ 2lb **15** Ran SP% **117.6**
Speed ratings (Par 101): **99,98,89,89,87 85,84,84,76,70 68,68,68,57,—**
toteswingers:1&2:£11.00, 2&3:£20.70, 1&3:£27.40 CSF £53.67 CT £822.75 TOTE £13.60: £3.80, £1.80, £7.30; EX 56.80 TRIFECTA Not won..
Owner P Saxon **Bred** Miss A M Rees **Trained** Caterham, Surrey

FOCUS
An ordinary handicap. The runners were spread across the track and the breakaway front pair had a sustained battle in the final furlong. The form cannot be taken literally.
Imjin River(IRE) Official explanation: jockeu said that the gelding bled from the nose

6940 NORFOLK AND SUFFOLK ANIMAL TRUST H'CAP — 6f 3y
5:20 (5:22) (Class 6) (0-60,60) 3-Y-O+ **£1,617** (£481; £240; £120) **Stalls** Centre

Form — RPR

-244 **1** **Dixie Gwalia**[68] 4950 3-8-10 **50**.............................. MartinLane 14 — 60
(David Simcock) *s.i.s: clsd gng wl to ld stands gp 2f out: drvn and hld on wl fr far side ldr cl home* **10/1**

220 **2** nk **Comrade Bond**[47] 5644 3-9-5 **59**.............................. TedDurcan 5 — 68
(Mark H Tompkins) *sn led quintet on far side: ev ch 1f out: drvn and kpt on wl ins fnl f: jst btn by stands' side ldr* **14/1**

3406 **3** ½ **Belinsky (IRE)**[14] 6609 4-9-5 **58**..............................(p) RobertWinston 10 — 65
(Mark Campion) *prom stands' side: drvn and ev ch 1f out: no ex fnl 100yds* **6/1**[2]

002 **4** ¾ **Shaws Diamond (USA)**[4] 6848 5-8-12 **51**............(v) RobbieFitzpatrick 2 — 56
(Derek Shaw) *sn chsng ldr on far side: rdn and kpt on wl ins fnl f* **13/2**[3]

2001 **5** nk **Full Shilling (IRE)**[10] 6696 3-9-6 **60**.............................. AdamKirby 9 — 64
(John Spearing) *chsd ldrs stands' side: rdn to chal over 1f out: nt qckn after* **5/1**[1]

0066 **6** ½ **Kyllachykov (IRE)**[14] 6602 3-8-6 **46** oh1......................(b) LeeNewman 8 — 48
(Robin Bastiman) *chsd ldrs: sn drvn along: nt qckn fr over 1f out* **14/1**

2044 **7** ¾ **Tenavon**[22] 6407 3-9-6 **60**.............................. ShaneKelly 12 — 60
(William Knight) *s.s: hdwy over 1f out: fin wl* **12/1**

0200 **8** 1½ **Errigal Lad**[83] 4434 6-8-12 **51**.............................. KellyHarrison 7 — 46
(Garry Woodward) *hanging and racing awkwardly in centre: drvn and btn wl over 1f out* **12/1**

4330 **9** 5 **Dictionary**[40] 5864 3-9-5 **59**..............................(tp) EddieAhern 4 — 38
(William Haggas) *last of far side quintet: no ch fr 1/2-way* **9/1**

2- **10** 1¼ **Little Village (IRE)**[158] 2080 5-8-8 **47**..........................(t) MartinHarley 16 — 22
(John C McConnell, Ire) *rdn and cl up on stands' side: wknd over 1f out* **7/1**

460 **11** 4 **Dolly Bay**[15] 6591 3-8-3 **46** oh1.............................. AdamBeschizza(3) 6 — —
(Julia Feilden) *3rd of five on far side early: outpcd fr 1/2-way* **40/1**

0-30 **12** 11 **Bianco Boy (USA)**[202] 1043 4-9-2 **55**.............................. SteveDrowne 13 — —
(John Best) *outpcd fr 1/2-way: t.o and eased 1f out* **40/1**

0P00 **13** ¾ **Musical Leap**[36] 5996 3-8-6 **46** oh1......................(bt) SilvestreDeSousa 1 — —
(Shaun Harris) *prom far side quintet tl 1/2-way: sn lost pl: t.o and eased 1f out* **100/1**

0054 **14** 4½ **Merito**[47] 5649 3-9-6 **60**..............................(b[1]) PaulHanagan 11 — —
(Kevin Ryan) *led stands' side gp for 4f (in front of far side runners): drvn and qckly lost pl: t.o and eased 1f out* **11/1**

1m 13.74s (-0.66) **Going Correction** -0.075s/f (Good)
WFA 3 from 4yo+ 1lb **14** Ran SP% **118.8**
Speed ratings (Par 101): **101,100,99,98,98 97,96,94,88,86 81,66,65,59**
toteswingers:1&2:£17.90, 2&3:£14.30, 1&3:£17.50 CSF £139.76 CT £947.31 TOTE £14.00: £4.80, £2.70, £1.60; EX 114.80 TRIFECTA Not won..
Owner Mrs Ann Simcock **Bred** Charlie Wyatt **Trained** Newmarket, Suffolk

FOCUS
An ordinary handicap. They split into two groups and there was a close finish between runners on opposite sides of the track. The first pair's best previous form had been over C&D, and the third is the best guide.
Merito Official explanation: vet said that the gelding had bled from the nose
T/Plt: £1,295.10 to a £1 stake. Pool of £64,668.95 - 36.45 winning tickets. T/Qpdt: £113.10 to a £1 stake. Pool of £6,361.76 - 41.60 winning tickets. SP

5529 DEAUVILLE (R-H)
Tuesday, October 18

OFFICIAL GOING: Turf: good to soft; fibresand: standard

6941a PRIX DES RESERVOIRS - HARAS D'ETREHAM (GROUP 3) (2YO FILLIES) (TURF) — 1m (R)
2:20 (12:00) 2-Y-O **£34,482** (£13,793; £10,344; £6,896; £3,448)

RPR

1 **Boldogsag (FR)**[10] 2-8-9 0.............................. Christophe-PatriceLemaire 7 — 105
(P Bary, France) *broke wl towards outside to r 3rd: then settled 5th following Mashoora: rdn 1 1/2f out: r.o wl u.p ins fnl f to get up fnl strides* **48/10**[3]

2 shd **Mashoora (IRE)**[59] 5296 2-8-9 0.............................. ChristopheSoumillon 4 — 105
(J-C Rouget, France) *settled 3rd on outside: rdn to ld 1 1/2f out: r.o wl ins fnl f: chal fnl 50yds: hdd cl home* **6/4**[1]

3 ¾ **Rajastani (IRE)**[40] 5873 2-8-9 0.............................. StephanePasquier 6 — 103
(S Wattel, France) *bkmarker fr s: pulling hrd: settled bef st: swtchd to outside: qcknd wl to go 3rd ins fnl f: r.o wl: nrest at fin* **14/5**[2]

4 1¾ **Brillante Etoile (FR)**[32] 2-8-9 0.............................. OlivierPeslier 5 — 99
(Y Durepaire, Spain) *settled towards rr: rdn over 1 1/2f out: nt qckn: styd on fnl f to go 4th 50yds: no threat to ldrs* **9/1**

5 hd **Gloomy Sunday (FR)**[44] 2-8-9 0.............................. PhilippeSogorb 1 — 99
(C Ferland, France) *settled 4th on rail: rdn 1 1/2f out: r.o fnl f wout threatening ldrs: lost 4th cl home* **73/10**

6 snk **Day Of Victory (FR)**[29] 2-8-9 0.............................. ThierryJarnet 3 — 98
(T Castanheira, France) *racd towards rr: rdn early in st: nt qckn: swtchd towards centre of trck ent fnl f: r.o wout threatening ldrs* **30/1**

7 *4* **Wafiyah (GER)**[45] 2-8-9 0 MaximeGuyon 8 89
(W Baltromei, Germany) *broke wl: sn led: rdn early in st: hdd 1 1/2f out: no ex: fdd* **13/1**

8 *hd* **Kapitala (FR)**[31] 2-8-9 0 IoritzMendizabal 2 89
(Andreas Lowe, Germany) *racd 2nd: rdn early in st: nt qckn: grad wknd* **33/1**

1m 41.9s (1.10) **8** Ran SP% **118.9**
WIN (incl. 1 euro stake): 5.80. PLACES: 1.30, 1.10, 1.20. DF: 7.60. SF: 20.40.
Owner Mme Georges Sandor **Bred** G Sandor **Trained** Chantilly, France

NOTEBOOK
Boldogsag(FR) made it three wins from three starts when she got up close home to deny the favourite. She was delivered late by Christophe Lemaire between horses and caught the favourite on the line. She only made her racecourse debut on September 17 but she has wasted little time in making her mark and looks capable of further progress.
Mashoora(IRE) cruised into contention with 2f to run and looked likely to bounce back to winning ways after finishing second last time out. However, she was forced to settle for second best again.
Rajastani(IRE), who sat last for the majority of the contest, finished well at the death.

6958a PRIX DE LIANGER (CONDITIONS) (4YO+) (FIBRESAND) 6f 110y
3:25 (12:00) 4-Y-O+ **£9,482** (£3,793; £2,844; £1,896; £948)

RPR

1 **Prime Spirit (IRE)**[41] 5-8-9 0 Roberto-CarlosMontenegro 7 92
(X Thomas-Demeaulte, France) **54/10**[2]

2 *1 ¾* **Dubawi Junior (IRE)**[56] 4-8-9 0 ChristopheSoumillon 14 87
(J-C Rouget, France) **7/1**

3 *shd* **Lixirova (FR)**[20] 4-8-6 0 MaximeGuyon 6 84
(D Smaga, France) **4/1**[1]

4 *snk* **Sumaro (GER)**[15] 6594 4-9-0 0 ASuborics 10 91
(W Hickst, Germany) **44/5**

5 *snk* **Ramble On (FR)**[418] 4-8-9 0 IoritzMendizabal 11 86
(G Botti, Italy) **8/1**

6 *1 ¾* **Gallery's Platine (FR)** 4-8-10 0 MathiasSautjeau 2 82
(Carmen Bocskai, Switzerland) **14/1**

7 *nse* **Eyes On Me (IRE)**[44] 5-8-3 0 TheoBachelot(3) 5 78
(J E Hammond, France) **22/1**

8 *1* **Tuaoi (USA)**[270] 257 6-8-9 0 (p) BriceRaballand 9 78
(Mlle A Voraz, France) **12/1**

9 *nk* **Reignier**[45] 5699 4-9-0 0 (p) StephanePasquier 4 82
(Mrs K Burke) *broke wl: racing freely: suffered interference after 2f and shuffled bk towards rr: rdn and r.o st: short of room 1f out: styd on* **6/1**[3]

10 *1 ¾* **Nareion (GER)**[176] 1575 5-8-9 0 ThierryThulliez 1 72
(W Baltromei, Germany) **35/1**

0 **Mister Thatcher (IRE)**[15] 6580 7-8-9 0 FergalLynch 8 —
(Mrs Annette McMahon-Reidy, France) **91/1**

0 **Molesne Bay (FR)**[372] 4-8-9 0 GaetanMasure 13 —
(D Allard, France) **96/1**

0 **Toxeas (FR)**[46] 4-8-13 0 (p) RomainAuray(5) 12 —
(J Heloury, France) **47/1**

0 **Rock Of Nassau (FR)**[15] 6593 5-8-9 0 (p) GregoryBenoist 3 —
(X Nakkachdji, France) **12/1**

1m 18.0s (78.00) **14** Ran SP% **117.1**
WIN (incl. 1 euro stake): 6.40. PLACES: 1.80, 2.30, 1.90. DF: 18.50. SF: 31.10.
Owner Prime Equestrian S.A.R.L. **Bred** Frank Gleeson **Trained** France

6816 KEMPTON (A.W) (R-H)
Wednesday, October 19

OFFICIAL GOING: Standard
Wind: Moderate behind

6942 FREE ENTRY FOR BETDAQ MEMBERS NURSERY 5f (P)
5:50 (5:51) (Class 6) (0-60,58) 2-Y-O **£1,617** (£481; £240; £120) **Stalls** Low

Form RPR

0455 **1** **Mr Hendrix**[14] 6620 2-9-1 **52** WilliamCarson 3 60
(Brett Johnson) *mde all: drvn out fnl f* **11/2**[2]

000 **2** *1 ¼* **Welease Bwian (IRE)**[36] 6019 2-8-12 **52** AdamBeschizza(3) 7 56
(Stuart Williams) *in tch: chsd ldrs 2f out: drvn to chse wnr ins fnl f: kpt on wl but no imp* **8/1**[3]

0602 **3** *¾* **Mount McLeod (IRE)**[14] 6627 2-9-2 **53** FergusSweeney 1 54
(Jamie Osborne) *s.i.s: t.k.h and hld up in rr: hdwy over 1f out: styd on wl to take 3rd wl ins fnl f: nt rch ldng duo* **5/2**[1]

0040 **4** *1* **Masivo Man (IRE)**[18] 6540 2-9-0 **51** (b) IanMongan 10 48
(Chris Dwyer) *chsd ldr: rdn and no imp over 1f out: wknd fnl 120yds* **14/1**

330 **5** *hd* **Finalist**[115] 3435 2-9-7 **58** ShaneKelly 5 57+
(Dean Ivory) *s.i.s: wl bhd and stl last 2f out: rapid hdwy and swtchd lft 1f out: swtchd rt and styd on strly ins fnl f: gng on cl home* **8/1**[3]

0200 **6** *shd* **Cataract**[14] 6628 2-8-13 **50** LukeMorris 6 46
(John Weymes) *chsd ldrs: drvn 2f out: wknd ins fnl f* **20/1**

0606 **7** *1 ¼* **Milwr**[9] 6763 2-8-1 **45** RaulDaSilva(7) 12 37
(Chris Dwyer) *racd towards outside and bhd: drvn and hdwy 1f out: styd on clsng stages: nvr a threat* **20/1**

0030 **8** *1 ¾* **Kaylee**[6] 6821 2-9-5 **56** TomMcLaughlin 2 42
(Gary Moore) *t.k.h: chsd ldrs: wknd ins fnl f* **11/2**[2]

6000 **9** *2 ¼* **Sea Poet**[10] 6724 2-9-0 **54** (v[1]) SeanLevey(3) 4 31
(John Bridger) *rdn and outpcd fr 1/2-way* **16/1**

4006 **10** *2 ¼* **J Cunningham**[40] 5896 2-8-8 **45** DavidProbert 11 14
(Mark Usher) *in rr: hanging rt and no ch fr 1/2-way* **25/1**

560 **11** *½* **No More Shoes (IRE)**[32] 6165 2-8-10 **47** (t) LiamKeniry 9 15
(Brendan Powell) *outpcd fr 1/2-way* **16/1**

60.68 secs (0.18) **Going Correction** -0.075s/f (Stan) **11** Ran SP% **113.4**
Speed ratings (Par 93): **95,93,91,90,89 89,87,84,81,77 76**
toteswingers:1&2:£12.60, 1&3:£2.40, 2&3:£9.10 CSF £45.55 CT £137.86 TOTE £14.30: £3.20, £3.90, £1.10; EX 80.60.
Owner Gayler William Chambers **Bred** C Lefevre **Trained** Ashtead, Surrey

FOCUS
A moderate handicap run at a reasonable gallop. The winner raced centre-to-far side in the straight. Ordinary form, but the time was decent.

NOTEBOOK
Mr Hendrix had the run of the race from a good draw at a track/trip that suits this style of racing and he showed improved form to score at the sixth attempt. Things were in his favour but he's lightly raced enough to be open to a bit more progress. (tchd 6-1)
Welease Bwian(IRE) ◆, gelded since his last run, has a bit of size and scope and, although easy in the market, showed improved form back in trip on this nursery debut. He's not the finished article by any means and he's capable of winning a race. (op 7-1)
Mount McLeod(IRE), who took a strong hold early on, fared the best of those to come from off the pace and, while she should be able to win over 5f when the leaders go off quickly, she'll be better suited by the return to 6f. Official explanation: jockey said filly was slowly away (op 10-3 tchd 9-4)
Masivo Man(IRE) wasn't disgraced from his double-figure draw after racing keenly but he's a moderate and inconsistent maiden who remains one to tread carefully with. (op 12-1)
Finalist ◆ was unable to go the early gallop on this first run for nearly four months, but who made up a good deal of late ground without being knocked about. He'll be suited by the return to 6f and is one to keep a close eye on. (tchd 10-1)
Kaylee, for whom the draw could be blamed on her previous outing, had no such excuse this time. She isn't fully exposed and is in good hands but is best watched in the short term. (op 9-2)

6943 BETDAQ MULTIPLES H'CAP 5f (P)
6:20 (6:20) (Class 6) (0-55,55) 3-Y-O+ **£1,617** (£481; £240; £120) **Stalls** Low

Form RPR

3300 **1** **Francis Albert**[11] 6694 5-9-1 **54** JimmyQuinn 4 65
(Michael Mullineaux) *s.i.s: in rr: hdwy on ins to chse ldrs 2f out: drvn and styd on strly to ld fnl 120yds: kpt on wl* **13/2**[2]

4604 **2** *1* **Argentine (IRE)**[11] 6696 7-8-13 **52** (b) TomEaves 5 59
(Ian Semple) *s.i.s: in rr: hdwy on ins 2f out: str run fnl f to take 2nd clsng stages: no imp on wnr* **7/1**[3]

5402 **3** *½* **Cliffords Reprieve**[14] 6619 3-9-2 **55** LiamKeniry 8 61
(Eric Wheeler) *sn led: drvn wl over 1f out: hdd fnl 120yds: one pce: ct for 2nd cl home* **7/1**[3]

3100 **4** *¾* **Porthgwidden Beach (USA)**[15] 6618 3-9-1 **54** (t) LeeNewman 6 57
(Anthony Middleton) *in tch: hdwy over 1f out: styd on wl clsng stages: nt rch ldrs* **8/1**

30 **5** *½* **Brian Sprout**[46] 5719 3-8-9 **48** LukeMorris 1 49
(John Weymes) *chsd ldrs on ins: rdn over 1f out: wknd fnl 120yds* **16/1**

3440 **6** *2 ¼* **Till Dawn (IRE)**[3] 6889 3-9-2 **55** NeilCallan 7 50+
(Tony Carroll) *in rr: hdwy and nt clr run appr fnl f: kpt on: nvr a threat* **7/2**[1]

0335 **7** *nk* **Cloth Ears**[14] 6619 5-8-7 **49** AdamBeschizza(3) 10 41
(Phil McEntee) *chsd ldrs: wknd ins fnl f* **16/1**

0234 **8** *nk* **Canadian Danehill (IRE)**[9] 6765 9-8-13 **52** (p) JimCrowley 2 43
(Robert Cowell) *racd towards outside: drvn along 2f out: sme hdwy fnl f* **8/1**

6000 **9** *2 ¼* **Fairy Tales**[56] 5381 3-8-13 **55** SeanLevey(3) 9 38
(John Bridger) *outpcd* **66/1**

-000 **10** *nk* **Papageno**[211] 941 4-8-9 **48** DavidProbert 3 30
(J R Jenkins) *spd 3f* **11/1**

6004 **11** *½* **Steel City Boy (IRE)**[7] 6802 8-9-2 **55** TomMcLaughlin 12 35
(Garry Woodward) *racd towards outside: outpcd* **9/1**

59.92 secs (-0.58) **Going Correction** -0.075s/f (Stan) **11** Ran SP% **114.4**
Speed ratings (Par 101): **101,99,98,97,96 93,92,92,88,87 87**
toteswingers:1&2:£7.00, 1&3:£7.80, 2&3:£7.50 CSF £50.02 CT £327.85 TOTE £4.50: £1.10, £4.40, £3.70; EX 36.60.
Owner Michael Mullineaux **Bred** R S And Mrs S H Kitching **Trained** Alpraham, Cheshire

FOCUS
A moderate handicap run at a decent gallop and one run three quarters of a second quicker than the juveniles in the opener. The winner raced centre-to-far side in the straight. The winner is rated to his best, with the next three close to their recent marks.
Argentine(IRE) Official explanation: trainer's rep said gelding bled from the nose

6944 BACK AND LAY AT BETDAQ.COM CLAIMING STKS 1m (P)
6:50 (6:50) (Class 6) 3-Y-O **£1,617** (£481; £240; £120) **Stalls** Low

Form RPR

3315 **1** **Poyle Punch**[123] 3178 3-9-7 **78** JimCrowley 2 82
(Ralph Beckett) *trckd ldrs: drvn to ld 1f out: hld on all out: jst lasted* **7/2**[1]

1410 **2** *nse* **Russian Ice**[34] 6089 3-8-10 **66** ShaneKelly 1 71
(Dean Ivory) *t.k.h: hld up in rr: hdwy on ins over 2f out: str run fnl f: fin fast: btn on nod* **14/1**

60 **3** *1 ½* **Exchange**[7] 6794 3-8-13 **70** KierenFallon 13 70
(Andrew Haynes) *led at stdy pce: drvn over 2f out: hdd 1f out: one pce ins fnl f* **16/1**

6513 **4** *1 ¼* **Hugely Exciting**[7] 6794 3-9-3 **70** (b) LiamKeniry 7 72
(J S Moore) *in tch: drvn over 2f out: kpt on fnl f: nt rch ldrs* **10/1**

2240 **5** *shd* **Sky Diamond (IRE)**[7] 6794 3-8-13 **69** (b) TomQueally 9 67+
(James Given) *in rr: hdwy fr 2f out: styd on fnl f: nt rch ldrs* **8/1**

4001 **6** *nk* **Safari Team (IRE)**[43] 5815 3-9-5 **78** (p) IanMongan 10 73
(Pat Phelan) *chsd ldrs: drvn over 2f out: one pce fnl f* **10/1**

3330 **7** *nse* **Ibiza Sunset (IRE)**[34] 6089 3-8-10 **69** LukeMorris 11 64
(Peter Winkworth) *chsd ldrs: drvn over 2f out: wknd ins fnl f* **6/1**[2]

3500 **8** *1 ½* **Tagansky**[28] 6255 3-8-12 **64** SebSanders 5 62
(Simon Dow) *in rr: drvn and hanging rt over 2f out: kpt on ins fnl f* **25/1**

2210 **9** *1 ¾* **Whodathought (IRE)**[9] 6755 3-9-0 **73** (bt) KieranO'Neill(3) 6 63
(Richard Hannon) *in tch: drvn along 3f out: styd on same pce fnl 2f* **15/2**[3]

5346 **10** *1 ¼* **Saucy Buck (IRE)**[34] 6090 3-8-13 **63** JimmyQuinn 12 56
(Ralph Smith) *in tch: drvn over 2f out: no imp: wknd fnl f* **28/1**

400 **11** *2 ¼* **Rafella (IRE)**[16] 6586 3-8-3 **65** DavidKenny(5) 3 46
(Michael Scudamore) *s.i.s: a towards rr* **50/1**

3105 **12** *1* **Social Forum (IRE)**[34] 6081 3-9-6 **77** NeilCallan 14 56
(David Elsworth) *chsd ldrs: wknd qckly over 1f out* **8/1**

555 **13** *16* **Rosairlie (IRE)**[21] 6465 3-8-4 **61** (b[1]) DavidProbert 8 —
(Harry Dunlop) *slowly away and detached: clsd on main gp off stdy pce after 2f: lost tch fr 3f out* **20/1**

1m 38.6s (-1.20) **Going Correction** -0.075s/f (Stan) **13** Ran SP% **115.2**
Speed ratings (Par 99): **103,102,101,100,100 99,99,98,96,95 93,92,76**
toteswingers:1&2:£9.50, 1&3:£16.70, 2&3:£17.90 CSF £50.40 TOTE £2.70: £1.10, £5.90, £9.00; EX 58.30.
Owner Cecil And Miss Alison Wiggins **Bred** Cecil And Miss Alison Wiggins **Trained** Kimpton, Hants

FOCUS
A fair but tightly knit race of its type but run at a steady gallop. The winner raced against the inside rail throughout and continues to improve. Sound form.
Rafella(IRE) Official explanation: jockey said filly was slowly away
Rosairlie(IRE) Official explanation: jockey said he lost an iron coming out of stalls

6945 BETDAQ MOBILE APPS MAIDEN STKS 7f (P)
7:20 (7:20) (Class 5) 2-Y-O **£2,264** (£673; £336; £168) **Stalls** Low

Form RPR

0 **1** **Awesome Pearl (USA)**[8] 6774 2-9-3 0 SebSanders 6 75+
(Sir Mark Prescott Bt) *racd in 4th but cl up: drvn and hdwy over 1f out: styd on to ld fnl 120yds: idled cl home: hld on all out* **10/1**[3]

2326 **2** *nse* **Tortoni (IRE)**[75] 4749 2-9-3 79 PaulHanagan 2 75
(Kevin Ryan) *led: t.k.h: rdn appr fnl f: hdd fnl 120yds: rallied last strides as wnr idled cl home: btn on nod* **9/4**[2]

3 *4* **Take A Note** 2-9-3 0 LiamKeniry 5 65+
(Patrick Chamings) *slowly away: t.k.h and sn chsng ldrs: chal over 1f out: wknd fnl 150yds* **16/1**

064 **4** *12* **Pilgrims Rest (IRE)**[10] 6726 2-9-3 0 KierenFallon 4 33
(Richard Hannon) *chsd ldr: drvn along ins fnl 3f: wknd over 1f out: eased whn btn ins fnl f* **8/13**[1]

1m 27.49s (1.49) **Going Correction** -0.075s/f (Stan) **4** Ran SP% **107.7**
Speed ratings (Par 95): **88,87,83,69**
CSF £30.96 TOTE £16.90; EX 29.80.
Owner Pearl Bloodstock Ltd **Bred** Centaur Farms Inc **Trained** Newmarket, Suffolk

FOCUS
The winner raced in the centre. An uncompetitive maiden run at a steady gallop so the bare form isn't entirely reliable and a race that took less winning than seemed likely with the market leader disappointing. The form is tentatively rated around the runner-up.

NOTEBOOK
Awesome Pearl(USA), well beaten after a slow start in testing ground on debut, was easy in the market but turned in a much-improved display, despite still displaying signs of inexperience, to show fair form on this all-weather debut. A stronger gallop would have suited better and, although this bare form looks dubious, he's the type physically to improve further.
Tortoni(IRE), gelded since a below-par run (reportedly upset in the preliminaries) in August, is a fair sort who was allowed an easy lead and ran creditably up in trip on this all-weather debut on this first outing for two and a half months. Things were in his favour but he's the best guide to this form and should be able to win a minor event. (op 2-1)
Take A Note, a half-brother to last year's 6f Polytrack winner Pomeroy, showed clear signs of ability on this racecourse debut, despite missing the break and after racing with the choke out. He should be all the better for this experience and may do better in ordinary handicaps in due course. (op 14-1)
Pilgrims Rest(IRE) had shown fair form up to 1m1f on turf but was a long way below that level (eased when no chance) in a race that turned into a test of speed on this all-weather debut over this shorter trip. A stiffer test on turf will suit better but it'll be an ordinary maiden he wins. Official explanation: trainer's rep had no explanation for the poor form shown (op 4-6 after 10-11 in places tchd 8-11)

6946 CONEXION COMMUNICATIONS LTD MAIDEN FILLIES' STKS 6f (P)
7:50 (7:50) (Class 5) 2-Y-O **£2,264** (£673; £336; £168) **Stalls** Low

Form RPR
02 **1** **Lollina Paulina**[84] 4430 2-9-0 0 PaulHanagan 8 72
(Kevin Ryan) *trckd ldr: edgd rt and rdn to ld appr fnl f: hld on wl* **4/1**[2]

6 **2** *3/4* **Jwala**[9] 6758 2-9-0 0 ShaneKelly 2 70
(Robert Cowell) *chsd ldrs: rdn to chal over 1f out: styd on ins fnl f: nt qckn fnl 120yds* **10/1**[3]

50 **3** *2 3/4* **Royale Ransom**[9] 6744 2-9-0 0 AdamKirby 4 62
(Clive Cox) *chsd ldrs: drvn and styd on to take one pce 3rd fnl 120yds* **14/1**

04 **4** *1* **Classic Falcon (IRE)**[27] 6274 2-9-0 0 KierenFallon 3 59
(William Haggas) *led: drvn over 2f out: hdd appr fnl f: wknd and lost 3rd fnl 120yds* **12/1**

435 **5** *1/2* **Gin Twist**[46] 5737 2-9-0 63 RichardKingscote 10 58
(Tom Dascombe) *t.k.h: towards rr: styd on fr over 1f out: kpt on: nvr gng pce to rch ldrs* **14/1**

6 *3/4* **Wiltshire Life (IRE)** 2-9-0 0 SteveDrowne 1 58+
(Jeremy Gask) *in rr: drvn and styd on fnl f: nt rch ldrs* **33/1**

0350 **7** *shd* **Emperors Pearl (IRE)**[67] 5052 2-9-0 65 RobertWinston 12 54
(Charles Hills) *stdd s: in rr: drvn and hdwy on outside: kpt on clsng stages* **12/1**

03 **8** *hd* **Athenian (IRE)**[15] 6612 2-9-0 0 SebSanders 5 54+
(Sir Mark Prescott Bt) *s.i.s: in rr: hdwy over 2f out: no imp on ldrs: one pce fr over 1f out* **20/1**

623 **9** *1* **Fine Painting (IRE)**[6] 6820 2-9-0 0 TomQueally 11 51
(Gary Moore) *sn chsng ldrs: drvn over 1f out: wknd ins fnl f* **5/4**[1]

10 *2 1/4* **Mary Frith** 2-9-0 0 LukeMorris 9 44
(Peter Winkworth) *s.i.s: in rr: rdn and flashed tail 1f out: hung lft fnl 120yds* **20/1**

11 *nk* **Marmalade Moon** 2-9-0 0 JimCrowley 7 43
(Robert Cowell) *chsd ldrs: wknd fr 2f out* **66/1**

1m 13.55s (0.45) **Going Correction** -0.075s/f (Stan) **11** Ran SP% **116.2**
Speed ratings (Par 92): **94,93,89,88,87 86,86,85,84,81 81**
toteswingers:1&2:£6.30, 1&3:£10.50, 2&3:£7.00 CSF £40.89 TOTE £6.30: £2.10, £4.10, £3.50; EX 57.20.
Owner The Paulina Partnership **Bred** Newsells Park Stud Limited **Trained** Hambleton, N Yorks

FOCUS
A modest and uncompetitive maiden in which the moderate gallop suited those up with the pace. The race took less winning than seemed likely with the market leader disappointing and the winner raced centre-to-far side in the straight. The standard of the form is set around the third.

NOTEBOOK
Lollina Paulina, returning after a break for this all-weather debut, had the run of the race and took advantage of her main market rival under-performing. She is a steadily progressive sort who has a good attitude, a bit of size and scope and may do better. (op 7-2 tchd 10-3)
Jwala was well placed given the way things unfolded and she left the bare facts of her first run a long way behind her on this all-weather debut. Her trainer has done well with fillies down the years and it will be interesting to see if this can be built on. (tchd 11-1)
Royale Ransom returned to form back on Polytrack, in the process shaping as though the return to 7f would be much more to her liking. Modest nurseries will be the way forward with her. (op 16-1)
Classic Falcon(IRE) was allowed an easy lead and ran her best race yet on this all-weather debut. She's clearly limited ability wise but is another that should benefit for the switch into run-of-the-mill nursery company.
Wiltshire Life(IRE) Official explanation: jockey said filly was denied a clear run
Athenian(IRE) was again well held but wasn't knocked about returned to Polytrack on this third, and qualifying run for a handicap mark. She is in good hands and should do better at some point. (op 16-1)
Fine Painting(IRE) admittedly wasn't ideally drawn but didn't get home after she again raced with the choke out. She is better than this but will have to settle better before she is a solid betting proposition. (tchd 6-4, 7-4 in a place and 15-8 in a place)

6947 CONEXION COMMUNICATIONS MEDIAN AUCTION MAIDEN STKS 1m 4f (P)
8:20 (8:23) (Class 5) 3-5-Y-O **£2,264** (£673; £336; £168) **Stalls** Centre

Form RPR
0 **1** **Winning Spark (USA)**[24] 6376 4-9-10 72 TomQueally 6 64+
(Gary Moore) *hld up in rr: stdy hdwy 2f out: trckd ldr 1f out: shkn up: pushed rt and qcknd to ld fnl 120yds: pushed out* **15/8**[1]

055 **2** *1/2* **Dollar Deal**[43] 5816 3-9-3 59 KierenFallon 4 63
(Luca Cumani) *trckd ldrs: led wl over 1f out: rdn: edgd rt and hdd fnl 120yds: nt pce of wnr* **10/3**[2]

52 **3** *6* **Ultimate Best**[20] 6475 3-8-12 0 JimmyQuinn 5 49
(Michael Mullineaux) *chsd ldrs: drvn along 3f out: styd on for wl hld 3rd fnl f* **6/1**

0-5 **4** *1/2* **Our Play (IRE)**[123] 3183 3-9-3 0 SteveDrowne 3 53
(Lydia Richards) *in tch: drvn along 4f out: kpt on to chse ldrs over 2f out: outpcd over 1f out* **10/1**

60-0 **5** *1 3/4* **Sunshine Buddy**[11] 6698 4-9-5 48 JamesMillman 2 45
(Rod Millman) *in tch: hdwy to chse ldrs over 2f out: wknd appr fnl f* **33/1**

02 **6** *3* **Magic Minstrel**[34] 6086 3-9-3 0 LiamKeniry 8 45
(Andrew Balding) *led after 1f: rdn along over 2f out: edgd rt and hdd wl over 1f out: wknd qckly* **4/1**[3]

00- **7** *1/2* **Princess Runner**[336] 7489 4-9-5 0 MartinHarley 1 39
(Des Donovan) *rdn along 4f out: a in rr* **50/1**

0/ **8** *14* **Sioux City Sue**[786] 5322 5-9-5 0 StephenCraine 7 17
(Jim Boyle) *chsd ldrs: drvn 4f out: wknd qckly 3f out* **33/1**

0 **9** *11* **Four Steps Back**[20] 6475 4-9-10 0 IanMongan 9 —
(Mark Usher) *reluctant to load: pressed ldrs: wknd 3f out* **25/1**

2m 35.48s (0.98) **Going Correction** -0.075s/f (Stan)
WFA 3 from 4yo+ 7lb **9** Ran SP% **112.9**
Speed ratings (Par 103): **93,92,88,88,87 85,84,75,68**
toteswingers:1&2:£1.90, 1&3:£2.60, 2&3:£3.20 CSF £7.62 TOTE £1.80: £1.02, £1.50, £2.30; EX 8.20.
Owner Mrs Elizabeth Kiernan Paul Chapman **Bred** Haras De Bernesq & Jean Zorbibe **Trained** Lower Beeding, W Sussex

FOCUS
Another uncompetitive and weak maiden and one run at a steady gallop to the intersection. The first two pulled clear of some very ordinary types and the winner raced centre-to-far side in the straight. The winner is a bit better than the bare form, which is limited by the fifth.

6948 BOOK YOUR CHRISTMAS PARTY AT KEMPTON H'CAP (DIV I) 1m (P)
8:50 (8:52) (Class 4) (0-85,85) 3-Y-O+ **£4,075** (£1,212; £606; £303) **Stalls** Low

Form RPR
4000 **1** **Veroon (IRE)**[25] 5059 5-9-1 79 (p) PaulHanagan 5 89
(James Given) *hld up in rr: hdwy on ins over 2f out: drvn to ld jst ins fnl f: styd on strly* **20/1**

0000 **2** *nk* **Norse Blues**[19] 6500 3-9-2 83 JamesDoyle 2 92
(Sylvester Kirk) *hld up in tch: hdwy over 1f out: styd on to go 2nd clsng stages: nt rch wnr* **16/1**

031 **3** *3/4* **Santefisio**[30] 6220 5-9-7 85 (p) TomQueally 12 92+
(Peter Makin) *hld up in rr: hdwy on ins fr 2f out: pressed ldrs fr 1f out: no imp on wnr and lost 2nd clsng stages* **9/2**[2]

0041 **4** *1* **Flowing Cape (IRE)**[18] 6542 6-9-5 83 (e[1]) GeorgeBaker 1 88
(Reg Hollinshead) *chsd ldrs: led appr fnl f: sn hdd: wknd fnl 50yds* **16/1**

2622 **5** *1 3/4* **Ree's Rascal (IRE)**[20] 6478 3-9-0 81 PatCosgrave 8 82
(Jim Boyle) *in rr: drvn and styd on fr over 1f out: kpt on clsng stages* **8/1**

0104 **6** *1/2* **Red Somerset (USA)**[30] 6219 8-8-12 79 JohnFahy[(3)] 6 79
(Mike Murphy) *chsd ldrs: drvn along fr over 3f out: styd wl there: styd on same pce fnl 2f* **14/1**

0000 **7** *hd* **Freeforaday (USA)**[30] 6219 4-9-2 80 LukeMorris 11 79
(John Best) *s.i.s: in rr: styd on fr over 1f out: kpt on clsng stages* **16/1**

4005 **8** *shd* **Moynahan (USA)**[10] 6727 6-9-4 82 (p) ChrisCatlin 4 81
(Paul Cole) *in tch: hdwy to chse ldrs fr 3f out: styd on same pce fr over 1f out* **7/1**[3]

0402 **9** *1/2* **Den's Gift (IRE)**[47] 5687 7-9-2 80 (b) AdamKirby 3 78
(Clive Cox) *led tl hdd appr fnl f: sn wknd* **8/1**

0060 **10** *12* **Big Bay (USA)**[68] 5014 5-8-12 79 (p) KieranO'Neill[(3)] 10 49
(Jane Chapple-Hyam) *chsd ldrs on outside: wknd over 2f out* **33/1**

050 **11** *1 1/4* **Rigolleto (IRE)**[26] 6290 3-9-4 85 TonyCulhane 14 52
(Mick Channon) *racd on outside: nvr bttr than mid-div: bhd fnl 3f* **16/1**

551 **12** *6* **Snow Magic (IRE)**[105] 3740 4-9-3 81 KierenFallon 9 35
(James Fanshawe) *towards rr: pushed along 3f out: sme hdwy whn hmpd over 2f out: no ch after and eased fnl f* **4/1**[1]

060 **13** *7* **Gaily Noble (IRE)**[54] 5451 5-8-13 77 FergusSweeney 13 15
(Andrew Haynes) *chsd ldrs towards outside: wknd wl over 2f out* **25/1**

200 **14** *12* **Round Won (USA)**[58] 5328 4-9-6 84 [1] JimCrowley 7 —
(William Knight) *chsd ldrs: wkng and rr whn bdly hmpd over 2f out* **25/1**

1m 37.60s ([illegible]) **Going Correction** -0.075s/f (Stan)
WFA 3 from 4yo+ 3lb **14** Ran SP% **118.5**
Speed ratings (Par 105): **108,107,106,105,104 103,103,103,102,90 89,83,76,64**
toteswingers:1&2:£45.30, 1&3:£30.60, 2&3:£30.10 CSF £293.92 CT £1748.89 TOTE £26.20: £6.00, £5.20, £1.50; EX 388.80.
Owner Danethorpe Racing Partnership **Bred** C M Farrell **Trained** Willoughton, Lincs

FOCUS
Mainly exposed sorts in the first division of a useful handicap. The gallop was a reasonable one and the winner raced just off the inside rail in the straight. He produced a 3lb personal best.
Snow Magic(IRE) Official explanation: jockey said filly had no more to give

6949 BOOK YOUR CHRISTMAS PARTY AT KEMPTON H'CAP (DIV II) 1m (P)
9:20 (9:21) (Class 4) (0-85,86) 3-Y-O+ **£4,075** (£1,212; £606; £303) **Stalls** Low

Form RPR
2001 **1** **Loyalty**[30] 6219 4-9-6 84 (v) JoeFanning 12 99+
(Derek Shaw) *s.i.s: in rr: hmpd after 2f: hdwy on outside to ld 1f out: sn clr: comf* **7/1**[2]

3151 **2** *3 1/2* **Tarooq (USA)**[7] 6797 5-9-2 80 6ex PaulHanagan 1 87+
(Richard Fahey) *in tch whn hmpd after 2f: n.m.r wl over 2f out: qcknd over 1f out and styd on wl to chse wnr fnl 120yds but nvr any ch* **3/1**[1]

0001 **3** *1 1/2* **Byrony (IRE)**[10] 6728 3-9-2 86 6ex KieranO'Neill[(3)] 14 90
(Richard Hannon) *chsd ldrs: led over 2f out: hdd 1f out: styd on same pce and lost 2nd fnl 120yds* **8/1**

0100 **4** *1 1/4* **Captain Macarry (IRE)**[9] 6759 6-9-4 82 (v) WilliamCarson 9 83
(Stuart Williams) *chsd ldrs: drvn and outpcd over 2f out: styd on again fnl f: nvr a threat to ldng trio* **16/1**

010 **5** *shd* **Islesman**[89] 4268 3-9-0 81 EddieAhern 2 83+
(Heather Main) *in rr: drvn and hdwy fr 2f out: styd on wl clsng stages* **20/1**

6304 **6** *nk* **Mazamorra (USA)**[50] 5608 4-8-13 77 (b[1]) AdamKirby 6 77
(Marco Botti) *chsd ldrs: drvn 2f out: styd on same pce fnl f* **7/1**[2]

6140 **7** *1/2* **Uncle Fred**[21] 6439 6-9-1 79 JimCrowley 8 78
(Patrick Chamings) *s.i.s: in rr: hmpd after 2f: hdwy over 2f out: sn chsng ldrs but no imp: wknd ins fnl f* **25/1**

0062 **8** *1 1/4* **Majestic Dream (IRE)**[21] 6457 3-9-1 85 (v) JohnFahy[(3)] 10 81
(Walter Swinburn) *chsd ldrs: drvn over 2f out: wknd fnl f* **15/2**[3]

1300 **9** *1/2* **Spa's Dancer (IRE)**[10] 6728 4-9-3 81 (b[1]) SebSanders 5 76
(J W Hills) *s.i.s: hmpd after 2f: racd wd and sme hdwy fr over 1f out* **14/1**

1110 **10** *2 1/2* **Blues Jazz**[32] 6174 5-8-11 80 GarryWhillans[(5)] 4 69
(Ian Semple) *chsd ldrs and pulling hrd in bhd ldrs after 2f whn hmpd: towards rr and nvr in contention after* **14/1**

1-00 **11** *1 ¼* **Hatta Stream (IRE)**[118] 3322 5-9-1 79........ RobertHavlin 13 65
(Lydia Pearce) *towards rr most of way* **66/1**

0010 **12** *3 ¼* **Reposer (IRE)**[46] 5717 3-9-2 83........ LukeMorris 11 61
(John Best) *sn led: hdd over 2f out sn wknd* **33/1**

3124 **13** *26* **Ongoodform (IRE)**[20] 6478 4-9-0 78........(b¹) KierenFallon 7 —
(Paul D'Arcy) *sn chsng ldrs: hung bdly lft and v wd bnd 3f out: no ch after: eased* **9/1**

-100 **14** *77* **Mullins Way (USA)**[18] 6533 3-9-3 84........ TonyCulhane 3
(Jo Hughes) *chsng ldrs whn bdly hmpd after 2f and virtually p.u after* **20/1**

1m 37.82s (-1.98) **Going Correction** -0.075s/f (Stan)
WFA 3 from 4yo+ 3lb **14** Ran SP% **119.9**
Speed ratings (Par 105): **106,102,101,99,99 99,98,97,97,94 93,90,64,—**
toteswingers:1&2:£6.80, 1&3:£9.10, 2&3:£5.30 CSF £26.19 CT £181.61 TOTE £10.60: £3.30, £1.10, £3.30; EX 23.40.
Owner Brian Johnson (Northamptonshire) **Bred** Ecoutila Partnership **Trained** Sproxton, Leics
■ Stewards' Enquiry : John Fahy four-day ban: careless riding (Nov 2-5)

FOCUS
Despite the muddling gallop, this was run at just a fractionally slower time than the first division and it threw up a ready winner (who came down the centre). A personal bedst from the winner, with the second close to his Lingfield form.
Ongoodform(IRE) Official explanation: jockey said colt hung left-handed
Mullins Way(USA) Official explanation: jockey said gelding lost its action
T/Jkpt: Not won. T/Plt: £925.10 to a £1 stake. Pool:£73,262.53 - 57.81 winning tickets T/Qpdt: £271.90 to a £1 stake. Pool:£6,983.53 - 19.00 winning tickets ST

6687 NEWMARKET (R-H)
Wednesday, October 19

OFFICIAL GOING: Good (8.1)
Stands' side of Rowley Mile track used with stalls on far side for all races.
Wind: fresh, behind Weather: bright and breezy

6950 EXPRESS COFFEE CARS MEDIAN AUCTION MAIDEN FILLIES' STKS 7f
1:30 (1:32) (Class 5) 2-Y-O **£3,234** (£962; £481; £240) **Stalls** Low

Form RPR

2 **1** **Diala (IRE)**[54] 5445 2-9-0 0........ EddieAhern 10 85+
(William Haggas) *in tch and a travelling wl: swtchd lft and hdwy to trck ldrs 2f out: pushed into ld 1f out: sn clr and r.o strly: readily* **6/4¹**

6 **2** *4* **Safarjal (IRE)**[48] 5655 2-9-0 0........ RichardHills 8 75+
(Charles Hills) *stdd s: hld up towards rr of main gp: stl plenty to do and pushed along 2f out: hdwy and 6th 1f out: styd on wl to go 2nd last strides: no ch w wnr* **13/2²**

2 **3** *hd* **Fulney**[15] 6603 2-9-0 0........ LukeMorris 16 74
(James Eustace) *chsd ldrs: wnt 2nd 4f out: ev ch and rdn 2f out: nt pce of wnr and btn 1f out: kpt on* **13/2²**

55 **4** *½* **Jellicle (IRE)**[21] 6440 2-9-0 0........ WilliamBuick 12 73
(John Gosden) *led: rdn and hung rt over 1f out: hdd 1f out: sn outpcd and no ch w wnr: continued to hang: plugged on same pce and lost 2 pls wl ins fnl f* **14/1**

5 *shd* **Safe House (IRE)** 2-9-0 0........ FrankieDettori 14 73+
(Mahmood Al Zarooni) *hmpd s: rcvrd and in tch in midfield after 1f: rdn and chsd ldrs wl over 1f out: outpcd by wnr and btn 1f out: kpt on same pce* **7/1³**

50 **6** *1 ¾* **Miss Cap Estel**[25] 6329 2-9-0 0........ JimmyFortune 6 68+
(Andrew Balding) *t.k.h: in tch: rdn and unable qck wl over 1f out: outpcd and btn 1f out: plugged on same pce fnl f* **10/1**

466 **7** *5* **Proud Pearl (USA)**[21] 6440 2-9-0 72........ MartinDwyer 7 55
(Brian Meehan) *w ldr tl 3f out: rdn and struggling whn edgd lft 2f out: wknd over 1f out* **25/1**

045 **8** *2 ¼* **Farleaze**[21] 6458 2-9-0 73........ ShaneKelly 4 49
(Brian Meehan) *in tch: rdn and struggling over 2f out: wknd 2f out: sn wl btn* **20/1**

9 *nk* **Lucertola** 2-9-0 0........ JimCrowley 15 48+
(Ralph Beckett) *hmpd s: rcvrd and in tch in midfield after 1f: chsd ldrs and rdn 2f out: edgd rt and wknd qckly over 1f out* **66/1**

10 *2 ½* **Dutch Diamond** 2-9-0 0........ NickyMackay 11 42
(John Gosden) *s.i.s: a towards rr: rdn and sme hdwy over 2f out: no imp and wl btn whn edgd lft over 1f out* **33/1**

0330 **11** *2* **City Dazzler (IRE)**[31] 6196 2-9-0 67........ RyanMoore 5 37
(Richard Hannon) *hld up in tch towards rr: rdn and struggling 3f out: wknd 2f out* **20/1**

12 *1 ¾* **Your Word** 2-9-0 0........ AdamKirby 3 32
(Clive Cox) *s.i.s: a pushed along in rr: lost tch over 2f out* **66/1**

0 **13** *3 ½* **Grand Liaison**[16] 6581 2-9-0 0........ IvaMilickova 2 23
(John Berry) *in tch: rdn and struggling 1/2-way: wknd 3f out: wl bhd fnl 2f* **200/1**

14 *1* **Choral Bee** 2-9-0 0........ DaneO'Neill 1 20+
(Henry Candy) *s.i.s: a in rr: lost tch wl over 2f out* **100/1**

005 **15** *½* **Bit A Craic**[50] 5605 2-9-0 46........(bt¹) KirstyMilczarek 13 19
(John Ryan) *chsd ldrs tl 1/2-way: wknd 3f out: sn bhd* **200/1**

16 *19* **Hikkaduwa** 2-9-0 0........ RussKennemore 9 —
(John Holt) *s.i.s: sn detached in last: t.o fr 1/2-way* **200/1**

1m 24.47s (-0.93) **Going Correction** -0.20s/f (Firm) **16** Ran SP% **116.7**
Speed ratings (Par 92): **97,92,92,91,91 89,83,81,80,78 75,73,69,68,68 46**
toteswingers:1&2:£3.30, 1&3:£3.00, 2&3:£6.70 CSF £9.46 TOTE £2.50: £1.10, £2.60, £2.50; EX 12.20 Trifecta £62.00 Pool: £792.48 - 9.45 winning units..
Owner Abdulla Al Khalifa **Bred** D Johnson **Trained** Newmarket, Suffolk

FOCUS
A maiden dominated by fillies who had shown plenty of ability and the time was 0.67 seconds quicker than the following colts and geldings version. They raced up the middle of the track. The winner was impressive in building on her debut form.

NOTEBOOK
Diala(IRE) was beaten less than a length by subsequent May Hill and Fillies' Mile winner Lyric Of Light on her debut over this trip on easy ground at the July course. She had been off for 54 days since then but showed she's gone the right way with a comfortable success, finding plenty after travelling strongly. There ought to be more to come and she looks pattern class. (op 5-4 tchd 13-8 in places and 7-4 in a place)
Safarjal(IRE), sixth in a good Salisbury maiden (one place behind Miss Cap Estel) over this trip on her debut, confirmed that promise despite being left with too much to do. She lost her place when the race got serious, maybe not handling the Dip, but finished nicely. Considering she had been absent for 48 days, she's entitled to come on for this, while a step up in trip will also help. (op 17-2)
Fulney was beaten only a nose under similar conditions on her debut at Leicester, but this was a stronger race. She again showed plenty of ability. (op 11-2)
Jellicle(IRE) disappointed on Polytrack last time, but she had shaped well enough on her debut at Yarmouth and this was more like it, although she hung under pressure. (tchd 16-1)
Safe House(IRE), who went to post early, fared best of the six newcomers, keeping on at the one pace having recovered into a handy position. A half-sister to a few winners, notably US 7f-1m Graded winner Rebellion, out of Challenge Stakes (this C&D) winner Last Resort, there should be better to come. (op 13-2)
Miss Cap Estel hasn't gone on from a promising debut. She was too lit up on easy ground when uppcd to 1m at Haydock last time, and although this was a bit better, she again didn't see her race out after being free early. Until she settles she won't fulfil her potential. (op 14-1)
Hikkaduwa Official explanation: jockey said filly moved poorly

6951 STERLING SOLUTIONS MAIDEN STKS (C&G) 7f
2:00 (2:03) (Class 4) 2-Y-O **£3,881** (£1,155; £577; £288) **Stalls** Low

Form RPR

2 **1** **Ellaal**[26] 6300 2-9-0 0........ RichardHills 16 83
(Charles Hills) *chsd ldr: rdn to ld narrowly and drew clr w runner-up over 1f out: kpt on wl fnl f: rdn out* **5/2²**

2 *shd* **Periphery (USA)** 2-9-0 0........ FrankieDettori 8 83+
(Mahmood Al Zarooni) *led: rdn and hdd over 1f out: clr w wnr and ev ch after: kpt on gamely but a jst hld* **11/2³**

3 *2 ½* **Forgotten Hero (IRE)** 2-9-0 0........ MichaelHills 5 81+
(Charles Hills) *s.i.s: in rr: stl last 3f out: effrt and nt clr run jst over 2f out: gd hdwy over 1f out: modest 5th and swtchd lft 1f out: r.o strly ins fnl f: nt rch ldrs* **18/1**

2 **4** *1 ½* **Opera Flute (IRE)**[10] 6725 2-9-0 0........ RyanMoore 3 72
(Richard Hannon) *chsd ldrs: rdn ent fnl 2f: outpcd by ldng pair and btn over 1f out: plugged on same pce after* **9/4¹**

60 **5** *nk* **Johnno**[68] 4995 2-9-0 0........ SebSanders 2 72
(J W Hills) *hld up towards rr: gd hdwy on far side over 2f out: disputing 3rd and no imp on ldng pair over 1f out: styd on same pce after* **25/1**

6 *4 ½* **Fast Or Free** 2-9-0 0........ JoeFanning 6 60+
(William Haggas) *chsd ldrs: rdn and struggling ent fnl 2f: wknd over 1f out* **40/1**

7 *hd* **Saloomy** 2-9-0 0........ WilliamBuick 4 59+
(David Simcock) *in tch towards rr: pushed along 1/2-way: sme hdwy over 1f out: nvr trbld ldrs* **10/1**

8 *hd* **Solemn Oath (USA)** 2-9-0 0........ JamieSpencer 15 59+
(Edward Vaughan) *s.i.s: bhd: swtchd lft and pushed along ent fnl 2f: kpt on but no ch w ldrs* **25/1**

0 **9** *1 ¼* **Mr Opulence**[21] 6463 2-9-0 0........ DaneO'Neill 14 56+
(Henry Candy) *s.i.s: in rr: pushed along and hdwy over 2f out: no imp and kpt on same pce fr wl over 1f out: nvr trbld ldrs* **80/1**

10 *1 ½* **Strictly Private** 2-9-0 0........ MartinDwyer 13 52
(Brian Meehan) *a towards rr: rdn and struggling 1/2-way: wl btn fnl 2f* **50/1**

11 *¾* **Man Of Ice** 2-9-0 0........ AdamKirby 7 50
(Jane Chapple-Hyam) *in tch in midfield: rdn and outpcd over 2f out: wknd 2f out* **100/1**

12 *1 ¾* **District Attorney (IRE)** 2-9-0 0........ PaulHanagan 9 45
(William Haggas) *in tch: rdn after 3f: struggling fr 1/2-way: wl btn fnl 2f* **10/1**

00 **13** *hd* **Like Clockwork**[99] 3954 2-8-7 0........ CharlesEddery⁽⁷⁾ 1 45
(Mark H Tompkins) *in tch: rdn and struggling 1/2-way: wknd wl over 2f out* **200/1**

14 *shd* **Bulldog Beasley (USA)** 2-9-0 0........ ShaneKelly 12 44
(Brian Meehan) *s.i.s: a in rr: nt clr run over 2f out: sn bhd* **66/1**

00 **15** *9* **Teacher (IRE)**[20] 6481 2-9-0 0........ LiamJones 10 21
(William Haggas) *chsd ldrs tl 1/2-way: sn lost pl: wl bhd fnl 2f* **66/1**

1m 25.14s (-0.26) **Going Correction** -0.20s/f (Firm) **15** Ran SP% **116.0**
Speed ratings (Par 97): **93,92,90,88,87 82,82,82,80,79 78,76,76,76,65**
toteswingers:1&2:£3.70, 1&3:£10.80, 2&3:£11.10 CSF £14.88 TOTE £3.60: £1.60, £1.30, £4.80; EX 15.00 Trifecta £105.80 Pool: £985.18 - 6.89 winning units..
Owner Hamdan Al Maktoum **Bred** W And R Barnett Ltd **Trained** Lambourn, Berks

FOCUS
Last year a division of this maiden was won by Western Aristocrat, a recent Grade 1 winner in the US. This latest edition looked a good race, although the time was 0.67 seconds slower than the opening fillies' maiden. The winner is rated just above her pre-race mark. Again the action unfolded up the middle.

NOTEBOOK
Ellaal, beaten 6l by Spiritual Star (well held in Dewhurst next time) over C&D on his debut, improved on that form with a hard-fought success, his experience crucial as he edged out a newcomer. A Derby entrant, he's clearly quite useful. (op 9-4 tchd 11-4)
Periphery(USA), out of the owner's Yorkshire Oaks winner Punctilious, travelled nicely up with the pace and kept on for pressure, but just found the winner, who had the benefit of a previous run, too strong. He looks a decent prospect. (op 9-2)
Forgotten Hero(IRE), a 110,000euros purchase, showed plenty of ability, running on from much further back than the front two after meeting trouble. He's potentially useful, but he had a cross-noseband fitted, was a bit keen early and his head was a touch high under pressure, so he'll have to prove he can go on from this. (op 20-1)
Opera Flute(IRE), a promising second on his debut over 6f at Goodwood (the fifth, from the same stable, won next time), ran okay without building on that form over this extra furlong. (op 5-2 tchd 11-4 in places)
Johnno showed up quite well after 68 days off. This was his third start and he could make a useful handicapper in due course. (tchd 22-1)
Fast Or Free, a 26,000gns half-brother to five winners, out of a 5f scorer, travelled well to a point.
Saloomy, a 55,000gns purchase, never threatened, but he's bred to do better being the first foal of a successful sprinter who is a sister to Abbaye winner Avonbridge. (op 14-1)
Solemn Oath(USA) ◆, a $60,000 half-brother to two winners in North American, raced off the pace after starting slowly and his rider was took a while to get serious, but the colt kept on without getting a hard ride. He has a fair amount of ability.
Strictly Private was extremely green, needing to be ridden along for most of the way, but he made modest late progress.

6952 EXPRESS CAFES HOUGHTON CONDITIONS STKS 1m
2:30 (2:31) (Class 2) 2-Y-O **£7,470** (£2,236; £1,118; £559; £279) **Stalls** Low

Form RPR

3242 **1** **Lord Ofthe Shadows (IRE)**[21] 6464 2-9-3 93........ RyanMoore 3 101
(Richard Hannon) *t.k.h: chsd ldr for 2f: chsd ldrs after tl rdn to chal ent fnl f: drvn to ld jst ins fnl f: styd on wl* **9/4²**

1233 **2** *1 ¾* **Leqqaa (USA)**[46] 5709 2-9-3 93........ RichardHills 1 97
(Mark Johnston) *led: rdn 3f out: hrd pressed ent fnl f: hdd jst ins fnl f: no ex and styd on same pce after* **13/8¹**

1210 **3** *6* **Jubilance (IRE)**[32] 6170 2-9-1 87........(v¹) WilliamBuick 2 81
(Jeremy Noseda) *chsd ldr after 2f: rdn and unable qck ent fnl 2f: edgd rt u.p and btn 1f out: fdd fnl 100yds* **10/3³**

1106 **4** *6* **Red Seventy**[27] 6270 2-9-8 98.. JimmyFortune 5 74
(Richard Hannon) *hld up in tch in last pair: rdn and little rspnse over 2f out: wl btn over 1f out* **11/2**

5L50 **5** *13* **Thecornishcockney**[34] 6100 2-8-12 74....................(b) StevieDonohoe 6 34
(John Ryan) *taken down early and ponied to s: stdd s: t.k.h and hld up in last pair: rdn wl over 2f out: sn btn and wl bhd* **50/1**

1m 36.62s (-1.98) **Going Correction** -0.20s/f (Firm) 2y crse rec **5** Ran SP% **109.3**
Speed ratings (Par 101): **101,99,93,87,74**
CSF £6.22 TOTE £2.80: £1.60, £1.30; EX 6.20.
Owner Richard Hitchcock Alan King **Bred** Max Morris **Trained** East Everleigh, Wilts

FOCUS
The stalls were on the far side, yet they all gradually edged left, ending up against the near rail. A small field for this conditions race, but Listed form in all but name. The winner is rated back to his best and the runner-up stepped up slightly on recent efforts.

NOTEBOOK
Lord Ofthe Shadows(IRE) was a bit keen early, but the race rather fell apart and he had enough left to readily take advantage. He probably won't be easy to place in Britain next year and it wouldn't surprise if he was sold to race abroad. (tchd 5-2)
Leqqaa(USA), third in Listed company on his last two starts, was hassled by Jubilance and readily swept aside late on. This was a disappointing performance from Mark Johnston's runner. (op 2-1)
Jubilance(IRE), who had a visor on for the first time, was in trouble when off the bridle over 3f out and ran a tame race on this step up in trip. (op 7-2)
Red Seventy had the same chance at the weights as Leqqaa but he ran a shocker. (op 9-2)

6953 WARRENS OF WARWICK MAIDEN STKS (DIV I) 1m
3:05 (3:06) (Class 4) 2-Y-O **£3,557** (£1,058; £529; £264) **Stalls** Low

Form RPR

1 **Kiz Kulesi** 2-9-3 0.. AhmedAjtebi 7 80+
(Mahmood Al Zarooni) *t.k.h: w ldr: ev ch and rn green over 1f out: rdn to ld 1f out: styd on strly fnl 150yds* **14/1**

2 *1 ½* **Danchai** 2-9-3 0.. TedDurcan 6 77+
(David Lanigan) *hld up in tch: rdn and hdwy 2f out: swtchd lft and hdwy to press ldrs over 1f out: edging rt 1f out: chsd wnr and styd on same pce fnl 150yds* **16/1**

03 **3** *2 ½* **Paloma's Prince (IRE)**[50] 5579 2-9-3 0........................... PatCosgrave 9 71
(Jim Boyle) *led: rdn and hrd pressed over 1f out: hdd 1f out: wknd fnl 150yds: eased cl home* **14/1**

0 **4** *½* **Autarch (USA)**[40] 5891 2-9-3 0... JimCrowley 4 70
(Amanda Perrett) *chsd ldrs: rdn over 2f out: unable qck over 1f out: plugged on same pce and no imp after* **40/1**

5 *½* **Silent Moment (USA)** 2-8-12 0..................................... FrankieDettori 2 64+
(Saeed Bin Suroor) *hld up in tch towards rr: hdwy to chse ldrs over 2f out: rdn and nt qckn over 1f out: styd on same pce* **5/4**[1]

0 **6** *5* **Opinion (IRE)**[35] 6064 2-9-3 0.. RyanMoore 1 59+
(Sir Michael Stoute) *in tch in midfield: rdn and chsd ldrs over 2f out: struggling and unable qck 2f out: wknd over 1f out* **8/1**[3]

0 **7** *½* **Kenmay (IRE)**[25] 6334 2-9-3 0.. MartinDwyer 11 56+
(Brian Meehan) *chsd ldrs: rdn and struggling 3f out: wknd 2f out* **33/1**

8 *1 ¼* **Al Mamzar (IRE)** 2-9-3 0.. JamieSpencer 12 53
(David Simcock) *t.k.h: hld up in tch: rdn over 2f out: sn btn* **10/1**

9 *½* **Northern Outlook** 2-9-3 0.. JimmyFortune 8 52+
(Andrew Balding) *s.i.s: sn niggled along in last trio: nvr trbld ldrs* **14/1**

10 *13* **Umayyad (IRE)** 2-9-3 0... WilliamBuick 13 22
(John Gosden) *wnt lft s: sn pushed along and rn green in rr: wl bhd fnl 2f* **5/1**[2]

11 *¾* **Phantom Ranch** 2-9-3 0... TomQueally 3 20
(Mark H Tompkins) *t.k.h: hld up in midfield: lost pl and struggling 4f out: wl bhd over 2f out* **100/1**

0 **12** *8* **Tarkoor**[26] 6300 2-9-3 0... RichardMullen 10 2
(Peter Chapple-Hyam) *in tch in midfield: rdn and struggling 3f out: sn wl btn and bhd fnl 2f: eased ins fnl f* **66/1**

13 *3 ½* **Daleel (IRE)** 2-9-3 0... RichardHills 5 —
(John Dunlop) *s.i.s: nvr gng wl and a bhd: lost tch 1/2-way: eased fnl f: t.o* **28/1**

1m 38.06s (-0.54) **Going Correction** -0.20s/f (Firm) **13** Ran SP% **118.5**
Speed ratings (Par 97): **94,92,90,89,89 84,83,82,81,68 68,60,56**
toteswingers:1&2:£23.30, 1&3:£20.90, 2&3:£28.00 CSF £209.36 TOTE £20.60: £4.90, £4.90, £2.80; EX 262.20 Trifecta £312.00 Pool: £045.00 - 2.00 winning units..
Owner Godolphin **Bred** Darley **Trained** Newmarket, Suffolk

FOCUS
The most notable winner of this maiden in the last decade was Proclamation, who won the following year's Sussex Stakes. The bare form of this running doesn't look all that strong and the time was 0.45 seconds slower than the second leg. A nice start from the winner though, with the third setting the standard. They raced up the middle of the track.

NOTEBOOK
Kiz Kulesi made a winning start despite being keen early and displaying an ungainly action. He was always up with the pace and won the in the manner of a galloper rather than a quickener. Related to some nice types in France, he is out of a winner at up to Group 2 level over 1m and he could be decent if strengthening up and learning to gallop in a more orthodox manner. (op 16-1)
Danchai, whose sales price decreased from 135,000gns to 95,000gns, made a pleasing introduction and should come on plenty. (op 14-1)
Paloma's Prince(IRE) had been absent since finishing a fair third on his second start in August. He confirmed he has plenty of ability, keeping on after being well placed. (tchd 12-1)
Autarch(USA) was beaten a long way into last on his debut at Sandown and this was a marked improvement. (op 33-1)
Silent Moment(USA), the only filly in the line-up, is a half-sister to multiple US Grade 1 dirt winner Congaree and was strongly supported in the market. However, she travelled just okay and was one-paced for pressure. Presumably she's thought capable of better. (op 7-4)
Opinion(IRE) weakened tamely, not building on his Yarmouth debut, and his yard remains without a winner in October. (op 6-1 tchd 17-2)
Kenmay(IRE) showed up well to a point and offered more than on his debut. (op 40-1 tchd 25-1)
Northern Outlook was not given anything like a hard ride on this debut and can do a lot better in time. (op 12-1)
Umayyad(IRE), a 150,000gns Montjeu colt, was never striding out well and William Buick seemed to be looking down in closing stages. Something might have been amiss. (op 13-2)
Daleel(IRE) Official explanation: jockey said colt moved poorly

6954 WARRENS OF WARWICK MAIDEN STKS (DIV II) 1m
3:40 (3:41) (Class 4) 2-Y-O **£3,557** (£1,058; £529; £264) **Stalls** Low

Form RPR

0 **1** **Pembrey**[95] 4080 2-9-3 0.. AhmedAjtebi 4 84
(Mahmood Al Zarooni) *chsd ldrs: rdn and effrt wl over 1f out: ev ch over 1f out: led ins fnl f: hld on wl towards fin* **20/1**

05 **2** *shd* **Mubaraza (IRE)**[68] 5013 2-9-3 0...................................... RichardHills 11 84
(John Dunlop) *pressed ldr thrght: rdn wl over 1f out: ev ch whn edgd rt and bmpd rival jst ins fnl f: kpt on wl towards fin: jst hld* **7/2**[2]

32 **3** *1 ¾* **Yaa Salam**[16] 6588 2-9-3 0... FrankieDettori 7 80
(Mahmood Al Zarooni) *chsd ldrs: rdn 3f out: ev ch 2f out: led narrowly over 1f out: wandered: bmpd rival and edgd lft jst ins fnl f: sn hdd: wknd fnl 50yds* **5/2**[1]

4 **4** *4* **Engrossing**[27] 6267 2-9-3 0.. PaulHanagan 2 71+
(David Elsworth) *t.k.h: hld up in midfield: effrt to chal ldrs over 1f out: sn no prog and btn 1f out* **7/2**[2]

2 **5** *1 ½* **Teide Peak (IRE)**[14] 6630 2-9-3 0.. JoeFanning 5 67
(Mark Johnston) *led: rdn 2f out: hdd and unable qck whn short of room over 1f out: sn btn: fdd fnl f* **9/1**

0 **6** *1* **Man Of Plenty**[35] 6059 2-9-3 0... DaneO'Neill 1 65+
(John Dunlop) *s.i.s: hld up in tch in last trio: rdn and struggling 3f out: no ch w ldrs but plugged on fnl 2f* **66/1**

7 *1 ½* **Between The Lines (IRE)** 2-9-3 0...................................... RyanMoore 8 62+
(Sir Michael Stoute) *chsd ldrs: rdn and struggling over 3f out: wknd over 2f out: wl btn fnl 2f* **20/1**

8 *3 ½* **Just When** 2-9-3 0.. JimmyFortune 9 54
(Andrew Balding) *v.s.a: hld up in last trio: rdn and struggling over 3f out: wknd and bhd fnl 2f* **25/1**

9 *nk* **Top Billing** 2-9-3 0... WilliamBuick 10 53
(John Gosden) *wnt rt s and s.i.s: hld up in last trio: struggling over 3f out: bhd fnl 2f* **13/2**[3]

10 *23* **Actor (IRE)** 2-9-3 0...(t) EddieAhern 3 —
(Jeremy Noseda) *in tch tl rdn and struggling over 3f out: wl bhd 2f out: t.o and eased ins fnl f* **25/1**

11 *1 ¼* **Princess Spirit** 2-8-12 0... MarcHalford 13 —
(Edward Creighton) *in tch in midfield tl lost pl 1/2-way: wl bhd fnl 2f: t.o and eased ins fnl f* **100/1**

1m 37.61s (-0.99) **Going Correction** -0.20s/f (Firm) **11** Ran SP% **116.0**
Speed ratings (Par 97): **96,95,94,90,88 87,86,82,82,59 58**
toteswingers:1&2:£19.30, 1&3:£8.90, 2&3:£3.10 CSF £83.31 TOTE £28.20: £4.60, £2.10, £1.10; EX 123.70 Trifecta £368.30 Pool: £1,115.02 - 2.24 winning units..
Owner Godolphin **Bred** Hascombe And Valiant Studs **Trained** Newmarket, Suffolk

FOCUS
The time was 0.45 seconds quicker than the first division. Again they tended to race up the middle. The form is rated slightly on the positive side with the first three all improvers.

NOTEBOOK
Pembrey had been absent since failing to beat a rival when favourite for his debut over 7f on easy ground at Haydock in July. He was dismissed in the betting this time, and his connections also had the market leader, but he kept finding for pressure. There may be more to come. (op 16-1)
Mubaraza(IRE) ◆ showed ability at the July course on his first two starts but had been off for 68 days. This was a promising return, just failing after being bumped by the third near the line, though he didn't look unlucky. He could be quite decent over middle-distances and maybe even further next year. (tchd 4-1)
Yaa Salam probably ran to a similar level as on his first two starts, but that wasn't good enough. (op 7-2)
Engrossing didn't build on the form of his recent C&D debut, racing a bit keenly and not going with the front three. (op 4-1)
Teide Peak(IRE), who ran green when runner-up on his debut under similar conditions at Nottingham, failed to go on from that, weakening disappointingly late on. (op 7-1)
Man Of Plenty ◆ caught the eye keeping on well much too late and is an interesting handicap prospect for longer trips next year. He needs one more run for a mark.

6955 THOROUGHBRED BREEDERS' ASSOCIATION CONDITIONS STKS 1m
4:10 (4:14) (Class 2) 3-Y-O+
£11,205 (£3,355; £1,677; £838; £419; £210) **Stalls** Low

Form RPR

4056 **1** **Inler (IRE)**[9] 6747 4-9-2 103...(b) JimmyFortune 5 108
(Brian Meehan) *mde all: clr after 2f: pressed and looked vulnerable 1f out: edgd lft but kpt on wl ins fnl f* **11/1**

1042 **2** *1* **Secrecy**[23] 6416 5-9-5 109... FrankieDettori 3 109
(Saeed Bin Suroor) *hld up in last trio: swtchd lft and hdwy 1/2-way: rdn to chse ldr 2f out: pressing wnr 1f out: no ex and hld fnl 100yds* **5/4**[1]

0112 **3** *2 ¾* **Stevie Thunder**[25] 6339 6-9-2 95............ PaulHanagan 1 00
(Ian Williams) *in tch in midfield: rdn and effrt over 2f out: 3rd and styd on same pce fr over 1f out* **7/2**[2]

10-0 **4** *2 ½* **Mantoba**[207] 998 3-8-13 105...(t) MartinDwyer 2 94
(Brian Meehan) *chsd ldr tl 1/2-way: rdn and outpcd over 2f out: plugged on same pce and no threat to ldrs fnl 2f* **16/1**

6-00 **5** *½* **Emirates Dream (USA)**[34] 6080 4-9-2 94...................(v1) WilliamBuick 4 92
(Saeed Bin Suroor) *hld up in last pair: effrt over 2f out: no prog 2f out and no threat to ldrs fr over 1f out* **10/1**

2000 **6** *2* **Tinkertown (IRE)**[53] 5466 3-8-13 96................................ JamieSpencer 6 88
(Roger Varian) *chsd ldrs: rdn and lost pl over 3f out: no prog u.p and wl hld 2f out* **11/1**

5254 **7** *2* **Fury**[95] 4096 3-8-13 104... KierenFallon 8 83
(William Haggas) *hld up in tch: hdwy to chse wnr 1/2-way tl rdn and fnd little over 2f out: lost 2nd 2f out and sn btn: wknd* **5/1**[3]

1m 35.18s (-3.42) **Going Correction** -0.20s/f (Firm)
WFA 3 from 4yo+ 3lb **7** Ran SP% **115.0**
Speed ratings (Par 109): **109,108,105,102,102 100,98**
toteswingers:1&2:£4.00, 1&3:£6.80, 2&3:£1.60 CSF £25.66 TOTE £14.50: £6.40, £1.10; EX 33.00 Trifecta £344.50 Pool: £1,527.31 - 3.28 winning units..
Owner Sangster Partnership **Bred** D And J Cantillon & C & K Canning **Trained** Manton, Wilts

FOCUS
Typically muddling conditions race form which shouldn't be taken too literally. The action unfolded far side.

NOTEBOOK
Inler(IRE) offered nothing in first-time blinkers in a similar race over 7f at Salisbury on his previous start, but he was helped by a combination of factors this time. The headgear was retained, he was up in trip and, most crucially of all, he was allowed an uncontested lead. He would have been 6lb worse off with the runner-up in a handicap and this might boost his confidence. (op 16-1)
Secrecy probably didn't run to his official mark of 109, but he deserves credit for being the only horse to get near front-running winner. (tchd 6-4 in a place and 13-8 in places)
Stevie Thunder, having his first start since running a fine second from a poor draw in the Cambridgeshire, wasn't obviously well placed considering he had plenty to find at the weights. He ran well, but would have been 11lb better off with the runner-up in a handicap, and 5lb better off with the winner.
Mantoba reportedly swallowed his tongue when last in the UAE Derby back in March. This was a respectable reintroduction. (op 12-1)
Emirates Dream(USA) raced keenly in a first-time visor (replacing cheekpieces) and carried his tail awkwardly. He looks best avoided for now. (op 12-1 tchd 14-1)

Fury showed no benefit for his three-month break and has totally lost his way. (tchd 9-2 and 11-2)

6956 MC SEAFOODS & NORFOLK ICE CREAM MAIDEN AUCTION STKS 1m
4:45 (4:45) (Class 5) 2-Y-O £3,234 (£962; £481; £240) Stalls Low

Form				RPR
00	1		**Bank On Me**[34] 6100 2-8-10 0 ....(t) RichardKingscote 13 (Philip McBride) *wnt lft s and s.i.s: sn rcvrd and chsd ldrs: led over 5f out: mde rest: rdn 2f out: clr over 1f out: tiring towards fin but a holding on* **25/1**	79
02	2	1 1/2	**Quizzed**[19] 6506 2-8-8 0 .... WilliamBuick 11 (Edward Vaughan) *chsd ldrs: rdn and sltly outpcd over 2f out: chsd clr wnr and drvn 1f out: kpt on fnl 100yds: nvr looked like getting to wnr* **3/1**[2]	74
653	3	1 3/4	**Haafhd Handsome**[9] 6743 2-8-10 0 .... RyanMoore 6 (Richard Hannon) *led tl over 5f out: chsd wnr after: rdn and nt qckn 2f out: plugged on same pce and no imp on wnr fr over 1f out: lost 2nd 1f out* **2/1**[1]	72
203	4	1 1/4	**Let Your Love Flow (IRE)**[19] 6506 2-8-7 0 .... JamesDoyle 5 (Sylvester Kirk) *in tch: rdn over 2f out: outpcd 2f out: 4th and wl hld over 1f out: plugged on ins fnl f* **12/1**	66
4	5	1/2	**Mr Fong**[11] 6697 2-8-13 0 .... MartinLane 8 (David Simcock) *in tch: rdn and effrt and rdn over 2f out: 5th and wl hld over 1f out: plugged on same pce after* **10/1**[3]	71
	6	2 3/4	**San Mambo** 2-8-13 0 .... AdamKirby 10 (Marco Botti) *in tch towards rr: rdn and effrt over 2f out: 6th and no threat to ldrs fr over 1f out* **10/1**[3]	65+
002	7	4 1/2	**Thecornishcowboy**[12] 6663 2-8-10 62 .... KirstyMilczarek 1 (John Ryan) *in tch: rdn and outpcd over 2f out: wkng whn n.m.r 2f out: wl btn over 1f out* **40/1**	51
	8	2	**Curly Come Home** 2-8-4 0 .... ChrisCatlin 12 (Chris Wall) *hld up in tch towards rr: rdn and effrt 3f out: sn struggling: wknd jst over 2f out: no ch over 1f out* **66/1**	41
40	9	1	**Marah Music**[33] 6123 2-9-0 0 .... SteveDrowne 3 (Peter Makin) *in tch in midfield on far side: rdn and outpcd wl over 2f out: wknd 2f out and no ch after* **16/1**	48
	10	2 3/4	**Underwritten** 2-8-11 0 .... JimmyFortune 4 (Andrew Balding) *s.i.s: a in rr: rdn and struggling 3f out: sn wl btn* **10/1**[3]	39+
5	11	1/2	**Shredding (IRE)**[28] 6244 2-8-12 0 .... PaulHanagan 9 (William Haggas) *chsd ldrs: rdn 3f out: struggling whn edgd rt and short of room jst over 2f out: sn wknd: wl btn and eased ins fnl f* **11/1**	42
00	12	3	**Search And Rescue (USA)**[19] 6506 2-8-11 0 .... DaneO'Neill 2 (J W Hills) *in tch towards rr on far side: rdn and struggling 3f out: sn wknd: wl bhd fnl 2f* **50/1**	31
	13	20	**Zarosa (IRE)** 2-7-12 0 .... HannahNunn(7) 7 (John Berry) *s.i.s: a in rr: lost tch 1/2-way: t.o* **100/1**	—

1m 38.33s (-0.27) **Going Correction** -0.20s/f (Firm) 13 Ran SP% 118.2
Speed ratings (Par 95): **93,91,89,88,88 85,80,78,77,75 74,71,51**
toteswingers:1&2:£22.60, 1&3:£14.50, 2&3:£2.90 CSF £96.72 TOTE £46.40: £8.30, £1.40, £1.40; EX 200.50 Trifecta £665.30 Pool: £1,330.69 - 1.48 winning units..
Owner PMRacing **Bred** Cheveley Park Stud Ltd **Trained** Newmarket, Suffolk

FOCUS
An auction maiden and the form doesn't look strong by Newmarket standards. The time was the slowest of the five 1m races, and they raced up the middle. The third and fourth help support the level of the form.

NOTEBOOK
Bank On Me had shown moderate form on his first two starts, but he improved a good deal for the first-time tongue-tie and won with more authority than the margin suggests, quickening well to go clear before idling. It's hard to know exactly what to make of this performance, but he looks of at least fair ability. (op 28-1 tchd 33-1 in places)
Quizzed plugged on but was always held. She now has the option of handicaps. (op 7-2)
Haafhd Handsome looked thoroughly awkward, carrying his head a bit high, wandering around and giving the odd flash of his tail. (tchd 7-4)
Let Your Love Flow(IRE) was held by Quizzed on their Wolverhampton meeting and so it proved.
Mr Fong travelled okay but was one-paced for pressure. He should find his level in handicaps. (op 12-1 tchd 9-1)
San Mambo, a 22,000gns half-brother to four winners, made a moderate introduction. (tchd 9-1)
Shredding(IRE) Official explanation: jockey said gelding lost its action

6957 THAI STREET CAFE NURSERY 1m 1f
5:20 (5:20) (Class 4) (0-85,84) 2-Y-O £3,881 (£1,155; £577; £288) Stalls Low

Form				RPR
1	1		**Main Sequence (USA)**[34] 6100 2-9-6 79 .... TedDurcan 3 (David Lanigan) *stdd s and dropped in bhd: hld up in rr: swtchd lft and effrt over 2f out: pressed ldrs and edgd rt over 1f out: led 1f out: flashed tail but readily drew clr fnl 150yds: comf* **7/2**[1]	90+
1	2	3 1/4	**Open Water (FR)**[35] 6059 2-9-6 79 .... JimmyFortune 7 (Andrew Balding) *in tch: effrt over 2f out: chsng ldrs and drvn over 1f out: no ch w wnr but kpt on to go 2nd fnl 50yds* **8/1**	81+
2133	3	3/4	**Mizbah**[36] 6031 2-9-3 76 .... (p) DaneO'Neill 1 (Saeed Bin Suroor) *led: rdn and hung lft over 1f out: hdd 1f out: nt pce of wnr and styd on same pce after: lost 2nd fnl 50yds* **12/1**	77
3011	4	1	**Poetic Lord**[10] 6724 2-9-11 84 6ex .... RyanMoore 13 (Richard Hannon) *chsd ldrs: wnt 2nd 3f out: ev ch whn n.m.r over 1f out: outpcd by wnr jst ins fnl f: kpt on same pce* **9/2**[2]	83
2332	5	hd	**Surfer (USA)**[29] 6230 2-9-6 79 .... AhmedAjtebi 6 (Mahmood Al Zarooni) *in tch: rdn: racd awkwardly and outpcd 2f out: styd on again ins fnl f: no ch w wnr* **12/1**	77+
01	6	2 1/4	**Fennell Bay (IRE)**[14] 6630 2-9-2 75 .... FrankieDettori 10 (Mahmood Al Zarooni) *chsd ldr tl 3f out: rdn and unable qck jst over 2f out: btn over 1f out: wknd fnl f* **8/1**	69
0511	7	nk	**Come On Blue Chip (IRE)**[12] 6667 2-9-7 80 .... (b) PaulHanagan 2 (Paul D'Arcy) *hld up in tch towards rr: rdn and effrt wl over 2f out: no imp tl plugged on ins fnl f: nvr threatened ldrs* **7/1**[3]	73
631	8	shd	**Winner's Wish**[23] 6400 2-9-6 79 .... WilliamBuick 11 (Jeremy Noseda) *in tch: rdn and unable qck wl over 2f out: outpcd and flashing tail u.p 2f out: kpt on same pce and no threat to ldrs after* **20/1**	72
2031	9	1 1/2	**That's Dangerous**[27] 6268 2-9-4 80 .... JohnFahy(3) 9 (Roger Charlton) *hld up in tch: effrt and clsd 3f out: rdn and struggling over 2f out: wknd 2f out* **12/1**	70
1500	10	7	**Pearl Charm (USA)**[39] 5931 2-9-6 79 .... RichardMullen 5 (Richard Hannon) *in tch towards rr: rdn and struggling 3f out: wknd u.p over 1f out: wl btn and eased ins fnl f* **40/1**	58
612	11	4 1/2	**Tingo In The Tale (IRE)**[54] 5446 2-9-5 78 .... JamesDoyle 12 (David Arbuthnot) *chsd ldrs: rdn and unable qck over 2f out: wknd wl over 1f out: wl btn and eased ins fnl f* **11/1**	48
044	12	15	**Tallevu (IRE)**[25] 6334 2-9-2 75 .... RichardKingscote 4 (Tom Dascombe) *chsd ldrs: rdn and losing pl 3f out: lost tch 2f out: t.o fnl f* **12/1**	12

1m 50.44s (-1.26) **Going Correction** -0.20s/f (Firm) 12 Ran SP% 121.4
Speed ratings (Par 97): **97,94,93,92,92 90,90,90,88,82 78,65**
toteswingers:1&2:£6.90, 1&3:£15.10, 2&3:£27.70 CSF £32.46 CT £315.21 TOTE £5.20: £2.30, £3.20, £5.00; EX 31.20 Trifecta £797.30 Part won. Pool: £1,077.52 - 0.54 winning units..
Owner Niarchos Family **Bred** Flaxman Holdings Ltd **Trained** Lambourn, Berks

FOCUS
Once more the action unfolded centre-field. This was a quality nursery - plenty of powerful connections were represented and seven of the first nine finishers had won last time. Solid form, with a nice performance from the winner.

NOTEBOOK
Main Sequence(USA) ◆ stayed on from well off the pace to make a winning debut at 50-1 over 1m at Yarmouth (third-placed Yaa Salam beaten favourite in 3.40 on this card) and repeated the trick to follow up. It was disconcerting he flashed his tail under pressure, but he has now twice shown he possess a well-above average sustained finishing kick, staying on most powerfully having taken a while to get going when first asked. He has the scope to make a fine older horse and should stay further, so it wouldn't surprise if he don't see him again this term and he turns up in something quite a bit better next year. (op 4-1 tchd 9-2)
Open Water(FR), a debut winner over 1m at Sandown, ran a solid race behind a potentially smart type. He could be one for valuable handicaps next year. (tchd 7-1)
Mizbah was allowed the run of the race in front and looks a bit flattered. (op 14-1)
Poetic Lord was on a hat-trick, but he had everything go his way when successful at Goodwood last time. Despite being 3lb well in, this was a tough ask under top weight and he performed creditably in defeat. (tchd 4-1)
Surfer(USA) carried his head high and is now 0-5. (tchd 14-1)
Fennell Bay(IRE) couldn't follow up his Nottingham maiden win. The form of that race was let down by the runner-up, Teide Park, who was only fifth in the 3.40 on this card. (op 15-2 tchd 7-1)
Come On Blue Chip(IRE) was on a hat-trick after two Polytrack wins, but he was up 10lb for the latest and faced with much stiffer company. He travelled strongly but found little. (op 8-1)
Winner's Wish couldn't muster the required pace and flashed her tail late on. (op 16-1)
Tingo In The Tale(IRE) travelled nicely enough but didn't stride out well in the closing stages. His maiden win came on soft ground. (op 14-1)
Tallevu(IRE) Official explanation: jockey said colt ran flat
T/Plt: £58.90 to a £1 stake. Pool:£74,408.85 - 920.70 winning tickets T/Qpdt: £21.80 to a £1 stake Pool:£4,267.62 - 144.80 w. tckts SP

6958a - (Foreign Racing) - See Page 1388

6941 DEAUVILLE (R-H)
Wednesday, October 19
OFFICIAL GOING: Turf: heavy: fibresand: standard

6959a PRIX DE LA FORET DE LYONS (H'CAP) (4YO+) (TURF) 6f 110y(S)
3:10 (12:00) 4-Y-0+ £8,620 (£3,448; £2,586; £1,724; £862)

			RPR
1		**Akton City (FR)**[19] 4-9-6 0 .... MaximeGuyon 9 (J-P Delaporte, France) **51/10**[1]	73
2	hd	**Baratom (FR)**[59] 5-9-6 0 .... AlexisBadel 6 (F-X De Chevigny, France) **21/1**	73
3	1	**Lisselan Prospect (USA)**[54] 6-9-0 0 ....(b) Roberto-CarlosMontenegro 7 (Mme J Bidgood, France) **23/1**	64
4	hd	**Gino Vanilli (FR)**[391] 7-9-0 0 .... FabriceVeron 17 (F Seguin, France) **9/1**[3]	63
5	snk	**Sky Skipper (IRE)**[19] 4-9-1 0 ....(b) MickaelBarzalona 5 (G Doleuze, France) **10/1**	64
6	1 1/4	**Prorisks (FR)**[132] 2867 5-9-1 0 .... Pierre-CharlesBoudot 13 (C Boutin, France) **19/1**	60
7	1/2	**Stay Cool (FR)**[60] 5-9-0 0 ....(b) GregoryBenoist 14 (D Smaga, France) **13/1**	58
8	3/4	**Montpazier (FR)**[1273] 7-8-11 0 ....(p) JohanVictoire 10 (W Walton, France) **9/1**[3]	53
9	nk	**Alpina (FR)**[60] 5-9-3 0 .... ThierryThulliez 11 (J-V Toux, France) **11/1**	58
10	snk	**Versaki (IRE)**[47] 5-8-6 0 ....(b) AntoineCoutier(3) 4 (J Clais, France) **23/1**	49
0		**Dawaraki (FR)**[539] 7-8-11 0 .... OlivierPeslier 16 (F Seguin, France) **15/1**	—
0		**Good Bye My Friend (FR)**[26] 5-8-13 0 ....(b[1]) BenjaminBoutin(5) 1 (C Boutin, France) **12/1**	—
0		**Swans A Swimming (IRE)**[138] 5-9-1 0 .... GaetanMasure 8 (Stal Garbo, Belgium) **36/1**	—
0		**Let It Rock (IRE)**[223] 831 4-9-3 0 .... DavyBonilla 15 (Mrs K Burke) *racd freely on wd outside: rdn over 2 1/2f out: no rspnse: wknd qckly* **22/1**	—
0		**Lisselan Rightcall (USA)**[41] 7-9-4 0 ....(b) ChristopheSoumillon 3 (Mme J Bidgood, France) **53/10**[2]	—
0		**Toccata Jem (FR)**[156] 4-9-0 0 .... AntoineHamelin 2 (D Sepulchre, France) **35/1**	—

1m 19.8s (2.60) 16 Ran SP% 118.5
WIN (incl. 1 euro stake): 6.10. PLACES: 2.50, 4.60, 4.90. DF: 71.50. SF: 98.00.
Owner J-P Delaporte **Bred** Pierre Camus Denais **Trained** France

6960 - 6966a (Foreign Racing) - See Raceform Interactive

GEELONG (L-H)
Wednesday, October 19
OFFICIAL GOING: Turf: good to soft

6967a CENTREBET GEELONG CUP (GROUP 3 H'CAP) (3YO+) (TURF) 1m 4f
6:00 (12:00) 3-Y-0+ £98,039 (£26,470; £13,235; £6,617; £3,676; £2,941)

			RPR
1		**Dunaden (FR)**[59] 5304 5-9-2 0 .... CraigAWilliams 8 (M Delzangles, France) *w.w towards rr: hdwy on outside over 2 1/2f out: r.o strly st to ld ins fnl f: pushed out* **5/1**[3]	117
2	3/4	**Tanby (AUS)**[11] 6711 5-8-5 0 ....(t) StevenKing 6 (Robert Hickmott, Australia) *chsd ldng pair: hrd rdn 1 1/2f out: r.o to go 2nd ins fnl f: no ex fnl 75yds* **21/10**[1]	105

3 ¾ **Bauer (IRE)**[11] 6711 8-8-11 **0**.......... DamienOliver 9 110
(Luca Cumani) *hld up in midfield: shuffled bk to rr of main gp 2f out: rdn and twice swtchd outside after 1 1/2f out (lost momentum 2nd time): 8th ent fnl f: styd on strly fnl 110yds: nrest at fin* **9/2**[2]

4 ½ **Showcause (AUS)**[193] 6-8-6 **0**..........(b) LukeNolen 13 104
(Frank Ritchie, New Zealand) *racd in midfield: scrubbed along over 2f out: 5th and u.p over 1 1/2f out: kpt on u.p: nt pce to chal* **12/1**

5 *shd* **Perfect Pecs (AUS)**[354] 7247 4-8-5 **0**..........(bt) DeanYendall 7 105
(Rick Hore-Lacy, Australia) *pressed ldr: led over 3f out: 2 l clr and rdn over 1 1/2f out: hdd ins fnl f: fdd fnl 75yds* **30/1**

6 *nk* **Back In Black (NZ)**[18] 6-8-5 **0**.......... CraigNewitt 5 102
(John Steffert, New Zealand) *settled towards rr on rail:* **30/1**

7 ¾ **Spechenka (AUS)**[18] 6-8-6 **0** ow1.......... MichaelWalker 10 102
(Ben Ahrens, Australia) *hld up towards rr: 9th and pushed along 2 1/2f out: effrt on outside 2f out: kpt on fnl f: nt pce to get on terms* **30/1**

8 *1* **I'm Jake (NZ)**[32] 6-8-5 **0**..........(v) DwayneDunn 1 99
(David Brideoake & David Feek, Australia) *racd keenly in bhd two ldrs: 4th and gng wl 2f out: rdn and nt qckn over 1 1/2f out: fdd fnl f* **8/1**

9 ¾ **Hume (NZ)**[25] 8-8-5 **0**..........(t) StephenBaster 12 98
(David Brideoake & David Feek, Australia) *hld up towards rr: hdwy on outside 2f out: rdn and no imp fnl 1 1/2f* **40/1**

10 *7* **Red Eye Special (NZ)**[18] 5-8-5 **0**..........(b) ChrisSymons 2 87
(Anthony Cummings, Australia) *racd in midfield: rdn and nt qckn 2f out: wknd u.p* **11/1**

11 *2* **Above Average (IRE)**[32] 5-8-5 **0**..........(t) LisaCropp 11 84
(Anthony Freedman, Australia) *hld up in rr: last 1 1/2f out: nvr a factor* **9/1**

12 *hd* **Diyaraka (FR)**[330] 7546 4-8-5 **0**.......... KerrinMcEvoy 4 83
(Michael Moroney, Australia) *chsd ldrs in tch: sltly hmpd over 2f out: sn rdn and btn* **100/1**

P **Rebel Soldier (IRE)**[25] 4-8-6 **0** ow1.......... JamesWinks 3 —
(David Hayes, Australia) *sn led on rail: hdd over 3f out: grad wknd: p.u fnl f* **70/1**

2m 30.14s (150.14) **13** Ran SP% **118.8**
PARI-MUTUEL (NSW TAB - all including au$1 stakes): WIN 5.90 PLACE 2.40, 1.40, 2.10; DF 10.60; SF 24.10.
Owner Pearl Bloodstock Ltd **Bred** Comte E Decazes **Trained** France

NOTEBOOK
Dunaden(FR) booked his place in the Melbourne Cup after an impressive staying performance. A first Australian runner for trainer Mikel Delzangles and owned by Pearl Bloodstock, he came with a sustained run down the centre in the home straight to land the spoils. He carried the same winning weight as Americain last year, and became the fourth overseas-trained horse to win the Geelong Cup in ten years. He was cut to 8-1 joint-favourite for the Melbourne Cup with last year's winner Americain.
Tanby(AUS) chased the leader but could not quite get to him but is assured a place in the Melbourne Cup field, and his performance can be considered all the more impressive as he was diagnosed with colic after the race.
Bauer(IRE) had been badly held up in the race, finishing with a late run to claim third, and has qualified 42nd on the entry list for the Melbourne Cup, so will struggle to get a run.

6810 BRIGHTON (L-H)

Thursday, October 20

OFFICIAL GOING: Good to firm (good in places)
Rail dolled out 5yds from 4.5f to 2.5f adding 11yds to all distances.
Wind: Moderate, half against Weather: Sunny

6968 BETFAIR RACING EXCELLENCE APPRENTICE TRAINING SERIES H'CAP 1m 3f 196y

2:00 (2:01) (Class 6) (0-55,55) 3-Y-O+ **£1,617** (£481; £240; £120) **Stalls** High

Form RPR
4004 **1** **Beauchamp Xiara**[14] 6657 5-8-9 **50**.......... NicoleNordblad(7) 7 55+
(Hans Adielsson) *prom: lost pl 3f out: rallied over 1f out: led ins fnl f: rdn out* **11/1**

0605 **2** *1 ¼* **Galloping Queen (IRE)**[44] 5815 3-8-4 **52**.......... MartinLeonard(7) 12 55
(Sheena West) [illegible] **10/1**

6200 **3** *hd* **Chantilly Dancer (IRE)**[64] 5178 5-8-12 **46** oh1.......... MatthewLawson 5 49
(Michael Quinn) *dwlt and rdn s: hdwy on ins rail over 2f out: drvn to chal 1f out: one pce* **20/1**

0006 **4** *2 ¼* **Silent Applause**[69] 5015 8-9-2 **50**.......... DavidKenny 11 49
(Dr Jon Scargill) *bhd: rdn 3f out: styd on fnl 2f: nvr nrr* **9/1**

331- **5** ¾ **Finch Flyer (IRE)**[278] 6020 4-9-0 **55**.......... RyanDuthie(7) 3 53
(Gary Moore) *towards rr: hdwy 3f out: chal 2f out: sn outpcd* **8/1**[3]

0630 **6** *1 ¼* **So Is She (IRE)**[12] 6698 3-8-8 **52**..........(p) NatashaEaton(3) 10 48
(Alan Bailey) *hld up in last: effrt in centre wd of others over 2f out: nvr able to chal* **17/2**

3445 **7** ¾ **Fastada (IRE)**[7] 6823 3-8-4 **48**..........(v) LukeRowe(3) 2 43
(Jonathan Portman) *w ldrs tl outpcd fnl 2f* **5/1**[2]

5040 **8** ½ **Visions Of Johanna (USA)**[6] 6833 6-9-4 **52**..........(t[1]) JustinNewman 1 46
(Richard Guest) *mde most tl 2f out: sn wknd* **5/1**[2]

0030 **9** *3 ¾* **Corlough Mountain**[55] 5421 7-8-9 **46** oh1.......... JackDuern(3) 9 34
(Paddy Butler) *mid-div tl rdn and btn 2f out* **50/1**

0502 **10** *3* **Laffraaj (IRE)**[17] 6585 3-8-1 **49** oh1 ow3.......... DavidWarren(7) 8 32
(Pat Eddery) *w ldrs tl wknd wl over 1f out* **12/1**

3624 **11** *3* **Zelos Diktator**[22] 6446 5-9-1 **54**..........(p) IanBurns(5) 6 33
(Gary Moore) *mid-div: sn pushed along: bhd fnl 3f* **4/1**[1]

2m 34.13s (1.43) **Going Correction** -0.05s/f (Good)
WFA 3 from 4yo+ 7lb **11** Ran SP% **116.8**
Speed ratings (Par 101): **93,92,92,90,90 89,88,88,85,83 81**
toteswingers:1&2:£27.60, 1&3:£48.00, 2&3:£41.50 CSF £115.38 CT £2167.79 TOTE £11.70: £2.40, £5.10, £7.90; EX 124.80 TRIFECTA Not won..
Owner Erik Penser **Bred** E Penser **Trained** Kingston Lisle, Oxon
■ A first winner for apprentice Nicole Nordblad.

FOCUS
A really moderate middle-distance contest to open the card with, which forms part of the Betfair apprentices' series. Weak form, the exposed third setting a poor standard.
Silent Applause Official explanation: vet said gelding lost left-hind shoe
Zelos Diktator Official explanation: jockey said gelding never travelled

6969 RICKY HATTON HERE 9TH NOVEMBER H'CAP 1m 1f 209y

2:30 (2:32) (Class 6) (0-65,71) 3-Y-O+ **£1,617** (£481; £240; £120) **Stalls** High

Form RPR
6501 **1** **Glass Mountain (IRE)**[10] 6764 3-9-9 **69** 6ex.......... MartinLane 7 78
(James Fanshawe) *hld up in rr: hdwy 3f out: wnt 2nd over 1f out: led fnl 100yds: pushed out* **3/1**[1]

5000 **2** *nk* **Wordiness**[22] 6461 3-8-11 **64**.......... MatthewLawson(5) 12 71
(Barry Brennan) *mid-div on outer: hdwy over 4f out: led 3f out: rdn and hdd fnl 100yds: nt qckn* **9/1**

4453 **3** *3 ¾* **Prince Of Thebes (IRE)**[7] 6811 10-8-10 **51** oh5.......... TomQueally 6 52
(Michael Attwater) *dwlt: bhd: drvn along 3f out: styd on fnl 2f: wnt 3rd ins fnl f: nvr nrr* **12/1**

501 **4** *1* **Penang Cinta**[7] 6811 8-9-5 **63** 6ex.......... RichardEvans(3) 10 62
(David Evans) *prom: hrd rdn 2f out: one pce* **11/2**[3]

0604 **5** *nk* **Red Yarn**[28] 6285 4-9-10 **65**..........(b) GeorgeBaker 9 63
(Gary Moore) *prom: led 5f out tl 3f out: outpcd and btn 2f out* **7/1**

0-63 **6** *4* **Dust Cloud (IRE)**[7] 6816 3-8-9 **55**.......... JimCrowley 1 45
(Peter Winkworth) *chsd ldrs tl wknd wl over 1f out* **8/1**

4455 **7** *2 ½* **Recalcitrant**[17] 6586 8-9-1 **59**.......... KieranO'Neill(3) 2 44
(Simon Dow) *led tl 5f out: racd wd of others in centre in st: wknd over 1f out* **4/1**[2]

1040 **8** *1 ¾* **Joan D'Arc (IRE)**[20] 6503 4-9-5 **60**.......... AdamKirby 8 42
(Noel Quinlan) *in tch tl wknd 3f out* **10/1**

5000 **9** *11* **Majestueux (USA)**[177] 1582 4-8-11 **52**.......... WilliamCarson 11 12
(Mark Hoad) *hld up towards rr: drvn along and hdwy over 3f out: wknd over 2f out* **33/1**

-010 **10** *1 ½* **Mister Bit (IRE)**[15] 6622 4-9-9 **64**..........(b) LukeMorris 5 21
(John Best) *mid-div: rdn 4f out: sn wknd* **10/1**

64R0 **11** *dist* **Negotiation (IRE)**[3] 6445 5-9-5 **63**..........(v) SeanLevey(3) 3 —
(Michael Quinn) *rel to r: a t.o* **20/1**

2m 3.48s (-0.12) **Going Correction** -0.05s/f (Good)
WFA 3 from 4yo+ 5lb **11** Ran SP% **127.6**
Speed ratings (Par 101): **98,97,94,93,93 90,88,87,78,77** —
toteswingers:1&2:£9.20, 1&3:£10.10, 2&3:£19.80 CSF £34.13 CT £303.00 TOTE £3.80: £1.30, £4.90, £3.00; EX 86.60 TRIFECTA Not won..
Owner Simon Gibson **Bred** C McEvoy **Trained** Newmarket, Suffolk
■ True To Form (5/2) was withdrawn on vet's advice. Deduct 25p in the £ under R4. New market formed.

FOCUS
This race lost two runners before anything significant had happened. True To Form was withdrawn while Negotiation took virtually no interest after leaving the stalls and tailed himself off. It's doubtful it took much winning but the winner stepped up on his Yarmouth win.

6970 BRITISH STALLION STUDS SUPPORTING BRITISH RACING EBF MAIDEN STKS 7f 214y

3:05 (3:05) (Class 4) 2-Y-O **£4,722** (£1,405; £702; £351) **Stalls** Centre

Form RPR
00 **1** **Jupiter Storm**[19] 6527 2-9-3 0.......... GeorgeBaker 3 87+
(Gary Moore) *led 4f: led 2f out: rdn clr 1f out: readily* **7/2**[2]

2 *2 ½* **Henry Clay** 2-9-3 0.......... AdamKirby 1 79+
(Mark Johnston) *hld up in 4th: rdn over 2f out: chsd wnr over 1f out: no imp* **5/1**

4433 **3** *2* **Humungosaur**[17] 6572 2-9-3 94.......... ChrisCatlin 6 75
(Paul Cole) *chsd ldrs: led 4f out tl 2f out: hung lft: one pce* **2/1**[1]

6205 **4** *5* **Breaking The Bank**[33] 6165 2-9-3 75..........(p) MartinDwyer 7 65
(William Muir) *hld up in rr: hdwy 3f out: wknd over 1f out* **5/1**

334 **5** *10* **Persidha**[22] 6449 2-8-12 69.......... DavidProbert 2 37
(Gay Kelleway) *trckd ldrs in 3rd: wknd wl over 1f out* **9/2**[3]

1m 35.2s (-0.80) **Going Correction** -0.05s/f (Good) **5** Ran SP% **107.1**
Speed ratings (Par 97): **102,99,97,92,82**
CSF £18.98 TOTE £4.40: £2.90, £3.20; EX 15.50.
Owner Heart Of The South Racing **Bred** Breeding Capital, Watership Down, Farish **Trained** Lower Beeding, W Sussex

FOCUS
A good maiden considering the official mark of the favourite, but slightly weakened when two likely candidates were forced to withdraw earlier in the day.

NOTEBOOK
Jupiter Storm raced prominently and found plenty when asked to extend. He once held an entry in the Group 1 Racing Post Trophy and, while that sort of level is a long way off, he looks worthy of being tried in a higher grade now. (op 5-1)
Henry Clay, a 115,000gns yearling, seemed to know his job and stayed on in good style after being held up to make a pleasing debut. (op 9-2)
Humungosaur, officially rated 94 (and 26lb higher on RPRs than the winner), his chance was obvious, but he showed little off the bridle and gave up what looked a decent winning chance, which is a touch worrying for a horse good enough to finish third in a Deauville Listed contest in August. It might be true that he wants easier ground, but he should still have been at least good enough to finish in the first two. (op 13-8 tchd 11-8)
Breaking The Bank had cheekpieces on for the first time but they didn't make a great deal of difference, and little attention should be paid to how close he got to the third. (op 11-2)
Persidha was up in trip and ran poorly. (tchd 4-1)

6971 BLAKES BUTCHER H'CAP 7f 214y

3:35 (3:35) (Class 6) (0-65,65) 3-Y-O+ **£1,617** (£481; £240; £120) **Stalls** Centre

Form RPR
6051 **1** **Methayel (IRE)**[7] 6813 3-9-3 **64** 6ex.......... TomQueally 1 76+
(Clive Brittain) *trckd ldng pair gng wl: led on bit 2f out: hrd rdn ins fnl f: r.o wl* **3/1**[1]

3403 **2** *1 ½* **Daffydowndilly**[17] 6591 3-8-13 **60**..........(t) JimCrowley 7 65
(Hughie Morrison) *bhd: rdn and hdwy 2f out: chsd wnr 1f out: nt qckn fnl 75yds* **18/1**

050 **3** *1* **On The Cusp (IRE)**[47] 5721 4-9-4 **62**..........(p) MartinHarley 11 65
(Richard Guest) *led tl 2f out: hung rt over 1f out: kpt on same pce* **16/1**

0060 **4** *shd* **Having A Ball**[106] 3741 7-8-7 **51** oh5.......... ChrisCatlin 2 54
(Jonathan Portman) *bhd: rdn over 2f out: styd on wl fnl f: nrly snatched 3rd* **40/1**

3056 **5** *nk* **Eager To Bow (IRE)**[13] 6664 5-9-6 **64**.......... GeorgeBaker 5 66
(Patrick Chamings) *hld up in 6th: hdwy 2f out: briefly wnt 2nd over 1f out: styd on same pce* **9/2**[2]

3042 **6** ¾ **Maz**[6] 6831 3-8-11 **61**.......... DominicFox(3) 9 61
(Alan Bailey) *towards rr: effrt and in tch 2f out: one pce fnl f* **9/2**[2]

2502 **7** *1 ¼* **Aviso (GER)**[7] 6814 7-8-11 **60**..........(p) MatthewCosham(5) 3 57
(David Evans) *chsd ldrs tl outpcd fnl 2f* **11/2**[3]

0300 **8** *2 ¼* **Inquisitress**[7] 6811 7-8-4 **51**.......... KieranO'Neill(3) 8 43
(John Bridger) *s.s: towards rr: hdwy over 2f out: wknd over 1f out* **14/1**

4200 **9** ¾ **Indian Violet (IRE)**[7] 6814 5-9-3 **61**.......... JamieGoldstein 10 52
(Ralph Smith) *hld up in 5th: hrd rdn and wknd 2f out* **11/1**

3102 **10** 1 ¼ **Twinkled**[13] 6664 3-8-11 **65**........ IanBurns(7) 12 53
(Michael Bell) *trckd ldr: rdn over 2f out: hld whn n.m.r over 1f out: sn lost pl* **8/1**

1m 34.88s (-1.12) **Going Correction** -0.05s/f (Good)
WFA 3 from 4yo+ 3lb **10** Ran SP% **116.4**
Speed ratings (Par 101): **103,101,100,100,100 99,98,95,95,93**
toteswingers:1&2:£7.80, 1&3:£12.40, 2&3:£24.30 CSF £61.12 CT £762.68 TOTE £5.20: £2.20, £4.70, £5.30; EX 31.60 Trifecta £438.10 Part won. Pool: £592.04 - 0.20 winning units..
Owner Saeed Manana **Bred** Lynchbages Edgeridge Ltd & Glenvale Stud **Trained** Newmarket, Suffolk

FOCUS
Modest form. It was a competitive enough race for the grade with the market leaders arriving in good form. The winner looked a bit better than the bare form.

6972 FROSTS FIREWORKS HERE 4TH NOVEMBER NURSERY 6f 209y
4:05 (4:09) (Class 5) (0-75,75) 2-Y-O **£2,264** (£673; £336; £168) **Stalls** Centre

Form RPR
104 **1** **Oscan (USA)**[12] 6699 2-9-6 **74**........ AhmedAjtebi 8 82+
(Mahmood Al Zarooni) *prom: drvn to ld over 1f out: rdn out* **10/3**[1]

0402 **2** 1 ¾ **Abhaath (USA)**[34] 6132 2-9-2 **70**........(p) TadhgO'Shea 11 74
(Saeed Bin Suroor) *mid-div on outer: hdwy 2f out: r.o to take 2nd nr fin* **15/2**

5612 **3** *nk* **Guava**[7] 6821 2-8-8 **65**........ SeanLevey(3) 5 68
(Richard Hannon) *prom: led over 2f out tl over 1f out: one pce* **7/1**[3]

045 **4** 1 ¼ **Manomine**[37] 6031 2-8-10 **64**........ TomQueally 3 64
(Clive Brittain) *mid-div: drvn to chse ldrs over 1f out: one pce* **8/1**

003 **5** *1* **Intomist (IRE)**[91] 4240 2-8-2 **61**........ NathanAlison(5) 13 58
(Jim Boyle) *dwlt: bhd: hdwy on inner 2f out: one pce fnl f* **16/1**

0520 **6** ½ **Royal Academician (USA)**[61] 5280 2-9-6 **74**........ GeorgeBaker 4 70
(Gary Moore) *trckd ldrs: rdn 2f out: no ex fnl f* **11/1**

0043 **7** ½ **True Prince (USA)**[38] 6001 2-8-1 **55**........ MartinLane 1 50
(Amanda Perrett) *in tch: drvn along 3f out: styd on same pce* **16/1**

1430 **8** 1 ¼ **Faraway**[12] 6699 2-8-11 **70**........(v) MatthewCosham(5) 7 61
(David Evans) *mid-div: rdn and no hdwy fnl 3f* **28/1**

0054 **9** *hd* **Pius Parker (IRE)**[7] 6817 2-8-6 **60**........ ChrisCatlin 12 51
(John Gallagher) *bhd: rdn over 2f out: nvr rchd ldrs* **28/1**

150 **10** *nk* **Uncle Roger (IRE)**[21] 6484 2-9-1 **69**........ LiamKeniry 9 59
(Eve Johnson Houghton) *towards rr: mod effrt whn n.m.r 2f out: nvr trbld ldrs* **28/1**

005 **11** 1 ½ **Roman Senate (IRE)**[37] 6018 2-7-9 **52**........(p) KieranO'Neill(3) 2 38
(Martin Bosley) *prom: led after 1f tl over 2f out: wknd over 1f out* **14/1**

4513 **12** *5* **Always Et Toujours**[16] 6599 2-9-7 **75**........ AdamKirby 10 48
(Mark Johnston) *led 1f: lost pl 4f out: sn struggling* **4/1**[2]

6000 **13** *7* **Superinjunction**[10] 6753 2-8-8 **62**........(b) MartinDwyer 6 17
(Brian Meehan) *prom tl wknd over 2f out* **100/1**

1m 23.1s **Going Correction** -0.05s/f (Good) **13** Ran SP% **116.6**
Speed ratings (Par 95): **98,96,95,94,93 92,91,90,90,89 88,82,74**
toteswingers:1&2:£5.80, 1&3:£7.60, 2&3:£8.00 CSF £26.61 CT £170.98 TOTE £6.10: £2.10, £2.60, £2.10; EX 18.30 Trifecta £45.20 Pool: £529.06 - 8.65 winning units..
Owner Godolphin **Bred** Darley **Trained** Newmarket, Suffolk

FOCUS
Competitive stuff, and most of these had a chance of sorts as they reached the home straight.

NOTEBOOK
Oscan(USA) came back to form at Wolverhampton last time when finishing fourth after a miserable effort in the Haynes, Hanson and Clark, and duly built on that to gain a cosy victory. His breeding suggests he'll have no problems getting further and he is a nice handicapper at least in the making. (op 9-2)
Abhaath(USA) was fitted with cheekpieces for the first time after a good run on his handicap debut last time, and followed his owner's first string home after taking a few strides to hit top gear. (op 8-1 tchd 6-1)
Guava, 3lb well in, hadn't run over this distance previously but she seemed to stay it well enough despite finishing behind the Godolphin pair. (tchd 13-2 and 15-2)
Manomine was being ridden along about 2f but kept on well inside the final furlong. (tchd 13-2)
Intomist(IRE) ◆, up in trip for his handicap debut, got behind early after starting slowly but found a nice passage up the inside rail to make his run. Although he didn't manage to threaten the places, this was a fair effort and he will be of interest for a race at a slightly lower level. Official explanation: jockey said colt was slowly away (op 9-1 tchd 20-1)
Royal Academician(USA) was slightly disappointing on his nursery debut last time at Sandown, but ran better up to a point here after travelling strongly. He may appreciate a flatter track or a bit shorter considering the pace he shows. (op 12-1 tchd 10-1)
Always Et Toujours had run well since going into handicaps, but he had noticeably sweated up around his neck and ran well below form. (tchd 7-2)

6973 DIGIBET.COM MEDIAN AUCTION MAIDEN STKS 6f 209y
4:40 (4:40) (Class 5) 2-Y-O **£2,264** (£673; £336; £168) **Stalls** Centre

Form RPR
0 **1** **Al Jabreiah**[70] 4961 2-8-12 0........ LiamJones 5 68+
(William Haggas) *in tch: pushed up to chse ldrs 4f out: rdn to chal ent fnl f: led last 75yds* **15/2**

0032 **2** ¾ **Siouxperhero (IRE)**[7] 6812 2-9-3 66........(b) MartinDwyer 6 70
(William Muir) *trckd ldr gng wl: shkn up to ld over 1f out: drvn along fnl f: hdd fnl 75yds* **10/11**[1]

4306 **3** *5* **Hi There (IRE)**[13] 6663 2-9-3 65........ DaneO'Neill 2 57
(J W Hills) *sn led: hdd over 1f out: no ex* **4/1**[2]

5630 **4** ¾ **Zigazag (IRE)**[81] 4581 2-9-3 61........ DavidProbert 4 54
(David Evans) *prom: drvn to chal over 1f out: wknd fnl f* **13/2**[3]

00 **5** *7* **Twenty One Choice (IRE)**[33] 6160 2-9-3 0........ JamesDoyle 1 36
(Ed de Giles) *t.k.h: chsd ldrs: j. path after 1f: rdn over 2f out: sn wknd* **16/1**

0000 **6** 2 ¼ **Cool Light**[22] 6458 2-8-12 50........ TomQueally 8 25
(Alan Jarvis) *t.k.h in rr: hrd rdn over 2f out: no rspnse* **14/1**

1m 23.67s (0.57) **Going Correction** -0.05s/f (Good) **6** Ran SP% **110.0**
Speed ratings (Par 95): **94,93,87,86,78 76**
toteswingers:1&2:£2.10, 1&3:£2.70, 2&3:£1.60 CSF £14.33 TOTE £11.00: £3.40, £1.20; EX 18.50 Trifecta £46.10 Pool: £739.33 - 11.86 winning units..
Owner Mohammed Jaber **Bred** Rabbah Bloodstock Limited **Trained** Newmarket, Suffolk

FOCUS
This was definitely a really weak affair.

NOTEBOOK
Al Jabreiah finished well beaten in a Newmarket maiden in August but improved considerably from that to take this in workmanlike style. She gave the impression she was still a bit green, so more improvement should be forthcoming. (op 17-2 tchd 9-1)
Siouxperhero(IRE) had been running okay recently, including at this course, but spurned another chance to gain a first win after travelling strongly for most of the race. He tended to edge left under maximum pressure but doesn't look irresolute. (op Evens tchd 5-6)
Hi There(IRE) had been given plenty of previous tries to shed his maiden tag, but didn't do a lot off the bridle after leading. (op 7-2 tchd 9-2)
Zigazag(IRE) had already been well beaten in a seller, so the fact he was easily held gives hope for the first two. (op 15-2)
Twenty One Choice(IRE) jumped a path after about 1f and tended to race too keenly under restraint early to give himself a chance of getting involved. (op 20-1 tchd 14-1)

6974 BRASSERIE ITALIAN MARINA SQUARE H'CAP 5f 213y
5:10 (5:10) (Class 4) (0-85,85) 3-Y-O+ **£3,234** (£962; £481; £240) **Stalls** Centre

Form RPR
000 **1** **Summerinthecity (IRE)**[26] 6331 4-9-7 **85**........ JamesDoyle 10 93
(Ed de Giles) *t.k.h in midfield: rdn and hdwy 2f out: str chal fnl f: led fnl 30yds* **8/1**

2060 **2** *nse* **We Have A Dream**[11] 6723 6-9-7 **85**........ MartinDwyer 6 93
(William Muir) *led: hld on gamely fnl f tl hdd last 30yds* **12/1**

631 **3** ½ **Earlsmedic**[57] 5387 6-8-7 **71**........(v) WilliamCarson 7 77
(Stuart Williams) *mid-div: hdwy to press ldrs over 1f out: hung lft u.p: chal fnl f: r.o* **15/2**[3]

1042 **4** *shd* **Psychic's Dream**[69] 5018 3-8-12 **77**........ MartinHarley 12 83
(Marco Botti) *sn chsng ldrs: drvn to chal between runners ins fnl f: r.o* **15/2**[3]

0405 **5** ¾ **New Leyf (IRE)**[21] 6478 5-9-7 **85**........(b) SteveDrowne 2 89
(Jeremy Gask) *towards rr: rdn and hdwy over 1f out: nrst fin* **10/1**

1323 **6** *nk* **Night Trade (IRE)**[29] 6246 4-9-2 **80**........ LukeMorris 11 83
(Ronald Harris) *mid-div: swtchd rt and hdwy jst over 1f out: kpt on u.p fnl f* **11/1**

6311 **7** ½ **Shifting Star (IRE)**[10] 6761 6-9-3 **84** 6ex........ SeanLevey(3) 8 85
(Walter Swinburn) *a.p: no ex fnl f* **4/1**[1]

1010 **8** 1 ¼ **Deerslayer (USA)**[10] 6761 5-9-1 **79**........(p) JimCrowley 14 76
(Amy Weaver) *w ldrs: hrd rdn over 1f out: sn wknd* **16/1**

4416 **9** ½ **Sluggsy Morant**[33] 6174 3-9-3 **82**........ DaneO'Neill 1 78
(Henry Candy) *bhd: hdwy and in tch over 1f out: hrd rdn: no imp* **11/2**[2]

0100 **10** *nk* **Serena's Pride**[61] 5268 3-8-11 **76**........ TomQueally 4 71
(Alan Jarvis) *t.k.h: chsd ldrs tl wknd 1f out* **28/1**

5511 **11** *hd* **Emiratesdotcom**[33] 6177 5-9-0 **78**........ FergusSweeney 3 72
(Milton Bradley) *dwlt: bhd: hrd rdn over 1f out: n.d* **12/1**

1106 **12** ¾ **Commandingpresence (USA)**[7] 6815 5-8-4 **71** oh2 KieranO'Neill(3) 13 63
(John Bridger) *dwlt: sn prom: wknd wl over 1f out* **40/1**

1000 **13** 2 ½ **Waabel**[10] 6761 4-8-11 **78**........ RobertLButler(3) 9 62
(Richard Guest) *a towards rr: n.d fnl 2f* **25/1**

69.61 secs (-0.59) **Going Correction** -0.05s/f (Good)
WFA 3 from 4yo+ 1lb **13** Ran SP% **118.4**
Speed ratings (Par 105): **101,100,100,100,99 98,98,96,95,95 95,94,90**
toteswingers:1&2:£20.40, 1&3:£15.60, 2&3:£23.20 CSF £97.60 CT £755.63 TOTE £10.30: £3.20, £3.70, £2.70; EX 94.00 TRIFECTA Not won..
Owner Ali Mortazavi **Bred** J Costello **Trained** Ledbury, Herefordshire

FOCUS
A decent sprint to conclude the meeting with and almost predictably a tight finish. Straightforward form with the runner-up the best guide.
T/Plt: £643.70 to a £1 stake. Pool of £79,098.06 - 89.70 winning tickets. T/Qpdt: £23.50 to a £1 stake. Pool of £6,474.43 - 203.38 winning tickets. LM

6871 WOLVERHAMPTON (A.W) (L-H)
Thursday, October 20

OFFICIAL GOING: Standard
Wind: Light behind Weather: Overcast

6975 ENJOY THE HORIZONS DINING EXPERIENCE CLAIMING STKS 5f 20y(P)
5:40 (5:41) (Class 6) 2-Y-O **£1,704** (£503; £251) **Stalls** Low

Form RPR
0216 **1** **Rougini (IRE)**[17] 6590 2-8-12 66........(v) AndrewElliott 2 71
(Mrs K Burke) *mde all: clr over 1f out: styd on wl* **7/2**[2]

0656 **2** *4* **Sonsie Lass**[33] 6178 2-8-8 53........ JoeFanning 10 53
(Keith Dalgleish) *prom: chsd wnr over 1f out: no imp ins fnl f* **40/1**

3643 **3** 1 ¾ **Dark Ages (IRE)**[16] 6597 2-9-2 65........ PaulHanagan 8 54
(Noel Quinlan) *chsd wnr over 3f: no ex fnl f* **15/2**

6200 **4** 2 ¼ **Courtland King (IRE)**[6] 6843 2-9-3 73........ PatCosgrave 3 47
(David Evans) *hld up: hdwy u.p over 1f out: nvr on terms* **11/2**[3]

1353 **5** 3 ¼ **The Dancing Lord**[8] 6786 2-9-0 73........ JakePayne(7) 1 40
(Bill Turner) *chsd ldrs tl rdn and wknd over 1f out* **11/2**[3]

1023 **6** 4 ½ **Mousie**[134] 2797 2-9-2 66........ NeilCallan 5 18
(Alan McCabe) *chsd ldrs: rdn 1/2-way: sn wknd* **16/1**

0250 **7** 4 ½ **Tyre Giant Dot Com**[14] 6652 2-8-12 62........(p) DaleSwift(3) 6 —
(Geoffrey Oldroyd) *hld up: wknd 1/2-way* **9/1**

8 *2* **Darleas Gift (IRE)** 2-9-2 0........ StephenCraine 4 —
(Kevin Ryan) *s.i.s: sn outpcd* **28/1**

2002 **9** *3* **Musical Valley**[19] 6540 2-9-3 73........(t) RichardKingscote 7 —
(Tom Dascombe) *dwlt: hdwy whn hung rt fr over 3f out: eased 1/2-way* **11/4**[1]

61.72 secs (-0.58) **Going Correction** -0.075s/f (Stan) **9** Ran SP% **113.2**
Speed ratings (Par 93): **101,94,91,88,83 75,68,65,60**
toteswingers:1&2:£10.70, 2&3:£15.80, 1&3:£3.80 CSF £120.43 TOTE £5.00: £2.00, £13.00, £2.80; EX 92.30.
Owner McKeown & Wotherspoon **Bred** John Graham **Trained** Middleham Moor, North Yorks

FOCUS
A weak juvenile seller.

NOTEBOOK
Rougini(IRE) ultimately made all for a comfortable success. She wasn't a factor in a fair nursery at Windsor last time, but got off the mark at the eighth attempt in a weak Redcar maiden the time before. A repeat of that form proved good enough here and she looked made for this track as she sped around the bend, so there should be more of these within her compass. (op 10-3 tchd 3-1)
Sonsie Lass looked outclassed at the weights, but it was her first run for a trainer making a name for himself this year and she ran a personal best in defeat. It was her first outing over the minimum (dam 5f AW winner) and she's capable of winning in this class. (op 33-1 tchd 28-1)
Dark Ages(IRE) had the blinkers left off on this return to Polytrack and drop in class. She could go with the winner turning for home, but kept on well enough and this is her sort of level. (op 6-1 tchd 8-1)
Courtland King(IRE) lacked the pace to challenge and again served notice he's flattered by his official mark. (op 7-1)

Musical Valley, well backed, ran right off the bend and lost any chance. Official explanation: jockey said gelding hung badly (op 3-1 tchd 10-3)

6976 WOLVERHAMPTON-RACECOURSE.CO.UK H'CAP 1m 4f 50y(P)
6:10 (6:10) (Class 4) (0-80,80) 3-Y-0+ **£2,911** (£866; £432; £216) **Stalls** Low

Form RPR
1555 **1** **Art Scholar (IRE)**[36] 6068 4-9-8 **76**................................ NeilChalmers 11 84
(Michael Appleby) *hld up: hdwy over 2f out: rdn to ld ins fnl f: r.o* **25/1**
4404 **2** 1 1/4 **Obsession (IRE)**[9] 6773 3-8-13 **74**..............................(v) JimmyFortune 3 80
(Jeremy Noseda) *a.p: pushed along over 4f out: rdn and edgd rt over 1f out: r.o* **8/1**
1600 **3** 1/2 **Lady of Burgundy**[24] 6410 5-8-13 **72**.......................... LeeNewnes(5) 10 77
(Mark Usher) *s.i.s: hld up: bhd 7f out: hdwy over 1f out: r.o to go 3rd nr fin: nt rch ldrs* **50/1**
0053 **4** nk **Rowan Tiger**[37] 6023 5-9-7 **75**.. PatCosgrave 4 80
(Jim Boyle) *chsd ldrs: rdn over 2f out: led over 1f out: hdd ins fnl f: sn hung lft and no ex* **16/1**
4022 **5** 3/4 **Vimiero (USA)**[3] 6922 4-9-9 **77**...................................... JamieSpencer 8 81
(Walter Swinburn) *stdd s: hld up: hdwy over 2f out: bmpd over 1f out: no ex ins fnl f* **6/4**[1]
00 **6** 6 **Red Anthem**[12] 6690 4-9-12 **80**......................................(p) SebSanders 7 74
(Gerard Butler) *hld up in tch: led over 2f out: rdn and hdd over 1f out: hmpd ins fnl f: sn hung lft and wknd* **12/1**
0000 **7** 5 **Admirable Duque (IRE)**[37] 6023 5-9-10 **78**....................(p) NeilCallan 1 66
(Dominic Ffrench Davis) *prom: rdn over 2f out: wknd over 1f out: eased ins fnl f* **33/1**
000 **8** 3/4 **L'Hermitage (IRE)**[7] 6822 3-8-13 **74**..........................(p) DarryllHolland 5 61
(Brian Meehan) *led after 1f: hdd 9f out: chsd ldr: rdn to ld over 3f out: hdd over 2f out: hmpd and wknd 1f out* **12/1**
1210 **9** 7 **Eagle Nebula**[29] 6254 7-9-5 **73**.................................... IanMongan 9 47
(Brett Johnson) *s.i.s: hld up: rdn over 1f out: n.d* **17/2**
0066 **10** nk **Mcbirney (USA)**[15] 6632 4-9-12 **80**............................... PaulHanagan 6 53
(Paul D'Arcy) *hld up: hdwy over 2f out: rdn and wknd over 1f out* **6/1**[2]
5006 **11** 1 **Laughing Jack**[14] 6658 3-9-2 **77**...................................(e) KierenFallon 2 48
(Ed Dunlop) *led 1f: chsd ldr tl led again 9f out: rdn and hdd over 3f out: wknd over 1f out* **15/2**[3]
531- **12** 22 **Honest Strike (USA)**[124] 3196 4-9-11 **79**......................... ShaneKelly 12 —
(Daniel Mark Loughnane, Ire) *chsd ldrs: rdn over 3f out: hmpd and wknd over 2f out: t.o* **25/1**

2m 38.18s (-2.92) **Going Correction** -0.075s/f (Stan)
WFA 3 from 4yo+ 7lb **12** Ran SP% **121.5**
Speed ratings (Par 105): **106,105,104,104,104 100,96,96,91,91 90,76**
toteswingers:1&2:£26.80, 2&3:£43.60, 1&3:£124.50 CSF £212.73 CT £9624.05 TOTE £49.20: £10.60, £1.40, £16.70; EX 185.90.
Owner Mrs J Scrivens **Bred** John Ramsbottom **Trained** Danethorpe, Notts

FOCUS
A fair handicap in which most of the runners arrived with something to prove. There was a sound pace on and a tight finish. The winner is rated in line with his earlier turf form this year.
Mcbirney(USA) Official explanation: jockey said gelding lost its action
Honest Strike(USA) Official explanation: jockey said gelding hung right

6977 BOOK NOW FOR CHRISTMAS MEDIAN AUCTION MDN STKS 1m 1f 103y(P)
6:40 (6:41) (Class 6) 2-Y-0 **£1,704** (£503; £251) **Stalls** Low

Form RPR
422 **1** **Amoralist**[24] 6400 2-9-3 82.. KierenFallon 3 74+
(Ed Dunlop) *chsd ldr tl led over 2f out: shkn up and c clr fr over 1f out: easily* **4/5**[1]
0006 **2** 3 3/4 **Vergrigio (IRE)**[7] 6812 2-9-3 55..(b) NeilCallan 7 65
(Brian Meehan) *chsd ldrs: rdn to go 2nd over 1f out: hung lft and no imp ins fnl f* **40/1**
5 **3** 5 **Mutual Regard (IRE)**[12] 6697 2-9-3 0.............................. SebSanders 2 55
(Sir Mark Prescott Bt) *prom: pushed along to chse wnr over 2f out tl over 1f out: sn wknd* **5/1**[3]
0 **4** 8 **Lithograph (USA)**[12] 6697 2-8-12 0............................... PaulHanagan 6 35
(Mahmood Al Zarooni) *sn led: rdn and hdd over 2f out: wknd over 1f out* **11/1**[?]
60 **5** 3/4 **Abundantly**[38] 6000 2-8-12 0... DarryllHolland 5 34
(Hughie Morrison) *hld up: stmbld after 1f: pushed along 7f out: n.d* **16/1**
00 **6** 11 **April Leyf (IRE)**[12] 6697 2-8-12 0............................... RobbieFitzpatrick 1 13
(Mark Brisbourne) *hld up: rdn and wknd over 2f out* **150/1**
7 40 **Mrs Awkward** 2-8-12 0... ShaneKelly 4 —
(Mark Brisbourne) *hld up: pushed along over 6f out: wknd 4f out: t.o* **66/1**

2m 2.68s (0.98) **Going Correction** -0.075s/f (Stan) **7** Ran SP% **109.4**
Speed ratings (Par 93): **92,88,84,77,76 66,31**
toteswingers:1&2:£5.70, 2&3:£5.60, 1&3:£1.30 CSF £33.91 TOTE £1.70: £1.10, £18.10; EX 19.40.
Owner Mrs Susan Roy **Bred** West Dereham Abbey Stud **Trained** Newmarket, Suffolk

FOCUS
Straightforward maiden form.

NOTEBOOK
Amoralist, a runner-up the last twice, wanted to go quicker than the modest early pace and Kieren Fallon got him nicely settled just off the leader. He was perfectly placed turning into the home straight and ultimately came away from his rivals without having to be fully extended. He was the clear form pick and this was a deserved success. (op 10-11 tchd 8-11)
Vergrigio(IRE) was having his sixth outing and, rated 55, he does little for this form. The longer trip evidently proved more suitable. (op 50-1)
Mutual Regard(IRE) looked a threat turning for home, but was trapped on the inside behind the tiring leader and allowed the winner first run. His finishing effort was laboured, though, and he probably needs more time. (tchd 11-2)
Lithograph(USA) was well backed to improve on his tame debut effort here behind the third last time out. He raced a lot more professionally, but was cooked at the top of the home straight and failed to get home. (op 9-4 tchd 2-1 and 3-1)
Abundantly never looked happy after clipping heels in the early parts. She kept on late and now qualifies for a mark. Official explanation: jockey said filly clipped heels shortly after start (op 20-1 tchd 22-1)

6978 WEATHERBYS BLOODSTOCK INSURANCE H'CAP 1m 1f 103y(P)
7:10 (7:12) (Class 5) (0-75,74) 3-Y-0 **£2,264** (£673; £336; £168) **Stalls** Low

Form RPR
5215 **1** **So Wise (USA)**[5] 6877 3-8-12 **65**..................................... PatCosgrave 6 79
(Keith Dalgleish) *a.p: chsd ldr 2f out: rdn to ld 1f out: r.o* **8/1**
5135 **2** 1 1/2 **Tornado Force (IRE)**[154] 2226 3-9-0 **67**........................ JimmyFortune 4 78
(Jeremy Noseda) *chsd ldr tl led wl over 2f out: rdn and hdd 1f out: styd on same pce* **12/1**
2150 **3** 2 **Spanish Plume**[13] 6674 3-9-7 **74**.............................. GrahamGibbons 11 81
(Reg Hollinshead) *hld up: hdwy 2f out: rdn over 1f out: styd on: nt rch ldrs* **10/1**
6503 **4** 1 1/4 **Jibaal (IRE)**[19] 6543 3-9-7 **74**.. JamieSpencer 10 78
(Marco Botti) *hld up in tch: rdn over 1f out: wknd ins fnl f* **11/2**[2]
034U **5** nk **Daruband**[26] 6136 3-9-6 **73**.. KierenFallon 12 77
(Alan McCabe) *stdd s: hld up: hdwy over 1f out: nt rch ldrs* **22/1**
5-42 **6** 1 1/2 **State Senator (USA)**[16] 6608 3-8-12 **65**.......................... SebSanders 8 66+
(Sir Mark Prescott Bt) *prom: nt clr run and lost pl over 2f out: n.d after* **2/1**[1]
5310 **7** 1/2 **Silver Alliance**[9] 6773 3-9-2 **72**... JohnFahy(3) 9 72
(Walter Swinburn) *s.i.s: hld up: nvr on terms* **13/2**[3]
30 **8** 1/2 **Polar Auroras**[17] 6587 3-8-10 **63**..................................... PaulHanagan 3 61
(Tony Carroll) *hld up: rdn over 3f out: n.d* **25/1**
0600 **9** 7 **Bilidn**[9] 6773 3-9-6 **73**.. NeilCallan 5 57
(Clive Brittain) *chsd ldrs: rdn over 3f out: wknd over 1f out* **11/1**
000 **10** 4 1/2 **Oasis Storm**[30] 6234 3-9-2 **69**.. TomEaves 1 43
(Michael Dods) *plld hrd: trckd ldrs: rdn over 3f out: wknd over 1f out* **14/1**
650 **11** 8 **Munaa's Dream**[16] 6609 3-8-0 **60** oh15......................... RaulDaSilva(7) 2 18
(Mrs K Burke) *set stdy pce tl qcknd 4f out: hdd wl over 2f out: wknd over 1f out* **100/1**

2m 1.46s (-0.24) **Going Correction** -0.075s/f (Stan) **11** Ran SP% **114.1**
Speed ratings (Par 101): **98,96,94,93,93 92,91,91,85,81 73**
toteswingers:1&2:£5.00, 2&3:£20.50, 1&3:£18.30 CSF £94.76 CT £966.26 TOTE £7.30: £2.50, £1.60, £3.70; EX 97.70.
Owner S Laffan **Bred** Juddmonte Farms Inc **Trained** Carluke, South Lanarkshire

FOCUS
This didn't look a bad 3-y-o handicap for the class, but few landed a blow as the first pair dominated in the home straight. Both showed improved form.
Polar Auroras Official explanation: jockey said filly was denied a clear run

6979 WEATHERBYS VAT SERVICES H'CAP (DIV I) 7f 32y(P)
7:40 (7:42) (Class 5) (0-75,75) 3-Y-0+ **£2,264** (£673; £336; £168) **Stalls** High

Form RPR
1150 **1** **Glenridding**[26] 6354 7-9-0 **68**.. FrederikTylicki 4 76
(James Given) *chsd ldr tl led 2f out: rdn out* **13/2**[3]
0010 **2** 1/2 **Needwood Ridge**[26] 6354 4-9-1 **69**..............................(bt) NeilCallan 12 76+
(Frank Sheridan) *s.i.s: hld up: rdn over 2f out: hdwy over 1f out: r.o* **12/1**
1014 **3** 1/2 **Master Of Dance (IRE)**[13] 6664 4-9-3 **71**.......................(p) JoeFanning 1 77
(Keith Dalgleish) *chsd ldrs: rdn over 1f out: styd on* **8/1**
4201 **4** 1 1/4 **Khajaaly (IRE)**[26] 6354 4-9-5 **73**................................... PaulHanagan 9 75
(Julia Feilden) *trckd ldrs: rdn over 1f out: no ex ins fnl f* **11/2**[2]
6160 **5** 1 3/4 **Downhill Skier (IRE)**[26] 6354 7-8-7 **68**........................... JackDuern(7) 2 66
(Mark Brisbourne) *mid-div: hdwy over 2f out: hmpd over 1f out: styd on* **28/1**
0120 **6** 3/4 **Master Leon**[56] 5403 4-8-11 **72**..............................(p) JustinNewman(7) 3 68
(Bryan Smart) *hld up: hmpd and r.o ins fnl f: nvr nrr* **12/1**
3122 **7** 1 3/4 **Katy's Secret**[36] 6065 4-9-2 **70**...................................... KierenFallon 7 61+
(William Jarvis) *hld up: nt clr run 1f out: nvr trbld ldrs* **11/4**[1]
3402 **8** hd **Ishiadancer**[26] 6354 6-9-3 **71**.. PatCosgrave 10 61
(Eric Alston) *led: rdn and hdd 2f out: wknd ins fnl f* **11/2**[2]
0600 **9** 1 3/4 **Ocean Legend (IRE)**[43] 5828 6-9-1 **72**................. MichaelO'Connell(3) 5 61
(Tony Carroll) *hld up: pushed along 1/2-way: hmpd ins fnl f: nvr trbld ldrs* **25/1**
605 **10** 2 **Conry (IRE)**[16] 6617 5-9-2 **70**... StephenCraine 6 50
(Patrick Morris) *dwlt: hld up: a in rr* **7/1**
3000 **11** 3/4 **Major Muscari (IRE)**[26] 6348 3-9-0 **73**............................ DaleSwift(3) 11 51
(Geoffrey Oldroyd) *chsd ldrs: rdn over 2f out: hung lft and wknd over 1f out* **25/1**

1m 28.85s (-0.75) **Going Correction** -0.075s/f (Stan)
WFA 3 from 4yo+ 2lb **11** Ran SP% **120.9**
Speed ratings (Par 103): **101,100,99,98,96 95,93,93,91,89 88**
toteswingers:1&2:£12.30, 2&3:£12.50, 1&3:£9.90 CSF £82.00 CT £655.37 TOTE £9.50: £2.70, £4.70, £2.10; EX 82.00.
Owner Tremousser Partnership **Bred** Bolton Grange **Trained** Willoughton, Lincs
■ Stewards' Enquiry : Jack Duern two-day ban: careless riding (Nov 3-4)

FOCUS
An open-looking handicap. It was run at a strong pace yet still it again paid to race handily. It was a second slower than the first division. The winner was probably the best guide.
Ocean Legend(IRE) Official explanation: jockey said gelding suffered interference in running

6980 WEATHERBYS VAT SERVICES H'CAP (DIV II) 7f 32y(P)
8:10 (8:10) (Class 5) (0-75,74) 3-Y-0+ **£2,264** (£673; £336; £168) **Stalls** High

Form RPR
0422 **1** **Chookie Royale**[5] 6869 3-9-4 **73**....................................(p) JoeFanning 1 86
(Keith Dalgleish) *a.p: chsd ldr over 1f out: rdn ins fnl f: r.o to ld nr fin* **11/2**[3]
0321 **2** 1/2 **Ducal**[14] 6653 3-9-2 **71**.. SebSanders 7 83
(Sir Mark Prescott Bt) *a.p: chsd ldr over 5f out: led 2f out: rdn and hdd nr fin* **7/2**[1]
3656 **3** 6 **Summer Dancer (IRE)**[25] 6381 7-9-3 **70**.................... MickyFenton 9 66
(Paul Midgley) *hld up: hdwy over 2f out: rdn over 1f out: styd on same pce ins fnl f* **16/1**
35-3 **4** 1/2 **Spin Cast**[20] 6505 3-8-12 **70**.. JohnFahy(3) 4 64
(Walter Swinburn) *hld up: hdwy over 1f out: edgd lft ins fnl f: nt trble ldrs* **7/1**
2010 **5** 2 1/4 **Blink Of An Eye**[22] 6442 3-9-4 **73**................................. JamieSpencer 3 61
(Michael Bell) *trckd ldrs: racd keenly: rdn and wknd over 1f out* **14/1**
1000 **6** 1/2 **Kings 'n Dreams**[22] 6467 4-9-4 **71**..............................(b) KierenFallon 8 58
(Dean Ivory) *hld up: rdn over 1f out: nvr nrr* **16/1**
1054 **7** 2 1/2 **Fleetwoodsands (IRE)**[23] 6434 4-9-0 **67**.............(t) RichardKingscote 2 47
(Milton Bradley) *led: rdn and hdd 2f out: wknd ins fnl f* **14/1**
0-32 **8** 1/2 **Quarrel (USA)**[10] 6759 4-9-5 **72**....................................(p) PaulHanagan 12 51
(William Haggas) *hld up: hdwy 5f out: rdn and wknd over 1f out* **9/2**[2]
2300 **9** 1 1/4 **Smalljohn**[147] 2431 5-9-0 **74**.................................(v) JustinNewman(7) 11 50
(Bryan Smart) *chsd ldrs: rdn 1/2-way: wknd over 1f out* **10/1**
5200 **10** 3 1/2 **Cuthbert (IRE)**[44] 5803 4-9-1 **68**..................................(v) ShaneKelly 5 34
(William Jarvis) *s.s: a in rr* **16/1**
0000 **11** 21 **City Legend**[104] 3830 3-9-3 **72**................................(bt) GrahamGibbons 6 —
(Alan McCabe) *a in rr: rdn over 4f out: wknd over 2f out: eased* **20/1**

1m 27.85s (-1.75) **Going Correction** -0.075s/f (Stan)
WFA 3 from 4yo+ 2lb **11** Ran SP% **113.1**
Speed ratings (Par 103): **107,106,99,99,96 95,93,92,91,87 63**
toteswingers:1&2:£5.40, 2&3:£29.20, 1&3:£18.50 CSF £23.97 CT £291.81 TOTE £8.10: £2.80, £2.40, £3.00; EX 34.40.
Owner Raeburn Brick Limited **Bred** D And J Raeburn **Trained** Carluke, South Lanarkshire

FOCUS
This second division of the 7f was also run at a strong pace and, always handy, the first pair pulled well clear late on. It was the pick of the four C&D times and the form is arguably worth the form at face value.
City Legend Official explanation: jockey said gelding never travelled

6981 ENJOY THE PARTY PACK GROUP OFFER MEDIAN AUCTION MAIDEN STKS 7f 32y(P)
8:40 (8:41) (Class 6) 3-5-Y-0 **£1,704** (£503; £251) **Stalls** High

Form RPR
22 **1** **Good Authority (IRE)**[14] 6653 4-9-5 70 DarryllHolland 5 77+
(Karen George) *s.i.s: sn hld up in tch: led over 1f out: shkn up and sn in command: eased nr fin* **8/11**[1]
5403 **2** *3 1/4* **Brick Dust (IRE)**[27] 6307 3-9-3 70 KierenFallon 7 68
(Luca Cumani) *chsd ldr: rdn and hung lft fr over 1f out: styd on same pce* **2/1**[2]
36 **3** *1 1/4* **Gold Tobougg**[69] 5007 3-8-12 0 PaulHanagan 4 60
(David Simcock) *hld up: hdwy over 2f out: rdn over 1f out: no ex ins fnl f* **6/1**[3]
0200 **4** *2* **Bambika**[2] 6929 3-8-9 55 JohnFahy(3) 8 54
(Jo Crowley) *prom: lost pl 5f out: hdwy over 2f out: no ex ins fnl f* **16/1**
46 **5** *1 3/4* **Royal Selection (IRE)**[75] 4796 3-8-5 0 JulieCumine(7) 3 50+
(Karen George) *stdd s: hld up and bhd: shkn up over 1f out: r.o ins fnl f: nvr nr to chal* **20/1**
0320 **6** *1/2* **Poppet's Joy**[9] 6767 3-8-12 53 GrahamGibbons 6 48
(Reg Hollinshead) *led: rdn and hdd over 1f out: wknd ins fnl f* **16/1**
0 **7** *3 1/4* **Bint Elnadim (IRE)**[5] 6874 3-8-12 0 RobbieFitzpatrick 1 39
(Derek Shaw) *s.i.s: hld up: nvr on terms* **66/1**
U60 **8** *10* **Kantata**[49] 5639 3-8-7 0 (b[1]) MatthewCosham(5) 9 12
(James Toller) *prom tl rdn and wknd over 2f out* **100/1**
5-65 **9** *4 1/2* **Jossy Johnston (IRE)**[81] 4576 3-9-3 52 PatCosgrave 2 —
(Eric Alston) *chsd ldrs tl wknd over 2f out* **33/1**

1m 29.28s (-0.32) **Going Correction** -0.075s/f (Stan)
WFA 3 from 4yo 2lb **9** Ran SP% **127.5**
Speed ratings (Par 101): **98,94,92,90,88 88,84,72,67**
toteswingers:1&2:£1.10, 2&3:£2.60, 1&3:£1.90 CSF £2.70 TOTE £1.60: £1.02, £1.50, £2.20; EX 3.30.
Owner Adrian Parr & Karen George **Bred** Mountarmstrong Stud **Trained** Higher Eastington, Devon
■ Stewards' Enquiry : Julie Cumine ten-day ban: failed to obtain best possible placing (Nov 3-5,9-12,14-16)

FOCUS
A very moderate maiden, run at a fair pace. It's doubtful the winner needed to improve.
Royal Selection(IRE) ◆ Official explanation: jockey said, regarding running and riding, that her orders were to drop the filly in, get to the rail and go the shortest route, it jumped out with the field and thereafter became detached but she did not want to roust it along as it was liable to race keenly.

6982 PARADE RESTAURANT H'CAP 7f 32y(P)
9:10 (9:10) (Class 7) (0-50,50) 3-Y-0+ **£1,533** (£452; £226) **Stalls** High

Form RPR
0040 **1** **Gala Spirit (IRE)**[16] 6618 4-9-2 **50** (p) PaulHanagan 11 59
(Peter Niven) *trckd ldr: plld hrd: led on bit 3f out: rdn clr over 1f out: r.o* **12/1**
3666 **2** *2* **Radiator Rooney (IRE)**[8] 6791 8-8-11 **48** AmyRyan(3) 7 52
(Patrick Morris) *s.i.s: hld up: hdwy over 1f out: r.o: nt rch wnr* **18/1**
014- **3** *nk* **Fearless Poet (IRE)**[307] 7910 3-9-0 **50** (p) TomEaves 5 53
(Bryan Smart) *mid-div: racd keenly: hdwy over 1f out: r.o: nrst fin* **6/1**[3]
0005 **4** *3/4* **Yungaburra (IRE)**[6] 6848 7-9-2 **50** (t[1]) JamesSullivan 3 51
(David C Griffiths) *hld up in tch: plld hrd: hdwy over 1f out: styd on* **7/1**
0400 **5** *3/4* **Lightning Spirit**[10] 6764 3-9-0 **50** (p) PatCosgrave 10 49
(Gary Moore) *pushed along in rr early: hld up: nt clr run over 1f out: r.o ins fnl f: nvr nrr* **9/2**[2]
030 **6** *nk* **Indian Dumaani**[27] 6310 4-8-9 **48** RyanPowell(5) 2 46
(David Bridgwater) *chsd ldrs: rdn over 1f out: no ex ins fnl f* **16/1**
5602 **7** *nk* **Dingaan (IRE)**[8] 6791 8-9-2 **50** RobbieFitzpatrick 8 47
(Peter Grayson) *s.i.s: hld up: nvr trbld ldrs* **7/1**
6045 **8** *2* **Titan Diamond (IRE)**[16] 6609 3-8-7 **50** RachealKneller(7) 1 42
(Mark Usher) *chsd ldrs: rdn over 1f out: wknd ins fnl f* **4/1**[1]
3000 **9** *6* **Dililah**[58] 5352 3-9-0 **50** ShaneKelly 9 26
(Linda Stubbs) *hld up in tch: rdn and wknd over 1f out* **40/1**
0260 **10** *2* **Cannon Bolt (IRE)**[47] 5725 3-9-0 **50** (b) LeeNewman 6 20
(Robin Bastiman) *sn led: hdd 3f out: wknd over 1f out* **8/1**
/000 **11** *3* **Bazguy**[218] 874 6-9-2 **50** (b) GrahamGibbons 4 12
(Garry Woodward) *chsd ldrs: rdn 1/2-way: wknd over 1f out* **25/1**

1m 29.64s (0.04) **Going Correction** -0.075s/f (Stan)
WFA 3 from 4yo+ 2lb **11** Ran SP% **113.7**
Speed ratings (Par 97): **96,93,93,92,91 91,90,88,81,79 76**
toteswingers:1&2:£20.10, 2&3:£13.20, 1&3:£11.60 CSF £201.72 CT £1444.92 TOTE £19.80: £5.00, £4.20, £2.30; EX 227.30.
Owner J M Cullinan **Bred** J Cullinan **Trained** Barton-le-Street, N Yorks

FOCUS
A bottom-drawer handicap and another wide-open race. Poor form, but sound enough.
T/Plt: £1,083.50 to a £1 stake. Pool of £78,443.64 - 52.85 winning tickets. T/Qpdt: £74.00 to a £1 stake. Pool of £10,809.80 - 108.00 winning tickets. CR

5926 DONCASTER (L-H)
Friday, October 21

OFFICIAL GOING: Good (good to soft in places on round course; 8.9)
Wind: moderate 1/2 against Weather: overcast

6983 E B F MERCEDES-BENZ OF DONCASTER FLEET MAIDEN STKS 7f
1:30 (1:31) (Class 5) 2-Y-0 **£3,299** (£981; £490; £245) **Stalls** High

Form RPR
00 **1** **Gregorian (IRE)**[34] 6170 2-9-3 0 WilliamBuick 6 85+
(John Gosden) *trckd ldng pair: smooth hdwy 2f out: led 1 1/2f out: rdn clr ent fnl f: styd on* **13/8**[1]
2 *4* **Shuja (USA)** 2-9-3 0 FrankieDettori 4 75
(Saeed Bin Suroor) *hld up in tch: hdwy over 2f out: rdn to chse ldrs over 1f out: styd on ins fnl f* **7/1**[3]
50 **3** *1/2* **Strada Facendo (USA)**[75] 4815 2-9-3 0 KierenFallon 3 73
(Luca Cumani) *trckd ldrs: hdwy 2f out: ch over 1f out: sn rdn and edgd lft ins fnl f: one pce* **8/1**
2222 **4** *1/2* **Choisan (IRE)**[13] 6702 2-9-3 79 DavidAllan 9 72
(Tim Easterby) *trckd ldrs: hdwy to chse ldr 1/2-way: effrt to dispute ld 1 1/2f out and ev ch tl rdn and one pce ent fnl f* **9/2**[2]
5 *1 3/4* **Princely Sum (IRE)** 2-9-0 0 LouisBeuzelin(3) 8 67+
(Sir Michael Stoute) *chsd ldrs: rdn along over 2f out: wknd over 1f out* **33/1**
6 *shd* **Razorbill (USA)** 2-9-3 0 MichaelHills 11 70+
(Charles Hills) *s.i.s and towards rr: stdy hdwy 3f out: chsd ldrs over 1f out: rdn and styng on whn hmpd ins fnl f: nt rcvr* **16/1**
030 **7** *2 1/2* **Vexillum (IRE)**[10] 6772 2-9-3 0 SamHitchcott 5 61
(Mick Channon) *sn led: rdn along 2f out: hdd 1 1/2f out and grad wknd* **100/1**
340 **8** *nk* **Right Regal (IRE)**[43] 5855 2-9-3 78 JamieSpencer 13 60
(Marco Botti) *hld up in midfield: hdwy and in tch 2f out: effrt whn n.m.r wl over 1f out: sn rdn and btn* **9/1**
9 *3* **Skirmish** 2-9-3 0 JoeFanning 1 52
(Mark Johnston) *wnt lft s: in tch: hdwy to chse ldrs wl over 2f out: sn rdn and wknd wl over 1f out* **25/1**
00 **10** *hd* **Kung Hei Fat Choy (USA)**[23] 6448 2-9-3 0 FrederikTylicki 16 52
(James Given) *midfield: rdn along and sme hdwy on outer 1/2-way: sn wknd* **40/1**
11 *2* **Young Freddie (IRE)** 2-9-3 0 TomEaves 10 46
(Bryan Smart) *chsd ldrs on outer: rdn along over 2f out: sn wknd* **80/1**
12 *2 1/2* **Running Reef (IRE)** 2-9-3 0 PJMcDonald 14 40
(Tracy Waggott) *a towards rr* **150/1**
00 **13** *nk* **Menelik (IRE)**[87] 4414 2-9-3 0 RichardKingscote 15 39
(Tom Dascombe) *a in rr* **25/1**
5 **14** *8* **Sirious Oss**[10] 6774 2-9-3 0 JamesSullivan 2 18
(Michael Easterby) *in rr: wl outpcd and bhd fr 1/2-way* **50/1**
0 **15** *1/2* **Rivington**[142] 2617 2-9-3 0 PaulHanagan 12 17
(Richard Fahey) *in tch on outer: pushed along 1/2-way: sn wknd* **33/1**
16 *13* **Jay Peas Jacko** 2-9-3 0 ShaneKelly 7 —
(Lucinda Featherstone) *chsd ldrs: rdn along and lost pl over 4f out: sn bhd* **250/1**

1m 25.89s (-0.41) **Going Correction** -0.20s/f (Firm) **16** Ran SP% **117.0**
Speed ratings (Par 95): **94,89,88,88,86 86,83,82,79,79 77,74,73,64,64 49**
toteswingers:1&2:£4.50, 1&3:£5.60, 2&3:£7.40 CSF £11.38 TOTE £2.30: £1.20, £2.50, £2.10; EX 17.30 Trifecta £101.80 Pool: £363.42 - 2.64 winning units..
Owner H R H Princess Haya Of Jordan **Bred** Rathasker Stud **Trained** Newmarket, Suffolk

FOCUS
This looked at least a fair maiden.

NOTEBOOK
Gregorian(IRE) was reported to have lost his action in the Dip when contesting a sales race at Newmarket on his second start, yet still ran to an RPR in the 80s. This was easier and he won despite proving awkward. Sweating beforehand, he displayed a significant knee action under pressure, and having quickened to go clear, he changed his legs and held his head high, having a good look around. He clearly has a decent amount of ability and it will be interesting to see which way he goes. (op 2-1)
Shuja(USA), from the first crop of Breeders' Cup Juvenile and Kentucky Derby winner Street Sense (yet to sire a winner in Britain), is out of Chesham winner Seba. He lacked acceleration but kept on to make a fair debut. (op 11-2)
Strada Facendo(USA) didn't go on from a promising debut when a beaten favourite at Leicester last time, but he had been given 75 days off. This was a respectable return, travelling as well as any for a long way, and he's one to keep in mind for handicaps. (tchd 15-2)
Choisan(IRE) showed speed but didn't see his race out. (op 4-1)
Princely Sum(IRE), a half-brother to last year's Rockfel winner (for these connections) Cape Dollar, was extremely weak in the market but showed ability.
Razorbill(USA) ◆ was staying on from a long way back when squeezed for room late on. He might have been second best otherwise and this was a promising start. (op 22-1)
Right Regal(IRE) again failed to confirm the promise of his first two starts. His finishing kick was particularly disappointing considering he travelled well, albeit he didn't get the best of runs through. (op 8-1)
Menelik(IRE) ◆ was again well held, but it might be worth noting his first two starts came in festival maidens (July meeting and Glorious Goodwood), and here he was returning from three months off. Handicaps are now an option and surely he can do better. (op 33-1)
Sirious Oss ran on from off an overly strong pace when fifth at Newcastle (1m, soft) on his debut, but he was never going this time, unsuited by much more of a speed test. He's probably one for handicaps.

6984 E B F SPIFFING CRABBIE'S ALCOHOLIC GINGER BEER MAIDEN FILLIES' STKS (DIV I) 1m (S)
2:00 (2:02) (Class 5) 2-Y-0 **£2,975** (£885; £442; £221) **Stalls** High

Form RPR
1 **Lacily (USA)** 2-9-0 0 FrankieDettori 10 80+
(Mahmood Al Zarooni) *hld up towards rr: hdwy to trck ldr over 2f out: shkn up and led last 100yds: pushed out* **11/8**[1]
0 **2** *1 1/4* **Amy Dorrit**[11] 6745 2-9-0 0 WilliamBuick 9 77+
(John Gosden) *trckd ldrs: t.k.h: led and qcknd pce 3f out: edgd lft and hdd ins fnl f: no ex* **11/2**[2]
5 **3** *3* **Cockney Rhyme**[8] 6818 2-9-0 0 EddieAhern 4 70
(Heather Main) *trckd ldrs: 3rd 2f out: kpt on same pce appr fnl f* **40/1**
04 **4** *nk* **Running Deer (IRE)**[23] 6458 2-9-0 0 TomQueally 5 69
(Sir Henry Cecil) *hld up in mid-div: effrt over 2f out: edgd lft over 1f out: kpt on* **15/2**
5 *1 1/4* **Openly** 2-8-11 0 LouisBeuzelin(3) 12 66
(James Fanshawe) *slowly away: in rr: edgd lft and kpt on 2f out: nvr trbld ldrs* **16/1**
6 *6* **Adeste** 2-9-0 0 KierenFallon 6 52+
(Sir Michael Stoute) *dwlt: hld up in rr: effrt over 2f out: sn lost pl* **10/1**
00 **7** *1/2* **Duchesse Satin (IRE)**[27] 6344 2-9-0 0 DavidAllan 7 51
(Tim Easterby) *hld up towards rr: crowded over 2f out: kpt on fnl f: nvr a factor* **100/1**
3 **8** *hd* **Inffiraaj (IRE)**[23] 6458 2-9-0 0 JamieSpencer 1 51
(Mick Channon) *set modest pce: hdd 3f out: lost pl over 1f out* **6/1**[3]
0 **9** *1/2* **Oops Caroline (IRE)**[10] 6776 2-9-0 0 DanielTudhope 2 50
(David O'Meara) *chsd ldrs on outer: drvn over 2f out: sn lost pl* **25/1**
10 *1 1/2* **Countess Ferrama** 2-9-0 0 MichaelHills 11 46
(William Haggas) *sn trcking ldrs: lost pl 2f out* **14/1**
40 **11** *8* **Sally Pepper (USA)**[23] 6458 2-9-0 0 JamesSullivan 8 28
(James Given) *t.k.h in rr: lost pl over 2f out: sn bhd* **40/1**

1m 42.18s (2.88) **Going Correction** -0.20s/f (Firm) **11** Ran SP% **114.9**
Speed ratings (Par 92): **77,75,72,72,71 65,64,64,64,62 54**
toteswingers:1&2:£2.90, 1&3:£12.00, 2&3:£21.30 CSF £8.28 TOTE £2.10: £1.10, £2.00, £6.50; EX 9.40 Trifecta £278.10 Pool: £627.73 - 1.67 winning units..
Owner Godolphin **Bred** Darley **Trained** Newmarket, Suffolk

The Form Book, Raceform Ltd, Compton, RG20 6NL

FOCUS
An interesting maiden, although the pace was steady until beyond halfway, resulting in a time 3.72 seconds slower than the second division. It was won by a smart prospect.
NOTEBOOK
Lacily(USA) ◆, by one of the best sires around in Elusive Quality (progeny include Raven's Pass and Sepoy), she's a half-sister to Group 3-winning stayer Ley Hunter, out of triple top-level winner (including Irish Oaks) Lailani. She had sufficient pace to remain on the bridle when the tempo increased before showing a good attitude when strongly pressed in the closing stages. From a stable with tremendous strength in depth in this division, she could be an Oaks filly. Her pedigree is a mix of speed and stamina, but that's no bad thing with Epsom in mind considering the last three Oaks winners were sired by (in chronological order) Danehill Dancer, Intikhab and Pivotal respectively. (op 2-1)
Amy Dorrit ◆'s trainer had sent out the runner-up in this race for the last two years and both subsequently finished in the top four in the Oaks, namely Izzi Top and Gertrude Bell. This one would have finished a lot closer on her debut at Salisbury had she not been denied a clear run and she showed herself to be quite decent. According to her trainer the filly "has done a lot of growing this year" and she should continue to progress. (op 7-1 tchd 5-1)
Cockney Rhyme hinted at ability over 7f on Polytrack first time up and this was better. (op 50-1)
Running Deer(IRE) lacked the pace to get involved and would have preferred a stronger end-to-end gallop, but she was going on nicely at the finish. (op 11-2)
Openly, out of a 1m2f winner, missed the break and lacked the speed of some, but she kept on. She can do better when faced with more of a test. (op 25-1)
Adeste, out of a maiden sister Moyglare winner Sequoyah and Fillies' Mile winner Listen, didn't have the pace to cope when the tempo lifted but made modest late progress. (op 8-1)
Inffiraaj(IRE), a well-held third on her debut over 1m at Nottingham (one place ahead of Running Order), was unsuited by making the running. She had her ears pricked, not focusing at all, and was totally caught out when the pace lifted. (op 9-2)

6985 E B F SPIFFING CRABBIE'S ALCOHOLIC GINGER BEER MAIDEN FILLIES' STKS (DIV II) 1m (S)
2:35 (2:36) (Class 5) 2-Y-O **£2,975** (£885; £442; £221) **Stalls** High

Form RPR
1 **Reckoning (IRE)** 2-9-0 0 .... JamieSpencer 7 92+
(Jeremy Noseda) *hld up in tch: gd hdwy on outer 3f out: led over 2f out and sn qcknd clr: rn green and hung bdly lft ent fnl f: kpt on* **9/1**
2 ¾ **Hepworth** 2-9-0 0 .... WilliamBuick 11 90+
(John Gosden) *hld up in rr: gd hdwy over 2f out: str run fr over 1f out: styd on strly ins fnl f* **9/1**
5 3 12 **Millymonkin**[10] 6776 2-8-7 0 .... DavidSimmonson(7) 8 63
(Michael Easterby) *outpcd and bhd: hdwy over 2f out: sn rdn and styd on wl fnl f* **20/1**
4 2 **Red Halo (IRE)** 2-9-0 0 .... KierenFallon 2 58+
(Sir Michael Stoute) *s.i.s and bhd: hdwy 3f out: rdn over 2f out: kpt on same pce appr fnl f* **9/2**[2]
0 5 shd **Maybeagrey**[13] 6702 2-9-0 0 .... DuranFentiman 4 58
(Tim Easterby) *chsd ldrs: rdn along over 2f out: grad wknd* **100/1**
0 6 ¾ **Dedication**[23] 6463 2-9-0 0 .... (t) FergusSweeney 10 56+
(Roger Charlton) *trckd ldrs: hdwy and cl up over 2f out: sn rdn and wknd wl over 1f out* **9/2**[2]
7 4 **Despatch** 2-9-0 0 .... StevieDonohoe 5 47
(Ralph Beckett) *s.i.s: sn in tch: rdn along over 3f out: sn wknd* **7/1**[3]
6U 8 ¾ **Bond Artist (IRE)**[37] 6047 2-8-11 0 .... DaleSwift(3) 1 45
(Geoffrey Oldroyd) *mde most tl rdn and hdd over 2f out: sn wknd* **10/1**
5 9 nk **Gabrial's Layla (IRE)**[27] 6322 2-9-0 0 .... JoeFanning 6 44
(Mark Johnston) *cl up: rdn to chal and ev ch over 2f out: wknd wl over 1f out* **16/1**
10 17 **Vena Amoris (USA)** 2-9-0 0 .... FrankieDettori 3 5
(Mahmood Al Zarooni) *s.i.s: a in rr* **3/1**[1]
00 11 23 **Bovs Castle**[17] 6603 2-9-0 0 .... ShaneKelly 9 —
(Lucinda Featherstone) *chsd ldrs: rdn along over 3f out: sn wknd* **200/1**

1m 38.46s (-0.84) **Going Correction** -0.20s/f (Firm) **11** Ran SP% **115.1**
Speed ratings (Par 92): **96,95,83,81,81 80,76,75,75,58 35**
toteswingers:1&2:£11.60, 1&3:£28.30, 2&3:£34.00 CSF £84.61 TOTE £9.70: £2.80, £2.50, £6.00; EX 78.00 TRIFECTA Not won..
Owner The Hon William Vestey **Bred** P A Byrne **Trained** Newmarket, Suffolk
FOCUS
The time was 3.72 seconds quicker than the slowly run first division.
NOTEBOOK
Reckoning(IRE), a 55,000gns half-sister to a 7f winner, out of a dual 1m scorer, won despite continually hanging left under pressure and handing the initiative to the runner-up. If she learns from this and proves more straightforward in future, she could be smart. (op 10-1 tchd 17-2)
Hepworth ◆, a half-sister to 1m4f AW winner Sagamore and Japanese 1m Group-placed Kyoei Basara (5f 2yo winner), stayed on powerfully to finish a long way clear of the rest, although she was a bit flattered to get so close. Her trainer has been known to run a good one in this maiden and she's another who might be smart. (op 13-2)
Millymonkin showed ability on her debut on testing ground at Newcastle and did so again. She looks one for handicaps over further in due course. (op 12-1)
Red Halo(IRE), a 200,000euros sister to a 1m winner, missed the break and ran extremely green, but showed ability. She can do better, especially when her yard return to form. (op 6-1)
Maybeagrey should find her level in handicaps. (op 80-1)
Dedication didn't improve as expected for better ground and a first-time tongue-tie. (op 6-1 tchd 13-2)
Vena Amoris(USA), a 90,000gns half-sister to a winner in the US, out of a stakes-placed performer in the US, ran as though something was amiss on her racecourse debut. (op 10-3 tchd 7-2)

6986 EARL OF DONCASTER HOTEL NURSERY 1m (S)
3:10 (3:11) (Class 4) (0-85,81) 2-Y-O **£3,881** (£1,155; £577; £288) **Stalls** High

Form RPR
565P 1 **Brimstone Hill (IRE)**[11] 6757 2-8-10 70 .... MichaelHills 8 77
(Charles Hills) *hld up in rr: hdwy over 2f out: chal over 1f out: styd on to ld last 100yds* **33/1**
3313 2 1¼ **Red Alpha (IRE)**[13] 6699 2-9-3 77 .... PaulHanagan 11 81
(Jeremy Noseda) *trckd ldrs: led over 2f out: hdd and no ex ins fnl f* **9/1**
4213 3 1¾ **Devdas (IRE)**[29] 6268 2-9-4 81 .... JohnFahy(3) 13 81
(Clive Cox) *hld up: hdwy to chal over 2f out: kpt on same pce fnl f* **6/1**[2]
6100 4 ¾ **Daghash**[20] 6527 2-9-5 79 .... TomQueally 9 77
(Clive Brittain) *dwlt: in rr: hmpd over 6f out: styd on fnl 2f: nt rch ldrs* **16/1**
2520 5 nk **The Blue Banana (IRE)**[12] 6724 2-9-5 79 .... ShaneKelly 3 77
(Brian Meehan) *dwlt: in rr: outpcd over 2f out: kpt on fnl f* **10/1**
41 6 1¼ **Never Perfect (IRE)**[15] 6644 2-9-3 77 .... JamieSpencer 6 72
(Tom Tate) *dwlt: swtchd lft after 1f: hdwy on outside over 4f out: rdn over 2f out: one pce* **11/2**[1]
244 7 hd **Gunner Will (IRE)**[53] 5541 2-9-6 80 .... TonyCulhane 10 74
(George Baker) *dwlt: in rr: styd on fnl 2f: nvr nr ldrs* **9/1**
343 8 4 **Buster Brown (IRE)**[20] 6532 2-9-1 75 .... FrederikTylicki 4 62
(James Given) *trckd ldrs: lost pl 2f out: in rr whn eased ins fnl f* **7/1**
2552 9 4½ **Courtesy Call (IRE)**[14] 6667 2-8-3 63 .... JoeFanning 1 41
(Mark Johnston) *chsd ldrs: chal on outer over 3f out: wknd over 1f out: sn eased* **11/1**
4511 10 hd **Fiction Or Fact (IRE)**[30] 6260 2-8-13 76 .... (p) AmyRyan(3) 5 50
(Kevin Ryan) *mid-div: swtchd lft over 6f out: drvn 4f out: lost pl over 2f out* **14/1**
135 11 6 **Dance The Rain**[41] 5931 2-9-2 76 .... TomEaves 2 40
(Bryan Smart) *trckd ldrs: led over 3f out: hdd and hung rt over 2f out: lost pl and eased 1f out* **16/1**
040 12 7 **Hareby (IRE)**[18] 6572 2-8-7 67 .... (b1) DavidAllan 12 11
(Tim Easterby) *mid-div: drvn over 2f out: sn lost pl: bhd whn eased fnl f* **33/1**
4031 13 19 **Stellar Express (IRE)**[9] 6806 2-9-1 75 6ex .... RobbieFitzpatrick 7 —
(Michael Appleby) *led: hung lft and hdd over 3f out: lost pl over 2f out: sn bhd: heavily eased fnl f: t.o: bit slipped* **13/2**[3]

1m 38.28s (-1.02) **Going Correction** -0.20s/f (Firm) **13** Ran SP% **117.2**
Speed ratings (Par 97): **97,95,94,93,92 91,91,87,83,82 76,69,50**
toteswingers:1&2:£43.60, 1&3:£28.90, 2&3:£9.90 CSF £302.38 CT £2037.98 TOTE £35.60: £7.10, £3.40, £2.20; EX 315.60 Trifecta £591.90 Part won. Pool of £799.88 - 0.50 winning units..

Owner H R Mould **Bred** Oscar Stud **Trained** Lambourn, Berks
■ Stewards' Enquiry : Jamie Spencer two-day ban: used whip with arm above shoulder (Nov 4-5)
FOCUS
The time was quicker than both divisions of the fillies' maiden.
NOTEBOOK
Brimstone Hill(IRE) was pulled up last time owing to a slipped saddle, but he was always travelling well on this occasion and found plenty, proving suited by the distance. This was his first success at the ninth attempt but clearly he's going the right way now. (op 40-1)
Red Alpha(IRE) seemed to get the trip okay but the winner was simply the better handicapped of the pair. (op 17-2 tchd 8-1 and 10-1)
Devdas(IRE), who got a bit warm, stuck on at the one pace after travelling well.
Daghash travelled better than most but couldn't quicken.
The Blue Banana(IRE) isn't straightforward, but this was better than his recent mulish display at Goodwood. (op 14-1)
Never Perfect(IRE)'s first two starts came on testing ground, including winning over 1m at Ayr (meeting later abandoned) last time, but he didn't prove as effective on this quicker surface in deeper company. (tchd 5-1 and 6-1)
Dance The Rain Official explanation: jockey said filly hung right-handed
Stellar Express(IRE) was 3lb well in under penalty picked up for her front-running Nottingham success, but dominating this field was tougher. Robbie Fitzpatrick reported the filly hung left throughout and the bit slipped through her mouth. Official explanation: jockey said filly hung left throughout and bit slipped through its mouth (tchd 6-1)

6987 RACING POST WEEKENDER OUT EVERY WEDNESDAY H'CAP 6f
3:45 (3:47) (Class 2) (0-105,105) 3-Y-O+ **£11,450** (£3,407; £1,702; £851) **Stalls** High

Form RPR
5003 1 **Bohemian Melody**[27] 6347 4-8-10 91 .... (b1) WilliamBuick 20 108+
(Marco Botti) *hld up towards rr: smooth hdwy to trck ldrs over 2f out: rdn to ld over 1f out: qcknd clr jst ins fnl f: kpt on* **12/1**[3]
4412 2 2¼ **Elusivity (IRE)**[21] 6500 3-8-10 92 .... JamieSpencer 10 102+
(Brian Meehan) *hld up in rr: hdwy 2f out: rdn to chse wnr ins fnl f: no imp towards fin* **7/1**[1]
0652 3 1½ **Mass Rally (IRE)**[27] 6331 4-8-10 91 .... (v) DanielTudhope 6 96
(Michael Dods) *hld up in tch: hdwy 2f out: rdn and styd on ins fnl f* **20/1**
5002 4 ¾ **Anne Of Kiev (IRE)**[20] 6531 6-9-7 102 .... (t) TomQueally 17 105
(Jeremy Gask) *awkward s and in rr: gd hdwy 2f out: rdn over 1f out: kpt on ins fnl f: nrst fin* **25/1**
3340 5 1¾ **Mac's Power (IRE)**[34] 6147 5-9-5 100 .... (t) KierenFallon 15 101+
(James Fanshawe) *hld up: hdwy 2f out: swtchd lft and rdn ent fnl f: kpt on* **8/1**[2]
0002 6 ½ **Seal Rock**[12] 6723 3-8-11 93 .... FergusSweeney 18 88
(Henry Candy) *prom: effrt and cl up over 2f out: rdn wl over 1f out: kpt on same pce* **8/1**[2]
4031 7 ½ **Advanced**[27] 6347 8-8-10 94 .... AmyRyan(3) 8 88
(Kevin Ryan) *cl up: effrt 2f out and ev ch tl rdn and one pce appr fnl f* **16/1**
1350 8 nk **El Viento (FR)**[34] 6145 3-8-10 92 .... (b) BarryMcHugh 12 85
(Richard Fahey) *trckd ldrs: hdwy over 2f out: ev ch 1 1/2f out: sn rdn and wknd ent fnl f* **40/1**
0006 9 hd **Capone (IRE)**[27] 6347 6-8-5 89 .... DominicFox(3) 21 81
(David Nicholls) *chsd ldrs on wd outside: rdn along over 2f out: wknd over 1f out* **33/1**
3032 10 ½ **Kaldoun Kingdom (IRE)**[13] 6706 6-9-2 97 .... PaulHanagan 14 88
(Richard Fahey) *trckd ldrs: hdwy and cl up over 2f out: rdn and led briefly wl over 1f out: sn hdd & wknd ins fnl f* **12/1**[3]
2610 11 ¾ **Bonnie Brae**[27] 6341 4-8-9 90 .... TedDurcan 4 78+
(David Elsworth) *hld up and bhd: hdwy 2f out: n.m.r and swtchd rt over 1f out: styng on whn nt clr run ent fnl f: one pce after* **33/1**
0410 12 ½ **Cheveton**[27] 6332 7-8-9 93 .... DaleSwift(3) 16 80
(Richard Price) *in tch: hdwy to chse ldrs over 2f out: sn rdn and btn over 1f out* **22/1**
1001 13 1¼ **Valery Borzov (IRE)**[27] 6331 7-8-9 93 .... LeeTopliss(3) 9 76
(Richard Fahey) *trckd ldrs: rdn along 2f out: sn wknd* **33/1**
2005 14 shd **Parisian Pyramid (IRE)**[13] 6706 5-8-13 94 .... StephenCraine 11 76
(Kevin Ryan) *cl up: rdn 2f out: sn wknd* **16/1**
5006 15 ½ **Secret Witness**[20] 6522 5-8-11 92 .... (b) JoeFanning 1 73
(Ronald Harris) *dwlt: in tch on wd outside: rdn along over 2f out and sn wknd* **16/1**
0053 16 nse **Star Rover (IRE)**[12] 6723 4-8-8 89 .... (v) StevieDonohoe 19 70
(David Evans) *chsd ldrs on outer to 1/2-way: sn wknd* **25/1**
2000 17 ½ **Iver Bridge Lad**[19] 6563 4-9-7 105 .... (b) MichaelO'Connell(3) 7 84
(John Ryan) *midfield: hdwy and in tch over 2f out: sn rdn and btn* **16/1**
0412 18 ¾ **Marvellous Value (IRE)**[34] 6145 6-8-11 92 .... TonyHamilton 5 69
(Michael Dods) *in tch: rdn along wl over 2f out: sn wknd* **16/1**
3005 19 nk **R Woody**[32] 6224 4-8-9 90 .... ShaneKelly 3 66
(Dean Ivory) *prom: rdn along 1/2-way: sn wknd* **16/1**
-250 20 nk **Madany (IRE)**[132] 2934 3-8-10 92 .... TadhgO'Shea 2 67
(Charles Hills) *in tch: rdn along wl over 2f out: sn wknd* **28/1**
1100 21 1½ **Grissom (IRE)**[34] 6145 5-8-11 92 .... DavidAllan 22 62
(Tim Easterby) *in tch on wd outside: rdn along over 2f out: sn wknd* **14/1**

0400 **22** *1* **Enderby Spirit (GR)**[69] 5060 5-8-10 **91**............................ TomEaves 13 58
(Bryan Smart) *cl up: rdn along wl over 2f out: sn wknd* **28/1**

1m 10.98s (-2.62) **Going Correction** -0.20s/f (Firm)
WFA 3 from 4yo+ 1lb **22** Ran SP% **127.0**
Speed ratings (Par 109): **109,106,104,103,100 100,99,98,98,98 97,96,94,94,93 93,93,92,91,91 89,88**
toteswingers:1&2:£18.20, 1&3:£60.70, 2&3:£91.00 CSF £82.05 CT £1735.34 TOTE £16.50: £3.60, £2.80, £5.30, £4.40; EX 119.00 Trifecta £1169.90 Part won. Pool of £1581.04 - 0.50 winning units..
Owner Mrs L Botti **Bred** Ivan W Allan **Trained** Newmarket, Suffolk

FOCUS
A red-hot sprint handicap. Somewhat surprisingly they all raced in one group for most of the way, and the main action was middle to stands' side. Only two of the first ten finishers were drawn in single figures. Improvement from the winner, with the race rated around the third.

NOTEBOOK
Bohemian Melody ◆ has looked potentially smart for a while now (he was really promising on Polytrack earlier in his career), but he's had a light campaign this time and was on the wrong wide at Ripon on his most recent start. There was no excuse this time, though, with him responding well to the first-time blinkers and quickening in the manner of a Group horse. It remains to be seen whether the headgear will continue to work so well, but he does look on the way to belatedly fulfilling his potential. He could be one for Dubai, especially considering he goes so well on synthetics. (op 11-1)

Elusivity(IRE) ◆ has a high cruising speed but tends to find only a brief burst of acceleration, and on his latest start he was picked off by a rival who challenged later, albeit it was the really smart Sirius Prospect (followed up off 7lb higher). Perhaps feeling he got there too soon last time, Jamie Spencer was anxious to deliver him as late as possible on this occasion, but consequently he was caught out when the winner quickened. He was up against another well-handicapped rival, though, and finished clear of the others off what was a 3lb higher mark. Like the winner, he has Group-race potential and may also be one for Dubai. (op 13-2 tchd 6-1)

Mass Rally(IRE) ◆ had to wait for a run before keeping on nicely behind two well-handicapped improvers. He was best of those from a single-figure draw and can surely end his losing run. (op 25-1)

Anne Of Kiev(IRE) recovered from a slow start to travel well, but she lost her place at a crucial stage and got going too late.

Mac's Power(IRE) ◆ was reported to have been unsuited by the soft ground in the Ayr Gold Cup on his previous start. Racing from a mark 10lb higher than when winning this last year, he got no run at all this time and otherwise would have finished a lot closer, although it's tough to say just where he would have ended up. (tchd 15-2)

Seal Rock, 2lb well in, fared best of those to chase the pace. (op 17-2 tchd 9-1)

Bonnie Brae ◆ got no run at all and should have finished a lot closer.

6988 RACING POST / SIS BETTING SHOP MANAGER H'CAP 1m 6f 132y
4:20 (4:21) (Class 4) (0-85,84) 3-Y-O+ **£4,528** (£1,347; £673; £336) **Stalls** Low

Form RPR
010 **1** **Gulf Of Naples (IRE)**[48] 5710 3-9-2 **81**........................ SamHitchcott 15 93+
(Mark Johnston) *mid-div: hdwy on outer over 3f out: led over 1f out: swvd rt 1f out: styd on wl* **20/1**

3000 **2** *2 ½* **Exemplary**[48] 5705 4-9-12 **82**.. JoeFanning 17 90
(Mark Johnston) *trckd ldrs: led over 2f out: hdd over 1f out: styd on same pce* **20/1**

3325 **3** *hd* **Moment Juste**[37] 6054 3-8-11 **76**...................................... WilliamBuick 3 84
(John Gosden) *chsd ldrs: drvn 4f out: outpcd over 2f out: kpt on fnl f* **10/1**

3322 **4** *1 ¼* **Bollin Greta**[34] 6151 6-10-0 **84**...(t) DavidAllan 4 90
(Tim Easterby) *hld up in rr: hdwy to chse ldrs over 3f out: kpt on same pce appr fnl f* **12/1**

112- **5** *1* **Switched Off**[202] 6322 6-9-0 **73**.............................. MichaelO'Connell(3) 5 78
(Ian Williams) *s.i.s: in rr: drvn and hdwy over 3f out: one pce over 1f out* **20/1**

5122 **6** *shd* **Mazagee (FR)**[11] 6749 3-9-3 **82**.. TedDurcan 8 87
(David Lanigan) *in rr: hdwy and swtchd ins over 3f out: kpt on one pce over 1f out* **7/2**[1]

5533 **7** *nk* **Gordonsville**[34] 6171 8-9-11 **81**................................... DanielTudhope 13 85
(Jim Goldie) *chsd ldrs: upsides 2f out: kpt on one pce* **16/1**

223 **8** *shd* **Wild Desert (FR)**[22] 6485 6-9-3 **78**.............................. LucyKBarry(5) 11 82
(Charlie Longsdon) *trckd ldr: led over 7f out: hdd over 2f out: fdd fnl f* **16/1**

0030 **9** *2 ¾* **Kings Troop**[14] 6676 5-9-10 **80**... TomQueally 12 81
(Alan King) *hld up in rr: hdwy over 3f out: kpt on fnl 2f: nvr nr ldrs* **33/1**

-465 **10** *2* **Hayzoom**[36] 6103 4-9-7 **77**..(p) FrankieDettori 10 75
(Peter Chapple-Hyam) *mid-div: hdwy to chse ldrs over 3f out: wknd fnl f* **10/1**

2512 **11** *nk* **Marcus Antonius**[9] 6798 4-8-9 **65**.................................... EddieAhern 19 63
(Jim Boyle) *swtchd lft after s: hdwy and mid-div 10f out: chsd ldrs and nt clr run over 2f out: wknd over 1f out* **14/1**

4152 **12** *2* **Wayward Glance**[28] 6294 3-9-4 **83**................................ JamieSpencer 9 78
(Michael Bell) *led tl over 7f out: chsd ldrs: wknd over 1f out* **7/1**[2]

6560 **13** *2 ½* **Spiekeroog**[13] 6707 5-8-8 **69**................................ AshleyMorgan(5) 7 61
(David O'Meara) *chsd ldrs: wknd over 1f out* **12/1**

0352 **14** *6* **Royal Trooper (IRE)**[27] 6333 5-9-13 **83**...................... FrederikTylicki 18 67
(James Given) *trckd ldrs on outside: dropped in rr bnd after 4f: hdwy over 5f out: lost pl 2f out* **9/1**[3]

1603 **15** *23* **Mungo Park**[48] 5714 3-8-13 **78**.. MichaelHills 14 32
(Mark Johnston) *chsd ldrs on outer: lost pl 4f out: bhd whn eased over 1f out* **16/1**

1124 **16** *4 ½* **Tweedledrum**[15] 3277 4-9-2 **79**............................... MichaelJMurphy(7) 2 27
(Tom Symonds) *in rr: hdwy on inner over 3f out: wknd over 2f out: eased 1f out* **25/1**

0200 **17** *13* **Time Square (FR)**[23] 6439 4-9-2 **72**................................(t) SebSanders 1 —
(Tony Carroll) *mid-div: reminders 4f out: sn lost pl: bhd whn eased* **66/1**

054/ **18** *3 ½* **Presque Perdre**[705] 2044 7-8-2 **65** oh18........................ JasonHart(7) 20 —
(George Moore) *s.s: swtchd lft after s: hdwy on outer over 6f out: lost pl 4f out: sn bhd: t.o whn eased* **50/1**

3m 6.57s (-0.83) **Going Correction** -0.20s/f (Firm)
WFA 3 from 4yo+ 9lb **18** Ran SP% **127.1**
Speed ratings (Par 105): **94,92,92,91,91 91,91,91,89,88 88,87,86,82,70 68,61,59**
toteswingers:1&2:£107.30, 1&3:£50.90, 2&3:£87.80 CSF £362.88 CT £4220.58 TOTE £36.20: £5.20, £4.80, £3.10, £3.00; EX 357.30 TRIFECTA Not won..
Owner Sheikh Hamdan Bin Mohammed Al Maktoum **Bred** Stone Ridge Farm **Trained** Middleham Moor, N Yorks

FOCUS
A fair staying handicap but it wasn't strong run and there was a bunch finish. The bare form is only ordinary for the grade, but the winner produced a clear personal best and could be a fair bit better than this.

6989 BENTLEY'S GENTLEMAN'S CLUB DONCASTER H'CAP 1m 2f 60y
4:55 (5:01) (Class 4) (0-85,85) 3-Y-O+ **£4,528** (£1,347; £673; £336) **Stalls** Low

Form RPR
0000 **1** **Dhaular Dhar (IRE)**[13] 6708 9-8-12 **79**........................ GaryBartley(3) 17 90
(Jim Goldie) *midfield: stdy hdwy 3f out: chsd ldrs whn n.m.r over 1f out: rdn and ev ch whn hmpd ent fnl f: sn led and styd on gamely* **28/1**

0205 **2** *hd* **Space War**[13] 6708 4-9-6 **84**.. JamesSullivan 15 95
(Michael Easterby) *t.k.h early: hld up towards rr: stdy hdwy over 3f out: effrt and edgd lft over 1f out: sn rdn and ev ch: edgd lft ins fnl f and no ex towards fin* **12/1**

2525 **3** *2* **Incendo**[20] 6528 5-9-7 **85**..(t) EddieAhern 8 92
(James Fanshawe) *trckd ldr: hdwy and cl up 2f out: rdn and ev ch over 1f out tl one pce ins fnl f* **14/1**

-210 **4** *1 ¼* **Jameel (USA)**[20] 6528 3-9-2 **85**..................................... FrankieDettori 14 89
(Saeed Bin Suroor) *trckd ldrs: hdwy 4f out: led 2f out: rdn over 1f out: hdd & wknd ins fnl f* **8/1**

004 **5** *nse* **All Annalena (IRE)**[27] 6330 5-9-6 **84**................................ TedDurcan 16 88
(Lucy Wadham) *a chsng ldrs: rdn along over 2f out: drvn over 1f out: kpt on same pce* **20/1**

1111 **6** *nk* **Camberley Two**[77] 4750 3-9-2 **85**................................ JamieSpencer 6 89
(Roger Charlton) *hld up towards rr: hdwy 3f out: rdn to chse ldrs wl over 1f out: kpt on same pce* **7/1**[2]

5001 **7** *½* **Tartan Gigha (IRE)**[10] 6773 6-9-3 **81** 6ex.......................... JoeFanning 1 84
(Mark Johnston) *trckd ldrs: effrt over 3f out: rdn along over 2f out: drvn and one pce appr fnl f* **11/1**

01- **8** *½* **Noguchi (IRE)**[347] 7382 6-9-5 **83**.................................... SebSanders 12 85
(Jeremy Noseda) *in tch: hdwy to chse ldrs over 3f out: rdn along and hld whn hmpd over 1f out: sn one pce* **33/1**

500 **9** *½* **Nice Style (IRE)**[27] 6339 6-9-7 **85**................................(t) TomQueally 7 86
(Jeremy Gask) *midfield: hdwy 4f out: effrt over 2f out: sn rdn and no imp appr fnl f* **15/2**[3]

0022 **10** *1 ½* **Jo'Burg (USA)**[13] 6708 7-9-4 **82**.............................. DanielTudhope 13 80+
(David O'Meara) *hld up towards rr: sme hdwy over 3f out: rdn along 2f out and sn no imp* **13/2**[1]

3322 **11** *shd* **Persian Peril**[38] 6024 7-9-6 **84**.. PJMcDonald 18 82+
(Alan Swinbank) *towards rr: sme hdwy over 2f out: sn rdn and n.d* **18/1**

021 **12** *nk* **New Hampshire (USA)**[126] 3135 3-9-2 **85**.................. WilliamBuick 20 82+
(John Gosden) *hld up and bhd: sme hdwy 3f out: rdn along 2f out: n.d* **11/1**

3113 **13** *¾* **Judicious**[38] 6024 4-9-2 **80**.. PaulQuinn 19 76+
(Geoffrey Harker) *hld up: a in rr* **20/1**

3100 **14** *hd* **Zebrano**[148] 2441 5-9-3 **81**......................................(b) FergusSweeney 4 77
(Andrew Haynes) *hld up: a towards rr* **66/1**

0045 **15** *4 ½* **Moheebb (IRE)**[20] 6544 7-9-2 **80**..................................(b) ShaneKelly 11 67
(Ruth Carr) *in tch: rdn along over 3f out: sn wknd* **40/1**

000- **16** *1 ¼* **Shadows Lengthen**[210] 7612 5-8-7 **78**..............(b) DavidSimmonson(7) 2 63
(Michael Easterby) *led: rdn along over 3f out: hdd 2f out and wknd qckly* **50/1**

3004 **17** *1* **Ginger Jack**[20] 6533 4-9-2 **80**.. DavidAllan 3 63
(Geoffrey Harker) *hld up: a bhd* **11/1**

0000 **18** *12* **Breakheart (IRE)**[36] 6078 4-9-1 **79**..............................(t) TonyHamilton 5 39
(Michael Dods) *chsd ldrs on inner: rdn along over 3f out: sn wknd* **20/1**

0030 **19** *6* **Oratory (IRE)**[16] 6631 5-9-2 **80**...................................... DuranFentiman 9 28
(Geoffrey Harker) *hld up: a bhd* **33/1**

2m 8.03s (-1.37) **Going Correction** -0.20s/f (Firm)
WFA 3 from 4yo+ 5lb **19** Ran SP% **122.8**
Speed ratings (Par 105): **97,96,95,94,94 93,93,93,92,91 91,91,90,90,86 85,85,75,70**
toteswingers:1&2:£102.20, 1&3:£83.60, 2&3:£29.60 CSF £303.36 CT £4869.97 TOTE £33.00: £5.20, £3.70, £4.10, £2.00; EX 538.00 TRIFECTA Not won..
Owner Jim Goldie Racing Club **Bred** Gainsborough Stud Management Ltd **Trained** Uplawmoor, E Renfrews

FOCUS
Another big-field handicap but it wasn't strong run. Sound enough form mongst the principals.
Dhaular Dhar(IRE) Official explanation: trainer said, regarding apparent improvement in form, that the horse was better suited by the way the race was run.

6990 PRICEWISE IN RACING POST ON SATURDAYS APPRENTICE H'CAP 1m (S)
5:25 (5:28) (Class 5) (0-75,78) 3-Y-O+ **£2,522** (£750; £375; £187) **Stalls** High

Form RPR
4022 **1** **Violent Velocity (IRE)**[31] 6231 8-9-1 **69**.................. MatthewLawson 11 80+
(John Quinn) *hld up: mid-div: hdwy over 3f out: led over 1f out: kpt on wl* **14/1**

2305 **2** *1 ¼* **Nolecce**[9] 6785 4-8-6 **63**..(p) JakePayne(3) 10 69
(Richard Guest) *trckd ldrs: led over 2f out: hdd over 1f out: styd on same pce fnl f* **25/1**

0652 **3** *nk* **Tewin Wood**[18] 6583 4-9-4 **75**................................ NatashaEaton(3) 15 80
(Alan Bailey) *chsd ldrs: led over 3f out: hdd over 2f out: kpt on same pce last 150yds* **10/1**

6000 **4** *2 ¾* **Chosen Forever**[15] 6658 6-8-11 **68**.................... GeorgeChaloner(3) 18 67
(Geoffrey Oldroyd) *racd stands' side: chsd ldrs: upsides 2f out: wknd fnl 150yds* **12/1**

0655 **5** *1 ¾* **Oh So Saucy**[55] 5496 7-8-13 **72**............................ DannyBrock(5) 8 67
(Chris Wall) *chsd ldrs: rdn over 2f out: kpt on fnl f* **8/1**[2]

2343 **6** *nk* **Ay Tay Tate (IRE)**[89] 4367 5-8-10 **64**........................ CharlesBishop 12 58
(David C Griffiths) *chsd ldrs: outpcd 3f out: kpt on over 1f out* **8/1**[2]

4043 **7** *½* **Muftarres (IRE)**[18] 6583 6-8-6 **67**..............................(b[1]) RichardOld(7) 9 60
(Paul Midgley) *hld up in rr: hdwy over 2f out: nvr nr ldrs* **14/1**

2003 **8** *2* **Climaxfortackle (IRE)**[7] 6830 3-8-9 **66**......................(v) DavidKenny 14 55
(Derek Shaw) *hld up in mid-div: hdwy over 2f out: one pce* **22/1**

3205 **9** *½* **Bloodsweatandtears**[20] 6543 3-9-0 **74** ow3.......(p) MichaelJMurphy(3) 4 61
(William Knight) *mid-div: rdn over 3f out: nvr a factor* **12/1**

003 **10** *1 ½* **Afrikaans (IRE)**[32] 6210 3-8-7 **64**................................ DarylByrne 2 48
(Mark Johnston) *chsd ldrs: drvn over 4f out: sn outpcd* **16/1**

6021 **11** *4* **The Osteopath (IRE)**[7] 6831 8-9-10 **78** 6ex...............(p) GarryWhillans 7 53
(Michael Dods) *chsd ldrs: effrt over 2f out: sn wknd* **15/2**[1]

3554 **12** *½* **Cyflymder (IRE)**[94] 4176 5-8-8 **65**........................ ThomasBrown(3) 19 39
(David C Griffiths) *racd stands' side: chsd ldrs: edgd lft after 3f: edgd rt 3f out: sn lost pl* **25/1**

0130 **13** *½* **Horatio Carter**[7] 6831 6-9-1 **69**..................................(p) LucyKBarry 13 41
(David O'Meara) *chsd ldrs: drvn 4f out: sn lost pl* **9/1**[3]

06/0 **14** ¾ **Miss Beat (IRE)**[151] 2366 5-9-0 **73**.................................... JasonHart(5) 6 44
(Declan Carroll) *s.i.s: hld up in rr: rdn and edgd rt over 3f out: wknd 2f out* **28/1**
1060 **15** 1½ **Gallego**[10] 6773 9-8-11 **65**.. RachealKneller 17 32
(Richard Price) *s.i.s: racd stands' side: sn bhd: sme late hdwy: nvr on terms* **25/1**
4035 **16** ¾ **Tapis Libre**[21] 6507 3-8-4 **66**................................ DavidSimmonson(5) 16 32
(Michael Easterby) *chsd ldrs: lost pl over 2f out* **16/1**
0000 **17** 5 **Cono Zur (FR)**[20] 6533 4-8-9 **68**..........................(b) ShirleyTeasdale(5) 1 22
(Ruth Carr) *led tl over 3f out: lost pl over 2f out* **16/1**
2060 **18** nk **Circus Star (USA)**[70] 5014 3-8-7 **64**................................ NathanAlison 5 17
(Brian Meehan) *hood removed v late: s.s: edgd lft and racd slone far side: sn bhd* **18/1**

1m 39.54s (0.24) **Going Correction** -0.20s/f (Firm)
WFA 3 from 4yo+ 3lb **18** Ran SP% **124.0**
Speed ratings (Par 103): **90,88,88,85,83 83,83,81,80,79 75,74,74,73,71 71,66,65**
toteswingers:1&2:£43.80, 1&3:£10.50, 2&3:£59.30 CSF £340.64 CT £3644.67 TOTE £11.90: £2.90, £5.60, £2.70, £3.30; EX 207.00 Trifecta £424.10 Part won. Pool of £573.12 - 0.10 winning units..
Owner Mrs S Quinn **Bred** Miss Jill Finegan **Trained** Settrington, N Yorks

FOCUS
A race for apprentices who had not ridden more than 25 winners. Plenty of runners but modest form. The winner is rated slightly better than the bare form. They were spread out across the track and up the middle was the place to be. Not many got involved.
Circus Star(USA) Official explanation: jockey said gelding was slowly away
T/Jkpt: Not won. T/Plt: £522.20 to a £1 stake. Pool of £91,721.67 - 128.20 winning tickets. T/Qpdt: £164.80 to a £1 stake. Pool of £7,129.38 - 32.00 winning tickets. JR

6160 NEWBURY (L-H)
Friday, October 21

OFFICIAL GOING: Good to firm (6.9)
Wind: Moderate ahead Weather: Overcast

6991 DOWNLOAD THE BLUE SQUARE BET APP EBF MAIDEN STKS (DIV I) 6f 110y
1:20 (1:22) (Class 4) 2-Y-O **£4,398** (£1,309; £654; £327) **Stalls** Centre

Form RPR
6 **1** **Usain Colt**[82] 4580 2-9-3 0... RichardHughes 11 86+
(Richard Hannon) *unf: scope: hld up in tch: pushed along and qcknd appr fnl f: r.o wl to ld fnl 120yds: edgd rt: readily* **3/1**[2]
2 2¼ **Swan Song** 2-8-12 0.. JimmyFortune 2 75+
(Andrew Balding) *neat: led over 4f out: drvn and styd on fnl f: hdd and outpcd by wnr fnl 120yds* **12/1**
02 **3** hd **Sheikh The Reins (IRE)**[20] 6525 2-9-3 0.................... RobertWinston 3 79
(John Best) *chsd ldr: drvn and ev ch fr 2f out: kpt on to press for 2nd fnl 120yds but no ch w wnr* **9/2**[3]
6 **4** 3 **Switzerland (IRE)**[20] 6525 2-9-3 0....................................... LukeMorris 7 71+
(Mark Johnston) *w'like: scope: chsd ldrs drvn over 2f out: styd on same pce fr over 1f out* **33/1**
5 **5** 2¾ **Forest Row**[161] 2049 2-9-3 0.. AdamKirby 1 63
(Clive Cox) *lw: s.i.s: sn rcvrd: chsd ldrs 2f out: wknd fnl f* **5/4**[1]
6 ½ **Daffyd** 2-9-3 0..(t) SteveDrowne 8 62
(Roger Charlton) *w'like: leggy: unruly paddock: hld up in rr: drvn and outpcd fnl 2f* **12/1**
7 ½ **Take Two** 2-9-3 0... RussKennemore 9 60
(John O'Shea) *unf: scope: slowly away: in rr: drvn and green fr 1/2-way but kpt on fnl f* **100/1**
0 **8** nk **Chambles**[22] 6480 2-8-9 0...................................... KieranO'Neill(3) 10 54
(Andrew Reid) *w'like: led tl over 4f out: drvn and edgd rt over 1f out: sn wknd* **100/1**
9 2¾ **Picture Dealer** 2-9-3 0.. RyanMoore 4 52+
(Gary Moore) *w'like: scope: attr: slowly away: in rr but sn in tch w main gp: wknd 2f out* **20/1**
0 **10** ½ **Silent Laughter**[81] 4614 2-8-12 0.. JimCrowley 5 45+
(Jonathan Portman) *athletic: chsd ldrs 4f* **100/1**
00 **11** 1¾ **Navajo Charm**[45] 5814 2-8-9 0................................ HarryBentley(3) 6 40
(Alan Jarvis) *chsd ldrs: drvn and wknd over 2f out* **66/1**

1m 19.66s (0.36) **Going Correction** -0.075s/f (Good) **11** Ran SP% **115.2**
Speed ratings (Par 97): **94,91,91,87,84 84,83,83,80,79 77**
toteswingers:1&2:£6.30, 1&3:£1.50, 2&3:£3.00 CSF £35.14 TOTE £3.40: £1.30, £2.40, £1.60; EX 37.00.
Owner Betfair/Birdcage Racing Club **Bred** Jenny Hall Bloodstock Ltd **Trained** East Everleigh, Wilts
■ A comeback winner for Richard Hughes, who had announced he would not ride until the new whip rules were amended.

FOCUS
The first division of a fairly ordinary maiden by the course's standards. The time was 0.12 seconds slower than the following race.

NOTEBOOK
Usain Colt swept through inside the final furlong for a stylish victory, winning with quite a bit in hand. A useful prospect who should stay 7f, he clearly has plenty of speed and it will be interesting to see if he turns up for a Newmarket conditions race open to both 2yo and 3yos at Newmarket in a couple of weeks, a race connections won with Paco Boy in 2007. (op 10-3 tchd 7-2)
Swan Song, a sister to a 5f Listed winner Loch Verdi and from the family of Lochsong, predictably showed speed and held on well for second, so should be winning a maiden, with a drop in trip possibly helping. (op 9-1)
Sheikh The Reins(IRE) ran another solid race and can be used to judge the form around. He looks capable of winning a maiden, possibly on the AW. (op 4-1 tchd 5-1 in a place)
Switzerland(IRE) improved markedly on his debut effort and should appreciate a stiffer test, especially once handicapping after another run.
Forest Row, a promising fifth in what is traditionally a decent maiden at the course back in May, proved solid at the head of the market, so it was most disappointing to see him run the way he did, finding little and fading. He's entitled to improve, but it doubtful this defeat was down to fitness. (op 6-4)
Daffyd, a half-brother to six winners, most notably Border Patrol and Eisteddfod, was wearing a tongue-tie for this debut and caused some trouble in the paddock beforehand. Not the best away, he stayed on late without being given a hard time and can be expected to improve markedly.
Take Two, although a half-brother to three jumps winners, showed a bit of ability on this racecourse debut, keeping on late having been slowly away and green. A stiffer test will suit and it'll be interesting to monitor his progress. (tchd 150-1 in a place)

6992 DOWNLOAD THE BLUE SQUARE BET APP EBF MAIDEN STKS (DIV II) 6f 110y
1:50 (1:51) (Class 4) 2-Y-O **£4,398** (£1,309; £654; £327) **Stalls** Centre

Form RPR
0 **1** **Priceless Jewel**[11] 6751 2-8-12 0.. JamesDoyle 7 77+
(Roger Charlton) *leggy: scope: attr: mde all: shkn up and qcknd 4 l clr appr fnl f: styd on strly clsng stages* **8/1**
2 2¼ **Tawaasul** 2-8-12 0... RichardHills 1 71+
(William Haggas) *str: trckd ldrs: pushed along: green and outpcd 2f out: styd on strly fnl f to take 2nd under hand riding fnl 120yds: gng on cl home* **5/1**[3]
0 **3** 2¼ **Fabled City (USA)**[12] 6725 2-9-3 0.. AdamKirby 6 69
(Clive Cox) *t.k.h and chsd ldrs: disp 2nd fr 2f out but nvr nr wnr: one pce and dropped to 3rd fnl 120yds* **6/1**
50 **4** hd **Aim Higher**[10] 6768 2-9-3 0.. RyanMoore 3 69
(John Gosden) *w'like: str: lw: chsd ldrs: disp 2nd fr 2f out: stl green and hung rt fnl f: wknd fnl 120yds* **11/4**[2]
5 1¾ **Typography** 2-9-3 0... MartinDwyer 5 64
(William Muir) *w'like: towards rr: drvn along over 2f out and one pce: kpt on ins fnl f: nt rch ldrs* **50/1**
03 **6** ½ **Emperor Vespasian**[23] 6464 2-9-3 0.............................. JimmyFortune 9 62
(Andrew Balding) *lw: chsd wnr pushed along 3f out: lost 2nd 2f out: sn outpcd but kpt on again clsng stages* **15/8**[1]
00 **7** 2¼ **Seraphiel**[23] 6463 2-9-3 0.. DaneO'Neill 4 56
(Chris Down) *in rr: hung rt to r alone towards stands' side fr 2f out: sme prog ins fnl f* **100/1**
0 **8** 1¼ **Glaze**[11] 6744 2-8-12 0... DarryllHolland 2 47
(Hughie Morrison) *stdd s: in rr but in tch: outpcd 2f out: mod prog again ins fnl f* **20/1**
9 27 **Miss Elliemay (IRE)** 2-8-12 0.. RussKennemore 8 —
(John O'Shea) *w'like: leggy: rdn 1/2-way: a bhd: eased fnl 2f: t.o* **100/1**

1m 19.54s (0.24) **Going Correction** -0.075s/f (Good) **9** Ran SP% **112.2**
Speed ratings (Par 97): **95,92,89,89,87 87,84,83,52**
toteswingers:1&2:£14.50, 1&3:£29.10, 2&3:£4.60 CSF £45.09 TOTE £10.50: £2.60, £1.70, £2.30; EX 71.40.
Owner B E Nielsen **Bred** Bjorn E Nielsen **Trained** Beckhampton, Wilts

FOCUS
It's doubtful there was much between the two divisions (winning time 0.12 seconds faster than division one.)

NOTEBOOK
Priceless Jewel ran out at least as impressive a winner as Usain Colt in division one, quickening well off the front and drawing clear, despite still looking green. Roger Charlton afterwards expressed his surprise at her poor debut showing, and this half-sister to the yard's top-notch sprinter Tante Rose looks to have a very bright future. (tchd 7-1)
Tawaasul, half-sister to 7f-1m winner Manaal, out of a 1,000 Guineas runner-up, made a highly satisfactory debut, staying on having initially been outpaced. She showed signs of greenness, so is entitled to improve, and can win a maiden. (tchd 6-1)
Fabled City(USA), again wearing the hood, proved one-paced under pressure. His dam won over 1m2f, so maybe a stiffer test will suit. (op 8-1)
Aim Higher ran his best race so far, but looked most awkward inside the final 2f, hanging both ways, probably through greenness, and Ryan Moore chose not to give him a corrective slap. He's clearly quite speedy and remains capable of better now handicapped, so should be given the benefit of the doubt for now. Official explanation: jockey said colt hung right (op 10-3 tchd 7-2)
Typography, already gelded, was green early, but did make some nice late headway and he can be found a race at a lesser track. (tchd 66-1)
Emperor Vespasian, who'd run previous winners close at Salisbury the time before, yet came up well short faced with this easier opportunity. He did have the run of the race the time before, so was perhaps flattered, and he may find himself high enough in the handicap with nurseries in mind. (op 6-4 tchd 11-8)

6993 BET AT BLUESQ.COM MAIDEN STKS (DIV I) 1m (S)
2:20 (2:23) (Class 5) 2-Y-O **£3,234** (£962; £481; £240) **Stalls** Centre

Form RPR
1 **Assizes** 2-9-3 0.. LukeMorris 8 82+
(Mark Johnston) *leggy: lengthy: scope: trckd ldrs: drvn to ld 1f out: pushed out* **15/2**
2 2¼ **Hallings Comet** 2-9-3 0... JimmyFortune 10 77+
(Andrew Balding) *leggy: athletic: s.i.s: in rr: hdwy over 2f out: styd on wl to chse wnr ins fnl f: kpt on but no imp* **8/1**
3 1¼ **Trader Jack** 2-9-3 0... SteveDrowne 3 76+
(Roger Charlton) *w'like: scope: gd bodied: s.i.s: in rr: hdwy and nt clr run over 2f out: drvn and styd on to take 3rd fnl 120yds: no imp on ldng duo* **6/1**[2]
4 1¼ **Mutasadder (USA)** 2-9-3 0... RichardHills 14 71+
(Roger Varian) *w'like: attr: lw: stdd s: in tch: drvn to chal over 1f out: wknd fnl 120yds* **8/1**
0 **5** ¾ **Turned To Gold (IRE)**[23] 6448 2-9-0 0...................... HarryBentley(3) 12 69
(Alan Jarvis) *str: lw: sn slt ld: hung lft fr over 3f out whn strly pressed: hdd over 2f out: sn drvn: ev ch over 1f out: wknd fnl 120yds* **25/1**
6 1 **Dream Tune** 2-9-3 0.. AdamKirby 1 67
(Clive Cox) *w'like: scope: chsd ldrs: chal 3f out: led over 2f out: hdd 1f out: wknd ins fnl f* **8/1**
0 **7** 2 **Wreaths Of Empire (IRE)**[25] 6400 2-9-3 0................. RichardHughes 7 62+
(Richard Hannon) *w'like: in rr: drvn and styd on fr 2f out: no imp on ldrs over 1f out and styd on same pce* **9/2**[1]
0 **8** 2¼ **Frederickthegreat**[22] 6481 2-9-3 0...............................(t) DarryllHolland 6 57+
(Hughie Morrison) *w'like: lw: in rr: stl last over 2f out whn drvn: styd on wl fnl f but nvr a threat* **25/1**
05 **9** 3¼ **Tectonic (IRE)**[42] 5875 2-9-3 0.. MartinDwyer 4 50
(Brian Meehan) *t.k.h: chsd ldrs: drvn and green fr over 2f out: sn wknd* **20/1**
10 2 **Unex Canaletto** 2-9-3 0.. ChrisCatlin 11 45
(Paul Cole) *w'like: t.k.h: chsd ldrs: wknd over 2f out* **16/1**
11 12 **Onertother** 2-9-3 0... MatthewDavies 2 18
(Joseph Tuite) *w'like: athletic: pressed ldrs 1/2-way: wknd over 2f out: hung rt whn no ch fnl f* **66/1**
12 hd **Superciliary** 2-9-3 0... JimCrowley 5 17
(Ralph Beckett) *str: lw: in tch: drvn along 3f out: wknd over 2f out* **13/2**[3]
13 4 **Tundridge** 2-9-3 0.. JamesDoyle 9 8
(Sylvester Kirk) *w'like: chsd ldrs over 4f* **25/1**

60 **14** *19* **Almirah**[102] 3917 2-8-12 0 ... MarcHalford 13 —
(Edward Creighton) *pressed ldrs: chalng whn edgd lft fr 3f out: wknd rapidly wl over 2f out* **150/1**

1m 40.49s (0.79) **Going Correction** -0.075s/f (Good) **14** Ran SP% **115.2**
Speed ratings (Par 95): **93,90,89,88,87 86,84,82,79,77 65,64,60,41**
toteswingers:1&2:£20.50, 1&3:£7.90, 2&3:£9.40 CSF £58.49 TOTE £9.30: £2.80, £2.70, £2.10; EX 84.00.

Owner Sheikh Hamdan Bin Mohammed Al Maktoum **Bred** Darley **Trained** Middleham Moor, N Yorks

FOCUS

This appeared the stronger of the two divisions of the 1m maiden and with those to have already run achieving little of note, it was predictably a clean sweep for newcomers.

NOTEBOOK

Assizes, a half-brother to 2yo 1m winner Dr Faustus, certainly knew his job and, having briefly been outpaced when the tempo lifted, he surged to the front over 1f out and went on to win with a bit in hand. Entitled to improve for the experience, he looks almost certain to appreciate the step up to 1m2f and it would be no surprise to see him run in the Zetland Stakes at Newmarket. (op 17-2 tchd 7-1)

Hallings Comet, nothing to get excited about on breeding, got a bump at the start and was soon in rear, but made good headway before the winner asserted late on. This was a nice beginning for him and he should stay 1m2f. (op 10-1)

Trader Jack, first foal of a half-sister to the yard's smart Al Kazeem, wasn't the best away and didn't receive much luck during the race. He was keeping on with purpose and natural progress should see him winning a maiden. (op 5-1)

Mutasadder(USA), half-brother to a 6f 2yo winner, has stamina on the dam's side of his pedigree, but having picked up to challenge, his effort petered out late on. He should learn and do better as a 3yo. (op 9-2)

Turned To Gold(IRE) showed the benefit of his debut experience, showing up well for a long way and looking a likely type for handicaps after another run. (op 40-1)

Dream Tune ◆, a 300,000euros Derby entrant with a blend of speed and stamina in his pedigree, fared better than the bare result, going to the front over 2f out before the lack of a run told. He ought to improve and is another likely sort to win a maiden. (op 15-2)

Wreaths Of Empire(IRE), well beaten over 1m2f at Bath on debut, was supported in the market, but lacked the pace to get involved over this shorter trip. (op 6-1)

Frederickthegreat was going on late but it's unclear what trip he needs from his pedigree. (op 33-1)

Tectonic(IRE), having his first start since leaving Sir Michael Stoute, was a touch keen and still looks inexperienced. He'll be one for ordinary handicaps. (op 33-1)

Onertother Official explanation: jockey said gelding hung right

Almirah Official explanation: jockey said filly hung left

6994 BET AT BLUESQ.COM MAIDEN STKS (DIV II) 1m (S)

2:55 (2:55) (Class 5) 2-Y-O **£3,234** (£962; £481; £240) **Stalls** Centre

Form RPR

1 **Waterclock (IRE)** 2-9-3 0 ... JamesDoyle 4 80+
(Roger Charlton) *leggy: in tch: pushed along 3f out: led wl over 1f out: drvn fnl f: jst hld on* **25/1**

55 **2** *shd* **Hefner (IRE)**[56] 5447 2-9-3 0 ... RichardHughes 1 80+
(Richard Hannon) *lw: chsd ldrs: chal 2f out: outpcd appr fnl f: rallied and str run fnl 150yds: fin strly and edgd lft clsng stages: jst failed* **6/1**[3]

3 *1 1/2* **Stencive** 2-9-3 0 ... RyanMoore 8 77+
(William Haggas) *w'like: attr: lw: hld up in rr: hdwy 3f out: styd on to chse wnr wl over 1f out: str chal ins fnl f: one pce and lost 2nd fnl 50yds* **9/2**[2]

0 **4** *7* **Arch Villain (IRE)**[9] 6795 2-9-3 0 ... JimCrowley 11 60+
(Amanda Perrett) *w'like: in rr: hdwy over 2f out: kpt on fnl f for wl-hld 4th* **50/1**

5 *2* **Captain Cat (IRE)** 2-9-3 0 ... GeorgeBaker 2 56
(Roger Charlton) *unf: trckd ldrs: led wl over 3f out: drvn and hdd wl over 1f out: sn wknd* **8/1**

6 **6** *1 1/4* **Sir Bedivere (IRE)**[34] 6160 2-9-3 0 ... MartinDwyer 3 53
(Brian Meehan) *lw: drvn and sn led: edgd rt to stands' side over 4f out and hdd wl over 3f out: wknd 2f out* **13/8**[1]

0 **7** *1 1/4* **Jarrah**[29] 6278 2-9-3 0 ... IanMongan 10 50
(Saeed Bin Suroor) *w'like: chsd ldrs: pushed along over 2f out: sn wknd* **12/1**

00 **8** *1 1/4* **Burnham**[12] 6726 2-9-3 0 ... DarryllHolland 12 47
(Hughie Morrison) *in rr: pushed along 3f out: mod prog fnl f* **25/1**

2 **9** *nk* **Hilali (IRE)**[15] 6652 2-9-3 0 ... LiamKeniry 13 47
(Gary Brown) *w'like: swtg: chsd ldrs: wknd and hung lft over 2f out* **20/1**

35 **10** *2 1/2* **Cape Rainbow**[23] 6464 2-9-3 0 ... DaneO'Neill 7 41
(Mark Usher) *lw: bhd most of way* **11/1**

0 **11** *1 1/4* **Hector's Chance**[43] 5861 2-9-3 0 ... FrankieMcDonald 6 38
(Heather Main) *w'like: attr: chsd ldrs over 5f: sn wknd* **100/1**

12 *3 1/4* **Micquus (IRE)** 2-9-3 0 ... NeilChalmers 5 30
(Andrew Balding) *green: mod prog over 3f out: sn wknd* **16/1**

1m 39.65s (-0.05) **Going Correction** -0.075s/f (Good) **12** Ran SP% **119.0**
Speed ratings (Par 95): **97,96,95,88,86 85,83,82,82,79 78,75**
toteswingers:1&2:£53.80, 1&3:£45.20, 2&3:£6.90 CSF £163.11 TOTE £25.50: £6.60, £2.30, £2.50; EX 251.70.

Owner Lady Rothschild **Bred** The Rt Hon Lord Rothschild **Trained** Beckhampton, Wilts

FOCUS

The front three drew clear in this second division and the time was 0.84 seconds quicker than the previous race. Still, there's a feeling the first leg of this maiden may prove the stronger.

NOTEBOOK

Waterclock(IRE), an already gelded son of Notnowcato, was dismissed in the market, but that didn't stop him making a successful debut, showing a likeable attitude when strongly challenged on either side in the final furlong. He's nothing out of the ordinary but should stay further and can make a decent handicapper next season. (op 20-1 tchd 18-1)

Hefner(IRE) improved for this first taste of fast ground, appreciating the return to 1m and staying on well to just miss out. He can win an ordinary maiden before going handicapping. (op 13-2)

Stencive, a 260,000gns half-brother to Joshua Tree, made good headway around runners and briefly looked the winner, but his effort flattened out late on. This was a promising start and he can improve to win a maiden. (op 6-1 tchd 13-2)

Arch Villain(IRE) improved massively on his debut effort a week earlier, for all he was still well held. He'll be one for handicaps next season. (op 40-1)

Captain Cat(IRE) travelled well and hit the front past halfway, but his inexperience told and he was ultimately well held. He looks to have scope and can improve. (tchd 9-1)

Sir Bedivere(IRE), a promising sixth in a decent maiden on debut, failed to build on that, dropping out having made most of the running. This clearly wasn't his form, but he's now left with a bit to prove. (op 2-1 tchd 9-4 in places)

6995 SIR GERALD WHENT MEMORIAL NURSERY 7f (S)

3:30 (3:30) (Class 4) (0-85,84) 2-Y-O **£3,881** (£1,155; £577; £288) **Stalls** Centre

Form RPR

1362 **1** **Poetic Dancer**[43] 5847 2-9-7 **84** ... AdamKirby 7 89
(Clive Cox) *lw: hld up in tch: swtchd rt and hdwy wl over 1f out: drvn and styd on wl fnl f: led nr fin* **7/1**

5611 **2** *1/2* **Red Quartet (IRE)**[14] 6670 2-9-0 **77** ... AndreaAtzeni 4 81
(Robert Eddery) *pressed ldrs: chal fr 2f out tl led appr fnl f: kpt on wl: hdd and no ex nr fin* **5/1**[1]

2231 **3** *1 1/2* **Van Der Art**[23] 6449 2-9-3 **83** ... HarryBentley(3) 2 83
(Alan Jarvis) *lw: s.i.s: sn rcvrd to chse ldrs: chal fr over 2f out tl over 1f out: styd on same pce ins fnl f* **8/1**

5436 **4** *3/4* **Opera Buff**[63] 5234 2-9-1 **78** ... LiamKeniry 5 76
(Sylvester Kirk) *chsd ldrs: drvn and outpcd wl over 1f out: styd on again ins fnl f: gng on again clsng stages* **9/1**

1645 **5** *nk* **Maroosh**[16] 6623 2-8-12 **75** ... MartinDwyer 1 72
(Brian Meehan) *pressed ldrs tl led over 2f out: hdd appr fnl f: styd on same pce* **14/1**

2464 **6** *nk* **Tina's Spirit (IRE)**[20] 6526 2-9-3 **83** ... (b) SeanLevey(3) 9 79
(Richard Hannon) *pressed ldrs: ev ch over 2f out: wknd fnl 120yds* **16/1**

5612 **7** *hd* **Amoure Medici**[13] 6699 2-8-12 **75** ... MartinLane 8 71
(Noel Quinlan) *s.i.s: in rr: hdwy over 2f out: nvr gng pce to press ldrs and one pce fnl f* **10/1**

3323 **8** *1/2* **Leenavesta (USA)**[71] 4955 2-8-3 **69** ... KieranO'Neill(3) 10 63
(Richard Hannon) *in rr: drvn along 1/2-way: styd on towards stands' side fnl f: nt rch ldrs* **14/1**

61 **9** *4 1/2* **Mr Maynard**[58] 5384 2-9-3 **80** ... RyanMoore 12 63
(Sir Michael Stoute) *lw: hld up in rr: hdwy over 2f out: nvr gng pce to rch ldrs: wknd fnl f* **11/2**[2]

061 **10** *7* **Main Focus (USA)**[135] 2817 2-9-3 **80** ... SteveDrowne 11 45+
(John Gosden) *plld hrd: chsd ldrs: wknd ins fnl 2f* **6/1**[3]

432 **11** *6* **Parisian Princess (IRE)**[39] 6000 2-9-3 **80** ... JimmyFortune 3 39
(George Baker) *t.k.h: led tl hdd over 2f out: sn wknd* **16/1**

6220 **12** *3 1/4* **Jay Bee Blue**[12] 6725 2-9-2 **79** ... JimCrowley 6 20
(Tom Dascombe) *rdn over 2f out: a bhd* **25/1**

1m 26.12s (0.42) **Going Correction** -0.075s/f (Good) **12** Ran SP% **118.0**
Speed ratings (Par 97): **94,93,91,90,90 90,89,89,84,76 69,65**
toteswingers:1&2:£7.10, 1&3:£8.70, 2&3:£8.80 CSF £41.68 CT £294.20 TOTE £7.30: £2.60, £2.50, £2.70; EX 44.20.

Owner The Laureates **Bred** Mrs Hugh Maitland-Jones **Trained** Lambourn, Berks

FOCUS

Quite a competitive nursery, though the pace was ordinary.

NOTEBOOK

Poetic Dancer, winner of a 6f maiden at the course in May, was up 5lb having narrowly been denied at Doncaster the time before, but she's clearly still progressing and stayed on strongly to defy top weight. Her dam was a 1m2f winner, so it's quite possible she'll improve again for a stiffer test, and there could be more to come. (op 6-1 tchd 5-1)

Red Quartet(IRE), chasing a hat-trick, was up 5lb and proved undone by this step up to 7f, just not being able to see it out as well as the winner. He remains on the up and could win again back in distance. (op 6-1)

Van Der Art, backed beforehand, wasn't helped with a slow start and proved one-paced in the latter stages. (op 12-1)

Opera Buff can have his effort upgraded as, having had to wait for a run, he was found wanting for pace on this drop in trip. He kept on late and will be of some interest returned to 1m. (op 10-1 tchd 11-1)

Maroosh continues to run well without suggesting he's up to winning off this mark.

Amoure Medici was unable to get into it from off the pace. (op 14-1)

Mr Maynard was unable to build on his Kempton maiden victory. He may do better next season when stepped up in trip. (op 5-1 tchd 6-1)

Main Focus(USA), off since winning a Kempton maiden in June, was far too keen and didn't get home. This should have taken the fizz out of him and he can leave this form behind if settling better. Official explanation: jockey said colt ran too free (op 5-1 tchd 9-2)

6996 PLAY RAINBOW RICHES AT BLUESQ.COM FILLIES' H'CAP 1m 2f 6y

4:05 (4:06) (Class 4) (0-85,85) 3-Y-O+ **£4,528** (£1,347; £673; £336) **Stalls** Low

Form RPR

0114 **1** **Jiwen (CAN)**[37] 6062 3-9-3 **83** ... RichardHills 14 92
(Roger Varian) *lw: hld up in rr: str run on outside fr over 2f out: edgd lft and fin wl fnl f: led last strides* **8/1**[2]

210 **2** *hd* **Fashionable Gal (IRE)**[27] 6330 4-9-1 **76** ... ChrisCatlin 5 85
(Neil King) *plld hrd: trckd ldrs: nt clr run 2f out: drvn and qcknd to ld appr fnl f: kpt on wl: ct last strides* **25/1**

1242 **3** *1* **Kenyan Cat**[27] 6330 4-9-3 **81** ... SeanLevey(3) 9 88+
(Ed McMahon) *swtg: mid-div: hdwy over 2f out: styd on to chse ldng duo ins fnl f: no ex clsng stages* **7/1**[1]

1504 **4** *3/4* **Gosbeck**[63] 5235 3-9-5 **85** ... DaneO'Neill 16 90
(Henry Candy) *lw: in rr: plenty to do whn plld to outside 2f out: rapid hdwy fnl f: fin wl* **7/1**[1]

1132 **5** *1/2* **Hunter Forward (AUS)**[16] 6632 5-9-2 **77** ... KirstyMilczarek 15 81
(Luca Cumani) *swtg: in rr: hdwy on outside over 2f out: styd on same pce ins fnl f* **12/1**

0322 **6** *hd* **Miss Aix**[31] 6241 3-9-0 **80** ... MartinDwyer 2 84
(Michael Bell) *chsd ldrs: drvn over 2f out: wknd ins fnl f* **16/1**

4631 **7** *1 3/4* **Always The Lady**[25] 6404 3-9-1 **81** ... AdamKirby 3 81
(Clive Cox) *chsd ldrs: drvn over 2f out: wkng whn n.m.r ins fnl f* **16/1**

F121 **8** *3/4* **Mrs Dee Bee (IRE)**[29] 6285 3-8-13 **79** ... RobertWinston 12 78
(Charles Hills) *chsd ldrs: drvn over 2f out: hung lft and wknd ins fnl f* **7/1**[1]

103 **9** *nk* **Tanaami (USA)**[23] 6457 3-9-0 **80** ... RobertHavlin 4 78
(Saeed Bin Suroor) *chsd ldr: led over 2f out: hdd appr fnl f: sn wknd* **8/1**[2]

0565 **10** *5* **Ken's Girl**[27] 6330 7-9-2 **77** ... IanMongan 1 65
(Stuart Kittow) *led tl hdd over 2f out: sn btn* **12/1**

2121 **11** *hd* **Destiny Of Dreams**[41] 5915 3-9-1 **81** ... JimmyFortune 13 69
(Jo Crowley) *chsd ldrs: drvn 3f out: wknd ins fnl 2f* **20/1**

3120 **12** *3 1/4* **Totheendoftheearth (IRE)**[23] 6457 3-9-0 **80** ... RyanMoore 8 61
(Sylvester Kirk) *hmpd on inner after 2f: in rr: plld hrd: sme hdwy over 2f out: nvr rchd ldrs and sn wknd* **10/1**[3]

1001 **13** *6* **Amoya (GER)**[21] 6507 4-8-12 **76** ... (t) AdamBeschizza(3) 10 45
(Philip McBride) *lw: plld hrd: sddle slipped: a bhd and no ch fnl 3f* **25/1**

331 **14** *3 1/2* **Fabulouslyspirited**[39] 5999 3-9-3 **83** ... JimCrowley 7 45
(Ralph Beckett) *mid-div: drvn and sme hdwy 4f out: chsd ldrs ins fnl 3f: wknd 2f out* **16/1**

0010 **15** *3 1/4* **Totally Ours**[13] 6708 4-9-6 **81**.......... DarryllHolland 6 37
(William Muir) *prom early: bhd fr 1/2-way* **25/1**

2m 6.52s (-2.28) **Going Correction** -0.075s/f (Good)
WFA 3 from 4yo+ 5lb **15** Ran SP% **118.1**
Speed ratings (Par 102): **106,105,105,104,104 103,102,101,101,97 97,94,90,87,84**
toteswingers:1&2:£25.60, 1&3:£5.00, 2&3:£32.50 CSF £198.91 CT £1452.12 TOTE £7.20: £2.20, £7.80, £2.70; EX 135.80.

Owner Hamdan Al Maktoum **Bred** Adena Springs **Trained** Newmarket, Suffolk

FOCUS
The early pace was a steady one in this handicap, which should have suited the prominent racers, but the winner, fourth and fifth came from the rear. The winner posted a 3lb personal best.

Amoya(GER) Official explanation: jockey said saddle slipped

6997 BLUE SQUARE SUPPORTING MARIE CURIE CANCER CARE H'CAP 1m 7y(R)

4:40 (4:40) (Class 5) (0-75,75) 3-Y-O **£2,587** (£770; £384; £192) **Stalls** Low

Form RPR

0123 **1** **Top Diktat**[37] 6069 3-9-5 **75**.......... RyanMoore 8 86
(Sir Michael Stoute) *in rr: nt clr run and swtchd rt to outside fr 2f out: str run fnl f: edgd lft: led last strides* **4/1**[1]

4111 **2** *hd* **Ellie In The Pink (IRE)**[34] 6167 3-9-0 **73**.......... HarryBentley(3) 9 84
(Alan Jarvis) *swtg: trckd ldrs: squeezed through over 1f out to ld jst ins fnl f: hdd last strides* **11/2**[2]

0306 **3** *3* **Danehill Dante (IRE)**[9] 6796 3-9-3 **73**.......... (b[1]) RichardHughes 12 77
(Richard Hannon) *in rr: hdwy and nt clr run fr ins fnl 2f: edgd lft sn after: styd on to chse ldrs ins fnl f but no imp* **8/1**

0000 **4** *nk* **Bajan Bear**[11] 6759 3-9-3 **73**.......... (p) DaneO'Neill 11 76
(Michael Blanshard) *s.i.s: in rr: swtchd to outside 2f out: sn rdn: hung rt and v wd ins fnl f: styd on wl clsng stages* **25/1**

1010 **5** *1/2* **Adorable Choice (IRE)**[31] 6234 3-9-1 **71**.......... (v) DarryllHolland 6 73
(Tom Dascombe) *led: pushed along over 2f out: hdd jst ins fnl f: wknd fnl 120yds* **22/1**

6102 **6** *nk* **Songburst**[9] 6797 3-9-2 **75**.......... KieranO'Neill(3) 7 76
(Richard Hannon) *chsd ldrs: rdn over 2f out: wknd fnl 120yds* **12/1**

5005 **7** *3/4* **Doricemay (IRE)**[37] 6062 3-9-3 **73**.......... AdamKirby 5 73
(Clive Cox) *towards rr: racd on outside: rdn and hdwy to chse ldrs fr 2f out: wknd ins fnl f* **7/1**

4464 **8** *1* **Great Shot**[9] 6797 3-9-4 **74**.......... JamesDoyle 1 71
(Sylvester Kirk) *lw: trckd ldrs: drvn to dispute 2nd 2f out: no imp: wknd fnl f* **6/1**[3]

1055 **9** *4* **Orientalist**[18] 6576 3-9-5 **75**.......... (p) LiamKeniry 2 63
(Eve Johnson Houghton) *chsd ldrs: drvn on ins whn bmpd wl over 1f out: sn btn* **18/1**

4210 **10** *1 1/2* **Swift Bird (IRE)**[25] 6409 3-9-4 **74**.......... (b) MartinLane 10 59
(Noel Quinlan) *chsd ldr tl 2f out: sn btn* **18/1**

2230 **11** *1/2* **Ferruccio (IRE)**[9] 6796 3-9-5 **75**.......... JimCrowley 4 58
(James Fanshawe) *chsd ldrs towards outside: rdn over 2f out: wknd over 1f out* **8/1**

-305 **12** *17* **Huwayit (IRE)**[9] 6796 3-9-0 **70**.......... MartinDwyer 3 14
(Clive Brittain) *nvr really travelling: sn drvn along towards rr: eased and no ch fnl 2f* **25/1**

1m 37.86s (-0.84) **Going Correction** -0.075s/f (Good) **12** Ran SP% **114.7**
Speed ratings (Par 101): **101,100,97,97,97 96,95,94,90,89 88,71**
toteswingers:1&2:£1.80, 1&3:£7.20, 2&3:£11.30 CSF £23.38 CT £164.27 TOTE £4.10: £1.80, £1.80, £3.20; EX 14.40.

Owner Mrs Denis Haynes **Bred** Wretham Stud **Trained** Newmarket, Suffolk

FOCUS
A fair handicap for the grade, and the form looks solid, with two in-form, progressive types pulling clear late on.

Adorable Choice(IRE) Official explanation: vet said filly had been struck into right hind

6998 WIN THOUSANDS OF SPORTS EXPERIENCES AT BLUESQ.COM APPRENTICE H'CAP 2m

5:15 (5:15) (Class 5) (0-75,73) 4-Y-O+ **£2,587** (£770; £384; £192) **Stalls** Low

Form RPR

11/0 **1** **Blimey O'Riley (IRE)**[30] 6249 6-9-5 **73**.......... CharlesEddery(5) 2 79
(Mark H Tompkins) *in rr but in tch: hdwy and drvn over 2f out: swtchd rt wl over 1f out: kpt on to ld fnl 75yds: all out* **8/1**

5204 **2** *1/2* **Double Handful (GER)**[12] 6722 5-9-6 **69**.......... AdamBeschizza 3 74
(Venetia Williams) *trckd ldr 7f out: chal 2f out tl led over 1f out: hdd and no ex fnl 75yds* **8/1**

2401 **3** *2* **Epsom Salts**[12] 6722 6-9-10 **73** 6ex.......... MatthewDavies 9 76
(Pat Phelan) *hld up in rr: hdwy on outside over 2f out: styd on to take 3rd fnl f: nt rch ldng duo* **15/2**

6052 **4** *3/4* **Sohcahtoa (IRE)**[12] 6722 5-9-4 **67**.......... HarryBentley 7 69
(Robert Mills) *in rr: hdwy over 2f out: nt clr run and swtchd lft wl over 1f out: styd on same pce ins fnl f* **10/3**[2]

0633 **5** *1/2* **Warne's Way (IRE)**[25] 6405 8-9-2 **72**.......... BrendanPowell(7) 1 73
(Brendan Powell) *disp ld 2f: styd chsng ldr tl led 9f out: drvn along 3f out: hdd over 1f out: wknd ins fnl f* **3/1**[1]

/05- **6** *3 1/2* **Sarando**[196] 7321 6-8-9 **61**.......... (tp) MatthewCosham(3) 6 58
(Paul Webber) *chsd ldrs: rdn and one pce fnl 2f* **5/1**[3]

0416 **7** *6* **Steady Gaze**[6] 6876 6-8-2 **56**.......... LukeRowe(5) 5 46
(Richard Rowe) *disp ld tl led after 2f: hdd 9f out: lost pl 5f out: rdn and rallied 3f out: wknd 2f out* **15/2**

3m 33.01s (1.01) **Going Correction** -0.075s/f (Good) **7** Ran SP% **110.5**
Speed ratings (Par 103): **94,93,92,92,92 90,87**
toteswingers:1&2:£5.80, 1&3:£5.20, 2&3:£5.20 CSF £63.42 CT £474.18 TOTE £9.80: £3.50, £3.20; EX 78.20.

Owner Trevor Benton **Bred** Mrs Ann Kennedy **Trained** Newmarket, Suffolk

■ Stewards' Enquiry : Charles Eddery 13-day ban: used whip with excessive frequency (Nov 4-5,9-12,14-19,22)

Adam Beschizza seven-day ban: used whip with excessive frequency (Nov 4-5,9-12,14)

FOCUS
A wide-open staying handicap. The form has been rated negatively.

T/Plt: £320.00 to a £1 stake. Pool of £57,703.34 - 131.61 winning tickets. T/Qpdt: £50.30 to a £1 stake. Pool of £5,420.56 - 79.70 winning tickets. ST

6975 WOLVERHAMPTON (A.W) (L-H)

Friday, October 21

OFFICIAL GOING: Standard
Wind: Fresh, behind Weather: Overcast

6999 ENJOY THE PARTY PACK GROUP OFFER CLASSIFIED STKS 5f 216y(P)

5:45 (5:45) (Class 6) 3-Y-O+ **£1,772** (£523; £261) **Stalls** Low

Form RPR

1600 **1** **Princess Dayna**[52] 5600 3-9-0 55.......... RichardKingscote 4 64
(Tom Dascombe) *chsd ldrs: rdn over 1f out: led and edgd rt ins fnl f: r.o wl* **16/1**

0145 **2** *2 1/2* **Circuitous**[13] 6696 3-9-0 55.......... (b) MartinHarley 7 56
(Keith Dalgleish) *led: rdn over 1f out: hdd and unable qck ins fnl f* **3/1**[1]

6650 **3** *shd* **Refusetosurrender (IRE)**[24] 6428 3-9-0 48.......... PatrickMathers 3 56
(Richard Fahey) *a.p: chsd ldr 2f out: sn rdn: styd on* **20/1**

65U6 **4** *1 1/4* **Chester Deelyte (IRE)**[31] 6238 3-9-0 48.......... (v) WilliamCarson 2 52
(Lisa Williamson) *hld up: hdwy over 1f out: r.o: nt rch ldrs* **40/1**

200 **5** *2* **Wandering Lad**[34] 6159 3-8-9 54.......... NeilFarley(5) 9 45
(Declan Carroll) *fly-jmpd s: in rr: hdwy over 1f out: styd on same pce fnl f* **14/1**

2260 **6** *3 1/4* **Hambleton**[55] 5490 4-8-10 54 ow2.......... JustinNewman(7) 11 37
(Bryan Smart) *sn pushed along in rr: hdwy over 3f out: rdn and wknd over 1f out* **9/2**[2]

0202 **7** *1 1/4* **Ivestar (IRE)**[28] 6304 6-8-10 53.......... (vt) JulieBurke(5) 13 31
(Ben Haslam) *s.s: hld up: rdn over 1f out: hung lft and styd on ins fnl f: nvr nrr* **5/1**[3]

0104 **8** *2 1/4* **Avon Light**[5] 6889 3-9-0 50.......... (p) LukeMorris 1 24
(Milton Bradley) *sn pushed along and prom: drvn over 2f out: wknd over 1f out* **5/1**[3]

3060 **9** *4* **Waterbury Girl**[8] 6816 3-8-11 52.......... DeclanCannon(3) 6 11
(Bryn Palling) *chsd ldr tl rdn over 2f out: wknd over 1f out* **50/1**

0060 **10** *3/4* **Future Impact (IRE)**[13] 6696 3-9-0 52.......... PatCosgrave 8 —
(Ed de Giles) *hld up: rdn and wknd over 1f out* **16/1**

400 **11** *6* **Chambers (IRE)**[17] 6609 5-9-1 53.......... AndrewMullen 5 —
(Eric Alston) *prom: rdn over 2f out: wkng whn hmpd wl over 1f out* **12/1**

1m 14.43s (-0.57) **Going Correction** -0.05s/f (Stan)
WFA 3 from 4yo+ 1lb **11** Ran SP% **111.8**
Speed ratings (Par 101): **101,97,97,95,93 88,87,84,78,77 69**
toteswingers: 1&2 £9.90, 1&3 £23.80, 2&3 £12.80 CSF £59.64 TOTE £14.40: £4.40, £2.60, £8.20; EX 67.30.

Owner T Dascombe **Bred** Mrs J A Chapman **Trained** Malpas, Cheshire

■ Stewards' Enquiry : William Carson three-day ban: careless riding (Nov 4,5,9)

FOCUS
Just a modest classified event, though it was soundly run. The winner rates a length personal best.

7000 NAME A RACE TO ENHANCE YOUR BRAND MAIDEN STKS 5f 216y(P)

6:20 (6:20) (Class 5) 2-Y-O **£2,264** (£673; £336; £168) **Stalls** Low

Form RPR

1 **Spykes Bay (USA)** 2-9-3 0.......... MartinHarley 1 73+
(Mrs K Burke) *led 1f: chsd ldrs: rdn to ld over 1f out: jst hld on* **10/3**[3]

063 **2** *hd* **Rio Grande**[47] 5756 2-9-3 72.......... PaulHanagan 5 72
(Ann Duffield) *a.p: chsd ldr over 3f out: led and edgd lft over 1f out: sn rdn and hdd: r.o* **9/4**[2]

3 *1 1/2* **Champagne Reefing (USA)** 2-9-3 0.......... PatCosgrave 7 67
(Jane Chapple-Hyam) *chsd ldrs: pushed along over 2f out: rdn and hung lft ins fnl f: r.o* **13/8**[1]

056 **4** *3 1/2* **Talya's Storm**[38] 6025 2-8-10 53.......... RaulDaSilva(7) 4 56
(Jeremy Gask) *s.i.s: hdwy over 3f out: rdn over 1f out: no ex fnl f* **25/1**

50 **5** *2 1/4* **Heidi's Delight (IRE)**[65] 5174 2-8-12 44.......... LukeMorris 3 44
(Ann Duffield) *s.i.s: sn pushed along in rr: nvr nrr* **66/1**

05 **6** *nk* **Gulf Storm (IRE)**[28] 6292 2-9-3 0.......... TomEaves 2 48
(Bryan Smart) *led 5f out: rdn and hdd over 1f out: wknd fnl f* **5/1**

0 **7** *10* **Dream Lioness**[52] 5590 2-8-7 0.......... JulieBurke(5) 6 —
(Ben Haslam) *sn outpcd* **33/1**

1m 15.34s (0.34) **Going Correction** -0.05s/f (Stan) **7** Ran SP% **116.9**
Speed ratings (Par 95): **95,94,92,88,85 84,71**
toteswingers: 1&2 £1.60, 1&3 £2.00, 2&3 £2.10 CSF £11.59 TOTE £4.50: £2.30, £1.90; EX 10.20.

Owner Mark Gittins **Bred** Brylynn Farm Inc **Trained** Middleham Moor, North Yorks

■ Stewards' Enquiry : Julie Burke five-day ban: hit filly when out of contention (Nov 4-5,9-11)

FOCUS
Hard to escape the conclusion that this was a pretty ordinary maiden.

NOTEBOOK
Spykes Bay(USA) ◆ made a pleasing winning start to his career, knuckling down well for pressure to always just hold the runner-up inside the final furlong. His yard has done pretty well with its juveniles this term and this American-bred can be expected to improve. (op 7-2)
Rio Grande, who'd left Jeremy Noseda after his York third, has the ability to win races, particularly if connections can really find the key to him, as he left the impression he's holding a bit back here, getting to the head of affairs hard on the bridle but carrying his head a bit awkwardly and wandering when pressure was finally applied. (op 15-8)
Champagne Reefing(USA), a son of Van Nistelrooy, had presumably been showing up well at home given his strength in the market but just lacked a bit of race sharpness, nudged along before most but sticking to his task well. He can only improve. (op 9-4)
Talya's Storm definitely has ability but ordinary handicaps will surely provide him with a more realistic chance of success.
Gulf Storm(IRE) faded after cutting out a lot of the running but at least can't get much of a mark and he's certainly bred to do better (Pivotal half-brother to a few winners). (op 11-2 tchd 6-1)

7001 HOTEL & CONFERENCING AT WOLVERHAMPTON H'CAP 7f 32y(P)

6:50 (6:50) (Class 6) (0-60,61) 3-Y-O+ **£1,908** (£563; £281) **Stalls** High

Form RPR

3324 **1** **Know No Fear**[6] 6877 6-9-3 **59**.......... (p) PaulHanagan 5 70
(Alastair Lidderdale) *hld up: hdwy over 2f out: rdn to ld and hung lft ins fnl f: r.o* **7/2**[1]

4221 **2** *3/4* **Scarborough Lily**[52] 5601 3-9-1 **59**.......... (b) NeilCallan 4 68
(Edward Vaughan) *hld up in tch: rdn: hung rt and ev ch ins fnl f: styd on* **6/1**[2]

5241 **3** *1 1/2* **Makyaal (IRE)**[8] 6816 3-9-2 **60** 6ex.......... (b) TadhgO'Shea 10 65
(John Dunlop) *s.i.s: hld up: hdwy and hung lft fr over 1f out: r.o: nt rch ldrs* **7/2**[1]

0444 **4** *1 1/4* **Galloping Minister (IRE)**[13] 6700 3-9-2 **60**.......... RichardKingscote 8 62
(Tom Dascombe) *a.p: rdn and ev ch 1f out: styd on same pce ins fnl f* **14/1**

1502 **5** *3/4* **Gazboolou**[9] 6784 7-9-0 **56** LukeMorris 3 56
(David Pinder) *chsd ldrs: rdn over 2f out: no ex ins fnl f* **15/2**[3]

4166 **6** *1* **Sopran Nad (ITY)**[43] 5843 7-9-0 **56** (b) DavidProbert 1 53
(Frank Sheridan) *chsd ldrs: rdn over 1f out: hung lft and no ex ins fnl f* **17/2**

2530 **7** *1/2* **Desert Falls**[3] 6930 5-9-2 **58** TonyCulhane 2 54
(Richard Whitaker) *led: rdn over 1f out: hdd and no ex ins fnl f* **14/1**

60-2 **8** *3/4* **Cheers**[210] 966 3-9-0 **58** FrankieMcDonald 9 52
(Oliver Sherwood) *hld up: nvr on terms* **20/1**

0034 **9** *1/2* **Unwrapit (USA)**[33] 6190 3-8-10 **61** ow2 (p) JustinNewman(7) 7 54
(Bryan Smart) *chsd ldr tl rdn over 1f out: wknd fnl f* **16/1**

5400 **10** *2 3/4* **Gemma's Delight (IRE)**[14] 6664 4-9-4 **60** (p) LiamJones 12 45
(James Unett) *hld up: racd keenly: hdwy over 2f out: wknd over 1f out* **16/1**

1m 29.18s (-0.42) **Going Correction** -0.05s/f (Stan)
WFA 3 from 4yo+ 2lb **10** Ran SP% **110.9**
Speed ratings (Par 101): **100,99,97,96,95 94,93,92,92,88**
toteswingers: 1&2 £3.40, 1&3 £2.30, 2&3 £2.40 CSF £22.59 CT £75.68 TOTE £3.50: £1.60, £2.40, £1.20; EX 21.30.
Owner C S J Beek **Bred** B Bargh **Trained** Eastbury, Berks

FOCUS
Three in-form horses came to the fore in this so it's probably form to view positively. The winner probably didn't need to match her latest effort.

7002 GREAT OFFERS AT WOLVERHAMPTON-RACECOURSE.CO.UK H'CAP 1m 5f 194y(P)
7:20 (7:20) (Class 5) (0-75,75) 3-Y-O+ **£2,522** (£750; £375; £187) **Stalls** Low

Form RPR

0221 **1** **Record Breaker (IRE)**[26] 6379 7-9-5 **70** (b) JoeFanning 12 79
(Mark Johnston) *hld up: pushed along over 6f out: hdwy over 1f out: led ins fnl f: styd on* **12/1**

0156 **2** *1/2* **Raktiman (IRE)**[25] 6405 4-9-2 **67** (p) RichardKingscote 7 75
(Tom Dascombe) *hld up: hdwy and edgd lft over 1f out: r.o* **20/1**

4242 **3** *1* **Reem Star**[12] 6729 3-9-1 **75** GeorgeBaker 13 82
(Ed Dunlop) *hld up: hdwy over 2f out: rdn and ev ch ins fnl f: styd on same pce* **13/2**[3]

4 *1/2* **In A Nutshell (IRE)**[38] 7359 4-9-0 **65** (p) KierenFallon 4 71
(C Byrnes, Ire) *s.i.s: sn prom: pushed along over 4f out: rdn and ev ch ins fnl f: styd on same pce* **7/2**[1]

503 **5** *1 1/4* **Ryton Runner (IRE)**[50] 5641 3-9-0 **74** NickyMackay 5 78
(John Gosden) *chsd ldrs: led over 2f out: rdn over 1f out: hdd and no ex ins fnl f* **7/2**[1]

6014 **6** *2 1/4* **Resplendent Ace (IRE)**[14] 6666 7-9-1 **66** PaulHanagan 8 67
(Karen Tutty) *hld up: hdwy over 2f out: rdn over 1f out: no ex fnl f* **20/1**

6550 **7** *1/2* **Pelham Crescent (IRE)**[5] 6893 8-9-10 **75** DavidProbert 6 75
(Bryn Palling) *s.i.s: hld up: rdn over 3f out: n.d* **16/1**

1036 **8** *nk* **Elrasheed**[21] 6499 3-9-0 **74** TadhgO'Shea 3 74
(John Dunlop) *prom: chsd ldr over 8f out: led wl over 2f out: sn rdn and hdd: wknd ins fnl f* **4/1**[2]

5024 **9** *1* **Sand Skier**[21] 6507 4-8-13 **71** NicoleNordblad(7) 2 69
(Hans Adielsson) *sn led: hdd over 11f out: chsd ldr to over 8f out: remained handy tl wknd ins fnl f* **22/1**

3050 **10** *6* **Dynamic Drive (IRE)**[44] 5837 4-9-5 **73** (p) DaleSwift(3) 11 63
(Walter Swinburn) *hld up: rdn over 1f out: n.d* **22/1**

3515 **11** *4 1/2* **Green Lightning (IRE)**[16] 6621 4-9-1 **66** (b) NeilCallan 10 50
(Mark Johnston) *mid-div: hdwy over 5f out: rdn over 2f out: wknd over 1f out* **9/1**

0036 **12** *16* **Jewelled Dagger (IRE)**[6] 6868 7-9-5 **70** TomEaves 9 31
(Keith Dalgleish) *chsd ldr tl led over 11f out: rdn and hdd wl over 2f out: sn wknd: t.o* **33/1**

620- **13** *2 3/4* **Spring Hawk (IRE)**[14] 6682 5-9-4 **69** (t) WilliamCarson 1 27
(T G McCourt, Ire) *chsd ldrs: pushed along over 6f out: rdn and wknd over 2f out: t.o* **50/1**

3m 1.74s (-4.26) **Going Correction** -0.05s/f (Stan)
WFA 3 from 4yo+ 9lb **13** Ran SP% **124.5**
Speed ratings (Par 103): **110,109,109,108,108 106,106,106,105,102 99,90,89**
toteswingers: 1&2 £21.90, 1&3 £10.40, 2&3 £27.10 CSF £239.77 CT £1714.14 TOTE £14.40: £4.90, £5.80, £2.40; EX 235.40.
Owner Triplin Racing **Bred** Sir E J Loder **Trained** Middleham Moor, N Yorks

FOCUS
Competitive stuff for the level and it was well run, the principals all coming from off the pace. Sound form even if the market principals were a shade disappointing.

7003 DINE IN HORIZONS H'CAP 1m 1f 103y(P)
7:50 (7:52) (Class 6) (0-60,60) 3-Y-O+ **£1,908** (£563; £281) **Stalls** Low

Form RPR

4202 **1** **Beach Babe**[6] 6872 3-9-2 **60** NickyMackay 4 71
(Jonathan Portman) *hld up: hdwy over 2f out: rdn and edgd lft fr over 1f out: r.o u.p to ld wl ins fnl f* **3/1**[1]

4000 **2** *1/2* **Royal Straight**[25] 6417 6-8-10 **55** (t) JulieBurke(5) 11 65
(Linda Perratt) *hld up: hdwy over 2f out: rdn to ld ins fnl f: sn hdd: styd on* **25/1**

31 **3** *2 1/4* **Pinotage**[3] 6926 3-9-0 **58** TonyCulhane 8 63
(Richard Whitaker) *hld up: rdn over 1f out: edgd lft and r.o ins fnl f: nt rch ldrs* **5/1**[2]

3050 **4** *3/4* **Ollon (USA)**[51] 5622 3-9-0 **58** PaulHanagan 7 62
(Richard Fahey) *hld up: hdwy over 2f out: rdn ins fnl f: styd on same pce* **8/1**

2440 **5** *nk* **Munaawer (USA)**[34] 6182 4-9-6 **60** (b) KierenFallon 10 63
(James Bethell) *hld up: plld hrd: hdwy over 3f out: led over 1f out: rdn: edgd lft and hdd ins fnl f: no ex* **8/1**

060 **6** *1/2* **Commerce**[23] 6468 4-9-4 **58** (p) GeorgeBaker 12 60
(Gary Moore) *led: hdd 7f out: chsd ldrs: led 3f out: rdn and hdd over 1f out: no ex ins fnl f* **20/1**

4055 **7** *2* **Ilie Nastase (FR)**[6] 6871 7-9-4 **58** (b) KirstyMilczarek 9 58+
(Conor Dore) *prom: gng wl whn nt clr run and lost pl 2f out: nt rcvr* **14/1**

001 **8** *1 1/2* **El Libertador (USA)**[7] 6845 5-9-6 **60** 6ex (b) LiamKeniry 5 55
(Eric Wheeler) *trckd ldrs: shkn up over 1f out: wknd fnl f* **17/2**

5503 **9** *4 1/2* **Nicholas Pocock (IRE)**[9] 6430 5-9-0 **57** (b) DaleSwift(3) 2 42
(Ian McInnes) *hld up: rdn over 2f out: no ch whn hung lft ins fnl f* **22/1**

0-26 **10** *6* **Daniel Thomas (IRE)**[13] 6698 9-9-0 **54** (bt) MartinHarley 13 27
(Richard Guest) *chsd ldrs: rdn over 2f out: wknd over 1f out* **18/1**

4350 **11** *2 1/4* **Duneen Dream (USA)**[123] 3235 6-9-1 **55** DavidProbert 1 23
(Nikki Evans) *chsd ldr tl led 7f out: rdn and hdd 3f out: wknd 2f out* **25/1**

12 *22* **My St Clair (IRE)**[12] 6732 6-9-2 **56** (p) NeilCallan 3 —
(C Byrnes, Ire) *prom: pushed along 5f out: wknd 3f out: t.o* **6/1**[3]

1m 59.65s (-2.05) **Going Correction** -0.05s/f (Stan)
WFA 3 from 4yo+ 4lb **12** Ran SP% **117.4**
Speed ratings (Par 101): **107,106,104,103,103 103,101,100,96,90 88,69**
toteswingers: 1&2 £21.30, 1&3 £2.90, 2&3 £24.60 CSF £90.89 CT £362.62 TOTE £2.80: £1.10, £12.80, £2.70; EX 108.60.
Owner Mrs R F Knipe **Bred** R F And S D Knipe **Trained** Compton, Berks
■ Stewards' Enquiry : Nicky Mackay seven-day ban: used whip with excessive frequency (Nov 4-5,9-12,14)

FOCUS
Just run-of-the-mill fare. The principals all came from out the back but that's not to say the gallop looked overly strong, although the time was good for the grade. The winner was close to her latest form.
Pinotage Official explanation: jockey said gelding suffered interference leaving stalls

7004 WOLVERHAMPTON HOLIDAY INN MEDIAN AUCTION MAIDEN STKS 1m 1f 103y(P)
8:20 (8:22) (Class 6) 3-5-Y-O **£1,772** (£523; £261) **Stalls** Low

Form RPR

5205 **1** **With Hindsight (IRE)**[25] 6402 3-9-3 **73** AdamKirby 6 74
(Clive Cox) *s.i.s: racd keenly and sn trcking ldrs: shkn up to ld over 1f out: hrd rdn ins fnl f: r.o* **11/10**[1]

32 **2** *2* **Double Trouble**[35] 6137 3-8-12 **0** AndreaAtzeni 4 65
(Marco Botti) *chsd ldr tl led over 2f out: rdn: edgd lft and hdd over 1f out: styd on same pce ins fnl f* **5/2**[2]

005 **3** *4 1/2* **Lucky Dime**[22] 6476 3-8-12 **45** LiamKeniry 10 56?
(Noel Quinlan) *chsd ldrs: rdn and hung lft fr over 1f out: wknd ins fnl f: wnt 3rd nr fin* **80/1**

5025 **4** *nk* **Mill Mick**[14] 6669 4-9-7 **65** (p) StephenCraine 3 60
(John Mackie) *led: hdd over 2f out: sn rdn: wknd ins fnl f: lost 3rd nr fin* **6/1**[3]

5 **5** *1* **Avison (IRE)**[36] 6097 3-9-3 **0** PaulHanagan 5 58
(Richard Fahey) *dwlt: hld up: swtchd rt over 1f out: r.o ins fnl f: nvr nr to chal* **10/1**

05 **6** *1 1/2* **Marshmallow**[27] 6324 3-8-12 **0** NickyMackay 8 50
(Chris Wall) *hld up: hdwy over 5f out: wknd 2f out* **8/1**

040 **7** *2 1/2* **Rasteau (IRE)**[23] 6459 3-8-12 **39** DavidKenny(5) 9 50?
(Tom Keddy) *hld up: pushed along and hdwy over 2f out: sn wknd* **150/1**

550/ **8** *14* **More For Less**[864] 2788 4-9-2 **50** JulieBurke(5) 7 20
(Owen Brennan) *hld up in tch: pushed along 1/2-way: wknd over 3f out* **100/1**

00-0 **9** *1 1/2* **Marafong**[28] 6295 4-9-7 **38** J-PGuillambert 11 17
(Brian Baugh) *hld up: rdn over 3f out: sn lost tch* **100/1**

2m 1.26s (-0.44) **Going Correction** -0.05s/f (Stan)
WFA 3 from 4yo+ 4lb **9** Ran SP% **114.6**
Speed ratings (Par 101): **99,97,93,92,92 90,88,76,74**
toteswingers: 1&2 £1.10, 1&3 £23.00, 2&3 £6.80 CSF £3.94 TOTE £2.80: £1.10, £1.20, £3.90; EX 4.40.
Owner Dennis Shaw **Bred** Thomas Doherty **Trained** Lambourn, Berks

FOCUS
Typically little depth to a race of this type at this time of year, and modest form.

7005 WOLVERHAMPTON-RACECOURSE.CO.UK H'CAP (DIV I) 1m 141y(P)
8:50 (8:51) (Class 6) (0-55,55) 3-Y-O+ **£1,567** (£462; £231) **Stalls** Low

Form RPR

0504 **1** **Valley Tiger**[7] 6845 3-8-12 **54** WilliamCarson 5 64
(William Muir) *hld up: hdwy over 2f out: rdn to ld ins fnl f: r.o* **13/2**[3]

6641 **2** *1 1/2* **Princess Gail**[15] 6657 3-8-12 **54** ShaneKelly 9 61
(Mark Brisbourne) *hld up in tch: led over 1f out: sn rdn: hdd ins fnl f: no ex nr fin* **4/1**[1]

34 **3** *2 3/4* **Yellow Printer**[13] 6698 5-9-3 **55** (b) AdamKirby 4 55
(Mark Gillard) *chsd ldrs: rdn over 1f out: styd on* **4/1**[1]

6200 **4** *1 1/4* **All In A Paddy**[28] 6310 3-8-9 **51** MartinLane 10 48
(Ed McMahon) *chsd ldrs: rdn over 2f out: hung lft fr over 1f out: styd on same pce fnl f* **16/1**

0000 **5** *1* **Querido (GER)**[16] 6624 7-8-11 **52** (tp) RobertLButler(3) 2 47
(Paddy Butler) *hld up in tch: rdn over 1f out: styd on same pce fnl f* **20/1**

1302 **6** *1* **One Of Twins**[20] 6545 3-8-13 **55** JamesSullivan 6 48
(Michael Easterby) *chsd ldr tl led over 7f out: rdn and hdd over 1f out: wknd ins fnl f* **5/1**[2]

5004 **7** *2 1/4* **Flying Cherry (IRE)**[36] 6084 4-8-5 **46** oh1 (t) JohnFahy(3) 8 34
(Jo Crowley) *hld up: rdn and swtchd lft over 1f out: nvr nrr* **12/1**

52-4 **8** *5* **Hilbre Court (USA)**[15] 6659 6-9-2 **54** J-PGuillambert 3 30
(Brian Baugh) *hld up: pushed along over 2f out: nvr on terms* **9/1**

0040 **9** *1 1/4* **Lennoxwood (IRE)**[25] 6411 3-8-6 **48** (be) RichardKingscote 1 21
(Mark Usher) *hld up: n.d* **20/1**

30-1 **10** *4 1/2* **Mnarani (IRE)**[138] 2746 4-9-3 **55** (b) MartinHarley 12 18
(Emmet Michael Butterly, Ire) *led 1f: chsd ldrs: ev ch over 2f out: sn rdn and nt run on* **7/1**

060 **11** *2 3/4* **Come And Go (UAE)**[37] 6070 5-8-13 **51** TomEaves 7 8
(Ian McInnes) *trckd ldrs: rdn over 2f out: wknd over 1f out* **28/1**

500- **12** *11* **Thatstheone**[391] 6369 3-8-10 **52** JoeFanning 13 —
(Bill Moore) *hld up: racd keenly: a in rr: wknd over 2f out* **66/1**

1m 50.39s (-0.11) **Going Correction** -0.05s/f (Stan)
WFA 3 from 4yo+ 4lb **12** Ran SP% **120.5**
Speed ratings (Par 101): **98,96,94,93,92 91,89,84,83,79 77,67**
toteswingers: 1&2 £6.60, 1&3 £6.80, 2&3 £6.10 CSF £31.81 CT £122.23 TOTE £8.10: £3.10, £1.40, £2.00; EX 40.60.
Owner Clive Edginton & Martin Graham **Bred** Usk Valley Stud **Trained** Lambourn, Berks

FOCUS
Ordinary fare, though it was soundly run. The time was similar to division I.

7006 WOLVERHAMPTON-RACECOURSE.CO.UK H'CAP (DIV II) 1m 141y(P)
9:20 (9:20) (Class 6) (0-55,55) 3-Y-O+ **£1,567** (£462; £231) **Stalls** Low

Form RPR

6434 **1** **Belle Park**[86] 4444 4-8-7 **52** JulieCumine(7) 6 61
(Karen George) *hld up: plld hrd: hdwy over 1f out: led ins fnl f: pushed out* **13/2**[3]

1030 **2** *nk* **Fair Breeze**[8] 6811 4-8-11 **49** RobertHavlin 8 57
(Richard Phillips) *hld up: hdwy on bit over 2f out: rdn to chse wnr ins fnl f: r.o* **10/1**

4256 **3** *3 1/4* **Deslaya (IRE)**[16] 6626 3-8-12 **54** NickyMackay 10 55
(Chris Wall) *prom: racd keenly: rdn and n.m.r over 1f out: styd on* **9/2**[2]

0500 **4** *1 3/4* **Shunkawakhan (IRE)**[13] 6698 8-8-9 **47** (tp) TomEaves 9 44
(Linda Perratt) *hld up: hdwy u.p over 1f out: r.o: nt rch ldrs* **25/1**

2055 **5** *hd* **Look For Love**[17] 6605 3-7-13 **48** ow1 .... JackDuern(7) 2 44
(Reg Hollinshead) *chsd ldrs: rdn over 1f out: no ex ins fnl f* **14/1**
0000 **6** *2* **Meydan Style (USA)**[22] 6494 5-8-9 **47** .... JoeFanning 1 39
(Bruce Hellier) *led: rdn over 1f out: hdd & wknd ins fnl f* **11/1**
0000 **7** *1 ¼* **Emerald Girl (IRE)**[11] 6764 4-8-13 **51** .... MartinHarley 3 40
(Richard Guest) *prom: rdn over 1f out: wkng whn hmpd ins fnl f* **16/1**
0453 **8** *6* **Whats For Pudding (IRE)**[7] 6847 3-8-7 **54** .... NeilFarley(5) 11 29
(Declan Carroll) *prom: rdn over 3f out: wknd over 1f out* **12/1**
0000 **9** *2 ¼* **Freedom Trail**[46] 5787 3-8-6 **48** .... FrederikTylicki 12 18
(Tim Fitzgerald) *chsd ldrs: rdn over 2f out: wknd over 1f out* **40/1**
056/ **10** *½* **Silly Dancer (IRE)**[47] 5767 8-9-3 **55** .... KieranFallon 5 24
(Adrian McGuinness, Ire) *half-rrd s: hld up: hdwy over 5f out: wknd over 1f out* **17/2**
0012 **11** *3 ¼* **Prime Circle**[15] 6659 5-9-1 **53** ....(p) AndrewMullen 7 14
(Alan Brown) *reluctant in rr: hdwy over 3f out: sn drvn along: wknd over 2f out* **3/1**[1]
4600 **12** *22* **Alqaahir (USA)**[22] 6486 9-9-0 **55** ....(p) RobertLButler(3) 4 —
(Paddy Butler) *hld up: hmpd over 7f out: rdn and wknd over 2f out* **25/1**

1m 50.33s (-0.17) **Going Correction** -0.05s/f (Stan)
WFA 3 from 4yo+ 4lb **12** Ran SP% **114.8**
Speed ratings (Par 101): **98,97,94,93,93 91,90,84,82,82 79,60**
toteswingers: 1&2 £5.90, 1&3 £5.50, 2&3 £4.30 CSF £66.16 CT £322.37 TOTE £6.40: £1.70, £4.40, £2.00; EX 60.20.
Owner R A Bimson **Bred** C A Green **Trained** Higher Eastington, Devon

FOCUS
As in the first division they went a good clip, setting it up for those coming from behind. The winner rates back to her best.
Prime Circle Official explanation: jockey said gelding never travelled
T/Plt: £20.30 to a £1 stake. Pool: £93,833.79. 3,363.73 winning tickets. T/Qpdt: £4.30 to a £1 stake. Pool: £10,067.24. 1,702.37 winning tickets. CR

7007 - 7009a (Foreign Racing) - See Raceform Interactive

6849 DUNDALK (A.W) (L-H)
Friday, October 21

OFFICIAL GOING: Standard

7010a DUNDALK STADIUM ON FACEBOOK H'CAP 7f (P)
7:35 (7:45) (70-100,98) 3-Y-0+ **£7,241** (£7,241; £1,551; £517)

RPR
1 **Flic Flac (IRE)**[7] 6854 3-9-1 87 .... PJSmullen 4 92
(D K Weld, Ire) *trckd ldrs: 5th 1/2-way: hdwy to ld narrowly 1f out: kpt on u.p ins fnl f: jnd on line* **6/1**[1]
1 *dht* **Sunset Beauty (IRE)**[12] 6732 4-8-12 82 ....(t) KJManning 5 87+
(J S Bolger, Ire) *in rr of mid-div: 10th ent st: 7th 1f out: hdwy between horses ins fnl f and kpt on wl to dispute on line* **6/1**[1]
3 *shd* **Obligada (IRE)**[97] 4115 3-8-12 89 .... SHJames(5) 3 94
(Kevin Prendergast, Ire) *mid-div: rdn to go 4th over 1f out: kpt on u.p ins fnl f: nt quite rch ldr* **16/1**
4 *½* **Collingwood (IRE)**[48] 5746 9-9-6 90 ....(t) WMLordan 14 93
(T M Walsh, Ire) *hld up: hdwy on outer fr 1f out: kpt on wl wout rching ldrs* **14/1**
5 *nse* **Duff (IRE)**[14] 6677 8-10-0 98 .... DPMcDonogh 6 101
(Edward Lynam, Ire) *a.p: 2nd 1/2-way: rdn in 3rd 1f out: kpt on same pce u.p ins fnl f* **7/1**[2]
6 *nk* **Queenie Keen (IRE)**[7] 6854 4-8-8 83 .... CPHoban(5) 9 85
(M Halford, Ire) *led: strly pressed fr 2f out: hdd 1f out: no ex u.p ins fnl f* **10/1**
7 *¾* **Lady Fashion**[7] 6854 3-9-12 98 .... FMBerry 10 98
(P D Deegan, Ire) *towards rr: sme hdwy on outer 1f out: kpt on ins fnl f: nt rch ldrs* **7/1**[2]
8 *shd* **Quinmaster (USA)**[26] 6388 9-8-13 83 ....(p) ShaneFoley 8 83
(M Halford, Ire) *towards rr: sme hdwy over 1f out: kpt on one pce* **25/1**
9 *nk* **Bawaardi (IRE)**[27] 6335 5-9-2 86 .... DavidNolan 12 85
(Richard Fahey) *chsd ldrs: outr appr st: rdn 2f out: no ex fnl f* **5/1**
10 *½* **Maundy Money**[19] 6560 8-8-9 86 .... CTKeane(7) 2 84
(David Marnane, Ire) *trckd ldrs: 3rd 1/2-way: no imp in 5th 1f out: no ex ins fnl f* **10/1**
11 *1 ½* **Iron Major (IRE)**[37] 6073 4-9-2 86 ....(tp) JMurtagh 7 80
(Edward Lynam, Ire) *a towards rr: nvr a factor* **8/1**[3]
12 *½* **He's Got Rhythm (IRE)**[2] 6960 6-8-12 82 .... CO'Donoghue 13 75
(David Marnane, Ire) *mid-div: 7th 1/2-way: hrd rdn and no ex over 1f out: wknd* **20/1**
13 *¾* **Luisant**[12] 6733 8-9-5 96 .... RDawson(7) 1 87
(J A Nash, Ire) *trckd ldrs on inner: 4th 1/2-way: no ex over 1f out: wknd* **9/1**
14 *4 ¼* **Casela Park (IRE)**[27] 6364 6-9-4 88 ....(b¹) BACurtis 11 67
(Jaclyn Tyrrell, Ire) *in rr of mid-div: sme hdwy on outer ent st: sn no ex* **14/1**

1m 22.7s (82.70)
WFA 3 from 4yo+ 2lb **14** Ran SP% **130.7**
CSF £19.30 CT £216.69; DF 21.70 TRIFECTA WIN: Sunset Beauty 3.60, Flic Flac 2.60; PL: SB 2.30, FF 2.10 Obligada 7.00.
Owner Moyglare Stud Farm **Bred** Moyglare Stud Farm **Trained** The Curragh, Co Kildare
Owner Patrick J Bolger **Bred** Patrick Bolger **Trained** Coolcullen, Co Carlow
■ Stewards' Enquiry : C O'Donoghue severe caution: used whip rapidly without giving regard to stride of the horse

NOTEBOOK
Flic Flac(IRE) sustained her effort well, coming through in the centre and seemingly getting her head in front on the line. Her head was certainly down but the spoils had to be shared. She seems to be developing a toughness which hasn't always been evident in the past and this surface certainly suits her well. (op 6/1 tchd 13/2)
Sunset Beauty(IRE) has kept her form well following a very notable hike in the handicap earlier in the summer. She came from mid-division to challenge in the straight and when seeing daylight inside the final furlong she really ran on strongly and deserved her share of the spoils. (op 6/1 tchd 13/2)
Obligada(IRE) didn't look likely to mount a challenge early in the straight. She had to be switched towards the outside from what was a good draw and came home very strongly inside the last.
Collingwood(IRE) did very much his best work at the finish. He's probably one of those horses for whom being drawn wide around here isn't a disadvantage as he has to be held up for a late run, and again he came fast and late but was a stride too late once again. (op 14/1 tchd 16/1)
Duff(IRE) ran a cracker. Tracking the pace he ran on with every chance inside the final furlong and lost nothing by being edged out inside the final hundred yards. He retains his appetite for racing. (op 9/1 tchd 13/2)
Queenie Keen(IRE) set off at a fair rate of knots, couldn't keep it up but only faded inside the last half-furlong. (op 8/1)
Lady Fashion was unable to negate the effects of her wide draw and ran respectably in the circumstances. (op 7/1 tchd 8/1)
Quinmaster(USA) kept on well inside the last having met a bit of trouble in running (op 33/1)
He's Got Rhythm(IRE) Official explanation: jockey said gelding hung in straight

7012a MERCURY STKS (LISTED RACE) 5f (P)
8:30 (8:46) 2-Y-0+ **£22,413** (£6,551; £3,103; £1,034)

RPR
1 **Nocturnal Affair (SAF)**[13] 6706 5-9-11 105 .... CO'Donoghue 6 104
(David Marnane, Ire) *trckd ldrs: 3rd travelling wl 2f out: hdwy to ld early fnl f: kpt on wl u.p* **5/2**[2]
2 *½* **Breathless Kiss (USA)**[13] 6706 4-9-8 ....(b) DPMcDonogh 4 99
(Kevin Ryan) *chsd ldrs: 6th 1f out: kpt on wl u.p ins fnl f: nt rch wnr* **20/1**
3 *½* **Balmont Mast (IRE)**[7] 6849 3-9-11 96 .... JMurtagh 13 100
(Edward Lynam, Ire) *trckd ldrs: 6th travelling wl 1/2-way: kpt on ins fnl f wout rching first 2* **15/2**
4 *shd* **Mayson**[20] 6522 3-9-11 .... DavidNolan 2 100
(Richard Fahey) *trckd ldrs: 4th 1/2-way: 3rd 1f out: no imp and kpt on one pce fnl f* **7/1**[3]
5 *½* **Chocolate Hills (FR)**[6] 6880 2-8-4 79 .... ShaneFoley 12 89
(G M Lyons, Ire) *in rr: sme hdwy and kpt on wl on outer ins fnl f: nt rch ldrs* **50/1**
6 *½* **Bannock (IRE)**[13] 6705 2-8-10 .... FMBerry 1 93+
(Mark Johnston) *led: strly pressed and hdd early fnl f: no ex* **15/8**[1]
7 *1* **The Reaper (IRE)**[14] 6677 3-9-11 99 ....(b) KLatham 9 93
(G M Lyons, Ire) *prom: 4th 2f out: no ex ins fnl f* **12/1**
8 *½* **Knock Stars (IRE)**[12] 6733 3-9-8 90 ....(t) BACurtis 11 88
(Patrick Martin, Ire) *towards rr: kpt on one pce fr over 1f out* **33/1**
9 *1 ¼* **Calm Bay (IRE)**[14] 6677 5-9-11 89 ....(bt) KJManning 5 86+
(H Rogers, Ire) *prom: 2nd 1/2-way: no ex ins fnl f* **33/1**
10 *1* **Timeless Call (IRE)**[14] 6677 3-9-8 93 .... NGMcCullagh 3 80
(Reginald Roberts, Ire) *mid-div: no imp in 8th whn short of room ins fnl f* **16/1**
11 *2 ½* **Srucahan (IRE)**[5] 6898 2-8-7 85 ....(b) WJSupple 7 68
(P D Deegan, Ire) *chsd ldrs: 7th 1/2-way: no ex fr over 1f out* **14/1**
12 *1* **Khaos (IRE)**[5] 6898 2-8-4 84 .... WMLordan 10 61
(P D Deegan, Ire) *a towards rr* **33/1**
13 *1 ¼* **Moonlit Garden (IRE)**[14] 6677 3-9-8 85 .... PJSmullen 8 63
(D K Weld, Ire) *a towards rr: nvr a factor* **33/1**

57.70 secs (57.70)
WFA 2 from 3yo+ 18lb **13** Ran SP% **126.3**
CSF £62.48 TOTE £2.40: £1.02, £4.00, £2.70; DF 70.30.
Owner Emma Bifova **Bred** T D Andrews **Trained** Bansha, Co Tipperary

FOCUS
The form is rated around around the second and fourth.

NOTEBOOK
Nocturnal Affair(SAF) ◆ won this race as a good horse should. He travelled very well in the race, came through to challenge a furlong out and quickened up well to go to win his race. Nice and uncomplicated and with more than a touch of class in a pretty sharp time. It was a thoroughly likeable performance. (op 3/1 tchd 9/4)
Breathless Kiss(USA) ran a very solid race indeed on paper but looked a lot less straightforward than the winner. racing in mid-division, he didn't give his rider much help up the straight as he consistently hung to his right but for all that he ran on strongly. Charting a straighter course would have seen him go quite close.
Balmont Mast(IRE) tracked the pace and looked to be really tanking behind the leaders turning in. He didn't pick up immediately but ran on inside the last to be nearest at the finish, and in terms of his time it would have compared well with the time he put up last week when winning so comprehensively. (op 8/1)
Mayson sustained his effort on the inside up the straight having been handy most of the way. Not quite good enough on the night, he was beaten only a length and it was a pretty smart effort. (op 4/1)
Chocolate Hills(FR) ◆ ran an encouraging race. He wasn't quickly away and really struggled to go the pace early on, but when realising what was involved he quickened in the straight and ran on very strongly. He also had to be switched to the wide outside. They could just have a very smart sprinter to go to war with next season.

7011 - 7014a (Foreign Racing) - See Raceform Interactive

6925 CLAIREFONTAINE (R-H)
Friday, October 21

OFFICIAL GOING: Turf: very soft

7015a PRIX DE L'ECOLE PRIMAIRE SAINTE-MARIE (PRIX DE LA FORET VERTE) (CONDITIONS) (4YO+) (LADY RIDERS) 1m
1:35 (12:00) 4-Y-0+ **£7,758** (£3,103; £2,327; £1,551; £775)

RPR
1 **Chemin Faisant (FR)**[1153] 7-9-0 0 ....(b) MlleAlexandraRosa(4) 5 64
(R Chotard, France) **17/2**
2 *1 ¾* **Kajima**[48] 5712 4-9-6 0 .... MissSallyAnnGrassick(5) 6 67
(R Pritchard-Gordon, France) **9/5**[1]
3 *2 ½* **Applique**[5] 4-9-7 0 .... MlleBlancheDeGranvilliers 2 57
(C Boutin, France) **78/10**
4 *1* **Tryst**[153] 6-9-4 0 .... MllePaulineBoisgontier 10 52
(J E Hammond, France) **5/2**[2]
5 *2* **Bold Marc (IRE)**[38] 6017 9-9-13 0 .... MissMPlat 1 56
(Mrs K Burke) *broke fast: settled in 2nd several l bhd clr ldr: swtchd to stands' rail ent st: u.p fr over 1 1/2f out: no ex: styd on fnl f* **11/2**[3]
6 *1 ½* **Babylona (FR)** 4-8-13 0 ....(b) KatjaMarkwalder(4) 8 43
(Philippe Le Geay, France) **34/1**
7 *2 ½* **Parvati (FR)**[23] 4-9-4 0 ....(b¹) MmeCatherineRieb-Menard 4 38
(Mlle V Dissaux, France) **34/1**
8 *3* **Northern Dream (FR)** 4-9-8 0 .... MlleBarbaraGuenet 3 35
(F Chappet, France) **23/1**
9 *1 ¾* **King Of Risk (FR)** 7-9-0 0 .... MlleFloraLePonner(4) 9 27
(P Le Ponner, France) **44/1**
10 *4* **Tequillo (FR)**[28] 6-9-4 0 ....(p) MlleHeleneCorcoral 7 18
(J Bertin, France) **36/1**

1m 47.6s (107.60) **10** Ran SP% **116.4**
WIN (incl. 1 euro stake): 9.50. PLACES: 1.90, 1.30, 2.00. DF: 11.90. SF: 37.00.
Owner Hubert Barbe **Bred** Michel Thiebaud **Trained** France

7016a PRIX JOURNEE DES ECOLES (PRIX DES GERBERAS) (CLAIMER) (3YO) (TURF) 1m 4f

2:05 (12:00) 3-Y-O **£6,896** (£2,758; £2,068; £1,379; £689)

RPR

1 **Poeme Du Berlais (FR)**[28] 3-9-1 0..............(p) PaulineProd'homme(5) 8 78
(D Prod'Homme, France) **7/1**

2 *5* **Layman Junior (FR)**[53] 3-9-2 0..................................(b) JohanVictoire 4 66
(D De Waele, France) **6/1**[3]

3 *nk* **Riquita (IRE)**[7] 3-8-13 0....................................(b) ChristopheSoumillon 6 63
(C Lerner, France) **14/5**[1]

4 *snk* **Allashka (FR)** 3-8-9 0.. AntoineHamelin(4) 1 62
(J-L Guillochon, France) **44/5**

5 *1 ½* **Bravo Biloute (FR)**[39] 3-8-6 0...............(p) MathieuTavaresDaSilva(5) 10 58
(S Jesus, France) **13/1**

6 *6* **Un Air De Danse (FR)**[29] 3-8-6 0..........................(b) TheoBachelot(5) 9 48
(S Wattel, France) **15/1**

7 *8* **Cold Case (FR)**[135] 3-8-8 0.................................... StephanePasquier 14 32
(F-X De Chevigny, France) **17/1**

8 *¾* **Red Chaparral (GER)**[130] 3-8-11 0..........................(b) MaximeGuyon 7 34
(W Baltromei, Germany) **13/1**

9 *2* **Catharos (FR)** 3-8-3 0.. CesarPasserat(5) 11 28
(Mali Droueche, France) **118/1**

10 *2* **Urlanie (FR)** 3-8-3 0.. StephaneLaurent(5) 2 25
(Mme A-E Gareau, France) **93/1**

U **Ulla**[16] 6622 3-8-13 0... RonanThomas 13 —
(Chris Wall) *broke wl on outside to r 3rd: dropped bk to 6th bef fnl turn: u.p whn swtchd towards stands' rail in st: no ex: fdd qckly* **11/2**[2]

0 **Birs**[53] 3-9-2 0... VincentVion 12 —
(B Beaunez, France) **55/1**

0 **Piccola Stella (FR)** 3-8-8 0................................(b[1]) MickaelBarzalona 5 —
(Alex Fracas, France) **13/1**

0 **Kalathir (FR)** 3-8-6 0 ow1............................ AlexandreChampenois(3) 3 —
(R Schoof, Belgium) **55/1**

2m 44.1s (6.20) **14** Ran SP% **117.4**
WIN (incl. 1 euro stake): 8.00. PLACES: 2.30, 2.00, 1.80. DF: 22.80. SF: 52.60.
Owner Victor Swimberghe **Bred** Mlle L Collet & Mlle C Collet **Trained** France

6983 DONCASTER (L-H)

Saturday, October 22

OFFICIAL GOING: Good (9.0)
Wind: Fresh 1/2 against Weather: Fine

7017 CROWNHOTEL-BAWTRY.COM H'CAP (DIV I) 1m 4f

1:30 (1:32) (Class 4) (0-85,85) 3-Y-O+ **£5,175** (£1,540; £769; £384) **Stalls** Low

Form RPR

-162 **1** **Direct Answer (USA)**[38] 6068 4-9-7 **80**...................... RichardMullen 18 91+
(Sir Michael Stoute) *trckd ldrs: hdwy to ld 2f out: rdn ent fnl f: kpt on wl towards fin* **10/1**

2123 **2** *hd* **A Boy Named Suzi**[29] 6294 3-9-2 **82**................................ LukeMorris 6 93+
(James Eustace) *hld up towards rr: gd hdwy wl over 2f out: rdn to chse wnr ent fnl f: sn chal and ev ch tl no ex nr fin* **8/1**[3]

3512 **3** *3* **Comedy Act**[7] 6868 4-9-4 **77**.. DanielTudhope 13 83
(David O'Meara) *hld up in rr: hdwy 3f out: swtchd rt and effrt 2f out: sn rdn and chsd ldrs ent fnl f: kpt on same pce* **14/1**

1032 **4** *1 ¼* **Romeo Montague**[27] 6375 3-9-5 **85**............................(b[1]) ChrisCatlin 10 89
(Ed Dunlop) *hld up in rr: gd hdwy on inner 3f out: rdn to chse ldrs over 1f out: kpt on same pce fnl f* **12/1**

2531 **5** *1 ½* **Eagle Rock (IRE)**[28] 6349 3-9-0 **80**.............................. AndrewMullen 1 82
(Tom Tate) *trckd ldng pair: effrt over 2f out: rdn wl over 1f out: grad wknd* **14/1**

6-25 **6** *nk* **Red Jade**[15] 6676 6-9-11 **84**.. PaulHanagan 5 85
(Richard Fahey) *in tch: hdwy to chse ldrs 3f out: rdn along 2f out: no imp appr fnl f* **7/1**[2]

2151 **7** *2 ¼* **Gunslinger (FR)**[27] 6376 6-9-6 **84**................................ DavidKenny(5) 16 82
(Michael Scudamore) *hld up in rr: hdwy on wd outside wl over 2f out: rdn and one pce fr wl over 1f out* **20/1**

00-0 **8** *shd* **Nezhenka**[8] 6832 4-9-10 **83**.................................. SilvestreDeSousa 11 80
(Mark Johnston) *towards rr: pushed along 4f out: rdn 3f out: n.d* **6/1**[1]

1P10 **9** *2 ¼* **Epic (IRE)**[15] 6676 4-9-3 **76**.. JimmyFortune 4 70
(Mark Johnston) *led: rdn along 3f out: hdd 2f out and sn wknd* **16/1**

-403 **10** *1 ¼* **Sea Of Galilee**[17] 6632 4-9-11 **84**.................................... DaneO'Neill 14 76
(Henry Candy) *hld up: sme hdwy over 3f out: sn rdn and n.d* **12/1**

1000 **11** *nk* **Mister Angry (IRE)**[23] 6485 4-9-7 **80**.................................. NeilCallan 3 71
(Mark Johnston) *chsd ldrs on inner: hdwy 3f out: rdn along wl over 1f out: sn wknd* **25/1**

0512 **12** *1* **Hot Spice**[18] 6607 3-9-0 **80**... TedDurcan 8 70
(John Dunlop) *hld up in rr: effrt and sme hdwy over 3f out: sn rdn and btn* **7/1**[2]

2251 **13** *2 ½* **Duquesa (IRE)**[12] 6756 3-8-2 **73**......................... MatthewCosham(5) 9 59
(David Evans) *towards rr whn hmpd on inner after 1f: a bhd after* **16/1**

2504 **14** *4 ½* **Royal Swain (IRE)**[34] 6191 5-9-4 **77**............................ PJMcDonald 17 55
(Alan Swinbank) *in tch: hdwy to chse ldrs over 3f out: rdn along wl over 2f out: sn wknd* **12/1**

210 **15** *28* **Baltic Light (USA)**[136] 2819 3-8-13 **79**......................... IanMongan 15 13
(Sir Henry Cecil) *chsd ldr: rdn along over 3f out: sn wknd* **25/1**

2m 29.89s (-5.01) **Going Correction** -0.275s/f (Firm)
WFA 3 from 4yo+ 7lb **15** Ran SP% **120.1**
Speed ratings (Par 105): **105,104,102,102,101 100,99,99,97,96 96,96,94,91,72**
toteswingers: 1&2 £18.50, 1&3 £26.10, 2&3 £22.90. CSF £84.64 CT £1125.36 TOTE £10.10: £3.90, £2.60, £6.20; EX 67.90 TRIFECTA Not won..
Owner K Abdulla **Bred** Juddmonte Farms Inc **Trained** Newmarket, Suffolk

FOCUS
The ground had dried out from the previous day's meeting to an official description of good. This was a decent, competitive handicap run at a solid gallop. The time was 0.28 seconds slower than the second leg. The form is basically sound.

7018 JOIN RACINGPOST.COM MEMBERS' CLUB H'CAP 5f

2:00 (2:05) (Class 2) (0-100,100) 3-Y-O+
£12,450 (£3,728; £1,864; £932; £466; £234) **Stalls** High

Form RPR

1000 **1** **Steps (IRE)**[13] 6723 3-8-10 **89**.. NeilCallan 10 97
(Roger Varian) *in tch: hdwy over 2f out: r.o to ld last 50yds* **25/1**

0060 **2** *nk* **Secret Witness**[1] 6987 5-8-13 **92**...........................(b) JimmyFortune 17 99
(Ronald Harris) *mid-div: gd hdwy stands' side over 1f out: styd on wl to chal ins fnl f: jst hld* **12/1**

0040 **3** *shd* **Face The Problem (IRE)**[66] 5180 3-8-9 **88**..................... ChrisCatlin 9 95
(Charles Hills) *in rr: hdwy on outside over 2f out: r.o to chal ins fnl f: no ex* **33/1**

305 **4** *nk* **Judge 'n Jury**[28] 6332 7-8-7 **86**.. LukeMorris 6 92
(Ronald Harris) *overall ldr centre: hdd and no ex last 50yds* **18/1**

0003 **5** *¾* **Barney McGrew (IRE)**[14] 6703 8-8-7 **86** oh1.............. BarryMcHugh 19 89
(Michael Dods) *s.i.s: hdwy 2f out: styd on wl ins fnl f* **12/1**

2034 **6** *nk* **Hazelrigg (IRE)**[28] 6332 6-8-8 **87** ow1.....................(be) PJMcDonald 12 89
(Tim Easterby) *chsd ldrs: edgd rt over 1f out: kpt on same pce* **16/1**

6233 **7** *hd* **Racy**[14] 6706 4-9-2 **95**.. PhillipMakin 7 96
(Kevin Ryan) *w ldr: kpt on same pce fnl f* **7/1**[1]

0203 **8** *1 ¾* **Singeur (IRE)**[7] 6865 4-9-2 **95**.....................................(b) LeeNewman 13 90
(Robin Bastiman) *in tch: effrt over 2f out: kpt on one pce* **10/1**[3]

3000 **9** *shd* **Ginger Ted (IRE)**[35] 6145 4-8-7 **86**...................(p) RobbieFitzpatrick 14 80
(Richard Guest) *s.i.s: styd on fnl 2f: nvr rchd ldrs* **22/1**

0224 **10** *nse* **Confessional**[21] 6522 4-9-6 **99**............................(be) SilvestreDeSousa 4 93
(Tim Easterby) *chsd ldrs on outside: one pce appr fnl f* **8/1**[2]

500 **11** *¾* **Piscean (USA)**[13] 6723 6-8-7 **86** oh1................................ JimmyQuinn 3 78
(Tom Keddy) *s.i.s: kpt on fnl 2f: nvr a factor* **50/1**

000 **12** *shd* **Medici Time**[33] 6224 6-8-8 **87**.......................................(v) TedDurcan 11 78
(Tim Easterby) *s.i.s: styd on fnl 2f: nvr a factor* **33/1**

0004 **13** *1* **Cocktail Charlie**[7] 6865 3-8-10 **89**...............................(b) DavidAllan 15 77
(Tim Easterby) *chsd ldrs: wknd over 1f out* **10/1**[3]

5010 **14** *1 ¾* **Foxy Music**[28] 6332 7-8-9 **88**...................................... GrahamGibbons 21 69
(Eric Alston) *led on stands' side: wknd over 1f out* **40/1**

4115 **15** *1 ½* **Dreamacha**[19] 6594 4-8-11 **90**..................................... WilliamCarson 20 66
(Stuart Williams) *in rr towards stands' side: swtchd lft over 1f out: nvr on terms* **16/1**

3621 **16** *½* **Marine Commando**[28] 6332 3-8-13 **92**............................ PaulHanagan 18 66
(Richard Fahey) *mid-div towards stands' side: effrt over 2f out: wknd over 1f out* **7/1**[1]

13-4 **17** *1 ¼* **Excel Bolt**[174] 1711 3-9-7 **100**.. TomEaves 16 70
(Bryan Smart) *chsd ldrs: wknd over 1f out* **28/1**

2266 **18** *shd* **Bathwick Bear (IRE)**[7] 6865 3-8-11 **90**.......................... AndreaAtzeni 2 59
(David Evans) *chsd ldrs on outside: lost pl over 2f out* **20/1**

0022 **19** *2* **Favourite Girl (IRE)**[7] 6865 5-9-0 **93**......................(v) DuranFentiman 1 55
(Tim Easterby) *chsd ldrs far side: lost pl 2f out* **12/1**

0030 **20** *1 ¼* **Swilly Ferry (USA)**[48] 5758 4-8-10 **89**......................(p) RobertWinston 22 47
(Charles Hills) *chsd ldr stands' side: wknd over 2f out* **16/1**

57.95 secs (-2.55) **Going Correction** -0.275s/f (Firm) **20** Ran SP% **127.0**
Speed ratings (Par 109): **109,108,108,107,106 106,105,103,102,102 101,101,99,97,94 93,91,91,88,86**
toteswingers: 1&2 £148.50, 1&3 £52.50, 2&3 £163.30. CSF £285.28 CT £9757.62 TOTE £35.10: £7.40, £3.60, £8.00, £5.40; EX 784.90 Trifecta £1811.20 Part won. Pool: £2,447.64 - 0.03 winning units..
Owner Michael Hill **Bred** Eamon Beston **Trained** Newmarket, Suffolk

FOCUS
They raced middle to stands' side in this typically competitive sprint handicap. The front-running fourth is probably the best guide.

NOTEBOOK
Steps(IRE) had struggled since winning back-to-back handicaps earlier in the year, though he had been denied a clear run on his two most recent starts. This wasn't just a return to form but a career best, and considering it was only his 12th start, maybe there's more to come. (tchd 22-1)
Secret Witness was just held after switching to the stands' rail with his challenge. This was a big improvement on his performance here over 6f of the previous day. (op 20-1)
Face The Problem(IRE) ◆ deserves extra credit as he'd been off for 66 days and had to make his challenge away from the pace.
Judge 'n Jury was contesting this race for the fourth year in succession. Racing from 19lb lower than for his success in the 2008 running, he showed tremendous pace but couldn't quite sustain it. (tchd 20-1)
Barney McGrew(IRE), 1lb out of the weights, compromised his chance with a slow start but finished strongly. (op 11-1)
Hazelrigg(IRE) tanked along as usual but didn't go any quicker off the bridle. He hasn't won since September 2010. (tchd 14-1)
Racy couldn't match his recent form. He remains with only a maiden win to his name. (op 15-2)
Ginger Ted(IRE) ◆, for whom this was more like it, maybe will be worth one last chance when returned to 6f with a bit of cut in the ground. (op 20-1)
Marine Commando, raised 4lb for ending a losing run over this trip on easy ground at Haydock, didn't pick up at all this time. He ran flat. (op 15-2 tchd 8-1)
Bathwick Bear(IRE)'s rider reported that the gelding was never travelling. Official explanation: jockey said gelding never travelled (tchd 22-1)

7019 BET THROUGH THE RACING POST APP STKS (REGISTERED AS THE DONCASTER STAKES) (LISTED RACE) 6f

2:30 (2:33) (Class 1) 2-Y-O **£12,728** (£4,813; £2,405; £1,201) **Stalls** High

Form RPR

4641 **1** **Gusto**[17] 6625 2-9-1 96.. DaneO'Neill 1 101
(Richard Hannon) *in tch: hdwy to trck ldrs 2f out: rdn ent fnl f: styd on wl to ld last 50yds* **8/1**

1016 **2** *nk* **Chunky Diamond (IRE)**[21] 6518 2-9-1 97.................. JimmyFortune 4 100
(Peter Chapple-Hyam) *hld up towards rr: gd hdwy on outer 2f out: rdn to ld jst ins fnl f: hdd and no ex last 50yds* **11/1**

0522 **3** *½* **Miss Lahar**[14] 6705 2-8-10 102.. MartinHarley 11 94
(Mick Channon) *trckd ldrs: smooth hdwy wl over 2f out: chal over 1f out: rdn to ld briefly ent fnl f: sn hdd and no ex* **9/2**[1]

21 **4** *2 ½* **Accession (IRE)**[36] 6127 2-9-1 85..................................... AdamKirby 3 91+
(Clive Cox) *towards rr: hdwy over 2f out: rdn over 1f out: styd on ins fnl f: nrst fin* **5/1**[2]

0140 **5** *hd* **Red Aggressor (IRE)**[14] 6692 2-9-1 90............................ NeilCallan 5 91
(Clive Brittain) *prom: cl up over 2f out: rdn to ld briefly 1 1/2f out: hdd 1f out and kpt on same pce* **25/1**

The Form Book, Raceform Ltd, Compton, RG20 6NL

10 **6** ½ **Dreamwriter (USA)**[51] 5656 2-8-10 0 KieranO'Neill 8 84
(Richard Hannon) *chsd ldrs: rdn along 2f out: kpt on same pce* **9/2**[1]

3123 **7** 2¼ **Son Du Silence (IRE)**[36] 6114 2-9-1 89 (b) PaulHanagan 9 82
(J S Moore) *led: rdn along over 2f out: hdd 1 1/2f out and sn wknd* **25/1**

2111 **8** *nse* **Ballesteros**[8] 6827 2-9-1 93 WilliamBuick 2 82
(Brian Meehan) *hld up: a in rr* **11/2**[3]

1000 **9** *8* **Cockney Fire**[21] 6535 2-8-10 85 AndreaAtzeni 7 53
(David Evans) *chsd ldr: rdn along wl over 2f out: sn wknd* **50/1**

1000 **10** *15* **West Leake Diman (IRE)**[14] 6688 2-9-1 107 RobertWinston 10 13
(Charles Hills) *trckd ldrs: hdwy to chse ldr 1/2-way: rdn along over 2f out and sn wknd* **5/1**[2]

1m 11.21s (-2.39) **Going Correction** -0.275s/f (Firm) 2y crse rec **10** Ran SP% **114.2**
Speed ratings (Par 103): **104,103,102,99,99 98,95,95,84,64**
toteswingers: 1&2 £13.00, 1&3 £7.60, 2&3 £9.40. CSF £87.94 TOTE £10.00: £3.20, £2.80, £2.10; EX 101.80 Trifecta £812.50 Pool: £1,098.03 - 64.00 winning units..
Owner Highclere Thoroughbred Racing-Rock Sand **Bred** New England, Mount Coote & P Barrett **Trained** East Everleigh, Wilts

■ Stewards' Enquiry : Dane O'Neill five-day ban: used whip with excessive frequency (Nov 5, 9-12)

FOCUS

A competitive juvenile Listed event run at a strong pace, and the time was a new juvenile course record. Solid form, up to scratch for the level.

NOTEBOOK

Gusto struggled in good company after an impressive maiden success, but he came good again in a Polytrack novice event on his most recent outing and built on that back on turf. He basically outstayed his main rivals and gave the impression 7f will be within reach. His rider picked up a five-day whip ban. (tchd 17-2)

Chunky Diamond(IRE), sixth in the Cornwallis last time, travelled well but simply found one too strong. He might prove best back over 5f. (op 14-1)

Miss Lahar has been running well in decent company since her maiden win, including finishing second in the Cornwallis (ahead of Chunky Diamond) two starts ago, and this was another fine effort, though she didn't pick up well enough after travelling easily. (tchd 4-1 and 5-1)

Accession(IRE) was up in grade after a Newbury maiden win and came up short, though this represents improvement. He's probably more of a 3-y-o prospect. (op 9-2 tchd 11-2)

Red Aggressor(IRE) had a bit to find but he ran respectably. (op 20-1)

Dreamwriter(USA) impressed when a wide-margin maiden winner on her debut and then got no run in a Listed race, but she hadn't been seen for 51 days. She was beaten by halfway this time, but might have had enough for the year. (op 11-2)

Ballesteros had progressed well to win his last three starts, though his best effort to date came over 5f on testing going. Up in class and faced with different conditions, he didn't travel with his usual fluency. (op 6-1)

West Leake Diman(IRE) looked flattered by his close-up seventh in the Middle Park and did nothing to alter that view, although he was eased late on, suggesting something might have been amiss. Robert Winston reported the colt ran flat. Official explanation: jockey said colt ran flat (op 11-2)

7020 RACING POST TROPHY (GROUP 1) (ENTIRE COLTS & FILLIES) 1m (S)

3:00 (3:04) (Class 1) 2-Y-O **£131,567** (£49,880; £24,963; £12,435; £6,240) **Stalls** High

Form RPR

1 **Camelot**[100] 4029 2-9-0 0 JPO'Brien 6 119+
(A P O'Brien, Ire) *hld up in rr: swtchd rt and smooth hdwy over 1f out: qcknd to ld last 150yds: smoothly wnt clr: v impressive* **10/11**[1]

63 **2** 2¼ **Zip Top (IRE)**[30] 6270 2-9-0 0 KJManning 5 111
(J S Bolger, Ire) *trckd ldrs: drvn over 2f out: rdn to ld over 1f out: hdd jst ins fnl f: styd on same pce* **8/1**

31 **3** *nk* **Fencing (USA)**[70] 5044 2-9-0 105 (t) WilliamBuick 4 111
(John Gosden) *hld up in rr: t.k.h: hdwy 2f out: chalng whn edgd rt jst ins fnl f: kpt on same pce* **9/4**[2]

4 2½ **Learn (IRE)**[79] 4733 2-9-0 0 CO'Donoghue 1 106+
(A P O'Brien, Ire) *set modest pce: qcknd over 2f out: hdd over 1f out: hld in 4th whn crowded jst ins fnl f* **7/1**[3]

1100 **5** *6* **Talwar (IRE)**[21] 6527 2-9-0 107 JimmyFortune 2 91
(Jeremy Noseda) *sn trcking ldr: t.k.h: drvn over 2f out: wknd over 1f out: eased clsng stages* **14/1**

1m 38.58s (-0.72) **Going Correction** -0.275s/f (Firm) **5** Ran SP% **113.4**
Speed ratings (Par 100): [illegible]
toteswingers: 1&2 £5.60. CSF £9.33 TOTE £2.00: £1.40, £3.00; EX 7.20.
Owner D Smith, Mrs J Magnier, M Tabor **Bred** Sheikh Abdulla Bin Isa Al-Khalifa **Trained** Ballydoyle, Co Tipperary

FOCUS

This top-class juvenile contest has gone to three Epsom Derby winners over the past decade, namely High Chaparral (2001), Motivator (2004) and Authorized (2006), while Brian Boru (2002) took this en route to his St Leger triumph. During the same period three also-rans subsequently placed at Epsom – The Great Gatsby (only fourth in 2002), Dylan Thomas (sixth in 2005), and Eagle Mountain (fourth in 2006). The last four runnings have not reached that standard, however. A field of five represented the poorest numerical turnout since American Post defeated three rivals in 2004, and the absence of Godolphin's highly regarded maiden winner Encke was disappointing. However, there was a highly promising winner and the form has some substance with the runner-up and third having both recorded three-figure RPRs last time. The time was nothing special on a day when some races dipped under standard, but the gallop, set by the winner's stablemate did not appear strong. The runner-up will be the key to the form and Camelot, an exciting prospect, was value for at least a length more and right up with this year's best juveniles.

NOTEBOOK

Camelot, absent since winning a standard maiden at Leopardstown (1m, good) on his debut in July, had been heavily punted and he became the first odds-on winner since American Post, producing an immensely promising performance. The true worth of the form will be a while in being established, but the winner could do no more than cruise along until scooting clear without needing anything like a hard ride. Another plus was his straightforward attitude. That can't always be said of Montjeu's progeny, but this was the sire's fourth success in the race. As well as this event often works out, still fresh in the memory are the subsequent records of more recent winners, some of whom were equally flashy in deeper fields (Crowded House and Ballydoyle's St Nicholas Abbey spring to mind), so top prices of 7-1 for the Guineas and 4-1 for the Derby don't appeal. However, it's worth noting the last horse to win this following a debut maiden success was Motivator, and anyone who's already on for the Classics has done well. He's clearly not short of tactical pace and as of yet there's no standout Guineas candidate, while he really ought to get 1m4f. (op Evens tchd 8-11and 6-5 in places)

Zip Top(IRE) reportedly didn't handle the downhill run when third in the Somerville Tattersall Stakes (fourth-placed Crusade won the Middle Park) over 7f at Newmarket last time, and he was supplemented for this. He was no match at all for the potentially high-class winner. (op 6-1 tchd 9-1)

Fencing(USA), absent since winning the Listed Washington Singer on his second start, resumed with a tongue-tie fitted for the first time. Up in trip, he was one-paced after being keen and is probably more of a 3-y-o prospect. (op 5-2 tchd 3-1 and 10-3 in a place)

Learn(IRE) looked out his depth, though he had been off since his maiden win in August. (op 8-1 tchd 10-1 and 6-1)

Talwar(IRE) has struggled since winning the Solario on soft ground. (op 16-1 tchd 20-1)

7021 JACK NOLAN 10TH ANNIVERSARY NURSERY 7f

3:35 (3:35) (Class 3) (0-95,92) 2-Y-O **£7,439** (£2,213; £1,106; £553) **Stalls** High

Form RPR

0241 **1** **Strictly Silver (IRE)**[36] 6110 2-8-7 81 DominicFox(3) 13 86+
(Alan Bailey) *hld up: gd hdwy over 2f out: chsd ldrs and swtchd lft over 1f out: rdn to ld wl ins fnl f: sn hung lft and styd on wl* **9/1**

11 **2** *nk* **Ortac Rock (IRE)**[35] 6166 2-8-12 86 SeanLevey(3) 14 90+
(Richard Hannon) *in tch: hdwy to trck ldrs 1/2-way: chal 2f out: rdn and edgd rt over 1f out: led jst ins fnl f: sn hdd and kpt on* **7/2**[1]

0530 **3** *nk* **Fulbright**[21] 6535 2-9-7 92 SilvestreDeSousa 11 95
(Mark Johnston) *chsd ldrs: cl up 1/2-way: led 3f out: rdn over 1f out: hdd jst ins fnl f: kpt on* **8/1**[3]

2113 **4** ½ **Deepsand (IRE)**[15] 6670 2-8-8 79 DavidAllan 12 81
(Tim Easterby) *hld up: hdwy 1/2-way: chsd ldrs over 2f out: rdn to chal over 1f out and ev ch tl nt qckn ins fnl f* **6/1**[2]

2110 **5** *hd* **Quick Bite (IRE)**[34] 6196 2-8-9 80 LukeMorris 7 82
(Hugo Palmer) *in tch: hdwy over 2f out: rdn to chse ldrs whn nt clr run over 1f out: sn swtchd lft and kpt on wl towards fin* **16/1**

2240 **6** 2¼ **Wolfgang (IRE)**[45] 5825 2-8-13 87 KieranO'Neill(3) 8 83
(Richard Hannon) *hld up in rr: hdwy over 2f out: sn rdn and kpt on fnl f: nrst fin* **12/1**

3450 **7** *nk* **Jack Who's He (IRE)**[21] 6535 2-9-2 87 (p) NeilCallan 4 82
(David Evans) *chsd ldrs: rdn along over 2f out: styng on whn n.m.r appr fnl f: one pce* **9/1**

1534 **8** ¾ **Satanic Beat (IRE)**[19] 6573 2-8-8 79 PJMcDonald 6 72
(Jedd O'Keeffe) *in tch: rdn along over 2f out: kpt on same pce* **11/1**

0251 **9** 1½ **Indepub**[18] 6599 2-8-7 81 AmyRyan(3) 9 70
(Kevin Ryan) *hld up: a in rr* **11/1**

3150 **10** *nk* **Vassaria (IRE)**[44] 5847 2-8-7 78 BarryMcHugh 3 66
(Michael Dods) *t.k.h early: cl up: rdn 2f out and grad wknd* **40/1**

2236 **11** *1* **Fayr Fall (IRE)**[14] 6699 2-8-3 74 DuranFentiman 1 60
(Tim Easterby) *cl up: led briefly 1/2-way: sn hdd and rdn: grad wknd* **20/1**

0015 **12** *3* **Holiday Reading (USA)**[14] 6699 2-8-4 75 AndreaAtzeni 2 53
(Brian Meehan) *led: hdd 1/2-way: rdn along wl over 2f out and sn wknd* **9/1**

1350 **13** 3¾ **Verbeeck**[15] 6670 2-8-13 84 (tp) RobertWinston 10 52
(Alan McCabe) *a in rr* **33/1**

015 **14** 1¼ **Bartley**[121] 3313 2-8-6 77 TomEaves 5 42
(Bryan Smart) *a towards rr: bhd fnl 2f* **33/1**

1m 25.26s (-1.04) **Going Correction** -0.275s/f (Firm) **14** Ran SP% **120.9**
Speed ratings (Par 99): **94,93,93,92,92 89,89,88,87,86 85,82,77,76**
toteswingers: 1&2 £9.30, 1&3 £11.20, 2&3 £6.80. CSF £39.13 CT £227.78 TOTE £11.00: £3.10, £1.70, £2.40; EX 62.40 Trifecta £281.40 Pool: £775.94 - 2.04 winning units..
Owner A J H **Bred** Langton Stud **Trained** Newmarket, Suffolk

■ Stewards' Enquiry : Dominic Fox five-day ban: used whip with excessive frequency (Nov 5,9-12)

FOCUS

A good nursery with some in-form, decent types dominant. Solid form with improvement from the winner. They raced middle to stands' side for much of the way.

NOTEBOOK

Strictly Silver(IRE), off the mark on easy ground at Ayr on his previous start, did well to follow up. Having again travelled like an above-average type, he had to wait for a run and then quickened well once the gap opened. He didn't help himself by hanging left when in the clear, ending up away from his main rivals, but had just enough in reserve to hold on. Worth more than the official margin suggests, there should be further improvement to come. His rider was the second on this card to pick up a five-day whip ban. (op 8-1)

Ortac Rock(IRE) came here 2-2, including getting away with a drop to 6f at Newbury last time, but he was just held off 4lb higher. He again stuck on in likeable fashion, though, and gives the impression he's far from the finished article. (op 9-2)

Fulbright improved for the step up in trip with a career-best under top weight. (op 10-1)

Deepsand(IRE), another up in trip, seemed to have his chance. (op 5-1)

Quick Bite(IRE) would have been closer with a better trip. Her winning form has come on testing ground and she could have more to offer. (op 14-1)

7022 CROWNHOTEL-BAWTRY.COM H'CAP (DIV II) 1m 4f

4:10 (4:10) (Class 4) (0-85,84) 3-Y-O+ **£5,175** (£1,540; £769; £384) **Stalls** Low

Form RPR

-010 **1** **Suhaili**[49] 5710 3-9-3 82 (t) WilliamBuick 7 93+
(Roger Varian) *trckd ldrs: rdn to chal over 2f out: styd on to ld last 50yds* **6/1**[1]

3343 **2** *nk* **Rio's Rosanna (IRE)**[5] 6918 4-9-2 74 RussKennemore 5 84
(Richard Whitaker) *dwlt: hld up in rr: gd hdwy to ld over 2f out: hdd: edgd rt and no ex clsng stages* **7/1**[2]

1202 **3** ¾ **Achalas (IRE)**[41] 5971 3-8-10 75 ow1 JamieSpencer 2 84
(Heather Main) *wnt rt s: in rr: hdwy over 3f out: chsng ldrs 1f out: no ex whn hmpd last 50yds* **14/1**

6002 **4** *2* **Tartan Gunna**[31] 6263 5-9-4 76 (b) SilvestreDeSousa 12 82
(Mark Johnston) *s.i.s: in rr: hdwy 3f out: chsng ldrs over 1f out: styd on same pce* **8/1**[3]

5103 **5** *1* **Lucky Windmill**[28] 6346 4-9-5 77 PJMcDonald 15 81
(Alan Swinbank) *hld up in mid-div: hdwy on outer to chal over 2f out: one pce fnl f* **12/1**

-000 **6** *shd* **Braveheart Move (IRE)**[14] 6690 5-9-11 83 RobertWinston 6 87
(Geoffrey Harker) *chsd ldrs: led 3f out: sn hdd: one pce* **11/1**

2030 **7** 2½ **Antigua Sunrise (IRE)**[14] 6708 5-9-1 80 LauraBarry(7) 16 80
(Richard Fahey) *in rr: hdwy and hung bdly rt over 2f out: racd alone stands' side: kpt on fnl f* **12/1**

0400 **8** *nse* **Greyfriars Drummer**[38] 6046 3-8-13 78 NeilCallan 1 78
(Mark Johnston) *dwlt: sn mid-div: drvn and hdwy on ins to chse ldrs over 3f out: edgd rt over 1f out: fdd* **18/1**

2640 **9** 1¾ **Ellemujie**[35] 6163 6-9-12 84 (p) AdamKirby 13 81
(Dean Ivory) *hld up in mid-div: hdwy over 3f out: chsng ldrs over 2f out: wknd fnl f* **14/1**

3660 **10** 4½ **Stagecoach Danman (IRE)**[28] 6333 3-9-1 80 JimmyFortune 3 70
(Mark Johnston) *chsd ldrs: drvn over 3f out: wknd over 1f out* **7/1**[2]

0-04 **11** 4½ **Rebel Dancer (FR)**[148] 2459 6-9-0 72 MartinLane 14 55
(Ian Williams) *s.i.s: nvr on terms* **16/1**

0104 **12** *nk* **Lady Chaparral**[57] 5435 4-9-12 84 TomEaves 10 66
(Michael Dods) *in tch: effrt over 3f out: wknd 2f out* **7/1**[2]

2 **13** 3½ **Kingston Tiger**[6] 5738 3-8-5 73 (v) AdamBeschizza(3) 4 49
(Michael Wigham) *in tch: drvn over 3f out: sn lost pl* **50/1**

00 **14** *6* **Jawaab (IRE)**[7] 5888 7-9-5 80 (e) RobertLButler(3) 17 47
(Richard Guest) *led 2f: chsd ldrs: lost pl over 3f out* **25/1**

1404 **15** *1¾* **Rock The Stars (IRE)**[24] 6465 4-9-4 **76**............................ DaneO'Neill 9 40
(J W Hills) *chsd ldrs: lost pl over 3f out: sn bhd* **16/1**

2m 29.61s (-5.29) **Going Correction** -0.275s/f (Firm)
WFA 3 from 4yo+ 7lb **15** Ran SP% **122.8**
Speed ratings (Par 105): **106,105,105,103,103 103,101,101,100,97 94,94,91,87,86**
toteswingers: 1&2 £9.30, 1&3 £16.20, 2&3 £18.80. CSF £46.63 CT £578.84 TOTE £7.70: £2.70, £3.00, £4.30; EX 52.00 Trifecta £243.40 Pool: £562.50 - 1.71 winning units..
Owner B E Nielsen **Bred** Mrs Rebecca Philipps **Trained** Newmarket, Suffolk

FOCUS
The time was 0.28 seconds quicker than the first division. The winner is on a good mark on a best view of his maiden form and could do better.

7023 RACING AND FOOTBALL OUTLOOK CONDITIONS STKS 7f
4:45 (4:46) (Class 3) 3-Y-0+
£8,092 (£2,423; £1,211; £605; £302; £152) **Stalls** High

Form RPR

6020 **1** **Mia's Boy**[7] 6862 7-8-11 **97**.. AndreaAtzeni 7 99
(Chris Dwyer) *hld up towards rr: gd hdwy 2f out: rdn over 1f out: styd on ins fnl f to ld last 50yds: jst hld on* **10/1**[3]

-121 **2** *shd* **Skilful**[28] 6335 3-8-9 **105**.. WilliamBuick 9 99+
(John Gosden) *led: pushed clr and edgd rt over 1f out: rdn and hung lft ins fnl f: hdd last 50yds: rallied nr line: jst hld* **1/1**[1]

005 **3** *1¾* **Redvers (IRE)**[23] 6477 3-8-9 **82**..............................(b[1]) StevieDonohoe 11 94
(Ralph Beckett) *trckd ldrs: hdwy 2f out: rdn over 1f out: styd on and ch ins fnl f: hld whn n.m.r nr line* **80/1**

3-00 **4** *1¼* **Zacynthus (IRE)**[105] 3864 3-8-9 **88**................................ RichardMullen 6 91
(Mahmood Al Zarooni) *trckd ldrs: hdwy 2f out: rdn over 1f out: one pce fnl f* **40/1**

0011 **5** *1¼* **Greensward**[28] 6326 5-8-11 **89**.. JimmyFortune 2 88
(Brian Meehan) *hld up in tch: hdwy over 2f out: rdn to chse ldrs over 1f out: kpt on same pce fnl f* **20/1**

3000 **6** *¾* **Point North (IRE)**[29] 6290 4-8-11 **83**............................(t) JamieSpencer 8 86
(Jeremy Noseda) *in rr tl styd on fnl 2f: n.d* **33/1**

3212 **7** *hd* **Smarty Socks (IRE)**[21] 6521 7-8-11 **102**..................... DanielTudhope 12 85
(David O'Meara) *towards rr: hdwy over 2f out: rdn wl over 1f out: no imp appr fnl f* **11/4**[2]

003 **8** *1¼* **Atlantis Star**[12] 6747 4-8-11 **94**.. TomEaves 13 82
(Mahmood Al Zarooni) *chsd ldrs: rdn along 2f out: grad wknd* **14/1**

2-00 **9** *2½* **Hung Parliament (FR)**[160] 2139 3-8-9 **102**...........[1] RichardKingscote 5 75
(Tom Dascombe) *midfield: rdn along over 2f out: no hdwy* **40/1**

1010 **10** *3½* **Polish World (USA)**[30] 6273 7-8-11 **86**........................ MickyFenton 14 65
(Paul Midgley) *prom: rdn along 3f out: sn wknd* **40/1**

-220 **11** *1½* **Afkar (IRE)**[38] 6069 3-8-9 **84**.. NeilCallan 3 61
(Clive Brittain) *chsd ldr: rdn along over 2f out: sn wknd* **33/1**

1103 **12** *2* **Hot Rod Mamma (IRE)**[15] 6672 4-8-6 **92**...................... BarryMcHugh 1 51
(Dianne Sayer) *wnt lft s: a towards rr* **20/1**

1000 **13** *4* **Below Zero (IRE)**[21] 6521 4-9-0 **103**.................................. IanMongan 4 48
(Mark Johnston) *chsd ldrs: rdn along over 2f out: sn wknd* **33/1**

1m 23.58s (-2.72) **Going Correction** -0.275s/f (Firm)
WFA 3 from 4yo+ 2lb **13** Ran SP% **119.3**
Speed ratings (Par 107): **104,103,101,100,99 98,97,96,93,89 87,85,81**
toteswingers: 1&2 £3.90, 1&3 £54.80, 2&3 £24.00. CSF £18.65 TOTE £11.10: £2.50, £1.10, £13.70; EX 26.40 Trifecta £1026.30 Pool: £1,858.47 - 1.34 winning units..
Owner Mrs Shelley Dwyer **Bred** Sir Eric Parker **Trained** Burrough Green, Cambs
■ Stewards' Enquiry : William Buick one-day ban: careless riding (Nov 5)

FOCUS
Typically confusing conditions race form, but it's taken at face value for now. The winner probably did not need to match this year's best.

NOTEBOOK
Mia's Boy would have been 8lb better off with the winner in a handicap, but 15lb worse off with the third. He won this in 2009 and was fourth last year, and clearly this track brings out the best in him. (op 17-2)
Skilful, a clear-cut winner off 93 over 1m on easy ground last time, had plenty of use made of him over this sharper test, but he was still found out. Despite hanging left late on, he was coming back at the winner near the line and was clear a few yards after the post. He didn't run to his official mark of 105 but has more to offer. (op 13-8 tchd 15-8 in places)
Redvers(IRE), who on all known form had no right to finish so close, seemingly improved significantly for first-time blinkers. (op 66-1)
Zacynthus(IRE) ran with credit after 105 days off, offering more than earlier in the season. (op 50-1)
Greensward was up in class after a couple of handicap wins. (op 16-1)
Smarty Socks(IRE), a good second off 101 in the Challenge Cup at Ascot last time, failed to find his customary late burst, although he didn't get much cover. He was probably a bit flat. (op 2-1)

7024 UNIVERSAL RECYCLING "HANDS AND HEELS" APPRENTICE SERIES FINAL H'CAP (RACING EXCELLENCE INITATIVE) 7f
5:20 (5:20) (Class 5) (0-75,75) 3-Y-0 **£2,911** (£866; £432; £216) **Stalls** High

Form RPR

144 **1** **Ted's Brother (IRE)**[7] 6867 3-9-1 **72**................................ JasonHart[(3)] 6 82+
(Richard Guest) *mid-div: hdwy over 2f out: led appr fnl f: hung rt: kpt on wl* **3/1**[1]

605 **2** *1* **Indieslad**[36] 6133 3-8-13 **67**......................................(p) GeorgeChaloner 19 74
(Ann Duffield) *chsd ldrs: effrt over 2f out: led over 1f out: sn hdd: kpt on same pce last 100yds* **22/1**

0300 **3** *¾* **Lizzie (IRE)**[18] 6604 3-8-9 **66**..(b) LauraBarry[(3)] 10 71
(Tim Easterby) *chsd ldrs: kpt on same pce last 150yds* **25/1**

6330 **4** *nse* **Showboating (IRE)**[10] 6801 3-9-6 **74**...............................(tp) NoraLooby 3 79
(Alan McCabe) *chsd ldrs: kpt on fnl f* **20/1**

-216 **5** *¾* **Formal Demand**[93] 4255 3-9-4 **72**............................ MichaelJMurphy 14 75
(Edward Vaughan) *hld up in mid-div: effrt over 2f out: hung rt and kpt on same pce fnl f* **9/1**[3]

2433 **6** *½* **Links Drive Lady**[18] 6604 3-8-13 **67**................................ NoelGarbutt 12 68
(Mark Rimmer) *chsd ldrs: led over 2f out: hdd over 1f out: crowded: one pce* **16/1**

0400 **7** *1* **Strictly Pink (IRE)**[37] 6081 3-9-4 **72**..........................(p) NatashaEaton 16 71
(Alan Bailey) *hld up in rr: hdwy 2f out: kpt on fnl 2f: nvr trbld ldrs* **16/1**

4000 **8** *3½* **Fieldgunner Kirkup (GER)**[27] 6382 3-9-6 **74**.............. GeorgeDowning 2 63
(David Barron) *s.i.s: sme hdwy over 2f out: nvr nr ldrs* **16/1**

0230 **9** *1¾* **Fluvial (IRE)**[22] 6511 3-8-13 **67**...................................... CharlesBishop 11 52
(Mark Johnston) *led tl over 2f out: wkng whn hmpd over 1f out* **14/1**

-112 **10** *hd* **Amelia's Surprise**[22] 6505 3-9-3 **74**.................................. IanBurns[(3)] 13 58
(Michael Bell) *mid-div: effrt over 3f out: wknd over 1f out* **10/1**

0065 **11** *6* **Adaria**[12] 6764 3-8-11 **65**...(p) JackDuern 18 33
(David C Griffiths) *chsd ldrs: hung lft over 2f out: wknd over 1f out* **11/1**

0006 **12** *1¾* **First Class Favour (IRE)**[7] 6869 3-8-13 **67**................ RachealKneller 5 30
(Tim Easterby) *chsd ldrs: lost pl over 1f out* **14/1**

0333 **13** *hd* **Auto Mac**[19] 6576 3-8-12 **69**...(b) TerenceFury[(3)] 1 32
(Neville Bycroft) *chsd ldrs: lost pl over 2f out* **25/1**

1000 **14** *1¾* **Last Destination (IRE)**[8] 6840 3-8-7 **66**................. DanielleMooney[(5)] 4 24
(Nigel Tinkler) *trckd ldrs: outpcd over 3f out: sn lost pl* **50/1**

3500 **15** *6* **Maggie Mey (IRE)**[8] 6831 3-8-13 **70**.................. DavidSimmonson[(3)] 17 12
(Paul Midgley) *chsd ldrs: sn drvn along: lost pl 3f out: sn bhd* **25/1**

2430 **16** *17* **Youhavecontrol (IRE)**[11] 6778 3-9-5 **73**.......................... RaulDaSilva 7 —
(Michael Dods) *rrd bdly s: a bhd: edgd lft and racd stands' side over 3f out: eased over 1f out: t.o* **7/1**[2]

5123 **17** *10* **Fairlie Dinkum**[122] 3278 3-9-6 **74**.................................. JustinNewman 9 —
(Bryan Smart) *s.i.s: in rr: drvn over 3f out: bhd whn eased over 1f out: t.o* **9/1**[3]

1m 25.59s (-0.71) **Going Correction** -0.275s/f (Firm) **17** Ran SP% **128.5**
Speed ratings (Par 101): **93,91,91,90,90 89,88,84,82,82 75,73,73,71,64 44,33**
toteswingers: 1&2 £24.30, 1&3 £25.30, 2&3 £51.00. CSF £83.77 CT £1522.88 TOTE £4.00: £1.40, £6.10, £6.70, £6.30; EX 107.90 TRIFECTA Not won..
Owner Maze Rattan Limited **Bred** T Counihan **Trained** Stainforth, S Yorks
■ Stewards' Enquiry : Laura Barry two-day ban: careless riding (Nov 5,9)

FOCUS
A modest handicap in which they raced middle to stands' side. It was competitive enough with a length personal best from the winner.
Formal Demand Official explanation: jockey said colt hung right final 2f
Youhavecontrol(IRE) Official explanation: jockey said gelding reared as stalls opened
Fairlie Dinkum Official explanation: jockey said filly missed the break and never travelled
T/Jkpt: Not won. T/Plt: £4,286.60 to a £1 stake. Pool of £127,600.95 - 21.73 winning tickets. T/Qpdt: £22.80 to a £1 stake. Pool of £8,619.25 - 278.90 winning tickets. JR

6991 NEWBURY (L-H)
Saturday, October 22

OFFICIAL GOING: Good to firm
Rail moved out between 1mile and 5f increasing distances by 32m on round course.
Wind: Moderate ahead Weather: Sunny

7025 JULIA TOOTH MEMORIAL EBF MAIDEN FILLIES' STKS (DIV I) 1m (S)
1:40 (1:42) (Class 4) 2-Y-0 **£4,398** (£1,309; £654; £327) **Stalls** Centre

Form RPR

5 **1** **Estrela**[24] 6462 2-9-0 0.. JamesDoyle 3 85+
(Roger Charlton) *racd wd 2f: mde virtually all: drvn clr appr fnl f: r.o strly* **6/1**[2]

5 **2** *4½* **Westwiththenight (IRE)**[36] 6128 2-9-0 0.............................. JMurtagh 16 75
(William Haggas) *pressed wnr: stl upsides whn pushed along fr 2f out: outpcd fnl f but kpt on wl for 2nd* **7/4**[1]

3 *1¾* **Caitlin** 2-9-0 0... DavidProbert 14 71
(Andrew Balding) *chsd ldrs: racd in 3rd fr over 2f out: kpt on fnl f but no imp on ldng duo and jst hld on to 3rd last strides* **14/1**

4 *shd* **Miracle Maid** 2-8-11 0... JohnFahy[(3)] 17 71+
(Clive Cox) *s.i.s: in rr: hdwy over 3f out: styd on to take 4th ins fnl f: clsng for 3rd last strides but no ch w ldng duo* **20/1**

5 *3* **Gallipot** 2-9-0 0... NickyMackay 6 70+
(John Gosden) *hld up in mid-div: n.m.r wl over 2f out: hdwy over 1f out: green but styd on wl in clsng stages: nvr a threat* **15/2**[3]

0 **6** *1½* **Kogershin (USA)**[18] 6603 2-9-0 0...................................... EddieAhern 10 60
(Jeremy Noseda) *chsd ldrs: drvn over 2f out: wknd fnl f* **12/1**

7 *2½* **Silence Is Easy** 2-9-0 0... SteveDrowne 2 55+
(William Muir) *in rr: pushed along and hdwy fr 2f out: styd on wl in clsng stages* **50/1**

8 *hd* **Virginia Gallica (IRE)** 2-9-0 0.. SebSanders 12 54+
(J W Hills) *in rr: pushed along 3f out: styd on wl in clsng stages* **50/1**

9 *nk* **Hunt A Mistress (IRE)** 2-9-0 0.. JoeFanning 5 55+
(Paul Cole) *in tch 1/2-way: one pce fnl 2f* **20/1**

0 **10** *½* **Angelic Note (IRE)**[28] 6329 2-9-0 0.................................... ShaneKelly 9 52
(Brian Meehan) *chsd ldrs: drvn over 3f out: wknd fr 2f out* **40/1**

11 *1¾* **Saint Hilary** 2-9-0 0... DarryllHolland 11 48+
(William Muir) *in rr tl styd on ins fnl f* **66/1**

12 *nk* **Simply** 2-9-0 0... TomQueally 7 48
(Eve Johnson Houghton) *s.i.s: towards rr most of way* **33/1**

13 *3¾* **Tearsforjoy (USA)** 2-9-0 0.. RichardHughes 13 39
(Richard Hannon) *a towards rr* **10/1**

14 *nk* **Bondi Mist (IRE)** 2-9-0 0.. JimCrowley 18 38
(Jonathan Portman) *chsd ldrs 5f* **100/1**

0 **15** *5* **Sea Fret**[13] 6726 2-9-0 0.. RobertHavlin 4 27
(Hughie Morrison) *chsd ldrs tl wknd over 2f out* **66/1**

16 *¾* **Absolutely Me (IRE)** 2-9-0 0... LiamKeniry 1 25
(Dominic Ffrench Davis) *a in rr* **66/1**

17 *10* **Tantrum (IRE)** 2-9-0 0.. RyanMoore 8 —
(Richard Hannon) *a bhd: eased whn no ch fnl 2f* **9/1**

1m 39.14s (-0.56) **Going Correction** -0.075s/f (Good) **17** Ran SP% **120.2**
Speed ratings (Par 94): **99,94,92,92,89 88,85,85,85,84 82,82,78,78,73 72,62**
toteswingers:1&2:£2.30, 2&3:£10.00, 1&3:£19.10 CSF £15.08 TOTE £6.80: £2.10, £1.50, £4.00; EX 13.90.
Owner Seasons Holidays **Bred** Chippenham Lodge Stud Ltd **Trained** Beckhampton, Wilts

FOCUS
After a dry night the ground remained good to firm. Very few had experience in the first division of this fillies' maiden but two of those, the market leaders, dominated throughout. The field raced up the stands' rail.n

NOTEBOOK
Estrela ◆, a half-sister to six winners, was slightly keen and just missed a place in the frame on her debut. Benefiting from that experience, she made virtually all the running and, going better than the favourite inside the last 2f, she asserted readily when asked in the last furlong. She looks capable of going on to better things, although much depends on how far she stays as her pedigree is a mix of speed and middle-distance performers. (op 11-2, tchd 7-1 in a place)
Westwiththenight(IRE), out of a Cheshire Oaks winner, never threatened seriously on debut in a conditions race over 7f here. Always upsides the winner, her rider started to niggle entering the last 2f and it was soon clear she was going to be second best. However, she was clear of the remainder and should have no trouble winning a maiden, possibly over a little further. (op 9-4 tchd 13-8)
Caitlin, a half-sister to a 7f-1m2f winner out of a 1m4f scorer, showed plenty of promise on her debut, as was the case with a couple of her stablemates the previous day. She was prominent throughout but could not go with the principals in the last 2f. She should benefit from the experience. (op 12-1)

Miracle Maid ◆, a half-sister to four winners at middle distances on the Flat and a couple over jumps, including Champion Hurdler Katchit and Miracle Seeker, ran a race full of promise, finishing well. Reportedly her blood had not been right earlier in the week but she had clearly recovered and is clearly well thought of, as she has an Irish Oaks entry. She can make her mark over middle-distances next season. (op 18-1)
Gallipot, the second foal of Sun Chariot winner Spinning Queen, also made a nice debut, especially as she got rather stuck behind the fourth when looking for a run. She was staying on steadily in the latter stages and will know more next time. (op 9-1 tchd 7-1)
Kogershin(USA) had shown some ability in a 7f fast ground Leicester maiden on her debut and put up a reasonable effort here, tracking the leaders before fading. She will be of interest in handicaps after one more run.

7026 WORTHINGTON'S HIGHFIELD SOCIAL CLUB STKS (REGISTERED AS HORRIS HILL) (GROUP 3) (C&G) 7f (S)

2:15 (2:16) (Class 1) 2-Y-O

£19,281 (£7,310; £3,658; £1,822; £914; £459) **Stalls** Centre

Form RPR
1212 **1** **Tell Dad**[21] 6527 2-8-12 100 EddieAhern 5 100
(Richard Hannon) *mde all: drvn along over 1f out: styd on strly fnl f: pushed out* **7/1**[2]
5336 **2** *2* **Saigon**[14] 6688 2-8-12 110 JMurtagh 7 99+
(James Toller) *hld up in rr: nt clr run and edgd lft fr 2f out: drvn: plenty to do and styd on strly fnl f to take 2nd cl home: no imp on wnr* **15/8**[1]
0200 **3** *hd* **Hazaz (IRE)**[21] 6527 2-8-12 89 SebSanders 10 94
(Clive Brittain) *chsd ldrs: wnt 2nd over 2f out: drvn and outpcd by wnr appr fnl f but kpt on: lost 2nd cl home* **40/1**
6111 **4** *½* **Producer**[27] 6372 2-8-12 88 RichardHughes 11 93
(Richard Hannon) *chsd ldrs: drvn to chse ldrs in 3rd over 1f out but no imp: styd on same pce in 4th* **8/1**[3]
1125 **5** *1 ¾* **Red Art (IRE)**[65] 5216 2-8-12 95 MichaelHills 4 88
(Charles Hills) *in rr: stl bhd whn bmpd 2f out: styd on fnl f: nvr gng pce to rch ldrs* **14/1**
466 **6** *2 ¼* **Strait Of Zanzibar (USA)**[42] 5951 2-8-12 0 (p) ShaneFoley 3 83
(K J Condon, Ire) *chsd ldrs: drvn along fr 3f out: styd on same pce fnl 2f* **20/1**
1033 **7** *hd* **Mehdi (IRE)**[21] 6527 2-8-12 100 (t) ShaneKelly 14 82
(Brian Meehan) *in tch 1/2-way: drvn to chse ldrs over 2f out: styd on same pce fr over 1f out* **10/1**
31 **8** *¾* **Nawwaar (USA)**[84] 4535 2-8-12 86 RichardHills 13 80
(John Dunlop) *hld up in rr: hdwy: drvn and sme hdwy 2f out: nvr rchd ldrs: wknd fnl f* **8/1**[3]
1005 **9** *1* **Wise Venture (IRE)**[11] 6766 2-8-12 84 HarryBentley 2 78
(Alan Jarvis) *chsd wnr to 3f out: wknd 2f out* **66/1**
1 **10** *hd* **Oxford Charley (USA)**[24] 6462 2-8-12 80 TomQueally 1 77
(Mikael Magnusson) *in rr: pushed lft ins fnl 2f: sn drvn and effrt over 1f out: wknd ins fnl f* **14/1**
501 **11** *1 ¼* **Right Divine (IRE)**[21] 6532 2-8-12 84 JimCrowley 6 74
(Brian Meehan) *in tch tl wknd fr 2f out* **33/1**
310 **12** *1 ¾* **Diamondhead (IRE)**[64] 5251 2-8-12 95 DarryllHolland 9 69
(Brian Meehan) *t.k.h in rr: drvn 2f out and little rspnse* **25/1**
1412 **13** *2 ¼* **Graphic (IRE)**[10] 6788 2-8-12 96 RyanMoore 12 63
(Richard Hannon) *chsd ldrs 3f out: wknd ins fnl 2f* **12/1**
2106 **14** *7* **Charitable Act (FR)**[21] 6527 2-8-12 90 SteveDrowne 15 45
(William Muir) *rdn over 2f out: towards rr most of way* **50/1**

1m 23.8s (-1.90) **Going Correction** -0.075s/f (Good) **14** Ran SP% **117.1**
Speed ratings (Par 105): **107,104,104,103,101 99,99,98,97,96 95,93,90,82**
toteswingers:1&2:£2.20, 2&3:£17.40, 1&3:£74.90 CSF £18.48 TOTE £5.50: £1.80, £1.30, £11.30; EX 20.10 Trifecta £746.10 Part won. Pool: £1,008.27 - 0.40 winning units..
Owner Andrew Tinkler **Bred** Wallace Holmes & Partners **Trained** East Everleigh, Wilts

FOCUS
The recent winners of this juvenile Group 3 have not really gone on to greater glory, the best of them being Beacon Lodge, who subsequently beat Sahpresa later in his career and was placed at Group 2 level. This looked just a fair renewal on paper. Tell Dad ran right up his mark with the third and fourth limiting the form.

NOTEBOOK
Tell Dad, a dual winner at 6-7f including a sales race and closely matched with Mehdi on recent runs in a similar contest, was up in grade. He set off in front and found plenty when asked to draw clear entering the last furlong. He is a really likeable type and a credit to his trainer, and deserved this Group victory, his handler's 117th 2yo winner of the season. He is in the sales next week but might not go now.
Saigon stood out on official ratings. However, the race was a story of woe for him, as he was held up early and repeatedly found his path blocked when looking for an opening in the second half of the race. He only got into the clear entering the last furlong, by which time the winner was gone beyond recall. He should have finished much closer. (op 11-4)
Hazaz(IRE) had gained just one placing in four starts but had run respectably in two sales races recently. Always in the leading group, he kept on going and was only just caught for second. Winning a maiden should prove a formality. (op 33-1)
Producer has progressed steadily, winning three 7f Epsom races on good and easy ground. Stepping up in grade, he showed up throughout but could not find a change of gear late on. He can improve next season, when a bit more ease in the ground should be in his favour.
Red Art(IRE), a dual 5f winner in June who had run well since over 6f, was up in trip and grade on his first start since August. He stayed on late having been at the back entering the last quarter-mile, having had to come around his rivals. (op 16-1)
Strait Of Zanzibar(USA), a 7f Listed winner at Tipperary but held in Group races either side, had cheekpieces replacing the blinkers he wore last time. He was under pressure some way out but kept responding.
Mehdi(IRE), a dual winner at 6f but beaten by a couple of today's opponents when placed in sales races the last twice over this trip, deserved a try at this level but was ultimately found out, having had his chance. (op 9-1)
Nawwaar(USA), who built on a promising debut when winning a 7f Goodwood maiden in July, had not been seen since. He made a brief effort from the rear after halfway but never got into contention. Richard Hills reported that the colt was never travelling. Official explanation: jockey said colt never travelled (op 13-2)

7027 WORTHINGTON'S CHAMPION SHIELD STKS (REGISTERED AS THE ST SIMON STAKES) (GROUP 3) 1m 4f 5y

2:45 (2:48) (Class 1) 3-Y-O+

£28,355 (£10,750; £5,380; £2,680; £1,345; £675) **Stalls** Low

Form RPR
11 **1** **Beaten Up**[43] 5888 3-8-10 98 JMurtagh 9 123+
(William Haggas) *t.k.h: hld up in rr: stdy hdwy on outside fr over 2f out to ld over 1f out: c clr ins fnl f: won gng away* **7/2**[3]
2122 **2** *4 ½* **Al Kazeem**[35] 6161 3-8-10 112 SteveDrowne 8 114
(Roger Charlton) *hld up in rr: stdy hdwy to ld 2f out: drvn and hdd appr fnl f: sn no ch w wnr but kpt on wl for clr 2nd* **5/2**[1]
5111 **3** *3 ½* **Barbican**[22] 6498 3-8-10 106 DarryllHolland 7 108
(Alan Bailey) *hld up towards rr tl impr qckly to chse ldr 5f out: chal fr 3f out to 2f out: wknd fnl f* **8/1**
0161 **4** *1* **Mohedian Lady (IRE)**[30] 6269 3-8-7 103 KierenFallon 3 104
(Luca Cumani) *chsd ldrs: rdn 4f out and outpcd fr 3f out: styd on again fnl f to take n.d 4th cl home* **3/1**[2]
-300 **5** *½* **Vulcanite (IRE)**[63] 5285 4-9-3 101 JimCrowley 2 106
(Ralph Beckett) *led: drvn along 3f out: hdd 2f out: wknd 1f out* **20/1**
-110 **6** *nk* **French Navy**[21] 6558 3-8-13 110 FrankieDettori 6 109
(Mahmood Al Zarooni) *chsd ldr to 5f out: styd chsng ldrs tl wknd 2f out* **11/2**
0305 **7** *2 ½* **Theology**[30] 6271 4-9-3 102 RyanMoore 5 102
(Jeremy Noseda) *chsd ldrs tl wknd qckly 2f out* **22/1**

2m 31.75s (-3.75) **Going Correction** -0.075s/f (Good)
WFA 3 from 4yo+ 7lb **7** Ran SP% **111.4**
Speed ratings (Par 113): **109,106,103,103,102 102,100**
toteswingers:1&2:£1.70, 2&3:£4.40, 1&3:£6.30 CSF £12.00 TOTE £3.70: £2.30, £1.60; EX 8.90 Trifecta £26.60 Pool: £1,461.46 - 40.61 winning units..
Owner B Haggas **Bred** J B Haggas **Trained** Newmarket, Suffolk

FOCUS
Formerly known as the St Simon Stakes, this is usually a pretty solid Group 3 with the last five winners all having been placed at Group 1 level formerly or subsequently. This looked a decent and interesting contest, with 3-y-os dominating in respect of runners and also the finish. The winner looks a Group 1 prospect for next year. The pace was moderate until the home turn.

NOTEBOOK
Beaten Up ◆ an unbeaten winner of a maiden in April and a classified stakes in September; both over 1m2f, was up in trip and grade but made light of it, despite pulling hard under restraint for a long way. He picked up really well when asked and scored in the style of a colt who can go on to much better things next season. (tchd 3-1 and 4-1 in places)
Al Kazeem had been runner-up in the Great Voltigeur and narrowly beaten by Green Destiny in the Arc trial here over 1m3f on his two previous starts and ran into another progressive rival. He came through looking the likely winner but could not respond when the winner pulled out of his slipstream. He deserves to pick up a Group race next year. (op 11-4, tchd 3-1 in places and 10-3 in a place)
Barbican had progressed really well this season, winning a Listed race last time over 1m6f. He ran his race on this drop in trip and is probably a reasonable guide to the form. (op 7-1 tchd 13-2)
Mohedian Lady(IRE) had progressed with racing to take a 1m4f fillies' Listed race last time. Up in grade back against colts, she was outpaced early in the straight before running on again. She will be of interest over this trip and further against her own sex next season. (tchd 10-3)
Vulcanite(IRE) was very progressive last season but had struggled to reproduce his form in Listed, Group races and the Ebor this time. He made the running and picked up the pace turning for home, but could not sustain his effort. (op 25-1 tchd 33-1)
French Navy's wins this season had been on good and easy ground at 1m2f. Up in trip on fast ground, he checked out pretty quickly in the straight. (op 13-2 tchd 7-1)
Theology was trying the shortest trip he has encountered this season and was up in grade. He was probably the most inconvenienced by the slow early pace. (op 16-1 tchd 25-1)

7028 TOTEPOOL STKS (REGISTERED AS THE RADLEY STAKES) (LISTED RACE) (FILLIES) 7f (S)

3:15 (3:20) (Class 1) 2-Y-O

£12,192 (£4,622; £2,313; £1,152; £578; £290) **Stalls** Centre

Form RPR
1312 **1** **Pimpernel (IRE)**[14] 6691 2-8-12 106 FrankieDettori 2 99+
(Mahmood Al Zarooni) *t.k.h and stdd in rr early: stdy hdwy fr 3f out to ld over 1f out: sn in command: easily* **1/1**[1]
1506 **2** *1 ¾* **Semayyel (IRE)**[14] 6705 2-8-12 90 TomQueally 14 90
(Clive Brittain) *reluctant to load: chsd ldrs: chal 2f out: kpt on to chse wnr ins fnl f: nvr any ch but hld on wl for 2nd* **40/1**
1 **3** *nk* **Fillionaire**[13] 6725 2-8-12 0 SamHitchcott 5 89
(Mick Channon) *in rr: drvn and hdwy fr 2f out: styd on fnl f to press for 2nd in clsng stages but no ch w wnr* **16/1**
1 **4** *1 ½* **Ultrasonic (USA)**[39] 6030 2-8-12 0 RyanMoore 4 85
(Sir Michael Stoute) *t.k.h in rr: hdwy over 2f out: drvn to chse ldrs over 1f out: no imp and styd on one pce* **9/2**[2]
3630 **5** *nk* **Mary Fildes (IRE)**[14] 6691 2-8-12 97 LiamKeniry 3 85
(J S Moore) *chsd ldrs: drvn and styd on same pce fnl 2f* **16/1**
01 **6** *½* **Way Too Hot**[80] 4662 2-8-12 84 KierenFallon 10 83
(Clive Cox) *towards rr: hdwy and drvn ins fnl 2f: one pce ins fnl f* **8/1**[3]
2531 **7** *1 ¾* **Self Centred**[28] 6322 2-8-12 84 MichaelHills 12 79
(Charles Hills) *chsd ldr tl led appr fnl 2f: hdd appr fnl f: sn btn* **25/1**
2514 **8** *nse* **My Queenie (IRE)**[36] 6128 2-8-12 89 EddieAhern 8 79
(Richard Hannon) *in tch: pushed along and nt much daylight and hanging lft fr ins fnl 2f: nver dangerous* **25/1**
0633 **9** *nk* **Millibar (IRE)**[12] 6742 2-8-12 71 TomMcLaughlin 1 78
(Nick Littmoden) *rrd stalls and slowly away: hdwy and in tch 2f out: styd on same pce fr over 1f out* **100/1**
5414 **10** *2* **Risky Art**[35] 6144 2-8-12 81 DarryllHolland 11 73
(Michael Easterby) *chsd ldrs: wknd appr fnl 2f* **25/1**
1056 **11** *2* **Mention (IRE)**[70] 5052 2-8-12 77 ShaneKelly 6 67
(Brian Meehan) *chsd ldrs over 4f* **66/1**
3251 **12** *nk* **Serene Oasis (IRE)**[7] 6866 2-8-12 74 TonyCulhane 7 67
(Mick Channon) *outpcd most of way* **66/1**
6201 **13** *¾* **Whimsical (IRE)**[24] 6440 2-8-12 85 RichardHughes 13 65
(Richard Hannon) *led tl hdd over 2f out: wknd qckly* **16/1**
0125 **14** *1* **Imelda Mayhem**[21] 6535 2-8-12 82 (p) JMurtagh 9 62
(J S Moore) *chsd ldrs over 4f* **25/1**

1m 24.6s (-1.10) **Going Correction** -0.075s/f (Good) **14** Ran SP% **118.7**
Speed ratings (Par 100): **103,101,100,98,98 98,96,95,95,93 91,90,89,88**
toteswingers:1&2:£16.10, 2&3:£125.40, 1&3:£6.60 CSF £67.40 TOTE £2.00: £1.20, £9.80, £3.60; EX 61.50 Trifecta £853.00 Pool: £1,348.69 - 1.17 winning units..
Owner Godolphin **Bred** Peter Harris **Trained** Newmarket, Suffolk
■ Stewards' Enquiry : Tom McLaughlin nine-day ban: used whip with excessive frequency (Nov 5,9-12,14-17)

FOCUS
This fillies' Listed contest has not produced any stars in recent seasons, the best recent winners being subsequent Group 3 scorers Lady Deauville and Summer Fete. This year's line-up looked modest for the grade, with only three of the runners officially rated 90 or above, although there were two once-raced unbeaten fillies with the potential to do better. The betting market featured only three and the time was 0.80secs slower than the earlier colts' Group 3. The easy winner did not need to match her last two efforts.

NOTEBOOK
Pimpernel(IRE) ◆, a three-time winner in six starts and runner-up in Rockfel last time, had a good deal in hand judged on official ratings and scored as the figures suggested, tracking the pace before coming through to score with the minimum of fuss. She heads for Dubai now for the carnival. (op 5-4)
Semayyel(IRE), a 7f winner on easy ground but held in Group races since, bounced back to earn some black type, despite being no match for the winner. (op 33-1)

Fillionaire ◆, a 55,000gns half-sister to a couple of winners, notably the very useful Pabusar, was a surprise winner on her debut over 6f. Up in grade on her second start, she ran creditably and picked up valuable black type. She might have more to offer next season. (tchd 14-1)
Ultrasonic(USA), a half-sister to a 1m2f winner, had scored on her debut over 6f on fast ground. Another stepping up in grade, she tracked the winner into contention but could not pick up as well as that rival, and just stayed on. This may have come a little early in her career and she might do better next season. (tchd 4-1 and 5-1)
Mary Fildes(IRE), an extended 5f winner and placed at Listed and Group 3 level, finished behind the winner in the Rockfel last time. She ran her race under a positive ride and was only edged out of the places late on. (op 20-1)
Way Too Hot, runner-up on her debut over C&D, has beaten beat a subsequent winner when taking her maiden on Polytrack next time. She came from the back to have her chance around 2f out but could find nothing extra off the bridle. (op 7-1)

7029 TOTESCOOP6 HBLB H'CAP — 1m 2f 6y
3:45 (3:48) (Class 2) 3-Y-0+

£31,125 (£9,320; £4,660; £2,330; £1,165; £585) Stalls Low

Form				RPR
2520	1		**Kirthill (IRE)**[35] 6163 3-8-8 **94** .... KierenFallon 5 (Luca Cumani) *mid-div: gd hdwy over 2f out: drvn to ld jst ins fnl f: rdn and sn hung lft: r.o strly* **11/2**[1]	104+
0061	2	3/4	**Pivotman**[26] 6409 3-8-7 **93** .... (t) JimCrowley 2 (Amanda Perrett) *led: drvn and styd on wl fr 2f out: hdd jst ins fnl f: nt gng pce of wnr but hld on wl for 2nd* **20/1**	101
662	3	nk	**Naqshabban (USA)**[35] 6163 3-9-2 **102** .... J-PGuillambert 1 (Luca Cumani) *chsd ldrs: drvn to chal 1f out: kpt on to press for 2nd ins fnl f: nt pce to trble wnr* **13/2**[2]	109
110-	4	shd	**Willing Foe (USA)**[350] 7350 4-9-2 **97** .... FrankieDettori 7 (Saeed Bin Suroor) *hld up in mid-div: nt clr run and edging rt fr over 2f out: gd hdwy appr fnl f: fin wl to cl on plcd horse nr fin but no ch w wnr* **8/1**[3]	104+
541	5	3	**Danderek**[32] 6241 5-8-7 **88** ow1 .... ShaneKelly 6 (Brian Meehan) *chsd ldr: rdn ins fnl 2f: wknd fnl f* **18/1**	89
6164	6	nk	**Circumvent**[15] 6672 4-9-5 **100** .... RyanMoore 15 (Paul Cole) *in rr: drvn and hdwy fr 2f out: kpt on fnl f: nvr a threat* **17/2**	100+
0461	7	3 1/2	**Oceanway (USA)**[14] 6704 3-8-11 **97** .... JoeFanning 13 (Mark Johnston) *chsd ldrs: drvn and wknd ins fnl 2f* **12/1**	90
4325	8	shd	**Classic Colori (IRE)**[22] 6496 4-8-7 **93** .... AshleyMorgan(5) 3 (David O'Meara) *chsd ldrs: drvn and wknd 2f out* **16/1**	86
0650	9	nse	**Resurge (IRE)**[35] 6163 6-9-2 **97** .... (v) FergusSweeney 16 (Stuart Kittow) *stdd s: in rr: drvn and styd on fr over 1f out: kpt on clsng stages* **22/1**	90
3100	10	1 3/4	**Glencadam Gold (IRE)**[107] 3774 3-8-9 **95** ow2 .... TomQueally 11 (Sir Henry Cecil) *racd on outside: in tch: wknd over 2f out* **14/1**	85
3004	11	nk	**Shavansky**[10] 6803 7-8-12 **93** .... JamesMillman 4 (Rod Millman) *chsd ldrs: wknd ins fnl 2f* **18/1**	82
6631	12	2 1/4	**Vainglory (USA)**[15] 6672 7-8-6 **92** .... LauraPike(5) 12 (David Simcock) *rdn wl over 2f out: a towards rr* **16/1**	77
0243	13	1 1/2	**Nanton (USA)**[21] 6519 9-9-10 **105** .... JMurtagh 8 (Jim Goldie) *in rr: hdwy 3f out: nvr rchd ldrs: sn wknd* **12/1**	87
0616	14	shd	**Colour Scheme (IRE)**[27] 6375 4-8-6 **87** .... (t) TadhgO'Shea 14 (Brian Meehan) *stdd s: stl towards rr whn hmpd 2f out: no ch after* **20/1**	68
2-40	15	1	**Togiak (IRE)**[15] 6672 4-8-8 **89** .... (p) SteveDrowne 9 (David Pipe) *bhd most of way* **22/1**	68
4000	U		**Right Step**[27] 6375 4-8-8 **92** .... HarryBentley(3) 10 (Alan Jarvis) *chsd ldrs: wkng whn hmpd: stmbld bdly and uns rdr 2f out* **14/1**	—

2m 6.85s (-1.95) **Going Correction** -0.075s/f (Good)
WFA 3 from 4yo+ 5lb — **16** Ran SP% **119.6**
Speed ratings (Par 109): **104,103,103,103,100 100,97,97,97,96 95,94,92,92,92** —
toteswingers:1&2:£33.90, 2&3:£35.50, 1&3:£10.10 CSF £118.74 CT £729.80 TOTE £5.90: £1.70, £4.60, £2.20, £2.40; EX 164.80 Trifecta £1499.30 Pool: £49,559.00 - 24.46 winning units..
Owner Leonidas Marinopoulos **Bred** Giacinto Guglielmi **Trained** Newmarket, Suffolk
■ Stewards' Enquiry : Frankie Dettori seven-day ban: careless riding (Nov 5,9-12,14-15)

FOCUS
A good, competitive handicap whose best recent winners have been subsequent Group 1 winner Rainbow Peak and Grade 1 winning hurdler Khyber Kim. The field raced in the centre of the track in the straight and the pace was not strong. The winner is a steady improver.

NOTEBOOK
Kirthill(IRE), a 1m winner who stays this trip but whose best form was on an easy surface, was favourite to make up for an unlucky run last time. He got a clear passage on this occasion, coming through towards the far side of the pack and doing enough, despite going left late on, to score. He looks the time his trainer might be able to improve again next year. (tchd 6-1)
Pivotman, raised 10lb for a runaway success on soft ground last time when fitted with a tongue tie for the first time, made the running on this very different going and stuck on gamely under pressure. He might have matured enough to be able to handle this faster surface again next year.
Naqshabban(USA), again ponied to the start, was a close second in a similar contest at the last meeting but had been raised 6lb for that. He was never far away and had every chance, but could not find an extra gear in the last furlong to trouble his stablemate. He might have preferred more ease in the ground. (tchd 6-1)
Willing Foe(USA), a three-time winner at 1m2f-1m4f last year, all on good ground, had not been seen since well beaten in the November Handicap last season. Gelded in the interim, he ran pretty well on this reappearance and could be the sort to make his mark at the Dubai Carnival in the new year. His rider picked up a seven-day ban for edging right and crossing Right Step, which caused the latter to clip heels and unseat his rider.
Danderek returned to form last time but had been put up 10lb as a result, giving him a lot to do off this mark. He ran well under a positive ride, only fading late on, and seems to be still progressing at the age of five. (op 16-1)
Circumvent, running well of late, stays this far and handles fast but best with cut. He ran on steadily from the rear but never got close enough to land a blow. (op 9-1 tchd 8-1)

7030 JULIA TOOTH MEMORIAL EBF MAIDEN FILLIES' STKS (DIV II) — 1m (S)
4:20 (4:24) (Class 4) 2-Y-0 — £4,398 (£1,309; £654; £327) Stalls Centre

Form				RPR
2	1		**Shirocco Star**[24] 6458 2-9-0 0 .... DarryllHolland 4 (Hughie Morrison) *trckd ldr: led appr fnl 2f: rdn and edgd rt fnl f: pushed out in clsng stages* **3/1**[1]	76+
0	2	1/2	**Varnish**[35] 6160 2-9-0 0 .... RichardHughes 8 (Richard Hannon) *trckd ldrs: nt clr run and swtchd lft off rails over 1f out: styd on to chse wnr ins fnl f: kpt on wl in clsng stages but a jst hld* **3/1**[1]	76+
	3	1	**Inchina** 2-9-0 0 .... JamesDoyle 2 (Roger Charlton) *chsd ldrs: pushed along: green and one pce 2f out: stl green and edgd rt 1f out whn bmpd: kpt on wl in clsng stages* **8/1**[3]	73+
0	4	1	**Lily Potts**[24] 6441 2-9-0 0 .... SteveDrowne 15 (Chris Down) *in rr: hdwy over 2f out: kpt on u.p fnl f: nosed into 4th last strides* **66/1**	70+
6	5	hd	**Derivatives (IRE)**[11] 6776 2-9-0 0 .... NickyMackay 5 (John Gosden) *chsd ldrs: chal over 1f out: rdn and hung rt fr over 1f out: one pce ins fnl f: lost 4th last strides* **5/1**[2]	70
0	6	4	**Supaheart**[12] 6745 2-9-0 0 .... RobertHavlin 7 (Hughie Morrison) *led tl hdd appr fnl 2f: hung rt and wknd over 1f out* **22/1**	61
0	7	3/4	**Excellent News (IRE)**[18] 6603 2-9-0 0 .... MichaelHills 3 (J W Hills) *chsd ldrs tl wknd ins fnl 2f* **50/1**	59
	8	1 1/2	**Kittens** 2-9-0 0 .... EddieAhern 1 (William Muir) *chsd ldrs over 5f* **20/1**	56
	9	3/4	**Ayla's Emperor** 2-9-0 0 .... SamHitchcott 17 (Mick Channon) *in rr: hrd drvn and sme hdwy on ins over 2f out: nvr beyond mid-div* **16/1**	54
	10	1/2	**Dusty Red** 2-9-0 0 .... JimCrowley 11 (William Knight) *s.i.s: sme hdwy whn hung lft and green 2f out: nvr in contention* **16/1**	53
00	11	1/2	**Velvet Star (IRE)**[24] 6458 2-9-0 0 .... (t) JoeFanning 14 (Paul Cole) *in rr: sme hdwy 2f out: sn hung lft and wknd* **50/1**	52
0	12	1/2	**White Flight**[12] 6744 2-9-0 0 .... FergusSweeney 13 (Jonathan Portman) *bhd most of way* **100/1**	53+
	13	5	**London Welsh** 2-9-0 0 .... TomQueally 9 (William Muir) *s.i.s: a towards rr* **25/1**	39
0	14	7	**Balaton**[18] 6603 2-9-0 0 .... ShaneKelly 6 (Brian Meehan) *chsd ldrs 5f* **33/1**	23
03	15	6	**Kylin**[12] 6751 2-9-0 0 .... RyanMoore 10 (Richard Hannon) *in tch early: wknd fr 3f out* **8/1**[3]	—

1m 40.69s (0.99) **Going Correction** -0.075s/f (Good) — **15** Ran SP% **123.0**
Speed ratings (Par 94): **92,91,90,89,89 85,84,83,82,81 81,80,75,68,62**
toteswingers:1&2:£2.60, 2&3:£5.30, 1&3:£3.50 CSF £10.29 TOTE £3.40: £1.50, £1.70, £3.00; EX 9.30.
Owner Helena Springfield Ltd **Bred** Meon Valley Stud **Trained** East Ilsley, Berks

FOCUS
More experience among the runners in this second leg of the fillies' maiden than in the first but the time was 1.55secs slower. The field raced towards the centre early before drifting to finish up near the stands' rail. They finished quite compressed and it's hard to rate the form any higher. The winner should have more to offer next year.

NOTEBOOK
Shirocco Star ◆, drawn widest of all, travelled well when a clear second-best on her debut over 1m at the end of last month. She built on that, despite being relatively weak in the market, going to the front over 2f out and staying on well to hold off the challengers in the closing stages. She looks sure to stay 1m2f at least next year, and might well develop into a Pattern-race filly. (op 15-8)
Varnish ◆ had shown promise under a positive ride on her debut in a 7f maiden here and was heavily backed against the favourite. Never far away, she was slightly outpaced and had to be switched when the leaders edged over to the stands' rail, and then stayed on well without quite looking as if she would catch the winner. However, it would have been close had she got a clear passage, and her winning turn should not be long delayed. (op 11-2)
Inchina ◆, a 360,000gns third foal of a 1m2f Listed winner from the family of Inchinor, made a promising debut against more experienced rivals. She had to be ridden to make ground but had every chance in the final furlong before giving best to the market leaders. She looks sure to go on from this and a maiden should be a formality. (op 17-2 tchd 9-1)
Lily Potts got the hang of things and stayed on late on her debut over 7f on Polytrack and did the same here on her first try on turf. She should be up to winning races if going on from her first two runs.
Derivatives(IRE), out of Nassau winner Favourable Terms, had missed the break and was never a threat on her debut. She was quite keen early here but ran well for much of the way, challenging the winner inside the last 2f before her earlier exertions told. (op 7-1)
Supaheart, who never got involved on her debut, was the stable second string on jockey bookings but ran pretty well from the front until tiring in the latter stages. She can make her mark in handicaps in due course.
Excellent News(IRE) missed the break and was outpaced on her debut but was much sharper this time, racing in the leading group until weakening in the last furlong and a half. (op 66-1 tchd 40-1)

7031 WORTHINGTON'S VICTORIA CLUB WHIZZ KIDS EBF AVONBRIDGE FILLIES' H'CAP — 7f (S)
4:55 (4:56) (Class 3) (0-95,92) 3-Y-0+ — £7,762 (£2,310; £1,154; £577) Stalls Centre

Form				RPR
2210	1		**Valencha**[7] 6862 4-9-2 **87** .... DarryllHolland 2 (Hughie Morrison) *awkward leaving stalls: hld up in rr: t.k.h: hdwy 2f out: rdn to chal ins fnl f: edgd rt and led clsng stages: all out* **13/2**[3]	96
0140	2	shd	**Entitled**[91] 4346 4-9-1 **86** .... RyanMoore 4 (Sir Michael Stoute) *hld up up rr: gd hdwy fr 2f out to take narrow ld jst ins fnl f: kpt on wl: hdd and no ex clsng stages* **7/2**[2]	95
2143	3	1 1/2	**Caelis**[44] 5862 3-8-5 **78** oh2 .... (v) NickyMackay 3 (Ralph Beckett) *chsd ldrs: wnt 2nd 3f out: slt ld appr fnl 2f: narrowly hdd ins fnl f: one pce fnl 120yds* **12/1**	83
0410	4	3/4	**Misplaced Fortune**[21] 6531 6-8-12 **86** .... (v) DaleSwift(3) 6 (Nigel Tinkler) *steadid s: hld up in tch: styd on to press ldrs whn pushed lft 1f out: styng on whn pushed rt ins fnl f: one pce* **22/1**	89
1030	5	1	**Deity**[27] 6383 3-8-12 **85** .... JMurtagh 10 (Jeremy Noseda) *t.k.h: sn led: drvn and narrowly hdd appr fnl 2f: stl ev ch whn edgd lft 1f out: wknd fnl 120yds* **20/1**	85
2242	6	1/2	**Romantic Wish**[32] 6239 3-8-13 **86** .... EddieAhern 5 (Robert Mills) *towards rr: drvn over 2f out: styd on fnl f: nvr gng pce to get into contention* **7/1**	85
0560	7	3	**Amitola (IRE)**[21] 6531 4-8-8 **82** .... HarryBentley(3) 12 (David Barron) *chsd ldrs: rdn over 2f out: wknd wl over 1f out* **25/1**	73
6655	8	1 1/4	**Perfect Silence**[7] 6862 6-8-12 **88** .... LucyKBarry(5) 11 (Clive Cox) *awkward leaving stalls: t.k.h: chsd ldrs 4f* **8/1**	75
0055	9	hd	**Gouray Girl (IRE)**[13] 6723 4-8-11 **85** .... (t) JohnFahy(3) 7 (Walter Swinburn) *rdn over 2f out: a struggling for pce and sn dropped away* **9/1**	72
2615	10	3/4	**Golden Delicious**[28] 6341 3-8-13 **86** .... RichardHughes 9 (Hughie Morrison) *chsd ldrs: rdn 3f out: wknd 2f out* **3/1**[1]	71
3450	11	2	**Ishbelle**[51] 5657 3-9-5 **92** .... (v) JimCrowley 8 (Ralph Beckett) *in rr: drvn along and no rspnse over 2f out* **25/1**	71

1m 24.72s (-0.98) **Going Correction** -0.075s/f (Good)
WFA 3 from 4yo+ 2lb — **11** Ran SP% **118.7**
Speed ratings (Par 104): **102,101,100,99,98 97,94,92,92,91 89**
toteswingers:1&2:£4.10, 2&3:£9.40, 1&3:£11.70 CSF £28.17 CT £226.23 TOTE £7.30: £2.40, £1.60, £3.30; EX 30.10.
Owner Pangfield Partners **Bred** T J Billington **Trained** East Ilsley, Berks

FOCUS
A decent fillies' handicap in which the pace held up best towards the centre of the track, although the time was slower than both the juvenile races over the trip. The form looks sound enough.

NOTEBOOK
Valencha is a progressive and generally consistent filly and she came from off the pace to snatch the race near the line. She had gone up 15lb since her win in June and should not go up much for this, so may not be finished yet. (op 9-1)
Entitled ◆, having her first start since July, was produced to win her race entering the final furlong only to be run out of it close home. She deserves to gain compensation for this defeat. (op 9-2)
Caelis ran a fine race from 2lb out of the handicap, doing best of those that raced prominently in the early stages and only backing out of things inside the last furlong. She has the option of switching back to Polytrack if the rains come. (tchd 14-1)
Misplaced Fortune was another to run well but all her wins have been at 6f and she might have not quite got home as strongly as the principals. (op 20-1 tchd 25-1)
Deity, having just her fifth start, has not really gone on from her debut success, but kept going pretty well after being quite keen while making the early running. (op 16-1)
Romantic Wish is usually consistent and had beaten today's third by 6l when scoring over C&D in June. However, she raced more towards the stands' side than the principals and could never land a blow. (op 15-2 tchd 8-1)
Gouray Girl(IRE) attempted to follow up her 2010 success in this off a 4lb lower mark, but she has not been in the same form this time and failed to get involved. (op 8-1 tchd 10-1)
Golden Delicious, who beat today's winner, her stablemate, at Ascot earlier in the season, was sent off favourite and raced prominently but faded out of contention over a furlong out and was allowed to come home in her own time. (op 7-2, tchd 4-1 in places)

7032 MAXWELL MORRISON 75TH BIRTHDAY LADY JOCKEYS' H'CAP (FOR LADY AMATEUR RIDERS) 1m 4f 5y
5:30 (5:30) (Class 5) (0-75,75) 4-Y-0+ **£2,807** (£870; £435; £217) **Stalls** Low

Form / RPR
4402 **1** **Shades Of Grey**[47] 5782 4-9-6 **63** MissRachelKing[(3)] 4 71
(Clive Cox) *chsd ldrs: pushed along to take slt ld over 2f out but strly pressed tl styd on ins fnl f: pushed out: jst hld on* **7/2**[1]
16-5 **2** *nk* **Sircozy (IRE)**[21] 1509 5-9-11 **70** MissHayleyMoore[(5)] 7 76
(Gary Moore) *mid-div: hdwy 3f out: swtchd rt 2f out: sn rdn then hung bdly rt: styd on wl ins fnl f: fin wl could nt quite get up* **12/1**
0342 **3** *1 ¾* **Stormy Morning**[7] 6870 5-9-7 **61** oh3 (p) MissLHorner 10 65
(Pat Eddery) *in rr: hdwy 4f out: pressed wnr 2f out tl one pce ins fnl f: one pce into 3rd fnl 50yds* **15/2**
6044 **4** *6* **Eastern Magic**[46] 5804 4-9-7 **61** MissADeniel 2 55
(Reg Hollinshead) *in tch: hdwy over 2f out: nvr rchd ldrs and kpt on for wl hld 4th fnl f* **9/2**[2]
0610 **5** *shd* **Bavarica**[44] 5866 9-9-13 **72** MissSBirkett[(5)] 5 66
(Julia Feilden) *s.i.s: in rr: hdwy 3f out to chse ldrs and edgd rt 2f out: sn wknd* **11/1**
02 **6** *1 ¼* **Strike Force**[15] 6669 7-10-0 **71** (t) MissALHutchinson[(3)] 3 63
(Clifford Lines) *in rr: drvn along: wd and mod hdwy over 2f out: nvr nr ldrs* **5/1**[3]
1330 **7** *2 ¼* **Megalala (IRE)**[41] 5971 10-10-6 **74** MissSBrotherton 9 62
(John Bridger) *led tl narrowly hdd appr fnl 2f: wknd over 1f out* **7/1**
30-0 **8** *½* **Honoured (IRE)**[23] 6486 4-9-0 **61** oh7 MissCHenderson[(7)] 6 48
(Nicky Henderson) *in tch: sme hdwy whn rdn: hung lft and wknd 2f out* **16/1**
0226 **9** *1 ¼* **Moody Tunes**[42] 5920 8-10-0 **75** MissALMurphy[(7)] 8 60
(Tom Dascombe) *chsd ldrs: wknd qckly over 2f out* **10/1**
5020 **10** *13* **Hurricane Thomas (IRE)**[7] 6870 7-9-2 **61** oh16 MissPhillipaTutty[(5)] 1 26
(Karen Tutty) *chsd ldrs: rdn 3f out: sn wknd* **28/1**
2m 36.94s (1.44) **Going Correction** -0.075s/f (Good) **10** Ran SP% **115.8**
Speed ratings (Par 103): **92,91,90,86,86 85,84,83,83,74**
toteswingers:1&2:£8.60, 2&3:£20.40, 1&3:£6.90 CSF £46.44 CT £297.67 TOTE £3.60: £1.90, £3.30, £2.70; EX 39.80.
Owner Dr and Mrs John Merrington **Bred** Theakston Stud **Trained** Lambourn, Berks
FOCUS
This amateur riders' handicap has proved a good warm-up race for jumpers, the last three winners having all been successful over hurdles or fences after winning this. Only two of this year's line-up fitted that description. It was slowly run and the winner did not need to improve much on her latest form.
T/Plt: £8.80 to a £1 stake. Pool of £105,656.51 - 8,756.34 winning tickets. T/Qpdt: £4.10 to a £1 Pool of £5,601.22 - 996.30 winning tickets. ST

6999 WOLVERHAMPTON (A.W) (L-H)
Saturday, October 22

OFFICIAL GOING: Standard
Wind: Fresh behind Weather: Cloudy with sunny spells

7033 STAY AT THE WOLVERHAMPTON HOLIDAY INN FILLIES' H'CAP 1m 1f 103y(P)
5:50 (5:50) (Class 5) (0-75,75) 3-Y-0+ **£2,911** (£866; £432; £216) **Stalls** Low

Form / RPR
4325 **1** **Convention**[31] 6255 3-9-0 **69** (b[1]) ChrisCatlin 11 77
(Ed Dunlop) *hld up: hdwy over 1f out: r.o u.p to ld wl ins fnl f* **13/2**[3]
/301 **2** *nk* **Wood Fairy**[97] 4128 5-8-12 **63** PaulHanagan 5 70
(Richard Fahey) *led: rdn ins fnl f: hdd nr fin* **5/1**[2]
-510 **3** *hd* **History Repeating**[26] 6402 3-8-3 **61** oh2 KieranO'Neill[(3)] 9 68
(Mark Usher) *hld up: pushed along over 2f out: hdwy over 1f out: rdn ins fnl f: r.o wl* **16/1**
0564 **4** *4* **Miss Chicane**[12] 6748 3-8-11 **66** LiamKeniry 2 65
(Walter Swinburn) *hld up in tch: racd keenly: nt clr run and swtchd lft over 1f out: styd on same pce fnl f* **10/1**
0424 **5** *hd* **Indian Valley (USA)**[21] 6543 4-9-7 **72** (b) LukeMorris 1 70
(Hugo Palmer) *chsd ldrs: rdn over 2f out: no ex fnl f* **5/1**[2]
400 **6** *1 ½* **Bella Noir**[28] 6330 4-9-10 **75** (v) MartinHarley 3 70
(Mrs K Burke) *hld up: pushed along over 2f out: nvr trbld ldrs* **10/1**
56/0 **7** *1* **Silly Dancer (IRE)**[1] 7006 8-8-10 **61** oh6 PatCosgrave 4 54
(Adrian McGuinness, Ire) *prom: rdn over 1f out: wknd fnl f* **22/1**
6323 **8** *½* **Ecossaise**[26] 6412 3-9-4 **73** SilvestreDeSousa 8 65
(Mark Johnston) *chsd ldr: rdn over 2f out: wknd fnl f* **9/4**[1]
0060 **9** *1 ¾* **Hip Hip Hooray**[5] 6924 5-9-0 **65** WilliamCarson 10 53
(Luke Dace) *hld up: rdn over 2f out: a in rr* **16/1**
2m 0.07s (-1.63) **Going Correction** -0.10s/f (Stan)
WFA 3 from 4yo+ 4lb **9** Ran SP% **111.7**
Speed ratings (Par 100): **103,102,102,99,98 97,96,96,94**
toteswingers:1&2:£4.70, 2&3:£26.00, 1&3:£13.40 CSF £37.18 CT £488.35 TOTE £4.20: £1.70, £1.90, £4.30; EX 14.80 Trifecta £250.90 Pool £3,828.74 - 11.29 winning units..
Owner St Albans Bloodstock LLP **Bred** Highclere Stud & Hmh Management **Trained** Newmarket, Suffolk
■ Stewards' Enquiry : Chris Catlin five-day ban: used whip with excessive frequency (Nov 5, 9-12)
FOCUS
A modest fillies' handicap but fairly sound form, rated around the first three.

7034 ENJOY THE RINGSIDE ENTERTAINMENT CLAIMING STKS 1m 141y(P)
6:20 (6:20) (Class 6) 3-Y-0+ **£1,704** (£503; £251) **Stalls** Low

Form / RPR
6214 **1** **Opus Maximus (IRE)**[8] 6831 6-8-12 67 (p) SophieDoyle[(3)] 1 69+
(Jennie Candlish) *hld up and bhd: hdwy over 1f out: swtchd lft ins fnl f: r.o to ld nr fin* **13/2**[3]
0224 **2** *hd* **Dream Of Fortune (IRE)**[15] 6669 7-9-1 62 (bt) PatCosgrave 7 68
(David Evans) *hld up: hdwy over 1f out: rdn and ev ch ins fnl f: r.o* **11/1**
4053 **3** *hd* **Empress Leizu (IRE)**[8] 6844 4-8-4 57 WilliamCarson 6 57
(Tony Carroll) *chsd ldr tl led over 2f out: rdn ins fnl f: hdd nr fin* **16/1**
0040 **4** *nse* **Wishformore (IRE)**[17] 6624 4-8-5 57 (p) RyanPowell[(5)] 3 63
(J S Moore) *chsd ldrs: rdn over 1f out: ev ch ins fnl f: r.o* **40/1**
5414 **5** *nk* **Ajdaad (USA)**[8] 6844 4-9-1 65 GrahamGibbons 11 67
(Alan McCabe) *hld up: hdwy over 1f out: rdn ins fnl f: r.o* **12/1**
3140 **6** *hd* **Charlie Cool**[21] 6533 8-9-9 90 (b) SilvestreDeSousa 4 75
(Ruth Carr) *hld up: hdwy over 2f out: rdn over 1f out: r.o* **7/2**[2]
5110 **7** *2 ½* **Bolodenka (IRE)**[56] 5485 9-8-13 72 PaulHanagan 5 59
(Richard Fahey) *prom: rdn over 1f out: no ex ins fnl f* **7/1**
0000 **8** *5* **Councellor (FR)**[10] 6797 9-8-13 72 (t) RobbieFitzpatrick 2 47
(Derek Shaw) *hld up in tch: pushed along over 2f out: wknd fnl f* **33/1**
0225 **9** *5* **Golden Creek (USA)**[34] 6188 3-9-5 72 (v[1]) LukeMorris 12 46
(Mrs K Burke) *led: hdd over 2f out: wknd over 1f out* **12/1**
5363 **10** *3 ½* **Twisted**[7] 6871 5-8-13 61 (b) JamesSullivan 13 28
(Michael Easterby) *s.i.s: sn mid-div: rdn over 2f out: wknd over 1f out: bhd whn hmpd ins fnl f* **20/1**
0414 **F** **Flowing Cape (IRE)**[3] 6948 6-9-9 83 GeorgeBaker 10 —
(Reg Hollinshead) *hld up: hdwy over 1f out: rdn and cl up whn broke leg and fell ins fnl f: fatally injured* **3/1**[1]
0450 **P** **Merton Lady**[59] 5389 3-8-4 60 FrankieMcDonald 9 —
(John Flint) *chsd ldrs: rdn over 2f out: wknd wl over 1f out: hung lft and p.u ins fnl f* **28/1**
1m 49.6s (-0.90) **Going Correction** -0.10s/f (Stan)
WFA 3 from 4yo+ 4lb **12** Ran SP% **116.2**
Speed ratings (Par 101): **100,99,99,99,99 99,96,92,88,84 —,—**
toteswingers:1&2:£13.50, 2&3:£17.00, 1&3:£18.50 CSF £70.96 TOTE £8.00: £2.10, £3.30, £4.90; EX 69.20 TRIFECTA Not won..
Owner Alan Baxter **Bred** Mrs Anne Marie Burns **Trained** Basford Green, Staffs
FOCUS
A blanket finish to this claimer but a race marred by a fatal injury.The winner did not have to run to his best to score, with the next three home slightly limiting the form.
Merton Lady Official explanation: vet said filly pulled up lame

7035 EVENTMASTERS HOSPITALITY "GOOD LUCK KIEREN" NURSERY 1m 141y(P)
6:50 (6:51) (Class 6) (0-65,64) 2-Y-0 **£1,704** (£503; £251) **Stalls** Low

Form / RPR
5030 **1** **Docs Legacy (IRE)**[28] 6345 2-9-2 **59** PaulHanagan 4 65
(Richard Fahey) *chsd ldrs: hung lft fr over 1f out: led ins fnl f: rdn out* **5/1**[2]
0206 **2** *1 ¼* **Priestley's Reward (IRE)**[10] 6807 2-9-6 **63** MartinHarley 5 66
(Mrs K Burke) *a.p: rdn and hung lft fr over 1f out: r.o* **12/1**
5502 **3** *nk* **Artistic Thread (IRE)**[4] 6937 2-8-13 **56** SebSanders 6 58
(Sir Mark Prescott Bt) *led: rdn and hdd ins fnl f: styd on same pce* **13/8**[1]
000 **4** *2 ¼* **Dalacara**[18] 6603 2-9-5 **62** LukeMorris 9 60
(Clive Cox) *chsd ldr over 6f out tl rdn over 1f out: no ex fnl f* **6/1**[3]
004 **5** *2 ¾* **Stag Hill (IRE)**[15] 6662 2-9-7 **64** JamesDoyle 2 56
(Sylvester Kirk) *s.i.s: hdwy 7f out: rdn over 1f out: styd on same pce* **14/1**
0600 **6** *1 ½* **Colourful Event (IRE)**[10] 6807 2-8-11 **54** (v) JoeFanning 3 43
(David Arbuthnot) *hld up: rdn over 2f out: nvr nrr* **33/1**
605 **7** *1* **Aglaja**[43] 5896 2-8-6 **52** SophieDoyle[(3)] 10 39
(Frank Sheridan) *hld up: pushed along 3f out: n.d* **66/1**
5125 **8** *1 ½* **King Kenobi (IRE)**[23] 6471 2-9-6 **63** (p) LiamKeniry 1 46
(J S Moore) *chsd ldr tl over 6f out: sn pushed along: rdn and wknd over 1f out* **10/1**
040 **9** *hd* **Hollywood All Star (IRE)**[23] 6474 2-8-6 **49** WilliamCarson 12 32
(William Muir) *hld up: rdn over 1f out: a in rr* **25/1**
030 **10** *1 ¼* **Ice Loch**[58] 5409 2-8-11 **54** JimmyQuinn 8 34
(Michael Blanshard) *hld up: effrt over 2f out: sn wknd* **28/1**
545 **11** *11* **Complex**[142] 2630 2-9-0 **57** SilvestreDeSousa 7 14
(David Evans) *hld up: pushed along 1/2-way: wknd over 2f out* **10/1**
1m 50.31s (-0.19) **Going Correction** -0.10s/f (Stan) **11** Ran SP% **113.3**
Speed ratings (Par 93): **96,94,94,92,90 88,87,86,86,85 75**
toteswingers:1&2:£6.40, 2&3:£6.30, 1&3:£2.30 CSF £58.24 CT £137.05 TOTE £5.80: £1.80, £3.60, £1.10; EX 73.60 Trifecta £621.60 Pool £3,309.96 - 3.94 winning units..
Owner D Bardsley **Bred** Miss Mary Davison **Trained** Musley Bank, N Yorks
FOCUS
A low-grade nursery and it paid not to be too far back. The form looks sound, rated around the placed horses.
NOTEBOOK
Docs Legacy(IRE) looks an improved performer for tackling longer trips in nurseries and he swooped past the long-time leader in the final furlong and kept on strongly to get off the mark in impressive style. There is more to come from this colt and he looks capable of winning off higher marks. (op 9-2)
Priestley's Reward(IRE) showed improved form on turf last time and backed that up with arguably a career-best effort on this all-weather debut. He made good headway and stayed on well down the middle of the track, suggesting he's capable of going one better soon. (tchd 11-1)
Artistic Thread(IRE) took them along at what looked a reasonable gallop but he couldn't resist the finishers in the final furlong and he has now been a beaten favourite on three of his last four starts. Although no match for the winner, he stuck to his task well enough to suggest he'll be able to get his head in front in a race of this nature.
Dalacara raced close to the pace but was being hard ridden two out and lacked a change of gear. He did keep on well enough though to this was an improvement on what he did in maidens. (op 15-2)

7036 EVENTMASTERS HOSPITALITY "GOOD LUCK SILVESTRE" CLAIMING STKS 1m 4f 50y(P)
7:20 (7:20) (Class 6) 3-Y-0+ **£1,874** (£553; £276) **Stalls** Low

Form / RPR
46 **1** **Ashammar (FR)**[24] 6445 6-9-7 68 (t) StevieDonohoe 8 70+
(Paul Webber) *hld up: hdwy over 2f out: led ins fnl f: r.o wl* **10/1**
2650 **2** *3* **Hallstatt (IRE)**[23] 5685 5-9-6 67 (t) GrahamGibbons 2 65
(John Mackie) *led: rdn and edgd rt over 1f out: hdd and unable qck ins fnl f* **13/2**
4032 **3** *2 ¾* **Potentiale (IRE)**[10] 6789 7-9-10 71 (b) SebSanders 9 64
(J W Hills) *hld up: rdn over 1f out: r.o ins fnl f: nt rch ldrs* **7/2**[2]

6640 **4** *2* **Graycliffe (IRE)**[18] 6613 5-9-6 46 StephenCraine 4 57
(Jennie Candlish) *prom: rdn over 2f out: styd on same pce fr over 1f out* **40/1**

00 **5** *1 ½* **Harrys Yer Man**[16] 6656 7-9-8 0 ShaneKelly 1 57?
(Mark Brisbourne) *chsd ldrs: rdn over 2f out: wknd fnl f* **100/1**

3050 **6** *shd* **Scamperdale**[24] 6445 9-9-12 88 PaulHanagan 6 60
(Brian Baugh) *prom: chsd ldr over 1f out: wknd ins fnl f* **2/1**[1]

0003 **7** *2* **Ahlawy (IRE)**[16] 6656 8-9-6 72 (tp) SilvestreDeSousa 3 51
(Frank Sheridan) *s.i.s: sn mid-div: rdn over 3f out: wknd over 1f out* **10/1**

3050 **8** *¾* **African Cheetah**[11] 6773 5-9-12 77 (t) LiamKeniry 11 56
(Reg Hollinshead) *chsd ldr tl rdn over 1f out: wknd fnl f* **5/1**[3]

0420 **9** *2* **Alhaque (USA)**[7] 6873 5-9-0 54 (bt) SophieDoyle(3) 10 44
(David Flood) *s.i.s: hld up: a in rr* **20/1**

0 **10** *14* **Mikeys Sister**[22] 6504 6-9-0 0 LukeMorris 5 18
(Tony Carroll) *hld up: a in rr* **66/1**

2m 41.38s (0.28) **Going Correction** -0.10s/f (Stan) **10 Ran SP% 113.4**
Speed ratings (Par 101): **95,93,91,89,88 88,87,86,85,76**
toteswingers:1&2:£6.40, 2&3:£5.70, 1&3:£6.30 CSF £69.40 TOTE £11.00: £2.40, £2.60, £1.30; EX 77.70 Trifecta £683.80 Pool £3,336.06 - 3.61 winning units..
Owner Paul Webber **Bred** H H The Aga Khan's Studs Sc **Trained** Mollington, Oxon

FOCUS
A muddling claimer with the form horses not at their best. The form is anchored by the fourth.
Scamperdale Official explanation: jockey said gelding stopped quickly

7037 EVENTMASTERS HOSPITALITY "GOOD LUCK PAUL" H'CAP 1m 4f 50y(P)
7:50 (7:50) (Class 6) (0-65,65) 3-Y-O **£2,070** (£616; £307; £153) **Stalls Low**

Form RPR

0561 **1** **Fascinating (IRE)**[7] 6873 3-9-7 65 SilvestreDeSousa 11 81
(Mark Johnston) *chsd ldr tl led over 3f out: rdn over 1f out: styd on* **10/11**[1]

363R **2** *¾* **Kalendar Girl (IRE)**[45] 5838 3-9-5 63 StevieDonohoe 8 78
(Willie Musson) *hld up: hdwy over 2f out: chsd wnr over 1f out: rdn and ev ch ins fnl f: styd on same pce* **10/1**[3]

2002 **3** *6* **Golestan Palace (IRE)**[14] 6701 3-8-12 56 (v) J-PGuillambert 6 61
(Ed Walker) *hld up: hdwy over 2f out: wnt 3rd over 1f out: sn rdn and no imp* **9/2**[2]

3434 **4** *7* **Joe Strummer (IRE)**[38] 6052 3-8-13 62 (t) MatthewLawson(5) 1 56
(Michael Bell) *hld up: nt clr run over 1f out: nvr on terms* **11/1**

-240 **5** *1* **Toucan Tango (IRE)**[115] 3518 3-9-1 59 ChrisCatlin 2 51
(Peter Chapple-Hyam) *chsd ldrs: rdn over 2f out: wknd sn after* **40/1**

5506 **6** *nk* **Nuba (IRE)**[21] 6545 3-8-7 51 (p) PaulHanagan 12 43
(Luke Dace) *prom: rdn over 2f out: wknd wl over 1f out* **16/1**

0050 **7** *2 ½* **Spartan King (IRE)**[17] 4927 3-8-11 55 MartinLane 9 43
(Ian Williams) *s.s: rdn over 2f out: sn wknd* **40/1**

0-46 **8** *nk* **Windsor Knights**[275] 234 3-9-0 58 (b) JamesDoyle 4 45
(Alastair Lidderdale) *hld up: effrt over 2f out: sn wknd* **50/1**

4444 **9** *11* **Miracle Play (IRE)**[14] 6701 3-8-13 60 (p) KieranO'Neill(3) 10 30
(David Evans) *led: hdd over 3f out: wknd wl over 1f out* **12/1**

0363 **10** *23* **Phoenix Flame**[26] 6415 3-8-7 51 oh1 (p) KierenFallon 7 —
(Alan McCabe) *chsd ldrs: pushed along 7f out: wknd over 2f out: t.o* **14/1**

2m 37.3s (-3.80) **Going Correction** -0.10s/f (Stan) **10 Ran SP% 115.1**
Speed ratings (Par 99): **108,107,103,98,98 97,96,96,88,73**
toteswingers:1&2:£2.40, 2&3:£6.00, 1&3:£2.30 CSF £10.81 CT £29.31 TOTE £2.00: £1.10, £2.90, £1.70; EX 11.50 Trifecta £47.30 Pool £3,723.12 - 58.24 winning units..
Owner Nabil Mourad **Bred** Trebles Holford Farm Thoroughbreds **Trained** Middleham Moor, N Yorks

FOCUS
The big gap between the front two and the third, who in turn was a long way clear of the rest, suggests this is decent form for the grade, with the time also backing up that impression. The third is probably the best guide to the level.

7038 D & G CONSULTANCY MAIDEN AUCTION STKS 5f 216y(P)
8:20 (8:20) (Class 6) 2-Y-O **£1,704** (£503; £251) **Stalls Low**

Form RPR

0230 **1** **Forest Edge (IRE)**[13] 6725 2-8-10 77 SilvestreDeSousa 4 71
(David Evans) *chsd ldr tl led 4f out: shkn up over 1f out: r.o: eased nr fin* **7/4**[1]

4335 **2** *2 ¼* **Half A Billion (IRE)**[18] 6598 2-9-0 69 TomEaves 6 66
(Michael Dods) *trckd ldrs: plld hrd: rdn over 1f out: styd on to go 2nd post: nt trble wnr* **3/1**[2]

0502 **3** *hd* **Ionwy**[14] 6695 2-8-5 56 FrankieMcDonald 5 56
(Derek Haydn Jones) *led 2f: chsd wnr: rdn over 1f out: styd on same pce ins fnl f: lost 2nd post* **7/1**[3]

5 **4** *½* **Jkt Prince (IRE)**[8] 6842 2-8-11 0 (b[1]) ShaneKelly 2 60
(Daniel Mark Loughnane, Ire) *prom: rdn over 1f out: styd on same pce ins fnl f* **15/2**

0 **5** *shd* **One More Roman (IRE)**[137] 2787 2-8-9 0 (bt[1]) LiamKeniry 3 58
(J S Moore) *s.i.s: hld up: rdn over 1f out: r.o ins fnl f: nrst fin* **12/1**

06 **6** *3 ¼* **Capriska**[9] 6818 2-8-5 0 JamieMackay 7 44
(Willie Musson) *s.i.s: a in rr* **33/1**

0 **7** *1* **Princess Kaiulani (IRE)**[16] 6654 2-8-9 0 PaulHanagan 8 44
(William Muir) *prom over 3f* **8/1**

P **Morethanyouknow (IRE)** 2-8-5 0 WilliamCarson 1 —
(John Spearing) *s.i.s: in rr and pushed along: p.u over 2f out* **28/1**

1m 15.34s (0.34) **Going Correction** -0.10s/f (Stan) **8 Ran SP% 110.8**
Speed ratings (Par 93): **93,90,89,89,88 84,83,—**
toteswingers:1&2:£2.20, 2&3:£1.80, 1&3:£2.30 CSF £6.46 TOTE £2.60: £1.20, £1.10, £1.10; EX 5.60 Trifecta £15.80 Pool £232.04 - 10.81 winning units..
Owner Peter Swinnerton **Bred** Alberto Panetta **Trained** Pandy, Monmouths

FOCUS
A modest maiden rated around those in the frame behind the winner. Easy form to assess.

NOTEBOOK
Forest Edge(IRE) had run some good races in defeat on turf and it's unlikely he showed improved form to get off the mark here as he set the standard with a mark of 77. He got the job done quite tidily in the end and it is unlikely his mark will increase given the standard of opposition, but whether he can be competitive in handicaps remains to be seen. (op 13-8)
Half A Billion(IRE) had a similar profile to the winner in that he was exposed after eight runs, and he is rated 8lb inferior to Forest Edge, so he probably ran to form here. The downside is that he ruined whatever chance he had by throwing his head around quite violently through the first couple of furlongs. (op 7-2)
Ionwy isn't capable of winning a maiden with a mark of just 56, but she appeared to show improved form when second in a handicap here last time, and her proximity to the runner-up and the winner suggests she might be a little better than that rating. In which case, she will be interesting back in a low-grade handicap.
Jkt Prince(IRE), on whom the first-time blinkers didn't really spark any major improvement, having tracked the winner into the straight and still looked to have plenty to offer, he didn't as much for pressure as looked likely. (op 8-1)
One More Roman(IRE) was noted putting in his best work at the finish and this was a major step forward from his debut. He could be interesting upped in trip, with the possibility of more to come. (op 14-1)

7039 LARKSHILL ENGINEERING H'CAP (DIV I) 5f 216y(P)
8:50 (8:50) (Class 5) (0-75,77) 3-Y-O+ **£1,940** (£577; £288; £144) **Stalls Low**

Form RPR

4554 **1** **Millyluvstobouggie**[24] 6442 3-9-1 75 LucyKBarry(5) 2 81
(Clive Cox) *chsd ldrs: led ins fnl f: rdn out* **5/1**[2]

0034 **2** *½* **Bahamian Lad**[43] 5881 6-8-10 64 (p) SilvestreDeSousa 5 68
(Reg Hollinshead) *a.p: rdn and ev ch ins fnl f: r.o* **5/1**[2]

4440 **3** *nse* **Diapason (IRE)**[18] 6604 5-9-2 70 (t) StephenCraine 1 74+
(Tom Dascombe) *hld up: nt clr run over 1f out tl r.o wl ins fnl f: nvr able to chal* **25/1**

-005 **4** *hd* **Johnstown Lad (IRE)**[8] 6849 7-9-2 70 (be) ShaneKelly 10 74
(Daniel Mark Loughnane, Ire) *hld up: rdn over 1f out: edgd lft and r.o ins fnl f: nt rch ldrs* **28/1**

0004 **5** *nse* **Sarah's Art (IRE)**[10] 6794 8-8-13 67 (t) RobbieFitzpatrick 3 70
(Derek Shaw) *hld up: hdwy and edgd lft over 1f out: r.o* **20/1**

6354 **6** *1 ¾* **Interchoice Star**[8] 6841 6-8-9 63 (p) WilliamCarson 9 61
(Ray Peacock) *sn led: rdn over 1f out: hdd and no ex ins fnl f* **14/1**

51 **7** *½* **Grandmas Dream**[9] 6815 3-9-8 77 (b) MartinHarley 4 73
(Richard Guest) *prom: lost pl over 2f out: rdn over 1f out: styd on* **8/1**

1631 **8** *1 ¼* **Colourbearer (IRE)**[16] 6655 4-9-4 72 (t) KierenFallon 7 64
(Milton Bradley) *s.i.s: hdwy on outer over 3f out: chsd ldr over 2f out tl no ex ins fnl f* **2/1**[1]

2500 **9** *1 ¼* **Ace Of Spies (IRE)**[30] 6282 6-8-11 65 (b) KirstyMilczarek 8 53
(Conor Dore) *led early: chsd ldrs tl wknd ins fnl f* **50/1**

55-5 **10** *½* **Ventura Cove (IRE)**[198] 1200 4-9-5 73 PaulHanagan 6 60
(Richard Fahey) *hld up: shkn up over 1f out: nvr trbld ldrs* **6/1**[3]

1m 14.16s (-0.84) **Going Correction** -0.10s/f (Stan)
WFA 3 from 4yo+ 1lb **10 Ran SP% 112.7**
Speed ratings (Par 103): **101,100,100,100,99 97,96,95,93,92**
toteswingers:1&2:£8.50, 2&3:£27.00, 1&3:£11.30 CSF £27.69 CT £560.63 TOTE £7.60: £2.20, £1.10, £10.20; EX 27.00 Trifecta £192.70 Pool £419.38 - 1.61 winning units..
Owner Ken Lock Racing **Bred** Ken Lock Racing **Trained** Lambourn, Berks
■ Stewards' Enquiry : Robbie Fitzpatrick one-day ban: careless riding (Nov 5)

FOCUS
Plenty of chances deep in the final furlong, and a bunch finish. It was the faster division but there are one or two doubts over the form.
Diapason(IRE) ◆ Official explanation: jockey said mare was denied a clear run
Ace Of Spies(IRE) Official explanation: jockey said gelding hung right

7040 LARKSHILL ENGINEERING H'CAP (DIV II) 5f 216y(P)
9:20 (9:21) (Class 5) (0-75,75) 3-Y-O+ **£1,940** (£577; £288; £144) **Stalls Low**

Form RPR

0002 **1** **Prince James**[31] 6266 4-8-8 62 GrahamGibbons 4 70
(Michael Easterby) *led 5f out: rdn over 1f out: jst hld on* **3/1**[1]

2342 **2** *shd* **Piddie's Power**[22] 6502 4-9-2 73 SeanLevey(3) 8 81
(Ed McMahon) *a.p: rdn to chse wnr over 1f out: ev ch ins fnl f: r.o* **6/1**

1150 **3** *1 ¼* **Darcey**[12] 6759 5-9-5 73 SilvestreDeSousa 5 77
(Amy Weaver) *sn pushed along and prom: hmpd and lost pl wl over 3f out: hdwy and nt clr run over 1f out: r.o* **9/2**[3]

5000 **4** *nk* **Blown It (USA)**[25] 6426 5-8-10 64 JoeFanning 3 67
(Keith Dalgleish) *hld up: r.o ins fnl f: nt rch ldrs* **9/1**

0005 **5** *1 ¾* **Red Cape (FR)**[22] 6502 8-9-7 75 (b) PJMcDonald 7 72
(Ruth Carr) *hld up: hdwy over 1f out: rdn: hung lft and wknd ins fnl f* **20/1**

2060 **6** *1 ½* **Elhamri**[43] 5895 7-8-11 65 KirstyMilczarek 1 58
(Conor Dore) *in tch: rdn over 1f out: no ex ins fnl f* **33/1**

1544 **7** *1 ½* **Whitecrest**[6] 6895 3-9-3 72 PatCosgrave 2 60
(John Spearing) *led 1f: chsd ldrs: rdn over 1f out: wknd ins fnl f* **7/1**

0001 **8** *5* **Haadeeth**[8] 6841 4-9-0 68 (b) PaulHanagan 10 40
(Richard Fahey) *prom: rdn and wknd over 1f out* **7/2**[2]

1103 **9** *5* **Lady Kildare (IRE)**[30] 6276 3-8-9 67 PatrickDonaghy(3) 9 23
(Jedd O'Keeffe) *chsd ldrs: rdn over 2f out: wknd over 1f out* **16/1**

1m 14.48s (-0.52) **Going Correction** -0.10s/f (Stan)
WFA 3 from 4yo+ 1lb **9 Ran SP% 115.8**
Speed ratings (Par 103): **99,98,97,96,94 92,90,83,77**
toteswingers:1&2:£2.70, 2&3:£9.70, 1&3:£4.90 CSF £21.46 CT £79.75 TOTE £2.50: £1.40, £4.00, £2.80; EX 24.40 Trifecta £253.30 Pool £585.42 - 1.71 winning units..
Owner A Saha **Bred** A C M Spalding **Trained** Sheriff Hutton, N Yorks

FOCUS
A modest sprint but the form is taken at face value rated around the placed horses. The slower division.
T/Plt: £55.80 to a £1 stake. Pool £76,512.13 - 1,000.95 winning tickets. T/Qpdt: £6.00 to a £1 stake. Pool £9,664.84 - 1,173.69 winning tickets. CR

7041 - 7042a (Foreign Racing) - See Raceform Interactive

6516 MOONEE VALLEY (L-H)
Saturday, October 22
OFFICIAL GOING: Turf: good to soft

7043a DRAKE INTERNATIONAL CUP (GROUP 2) 1m 4f 110y
6:00 (6:00) 4-Y-O+
£113,071 (£29,411; £14,705; £7,352; £4,084; £3,267)

RPR

1 **Americain (USA)**[62] 5304 6-9-2 GeraldMosse 3 119+
(A De Royer-Dupre, France) **5/2**[1]

2 *2 ¼* **Tullamore (NZ)**[7] 6886 5-9-0 NashRawiller 5 112
(Gai Waterhouse, Australia) **3/1**[2]

3 *1 ¼* **Illo (GER)**[104] 5-8-13 LukeNolen 8 109
(Bart Cummings, Australia) **15/2**

4 *½* **Anudjawun (NZ)**[14] 6711 6-8-9 (b) MichaelRodd 9 104
(Shaun Dwyer, Australia) **20/1**

5 *hd* **Shewan (AUS)**[14] 6711 5-9-0 ChrisSymons 7 109
(Robert Smerdon, Australia) **9/2**[3]

6 *2 ¾* **Harris Tweed (NZ)**[35] 6-8-11 (bt) BradRawiller 4 102
(Murray Baker, New Zealand) **25/1**

7 *hd* **Paddy O'Reilly (NZ)**[182] 6-8-11 (vt) CraigAWilliams 1 102
(Robert Smerdon, Australia) **17/1**

8 *6* **Swooper (AUS)** 7-8-7 BenMelham 2 89
(Darryl Dodson, Australia) **20/1**

9 *½* **Pergola (NZ)**[222] 7-8-9 (b) JamesWinks 10 90
(Colin & Cindy Alderson, Australia) **60/1**

The Form Book, Raceform Ltd, Compton, RG20 6NL

10 *12* **Lalla Rookh (AUS)**[167] 4-8-0 ....(p) ClareLindop 6 63
(Leon Macdonald & Andrew Gluyas, Australia) **17/1**
2m 36.41s (156.41) **10** Ran SP% **109.6**

Owner G T Ryan, K L Bamford, & Mrs C O Bamford **Bred** Wertheimer Et Frere **Trained** Chantilly, France

NOTEBOOK
Americain(USA) was tucked away on the inside and for a moment it looked as though he had nowhere to go, but Mosse didn't panic and the pair came home convincing winners. He receives no penalty for this success and, despit carrying top weight at Flemington, will take a lot of beating in the Melbourne Cup.
Tullamore(NZ) is a solid marker to rate the race though considering he was third in the Caulfield Cup, which helps to make Americain's effort look decent.
Illo(GER) will have pleased connections on his first outing for them since leaving Germany, but whether he can reverse form with the winner here if they meet at Flemington is open to question, even though the legendary Bart Cummings has been known to perform the odd miracle.

7044a TATTS COX PLATE (GROUP 1) (3YO+) (TURF) 1m 2f 44y
7:35 (12:00) 3-Y-0+
£1,209,150 (£287,581; £143,790; £84,967; £71,895; £65,359)

RPR
1 **Pinker Pinker (AUS)**[21] 4-8-10 0....................(b) CraigAWilliams 12 118
(Greg Eurell, Australia) *hld up towards rr: shkn up and hdwy on ins over 2 1/2f out: 4th and running on 1 1/2f out: swtchd outside ent fnl f and r.o wl u.p to ld fnl 50yds* **25/1**
2 *1 1/4* **Jimmy Choux (NZ)**[21] 4-9-1 0.................... JonathanRiddell 10 120+
(John Bary, New Zealand) *broke out of stall bef s: settled in 4th wl in tch: wnt 3rd on outside of two ldrs ins fnl 2f: led under 1 1/2f out: rdn and nt qckn appr fnl 110yds: hdd fnl 50yds: no ex* **11/2**[2]
3 *snk* **Rekindled Interest (AUS)**[20] 4-9-1 0....................(b[1]) DwayneDunn 3 120
(Jim Conlan, Australia) *midfield: 6th on ins 4f out: pushed along and briefly short of room 2f out: swtchd outside and bmpd between horses 1 1/2f out: 4th and in clr over 1f out: r.o u.p fnl f* **9/1**[3]
4 *nk* **Wall Street (NZ)**[14] 6714 7-9-4 0....................(t) DarrenBeadman 7 122
(Jeff Lynds, New Zealand) *unsettled in stalls: dwlt: hld up in rr: sltly hmpd 4f out: hdwy on wd outside over 2 1/2f out: wdst of all fnl turn 1 1/2f out: 8th ent fnl f: styd on u.p: run flattened out fnl 50yds* **80/1**
5 *shd* **Secret Admirer (AUS)**[21] 4-8-10 0.................... BrentonAvdulla 8 114
(Grahame Begg, Australia) *hld up in rr: pushed along and hdwy on outside over 2 1/2f out: 6th and styng on u.p ent fnl f: nt pce to chal ldrs* **12/1**
6 *2* **Efficient (NZ)**[20] 8-9-4 0.................... StevenKing 5 118
(Robert Hickmott, Australia) *w.w towards rr: prog 4f out to go 7th: cl 4th and pushed along 2 1/2f out: rdn and nt qckn fr 1 1/2f out* **18/1**
7 *1/2* **King's Rose (NZ)**[14] 6714 4-8-10 0....................(p) LukeNolen 2 109+
(Peter G Moody, Australia) *prom: lost pl 2f out: 8th and short of room sn after: one pce fnl f* **10/1**
8 *shd* **Helmet (AUS)**[14] 6715 3-7-11 0....................(p) KerrinMcEvoy 11 112+
(Peter Snowden, Australia) *broke wl: led and sn swtchd to ins rail: pressed 3f out: hdd ins fnl 1 1/2f: wknd fnl f* **9/5**[1]
9 *2* **Sincero (AUS)**[14] 6713 4-9-1 0....................(b) ChrisO'Brien 6 110
(Stephen Farley, Australia) *racd in midfield: pushed along but short of room 3f out: forced wd fnl bnd: sme hdwy fnl f: n.d* **25/1**
10 *hd* **Glass Harmonium (IRE)**[20] 5-9-4 0....................(t) DamienOliver 4 113
(Michael Moroney, Australia) *fractious in stalls: missed break: a among bkmarkers: rdn over 1 1/2f out: no imp* **9/1**[3]
11 *hd* **Playing God (AUS)**[14] 6713 4-9-1 0.................... StevenParnham 15 109
(Neville Parnham, Australia) *hld up towards rr: effrt into midfield 3f out: sn rdn: nt qckn u.p fnl 1 1/2f* **70/1**
12 *2* **Shamrocker (NZ)**[20] 4-8-10 0.................... StevenArnold 1 100
(Danny O'Brien, Australia) *midfield: rdn and nt qckn over 3f out: btn fnl 1 1/2f* **50/1**
13 *1* **Avienus (AUS)**[14] 6713 6-9-0 0....................(b) BradRawiller 14 102
(Mark C Webb, Australia) *racd keenly: chsd ldng gp: wknd fnl 1 1/2f* **70/1**
14 *1* **Lion Tamer (NZ)**[14] 6713 4-9-1 0....................(bt) HughBowman 16 101
(Murray & Bjorn Baker, New Zealand) *trckd ldrs: pressed ldr 3f out: rdn and wknd over 1 1/2f out* **12/1**
2m 5.39s (125.39)
WFA 3 from 4yo+ 5lb **14** Ran SP% **114.5**
PARI-MUTUEL (NSW TAB - all including au$1 stakes): WIN 21.40 PLACE 4.60, 2.30, 3.40; DF 80.00; SF 159.60.
Owner M D Kirby Nominees Pty Ltd **Bred** W Giovas & C Gordon **Trained** Australia

NOTEBOOK
Pinker Pinker(AUS), who'd only won up to 1m previously, was given a terrific ride by Craig Williams, who won the Caulfield Cup the previous weekend, as he sat and waited for the gap that took his mount to the front. In winning, she reversed form with a couple she met here.
Jimmy Choux(NZ), New Zealand's star performer, looked like winning as they got into the final stages but wasn't able to hang on. It's was a fine effort from a wide draw.
Rekindled Interest(AUS) loves it at this course (2/3 prior to this run) and kept on well late on in first-time blinkers after meeting some traffic on the final bend.
King's Rose(NZ) had the perfect trip all the way round, but Luke Nolen chose to go outside turning in, which saw his mount run into a bit of trouble. King's Rose had beaten the winner the last time they met (identical weights that day as well) and her moving out left the way clear for Pinker Pinker to take what would have been her route.
Helmet(AUS), taking on his elders for the first time, managed to get to the head of affairs from his wide stall but ran like a horse that didn't stay.
Glass Harmonium(IRE) fluffed the start, having had a good draw for a pacesetter, and never got into the race.
Shamrocker(NZ)'s jockey said aftewards that his mount wants 2m and Flemington.

6904 SAN SIRO (R-H)
Saturday, October 22

OFFICIAL GOING: Turf: good

7045a PREMIO ST LEGER ITALIANO (GROUP 3) (3YO+) (TURF) 1m 6f
3:50 (12:00) 3-Y-0+ **£34,482** (£15,172; £8,275; £4,137)

RPR
1 **Altano (GER)**[34] 6200 5-8-13 0.................... JBojko 4 108
(A Wohler, Germany) *hld up towards rr: shkn up and hdwy 3 1/2f out: led over 2f out: rdn clr fnl f* **151/10**
2 *8* **Leo Gali (IRE)**[68] 4-8-9 0.................... MircoDemuro 7 92
(Vaclav Luka II, Czech Republic) *w.w in rr: hdwy on outside over 4f out: sn rdn: styd on u.p to ld briefly ins fnl 2 1/2f: hdd appr fnl 2f: one pce fnl f to hold on for 2nd* **69/10**
3 *1/2* **Lacateno**[16] 6661 4-8-13 0.................... AStarke 6 96
(W Hickst, Germany) *settled in midfield: pushed along and outpcd 4f out: kpt on u.p to go 4th ins fnl 2f: plugged on to take 3rd fnl 75yds* **11/2**[3]
4 *3/4* **Oriental Fox (GER)**[55] 3-8-5 0.................... RoystonFfrench 2 96
(Carmen Bocskai, Switzerland) *a.p: 2nd and hrd rdn ins fnl 3f: wknd u.p fnl 1 1/2f* **127/20**
5 *6* **Caudillo (GER)**[20] 6569 8-8-13 0.................... LManiezzi 9 86
(Dr A Bolte, Germany) *midfield: rdn and no imp 3 1/2f out: wknd ins fnl 1 1/2f* **15/4**[2]
6 *3* **Alla Prossima**[30] 3-8-2 0.................... DPorcu 10 80
(S Smrczek, Germany) *hld up and racd keenly: last 3f out: rdn and no imp* **67/1**
7 *1 1/4* **Frantic Storm (GER)**[475] 5-8-13 0.................... CristianDemuro 1 80
(Frau J Mayer, Germany) *led: hdd 4f out: sn hrd rdn: wknd fnl 2f* **30/1**
8 *3 1/2* **Fair Boss (IRE)**[34] 6200 3-8-5 0.................... APietsch 5 76
(W Hickst, Germany) *chsd ldrs: lost pl 6f out: rallied u.p on rail 3 1/2f out to chse ldng gp: wknd fr 2f out* **29/20**[1]
9 *6* **Orsino (GER)**[20] 6569 4-8-13 0.................... MEsposito 8 67
(R Rohne, Germany) *chsd ldr: led 4f out: hdd ins fnl 2 1/2f: sn rdn and btn* **79/10**
10 *1 1/4* **Tarkheena Prince (USA)**[244] 628 6-8-13 0.... PierantonioConvertino 3 65
(C Von Der Recke, Germany) *hld up towards rr: hdwy into 5th 5f out: sn rdn: wknd fnl 2 1/2f: eased fr 1 1/2f out* **758/100**
2m 53.6s (173.60)
WFA 3 from 4yo+ 9lb **10** Ran SP% **137.3**
WIN (incl. 1 euro stake): 16.05. PLACES: 4.63, 3.18, 2.66. DF: 58.34.
Owner Frau Dr I Hornig **Bred** Gestut Hof Ittlingen **Trained** Germany
■ Eight of the ten runners came from Germany, with none from Italy.

NOTEBOOK
Altano(GER), sixth to Fox Hunt in the German Leger, routed the opposition.

7046 - (Foreign Racing) - See Raceform Interactive

2134 CAPANNELLE (R-H)
Sunday, October 23

OFFICIAL GOING: Turf: soft

7047a LONGINES LYDIA TESIO (GROUP 1) (3YO+ FILLIES & MARES) (TURF) 1m 2f
4:05 (12:00) 3-Y-0+ **£116,379** (£51,206; £27,931; £13,965)

RPR
1 **Quiza Quiza Quiza**[22] 5-9-0 0.................... FabioBranca 1 112
(L Riccardi, Italy) *hld up towards rr: rdn and hdwy 2f out: r.o u.p fnl f: led fnl 25yds* **57/10**
2 *1/2* **Beatrice Aurore (IRE)**[61] 5366 3-8-10 0.................... MircoDemuro 2 112
(John Dunlop) *hld up in rr: pushed along and hdwy on ins 2 1/2f out: led over 1f out: r.o u.p fnl f: hdd fnl 25yds: no ex* **9/2**[3]
3 *1 1/2* **Kapitale (GER)**[28] 6395 3-8-10 0.................... JohanVictoire 8 105
(A Wohler, Germany) *prom: rdn to ld over 2 1/2f out: hdd over 1f out: kpt on one pce fnl f* **101/10**
4 *2 1/2* **Djumama (IRE)**[21] 6568 3-8-10 0.................... DarioVargiu 3 104
(Andreas Lowe, Germany) *settled midfield on ins: 5th and scrubbed along over 2f out: sn rdn and nt qckn: styd on ins fnl f: nt pce to chal ldrs: tk 4th on line* **13/5**[1]
5 *shd* **Elle Shadow (IRE)**[57] 5497 4-9-0 0.................... AStarke 5 103
(P Schiergen, Germany) *plld hrd in ld early: sn hld up under restraint bhd ldng gp: effrt on outside over 2f out: 4th and rdn ins fnl 2f: fdd fnl f* **23/5**
6 *1/2* **Not For Sale (GER)**[14] 6739 4-9-0 0.................... EFrank 10 102
(T Mundry, Germany) *settled towards rr: prog to chse ldrs over 2f out: sn hrd rdn: nt qckn: wknd fnl 100yds* **14/1**
7 *5* **Modeyra**[22] 6557 4-9-0 0.................... FrankieDettori 7 92
(Saeed Bin Suroor) *trckd ldr: rdn over 2f out: wknd fnl f* **29/10**[2]
8 *2 1/2* **Night Of Dubai (IRE)**[49] 3-8-10 0.................... MEsposito 9 88
(Mario Hofer, Germany) *sn led: hdd over 2 1/2f out: rdn and dropped away ins fnl 2f: eased fnl f* **34/1**
9 *nk* **Oeuvre D'Art (IRE)**[14] 6739 3-8-10 0.................... UmbertoRispoli 11 87
(B Grizzetti, Italy) *hld up: no imp fnl 2f* **14/1**
10 *1* **Malagenia (IRE)**[29] 6370 3-8-10 0.................... CristianDemuro 6 85
(L Riccardi, Italy) *w.w towards rr: nvr on terms* **14/1**
11 *1 1/4* **Shamal Sally (USA)**[14] 6739 4-9-0 0.................... ZSmida 12 82
(Zuzana Kubovicova, Salvador) *chsd ldrs on outside: 5th and gng wl enough 2 1/2f out: rdn and wknd fr 2f out* **62/1**
12 *4 1/4* **She Is Great (IRE)**[14] 6739 4-9-0 0.................... PierantonioConvertino 4 73
(B Grizzetti, Italy) *hld up in fnl 3rd: rdn and wknd fnl 2f: eased fr 1f out* **38/1**
(-123.30)
WFA 3 from 4yo+ 5lb **12** Ran SP% **140.4**
WIN (incl. 1 euro stake); 3.34 (Quiza Quiza Quiza coupled with Malagenia).. PLACES: 2.59, 2.41, 4.00. DF: 25.62.
Owner Riccardo Cantoni **Bred** Ricardo Cantoni **Trained** Italy

NOTEBOOK
Quiza Quiza Quiza, a tough mare well at home in the rain-softened ground, stayed on well to snatch the race late on.
Beatrice Aurore(IRE) was collared late on and denied this Group 1 prize. Unlike the winner, she would have preferred a sounder surface.
Modeyra was in the firing line until the final two furlongs, at which point her tank was empty.

4839 DUSSELDORF (R-H)

Sunday, October 23

OFFICIAL GOING: Turf: soft

7048a GROSSER PREIS DER LANDESHAUPTSTADT DUSSELDORF (GROUP 3) (3YO+) (TURF) — 1m 110y

3:30 (3:40) 3-Y-0+

£27,586 (£9,482; £4,741; £2,586; £1,724; £1,293)

RPR

1 — **Alianthus (GER)**52 5664 6-9-6 0 ... FilipMinarik 2 — 114
(J Hirschberger, Germany) *broke wl: settled bhd ldr: travelling wl: gd prog through fnl turn: tk ld under 2f out: r.o wl u.p: kpt on: comf* — **2/5**1

2 — *1* — **Empire Storm (GER)**20 6595 4-9-2 0 ... EPedroza 7 — 108
(A Wohler, Germany) *hld up in 4th: travelling wl: sn mde move ent st: r.o wl u.p: looked threatening ins fnl f: chsd wnr home* — **53/10**2

3 — *1 1/4* — **Neatico (GER)**35 6201 4-9-2 0 ... KClijmans 6 — 105
(P Schiergen, Germany) *settled 2nd last: mde gd prog down bk st: qcknd wl into st: r.o wl fnl 2f* — **133/10**

4 — *2 1/2* — **Apollo Star (GER)**770 9-9-2 0 ... StefanieHofer 8 — 100
(F Holcak, Czech Republic) *broke fast: sent to ld: set gd pce: led into st: r.o but hdd under 2f out: no threat to first three* — **114/10**

5 — *1 1/2* — **Auvano (GER)**20 6595 7-9-2 0 ... APietsch 3 — 96
(R Dzubasz, Germany) *settled in midfield: travelling wl: rdn early in st: mde no real imp* — **89/10**3

6 — *hd* — **Combat Zone (IRE)**29 6339 5-9-2 0 ... THellier 5 — 96
(Mario Hofer, Germany) *bkmarker fr s: styd on st: passed btn horses* — **111/10**

7 — *7* — **Big Hunter (FR)**56 5530 4-9-2 0 ... DavidBreux 4 — 81
(E Kurdu, Germany) *settled 5th: r.o early in st but sn wknd* — **227/10**

8 — *4 1/2* — **Le Big (GER)**35 6201 7-9-2 0 ... AHelfenbein 1 — 71
(U Stoltefuss, Germany) *broke fast: a.p: travelling wl ent st: rdn and sn wknd* — **112/10**

1m 45.56s (-2.02) — **8** Ran SP% **133.1**
WIN (incl. 10 euro stake): 14. PLACES: 10, 11, 14. SF: 40.
Owner Baron G Von Ullmann **Bred** Gestut Karlshof **Trained** Germany

NOTEBOOK
Alianthus(GER) confirmed his position as Germany's top miler with a comfortable victory. He has been a revelation since being switched to a mile and has now won seven of his last ten starts, including this event last year, and was runner-up on the other three occasions. A trip to the Hong Kong international meeting at the end of the year is possibly on the agenda.

6902 LONGCHAMP (R-H)

Sunday, October 23

OFFICIAL GOING: Turf: good

7049a PRIX ROYAL-OAK (GROUP 1) (3YO+) (TURF) — 1m 7f 110y

2:08 (12:00) 3-Y-0+ **£123,146** (£49,267; £24,633; £12,306; £6,163)

RPR

1 — **Be Fabulous (GER)**17 6661 4-9-1 0 ... MaximeGuyon 8 — 111
(A Fabre, France) *w.w in midfield: a travelling wl: prog on outside ins fnl 2f: rdn to ld 140yds out: sn clr: pushed out: comf* — **6/1**2

2 — *1 3/4* — **Miss Lago (IRE)**22 6555 3-8-6 0 ... AnthonyCrastus 3 — 110+
(E Lellouche, France) *settled towards rr: hdwy and rdn 2f out: disputing 6th 1f out: r.o wl fnl f: nrest at fin* — **8/1**

3 — *hd* — **Shankardeh (IRE)**22 6555 3-8-6 0 ... Christophe-PatriceLemaire 2 — 110+
(M Delzangles, France) *settled midfield: 6th and shkn up on rail ins fnl 2 1/2f: styd on u.p fr 1 1/2f out: nt pce to chal wnr* — **9/2**1

4 — *nse* — **Tac De Boistron (FR)**17 6661 4-9-4 0 ... ChristopheSoumillon 5 — 112
(A Lyon, France) *trckd tres rock danon in 4th: rdn 2 1/2f out: 3rd and styng on ins eventual wnr fr 1 1/2f out: effrt flattened out fnl 75yds and lost two pls cl home* — **12/1**

5 — *2* — **Cavalryman**70 5092 5-9-4 0 ...(b) MickaelBarzalona 14 — 110
(Saeed Bin Suroor) *prom racing keenly: led sn after ent bk st: sn in clr ld: pushed along over 2f out: styd on wout qckning: hdd fnl 140yds: no ex* — **16/1**

6 — *nk* — **Shamanova (IRE)**22 6557 4-9-1 0 ... JMurtagh 12 — 106
(A De Royer-Dupre, France) *missed break: rousted along to take up midfield position: rdn 2f out: kpt on at one pce: nvr able to chal* — **6/1**2

7 — *1 1/2* — **Electrolyser (IRE)**17 6661 6-9-4 0 ... IoritzMendizabal 4 — 107
(Clive Cox) *led: hdd sn after ent bk st: styd clr 2nd tl rdn and nt qckn 1 1/2f out: one pce fnl f* — **20/1**

8 — *2* — **Tres Rock Danon (FR)**21 6562 5-9-4 0 ... ASuborics 13 — 105
(W Hickst, Germany) *hdd main pack bhd two clr ldrs: rdn and nt qckn over 2f out: wknd fnl f* — **7/1**3

9 — *snk* — **Silver Valny (FR)**21 6562 5-9-4 0 ... ThomasMessina 6 — 105
(Mlle M-L Mortier, France) *hld up towards rr: scrubbed along 2 1/2f out: no imp fnl 1 1/2f* — **14/1**

10 — *4* — **Gentoo (FR)**21 6562 7-9-4 0 ...(p) OlivierPeslier 7 — 100
(A Lyon, France) *hld up towards rr: rdn on outside over 2f out: nvr in contention* — **9/1**

11 — *1 1/2* — **Maria Royal (IRE)**21 6562 4-9-1 0 ... GregoryBenoist 9 — 95
(A De Royer-Dupre, France) *bhd: sme mod late hdwy: nvr a factor* — **16/1**

12 — *1/2* — **Gradara**25 6470 4-9-1 0 ... StephanePasquier 1 — 95
(S Wattel, France) *racd in middle 3rd: rdn and no hdwy fnl 2 1/2f: eased fnl f* — **16/1**

13 — *8* — **Celtic Celeb (IRE)**21 6562 4-9-4 0 ... ThierryJarnet 10 — 88
(F Doumen, France) *settled midfield on outside: rdn and no imp 2f out: sn wknd: eased fnl f* — **20/1**

14 — *10* — **Balaythous (FR)**17 6661 5-9-4 0 ... FlavienPrat 11 — 76
(Mlle B Renk, France) *a in rr: last st: sn hrd rdn: wknd over 1 1/2f out: eased fnl f* — **14/1**

3m 21.47s (-0.03) **Going Correction** +0.425s/f (Yiel)
WFA 3 from 4yo+ 9lb — **14** Ran SP% **128.6**
Speed ratings: **117,116,116,116,115 114,114,113,113,111 110,110,106,101**
WIN (incl. 1 euro stake): 5.20. PLACES: 2.10, 2.30, 2.00. DF: 19.50. SF: 42.50.
Owner Godolphin SNC **Bred** Gestut Karlshof **Trained** Chantilly, France

FOCUS
Coming three weeks after the Prix du Cadran (the French Gold Cup), the Prix Royal-Oak (French St Leger) over 1m71/2f has a rollcall of recent winners that includes Ask, Yeats, Allegretto, Westerner and Mr Dinos. While those five landed the race among a haul of big successes throughout their careers, the 14 who went to post this time could hardly be described as prolific winners at the highest grade.

NOTEBOOK
Be Fabulous(GER), representing Godolphin's French arm, gave master trainer Andre Fabre a seventh win in the Prix Royal-Oak and a first since Amilynx completed back-to-back wins in the race in 2000. One of six fillies in the race, she came with a powerful late charge to win comfortably.
Miss Lago(IRE) has won only one race, in maiden company, but she was an eye-catching second in Listed company behind Shankardeh over course and distance last time. She looks an out-and-out stayer who was flying at the end and it would be a huge surprise if she was not to add to her tally when she stays in training next year.
Shankardeh(IRE) ran close to her Prix Chaudenay form with Miss Lago. She is a consistent sort with plenty still to give.
Tac De Boistron(FR), fourth behind Be Fabulous last time, had to settle for the same position again. He raced prominently but was unable to go with the winner on ground that would have been plenty quick enough for him.
Cavalryman was blinkered for this step up in trip. He opened up a decent advantage down the back straight and, just for a moment, looked as though he may have slipped the field, but he was cut down inside the last and, tiring, was run out of the places.
Electrolyser(IRE), who raced prominently, found a few too good but was not discredited. He could head to the sales next week.
Tres Rock Danon(FR), second in the Prix du Cadran, has had a successful season. This may have been one race too many for him and he was eased when beaten.
Gentoo(FR), last year's winner, could never land a blow. The ground was against him.

6766 LEICESTER (R-H)

Monday, October 24

OFFICIAL GOING: Good to firm (watered; 7.7)

False rail from round course bend all the way up the home straight, adding 10yds to races on round course.

Wind: Fresh half-against Weather: Overcast

7050 SIS LIVE H'CAP (DIV I) — 1m 60y

1:30 (1:30) (Class 4) (0-80,79) 3-Y-0+ **£3,969** (£1,188; £594; £297; £148) **Stalls** Low

Form — RPR

3420 — **1** — **Uppercut**37 6167 3-9-3 **78** ... FergusSweeney 2 — 88
(Stuart Kittow) *chsd ldrs: rdn to ld over 1f out: styd on* — **5/1**2

0122 — **2** — *hd* — **Yojimbo (IRE)**15 6728 3-9-4 **79** ... RyanMoore 6 — 88
(Mick Channon) *led: hdd 7f out: chsd ldr: pushed along over 2f out: rdn and ev ch fr over 1f out: styd on* — **9/4**1

5500 — **3** — *3* — **Chosen Character (IRE)**15 6727 3-9-1 **76** ...(vt) StephenCraine 5 — 78
(Tom Dascombe) *s.i.s: hld up: hdwy over 2f out: rdn over 1f out: styd on to go 3rd ins fnl f: nt rch ldrs* — **9/1**

-006 — **4** — *1 1/2* — **Avertis**14 6759 6-8-11 **74** ...(tp) AmyScott(5) 4 — 73
(Alastair Lidderdale) *chsd ldr tl led 7f out: pushed along and hdd over 1f out: no ex ins fnl f* — **14/1**

1614 — **5** — *3/4* — **West End Lad**19 6632 8-9-6 **78** ...(b) RussKennemore 9 — 75
(Roy Bowring) *chsd ldrs: pushed along over 3f out: styd on same pce appr fnl f* — **10/1**

5131 — **6** — *nk* — **Jordaura**28 6401 5-9-5 **77** ... RobertWinston 8 — 74
(Gay Kelleway) *hld up: hdwy u.p and hung lft over 1f out: nt trble ldrs* — **8/1**

4100 — **7** — *1/2* — **Daneside (IRE)**10 6830 4-8-9 **72** ... MatthewLawson(5) 10 — 67
(Gary Harrison) *hld up: effrt over 2f out: nvr on terms* — **7/1**3

2020 — **8** — *5* — **All Right Now**51 5717 4-8-11 **72** ... HarryBentley(3) 3 — 56
(Derek Haydn Jones) *hld up in tch: rdn and hung lft over 2f out: sn wknd* — **25/1**

2110 — **9** — *1 3/4* — **Mrs Greeley**37 6167 3-9-1 **76** ... WilliamCarson 11 — 56
(Eve Johnson Houghton) *s.i.s: swtchd rt sn after s: hld up: nvr on terms* — **12/1**

2000 — **10** — *9* — **My Kingdom (IRE)**14 6762 5-9-7 **79** ...(t) JoeFanning 1 — 38
(Patrick Morris) *hld up: lost tch fnl 2f: eased* — **22/1**

1m 43.88s (-1.22) **Going Correction** -0.15s/f (Firm)
WFA 3 from 4yo+ 3lb — **10** Ran SP% **112.7**
Speed ratings (Par 105): **100,99,96,95,94 94,93,88,87,78**
toteswingers:1&2:£2.70, 1&3:£5.20, 2&3:£5.20 CSF £15.98 CT £96.19 TOTE £5.20: £2.30, £1.50, £2.00; EX 22.90.
Owner H A Cushing **Bred** The Hon Mrs R Pease **Trained** Blackborough, Devon

FOCUS
Times seemed to confirm the ground was riding fast, with Ryan Moore confirming it to be 'good to firm' following this opening contest. The opening division of this ordinary handicap was dominated by 3-y-os. The form is rated around the first three.
Jordaura Official explanation: jockey said gelding hung left

7051 HAYMARKET NURSERY — 7f 9y

2:00 (2:01) (Class 6) (0-65,65) 2-Y-0 **£1,617** (£481; £240; £120) **Stalls** High

Form — RPR

0405 — **1** — **Love Tale**32 6284 2-9-0 **58** ... FergusSweeney 7 — 64
(Mark Rimell) *a.p: led over 1f out: rdn and hung lft ins fnl f: styd on* — **16/1**

0010 — **2** — *1 1/4* — **Inniscastle Boy**25 6487 2-9-5 **63** ... WilliamCarson 2 — 65
(William Muir) *mid-div: sn pushed along: hdwy over 1f out: r.o to go 2nd wl ins fnl f: nt rch wnr* — **22/1**

6064 — **3** — *1 1/4* — **Ishiamiracle**11 6819 2-9-2 **60** ... DavidProbert 3 — 59
(Andrew Balding) *a.p: rdn over 1f out: styd on same pce ins fnl f* — **11/1**

0340 — **4** — *1 1/4* — **Findhornbay**21 6573 2-9-6 **64** ... JoeFanning 5 — 60
(Mark Johnston) *led: rdn and hdd over 1f out: no ex ins fnl f* — **11/1**

0544 — **5** — *1/2* — **Steady The Buffs**12 6786 2-9-7 **65** ...(b) LukeMorris 13 — 59
(Hugo Palmer) *chsd ldrs: rdn over 1f out: styd on same pce fnl f* — **20/1**

003 — **5** — *dht* — **Emman Bee (IRE)**21 6581 2-9-6 **64** ... FrankieMcDonald 14 — 59
(John Gallagher) *mid-div: hdwy u.p over 1f out: nt clr run ins fnl f: styd on* — **14/1**

0506 — **7** — *3/4* — **Siberian Belle (IRE)**27 6424 2-8-9 **53** ... TonyHamilton 10 — 47
(Richard Fahey) *sn pushed along in rr: r.o ins fnl f: nvr nrr* — **22/1**

053 — **8** — *1/2* — **Gabrial's Bounty (IRE)**19 6620 2-9-4 **62** ... SamHitchcott 8 — 53
(Mick Channon) *hld up: rdn over 2f out: hdwy over 1f out: nt rch ldrs* — **13/2**1

0200 — **9** — *3/4* — **Dine Out**15 6724 2-9-5 **63** ...(b1) TomQueally 1 — 52
(Mark H Tompkins) *s.i.s: outpcd: swtchd lft over 1f out: r.o ins fnl f: nrst fin* — **28/1**

0001 **10** *hd* **Lady Advocate (IRE)**[56] 5555 2-9-0 **58**....................(b) RobertWinston 12 47
(Tim Easterby) *w ldr: pushed along over 2f out: rdn over 1f out: wknd ins fnl f* **14/1**

060 **11** *1* **Roll Of Thunder**[26] 6448 2-8-11 **58**.................................. DaleSwift(3) 16 44
(John Quinn) *prom: rdn 1/2-way: wknd fnl f* **17/2**[3]

006 **12** *1 1/4* **Emirates Jack (IRE)**[21] 6581 2-9-4 **62**........................ TonyCulhane 18 45
(George Baker) *hld up: shkn up and hung rt fr over 2f out: nvr trbld ldrs* **14/1**

405 **13** *1 1/2* **Samasana (IRE)**[11] 6812 2-8-5 **52**.................. HarryBentley(3) 4 31
(Ian Wood) *chsd ldrs: rdn over 1f out: sn wknd* **9/1**

6005 **14** *2 1/2* **Perfect Day (IRE)**[11] 6821 2-8-13 **57**.............................. TedDurcan 15 29
(Paul Cole) *s.i.s: outpcd* **12/1**

060 **15** *3/4* **Kieron's Rock (IRE)**[20] 6598 2-9-4 **65**.................... PatrickDonaghy(3) 6 36
(Jedd O'Keeffe) *prom: rdn over 1f out: wknd fnl f* **25/1**

3405 **16** *5* **Fairy Moss (IRE)**[81] 4708 2-8-8 **52**................................ AndreaAtzeni 9 10
(David Evans) *mid-div: sn pushed along: wknd 3f out* **33/1**

040 **17** *16* **Authora (IRE)**[31] 6291 2-9-7 **65**.. RyanMoore 17 —
(Richard Hannon) *hld up: rdn over 2f out: sn wknd and eased* **7/1**[2]

1m 25.68s (-0.52) **Going Correction** -0.15s/f (Firm) **17** Ran SP% **120.3**
Speed ratings (Par 93): **96,94,93,91,91 91,90,89,88,88 87,86,84,81,80 74,56**
toteswingers:1&2:£106.00, 1&3:£22.70, 2&3:£36.90 CSF £339.35 CT £3999.98 TOTE £22.60: £4.90, £4.70, £3.10, £3.00; EX 783.90.
Owner Mark Rimell **Bred** Witney And Warren Enterprises Ltd **Trained** Leafield, Oxon

FOCUS
A wide-open nursery, with it being 13-2 the field, but not that many got into it. The form is limited by the winner, despite that one recording a personal-best.

NOTEBOOK
Love Tale, back up to 7f, was always travelling well just in behind the leaders and found plenty when asked to go and win the race. Scoring off a mark of just 58, she looks capable of better and can probably win again. (op 14-1)
Inniscastle Boy, 3lb higher than when winning at Kempton, bounced back from a poor effort at Wolverhampton and may improve again for 1m. (op 25-1)
Ishiamiracle ran another solid race and could also benefit from 1m, her half-sister having won over that trip. (op 10-1)
Findhornbay appeared to not quite last home on this step up to 7f. A similarly positive ride returned to 6f may result in a victory. (op 9-1)
Emman Bee(IRE) looked on a stiff enough mark for this nursery debut, but ran a race full of promise, keeping on late and looking unlucky not to finish closer. There could be more to come. Official explanation: jockey said filly missed the break
Gabrial's Bounty(IRE), back up to 7f for this handicap debut, never got into it but wasn't favoured in being held up and can leave this form behind in time. (op 7-1 tchd 6-1)
Authora(IRE) showed little on this nursery debut, but is presumably thought capable of better. (tchd 13-2 and 15-2)

7052 BRITISH STALLION STUDS SUPPORTING BRITISH RACING E B F FOSSE WAY MAIDEN STKS 5f 218y
2:30 (2:30) (Class 4) 2-Y-O **£4,334** (£1,289; £644; £322) **Stalls** High

Form RPR

0 **1** **Dakota Canyon (IRE)**[13] 6768 2-9-3 0........................... TonyHamilton 1 76+
(Richard Fahey) *a.p: pushed along over 2f out: rdn and r.o to ld towards fin* **14/1**

43 **2** *hd* **Kyleakin Lass**[26] 6449 2-8-12 0.. TomQueally 2 70
(Ian Wood) *led 1f: trckd ldrs: led over 1f out: rdn and edgd rt ins fnl f: hdd towards fin* **4/1**[3]

5 **3** *2* **Peter Anders**[26] 6448 2-9-3 0.. JoeFanning 6 69+
(Mark Johnston) *s.i.s: sn prom: pushed along over 2f out: styd on: nt rch ldrs* **3/1**[2]

43 **4** *1 1/2* **Springheel Jake**[10] 6836 2-9-3 0... DavidNolan 3 64
(Ann Duffield) *chsd ldr: rdn and ev ch 2f out: no ex ins fnl f* **10/1**

2 **5** *nk* **Madgenta (IRE)**[14] 6751 2-8-12 0.. RyanMoore 4 58
(Richard Hannon) *led 5f out: rdn: edgd rt and hdd over 1f out: no ex ins fnl f* **13/8**[1]

6 **6** *4 1/2* **Tioman Pearl**[19] 6629 2-9-3 0.. NeilCallan 7 48
(Roger Varian) *chsd ldrs: rdn over 1f out: wknd fnl f* **14/1**

7 *2 1/2* **Desert Red (IRE)** 2-8-12 0.. PatCosgrave 8 35
(George Baker) [illegible] *wknd wl over 1f out* **28/1**

00 **8** *7* **Moataz (USA)**[13] 6768 2-8-12 0.. DarylByrne(5) 5 18
(Mark Johnston) *hld up: racd keenly: pushed along 1/2-way: wknd 2f out* **66/1**

1m 12.8s (-0.20) **Going Correction** -0.15s/f (Firm) **8** Ran SP% **110.5**
Speed ratings (Par 97): **95,94,92,90,89 83,80,71**
toteswingers:1&2:£7.70, 1&3:£6.40, 2&3:£2.70 CSF £64.52 TOTE £21.60: £2.90, £1.90, £1.30; EX 96.80.
Owner Mrs Una Towell **Bred** P J Towell **Trained** Musley Bank, N Yorks

FOCUS
A fair maiden likely to produce winners, though the time was 0.35 seconds slower than the later fillies' maiden, which looked modest. The form is straightforward but limited, rated around the runner-up and fourth.

NOTEBOOK
Dakota Canyon(IRE), a half-brother to a 6f 2-y-o Listed winner, offered little encouragement here on his debut over 7f, but knew considerably more on this occasion and, having moved up going well, simply outstayed the runner-up. He's very much the type to do better at three, and could develop into a useful handicapper. (op 20-1)
Kyleakin Lass again displayed plenty of speed, travelling strongly up on the pace, but she was soon challenged by the winner, having gone on, and couldn't quite see it out as well. She's shown more than enough to win a standard maiden and, given her pedigree, a return to slower conditions should suit, as may a drop to 5f. (op 11-4)
Peter Anders ◆, who was well backed, is bred to want further, but still stepped up on his debut effort. Slower conditions will help and he looks a certain future winner. (op 9-2)
Springheel Jake is now qualified for a mark and should fare better in handicaps. (op 17-2)
Madgenta(IRE) had made such a promising debut at Windsor, but this time dropped away having been made plenty of use of. She wasn't her at her best and deserves another chance. (tchd 5-4)
Tioman Pearl looks one for low-grade handicaps next season. (op 12-1)

7053 SIR GORDON RICHARDS CONDITIONS STKS 1m 3f 183y
3:00 (3:00) (Class 3) 3-Y-O+ **£6,490** (£1,942; £971; £486; £242) **Stalls** Low

Form RPR

013 **1** **Sadeek's Song (USA)**[16] 6704 3-8-13 **92**........................... RyanMoore 5 107
(Mahmood Al Zarooni) *a.p: chsd ldr over 8f out: led over 3f out: rdn over 1f out: styd on wl* **4/1**[2]

4344 **2** *1 1/2* **Colombian (IRE)**[43] 5987 3-8-13 **115**.............................. WilliamBuick 4 105
(John Gosden) *chsd ldr over 3f: remained handy: chsd wnr 3f out: ev ch over 1f out: hung rt and styd on same pce ins fnl f* **4/6**[1]

6002 **3** *2 3/4* **Al Shemali**[31] 6301 7-9-8 **103**... AhmedAjtebi 2 102
(Mahmood Al Zarooni) *prom: pushed along over 3f out: rdn over 1f out: styd on same pce* **10/1**

1 **4** *3/4* **Late Telegraph (IRE)**[55] 5585 3-8-13 **90**............................. TomQueally 3 99
(Sir Henry Cecil) *s.i.s: hld up: hdwy over 3f out: rdn over 1f out: no ex fnl f* **11/2**[3]

2404 **5** *4* **Borug (USA)**[30] 6342 3-8-9 **86**... TedDurcan 1 89
(Saeed Bin Suroor) *hld up: hdwy over 5f out: rdn and wknd over 1f out* **22/1**

6 *19* **Cloudy Spirit**[170] 6-8-11 0.. DavidProbert 6 58
(Reg Hollinshead) *led: rdn and hdd over 3f out: wknd over 2f out* **66/1**

2m 33.02s (-0.88) **Going Correction** -0.15s/f (Firm)
WFA 3 from 6yo+ 7lb **6** Ran SP% **110.3**
Speed ratings (Par 107): **96,95,93,92,90 77**
toteswingers:1&2:£1.90, 1&3:£2.40, 2&3:£1.20 CSF £6.82 TOTE £5.40: £1.50, £1.20; EX 6.50.
Owner Godolphin **Bred** Darley **Trained** Newmarket, Suffolk

FOCUS
An interesting conditions event rated at something like face value, apart from the runner-up 12lb off his French Group form.

NOTEBOOK
Sadeek's Song(USA) confirmed the good impression he created when a running-on third at York the time before, relishing the step up to 1m4f. Soon prominent, the son of Kingmambo looked vulnerable when the favourite drew alongside, seemingly travelling the better, but he responded well and really grabbed the ground late on. This was just his fourth start and he looks capable of winning at Listed/Group3 level at least, with a trip to the Dubai Carnival surely on the cards. (op 5-1)
Colombian(IRE)'s placed efforts in several notable French Group races this season looked easily the best form on offer, and he had an obvious chance on official figures. He'd missed the Group 3 St Simon Stakes at the weekend on account of the ground being quick, but it was similar here and, having travelled up well, he appeared to be outstayed by the winner. Perhaps he was reluctant to fully let himself down on the ground, but either way he was disappointing and clearly has a bit to prove. (tchd 8-11)
Al Shemali ran about as well as could have been expected considering the weight he was conceding to the 3-y-os. (op 9-1 tchd 17-2)
Late Telegraph(IRE), a once-raced maiden winner who wore a hood on his debut, showed ability whilst not looking as battle-hardened as some. Rated 90, he remains capable of better and is with the right trainer. (tchd 5-1 and 6-1)
Borug(USA) faced a tough task, but isn't progressing. His rating will continue to tumble, though, and he may soon be of some interest switched back to handicaps. (op 18-1)

7054 SIS LIVE H'CAP (DIV II) 1m 60y
3:30 (3:30) (Class 4) (0-80,80) 3-Y-O+ **£3,969** (£1,188; £594; £297; £148) **Stalls** Low

Form RPR

0351 **1** **Iron Step**[47] 5835 3-9-2 **78**..(t) WilliamBuick 8 88+
(Nicky Vaughan) *chsd ldr tl led over 1f out: sn rdn: r.o* **10/1**

3110 **2** *1 1/2* **Moone's My Name**[40] 6062 3-9-3 **79**................................... JimCrowley 2 85
(Ralph Beckett) *chsd ldrs: rdn over 1f out: r.o* **7/1**

1256 **3** *1/2* **Bakoura**[40] 6062 3-9-0 **76**.. RichardHills 6 81+
(John Dunlop) *s.i.s: hld up: hdwy over 1f out: edgd rt: r.o: nt rch ldrs* **9/2**[2]

0046 **4** *shd* **Amethyst Dawn (IRE)**[39] 6079 5-9-5 **78**............................ TedDurcan 7 83
(Tim Easterby) *led: rdn and hdd over 1f out: styd on* **12/1**

0210 **5** *3/4* **Quadrant (IRE)**[26] 6457 3-9-4 **80**.........................(b) RyanMoore 5 83
(Brian Meehan) *a.p: pushed along over 3f out: styd on* **6/1**[3]

-220 **6** *3* **Present Danger**[40] 6062 3-9-0 **76**................................ RobertWinston 4 72
(Tom Dascombe) *hld up: pushed along over 3f out: rdn and swtchd lft over 1f out: hung rt and styd on ins fnl f: nvr nrr* **4/1**[1]

0050 **7** *2 1/4* **Follow The Flag (IRE)**[15] 6727 7-8-4 **66**........................(p) JohnFahy(3) 1 57
(Alan McCabe) *hld up: rdn over 1f out: n.d* **12/1**

-022 **8** *4* **Little Curtsey**[25] 6477 3-9-3 **79**.. JoeFanning 9 61
(Hughie Morrison) *trckd ldrs: racd keenly: effrt and n.m.r over 1f out: wknd ins fnl f* **9/2**[2]

0-00 **9** *4* **Elkmait**[25] 6477 3-9-1 **77**.. TomQueally 3 49
(Clive Brittain) *hld up: pushed along over 3f out: wknd 2f out* **33/1**

2000 **10** *1* **Taqaat (USA)**[34] 6239 3-8-13 **75**... LukeMorris 10 45
(Tim McCarthy) *chsd ldrs: rdn over 2f out: wknd over 1f out* **66/1**

402 **11** *14* **Russian Affair**[14] 6750 3-8-10 **72**.. NeilCallan 11 —
(Roger Varian) *sn pushed along in rr: hung rt and reminder 6f out: bhd whn rdn and hung rt over 2f out* **18/1**

1m 44.21s (-0.89) **Going Correction** -0.15s/f (Firm)
WFA 3 from 5yo+ 3lb **11** Ran SP% **117.3**
Speed ratings (Par 105): **98,96,96,95,95 92,89,85,81,80 66**
toteswingers:1&2:£7.70, 1&3:£7.40, 2&3:£7.50 CSF £78.15 CT £370.80 TOTE £14.40: £4.00, £1.10, £3.00; EX 72.30.
Owner Andrew Tinkler **Bred** Brook Stud Bloodstock Ltd **Trained** Helshaw Grange, Shropshire

FOCUS
The time of this second division was 0.33 seconds slower than the first. The form is rated around the placed horses.
Little Curtsey Official explanation: vet said filly bled from the nose

7055 GUMLEY CLAIMING STKS 7f 9y
4:00 (4:00) (Class 6) 3-4-Y-O **£1,617** (£481; £240; £120) **Stalls** High

Form RPR

01/0 **1** **Regency Art (IRE)**[61] 5371 4-8-5 62................................. JoeFanning 11 76+
(David Nicholls) *chsd ldrs: led over 1f out: shkn up: styd on wl* **8/1**

2203 **2** *1 3/4* **Cootehill Lass (IRE)**[27] 6433 3-8-4 70.......................(p) AndreaAtzeni 4 70
(David Evans) *hld up: pushed along 1/2-way: hdwy over 2f out: edgd rt and styd on to go 2nd ins fnl f: nt rch wnr* **11/4**[2]

4406 **3** *1/2* **Tro Nesa (IRE)**[24] 6502 3-7-12 68..................................... NickyMackay 3 63
(Ann Duffield) *prom: pushed along over 2f out: styd on* **11/1**

1622 **4** *nk* **Boy The Bell**[20] 6617 4-8-5 73.. DavidProbert 10 67
(Brian Ellison) *led to 1/2-way: rdn over 2f out: ev ch over 1f out: no ex ins fnl f* **9/4**[1]

1035 **5** *1 3/4* **Flying Phoenix**[6] 6936 3-7-9 63............................(b) NataliaGemelova(3) 9 58
(Gay Kelleway) *hld up: plld hrd: hdwy: swtchd rt and nt clr run over 1f out and ins fnl f: nt trble ldrs* **12/1**

1230 **6** *1 1/4* **My Lord**[13] 6767 3-9-1 67... LukeMorris 1 71?
(Ronald Harris) *hld up in tch: rdn and ev ch over 1f out: wknd ins fnl f* **22/1**

3000 **7** *1 3/4* **Matavia Bay (IRE)**[14] 6752 3-8-6 60.............................. HarryBentley(3) 2 60
(Alan Jarvis) *chsd ldrs: led 1/2-way: hdd over 1f out: wknd fnl f* **12/1**

1600 **8** *1 3/4* **Layla Jamil (IRE)**[14] 6759 3-8-4 73 ow1............................ JohnFahy(3) 6 54
(Mick Channon) *chsd ldrs: rdn over 2f out: wknd fnl f* **13/2**[3]

3002 **9** *4 1/2* **Dimaire**[13] 6767 4-8-2 55 ow2.. FrankieMcDonald 7 34
(Derek Haydn Jones) *plld hrd and prom: outpcd 1/2-way: n.d after* **28/1**

0006 **10** *3 1/2* **Gertmegalush (IRE)**[39] 6091 4-8-5 57.............................. WilliamCarson 8 28
(John Harris) *s.i.s: sn pushed along in rr: lost tch fnl 2f* **40/1**

0430 **11** *6* **Sophie's Beau (USA)**[20] 6618 4-8-4 50........................ ChrisDCogan(5) 5 16
(Michael Chapman) *s.s: hdwy to join ldrs over 4f out: wknd over 2f out*
80/1

1m 24.72s (-1.48) **Going Correction** -0.15s/f (Firm)
WFA 3 from 4yo 2lb **11** Ran SP% **117.1**
Speed ratings (Par 101): **102,100,99,99,97 95,93,91,86,82 75**
toteswingers:1&2:£5.50, 1&3:£9.80, 2&3:£7.40 CSF £29.27 TOTE £10.80: £2.30, £1.70, £2.90; EX 39.30.Layla Jamil was claimed by Mr A Bailey for £10,000. Regency Art was claimed by Mr R A Harris for £6,000.
Owner D Nicholls **Bred** Rathasker Stud **Trained** Sessay, N Yorks

FOCUS
This looked a competitive claimer on paper but Regency Art won easily. The third is the best guide to the level.

7056 HOBY MEDIAN AUCTION MAIDEN FILLIES' STKS 5f 218y
4:30 (4:30) (Class 5) 2-Y-O **£2,264** (£673; £336; £168) **Stalls** High

Form RPR
035 **1** **Tinzapeas**[14] 6742 2-9-0 62.. NeilCallan 8 72
(Mick Channon) *chsd ldrs: led over 1f out: rdn and edgd rt ins fnl f: jst hld on*
14/1

44 **2** *nk* **Fanoos**[14] 6758 2-9-0 0.. RichardHills 11 71
(John Gosden) *prom: swtchd rt over 1f out: rdn to chse wnr ins fnl f: r.o*
6/4[1]

40 **3** *2 1/4* **Little Rainbow**[23] 6524 2-9-0 0.. AdamKirby 10 64
(Clive Cox) *chsd ldr tl led over 3f out: rdn and hdd over 1f out: styd on same pce ins fnl f*
9/2[2]

0 **4** *2 1/4* **Miriam's Song**[52] 5681 2-9-0 0.. FergusSweeney 3 58
(Stuart Kittow) *prom: rdn over 1f out: styd on same pce*
12/1

5 *hd* **Tenderly Place** 2-8-11 0.. HarryBentley(3) 7 57+
(William Knight) *s.s: hdwy over 2f out: styd on same pce fnl f*
33/1

6 *3 1/4* **Betty Brook (IRE)** 2-9-0 0.. TomMcLaughlin 2 47
(Nick Littmoden) *in rr: hdwy over 1f out: edgd lft ins fnl f: nt trble ldrs* **50/1**

00 **7** *3* **How Sweet It Is (IRE)**[147] 2542 2-9-0 0.. TomQueally 12 38
(James Bethell) *mid-div: pushed along over 3f out: rdn and wknd over 1f out*
7/1

00 **8** *1 3/4* **Aubrietia**[14] 6758 2-9-0 0.. TedDurcan 6 33
(Edward Vaughan) *hld up: rdn over 2f out: n.d*
50/1

0 **9** *6* **Throne**[20] 6603 2-9-0 0.. RyanMoore 4 15
(Richard Hannon) *s.i.s: a in rr*
11/2[3]

3540 **10** *1 3/4* **Maltease Ah**[82] 4662 2-9-0 65..(p) JimCrowley 13 10
(Andrew Reid) *led: hdd over 3f out: wknd 2f out*
16/1

11 *17* **Miss Boom Boom** 2-9-0 0.. AndreaAtzeni 1 —
(Chris Dwyer) *s.s: outpcd*
100/1

1m 12.45s (-0.55) **Going Correction** -0.15s/f (Firm) **11** Ran SP% **114.2**
Speed ratings (Par 92): **97,96,93,90,90 86,82,79,71,69 46**
toteswingers:1&2:£6.40, 1&3:£9.60, 2&3:£2.90 CSF £34.01 TOTE £15.50: £3.10, £1.50, £1.70; EX 41.60.
Owner M Channon **Bred** Mike Channon Bloodstock Ltd **Trained** West Ilsley, Berks

FOCUS
Few got into what had looked a modest maiden, the winner boasting a rating of just 62. The time was 0.35 seconds faster than the earlier juvenile maiden over the same trip. The form looks limited.

NOTEBOOK
Tinzapeas, racing over 6f for the first time, looked vulnerable as the favourite switched to challenge, but kept pulling out more against the rail and deservedly held on. It's probable she'll prove best back over further in handicaps. (op 16-1)
Fanoos still appears quite weak. She rated the one to beat in modest company, and perhaps would have prevailed under a better ride, Richard Hills getting himself caught in behind runners before having to switch. That said, she had her chance and it's likely she'll do better next year. (op 13-8 tchd 11-8)
Little Rainbow, well beaten in an Ascot sales race the time before, appreciated the return to maiden company and looks one for low-grade handicaps now qualified. (op 6-1)
Miriam's Song improved on her initial effort and is another handicap prospect. (op 16-1 tchd 10-1)
Tenderly Place, whose dam was a 5f winner, looked in need of the experience so shaped quite well considering. (op 22-1)
Betty Brook(IRE) (op 33-1)
How Sweet It Is(IRE) needed this for a mark and never threatened. (op 13-2)
Throne was never in the race following a sluggish start, Ryan Moore giving this green filly an educational ride with the future in mind. She'll be one for next season. Official explanation: jockey said filly never travelled (op 9-2)
Miss Boom Boom Official explanation: jockey said filly missed the break

7057 AMATEUR JOCKEYS' ASSOCIATION INSURE THEIR MEMBERS H'CAP (FOR GENTLEMEN AMATEUR RIDERS) 7f 9y
5:00 (5:07) (Class 5) (0-70,68) 3-Y-O+ **£2,305** (£709; £354) **Stalls** High

Form RPR
0000 **1** **Steed**[14] 6759 4-10-9 68..(b) MrFMitchell(5) 9 83
(Richard Guest) *chsd ldrs: led over 1f out: pushed out*
14/1

5056 **2** *2 1/4* **Hayek**[39] 6081 4-10-1 60..(b) MrWEasterby(5) 4 69
(Tim Easterby) *a.p: rdn to chse wnr fnl f: styd on*
9/1

5316 **3** *3 3/4* **No Larking (IRE)**[42] 5992 3-10-11 67.. MrSWalker 5 66
(Henry Candy) *chsd ldrs: pushed along 1/2-way: rdn over 1f out: styd on same pce fnl f*
11/2[2]

3032 **4** *shd* **Flying Applause**[13] 6777 6-10-10 67..(bt) MrCMartin(3) 6 66
(Roy Bowring) *s.i.s: hld up: hdwy over 2f out: swtchd lft over 1f out: styd on*
9/1

0524 **5** *4* **Half A Crown (IRE)**[20] 6610 6-10-0 59 ow1.. MrJackSalmon(5) 10 47
(Peter Salmon) *chsd ldr: ev ch over 1f out: wknd ins fnl f*
20/1

6040 **6** *1* **Golden Taurus (IRE)**[17] 6664 3-10-9 65.. MrMarioBaratti 12 50
(J W Hills) *s.i.s: hld up: hdwy over 1f out: nt trble ldrs*
33/1

0140 **7** *1/2* **Divertimenti (IRE)**[12] 6802 7-10-5 64..(b) MrOGarner(5) 7 48
(Roy Bowring) *led: rdn and hdd over 1f out: sn wknd*
18/1

2510 **8** *nk* **George Thisby**[26] 6468 5-10-8 67.. MrPMillman(5) 15 50
(Rod Millman) *sn pushed along in rr: r.o ins fnl f: nvr nrr*
8/1[3]

1650 **9** *3/4* **Mazovian (USA)**[26] 6456 3-10-3 66.. MrRyanClark(7) 11 47
(Michael Chapman) *chsd ldrs: rdn 1/2-way: wknd over 1f out*
40/1

4014 **10** *1 3/4* **Prince Of Passion (CAN)**[10] 6847 3-10-3 62.. JamesBest(3) 17 38
(Derek Shaw) *s.i.s: sn mid-div: rdn over 2f out: n.d*
14/1

5365 **11** *3/4* **Merrjanah**[119] 3470 3-9-13 62.. MrAFrench(7) 3 36
(John Wainwright) *s.i.s: nvr nrr*
28/1

5100 **12** *1/2* **Sofias Number One (USA)**[13] 6777 3-9-11 60..(bt[1]) MrSAHuggan(7) 13 33
(Roy Bowring) *reluctant to post: s.i.s: outpcd: swtchd lft to r alone 3f out: nvr on terms*
25/1

6030 **13** *nk* **Heezararity**[21] 6583 3-10-12 68.. JackQuinlan 16 40
(Stuart Kittow) *sn pushed along in rr: n.d*
5/1[1]

603 **14** *nk* **Exchange**[5] 6944 3-10-5 68.. MrEdwardSibbick(7) 18 39
(Andrew Haynes) *prom: rdn over 2f out: wknd over 1f out*
16/1

-054 **15** *1 1/4* **Spiritual Art**[138] 2824 5-10-3 60..(t) MrMEnnis(3) 2 28
(Luke Dace) *hld up: wknd over 1f out*
25/1

0500 **16** *1 1/4* **Stamp Duty (IRE)**[30] 6343 3-9-11 60.. MrAaronJames(7) 14 24
(Suzzanne France) *prom over 4f*
33/1

4300 **17** *8* **Hand Painted**[25] 6479 5-10-3 62..(p) MrBJPoste(5) 8 —
(Anthony Middleton) *s.i.s: a in rr*
22/1

0116 **18** *3 1/4* **Mr Udagawa**[27] 6435 5-10-8 67..(p) MrRJWilliams(5) 1 —
(Bernard Llewellyn) *mid-div: sn pushed along: wknd over 2f out*
12/1

1m 24.5s (-1.70) **Going Correction** -0.15s/f (Firm)
WFA 3 from 4yo+ 2lb **18** Ran SP% **123.9**
Speed ratings (Par 103): **103,100,96,96,91 90,89,89,88,86 85,85,84,84,83 81,72,68**
toteswingers:1&2:£35.00, 1&3:£25.40, 2&3:£9.20 CSF £121.00 CT £795.53 TOTE £18.30: £3.80, £2.80, £2.00, £1.40; EX 204.90.
Owner EERC & Alison Ibbotson **Bred** Rosyground Stud **Trained** Stainforth, S Yorks

FOCUS
A competitive amateur riders' handicap, or at least it was on paper. The winner is rated close to his turf best with the runner-up to his mark.
Flying Applause Official explanation: jockey said gelding lost its tongue strap in running
T/Plt: £118.90 to a £1 stake. Pool:£53,268.85 - 327.04 winning tickets T/Qpdt: £17.80 to a £1 stake. Pool:£4,637.57 - 191.90 winning tickets CR

[6833] REDCAR (L-H)
Monday, October 24

OFFICIAL GOING: Good (good to firm in places; 8.6)
Wind: fresh 1/2 behind Weather: fine but very windy

7058 BRITISH STALLION STUDS SUPPORTING BRITISH RACING E B F MAIDEN FILLIES' STKS 6f
1:40 (1:40) (Class 5) 2-Y-O **£2,975** (£885; £442; £221) **Stalls** Centre

Form RPR
0342 **1** **Takealookatmenow (IRE)**[10] 6836 2-9-0 67.. AdrianNicholls 12 66+
(David Nicholls) *trckd ldrs: led over 3f out: pushed out*
11/4[1]

0 **2** *2 1/2* **Sweetnessandlight**[20] 6612 2-9-0 0.. MichaelStainton 10 58
(Jason Ward) *dwlt: sn chsng ldrs: styd on to take 2nd nr fin*
100/1

6434 **3** *3/4* **Headstight (IRE)**[10] 6836 2-9-0 53.. MickyFenton 4 56
(Paul Midgley) *chsd ldrs: swtchd lft jst ins fnl f: kpt on same pce*
16/1

4 *1/2* **It's My Time** 2-9-0 0.. MartinLane 2 54
(David Simcock) *s.i.s: hdwy over 2f out: kpt on fnl f*
6/1

5 *7* **Twilight Allure**[77] 2-8-11 0.. AmyRyan(3) 5 32
(Kevin Ryan) *chsd ldrs: wknd over 1f out*
33/1

6 *2 1/2* **Champagne Katie** 2-9-0 0.. TomEaves 3 24
(Bryan Smart) *towards rr: reminders 3f out: nvr nr ldrs*
9/1

00 **7** *1/2* **Naturalmente (IRE)**[11] 6820 2-9-0 0.. FrederikTylicki 9 22
(Kevin Ryan) *led over 2f: wknd over 1f out*
25/1

3 **8** *1/2* **Lady Mandy**[19] 6629 2-9-0 0.. PaulHanagan 6 20
(Richard Fahey) *sn outpcd and bhd: nvr on terms*
11/2[3]

06 **9** *nk* **Brave One (IRE)**[20] 6598 2-8-7 0.. ShirleyTeasdale(7) 8 19
(David Nicholls) *in rr: rdn 3f out: hung lft: sn bhd*
50/1

10 *1* **Italian Ice** 2-9-0 0.. DavidAllan 1 16
(Bryan Smart) *chsd ldrs on outer: drvn 3f out: wknd over 1f out*
16/1

0 **11** *1/2* **Lady Kashaan (IRE)**[26] 6448 2-9-0 0.. PJMcDonald 7 15
(Alan Swinbank) *in rr: bhd fnl 3f*
20/1

5 **12** *14* **Hurriya**[20] 6612 2-9-0 0..(p) KierenFallon 13 —
(Saeed Bin Suroor) *chsd ldrs: lost pl over 2f out: bhd whn eased ins fnl f*
4/1[2]

13 *2 1/2* **Solange (IRE)** 2-9-0 0.. DuranFentiman 11 —
(Tim Easterby) *s.s: a wl bhd: eased over 1f out*
33/1

1m 10.84s (-0.96) **Going Correction** -0.075s/f (Good) **13** Ran SP% **115.5**
Speed ratings (Par 92): **103,99,98,98,88 85,84,84,83,82 81,62,59**
toteswingers:1&2:£34.80, 1&3:£5.90, 2&3:£106.60 CSF £358.07 TOTE £3.40: £1.10, £30.00, £3.40; EX 152.40 TRIFECTA Not won..
Owner D Nicholls & Mrs S J Barker **Bred** Ian W Glenton **Trained** Sessay, N Yorks

FOCUS
This was a weak fillies' maiden and few landed a blow from off the pace, with the first four coming clear. The winner is rated just below her mark with minor improvement from the moderate third.

NOTEBOOK
Takealookatmenow(IRE) had made the frame in three of her four previous outings and she deservedly opened her account, completing the task in straightforward fashion. She was always perfectly placed and put the race to bed nearing the furlong pole. This daughter of Moss Vale set a clear standard here and it's unlikely she had to improve, but she ought to find her level in handicaps from here on. (op 15-8, tchd 3-1 in a place)
Sweetnessandlight showed the clear benefit of her debut experience on Fibresand and posted a greatly improved effort. She qualifies for nurseries after her next assignment
Headstight(IRE), having her seventh outing, finished a little closer to the winner than when beaten five lengths behind her over C&D ten days earlier and, rated 53, puts the form into perspective. (op 14-1)
It's My Time ◆ was solid enough in the betting for her racecourse debut without being strongly fancied. She was the only one to make an impact from off the pace and really caught the eye from 2f out. Back her next time if tried over a stiffer test. (tchd 5-1)
Twilight Allure shaped as though she'd come on for this return from a 77-day break.
Champagne Katie, well-bred, attracted good support beforehand but clearly needed the initial experience. (op 11-1 tchd 12-1)
Lady Mandy was never in the hunt and needs further. (op 6-1 tchd 7-1)
Hurriya raced in cheekpieces on this switch to turf and was most disappointing. (op 9-2 tchd 3-1)

7059 VOLTIGEUR RESTAURANT 2 COURSE SPECIAL £10.95 NURSERY 5f
2:10 (2:12) (Class 6) (0-65,65) 2-Y-O **£1,617** (£481; £240; £120) **Stalls** Centre

Form RPR
004 **1** **Emily Hall**[30] 6344 2-8-1 45.. DuranFentiman 10 50
(Bryan Smart) *in rr: gd hdwy stands' side over 1f out: styd on strly to ld nr fin*
33/1

6456 **2** *3/4* **Triggerlo**[29] 6384 2-8-12 56.. KierenFallon 13 58
(Mick Channon) *mid-div: drvn over 2f out: styd on wl fnl f: tk 2nd nr fin*
12/1

0404 **3** *nk* **Princess Banu**[16] 6695 2-9-2 60.. ChrisCatlin 15 61
(Mick Channon) *w ldrs: led last 100yds: hdd nr fin*
25/1

6561 **4** *1/2* **Uncle Timmy**[20] 6597 2-8-8 52.. PaulHanagan 2 51
(John Quinn) *chsd ldrs: kpt on same pce last 100yds*
8/1[3]

5040 **5** *nk* **Bitter Lemon**[11] 6821 2-8-10 57.. AmyRyan(3) 8 55
(Kevin Ryan) *mid-div: hdwy over 2f out: chsng ldrs over 1f out: styd on same pce*
20/1

065 **6** *hd* **Chicarito**[21] 6579 2-9-4 **62**....(p) IanMongan 5 59
(John Gallagher) *w ldrs: led over 1f out: hdd ins fnl f: no ex* **20/1**

0361 **7** *hd* **Wake Up Sioux (IRE)**[29] 6384 2-8-9 **56**.... AdamBeschizza(3) 14 53
(David C Griffiths) *in rr: hdwy over 2f out: styd on fnl f* **14/1**

23 **8** *3/4* **Red Shadow**[9] 6863 2-8-13 **57**.... AndrewMullen 16 51
(Alan Brown) *chsd ldrs: kpt on one pce over 1f out* **16/1**

2005 **9** *1/2* **Koalition (IRE)**[7] 6912 2-8-9 **58**....(v1) AshleyMorgan(5) 18 50
(David O'Meara) *chsd ldrs: kpt on one pce over 1f out* **22/1**

3424 **10** *1 1/2* **Wish Again (IRE)**[19] 6627 2-9-0 **58**.... AdrianNicholls 3 45
(David Nicholls) *led: hdd over 1f out: sn wknd* **6/1**[2]

50 **11** *1 1/2* **Verus Delicia (IRE)**[20] 6598 2-8-1 **50**.... NeilFarley(5) 7 31
(Patrick Morris) *mid-div: wknd 2f out* **20/1**

630 **12** *nk* **Made In The Shade**[154] 2346 2-8-8 **57**.... LMcNiff(5) 17 37
(Paul Midgley) *mid-div: drvn over 2f out: nvr a factor* **28/1**

2310 **13** *1 1/4* **Balm**[10] 6843 2-9-7 **65**.... PaddyAspell 9 41
(Patrick Morris) *mid-div: hdwy to chse ldrs over 2f out: wknd over 1f out* **33/1**

045 **14** *1 1/2* **Holy Angel (IRE)**[37] 6152 2-9-2 **60**....(b1) DavidAllan 19 30
(Tim Easterby) *chsd ldrs: lost pl over 1f out* **5/1**[1]

2323 **15** *1 1/4* **Regal Lady**[10] 6843 2-9-5 **63**....(p) FrederikTylicki 11 29
(David Brown) *dwlt: nvr a factor* **10/1**

005 **16** *1 3/4* **Phoenician Blaze**[10] 6836 2-8-9 **53**.... MartinLane 6 13
(Tim Etherington) *a in rr* **20/1**

5624 **17** *3/4* **Celestial Dawn**[36] 6186 2-8-12 **56**.... PJMcDonald 4 13
(John Weymes) *s.i.s: a towards rr* **6/1**[2]

6403 **18** *21* **Dolly Danca**[12] 6800 2-8-12 **56**.... MickyFenton 12 —
(Paul Midgley) *in rr: sddle slipped and heavily eased over 2f out: virtually p.u: t.o* **25/1**

58.01 secs (-0.59) **Going Correction** -0.075s/f (Good) **18** Ran SP% **126.1**
Speed ratings (Par 93): **101,99,99,98,98 97,97,96,95,93 90,90,88,85,83 80,79,46**
toteswingers:1&2:£74.00, 1&3:£152.60, 2&3:£56.60 CSF £351.90 CT £9708.35 TOTE £40.30: £6.10, £3.80, £6.40, £1.70; EX 676.20 TRIFECTA Not won..
Owner R & E Hall & Son **Bred** R & E Hall & Son **Trained** Hambleton, N Yorks

FOCUS
A low-grade nursery, run at a solid pace and the form is limited.

NOTEBOOK
Emily Hall came from near last to first in the second half of proceedings and opened her account at the fourth time of asking. She was dropping back in trip for this nursery debut and therefore it wasn't surprising to see her outpaced early. She really ate up the ground when switching nearside from 2f out, though, and there should be some more to come in this sphere back up in trip (tchd 40-1)
Triggerlo was another that got markedly outpaced before staying on strongly. He helps to set the level and looks well worth another try over further. (op 14-1)
Princess Banu, stablemate of the runner-up, fared best of those racing handily and she too can be used to rate the form around.
Uncle Timmy, somewhat free to post, held every chance and is evidently still on a workable mark.
Bitter Lemon left the impression the drop in trip went against him back on turf.
Chicarito was equipped with cheekpieces on this nursery debut and, despite wandering under pressure late on, posted his best effort so far under an aggressive ride. (op 16-1)
Wake Up Sioux(IRE), just 1lb higher, got going too late in the day. (op 11-1)
Holy Angel(IRE) wore blinkers for this switch to a nursery and didn't look to have an obvious excuse. (op 15-2)
Dolly Danca Official explanation: jockey said filly lost its action and saddle slipped

7060 EUROPEAN BREEDERS' FUND - DOUBLE TRIGGER MAIDEN STKS (FOR THE DOUBLE TRIGGER TROPHY) 1m 1f
2:40 (2:44) (Class 5) 2-Y-O **£2,975** (£885; £442; £221) **Stalls** Low

Form RPR

3 **1** **Future Security (IRE)**[13] 6774 2-9-3 0.... PaulHanagan 6 80+
(Saeed Bin Suroor) *chsd ldrs: t.k.h: drvn and outpcd over 5f out: hdwy and 3rd over 2f out: edgd lft: styd on to ld nr fin* **11/2**[3]

33 **2** *nk* **Zaeem**[13] 6771 2-9-3 0.... KierenFallon 9 79
(Mahmood Al Zarooni) *trckd ldr: led over 3f out: jnd 1f out: no ex and hdd towards fin* **11/4**[2]

5 **3** *1* **Touch Gold (IRE)**[30] 6334 2-9-3 0.... IanMongan 8 77+
(Sir Henry Cecil) *trckd ldrs: wnt 2nd over 2f out: upsides 1f out: kpt on same pce last 50yds* **4/5**[1]

0 **4** *13* **Queen's Estate (GER)**[13] 6774 2-9-3 0.... FrederikTylicki 10 51
(Mark Johnston) *led 1f: chsd ldrs: wknd 2f out* **20/1**

0 **5** *2 1/4* **Flashman**[16] 6697 2-9-0 0.... LeeTopliss(3) 7 47
(Richard Fahey) *restless in stalls: mid-div: sn pushed along: sme hdwy 4f out: nvr a factor* **50/1**

4 **6** *1 1/4* **Gucci D'Oro (USA)**[43] 5959 2-9-3 0.... MartinLane 11 44
(David Simcock) *in rr: reminder over 4f out: kpt on fnl 2f: nvr a factor* **18/1**

7 *12* **Border Hill Jack** 2-9-3 0.... LeeNewman 5 20
(Robin Bastiman) *s.i.s: nvr on terms* **100/1**

8 *1 3/4* **Oxbow (IRE)** 2-9-3 0.... ChrisCatlin 4 17
(Mahmood Al Zarooni) *chsd ldrs: edgd rt over 2f out: sn wknd* **20/1**

9 *2 1/4* **Sweet Grace** 2-8-12 0.... MichaelStainton 2 —
(David Brown) *rrd over bkwards bhd stalls: led after 1f: hdd over 3f out: wknd 2f out* **100/1**

0 **10** *10* **Vamoose**[13] 6774 2-9-3 0.... TomEaves 1 —
(Kevin Ryan) *s.i.s: reminders after s: bhd fnl 6f* **100/1**

0 **11** *18* **Beyond Hubris (IRE)**[121] 3382 2-9-3 0....(b1) MickyFenton 3 —
(Tom Tate) *dwlt: in rr: pushed along and bhd 6f out: t.o* **40/1**

1m 54.71s (1.71) **Going Correction** -0.075s/f (Good) **11** Ran SP% **119.8**
Speed ratings (Par 95): **89,88,87,76,74 73,62,60,58,50 34**
toteswingers:1&2:£1.70, 1&3:£2.30, 2&3:£1.90 CSF £20.59 TOTE £6.60: £2.00, £1.10, £1.10; EX 11.80 Trifecta £38.40 Pool £765.64 - 14.75 winning units..
Owner Godolphin **Bred** Mrs Vanessa Hutch **Trained** Newmarket, Suffolk

FOCUS
There was a fair pace on and the principals came clear from 2f out in a tight finish. The form is rated on the positive side.

NOTEBOOK
Future Security(IRE) responded to pressure late in the day and just got there where it mattered. Despite showing promise behind a useful prospect at Newcastle on his debut 13 days earlier, he still showed distinct signs of inexperience here and had plenty on his plate 4f out. He was expertly handled from thereon, however, and won a little cosily. A stiffer test should see him come into his own next year. (op 6-1)
Zaeem, who set the standard, was Godolphin's number one hope according to the betting and was sent on for home around 3f out. He only got picked off right at the finish and fully deserves to find an opening. (op 7-2)
Touch Gold(IRE) ◆ did look very short in the betting. He travelled up well in the home straight and threw down a decent challenge, but ultimately paid for refusing to settle early on. He should soon make amends. (op 8-11 tchd 10-11)
Queen's Estate(GER) was left behind by the first three before the 2f and was a tired horse at the finish. He needs more time. (tchd 22-1)

7061 SUBSCRIBE TO RACING UK (S) STKS 1m 2f
3:10 (3:10) (Class 6) 3-5-Y-O **£1,704** (£503; £251) **Stalls** Low

Form RPR

4230 **1** **Valantino Oyster (IRE)**[20] 6601 4-9-1 61.... PatrickMathers 4 69
(Tracy Waggott) *drvn to chse ldrs: led over 3f out: sn rdn: all out* **8/1**[3]

001 **2** *nse* **True To Form (IRE)**[9] 6872 4-9-6 74....(p) KierenFallon 12 74
(George Baker) *mid-div: effrt over 3f out: wnt 2nd 2f out: sn upsides: jst failed* **11/10**[1]

4000 **3** *10* **Christmas Light**[7] 6918 4-9-1 68....(p) DanielTudhope 14 49
(David O'Meara) *hld up towards rr: effrt over 3f out: hung lft and modest 3rd over 1f out* **9/2**[2]

6005 **4** *12* **Child Of Our Time (IRE)**[49] 5791 4-8-10 46.... DavidAllan 6 20
(Tracy Waggott) *s.i.s: kpt on fnl 2f: tk poor 4th towards fin* **12/1**

4212 **5** *3/4* **Chilledtothebone**[54] 5631 3-8-10 65....(tp) TomEaves 10 23
(Linda Stubbs) *hld up in mid-div: hdwy over 3f out: wknd over 1f out* **8/1**[3]

-600 **6** *1/2* **Convitezza**[27] 6049 5-8-10 32....(t) PaddyAspell 9 17
(Mike Sowersby) *in rr: kpt on fnl 2f: nvr on terms* **150/1**

/060 **7** *nk* **Freddie Bolt**[75] 4904 5-9-1 43....(p) LeeNewman 2 22
(Frederick Watson) *s.i.s: sn chsng ldrs: one pce fnl 3f* **100/1**

5346 **8** *3 1/2* **Goodmanyourself**[23] 6536 3-8-10 45....(b1) MickyFenton 5 15
(Paul Midgley) *led and sn clr: hdd over 3f out: sn lost pl* **25/1**

0514 **9** *4* **Fairy Mist (IRE)**[31] 6310 4-9-1 51....(p) FrederikTylicki 3 —
(Brian Rothwell) *chsd clr ldr: wknd 2f out* **12/1**

5600 **10** *2* **Valentine's Gift**[23] 6536 3-8-10 50.... ChrisCatlin 1 —
(Neville Bycroft) *dwlt: a in rr* **25/1**

0 **11** *3* **Eyeforglory**[33] 6264 5-8-10 0.... DuranFentiman 7 —
(Suzzanne France) *in rr: drvn 7f out* **66/1**

00-0 **12** *25* **Moonbalej**[10] 6833 4-8-10 50....(v) JulieBurke(5) 11 —
(Wilf Storey) *mid-div: lost pl over 3f out: sn bhd: virtually p.u: t.o* **66/1**

2m 5.40s (-1.70) **Going Correction** -0.075s/f (Good)
WFA 3 from 4yo+ 5lb **12** Ran SP% **115.7**
Speed ratings (Par 101): **103,102,94,85,84 84,84,81,78,76 74,54**
toteswingers: 1&2 £4.30, 1&3 £5.40, 2&3 £2.80 CSF £16.31 TOTE £11.80: £2.50, £1.20, £1.60; EX 33.20 Trifecta £105.80 Pool £772.74 - 5.40 winning units..There was no bid for the winner. True To Form was subject to a friendly claim.
Owner Mrs J Waggott **Bred** Des Vere Hunt Farm Co And Jack Ronan **Trained** Spennymoor, Co Durham
■ Stewards' Enquiry : Patrick Mathers seven-day ban: used whip with excessive frequency (Nov 9-12,14-16)

FOCUS
A weak seller and a very tight finish with the winner rated back to his winning Ripon form.

7062 MARKET CROSS JEWELLERS H'CAP 1m 6f 19y
3:40 (3:40) (Class 5) (0-70,70) 3-Y-O **£2,102** (£625; £312; £156) **Stalls** Low

Form RPR

2022 **1** **Body Language (IRE)**[21] 6577 3-9-5 **68**....(p) PaulHanagan 12 77+
(Ann Duffield) *trckd ldr: effrt over 3f out: chal over 1f out: led jst ins fnl f: kpt on* **7/2**[1]

4221 **2** *3/4* **Singzak**[20] 6601 3-9-7 **70**.... PaddyAspell 11 78+
(Michael Easterby) *led: qcknd over 4f out: jnd over 1f out: hdd jst ins fnl f: no ex* **9/2**[2]

4616 **3** *4 1/2* **Ad Value (IRE)**[20] 6600 3-8-8 **56** ow1.... PJMcDonald 8 59
(Alan Swinbank) *mid-div: hdwy over 3f out: kpt on to take 3rd last 50yds* **8/1**

0211 **4** *1* **Damascus Symphony**[13] 6775 3-9-4 **67**.... KierenFallon 4 67
(James Bethell) *hld up towards rr: hdwy over 3f out: hung lft and one pce fnl 2f* **9/2**[2]

0201 **5** *2 1/2* **Tigerino (IRE)**[9] 6876 3-8-2 **51** oh1.... DuranFentiman 10 48
(Chris Fairhurst) *hld up in mid-div: hdwy 3f out: nvr trbld ldrs* **12/1**

2413 **6** *1 1/4* **Lady Barastar (IRE)**[14] 6756 3-9-2 **68**.... AdamBeschizza(3) 7 63
(Walter Swinburn) *s.i.s: hld up in rr: effrt over 3f out: kpt on: nvr nr ldrs* **15/2**[3]

5000 **7** *1 1/4* **Dissetti (IRE)**[11] 6823 3-8-3 **52** ow1....(t) ChrisCatlin 6 45
(Sir Mark Prescott Bt) *hld up: hdwy 9f out: hmpd 3f out: one pce* **14/1**

4300 **8** *4 1/2* **Madrasa (IRE)**[13] 6775 3-8-7 **56**....(t) TomEaves 3 43
(Keith Reveley) *mid-div: drvn over 4f out: wkng whn n.m.r on inner 3f out* **12/1**

1025 **9** *1/2* **Hal Of A Lover**[12] 5489 3-8-10 **59**.... DanielTudhope 1 45
(David O'Meara) *in tch: wnt modest 3rd 3f out: wknd over 1f out* **25/1**

2155 **10** *2 3/4* **Silver Tigress**[39] 6082 3-8-10 **59**.... PatrickMathers 2 41
(George Moore) *stdd s: hld up in rr: effrt and sme hdwy over 3f out: wknd fnl 2f* **25/1**

0320 **11** *24* **Srimenanti**[9] 6870 3-8-8 **57**....(p) FrederikTylicki 5 —
(Brian Rothwell) *chsd ldrs: pushed along 9f out: lost pl over 3f out: sn bhd: eased: t.o* **25/1**

3m 4.74s (0.04) **Going Correction** -0.075s/f (Good) **11** Ran SP% **115.1**
Speed ratings (Par 101): **96,95,93,92,91 90,89,86,86,85 71**
toteswingers: 1&2 £3.60, 1&3 £9.10, 2&3 £9.70 CSF £17.82 CT £114.10 TOTE £4.10: £1.30, £1.70, £3.00; EX 20.20 Trifecta £122.40 Pool £875.15 - 5.29 winning units..
Owner Mrs Anne Morrissey **Bred** Michael Morrissey **Trained** Constable Burton, N Yorks

FOCUS
This moderate 3-y-o staying handicap appeared to be run at a sound pace, but the first pair dominated from the outset. The form makes sense but is not rated too positively.

7063 BOOK YOUR CHRISTMAS PARTIES @ REDCAR RACECOURSE MAIDEN STKS 7f
4:10 (4:14) (Class 5) 3-Y-O+ **£2,102** (£625; £312; £156) **Stalls** Centre

Form RPR

0220 **1** **Hoppy's Flyer (FR)**[10] 6840 3-8-12 66.... MickyFenton 11 58
(Paul Midgley) *hld up towards rr: hdwy 2f out: r.o to ld ins fnl f: hld on towards fin* **9/2**[3]

2 *nk* **True Satire** 3-8-12 0.... IvaMilickova 16 57
(Jane Chapple-Hyam) *w ldrs: rdn and hung lft over 1f out: kpt on towards fin* **20/1**

3 **3** *1 1/4* **Pulsatilla**[94] 4286 3-8-12 0.... TomEaves 10 54
(Bryan Smart) *trckd ldrs: effrt 2f out: styd on same pce last 100yds* **9/1**

05 **4** *nse* **Ornithologist (USA)**[12] 6804 3-9-3 0.... DanielTudhope 15 58
(David O'Meara) *in rr: hdwy 2f out: styng on at fin* **8/1**

30 **5** *nse* **Darsan (IRE)**[25] 6473 3-8-12 0.... ChrisCatlin 6 53
(Chris Wall) *chsd ldrs: effrt over 1f out: kpt on ins fnl f* **10/3**[1]

0240 **6** *1/2* **Billy Cadiz**[33] 6262 6-8-12 44.... JacobButterfield(7) 3 57
(Mark Campion) *mde most: hdd last 150yds: no ex* **25/1**

0000 **7** *2* **Fama Mac**[58] 5470 4-9-5 50 .... IanMongan 14 52?
(Neville Bycroft) *chsd ldrs: one pce fnl 2f* **25/1**
6420 **8** *hd* **Andiamo Via**[63] 5314 4-9-5 58 .... PJMcDonald 1 51
(Michael Smith) *wknd last 75yds* **4/1**[2]
3- **9** *3 1/4* **Menha**[428] 5324 3-8-7 0 .... JulieBurke(5) 12 37
(John Gallagher) *gave problems and uns rdr in stalls: trckd ldrs: wknd over 1f out* **9/1**
45 **10** *1* **Think**[49] 5792 4-9-5 0 .... PaddyAspell 7 40
(Clive Mulhall) *in rr: nvr a factor* **25/1**
0060 **11** *shd* **Blue Rum (IRE)**[20] 6602 4-9-0 45 .... AdamCarter(5) 4 39
(Alan Kirtley) *w ldrs: wknd over 1f out* **66/1**
12 *1/2* **Crystal Child** 3-8-12 0 .... DuranFentiman 5 33
(Brian Rothwell) *a towards rr* **66/1**
00-0 **13** *9* **Zoom In**[150] 2465 3-8-12 45 ....(t) DanielleMcCreery(5) 13 14
(Lee James) *s.s: bhd fnl 3f* **100/1**
14 *1/2* **Ripristini (IRE)** 3-9-3 0 .... FrederikTylicki 2 12
(Patrick Holmes) *in rr: bhd fnl 3f* **16/1**
15 *15* **Cara's Delight (AUS)** 4-9-0 0 .... LeeNewman 8 —
(Frederick Watson) *s.s: a bhd: t.o* **100/1**

1m 24.1s (-0.40) **Going Correction** -0.075s/f (Good)
WFA 3 from 4yo+ 2lb **15** Ran SP% **119.5**
Speed ratings (Par 103): **99,98,97,97,97 96,94,94,90,89 89,88,78,77,60**
toteswingers: 1&2 £21.30, 1&3 £27.80, 2&3 £7.50 CSF £97.39 TOTE £3.30: £1.30, £9.30, £3.00; EX 141.60 Trifecta £460.50 Part won. Pool £622.43 - 0.93 winning units..
Owner Gap Personnel **Bred** Georges Sandor **Trained** Westow, N Yorks
■ Stewards' Enquiry : Iva Milickova nine-day ban: used whip with excessive frequency (Nov 9-12,14-18)

FOCUS
A very weak maiden with the majority of the principals well below their best marks and the sixth and seventh holding the form down.

7064 FOLLOW REDCARRACING ON FACEBOOK & TWITTER APPRENTICE H'CAP (DIV I) 6f
4:40 (4:44) (Class 6) (0-65,65) 3-Y-O+ **£1,293** (£385; £192; £96) **Stalls** Centre

Form RPR
050 **1** **Henry Morgan**[13] 6779 4-9-0 **61** .... JustinNewman(3) 11 70
(Bryan Smart) *tubed: s.i.s: hdwy 2f out: styd on to ld clsng stages* **5/2**[1]
4205 **2** *hd* **Winning Draw (IRE)**[20] 6615 3-8-2 **54** ....(b) RichardOld(7) 2 62
(Paul Midgley) *mde most: hdd and no ex clsng stages* **8/1**
0110 **3** *1 1/4* **Secret City (IRE)**[13] 6779 5-9-7 **65** ....(b) LMcNiff 6 69
(Robin Bastiman) *chsd ldrs: upsides over 1f out: kpt on same pce last 100yds* **5/1**[2]
061 **4** *1/2* **Bond Blade**[20] 6615 3-9-4 **63** .... AdamCarter 9 65
(Geoffrey Oldroyd) *chsd ldrs: kpt on same pce fnl f* **10/1**
4530 **5** *1/2* **Lady Del Sol**[10] 6840 3-8-10 **60** ....(p) GeorgeChaloner(5) 5 61
(Marjorie Fife) *s.s: hdwy over 2f out: upsides over 1f out: kpt on same pce* **6/1**[3]
1006 **6** *3/4* **Ryedane (IRE)**[33] 6266 9-9-1 **64** ....(b) DavidSimmonson(5) 3 62
(Tim Easterby) *in rr: kpt on fnl 2f: nvr trbld ldrs* **20/1**
0302 **7** *nk* **Fair Bunny**[54] 5620 4-8-7 **51** oh4 ....(b) NeilFarley 1 48
(Alan Brown) *w ldr: one pce over 1f out* **20/1**
0000 **8** *4 1/2* **Durham Express (IRE)**[18] 6646 4-8-11 **55** .... AshleyMorgan 8 38
(Michael Dods) *w ldrs: wknd over 1f out* **20/1**
5004 **9** *hd* **Eqtiraab (IRE)**[10] 6834 3-9-5 **64** ....(b[1]) BrianToomey 7 46
(Tony Coyle) *dwlt: effrt over 2f out: wknd over 1f out* **11/1**
034 **10** *4 1/2* **Andrasta**[47] 5824 6-8-7 **51** .... JulieBurke 4 19
(Alan Berry) *led to s: chsd ldrs: outpcd 2f out: sn wknd* **25/1**
2605 **11** *8* **Tombellini (IRE)**[37] 6158 4-8-7 **56** .... ShirleyTeasdale(5) 10 —
(David Nicholls) *dwlt: in rr: lost pl 2f out: sn bhd* **8/1**

1m 11.39s (-0.41) **Going Correction** -0.075s/f (Good)
WFA 3 from 4yo+ 1lb **11** Ran SP% **117.3**
Speed ratings (Par 101): **99,98,97,96,95 94,94,88,88,82 71**
toteswingers: 1&2 £7.20, 1&3 £4.70, 2&3 £8.30 CSF £21.20 CT £96.37 TOTE £4.70: £1.80, £2.90, £2.30; EX 28.00 Trifecta £302.60 Pool £744.35 - 1.82 winning units..
Owner Mrs F Denniff **Bred** A S Denniff **Trained** Hambleton, N Yorks

FOCUS
An ordinary sprint handicap, confined to apprentice riders and rated around the placed horses to previous course form.

7065 FOLLOW REDCARRACING ON FACEBOOK & TWITTER APPRENTICE H'CAP (DIV II) 6f
5:10 (5:10) (Class 6) (0-65,64) 3-Y-O+ **£1,293** (£385; £192; £96) **Stalls** Centre

Form RPR
0000 **1** **Insolenceofoffice (IRE)**[10] 6840 3-9-0 **58** ....(p) LMcNiff 2 67
(Bruce Hellier) *w ldrs: led over 1f out: kpt on wl* **10/1**
3000 **2** *1 1/2* **Greenhead High**[12] 6802 3-8-6 **55** .... ShirleyTeasdale(5) 8 59
(David Nicholls) *w ldrs: styd on same pce last 100yds* **14/1**
6430 **3** *3/4* **Red Scintilla**[26] 6450 4-8-5 **55** ....(p) DanielleMooney(7) 6 57
(Nigel Tinkler) *dwlt: hld up in rr: effrt 2f out: hung lft: styd on fnl f* **11/2**[3]
0054 **4** *1/2* **Sonny Red (IRE)**[28] 6414 7-9-2 **62** .... JustinNewman(3) 5 62
(David Nicholls) *chsd ldrs: kpt on same pce last 150yds* **10/3**[1]
0040 **5** *3/4* **Choc'A'Moca (IRE)**[18] 6646 4-9-0 **62** ....(v) DavidSimmonson(5) 11 60
(Paul Midgley) *racd along stands' side: in rr: edgd lft over 2f out: chsng ldrs over 1f out: kpt on same pce* **12/1**
0000 **6** *nk* **Rainy Night**[12] 6802 5-9-4 **64** ....(v) LucyKBarry(3) 4 61
(Reg Hollinshead) *chsd ldrs: one pce appr fnl f* **13/2**
4432 **7** *3/4* **Arch Walker (IRE)**[101] 4041 4-9-3 **63** ....(b[1]) CharlesBishop(3) 9 57
(John Weymes) *mde most: hdd over 1f out: wknd last 150yds* **7/2**[2]
-000 **8** *2 3/4* **Spirit Of Dixie**[10] 6848 4-8-7 **50** oh2 .... NeilFarley 1 36
(Noel Wilson) *w ldrs: lost pl over 1f out* **33/1**
0005 **9** *8* **Future Gem**[26] 6454 5-8-3 **51** oh5 ow1 ....(p) GeorgeChaloner(5) 3 11
(David Thompson) *dwlt: sme hdwy over 2f out: sn wknd: eased whn bhd* **66/1**
440 **10** *3 1/2* **Royal Blade (IRE)**[28] 6414 4-9-3 **60** .... JulieBurke 10 —
(Alan Berry) *in rr: lost pl over 1f out: eased whn bhd* **8/1**

1m 11.62s (-0.18) **Going Correction** -0.075s/f (Good)
WFA 3 from 4yo+ 1lb **10** Ran SP% **113.0**
Speed ratings (Par 101): **98,96,95,94,93 92,91,88,77,72**
toteswingers: 1&2 £25.50, 1&3 £13.30, 2&3 £20.00 CSF £136.02 CT £870.17 TOTE £14.40: £3.50, £4.50, £2.80; EX 173.10 TRIFECTA Not won..
Owner CCCNLP **Bred** Gerard Kennedy **Trained** Garstang, Lancs
■ Stewards' Enquiry : Shirley Teasdale seven-day ban: used whip with excessive frequency (Nov 9-12,14-15,tbn)

FOCUS
The second division of the apprentice handicap was another ordinary event. The pair of 3-y-os filled the first two places and the third looks the best guide.

T/Jkpt: Not won. T/Plt: £69.80 to a £1 stake. Pool:£49,404.47 - 516.33 winning tickets T/Qpdt: £7.10 to a £1 stake. Pool:£4,575.20 - 475.90 winning tickets WG

6611 SOUTHWELL (L-H)
Monday, October 24

OFFICIAL GOING: Standard
Wind: Fresh against Weather: Fine, dry and blustery

7066 BRAMLEY APPLE MEDIAN AUCTION MAIDEN STKS 1m (F)
2:20 (2:21) (Class 6) 2-Y-O **£1,704** (£503; £251) **Stalls** Low

Form RPR
6 **1** **Halling's Quest**[26] 6463 2-9-3 0 .... RobertHavlin 6 86+
(Hughie Morrison) *trckd ldng pair: cl up 3f out: led 2f out: rdn clr appr fnl f: styd on wl* **6/5**[1]
2 *8* **Third Half** 2-9-3 0 .... SebSanders 2 67
(Tom Dascombe) *cl up on inner: led after 2f: rdn along and hdd 2f out: kpt on same pce appr fnl f* **9/2**[3]
3 *1 3/4* **Burnhope** 2-9-0 0 .... BillyCray(3) 5 63
(David Nicholls) *led 2f: cl up: rdn and ev ch 2f out: one pce appr fnl f* **16/1**
02 **4** *17* **Hunting Gonk**[18] 6644 2-9-3 0 .... JamesSullivan 4 23
(James Given) *chsd ldrs: rdn along 1/2-way: outpcd fr over 3f out* **7/2**[2]
00 **5** *5* **Tresabella**[48] 5806 2-8-12 0 .... NeilChalmers 1 7
(Michael Appleby) *chsd ldrs: rdn along 1/2-way: sn outpcd* **80/1**
6 *7* **Baileys Dutch** 2-9-3 0 .... LiamJones 3 —
(Mark Johnston) *dwlt and sltly hmpd s: sn rdn along and outpcd: a bhd* **5/1**

1m 45.27s (1.57) **Going Correction** +0.425s/f (Slow) **6** Ran SP% **109.6**
Speed ratings (Par 93): **109,101,99,82,77 70**
toteswingers:1&2:£2.00, 1&3:£7.00, 2&3:£8.40 CSF £6.63 TOTE £2.00: £1.40, £1.80; EX 10.30.
Owner The Fairy Story Partnership **Bred** Deepwood Farm Stud **Trained** East Ilsley, Berks

FOCUS
An interesting maiden and the time was 0.90 seconds quicker than the later Class 5 handicap for older horses, which helps back up the form.

NOTEBOOK
Halling's Quest won in good style and readily confirmed the promise he showed on his debut at Salisbury. He had the benefit of experience over the runner-up and third and it's hard to know exactly what he achieved, but he looks pretty useful. (op 9-4)
Third Half is a half-brother to the stable's St Leger runner-up Brown Panther (made winning debut here), but he lacks size and has already been gelded. He knew enough to lead early but was no match at all for the winner. (op 11-4)
Burnhope, out of a dual 5f winner, has already been gelded but showed ability. (op 12-1 tchd 11-1)
Hunting Gonk was never going and failed to get near his turf form. This was especially disappointing considering his dam was a three-time winner here. The representative of James Given reported the colt would not face the kickback. Official explanation: trainer's rep said colt would not face the kickback (op 3-1 tchd 4-1)
Baileys Dutch showed nothing on this debut. (op 6-1 tchd 9-2)

7067 FOLLOW AT THE RACES ON TWITTER NOVICE STKS 6f (F)
2:50 (2:50) (Class 5) 2-Y-O **£2,264** (£673; £336; £168) **Stalls** Low

Form RPR
3422 **1** **Quite A Thing**[9] 6863 2-9-2 84 .... SebSanders 3 76
(Sir Mark Prescott Bt) *sn pushed and niggled along in rr: swtchd outside and hdwy 1/2-way: rdn 2f out: chsd ldng pair and edgd lft ent fnl f: styd on strly to ld last 100yds* **8/11**[1]
0 **2** *1 1/2* **Wicked Wench**[14] 6744 2-8-10 0 ow1 .... StevieDonohoe 6 66
(Jo Hughes) *dwlt: sn in tch: hdwy to chse ldr 3f out: rdn to chal 1f out: led briefly ins fnl f: hdd and no ex last 100yds* **14/1**
2361 **3** *1 1/2* **Scrooby Doo**[20] 6612 2-8-11 70 .... BillyCray(3) 5 65
(David Nicholls) *led: qcknd clr 3f out: rdn wl over 1f out: edgd lft and jnd ent fnl f: sn hdd and one pce* **5/2**[2]
64 **4** *2 1/4* **Le King Beau (USA)**[10] 6837 2-9-0 0 .... BarryMcHugh 1 58
(Tony Coyle) *trckd ldrs: effrt 3f out: rdn 2f out and kpt on same pce* **8/1**[3]
0236 **5** *11* **Mousie**[4] 6975 2-8-11 66 .... MartinHarley 4 22
(Alan McCabe) *cl up: rdn along bef 1/2-way: sn wknd* **25/1**

1m 19.23s (2.73) **Going Correction** +0.425s/f (Slow) **5** Ran SP% **108.1**
Speed ratings (Par 95): **98,96,94,91,76**
CSF £11.47 TOTE £1.80: £1.20, £6.00; EX 10.40.
Owner Lady Fairhaven & The Hon C & H Broughton **Bred** Whitsbury Manor Stud & Pigeon House Stud **Trained** Newmarket, Suffolk

FOCUS
A weak novice event run at a quick pace and the third and fourth help set the level.

NOTEBOOK
Quite A Thing won despite not facing the kickback after a slow start and then taking an age to get into her stride when in the clear up the straight. She was matched at 140 on Betfair, but was helped by the leaders weakening and she didn't have to run to form. (tchd 4-6 and 4-5)
Wicked Wench, carrying 1lb overweight, stepped up on her Salisbury debut. (tchd 16-1)
Scrooby Doo, off the mark in a weak C&D maiden last time, failed to see her race out this time after setting a good pace. (op 11-4 tchd 9-4)
Le King Beau(USA) struggled on this drop in trip and switch to Fibresand. Handicaps are now an option.

7068 EXCLUSIVE BREEDERS CUP COVERAGE ON ATR H'CAP 1m (F)
3:20 (3:21) (Class 5) (0-70,70) 3-Y-O+ **£2,264** (£673; £336; £168) **Stalls** Low

Form RPR
0302 **1** **Dr Red Eye**[38] 6116 3-9-1 **70** .... BillyCray(3) 2 85+
(David Nicholls) *trckd ldrs on inner: hdwy to ld 2f out: rdn clr over 1f out: kpt on strly* **4/1**[1]
2233 **2** *4* **Elusive Warrior (USA)**[20] 6617 8-8-2 **58** ....(p) NoraLooby(7) 11 62
(Alan McCabe) *trckd ldrs: effrt on outer over 2f out: rdn wl over 1f out: kpt on ins fnl f: tk 2nd nr fin: no ch w wnr* **10/1**
4020 **3** *hd* **Tobrata**[100] 4111 5-8-9 **58** .... BarryMcHugh 4 62
(Mel Brittain) *towards rr: hdwy 2f out: rdn over 1f out: styd on ins fnl f: tk 3rd nr fin* **11/2**[3]
0503 **4** *nk* **On The Cusp (IRE)**[4] 6971 4-9-3 **66** ....(p) MartinHarley 7 69
(Richard Guest) *sn led: rdn along and hdd 2f out: wknd ent fnl f: lost 2nd nr fin* **5/1**[2]
4206 **5** *10* **Kishanda**[12] 6785 3-8-9 **61** .... RobertHavlin 9 41+
(Hughie Morrison) *hmpd and squeezed out s: bhd tl hdwy over 2f out: sn rdn and kpt on fnl f: nvr nr ldrs* **9/1**
2250 **6** *3/4* **San Antonio**[138] 2816 11-8-12 **68** ....(b) ChristyMews(7) 12 46
(Pam Sly) *bhd: swtchd rt and hdwy 2f out: styd on fnl f: nvr nr ldrs* **33/1**

315 **7** *1¾* **Desert Icon (IRE)**[12] 6794 5-9-4 **67**........................(bt) StephenCraine 10 41
(David Flood) *cl up: effrt over 2f out and sn rdn: ev ch tl wknd wl over 1f out* **20/1**

3461 **8** *3* **Emeralds Spirit (IRE)**[27] 6430 4-8-12 **61**.................... JamesSullivan 13 28
(John Weymes) *towards rr: hdwy and in tch 3f out: sn rdn: edgd lft and wknd* **20/1**

0444 **9** *3¾* **Anjomarba (IRE)**[11] 6814 4-9-4 **67**................................ KirstyMilczarek 5 26
(Conor Dore) *broke wl: chsd ldrs tl lost pl after 2f: bhd fr 1/2-way* **20/1**

2406 **10** *2* **Double Duchess**[37] 6181 3-8-11 **63**............................. MatthewDavies 3 17
(Paul D'Arcy) *a towards rr* **11/1**

0413 **11** *5* **Knowe Head (NZ)**[30] 6357 4-9-1 **64**.................................... LiamJones 1 —
(James Unett) *midfield: hdwy to chse ldrs 3f out: rdn over 2f out and sn wknd* **6/1**

0004 **12** *10* **Petomic (IRE)**[9] 6871 6-8-8 **57**................................(p) RobbieFitzpatrick 6 —
(Richard Guest) *chsd ldrs: rdn along wl over 2f out: sn wknd* **25/1**

400 **13** *19* **Neat Sweep (IRE)**[153] 2392 3-9-1 **67**........................... StevieDonohoe 8 —
(Alan McCabe) *a in rr: bhd fnl 3f* **40/1**

1m 46.17s (2.47) **Going Correction** +0.425s/f (Slow)
WFA 3 from 4yo+ 3lb **13** Ran SP% **117.3**
Speed ratings (Par 103): **104,100,99,99,89 88,87,84,80,78 73,63,44**
toteswingers:1&2:£12.30, 1&3:£6.20, 2&3:£9.50 CSF £38.66 CT £229.71 TOTE £6.50: £2.40, £4.20, £2.60; EX 36.30.
Owner The Red Eye Partnership **Bred** G E Amey **Trained** Sessay, N Yorks

FOCUS

A modest handicap won in convincing fashion. The solid runner-up is the best guide to the level.

Kishanda Official explanation: jockey said filly suffered interference at start

Anjomarba(IRE) Official explanation: jockey said filly never travelled

7069 ATTHERACES.COM EXCLUSIVE HUGH TAYLOR TIPPING MAIDEN STKS 7f (F)

3:50 (3:53) (Class 5) 3-Y-0+ **£2,385** (£704; £352) **Stalls** Low

Form RPR

1 **Take Cover** 4-9-5 0.. SebSanders 6 66
(George Margarson) *dwlt: sn trcking ldrs: hdwy 3f out: led wl over 1f out: sn clr: pushed out* **13/8[1]**

4 **2** *1½* **Enchanted Dream**[54] 5626 3-8-12 0............................... BarryMcHugh 3 57
(George Margarson) *pushed along and outpcd towards rr: swtchd wd and hdwy over 2f out: rdn over 1f out: styd on fnl f: nt rch wnr* **5/1[3]**

6600 **3** *6* **Carrside Lady**[39] 6096 5-9-0 35................................(b) LiamKeniry 5 41
(Garry Woodward) *cl up: led after 3f: rdn over 2f out: hdd wl over 1f out: kpt on same pce* **14/1**

00 **4** *4* **Apassionforfashion**[59] 5443 3-8-12 0............................ JamesSullivan 2 30
(Bryan Smart) *s.i.s and bhd: hdwy over 2f out: sn rdn and plugged on same pce: nvr nr ldrs* **20/1**

3003 **5** *3* **Totally Trusted**[20] 6616 3-8-5 58.................................. LeonnaMayor(7) 8 22
(David Nicholls) *dwlt: sn chsng ldrs on outer: rdn along over 2f out: hung lft wl over 1f out and sn wknd* **9/4[2]**

0-0 **6** *4½* **Callisto Light**[42] 5999 4-9-0 0... LiamJones 4 10
(George Prodromou) *chsd ldrs: rdn along 3f out: sn outpcd* **7/1**

0666 **7** *3* **Mrs Medley**[41] 6034 5-8-11 30.. BillyCray(3) 1 —
(Garry Woodward) *led 3f: cl up: rdn along 3f out: sn wknd* **100/1**

0005 **8** *3* **Gessabelle**[9] 6874 4-9-0 42..(t) KirstyMilczarek 7 —
(Phil McEntee) *in tch: rdn along 1/2-way: sn lost pl and bhd* **33/1**

1m 34.04s (3.74) **Going Correction** +0.425s/f (Slow)
WFA 3 from 4yo+ 2lb **8** Ran SP% **113.4**
Speed ratings (Par 103): **95,93,86,81,78 73,69,66**
toteswingers:1&2:£2.50, 1&3:£5.60, 2&3:£5.90 CSF £10.01 TOTE £2.90: £1.40, £1.80, £4.10; EX 7.40.
Owner Norcroft Park Stud **Bred** Norcroft Park Stud **Trained** Newmarket, Suffolk

FOCUS

A weak maiden but there was enough to like about the two George Margarson runners, who share the same dam and filled the first couple of places. The runner-up is probably the best guide to the level

7070 SIS LIVE H'CAP 1m 4f (F)

4:20 (4:20) (Class 5) (0-75,72) 3-Y-0+ **£2,264** (£673; £336; £168) **Stalls** Low

Form RPR

401- **1** **Marsh Warbler**[223] 6652 4-9-10 **70**.............................. BarryMcHugh 7 83
(Brian Ellison) *hld up and bhd: stdy hdwy over 4f out: chsd ldrs over 2f out: styd on wl to ld ins fnl f* **7/4[1]**

0302 **2** *3¼* **Amazing Blue Sky**[7] 6916 5-9-3 **63**............................ JamesSullivan 9 71
(Ruth Carr) *cl up: led over 3f out: rdn clr 2f out: hdd and no ex ins fnl f* **8/1[3]**

-631 **3** *9* **Hit The Switch**[144] 2656 5-9-4 **64**................................ StephenCraine 10 57
(Jennie Candlish) *trckd ldrs: hdwy over 4f out: rdn along over 2f out: sn one pce* **4/1[2]**

5000 **4** *4½* **Montegonian (USA)**[12] 6797 3-9-3 **70**............................ SebSanders 1 56
(Marcus Tregoning) *led: rdn along and hdd over 3f out: grad wknd* **12/1**

2100 **5** *9* **Calculating (IRE)**[17] 6666 7-9-6 **71**................................ LeeNewnes(5) 3 43
(Mark Usher) *s.i.s: a in rr* **16/1**

0146 **6** *10* **Resplendent Ace (IRE)**[3] 7002 7-9-3 **66**................. DeclanCannon(3) 5 22
(Karen Tutty) *chsd ldrs: rdn along 4f out: wknd over 3f out* **11/1**

-450 **7** *8* **Bariolo (FR)**[24] 6503 7-9-2 **62**... LiamKeniry 4 —
(Noel Chance) *chsd ldrs: rdn along over 4f out: sn outpcd* **20/1**

4221 **8** *2¼* **Baileys Agincourt**[209] 1028 3-9-1 **68**.................................. LiamJones 8 —
(Mark Johnston) *dwlt: a in rr: rdn along 1/2-way: t.o fnl 3f* **8/1[3]**

2432 **9** *43* **Lady Elsie**[57] 5512 3-9-5 **72**.. MartinHarley 2 —
(Alan McCabe) *prom: rdn along 5f out: sn wknd* **14/1**

6650 **P** **Kingaroo (IRE)**[9] 6870 5-8-9 **58**.. BillyCray(3) 6 —
(Garry Woodward) *towards rr and sn pushed along: rdn along bef 1/2-way: bhd and wd st: p.u 1f out* **22/1**

2m 45.26s (4.26) **Going Correction** +0.425s/f (Slow)
WFA 3 from 4yo+ 7lb **10** Ran SP% **116.3**
Speed ratings (Par 103): **102,99,93,90,84 78,72,71,42,—**
toteswingers:1&2:£5.60, 1&3:£2.70, 2&3:£5.10 CSF £16.30 CT £50.31 TOTE £1.60: £1.10, £2.90, £2.30; EX 21.50.
Owner Dan Gilbert & Kristian Strangeway **Bred** Darley **Trained** Norton, N Yorks

FOCUS

A modest handicap run at an overly strong gallop. The winner is rated to his old turf best with the runner-up in line with recent turf efforts at this trip.

Baileys Agincourt Official explanation: jockey said gelding never travelled

Lady Elsie Official explanation: trainer said filly was unsuited by the Fibresand surface

7071 PHRUIT'S PHINEST PHURLONGS APPRENTICE H'CAP 6f (F)

4:50 (4:50) (Class 6) (0-55,61) 3-Y-0+ **£1,704** (£503; £251) **Stalls** Low

Form RPR

6001 **1** **Princess Dayna**[3] 6999 3-9-2 **61** 6ex......................... BrendanPowell(5) 8 72
(Tom Dascombe) *trckd ldrs: hdwy 2f out: effrt to chal and n.m.r over 1f out: rdn to ld jst ins fnl f: styd on wl* **9/2[3]**

2405 **2** *1¾* **Fluctuation (IRE)**[20] 6618 3-8-12 **52**........................(v) DarylByrne 11 57
(Ian Williams) *dwlt and towards rr: hdwy over 2f out: rdn to chal over 1f out: led briefly ent fnl f: sn hdd: kpt on same pce* **6/1**

0502 **3** *hd* **Lethal**[20] 6618 8-8-11 **50**..(p) DavidKenny 1 54
(Richard Price) *trckd ldrs on inner: hdwy 3f out: cl up 2f out: rdn and ev ch whn edgd rt over 1f out: kpt on same pce fnl f* **12/1**

0044 **4** *¾* **Gracie's Gift (IRE)**[18] 6646 9-8-13 **52**............................(v) RaulDaSilva 5 54
(Richard Guest) *chsd ldrs: swtchd rt and hdwy wl over 1f out: sn rdn: styd on ins fnl f* **7/1**

4404 **5** *2½* **Stylistickhill (IRE)**[20] 6618 3-9-0 **54**........................(t) LeonnaMayor 3 48
(David Nicholls) *towards rr: hdwy on inner 2f out: sn rdn and kpt on appr fnl f: nrst fin* **4/1[2]**

0000 **6** *nk* **Scruffy Skip (IRE)**[55] 5601 6-8-4 **48**...........................(p) DanielHarris(5) 6 41
(Christine Dunnett) *led: rdn 2f out: drvn and hdd ent fnl f: sn wknd* **25/1**

6503 **7** *2* **Refusetosurrender (IRE)**[3] 6999 3-8-3 **48**.................(p) LauraBarry(5) 4 35
(Richard Fahey) *towards rr: sme hdwy on outer wl over 1f out: sn rdn and no imp* **11/4[1]**

1400 **8** *½* **Wotatomboy**[6] 6931 5-8-6 **48**.. LukeRowe(3) 9 33
(Richard Whitaker) *towards rr: sme hdwy on outer 2f out: rdn wl over 1f out: sn btn* **16/1**

0000 **9** *1* **Bird Dog**[34] 6238 5-8-2 **46** oh1......................................(v) DannyBrock(5) 12 28
(Phil McEntee) *chsd ldrs: rdn along over 2f out: wknd wl over 1f out* **100/1**

0000 **10** *1¼* **Norton Girl**[68] 5165 3-8-9 **49**.. GarryWhillans 10 27
(Michael Herrington) *dwlt: a in rr* **16/1**

530 **11** *8* **Tenancy (IRE)**[12] 6791 7-8-7 **49**.. JakePayne(3) 2 —
(Shaun Harris) *cl up: rdn along over 2f out: sn wknd* **16/1**

6006 **12** *nk* **Lujiana**[26] 6454 6-8-6 **50**... JasonHart(5) 7 —
(Mel Brittain) *a towards rr* **25/1**

1m 19.79s (3.29) **Going Correction** +0.425s/f (Slow)
WFA 3 from 5yo+ 1lb **12** Ran SP% **125.7**
Speed ratings (Par 101): **95,92,92,91,88 87,85,84,83,81 70,70**
toteswingers:1&2:£8.60, 1&3:£6.50, 2&3:£7.50 CSF £33.40 CT £320.91 TOTE £5.10: £1.70, £2.90, £2.30; EX 37.90.
Owner T Dascombe **Bred** Mrs J A Chapman **Trained** Malpas, Cheshire

FOCUS

A moderate sprint handicap rated around the placed horses.

T/Plt: £36.70 to a £1 stake. Pool:£53,838.97 - 1,070.37 winning tickets T/Qpdt: £13.60 to a £1 stake. Pool:£4,908.00 - 265.70 winning tickets JR

6863 CATTERICK (L-H)

Tuesday, October 25

OFFICIAL GOING: Soft (6.3)

7072 COWTHORPE MEDIAN AUCTION MAIDEN STKS 5f 212y

1:50 (1:54) (Class 6) 2-Y-0 **£1,704** (£503; £251) **Stalls** Low

Form RPR

4232 **1** **Idler (IRE)**[20] 6629 2-9-3 76.. SilvestreDeSousa 4 63
(Mark Johnston) *sn led: rdn wl over 1f out: kpt on* **1/2[1]**

0 **2** *¾* **Colbyor**[61] 5398 2-9-3 0.. TonyHamilton 12 61
(Richard Fahey) *chsd ldrs on outer: hdwy to chse wnr over 2f out: rdn to chal over 1f out: ev ch tl one pce ins fnl f* **10/1**

03 **3** *2½* **Sir Windsorlot (IRE)**[54] 5646 2-9-3 0.................................. TomEaves 2 53+
(John Quinn) [illegible] *after 2f: outpcd rt and rdn to chse ldng pair whn edgd lft ent fnl f: sn no imp* **9/2[2]**

5060 **4** *1* **Only Orsenfoolsies**[105] 3948 2-9-3 47.......................... FrederikTylicki 7 50
(Micky Hammond) *cl up: rdn along wl over 2f out: grad wknd* **100/1**

6600 **5** *2¾* **Villa Reigns**[10] 6866 2-9-3 51..(p) LukeMorris 6 42
(John Weymes) *chsd ldrs: rdn and wandered wl over 1f out: sn wknd* **66/1**

6 *2¼* **Forever Janey** 2-8-12 0.. JamesSullivan 3 30+
(Paul Green) *towards rr: hdwy 2f out: kpt on same pce* **33/1**

04 **7** *5* **Gone By Sunrise**[28] 6425 2-9-3 0.................................... PaulHanagan 1 20
(Richard Fahey) *chsd ldrs: rdn along 1/2-way: sn wknd* **9/1[3]**

600 **8** *nk* **Pavers Star**[17] 6702 2-9-3 0..(v[1]) DanielTudhope 8 19
(Noel Wilson) *prom: rdn along wl over 2f out: grad wknd* **150/1**

60 **9** *3¾* **Whip It In (IRE)**[18] 6673 2-8-12 0...................................... MickyFenton 5 3
(Paul Midgley) *s.i.s: a in rr* **20/1**

10 *¾* **Niceonemyson** 2-9-3 0.. PaddyAspell 11 6
(Christopher Wilson) *a in rr* **50/1**

00 **11** *9* **Confused Sphere (IRE)**[17] 6702 2-9-3 0...................... DuranFentiman 10 —
(Noel Wilson) *dwlt: a in rr* **100/1**

0000 **12** *23* **Cherchedi (IRE)**[27] 6449 2-8-7 33...................................... JulieBurke(5) 9 —
(Alan Berry) *s.i.s: a bhd: t.o fr 1/2-way* **200/1**

1m 20.39s (6.79) **Going Correction** +0.85s/f (Soft) **12** Ran SP% **118.2**
Speed ratings (Par 93): **88,87,83,82,78 75,69,68,63,62 50,19**
toteswingers: 1&2 £1.60, 1&3 £4.70, 2&3 £1.90 CSF £6.44 TOTE £1.40: £1.02, £3.10, £1.40; EX 7.00.
Owner Sheikh Hamdan Bin Mohammed Al Maktoum **Bred** Darley **Trained** Middleham Moor, N Yorks

FOCUS

The ground had eased from that forecast and was officially given as soft (GoingStick 6.3), though the jockeys in the opener described it as "heavy". Despite the conditions, the jockeys decided to stay towards the inside in the home straight. An uncompetitive maiden that went the way of the short-priced favourite, though it wasn't easy. The fourth and fifth set a solid but limited level.

NOTEBOOK

Idler(IRE) had made the frame in his first four starts and set the standard with a mark of 76. In front after a furlong, he made all from that point but he looked tired in the closing stages and had little in reserve at the line. This looked as far as he wanted to go in the conditions and will probably need to improve to defy this sort of mark in handicaps. (op 8-15 tchd 8-13)

Colbyor, well beaten on his Carlisle debut in August, looked the stable's second string on jockey bookings, but that proved not to be the case and he didn't go unbacked. Always handy, he never gave the favourite much peace and was coming back again at the line. This was a good effort from the outside stall and he should be able to find a small race. (op 14-1)

Sir Windsorlot(IRE) had missed the break in his first two starts, but showed definite promise last time and this extra furlong promised to suit. However, despite breaking much better he became outpaced mid-race and hung when rallying inside the last 2f. At least he can now be handicapped. (op 4-1)
Only Orsenfoolsies, returning from 105 days off and rated just 47 having been unplaced on his first five starts, ran well for a long way but his proximity does little for the form. (op 66-1)
Villa Reigns, rated 51 after finishing unplaced in his first five starts, also ran well for a long way but he hung badly over a furlong from home despite the application of cheekpieces. Official explanation: jockey said gelding hung left throughout
Forever Janey, retained for just 800gns as a yearling, is out of a half-sister to a couple of winning sprinters. She made a little bit of late headway. (op 40-1)

7073 GO RACING AT WETHERBY THIS FRIDAY H'CAP — 5f 212y
2:20 (2:20) (Class 5) (0-75,73) 3-Y-O — **£2,070** (£616; £307; £153) **Stalls** Low

Form — RPR

2600 **1** — **Rowan Spirit (IRE)**[11] 6840 3-9-0 **66** .... GrahamGibbons 3 — 76
(Mark Brisbourne) *trckd ldrs: smooth hdwy and cl up 2f out: rdn to ld over 1f out: edgd lft ins fnl f: kpt on* **8/1**

1116 **2** *1 1/2* **Deliberation (IRE)**[37] 6190 3-9-2 **73** .... JulieBurke(5) 7 — 78
(Kevin Ryan) *cl up: led 1/2-way: c wd to stands' rail and sn rdn: hdd over 1f out: edgd lft and one pce fnl f* **9/2[2]**

233 **3** *nk* **Cool Rhythm**[11] 6834 3-9-3 **69** .... DanielTudhope 5 — 73
(David O'Meara) *in tch: hdwy to chse ldrs 2f out: swtchd lft and rdn over 1f out: styng on whn swtchd rt ins fnl f: nrst fin* **11/2[3]**

2115 **4** *1/2* **Meandmyshadow**[10] 6869 3-9-2 **68** .... SilvestreDeSousa 8 — 71
(Alan Brown) *chsd ldng pair: rdn along wl over 1f out: kpt on same pce* **6/1**

6302 **5** *5* **Black Annis Bower**[13] 6801 3-9-4 **70** .... JamesSullivan 2 — 57
(Michael Easterby) *midfield: rdn along 1/2-way: nvr a factor* **9/4[1]**

3055 **6** *1 1/2* **Belle Bayardo (IRE)**[9] 6895 3-9-7 **73** .... LukeMorris 6 — 55
(Ronald Harris) *dwlt: a in rr* **10/1**

200 **7** *2 3/4* **Crimson Knot (IRE)**[39] 6112 3-9-7 **73** .... PaulHanagan 1 — 46
(Alan Berry) *a in rr* **15/2**

3000 **8** *3 3/4* **Bay Of Fires (IRE)**[31] 6343 3-8-10 **67** .... AshleyMorgan(5) 4 — 28
(David O'Meara) *led: rdn along and hdd wl over 2f out: sn wknd* **18/1**

1m 18.06s (4.46) **Going Correction** +0.85s/f (Soft) — **8** Ran SP% **115.9**
Speed ratings (Par 101): **104,102,101,100,94 92,88,83**
toteswingers: 1&2 £9.10, 1&3 £8.80, 2&3 £2.60 CSF £44.37 CT £218.33 TOTE £11.10: £3.10, £2.20, £1.10; EX 41.10.
Owner Deva Racing Captain Rio Partnership **Bred** Secret Justice Syndicate **Trained** Great Ness, Shropshire

FOCUS
An ordinary sprint handicap and this time the field came over to the stands' rail, which set the trend for the rest of the meeting. Few got into it, however, with a group of four in a clear advantage over the other quartet at halfway.
Rowan Spirit(IRE) Official explanation: trainer said, regarding apparent improvement in form, that the gelding had appreciated the drop back to 6f and the soft ground.
Black Annis Bower Official explanation: jockey said filly never travelled
Crimson Knot(IRE) Official explanation: jockey said filly hung left throughout

7074 TURFTV.CO.UK H'CAP (DIV I) — 7f
2:50 (2:52) (Class 4) (0-85,85) 3-Y-O+ — **£4,075** (£1,212; £606; £303) **Stalls** Low

Form — RPR

2000 **1** — **Clockmaker (IRE)**[18] 6672 5-9-7 **85** .... GrahamGibbons 5 — 95
(Tim Easterby) *cl up on inner: led wl over 2f out and wd st: rdn over 1f out: kpt on wl fnl f* **14/1**

5500 **2** *1 1/4* **Powerful Presence (IRE)**[17] 6708 5-8-13 **77** .... DanielTudhope 14 — 84
(David O'Meara) *trckd ldrs: hdwy 2f out: rdn to chal over 1f out and ev ch tl no ex wl ins fnl f* **11/2[3]**

1224 **3** *2* **Fast Shot**[55] 5621 3-9-3 **83** .... DavidAllan 15 — 84
(Tim Easterby) *cl up on outer: hdwy and wd st: cl up 2f out: rdn wl over 1f out and ev ch tl one pce ins fnl f* **9/1**

-031 **4** *1 1/2* **Makbullet**[10] 6867 4-8-7 **71** oh2 .... PaulHanagan 2 — 68
(Michael Smith) *trckd ldrs on inner: hdwy over 2f out: rdn over 1f out: one pce ent fnl f* **4/1[1]**

0006 **5** *nk* **Orpsie Boy (IRE)**[15] 6761 8-9-1 **82** .... DaleSwift(3) 4 — 78
(Ruth Carr) *hld up in rr: hdwy wl over 1f out: swtchd lft and rdn ent fnl f: kpt on* **20/1**

1123 **6** *2* **Kingswinford (IRE)**[24] 6541 5-8-11 **82** .... JustinNewman(7) 7 — 73
(Brian Ellison) *chsd ldrs: rdn along wl over 1f out: wknd ent fnl f* **5/1[2]**

0015 **7** *3/4* **Frognal (IRE)**[13] 6794 5-9-0 **78** ....(bt) MartinHarley 12 — 67
(Richard Guest) *bhd: hdwy wl over 1f out: sn swtchd rt and rdn: no imp fnl f* **40/1**

2006 **8** *2 3/4* **Gap Princess (IRE)**[47] 5862 7-9-0 **78** .... SilvestreDeSousa 3 — 60
(Geoffrey Harker) *midfield: hdwy on inner wl over 2f out: rdn to chse ldrs over 1f out: sn btn* **16/1**

4540 **9** *3/4* **Breezolini**[11] 6840 3-8-12 **71** oh3 ....(v) AmyRyan(3) 10 — 50
(Richard Whitaker) *towards rr: hdwy 2f out: sn rdn and n.d* **28/1**

0016 **10** *1* **Keys Of Cyprus**[11] 6830 9-8-12 **73** .... ShirleyTeasdale(7) 9 — 50
(David Nicholls) *chsd ldrs: rdn along 2f out: wknd over 1f out* **11/1**

0030 **11** *3 1/2* **Cornus**[15] 6762 9-8-8 **75** ....(be) DeclanCannon(3) 6 — 42
(Alan McCabe) *a towards rr* **25/1**

6250 **12** *3/4* **Lucky Numbers (IRE)**[8] 6913 5-9-7 **85** .... JamesSullivan 8 — 50
(Paul Green) *nvr bttr than midfield* **16/1**

0000 **13** *5* **Gallagher**[17] 6703 5-9-2 **80** ....(t) PJMcDonald 11 — 32
(Ruth Carr) *dwlt: hdwy on outer and in tch after 2f: rdn along wl over 2f out and sn wknd* **16/1**

0020 **14** *5* **My Gacho (IRE)**[39] 6113 9-8-13 **77** ....(v) AdrianNicholls 13 — 15
(David Nicholls) *led: rdn along and hdd wl over 2f out: wknd wl over 1f out* **20/1**

1004 **15** *hd* **Mandalay King (IRE)**[39] 6113 6-8-7 **76** .... JulieBurke(5) 1 — 14
(Marjorie Fife) *a bhd* **16/1**

1m 32.01s (5.01) **Going Correction** +0.85s/f (Soft)
WFA 3 from 4yo+ 2lb — **15** Ran SP% **119.8**
Speed ratings (Par 105): **105,103,101,99,99 96,96,92,92,90 86,86,80,74,74**
toteswingers: 1&2 £15.30, 1&3 £18.40, 2&3 £9.30 CSF £82.00 CT £764.27 TOTE £21.40: £6.10, £2.70, £3.60; EX 117.90.
Owner Middleham Park Racing XI & Partners **Bred** Lemongrove Stud & Brendan Arthur **Trained** Great Habton, N Yorks

FOCUS
A competitive handicap.
Clockmaker(IRE) Official explanation: trainer's rep said he could offer no explanation for the apparent improvement in form
Lucky Numbers(IRE) Official explanation: jockey said gelding suffered interference in running
My Gacho(IRE) Official explanation: jockey said gelding hung left and lost its action
Mandalay King(IRE) Official explanation: jockey said gelding never travelled

7075 CATTERICKBRIDGE.CO.UK H'CAP — 1m 7f 177y
3:20 (3:20) (Class 5) (0-70,73) 3-Y-O+ — **£2,070** (£616; £307; £153) **Stalls** Low

Form — RPR

0055 **1** — **Gaselee (USA)**[14] 6780 5-9-9 **65** .... GrahamGibbons 9 — 83
(Rae Guest) *mde all: pushed clr over 1f out: heavily eased last 100yds* **5/1[3]**

4130 **2** *13* **Mohawk Ridge**[27] 6451 5-9-11 **70** .... LeeTopliss(3) 3 — 72
(Michael Dods) *trckd ldrs: wnt 2nd over 4f out: kpt on: no ch w wnr* **9/2[2]**

2264 **3** *13* **White Deer (USA)**[26] 6493 7-9-7 **63** ....(p) RobertWinston 8 — 49
(Geoffrey Harker) *hld up in rr: hdwy over 5f out: wnt modest 3rd over 2f out: one pce* **22/1**

344 **4** *2* **Tricksofthetrade (IRE)**[21] 6614 5-10-0 **70** .... PJMcDonald 1 — 54
(Alan Swinbank) *chsd ldrs: outpcd over 3f out: wknd over 1f out* **13/2**

46-0 **5** *1* **High Ransom**[200] 1215 4-9-10 **66** .... FrederikTylicki 13 — 49
(Micky Hammond) *in rr: kpt on fnl 2f: nvr nr ldrs* **16/1**

645 **6** *4 1/2* **Bijou Dan**[28] 5369 10-9-5 **61** .... AndrewMullen 12 — 38
(George Moore) *in rr: sn pushed along: kpt on fnl 3f: nvr on terms* **20/1**

4001 **7** *1 1/4* **Descaro (USA)**[8] 6915 5-10-3 **73** 6ex ....(v) SilvestreDeSousa 2 — 49
(David O'Meara) *hld up in mid-div: effrt over 5f out: sn btn* **4/1[1]**

3-00 **8** *2 1/2* **I Got Music**[180] 1458 4-8-6 **51** oh2 .... DeclanCannon(3) 7 — 24
(Keith Reveley) *hld up: sme hdwy over 5f out: nvr on terms* **20/1**

0000 **9** *13* **Sirgarfieldsobers (IRE)**[8] 6916 5-9-7 **70** .... JasonHart(7) 4 — 27
(Declan Carroll) *s.s: t.k.h detached in last: gd hdwy over 7f out: sn chsng ldrs: wknd over 4f out: sn wl bhd* **22/1**

6315 **10** *12* **Evergreen Forest (IRE)**[13] 6789 3-9-3 **69** ....(b) PaulHanagan 5 — 12
(Alastair Lidderdale) *t.k.h: trckd ldrs: lost pl over 5f out: wl bhd whn eased over 2f out* **4/1[1]**

6400 **11** *33* **Quaestor (IRE)**[28] 4612 4-8-9 **51** oh6 ....(p) LukeMorris 10 — —
(Andrew Crook) *chsd ldrs: drvn over 5f out: sn lost pl and bhd: t.o over 3f out: virtually p.u* **100/1**

330/ **12** *19* **Lazy Darren**[684] 2666 7-9-9 **65** .... TonyHamilton 11 — —
(Chris Grant) *chsd ldrs: racd wd: lost pl over 6f out: t.o 4f out: virtually p.u* **40/1**

3m 47.75s (15.75) **Going Correction** +0.85s/f (Soft)
WFA 3 from 4yo+ 10lb — **12** Ran SP% **115.7**
Speed ratings (Par 103): **94,87,81,80,79 77,76,75,68,62 46,36**
toteswingers: 1&2 £4.70, 1&3 £20.80, 2&3 £12.50 CSF £24.35 CT £453.23 TOTE £6.90: £2.30, £2.40, £5.20; EX 27.60.
Owner Mrs Paula Smith **Bred** Flaxman Holdings Ltd **Trained** Newmarket, Suffolk

FOCUS
A war of attrition in the conditions and there will be 3m chases run around here this winter in which the field finish closer together.

7076 TURFTV.CO.UK H'CAP (DIV II) — 7f
3:50 (3:50) (Class 4) (0-85,85) 3-Y-O+ — **£4,075** (£1,212; £606; £303) **Stalls** Low

Form — RPR

0101 **1** — **Beckermet (IRE)**[10] 6869 9-8-12 **76** .... PJMcDonald 11 — 90
(Ruth Carr) *prom: hdwy to ld wl over 2f out and wd st to stands' rail: rdn along wl over 1f out: kpt on strly fnl f* **13/2[1]**

6654 **2** *1* **Sam Nombulist**[40] 6081 3-8-2 **71** oh4 ....(v) AmyRyan(3) 6 — 82
(Richard Whitaker) *prom: chsd wnr over 2f out: rdn and carried hd high over 1f out: kpt on fnl f* **9/1[3]**

0500 **3** *1 3/4* **Ballista (IRE)**[16] 6723 3-9-4 **84** .... RichardKingscote 3 — 90
(Tom Dascombe) *trckd ldrs: hdwy 2f out: rdn to chse ldng pair wl over 1f out: no imp ins fnl f* **9/1[3]**

-000 **4** *3* **Madam Macie (IRE)**[40] 6094 4-8-13 **77** .... SilvestreDeSousa 10 — 75
(David O'Meara) *chsd ldrs on outer: hdwy over 2f out: rdn wl over 1f out: kpt on same pce* **7/1[2]**

504 **5** *3/4* **Clumber Place**[10] 6869 5-8-7 **71** oh4 .... PaulHanagan 9 — 67
(Richard Guest) *chsd ldrs: rdn along wl over 1f out: kpt on same pce fnl f* **14/1**

5210 **6** *1 1/2* **Illustrious Prince (IRE)**[40] 6081 4-8-12 **81** .... NeilFarley(5) 8 — 73
(Declan Carroll) *in rr and pushed along: hdwy over 2f out: rdn wl over 1f out and sn no imp* **10/1**

5020 **7** *3/4* **Dorback**[17] 6703 4-9-2 **80** .... DanielTudhope 14 — 70
(Noel Wilson) *chsd ldrs: rdn 2f out: wknd appr fnl f* **18/1**

0444 **8** *1/2* **No Poppy (IRE)**[22] 6576 3-8-8 **79** .... AdamCarter(5) 15 — 68
(Tim Easterby) *dwlt and in rr: sme hdwy wl over 1f out: n.d* **14/1**

2140 **9** *7* **Another Citizen (IRE)**[39] 6113 3-8-12 **78** .... DavidAllan 1 — 48
(Tim Easterby) *prom on inner: effrt over 2f out: rdn wl over 1f out and sn wknd* **10/1**

0005 **10** *1/2* **Mon Brav**[39] 6113 4-9-4 **85** .... DaleSwift(3) 7 — 53
(Brian Ellison) *sn rdn along: a in rr* **10/1**

05-6 **11** *hd* **Regeneration (IRE)**[26] 6477 5-8-9 **78** .... DarylByrne(5) 5 — 46
(Michael Bell) *in tch: pushed along wl over 2f out: sn rdn and wknd* **28/1**

0001 **12** *2* **Celtic Sultan (IRE)**[26] 6478 7-9-4 **82** .... MickyFenton 12 — 45
(Tom Tate) *a in rr* **12/1**

0000 **13** *1/2* **Mujaadel (USA)**[24] 6533 6-8-9 **76** ow2 ....(p) MichaelO'Connell(3) 13 — 37
(David Nicholls) *s.i.s: a in rr* **14/1**

0300 **14** *8* **Klynch**[39] 6113 5-9-6 **84** ....(b) JamesSullivan 4 — 24
(Ruth Carr) *led: rdn along and hdd wl over 2f out: sn wknd* **22/1**

1m 32.79s (5.79) **Going Correction** +0.85s/f (Soft)
WFA 3 from 4yo+ 2lb — **14** Ran SP% **118.1**
Speed ratings (Par 105): **100,98,96,93,92 90,90,89,81,80 80,78,77,68**
toteswingers: 1&2 £9.80, 1&3 £9.70, 2&3 £17.30 CSF £62.00 CT £546.82 TOTE £6.20: £2.60, £3.30, £4.80; EX 75.80.
Owner Shopping, Shoes & Champers Partnership **Bred** Fritz Von Ball Moss **Trained** Huby, N Yorks

FOCUS
Like the first division, a competitive handicap, though the winning time was 0.78 seconds slower than the first leg.
Mon Brav Official explanation: jockey said gelding never travelled
Mujaadel(USA) Official explanation: jockey said gelding was unsuited by the soft ground

7077 RACING UK ON SKY 432 H'CAP (DIV I) — 1m 3f 214y
4:20 (4:20) (Class 6) (0-60,60) 3-Y-O+ — **£1,704** (£503; £251) **Stalls** Low

Form — RPR

4050 **1** — **Illustration (IRE)**[10] 6872 3-8-11 **52** .... SilvestreDeSousa 13 — 71+
(Mark Johnston) *mid-div: sn pushed along: hrd drvn over 6f out: sn chsng ldrs: wnt cl 2nd over 4f out: led over 2f out: forged clr: eased towards fin* **5/1[2]**

0500 **2** *7* **Dubara Reef (IRE)**[10] 6870 4-9-7 **55** ....(v[1]) JamesSullivan 15 — 60
(Paul Green) *drvn to chse ldrs: 3rd and one pce over 2f out* **12/1**

4000 **3** *1 1/4* **Donna Elvira**[38] 6157 4-9-3 **51** .... TonyHamilton 8 — 54
(Edwin Tuer) *led: hdd over 2f out: kpt on same pce* **10/1**

The Form Book, Raceform Ltd, Compton, RG20 6NL

2-00 **4** *11* **Flora's Pride**[118] 3510 7-8-12 **51**........ ShaneBKelly(5) 2 36
(Keith Reveley) *in rr: hdwy over 4f out: nvr a factor* **10/1**

3304 **5** *2 1/2* **Bavarian Nordic (USA)**[29] 6419 6-9-6 **59** ow1........(v) BrianToomey(5) 7 40
(Richard Whitaker) *hld up in mid-div: effrt over 3f out: one pce* **9/1**

1436 **6** *7* **Ferney Boy**[25] 6503 5-9-3 **51**........ RobertWinston 9 21
(Chris Fairhurst) *in rr-div: hdwy on outer over 5f out: sn chsng ldrs: hung rt over 1f out: sn eased* **4/1**[1]

-006 **7** *1/2* **Hammer**[10] 6870 6-8-5 **46** oh1........ JordanNason(7) 4 15
(Geoffrey Harker) *trckd ldrs: drvn and outpcd over 3f out: hung lft 2f out* **28/1**

1320 **8** *1 3/4* **Daytime Dreamer (IRE)**[11] 6838 7-9-12 **60**........ PJMcDonald 14 27
(Martin Todhunter) *mid-div: drvn over 6f out: rdn over 4f out: sn btn* **14/1**

0330 **9** *8* **Drawback (IRE)**[10] 6870 8-8-10 **49**........(p) MatthewLawson(5) 3 —
(Barry Brennan) *chsd ldrs: drvn over 6f out: lost pl over 3f out* **16/1**

4-60 **10** *3 1/4* **Ergo (FR)**[8] 6916 7-9-12 **60**........(p) PaddyAspell 10 —
(James Moffatt) *a towards rr: nvr a factor* **50/1**

000 **11** *33* **Mainland (USA)**[13] 4902 5-9-7 **55**........(t) TomEaves 11 —
(Robert Johnson) *hld up in rr: bhd fnl 3f: eased: t.o* **80/1**

0335 **12** *18* **They All Laughed**[21] 6600 8-9-0 **48**........(p) PaulHanagan 12 —
(Marjorie Fife) *detached in last: drvn after 3f: nt keen and sn bhd: t.o whn eased 3f out* **17/2**

/006 **13** *18* **Circus Polka (USA)**[10] 6871 7-8-8 **47**........ JulieBurke(5) 6 —
(Owen Brennan) *chsd ldrs: lost pl over 4f out: eased whn bhd over 2f out: sn t.o* **33/1**

0054 **P** **Child Of Our Time (IRE)**[1] 7061 4-8-12 **46**........ DavidAllan 1 —
(Tracy Waggott) *chsd ldrs: lost pl over 3f out: bhd whn eased over 2f out: sn t.o: p.u ins fnl f* **11/2**[3]

2m 51.97s (13.07) **Going Correction** +0.85s/f (Soft)
WFA 3 from 4yo+ 7lb **14** Ran SP% **120.6**
Speed ratings (Par 101): **90,85,84,77,75 70,70,69,64,61 39,27,15,—**
toteswingers: 1&2 £12.10, 1&3 £11.70, 2&3 £16.70 CSF £62.55 CT £588.53 TOTE £9.00: £2.80, £5.00, £5.30; EX 107.70.
Owner Sheikh Hamdan Bin Mohammed Al Maktoum **Bred** Moyglare Stud Farm Ltd **Trained** Middleham Moor, N Yorks

FOCUS
A basement handicap in which they finished spread out all over North Yorkshire. Only the winner has any pretensions to being any better than this grade.
They All Laughed Official explanation: jockey said gelding never travelled
Child Of Our Time(IRE) Official explanation: jockey said filly lost its action

7078 RACING UK ON SKY 432 H'CAP (DIV II) 1m 3f 214y
4:50 (4:51) (Class 6) (0-60,60) 3-Y-O+ **£1,704** (£503; £251) **Stalls** Low

Form RPR

0061 **1** **Vittachi**[10] 6870 4-9-7 **55**........ PaulHanagan 15 66
(Alistair Whillans) *trckd ldrs: hdwy on outer 4f out: led wl over 2f out and wd st to stands' rail: rdn wl over 1f out: kpt on strly u.p fnl f* **11/4**[1]

6045 **2** *1 1/4* **Strong Knight**[13] 5823 4-8-13 **47**........ DuranFentiman 8 56
(Tim Walford) *hld up in tch: hdwy 5f out: chsd ldrs over 2f out: swtchd lft and rdn over 1f out: sn chal and ev ch tl no ex wl ins fnl f* **9/2**[2]

5000 **3** *1 3/4* **Ananda Kanda (USA)**[24] 6546 4-9-5 **56**........ DaleSwift(3) 14 62
(Brian Ellison) *a.p: cl up 3f out: rdn 2f out and ev ch tl one pce ins fnl f* **11/1**

45 **4** *1 1/2* **C P Joe (IRE)**[22] 6584 3-9-3 **58**........ SilvestreDeSousa 13 62+
(Paul Green) *hld up in midfield: stdy hdwy over 4f out: chsd ldrs over 2f out: rdn over 1f out: sn one pce* **15/2**

/5-6 **5** *9* **Sory**[14] 6781 4-9-6 **54**........ JamesSullivan 7 43
(Tina Jackson) *hld up towards rr: hdwy over 4f out: rdn wl over 2f out: kpt on: nt rch ldrs* **33/1**

6000 **6** *3/4* **Applaude**[18] 6235 6-8-13 **47**........(b) MichaelStainton 1 35
(Jason Ward) *hld up towards rr: hdwy over 4f out: rdn along 3f out: n.d* **33/1**

0-00 **7** *3/4* **Mecox Bay (IRE)**[157] 2312 4-9-12 **60**........(p) NeilChalmers 6 47
(Michael Appleby) *led: rdn along 4f out: hdd wl over 2f out and sn wknd* **16/1**

-006 **8** *2 1/2* **Kathlatino**[17] 5107 4-9-2 **50**........ TomEaves 2 33
(Micky Hammond) *chsd ldrs: rdn along over 4f out: sn wknd* **16/1**

6000 **9** *nk* **Without Equal**[25] 5650 5-9-3 **51**........ BarryMcHugh 4 34
(David Thompson) *a in rr* **66/1**

120- **10** *12* **Al Shababiya (IRE)**[373] 6955 4-9-10 **58**........ DanielTudhope 12 21
(Alison Thorpe) *a in rr* **5/1**[3]

1050 **11** *3 3/4* **Obara D'Avril (FR)**[21] 6613 9-8-12 **46**........(p) TonyHamilton 3 —
(Simon West) *chsd ldrs: rdn along over 3f out: sn wknd* **18/1**

3450 **12** *11* **Northumberland**[41] 6050 5-8-9 **46** oh1........ DeclanCannon(3) 11 —
(Owen Brennan) *chsd ldrs: rdn along over 5f out: sn wknd* **40/1**

005 **13** *47* **Ritsi**[29] 6419 8-8-7 **46** oh1........ JulieBurke(5) 9 —
(Marjorie Fife) *v.s.a and lost 15 l s: a bhd* **16/1**

2m 53.23s (14.33) **Going Correction** +0.85s/f (Soft)
WFA 3 from 4yo+ 7lb **13** Ran SP% **114.3**
Speed ratings (Par 101): **86,85,84,83,77 76,76,74,74,66 63,56,24**
toteswingers: 1&2 £2.90, 1&3 £9.20, 2&3 £13.50 CSF £13.07 CT £115.30 TOTE £4.30: £2.30, £1.10, £2.60; EX 10.20.
Owner Sutherland Five **Bred** London Thoroughbred Services Ltd **Trained** Newmill-On-Slitrig, Borders

FOCUS
Another moderate handicap in which the conditions proved too much for a few. The winning time was 1.26 seconds slower than the first division.
Ritsi Official explanation: jockey said gelding was slow away

7079 JUMP SEASON NEXT H'CAP 5f
5:20 (5:24) (Class 6) (0-65,62) 3-Y-O+ **£2,726** (£805; £402) **Stalls** Low

Form RPR

4250 **1** **Mottley Crewe**[13] 6793 4-9-7 **62**........(b[1]) MartinHarley 5 70
(Richard Guest) *overall ldr stands' side: kpt on fnl f: all out* **10/1**

0452 **2** *nk* **Bailadeira**[11] 6839 3-8-11 **55**........ MichaelO'Connell(3) 7 62
(Tim Etherington) *chsd overall ldrs stands' side: kpt on ins fnl f: jst hld* **25/1**

1503 **3** *hd* **Suddenly Susan (IRE)**[21] 6615 3-8-7 **55**........(b) LeonnaMayor(7) 11 61
(David Nicholls) *racd stands' side: chsd ldrs: edgd lft ins fnl f: no ex nr fin* **14/1**

0366 **4** *3/4* **Prince Of Vasa (IRE)**[34] 6261 4-9-5 **60**........ AdrianNicholls 9 64
(Michael Smith) *chsd ldrs stands' side: hung bdly lft fnl f and ended up far side: kpt on towards fin* **12/1**

4601 **5** *nk* **El Dececy (USA)**[9] 6889 7-9-1 **56** 6ex........(t) SilvestreDeSousa 13 59
(Richard Guest) *chsd ldrs stands' side: kpt on ins fnl f* **5/2**[1]

0405 **6** *1/2* **Garstang**[26] 6491 8-8-10 **51**........(b) NeilChalmers 8 52
(Bruce Hellier) *in rr stands' side: styd on fnl 2f: nt rch ldrs* **20/1**

5260 **7** *3/4* **Bertbrand**[189] 1464 6-8-7 **48**........(v) JamesSullivan 6 46
(Ian McInnes) *racd stands' side: mid-div: kpt on fnl f: nvr a threat* **80/1**

1252 **8** *hd* **Spirit Of Coniston**[13] 6802 8-9-7 **62**........ MickyFenton 1 59
(Paul Midgley) *racd far side: chsd ldr: hung lft and led that side over 1f out: kpt on same pce* **8/1**

2314 **9** *1 3/4* **Surely This Time (IRE)**[27] 6456 3-9-7 **62**........(bt) PaulHanagan 2 53
(Kevin Ryan) *led and clr of three other far side: edgd rt over 2f out: hdd over 1f out: sn wknd* **4/1**[2]

210 **10** *1/2* **Ingenti**[11] 6840 3-9-0 **55**........ PaddyAspell 12 44
(Christopher Wilson) *s.i.s: racd stands' side: a towards rr* **18/1**

-45 **11** *3/4* **Danum Dancer**[21] 6602 7-9-0 **55**........(b) GrahamGibbons 3 41
(Neville Bycroft) *s.i.s: racd far side: nvr gng pce and nvr on terms* **13/2**[3]

5000 **12** *2* **Avertuoso**[13] 6802 7-9-2 **57**........(v) TomEaves 10 36
(Bryan Smart) *racd stands' side: sn drvn along and a in rr* **12/1**

-000 **13** *2 3/4* **Drumpellier (IRE)**[21] 6618 4-8-7 **48**........(p) DuranFentiman 4 17
(Simon West) *racd far side: chsd ldr: wknd 2f out* **33/1**

63.38 secs (3.58) **Going Correction** +0.75s/f (Yiel) **13** Ran SP% **122.2**
Speed ratings (Par 101): **101,100,100,99,98 97,96,96,93,92 91,88,83**
CSF £246.96 CT £3576.79 TOTE £8.10: £2.10, £7.00, £5.90; EX 259.50.
Owner Rakebackmypoker.com **Bred** Longdon Stud Ltd **Trained** Stainforth, S Yorks
■ Stewards' Enquiry : Michael O'Connell two-day ban: careless riding (Nov 9-10)

FOCUS
A modest sprint handicap in which those that raced prominently towards the nearside of the track dominated. The quartet that raced far side never had a prayer, even though Surely This Time soon blazed off into a clear advantage, but he folded tamely and couldn't even manage to win the race on that side, that honour going to course-specialist Spirit Of Coniston back in eighth.
T/Plt: £660.40 to a £1 stake. Pool:£49,849.60 - 55.10 winning tickets T/Qpdt: £220.30 to a £1 stake. Pool:£4,660.63 - 15.65 winning tickets JR

6933 YARMOUTH (L-H)
Tuesday, October 25

OFFICIAL GOING: Good to soft changing to soft after race 1 (1:30)
Wind: light across Weather: rain clearing

7080 BRITISH STALLION STUDS EBF MAIDEN STKS 7f 3y
1:30 (1:32) (Class 5) 2-Y-O **£2,911** (£866; £432; £216) **Stalls** Centre

Form RPR

2 **1** **Rewarded**[38] 6160 2-9-3 0........ KirstyMilczarek 4 83+
(James Toller) *t.k.h: trckd ldrs: pushed along to chse ldr 2f out: led ins fnl f: r.o wl: pushed out* **3/1**[1]

3 **2** *1 1/4* **Flaxen Flare (IRE)**[14] 6768 2-9-3 0........ JimmyFortune 5 80
(Andrew Balding) *chsd ldr tl pushed ahd over 2f out: rdn 2f out: hdd ins fnl f: kpt on for clr 2nd but a hld by wnr* **7/1**

3 *4 1/2* **Qaadira (USA)** 2-8-12 0........ RichardHills 2 64+
(John Gosden) *s.i.s: sn rcvrd and in tch in midfield: hdwy over 2f out: rdn and chsd ldng pair over 1f out: kpt on same pce and no imp fnl f* **5/1**[3]

4 *1 3/4* **Commend** 2-9-3 0........ RyanMoore 9 64+
(Sir Michael Stoute) *in tch in midfield: pushed along and outpcd 1/2-way: rallied and swtchd rt over 1f out: kpt on wl ins fnl f: nvr trbld ldrs* **7/2**[2]

5 *hd* **Invisible Hunter (USA)** 2-9-3 0........ FrankieDettori 13 64+
(Saeed Bin Suroor) *hld up towards rr: switching lft and hdwy over 2f out: pushed along and kpt on wl fr over 1f out: nvr trbld ldrs* **15/2**

54 **6** *1 3/4* **Peak Storm**[14] 6768 2-9-3 0........ MartinLane 8 59
(John Gallagher) *chsd ldrs: rdn and unable qck ent fnl 2f: drvn and wknd over 1f out* **16/1**

35 **7** *2* **Excellent Jem**[20] 6629 2-9-3 0........ NeilCallan 16 54
(George Margarson) *t.k.h: led tl hdd and rdn over 2f out: wknd u.p over 1f out* **50/1**

8 *1 3/4* **Sea Fever (IRE)** 2-9-3 0........ KierenFallon 6 50+
(Luca Cumani) *chsd ldng pair tl rdn and unable qck over 2f out: btn wl over 1f out: wknd and nt given a hrd time after* **10/1**

9 *3 1/2* **Pink Belini** 2-8-12 0........ LiamKeniry 1 36
(Alan McCabe) *hld up toward rr: pushed along 4f out: sn struggling: wl btn fnl 2f* **100/1**

26 **10** *nk* **Shomberg**[34] 6244 2-9-3 0........ TomQueally 14 41
(Mark H Tompkins) *in tch in midfield: rdn and wknd over 2f out: no ch fr wl over 1f out* **33/1**

11 *1* **Perfect Example (IRE)** 2-8-12 0........ JamieSpencer 12 33
(Peter Chapple-Hyam) *s.i.s: a towards rr: no ch fnl 2f* **33/1**

0 **12** *4* **Retromania (IRE)**[7] 6927 2-9-3 0........ SteveDrowne 15 28
(John Best) *s.i.s: a towards rr: lost tch 3f out* **100/1**

13 *11* **Critical Point** 2-9-3 0........ StevieDonohoe 7 —
(Sir Mark Prescott Bt) *s.i.s: a struggling in rr and sn rdn along: lost tch 1/2-way: t.o* **40/1**

14 *4 1/2* **Derek The Diamond** 2-9-3 0........ DavidProbert 10 —
(J R Jenkins) *s.i.s: t.k.h early: hld up towards rr: struggling 1/2-way: sn lost tch: t.o* **100/1**

15 *4 1/2* **Waldstein** 2-9-3 0........ RobertHavlin 11 —
(Andrew Haynes) *s.i.s: a bhd: lost tch 4f out: t.o and eased fnl f* **200/1**

1m 28.54s (1.94) **Going Correction** +0.175s/f (Good) **15** Ran SP% **116.9**
Speed ratings (Par 95): **95,93,88,86,86 84,81,79,75,75 74,69,57,52,47**
toteswingers:1&2:£5.70, 1&3:£4.60, 2&3:£7.90 CSF £22.65 TOTE £4.40: £1.50, £2.80, £2.20; EX 18.10 Trifecta £214.20 Part won. Pool £289.47 - 0.74 winning units..
Owner P C J Dalby & R D Schuster **Bred** Edward David Kessly **Trained** Newmarket, Suffolk

FOCUS
This looked a good juvenile maiden, although conditions wouldn't have suited all. They raced up the middle and the first two help set the level.

NOTEBOOK
Rewarded was runner-up to a potentially high-class colt on his debut at Newbury (Godolphin's Mighty Ambition) and he gave that form another boost with a straightforward success. His stamina was key, the soft ground making this a good test, and he'll appreciate further in due course. He's a nice 3-y-o in the making. (op 11-4 tchd 7-2 in places)
Flaxen Flare(IRE), third on his debut at Leicester, improved on that form by pulling clear of the others. He looks pretty useful. (op 4-1)
Qaadira(USA), the first foal of a 7f-1m2f (including US Grade 2) winner, had a sheepskin noseband fitted. She recovered well from a slow start but couldn't go with the front two, who both had the benefit of experience. There should be plenty more to come. (tchd 9-2)
Commend, out of an unraced half-sister to numerous winners, was strongly supported but needed the run. He took an age to pick up but was going on at the finish and should be suited by further. (op 7-1)
Invisible Hunter(USA), a $150,000 half-brother to winners in the US, has quite a fluent action and probably wouldn't want the ground much softer. He ran green under pressure and was another going on at the line. (op 13-2 tchd 6-1)
Peak Storm was only a short-head behind Flaxen Lake last time but didn't progress like that rival. Handicaps are now an option. (tchd 18-1)

Sea Fever(IRE) ◆, a 115,000gns half-brother to Wigmore Hall, wasn't given a hard ride and can do much better in the long term. (op 14-1 tchd 9-1)
Shomberg Official explanation: jockey said colt hung left

7081 ODDSCHECKER.COM NURSERY 7f 3y
2:00 (2:01) (Class 5) (0-75,75) 2-Y-O £2,264 (£673; £336; £168) **Stalls** Centre

Form RPR
044 **1** **Master Of Ages (IRE)**[133] 3016 2-9-3 **71**............ JoeFanning 6 81+
(Mark Johnston) *racd towards far side: mde all: shkn up and drew clr over 1f out: r.o wl: readily* **12/1**
043 **2** *4* **Altona (IRE)**[15] 6745 2-9-2 **70**............ TonyCulhane 4 69
(Mick Channon) *hld up towards far side: effrt 2f out: rdn and styd on to take 2nd last 100yds: no ch w wnr* **6/1**[3]
0450 **3** *1* **Abshir Zain (IRE)**[26] 6484 2-8-12 **66**............(b) TomQueally 5 63
(Clive Brittain) *s.i.s: in tch towards far side: prog to chse wnr 2f out: no imp: lost 2nd last 100yds* **16/1**
2323 **4** *nk* **Alice Rose (IRE)**[83] 4682 2-8-13 **67**............ NickyMackay 10 63
(Rae Guest) *hld up nr side: rdn and prog to ld gp over 1f out: edgd lft but styd on: nt on terms* **7/1**
0246 **5** *1 ¼* **Zain Point (IRE)**[10] 6866 2-8-12 **66**............(t) SteveDrowne 8 59
(Gerard Butler) *hld up nr side: effrt over 2f out: hanging lft but kpt on fnl f: nvr on terms* **11/1**
442 **6** *1* **Traveller's Tales**[15] 6745 2-9-7 **75**............ RyanMoore 3 65
(Richard Hannon) *racd towards far side: mostly chsd wnr to 2f out: wknd qckly* **3/1**[1]
004 **7** *1* **Chatterati (USA)**[27] 6441 2-9-2 **70**............ FrankieDettori 12 58
(Mahmood Al Zarooni) *trckd ldr nr side: led gp 3f out to over 1f out: wknd qckly fnl f* **11/2**[2]
15 **8** *4* **Four Better**[15] 6757 2-9-2 **73**............ SophieDoyle(3) 11 51
(Jamie Osborne) *led nr side quartet to 3f out: wknd rapidly over 1f out* **6/1**[3]
031 **9** *½* **The New Black (IRE)**[109] 3816 2-8-11 **65**............ DavidProbert 1 41
(Gay Kelleway) *racd towards far side: in tch tl wknd qckly 2f out* **20/1**
5500 **10** *1* **Atlantis Crossing (IRE)**[7] 6937 2-7-10 **53**............ NataliaGemelova(3) 2 27
(Jim Boyle) *in tch towards far side: effrt to dispute 2nd 3f out to 2f out: wknd rapidly* **16/1**

1m 28.62s (2.02) **Going Correction** +0.175s/f (Good) **10** Ran SP% **114.0**
Speed ratings (Par 95): **95,90,89,88,87 86,85,80,80,78**
toteswingers:1&2:£15.30, 1&3:£35.00, 2&3:£24.90 CSF £80.43 CT £1158.71 TOTE £18.50: £3.20, £2.80, £4.30; EX 135.10 TRIFECTA Not won..
Owner Sheikh Hamdan Bin Mohammed Al Maktoum **Bred** Darley **Trained** Middleham Moor, N Yorks

FOCUS
They split into two groups, the majority racing up the middle and four runners positioned towards the stands' side. The form is modest and somewhat limited.

NOTEBOOK
Master Of Ages(IRE), who stayed up the centre, was allowed an uncontested lead so this is form to treat with a bit of caution. The winner clearly had much go his way, though he was completely unexposed after three runs over shorter and had been gelded since last seen in June. The ground evidently suited and he could have a profitable end to the year.
Altona(IRE) finished one place behind Traveller's Tales at Salisbury last time, but she proved better suited by these conditions than the Hannon filly and the extra emphasis on stamina was in her favour. (op 7-1 tchd 15-2)
Abshir Zain(IRE) has been given a chance by the handicapper and offered a bit more.
Alice Rose(IRE) fared best of those who raced towards the stands' side, although she didn't help herself by going left under pressure late on. (op 13-2 tchd 6-1 and 15-2)
Zain Point(IRE) travelled well in the stands' side group and offered a bit of encouragement. (op 10-1)
Traveller's Tales couldn't match her maiden form (ahead of Altona last time) and was presumably unsuited by the conditions. (op 11-4)
Chatterati(USA) is another who might not have appreciated the ground. (tchd 13-2)

7082 BRITISH STALLION STUDS SUPPORTING BRITISH RACING EBF MAIDEN STKS (DIV I) 1m 3y
2:30 (2:31) (Class 5) 2-Y-O £2,911 (£866; £432; £216) **Stalls** Centre

Form RPR
1 **Swedish Sailor** 2-9-3 0............ FrankieDettori 2 84+
(Mahmood Al Zarooni) *mde virtually all: gng best ent fnl 2f: pushed along and readily c clr over 1f out: pushed out: easily* **7/2**[1]
2 *5* **Noble Mission** 2-9-3 0............ TomQueally 15 73+
(Sir Henry Cecil) *racd on stands' rail: hld up towards rr: swtchd lft to join main gp and hdwy over 2f out: rdn and outpcd by wnr over 1f out: swtchd lft ins fnl f and kpt on to go 2nd towards fin: no ch w wnr* **6/1**
3 *½* **Frasers Hill** 2-9-3 0............ NeilCallan 12 72+
(Roger Varian) *t.k.h: hld up in tch: hdwy 3f out: chsd wnr and rdn 2f out: drvn and btn over 1f out: wknd fnl 75yds and lost 2nd towards fin* **5/1**[3]
4 **4** *nk* **Commitment**[24] 6529 2-9-3 0............ KierenFallon 13 71+
(Luca Cumani) *racd against stands' rail thrght: w ldrs: rdn and outpcd 2f out: 4th and no ch w wnr 1f out: kpt on again fnl 100yds* **4/1**[2]
65 **5** *2 ¾* **Counsel (IRE)**[22] 6588 2-9-3 0............ RyanMoore 6 65+
(Sir Michael Stoute) *in tch: rdn and unable qck ent fnl 2f: sn outpcd: 5th and wl btn 1f out* **8/1**
42 **6** *3 ½* **Dutch Master**[15] 6742 2-9-3 0............ JimmyFortune 4 57
(Andrew Balding) *pressed ldrs: rdn over 2f out: struggling u.p ent fnl 2f: wknd over 1f out* **9/1**
7 *¾* **Inthar (USA)** 2-9-3 0............ TedDurcan 5 56
(Saeed Bin Suroor) *in tch: rdn and outpcd 2f out: wknd qckly wl over 1f out* **16/1**
8 *nk* **Eagle Power (IRE)** 2-9-3 0............ EddieAhern 14 55
(James Fanshawe) *dwlt: hld up towards rr: rdn and struggling over 2f out: no ch w ldrs fnl 2f: plugged on past btn horses fnl f* **28/1**
0 **9** *nk* **Storm King**[14] 6771 2-9-3 0............ MartinLane 10 54
(George Margarson) *chsd ldrs: rdn and struggling over 2f out: wknd 2f out* **66/1**
10 *shd* **Little Red Minx (IRE)** 2-8-12 0............ RobertHavlin 9 49
(Peter Chapple-Hyam) *s.i.s: hld up in rr of main gp: rdn and wknd over 2f out: no ch fnl 2f* **100/1**
11 *2 ½* **Nordic Quest (IRE)** 2-9-3 0............ JamieSpencer 7 49
(Gerard Butler) *s.i.s: hld up towards rr: rdn and struggling over 2f out: sn wl btn* **20/1**
12 *5* **Three Bards (IRE)** 2-9-3 0............ JoeFanning 1 38
(Mark Johnston) *chsd ldrs tl over 2f out: sn wknd: wl bhd ins fnl f* **20/1**
0 **13** *1 ¼* **Gabrial The Prince (IRE)**[34] 6245 2-9-3 0............ StevieDonohoe 3 35
(David Simcock) *s.i.s: sn rcvrd and in tch in midfield: rdn and wknd 3f out: bhd fnl 2f* **100/1**
00 **14** *16* **Pre Catalan**[27] 6440 2-8-12 0............ TomMcLaughlin 11 —
(Ed Dunlop) *hld up in rr of main gp: rdn and wknd qckly 3f out: sn bhd: eased ins fnl f: t.o* **100/1**
15 *4* **Hard Road** 2-9-3 0............ ChrisCatlin 16 —
(Chris Wall) *s.i.s: sn rdn and a toiling in rr: lost tch 1/2-way: t.o fnl 3f* **100/1**

1m 42.3s (1.70) **Going Correction** +0.175s/f (Good) **15** Ran SP% **118.6**
Speed ratings (Par 95): **98,93,92,92,89 85,85,84,84,84 82,77,75,59,55**
toteswingers:1&2:£4.00, 1&3:£6.40, 2&3:£7.50 CSF £22.48 TOTE £5.80: £1.20, £2.50, £1.40; EX 30.40 Trifecta £170.30 Pool £545.49 - 2.37 winning units..
Owner Godolphin **Bred** Darley **Trained** Newmarket, Suffolk

FOCUS
This maiden went to Sea Moon last year, and in 1998 it was won by the great Dubai Millennium. The winner was impressive.

NOTEBOOK
Swedish Sailor ◆, a half-brother to among others 1m4f Group 3 scorer Synopsis, was well suited by the ground, as well as the resulting stamina test, and is a nice middle-distance prospect. (op 6-1)
Noble Mission is a brother to the brilliant Frankel, as well as a half-brother to Bullet Train, who took the 2009 running of this race. It's doubtful he was helped by being taken to race with only one rival Commitment against the stands' rail after a furlong or so, while the majority raced up the middle, especially as he ended up switching back towards the centre with his challenge, but regardless, this was a promising start. He's not unlike his brother to look at, though is weaker behind at present. From a form perspective, judged on his own merits rather than comparing him to his famous sibling, he travelled like a colt with above-average ability. (op 5-1 tchd 7-1)
Frasers Hill's sales price increased from 55,000gns as a foal to 300,000gns as a yearling. A half-brother to 1m2f Group 3 winner Shimraan, he showed plenty of ability. (op 11-4)
Commitment, a well-held fourth behind the smart-looking Encke on his debut at Newmarket, severely compromised his chance by playing up and sweating beforehand. He ran better than expected in the circumstances and could be quite useful if more relaxed in future. (op 5-1)
Counsel(IRE) ◆ was again well held, but he travelled nicely to a point and has now qualified for a handicap mark. Out of a sister to St Leger winner Brian Boru, he can progress over further next year. (op 9-1)
Dutch Master found this tougher than his first two starts. (op 8-1 tchd 15-2)

7083 BRITISH STALLION STUDS SUPPORTING BRITISH RACING EBF MAIDEN STKS (DIV II) 1m 3y
3:00 (3:01) (Class 5) 2-Y-O £2,911 (£866; £432; £216) **Stalls** Centre

Form RPR
4 **1** **Handsome Man (IRE)**[14] 6774 2-9-3 0............ KierenFallon 11 79+
(Saeed Bin Suroor) *trckd overall ldr nr side: led over 2f out: drvn and clr of rest of gp over 1f out: hld on wl fr far side ldr* **7/2**[1]
2 *½* **Moshaagib (USA)** 2-9-3 0............ RichardHills 5 75+
(John Gosden) *hld up in rr far side: clsd over 2f out: led gp ins fnl f: shkn up and r.o wl: jst hld* **11/2**[2]
3 *2 ½* **Mossbrae** 2-9-3 0............ NeilCallan 1 70+
(Roger Varian) *wl in tch far side: clsd to chal 2f out: led gp briefly 1f out and wl on terms w nr side wnr: one pce* **12/1**
4 *1* **Ruban (IRE)** 2-9-3 0............ FrankieDettori 2 68+
(Mahmood Al Zarooni) *led gp towards far side and wl on terms: hdd and no ex 1f out* **7/2**[1]
5 *2 ¾* **Bonnet De Douche (IRE)** 2-8-12 0............ RobertHavlin 15 57
(Peter Chapple-Hyam) *trckd ldrs nr side: cl enough over 2f out: chsd wnr fnl 2f but sn lft bhd* **100/1**
6 *1 ¼* **Cyrus Sod** 2-9-3 0............ MartinLane 8 59
(David Simcock) *chsd nr side ldrs: outpcd and rdn over 2f out: plugged on fnl f* **66/1**
7 *½* **Sun Central (IRE)** 2-9-3 0............ ShaneKelly 10 58+
(William Haggas) *hld up wl in rr nr side: swtchd lft over 2f out: rn green and hanging over 1f out: styd on quite takingly nr fin* **12/1**
6 **8** *nk* **Supreme Rock**[13] 6792 2-9-3 0............ JamieSpencer 12 57
(Jim Boyle) *wl on terms towards nr side: rdn and w wnr jst over 2f out: wknd over 1f out* **33/1**
50 **9** *shd* **Ukrainian (IRE)**[24] 6527 2-9-3 0............ JoeFanning 14 57
(Mark Johnston) *mde most on nr side to over 2f out: wknd* **25/1**
05 **10** *hd* **Romantic (IRE)**[57] 5564 2-9-3 0............ TomQueally 3 57
(Sir Henry Cecil) *wl on terms towards nr side: shkn up over 2f out: grad fdd* **9/1**[3]
0 **11** *nk* **Rye House (IRE)**[33] 6267 2-9-3 0............ RyanMoore 6 58+
(Sir Michael Stoute) *towards rr: c towards nr side fr 1/2-way: pushed along 3f out: in rr whn nt clr run over 1f out: kpt on* **12/1**
12 *½* **Blazing Speed** 2-9-3 0............ EddieAhern 9 55
(James Fanshawe) *trckd ldrs nr side: shkn up over 2f out: steadily wknd* **12/1**
13 *22* **Ze King** 2-9-3 0............ ChrisCatlin 7 6
(Chris Wall) *in tch over 4f: sn wknd: t.o* **150/1**
14 *13* **Tis Rock 'N' Roll (USA)** 2-9-3 0............ TedDurcan 4 —
(David Lanigan) *racd towards far side: in tch to 1/2-way: wknd: t.o* **10/1**

1m 43.28s (2.68) **Going Correction** +0.175s/f (Good) **14** Ran SP% **119.6**
Speed ratings (Par 95): **93,92,90,89,86 85,84,84,84,83 83,83,61,48**
toteswingers:1&2:£4.70, 1&3:£11.40, 2&3:£14.40 CSF £21.36 TOTE £5.40: £1.80, £2.00, £4.80; EX 33.00 Trifecta £360.90 Pool £565.82 - 1.16 winning units..
Owner Godolphin **Bred** Bloomsbury Stud **Trained** Newmarket, Suffolk

FOCUS
Division two of what can be a good maiden. Considering the ground was deteriorating as the meeting progressed, time comparisons would be misleading. They raced middle to stands' side and the winner put up an improved effort.

NOTEBOOK
Handsome Man(IRE) handled similarly testing ground okay when fourth on his debut at Newcastle (third-placed finisher from same stable won next time) and showed a good attitude to confirm that promise. He raced with the main pace for much of the way (towards the near side), but any potential advantage disappeared when his main rivals emerged away towards the centre of the track and he had to work hard, pulling clear of his bunch. His performance probably deserves upgrading. (tchd 4-1)
Moshaagib(USA), a $500,000 brother to a smart performer at around 1m2f in the US, had to be niggled along a fair way out but gradually got the idea and fared best of the four runners who ended up centre-field. (op 7-1 tchd 8-1)
Mossbrae, a 65,000gns purchase, has already been gelded. He travelled well to a point and, considering there's plenty of stamina on the dam's side of his pedigree, he should do better over further in due course. (op 11-1)
Ruban(IRE) was sold for just 9,000gns as a foal but fetched 100,000gns this April. He showed plenty of ability and should build on this. (op 4-1 tchd 3-1)
Bonnet De Douche(IRE) made a fine debut considering she was the only filly in the line-up.
Sun Central(IRE) ◆, a half-brother to among others George Washington and Grandera, very much caught the eye going on well near the finish, having looked badly in need of the experience. (op 16-1)

FOCUS
The first pair came right away in a driving finish in this moderate sprint maiden and the form looks straightforward, with the third the best guide.

7094 BETDAQ MULTIPLES BRITISH STALLION STUDS E B F MAIDEN STKS 1m (P)
7:05 (7:06) (Class 5) 2-Y-O **£2,911** (£866; £432; £216) **Stalls** Low

Form RPR

53 **1** **Holly Martins**[14] 6792 2-8-10 0 ....(t) NicoleNordblad(7) 9 76
(Hans Adielsson) *mde all: pushed along and kpt on wl fr over 2f out: hrd pressed fnl f: hld together and a fending off runner-up* **20/1**

6 **2** *hd* **Dynastic**[42] 6059 2-9-3 0 .... RyanMoore 2 76+
(Sir Michael Stoute) *hld up in midfield: prog 3f out: chsd wnr over 1f out: drvn to chal fnl f: a jst hld nr fin* **9/4**[2]

3 **3** *2 ½* **Circus Mondao (USA)**[28] 6462 2-9-3 0 .... FrankieDettori 10 70
(Mahmood Al Zarooni) *trckd wnr after 2f: rdn over 2f out: nt qckn and lost 2nd over 1f out: one pce after* **10/11**[1]

0 **4** *5* **Attraction Ticket**[25] 6529 2-9-3 0 .... MartinLane 6 59+
(David Simcock) *racd wd in midfield: drvn over 2f out: hanging but kpt on one pce after: nvr on terms* **50/1**

00 **5** *2* **Retromania (IRE)**[1] 7080 2-9-3 0 .... LukeMorris 4 54
(John Best) *wl in rr: rdn in 9th over 4f out and struggling to stay in tch: passed wkng rivals 2f out: nvr on terms* **100/1**

0 **6** *hd* **Tazweed (IRE)**[14] 6795 2-9-3 0 .... NeilCallan 7 54
(Roger Varian) *wl in rr: pushed along in 10th and struggling over 4f out: sme prog fnl 2f: kpt on but nvr on terms* **25/1**

7 *hd* **Samedi** 2-8-12 0 .... SilvestreDeSousa 5 48
(Mark Johnston) *chsd ldrs: rdn and cl enough over 2f out: wknd qckly jst over 1f out* **14/1**

54 **8** *2 ¾* **Yes It's The Boy (USA)**[23] 6579 2-9-3 0 ....(t) J-PGuillambert 3 47
(Ed Walker) *plld hrd: chsd wnr 2f: styd handy tl wknd qckly wl over 1f out* **25/1**

9 *5* **Letham Cottage** 2-9-3 0 .... JamesDoyle 13 35
(David Evans) *chsd ldrs: rdn over 3f out: wknd over 2f out* **100/1**

10 *8* **Graylyn Olivaa** 2-9-3 0 .... AndreaAtzeni 1 17
(Robert Eddery) *chsd ldrs: rdn 1/2-way: sn wknd: t.o* **66/1**

0 **11** *½* **Silver Native (IRE)**[93] 4384 2-9-3 0 .... AdamKirby 11 16
(Mike Murphy) *a wl in rr: rdn in 11th and struggling over 4f out: t.o* **100/1**

12 *8* **Quernstone (USA)** 2-9-3 0 .... AhmedAjtebi 12 —
(Mahmood Al Zarooni) *s.i.s: rn green and mostly in last pair: a wl bhd: t.o* **10/1**[3]

13 *12* **Vagabond King** 2-9-3 0 .... MarcHalford 8 —
(Edward Creighton) *s.v.s: rn green and a in last pair: t.o* **100/1**

1m 39.37s (-0.43) **Going Correction** -0.075s/f (Stan) **13 Ran SP% 118.8**
Speed ratings (Par 95): **99,98,96,91,89 89,88,86,81,73 72,64,52**
toteswingers: 1&2 £7.60, 1&3 £5.30, 2&3 £1.10 CSF £62.98 TOTE £34.20: £3.50, £1.02, £1.30; EX 78.80.
Owner The Third Man **Bred** Biddestone Stud **Trained** Kingston Lisle, Oxon

FOCUS
There was a proper turn up in this juvenile maiden. The form is rated around the principals.

NOTEBOOK
Holly Martins made all to deny the big two in the market. He showed an engine when third over this trip at Lingfield last time, but didn't look willing in a first-time hood that day. The decision to send him from the front this time worked the oracle, though, and his latent ability saw him just last home. Much depends on his temperament regards his future, but this is clearly the way to ride him.
Dynastic was expected to step up markedly on his debut form at Sandown. He looked the one to be on around 1f out, but couldn't master the runner-up at the finish. Had he been able to sit more handily he would have surely prevailed and he will no doubt be winning races as he matures. (op 7-4)
Circus Mondao(USA) was the big disappointment, having gone close on his debut at Salisbury last month. He sat a lot more handily here, trying to negate his wide draw, and was in the ideal position turning for home. Frankie Dettori sent out distress signals 2f out, however, and he proved laboured under pressure. (op 11-10)
Attraction Ticket was doing some fair work late on and looks sure to come on again for the experience. (op 40-1)
Tazweed(IRE) again proved distinctly green, but the penny finally dropped late on and he's one to keep an eye on. (op 33-1)
Graylyn Olivaa Official explanation: jockey said colt ran green
Silver Native(IRE) Official explanation: jockey said colt ran green
Quernstone(USA) Official explanation: jockey said colt ran green

7095 BETDAQ MOBILE APPS NURSERY 1m (P)
7:35 (7:36) (Class 4) (0-85,84) 2-Y-O **£3,428** (£1,020; £509; £254) **Stalls** Low

Form RPR

4312 **1** **Venetian View (IRE)**[27] 6484 2-9-5 **82** .... RyanMoore 7 86
(Gary Moore) *hld up in last trio as ldrs set str pce: wound up fr 2f out: gd prog fnl f: r.o to ld last 50yds* **10/3**[1]

436 **2** *½* **Jack Of Diamonds (IRE)**[25] 6524 2-8-12 **75** .... DaneO'Neill 9 78
(Roger Teal) *sn trckd ldng pair on outer: chal 2f out: rdn to ld jst over 1f out and looked like holding on: hdd last 50yds* **16/1**

421 **3** *shd* **Ahzeemah (IRE)**[14] 6795 2-9-2 **79** ....(p) TedDurcan 8 82
(Saeed Bin Suroor) *hld up in last trio: rdn and hanging over 2f out: picked up over 1f out and followed wnr through fnl f: nrly snatched 2nd* **9/1**[3]

14 **4** *½* **Three Am Tour (IRE)**[38] 6196 2-9-7 **84** .... RichardHughes 2 85
(Richard Hannon) *hld up in last trio: looking for room over 2f out: swtchd sharply rt wl over 1f out and prog: clsd on ldrs fnl f: nt qckn last 75yds* **9/1**[3]

402 **5** *¾* **Curzon Line**[14] 6795 2-9-1 **78** .... FrankieDettori 6 78
(Mahmood Al Zarooni) *chsd ldr's str pce: rdn to ld over 2f out: hdd jst over 1f out: lost pls last 100yds* **9/2**[2]

21 **6** *nk* **Gassin Golf**[71] 5142 2-9-0 **77** .... SebSanders 5 76+
(Sir Mark Prescott Bt) *slowest away and rousted along to rch midfield: drvn over 2f out: tried to cl over 1f out: one pce fnl f* **9/2**[2]

6326 **7** *1 ¾* **Goldream**[15] 6774 2-9-3 **80** .... KierenFallon 3 75
(Luca Cumani) *chsd ldrs: rdn over 3f out: struggling to hold pl over 2f out: tried to cl again over 1f out: fdd ins fnl f* **9/2**[2]

261 **8** *3 ½* **Halling Dancer**[27] 6474 2-9-1 **78** .... NeilCallan 1 65
(John Akehurst) *prom: rdn wl over 2f out: nt qckn wl over 1f out: wknd* **10/1**

001 **9** *3 ¾* **Bounty Seeker (USA)**[77] 4919 2-9-1 **78** .... SilvestreDeSousa 4 56
(Mark Johnston) *led at str pce: urged along fr 1/2-way: hdd over 2f out: wknd over 1f out* **16/1**

1m 39.28s (-0.52) **Going Correction** -0.075s/f (Stan) **9 Ran SP% 118.5**
Speed ratings (Par 97): **99,98,98,97,97 96,95,91,87**
toteswingers: 1&2 £15.20, 1&3 £5.90, 2&3 £7.20 CSF £60.42 CT £364.55 TOTE £4.50: £1.10, £7.50, £4.10; EX 62.90.
Owner R A Green **Bred** J F Tuthill **Trained** Lower Beeding, W Sussex

FOCUS
This looked an above-average nursery. There was a sound pace on and, despite there being any amount of chances inside the final furlong, the best horse came through the win. The form is rated slightly positively.

NOTEBOOK
Venetian View(IRE) got back to winning ways under a cracking ride and is now 2-2 at this venue. Ryan Moore bided his time and was last turning for home, but produced him with perfect timing towards the outside. He obviously loves this surface and there should be more to come over this trip. (op 3-1 tchd 7-2)
Jack Of Diamonds(IRE) ◆, drawn widest, took it up at the furlong pole and ran a big race. He wasn't able to reverse previous 7f course form with the winner despite being on 7lb better terms, but there is no doubt a race for him round here back over 7f.
Ahzeemah(IRE), back up in trip for his nursery bow, came from a similar position as the winner and made his challenge widest of all in the home straight. He took a long time to hit top gear and would have been second in another stride. He confirmed his winning Lingfield form with his owner's Curzon Line, who was ahead of him in the betting and 1lb better off. (tchd 10-1)
Three Am Tour(IRE), a maiden winner here on her penultimate outing, proved keen under restraint and that didn't help her get home over this extra furlong. (op 10-1 tchd 12-1)
Gassin Golf looked potentially well treated on this nursery debut. He again missed the kick, though, and being rushed up to recover likely cost him at the business end. (op 5-1)
Goldream, given a suicidal ride on turf last time, was solid in the betting for this switch to a nursery and return to Polytrack. He responded to pressure off the home turn, but petered out late on and looks worth dropping back a furlong. (tchd 5-1)

7096 CONEXION COMMUNICATIONS CLASSIFIED STKS 7f (P)
8:05 (8:07) (Class 6) 3-Y-0+ **£1,617** (£481; £240; £120) **Stalls** Low

Form RPR

650 **1** **Demoiselle Bond**[35] 6257 3-9-0 45 .... SteveDrowne 2 56
(Lydia Richards) *mde all: rdn and edgd lft fr over 2f out: 2 l clr over 1f out: kpt on* **100/1**

0044 **2** *1 ¼* **Miss Villefranche**[59] 5515 3-9-0 55 ....(v) AdamKirby 7 53+
(Michael Bell) *dwlt: wl in rr: stdy prog fr 1/2-way: rdn over 1f out: wnt 2nd jst ins fnl f: no imp on wnr nr fin* **7/1**[3]

024 **3** *nk* **Shaws Diamond (USA)**[8] 6940 5-9-2 54 ....(v) RobbieFitzpatrick 12 52
(Derek Shaw) *mostly chsd wnr: drvn and no imp over 2f out: lost 2nd ins fnl f: kpt on* **9/1**

04 **4** *nse* **Khaki (IRE)**[13] 6816 3-9-0 53 .... SilvestreDeSousa 5 52
(David Evans) *chsd ldrs: urged along fr 4f out: drvn to dispute 2nd 2f out: one pce after* **14/1**

343 **5** *1 ¼* **Yellow Printer**[5] 7005 5-9-2 55 ....(b) FergusSweeney 11 49+
(Mark Gillard) *wl in rr: rdn on outer over 2f out: styd on fr jst over 1f out: nrst fin* **11/2**[2]

0330 **6** *2 ¼* **Qaraqum (USA)**[16] 6746 4-9-2 55 .... KierenFallon 8 43
(Denis Coakley) *prom: shkn up to dispute 2nd 2f out: nt qckn over 1f out: eased whn btn ins fnl f* **11/2**[2]

0320 **7** *½* **Princess Willow**[14] 6784 3-9-0 55 .... SamHitchcott 6 41
(John E Long) *chsd ldrs: rdn over 2f out: nt qckn wl over 1f out: fdd fnl f* **16/1**

5450 **8** *2* **Harvest Mist (IRE)**[10] 6889 3-9-0 55 .... NeilChalmers 14 36
(Michael Blanshard) *rring in stalls: awkward s: wl in rr: no prog over 2f out: modest late prog* **25/1**

2614 **9** *3 ¼* **Love Nest**[21] 6626 3-9-0 55 .... EddieAhern 9 27
(John Dunlop) *settled towards rr: effrt over 2f out: tried to cl on ldrs over 1f out: wknd fnl f* **7/2**[1]

0350 **10** *hd* **Queen's Choice (IRE)**[50] 5803 3-9-0 50 .... StephenCraine 3 26
(Anabel K Murphy) *dwlt: wl in rr: effrt towards inner over 2f out: sme prog over 1f out: sn wknd* **40/1**

065 **11** *2 ¾* **Treasure Act**[16] 6754 3-9-0 55 .... LiamKeniry 4 19
(Patrick Chamings) *in tch tl wknd over 2f out* **12/1**

0000 **12** *12* **Sylas Ings**[95] 4321 3-9-0 55 .... IanMongan 1 —
(Pat Phelan) *v restless in stalls: nvr gng wl and t.o after 3f* **15/2**

0-00 **13** *4 ½* **Emerald Royal**[245] 655 3-9-0 47 ....(t) MarcHalford 13 —
(Edward Creighton) *prom tl wknd rapidly 3f out: t.o* **80/1**

1m 25.72s (-0.28) **Going Correction** -0.075s/f (Stan)
WFA 3 from 4yo+ 2lb **13 Ran SP% 116.0**
Speed ratings (Par 101): **98,96,96,96,94 92,91,89,85,85 82,68,63**
toteswingers: 1&2 £87.70, 1&3 £26.80, 2&3 £7.60 CSF £690.48 TOTE £202.00: £43.70, £3.00, £2.80; EX 1575.70.
Owner The Demoiselle Bond Partnership **Bred** Mrs Lydia Richards **Trained** Funtington, W Sussex

FOCUS
An ordinary contest and a typically tight affair of its type. The fourth is rated to his latest mark in a similar contest.
Demoiselle Bond Official explanation: trainer said, regarding apparent improvement in form, that the filly was suited by being able to make the running.
Harvest Mist(IRE) Official explanation: jockey said filly reared as stalls opened
Sylas Ings Official explanation: jockey said gelding never travelled

7097 RACING@SKYSPORTS.COM H'CAP 7f (P)
8:35 (8:37) (Class 5) (0-75,75) 3-Y-0+ **£2,264** (£673; £336; £168) **Stalls** Low

Form RPR

4660 **1** **Al Aqabah (IRE)**[14] 6796 6-9-2 **70** ....(b) SilvestreDeSousa 11 80
(Brian Gubby) *prom: chsd ldr over 1f out: drvn into narrow ld ins fnl f: asserted nr fin* **13/2**[3]

2200 **2** *½* **Sermons Mount (USA)**[10] 6895 5-9-1 **72** .... JohnFahy(3) 12 81
(Peter Hedger) *t.k.h: trckd ldr: drvn ahd 2f out: hdd ins fnl f: no ex nr fin* **12/1**

3150 **3** *1 ¼* **Requisite**[35] 6256 6-9-7 **75** ....(b) JamesDoyle 1 81+
(Ian Wood) *hld up in last trio: stl plenty to do over 2f out: gd prog over 1f out: wnt 3rd ins fnl f: nvr cl enough to chal* **10/1**

1530 **4** *1* **Stonecrabstomorrow (IRE)**[8] 6931 8-8-6 **65** .... MarkCoumbe(5) 7 68+
(Michael Attwater) *settled wl in rr: rdn over 2f out: prog over 1f out: styd on to take 4th nr fin* **20/1**

3034 **5** *hd* **Sakhee's Pearl**[35] 6256 5-9-7 **75** ....(b) IanMongan 13 77
(Jo Crowley) *chsd ldrs on outer: drvn 2f out and tried to cl: kpt on same pce fr over 1f out* **5/1**[2]

0500 **6** *shd* **Copperwood**[32] 6354 6-9-0 **68** .... DaneO'Neill 9 70
(Michael Blanshard) *hld up in midfield: effrt and swtchd rt wl over 1f out: tried to cl sn after: one pce fnl f* **11/1**

4033 **7** *1 ½* **Speak The Truth (IRE)**[14] 6793 5-8-3 **62** .... NathanAlison(5) 8 60
(Jim Boyle) *chsd ldng pair: rdn over 2f out: wknd fnl f* **8/1**

2141 **8** *1 ½* **Elsie's Orphan**[72] 5100 4-9-5 **73** .... LiamKeniry 10 67
(Patrick Chamings) *s.i.s: sn in midfield: effrt over 2f out: no prog and btn over 1f out* **4/1**[1]

0000 **9** *3/4* **City Legend**[6] 6980 3-8-13 **72**....................(vt) KieranO'Neill(3) 3 64
(Alan McCabe) *led but needed plenty of urging to stay there: hdd 2f out: wknd over 1f out* **33/1**

5000 **10** *3* **Sir Mozart (IRE)**[23] 6583 8-8-13 **67**.................... MartinHarley 2 51
(Barney Curley) *hld up in rr: shuffled along fr 2f out: nvr nr ldrs: capable of bttr* **20/1**

0000 **10** *dht* **Bassett Road (IRE)**[16] 6762 3-9-5 **75**.................... ShaneKelly 6 59
(Willie Musson) *chsd ldrs: rdn and effrt towards inner 2f out: wknd over 1f out* **10/1**

/0-4 **12** *1* **Mac Tiernan (IRE)**[32] 6360 4-9-1 **69**.................... AdamKirby 5 50
(Pat Murphy) *a towards rr: shkn up and no prog 2f out: wl btn over 1f out* **28/1**

0660 **13** *8* **Bubbly Braveheart (IRE)**[14] 6794 4-8-3 **62**.......... JemmaMarshall(5) 4 22
(Pat Phelan) *a struggling in rr: t.o* **20/1**

1m 24.84s (-1.16) **Going Correction** -0.075s/f (Stan)
WFA 3 from 4yo+ 2lb **13** Ran SP% **116.0**
Speed ratings (Par 103): **103,102,101,99,99 99,97,96,95,91 91,90,81**
toteswingers: 1&2 £21.70, 1&3 £20.50, 2&3 £48.60 CSF £72.25 CT £799.38 TOTE £7.10: £3.40, £6.90, £5.10; EX 121.60.
Owner Brian Gubby **Bred** Ocal Bloodstock **Trained** Bagshot, Surrey

FOCUS
A modest handicap that looked wide-open. There was a solid pace on and the first two are rated as running slight personal bests with the third a shade off his best from the rear.
Mac Tiernan(IRE) Official explanation: jockey said gelding ran too free

7098 CONEXION COMMUNICATIONS H'CAP 1m (P)
9:05 (9:05) (Class 5) (0-75,75) 3-Y-O+ **£2,264** (£673; £336; £168) **Stalls** Low

Form RPR

0000 **1** **The Which Doctor**[14] 6797 6-8-11 **65**....................(e) MartinHarley 12 75
(Richard Guest) *hld up in rr: stdy prog fr over 2f out: rdn to ld over 1f out: hld on nr fin* **20/1**

0432 **2** *nk* **Change The Subject (USA)**[45] 5960 3-9-2 **73**.................... MartinLane 1 82
(David Simcock) *chsd ldr 3f: styd prom: rdn to go 2nd again 2f out: upsides over 1f out: chsd wnr after: styd on but jst hld nr fin* **6/1[3]**

0-40 **3** *1/2* **Peponi**[20] 6658 5-9-5 **73**.................... SteveDrowne 3 81
(Peter Makin) *mde most: rdn and hdd over 1f out: kpt on wl fnl f but a hld after* **7/1**

54-0 **4** *2 3/4* **Reverend Green (IRE)**[28] 6439 5-9-7 **75**.................... DaneO'Neill 2 77
(Chris Down) *trckd ldrs: rdn and nt qckn 2f out: one pce and no imp after* **15/2**

1101 **5** *3 1/4* **Catchanova (IRE)**[23] 6586 4-9-7 **75**.................... SebSanders 5 69
(Eve Johnson Houghton) *trckd ldrs: rdn and nt qckn 2f out: wknd over 1f out* **5/2[1]**

5000 **6** *shd* **Fault**[11] 6878 5-8-2 **61**.................... AmyScott(5) 11 55
(Alastair Lidderdale) *t.k.h on outer: prog to chse ldr after 3f to 2f out: fdd* **33/1**

503 **7** *2 3/4* **Rock Anthem (IRE)**[9] 6924 7-8-8 **62**.................... SilvestreDeSousa 8 49
(Mike Murphy) *t.k.h: hld up towards rr: rdn and nt qckn over 2f out: wl hld after* **3/1[2]**

0504 **8** *2 3/4* **Mcconnell (USA)**[29] 6433 6-9-4 **72**.................... AmirQuinn 7 53
(Gary Moore) *wl in tch in midfield tl wknd over 2f out* **33/1**

3000 **9** *5* **Rezwaan**[14] 6796 4-9-5 **73**....................(b) ShaneKelly 6 43
(Murty McGrath) *hld up in rr: pushed along on inner over 2f out: sn no prog: wknd over 1f out* **33/1**

3000 **10** *8* **Douze Points (IRE)**[47] 5879 5-9-7 **75**.................... AdamKirby 4 26
(Pat Murphy) *hld up in rr: last and struggling 1/2-way: wd bnd 3f out: wl bhd after: t.o* **14/1**

0-00 **11** *2* **Striking Priorite**[28] 6453 3-8-1 **61** oh3.................... KieranO'Neill(3) 9 —
(Tim Fitzgerald) *hld up in rr: rdn and struggling 3f out: t.o* **33/1**

1m 39.0s (-0.80) **Going Correction** -0.075s/f (Stan)
WFA 3 from 4yo+ 3lb **11** Ran SP% **115.3**
Speed ratings (Par 103): **101,100,100,97,94 94,91,88,83,75 73**
toteswingers: 1&2 £26.90, 1&3 £131.80, 2&3 £6.60 CSF £127.21 CT £948.09 TOTE £28.00: £9.30, £2.50, £3.60; EX 225.50.
Owner Rakebackmypoker.com **Bred** Limestone And Tara Studs **Trained** Stainforth, S Yorks

FOCUS
Another modest handicap. It was run at routine sort of pace and the principals dominated the final furlong. The winner is rated to this year's form backed up by the placed horses.
T/Plt: £207.40 to a £1 stake. Pool: £58,402.51. 205.50 winning tickets. T/Qpdt: £27.40 to a £1 stake. Pool: £9,136.43. 245.90 winning tickets. JN

6379 MUSSELBURGH (R-H)
Wednesday, October 26
OFFICIAL GOING: Good (good to soft in places on straight course; 6.4)
Wind: Light, half against Weather: Sunny

7099 WILLIAM HILL SCOTTISH CUP (S) H'CAP 1m 1f
2:10 (2:10) (Class 6) (0-65,65) 3-Y-O+ **£1,617** (£481; £240; £120) **Stalls** Low

Form RPR

0002 **1** **Royal Straight**[5] 7003 6-8-9 **55**....................(t) JulieBurke(5) 10 69+
(Linda Perratt) *t.k.h: hld up: smooth hdwy over 2f out: edgd rt and led over 1f out: sn rdn clr: kpt on strly: eased nr fin* **11/2[2]**

0450 **2** *1 1/4* **Monthly Medal**[15] 6777 8-9-3 **58**....................(t) JamesSullivan 9 66
(Wilf Storey) *t.k.h: hld up towards rr: hdwy over 2f out: effrt and chsd wnr over 1f out: hung rt and kpt on fnl f: nt rch eased-down wnr* **25/1**

5250 **3** *7* **Military Call**[11] 6872 4-8-12 **60**....................(v[1]) JustinNewman(7) 8 53
(Alistair Whillans) *trckd ldrs: ev ch gng wl over 2f out: rdn over 1f out: kpt on same pce* **8/1[3]**

3255 **4** *1 1/4* **Goninodaethat**[29] 6430 3-8-9 **54**.................... LeeNewman 5 44
(Jim Goldie) *t.k.h: led tl rdn and hdd over 1f out: nt qckn* **5/1[1]**

5262 **5** *3/4* **Whispering Spirit (IRE)**[27] 6490 5-9-6 **61**....................(v) FrederikTylicki 4 49
(Ann Duffield) *prom: effrt and rdn on outside 2f out: sn no ex* **11/2[2]**

0260 **6** *hd* **Bright Applause**[15] 6775 3-9-1 **60**.................... TomEaves 7 48
(Tracy Waggott) *dwlt: hld up towards rr: effrt whn nt clr run briefly 2f out: sn no imp* **9/1**

4000 **7** *3 1/4* **Kalahaag (IRE)**[27] 6472 3-8-10 **58**....................(p) BillyCray(3) 1 39
(David Nicholls) *trckd ldrs: rdn over 2f out: wknd over 1f out* **16/1**

0060 **8** *14* **Just Five (IRE)**[22] 6616 5-9-10 **65**....................(v[1]) PhillipMakin 12 15
(John Weymes) *t.k.h: hld up in midfield: outpcd over 2f out: edgd rt and sn btn: t.o* **40/1**

0002 **9** *12* **Let's Face Facts**[71] 5153 4-8-13 **54**.................... DanielTudhope 14 —
(Jim Goldie) *bhd on outside: struggling after 3f: nvr on terms: t.o* **11/1**

2330 **10** *2* **Jupiter Fidius**[28] 6452 4-9-5 **60**....................(p) PaulHanagan 13 —
(Kate Walton) *in midfield on outside: struggling and hung rt over 2f out: sn btn: t.o* **11/2[2]**

030 **11** *1* **Aqua Lad**[11] 6868 3-9-1 **60**.................... JoeFanning 3 —
(Mark Johnston) *towards rr: rdn and edgd lft 3f out: sn btn: t.o* **18/1**

05-6 **12** *17* **Number One Guy**[11] 6872 4-9-0 **60**.................... AdamCarter(5) 11 —
(Philip Kirby) *hld up: struggling over 4f out: sn btn: t.o* **25/1**

1m 54.79s (0.89) **Going Correction** +0.10s/f (Good)
WFA 3 from 4yo+ 4lb **12** Ran SP% **113.5**
Speed ratings (Par 101): **100,98,92,91,90 90,87,75,64,62 62,46**
toteswingers:1&2:£47.70, 1&3:£16.80, 2&3:£42.60 CSF £134.31 CT £1087.26 TOTE £6.90: £2.10, £10.20, £3.40; EX 237.60.There was no bid for the winner
Owner Ken McGarrity **Bred** Brook Stud Bloodstock & Leydens Farm Stud **Trained** East Kilbride, S Lanarks

FOCUS
On a lovely late autumn day the ground had dried out and was described as 'soft' and 'good to soft', but the winning time of the first suggested it was riding just on the slow side of good. A standard selling handicap run at a sound pace with the winner to this year's best.

7100 TURFTV H'CAP 5f
2:40 (2:40) (Class 6) (0-60,60) 3-Y-O+ **£1,617** (£481; £240; £120) **Stalls** High

Form RPR

5010 **1** **Here Now And Why (IRE)**[51] 5787 4-9-1 **54**.................... RobertWinston 5 64+
(Ian Semple) *in tch: effrt and drvn over 1f out: led ins fnl f: kpt on u.p* **5/1[2]**

224 **2** *3/4* **Cayman Fox**[28] 6454 6-9-5 **58**.................... PJMcDonald 3 66
(Linda Perratt) *cl up: effrt and ev ch over 1f out to ins fnl f: kpt on fin* **16/1**

0055 **3** *hd* **Berbice (IRE)**[15] 6779 6-9-6 **59**....................(b) PaulHanagan 4 66
(Linda Perratt) *dwlt: hld up: smooth hdwy to dispute ld ins fnl f: sn rdn: fnd little* **5/1[2]**

5020 **4** *2 1/4* **Sandwith**[56] 5620 8-8-13 **55**....................(b) GaryBartley(3) 12 54
(George Foster) *t.k.h: cl up: led 2f out to ins fnl f: kpt on same pce* **12/1**

1206 **5** *nk* **Mission Impossible**[15] 6778 6-9-7 **60**....................(p) PatrickMathers 10 58
(Tracy Waggott) *in tch: drvn along 1/2-way: edgd rt over 1f out: no imp fnl f* **9/2[1]**

4502 **6** *nk* **Triskaidekaphobia**[22] 6602 8-8-10 **49**....................(t) JamesSullivan 7 46
(Wilf Storey) *cl up: rdn and lost pl 2f out: styd on ins fnl f: nvr able to chal* **20/1**

500 **7** *nk* **Boucher Garcon (IRE)**[48] 5865 3-8-3 **47**.................... NeilFarley(5) 14 43
(Declan Carroll) *led to 2f out: sn drvn along and kpt on same pce* **16/1**

0006 **8** *1/2* **Carrie's Magic**[30] 6414 4-9-2 **60**....................(b) GarryWhillans(5) 1 54
(Alistair Whillans) *dwlt: bhd on outside: effrt 1/2-way: no imp over 1f out* **20/1**

0510 **9** *1* **Distant Sun (USA)**[18] 6694 7-9-5 **58**....................(p) PhillipMakin 2 48
(Linda Perratt) *in tch: drvn along 1/2-way: no ex over 1f out* **12/1**

0600 **10** *1 1/4* **Hitches Dubai (BRZ)**[35] 6266 6-8-7 **46**.................... JoeFanning 11 32
(Geoffrey Harker) *bhd and sn outpcd: nvr on terms* **25/1**

0060 **11** *5* **Ya Boy Sir (IRE)**[31] 6386 4-8-7 **46** oh1....................(b) PaddyAspell 13 14
(Ian Semple) *in tch: struggling 2f out: btn fnl f* **33/1**

4030 **12** *1 1/4* **Hygrove Gal**[10] 6889 3-9-2 **55**.................... TomEaves 8 18
(Bryan Smart) *bhd and sn struggling: no ch fr 1/2-way* **14/1**

3213 **13** *3 3/4* **Novalist**[49] 5824 3-9-3 **56**....................(b) LeeNewman 9 —
(Robin Bastiman) *towards rr and sn pushed along: nvr on terms* **6/1[3]**

61.75 secs (1.35) **Going Correction** +0.20s/f (Good) **13** Ran SP% **115.9**
Speed ratings (Par 101): **97,95,95,91,91 90,90,89,88,86 78,76,70**
toteswingers:1&2:£14.30, 1&3:£7.10, 2&3:£8.00 CSF £74.83 CT £337.32 TOTE £5.90: £1.80, £4.00, £2.20; EX 72.70.
Owner Kenman Properties **Bred** Mrs Sandra McCarthy **Trained** Carluke, S Lanarks
■ Stewards' Enquiry : Robert Winston seven-day ban: used whip with excessive frequency (Nov 10,12-14,17)

FOCUS
A low-grade sprint handicap and the pace was strong. The runner-up is rated in line with his recent best.
Novalist Official explanation: jockey said gelding hit its head on stall gates

7101 BRITISH STALLION STUDS SUPPORTING BRITISH RACING E B F MAIDEN STKS 1m
3:15 (3:15) (Class 4) 2-Y-O **£5,175** (£1,540; £769; £384) **Stalls** Low

Form RPR

2224 **1** **Choisan (IRE)**[5] 6983 2-9-3 79.................... DavidAllan 7 81
(Tim Easterby) *mde all: rdn and clr 1f out: kpt on strly* **2/1[1]**

2 *1 1/2* **Golden Halo (IRE)**[30] 6420 2-9-3 0.................... PaulHanagan 6 78
(David Marnane, Ire) *t.k.h: sn cl up: hung lft and wnt 2nd over 1f out: kpt on ins fnl f: nt rch wnr* **7/2[2]**

3 *3/4* **Sparkling Portrait** 2-9-3 0.................... TonyHamilton 2 76+
(Richard Fahey) *dwlt: hld up: effrt and rn green on outside 2f out: kpt on fnl f: bttr for r* **25/1**

4 **4** *3 3/4* **Clon Brulee (IRE)**[28] 6448 2-9-3 0.................... LeeNewman 5 67
(David Barron) *in tch: pushed along over 3f out: no imp fr 2f out* **10/1**

5 **5** *2* **No Time To Cry**[12] 6837 2-8-12 0.................... FrederikTylicki 3 58
(Ann Duffield) *in tch: drvn along over 3f out: outpcd fr 2f out* **50/1**

4 **6** *nk* **Brockwell**[18] 6702 2-9-3 0.................... RichardKingscote 4 62
(Tom Dascombe) *hld up on outside: struggling over 2f out: sn btn* **7/2[2]**

4 **7** *6* **Star Date (IRE)**[15] 6772 2-9-3 0.................... TomEaves 1 48
(Gerard Butler) *t.k.h: hld up: drvn along over 2f out: btn over 1f out* **9/2[3]**

06 **8** *hd* **Lost Highway (IRE)**[15] 6772 2-8-12 0.................... JoeFanning 8 43
(Mark Johnston) *chsd wnr: rdn and edgd lft 2f out: sn btn* **25/1**

1m 42.66s (1.46) **Going Correction** +0.10s/f (Good) **8** Ran SP% **114.7**
Speed ratings (Par 97): **96,94,93,90,88 87,81,81**
toteswingers:1&2:£1.40, 1&3:£11.50, 2&3:£15.30 CSF £9.03 TOTE £3.20: £1.50, £1.10, £7.40; EX 11.40.
Owner Croft, Taylor, Hebdon & Hernon **Bred** David A Cahill **Trained** Great Habton, N Yorks

FOCUS
A 1m maiden run at a steady pace to past halfway. The winner is rated to his mark backed up by the runner-up and the form looks quite solid.

NOTEBOOK
Choisan(IRE), placed in six of his previous nine starts, and with an official rating of 79, set his own pace. He wound it up in the final 3f and came home straight as a die against the running rail, always looking in command. He will stay further but whether he can defy this sort of mark in handicap company remains to be seen. (tchd 5-2)
Golden Halo(IRE), who improved on his initial effort when going down by a head in a 7f Roscommon maiden, is not very big. He pulled hard upsides the winner and then hung badly left. He was closing the gap at the line but does not look straightforward. (op 3-1 tchd 5-2)
Sparkling Portrait, neglected by Paul Hanagan, showed a fair level of ability on her debut. Settled in the rear, she had to be switched inside late on after not being helped by the errant runner-up. She looks sure to improve and make her mark at three.
Clon Brulee(IRE), out of a mare that won over 1m4f, again showed ability without being in any way knocked about. He needs another run to qualify for a handicap mark. (tchd 11-1)

No Time To Cry, blanketed for stalls entry, again showed ability but will not be the finished article until next year.
Brockwell, a strong finishing fourth behind the winner on his debut at York, is quite a big individual. He struggled to keep up once in line for home and will show to much better effect next year. (op 9-2)
Star Date(IRE), who showed ability on his debut at Leicester, failed to build on that but is another who will show his true potential at three. (op 6-1 tchd 13-2)
Lost Highway(IRE) has plenty of size about her. She dropped right away late on but this third outing qualifies her for a handicap mark. (op 28-1)

7102 WILLIAM HILL SCOTTISH CUP H'CAP (FOR THE WILLIE PARK TROPHY) 2m
3:50 (3:50) (Class 4) (0-85,87) 3-Y-0+ **£5,175** (£1,540; £769; £384) **Stalls** High

Form RPR
2035 **1** **Los Nadis (GER)**[18] 6707 7-9-1 **72**.................. LeeNewman 9 83
(Jim Goldie) *cl up: rdn to ld over 1f out: styd on wl fnl f* **11/1**
5330 **2** *2* **Gordonsville**[5] 6988 8-9-10 **81**.................. JamesSullivan 2 89
(Jim Goldie) *in tch: hdwy to chse wnr over 1f out: kpt on same pce ins fnl f* **8/1**
3506 **3** *5* **Dazzling Light (UAE)**[74] 5035 6-9-1 **75**.................. GaryBartley(3) 6 77
(Jim Goldie) *hld up: hdwy over 2f out: rdn and kpt on fnl f: no imp* **12/1**
360- **4** *3* **Bogside Theatre (IRE)**[249] 2938 7-9-5 **76**.................. DanielTudhope 7 75
(David O'Meara) *led after 2f: clr after 4f: rdn over 3f out: hdd over 1f out: sn outpcd* **16/1**
5010 **5** *1 ¼* **Bollin Judith**[40] 6115 5-9-7 **85**..................(t) JustinNewman(7) 3 82
(Tim Easterby) *hld up in tch: rdn on outside over 2f out: sn no imp* **10/1**
0310 **6** *1 ½* **Bowdler's Magic**[18] 6690 4-10-2 **87**.................. JoeFanning 4 82
(Mark Johnston) *prom: rdn over 2f out: wknd over 1f out* **11/2**[2]
1234 **7** *14* **Beat The Shower**[18] 6707 5-9-5 **76**.................. RobertWinston 1 54
(Peter Niven) *hld up: rdn and outpcd over 2f out: edgd lft and sn btn* **13/2**[3]
1463 **8** *7* **Mason Hindmarsh**[34] 6279 4-8-9 **66**.................. FrederikTylicki 11 36
(Karen McLintock) *led 2f: cl up tl rdn and wknd over 2f out* **25/1**
0-00 **9** *2 ½* **Lochiel**[38] 6191 7-8-9 **66** oh1.................. TomEaves 10 33
(Ian Semple) *t.k.h: hld up: rdn 3f out: edgd rt and sn btn* **66/1**
4511 **10** *2 ½* **Lexington Bay (IRE)**[32] 6333 3-9-4 **85**.................. PaulHanagan 5 49
(Richard Fahey) *t.k.h: hld up: rdn along over 3f out: hung lft over 2f out: sn btn* **9/5**[1]

3m 32.19s (-1.31) **Going Correction** +0.10s/f (Good)
WFA 3 from 4yo+ 10lb **10** Ran SP% **111.9**
Speed ratings (Par 105): **107,106,103,102,101 100,93,90,88,87**
toteswingers:1&2:£10.50, 1&3:£25.70, 2&3:£27.90 CSF £91.96 CT £1065.34 TOTE £12.30: £3.50, £2.70, £3.80; EX 87.50.
Owner Ian G M Dalgleish **Bred** Stiftung Gestut Fahrhof **Trained** Uplawmoor, E Renfrews

FOCUS
A decent handicap run at a true pace, which proved a triumph for Jim Goldie, who was responsible for the first three home. The runner-up looks a sound guide to the form.
Lexington Bay(IRE) Official explanation: jockey said gelding never travelled

7103 SCOTTISH RACING YOUR BETTER BET NURSERY 5f
4:25 (4:25) (Class 4) (0-85,83) 2-Y-0 **£3,881** (£1,155; £577; £288) **Stalls** High

Form RPR
1210 **1** **Free Zone**[25] 6535 2-9-7 **83**.................. TomEaves 5 87
(Bryan Smart) *mde virtually all: drvn ins fnl f: edgd rt and hld on wl towards fin* **9/4**[1]
4101 **2** *hd* **I'll Be Good**[11] 6863 2-8-13 **78**.................. GaryBartley(3) 3 81
(Robert Johnson) *prom: hdwy over 1f out: rdn: edgd lft and disp ld ins fnl f: kpt on: hld nr fin* **9/4**[1]
0020 **3** *4* **Busy Bimbo (IRE)**[19] 6673 2-7-12 **60** oh2.................. JamesSullivan 6 49
(Alan Berry) *n.m.r sn after s: sn outpcd: hdwy on outside over 1f out: kpt on fnl f: nt pce of first two* **16/1**
6240 **4** *1 ½* **Celestial Dawn**[2] 7059 2-7-7 **60** oh4.................. NeilFarley(5) 4 43
(John Weymes) *chsd ldrs: rdn 1/2-way: wknd fnl f* **17/2**
3230 **5** *1 ½* **Regal Lady**[2] 7059 2-8-1 **63**..................(p) PaulHanagan 7 41
(David Brown) *in tch: rdn and hung rt 2f out: sn btn* **13/2**[3]
1040 **6** *3 ¼* **Profile Star (IRE)**[102] 4094 2-8-13 **75**.................. LeeNewman 1 41
(David Barron) *w wnr tl rdn and wknd appr fnl f* **4/1**[2]

60.92 secs (0.52) **Going Correction** [illegible] **6** Ran SP% [illegible]
Speed ratings (Par 97): **103,102,96,93,91 86**
toteswingers:1&2:£1.60, 1&3:£5.00, 2&3:£5.20 CSF £7.24 TOTE £2.40: £1.10, £1.30; EX 5.00.
Owner Fromthestables.com Racing **Bred** R G Levin **Trained** Hambleton, N Yorks

FOCUS
The two at the head of the weights in this handicap pulled right away in the end. the form looks straightforward but limited.

NOTEBOOK
Free Zone, who took a nursery at Chester from a 4lb lower mark, failed to make an impact in the Two-Year-Old Trophy at Redcar. A close-coupled, most likeable type, he won the battle for the lead and then had to dig deep under a forceful ride. (op 2-1 tchd 15-8)
I'll Be Good has progressed nicely, taking a maiden at Hamilton on his ninth start and followed that up two outings later at Catterick. Raised 4lb for that, he had a good tow into the race from the two pacesetters and, after going head-to-head, just came off second-best. (op 2-1)
Busy Bimbo(IRE), with the cheekpieces experiment aborted, lost valuable ground at the start and had to make her effort wide. She had just missed out from a 2lb lower mark over this C&D two outings previously, and this half-sister to grand stable-servant Look Busy can find an opening.
Celestial Dawn, having her second start in three days, was soon outpaced. (op 9-1 tchd 10-1)
Regal Lady, who had also finished well beaten at Redcar earlier in the week, was struggling from halfway. (op 8-1 tchd 6-1)
Profile Star(IRE), off the mark at Thirsk in April, didn't really progress. Back after a break of 102 days, he matched strides with the winner but dropped out quickly and was eased right up. (op 11-2 tchd 6-1)

7104 CUNDALL JOHNSTON AND PARTNERS H'CAP 5f
4:55 (4:55) (Class 5) (0-75,75) 3-Y-0+ **£2,264** (£673; £336; £168) **Stalls** High

Form RPR
0500 **1** **Captain Royale (IRE)**[15] 6779 6-8-9 **68**..................(p) ShaneBKelly(5) 8 82
(Tracy Waggott) *cl up: hdwy against stands' rail to ld over 1f out: kpt on strly fnl f* **9/1**
6610 **2** *2 ½* **Go Go Green (IRE)**[40] 6112 5-9-4 **72**.................. DanielTudhope 1 77
(Jim Goldie) *bhd and sn outpcd: hdwy and swtchd lft ins fnl f: kpt on to take 2nd towards fin: no ch w wnr* **16/1**
4114 **3** *hd* **Two Turtle Doves (IRE)**[29] 6436 5-8-5 **64**.................. NeilFarley(5) 2 68
(Michael Mullineaux) *bhd and sn outpcd: hdwy on outside over 1f out: styd on fnl f: nrst fin* **12/1**
0543 **4** *½* **Crimson Cloud**[75] 4988 3-9-0 **68**.................. PaulHanagan 7 70
(Richard Fahey) *t.k.h: w ldrs: ev ch tl kpt on same pce ins fnl f* **9/1**
0650 **5** *½* **Tillys Tale**[37] 6212 4-9-1 **69**..................(p) JoeFanning 6 69
(Paul Midgley) *cl up: rdn and edgd rt over 1f out: kpt on same pce ins fnl f* **16/1**
6034 **6** *hd* **Tadalavil**[15] 6778 6-8-8 **62**.................. TomEaves 12 62
(Linda Perratt) *hld up in midfield: rdn and hdwy appr fnl f: kpt on: nvr able to chal* **10/1**
3230 **7** *shd* **Sleepy Blue Ocean**[40] 6112 5-9-3 **71**..................(p) RobertWinston 5 70
(John Balding) *in tch: effrt and drvn over 1f out: kpt on same pce ins fnl f* **13/2**[3]
2036 **8** *nk* **Rothesay Chancer**[40] 6112 3-9-4 **75**.................. GaryBartley(3) 4 73
(Jim Goldie) *hld up in midfield on outside: effrt and rdn over 1f out: nt qckn ins fnl f* **4/1**[1]
4214 **9** *2* **Tongalooma**[30] 6418 5-9-2 **70**.................. PJMcDonald 11 61
(James Moffatt) *midfield: rdn and edgd rt over 1f out: nvr able to chal* **6/1**[2]
2340 **10** *1* **Sands Of Dee (USA)**[71] 5148 4-8-12 **69**.................. BillyCray(3) 10 56
(David Nicholls) *bhd and sn outpcd: nvr able to chal* **12/1**
0000 **11** *1 ¼* **Gottcher**[14] 6801 3-9-0 **68**.................. LeeNewman 13 51
(David Barron) *led to over 1f out: edgd rt and sn btn* **25/1**
0640 **12** *4 ½* **Senate Majority**[25] 6537 4-8-12 **66**..................(b) DavidAllan 3 33
(Tim Easterby) *midfield on outside: struggling wl over 1f out: sn btn* **20/1**

60.93 secs (0.53) **Going Correction** +0.20s/f (Good) **12** Ran SP% **112.5**
Speed ratings (Par 103): **103,99,98,97,97 96,96,96,92,91 89,82**
toteswingers:1&2:£31.80, 1&3:£16.00, 2&3:£16.70 CSF £136.86 CT £1740.96 TOTE £12.20: £3.50, £6.10, £5.40; EX 217.60.
Owner H Conlon **Bred** Skymarc Farm Inc **Trained** Spennymoor, Co Durham

FOCUS
A wide open sprint handicap. Plenty were in contention before the winner pulled clear late on. The placed horses are rated close to their marks and set the level.

7105 RACING UK AMATEUR RIDERS' H'CAP 2m
5:25 (5:25) (Class 6) (0-65,62) 3-Y-0+ **£1,559** (£483; £241; £121) **Stalls** High

Form RPR
31 **1** **Strikemaster (IRE)**[22] 6600 5-10-6 **54**..................(t) MrAaronJames(7) 4 67
(Lee James) *hld up: hdwy over 3f out: led over 1f out: pushed clr* **9/2**[2]
113 **2** *5* **La Bacouetteuse (FR)**[30] 6419 6-10-13 **61**..........(p) MissSMDoolan(7) 5 68
(Iain Jardine) *t.k.h: in tch: outpcd over 3f out: rallied to chse (clr) wnr ins fnl f: r.o* **10/3**[1]
1134 **3** *2* **Soprano (GER)**[40] 6115 9-11-0 **62**.................. MrBInglis(7) 2 67
(Jim Goldie) *in tch: outpcd over 6f out: rallied over 2f out: kpt on fnl f: nrst fin* **10/3**[1]
0506 **4** *6* **Abernethy (IRE)**[30] 6415 3-9-1 **45**..................(t) MrJHamilton(7) 10 42
(Linda Perratt) *t.k.h: hld up: hdwy to ld over 2f out: hdd over 1f out: wknd ins fnl f* **25/1**
0460 **5** *6* **Sergeant Pink (IRE)**[70] 5166 5-10-9 **57**.................. MissNSayer(7) 3 47
(Dianne Sayer) *t.k.h: hld up: outpcd over 4f out: sme late hdwy: nvr on terms* **16/1**
34 **6** *½* **Mighty Whitey (IRE)**[30] 6417 5-11-1 **61**..................(t) MrSFox(5) 7 51
(Noel C Kelly, Ire) *plld hrd in rr: hdwy on outside to ld 1/2-way: hung lft and hdd over 2f out: wknd over 1f out* **5/1**[3]
7 *1 ¼* **Red Kingdom (IRE)**[13] 5403 7-9-11 **45**.................. MissRobynGray(7) 11 33
(Dianne Sayer) *t.k.h: in tch: lost pl 1/2-way: sn struggling: n.d after* **50/1**
050 **8** *nk* **Eila Wheeler**[15] 6781 4-9-13 **45**.................. MrTSpeke(5) 8 33
(Robert Johnson) *chsd ldrs: c v wd bnd ent st: wknd fnl 2f* **40/1**
05-5 **9** *5* **Antoella (IRE)**[220] 324 4-10-4 **45**.................. MrTomDavid 1 27
(Philip Kirby) *plld hrd: led at stdy gallop: hdd 1/2-way: rdn and wknd over 2f out* **12/1**
6/35 **10** *3 ¼* **Elk Trail (IRE)**[43] 6029 6-10-12 **56**.................. MissMMullineaux(3) 6 34
(Michael Mullineaux) *cl up tl rdn and wknd over 2f out* **15/2**

3m 43.17s (9.67) **Going Correction** +0.10s/f (Good)
WFA 3 from 4yo+ 10lb **10** Ran SP% **114.6**
Speed ratings (Par 101): **79,76,75,72,69 69,68,68,65,64**
toteswingers:1&2:£2.60, 1&3:£2.20, 2&3:£2.90 CSF £19.22 CT £55.60 TOTE £5.20: £1.90, £1.10, £2.20; EX 18.00.
Owner Mrs Carol Lloyd-James **Bred** Dr Peter Harms **Trained** Norton, N Yorks

FOCUS
The early pace in this low-grade handicap was very steady and in the end they were spread right across the track. The placed horses are [illegible] set the level.
[illegible] to a £1 stake. Pool:£51,691.01 - 23.00 winning tickets T/Qpdt: £137.40 to a £1 stake. Pool:£4,048.61 - 21.80 winning tickets RY

6800 NOTTINGHAM (L-H)
Wednesday, October 26

OFFICIAL GOING: Good to firm (7.7)
All races on outer course. Stands' bend out 3m, far bend out 6m, far side home straight rail moved out 3m inc. dist. on round course by 31yds.
Wind: Virtually nil Weather: Fine and dry

7106 ROSELAND GROUP LTD H'CAP 5f 13y
1:30 (1:33) (Class 5) (0-70,70) 3-Y-0+ **£2,264** (£673; £336; £168) **Stalls** High

Form RPR
0305 **1** **Style And Panache (IRE)**[14] 6801 3-9-5 **69**.........(p) SilvestreDeSousa 6 78
(David Evans) *trckd ldrs: hdwy 1/2-way: led 1 1/2f out: rdn and styd on wl fnl f* **12/1**
0240 **2** *¾* **Ishetoo**[27] 6491 7-9-5 **69**..................(p) TomQueally 4 75
(Ollie Pears) *towards rr: gd hdwy wl over 1f out: rdn and styd on wl fnl f: nrst fin* **11/1**
106 **3** *¾* **Lord Of The Reins (IRE)**[8] 6932 7-9-1 **68**.................. KieranO'Neill(3) 1 72
(P J O'Gorman) *trckd ldrs: hdwy over 2f out: rdn and ev ch over 1f out: kpt on* **12/1**
0042 **4** *nse* **Igoyougo**[25] 6537 5-9-5 **69**.................. PaulQuinn 8 72
(Noel Wilson) *trckd ldrs: hdwy 2f out: rdn and ev ch ent fnl f: sn no ex* **8/1**[3]
0406 **5** *hd* **Above The Stars**[14] 6801 3-9-3 **70**.................. LeeTopliss(3) 14 73+
(Richard Fahey) *midfield: hdwy 2f out: sn rdn and kpt on ins fnl f: nrst fin* **6/1**[1]
0000 **6** *nse* **Mey Blossom**[25] 6537 6-9-0 **64**.................. TonyCulhane 11 67
(Richard Whitaker) *towards rr: gd hdwy wl over 1f out: styd on strly ins fnl f: nrst fin* **22/1**
6351 **7** *¾* **Cape Royal**[14] 6802 11-9-3 **70**..................(tp) SeanLevey(3) 5 70
(Milton Bradley) *chsd ldrs: rdn over 1f out: kpt on same pce* **14/1**
0000 **8** *2 ¼* **Not My Choice (IRE)**[16] 6759 6-9-6 **70**..................(t) MichaelStainton 15 62
(David C Griffiths) *nvr bttr than midfield* **40/1**

2353 **9** ¾ **Tislaam (IRE)**[21] 6634 4-9-4 **68**................................(be[1]) MartinHarley 13 57
(Alan McCabe) *nvr nr ldrs* **7/1**[2]
4050 **10** *nk* **Estonia**[8] 6932 4-9-3 **67**.. LukeMorris 10 55
(Michael Squance) *nvr bttr than midfield* **22/1**
0000 **11** 1 ¼ **Desert Strike**[34] 6276 5-8-13 **70**.......................................(p) RyanTate[(7)] 7 53
(Alan McCabe) *v.s.a: a in rr* **22/1**
400 **12** ½ **Cruise Tothelimit (IRE)**[37] 6212 3-9-5 **69**.......................... ShaneKelly 2 51
(Mark Brisbourne) *cl up: rdn wl over 1f out: sn wknd* **12/1**
1643 **13** 1 ½ **Atlantic Cycle (IRE)**[40] 6119 4-9-3 **67**............................(t) LiamKeniry 12 43
(Milton Bradley) *wnt rt and hmpd s: a in rr* **16/1**
5406 **14** *shd* **Ridley Didley (IRE)**[11] 6875 6-9-2 **66**.......................... AdrianNicholls 17 42
(Noel Wilson) *qckly away and led: rdn and edgd lft over 2f out: hdd wl over 1f out and sn wknd* **16/1**
0005 **15** 1 ¾ **Nomoreblondes**[25] 6537 7-9-1 **70**......................................(v) LMcNiff[(5)] 3 40
(Paul Midgley) *cl up: rdn 2f out and sn wknd* **14/1**
0261 **16** 1 ½ **The Strig**[16] 6765 4-9-1 **65**...(v) WilliamCarson 9 29
(Stuart Williams) *chsd ldrs: rdn along 1/2-way: sn wknd* **8/1**[3]

61.45 secs (0.45) **Going Correction** +0.175s/f (Good) **16** Ran SP% **121.0**
Speed ratings (Par 103): **103,101,100,100,100 100,98,95,94,93 91,90,88,88,85 83**
toteswingers:1&2:£26.50, 1&3:£28.10, 2&3:£32.00 CSF £130.30 CT £1029.58 TOTE £11.90: £2.20, £3.70, £3.60, £2.10; EX 135.30 TRIFECTA Not won..
Owner Roger Ambrose,Sean Ambrose & Bill Reilly **Bred** Rathasker Stud **Trained** Pandy, Monmouths

FOCUS
Following 3mm of rain overnight the ground was good to firm (GoingStick 7.7). The stands' bend was out 3 metres and the far bend 6 metres, while the far side home straight rail had been moved 3m to narrow the straight, increasing circuit distances by approximately 31yds. A wide open sprint handicap and they were spread right across the track. There didn't appear to be a draw bias and this form looks sound, rated around the first four.
Desert Strike Official explanation: jockey said gelding missed the break and hung right

7107 NOTTINGHAMRACECOURSE.CO.UK H'CAP 2m 9y
2:00 (2:00) (Class 6) (0-65,64) 3-Y-0+ **£1,681** (£500; £250; £125) **Stalls** Low

Form RPR
1023 **1** **Brasingaman Eric**[12] 6838 4-9-9 **59**.............................. JimmyFortune 8 68
(George Moore) *mde all: rdn over 2f out: kpt on gamely fnl f* **9/2**[3]
605 **2** ½ **Riviera Stars**[13] 6810 3-9-4 **64**.. JamieSpencer 10 72
(Michael Bell) *trckd ldrs: hdwy 3f out: rdn to chse wnr 2f out: drvn and kpt on ins fnl f* **5/1**
4466 **3** 1 ¾ **Sancho Panza**[17] 6722 4-9-10 **63**..........................(p) AdamBeschizza[(3)] 1 69
(Julia Feilden) *trckd ldrs: lost pl and rr over 5f out: hdwy 3f out: rdn to chse ldrs over 2f out: kpt on fnl f* **4/1**[2]
4040 **4** 1 ¼ **Simple Jim (FR)**[12] 6838 7-9-4 **54**............................ SilvestreDeSousa 4 59
(David O'Meara) *hld up in rr: hdwy on outer 4f out: pushed along to chse ldrs wl over 2f out: no imp fnl f* **7/2**[1]
0660 **5** 2 ¼ **Carnac (IRE)**[17] 6722 5-9-0 **50**...(p) MartinHarley 5 52
(Alan McCabe) *hld up: stdy hdwy on inner 4f out: effrt and n.m.r wl over 2f out: sn rdn and no imp* **12/1**
040- **6** 5 **Akula (IRE)**[224] 6132 4-9-8 **58**.. TomQueally 11 54
(Mark H Tompkins) *trckd wnr: rdn along over 3f out: grad wknd* **6/1**
50-5 **7** 2 ½ **Highland Cadett**[23] 6582 4-8-2 **45**............................ RachealKneller[(7)] 3 38
(Pam Ford) *chsd ldng pair: pushed along 6f out: rdn and edgd rt over 3f out: sn wknd* **125/1**
5010 **8** 3 ¾ **Zefooha (FR)**[26] 5651 7-9-13 **63**....................................(p) DuranFentiman 2 51
(Tim Walford) *hld up towards rr: hdwy on outer 6f out: rdn along over 3f out: sn wknd* **10/1**
2006 **9** 15 **Motirani**[41] 6104 4-9-12 **62**...(p) ChrisCatlin 6 32
(Lydia Pearce) *trckd ldrs: pushed along 1/2-way: rdn 4f out: sn wknd* **25/1**

3m 40.04s (9.74) **Going Correction** +0.40s/f (Good)
WFA 3 from 4yo+ 10lb **9** Ran SP% **112.8**
Speed ratings (Par 101): **91,90,89,89,88 85,84,82,75**
toteswingers:1&2:£3.40, 1&3:£5.50, 2&3:£5.20 CSF £26.51 CT £95.61 TOTE £6.10: £2.00, £1.80, £1.50; EX 25.70 Trifecta £314.00 Pool £916.63 - 2.16 winning units..
Owner R Morgan **Bred** Mrs Heather Morgan **Trained** Middleham Moor, N Yorks

FOCUS
A moderate handicap in which the winner benefited from an easy lead. He's worth a length personal best.

7108 REWARDS4RACING.COM (S) STKS 1m 75y
2:30 (2:30) (Class 6) 2-Y-0 **£1,681** (£500; £250; £125) **Stalls** Centre

Form RPR
0 **1** **Artlana**[53] 5727 2-8-7 0 ow1.. BarryMcHugh 14 58
(Julie Camacho) *towards rr: stdy hdwy on inner wl over 2f out: rdn over 1f out: styd on ins fnl f to ld last 100yds* **33/1**
4033 **2** 1 ½ **Emerald Smile (IRE)**[34] 6280 2-8-6 52.............................. LukeMorris 9 54
(J S Moore) *chsd ldrs: hdwy on outer 3f out: led over 2f out and sn edgd lft: rdn: carried hd high and hung lft ent fnl f: hdd and no ex last 100yds* **8/1**[3]
0300 **3** ¾ **Angel Cake (IRE)**[35] 6260 2-8-3 60............................ KieranO'Neill[(3)] 11 52
(Amy Weaver) *hld up: hdwy on outer over 3f out: rdn to chse ldrs and edgd lft 2f out: one pce fnl f* **6/1**[2]
6554 **4** 1 ¼ **Jaci Uzzi (IRE)**[16] 6760 2-8-6 49.............................. SilvestreDeSousa 5 49
(David Evans) *sn led: rdn along 3f out: hdd over 2f out: one pce ent fnl f* **6/1**[2]
2054 **5** ¾ **Ciara Boo (IRE)**[99] 4178 2-8-3 55...............................(t) SophieDoyle[(3)] 12 48
(David Evans) *in rr: hdwy on outer over 2f out: sn rdn and styd on fnl f: nrst fin* **28/1**
0456 **6** 2 **Loxton Lad (IRE)**[16] 6757 2-8-11 59.................................. JamesDoyle 8 48
(Roger Charlton) *trckd ldng pair: effrt over 3f out: rdn wl over 2f out: kpt on same pce appr fnl f* **6/4**[1]
00 **7** 1 **Malvesi**[12] 6836 2-8-11 0.. GrahamGibbons 2 46
(Ann Duffield) *dwlt and in rr: sme hdwy over 2f out: sn rdn and nvr rchd ldrs* **11/1**
05 **8** 1 ½ **Notnowstanley**[55] 5637 2-8-6 0.. RyanPowell[(5)] 1 42
(J S Moore) *nvr bttr than midfield* **66/1**
0050 **9** 2 ½ **Bit A Craic**[7] 6950 2-8-6 46.................................(bt) KirstyMilczarek 4 32
(John Ryan) *chsd ldrs: rdn along over 3f out: sn wknd* **50/1**
0405 **10** 3 ½ **Arrowroot**[12] 6835 2-8-11 49..(b) DuranFentiman 7 29
(Tim Easterby) *prom: cl up 1/2-way: rdn wl over 2f out and sn wknd* **25/1**
000 **11** 18 **Silver Six**[43] 6018 2-8-11 50..(v[1]) SamHitchcott 10 —
(Mick Channon) *a towards rr* **20/1**
0000 **12** 1 ¼ **King Fong**[22] 6611 2-8-4 48.. BradleyBosley[(7)] 6 —
(John Ryan) *a in rr* **100/1**
4040 **13** *8* **Dutchman's Field**[14] 6807 2-8-11 55..........................(b[1]) AdrianNicholls 3 —
(David Nicholls) *s.i.s: a in rr* **20/1**

1m 50.11s (4.51) **Going Correction** +0.40s/f (Good) **13** Ran SP% **112.2**
Speed ratings (Par 93): **93,91,90,89,88 86,85,84,81,78 60,59,51**
toteswingers:1&2:£36.00, 1&3:£40.20, 2&3:£5.20 CSF £244.88 TOTE £70.70: £13.10, £2.40, £1.80; EX 211.10 TRIFECTA Not won..There was no bid for the winner.
Owner G B Turnbull Ltd **Bred** G B Turnbull Ltd **Trained** Norton, N Yorks

FOCUS
The leaders went off too fast here and that set things up for a closer. The form is limited by the proximity of the runner-up and fourth.

NOTEBOOK
Artlana, who showed little on her debut, looked a lot more professional in this lower grade and, ridden with patience in midfield off the strong pace, stayed on up the far rail to win a shade cosily. This wasn't much of a race but she's likely to be kept on the go on the AW and it wouldn't be a surprise to see her win a little nursery. (op 40-1)
Emerald Smile(IRE) sat just off the pace and had every chance in the straight, but not for the first time she carried her head a touch high under pressure. (op 7-1)
Angel Cake(IRE) was officially best in at the weights, and she was ridden with restraint off a strong pace, so can't have any excuses. (op 8-1 tchd 17-2)
Jaci Uzzi(IRE), given a more positive ride down in trip, was hassled by Arrowroot on the front end and had too much use made of her. (op 11-2 tchd 9-2)
Ciara Boo(IRE), dropped out in last, wasn't travelling early but flashed home in the closing stages. She might not be one to give up on.
Loxton Lad(IRE) paid for chasing the strong gallop set by the two leaders. (op 15-8)
Dutchman's Field Official explanation: jockey said gelding had no more to give

7109 E B F OATH COLTS AND GELDINGS MAIDEN STKS 1m 75y
3:05 (3:06) (Class 4) 2-Y-0 **£4,528** (£1,347; £673; £336) **Stalls** Centre

Form RPR
03 **1** **Moidore**[15] 6772 2-9-0 0.. SteveDrowne 12 82+
(Roger Charlton) *mde all: rdn 2f out: clr appr fnl f: kpt on strly* **6/4**[1]
05 **2** 5 **Aleksandar**[27] 6483 2-9-0 0.. KirstyMilczarek 9 69
(Luca Cumani) *trckd ldrs: hdwy over 3f out: swtchd rt and rdn 2f out: chsd wnr ent fnl f: kpt on same pce* **28/1**
3 ¾ **Cameron Highland (IRE)** 2-9-0 0...................................... NeilCallan 4 67+
(Roger Varian) *hld up in tch: gd hdwy 4f out: effrt over 2f out and sn ev ch: rdn: edgd lft and green over 1f out: one pce after* **4/1**[2]
04 **4** 2 ¼ **Autarch (USA)**[7] 6953 2-9-0 0.. JimmyFortune 10 62
(Amanda Perrett) *chsd ldrs on inner: rdn along over 2f out: sn one pce* **11/2**[3]
0 **5** 1 ½ **Leitrim King (IRE)**[25] 6529 2-9-0 0...................................... ShaneKelly 8 58
(William Haggas) *in tch: hdwy 3f out: chsd ldrs over 2f out: sn rdn and one pce* **11/1**
0 **6** 1 ¾ **Exning Halt**[100] 4159 2-9-0 0.. EddieAhern 2 54
(James Fanshawe) *hld up in rr: sme late hdwy* **33/1**
7 *hd* **Ace Of Valhalla** 2-9-0 0.. TomQueally 3 54
(Sir Henry Cecil) *hld up in rr: sme late hdwy* **9/1**
8 2 ¾ **Dylans Verse (IRE)** 2-9-0 0.. DavidProbert 7 47
(Reg Hollinshead) *a in rr* **100/1**
00 **9** 5 **Youcouldbelucky (USA)**[28] 6447 2-9-0 0............. SilvestreDeSousa 11 36
(Mark Johnston) *cl up: rdn along 1/2-way: sn wknd* **20/1**
10 *11* **Dancing Lancer** 2-8-11 0.. MichaelO'Connell[(3)] 5 11
(Kate Walton) *s.i.s: a outpcd and bhd* **100/1**
06 **11** ½ **Ali Hope (IRE)**[45] 5959 2-9-0 0.......................................(b[1]) JamesDoyle 6 9
(Roger Charlton) *chsd ldrs: rdn along over 3f out: sn wknd* **100/1**
12 ¾ **Gabrial's King (IRE)**[26] 6508 2-9-0 0.................................. JamieSpencer 1 8
(Ian Williams) *dwlt: a in rr* **14/1**

1m 48.96s (3.36) **Going Correction** +0.40s/f (Good) **12** Ran SP% **114.5**
Speed ratings (Par 97): **99,94,93,91,89 87,87,84,79,68 68,67**
toteswingers:1&2:£11.60, 1&3:£2.50, 2&3:£24.90 CSF £58.85 TOTE £2.50: £1.30, £7.40, £1.40; EX 52.60 Trifecta £445.30 Pool £878.71 - 1.46 winning units..
Owner The Queen **Bred** The Queen **Trained** Beckhampton, Wilts

FOCUS
No more than a fair maiden, and although the winner was quite impressive the race looked to lack depth.

NOTEBOOK
Moidore made just about all the running. His third at Leicester set the standard and, having enjoyed the run of things, he could do no more than run out a cosy winner. His pedigree suggests he'll be a 1m4f horse next year, and he can be expected to kick off life in handicaps off a mark in the low-80s. (op 2-1)
Aleksandar couldn't stay with the winner inside the last but this was a solid third run, and handicaps now beckon for him too. He's another who will get further next year. (op 25-1)
Cameron Highland(IRE) didn't get the clearest of runs but, once switched out wide, his effort flattened out. This was still a perfectly acceptable debut effort, though, and this 310,000gns purchase can win a maiden before the year is out if his connections decide to persevere with him. (tchd 7-2)
Autarch(USA) took a step back from his Newmarket fourth, but he's another now eligible for a mark and can be expected to do better in that sphere. (tchd 9-2)
Leitrim King(IRE) is the sort that can be expected to do better next year. (tchd 12-1)
Exning Halt again looked green. (op 28-1)
Ace Of Valhalla, a half-brother to Group 3 winner Trick Or Treat, also looked in need of the experience. (op 13-2 tchd 10-1)

7110 NOTTINGHAM RACECOURSE HOSPITALITY H'CAP 1m 75y
3:40 (3:40) (Class 4) (0-85,85) 3-Y-0+ **£4,204** (£1,251; £625; £312) **Stalls** Centre

Form RPR
2360 **1** **Fantasy Gladiator**[34] 6273 5-9-1 **79**..............................(p) TomQueally 12 89
(Robert Cowell) *racd keenly: hld up in rr: swtchd rt over 2f out: sn gd hdwy on outer: chal jst ins fnl f: kpt on: led post* **25/1**
0000 **2** *nse* **Kay Gee Be (IRE)**[14] 6803 7-9-3 **84**.................................... LeeTopliss[(3)] 7 94
(Richard Fahey) *hld up: pushed along and gd hdwy over 2f out: led over 1f out: strly pressed thrght fnl f: kpt on: hdd post* **12/1**
0536 **3** *hd* **Chapter And Verse (IRE)**[17] 6728 5-9-4 **82**.......................... TonyCulhane 6 91
(Mike Murphy) *racd keenly: hld up: pushed along and gd hdwy 2f out: rdn and ev ch jst ins fnl f: kpt on: jst hld* **8/1**[2]
4000 **4** 6 **Desert Romance (IRE)**[14] 6803 5-9-1 **84**.................(p) AshleyMorgan[(5)] 2 80
(David O'Meara) *led: rdn whn hdd over 1f out: no ex* **10/1**
0061 **5** *shd* **Nazreef**[17] 6727 4-9-5 **83**...(bt) RobertHavlin 8 78+
(Hughie Morrison) *dwlt: sn midfield: hdwy over 2f out: rdn and ev ch 2f out: one pce fr over 1f out* **9/1**[3]
6523 **6** ½ **Tewin Wood**[5] 6990 4-8-4 **75**...................................... NatashaEaton[(7)] 1 69
(Alan Bailey) *trckd ldrs: rdn over 2f out: sn one pce* **10/1**
0003 **7** 1 ¾ **Just Bond (IRE)**[25] 6533 9-9-4 **85**...................................... DaleSwift[(3)] 11 75
(Geoffrey Oldroyd) *hld up: pushed along over 2f out: kpt on fnl f: n.d* **14/1**
0303 **8** 1 ½ **Mahadee (IRE)**[17] 6727 6-9-1 **82**................................(p) HarryBentley[(3)] 3 69
(Ed de Giles) *midfield: pushed along 3f out: sn no prog* **22/1**

0-00 **9** *1* **King Of Windsor (IRE)**[39] 6173 4-9-2 **80**..............(b[1]) StevieDonohoe 14 64
(Ralph Beckett) *hld up: bhd tl sme late hdwy* **22/1**

0055 **10** *3/4* **Willow Dancer (IRE)**[17] 6728 7-9-3 **81**..................(p) EddieAhern 16 64
(Walter Swinburn) *in tch: smooth hdwy 3f out: rdn to chal 2f out: wknd over 1f out* **16/1**

020 **11** *1/2* **Nelson's Bounty**[33] 6302 4-9-5 **83**................................ NeilCallan 13 65
(Paul D'Arcy) *midfield: rdn to chse ldrs over 2f out: wknd over 1f out* **12/1**

1000 **12** *2* **Daneside (IRE)**[2] 7050 4-8-3 **72**............................ MatthewLawson(5) 10 49
(Gary Harrison) *prom on outer: pushed along over 3f out: wknd over 1f out* **14/1**

1640 **13** *2* **Karaka Jack**[40] 6113 4-9-2 **83**................................ MichaelO'Connell(3) 5 55
(David Nicholls) *midfield: pushed along over 3f out: sn no imp: wknd over 1f out* **12/1**

0250 **14** *12* **Venutius**[33] 6290 4-9-5 **83**.. GrahamGibbons 9 28
(Ed McMahon) *w ldr: pushed along over 3f out: wknd over 2f out* **10/1**

3313 **15** *15* **Ampleforth**[21] 6631 3-8-9 **76**.................................... SilvestreDeSousa 4 —
(Mark Johnston) *trckd ldrs: pushed along 5f out: lost pl over 3f out: wknd wl over 2f out* **9/2[1]**

1m 47.71s (2.11) **Going Correction** +0.40s/f (Good)
WFA 3 from 4yo+ 3lb **15** Ran SP% **121.4**
Speed ratings (Par 105): **105,104,104,98,98 98,96,94,93,93 92,90,88,76,61**
toteswingers:1&2:£56.80, 1&3:£26.70, 2&3:£19.20 CSF £294.96 CT £2687.38 TOTE £36.20: £8.60, £5.40, £1.60; EX 368.00 Trifecta £444.20 Part won. Pool £600.39 - 0.63 winning units..
Owner The Fantasy Fellowship **Bred** R S A Urquhart **Trained** Six Mile Bottom, Cambs

FOCUS
There was a decent enough pace to this handicap and the first three came from the back. The first three finished clear and the form is rated around the trio.
Nazreef Official explanation: jockey said gelding stumbled leaving stalls
Ampleforth Official explanation: trainer's rep had no explanation for the poor form shown

7111 ROSELAND GROUP LTD MAIDEN STKS — 1m 75y
4:15 (4:15) (Class 5) 3-Y-O **£2,264** (£673; £336; £168) **Stalls** Centre

Form RPR

323 **1** **Kahraba (USA)**[36] 6242 3-8-12 80............................ SilvestreDeSousa 7 78
(Saeed Bin Suroor) *cl up: pushed along over 3f out: rdn 2f out: kpt on u.p to ld ins fnl f* **11/8[1]**

3533 **2** *1 1/2* **Shuhra (IRE)**[28] 6459 3-8-12 72.. RichardHills 2 75
(William Haggas) *led: pushed along wl over 2f out: rdn over 1f out: hdd and no ex ins fnl f* **4/1[2]**

3 *10* **Bravestofthebrave (USA)** 3-9-3 0................................ RobertHavlin 5 57+
(John Gosden) *s.i.s: green and pushed along in rr: hdwy 1/2-way: rdn over 2f out: kpt on: no imp on ldng duo* **9/2[3]**

4 *nk* **Rex Romanorum (IRE)**[360] 7257 3-9-3 0.................... DuranFentiman 9 56
(Patrick Holmes) *prom on outer: rdn along over 3f out: kpt on same pce* **33/1**

0 **5** *2 3/4* **Dicey Vows (USA)**[28] 6459 3-9-0 0.............................. HarryBentley(3) 10 50
(Alan Jarvis) *a midfield* **100/1**

6 *2 3/4* **Nonaynever** 3-9-3 0.. JimmyFortune 8 44
(Jeremy Noseda) *a towards rr* **13/2**

-5 **7** *1/2* **Archelao (IRE)**[16] 6750 3-9-3 0.................................... RichardMullen 3 43
(Marcus Tregoning) *in tch: rdn along over 3f out: sn no hdwy* **25/1**

8 *1* **Sondray** 3-8-12 0.. ChrisCatlin 4 35
(Jo Crowley) *a towards rr* **66/1**

0 **9** *8* **First Class**[23] 6591 3-9-3 0.. TomQueally 1 22
(Rae Guest) *chsd ldng pair on inner: rdn along 1/2-way: sn outpcd* **33/1**

10 *2 1/4* **Refractor (IRE)** 3-9-3 0.. EddieAhern 12 17
(James Fanshawe) *a in rr* **22/1**

11 *4 1/2* **Mon Petit Bijou** 3-8-12 0.. SaleemGolam 11 —
(Lydia Pearce) *dwlt: a bhd* **100/1**

66- **12** *18* **Tagena (IRE)**[540] 1793 3-8-12 0.................................... DavidProbert 6 —
(Richard Price) *chsd ldrs: rdn along 1/2-way: sn wknd* **66/1**

1m 48.69s (3.09) **Going Correction** +0.40s/f (Good) **12** Ran SP% **112.7**
Speed ratings (Par 101): **100,98,88,88,85 82,82,81,73,70 66,48**
toteswingers:1&2:£2.00, 1&3:£2.40, 2&3:£3.10 CSF £5.80 TOTE £2.20: £1.20, £1.50, £1.80; EX 5.80 Trifecta £15.50 Pool £1,086.29 - 51.59 winning units..
Owner Godolphin **Bred** Stonerside Stable **Trained** Newmarket, Suffolk

FOCUS
An ordinary maiden and only two mattered from a long way out. It's doubtful they improved however, as the form of those behind looks poor.

7112 AJA LADIES' GRAND FINALE H'CAP (FOR LADY AMATEUR RIDERS) (DIV I) — 1m 2f 50y
4:45 (4:45) (Class 6) (0-65,65) 3-Y-O+ **£1,622** (£503; £251; £125) **Stalls** Low

Form RPR

1404 **1** *2 1/4* **Ice Nelly (IRE)**[14] 6799 3-9-10 **64**............................ MissNDumelow(5) 1 71
(Hughie Morrison) *hld up in rr: hdwy on wd outside 2f out: rdn over 1f out: styd on ins fnl f: tk 2nd nr fin: fin 2nd plcd 1st* **5/1[2]**

2523 **2** *1/2* **Petsas Pleasure**[16] 6764 5-10-5 **63**................................ MissLHorner 12 69
(Ollie Pears) *hld up in rr: stdy hdwy on wd outside over 2f out: rdn to chse wnr ent fnl f: sn one pce: fin 3rd: plcd 2nd* **9/2[1]**

0650 **3** *1 1/2* **Kool Shuffle (GER)**[74] 5031 3-9-4 **53**........................ MissSBrotherton 4 56
(Tom Tate) *led 3f: chsd ldrs on inner: rdn along over 2f out: kpt on same pce: fin 4th: plcd 3rd* **7/1[3]**

0602 **4** *1 1/4* **Call Of Duty (IRE)**[12] 6833 6-9-11 **58**........................ MissECSayer(3) 15 58
(Dianne Sayer) *hld up towards rr: hdwy 3f out: rdn to chse ldrs over 1f out: sn one pce: fin 5th: plcd 4th* **8/1**

0052 **5** *1/2* **Sail Home**[27] 6486 4-9-11 **60**.................................... MissSBirkett(5) 5 60
(Julia Feilden) *cl up: led after 3f: rdn along wl over 2f: hdd over 1f out: wknd: fin 6th: plcd 5th* **10/1**

0426 **6** *nk* **Maz**[6] 6971 3-9-6 **62**..(p) MissAlexOwen(7) 8 61
(Alan Bailey) *trckd ldrs: hdwy 3f out: ev ch 2f out: sn rdn and one pce appr fnl f: fin 7th: plcd 6th* **17/2**

6646 **7** *1/2* **Marino Prince (FR)**[76] 4944 6-9-3 **52**.................. MissPhillipaTutty(5) 11 50
(Joanne Foster) *hld up: hdwy and in tch 3f out: rdn along over 2f out: sn one pce: fin 8th: plcd 7th* **33/1**

2655 **8** *2* **Only You Maggie (IRE)**[10] 6894 4-10-0 **65**............(v) MissMHooper(7) 3 60
(Gary Harrison) *trckd ldrs: swtchd lft and hdwy 3f out: rdn 2f out: grad wknd: fin 9th: plcd 8th* **16/1**

0200 **9** *2* **Hurricane Thomas (IRE)**[4] 7032 7-9-2 **51** oh6........... MissGTutty(5) 10 42
(Karen Tutty) *cl up: rdn along wl over 2f out: grad wknd: fin 10th: plcd 9th* **14/1**

0460 **10** *19* **Alternative Choice (USA)**[11] 6873 5-9-10 **54**(b[1]) MrsEmmaLittmoden 14 —
(Nick Littmoden) *in tch: rdn along 3f out: sn wknd: fin 11th: plcd 10th* **18/1**

0000 **11** *3 3/4* **Charlietoo**[27] 6494 5-9-4 **51** oh5......................... MissHannahWatson(3) 2 —
(Pam Ford) *a towards rr: fin 12th: plcd 11th* **100/1**

0001 **D** **My Mate Jake (IRE)**[12] 6833 3-9-11 **65**............... MissAZetterholm(5) 13 74
(James Given) *in tch: hdwy to trck ldrs 3f out: led appr fnl f: sn rdn and kpt on wl: fin 1st: disq. and plcd last: failed to draw correct weight* **5/1[2]**

2m 16.77s (5.07) **Going Correction** +0.40s/f (Good)
WFA 3 from 4yo+ 5lb **12** Ran SP% **116.5**
Speed ratings (Par 101): **93,92,91,90,90 89,89,87,86,71 68,95**
toteswingers:1&2:£3.90, 1&3:£9.30, 2&3:£5.90 CSF £27.21 CT £158.46 TOTE £5.40: £2.00, £1.50, £2.30; EX 19.50 Trifecta £138.30 Pool £618.64 - 3.31 winning units..
Owner Lady Hardy **Bred** Lady Hardy **Trained** East Ilsley, Berks
■ Stewards' Enquiry : Miss A Zetterholm five-day ban: failed to draw correct weight (Nov 16,22,28,29,Dec 19)

FOCUS
It was faster than division II and the form makes plenty of sense. The disqualified winner rates back to his juvenile form.

7113 AJA LADIES' GRAND FINALE H'CAP (FOR LADY AMATEUR RIDERS) (DIV II) — 1m 2f 50y
5:15 (5:15) (Class 6) (0-65,64) 3-Y-O+ **£1,622** (£503; £251; £125) **Stalls** Low

Form RPR

2400 **1** **Rockweiller**[51] 5791 4-10-1 **58**................................(v) MissSBrotherton 12 66
(Steve Gollings) *led: rdn whn hdd over 2f out: rallied to ld again towards fin* **5/1[2]**

6340 **2** *shd* **Wom**[42] 6052 3-9-2 **55**..(be) MissBAndrews(5) 9 63
(Pam Sly) *racd keenly: w ldr: rdn to ld over 2f out: kpt on: hdd nr fin* **7/1[3]**

0445 **3** *1* **Entrance**[54] 5666 3-9-4 **57**.. MissSBirkett(5) 3 63+
(Julia Feilden) *racd keenly: hld up: stl plenty to do whn briefly short room 2f out: kpt on wl fr over 1f out: wnt 3rd cl home* **9/1**

0100 **4** *nk* **Harare**[12] 6833 10-9-4 **52**..(v) MissGTutty(5) 11 57
(Karen Tutty) *t.k.h in midfield: hdwy to go 3rd 2f out: kpt on: lost 3rd cl home* **14/1**

0600 **5** *3 1/2* **Gallego**[5] 6990 9-10-7 **64**.. MissGAndrews 6 63
(Richard Price) *s.i.s: hld up and keen: hdwy on outer into midfield 5f out: pushed along over 3f out: kpt on one pce* **12/1**

030/ **6** *shd* **Baan (USA)**[69] 7084 8-9-12 **62**................................ MissCAMadgin(7) 14 61
(James Eustace) *racd keenly: hld up in rr: pushed along over 2f out: hdwy over 1f out: kpt on: eased fnl 50yds* **15/2**

1013 **7** *shd* **Market Puzzle (IRE)**[12] 6833 4-9-11 **59**....(p) MissBeckyBrisbourne(5) 13 57
(Mark Brisbourne) *racd keenly: trckd ldrs: outpcd by ldng pair 3f out: plugged on fr over 1f out* **4/1[1]**

-000 **8** *2 1/4* **Ptolomeos**[49] 5823 8-9-0 **50** oh5............................ MissECrossman(7) 4 44
(Sean Regan) *slowly away: sn plld way into midfield: rdn over 2f out: no imp* **66/1**

3035 **9** *1 1/2* **Granny Anne (IRE)**[56] 5631 3-8-10 **51**.......................... MrsRWilson(7) 7 42
(Paul D'Arcy) *midfield: pushed along over 3f out: nvr threatened* **10/1**

3335 **10** *3 1/4* **Talk Of Saafend (IRE)**[58] 4982 6-9-6 **52**..................... MissECSayer(3) 1 37
(Dianne Sayer) *s.i.s: hld up: nvr threatened* **12/1**

0300 **11** *2 1/4* **Guga (IRE)**[36] 6236 5-9-8 **58**.................................(b) MissABlakemore(5) 5 39
(John Mackie) *racd keenly: trckd ldrs: rdn over 3f out: wknd over 1f out* **16/1**

00-0 **12** *3/4* **Nippy Nikki**[96] 4284 3-8-9 **50** oh5.............................. MissHMillward(7) 8 29
(John Norton) *t.k.h in midfield: wknd over 3f out* **100/1**

5030 **13** *10* **Wrecking Crew (IRE)**[27] 6486 7-9-8 **56**.................... MrsDBamonte(5) 10 16
(Rod Millman) *plld hrd: trckd ldrs on outer: wknd 3f out* **12/1**

2m 17.8s (6.10) **Going Correction** +0.40s/f (Good)
WFA 3 from 4yo+ 5lb **13** Ran SP% **118.1**
Speed ratings (Par 101): **91,90,90,89,87 87,86,85,83,81 79,78,70**
toteswingers:1&2:£12.00, 1&3:£7.60, 2&3:£14.30 CSF £39.50 CT £310.11 TOTE £4.40: £2.30, £2.10, £2.30; EX 52.30 Trifecta £233.80 Part won. Pool £315.95 - 0.30 winning units..
Owner P Whinham **Bred** Exors Of The Late Mrs E A Hankinson **Trained** Scamblesby, Lincs
■ Stewards' Enquiry : Miss A Blakemore three-day ban: used whip without giving gelding time to respond (Nov 16,22,28)

FOCUS
The slower of the two divisions by 1.03sec and very few got into it. It looked the lesser race and the form is less solid.
T/Jkpt: Not won. T/Plt: £108.00 to a £1 stake. Pool:£57,259.92 - 386.81 winning tickets T/Qpdt: £22.00 to £1. Pool: £3,704.72 - 124.14 w. tckts JR 7114a - (Foreign Racing) - See RI

BENDIGO
Wednesday, October 26
OFFICIAL GOING: Turf: good

7115a JAYCO BENDIGO CUP (LISTED H'CAP) (TURF) — 1m 4f
6:00 (12:00) 3-Y-0+
£80,718 (£23,529; £11,764; £5,882; £3,267; £2,614)

RPR

1 **Tanby (AUS)**[7] 6967 5-8-7 **0**..(t) StevenKing 4 111
(Robert Hickmott, Australia) **3/1[2]**

2 *1 3/4* **At First Sight (IRE)**[39] 4-9-2 **0**.................................... NicholasHall 5 117+
(Robert Hickmott, Australia) **2/1[1]**

3 *1 1/4* **Western Symbol (NZ)** 5-8-5 **0**.................................(b) KerrinMcEvoy 1 104
(Gai Waterhouse, Australia) **9/1[3]**

4 *1/2* **Boom 'n' Zoom (AUS)** 6-8-8 **0**.................................(b) CraigNewitt 7 106
(Ken Keys, Australia) **9/1[3]**

5 *hd* **Olympic Win (NZ)**[226] 6-8-5 **0**..................................(t) ChrisSymons 2 103
(Robert Smerdon, Australia) **18/1**

6 *1 1/4* **Back In Black (NZ)**[7] 6967 6-8-6 **0** ow1......................... DannyNikolic 3 102
(John Steffert, New Zealand) **19/1**

7 *3/4* **Sunset Cafe (AUS)** 5-8-5 **0**......................................(p) StephenBaster 9 99
(Leon Corstens, Australia) **80/1**

8 *nk* **Sahara Sun (CHI)**[18] 6713 4-8-11 **0**...........................(t) DwayneDunn 10 105
(Luca Cumani) *pushed along fr s to chse ldrs: sn settled 5th: shkn up on outside 2 1/2f out: hrd rdn and nt qckn fr 2f out: kpt on at one pce fnl f* **10/1**

9 *nk* **Dream Pedlar (AUS)**[11] 6886 7-8-11 **0**..................(b) CraigAWilliams 11 105
(Troy Blacker, Australia) **15/1**

10 *hd* **Innocent Lady (NZ)**[26] 5-8-6 **0** ow1............................... JamesWinks 6 99
(Graeme & Mark Sanders, New Zealand) **30/1**

11 *5* **Two For Tea (NZ)**[18] 6711 5-8-5 **0**.............................(t) MichaelWalker 12 90
(Gai Waterhouse, Australia) **40/1**

12 3 3/4 **Cosmonaut (AUS)**[26] 4-8-5 0 ...... LukeNolen 8 84
(Bart Cummings, Australia) 12/1
2m 28.72s (148.72) **12** Ran SP% **118.5**
PARI-MUTUEL (NSW TAB - all including au$1 stakes): WIN 3.70 PLACE 1.60, 1.50, 2.80; DF 4.30; SF 8.00.
Owner N & Mr & Mrs L J Williams **Bred** S Bennetts **Trained** Australia

7091 KEMPTON (A.W) (R-H)

Thursday, October 27

OFFICIAL GOING: Standard

Wind: Light, behind. Weather: Gloomy

7116 BLUESQ.COM CLAIMING STKS 5f (P)

5:30 (5:30) (Class 5) 3-Y-0+ **£2,264** (£673; £336; £168) **Stalls** Low

Form RPR

2042 **1** **Lucky Art (USA)**[12] 6875 5-8-12 78 ...... JustinNewman(7) 1 84
(Conor Dore) *wl away fr prime draw: mde all and mostly 2 l clr: rdn and styd on wl fnl f* **5/1**[2]

4656 **2** 1 3/4 **Osiris Way**[57] 5627 9-9-8 77 ...... JohnFahy(3) 8 83
(Patrick Chamings) *mostly chsd wnr: rdn over 1f out: kpt on but no imp* **16/1**

6050 **3** 1/2 **Steelcut**[27] 6502 7-8-13 67 ......(p) LukeMorris 4 69
(David Evans) *towards rr and off the pce: latched on to bk of ldng gp 2f out: urged along and styd on wl fnl f to take 3rd post* **14/1**

0/21 **4** hd **Master Of Disguise**[12] 6875 5-9-1 85 ......(t) SilvestreDeSousa 5 71
(Brian Baugh) *chsd ldrs: effrt 2f out: nt qckn over 1f out: styd on fnl f: n.d* **15/8**[1]

510 **5** shd **Grandmas Dream**[5] 7039 3-9-0 77 ......(b) MartinHarley 3 69
(Richard Guest) *trckd ldrs on inner: rdn and nt qckn over 1f out: styd on same pce after* **15/2**

0015 **6** shd **Penny's Pearl (IRE)**[13] 6841 3-8-6 62 ...... AndreaAtzeni 2 61
(David Evans) *prom: disp 2nd fr 1/2-way to over 1f out: one pce* **14/1**

6240 **7** 4 **Atlantic Beach**[56] 5658 6-9-3 66 ...... LiamKeniry 12 58
(Milton Bradley) *chsd ldrs: rdn and nt qckn wl over 1f out: wknd fnl f* **25/1**

2020 **8** 2 1/4 **Fol Hollow (IRE)**[10] 6913 6-9-11 81 ...... AdrianNicholls 7 58
(David Nicholls) *sn hld up in rr: urged along and wl outpcd sn after 1/2-way: nvr on terms after* **11/2**[3]

5000 **9** 1/2 **Oldjoesaid**[10] 6917 7-9-11 80 ......(b) PhillipMakin 10 56
(Kevin Ryan) *hld up in last pair: outpcd 1/2-way: no ch after: styd on ins fnl f* **9/1**

3/00 **10** 10 **Lady Royal Oak (IRE)**[24] 6593 4-9-0 60 ...... KirstyMilczarek 11 9
(Olivia Maylam) *t.k.h: racd wd in midfield: hanging bnd over 3f out: wknd 2f out: t.o* **66/1**

3200 **11** 1 1/2 **Lesley's Choice**[12] 6875 5-9-11 77 ......(p) AdamKirby 6 14
(Paul Rich) *a wl in rr: outpcd and struggling fr 1/2-way: t.o* **25/1**

58.96 secs (-1.54) **Going Correction** -0.10s/f (Stan) **11** Ran SP% **117.0**
Speed ratings (Par 103): **108,105,104,104,103 103,97,93,92,76 74**
Tote Swingers:1&2:£15.80, 2&3:£16.60, 1&3:£16.70 CSF £79.46 TOTE £3.10: £1.10, £5.70, £4.80; EX 94.50.Grandmas Dream was claimed by Richard Fahey for £9,000.
Owner Chris McHugh **Bred** Gaines-Gentry Thoroughbreds **Trained** Cowbit, Lincs

FOCUS
A fair race of its type. Although the gallop to the home turn was an ordinary one (favouring those close to the pace), the final time was only half a second outside the course record. The winner raced close to the inside rail throughout. The form could be rated higher.
Lady Royal Oak(IRE) Official explanation: jockey said filly ran too freely

7117 BLUE SQUARE CLAIMING STKS 1m 2f (P)

6:00 (6:00) (Class 6) 2-Y-0 **£1,617** (£481; £240; £120) **Stalls** Low

Form RPR

2062 **1** **Priestley's Reward (IRE)**[5] 7035 2-9-6 63 ...... MartinHarley 4 66
(Mrs K Burke) *hld up in 5th and off the pce: prog 3f out: clsd to dispute ld 1f out: drvn and gained upper hand nr fin* **7/2**[2]

1541 **2** nk **Snowed In (IRE)**[28] 6471 2-9-2 70 ...... LukeMorris 2 61
(J S Moore) *trckd clr ldr: clsd 3f out: rdn to dispute ld 1f out: edgd rt and nt qckn nr fin* **4/7**[1]

4365 **3** 1 3/4 **Manderston**[17] 6763 2-8-10 54 ...... SilvestreDeSousa 7 52
(Mark Johnston) *led and sn 4 l clr: c bk to rivals fr 3f out: hdd and one pce 1f out* **12/1**

2050 **4** 2 1/2 **Rafaella**[17] 6743 2-8-8 62 ...... JohnFahy(3) 1 48
(Harry Dunlop) *chsd clr ldng pair: clsd 3f out: rdn and nt qckn 2f out: one pce after* **7/1**[3]

000 **5** 10 **Cotes Du Rhone (IRE)**[66] 5325 2-8-12 27 ......(p) AndreaAtzeni 3 30
(David Evans) *nvr gng wl: drvn to dispute 3rd briefly 3f out: wknd 2f out: t.o* **66/1**

0000 **6** 11 **Hawkino (IRE)**[9] 6937 2-9-0 53 ...... RobbieFitzpatrick 8 11
(Derek Shaw) *stdd s: hld up last: wknd over 2f out: t.o: lame* **50/1**

2m 11.49s (3.49) **Going Correction** -0.10s/f (Stan) **6** Ran SP% **109.5**
Speed ratings (Par 93): **82,81,80,78,70 61**
Tote Swingers:1&2:£1.40, 2&3:£1.60, 1&3:£2.50 CSF £5.56 TOTE £3.40: £1.40, £1.10; EX 7.50.
Owner P Dean & Mrs E Burke **Bred** Michael Mullins **Trained** Middleham Moor, North Yorks

FOCUS
An uncompetitive claimer run at just an ordinary gallop, and weak form. The winner edged towards the far rail in the closing stages.

NOTEBOOK
Priestley's Reward(IRE), who had a little bit to find strictly at the weights in relation to the runner-up, appreciated the step up to this trip and showed improved form to get off the mark, despite edging towards the far rail late on. A stronger gallop would have suited and he may be capable of a little better. (op 10-3 tchd 4-1)
Snowed In(IRE), the pick of the weights, was well supported and had the run of the race but was just touched off returned to this longer trip. He's a reliable yardstick who should continue to go well. (op 4-6 tchd 4-5 in a place)
Manderston's form has a very uneven look to it but he was allowed an easy lead and returned to something like his best upped to this trip for the first time. However this could flatter him and he wouldn't be one to go in head down for next time. (op 10-1)
Rafaella wasn't totally disgraced in terms of form on this first run on sand and on this first run over this trip but was again some way below her encouraging debut effort and she will have to settle much better before she is a betting proposition. (op 13-2 tchd 15-2)
Hawkino(IRE) Official explanation: vet said gelding was lame right-hind

7118 PLAY CLEOPATRA AT BLUESQ.COM MAIDEN FILLIES' STKS 1m (P)

6:30 (6:33) (Class 5) 2-Y-0 **£2,264** (£505; £505; £168) **Stalls** Low

Form RPR

6 **1** **Dreams Of Fire (USA)**[17] 6744 2-9-0 0 ...... RyanMoore 3 79
(Sir Michael Stoute) *trckd ldrs in 6th: prog and shkn up to dispute 2nd 2f out: looked hld tl styd on ins fnl f to ld last strides* **6/1**[3]

42 **2** 1/2 **Dulkashe (IRE)**[16] 6776 2-9-0 0 ...... KierenFallon 2 78
(Luca Cumani) *prom: shkn up to chse ldr wl over 2f out: no imp over 1f out: styd on ins fnl f: a hld* **9/4**[1]

3 **2** dht **Eluding**[23] 6603 2-9-0 0 ...... FrankieDettori 1 78
(Mahmood Al Zarooni) *led: looked to be gng best 2f out: stl 2 l clr ins fnl f: wknd and hdd last strides* **3/1**[2]

4 nk **Popular** 2-9-0 0 ...... TomQueally 6 79+
(Sir Henry Cecil) *s.s: rcvrd into midfield: hdwy 3f out: trying to cl on ldrs whn nt clr run and swtchd rt 1f out: pushed along and styd on: nrst fin* **10/1**

5 1/2 **Bon Allumage** 2-9-0 0 ...... IanMongan 7 76
(Sir Henry Cecil) *trckd ldrs in 5th: pushed along 2f out: stl chsng over 1f out: kpt on: nvr quite able to chal* **25/1**

0 **6** 4 1/2 **Layali Dubai (USA)**[29] 6458 2-9-0 0 ...... SilvestreDeSousa 5 67
(Saeed Bin Suroor) *in tch in midfield: outpcd by ldrs over 2f out: shkn up and kpt on over 1f out: eased ins fnl f* **8/1**

7 2 1/2 **Hello Dubai** 2-9-0 0 ...... LiamKeniry 10 60+
(David Simcock) *s.s: wl in rr and rn green: prog over 2f out: rchd 7th over 1f out and shkn up: no imp after* **66/1**

8 3 1/2 **Zowaina** 2-9-0 0 ...... AndreaAtzeni 9 52+
(Roger Varian) *sed slowest of all: detached in last pair early: sme prog 3f out: nvr on terms* **25/1**

0 **9** 4 1/2 **Adelindus**[17] 6745 2-9-0 0 ...... AdamKirby 4 42
(Walter Swinburn) *sn towards rr: shkn up and outpcd fr over 2f out: no ch after* **66/1**

10 2 1/4 **Paradise Sea (USA)** 2-9-0 0 ...... PaulHanagan 8 36
(Mikael Magnusson) *mostly chsd ldr to wl over 2f out: wknd qckly* **7/1**

11 6 **Sea Anemone** 2-9-0 0 ...... JimmyFortune 14 23
(Andrew Balding) *a towards rr: wknd over 2f out* **66/1**

0 **12** 1/2 **Authoritarian**[23] 6603 2-9-0 0 ...... RichardHughes 11 22
(Richard Hannon) *racd wd: pressed ldrs to over 2f out: wknd rapidly* **25/1**

0 **13** 13 **Hip Hop**[29] 6441 2-9-0 0 ...... DaneO'Neill 13 —
(Brett Johnson) *sn toiling in last pair: t.o 3f out* **66/1**

14 9 **Asparella** 2-9-0 0 ...... ShaneKelly 12 —
(Murty McGrath) *a wl in rr: wknd 3f out: t.o* **66/1**

1m 38.96s (-0.84) **Going Correction** -0.10s/f (Stan) **14** Ran SP% **121.8**
Speed ratings (Par 92): **100,99,99,99,98 94,91,88,83,81 75,74,61,52**
Place: Dulkashe £1.90, Eluding £1.10; CSF: DOF & Dulkashe £10.10, DOF & E £16.20; Exacta: DOF & D £9.51, DOF & E £11.65; Tote Swingers:1&2:£3.10, 2&2:£2.20, 1&2:£3.40 TOTE £7.10: £2.40.
Owner Niarchos Family **Bred** Flaxman Holdings Limited **Trained** Newmarket, Suffolk

FOCUS
An interesting fillies' maiden featuring a couple that had shown fair form and a couple of well-bred newcomers. The gallop was only an ordinary one and the first five finished in a heap but this race should throw up winners, particularly the fourth. The principals came down the centre in the straight.

NOTEBOOK
Dreams Of Fire(USA) ◆, closely related to Derby winner Kris Kin, stepped up a fair bit on her debut run at Salisbury over this longer trip to get off the mark on this first run on an artificial surface. She should stay at least 1m2f next season and she appeals as the sort to win more races. (op 8-1)
Dulkashe(IRE) had shown a fair level of form on two turf starts and she reproduced that level on this all-weather debut. She remains capable of picking up a similar event around this trip on either turf or Polytrack at some stage. (op 5-2 tchd 11-4)
Eluding, from a yard going well, attracted support and ran as well as she had on her debut at Leicester over this longer trip on this Polytrack debut after being allowed to do her own in thing in front. She too is sure to pick up an ordinary event. (op 5-2 tchd 11-4)
Popular ◆, a sister to the yard's high-class middle-distance performer Midday, shaped with plenty of promise on this racecourse debut. She fared the best of those to come from off the pace, she wasn't knocked about after meeting trouble and should win a similar event at the very least. Official explanation: jockey said filly was denied a clear run (op 8-1)
Bon Allumage, the first foal of the yard's former 1m4f Listed winner Brisk Breeze, showed a fair level of form on this racecourse debut. She will be suited by at least 1m2f next year and she's sure to improve for this experience and win a race. (op 20-1)
Layali Dubai(USA) proved a shade disappointing in view of her price on her debut at Nottingham but she fared better this time. She may do better over a bit further once qualified for a handicap mark. (op 12-1)
Hello Dubai, a 30,000gns half-sister to a couple of useful sorts up to 1m, was green but should improve for this debut experience. (op 50-1)
Zowaina, a half-sister to the yard's useful 1m4f debut maiden winner Shubaat, should improve for this experience. Official explanation: jockey said filly was slowly away
Paradise Sea(USA), well supported throughout the day but easy to back before the off, shaped as though this debut run was needed. This $140,000 half-sister to high-class David Junior should come on a fair bit for this run. (op 5-1)

7119 WIN THOUSANDS OF SPORTS EXPERIENCES AT BLUESQ.COM H'CAP 1m (P)

7:00 (7:00) (Class 7) (0-50,50) 3-Y-0+ **£1,455** (£433; £216; £108) **Stalls** Low

Form RPR

4005 **1** **Lightning Spirit**[7] 6982 3-9-0 **50** ......(p) RyanMoore 9 59
(Gary Moore) *chsd ldrs in 4th: rdn over 2f out: prog to ld over 1f out: styd on* **5/2**[1]

0310 **2** 3/4 **Tinkerbell Will**[60] 5515 4-9-2 **49** ...... SamHitchcott 4 56
(John E Long) *towards rr on inner: urged along and prog wl over 2f out: styd on to take 2nd 1f out: a hld* **10/1**

5-00 **3** 1 **Fayre Bella**[15] 6791 4-8-12 **48** ...... JohnFahy(3) 2 53
(John Gallagher) *chsd ldng pair: rdn over 2f out: tried to chal over 1f out: one pce fnl f* **20/1**

5050 **4** 1/2 **Endaxi Mana Mou**[26] 6545 3-9-0 **50** ......(b) LiamKeniry 7 54
(Noel Quinlan) *hld up in midfield: rdn and nt qckn over 2f out: styd on fr over 1f out: nrst fin* **20/1**

0326 **5** 1 1/4 **Queenie's Star (IRE)**[42] 6083 4-8-10 **48** ...... MarkCoumbe(5) 11 49
(Michael Attwater) *wl in rr: shkn up over 2f out: prog wl over 1f out: styd on: nvr able to chal* **5/1**[2]

2400 **6** 1 **Carlitos Spirit (IRE)**[20] 5822 7-9-0 **50** ......(v) PaulPickard(3) 6 48
(Ian McInnes) *chsd ldrs in 5th: effrt on inner over 2f out: nt qckn over 1f out: fdd* **11/1**

450 **7** *hd* **My Flame**[42] 6083 6-9-0 **47**.......................... FergusSweeney 13 45
(J R Jenkins) *trckd ldr: led over 3f out: hdd & wknd over 1f out* **8/1**

0005 **8** *1* **Hi Spec (IRE)**[21] 6657 8-9-0 **47** ow1..........................(tp) AdamKirby 8 43
(Mandy Rowland) *s.s: mostly in last pair: shkn up and sme prog 2f out: rchd 8th 1f out: no hdwy after* **11/1**

4360 **9** *9* **Farmers Dream (IRE)**[34] 6309 4-9-0 **47**............ SilvestreDeSousa 14 22
(Richard Price) *nvr beyond midfield on outer: wknd jst over 2f out* **8/1**

0000 **10** *1* **Emerald Girl (IRE)**[1] 7091 4-9-2 **49**.......................... MartinHarley 12 22
(Richard Guest) *s.s: a in rr: brief effrt over 3f out: wknd over 2f out* **15/2**[3]

0/0- **11** *hd* **What's For Tea**[39] 983 6-8-10 **46**....................(v[1]) RobertLButler(3) 3 18
(Paddy Butler) *a in rr: struggling over 3f out: bhd after* **50/1**

0050 **12** *nk* **Indian Wish (USA)**[65] 5352 3-8-9 **50**.......................... LauraPike(5) 1 21
(Tim McCarthy) *led to over 3f out: wknd rapidly 2f out* **25/1**

1m 39.49s (-0.31) **Going Correction** -0.10s/f (Stan)
WFA 3 from 4yo+ 3lb **12** Ran SP% **120.3**
Speed ratings (Par 97): **97,96,95,94,93 92,92,91,82,81 81,80**
Tote Swingers:1&2:£6.00, 2&3:£45.70, 1&3:£17.60 CSF £27.62 CT £429.18 TOTE £2.30: £1.10, £3.70, £8.20; EX 24.40.
Owner Heart Of The South Racing **Bred** John And Caroline Penny **Trained** Lower Beeding, W Sussex

FOCUS
A low-grade handicap in which the gallop was only fair. The winner came down the centre in the straight and she and the second showed fair form for the grade.

7120 BET AT BLUESQ.COM ON YOUR MOBILE H'CAP 2m (P)
7:30 (7:30) (Class 4) (0-80,83) 3-Y-O+ **£4,075** (£1,212; £606; £303) **Stalls** Low

Form RPR

2433 **1** **Spice Fair**[17] 6749 4-10-1 **81**.......................... JimmyFortune 4 92
(Mark Usher) *hld up last: stl there 3f out: gd prog after to chse ldr fnl f: drvn and r.o to ld last 50yds: gd ride* **8/1**[2]

4134 **2** *nk* **Palazzo Bianco**[13] 6832 3-9-7 **83**.......................... RobertHavlin 6 94
(John Gosden) *trckd ldng pair: wnt 2nd 2f out: drvn ahd over 1f out: r.o but hdd last 50yds* **15/8**[1]

1316 **3** *4* **Susan Stroman**[54] 5714 3-9-0 **76**.......................... JamieSpencer 3 82
(Ed Dunlop) *trckd ldrs: disp 5th after 5f: effrt towards inner over 2f out and sn cl enough: styd on same pce fr over 1f out* **8/1**[2]

0310 **4** *nk* **Where's Susie**[31] 6405 6-9-10 **76**.......................... DaneO'Neill 7 82
(Michael Madgwick) *hld up in last trio: rdn and prog on outer fr over 2f out: styd on fnl f: nvr able to threaten* **25/1**

0002 **5** *½* **Phonic (IRE)**[22] 6622 4-8-12 **64**.......................... EddieAhern 10 69
(John Dunlop) *hld up disputing 9th: prog over 3f out: rdn over 2f out: styd on after but nvr gng pce to rch ldrs* **14/1**

3200 **6** *2¾* **Huff And Puff**[17] 6749 4-9-13 **79**.......................... KierenFallon 11 81
(Amanda Perrett) *hld up in midfield tl prog to dispute 3rd after 5f: drvn wl over 2f out: wknd over 1f out* **8/1**[2]

3420 **7** *4* **Rosewood Lad**[18] 6722 4-9-8 **74**.......................... PaulHanagan 9 71
(J S Moore) *hld up disputing 7th: effrt wl over 2f out: sn no prog: wknd over 1f out* **20/1**

1010 **8** *4½* **May Contain Nuts**[19] 6707 3-9-0 **76**.......................... FergusSweeney 5 68
(Brendan Powell) *trckd ldr: led over 2f out: hdd & wknd over 1f out* **25/1**

2230 **9** *2* **Wild Desert (FR)**[6] 6988 6-9-7 **78**.......................... LucyKBarry(5) 1 67
(Charlie Longsdon) *led at decent pce to over 2f out: wknd qckly over 1f out* **12/1**

0-10 **10** *10* **Jasmeno**[11] 6893 4-9-5 **71**..........................(t) RichardHughes 8 48
(Hughie Morrison) *trckd ldrs: disp 5th after 5f: rdn wl over 2f out: sn wknd and eased* **9/1**[3]

0106 **11** *14* **Strewth (IRE)**[24] 6584 3-8-9 **71**.......................... LukeMorris 12 31
(John Best) *dwlt: a in last trio: rdn and wknd 3f out* **33/1**

/5-0 **12** *1* **No Rules**[18] 6722 6-8-13 **65**.......................... TomQueally 13 24
(Mark H Tompkins) *towards rr disputing 9th: no prog 3f out: sn wknd* **16/1**

021 **13** *48* **Morar**[80] 4844 5-9-12 **78**.......................... IanMongan 2 —
(Laura Mongan) *settled disputing 7th: first one u.p over 4f out: sn wknd and eased: t.o* **16/1**

3m 24.7s (-5.40) **Going Correction** -0.10s/f (Stan) course record
WFA 3 from 4yo+ 10lb **13** Ran SP% **119.6**
Speed ratings (Par 105): **109,108,106,106,106 105,103,100,99,94 87,87,63**
Tote Swingers:1&2:£4.90, 2&3:£5.40, 1&3:£9.30 CSF £[illegible] CT £[illegible]100.18 TOTE £[illegible]: £3.00, £1.[illegible], £3.10, EX 29.40.
Owner Saxon House Racing **Bred** Mrs D Hughes **Trained** Upper Lambourn, Berks
■ Stewards' Enquiry : Robert Havlin five-day ban: used whip with excessive frequency (Nov 10-12,14,15)

FOCUS
A fair handicap in which a reasonable gallop resulted in a new course record. This form looks reliable and the winner came down the centre in the straight. He recorded another personal best.
Morar Official explanation: vet said mare returned distressed

7121 ENHANCED SP'S AT BLUESQ.COM H'CAP (DIV I) 1m 4f (P)
8:00 (8:01) (Class 6) (0-65,71) 3-Y-O+ **£1,617** (£481; £240; £120) **Stalls** Centre

Form RPR

5611 **1** **Fascinating (IRE)**[5] 7037 3-9-11 **71** 6ex.......................... SilvestreDeSousa 4 87+
(Mark Johnston) *s.i.s: sn trckd ldrs: rousted along whn pce lifted over 3f out: prog on inner to ld over 2f out and sn drvn clr: in n.d after* **4/6**[1]

02 **2** *5* **Fellisha (IRE)**[9] 6926 3-8-2 **55**.......................... RaulDaSilva(7) 9 61
(Andrew Heffernan, Ire) *hld up last: prog whn hmpd over 2f out: styd on again fr wl over 1f out: wnt 2nd ins fnl f: no ch w wnr* **9/1**[3]

3000 **3** *1½* **Buddy Holly**[15] 6789 6-9-12 **65**.......................... AndreaAtzeni 3 68
(Robert Eddery) *trckd ldr after 1f to wl over 2f out: outpcd u.p: kpt on to take modest 2nd briefly 1f out: no ch w wnr* **14/1**

3350 **4** *¾* **Miss Bounty**[9] 6926 6-9-2 **55**.......................... MatthewDavies 7 57
(Jim Boyle) *hld up in last trio: rdn 3f out: styd on u.p on outer fnl 2f: no threat* **25/1**

616- **5** *nk* **Lucas Pitt**[327] 7704 4-8-10 **54**.......................... DavidKenny(5) 11 56
(Michael Scudamore) *hld up in last pair: drvn 3f out: styd on fnl 2f on outer: nrst fin but n.d* **10/1**

40 **6** *2¼* **Robby Bobby**[80] 4847 6-9-6 **59**.......................... IanMongan 8 57
(Laura Mongan) *hld up towards rr: gng bttr than most over 3f out: prog over 2f out but sn drvn and outpcd: clsd to dispute 2nd 1f out: wknd qckly last 150yds* **33/1**

4002 **7** *1* **Bin End**[22] 6621 5-9-3 **61**.......................... LeeNewnes(5) 6 57
(Barry Brennan) *in tch: rdn over 3f out: in pack chsng clr wnr over 1f out: wknd* **8/1**[2]

2345 **8** *2* **Corvette**[11] 6891 3-9-3 **63**..........................(v) PaulHanagan 12 56
(J R Jenkins) *led after 1f: set mod pce tl kicked on 4f out: hdd over 2f out: lost 2nd and wknd rapidly 1f out* **12/1**

0135 **9** *19* **Prince Blue**[22] 6622 4-8-13 **52**.......................... SamHitchcott 5 15
(John E Long) *led 1f: prom tl wknd rapidly 3f out: t.o* **16/1**

0260 **10** *28* **Barodine**[30] 6438 8-9-2 **58**.......................... HarryBentley(3) 2 —
(Ron Hodges) *trckd ldrs tl wknd rapidly over 3f out: wl t.o* **50/1**

2m 34.23s (-0.27) **Going Correction** -0.10s/f (Stan)
WFA 3 from 4yo+ 7lb **10** Ran SP% **119.2**
Speed ratings (Par 101): **96,92,91,91,90 89,88,87,74,56**
Tote Swingers:1&2:£2.90, 2&3:£7.80, 1&3:£3.60 CSF £7.61 CT £51.23 TOTE £1.80: £1.10, £1.80, £4.20; EX 4.20.
Owner Nabil Mourad **Bred** Trebles Holford Farm Thoroughbreds **Trained** Middleham Moor, N Yorks

FOCUS
A modest handicap and a steady gallop but a race won in convincing fashion by the most progressive winner, who raced close to the inside rail in the straight. He is much improved but will be hit hard for this.
Prince Blue Official explanation: jockey said gelding hung left
Barodine Official explanation: vet said gelding bled from the nose

7122 ENHANCED SP'S AT BLUESQ.COM H'CAP (DIV II) 1m 4f (P)
8:30 (8:30) (Class 6) (0-65,65) 3-Y-O+ **£1,617** (£481; £240; £120) **Stalls** Centre

Form RPR

0042 **1** **Ninfea (IRE)**[14] 6811 3-9-0 **60**..........................(p) LiamKeniry 4 68
(Sylvester Kirk) *trckd ldrs: rdn and outpcd over 2f out: wnt 3rd over 1f out but stl plenty to do: styd on wl fnl f to ld last strides* **4/1**[2]

0313 **2** *¾* **Fifty Cents**[15] 6790 7-9-3 **56**..........................(p) KierenFallon 3 63
(Brendan Powell) *led at modest pce: kicked on over 3f out: drvn and pressed 2f out: beat off rival 1f out and looked sure to win: collared last strides* **3/1**[1]

0000 **3** *1¼* **Honourable Knight (IRE)**[12] 6871 3-8-9 **55**............(be[1]) DavidProbert 5 60
(Mark Usher) *hld up in last pair in slowly run r: rdn 3f out: prog u.p 2f out: styd on wl fnl f: snatched 3rd last stride* **10/1**

2000 **4** *nse* **Beat Route**[15] 6789 4-9-7 **65**.......................... JemmaMarshall(5) 8 70
(Michael Attwater) *t.k.h: trckd ldr: shkn up to chal 2f out and clr of rest: nt qckn over 1f out: lost 2 pls nr fin* **7/1**[3]

204 **5** *9* **Naheell**[222] 917 5-9-6 **59**..........................(p) SilvestreDeSousa 1 50
(George Prodromou) *dwlt: sn trckd ldrs: rdn 3f out: lft bhd fr 2f out* **14/1**

0550 **6** *shd* **Ilie Nastase (FR)**[6] 7003 7-8-11 **57**..........................(b) JustinNewman(7) 7 47
(Conor Dore) *t.k.h: hld up in tch: struggling once pce lifted over 3f out: wl btn 2f out* **9/1**

0640 **7** *shd* **Divine Rule (IRE)**[14] 6240 3-8-11 **57**..........................(p) FergusSweeney 11 47
(Laura Mongan) *hld up in last in slowly run r: effrt on inner over 2f out but already outpcd: no ch after* **20/1**

4060 **8** *¾* **Beckfield Dancer**[22] 6622 3-8-5 **51** oh3.......................... PaulHanagan 2 40
(Stuart Williams) *trckd ldng pair: rdn and nt qckn wl over 2f out: wknd and lost 3rd over 1f out* **16/1**

2546 **9** *4½* **Rodrigo De Freitas (IRE)**[15] 6789 4-9-6 **59**..........................(v) TomQueally 10 41
(Jim Boyle) *trckd ldrs: rdn and fnd nil over 2f out: sn wknd* **8/1**

0 **10** *14* **Green To Gold (IRE)**[15] 6790 6-9-10 **63**.......................... JamieSpencer 6 22
(Don Cantillon) *racd wd: hld up in tch: wknd 3f out: t.o* **10/1**

2m 34.33s (-0.17) **Going Correction** -0.10s/f (Stan)
WFA 3 from 4yo+ 7lb **10** Ran SP% **114.1**
Speed ratings (Par 101): **96,95,94,94,88 88,88,88,85,75**
Tote Swingers:1&2:£1.80, 2&3:£10.00, 1&3:£8.60 CSF £16.00 CT £109.85 TOTE £5.20: £1.50, £1.30, £3.70; EX 16.10.
Owner Miss A Jones **Bred** Kilco Builders **Trained** Upper Lambourn, Berks

FOCUS
A modest handicap in which the gallop was on the steady side. The first four, who pulled clear, came down the centre in the straight. the runner-up is the best guide to the form, which looks a little shaky.

7123 BLUE SQUARE MINI ROULETTE H'CAP 6f (P)
9:00 (9:00) (Class 6) (0-60,60) 3-Y-O+ **£1,617** (£481; £240; £120) **Stalls** Low

Form RPR

6006 **1** **Mambo Spirit (IRE)**[28] 6479 7-9-3 **60**.......................... DaneO'Neill 3 7[illegible]+
(Tony Newcombe) *[illegible] prog on inner fr 2f out: shkn up to ld 1f out against rail: a in command fnl f* **3/1**[1]

4063 **2** *¾* **Belinsky (IRE)**[9] 6940 4-9-1 **58**.......................... PaulHanagan 8 68
(Mark Campion) *led: rdn 2f out: edgd lft and hdd 1f out: r.o but safely hld* **10/3**[2]

3636 **3** *2¾* **Valeo Si Vales (IRE)**[13] 6848 3-9-1 **59**..........................(b) FergusSweeney 9 60
(Jamie Osborne) *hld up in last pair: shkn up over 1f out: r.o fnl f to take 3rd nr fin: no ch to rch ldng pair* **13/2**

1020 **4** *nk* **The Name Is Frank**[29] 6444 6-9-2 **59**..........................(p) DavidProbert 1 59
(Mark Gillard) *plld hrd: pressed ldng pair: chal 2f out: cl 3rd but hld whn squeezed out jst over 1f out: outpcd after: lost 3rd nr fin* **7/1**

0511 **5** *nk* **Vhujon (IRE)**[15] 6784 6-9-0 **57**.......................... RobbieFitzpatrick 2 56
(Peter Grayson) *hld up in last pair: effrt 2f out: styd on fnl f: nrst fin but no ch* **9/2**[3]

5005 **6** *½* **Brandywell Boy (IRE)**[9] 6931 8-9-0 **60**.......................... BillyCray(3) 4 57
(Dominic Ffrench Davis) *pressed ldng pair: rdn 2f out: fdd over 1f out* **14/1**

0003 **7** *2* **Morermaloke**[21] 6655 3-8-12 **59**..........................(p) PaulPickard(3) 5 50
(Ian McInnes) *hld up in midfield: effrt over 2f out: nt qckn and no imp on ldrs 1f out: wknd qckly last 100yds* **12/1**

4433 **8** *2* **Catalinas Diamond (IRE)**[9] 6931 3-9-1 **59**..........................(t) SteveDrowne 6 44
(Pat Murphy) *pressed ldng pair: poised to chal 2f out: sn shkn up and fnd nil: wknd tamely fnl f* **15/2**

000 **9** *12* **Cranworth Quest (IRE)**[66] 5317 3-9-0 **58**.......................... MartinLane 12 —
(Tim Etherington) *gd spd fr wd draw to join ldr: wknd rapidly 2f out: t.o* **33/1**

1m 12.31s (-0.79) **Going Correction** -0.10s/f (Stan)
WFA 3 from 4yo+ 1lb **9** Ran SP% **121.2**
Speed ratings (Par 101): **101,100,96,95,95 94,92,89,73**
Tote Swingers:1&2:£4.10, 2&3:£3.90, 1&3:£5.60 CSF £13.92 CT £62.43 TOTE £3.10: £1.30, £1.10, £2.80; EX 18.30.
Owner A G Newcombe **Bred** R Warren **Trained** Yarnscombe, Devon

FOCUS
A moderate handicap run at a reasonable gallop. The winner raced against the inside rail in the straight and the form looks sound. The winner looks very well handicapped.
T/Plt: £21.00 to a £1 stake. Pool £72,622.85. 2,517.47 winning tickets T/Qpdt: £4.00 to a £1 stake. Pool £11,264.01. 2,040.18 winning tickets JN

[6926] LINGFIELD (L-H)
Thursday, October 27

OFFICIAL GOING: Standard
Wind: Light, across. Weather: light cloud, bright spells

7124 EBF WEATHERBYS PRIVATE BANKING MAIDEN FILLIES' STKS (DIV I) 7f (P)
1:40 (1:43) (Class 5) 2-Y-O **£3,234** (£962; £481; £240) **Stalls** Low

Form RPR

0 1 **Cantal**[40] 6168 2-9-0 0.............................. RyanMoore 11 74+
(Sir Michael Stoute) *pressed ldr: rdn to ld jst over 1f out: kpt on wl ins fnl f: hrd pressed fnl 75yds: jst hld on* **4/1**[2]

2 *nse* **Srinagar Girl** 2-9-0 0.............................. TomQueally 5 74+
(Sir Henry Cecil) *t.k.h: hld up wl in tch: swtchd rt and effrt wl over 1f out: chsd wnr jst ins fnl f: r.o wl and str chal fnl 75yds: jst failed* **25/1**

0 3 *2 ¼* **Al Andaleeb (USA)**[62] 5444 2-9-0 0.............................. FrankieDettori 4 68
(Saeed Bin Suroor) *led: rdn and hdd jst over 1f out: no ex and outpcd fnl 100yds* **8/1**

5 4 *nk* **Strathnaver**[23] 6603 2-9-0 0.............................. KierenFallon 1 67+
(Ed Dunlop) *s.i.s: sn rcvrd and in tch in midfield on inner: swtchd rt over 2f out: rdn and hdwy over 1f out: kpt on but nt pce to rch ldrs* **7/1**

6 5 *2 ½* **Shabora (IRE)**[23] 6603 2-9-0 0.............................. AndreaAtzeni 6 61
(Roger Varian) *s.i.s: in tch in rr: shkn up and hdwy on inner 2f out: no imp and styd on same pce fnl f* **13/2**[3]

00 6 *nk* **Moody Dancer**[40] 6169 2-9-0 0.............................. WilliamCarson 3 60
(William Muir) *chsd ldrs: rdn and unable qck wl over 1f out: swtchd rt and outpcd over 1f out: wknd 1f out* **100/1**

2 7 *1 ¾* **Scarlet Belle**[17] 6744 2-9-0 0.............................. RichardMullen 7 55
(Marcus Tregoning) *in tch: rdn and outpcd 2f out: no threat to ldrs after* **14/1**

4 8 *1* **Pearl War (USA)**[62] 5444 2-9-0 0.............................. EddieAhern 10 53
(William Haggas) *hld up in tch towards rr: rdn and unable qck 2f out: wknd over 1f out* **7/4**[1]

6 9 *½* **Mandianna (IRE)**[17] 6751 2-9-0 0.............................. FergusSweeney 8 52
(Jo Crowley) *chsd ldrs: rdn and unable qck ent fnl 2f: wknd over 1f out* **33/1**

10 *½* **So Cheeky** 2-9-0 0.............................. RichardHughes 9 50
(Richard Hannon) *s.i.s: a towards rr and sn swtchd rt: rdn and no prog over 2f out: one pce and n.d after* **25/1**

1m 25.13s (0.33) **Going Correction** -0.025s/f (Stan) **10** Ran SP% **111.6**
Speed ratings (Par 92): **97,96,94,94,91 90,88,87,87,86**
Tote Swingers:1&2:£19.50, 2&3:£31.50, 1&3:£5.90 CSF £98.99 TOTE £5.70: £1.80, £5.30, £2.50; EX 141.00 Trifecta £381.20 Part won. Pool £515.19 - 0.44 winning units..
Owner Cheveley Park Stud **Bred** Cheveley Park Stud Ltd **Trained** Newmarket, Suffolk

FOCUS
A fair maiden with several top stables represented, and the market got it right. It's hard to rate the form any higher.

NOTEBOOK
Cantal failed to get home over 1m on her Newmarket debut, but she was sent off very well backed here. Always in a good position, she took over in front over a furlong from home but would have been caught in another stride. The form may not be great, but getting a win out of this half-sister to the Group 3 winner Evasive was probably the main thing. (op 8-1)
Srinagar Girl, a 50,000gns half-sister to two winners at up to 1m2f and by a sire with a superb record on sand, only just failed to get up and may have done so with previous experience. An all-weather maiden should be a formality should connections wish. (op 20-1)
Al Andaleeb(USA) failed to beat a rival on her Newmarket debut in August and did better here, leading until over a furlong from home, but this shows that she does have her limitations. (tchd 9-1)
Strathnaver, a fair fifth of 17 on her Leicester debut earlier this month, was weak in the market and lost ground at the start, so didn't fare badly in the circumstances. She may be one for handicaps. (op 9-2)
Shabora(IRE), just behind Strathnaver on her Leicester debut, was another to miss the break before making some late progress and looks another that needs a bit more time. (tchd 11-2)
Pearl War(USA) was disappointing considering the promise she showed on her debut. Official explanation: trainer had no explanation for the poor form shown (op 15-8 tchd 13-8)

7125 EBF WEATHERBYS PRIVATE BANKING MAIDEN FILLIES' STKS (DIV II) 7f (P)
2:10 (2:10) (Class 5) 2-Y-O **£3,234** (£962; £481; £240) **Stalls** Low

Form RPR

32 1 **Rhagori**[29] 6455 2-9-0 0.............................. JimCrowley 3 72+
(Ralph Beckett) *chsd ldrs: rdn to chal jst over 1f out: drvn to ld jst ins fnl f: r.o wl* **9/4**[1]

4454 2 *1* **Miss Astragal (IRE)**[61] 5475 2-9-0 73.............................. RichardHughes 6 69
(Richard Hannon) *s.i.s: in tch in last quartet: pushed along 3f out: effrt and n.m.r over 1f out: swtchd rt 1f out: r.o wl to go 2nd towards fin: nt rch wnr* **5/2**[2]

6 3 *¾* **Brief Chat (USA)**[17] 6745 2-9-0 0.............................. JimmyFortune 7 67
(Amanda Perrett) *led for 1f: chsd ldr after: rdn to ld 1f out: sn hdd and styd on same pce fnl 150yds* **8/1**

5 4 *½* **Al Wajba (USA)**[26] 6525 2-9-0 0.............................. EddieAhern 5 66+
(William Haggas) *in tch on outer: wnt wd and lost grnd bnd wl over 1f out: rallied 1f out: styd on wl fnl f: nt rch ldrs* **15/2**

6 5 *½* **Sugar Loaf**[75] 5048 2-9-0 0.............................. WilliamCarson 9 64
(William Muir) *s.i.s: bhd: rdn over 4f out: hdwy over 1f out: drvn ins fnl f: styd on same pce and no imp fnl 100yds* **28/1**

6 *shd* **Miss Blakeney** 2-9-0 0.............................. RichardMullen 8 64+
(Marcus Tregoning) *rn green and pushed along at times: in tch in rr: nt clr run 2f out: hdwy whn swtchd lft 1f out: r.o fnl f: nt rch ldrs* **11/1**

0004 7 *¾* **Street Angel (IRE)**[30] 6424 2-9-0 44..............................(b[1]) SilvestreDeSousa 1 62
(Alan Bailey) *chsd ldr tl led after 1f: rdn ent fnl 2f: hdd 1f out: no ex fnl f* **40/1**

04 8 *¾* **Aiaam Al Wafa (IRE)**[17] 6744 2-9-0 0.............................. TedDurcan 4 60
(David Lanigan) *in tch towards rr: shkn up and nt clr run wl over 1f out: hdwy on inner over 1f out: no imp ins fnl f* **6/1**[3]

0 9 *1 ½* **Song Of Joy (IRE)**[138] 2914 2-9-0 0.............................. LukeMorris 2 56
(Paul D'Arcy) *chsd ldrs: rdn and unable qck 2f out: wknd fnl f* **66/1**

66 10 *16* **Saucy Cat (IRE)**[15] 6795 2-9-0 0.............................. ShaneKelly 10 15
(Murty McGrath) *s.i.s: t.k.h and sn rcvrd to chse ldrs: wknd qckly 2f out: wl bhd and eased ins fnl f* **50/1**

1m 26.15s (1.35) **Going Correction** -0.025s/f (Stan) **10** Ran SP% **114.2**
Speed ratings (Par 92): **91,89,89,88,87 87,86,86,84,66**
Tote Swingers:1&2:£1.90, 2&3:£6.70, 1&3:£7.00 CSF £7.61 TOTE £3.50: £1.50, £2.10, £3.90; EX 8.80 Trifecta £52.60 Pool £345.93 - 4.86 winning units..
Owner Landmark Racing Limited **Bred** P T Tellwright **Trained** Kimpton, Hants

FOCUS
Probably the weaker of the two divisions with the 44-rated Street Angel making much of the running until inside the last furlong and the field finishing in more of a heap. The winning time was over a second slower than the first leg. The first two help set the level.

NOTEBOOK
Rhagori, placed in her first two starts though beaten at odds-on on the second occasion, quickened up well to hit the front inside the last furlong and appeared to appreciate the surface. She should have a future in handicaps. (tchd 11-4)
Miss Astragal(IRE) was rated 73 after showing ability in turf maidens, but she wasn't best away here and her finishing effort was too late. She has the ability to win a race, but has little in the way of scope. (tchd 2-1)
Brief Chat(USA), a fair sixth of 13 on her Salisbury debut, was always up there and had every chance until the very latter stages. Handicaps are likely to bring out the best in her. (op 9-1 tchd 10-1 and 15-2)
Al Wajba(USA) ◆, a well-beaten fifth of seven on her Newmarket debut, travelled well off the pace but lost ground on the home bend and soon had plenty to do. She finished well, however, and is one to keep onside. (op 8-1 tchd 9-1 and 7-1)
Sugar Loaf, a very well-beaten sixth of seven on her Newbury debut, didn't run badly considering she was off the bridle a long way out. She looks one for handicaps in due course. (op 50-1)
Miss Blakeney, a half-sister to three winners in France and the only newcomer in the field, looked to need the experience but was doing some pleasing late work and should come on for the run. (op 12-1 tchd 10-1)

7126 BRITISH STALLION STUDS SUPPORTING BRITISH RACING EBF MAIDEN STKS 7f (P)
2:40 (2:40) (Class 5) 2-Y-O **£3,557** (£1,058; £529; £264) **Stalls** Low

Form RPR

4332 1 **Grizzle**[13] 6829 2-9-3 82.............................. FrankieDettori 3 80
(Mahmood Al Zarooni) *in tch: rdn and effrt on inner over 1f out: qcknd to ld ins fnl f: r.o wl: pushed out* **15/8**[1]

04 2 *1* **Protanto (IRE)**[43] 6064 2-9-3 0.............................. TedDurcan 7 77+
(David Lanigan) *racd in midfield: rdn over 1f out: r.o strly ins fnl f to go 2nd cl home: nt rch wnr* **16/1**

2 3 *nk* **Kinloch Castle**[12] 6866 2-9-3 0.............................. SilvestreDeSousa 11 77
(Mark Johnston) *led on outer: rdn 2f out: hdd jst over 1f out: chsd wnr and styd on same pce fnl 100yds: lost 2nd cl home* **4/1**[2]

03 4 *1 ¾* **Impel (IRE)**[18] 6725 2-9-3 0.............................. RichardHughes 1 72
(Richard Hannon) *w ldr: rdn and led narrowly jst over 1f out: hdd ins fnl f: sn btn: fdd fnl 75yds* **11/2**[3]

3 5 *½* **Isthmus**[28] 6481 2-9-3 0.............................. TomQueally 4 71+
(Amanda Perrett) *chsd ldrs: rdn and unable qck over 1f out: drvn and kpt on same pce ins fnl f* **16/1**

00 6 *2 ½* **Fisher**[38] 6214 2-9-3 0.............................. DaneO'Neill 5 64
(Richard Hannon) *racd off the pce in midfield: clsd 3f out: rdn and no imp 2f out: styd on same pce and no threat to ldrs after* **66/1**

4 7 *¾* **Maistro (IRE)**[28] 6474 2-9-3 0.............................. KierenFallon 6 62
(Luca Cumani) *racd in last trio: pushed along on outer wl over 2f out: no prog and edging lft over 1f out: n.d* **8/1**

5 8 *3 ¼* **Mokbil (IRE)**[16] 6768 2-9-3 0.............................. RichardHills 10 54
(Roger Varian) *t.k.h: chsd ldrs: rdn and unable qck 2f out: wknd qckly over 1f out: wl btn and eased wl ins fnl f* **11/2**[3]

9 *1 ¼* **Welsh Bard (IRE)** 2-9-3 0.............................. SebSanders 8 51
(Sir Mark Prescott Bt) *s.i.s: sn rdn along in last pair: n.d* **50/1**

10 *4 ½* **Mr Fickle (IRE)** 2-9-3 0.............................. AmirQuinn 9 39
(Gary Moore) *s.i.s: a last: lost tch wl over 1f out* **100/1**

1m 24.83s (0.03) **Going Correction** -0.025s/f (Stan) **10** Ran SP% **112.9**
Speed ratings (Par 95): **98,96,96,94,93 91,90,86,85,79**
Tote Swingers:1&2:£8.00, 2&3:£10.00, 1&3:£2.20 CSF £34.80 TOTE £2.60: £1.10, £3.90, £1.70; EX 36.80 Trifecta £238.90 Pool £662.02 - 2.05 winning units..
Owner Godolphin **Bred** Darley **Trained** Newmarket, Suffolk

FOCUS
A maiden contested only by colts and geldings this time, several of whom had already shown ability. Those that raced handily were at an advantage and the winning time was faster than both divisions of the fillies' maiden. Fair form, which looks sound.

NOTEBOOK
Grizzle was rated 82 after making the frame in his first five starts and, having always been travelling well just behind the leaders, made full use of the gap that appeared against the rail inside the last furlong. It will be interesting to see if connections try and win a handicap with him on this surface. (op 5-2)
Protanto(IRE)showed some ability on his first two starts and this was his best effort yet. Held up in the rear group, he ran on strongly down the outside off the final bend and on this evidence 1m will suit. Handicaps now become an option. (op 14-1)
Kinloch Castle, clear of the rest when narrowly beaten by a 71-rated rival on his Catterick debut, was always at the sharp end and had every chance, but the way he hung under pressure a furlong from home suggests that he is still far from the finished article. (op 6-1)
Impel(IRE) helped force the pace and grabbed the lead on his own over a furlong out, but it wasn't for long once the winner was unleashed on his inside. He can now go the nursery route. (op 4-1)
Isthmus, a fair third of nine on his Warwick debut, had every chance but became outpaced when things quickened up over a furlong from home. He is another likely to do better in handicaps. (op 10-1)
Maistro(IRE) was disappointing having come off the bridle a fair way out. (op 7-1 tchd 9-1)
Mokbil(IRE) was another to disappoint, fading tamely. (op 5-1)

7127 JOIN HOT TO TROT RACING CLUB H'CAP 7f (P)
3:10 (3:10) (Class 3) (0-95,95) 3-Y-0+ **£6,663** (£1,982; £990; £495) **Stalls** Low

Form RPR

0056 1 **Citrus Star (USA)**[33] 6341 4-9-4 92.............................. TedDurcan 14 105
(Chris Wall) *stdd and dropped in bhd after s: hld up in last quartet: rdn and effrt towards inner over 1f out: rdn to ld jst ins fnl f: r.o strly and drew clr fnl 100yds* **13/2**[3]

5000 2 *2 ½* **Seek The Fair Land**[17] 6761 5-8-11 85.............................. EddieAhern 6 91
(Jim Boyle) *chsd ldrs: rdn to chse ldr over 1f out: ev ch ins fnl f: nt pce of wnr ins fnl f: kpt on* **8/1**

0001 3 *½* **Steed**[3] 7057 4-9-3 94 6ex..............................(b) RobertLButler(3) 9 99
(Richard Guest) *in tch: rdn and unable qck over 1f out: rallied and bmpd 1f out: styd on wl ins fnl f: no threat to wnr* **16/1**

5066 4 *1* **Janood (IRE)**[19] 6704 3-9-3 93..............................(b[1]) FrankieDettori 8 95
(Saeed Bin Suroor) *in tch: hdwy to chse ldrs over 2f out: rdn and nt qckn over 1f out: one pce and no threat to wnr ins fnl f* **11/2**[2]

-210 5 *1 ¼* **Hazzard County (USA)**[229] 846 7-9-0 95.............................. AliceHaynes(7) 4 94
(David Simcock) *hld up in last quartet: rdn and hdwy towards inner over 1f out: kpt on ins fnl f: nvr able to chal* **16/1**

0600 6 *½* **Judd Street**[18] 6728 9-8-9 83..............................(vt) KierenFallon 2 81
(Eve Johnson Houghton) *t.k.h: chsd ldrs: rdn and unable qck over 1f out: plugged on same pce fnl f* **22/1**

0602 **7** *nk* **We Have A Dream**[7] 6974 6-8-11 **85** ow1.................... RichardHughes 1 82
(William Muir) *led: rdn and hdd jst ins fnl f: wknd fnl 100yds* **14/1**

3-02 **8** *hd* **Call To Reason (IRE)**[33] 6335 4-8-12 **86**......................... RyanMoore 11 85+
(Jeremy Noseda) *in tch in midfield: nt clr run wl over 1f out: stl plenty to do whn bmpd 1f out: nt clr run again ins fnl f tl fnl 100yds: nvr able to chal* **10/3**[1]

1060 **9** *1 ½* **Shamir**[54] 5712 4-9-0 **88**... IanMongan 3 80
(Jo Crowley) *hld up in last quartet: hdwy towards inner over 1f out: kpt on but nvr threatened ldrs* **10/1**

0204 **10** *½* **Mac Gille Eoin**[18] 6723 7-8-13 **87**...................................... JimCrowley 7 78
(John Gallagher) *t.k.h: hld up in tch in midfield: rdn and no prog over 1f out: wknd fnl f* **20/1**

6000 **11** *½* **Mr Willis**[77] 4962 5-9-1 **89**.. MarcHalford 5 79
(Terry Clement) *s.i.s: hld up in rr: c v wd bnd wl over 1f out: sn rdn: kpt on but n.d* **33/1**

0050 **12** *nse* **R Woody**[6] 6987 4-9-2 **90**.. ShaneKelly 13 79
(Dean Ivory) *pressed ldr tl over 1f out: wknd fnl f* **16/1**

0530 **13** *6* **Star Rover (IRE)**[6] 6987 4-9-2 **90**.........................(v) SilvestreDeSousa 10 63
(David Evans) *chsd ldrs on outer: lost pl ent fnl 2f: wl bhd fnl f* **9/1**

1m 23.26s (-1.54) **Going Correction** -0.025s/f (Stan)
WFA 3 from 4yo+ 2lb **13** Ran SP% **118.4**
Speed ratings (Par 107): **107,104,103,102,101 100,100,99,98,97 97,96,90**
Tote Swingers:1&2:£13.50, 2&3:£22.40, 1&3:£22.10 CSF £55.68 CT £831.79 TOTE £8.90: £2.90, £3.30, £5.80; EX 73.50 Trifecta £553.90 Pool £800.54 - 1.00 winning units..
Owner Induna Racing Partners Two **Bred** Stephen McDonald **Trained** Newmarket, Suffolk

FOCUS
A decent and competitive handicap and the form looks solid despite the third running surprisingly well.

NOTEBOOK
Citrus Star(USA) ◆ had finished unplaced in all nine starts since his last win and was making his all-weather debut. The outside stall was a problem too and he was unsurprisingly tucked in, but despite still having plenty to do turning in he was still travelling well and produced a telling turn of foot towards the inside to hit the front a furlong from home. The way he handled the surface suggested he had been waiting for it all his life and he is probably capable of even better. He will run in a conditions race in a fortnight's time. (tchd 7-1)
Seek The Fair Land came into this on a losing run of 23, but all five of his wins had come over 7f on Polytrack (two here) and he was 1lb below the last of them. Well backed, he was produced with his effort at the same time as the winner and, although unable to match him, finished a clear second best. There will be other days. (op 10-1 tchd 15-2)
Steed, carrying a 6lb penalty for his Leicester success three days earlier, was finishing better than anything down the wide outside. He won't find many options on his beloved Fibresand off this sort of mark, but he has won on Polytrack and this effort suggests he may be able to find another race on this surface. (tchd 14-1)
Janood(IRE), whose stable had won the last two runnings of this race, was tried in blinkers having disappointed since returning to this country. He had every chance up the home straight, but lacked the pace to take advantage. (op 15-2)
Hazzard County(USA) ◆ was returning from 229 days off, though he has won following a lengthy absence in the past. He isn't the easiest of rides and needs producing at just the right time, but this was still a pleasing return and he was by no means given a hard ride by his apprentice. (op 12-1)
Judd Street has dropped 16lb in the weights since his reappearance for a reason, but this wasn't a bad effort, especially as he met trouble on the home bend. (tchd 20-1)
We Have A Dream, trying this trip for the first time on his 62nd start, made much of the running but patently failed to stay.
Call To Reason(IRE), still comparatively lightly raced, didn't perform very well in her only previous try on Polytrack. She didn't have much room to play with from over a furlong out, but wasn't unlucky. Her rider reported that the filly was denied a clear run. Official explanation: jockey said filly was denied a clear run (op 11-4 tchd 7-2)

7128 EBF NORMANDIE STUD FLEUR DE LYS FILLIES' STKS (LISTED RACE) 1m (P)

3:40 (3:41) (Class 1) 3-Y-O+

£17,013 (£6,450; £3,228; £1,608; £807; £405) **Stalls** High

Form RPR

3001 **1** **Clinical**[32] 6394 3-9-0 103.. SebSanders 10 105
(Sir Mark Prescott Bt) *w ldr tl rdn to ld wl over 1f out: hld on wl u.p towards fin* **7/1**

1440 **2** *nk* **Sooraah**[34] 6297 4-9-3 97 RyanMoore 4 101+
(William Haggas) *in tch: rdn and hdwy ent fnl f: chsd wnr fnl 75yds: r.o wl and str chal towards fin: nt quite rch wnr* **4/1**[1]

2-02 **3** *1 ¾* **Mosqueras Romance**[46] 5980 5-9-0 100........................... AdamKirby 8 97
(Marco Botti) *in tch: rdn and effrt to chse ldrs over 1f out: kpt on same pce ins fnl f* **6/1**

6521 **4** *½* **Avon Lady**[16] 6770 4-9-0 94.. EddieAhern 3 96
(James Fanshawe) *chsd ldng pair: drvn and effrt over 1f out: styd on same pce ins fnl f* **12/1**

1-02 **5** *½* **Zoowraa**[16] 6770 3-8-11 100... FrankieDettori 12 95
(Mahmood Al Zarooni) *in tch: rdn and outpcd over 1f out: rallied and styd on again fnl 100yds: nt pce to chal ldrs* **5/1**[3]

-103 **6** *hd* **The Shrew**[34] 6297 3-8-11 98... PaulHanagan 1 94
(John Gosden) *led: rdn and hdd wl over 1f out: outpcd and btn 1f out: styd on same pce after* **9/2**[2]

0154 **7** *½* **Conciliatory**[32] 6394 4-9-0 93.................................(p) SilvestreDeSousa 6 93
(Rae Guest) *in tch in midfield: rdn and hdwy on inner over 1f out: one pce and no imp ins fnl f* **20/1**

5000 **8** *¾* **Night Lily (IRE)**[34] 6302 5-9-0 90....................................... LukeMorris 5 91
(Paul D'Arcy) *hld up in last pair: pushed along over 2f out: kpt on u.p ins fnl f: nvr trbld ldrs* **10/1**

5-10 **9** *1 ¾* **Kameruka**[16] 6783 5-9-0 93... RichardHughes 9 87
(R Pritchard-Gordon, France) *hld up in last trio: effrt on outer wl over 1f out: no imp: nvr trbld ldrs* **25/1**

3000 **10** *nk* **Kinky Afro (IRE)**[11] 6909 4-9-0 91.................................(p) LiamKeniry 7 87
(J S Moore) *in tch in midfield: rdn and unable qck over 2f out: no hdwy and btn fr wl over 1f out* **66/1**

R420 **P** **Jacqueline Quest (IRE)**[49] 5848 4-9-0 102...................... KierenFallon 11 —
(Ian Williams) *virtually ref to r: eventually exited stalls and immediately p.u* **10/1**

1m 35.96s (-2.24) **Going Correction** -0.025s/f (Stan) course record
WFA 3 from 4yo+ 3lb **11** Ran SP% **117.6**
Speed ratings (Par 108): **110,109,107,107,106 106,106,105,103,103** —
Tote Swingers:1&2:£7.50, 2&3:£6.40, 1&3:£7.30 CSF £34.45 TOTE £11.40: £3.40, £1.80, £1.30; EX 65.00 Trifecta £586.50 Pool £800.54 - 1.01 winning units..
Owner Cheveley Park Stud **Bred** Cheveley Park Stud Ltd **Trained** Newmarket, Suffolk

FOCUS
An ordinary race of its type, though the first two fillies had been successful at this level before. Unfortunately, not for the first time Jacqueline Quest refused to come out of the stalls. The winner is rated to her Cologne level, with the second a bit better than the bare form.

NOTEBOOK
Clinical was penalised 3lb after winning a soft-ground Listed race in Germany last month, but had no problems with these very different conditions. She was always in a handy position behind the leader before taking over in front approaching the furlong pole and rather got first run on the second filly. This will have boosted her value further. (op 6-1 tchd 15-2)
Sooraah, also carrying a 3lb penalty for winning a Listed race at Ascot in July, was given much more to do than the winner and finished with a real flourish, but her effort was always going to fall a couple of strides short. (op 6-1)
Mosqueras Romance, runner-up in five Listed events including by a short-head in this race last year, had every chance to break her hoodoo at this level, but couldn't quicken sufficiently and the wait continues. (op 5-1 tchd 13-2)
Avon Lady narrowly defeated Zoowraa at Leicester earlier this month and was travelling better than anything behind the leaders turning for home, but lacked the turn of foot to capitalise. (op 14-1 tchd 11-1)
Zoowraa, from the stable that had taken the last two runnings of this race, had her chance but her finishing effort wasn't convincing and she has become very disappointing after looking so promising this time last year. (tchd 6-1)
The Shrew was having her first start since finishing well beaten in the 1,000 Guineas when third in a Newmarket Listed event last month and had the run of the race out in front, but was comfortably picked off. (op 5-1)
Conciliatory finished over 2l behind Clinical in Germany, but was beaten further this time. (op 22-1 tchd 25-1 and 16-1)
Night Lily(IRE) had plenty to find on these terms and didn't find her stride until it was too late. (op 16-1)

7129 EBF COCKNEY REBEL - A LEADING FIRST SEASON SIRE RIVER EDEN FILLIES' STKS (LISTED RACE) 1m 5f (P)

4:10 (4:11) (Class 1) 3-Y-O+

£17,013 (£6,450; £3,228; £1,608; £807; £405) **Stalls** Low

Form RPR

2604 **1** **Charleston Lady**[26] 6530 3-8-8 95.................................(b[1]) JimCrowley 1 99
(Ralph Beckett) *bhd: swtchd to outer and hdwy on bnd 2f out: str run ins fnl f to ld last strides* **14/1**

6024 **2** *hd* **Roxy Flyer (IRE)**[35] 6269 4-9-2 93................................... RyanMoore 10 99
(Amanda Perrett) *hld up in last pair: swtchd to outer and gd hdwy over 2f out: led but hung lft over 1f out: kpt on u.p tl hdd and no ex last strides* **7/1**[3]

0336 **3** *nk* **Cill Rialaig**[12] 6859 6-9-2 104... RichardHughes 3 98+
(Hughie Morrison) *in tch in midfield: hdwy to trck ldrs and travelling wl on inner over 2f out: nt clr run 2f out: drvn and ev ch ins fnl f: no ex cl home* **9/4**[1]

1535 **4** *nk* **Twin Soul (IRE)**[27] 6498 3-8-8 79..................................... DavidProbert 6 98+
(Andrew Balding) *in tch in midfield: hdwy whn nt clr run and hmpd 1f out: sn swtchd rt and rallied u.p: kpt on wl and pressing ldrs towards fin* **16/1**

3360 **5** *1 ¼* **Western Pearl**[18] 6736 4-9-2 92..................................... JamieSpencer 2 97+
(William Knight) *hld up in last trio: n.m.r over 2f out: hdwy towards inner over 1f out: chsng ldrs whn nt clr run and hmpd jst ins fnl f: styd on same pce after* **16/1**

4316 **6** *3* **Zafarana**[46] 5963 3-8-8 83.. KierenFallon 5 92
(Ed Dunlop) *t.k.h: in tch in midfield: effrt whn nt clr run wl over 1f out: nt rcvr and styd on same pce after* **25/1**

2120 **7** *1* **Highest**[133] 3065 3-8-8 95... EddieAhern 4 93+
(John Gosden) *in tch: rdn to chse ldrs over 1f out: keeping on same pce whn nt clr run and hmpd 1f out: nt rcvr and nt pushed after* **7/1**[3]

00/5 **8** *2 ½* **Bolivia (GER)**[41] 6125 5-9-2 95.. PaulHanagan 11 86
(Lucy Wadham) *taken down early: chsd ldr tl led over 10f out: rdn over 3f out: drvn over 2f out: hdd over 1f out: sn wknd* **14/1**

0121 **9** *2 ½* **Qushchi**[40] 6172 3-8-8 96.. TomQueally 8 83
(William Jarvis) *chsd ldrs: rdn and nt qckning whn n.m.r wl over 1f out: sn wknd* **3/1**[2]

0223 **10** *2 ½* **Quiz Mistress**[23] 6607 3-8-8 77................................ SilvestreDeSousa 9 79
(Gerard Butler) *in tch in midfield: rdn and unable qck 2f out: wknd over 1f out* **25/1**

1155 **11** *3 ¾* **Sharp Relief (IRE)**[18] 6729 3-8-8 72................................ RobertHavlin 7 73+
([illegible]) *[illegible] struggling whn nt clr run and snatched up over 1f out: sn btn and bhd fnl f* **100/1**

2m 42.3s (-3.70) **Going Correction** -0.025s/f (Stan) course record
WFA 3 from 4yo+ 8lb **11** Ran SP% **114.5**
Speed ratings (Par 108): **110,109,109,109,108 106,106,104,103,101 99**
Tote Swingers:1&2:£11.70, 2&3:£4.60, 1&3:£8.00 CSF £104.22 TOTE £18.60: £4.80, £1.80, £1.20; EX 100.80 Trifecta £447.80 Pool £877.47 - 1.45 winning units..
Owner R A Pegum **Bred** Mrs J Chandris **Trained** Kimpton, Hants

FOCUS
Another ordinary Listed event. All 11 fillies were still within a few lengths of each other coming to the last furlong and things got tight for some. The form is taken at face value although there are one or two doubts.

NOTEBOOK
Charleston Lady did well to win this as she had to come from last place and was forced to circle the entire field rounding the home bend to get a run, but considering a few who made their efforts more towards the inner got into trouble, it was a wise move, and she put her head in front a few strides from the line. The first time-blinkers may well have helped and she is now due to head for the sales. (tchd 16-1)
Roxy Flyer(IRE), sixth in this last year, also made her effort from off the pace on the wide outside on the home bend, but before the winner. In front over a furlong out, she gave her rival something to aim at and she was collared close home. (op 8-1 tchd 17-2)
Cill Rialaig had upwards of 8lb in hand of these rivals at the weights following her very respectable sixth of ten behind Dancing Rain in the big fillies and mares race at Ascot 12 days earlier. She had run well in her only previous try on Polytrack when still a maiden, so the surface shouldn't have been an issue, but she didn't enjoy the smoothest of trips and was forced to follow a route tight against the inside rail. She tried hard, but didn't have a lot of room to play with on the inside in the home straight and was just outpaced by two rivals who made their efforts much wider. (op 2-1 tchd 7-4 and 5-2 in a place)
Twin Soul(IRE), successful in her last three starts on Polytrack, was one of those not to enjoy much room in the home straight and had to be switched right, but stayed on well. She faced a very stiff task on these terms, but may have blown her handicap mark with this effort. (tchd 20-1)
Western Pearl, ninth in this last year, also didn't have a lot of room to play with in the straight and can be given some extra credit. (op 20-1 tchd 22-1)
Zafarana seemed to relish the Polytrack when winning her maiden at Kempton two starts back, but she had plenty on at these weights. She became short of room rounding the home bend, but didn't exactly take off once in the clear. (tchd 28-1)
Highest, not seen since running poorly in the Ribblesdale, had her chance but either didn't stay or blew up. Her rider reported that the filly was denied a clear run. Official explanation: jockey said filly was denied a clear run (tchd 15-2)

Sharp Relief(IRE) Official explanation: jockey said filly suffered interference in running

7130 RIDE SIERRA NEVADA FOR MARIE CURIE H'CAP — 1m 2f (P)

4:40 (4:40) (Class 5) (0-75,75) 3-Y-0+ — £2,385 (£704; £352) — Stalls Low

Form — RPR

3641 **1** **Green Wadi**[15] 6789 6-9-5 **73**.........(p) RyanMoore 12 — 82
(Gary Moore) *in tch in midfield: rdn and effrt to press ldrs over 1f out: led ins fnl f: drvn and hld on wl fnl 100yds* **13/2**[3]

0003 **2** *hd* **Nibani (IRE)**[15] 6785 4-8-11 **70**.........(p) AmyScott(5) 4 — 79
(Alastair Lidderdale) *hld up in tch in rr: hdwy on outer over 2f out: rdn over 1f out: ev ch ins fnl f: kpt on but hld towards fin* **20/1**

4006 **3** *2 1/4* **Hurricane Spirit (IRE)**[15] 6797 7-9-4 **72**.........(b) SteveDrowne 5 — 76
(Terry Clement) *dwlt: pushed along early: in tch towards rr: hdwy over 1f out: running on whn nt clr run and swtchd rt ins fnl f: r.o to go 3rd towards fin* **20/1**

4325 **4** *shd* **Birdolini**[29] 6457 3-9-0 **73**......... FergusSweeney 13 — 77
(Alan King) *hld up in tch in last quartet: c wd and effrt over 1f out: r.o wl ins fnl f: nt rch ldrs* **11/2**[2]

5504 **5** *hd* **Choral Festival**[24] 6592 5-8-12 **69**......... SeanLevey(3) 11 — 73
(John Bridger) *in tch in midfield: rdn and effrt 2f out: no imp tl r.o wl u.p fnl 100yds: nt rch ldrs* **18/1**

0206 **6** *nk* **Understory (USA)**[37] 6241 4-9-6 **74**......... KierenFallon 10 — 77
(Tim McCarthy) *chsd ldr tl led 8f out and set stdy gallop: qcknd 3f out: rdn over 1f out: hdd ins fnl f: no ex and sn btn: wknd towards fin* **18/1**

1406 **7** *nk* **Gala Casino Star (IRE)**[36] 6263 6-9-6 **74**......... PaulHanagan 2 — 76
(Richard Fahey) *chsd ldrs: drvn and ev ch over 1f out tl unable qck ins fnl f: wknd fnl 100yds* **14/1**

3264 **8** *nse* **Billion Dollar Kid**[10] 6924 6-9-2 **70**.........(tp) RichardKingscote 6 — 72
(Jo Davis) *chsd ldrs: shuffled bk but stl wl in tch 4f out: hdwy u.p over 1f out: no ex and one pce ins fnl f* **12/1**

0263 **9** *1 3/4* **Heatherbird**[43] 6063 3-8-12 **74**......... HarryBentley(3) 9 — 73
(William Jarvis) *taken down early: hld up in tch towards rr: rdn and no imp over 1f out: kpt on ins fnl f but no threat to ldrs* **11/2**[2]

5600 **10** *1/2* **Kiss A Prince**[29] 6469 5-9-4 **72**.........(b) ShaneKelly 1 — 70
(Dean Ivory) *dwlt: sn rcvrd: t.k.h: in tch in midfield: effrt on inner over 1f out: wknd ins fnl f* **17/2**

4-00 **11** *1 1/2* **Flag Of Glory**[136] 2999 4-9-4 **72**......... WilliamCarson 7 — 67
(Peter Hiatt) *in tch: chsd ldrs 4f out tl unable qck u.p wl over 1f out: wknd fnl f* **33/1**

01 **12** *11* **Medal Of Valour (JPN)**[24] 6578 3-9-2 **75**......... SilvestreDeSousa 3 — 48
(Mark Johnston) *led tl 8f out: chsd ldr after tl ent fnl 2f: sn lost pl: bhd fnl f* **11/4**[1]

2m 5.93s (-0.67) **Going Correction** -0.025s/f (Stan)
WFA 3 from 4yo+ 5lb — **12** Ran SP% **118.6**
Speed ratings (Par 103): **101,100,99,98,98 98,98,98,96,96 95,86**
Tote Swingers:1&2:£21.00, 2&3:£59.60, 1&3:£19.30 CSF £132.26 CT £2458.75 TOTE £6.40: £2.80, £7.30, £6.70; EX 148.50 TRIFECTA Not won..
Owner Andrew Bradmore **Bred** Mrs P A Clark **Trained** Lower Beeding, W Sussex

FOCUS
An ordinary handicap and a lack of pace resulted in a typical Lingfield bunched finish. The winner's best form since he was a 2yo.
Heatherbird Official explanation: jockey said filly ran too free
Medal Of Valour(JPN) Official explanation: trainer's rep said colt was unsuited by the Polytrack surface

7131 PLAWHATCH APPRENTICE H'CAP — 7f (P)

5:10 (5:11) (Class 6) (0-60,65) 3-Y-0+ — £1,704 (£503; £251) — Stalls Low

Form — RPR

6053 **1** **Rio Royale (IRE)**[17] 6746 5-9-0 **58**.........(b[1]) LukeRowe(5) 14 — 70
(Amanda Perrett) *chsd ldrs: wnt 2nd over 2f out: rdn to ld over 1f out: clr ins fnl f: rdn out* **7/1**[2]

0400 **2** *1 3/4* **Lennoxwood (IRE)**[6] 7005 3-8-4 **48**.........(be) RachealKneller(3) 4 — 55
(Mark Usher) *in tch: rdn and effrt over 1f out: chsd wnr ins fnl f: kpt on* **16/1**

4301 **3** *nk* **Fedora (IRE)**[22] 6626 5-9-1 **57**.........(t) RaulDaSilva(3) 6 — 63
(Olivia Maylam) *hld up in midfield: clsd over 2f out: rdn over 1f out: wnt 3rd ins fnl f: kpt on and pressing for 2nd cl home: no threat to wnr* **5/1**[1]

6600 **4** *1 1/4* **Pipers Piping (IRE)**[122] 3468 5-9-6 **59**......... AmyScott 9 — 62+
(Alastair Lidderdale) *hld up wl off the pce in last quartet: clsd over 2f out: c wd and hdwy over 1f out: r.o wl fnl f: nt rch ldrs* **10/1**

2000 **5** *2* **Indian Violet (IRE)**[7] 6971 5-9-0 **60**......... DanielCremin(7) 13 — 58+
(Ralph Smith) *stdd after s: hld up wl off the pce in last quartet: clsd over 2f out: rdn and hdwy over 1f out: edgd lft but kpt on ins fnl f: nvr trbld ldrs* **12/1**

0021 **6** *1/2* **Seneschal**[9] 6931 10-9-9 **65** 6ex......... LucyKBarry(3) 12 — 61
(Adrian Chamberlain) *chsd ldrs: wnt 2nd over 3f out: led over 2f out: rdn and hdd over 1f out: wknd fnl f* **7/1**[2]

3000 **7** *1* **Inquisitress**[7] 6971 7-8-7 **46** oh1......... RyanPowell 5 — 40
(John Bridger) *dwlt: pushed along early and wl off the pce in last quartet: hdwy on inner over 1f out: no imp u.p fnl f* **20/1**

2505 **8** *shd* **Karate (IRE)**[13] 6847 3-8-12 **58**......... NicoleNordblad(5) 2 — 51
(Hans Adielsson) *led tl 5f out: chsd ldrs after: nt clr run and shuffled bk over 2f out: rdn and wknd over 1f out* **7/1**[2]

5320 **9** *hd* **Kai Mook**[22] 6624 4-9-7 **60**.........(bt) MatthewLawson 3 — 53
(Roger Ingram) *racd off the pce in midfield: rdn and hdwy 3f out: no imp over 1f out: btn whn carried lft ins fnl f* **8/1**[3]

5000 **10** *1/2* **Royal Acclamation (IRE)**[21] 6659 6-8-8 **50**......... DavidKenny(3) 11 — 41
(Michael Scudamore) *racd off the pce in midfield: reminder over 4f out: rdn and no imp over 1f out: plugged on same pce fnl f* **50/1**

4555 **11** *1* **Jackie Love (IRE)**[28] 6472 3-8-3 **49**.........(b) NatashaEaton(5) 7 — 38
(Olivia Maylam) *stdd s: t.k.h: hld up wl off the pce in last: styd on fnl f: n.d* **12/1**

2005 **12** *1 1/4* **Cavalry Guard (USA)**[156] 2385 7-8-7 **46** oh1......... MatthewCosham 8 — 31
(Tim McCarthy) *w ldrs tl led 5f out: hdd over 2f out: sn lost pl: wl btn 1f out* **33/1**

1322 **13** *9* **Bold Ring**[75] 5040 5-9-0 **58**......... JadeMuggeridge(5) 10 — 19
(Edward Creighton) *racd off the pce in midfield: rdn and lost pl over 2f out: bhd fnl 2f* **7/1**[2]

1m 24.91s (0.11) **Going Correction** -0.025s/f (Stan)
WFA 3 from 4yo+ 2lb — **13** Ran SP% **117.8**
Speed ratings (Par 101): **98,96,95,94,91 91,90,90,89,89 88,86,76**
Tote Swingers:1&2:£23.20, 2&3:£20.50, 1&3:£9.60 CSF £109.85 CT £632.42 TOTE £9.60: £4.80, £6.10, £2.20; EX 148.30 TRIFECTA Not won..
Owner Mrs Amanda Perrett **Bred** Glending Bloodstock **Trained** Pulborough, W Sussex

FOCUS
There was a disputed lead in this moderate apprentice handicap and the field was very well spread out after a couple of furlongs, but the leading group still provided the first three home. The winner is rated back to something like last winter's form.
Bold Ring Official explanation: jockey said mare became upset in stalls
T/Jkpt: Not won. T/Plt: £179.60 to a £1 stake. Pool £74,471.01. 302.55 winning tickets. T/Qpdt: £17.90 to a £1 stake. Pool £6,850.30. 282.90 winning tickets. SP

6950 NEWMARKET (R-H)

Friday, October 28

OFFICIAL GOING: Good (8.1)
Stands' side track used with stalls on Far side except 12f &16f: centre.
Wind: virtually nil Weather: sunny

7132 PRESTIGE VEHICLES E B F "SLEEPING INDIAN" MAIDEN STKS — 6f

1:20 (1:22) (Class 4) 2-Y-0 — £4,528 (£1,347; £673; £336) — Stalls Low

Form — RPR

1 **Muaamara** 2-8-12 0......... SamHitchcott 7 — 82+
(Mick Channon) *hld up in tch: gng wall but nt clr run bhd wall of horses over 1f out: sn swtchd lft and hdwy ent fnl f: chal ins fnl f: led fnl 75yds: r.o wl* **13/2**

2 *1/2* **Vivid Blue** 2-8-12 0......... PaulHanagan 3 — 80+
(William Haggas) *in tch: swtchd to far rail 4f out: hdwy to chal over 1f out: rdn to ld 1f out: hdd fnl 75yds: no ex* **6/1**[3]

24 **3** *6* **Opera Flute (IRE)**[9] 6951 2-9-3 0......... RichardHughes 1 — 67
(Richard Hannon) *sn pushed into ld: rdn ent fnl 2f: hdd over 1f out: stl pressing ldrs 1f out: sn btn and fdd ins fnl f* **4/6**[1]

46 **4** *1* **Glen Ellyn**[11] 6912 2-9-3 0......... SilvestreDeSousa 5 — 64
(Mark Johnston) *chsd ldr: ev ch over 2f out: drvn to ld over 1f out: hdd 1f out: sn btn and fdd ins fnl f* **11/2**[2]

0 **5** *1 1/2* **Sarah Berry**[18] 6758 2-8-12 0......... AndreaAtzeni 2 — 55
(Chris Dwyer) *in tch: pushed along and struggling 1/2-way: outpcd and wl btn 2f out: plugged on fnl f* **100/1**

00 **6** *nk* **Titus Bolt (IRE)**[16] 6795 2-9-3 0......... StephenCraine 4 — 59
(Jim Boyle) *chsd ldrs: rdn over 1f out: sn btn: fdd and edgd rt fnl f* **25/1**

7 *29* **Vicgernic** 2-9-3 0......... TomQueally 6 — —
(Gary Moore) *s.i.s: sn outpcd and detached in last: t.o fr 1/2-way* **20/1**

1m 12.67s (0.47) **Going Correction** +0.075s/f (Good) — **7** Ran SP% **112.6**
Speed ratings (Par 97): **99,98,90,89,87 86,47**
ToteSwingers:1&2:£2.70, 2&3:£1.80, 1&3:£1.90 CSF £41.90 TOTE £8.10: £5.00, £3.40; EX 40.00 Trifecta £99.80 Pool: £671.73 - 4.98 winning units..
Owner M Al-Qatami & K M Al-Mudhaf **Bred** R J Cornelius **Trained** West Ilsley, Berks

FOCUS
The market for this maiden was dominated by a couple of horses with previous experience, but the finish was fought out by two newcomers. The winner impressed but the winner was again below his debut form.

NOTEBOOK
Muaamara, who got upset beforehand and was withdrawn before her intended debut at York earlier in the month, was better behaved here. She could be seen travelling strongly in behind the leaders 2f out but no gap opened up and she was forced to switch around horses, handing first run to her main rival, who got an uninterrupted run up the rail, but she picked up well once in the clear and won a shade cosily in the end. Her dam stayed 1m2f so she should get further in time. (op 15-2)
Vivid Blue raced a little green early, but came with a good run out of the Dip alongside the far rail. She couldn't hold off the winner, but it was a good effort on her debut and her pedigree suggests she'll get a mile in time. (op 7-1)
Opera Flute(IRE) took a step backwards when upped to 7f here last time, but the money for him suggested much better was expected back over 6f. However, he disappointed, coming under pressure at halfway and lacking the pace of the first two. At least handicaps are now an option. (tchd 8-11)
Glen Ellyn came to challenge 2f out, but found little from the exit of the Dip and ultimately finished well held. This was still a step up on his first two efforts, though. He's bred for further next year. (tchd 5-1)
Sarah Berry, who got warm beforehand, was struggling from an early stage.
Titus Bolt(IRE), who showed some speed, dropped out quickly approaching the last. He's another now eligible to run in handicap company, which should prove more suitable. (op 28-1)

7133 CHRISTINE KILKER MEMORIAL E B F MAIDEN STKS (C&G) (DIV I) — 7f

1:50 (1:52) (Class 4) 2-Y-0 — £4,204 (£1,251; £625; £312) — Stalls Low

Form — RPR

1 **Beaufort Twelve** 2-8-11 0......... HarryBentley(3) 10 — 85+
(William Jarvis) *chsd ldrs: pushed along over 1f out: rdn and hdwy to ld 1f out: in command whn rn green and idled fnl 75yds: pushed out* **33/1**

4 **2** *1 1/4* **Qannaas (USA)**[29] 6481 2-9-0 0......... RichardHills 3 — 82
(Charles Hills) *chsd ldr: upsides and rdn 2f out: chsd wnr and kpt on but a readily hld fnl f* **11/4**[2]

4222 **3** *1 1/2* **Fa'lz (IRE)**[27] 6532 2-9-0 **81**......... FrankieDettori 4 — 78
(Saeed Bin Suroor) *led: rdn over 1f out: hdd 1f out: no ex and wknd ins fnl f* **7/4**[1]

4 *nk* **Press Baron** 2-9-0 0......... SebSanders 6 — 77+
(J W Hills) *stdd s: hld up in tch towards rr: hdwy 1/2-way: rdn and chsd ldng trio over 1f out: swtchd lft and styd on ins fnl f* **66/1**

5 *1* **Uriah Heep (FR)** 2-9-0 0......... RyanMoore 12 — 75
(Sir Michael Stoute) *pushed along early: in tch in midfield: rdn and chsd ldrs 2f out: edgd rt and unable qck over 1f out: kpt on same pce ins fnl f* **4/1**[3]

6 *nk* **Alraased (USA)** 2-9-0 0......... TadhgO'Shea 7 — 74+
(John Dunlop) *stdd s: plld hrd: hld up in rr: hdwy 4f out: rdn and edging rt over 1f out: kpt on but no threat to wnr ins fnl f* **25/1**

0 **7** *10* **Royal Prospector**[42] 6127 2-9-0 0......... RichardHughes 5 — 48
(Richard Hannon) *in tch: lost pl 1/2-way and rdn 3f out: lost tch w ldrs 2f out and no ch after* **11/1**

0 **8** *2 1/2* **Petrol**[10] 6935 2-8-7 0......... HayleyBurton(7) 8 — 41
(Luca Cumani) *stdd s: hld up in last trio: losing tch and edgd rt wl over 2f out: wl btn after* **100/1**

9 *nse* **Noble Thought (IRE)** 2-9-0 0......... PaulHanagan 9 — 41
(William Haggas) *in tch: hanging rt and reminder after 2f: rdn and struggling 1/2-way: lost tch w ldrs and wl btn 2f out* **12/1**

0 **10** *1 1/2* **Bulldog Beasley (USA)**[9] 6951 2-9-0 0......... ShaneKelly 1 — 37
(Brian Meehan) *in tch: rdn and struggling 3f out: sn lost tch w ldrs: wl bhd over 1f out* **50/1**

The Form Book, Raceform Ltd, Compton, RG20 6NL

11 3/4 **Chankillo** 2-9-0 0 .... TomQueally 2 35
(Mark H Tompkins) *s.i.s: a bhd: losing tch whn n.m.r wl over 2f out: sn wl bhd* **66/1**

1m 25.8s (0.40) **Going Correction** +0.075s/f (Good) **11** Ran SP% **111.8**
Speed ratings (Par 97): **100,98,96,96,95 95,83,80,80,78 78**
ToteSwingers:1&2:£12.50, 2&3:£11.60, 1&3:£11.20 CSF £115.21 TOTE £45.80: £7.40, £1.10, £1.10; EX 147.40 TRIFECTA Not won..

Owner Tony Foster & John Kelsey-Fry **Bred** Limestone Stud **Trained** Newmarket, Suffolk

FOCUS
Neither of the first two in the betting set that high a standard but it was still a bit of a surprise result. The time was decent and the form is taken at something like face value.

NOTEBOOK
Beaufort Twelve, a son of Hurricane Run out of a mare who was a smart 2yo (won Group 3 Firth Of Clyde Stakes and runner-up in the Rockfel) for Sir Mark Prescott, knew his job, breaking well and never far off the pace. He lengthened well out of the Dip, won nicely in the end, and has the potential to develop into a useful type next year, but connections could do with the handicapper not rating the third as having run to his official mark. (op 40-1)

Qannaas(USA) ran with promise on his debut at Warwick, but that wasn't much of a race and more was required here. He may have stepped up ever so slightly, but his pedigree suggests he'll be of more interest if tried on the AW. (op 10-3 tchd 5-2)

Fa'lz(IRE) looks flattered by his official mark of 81 and it's unlikely that he ran to that level here. Having set out to make all, he found nothing when challenged. (op 6-4 tchd 9-4)

Press Baron was given a waiting ride and got plenty of cover before being asked for his effort, at which point he began to run a little green. He was keeping on at the finish, though, and as a half-brother to four winners he should make his mark next year.

Uriah Heep(FR), who was a little green early, ran all right on his debut, although his Derby entry looks rather fanciful on this evidence. He should do better next year. (tchd 10-3)

Alraased(USA) ◆ is probably the one to take from the race, as he did hardly anything right on his debut yet still finished fairly close up at the finish. He gave lengths away when walking out of the stalls, then pulled hard, before running green when asked to make a forward move. He should come on plenty for this experience and do much better next year.

7134 CHRISTINE KILKER MEMORIAL E B F MAIDEN STKS (C&G) (DIV II) 7f
2:25 (2:27) (Class 4) 2-Y-0 **£4,204** (£1,251; £625; £312) **Stalls** Low

Form RPR

1 **Better Announce (IRE)** 2-9-0 0 .... RichardHughes 7 79+
(Ed Walker) *chsd ldr: rdn to chal and carried lft fr wl over 1f out: kpt on wl to ld wl ins fnl f: eased cl home* **7/2**[1]

2 1/2 **Moodhill** 2-9-0 0 .... RichardHills 1 78+
(Charles Hills) *sn led: edgd lft fr wl over 1f out: rdn and continued to edge lft 1f out: hdd and no ex wl ins fnl f* **9/2**[3]

04 3 nk **Mawaqeet (USA)**[14] 6828 2-9-0 0 .... TadhgO'Shea 10 77+
(Sir Michael Stoute) *hld up in rr: rdn 3f out: stl plenty to do and hdwy over 1f out: edgd rt 1f out: chsd ldng pair ins fnl f: kpt on* **6/1**

4 3 3/4 **Paramythi (IRE)** 2-9-0 0 .... J-PGuillambert 8 67
(Luca Cumani) *in tch: rdn and unable tp qckn ent fnl 2f: no threat to ldrs but kpt on again ins fnl f* **14/1**

5 nk **Lothian Sky (IRE)** 2-9-0 0 .... SteveDrowne 4 66
(William Jarvis) *wnt lft s: hld up towards rr: rdn and hdwy on far side 2f out: styd on but no threat to ldng trio fnl f* **33/1**

6 nse **Restaurateur (IRE)** 2-9-0 0 .... JimmyFortune 11 66+
(Andrew Balding) *v.s.a: in rr: hdwy and pushed along 3f out: chsng ldrs whn sltly hmpd over 1f out: no prog after and btn 1f out* **4/1**[2]

0 7 3/4 **District Attorney (IRE)**[9] 6951 2-9-0 0 .... PaulHanagan 9 64
(William Haggas) *in tch: lost pl and rdn along 1/2-way: plugged on same pce and no threat to ldrs fnl 2f* **5/1**

8 nk **Infinite Jest** 2-9-0 0 .... SebSanders 2 64
(J W Hills) *in tch: chsd ldng pair over 2f out: rdn and unable qck 2f out: outpcd and btn 1f out: wknd fnl f* **20/1**

9 1 **Harlestone Wood** 2-9-0 0 .... TedDurcan 3 61
(John Dunlop) *s.i.s: hld up in rr: hdwy 1/2-way: chsng ldrs and rdn 2f out: wknd over 1f out* **20/1**

0 10 9 **Ben Croy**[16] 6805 2-9-0 0 .... ShaneKelly 5 38
(Brian Meehan) *squeezed for room leaving stalls and s.i.s: t.k.h: hld up towards rr: hdwy into midfield 4f out: wknd qckly 2f out* **20/1**

0 11 13 **Tiger Would**[16] 6805 2-9-0 0 .... NickyMackay 6 —
(David Elsworth) *wnt rt s: sn rcvrd to chse ldrs: wknd over 2f out: wl bhd fnl f: t.o* **100/1**

1m 27.54s (2.14) **Going Correction** +0.075s/f (Good) **11** Ran SP% **116.2**
Speed ratings (Par 97): **90,89,89,84,84 84,83,83,82,71 56**
ToteSwingers:1&2:£4.30, 2&3:£3.80, 1&3:£5.60 CSF £17.61 TOTE £3.90: £1.60, £1.10, £2.40; EX 19.50 Trifecta £138.40 Pool: £961.84 - 5.14 winning units..

Owner Ms A A Yap **Bred** Marston Stud And Fleming Thoroughbreds **Trained** Newmarket, Suffolk

FOCUS
The winning time for the second division of this maiden was 1.74sec slower than the first leg. The first two and the sixth ended up more towards the stands' side and it was a nice start from the winner.

NOTEBOOK
Better Announce(IRE), for whom the market spoke, had been available at prices as big as 10-1 in the morning, and this half-brother to three winners, including the smart pair Humungous and Amazing Beauty, made a winning debut in gritty fashion, seeing out his race well to get the better of Moodhill, who had carried him over towards the stands' side on the climb out of the Dip. The winner should get further in time. (op 4-1)

Moodhill, a half-brother to four winners, held the call for much of the race, but began to edge left from the exit of the Dip and was eventually run out of it. He probably has the ability to win an ordinary maiden next spring. (op 7-2 tchd 10-3)

Mawaqeet(USA) ◆ got outpaced at halfway before staying on well through the closing stages to finish well clear of the bunch up the centre of the track. This was a step up on his previous efforts and the better ground was clearly in his favour. He could be an interesting type for middle-distance handicaps next year. (op 7-1 tchd 15-2)

Paramythi(IRE) kept on under hands-and-heels riding in the closing stages to take fourth. His pedigree suggests he'll be a 1m4f-plus horse next year, and this was a perfectly satisfactory debut effort. (op 10-1)

Lothian Sky(IRE) kept on towards the far side but could never land a serious blow. He's by Authorized out of a mare who stayed 1m6f, so it won't be until he steps up to middle distances next year that we'll see the best of him. Official explanation: jockey said colt hung left (op 20-1)

Restaurateur(IRE) missed the break badly and had ground to make up on the field from early on. He didn't run badly in the circumstances and this half-brother to six winners should do better in time. (op 5-1 tchd 13-2 in a place)

District Attorney(IRE) improved on his debut effort but needs another run before he's eligible for handicaps. (op 8-1)

7135 "DUBAWI" E B F BOSRA SHAM FILLIES' STKS (LISTED RACE) 6f
3:00 (3:01) (Class 1) 2-Y-O
£12,192 (£4,622; £2,313; £1,152; £578; £290) **Stalls** Low

Form RPR

1531 1 **Artistic Jewel (IRE)**[30] 6466 2-8-12 92 .... GrahamGibbons 12 98+
(Ed McMahon) *racd in centre tl gps merged over 2f out: chsd ldrs: wnt 2nd over 3f out: rdn to ld and edging rt over 1f out: drvn and clr ins fnl f: in command but kpt up to work fnl f: r.o strly* **4/1**[2]

1232 2 3 1/2 **Excelette (IRE)**[27] 6535 2-8-12 98 .... TomEaves 9 88
(Bryan Smart) *racd in centre tl gps merged over 2f out: overall ldr: rdn and edging rt whn hdd over 1f out: outpcd and no threat to wnr ins fnl f: kpt on gamely to hold 2nd* **7/2**[1]

12 3 1/2 **Radio Gaga**[21] 6670 2-8-12 84 .... RichardMullen 13 86
(Ed McMahon) *racd in centre tl gps merged over 2f out: towards rr: rdn over 3f out: hdwy u.p over 1f out: styd on wl to go 3rd towards fin: no ch w wnr* **6/1**[3]

3300 4 nk **Hidden Passion (USA)**[27] 6535 2-8-12 85 .... (t) JamieSpencer 1 85
(Brian Meehan) *taken down early and ponied to s: racd on far side tl gps merged over 2f out: chsd overall ldrs: rdn and nt pce of wnr wl over 1f out: kpt on same pce fnl f* **28/1**

5223 5 nk **Miss Lahar**[6] 7019 2-8-12 102 .... MartinHarley 4 84
(Mick Channon) *racd on far side tl gps merged over 2f out: chsd ldrs: drvn to chse ldrs and unable qck over 1f out: no threat to wnr and plugged on same pce fnl f* **7/2**[1]

410 6 nk **Villeneuve**[35] 6296 2-8-12 83 .... RyanMoore 3 83
(William Muir) *racd far side tl gps merged over 2f out: bhd: rdn and wl bhd over 3f out: hdwy over 1f out: styd on wl ins fnl f: nvr trbld ldrs* **20/1**

3524 7 nk **Misty Conquest (IRE)**[41] 6146 2-8-12 97 .... RichardKingscote 2 82
(Tom Dascombe) *racd on far side tl gps merged over 2f out: racd in midfield: rdn and unable qck wl over 2f out: kpt on u.p but no threat to wnr fnl f* **15/2**

62 8 2 3/4 **Jwala**[9] 6946 2-8-12 0 .... ShaneKelly 11 74
(Robert Cowell) *racd in centre tl gps merged over 2f out: hld up in midfield: rdn and fnd little ent fnl 2f: edgd rt and btn over 1f out* **50/1**

0301 9 1 3/4 **Judas Jo (FR)**[47] 5983 2-8-12 79 .... RobertWinston 14 69
(Gay Kelleway) *racd in centre tl gps merged over 2f out: hld up in rr: rdn and effrt over 2f out: no real prog: nvr trbld ldrs* **66/1**

2106 10 1/2 **Besito (IRE)**[41] 6146 2-8-12 83 .... KierenFallon 6 67
(William Jarvis) *racd on far side tl gps merged over 2f out: chsd ldrs: rdn and struggling ent fnl 2f: wknd over 1f out* **16/1**

15 11 1 **Alice's Dancer (IRE)**[32] 6413 2-8-12 79 .... WilliamCarson 10 64
(William Muir) *racd in centre tl gps merged over 2f out: chsd ldr tl over 3f out: wknd u.p 2f out* **33/1**

2 12 18 **Subtle Knife**[24] 6612 2-8-12 0 .... SilvestreDeSousa 7 10
(Giles Bravery) *racd on far side tl gps merged over 2f out: in tch in midfield: rdn and struggling 1/2-way: sn wknd: wl bhd and eased ins fnl f* **40/1**

0431 13 30 **Idols Eye**[45] 6026 2-8-12 72 .... RichardHughes 8 —
(Richard Hannon) *racd in centre tl gps merged over 2f out: a in rr: lost tch over 2f out: sn eased and virtually p.u fr over 1f out: t.o* **33/1**

16 R **Daraa (IRE)**[55] 5698 2-8-12 0 .... TomQueally 5 —
(Clive Brittain) *ref to r* **50/1**

1m 11.95s (-0.25) **Going Correction** +0.075s/f (Good) **14** Ran SP% **118.3**
Speed ratings (Par 100): **104,99,98,98,97 97,97,93,91,90 89,65,25,—**
ToteSwingers:1&2:£4.80, 2&3:£5.50, 1&3:£5.80 CSF £16.56 TOTE £5.70: £2.10, £1.60, £2.40; EX 25.10 Trifecta £96.60 Pool: £1,441.18 - 11.03 winning units..

Owner R L Bedding **Bred** Jim McDonald **Trained** Lichfield, Staffs

FOCUS
Not the strongest of Listed races. The field split into two groups that raced only slightly apart, before merging late on. The first three came from the group that raced more towards the centre. The form seems sound enough.

NOTEBOOK
Artistic Jewel(IRE) put up a taking performance to back up her win in a small-field conditions race at Salisbury (fourth won twice since, including in Listed company) in contrasting conditions. She won despite the soft ground last time and looked far more comfortable on this faster surface, stretching right away in the closing stages. She looks the type who could go on to better things over this distance next year. (op 9-2 tchd 7-2)

Excelette(IRE), runner-up in the Two-Year-Old Trophy last time out, showed speed throughout and is probably a fair guide to the level of form as she's been very consistent since stepping up in class. (tchd 3-1 and 4-1)

Radio Gaga, one of the least exposed runners in the line-up and a stablemate of the winner, was beaten into second in a nursery off 82 last time out, but is clearly improving fast. She stayed on nicely for third and should get further next year. (op 13-2 tchd 7-1)

Hidden Passion(USA), who was first home from the group that raced more towards the far side early, had a bit to find at this level and ran about as well as could be expected. (op 25-1)

Miss Lahar, who was the highest-rated filly in the field, was below her best and has yet to truly convince beyond 5f. (op 4-1 tchd 10-3)

Villeneuve, who lost her action on fast ground here last time, got unbalanced running into the Dip but stayed on quite well once she hit the rising ground. There should be better to come from her and, as she's out of a mare who won over 1m4f, a longer trip is likely to help in future. (op 18-1)

Misty Conquest(IRE) was below her best, although she's been on the go for a long time and perhaps this was just one race too many for her. (op 8-1 tchd 17-2)

Idols Eye Official explanation: trainer's rep said filly finished lame

7136 E B F "ARCHIPENKO" FILLIES' H'CAP 1m 4f
3:35 (3:40) (Class 3) (0-90,89) 3-Y-O+
£7,158 (£2,143; £1,071; £535; £267; £134) **Stalls** Centre

Form RPR

2226 1 **Hawaafez**[133] 3108 3-9-1 85 .... RichardHills 6 104+
(Marcus Tregoning) *t.k.h: hld up in tch: c stands' side st: led gng strly over 2f out: sn clr and in n.d fnl 2f: eased towards fin* **7/2**[1]

5236 2 7 **Moment Of Time**[48] 5911 3-9-5 89 .... JimmyFortune 7 95+
(Andrew Balding) *hld up in tch: c stands' side st: rdn and effrt over 2f out: wnt 2nd but no ch w wnr over 1f out: edgd lft and no imp after* **17/2**

214 3 8 **Miss Topsy Turvy (IRE)**[18] 6749 3-8-6 76 .... TedDurcan 8 69
(John Dunlop) *hld up in last trio: c to stands' side st: hdwy to chse ldrs 4f out: rdn and chse clr wnr 2f out: no imp and lost 3rd over 1f out: wl btn and hung on for 3rd cl home* **5/1**[2]

11 4 hd **Just Lille (IRE)**[46] 6006 8-9-12 89 .... (p) PaulHanagan 12 82
(Ann Duffield) *chsd ldrs: c stands' side st: rdn and btn 3f out: 4th and no ch over 1f out: pressing for modest 3rd cl home* **16/1**

1401 **5** *6* **Milnagavie**[86] 4660 4-9-10 **87** RichardHughes 4 70
(Richard Hannon) *chsd ldr: c stands' side st: rdn to ld overall wl over 2f out: sn hdd and no ch w wnr: wknd 2f out* **8/1**

1612 **6** *hd* **Jeu De Vivre (IRE)**[33] 6385 3-8-12 **82** SilvestreDeSousa 1 65+
(Mark Johnston) *hld up in midfield: styd far side st: rdn and effrt 4f out: wknd and wl btn 2f out* **8/1**

2500 **7** *½* **Kathleen Frances**[55] 5729 4-9-2 **79** TomQueally 11 61
(Mark H Tompkins) *hld up in rr: c stands' side st: rdn and wl btn over 3f out: no ch but plugged on past btn horses fr over 1f out* **10/1**

-030 **8** *1* **Encore Une Annee**[35] 6294 3-8-7 **77** (bt[1]) JimCrowley 2 58
(Ralph Beckett) *hld up in last trio: c stands' side st: rdn and effrt 4f out: wknd wl over 2f out: sn wl btn* **12/1**

4210 **9** *4 ½* **Vita Lika**[21] 6674 3-8-8 **78** JamieSpencer 13 51
(Brian Meehan) *led: styd far side st: rdn and hdd wl over 2f out: sn wknd and wl bhd: eased fnl f* **7/1**[3]

0430 **10** *¾* **Misty Isles**[18] 6755 3-8-5 **75** oh3 FrankieMcDonald 9 47
(Heather Main) *awkward leaving stalls: t.k.h: hld up in tch: c stands' side st: rdn and wknd 4f out: wl bhd fnl 2f* **28/1**

223 **11** *17* **Sweet Lavender (IRE)**[24] 6614 3-8-5 **75** oh1 (v[1]) NickyMackay 10 20
(Saeed Bin Suroor) *in tch: c stands' side st: wknd over 4f out: t.o fnl 2f* **16/1**

2m 32.01s (0.01) **Going Correction** +0.075s/f (Good)
WFA 3 from 4yo+ 7lb 11 Ran SP% **116.1**
Speed ratings (Par 104): **102,97,92,91,87 87,87,86,83,83 71**
ToteSwingers:1&2:£7.80, 2&3:£10.50, 1&3:£4.90 CSF £32.97 CT £148.85 TOTE £4.10: £1.60, £3.70, £2.10; EX 35.90 Trifecta £136.70 Pool: £1,047.46 - 5.67 winning units..
Owner Hamdan Al Maktoum **Bred** Shadwell Estate Co Ltd **Trained** Lambourn, Berks

FOCUS
Most of the field edged over to the stands' side in the straight and the two that stayed on the far side (Vita Lika and Jeu De Vivre) finished well held. Late-season fillies' form, with improvement from the impressive winner.

NOTEBOOK
Hawaafez hadn't been seen since finishing in mid-division in the Queen's Vase back in June, but there was good support for her in the market, suggesting that she was back in good heart and expected to go close. Runner-up when taking on colts over this C&D off the same mark earlier in the campaign, she was potentially well handicapped, and the race itself revealed that she was chucked in, having clearly improved considerably since she was last seen. Always travelling strongly, she quickly put distance between herself and the rest of the stands'-side group heading to the final furlong, and won in the manner of a filly who will soon be chasing black type again. (op 11-2)

Moment Of Time was well below form on easy ground at Bath last time but bounced back in some style returned to a quicker surface. She was unlucky to bump into a rival who it turned out was thrown in at the weights, but she beat the rest handily. She should be able to win a Polytrack maiden if connections decide to persevere with her this year. (op 10-1 tchd 11-1)

Miss Topsy Turvy(IRE), who put up a career-best last time out, stayed on along the stands' rail and helps give the form a solid look. (tchd 11-2)

Just Lille(IRE) didn't run badly on her return to handicap company. Her current mark doesn't make things easy for her, though. (op 9-1 tchd 8-1)

Milnagavie, raised 5lb for her latest win on the Polytrack back in August, might yet have more to offer back on the artificial surface. (tchd 17-2)

7137 BETFAIR RACING EXCELLENCE APPRENTICE JOCKEYS' TRAINING SERIES FINAL (H'CAP) 1m

4:10 (4:11) (Class 5) (0-75,74) 3-Y-O **£5,175** (£1,540; £769; £384) **Stalls** Low

Form RPR

0003 **1** **May Be Some Time**[30] 6468 3-8-10 **63** MatthewCosham 2 73+
(Stuart Kittow) *in tch in midfield: effrt and swtchd rt over 1f out: rdn to ld ins fnl f: styd on wl* **9/2**[1]

4635 **2** *1* **Conducting**[16] 6799 3-8-7 **65** NicoleNordblad[(5)] 11 71+
(Gay Kelleway) *wnt lft s: sn stdd and swtchd rt: hld up wl bhd: stl plenty to do but travelling wl 2f out: hdwy over 1f out: pushed along ent fnl f: chsd wnr ins fnl f: no imp fnl 75yds* **5/1**[2]

3511 **3** *1 ½* **Quite A Catch (IRE)**[56] 5673 3-9-2 **69** (v) JustinNewman 9 72
(Jonathan Portman) *led and swtchd lft to r against stands' rail sn after s: rdn 2f out: hrd pressed over 1f out: hdd ins fnl f: no ex and kpt on same pce after* **9/2**[1]

3403 **4** *nse* **Isingy Red (FR)**[16] 6796 3-9-3 **70** NathanAlison 7 73
(Jim Boyle) *hld up towards rr: grad swtchd to r against stands' rail: rdn and hdwy over 2f out: ev ch over 1f out: styd on same pce ins fnl f* **14/1**

616 **5** *¾* **National Hope (IRE)**[24] 6617 3-9-0 **67** (tp) DavidKenny 5 68
(George Baker) *in tch in midfield: rdn and effrt over 2f out: ev ch u.p over 1f out: no ex jst ins fnl f: wknd fnl 100yds* **20/1**

-040 **6** *2* **Menadati (USA)**[19] 6727 3-9-6 **73** LucyKBarry 4 70
(Peter Hiatt) *chsd ldr: rdn 2f out: ev ch over 1f out: no ex u.p jst ins fnl f: wknd fnl 150yds* **8/1**[3]

0560 **7** *4 ½* **Flashbang**[24] 6604 3-9-0 **67** CharlesBishop 10 53
(Paul Cole) *short of room and stdd after s: hld up towards rr: hdwy into midfield 1/2-way: effrt over 2f out: rdn and ev ch over 1f out tl 1f out: fdd fnl f* **16/1**

2-30 **8** *6* **Ice Cold Bex**[133] 3133 3-9-6 **73** MatthewLawson 3 45
(Philip McBride) *chsd ldrs tl 3f out: sn struggling u.p: wknd 2f out: wl btn fnl f* **12/1**

6461 **9** *3 ¾* **Lieutenant Kojak**[21] 6668 3-9-4 **74** NoelGarbutt[(3)] 1 38
(Peter Charalambous) *chsd ldrs: rdn and unable qck 3f out: wknd wl over 1f out: wl bhd fnl f* **8/1**[3]

5165 **10** *2 ½* **Muhandis (IRE)**[134] 3081 3-9-0 **74** RichardOld[(7)] 6 32
(Nick Littmoden) *in tch in midfield: rdn and struggling whn hung rt over 2f out: wknd 2f out: no ch 1f out* **28/1**

2300 **11** *1* **Cristaliyev**[16] 6794 3-8-1 **61** (p) DanielCremin[(7)] 12 17
(Jim Boyle) *pushed lft s and slowly away: in rr: swtchd to r towards stands' rail after 1f: effrt u.p over 2f out: hung rt and wknd 2f out: sn bhd* **40/1**

1105 **12** *24* **Mystic Edge**[61] 5518 3-9-0 **72** IanBurns[(5)] 8 —
(Michael Bell) *in tch in midfield: rdn and struggling 3f out: sn wknd: t.o and eased ins fnl f* **12/1**

1m 40.56s (1.96) **Going Correction** +0.075s/f (Good) **12** Ran SP% **113.8**
Speed ratings (Par 101): **93,92,90,90,89 87,83,77,73,70 69,45**
ToteSwingers:1&2:£5.20, 2&3:£5.80, 1&3:£3.40 CSF £24.65 CT £107.01 TOTE £6.60: £1.50, £1.10, £2.80; EX 34.90 Trifecta £110.00 Pool: £741.78 - 4.99 winning units..
Owner Dr G S Plastow **Bred** D R Tucker **Trained** Blackborough, Devon

FOCUS
An ordinary apprentices' handicap. The winner is rated to the level of his latest Salisbury form.

7138 NGK SPARK PLUGS CONDITIONS STKS 6f

4:45 (4:45) (Class 3) 2-3-Y-0
£7,158 (£2,143; £1,071; £535; £267; £134) **Stalls** Low

Form RPR

214 **1** **Heyward Girl (IRE)**[23] 6625 2-7-12 80 AndreaAtzeni 6 82
(Robert Eddery) *mde all: rdn wl over 1f out: kpt finding ex: hld on gamely u.p towards fin* **13/2**

411 **2** *nk* **Billyrayvalentine (CAN)**[38] 6237 2-8-3 81 (t) PaulHanagan 5 86+
(George Baker) *stdd s: t.k.h: hld up in last: switching rt and effrt over 1f out: str chal ins fnl f: r.o but hld towards fin* **9/4**[2]

005 **3** *½* **Parc De Launay**[21] 6670 2-8-7 89 ow1 JamieSpencer 2 89
(Tom Tate) *hld up in tch in last pair: rdn and effrt over 1f out: hanging rt and unable qck 1f out: styd on u.p fnl 100yds: nvr looked like getting to wnr* **15/8**[1]

0600 **4** *4 ½* **Avonmore Star**[30] 6467 3-9-11 79 RichardHughes 3 79
(Richard Hannon) *restless in stalls: in tch: hdwy to chse ldrs 1/2-way: rdn to chse wnr 2f out tl ins fnl f: sn btn and fdd* **18/1**

0110 **5** *hd* **Bop It**[27] 6535 2-8-6 84 (t) TomEaves 7 73
(Bryan Smart) *t.k.h: chsd ldrs: wnt 2nd 1/2-way tl rdn and fnd little 2f out: wknd over 1f out* **10/1**

312- **6** *43* **Zabeel Park (USA)**[454] 4611 3-9-6 93 FrankieDettori 1 —
(Saeed Bin Suroor) *chsd ldr tl 1/2-way: lost pl and dropped to last ent fnl 2f: eased and virtually p.u fr over 1f out: t.o* **11/2**[3]

1m 12.79s (0.59) **Going Correction** +0.075s/f (Good) **6** Ran SP% **108.6**
Speed ratings: **99,98,97,91,91 34**
ToteSwingers:1&2:£3.20, 2&3:£1.60, 1&3:£3.20 CSF £20.11 TOTE £8.10: £3.80, £1.10; EX 19.60.
Owner Phillips,Donaldson,Matthews,Smith & Kerve **Bred** Ballykilbride Stud **Trained** Newmarket, Suffolk

FOCUS
Most of these didn't look comfortable on the ground or track, but the exception was the winner. The form is rated through the runner-up.

NOTEBOOK
Heyward Girl(IRE) bounced off the fast ground and made every yard. Getting weight from all her rivals, she was representing an age-group now responsible for nine of the last ten winners of this race, and she stepped up on her recent Polytrack form back on turf. She could well have more to offer, as she's relatively lightly raced. (tchd 7-1 in a place)

Billyrayvalentine(CAN)'s Folkestone win didn't amount to much, but he'd created a good impression. Held up at the back of the field off a gallop that wasn't overly strong, he was asked to make up a lot of ground in a short space of time. He did well to get as close as he did, without looking entirely comfortable on the ground. (op 11-4 tchd 2-1 and 5-2 in a place)

Parc De Launay, who was pulled out of the Two-Year-Old Trophy earlier in the season because of fast ground, got unbalanced running into the Dip and didn't look comfortable on this surface. He can do better when reverting to easier ground. (op 5-2 tchd 11-4)

Avonmore Star has struggled since the spring and faced a difficult task on these terms giving plenty of weight to all his rivals. Restless in the stalls, he showed speed until finding the weight telling in the closing stages. (op 12-1)

Bop It was another who seemed to get unbalanced and looked uncomfortable on the track. (op 6-1 tchd 11-2)

Zabeel Park(USA), not seen since finishing second in a French Listed race last July, stopped very quickly and presumably something was amiss. Official explanation: jockey said filly lost its action (tchd 7-2 in places)

7139 RACING UK H'CAP 2m

5:20 (5:23) (Class 3) (0-90,92) 3-Y-0+ **£7,439** (£2,213; £1,106; £553) **Stalls** Centre

Form RPR

0101 **1** **Gulf Of Naples (IRE)**[7] 6988 3-9-1 **87** 6ex SilvestreDeSousa 6 96+
(Mark Johnston) *chsd ldrs: wnt 2nd briefly over 3f out: pressed ldr ent fnl 2f: rdn to ld 1f out: styd on wl and a in command fnl f: rdn out* **9/4**[1]

0524 **2** *1 ½* **Sohcahtoa (IRE)**[7] 6998 5-8-9 **71** oh1 JimCrowley 7 78
(Robert Mills) *stdd s: hld up in rr: smooth hdwy 3f out: drvn ent fnl f: chsd wnr jst ins fnl f: r.o but no imp on wnr* **25/1**

0022 **3** *shd* **Dark Ranger**[41] 6171 5-8-8 **73** SeanLevey[(3)] 12 80
(Tim Pitt) *t.k.h: hld up in last trio: clsd and in tch 6f out: squeezed between horses and hdwy ent fnl 2f: drvn to chse ldrs over 1f out: kpt on ins fnl f but no imp on wnr* **17/2**

3026 **4** *3* **Stentorian (IRE)**[24] 6601 3-8-1 **73** (b) AndreaAtzeni 10 76
(Mark Johnston) *chsd ldrs: swtchd rt and wnt 2nd 3f out: pushed into ld over 2f out: rdn and hdd 1f out: wknd fnl 100yds* **25/1**

6401 **5** *4 ½* **Hawridge King**[30] 6469 9-8-11 **73** ow1 (v) RichardHughes 1 71
(Stuart Kittow) *led: clr 10f out: hdd and rdn over 2f out: sn outpcd: wknd over 1f out* **16/1**

0/31 **6** *nk* **Orsippus (USA)**[20] 6707 5-8-9 **71** PaulHanagan 2 69
(Michael Smith) *t.k.h early: hld up in midfield: clsd 6f out: chsd ldrs and rdn over 2f out: sn struggling: wknd over 1f out* **7/1**[3]

1/01 **7** *½* **Blimey O'Riley (IRE)**[7] 6998 6-8-11 **73** TomQueally 11 70
(Mark H Tompkins) *hld up in last trio: clsd and in tch 6f out: n.m.r over 2f out: sn rdn and no prog: no ch w ldrs fnl 2f* **9/1**

205 **8** *½* **Defence Of Duress (IRE)**[14] 6832 3-8-7 **79** JamieSpencer 5 75
(Tom Tate) *hld up in midfield: rdn and unable qck whn bmpd and wnt lft ent fnl 2f: no hdwy and btn whn hung rt over 1f out* **10/3**[2]

6050 **9** *2 ¾* **Magicalmysterytour (IRE)**[12] 6893 8-9-1 **77** StevieDonohoe 8 70
(Willie Musson) *hld up in tch in midfield: shuffled bk to rr but stl in tch 4f out: rdn and no hdwy over 2f out: sn wl btn* **16/1**

0030 **10** *35* **Trovare (USA)**[17] 5448 4-9-5 **81** RyanMoore 4 32
(Amanda Perrett) *t.k.h: chsd ldr tl rdn and struggling whn bmpd over 3f out: sn dropped out: lost tch 2f out: t.o and eased fnl f* **12/1**

3m 28.76s (-1.74) **Going Correction** +0.075s/f (Good)
WFA 3 from 4yo+ 10lb **10** Ran SP% **114.0**
Speed ratings (Par 107): **107,106,106,104,102 102,102,101,100,82**
ToteSwingers:1&2:£13.50, 2&3:£19.40, 1&3:£5.30 CSF £62.15 CT £401.73 TOTE £2.80: £1.10, £5.60, £3.00; EX 70.80 Trifecta £447.00 Pool: £1,574.90 - 2.61 winning units..
Owner Sheikh Hamdan Bin Mohammed Al Maktoum **Bred** Stone Ridge Farm **Trained** Middleham Moor, N Yorks

FOCUS
The whole field came stands' side in the straight this time. The market liked the less-exposed 3yos, and one of them came out on top. An ordinary race for the grade but it's hard to knock the winner.

NOTEBOOK
Gulf Of Naples(IRE) was 1lb well in under his penalty for scoring at Doncaster a week earlier, and proved himself to be ahead of the handicapper with a gutsy win. The extra distance was only in his favour and the chances are he'll improve again for another winter on his back - half-brother Dream Eater only reached his peak as a 5yo. (tchd 15-8 and 5-2 in places and 11-4 in a place)

Sohcahtoa(IRE) is on a competitive mark and stays this trip well, but he's not a winner. If pressed, he'll always gladly defer.

Dark Ranger, runner-up in the Cesarewitch Trial over 2f further here last month, was just 3lb higher and looked to hold solid claims. He was keeping on steadily at the finish after getting slightly tapped for toe, but never really looked like getting there. If anything this trip looked a little on the short side for him. (op 8-1 tchd 9-1)
Stentorian(IRE) was last off the bridle but ultimately he didn't see out the trip on this 4f step up in distance. Things might be different dropped to 1m6f.
Hawridge King, who was given a positive ride, repeated last year's fifth-place finish. (op 12-1)
Orsippus(USA), who was put up 8lb for his win at York last time, paid for racing keenly early. (op 13-2 tchd 6-1)
Blimey O'Riley(IRE) got to race off the same mark as when taking an apprentices' event at Newbury a week earlier and was officially 3lb well in, but he was weak in the betting and struggled to pick up under pressure in this hotter company. (op 7-1 tchd 10-1)
Defence Of Duress(IRE) was disappointing. He failed to pick up when his rider went for him and then got unbalanced running into the Dip. (op 11-2 tchd 6-1)
T/Plt: £46.50 to a £1 stake. Pool:£64,746.34 - 1,015.22 winning tickets. T/Qpdt: £4.20 to a £1 stake. Pool:£8,051.36 - 1,412.65 winning tickets. SP

7033 WOLVERHAMPTON (A.W) (L-H)
Friday, October 28

OFFICIAL GOING: Standard
Wind: Fresh behind Weather: Cloudy with sunny spells

7140 CLEVELAND SUITE NOVICE STKS 7f 32y(P)
5:40 (5:41) (Class 5) 2-Y-O £2,264 (£673; £336; £168) Stalls High

Form RPR
5312 1 **Blodwen Abbey**[14] 6843 2-8-8 73 AdamBeschizza(3) 1 75
(James Unett) *sn led: clr over 2f out: rdn over 1f out: styd on* 3/1[2]
51 2 1 ¾ **Purple 'n Gold (IRE)**[22] 6654 2-9-2 78 MatthewDavies 5 76+
(George Baker) *chsd ldrs: pushed along 3f out: sn outpcd: styd on u.p fr over 1f out: wnt 2nd ins fnl f: nt rch wnr* 10/11[1]
0530 3 2 ¼ **Lolita Lebron (IRE)**[25] 6573 2-9-0 68 DuranFentiman 3 68
(Lawrence Mullaney) *led early: chsd wnr: pushed along 1/2-way: rdn over 1f out: styd on same pce: lost 2nd ins fnl f* 16/1
240 4 1 ¼ **Alhira**[45] 6030 2-8-9 69 MartinLane 4 60
(David Simcock) *hld up: hdwy over 2f out: rdn over 1f out: no ex* 7/2[3]
0020 5 6 **Thecornishcowboy**[9] 6956 2-9-0 62 AdamKirby 2 50
(John Ryan) *chsd ldrs: pushed along 1/2-way: wknd over 2f out* 18/1
1m 29.96s (0.36) **Going Correction** -0.025s/f (Stan) **5** Ran SP% **110.8**
Speed ratings (Par 95): **96,94,91,90,83**
CSF £6.22 TOTE £4.70: £1.40, £1.10; EX 7.10.
Owner J M Davies **Bred** Bearstone Stud **Trained** Tedsmore Hall, Shropshire

FOCUS
Form to treat with caution. The winner was allowed a soft lead and although he rates a minor improver he might well have been flattered.
NOTEBOOK
Blodwen Abbey was allowed an uncontested lead. Although a bit free, her speed was key and she had been able to save plenty. She might be a bit flattered and her stamina will tested more severely in due course.
Purple 'n Gold(IRE) won a 6f maiden here last time and his breeding suggested he'd improve again for this trip, but he was weak in the market and ran a lazy race. He was sluggishly away from the stalls and that set the theme, the colt taking an age to pick up for pressure. In fairness he had little chance with the winner considering how the race played out, but he'll have to be sharper when faced with better company. (op 4-6)
Lolita Lebron(IRE) ran her race but wasn't good enough. (tchd 20-1)
Alhira continues to go the wrong way. Her rider had to dismount down at the start, and in the race itself after seemingly travelling okay, she found nothing for pressure. (op 11-2 tchd 6-1)

7141 AT THE RACES SKY 415 FILLIES' H'CAP 7f 32y(P)
6:10 (6:11) (Class 5) (0-75,75) 3-Y-O+ £2,522 (£750; £375; £187) Stalls High

Form RPR
0010 1 **Supreme Spirit (IRE)**[17] 6779 4-9-5 73 (b) IanMongan 2 83
(George Margarson) *a.p: chsd ldr over 1f out: rdn to ld ins fnl f: r.o* 16/1
-530 2 ¾ **Swift Breeze**[36] 6285 3-8-11 67 ShaneKelly 7 75
(William Haggas) *s.i.s: hld up: hdwy 3f out: rdn and ev ch ins fnl f: edgd rt: styd on* 12/1
2443 3 3 ¾ **Wadha (IRE)**[14] 6839 3-9-0 70 KierenFallon 4 68
(Saeed Bin Suroor) *chsd ldrs: rdn over 1f out: styd on same pce fnl f* 6/1[3]
1120 4 nk **Amelia's Surprise**[6] 7024 3-9-4 74 AdamKirby 10 71
(Michael Bell) *hld up: hdwy over 1f out: sn rdn: r.o* 5/2[1]
1340 5 1 ½ **Orpens Peach (IRE)**[45] 6041 4-8-9 63 MartinHarley 3 56+
(Seamus Fahey, Ire) *led: rdn over 1f out: hdd & wknd ins fnl f* 8/1
120U 6 ¾ **Just The Tonic**[13] 6869 4-8-9 68 JulieBurke(5) 11 59
(Marjorie Fife) *s.s: hld up: r.o ins fnl f: nvr nrr* 25/1
5124 7 1 **Libys Dream (IRE)**[10] 6931 3-8-10 66 MartinLane 5 54+
(Michael Mullineaux) *mid-div and sn pushed along: outpcd over 2f out: n.d after: no ch whn rdn and hung lft ins fnl f* 4/1[2]
2202 8 2 **Vizean (IRE)**[14] 6834 3-8-8 67 DaleSwift(3) 6 50
(John Mackie) *chsd ldr tl rdn and wknd over 1f out* 8/1
5400 9 shd **Breezolini**[3] 7074 3-8-9 68 (v) AmyRyan(3) 8 51
(Richard Whitaker) *sn pushed along and a in rr* 17/2
0360 10 6 **Green Apple**[12] 6895 3-9-2 72 LukeMorris 9 38
(Peter Makin) *chsd ldrs: rdn over 2f out: hung lft and wknd over 1f out* 16/1
1m 28.76s (-0.84) **Going Correction** -0.025s/f (Stan)
WFA 3 from 4yo+ 2lb **10** Ran SP% **118.9**
Speed ratings (Par 100): **103,102,97,97,95 94,93,91,91,84**
ToteSwingers: 1&2 £29.30, 1&3 £16.30, 2&3 £14.30 CSF £196.61 CT £1321.10 TOTE £16.90: £6.40, £5.80, £2.10; EX 195.60.
Owner Mrs C C Regalado-Gonzalez **Bred** Jill Finnegan And Noel Cogan **Trained** Newmarket, Suffolk

FOCUS
A fair fillies' handicap for the grade, run at a good pace. The form looks sound.

7142 ENJOY THE PARTY PACK GROUP OFFER MEDIAN AUCTION MAIDEN STKS 7f 32y(P)
6:40 (6:44) (Class 6) 2-Y-O £1,704 (£503; £251) Stalls High

Form RPR
5 1 **Gloriam (USA)**[77] 4996 2-9-3 0 MartinLane 6 79+
(David Simcock) *a.p: chsd ldr over 5f out: led over 2f out: pushed clr fr over 1f out* 4/9[1]
4 2 6 **Safari Sunseeker (IRE)**[12] 6890 2-9-3 0 LukeMorris 9 63
(Peter Winkworth) *chsd ldrs: pushed along 1/2-way: chsd wnr and edgd lft 2f out: sn rdn: styd on same pce* 4/1[2]
3 1 ½ **Hurler And Farmer (IRE)** 2-9-0 0 LeeTopliss(3) 8 60+
(Richard Fahey) *prom: pushed along whn hmpd 2f out: hung lft over 1f out: styd on to go 3rd wl ins fnl f: nt trble ldrs* 10/1
04 4 1 **Good Luck Charm**[10] 6928 2-9-3 0 AdamKirby 10 57
(Gary Moore) *hld up: hdwy over 2f out: shkn up over 1f out: no ex: lost 3rd wl ins fnl f* 5/1[3]
0 5 3 **Ypres**[13] 6866 2-9-3 0 MichaelStainton 1 51
(Jason Ward) *chsd ldrs: rdn whn hmpd 2f out: wknd over 1f out* 50/1
6 nk **Hill Of Dreams (IRE)** 2-8-12 0 ShaneKelly 11 44
(Dean Ivory) *s.i.s: hld up: effrt over 2f out: n.d* 20/1
0 7 19 **Jay Peas Jacko**[7] 6983 2-9-3 0 TomMcLaughlin 3 —
(Lucinda Featherstone) *led over 4f: hmpd and wknd 2f out: t.o* 100/1
8 15 **Bonnie Blade** 2-8-12 0 WilliamCarson 4 —
(James Unett) *unruly to post: s.i.s: a in rr: bhd fr 1/2-way: t.o* 50/1
9 13 **Highest Red** 2-9-3 0 FergusSweeney 12 —
(Andrew Haynes) *s.i.s: a in rr: bhd fnl 4f: t.o* 20/1
1m 30.14s (0.54) **Going Correction** -0.025s/f (Stan) **9** Ran SP% **129.4**
Speed ratings (Par 93): **95,88,86,85,81 81,59,42,27**
ToteSwingers: 1&2 £1.10, 1&3 £2.10, 2&3 £4.30 CSF £3.14 TOTE £1.60: £1.02, £1.10, £3.70; EX 2.90.
Owner H E Sheikh Sultan Bin Khalifa Al Nahyan **Bred** Robert Pierz **Trained** Newmarket, Suffolk
■ Stewards' Enquiry : Michael Stainton two-day ban: careless riding (Nov 11-12)

FOCUS
An ordinary juvenile maiden and the time was the slowest of the three 7f races. The winner improved and can do better still.
NOTEBOOK
Gloriam(USA) had twice been a non-runner since shaping well behind the highly regarded Top Offer on his debut in August, but he was heavily backed and gained a straightforward success. A good-looking type with scope, he should make at least a useful handicapper. (op 4-7 tchd 8-13 and 8-11 in places)
Safari Sunseeker(IRE) ran to just a moderate level on his debut at Bath, but it was a promising introduction and he showed he's very much gone the right way. He was always held by the winner, but displayed a good attitude to take a clear second and is up to winning a similar race. (tchd 7-2)
Hurler And Farmer(IRE), whose dam was placed over 7f-1m2f, didn't get the best of runs into the straight but finished nicely and has plenty of ability.
Good Luck Charm seemed to travel okay but his finishing effort was tame. This performance did not confirm the promise of his improved effort over 1m at Lingfield last time. (op 7-2)

7143 AT THE RACES VIRGIN 534 NURSERY 5f 20y(P)
7:10 (7:11) (Class 6) (0-60,59) 2-Y-O £1,908 (£563; £281) Stalls Low

Form RPR
0212 1 **Look Here's Lady**[24] 6597 2-9-6 58 GrahamGibbons 5 65
(Ed McMahon) *mde all: rdn over 1f out: r.o u.p* 11/4[1]
045 2 ¾ **M J Woodward**[24] 6597 2-8-12 50 SilvestreDeSousa 6 54
(Paul Green) *chsd wnr 2f: sn pushed along: rdn and r.o to go 2nd wl ins fnl f* 7/1
040 3 1 **Claretintheblood (IRE)**[22] 6654 2-9-0 55 LeeTopliss(3) 1 56
(Richard Fahey) *a.p: chsd wnr over 1f out: sn rdn and ev ch: styd on same pce ins fnl f* 10/1
6023 4 hd **Mount McLeod (IRE)**[9] 6942 2-9-1 53 FergusSweeney 2 54
(Jamie Osborne) *hld up: swtchd rt and hdwy over 1f out: r.o: nt rch ldrs* 4/1[2]
4562 5 1 ½ **Triggerlo**[4] 7059 2-9-4 56 MartinHarley 10 51
(Mick Channon) *hld up: pushed along 3f out: hdwy u.p over 1f out: nt trble ldrs* 9/2[3]
6562 6 ¾ **Sonsie Lass**[8] 6975 2-9-1 53 JoeFanning 3 45
(Keith Dalgleish) *plld hrd and prom: rdn over 1f out: no ex fnl f* 11/2
2006 7 nk **Cataract**[9] 6942 2-8-12 50 (v[1]) LukeMorris 11 41
(John Weymes) *sn pushed along in rr: r.o ins fnl f: nvr nrr* 33/1
0000 8 1 ½ **Bolshoi Melody**[15] 6821 2-9-1 53 AdamKirby 9 38
(Jeremy Gask) *prom: rdn 1/2-way: hung lft and wknd ins fnl f* 28/1
4006 9 5 **Burnwynd Spirit (IRE)**[14] 6842 2-9-0 52 JamesSullivan 4 19
(Ian Semple) *prom: chsd wnr 3f out tl rdn wl over 1f out: wknd fnl f* 25/1
0440 10 25 **Copper Falls**[74] 5099 2-9-4 56 KierenFallon 8 —
(Brendan Powell) *s.s: outpcd: t.o* 14/1
63.28 secs (0.98) **Going Correction** -0.025s/f (Stan) **10** Ran SP% **118.7**
Speed ratings (Par 93): **91,89,88,87,85 84,83,81,73,33**
ToteSwingers: 1&2 £3.20, 1&3 £4.80, 2&3 £13.90 CSF £22.62 CT £176.02 TOTE £2.80: £1.10, £2.80, £3.80; EX 27.10.
Owner S L Edwards **Bred** S L Edwards **Trained** Lichfield, Staffs

FOCUS
A moderate but reasonably competitive nursery. Not form to be positive about but it appears sound enough. The winner is going the right way.
NOTEBOOK
Look Here's Lady continued her steady progression with a straightforward success, readily confirming recent Catterick placings with the runner-up. (op 3-1 tchd 5-2)
M J Woodward simply lacked the pace of the winner, having to be driven to hold his position before the straight. Only moderate, it's questionable whether he'd benefit from an extra furlong and perhaps some headgear will help sharpen him up. Silvestre de Sousa reported the colt hung right-handed. Official explanation: jockey said colt hung right-handed (op 13-2 tchd 8-1)
Claretintheblood(IRE) offered encouragement on her nursery debut, although she was well drawn. (op 12-1 tchd 9-1)
Mount McLeod(IRE) is in danger of becoming frustrating, if she isn't already, with this the third straight race she's been unable to show her best. Much like at Kempton last time, she started too sluggishly to get a handy position and was keen. Once in the straight, she was full of running when having to switch around a rival and got going too late. (op 10-3)
Triggerlo wasn't helped by his wide draw. (op 11-2 tchd 6-1)
Sonsie Lass couldn't get to the front and was too keen. (op 9-2)
Copper Falls Official explanation: jockey said filly lost its action

7144 EXCLUSIVE BREEDERS' CUP COVERAGE ON ATR H'CAP 1m 1f 103y(P)
7:40 (7:41) (Class 6) (0-60,64) 3-Y-O £1,908 (£563; £281) Stalls Low

Form RPR
4362 1 **Love Your Looks**[15] 6816 3-9-5 57 TonyCulhane 5 73+
(Mike Murphy) *s.i.s: hld up: hdwy over 2f out: shkn up to ld over 1f out: styd on wl: eased nr fin* 11/2
313 2 2 ¾ **Pinotage**[7] 7003 3-9-1 58 JustinNewman(5) 2 67
(Richard Whitaker) *chsd ldr tl led over 3f out: rdn and hdd over 1f out: swished tail and no ex fnl f* 7/4[1]
0523 3 4 **Eastward Ho**[14] 6845 3-9-2 54 SilvestreDeSousa 9 55
(Jason Ward) *hld up: pushed along over 2f out: hdwy over 1f out: nvr nrr* 9/2[3]
5402 4 nk **Bedibyes**[15] 6813 3-9-0 55 RobertLButler(3) 7 55
(Richard Mitchell) *s.i.s: pushed along and hdwy over 1f out: rdn ins fnl f: n.d* 20/1

400 **5** 14 **Crystal Sky (IRE)**[44] 6067 3-9-6 **58** .... FergusSweeney 6 29
(Andrew Haynes) *prom: rdn over 2f out: wknd over 1f out* **25/1**
00 **6** 4 **Skystream (IRE)**[22] 6653 3-8-9 **52** .... GarryWhillans(5) 8 14
(Ian Semple) *chsd ldrs: rdn over 3f out: wknd over 1f out* **25/1**
2331 **7** 8 **If What And Maybe**[3] 7085 3-9-12 **64** 6ex ....(v) AdamKirby 3 —
(John Ryan) *sn pushed along and prom: rdn and wknd over 2f out* **4/1**[2]
0063 **8** 8 **Tawseef (IRE)**[15] 6813 3-9-4 **56** .... WilliamCarson 1 —
(Roy Brotherton) *led: hdd over 3f out: sn rdn: wknd over 2f out* **7/1**

2m 1.39s (-0.31) **Going Correction** -0.025s/f (Stan) **8** Ran SP% **114.9**
Speed ratings (Par 99): **100,97,94,93,81 77,70,63**
ToteSwingers: 1&2 £2.50, 1&3 £2.70, 2&3 £5.00 CSF £15.28 CT £45.62 TOTE £6.60: £1.80, £1.10, £1.90; EX 21.30.
Owner M Murphy **Bred** Ellis Stud And Bellow Hill Stud **Trained** Westoning, Beds

FOCUS
A reasonable race for the grade, and sound form, rated though the runner-up. A biggish personal best from the winner.

7145 THE HORIZONS RESTAURANT, THE PLACE TO DINE H'CAP 2m 119y(P)
8:10 (8:10) (Class 6) (0-60,57) 3-Y-O+ **£1,704** (£503; £251) **Stalls** Low

Form RPR
4522 **1** **The Absent Mare**[23] 5898 3-8-10 **49** .... MartinLane 7 59
(Robin Dickin) *hld up: hdwy 3f out: rdn to ld ins fnl f: styd on wl* **7/1**[3]
2015 **2** 1 3/4 **Tigerino (IRE)**[4] 7062 3-8-11 **50** .... DuranFentiman 2 58
(Chris Fairhurst) *chsd ldrs: led over 2f out: rdn over 1f out: hdd and unable qck ins fnl f* **2/1**[1]
0-60 **3** 2 **Smart George (IRE)**[181] 1683 3-9-2 **55** ....(bt[1]) SilvestreDeSousa 6 61
(Paul W Flynn, Ire) *chsd ldr tl led over 3f out: rdn and hdd over 2f out: no ex ins fnl f* **7/2**[2]
0521 **4** 15 **Blue Cossack (IRE)**[15] 6823 3-9-4 **57** ....(be) LiamKeniry 1 45
(Mark Usher) *s.s: hld up: rdn and wknd over 2f out* **7/2**[2]
110/ **5** nk **Hamalka (IRE)**[23] 6640 6-10-0 **57** .... MartinHarley 5 44
(P Cluskey, Ire) *prom tl rdn and wknd over 2f out* **17/2**
3/50 **6** 13 **Tobago Bay**[157] 2377 6-9-8 **51** ....(b) JamieGoldstein 4 23
(Gary Moore) *led: rdn and hdd over 3f out: wknd over 2f out: t.o* **8/1**
0050 **7** 43 **Ritsi**[3] 7078 8-8-11 **45** ....(p) JulieBurke(5) 3 —
(Marjorie Fife) *prom: pushed along over 5f out: wknd 4f out: t.o* **25/1**

3m 42.4s (0.60) **Going Correction** -0.025s/f (Stan)
WFA 3 from 6yo+ 10lb **7** Ran SP% **115.8**
Speed ratings (Par 101): **97,96,95,88,88 81,61**
ToteSwingers: 1&2 £3.00, 1&3 £3.00, 2&3 £2.40 CSF £22.02 TOTE £8.50: £3.90, £1.10; EX 8.80.
Owner J C Clemmow **Bred** Beautiful Losers Bloodstock & R Hobson **Trained** Atherstone on Stour, Warwicks

FOCUS
Not a bad staying handicap for the grade. The pace was decent and the form looks sound.

7146 ESPN BREEDERS' CUP COVERAGE ON ATR H'CAP 1m 141y(P)
8:40 (8:41) (Class 5) (0-70,69) 3-Y-O+ **£2,264** (£673; £336; £168) **Stalls** Low

Form RPR
0221 **1** **Zafeen's Pearl**[13] 6877 4-9-7 **69** .... ShaneKelly 12 82+
(Dean Ivory) *hld up: hdwy 5f out: shkn up to ld wl ins fnl f: readily* **2/1**[1]
420 **2** 1 **Sweet Secret**[30] 6468 4-9-3 **65** ....(p) AdamKirby 1 73
(Jeremy Gask) *led: rdn over 1f out: hdd wl ins fnl f* **10/1**
6041 **3** 3/4 **Saharia (IRE)**[14] 6844 4-9-0 **67** ....(v) MarkCoumbe(5) 10 73
(Michael Attwater) *hld up: hdwy over 5f out: rdn and ev ch ins fnl f: styd on same pce* **9/1**
0221 **4** shd **Violent Velocity (IRE)**[7] 6990 8-9-7 **69** .... PaulHanagan 3 75
(John Quinn) *prom: pushed along over 2f out: r.o* **4/1**[2]
2033 **5** 1/2 **Carcinetto (IRE)**[13] 6877 9-9-3 **65** .... SilvestreDeSousa 9 70+
(David Evans) *hld up: swtchd rt over 1f out: r.o ins fnl f: nvr nrr* **8/1**
3120 **6** 1/2 **Chookie Avon**[22] 6646 4-9-0 **62** ....(p) JoeFanning 2 66
(Keith Dalgleish) *hld up: plld hrd: hdwy over 1f out: sn rdn: styd on same pce ins fnl f* **16/1**
3006 **7** 2 1/2 **Come On Safari (IRE)**[25] 6587 4-9-3 **65** .... MartinHarley 7 63
(Joseph Tuite) *hld up in tch: lost pl 5f out: hdwy over 1f out: no imp ins fnl f* **14/1**
0600 **8** 3 3/4 **Forward Feline (IRE)**[31] 6434 5-9-3 **65** .... DavidProbert 6 54
(Bryn Palling) *s.i.s: sn prom: lost pl 4f out: n.d after* **28/1**
0005 **9** 1 **Qeethaara (USA)**[13] 6878 7-8-12 **63** .... RyanClark(3) 4 50
(Mark Brisbourne) *chsd ldr 2f: remained handy tl rdn and wknd over 1f out* **20/1**
0001 **10** 3/4 **Without Prejudice (USA)**[52] 5803 6-9-7 **69** .... GrahamGibbons 13 54
(Michael Easterby) *s.s: swtchd lft sn after s: hld up: rdn over 1f out: n.d* **15/2**[3]
6000 **11** 1 3/4 **Lastkingofscotland (IRE)**[16] 6794 5-9-5 **67** ....(b) KirstyMilczarek 8 48
(Conor Dore) *prom tl rdn and wknd over 2f out* **33/1**
2010 **12** 5 **Aussie Blue (IRE)**[13] 6878 7-9-2 **64** .... TonyCulhane 5 34
(Richard Whitaker) *chsd ldr 6f out tl rdn over 2f out: wknd over 1f out* **20/1**

1m 50.75s (0.25) **Going Correction** -0.025s/f (Stan) **12** Ran SP% **123.8**
Speed ratings (Par 103): **97,96,95,95,94 94,92,88,88,87 85,81**
ToteSwingers: 1&2 £5.40, 1&3 £6.90, 2&3 £15.00 CSF £23.32 CT £159.81 TOTE £3.50: £2.10, £5.30, £5.00; EX 24.20.
Owner Heather Yarrow & Lesley Ivory **Bred** Mr And Mrs L Baker **Trained** Radlett, Herts

FOCUS
A modest handicap and the pace seemed to slow early in the back straight. Orinary form, rated around the second and third, with the winner better than the bare form.
Without Prejudice(USA) Official explanation: jockey said gelding missed the break
T/Plt: £26.10 to a £1 stake. Pool:£75,185.50 - 2,102.01 winning tickets. T/Qpdt: £5.80 to a £1 stake Pool: £9,386.17 - 1,188.36 w. tckts CR

7147 - 7148a - (Foreign Racing) - See RI

7007 DUNDALK (A.W) (L-H)
Friday, October 28

OFFICIAL GOING: Standard

7149a WINTER RACING AT DUNDALK H'CAP 6f (P)
6:55 (6:58) 3-Y-O+ **£11,206** (£3,275; £1,551; £517)

RPR
1 **Bajan Tryst (USA)**[20] 6706 5-9-9 97 .... DPMcDonogh 12 102
(Kevin Ryan) *chsd ldr in 2nd: rdn to ld 1f out: kpt on wl u.p fnl f* **10/1**
2 nk **The Reaper (IRE)**[7] 7012 3-9-3 99 ....(b) DJBenson(7) 3 103
(G M Lyons, Ire) *chsd ldrs: 3rd 1/2-way: rdn in cl 5th 2f out: 4th 1f out: kpt on fnl f* **9/1**
3 shd **Five Star Junior (USA)**[50] 5852 5-9-9 97 .... JMurtagh 1 101
(Linda Stubbs) *hld up towards rr: hdwy in centre under 2f out: rdn into 6th under 1f out: kpt on fnl f* **11/4**[1]
4 1/2 **What About You (IRE)**[97] 4333 3-8-11 86 ....(b) CO'Donoghue 9 88
(Richard Fahey) *led: rdn and hdd 1f out: no ex and kpt on same pce fnl f* **11/2**[2]
5 hd **Luisant**[7] 7010 8-9-5 93 .... KJManning 4 94
(J A Nash, Ire) *chsd ldrs: 5th 1/2-way: rdn into 3rd 1f out: no ex ins fnl f: kpt on same pce* **16/1**
6 hd **Johannes (IRE)**[54] 5758 8-9-1 89 .... JPO'Brien 8 90
(Richard Fahey) *hld up towards rr: hdwy wd under 2f out: rdn and clsr 1f out: no ex ins fnl f: kpt on same pce* **11/2**[2]
7 nk **Gossamer Seed (IRE)**[19] 6733 3-9-0 94 ....(t) RPWhelan(5) 7 94
(John Joseph Murphy, Ire) *chsd ldrs early: 8th 1/2-way: rdn 2f out: styd on into 5th 1f out: no ex fnl f* **14/1**
8 shd **Quinmaster (USA)**[7] 7010 9-8-9 83 ....(p) ShaneFoley 6 83
(M Halford, Ire) *hld up towards rr: hdwy wd under 2f out: rdn and clsr 1f out: no ex ins fnl f: kpt on same pce* **14/1**
9 3/4 **Knock Stars (IRE)**[7] 7012 3-9-1 90 ....(t) SeamieHeffernan 5 87
(Patrick Martin, Ire) *in rr of mid-div: rdn and jst bhd ldrs 1f out: no ex ins fnl f* **20/1**
10 1/2 **Peahen**[33] 6388 3-9-8 100 ....(b[1]) EJMcNamara(3) 11 96
(G M Lyons, Ire) *dwlt: towards rr: wd and hdwy under 2f out: rdn and clsr 1f out: no ex ins fnl f* **20/1**
11 nk **Six Of Hearts**[21] 6677 7-9-12 105 ....(b) SHJames(5) 10 100
(Cecil Ross, Ire) *chsd ldrs: 7th 1/2-way: rdn 2f out: no ex 1f out: kpt on same pce* **16/1**
12 1 1/2 **Tornadodancer (IRE)**[21] 6677 8-8-12 86 ....(b) BACurtis 13 76
(T G McCourt, Ire) *chsd ldrs: 4th 1/2-way: rdn in 3rd 2f out: no ex over 1f out* **16/1**
13 hd **My Girl Anna (IRE)**[9] 6960 4-8-4 85 .... SAGray(7) 2 74
(Muredach Kelly, Ire) *mid-div best: rdn and no imp 2f out: kpt on one pce* **9/1**
14 3 1/4 **Flic Flac (IRE)**[7] 7010 3-9-1 90 .... PJSmullen 14 69
(D K Weld, Ire) *chsd ldrs: 6th 1/2-way: rdn in 4th 2f out: no ex over 1f out: eased fnl f* **13/2**[3]

1m 11.1s (71.10)
WFA 3 from 4yo+ 1lb **14** Ran SP% **140.4**
CSF £113.49 CT £337.80 TOTE £18.50: £8.00, £5.50, £2.10; DF 134.50.
Owner Mrs Margaret Forsyth & Mrs R G Hillen **Bred** William Patterson & James Glenn **Trained** Hambleton, N Yorks

■ Stewards' Enquiry : R P Whelan severe caution: use of whip
C O'Donoghue three-day ban: careless riding (Nov 11, 18, 25); severe caution: failed to keep a straight linr to marker poles

FOCUS
They finished in a bit of a heap in this race but not very many horses got into it. The form is rated around the third and fourth.

NOTEBOOK
Bajan Tryst(USA) negated the effect of his poor draw by being smartly away and Declan McDonogh was eventually able to manoeuvre him to the inner. From there he kept up the gallop strongly under pressure and really responded gamely. It was a tough and honest performance which just about deserved the reward it got. (op 8/1)
The Reaper(IRE) is responding well to being upped in class. He was on the inside and no more than a length or so off the pace the whole way while often looking as though he was in danger of meeting trouble in running. He ran on well under pressure, and has a fair chance of winning a race like this. (op 9/1 tchd 8/1)
Five Star Junior(USA) was towards the back and looked to be struggling to get into it. He picked up well when switched for his effort in the straight but never looked like getting to the winner. (op 6/1)
What About You(IRE) showed tremendous pace while getting a soft enough lead for a race of this nature. He just ran out of steam inside the last but it was still a very decent effort. (op 15/2 tchd 5/1)
Luisant was prominent early on and, in the end, kept on well having looked to be struggling turning into the straight. (op 14/1)

7150a BOOKINGS@DUNDALKSTADIUM.COM H'CAP 1m (P)
7:25 (7:26) (60-80,83) 3-Y-O+ **£5,948** (£1,379; £603; £344)

RPR
1 **Katherine Lee (IRE)**[7] 7008 3-9-9 78 .... JMurtagh 6 84
(M Halford, Ire) *mde all: rdn and chal 1f out: kpt on wl u.p fnl f* **9/2**[1]
2 hd **Tarrsille (IRE)**[50] 5872 5-9-4 77 ....(t) GJPhillips(7) 11 83
(G M Lyons, Ire) *chsd ldrs: 4th 1/2-way: rdn in 5th 2f out: 4th 1f out: kpt on fnl f to press wnr closing stages* **14/1**
3 1 1/2 **Six Silver Lane**[57] 5662 3-9-9 78 ....(p) JPO'Brien 3 81
(Ms Joanna Morgan, Ire) *chsd ldrs: 5th 1/2-way: rdn into 3rd 2f out: kpt on same pce fr over 1f out* **8/1**
4 hd **If Per Chance (IRE)**[24] 6140 6-9-6 77 ....(p) CPHoban(5) 2 79
(M Halford, Ire) *hld up towards rr: hdwy in 8th 2f out: rdn into 6th 1f out: kpt on same pce fnl f* **20/1**
5 shd **Golden Shoe (IRE)**[14] 6853 3-9-10 79 .... KJManning 10 81
(J T Gorman, Ire) *chsd ldrs: 3rd 1/2-way: 2nd 3f out: rdn to chal 1f out: no ex ins fnl f* **5/1**[2]
6 1 3/4 **Mountain Coral (IRE)**[54] 5762 7-9-7 80 .... CTKeane(7) 9 78
(F Oakes, Ire) *chsd ldrs: 7th 1/2-way: rdn 2f out: 5th 1f out: no ex ins fnl f: kpt on same pce* **18/1**
7 1 3/4 **Fishforcompliments**[33] 6381 7-9-13 79 ....(p) PJSmullen 5 73
(Richard Fahey) *chsd ldrs: 6th 1/2-way: rdn 2f out: no ex over 1f out: kpt on same pce* **13/2**[3]
8 nk **Crystal Morning (IRE)**[14] 6853 3-9-9 78 .... ShaneFoley 13 71
(Mrs John Harrington, Ire) *hld up towards rr: rdn and no imp 2f out: kpt on one pce fr over 1f out* **11/1**
9 3/4 **Truly Genius (IRE)**[14] 6853 3-9-6 80 ....(b[1]) SHJames(5) 1 71
(C P Donoghue, Ire) *mid-div: 8th 1/2-way: rdn and no imp 2f out: kpt on one pce* **5/1**[2]
10 nk **Romeo's On Fire (IRE)**[14] 6849 7-9-9 78 .... EJMcNamara(3) 14 69
(G M Lyons, Ire) *in rr of mid-div thrght: nvr a factor* **22/1**
11 nk **Rambling Dancer (IRE)**[145] 2747 7-9-8 77 .... SMGorey(3) 12 67
(Mrs Valerie Keatley, Ire) *in rr of mid-div thrght: nvr a factor* **16/1**
12 1 3/4 **Cheers Buddy (IRE)**[27] 5978 3-9-11 80 ....(b) SeamieHeffernan 4 66
(Paul Hennessy, Ire) *chsd ldr in 2nd: rdn in 4th 2f out: no ex and wknd* **33/1**
13 4 3/4 **World Ruler**[34] 6364 6-10-0 80 .... CO'Donoghue 7 55
(David Marnane, Ire) *mid-div: 9th 1/2-way: rdn and no ex 2f out: wknd* **15/2**

14 3 3/4 **Insieme (IRE)**[235] 791 3-9-5 79.. RPWhelan[(5)] 8 45
(Paul Cashman, Ire) *a towards rr* **16/1**

1m 38.0s (98.00)
WFA 3 from 5yo+ 3lb **14** Ran SP% **131.8**
CSF £74.00 CT £530.73 TOTE £5.30: £2.40, £6.10, £3.70; DF 82.20.
Owner Gerard P Callanan **Bred** Gerard Callinan **Trained** Doneany, Co Kildare
■ Stewards' Enquiry : S M Gorey one-day ban: continued to hit his mount afyer his chance of winning or being placed had clearly gone (Nov 11)
S H James severe caution: failed to report that his mount hung

FOCUS
An ordinary handicap run at a decent gallop. The fifth is the best guide.

NOTEBOOK
Katherine Lee(IRE) probably didn't need to improve a whole lot to win this. Making all at a decent clip, she was brought towards the centre of the track in the straight and from there she kept battling and pulled out plenty to repel her rivals. She's probably still reasonably handicapped and her liking for this surface will give her a chance of following up. (op 5/1)
Tarrsille(IRE) is one of those horses that seems to have been around for much longer than he has and this was probably his best effort for a while. Racing just off the pace, he sustained his effort towards the outside in the last furlong and a half and only narrowly failed to get up. It looks as though he may well be back on a winning mark if the handicapper is kind to him. (op 16/1)
Six Silver Lane ◆ ran a cracker. He raced in a handy position most of the way and had pretty much every chance when challenging between horses in the straight. His effort just flattened out well inside the last furlong in the manner of a horse that may have just needed it a fraction. (op 7/1)
If Per Chance(IRE) got the handicapper's kiss of death last year and has lost his way, but this was far more promising. On the inside rail, he kept on from mid-division inside the final furlong under mostly hands and heels and might not be too far off winning again.
Golden Shoe(IRE) has been consistent of late and ran another decent race here. He was close to the pace most of the way and kept going under pressure, but just ran out of steam well inside the last. (op 7/1)

7151 - 7154a - (Foreign Racing) - See Raceform Interactive

7049 LONGCHAMP (R-H)
Friday, October 28

OFFICIAL GOING: Turf: good to soft

7155a CRITERIUM DE VITESSE (LISTED RACE) (2YO) (TURF) 5f (S)
1:20 (12:00) 2-Y-O **£23,706** (£9,482; £7,112; £4,741; £2,370)

RPR
1 **Stepper Point**[60] 5562 2-9-2 0.. ChristopheSoumillon 5 105
(William Muir) *broke wl: sn led on ins rail: rdn 1 1/2f out: sn wnt clr: easily* **2/1**[1]
2 3 1/2 **Sea Trial (FR)**[25] 2-9-2 0.. JohanVictoire 9 92
(Mme C Head-Maarek, France) **11/2**[2]
3 2 1/2 **Nadeaud (FR)**[30] 2-8-13 0.. ThierryJarnet 11 80
(D Guillemin, France) **15/1**
4 1 1/4 **Bandidazo (USA)**[30] 2-9-2 0..(b[1]) Pierre-CharlesBoudot 1 79
(A Fabre, France) **23/1**
5 2 1/2 **Arabian Falcon**[57] 2-9-2 0..(p) FilipMinarik 8 70
(A Kleinkorres, Germany) **78/10**
6 hd **Paker (IRE)** 2-9-2 0..(b[1]) FabriceVeron 6 69
(W Olkowski, Poland) **17/1**
7 3/4 **Picante (IRE)**[10] 2-8-13 0.. AnthonyCrastus 2 63
(C Boutin, France) **35/1**
8 2 1/2 **Vital Wave (IRE)**[25] 2-9-2 0.. MickaelBarzalona 4 57
(E J O'Neill, France) **12/1**
9 1 **Chapman (GER)**[75] 2-9-2 0.. OlivierPeslier 10 54
(P Schiergen, Germany) **58/10**[3]
10 4 **Luv U Forever**[20] 6705 2-8-13 0.. MaximeGuyon 12 36
(Jo Hughes) *broke wl on wd outside: had to be shkn up at 1/2-way: nt qckn: fdd: eased fnl f* **15/2**
11 **Misedargent (FR)**[16] 6808 2-8-13 0.. StephanePasquier 3 36
(C Boutin, France) **29/1**

55.55 secs (-0.75) **11** Ran SP% **116.3**
WIN (incl. 1 euro stake): 3.00. PLACES: 1.50, 1.90, 3.30. DF: 8.50. SF: 10.20.
Owner C L A Edginton **Bred** Whitsbury Manor Stud **Trained** Lambourn, Berks

NOTEBOOK
Stepper Point, last seen bolting up in a nursery at Warwick in August, was being prepared for Ayr but pulled a muscle in his ribs and was given some time off. Bouncing out well, he showed tons of speed here and won as he liked. He should have plenty more to offer at three.

7156a PRIX CASIMIR DELAMARRE (LISTED RACE) (3YO FILLIES) (TURF) 1m 1f
2:55 (12:00) 3-Y-O **£23,706** (£9,482; £7,112; £4,741; £2,370)

RPR
1 **Giofra** 3-9-0 0.. MaximeGuyon 10 107
(A De Royer-Dupre, France) **114/10**
2 3 **Acacalia (GER)** 3-9-0 0.. FilipMinarik 6 101
(C Sprengel, Germany) **16/1**
3 1/2 **Private Eye (FR)**[48] 5958 3-9-0 0.. OlivierPeslier 1 100
(E Libaud, France) **9/1**
4 nk **La Mouche**[36] 6288 3-9-0 0.. GregoryBenoist 3 99
(E Lellouche, France) **13/1**
5 nk **Malicia (USA)**[90] 4570 3-9-0 0.. Roberto-CarlosMontenegro 9 98
(X Thomas-Demeaulte, France) **8/1**
6 hd **Psireve (FR)**[49] 5910 3-9-0 0.. TonyPiccone 12 98
(J-M Capitte, France) **28/1**
7 3/4 **Vigee Le Brun (USA)** 3-9-0 0.. ChristopheSoumillon 7 96
(M Delzangles, France) **3/1**[1]
8 nse **Poplin**[27] 6530 3-9-0 0.. ThierryThulliez 5 96
(Luca Cumani) *settled bhd ldrs in 4th on outer: travelling wl: rdn 2f out: nt pce to chal: styd u.p fnl f* **19/5**[2]
9 1 1/2 **Riqa**[36] 6288 3-9-0 0.. ThierryJarnet 4 93
(F Head, France) **9/2**[3]
10 1 1/2 **Triveni (FR)**[145] 2750 3-9-0 0.. AlexisBadel 8 90
(Mme M Bollack-Badel, France) **54/1**
11 **Overturned**[30] 3-9-0 0.. MickaelBarzalona 2 —
(E J O'Neill, France) **18/1**

1m 56.42s (4.82) **11** Ran SP% **116.7**
WIN (incl. 1 euro stake): 12.40. PLACES: 4.20, 5.10, 3.10. DF: 83.30. SF: 242.40.
Owner Haras De La Perelle **Bred** Haras De La Perelle **Trained** Chantilly, France

6644 AYR (L-H)
Saturday, October 29

OFFICIAL GOING: Heavy (6.9)
All races on hurdles track. With the unusual course configeration no speed figures have been calculated for this meeting.
Wind: Strong, half behind Weather: Overcast, showers

7157 JOHN SMITH'S NURSERY 1m 1f
1:50 (1:50) (Class 5) (0-75,73) 2-Y-O **£2,264** (£673; £336; £168) **Stalls** High

Form RPR
0301 **1** **Docs Legacy (IRE)**[7] 7035 2-8-13 65.. PaulHanagan 2 68+
(Richard Fahey) *chsd ldrs: pushed along over 3f out: edgd rt and led over 1f out: drvn out fnl f* **15/8**[1]
4433 **2** 2 1/2 **Joshua The First**[23] 6644 2-9-3 69.. DavidAllan 4 67
(Keith Dalgleish) *prom: effrt and hung lft 2f out: hdwy to chse wnr ins fnl f: kpt on: no imp* **7/2**[3]
0045 **3** 1 3/4 **I'm Harry**[19] 6753 2-9-5 71.. RobertWinston 3 66
(Charles Hills) *pressed ldr: drvn along over 3f out: kpt on same pce fnl f* **4/1**
4332 **4** 5 **Dubious Escapade (IRE)**[12] 6911 2-8-13 65.. TomEaves 1 50
(Ann Duffield) *led: rdn and hdd over 1f out: sn btn* **5/2**[2]
0540 **5** dist **Come To Mind**[36] 6293 2-7-9 52 oh5 ow2.. NeilFarley[(5)] 6 —
(Alan Berry) *bhd and niggled after 3f: struggling over 4f out: virtually p.u fnl 2f* **50/1**

2m 13.84s (133.84) **5** Ran SP% **107.5**
CSF £8.28 TOTE £2.40: £1.60, £1.40; EX 10.80.
Owner D Bardsley **Bred** Miss Mary Davison **Trained** Musley Bank, N Yorks
■ Stewards' Enquiry : Paul Hanagan five-day ban: used whip with excessive frequency (Nov12,14-17)

FOCUS
A real test for these juveniles in the conditions. The winner was suited by the ground and the form could be rated a little higher.

NOTEBOOK
Docs Legacy(IRE) proved best equipped to deal with the testing conditions. A winner over 8.6f at Wolverhampton last time, he's out of a German mare who herself is a half-sister to six winners, including Lightning Strike, who won at up to 2m, so the stamina is there in his pedigree. He wasn't going best turning in but saw his race out the strongest, which is what counted. (op 2-1)
Joshua The First is fully exposed but had at least some experience of running in this sort of ground and he ran another fair race. (tchd 3-1)
I'm Harry has some soft-ground influences in his pedigree and didn't run badly. (op 11-2)
Dubious Escapade(IRE) went from travelling best into the straight to falling in a hole 2f out. Clearly it was too great a test for her. (op 2-1)

7158 MISS ELLIE MAIDEN STKS 1m 1f
2:25 (2:25) (Class 5) 3-Y-O+ **£2,264** (£673; £336; £168) **Stalls** High

Form RPR
5- **1** **Mama Sox (IRE)**[74] 5158 3-8-7 67..(t) CharlesBishop[(5)] 8 63
(John C McConnell, Ire) *t.k.h: trckd ldrs: hdwy to ld over 2f out: hrd pressed fnl f: jst hld on* **11/4**[1]
55 **2** nse **Avison (IRE)**[8] 7004 3-9-3 0.. PaulHanagan 10 68
(Richard Fahey) *prom: hdwy over 2f out: chal and drvn fnl f: kpt on: jst failed* **7/2**[2]
6030 **3** 8 **Spread Boy (IRE)**[15] 6833 4-9-7 49.. TomEaves 5 50
(Alan Berry) *in tch: hdwy and ev ch over 2f out: sn rdn: outpcd by ldng pair appr fnl f* **9/1**
5 **4** 6 **Lady Gargoyle**[40] 6210 3-8-13 0 ow1.. DanielTudhope 7 33
(Jim Goldie) *hld up: outpcd over 3f out: sme late hdwy: nvr on terms* **9/1**
5050 **5** 2 1/4 **Miss Pronounce**[40] 6208 3-8-12 38.. PaddyAspell 9 27
(Linda Perratt) *cl up: rdn over 3f out: wknd over 2f out* **40/1**
0040 **6** 4 **Eqtiraab (IRE)**[5] 7064 3-9-3 64..(b) BarryMcHugh 6 23
(Tony Coyle) *cl up: led over 3f out to over 2f out: sn rdn and wknd* **7/2**[2]
-000 **7** 39 **Supreme Seductress (IRE)**[31] 6459 3-8-12 60.. RobertWinston 2 —
(Charles Hills) *led: rdn and hdd over 3f out: lost tch fnl 2f: t.o* **9/2**[3]

2m 16.07s (136.07)
WFA 3 from 4yo 4lb **7** Ran SP% **111.7**
toteswingers:1&2:£1.90, 1&3:£5.70, 2&3:£6.10 CSF £11.96 TOTE £4.20: £2.60, £2.00; EX 13.10.
Owner David P McConnell **Bred** John O'Connor **Trained** Stamullen, Co Meath

FOCUS
Ordinary maiden form with the winner not needing to run to her Irish form while the runner-up seems to be progressing.

7159 PLUMBSTORE H'CAP 1m 1f
2:55 (2:55) (Class 6) (0-60,60) 3-Y-O+ **£1,617** (£481; £240; £120) **Stalls** High

Form RPR
0002 **1** **Funky Munky**[14] 6430 6-8-12 **48**..(p) PJMcDonald 10 56
(Alistair Whillans) *trckd ldrs: led over 3f out: sn hrd pressed: rdn and hld on wl fnl f* **10/1**
4 **2** 1/2 **Pacey Outswinger (IRE)**[32] 6430 4-8-10 **46** oh1.. PaulHanagan 8 53
(John C McConnell, Ire) *hld up in tch: hdwy and ev ch over 2f out: rdn over 1f out: kpt on fnl f: hld nr fin* **8/1**
0603 **3** 2 **Aerodynamic (IRE)**[18] 6777 4-9-10 **60**.. PaddyAspell 11 63
(Clive Mulhall) *hld up on outside: smooth hdwy to trck ldrs 3f out: rdn 2f out: kpt on same pce fnl f* **2/1**[1]
0 **4** 8 **Sultana Belle (IRE)**[32] 6430 3-8-6 **46** oh1..(p) BarryMcHugh 6 31
(Lee Smyth, Ire) *bhd: outpcd 4f out: rallied 3f out: plugged on same pce fr 2f out* **66/1**
4326 **5** 6 **Henrys Gift (IRE)**[43] 6116 3-9-1 **55**.. TomEaves 4 27
(Michael Dods) *led: rdn and hdd over 3f out: wknd fr 2f out* **16/1**
0563 **6** 7 **Little Book**[32] 6428 3-8-13 **53** ow1.. DanielTudhope 3 9
(Jim Goldie) *hld up: shortlived effrt wl over 2f out: btn over 1f out* **15/2**[3]
5406 **7** 2 **Spavento (IRE)**[15] 6831 5-9-9 **59**.. DavidAllan 9 11
(Eric Alston) *prom: struggling over 3f out: nvr on terms* **12/1**
0-00 **8** 16 **Newport Arch**[31] 6452 3-9-0 **57**..(v[1]) MichaelO'Connell[(3)] 5 —
(John Quinn) *hld up towards rr: struggling over 3f out: btn fnl 2f: t.o* **14/1**
0640 **9** 4 1/2 **Hits Only Jude (IRE)**[32] 6430 8-9-3 **60**..(v) JasonHart[(7)] 2 —
(Declan Carroll) *cl up tl rdn and wknd 3f out: t.o* **25/1**
33-0 **10** 43 **Highkingofireland**[15] 6830 5-9-9 **59**.. RobertWinston 1 —
(Mrs K Burke) *in tch on ins: lost pl 4f out: sn struggling: t.o* **4/1**[2]

246/ **11** *9* **Key News (IRE)**[33] 6422 6-9-2 55 .... APThornton(3) 7 —
(Patrick Martin, Ire) *hld up in tch: struggling over 3f out: virtually p.u fnl 2f* **12/1**

2m 11.98s (131.98)
WFA 3 from 4yo+ 4lb **11** Ran SP% **118.6**
toteswingers:1&2:£22.80, 1&3:£2.80, 2&3:£8.70 CSF £88.38 CT £227.34 TOTE £6.60: £2.20, £3.10, £1.30; EX 46.40.
Owner The Twelve Munkys **Bred** Mrs S Corbett **Trained** Newmill-On-Slitrig, Borders

FOCUS
A moderate handicap best rated around the placed horses.
Highkingofireland Official explanation: jockey said gelding lost its action

7160 JOHN SMITH'S H'CAP 1m 1f
3:30 (3:30) (Class 4) (0-80,80) 3-Y-O **£4,204** (£1,251; £625; £312) **Stalls** High

Form RPR
5102 **1** **Neutrafa (IRE)**[34] 6383 3-9-0 76 .... MichaelO'Connell(3) 5 86+
(John Mackie) *trckd ldr: led over 2f out: sn pushed clr: kpt on wl fnl f* **11/10**[1]

6002 **2** *3* **Persian Herald**[31] 6465 3-9-0 73 .... TomEaves 1 74
(William Muir) *hld up in tch: rdn over 2f out: hdwy to chse (clr) wnr over 1f out: no imp fnl f* **5/1**[3]

4024 **3** *8* **Triple Eight (IRE)**[26] 6582 3-9-2 80 ....(p) GarryWhillans(5) 4 63
(Philip Kirby) *led to over 2f out: lost 2nd over 1f out: sn btn* **9/1**

2520 **4** *4 1/2* **Retreat Content (IRE)**[84] 4784 3-8-8 67 .... BarryMcHugh 3 41
(Linda Perratt) *in tch: shortlived effrt over 2f out: btn over 1f out* **9/2**[2]

4040 **5** *21* **Goldenveil (IRE)**[41] 6191 3-9-4 77 .... PaulHanagan 2 —
(Richard Fahey) *trckd ldrs: struggling 3f out: sn btn: t.o* **9/2**[2]

2m 14.74s (134.74) **5** Ran SP% **110.6**
CSF £7.02 TOTE £1.80: £1.10, £2.40; EX 5.00.
Owner Tony Ashley **Bred** Twelve Oaks Stud & Deerpark Stud **Trained** Church Broughton , Derbys

FOCUS
An oedinary handicap and the market got it right.

7161 JOHN SMITH'S NO NONSENSE H'CAP 1m 1f
4:05 (4:05) (Class 3) (0-90,87) 3-Y-O+ **£5,822** (£1,732; £865; £432) **Stalls** High

Form RPR
-050 **1** **European Dream (IRE)**[181] 1713 8-8-13 77 ....(p) RobertLButler(3) 9 88
(Richard Guest) *hld up: rdn and hdwy over 2f out: led ins fnl f: kpt on wl* **11/1**

5411 **2** *3/4* **Scrapper Smith (IRE)**[44] 6080 5-9-7 87 .... GarryWhillans(5) 1 96
(Alistair Whillans) *hld up: hdwy over 2f out: effrt u.p and wnt 2nd ins fnl f: kpt on* **10/3**[1]

1-06 **3** *2 1/4* **Flipping**[36] 6290 4-9-2 77 .... GrahamGibbons 8 81
(Eric Alston) *led: clr over 3f out: rdn 2f out: hdd ins fnl f: no ex* **6/1**

0210 **4** *6* **The Osteopath (IRE)**[8] 6990 8-9-2 77 ....(p) TomEaves 5 68
(Michael Dods) *chsd ldrs: effrt and chsd wnr over 1f out to ent fnl f: sn wknd* **14/1**

0500 **5** *4 1/2* **Daring Dream (GER)**[42] 6148 6-9-2 77 .... DanielTudhope 10 58
(Jim Goldie) *dropped to rr gp after 2f: rdn and hung lft over 2f out: nvr rchd ldrs* **11/1**

1132 **6** *4 1/2* **Swiftly Done (IRE)**[44] 6078 4-9-5 85 ....(b) NeilFarley(5) 7 56
(Declan Carroll) *chsd ldrs: wnt 2nd 3f out to over 1f out: sn wknd* **9/2**[3]

4045 **7** *4 1/2* **Arabian Spirit**[22] 6672 6-9-12 87 ....(p) PaulHanagan 3 48
(Richard Fahey) *chsd wnr: rdn over 3f out: wknd over 2f out* **7/2**[2]

4030 **8** *42* **Silver Rime (FR)**[42] 6148 6-9-1 83 .... RossSmith(7) 11 —
(Linda Perratt) *dwlt: bhd: struggling over 3f out: sn lost tch: t.o* **14/1**

2-05 **9** *7* **Full Toss**[32] 6429 5-8-7 75 .... JasonHart(7) 4 —
(Jim Goldie) *sn bhd: struggling over 4f out: lost tch over 3f out: t.o* **25/1**

2m 14.52s (134.52) **9** Ran SP% **111.6**
toteswingers:1&2:£18.90, 1&3:£15.70, 2&3:£4.80 CSF £45.46 CT £240.88 TOTE £13.90: £3.70, £1.60, £2.10; EX 61.10.
Owner You Trotters **Bred** Limetree Stud Ltd **Trained** Stainforth, S Yorks

FOCUS
This looked quite a competitive heat and it was run at a good gallop, given the conditions. The winner is rated back to his 2009 form with the second progressive and the third slightly below his best from the front.

NOTEBOOK
European Dream(IRE) has always appreciated getting his toe in and, back with Richard Guest and having his first start since May, he returned to winning form, benefiting from sitting well off the pace in the early stages and being brought with his challenge between horses inside the last. He's fairly handicapped over hurdles at the moment so could strike in that sphere if building on this. (op 8-1)
Scrapper Smith(IRE), at home in soft ground, was chasing a hat-trick off a 2lb higher mark. Like the winner, he benefited from sitting well off the strong pace up front and had every chance. (tchd 3-1 and 7-2)
Flipping ◆ went too fast early and set things up for a closer. The fact that he was able to hang on for third suggests he would have won with a slightly less aggressive ride, and he's clearly on a mark he should be able to win off, granted this sort of ground. Connections will have to wait for next spring now, however. (op 13-2)
The Osteopath(IRE) was one of the trio who chased the strong pace set by the third, so can have his effort upgraded slightly.
Daring Dream(GER) raced with the first two in the group that was ridden with more patience. He's been out of form lately, though. (tchd 12-1)
Swiftly Done(IRE) chase the leader and paid the price.
Arabian Spirit also did too much too soon. (op 9-2)

7162 JOHN SMITH'S EXTRA SMOOTH H'CAP 1m 7f
4:40 (4:43) (Class 4) (0-85,85) 3-Y-O+ **£4,204** (£1,251; £625; £312) **Stalls** Far side

Form RPR
3-02 **1** **Sphinx (FR)**[43] 6115 13-8-13 70 ....(b) PaulHanagan 2 78
(Edwin Tuer) *in tch: smooth hdwy to ld over 2f out: rdn and r.o strly fr over 1f out* **5/4**[1]

5034 **2** *4* **Chookie Hamilton**[15] 6838 7-9-3 74 .... DavidAllan 3 77
(Keith Dalgleish) *trckd ldrs: chal over 3f out to over 2f out: kpt on same pce fnl f* **12/1**

0150 **3** *2 3/4* **The Oil Magnate**[18] 6780 6-9-0 71 .... TomEaves 6 70
(Michael Dods) *hld up last but in tch: effrt over 2f out: no imp fr over 1f out* **6/1**[3]

0214 **4** *6* **Pertemps Networks**[22] 6676 7-9-6 77 .... GrahamGibbons 1 68
(Michael Easterby) *led at stdy gallop: rdn and hdd over 2f out: wknd over 1f out* **5/2**[2]

6/ **5** *3 3/4* **Vivaldi (IRE)**[50] 5907 6-9-7 85 .... LAMcKenna(7) 4 72
(J J Lambe, Ire) *in tch: rdn over 2f out: wknd wl over 1f out* **28/1**

-006 **6** *13* **Graceful Descent (FR)**[42] 6151 6-9-3 74 .... DanielTudhope 5 44
(Jim Goldie) *t.k.h: trckd ldrs: struggling wl over 2f out: sn btn: t.o* **6/1**[3]

3m 58.2s (37.80) **6** Ran SP% **112.7**
toteswingers:1&2:£2.40, 1&3:£1.80, 2&3:£5.20 CSF £17.59 TOTE £2.20: £1.40, £2.70; EX 12.40.
Owner Ontoawinner **Bred** Martyn Arbib **Trained** Great Smeaton, N Yorks

FOCUS
There was a flip start to this stayers' event and they went steady early. The winner is rated to form with the rest below their best.

7163 SANDY ABBOTT 60TH BIRTHDAY H'CAP 1m 6f
5:15 (5:16) (Class 5) (0-70,70) 3-Y-O+ **£2,264** (£673; £336; £168) **Stalls** Far side

Form RPR
4615 **1** **River Dragon (IRE)**[12] 6915 6-9-2 63 .... BarryMcHugh 3 70
(Tony Coyle) *mde virtually all: niggled over 4f out: rdn over 2f out: hld on wl fnl f* **2/1**[2]

-553 **2** *1 3/4* **Lady Bluesky**[18] 6780 8-8-11 63 .... GarryWhillans(5) 5 68
(Alistair Whillans) *pressed wnr: rdn and ev ch over 2f out: kpt on same pce ins fnl f* **7/4**[1]

0302 **3** *nk* **Pokfulham (IRE)**[33] 6419 5-9-4 65 ....(v) DanielTudhope 4 70
(Jim Goldie) *t.k.h: prom: effrt over 2f out: edgd lft and kpt on same pce ins fnl f* **7/2**[3]

52/1 **4** *39* **Hunting Tower**[31] 6451 7-9-9 70 ....(t) PaulHanagan 1 20
(J J Lambe, Ire) *trckd ldrs: struggling 3f out: sn btn* **11/2**

3m 39.8s (219.80) **4** Ran SP% **107.3**
CSF £5.78 TOTE £2.50; EX 6.20.
Owner Brian Kerr & Tony Coyle **Bred** Barronstown Stud And Cobra Bloodstock **Trained** Norton, N Yorks

FOCUS
Another flip start and a steady early gallop. The winner was back to form, rated to a similar mark as when beating the second at Newcastle.
T/Plt: £10.90 to a £1 stake. Pool:£46,729.61 - 3.124.57 winning tickets. T/Qpdt: £4.90 to a £1 stake. Pool:£2,777.53 - 414.40 winning tickets. RY

7132 NEWMARKET (R-H)
Saturday, October 29

OFFICIAL GOING: Good (8.4)
Stands' side track used with stalls on stands' side for all races.
Wind: Fairly light, across Weather: Light cloud, bright spells

7164 E B F "MAKFI" MAIDEN FILLIES' STKS (DIV I) 7f
1:00 (1:01) (Class 4) 2-Y-O **£4,398** (£1,309; £654; £327) **Stalls** High

Form RPR
1 **Starscope** 2-9-0 0 .... NickyMackay 6 86+
(John Gosden) *dwlt: sn rcvrd and in tch in midfield: rn green and edgd rt over 2f out: shkn up to chse ldrs 2f out: rdn to ld over 1f out: styd on strly and drew clr fnl f: rdn out* **20/1**

30 **2** *2 3/4* **Coplow**[28] 6526 2-9-0 0 .... RichardHughes 5 79
(Richard Hannon) *dwlt: t.k.h early: hld up in tch: hdwy to ld and crossed to stands' rail 5f out: rdn and hdd over 1f out: nt pce of wnr and styd on same pce fnl f* **7/4**[1]

53 **3** *1 1/2* **Cockney Rhyme**[8] 6984 2-9-0 0 .... EddieAhern 11 75
(Heather Main) *chsd ldrs: nt clr run and swtchd rt wl over 1f out: kpt on u.p but no threat to wnr ins fnl f* **20/1**

022 **4** *3/4* **Balady (IRE)**[35] 6329 2-9-0 83 .... RichardHills 3 73
(John Dunlop) *in tch: hdwy to press ldr over 4f out: ev ch and rdn over 1f out: unable qck and btn jst ins fnl f: wknd fnl 100yds* **9/4**[2]

0 **5** *1 3/4* **Top Frock (IRE)**[31] 6463 2-9-0 0 .... AdamKirby 7 69
(Clive Cox) *taken down early: led for 2f: chsd ldrs after: rdn and unabe to qckn 2f out: sn outpcd and btn 1f out* **25/1**

6 *nk* **Valley Queen** 2-9-0 0 .... DaneO'Neill 9 68
(Mark Usher) *dwlt and flashing tail early: in tch in midfield: rdn and outpcd over 2f out: no threat to ldrs fnl 2f* **150/1**

7 *3/4* **Saaboog** 2-9-0 0 .... TedDurcan 2 68+
(David Lanigan) *hld up in last trio: outpcd 1/2-way: sme prog but no threat to ldrs whn hmpd and swtchd rt wl over 1f out: nvr trbld ldrs* **18/1**

3 **8** *1/2* **Frosty Secret**[30] 6480 2-9-0 0 .... LukeMorris 10 65
(Jane Chapple-Hyam) *chsd ldrs: rdn and struggling 1/2-way: wknd over 2f out* **20/1**

9 *2 1/4* **Muzdaan (IRE)** 2-9-0 0 .... AndreaAtzeni 12 59
(Roger Varian) *in tch in midfield: rdn and outpcd 1/2-way: bhd fnl 2f* **12/1**

10 *1 1/4* **Fleur De Cactus (IRE)** 2-9-0 0 .... RyanMoore 8 55
(Sir Michael Stoute) *a in rr: rdn and struggling 1/2-way: n.d after* **15/2**[3]

11 *1 3/4* **Proximity** 2-9-0 0 .... RichardMullen 1 51
(Sir Michael Stoute) *dwlt: hld up towards rr: outpcd 1/2-way and n.d after* **20/1**

12 *1 1/4* **Astrogold** 2-9-0 0 .... TomQueally 13 48
(Mark H Tompkins) *a in rr: rn green and outpcd 1/2-way: bhd over 2f out* **80/1**

1m 26.15s (0.75) **Going Correction** -0.05s/f (Good) **12** Ran SP% **116.6**
Speed ratings (Par 94): **93,89,88,87,85 84,84,83,80,79 77,76**
toteswingers:1&2:£14.10, 1&3:£34.90, 2&3:£7.30 CSF £51.26 TOTE £29.20: £5.40, £1.20, £3.60; EX 108.90 TRIFECTA Not won..
Owner Cheveley Park Stud **Bred** Cheveley Park Stud Ltd **Trained** Newmarket, Suffolk

FOCUS
Sariska took a division of this fillies' maiden in 2008 and Dar Re Mi was narrowly beaten on her debut the year before. The winner of this year's first division certainly made the best possible start. The stalls were placed against the stands' rail and the field stayed there. The winner was quite impressive and can rate higher but the third looks the best guide at this stage.

NOTEBOOK
Starscope ◆, out of a winning half-sister to Medicean, was full of herself behind the stalls beforehand and saw a lot of daylight on the outside of the field once under way, but she produced a telling turn of foot to hit the front before the furlong pole and soon bounded clear. She looks a nice prospect for next year and is a top-priced 33-1 for the 1000 Guineas. The extra furlong won't be a problem. (op 25-1)
Coplow hung badly due to a cut mouth when a disappointing third-favourite for the Tattersalls Millions 2yo Fillies' Trophy here earlier in the month, but her jockey was very bullish about her chances here beforehand. She did well to cross over from her low draw in front and took some passing, but she came up against an unexposed rival who proved much too good. She now gets a mark. (op 15-8 tchd 2-1)
Cockney Rhyme had shown ability in her first two starts, even though it looked as though she might have been flattered by her 40-1 third of 11 at Doncaster last time due to a slow pace, but this staying-on performance suggests otherwise and she can now be handicapped. (op 28-1)

Balady(IRE) set the standard with an official mark of 83 having finished runner-up in her two previous starts, but she had every chance before tiring and doesn't seem to be moving forward. (tchd 5-2 and 11-4 in a place)

Top Frock(IRE) didn't get home over 1m on her Salisbury debut and ran a bit better over this shorter trip, but she looks one for handicaps later on. (op 33-1 tchd 20-1)

Valley Queen ◆, half-sister to a winner over 1m2f, looked very green beforehand but she was noted staying on in pleasing fashion towards the end and her trainer expects her to be a much stronger filly next year.

Saaboog ◆, an 80,000gns filly out of a 6f winner, was never going to win but she may have been a bit closer with a clearer run and her rider was by no means hard on her. She is one to note for next year. (op 20-1 tchd 14-1)

Frosty Secret, green when third of ten on her Warwick debut, didn't step up from that and was in trouble a long way out. (op 18-1 tchd 16-1)

Proximity, a sister to the smart Confront and a half-sister to three other winners, was far too green to do herself justice on this debut. (tchd 22-1 and 28-1 in places)

7165 E B F "MAKFI" MAIDEN FILLIES' STKS (DIV II) 7f

1:30 (1:32) (Class 4) 2-Y-O **£4,398** (£1,309; £654; £327) **Stalls** High

Form RPR

1 **The Fugue** 2-9-0 0 RobertHavlin 10 90+
(John Gosden) *dwlt: racd in centre: hld up towards rr: stdy prog fr 4f out: chsd ldr 2f out: drew clr of field and chal over 1f out: led ins fnl f: styd on wl: pushed out* **14/1**

6 2 1 ½ **Salacia (IRE)**[11] 6933 2-9-0 0 FrankieDettori 8 86
(Mahmood Al Zarooni) *racd in centre: led: clr 1/2-way: hrd pressed and rdn over 1f out: hdd ins fnl f: no ex but kpt on for clr 2nd: 2nd of 9 in gp* **3/1**[2]

0 3 7 **Dutch Diamond**[10] 6950 2-9-0 0 NickyMackay 6 68
(John Gosden) *racd in centre: in tch: rdn to chse ldng pair but outpcd 2f out: no imp and wl btn after: 3rd of 9 in gp* **16/1**

32 4 ¾ **No Compromise**[19] 6743 2-9-0 0 JimmyFortune 13 66
(Hughie Morrison) *racd on stands' rail chsd ldrs overall: rdn and unable qck over 2f out: 4th and wl btn over 1f out: 1st of 3 in gp* **11/4**[1]

5 ¾ **Keene Dancer** 2-9-0 0 RyanMoore 12 64
(Sir Michael Stoute) *hld up on stands' side tl swtchd to centre gp over 4f out: outpcd and rdn 1/2-way: plugged on but no ch w ldrs fnl 2f: 4th of 9 in gp* **15/2**[3]

6 ¾ **Pomarine (USA)** 2-9-0 0 TomQueally 7 62+
(Amanda Perrett) *racd in centre: t.k.h: hld up in midfield: rdn and outpcd 1/2-way: no threat to ldrs but kpt on again ins fnl f: 5th of 9 in gp* **25/1**

0 7 nse **Santarini (IRE)**[93] 4471 2-9-0 0 RichardHughes 4 63
(Richard Hannon) *racd in centre: chsd ldr tl over 2f out: sn outpcd and btn: wkng whn hmpd wl over 1f out: 6th of 9 in gp* **15/2**[3]

8 nk **Al Baidaa** 2-9-0 0 AndreaAtzeni 5 61
(Roger Varian) *racd in centre: in tch in midfield: rdn and outpcd 3f out: no threat to ldrs and plugged on same pce fnl 2f: 7th of 9 in gp* **12/1**

00 9 3 **Melodrama (IRE)**[11] 6928 2-9-0 0 TedDurcan 2 53
(David Lanigan) *racd in centre: a towards rr: rdn and stuggling 1/2-way: no ch after: 8th of 9 in gp* **50/1**

10 hd **Heyaaraat (IRE)** 2-9-0 0 RichardHills 11 53
(Charles Hills) *racd on stands' rail: in tch overall: rdn and effrt over 2f out: wknd qckly wl over 1f out: 2nd of 3 in gp* **8/1**

11 2 **Cape Crossing** 2-9-0 0 DavidProbert 9 48
(Andrew Balding) *racd on stands' rail: hld up in tch: hdwy and rdn 1/2-way: wknd 2f out: 3rd of 3 in gp* **16/1**

12 46 **Chateau Lola** 2-9-0 0 DaneO'Neill 1 —
(Derek Shaw) *racd in centre: s.i.s: sn outpcd: t.o fr 1/2-way: 9th of 9 in gp* **100/1**

1m 25.39s (-0.01) **Going Correction** -0.05s/f (Good) **12** Ran SP% **119.2**
Speed ratings (Par 94): **98,96,88,87,86 85,85,85,81,81 79,26**
toteswingers: 1&2 £11.90, 1&3 £35.40, 2&3 £15.90. CSF £55.70 TOTE £21.20: £5.60, £1.70, £3.30; EX 94.40 Trifecta £637.20 Part won. Pool: £861.19 - 0.72 winning units..
Owner Lord Lloyd-Webber **Bred** Watership Down Stud **Trained** Newmarket, Suffolk

FOCUS

Only five of the runners had previous experience in this second leg of this fillies' maiden but the time was 0.76secs faster than the first division. The first two came well clear and the form looks decent.

NOTEBOOK

The Fugue ◆, a half-sister to a winner at up to 2m out of a Ribblesdale runner-up who is a half-sister to Summoner and Compton Admiral, looked sure to benefit from the outing beforehand and was tardy leaving the stalls. However, she moved up to track the leader going well, and from the Dip it was clear that she was going to reel in the leader. She looks sure to improve with time and a longer distance, and could possibly make up into a Group-class performer next season, although quotes of between 20-1 and 33-1 for the Oaks are not particularly generous at this stage.

Salacia(IRE), a half-sister to decent winners at 6f-1m4f had made a promising debut over a 1m at Yarmouth but did not get home there. The drop in trip here was in her favour but she probably again did too much early, as she was clear 2f out before being run down. That said, she finished some way in front of the rest. (op 9-2 tchd 5-1)

Dutch Diamond was slowly away and well beaten in a maiden here earlier in the month but had clearly come on for that and ran creditably, staying on after coming under pressure around 3f from home. (op 22-1 tchd 25-1 in a place)

No Compromise had made a promising debut over 7f on Polytrack but was touched off after looking the winner at Salisbury next time. She set the standard on that form and led the trio up the stands' rail, but was never on terms with the group in the centre and finished well held. At least she qualifies for handicaps now. (op 5-2 tchd 3-1)

Keene Dancer, the third foal of Prix de L'Opera winner Kinnaird and a half-sister to a 1m4f AW winner, made a promising debut staying on steadily late and should benefit from the experience. (op 9-1)

Santarini(IRE) was well backed but finished last of 17 on her debut in a Goodwood maiden and had been off since. She tracked the leader before losing her place over 2f out but then ran on again. (op 6-1 tchd 11-2)

Heyaaraat(IRE), a 48,000gns first foal of a half-sister to eight winners from a high-class staying family of the Aga Khan's, travelled quite well in the nearside trio but appeared to hang in the final quarter-mile. (op 15-2)

7166 NOVAE BLOODSTOCK INSURANCE BEN MARSHALL STKS (LISTED RACE) 1m

2:05 (2:05) (Class 1) 3-Y-0+

£17,013 (£6,450; £3,228; £1,608; £807; £405) **Stalls** High

Form RPR

0422 1 **Secrecy**[10] 6955 5-9-0 109 (p) KierenFallon 3 111
(Saeed Bin Suroor) *racd in centre: mde virtually all: clr w rival 3f out: rdn and hung rt fr 2f out: clr over 1f out: styd on wl* **9/2**[2]

1-41 2 4 ½ **Samurai Sword**[176] 1843 3-8-11 94 SilvestreDeSousa 9 101+
(Mahmood Al Zarooni) *racd on stands' side: hld up towards rr: rdn and hung rt to join main gp fr over 2f out: 6th and wl btn over 1f out: kpt on to go 2nd towards fin: no ch w wnr* **6/1**[3]

0400 3 ½ **Maali (IRE)**[21] 6693 3-8-11 94 (bt) TomQueally 7 100
(Clive Brittain) *racd in centre: racd in midfield: rdn to chse clr ldng trio 2f out: plugged on but no threat to wnr* **33/1**

12-1 4 shd **Ecliptic (USA)**[19] 6747 3-8-11 107 FrankieDettori 5 99
(Mahmood Al Zarooni) *taken down early: racd in centre: stdd s: t.k.h and hld up towards rr: rdn and effrt over 2f out: 4th and wl btn over 1f out: kpt on to chse clr wnr ins fnl f: no imp and lost 2 pls cl home* **5/6**[1]

0500 5 3 ¾ **Loving Spirit**[37] 6273 3-8-11 90 (b[1]) RobertHavlin 1 91
(James Toller) *racd in centre: t.k.h: sn chsng wnr: clr of field 3f out: rdn and edgd rt fr 2f out: swtchd lft and btn over 1f out: fdd ins fnl f* **28/1**

-150 6 3 ¼ **Confront**[92] 4494 6-9-0 107 RyanMoore 2 83
(Sir Michael Stoute) *racd in centre: hld up towards rr: rdn and effrt wl over 2f out: no imp and wl btn 2f out* **13/2**

050 7 2 ¾ **Mac Love**[79] 4972 10-9-0 102 SteveDrowne 6 77
(Roger Charlton) *racd in centre: stdd s: t.k.h: hld up in rr: rdn and no hdwy wl over 2f out: wl btn fnl 2f* **28/1**

4000 8 ¾ **Irish Flame (SAF)**[217] 1001 5-9-0 111 RichardHughes 8 75
(M F De Kock, South Africa) *racd on stands' side: chsd overall ldrs: rdn and struggling 3f out sn hung rt and jnd main gp: wknd over 2f out* **16/1**

53- 9 4 **Ocean Bay**[462] 4375 3-8-12 95 ow1 AdamKirby 4 67
(John Ryan) *racd in centre: in tch in midfield: rdn and struggling over 3f out: wknd wl over 2f out* **66/1**

1m 36.7s (-1.90) **Going Correction** -0.05s/f (Good)
WFA 3 from 5yo+ 3lb **9** Ran SP% **117.6**
Speed ratings (Par 111): **107,102,102,101,98 94,92,91,87**
toteswingers: 1&2 £3.30, 1&3 £11.90, 2&3 £17.00. CSF £30.89 TOTE £5.60: £1.50, £2.00, £4.80; EX 25.70 Trifecta £430.30 Pool: £1,529.55 - 2.63 winning units..
Owner Godolphin **Bred** Whatton Manor Stud **Trained** Newmarket, Suffolk

FOCUS

A fair Listed race in which 3yos had taken six of the previous eight runnings, but this was one for the older brigade. The main group raced down the centre of the track early, whilst two stayed against the stands' rail, but all the runners gradually edged to their right and ended up closer to the far rail. Godolphin were strongly represented here (as they often are in such races at this time of year) with three of the nine runners spread between their two trainers, and they ended up first, second and fourth. There are doubts over this form with the third and fifth not convincing as having shown improved form.

NOTEBOOK

Secrecy, whose participation depended on the ground being suitable, had cheekpieces on for the first time and was ridden very differently to when runner-up over C&D ten days earlier. Soon at the head of the main group out in the centre, he hung way to his right inside the last 2f, but was already clear by that stage and never looked like being caught. (tchd 4-1)

Samurai Sword ◆, last seen winning an Ascot handicap off 85 in May, started off by tracking Irish Flame (the pair racing by themselves against the stands' rail) before edging over to join the other runners inside the last 2f. He didn't appear to handle the Dip too well, but ran on again up the rising ground to just grab second. He looks the type for a Dubai campaign in the new year. (op 9-1)

Maali(IRE), 0-7 coming into this having faced some stiff tasks in recent months, faced another one here but plugged on to grab third and record probably his best effort yet. He could probably do with a confidence-booster back in a maiden, however.

Ecliptic(USA) made a successful return from 458 days off at Salisbury earlier this month, but merely plugged on again after getting outpaced 2f from home on this occasion. The dreaded 'bounce' may have been a factor. (op 10-11 tchd evens and 4-5 in places)

Loving Spirit, disappointing since finishing ninth in the 2000 Guineas and worst off at the weights, may have done too much early in the first-time blinkers. (op 33-1)

Confront hadn't been seen since finishing well beaten in a handicap at Glorious Goodwood, but has won twice following much longer absences so this timid effort may suggest that he is just not as good as he was. (tchd 7-1)

Mac Love, a remarkable 10-y-o having his 74th start, never got into the race and time may finally be catching up with him. (op 25-1)

Irish Flame(SAF), having his first start in this country and not seen since finishing seventh behind Rewilding in the Sheema Classic, was the one to beat on official ratings but he faded tamely after leading the eventual runner-up against the stands' rail to the 2f pole and then hanging. His trainer was worried about the trip perhaps being too short and the Hong Kong Vase is apparently his target, but it would still have been nice to see more from him here. Official explanation: jockey said horse hung right (op 12-1)

Ocean Bay was returning from an absence of 462 days after three outings at two and appeared to blow up. Connections had an eye on a race in France next month for him, but he will need to step up considerably from this.

7167 LAUNDRY COTTAGE STUD FARM ZETLAND CONDITIONS STKS 1m 2f

2:40 (2:40) (Class 3) 2-Y-O

£7,158 (£2,143; £1,071; £535; £267; £134) **Stalls** High

Form RPR

01 1 **Mojave (IRE)**[18] 6772 2-9-0 85 FrankieDettori 3 97
(Mahmood Al Zarooni) *taken down early: racd towards centre: chsd ldrs: rdn to ld 2f out: sn edgd lft u.p: clr 1f out: fnd ex whn pressed fnl 75yds: styd on* **2/1**[1]

0212 2 ¾ **Repeater**[25] 6606 2-9-0 86 SebSanders 6 96
(Sir Mark Prescott Bt) *stdd s: hld up in rr: clsd 5f out: rdn to chse clr wnr over 1f out: edgd lft but styd on fnl f: swtchd rt and pressing wnr fnl 75yds: no ex and hld towards fin* **11/4**[2]

151 3 6 **Rougemont (IRE)**[25] 6606 2-9-3 85 RichardHughes 5 87
(Richard Hannon) *in tch: rdn and unable qck 3f out: 6th and wl hld over 1f out: plugged on u.p to go modest 3rd ins fnl f: no ch w ldng pair* **6/1**

2003 4 1 **Hazaz (IRE)**[7] 7026 2-9-0 101 TomQueally 7 83
(Clive Brittain) *hld up in tch: rdn and effrt over 2f out: no imp and no threat to ldng pair over 1f out: plugged on fnl f* **4/1**[3]

0310 5 4 ½ **Stellar Express (IRE)**[8] 6986 2-8-9 78 NeilChalmers 4 69
(Michael Appleby) *led and crossed to r on stands' rail: rdn and hdd 2f out: sn outpcd and btn: fdd fnl f* **28/1**

001 6 nk **Bank On Me**[10] 6956 2-9-0 82 (t) RyanMoore 2 73
(Philip McBride) *racd towards centre: chsd ldrs tl rdn and wknd over 2f out* **11/1**

02 7 13 **Ocean Tempest**[96] 4390 2-9-0 0 KierenFallon 8 49
(John Ryan) *hld up in tch towards rr: rdn and wknd over 2f out: sn bhd* **16/1**

8 dist **Orinocco** 2-8-12 0 ow1 AdamKirby 1 —
(John Ryan) *sn detached in last: t.o and virtually p.u fnl 3f* **100/1**

2m 4.99s (-0.81) **Going Correction** -0.05s/f (Good) **8** Ran SP% **112.9**
Speed ratings (Par 99): **101,100,95,94,91 90,80,—**
toteswingers: 1&2 £2.10, 1&3 £3.00, 2&3 £3.00. CSF £7.40 TOTE £2.60: £1.10, £1.30, £2.20; EX 8.50 Trifecta £15.50 Pool: £1,050.07 - 49.91 winning units..
Owner Godolphin **Bred** Mrs Eithne Hamilton **Trained** Newmarket, Suffolk

FOCUS
By far the best recent winner of this conditions stakes was the subsequent dual Champion Stakes and multiple Group 1 winner Twice Over. None of this year's runners looked likely to emulate that one but it looked an interesting contest just the same. As usual it proved a real stamina test for these juveniles and two drew clear. The first two looks improvers and the form should prove sound.

NOTEBOOK
Mojave(IRE) ◆, a 200,000gns half-brother to six winners, including the high-class Dubai Prince, had stepped up on his debut to win a 1m Leicester maiden and built on that over this longer trip. Always travelling well up the centre, he went on going into the Dip and stayed on strongly to hold off the runner-up. He clearly gets the stamina from his dam, who stayed 1m5f, and can develop into a decent middle-distance performer next season. (op 9-4)

Repeater, a dual winner before being narrowly beaten by Rougemont over this trip last time, was 3lb better off with that rival and more than reversed the form with a truer gallop this time. He came through to chase the winner and was gradually closing on the climb to the line. He looks a dour galloper and should get staying trips. (op 10-3 tchd 7-2)

Rougemont(IRE), a dual winner including at this trip on fast ground, was 3lb worse off with Repeater having narrowly defeated that colt last time. However, he came under pressure some way from home and could only stay on at the one pace. (tchd 11-2)

Hazaz(IRE) posted his best effort when third in the Group 3 Horris Hill the previous week, which gave him a clear chance on official ratings. However, he was also taking a big step up in distance and never got seriously into contention. (op 7-2)

Stellar Express(IRE), a dual winner at up to 1m on fast and easy ground, had a fair bit to find on the ratings. She cut out the running until headed by the winner but was quickly beaten. (op 25-1)

Bank On Me improved for the fitting of a tongue tie when taking a maiden over 1m here earlier in the month but did not appear to last home over this longer distance, although he was probably outclassed in any case. (op 12-1 tchd 10-1)

Orinocco Official explanation: jockey said colt moved poorly

7168 HOME OF RACING H'CAP — 1m
3:15 (3:16) (Class 3) (0-95,95) 3-Y-0+

£8,092 (£2,423; £1,211; £605; £302; £152) **Stalls** High

Form — RPR

1- **1** **Farhh**[462] 4375 3-8-13 **90** SilvestreDeSousa 7 107+
(Saeed Bin Suroor) *racd on far side: hld up in tch: hdwy and nt clr run wl over 1f out: rdn to chse ldr jst over 1f out: led ins fnl f: sn in command and r.o strly: readily* **12/1**[3]

00 **2** 2 ½ **Roayh (USA)**[21] 6704 3-9-1 **92** FrankieDettori 11 100
(Saeed Bin Suroor) *racd far side: hld up in tch: hdwy to press ldrs 2f out: rdn to ld over 1f out: hdd and nt pce of wnr ins fnl f: styd on same pce: 2nd of 12 in gp* **16/1**

2632 **3** nk **Double Dealer**[50] 5892 3-8-12 **89** EddieAhern 5 101+
(Mahmood Al Zarooni) *racd far side: hld up in tch towards rr: hdwy 2f out: nt clr run over 1f out: swtchd rt and r.o wl ins fnl f: pressing for 2nd cl home: 3rd of 12 in gp* **11/1**[2]

1111 **4** 1 ½ **Diverting**[26] 6574 3-8-9 **86** LeeNewman 8 90
(William Jarvis) *racd far side: hld up in tch towards rr: rdn and hdwy over 2f out: n.m.r over 1f out: chsd ldng pair 1f out: styd on same pce after: 4th of 12 in gp* **16/1**

50-0 **5** shd **Mull Of Killough (IRE)**[35] 6335 5-9-4 **92** TonyHamilton 20 96+
(Richard Fahey) *racd in centre: hld up in tch: hdwy 3f out: rdn to ld gp and chsd ldrs overall 2f out: edgd rt u.p and styd on same pce fnl f: 1st of 8 in gp* **25/1**

022 **6** 2 **Robemaker**[36] 6290 3-9-0 **91** RobertHavlin 12 90
(John Gosden) *racd far side: in tch in midfield: rdn and effrt to chse ldrs 2f out: unable qck over 1f out: plugged on same pce and no threat to ldrs fnl f: 5th of 12 in gp* **14/1**

3033 **7** hd **Viva Vettori**[21] 6708 7-8-11 **85** (p) NickyMackay 9 84
(David Elsworth) *racd on far side: stdd s: hld up in rr: switching lft and effrt wl over 1f out: styng on whn swtchd lft again ins fnl f: kpt on: nt rch ldrs: 6th of 12 in gp* **16/1**

5-10 **8** 1 **Alakhan (IRE)**[36] 6290 5-8-12 **86** TomQueally 19 82
(Ian Williams) *racd in centre: hld up towards rr: hdwy 3f out: rdn and chsd gp ldr 2f out: edgd rt and styd on same pce fr over 1f out: 2nd of 8 in gp* **25/1**

5040 **9** 2 **Duster**[14] 6862 4-8-12 **86** RichardHughes 1 78
(Hughie Morrison) *racd on far side: overall ldr tl rdn and hdd over 1f out: wknd fnl f: 7th of 12 in gp* **22/1**

14 **10** shd **Dubawi Sound**[34] 6374 3-8-11 **88** JimmyFortune 10 79+
(Roger Varian) *racd on far side: awkward leaving stalls and s.i.s: hld up bhd: hdwy over 3f out: effrt to chse ldrs over 2f out: wknd over 1f out: 8th of 12 in gp* **3/1**[1]

4001 **11** 2 **Oriental Scot**[36] 6290 4-8-10 **84** JoeFanning 2 71
(William Jarvis) *racd on far side: awkward leaving stalls and s.i.s: hld up in rr: switching lft over 2f out: kpt on fnl f: nvr trbld ldrs: 9th of 12 in gp* **25/1**

6110 **12** ½ **Directorship**[14] 6862 5-9-2 **90** FergusSweeney 15 76
(Patrick Chamings) *racd in centre: hld up in rr: rdn and effrt 3f out: no prog u.p wl over 1f out: n.d after: 3rd of 8 in gp* **16/1**

2200 **13** ¾ **Afkar (IRE)**[7] 7023 3-8-5 **82** (b[1]) ChrisCatlin 3 66
(Clive Brittain) *racd on far side: chsd overall ldr 2f out: sn wknd: 10th of 12 in gp* **50/1**

3110 **14** shd **Stage Attraction (IRE)**[98] 4313 3-8-10 **87** DavidProbert 18 71
(Andrew Balding) *racd in centre: in tch: rdn 3f out: wknd u.p 2f out: 4th of 8 in gp* **16/1**

0364 **15** nk **Tuscania**[29] 6495 3-8-11 **88** RyanMoore 4 71
(Sir Michael Stoute) *racd on far side: chsd ldrs tl wknd u.p 2f out: no ch fnl f: 11th of 12 in gp* **14/1**

1150 **16** hd **Making Eyes (IRE)**[35] 6330 3-8-8 **85** KierenFallon 17 68
(Hugo Palmer) *racd in centre: led gp and chsd ldrs overall tl over 2f out: sn wknd u.p: 5th of 8 in gp* **12/1**[3]

0616 **17** 1 ½ **Indian Jack (IRE)**[29] 6495 3-8-12 **89** RichardMullen 13 68
(Alan Bailey) *racd in centre: midfield overall: rdn and no hdwy over 3f out: wknd over 2f out: 6th of 8 in gp* **16/1**

0044 **18** ¾ **Benandonner (USA)**[28] 6541 8-8-13 **87** MartinLane 14 64
(Mike Murphy) *racd in centre: chsd ldrs: rdn 1/2-way: wknd over 2f out: 7th of 8 in gp* **33/1**

01-0 **19** ¾ **Make A Dance (USA)**[181] 1719 3-8-9 **86** MichaelHills 6 62
(Charles Hills) *racd on far side: chsd ldrs tl wknd u.p over 2f out: bhd fnl f: 12th of 12 in gp* **16/1**

-416 **20** 6 **Justonefortheroad**[170] 2031 5-9-4 **95** LeeTopliss(3) 16 57
(Richard Fahey) *racd in centre: hld up towards rr: rdn and struggling over 3f out: wknd over 2f out: 8th of 8 in gp* **20/1**

1m 36.28s (-2.32) **Going Correction** -0.05s/f (Good)
WFA 3 from 4yo+ 3lb **20** Ran SP% **128.8**
Speed ratings (Par 107): **109,106,106,104,104 102,102,101,99,99 97,96,96,95,95 95,93,93,92,86**
toteswingers: 1&2 £24.60, 1&3 £10.60, 2&3 £34.00. CSF £180.84 CT £2204.46 TOTE £12.80: £2.60, £4.00, £3.00, £3.50; EX 149.60 Trifecta £852.00 Pool: £1,957.41 - 1.70 winning units..
Owner Godolphin **Bred** Darley **Trained** Newmarket, Suffolk

FOCUS
Not surprisingly in a big field like this, the runners split into two groups with 12 racing against the far rail whilst the other eight raced centre-to-stands side. The far-side group provided the first four horses home and the leaders on both flanks may have gone off too quick, as none of them figured in the finish. A triumph for Godolphin with a 1-2-3 and the runner-up is probably the best guide, with the fourth and fifth close to form.

NOTEBOOK
Farhh ◆ was unraced since bolting up on his debut in a seven-runner maiden on the July Course 462 days earlier and the handicapper didn't have much to go on, so with hindsight a mark of 90 greatly underestimated his ability, especially as he gave most of his rivals a start here. He travelled very smoothly once under way, however, and his rider did well to weave him through the gaps before nailing his stable companion inside the last furlong and winning going away. He looks more than capable of winning something much better than this if kept sound. (op 11-1 tchd 9-1)

Roayh(USA), a smart juvenile but disappointing in four previous starts this year, seemed to be helped by this drop in trip and looked the likely winner when leading over a furlong out, but his much less-exposed stablemate then proved different gear.

Double Dealer ◆ was surrounded by subsequent winners when narrowly beaten at Sandown last month, but the handicapper noticed and hit him with a 6lb rise. However, he may have been unlucky not to go even closer here as, after travelling powerfully, he had nowhere to go between the 2f and 1f markers and by the time he saw daylight against the far rail, it was too late. Official explanation: jockey said colt was denied a clear run

Diverting has been a revelation in recent months and was bidding for a five-timer off a 5lb higher mark. She was having to be niggled along from some way out, but responded in typically game fashion and lost little in defeat. (tchd 18-1 in a place)

Mull Of Killough(IRE) ◆ showed little on his return from 465 days off and debut for the yard at Haydock last month, but this was a big improvement especially as he did much the best of those that raced in the nearside group. Third in last year's Lincoln for John Spearing, it will be interesting to see if his new yard aims him at the Doncaster feature again next spring. (tchd 33-1 in a place)

Robemaker had every chance on ground that would have been quick enough for him and reversed last month's narrow defeat by Oriental Scot on 1lb better terms.

Viva Vettori was slow to break and made some late headway, but he is now 0-27 on turf and probably needs further than this now.

Alakhan(IRE) ◆ may have 'bounced' when well-beaten at Haydock last month having made a successful return from 522 days off at Chester a fortnight earlier. Not much went right for him here as he was slow to break and found himself in the disadvantaged stands' side group. He also appeared to get unbalanced in the Dip, but finished well and this lightly raced 5-y-o still has more to offer. (op 28-1)

Dubawi Sound ◆ was a disappointing favourite at Epsom last month when reappearing from an absence of 162 days since his successful debut, but he didn't seem to handle the track. Slow to break, he then took a strong hold and an effort coming to the last 2f amounted to little. It may be best to forgive him this too, and he could do better still as a 4-y-o. (op 7-2 tchd 4-1)

Make A Dance(USA), winner of the first division of the fillies' maiden on this card last year, hadn't been seen since finishing 16th of the 18 runners in the 1000 Guineas, but she ran here as though the outing was needed. (op 11-1)

7169 E B F "MOUNT NELSON" MONTROSE FILLIES' STKS (LISTED RACE) — 1m
3:55 (3:55) (Class 1) 2-Y-0

£12,192 (£4,622; £2,313; £1,152; £578; £290) **Stalls** High

Form — RPR

41 **1** **Coquet**[21] 6697 2-8-12 75 RobertHavlin 11 95
(Hughie Morrison) *in tch: hdwy to chse ldr 3f out: rdn and chal over 1f out: led ins fnl f: battled on gamely and hld on wl fnl 100yds* **20/1**

1 **2** ½ **Abishena (IRE)**[25] 6603 2-8-12 79 SilvestreDeSousa 4 94
(Mark Johnston) *hld up in tch towards rr: hdwy over 2f out: chsd ldrs u.p over 1f out: wnt 2nd and pressing wnr ins fnl f: kpt on wl but hld towards fin* **4/1**[2]

2321 **3** ½ **Esentepe (IRE)**[53] 5807 2-8-12 80 DaneO'Neill 7 93
(Richard Hannon) *hld up in tch towards rr: rdn and effrt 2f out: hdwy u.p to chse ldrs 1f out: kpt on wl fnl f but no imp fnl 75yds* **14/1**

31 **4** 1 **Gifted Girl (IRE)**[93] 4471 2-8-12 83 KierenFallon 2 90
(Paul Cole) *dwlt: sn rcvrd and in tch: led and edgd lft 4f out: rdn and hrd pressed over 1f out: hdd jst ins fnl f: no ex and styd on same pce after* **8/1**[3]

01 **5** hd **Graser (IRE)**[16] 6818 2-8-12 76 AdamKirby 9 90
(Marco Botti) *hld up towards rr: stl plenty to do 2f out: switching rt u.p and hdwy over 1f out: kpt on ins fnl f: nt gng pce to rch ldrs* **14/1**

2210 **6** 2 **Na Zdorovie**[50] 5885 2-8-12 86 MichaelHills 3 85
(Charles Hills) *led tl 4f out: chsd ldrs after: rdn over 2f out: wknd jst over 1f out* **20/1**

1 **7** 4 **Oojooba**[35] 6329 2-8-12 88 RyanMoore 1 76
(Roger Varian) *chsd ldrs: rdn and unable qck ent fnl 2f: wknd over 1f out* **11/4**[1]

1 **8** 1 ¼ **Tactfully (IRE)**[31] 6458 2-8-12 85 FrankieDettori 6 73
(Mahmood Al Zarooni) *in tch in midfield: rdn over 3f out: nvr looked happy after and outpcd 3f out: wknd 2f out* **11/4**[1]

01 **9** nk **Amthal (IRE)**[16] 6819 2-8-12 66 SebSanders 8 73
(Clive Brittain) *stdd s: hld up in rr: effrt towards centre and rdn over 2f out: no prog and wknd wl over 1f out* **66/1**

5314 **10** 3 ½ **Dare To Dream**[35] 6340 2-8-12 78 RichardHughes 12 65
(Richard Hannon) *t.k.h: hld up in tch tl rdn and struggling over 3f out: bhd fnl 2f* **20/1**

661 **11** 14 **Pretty Pebble (IRE)**[30] 6480 2-8-12 74 MartinDwyer 10 40
(Brian Meehan) *t.k.h: chsd ldr tl 5f out: lost pl qckly 2f out: sn bhd: eased ins fnl f* **33/1**

1m 38.05s (-0.55) **Going Correction** -0.05s/f (Good) **11** Ran SP% **116.5**
Speed ratings (Par 100): **100,99,99,98,97 95,91,90,90,86 72**
toteswingers: 1&2 £14.40, 1&3 £21.40, 2&3 £10.90. CSF £92.68 TOTE £24.00: £5.00, £1.90, £3.40; EX 161.20 Trifecta £1095.20 Part won. Pool: £1,480.12 - 0.40 winning units..
Owner Hon Mary Morrison & Partners **Bred** Meon Valley Stud **Trained** East Ilsley, Berks
■ Stewards' Enquiry : Robert Havlin 14-day ban: used whip with excessive frequency (Nov 16-19,22-26,28-30,Dec 1-2)
Silvestre De Sousa five-day ban: used whip with excessive frequency (Nov 12,14-17)

FOCUS
The last two winners of this Listed contest have gone on to score at the highest level, both this season, with Timepiece winning the Falmouth Stakes and Blue Bunting taking the 1,000 Guineas, Irish and Yorkshire Oaks. This did not look that strong a field, with the highest official rating being 88, although nine of the 11 had won their previous start and the other two scored on their penultimate outing. The form looks weak for the grade and is rated cautiously, although there were several improvers.

NOTEBOOK
Coquet ◆ had finished fourth in a 1m Polytrack maiden on her debut and then followed up in a similar race at Wolverhampton. Making her turf debut, she responded well to pressure to hit the front entering the last furlong and then held off the challengers on her outside. She has a quality pedigree and her stud value is assured, but she might be open to improvement over further next season. Her rider picked up a 14-day ban for using his whip with excessive frequency. (op 16-1)
Abishena(IRE) overcame a slow start and a stumble to win a 7f maiden on her debut and put up a decent performance here, challenging from 2f out and finding more for pressure up the hill, although her pedigree suggests this may be near the limit of her stamina. Her rider picked up a five-day ban for excessive use of the whip. (op 6-1)
Esentepe(IRE) finished in the frame on all her starts before getting off the mark at the eighth attempt at Leicester last month. Stepping up in grade, she ran a decent race having been posted on the wide outside throughout. She earned valuable black type here and is probably a fair guide to the level. (op 16-1)
Gifted Girl(IRE) got off the mark next time at Goodwood in July but had been off since. She came through to show ahead around 3f out but had to give best on the rise to the line. She might be able to build on this although her rider reported that the filly hung left. Official explanation: jockey said filly hung left (op 15-2 tchd 7-1)
Graser(IRE) had improved on her debut effort to win a 7f Polytrack maiden and built on that again here. She had to give best to the winner when both went for a gap around 2f out but then ran on once in the clear, although without seriously threatening the principals. She is bred to stay a good deal further in time and may have more to offer next season. (op 18-1 tchd 20-1)
Na Zdorovie won a Chester maiden before being outclassed in the May Hill next time. She made the running here but looked set to drop away when headed only to run on again in the latter stages. (op 18-1)
Oojooba, a daughter of 1000 Guineas heroine Ameerat, had been a good winner on her debut over 1m on easy ground. She seemed to travel well enough in the slipstream of the leaders but failed to pick up when asked. (op 5-2 tchd 9-4 and 3-1 in a place)
Tactfully(IRE) easily beat a subsequent winner in a Nottingham maiden on her debut but she was one of the first to come under riding soon after halfway and could not respond. (tchd 3-1 and 10-3 in places)
Amthal(IRE) improved considerably for her debut run when winning a 7f maiden on Polytrack but missed the break and her rider reported that the filly lost her action. Official explanation: jockey said filly lost its action
Pretty Pebble(IRE) Official explanation: jockey said filly had no more to give

7170 JAMES SEYMOUR STKS (LISTED RACE) 1m 2f
4:25 (4:25) (Class 1) 3-Y-0+
£17,013 (£6,450; £3,228; £1,608; £807; £405) **Stalls** High

Form / RPR

3302 **1** **Slumber**[49] 5934 3-8-12 103 .... MichaelHills 8 114
(Charles Hills) *racd alone against stands' rail pressed overall ldr: led 3f out: rdn and kpt on wl fr over 1f out* **5/1**[3]

1322 **2** *1 3/4* **Dux Scholar**[21] 6693 3-9-2 112 .... RyanMoore 3 115
(Sir Michael Stoute) *swtchd to r on far side: in tch: rdn over 2f out: chsd wnr over 1f out: kpt on but no imp ins fnl f* **2/1**[1]

50 **3** *3 3/4* **Classic Punch (IRE)**[37] 6277 8-9-3 99 .... RichardHughes 7 103
(David Elsworth) *led and swtchd to r on far side: led tl 3f out: rdn and outpcd over 1f out: 3rd and kpt on same pce fnl f* **25/1**

2021 **4** *shd* **Jet Away**[22] 6671 4-9-3 114 .... TomQueally 5 103
(Sir Henry Cecil) *stdd s: t.k.h: swtchd to r on far side after s: hld up in last trio: effrt and rdn over 2f out: no imp on wnr and edgd rt over 1f out* **5/2**[2]

5 **5** *2 3/4* **Retrieve (AUS)**[21] 6693 4-9-3 112 .... (t) FrankieDettori 1 98
(Saeed Bin Suroor) *swtchd to r on far side: hld up in last trio: rdn and no imp over 2f out: 5th and wl btn over 1f out* **6/1**

051 **6** *12* **Honour System (IRE)**[233] 827 4-9-3 104 .... KierenFallon 2 74
(Saeed Bin Suroor) *swtchd to r on far side: chsd ldrs tl over 2f out: sn wknd: wl bhd and eased ins fnl f* **28/1**

-006 **7** *16* **Dangerous Midge (USA)**[22] 6671 [illegible] .... [illegible] 1 [illegible]
(Brian Meehan) *stdd and swtchd to r on far side after s: hld up in last trio: dropped to last and rdn 4f out: no rspnse: lost tch 2f out: eased fnl f: t.o* **10/1**

2m 3.21s (-2.59) **Going Correction** -0.05s/f (Good)
WFA 3 from 4yo+ 5lb **7** Ran SP% **109.2**
Speed ratings (Par 111): **108,106,103,103,101 91,78**
toteswingers: 1&2 £2.20, 1&3 £7.70, 2&3 £6.80. CSF £14.02 TOTE £5.90: £2.80, £2.00; EX 14.60 Trifecta £97.90 Pool: £1,972.58 - 14.90 winning units..
Owner K Abdulla **Bred** Millsec Limited **Trained** Lambourn, Berks

FOCUS
This race was won by the subsequent Group 1-winner Timepiece last year and her owner Prince Khalid Abdullah was responsible for three of the seven runners here (with different trainers). They eventually finished first, second and fourth, but this race was noteworthy for the tactics employed. Whilst Richard Hughes aboard established pacemaker Classic Punch went straight for the far rail, the winner ran a solo up the stands' rail. The form is taken at face value with the placed horses basically to form.

NOTEBOOK
Slumber's rider decided to race alone up the stands' rail and the tactic worked a treat. He had no trouble keeping pace with the far-side group and it then became obvious that he was holding the upper hand from some way out. Placed three times from four starts in Group 3 company this season, the drop in class helped and he deserved this, but there has to be a big question mark against the form in view of the way the race was run. (op 13-2 tchd 7-1)
Dux Scholar, in the frame in all ten previous outings and placed in three Group 3 contests since winning a Newbury Listed event, moved to the front of the far-side group 2f out did his best to get on terms with the winner, but hung away to his left and was never getting there. (op 5-2 tchd 11-4 in a place)
Classic Punch(IRE) has a fine record on the July Course and can be a hard horse to catch when allowed an uncontested lead, but he was worst in the weights so this effort, in which he led the far-side group to the 2f pole, may flatter him. (op 20-1 tchd 16-1)
Jet Away, back up to Listed company following his very impressive success in a York conditions event earlier this month, didn't travel anything like as well here as he did then, racing keenly early and then looking ill-at-ease on the track when asked for his effort. (op 15-8)
Retrieve(AUS) finished a creditable fifth of ten in the Darley Stakes on his debut for Godolphin here earlier this month, but didn't step up from that. His best form in Australia was with cheekpieces alongside the tongue-tie, but he still has it all to prove. (op 9-2 tchd 13-2)
Honour System(IRE), not seen since winning a Meydan handicap in March, chased the leader in the far-side group for a long way but then appeared to blow up. (op 25-1)
Dangerous Midge(USA), winner of the Breeders' Cup Turf a year ago, ran another shocker and appears to have lost the plot completely. (op 16-1 tchd 18-1 in a place)

7171 RACING UK H'CAP 7f
5:00 (5:01) (Class 4) (0-85,84) 3-Y-0+ **£5,175** (£1,540; £769; £384) **Stalls** High

Form / RPR

5315 **1** **Yair Hill (IRE)**[29] 6495 3-9-2 **81** .... TedDurcan 20 93+
(John Dunlop) *hld up towards rr: hdwy against stands' rail 2f out: swtchd rt and rdn to chse ldr 1f out: led ins fnl f: r.o wl* **12/1**

1011 **2** *1* **Beckermet (IRE)**[4] 7076 9-9-5 **82** 6ex .... SilvestreDeSousa 19 91
(Ruth Carr) *broke wl: led: rdn wl over 1f out: hdd and nt pce of wnr ins fnl f: kpt on* **7/1**[2]

5600 **3** *nk* **Amitola (IRE)**[7] 7031 4-9-3 **80** .... LeeNewman 4 88+
(David Barron) *racd alone on far side: a.p: rdn and pressing ldrs over 1f out: kpt on same pce ins fnl f* **22/1**

1623 **4** *3/4* **Rondeau (GR)**[34] 6378 6-9-6 **83** .... JimCrowley 10 89+
(Patrick Chamings) *stdd s: hld up bhd: hdwy over 1f out: r.o ins fnl f: nt rch ldrs* **18/1**

560- **5** *3/4* **Simayill**[392] 6559 3-9-0 **79** .... MartinDwyer 7 83
(Clive Brittain) *chsd ldrs: rdn over 2f out: unable qck u.p over 1f out: kpt on same pce fnl f* **33/1**

6006 **6** *1 1/2* **Amwell Pinot**[53] 5811 3-8-10 **78** .... (v) DominicFox[(3)] 13 78
(Alan Bailey) *in tch in midfield: rdn 3f out: unable qck u.p 2f out: kpt on u.p fnl f but nvr gng pce to threaten ldrs* **25/1**

0003 **7** *shd* **King Of Eden (IRE)**[35] 6327 5-9-6 **83** .... ShaneKelly 18 83
(Eric Alston) *hld up in midfield: rdn and effrt over 1f out: unable qck 1f out: kpt on same pce ins fnl f: nvr gng pce to chal ldrs* **20/1**

-205 **8** *hd* **Prince Of Burma (IRE)**[121] 3557 3-8-13 **78** .... J-PGuillambert 11 77
(Jeremy Gask) *hld up towards rr: hdwy 2f out: nt clr run and swtchd lft ent fnl f: styd on but nvr gng pce to threaten ldrs* **20/1**

5305 **9** *shd* **Sunrise Safari (IRE)**[12] 6920 8-8-9 **75** .... (v) LeeTopliss[(3)] 14 74
(Richard Fahey) *taken down early: chsd ldrs: rdn to chse ldr wl over 1f out tl 1f out: no ex and btn ins fnl f: wknd fnl 75yds* **20/1**

03/6 **10** *1* **Sos Brillante (CHI)**[44] 6088 6-9-0 **84** .... NoelGarbutt[(7)] 17 80
(Terry Clement) *in tch: rdn over 2f out: unable qck and n.m.r wl over 1f out: one pce and no threat to ldrs fnl f* **66/1**

5346 **11** *nk* **Arctic Lynx (IRE)**[56] 5718 4-9-0 **77** .... SteveDrowne 9 73+
(John Best) *t.k.h early: hld up towards rr: rdn and effrt wl over 2f out: kpt on ins fnl f: nvr trbld ldrs* **25/1**

1 **12** *1 1/4* **Intercept (IRE)**[30] 6473 3-9-1 **80** .... RyanMoore 1 72+
(John Gosden) *swtchd lft after s: in tch: rdn ent fnl 2f: rn green wl over 1f out: btn ent fnl f: wknd fnl f* **4/1**[1]

0500 **13** *3/4* **Rocket Rob (IRE)**[19] 6761 5-9-1 **78** .... StevieDonohoe 15 68
(Willie Musson) *hld up in rr: rdn and effrt 2f out: sme hdwy fnl f: nvr trbld ldrs* **25/1**

0230 **14** *nse* **Big Noise**[34] 6378 7-9-2 **82** .... (b[1]) SeanLevey[(3)] 8 72
(Dr Jon Scargill) *in tch in midfield: rdn and effrt wl over 2f out: no prog u.p and btn over 1f out* **18/1**

2321 **15** *hd* **Mingun Bell (USA)**[39] 6239 4-9-2 **79** .... TomQueally 2 68+
(Ed de Giles) *s.i.s: swtchd lft after s: hld up in tch towards rr: swtchd rt and effrt 2f out: no imp: no threat to ldrs after* **14/1**

400 **16** *1 1/2* **Namwahjobo (IRE)**[43] 6113 3-8-12 **80** .... JohnFahy[(3)] 12 65
(Jim Goldie) *a in rr: rdn and no prog 3f out: plugged on same pce u.p fr over 1f out: n.d* **12/1**

0002 **17** *2 3/4* **Rash Judgement**[38] 6246 6-8-13 **76** .... KierenFallon 3 54
(Stuart Kittow) *taken down early: swtchd lft after s: chsd ldrs: rdn wl over 2f out: wknd over 1f out* **12/1**

2340 **18** *1 1/2* **River Falcon**[43] 6113 11-9-0 **77** .... RobertHavlin 6 51
(Jim Goldie) *a in rr: n.d* **25/1**

6120 **19** *1 1/4* **Dasho**[31] 6467 3-8-11 **76** .... KellyHarrison 16 47
(Olivia Maylam) *taken down early: t.k.h: chsd ldr tl wl over 1f out: sn wknd* **33/1**

3-14 **20** *2 1/4* **Rossetti**[175] 1916 3-9-2 **81** .... EddieAhern 5 45
(James Fanshawe) *swtchd lft after s: in tch in midfield: rdn and lost pl over 2f out: bhd over 1f out* **9/1**[3]

1m 25.14s (-0.26) **Going Correction** -0.05s/f (Good)
WFA 3 from 4yo+ 2lb **20** Ran SP% **124.2**
Speed ratings (Par 105): **99,97,97,96,95 94,93,93,93,92 92,90,89,89,89 87,84,83,81,79**
toteswingers: [illegible] CSF £77.49 CT £1894.92 TOTE £13.30: £3.30, £2.00, £4.80, £3.70; EX 119.40 Trifecta £830.20 Pool: £1,133.14 - 1.01 winning units..
Owner The Earl Cadogan **Bred** The Earl Cadogan **Trained** Arundel, W Sussex

FOCUS
A very competitive handicap to finish the Newmarket season, with just 8lb covering the entire field on official ratings, not including weight-for-age allowances. The form is ordinary for the grade with the placed horses helping to set the level.
T/Jkpt: Not won. T/Plt: £556.50 to a £1 stake. Pool:£88,635.85 - 116.25 winning tickets. T/Qpdt: £53.70 to a £1 stake. Pool:£7,361.49 - 101.30 winning tickets. SP

7140 WOLVERHAMPTON (A.W) (L-H)
Saturday, October 29

OFFICIAL GOING: Standard
Wind: Fresh behind Weather: Overcast

7172 LADBROKES H'CAP (DIV I) 5f 216y(P)
5:50 (5:50) (Class 5) (0-70,73) 3-Y-0+ **£1,704** (£503; £251) **Stalls** Low

Form / RPR

0004 **1** **Frequency**[18] 6779 4-9-7 **70** .... (b) JoeFanning 4 79+
(Keith Dalgleish) *a.p: nt clr run over 1f out: led ins fnl f: r.o* **7/2**[2]

0006 **2** *1 1/2* **Mey Blossom**[3] 7106 6-9-1 **64** .... TonyCulhane 11 68
(Richard Whitaker) *hld up: rdn over 1f out: r.o wl ins fnl f: wnt 2nd nr fin: nt rch wnr* **11/1**

0045 **3** *nk* **Sarah's Art (IRE)**[7] 7039 8-8-13 **67** .... (t) MarkCoumbe[(5)] 10 70
(Derek Shaw) *a.p: chsd ldr over 1f out: rdn to ld ins fnl f: sn hdd and unable qck* **9/1**[3]

0060 **4** *nk* **Loyal Royal (IRE)**[11] 6931 8-9-4 **67** .... (bt) RichardKingscote 3 69
(Milton Bradley) *dwlt: hld up: swtchd lft over 1f out: r.o wl ins fnl f: nt rch ldrs* **28/1**

6563 **5** *1* **Volito**[11] 6930 5-9-0 **63** .... LiamKeniry 12 62
(Anabel K Murphy) *s.s: hld up: r.o ins fnl f: nrst fin* **9/1**[3]

2256 **6** *nk* **Adventure Story**[23] 6655 4-9-1 **64** .... FergusSweeney 5 62
(Peter Makin) *chsd ldr over 3f: rdn over 1f out: styd on same pce ins fnl f* **9/1**[3]

2040 **7** *1/2* **Sir Nod**[22] 6665 9-9-7 **70** .... TonyHamilton 13 67
(Julie Camacho) *sn led: rdn over 1f out: hdd and no ex ins fnl f* **14/1**

0365 **8** ½ **Athaakeel (IRE)**[13] 6889 5-9-1 **64**....(b) LukeMorris 7 59
(Ronald Harris) *hld up: hdwy and nt clr run over 1f out: swtchd rt: no ex ins fnl f* **16/1**

1162 **9** ¾ **Deliberation (IRE)**[4] 7073 3-9-1 **68**.... AmyRyan(3) 9 61
(Kevin Ryan) *mid-div: hdwy over 2f out: rdn over 1f out: nt clr run and no ex ins fnl f* **5/2**[1]

0056 **10** 2 ½ **Overwhelm**[131] 3239 3-8-13 **66**.... KieranO'Neill(3) 8 51
(Andrew Reid) *trckd ldrs: plld hrd: pushed along to chse ldr over 2f out to over 1f out: wknd ins fnl f* **20/1**

4530 **11** 2 **Chjimes (IRE)**[11] 6932 7-9-6 **69**....(b) KirstyMilczarek 6 47
(Conor Dore) *s.i.s: sn pushed along in rr: wknd over 1f out* **16/1**

1m 15.38s (0.38) **Going Correction** +0.05s/f (Slow)
WFA 3 from 4yo+ 1lb **11** Ran SP% **115.8**
Speed ratings (Par 103): **99,97,96,96,94 94,93,93,92,88 86**
toteswingers:1&2:£8.90, 2&3:£13.70, 1&3:£6.60 CSF £41.28 CT £327.00 TOTE £4.00: £1.40, £4.00, £2.40; EX 39.70.
Owner Mrs Francesca Mitchell **Bred** Manor Farm Stud (rutland) **Trained** Carluke, South Lanarkshire

FOCUS
They went off fast in this sprint handicap and the first three came from off the pace. The form is modest rated around those in the frame behind the winner.

7173 LADBROKES H'CAP (DIV II) 5f 216y(P)
6:20 (6:20) (Class 5) (0-70,71) 3-Y-0+ **£1,704** (£503; £251) **Stalls** Low

Form RPR

000 **1** **Caledonia Princess**[28] 6537 5-9-7 **70**.... FrederikTylicki 2 79
(Jo Hughes) *hld up in tch: racd keenly: n.m.r over 1f out: r.o to ld wl ins fnl f* **16/1**

0004 **2** 1 ½ **Blown It (USA)**[7] 7040 5-9-0 **63**.... JoeFanning 1 67
(Keith Dalgleish) *chsd ldrs: led ins fnl f: sn hung lft and hdd: styd on same pce* **4/1**[1]

0022 **3** 1 **Roman Strait**[11] 6930 3-9-4 **68**.... LiamKeniry 11 69+
(Michael Blanshard) *hld up: rdn over 1f out: r.o wl ins fnl f: nrst fin* **9/2**[2]

0600 **4** nse **Dead Cool**[11] 6930 3-9-4 **68**....(p) NickyMackay 4 69
(Hughie Morrison) *hld up: hdwy over 2f out: rdn over 1f out: styd on* **14/1**

0330 **5** nse **Methaaly (IRE)**[22] 6665 8-9-7 **70**....(be) JimmyQuinn 12 71
(Michael Mullineaux) *dwlt: hld up: hdwy over 1f out: sn rdn: r.o* **20/1**

1120 **6** ¾ **Efistorm**[11] 6931 10-9-2 **65**.... KirstyMilczarek 9 63
(Conor Dore) *prom: nt clr run and lost pl wl over 1f out: swtchd rt: r.o u.p ins fnl f* **12/1**

6114 **7** ½ **Riflessione**[19] 6752 5-9-4 **67**....(b) LukeMorris 10 64
(Ronald Harris) *trckd ldrs: plld hrd: rdn to ld and hung rt over 1f out: hdd and no ex ins fnl f* **13/2**[3]

2536 **8** 1 ¼ **Pose (IRE)**[19] 6746 4-8-8 **62**....(t) MatthewLawson(5) 3 55
(Roger Ingram) *s.s: outpcd: r.o ins fnl f: nvr nrr* **22/1**

4403 **9** hd **Diapason (IRE)**[7] 7039 5-9-8 **71**....(t) StephenCraine 13 63
(Tom Dascombe) *hld up: hdwy over 2f out: rdn over 1f out: wknd ins fnl f* **10/1**

2240 **10** nk **Brynfa Boy**[17] 6793 5-9-2 **68**....(t) KieranO'Neill(3) 5 59
(Patrick Morris) *hld up: effrt over 1f out: rdn and wknd ins fnl f* **7/1**

0050 **11** nse **Tom Sawyer**[17] 6801 3-9-6 **70**....(p) TonyHamilton 8 61
(Julie Camacho) *chsd ldrs: rdn over 1f out: wknd ins fnl f* **12/1**

5000 **12** 4 **Ace Of Spies (IRE)**[7] 7039 6-8-10 **64**....(b) DavidKenny(5) 6 42
(Conor Dore) *led: pushed along over 2f out: rdn and hdd over 1f out: wknd ins fnl f* **50/1**

266 **13** 2 **Rohlindi**[79] 4970 3-9-1 **65**.... FergusSweeney 7 37
(Jeremy Gask) *prom: pushed along over 2f out: wknd over 1f out* **20/1**

1m 15.17s (0.17) **Going Correction** +0.05s/f (Slow)
WFA 3 from 4yo+ 1lb **13** Ran SP% **116.9**
Speed ratings (Par 103): **100,98,96,96,96 95,94,93,92,92 92,87,84**
toteswingers:1&2:£18.20, 2&3:£3.50, 1&3:£19.70 CSF £73.60 CT £355.11 TOTE £20.40: £5.60, £1.10, £1.20; EX 146.00.
Owner Isla & Colin Cage **Bred** Mrs I M Cage And C J Cage **Trained** Lambourn, Berks

FOCUS
The second division of an average handicap but slightly faster than the first leg. The runner-up sets the standard rated to his latest C&D form.
Riflessione Official explanation: jockey said gelding hung right-handed

7174 LADBROKES.COM MEDIAN AUCTION MAIDEN STKS 5f 216y(P)
6:50 (6:51) (Class 6) 2-Y-0 **£1,617** (£481; £240; £120) **Stalls** Low

Form RPR

32 **1** **Desert Philosopher**[12] 6912 2-9-3 0.... PhillipMakin 1 80
(Kevin Ryan) *mde all: rdn over 1f out: jst hld on* **4/5**[1]

5 **2** ½ **Decision By One**[23] 6654 2-9-3 0.... RichardKingscote 4 79
(Tom Dascombe) *chsd wnr: rdn and edgd lft over 1f out: r.o* **7/2**[2]

6 **3** 4 ½ **Words Come Easy**[57] 5689 2-8-9 0.... AdamBeschizza(3) 7 60
(Philip McBride) *hld up: pushed along over 2f out: r.o ins fnl f: wnt 3rd post: nvr nrr* **10/1**

0 **4** nk **Naughtical**[12] 6919 2-8-12 0.... SebSanders 5 59
(J W Hills) *chsd ldrs: rdn over 1f out: wknd ins fnl f: lost 3rd post* **40/1**

42 **5** 2 ¾ **Tiablo (IRE)**[16] 6819 2-8-12 0.... MartinLane 6 51
(David Simcock) *chsd ldrs: rdn and hung lft over 1f out: wknd fnl f* **5/1**[3]

56 **6** 4 ½ **Zafonic Star**[51] 5863 2-9-0 0.... RyanClark(3) 3 42
(Ian Williams) *s.s: hld up: shkn up and wknd over 2f out* **12/1**

0 **7** 7 **Lana Mae**[23] 6654 2-8-12 0.... LukeMorris 8 16
(Jeremy Gask) *hld up: racd keenly: wknd 1/2-way* **50/1**

0 **8** 60 **Midnight Diva**[35] 6352 2-8-12 0.... TomMcLaughlin 2 —
(Christopher Kellett) *sn outpcd: t.o* **150/1**

1m 15.62s (0.62) **Going Correction** +0.05s/f (Slow) **8** Ran SP% **116.3**
Speed ratings (Par 93): **97,96,90,89,86 80,70,—**
toteswingers:1&2:£1.60, 2&3:£5.10, 1&3:£2.90 CSF £3.93 TOTE £1.80: £1.10, £2.20, £3.50; EX 4.80.
Owner Ahmad Al Shaikh **Bred** Wood Hall Stud Limited **Trained** Hambleton, N Yorks

FOCUS
There was not much strength in depth in this maiden but the favourite put in a professional display to hold off his main market rival who was clear of the rest. The winner looks the best guide to the level.

NOTEBOOK
Desert Philosopher was unable to reel in wind-assisted front-runners when third at Warwick before a solid second over 6f at Pontefract where he pulled 5l clear of the rest. He had leading form claims switched to AW and showed a good attitude to get off the mark under an attacking ride. His future will depend on what mark he receives for handicaps but he is a likeable and quietly progressive type. (op 10-11 tchd 11-10 and Evens in places)

Decision By One, an eye-catching fifth of 13 from a tough draw in a similar contest over C&D on debut this month, was a bit keen in the slipstream of the winner in the early stages but he kept battling and did well to go close. A half-brother to prolific sprint winner Taurus Twins, out of a sprint winning half-sister to numerous minor winners at 1m-2m, he should continue to get better with practice.
Words Come Easy shaped with a bit of promise when sixth in a 6f Kempton maiden on debut and it was a similar story here from a half-sister to highly progressive 6f-7f winner Audacity Of Hope. (tchd 12-1)
Naughtical beat one rival after missing the break on her debut at Windsor but she showed some ability in an improved second run. She is out of a half-sister to several 1m-1m6f Flat/2m hurdle winners and should do better over a stiffer test next season.
Tiablo(IRE) nearly defied a market drift when just caught in an ordinary 7f Kempton maiden on her second start. She had fair form claims but looked short of pace back sprinting. (op 4-1 tchd 11-2)

7175 LADBROKES GAME ON H'CAP (DIV I) 7f 32y(P)
7:20 (7:20) (Class 5) (0-70,71) 3-Y-0+ **£1,940** (£577; £288; £144) **Stalls** High

Form RPR

1206 **1** **Chookie Avon**[1] 7146 4-8-13 **62**....(p) JoeFanning 4 74
(Keith Dalgleish) *a.p: shkn up over 1f out: styd on to ld towards fin* **8/1**

-150 **2** nk **Woolfall Sovereign (IRE)**[224] 915 5-9-0 **70** ow1 MichaelJMurphy(7) 3 81
(George Margarson) *chsd ldrs: rdn over 1f out: led ins fnl f: hdd towards fin* **7/1**

0051 **3** 2 **Global Village (IRE)**[22] 6664 6-9-3 **66**.... SebSanders 5 72
(Brian Ellison) *chsd ldr tl led over 2f out: rdn over 1f out: hdd and no ex ins fnl f* **11/4**[1]

1501 **4** ¾ **Glenridding**[9] 6979 7-9-8 **71**.... FrederikTylicki 9 75
(James Given) *sn pushed along and prom: chsd ldr 2f out: sn rdn: no ex ins fnl f* **9/2**[2]

0430 **5** 1 **Muftarres (IRE)**[8] 6990 6-9-3 **66**....(b) RussKennemore 1 67
(Paul Midgley) *hld up: rdn over 1f out: r.o ins fnl f: nrst fin* **13/2**[3]

1510 **6** 1 ¼ **This Ones For Eddy**[50] 5902 6-8-13 **62**.... LukeMorris 2 60
(John Balding) *hld up: pushed along 3f out: r.o ins fnl f: nvr nrr* **16/1**

102 **7** nk **Needwood Ridge**[9] 6979 4-9-7 **70**....(bt) DaneO'Neill 11 67
(Frank Sheridan) *dwlt: hld up: hdwy over 2f out: sn rdn: styng on same pce whn edgd lft fnl f* **7/1**

2103 **8** nk **Spinning Ridge (IRE)**[22] 6664 6-8-13 **62**....(v) DavidProbert 10 58
(Ronald Harris) *s.i.s: hld up: rdn over 1f out: n.d* **12/1**

0060 **9** 15 **Dhhamaan (IRE)**[14] 6867 6-9-4 **67**....(b) JamesSullivan 6 23
(Ruth Carr) *led over 4f: wknd over 1f out* **28/1**

10 3 ¾ **Give Me Shelter (IRE)**[29] 6510 3-9-1 **66**.... MartinHarley 8 12
(Bernard Anthony Heffernan, Ire) *hld up: plld hrd: wknd 2f out* **50/1**

1m 29.1s (-0.50) **Going Correction** +0.05s/f (Slow)
WFA 3 from 4yo+ 2lb **10** Ran SP% **113.3**
Speed ratings (Par 103): **104,103,101,100,99 97,97,97,80,75**
toteswingers:1&2 £12.80, 2&3 £5.70, 1&3 £3.40 CSF £61.06 CT £192.64 TOTE £11.20: £2.30, £1.90, £2.30; EX 69.80.
Owner Carleton Boys Of Carlisle **Bred** D And J Raeburn **Trained** Carluke, South Lanarkshire
■ Stewards' Enquiry : Michael J Murphy five-day ban: used whip with excessive frequency (Nov 12,14-17)

FOCUS
There was a tight finish in this handicap which was run at a decent pace. The first two recorded personal bests with the fourth close to his latest C&D win.
Muftarres(IRE) Official explanation: jockey said gelding was denied a clear run

7176 LADBROKES GAME ON H'CAP (DIV II) 7f 32y(P)
7:50 (7:50) (Class 5) (0-70,70) 3-Y-0+ **£1,940** (£577; £288; £144) **Stalls** High

Form RPR

-005 **1** **Bavarian Princess (USA)**[28] 6541 3-8-13 **64**.... MartinHarley 6 75
(Mrs K Burke) *a.p: rdn over 1f out: r.o to ld wl ins fnl f* **7/1**

0505 **2** ½ **Striker Torres (IRE)**[25] 6616 5-9-0 **66**.... DaleSwift(3) 4 76
(Geoffrey Oldroyd) *led: rdn 1f out: hdd wl ins fnl f* **5/1**[3]

0040 **3** 1 ½ **Lord Of The Dance (IRE)**[49] 5924 5-9-3 **66**.... TomMcLaughlin 8 72
(Mark Brisbourne) *a.p: rdn to chse ldr 2f out: edgd lft over 1f out: styd on same pce ins fnl f* **9/2**[2]

4541 **4** 2 ¾ **Tourist**[17] 6794 6-9-3 **69**.... RyanClark(3) 10 68
(Ian Williams) *hld up: hdwy over 1f out: r.o: nt rch ldrs* **7/2**[1]

5020 **5** 1 **Aviso (GER)**[9] 6971 7-8-13 **62**....(p) FergusSweeney 7 58
(David Evans) *chsd ldr tl rdn 2f out: wknd ins fnl f* **5/1**[3]

5050 **6** 2 ½ **Silly Billy (IRE)**[19] 6746 3-8-6 **62**.... JemmaMarshall(5) 5 51
(Sylvester Kirk) *hld up: nvr on terms* **16/1**

050 **7** ½ **Conry (IRE)**[9] 6979 5-9-5 **68**.... StephenCraine 2 56
(Patrick Morris) *prom: pushed along over 2f out: wknd over 1f out* **11/1**

6563 **8** ¾ **Summer Dancer (IRE)**[9] 6980 7-9-7 **70**.... MickyFenton 9 56
(Paul Midgley) *hld up: plld hrd: wknd over 1f out* **13/2**

0000 **9** 10 **Beauchamp Yorker**[17] 6797 4-8-8 **64**....(bt[1]) NicoleNordblad(7) 3 23
(Hans Adielsson) *chsd ldrs: lost pl over 5f out: wknd 3f out* **10/1**

1m 29.58s (-0.02) **Going Correction** +0.05s/f (Slow)
WFA 3 from 4yo+ 2lb **9** Ran SP% **122.9**
Speed ratings (Par 103): **102,101,99,96,95 92,92,91,79**
toteswingers:1&2:£6.20, 2&3:£5.40, 1&3:£6.20 CSF £44.72 CT £181.52 TOTE £8.80: £3.50, £2.80, £1.30; EX 56.10.
Owner Aricabeau Syndicate II & Partners **Bred** Maura Gittens **Trained** Middleham Moor, North Yorks

FOCUS
The pace was not very strong in this second division of a minor handicap and the hold-up performers were probably at a disadvantage. The form makes a fair bit of sense and looks sound enough.
Bavarian Princess(USA) Official explanation: trainer's rep said, regarding apparent improvement in form, that the filly had been continuously improving since arriving from Ireland and seems to show its best on the polytrack.

7177 THE BLACK COUNTRY'S ONLY RACECOURSE MAIDEN AUCTION STKS 1m 141y(P)
8:20 (8:20) (Class 5) 2-Y-0 **£1,704** (£503; £251) **Stalls** Low

Form RPR

6 **1** **Feisty Champion (IRE)**[19] 6742 2-8-12 0.... SebSanders 12 70+
(J W Hills) *s.i.s: hld up: pushed along 6f out: hdwy over 1f out: rdn: edgd lft and led wl ins fnl f: r.o* **5/1**[3]

6 **2** 1 ¼ **Hallmark Star**[18] 6771 2-9-1 0.... DaneO'Neill 5 70
(Gerard Butler) *a.p: swtchd lft over 1f out: rdn to ld ins fnl f: sn hdd and unable qck* **7/4**[1]

3 **3** ½ **Bursting Bubbles (IRE)**[16] 6818 2-8-4 0.... ChrisCatlin 2 58
(Ed Dunlop) *chsd ldr: rdn and ev ch fr over 1f out tl no ex wl ins fnl f* **5/1**[3]

4654 **4** ½ **Bogey Hole (IRE)**[19] 6763 2-8-4 50.... KieranO'Neill(3) 1 60
(Nikki Evans) *led: rdn over 1f out: hdd and unable qck ins fnl f* **25/1**

4430 **5** *1 1/2* **Landown Littlerock**[17] 6806 2-8-9 65 .... LukeMorris 9 58
(Reg Hollinshead) *hld up: hdwy 1/2-way: pushed along over 2f out: rdn and hung lft over 1f out: no ex fnl f* **4/1**[2]

00 **6** *3/4* **Jericho (IRE)**[18] 6771 2-9-1 0 .... FergusSweeney 6 63
(Jamie Osborne) *s.s: hld up: hdwy over 1f out: r.o: nt rch ldrs* **11/1**

0 **7** *9* **Swift Winged**[11] 6928 2-8-4 0 .... NickyMackay 8 31
(Hughie Morrison) *hld up: pushed along over 2f out: sn wknd* **11/1**

00 **8** *3* **Isola Bella**[43] 6117 2-8-4 0 .... RossAtkinson(3) 10 27
(Jonathan Portman) *hld up: plld hrd: rdn and wknd over 2f out* **40/1**

56 **9** *1 1/4* **Elammato (IRE)**[109] 3947 2-8-9 0 .... JamesSullivan 4 26
(Lisa Williamson) *chsd ldrs: pushed along over 3f out: wknd over 1f out* **100/1**

1m 52.31s (1.81) **Going Correction** +0.05s/f (Slow) **9** Ran SP% **113.6**
Speed ratings (Par 95): **93,91,91,91,89 89,81,78,77**
toteswingers:1&2:£3.40, 2&3:£2.30, 1&3:£3.40 CSF £13.76 TOTE £10.30: £3.30, £1.10, £1.10; EX 20.50.
Owner Eddie M C Wong **Bred** Mrs E Comer **Trained** Upper Lambourn, Berks

FOCUS
An ordinary maiden auction run at a stop-start gallop. The form is rated around the front pair but is slightly fluid.

NOTEBOOK
Feisty Champion(IRE), a 33-1 sixth of 11 at Salisbury on debut, still looked inexperienced and took time to find top gear but he powered home out wide to get off the mark in an improved second run. A half-brother to 1m-1m4f Flat/2m-2m4f hurdle winner Diyla, out of a 1m5f winner, he looks a willing type and should continue to progress with time and distance. (tchd 6-1)
Hallmark Star showed promise when 40-1 sixth of 11 in a 1m Leicester maiden on debut. He was strong in the market and travelled well for a long way but couldn't fight off a fast finisher. A half-brother to seven winners, notably 1m/1m2f Listed winner Inglenook, he is a scopey type who should continue to progress. (op 9-4 tchd 5-2)
Bursting Bubbles(IRE), just over 6l third at 20-1 in a 7f Kempton maiden on debut, raced near the pace and stuck well to her task in another encouraging run. Related to stacks of winners, including useful 1m2f-2m scorer Downhiller, she should continue to go the right way. (op 11-4)
Bogey Hole(IRE) seemed to excel herself with plenty to find back in a maiden, but this 50-rated filly was allowed to dictate and her proximity casts a shadow over the form.
Landown Littlerock was well below form on nursery debut last time and this 65-rated performer couldn't make an impact back in a maiden. (op 9-2 tchd 100-30)

7178 BET IN PLAY AT LADBROKES.COM H'CAP 1m 1f 103y(P)
8:50 (8:50) (Class 5) (0-70,71) 3-Y-0+ **£2,264** (£673; £336; £168) **Stalls** Low

Form RPR

2151 **1** **So Wise (USA)**[9] 6978 3-9-7 **71** .... JoeFanning 11 89+
(Keith Dalgleish) *a.p: led 3f out: clr over 1f out: readily* **3/1**[1]

022 **2** *2 3/4* **Fellisha (IRE)**[2] 7121 3-8-2 **59** .... RaulDaSilva(7) 12 66
(Andrew Heffernan, Ire) *hld up: racd keenly: hdwy over 2f out: rdn to go 2nd ins fnl f: no ch w wnr* **9/1**

2242 **3** *4* **Dream Of Fortune (IRE)**[7] 7034 7-9-3 **66** ....(bt) RichardEvans(3) 5 65
(David Evans) *prom: rdn over 1f out: wknd ins fnl f* **12/1**

0450 **4** *1 3/4* **Moheebb (IRE)**[8] 6989 7-9-4 **67** ....(b) DaleSwift(3) 3 62
(Ruth Carr) *s.i.s and sn drvn along in rr: styd on ins fnl f: nvr nrr* **16/1**

2002 **5** *3/4* **Celtic Step**[14] 6871 7-8-9 **58** .... LeeTopliss(3) 4 51
(Peter Niven) *hld up: styd on ins fnl f: nvr nrr* **20/1**

5202 **6** *3* **Stargazing (IRE)**[66] 5391 5-9-3 **63** .... AdamKirby 10 50
(Marco Botti) *chsd ldr tl rdn over 2f out: wknd over 1f out* **11/2**[3]

4/23 **7** *1/2* **Agilete**[53] 5815 9-9-7 **67** .... ChrisCatlin 6 53
(Lydia Pearce) *mid-div: hdwy over 3f out: rdn and wknd over 1f out* **20/1**

0540 **8** *1 3/4* **Fleetwoodsands (IRE)**[9] 6980 4-9-5 **65** ....(t) RichardKingscote 9 47
(Milton Bradley) *hld up: nvr on terms* **16/1**

0014 **9** *2 3/4* **You've Been Mowed**[14] 6878 5-8-8 **61** .... BrendanPowell(7) 8 38
(Richard Price) *led over 6f: wknd 2f out* **16/1**

5351 **10** *3/4* **Frontline Phantom (IRE)**[26] 6589 4-9-7 **67** ....(p) MartinHarley 1 42
(Mrs K Burke) *chsd ldrs: pushed along over 3f out: wknd over 2f out* **8/1**

0000 **11** *6* **Barton Bounty**[128] 3317 4-8-4 **57** .... FrancescaWolter(7) 2 19
(Peter Niven) *hld up: a in rr: wknd over 3f out* **33/1**

0032 **P** **Nibani (IRE)**[2] 7130 4-9-10 **70** ....(p) FergusSweeney 7 —
(Alastair Lidderdale) *hld up: a in rr: p.u wl over 3f out* **5/1**[2]

2m 0.94s (-0.76) **Going Correction** +0.05s/f (Slow)
WFA 3 from 4yo+ 4lb **12** Ran SP% **116.0**
Speed ratings (Par 103): **105,102,99,97,96 94,93,92,89,89 83,—**
toteswingers:1&2:£5.10, 2&3:£12.40, 1&3:£7.30 CSF £28.67 CT £284.49 TOTE £5.00: £2.00, £2.70, £3.10; EX 35.60.
Owner S Laffan **Bred** Juddmonte Farms Inc **Trained** Carluke, South Lanarkshire

FOCUS
A progressive 3-y-o hammered his rivals in this handicap which was run at a decent pace. The third looks the best guide to the level.
Stargazing(IRE) Official explanation: jockey said mare stopped quickly
Nibani(IRE) Official explanation: jockey said gelding lost its action in back straight but appeared sound when pulled up

7179 ENJOY THE PARTY PACK GROUP OFFER MAIDEN STKS 1m 1f 103y(P)
9:20 (9:20) (Class 5) 3-Y-0+ **£2,911** (£866; £432; £216) **Stalls** Low

Form RPR

2034 **1** **Ajeeb (USA)**[52] 5837 3-9-3 78 .... MartinLane 7 83
(David Simcock) *wnt rt s: led after 1f: clr over 1f out: rdn out* **13/8**[1]

03 **2** *1 1/4* **Martine's Spirit (IRE)**[17] 6804 3-8-12 0 .... ChrisCatlin 3 75
(William Haggas) *led 1f: chsd ldrs: rdn over 2f out: styd on* **11/4**[2]

0 **3** *1/2* **Silver Blossom (IRE)**[17] 6804 3-8-12 0 .... DavidProbert 2 74
(Andrew Balding) *hld up: r.o u.p ins fnl f: nt rch ldrs* **4/1**[3]

4 *1 1/4* **Daring Indian**[186] 3-9-0 0 .... RyanClark(3) 4 77
(Ian Williams) *prom: racd keenly: rdn over 2f out: styd on* **16/1**

4U5 **5** *2 1/4* **Daruband**[9] 6978 3-9-3 71 ....(p) MartinHarley 1 72
(Alan McCabe) *hld up in tch: rdn over 2f out: no ex fnl f* **5/1**

0 **6** *35* **Mustafeed (USA)**[15] 6834 3-9-3 0 .... JoeFanning 6 —
(Keith Dalgleish) *plld hrd and prom: trckd wnr over 6f out tl wknd over 2f out: t.o* **14/1**

2m 1.41s (-0.29) **Going Correction** +0.05s/f (Slow) **6** Ran SP% **114.0**
Speed ratings (Par 103): **103,101,101,100,98 67**
toteswingers:1&2:£1.90, 2&3:£1.90, 1&3:£1.90 CSF £6.50 TOTE £2.50: £2.20, £2.30; EX 8.40.
Owner Ahmad Al Shaikh **Bred** Timothy C Thornton & Brereton C Jones **Trained** Newmarket, Suffolk

FOCUS
The 78-rated winner put in a resolute front-running display to score in this maiden. The fifth helps set the level.
T/Plt: £25.00 to a £1 stake. Pool £90,241.00 - 2,630.39 winning tickets. T/Qpdt: £6.40 to a £1 stake. Pool £9,199.97 - 1,057.58 winning tickets. CR

7180 - 7184a, 7186 - 7188a - (Foreign Racing) - See Raceform Interactive

5741 LEOPARDSTOWN (L-H)
Sunday, October 30

OFFICIAL GOING: Yielding (yielding to soft in places)

7185a JRA KILLAVULLAN STKS (GROUP 3) 7f
1:30 (1:31) 2-Y-O **£26,616** (£7,780; £3,685; £1,228)

RPR

1 **Nephrite**[35] 6387 2-9-1 .... JPO'Brien 3 108+
(A P O'Brien, Ire) *settled off str pce in 4th: smooth hdwy to cl ent st: rdn to chal over 1f out: led over 100yds out and kpt on wl* **13/8**[2]

2 *1 1/2* **Born To Sea (IRE)**[50] 5950 2-9-1 .... JMurtagh 2 104+
(John M Oxx, Ire) *settled off str pce in 3rd: clsd ent st: rdn to ld briefly early fnl f: no imp on wnr fnl 100yds: lame post-r* **8/11**[1]

3 *2 3/4* **Aaraas**[127] 3416 2-8-12 93 .... DPMcDonogh 6 94+
(Kevin Prendergast, Ire) *hld up in rr: rdn ent st: 6th 1f out: kpt on u.p wout troubling first 2* **20/1**

4 *nk* **Ishvana (IRE)**[105] 4131 2-8-12 .... SeamieHeffernan 7 93
(A P O'Brien, Ire) *trckd ldr in 2nd and sn clr of remainder: pushed along appr st: dropped to 4th u.p 1f out: no imp ins fnl f* **25/1**

5 *1 1/4* **Vault (IRE)**[23] 6680 2-9-1 98 .... WMLordan 5 93
(A P O'Brien, Ire) *led at a str pce: strly pressed and hdd early fnl f: no ex and wknd* **33/1**

6 *1* **Seanie (IRE)**[23] 6680 2-9-1 98 .... PJSmullen 1 90
(David Marnane, Ire) *chsd clr ldrs in 6th: sme hdwy in 5th early st: no ex fr over 1f out* **16/1**[3]

7 *6* **While You Wait (IRE)**[25] 6639 2-9-1 .... KJManning 4 75
(J S Bolger, Ire) *chsd clr ldrs in 5th: nvr a factor: no ex under 2f out* **66/1**

1m 29.53s (0.83) **Going Correction** +0.275s/f (Good) **7** Ran SP% **114.9**
Speed ratings: **106,104,101,100,99 98,91**
CSF £3.06 TOTE £2.70: £1.30, £1.02; DF 3.80.
Owner Michael Tabor **Bred** Templeton Stud & Cheveley Park Stud Ltd **Trained** Ballydoyle, Co Tipperary

FOCUS
This was billed as the second instalment of the Born To Sea series, but the sequel wasn't as impressive as the original episode.

NOTEBOOK
Nephrite ◆ emerged with an enhanced reputation. There was no fluke about the performance either as Vault and Ishvana set a scorching early gallop. Like on his Curragh debut over 6f Nephrite travelled smoothly throughout and seemed to improve into contention with consummate ease entering the home straight. His confident rider gave the son of Pivotal one flick of the whip over 1f out and he responded in the manner of a top juvenile, quickening away from his more esteemed market rival. (op 2/1)
Born To Sea(IRE) was unable to maintain his unbeaten record. However, the defeat shouldn't be greeted with too much discontent as the ground was softer than ideal and his trainer revealed afterwards that he was unable to display his turn of foot on the easy surface. After settling well in third, the son of Invincible Spirit began to make ground on the pacesetters entering the home straight and hit the front passing the 1f pole. It soon became apparent that Nephrite had his measure quite easily and he was unable to put up a fight. He was also found to be lame post race. Official explanation: vet said colt was found to be lame post-race (op 8/13)
Aaraas plugged on up the home straight and gave the impression that 1m at the very least would be her optimum trip.
Ishvana(IRE) tracked the tearaway Vault and did well to finish as close as she did in the circumstances.
Vault(IRE) ensured the contest was run at a good clip, but he paid the price in the home straight and folded tamely when passed.

7189a DERRINSTOWN STUD APPRENTICE H'CAP FINAL 1m
3:40 (3:42) 3-Y-0+ **£14,008** (£4,094; £1,939; £646)

RPR

1 **Take It To The Max**[45] 6079 4-9-5 88 ....(p) LFRoche 12 100
(Richard Fahey) *sn led and mde virtually all: asserted over 1f out and kpt on wl ins fnl f* **9/2**[1]

2 *3* **Elusive Award (USA)**[9] 7013 4-8-11 84 ....(b) SAGray(4) 15 89+
(Andrew Oliver, Ire) *towards rr: sme hdwy between horses over 1f out: kpt on wl ins fnl f to go 2nd cl home: nrest at fin* **16/1**

3 *hd* **Ted Dolly (IRE)**[8] 6560 7-8-11 80 .... GFCarroll 5 85
(Ms Joanna Morgan, Ire) *mid-div: hdwy on outer early st: wnt 3rd ins fnl f: kpt on same pce but no imp on wnr* **11/1**

4 *nse* **Fred Fenster (IRE)**[11] 6964 3-9-7 93 .... JPO'Brien 8 97
(Edward Lynam, Ire) *hld up towards rr: gd hdwy on inner early st: wnt 2nd 1f out but sn no imp on wnr: kpt on one pce* **6/1**[2]

5 *1 1/2* **Castle Bar Sling (USA)**[44] 6141 6-9-10 97 .... MMMonaghan(4) 17 98
(T J O'Mara, Ire) *towards rr: sme hdwy fr early st: kpt on wl wout threatening* **20/1**

6 *hd* **Extraterrestrial**[23] 6672 7-9-10 93 .... EJMcNamara 11 94
(Richard Fahey) *hld up in rr: kpt on wl in st wout rching ldrs* **8/1**[3]

7 *nk* **Shirley Blake (IRE)**[47] 6040 4-8-13 82 .... BACurtis 13 82
(Paul Cashman, Ire) *chsd ldrs: 7th 1/2-way: pushed along ent st: 4th over 1f out: no ex ins fnl f* **10/1**

8 *nk* **New Magic (IRE)**[15] 6884 4-9-0 85 ....(t) CPHoban(2) 16 84
(Dermot Anthony McLoughlin, Ire) *in rr of mid-div: nvr a factor: kpt on one pce in st* **25/1**

9 *hd* **Tobar Na Gaoise (IRE)**[75] 5158 3-8-10 89 .... DAParkes(7) 4 88
(J S Bolger, Ire) *prom: 4th 1/2-way: 2nd ent st: no ex fr 1f out: wknd* **14/1**

10 *1/2* **Money Trader (IRE)**[126] 3440 4-8-8 81 .... CTKeane(4) 7 79
(J T Gorman, Ire) *chsd ldrs: 9th 1/2-way: 5th over 1f out: no ex ins fnl f* **33/1**

11 *nk* **Adam's Return (IRE)**[49] 5978 5-8-1 74 .... SamanthaBell(4) 3 71
(W T Farrell, Ire) *in rr of mid-div: nvr a factor: sme hdwy fr early st: kpt on one pce* **10/1**

12 *nse* **Balladiene (IRE)**[21] 6732 5-8-4 77 .... RDawson(4) 14 74
(Jarlath P Fahey, Ire) *prom: chsd ldrs 1/2-way: rdn and no ex appr st: wknd* **10/1**

13 *hd* **Boom To Bust (IRE)**[16] 6853 3-8-6 85 .... MeganCarberry(7) 9 81
(G M Lyons, Ire) *chsd ldrs: 7th appr st: no ex fr over 1f out* **20/1**

14 *1 3/4* **Maal (IRE)**[25] 6640 8-8-0 76 .... DHBergin(7) 2 68
(David Marnane, Ire) *in rr of mid-div: sme hdwy early st: no ex fr 1f out* **25/1**

15 *1 3/4* **Star Links (USA)**[44] 6141 5-8-11 84 ....(b) RossCoakley(4) 10 72
(S Donohoe, Ire) *mid-div: 9th ent st: no ex fr over 1f out* **12/1**

16 1 1/4 **Winning Impact (IRE)**[34] 6421 4-8-12 81 .... SHJames 6 66
(J G Coogan, Ire) *chsd ldrs: 8th 1/2-way: 5th ent st: no ex over 1f out: wknd* **16/1**

17 3 1/2 **Toufan Express**[28] 6560 9-8-11 84 ow1 .... DJBenson(4) 18 61
(Adrian McGuinness, Ire) *prom: 3rd 1/2-way: rdn along ent st: no ex over 1f out: eased whn btn ins fnl f* **16/1**

18 4 1/2 **Maundy Money**[9] 7010 8-9-3 86 .... ShaneFoley 1 53
(David Marnane, Ire) *mid-div: no threat under 2f out: eased whn btn* **16/1**

19 3 **Royal Intruder**[36] 6360 6-8-2 75 .... GJPhillips(4) 19 35
(S Donohoe, Ire) *chsd ldrs: 5th 1/2-way: pushed along in 8th ent st: sn no ex: eased whn btn fnl f* **25/1**

20 4 1/2 **Independent Girl (IRE)**[11] 6964 3-8-0 76 oh1(p) KatherineSO'Brien(4) 20 26
(Ms Joanna Morgan, Ire) *mid-div on outer: sn hdwy racing keenly to trck ldrs: 2nd 1/2-way: no ex early st and wknd: eased* **20/1**

1m 41.83s (0.63) **Going Correction** +0.275s/f (Good)
WFA 3 from 4yo+ 3lb **20** Ran SP% **145.8**
Speed ratings: **107,104,103,103,102 102,101,101,101,100 100,100,100,98,96 95,91,87,84,79**
CSF £83.82 CT £832.56 TOTE £5.80: £1.80, £4.60, £1.80, £2.30; DF 177.50.
Owner Mrs Phillipa Davies **Bred** Whatton Manor Stud **Trained** Musley Bank, N Yorks

FOCUS
This looked the trickiest puzzle of the afternoon for punters to solve but they got it spot-on in the end as British raider Take It To The Max was supported into favouritism and duly obliged in the manner of a very well-handicapped horse. The placed horses are rated to their recent best.

NOTEBOOK
Take It To The Max has been a model of consistency this season and had already won three times coming into this. His rider kept things simple here and was soon at the head of affairs. It became apparent early in the home straight that he was travelling best of all and he stayed on well for a most comfortable success. (op 5/1 tchd 11/2)
Elusive Award(USA) came with a late rattle to grab a slice of the place money. He needs to be held up and his rider did a good job in getting him settled, but the winner just had too much in hand and he was unable to reel him in.
Ted Dolly(IRE) has been busy over the last few months, but he ran another solid race here and was unlucky not to finish a little closer. After being towards the inside approaching the home straight his rider was forced to switch to the wide outside to mount a challenge, but by that stage the winner had flown. After making an encouraging debut over hurdles at Galway he may return to that sphere now. (op 14/1)
Fred Fenster(IRE) has gone up 20lb for his wide-margin victories at Cork and Navan and the hike just proved too much. Held up in the early stages, he made his challenge towards the inside in the home straight on ground that was possibly slower than the outer and was unable to mount a serious challenge. (op 11/2 tchd 5/1)
Castle Bar Sling(USA) was left with a mountain to climb entering the home straight but he did stay on well to grab fifth.
Extraterrestrial was another to make late progress from a long way back. (op 8/1 tchd 7/1)

7190 - 7191a (Foreign Racing) - See Raceform Interactive

7090 SAINT-CLOUD (L-H)
Sunday, October 30

OFFICIAL GOING: Turf: very soft

7192a CRITERIUM INTERNATIONAL (GROUP 1) (2YO COLTS & FILLIES) (TURF) 1m
1:30 (12:00) 2-Y-O **£123,146** (£49,267; £24,633; £12,306; £6,163)

RPR

1 **French Fifteen (FR)**[24] 6660 2-9-0 0 .... ThierryThulliez 9 115
(N Clement, France) *hld up towards rr: patiently rdn early in st: swtchd to outer over 1 1/2f out: qcknd wl: r.o strly fnl f to ld 50yds out: comf* **7/1**

2 1 1/4 **Pakal (GER)**[21] 2-9-0 0 .... OlivierPeslier 7 112
(Mario Hofer, Germany) *joint ldr on settling: nt qckn over 1 1/2f out: rallied and r.o wl ent fnl f: tk ld 1f out: r.o wl: hdd fnl 50yds out* **14/1**

3 1/2 **Bonfire**[32] 6463 2-9-0 0 .... JimmyFortune 1 114+
(Andrew Balding) *settled towards rr on inner: short of room early in st: r.o wl whn fnd opening under 1f out: fin strly: tk 3rd fnl strides: unlucky nt to fin clsr* **13/2**[3]

4 shd **Learn (IRE)**[8] 7020 2-9-0 0 .... CO'Donoghue 10 111
(A P O'Brien, Ire) *racd 3rd on settling: qcknd to ld over 1 1/2f out: r.o wl: hdd 1f out: styd on: lost 3rd fnl strides* **4/1**[1]

5 3/4 **Kendam (FR)**[18] 6808 2-8-10 0 .... MaximeGuyon 2 105
(H-A Pantall, France) *settled 5th on rail: rdn early in st: r.o wl u.str.p fnl f wout troubling ldrs* **8/1**

6 2 1/2 **Veneto (FR)**[28] 6565 2-9-0 0 .... StephanePasquier 8 104
(B De Montzey, France) *w.w in midfield: rdn over 1 1/2f out on outside: no ex* **12/1**

7 snk **Saint Pellerin (GER)**[43] 6184 2-9-0 0 .... GregoryBenoist 4 104
(J-C Rouget, France) *settled 4th: r.o u.p in st: nt qckn 1f out: styd on one pce* **4/1**[1]

8 nk **Vasco Bere (FR)**[30] 2-9-0 0 .... ThierryJarnet 11 103
(F Head, France) *settled towards rr: rdn early in st: mde no imp* **20/1**

9 snk **Ice Cool (FR)**[24] 6660 2-9-0 0 .... MickaelBarzalona 5 103
(W Hefter, Germany) *towards rr on inner: rdn but nt qckn in st: no imp fnl 1 1/2f* **14/1**

10 2 **Swing Alone (IRE)**[22] 6692 2-9-0 0 .... RobertWinston 6 98
(Gay Kelleway) *joint ldr on settling: rdn early in st: led 2f out: hdd over 1 1/2f out: sn wknd* **50/1**

11 1 1/2 **Salair Haut (IRE)**[24] 2-9-0 0 .... ChristopheSoumillon 3 95
(M Delzangles, France) *racd in midfield: sn wknd ent st* **6/1**[2]

1m 43.5s (-4.00) **11** Ran SP% **119.0**
WIN (incl. 1 euro stake): 11.30. PLACES: 3.40, 4.00, 4.20. DF: 41.40. SF: 89.20.
Owner Raymond Tooth **Bred** G Forien & Mme G Forien **Trained** Chantilly, France

FOCUS
Not a strong race for the grade and the field finished quite well bunched after the early pace had been steady.

NOTEBOOK
French Fifteen(FR) has been progressing well at a lower level, taking second in a Group 3 over this same C&D last time, and he produced a much-improved display to win this, swooping late and wide to get well on top close home. The key point in the race came over 1f out when, having found himself short of room, his rider switched him out, whilst the similarly strong travelling Bonfire had to stay inside and continued to find trouble. It was circumstance rather than jockey error, and it's likely there'd have been little between the two.
Pakal(GER) appeared to run right up to his best under a positive ride, sticking on well for pressure against the rail.
Bonfire impressed with the way he powered clear late on when winning his maiden at Salisbury and, with conditions similar, he was entitled to put up a good show. He became short of room soon after turning in, however, and by the time he found daylight, the race was over. The way he finished very much suggested he'd have gone close to winning, and although no doubt disappointed, connections have a bright middle-distance prospect for next season.
Learn(IRE), whose trainer had won this three times in the previous five years, was fourth in the Racing Post Trophy the previous weekend. He got warm beforehand and, despite going on inside the final 2f, always looked likely to be swamped.

7193a PRIX PERTH (GROUP 3) (3YO+) (TURF) 1m
2:40 (12:00) 3-Y-O+ **£34,482** (£13,793; £10,344; £6,896; £3,448)

RPR

1 **Cityscape**[36] 6369 5-9-4 0 .... SteveDrowne 11 121+
(Roger Charlton) *broke wl to r 2nd on outer: sent to ld after 2f: rdn early in st: qcknd wl to go clr 1 1/2f out: r.o wl: easily* **7/4**[1]

2 2 **Sommerabend**[42] 6201 4-9-6 0 .... MaximeGuyon 7 114
(U Stoltefuss, Germany) *racd 3rd for 2f: pursued eventual wnr into st: r.o gamely fnl quarter m to hold 2nd* **9/1**

3 3/4 **Akarlina (FR)**[23] 6686 5-9-1 0 .... ThierryThulliez 2 108
(N Clement, France) *led for 2f: settled in 2nd: relegated to 3rd ent st: r.o wl fnl 1 1/2f to a hold 3rd* **14/1**

4 3/4 **Skins Game**[42] 6206 5-9-4 0 .... ChristopheSoumillon 5 109
(J-C Rouget, France) *settled in midfield: r.o wl st to go 4th ins fnl f* **10/1**

5 2 **Liang Kay (GER)**[100] 6-9-1 0 .... StephanePasquier 1 101
(A De Royer-Dupre, France) *a.p: r.o wl fnl 1 1/2f wout troubling ldrs* **14/1**

6 snk **Polytechnicien (USA)**[106] 4120 5-9-4 0 .... OlivierPeslier 3 104
(A Fabre, France) *settled towards rr on inner: short of room whn looking for opening 2f out: r.o fnl f wout making any imp on ldrs* **13/2**[3]

7 shd **Nova Hawk**[18] 6809 3-8-8 0 .... GregoryBenoist 4 97
(Rod Collet, France) *settled towards rr: hrd rdn over 1 1/2f out: no imp* **4/1**[2]

8 hd **Red Dubawi (IRE)**[76] 5128 3-8-11 0 .... FabienLefebvre 8 99
(A De Royer-Dupre, France) *racd towards rr: r.o late on wd outside: clst at fin* **14/1**

9 1/2 **Verglacial (IRE)**[36] 6397 4-9-1 0 .... TonyPiccone 10 99
(C Lerner, France) *a towards rr: nvr a factor* **33/1**

10 3/4 **Zinabaa (FR)**[29] 6556 6-9-4 0 .... YannickLetondeur 12 100
(M Mace, France) *racd in midfield on outer: rdn early in st: no ex* **10/1**

0 **Glad Sky**[19] 6783 5-9-1 0 .... AnthonyCrastus 6 —
(J-L Pelletan, France) *prom early: rdn and no prog in st* **33/1**

0 **Rockatella (IRE)**[57] 5753 4-8-11 0 .... MickaelBarzalona 9 —
(W Hefter, Germany) *racd in midfield: rdn and sn wknd in st* **33/1**

1m 43.8s (-3.70)
WFA 3 from 4yo+ 3lb **12** Ran SP% **126.7**
WIN (incl. 1 euro stake): 2.80. PLACES: 1.60, 3.00, 3.50. DF: 13.20. SF: 14.80.
Owner K Abdulla **Bred** Juddmonte Farms Ltd **Trained** Beckhampton, Wilts

NOTEBOOK
Cityscape loves to get his toe in and, with no pace on early, he was allowed to stride on and make his own way home. He won easily in the end and there's a chance he could go for the Hong Kong Mile next. He is likely to stay in training next year.

7172 WOLVERHAMPTON (A.W) (L-H)
Monday, October 31

OFFICIAL GOING: Standard
Wind: Fresh half-behind Weather: Overcast with the odd spot of rain

7194 BOOK NOW FOR CHRISTMAS MAIDEN STKS 5f 20y(P)
2:15 (2:15) (Class 5) 2-Y-O **£1,908** (£563; £281) **Stalls** Low

Form RPR

24 1 **Exceedance**[15] 6892 2-9-3 0 .... (t) TomEaves 6 81+
(Bryan Smart) *mde virtually all: racd keenly: clr 1/2-way: shkn up over 1f out: r.o* **11/10**[1]

5 2 3 **Littlesuzie**[15] 6892 2-8-5 0 .... NicoleNordblad(7) 9 66
(Hans Adielsson) *sn chsng wnr: pushed along over 1f out: no imp fnl f* **6/1**[3]

05 3 nk **Crazy Too (IRE)**[21] 6758 2-8-12 0 .... PaulHanagan 7 65
(David Simcock) *hld up: hdwy 1/2-way: rdn over 1f out: styd on same pce ins fnl f* **85/40**[2]

0 4 4 1/2 **Marmalade Moon**[12] 6946 2-8-12 0 .... JimCrowley 1 48
(Robert Cowell) *chsd ldrs: rdn over 1f out: no ex fnl f* **18/1**

00 5 1 3/4 **Princess Kaiulani (IRE)**[9] 7038 2-8-12 0 .... WilliamCarson 5 42
(William Muir) *sn outpcd: mod late hdwy: nvr nrr* **20/1**

00 6 3/4 **Rivington**[10] 6983 2-9-3 0 .... TonyHamilton 3 44
(Richard Fahey) *hld up: rdn 1/2-way: n.d* **25/1**

250 7 3 1/4 **Launch On Line**[175] 1957 2-8-12 70 .... LukeMorris 8 28
(Bill Turner) *chsd ldrs to 1/2-way* **16/1**

0 8 3 1/2 **Stoneacre Wigan**[53] 5863 2-9-3 0 .... StephenCraine 2 20
(Peter Grayson) *hld up: wknd 1/2-way* **100/1**

62.95 secs (0.65) **Going Correction** -0.025s/f (Stan) **8** Ran SP% **114.6**
Speed ratings (Par 95): **93,88,87,80,77 76,71,65**
toteswingers:1&2:£2.20, 1&3:£1.50, 2&3:£1.90 CSF £8.34 TOTE £2.40: £1.20, £1.50, £1.10; EX 9.90 Trifecta £12.40 Pool: £575.05 - 34.10 winning units..
Owner Andrew Tinkler **Bred** A S Denniff **Trained** Hambleton, N Yorks

FOCUS
An uncompetitive maiden which few ever got into. The winner may do better still when the emphasis is on speed. The form looks quite straightforward.

NOTEBOOK
Exceedance had shown plenty of ability in his first two starts on turf (which came 149 days apart) and having soon got himself to the front never looked in much danger once clear turning in. He did edge away to his right in the straight and had to be kept up to his work, but his future will depend on the mark he is now given. (op 10-11)
Littlesuzie finished just a length behind Exceedance on her Bath debut earlier this month after getting hampered, but despite having every chance she was beaten further by him this time. (tchd 13-2)
Crazy Too(IRE), unplaced in two 6f Yarmouth maidens, was the only one to make any real impression from off the pace. Her dam was a Listed winner over 1m4f, so a return to further will be in her favour and she now gets a mark. (op 5-2 tchd 11-4 and 2-1)
Marmalade Moon lasted longer than when last of 11 on her Kempton debut 12 days earlier and is likely to improved again from this. (op 20-1 tchd 16-1)
Princess Kaiulani(IRE), well beaten in two 6f maidens here, will have more options now that she gets a mark (tchd 18-1)

Launch On Line, returning from 175 days off, continues to disappointed since her promising Lingfield debut.

7195 BREEDERS' CUP ONLY ON ATR H'CAP 1m 5f 194y(P)
2:50 (3:15) (Class 6) (0-60,58) 3-Y-0+ **£1,704** (£503; £251) **Stalls** Low

Form RPR

1 **The Drunken Dr (IRE)**[43] 6198 3-8-12 **52**....(b) MartinHarley 13 63
(Niall Moran, Ire) *hld up: hdwy over 3f out: sn rdn: led ins fnl f: hung lft nr fin: all out* **8/1**

550 **2** *hd* **Rosairlie (IRE)**[12] 6944 3-9-4 **58**.... LukeMorris 8 69
(Harry Dunlop) *hld up: hdwy over 2f out: rdn and hung lft fr over 1f out: styd on: n.m.r nr fin* **25/1**

0535 **3** *3* **Black Iceman**[28] 6585 3-8-9 **49**.... LiamKeniry 3 56
(Lydia Pearce) *mid-div: hdwy 1/2-way: led over 2f out: rdn and hung lft over 1f out: hdd and unable qck ins fnl f* **10/1**

4054 **4** *1 1/2* **Maslak (IRE)**[16] 6870 7-9-13 **58**.... ChrisCatlin 6 63
(Peter Hiatt) *chsd ldrs: ev ch 2f out: sn rdn: no ex fnl f* **14/1**

6605 **5** *2* **Carnac (IRE)**[5] 7107 5-9-7 **52**....(p) ShaneKelly 10 54
(Alan McCabe) *s.i.s: hdwy to chse ldr 10f out: led 3f out: rdn and hdd 2f out: wknd ins fnl f* **10/1**

0-00 **6** *1/2* **Layla's Boy**[24] 6666 4-9-9 **54**....(t) GrahamGibbons 1 55
(John Mackie) *mid-div: hdwy 1/2-way: rdn over 1f out: wknd ins fnl f* **17/2**

16-4 **7** *9* **Kickahead (USA)**[16] 6873 9-9-4 **52**....(t) RyanClark(3) 12 41
(Ian Williams) *prom: lost pl 8f out: hdwy u.p over 2f out: sn wknd* **13/2**[3]

5354 **8** *3 1/2* **Dhampas**[18] 6823 3-8-6 **46**....(b) NickyMackay 11 30
(Jim Boyle) *sn prom: led over 11f out: clr 6f out: hdd 3f out: wknd wl over 1f out* **9/2**[2]

6404 **9** *11* **Graycliffe (IRE)**[9] 7036 5-9-12 **57**.... StephenCraine 4 26
(Jennie Candlish) *rrd s: a in rr: t.o* **22/1**

23 **10** *2* **Locum**[16] 6873 6-9-11 **56**.... PaulHanagan 5 22
(Mark H Tompkins) *hld up: rdn and wknd over 2f out: t.o* **85/40**[1]

50/0 **11** *62* **More For Less**[10] 7004 4-8-12 **46**.... PaulPickard(3) 9 —
(Owen Brennan) *chsd ldrs: lost pl over 11f out: bhd and rdn 7f out: t.o* **100/1**

4200 **12** *3/4* **Bute Street**[35] 6405 6-9-9 **57**.... HarryBentley(3) 7 —
(Ron Hodges) *hld up: rdn over 4f out: sn wknd: t.o* **12/1**

222- **13** *15* **Sassanian (IRE)**[419] 3213 4-9-12 **57**.... AndreaAtzeni 2 —
(Nikki Evans) *led: hdd over 11f out: pushed along over 9f out: rdn and wknd 5f out: t.o* **33/1**

3m 4.81s (-1.19) **Going Correction** -0.025s/f (Stan)
WFA 3 from 4yo+ 9lb **13** Ran SP% **129.8**
Speed ratings (Par 101): **102,101,100,99,98 97,92,90,84,83 47,47,38**
toteswingers:1&2:£46.80, 1&3:£20.00, 2&3:£70.60 CSF £208.58 CT £2059.82 TOTE £11.10: £3.50, £9.50, £2.70; EX 392.20 Trifecta £346.80 Part won. Pool: £468.77 - 0.62 winning units..
Owner Edric Browne **Bred** L Mulryan **Trained** Strokestown, Co Roscommon

FOCUS
A moderate staying handicap and a race of changing fortunes. A fair time for the grade and sound form.
Sassanian(IRE) Official explanation: jockey said gelding was never travelling

7196 HOTEL & CONFERENCING AT WOLVERHAMPTON (S) STKS 7f 32y(P)
3:20 (3:55) (Class 6) 2-Y-O **£1,533** (£452; £226) **Stalls** High

Form RPR

0140 **1** **Adranian (IRE)**[23] 6699 2-9-2 68....(v) AdamKirby 7 68
(David Evans) *hld up: hdwy over 2f out: rdn to ld ins fnl f: r.o* **5/1**[3]

644 **2** *1 1/2* **Le King Beau (USA)**[7] 7067 2-8-11 0.... BarryMcHugh 1 59
(Tony Coyle) *chsd ldrs: led 2f out: sn rdn and edgd rt: hdd and unable qck ins fnl f* **3/1**[2]

6220 **3** *1 1/4* **Make Up**[44] 6144 2-8-6 54.... DuranFentiman 6 51
(Noel Wilson) *sn pushed along in rr: hdwy over 1f out: sn rdn: r.o* **20/1**

6 **4** *2 1/4* **Can Do Les (IRE)**[135] 3194 2-8-11 0.... JoeFanning 2 51
(Keith Dalgleish) *a.p: rdn over 1f out: styd on same pce fnl f* **7/1**

3535 **5** *3/4* **The Dancing Lord**[11] 6975 2-8-9 71.... RyanWhile(7) 4 54
(Bill Turner) *sn prom: chsd ldr over 5f out: led over 3f out: hdd 2f out: sn rdn: edgd rt over 1f out: wknd ins fnl f* **8/1**

3652 **6** *nk* **Artists Corner**[17] 6835 2-8-11 58....(b) TonyHamilton 9 48
(Richard Fahey) *s.s: hdwy on outer over 2f out: rdn over 1f out: wknd and edgd lft ins fnl f* **8/1**

3345 **7** *1* **Persidha**[11] 6970 2-8-6 67.... PaulHanagan 3 41
(Gay Kelleway) *hld up in tch: pushed along over 2f out: n.m.r over 1f out: wknd fnl f* **5/2**[1]

0300 **8** *1 3/4* **Ice Loch**[9] 7035 2-8-11 53....(b1) LukeMorris 11 43
(Michael Blanshard) *sn pushed along in rr: hdwy over 5f out: ev ch 2f out: sn rdn and edgd rt: wknd fnl f* **33/1**

3006 **9** *54* **Storm Fairy**[48] 6021 2-8-6 45.... WilliamCarson 12 —
(Mrs K Burke) *chsd ldrs tl rdn and wknd over 2f out: t.o* **33/1**

00 **10** *1 3/4* **Clouds Of Glory**[15] 6892 2-8-3 0.... HarryBentley(3) 10 —
(Ron Hodges) *led 4f: sn rdn and wknd* **100/1**

1m 30.57s (0.97) **Going Correction** -0.025s/f (Stan) **10** Ran SP% **116.6**
Speed ratings (Par 93): **93,91,89,87,86 86,84,82,21,19**
toteswingers:1&2:£4.10, 1&3:£11.60, 2&3:£11.90 CSF £19.77 TOTE £7.60: £2.00, £1.70, £2.70; EX 30.10 TRIFECTA Not won..There was no bid for the winner. Le King Beau was claimed by W R Muir for £6,000.
Owner Cos We Can Partnership **Bred** Hugh O'Brien **Trained** Pandy, Monmouths
■ Stewards' Enquiry : Ryan While two-day ban: careless riding (Nov 14-15)

FOCUS
A moderate seller and something of a rough race with the hanging Le King Beau edging right off the home bend and forcing several of his rivals wide. Sound form for the grade.

NOTEBOOK
Adranian(IRE) had twice struggled in handicaps since winning a C&D claimer last month, but the drop in class under conditions he is proven under did the trick and, having been held up early, he led a furlong out and won going away. (op 9-2)
Le King Beau(USA) found 1m too far two starts back and 6f inadequate last time, so the return to this trip promised to suit and he attracted support. In front just after halfway, he didn't handle the turn for home too well and hung out into the centre of the track, but still held the lead until the winner was unleashed. He was claimed by William Muir and can win a seller. (op 7-2)
Make Up, last of eight on her debut for the yard in an Ayr nursery last time, had previously finished runner-up in a couple of sellers for Richard Hannon. She didn't perform badly on these disadvantageous terms, but wasn't as inconvenienced by the hanging runner-up as some of her rivals.
Can Do Les(IRE), making his debut for the yard after a break having finished well beaten in three turf maidens in Ireland, also appeared to enjoy a clear run. (op 17-2)
The Dancing Lord had a decent chance at the weights, but he was having his first try at 7f and didn't appear to see it out. (tchd 9-1)
Artists Corner had a bit to find with a few of these at the weights, but can be forgiven this to a degree as she gave her rivals a start and was forced widest off the home turn.
Persidha, a tailed-off last of five over 1m at Brighton last time, was still best in at the weights on account of her previous efforts but, although briefly short of room after turning in, she was in no way unlucky. (op 9-4)
Clouds Of Glory's rider reported that the filly hung right-handed. Official explanation: jockey said filly hung right-handed

7197 BREEDERS' CUP LIVE ATR SKY 415 MAIDEN STKS 7f 32y(P)
3:55 (4:33) (Class 5) 2-Y-O **£1,908** (£563; £281) **Stalls** High

Form RPR

605 **1** **Johnno**[12] 6951 2-9-3 74.... DaneO'Neill 11 74+
(J W Hills) *s.i.s: hld up: hdwy over 2f out: led ins fnl f: r.o: readily* **3/1**[3]

05 **2** *1 3/4* **Andalieb**[55] 5801 2-9-3 0.... PaulHanagan 3 70
(David Simcock) *chsd ldrs: rdn and ev ch 1f out: styd on same pce* **5/2**[1]

3262 **3** *1 1/2* **Tortoni (IRE)**[12] 6945 2-9-3 79.... PhillipMakin 6 66
(Kevin Ryan) *led: rdn over 1f out: hdd and unable qck ins fnl f* **11/4**[2]

44 **4** *2 1/2* **Hey Fiddle Fiddle (IRE)**[48] 6019 2-8-7 0.... MatthewLawson(5) 7 55+
(Charles Hills) *w ldr: rdn and ev ch over 1f out: no ex fnl f* **8/1**

0 **5** *2 1/4* **Beauchamp Orange**[33] 6440 2-8-5 0....(b1) NicoleNordblad(7) 12 49
(Hans Adielsson) *s.i.s: hdwy over 2f out: styd on: nt trble ldrs* **25/1**

6 *4* **Fistful Of Dollars (IRE)** 2-9-3 0.... FergusSweeney 5 45
(Jamie Osborne) *hld up: pushed along 1/2-way: sn wknd* **16/1**

06 **7** *2 1/2* **Compton Air (USA)**[42] 6216 2-9-3 0....(t) JimCrowley 2 38
(Hans Adielsson) *mid-div: effrt over 2f out: slipped wl over 1f out: sn wknd* **12/1**

8 *6* **Foursquare Funtime** 2-9-3 0.... AdamKirby 4 24
(Reg Hollinshead) *s.i.s: outpcd* **50/1**

9 *2* **Morna's Glory** 2-8-9 0.... HarryBentley(3) 9 14
(Ron Hodges) *prom tl wknd over 2f out* **66/1**

0 **10** *1 1/4* **Minty Jones**[17] 6842 2-8-10 0.... NoelGarbutt(7) 10 16
(Michael Mullineaux) *hld up: hdwy 4f out: wknd over 2f out* **150/1**

0 **11** *2 1/2* **Critical Point**[6] 7080 2-9-3 0.... SebSanders 1 10
(Sir Mark Prescott Bt) *sn outpcd* **22/1**

0 **12** *11* **Mrs Awkward**[11] 6977 2-8-12 0.... ShaneKelly 8 —
(Mark Brisbourne) *chsd ldrs tl wknd over 2f out: t.o* **150/1**

1m 30.23s (0.63) **Going Correction** -0.025s/f (Stan) **12** Ran SP% **117.9**
Speed ratings (Par 95): **95,93,91,88,85 81,78,71,69,67 65,52**
toteswingers:1&2:£66.00, 1&3:£11.70, 2&3:£21.10 CSF £10.42 TOTE £5.00: £1.70, £1.20, £1.80; EX 16.00 Trifecta £42.80 Pool: £620.36 - 10.71 winning units..
Owner Gary And Linnet Woodward **Bred** Gestut Sohrenhof **Trained** Upper Lambourn, Berks

FOCUS
A routine Polytrack maiden, dominated by the market principals. The winning time was 0.34 seconds quicker than the seller. The winner is improving with racing and the second produced a small step up.

NOTEBOOK
Johnno improved on his third start when fifth of 15 at Newmarket earlier this month and took another step forward. He wasn't best away from his wide draw, but travelled into the race smoothly and maintained his effort around the outside to hit the front inside the last furlong. He should have a future in handicaps. (op 11-4 tchd 10-3)
Andalieb was always in a good position and had every chance on the inside a furlong out, but couldn't match the finishing pace of the winner. He has improved with each outing and will have more options now that he gets a mark. (op 3-1)
Tortoni(IRE), placed in five of his six previous starts, was probably not helped by the close attentions of Hey Fiddle Fiddle from the off, which may have softened him up for the closing stages. He has had enough chances now, however, and would have been 5lb worse off with the winner in a handicap. (op 5-2 tchd 9-4)
Hey Fiddle Fiddle(IRE) was a disappointing favourite at Folkestone last time following her promising Windsor debut and she didn't get home here after disputing the early advantage. (tchd 9-1)
Beauchamp Orange showed some ability when eighth of 13 on her Kempton debut last month and had blinkers on this time. She took a while to get into her stride early, but came home well enough and she gives the impression she is capable of better. (op 33-1)
Fistful Of Dollars(IRE), a 42,000gns half-brother to five winners including the Listed winner Troubadour, is by a sire with a decent record on Polytrack and this experience shouldn't be lost on him.

7198 ENJOY THE PARTY PACK GROUP OFFER H'CAP 1m 141y(P)
4:30 (5:00) (Class 6) (0-65,65) 3-Y-O **£1,704** (£503; £251) **Stalls** Low

Form RPR

4045 **1** **Stylistickhill (IRE)**[7] 7071 3-8-7 **54**....(t) BillyCray(3) 4 64+
(David Nicholls) *s.i.s: hld up: hdwy over 2f out: hmpd sn after: rdn ins fnl f: r.o to ld towards fin* **14/1**

2400 **2** *1/2* **McCool Bannanas**[44] 6181 3-8-12 **59**.... AdamBeschizza(3) 2 67
(James Unett) *s.i.s: hld up: hdwy over 2f out: rdn ins fnl f: r.o* **20/1**

6412 **3** *nk* **Princess Gail**[10] 7005 3-8-11 **55**.... ShaneKelly 11 62
(Mark Brisbourne) *hld up: hdwy over 2f out: led ins fnl f: sn rdn: hdd towards fin* **4/1**[2]

002 **4** *2* **Loves Theme (IRE)**[6] 7085 3-8-9 **60**....(b) NatashaEaton(7) 12 62
(Alan Bailey) *prom: chsd ldr over 6f out: led wl over 2f out: rdn and hdd ins fnl f: no ex* **11/1**

6036 **5** *nk* **Lady Gar Gar**[54] 5821 3-9-4 **65**....(v1) DaleSwift(3) 9 67
(Geoffrey Oldroyd) *prom: rdn to chse ldr over 1f out tl styd on same pce fnl f* **8/1**[3]

1310 **6** *nk* **Appyjack**[14] 6923 3-9-4 **62**.... LukeMorris 10 63
(Tony Carroll) *chsd ldrs: rdn over 1f out: no ex ins fnl f* **10/1**

35-5 **7** *4* **Starstuded (IRE)**[28] 6578 3-9-4 **62**.... PaulHanagan 6 54
(William Haggas) *hld up: hdwy over 2f out: wknd over 1f out* **4/1**[2]

1660 **8** *1 1/4* **Catallout (IRE)**[16] 6869 3-9-0 **65**.... JasonHart(7) 3 54
(Declan Carroll) *hld up: rdn over 2f out: nvr on terms* **16/1**

6001 **9** *nk* **Shelovestobouggie**[16] 6878 3-9-5 **63**....(t) AndreaAtzeni 7 51
(Marco Botti) *hld up in tch: rdn over 1f out: edgd lft and wknd fnl f* **7/2**[1]

5340 **10** *1 1/4* **Nicola's Dream**[19] 6799 3-9-5 **63**....(p) TonyHamilton 5 48
(Richard Fahey) *chsd ldrs: lost pl 6f out: wknd over 2f out* **16/1**

5-50 **11** *9* **Lady Deanie (IRE)**[175] 1958 3-8-9 **53**.... RichardKingscote 8 18
(Bryn Palling) *sn led: hdd wl over 2f out: wknd over 1f out* **66/1**

6500 **12** *23* **Illawalla**[75] 5165 3-8-7 **51** oh6....(p) JamesSullivan 1 —
(Hugh McWilliams) *chsd ldrs: rdn over 3f out: sn wknd: t.o* **100/1**

1m 50.41s (-0.09) **Going Correction** -0.025s/f (Stan) **12** Ran SP% **116.4**
Speed ratings (Par 99): **99,98,98,96,96 95,92,91,91,89 81,61**
toteswingers:1&2:£3.60, 1&3:£7.10, 2&3:£10.80 CSF £259.38 CT £1352.32 TOTE £13.10: £2.70, £6.50, £1.50; EX 266.80 Trifecta £460.90 Part won. Pool: £622.97 - 0.20 winning units..
Owner Paul Dixon & The Tickhill Racing Partner **Bred** Eamon Reilly **Trained** Sessay, N Yorks

FOCUS
A modest handicap in which the first three horses all came from well off the pace. The form looks sound, with a clear personal best from the winner who looked a bit better than the bare form.

Starstuded(IRE) Official explanation: jockey said filly hung left throughout

7199 BREEDERS' CUP LIVE ATR VIRGIN 534 H'CAP — 1m 141y(P)
5:00 (5:30) (Class 4) (0-80,80) 3-Y-O+ — **£2,911** (£866; £432; £216) **Stalls** Low

Form — RPR

0601 **1** — **Gritstone**[24] 6669 4-9-3 **75** .... PaulHanagan 4 — 88
(Richard Fahey) *a.p: rdn to ld ins fnl f: r.o* **6/5**[1]

5631 **2** 1 1/4 **Elijah Pepper (USA)**[30] 6543 6-9-4 **76** .... GrahamGibbons 13 — 86
(David Barron) *chsd ldrs: rdn to ld 1f out: sn hdd: styd on same pce* **6/1**[2]

1050 **3** 1 1/2 **Munsarim (IRE)**[23] 6708 4-9-6 **78** .... JoeFanning 11 — 85
(Keith Dalgleish) *hld up: hdwy over 2f out: rdn over 1f out: r.o* **8/1**

0360 **4** 1/2 **Kidlat**[62] 5608 6-9-5 **77** .... AdamKirby 9 — 82
(Alan Bailey) *sn pushed along and prom: led over 7f out: clr over 6f out: rdn and hdd 1f out: no ex ins fnl f* **16/1**

5224 **5** shd **Lockantanks**[17] 6830 4-9-3 **75** .... NeilChalmers 3 — 80
(Michael Appleby) *chsd ldrs: lost pl 1/2-way: hdwy over 2f out: rdn over 1f out: styd on same pce ins fnl f* **13/2**[3]

0316 **6** 1 1/2 **Mishrif (USA)**[32] 6478 5-9-4 **76** ....(b) ShaneKelly 8 — 78
(J R Jenkins) *prom: rdn over 2f out: styd on* **16/1**

0000 **7** 1 3/4 **Snow Dancer (IRE)**[37] 6330 7-9-7 **79** .... PhillipMakin 7 — 77
(Hugh McWilliams) *s.i.s: in rr: rdn over 2f out: r.o ins fnl f: nrst fin* **12/1**

5500 **8** 1 1/2 **Tiradito (USA)**[32] 6478 4-9-1 **78** ....(p) MarkCoumbe(5) 5 — 72
(Michael Attwater) *hld up: rdn over 1f out: nvr on terms* **25/1**

5060 **9** 2 3/4 **Avonrose**[17] 6831 4-9-0 **77** .... NeilFarley(5) 2 — 65
(Derek Shaw) *hld up: rdn over 2f out: n.d* **33/1**

0000 **10** 5 **Vitznau (IRE)**[42] 6219 7-8-11 **72** .... HarryBentley(3) 12 — 48
(Robert Cowell) *s.i.s: swtchd lft sn after s: hdwy 4f out: rdn and wknd over 1f out* **14/1**

0600 **11** 1/2 **Titan Triumph**[173] 2000 7-9-8 **80** ....(t) JimCrowley 1 — 55
(William Knight) *hld up: rdn over 2f out: a in rr* **28/1**

6150 **12** 3/4 **Invincible Force (IRE)**[14] 6917 7-9-7 **79** ....(b) JamesSullivan 10 — 53
(Paul Green) *led: hdd over 7f out: chsd ldr tl rdn over 2f out: wknd over 1f out* **50/1**

1m 49.14s (-1.36) **Going Correction** -0.025s/f (Stan) — 12 Ran SP% **122.5**
Speed ratings (Par 105): **105,103,102,102,102 100,99,97,95,90 90,89**
toteswingers:1&2:£3.60, 1&3:£7.10, 2&3:£10.80 CSF £8.36 CT £45.12 TOTE £2.50: £1.50, £1.80, £2.60; EX 11.00 Trifecta £235.90 Pool: £580.35 - 1.82 winning units..
Owner The Living Legend Racing Partnership **Bred** D W Armstrong **Trained** Musley Bank, N Yorks
■ Stewards' Enquiry : Jim Crowley five-day ban: used whip when out of contention (Nov 14-18)

FOCUS
A fair handicap with a decent pace set by Kidlat and the winning time was 1.27 seconds faster than the preceding Class 6 event. The form looks solid, the winner back to his 3yo best.

7200 ATR BREEDERS' CUP MEGASITE NOW LIVE H'CAP — 1m 4f 50y(P)
5:30 (6:00) (Class 5) (0-70,70) 3-Y-O+ — **£2,045** (£603; £302) **Stalls** Low

Form — RPR

1435 **1** — **Waahej**[14] 6918 5-9-0 **66** .... LauraPike(5) 9 — 79
(Peter Hiatt) *hld up: hdwy to ld 2f out: sn rdn clr* **5/1**[3]

2036 **2** 7 **Viva Diva**[24] 6666 3-9-2 **70** .... ShaneKelly 11 — 74+
(David Lanigan) *chsd ldrs: n.m.r and lost pl 3f out: rallied over 1f out: styd on to go 2nd ins fnl f: no ch w wnr* **9/2**[2]

6/00 **3** 3 **Miss Beat (IRE)**[10] 6990 5-8-13 **65** .... NeilFarley(5) 3 — 62
(Declan Carroll) *hld up: racd keenly: hdwy 4f out: led 3f out: hdd 2f out: wknd fnl f* **20/1**

4006 **4** 1/2 **Irish Jugger (USA)**[30] 6546 4-9-4 **65** .... JamesMillman 2 — 61
(Rod Millman) *hld up: styd on ins fnl f: nrst fin* **20/1**

6313 **5** 1/2 **Hit The Switch**[7] 7070 5-9-3 **64** ....(p) StephenCraine 5 — 59
(Jennie Candlish) *led: hdd 3f out: wknd over 1f out* **8/1**

5662 **6** hd **Alhaban (IRE)**[17] 6844 5-9-5 **66** ....(p) LukeMorris 1 — 61
(Ronald Harris) *hld up: rdn over 1f out: nvr on terms* **16/1**

0254 **7** 1 1/4 **Mill Mick**[10] 7004 4-9-2 **63** ....(p) PaulHanagan 4 — 56
(John Mackie) *prom: rdn over 2f out: wknd over 1f out* **9/1**

-000 **8** 2 1/4 **Irons On Fire (USA)**[89] 4664 3-9-0 **68** .... DaneO'Neill 7 — 57
(George Baker) *s.i.s: n.d* **33/1**

1622 **9** 1 1/4 **Ghufa (IRE)**[53] 5866 7-9-8 **69** .... ChrisCatlin 10 — 56
(Lydia Pearce) *hld up: rdn over 1f out: nvr nrr* **5/1**[3]

0060 **10** 7 **Saint Thomas (IRE)**[27] 6601 4-9-5 **66** .... GrahamGibbons 12 — 42
(John Mackie) *chsd ldrs: rdn over 2f out: wknd wl over 1f out* **4/1**[1]

3055 **11** 1 1/2 **Spring Secret**[20] 6773 5-9-1 **62** .... RichardKingscote 8 — 36
(Bryn Palling) *chsd ldr: rdn over 2f out: sn wknd* **9/1**

2m 39.87s (-1.23) **Going Correction** -0.025s/f (Stan)
WFA 3 from 4yo+ 7lb — 11 Ran SP% **121.0**
Speed ratings (Par 103): **103,98,96,96,95 95,94,93,92,87 86**
toteswingers:1&2:£5.40, 1&3:£22.50, 2&3:£31.00 CSF £27.91 CT £424.66 TOTE £7.20: £2.00, £1.80, £8.00; EX 34.10 TRIFECTA Not won..
Owner Monarch Hose & Hydraulics / P W Hiatt **Bred** David John Brown **Trained** Hook Norton, Oxon
■ Stewards' Enquiry : Luke Morris caution: careless riding

FOCUS
An ordinary middle-distance handicap which turned into a one-horse race. The winner is rated around last season's wide-margin Polytrack win but the race rather fell apart and he may not have had to improve that much on recent form.
T/Jkpt: Not won. T/Plt: £124.80 to a £1 stake. Pool:£73,951.80 - 432.43 winning tickets T/Qpdt: £10.10 to a £1 stake. Pool:£8,050.82 - 587.54 winning tickets CR

7116 KEMPTON (A.W) (R-H)
Tuesday, November 1

OFFICIAL GOING: Standard
Wind: virtually nil Weather: bright

7201 32REDPOKER.COM H'CAP — 5f (P)
2:30 (2:31) (Class 6) (0-65,65) 3-Y-O+ — **£1,617** (£481; £240; £120) **Stalls** Low

Form — RPR

0500 **1** — **Estonia**[6] 7106 4-9-7 **65** .... AdamKirby 6 — 73
(Michael Squance) *taken down early: hld up in midfield: nt clr run jst over 1f out: squeezed between horses and hdwy 1f out: ev ch ins fnl f: r.o wl to ld nr fin* **5/1**[1]

050 **2** nk **Alis Aquilae (IRE)**[59] 5732 5-9-7 **65** .... StevieDonohoe 1 — 72
(Tim Etherington) *broke wl but sn pushed along and dropped to last trio: in tch: hdwy on inner to chse ldrs 1f out: swtchd lft and rdn to ld ins fnl f: r.o tl hdd and no ex nr fin* **5/1**[1]

1100 **3** 3/4 **Crimson Queen**[33] 6479 4-9-5 **63** .... IanMongan 4 — 67
(Roy Brotherton) *in tch in midfield: rdn and effrt over 1f out: chsd ldrs and drvn 1f out: kpt on same pce fnl 100yds* **7/1**[3]

4015 **4** hd **Howyadoingnotsobad (IRE)**[26] 6655 3-9-0 **58** .... TomMcLaughlin 5 — 62
(Karen George) *led: rdn over 1f out: hdd ins fnl f: no ex and one pce fnl 150yds* **6/1**[2]

1344 **5** 3/4 **Dorothy's Dancing (IRE)**[73] 5279 3-9-1 **59** ....(p) FergusSweeney 2 — 60
(Gary Moore) *t.k.h: chsd ldrs: rdn to ld 1f out: hdd ins fnl f: wknd fnl 75yds* **11/1**

4135 **6** 2 1/2 **Griffin Point (IRE)**[20] 6802 4-9-4 **62** .... MartinDwyer 8 — 54
(William Muir) *chsd ldr tl jst over 1f out: wknd ins fnl f* **6/1**[2]

6002 **7** 1/2 **Black Baccara**[14] 6931 4-9-0 **61** ....(be) RyanClark(3) 9 — 51
(Phil McEntee) *in tch in midfield: rdn and effrt over 1f out: no imp 1f out: wknd ins fnl f* **9/1**

/000 **8** nk **Lady Royal Oak (IRE)**[5] 7116 4-9-2 **60** .... KirstyMilczarek 10 — 49
(Olivia Maylam) *led rdrless to s: stdd s: hld up in rr: rdn and sme hdwy over 1f out: kpt on but nvr trbld ldrs* **50/1**

2610 **9** 3/4 **The Strig**[6] 7106 4-9-7 **65** ....(v) WilliamCarson 11 — 51+
(Stuart Williams) *pressed ldrs on outer: rdn ent fnl 2f: unable qck u.p 1f out: wknd fnl f* **7/1**[3]

2512 **10** 1 1/4 **Jimmy Ryan (IRE)**[88] 4759 10-9-2 **60** ....(t) SebSanders 12 — 42
(Tim McCarthy) *taken down early: a towards rr: edgd rt and wknd over 1f out* **20/1**

0060 **11** 1 1/4 **Dolly Parton (IRE)**[22] 6746 3-8-10 **57** ....(v) SeanLevey(3) 3 — 34
(John Bridger) *in rr fr 1/2-way: wknd over 1f out* **50/1**

59.75 secs (-0.75) **Going Correction** -0.125s/f (Stan) — 11 Ran SP% **113.9**
Speed ratings (Par 101): **101,100,99,99,97 93,92,91,89 87**
toteswingers:1&2:£8.00, 2&3:£10.40, 1&3:£9.60 CSF £27.88 CT £175.73 TOTE £5.40: £1.50, £3.90, £4.10; EX 46.30.
Owner Miss K Squance **Bred** Millsec Limited **Trained** Newmarket, Suffolk

FOCUS
A moderate sprint handicap. The first two came from off the pace and the winner is rated back to her best.

7202 £32 FREE AT 32RED.COM H'CAP (DIV I) — 1m 2f (P)
3:00 (3:01) (Class 6) (0-65,71) 3-Y-O+ — **£1,617** (£481; £240; £120) **Stalls** Low

Form — RPR

0000 **1** — **Lisahane Bog**[20] 6790 4-9-7 **65** ....(b) JohnFahy(3) 2 — 79
(Peter Hedger) *rdn along early: chsd ldr tl 9f out: rdn to ld 2f out: sn lft wl clr: styd on wl* **4/1**[1]

0310 **2** 6 **Abigails Angel**[27] 6622 4-9-3 **58** .... IanMongan 6 — 60
(Brett Johnson) *dwlt: rdn along early: hld up: rdn and hdwy over 2f out: lft 3rd wl over 1f out: chsd clr wnr over 1f out: no imp* **11/2**[3]

0005 **3** 3 1/4 **Gallantry**[27] 6624 9-9-2 **57** .... TomMcLaughlin 10 — 53
(Paul Howling) *stdd s: hld up in rr: hdwy and lft modest 4th wl over 1f out: no ch w wnr but r.o ins fnl f to snatch 3rd towards fin* **14/1**

0001 **4** nk **The Which Doctor**[6] 7098 6-10-2 **71** 6ex....(e) MartinHarley 11 — 66
(Richard Guest) *s.i.s and rdn along early: racd in last trio: hdwy over 4f out: lft modest 3rd wl over 1f out: no imp: lost 3rd nr fin* **9/2**[2]

0000 **5** 7 **Missionaire (USA)**[20] 6789 4-9-8 **63** ....(p) JimCrowley 12 — 44
(Tony Carroll) *racd in midfield: rdn and effrt on outer over 2f out: carried wd and outpcd 2f out and wl btn after* **20/1**

5565 **6** 1/2 **Novel Dancer**[88] 4755 3-9-6 **65** .... SteveDrowne 7 — 45
(Lydia Richards) *rdn along thrght: racd in last trio: wknd ent fnl 2f: no ch after* **12/1**

6510 **7** 1 **Genes Of A Dancer (AUS)**[20] 6784 5-9-0 **60** ow3.... LucyKBarry(5) 3 — 38
(Adrian Chamberlain) *hld up towards rr: hdwy on outer over 2f out: carried v wd and outpcd 2f out: wl btn after* **9/2**[2]

0206 **8** 2 1/2 **Kassiodor (GER)**[249] 684 4-9-2 **57** ....[1] TomQueally 4 — 30
(Barney Curley) *taken down early: led: hdd 2f out: sn hung bdly lft and reluctant: wl btn after* **12/1**

460- **9** 2 1/2 **Dazzling Begum**[396] 6538 6-8-11 **52** .... LiamKeniry 8 — 20
(Des Donovan) *a towards rr: rdn and struggling whn hmpd 2f out: sn wknd* **25/1**

5455 **10** 1/2 **Ocean Of Peace (FR)**[136] 3176 8-8-9 **57** .... KirstenSmith(7) 1 — 24
(Martin Bosley) *in tch in midfield: rdn and losing pl over 3f out: wknd and bhd whn hmpd 2f out* **12/1**

0000 **11** 72 **Dark Pegasus**[26] 6653 3-8-6 **51** oh6.... NickyMackay 9 — —
(Karen George) *chsd ldrs tl lost pl rapidly 4f out: t.o and eased fr over 2f out* **80/1**

000- **U** — **Whodunit (UAE)**[515] 2714 7-9-3 **58** ....(b) ChrisCatlin 5 — —
(Peter Hiatt) *chsd ldrs tl wnt 2nd 9f out: rdn and struggling whn hmpd, stmbld and uns rdr 2f out* **25/1**

2m 5.83s (-2.17) **Going Correction** -0.125s/f (Stan)
WFA 3 from 4yo+ 4lb — 12 Ran SP% **115.2**
Speed ratings (Par 101): **103,98,95,95,89 89,88,86,84,84 26,—**
toteswingers:1&2:£5.40, 2&3:£9.60, 1&3:£9.60 CSF £23.81 CT £278.81 TOTE £5.70: £2.80, £1.70, £4.80; EX 34.80.
Owner P C F Racing Ltd **Bred** J J Whelan **Trained** Dogmersfield, Hampshire

FOCUS
A moderate handicap and a rough race. It was a bit slower than division II. It looks safe to rate the winner back to his old best but nothing else ran to form.
Novel Dancer Official explanation: jockey said that the gelding suffered interference in running
Kassiodor(GER) Official explanation: jockey said that the gelding hung left throughout

7203 £32 FREE AT 32RED.COM H'CAP (DIV II) — 1m 2f (P)
3:30 (3:33) (Class 6) (0-65,65) 3-Y-O+ — **£1,617** (£481; £240; £120) **Stalls** Low

Form — RPR

3300 **1** — **Megalala (IRE)**[10] 7032 10-9-4 **62** .... KieranO'Neill(3) 9 — 75
(John Bridger) *mde all: rdn and styd on wl fr over 1f out: clr ins fnl f: rdn out* **14/1**

1024 **2** 3 **Colinca's Lad (IRE)**[42] 6241 9-8-12 **58** .... RosieJessop(5) 2 — 65
(Peter Charalambous) *chsd ldrs: chsd wnr over 4f out: drvn and styd on same pce fr over 1f out* **7/1**

1546 **3** 1/2 **Cane Cat (IRE)**[38] 6357 4-8-11 **59** ....(t) GeorgeDowning(7) 7 — 65
(Tony Carroll) *hld up in last quartet: rdn and hdwy over 2f out: chsd ldng pair over 1f out: kpt on ins fnl f but no threat to wnr* **16/1**

0652 **4** 3 3/4 **Rosco Flyer (IRE)**[20] 6790 5-9-9 **64** ....(b) AdamKirby 5 — 63
(Roger Teal) *s.i.s: towards rr: rdn 1/2-way: hdwy on outer over 2f out: no prog u.p over 1f out: wl btn 1f out* **9/4**[1]

0101 **5** hd **Bennelong**[17] 6871 5-9-3 **65** .... LukeRowe(7) 10 — 63
(Richard Rowe) *hld up in last pair: hdwy on wd outside over 2f out: no imp over 1f out: nvr trbld ldrs* **16/1**

0062 **6** 2 3/4 **Rainsborough**[6] 7091 4-8-10 **51** oh1.... JimCrowley 6 — 44
(Peter Hedger) *hld up in midfield: hdwy to chse ldng pair over 3f out: rdn and fnd little wl over 1f out: sn wknd* **13/2**[3]

043 **7** 3 3/4 **Nina Rose**[27] 6624 4-8-13 **57** .... JohnFahy(3) 4 — 42
(Clive Cox) *in tch in midfield: rdn 5f out: wknd wl over 1f out* **9/2**[2]

000 **8** *4 1/2* **Saviour Sand (IRE)**[17] 6872 7-9-2 57......................(t) KirstyMilczarek 11 33
(Olivia Maylam) *stdd s: hld up in last pair: rdn and btn over 2f out: no ch fnl 2f* **50/1**

2000 **9** *nk* **Cloudy Bay (USA)**[26] 6656 4-9-0 60..........................(p) RyanPowell(5) 1 36
(John Flint) *in tch in midfield: rdn and struggling over 2f out: wknd 2f out* **12/1**

501 **10** *9* **Phluke**[31] 6538 10-9-2 57.............................. FergusSweeney 3 15
(Eve Johnson Houghton) *chsd ldrs: nt clr run and shuffled bk to rr over 2f out: no ch and eased fr over 1f out* **12/1**

606 **11** *6* **Commerce**[11] 7003 4-9-1 56..(p) LiamKeniry 8 —
(Gary Moore) *chsd wnr tl over 4f out: dropped out qckly over 2f out: wl bhd fnl 2f: t.o* **14/1**

2m 5.51s (-2.49) **Going Correction** -0.125s/f (Stan) 11 Ran SP% **117.2**
Speed ratings (Par 101): **104,101,101,98,98 95,92,89,89,81 77**
toteswingers:1&2:£13.40, 2&3:£25.90, 1&3:£41.00 CSF £108.39 CT £1597.57 TOTE £21.90: £5.10, £1.90, £6.90; EX 151.70.
Owner Tommy Ware **Bred** Joseph Gallagher **Trained** Liphook, Hants

FOCUS
Very few ever got into this with the first two horses at the sharp end throughout. The winning time was 0.32 seconds faster than the first division. The first two both ran Polytrack personal bests.
Rosco Flyer(IRE) Official explanation: jockey said that the gelding was slowly away
Bennelong Official explanation: jockey said that the gelding was awkward on the final bend
Phluke Official explanation: jockey said that the gelding was never travelling

7204 32RED.COM H'CAP 1m 2f (P)
4:00 (4:02) (Class 4) (0-85,84) 3-Y-O £4,075 (£1,212; £606; £303) **Stalls** Low

Form RPR
5311 **1** **Proud Chieftain**[88] 4763 3-9-4 81.............................. JimCrowley 1 93+
(Clifford Lines) *hld up in midfield: travelling wl but nt clr run over 2f out: rdn and gd hdwy on inner to ld over 1f out: r.o wl fnl f: rdn out* **4/1**[2]

0210 **2** *1/2* **New Hampshire (USA)**[11] 6989 3-9-7 84...................... NickyMackay 5 95+
(John Gosden) *in tch in midfield: rdn 3f out: hdwy on outer to chse ldr and edgd rt over 1f out: ev ch thrght fnl f: r.o but a hld* **4/1**[2]

231- **3** *hd* **Auden (USA)**[397] 6504 3-9-4 81.............................. IanMongan 2 93+
(Mahmood Al Zarooni) *chsd ldrs: nt clr run and swtchd lft over 1f out: hdwy to chse ldng pair 1f out: kpt on wl u.p but nvr quite getting to wnr* **3/1**[1]

3- **4** *6* **Beginnings (USA)**[126] 3-9-0 77.............................. SebSanders 7 76
(Lydia Pearce) *hld up in last trio: rdn and hdwy on inner over 1f out: outpcd by ldrs 1f out: 4th and wl hld fnl f* **100/1**

-200 **5** *2 1/2* **If You Whisper (IRE)**[33] 6477 3-8-12 75.................. TonyCulhane 9 69
(Mike Murphy) *stdd s: hld up in last trio: hdwy on outer over 4f out: chsd ldrs 3f out: drvn and no ex over 1f out: wknd 1f out* **12/1**

41- **6** *1 1/4* **Inimitable Romanee (USA)**[387] 6770 3-9-0 77......... JimmyFortune 10 68
(Amanda Perrett) *chsd ldr: rdn and unable qck wl over 1f out: wkng whn short of room and hmpd over 1f out: sn wknd* **12/1**

520 **7** *nk* **Grand Theft Equine**[37] 6377 3-8-10 73...................... DaneO'Neill 3 64
(Jim Boyle) *led tl rdn and hdd over 1f out: btn 1f out: wknd qckly fnl f* **16/1**

4662 **8** *hd* **Tasfeya**[22] 6755 3-9-2 79.............................. AdamKirby 8 69
(John Akehurst) *chsd ldrs: rdn and unable qck 2f out: struggling whn hmpd jst over 1f out: wknd ins fnl f* **11/2**[3]

0652 **9** *1* **Balandra**[36] 6404 3-9-2 79..............................(t) KirstyMilczarek 6 67
(Luca Cumani) *s.i.s: racd in last trio: hdwy on outer over 4f out: squeezed for room and lost pl 4f out: bhd and hung lft over 2f out: sn lost tch* **12/1**

5300 **10** *1/2* **Buxfizz (USA)**[30] 5547 3-9-1 78.............................. TomQueally 4 65
(Robert Mills) *a in rr: rdn and btn over 2f out: sn bhd* **33/1**

2m 5.38s (-2.62) **Going Correction** -0.125s/f (Stan) 10 Ran SP% **113.3**
Speed ratings (Par 104): **105,104,104,99,97 96,96,96,95,95**
toteswingers:1&2:£4.10, 2&3:£3.50, 1&3:£4.20 CSF £19.74 CT £53.26 TOTE £5.20: £2.30, £2.50, £1.40; EX 21.70.
Owner Prima Racing Partnership **Bred** John James **Trained** Exning, Suffolk

FOCUS
A decent handicap for the grade and, with the pace honest, the winning time was quicker than both divisions of the class 6 handicap for older horses. The top three in the weights (all by sires with good records around here) dominated the finish and the form looks solid. The first three could be underrated here.

7205 32RED CASINO NURSERY 7f (P)
4:30 (4:30) (Class 5) (0-75,75) 2-Y-O £2,264 (£673; £336; £168) **Stalls** Low

Form RPR
035 **1** **Young Prince (IRE)**[43] 6214 2-9-4 72.............................. JimCrowley 4 80+
(Robert Mills) *in tch in midfield: rdn and effrt 2f out: qcknd to chal 1f out: led ins fnl f: r.o wl* **7/1**

0415 **2** *1 1/2* **Shannon Spree**[54] 5844 2-8-11 68.............................. KieranO'Neill(3) 10 70
(Richard Hannon) *sn pushed along in last trio: rdn and gd hdwy on inner 2f out: chsd wnr ins fnl f: r.o but no imp* **12/1**

4022 **3** *1 3/4* **Abhaath (USA)**[12] 6972 2-9-4 72..............................(p) RichardHills 11 70
(Saeed Bin Suroor) *led: rdn and fnd ex ent fnl 2f: hdd ins fnl f: nt gng pce of ldng pair after* **5/1**[2]

13 **4** *1/2* **Anginola (IRE)**[20] 6806 2-8-12 66.............................. TomQueally 5 62
(Joseph Tuite) *in tch: rdn and effrt 2f out: styd on u.p ins fnl f: nvr gng pce to chal ldrs* **7/2**[1]

0402 **5** *1 3/4* **Trusting (IRE)**[19] 6817 2-8-4 58 ow1.............................. ChrisCatlin 8 50
(Eve Johnson Houghton) *chsd ldrs: rdn and unable qck jst over 2f out: outpcd over 1f out: wknd ins fnl f* **20/1**

0510 **6** *nk* **Plym**[22] 6753 2-9-0 68.............................. JimmyFortune 2 59
(Richard Hannon) *sn bustled along to press ldr: rdn and unable qck over 2f out: wknd 1f out* **10/1**

6040 **7** *3/4* **Whinging Willie (IRE)**[37] 6372 2-9-4 72...................... FergusSweeney 6 61
(Gary Moore) *in tch in last trio: rdn and no imp over 2f out: styd on ins fnl f: nvr trbld ldrs* **14/1**

0230 **8** *1* **Represent (IRE)**[14] 6935 2-8-11 65.............................. TonyCulhane 9 51
(Mick Channon) *in tch in midfield: swtchd lft and effrt over 2f out: no imp and no threat to ldrs fnl 2f* **20/1**

0322 **9** *hd* **Siouxperhero (IRE)**[12] 6973 2-9-2 70..........................(b) MartinDwyer 7 56
(William Muir) *s.i.s: in tch in rr: rdn and effrt jst over 2f out: no real imp and nvr trbld ldrs* **13/2**

6006 **10** *nk* **Colourful Event (IRE)**[10] 7035 2-8-0 54 oh2 ow2.(v) FrankieMcDonald 1 39
(David Arbuthnot) *chsd ldrs: unable qck u.p over 2f out: wknd over 1f out* **50/1**

002 **11** *1* **Captivity**[24] 6697 2-9-7 75.............................. IanMongan 13 57
(Mahmood Al Zarooni) *chsd ldng pair: rdn and fnd little jst over 2f out: wknd 1f out* **11/2**[3]

1m 25.34s (-0.66) **Going Correction** -0.125s/f (Stan) 11 Ran SP% **115.0**
Speed ratings (Par 96): **98,96,94,93,91 91,90,89,89,88 87**
toteswingers:1&2:£16.70, 2&3:£10.80, 1&3:£7.80 CSF £83.38 CT £465.15 TOTE £10.30: £2.20, £2.80, £1.60; EX 106.10.
Owner Mrs B B Mills **Bred** J C Carr **Trained** Headley, Surrey

FOCUS
An ordinary nursery with a disputed lead. The winner impressed and can rate higher, and the form is solid in behind.

NOTEBOOK
Young Prince(IRE) was making his handicap debut after showing ability in a couple of maidens here and made light of his opening mark of 72. He showed a decent turn of foot to lead at the furlong pole and has the scope to progress in this sphere. (op 13-2)
Shannon Spree, 1-1 on Polytrack with her win coming over 1m here, did well to finish as close as she did as she wasn't travelling at all well from an early stage and had to be shoved along to stay in touch, but she ran on well when switched to the far rail after the intersection. A return to further will help her. (op 16-1)
Abhaath(USA) ran well to finish runner-up in his last two starts and performed well again, especially as he was given no peace up front by Plym early on and though in front on his own coming to the last furlong, was soon overhauled. (op 9-2)
Anginola(IRE) was unfortunate not to come into this 2-2 at the track, but on this occasion she took too long to pick up. She probably needs the extra furlong now.
Trusting(IRE) stepped up from her turf efforts when narrowly beaten in a C&D nursery last time, but although she ran creditably she found this tougher.
Whinging Willie(IRE), making his AW debut, was noted making some late headway and is worth keeping an eye on if returned to Polytrack. (op 16-1)
Siouxperhero(IRE), in the frame six times from ten starts but beaten at odds-on last time, had little chance after fluffing the start. Official explanation: jockey said that the colt reared and was slowly away (op 8-1)

7206 32REDBET.COM H'CAP 1m 4f (P)
5:00 (5:01) (Class 6) (0-55,55) 4-Y-O+ £1,617 (£481; £240; £120) **Stalls** Centre

Form RPR
-600 **1** **Shalambar (IRE)**[20] 6790 5-9-2 55.............................. JimCrowley 1 64+
(Tony Carroll) *sn pushed along to press ldr: led 5f out: mde rest: rdn and wnt clr over 2f out: kpt on ins fnl f: rdn out* **3/1**[1]

0040 **2** *2 3/4* **Suhailah**[14] 6926 5-8-5 49.............................. MarkCoumbe(5) 10 54
(Michael Attwater) *in tch in midfield: rdn and hdwy to chse wnr 2f out: kpt on fnl f but nvr gng to rch wnr* **16/1**

0041 **3** *1 1/4* **Beauchamp Xiara**[12] 6968 5-8-7 53...................... NicoleNordblad(7) 13 56
(Hans Adielsson) *hld up last quartet: pushed along and hdwy 2f out: styd on ins fnl f: wnt 3rd cl home: no ch* **8/1**[3]

2205 **4** *1/2* **Croix Rouge (USA)**[6] 7091 9-9-2 55...................... JamieGoldstein 3 57
(Ralph Smith) *in tch in midfield: rdn and effrt over 2f out: kpt on u.p ins fnl f: nvr gng pce to rch wnr* **16/1**

3350 **5** *3/4* **Laconicos (IRE)**[17] 6873 9-8-11 55..........................(t) LauraPike(5) 5 56
(William Stone) *taken down early: t.k.h: hld up in last quartet: rdn and effrt over 1f out: styd on wl ins fnl f: nvr trbld ldrs* **11/1**

6600 **6** *nk* **Musashi (IRE)**[6] 7091 6-9-2 55.............................. IanMongan 4 56
(Laura Mongan) *hld up in last quartet: nt clr run over 2f out: swtchd ins and effrt 2f out: hdwy u.p over 1f out: kpt on but no ch w wnr* **14/1**

0330 **7** *1/2* **Holden Eagle**[62] 5612 6-9-2 55.............................. DaneO'Neill 14 55
(Tony Newcombe) *t.k.h: chsd ldrs: rdn and unable qck jst over 2f out: plugged on same pce and no threat to wnr fnl 2f* **9/1**

5005 **8** *2* **Regal Rave (USA)**[19] 6811 4-8-8 50..........................(v) JohnFahy(3) 6 47
(Peter Hedger) *t.k.h: hld up in midfield: rdn and unable qck over 2f out: no ch w wnr fnl 2f* **8/1**[3]

6240 **9** *2 1/2* **Zelos Diktator**[12] 6968 5-9-0 53..............................(p) TomQueally 2 46
(Gary Moore) *in tch: rdn and lost pl over 2f out: no ch w wnr fnl 2f* **11/2**[2]

2050 **10** *2 3/4* **Vinces**[19] 6811 7-8-12 51..............................(b[1]) MartinDwyer 9 39
(Tim McCarthy) *dwlt: rcvrd and racd in midfield after 2f: chsd wnr over 4f out: rdn and outpcd over 2f out: wknd wl over 1f out* **25/1**

6506 **11** *2 3/4* **Sunset Boulevard (IRE)**[14] 6926 8-9-2 55...............(b) MartinHarley 12 39
(Paddy Butler) *hld up in last quartet: rdn and no prog on outer over 2f out: sn wknd* **25/1**

2003 **12** *5* **Chantilly Dancer (IRE)**[12] 6968 5-8-2 46............... MatthewLawson(5) 7 22
(Michael Quinn) *a bhd: rdn and wd bnd 3f out: sn lost tch* **20/1**

6200 **13** *1 1/4* **Miss Whippy**[28] 6600 4-8-10 49.............................. KirstyMilczarek 11 23
(Paul Howling) *led: hdd 5f out: rdn and flshing tail over 3f out: wknd wl over 2f out: bhd over 1f out* **25/1**

2m 34.14s (-0.36) **Going Correction** -0.125s/f (Stan) 13 Ran SP% **115.7**
Speed ratings (Par 101): **96,94,93,93,92 92,91,90,88,87 85,81,81**
CSF £49.48 CT £343.90 TOTE £2.40: £1.10, £6.50, £3.30; EX 62.80.
Owner B J Millen **Bred** His Highness The Aga Khan's Studs S C **Trained** Cropthorne, Worcs

FOCUS
A very moderate handicap run at a pedestrian pace, little more than a banded contest, but notable for a gamble landed. The winner has dropped a long way in the weights and could be capable of better. The form looks sound enough.
Shalambar(IRE) Official explanation: jockey said, regarding the apparent improvement of form, that the drop in grade and the step up in trip helped

7207 32REDBINGO.COM MEDIAN AUCTION MAIDEN STKS 1m (P)
5:30 (5:34) (Class 6) 3-5-Y-O £1,617 (£481; £240; £120) **Stalls** Low

Form RPR
62 **1** **Mad Ginger Alice**[25] 6668 3-8-12 0.............................. KirstyMilczarek 6 61+
(Olivia Maylam) *mde all: rdn over 2f out: styd on wl ins fnl f: rdn out* **11/4**[2]

465 **2** *1* **Royal Selection (IRE)**[12] 6981 3-8-12 0...................... TomMcLaughlin 5 59+
(Karen George) *hld up in tch: carried wd bnd 3f out: effrt to chse wnr 2f out: edgd lft and kpt on u.p 1f out: no imp fnl 75yds* **9/4**[1]

3 *1 3/4* **Chasin' Rainbows** 3-8-12 0.............................. LiamKeniry 7 55
(Sylvester Kirk) *s.i.s: in tch in last trio: rdn and effrt over 2f out: hdwy over 1f out: kpt on steadily ins fnl f* **11/2**

50 **4** *3/4* **Pacific Reach**[52] 5911 3-9-3 0..............................(t) JimmyFortune 4 58
(Andrew Balding) *chsd ldng pair: chsd wnr 3f out: rdn and unable qck over 2f out: outpcd and btn 1f out: plugged on but no threat to ldrs ins fnl f* **3/1**[3]

5 *3 3/4* **Bon Royale** 3-8-12 0.............................. ChrisCatlin 1 44
(Phil McEntee) *chsd ldr for 1f: stdd and hld up in tch after: rdn and effrt ent fnl 2f: wknd over 1f out* **14/1**

0- **6** *5* **Harlequin Girl**[413] 6058 3-8-9 0.............................. DominicFox(3) 8 32
(Terry Clement) *chsd ldr after 1f: hung lft bnd 3f out and lost 2nd: wknd over 2f out* **40/1**

7 7 **Bondie** 3-9-0 0.. KieranO'Neill(3) 3 20
(John Bridger) *slowly away: in tch in rr: rdn 1/2-way: wknd 2f out* **16/1**

1m 41.26s (1.46) **Going Correction** -0.125s/f (Stan) 7 Ran SP% **112.8**
Speed ratings (Par 101): **87,86,84,83,79 74,67**
toteswingers:1&2:£1.50, 2&3:£2.70, 1&3:£2.70 CSF £9.11 TOTE £3.10: £1.10, £1.90; EX 5.40.
Owner A C Maylam **Bred** Mrs P A Clark **Trained** Epsom, Surrey

FOCUS
A weak maiden run in a slow time. A small step up from the winner.

7208 32RED H'CAP 1m (P)
6:00 (6:00) (Class 5) (0-70,70) 3-Y-0+ **£2,264** (£673; £336; £168) **Stalls** Low

Form RPR
034 **1** **Full Bloom**[29] 6583 3-9-2 **70**..(p) KieranO'Neill(3) 4 79
(Gerard Butler) *in tch in midfield: rdn over 3f out: hdwy and chsd ldr ent fnl f: led ins fnl f: r.o strly and sn in command* **6/1**[3]

01 **2** 1 1/2 **Princess Icicle**[61] 5639 3-9-5 **70**.. DaneO'Neill 1 75
(Jo Crowley) *chsd ldrs: wnt 2nd over 2f out: rdn to ld 2f out: hdd ins fnl f: nt gng pce of wnr after* **10/3**[1]

4030 **3** *hd* **Cool Hand Jake**[55] 5835 5-9-6 **69**.. TomQueally 11 74
(Peter Makin) *in tch in last trio on outer: rdn over 2f out: hdwy over 1f out: chsd ldng pair and drvn ins fnl f: kpt on and pressing for 2nd cl home* **7/2**[2]

300 **4** 1 1/4 **Polar Auroras**[12] 6978 3-8-10 **61**.. JimCrowley 9 63
(Tony Carroll) *hld up in last pair: rdn and hdwy on inner jst over 2f out: kpt on same pce ins fnl f* **20/1**

5620 **5** 1 3/4 **Sasheen**[16] 6888 4-9-6 **69**.. FergusSweeney 5 67
(Jeremy Gask) *chsd ldr tl rdn to ld over 2f out: hdd 2f out and unable qck over 1f out: wknd 1f out* **8/1**

5340 **6** *nk* **Hereford Boy**[55] 5835 7-9-5 **68**..(p) AdamKirby 6 65
(Dean Ivory) *hld up in midfield: nt clr run fr over 2f out: switching lft and fnlly clr run jst over 1f out: kpt on but nvr able to chal* **8/1**

0140 **7** 1 **Prince Of Passion (CAN)**[8] 7057 3-8-6 **62**........(t) MatthewCosham(5) 2 57
(Derek Shaw) *chsd ldrs: rdn and effrt to chse ldng pair 2f out: sn unable qck and drvn: wknd ent fnl f* **14/1**

2200 **8** 3 **Blue Deer (IRE)**[20] 6797 3-9-2 **67**.. StevieDonohoe 8 55
(John Akehurst) *hld up in rr: struggling over 3f out: n.d* **25/1**

0040 **9** 1 **Mister Green (FR)**[164] 2304 5-9-6 **69**........................(bt) TonyCulhane 7 55
(David Flood) *s.i.s: sn rcvrd and in tch in midfield: short-lived effrt u.p on inner over 2f out: wknd wl over 1f out* **6/1**[3]

4341 **10** 6 **Belle Park**[11] 7006 4-8-0 **56**.. JulieCumine(7) 3 28
(Karen George) *led tl over 2f out: wknd 2f out: fdd ins fnl f* **10/1**

1m 38.65s (-1.15) **Going Correction** -0.125s/f (Stan)
WFA 3 from 4yo+ 2lb 10 Ran SP% **120.5**
Speed ratings (Par 103): **100,98,98,97,95 95,94,91,90,84**
toteswingers:1&2:£4.00, 2&3:£3.00, 1&3:£6.20 CSF £27.27 CT £84.70 TOTE £4.50: £1.40, £1.60, £1.80; EX 27.90.
Owner Shoreham Stud **Bred** Heather Raw **Trained** Newmarket, Suffolk

FOCUS
An ordinary handicap run at a fair pace. The form looks sound.
T/Jkpt: Not won. T/Plt: £100.90 to a £1 stake. Pool of £71,987.71 - 520.73 winning tickets.
T/Qpdt: £91.00 to a £1 stake. Pool of £5,635.34 - 45.80 winning tickets. SP

7058 REDCAR (L-H)
Tuesday, November 1

OFFICIAL GOING: Good (good to firm in places; 8.8)
Wind: fresh 1/2 behind Weather: fine

7209 BRITISH STALLION STUDS SUPPORTING BRITISH RACING EBF MAIDEN STKS (DIV I) 7f
12:40 (12:42) (Class 5) 2-Y-O **£2,652** (£789; £394; £197) **Stalls** Centre

Form RPR
6 **1** **Starboard**[59] 5697 2-9-3 0.. RobertHavlin 8 89+
(John Gosden) *dwlt and towards rr: smooth hdwy 1/2-way: swtchd rt and led 2f out: pushed clr appr fnl f: easily* **1/2**[1]

2 5 **Galician** 2-8-12 0.. FrederikTylicki 2 69+
(Mark Johnston) *trckd ldr: effrt 2f out: rdn to chse wnr over 1f out: kpt on same pce* **16/1**

3 4 **Dos Amigos (IRE)** 2-9-3 0.. TonyHamilton 11 62
(Michael Dods) *s.i.s and towards rr: hdwy 1/2-way: rdn wl over 1f out: styd on: nrst fin* **100/1**

4 2 1/4 **Cardinal Walter (IRE)** 2-9-3 0.. MartinLane 6 56
(David Simcock) *in tch: pushed along and outpcd 1/2-way: rdn wl over 2f out: styd on wl appr fnl f: nrst fin* **10/1**[3]

5 1 **Sky Crossing** 2-9-3 0.. JamesSullivan 9 53
(James Given) *led: rdn along and hdd 2f out: wknd over 1f out* **20/1**

02 **6** *nk* **Scrupul (IRE)**[25] 6675 2-9-3 0.. J-PGuillambert 5 52
(Luca Cumani) *t.k.h early: trckd ldrs: effrt wl over 2f out: sn rdn and wknd over 1f out* **5/1**[2]

0 **7** 3 **Vite (IRE)**[31] 6532 2-9-3 0.. TomEaves 1 45
(Bryan Smart) *chsd ldrs: rdn along wl over 2f out: grad wknd* **33/1**

0 **8** 5 **Duke Liam (IRE)**[15] 6912 2-8-10 0.. ShirleyTeasdale(7) 12 32
(David Nicholls) *chsd ldrs: rdn along over 2f out: sn wknd* **100/1**

6 **9** 3 **Shatter (IRE)**[14] 6935 2-8-12 0.. ShaneKelly 3 19
(William Haggas) *dwlt: a towards rr* **12/1**

10 1 3/4 **Moorside Magic** 2-8-12 0.. PaulHanagan 7 14
(Richard Fahey) *s.i.s and wnt lft s: a in rr* **25/1**

0 **11** 3 **Willy McBay**[18] 6825 2-9-3 0.. AndrewMullen 4 11
(George Moore) *in tch: rdn along bef 1/2-way: sn wknd and bhd* **200/1**

0 **12** 8 **Niceonemyson**[7] 7072 2-9-3 0.. PaddyAspell 10 —
(Christopher Wilson) *chsd ldrs: rdn along 1/2-way: sn wknd* **200/1**

1m 24.73s (0.23) **Going Correction** +0.15s/f (Good) 12 Ran SP% **116.8**
Speed ratings (Par 96): **104,98,93,91,90 89,86,80,77,75 71,62**
toteswingers:1&2:£4.90, 2&3:£83.30, 1&3:£25.90 CSF £10.63 TOTE £1.40: £1.10, £4.00, £20.10; EX 13.20 Trifecta £371.70 Part won. Pool of £502.42 - 0.43 winning units..
Owner K Abdulla **Bred** Juddmonte Farms Ltd **Trained** Newmarket, Suffolk

FOCUS
An interesting maiden won in good style by the potentially smart Starboard, who recorded a time a full second quicker than the next leg. The time was also faster than the Class 5 handicap for 3yos. The winner built on his debut promise but the depth of the race is in question.

NOTEBOOK
Starboard ◆ managed only sixth on his debut at Ascot, but was sent off just 2-1 that day and the race has worked out well. Despite starting a bit sluggishly this time, he moved into contention going easily and drew clear with significant ease. He's one to keep in mind for next year. (op 4-7 tchd 8-13)

Galician, a half-sister to five winners in Australia, including Queensland Oaks (1m4f) winner Allow, out of a 1m2f winner in Britain, shaped well. She finished nicely clear of the others.

Dos Amigos(IRE), an 8,500euros purchase, wasn't best away but was going on at the finish. He should make a fair handicapper in due course.

Cardinal Walter(IRE), a 160,000euros purchase, is a half-brother to some decent winners, notably Manieree, who won the 1m2f Group 2 Blandford Stakes this year. This was a satisfactory debut and he can do better when faced with more of a stamina test. (tchd 9-1)

Sky Crossing seemed to know his job but got tired. He showed ability and can do better. (tchd 80-1)

Scrupul(IRE), runner-up over 1m at York on his second start, didn't build on that form but will be interesting when switching to handicaps. (op 9-2)

7210 BRITISH STALLION STUDS SUPPORTING BRITISH RACING EBF MAIDEN STKS (DIV II) 7f
1:10 (1:10) (Class 5) 2-Y-O **£2,652** (£789; £394; £197) **Stalls** Centre

Form RPR
242 **1** **Personal Touch**[43] 6207 2-9-3 73.. PaulHanagan 7 75
(Richard Fahey) *w ldrs: narrow ld over 1f out: edgd lft ins fnl f: all out* **2/1**[2]

53 **2** *nse* **Peter Anders**[8] 7052 2-9-3 0.. FrederikTylicki 6 75
(Mark Johnston) *led: narrowly hdd over 1f out: carried lft fnl 75yds: jst failed* **8/11**[1]

05 **3** 6 **Maybeagrey**[11] 6985 2-8-12 0.. DuranFentiman 5 54+
(Tim Easterby) *sn outpcd: hdwy 3f out: kpt on to take 3rd 1f out: nvr nr 1st 2* **16/1**

4 3 1/4 **Red Hot Secret** 2-8-12 0.. MickyFenton 4 46+
(Jeremy Gask) *chsd ldrs: drvn over 3f out: edgd lft over 1f out: sn wknd* **25/1**

00 **5** 5 **Blackamoor Zara**[18] 6837 2-8-8 0 ow1.. LMcNiff(5) 11 34
(Bruce Hellier) *wnt rt s: sn mid-div: nvr trbld ldrs* **200/1**

6 **6** 2 1/2 **Bond Style**[102] 4292 2-9-3 0.. TomEaves 3 31
(Bryan Smart) *chsd ldrs: wknd over 1f out* **12/1**[3]

7 3/4 **Rhyme Royal** 2-8-12 0.. JamesSullivan 8 24
(James Given) *s.i.s: nvr on terms* **66/1**

0 **8** 1 1/4 **Release The Funds (IRE)**[15] 6912 2-8-10 0.......... ShirleyTeasdale(7) 9 26
(David Nicholls) *chsd ldrs: wknd over 2f out* **66/1**

9 12 **Madam Lilibet (IRE)** 2-8-12 0.. PJMcDonald 2 —
(Sharon Watt) *s.s: sn t.o* **80/1**

10 3 1/4 **Sleepy Lucy** 2-8-9 0.. RobertLButler(3) 10 —
(Richard Guest) *s.s: hdwy into mid-div: over 3f out: wknd 2f out* **50/1**

1m 25.73s (1.23) **Going Correction** +0.15s/f (Good) 10 Ran SP% **115.3**
Speed ratings (Par 96): **98,97,91,87,81 78,77,76,62,59**
toteswingers:1&2:£1.10, 2&3:£2.90, 1&3:£3.20 CSF £3.63 TOTE £1.60: £1.10, £1.10, £3.70; EX 3.70 Trifecta £14.10 Pool: £636.79 - 33.32 winning units..
Owner Nicholas Wrigley & Kevin Hart **Bred** Cheveley Park Stud Ltd **Trained** Musley Bank, N Yorks

FOCUS
The time was exactly a second slower than the first division, but that race was won by a potentially smart sort. The first pair were clear and the winner is rated to his mark.

NOTEBOOK
Personal Touch, runner-up to a useful type in a three-runner maiden over 6f on his third start, proved effective over this longer trip, finding enough despite edging left under pressure. He looks a fair handicapper in the making. (op 11-8)

Peter Anders, back up in trip after a running-on third over 6f at Leicester on his second start, had his chance but was intimidated by the winner, who edged left. He now has the option of handicaps. (op 6-5)

Maybeagrey seemed unsuited by the drop in trip, but she fared best of the fillies and is now eligible for a handicap mark. (op 18-1)

Red Hot Secret, a half-sister to 6f winner Dark Secret, and 1m scorer Heaven Bound, is out of a 1m winner. She went left when getting noticeably tired late on and should come on plenty for the run.

Blackamoor Zara showed her first sign of ability.

7211 HOLD YOUR CHRISTMAS PARTY HERE (S) STKS 1m
1:40 (1:40) (Class 6) 3-5-Y-O **£1,704** (£503; £251) **Stalls** Centre

Form RPR
-536 **1** **Elspeth's Boy (USA)**[65] 5516 4-9-0 75.. PaulHanagan 12 67
(Philip Kirby) *hld up towards rr: hdwy 2f out: rdn to chse ldr ins fnl f: styd on to ld nr fin* **9/2**[3]

0143 **2** *nk* **Master Of Dance (IRE)**[12] 6979 4-9-6 71........................(p) TomEaves 3 73
(Keith Dalgleish) *trckd ldrs: hdwy on outer 1/2-way: led wl over 1f out: rdn ent fnl f: hdd and no ex nr fin* **9/4**[2]

4546 **3** 2 1/2 **American Lover (FR)**[19] 6816 4-8-9 54.. PaddyAspell 4 56
(John Wainwright) *chsd ldrs: hdwy 1/2-way: cl up 3f out: led 2f out: sn rdn and hdd over 1f out: kpt on same pce* **22/1**

0355 **4** 1 3/4 **Flying Phoenix**[8] 7055 3-8-10 59........................(b) NataliaGemelova(3) 6 58
(Gay Kelleway) *hld up: hdwy over 2f out: rdn wl over 1f out: kpt on fnl f: nrst fin* **11/1**

1236 **5** 1 1/2 **Kingswinford (IRE)**[7] 7074 5-9-1 82.. JustinNewman(5) 13 60
(Brian Ellison) *in tch: effrt to chse ldrs over 2f out: sn rdn and no imp* **5/4**[1]

0000 **6** 1 1/4 **Spirit Of Dixie**[8] 7065 4-8-9 48.. PaulQuinn 11 46?
(Noel Wilson) *prom: led 3f out: sn rdn and hdd 2f out: grad wknd* **66/1**

6006 **7** 5 **Convitezza**[8] 7061 5-8-9 32..(t) PatrickMathers 9 34?
(Mike Sowersby) *towards rr: effrt and sme hdwy 3f out: rdn over 2f out and n.d* **150/1**

023 **8** 3 1/2 **Why So Serious**[63] 5599 5-8-7 47.. HannahNunn(7) 1 31
(Peter Salmon) *chsd ldrs on outer: rdn along over 3f out: sn wknd* **33/1**

3460 **9** 1 1/4 **Goodmanyourself**[8] 7061 3-8-12 45........................(b) MickyFenton 10 28
(Paul Midgley) *sn led hung rt and swtchd to r nr stands' rail: rdn along over 3f out: sn hdd & wknd* **33/1**

6000 **10** 23 **Honest Buck**[57] 5789 4-9-0 47..(p) FrederikTylicki 14 —
(Kate Walton) *prom: rdn along over 3f out: sn wknd* **50/1**

1m 38.46s (0.46) **Going Correction** +0.15s/f (Good)
WFA 3 from 4yo+ 2lb 10 Ran SP% **116.1**
Speed ratings (Par 101): **103,102,100,98,96 95,90,87,85,62**
.There was no bid for the winner. Master of Dance was subject to a friendly claim. \n\x\x

Owner Preesall Garage **Bred** S M D Ltd **Trained** Castleton, N Yorks

FOCUS
A modest seller with the favourite disappointing. The form is rated around the second and third, with the winner a stone off his reappearance effort.

Goodmanyourself Official explanation: jockey said that the gelding hung right throughout

7212 REDCARRACING ON FACEBOOK & TWITTER H'CAP 1m 6f 19y
2:10 (2:11) (Class 6) (0-65,63) 3-Y-0 **£1,704** (£503; £251) **Stalls** Low

Form RPR

0402 **1** **Rose Of Sarratt (IRE)**[42] 6240 3-9-6 **62**........................ PaulHanagan 11 74+
(Rae Guest) *trckd ldrs: led after 5f: wnt clr over 3f out: rdn 2f out: all out* **7/2**[2]

3000 **2** *hd* **Madrasa (IRE)**[8] 7062 3-9-0 **56**......................................(bt[1]) TomEaves 8 68
(Keith Reveley) *hld up in rr: hdwy and nt clr run 3f out: chsd wnr over 2f out: hung lft over 1f out: no ex last 50yds* **12/1**

6163 **3** *10* **Ad Value (IRE)**[8] 7062 3-9-0 **56**....................................... PJMcDonald 3 54
(Alan Swinbank) *trckd ldrs: t.k.h: effrt and swtchd lft over 3f out: kpt on to take modest 3rd nr fin* **11/4**[1]

2 **4** *nse* **Miss Mysterious (FR)**[21] 6781 3-8-9 **51**........................ FrederikTylicki 1 49
(Kate Walton) *led after 1f: hdd after 5f: chsd wnr: one pce fnl 3f* **12/1**

006 **5** *4 ½* **Labroc (IRE)**[38] 6349 3-9-4 **60**... ShaneKelly 5 52
(William Haggas) *chsd ldrs: edgd rt and effrt over 3f out: wknd 2f out* **16/1**

4302 **6** *3* **Lord Of The Storm**[21] 6769 3-8-4 **53**..............................(t) JakePayne(7) 7 40
(Bill Turner) *mid-div: drvn over 5f out: hmpd over 3f out: nvr nr ldrs* **12/1**

6060 **7** *hd* **Red Lite (IRE)**[55] 5823 3-8-8 **50**...................................... JamesSullivan 4 37
(Wilf Storey) *in rr: hdwy over 3f out: wknd 2f out* **33/1**

-500 **8** *1* **Willow's Wish**[21] 6780 3-8-3 **45**...................................... AndrewMullen 14 31
(George Moore) *chsd ldrs: wknd over 2f out* **25/1**

00-0 **9** *1 ¾* **Old Boy Ted**[24] 6701 3-8-10 **52**... DavidAllan 2 35
(Mark H Tompkins) *in rr: effrt 4f out: nvr a factor* **16/1**

36-6 **10** *20* **Blake Dean**[30] 2058 3-9-7 **63**.....................................(p) DanielTudhope 12 18
(Ben Haslam) *in rr div: drvn over 5f out: bhd fnl 4f: t.o* **16/1**

056 **11** *12* **Marshmallow**[11] 7004 3-9-1 **57**.. TedDurcan 13 —
(Chris Wall) *t.k.h: led 1f: chsd ldrs: wknd 3f out: sn bhd: t.o* **9/2**[3]

000 **12** *6* **Sendarose (IRE)**[57] 5792 3-8-3 **45**................................ DuranFentiman 10 —
(Tim Easterby) *in rr: drvn 4f out: sn bhd: t.o* **22/1**

3m 7.99s (3.29) **Going Correction** +0.15s/f (Good) **12** Ran SP% **118.9**
Speed ratings (Par 98): **96,95,90,90,87 85,85,85,84,72 65,62**
toteswingers:1&2:£10.00, 2&3:£7.50, 1&3:£2.80 CSF £44.39 CT £133.46 TOTE £4.90: £1.60, £7.10, £1.10; EX 55.40 Trifecta £106.70 Pool: £532.34 - 3.69 winning units..
Owner E P Duggan **Bred** Commonwealth **Trained** Newmarket, Suffolk
■ Stewards' Enquiry : P J McDonald one-day ban: careless riding (15 Nov)

FOCUS
A moderate staying handicap but two runners finished well clear. The winner was at least unexposed.

7213 SUBSCRIBE TO RACING UK H'CAP 7f
2:40 (2:40) (Class 5) (0-75,74) 3-Y-0 **£2,264** (£673; £336; £168) **Stalls** Centre

Form RPR

2101 **1** **Green Howard**[18] 6840 3-9-7 **74**..................................... DanielTudhope 8 85
(Robin Bastiman) *hld up in rr: stdy hdwy wl over 2f out: rdn to ld ent fnl f: edgd lft and kpt on* **3/1**[1]

2021 **2** *½* **Comrade Bond**[7] 7084 3-8-13 **66** 6ex.............................. TedDurcan 10 75
(Mark H Tompkins) *trckd ldrs: hdwy and cl up wl over 2f out: rdn to ld wl over 1f out: hdd ent fnl f: kpt on* **3/1**[1]

0000 **3** *2 ½* **Fieldgunner Kirkup (GER)**[10] 7024 3-9-5 **72**..............(b) LeeNewman 6 75
(David Barron) *trckd ldrs: effrt over 2f out: rdn wl over 1f out: kpt on same pce fnl f* **7/1**[2]

4340 **4** *1 ½* **Fenella Fudge**[34] 6450 3-8-12 **65**..................................(b) PaulHanagan 4 63
(James Given) *cl up: led 4f out: rdn along wl over 2f out: sn hdd and kpt on same pce appr fnl f* **7/1**[2]

5000 **5** *1 ½* **Alluring Star**[17] 6867 3-8-12 **65**..................................... JamesSullivan 9 59
(Michael Easterby) *led 3f: cl up and rdn along wl over 2f out: grad wknd* **25/1**

0105 **6** *1 ½* **Thatcherite (IRE)**[32] 6505 3-9-4 **71**..............................(t) StephenCraine 1 61
(Tony Coyle) *hld up in rr: hdwy over 3f out: chsd ldrs 2f out: sn rdn and no imp* **9/1**

2000 **7** *1 ¼* **Cottam Stella**[18] 6840 3-8-2 **60** oh11..............................(t) NeilFarley(5) 2 47
(Mel Brittain) *chsd ldrs on wd outside: rdn along over 3f out: grad wknd* **66/1**

444- **8** *6* **Indian Arrow**[326] 7802 3-9-1 **68**... TomEaves 5 39
(John Quinn) *a towards rr* **40/1**

4560 **9** *1 ¾* **Bachelor Knight (IRE)**[41] 6266 3-8-8 **61**...................(t) BarryMcHugh 11 27
(Suzzanne France) *in tch: rdn along over 3f out: sn wknd* **66/1**

655 **10** *1 ½* **Maven**[18] 6834 3-8-7 **60**.. DavidAllan 3 22
(Tim Easterby) *chsd ldrs: rdn along over 3f out: sn wknd* **15/2**[3]

5110 **11** *½* **Sabratha (IRE)**[59] 5722 3-9-0 **70**... JulieBurke(3) 7 31
(Linda Perratt) *in tch: rdn along over 3f out: sn wknd* **17/2**

1m 25.09s (0.59) **Going Correction** +0.15s/f (Good) **11** Ran SP% **116.6**
Speed ratings (Par 102): **102,101,98,96,95 93,92,85,83,81 80**
totewingers:1&2:£2.80, 2&3:£6.20, 1&3:£5.40 CSF £10.58 CT £56.65 TOTE £4.80: £1.90, £1.60, £1.70; EX 10.10 Trifecta £73.40 Pool: £490.42 - 4.94 winning units..
Owner Ms M Austerfield **Bred** Miss A J Rawding & P M Crane **Trained** Cowthorpe, N Yorks

FOCUS
A couple of in-form runners dominated. They were closely matched on lines through Beautiful Day and both improved on recent efforts.

7214 VOLTIGEUR RESTAURANT 2 COURSE SPECIAL £10.95 CLAIMING STKS 1m 2f
3:10 (3:11) (Class 6) 3-4-Y-0 **£1,704** (£503; £251) **Stalls** Low

Form RPR

4164 **1** **Tiger Webb**[64] 5546 3-9-6 82....................................... GrahamGibbons 5 76
(Michael Easterby) *trckd ldrs: wnt 2nd 3f out: chal over 1f out: kpt on to ld last 30yds* **4/1**[3]

5323 **2** *hd* **Key Breeze**[25] 6669 4-9-5 68..(t) PaulHanagan 2 71
(Kevin Ryan) *hld up in mid-div: hdwy on outside over 3f out: chal over 1f out: kpt on to take 2nd cl home: jst hld* **7/2**[2]

5211 **3** *½* **Yorksters Prince (IRE)**[31] 6536 4-9-9 64.....................(b) BarryMcHugh 4 74
(Tony Coyle) *led: jnd over 1f out: hdd towards fin* **11/4**[1]

3330 **4** *3* **Auto Mac**[10] 7024 3-9-3 67...................................... DuranFentiman 6 66
(Neville Bycroft) *chsd ldrs: upsides over 1f out: one pce* **25/1**

4130 **5** *¾* **Shabak Hom (IRE)**[21] 6773 4-9-5 74...................................... MartinLane 7 63
(David Simcock) *s.s: detached in last pair: hdwy 3f out: kpt on: nvr rchd ldrs* **9/2**

6224 **6** *nk* **Boy The Bell**[8] 7055 4-8-9 73.. PaulPickard(3) 3 55
(Brian Ellison) *hld up in rr: drvn over 3f out: kpt on one pce fnl 2f* **9/2**

00-P **7** *17* **Jan Smuts (IRE)**[22] 6750 3-8-11 0.................................... JamesSullivan 9 24
(Wilf Storey) *rrd s: detached in last 2: nvr on terms* **150/1**

0-00 **8** *8* **Stay On Track (IRE)**[26] 6659 4-8-12 45........................ KellyHarrison 1 —
(Garry Woodward) *t.k.h: w ldr: lost pl over 2f out* **150/1**

00 **9** *26* **Camina**[47] 6096 3-8-7 0 ow1..(v[1]) DavidAllan 8 —
(Michael Smith) *mid-div: lost pl over 6f out: bhd fnl 4f: t.o* **150/1**

2m 8.89s (1.79) **Going Correction** +0.15s/f (Good)
WFA 3 from 4yo 4lb **9** Ran SP% **111.1**
Speed ratings (Par 101): **98,97,97,95,94 94,80,74,53**
toteswingers:1&2:£3.60, 2&3:£2.60, 1&3:£2.90 CSF £17.22 TOTE £3.80: £2.20, £1.10, £1.40; EX 13.90 Trifecta £25.70 Pool: £896.86 - 25.74 winning units..Boy The Bell was claimed by O Pears for £3000.
Owner Backup Technology & Steve Hull 1 **Bred** Meon Valley Stud **Trained** Sheriff Hutton, N Yorks
■ Stewards' Enquiry : Graham Gibbons five-day ban: used whip with excessive frequency (15-19 Nov)

FOCUS
A muddling claimer run in a time 0.50 seconds slower than the following Class 5 handicap, which looked to be modestly run. The winner was 10lb off his summer form for Henry Cecil but there's a chance the third is a bit flattered by this seeming improvement.
Stay On Track(IRE) Official explanation: jockey saif that the gelding lost his action

7215 ANNUAL BADGES MAKE GREAT CHRISTMAS PRESENTS H'CAP 1m 2f
3:40 (3:43) (Class 5) (0-70,70) 3-Y-0+ **£2,264** (£673; £336; £168) **Stalls** Low

Form RPR

4002 **1** **Law To Himself (IRE)**[15] 6918 4-9-6 **66**........................... PJMcDonald 1 75
(Alan Swinbank) *mde all: rdn wl over 1f out: kpt on gamely ins fnl f* **9/1**[3]

0350 **2** *½* **Tapis Libre**[11] 6990 3-9-1 **65**.. PaddyAspell 6 73
(Michael Easterby) *trckd ldrs on inner: hdwy 3f out: swtchd rt and rdn to chse wnr over 1f out: chal ent fnl f and ev ch tl one pce fnl 100yds* **25/1**

-043 **3** *1 ¾* **Zenarinda**[105] 4180 4-9-4 **64**.. TedDurcan 3 69
(Mark H Tompkins) *midfield: smooth hdwy to trck ldrs 3f out: n.m.r and swtchd lft to rails wl over 1f out: sn rdn and kpt on fnl f* **20/1**

0050 **4** *1* **The Galloping Shoe**[17] 5724 6-9-5 **70**........................ GarryWhillans(5) 9 73+
(Alistair Whillans) *hld up towards rr: hdwy on wd outside wl over 2f out: rdn to chse ldrs over 1f out: kpt on same pce* **9/1**[3]

1455 **5** *2 ¾* **Eijaaz (IRE)**[17] 6868 10-9-1 **61**......................................(p) DanielTudhope 5 58
(Geoffrey Harker) *hld up towards rr: stdy hdwy on outer 3f out: rdn wl over 1f out: kpt on fnl f: nrst fin* **25/1**

0200 **6** *¾* **White Diamond**[15] 6916 4-9-7 **70**..................................(p) DaleSwift(3) 14 66
(Malcolm Jefferson) *cl up on outer: pushed along over 3f out: rdn over 2f out: grad wknd* **40/1**

1531 **7** *¾* **Kodicil (IRE)**[15] 6916 3-9-2 **66**....................................(p) DuranFentiman 7 60
(Tim Walford) *cl up: pushed along over 3f out: rdn over 2f out: grad wknd* **6/1**[2]

0253 **8** *½* **Brockfield**[15] 6916 5-9-3 **63**... DavidAllan 8 56+
(Mel Brittain) *plld hrd: trckd ldrs: chsd ldng pair 3f out: sn rdn and grad wknd* **10/1**

0540 **9** *½* **Spes Nostra**[25] 6674 3-9-6 **70**... TomEaves 12 62
(David Barron) *trckd ldrs on outer: pushed along 3f out: rdn over 2f out and grad wknd* **20/1**

0160 **10** *shd* **Black Coffee**[39] 6295 6-9-6 **66**.......................................(b) ShaneKelly 15 58
(Mark Brisbourne) *dwlt and towards rr: sme hdwy on inner wl over 2f out: swtchd rt to outer over 1f out: sn rdn and no imp fnl f* **25/1**

1556 **11** *shd* **Muwalla**[67] 5441 4-9-4 **64**... TonyHamilton 2 56
(Chris Grant) *in tch on inner: pushed along over 3f out: rdn over 2f out and sn no hdwy* **20/1**

0104 **12** *¾* **Dean Iarracht (IRE)**[18] 6833 5-8-12 **58**.....................(p) FrederikTylicki 10 48
(Tracy Waggott) *s.i.s: a in rr* **16/1**

0500 **13** *1 ½* **Hydrant**[32] 6507 5-9-7 **67**... AndrewMullen 13 54
(Peter Salmon) *chsd ldrs: rdn along over 3f out: sn wknd* **33/1**

0011 **14** *1 ¼* **My Mate Jake (IRE)**[6] 7112 3-9-1 **65**................................. PaulHanagan 4 50
(James Given) *a towards rr* **7/4**[1]

0000 **15** *24* **Sirgarfieldsobers (IRE)**[7] 7075 5-9-1 **68**........................ JasonHart(7) 11 5
(Declan Carroll) *s.i.s: in rr and wd st: sn bhd* **50/1**

2m 8.39s (1.29) **Going Correction** +0.15s/f (Good)
WFA 3 from 4yo+ 4lb **15** Ran SP% **118.8**
Speed ratings (Par 103): **100,99,98,97,95 94,94,93,93,93 93,92,91,90,71**
toteswingers:1&2:£63.60, 2&3:£82.50, 1&3:£17.70 CSF £217.09 CT £4321.87 TOTE £11.60: £2.70, £12.60, £5.80; EX 318.60 TRIFECTA Not won..
Owner A Mallen **Bred** C Lilburn **Trained** Melsonby, N Yorks

FOCUS
The time was 0.50 seconds quicker than the claimer, but that's possibly a bit misleading as the pace looked slow here and the winner made all. He rates back to his best.
My Mate Jake(IRE) Official explanation: jockey said that the gelding was never travelling

7216 THANKS & SEE YOU NEXT SEASON H'CAP 6f
4:10 (4:11) (Class 6) (0-60,60) 3-Y-0+ **£1,704** (£503; £251) **Stalls** Centre

Form RPR

5245 **1** **Half A Crown (IRE)**[8] 7057 6-9-4 **58**.............................. AndrewMullen 18 65
(Peter Salmon) *chsd ldrs stands' side: led over 1f out: hld on towards fin* **20/1**

3546 **2** *nk* **Interchoice Star**[10] 7039 6-9-1 **55**.....................................(p) TomEaves 20 61
(Ray Peacock) *racd stands' side: in rr-div: hdwy over 2f out: chsng ldrs over 1f out: kpt on towards fin* **20/1**

-005 **3** *hd* **Transmit (IRE)**[21] 6777 4-9-6 **60**.. DavidAllan 17 65
(Tim Easterby) *chsd ldrs stands' side: led over 2f out: hdd over 1f out: kpt on wl towards fin* **12/1**

2065 **4** *½* **Mission Impossible**[6] 7100 6-9-6 **60**......................(p) PatrickMathers 19 64
(Tracy Waggott) *chsd ldrs: kpt on wl ins fnl f* **25/1**

0001 **5** *1 ¼* **Insolenceofoffice (IRE)**[8] 7065 3-8-13 **58**........................(p) LMcNiff(5) 9 58+
(Bruce Hellier) *w ldrs towards far side: kpt on same pce appr fnl f* **8/1**[3]

5000 **6** *nse* **Schoolboy Champ**[35] 6430 4-9-2 **56**.................................... ShaneKelly 3 56
(Mark Brisbourne) *mid-div: towards far side: hdwy over 2f out: kpt on ins fnl f* **25/1**

5100 **7** *1* **Distant Sun (USA)**[6] 7100 7-8-13 **58**......................(p) ShaneBKelly(5) 12 54
(Linda Perratt) *chsd ldrs: one pce over 1f out* **40/1**

1640 **8** *½* **Edgware Road**[21] 6777 3-9-6 **60**......................................(v) PaulHanagan 6 55
(Keith Dalgleish) *mid-div: kpt on fnl 2f: nvr rchd ldrs* **15/2**[2]

0060 **9** *½* **Carrie's Magic**[6] 7100 4-9-1 **60**..........................(b) GarryWhillans(5) 13 53
(Alistair Whillans) *mid-div: kpt on fnl 2f: nvr a threat* **25/1**

6015 **10** *nk* **El Decency (USA)**[7] 7079 7-9-5 **59**.....................................(t[1]) TedDurcan 2 51
(Richard Guest) *mid-div: hdwy far side to chse ldrs over 1f out: hung rt: heavily eased whn wl hld last 75yds* **6/1**[1]

0002 **11** *½* **Greenhead High**[8] 7065 3-8-8 **55**............................. ShirleyTeasdale(7) 1 46
(David Nicholls) *overall ldrs far side: hdd over 3f out: wknd over 1f out: edgd rt ins fnl f* **20/1**

2220 **12** *½* **Mucky Molly**[24] 6694 3-9-2 **56**.. KellyHarrison 7 45
(Olivia Maylam) *mid-div: effrt over 2f out: nvr a factor* **16/1**

5305 **13** ¾ **Lady Del Sol**[8] 7064 3-9-6 **60**....(p) DanielTudhope 5 47
(Marjorie Fife) *mid-div towards far side: edgd rt 2f out: hmpd ins fnl f: nvr a factor* **14/1**
3664 **14** *nk* **Prince Of Vasa (IRE)**[7] 7079 4-9-3 **60**.... PaulPickard(3) 16 46
(Michael Smith) *chsd ldrs: wkng whn hmpd over 1f out* **10/1**
-450 **15** *shd* **Danum Dancer**[7] 7079 7-9-1 **55**....(b) BarryMcHugh 10 40
(Neville Bycroft) *s.i.s: nvr on terms* **18/1**
4502 **16** *nse* **Monthly Medal**[6] 7099 8-9-4 **58**....(t) JamesSullivan 4 43
(Wilf Storey) *in rr far side: hung lft over 2f out: nvr on terms* **10/1**
2020 **17** *5* **Ivestar (IRE)**[11] 6999 6-9-4 **58**....(vt) PJMcDonald 14 27
(Ben Haslam) *v.s.a: a bhd* **33/1**
2052 **18** *1 ¼* **Winning Draw (IRE)**[8] 7064 3-9-0 **54**....(b) MickyFenton 15 19
(Paul Midgley) *w ldrs: wknd 2f out: sn eased* **14/1**
0000 **19** *1 ¾* **Milton Of Campsie**[18] 6847 6-9-5 **59**.... StephenCraine 11 19
(Richard Guest) *s.i.s: sn chsng ldrs: wkng whn hmpd over 1f out* **20/1**

1m 12.35s (0.55) **Going Correction** +0.15s/f (Good) **19** Ran SP% **123.5**
Speed ratings (Par 101): **102,101,101,100,99 98,97,96,96,95 95,94,93,93,93 92,86,84,82**
toteswingers:1&2:£28.80, 2&3:£44.60, 1&3:£24.00 CSF £351.69 CT £2706.73 TOTE £16.80: £2.90, £6.00, £2.40, £6.40; EX 651.20 TRIFECTA Not won..
Owner Viscount Environmental **Bred** Burns Farm Stud **Trained** Kirk Deighton, West Yorks

FOCUS

Unusually, the top four stalls provided the top four finishers. Modest form with a small personal best from the winner.

El Dececy(USA) Official explanation: jockey said that the gelding hung right in the final furlong
Winning Draw(IRE) Official explanation: jockey said that the filly lost her action
T/Plt: £5.60 to a £1 stake. Pool of £48,619.60 - 6,307.57 winning tickets. T/Qpdt: £2.90 to a £1 stake. Pool of £3,827.54 - 967.44 winning tickets. WG

7047 CAPANNELLE (R-H)

Tuesday, November 1

OFFICIAL GOING: Turf: soft

7217a PREMIO GUIDO BERARDELLI (GROUP 3) (2YO) (TURF) 1m 1f

3:15 (12:00) 2-Y-O **£34,482** (£15,172; £8,275; £4,137)

RPR

1 **Duck Feet (IRE)**[44] 2-8-11 0.... CColombi 7 —
(S Botti, Italy) *broke wl: settled in midfield: tk clsr order 2 1/2f out: rdn 2f out and r.o to ld appr fnl f: rdn out* **39/20**[2]
2 *1 ¼* **Lui E La Luna**[23] 6740 2-8-11 0.... FabioBranca 4 —
(B Grizzetti, Italy) *trckd ldrs: rdn and led 2f out: hdd appr fnl f: kpt on u.p* **9/5**[1]
3 *1 ¼* **Mamath (IRE)** 2-8-11 0.... GBietolini 5 —
(R Brogi, Italy) *hld up towards rr: hdwy over 2 1/2f out: 5th and rdn 1 1/2f out: styd on u.p fnl f: run flattened out last 75yds* **219/10**
4 *1 ½* **Blu Petraeus (IRE)** 2-8-11 0.... CristianDemuro 3 —
(Vittorio Caruso, Italy) *led: hdd 2f out: sn rdn: one pce fnl f* **131/10**
5 *snk* **Royal Approval (ITY)**[23] 6740 2-8-11 0.... CFiocchi 9 —
(Maria Rita Salvioni, Italy) *hld up towards rr: 8th and pushed along ins fnl 3f: styd on u.p ins fnl 1 1/2f: nvr on terms* **24/1**
6 *4* **Shukal (ITY)** 2-8-11 0.... MircoDemuro 6 —
(S Botti, Italy) *midfield: gradual hdwy to go 2nd 2 1/2f out: sn rdn and wknd fnl 2f* **21/10**[3]
7 *½* **Teixidor (ITY)** 2-8-11 0.... SSulas 1 —
(Ottavio Di Paolo, Italy) *hld up towards rr: rdn and no imp fnl 3f* **43/5**
8 *3* **Golden Heliostatic (IRE)** 2-8-11 0.... MBelli 8 —
(G Fratini, Italy) *chsd ldr: rdn and wknd ins fnl 3f* **51/1**
9 *3* **Hachico**[37] 2-8-11 0.... GMarcelli 2 —
(A Candi, Italy) *missed break and sn bhd: nvr in contention* **238/10**

(-114.70) **9** Ran SP% **133.7**
WIN (incl. 1 euro stake): 2.94. PLACES: 1.31, 1.46, 2.77. DF: 3.64.
Owner Dioscuri Srl **Bred** K & Mrs Cullen **Trained** Italy

7181 FLEMINGTON (L-H)

Tuesday, November 1

OFFICIAL GOING: Turf: good

7218a EMIRATES MELBOURNE CUP (GROUP 1 H'CAP) (3YO+) (TURF) 2m

4:00 (12:00) 3-Y-0+

£2,483,660 (£588,235; £294,117; £163,398; £114,379; £81,699)

RPR

1 **Dunaden (FR)**[13] 6967 5-8-8 **0** 1ex.... Christophe-PatriceLemaire 13 121
(M Delzangles, France) *hld up towards rr: smooth hdwy over 2f out: drvn and led last 50yds: jst hld on* **15/2**[2]
2 *nse* **Red Cadeaux**[52] 5952 5-8-6 **0**.... MichaelRodd 15 119
(Ed Dunlop) *hld up: checked after 4f: smooth hdwy on outside 3f out: qcknd to ld ent fnl f: sn rdn: hdd last 50yds: rallied: jst failed* **30/1**
3 *1 ¼* **Lucas Cranach (GER)**[17] 6886 4-8-6 **0**....(p) CoreyBrown 11 118
(Anthony Freedman, Australia) *hld up in midfield: smooth hdwy over 2f out: led appr fnl f to ent fnl f: kpt on: hld nr fin* **12/1**
4 *nk* **Americain (USA)**[10] 7043 6-9-2 **0**.... GeraldMosse 14 127
(A De Royer-Dupre, France) *hld up: effrt and plenty to do on wd outside over 2f out: edgd lft and kpt on strly fnl f: nrst fin* **4/1**[1]
5 *1 ¼* **Manighar (FR)**[17] 6886 5-8-7 **0**....(b[1]) DamienOliver 20 117
(Luca Cumani) *prom on outside: hdwy to chse ldr after 4f to 1/2-way: shkn up to ld 2f out: hdd appr fnl f: kpt on same pce last 100yds* **40/1**
6 *hd* **Lost In The Moment (IRE)**[31] 6519 4-8-5 **0**....(p) WilliamBuick 3 115
(Saeed Bin Suroor) *hld up in midfield: hdwy to chse ldrs over 1f out: sn rdn: kpt on same pce ins fnl f* **30/1**
7 *shd* **Fox Hunt (IRE)**[44] 6200 4-8-6 **0** 1ex....(v) SilvestreDeSousa 18 116
(Mark Johnston) *t.k.h towards rr: outpcd whn n.m.r 3f out: hdwy over 1f out: edgd lft and kpt on wl fnl f: nrst fin* **30/1**
8 *¾* **Niwot (AUS)**[3] 7-8-0 **0**.... DeanYendall 9 109
(Michael, Wayne & John Hawkes, Australia) *t.k.h: chsd ldr 4f: prom tl rdn and no ex fr over 1f out* **8/1**[3]
9 *hd* **Unusual Suspect (USA)**[17] 6886 7-8-7 **0**....(v) BradRawiller 7 116
(Michael Kent, Australia) *t.k.h: hld up towards rr: plenty to do 3f out: hdwy and angled rt over 1f out: kpt on fnl f: nvr able to chal* **30/1**
10 *2 ¾* **At First Sight (IRE)**[6] 7115 4-8-4 **0**.... StevenKing 10 110
(Robert Hickmott, Australia) *t.k.h: chsd ldrs: rdn over 2f out: outpcd over 1f out: btn fnl f* **9/1**
11 *nse* **Precedence (NZ)**[3] 7182 6-8-6 **0**....(b) DarrenBeadman 2 111
(Bart Cummings, Australia) *plld hrd in tch: hdwy to chse ldr 1/2-way: led 3f out to over 2f out: sn rdn: wknd ins fnl f* **50/1**
12 *1* **Drunken Sailor (IRE)**[17] 6886 6-8-7 **0**....(b) DwayneDunn 8 111
(Luca Cumani) *s.i.s: plld hrd in midfield on ins: hdwy and cl up 2f out: sn rdn: wknd ins fnl f* **40/1**
13 *nk* **The Verminator (AUS)**[3] 7182 5-8-3 **0** 5ex....(b) CraigNewitt 4 107
(Chris Waller, Australia) *t.k.h: trckd ldrs tl rdn and wknd wl over 1f out* **100/1**
14 *shd* **Tullamore (NZ)**[10] 7043 5-8-3 **0**.... ChrisMunce 12 107
(Gai Waterhouse, Australia) *s.i.s: swtchd to ins after 1f: hld up: stdy hdwy into midfield 1/2-way: effrt over 2f out: btn over 1f out* **20/1**
15 *shd* **Moyenne Corniche**[24] 6711 6-8-3 **0**.... BrettPrebble 16 107
(Brian Ellison) *t.k.h: swtchd to ins rail after 1f: hld up: squeezed through and in tch after 4f: efft over 2f out: rdn over 1f out: sn btn* **30/1**
16 *nse* **Saptapadi (IRE)**[17] 6886 5-8-3 **0**.... ChrisSymons 21 107
(Brian Ellison) *swtchd to ins after 1f: hld up: checked after 4f: rdn along over 2f out: nvr on terms* **80/1**
17 *½* **Older Than Time (AUS)**[3] 5-8-0 **0**....(b) TimothyClark 19 103
(Gai Waterhouse, Australia) *hld up and bhd: drvn along 3f out: nvr able to chal* **100/1**
18 *nk* **Hawk Island (IRE)**[17] 6886 6-8-5 **0**....(t) GlynSchofield 17 108
(Chris Waller, Australia) *s.i.s and sn swtchd to ins: hld up: hmpd and lost grnd after 4f: rdn over 2f out: btn over 1f out* **150/1**
19 *6* **Illo (GER)**[10] 7043 5-8-5 **0**.... JimCassidy 1 101
(Bart Cummings, Australia) *t.k.h: led at modest gallop: clr after 6f to 1/2-way: hdd 3f out: rdn and wknd over 1f out* **20/1**
20 *1 ¾* **Jukebox Jury (IRE)**[52] 5952 5-9-0 **0**.... NeilCallan 6 108
(Mark Johnston) *sn pushed along and in tch: effrt and drvn along over 2f out: wknd over 1f out: fin lame* **14/1**
21 *nk* **Shamrocker (NZ)**[10] 7044 4-8-3 **0**.... LukeNolen 23 101
(Danny O'Brien, Australia) *hld up in midfield on outside: struggling wl over 2f out: sn btn* **40/1**
22 *nse* **Glass Harmonium (IRE)**[3] 7182 5-8-7 **0**....(t) LisaCropp 22 101
(Michael Moroney, Australia) *missed break: hld up in last: rdn along on ins wl over 2f out: nvr on terms* **30/1**
23 *8 ½* **Modun (IRE)**[59] 5711 4-8-5 **0**.... KerrinMcEvoy 5 90
(Saeed Bin Suroor) *on toes in preliminaries: hld up in midfield on outside: rdn along wl over 2f out: wknd wl over 1f out* **30/1**

3m 20.84s (1.20) **23** Ran SP% **112.5**
PARI-MUTUEL (NSW TAB - all including au$1 stakes): WIN 9.10 PLACE 3.40, 14.30, 4.40; DF 232.80; SF 364.40.
Owner Pearl Bloodstock Ltd **Bred** Comte E Decazes **Trained** France

FOCUS

Considering how many of these either raced or started their career in the northern hemisphere, this contest had a distinctly European feel about it and, as it turned out, the first seven home represented that region in one way or another. Rock-solid form.

NOTEBOOK

Dunaden(FR) was moved into a fine position just before turning in, but the combination looked to be held by the runner-up at one stage late on as he went past. However, the horse found a bit extra for strong driving and got up by a narrow margin. It was terrible luck on Craig Williams, who rode Dunaden to win the Geelong Cup but was suspended from taking this ride, as he would have completed the Caulfield Cup, Cox Plate and Melbourne Cup treble in one season, but it was a second successive victory for a French trainer/jockey combination.

Red Cadeaux has been a capable performer in Group company and handicaps, so was entitled to respect on this season's form against plenty he took on here. Four places in front of the winner in the Prix Kergorlay, this was agony for his backers, as he hit the front possibly a shade too early in hindsight and was beaten by pixels (officially a nose) in the photograph, the closest finish in the 151-year history of the race. Ironically, considering the recent whip row here, his jockey got a ban for excessive use. Had he held on, he would have been the first horse since Vintage Crop to take this without an Australian prep and gone down in history as the first horse to win for Britain.

Lucas Cranach(GER)'s standout European form was when chasing home Arc winner Danedream in Germany after being poorly placed in a slowly-run contest. He made a decent start to his career in Australia after being purchased by new connections with a solid fifth in the Caulfield Cup, despite going wide and overcoming a late injury scare, and ran a cracker here, albeit with no obvious excuses. His jockey was handed a 13-day ban for careless riding early in the race.

Americain(USA), who had been re-plated after tearing off a shoe in morning exercise, was so impressive when taking last year's race, so clearly had all the right equipment in his armoury to go close again. He showed his customary change-of-gear when winning the Group 2 Drake International Cup at Moonee Valley (1m4f) recently, where things didn't go his way for a while, and he finished off strongly again here after finding himself thrown the furthest wide turning in - he looked to be beaten the same distance by the first three as he was behind them off the final bend. Reports before the race seemed to indicate the horse will now remain in Australia to take in a couple more high-profile races before retiring to stud.

Manighar(FR) didn't seem to get the best ride in this race last season when he was heavily restrained in rear for much of the early part before finishing seventh. Blinkers were fitted for the first time in an attempt to sharpen him up and, after being ridden prominently, he kept on really well after holding every chance down the home straight.

Lost In The Moment(IRE)'s form had been consistent since heading back from Dubai, including when runner-up in the Goodwood Cup, and he did best of those who took part in the Ebor back in August.

Fox Hunt(IRE) is a typically tough and genuine sort from the Johnston stable. He was having his 12th start of the season, the first of which came in February. The winner of the German St Leger on his previous outing, he sat with the first, second and fourth for much of the race towards the rear, but became outpaced at the top of the home straight, after being squeezed for room, before running on really strongly.

Niwot(AUS) instantly became interesting when winning the Lexus Stakes convincingly three days ago. A previous C&D winner, he probably wanted a stronger gallop to chase, as he didn't have the same speed that some possess when the tempo increased.

Unusual Suspect(USA), a Grade 1 winner in America over 1m4f, was specifically purchased to win this by current connections, and they deliberately swerved the Mackinnon Stakes the previous Saturday to keep him fresh. His jockey somehow managed to turn a good position into a poor one within a furlong or two of the start and, although he stayed on powerfully in the latter stages, he was never a threat.

Drunken Sailor(IRE), who took a grip early, shaped well in the Caulfield Cup but his jockey reported afterwards here that he felt his mount didn't stay.

Moyenne Corniche looked to be racing freely while the field headed down the back straight and didn't have anything left off the bridle.

Saptapadi(IRE) didn't have a great draw for this and never really featured.

Jukebox Jury(IRE) had returned to his best after being tried over staying distances. Things looked promising while he was racing towards the front, but he soon came under pressure and emptied quite quickly. He was found to be lame post-race.

Modun(IRE) never settled and, as a result had no chance of seeing out the trip.

6808 MAISONS-LAFFITTE (R-H)

Tuesday, November 1

OFFICIAL GOING: Turf: soft changing to very soft after race 1 (12.20)

7219a PRIX MIESQUE (GROUP 3) (2YO FILLIES) (TURF) 7f (S)
1:20 (12:00) 2-Y-O £34,482 (£13,793; £10,344; £6,896; £3,448)

RPR
1 **Topeka (IRE)**46 6143 2-8-11 0 ChristopheSoumillon 2 104+
(Robert Collet, France) *settled in 4th following ldr Cool Wave: shkn up 2f out and swtchd to stands' rail 1 1/2f out: qcknd wl: tk ld 1f out: wnt clr: easily* **13/10**1
2 2 **Barbayam**29 2-8-11 0 OlivierPeslier 7 99
(F Head, France) *racd freely in 2nd on outside: picked up wl 1 1/2f out to take ld: hdd 1f out: styd on to be clr 2nd* **14/1**
3 2 1/2 **Tibaldi (FR)**24 2-8-11 0 JohanVictoire 6 93
(Mme C Head-Maarek, France) *followed Barbayam on outside in 6th: rdn over 1 1/2f out: styd on u.p fnl f to go clr 3rd* **48/10**3
4 2 **Survey (GER)**23 2-8-11 0 StefanieHofer 5 88
(Mario Hofer, Germany) *prom fr s: 2nd ent fnl 1 1/2f out: rdn but nt qckn fnl f: styd on one pce* **33/10**2
5 2 1/2 **Cool Wave**16 6904 2-8-11 0 DarioVargiu 3 82
(B Grizzetti, Italy) *sn led: stl in front 2f out: hdd 1 1/2f out: rdn but no ex: styd on one pce fnl f* **10/1**
6 2 1/2 **Nimohe (FR)**54 5873 2-8-11 0 MickaelBarzalona 4 75
(J Heloury, France) *settled in midfield: rdn but no ex fr 2f out: styd on one pce fnl f* **22/1**
7 1 3/4 **Dutchessa**30 2-8-11 0 MaximeGuyon 1 71
(C Ferland, France) *racd towards rr: rdn but no ex fr 2f out: nvr a factor thereafter: eased fnl f* **11/1**
8 2 1/2 **Manuka (USA)**21 2-8-11 0 GregoryBenoist 8 65
(D Smaga, France) *racd towards rr: rdn over 2f out: no ex: nvr figured thereafter: eased fnl f* **18/1**

1m 28.9s (0.60) **8** Ran SP% **117.7**
WIN (incl 1 euro stake): 2.30. PLACES: 1.30, 2.40, 1.60. DF: 12.60. SF: 20.30..
Owner G A Oldham **Bred** Citadel Stud Establishment **Trained** Chantilly, France

NOTEBOOK
Topeka(IRE) appreciated the testing ground and collected her fourth win on the bounce with ease. She had a breathing problem when beaten second time up, but has otherwise proved very progressive, and she'll now be trained with the Classics in mind. She's likely to return in the Prix Imprudence, and will be entered in both the 1,000 Guineas and the Pouliches.

7220a CRITERIUM DE MAISONS-LAFFITTE (GROUP 2) (2YO) (TURF) 6f (S)
1:50 (12:00) 2-Y-O £93,362 (£36,034; £17,198; £11,465; £5,732)

RPR
1 **Restiadargent (FR)**49 6042 2-8-10 0 MaximeGuyon 10 112+
(H-A Pantall, France) *settled bhd ldrs on outside: qcknd wl over 1 1/2f out: led 1f out: sn wnt clr: impressive* **3/1**2
2 5 **Vaniloquio (IRE)**21 6782 2-9-0 0 ThierryThulliez 8 101
(N Clement, France) *settled towards rr: picked up wl over 1 1/2f out: r.o wl fnl f: tk 2nd on line* **63/10**3
3 snk **Dont Teutch (FR)**20 6808 2-8-10 0 GregoryBenoist 9 97
(D Smaga, France) *broke wl: swtchd to stands' rail: racd alone: a.p: led ent fnl 1 1/2f: hdd 1f out: r.o wl: lost 2nd on line* **30/1**
4 nk **Chica Loca (FR)**20 6808 2-8-10 0 MickaelBarzalona 1 96
(M Figge, Germany) *racd towards rr on outside: shkn up 2f out: styd on wl fnl f* **15/2**
5 1 1/2 **Murano (IRE)**42 6243 2-9-0 0 OlivierPeslier 7 95
(B De Montzey, France) *sn prom on outside: led after 2f: stl in front 2f out: rdn and hdd over 1 1/2f out: styd on fnl f* **13/1**
6 snk **Bannock (IRE)**11 7012 2-9-0 0 JoeFanning 6 95
(Mark Johnston) *sn prom: rdn and u.p 2f out: nt qckn: styd on one pce fnl f* **18/1**
7 snk **Calahorra (FR)**20 6808 2-8-10 0 ThierryJarnet 2 90
(C Baillet, France) *towards rr: rdn 2f out: no ex: styd on fnl f* **30/1**
8 nk **Bogart**31 6535 2-9-0 0 PhillipMakin 4 93
(Kevin Ryan) *prom fr s: u.p 2f out: nt qckn: styd on one pce fnl f* **5/2**1
9 8 **Choisir Shadow (IRE)**23 2-8-10 0 DarioVargiu 3 65
(B Grizzetti, Italy) *prom fr s: shkn up over 2f out: no ex: nvr a factor thereafter* **11/1**
10 7 **Silverheels (IRE)**31 6535 2-9-0 0 ChristopheSoumillon 5 48
(Paul Cole) *towards rr fr s: rdn but no ex fr over 2 1/2f out: eased fr 1 1/2f out* **73/10**

1m 14.4s (1.00) **10** Ran SP% **118.3**
WIN (incl 1 euro stake): 4.00. PLACES: 1.70, 2.00, 5.00. DF: 13.40. SF: 31.10..
Owner Guy Pariente **Bred** G Pariente **Trained** France

NOTEBOOK
Restiadargent(FR), winner of the Group 3 Prix d'Arenberg last time out, ran out an impressive winner. She'll be given a chance to stay further in the Prix Imprudence next spring, but is likely to be a sprinter next year.
Bannock(IRE) ran well to a point, but the soft ground got to him in the end.
Bogart didn't appreciate the testing ground and was below his best.

7221a PRIX DE SEINE-ET-OISE (GROUP 3) (3YO+) (TURF) 6f (S)
2:20 (12:00) 3-Y-O+ £34,482 (£13,793; £10,344; £6,896; £3,448)

RPR
1 **Iver Bridge Lad**11 6987 4-8-11 0 (b) MichaelO'Connell 15 114
(John Ryan) *w.w in outside gp: qcknd wl 1f out: r.o strly to take ld 100yds out: sn clr: easily* **70/1**
2 2 1/2 **Fred Lalloupet**27 6643 4-8-11 0 AnthonyCrastus 5 106
(D Smaga, France) *led small gp on stands' rail: stl led 1f out: r.o wl: hdd 100yds out: r.o to hold 2nd on line* **25/1**
3 shd **Definightly**51 5979 5-8-11 0 (b) ThierryThulliez 11 106
(Roger Charlton) *sn led gp on outside: hdd 1f out: r.o wl ins fnl f: narrowly missed 2nd* **53/10**3
4 1 1/2 **Secret Asset (IRE)**30 6563 6-8-11 0 LukeMorris 14 101
(Jane Chapple-Hyam) *a.p in outside gp: r.o wl fnl f to take 4th* **8/1**
5 1 **Kalahari Gold (IRE)**27 6643 6-8-11 0 OlivierPeslier 1 98
(F Rohaut, France) *w.w amongst small gp on stands' rail: r.o wl fnl f* **12/1**
6 shd **Spectacle Du Mars (FR)**30 6563 4-8-11 0 GregoryBenoist 16 97
(X Nakkachdji, France) *a.p in outer gp: nt qckn ins fnl f* **22/1**
7 nk **Total Gallery (IRE)**149 2754 5-8-11 0 StephanePasquier 12 96
(Henry Candy) *a.p in outer gp: rdn but no ex ins fnl f* **23/1**
8 shd **Mar Adentro (FR)**30 6563 5-8-11 0 (p) ThierryJarnet 6 96
(R Chotard, France) *led small gp in centre of trck: rdn but no ex fnl 1 1/2f* **17/2**
9 1 1/4 **Mirza**45 6145 4-8-11 0 PhillipMakin 9 92
(Rae Guest) *prom amongst gp on outside: nt qckn fr 1 1/2f out* **61/1**
10 hd **Amico Fritz (GER)**65 5528 5-9-0 0 MaximeGuyon 8 94
(H-A Pantall, France) *w.w in outside gp: briefly threatened 1 1/2f out: no ex* **18/1**
0 **Mariol (FR)**27 6643 8-8-11 0 SebastienMaillot 4 —
(Robert Collet, France) *w.w in small gp in centre of trck: no prog fr 1 1/2f out* **33/1**
0 **Marchand D'Or (FR)**30 6566 8-9-0 0 DavyBonilla 7 —
(M Delzangles, France) *settled towards rr in centre of trck: proged 2f out but then effrt sn flattened out: eased fnl f* **48/10**2
0 **Clairvoyance (IRE)**65 5528 4-8-8 0 MickaelBarzalona 3 —
(H-A Pantall, France) *w.w in small gp in centre of trck: no prog fnl 2f* **13/1**
0 **Birthday Lion (GER)**29 6594 6-8-11 0 GaetanMasure 13 —
(U Stoltefuss, Germany) *prom amongst gp on outside: wknd qckly over 1f out* **55/1**
0 **Split Trois (FR)**65 5532 3-8-8 0 Pierre-CharlesBoudot 10 —
(Y De Nicolay, France) *w.w in small gp in centre of trck: nvr a factor* **51/1**
0 **Faustina (FR)**20 6809 3-8-8 0 ChristopheSoumillon 2 —
(J E Hammond, France) *w.w in small gp on stands' rail: no prog fr 2f out: a bhd* **43/10**1

1m 14.1s (0.70) **16** Ran SP% **115.8**
WIN (incl 1 euro stake): 70.90. PLACES: 18.50, 7.60, 2.40. DF: 727.90. SF: 1443.60..
Owner The Iver Lads **Bred** Jcs Wilson Bloodstock **Trained** Newmarket, Suffolk

NOTEBOOK
Iver Bridge Lad was the outsider of the entire field but he proved very much at home in the conditions and came home a clear winner. Connections are hoping that by winning this Group race he'll now receive an invitation for the Hong Kong Sprint, although the main plan is to take him back to Meydan next year.
Definightly appreciates this sort of ground and looked to run up to her recent best in defeat.
Secret Asset(IRE) ran well considering this wouldn't be his ideal ground.
Total Gallery(IRE) can go well fresh, but this wasn't one of his better efforts.
Mirza was up in grade and wasn't disgraced.

7201 KEMPTON (A.W) (R-H)

Wednesday, November 2

OFFICIAL GOING: Standard
Wind: fresh, half behind Weather: dry, light rain after race 4

7222 FREE ENTRY FOR BETDAQ MEMBERS NURSERY (DIV I) 1m (P)
4:40 (4:42) (Class 6) (0-65,65) 2-Y-O £1,617 (£481; £240; £120) Stalls Low

Form RPR
004 1 **Night Flash (GER)**27 6644 2-9-0 **58** MartinHarley 1 64
(James Given) *broke fast: led for 1f: chsd ldrs after: rdn and chal over 1f out: led 1f out: r.o wl and drew clr fnl 100yds* **8/1**
0102 2 1 3/4 **Inniscastle Boy**9 7051 2-9-5 **63** MartinDwyer 11 65
(William Muir) *t.k.h: chsd ldrs: wnt 2nd after 2f: rdn and ev ch 2f out: nt pce of wnr and carried lft ins fnl f: wnt 2nd on post* **5/1**2
046 3 nse **Compton Rainbow**17 6892 2-9-2 **60** 1 WilliamCarson 8 62
(Hans Adielsson) *led after 1f and set stdy gallop: rdn and qcknd over 2f out: hdd 1f out: edgd lft fnl f and outpcd by wnr fnl 100yds: lost 2nd on post* **15/2**3
2000 4 3 1/4 **Dickens Rules (IRE)**21 6806 2-9-4 **62** LiamKeniry 6 57
(Sylvester Kirk) *t.k.h: chsd ldrs: rdn and effrt over 2f out: drvn and unable qck over 1f out: wknd ins fnl f* **12/1**
0601 5 2 **Camrock Star (IRE)**23 6763 2-9-6 **64** SilvestreDeSousa 9 54+
(David Evans) *t.k.h: hld up in last trio: rdn and hanging rt over 2f out: outpcd and drvn 2f out: wknd over 1f out* **9/1**
050 6 1/2 **Swift Cat**24 6725 2-9-4 **65** HarryBentley(3) 2 54
(John Best) *in tch in midfield: rdn and unable qck over 2f out: wknd over 1f out* **15/2**3
0430 7 2 3/4 **True Prince (USA)**13 6972 2-8-11 **55** SebSanders 3 37
(Amanda Perrett) *chsd ldrs: rdn and unable qck wl over 2f out: wknd 2f out* **4/1**1
3366 8 nk **Kyllasie**34 6480 2-9-4 **65** KieranO'Neill(3) 7 47
(Richard Hannon) *dropped to last pair sn after s: in tch: rdn and effrt on inner jst over 2f out: no prog and wknd over 1f out* **11/1**
0043 9 1/2 **She's Flawless (USA)**19 6846 2-8-8 **52** (b) ShaneKelly 4 33
(Brian Meehan) *stdd s: hld up in tch in rr: rdn and no hdwy over 2f out: n.d* **9/1**
4004 10 1 1/4 **Denton Dancer**30 6581 2-9-6 **64** (p) LukeMorris 5 42
(James Eustace) *t.k.h: hld up towards rr: rdn and unable qck over 2f out: wknd 2f out* **16/1**

1m 41.45s (1.65) **Going Correction** -0.05s/f (Stan) **10** Ran SP% **113.2**
Speed ratings (Par 94): **89,87,87,83,81 81,78,78,77,76**
toteswingers:1&2:£8.00, 1&3:£9.40, 2&3:£9.40 CSF £46.30 CT £318.39 TOTE £10.40: £4.80, £2.20, £3.70; EX 62.40.
Owner Danethorpe Racing Partnership **Bred** Gestut Etzean **Trained** Willoughton, Lincs

FOCUS
They went a steady pace in this moderate nursery and few landed a blow as those racing handily sprinted away in the home straight. The winner improved but was always well placed close to the slow pace.

NOTEBOOK
Night Flash(GER) was always in the firing line and came away readily when asked to get on top nearing the furlong marker. This was his nursery and AW debut so he's clearly been entered on a decent mark. No doubt he got the run of the race, but there could well be more to come. (op 7-1)
Inniscastle Boy was another that raced handily and probably ran up to his previous level, getting the extra furlong well enough. He rates the best guide for the form. (op 9-2 tchd 11-2)
Compton Rainbow, stoutly bred on the dam's side, was up in trip for this handicap debut and posted her most encouraging effort to date. She was able to dictate the pace, though. (op 17-2)
Dickens Rules(IRE) shaped better again but was close enough if good enough 2f out. (op 16-1)
Camrock Star(IRE) wasn't suited by how this panned out and is probably worth another chance. (op 13-2)
True Prince(USA) was well backed, but he dropped out tamely. (op 6-1)

Denton Dancer Official explanation: jockey said gelding ran too free

7223 FREE ENTRY FOR BETDAQ MEMBERS NURSERY (DIV II) 1m (P)

5:10 (5:10) (Class 6) (0-65,65) 2-Y-O **£1,617** (£481; £240; £120) **Stalls** Low

Form RPR

5463 **1** **Next Cry (USA)**[23] 6757 2-9-4 **65**.................... KieranO'Neill(3) 2 72+
(Richard Hannon) *chsd ldrs: rdn to chal over 1f out: led ins fnl f: styd on wl to ld fnl 75yds* **10/3**[2]

306 **2** 1 ½ **Fairyinthewind (IRE)**[47] 6131 2-9-2 **60**.................... EddieAhern 8 64
(Paul D'Arcy) *chsd ldrs: rdn and effrt on inner jst over 1f out: ev ch over 1f out: led 1f out: hdd ins fnl f: nt pce of wnr fnl 75yds* **11/2**[3]

0035 **3** 2 ¼ **Emman Bee (IRE)**[9] 7051 2-9-6 **64**.................... FrankieMcDonald 3 62
(John Gallagher) *led: flashing tail over 3f out: rdn and fnd ex over 2f out: hrd pressed over 1f out: hdd 1f out: wknd ins fnl f* **20/1**

0010 **4** 6 **Coach Montana (IRE)**[15] 6937 2-8-13 **57**.................... IvaMilickova 7 42
(Jane Chapple-Hyam) *chsd ldr tl over 2f out: sn unable qck and rdn: outpcd and wl hld over 1f* **20/1**

6445 **5** 3 ¼ **Chrissycross (IRE)**[30] 6581 2-9-3 **64**.................... HarryBentley(3) 6 41
(Roger Teal) *a same pl: rdn and struggling over 3f out: wknd over 2f out and wl btn fnl 2f* **20/1**

0015 **6** 1 ½ **Remember Rocky**[23] 6760 2-8-9 **58**.................... MatthewLawson(5) 1 32
(Steve Gollings) *a towards rr: rdn and outpcd over 3f out: drvn and no prog over 2f out: no ch fnl 2f* **7/1**

0045 **7** hd **Stag Hill (IRE)**[11] 7035 2-9-5 **63**.................... LiamKeniry 10 36
(Sylvester Kirk) *hld up in tch on outer: rdn and struggling over 3f out: sn outpcd and wl btn over 2f out* **14/1**

0026 **8** 1 ¾ **Doc Hill**[15] 6927 2-8-9 **53**.................... LukeMorris 5 22
(Michael Blanshard) *dwlt: a towards rr: rdn and outpcd over 3f out: wl bhd fnl 2f* **16/1**

0364 **9** 3 ¼ **Baileys Over Ice**[21] 6806 2-9-7 **65**.................... PaulHanagan 4 27
(James Given) *sn pushed along: a in rr: lost tch 3f out: wl bhd over 2f out* **8/1**

5520 **10** ½ **Courtesy Call (IRE)**[12] 6986 2-9-4 **62**.................... SilvestreDeSousa 9 23
(Mark Johnston) *sn pushed along and dropped to rr: a bhd: rdn and toiling over 3f out: drvn and lost tch wl over 2f out* **11/4**[1]

1m 39.56s (-0.24) **Going Correction** -0.05s/f (Stan) **10** Ran SP% **115.6**
Speed ratings (Par 94): **99,97,95,89,86 84,84,82,79,78**
toteswingers:1&2:£4.10, 1&3:£13.40, 2&3:£17.70 CSF £21.06 CT £313.75 TOTE £3.40: £1.10, £3.00, £6.50; EX 23.20.
Owner William Stobart **Bred** G Watts Humphrey Jr Et Al **Trained** East Everleigh, Wilts

FOCUS
This second division of the moderate nursery was another race where the principals came clear as those held up again struggled. A sound pace, and straightforward, solid form.

NOTEBOOK
Next Cry(USA) hit top gear when given a few reminders entering the final furlong and was nicely on top at the finish. He had been threatening to open his account of late and shaped very much on his previous outing in a 7f maiden here in August that an AW nursery should be within his compass. He's a likeable sort. (op 9-2)
Fairyinthewind(IRE) ◆ was nicely positioned despite her wide draw and travelled sweetly into the home straight. She looked the most likely winner when quickening on the inside 2f out, but ultimately got outstayed by the winner. It was her first run beyond 6f and she's evidently started life in this sphere on a workable mark so a drop back to 7f can do the trick. (op 4-1)
Emman Bee(IRE) proved keen from the front, but was at a big advantage being up there and returned to the form of his penultimate third at Warwick. He's another that got outstayed, though. (op 16-1)
Coach Montana(IRE) raced one off the early leader, but proved woefully one-paced after turning in. (op 28-1 tchd 33-1)
Courtesy Call(IRE) was undone by the draw, but still turned in a disappointing effort. (op 10-3 tchd 7-2 in places)

7224 BACK AND LAY AT BETDAQ.COM H'CAP 6f (P)

5:40 (5:41) (Class 6) (0-55,59) 3-Y-O+ **£1,617** (£481; £240; £120) **Stalls** Low

Form RPR

3320 **1** **Doctor Hilary**[23] 6746 9-9-2 **55**....................(v) RobertHavlin 1 67
(Mark Hoad) *chsd ldr: drew clr w ldr 2f out: pushed ahd over 1f out: r.o strly and clr fnl f: readily* **7/2**[1]

2221 **2** 2 ¼ **Bateleur**[8] 7086 7-9-1 **59** 6ex.................... CharlesBishop(5) 3 64
(Mick Channon) *t.k.h early: rdn and outpcd ent fnl 2f: rallied and styd on ins fnl f: chsd wnr fnl 75yds: no threat to wnr* **4/1**[2]

0406 **3** 1 ¾ **Memphis Man**[16] 6920 8-8-13 **52**.................... SilvestreDeSousa 6 51
(David Evans) *taken down early: t.k.h: hld up in tch: rdn and chsd clr ldng pair wl over 1f out: plugged on but no ch w wnr* **11/2**[3]

3003 **4** ¾ **The Jailer**[40] 6304 8-8-11 **55**.................... RyanPowell(5) 9 52
(John O'Shea) *led and crossed to ins sn after s: rdn and drew clr w wnr 2f out: hdd over 1f out: sn drvn and btn 1f out: wknd and lost 2 pls fnl 75yds* **12/1**

0054 **5** shd **Yungaburra (IRE)**[13] 6982 7-8-11 **50**....................(tp) TomMcLaughlin 2 46
(David C Griffiths) *led rdrless to s: t.k.h: hld up in last quartet: rdn and effrt on inner jst over 2f out: styd on ins fnl f: no ch w wnr* **13/2**

0006 **6** ¾ **Young Simon**[134] 3254 4-8-11 **53**....................(v) KieranO'Neill(3) 8 47
(George Margarson) *sltly hmpd s: hld up in last pair: swtchd ins and effrt jst over 2f out: kpt on but nvr nr wnr* **6/1**

6000 **7** 1 **Super Frank (IRE)**[35] 6444 8-9-2 **55**....................(b) JamieGoldstein 4 46
(Zoe Davison) *hld up in last quartet: rdn and effrt over 2f out: sn drvn and no imp: nvr trbld ldrs* **28/1**

000 **8** 3 ½ **Namir (IRE)**[36] 6436 9-9-2 **55**....................(vt) JimCrowley 10 35
(James Evans) *taken down early: t.k.h: hld up in midfield: rdn and nt qckn over 2f out: wknd 2f out* **25/1**

0000 **9** 1 ¼ **Fairy Tales**[14] 6943 3-8-10 **52**.................... SeanLevey(3) 7 28
(John Bridger) *chsd ldrs: rdn and unable qck over 2f out: sn struggling and wknd 2f out* **25/1**

1004 **10** ½ **Porthgwidden Beach (USA)**[14] 6943 3-9-0 **53**............(t) LiamKeniry 11 27
(Anthony Middleton) *stdd after s: t.k.h: hld up in last quartet: wd bnd 3f out and sn rdn: no hdwy: wl btn fnl 2f* **9/1**

1m 12.3s (-0.80) **Going Correction** -0.05s/f (Stan) **10** Ran SP% **114.1**
Speed ratings (Par 101): **103,100,97,96,96 95,94,89,87,87**
toteswingers:1&2:£4.10, 1&3:£4.30, 2&3:£3.50 CSF £16.53 CT £74.15 TOTE £5.00: £1.40, £1.30, £2.10; EX 19.50.
Owner J Baden White **Bred** The Lavington Stud **Trained** Lewes, E Sussex

FOCUS
This was an open-looking sprint, but once more it was a race where it paid to be handy.

Porthgwidden Beach(USA) Official explanation: jockey said filly ran too free

7225 BETDAQ MULTIPLES/BRITISH STALLION STUDS E B F MAIDEN STKS 6f (P)

6:10 (6:10) (Class 5) 2-Y-O **£3,169** (£943; £471; £235) **Stalls** Low

Form RPR

25 **1** **Intuition**[19] 6828 2-9-3 0.................... PaulHanagan 2 71+
(Richard Hannon) *racd off the pce in midfield: rdn along 1/2-way: no imp and looked wl hld tl str run on inner ins fnl f: clsd rapidly on tiring ldr fnl 100yds and led on post* **2/1**[2]

2304 **2** nse **Lady Gibraltar**[48] 6075 2-8-9 70....................(v) HarryBentley(3) 8 66
(Alan Jarvis) *racd freely: sn led and clr: rdn over 1f out: stl abt 5 l clr 1f out: tiring and pushed along and edgd lft off rail ins fnl f: hdd on post* **10/1**

4333 **3** nk **Poker Hospital**[16] 6921 2-8-12 74....................(p) SilvestreDeSousa 4 65
(George Baker) *led: sn hdd and chsd clr ldr: rdn and no prog over 2f out: drvn and stl no imp over 1f out: clsd on tired ldr fnl 100yds: styd on* **7/4**[1]

00 **4** nk **Bareback (IRE)**[24] 6725 2-9-3 0.................... LukeMorris 5 69
(John Best) *chsd ldng pair: pushed along over 3f out: drvn over 1f out and stl no imp on ldr tl styd on ins fnl f* **16/1**

60 **5** 1 ½ **Princess Maya**[23] 6745 2-8-12 0.................... DaneO'Neill 9 59
(Jo Crowley) *chsd ldng trio: rdn and no imp over 2f out: 5th and wl hld 1f out: styd on fnl f* **11/2**[3]

6 2 **Nicholascopernicus (IRE)** 2-9-3 0.................... J-PGuillambert 3 58+
(Ed Walker) *s.i.s: racd wl off the pce in last trio: rdn over 3f out: sme hdwy but stl plenty to do over 2f out: kpt on ins fnl f* **10/1**

7 6 **Graylyn Valentino** 2-9-3 0.................... MartinLane 7 39
(Robin Dickin) *v.s.a: a wl off the pce in last trio: n.d* **40/1**

050 **8** ¾ **Meet Joe Black (IRE)**[28] 6630 2-9-3 41.................... TomMcLaughlin 1 36
(David Evans) *s.i.s: early reminders and sn outpcd in rr: nvr trbld ldrs* **66/1**

1m 13.06s (-0.04) **Going Correction** -0.05s/f (Stan) **8** Ran SP% **113.1**
Speed ratings (Par 96): **98,97,97,97,95 92,84,83**
toteswingers:1&2:£4.40, 1&3:£1.20, 2&3:£2.50 CSF £21.84 TOTE £3.20: £1.10, £3.00, £1.60; EX 17.90.
Owner Sir Robert Ogden **Bred** Mickley Stud & D Mossop **Trained** East Everleigh, Wilts

FOCUS
A modest juvenile maiden and they were strung out early. The first four were very closely covered at the finish. The winner could do better, but the runner-up stopped and this looks a race to view negatively.

NOTEBOOK
Intuition looked a most unlikely winner around 2f out, but as the runner-up began to slow inside the closing stages he picked up strongly on the inside and just got up at the business end. He got markedly outpaced, but it was his first run as a sprinter and he clearly wants a stiffer test. A sound surface is also important to his cause and he has the scope to rate higher. (tchd 15-8 and 9-4 in places)
Lady Gibraltar had run very disappointingly the last twice, including in the visor last time out. She shot clear into the home straight on this AW debut, though, and was still around five lengths clear at the furlong marker. Her rider appeared confident she had done enough as she began to wilt late on, however, and could have been much harder on her. That saw her get mugged right on the line and this was probably a missed opportunity. (tchd 11-1)
Poker Hospital raced closest to the tearaway leader, but hit a flat spot after straightening for home and that cost him as he wasn't beaten at all far. It's not hard to see why he wears cheekpieces. (op 13-8 tchd 6-4)
Bareback(IRE), representing last year's winning stable, kept on to post by far his best effort to date and is now eligible for nurseries. (op 25-1)
Nicholascopernicus(IRE) wasn't able to go the pace after a tardy start on this belated racecourse debut, but is bred to stay further and caught the eye somewhat under an educational ride. He's one to keep an eye on. (op 8-1)

7226 BETDAQ MOBILE APPS FLOODLIT STKS (LISTED RACE) 1m 4f (P)

6:40 (6:43) (Class 1) 3-Y-O+

£17,013 (£6,450; £3,228; £1,608; £807; £405) **Stalls** Centre

Form RPR

5006 **1** **Prince Bishop (IRE)**[53] 5921 4-9-3 110....................(v) SilvestreDeSousa 3 110
(Saeed Bin Suroor) *hld up in tch: hdwy to join ldr on bit and wnt clr of field 2f out: pushed to ld 1f out and sn readily drew clr: eased towards fin: easily* **6/1**[3]

4110 **2** 3 ¾ **Parlour Games**[60] 5700 3-8-11 95.................... PaulHanagan 5 103
(Mahmood Al Zarooni) *stdd s: hld up in last pair: rdn and effrt on outer over 2f out: chsd clr ldng pair 2f out: no ch w wnr but kpt on ins fnl f to go 2nd last strides* **7/4**[1]

4540 **3** hd **Laaheb**[118] 3775 5-9-3 113.................... RichardHills 7 103
(Roger Varian) *chsd ldrs tl wnt 2nd over 6f out: led over 2f out and sn rdn clr of field w wnr: hdd 1f out and sn btn: lost 2nd last strides* **15/8**[2]

-006 **4** 3 **Precision Break (USA)**[41] 6271 6-9-3 94.................... MartinLane 1 98
(David Simcock) *chsd ldr tl over 6f out: chsd ldrs after: rdn wl over 2f out: outpcd and btn 2f out: 4th and wl hld after* **16/1**

3465 **5** 5 **Crocus Rose**[67] 5471 5-8-12 80.................... LukeMorris 4 85?
(Harry Dunlop) *in tch: rdn over 3f out: outpcd and btn 2f out: 5th and no ch after* **100/1**

0421 **6** 1 ½ **Spensley (IRE)**[61] 5693 5-9-3 91.................... EddieAhern 6 88
(James Fanshawe) *stdd and dropped in bhd after s: hld up in last: rdn and effrt over 2f out: no imp and sn btn: no ch fnl 2f* **15/2**

0233 **7** 12 **Woolfall Treasure**[33] 6103 6-9-3 97....................(v) DaneO'Neill 2 68
(Gary Moore) *led: rdn and hdd over 2f out: sn wknd: wl bhd over 1f out: eased ins fnl f* **25/1**

2m 29.33s (-5.17) **Going Correction** -0.05s/f (Stan) course record
WFA 3 from 4yo+ 6lb **7** Ran SP% **107.9**
Speed ratings (Par 111): **115,112,112,110,107 106,98**
toteswingers:1&2:£2.10, 1&3:£2.10, 2&3:£1.80 CSF £15.03 TOTE £4.20: £1.70, £1.90; EX 14.50.
Owner Godolphin **Bred** Thurso Limited **Trained** Newmarket, Suffolk

FOCUS
A very mixed bunch made up this Listed event. It was run at a solid pace and that resulted in a course record time.

NOTEBOOK
Prince Bishop(IRE), gelded since his last outing, enhanced his trainer's decent record in the race with a comfortable success. He had disappointed previously this year, but didn't have much to beat according to official figures on this Polytrack debut and the surface proved up his street. It was his first success since narrowly beating this season's Champion Stakes winner Cirrus Des Aigles at Longchamp on his final outing last term, being gelded has obviously helped and he's evidently developed into an end-of-season performer. (op 11-2)
Parlour Games had something to find on this debut in Listed company, but was heavily backed. He took time to settle under restraint and it was clear 2f out he was beat. He did keep on gamely, however, and looks much more of a stayer. (op 2-1)

Laaheb was best in at the weights and appeared as though he may end his losing run when hitting top gear in the home straight. He proved a sitting duck for the winner, though, and perhaps this first outing since July was needed. (op 6-4 tchd 2-1)
Precision Break(USA) won his only previous outing here and wasn't disgraced back down in trip, but did get outclassed. (op 12-1)

7227 TFM NETWORKS H'CAP — 1m (P)
7:10 (7:11) (Class 4) (0-85,85) 3-Y-0+ — **£4,075** (£1,212; £606; £303) **Stalls** Low

Form — RPR

1026 **1** **Songburst**[12] 6997 3-8-6 **75** KieranO'Neill(3) 8 — 84
(Richard Hannon) *sn led and set stdy gallop tl hdd 5f out: chsd ldrs after: rdn and effrt 2f out: drvn and ev ch fnl f: edgd lft fnl 100yds but kpt on wl to ld last stride* **13/2**[2]

4531 **2** *shd* **George Guru**[21] 6796 4-8-10 **79** MarkCoumbe(5) 13 — 87
(Michael Attwater) *hld up in tch on outer: hdwy to ld 5f out: rdn over 2f out: edgd lft over 1f out but kpt on gamely u.p tl hdd last stride* **17/2**

0001 **3** *1/2* **Veroon (IRE)**[14] 6948 5-9-4 **82** (p) PaulHanagan 3 — 89+
(James Given) *hmpd after 1f: hld up in last quartet: stl plenty to do and rdn jst over 2f out: swtchd ins and str run wl over 1f out: chal ins fnl f: r.o* **7/1**[3]

105 **4** *2* **Islesman**[14] 6949 3-9-0 **80** EddieAhern 9 — 85+
(Heather Main) *hld up in tch: rdn jst over 2f out: hdwy u.p over 1f out: pressing ldrs and keeping on whn squeezed for room and hmpd wl ins fnl f: forced to ease and nt rcvr* **12/1**

221 **5** *1 1/4* **Good Authority (IRE)**[13] 6981 4-8-11 **75** TomMcLaughlin 7 — 74+
(Karen George) *in tch towards rr: hmpd 6f out: rdn and effrt ent fnl 2f: kpt on ins fnl f: nvr threatened ldrs* **11/1**

4010 **6** *1/2* **Kakapuka**[38] 6378 4-9-3 **81** LukeMorris 11 — 79
(Anabel K Murphy) *chsd ldrs: rdn and effrt over 2f out: unable qck u.p over 1f out: wknd ins fnl f* **33/1**

1104 **7** *1/2* **Queen Of Cash (IRE)**[53] 5920 3-9-4 **84** RobertHavlin 6 — 81
(Hughie Morrison) *broke wl: led briefly: sn stdd and hld up in tch: rdn and effrt ent fnl 2f: no imp over 1f out: styd on same pce fnl f* **11/2**[1]

1015 **8** *nse* **Catchanova (IRE)**[7] 7098 4-8-11 **75** SebSanders 5 — 72+
(Eve Johnson Houghton) *hmpd sn after s: hld up in last pair: rdn and effrt over 2f out: styd on ins fnl f: nvr threatened ldrs* **12/1**

0002 **9** *1 1/4* **Norse Blues**[14] 6948 3-9-5 **85** LiamKeniry 10 — 79
(Sylvester Kirk) *chsd ldrs: rdn and unable qck over 2f out: wknd over 1f out* **15/2**

0300 **10** *6* **Gallant Eagle (IRE)**[16] 6924 4-9-2 **80** MartinHarley 1 — 60+
(Ed de Giles) *hld up in last quartet: hmpd after 1f and dropped to last pair after: rdn and no prog over 2f out: wl btn fnl 2f* **16/1**

5236 **11** *nk* **Wiqaaya (IRE)**[63] 5635 3-9-2 **82** RichardHills 2 — 61
(Ed Dunlop) *hld up in last quartet: rdn and short-lived effrt ent fnl 2f: sn btn* **12/1**

3130 **12** *13* **Ampleforth**[7] 7110 3-8-10 **76** SilvestreDeSousa 4 — 25
(Mark Johnston) *in tch in midfield: nvr really travelling and rdn along at times: drvn and btn 2f out: wl btn and eased ins fnl f* **15/2**

1m 39.31s (-0.49) **Going Correction** -0.05s/f (Stan)
WFA 3 from 4yo+ 2lb — **12 Ran SP% 115.5**
Speed ratings (Par 105): **100,99,99,97,96 95,95,95,93,87 87,74**
toteswingers:1&2:£16.30, 1&3:£12.80, 2&3:£12.60 CSF £59.19 CT £405.40 TOTE £5.80: £2.60, £7.70, £5.20; EX 88.60.
Owner Axom (XXIV) **Bred** Paulyn Limited **Trained** East Everleigh, Wilts
■ Stewards' Enquiry : Kieran O'Neill two-day ban: careless riding (Nov 16-17)

FOCUS
A very competitive handicap. It was run at an uneven pace, though, and again those racing handily held an advantage.
George Guru ◆ Official explanation: jockey said gelding hung left throughout

7228 RACING@SKYSPORTS.COM H'CAP — 1m (P)
7:40 (7:40) (Class 6) (0-65,65) 3-Y-0+ — **£1,617** (£481; £240; £120) **Stalls** Low

Form — RPR

0000 **1** **Mountrath**[24] 6728 4-9-5 **63** (v) AdamKirby 10 — 73
(Gary Moore) *hld up in last trio: rdn and hdwy over 1f out: led ins fnl f: r.o wl and sn in command: eased cl home* **12/1**

0604 **2** *1 1/2* **Having A Ball**[13] 6971 7-8-10 **54** ChrisCatlin 3 — 60
(Jonathan Portman) *bustled along leaving stalls: sn in tch: rdn and effrt ent fnl 2f: ev ch u.p 1f out: nt pce of wnr fnl 100yds: kpt on* **20/1**

5025 **3** *nk* **Gazboolou**[12] 7001 7-8-13 **57** LukeMorris 4 — 62
(David Pinder) *hld up in last quartet: swtchd ins and gd hdwy jst over 2f out: pressed ldrs over 1f out: kpt on ins fnl f* **16/1**

0016 **4** *1/2* **Princess Lexi (IRE)**[131] 3338 4-8-11 **58** HarryBentley(3) 12 — 62+
(William Knight) *chsd ldrs: rdn to ld wl over 1f out: hrd pressed over 1f out: hdd and nt pce of wnr ins fnl f: lost 2 pls fnl 75yds* **7/1**[2]

4402 **5** *3/4* **Woolston Ferry (IRE)**[18] 6877 5-9-5 **63** WilliamCarson 13 — 65+
(David Pinder) *v.s.a and lost abt 10 l: clsd and in tch but stl last 5f out: swtchd sharply lft and rdn over 2f out: hdwy over 1f out: styd on wl ins fnl f: nvr able to chal* **15/2**[3]

6050 **6** *1/2* **Isdaal**[100] 4394 4-9-4 **62** ShaneKelly 5 — 63
(Kevin Morgan) *in tch in midfield: rdn over 2f out: keeping on whn hmpd over 1f out: styd on fnl 150yds: nvr able to chal* **20/1**

2640 **7** *shd* **Super Duplex**[14] 6592 4-9-1 **64** JemmaMarshall(5) 1 — 65
(Pat Phelan) *stdd s: hld up in last pair: pushed along and hdwy towards inner over 1f out: styd on ins fnl f: nvr threatened ldrs* **8/1**

1020 **8** *1* **Jonnie Skull (IRE)**[19] 6848 5-9-2 **60** (vt) SilvestreDeSousa 8 — 59
(Phil McEntee) *led: rdn over 2f out: hdd wl over 1f out: wknd fnl f* **12/1**

5522 **9** *1/2* **Compton Blue**[24] 6727 5-9-4 **65** (b) KieranO'Neill(3) 7 — 63
(Richard Hannon) *in tch in midfield: rdn 1/2-way: drvn and no imp 2f out: styd on same pce and nvr threatened ldrs* **11/4**[1]

5210 **10** *9* **Pearl Opera**[20] 6813 3-8-12 **58** EddieAhern 9 — 35
(Denis Coakley) *chsd ldrs: wnt 2nd 3f out: rdn jst over 2f out: fnd little and sn btn: wl btn and eased ins fnl f* **7/1**[2]

1603 **11** *1 1/4* **Escape Artist**[42] 6264 4-8-9 **56** (vt[1]) SeanLevey(3) 6 — 30
(John Bridger) *t.k.h: chsd ldr tl 3f out: rdn and lost pl over 2f out: wl bhd over 1f out* **16/1**

440 **12** *3 1/2* **Army Of Stars (IRE)**[26] 6664 5-8-13 **60** (b) RyanClark(3) 11 — 26
(Michael Blake) *chsd ldrs: rdn and struggling over 3f out: wknd and bhd fnl 2f* **25/1**

1m 38.85s (-0.95) **Going Correction** -0.05s/f (Stan)
WFA 3 from 4yo+ 2lb — **12 Ran SP% 115.1**
Speed ratings (Par 101): **102,100,100,99,98 98,98,97,96,87 86,83**
toteswingers:1&2:£61.40, 1&3:£37.30, 2&3:£35.80 CSF £228.00 CT £3853.33 TOTE £12.10: £3.30, £3.50, £6.20; EX 377.10.
Owner David Phelan **Bred** A G Antoniades **Trained** Lower Beeding, W Sussex

FOCUS
A moderate handicap, run at a fair pace.
Army Of Stars(IRE) Official explanation: jockey said horse stopped quickly

7229 SKYSPORTS.COM RACING H'CAP — 7f (P)
8:10 (8:10) (Class 6) (0-55,55) 3-Y-0+ — **£1,617** (£481; £240; £120) **Stalls** Low

Form — RPR

0452 **1** **Yakama (IRE)**[23] 6764 6-9-0 **53** (p) SebSanders 1 — 61
(Christine Dunnett) *hld up in tch in midfield: hdwy to press ldrs over 1f out: rdn to ld 1f out: hld on wl fnl f* **10/1**

6020 **2** *nk* **Dingaan (IRE)**[13] 6982 8-9-0 **53** SilvestreDeSousa 4 — 60
(Peter Grayson) *t.k.h: hld up in tch towards rr: gd hdwy 2f out: chal 1f out: ev ch fnl f: r.o but a jst hld* **7/1**[3]

0400 **3** *1* **Cut And Thrust (IRE)**[21] 6784 5-9-2 **55** AdamKirby 12 — 59
(Mark Wellings) *rdr struggling to remove hood at s: hld up in tch: rdn and gd hdwy on inner over 1f out: chsd ldng pair ins fnl f: kpt on but no imp fnl 75yds* **12/1**

304 **4** *2 1/2* **Tudor Prince (IRE)**[21] 6784 7-9-1 **54** DavidProbert 8 — 52
(Tony Carroll) *t.k.h: chsd ldrs: wnt 2nd 4f out: rdn to ld 2f out: hdd 1f out: wknd ins fnl f* **9/2**[1]

025 **5** *1 3/4* **Blue Noodles**[21] 6784 5-9-2 **55** (p) PaddyAspell 7 — 48
(John Wainwright) *chsd ldr tl 4f out: rdn and unable qck over 2f out: btn over 1f out: wknd fnl f* **8/1**

6524 **6** *1/2* **Ad Vitam (IRE)**[20] 6813 3-8-12 **52** (vt) MichaelStainton 14 — 43
(David C Griffiths) *t.k.h: hld up in tch on outer: lost pl bnd 3f out: rdn and no imp over 2f out: edgd rt over 1f out: styd on past btn horses fnl f: nvr trbld ldrs* **10/1**

0200 **7** *1 1/4* **Peter Tchaikovsky**[19] 6848 5-9-2 **55** LukeMorris 10 — 43
(Ian McInnes) *t.k.h: chsd ldrs: rdn and unable qck over 2f out: btn over 1f out: wknd fnl f* **12/1**

2634 **8** *nse* **Anrheg**[23] 6746 3-8-13 **53** DaneO'Neill 5 — 41
(David Brown) *t.k.h: hld up in tch: rdn and unable qck over 2f out: outpcd and btn over 1f out* **6/1**[2]

1000 **9** *nk* **Litotes**[53] 5944 3-8-6 **51** (p[1]) MarkCoumbe(5) 9 — 38
(Michael Attwater) *led: rdn and hdd 2f out: sn unable qck: wknd over 1f out* **20/1**

2/3- **10** *1* **Vigano (IRE)**[150] 2746 6-9-0 **53** (b) BACurtis 6 — 37
(Jaclyn Tyrrell, Ire) *in tch in midfield: rdn and unable qck over 2f out: sn outpcd and no threat to ldrs fnl 2f* **6/1**[2]

0444 **11** *2 1/2* **Gracie's Gift (IRE)**[9] 7071 9-8-13 **52** (v) PaulHanagan 11 — 30
(Richard Guest) *hld up in tch in last quartet: rdn and no prog over 2f out: nvr trbld ldrs* **14/1**

0000 **12** *4 1/2* **Spring Buck (IRE)**[23] 6746 6-8-11 **50** (bt[1]) ChrisCatlin 2 — 16
(Paul Cole) *s.i.s: a bhd: rdn and lost tch over 2f out* **33/1**

1m 26.56s (0.56) **Going Correction** -0.05s/f (Stan)
WFA 3 from 5yo+ 1lb — **12 Ran SP% 118.3**
Speed ratings (Par 101): **94,93,92,89,87 87,85,85,85,84 81,76**
toteswingers:1&2:£9.50, 1&3:£25.50, 2&3:£25.90 CSF £78.22 CT £873.04 TOTE £12.60: £4.20, £3.60, £5.80; EX 62.30.
Owner Mrs Christine Dunnett **Bred** Azienda Agricola Robiati Angelo **Trained** Hingham, Norfolk
■ Stewards' Enquiry : Paddy Aspell one-day ban: careless riding (Nov 16)

FOCUS
A tight handicap, run at an average pace. Weak form.
T/Plt: £48.60 to a £1 stake. Pool:£81,367.20 - 1,220.02 winning tickets T/Qpdt: £10.70 to a £1 stake. Pool:£8,385.21 - 577.60 winning tickets SP

7106 NOTTINGHAM (L-H)
Wednesday, November 2

OFFICIAL GOING: Soft (good to soft in places)
All races on outer course. Stands bend out 3m, far bend out 8m, far side home straight rail moved out 3m increasing distances on Round course by 38yds.

7230 PHS WASHROOMS H'CAP — 5f 13y
12:25 (12:26) (Class 6) (0-55,55) 3-Y-0+ — **£1,617** (£481; £240; £120) **Stalls** High

Form — RPR

3020 **1** **Fair Bunny**[9] 7064 4-8-8 **47** (b) AndrewMullen 5 — 56
(Alan Brown) *prom centre: hdwy to ld wl over 1f out: rdn: edgd rt and hdd briefly ent fnl f: sn led again and kpt on wl* **11/2**[2]

1004 **2** *1 1/4* **Inde Country**[76] 5215 3-8-9 **48** (t) LukeMorris 3 — 53
(Nicky Vaughan) *midfield centre: hdwy 1/2-way: rdn to ld briefly ent fnl f: sn hdd: drvn and no ex last 100yds* **20/1**

24 **3** *hd* **Avonvalley**[43] 6238 4-8-9 **48** FergusSweeney 17 — 52
(Peter Grayson) *racd towards stands' rail: hld up in tch: hdwy wl over 1f out: sn rdn and edgd lft ent fnl f: styd on: nrst fin* **9/2**[1]

P000 **4** *2* **Musical Leap**[15] 6940 3-8-7 **46** oh1 (bt) JamieMackay 7 — 43
(Shaun Harris) *hld up towards rr: hdwy in centre wl over 1f out: rdn and styd on fnl f: nrst fin* **100/1**

000 **5** *3/4* **Boucher Garcon (IRE)**[7] 7100 3-8-3 **47** NeilFarley(5) 1 — 41
(Declan Carroll) *racd towards far rail: prom: rdn 2f out: grad wknd appr fnl f* **10/1**

0000 **6** *1* **Drumpellier (IRE)**[8] 7079 4-8-9 **51** ow3 (b[1]) PaulPickard(3) 8 — 41
(Simon West) *cl up centre: rdn 2f out: grad wknd* **20/1**

0005 **7** *nk* **Replicator**[21] 6791 6-8-5 **47** (e) DominicFox(3) 6 — 36
(Patrick Gilligan) *chsd ldrs centre: rdn along 2f out: no imp* **18/1**

4056 **8** *1/2* **Garstang**[8] 7079 8-8-12 **51** (b) NeilChalmers 10 — 38
(Bruce Hellier) *dwlt and in rr: sme hdwy 2f out: sn rdn and n.d* **8/1**

4406 **9** *1 1/4* **Till Dawn (IRE)**[14] 6943 3-9-0 **53** (b[1]) DavidProbert 15 — 36
(Tony Carroll) *racd towards stands' side: chsd ldrs: rdn along 1/2-way: sn wknd* **9/1**

3504 **10** *1 1/4* **Cloth Ears**[8] 7086 5-8-6 **48** (b) AdamBeschizza(3) 11 — 26
(Phil McEntee) *racd nr stands' rail: overall ldr: rdn along over 2f out: sn hdd and grad wknd* **6/1**[3]

0405 **11** *1/2* **Fathey (IRE)**[49] 6070 5-8-2 **46** oh1 (t) MatthewLawson(5) 16 — 23
(Charles Smith) *racd towards stands' rail: chsd ldrs to 1/2-way: sn wknd* **14/1**

-000 **12** *3* **Bombay Mist**[23] 6765 4-8-7 **46** oh1 (e) JamesSullivan 14 — 12
(Richard Guest) *chsd ldrs towards stands' rail: swtchd lft after 1f: rdn along 1/2-way: sn wknd* **66/1**

6000 **13** *3 3/4* **Ronnie Howe**[167] 2237 7-8-10 **49** oh1 ow3 (bt) RussKennemore 9 — —
(Roy Bowring) *prom centre: rdn along 1/2-way: sn wknd* **33/1**

0300 **14** *3/4* **Quadra Hop (IRE)**[133] 3272 3-9-0 **53** (t) EddieAhern 4 — —
(Bryn Palling) *racd towards far side: a towards rr* **22/1**

2600 **15** *15* **Bertbrand**[8] 7079 6-8-9 **48**...(v) PaulHanagan 2 —
(Ian McInnes) *racd towards far side: a in rr: bhd and eased fnl f* **12/1**
63.06 secs (2.06) **Going Correction** +0.45s/f (Yiel) **15** Ran SP% **117.0**
Speed ratings (Par 101): **101,99,98,95,94 92,92,91,89,87 86,81,75,74,50**
toteswingers:1&2:£12.00, 1&3:£2.50, 2&3:£12.20 CSF £118.16 CT £548.69 TOTE £6.50: £1.30, £6.40, £1.70; EX 112.00 TRIFECTA Not won..
Owner Mrs Susan Johnson **Bred** Mrs S Johnson **Trained** Yedingham, N Yorks

FOCUS
Various rails were moved, adding approximately 28 yards to races on the round course. Following a dry night and bright morning the ground was changed to soft, good to soft in places. Andrew Mullen, who rode the winner, described conditions as "soft". Mainly exposed sorts in a moderate handicap and one run at a decent gallop. The field fanned across the course and, although the first two home raced in the centre, the proximity of the third (stands side) and fifth (far side) suggests there was little or no advantage.
Bertbrand Official explanation: trainer said gelding was unsuited by the soft, good to soft in places ground

7231 PHS COMPLIANCE NURSERY 5f 13y
12:55 (12:56) (Class 5) (0-70,70) 2-Y-O **£2,264** (£673; £336; £168) **Stalls** High

Form RPR
5614 **1** **Uncle Timmy**[9] 7059 2-8-3 **52**... JoeFanning 5 60+
(John Quinn) *chsd ldrs: swtchd rt over 1f out: sn led: drew clr* **4/1**[1]
0600 **2** *3* **Tangtastic (IRE)**[49] 6053 2-8-0 **49** oh1 ow2... FrankieMcDonald 2 46
(Edward Creighton) *chsd ldrs: kpt on fnl f: no imp* **16/1**
4043 **3** *2 ¼* **Princess Banu**[9] 7059 2-8-11 **60**... ChrisCatlin 1 49
(Mick Channon) *led tl 1f out: one pce* **9/2**[2]
500 **4** *1 ¼* **Verus Delicia (IRE)**[9] 7059 2-8-1 **50**... PaulHanagan 6 36+
(Patrick Morris) *hld up: hdwy over 2f out: edgd lft 1f out: kpt on* **16/1**
230 **5** *¾* **Red Shadow**[9] 7059 2-8-8 **57**... AndrewMullen 3 39
(Alan Brown) *chsd ldrs: wknd fnl f* **9/2**[2]
056 **6** *3 ¼* **Gulf Storm (IRE)**[12] 7000 2-8-11 **60**... TomEaves 10 30
(Bryan Smart) *rrd at s: kpt on fnl 2f: nvr a factor* **6/1**[3]
0020 **7** *hd* **Musical Valley**[13] 6975 2-9-7 **70**...(t) RichardKingscote 4 39
(Tom Dascombe) *s.i.s: sme hdwy 2f out: hung rt: nvr nr ldrs* **12/1**
100 **8** *1* **Roy's Legacy**[19] 6843 2-9-2 **65**...(t) PhillipMakin 7 31
(Shaun Harris) *s.i.s: nvr nr ldrs* **9/1**
4435 **9** *2 ¾* **White Spirit (IRE)**[56] 5833 2-9-2 **65**... AndreaAtzeni 12 21
(Marco Botti) *mid-div: lost pl 2f out* **10/1**
0000 **10** *1 ¼* **Doctor Dalek (IRE)**[40] 6308 2-8-7 **56**... DavidProbert 9 —
(Edward Creighton) *prom: wknd 2f out* **33/1**
000 **11** *nse* **Fouracres**[40] 6308 2-7-9 **47** oh2... DominicFox(3) 8 —
(Michael Appleby) *chsd ldrs: lost pl over 2f out* **100/1**
6400 **12** *11* **Nellie Pickersgill**[43] 6232 2-8-4 **53**... DuranFentiman 11 —
(Tim Easterby) *mid-div: lost pl over 2f out: eased whn bhd* **40/1**
63.07 secs (2.07) **Going Correction** +0.45s/f (Yiel) **12** Ran SP% **115.6**
Speed ratings (Par 96): **101,96,92,90,89 84,83,82,77,75 75,58**
toteswingers:1&2:£17.80, 1&3:£2.40, 2&3:£16.70 CSF £66.87 CT £299.69 TOTE £5.30: £2.10, £7.40, £1.70; EX 74.40 TRIFECTA Not won..
Owner Mrs Alurie O'Sullivan **Bred** Mrs A M O'Sullivan **Trained** Settrington, N Yorks

FOCUS
A moderate nursery and, although the pace in the conditions seemed reasonable, those attempting to come from behind were at a disadvantage. The field raced centre-to-stands' side with four of the first five home racing down the centre. Form to view negatively overall.

NOTEBOOK
Uncle Timmy ◆ is a progressive sort who had no problems with these conditions and turned in his best effort after attracting support to score with plenty in hand. He'll be up in the weights for this but may be capable of better. (op 9-2)
Tangtastic(IRE) hadn't shown much on turf and Polytrack but she posted her best effort dropped a fair way in distance, despite being out of the handicap and her rider posting 2lb overweight. It remains to be seen whether this can be built on. (op 18-1 tchd 14-1)
Princess Banu, who will be 1lb higher in future, was having her first run in ground this testing and extended her run of creditable efforts. She's had plenty of chances since her maiden win in April but she should continue to run well. (op 4-1 tchd 7-2)
Verus Delicia(IRE), who raced just away from the first three (and hung towards stands rail when asked for an effort), seems to like give in the ground and ran her best race since her debut. She'll be 5lb lower in future and isn't one to write off. (op 14-1)
Red Shadow had conditions to suit but, while not totally disgraced, she wasn't at her very best for the second time in succession. She has yet to win and isn't one for maximum faith at this stage. (op 6-1 tchd 4-1)
Musical Valley Official explanation: jockey said gelding hung badly right

7232 PHS WATERLOGIC MAIDEN STKS (DIV I) 1m 75y
1:30 (1:34) (Class 5) 2-Y-O **£2,264** (£673; £336; £168) **Stalls** Centre

Form RPR
1 **Colima (IRE)** 2-8-12 0... JimCrowley 8 80+
(Ralph Beckett) *prom: hdwy to ld wl over 2f out: rdn clr wl over 1f out: kpt on strly* **11/1**
3 **2** *2* **Key Appointment**[19] 6828 2-9-3 0... MickyFenton 15 81+
(Tom Tate) *trckd ldrs: hdwy 3f out: chsd wnr wl over 1f out: rdn and kpt on ins fnl f* **11/4**[1]
3 *2 ¼* **Croftamie** 2-8-12 0... JoeFanning 14 71+
(Mark Johnston) *dwlt: sn in tch: hdwy over 3f out: rdn to chse ldng pair and edgd lft wl over 1f out: kpt on same pce* **33/1**
4 *2 ¾* **Aquilla (IRE)** 2-8-12 0... EddieAhern 5 65+
(Sir Henry Cecil) *in tch: hdwy on inner to chse ldrs over 3f out: rdn 2f out: kpt on same pce* **11/1**
5 *2* **Energize (FR)** 2-9-3 0... JimmyFortune 11 66+
(Sir Michael Stoute) *hld up in tch: hdwy over 3f out: effrt to chse ldrs 2f out: sn rdn and one pce* **11/1**
5 **6** *2* **Grey Mirage**[28] 6630 2-9-3 0... AdamKirby 9 61
(Marco Botti) *midfield: hdwy to trck ldrs over 3f out: chsd ldrs over 2f out: sn rdn and no imp* **7/2**[2]
7 *1* **Sunpass** 2-9-3 0... NickyMackay 6 59
(John Gosden) *midfield: green and n.m.r whn lost pl after 2f: sme hdwy over 2f out: nvr nr ldrs* **4/1**[3]
8 *1 ½* **Homeric (IRE)** 2-9-3 0... TedDurcan 3 56+
(Ed Dunlop) *hld up towards rr: hdwy on inner 1/2-way: chsd ldrs 3f out: rdn over 2f out: sn wknd* **25/1**
0 **9** *2 ¼* **Curly Come Home**[14] 6956 2-8-12 0... ChrisCatlin 2 46
(Chris Wall) *prom: rdn along over 3f out: wknd fnl 2f* **100/1**
10 *¾* **Our Ivor** 2-9-3 0... NeilChalmers 7 49
(Michael Appleby) *a towards rr* **100/1**
0 **11** *nse* **Ze King**[8] 7083 2-9-3 0... LukeMorris 16 49
(Chris Wall) *midfield on outer: rdn along over 3f out: nvr a factor* **100/1**
6 **12** *hd* **Tantamount**[19] 6828 2-9-3 0... SteveDrowne 17 49
(Roger Charlton) *dwlt: sn in midfield: effrt 3f out: rdn along over 2f out: n.d* **20/1**
0 **13** *½* **Underwritten**[14] 6956 2-9-3 0... DavidProbert 13 47
(Andrew Balding) *led: rdn along 4f out: hdd 3f out and wknd qckly* **50/1**
14 *2 ¾* **Attwaal (IRE)** 2-9-3 0... AndreaAtzeni 12 41
(Roger Varian) *s.i.s: green and sn rdn along: a in rr* **16/1**
15 *5* **Galletto (IRE)** 2-9-3 0... J-PGuillambert 4 30
(Luca Cumani) *s.i.s: a in rr* **33/1**
0 **16** *2 ¾* **Blue Pencil**[19] 6825 2-9-3 0... FrankieMcDonald 1 24
(Paul Fitzsimons) *trckd ldr: cl up 1/2-way: led over 3f out: sn rdn and hdd wl over 2f out: sn wknd* **100/1**
17 *6* **Totom Chief** 2-9-3 0... StevieDonohoe 10 11
(Gay Kelleway) *s.i.s: a in rr* **100/1**
1m 53.33s (7.73) **Going Correction** +0.775s/f (Yiel) **17** Ran SP% **121.2**
Speed ratings (Par 96): **92,90,87,85,83 81,80,78,76,75 75,75,74,72,67 64,58**
toteswingers:1&2:£8.20, 1&3:£44.50, 2&3:£16.80 CSF £38.58 TOTE £16.80: £3.60, £1.60, £8.00; EX 56.30 TRIFECTA Not won..
Owner Mr and Mrs David Aykroyd **Bred** Sir Eric Parker **Trained** Kimpton, Hants

FOCUS
A race that has thrown up a couple of smart types, notably St Leger-placed Regal Flush in 2006 and Burj Nahaar in 2009. Division one of this renewal featured a couple that had shown promise first time along with a host of well-bred newcomers from powerful yards. Although the pace was an ordinary one, the field (raced in the centre in the straight) finished well strung out and this race should throw up winners. Pace held up well in this race.

NOTEBOOK
Colima(IRE) ◆, a 170,000gns half-sister to smart Flat/very useful hurdler Eradicate and to useful dual Flat winner Huff And Puff, was fairly easy in the market but created a favourable impression, in doing so showing useful form, on this racecourse debut. She's the type to improve again, should have no problems with middle distances next year and should be able to hold her own in stronger company. (op 14-1 tchd 10-1)
Key Appointment had shown promise at a fair level on his debut in testing ground at Haydock and he bettered that effort after again travelling strongly. He should stay 1m2f, is open to improvement and is sure to win a race. (op 5-2)
Croftamie, who cost only 3,500 but whose dam is from the same family as high-class (around 1m) Cesare, showed her inexperience but also showed a fair level of form on this racecourse debut. She is open to improvement and is sure to pick up a race at some point. (op 25-1)
Aquilla(IRE) ◆, a 260,000gns yearling and half-sister to smart (up to 1m2f) Puncher Clynch, was easy in the market but shaped pleasingly without being at all knocked about on this racecourse debut. She's open to plenty of further progress and appeals as the sort to win races. (op 8-1 tchd 12-1)
Energize(FR), a 130,000euro purchase whose dam is a half-sister to top-class Six Perfections, was nibbled at in the market and showed ability on this racecourse debut. He shapes as though he'll stay a bit further and is sure to come on for this run. (op 14-1)
Grey Mirage, as he has done on his debut, attracted support and travelled well for a long way but failed to find as much as seemed likely when asked for an effort. He'll be of more interest back on quicker ground once qualified for a handicap mark. (op 4-1 tchd 9-2)
Sunpass, the first foal of a 1m2f winner, herself a half-sister to Italian Group 1 winner Nayyara, attracted support and showed ability at an ordinary level after racing with the choke out. She should be able to improve on these bare facts. (op 11-2)
Tantamount wasn't knocked about and should fare better in handicaps in due course. Official explanation: jockey said colt hung right (tchd 16-1)
Attwaal(IRE), who has several winners in his pedigree, was fairly easy in the market and was too green to do himself justice on this racecourse debut. (op 12-1)

7233 PHS WATERLOGIC MAIDEN STKS (DIV II) 1m 75y
2:00 (2:01) (Class 5) 2-Y-O **£2,264** (£673; £336; £168) **Stalls** Centre

Form RPR
2 **1** **Cubanita**[35] 6463 2-8-12 0... JimCrowley 3 81+
(Ralph Beckett) *trckd ldr: led 3f out: styd on wl fnl f: drvn out* **15/8**[1]
3 **2** *1 ¼* **Anomaly**[41] 6267 2-9-3 0... PaulHanagan 6 82
(Mahmood Al Zarooni) *trckd ldrs: drvn over 2f out: kpt on same pce and chsd wnr fnl 150yds* **9/4**[2]
6 **3** *¾* **Poetic Power (IRE)**[28] 6630 2-9-3 0... NickyMackay 9 80
(David Elsworth) *trckd ldrs: wnt cl 2nd over 2f out: kpt on same pce fnl f* **28/1**
4 *2 ¼* **Morant Bay (IRE)** 2-8-12 0... IanMongan 10 70+
(Sir Henry Cecil) *chsd ldrs: one pce fnl 2f* **33/1**
2 **5** *4* **Lelaps (USA)**[19] 6828 2-9-3 0... AdamKirby 14 66+
(Marco Botti) *s.i.s: in rr: drvn 4f out: kpt on: nvr rchd ldrs* **4/1**[3]
6 *1 ¼* **Dark Stranger (USA)** 2-9-3 0... RobertHavlin 15 63
(John Gosden) *sn chsng ldrs: wknd over 1f out* **25/1**
7 *nk* **Rose Season** 2-8-12 0... AndreaAtzeni 4 57+
(Roger Varian) *s.i.s: kpt on fnl 3f: nvr nr ldrs* **50/1**
8 *4 ½* **Sequence (IRE)** 2-8-12 0... JimmyFortune 16 47+
(Sir Michael Stoute) *s.i.s: in rr: hung lft marooned far side once in home st: kpt on 2f out: will do bttr* **16/1**
0 **9** *2 ¾* **Choral Bee**[14] 6950 2-8-12 0... DaneO'Neill 12 41
(Henry Candy) *chsd ldrs: wknd over 2f out* **100/1**
10 *2 ¼* **Dark Orchid** 2-8-12 0... TedDurcan 13 35
(Peter Chapple-Hyam) *in rr: sme hdwy 2f out: nvr on terms* **33/1**
11 *½* **Pentameter** 2-9-3 0... EddieAhern 7 39+
(Amanda Perrett) *sn prom: lost pl over 2f out* **66/1**
25 **12** *¾* **Teide Peak (IRE)**[14] 6954 2-9-3 0... JoeFanning 5 38
(Mark Johnston) *led tl 3f out: wknd 2f out* **12/1**
0 **13** *5* **Dylans Verse (IRE)**[7] 7109 2-9-3 0... PhillipMakin 2 26
(Reg Hollinshead) *mid-div: hdwy 4f out: wknd over 2f out* **100/1**
0 **14** *6* **Micquus (IRE)**[12] 6994 2-9-3 0... DavidProbert 1 12
(Andrew Balding) *in rr: hdwy 4f out: lost pl over 2f out* **100/1**
0 **15** *1* **Hard Road**[8] 7082 2-9-3 0... ChrisCatlin 17 10
(Chris Wall) *s.s: sn detached in last* **150/1**
0 **16** *nk* **Run Richard Run**[41] 6278 2-9-3 0... TomEaves 8 9
(Bryan Smart) *lost pl after 2f: sn bhd* **100/1**
0 **17** *1 ½* **Thane Of Cawdor (IRE)**[21] 6805 2-9-3 0... MickyFenton 11 6
(Tom Tate) *in rr: sme hdwy wd outside 3f out: sn lost pl* **66/1**
1m 51.35s (5.75) **Going Correction** +0.775s/f (Yiel) **17** Ran SP% **121.9**
Speed ratings (Par 96): **102,100,100,97,93 92,92,87,84,82 82,81,76,70,69 69,67**
toteswingers:1&2:£2.10, 1&3:£19.20, 2&3:£19.80 CSF £5.59 TOTE £3.60: £1.90, £1.10, £8.50; EX 5.60 Trifecta £143.00 Pool of £656.48 - 2.93 winning units..
Owner Miss K Rausing **Bred** Miss K Rausing **Trained** Kimpton, Hants

FOCUS
Division two of a useful-looking maiden and one in which the market leaders came to the fore in the closing stages. The gallop was just an ordinary one (though two seconds quicker than division one) and the field raced in the centre in the home straight. This should also throw up winners and the form has a sound feel.

NOTEBOOK

Cubanita ◆ had shown plenty of promise on her debut when chasing home Bonfire (unlucky in French Group 1 last weekend) and she duly stepped up on that effort, in the process showing a good attitude. She'll be well suited by middle distances next year and, as with her stablemate, who won of the first division, looks the type to hold her own at a higher level. (op 7-4 tchd 2-1)

Anomaly showed useful form on his debut when a close third on fast ground and he wasn't far off that level in these very different conditions. He should stay 1m2f and is sure to win a similar event at the very least. (op 11-4)

Poetic Power(IRE) had shown only a moderate level of form on his debut but he was well placed throughout and duly stepped up a fair way on that level in this much softer ground. There is plenty of stamina in his pedigree (dam an unraced sister to top-class stayer Yeats) and he's sure to win a race granted a suitable test. (op 25-1)

Morant Bay(IRE), a 50,000euro yearling and half-sister to a winner in Hong Kong out of a juvenile Group 3 1m winner in France, shaped with promise on this racecourse debut. She should stay 1m2f and is entitled to improve for this experience. (op 25-1)

Lelaps(USA), who finished just in front of Key Appointment (second in first division) on his debut at Haydock, failed to build on that but looks a bit better than the bare result suggests given he was held up in a race that favoured the prominent-racers. He's well worth another chance in ordinary company. (op 9-2)

Dark Stranger(USA), the first foal of a winner in the US, showed ability, despite his greenness and despite looking less than happy in these conditions on this racecourse debut. However, he is entitled to improve for the experience and is sure to pick up a race at some point. (tchd 28-1)

Rose Season, who has several (including smart) winners in her pedigree up to 2m, showed ability and should improve for this experience.

Sequence(IRE) takes the eye on pedigree given she's a half-sister to Derby and Arc winner Sinndar and she should be able to leave these bare facts behind at some point next year. Official explanation: jockey said filly hung left (tchd 20-1)

7234 PHS TREADSMART CONDITIONS STKS — 1m 75y

2:30 (2:34) (Class 3) 3-Y-O+

£6,411 (£1,919; £959; £479; £239; £120) **Stalls** Centre

Form				RPR
4100	**1**		**King Torus (IRE)**[25] 6693 3-9-4 108 ... JimCrowley 8 (Richard Hannon) *hung bdly rt and racd wd for first f: trckd ldrs: hdwy 3f out: rdn to chal wl over 1f out: styd on u.p to ld last 100yds* **9/2**[2]	100
2010	**2**	1 ¼	**Sarrsar**[46] 6150 4-8-10 103 ...(v) PaulHanagan 7 (Saeed Bin Suroor) *chsd clr ldr: tk clsr order 3f out: led 2f out: jnd and rdn over 1f out: hdd and no ex last 100yds* **2/1**[1]	87
6145	**3**	1 ½	**West End Lad**[9] 7050 8-8-10 78 ...(b) RussKennemore 5 (Roy Bowring) *led and sn clr: pushed along 3f out: rdn and hdd 2f out: kpt on u.p fnl f* **16/1**	84
1225	**4**	2 ¼	**Focail Eile**[19] 6830 6-8-10 75 ... FrederikTylicki 4 (John Ryan) *trckd ldrs: hdwy over 3f out: rdn along over 2f out: wandered over 1f out and sn btn* **10/1**	79
-000	**5**	8	**Hung Parliament (FR)**[11] 7023 3-8-8 99 ... RichardKingscote 2 (Tom Dascombe) *a in rr* **14/1**	60
1030	**6**	9	**Hot Rod Mamma (IRE)**[11] 7023 4-8-5 92 ... DuranFentiman 3 (Dianne Sayer) *dwlt and in rr: hdwy to chse ldrs over 3f out: rdn 2f out: sn btn and eased fnl f* **9/1**[3]	35

1m 50.74s (5.14) **Going Correction** +0.775s/f (Yiel)
WFA 3 from 4yo+ 2lb — **6** Ran SP% **83.2**
Speed ratings (Par 107): **105,103,102,100,92 83**
toteswingers:1&2:£1.30, 1&3:£4.40, 2&3:£4.20 CSF £7.55 TOTE £4.20: £2.20, £1.10; EX 7.40 Trifecta £31.50 Pool of £283.50 - 6.64 winning units..
Owner Sir Robert Ogden **Bred** Whisperview Trading Ltd **Trained** East Everleigh, Wilts
■ Stevie Thunder (9/4) was withdrawn after failing to enter the stalls. Deduct 30p in the £ under R4.

FOCUS

Not a strong race for the money and one in which market leader Stevie Thunder failed to go into the stalls. The finish was dominated by the two smart sorts but just an ordinary gallop and the proximity of the 78-rated third and 75-rated fourth suggests this race is dubious as a literal form-guide.

NOTEBOOK

King Torus(IRE) had been well beaten on his only previous attempt in soft (French Group 1 last autumn) and looked to have a bit to find conceding weight all round but he showed a more tenacious attitude than his main rival to notch his fifth career win (from only ten starts). Although this form looks shaky, he may do better if kept in training returned to a sound surface next year. (tchd 4-1 and 5-1)

Sarrsar, the clear pick of the weights, looked to have plenty in his favour and, although he fared better than at Ayr (tailed off) on his previous start, he didn't look to be giving his rider maximum assistance at any stage. He's clearly capable of scoring at this level but doesn't look one to be taking too short a price about. (op 9-4)

West End Lad, second in this race last year when the market leaders underperformed, ran very well in the face of a stiff task but, from a handicapping point of view, he's almost certainly better judged by his proximity to the fourth home than he is to the winner and runner-up. His short-term future lies with the assessor. (op 18-1 tchd 20-1)

Focail Eile, who has shown improved form this season, was another who ran creditably in the face of a stiff task. He's flattered by his proximity behind a couple of smart sorts but should continue to run well if switched back to sand, assuming the handicapper doesn't overreact. (op 14-1 tchd 9-1)

Hung Parliament(FR), who proved troublesome at the start, didn't look the easiest of rides with the hood again fitted and was again a long way below the smart form he showed as a juvenile. He remains one to tread very carefully with. (op 16-1)

Hot Rod Mamma(IRE), who improved out of all recognition in summer, got very stirred up in the stalls and was a long way below her best for the third time in her last four starts. She's probably had enough for now but may find things tough from a mark in the 90's next year. (op 11-1)

7235 PHS DIRECT H'CAP — 1m 75y

3:05 (3:05) (Class 5) (0-70,69) 3-Y-O — **£2,264** (£673; £336; £168) **Stalls** Centre

Form				RPR
2135	**1**		**Watts Up Son**[18] 6867 3-8-11 66 ...(bt) JasonHart(7) 12 (Declan Carroll) *led on outside: crossed to rail after 2f: mde rest: rdn clr over 2f out: hung rt towards fin: unchal* **8/1**	74
0000	**2**	1 ¼	**Uncle Dermot (IRE)**[21] 6799 3-9-2 64 ... DaneO'Neill 7 (Brendan Powell) *dwlt: in rr: hdwy 4f out: hung lft and chsd wnr over 2f out: styd on same pce last 100yds* **16/1**	69
5460	**3**	½	**Frozen Over**[16] 6924 3-9-5 67 ... FergusSweeney 11 (Stuart Kittow) *dwlt: hld up towards rr: hdwy on outside 3f out: kpt on same pce fnl f* **7/1**[3]	71
4205	**4**	hd	**Barista (IRE)**[19] 6840 3-9-7 69 ... SamHitchcott 6 (Mick Channon) *mid-div: hdwy to chse ldrs over 3f out: kpt on same pce fnl f* **11/1**	72
0060	**5**	2 ½	**First Class Favour (IRE)**[11] 7024 3-9-3 65 ... TedDurcan 1 (Tim Easterby) *hld up in rr: kpt on fnl 2f: nvr a factor* **10/1**	63
1402	**6**	5	**Blue Maisey**[17] 6888 3-9-7 69 ... SteveDrowne 5 (Peter Makin) *sn chsng ldrs: wknd over 1f out* **13/2**[2]	55
0300	**7**	3 ½	**Heezararity**[9] 7057 3-9-6 68 ... IanMongan 10 (Stuart Kittow) *chsd ldrs: lost pl over 1f out* **15/2**	46
5500	**8**	4 ½	**Bodie**[155] 2598 3-8-9 57 ... MickyFenton 2 (Pam Sly) *s.i.s: in rr: sme hdwy and swtchd lft over 3f out: sn wknd* **40/1**	25
2405	**9**	2 ¾	**Sky Diamond (IRE)**[14] 6944 3-9-5 67 ...(b) PaulHanagan 8 (James Given) *chsd ldrs: drvn over 3f out: lost pl 2f out* **12/1**	28
1011	**10**	27	**Smart Step**[19] 6830 3-9-5 67 ... JoeFanning 9 (Mark Johnston) *anticipated s: chsd ldrs: wnt 2nd over 4f out: drvn over 3f out: lost pl over 2f out: eased: t.o* **9/4**[1]	—
0-60	**11**	10	**Calico Bay (IRE)**[22] 6767 3-8-7 55 oh10 ...(v[1]) AndrewMullen 3 (Alan McCabe) *s.i.s: hdwy 7f out: lost pl over 4f out: t.o 3f out: sn eased* **100/1**	—

1m 51.86s (6.26) **Going Correction** +0.775s/f (Yiel) — **11** Ran SP% **113.9**
Speed ratings (Par 102): **99,97,97,97,94 89,86,81,78,51 41**
toteswingers:1&2:£26.30, 1&3:£10.30, 2&3:£25.80 CSF £124.14 CT £950.86 TOTE £11.60: £3.40, £5.00, £3.30; EX 200.70 TRIFECTA Not won..
Owner L Ibbotson, D Watts & J Syme **Bred** West Dereham Abbey Stud **Trained** Sledmere, E Yorks

FOCUS

A modest handicap run at a reasonable gallop but one that took less winning than seemed likely with the market leader disappointing. The field came down the centre and, as in previous races on this card, attempting to come from behind proved difficult.

Smart Step Official explanation: jockey said filly lost her action

7236 B&M INSTALLATIONS H'CAP (DIV I) — 1m 2f 50y

3:40 (3:40) (Class 5) (0-75,75) 3-Y-O+ — **£2,264** (£673; £336; £168) **Stalls** Low

Form				RPR
4021	**1**		**Carinya (IRE)**[17] 6888 3-9-3 72 ... TomEaves 4 (Amy Weaver) *hld up towards rr: wd st and stdy hdwy over 3f out: swtchd lft and effrt over 1f out: rdn to chal ent fnl f: styd on wl to ld last 75yds* **7/1**[3]	85
1254	**2**	½	**Carragold**[40] 6302 5-9-0 65 ... DuranFentiman 13 (Mel Brittain) *midfield and sn pushed along on outer: rdn along and wd st: hdwy on stands' rails and cl up over 3f out: led wl over 2f out: rdn wl over 1f out: hdd and no ex last 75yds* **11/4**[1]	77
5301	**3**	5	**Focail Maith**[21] 6799 3-9-4 73 ... FrederikTylicki 14 (John Ryan) *in tch: hdwy to chse ldrs 4f out: rdn 2f out and ch tl one pce ent fnl f* **8/1**	76
5650	**4**	nk	**Ken's Girl**[12] 6996 7-9-10 75 ... IanMongan 9 (Stuart Kittow) *cl up: wd st: effrt 3f out: rdn over 2f out and ev ch tl wknd appr fnl f* **13/2**[2]	77
230	**5**	4 ½	**Spyder**[42] 6248 3-9-4 73 ...(b) AdamKirby 3 (Jane Chapple-Hyam) *reminders s and sn led: rdn wl over 3f out: hdd wl over 2f out and sn one pce* **10/1**	66
1120	**6**	½	**Peachez**[17] 6893 3-8-11 71 ...(p) AmyScott(5) 6 (Alastair Lidderdale) *s.i.s and bhd: hdwy wl over 2f out: sn rdn and styd on appr fnl f: nt rch ldrs* **10/1**	63
3110	**7**	½	**Not Til Monday (IRE)**[137] 3157 5-9-8 73 ...(v) JimmyFortune 12 (J R Jenkins) *chsd ldrs on outer: wd st: rdn along 3f out: grad wknd fr over 2f out* **16/1**	64
4/0-	**8**	2	**Henry San (IRE)**[439] 5266 4-9-5 70 ... FergusSweeney 11 (Alan King) *in tch: rdn along 3f out: sn no imp* **33/1**	58
023/	**9**	11	**Garter Knight**[642] 7246 5-8-11 62 ... MickyFenton 5 (Pam Sly) *a towards rr* **33/1**	29
3000	**10**	17	**Cairncross (IRE)**[17] 6888 3-8-12 67 ... JoeFanning 10 (Mark Johnston) *a towards rr: bhd and eased fnl 2f* **16/1**	—
2260	**11**	3 ¾	**Moody Tunes**[11] 7032 8-9-9 74 ... RichardKingscote 8 (Tom Dascombe) *cl up: rdn along over 3f out: sn wknd* **14/1**	—
4000	**12**	3	**Osgood**[18] 6869 4-9-6 71 ... SamHitchcott 2 (Mick Channon) *chsd ldrs on inner: rdn along over 3f out: sn wknd* **16/1**	—
0050	**13**	7	**Burns Night**[19] 6830 5-9-6 71 ... DanielTudhope 7 (Geoffrey Harker) *a towards rr: bhd fnl 3f* **25/1**	—
-040	**14**	9	**Mafeteng**[42] 6248 3-8-13 68 ... TedDurcan 1 (John Dunlop) *a towards rr: bhd fnl 3f* **20/1**	—

2m 18.46s (6.76) **Going Correction** +0.775s/f (Yiel)
WFA 3 from 4yo+ 4lb — **14** Ran SP% **120.6**
Speed ratings (Par 103): **103,102,98,98,94 94,93,92,83,69 66,64,58,51**
toteswingers:1&2:£2.90, 1&3:£8.70, 2&3:£6.00 CSF £25.27 CT £160.90 TOTE £5.50: £2.30, £1.30, £2.30; EX 25.70 Trifecta £20.20 Pool of £626.74 - 22.92 winning units..
Owner Robert Boyd **Bred** E O'Gorman **Trained** Newmarket, Suffolk

FOCUS

Division one of a fair handicap. A decent gallop saw those ridden patiently come to the fore late on and the field raced centre-to-stands' side in the straight.

7237 B&M INSTALLATIONS H'CAP (DIV II) — 1m 2f 50y

4:10 (4:10) (Class 5) (0-75,75) 3-Y-O+ — **£2,264** (£673; £336; £168) **Stalls** Low

Form				RPR
0023	**1**		**Hidden Glory**[22] 6773 4-9-5 70 ...(b) FrederikTylicki 13 (James Given) *hld up in mid-div: hdwy 3f out: led over 1f out: styd on wl* **10/1**	80
2530	**2**	2 ¼	**Brockfield**[1] 7215 5-8-12 63 ... DuranFentiman 2 (Mel Brittain) *trckd ldrs: led after 2f: hdd over 1f out: kpt on same pce* **7/2**[1]	69
1466	**3**	½	**Dazzling Valentine**[174] 2018 3-9-1 73 ... DominicFox(3) 11 (Alan Bailey) *in rr: hdwy over 3f out: styd on same pce fnl f* **33/1**	78
-031	**4**	3 ¾	**Brigadoon**[16] 6918 4-9-8 73 ... LeeNewman 12 (William Jarvis) *rr-div: sn pushed along: hdwy 4f out: sn chsng ldrs: one pce fnl 2f* **9/2**[2]	71
4-60	**5**	1 ¾	**Hidden Fire**[27] 6658 4-9-6 71 ... NickyMackay 1 (David Elsworth) *hld up towards rr: hdwy over 3f out: chsd ldr over 2f out: wknd over 1f out* **13/2**[3]	65
3436	**6**	2	**Ay Tay Tate (IRE)**[12] 6990 5-8-13 64 ... SteveDrowne 9 (David C Griffiths) *chsd ldrs: sn drvn along: wknd over 1f out* **9/1**	55
3022	**7**	1 ¾	**Amazing Blue Sky**[9] 7070 5-9-10 75 ... JamesSullivan 8 (Ruth Carr) *led 1f: chsd ldrs: wknd over 1f out* **12/1**	62
0114	**8**	10	**Count Ceprano (IRE)**[79] 5110 7-9-4 69 ... ChrisCatlin 10 (Lydia Pearce) *rr-div: effrt 4f out: wknd over 2f out* **28/1**	37
0560	**9**	34	**Botanist**[30] 6592 4-9-1 66 ...(t) StevieDonohoe 5 (Tobias B P Coles) *sn chsng ldrs: lost pl 3f out: sn bhd and eased: t.o* **18/1**	—
0500	**10**	¾	**African Cheetah**[11] 7036 5-9-3 68 ...(t) IanMongan 7 (Reg Hollinshead) *in rr: hdwy over 3f out: sn wknd: eased whn bhd: t.o* **25/1**	—
3110	**11**	¾	**Desert Vision**[26] 6676 7-9-2 74 ...(bt) DavidSimmonson(7) 6 (Michael Easterby) *w ldrs: led after 1f: hdd after 2f: lost pl 3f out: sn bhd: eased: t.o* **16/1**	—

0000 **12** *5* **Best Prospect (IRE)**[59] 5757 9-9-3 68 ....(vt) PhillipMakin 3 —
(Michael Dods) *dwlt: hld up in rr: sme hdwy 3f out: sn wknd and eased: virtually p.u: t.o* **22/1**
5544 **13** *4 1/2* **Crystal Etoile**[30] 6586 3-8-13 68 .... JimmyFortune 4 —
(Sir Michael Stoute) *mid-div: drvn and lost pl 4f out: sn wl bhd: virtually p.u: t.o* **7/1**

2m 19.57s (7.87) **Going Correction** +0.775s/f (Yiel)
WFA 3 from 4yo+ 4lb **13** Ran SP% **118.7**
Speed ratings (Par 103): **99,97,96,93,92 90,89,81,54,53 53,49,45**
toteswingers:1&2:£7.80, 1&3:£41.80, 2&3:£25.00 CSF £42.67 CT £1138.83 TOTE £11.50: £3.50, £2.10, £7.00; EX 40.10 Trifecta £507.30 Part won. Pool of £685.62 - 0.43 winning units..
Owner Danethorpe Racing Partnership **Bred** P Balding **Trained** Willoughton, Lincs

FOCUS
Mainly exposed sorts in division two and the runners again came centre-to-stands' side in the straight. The gallop was a reasonable one.
Crystal Etoile Official explanation: trainer's rep had no explanation for the poor form shown
T/Jkpt: Not won. T/Plt: £60.30 to a £1 stake. Pool:£53,541.92 - 647.28 winning tickets T/Qpdt: £21.00 to £1 Pool: £4,150.53 - 145.70 w. tckts JR

7239a - (Foreign Racing) - See RI

3532 COMPIEGNE (L-H)
Wednesday, November 2

OFFICIAL GOING: Turf: heavy

7238a PRIX DE FRANCIERES (CONDITIONS) (2YO) (TURF) 7f
12:00 (12:00) 2-Y-O **£9,482** (£3,793; £2,844; £1,896; £948)

RPR
1 **Meniska (FR)**[40] 2-8-10 0 .... ChristopheSoumillon 6 78
(C Laffon-Parias, France) **21/10**[1]
2 *2* **Small Frida (FR)**[30] 2-8-13 0 .... MaximeGuyon 8 76
(Mme Pia Brandt, France) **5/2**[2]
3 *2 1/2* **Singapore Sling (FR)**[22] 2-8-11 0 .... AnthonyCrastus 4 68
(A Bonin, France) **7/1**
4 *2* **Stormy Whatever (FR)**[27] 6645 2-9-0 0 .... StephanePasquier 3 66
(James Given) *hld up toward rr: outpcd 2 1/2f out: styd on fnl f: nvr on terms* **3/1**[3]
5 *2* **Countrystar (FR)**[47] 2-8-11 0 .... FlavienPrat 7 58
(C Boutin, France) **29/1**
6 *3* **Questor (FR)**[82] 2-8-13 0 .... PierreHouel(7) 2 59
(M Boutin, France) **10/1**
7 *3* **Lady Rocket (FR)**[5] 2-8-3 0 ow1 .... BenjaminBoutin(6) 1 41
(C Boutin, France) **38/1**
8 *15* **Finisterien (IRE)**[14] 2-9-6 0 .... FranckBlondel 5 14
(J-V Toux, France) **16/1**

1m 32.19s (92.19) **8** Ran SP% **119.2**
PARI-MUTUEL (all including 1 euro stakes): WIN 3.10; PLACE 1.30, 1.20, 1.70; DF 4.60; SF 9.90.
Owner Leonidas Marinopoulos **Bred** 6 C Racing Ltd **Trained** Chantilly, France

7066 SOUTHWELL (L-H)
Thursday, November 3

OFFICIAL GOING: Standard
Wind: Light half against Weather: Overcast

7240 VISIT ATTHERACES.COM/BREEDERSCUP MEDIAN AUCTION MAIDEN STKS 7f (F)
12:40 (12:42) (Class 6) 2-Y-O **£1,704** (£503; £251) **Stalls** Low

Form RPR
23 **1** **Kinloch Castle**[7] 7126 2-9-3 0 .... SilvestreDeSousa 6 81+
(Mark Johnston) *pushed along on outer to ld after 1f: rdn clr wl over 1f out: easily* **4/11**[1]
0643 **2** *7* **Ishiamiracle**[10] 7051 2-8-5 60 .... LeonnaMayor(7) 2 57
(Phil McEntee) *led 1f: trckd ldrs: effrt over 2f out: rdn wl over 1f out: styd on to take 2nd ins fnl f: no ch w wnr* **28/1**
3 *2 1/2* **Don Libre** 2-9-3 0 ....(t) ChrisCatlin 1 59+
(Paul Cole) *in rr: green: outpcd and bhd after 3f: hdwy 2f out: styd on wl ins fnl f: tk 3rd nr fin* **20/1**
3 **4** *1* **Burnhope**[10] 7066 2-9-3 0 .... PaulHanagan 5 53
(David Nicholls) *cl up: hdwy and cl up 3f out: rdn 2f out: sn edgd lft and grad wknd* **9/2**[2]
53 **5** *8* **Mutual Regard (IRE)**[14] 6977 2-9-3 0 .... SebSanders 4 32
(Sir Mark Prescott Bt) *in tch: rdn along 1/2-way: sn outpcd* **8/1**[3]
00 **6** *4* **Kian's Joy**[17] 6912 2-9-3 0 .... TonyHamilton 7 22
(Jedd O'Keeffe) *s.i.s: a in rr* **100/1**
00 **7** *28* **Avonbridge Lad**[23] 6774 2-9-3 0 .... AndrewMullen 3 —
(Alan Brown) *chsd ldrs: cl up 1/2-way: rdn along 3f out: sn wknd: bhd and eased over 1f out* **150/1**

1m 30.19s (-0.11) **Going Correction** 0.0s/f (Stan) **7** Ran SP% **112.5**
Speed ratings (Par 94): **100,92,89,88,78 74,42**
CSF £17.95 TOTE £1.20: £1.10, £5.60; EX 10.80.
Owner Sheikh Hamdan Bin Mohammed Al Maktoum **Bred** Whatton Manor Stud **Trained** Middleham Moor, N Yorks

FOCUS
A run-of-the-mill median auction maiden.

NOTEBOOK
Kinloch Castle, in the frame in stronger events on his two previous starts, registered an easy success. Fast away, he grabbed the lead after 2f and was always in command thereafter. He drew well clear under hands and heels in the home straight and can win again. (op 1-2)
Ishiamiracle, having her sixth run and officially rated 60, looks a reasonable guide to the form. She was always in the first four and stayed on bravely in the closing stages. A small handicap should eventually come her way. (op 25-1)
Don Libre, a newcomer related to a German Listed winner, showed a hint of promise. Well adrift early on, he overtook several rivals in the home straight and will probably appreciate a longer trip. (op 16-1)
Burnhope, third over 1m here ten days earlier, was disappointing. Second in the early stages, and again 2f out, he faded at the business end. (op 4-1)
Mutual Regard(IRE), dropping in trip on this third run, was always in about the same place. He will need to do much better to land a maiden. (tchd 9-1)
Kian's Joy was never in serious contention and has now run three times without showing startling ability.
Avonbridge Lad, well beaten in two previous starts, showed speed until halfway but then dropped away tamely.

7241 BREEDERS' CUP LIVE ON AT THE RACES CLAIMING STKS 1m 3f (F)
1:10 (1:10) (Class 6) 3-Y-O+ **£1,704** (£503; £251) **Stalls** Low

Form RPR
5060 **1** **La Estrella (USA)**[26] 6690 8-9-11 84 .... DaneO'Neill 2 87
(Don Cantillon) *trckd ldrs on inner: effrt and nt clr run 3f out: hdwy to chse ldr wl over 1f out: rdn and styd on wl fnl f to ld last 40yds* **8/11**[1]
2065 **2** *1/2* **Kishanda**[10] 7068 3-8-5 61 .... ChrisCatlin 3 71
(Hughie Morrison) *trckd ldrs: hdwy over 4f out: led 3f out: sn clr: rdn wl over 1f out: hdd and no ex last 40yds* **12/1**
4601 **3** *9* **Mazij**[16] 6936 3-8-8 62 .... WilliamCarson 5 58
(Peter Hiatt) *prom: rdn to chse ldr over 2f out: drvn and kpt on same pce fr wl over 1f out* **20/1**
-110 **4** *1 1/4* **Dontpaytheferryman (USA)**[12] 1387 6-9-10 82 .... PaulHanagan 4 67
(Brian Ellison) *hld up towards rr: hdwy over 4f out: rdn to chse ldrs wl over 2f out: sn one pce* **4/1**[3]
0000 **5** *3/4* **Kalahaag (IRE)**[8] 7099 3-8-1 58 ow1 .... BillyCray(3) 7 50
(David Nicholls) *in rr: sme hdwy 3f out: sn rdn and n.d* **33/1**
-06 **6** *4 1/2* **Seawood**[107] 4180 5-9-0 0 .... RussKennemore 6 47
(Roy Bowring) *a towards rr* **100/1**
0400 **7** *17* **Visions Of Johanna (USA)**[14] 6968 6-8-13 59 ..(vt[1]) SilvestreDeSousa 1 16
(Richard Guest) *cl up: led 1/2-way: rdn along and hdd 3f out: sn wknd* **16/1**
051 **8** *14* **Uphold**[28] 6656 4-9-12 85 ....(v) AdamKirby 8 —
(Gay Kelleway) *led: pushed along and hdd 1/2-way: cl up tl rdn 3f out and sn wknd* **7/2**[2]

2m 26.08s (-1.92) **Going Correction** 0.0s/f (Stan)
WFA 3 from 4yo+ 5lb **8** Ran SP% **122.4**
Speed ratings (Par 101): **106,105,99,98,97 94,82,71**
toteswingers:1&2:£3.30, 2&3:£14.20, 1&3:£7.50 CSF £12.94 TOTE £1.60: £1.10, £2.70, £4.90; EX 13.30 Trifecta £196.80 Pool: £500.03 - 1.88 winning units..Kishanda was claimed by G Kelleway for £7000.
Owner Don Cantillon **Bred** Five Horses Ltd And Theatrical Syndicate **Trained** Newmarket, Suffolk

FOCUS
A claimer in which the contestants' form varied widely. The winner was close to form despite below-par runs from the fourth and eighth.
Uphold Official explanation: jockey said gelding stopped quickly

7242 $26M BREEDERS' CUP NOV 4TH AND 5TH NURSERY 7f (F)
1:40 (1:42) (Class 6) (0-60,60) 2-Y-O **£2,045** (£603; £302) **Stalls** Low

Form RPR
0000 **1** **Mick Slates (IRE)**[22] 6806 2-8-1 45 .... NeilFarley(5) 10 51
(Declan Carroll) *prom: hdwy to ld wl over 2f out: rdn clr over 1f out: kpt on* **16/1**
6020 **2** *1 1/4* **Man Of My Word**[22] 6806 2-9-4 60 .... BillyCray(3) 9 63
(David Nicholls) *midfield: hdwy on inner wl over 1f out: sn rdn and styd on ins fnl f: nt rch wnr* **9/1**
4000 **3** *1 3/4* **Percythepinto (IRE)**[16] 6937 2-9-4 57 ....(t) TonyCulhane 12 58+
(George Baker) *dwlt: sn in midfield: hdwy over 2f out: rdn wl over 1f out: chsd ldng pair ent fnl f: kpt on* **11/4**[1]
4061 **4** *3 3/4* **Red Tyke (IRE)**[37] 6424 2-8-10 49 .... TomEaves 4 37
(John Quinn) *trckd ldrs: hdwy to chse wnr 2f out: rdn over 1f out and sn one pce* **9/2**[2]
4050 **5** *2 1/2* **Samasana (IRE)**[10] 7051 2-8-13 52 .... MartinLane 8 34
(Ian Wood) *dwlt and towards rr: wd st and hdwy over 2f out: rdn over 1f out: kpt on ins fnl f: nrst fin* **22/1**
3500 **6** *3/4* **The Name Is Don (IRE)**[18] 6890 2-9-6 59 .... AdamKirby 5 39
(Mark Gillard) *towards rr: wd st: hdwy on outer over 2f out: rdn and edgd lft over 1f out: nrst fin* **16/1**
0000 **7** *2* **Quiet Appeal (IRE)**[28] 6645 2-8-10 49 .... SilvestreDeSousa 14 24
(Mark Johnston) *ponied to s: towards rr: hdwy on outer 1/2-way: rdn to chse ldrs over 2f out: wknd over 1f out* **20/1**
0050 **8** *1 1/4* **Phoenician Blaze**[10] 7059 2-8-11 53 .... MichaelO'Connell(3) 7 25
(Tim Etherington) *led 2f: prom tl rdn 2f out and grad wknd* **20/1**
650 **9** *1* **More Bottle (IRE)**[36] 6448 2-9-0 53 .... MickyFenton 13 22
(Tom Tate) *in tch: hdwy 3f out and sn chsng ldrs: rdn over 2f out and sn wknd* **25/1**
0050 **10** *1 1/2* **Perfect Day (IRE)**[10] 7051 2-9-4 57 ....(b) ChrisCatlin 3 22
(Paul Cole) *a towards rr* **14/1**
5454 **11** *3/4* **New Romantic**[20] 6846 2-9-1 54 .... PaulHanagan 11 17
(Julie Camacho) *in tch: hdwy to chse ldrs wl over 2f out: sn rdn and wknd* **7/1**[3]
000 **12** *2 1/2* **Son Of May**[40] 6334 2-9-2 55 ....(b) StevieDonohoe 1 12
(Jo Hughes) *a towards rr* **10/1**
0050 **13** *2* **Koalition (IRE)**[10] 7059 2-9-0 58 .... AshleyMorgan(5) 2 9
(David O'Meara) *chsd ldrs on inner: rdn along 3f out: sn wknd* **14/1**
0000 **14** *8* **Ooi Long**[49] 6099 2-8-7 46 .... NickyMackay 6 —
(Mark Rimmer) *cl up: led after 2f: rdn along 3f out: sn hdd & wknd* **50/1**

1m 31.22s (0.92) **Going Correction** 0.0s/f (Stan) **14** Ran SP% **121.2**
Speed ratings (Par 94): **94,92,90,86,83 82,80,78,77,76 75,72,70,60**
toteswingers:1&2:£32.10, 2&3:£9.00, 1&3:£21.10 CSF £143.35 CT £526.00 TOTE £24.00: £8.00, £3.00, £1.80; EX 306.10 TRIFECTA Not won..
Owner Ormskirk **Bred** Peter McCutcheon **Trained** Sledmere, E Yorks

FOCUS
A low-grade nursery, with the top weight rated 60, and it seemed to pay to be prominent from the outset.

NOTEBOOK
Mick Slates(IRE), having his first run over 7f, notched a game first success. Always in the first three, he was out in front before the 2f marker and battled on resolutely when the runner-up launched a challenge. His immediate future now depends on the handicapper's reaction. Official explanation: trainer's rep said, regarding apparent improvement in form, that it was the gelding's first run on Fibresand and appeared suited by the drop in trip. (op 18-1 tchd 20-1)
Man Of My Word, well backed at each-way prices, was always in the first half-dozen. He was fifth 2f out and stayed on strongly, but could not quite get to the winner. This trip was no problem for him. (op 16-1)
Percythepinto(IRE), supported in the morning and sent off favourite, arguably lost his winning chance with a slow start. He overtook several rivals in the home straight, but never seemed likely to trouble the principals. (op 3-1 tchd 5-2, 7-2 in a place)
Red Tyke(IRE), 2lb higher than when scoring at Ayr last time out, broke quickly and was always in the first four. Second at the 2f pole, he faded late on and did not quite match his previous winning form. (op 6-1)
Samasana(IRE), a maiden having her 11th run, was another to lose ground at the start. Considering that disadvantage, she performed creditably. (op 20-1 tchd 25-1)

The Name Is Don(IRE), trying this trip for the first time, was never in meaningful contention. (op 18-1)

7243 EXCLUSIVE BREEDERS' CUP COVERAGE ON ATR H'CAP 7f (F)
2:10 (2:16) (Class 5) (0-75,79) 3-Y-0+ **£2,264** (£673; £336; £168) **Stalls** Low

Form RPR

3101 **1** **Eastern Hills**[30] 6617 6-9-6 **74**........(p) MartinHarley 6 87
(Alan McCabe) *cl up: led wl over 2f out: jnd and rdn over 1f out: kpt on gamely towards fin* **9/1**

5002 **2** *hd* **Powerful Presence (IRE)**[9] 7074 5-9-7 **75**........ SilvestreDeSousa 10 87
(David O'Meara) *trckd ldrs: hdwy to chse wnr over 2f out: rdn to chal jst over 1f out: ev ch ins fnl f: no ex towards fin* **13/8**[1]

6515 **3** *2 ¾* **Bianca De Medici**[50] 6065 4-9-6 **74**........ PaulHanagan 5 79
(Hughie Morrison) *in tch: hdwy 3f out: rdn to chse ldng pair over 1f out: kpt on same pce ins fnl f* **6/1**[2]

0052 **4** *5* **J R Hartley**[30] 6616 3-9-1 **75**........(p) JustinNewman(5) 8 67
(Bryan Smart) *in tch: hdwy 1/2-way: effrt to chse ldrs 2f out: sn rdn and no imp* **13/2**[3]

2332 **5** *¾* **Elusive Warrior (USA)**[10] 7068 8-8-0 **61** oh3........(p) NoraLooby(7) 1 51
(Alan McCabe) *cl up on inner: rdn along 3f out: grad wknd fr over 2f out* **16/1**

0000 **6** *2 ¼* **Councellor (FR)**[12] 7034 9-8-13 **67**........(t) RobbieFitzpatrick 7 52
(Derek Shaw) *bhd tl styd on fnl 2f: nvr a factor* **50/1**

0101 **7** *1* **Supreme Spirit (IRE)**[6] 7141 4-9-11 **79** 6ex........(b) IanMongan 9 61
(George Margarson) *dwlt and in rr: swtchd to inner and hdwy 2f out: plugged on u.p fnl f:* **8/1**

0000 **8** *2 ½* **Not My Choice (IRE)**[8] 7106 6-9-2 **70**........(t) MichaelStainton 2 45
(David C Griffiths) *in rr fr 1/2-way* **33/1**

4000 **9** *17* **One Way Or Another (AUS)**[18] 6895 8-9-2 **70**........ AdamKirby 4 —
(Jeremy Gask) *in tch: wd st: sn rdn and outpcd* **9/1**

0600 **10** *2 ¼* **Luv U Too**[20] 6830 3-9-3 **72**........(b[1]) StevieDonohoe 14 —
(Jo Hughes) *sn led: rdn along and hdd wl over 2f out: sn wknd* **25/1**

4000 **11** *6* **Fantasy Fry**[128] 3493 3-9-4 **73**........(t) RichardKingscote 12 —
(Tom Dascombe) *a in rr* **40/1**

1m 29.42s (-0.88) **Going Correction** 0.0s/f (Stan)
WFA 3 from 4yo+ 1lb **11** Ran SP% **113.9**
Speed ratings (Par 103): **105,104,101,95,95 92,91,88,69,66 59**
toteswingers:1&2:£4.50, 2&3:£2.50, 1&3:£7.40 CSF £22.54 CT £98.41 TOTE £11.00: £2.80, £1.30, £2.10; EX 27.20 Trifecta £65.80 Pool: £803.91 - 9.04 winning units..Ishiadancer was withdrawn. Price at time of withdrawal 16/1. Rule 4 does not apply.
Owner Charles Wentworth **Bred** Azienda Agricola Patrizia **Trained** Averham Park, Notts

FOCUS
A competitive handicap. The winner took another step up and the first three were clear.

7244 ATR BREEDERS' CUP MEGASITE NOW LIVE H'CAP 2m (F)
2:40 (2:41) (Class 5) (0-75,71) 3-Y-0+ **£2,264** (£673; £336; £168) **Stalls** Low

Form RPR

2326 **1** **First Rock (IRE)**[23] 6780 5-8-13 **61**........ GarryWhillans(5) 7 71+
(Alan Swinbank) *trckd ldrs: smooth hdwy to join ldr 3f out: sn led and pushed clr: styd on wl* **5/2**[1]

1005 **2** *2 ¾* **Calculating (IRE)**[10] 7070 7-9-9 **71**........ LeeNewnes(5) 5 76
(Mark Usher) *hld up: hdwy to trck ldrs after 6f: pushed along and outpcd 4f out: rdn wl over 2f out: styd on appr fnl f: nt rch wnr* **9/1**

025 **3** *3 ¼* **Midnight Waltz**[42] 6286 3-9-2 **68**........ SebSanders 1 69
(Sir Mark Prescott Bt) *led: rdn along over 3f out: hdd wl over 2f out: wknd wl over 1f out: lost 2nd wl ins fnl f* **5/2**[1]

20-0 **4** *15* **Al Shababiya (IRE)**[9] 7078 4-9-8 **65**........ DanielTudhope 3 48
(Alison Thorpe) *prom: effrt to chse ldr 4f out: rdn along 3f out: outpcd fnl 2f* **20/1**

003/ **5** *76* **Actodos (IRE)**[769] 6258 7-9-6 **63**........ DaneO'Neill 6 —
(Tony Newcombe) *prom: chsd ldr after 5f tl rdn along and wknd 4f out: sn bhd: t.o fnl 2f* **7/1**[3]

6212 **6** *20* **Dark Spirit (IRE)**[63] 4887 3-9-5 **71**........ PaulHanagan 4 —
(Alison Thorpe) *in tch: rdn along over 5f out: sn wknd and bhd: t.o fnl 3f* **5/1**[2]

50/4 **7** *49* **Indian Pipe Dream (IRE)**[68] 639 9-9-8 **65**........ SilvestreDeSousa 9 —
[illegible]

3m 45.54s (0.04) **Going Correction** 0.0s/f (Stan)
WFA 3 from 4yo+ 9lb **7** Ran SP% **109.4**
Speed ratings (Par 103): **99,97,96,88,50 40,16**
toteswingers:1&2:£5.60, 2&3:£4.60, 1&3:£2.40 CSF £23.75 CT £54.61 TOTE £3.90: £2.80, £5.90; EX 29.90 Trifecta £191.50 Pool: £792.29 - 3.06 winning units..
Owner United Five Racing **Bred** K Molloy **Trained** Melsonby, N Yorks

FOCUS
A moderate handicap where the first three were clear. The winner rates a personal best to reverse C&D form with the runner-up.
Dark Spirit(IRE) Official explanation: jockey said filly never travelled
Indian Pipe Dream(IRE) Official explanation: jockey said gelding never travelled

7245 TOP TIPS AT THEBETTINGMAN.NET MAIDEN STKS 5f (F)
3:10 (3:11) (Class 5) 3-Y-0+ **£2,385** (£704; £352) **Stalls** High

Form RPR

00 **1** **Nially Noo**[51] 6027 3-9-0 0........ LeeTopliss(3) 10 73
(Derek Shaw) *mde all: rdn wl over 1f out: edgd lft and kpt on wl ins fnl f* **14/1**

0-30 **2** *1 ½* **Excellent Aim**[148] 2829 4-9-3 57........ IanMongan 2 67
(George Margarson) *chsd ldrs: hdwy over 2f out: rdn over 1f out: kpt on fnl f* **5/1**[3]

4522 **3** *½* **Bailadeira**[9] 7079 3-8-9 55........ MichaelO'Connell(3) 1 60
(Tim Etherington) *trckd ldrs: hdwy and cl up 1/2-way: rdn to chse wnr wl over 1f out: one pce fnl f* **4/1**[2]

0-60 **4** *6* **Good Timin'**[9] 7086 3-9-3 57........(v) GrahamGibbons 5 44
(David Brown) *in tch: hdwy over 2f out: rdn along wl over 1f out: no imp appr fnl f* **7/1**

22 **5** *2* **Coastal Passage**[19] 6874 3-9-3 0........(p) SilvestreDeSousa 4 36
(John Balding) *chsd ldrs: rdn along 3f out: outpcd fr 1/2-way* **11/8**[1]

0004 **6** *½* **Musical Leap**[1] 7230 3-9-3 35........(bt) JamieMackay 9 35
(Shaun Harris) *towards rr tl sme late hdwy* **66/1**

00-4 **7** *nk* **Cerejeira (IRE)**[20] 6839 3-8-12 46........ DavidAllan 13 29
(Eric Alston) *cl up: rdn along 1/2-way: grad wknd* **20/1**

/5-0 **8** *4 ½* **Manana Manana**[59] 5787 5-9-3 47........(t) TonyCulhane 12 17
(Richard Guest) *midfield: nvr a factor* **33/1**

0000 **9** *1* **Beating Harmony**[33] 6545 3-9-3 48........ RobbieFitzpatrick 8 14
(Michael Appleby) *a outpcd in rr* **50/1**

10 *2 ¼* **Lady Libby Lamb** 3-8-12 0........ MichaelStainton 6 —
(David C Griffiths) *s.i.s: a in rr* **100/1**

060 **11** *3 ¼* **Grayfriars**[43] 6251 3-8-10 45........ JasonHart(7) 3 —
(J R Jenkins) *dwlt: a bhd* **66/1**

0 **12** *3 ½* **Irish Law**[20] 6839 3-9-0 0........ RobertLButler(3) 14 —
(John Balding) *chsd ldrs: rdn along bef 1/2-way: sn wknd* **100/1**

60.95 secs (1.25) **Going Correction** +0.325s/f (Slow) **12** Ran SP% **112.6**
Speed ratings (Par 103): **103,100,99,90,87 86,85,78,76,73 68,62**
toteswingers:1&2:£11.00, 2&3:£3.60, 1&3:£11.00 CSF £75.78 TOTE £25.50: £4.30, £1.50, £1.10; EX 105.90 Trifecta £532.30 Not won. Pool: £719.44 - 0.10 winning units..
Owner Market Avenue Racing Club Ltd **Bred** C J Mills **Trained** Sproxton, Leics
■ Stewards' Enquiry : Michael Stainton five-day ban: used whip when out of contention (Nov 17-19,22-23)

FOCUS
No obvious depth to this modest sprint maiden. The favourite disappointed and the winner showed his first form.

7246 60% AND STILL SMILING H'CAP (DIV I) 1m (F)
3:40 (3:41) (Class 6) (0-52,52) 3-Y-0+ **£1,704** (£503; £251) **Stalls** Low

Form RPR

0500 **1** **Putin (IRE)**[21] 6816 3-8-7 **52**........(p) LeonnaMayor(7) 14 62
(Phil McEntee) *cl up: led after 2f: rdn wl over 1f out: kpt on wl ins fnl f* **16/1**

6306 **2** *2* **So Is She (IRE)**[14] 6968 3-8-9 **50**........(b) DominicFox(3) 11 55+
(Alan Bailey) *towards rr: gd hdwy on inner wl over 1f out: rdn and styd on strly fnl f: tk 2nd nr line* **8/1**

0050 **3** *nse* **Spahi (FR)**[59] 5788 5-8-12 **48**........ DanielTudhope 12 53
(David O'Meara) *midfield: hdwy over 3f out: chsd wnr 2f out: sn rdn and edgd lft appr fnl f: one pce* **5/1**[2]

3006 **4** *nse* **Riczar**[23] 6767 3-8-8 **46** oh1........ RichardKingscote 9 51
(Tom Dascombe) *trckd ldrs: hdwy over 2f out: rdn to chse wnr ent fnl f: kpt on same pce* **25/1**

0504 **5** *7* **Endaxi Mana Mou**[7] 7119 3-8-12 **50**........(b) MartinLane 6 39
(Noel Quinlan) *in tch: hdwy on inner 3f out: sn chsng ldrs: rdn 2f out: grad wknd* **8/1**

6 *2 ¾* **Oxford Gold (IRE)**[78] 5188 4-8-11 **47**........(bt) JamieSpencer 10 29
(Edward Vaughan) *dwlt and in rr tl styd on fnl 2f: n.d* **9/4**[1]

-260 **7** *4 ½* **Daniel Thomas (IRE)**[13] 7003 9-9-2 **52**........(t[1]) MartinHarley 1 24
(Richard Guest) *cl up on inner: chsd wnr 3f out: rdn 2f out: grad wknd* **7/1**[3]

000/ **8** *9* **Marina's Ocean**[691] 7726 7-8-10 **46** oh1........ RussKennemore 8 —
(Roy Bowring) *nvr nr ldrs* **80/1**

0 **9** *¾* **Mujady Star (IRE)**[28] 6659 3-8-6 **47**........(t) NataliaGemelova(3) 7 —
(Kevin M Prendergast) *a towards rr* **20/1**

0503 **10** *½* **Storm Runner (IRE)**[9] 7084 3-8-13 **51**........ SebSanders 4 —
(George Margarson) *a towards rr* **11/1**

5140 **11** *4* **Fairy Mist (IRE)**[10] 7061 4-8-8 **51**........(p) JasonHart(7) 5 —
(Brian Rothwell) *a towards rr* **9/1**

0060 **12** *23* **Chardonnay Star (IRE)**[20] 6839 4-8-10 **46** oh1........ DavidAllan 13 —
(Colin Teague) *a towards rr* **100/1**

030 **13** *10* **Back For Tea (IRE)**[132] 3363 3-8-10 **48**........(t) MickyFenton 3 —
(K F Clutterbuck) *prom: rdn along 1/2-way and sn wknd* **33/1**

60-0 **14** *2 ½* **Countrycraft**[296] 120 4-8-10 **46** oh1........ LeeNewman 2 —
(Sally Hall) *led 2f: prom tl rdn along over 3f out and sn wknd* **66/1**

1m 44.27s (0.57) **Going Correction** 0.0s/f (Stan)
WFA 3 from 4yo+ 2lb **14** Ran SP% **121.6**
Speed ratings (Par 101): **97,95,94,94,87 85,80,71,70,70 66,43,33,30**
toteswingers:1&2:£33.70, 2&3:£13.40, 1&3:£17.80 CSF £133.57 CT £555.72 TOTE £22.60: £6.20, £1.90, £2.50; EX 135.60 TRIFECTA Not won..
Owner S Jakes **Bred** D Llewelyn & J Runeckles **Trained** Newmarket, Suffolk
■ Stewards' Enquiry : Daniel Tudhope five-day ban: used whip with excessive frequency (Nov 17-19,22-23)

FOCUS
The first division of a poor handicap, but seemingly competitive on paper. It was slightly the slower division. The third and fourth set the standard.

7247 60% AND STILL SMILING H'CAP (DIV II) 1m (F)
4:10 (4:10) (Class 6) (0-52,52) 3-Y-0+ **£1,704** (£503; £251) **Stalls** Low

Form RPR

4040 **1** **Minortransgression (USA)**[44] 6236 4-9-1 **51**........ SebSanders 1 66
(Paul Rich) *trckd ldrs on inner: gd hdwy 2f out: led appr fnl f: rdn clr* **13/2**

14-3 **2** *5* **Fearless Poet (IRE)**[14] 6982 3-8-12 **50**........(p) TomEaves 13 53
(Bryan Smart) *cl up: led 3f out: rdn 2f out: hdd appr fnl f: kpt on same pce* **5/2**[1]

065 **3** *hd* **Marina Ballerina**[83] 5021 3-8-10 **48** ow1........ RussKennemore 9 51+
(Roy Bowring) *s.i.s and in rr: rdn 2f out: styd on strly fnl f: tk 3rd on line* **10/1**

0006 **4** *nk* **Scruffy Skip (IRE)**[10] 7071 6-8-12 **48**........(p) TomMcLaughlin 4 50
(Christine Dunnett) *led 1f: prom: rdn 2f out: ch tl one pce fnl f: lost 3rd on line* **20/1**

0523 **5** *¾* **Spacecraft (IRE)**[65] 5601 4-8-10 **46** oh1........ GrahamGibbons 2 46
(Christopher Kellett) *dwlt: hdwy to trck ldrs after 2f: effrt to chse ldr 3f out: rdn 2f out: sn one pce* **11/2**[3]

0056 **6** *1* **Scoglio**[28] 6659 3-8-11 **52**........(p) PatrickDonaghy(3) 8 50
(Frank Sheridan) *towards rr: hdwy 3f out: chsd ldrs whn n.m.r and swtchd rt over 1f out: sn one pce* **15/2**

5406 **7** *1 ½* **Raghdaan**[36] 6446 4-8-12 **48**........ ChrisCatlin 11 42
(Peter Hiatt) *dwlt and rr tl styd on fnl 2f: n.d* **9/2**[2]

000 **8** *2* **Nha Trang (IRE)**[83] 4985 4-8-10 **46** oh1........ NeilChalmers 3 36
(Michael Appleby) *nvr nr ldrs* **50/1**

-604 **9** *6* **Penderyn**[68] 5470 4-8-10 **46** oh1........ RobbieFitzpatrick 7 22
(Charles Smith) *chsd ldrs on outer: rdn along wl over 2f out: sn wknd* **50/1**

0000 **10** *nse* **Emerald Girl (IRE)**[7] 7119 4-8-11 **47**........(b[1]) MartinHarley 12 23
(Richard Guest) *a towards rr* **16/1**

00-4 **11** *10* **Looney Les (IRE)**[63] 5212 3-8-9 **47** oh1 ow1........(b[1]) StevieDonohoe 6 —
(Jo Hughes) *dwlt: sn in tch: rdn along over 3f out: sn wknd* **20/1**

0-00 **12** *38* **Sandy Lonnen**[20] 6833 3-8-9 **50**........ JulieBurke(3) 5 —
(Colin Teague) *cl up: led after 1f: rdn along and hdd 3f out: sn wknd* **33/1**

1m 44.11s (0.41) **Going Correction** 0.0s/f (Stan)
WFA 3 from 4yo+ 2lb **12** Ran SP% **118.6**
Speed ratings (Par 101): **97,92,91,91,90 89,88,86,80,80 70,32**
toteswingers:1&2:£6.20, 2&3:£7.80, 1&3:£11.70 CSF £21.78 CT £165.50 TOTE £6.90: £1.80, £2.10, £3.60; EX 28.10 Trifecta £387.90 Part won. Pool: £524.25 - 0.10 winning units..
Owner G A Morgan **Bred** Padua Stables **Trained** Newport, Gwent

FOCUS
Arguably weaker than the first division, but the time was slightly quicker. The form is rated around the runner-up, with the winner back close to his form this time last year.

Minortransgression(USA) Official explanation: trainer said, regarding apparent improvement in form, that the gelding appeared to be suited by the Fibresand.
T/Plt: £57.70 to a £1 stake. Pool of £47,138.02 - 595.51 winning tickets. T/Qpdt: £26.80 to a £1 stake. Pool of £4,083.25 - 112.70 winning tickets. JR

7194 WOLVERHAMPTON (A.W) (L-H)
Thursday, November 3

OFFICIAL GOING: Standard
Wind: Fresh half-behind Weather: Overcast

7248 ESPN BREEDERS' CUP COVERAGE ON ATR MAIDEN AUCTION STKS 5f 216y(P)
4:30 (4:33) (Class 6) 2-Y-O £1,704 (£503; £251) Stalls Low

Form | | | | RPR
3 **1** **Compton Ashdown**35 6492 2-8-5 0 NicoleNordblad(7) 1 64
(Hans Adielsson) *mde all: rdn over 1f out: jst hld on* 5/13
0 **2** *hd* **Cone Donkey (IRE)**43 6259 2-8-8 0 JoeFanning 7 59
(Bryan Smart) *chsd wnr: rdn over 1f out: r.o* 8/1
60 **3** *1 1/2* **Seattle Sounder (IRE)**20 6836 2-9-1 0 DavidNolan 8 62
(Ann Duffield) *s.i.s: hdwy 4f out: pushed along over 2f out: hrd rdn and hung lft ins fnl f: styd on* 9/1
0260 **4** *1 1/2* **Rockme Cockney**21 6819 2-8-9 70 SteveDrowne 4 51
(Jeremy Gask) *chsd ldrs: rdn over 2f out: styd on same pce ins fnl f* 5/13
5 *2* **Incendiary (IRE)** 2-9-2 0 MichaelHills 2 52
(Hugo Palmer) *chsd ldrs: rdn over 1f out: no ex fnl f* 13/81
000 **6** *3 1/2* **Skyblue**16 6935 2-8-7 0 (t) AndreaAtzeni 5 33
(Tobias B P Coles) *s.s: rdn over 2f out: nvr on terms* 66/1
3660 **7** *1/2* **Trioomph**19 6864 2-8-6 62 PaulHanagan 6 30
(James Given) *sn pushed along in rr: rdn over 2f out: sn outpcd* 9/22

1m 15.82s (0.82) **Going Correction** 0.0s/f (Stan) 7 Ran SP% 112.2
Speed ratings (Par 94): **94,93,91,89,87 82,81**
toteswingers:1&2:£4.60, 2&3:£9.20, 1&3:£8.40 CSF £41.61 TOTE £5.00: £2.50, £4.20; EX 47.20.
Owner Erik Penser **Bred** Wayne And Hilary Thornton **Trained** Kingston Lisle, Oxon
■ Stewards' Enquiry : Joe Fanning five-day ban: used whip with excessive frequency (Nov 17-19,22-23)

FOCUS
An ordinary maiden run at a steady pace.

NOTEBOOK
Compton Ashdown was an encouraging 66-1 third in a 5f maiden here on debut in September, and confirmed that promise by making all stepped up to 6f. The form does not look very solid and he didn't have much in hand in the end but he is a scopey and uncomplicated type who could continue to progress and should stay further than this. (op 9-2 tchd 4-1)
Cone Donkey(IRE) struggled in a 7f Redcar maiden on debut but she showed a good attitude and plenty of improvement to go close dropped to 6f on AW.
Seattle Sounder(IRE) did not really seen out his races in two previous 6f-7f maidens but he was supported at biggish prices and shaped well this time. He is a half-brother to prolific minor 1m winner Kilmannin and could be one to keep an eye on when sent handicapping. (op 16-1)
Rockme Cockney was caught out when the pace increased before staying on again. She has an official rating of 70 and went close in a Thirsk maiden on her third start but she has not managed to get near that form in three runs since. (tchd 9-2)
Incendiary(IRE) is out of an unplaced half-sister to high-class miler Ventiquattrofogli and was a huge market mover throughout the day, but he couldn't make an impact on debut. (tchd 15-8)
Trioomph was below form on nursery debut last time and this 62-rated filly was very laboured and held her head at an awkward angle back sprinting in a maiden on AW debut. (tchd 4-1 and 5-1)

7249 32RED MAIDEN STKS 7f 32y(P)
5:00 (5:01) (Class 5) 3-Y-O+ £2,264 (£673; £336; £168) Stalls High

Form | | | | RPR
2323 **1** **Chokidar (IRE)**28 6653 3-9-3 70 (b) FrederikTylicki 5 78
(David Nicholls) *chsd ldrs: led over 1f out: rdn clr* 6/42
00 **2** *6* **Bint Elnadim (IRE)**14 6981 3-8-12 0 JimmyQuinn 6 57
(Derek Shaw) *hld up: hdwy over 2f out: rdn over 1f out: styd on to go 2nd nr fin: no ch w wnr* 80/1
034- **3** *3/4* **Red Lover**377 7058 3-9-3 79 PaulHanagan 7 60
(Ed Dunlop) *s.i.s: hld up: racd keenly: pushed along over 2f out: hdwy over 1f out: styd on to go 3rd nr fin: nvr nrr* 1/11
3-0 **4** *1/2* **Menha**10 7063 3-8-12 0 SilvestreDeSousa 3 53
(John Gallagher) *sn led: rdn and hdd over 1f out: wknd ins fnl f: lost 2 pls nr fin* 9/13
06 **5** *1 1/2* **Mustafeed (USA)**5 7179 3-9-3 0 JoeFanning 1 54
(Keith Dalgleish) *trckd ldr: plld hrd: rdn over 1f out: wknd ins fnl f* 25/1
6 *4 1/2* **Aqua Ardens (GER)** 3-9-3 0 StephenCraine 2 42
(George Baker) *prom: pushed along over 3f out: wknd 2f out* 33/1
7 *3 3/4* **Mataajir (USA)**404 6383 3-8-12 0 MarkCoumbe(5) 10 32
(Derek Shaw) *bhd and pushed along 5f: n.d* 25/1
00- **8** *2 1/2* **Laser Blazer**323 7873 3-9-3 0 AdamKirby 4 25
(Jeremy Gask) *hld up: rdn over 2f out: a in rr* 33/1
-000 **9** *3 3/4* **Lucky Tricks**38 6411 3-8-12 34 (t) SteveDrowne 9 —
(Jeremy Gask) *prom: pushed along 1/2-way: wknd over 2f out* 66/1
60 **10** *9* **Career Quest**19 6874 3-8-12 0 J-PGuillambert 11 —
(Bill Moore) *hld up: pushed along 1/2-way: sn wknd: t.o* 100/1

1m 29.37s (-0.23) **Going Correction** 0.0s/f (Stan)
WFA 3 from 5yo 1lb 10 Ran SP% 117.3
Speed ratings (Par 103): **101,94,93,92,91 85,81,78,74,64**
toteswingers:1&2:£16.50, 2&3:£11.60, 1&3:£1.10 CSF £127.00 TOTE £2.30: £1.10, £13.10, £1.02; EX 121.70.
Owner Paul J Dixon **Bred** Jeremy Gompertz **Trained** Sessay, N Yorks

FOCUS
The well-backed 70-rated second favourite was a runaway winner in this maiden. It was a weak race and it's doubtful she had to improve.

7250 VISIT ATTHERACES.COM/BREEDERSCUP MAIDEN FILLIES' STKS 1m 141y(P)
5:30 (5:31) (Class 5) 3-Y-O+ £2,264 (£673; £336; £168) Stalls Low

Form | | | | RPR
0-34 **1** **Whey Sauce (JPN)**156 2596 3-8-12 85 RobertHavlin 6 84
(Peter Chapple-Hyam) *a.p: chsd ldr over 6f out: led 2f out: styd on wl* 5/13
35 **2** *1/2* **Shieldmaiden (USA)**141 3043 3-8-12 0 SilvestreDeSousa 11 83
(Mark Johnston) *s.i.s: hld up: hdwy to ld over 7f out: pushed along and hdd 2f out: rdn and ev ch ins fnl f: styd on* 12/1
0-2 **3** *5* **Fakhuur**35 6473 3-8-12 0 MartinDwyer 2 71
(Clive Brittain) *sn led: hdd over 7f out: chsd ldrs: rdn over 1f out: styd on same pce* 4/12
4 *1 1/4* **Aqua Aura (USA)** 3-8-12 0 PaulHanagan 1 68+
(Saeed Bin Suroor) *s.i.s: sn prom: pushed along over 2f out: no ex fnl f over 1f out* 11/101
5 *1/2* **Stars In Your Eyes** 3-8-12 0 NickyMackay 7 67+
(John Gosden) *hld up: hdwy over 1f out: nvr nrr* 14/1
6 *1 1/2* **Placere (IRE)**25 6735 3-8-12 0 LukeMorris 3 64
(Richard Brabazon, Ire) *chsd ldrs: pushed along 1/2-way: wknd over 1f out* 25/1
0-34 **7** *7* **Moon Over Water (IRE)**22 6804 3-8-12 64 AndreaAtzeni 12 47
(Roger Varian) *hld up in tch: racd keenly: pushed along over 3f out: wknd over 2f out* 11/1
0 **8** *3 1/4* **Crystal Child**10 7063 3-8-12 0 DuranFentiman 5 40
(Brian Rothwell) *hld up: effrt over 3f out: sn wknd* 100/1
9 *10* **Fifth Auntie** 4-8-8 0 BrendanPowell(7) 4 17
(J R Jenkins) *hld up: rdn over 3f out: wknd over 2f out* 100/1
10 *11* **Bold Ambition (IRE)** 3-8-12 0 JamesSullivan 8 —
(Ruth Carr) *hld up: a in rr: wknd 3f out: t.o* 100/1
11 *1/2* **Always A Way** 3-8-12 0 (t) EddieAhern 10 —
(Mikael Magnusson) *s.i.s: a in rr: wknd 3f out: t.o* 50/1

1m 49.83s (-0.67) **Going Correction** 0.0s/f (Stan)
WFA 3 from 4yo 3lb 11 Ran SP% 115.8
Speed ratings (Par 100): **102,101,97,96,95 94,88,85,76,66 66**
toteswingers:1&2:£6.50, 2&3:£6.00, 1&3:£3.60 CSF £59.89 TOTE £4.30: £1.10, £4.20, £1.10; EX 42.70.
Owner A Black **Bred** Shadai Corporation Inc **Trained** Newmarket, Suffolk

FOCUS
A fair fillies' maiden for the track and time of year. The well-backed Godolphin favourite couldn't make an impact but the first two had a good battle and pulled clear. The winner was the form choice but did not need to match her Musidora figure.

7251 VISIT ATR BREEDERS' CUP MEGASITE NURSERY (DIV I) 5f 216y(P)
6:00 (6:00) (Class 6) (0-65,65) 2-Y-O £1,704 (£503; £251) Stalls Low

Form | | | | RPR
5000 **1** **Atlantis Crossing (IRE)**9 7081 2-8-3 52 (b1) NathanAlison(5) 11 57
(Jim Boyle) *s.i.s: hmpd over 5f out: plld hrd and hdwy over 4f out: led ins fnl f: rdn out* 22/1
452 **2** *1 1/2* **M J Woodward**6 7143 2-8-6 50 JamesSullivan 4 50
(Paul Green) *chsd ldr: rdn and ev ch ins fnl f: styd on same pce* 3/11
05 **3** *3/4* **Heidi's Delight (IRE)**13 7000 2-8-3 47 PaulHanagan 5 45
(Ann Duffield) *chsd ldrs: rdn over 2f out: styd on same pce ins fnl f* 14/1
355 **4** *1/2* **Gin Twist**15 6946 2-9-4 62 RichardKingscote 1 58
(Tom Dascombe) *chsd ldrs: led over 1f out: rdn and hdd ins fnl f: no ex* 7/1
0000 **5** *1 1/2* **Songbird Blues**20 6846 2-8-8 52 LukeMorris 13 45
(Mark Usher) *hld up: hdwy and nt clr run over 1f out: r.o u.p ins fnl f: nt rch ldrs* 11/1
5640 **6** *2 3/4* **Stepharlie**17 6912 2-8-13 62 JustinNewman(5) 10 46
(Bryan Smart) *chsd ldrs: pushed along over 2f out: styd on same pce fr over 1f out* 10/1
3560 **7** *1 1/4* **Monumental Man**28 6654 2-9-6 64 (tp) ShaneKelly 9 44
(James Unett) *s.i.s: nvr nrr* 16/1
3404 **8** *1 1/2* **Findhornbay**10 7051 2-9-6 64 SilvestreDeSousa 8 39
(Mark Johnston) *chsd ldrs: rdn over 2f out: wknd fnl f* 5/12
6304 **9** *1* **Zigazag (IRE)**14 6973 2-9-0 58 AdamKirby 7 30
(David Evans) *half-rrd s: in rr: rdn over 1f out: nvr on terms* 6/13
060 **10** *1/2* **Liquid Sunshine**21 6819 2-8-9 53 LiamKeniry 2 24
(Sylvester Kirk) *sn led: rdn and hdd over 1f out: wknd ins fnl f* 10/1
000 **11** *8* **Four Poorer (IRE)**59 5779 2-8-1 45 FrankieMcDonald 6 —
(Jamie Osborne) *s.i.s: outpcd* 66/1

1m 16.02s (1.02) **Going Correction** 0.0s/f (Stan) 11 Ran SP% 113.4
Speed ratings (Par 94): **93,91,90,89,87 83,82,80,78,78 67**
toteswingers:1&2:£32.00, 2&3:£10.80, 1&3:£53.80 CSF £84.23 CT £997.74 TOTE £29.60: £15.60, £1.10, £4.60; EX 134.10.
Owner Booth, O'Dwyer, Hegarty & Taylor **Bred** J K Thoroughbreds & P Doyle Bloodstock **Trained** Epsom, Surrey

FOCUS
A low-grade nursery run at a decent pace.

NOTEBOOK
Atlantis Crossing(IRE) showed generally regressive form in five previous starts and was sent off at a big price but first-time blinkers and a drop back to sprinting on his AW debut helped galvanize him, and he powered through a late gap to register a first win with quite a bit in hand. An Elusive City colt who is out of a triple 6f winner, he has potential for further improvement as a sprinter if the headgear continues to work. Official explanation: trainer's rep said, regarding apparent improvement in form, that the colt appeared to benefit from the first-time blinkers. (op 25-1 tchd 28-1)
M J Woodward couldn't repel a strong finishing rival but this was another creditable effort from a quietly progressive colt who has gone close in 5f/6f nurseries on his last four starts. (op 4-1)
Heidi's Delight(IRE) was well held at 20-1 or bigger in four maidens, but she broke much better and showed quite a bit of improvement in this placed effort on her nursery debut. (op 9-1)
Gin Twist is 0-10 and can put a dent in her chance by taking a strong hold but she travelled well for a long way before her effort flattened out and could make an impact back at 5f next time. (op 6-1)
Songbird Blues had not found much progress in five previous runs but she was backed at big prices and stayed on well after finding some trouble. (op 14-1)
Monumental Man Official explanation: jockey said gelding suffered interference in running
Findhornbay travelled well for a long way before fading into fourth in a 7f Leicester nursery last time. The drop back to 6f looked likely to suit but she dropped out after running wide around the final turn. (op 4-1 tchd 7-2)
Zigazag(IRE) didn't get the best of runs after a slow start but was ultimately well held off a sliding mark and is now 0-8. (op 8-1)

7252 VISIT ATR BREEDERS' CUP MEGASITE NURSERY (DIV II) 5f 216y(P)
6:30 (6:30) (Class 6) (0-65,65) 2-Y-O £1,704 (£503; £251) Stalls Low

Form | | | | RPR
5626 **1** **Sonsie Lass**6 7143 2-8-8 52 JoeFanning 4 59
(Keith Dalgleish) *disp ld 1f: trckd ldrs: rdn to ld ins fnl f: r.o* 8/1
0234 **2** *nk* **Mount McLeod (IRE)**6 7143 2-8-9 53 FergusSweeney 8 59
(Jamie Osborne) *hld up: hdwy over 2f out: rdn over 1f out: r.o* 11/41
2500 **3** *1* **Monty Fay (IRE)**33 6539 2-8-11 55 PaulHanagan 3 58
(Derek Haydn Jones) *led 5f out: rdn over 1f out: hdd and unable qck ins fnl f* 8/1
4160 **4** *1/2* **Sweet Ovation**29 6627 2-8-12 56 DavidProbert 11 58
(Mark Usher) *s.i.s: hdwy over 4f out: rdn and ev ch over 1f out: styd on same pce ins fnl f* 12/1

5135 **5** 1¼ **First Rebellion**[29] 6627 2-8-5 **49**...............................(p) SilvestreDeSousa 2 47
(Tony Carroll) *sn led: hdd 5f out: chsd ldrs: rdn over 1f out: no ex ins fnl f* **9/1**

0564 **6** 4½ **Talya's Storm**[13] 7000 2-8-7 **58**.............................. RaulDaSilva(7) 5 42
(Jeremy Gask) *s.i.s: hdwy over 4f out: hmpd and lost pl wl over 2f out: n.d after* **16/1**

0402 **7** ¾ **Welsh Royale**[35] 6489 2-9-5 **63**.............................. WilliamCarson 7 45
(William Muir) *sn outpcd: rdn over 1f out: nvr nrr* **4/1**[2]

0052 **8** ½ **King's Future**[22] 6787 2-9-7 **65**...............................(p) LukeMorris 6 46
(John Akehurst) *mid-div: hdwy over 2f out: rdn and wknd over 1f out* **15/2**[3]

0000 **9** 2¼ **Ferdy (IRE)**[29] 6627 2-8-1 **45**.............................. JamesSullivan 10 19
(Paul Green) *chsd ldrs: bmpd and lost pl wl over 3f out: n.d after* **50/1**

160 **10** ½ **Pendle Lady (IRE)**[118] 3810 2-9-6 **64**.............................. ShaneKelly 12 36
(Mark Brisbourne) *s.i.s: outpcd* **16/1**

0006 **11** *hd* **Our Monica (IRE)**[30] 6597 2-8-1 **45**.............................. AndreaAtzeni 1 17
(Ann Duffield) *s.i.s: hdwy over 4f out: pushed along over 2f out: wknd over 1f out* **25/1**

1m 15.34s (0.34) **Going Correction** 0.0s/f (Stan) **11** Ran SP% **115.9**
Speed ratings (Par 94): **97,96,95,94,92 86,85,85,82,81 81**
toteswingers:1&2:£6.60, 2&3:£6.50, 1&3:£14.70 CSF £29.73 CT £188.52 TOTE £12.00: £3.70, £2.20, £3.60; EX 31.90.
Owner J S Morrison **Bred** Baldernock Bloodstock Ltd **Trained** Carluke, South Lanarkshire

FOCUS
The first five pulled well clear in the second division of a minor nursery.

NOTEBOOK
Sonsie Lass travelled enthusiastically near the pace and showed a good attitude to hold off a fast finisher and get off the mark on the seventh attempt. She has looked headstrong at times but seems to be learning to settle better and could find further progress in sprint handicaps. (op 15-2 tchd 9-1)
Mount McLeod(IRE) did not get much luck when in the frame in sprint nurseries on her last three starts and she finished fast again but was just held. (op 9-4 tchd 3-1)
Monty Fay(IRE) had gone backwards since a close call at 33-1 in a C&D maiden on his second start but the handicapper had quickly dropped him 11lb in the weights and this was much better from a market springer. (op 12-1)
Sweet Ovation was forced wide for most of the way but did well to hang in there in her best effort since getting off the mark off 3lb lower in a Chepsow nursery in August. Her slow starting style can be a problem but she may be able to win again when things go her way. (tchd 11-1)
First Rebellion seemed to respond well to cheekpieces, putting in his third respectable run since winning off a mark of 45 at Chepstow in August. (op 8-1)
Welsh Royale chased home a progressive wide-margin subsequent winner when 16-1 second off 3lb lower on 7f nursery debut here last time. He was well backed but was toiling some way out and the drop back in trip probably backfired. (op 11-2)

7253 BOOK NOW FOR CHRISTMAS CLAIMING STKS 5f 216y(P)
7:00 (7:00) (Class 6) 3-Y-O+ **£1,704** (£503; £251) **Stalls** Low

Form RPR

3150 **1** **Desert Icon (IRE)**[10] 7068 5-8-11 67..........................(bt) TonyCulhane 7 78
(David Flood) *s.s: hdwy over 1f out: rdn to ld ins fnl f: r.o* **40/1**

0000 **2** 1¼ **Ivory Silk**[24] 6761 6-9-2 79.............................. AdamKirby 6 79
(Jeremy Gask) *hld up: hdwy over 1f out: sn rdn: r.o* **14/1**

3110 **3** 1 **Lewyn**[206] 1274 4-8-0 75..............................(bt) RaulDaSilva(7) 8 67+
(Jeremy Gask) *chsd ldrs: swtchd rt over 1f out: r.o* **20/1**

0064 **4** *shd* **Evens And Odds (IRE)**[19] 6875 7-8-12 92..................(t) PaulHanagan 9 71
(Kevin Ryan) *prom: pushed along over 2f out: rdn and r.o wl towards fin* **6/5**[1]

6030 **5** *nk* **Dominium (USA)**[24] 6762 4-9-4 77..............................(b) SteveDrowne 3 77
(Jeremy Gask) *mid-div: hdwy over 1f out: sn rdn: ev ch ins fnl f: unable qck* **16/1**

1260 **6** 1¼ **Apache Ridge (IRE)**[101] 4378 5-8-11 75......................(p) JoeFanning 12 66
(Keith Dalgleish) *hld up: hdwy over 1f out: edgd lft and styd on same pce ins fnl f* **14/1**

0020 **7** 1¼ **Tombi (USA)**[40] 6351 7-9-4 80.............................. MichaelO'Connell(3) 2 72
(Ollie Pears) *led: rdn over 1f out: hdd and no ex ins fnl f* **11/2**[3]

0055 **8** *hd* **Red Cape (FR)**[12] 7040 8-8-13 74..............................(b) JamesSullivan 11 63
(Ruth Carr) *chsd ldr: rdn and ev ch ins fnl f: no ex* **33/1**

/214 **9** 2 **Master Of Disguise**[7] 7116 5-8-13 85..................(t) SilvestreDeSousa 10 58
(Brian Baugh) *chsd ldrs: rdn over 1f out: wknd ins fnl f* **7/2**[2]

0000 **10** 2¼ **Desert Strike**[8] 7106 5-9-1 78..............................(p) MartinHarley 5 51
(Alan McCabe) *s.s: bhd and nt clr run over 2f out: n.d* **25/1**

00-0 **11** 19 **Thatstheone**[13] 7005 3-8-6 46.............................. JimmyQuinn 4 —
(Bill Moore) *sn pushed along in rr: wknd over 2f out* **100/1**

1m 14.37s (-0.63) **Going Correction** 0.0s/f (Stan) **11** Ran SP% **117.3**
Speed ratings (Par 101): **104,102,101,100,100 98,97,96,94,91 65**
toteswingers:1&2:£64.00, 2&3:£18.90, 1&3:£59.50 CSF £492.50 TOTE £52.50: £10.20, £2.20, £4.00; EX 545.50.Evens And Odds was claimed by R Teatum for £6000.
Owner Charlie Adam **Bred** Lynch Bages Ltd & Samac Ltd **Trained** Exning, Suffolk

FOCUS
The hot favourite was laboured in this decent claimer and the runner with the second lowest official rating in the line up came from a long way back to spring a surprise. The winner is rated back to last year's best.

7254 32RED.COM H'CAP 1m 5f 194y(P)
7:30 (7:31) (Class 5) (0-70,69) 3-Y-O+ **£2,264** (£673; £336; £168) **Stalls** Low

Form RPR

0010 **1** **Quinsman**[84] 4974 5-9-12 **67**.............................. LiamKeniry 7 76
(J S Moore) *hld up: hdwy over 3f out: chsd ldr over 2f out: sn rdn: styd on u.p to ld wl ins fnl f* **9/2**[2]

0506 **2** ¾ **Mr Plod**[65] 5588 6-8-13 **54**..............................(p) MartinDwyer 6 62
(Andrew Reid) *a.p: chsd ldr over 10f out: led 6f out: rdn over 1f out: hdd wl ins fnl f* **13/2**[3]

4P35 **3** 3¼ **Little Jazz**[24] 6756 3-9-3 **66**.............................. SilvestreDeSousa 5 70
(Paul D'Arcy) *hld up: hdwy over 2f out: rdn over 1f out: eased whn btn wl ins fnl f* **7/4**[1]

1036 **4** 19 **Soundbyte**[39] 6376 6-9-11 **66**.............................. PaulHanagan 8 42
(John Gallagher) *hld up: hdwy over 4f out: rdn and wknd wl over 1f out* **9/2**[2]

-000 **5** 3 **Mecox Bay (IRE)**[9] 7078 4-9-5 **60**..............................(p) NeilChalmers 4 32
(Michael Appleby) *led 8f: rdn and wknd over 2f out* **14/1**

00-0 **6** 3¼ **Princess Runner**[15] 6947 4-8-9 **50** oh5.............................. MartinHarley 2 18
(Des Donovan) *s.i.s: sn prom: chsd ldr over 4f out tl rdn over 2f out: sn wknd* **10/1**

2045 **7** *shd* **Mustajed**[28] 6656 10-9-7 **62**.............................. JamesMillman 3 30
(Rod Millman) *hld up: rdn over 3f out: sn wknd* **10/1**

2000 **8** 9 **Time Square (FR)**[13] 6988 4-10-0 **69**..............................(t) LukeMorris 1 24
(Tony Carroll) *plld hrd: trckd ldr tl over 10f out: remained handy: rdn over 3f out: wknd over 2f out: t.o* **16/1**

3m 5.88s (-0.12) **Going Correction** 0.0s/f (Stan)
WFA 3 from 4yo+ 8lb **8** Ran SP% **116.8**
Speed ratings (Par 103): **100,99,97,86,85 83,83,78**
toteswingers:1&2:£7.60, 2&3:£2.20, 1&3:£3.20 CSF £34.40 CT £69.92 TOTE £3.50: £1.10, £2.70, £1.10; EX 28.50.
Owner J S Moore **Bred** Mr & Mrs G Middlebrook **Trained** Upper Lambourn, Berks

FOCUS
They finished well strung out in this staying handicap with the first three well clear. The winner got closer to last autumn's mark.
Time Square(FR) Official explanation: jockey said gelding had no more to give

7255 EXCLUSIVE BREEDERS' CUP COVERAGE ON ATR H'CAP 1m 4f 50y(P)
8:00 (8:01) (Class 5) (0-75,75) 3-Y-O **£2,264** (£673; £336; £168) **Stalls** Low

Form RPR

3314 **1** **Alshazah**[21] 6822 3-9-7 **75**.............................. JamesMillman 5 85+
(Rod Millman) *s.i.s: hld up: hdwy over 4f out: led 1f out: styd on wl* **11/4**[1]

3213 **2** 3 **Hygrove Welshlady (IRE)**[23] 6775 3-8-8 **69**........... BrendanPowell(7) 7 74
(J W Hills) *a.p: chsd ldr over 2f out: led wl over 1f out: rdn and hdd 1f out: styd on same pce* **12/1**

0444 **3** *nk* **Perilously (USA)**[22] 6790 3-8-12 **66**.............................. PaulHanagan 9 71
(Jeremy Noseda) *hld up: hdwy over 2f out: rdn and hung lft fr over 1f out: styd on same pce fnl f* **12/1**

2055 **4** ¾ **Dark Dune (IRE)**[20] 6838 3-9-1 **69**.............................. DavidAllan 10 74+
(Tim Easterby) *s.i.s: hld up: nt clr run wl over 1f out: hung lft and r.o ins fnl f: nt rch ldrs* **16/1**

5103 **5** 1¼ **History Repeating**[12] 7033 3-8-1 **62**.............................. RachealKneller(7) 3 64
(Mark Usher) *hld up: nt clr run over 2f out: hdwy and n.m.r over 1f out: r.o: nt rch ldrs* **12/1**

2510 **6** *hd* **Duquesa (IRE)**[12] 7017 3-9-5 **73**.............................. AdamKirby 8 74
(David Evans) *hld up: hdwy u.p over 1f out: styd on same pce fnl f* **8/1**

6004 **7** 6 **Circle Of Angels**[18] 6894 3-8-10 **64**.............................. JoeFanning 2 56
(Ian Williams) *chsd ldrs: rdn over 2f out: wknd over 1f out* **25/1**

-324 **8** 6 **Waltzing Cat (USA)**[43] 6255 3-8-12 **66**..........................(t) SebSanders 1 48
(Sir Mark Prescott Bt) *chsd ldr: hmpd after 1f: led over 3f out: rdn and hdd wl over 1f out: sn hung lft: wknd fnl f* **6/1**

4014 **9** 11 **Deceptive**[22] 6789 3-9-5 **73**.............................. SteveDrowne 6 37
(Roger Charlton) *chsd ldrs: pushed along over 3f out: wknd wl over 1f out* **7/2**[2]

323 **10** 8 **Eyedoro (USA)**[21] 6810 3-9-7 **75**.............................. SilvestreDeSousa 4 27
(Mark Johnston) *sn led: hdd over 3f out: wknd and eased over 1f out: t.o* **9/2**[3]

2m 40.23s (-0.87) **Going Correction** 0.0s/f (Stan) **10** Ran SP% **125.3**
Speed ratings (Par 102): **102,100,99,99,98 98,94,90,83,77**
toteswingers:1&2:£11.20, 2&3:£24.70, 1&3:£8.90 CSF £40.94 CT £361.48 TOTE £3.30: £1.10, £7.30, £6.60; EX 53.60.
Owner The Links Partnership **Bred** Brookside Breeders Club **Trained** Kentisbeare, Devon

FOCUS
This looked a competitive middle-distance handicap but the favourite scored in decisive style from off the steady pace. This was another step forward and he may do a bit better yet. The next three ran basically to their marks.
Dark Dune(IRE) Official explanation: jockey said gelding was denied a clear run
T/Jkpt: Not won. T/Plt: £303.50 to a £1 stake. Pool of £74,874.74 - 180.05 winning tickets.
T/Qpdt: £89.70 to a £1 stake. Pool of £9,930.08 - 81.90 winning tickets. CR

7192 SAINT-CLOUD (L-H)
Thursday, November 3

OFFICIAL GOING: Turf: heavy

7256a PRIX D'HERBEVILLE (CLAIMER) (4YO+) (TURF) 1m
3:20 (12:00) 4-Y-O+ **£7,758** (£3,103; £2,327; £1,551; £775)

RPR

1 **Earl Of Fire (GER)**[75] 6-9-5 0.............................. SylvainRuis 8 90
(Alex Fracas, France) **9/2**[1]

2 5 **Peter Spring (FR)**[153] 7-8-11 0..............................(b) FabienLefebvre 16 71
(N Madamet, France) **24/1**

3 ¾ **Simbad (FR)**[1267] 7-8-11 0..............................(b[1]) FranckBlondel 4 69
(Hanne Bechmann, Denmark) **11/1**

4 1 **Arrivederla (IRE)**[20] 5-8-8 0..............................(p) JohanVictoire 14 63
(Mme J Bidgood, France) **18/1**

5 1½ **Eragons Dream (IRE)**[20] 4-9-1 0.............................. StephanePasquier 1 67
(P Bary, France) **10/1**[3]

6 1 **Beagle Boy (IRE)**[57] 4-8-11 0..............................(b) GaetanMasure 5 61
(A Wohler, Germany) **13/1**

7 1 **Nightdance Victor (GER)**[20] 4-9-6 0.............................. AStarke 15 67
(P Schiergen, Germany) **10/1**[3]

8 ¾ **Tiberina (IRE)**[57] 6-8-7 0.............................. MathieuTavaresDaSilva(6) 12 59
(R Le Gal, France) **19/1**

9 1½ **Peinture Texane (FR)**[153] 5-8-11 0.............................. DavyBonilla 11 53
(M Boutin, France) **10/1**[3]

10 *nk* **Celtie Rod (IRE)**[16] 7-9-1 0.............................. ThierryJarnet 3 57
(X Nakkachdji, France)

0 **Magic Cat**[47] 6150 5-9-5 0.............................. MatthieuAutier(3) 17 —
(Mrs K Burke) *broke wl on outside: settled midfield: sn u.p ent st: no ex: styd on one pce tl eased fnl 100yds* **73/10**[2]

0 **Rock Of Nassau (FR)**[16] 6958 5-9-4 0..............................(p) GregoryBenoist 13 —
(X Nakkachdji, France) **20/1**

0 **Isle Of Pearl (IRE)**[44] 4-8-0 0..............................(p) PierreTomas(8) 7 —
(Y De Nicolay, France) **15/1**

0 **Morning Glory (FR)**[62] 4-8-8 0.............................. AnthonyCrastus 9 —
(Y De Nicolay, France) **36/1**

0 **Babylona (FR)**[13] 7015 4-8-6 0..............................(b) StephaneLaurent(5) 6 —
(Philippe Le Geay, France) **64/1**

P **Galma (FR)**[364] 8-8-7 0.............................. StevanBourgois(8) 10 —
(Robert Collet, France) **37/1**

1m 45.5s (-2.00) **16** Ran SP% **105.1**
WIN (incl 1 euro stake): 5.50. PLACES: 2.50, 6.30, 3.70. DF: 80.90. SF: 93.90.
Owner Ecurie White Star **Bred** Frau M Haller **Trained** France

6406FFOS LAS (L-H)

Friday, November 4

OFFICIAL GOING: Soft (heavy in places in back straight) changing to heavy after race 2 (1.00)

Wind: Light against Weather: cloudy, brighter spells and showers threatening

7257 IWEC INTERNATIONAL MEDIAN AUCTION MAIDEN STKS (DIV I) 1m (R)

12:30 (12:30) (Class 5) 2-Y-O **£2,522** (£750; £375; £187)

Form RPR

3 **1** **Trader Jack**[14] 6993 2-9-3 0 SteveDrowne 5 83+
(Roger Charlton) *chsd ldr: led on bit 3f out: pushed along and readily wnt clr over 1f out: eased towards fin: easily* **10/11**[1]

2 *3 ½* **Lycidas (GER)** 2-9-3 0 StevieDonohoe 7 71+
(Tobias B P Coles) *t.k.h: hld up in tch: rdn and effrt over 2f out: chsd clr wnr over 1f out: kpt on but no imp* **33/1**

00 **3** *1 ¼* **Fine Resolve**[17] 6928 2-9-3 0 LiamKeniry 2 69+
(Andrew Balding) *in tch: pushed along and outpcd 3f out: swtchd rt and rallied over 1f out: styd on and edgd lft fnl f: no threat to wnr* **16/1**

0 **4** *6* **Take Two**[14] 6991 2-9-3 0 RussKennemore 8 55
(John O'Shea) *t.k.h: hld up in tch: rdn and effrt to chse wnr ent fnl 2f: outpcd and btn over 1f out: wknd fnl f* **8/1**[3]

0 **5** *¾* **Isobella**[22] 6818 2-8-12 0 RobertHavlin 3 49
(Hughie Morrison) *in tch in midfield: hdwy to chse ldrs 3f out: rdn and no ex jst over 2f out: wknd over 1f out* **33/1**

6 *1 ¾* **Queen's Star** 2-8-12 0 DavidProbert 4 45+
(Andrew Balding) *hld up towards rr: rdn and struggling 3f out: n.d but plugged on fr over 1f out* **12/1**

0 **7** *2 ¾* **Delishuss**[49] 6117 2-8-12 0 MartinLane 11 39
(Dominic Ffrench Davis) *chsd ldng pair tl 1/2-way: rdn and struggling over 3f out: sn wknd* **100/1**

8 *hd* **Tigresa (IRE)** 2-8-12 0 SilvestreDeSousa 6 38
(Mark Johnston) *led tl hdd and rdn 3f out: wknd u.p 2f out* **13/2**[2]

0 **9** *2 ¾* **Ayla's Emperor**[13] 7030 2-8-12 0 SamHitchcott 10 32
(Mick Channon) *in tch in midfield on outer: rdn and struggling over 3f out: wknd over 2f out* **17/2**

10 *9* **Kings Apollo** 2-9-3 0 EddieAhern 9 18
(Tom Symonds) *a in rr: rdn and toiling 1/2-way: lost tch 3f out* **28/1**

00 **11** *3 ¾* **Lady Jane Grace (IRE)**[123] 3686 2-8-12 0 AndreaAtzeni 12 —
(David Evans) *a in rr: rdn and btn 1/2-way* **100/1**

12 *27* **Make Me Smyle** 2-9-3 0 LukeMorris 1 —
(Stuart Kittow) *s.i.s: a in rr: lost tch 1/2-way t.o* **14/1**

1m 51.1s (10.10) **Going Correction** +1.10s/f (Soft) **12** Ran SP% **118.9**

Speed ratings (Par 96): **93,89,88,82,81 79,77,76,74,65 61,34**

toteswingers:1&2:£8.10, 2&3:£43.50, 1&3:£7.50 CSF £49.84 TOTE £2.00: £1.10, £5.20, £6.70; EX 28.80 Trifecta £276.20 Part won. Pool: £373.35 - 0.62 winning units..

Owner D J Deer **Bred** D J And Mrs Deer **Trained** Beckhampton, Wilts

FOCUS

The jockeys reported that the ground was riding heavy all round. This race was started by flag due to wet ground by the mile marker. They went a steady pace and came down the middle of the track in the home straight. The time was over 12 secs outside the standard, and half a second slower than division two.

NOTEBOOK

Trader Jack ◆ set the standard on his debut third at Newbury. That came on fast ground, but these conditions posed him no problems and he won very easily indeed. The opposition did not amount to much but he should hold his own in better company. (op 6-5 tchd 5-4 in places)

Lycidas(GER), keen to get on with things early, tracked the leaders and came through for second without troubling the favourite. A half-brother to several winners, including Prix de l'Opera scorer Lady Marian, he should be up to winning a maiden. (op 22-1)

Fine Resolve ran a better race back on turf and with the tongue strap left off, pushed into third late on despite looking like he wanted to hang. He's qualified for handicaps now. (op 20-1)

Take Two is bred to need a trip - he's a half-brother to smart jumper My Petra - and he improved on what he showed on his debut. However, his stamina was on the wane late on in this ground. (tchd 15-2)

Isobella showed a lot more than she had on her debut on Polytrack last month, when she finished a long last. (op 40-1)

Queen's Star, a stablemate of the third, should do better in time. She is a grand-daughter of Ascot Gold Cup winner Indian Queen, who raced in the same colours. David Probert reported that the filly ran green. Official explanation: jockey said filly ran green

Tigresa(IRE) made the running until the winner eased past and was held together when beaten. A relatively cheap buy at 8,000gns, she is out of an unraced sister to Godolphin's smart 7f-1m performer Caradak. (op 9-2)

7258 IWEC INTERNATIONAL MEDIAN AUCTION MAIDEN STKS (DIV II) 1m (R)

1:00 (1:00) (Class 5) 2-Y-O **£2,522** (£750; £375; £187)

Form RPR

0 **1** **Knave Of Clubs (IRE)**[27] 6697 2-9-3 0 SteveDrowne 10 77
(Peter Makin) *racd wdst thrght: swtchd rt and racing towards stands' rail fr 1/2-way: rdn over 2f out: hdwy over 1f out: chal ins fnl f: styd on wl to ld cl home* **12/1**

4364 **2** *nk* **Opera Buff**[14] 6995 2-9-3 77 LiamKeniry 5 76
(Sylvester Kirk) *chsd ldr: upsides and travelling wl over 2f out: rdn to ld narrowly 2f out: drvn 1f out: hdd and no ex cl home* **9/4**[1]

0 **3** *½* **Villa Royale**[24] 6771 2-8-12 0 SilvestreDeSousa 11 70
(Harry Dunlop) *led: rdn over 2f out: hdd 2f out: battled on wl and ev ch after: no ex fnl 50yds* **6/1**[3]

4 *2 ½* **Dora's Gift** 2-8-12 0 RobertHavlin 8 64+
(Hughie Morrison) *pushed along towards rr: hdwy into midfield 5f out: chsd ldrs over 2f out: styd on same pce fr over 1f out* **15/2**

42 **5** *nk* **Sunley Pride**[34] 6529 2-9-3 0 SamHitchcott 6 69
(Mick Channon) *chsd ldrs: wnt 3rd and travelling wl over 2f out: rdn and unable qck 2f out: outpcd and btn over 1f out: styd on same pce after* **5/2**[2]

6 *1 ½* **Autumn Fire** 2-8-12 0 DavidProbert 7 60
(Andrew Balding) *in tch: hdwy to chse ldrs 3f out: rdn along and unable qck jst over 2f out: outpcd and btn over 1f out: styd on same pce after* **15/2**

7 *5* **Silent Energy (IRE)** 2-9-3 0 LukeMorris 4 54
(Ronald Harris) *chsd ldrs: rdn 5f out: drvn and unable qck over 2f out: wknd wl over 1f out* **33/1**

8 *8* **Sunny Bank** 2-8-10 0 ThomasBrown(7) 2 37
(Andrew Balding) *bhd: detached in last pair 5f out: lost tch 1/2-way* **14/1**

0060 **9** *4* **Three Tenors**[36] 6471 2-8-12 46 (b[1]) MatthewLawson(5) 9 28
(Gary Harrison) *bhd: detached in last pair 5f out: short-lived effrt u.p over 3f out: sn wknd* **100/1**

0 **10** *19* **Letham Cottage**[9] 7094 2-9-3 0 AndreaAtzeni 3 —
(David Evans) *pushed along towards rr 5f out: lost tch over 2f out: eased fnl f: t.o* **50/1**

11 *15* **Ewenny Star** 2-8-9 0 DeclanCannon(3) 1 —
(Bryn Palling) *t.k.h early: in tch on inner tl wknd over 3f out: wl bhd and eased 2f out: t.o* **50/1**

1m 50.6s (9.60) **Going Correction** +1.10s/f (Soft) **11** Ran SP% **119.4**

Speed ratings (Par 96): **96,95,95,92,92 90,85,77,73,54 39**

toteswingers:1&2:£6.50, 2&3:£4.70, 1&3:£10.60 CSF £39.52 TOTE £16.20: £3.20, £1.60, £2.30; EX 57.60 Trifecta £318.60 Part won. Pool: £430.63 - 0.40 winning units..

Owner J P Carrington **Bred** Bakewell Bloodstock **Trained** Ogbourne Maisey, Wilts

FOCUS

Also started by flag, this looked the stronger division on paper and the time was half a second quicker. The runners again came towards the centre in the straight.

NOTEBOOK

Knave Of Clubs(IRE), lining up on the outside, was brought wide on the home turn which left him with a lot to do in the straight. Racing on the best of the ground, and with his tongue lolling out, he produced a sustained run to get up. This half-brother to the yard's useful filly Harvest Queen had been comfortably held on his debut on Polytrack, but improved considerably here. (tchd 14-1)

Opera Buff, a consistent sort with a BHA rating of 77, travelled up well but had to be stoked up to get the better of the third, and could not hold off the winner's late burst. This was a missed opportunity but conditions were not ideal for him. (tchd 5-2)

Villa Royale, a half-sister to her owner's smart filly Ceilidh House, was well held on her debut last month. Lining up near the outer but coming over to lead, she battled on well and was only quelled deep inside the last. (op 8-1)

Dora's Gift was under pressure early in the long home straight but was staying on. This half-sister to the useful Traphalgar ought to pay her way. (op 9-1)

Sunley Pride was runner-up to the highly regarded Encke on his second start at Newmarket but let that form down, not finding a great deal after moving nicely in behind the leaders. The ground was an obvious excuse. (op 9-4)

Autumn Fire is a half-sister to four winners in the royal colours, most notably Banknote, and will improve for the run. (op 7-1 tchd 8-1)

Silent Energy(IRE) wasn't discredited on this debut but may need more time. (op 40-1)

7259 O'BRIEN CHARTERED ACCOUNTANTS NURSERY 1m (R)

1:30 (1:30) (Class 4) (0-85,81) 2-Y-O **£3,881** (£1,155; £577; £288)

Form RPR

3422 **1** **Takeitfromalady (IRE)**[23] 6807 2-8-10 **70** (b[1]) JimCrowley 4 75+
(Ralph Beckett) *hld up in last pair: racd against stands' rail in st: hdwy to ld travelling wl over 2f out: clr 1f out: eased towards fin* **9/4**[1]

000 **2** *2 ¾* **Captain Cardington (IRE)**[55] 5931 2-8-8 **68** TonyCulhane 8 66
(Mick Channon) *chsd ldrs: rdn and lost pl 5f out: rallied and edging lft u.p wl over 2f out: chsd wnr ins fnl f: plugged on* **10/1**[3]

3150 **3** *4* **New Decade**[23] 6806 2-8-5 **65** SilvestreDeSousa 6 54
(Mark Johnston) *led: rdn and hdd over 2f out: btn over 1f out: lost 2nd and wknd ins fnl f* **11/2**[2]

1051 **4** *6* **Basantee**[21] 6826 2-9-7 **81** RichardKingscote 9 57
(Tom Dascombe) *chsd ldr: rdn over 3f out: lost 2nd wl over 2f out and sn struggling: wknd wl over 1f out* **9/4**[1]

036 **5** *6* **Raspberry Fizz**[23] 6806 2-7-12 **61** oh6 ow3 (b) HarryBentley(3) 5 24
(Eve Johnson Houghton) *in tch: hdwy to chse ldr 1/2-way: struggling and losing pl whn short of room wl over 2f out: sn wknd* **14/1**

4156 **6** *18* **Al's Memory (IRE)**[21] 6829 2-9-3 **77** AndreaAtzeni 7 —
(David Evans) *chsd ldrs tl rdn and wknd wl over 2f out: wl btn and eased over 1f out* **11/2**[2]

000 **7** *1* **Imperial Stargazer**[26] 6726 2-8-7 **67** SamHitchcott 2 —
(Mick Channon) *a in rr and nvr gng wl: rdn and lost tch over 3f out* **10/1**[3]

1m 50.2s (9.20) **Going Correction** +1.10s/f (Soft) **7** Ran SP% **117.2**

Speed ratings (Par 98): **98,95,91,85,79 61,60**

toteswingers:1&2:£5.90, 2&3:£10.90, 1&3:£2.90 CSF £27.90 CT £113.01 TOTE £2.40: £1.20, £8.70; EX 33.10 Trifecta £104.80 Pool: £279.26 - 1.97 winning units..

Owner R Roberts **Bred** Sean Collins **Trained** Kimpton, Hants

FOCUS

The official going description was changed to Heavy before this race, which was started by flag. This time the field came over to the stands' side in the straight. The pace was fair and the time was marginally the quickest of the three mile races.

NOTEBOOK

Takeitfromalady(IRE) secured the best strip of ground alongside the stands' fence and ran out a pretty comfortable winner. He came here in good heart, having finished runner-up in a pair of nurseries over this trip, and was sharpened up by the blinkers. (op 2-1)

Captain Cardington(IRE) stayed on for pressure without troubling the winner. He had finished last on his two most recent starts, but had been gelded since his latest run and had also been dropped 4lb. (op 12-1 tchd 14-1)

New Decade, another who has been given some assistance by the handicapper, made the running before fading. His win came on Fibresand and each of his five runs on turf has been on easy ground or worse. (op 7-1)

Basantee was not inconvenienced by the conditions, but she wasn't able to lead this time and she had been brushed aside with a quarter-mile left. (op 11-4)

Al's Memory(IRE) was not disgraced in heavy ground at Haydock, but after racing furthest from the rail in the straight here he dropped right away. (op 5-1 tchd 6-1)

7260 SIX IN SIX MAIDEN STKS 6f

2:00 (2:02) (Class 5) 3-4-Y-O **£2,587** (£770; £384; £192) **Stalls** High

Form RPR

1 **Rivas Rhapsody (IRE)** 3-8-12 0 SilvestreDeSousa 6 66+
(Ian Wood) *t.k.h: hld up wl in tch: swtchd lft and effrt ent fnl 2f: led ins fnl f: r.o strly and drew clr fnl 100yds: comf* **11/4**[2]

0000 **2** *3 ¼* **Welsh Dancer**[19] 6889 3-9-3 45 LukeMorris 9 58
(Ronald Harris) *led: rdn ent fnl 2f: hdd ins fnl f: nt gng pce of wnr fnl 100yds* **20/1**

6656 **3** *2 ½* **Hollie**[9] 7093 3-8-12 60 SteveDrowne 1 45
(Peter Makin) *taken down early: wnt lft s: sn in tch: wnt 2nd over 2f out: rdn and ev ch 2f out: no ex and btn over 1f out: wknd ins fnl f* **9/1**

56-0 **4** *shd* **Yashila (IRE)**[188] 1682 3-8-12 75 LiamKeniry 8 45
(J S Moore) *hld up in tch: pushed along and effrt over 2f out: outpcd and btn over 1f out: hung lft and wl hld ins fnl f* **9/2**[3]

5 *¾* **Ready When You Are (IRE)**[334] 7749 3-8-12 0 (b[1]) JimCrowley 5 42
(Ralph Beckett) *hld up in tch in rr: hdwy over 2f out: nt clr run 2f out: rdn and fnd nil jst over 1f out: wl hld fnl f* **2/1**[1]

055 **6** *1 ¼* **Bunkered Again**[32] 6591 4-8-5 41 (t) RaulDaSilva(7) 4 38
(Jeremy Gask) *hld up in tch: rdn and effrt jst over 2f out: wknd over 1f out* **25/1**

7 ¾ **Clear Spring (IRE)** 3-9-3 0 MartinHarley 3 41
(John Spearing) *s.i.s: pushed along in rr thrght: nvr trbld ldrs* **15/2**

0600 8 9 **Waterbury Girl**[14] 6999 3-8-9 47 DeclanCannon(3) 2 —
(Bryn Palling) *chsd ldr tl over 2f out: sn struggling and losing pl: wl bhd fnl f* **33/1**

3550 P **Lady Excellentia (IRE)**[19] 6889 3-8-12 42 DavidProbert 7 —
(Ronald Harris) *plld hrd: hld up in tch: lost action and eased 4f out: p.u and dismntd 1/2-way* **20/1**

1m 16.01s (6.01) **Going Correction** +0.775s/f (Yiel) **9** Ran SP% **116.3**
Speed ratings (Par 103): **90,85,82,82,81 79,78,66,—**
toteswingers:1&2:£12.30, 2&3:£17.30, 1&3:£4.30 CSF £59.38 TOTE £3.50: £1.70, £7.20, £1.60; EX 51.80 Trifecta £565.70 Pool: £764.54 - 0.10 winning units..
Owner D Hefin Jones **Bred** D Hefin Jones **Trained** Upper Lambourn, Berks

FOCUS
A weak sprint maiden and not form to treat too positively, but the winner did it well and shouldn't be overfaced for handicaps.
Waterbury Girl Official explanation: jockey said that the filly ran too freely

7261 EGAN WASTE NURSERY 5f
2:30 (2:31) (Class 4) (0-85,85) 2-Y-O **£3,780** (£1,131; £565; £283; £141) **Stalls** High

Form RPR

1 1 **Rafeej**[19] 6892 2-8-11 75 SilvestreDeSousa 2 89+
(Mark Johnston) *in tch: rdn 1/2-way: hdwy to ld 2f out: rn green and hung rt wl over 1f out: clr ent fnl f: r.o wl: eased towards fin* **9/4**[1]

4551 2 4½ **Ashpan Sam**[45] 6232 2-8-9 73 LukeMorris 1 70
(John Spearing) *stdd s: hld up in tch in rr: rdn 1/2-way: hung lft and hdwy 2f out: no threat to wnr but kpt on ins fnl f to go 2nd cl home* **8/1**

4514 3 hd **Bubbly Ballerina**[41] 6323 2-9-3 84 DominicFox(3) 7 80
(Alan Bailey) *pressed ldrs: rdn 2f out: chsd clr wnr over 1f out: no imp and wl hld after: lost 2nd cl home* **13/2**

5213 4 nk **Planet I T (IRE)**[21] 6827 2-9-7 85 LiamKeniry 6 80
(Mark Usher) *in tch: rdn and effrt jst over 2f out: no threat to wnr but kpt on and pressing for placings ins fnl f* **3/1**[2]

0610 5 ¾ **Main Focus (USA)**[14] 6995 2-9-2 80 RobertHavlin 4 72
(John Gosden) *taken down early: racd keenly: led after 1f tl 2f out: sn outpcd by wnr and lost 2nd over 1f out: btn and plugged on same pce fnl f* **11/2**[3]

2300 6 4½ **Middleton Flyer (IRE)**[21] 6827 2-8-6 70 AndreaAtzeni 5 48
(David Evans) *led for 1f: rdn and struggling 1/2-way: wknd wl over 1f out* **7/1**

3000 7 7 **Signifer (IRE)**[21] 6827 2-9-7 85 TonyCulhane 3 36
(Mick Channon) *t.k.h: chsd ldrs tl over 2f out: wknd qckly wl over 1f out: wl bhd fnl f* **10/1**

60.94 secs (2.64) **Going Correction** +0.775s/f (Yiel) **7** Ran SP% **117.2**
Speed ratings (Par 98): **109,101,101,101,99 92,81**
toteswingers:1&2:£4.80, 2&3:£8.30, 1&3:£4.30 CSF £21.80 TOTE £2.30: £1.10, £6.30; EX 23.50.
Owner Hamdan Al Maktoum **Bred** Whatton Manor Stud **Trained** Middleham Moor, N Yorks

FOCUS
An ordinary nursery in which they kept a little away from the stands' rail.

NOTEBOOK
Rafeej ♦ quickened up in good style to lead and was pulling clear when edging to his right then drifting into the centre again. Successful in a Bath maiden on his only previous start, he did this in very taking fashion despite giving the impression that he'd prefer better ground, and looks one to keep on-side. (op 5-2 tchd 11-4)
Ashpan Sam stayed on for pressure once switched to the outer again, posting a fair effort on this nursery debut. He'd been raised 11lb for his maiden win, which came on a fast surface. (op 15-2 tchd 9-1)
Bubbly Ballerina, whose last four runs had all been at Chester, had the cheekpieces off and was dropping in trip. Racing on the stands' side of the group, she ran a solid race but lacked a change of gear. (tchd 15-2 and 8-1 in places)
Planet I T(IRE) remained towards the near side and stayed on without troubling the leaders. He did confirm his Haydock superiority over Middleton Flyer and Signifer, both of whom have had very busy seasons. (op 10-3)
Main Focus(USA), back in trip, raced keenly up with the pace before weakening in ground that was no good to him. (op 7-1)

7262 RONALD JESSETT MEMORIAL H'CAP 6f
3:00 (3:03) (Class 4) (0-85,85) 3-Y-O+ **£4,528** (£1,347; £673; £336) **Stalls** High

Form RPR

1 **Colour Of Love (IRE)**[21] 6853 3-9-2 83 (b) SeanLevey(3) 12 92
(W McCreery, Ire) *in tch: rdn and hdwy over 2f out: chsd ldr over 1f out: led ins fnl f: r.o wl* **14/1**

6234 2 ¾ **Jack My Boy (IRE)**[25] 6761 4-8-13 77 (v) AndreaAtzeni 13 84
(David Evans) *chsd ldr tl over 2f out: outpcd and rdn wl over 1f out: rallied and styd on wl ins fnl f: wnt 2nd again cl home* **15/2**[3]

4400 3 nk **Galatian**[37] 6467 4-8-13 77 (v[1]) JamesMillman 3 83
(Rod Millman) *chsd ldrs: led gng wl 2f out: rdn over 1f out: hdd ins fnl f: no ex: lost 2nd cl home* **10/1**

2241 4 ½ **Flameoftheforest (IRE)**[24] 6779 4-9-0 81 (p) HarryBentley(3) 7 85
(Ed de Giles) *hld up towards rr: hdwy 2f out: chsd ldng trio ent fnl f: kpt on same pce ins fnl f* **11/2**[1]

5230 5 3¾ **Macdillon**[37] 6467 5-9-0 78 LiamKeniry 9 70
(Stuart Kittow) *in tch: chsd ldrs and rdn 2f out: outpcd and btn over 1f out: wknd fnl f* **9/1**

0050 6 hd **Dickie Le Davoir**[18] 6913 7-8-13 80 (b) RobertLButler(3) 10 72
(Richard Guest) *towards rr: rdn and hdwy 2f out: hung lft and plugged on same pce fr over 1f out* **25/1**

2500 7 ½ **Lucky Numbers (IRE)**[10] 7074 5-9-6 84 JamesSullivan 6 74
(Paul Green) *in tch: rdn to chse ldrs 2f out: struggling and btn over 1f out: wknd fnl f* **14/1**

3631 8 nk **Camache Queen (IRE)**[37] 6467 3-9-1 79 EddieAhern 14 68
(Denis Coakley) *in tch in midfield: rdn and effrt over 2f out: wknd over 1f out* **13/2**[2]

005 9 3¼ **West Coast Dream**[41] 6331 4-9-7 85 SilvestreDeSousa 11 64
(Roy Brotherton) *led tl 2f out: sn rdn and no ex: wknd over 1f out* **11/2**[1]

0150 10 2 **Frognal (IRE)**[10] 7074 5-9-0 78 (bt) MartinHarley 4 50
(Richard Guest) *hld up towards rr: hdwy over 2f out: rdn and no prog over 1f out: sn wknd* **33/1**

3236 11 10 **Night Trade (IRE)**[15] 6974 4-9-2 80 LukeMorris 15 20
(Ronald Harris) *in tch in midfield: rdn and no hdwy ent fnl 2f: wknd qckly wl over 1f out: bhd and eased ins fnl f* **10/1**

104 12 12 **Bravo King (IRE)**[41] 6327 3-9-4 82 (e[1]) JimCrowley 1 —
(Richard Guest) *racd alone towards far side: in tch: rdn and struggling 3f out: wknd and bhd over 1f out: eased ins fnl f* **12/1**

2133 13 1 **Celtic Sixpence (IRE)**[25] 6762 3-9-1 79 MartinLane 8 —
(Noel Quinlan) *chsd ldrs tl 1/2-way: sn lost pl: wl bhd and eased ins fnl f* **9/1**

1m 13.81s (3.81) **Going Correction** +0.775s/f (Yiel) **13** Ran SP% **121.9**
Speed ratings (Par 105): **105,104,103,102,97 97,97,96,92,89 76,60,58**
CSF £117.64 CT £1152.86 TOTE £20.70: £7.50, £3.00, £6.40; EX 222.90 TRIFECTA Not won..
Owner GAA Legends Syndicate **Bred** Liam Queally **Trained** The Curragh, Co.Kildare
■ Stewards' Enquiry : Sean Levey five-day ban: used whip with excessive frequency (Nov 18-19,22-24)

FOCUS
An open sprint handicap which went to the Irish contender. Not many showed their form but the winner rates a personal best.

7263 GORREL EQUIPMENT SOLUTIONS LTD H'CAP 1m 2f (R)
3:30 (3:32) (Class 6) (0-65,65) 3-Y-O+ **£1,811** (£539; £269; £134) **Stalls** Low

Form RPR

5034 1 **On The Cusp (IRE)**[11] 7068 4-9-7 62 (p) MartinHarley 10 74
(Richard Guest) *t.k.h: w ldr tl led 6f out: mde rest: rdn and drew clr wl over 2f out: in command over 1f out: eased towards fin* **11/2**[2]

0301 2 3¾ **Taste The Wine (IRE)**[10] 6486 5-9-9 64 DavidProbert 14 68
(Bernard Llewellyn) *hld up in tch towards rr: rdn and hdwy into 6th 2f out: plugged on u.p to chse wnr fnl 100yds: no imp on wnr* **15/2**

2040 3 1¾ **Lakota Ghost (USA)**[17] 6926 3-9-1 60 EddieAhern 1 61
(Seamus Durack) *chsd ldrs: rdn and outpcd over 3f out: kpt on u.p to chse wnr over 1f out: no imp: lost 2nd fnl 100yds* **7/1**

5534 4 1¼ **Disturbia (IRE)**[9] 7091 3-8-6 51 oh4 LukeMorris 7 49
(J W Hills) *hld up in tch: rdn and effrt over 3f out: 5th and no prog whn edgd rt 2f out: plugged on same pce fnl f* **8/1**

503 5 1 **Cardi King**[36] 6475 3-9-0 59 JimCrowley 13 55
(Ian Wood) *hld up in tch in rr: gd hdwy to chse ldrs over 3f out: chsd wnr and rdn 3f out: no prog and btn 2f out: wknd ins fnl f* **10/1**

3616 6 6 **Monster Munchie (JPN)**[28] 6669 3-9-1 63 HarryBentley(3) 6 47
(William Knight) *chsd ldrs: rdn and lost pl over 3f out: no ch fnl 2f* **5/1**[1]

3521 7 ½ **Sweet World**[26] 6438 7-9-10 65 MartinLane 3 48
(Bernard Llewellyn) *hld up in tch in rr: rdn and effrt in centre 3f out: no real prog: wl btn fnl 2f* **7/1**

0303 8 5 **Corrib (IRE)**[19] 6888 8-8-11 55 (p) DeclanCannon(3) 9 28
(Bryn Palling) *chsd ldrs: wnt 2nd over 3f out tl 3f out: wknd 2f out: bhd fnl f* **14/1**

0-60 9 18 **Curlew (IRE)**[77] 5231 5-9-7 62 JamesMillman 12 —
(Chris Down) *chsd ldrs tl lost pl qckly over 3f out: t.o fnl 2f: t.o* **40/1**

0130 10 1¾ **Market Puzzle (IRE)**[9] 7113 4-8-11 59 (p) RachealKneller(7) 2 —
(Mark Brisbourne) *hld up in tch in rr: pushed and effrt 3f out: no prog and sn wl bhd: eased ins fnl f: t.o* **13/2**[3]

11 10 **Strut In Style (IRE)**[23] 6198 3-8-9 57 (b[1]) KieranO'Neill(3) 5 —
(W McCreery, Ire) *led tl 6f out: chsd wnr tl over 3f out: sn wknd: t.o fnl 2f: eased ins fnl f* **12/1**

2m 25.2s (15.80) **Going Correction** +1.325s/f (Soft)
WFA 3 from 4yo+ 4lb **11** Ran SP% **119.1**
Speed ratings (Par 101): **89,86,84,83,82 78,77,73,59,57 49**
toteswingers:1&2:£8.30, 2&3:£11.00, 1&3:£9.40 CSF £47.17 CT £296.87 TOTE £6.90: £2.30, £2.80, £2.40; EX 59.90 Trifecta £342.00 Pool: £485.32 - 1.05 winning units..
Owner Rakebackmypoker.com **Bred** J Stan Cosgrove **Trained** Stainforth, S Yorks
■ Stewards' Enquiry : David Probert nine-day ban: used whip with excessive frequency (Nov 18-19,22-26,28-29)

FOCUS
A modest handicap in which the field came to the stands' side once in line for home. There are doubts over plenty in the bad ground but the easy winner is rated to his AW best.
Corrib(IRE) Official explanation: jockey said that the mare was unsuited by the heavy ground

7264 DIGIBET.COM APPRENTICE H'CAP 1m 4f (R)
4:00 (4:00) (Class 6) (0-65,65) 3-Y-O+ **£1,811** (£539; £269; £134) **Stalls** Low

Form RPR

454 1 **C P Joe (IRE)**[10] 7078 3-8-9 58 (v) MatthewLawson(3) 11 68
(Paul Green) *hld up in rr: pushed along and gd hdwy to chse ldrs over 3f out: wnt 2nd 2f out: led over 1f out: clr and styd on wl ins fnl f* **14/1**

0036 2 5 **Sistine**[87] 4878 3-9-0 60 SeanLevey 13 62
(Nicky Henderson) *hld up in tch towards rr: c towards stands' rail and hdwy to chse ldrs over 3f out: wnt 2nd over 2f out: led 2f out tl over 1f out: no ex and plugged on same pce fnl f* **8/1**

0041 3 5 **Rock Peak (IRE)**[85] 4951 6-9-0 54 (b) LouisBeuzelin 8 48
(Bernard Llewellyn) *in tch: hdwy to chse ldrs and c to stands' rail in st: led 3f out: rdn and hdd 2f out: sn wknd* **22/1**

0000 4 6 **Admirable Duque (IRE)**[15] 6976 5-9-5 64 (b) LucyKBarry(5) 1 48
(Dominic Ffrench Davis) *chsd ldrs: wnt 2nd 8f out tl led and styd on inner 4f out: rdn and hdd 3f out: wknd 2f out* **14/1**

2012 5 6 **Aegean Destiny**[52] 6029 4-9-4 63 MichaelJMurphy(5) 10 38
(John Mackie) *hld up in tch towards rr: nt clr run 5f out: rdn and hdwy over 3f out: no prog over 2f out: 5th and wl btn fnl 2f* **3/1**[1]

5002 6 ¾ **Dubara Reef (IRE)**[10] 7077 4-9-1 55 (v) JamesSullivan 9 29
(Paul Green) *led for 2f: sn rdn along but styd prom: wknd 3f out: 6th and no ch fnl 2f* **10/1**

-315 7 11 **Passion Play**[34] 6546 3-9-5 65 HarryBentley 7 21
(William Knight) *t.k.h: chsd ldrs tl lost pl 4f out: no ch fnl 3f* **10/1**

16-5 8 1¼ **Lucas Pitt**[8] 7121 4-8-9 54 DavidKenny(5) 4 8
(Michael Scudamore) *in tch in midfield: rdn and struggling 4f out: wknd and wl btn over 2f out* **12/1**

3430 9 3½ **Transfer**[24] 6773 6-9-11 65 RyanClark 6 13
(Richard Price) *t.k.h: chsd ldrs tl led after 2f: rdn and hdd 4f out: sn wknd: wl bhd fnl 3f: t.o* **7/1**[3]

10 ½ **Snuggle Up (IRE)**[21] 6855 3-8-6 52 (t) KieranO'Neill 5 —
(W McCreery, Ire) *hld up in tch in last quartet: rdn and btn 4f out: wl bhd fnl 3f* **5/1**[2]

0550 11 7 **Spring Secret**[4] 7200 5-9-6 65 ThomasBrown(5) 12 —
(Bryn Palling) *chsd ldrs tl rdn and lost pl 4f out: sn bhd: t.o fnl 3f* **7/1**[3]

5456 12 60 **Madam Tessa (IRE)**[25] 6748 3-9-0 60 DeclanCannon 2 —
(Bryn Palling) *hld up in midfield: hmpd and struggling 5f out: lost tch 4f out: sn wl t.o* **50/1**

00-0 13 36 **Great Show**[24] 6767 4-8-6 51 oh6 (t) RachealKneller(5) 3 —
(Bernard Llewellyn) *a in rr: rdn and struggling 6f out: lost tch and wl t.o fnl 4f* **100/1**

2m 52.78s (15.38) **Going Correction** +1.325s/f (Soft)
WFA 3 from 4yo+ 6lb **13** Ran SP% **124.3**
Speed ratings (Par 101): **101,97,94,90,86 85,78,77,75,75 70,30,6**
toteswingers:1&2:£22.50, 2&3:£15.60, 1&3:£30.00 CSF £125.43 CT £2486.15 TOTE £19.20: £5.80, £2.40, £5.20; EX 99.90 TRIFECTA Not won..

Owner Gary Williams **Bred** David And Elizabeth Kennedy **Trained** Lydiate, Merseyside

FOCUS

A moderate handicap for apprentice riders, run on the worst of the ground. The runners were spread across the course in the home straight and came home at wide intervals. Not form to take literally.

T/Plt: £313.60 to a £1 stake. Pool of £50,761.58 - 118.16 winning tickets. T/Qpdt: £182.30 to a £1 stake. Pool of £3,695.38 - 15.00 winning tickets. SP

7248 WOLVERHAMPTON (A.W) (L-H)

Friday, November 4

OFFICIAL GOING: Standard

Wind: Light behind Weather: Early rain clearing

7265 ATR BREEDERS' CUP MEGASITE NOW LIVE APPRENTICE H'CAP 5f 216y(P)

4:30 (4:31) (Class 5) (0-70,76) 3-Y-O+ **£2,522** (£750; £375; £187) **Stalls** Low

Form RPR

0066 **1** **Ryedane (IRE)**[11] 7064 9-8-12 **64**................................(b) AdamCarter(3) 4 73
(Tim Easterby) *s.i.s: hld up: hdwy over 2f out: rdn over 1f out: hung lft ins fnl f: r.o to ld post* **20/1**

0010 **2** *shd* **Haadeeth**[13] 7040 4-9-0 **68**................................(b) GeorgeChaloner(5) 13 78+
(Richard Fahey) *a.p: led wl over 1f out: pushed clr fnl f: hdd post* **10/1**

3305 **3** *1 1/2* **Methaaly (IRE)**[6] 7173 8-9-2 **70**................................(be) NoelGarbutt(5) 8 74
(Michael Mullineaux) *s.i.s: hdwy over 1f out: hung lft ins fnl f: r.o: nt rch ldrs* **11/1**

0342 **4** *2* **Bahamian Lad**[13] 7039 6-8-13 **65**................................(p) LMcNiff(3) 10 63
(Reg Hollinshead) *chsd ldrs: rdn over 1f out: styd on same pce fnl f* **5/1**[2]

0062 **5** *1 3/4* **Mey Blossom**[6] 7172 6-9-1 **64**................................(p) AmyRyan 6 56
(Richard Whitaker) *mid-div: pushed along over 2f out: rdn over 1f out: styd on u.p: nt trble ldrs* **6/1**[3]

0041 **6** *nk* **Frequency**[6] 7172 4-9-13 **76** 6ex................................(b) PaulPickard 9 67
(Keith Dalgleish) *hld up: hdwy over 2f out: rdn over 1f out: no ex ins fnl f* **4/1**[1]

500 **7** *nk* **Kipchak (IRE)**[21] 6841 6-8-10 **62**................................(b) RyanPowell(3) 7 52
(Conor Dore) *chsd ldr: led 4f out: rdn and hdd over 2f out: no ex fnl f* **50/1**

0263 **8** *hd* **Meia Noite**[27] 6694 4-8-4 **60**................................ DannyBrock(7) 11 50
(Chris Wall) *chsd ldrs: led over 2f out: hdd wl over 1f out: wknd ins fnl f* **7/1**

1000 **9** *1/2* **Distant Sun (USA)**[3] 7216 7-8-10 **62**................................(p) ShaneBKelly(3) 3 50
(Linda Perratt) *hld up: plld hrd: n.d* **12/1**

0606 **10** *nk* **Elhamri**[13] 7040 7-9-0 **63**................................ MatthewDavies 5 50
(Conor Dore) *chsd ldrs: rdn over 1f out: btn whn nt clr run ins fnl f* **18/1**

0000 **11** *3/4* **Dream Catcher (FR)**[19] 6895 3-9-3 **69**................................ JamesRogers(3) 1 54
(David Pinder) *led: hdd 4f out: rdn over 2f out: wknd fnl f* **11/1**

0400 **12** *1* **Sir Nod**[6] 7172 9-9-7 **70**................................ LeeTopliss 2 51
(Julie Camacho) *prom: nt clr run and lost pl over 2f out: n.d after* **12/1**

1m 14.58s (-0.42) **Going Correction** -0.025s/f (Stan) **12** Ran SP% **116.6**

Speed ratings (Par 103): **101,100,98,96,93 93,93,92,92,91 90,89**

toteswingers:1&2:£26.40, 2&3:£14.60, 1&3:£27.10 CSF £204.04 CT £2345.71 TOTE £28.40: £6.60, £5.30, £3.30; EX 270.40.

Owner Ryedale Partners No 5 **Bred** Tally-Ho Stud **Trained** Great Habton, N Yorks

FOCUS

An ordinary apprentice handicap which looked pretty open on paper. It was sound run and the winner is rated to this year's turf form.

Distant Sun(USA) Official explanation: jockey said that the gelding hung right-handed

7266 EXCLUSIVE BREEDERS' CUP COVERAGE ON ATR H'CAP 5f 20y(P)

5:00 (5:02) (Class 6) (0-60,60) 3-Y-O+ **£1,704** (£503; £251) **Stalls** Low

Form RPR

0005 **1** **Perlachy**[27] 6694 7-9-3 **56**................................(v) KellyHarrison 12 65
(Ronald Harris) *hld up: hdwy over 1f out: rdn ins fnl f: r.o to ld nr fin* **22/1**

413 **2** *1* **Rightcar**[48] 6176 4-8-13 **52**................................ RobbieFitzpatrick 8 57
(Peter Grayson) *hld up: hdwy over 1f out: sn rdn: r.o* **16/1**

0000 **3** *1/2* **Grand Stitch (USA)**[23] 6802 5-9-0 **58**................................(v) NeilFarley(5) 2 61+
(Declan Carroll) *chsd ldr tl led 3f out: rdn clr 1f out: hdd nr fin* **11/1**

1452 **4** *3/4* **Circuitous**[14] 6999 3-9-0 **53**................................(b) JoeFanning 4 54
(Keith Dalgleish) *s.i.s: hdwy over 1f out: r.o: nt rch ldrs* **9/2**[1]

2242 **5** *nk* **Cayman Fox**[9] 7100 6-9-2 **58**................................ DaleSwift(3) 7 57
(Linda Perratt) *a.p: rdn 1/2-way: r.o* **9/1**

0101 **6** *3/4* **Here Now And Why (IRE)**[9] 7100 4-9-4 **60** 6ex........... LeeTopliss(3) 10 57
(Ian Semple) *prom: rdn over 1f out: styd on* **11/2**[2]

0004 **7** *hd* **Fear Nothing**[29] 6655 4-9-5 **58**................................(b) TomEaves 9 54
(Ian McInnes) *chsd ldrs: rdn over 1f out: styd on* **16/1**

0030 **8** *1 1/4* **Morermaloke**[8] 7123 3-9-3 **59**................................(p) PaulPickard(3) 6 51
(Ian McInnes) *outpcd: r.o ins fnl f: nrst fin* **14/1**

0000 **9** *1 1/2* **Avertuoso**[10] 7079 7-8-13 **57**................................(v) JustinNewman(5) 5 43
(Bryan Smart) *mid-div: rdn 1/2-way: styd on same pce fr over 1f out* **12/1**

6502 **10** *1/2* **Kinlochrannoch**[35] 6501 3-9-7 **60**................................(p) PaulHanagan 3 44
(Ben Haslam) *led: hdd 3f out: rdn over 1f out: wknd ins fnl f* **13/2**[3]

0-53 **11** *3/4* **Itum**[44] 6251 4-9-3 **56**................................ PhillipMakin 13 38
(Christine Dunnett) *s.i.s: outpcd* **14/1**

3001 **12** *3/4* **Francis Albert**[16] 6943 5-9-5 **58**................................ JimmyQuinn 1 37
(Michael Mullineaux) *prom: rdn over 1f out: wkng whn n.m.r ins fnl f* **7/1**

61.82 secs (-0.48) **Going Correction** -0.025s/f (Stan) **12** Ran SP% **114.9**

Speed ratings (Par 101): **102,100,99,98,97 96,96,94,92,91 90,88**

toteswingers:1&2:£30.30, 2&3:£17.00, 1&3:£47.80 CSF £326.33 CT £4083.53 TOTE £20.90: £4.40, £4.20, £3.60; EX 180.10.

Owner Mrs N Macauley **Bred** J James **Trained** Earlswood, Monmouths

FOCUS

Quite competitive for the grade. The leaders went too fast and the race was set up for a closer. The winner took advantage of a lenient mark.

Francis Albert Official explanation: jockey said that the gelding hung right-handed

7267 32RED MEDIAN AUCTION MAIDEN STKS 5f 20y(P)

5:35 (5:35) (Class 6) 2-Y-O **£1,704** (£503; £251) **Stalls** Low

Form RPR

62 **1** **Code Six (IRE)**[23] 6800 2-8-12 0................................ TomEaves 8 65
(Bryan Smart) *mde virtually all: rdn ins fnl f: r.o* **4/1**[2]

02 **2** *1/2* **Colbyor**[10] 7072 2-9-3 0................................ PaulHanagan 5 68
(Richard Fahey) *a.p: pushed along 1/2-way: chsd wnr over 1f out: sn rdn: r.o* **6/4**[1]

6 **3** *1 1/2* **Betty Brook (IRE)**[11] 7056 2-8-5 0................................ RichardOld(7) 3 58
(Nick Littmoden) *hld up: racd keenly: hdwy over 1f out: r.o* **28/1**

06 **4** *1 3/4* **I See You**[68] 5514 2-8-12 0................................ BarryMcHugh 2 51
(George Margarson) *s.i.s: hld up: plld hrd: shkn up 2f out: r.o ins fnl f: nt trble ldrs* **4/1**[2]

000 **5** *1 1/2* **Musical Strike**[19] 6890 2-9-3 42................................ RobbieFitzpatrick 9 51
(Shaun Harris) *in rr: hdwy over 1f out: styd on same pce ins fnl f* **300/1**

0 **6** *3* **Darleas Gift (IRE)**[15] 6975 2-8-12 0................................ PhillipMakin 4 35
(Kevin Ryan) *chsd ldrs: rdn 1/2-way: wknd fnl f* **66/1**

5400 **7** *hd* **Maltease Ah**[11] 7056 2-8-12 65................................(p) KirstyMilczarek 10 34
(Andrew Reid) *led early: chsd wnr tl rdn over 1f out: wknd ins fnl f* **16/1**

4330 **8** *3/4* **Red Socks (IRE)**[134] 3308 2-9-0 64................................ NataliaGemelova(3) 1 37
(Gay Kelleway) *chsd ldrs: rdn over 1f out: wknd ins fnl f* **5/1**[3]

0 **9** *1* **Salaaheb (IRE)**[31] 6603 2-8-7 0................................ JemmaMarshall(5) 7 28
(Alastair Lidderdale) *sn pushed along and a in rr* **20/1**

62.15 secs (-0.15) **Going Correction** -0.025s/f (Stan) **9** Ran SP% **112.6**

Speed ratings (Par 94): **100,99,96,94,91 86,86,85,83**

toteswingers:1&2:£2.40, 2&3:£12.30, 1&3:£20.40 CSF £9.88 TOTE £5.10: £1.90, £1.30, £4.30; EX 12.90.

Owner Woodcock Electrical Limited **Bred** Miss Tamaria Butler **Trained** Hambleton, N Yorks

FOCUS

A modest maiden.

NOTEBOOK

Code Six(IRE), as she had done at Nottingham, showed good early pace to lead and maintained her advantage well enough to hold off the favourite close home. She's a speedy type, well suited to a sharp or easy 5f, and should pay her way in handicaps. (op 7-2)

Colbyor was well enough placed turning in and stayed on well, but he couldn't quite catch the leader. A reproduction of this effort would be good enough to win many bog-standard maidens round here. (op 11-10 tchd 13-8)

Betty Brook(IRE) stepped up on her debut effort at Leicester and will be an interesting type for handicaps after one more outing. Her pedigree suggests another furlong won't do any damage. (op 33-1)

I See You didn't break particularly well and as a result met trouble in running. She stayed on once in the clear and might have more to offer in handicaps. (op 11-2)

Musical Strike, sent off at 300-1, had shown precious little in his previous three starts and his performance is the anchor to the form. (op 200-1)

Red Socks(IRE) was disappointing returned to the AW as a reproduction of his previous form on the surface should have seen him fighting it out for a place. Perhaps he needed the run following a 134-day absence. (op 7-1)

7268 BREEDERS' CUP ONLY ON ATR H'CAP (DIV I) 7f 32y(P)

6:10 (6:10) (Class 6) (0-62,68) 3-Y-O+ **£1,567** (£462; £231) **Stalls** High

Form RPR

0553 **1** **Berbice (IRE)**[9] 7100 6-9-3 **61**................................ PaulHanagan 3 68
(Linda Perratt) *hld up: hdwy over 1f out: r.o to ld last stride* **11/1**

0011 **2** *nse* **Michael's Nook**[21] 6847 4-8-8 **57**................................ LMcNiff(5) 7 64
(David Barron) *a.p: chsd ldr 2f out: rdn over 1f out: r.o* **5/2**[1]

2061 **3** *nk* **Chookie Avon**[6] 7175 4-9-10 **68** 6ex................................(p) JoeFanning 2 74
(Keith Dalgleish) *hld up in tch: rdn over 1f out: r.o* **4/1**[2]

0401 **4** *nse* **Gala Spirit (IRE)**[15] 6982 4-8-11 **55**................................(p) TomEaves 8 61
(Peter Niven) *led: rdn over 1f out: hdd last stride* **14/1**

6004 **5** *1/2* **Pipers Piping (IRE)**[8] 7131 5-8-10 **59**................................(p) AmyScott(5) 5 64+
(Alastair Lidderdale) *hld up: hdwy over 1f out: sn rdn: r.o wl* **13/2**[3]

5550 **6** *1 3/4* **Jackie Love (IRE)**[8] 7131 3-8-6 **51** oh2................................(v) KirstyMilczarek 1 51
(Olivia Maylam) *s.i.s: hld up: hdwy over 1f out: sn rdn: styd on same pce ins fnl f* **50/1**

5164 **7** *3/4* **Pytheas (USA)**[21] 6848 4-8-10 **59**................................(p) MarkCoumbe(5) 6 57
(Michael Attwater) *chsd ldrs: rdn over 1f out: styd on same pce fnl f* **14/1**

0011 **8** *1 1/4* **Princess Dayna**[11] 7071 3-8-12 **57**................................ RichardKingscote 9 52
(Tom Dascombe) *hld up: rdn over 1f out: nt trble ldrs* **7/1**

4530 **9** *nk* **Whats For Pudding (IRE)**[14] 7006 3-8-1 **51**................................ NeilFarley(5) 12 45
(Declan Carroll) *chsd ldr tl rdn over 2f out: no ex fnl f* **25/1**

5106 **10** *1/2* **This Ones For Eddy**[6] 7175 6-9-4 **62**................................ GrahamGibbons 11 54
(John Balding) *hld up: nvr on terms* **20/1**

0260 **11** *nk* **Bonnie Prince Blue**[24] 6777 8-8-13 **60**................................(b) DaleSwift(3) 4 52
(Ian McInnes) *hld up: rdn over 1f out: n.d* **25/1**

0205 **12** *1 1/4* **Aviso (GER)**[6] 7176 7-9-4 **62**................................(v[1]) TomMcLaughlin 10 50
(David Evans) *hld up: plld hrd: a in rr* **16/1**

1m 29.65s (0.05) **Going Correction** -0.025s/f (Stan)

WFA 3 from 4yo+ 1lb **12** Ran SP% **116.4**

Speed ratings (Par 101): **98,97,97,97,96 94,94,92,92,91 91,90**

toteswingers:1&2:£6.30, 2&3:£2.90, 1&3:£7.00 CSF £36.30 CT £135.29 TOTE £11.00: £4.10, £1.30, £2.10; EX 52.50.

Owner Ken McGarrity **Bred** William Flynn **Trained** East Kilbride, S Lanarks

FOCUS

The early pace wasn't great here and it turned into a bit of a sprint from the turn in. It was slightly slower than division II. The winenr had slipped to a good mark.

7269 BREEDERS' CUP ONLY ON ATR H'CAP (DIV II) 7f 32y(P)

6:40 (6:42) (Class 6) (0-62,62) 3-Y-O+ **£1,567** (£462; £231) **Stalls** High

Form RPR

0312 **1** **Trojan Rocket (IRE)**[21] 6841 3-9-2 **61**................................ SilvestreDeSousa 6 73
(George Prodromou) *hld up: hdwy 2f out: rdn to ld ins fnl f: r.o* **3/1**[3]

3241 **2** *1/2* **Know No Fear**[14] 7001 6-9-4 **62**................................(p) PaulHanagan 7 72
(Alastair Lidderdale) *hld up: hdwy over 1f out: rdn to chse wnr ins fnl f: edgd lft: r.o* **11/4**[2]

3015 **3** *2 1/4* **Diamond Run**[36] 6488 3-9-1 **60**................................ DaneO'Neill 5 64
(J W Hills) *chsd ldr tl led over 1f out: sn rdn: hdd and unable qck ins fnl f* **2/1**[1]

4306 **4** *4* **Norcroft**[17] 6939 9-8-0 **51** oh2................................(p) DanielHarris(7) 4 44
(Christine Dunnett) *hld up: rdn over 2f out: styd on: nt trble ldrs* **33/1**

000 **5** *1 1/2* **Adam De Beaulieu (USA)**[97] 4563 4-9-4 **62**................................(tp) PhillipMakin 3 51
(Ben Haslam) *chsd ldrs: rdn over 2f out: wknd over 1f out* **18/1**

2200 **6** *1/2* **Mucky Molly**[3] 7216 3-8-11 **56**................................ KirstyMilczarek 8 44
(Olivia Maylam) *hld up: hdwy over 2f out: rdn over 1f out: sn wknd* **14/1**

0503 **7** *2* **Desert Auction (IRE)**[36] 6490 4-9-4 **62**................................ TomEaves 2 45
(Ian Semple) *hld up: pushed along 1/2-way: n.d* **17/2**

0006 **8** *1 1/2* **Fault**[9] 7098 5-8-12 **61**................................(tp) AmyScott(5) 1 40
(Alastair Lidderdale) *led: rdn and hdd over 1f out: wknd fnl f* **12/1**

6016 **9** *2* **Bathwick Xaara**[39] 6408 4-8-9 **56**................................ RossAtkinson(3) 10 29
(Jonathan Portman) *chsd ldrs: rdn over 2f out: wknd wl over 1f out* **25/1**

1m 28.99s (-0.61) **Going Correction** -0.025s/f (Stan)

WFA 3 from 4yo+ 1lb **9** Ran SP% **121.9**

Speed ratings (Par 101): **102,101,98,94,92 92,89,88,85**

toteswingers:1&2:£1.80, 2&3:£2.00, 1&3:£2.70 CSF £12.51 CT £20.61 TOTE £4.20: £1.70, £1.70, £1.10; EX 10.10.

Owner G D J Linder **Bred** J G F Fox **Trained** East Harling, Norfolk

FOCUS
There was a good gallop to this second division, thanks to Fault, who went off at a fast pace, resulting in a winning time 0.66sec quicker than the steadily run first division. The winner earned a 6lb personal best.

7270 BREEDERS' CUP LIVE ON AT THE RACES CLASSIFIED STKS 1m 141y(P)
7:10 (7:11) (Class 6) 3-Y-O+ **£1,908** (£563; £281) **Stalls** Low

Form RPR
0442 **1** **Miss Villefranche**[9] 7096 3-9-0 55..............................(v) StevieDonohoe 3 62
(Michael Bell) *hld up in tch: rdn to ld ins fnl f: styd on* **5/1**[3]
0066 **2** ½ **Excellent Vision**[15] 6657 4-9-3 51...........................(t) RichardKingscote 9 61+
(Milton Bradley) *s.i.s: hld up: hdwy and swtchd rt over 1f out: rdn ins fnl f: r.o* **9/1**
0-04 **3** 2 **Dashing Eddie (IRE)**[10] 7085 3-9-0 51........................... PhillipMakin 13 56
(Kevin Ryan) *sn led: rdn over 1f out: hdd and unable qck ins fnl f* **4/1**[1]
044 **4** 1½ **Khaki (IRE)**[9] 7096 3-9-0 53...................................... SilvestreDeSousa 5 53
(David Evans) *chsd ldrs: pushed along over 2f out: rdn and nt clr run over 1f out: styd on same pce ins fnl f* **7/1**
0302 **5** nk **Fair Breeze**[14] 7006 4-9-3 52.. RobertHavlin 1 52
(Richard Phillips) *hld up in tch: rdn over 1f out: styd on same pce fnl f* **5/1**[3]
00/0 **6** 1½ **Bertie Boo**[20] 6877 6-9-3 40.. NeilChalmers 7 49
(Michael Appleby) *sn chsng ldr: rdn over 2f out: no ex fnl f* **40/1**
0243 **7** nk **Shaws Diamond (USA)**[9] 7096 5-9-3 54.....................(v) PaulHanagan 10 48
(Derek Shaw) *trckd ldrs: racd keenly: outpcd over 2f out: styd on ins fnl f* **9/2**[2]
1004 **8** 2¼ **Freda's Rose (IRE)**[44] 6262 7-8-12 55................................ LMcNiff(5) 4 43
(Owen Brennan) *s.i.s: hld up: nvr nrr* **8/1**
206 **9** 2¼ **Gay Gallivanter**[22] 6813 3-9-0 54................................ TomMcLaughlin 6 38
(Michael Quinn) *prom: rdn over 2f out: sn wknd* **20/1**
3500 **10** nse **Queen's Choice (IRE)**[9] 7096 3-9-0 50..................... StephenCraine 8 38
(Anabel K Murphy) *hld up: rdn over 3f out: wknd over 2f out* **40/1**
6000 **11** 11 **Lough Corrib (USA)**[22] 6813 3-9-0 54...................(p) KirstyMilczarek 11 —
(Alastair Lidderdale) *s.i.s: hld up: hdwy over 4f out: wknd over 2f out: sddle slipped* **25/1**

1m 51.97s (1.47) **Going Correction** -0.025s/f (Stan)
WFA 3 from 4yo+ 3lb **11** Ran SP% **118.6**
Speed ratings (Par 101): **92,91,89,88,88 86,86,84,82,82 72**
toteswingers:1&2:£12.10, 2&3:£7.40, 1&3:£4.90 CSF £47.62 TOTE £5.70: £2.50, £2.80, £1.10; EX 55.20.
Owner J L C Pearce **Bred** J L C Pearce **Trained** Newmarket, Suffolk

FOCUS
All bar Bertie Boo were within 5lb of each other on adjusted ratings, so it was a competitive heat on paper. The early pace wasn't that strong. The form makes sense amongst the principals.
Lough Corrib(USA) Official explanation: jockey said that the gelding ran too freely

7271 32RED.COM MEDIAN AUCTION MAIDEN STKS 1m 1f 103y(P)
7:40 (7:40) (Class 6) 3-5-Y-O **£1,704** (£503; £251) **Stalls** Low

Form RPR
2626 **1** **Ela Gonda Mou**[34] 6530 4-8-10 70................................ RosieJessop(5) 6 56+
(Peter Charalambous) *led over 8f out: sn wl clr: shkn up over 1f out: unchal* **4/5**[1]
05 **2** 3½ **Thackeray**[24] 6781 4-9-6 0.. KellyHarrison 4 53
(Chris Fairhurst) *hld up: hdwy over 6f out: chsd wnr over 4f out: rdn and hung lft over 1f out: no imp* **18/1**
0565 **3** 2½ **Baby Driver**[18] 6923 3-9-3 48..................................(t[1]) RichardKingscote 2 48
(Tom Dascombe) *stdd s: hld up: plld hrd: pushed along 3f out: rdn over 1f out: styd on to go 3rd wl ins fnl f: nvr nrr* **9/1**
4500 **4** nk **Northumberland**[10] 7078 5-9-1 42.. LMcNiff(5) 5 47?
(Owen Brennan) *led 1f: chsd wnr to over 4f out: outpcd 3f out: styd on ins fnl f* **66/1**
6002 **5** 1 **Roman Flame**[49] 6122 3-8-12 58.............................. SilvestreDeSousa 1 40
(Michael Quinn) *hld up: hdwy over 3f out: rdn over 2f out: wknd fnl f* **7/2**[2]
2-4 **6** 40 **Fonnie (IRE)**[28] 6668 3-8-12 0.. PaulHanagan 3 —
(Rae Guest) *chsd ldrs: pushed along 1/2-way: wknd over 3f out: t.o* **7/1**[3]

2m 1.22s (-0.48) **Going Correction** -0.025s/f (Stan)
WFA 3 from 4yo+ 3lb **6** Ran SP% **107.0**
Speed ratings (Par 101): **101,97,95,95,94 58**
toteswingers:1&2:£5.60, 2&3:£6.60, 1&3:£1.80 CSF £15.33 TOTE £1.80: £1.10, £7.70; EX 13.90.
Owner P Charalambous **Bred** Peter Charles **Trained** Newmarket, Suffolk

FOCUS
A poor maiden and the result was soon in no doubt. The form is severely limited by the fourth.

7272 VISIT ATTHERACES.COM/BREEDERSCUP H'CAP 1m 4f 50y(P)
8:15 (8:15) (Class 4) (0-85,84) 3-Y-O+ **£3,234** (£962; £481; £240) **Stalls** Low

Form RPR
-051 **1** **Raucous Behaviour (USA)**[37] 6445 3-8-12 **78**........ SilvestreDeSousa 4 86
(George Prodromou) *prom: chsd ldr 10f out: led over 3f out: rdn over 1f out: styd on* **8/1**
2150 **2** ¾ **Brouhaha**[18] 6922 7-9-6 **80**.. RichardKingscote 2 87
(Tom Dascombe) *a.p: rdn over 1f out: r.o: wnt 2nd post: nt rch wnr* **12/1**
0240 **3** hd **Destiny Of A Diva**[30] 6631 4-9-10 **84**.......................... GrahamGibbons 8 91
(Reg Hollinshead) *a.p: chsd wnr over 2f out: rdn over 1f out: styd on: lost 2nd post* **8/1**
5551 **4** 1½ **Art Scholar (IRE)**[15] 6976 4-9-5 **79**................................ NeilChalmers 7 83
(Michael Appleby) *hld up: hdwy over 1f out: sn rdn: r.o: nt rch ldrs* **3/1**[2]
3432 **5** hd **Rio's Rosanna (IRE)**[13] 7022 4-9-4 **78**...................... RussKennemore 9 82
(Richard Whitaker) *hld up: hdwy over 3f out: rdn over 1f out: styd on same pce ins fnl f* **11/4**[1]
1263 **6** 6 **Broughtons Paradis (IRE)**[18] 6922 5-8-10 **70**.......... StevieDonohoe 10 64
(Willie Musson) *s.s: hld up: hdwy over 1f out: nvr nrr* **10/1**
000 **7** 9 **Jawaab (IRE)**[6] 7022 7-9-5 **82**..................................(e) RobertLButler(3) 5 62
(Richard Guest) *led after 1f: hdd over 3f out: sn rdn: wknd 2f out* **28/1**
0300 **8** ½ **Antigua Sunrise (IRE)**[13] 7022 5-9-5 **79**........................ PaulHanagan 1 58
(Richard Fahey) *led 1f: chsd ldrs: pushed along 4f out: wknd 2f out* **15/2**[3]
0-00 **9** 1¼ **Effervesce (IRE)**[18] 6922 4-8-10 **70** oh3............................ RobertHavlin 6 47
(David Pipe) *s.s: a in rr* **8/1**
1113 **10** 6 **Stanley Rigby**[234] 858 5-9-0 **74**.. BarryMcHugh 3 42
(Richard Fahey) *hld up: wknd over 2f out* **22/1**

2m 38.29s (-2.81) **Going Correction** -0.025s/f (Stan)
WFA 3 from 4yo+ 6lb **10** Ran SP% **121.3**
Speed ratings (Par 105): **108,107,107,106,106 102,96,95,95,91**
toteswingers:1&2 £5.60, 2&3 £6.60, 1&3 £1.80 CSF £103.43 CT £805.37 TOTE £10.90: £2.80, £4.40, £2.40; EX 112.00.
Owner Matt Bartram **Bred** Stonerside Stable **Trained** East Harling, Norfolk

FOCUS
A fair handicap which was sound run. The winner rates a 4lb personal best.
T/Jkpt: Not won. T/Plt: £152.90 to a £1 stake. Pool £86,017.97 - 410.54 winning units T/Qpdt: £4.40 to a £1 stake. Pool £11,512.86 - 1,914.21 winning units CR

7147 DUNDALK (A.W) (L-H)
Friday, November 4

OFFICIAL GOING: Standard

7273a IRISH STALLION FARMS EUROPEAN BREEDERS FUND 2YO MAIDEN 6f (P)
6:20 (6:23) 2-Y-O **£7,732** (£1,793; £784; £448)

RPR
1 **Piri Wango (IRE)** 2-9-5 .... KLatham 10 82+
(G M Lyons, Ire) *mid-div: 9th 1/2-way: rdn and hdwy under 2f out: 6th 1f out: styd on to ld last 100yds: kpt on wl* **10/1**
2 1¾ **Pyrenean Music (IRE)**[28] 6679 2-9-5 .... KJManning 12 77
(David Wachman, Ire) *chsd ldrs: 6th 1/2-way: rdn in 5th 2f out: kpt on fnl f to dispute briefly last 100yds: no ex cl home* **14/1**
3 1½ **Fast Finian (IRE)**[20] 6880 2-9-5 .... GFCarroll 14 73
(M Halford, Ire) *towards rr: late hdwy in 8th 1f out: kpt on wl fnl f* **8/1**
4 nse **Wasabi's House (IRE)** 2-9-0 .... JMurtagh 6 73+
(John M Oxx, Ire) *mid-div: 8th 1/2-way: 7th travelling wl 1f out: nt clr run ins fnl f* **7/1**[3]
5 ½ **Harry Trotter (IRE)**[105] 4297 2-9-5 78........................ CO'Donoghue 13 71
(David Marnane, Ire) *chsd ldr in 2nd: rdn to ld 1f out: hdd fnl 100yds and no ex* **10/1**
6 2 **Yeeoow (IRE)**[19] 6892 2-9-5 .... DPMcDonogh 8 65
(Mrs K Burke) *chsd ldrs: 4th 1/2-way: rdn 2f out: kpt on same pce fr over 1f out* **5/1**[2]
7 nk **Nero Emperor (IRE)**[190] 1639 2-9-5 .... WMLordan 11 69+
(T Stack, Ire) *sn chsd ldrs: 3rd 1/2-way: rdn to chal in 2nd 1f out: no ex ins fnl f* **9/2**[1]
8 shd **Ultra Steps (IRE)**[121] 3749 2-9-0 .... CDHayes 5 59
(Adrian McGuinness, Ire) *mid-div best: rdn and no imp over 2f out: kpt on one pce* **66/1**
9 1 **Two Cities (IRE)** 2-9-5 .... NGMcCullagh 2 61
(David Wachman, Ire) *mid-div: 7th 1/2-way: rdn and no imp 2f out: kpt on one pce* **20/1**
10 nk **Srucahan (IRE)**[14] 7012 2-9-5 85.....................................(b) PJSmullen 1 60
(P D Deegan, Ire) *led: rdn and hdd 1f out: no ex and wknd* **5/1**[2]
11 nse **Queenscliff (IRE)** 2-9-0 .... MCHussey 7 55
(David Wachman, Ire) *in rr of mid-div thrght: nvr a factor* **33/1**
12 2½ **Brog Deas (IRE)**[42] 6313 2-9-5 .... DMGrant 9 52
(Patrick J Flynn, Ire) *a towards rr* **33/1**
13 ¾ **Reaching (IRE)** 2-9-0 .... SeamieHeffernan 3 45
(A P O'Brien, Ire) *chsd ldrs: 5th 1/2-way: rdn and no ex 2f out: wknd* **8/1**
14 nk **Pearl Of Romance (IRE)**[21] 6850 2-8-9 .... LFRoche(5) 4 44
(W McCreery, Ire) *s.i.s: a towards rr* **28/1**

1m 11.8s (71.80) **14** Ran SP% **126.7**
CSF £142.03 TOTE £13.60: £4.30, £7.90, £4.00; DF 293.40.
Owner David Spratt **Bred** Michael Kinane **Trained** Dunsany, Co. Meath

NOTEBOOK
Piri Wango(IRE) ◆ was one of five newcomers and produced a performance of some potential. Drawn in stall ten, his rider was unable to get any cover and turned into the home straight widest of all. But despite covering more ground than his opponents, he came with a persistent challenge down the outside and won going away after hitting the front 100 yards out. His trainer was very complimentary after the race and suggested you won't see the best of him until he goes over 1m so he is an exciting prospect for next year. (op 6/1)
Pyrenean Music(IRE) was a little disappointing at this venue last month but this proved that his promising Gowran Park debut was no fluke with a sound performance here. Never far off the pace, he came with his challenge 1f out and momentarily looked the likeliest winner before the winner came and spoiled the party. (op 12/1)
Fast Finian(IRE) was given a patient ride and stayed on strongly to snatch third close home without ever looking a potential threat. (op 8/1 tchd 9/1)
Wasabi's House(IRE) ◆ appeared to be still full of running 1f out but the gaps never appeared and Murtagh was forced to sit and suffer. She could develop into a nice three-year next season. Official explanation: jockey said filly ran short of room in the closing stages (op 6/1 tchd 8/1)
Harry Trotter(IRE) raced close to the pace throughout and got his head in-front over 1f out but was swallowed up by the fast-finishing pair to his outside. (op 10/1 tchd 11/1)
Yeeoow(IRE) was another to race prominently but lacked a turn of foot when the race began in earnest. Official explanation: jockey said colt stumbled badly on leaving the stalls (op 5/1 tchd 11/2)
Nero Emperor(IRE) ◆ ran better than his finishing position suggests. Not seen since finishing fourth in a Tipperary maiden back in April, the son of Holy Roman Emperor was very keen early on and pulled his way to front early in the home straight. It was hardly surprising that there wasn't enough juice left in the tank to sustain that challenge and, once his chance had gone, his rider accepted the situation. (op 4/1 tchd 5/1)

7275a FOLLOW DUNDALK ON FACEBOOK 2YO CLAIMING RACE 7f (P)
7:20 (7:21) 2-Y-O **£4,163** (£965; £422; £241)

RPR
1 **Mr Red Clubs (IRE)**[5] 7186 2-9-0 73.................................... JMurtagh 5 71
(Paul W Flynn, Ire) *chsd ldrs early: 7th 1/2-way: rdn into 4th 2f out: 2nd and no imp on ldr 1f out: r.o strly clsng stages to ld last strides* **2/1**[1]
2 nk **Catfromtherock (IRE)**[14] 7011 2-9-0 67.......................... CO'Donoghue 7 70
(David Marnane, Ire) *attempted to make all: asserted over 1f out: rdn ins fnl f: hdd dying strides* **13/2**[2]
3 1¾ **Perla Du Ma (IRE)**[7] 7147 2-9-5 73.. KLatham 1 70
(G M Lyons, Ire) *hld up towards rr: hdwy into 5th 2f out: rdn in 4th 1f out: kpt on same pce fnl f* **12/1**
4 hd **Cheerful Giver (IRE)**[76] 5293 2-9-0 80..........................(bt[1]) KJManning 4 65
(J S Bolger, Ire) *chsd ldrs: 3rd 1/2-way: rdn in 2nd 2f out: no ex in 3rd 1f out: kpt on same pce fnl f* **13/2**[2]
5 1¾ **Ok Annie (IRE)**[28] 6681 2-8-2 68....................................... CPHoban(5) 2 53
(Patrick Martin, Ire) *chsd ldrs: 6th 1/2-way: rdn into 3rd 2f out: no ex in 5th 1f out: kpt on same pce fnl f* **10/1**
6 nk **Angels Art (IRE)**[7] 7147 2-7-13 73.................................(t) GJPhillips(7) 3 51
(G M Lyons, Ire) *mid-div: hdwy into 6th 2f out: rdn and no imp over 1f out: kpt on same pce* **12/1**

7 ½ **Roman Locket (IRE)**[19] 6897 2-8-9 .... CDHayes 6 53
(Andrew Oliver, Ire) *towards rr: rdn and no imp 2f out: mod 9th 1f out: kpt on one pce* **12/1**

8 ½ **Athlumney Lass (IRE)**[5] 7186 2-8-8 69.............................(p) DMGrant 12 51
(H Rogers, Ire) *chsd ldr in 2nd: rdn and lost pl over 2f out: kpt on one pce in 7th 1f out* **12/1**

9 2 **Hazel Wand (IRE)**[16] 6963 2-8-9 .... DPMcDonogh 11 46
(Kevin Prendergast, Ire) *mid-div: rdn and no imp 2f out: kpt on one pce* **14/1**

10 3 ½ **Class Monitor**[30] 6628 2-8-11 ....(b[1]) PJSmullen 9 39
(Mrs K Burke) *chsd ldrs: 5th 1/2-way: rdn and dropped to 8th 2f out: kpt on one pce fr over 1f out* **8/1[3]**

11 ½ **Ruhar (IRE)**[21] 6851 2-8-9 .... WMLordan 8 35
(W McCreery, Ire) *a towards rr* **20/1**

12 3 ¼ **Linenhall Lady (IRE)**[19] 6897 2-8-2 .... LFRoche(5) 14 25
(M J Grassick, Ire) *mid-div best: rdn and no ex ent st* **25/1**

13 1 ½ **Unescorted (IRE)**[7] 7147 2-8-6 .... NGMcCullagh 13 19
(M J Grassick, Ire) *t.k.h to chse ldrs: 4th 1/2-way: wknd ent st* **16/1**

14 4 ½ **Adelais (IRE)** 2-8-13 ....(p) BACurtis 10 14
(Ms Joanna Morgan, Ire) *a towards rr* **40/1**

1m 25.5s (85.50) **14 Ran SP% 134.6**
CSF £16.16 TOTE £3.40: £1.40, £2.80, £3.20; DF 20.00.
Owner Miss C Howes **Bred** Tally-Ho Stud **Trained** Colehill, Co Longford

NOTEBOOK
Mr Red Clubs(IRE) went in pursuit of the trailblazing Catfromtherock 2f out but his chase looked to be in vain as he was still 2l in arrears well inside the final furlong. But he managed to conjure one last-gasp effort from the son of Red Clubs and got his head where it mattered. (op 5/2)
Catfromtherock(IRE) led everywhere bar on the line. After assuming the pacesetting duties, the son of One Cool Cat had everything in trouble passing the 2f pole and looked sure to break his duck when holding a 2l lead well inside the final furlong. But he got tired close home and paid the ultimate penalty. He looks to have enough pace to cope with 6f. (op 6/1)
Perla Du Ma(IRE) was beaten only 4l when sixth here over 5f last week and seemed to stay the extra 2f well enough here, although he never got close enough to get involved with the front two. (op 11/1)
Cheerful Giver(IRE) was the highest rated of these after acquiring a mark of 80. But he came here fully exposed and it was no surprise to see him get outpaced after entering the home straight before staying on at the one pace to finish fourth. (op 6/1 tchd 13/2)
Ok Annie(IRE) tracked the pace but came under pressure 2f out and just plugged on without troubling the principals.
Angels Art(IRE) made a promising start to her career but had a regressive profile coming into this and could stay on only at the one pace after travelling smoothly into the home straight.

7277a IRISH STALLION FARMS EUROPEAN BREEDERS FUND COOLEY FILLIES STKS (LISTED RACE) 1m (P)
8:20 (8:22) 3-Y-O+ **£28,017** (£8,189; £3,879; £1,293)

RPR

1 **Clinical**[8] 7128 3-9-3 .... SebSanders 7 103
(Sir Mark Prescott Bt) *chsd ldr in 2nd: impr to ld 2f out: rdn and kpt on wl u.p fr over 1f out: all out cl home: jst hld on* **6/4[1]**

2 nse **Night Lily (IRE)**[8] 7128 5-9-2 .... WMLordan 1 100
(Paul D'Arcy) *mid-div: 7th 1/2-way: rdn in 6th 2f out: 3rd 1f out: r.o wl fnl f: jst failed* **14/1**

3 ¾ **Atlantic Swing (USA)**[5] 7187 3-9-0 91.................................. JMurtagh 4 98
(John M Oxx, Ire) *mid-div: rdn 2f out: styd on into 4th 1f out: kpt on same pce fnl f* **10/1**

4 1 **Duchess Of Foxland (IRE)**[19] 6899 4-9-2 98.......... SeamieHeffernan 6 95
(Mark L Fagan, Ire) *chsd ldrs: 3rd 1/2-way: rdn to chal 2f out: 2nd 1f out: no ex ins fnl f: kpt on same pce* **12/1**

5 nk **Rose Bonheur**[34] 6520 3-9-3 107................................. DPMcDonogh 12 97+
(Kevin Prendergast, Ire) *hld up towards rr: rdn in 10th over 1f out: kpt on fnl f* **7/1[3]**

6 hd **Gossamer Seed (IRE)**[7] 7149 3-9-0 93................................(t) BACurtis 5 94+
(John Joseph Murphy, Ire) *hld up towards rr: rdn in 9th 1f out: kpt on fnl f* **25/1**

7 ¾ **Face Reality (USA)**[78] 5228 3-9-0 98 .... CO'Donoghue 14 92
(David Marnane, Ire) *hld up towards rr: hdwy in 9th 2f out: rdn into 7th 1f out: no ex ins fnl f* **20/1**

8 1 ¼ **Sunset Beauty (IRE)**[14] 7010 4-9-2 85............................(t) KJManning 9 89
(J S Bolger, Ire) *chsd ldrs: 4th 1/2-way: rdn 2f out: no ex in 6th 1f out: kpt on one pce* **14/1**

9 shd **Mosqueras Romance**[8] 7128 5-9-2 ....(b[1]) AdamKirby 11 88
(Marco Botti) *mid-div early: 6th 1/2-way: rdn in 5th 2f out: no ex over 1f out: kpt on one pce* **13/2[2]**

10 ¾ **Katherine Lee (IRE)**[7] 7150 3-9-0 82.................................. ShaneFoley 2 86
(M Halford, Ire) *led: rdn and hdd 2f out: no ex over 1f out* **20/1**

11 ½ **Enchanted Evening (IRE)**[20] 6882 5-9-2 87...................(b) PJSmullen 3 85
(D K Weld, Ire) *chsd ldrs: 5th 1/2-way: rdn and no ex 2f out* **20/1**

12 ¾ **Miranda's Girl (IRE)**[14] 7008 6-9-2 83.............................(b) RPCleary 8 83
(Thomas Cleary, Ire) *chsd ldrs early: 8th 1/2-way: rdn and no ex ent st* **25/1**

13 1 **Blue Moon**[21] 6854 4-9-2 .... GFCarroll 13 80
(Kevin Ryan) *mid-div: rdn and no ex ent st* **7/1[3]**

14 6 **Obligada (IRE)**[14] 7010 3-9-0 90.. CDHayes 10 64
(Kevin Prendergast, Ire) *mid-div: rdn and no ex ent st* **20/1**

1m 35.8s (95.80)
WFA 3 from 4yo+ 2lb **14 Ran SP% 135.2**
CSF £26.06 TOTE £2.40: £2.20, £2.90, £3.30; DF 58.20.
Owner Cheveley Park Stud **Bred** Cheveley Park Stud Ltd **Trained** Newmarket, Suffolk
■ Stewards' Enquiry : Seb Sanders two-day ban: used whip with excessive frequency and used whip rapidly without giving regard to the stride of the horse (Nov 18, 25)
D P McDonogh one-day ban: used whip rapidly without giving regard to the stride of the horse (Nov 18)

FOCUS
A Listed contest that was worthy of the lucrative pot and produced a thrilling finish between two British raiders. The form is rated around the third.

NOTEBOOK
Clinical chased the pacesetting Katherine Lee before hitting the front 2f out. That looked to be the decisive move as she put daylight between herself and the rest of the pack, and a comfortable success looked on the cards. But it was a nail-biting final furlong for favourite backers as Night Lily came with a wet sail up the inside and only failed to get up by the minimum of margins. (op 9/4)
Night Lily(IRE) was beaten over 4l by Clinical last time but she fared much better here and would have been in front in another stride. Still in mid-division 2f out, she produced a power-packed finish and gave the impression that 1m was very much on the short side. (op 14/1 tchd 12/1)
Atlantic Swing(USA) was turned out quickly after disappointing over 1m2f at Leopardstown last Sunday and produced a much-improved effort. She came under pressure 2f out but kept going and was gaining on the winner at the finish. She could blossom next year over further if wintering well.
Duchess Of Foxland(IRE) hadn't been beaten far on her last couple of runs and she produced another solid effort here, staying on well in the closing stages to grab fourth.
Rose Bonheur has enjoyed a fantastic season and was back trying 1m here after flourishing over shorter. It wasn't surprising to see her held up out the back, but her rider was forced to make his challenge widest of all in the home straight and she never looked like getting there. (op 6/1)
Gossamer Seed(IRE) was another to be given a lot to do and stayed on well when the race was over. (op 20/1)

7274, 7276, 7278 - 7279a (Foreign Racing) - See Raceform Interactive

1921 CHURCHILL DOWNS (L-H)
Friday, November 4

OFFICIAL GOING: Dirt: muddy changing to standard; turf: good

7280a SENTIENT JET BREEDERS' CUP JUVENILE SPRINT (CONDITIONS) (2YO) (DIRT) 6f (D)
8:10 (8:12) 2-Y-O **£173,076** (£57,692; £31,730; £19,230; £9,615)

RPR

1 **Secret Circle (USA)**[25] 2-8-10 0...(b) RBejarano 6 112
(Bob Baffert, U.S.A) *w ldr: rdn to ld over 2f out: arnd 3 l clr over 1f out: edgd rt then lft ins fnl f: hld on towards fin* **4/7[1]**

2 1 **Shumoos (USA)**[41] 6337 2-8-7 0.. GKGomez 5 106
(Brian Meehan) *hld up: sn wl bhd: stl last 1/2-way: gd hdwy on inner wl over 1f out: wnt 2nd jst ins fnl f: kpt on strly: nt quite rch wnr* **12/1**

3 4 ½ **Holdin Bullets (USA)**[197] 2-8-10 0....................................(b) JASanchez 7 95
(Wesley A Ward, U.S.A) *prom: rdn over 2f out: kpt on but no match for ldng pair ins fnl f* **16/1**

4 1 ¾ **Seeker (USA)**[33] 2-8-10 0.. JRLeparoux 1 90
(Steven Asmussen, U.S.A) *sn pushed along to keep in tch: kpt on fr over 1f out: nvr threatened ldrs* **9/1[2]**

5 2 ¾ **Jake Mo (USA)**[28] 2-8-10 0.. MESmith 8 81
(Allen Milligan, U.S.A) *s.i.s: sn outpcd in rr: hdwy 2f out: kpt on: nvr trbld ldrs* **33/1**

6 1 ¾ **Sum Of The Parts (USA)**[28] 2-8-10 0.................................... RMaragh 2 76
(Thomas Amoss, U.S.A) *chsd ldrs on inner: wknd over 1f out* **16/1**

7 1 ¾ **Trinniberg (USA)**[33] 2-8-10 0....................................(b) CVelasquez 4 71
(Bisnath Parboo, U.S.A) *led narrowly: rdn whn hdd over 2f out: wknd over 1f out* **10/1[3]**

8 ½ **Blacky The Bull (USA)**[27] 2-8-10 0.................................. PValenzuela 3 69
(Jeff Bonde, U.S.A) *dwlt: a outpcd towards rr* **33/1**

9 5 ¾ **Vexor (USA)**[33] 2-8-10 0.. DCohen 9 51
(John C Kimmel, U.S.A) *chsd ldrs on outer: wknd wl over 1f out* **9/1[2]**

1m 10.52s (1.12) **9 Ran SP% 118.1**
PARI-MUTUEL (all including $2 stakes): WIN 2.80; PLACE (1-2) 2.40, 8.20; SHOW (1-2-3) 2.10, 5.60, 6.20; SF 28.00.
Owner Karl Watson, Michael E Pegram & Paul Weitman **Bred** Willmott Stables **Trained** USA

FOCUS
There are plenty who don't agree with the continued expansion of the Breeders' Cup, but the Juvenile Sprint, run for the first time this season, provides a year-end target for the speediest 2yos around. This wasn't a strong first running, but it produced a smart winner.

NOTEBOOK
Secret Circle(USA) made it 3-3 despite facing competition for the lead in a race run at what would usually be overly quick fractions. They went 20.96 seconds for the first quarter and 44.55 at the four-furlong point. While he was helped by the field lacking depth, it was still immensely impressive that he was able to hold on, and that's despite hanging right in the closing stages. His waywardness probably shouldn't be overplayed as he's a young horse and had been clear of his rivals for quite a while. Bob Baffert indicated he would see if Secret Circle could stretch out for longer distances, doubtless encouraged by victory at the home of the Kentucky Derby.
Shumoos(USA), trying dirt for the first time and using Lasix, couldn't go the early pace but was helped by racing so far back. She may also have been aided by sticking tight against the inside rail when staying on and is surely flattered. It was reported she would remain in the US with Ben Cecil.
Holdin Bullets(USA) had been absent since winning on his debut over the Keeneland Polytrack in April. He had reportedly been entered at Chantilly and Royal Ascot when shipped over to Europe but didn't run. This was a fine effort for one so light on racing.
Seeker(USA) stuck on from off the pace but didn't have the required speed.

7281a BREEDERS' CUP JUVENILE FILLIES TURF (GRADE 2) (2YO FILLIES) (TURF) 1m (T)
8:50 (8:51) 2-Y-O **£346,153** (£115,384; £63,461; £38,461; £19,230)

RPR

1 **Stephanie's Kitten (USA)**[28] 6685 2-8-10 0.................... JRVelazquez 5 111
(Wayne Catalano, U.S.A) *prom: rdn along 2f out: edgd lft and chsd ldr 1f out: qcknd to ld last 25yds: kpt on wl* **8/1[3]**

2 ¾ **Stopshoppingmaria (USA)**[27] 6717 2-8-10 0............... JJCastellano 4 109
(Todd Pletcher, U.S.A) *dictated modest gallop against ins rail: rdn and qcknd ent st: hdd and no ex last 25yds* **9/1**

3 1 ¼ **Sweet Cat (USA)**[22] 2-8-10 0.. GKGomez 6 106
(Todd Pletcher, U.S.A) *trckd ldr: drvn along fr 2f out: lost 2nd 1f out: kpt on u.p ins fnl f* **12/1**

4 nk **Up (IRE)**[35] 6509 2-8-10 0.. RyanMoore 3 105
(A P O'Brien, Ire) *midfield on ins: effrt whn n.m.r 2f out: swtchd rt and hdwy over 1f out: kpt on u.p fnl f: nrst fin* **10/1**

5 ¾ **Hard Not To Like (CAN)**[20] 2-8-10 0...................................... MESmith 8 104
(Gail Cox, Canada) *midfield on outside: stdy hdwy 3f out: drvn over 2f out: kpt on same pce fnl f* **33/1**

6 1 **Somali Lemonade (USA)**[22] 2-8-10 0...................................... ASolis 14 101
(Michael Matz, U.S.A) *t.k.h: hld up off modest gallop: rdn and hdwy on outside wl over 1f out: kpt on fnl f: nvr any ch of rching ldrs* **9/2[2]**

7 hd **Pure Gossip (USA)**[33] 2-8-10 0.. RCuratolo 9 101
(Philip M Serpe, U.S.A) *midfield: rdn and outpcd over 2f out: rallied over 1f out: kpt on fnl f: no imp* **12/1**

8 1 **Elusive Kate (USA)**[33] 6564 2-8-10 0................................ WilliamBuick 10 99
(John Gosden) *hld up off modest gallop on outside: rdn and outpcd over 2f out: hung lft over 1f out: nvr able to chal* **10/3[1]**

9 ½ **Dayatthespa (USA)**[48] 2-8-10 0.. RADominguez 2 97
(Chad C Brown, U.S.A) *trckd ldrs on ins: rdn over 2f out: wknd over 1f out* **9/1**

10 ½ **Royal Bonnie (USA)**[33] 2-8-10 0.. CVelasquez 7 96
(George Weaver, U.S.A) *t.k.h early: trckd ldrs: drvn over 2f out: wknd over 1f out* **50/1**

11 1 ¼ **Customer Base (USA)**[16] 2-8-10 0...................................... JRLeparoux 13 93
(Thomas F Proctor, U.S.A) *t.k.h: hld up and bhd on outside off modest gallop: swtchd lft 1/2-way: rdn over 2f out: sn btn* **25/1**

The Form Book, Raceform Ltd, Compton, RG20 6NL

12 *hd* **My Gi Gi (USA)**[32] 6596 2-8-10 0.. RBejarano 1 93
(Brian Koriner, U.S.A) *s.i.s: hld up off modest gallop against ins rail: rdn over 2f out: nvr on terms* **33/1**

13 *3/4* **Ann Of The Dance (USA)**[28] 6685 2-8-10 0.................... CNakatani 11 91
(Martin D Wolfson, U.S.A) *hld up and bhd off modest gallop: drvn on wd outside over 2f out: nvr on terms* **50/1**

14 *1 1/2* **Dear Lavinia (USA)**[22] 6824 2-8-10 0....... Christophe-PatriceLemaire 12 88
(J-C Rouget, France) *dwlt: t.k.h towards rr: struggling over 2f out: sn btn* **14/1**

1m 38.9s (4.07) **14** Ran SP% **117.2**
PARI-MUTUEL (all including $2 stakes): WIN 14.20; PLACE (1-2) 6.60, 9.20; SHOW (1-2-3) 5.20, 7.60, 9.40; SF 106.20.
Owner Kenneth L & Sarah K Ramsey **Bred** Kenneth L & Sarah K Ramsey **Trained** USA

FOCUS
The pace wasn't that strong - they went 24.57, 50.55 and 1.15.71 for the first three quarters respectively.

NOTEBOOK
Stephanie's Kitten(USA), seemingly the choice of John Velazquez of the two Todd Pletcher runners, had won a Grade 1 on Polytrack at Keeneland last time and continued her progression with a likeable performance. The modest pace was far from ideal, yet she picked up sufficiently. She could be one for next year's Filly & Mare Turf.
Stopshoppingmaria(USA), on her turf debut, took them along and she gave it a good shot. She came here instead of re-opposing My Miss Aurelia in the dirt equivalent, having been no match for that rival in the Frizette last time.
Sweet Cat(USA), a stablemate of the runner-up and by the same sire as the winner, had every chance but couldn't pick up sufficiently.
Up(IRE), using Lasix, didn't show enough early pace to make use of her low draw. She had a ground-saving trip, but by the time she was switched into the clear there was only a furlong to run and she got going too late. This was a big step up from her Dundalk maiden win and there might be more to come, but she's not very big.
Hard Not To Like(CAN) was not well ridden, being taken much wider than seemed necessary. It was no surprise she faded in the straight and her performance wants upgrading.
Somali Lemonade(USA) was dropped in from the widest draw and saved ground until the final bend, but the steady pace gave her little hope of making a telling impression. She had Sweet Cat behind when winning a Grade 3 last time.
Elusive Kate(USA) might be flattered by her Marcel Boussac win, but she shouldn't be judged harshly on this effort. Drawn on the outside, she was bumped on the first bend and was wide throughout. It was also reported she wasn't helped by loose ground. She didn't use Lasix.
Dayatthespa(USA) was disappointing considering she was favourably drawn and had Stephanie's Kitten behind last time.

7282a SENTIENT JET BREEDERS' CUP FILLY & MARE SPRINT (GRADE 1) (3YO+ FILLIES & MARES) (DIRT) 7f

9:30 (9:32) 3-Y-0+ **£346,153** (£115,384; £63,461; £38,461; £19,230)

RPR

1 **Musical Romance (USA)**[27] 4-8-12 0................................(b) JCLeyva 5 119
(William Kaplan, U.S.A) *trckd ldrs: rdn over 1f out: led jst ins fnl f: kpt on wl* **14/1**

2 *1 1/4* **Switch (USA)**[27] 4-8-12 0.. JRosario 6 116
(John W Sadler, U.S.A) *hld up in rr: hdwy towards outer 2f out: kpt on wl* **3/1**[2]

3 *hd* **Her Smile (USA)**[47] 3-8-10 0.. JRVelazquez 11 114
(Todd Pletcher, U.S.A) *hld up: hdwy over 2f out: chsd ldrs over 1f out: kpt on fnl f* **20/1**

4 *2 1/2* **Pomeroys Pistol (USA)**[41] 3-8-10 0............................. JJCastellano 12 108
(Amy Tarrant, U.S.A) *chsd ldrs: rdn and ev ch over 1f out: no ex ins fnl f* **9/1**[3]

5 *1/2* **Turbulent Descent (USA)**[90] 3-8-10 0.................................. DFlores 3 106
(Mike Puype, U.S.A) *squeezed out s: racd keenly: hld up in tch: angled towards outer 4f out: sn trckd ldrs: led over 1f out: sn rdn: hdd jst ins fnl f: wknd fnl 100yds* **7/4**[1]

6 *2 3/4* **Champagne D'Oro (USA)**[34] 6554 4-8-12 0....................... CNakatani 4 100
(Eric J Guillot, U.S.A) *in tch: rdn over 2f out: one pce* **25/1**

7 *8 1/4* **Golden Mystery (USA)**[34] 5-8-12 0............................... KCarmouche 9 78
(Juan Carlos Guerrero, U.S.A) *led narrowly: hdd over 2f out: wknd over 1f out* **25/1**

8 *nk* **Irish Gypsy (USA)**[75] 5-8-12 0..(b) MGarcia 1 77
(Bob Baffert, U.S.A) *hld up in tch towards inner: rdn over 2f out: sn btn* **25/1**

9 *3 3/4* **Tanda (USA)**[35] 4-8-12 0.. JTalamo 8 67
(Mike Mitchell, U.S.A) *midfield on outer: dropped towards rr over 3f out: nvr a factor after* **14/1**

10 *1 3/4* **Tamarind Hall (USA)**[41] 4-8-12 0... DCohen 10 62
(Jeremiah C Englehart, U.S.A) *prom: led over 2f out: rdn whn hdd over 1f out: wknd* **20/1**

11 *2 1/4* **Great Hot (BRZ)**[13] 3-8-10 0 ow2............................ ChantalSutherland 2 55
(A C Avila, U.S.A) *midfield: wknd over 2f out* **14/1**

12 *22* **Tar Heel Mom (USA)**[41] 6-8-12 0.. ASolis 7 —
(Stanley M Hough, U.S.A) *midfield towards outer: lost pl over 3f out: sn bhd* **20/1**

1m 23.47s (83.47)
WFA 3 from 4yo+ 1lb **12** Ran SP% **117.2**
PARI-MUTUEL (all including $2 stakes): WIN 42.40; PLACE (1-2) 15.60, 4.80; SHOW (1-2-3) 8.60, 3.40, 12.40; SF 177.00.
Owner Pinnacle Racing Stable & William A Kaplan **Bred** Ocala Stud **Trained** North America

FOCUS
The favourite was unable to show her best and this isn't strong form, but the winner is progressive and the second ran to her best. They went 22.40 for the first quarter and 45.71 for the half.

NOTEBOOK
Musical Romance(USA) made her bid tight against the inside rail, which certainly wasn't playing slow. This was a career best.
Switch(USA), runner-up in this last year, repeated the trick but wasn't helped by being set plenty to do. She might have been flattening out in the final strides, but that's understandable.
Her Smile(USA) also came from off the pace, but she wasn't as far back as Switch.
Pomeroys Pistol(USA) had no excuse.
Turbulent Descent(USA), having been squeezed out at the start, she raced too keenly and was soon short of room again. She still didn't relax, though, and tanked her way to the front entering the straight. Her exertions soon told.

7283a GREY GOOSE BREEDERS' CUP JUVENILE FILLIES (GRADE 1) (2YO FILLIES) (DIRT) 1m 110y(D)

10:10 (10:12) 2-Y-0 **£692,307** (£230,769; £126,923; £76,923; £38,461)

RPR

1 **My Miss Aurelia (USA)**[27] 6717 2-8-10 0........................... CNakatani 9 120
(Steven Asmussen, U.S.A) *trckd ldr gng wl: led 2f out: 3 l clr whn rdn and edgd both ways over 1f out: drvn and kpt on strly fnl f* **5/2**[1]

2 *3* **Grace Hall (USA)**[34] 2-8-10 0.. RADominguez 5 113
(Anthony Dutrow, U.S.A) *hld up in midfield: stdy hdwy over 3f out: drvn and hdwy to chse wnr over 1f out: edgd lft: kpt on fnl f: nt gng pce to chal wnr* **7/2**[2]

3 *6* **Weemissfrankie (USA)**[32] 6596 2-8-10 0......................... RBejarano 11 100
(Peter Eurton, U.S.A) *midfield on outside: rdn 3f out: hdwy 2f out: edgd lft and kpt on fnl f: nt pce of first two* **7/1**[3]

4 *1 1/4* **Self Preservation (USA)**[32] 6596 2-8-10 0........................... JRosario 6 97
(B Cecil, U.S.A) *broke wl: blkd after 1f and sn dropped to midfield: outpcd 4f out: hdwy and edgd lft over 1f out: kpt on: nvr rchd ldrs* **40/1**

5 *1 1/2* **Questing**[42] 6296 2-8-10 0.. WilliamBuick 1 97+
(John Gosden) *midfield on ins: rdn whn n.m.r briefly over 2f out: hung lft u.p over 1f out: nvr able to chal* **16/1**

6 *1* **Miss Netta (USA)**[27] 6717 2-8-10 0.. RMaragh 4 92
(Kiaran McLaughlin, U.S.A) *t.k.h: hld up towards rr: hdwy and in tch 2f out: no further imp and btn fnl f* **8/1**

7 *3* **Northern Passion (CAN)**[48] 2-8-10 0.................................. LContreras 10 85
(Mark Casse, Canada) *sn bhd: rdn along and effrt over 2f out: no imp whn checked over 1f out: sn btn* **14/1**

8 *2 1/4* **Putthebabiesdown (USA)**[28] 6685 2-8-10 0.......................... AGarcia 7 80
(Kenneth McPeek, U.S.A) *hld up towards rr: drvn along 3f out: hdwy and hung lft over 1f out: sn no imp* **40/1**

9 *1 1/2* **Frolic's Revenge (USA)**[28] 6685 2-8-10 0...................... JRVelazquez 12 77
(Milton W Wolfson, U.S.A) *towards rr on outside: struggling over 3f out: btn fnl 2f* **50/1**

10 *3/4* **Say A Novena (USA)**[34] 2-8-10 0..................................... ElvisTrujillo 13 75
(Edward Plesa Jr, U.S.A) *trckd ldrs on outside: effrt over 2f out: edgd lft u.p and wknd over 1f out* **50/1**

11 *hd* **Candrea (USA)**[32] 6596 2-8-10 0.. MGarcia 2 75
(Bob Baffert, U.S.A) *led at ordinary gallop against ins rail: rdn and hdd 2f out: wknd over 1f out* **9/1**

12 *1 3/4* **Awesome Belle (USA)**[20] 2-8-10 0..................................(b) LJurado 14 71
(Stanley I Gold, U.S.A) *racd wd: sn bhd: struggling over 3f out: nvr on terms* **25/1**

13 *11 1/2* **Rocket Twentyone (CAN)**[55] 2-8-10 0................................. ERazoJr 3 45
(W T Howard, U.S.A) *prom on ins: drvn along over 2f out: sn wknd* **33/1**

14 *15* **Homecoming Queen (IRE)**[26] 6731 2-8-10 0................. RyanMoore 8 12
(A P O'Brien, Ire) *s.i.s: a detached and drvn along: nvr on terms* **20/1**

1m 46.0s (1.63) **14** Ran SP% **117.3**
PARI-MUTUEL (all including $2 stakes): WIN 6.20; PLACE (1-2) 4.00, 4.60; SHOW (1-2-3) 3.00, 3.20, 3.60; SF 24.80.
Owner Stonestreet Stables & George Bolton **Bred** Stonestreet Thoroughbred Holdings **Trained** USA

FOCUS
This was a strong edition of the Juvenile Fillies with the first three finishers each having won their first three starts, and the winner looks top class. The pace was solid but not too fast - they went 23.20 for the first quarter, 47.19 for the half and clocked 1:13.08 at the six-furlong point.

NOTEBOOK
My Miss Aurelia(USA) did well to draw away from such a good-looking field, gaining the second Grade 1 of her career. Her previous top-level success came in the Frizette when she recorded a time 0.33 seconds quicker time Union Rags managed in the Champagne Stakes on the same card. It will be interesting to see if her connections are willing to take on the colts by aiming the filly at next year's Kentucky Derby. We now know the track suits.
Grace Hall(USA) would herself have been a pretty high-class winner of this in many other years. Having raced further back than My Miss Aurelia, she kept on well but surprisingly still looked a bit green and was always held.
Weemissfrankie(USA), unbeaten in California, including the Grade 1 Oak Leaf last time, had a wide trip throughout and her performance needs upgrading.
Self Preservation(USA) didn't have the mid-race speed to hold her position and then ran on all too late.
Questing, trying dirt for the first time and using Lasix, wasn't sharp enough to get a handy position from the inside stall, but she was going just fine in mid-division until squeezed up against the rail leaving the back straight. She was then blocked when trying to recover but there was much to like about how well she kept on when eventually in the clear and there's a case to be made for saying she was third best. Surely she's worth another try on this surface.
Miss Netta(USA) didn't make the anticipated improvement from the Frizette, when she missed the break. She might not be one to give up on just yet, though, as she still looked pretty raw.
Homecoming Queen(IRE), who used Lasix on her dirt debut, was never going.

7284a EMIRATES AIRLINE BREEDERS' CUP FILLY & MARE TURF (GRADE 1) (3YO+ FILLIES & MARES) (TURF) 1m 3f (T)

10:50 (10:53) 3-Y-0+ **£692,307** (£230,769; £126,923; £76,923; £38,461)

RPR

1 **Perfect Shirl (USA)**[47] 4-8-12 0....................................... JRVelazquez 7 116
(Roger L Attfield, Canada) *midfield: rdn and hdwy over 1f out: kpt on: led fnl 75yds* **20/1**

2 *3/4* **Nahrain**[33] 6568 3-8-8 0.. FrankieDettori 5 116
(Roger Varian) *in tch: chal 2f out: rdn to ld narrowly appr fnl f: kpt on: hdd fnl 75yds* **3/1**[2]

3 *nse* **Misty For Me (IRE)**[62] 5745 3-8-8 0................................ RyanMoore 11 116+
(A P O'Brien, Ire) *stmbld s: racd keenly in rr: pushed along and stl last 2f out: hdwy on outer over 1f out: kpt on fnl f: nrst fin* **9/2**[3]

4 *hd* **Distorted Legacy (USA)**[34] 6547 4-8-12 0............................ RMaragh 9 114
(Angel Penna Jr, U.S.A) *midfield: pushed along and sltly outpcd 2f out: hdwy appr fnl f: kpt on: nrst fin* **33/1**

5 *hd* **Aruna (USA)**[26] 6738 4-8-12 0... JRLeparoux 6 114
(H Graham Motion, U.S.A) *racd keenly: hld up: pushed along and hdwy over 1f out: n.m.r appr fnl f: and again ins fnl f: kpt on: looked unlucky* **8/1**

6 *1 1/2* **Dubawi Heights**[33] 6571 4-8-12 0... JRosario 1 111
(Simon Callaghan, U.S.A) *racd keenly: led at stdy pce: rdn whn hdd appr fnl f: no ex* **8/1**

7 *nse* **Shared Account (USA)**[47] 5-8-12 0... EPrado 8 111
(H Graham Motion, U.S.A) *trckd ldrs: ev ch over 1f out: no ex fnl 100yds* **16/1**

8 *nk* **Cambina (IRE)**[33] 6571 3-8-8 0.. GKGomez 4 112
(Jeff Bonde, U.S.A) *racd keenly: hld up: sme late hdwy: nvr threatened ldrs* **25/1**

9 *1 1/4* **Harmonious (USA)**[33] 6571 4-8-12 0..................................... MGarcia 3 108
(John Shirreffs, U.S.A) *midfield towards inner: pushed along over 2f out: no imp* **20/1**

10 *1 1/2* **Stacelita (FR)**[34] 6547 5-8-12 0.. RADominguez 2 106
(Chad C Brown, U.S.A) *trckd ldrs: short of room on inner over 1f out: wknd ins fnl f* **5/2**[1]

11 *nk* **Dynaslew (USA)**34 6547 5-8-12 0....................................(b) CNakatani 10 105
(Seth Benzel, U.S.A) *trckd ldr: rdn 2f out: wknd appr fnl f* **40/1**

2m 18.62s (138.62)
WFA 3 from 4yo+ 5lb **11** Ran SP% **118.6**
PARI-MUTUEL (all including $2 stakes): WIN 57.60; PLACE (1-2) 18.60, 5.00; SHOW (1-2-3) 11.60, 3.80, 5.20; SF 324.00.

Owner Charles E Fipke **Bred** Charles Fipke **Trained** Canada

FOCUS
One of the leading fancies, Announce, was withdrawn shortly before the start having played up when out on the track and even backed into the side of an ambulance. According to one of the vets the filly sustained a small laceration over her right-hind hock, but her rider Maxime Guyon looked less than pleased with the decision. This is not form to take literally. When the pace is muddling around this seven-furlong oval, track position is crucial and the best horse won't always win. That was the case here with several finding trouble, and speed proved more important than stamina. Consequently, distances were compressed.

NOTEBOOK
Perfect Shirl(USA) enjoyed a better trip than some and made the most of it to land the upset. Her pre-race form did not match up to the best of these and she's surely flattered.

Nahrain, racing on Lasix for the first time in her bid to go 5-5, had a smooth trip but lacked the winner's pace. This was a tough gig for one so inexperienced and she might return an even better filly if kept in training.

Misty For Me(IRE), who like the runner-up was getting Lasix for the first time, did extremely well to go so close. Her race looked as good as over soon after the start as she stumbled on coming out of the stalls, and was then wide on the first bend before tucking in well off the pace. She was still last of all on the final turn but finished extremely well, briefly looking as though she'd get up for a most unlikely victory. Her performance is all the more creditable considering she'd been absent for two months.

Distorted Legacy(USA) had a wide trip pretty much throughout and did well to finish so close.

Aruna(USA) was travelling well but had nowhere to go for much of the closing stages. There's no way of telling where she would have finished with a clear run, but it's quite possible she would have won.

Dubawi Heights raced a bit freely in front and didn't see her race out.

Shared Account(USA), last year's winner, was a bit wider than ideal with no cover and her run soon flattened out in the straight.

Stacelita(FR), who sported an unusual blinker to protect an injured left eye, had nowhere to go when looking to make a move early in the straight, but she didn't pick up once she had room. This was the deepest field she'd faced since switching to the US, and a relative sprint finish on drying ground was no use to a mare who lacks a change of pace.

Dynaslew(USA) was dismounted soon after passing the line and it looked as though she had bled.

7285a BREEDERS' CUP LADIES' CLASSIC (GRADE 1) (3YO+ FILLIES & MARES) (DIRT) 1m 1f (D)
11:30 (9:32) 3-Y-O+ **£692,307** (£230,769; £126,923; £76,923; £38,461)

RPR

1 **Royal Delta (USA)**34 6551 3-8-9 0.. JLezcano 6 123+
(William Mott, U.S.A) *prom: drvn along on outside over 2f out: gd hdwy to ld ins fnl f: sn clr: eased nr fin* **9/4**1

2 *2 ½* **It's Tricky (USA)**34 3-8-9 0.. RADominguez 3 117
(Kiaran McLaughlin, U.S.A) *trckd ldrs on ins: wnt 2nd over 2f out: drvn to ld briefly ins fnl f: kpt on same pce towards fin* **11/2**3

3 *2 ¼* **Pachattack (USA)**26 6738 5-8-12 0....................................(b) RMaragh 2 112
(Gerard Butler) *prom: drvn and outpcd over 2f out: rallied fnl f to go 3rd towards fin: no ch w first two* **16/1**

4 *¾* **Ultra Blend (USA)**34 6554 5-8-12 0.. DFlores 7 111
(Art Sherman, U.S.A) *fractious in stalls: hld up off modest gallop: rdn and plenty to do over 2f out: gd hdwy on outside over 1f out: kpt on: nvr any ch of rching ldrs* **13/2**

5 *½* **Plum Pretty (USA)**34 3-8-9 0... RBejarano 8 110
(Bob Baffert, U.S.A) *led: sn crossed over to ins rail and stdd pce: rdn over 2f out: hdd ins fnl f: sn no ex: wknd and lost two pls towards fin* **11/4**2

6 *½* **Ask The Moon (USA)**34 6554 6-8-12 0.......................... JJCastellano 5 109
(Martin D Wolfson, U.S.A) *trckd ldr to over 2f out: edgd lft and outpcd over 1f out* **12/1**

7 *3* **Super Espresso (USA)**26 6738 4-8-12 0..................(b) JRVelazquez 9 102
(Todd Pletcher, U.S.A) *hld up in tch on outside: drvn along and outpcd over 2f out: edgd lft: btn over 1f out* **33/1**

8 *2 ½* **Satans Quick Chick (USA)**34 6551 5-8-12 0.......................... EPrado 4 97
(Eric R Reed, U.S.A) *sat last off modest pce: rdn along and struggling over 2f out: nvr on terms* **66/1**

9 *11 ¾* **Miss Match (ARG)**33 6570 6-8-12 0...................................(b) GKGomez 1 72
(Neil Drysdale, U.S.A) *in tch on ins: lost pl after 2f: struggling 4f out: lost tch fnl 2f* **11/1**

1m 50.78s (110.78)
WFA 3 from 4yo+ 3lb **9** Ran SP% **112.5**
PARI-MUTUEL (all including $2 stakes): WIN 6.40; PLACE (1-2) 4.00, 5.00; SHOW (1-2-3) 3.20, 3.80, 6.00; SF 32.00.

Owner Palides Investments NV Inc **Bred** Palides Investments N V Inc **Trained** USA

FOCUS
Sectionals of 24.18, 49.00, 1:13.72 and 1:38.12 theoretically should have put the race on a plate for Plum Pretty, who didn't face any pressure for the lead. However, this proved to be more of a test than the clock suggested, with the track seemingly quite demanding, and Bob Baffert's filly faded badly in the straight.

NOTEBOOK
Royal Delta(USA) was no match for Havre De Grace in the Beldame last time, although she didn't give her true running that day, maybe not helped by a wet track. Whatever, the absence of her old rival made this easier and her proven stamina was a major asset as she confirmed herself the best 3yo filly in the US. She will be offered during the Keeneland November breeding stock sale.

It's Tricky(USA) was well enough placed but the winner is the stronger stayer of the pair, and probably the better filly regardless.

Pachattack(USA), part of Gerard Butler's North American string, ran as well as could have been expected to pick up some more Grade 1-placed black type. Her connections really have made the most of this filly and they deserve credit.

Ultra Blend(USA) got a bit too far back and ran out of racetrack.

Plum Pretty(USA) won the Kentucky Oaks over C&D earlier in the year, but on that occasion the final time was 1.27 seconds quicker than it was here and she doesn't have the stamina reserves one might expect for a daughter of Medaglia D'Oro out of an A.P. Indy mare.

Ask The Moon(USA) didn't go to front as expected and wasn't good enough when it mattered.

7286 - 7291a (Foreign Racing) - See Raceform Interactive

7017 DONCASTER (L-H)
Saturday, November 5

OFFICIAL GOING: Straight course - good to soft (soft in places); round course - soft (good to soft in places) changing to soft after race 1 (12.15)
Wind: light 1/2 against Weather: overcast, light drizzle

7292 BETFRED COCK O'THE NORTH E B F MAIDEN STKS (DIV I) 6f
12:15 (12:17) (Class 5) 2-Y-O **£3,234** (£962; £481; £240) **Stalls** High

Form RPR

0 1 **Tartiflette**26 6751 2-8-12 0.. GrahamGibbons 10 79
(Ed McMahon) *trckd ldrs: hdwy 2f out: rdn to chal ent fnl f: sn led and kpt on wl towards fin* **20/1**

2 *nk* **Pacific Heights (IRE)**22 6851 2-9-3 0................................. MartinLane 5 83
(Tim Pitt) *in tch: hdwy 2f out: rdn over 1f out: styd on to chal ins fnl f and ev ch tl no ex towards fin* **11/1**

554 3 *2* **Jellicle (IRE)**17 6950 2-8-12 77.. RobertHavlin 9 72
(John Gosden) *cl up: led wl over 1f out: rdn and hdd jst ins fnl f: one pce* **9/2**1

4 *½* **Mrs Huffey** 2-8-12 0.. FergusSweeney 11 71+
(Henry Candy) *towards rr: swtchd lft and hdwy 2f out: rdn over 1f out: styd on ins fnl f: nrst fin* **5/1**2

42 5 *hd* **Tango Sky (IRE)**129 3511 2-9-3 0.. JimCrowley 16 75
(Ralph Beckett) *trckd ldrs: hdwy 2f out: rdn and ch whn edgd lft appr fnl f: kpt on same pce* **5/1**2

6 *1* **Rugosa** 2-8-12 0.. MichaelHills 8 67+
(Charles Hills) *dwlt: sn trcking ldrs: effrt and hdwy 2f out: rdn over 1f out: kpt on same pce* **17/2**

66 7 *¾* **Tioman Pearl**12 7052 2-9-3 0.. AndreaAtzeni 2 70
(Roger Varian) *hld up: swtchd rt and hdwy 1/2-way: chsd ldrs 2f out: rdn over 1f out and kpt on same pce* **25/1**

8 *1 ¼* **Scarabocio** 2-9-3 0...1 JimmyFortune 14 66
(Peter Chapple-Hyam) *towards rr: hdwy 1/2-way: chsd ldrs and swtchd rt to stands' rails over 1f out: kpt on same pce* **13/2**3

0 9 *1 ¾* **Chart**24 6800 2-9-3 0.. LeeNewman 12 61
(William Jarvis) *racd freely: cl up: led 1/2-way: hdd wl over 1f out: sn edgd rt and wknd* **50/1**

10 *3 ¾* **Lady Cricketer** 2-8-12 0.. LukeMorris 3 45
(Jane Chapple-Hyam) *midfield: rdn along 1/2-way: nvr a factor* **50/1**

5 11 *nk* **Kathleensluckylad (IRE)**35 6532 2-9-3 0........................ PhillipMakin 7 49
(Kevin Ryan) *led: hdd 1/2-way and sn pushed along: wknd 2f out* **12/1**

12 *1 ½* **Silver Lace (IRE)** 2-8-12 0.. TedDurcan 13 39
(Chris Wall) *green: a towards rr* **50/1**

13 *1* **Pearl Frost** 2-9-3 0.. StevieDonohoe 1 41
(Ralph Beckett) *s.i.s: green and sn rdn along: a bhd* **14/1**

30 14 *¾* **Lady Mandy**12 7058 2-8-12 0.. PaulHanagan 15 34
(Richard Fahey) *in tch: rdn along 1/2-way: sn wknd* **16/1**

00 15 *¾* **Clapped**28 6697 2-9-3 0.. SteveDrowne 4 37
(Edward Vaughan) *a in rr* **150/1**

0 16 *11* **Graylyn Olivaa**10 7094 2-9-0 0.................................. MichaelO'Connell(3) 6 4
(Robert Eddery) *towards rr: rdn along 1/2-way: sn bhd* **150/1**

1m 15.42s (1.82) **Going Correction** +0.375s/f (Good) **16** Ran SP% **119.8**
Speed ratings (Par 96): **102,101,98,98,98 96,95,94,91,86 86,84,82,81,80 66**
toteswingers:1&2:£45.70, 2&3:£6.20, 1&3:£20.30 CSF £216.10 TOTE £30.70: £7.80, £3.70, £1.80; EX 333.60 TRIFECTA Not won..

Owner A Buxton **Bred** Andrew Buxton **Trained** Lichfield, Staffs

FOCUS
The ground was described as good to soft, soft in places on the straight course and the jockeys suggested it was soft. It was officially changed to soft after this race. The first division of this juvenile maiden and just fair form among those with previous experience. Big improvement from the winner, but not a race to be with.

NOTEBOOK
Tartiflette, slowly away and outpaced in a 6f fast-ground maiden last month, had clearly come on a ton for that and handled this easier ground well, tracking the leaders until coming through to take over entering the last furlong and finding extra under pressure to hold off the runner-up. She can improve again with another winter under her belt. (op 16-1)

Pacific Heights(IRE), well beaten on her debut in a Dundalk maiden for Aidan O'Brien, was sold for 20,000gns soon after but ran well on this debut for a new yard. He tracked the pace before challenging throughout the last furlong but could not get past the winner. He can win a similar contest. (op 22-1)

Jellicle(IRE) had posted fair efforts in three maidens on a sound surface and Polytrack but did not quite get home on this easier surface despite the drop in trip. Officially rated 77, she probably sets the standard. (op 4-1)

Mrs Huffey ◆, a 32,000gns first foal of a sister to Queen Mary winner Shining Hour, was well backed on this debut but missed the break and had to come around her field before staying on late. She should be much sharper next time. (op 9-2)

Tango Sky(IRE) had shown fair form in maidens in the first half of the year but had not run since June, having been gelded during his absence. He was never far away but tended to lug in behind the winner in the closing stages and was not given a hard time when held. His rider reported that the gelding hung left. He now qualifies for a handicap mark. Official explanation: jockey said that the gelding hung left (op 9-2 tchd 11-2)

Rugosa, the fourth foal of a sister to a Listed winner from the family of Xaar, was another to run well on her debut, having missed the break, and should be better for the experience. (op 11-1)

Tioman Pearl had shown moderate form in 6f maidens on fast ground and kept on in the closing stages. He now qualifies for a mark and can do better in handicaps in due course. (op 22-1)

Scarabocio, wearing a hood on this debut, ran quite well racing nearest the stands' side and is another who is likely to improve for the outing. (op 15-2)

Clapped Official explanation: jockey said that the gelding had a breathing problem

7293 BETFRED COCK O'THE NORTH E B F MAIDEN STKS (DIV II) 6f
12:50 (12:52) (Class 5) 2-Y-O **£3,234** (£962; £481; £240) **Stalls** High

Form RPR

1 **Brick Tops** 2-8-12 0.. JimCrowley 12 76+
(Ralph Beckett) *trckd ldrs: smooth hdwy over 2f out: led appr fnl f: pushed out* **6/1**3

6 2 *¾* **Hawks Reef**22 6836 2-9-3 0.. PaulHanagan 9 78
(Richard Fahey) *led: pushed along 2f out: sn rdn and hdd over 1f out: no ex wl ins fnl f* **8/1**

3 *1* **Shame On You (IRE)** 2-8-12 0.. MichaelHills 7 70+
(Charles Hills) *s.i.s and bhd: hdwy 1/2-way: sn swtchd rt and effrt to chse ldrs over 1f out: rdn and styd on fnl f: nrst fin* **5/1**2

4 *½* **Henry Allingham** 2-9-3 0.. AndreaAtzeni 16 74
(Roger Varian) *chsd ldrs: hdwy 2f out: rdn over 1f out: kpt on same pce* **12/1**

5 1 1/2 **Panzanella** 2-8-12 0 .... RobertHavlin 8 64+
(John Gosden) *s.i.s and towards rr: hdwy 1/2-way: trckd ldrs 2f out: effrt: n.m.r and green over 1f out: kpt on fnl f* **5/1[2]**

6 3 1/2 **Yojojo (IRE)** 2-8-12 0 .... DavidProbert 2 54+
(Gay Kelleway) *t.k.h in midfield: hdwy on wd outside over 2f out: rdn and edgd lft wl over 1f out: styd on fnl f: nrst fin* **40/1**

03 7 hd **Red Bay**[20] 6890 2-9-3 0 .... LukeMorris 6 58
(Jane Chapple-Hyam) *prom: effrt to chal 2f out: sn rdn and wknd appr fnl f* **14/1**

4 8 nk **Kyllachy Dancer**[129] 3504 2-8-7 0 .... SHJames(5) 3 52
(John Quinn) *in tch: rdn along 2f out: sn one pce* **12/1**

04 9 nk **Foot Tapper**[18] 6935 2-9-3 0 .... TedDurcan 10 56
(Chris Wall) *trckd ldrs: rdn 2f out: grad wknd* **14/1**

3000 10 nse **Medam**[18] 6935 2-8-12 50 .... (t) JamieMackay 14 51
(Shaun Harris) *s.i.s and bhd: gd hdwy to trck ldrs after 2f: rdn 2f out: grad wknd* **100/1**

2 11 2 3/4 **Iffraam (IRE)**[157] 2617 2-9-3 0 .... TomEaves 5 48
(Michael Dods) *chsd ldrs: rdn along wl over 2f out: sn wknd* **9/2[1]**

12 3 **Choccywoccydoodah** 2-8-12 0 .... JamesSullivan 11 34
(James Given) *midfield: rdn along 1/2-way: sn wknd* **33/1**

0 13 1 1/2 **Chateau Lola**[7] 7165 2-8-7 0 .... (v[1]) MarkCoumbe(5) 15 29
(Derek Shaw) *cl up: rdn along over 2f out: sn wknd* **100/1**

0 14 1/2 **Forget Me Not Lane (IRE)**[29] 6673 2-9-3 0 .... PhillipMakin 4 33
(Kevin Ryan) *a in rr* **14/1**

15 1 3/4 **Luna Vale** 2-8-12 0 .... MartinLane 1 23
(Robert Eddery) *nvr bttr than midfield* **100/1**

1m 16.51s (2.91) **Going Correction** +0.375s/f (Good) **15** Ran SP% **120.6**
Speed ratings (Par 96): **95,94,92,92,90 85,85,84,84,84 80,76,74,73,71**
toteswingers:1&2:£12.90, 2&3:£9.40, 1&3:£6.60 CSF £52.45 TOTE £7.80: £3.00, £2.70, £1.90; EX 68.70 Trifecta £217.00 Part won. Pool: £293.26 - 0.93 winning units..
Owner Favourites Racing XIX **Bred** Yeguada De Milagro & Balmerino B/Stock **Trained** Kimpton, Hants

FOCUS
The second division of this maiden and the slower of the two by 1.09sec. The winner is sure to rate higher than the bare form.

NOTEBOOK
Brick Tops, who cost 95,000gns as a foal and changed hands for 80,000gns in May, travelled well off the pace and came to challenge going strongly. In the end she was made to battle by the more experienced runner-up, but she won a shade cosily and looks one with a future. She shouldn't have any problem getting another furlong. (op 13-2 tchd 7-1)
Hawks Reef raced a shade keenly in front but battled on well when the winner came alongside. This was a step up on his debut effort and he looks the type who will pay his way in sprint handicaps next season. (op 9-1 tchd 7-1)
Shame On You(IRE), who cost 75,000gns, was out the back and ran green for much of the race, but she was staying on nicely at the finish and looks the type to benefit considerably from this experience. She should get further next year. (op 7-2)
Henry Allingham, a half-brother to useful sprinter Harry Patch, showed speed and kept on pretty well. His three winning siblings acted well on Polytrack so that might be an option for connections. (tchd 11-1)
Panzanella, a Dansili filly out of French 1,000 Guineas winner Zenda, was going as strongly as the winner 2f out but found less off the bridle, running green when let down. She looks the type to do better next year. (op 8-1)
Yojojo(IRE), who missed her intended debut at Leicester last month on account of the fast ground, looked in need of this experience-wise as she wandered about under pressure. She can do better in time. (op 100-1)
Red Bay is now eligible for a handicap mark and should have better opportunities in that sphere.
Kyllachy Dancer didn't see out her race over this extra furlong on this softer ground. (op 11-1 tchd 14-1)
Iffraam(IRE), who had been off the track for five months, was struggling at halfway and failed to replicate the performance he put up on his debut. (tchd 4-1 and 5-1)

7294 BETFRED MOBILE NURSERY 6f
1:25 (1:26) (Class 5) (0-75,74) 2-Y-O **£2,911** (£866; £432; £216) **Stalls** High

Form RPR

316 1 **Royal Reyah**[27] 6724 2-8-13 66 .... FergusSweeney 16 75
(Stuart Kittow) *in rr: hdwy over 2f out: edgd rt jst ins fnl f: styd on to ld last 50yds* **7/1[2]**

0261 2 3/4 **Master Bond**[22] 6836 2-9-6 73 .... TomEaves 17 79
(Bryan Smart) *chsd ldrs: led jst ins fnl f: crowded: hdd and no ex last 50yds* **5/1[1]**

2020 3 1 3/4 **Blue Shoes (IRE)**[30] 6645 2-8-13 66 .... DavidAllan 14 67
(Tim Easterby) *chsd ldrs: led over 2f out: hdd jst ins fnl f: styd on same pce* **14/1**

2035 4 1 **Whisky Bravo**[19] 6921 2-8-13 66 .... SteveDrowne 13 64
(David Brown) *s.i.s: hdwy over 2f out: kpt on same pce fnl f* **11/1**

056 5 1 1/2 **Generalyse**[27] 6725 2-9-6 73 .... AdamKirby 7 67
(Ben De Haan) *hld up in midfield: hdwy over 2f out: kpt on same pce over 1f out* **16/1**

4051 6 1/2 **Love Tale**[12] 7051 2-8-11 64 .... LukeMorris 2 56
(Mark Rimell) *chsd ldrs: edgd rt 2f out: one pce fnl 2f* **20/1**

6123 7 2 1/2 **Guava**[16] 6972 2-8-13 66 .... MartinHarley 4 51
(Richard Hannon) *chsd ldrs: one pce whn nt clr run over 1f out* **8/1[3]**

6525 8 3/4 **Silvas Romana (IRE)**[30] 6645 2-9-7 74 .... ShaneKelly 12 56
(Mark Brisbourne) *towards rr: effrt over 2f out: kpt on: nvr nr ldrs* **16/1**

061 9 1 3/4 **Wordismybond**[33] 6581 2-9-3 70 .... JimmyFortune 10 47
(Peter Makin) *hld up towards rr: hdwy and nt clr run over 2f out: sn hmpd: hmpd over 1f out: nt clr run and eased 100yds out* **12/1**

3230 10 hd **Leenavesta (USA)**[15] 6995 2-8-13 69 .... KieranO'Neill(3) 11 45
(Richard Hannon) *chsd ldrs: outpcd over 2f out: no threat after* **12/1**

1000 11 1 **Roy's Legacy**[3] 7231 2-8-12 65 .... (t) GrahamGibbons 1 38
(Shaun Harris) *chsd ldrs: wknd over 1f out* **28/1**

0403 12 nk **Claretintheblood (IRE)**[8] 7143 2-8-2 55 .... PaulHanagan 8 28
(Richard Fahey) *chsd ldrs: wknd over 1f out* **12/1**

0060 13 3/4 **Bountiful Catch**[23] 6821 2-8-0 53 .... JimmyQuinn 5 23
(Pam Sly) *t.k.h: chsd ldrs: lost pl over 1f out* **22/1**

5400 14 6 **Alnair (IRE)**[30] 6645 2-8-9 62 .... EddieAhern 3 14
(Declan Carroll) *led tl over 2f out: sn wknd* **20/1**

0300 15 1/2 **Vexillum (IRE)**[15] 6983 2-9-0 67 .... SamHitchcott 6 18
(Mick Channon) *chsd ldrs: wkng whn edgd lft 2f out* **22/1**

2601 16 6 **First Phase**[30] 6645 2-8-11 64 .... DuranFentiman 9 —
(Mel Brittain) *in rr: sme hdwy over 2f out: sn wknd* **16/1**

5010 17 5 **True Bond**[72] 5399 2-8-10 63 .... SilvestreDeSousa 15 —
(Geoffrey Oldroyd) *chsd ldrs: lost pl over 2f out: bhd whn eased* **20/1**

1m 16.06s (2.46) **Going Correction** +0.375s/f (Good) **17** Ran SP% **122.4**
Speed ratings (Par 96): **98,97,94,93,91 90,87,86,84,83 82,82,81,73,72 64,57**
CSF £36.54 CT £367.92 TOTE £8.00: £2.70, £1.90, £2.20, £2.90; EX 49.60 Trifecta £200.40 Pool: £503.87 - 1.86 winning units..
Owner B Hopkins, M Harris & R Perry **Bred** Hopkins, Kittow & Mrs Perry **Trained** Blackborough, Devon
■ Stewards' Enquiry : Fergus Sweeney caution: careless riding.

FOCUS
A competitive if modest nursery but the closing stages were dominated by the market leaders. The time was slower than the first division of the earlier maiden but quicker than the second leg. High numbers came out on top but the form seems pretty solid.

NOTEBOOK
Royal Reyah, a winner over an extended 5f on good ground but untried on softer, was making his handicap debut. He coped with the ground well - his dam is a daughter of the soft-ground influence Efisio - and proved stronger than the favourite in the last furlong, having tracked that rival throughout. There could be more to come from him. (op 8-1)
Master Bond, who got off the mark at the fourth attempt in a 6f Redcar maiden, is suited by soft ground and travelled well, but could not hold off the winner in the last furlong. He was clear of the rest and is capable of winning similar races off this mark. (op 9-2 tchd 4-1)
Blue Shoes(IRE) has had plenty of racing but is well suited by a soft surface and this trip. Although beaten a long way last time on heavy, she bounced back here and was only worn down by two progressive colts in the closing stages. He looks a fair guide to the level. (op 12-1)
Whisky Bravo ◆'s only win was over 5f on Fibresand but he had run well on easy ground on turf. He caught the eye here, as he missed the break quite badly but was staying on in good fashion in the latter stages. He would be interesting if returned to Southwell before the end of the year. (op 16-1)
Generalyse had shown fair form in maidens on the last two of his three starts and was making his handicap debut. He got into contention at around the quarter-mile pole but could not sustain the effort. Better ground might suit him and he looks the type to improve over the winter.
Love Tale had shown steady improvement before winning a 7f fast-ground nursery last time off 6lb lower. She faced a drop in trip and a much softer surface but ran creditably and appears on the upgrade. (op 16-1)
Guava won a 6f fast-ground nursery off 6lb lower but had run well in two starts since. She stayed on late but looked less effective on this softer surface. (op 9-1 tchd 10-1)
Wordismybond Official explanation: jockey said that the colt suffered interference in running

7295 BETFRED THE BONUS KING H'CAP 7f
2:00 (2:01) (Class 2) (0-105,103) 3-Y-0+ **£12,938** (£3,850; £1,924; £962) **Stalls** High

Form RPR

6100 1 **Bonnie Brae**[15] 6987 4-8-11 90 .... TedDurcan 2 103
(David Elsworth) *midfield: hdwy on outer wl over 2f out: rdn to chal over 1f out: led ins fnl f: styd on wl* **16/1**

0000 2 1 **Docofthebay (IRE)**[21] 6862 7-8-10 89 .... (b) FrederikTylicki 1 99
(David Nicholls) *trckd ldrs: effrt 2f out: rdn and n.m.r over 1f out: led briefly ent fnl f: sn hdd and ev ch tl no ex last 100yds* **16/1**

0230 3 2 **The Confessor**[21] 6862 4-8-11 90 .... FergusSweeney 9 95
(Henry Candy) *cl up travelling wl: effrt to chal over 2f out: rdn and ev ch over 1f out: one pce ins fnl f* **8/1[1]**

0010 4 nk **Valery Borzov (IRE)**[15] 6987 7-8-11 93 .... LeeTopliss(3) 6 97
(Richard Fahey) *led: rdn wl over 1f out: hdd ent fnl f: one pce* **33/1**

4200 5 hd **Prime Exhibit**[29] 6672 6-8-10 89 .... PaulHanagan 3 93
(Richard Fahey) *in tch: hdwy to chse ldrs over 2f out: rdn wl over 1f out: kpt on fnl f* **8/1[1]**

6523 6 3/4 **Mass Rally (IRE)**[15] 6987 4-8-12 91 .... (v) DanielTudhope 13 93+
(Michael Dods) *towards rr: hdwy over 2f out: rdn wl over 1f out: styd on fnl f: nrst fin* **11/1[3]**

0310 7 1 1/4 **Advanced**[15] 6987 8-8-12 94 .... AmyRyan(3) 16 92
(Kevin Ryan) *prom: rdn along 2f out: grad wknd* **22/1**

6550 8 nk **Perfect Silence**[14] 7031 6-8-1 87 .... NicoleNordblad(7) 20 85
(Clive Cox) *racd towards stands' rail: chsd ldrs: rdn along 2f out: sn one pce* **14/1**

2064 9 1 **Axiom**[21] 6862 7-9-1 101 ow1 .... MichaelJMurphy(7) 5 96
(Ed Walker) *towards rr: hdwy over 2f out: rdn wl over 1f out: kpt on fnl f: nvr nr ldrs* **12/1**

2010 10 3 **Kiwi Bay**[21] 6862 6-8-11 90 .... TomEaves 8 77
(Michael Dods) *dwlt and towards rr: hdwy over 2f out: styd on appr fnl f: nvr nr ldrs* **22/1**

4100 11 1 3/4 **Cheveton**[15] 6987 7-8-10 92 .... DaleSwift(3) 7 75
(Richard Price) *chsd ldrs: rdn along over 2f out: sn wknd* **[illegible]**

0005 12 2 **Masked Dance (IRE)**[49] 6148 4-8-11 90 ow1 .... (p) PhillipMakin 15 67
(Kevin Ryan) *in tch: rdn along over 2f out: sn wknd* **33/1**

0050 13 nk **Captain Bertie (IRE)**[43] 6290 3-8-6 86 .... LukeMorris 18 63
(Charles Hills) *racd towards stands' rail: a towards rr* **12/1**

2101 14 1 1/2 **Valencha**[14] 7031 4-8-12 91 .... JimmyFortune 17 64
(Hughie Morrison) *racd towards stands' rail: a towards rr* **14/1**

0050 15 1 1/4 **Parisian Pyramid (IRE)**[15] 6987 5-9-0 93 .... PJSmullen 11 62
(Kevin Ryan) *nvr bttr than midfield* **16/1**

1030 16 hd **Casual Glimpse**[35] 6521 3-9-6 103 .... KieranO'Neill(3) 22 72
(Richard Hannon) *racd towards stands' rail: in tch: rdn along over 2f out: sn wknd* **33/1**

0001 17 6 **Clockmaker (IRE)**[11] 7074 5-8-11 90 .... GrahamGibbons 19 43
(Tim Easterby) *a towards rr: bhd fnl 2f* **16/1**

1402 18 4 **Entitled**[14] 7031 4-8-10 89 .... DavidProbert 10 32
(Sir Michael Stoute) *s.i.s: racd towards stands' rail: a in rr* **9/1[2]**

5030 19 4 **Crown Counsel (IRE)**[21] 6862 3-8-11 91 .... SilvestreDeSousa 4 24
(Mark Johnston) *cl up: effrt over 2f out: sn rdn and wknd* **33/1**

001 20 1/2 **Summerinthecity (IRE)**[16] 6974 4-8-9 88 .... MartinHarley 14 19
(Ed de Giles) *a in rr* **20/1**

3305 21 8 **Masaya**[53] 6035 3-9-0 94 .... MartinDwyer 12 —
(Clive Brittain) *chsd ldrs: rdn along 1/2-way: sn lost pl and bhd* **33/1**

1m 27.26s (0.96) **Going Correction** +0.375s/f (Good)
WFA 3 from 4yo+ 1lb **21** Ran SP% **124.4**
Speed ratings (Par 109): **109,107,105,105,105 104,102,102,101,97 95,93,93,91,90 89,82,78,73,73 64**
toteswingers:1&2:£108.50, 2&3:£42.00, 1&3:£0.00 CSF £219.05 CT £2222.23 TOTE £20.40: £5.10, £4.30, £2.40, £10.40; EX 327.40 Trifecta £804.50 Part won. Pool: £1087.28 - 0.10 winning units..
Owner Mrs T A Foreman **Bred** Rosyground Stud **Trained** Newmarket, Suffolk

FOCUS
A fiercely competitive handicap and the action developed centre to far side. It was well run and the winner rates a clear personal best, with the form looking quite sound among the principals.

NOTEBOOK
Bonnie Brae got no run here on her previous start but things panned out far more kindly this time, as she was delivered towards the far side unimpeded and quickened up well when asked to go on. She likes to get her toe in and no doubt the priority will be to get some black type with her now.
Docofthebay(IRE), fifth in this race last year off 6lb higher, is on a mark he off which should be competitive and, having tracked the pace going well, he stayed on in good style to take second, only being seen off by a progressive rival.

The Confessor doesn't mind this sort of ground. Always close to the front, he kept on well for pressure and posted a solid effort, but the handicapper looks to just about have his measure. (op 10-1 tchd 15-2)

Valery Borzov(IRE) ran well over a trip which is probably a little beyond his ideal distance. He's another who has little margin off his current mark, though.

Prime Exhibit, back over his ideal distance, has no problem with soft ground and kept on reasonably well. (op 9-1)

Mass Rally(IRE) didn't enjoy much luck in running when looking for a way through from the back of the field. That said, he's not the most straightforward. (tchd 12-1)

Advanced is a consistent sort in these types of events but it was no surprise to see him find a few too good. (op 25-1)

Perfect Silence did best of the six that raced more towards the stands' side early on. She probably deserves a bit of a bump for that. (op 20-1)

Axiom ran a decent race at Ascot last time but was keeping on all too late on this occasion. The handicapper continues to have a pretty good handle on him. (op 11-1 tchd 10-1)

Captain Bertie(IRE) has been very in and out this season. (op 14-1)

Entitled, despite being by Pivotal, may not have been at home on the ground. Official explanation: jockey said that the filly was unsuited by the Soft going (tchd 10-1)

7296 BETFRED GOALS GALORE E B F "SIR PERCY" GILLIES FILLIES' STKS (LISTED RACE) — 1m 2f 60y

2:35 (2:36) (Class 1) 3-Y-O+ — **£17,760** (£6,717; £3,357; £1,677) **Stalls** Low

Form — RPR

4253 **1** **Mirror Lake**[45] 6247 4-9-0 99 .... MartinDwyer 4 101
(Amanda Perrett) *chsd ldrs: edgd rt and led last 100yds: hld on towards fin* **7/1**[3]

3011 **2** *nk* **Principal Role (USA)**[35] 6530 4-9-3 114 .... IanMongan 19 103
(Sir Henry Cecil) *hld up in tch: stdy hdwy over 2f out: led briefly jst ins fnl f: edgd rt and no ex towards fin* **11/4**[1]

36 **3** *3/4* **Ceilidh House**[56] 5934 4-9-0 102 .... (t) JimCrowley 10 99
(Ralph Beckett) *hld up in rr: gd hdwy on outside over 2f out: chal 1f out: edgd lft: no ex last 50yds* **11/2**[2]

1010 **4** *3/4* **Tameen**[45] 6249 3-8-10 88 .... RichardHills 18 99+
(John Dunlop) *in rr: hdwy over 3f out: hrd rdn and styd on wl whn nt clr run clsng stages* **16/1**

1001 **5** *nk* **Askaud (IRE)**[42] 6330 3-8-10 89 .... (p) FrederikTylicki 9 97
(David Nicholls) *chsd ldrs: led over 2f out: hdd jst ins fnl f: kpt on same pce* **16/1**

6 *3* **Famusa**[132] 4-9-0 99 .... AdamKirby 3 91
(Marco Botti) *in tch: pushed along over 4f out: one pce fnl 2f* **9/1**

1221 **7** *1* **Satwa Pearl**[55] 5962 5-9-0 82 .... PaulHanagan 1 89
(Ed Dunlop) *s.i.s: hdwy over 3f out: one pce fnl 2f* **16/1**

6033 **8** *4* **Bea Remembered**[35] 6530 4-9-0 95 .... (t) ShaneKelly 11 81
(Brian Meehan) *dwlt: hld up in rr: hdwy over 3f out: nvr rchd ldrs* **16/1**

0464 **9** *1 3/4* **Amethyst Dawn (IRE)**[12] 7054 5-9-0 77 .... DavidAllan 14 78
(Tim Easterby) *led: hdd over 2f out: wknd over 1f out* **40/1**

6310 **10** *1/2* **Always The Lady**[15] 6996 3-8-10 81 .... TedDurcan 5 77
(Clive Cox) *chsd ldrs: wknd over 1f out* **25/1**

1213 **11** *1 1/4* **Captivator**[52] 6066 4-9-0 94 .... EddieAhern 7 75
(James Fanshawe) *hld up in mid-div: effrt 3f out: wknd over 1f out* **9/1**

0054 **12** *1 1/4* **Starkat**[69] 5518 5-9-0 69 .... BarryMcHugh 6 72
(George Margarson) *in rr div: nvr on terms* **100/1**

1434 **13** *6* **The Only Key**[50] 6124 5-9-0 84 .... LukeMorris 8 61
(Jane Chapple-Hyam) *chsd ldrs: rdn over 3f out: lost pl over 2f out* **16/1**

030 **14** *1 3/4* **Silver Grey (IRE)**[19] 6922 4-9-0 82 .... (p) MartinLane 20 58
(Roger Ingram) *drvn to chse ldrs: lost pl over 2f out* **50/1**

2101 **15** *2 1/2* **Lucky Legs (IRE)**[26] 6755 3-8-10 82 .... MichaelHills 15 53
(Charles Hills) *in rr: bhd fnl 2f* **33/1**

0/50 **16** *9* **Bolivia (GER)**[9] 7129 5-9-0 92 .... SteveDrowne 16 36
(Lucy Wadham) *chsd ldrs: hung lft 4f out: sn lost pl and bhd* **28/1**

3100 **17** *47* **Rougette**[78] 5255 3-8-10 85 .... JimmyFortune 2 —
(Charles Hills) *in rr: heavily eased over 2f out: virtually p.u: t.o* **40/1**

2m 13.31s (3.91) **Going Correction** +0.375s/f (Good)
WFA 3 from 4yo+ 4lb — **17** Ran SP% **122.0**
Speed ratings (Par 108): **99,98,98,97,97 94,94,90,89,89 88,87,82,80,78 71,34**
toteswingers:1&2:£7.10, 2&3:£6.40, 1&3:£11.50 CSF £24.74 TOTE £7.20: £3.10, £1.70, £2.50; EX 27.90 Trifecta £92.40 Pool : £1361.20 - 10.89 winning units..
Owner K Abdulla **Bred** Millsec Limited **Trained** Pulborough, W Sussex

■ Stewards' Enquiry : Richard Hills nine-day ban: excessive use of the whip (Nov 19, 22-26, 28-30)

FOCUS

Varying levels of ability in this fillies' Listed race. The form is unlikely to prove too solid, with the ground adding to the doubts, and the first three are rated below their best.

NOTEBOOK

Mirror Lake, a triple winner at around this trip who goes well on easy ground and stays further, was the owner's second-string but proved just the stronger. Always tracking the leading group, she was briefly short of room around 2f out but, once in the clear, she found plenty for pressure and just got the better of the favourite. (op 10-1)

Principal Role(USA), a specialist at this trip, handles fast and easy ground and came into this in form and a standout on official ratings. Drawn wide and a little keen in the early stages, she moved up looking as if she would justify favouritism but came under pressure 2f out. She ran on gamely but was just denied and lost nothing in defeat. (op 5-2 tchd 3-1)

Ceilidh House was bidding to repeat her success of 12 months previously. She looked as though she was going to succeed when sweeping down the outside to hit the front, but the Abdulla pair on her inside rallied and she had no more to offer inside the last furlong. (op 5-1)

Tameen ◆, a progressive filly who stays 1m4f, had a good bit to find off a mark of 88. She was held up at the back early but stayed on really well in the last quarter-mile to finish on the heels of the principals. A return to further will be in her favour and she could make her mark at this level if kept in training.

Askaud(IRE), a decent handicapper at up to this trip on easy ground, had improved for the fitting of cheekpieces. She had a lot to do on the ratings but performed creditably, fading out of contention only entering the last furlong.

Famusa, a multiple winner in Italy on soft ground and Listed placed at 1m3f, was having her first run for a new trainer. She was being pushed along turning for home but kept staying on in the straight. Given time to acclimatise, she can hold her own at this level next season. (op 11-1)

Satwa Pearl, ex-French, had shown steady improvement for her current yard, winning over 1m2f on easy ground last time. Another with a lot to find, she moved up halfway down the straight but could not sustain the effort.

Captivator had done really well since a hood was fitted but her effort in the straight was short-lived here and the ground might have been too soft. (tchd 10-1)

7297 BETFRED NOVEMBER H'CAP — 1m 4f

3:10 (3:11) (Class 2) 3-Y-O+
£40,462 (£12,116; £6,058; £3,029; £1,514; £760) **Stalls** Low

Form — RPR

4236 **1** **Zuider Zee (GER)**[51] 6103 4-8-13 **93** .... RobertHavlin 20 108
(John Gosden) *hld up: smooth hdwy over 4f out: chsd ldng pair 3f out: led wl over 1f out: clr appr fnl f: styd on strly* **8/1**[2]

10-4 **2** *6* **Willing Foe (USA)**[14] 7029 4-9-4 **98** .... IanMongan 5 103+
(Saeed Bin Suroor) *trckd ldrs: hdwy 4f out: led wl over 2f out: rdn and hdd wl over 1f out: edgd lft fnl f: no ch w wnr* **11/1**

0000 **3** *1 1/4* **Merchant Of Dubai**[49] 6163 6-8-13 **93** .... DanielTudhope 16 96+
(Jim Goldie) *hld up towards rr: hdwy 4f out: n.m.r wl over 2f out: sn rdn: styd on wl appr fnl f: nrst fin* **16/1**

20-0 **4** *3/4* **Hanoverian Baron**[176] 2071 6-8-11 **91** .... DavidProbert 22 93
(Tony Newcombe) *hld up in midfield: hdwy 4f out: chsd ldrs over 2f out: rdn wl over 1f out: sn no imp: lost 3rd ins fnl f* **20/1**

0601 **5** *1* **Classic Vintage (USA)**[55] 5963 5-9-1 **95** .... (b) JimCrowley 13 96
(Amanda Perrett) *midfield: hdwy 4f out: effrt whn n.m.r wl over 2f out: sn rdn and kpt on: nrst fin* **20/1**

4112 **6** *1 1/4* **Scrapper Smith (IRE)**[7] 7161 5-8-7 **90** .... DaleSwift(3) 2 89
(Alistair Whillans) *midfield: hdwy on inner 5f out: effrt 3f out: rdn and kpt on fnl 2f: nrst fin* **14/1**

0010 **7** *1 1/2* **Crackentorp**[63] 5705 6-8-12 **92** .... DavidAllan 19 88
(Tim Easterby) *hld up in rr: hdwy 4f out: rdn along wl over 2f out: plugged on: nvr gng pce to rch ldrs* **33/1**

4000 **8** *2 1/2* **The Betchworth Kid**[35] 6528 6-8-13 **98** .... LucyKBarry(5) 21 90
(Alan King) *hld up and bhd: hdwy 4f out: rdn and edgd lft over 2f out: plugged on: nvr a factor* **16/1**

1222 **9** *1 1/2* **Kiama Bay (IRE)**[56] 5921 5-9-0 **99** .... SHJames(5) 11 89
(John Quinn) *hld up: sme hdwy 3f out: n.d* **10/1**[3]

-106 **10** *1/2* **Pekan Star**[91] 4801 4-8-13 **93** .... AndreaAtzeni 14 82
(Roger Varian) *midfield: effrt over 3f out: sn rdn along and no hdwy* **13/2**[1]

2200 **11** *2* **Montaff**[77] 5285 5-9-10 **104** .... SamHitchcott 12 90
(Mick Channon) *in tch: rdn along 4f out: wknd 3f out* **40/1**

6500 **12** *nse* **Resurge (IRE)**[14] 7029 6-9-1 **95** .... FergusSweeney 8 81
(Stuart Kittow) *hld up: a towards rr* **33/1**

4610 **13** *shd* **Oceanway (USA)**[14] 7029 3-8-11 **97** .... SilvestreDeSousa 1 83
(Mark Johnston) *chsd ldrs on inner: rdn along 3f out: wknd fnl 2f* **20/1**

0605 **14** *1 1/4* **Harlestone Times (IRE)**[57] 5883 4-9-5 **99** .... TedDurcan 3 83
(John Dunlop) *hld up: a in rr* **16/1**

-106 **15** *hd* **Tepmokea (IRE)**[20] 6900 5-9-1 **95** .... PaulHanagan 23 78
(Richard Fahey) *racd wd: a towards rr* **22/1**

0013 **16** *2* **Status Symbol (IRE)**[42] 6333 6-8-10 **90** .... (t) EddieAhern 4 70
(Giles Bravery) *led: rdn clr 4f out: hdd wl over 2f out: wknd qckly* **14/1**

5004 **17** *1* **Itlaaq**[35] 6528 5-8-12 **92** .... (t) GrahamGibbons 7 70
(Michael Easterby) *n.d* **33/1**

1000 **18** *3* **Burj Nahar**[58] 5853 4-9-3 **97** .... (t) RichardHills 10 71
(Saeed Bin Suroor) *a towards rr* **25/1**

5010 **19** *1/2* **Bramalea**[44] 6269 6-8-10 **90** .... JimmyQuinn 6 63
(Hughie Morrison) *prom on inner: rdn along 4f out: sn wknd* **25/1**

-151 **20** *5* **Samsons Son**[45] 6249 7-8-10 **90** .... JimmyFortune 15 55
(Alan King) *towards rr fr 1/2-way* **12/1**

0151 **21** *9* **Demolition**[24] 6803 7-8-13 **93** .... PJSmullen 9 43
(Noel Wilson) *chsd ldr: rdn along 4f out: wknd 3f out* **20/1**

0/43 **22** *12* **Enroller (IRE)**[55] 5963 6-8-11 **91** .... SteveDrowne 17 22
(William Muir) *racd wd: midfield: hdwy and in tch 5f out: rdn along over 3f out: sn wknd and bhd* **20/1**

1400 **U** **Ile De Re (FR)**[30] 6661 5-8-13 **93** .... MartinLane 18 —
(Ian Williams) *hld up towards rr whn hmpd and uns rdr after 2f* **22/1**

2m 36.49s (1.59) **Going Correction** +0.375s/f (Good)
WFA 3 from 4yo+ 6lb — **23** Ran SP% **132.0**
Speed ratings (Par 109): **109,105,104,103,103 102,101,99,98,98 96,96,96,95,95 94,93,91,91,88 82,74,—**
toteswingers:1&2:£55.90, 2&3:£55.80, 1&3:£45.90 CSF £77.44 CT £1422.89 TOTE £9.50: £2.60, £3.10, £4.40, £6.70; EX 72.50 Trifecta £2280.20 Pool: £32342.89 - 10.49 winning units..
Owner H R H Princess Haya Of Jordan **Bred** Graf U Grafin V Stauffenberg **Trained** Newmarket, Suffolk

FOCUS

Nine of the previous ten winners of the November Handicap were aged three or four, and although there were only six representatives from those age-groups in the race this time around they included the first two home. The form is not rated too positively but the winner rates a clear personal best.

NOTEBOOK

Zuider Zee(GER) apparently didn't like the ground at Yarmouth last time but he'd been running well prior to that and he really took to these conditions, joining the runner-up with 2f to run and then powering away (stays 1m6f) to score in emphatic style. It's possible he could make up into a stayer next year. (op 12-1)

Willing Foe(USA) was well fancied for this race last year but ran a shocker. Off for the best part of a year afterwards, he ran well on his reappearance at Newbury a fortnight ago, and only the impressive winner was too good for him here. It wouldn't be a surprise to see him rock up at the Dubai carnival. (tchd 9-1)

Merchant Of Dubai didn't run well at Newbury last time but he bounced back to form here, staying on well from off the pace. The last two years he's run his best race first time out, so he could be one to bear in mind next spring.

Hanoverian Baron, absent since May, has won fresh before and also has form in soft ground. He didn't look to be that well handicapped, though, and in the circumstances he ran a solid race.

Classic Vintage(USA), who won from the front last time out, was ridden with more patience here and stayed on late to take fifth, one place worse than he achieved in this race last year. (op 18-1)

Scrapper Smith(IRE) is at the top of his game at the moment and got the longer trip fine, but he just found the competition a shade tougher here than of late. (op 16-1)

Crackentorp, returning from a two-month break, stayed on from well back but was never a real threat. (op 40-1)

The Betchworth Kid, who was second in this race last year, was another who was keeping on all too late. (op 20-1)

Kiama Bay(IRE) has had a great season but this looked just one race too many at the end of a campaign which began on the AW back in January. (op 12-1)

Pekan Star looked interesting on paper up in trip on softer ground having been gelded since he last ran, but he wouldn't settle early and hung badly under pressure in the straight, looking thoroughly uncooperative. He looks one to avoid now. (op 8-1)

Oceanway(USA) Official explanation: jockey said that the filly had no more to give

Status Symbol(IRE) took them along and kicked clear early in the straight. That was much too soon as he began to paddle going to 2f out and soon dropped right out. He goes well on Polytrack and will be one to look out for in the few races he's eligible to run in on that surface these days. (op 16-1)

Burj Nahar has been very disappointing since winning on his reappearance, and the softer ground failed to bring about improvement.
Bramalea Official explanation: jockey said that the mare hung right
Enroller(IRE) Official explanation: jockey said that the gelding hung right

7298 BETFRED 1350 SHOPS NATIONWIDE WENTWORTH STKS (LISTED RACE) 6f
3:40 (3:44) (Class 1) 3-Y-O+ **£17,760** (£6,717; £3,357; £1,677) **Stalls** High

Form RPR
0111 **1** **Sirius Prospect (USA)**^{28} 6706 3-9-3 110 ShaneKelly 11 106+
(Dean Ivory) *hld up in rr: gd hdwy 2f out: chsd ldr 1f out: r.o to ld towards fin* **9/2**^{3}
3034 **2** *nk* **Mayson**^{15} 7012 3-9-3 100 PaulHanagan 2 105
(Richard Fahey) *led: kpt on wl ins fnl f: hdd nr fin* **12/1**
0021 **3** *3 ½* **Doc Hay (USA)**^{19} 6913 4-9-3 85 JimCrowley 1 94
(Keith Dalgleish) *hld up in rr: hdwy over 2f out: edgd rt and chsd ldng pair 1f out: kpt on same pce* **33/1**
1321 **4** *2 ½* **Eton Rifles (IRE)**^{27} 6733 6-9-6 106 SilvestreDeSousa 6 89
(Stuart Williams) *trckd ldrs: t.k.h: nt clr run over 2f out: swtchd rt over 1f out: styd on* **7/2**^{2}
3/60 **5** *hd* **Sos Brillante (CHI)**^{7} 7171 6-8-13 80 ow1 IanMongan 14 81
(Terry Clement) *in rr: hdwy stands' side over 1f out: styd on wl towards fin* **100/1**
1503 **6** *nk* **Requisite**^{10} 7097 6-8-12 75 (b) EddieAhern 5 79
(Ian Wood) *in rr: styd on fnl 2f: edgd lft 1f out: nvr nr ldrs* **125/1**
0602 **7** *nse* **Secret Witness**^{14} 7018 5-9-3 94 (b) LukeMorris 4 84
(Ronald Harris) *chsd ldrs: kpt on same pce fnl 2f* **25/1**
5602 **8** *1* **Haajes**^{19} 6913 7-9-3 82 MickyFenton 15 81
(Paul Midgley) *hld up stands' side: swtchd lft after 1f: kpt on fnl 2f: nvr nr ldrs* **80/1**
5150 **9** *¾* **Prime Defender**^{21} 6858 7-9-3 108 SebSanders 16 78
(Charles Hills) *racd stands' side: mid-div: swtchd lft after 2f: nvr nr ldrs* **18/1**
5621 **10** *hd* **Our Jonathan**^{49} 6147 4-9-3 114 PJSmullen 13 78
(Kevin Ryan) *hld up in mid-div towards stands' side: effrt 2f out: sn wknd* **11/4**^{1}
0001 **11** *2* **Iver Bridge Lad**^{4} 7221 4-9-9 104 (b) MichaelO'Connell 10 77
(John Ryan) *chsd ldrs: wknd over 1f out* **12/1**
0103 **12** *6* **Libranno**^{21} 6858 3-9-9 112 JimmyFortune 9 58
(Richard Hannon) *chsd ldrs: effrt over 2f out: lost pl over 1f out* **9/1**
1103 **13** *2* **Lady Paris (IRE)**^{48} 6189 3-8-12 87 TomEaves 8 41
(Bryan Smart) *chsd ldrs: lost pl 2f out* **50/1**
0220 **14** *3* **Favourite Girl (IRE)**^{14} 7018 5-8-12 92 (p) DuranFentiman 3 31
(Tim Easterby) *chsd ldr: wknd 2f out* **33/1**
0454 **15** *nk* **Dawn Eclipse (IRE)**^{34} 6561 6-8-12 100 (p) BACurtis 7 30
(T G McCourt, Ire) *s.s: a in rr* **40/1**
0205 **16** *nk* **Aneedah (IRE)**^{35} 6531 3-8-12 97 (p) RobertHavlin 12 29
(John Gosden) *s.i.s: a in rr* **16/1**

1m 13.82s (0.22) **Going Correction** +0.375s/f (Good) **16** Ran SP% **120.7**
Speed ratings (Par 111): **113,112,107,104,104 103,103,102,101,101 98,90,87,83,83 83**
toteswingers:1&2:£13.90, 2&3:£50.50, 1&3:£52.40 CSF £54.09 TOTE £5.60: £2.20, £3.60, £9.70; EX 104.10 Trifecta £1781.80 Part won. Pool of £2407.96 - 0.63 winning units..
Owner Miss N Yarrow **Bred** Brookdale And Dr Ted Folkerth **Trained** Radlett, Herts

FOCUS
A decent renewal of this Listed sprint in which half the field were rated 100 or more. In the end two of the 3yos came right away and the time was 1.6secs faster than the quicker of the three juvenile races at the trip. Sirius Prospect did not need to match his latest effort but looked a bit better than the bare form.

NOTEBOOK
Sirius Prospect(USA) ◆, a highly progressive sprinter who stays 7f and handles easy ground, justified his rating of 110 in winning his first Listed race here. Held up early, he lengthened really well to cut down the long-time leader inside the final furlong. Although the margin was narrow, his rider never got serious with him and he was value for further. He can be given extra credit as he raced away from where the pace was and gave the runner-up a good start. He is certainly living up to his name and he looks sure to be a major player in Group races next season. He will need to step up again, but looks more than capable of doing so and the Golden Jubilee could be an ideal first target next season. (tchd 5-1)
Mayson had won at 6f on easy ground but had not scored since August 2010. However, he had run some good races and set off in front here. He was clear well over a furlong from home and looked like making all, only to be run down by the improving winner inside the last furlong. He deserves credit as he fought back when challenged and probably ran into a Group horse in the making. (op 16-1)
Doc Hay(USA), all of whose wins have been at 5f, was up in grade and trip. He raced on the outside of his field before staying on late without troubling the principals, as befits a horse that likes a stiff track. His rookie trainer has done really well with him, having managed to win four times since June, but after this good performance much depends on how the handicapper reacts. (tchd 40-1)
Eton Rifles(IRE), a progressive sort who is effective at 6f-7f and had won a Listed race last time on soft, travelled well in behind the leaders but found himself stuck behind a wall of horses just as the race was developing over 2f out. He had to be switched to get an opening and could stay on only once the race was over. (op 13-2)
Sos Brillante(CHI), whose best effort so far in this country was on her turf debut over 7f the previous week, ran above herself, staying on late up the stands' side. (tchd 125-1)
Requisite had masses to do off a rating of 75 and was another to run really well, staying on and ending up third in a four-horse battle for fourth place. (op 100-1)
Secret Witness goes well at this course, winning over 5f in August and being narrowly beaten at the last meeting. He ran another fine race, despite being up in trip and grade, before tiring late on.
Prime Defender, an impressive winner of the Ayr Gold Cup on soft ground on his previous start, had conditions to suit but faded out of contention after being close enough 2f out. The trainer reported that the gelding twisted his near-fore shoe. (op 16-1 tchd 20-1)
Our Jonathan Official explanation: jockey said that the gelding twisted his near-fore shoe (op 3-1)
Iver Bridge Lad showed up until fading under pressure in the last quarter-mile. He might have found this coming too soon after winning at Maisons-Laffitte earlier in the week. His rider reported that the colt ran flat. Official explanation: jockey said that the colt ran flat (op 11-1)
Libranno, another who showed up for a fair way probably found the ground softer than ideal. (op 13-2)

7299 BETFRED.COM APPRENTICE H'CAP 7f
4:10 (4:12) (Class 5) (0-75,75) 3-Y-O+ **£2,911** (£866; £432; £216) **Stalls** High

Form RPR
6542 **1** **Sam Nombulist**^{11} 7076 3-9-3 **74** (v) AmyRyan 17 86
(Richard Whitaker) *racd stands' side: chsd ldrs: led over 2f out: styd on wl ins fnl f: rdn out* **8/1**^{3}
1620 **2** *2 ¾* **Deliberation (IRE)**^{7} 7172 3-8-13 **73** SHJames$^{(3)}$ 14 78
(Kevin Ryan) *racd stands' side: chsd ldrs: wnt 2nd over 1f out: no imp* **16/1**
4040 **3** *6* **Caldercruix (USA)**^{20} 6895 4-8-10 **71** (v) RaulDaSilva$^{(5)}$ 10 60
(James Evans) *led: hdd over 2f out: one pce over 1f out* **25/1**
5236 **4** *1 ¼* **Tewin Wood**^{10} 7110 4-8-13 **74** NatashaEaton$^{(5)}$ 5 60
(Alan Bailey) *chsd ldrs: hrd rdn and kpt on one pce over 1f out* **9/1**
2254 **5** *1 ½* **Focail Eile**^{3} 7234 6-9-5 **75** MichaelO'Connell 11 57
(John Ryan) *mid-div: hdwy over 2f out: kpt on same pce over 1f out* **8/1**^{3}
530 **6** *shd* **Junket**^{73} 5383 4-8-12 **73** JustinNewman$^{(5)}$ 16 55
(Dr Jon Scargill) *in rr: drvn over 3f out: kpt on fnl 2f: nvr nr ldrs* **8/1**^{3}
0340 **7** *¾* **Northern Fling**^{35} 6533 7-8-12 **73** JasonHart$^{(5)}$ 9 53
(Jim Goldie) *mid-div: hdwy on outer 3f out: one pce fnl 2f* **16/1**
2211 **8** *hd* **Zafeen's Pearl**^{8} 7146 4-8-12 **75** PaulBooth$^{(7)}$ 12 54+
(Dean Ivory) *slowly away: t.k.h in rr: hmpd and lost pl over 4f out: swtchd stands' side: kpt on fnl 2f* **9/2**^{1}
6363 **9** *3 ½* **Jungle Bay**^{26} 6759 4-9-4 **74** (p) LouisBeuzelin 2 44
(Jane Chapple-Hyam) *chsd ldrs: drvn over 3f out: lost pl over 1f out* **7/1**^{2}
6630 **10** *¾* **Dancing Maite**^{25} 6778 6-8-9 **70** DavidKenny$^{(5)}$ 6 38
(Roy Bowring) *dwlt: hld up: hdwy to chse ldrs over 2f out: wknd over 1f out* **14/1**
3050 **11** *1* **Sunrise Safari (IRE)**^{7} 7171 8-9-4 **74** (v) LeeTopliss 8 40
(Richard Fahey) *chsd ldrs: wknd over 1f out* **16/1**
-000 **12** *hd* **Signore Momento (IRE)**^{25} 6778 5-8-10 **71** (bt^{1}) DarylByrne$^{(5)}$ 3 36
(Amy Weaver) *chsd ldrs on outer: wknd 2f out* **25/1**
5504 **13** *2 ½* **Rough Rock (IRE)**^{26} 6759 6-9-4 **74** KieranO'Neill 7 33
(Chris Dwyer) *s.i.s: hdwy over 2f out: sn wknd* **16/1**
5030 **14** *9* **Kerrys Requiem (IRE)**^{75} 5314 5-9-3 **73** (p) SeanLevey 15 8
(Tim Pitt) *chsd ldrs: lost pl 2f out: bhd whn eased ins fnl f* **16/1**
4125 **15** *4 ½* **Goal (IRE)**^{89} 4854 3-9-3 **74** RyanClark 1 —
(Richard Guest) *in rr: hdwy 4f out: lost pl over 2f out: bhd whn eased ins fnl f* **14/1**

1m 29.15s (2.85) **Going Correction** +0.375s/f (Good)
WFA 3 from 4yo+ 1lb **15** Ran SP% **124.5**
Speed ratings (Par 103): **98,94,88,86,84 84,83,83,79,78 77,77,74,64,59**
toteswingers:1&2:£26.10, 2&3:£70.80, 1&3:£35.70 CSF £133.44 CT £3112.84 TOTE £8.60: £3.20, £6.10, £11.20; EX 122.00 TRIFECTA Not won..
Owner Wham Partnership **Bred** R F And S D Knipe **Trained** Scarcroft, W Yorks
■ Stewards' Enquiry : Natasha Eaton five-day ban: used whip with excessive frequency (Nov 19,22-25)

FOCUS
The final race of the turf season and the race developed more towards the stands' side, with the first two pulling nicely clear. The pace held up pretty well and the winner is rated in line with her latest form.
T/Jkpt: Not won. T/Plt: £261.10 to a £1 stake. Pool of £136,986.31- 382.86 winning tickets. T/Qpdt: £65.00 to a £1 stake. Pool of £11,507.83 - 130.90 winning tickets. JR

7280 CHURCHILL DOWNS (L-H)
Saturday, November 5
OFFICIAL GOING: Dirt: standard changing to fast; turf: good changing to firm

7300a BREEDERS' CUP MARATHON (GRADE 2) (3YO+) (DIRT) 1m 6f
5:20 (5:20) 3-Y-O+ **£173,076** (£57,692; £31,730; £19,230; £9,615)

RPR
1 **Afleet Again (USA)**^{27} 4-9-0 0 (b) CVelasquez 8 118
(Robert E Reid Jr, U.S.A) *hld up: hdwy on outer over 2f out: sn chsng ldrs: led ins fnl f: styd on wl* **33/1**
2 *2 ¼* **Birdrun (USA)**^{35} 6552 5-9-0 0 JRVelazquez 1 115
(William Mott, U.S.A) *trckd ldrs: drvn to chal wl over 1f out: kpt on but no ch w wnr fnl 100yds* **6/1**^{2}
3 *hd* **Giant Oak (USA)**^{28} 5-9-0 0 (b) SXBridgmohan 5 115
(Chris Block, U.S.A) *midfield: hdwy over 2f out: led 1f out: sn hdd: kpt on at one pce* **7/1**
4 *3 ¼* **Pleasant Prince (USA)**^{51} 4-9-0 0 JRosario 4 110
(Wesley A Ward, U.S.A) *led: rdn whn hdd over 2f out: sn outpcd: plugged on again fnl f* **14/1**
5 *1 ¼* **Cease (USA)**^{28} 4-9-0 0 GKGomez 9 108
(Albert M Stall Jr, U.S.A) *trckd ldrs: hdwy to ld over 2f out: hdd 1f out: wknd* **13/2**^{3}
6 *10 ¾* **Eldaafer (USA)**^{56} 6-9-0 0 (b) JJCastellano 10 93
(Diane Alvarado, U.S.A) *in tch: rdn and ev ch 2f out: wknd appr fnl f* **10/1**
7 *9 ½* **Baryshnikov (USA)**^{42} 5-9-0 0 (b) MESmith 2 80
(Michael J Maker, U.S.A) *prom: wknd over 2f out* **25/1**
8 *11* **Brigantin (USA)**^{34} 6562 4-9-0 0 JRLeparoux 6 65
(A Fabre, France) *hld up in rr: nvr threatened* **7/1**
9 *1 ¾* **Harrison's Cave**^{17} 6966 3-8-10 0 RyanMoore 7 66
(A P O'Brien, Ire) *in tch: wknd qckly over 3f out* **20/1**
P **Meeznah (USA)**^{21} 6859 4-8-11 0 TomQueally 3 —
(David Lanigan) *trckd ldrs on inner: pushed along and lost pl 9f out: t.o 5f out: eased over 3f out: sn p.u* **7/1**
P **A. U. Miner (USA)**^{35} 6552 6-9-0 0 CHBorel 11 —
(Clark Hanna, U.S.A) *hld up in rr: hdwy over 3f out: wnt wrong and p.u and dismntd over 2f out* **7/2**^{1}

3m 0.39s (180.39)
WFA 3 from 4yo+ 8lb **11** Ran SP% **114.6**
PARI-MUTUEL (all including $2 stakes): WIN 85.20; PLACE (1-2) 35.80, 7.20; SHOW (1-2-3) 13.80, 5.80, 6.80; SF 668.40.
Owner Kasey K King Racing Stable LLC **Bred** Roll Z Dice Racing Stable **Trained** USA

FOCUS
A race not worthy of its Breeders' Cup title. Very few North American horses are bred for this sort of distance and the Europeans are used to racing on turf. The pace was strong for the distance with the sectionals 23.47, 48.05, 1:12.65, and 1:38.97.

NOTEBOOK
Afleet Again(USA) couldn't be fancied on recent form, but he was pretty smart last year when contesting races such as the Haskell and Travers, albeit he was well held in both. A dour closer with a long stride, the race set up well for him.
Birdrun(USA) deserves credit as he sat closer to the hot pace than the winner.
Giant Oak(USA) has the talent to win a race like this, but his strike-rate is poor. In fairness, the trip probably stretches him.
Pleasant Prince(USA) went off too fast.
Cease(USA) lacked the experience of some of these and had stamina to prove. He went well for a long way and has the potential to do better in due course, most likely back over shorter distances.
Eldaafer(USA), last year's winner, hasn't been in the same form this time around.
Brigantin(USA) stays extremely well on turf, as he showed when third in the Prix du Cadran last time, but he didn't take to dirt. He didn't use Lasix.
Harrison's Cave was another turf runner who didn't act on the surface. He used Lasix.

Meeznah(USA), using Lasix for the first time, struggled badly on her first dirt start. After being pulled up she was taken away in a horse ambulance, but an initial examination found no sign of injury and she was thought to be suffering from fatigue.
A. U. Miner(USA), unlucky in this last year, was beginning to make a move when sadly going wrong shortly before the straight. He reportedly suffered bilateral sesamoid fractures in the left front fetlock joint. There was no immediate word on his status.

7301a BREEDERS' CUP JUVENILE TURF (GRADE 1) (2YO COLTS & GELDINGS) (TURF) 1m (T)

6:02 (6:06) 2-Y-O **£346,153** (£115,384; £63,461; £38,461; £19,230)

RPR

1 **Wrote (IRE)**[42] 6336 2-8-10 0 RyanMoore 5 115
(A P O'Brien, Ire) *midfield on inner: hdwy over 2f out: sn chsng ldrs: led jst ins fnl f: kpt on to go clr fnl 100yds* **9/1**

2 2 1/4 **Excaper (USA)**[27] 2-8-10 0 (b) EmmaJayneWilson 11 110
(Ian Black, Canada) *trckd ldr: rdn over 2f out: led 1f out: sn hdd: kpt on but no ch w wnr* **33/1**

3 nse **Farraaj (IRE)**[44] 6270 2-8-10 0 NeilCallan 4 110
(Roger Varian) *trckd ldrs: rdn to ld narrowly 2f out: hdd 1f out: kpt on* **13/2**[2]

4 1 1/4 **Lucky Chappy (IRE)**[27] 2-8-10 0 JRosario 12 107
(H Graham Motion, U.S.A) *hld up: rdn and hdwy on outer 2f out: kpt on wl fnl f: nvr nrr* **14/1**

5 hd **Animal Spirits (USA)**[27] 2-8-10 0 RAlbarado 10 106+
(Albert M Stall Jr, U.S.A) *hld up: hdwy over 1f out: kpt on fnl f: nvr nrr* **10/1**

6 hd **Daddy Nose Best (USA)**[49] 2-8-10 0 JRLeparoux 9 106
(Steven Asmussen, U.S.A) *hld up in midfield: rdn over 2f out: kpt on: nvr trbld ldrs* **33/1**

7 3/4 **Finale (USA)**[49] 2-8-10 0 JRVelazquez 13 104+
(Todd Pletcher, U.S.A) *in tch on outer: rdn over 2f out: no ex ins fnl f: short of room nr line* **4/1**[1]

8 1 3/4 **Caspar Netscher**[28] 6688 2-8-10 0 KierenFallon 7 100
(Alan McCabe) *t.k.h in midfield: rdn and hdwy on inner over 1f out: wknd ins fnl f* **7/1**[3]

9 nk **Shkspeare Shaliyah (USA)**[34] 2-8-10 0 ASolis 3 99
(Doodnauth Shivmangal, U.S.A) *hld up: sme late hdwy: nvr threatened ldrs* **10/1**

10 nse **Fantastic Song (USA)**[34] 2-8-10 0 JJCastellano 2 99
(Chad C Brown, U.S.A) *hld up: sme late hdwy: nvr threatened ldrs* **25/1**

11 4 1/4 **Coalport (USA)**[27] 2-8-10 0 JAlvarado 6 89
(Wayne Catalano, U.S.A) *midfield: rdn over 2f out: wknd over 1f out* **25/1**

12 nk **State Of Play (USA)**[65] 2-8-10 0 RADominguez 14 88
(H Graham Motion, U.S.A) *in tch: rdn over 2f out: wknd over 1f out* **8/1**

13 3 3/4 **Majestic City (USA)**[28] 6720 2-8-10 0 (b) GKGomez 8 80
(Peter Miller, U.S.A) *led: rdn whn hdd 2f out: sn wknd* **7/1**[3]

14 1 3/4 **Tequila Factor (USA)**[21] 2-8-10 0 (b) RBejarano 15 75
() *in tch towards outer: lost pl over 2f out: sn wknd* **66/1**

1m 37.41s (2.58) **14 Ran SP% 119.4**
PARI-MUTUEL (all including $2 stakes): WIN 25.20; PLACE (1-2) 13.80, 30.40; SHOW (1-2-3) 8.60, 15.80, 7.80; SF 964.00.
Owner Mrs John Magnier, M Tabor & D Smith **Bred** Speers Bloodstock Ltd **Trained** Ballydoyle, Co Tipperary

FOCUS
They went a solid pace.

NOTEBOOK
Wrote(IRE), the Royal Lodge third, enjoyed a nice run through the race, saved ground on the inside throughout, and picked up well once switched entering the straight. He was pulling clear at the line, appreciating every yard of the 1m trip, and has the pedigree and look of a colt who'll appreciate middle distances next season. The slightly easier ground compared with Newmarket probably suited him, but he was on Lasix and it remains to be seen if he can translate this improvement back to Europe.
Excaper(USA), second and fourth in Canadian Grade 3s on his last two starts, crossed over from his wide draw to take up a position chasing the leader and was the first to kick for home on turning in. He battled on well but the winner saw it out so much better.
Farraaj(IRE), runner-up in a Newmarket Group 3 last time, was up a furlong in distance and, despite getting a nice run through the race on the rail and having every chance in the straight, he couldn't pick up when required. His pedigree suggests this might be as far as he needs to go, and he might prove to be at his best over 7f.
Lucky Chappy(IRE) swung wide off the bend into the straight and was brought with an uninterrupted challenge down the centre of the track.
Animal Spirits(USA) got into a fair amount of trouble as he fought for room more towards the inner.
Daddy Nose Best(USA), in common with the runner-up, reversed last-time-out form with \bFinale\p, but the favourite was poorly drawn, trapped much wider than ideal and ran better than his finishing position might suggest.
Caspar Netscher, who was keen early, didn't get home and looked to be found out by the greater test of stamina. Connections blamed the rain-softened ground, though.

7302a SENTIENT JET BREEDERS' CUP SPRINT (GRADE 1) (3YO+) (DIRT) 6f (D)

6:37 (6:40) 3-Y-0+ **£519,230** (£173,076; £95,192; £57,692; £28,846)

RPR

1 **Amazombie (USA)**[28] 5-9-0 0 MESmith 7 121+
(Bill Spawr, U.S.A) *midfield: rdn and hdwy over 2f out: chsd ldr over 1f out: led ins fnl f: kpt on* **6/1**

2 nk **Force Freeze (USA)**[35] 6549 6-9-0 0 JRVelazquez 6 120
(Peter R Walder, U.S.A) *prom: led over 2f out: rdn over 1f out: hdd ins fnl f: kpt on* **12/1**

3 2 1/4 **Jackson Bend (USA)**[35] 6550 4-9-0 0 CNakatani 5 113+
(Nicholas Zito, U.S.A) *hld up: rdn and gd hdwy on outer over 1f out: wnt 3rd jst ins fnl f: kpt on wl: nt quite rch ldng pair* **3/1**[1]

4 5 1/4 **Aikenite (USA)**[29] 4-9-0 0 JJCastellano 3 96
(Todd Pletcher, U.S.A) *outpcd in rr tl kpt on fr over 1f out: wnt 4th post* **14/1**

5 nse **Hamazing Destiny (USA)**[29] 5-9-0 0 RAlbarado 4 96
(D Wayne Lukas, U.S.A) *midfield: sme hdwy on inner over 1f out: one pce fnl f: lost 4th post* **12/1**

6 1 **Apriority (USA)**[35] 6549 4-9-0 0 (b) JRosario 9 93
(David Fawkes, U.S.A) *hld up: sme hdwy on outer over 1f out: no further imp fnl f* **25/1**

7 1/2 **Big Drama (USA)**[62] 5-9-0 0 (b) RADominguez 8 91
(David Fawkes, U.S.A) *chsd ldrs towards outer: wknd appr fnl f* **4/1**[2]

8 4 **Giant Ryan (USA)**[35] 6549 5-9-0 0 CVelasquez 2 78+
(Bisnath Parboo, U.S.A) *w ldr: rdn over 2f out: wknd wl over 1f out* **6/1**

9 4 3/4 **Euroears (USA)**[35] 6549 7-9-0 0 RBejarano 1 63+
(Bob Baffert, U.S.A) *sn pushed along to ld narrowly: hdd over 2f out: sn wknd* **11/2**[3]

69.17 secs (-0.23) **9 Ran SP% 114.9**
PARI-MUTUEL (all including $2 stakes): WIN 17.80; PLACE (1-2) 7.40, 7.00; SHOW (1-2-3) 5.00, 5.00, 3.20; SF 145.20.
Owner Thomas C Sanford & William Spawr **Bred** Gregg Anderson **Trained** North America

FOCUS
As expected the lead was contested and they went 21.12 for the first quarter and 44.41 for the half. That set it up for a closer.

NOTEBOOK
Amazombie(USA) followed up his win in the Grade 1 Ancient Title, helped by sitting off the overly hot pace. Everything went his way.
Force Freeze(USA) deserves enormous credit as he was one of three runners to force the pace. He was nothing special when trained in Dubai, but has proved himself a high-class sprinter since returning to the US and he can be considered the best horse on the day.
Jackson Bend(USA) had shown improved form over 7f-1m this year and was expected to be suited by a furiously run race at this trip, but he simply didn't have the pace. His first preference at the entry stage was for the Dirt Mile and on reflection that's the race he should have gone for.
Aikenite(USA) was a bit out of his depth and couldn't muster the required pace.
Hamazing Destiny(USA) couldn't repeat the form he showed when runner-up in this last year.
Big Drama(USA), last year's winner, has managed only two runs this year and missed his intended prep in the Vosburgh with a setback. His chance was compromised by the overly strong pace.
Giant Ryan(USA) was disappointing considering he had Force Freeze behind in second when taking the Vosburgh, although that win was gained on a muddy track.
Euroears(USA) wasn't fast away from the unhelpful inside stall and had to be driven along to go to the front. He faced competition once there and had little hope of sustaining a worthwhile effort.

7303a BREEDERS' CUP TURF SPRINT (GRADE 2) (3YO+) (TURF) 5f

7:21 (7:23) 3-Y-0+ **£346,153** (£115,384; £63,461; £38,461; £19,230)

RPR

1 **Regally Ready (USA)**[20] 6908 4-9-0 0 (b) CNakatani 8 122
(Steven Asmussen, U.S.A) *w ldr: led over 2f out: rdn over 1f out: kpt on wl* **7/2**[1]

2 1 1/2 **Country Day (USA)**[28] 5-9-0 0 JamesGraham 11 117
(Steve Margolis, U.S.A) *sn prom: rdn over 2f out: kpt on: wnt 2nd fnl 100yds* **33/1**

3 3/4 **Perfect Officer (USA)**[28] 5-9-0 0 KCarmouche 4 114
(Michael V Pino, U.S.A) *chsd ldrs towards inner: rdn over 2f out: kpt on: wnt 3rd fnl 75yds* **12/1**

4 1/2 **Great Attack (USA)**[28] 4-9-0 0 (b) JASanchez 5 112
(Wesley A Ward, U.S.A) *prom: chsd wnr over 1f out: no ex and lost 2 pls fnl 100yds* **33/1**

5 nk **Caracortado (USA)**[69] 4-9-0 0 JTalamo 13 111
(Michael Machowsky, U.S.A) *chsd ldrs on outer: rdn over 2f out: kpt on* **13/2**[3]

6 1 1/4 **Rapport (USA)**[28] 4-8-11 0 BHernandezJr 9 104
(Ronny Werner, U.S.A) *led narrowly: hdd over 2f out: remained prom tl wknd ins fnl f* **33/1**

7 2 3/4 **Camp Victory (USA)**[25] 4-9-0 0 (b) JRLeparoux 12 97
(Mike Mitchell, U.S.A) *dwlt: hld up: hdwy into midfield and swtchd to inner over 2f out: kpt on one pce* **10/1**

8 1/2 **Chamberlain Bridge (USA)**[61] 7-9-0 0 (b) HJTheriotll 14 95
(W Bret Calhoun, U.S.A) *in tch on outer: outpcd over 2f out: nvr threatened to get bk on terms* **9/1**

9 3/4 **Holiday For Kitten (USA)**[28] 3-8-9 0 (b) JRosario 2 87
(Wesley A Ward, U.S.A) *hld up: nvr threatened* **20/1**

10 nse **Grand Adventure (USA)**[20] 6908 5-9-0 0 JJCastellano 1 92
(Mark Frostad, Canada) *hld up: n.d* **20/1**

11 2 3/4 **Hoofit (NZ)**[29] 4-9-0 0 EPrado 7 82
(H Graham Motion, U.S.A) *midfield: wnt v wd on bnd 3f out: no ch after* **10/1**

12 nk **California Flag (USA)**[25] 7-9-0 0 (b) PValenzuela 6 81
(Brian Koriner, U.S.A) *midfield: wknd over 1f out* **12/1**

13 1 1/4 **Broken Dreams (USA)**[36] 5-8-11 0 (b) GKGomez 3 74
(Thomas F Proctor, U.S.A) *hld up: a towards rr* **16/1**

14 1 3/4 **Havelock (USA)**[28] 4-9-0 0 RAlbarado 10 70
(Darrin Miller, U.S.A) *midfield: carried v wd on bnd 3f out: no ch after* **5/1**[2]

56.48 secs (56.48) **14 Ran SP% 120.0**
PARI-MUTUEL (all including $2 stakes): WIN 6.60; PLACE (1-2) 4.60, 24.00; SHOW (1-2-3) 3.00, 14.20, 6.00; SF 188.20.
Owner Vinery Stables **Bred** Grapestock Llc **Trained** USA

FOCUS
No European interest here and, unusually for this race, few got involved.

NOTEBOOK
Regally Ready(USA), who beat Bated Breath to take a Canadian Grade 1 last time out, broke well from stall eight and soon held a prominent position to the leader's inside. Cutting the corner into the straight, he held his pursuers comfortably at bay inside the last and won quite cosily. The early speed he showed to bag the ideal pitch going into the first turn won him the day and this performance confirmed him to be North America's top turf sprinter.
Country Day(USA) wasn't ideally drawn but he showed good speed to chase the leaders and cornered the bend into the straight well. This was a fine effort in defeat.
Perfect Officer(USA) saved plenty of ground hugging the rail into the straight and had no excuses. He looks ot have run close to his best in defeat.
Great Attack(USA) had a nice position going into the first turn but didn't corner it well at all and did no favours to those on his outer when hampering California Flag, who in turn bumped Hoofit and Havelock, forcing them wide.
Caracortado(USA) ran well considering he was drawn badly and ended up being trapped wide throughout.
Rapport(USA) looked up against it in this company and, although she showed good early speed to lead, she was comfortably seen off with over a furlong to run.
Chamberlain Bridge(USA) finished fast and late to take this race last year, but he hasn't been in the same form this time around.
Havelock(USA) had beaten the runner-up, third and fourth when successful in a Keeneland Grade 3 last time out, so on that form he should have been involved in the finish, but he didn't get a good trip, as he was badly hampered going into the first turn and pushed very wide. His race was immediately lost at that point and his rider took things easy afterwards.

7304a BREEDERS' CUP DIRT MILE (GRADE 1) (3YO+) (DIRT) 1m

8:01 (8:03) 3-Y-0+ **£346,153** (£115,384; £63,461; £38,461; £19,230)

RPR

1 **Caleb's Posse (USA)**[35] 3-8-11 0 RMaragh 8 127
(Donnie K Von Hemel, U.S.A) *hld up in rr: rapid hdwy on outer over 1f out: led ins fnl f: kpt on to go clr fnl 100yds* **7/1**

2 4 **Shackleford (USA)**35 3-8-11 0........ JLCastanon 2 118
(Dale Romans, U.S.A) *trckd ldr: led over 2f out: rdn over 1f out: hdd ins fnl f: sn no ch w wnr* **7/1**

3 1 ¾ **Tres Borrachos (USA)**34 6570 6-9-0 0........ JRosario 4 115
(Martin F Jones, U.S.A) *hld up in rr: pushed along and stl last 2f out: kpt on fr over 1f out: wnt 3rd post* **33/1**

4 ½ **Trappe Shot (USA)**35 6549 4-9-0 0........ JRVelazquez 9 114
(Kiaran McLaughlin, U.S.A) *in tch: rdn and hdwy over 1f out: wnt 3rd jst ins fnl f: one pce: lost 3rd post* **4/1**2

5 2 ½ **Tapizar (USA)**28 3-8-11 0........ GKGomez 3 107
(Steven Asmussen, U.S.A) *chsd ldrs on outer: wknd ins fnl f*

6 2 ¾ **Jersey Town (USA)**35 6550 5-9-0 0........ CVelasquez 7 102
(Barclay Tagg, U.S.A) *in tch: hdwy to chse ldrs wl over 1f out: wknd ins fnl f* **16/1**

7 hd **Wilburn (USA)**35 3-8-11 0........ JRLeparoux 5 100
(Steven Asmussen, U.S.A) *midfield towards inner: hdwy to chse ldrs over 2f out: wknd over 1f out* **5/2**1

8 nk **The Factor (USA)**28 3-8-11 0........ MGarcia 1 100
(Bob Baffert, U.S.A) *led: hdd over 2f out: sn wknd* **6/1**3

9 2 **Irrefutable (USA)**28 5-9-0 0........ RBejarano 6 96
(Bob Baffert, U.S.A) *midfield: outpcd over 3f out: wknd over 1f out* **12/1**

1m 34.59s (94.59)
WFA 3 from 4yo+ 2lb **9 Ran SP% 111.0**
PARI-MUTUEL (all including $2 stakes): WIN 15.60; PLACE (1-2) 7.00, 6.40; SHOW (1-2-3) 4.80, 4.80, 10.80; SF 112.80.
Owner McNeill Stables LLC & Cheyenne Stables LLC **Bred** Don C McNeill **Trained** USA

FOCUS
The pace was too fast with The Factor taking them along in splits of 22.49, 45.36 and 1:09.52.

NOTEBOOK
Caleb's Posse(USA) had the race fall kindly for him and he won emphatically. He denied narrowly Uncle Mo over 7f in the King's Bishop earlier in the season and was suited by the return to a one-turn race after failing behind Wilburn in the Indiana Derby last out.
Shackleford(USA) is a tremendously tough horse. He's had an extremely hard campaign, including taking in all three legs of the Triple Crown (won the Preakness), and he ran another fine race. This looked his for the taking when he was still going well early in the straight, but he had chased the strong pace and paid for it late on.
Tres Borrachos(USA) doesn't win very often but he benefited from sitting well off the pace and stayed on past beaten rivals.
Trappe Shot(USA) didn't improve for the step back up in trip and was disappointing. His form has dipped lately.
Tapizar(USA) wasn't able to dominate and was comfortably held.
Wilburn(USA) probably found this coming a bit too soon in his development, and the switch from a two-turn race to what was effectively an extended sprint did not suit. He remains a fine prospect.
The Factor(USA) came here instead of going for the Sprint in the hope of getting an easy time on the lead, but that didn't materialise as he was pressed throughout by Shackleford.

7305a EMIRATES AIRLINE BREEDERS' CUP TURF (GRADE 1) (3YO+) (TURF) 1m 4f (T)

8:45 (8:47) 3-Y-O+ **£1,038,461** (£346,153; £190,384; £115,384; £57,692)

RPR

1 **St Nicholas Abbey (IRE)**34 6567 4-9-0 0........ JPO'Brien 1 124+
(A P O'Brien, Ire) *hld up: hdwy and angled to outside wl over 1f out: drvn and qcknd to ld ins fnl f: sn clr: readily* **5/1**3

2 2 ¼ **Sea Moon**56 5928 3-8-10 0........ RyanMoore 7 122+
(Sir Michael Stoute) *s.i.s: hld up: hdwy to trck ldrs over 2f out: drvn and ev ch ent fnl f: kpt on: nt pce of wnr* **7/2**2

3 1 **Brilliant Speed (USA)**28 6716 3-8-10 0........ JRVelazquez 8 121
(Thomas Albertrani, U.S.A) *t.k.h: prom on outside: hdwy to ld 2f out: sn rdn and edgd lft: hdd ins fnl f: sn no ex* **33/1**

4 3 **Sarafina (FR)**34 6567 4-8-11 0........ Christophe-PatriceLemaire 2 111
(A De Royer-Dupre, France) *hld up in tch: hdwy to trck ldrs whn nt clr run briefly wl over 1f out: sn rdn: kpt on same pce fnl f* **2/1**1

5 6 ¼ **Stately Victor (USA)**34 4-9-0 0........(b) MESmith 4 104
(Michael J Maker, U.S.A) *hld up on outside: struggling wl over 2f out: sn btn* **40/1**

6 hd **Midday**21 6861 5-8-11 0........ TomQueally 9 101
(Sir Henry Cecil) *trckd ldrs on ins: drvn over 2f out: wknd over 1f out* **6/1**

7 ¾ **Await The Dawn (USA)**80 5183 4-9-0 0........ JRLeparoux 6 102
(A P O'Brien, Ire) *led at stdy gallop on ins: rdn and hdd 2f out: wknd appr fnl f* **7/1**

8 5 ¼ **Teaks North (USA)**84 5076 4-9-0 0........(b) JJCastellano 5 94
(Justin Sallusto, U.S.A) *t.k.h: hld up in tch on ins: n.m.r briefly over 2f out: sn rdn and btn* **33/1**

9 1 **Dean's Kitten (USA)**35 6548 4-9-0 0........(b) RADominguez 3 92
(Michael J Maker, U.S.A) *t.k.h: trckd ldr: rdn and ev ch 2f out: sn wknd* **14/1**

2m 28.85s (148.85)
WFA 3 from 4yo+ 6lb **9 Ran SP% 114.0**
PARI-MUTUEL (all including $2 stakes): WIN 15.60; PLACE (1-2) 7.20, 5.00; SHOW (1-2-3) 5.40, 4.20, 7.00; SF 76.20.
Owner D Smith, Mrs J Magnier, M Tabor **Bred** Barton Bloodstock & Villiers Synd **Trained** Ballydoyle, Co Tipperary

FOCUS
The one race on the card that can generally be relied on to be dominated by European-trained horses and St Nicholas Abbey led home a 1-2 for the visitors this time around.

NOTEBOOK
St Nicholas Abbey(IRE) wasn't sure to appreciate this tight track, but one of his most impressive wins to date came at Chester earlier this year, when he quickened away for a wide-margin win, and clearly connections had no fear that he would lack the acceleration needed, as he was dropped in, while his stablemate Await The Dawn took up pacemaking duties in a race where there was no obvious front-runner. Saving ground towards the inside, the only moment of worry for him was when it looked as if he might be denied a clear run turning in, but once switched out he quickened in tremendous style and won with ease. He's always had the potential to be top class (champion 2yo in his day) and could well improve again if kept in training as a 5yo, although one wonders how much he was aided by the use of Lasix here. His rider Joseph O'Brien (18), who rode a cool race, became the youngest jockey to win at the Breeders' Cup.
Sea Moon was slow out of the gates and trailed the field early, but he made good headway around the turn into the straight and was well placed turning in. He picked up well when Ryan Moore asked him to quicken but nowhere near as well as the winner, who flew past him on the outside. This was just his sixth career start and, knowing what we do about Sir Michael Stoute's record with older horses, he looks an exciting prospect for next season, when all the top 1m4f races should be open to him.
Brilliant Speed(USA), third in the Belmont Stakes earlier in the year, has since won a Grade 3 and finished runner-up to Jeremy Noseda's Western Aristocrat in a Grade 1 on turf. That latter race was over 1m1f and the return to the Belmont distance saw him improve and deny the Europeans the trifecta.
Sarafina(FR) looked to be going well enough turning in but, when required to make her move, her trademark turn of foot was missing. The Arc had been her big target all season and this was clearly something of an afterthought. Coupled with the race coming at the end of a long season, she can be excused being below her best.
Stately Victor(USA), held up in rear, was outpaced leaving the back straight and merely plugged on past a few beaten horses late on.
Midday, runner-up in the Filly & Mare Turf here last year, played up a bit beforehand. She's had a long, hard season, and this was clearly not her true form. A tough and consistent mare at the top level (winner of six Group/Grade 1 races), she's likely to retire to the paddocks now.
Await The Dawn(USA) was apparently lucky to survive an illness after disappointing at York in August. This was a tough race in which to make his return, and he shouldn't be judged too harshly.

7306a GREY GOOSE BREEDERS' CUP JUVENILE (GRADE 1) (2YO COLTS & GELDINGS) (DIRT) 1m 110y(D)

9:25 (9:28) 2-Y-O **£692,307** (£230,769; £126,923; £76,923; £38,461)

RPR

1 **Hansen (USA)**42 2-8-10 0........(b) RADominguez 5 120
(Michael J Maker, U.S.A) *mde all at decent gallop: rdn 2f out: hld on gamely u.p fnl f* **8/1**3

2 hd **Union Rags (USA)**28 6718 2-8-10 0........ JJCastellano 10 120+
(Michael Matz, U.S.A) *midfield on outside: hdwy over 2f out: chsng wnr whn rdn and veered both ways fr over 1f out: kpt on wl u.p fnl f: jst hld* **7/4**1

3 1 **Creative Cause (USA)**35 6553 2-8-10 0........(b) JRosario 7 118
(Mike Harrington, U.S.A) *trckd ldrs: effrt and disp 2nd pl over 2f out to over 1f out: sn drvn and edgd lft: kpt on fnl f* **6/1**2

4 5 **Dullahan (USA)**28 6720 2-8-10 0........ KDesormeaux 2 108
(Dale Romans, U.S.A) *bhd and sn outpcd: hdwy whn plenty to do over 1f out: hung lft u.p and styd on wl fnl f: nvr able to chal* **16/1**

5 nk **Take Charge Indy (USA)**28 6720 2-8-10 0........(b) JamesGraham 1 107
(Patrick Byrne, U.S.A) *midfield on ins: hdwy and prom over 2f out: outpcd fr over 1f out* **33/1**

6 2 ¼ **Crusade (USA)**28 6688 2-8-10 0........ JRLeparoux 3 103
(A P O'Brien, Ire) *s.i.s: bhd and outpcd: hdwy u.p 2f out: kpt on fnl f: nvr on terms* **14/1**

7 ½ **Fort Loudon (USA)**21 2-8-10 0........(b) LJurado 12 102
(Stanley I Gold, U.S.A) *t.k.h: in tch on outside: struggling over 2f out: hung lft and wknd over 1f out* **33/1**

8 2 **Optimizer (USA)**28 6720 2-8-10 0........(b1) RAlbarado 13 98
(D Wayne Lukas, U.S.A) *s.i.s: hld up: hdwy towards ins into midfield 1/2-way: rdn over 2f out: hung lft and wknd over 1f out* **33/1**

9 ½ **Speightscity (USA)**64 2-8-10 0........ CNakatani 8 97
(Gary Contessa, U.S.A) *trckd ldr to 2f out: sn rdn: wknd over 1f out* **33/1**

10 6 ½ **Drill (USA)**35 6553 2-8-10 0........ MGarcia 4 84
(Bob Baffert, U.S.A) *sn bhd on outside: struggling wl over 3f out: nvr on terms* **10/1**

11 1 ¼ **Alpha (USA)**28 6718 2-8-10 0........ GKGomez 9 81
(Kiaran McLaughlin, U.S.A) *t.k.h in midfield: drvn and outpcd over 3f out: btn fnl 2f* **12/1**

12 hd **Daddy Long Legs (USA)**42 6336 2-8-10 0........ RyanMoore 11 81
(A P O'Brien, Ire) *s.i.s: bhd and outpcd: lost tch fr 3f out: t.o* **6/1**2

13 ¾ **Prospective (USA)**27 2-8-10 0........ LContreras 6 80
(Mark Casse, Canada) *t.k.h in midfield: angled to outside after 3f: struggling wl over 2f out: sn btn* **33/1**

1m 44.44s (0.07) **13 Ran SP% 120.1**
PARI-MUTUEL (all including $2 stakes): WIN 16.20; PLACE (1-2) 6.60, 3.20; SHOW (1-2-3) 4.60, 2.20, 3.60; SF 46.20.
Owner Kendall Hansen MD & Sky Chai Racing **Bred** Dr Kendall Hansen **Trained** USA

FOCUS
The winner made all, going 23.26 for the first quarter, 47.39 for the half and 1:12.24 at the six-furlong point.

NOTEBOOK
Hansen(USA) was hard to assess after two wide-margin wins in relatively minor company on Polytrack at Turfway Park, but he had no problems handling dirt and proved himself an extremely talented colt. He was, however, helped by the favourite suffering a wide trip and he lacks the size of some of these.
Union Rags(USA), who came here after taking the Champagne Stakes, surely would have won had he not endured such a wide trip. That said, he might still have been good enough had he not wandered around a bit under pressure. He might not be the superstar that people were hoping for, but he has the scope to make an even better older horse.
Creative Cause(USA) held a good position throughout and there seemed to be no excuses. However, it might be worth noting he was kicked by a lead horse during the week.
Dullahan(USA), back on dirt after winning a Grade 1 on synthetics, made up significant ground in the straight. It remains to be seen whether this is his ideal surface, but he looks a colt with an extremely bright future.
Take Charge Indy(USA) ran a fine race considering this was his first try on dirt.
Crusade(USA), who used Lasix, never had a chance on his dirt debut after missing the break, and anyway the trip didn't seem to suit. He's sprint bred.
Daddy Long Legs(USA), who also used Lasix, never looked like adding to his Royal Lodge win. He seemed to be climbing a bit early on, not facing the kickback, and seemingly didn't take to the surface.

7307a TVG BREEDERS' CUP MILE (GRADE 1) (3YO+) (TURF) 1m (T)

10:07 (10:09) 3-Y-O+ **£692,307** (£230,769; £126,923; £76,923; £38,461)

RPR

1 **Court Vision (USA)**48 6204 6-9-0 0........(b) RAlbarado 9 123
(Dale Romans, U.S.A) *hld up and bhd: gd hdwy on outside wl over 1f out: edgd lft and led last 100yds: kpt on wl u.p: jst hld on* **50/1**

2 nse **Turallure (USA)**48 6204 4-9-0 0........ JRLeparoux 13 123
(Charles Lopresti, U.S.A) *hld up and bhd: gd hdwy on wd outside wl over 1f out: sn rdn: edgd lft and kpt on wl towards fin: jst failed* **12/1**

3 1 **Goldikova (IRE)**34 6566 6-8-11 0........ OlivierPeslier 1 118+
(F Head, France) *trckd ldrs on ins: effrt and swtchd rt over 1f out: qcknd to ld 1f out: drvn and hdd last 100yds: hld towards fin* **5/4**1

4 1 ½ **Gio Ponti (USA)**28 6721 6-9-0 0........ RADominguez 5 117
(Christophe Clement, U.S.A) *hld up on ins: hdwy whn rdn and edgd lft over 1f out: kpt on fnl f: no imp towards fin* **9/1**

5 2 **Mr. Commons (USA)**27 3-8-11 0........ MESmith 4 112
(John Shirreffs, U.S.A) *t.k.h: in tch: effrt and rdn on outside whn blkd wl over 1f out: edgd lft and one pce fnl f* **33/1**

6 1 **Sidney's Candy (USA)**28 6721 4-9-0 0........ JRVelazquez 10 110
(Todd Pletcher, U.S.A) *cl up: rdn and led 2f out: sn edgd lft: hdd 1f out: btn last 100yds* **28/1**

7 *nk* **Jeranimo (USA)**[27] 5-9-0 0 MGarcia 7 110
(Michael Pender, U.S.A) *pressed ldr: effrt and disp ld 2f out: wknd ins fnl f* **33/1**

8 *1¼* **Byword**[35] 6558 5-9-0 0 MaximeGuyon 8 107
(A Fabre, France) *midfield: effrt and pushed along whn n.m.r briefly 2f out: no imp fnl f* **8/1**[3]

9 *2½* **Zoffany (IRE)**[28] 6721 3-8-11 0 RyanMoore 2 100
(A P O'Brien, Ire) *hld up: rdn and hdwy on ins whn nt clr run briefly and blkd over 1f out: sn no imp* **18/1**

10 *½* **Strong Suit (USA)**[28] 6687 3-8-11 0 RichardHughes 11 99
(Richard Hannon) *stdd s: hld up: effrt towards outside whn nt clr run wl over 1f out: sn btn* **13/2**[2]

11 *2½* **Compliance Officer (USA)**[14] 5-9-0 0 (b) ASolis 12 94
(Bruce R Brown, U.S.A) *in tch on outside: effrt over 2f out: checked wl over 1f out: sn wknd* **40/1**

12 *5½* **Get Stormy (USA)**[28] 6721 5-9-0 0 GKGomez 6 81
(Thomas Bush, U.S.A) *led to 2f out: sn rdn and wknd: eased whn btn fnl f* **33/1**

13 *3* **Courageous Cat (USA)**[48] 6204 5-9-0 0 PValenzuela 3 74
(William Mott, U.S.A) *t.k.h: prom: pushed along whn hmpd wl over 1f out: sn bmpd and lost pl: eased* **12/1**

1m 37.05s (2.22)
WFA 3 from 4yo+ 2lb **13** Ran SP% **116.2**
PARI-MUTUEL (all including $2 stakes): WIN 131.60; PLACE (1-2) 48.60, 10.00; SHOW (1-2-3) 21.40, 7.00, 2.40; SF 1,979.60.
Owner Spendthrift Farm LLC **Bred** W S Farish & Kilroy Thoroughbred Partnership **Trained** USA

NOTEBOOK
Court Vision(USA) benefited from being held up in a race run at a strong early gallop. The outsider of the entire field, he was beaten 2l into fifth in this race last year and hadn't shown a great deal earlier this season (only seventh behind Turallure in the Woodbine Mile last time), but he finished well from off the pace and held on by the narrowest of margins at the line.
Turallure(USA) showed when taking the Grade 1 Woodbine Mile last time out that he has a fast finish in him, and this race set up perfectly for his style of running. Closing widest and latest of all, he was in front a stride after the line.
Goldikova(IRE) was attempting to notch a record fourth success at the Breeders' Cup, and despite having tasted defeat more regularly this year than has been the case in past seasons, her trainer was confident beforehand that she was as good as ever. Being drawn in stall one was a potential problem but she broke well and held her position on the rail into the first turn. Things got very tight turning into the straight, though, and when Peslier angled her out, she hampered Courageous Cat, who in turn hampered Byword and forced Strong Suit to be snatched up. She picked up well to take the measure of the leaders but the early fractions, which she raced with, had been too strong, and she was cut down close home by a couple of rivals who had been held up in rear. The interference she caused would have normally seen her disqualified, but the stewards, in what appeared an act of kindness, let the result stand. The winner of 14 Group/Grade 1 races, she retires to the paddocks as one of the greatest racemares of all time.
Gio Ponti(USA) got trapped with little room to play with turning in, and the winner crossed in front of him half a furlong out, which didn't help. He posted a sound effort, though, and is just a thoroughly consistent performer in this type of event.
Mr. Commons(USA), who has yet to win in Graded company, did best of the three 3yos in the race. He was caught a little wider than ideal, so didn't run badly considering his inexperience, and he could well be the type to return next year and do even better; his sire Artie Schiller won this race as a 4yo in 2005.
Sidney's Candy(USA) paid for chasing the strong gallop set by Get Stormy and he hit the wall with a furlong to run.
Byword should have been suited by the strong gallop as he was dropping back in distance from 1m2f, but things got a bit tight for him rounding the turn into the straight and then, just as he went for a run between horses on straightening up, the gap closed on him quickly and his momentum was halted. Any chance he had was lost there, but in an ideal world he needs a bit further than this.
Zoffany(IRE) had been disappointing in his previous two starts, including when running a shocker on his last visit to America. It was suggested by Aidan O'Brien that the colt may have had a bad reaction to first-time Lasix on that occasion, but he was on the medication again here. Held up out the back along with the winner and runner-up, the race was set up for a closer like him, so his tame finish, albeit having been hampered, suggests he might have a problem.
Strong Suit(USA), who had his stamina to prove over this longer trip, was poorly drawn. Keen early, he got bumped and lost his footing momentarily heading to the first bend. Caught wide afterwards, he was struggling to pick up when snatched up to avoid trouble early in the straight. Richard Hughes reported that the colt wasn't happy on the loose ground.
Courageous Cat(USA), who was narrowly beaten by Turallure in the Woodbine Mile last time out, was taken out when Olivier Peslier switched Goldikova sharply right early in the straight. His race was immediately over at that point.

7308a BREEDERS' CUP CLASSIC (GRADE 1) (3YO+) (DIRT) 1m 2f (D)
11:00 (11:03) 3-Y-O+ **£1,730,769** (£576,923; £317,307; £192,307; £96,153)

RPR

1 **Drosselmeyer (USA)**[35] 6552 4-9-0 0 MESmith 2 126
(William Mott, U.S.A) *sn wl bhd: pushed along and plenty to do over 2f out: gd hdwy on outside over 1f out: styd on strly u.p: led towards fin* **20/1**

2 *1½* **Game On Dude (USA)**[34] 6570 4-9-0 0 (b) ChantalSutherland 7 123
(Bob Baffert, U.S.A) *led: hrd pressed and rdn fr over 2f out: edgd lft u.p ins fnl f: kpt on: hdd towards fin* **14/1**

3 *1* **Ruler On Ice (USA)**[42] 3-8-10 0 (b) GKGomez 3 121
(Kelly Breen, U.S.A) *sn wl bhd: drvn and hdwy nr ins over 1f out: edgd rt and kpt on strly fnl f: nt rch first two* **14/1**

4 *½* **Havre De Grace (USA)**[35] 6551 4-8-11 0 RADominguez 9 117
(J Larry Jones, U.S.A) *hld up in tch on outside: effrt and hrd rdn over 1f out: kpt on fnl f: nvr able to chal* **4/1**[1]

5 *hd* **Flat Out (USA)**[35] 6552 5-9-0 0 ASolis 1 120
(Charles L Dickey, U.S.A) *chsd main gp on outside: drvn along over 2f out: kpt on u.p fnl f: no imp towards fin* **4/1**[1]

6 *nk* **So You Think (NZ)**[21] 6861 5-9-0 0 (b) RyanMoore 4 119
(A P O'Brien, Ire) *t.k.h early: trckd ldrs: effrt and drvn on ins over 1f out: no ex ins fnl f* **4/1**[1]

7 *nk* **To Honor And Serve (USA)**[42] 3-8-10 0 JLezcano 12 118
(William Mott, U.S.A) *prom on outside: rdn and effrt 2f out: no ex u.p ins fnl f* **11/1**[3]

8 *½* **Ice Box (USA)**[35] 6552 4-9-0 0 CNakatani 5 117
(Nicholas Zito, U.S.A) *s.i.s: sn wl bhd: hdwy on wd outside over 1f out: sn rdn: no imp fnl f* **40/1**

9 *1¼* **Rattlesnake Bridge (USA)**[42] 3-8-10 0 CHBorel 6 115
(Kiaran McLaughlin, U.S.A) *t.k.h: sn last and detached: rdn over 2f out: edgd rt and styd on fnl f: nvr able to chal* **33/1**

10 *1½* **Uncle Mo (USA)**[35] 6550 3-8-10 0 JRVelazquez 11 112
(Todd Pletcher, U.S.A) *t.k.h: trckd ldr: rdn and ev ch over 2f out: wknd ins fnl f* **11/2**[2]

11 *nse* **Stay Thirsty (USA)**[35] 6552 3-8-10 0 JJCastellano 8 112
(Todd Pletcher, U.S.A) *trckd ldrs: rdn over 2f out: edgd lft and wknd over 1f out* **14/1**

12 *¾* **Headache (USA)**[28] 5-9-0 0 (b) PLopez 10 110
(Michael J Maker, U.S.A) *hld up bhd ldng gp on outside: drvn along and hung rt bnd ent st: sn wknd* **40/1**

2m 4.27s (3.08)
WFA 3 from 4yo+ 4lb **12** Ran SP% **116.3**
PARI-MUTUEL (all including $2 stakes): WIN 31.60; PLACE (1-2) 13.20, 13.60; SHOW (1-2-3) 8.80, 9.20, 9.80; SF 444.80.
Owner WinStar Farm LLC **Bred** Aaron U Jones & Marie D Jones **Trained** USA

FOCUS
Having threatened for much of the season to be one of the less memorable runnings of the Classic, the race ultimately attracted some star names in Havre De Grace, So You Think and Uncle Mo. However, all three had something to prove and as it turned out they all flopped meaning it was indeed a forgettable contest. The opening sectionals were 23.61, 47.84 and 1:12.82 - a fair gallop that didn't favour a particular run style.

NOTEBOOK
Drosselmeyer(USA) had a setback after winning last year's Belmont Stakes (form worked out really well) and had struggled to rediscover his best since returning. However, he recorded a career-best Beyer speed figure when runner-up in the Jockey Club Gold Cup last time and built on that to record a victory that would have seemed most unlikely when he was switched to turf (failed to beat a rival) as recently as August. The surface was riding on the slow side and that meant his stamina was a key asset. Interestingly, Drosselmeyer had Mike Smith aboard for the first time since his Belmont Stakes triumph and full credit to the rider for gaining some sort of redemption 12 months on from Zenyatta's agonising defeat in this race. It was reported beforehand that this was to be the winner's last race.
Game On Dude(USA), fourth to Drosselmeyer in that aforementioned Belmont Stakes, ran a really game race from the front. He looked in serious trouble when joined by Uncle Mo leaving the back straight, but just kept finding for pressure.
Ruler On Ice(USA) was another suited by the stamina test, but he got going too late.
Havre De Grace(USA), who came here instead of sticking against her own sex in the Ladies Classic, didn't run up to her best. The distance didn't seem an issue as she kept plugging away, but she never threatened to muster the required pace. She may stay in training.
Flat Out(USA) was disappointing considering he had Drosselmeyer behind when taking the Jockey Club Gold Cup last time. His jockey got him unbalanced early in the straight and he didn't pick up well enough.
So You Think(NZ) had blinkers on for the first time since he raced in Australia, and also used Lasix for this dirt debut. He broke alertly and was well placed for much of the way, but he showed a high knee action in the straight and didn't seem to be getting over the surface all that efficiently when under pressure. This was also the end of a long season. He stays in training and might be dropped back to 1m next year.
Uncle Mo(USA) came into the race with a far-from-ideal preparation for tackling a distance his breeding suggested would stretch him and he gradually faded in the straight after having his chance.
Stay Thirsty(USA) reverses his best for Saratoga.

7309a (Foreign Racing) - See Raceform Interactive

7218 FLEMINGTON (L-H)
Saturday, November 5
OFFICIAL GOING: Turf: good to soft changing to good

7310a QUEEN ELIZABETH STKS (GROUP 3 H'CAP) (3YO+) 1m 5f
5:30 (12:00) 3-Y-O+

£99,019 (£29,411; £14,705; £7,352; £4,084; £3,267)

RPR

1 **Ironstein (AUS)**[35] 6-8-7 0 (p) BrentonAvdulla 9 111+
(Gerald Ryan, Australia) **19/1**

2 *2¼* **Shootoff (NZ)**[21] 6886 4-9-0 0 (b) KerrinMcEvoy 6 117
(Graeme Rogerson, Australia) **17/2**[3]

3 *2¼* **Paddy O'Reilly (NZ)**[14] 7043 6-8-9 0 (vt) NashRawiller 3 106
(Robert Smerdon, Australia) **19/1**

4 *1* **Bauer (IRE)**[17] 6967 8-9-0 0 MichaelRodd 5 110
(Luca Cumani) *trckd ldrs on rail: 3rd and rdn 2f out: one pce fnl 1 1/2f* **11/10**[1]

5 *shd* **Anudjawun (NZ)**[7] 6-8-7 0 MarkZahra 8 103
(Shaun Dwyer, Australia) **12/1**

6 *¾* **Sahara Sun (CHI)**[10] 7115 4-8-10 0 (t) DwayneDunn 10 106
(Luca Cumani) *racd 5th on outside: hdwy to go 3rd appr 5f out: rdn and nt qckn 2f out: kpt on fnl f* **40/1**

7 *hd* **Montgomery (NZ)** 6-8-7 0 (t) PeterMertens 7 101
(Colin & Cindy Alderson, Australia) **30/1**

8 *1* **Back In Black (NZ)**[10] 7115 6-8-8 0 ow1 DannyNikolic 13 101
(John Steffert, New Zealand) **50/1**

9 *¾* **Macedonian (NZ)**[7] 6-8-8 0 (b) LukeNolen 2 100
(Peter G Moody, Australia) **11/2**[2]

10 *hd* **Boom 'n' Zoom (AUS)**[10] 7115 6-8-9 0 (b) CraigNewitt 1 100
(Ken Keys, Australia) **14/1**

11 *¾* **Home On A Wing (AUS)**[35] 5-8-7 0 (b) DeanYendall 4 97
(Anthony Cummings, Australia) **50/1**

12 *¾* **Raffaello (AUS)**[7] 7-8-8 0 (b) NikitaMcLean 11 97
(Patrick F Ryan, Australia) **40/1**

13 *1¾* **Tactic**[7] 5-8-8 0 (be) NicholasHall 12 94
(David Hayes, Australia) **100/1**

14 *3¾* **Spechenka (AUS)**[7] 6-8-7 0 ChrisMunce 14 88
(Ben Ahrens, Australia) **40/1**

2m 44.81s (164.81) **14** Ran SP% **113.3**
PARI-MUTUEL (NSW TAB - all including au$1 stakes): WIN 17.70 PLACE 3.70, 2.70, 4.70; DF 65.30; SF 205.80.
Owner I C Burford, Strawberry Hill Stud Syndicate et al **Bred** Strawberry Hill Stud **Trained** Australia

NOTEBOOK
Bauer(IRE) was well placed turning in but lacked a change of gear when it was required. He has been retired.
Sahara Sun(CHI) was caught one-paced and continues to disappoint.

The Form Book, Raceform Ltd, Compton, RG20 6NL

7045 SAN SIRO (R-H)
Saturday, November 5

OFFICIAL GOING: Turf: soft

7311a PREMIO CHIUSURA (GROUP 3) (2YO+) (TURF) 7f
3:05 (12:00) 2-Y-O+ £34,482 (£15,172; £8,275; £4,137)

RPR

1 **Konig Concorde (GER)**[25] 6783 6-9-4 0 FilipMinarik 6 110
(C Sprengel, Germany) *trckd ldrs: led 1/2-way: wnt clr over 2f: sn hrd rdn: r.o wl* 67/10

2 2 1/2 **Blu Constellation (ITY)**[112] 4121 3-9-4 0 MircoDemuro 4 104
(Vittorio Caruso, Italy) *hld up towards rr: hdwy to chse wnr over 2f out: ev ch appr fnl f: sn rdn: nt qckn: eased whn hld cl home* 4/6[1]

3 1 1/2 **Exciting Life (IRE)**[33] 6594 3-9-4 0 AStarke 3 100
(P Schiergen, Germany) *hld up in rr: tk clsr order 1/2-way: hrd rdn and tk 3rd ins fnl 2f: kpt on u.p fnl f: nvr on terms* 161/10

4 3 **Stark Danon (FR)**[48] 3-9-6 0 ASuborics 9 94
(W Hickst, Germany) *w.w towards rr: midfield on outside 2 1/2f out: effrt 1 1/2f out: sn rdn: one pce fnl f* 59/10[3]

5 3 1/2 **Smooth Operator (GER)**[20] 6906 5-9-8 0 (b) THellier 1 85
(Mario Hofer, Germany) *hld up in midfield on ins: outpcd over 2f out: sn rdn and kpt on at one pce: nvr in contention* 39/10[2]

6 4 **Le Big (GER)**[13] 7048 7-9-4 0 CristianDemuro 5 71
(U Stoltefuss, Germany) *racd keenly in midfield: wnt 3rd over 2f out: sn rdn and nt qckn: wknd nring fnl f* 113/10

7 10 **Bohemian Rhap (IRE)** 2-7-12 0 FBossa 10 45
(B Grizzetti, Italy) *chsd ldrs: rdn and dropped away qckly fr over 2f out* 37/1

8 hd **Abaton**[20] 6905 5-9-4 0 SUrru 2 43
(Vittorio Caruso, Italy) *led: hdd 1/2-way: sn rdn: wknd fr 2f out: eased fnl f* 4/6[1]

9 4 **Laddove (ITY)**[146] 4-9-4 0 DarioVargiu 7 32
(M Gasparini, Italy) *pressed ldr: lost pl over 2f out: rdn and wknd fnl 1 1/2f* 33/1

10 2 **Paris To Peking (ITY)**[153] 3-9-1 0 UmbertoRispoli 8 25
(S Botti, Italy) *tk a gd hold in midfield: rdn and no imp 2 1/2f out: wknd fnl 1 1/2f* 156/10

1m 35.4s (7.20)
WFA 2 from 3yo 21lb 3 from 4yo+ 1lb 10 Ran SP% 193.4
WIN (incl. 1 euro stake): 7.68. PLACES: 1.92, 1.23, 2.69. DF: 5.89.
Owner Wolfgang Frohlich **Bred** Gestut Elsetal **Trained** Germany

LE CROISE-LAROCHE
Saturday, November 5

OFFICIAL GOING: Turf: very soft

7312a PRIX DE WEPPES (CLAIMER) (2YO) (TURF) 1m 1f
4:05 (12:00) 2-Y-O £6,465 (£2,586; £1,939; £1,293; £646)

RPR

1 **Lady Jourdain (IRE)**[19] 6925 2-9-7 0 HarryBentley 6 71
(Mrs K Burke) *broke wl: racd cl 2nd: gng wl: rdn ent st: u.p to take ld 1f out: r.o wl* 19/5[2]

2 3/4 **Inches Away (FR)**[19] 6925 2-8-8 0 (b) TheoBachelot 2 56
(S Wattel, France) 15/2[3]

3 1/2 **Super Du Wal (FR)**[50] 2-8-11 0 (b[1]) SylvainRuis 7 58
(S Jesus, France) 24/1

4 1 1/2 **Valensole (FR)**[46] 2-8-13 0 BriceRaballand 12 57
(P Lacroix, France) 13/1

5 3/4 **Medibah (FR)**[18] 2-8-8 0 StephanePasquier 14 51
(D Wattel, France) 15/2[3]

6 4 **Bouncing Lily (FR)**[19] 6925 2-9-3 0 ChristopheSoumillon 8 51
(C Boutin, France) 23/10[1]

7 1 **Sherky (FR)**[17] 2-8-10 0 EddyHardouin[(6)] 13 48
(Robert Collet, France) 12/1

8 1/2 **My Tendresse (FR)**[19] 6925 2-8-7 0 (b[1]) FlavienMasse[(6)] 10 44
(P Demercastel, France) 67/1

9 3/4 **Primo Paco (FR)**[50] 2-8-8 0 ThibaultSpeicher[(8)] 11 46
(M Boutin, France) 30/1

10 6 **Vaiara (FR)**[162] 2-8-5 0 MatthieuAutier[(3)] 1 25
(P Lacroix, France) 62/1

0 **Victoria Lagrange (FR)**[19] 6925 2-8-8 0 (p) TonyPiccone 3 —
(C Lerner, France) 10/1

0 **Birdie For Diki (GER)** 2-9-2 0 (p) DavidBreux 4 —
(R Rohne, Germany) 11/1

0 **Fleur De General (FR)** 2-8-13 0 SHellyn 5 —
(R Roels, Germany) 75/1

2m 1.30s (121.30) 13 Ran SP% 118.5
WIN (incl. 1 euro stake): 4.80. PLACES: 2.40, 2.60, 5.40. DF: 22.30. SF: 39.00.
Owner Mrs Elaine M Burke **Bred** Tally-Ho Stud **Trained** Middleham Moor, North Yorks

7313a GRAND PRIX DU NORD (LISTED RACE) (3YO) (TURF) 1m 2f 110y
5:05 (12:00) 3-Y-O £23,706 (£9,482; £7,112; £4,741; £2,370)

RPR

1 **Colombian (IRE)**[12] 7053 3-9-2 0 ChristopheSoumillon 3 109
(John Gosden) *broke wl: sn led: gng easily: set mod pce: rdn 1 1/2f out: sn wnt clr: eased down fnl 50yds: easily* 1/1[1]

2 3 **Simba (FR)**[25] 6783 3-9-2 0 TonyPiccone 7 103
(C Lerner, France) 23/1

3 1 **Mighty Mouse (GER)**[34] 3-9-2 0 DPorcu 9 101
(P Vovcenko, Germany) 39/1

4 1/2 **Petit Chevalier (FR)**[16] 7114 3-9-2 0 ThierryThulliez 8 100
(W Baltromei, Germany) 31/1

5 1 1/2 **Staros (IRE)**[29] 6686 3-9-2 0 Pierre-CharlesBoudot 2 97
(E Lellouche, France) 13/2

6 6 **War Is War (IRE)**[28] 6709 3-9-2 0 MickaelBarzalona 1 85
(E J O'Neill, France) 15/1

7 shd **Un Jour (FR)**[53] 3-8-13 0 SebastienMaillot 6 82
(Mlle Valerie Boussin, France) 5/1[2]

8 nse **Rich Coast**[30] 3-9-2 0 StephanePasquier 4 85
(P Bary, France) 58/10[3]

9 8 **Signorella**[178] 3-8-13 0 GregoryBenoist 5 67
(M Delzangles, France) 11/1

2m 18.6s (138.60) 9 Ran SP% 119.1
WIN (incl. 1 euro stake): 2.00. PLACES: 1.50, 4.10, 7.00. DF: 26.70. SF: 26.80.
Owner H R H Princess Haya Of Jordan **Bred** Smythson **Trained** Newmarket, Suffolk

NOTEBOOK
Colombian(IRE), beaten at odds-on last time, enjoyed the run of things and finally gained reward for some consistent efforts in good company this year.

7314a PRIX DE DOUAI (CLAIMER) (4YO+) (LADY RIDERS) (TURF) 1m 1f
6:15 (12:00) 4-Y-O+ £5,603 (£2,241; £1,681; £1,120; £560)

RPR

1 **El Abrego (GER)** 5-9-7 0 MllePaulineBoisgontier 15 74
(A Wohler, Germany) 3/1[1]

2 4 **Barosch (IRE)** 5-9-3 0 (p) MlleMarieRollando[(4)] 12 66
(Mario Hofer, Germany) 16/1

3 1/2 **Fitz**[40] 6411 5-9-7 0 MlleDelphineGarcia-Dubois 6 65
(Matthew Salaman) *bkmarker fr s: mde gd prog towards end of bk st: u.p over 1 1/2f out: r.o fnl f* 9/1

4 3/4 **Barreq (USA)**[470] 4339 4-9-11 0 MlleJadeyPietrasiewicz 4 67
(Mario Hofer, Germany) 9/2[2]

5 snk **Glamour Profession (IRE)**[58] 4-9-11 0 MmeAngelinaBatist 7 67
(Mme J Hendriks, Holland) 16/1

6 1 **Hot Spot (FR)**[22] 7-9-11 0 MissMPlat 10 65
(S Cerulis, France) 6/1[3]

7 1/2 **Centeo (SPA)**[192] 6-9-7 0 MlleStephanieHusser 14 60
(L De Clerck, France) 20/1

8 1 **The Desert Saint**[9] 5-9-0 0 (p) MlleCamillePeltier[(4)] 13 55
(B Dutruel, France) 23/1

9 8 **Kite Hunter (IRE)**[68] 4-9-7 0 (p) MlleBlancheDeGranvilliers 11 41
(C Boutin, France) 11/1

10 nk **Spirit Of Music (FR)**[1209] 8-9-3 0 (b) MmeSophieGillet[(4)] 5 40
(D Considerant, Belgium) 46/1

0 **Manjam (IRE)**[111] 1139 7-9-0 0 (b[1]) MlleMarieArtu[(4)] 8 —
(Braem Horse Racing Sprl, Belgium) 41/1

0 **Bold Marc (IRE)**[15] 7015 9-9-6 0 MissRachelKing 1 —
(Mrs K Burke) *broke wl to ld: clr ent st: sn rdn: hdd over 1f out: wknd qckly* 14/1

0 **Giant Generation (GER)**[18] 7-10-0 0 MmeCatherineRieb-Menard 9 —
(G Martin, Austria) 21/1

0 **Nice Land (GER)**[64] 7-9-4 0 (b) MlleHeleneCorcoral 2 —
(Frau P Bastiaens-Vancauwenbergh, Germany) 14/1

1m 58.0s (118.00) 14 Ran SP% 118.9
WIN (incl. 1 euro stake): 4.00. PLACES: 1.70, 4.70, 3.10. DF: 37.30. SF: 67.00.
Owner Hannes K Gutschow **Bred** H K Gutschow **Trained** Germany

7315a PRIX HECTOR FRANCHOMME (H'CAP) (4YO+) (TURF) 5f 110y
6:55 (12:00) 4-Y-O+ £6,896 (£2,758; £2,068; £1,379; £689)

RPR

1 **Lisselan Hurricane (USA)**[115] 5-8-8 0 StephaneLaurent[(3)] 14 67
(Y Marie-Nelly, France) 32/1

2 nk **Salut Thomas (FR)**[28] 9-8-4 0 (b) SylvainRuis 8 59
(M Boutin, France) 3/1[1]

3 1 1/2 **La Biriquina (USA)**[71] 6-8-4 0 (p) FlavienPrat 9 54
(T Doumen, France) 13/1

4 nse **Swans A Swimming (IRE)**[17] 6959 5-8-11 0 GaetanMasure 6 61
(Stal Garbo, Belgium) 30/1

5 1/2 **Ceodora (GER)**[28] 6-9-6 0 (p) ChristopheSoumillon 12 68
(P Monfort, France) 19/5[2]

6 1 1/2 **Quambona (FR)**[212] 7-8-7 0 (b) MlleChloeSuain 4 50
(Ecurie'T Heyveld, Belgium) 35/1

7 2 1/2 **Kielder (IRE)**[36] 4-9-0 0 (b) AurelienLemaitre 10 49
(Braem Horse Racing Sprl, Belgium) 15/1

8 shd **Raj Love Royale (FR)**[9] 6-8-0 0 JeromeClaudic 13 35
(J Phelippon, France) 9/1

9 3/4 **Postsprofit (IRE)**[115] 7-8-0 0 DavidBreux 15 32
(Mme A-M Verschueren, France) 13/1

10 1/2 **Roi Dana (FR)**[746] 6-8-0 0 DelphineSantiago 5 31
(R Ducasteele, France) 83/10[3]

0 **Rogalt (IRE)**[33] 6593 5-9-6 0 (b) SHellyn 11 —
(R Houthoofd, Belgium) 16/1

0 **Email Exit (IRE)**[36] 4-8-2 0 (b) MatthieuAutier 2 —
(C Plisson, France) 31/1

0 **Let It Rock (IRE)**[17] 6959 4-9-0 0 HarryBentley 3 —
(Mrs K Burke) *broke wl towards ins: racd bhd ldrs: rdn bef st: no ex u.p 1 1/2f out: sn wknd: dropped rt out: eased ins fnl f* 38/1

0 **Zenside (IRE)**[99] 5-8-5 0 (b) AlexisBadel 7 —
(Mlle A Voraz, France) 19/1

0 **Kaldougold (BEL)**[846] 3934 4-8-8 0 AnthonyDeau 1 —
(Andre Hermans, Belgium) 20/1

68.20 secs (68.20) 15 Ran SP% 117.5
WIN (incl. 1 euro stake): 32.50. PLACES: 8.20, 1.90, 4.00. DF: 42.00. SF: 131.40.
Owner Yann Marie-Nelly **Bred** Lisselan Farms & D C Blackburn **Trained** France

7316 - 7321a (Foreign Racing) - See Raceform Interactive

7184 LEOPARDSTOWN (L-H)
Sunday, November 6

OFFICIAL GOING: Yielding (yielding to soft in places)

7322a LEOPARDSTOWN NOVEMBER (PREMIER H'CAP) 2m
4:05 (4:07) 3-Y-O+
£31,034 (£9,827; £4,655; £1,551; £1,034; £517) Stalls Far side

RPR

1 **Hidden Universe (IRE)**[32] 6637 5-8-13 90 PJSmullen 4 94+
(D K Weld, Ire) *chsd ldrs: 5th 1/2-way: rdn 2f out: styd on to ld 1f out: kpt on wl u.p fnl f* 7/2[1]

2 3/4 **Pozyc (FR)**[8] 4568 5-8-4 81 oh2 NGMcCullagh 3 84
(W P Mullins, Ire) *mid-div: rdn into 6th 2f out: 4th 1f out: kpt on wl fnl f to press wnr cl home* 12/1

3 ½ **Highly Efficient**[21] 6900 3-8-4 90 oh1 .... BACurtis 12 92
(Thomas Mullins, Ire) *chsd ldrs: 2nd 1/2-way: impr to ld and dispute 3f out: rdn and hdd 1f out: kpt on fnl f: no ex cl home* **11/2**[3]

4 1 ¾ **Tawaagg**[21] 6900 7-7-13 81 oh2 .... CPHoban(5) 6 82
(W P Mullins, Ire) *mid-div: rdn in 7th 2f out: 5th 1f out: kpt on fnl f* **14/1**

5 hd **Dibella (IRE)**[167] 7141 4-7-11 81 oh7 .... MMMonaghan(7) 10 81
(Paul Nolan, Ire) *hld up towards rr: hdwy in 10th 3f out: rdn into cl 4th on inner 2f out: disp 1 1/2f out: hdd 1f out: no ex ins fnl f* **25/1**

6 2 ¾ **Rising Wind (IRE)**[28] 6734 3-8-5 91 .... CDHayes 11 88
(Kevin Prendergast, Ire) *mid-div: rdn in 10th 2f out: kpt on same pce fr over 1f out* **7/1**

7 hd **What A Charm (IRE)**[28] 6736 4-10-0 105 .... (p) JMurtagh 2 102
(John M Oxx, Ire) *led: disp 3f out: rdn in 2nd 2f out: no ex over 1f out* **7/1**

8 4 ¼ **Waydownsouth (IRE)**[23] 6856 4-9-1 99 .... DJBenson(7) 7 91
(Patrick J Flynn, Ire) *hld up towards rr: hdwy ent st: 9th 2f out: rdn and no ex over 1f out* **28/1**

9 2 ¾ **Pond Cottage (IRE)**[14] 7046 4-8-7 84 .... WMLordan 16 73
(Ms Joanna Morgan, Ire) *mid-div: rdn into 8th 2f out: no ex over 1f out* **16/1**

10 6 ½ **Domination**[18] 6966 4-8-4 81 oh3 .... (p) ShaneFoley 14 63
(C Byrnes, Ire) *mid-div: rdn into 8th 3f out: no ex st* **5/1**[2]

11 1 **Dayia (IRE)**[29] 6690 7-9-2 93 .... SeamieHeffernan 8 74
(Lydia Pearce) *chsd ldrs: 4th 1/2-way: rdn into cl 3rd on inner 2f out: no ex over 1f out: wknd* **20/1**

12 3 ¾ **Solo Performer (IRE)**[16] 7013 6-8-11 88 .... (b) KJManning 15 65
(H Rogers, Ire) *towards rr for most: nvr a factor* **25/1**

13 1 **Deutschland (USA)**[14] 7046 8-8-10 87 .... (t) GFCarroll 1 63
(W P Mullins, Ire) *towards rr for most: nvr a factor* **14/1**

14 ¾ **Whatuthink (IRE)**[14] 7046 9-8-6 83 .... SilvestreDeSousa 13 58
(Oliver McKiernan, Ire) *chsd ldrs: 3rd 1/2-way: rdn and wknd over 3f out* **16/1**

15 hd **Prince Chaparral (IRE)**[10] 6513 5-9-0 91 .... DMGrant 5 66
(Patrick J Flynn, Ire) *in rr of mid-div: rdn into 8th 2f out: no ex over 1f out and wknd* **14/1**

16 18 **Admiral Barry (IRE)**[28] 6734 6-9-5 96 .... DPMcDonogh 9 51
(Eoin Griffin, Ire) *chsd ldrs: 6th 1/2-way: wknd over 3f out: eased st* **16/1**

3m 35.63s (4.63) **Going Correction** +0.525s/f (Yiel)
WFA 3 from 4yo+ 9lb **16** Ran SP% **140.5**
Speed ratings: **109,108,108,107,107 106,105,103,102,99 98,96,96,95,95 86**
Daily Double: Not won. Pick Six: Not won. CSF £52.86 CT £251.66 TOTE £4.20: £1.70, £3.60, £2.20, £3.10; DF 54.60.
Owner Dr R Lambe **Bred** Moyglare Stud Farm Ltd **Trained** The Curragh, Co Kildare

NOTEBOOK
Hidden Universe(IRE) did not look a blot off 90 for this handicap debut but he justified his trainer's confidence with a game success. It sets him up nicely for a hurdling campaign. It would be wrong to say he travelled like a dream but he looked the likely winner before the 3f pole and came up the near side under Pat Smullen. Hidden Universe was strongly challenged in the closing stages but kept finding. Dermot Weld believes that two miles is also his hurdling trip but there must be every chance he gets further jumping. His best days in that sphere are likely yet to come. (op 7/2 tchd 3/1)
Pozyc(FR) ran a blinder and was staying on all the way to the line. He has developed into a useful dual-purpose type and one is tempted to say he is still favourably treated when he goes back hurdling.
Highly Efficient was a little keen stepped up to this trip and pulled his way to second at halfway. He stayed the trip pretty well and is likely to go hurdling shortly. Given that he was running off 90, he has a fair bit of jumping potential. (op 6/1 tchd 5/1)
Tawaagg, behind the third at Naas, ran a similar race and stayed the trip surprisingly well. He is another who will presumably go back jumping and connections will perhaps be tempted by another tilt at the MCR Hurdle.
Dibella(IRE), settled out the back, performed surprisingly well from 7lb out of the handicap. She should have races in her off 112 hurdling and is lightly raced. (op 33/1)
Rising Wind(IRE) never threatened but edged front-runner What A Charm for sixth. (op 9/1)
What A Charm(IRE) was probably found out by her big weight. (op 7/1 tchd 6/1)
T/Jkpt: Not won. T/Plt: @357.30. Pool of @20,189.99 - 42.38 winning tickets. II

7217 CAPANNELLE (R-H)
Sunday, November 6

OFFICIAL GOING: Turf: soft

7323a PREMIO RIBOT (GROUP 2) (3YO+) (TURF) 1m
2:40 (12:00) 3-Y-0+ **£60,344** (£26,551; £14,482; £7,241)

RPR

1 **Vanjura (GER)**[43] 6369 4-8-13 0 .... APietsch 9 109
(R Dzubasz, Germany) *trckd ldr: rdn to chal over 2f out: led ins fnl f: r.o* **11/10**[1]

2 1 **Emerald Commander (IRE)**[44] 6298 4-9-2 0 .... FrankieDettori 2 110
(Saeed Bin Suroor) *led at mod pce: rdn over 3f out: hdd ins fnl f: kpt on* **29/10**[2]

3 nk **Marcret (ITY)**[21] 6905 4-9-2 0 .... UmbertoRispoli 4 109
(S Botti, Italy) *hld up: hdwy on inner over 4f out: short of room and had to switch over 2f out: r.o ins fnl f: nvr nrr* **139/10**

4 2 **Regarde Moi**[14] 3-9-1 0 .... FabioBranca 8 106
(S Botti, Italy) *midfield: rdn over 3f out: kpt on but nt pce to chal* **13/2**

5 ½ **Indomito (GER)**[49] 6201 5-9-2 0 .... EPedroza 1 104
(A Wohler, Germany) *trckd ldrs: racd keenly: rdn wl over 4f out: outpcd ins fnl 2f: kpt on* **105/10**

6 10 **Passaggio (ITY)**[14] 3-9-1 0 .... APolli 6 82
(A Cascio, Italy) *hld up in rr: hdwy on outside over 4f out: rdn to chal over 3f out: wknd ins fnl 2f: wl hld* **26/1**

7 1 ½ **Ransom Hope**[14] 6-9-2 0 .... CristianDemuro 5 77
(L Riccardi, Italy) *hld up: rdn and no prog over 3f out: wknd* **83/10**

8 nse **Le Vie Infinite (IRE)**[21] 6905 4-9-2 0 .... DarioVargiu 3 77
(R Brogi, Italy) *trckd ldr: racd keenly: rdn and outpcd over 3f out: wknd and eased* **61/10**[3]

9 3 ½ **Turati**[189] 5-9-2 0 .... MircoDemuro 10 69
(E Botti, Italy) *hld up: rdn over 4f out: jockey looking down and eased over 2f out* **83/10**

10 3 ½ **Silver Arrow (ITY)**[107] 6-9-2 0 .... CFiocchi 7 61
(Maria Rita Salvioni, Italy) *midfield: rdn and lost pl wl over 4f out: steadily wknd and wl btn* **25/1**

1m 37.8s (-2.00)
WFA 3 from 4yo+ 2lb **10** Ran SP% **145.1**
WIN (incl. 1 euro stake): 2.10. PLACES: 1.10, 1.30, 1.80. DF: 5.90.
Owner M Barth **Bred** J-C Haimet & J-P Liberge **Trained** Germany

7324a PREMIO ROMA GBI RACING (GROUP 1) (3YO+) (TURF) 1m 2f
3:15 (12:00) 3-Y-0+ **£116,379** (£51,206; £27,931; £13,965)

RPR

1 **Zazou (GER)**[34] 6595 4-9-2 0 .... MickaelBarzalona 2 119
(W Hickst, Germany) *midfield: hdwy over 3f out: str run to ld 2f out: strly pressed ins fnl f: all out: jst hld on* **83/10**

2 shd **Rio De La Plata (USA)**[36] 6556 6-9-2 0 .... FrankieDettori 10 119+
(Saeed Bin Suroor) *hld up: hdwy on outer over 2f out: chsd clr ldr ins fnl f: kpt on: jst failed* **7/10**[1]

3 2 ½ **Voila Ici (IRE)**[21] 6907 6-9-2 0 .... MircoDemuro 1 114
(Vittorio Caruso, Italy) *hld up: rdn to chal 4f out: outpcd by ldng duo 2f out: kpt on ins fnl f to take 3rd last strides* **37/10**[2]

4 hd **Russian Tango (GER)**[34] 6595 4-9-2 0 .... EPedroza 4 114
(A Wohler, Germany) *trckd ldrs: rdn to chal 3f out: led ins fnl 2f: sn hdd and outpcd: kpt on ins fnl f: jst ct for 3rd* **93/10**

5 1 ¾ **Mawingo (GER)**[126] 3672 3-9-0 0 .... ADeVries 7 112
(J Hirschberger, Germany) *hld up: hdwy on inner over 3f out: outpcd over 2f out: kpt on* **77/10**[3]

6 2 ½ **Lindenthaler (GER)**[34] 6595 3-9-0 0 .... CristianDemuro 5 107
(P Schiergen, Germany) *trckd ldrs: 3rd and travelling wl ins fnl 4f: rdn over 2 1/2f out: grad wknd: kpt on again fnl 100yds* **17/1**

7 ½ **Lord Chaparral (IRE)**[21] 6907 4-9-2 0 .... DarioVargiu 6 104
(R Brogi, Italy) *led: rdn and hdd over 2f out: wknd ins fnl f* **12/1**

8 10 **Inorato (IRE)**[14] 3-9-0 0 .... UmbertoRispoli 8 86
(F & L Camici, Italy) *hld up in rr: rdn and no rspnse over 3f out: wknd and eased ins fnl 2f* **221/10**

9 8 **Branderburgo (IRE)**[36] 4-9-2 0 .... GBietolini 3 68
(L Riccardi, Italy) *trckd ldrs: lost pl over 3f out: wknd ins fnl 2f: eased rt down ins fnl f* **40/1**

(-123.30)
WFA 3 from 4yo+ 4lb **9** Ran SP% **132.1**
WIN (incl. 1 euro stake): 9.30. PLACES: 1.80, 1.10, 1.40. DF: 28.90.
Owner WH Sport International **Bred** Gestut Fahrhof **Trained** Germany

1433 KREFELD (R-H)
Sunday, November 6

OFFICIAL GOING: Turf: good

7325a GERMAN RACING - HERZOG VON RATIBOR-RENNEN (GROUP 3) (2YO) (TURF) 1m 110y
2:00 (2:10) 2-Y-0 **£27,586** (£9,482; £4,741; £2,586; £1,724)

RPR

1 **Pastorius (GER)**[42] 2-9-2 0 .... THellier 3 —
(Mario Hofer, Germany) *broke wl: settled 4th on ins: mde move ent st: r.o wl u.p in battle w black arrow: tk ld jst ins fnl f: r.o wl: comf* **2/1**[3]

2 1 ½ **Black Arrow (IRE)**[42] 2-9-2 0 .... JBojko 4 —
(A Wohler, Germany) *broke wl: racd bhd ldr: gd prog on turn into st: r.o wl u.p: battled w pastorius tl ins fnl f: r.o but a being hld by wnr* **8/5**[1]

3 1 ½ **Laeyos (GER)** 2-8-13 0 .... ThierryThulliez 1 —
(Markus Klug, Germany) *broke fast: sn led: set gd pce: led into st: r.o but hdd 1f out: no answer to first two* **76/10**

4 4 **Dabbitse (GER)** 2-8-13 0 .... AStarke 5 —
(C Zschache, Germany) *racd in 3rd: shkn up ent st but nt pce to go w ldrs: styd on one pce* **66/10**

5 2 **Energizer (GER)**[21] 6901 2-9-2 0 .... FilipMinarik 2 —
(J Hirschberger, Germany) *bkmarker fr s: threatened briefly ent st but sn rdn and wknd* **9/5**[2]

1m 50.95s (4.35) **5** Ran SP% **132.3**
WIN (incl. 10 euro stake): 30. PLACES: 14, 13. SF: 81.
Owner Stall Antanando **Bred** Franz Prinz Von Auersperg & Florian Haffa **Trained** Germany

7219 MAISONS-LAFFITTE (R-H)
Monday, November 7

OFFICIAL GOING: Turf: heavy

7326a PRIX PHARAMOND (CONDITIONS) (2YO) (TURF) 6f (S)
12:30 (12:00) 2-Y-0 **£12,500** (£5,000; £3,750; £2,500; £1,250)

RPR

1 **Paris Blue (FR)**[52] 2-9-2 0 .... MaximeGuyon 3 88
(J-L Pelletan, France) **13/5**[1]

2 ¾ **Fragment (IRE)**[30] 2-8-6 0 .... StephanePasquier 4 76
(R Pritchard-Gordon, France) **13/2**[3]

3 3 **Slipstick (IRE)**[20] 2-8-13 0 .... Pierre-CharlesBoudot 2 74
(J-M Capitte, France) **12/1**

4 3 ½ **Stormy Whatever (FR)**[5] 7238 2-8-13 0 .... FrederikTylicki 12 63
(James Given) *broke wl on wd outside: racd in 3rd: rdn to take ld 2 1/2f out: hdd 2f out: u.p but no ex 1 1/2f out: rallied ins fnl f to take 4th on line* **10/1**

5 snk **Portovino (FR)**[67] 2-8-9 0 .... ChristopheSoumillon 1 59
(E J O'Neill, France) **4/1**[2]

6 ¾ **Bonne Idee (FR)**[15] 2-8-13 0 .... ThierryJarnet 10 61
(F Head, France) **4/1**[2]

7 3 ½ **Sturmwolke (IRE)** 2-8-6 0 .... AndreBest 8 43
(M Figge, Germany) **8/1**

8 9 **Cattiva (FR)** 2-8-9 0 .... JeremyCrocquevieille 7 19
(Mme B Valenti, Spain) **19/1**

9 9 **Finisteria (FR)**[30] 2-8-6 0 .... (p) FabriceVeron 9 —
(Mme C Barande-Barbe, France) **35/1**

1m 17.8s (4.40) **9** Ran SP% **116.8**
WIN (incl. 1 euro stake): 3.60. PLACES: 1.50, 2.40, 2.70. DF: 13.90. SF: 24.10.
Owner Cecil Motschmann **Bred** Ecurie Des Monceaux & Skymarc Farm **Trained** France

The Form Book, Raceform Ltd, Compton, RG20 6NL

[7222]KEMPTON (A.W) (R-H)

Wednesday, November 9

OFFICIAL GOING: Standard

Wind: Light, half behind Weather: Fine

7327 FREE ENTRY FOR BETDAQ MEMBERS MEDIAN AUCTION MAIDEN STKS 1m 2f (P)

4:20 (4:21) (Class 6) 3-4-Y-O **£1,617** (£481; £240; £120) **Stalls** Low

Form RPR

1 **Camborne** 3-9-3 0 WilliamBuick 2 75+
(John Gosden) *s.i.s: pushed along in last early and rapid prog to chse ldr after 2f: shkn up to ld 2f out: rn green and jnd ins fnl f: rdn and fought on wl* **6/4**[1]

0 2 *hd* **Refractor (IRE)**[14] 7111 3-9-3 0 MartinLane 4 74
(James Fanshawe) *hld up in last pair: prog 3f out: hdwy to take 2nd jst over 1f out: rdn to chal and upsides ins fnl f: r.o but jst denied* **9/1**

5200 3 *8* **Grand Theft Equine**[8] 7204 3-9-3 73 EddieAhern 8 58
(Jim Boyle) *led: rdn and hdd 2f out: brushed aside fnl f* **10/3**[2]

3450 4 *2 1/4* **Corvette**[13] 7121 3-8-12 61 (v) ShaneKelly 7 48
(J R Jenkins) *prom: wl in tch in 3rd over 2f out: wknd over 1f out* **10/3**[2]

0400 5 *nse* **Rasteau (IRE)**[19] 7004 3-9-0 40 RyanClark(3) 3 53?
(Tom Keddy) *chsd ldrs: rdn over 3f out: outpcd over 2f out: nvr on terms after* **25/1**

00 6 *9* **Grand Sort**[28] 6804 3-9-3 0 FergusSweeney 6 35
(Tony Newcombe) *prom tl wknd wl over 2f out* **66/1**

0 7 *shd* **Dawn Story**[133] 3519 3-8-12 0 RobertHavlin 1 30
(Hughie Morrison) *a towards rr: struggling 3f out: sn wknd* **8/1**[3]

0 8 *3/4* **Turbulent Priest**[55] 6085 3-9-3 0 JamieGoldstein 9 33
(Zoe Davison) *s.i.s: sn in tch: rdn and wknd 3f out* **66/1**

0 9 *22* **Bondie**[8] 7207 3-8-12 0 RosieJessop(5) 5 —
(John Bridger) *sn struggling in last: lost tch 1/2-way: t.o* **66/1**

2m 6.69s (-1.31) **Going Correction** -0.10s/f (Stan) **9** Ran SP% **115.6**

Speed ratings (Par 101): **101,100,94,92,92 85,85,84,67**

toteswingers:1&2:£4.40, 2&3:£3.80, 1&3:£1.70 CSF £16.40 TOTE £2.80: £1.30, £3.70, £1.30; EX 11.30.

Owner H R H Princess Haya Of Jordan **Bred** Southill Stud **Trained** Newmarket, Suffolk

FOCUS

A weak maiden and the time was 1.98 seconds slower than the following Class 4 handicap, so it's hard to know exactly what the front two achieved in pulling so far clear but it was still a good effort from the winner. It was a race notable for a tremendously pro-active ride from the increasingly impressive William Buick.

7328 BETDAQ MULTIPLES H'CAP 1m 2f (P)

4:50 (4:50) (Class 4) (0-85,85) 3-Y-0+ **£4,075** (£1,212; £606; £303) **Stalls** Low

Form RPR

1206 1 **Mountain Range (IRE)**[54] 6130 3-9-3 **82** EddieAhern 5 92+
(John Dunlop) *hld up last: stl only 11th 3f out: gd prog fr 2f out: produced to ld 1f out: rdn and styd on wl* **8/1**

1005 2 *3/4* **Emerald Wilderness (IRE)**[23] 6922 7-9-4 **82** (p) JohnFahy(3) 9 90
(Robert Cowell) *dwlt: hld up in rr: sme prog on outer 4f out: drvn and hdwy wl over 1f out: c to chal 1f out: r.o but a hld* **16/1**

6400 3 *nse* **Ellemujie**[18] 7022 6-9-8 **83** (p) AdamKirby 3 91
(Dean Ivory) *patiently rdn in rr: stl there over 2f out: prog on outer over 1f out: drvn and styd on: nvr quite able to chal* **12/1**

01-0 4 *1 3/4* **Noguchi (IRE)**[19] 6989 6-9-6 **81** SebSanders 8 87
(Jeremy Noseda) *trckd ldrs: lost pl sltly fr 1/2-way: trapped bhd rivals 2f out on inner: nt clr run over 1f out: one pce whn in the clr fnl f* **3/1**[2]

3604 5 *nse* **Kidlat**[9] 7199 6-9-2 **77** IanMongan 6 81
(Alan Bailey) *rousted along fr s: chsd ldr after 2f tl 4f out: tried to hold pl after: drvn and effrt 2f out: cl up 1f out: outpcd* **20/1**

0100 6 *5* **Totally Ours**[19] 6996 4-9-8 **83** SteveDrowne 12 77
(William Muir) *prog arnd rivals to go prom after 4f: drvn wl over 1f out: sn wknd* **25/1**

2020 7 *hd* **If I Were A Boy (IRE)**[20] 6306 4-8-11 **72** (p) ShaneKelly 2 66
(Dominic Ffrench Davis) *led: hrd pressed over 2f out: hdd & wknd 1f out* **16/1**

4553 8 *2 1/4* **Young Dottie**[37] 6587 5-8-11 **77** JemmaMarshall(5) 1 67
(Pat Phelan) *trckd ldr 2f: styd handily plcd on inner: effrt 2f out: cl up jst over 1f out: wknd* **33/1**

5253 8 *dht* **Incendo**[19] 6989 5-9-10 **85** (t) MartinLane 7 75
(James Fanshawe) *prog to press ldr after 4f: drvn over 2f out: stl chalng over 1f out: sn wknd* **13/2**[3]

0000 10 *1 1/4* **Tinshu (IRE)**[23] 6922 5-9-6 **81** FergusSweeney 10 68
(Derek Haydn Jones) *prog arnd rivals to go prom after 4f: rdn over 2f out: wknd over 1f out* **16/1**

31-3 11 *1 1/2* **Auden (USA)**[8] 7204 3-9-2 **81** WilliamBuick 4 65
(Mahmood Al Zarooni) *prom: lost pl in general changing of pls after 4f: rdn 3f out: wknd 2f out* **11/8**[1]

1-55 12 *28* **Aurora Sky (IRE)**[12] 2156 5-8-13 **74** (t) LiamKeniry 11 —
(Liam Corcoran) *in tch to 4f out: sn wknd rapidly: t.o* **66/1**

2m 4.71s (-3.29) **Going Correction** -0.10s/f (Stan)

WFA 3 from 4yo+ 4lb **12** Ran SP% **129.9**

Speed ratings (Par 105): **109,108,108,106,106 102,102,100,100,99 98,76**

CSF £134.86 CT £1567.97 TOTE £5.20: £1.20, £4.90, £3.90; EX 131.60.

Owner Sir Philip Wroughton **Bred** Holborn Trust Co **Trained** Arundel, W Sussex

FOCUS

The lead was contested and the pace looked honest, with the first four finishers still in the second half of the field rounding the final bend. The time supports the visual impression, being 1.98 seconds quicker than the opening maiden, as well as the only race on the card to dip under standard. The favourite ran poorly, but this still looks good form for the grade.

7329 BACK AND LAY AT BETDAQ.COM E B F MAIDEN STKS (DIV I) 7f (P)

5:20 (5:21) (Class 5) 2-Y-0 **£2,846** (£847; £423; £211) **Stalls** Low

Form RPR

023 1 **Sheikh The Reins (IRE)**[19] 6991 2-9-3 81 SteveDrowne 5 75+
(John Best) *mde all: shkn up 2f out: edgd lft but kpt on fr over 1f out: a holding rivals* **5/4**[1]

00 2 *1/2* **Royal Prospector**[12] 7133 2-9-3 0 JimCrowley 11 74
(Richard Hannon) *sn chsd ldng pair: rdn over 2f out: wnt 2nd over 1f out: grad clsd nr fin: a hld* **10/1**

5 3 *3/4* **Typography**[19] 6992 2-9-3 0 SebSanders 8 72
(William Muir) *s.i.s: sn in midfield: rdn over 2f out: prog over 1f out: styd on and clsd on ldng pair fnl f: nvr able to chal* **7/1**

00 4 *1 1/2* **Poetry Writer**[51] 6214 2-9-3 0 NeilChalmers 9 68
(Michael Blanshard) *chsd ldrs: rdn over 2f out: effrt over 1f out: one pce fnl f* **33/1**

04 5 *nk* **Arch Villain (IRE)**[19] 6994 2-9-3 0 EddieAhern 2 67+
(Amanda Perrett) *settled in midfield: effrt over 2f out: prog and rdn over 1f out: kpt on same pce fnl f* **13/2**[3]

6 *1 1/2* **Glaisdale** 2-8-12 0 (b[1]) RobertHavlin 10 58
(James Toller) *dwlt: t.k.h and hld up in rr running green: pushed along over 2f out: kpt on steadily fr over 1f out* **25/1**

05 7 *3 1/2* **Sarah Berry**[12] 7132 2-8-12 0 AndreaAtzeni 6 49
(Chris Dwyer) *chsd wnr: rdn over 2f out: sltly checked over 1f out: wknd rapidly* **66/1**

30 8 *2 1/2* **Polydamos**[144] 3152 2-9-3 0 LukeMorris 7 48
(Harry Dunlop) *a towards rr: rdn and no prog over 2f out: n.d after* **7/2**[2]

0 9 *7* **Hardy Plume**[30] 6742 2-9-3 0 ShaneKelly 1 29
(Denis Coakley) *chsd ldrs tl wknd qckly over 2f out* **33/1**

0 10 *2 1/2* **Derek The Diamond**[15] 7080 2-9-3 0 FergusSweeney 3 23
(J R Jenkins) *sn last: struggling after 3f: nvr a factor* **66/1**

0 11 *1* **Hearduthefirsttime (IRE)**[22] 6935 2-9-3 0 MickyFenton 12 20
(Barney Curley) *a in rr: wl btn 3f out* **50/1**

1m 26.42s (0.42) **Going Correction** -0.10s/f (Stan) **11** Ran SP% **116.3**

Speed ratings (Par 96): **93,92,91,89,89 87,83,80,72,70 68**

toteswingers:1&2:£3.80, 2&3:£10.40, 1&3:£2.70 CSF £14.31 TOTE £2.20: £1.50, £3.70, £3.00; EX 16.50.

Owner Splinter Group **Bred** M Enright **Trained** Hucking, Kent

FOCUS

A modest maiden run in a time 1.41 seconds slower than the following division. The winner was always in command and the next four all improved; the question is by how much?

NOTEBOOK

Sheikh The Reins(IRE) confirmed the promise of his first three starts with a straightforward success, not having to run up to his official mark of 81. He should make a fair handicapper. (op 11-8 tchd 6-5)

Royal Prospector stepped up on his first two performances and now has the option of handicaps. (op 11-1)

Typography didn't really build on the form of his Newbury debut. (op 13-2)

Poetry Writer hinted at ability on his first two starts, including over C&D, and did so again after 51 days off. He can now switch to handicaps. (op 40-1)

Arch Villain(IRE) is yet another who can now switch to handicaps. (op 15-2 tchd 8-1)

Glaisdale showed ability after a slow start and her performance was all the more encouraging considering she's bred to want quite a bit further on both sides of her pedigree (dam won over 2m, and over hurdles). However, the fitting of blinkers for her debut was a bit off-putting and she's not that big.

Polydamos had been absent since finishing down the field in the Chesham, having earlier shaped well on his debut at Sandown, and this was a disappointing reintroduction. He has a lot to prove. (op 3-1 tchd 4-1)

7330 BACK AND LAY AT BETDAQ.COM E B F MAIDEN STKS (DIV II) 7f (P)

5:50 (5:55) (Class 5) 2-Y-0 **£2,846** (£847; £423; £211) **Stalls** Low

Form RPR

1 **Rassam (IRE)** 2-9-3 0 WilliamBuick 7 91+
(Saeed Bin Suroor) *prog to ld after 2f: mde rest: clr whn shkn up and edgd lft over 1f out: fine debut* **4/7**[1]

2 *7* **Haaf A Sixpence** 2-9-3 0 JimCrowley 6 71+
(Ralph Beckett) *prog to chse wnr over 4f out: lft bhd fr 2f out: hld on for 2nd nr fin* **8/1**[3]

03 3 *1/2* **Fabled City (USA)**[19] 6992 2-9-3 0 AdamKirby 3 70
(Clive Cox) *prog to chse ldng trio 1/2-way: drvn over 2f out: chal for 3rd over 1f out: pushed along and kpt on same pce fnl f* **4/1**[2]

0 4 *1 1/4* **Nassau Storm**[153] 2837 2-9-3 0 ShaneKelly 2 66
(William Knight) *led 2f: sn lost pl and dropped to 5th 1/2-way: rdn over 2f out: kpt on fnl f* **25/1**

5 *nk* **Kalokagathia (IRE)** 2-9-3 0 IanMongan 1 65+
(Jo Crowley) *towards rr: prog to go 6th 1/2-way: nt on terms w those chsng clr wnr over 1f out: styd on fnl f: nt disgracd* **25/1**

00 6 *1 3/4* **Kinglami**[86] 5111 2-9-3 0 LukeMorris 11 61
(Brian Gubby) *prog to chse ldng pair over 4f out: rdn over 2f out: wknd ins fnl f* **50/1**

0 7 *15* **Infinite Jest**[12] 7134 2-9-3 0 EddieAhern 12 22
(J W Hills) *wl in rr: t.o last 3f out: passed 4 rivals fnl 75yds* **11/1**

0 8 *nk* **My Lady Picolla**[22] 6927 2-8-12 0 RobertHavlin 5 16
(Dr Jon Scargill) *a in rr: wl bhd over 2f out* **100/1**

0 9 *hd* **Welsh Bard (IRE)**[13] 7126 2-9-3 0 SebSanders 10 21
(Sir Mark Prescott Bt) *a wl in rr: t.o in last pair over 2f out* **33/1**

10 *1/2* **Cape Joy (IRE)** 2-8-12 0 SteveDrowne 4 14
(Richard Hannon) *dwlt: a wl in rr: bhd fnl 2f* **12/1**

00 11 *3/4* **Hip Hop**[13] 7118 2-8-9 0 KierenFox(3) 8 12
(Brett Johnson) *chsd ldr 2f: lost pl rapidly: wknd as rapidly 3f out: wl bhd after* **100/1**

1m 25.01s (-0.99) **Going Correction** -0.10s/f (Stan) **11** Ran SP% **125.4**

Speed ratings (Par 96): **101,93,92,91,90 88,71,71,70,70 69**

toteswingers:1&2:£3.60, 2&3:£4.20, 1&3:£1.60 CSF £6.48 TOTE £1.70: £1.10, £1.60, £1.50; EX 10.10.

Owner Godolphin **Bred** Ben Sangster **Trained** Newmarket, Suffolk

■ Stewards' Enquiry : Shane Kelly one-day ban: use of whip (23-24 Nov)

FOCUS

The time was 1.41 seconds quicker than the first division. The easy winner impressed and this is decent form which fits in with the third.

NOTEBOOK

Rassam(IRE) is pretty decent, winning by a wide margin on his debut. However, he looked a highly strung colt, racing freely despite the fitting of a cross-noseband, and also carried his head a bit high under pressure. A 150,000gns half-brother to dual 1m Listed winner Wasseema, he could be quite smart if going the right way and perhaps he'll be considered for Dubai, but his next run will tell us more. (op 8-11 tchd 5-6)

Haaf A Sixpence went unsold for £400 at Ascot in January, but he has ability. (op 9-1 tchd 10-1)

Fabled City(USA) didn't go on from his recent third at Newbury, although the form of that race had earlier taken a knock when the fifth, Typography, was well held in the first division of this race. (op 7-2 tchd 3-1)

Nassau Storm had been off for 153 days and might be better for the run.

Kalokagathia(IRE), whose sales price increased from 10,000euros to £20,000, is a half-brother to a 1m2f winner and kept on okay in the closing stages.

7331 BETDAQ MOBILE APPS H'CAP 2m (P)
6:20 (6:21) (Class 6) (0-60,61) 3-Y-O+ £1,617 (£481; £240; £120) Stalls Low

Form RPR

5221 **1** **The Absent Mare**^{10} 7145 3-8-12 **53**.............................. MartinLane 12 64+
(Robin Dickin) *s.i.s: hld up: last tl prog wl over 2f out: clsd to ld jst over 1f out: rdn clr* **13/2**^{3}

6001 **2** *4* **Shalambar (IRE)**^{8} 7206 5-10-1 **61** 6ex.............................. JimCrowley 8 67
(Tony Carroll) *led after 1f: wound up the pce fr 4f out: drvn over 2f out: hdd and outpcd jst over 1f out* **6/4**^{1}

1003 **3** *1/2* **Galiotto (IRE)**^{29} 3946 5-9-6 **52**................................(b) FergusSweeney 6 57
(Gary Moore) *hld up in last trio: pushed along 4f out: prog over 2f out: tried to chal over 1f out: sn outpcd but kpt on* **12/1**

3301 **4** *3* **Henry Holmes**^{28} 6798 8-9-4 **50**.............................. SteveDrowne 7 52
(Lydia Richards) *t.k.h: led 1f: restrained bhd ldrs: rdn over 3f out: steadily outpcd over 2f out* **7/1**

1162 **5** *1 3/4* **Red Current**^{25} 6876 7-9-7 **58**.............................. DavidKenny$^{(5)}$ 2 58
(Michael Scudamore) *hld up disputing 4th: prog to chse ldr wl over 2f out: sn rdn to chal: nt qckn and lost 2nd over 1f out: fdd* **14/1**

5502 **6** *hd* **Rosairlie (IRE)**^{9} 7195 3-9-3 **58**.............................. LukeMorris 4 57
(Harry Dunlop) *chsd ldrs disputing 4th: drvn over 3f out: sn lost pl and struggling* **9/2**^{2}

2036 **7** *8* **Delorain (IRE)**^{15} 7087 8-9-0 **51**................................(v) LauraPike$^{(5)}$ 3 41
(William Stone) *chsd ldr after 3f to over 3f out: sn wknd* **9/1**

406 **8** *6* **Robby Bobby**^{13} 7121 6-9-11 **57**.............................. IanMongan 1 40
(Laura Mongan) *hld up in last trio: effrt and in tch bhd ldrs over 2f out: wknd rapidly over 1f out* **20/1**

3m 29.91s (-0.19) **Going Correction** -0.10s/f (Stan)
WFA 3 from 4yo+ 9lb **8** Ran SP% **113.1**
Speed ratings (Par 101): **96,94,93,92,91 91,87,84**
toteswingers:1&2:£3.00, 2&3:£10.00, 1&3:£10.80 CSF £16.32 CT £113.63 TOTE £8.40: £2.40, £1.02, £4.20; EX 23.20.
Owner J C Clemmow **Bred** Beautiful Losers Bloodstock & R Hobson **Trained** Atherstone on Stour, Warwicks

FOCUS
An ordinary staying handicap and the pace appeared fair after a furlong or so. The winner improved again for the trip.

7332 BACCES 40TH ANNIVERSARY CELEBRATION (S) STKS 6f (P)
6:50 (6:51) (Class 6) 3-Y-O+ £1,617 (£481; £240; £120) Stalls Low

Form RPR

3636 **1** **Lutine Charlie (IRE)**^{28} 6793 4-9-0 62..............................(p) KierenFox$^{(3)}$ 5 76
(Ronald Harris) *chsd clr ldrs in 4th: clsd fr 2f out: rdn to ld 1f out: styd on wl* **12/1**

0200 **2** *1 1/2* **Dorback**^{15} 7076 4-9-3 78.............................. FergusSweeney 11 71+
(Noel Wilson) *sltly awkward s: hld up last: plenty to do whn asked to make prog over 2f out: swtchd to inner and styd on thrght fnl 2f to take 2nd last 75yds: no ch to chal* **7/2**^{1}

420 **3** *1/2* **Silver Turn**^{22} 6929 3-9-3 69.............................. J-PGuillambert 4 70
(Jeremy Gask) *chsd clr ldr: clsd to chal jst as wnr flew past 1f out: kpt on same pce after* **20/1**

0000 **4** *1 3/4* **Oldjoesaid**^{13} 7116 7-9-8 76................................(b) StephenCraine 1 69
(Kevin Ryan) *led at str pce and stretched field out: hdd & wknd 1f out* **8/1**^{3}

00-0 **5** *1/2* **My Best Bet**^{49} 6256 5-8-7 76.............................. MarkCoumbe$^{(5)}$ 6 57+
(Derek Shaw) *hld up in 7th: effrt over 2f out: styd on fr over 1f out: nvr gng pce to threaten* **9/1**

2306 **6** *3 1/2* **My Lord**^{16} 7055 3-9-8 75.............................. LukeMorris 7 56
(Ronald Harris) *chsd clr ldng pair to 2f out: steadily wknd u.p over 1f out* **11/2**^{2}

3600 **7** *2 1/4* **Green Apple**^{12} 7141 3-9-3 67..............................(p) SteveDrowne 9 44
(Peter Makin) *chsd ldrs in 5th: rdn over 2f out and no prog: wl btn over 1f out* **9/1**

1103 **8** *2 1/4* **Lewyn**^{6} 7253 4-8-10 75................................(bt) RaulDaSilva$^{(7)}$ 8 37
(Jeremy Gask) *towards rr in 6th: rdn and effrt over 2f out: no prog over 1f out: wknd* **7/2**^{1}

1436 **9** *6* **Liberal Lady**^{113} 4182 3-8-12 59.............................. MatthewLawson$^{(5)}$ 3 18
(Ralph Smith) *restless stalls: a in rr: struggling fr 1/2-way: t.o* **20/1**

520R **R** **Timeteam (IRE)**^{28} 6793 5-9-3 65..............................(b^{1}) AdamKirby 10 —
(K F Clutterbuck) *ref to r: tk no part* **12/1**

1m 11.87s (-1.23) **Going Correction** -0.10s/f (Stan) **10** Ran SP% **115.8**
Speed ratings (Par 101): **104,102,101,99,98 93,90,87,79,—**
toteswingers:1&2:£10.80, 2&3:£27.20, 1&3:£47.80 CSF £53.49 TOTE £15.70: £4.90, £2.00, £5.80; EX 66.80.There was no bid for the winner.
Owner Jason Tucker **Bred** Patrice O'Connell **Trained** Earlswood, Monmouths

FOCUS
The pace looked a bit too strong courtesy of Oldjoesaid and the field were soon strung out. A fair race for the grade on paper, rated around the winner to his best form since he was a 2yo.

7333 SIRIO/HTC HEALTH H'CAP 1m 4f (P)
7:20 (7:22) (Class 6) (0-55,55) 3-Y-O £1,617 (£481; £240; £120) Stalls Centre

Form RPR

0003 **1** **Honourable Knight (IRE)**^{13} 7122 3-9-1 **54**..............(be) SteveDrowne 4 61
(Mark Usher) *wl plcd bhd ldrs: rousted along over 3f out and briefly short of room: prog over 2f out: drvn to ld over 1f out: asserted fnl f* **9/2**^{1}

623 **2** *1 1/2* **Dolly Colman (IRE)**^{68} 5665 3-8-8 **47**.............................. LukeMorris 11 52
(Michael Blake) *hld up in last trio: hdwy and nt clr run over 2f out: prog to dispute ld wl over 1f out: nt qckn and hld fnl f* **10/1**

0054 **3** *hd* **Sir Randolf (IRE)**^{14} 7092 3-8-11 **50**..............................(t) JimCrowley 9 56
(Sylvester Kirk) *hld up in last trio: looking for room over 2f out: prog wl over 1f out: styd on to take 3rd nr fin: nvr able to chal* **8/1**

203 **4** *1/2* **Avon Supreme**^{15} 7085 3-9-0 **53**.............................. StevieDonohoe 3 57
(Gay Kelleway) *hld up in midfield: prog on outer over 2f out: disp ld wl over 1f out: sn nt qckn: one pce fnl f* **10/1**

3062 **5** *hd* **So Is She (IRE)**^{6} 7246 3-8-12 **51** ow1..............................(p) IanMongan 1 55
(Alan Bailey) *settled in midfield: lost pl and n.m.r over 2f out: rallied over 1f out: kpt on fnl f* **13/2**^{3}

6 *2 1/2* **The Catenian (IRE)**^{66} 5768 3-8-7 **46** oh1.............................. JimmyQuinn 6 46
(Eoin Doyle, Ire) *s.i.s: swtchd to inner in midfield: n.m.r over 2f out and swtchd rt jst over 2f out: no imp over 1f out* **11/2**^{2}

-460 **7** *1 1/2* **Windsor Knights**^{18} 7037 3-9-1 **54**..............................(b) RichardKingscote 14 51
(Alastair Lidderdale) *hld up last: stl only one bhd him over 2f out: shkn up and passed wkng rivals to go 7th fnl f: nvr on terms* **25/1**

3026 **8** *4 1/2* **Lord Of The Storm**^{8} 7212 3-8-5 **47**..............................(t) KierenFox$^{(3)}$ 2 37
(Bill Turner) *chsd clr ldr 4f: styd prom tl wknd over 2f out* **13/2**^{3}

4000 **9** *1 3/4* **Harry Lime**^{15} 7085 3-9-2 **55**..............................(p) AndreaAtzeni 5 42
(Chris Dwyer) *nvr beyond midfield: rdn and no prog over 2f out: wl btn over 1f out* **25/1**

6330 **10** *1* **Like A Boy**^{39} 6545 3-8-13 **52**.............................. SebSanders 7 38
(Bill Turner) *wl plcd bhd clr ldrs: rdn and lost pl over 2f out: wl btn over 1f out* **12/1**

0606 **11** *1/2* **Farmers Hill**^{14} 7091 3-8-8 **47** oh1 ow1..............................(b) FergusSweeney 12 32
(Mark Hoad) *prom: chsd clr ldr after 4f to over 2f out: wknd qckly* **14/1**

6400 **12** *8* **Divine Rule (IRE)**^{13} 7122 3-8-9 **55**.............................. CharlotteJenner$^{(7)}$ 10 27
(Laura Mongan) *led and sn wl clr: hdd & wknd rapidly wl over 1f out* **16/1**

006 **13** *54* **Suffolini**^{41} 6475 3-8-4 **46** oh1.............................. JohnFahy$^{(3)}$ 8 —
(William Stone) *wl in rr and nt gng wl: effrt on wd outside 4f out: sn wknd: t.o* **66/1**

2m 33.78s (-0.72) **Going Correction** -0.10s/f (Stan) **13** Ran SP% **119.0**
Speed ratings (Par 98): **98,97,96,96,96 94,93,90,89,88 88,83,47**
toteswingers:1&2:£6.50, 2&3:£19.70, 1&3:£10.00 CSF £48.54 CT £355.01 TOTE £4.60: £1.80, £4.10, £2.30; EX 75.50.
Owner Bryan Fry **Bred** Mohammed Al Sulaim **Trained** Upper Lambourn, Berks
■ Stewards' Enquiry : Richard KingscoteM £140 fine: failed to weigh out

FOCUS
The pace was unusually strong by Polytrack standards and this was a proper test. Sound if limited form.

7334 CONEXION COMMUNICATIONS H'CAP 1m (P)
7:50 (7:50) (Class 5) (0-75,75) 3-Y-O £2,264 (£673; £336; £168) Stalls Low

Form RPR

2206 **1** **Present Danger**^{16} 7054 3-9-7 **75**.............................. RichardKingscote 2 86
(Tom Dascombe) *trckd ldrs: prog on inner over 2f out: led over 1f out: edgd lft and swished tail: styd on wl* **5/1**^{2}

3033 **2** *2 1/4* **Choral**^{55} 6089 3-9-5 **73**.............................. SteveDrowne 9 79
(Richard Hannon) *prom: trckd ldr 5f out: rdn to chal and upsides over 1f out: chsd wnr after: one pce* **9/2**^{1}

634 **3** *1 1/2* **Drakes Drum**^{30} 6750 3-8-13 **70**.............................. JohnFahy$^{(3)}$ 4 73
(Clive Cox) *racd freely: led: drvn over 2f out: hdd and nt qckn over 1f out: clung on for 3rd* **13/2**

0511 **4** *1/2* **Methayel (IRE)**^{20} 6971 3-9-0 **68**.............................. SebSanders 8 69
(Clive Brittain) *stdd s: in tch: prog on outer to go prom over 3f out: rdn over 2f out: one pce* **11/2**^{3}

5302 **5** *1 3/4* **Swift Breeze**^{12} 7141 3-9-3 **71**.............................. ShaneKelly 7 68
(William Haggas) *dwlt: hld up in last pair: prog 1/2-way: rdn and nt qckn 2f out: no imp after* **11/2**^{3}

0406 **6** *hd* **Menadati (USA)**^{12} 7137 3-9-3 **71**.............................. LukeMorris 3 68
(Peter Hiatt) *s.s: hld up in last pair: rdn over 2f out: no real prog* **7/1**

4034 **7** *1 1/2* **Isingy Red (FR)**^{12} 7137 3-9-1 **69**.............................. StephenCraine 5 62
(Jim Boyle) *t.k.h: hld up in rr: wd bnd 3f out: rdn and nt qckn over 2f out: sn no ch* **13/2**

6-26 **8** *1 3/4* **Matilda's Waltz**^{152} 2891 3-9-1 **69**..............................(b^{1}) JimCrowley 6 58
(Ralph Beckett) *hld up in tch: lost pl sn after 1/2-way: rdn over 2f out: no prog and btn after* **12/1**

6530 **9** *24* **Levantera (IRE)**^{43} 6438 3-8-7 **61**.............................. MichaelStainton 1 —
(Paul Howling) *rousted along fr s but unable to ld: chsd ldr 3f: wknd over 3f out: t.o* **33/1**

1m 38.9s (-0.90) **Going Correction** -0.10s/f (Stan) **9** Ran SP% **115.4**
Speed ratings (Par 102): **100,97,96,95,94 93,92,90,66**
toteswingers:1&2:£3.10, 2&3:£6.50, 1&3:£8.70 CSF £27.76 CT £148.53 TOTE £6.50: £2.50, £1.20, £2.80; EX 34.80.
Owner A Black & M Owen **Bred** Watership Down Stud **Trained** Malpas, Cheshire

FOCUS
A modest handicap and they didn't seem to go that quick. Sound enough form judged around the runner-up.
T/Plt: £127.90 to a £1 stake. Pool of £64,691.08 - 369.19 winning tickets. T/Qpdt: £8.20 to a £1 stake. Pool of £10,173.32 - 913.84 winning tickets. JN

7240 SOUTHWELL (L-H)
Wednesday, November 9

OFFICIAL GOING: Standard
Wind: Virtually nil Weather: Overcast

7335 I LOVE BETDAQ MAIDEN AUCTION STKS 5f (F)
1:00 (1:00) (Class 6) 2-Y-O £1,704 (£503; £251) Stalls High

Form RPR

02 **1** **Wicked Wench**^{16} 7067 2-8-4 0.............................. JoeFanning 4 65+
(Jo Hughes) *mde virtually all: rdn over 1f out: kpt on* **4/5**^{1}

250 **2** *2* **Bengaline**^{33} 6673 2-8-10 68.............................. BillyCray$^{(3)}$ 1 65
(David Nicholls) *cl up: rdn wl over 1f out: ev ch tl one pce ent fnl f* **6/4**^{2}

3 *1* **Ambitious Icarus** 2-8-9 0.............................. RobbieFitzpatrick 2 56
(Richard Guest) *green and dwlt: sn chsng ldng pair: rdn wl over 1f out: kpt on fnl f: nrst fin* **40/1**

2200 **F** **Beechey's Beauty**^{95} 4809 2-8-4 60..............................(be^{1}) LeonnaMayor$^{(7)}$ 3 —
(Phil McEntee) *sn outpcd: bhd fr 1/2-way: collapsed and fell over 1f out: fatally injured* **11/1**^{3}

60.54 secs (0.84) **Going Correction** +0.025s/f (Slow) **4** Ran SP% **106.3**
Speed ratings (Par 94): **94,90,89,—**
CSF £2.16 TOTE £2.10; EX 2.50.
Owner James Hearne **Bred** Rainsbrook Bloodstock **Trained** Lambourn, Berks

FOCUS
A poor maiden, which looked a match, was marred by the death of Beechey's Beauty. The winner seemingly confirmed her recent improved course form, and the race could be rated 6-7lb higher.

NOTEBOOK
Wicked Wench had split a couple of previous winners when runner-up in a 6f novice event here last time and found this task rather easier. Up there from the start, she forged ahead of her market rival from over a furlong from home and, with further progress possible, should have a future in low-grade handicaps on the all-weather. (op 8-11)
Bengaline ran by far his best previous race when runner-up in a C&D maiden in August and tried to keep the filly honest for as long as possible, but his unexposed rival prove too strong. His mark of 68 provides the benchmark. (op 2-1)

Ambitious Icarus, a £1,200 gelding out of a half-sister to three winners at up to 1m2f (one also scored over hurdles), was last of the three finishers but wasn't totally disgraced. He looks well worth another go under these conditions and may appreciate a bit further. (op 25-1)

7336 32RED.COM NURSERY — 1m (F)

1:30 (1:31) (Class 5) (0-70,70) 2-Y-O — **£2,385** (£704; £352) Stalls Low

Form	Pos	Dist	Horse / Comment	Jockey	RPR
5303	**1**		**Finbar**[28] 6807 2-9-4 **67** (James Given) *cl up: chal over 2f out: rdn to ld over 1f out: sn clr* **5/2**[1]	FrederikTylicki 3	77+
6432	**2**	4 ½	**Ishiamiracle**[6] 7240 2-8-4 **60** (Phil McEntee) *led: rdn along and jnd over 2f out: hdd over 1f out: kpt on same pce* **12/1**	LeonnaMayor(7) 5	60
0006	**3**	5	**Season Spirit**[26] 6825 2-8-9 **58** (James Given) *dwlt: hdwy on outer to chse ldrs over 3f out: wd st and rdn over 2f out: styd on ins fnl f: tk 3rd on line* **25/1**	TomEaves 7	46
006	**4**	shd	**Fisher**[13] 7126 2-9-5 **68** (Richard Hannon) *sn pushed along towards rr: hdwy 3f out: rdn 2f out: sn chsng ldng pair: one pce fnl f: lost 3rd on line* **13/2**	PhillipMakin 6	56
454	**5**	1 ½	**Manomine**[20] 6972 2-9-0 **63** (Clive Brittain) *chsd ldrs: hdwy 3f out: rdn over 2f out: sn one pce* **9/2**[3]	J-PGuillambert 2	47
01	**6**	1 ½	**Artlana**[14] 7108 2-8-8 **57** (Julie Camacho) *sn rdn along and a in rr* **12/1**	BarryMcHugh 4	38
1503	**7**	2	**New Decade**[5] 7259 2-9-7 **70** (Mark Johnston) *trckd ldrs: effrt wl over 2f out: sn rdn and wknd* **3/1**[2]	JoeFanning 8	46
2310	**8**	1 ¼	**Sheila's Buddy**[39] 6524 2-9-6 **69** (J S Moore) *chsd ldrs on inner: rdn along 3f out: sn wknd* **14/1**	LiamKeniry 1	43

1m 42.53s (-1.17) **Going Correction** -0.125s/f (Stan) — **8** Ran SP% **111.0**
Speed ratings (Par 96): **100,95,90,90,88 87,85,84**
toteswingers:1&2:£8.90, 2&3:£19.90, 1&3:£8.20 CSF £31.18 CT £577.30 TOTE £3.80: £1.50, £3.50, £4.50; EX 26.10 Trifecta £165.20 Pool: £288.00 - 1.29 winning units..
Owner Elite Racing Club **Bred** Elite Racing Club **Trained** Willoughton, Lincs

FOCUS

An ordinary nursery and they finished spread out. It was not much of a race but the winner did it well. However his opportunities to run here may be limited now.

NOTEBOOK

Finbar was making his all-weather debut after finishing third in a Nottingham nursery last month that has worked out well, but he is by a sire with a marvellous record around here and he relished the surface, pulling right away after leading over a furlong out. He can expect a hefty rise for this, but still has improvement to come. (op 9-4 tchd 11-4)

7337 CONNOLLY'S REDMILLS "PURE NUTRITION" NURSERY — 6f (F)

2:00 (2:00) (Class 5) (0-70,68) 2-Y-O — **£2,385** (£704; £352) Stalls Low

Form	Pos	Dist	Horse / Comment	Jockey	RPR
434	**1**		**Springheel Jake**[16] 7052 2-9-4 **68** (Ann Duffield) *trckd ldrs: pushed along wl over 2f out: hdwy to ld 1 1/2f out: sn rdn: edgd lft ins fnl f: kpt on wl* **4/1**[3]	DaleSwift(3) 7	75+
2342	**2**	1	**Mount McLeod (IRE)**[11] 7252 2-8-3 **53** (Jamie Osborne) *dwlt: sn trcking ldrs on inner: hdwy 2f out: chal wl over 1f out: sn rdn and ev ch tl no ex last 100yds* **11/4**[1]	SophieDoyle(3) 1	54
0600	**3**	1 ½	**Bountiful Catch**[4] 7294 2-8-6 **53** (Pam Sly) *towards rr: hdwy over 2f out: rdn wl over 1f out: kpt on fnl f* **18/1**	JimmyQuinn 2	50
4503	**4**	2 ½	**Abshir Zain (IRE)**[15] 7081 2-9-4 **65** (Clive Brittain) *in rr: hdwy wl over 2f out: rdn wl over 1f out: kpt on same pce* **4/1**[3]	(b) FrederikTylicki 6	54
0035	**5**	1 ½	**Intomist (IRE)**[20] 6972 2-8-12 **59** (Jim Boyle) *dwlt: sn chsng ldr: cl up 1/2-way: led over 2f out: sn rdn and hdd 1 1/2f out: grad wknd* **10/3**[2]	(b[1]) StephenCraine 5	44
4040	**6**	3 ½	**Findhornbay**[6] 7251 2-9-0 **61** (Mark Johnston) *ponied to s: led: rdn along and hdd over 2f out: sn wknd* **15/2**	JoeFanning 4	35
0500	**7**	10	**Point At Issue (IRE)**[23] 6912 2-8-6 **53** (David Nicholls) *sn outpcd and bhd fr 1/2-way* **25/1**	PaulQuinn 3	—

1m 16.52s (0.02) **Going Correction** -0.125s/f (Stan) — **7** Ran SP% **110.6**
Speed ratings (Par 96): **94,92,90,87,85 80,67**
toeswingers:1&2:£1.90, 2&3:£8.00, 1&3:£7.00 CSF £14.37 TOTE £6.90: £2.90, £2.10; EX 18.50.

Owner Jimmy Kay **Bred** Mrs T Brudenell **Trained** Constable Burton, N Yorks

FOCUS

Another ordinary nursery. Straightforward form, rated around the second, with the winner well on top of a weakish field.

NOTEBOOK

Springheel Jake was making his all-weather/nursery debuts after showing ability in three turf maidens last month. He wasn't travelling as well as some straightening up for home, but showed a decent attitude to squeeze through between a couple of rivals and lead over a furlong out. The surface was no problem at all and he looks well worth returning here. (op 9-2 tchd 5-1)

Mount McLeod(IRE), in the frame in her last four outings on turf and Polytrack, missed the break but was still on the bridle when delivered with her effort passing the 2f pole. However, she didn't find as much as the winner once under pressure and she is beginning to run out of excuses. (tchd 5-2 and 3-1)

Bountiful Catch had shown precious little in five previous outings and this staying-on effort on his Fibresand debut was an improvement, but he will need to step up again to win a race. (tchd 20-1)

Abshir Zain(IRE), trying his shortest trip to date on this all-weather debut, struggled to go the pace and was getting all the kickback, but didn't find a lot when switched to the inside rail. (op 6-1)

Intomist(IRE), blinkered for the first time, was always up there and still had every chance passing the 2f pole, but didn't get home. His rider reported that the colt stopped quickly and the Stewards ordered him to be routine tested. Official explanation: jockey said that the colt stopped quickly (op 5-2)

7338 32REDBINGO.COM (S) STKS — 1m (F)

2:30 (2:30) (Class 6) 2-Y-O — **£1,704** (£503; £251) Stalls Low

Form	Pos	Dist	Horse / Comment	Jockey	RPR
0003	**1**		**Percythepinto (IRE)**[6] 7242 2-8-6 57 (George Baker) *sn cl up: led on bit over 2f out: pushed clr wl over 1f out: easily* **4/11**[1]	(t) DavidKenny(5) 2	61
0400	**2**	3 ¾	**Dutchman's Field**[14] 7108 2-8-8 52 (David Nicholls) *led: pushed along and jnd 3f out: rdn and hdd over 2f out: sn edgd lft and one pce* **12/1**[3]	BillyCray(3) 4	50
050	**3**	15	**Notnowstanley**[14] 7108 2-8-11 43 (J S Moore) *reminders s and chsd ldrs: effrt 3f out: sn rdn and outpcd fr over 2f out* **14/1**	(b[1]) GrahamGibbons 1	14
000	**4**	3 ¾	**Malvesi**[14] 7108 2-8-11 53 (Ann Duffield) *pushed along s and sn cl up on outer: rdn along 1/2-way: outpcd fnl 3f* **9/2**[2]	TomEaves 6	5
4305	**5**	28	**River Nova**[58] 6002 2-8-6 49 (Alan Berry) *in rr: outpcd after 2f and sn bhd: t.o fnl 3f* **25/1**	BarryMcHugh 3	—

1m 44.18s (0.48) **Going Correction** -0.125s/f (Stan) — **5** Ran SP% **109.7**
Speed ratings (Par 94): **92,88,73,69,41**
CSF £5.83 TOTE £1.30: £1.10, £2.80; EX 6.00.The winner was bought in 8,250gns.
Owner Seaton Partnership **Bred** Stone Ridge Farm **Trained** Whitsbury, Hants

FOCUS

There won't be many more uncompetitive races than this run around here during the winter. That said, the winner is rated back to his best.

NOTEBOOK

Percythepinto(IRE) finished third when gambled for a 7f nursery here six days earlier and probably blew his chance at the start there, but he broke much better this time. With his rider looking around for dangers turning in, he only had to be shaken up to see off his only conceivable danger and couldn't have done it more easily. Retained for 8,250gns at the auction, he may turn out again at Kempton on Thursday evening. (op 2-5 tchd 4-9 and 1-2 in places)

Dutchman's Field ran his best race so far on Polytrack at Kempton in September and tried to make all here, but was completely outclassed by the winner inside the last 2f. It will be a poor race he wins.

Notnowstanley was tried in first-time blinkers but they had little effect. (op 11-1)

Malvesi showed nothing on this all-weather debut. (op 5-1 tchd 11-2)

7339 32RED H'CAP — 1m (F)

3:00 (3:00) (Class 4) (0-85,84) 3-Y-O+ — **£4,851** (£1,443; £721; £360) Stalls Low

Form	Pos	Dist	Horse / Comment	Jockey	RPR
0006	**1**		**Everymanforhimself (IRE)**[39] 6542 7-9-0 **77** (Kevin Ryan) *trckd ldrs: smooth hdwy wl over 2f out: led wl over 1f out: rdn clr appr fnl f: kpt on strly* **25/1**	(b) PhillipMakin 8	94
0200	**2**	6	**All Right Now**[16] 7050 4-8-13 **76** (Derek Haydn Jones) *prom: effrt and cl up over 2f out: sn rdn and ev ch tl one pce appr fnl f* **12/1**	FrederikTylicki 7	79
1063	**3**	¾	**Piceno (IRE)**[25] 6867 3-8-12 **77** (David Nicholls) *led: rdn along and edgd lft 2f out: sn hdd: kpt on same pce appr fnl f* **10/1**	(b) GrahamGibbons 1	78
0022	**4**	¾	**Powerful Presence (IRE)**[6] 7243 5-9-0 **77** (David O'Meara) *in tch on outer: hdwy to chse ldrs 2f out: sn rdn and edgd lft: no imp appr fnl f* **11/4**[1]	DanielTudhope 14	77+
0600	**5**	1 ¼	**Sam Sharp (USA)**[60] 5940 5-9-7 **84** (Ian Williams) *chsd ldrs on inner: rdn along over 2f out: grad wknd* **10/1**	RichardKingscote 3	81
1011	**6**	½	**Eastern Hills**[6] 7243 6-8-10 **80** 6ex (Alan McCabe) *in tch: hdwy to chse ldrs 2f out: sn rdn and no imp* **8/1**[3]	(p) RyanTate(7) 11	76
3021	**7**	3 ½	**Dr Red Eye**[16] 7068 3-8-11 **79** (David Nicholls) *chsd ldrs: rdn along wl over 2f out: wknd wl over 1f out* **6/1**[2]	BillyCray(3) 2	67
0500	**8**	1	**Follow The Flag (IRE)**[16] 7054 7-8-12 **75** (Alan McCabe) *in rr tl sme late hdwy* **20/1**	(p) PaddyAspell 5	60
1354	**9**	10	**Koo And The Gang (IRE)**[69] 5648 4-8-10 **76** (Brian Ellison) *blind removed late and dwlt: a towards rr* **8/1**[3]	PaulPickard(3) 4	38
1206	**10**	2 ¾	**Master Leon**[20] 6979 4-8-9 **72** (Bryan Smart) *in rr and sn swtchd to outer: nvr a factor* **33/1**	(p) TomEaves 9	28
0000	**11**	13	**Douze Points (IRE)**[14] 7098 5-8-8 **71** (Pat Murphy) *a in rr* **100/1**	FrankieMcDonald 6	—
2104	**12**	½	**The Osteopath (IRE)**[11] 7161 8-8-13 **76** (Michael Dods) *a towards rr* **50/1**	(p) TonyHamilton 12	—
-063	**13**	½	**Flipping**[11] 7161 4-9-0 **77** (Eric Alston) *prom: rdn along 3f out: sn wknd* **16/1**	DavidAllan 10	—
3310	**14**	23	**Fabulouslyspirited**[19] 6996 3-9-4 **83** (Ralph Beckett) *towards rr: pushed along 3f out: sn wknd and bhd whn eased over 1f out* **12/1**	StevieDonohoe 13	—

1m 40.3s (-3.40) **Going Correction** -0.125s/f (Stan)
WFA 3 from 4yo+ 2lb — **14** Ran SP% **117.1**
Speed ratings (Par 105): **112,106,105,104,103 102,99,98,88,85 72,72,71,48**
toteswingers:1&2:£72.80, 2&3:£31.00, 1&3:£49.40 CSF £282.50 CT £3261.65 TOTE £41.30: £12.40, £5.70, £5.50; EX 307.00 TRIFECTA Not won..
Owner Mrs J Ryan **Bred** Denis McDonnell **Trained** Hambleton, N Yorks

FOCUS

A competitive handicap for the track and grade and the form should stand up. The winner is rated to last winter's form.

Piceno(IRE) Official explanation: jockey said that the gelding hung left-handed

Powerful Presence(IRE) Official explanation: jockey said that the gelding hung right-handed

7340 32REDPOKER.COM H'CAP — 1m 6f (F)

3:30 (3:30) (Class 6) (0-60,60) 3-Y-O+ — **£1,704** (£503; £251) Stalls Low

Form	Pos	Dist	Horse / Comment	Jockey	RPR
4200	**1**		**Mediterranean Sea (IRE)**[35] 6621 5-9-12 **60** (J R Jenkins) *hld up towards rr: hdwy on inner and in tch 1/2-way: trckd ldrs over 3f out: swtchd rt and effrt to chal wl over 1f out: sn led and rdn clr ent fnl f: styd on* **3/1**[1]	FrederikTylicki 1	69+
0005	**2**	5	**Mecox Bay (IRE)**[6] 7254 4-9-0 **55** (Michael Appleby) *a.p: cl up 4f out: rdn to ld briefly 2f out: sn hdd and kpt on same pce appr fnl f* **14/1**	JackDuern(7) 2	57
0065	**3**	2 ¼	**Labroc (IRE)**[8] 7212 3-9-4 **60** (William Haggas) *in tch: trckd ldrs 1/2-way: effrt 3f out: rdn along over 2f out: styd on same pce appr fnl f* **5/1**[3]	JoeFanning 3	59
346	**4**	2 ¼	**Mighty Whitey (IRE)**[14] 7105 5-9-7 **60** (Noel C Kelly, Ire) *led: pushed along over 3f out: rdn over 2f out: hdd 1 1/2f out and grad wknd* **13/2**	(e[1]) LMcNiff(5) 8	56
3300	**5**	18	**Short Supply (USA)**[25] 6870 5-9-6 **54** (Tim Walford) *prom: pushed along 4f out: rdn 3f out: outpcd fnl 2f* **5/1**[3]	(b[1]) GrahamGibbons 7	25
5000	**6**	15	**Willow's Wish**[8] 7212 3-8-4 **46** oh1 (George Moore) *chsd ldrs: rdn along and lost pl over 4f out: sn bhd* **50/1**	AndrewMullen 4	—
3253	**7**	30	**Revolutionary**[14] 5415 3-9-0 **56** (Alison Thorpe) *a towards rr: rdn along 1/2-way: sn bhd and t.o fnl 3f* **10/1**	(b[1]) TomEaves 6	—
523	**8**	57	**Ultimate Best**[21] 6947 3-9-2 **58** (Michael Mullineaux) *a in rr: lost tch 5f out: t.o and eased fnl 3f* **7/2**[2]	JimmyQuinn 5	—

3m 7.96s (-0.34) **Going Correction** -0.125s/f (Stan)
WFA 3 from 4yo+ 8lb — **8** Ran SP% **111.6**
Speed ratings (Par 101): **95,92,90,89,79 70,53,21**
toteswingers:1&2:£8.00, 2&3:£12.40, 1&3:£3.50 CSF £42.95 CT £197.87 TOTE £3.70: £1.20, £5.40, £2.60; EX 48.50 Trifecta £234.70 Pool: £586.92 - 1.85 winning units..
Owner Mrs Wendy Jenkins **Bred** D H W Dobson **Trained** Royston, Herts

FOCUS

This was a poor staying handicap and a few of these appeared to hate the experience. It was quite well run and the winner is arguably worth a little more.

Ultimate Best Official explanation: jockey said that the filly was never travelling

7341 32RED CASINO H'CAP 6f (F)
4:00 (4:01) (Class 5) (0-75,75) 3-Y-0+ **£2,385** (£704; £352) **Stalls** Low

Form RPR

0063 **1** **Punching**[15] 7086 7-9-0 **68** KirstyMilczarek 11 80
(Conor Dore) *trckd ldr: cl up 1/2-way: led 2f out: sn rdn and hdd over 1f out: rallied gamely ins fnl f to ld last 50yds* **13/2**[3]

6001 **2** *nk* **Rowan Spirit (IRE)**[15] 7073 3-9-4 **72** GrahamGibbons 12 83
(Mark Brisbourne) *prom: hdwy and cl up over 2f out: rdn to ld over 1f out: hdd and no ex last 50yds* **8/1**

0603 **3** *2 1/4* **Spitfire**[57] 6022 6-9-1 **69** FrederikTylicki 14 73
(J R Jenkins) *towards rr: wd st: gd hdwy wl over 1f out: sn rdn and styd on wl fnl f: nrst fin* **7/1**

2300 **4** *1 3/4* **Sleepy Blue Ocean**[14] 7104 5-9-6 **74** (p) BarryMcHugh 13 72
(John Balding) *chsd ldrs: hdwy over 2f out: rdn wl over 1f out: kpt on same pce* **11/2**[2]

5061 **5** *1* **Equuleus Pictor**[43] 6436 7-9-7 **75** (p) PhillipMakin 2 70
(John Spearing) *chsd ldrs on inner: rdn along 2f out: one pce appr fnl f* **9/2**[1]

3400 **6** *1 1/4* **Sands Of Dee (USA)**[14] 7104 4-8-6 **63** (b) BillyCray(3) 4 54
(David Nicholls) *chsd ldrs on inner: rdn along wl over 2f out: kpt on same pce* **10/1**

2246 **7** *3* **Arrivaderci**[22] 6929 3-8-3 **64** ow1 (e[1]) JasonHart(7) 9 46
(Richard Guest) *in tch: rdn over 2f out: sn no imp* **16/1**

0020 **8** *3/4* **Black Baccara**[8] 7201 4-8-7 **61** (be) JoeFanning 8 40
(Phil McEntee) *led: rdn along and hdd 2f out: sn wknd* **22/1**

0450 **9** *nk* **Dunseverick (IRE)**[55] 6089 3-9-0 **68** TonyCulhane 1 46
(David Flood) *a towards rr* **9/1**

0453 **10** *hd* **Sarah's Art (IRE)**[11] 7172 8-8-13 **67** (t) RobbieFitzpatrick 7 45
(Derek Shaw) *a towards rr* **25/1**

0-40 **11** *1 1/4* **Mac Tiernan (IRE)**[14] 7097 4-8-11 **65** FrankieMcDonald 6 39
(Pat Murphy) *s.i.s: a towards rr* **33/1**

414- **12** *1 1/4* **Efisio Princess**[491] 3761 8-8-11 **68** NataliaGemelova(3) 5 38
(John E Long) *dwlt and towards rr: wd st and hdwy on outer over 2f out: rdn wl over 1f out: sn btn* **22/1**

3046 **13** *8* **Red Roar (IRE)**[29] 6779 4-8-13 **67** TomEaves 10 11
(Alan Berry) *a towards rr* **16/1**

1m 15.45s (-1.05) **Going Correction** -0.125s/f (Stan) **13** Ran SP% **116.8**
Speed ratings (Par 103): **102,101,98,96,94 93,89,88,87,87 85,84,73**
toteswingers:1&2:£11.90, 2&3:£10.00, 1&3:£8.30 CSF £53.45 CT £294.13 TOTE £5.40: £2.00, £2.70, £2.20; EX 35.60 Trifecta £137.20 Pool: £584.33 - 3.15 winning units..
Owner Liam Breslin **Bred** Cheveley Park Stud Ltd **Trained** Cowbit, Lincs

FOCUS
An ordinary, but quite competitive sprint handicap in which the four highest-drawn horses filled the first four places. The winner goes well here and is rated back to something like his best to beat the improved runner-up.
T/Plt: £137.10 to a £1 stake. Pool of £52,445.92 - 279.09 winning tickets. T/Qpdt: £35.60 to a £1 stake. Pool of £3,436.91 - 71.30 winning tickets. JR

7327 KEMPTON (A.W) (R-H)
Thursday, November 10

OFFICIAL GOING: Standard
Wind: Light, across Weather: Fine

7342 ENHANCED SPS AT BLUESQ.COM NURSERY 1m (P)
4:20 (4:21) (Class 6) (0-60,64) 2-Y-0 **£1,617** (£481; £240; £120) **Stalls** Low

Form RPR

3062 **1** **Fairyinthewind (IRE)**[8] 7223 2-9-7 **60** LukeMorris 2 71+
(Paul D'Arcy) *hld up in midfield: smooth prog over 2f out: led over 1f out: shkn up and sn clr: eased last 75yds* **2/1**[1]

000 **2** *4* **Auntie Kathryn (IRE)**[58] 6018 2-8-9 **48** (v[1]) WilliamCarson 1 48
(Stuart Williams) *s.i.s: hld up in rr: swtchd lft over 2f out: rdn and prog wl over 1f out: styd on to take 2nd last 150yds: no ch w wnr* **25/1**

235 **3** *2* **Ermyn Flyer**[28] 6817 2-9-4 **57** IanMongan 6 52
(Pat Phelan) *trckd ldng pair: rdn over 2f out: outpcd by wnr over 1f out: disp one pce 2nd briefly ins fnl f* **8/1**[3]

5060 **4** *2 1/4* **House Limit (IRE)**[28] 6817 2-8-12 **51** (b[1]) EddieAhern 10 41
(Harry Dunlop) *t.k.h: pressed ldr: rdn to chal and upsides whn wnr cruised by over 1f out: wknd* **25/1**

000 **5** *1 1/2* **No Plan B (IRE)**[41] 6506 2-9-4 **57** MartinLane 5 44
(Noel Quinlan) *trckd ldrs: rdn and nt qckn over 2f out: one pce and no imp after* **12/1**

0463 **6** *1 1/2* **Compton Rainbow**[8] 7222 2-9-0 **60** (t) NicoleNordblad(7) 7 43
(Hans Adielsson) *t.k.h: led to over 1f out: wknd* **8/1**[3]

000 **7** *1 1/4* **Leading Star**[112] 4245 2-8-11 **50** FrankieMcDonald 4 30
(Michael Madgwick) *a abt same pl: rdn and no prog over 2f out: wl btn after* **100/1**

004 **8** *1/2* **Quixote**[38] 6572 2-9-6 **59** SebSanders 13 38
(Clive Brittain) *racd wd in midfield: shkn up over 2f out: sn wknd* **8/1**[3]

0060 **9** *3* **Emirates Jack (IRE)**[17] 7051 2-9-4 **57** TonyCulhane 3 29
(George Baker) *restrained into last sn after s and detached fr rest: styd there tl nudged along and passed wkng rivals fnl f: nvr remotely involved* **9/1**

060 **10** *3/4* **La Sonadora**[31] 6742 2-9-1 **54** SteveDrowne 12 24
(John Spearing) *reluctant to enter stalls: hld up in rr: nt looking keen bef 1/2-way: nvr a factor* **66/1**

0545 **11** *2 3/4* **Ciara Boo (IRE)**[15] 7108 2-8-13 **52** (t) AdamKirby 8 16
(David Evans) *reminder in midfield after 3f: sn struggling: wl bhd fnl 2f* **20/1**

0031 **12** *6* **Percythepinto (IRE)**[1] 7338 2-9-5 **63** 6ex (t) DavidKenny(5) 11 13
(George Baker) *prom to 3f out: wknd qckly and eased* **4/1**[2]

1m 39.6s (-0.20) **Going Correction** -0.10s/f (Stan) **12** Ran SP% **119.3**
Speed ratings (Par 94): **97,93,91,88,87 85,84,84,81,80 77,71**
toteswingers: 1&2 £19.60, 1&3 £4.00, 2&3 £41.90. CSF £66.30 CT £352.17 TOTE £2.70: £1.10, £14.10, £1.50; EX 57.80.
Owner Spittinginthewind Partnership **Bred** J Cullinan **Trained** Newmarket, Suffolk

FOCUS
A moderate handicap run at a reasonable gallop. The winner raced towards the inside in the last quarter mile.

NOTEBOOK
Fairyinthewind(IRE) is an unexposed sort who turned in her best effort to win with plenty in hand. She is due to go up 2lb even before this win is taken into account but she's a strong traveller and one lightly raced enough to be open to further progress on Polytrack. (op 13-8)
Auntie Kathryn(IRE), tried visored, hadn't shown much in turf maidens but shaped with much more encouragement after coming widest on this all-weather and handicap debut, despite losing ground at the start and racing with the choke out. There is a race to be won with her. (op 33-1)
Ermyn Flyer has yet to win but she is a fairly consistent sort who ran creditably upped to this trip for the first time and she didn't fail through lack of stamina. She doesn't look to have much in hand of her mark at present but she should continue to give a good account. (op 5-1)
House Limit(IRE), fitted with first-time blinkers, wasn't totally disgraced on his first start over this trip after helping to force a reasonable gallop. This was his best effort since his debut but he'll have to show a bit more before he's a solid betting proposition.
Emirates Jack(IRE) Official explanation: jockey said gelding hung right throughout
Ciara Boo(IRE) Official explanation: jockey said filly never travelled
Percythepinto(IRE), penalised for his win in uncompetitive selling company at Southwell the previous day, was the disappointment. Although he has run well on Polytrack, he didn't look happy on the surface this time and will be of more interest back on Fibresand. (op 11-2)

7343 BLUE SQUARE/BRITISH STALLION STUDS E B F MAIDEN FILLIES' STKS (DIV I) 1m (P)
4:50 (4:51) (Class 5) 2-Y-O **£2,846** (£847; £423; £211) **Stalls** Low

Form RPR

25 **1** **Madgenta (IRE)**[17] 7052 2-9-0 0 ShaneKelly 5 74
(Richard Hannon) *trckd ldrs on inner: prog 3f out: clsd to ld over 1f out: rdn out* **10/1**

2 *1 1/4* **Tajriba (IRE)** 2-9-0 0 EddieAhern 11 71
(Saeed Bin Suroor) *dwlt: prog fr rr on outer fr 1/2-way: trckd ldrs over 2f out: rdn to chal and upsides over 1f out: one pce* **3/1**[2]

4646 **3** *shd* **Tina's Spirit (IRE)**[20] 6995 2-8-11 82 (b) JohnFahy(3) 4 71
(Clive Cox) *trckd ldrs: nt clr run briefly over 2f out: prog wl over 1f out: styd on same pce to press for 2nd nr fin* **6/1**[3]

0 **4** *1* **Virginia Gallica (IRE)**[19] 7025 2-9-0 0 SebSanders 2 69
(J W Hills) *trckd ldng pair: chsd ldr over 2f out: chal over 1f out: fdd fnl f* **50/1**

055 **5** *1* **Winter Dress**[43] 6463 2-9-0 66 AdamKirby 3 66
(Roger Teal) *led: rdn and hung lft fr over 2f out: hdd and fdd over 1f out* **25/1**

02 **6** *3/4* **Amy Dorrit**[20] 6984 2-9-0 0 WilliamBuick 8 67
(John Gosden) *t.k.h: trckd ldrs: nt qckn wl over 2f out and struggling after: kpt on fnl f on wd outside* **2/1**[1]

6 **7** *1 1/4* **Miss Blakeney**[14] 7125 2-8-11 0 SophieDoyle(3) 10 63+
(Marcus Tregoning) *racd on outer in midfield: pushed along over 3f out: outpcd over 2f out: styd on fnl f* **14/1**

65 **8** *3 1/4* **Sugar Loaf**[14] 7125 2-9-0 0 WilliamCarson 6 54
(William Muir) *broke wl but restrained into midfield: rdn 3f out: sn outpcd: n.d after* **25/1**

9 *nk* **Narla** 2-9-0 0 IanMongan 14 54+
(Sir Henry Cecil) *sn restrained into last quartet: pushed along over 2f out: sme late prog* **25/1**

00 **10** *nk* **Song Of Joy (IRE)**[14] 7125 2-9-0 0 LukeMorris 7 53
(Paul D'Arcy) *wl in rr: drvn and modest prog 2f out: sn no hdwy* **100/1**

4 **11** *3 1/2* **Fleur De La Vie (IRE)**[73] 5537 2-9-0 0 JimCrowley 9 45
(Ralph Beckett) *hld up in last quartet: reminders over 2f out and no prog* **11/1**

50 **12** *1/2* **Stickleback**[55] 6117 2-9-0 0 MartinLane 13 44
(Harry Dunlop) *dwlt: sn pushed along: a in rr: bhd fnl 3f* **100/1**

04 **13** *2 1/2* **Lily Potts**[19] 7030 2-9-0 0 SteveDrowne 12 38
(Chris Down) *mostly chsd ldr to over 2f out: wknd qckly and eased* **20/1**

14 *2* **Al Karlovyyh (IRE)** 2-9-0 0 J-PGuillambert 1 33
(Clive Brittain) *dwlt: nvr beyond midfield: pushed along over 3f out: sn wknd* **50/1**

1m 40.13s (0.33) **Going Correction** -0.10s/f (Stan) **14** Ran SP% **118.9**
Speed ratings (Par 93): **94,92,92,91,90 89,88,85,85,84 81,80,78,76**
toteswingers: 1&2 £6.90, 1&3 £5.40, 2&3 £4.00. CSF £36.83 TOTE £6.70: £1.50, £2.00, £1.20; EX 55.60.
Owner Arlington Bloodstock **Bred** Peter Hodgson And Star Pointe Limited **Trained** East Everleigh, Wilts

FOCUS
Not too much in the way of strength-in-depth and a disappointing run from the market leader but the proximity of a reliable yardstick in third confirms this is fair form. The gallop was an ordinary one and the winner came down the centre.

NOTEBOOK
Madgenta(IRE) appreciated the extra 2f of this contest and turned in her best effort on this all-weather debut. This wasn't the best quality maiden ever staged at this course but she may well fare better in ordinary handicaps. (op 8-1)
Tajriba(IRE), a 200,000 yearling who is closely related to heavy-ground Irish I,000 Guineas winner Nightime and who is a half-sister to a couple of very useful sorts up to 1m1f, attracted support shaped pleasingly after racing wide on this racecourse debut to fare the best of those held up. She is sure to pick up a similar event. (op 10-3 tchd 11-4)
Tina's Spirit(IRE), up in trip, was well placed throughout and she's a good guide to this form after giving it her best shot returned to Polytrack. She's not as good as her rating suggests and is likely to remain vulnerable against the more progressive sorts in this grade but she should pick up a small event. (op 11-2 tchd 5-1)
Virginia Gallica(IRE) had hinted at ability in a Newbury maiden on debut and duly stepped up a fair way on that level. She's open to further progress, will have no problems with at least 1m2f in due course and she's capable of winning races. (op 66-1)
Winter Dress, from a yard that has been very quiet, ran as well as she ever has done after going from the front in a race that suited the prominent-racers. Her best chance of success will surely lie in run-of-the-mill handicap company. Official explanation: jockey said filly hung left (op 20-1)
Amy Dorrit had strong claims on her Doncaster form but she raced with the choke out and was a fair way below that level on this all-weather debut. However she is in good hands and will be worth another chance at some point. (op 15-8 tchd 9-4)
Miss Blakeney, who wasn't knocked about, ran to a similar level as over a furlong shorter on her debut. She too will be of much more interest once qualified for a handicap mark.
Narla is related to several winners, including 1m4f Group 3 winner The Geezer. She hinted at ability without being knocked about and will be of more interest over further next year.
Lily Potts Official explanation: jockey said filly had no more to give

7344 BLUE SQUARE/BRITISH STALLION STUDS E B F MAIDEN FILLIES' STKS (DIV II) 1m (P)
5:20 (5:20) (Class 5) 2-Y-O **£2,846** (£847; £423; £211) **Stalls** Low

Form RPR

1 **Tumooh (IRE)** 2-9-0 0 EddieAhern 3 75+
(Saeed Bin Suroor) *settled in midfield: pushed along and nt enough prog fr 2f out: suddenly picked up wl fnl f: r.o to ld last strides* **3/1**[1]

2 *1/2* **Isatis** 2-9-0 0 IanMongan 2 72+
(Sir Henry Cecil) *patiently rdn on inner: prog over 2f out: wnt 2nd 1f out and clsd qckly on ldr: led last 100yds: hdd fnl strides* **7/2**[2]

542 **3** *1* **Miss Astragal (IRE)**[14] 7125 2-9-0 73................................ JimCrowley 8 70
(Richard Hannon) *prom: rdn to chse ldr over 2f out: no imp and lost 2nd 1f out: styd on* **4/1**[3]

65 **4** *nse* **Derivatives (IRE)**[19] 7030 2-9-0 0.................................. WilliamBuick 12 70
(John Gosden) *racd wd early tl led after 2f and crossed to rail: kicked on over 2f out: at least 2 l clr 1f out: folded and hdd last 100yds* **3/1**[1]

5 *3* **Ice On Fire** 2-9-0 0.. LukeMorris 1 63
(Philip McBride) *s.s: mostly in last trio: urged along over 2f out: styd on to take 5th ins fnl f* **33/1**

00 **6** *hd* **Excellent News (IRE)**[19] 7030 2-9-0 0............................. SebSanders 5 63
(J W Hills) *towards rr: pushed along over 2f out: shkn up and kpt on fr over 1f out: n.d* **33/1**

0 **7** *½* **Silence Is Easy**[19] 7025 2-9-0 0..................................... SteveDrowne 7 61
(William Muir) *mostly in midfield: pushed along and outpcd over 2f out: kpt on fr over 1f out* **14/1**

8 *1 ¼* **Mishhar (IRE)** 2-9-0 0.. J-PGuillambert 10 59
(Clive Brittain) *racd wd in midfield: pushed along over 3f out: nvr gng pce to threaten but kpt on fr over 1f out* **33/1**

9 *½* **Sigurwana (USA)** 2-9-0 0.. WilliamCarson 6 57
(William Haggas) *led at modest pce for 2f: sn in 3rd: steadily wknd fnl 2f* **20/1**

10 *5* **Discern** 2-9-0 0... MartinLane 13 46
(James Fanshawe) *sed v awkwardly: a in last trio: struggling sn after 1/2-way: nvr on terms* **33/1**

00 **11** *3 ¼* **Enthrall (IRE)**[42] 6474 2-9-0 0.. ShaneKelly 11 38
(Denis Coakley) *prom: chsd ldr over 4f out to over 2f out: wknd and eased* **66/1**

00 **12** *3 ¾* **You Got The Love**[35] 6654 2-9-0 0........................... FergusSweeney 14 30
(Jeremy Gask) *a in rr: struggling fr 1/2-way* **66/1**

1m 40.77s (0.97) **Going Correction** -0.10s/f (Stan) **12** Ran SP% **118.4**
Speed ratings (Par 93): **91,90,89,89,86 86,85,84,84,79 75,72**
toteswingers: 1&2 £2.40, 1&3 £3.20, 2&3 £2.70. CSF £12.72 TOTE £6.00: £1.10, £3.20, £2.30; EX 16.60.
Owner Godolphin **Bred** Shadwell Estate Company Limited **Trained** Newmarket, Suffolk

FOCUS
Division two of a fair maiden. The gallop was no more than fair and the first four, who pulled clear, raced down the centre in the straight.

NOTEBOOK
Tumooh(IRE) ◆, a well-backed half-sister to very useful (up to 1m4f) Mooakada whose dam is from the family of 1000 Guineas winner Shadayid, created a favourable impression on this racecourse debut and is probably a fair bit better than these bare facts give her credit for. A better gallop over a bit further will suit ideally and she's the type to hold her own in stronger company. (op 9-2)
Isatis ◆, a 17,000gns half-sister to fair 6f Polytrack winner Mawjoodah, was solid at the head of the market and showed more than enough on this racecourse debut to suggest a similar event can be found on this surface. (op 3-1 tchd 5-2)
Miss Astragal(IRE) has had a few chances and is vulnerable to the better types in this grade but she's a reliable yardstick who looks the best marker to the worth of this form. She pulled clear of the rest and should be able to pick up a small event at some point. (op 7-2)
Derivatives(IRE) has improved steadily with every start and, although racing with the choke out early on, ran her best effort on this all-weather debut. She should be able to pick up an uncompetitive maiden or an ordinary handicap in due course. (op 11-4 tchd 7-2)
Ice On Fire, a half-sister to winners from 6f-1m4f, showed ability at a modest level, despite her inexperience, on this racecourse debut. A stronger overall gallop would have suited but she'll be of most interest once qualified for a mark.
Excellent News(IRE) finished a similar distance behind the fourth as she had at Newbury on her previous start and she's another that will be of most interest switched to ordinary handicaps away from progressive types.
Silence Is Easy attracted support at a price and bettered the form shown at Newbury on her debut. She should stay 1m2f and is open to improvement. (op 20-1 tchd 25-1 in a place)
Mishhar(IRE), who has several winners up to middle-distances in her pedigree, showed ability at a modest level, despite running green, on this racecourse debut. She's open to improvement and should be able to pick up a race granted a stiffer test of stamina.

7345 DOWNLOAD THE BLUE SQUARE BET APP MEDIAN AUCTION MAIDEN STKS 6f (P)
5:50 (5:53) (Class 6) 2-Y-O £1,617 (£481; £180; £180) **Stalls** Low

Form RPR

3 **1** **Fortrose Academy (IRE)**[175] 2214 2-9-3 0...................... LiamKeniry 3 74
(Andrew Balding) *trckd ldr: led over 2f out: rdn and edgd rt fnl f: asserted last 100yds* **7/2**[2]

22 **2** *1* **Gabriel's Lad (IRE)**[40] 6539 2-9-3 0................................ EddieAhern 5 71
(Denis Coakley) *trckd ldrs: prog on inner over 2f out: chsd wnr over 1f out: trying to chal whn sltly tightened up ins fnl f: no ex* **9/4**[1]

6 **3** *2* **Wiltshire Life (IRE)**[22] 6946 2-8-12 0............................ SteveDrowne 1 60
(Jeremy Gask) *chsd ldrs: rdn over 2f out: nt qckn and outpcd over 1f out: kpt on* **5/1**

3 *dht* **Topflight Princess** 2-8-12 0.. FergusSweeney 2 60
(Jeremy Gask) *s.s: sn in tch: outpcd over 2f out whn sing to make prog: jst pushed along and styd on steadily to dispute 3rd fnl f* **33/1**

5 *2* **Triple Salchow** 2-8-12 0.. FrankieMcDonald 6 54+
(Alastair Lidderdale) *awkward s: wl in rr: urged along fnl 2f and kpt on to take 5th ins fnl f* **66/1**

04 **6** *¾* **Lady Arabella (IRE)**[23] 6927 2-8-7 0.................... JemmaMarshall(5) 11 52
(Alastair Lidderdale) *chsd ldrs: rdn over 2f out: one pce and no imp* **16/1**

7 *nk* **Nevaeh** 2-8-12 0.. LukeMorris 10 51+
(Pat Eddery) *s.s: rn green in last pair: urged along sn after 1/2-way: styd on quite takingly fnl f* **33/1**

8 *¾* **Make A Fuss** 2-8-12 0.. StephenCraine 4 49
(Sylvester Kirk) *a towards rr: shkn up and no prog over 2f out: sn outpcd* **50/1**

0 **9** *shd* **Johnny Splash (IRE)**[55] 6118 2-9-0 0............................. JohnFahy(3) 12 53
(Roger Teal) *fast away fr wdst draw: led to over 2f out: wknd* **20/1**

10 *1 ¼* **Bella Ophelia (IRE)** 2-8-12 0.. SebSanders 9 45
(Hughie Morrison) *racd wd in rr: pushed along over 2f out: no real prog* **11/1**

11 *nk* **Percival Provost** 2-8-12 0.. JimCrowley 8 44
(Ralph Beckett) *chsd ldrs tl wknd over 2f out* **4/1**[3]

12 *3 ¾* **Absolute Bearing (IRE)** 2-9-3 0.. MartinLane 7 37
(Tim Etherington) *s.s: a struggling in last* **50/1**

1m 13.27s (0.17) **Going Correction** -0.10s/f (Stan) **12** Ran SP% **119.9**
Speed ratings (Par 94): **94,92,90,90,87 86,85,84,84,83 82,77**
Places: £1.20, £1.10, Topflight Princess £10.00, Wiltshire Life £0.80; toteswingers: 1&2 £2.60, 1&TP £17.70, 1&WL £1.60, 2& TP £13.10, 2&WL £1.10. CSF £11.26 TOTE £3.00; EX 11.80.
Owner Evan M Sutherland **Bred** L K I Bloodstock & Diomed Bloodstock **Trained** Kingsclere, Hants
■ Stewards' Enquiry : Liam Keniry two-day ban: careless riding (Nov 24-25)

FOCUS
An ordinary and uncompetitive maiden run at a reasonable gallop. The winner edged towards the far rail in the closing stages.

NOTEBOOK
Fortrose Academy(IRE), who shaped well on turf in May, was easy to back near the off on this all-weather debut and first run for nearly six months (sustained stress fracture of hind leg) but he confirmed he retains all his ability, despite racing with the choke out. He may progress further in handicaps. (op 11-4 tchd 9-2)
Gabriel's Lad(IRE) is bordering on fair and he bettered the form of his all-weather debut in this uncompetitive event, with the interference suffered late on making no difference to the result. He should be able to pick up a similar event. (tchd 2-1 and 11-4)
Wiltshire Life(IRE) attracted support and bettered the form of her debut effort at this course. She'll be of more interest once handicapped. (op 8-1 tchd 4-1)
Topflight Princess, a 7,500 first foal of a dual 5f winner, showed ability at a modest level on this racecourse debut after racing with the choke out. She should be able to step up on these bare facts in due course. (op 8-1 tchd 4-1)
Triple Salchow, who cost only 1000GBP and is the first foal of an unraced dam, hinted at ability on this racecourse debut. She's likely to remain vulnerable in this grade. (op 100-1)
Lady Arabella(IRE) failed to build on her latest effort returned to sprinting. She'll be seen to better effect in ordinary handicaps over a bit further.
Percival Provost, the first foal of a 5f juvenile winner, attracted support but was soundly beaten on this racecourse debut. (op 9-2)

7346 WIN THOUSANDS OF SPORTS TICKETS AT BLUESQ.COM H'CAP 1m 4f (P)
6:20 (6:21) (Class 5) (0-70,72) 3-Y-0+ £2,264 (£673; £336; £168) **Stalls** Centre

Form RPR

1015 **1** **Bennelong**[9] 7203 5-9-4 **65**.. AmirQuinn 6 76+
(Richard Rowe) *trckd ldrs in 5th: cruising whn prog over 2f out: led jst over 1f out: rdn and fnd enough to assert* **16/1**

0240 **2** *1* **Sand Skier**[20] 7002 4-9-2 **70**.................................. NicoleNordblad(7) 13 80
(Hans Adielsson) *hld up in midfield in 8th: prog and reminder 2f out: r.o over 1f out to take 2nd nr fin* **11/1**

4351 **3** *½* **Waahej**[10] 7200 5-9-6 **72** 6ex... LauraPike(5) 4 81
(Peter Hiatt) *hld up in last pair and wl off the pce: brought wd and gd prog fr jst over 2f out: styd on fnl f: tk 3rd post* **4/1**[1]

0004 **4** *shd* **Beat Route**[14] 7122 4-8-12 **64**.................................. JemmaMarshall(5) 1 72
(Michael Attwater) *trckd ldng pair: effrt to ld over 2f out: hdd jst over 1f out: no ch w wnr and lost 2 pls nr fin* **11/1**

6524 **5** *2* **Rosco Flyer (IRE)**[9] 7203 5-9-3 **64**................................(b) AdamKirby 2 69
(Roger Teal) *chsd ldrs disputing 6th: drvn 3f out: styd on to take 5th fnl f: nvr able to chal* **13/2**[2]

00 **6** *5* **Archie Rice (USA)**[59] 6005 5-9-5 **66**................................ JimmyQuinn 5 63
(Tom Keddy) *settled in abt 7th: effrt on inner over 2f out: tried to cl on ldrs over 1f out: sn wknd* **20/1**

0-54 **7** *1 ¾* **Our Play (IRE)**[22] 6947 3-9-3 **70**.................................... SteveDrowne 10 64
(Lydia Richards) *off the pce in 9th: urged along 1/2-way: tried to mount an effrt over 2f out: sn no hdwy* **40/1**

4021 **8** *1 ¼* **Shades Of Grey**[19] 7032 4-9-3 **67**................................... JohnFahy(3) 12 59
(Clive Cox) *trckd ldng trio: rdn over 2f out: wknd over 1f out* **9/1**

3001 **9** *1 ½* **Megalala (IRE)**[9] 7203 10-9-7 **68** 6ex............................ NeilChalmers 3 58
(John Bridger) *led at gd pce: hdd over 2f out: wknd over 1f out* **11/1**

/2-0 **10** *3 ½* **Sumani (FR)**[55] 6121 5-9-3 **64**..[1] LukeMorris 11 48
(Simon Dow) *chsd ldrs disputing 6th: drvn 4f out: no prog over 2f out: wknd* **20/1**

2000 **11** *nk* **Addikt (IRE)**[34] 6669 6-9-3 **69**.................................... DavidKenny(5) 8 53
(Michael Scudamore) *s.s: wl off the pce in last pair: reminders over 5f out: no prog and wl btn 3f out* **40/1**

0004 **12** *2 ½* **Montegonian (USA)**[17] 7070 3-9-0 **67**............................. SebSanders 9 47
(Marcus Tregoning) *hld up in 12th: rdn 4f out: no prog* **7/1**[3]

0362 **13** *3 ½* **Viva Diva**[10] 7200 3-9-3 **70**.. EddieAhern 14 44
(David Lanigan) *a in last quartet: struggling over 3f out* **13/2**[2]

6460 **14** *1* **Green Earth (IRE)**[23] 6931 4-9-7 **68**................................ IanMongan 7 41
(Pat Phelan) *pressed ldr to over 2f out: wknd rapidly* **16/1**

2m 31.96s (-2.54) **Going Correction** -0.10s/f (Stan)
WFA 3 from 4yo+ 6lb **14** Ran SP% **120.3**
Speed ratings (Par 103): **104,103,103,102,101 98,97,96,95,92 92,91,88,88**
toteswingers: 1&2 £53.70, 1&3 £18.80, 2&3 £12.80. CSF £174.21 CT £849.22 TOTE £27.40: £11.40, £7.00, £2.10; EX 194.50.
Owner Miss Victoria Baalham **Bred** The National Stud **Trained** Sullington, W Sussex

FOCUS
Exposed performers in a modest handicap. The gallop was an ordinary one and the first five finished clear, showing solid form. The winner came down the centre in the straight.

7347 PLAY RAINBOW RICHES AT BLUESQ.COM CONDITIONS STKS 1m 3f (P)
6:50 (6:51) (Class 4) 3-Y-0+ £4,075 (£1,212; £606; £303) **Stalls** Low

Form RPR

0000 **1** **Irish Flame (SAF)**[12] 7166 5-9-6 111................................... LukeMorris 5 116
(M F De Kock, South Africa) *hld up in 5th: prog over 3f out: chsd ldr over 2f out: rdn to ld jst over 1f out: styd on wl* **5/1**[3]

-433 **2** *3 ¼* **Treasury Devil (USA)**[34] 6671 3-8-8 100....................(b[1]) WilliamBuick 4 103
(John Gosden) *pressed ldr early then settled in 2nd: pressed for position so moved up to ld 3f out: drvn 2f out: hdd and outpcd jst over 1f out* **13/8**[1]

14 **3** *4 ½* **Late Telegraph (IRE)**[17] 7053 3-8-11 95............................ IanMongan 7 98
(Sir Henry Cecil) *t.k.h: hld up in 4th: moved up to chal on outer 3f out: nt qckn and lost 2nd over 2f out: one pce after* **11/4**[2]

4216 **4** *2 ¼* **Spensley (IRE)**[8] 7226 5-8-13 91..................................... JimCrowley 6 91
(James Fanshawe) *hld up in last pair: rdn over 3f out: no imp on ldrs over 2f out: plugged on* **15/2**

1230 **5** *9* **Sir Boss (IRE)**[152] 2932 6-8-13 87.....................................[1] JimmyQuinn 2 75
(Michael Mullineaux) *chsd ldng pair to over 3f out: sn rdn: wknd over 2f out* **25/1**

5045 **6** *1 ¼* **Choral Festival**[14] 7130 5-8-8 68..................................... NeilChalmers 3 68
(John Bridger) *a in last pair: struggling and detached over 3f out: no ch after* **100/1**

4015 **7** *2 ¼* **Milnagavie**[13] 7136 4-8-8 87.. SteveDrowne 1 64
(Richard Hannon) *led: tried to set modest pce but buzzed up by rival after 1f and set gd gallop: hdd & wknd 3f out* **7/1**

2m 16.98s (-4.92) **Going Correction** -0.10s/f (Stan) course record
WFA 3 from 4yo+ 5lb **7** Ran SP% **110.5**
Speed ratings (Par 105): **113,110,107,105,99 98,96**
toteswingers: 1&2 £1.50, 1&3 £2.80, 2&3 £1.90. CSF £12.64 TOTE £6.80: £6.10, £1.10; EX 13.50.
Owner L M Nestadt, B Kantor et al **Bred** Millennium Stud **Trained** South Africa

FOCUS
A decent conditions event in which the two smart performers filled the first two places. Although the gallop to the home straight was just an ordinary one, the pace really picked up thereafter and this was run in course record time. The winner raced near the inside rail in the closing stages and rates back to something like his South African form.

7348 BET AT BLUESQ.COM H'CAP — 7f (P)
7:20 (7:20) (Class 5) (0-75,74) 3-Y-O — £2,264 (£673; £336; £168) Stalls Low

Form				RPR
1301	1		**Numeral (IRE)**[43] 6442 3-9-7 **74** .... JimCrowley 1 (Richard Hannon) *cl up: trckd ldr 4f out: led over 2f out: edgd lft and drvn over 1f out: styd on wl* **4/5**[1]	83+
1340	2	1 ½	**Justbookie Dot Com (IRE)**[27] 6830 3-9-3 **73** ....(v) RichardEvans(3) 8 (David Evans) *hld up in last: prog wl over 2f out: drvn over 1f out: edgd lft but styd on to take 2nd last 100yds* **13/2**[3]	78
3015	3	½	**One Cool Chick**[31] 6746 3-8-7 **60** oh3 .... NeilChalmers 4 (John Bridger) *stdd s: hld up in last pair: prog to chse ldng pair over 2f out: drvn to chse wnr over 1f out and edgd lft: one pce and lost 2nd last 100yds* **25/1**	64
501	4	3 ¼	**Demoiselle Bond**[15] 7096 3-8-8 **61** oh2 ow1 .... SteveDrowne 2 (Lydia Richards) *led: shifted lft and hdd over 2f out: continued to edge lft and lost 2nd over 1f out: fdd* **12/1**	56
-050	5	½	**Malpas Missile (IRE)**[133] 3549 3-9-5 **72** .... RichardKingscote 6 (Tom Dascombe) *hld up in 6th: no prog over 2f out: rdn and one pce over 1f out* **10/1**	66
4000	6	2 ¾	**Strictly Pink (IRE)**[19] 7024 3-9-4 **71** ....(p) IanMongan 9 (Alan Bailey) *cl up: disp 2nd over 3f out: drvn over 2f out: steadily wknd* **5/1**[2]	57
0000	7	5	**Bassett Road (IRE)**[15] 7097 3-9-5 **72** .... StevieDonohoe 7 (Willie Musson) *chsd ldr 3f: wd and lost grnd qckly: last 3f out: wl btn after* **9/1**	45
0000	8	nk	**City Legend**[15] 7097 3-9-0 **67** ....(vt) LukeMorris 5 (Alan McCabe) *cl up: rdn to dispute 2nd briefly over 3f out: wknd u.p over 2f out* **16/1**	39

1m 25.07s (-0.93) **Going Correction** -0.10s/f (Stan) — 8 Ran SP% **122.1**
Speed ratings (Par 102): **101,99,98,95,94 91,85,85**
toteswingers: 1&2 £2.20, 1&3 £9.20, 2&3 £9.00. CSF £7.44 CT £83.66 TOTE £2.30: £1.50, £2.70, £4.60; EX 9.80.

Owner Highclere Thoroughbred Racing-Flying Fox **Bred** Tinnakill Bloodstock & Forenaghts Stud **Trained** East Everleigh, Wilts

FOCUS
Not the most competitive of handicaps but one run at a reasonable gallop. The first three, who pulled clear, came down the centre in the straight. The winner is a bit more convincing than the bare form.

7349 BET AT BLUESQ.COM ON YOUR MOBILE H'CAP — 6f (P)
7:50 (7:50) (Class 6) (0-65,65) 3-Y-O+ — £1,617 (£481; £240; £120) Stalls Low

Form				RPR
04	1		**Qubuh (IRE)**[27] 6840 3-9-1 **64** .... TomEaves 1 (Linda Stubbs) *trckd ldng trio: burst through to ld over 2f out: hrd pressed and drvn over 1f out: battled on wl: jst hld on* **4/1**[1]	72
0000	2	hd	**Lastkingofscotland (IRE)**[13] 7146 5-8-7 **63** ....(b) NoelGarbutt(7) 4 (Conor Dore) *bmpd and hmpd s: wl off the pce in last pair: prog on inner over 2f out: rdn over 1f out: styd on wl fnl f: tk 2nd nr fin and jst failed to catch wnr* **12/1**	71+
2000	3	½	**Custom House (IRE)**[28] 6814 3-8-12 **64** ....(b[1]) NataliaGemelova(3) 3 (John E Long) *wnt sharply lft s: hld up in midfield: prog on inner to go 2nd wl over 1f out: sn chalng and upsides: nt qckn last 100yds: lost 2nd nr fin* **13/2**[3]	70
1143	4	1	**Two Turtle Doves (IRE)**[15] 7104 5-9-1 **64** .... JimmyQuinn 10 (Michael Mullineaux) *trckd ldng trio: effrt over 2f out: tried to cl over 1f out: styd on same pce fnl f* **10/1**	67
4200	5	½	**Co Dependent (USA)**[29] 6793 5-8-13 **65** .... SophieDoyle(3) 9 (Jamie Osborne) *stdd s: hld up in last pair and wl off the pce: stl in last pair 2f out: gd prog over 1f out: rdn and threatened to cl ent fnl f: one pce last 150yds* **7/1**	66
5200	6	1 ¾	**Diamond Vine (IRE)**[25] 6895 3-9-2 **65** ....(p) LiamKeniry 2 (Ronald Harris) *trckd ldng trio: pushed along 3f out: lost pl over 2f out: kpt on same pce fr over 1f out* **8/1**	61
4440	7	2 ¼	**Anjomarba (IRE)**[17] 7068 4-8-10 **64** .... DavidKenny(5) 5 (Conor Dore) *racd on inner: disp ld to wl over 1f out: steadily wknd* **10/1**	52
0306	8	nk	**Dvinsky (USA)**[23] 6931 10-9-1 **64** ....(b) ShaneKelly 8 (Paul Howling) *urged along to dispute ld: hdd over 2f out: steadily wknd* **12/1**	51
0015	9	¾	**Insolenceofoffice (IRE)**[9] 7216 3-8-9 **63** ....(p) LMcNiff(5) 11 (Bruce Hellier) *racd wd in midfield and chsd along: struggling over 2f out* **11/2**[2]	48
0160	10	3 ½	**Mary's Pet**[25] 6889 4-9-1 **64** .... StevieDonohoe 6 (John Akehurst) *a in last trio: struggling over 2f out* **20/1**	38
2250	11	5	**Court Applause (IRE)**[134] 3523 3-9-0 **63** .... WilliamCarson 12 (William Muir) *racd wdst of all in trio disputing ld: hdd over 2f out: wknd rapidly* **11/1**	21

1m 12.6s (-0.50) **Going Correction** -0.10s/f (Stan) — 11 Ran SP% **119.0**
Speed ratings (Par 101): **99,98,98,96,96 93,90,90,89,84 78**
toteswingers: 1&2 £24.20, 1&3 £10.00, 2&3 £11.00. CSF £54.01 CT £256.54 TOTE £3.30: £1.10, £5.90, £4.00; EX 117.90.

Owner D M Smith **Bred** Irish National Stud **Trained** Norton, N Yorks

FOCUS
A modest handicap run at a sound pace throughout. The winner raced towards the centre in the straight. Ordinary straightforward form.

T/Jkpt: Not won. T/Plt: £40.70 to a £1 stake. Pool of £64,536.36 - 1,155.67 winning tickets. T/Qpdt: £8.20 to a £1 stake. Pool of £8,575.83 - 770.93 winning tickets. JN

7335 SOUTHWELL (L-H)
Thursday, November 10

OFFICIAL GOING: Standard
Wind: Light against Weather: Overcast, sunny periods

7350 SOUTHWELL RACECOURSE "WHAT A COURSE" MAIDEN AUCTION STKS — 7f (F)
12:20 (12:21) (Class 6) 2-Y-O — £1,617 (£481; £240; £120) Stalls Low

Form				RPR
324	1		**No Compromise**[12] 7165 2-8-8 71 .... RichardKingscote 3 (Hughie Morrison) *trckd ldr: smooth hdwy to ld 2f out: pushed clr over 1f out: kpt on* **13/8**[1]	80+
4422	2	6	**Enery (IRE)**[29] 6792 2-8-13 72 .... TomEaves 2 (Mahmood Al Zarooni) *chsd ldrs and sn rdn along: outpcd wl over 2f out: styd on appr fnl f: tk 2nd nr fin: no ch w wnr* **11/4**[2]	69
426	3	nk	**Dutch Master**[16] 7082 2-8-11 77 .... LiamKeniry 4 (Andrew Balding) *prom: effrt over 2f out: rdn to chse wnr wl over 1f out: one pce and lost 2nd nr fin* **3/1**[3]	67
4322	4	7	**Ishiamiracle**[1] 7336 2-8-4 60 .... KirstyMilczarek 5 (Phil McEntee) *led: rdn along 3f out: hdd 2f out: grad wknd* **15/2**	41
	5	6	**Red Hermes (IRE)** 2-8-4 0 .... JimmyQuinn 6 (Mark H Tompkins) *dwlt: in tch whn green and rn wd home bnd and sn outpcd: wandered bdly over 1f out* **33/1**	26
	6	3 ¼	**Spartilla** 2-8-9 0 .... FrederikTylicki 7 (James Given) *dwlt: green and sn chsd along: outpcd and bhd fr 1/2-way* **28/1**	22
	7	33	**There's No Rules** 2-8-9 0 .... RobbieFitzpatrick 1 (Richard Guest) *dwlt: green and outpcd in rr: bhd fr 1/2-way* **80/1**	—

1m 27.73s (-2.57) **Going Correction** -0.25s/f (Stan) — 7 Ran SP% **109.2**
Speed ratings (Par 94): **104,97,96,88,81 78,40**
toteswingers: 1&2 £1.60, 1&3 £1.90, 2&3 £1.80. CSF £5.64 TOTE £2.10: £1.20, £2.20; EX 6.20.

Owner Mouse Hamilton-Fairley **Bred** The Hon Mrs E J Wills **Trained** East Ilsley, Berks

FOCUS
No more than a fair maiden auction won easily by the runner with the best form. For the grade, the gallop was a good one.

NOTEBOOK
No Compromise's form hasn't looked particularly progressive but it was still the best on offer and, back on the all-weather for the first time since her debut, she showed what she is capable of under seemingly ideal conditions given she doesn't look the best of movers, a good gallop and an easy surface. This win might not have done her handicap mark much good but, despite being by Avonbridge, she shapes as though she'll stay a mile. Official explanation: jockey said that the filly ran green (op 7-4 tchd 15-8 and 6-4)

Enery(IRE) ran below his best seeming unsuited by a combination of the surface and the drop back to 7f, never travelling at any point and only securing second late on. (op 5-2 tchd 9-4 and 3-1)

Dutch Master had run easily his best race so far on his only time away from soft ground, so it's likely he wasn't at his best either in being beaten so far in third, well held from early in the straight. (op 7-2)

Ishiamiracle was making a quick reappearance after finishing second off a mark of 60 in a nursery here the previous day and didn't run as badly as the distance she was beaten would suggest, as the good gallop she set took its toll late on. (op 7-1 tchd 8-1)

Red Hermes(IRE), a fourth foal of a mare still looking for her first winner, showed promise but she also looked far from an easy ride, running wide on the bend and then hanging badly in the straight. Official explanation: jockey said filly ran green

7351 32RED ALL-WEATHER "HANDS AND HEELS" APPRENTICE SERIES H'CAP (RACING EXCELLENCE INITIATIVE) — 7f (F)
12:50 (12:50) (Class 6) (0-60,60) 3-Y-O+ — £1,704 (£503; £251) Stalls Low

Form				RPR
4020	1		**Lujano**[56] 6098 6-8-10 **54** .... JacobButterfield(5) 8 (Ollie Pears) *chsd ldrs: hdwy 3f out: swtchd rt and chal 2f out: led over 1f out: jst hld on* **9/2**[2]	64+
2406	2	shd	**Billy Cadiz**[17] 7063 6-8-10 **49** .... GeorgeChaloner 12 (Mark Campion) *midfield: hdwy 2f out: rdn and n.m.r ent fnl f: styd on strly: jst failed* **9/1**	58+
3064	3	1	**Norcroft**[6] 7269 9-8-5 **49** ....(p) DanielHarris(5) 9 (Christine Dunnett) *dwlt and towards rr: hdwy wl over 2f out: rdn over 1f out: kpt on fnl f* **11/1**	54
2212	4	nk	**Scarborough Lily**[20] 7001 3-9-6 **60** ....(b) MichaelJMurphy 10 (Edward Vaughan) *hld up: hdwy 2f out: rdn to chse ldrs over 1f out: kpt on ins fnl f* **4/1**[1]	64
4000	5	1 ¼	**Wotatomboy**[17] 7071 5-8-8 **47** ....(v) NoraLooby 11 (Richard Whitaker) *led: rdn along wl over 2f out: hdd over 1f out and grad wknd* **50/1**	48
0200	6	1 ¼	**Jonnie Skull (IRE)**[8] 7228 5-9-7 **60** ....(vt) JasonHart 3 (Phil McEntee) *cl up on inner: rdn along 2f out: grad wknd* **6/1**[3]	57
0060	7	2	**Takajan (IRE)**[27] 6841 4-9-7 **60** .... JackDuern 2 (Mark Brisbourne) *dwlt and towards rr tl sme late hdwy* **12/1**	52
0006	8	¾	**Spirit Of Dixie**[9] 7211 4-8-8 **47** ....(p) NatashaEaton 13 (Noel Wilson) *prom: rdn along over 2f out: sn wknd* **50/1**	37
5001	9	2 ¾	**Putin (IRE)**[7] 7246 3-9-1 **58** 6ex ....(p) DannyBrock(3) 5 (Phil McEntee) *trckd ldrs: pushed along 3f out: rdn over 2f out and sn wknd* **6/1**[3]	41
0035	10	8	**Totally Trusted**[17] 7069 3-9-4 **58** .... GeorgeDowning 6 (David Nicholls) *a towards rr* **16/1**	19
2000	11	5	**Eshoog (IRE)**[27] 6841 3-9-1 **60** .... HayleyBurton(5) 1 (Phil McEntee) *chsd ldrs: rdn along 3f out: sn wknd* **33/1**	7
4303	U		**Red Scintilla**[17] 7065 4-8-9 **55** ....(p) DanielleMooney(7) 4 (Nigel Tinkler) *in rr whn hmpd and uns rdr after 1f* **12/1**	—

1m 29.92s (-0.38) **Going Correction** -0.25s/f (Stan)
WFA 3 from 4yo+ 1lb — 12 Ran SP% **113.2**
Speed ratings (Par 101): **92,91,90,90,88 87,85,84,81,72 66,—**
toteswingers: 1&2 £8.10, 1&3 £9.20, 2&3 £15.90. CSF £42.05 CT £413.10 TOTE £7.40: £2.60, £3.50, £4.80; EX 49.90 TRIFECTA Not won..

Owner David Scott and Co (Pattern Makers) Ltd **Bred** D Scott **Trained** Norton, N Yorks

■ Stewards' Enquiry : Hayley Burton two-day ban: failed to weigh in (Nov 24-25)
George Downing four-day ban: careless riding (Nov 24-26,28)

FOCUS
A modest 'hands and heels' apprentice handicap in which solid recent form was thin on the ground. The gallop was once again a good one but it was the slowest of the four C&D times. The winner is rated slightly better than the bare form.

7352 32REDBET CLAIMING STKS — 7f (F)
1:20 (1:21) (Class 6) 3-Y-O+ — £1,617 (£481; £240; £120) Stalls Low

Form — RPR

1656 **1** **Jobe (USA)**[69] 5682 5-9-2 78 (p) PhillipMakin 6 — 88
(Kevin Ryan) *chsd ldng pair: hdwy 2f out: rdn to ld over 1f out: jst hld on* **5/1**[3]

066 **2** *hd* **Salerosa (IRE)**[136] 3473 6-8-1 75 (p) DuranFentiman 8 — 72
(Ann Duffield) *hld up in midfield: smooth hdwy over 2f out: trckd ldrs on bit 1 1/2f out: rdn to chse wnr ins fnl f: kpt on wl: jst failed* **15/2**

6400 **3** *4 1/2* **Hits Only Jude (IRE)**[12] 7159 8-8-3 71 (v) JasonHart(7) 11 — 69
(Declan Carroll) *sn rdn along and in rr: hdwy whn carried lft wl over 1f out: sn rdn: styd on wl fnl f: nrst fin* **33/1**

2246 **4** *3/4* **Boy The Bell**[9] 7214 4-8-8 73 BarryMcHugh 7 — 65
(Ollie Pears) *chsd ldrs: rdn along 2f out: kpt on same pce appr fnl f* **9/2**[2]

0004 **5** *nse* **Lovelace**[40] 6542 7-8-10 83 TonyHamilton 13 — 67
(Richard Fahey) *dwlt: sn in midfield: hdwy 2f out: sn rdn and hung lft: drvn and kpt on fnl f:* **7/2**[1]

0041 **6** *3 1/4* **Brio**[30] 6767 3-8-5 62 (v) JoeFanning 2 — 54
(Alan McCabe) *cl up: rdn to ld 2f out: hdd over 1f out: wknd ent fnl f* **12/1**

6000 **7** *1* **Jibouti (IRE)**[23] 6939 3-8-5 52 (b1) KirstyMilczarek 14 — 52
(Clive Brittain) *in tch: hdwy to chse ldrs 3f out: rdn over 2f out and sn wknd* **66/1**

0004 **8** *2 1/2* **Watch Chain (IRE)**[37] 6616 4-8-8 59 (p) AndrewMullen 9 — 47
(Alan McCabe) *nvr bttr than midfield* **20/1**

2250 **9** *3/4* **Golden Creek (USA)**[19] 7034 3-8-6 70 (v) MatthewLawson(5) 1 — 49
(Mrs K Burke) *led: rdn along 3f out: hdd 2f out and wknd qckly* **11/2**

0- **10** *5* **Bahri Beat (IRE)**[359] 7471 3-8-9 0 PaddyAspell 10 — 33
(John Norton) *a towards rr* **200/1**

2000 **11** *1/2* **Lesley's Choice**[14] 7116 5-9-3 74 (p) SophieDoyle(3) 4 — 42
(Paul Rich) *a towards rr* **50/1**

-000 **12** *hd* **Mi Regalo**[28] 6815 3-8-2 72 (p) NataliaGemelova(3) 5 — 28
(Phil McEntee) *a towards rr* **25/1**

0-00 **13** *5* **Autumn Blades (IRE)**[90] 4993 6-8-12 92 (b) TomEaves 3 — 20
(Ruth Carr) *dwlt: hdwy and in tch 4f out: rdn 3f out and sn wknd* **10/1**

0050 **P** **Le Reveur**[26] 6877 9-8-6 45 RobbieFitzpatrick 12 — —
(Richard Guest) *towards rr whn p.u after 2f: lame* **150/1**

1m 28.27s (-2.03) **Going Correction** -0.25s/f (Stan)
WFA 3 from 4yo+ 1lb — **14** Ran SP% **117.2**
Speed ratings (Par 101): **101,100,95,94,94 91,89,87,86,80 79,79,73,—**
toteswingers: 1&2 £9.60, 1&3 £27.40, 2&3 £37.10. CSF £39.18 TOTE £7.00: £2.50, £3.20, £11.30; EX 43.10 TRIFECTA Not won..
Owner Mrs Angie Bailey **Bred** David Garvin **Trained** Hambleton, N Yorks

FOCUS
A decent field considering the prize-money on offer and another race run at a good clip. The time was modest and the form is rated around the second and third.
Le Reveur Official explanation: jockey said gelding felt wrong and pulled up

7353 32REDPOKER.COM (S) STKS — 6f (F)
1:50 (1:50) (Class 6) 2-Y-O — £1,617 (£481; £240; £120) Stalls Low

Form — RPR

2203 **1** **Make Up**[10] 7196 2-8-6 54 BarryMcHugh 5 — 60
(Noel Wilson) *trckd ldrs: hdwy to chse ldng pair 1/2-way: effrt on outer over 2f out: rdn to ld wl over 1f out: styd on wl* **9/1**

04 **2** *2 1/2* **Smacker (IRE)**[29] 6800 2-8-11 0 JoeFanning 3 — 58
(Hughie Morrison) *trckd ldr: smooth hdwy to chal over 2f out: shkn up and ev ch wl over 1f out: sn rdn and kpt on same pce* **5/4**[1]

5355 **3** *3 3/4* **The Dancing Lord**[10] 7196 2-8-9 71 RyanWhile(7) 1 — 57+
(Bill Turner) *in tch on inner: hdwy 2f out: sn rdn: styd on to take 3rd ins fnl f* **7/1**[3]

2430 **4** *3* **Thorpe Bay**[27] 6846 2-8-11 62 (b) FrederikTylicki 9 — 37
(Mark Rimmer) *led: rdn and jnd over 2f out: hdd wl over 1f out and sn one pce* **5/1**[2]

0040 **5** *4* **I'm A Doughnut**[30] 6627 2-8-11 59 (p) RichardKingscote 6 — 25
(Tom Dascombe) *towards rr: rdn over 2f out: nvr nr ldrs* **14/1**

6 *1 1/2* **Ficelle (IRE)** 2-8-3 0 ow2 MatthewLawson(5) 10 — 18
(Mrs K Burke) *v.s.a and lost many l s: bhd tl sme late hdwy* **33/1**

6526 **7** *2 1/4* **Artists Corner**[10] 7196 2-8-11 58 (v1) TonyHamilton 7 — 14
(Richard Fahey) *v.s.a and lost many l s: a bhd* **8/1**

1350 **8** *6* **Miserere Mei (IRE)**[59] 6001 2-8-4 62 (e1) JasonHart(7) 2 — —
(Richard Guest) *chsd ldrs: hdwy 3f out: rdn 2f out: sn wknd and heavily eased fnl f* **12/1**

06 **9** *2* **Darleas Gift (IRE)**[6] 7267 2-8-6 0 DuranFentiman 4 — —
(Kevin Ryan) *chsd ldrs to 1/2-way: sn wknd* **50/1**

1m 15.18s (-1.32) **Going Correction** -0.25s/f (Stan) — **9** Ran SP% **114.0**
Speed ratings (Par 94): **98,94,89,85,80 78,75,67,64**
toteswingers: 1&2 £4.70, 1&3 £6.20, 2&3 £2.50. CSF £20.37 TOTE £8.40: £2.70, £1.20, £2.90; EX 31.60 Trifecta £132.80 Pool: £463.20 - 2.58 winning units..The winner was bought in for 7,250gns.
Owner Ms Sara Hattersley **Bred** Brook Stud Bloodstock Ltd **Trained** Sandhutton, N Yorks

FOCUS
A modest seller run once again at a good pace and in which few ever got involved.

NOTEBOOK
Make Up had hitherto looked exposed at this level but her first try of the surface took her form to a new level and she won it nicely after travelling well throughout. She looks to have a fair amount of speed and may be better kept to this trip than 7f, though she'll find things harder back in a handicap off her revised mark. She was bought in for 7,250 gns. (op 8-1)
Smacker(IRE) had to be of interest dropped steeply in class and representing a yard with an excellent record here, and was duly sent off a short-priced favourite, but that he wasn't able to get his head in front rather exposes his own limitations. That said, he'll probably be better suited by 7f. (op 15-8 tchd 2-1)
The Dancing Lord started a big price for one with easily the highest BHA rating and left the impression he wasn't seen to best advantage, with his apprentice rider never seeming able to ride him out properly for whatever reason. (op 9-2)
Thorpe Bay was having his first experience of the surface, but it seemed more that he's something of a free-going sort as well as a dubious stayer that saw him folding tamely after setting a good pace. (op 6-1 tchd 9-2)
I'm A Doughnut fared little better dropped in grade and tried in cheekpieces. (op 16-1)
Ficelle(IRE), a newcomer, showed some promise after a very slow start, making ground into sixth, and not hard ridden either, after being in a hopeless position turning for home. Official explanation: jockey said filly hung left-handed (op 25-1 tchd 22-1)
Artists Corner Official explanation: jockey said filly was slowly away

7354 32RED CASINO MAIDEN STKS — 7f (F)
2:20 (2:22) (Class 5) 3-Y-O — £2,385 (£704; £352) Stalls Low

Form — RPR

0064 **1** **Riczar**[7] 7246 3-8-12 44 RichardKingscote 4 — 63
(Tom Dascombe) *mde most: rdn clr over 2f out: kpt on wl* **20/1**

33 **2** *3 1/2* **Pulsatilla**[17] 7063 3-8-12 0 TomEaves 8 — 54
(Bryan Smart) *cl up: disp ld 1/2-way: rdn and ev ch 2f out: kpt on same pce appr fnl f* **9/1**

2000 **3** *1 1/2* **Afkar (IRE)**[12] 7168 3-9-3 79 FrederikTylicki 3 — 55
(Clive Brittain) *chsd ldrs: effrt over 2f out: rdn wl over 1f out and sn one pce* **10/11**[1]

4 *3/4* **Community (USA)** 3-8-5 0 LeonnaMayor(7) 2 — 48+
(Phil McEntee) *hld up in tch: swtchd outside and sme hdwy wl over 1f out: sn no imp* **9/2**[2]

5 *3/4* **Schoolmaster** 3-9-3 0 JoeFanning 10 — 51
(Giles Bravery) *trckd ldrs: hdwy wl over 2f out: rdn wl over 1f out: sn one pce* **20/1**

00 **6** *3* **First Class**[15] 7111 3-9-3 0 GrahamGibbons 9 — 43
(Rae Guest) *chsd ldrs: rdn and edgd lft 2f out: sn btn* **20/1**

0-60 **7** *3 1/2* **Cairanne**[16] 7084 3-8-12 41 JimmyQuinn 7 — 29
(Tom Keddy) *nvr nr ldrs* **100/1**

42 **8** *3 1/4* **Enchanted Dream**[17] 7069 3-8-12 0 BarryMcHugh 1 — 21
(George Margarson) *a towards rr* **7/1**[3]

9 *3 1/2* **Field Finner** 3-8-9 0 BillyCray(3) 5 — 12
(David Nicholls) *s.i.s: a bhd* **28/1**

0000 **10** *17* **Pronounce**[27] 6845 3-9-3 37 RobbieFitzpatrick 6 — —
(Michael Appleby) *sn rdn along and a bhd* **150/1**

1m 28.77s (-1.53) **Going Correction** -0.25s/f (Stan) — **10** Ran SP% **112.5**
Speed ratings (Par 102): **98,94,92,91,90 87,83,79,75,56**
toteswingers: 1&2 £5.30, 1&3 £6.10, 2&3 £2.50. CSF £166.82 TOTE £22.20: £3.70, £1.10, £1.20; EX 49.20 Trifecta £380.60 Part won. Pool: £514.39 - 0.93 winning units..
Owner Richard Woods **Bred** Baroness Bloodstock & Redmyre Bloodstock **Trained** Malpas, Cheshire
■ Stewards' Enquiry : Leonna Mayor seven-day ban: used whip with excessive frequency (Nov 24-26,28-Dec 1)

FOCUS
Just a modest maiden in all probability with the favourite well below his best. The pace didn't pick up in earnest until straightening for home and little got involved from behind. The form is rated tentatively around the runner-up.

7355 32RED.COM H'CAP (DIV I) — 5f (F)
2:50 (2:53) (Class 4) (0-80,80) 3-Y-O+ — £4,075 (£1,212; £606; £303) Stalls High

Form — RPR

61U0 **1** **Monsieur Jamie**[52] 6217 3-9-4 77 JoeFanning 7 — 89
(J R Jenkins) *a.p: cl up 1/2-way: led appr fnl f: sn rdn and r.o* **11/2**[2]

6050 **2** *1 1/4* **Lenny Bee**[24] 6917 5-9-2 80 (t) JustinNewman(5) 3 — 87
(Deborah Sanderson) *chsd ldrs: hdwy 2f out: sn rdn and edgd lft over 1f out: kpt on fnl f* **7/2**[1]

0102 **3** *nk* **Dancing Freddy (IRE)**[24] 6917 4-8-13 75 (tp) RobertLButler(3) 10 — 81
(Richard Guest) *trckd ldrs: swtchd rt and hdwy wl over 1f out: rdn and kpt on fnl f* **9/1**

4065 **4** *nse* **Above The Stars**[15] 7106 3-8-11 70 BarryMcHugh 9 — 76
(Richard Fahey) *trckd ldrs: hdwy 2f out: rdn over 1f out: kpt on fnl f* **8/1**

2306 **5** *1/2* **Island Legend (IRE)**[143] 3222 5-9-7 80 (p) RichardKingscote 8 — 84
(Milton Bradley) *led: rdn wl over 1f out: hdd appr fnl f: wknd* **14/1**

4111 **6** *3/4* **Captain Scooby**[44] 6427 5-8-13 79 (e1) JasonHart(7) 2 — 80
(Richard Guest) *chsd ldrs: hdwy whn n.m.r over 1f out: sn rdn and one pce* **12/1**

1400 **7** *3/4* **Soopacal (IRE)**[161] 2632 6-8-7 66 TomEaves 1 — 65
(Michael Herrington) *dwlt: hdwy on outer and in tch 1/2-way: sn rdn along and kpt on same pce appr fnl f* **16/1**

6640 **8** *3/4* **Prince Of Vasa (IRE)**[9] 7216 4-8-7 66 oh6 AdrianNicholls 12 — 62
(Michael Smith) *towards rr tl styd on appr fnl f: nrst fin* **25/1**

1120 **9** *1* **Six Wives**[34] 6665 4-8-11 73 BillyCray(3) 4 — 65
(David Nicholls) *s.i.s: hdwy and in tch 1/2-way: sn rdn and wknd* **7/1**[3]

0000 **10** *1 3/4* **Noodles Blue Boy**[24] 6917 5-9-6 79 TonyHamilton 6 — 65
(Ollie Pears) *chsd ldrs to 1/2-way: sn wknd* **12/1**

6505 **11** *1 3/4* **Tillys Tale**[15] 7104 4-8-9 68 (p) MickyFenton 5 — 48
(Paul Midgley) *chsd ldrs to 1/2-way: sn wknd* **16/1**

4600 **12** *3* **On The High Tops (IRE)**[47] 6350 3-9-0 73 (b1) AndrewMullen 13 — 42
(Ruth Carr) *cl up: rdn along 1/2-way: sn wknd* **33/1**

6000 **13** *1/2* **Lucky Mellor**[57] 6056 4-8-13 72 PaddyAspell 11 — 39
(Barry Murtagh) *towards rr: bhd fr 1/2-way* **22/1**

59.52 secs (-0.18) **Going Correction** -0.025s/f (Stan) — **13** Ran SP% **116.2**
Speed ratings (Par 105): **100,98,97,97,96 95,94,93,91,88 85,81,80**
toteswingers: 1&2 £5.40, 1&3 £8.10, 2&3 £8.30. CSF £23.60 CT £177.24 TOTE £5.50: £1.90, £2.50, £3.10; EX 26.80 Trifecta £130.80 Pool: £394.32 - 2.23 winning units..
Owner Mark Goldstein & Stephen Pettman **Bred** Greg Parsons **Trained** Royston, Herts

FOCUS
A fair sprint handicap in which few came here at the top of their game but there are reasons for thinking the first two are well handicapped. The action unfolded down the centre. The time was slow compatred with division II and the form is straightforward.

7356 32RED.COM H'CAP (DIV II) — 5f (F)
3:20 (3:21) (Class 4) (0-80,80) 3-Y-O+ — £4,075 (£1,212; £606; £303) Stalls High

Form — RPR

5434 **1** **Crimson Cloud**[15] 7104 3-8-12 71 (b1) TonyHamilton 10 — 85
(Richard Fahey) *cl up: led after 2f: rdn wl over 1f out: drvn out towards fin* **18/1**

2501 **2** *1* **Mottley Crewe**[16] 7079 4-8-4 70 (b) NoraLooby(7) 3 — 80
(Richard Guest) *prom: effrt 2f out and sn ev ch: rdn over 1f out: no ex last 100yds* **16/1**

6310 **3** *2* **Colourbearer (IRE)**[19] 7039 4-8-13 72 (t) RichardKingscote 8 — 75
(Milton Bradley) *in tch: hdwy 2f out: rdn to chse ldng pair over 1f out: no imp ins fnl f* **9/2**[1]

1051 **4** *1 1/4* **Forever's Girl**[40] 6537 5-9-4 80 DaleSwift(3) 2 — 78
(Geoffrey Oldroyd) *dwlt and towards rr: hdwy 2f out: rdn and kpt on appr fnl f: nrst fin* **6/1**[2]

0-24 **5** *2 1/2* **Trade Secret**[52] 6212 4-9-1 74 DuranFentiman 1 — 63
(Mel Brittain) *in tch: hdwy 2f out: sn rdn and one pce* **8/1**

0506 **6** *1* **Dickie Le Davoir**[6] 7262 7-8-4 70 (be) JasonHart(7) 4 — 56
(Richard Guest) *s.i.s and in rr tl styd on appr fnl f: nrst fin* **17/2**

5600 **7** *1/2* **Bookiesindex Boy**[37] 6616 7-8-7 66 oh2 (bt) JoeFanning 12 — 50
(J R Jenkins) *nvr bttr than midfield* **14/1**

0400 **8** ½ **Nadeen (IRE)**[40] 6537 4-8-10 **69** AdrianNicholls 9 51
(Michael Smith) *a towards rr* **8/1**
5003 **9** *nse* **Hotham**[24] 6913 8-9-6 **79** BarryMcHugh 5 61
(Noel Wilson) *dwlt: sn in tch: rdn over 2f out and sn wknd* **12/1**
12-0 **10** *2* **Jameela Girl**[47] 6348 3-9-5 **78** GrahamGibbons 7 53
(Robert Cowell) *chsd ldrs: rdn 1/2-way: sn wknd* **25/1**
0421 **11** *1 ½* **Lucky Art (USA)**[14] 7116 5-9-0 **78** JustinNewman(5) 11 47
(Conor Dore) *led 2f: rdn along over 2f out and sn wknd* **7/1**[3]
0000 **12** *9* **Cadeaux Pearl**[33] 6703 3-9-4 **80** (b) BillyCray(3) 6 17
(David Nicholls) *dwlt: a towards rr* **9/1**

58.29 secs (-1.41) **Going Correction** -0.025s/f (Stan) **12** Ran SP% **117.1**
Speed ratings (Par 105): **110,108,105,103,99 97,96,96,95,92 90,75**
toteswingers: 1&2 £45.30, 1&3 £29.40, 2&3 £23.40. CSF £275.03 CT £1545.99 TOTE £22.50: £5.70, £6.10, £1.90; EX 255.50 Trifecta £174.20 Pool: £466.29 - 1.98 winning units..
Owner R A Fahey **Bred** Mrs Sheila Oakes **Trained** Musley Bank, N Yorks

FOCUS
The less competitive of the two divisions and a race dominated by the first two from the off. However it was the faster division and the form is rated on the positive side with personal bests from the first two.
Jameela Girl Official explanation: jockey said filly had a breathing problem

7357 32REDBINGO.COM H'CAP — 1m 4f (F)
3:50 (3:50) (Class 6) (0-60,60) 3-Y-0+ — £1,704 (£503; £251) Stalls Low

Form RPR
01-6 **1** **Gosforth Park**[30] 6775 5-9-4 **54** DuranFentiman 7 65
(Mel Brittain) *trckd ldrs on inner: smooth hdwy to chse ldng pair 3f out: effrt wl over 1f out: chal ent fnl f and sn rdn: styd on wl to ld last 75yds* **6/1**[3]
230 **2** ½ **Locum**[10] 7195 6-9-6 **56** DavidAllan 8 66
(Mark H Tompkins) *trckd ldrs: hdwy 5f out and sn cl up: led 3f out: rdn over 1f out: jnd ins fnl f: hdd and no ex last 75yds* **7/1**
0544 **3** *5* **Maslak (IRE)**[10] 7195 7-9-5 **58** RyanClark(3) 2 60
(Peter Hiatt) *trckd ldrs: pushed along over 4f out: outpcd over 3f out: hdwy 2f out: rdn and kpt on to take 3rd ins fnl f* **7/2**[1]
0452 **4** ½ **Strong Knight**[16] 7078 4-9-0 **50** GrahamGibbons 12 51
(Tim Walford) *trckd ldrs: cl up 1/2-way: led 4f out: hdd 3f out and sn rdn: grad wknd fnl 2f* **9/2**[2]
5 *1* **Faranadooney (USA)**[27] 6855 4-9-0 **50** (bt) MickyFenton 5 50
(Ms Joanna Morgan, Ire) *midfield: hdwy on outer over 3f out: rdn to chse ldrs 2f out: no imp* **12/1**
0005 **6** *1 ¾* **Kalahaag (IRE)**[7] 7241 3-8-9 **54** BillyCray(3) 1 51
(David Nicholls) *hld up in rr: hdwy on inner 3f out: rdn over 2f out: plugged on same pce* **11/1**
0003 **7** *5* **Donna Elvira**[16] 7077 4-9-0 **50** TonyHamilton 3 39
(Edwin Tuer) *led: rdn along over 4f out: sn hdd & wknd* **12/1**
3464 **8** *10* **Mighty Whitey (IRE)**[1] 7340 5-9-5 **60** (t) LMcNiff(5) 11 33
(Noel C Kelly, Ire) *s.i.s: a in rr* **15/2**
0300 **9** *2 ¾* **Aqua Lad**[15] 7099 3-9-1 **57** JoeFanning 4 25
(Mark Johnston) *in tch: rdn along over 4f out: sn wknd* **16/1**
10 *shd* **Erycina (IRE)**[154] 2863 3-8-8 **50** PaulQuinn 10 18
(Noel Wilson) *a in rr* **66/1**
60-0 **11** *12* **Dazzling Begum**[9] 7202 6-9-2 **52** AndreaAtzeni 9 —
(Des Donovan) *trckd ldr: pushed along 5f out: rdn and wknd over 3f out* **20/1**

2m 38.53s (-2.47) **Going Correction** -0.25s/f (Stan)
WFA 3 from 4yo+ 6lb **11** Ran SP% **114.8**
Speed ratings (Par 101): **98,97,94,94,93 92,88,82,80,80 72**
toteswingers: 1&2 £6.90, 1&3 £6.20, 2&3 £6.40. CSF £46.47 CT £169.07 TOTE £7.40: £2.20, £3.60, £1.30; EX 47.40 Trifecta £77.80 Pool: £431.30 - 4.10 winning units..
Owner Mel Brittain **Bred** C A Cyzer **Trained** Warthill, N Yorks

FOCUS
A modest finale run at just a fair pace and it appeared an advantage to race prominently. The winner rated a 4lb personal best.
Kalahaag(IRE) Official explanation: jockey said filly hung right-handed
T/Plt: £81.90 to a £1 stake. Pool of £55,263.12 - 492.15 winning tickets. T/Qpdt: £11.60 to a £1 stake. Pool of £4,469.66 - 283.30 winning tickets. JR

7124 LINGFIELD (L-H)
Friday, November 11

OFFICIAL GOING: Standard
Wind: medium, half behind Weather: overcast

7358 SINGAPORE TURF CLUB NURSERY — 7f (P)
12:50 (12:50) (Class 5) (0-75,75) 2-Y-0 — £2,385 (£704; £352) Stalls High

Form RPR
631 **1** **Asifa (IRE)**[43] 6481 2-9-7 **75** (p) WilliamBuick 8 84
(Saeed Bin Suroor) *sn led: rdn and edging rt fr over 1f out: clr ins fnl f: styd on wl: rdn out* **5/2**[1]
2205 **2** *2 ¾* **Not Bad For A Boy (IRE)**[27] 6866 2-9-1 **69** AdamKirby 1 71
(Richard Hannon) *trckd ldrs on inner: rdn and chsd wnr over 1f out: kpt on same pce and no imp u.p ins fnl f* **10/1**
000 **3** ½ **All Nighter (IRE)**[33] 6725 2-9-2 **70** ShaneKelly 6 71
(Brian Meehan) *stdd s: hld up wl in tch in last trio: rdn and hdwy on inner over 1f out: chsd ldng pair and styd on same pce u.p ins fnl f* **20/1**
0261 **4** *2 ¼* **Cresta Star**[44] 6441 2-9-7 **75** JimCrowley 10 70
(Richard Hannon) *pushed along early and sn chsng wnr: rdn and unable qck 2f out: 4th and btn 1f out: plugged on same pce fnl f* **8/1**
002 **5** *1 ¾* **Rocky Reef**[35] 6662 2-9-0 **68** LiamKeniry 7 58
(Andrew Balding) *dwlt: pushed along early: in tch in last rio: rdn and effrt jst over 2f out: no imp and styd on same pce fr over 1f out* **7/1**
0223 **6** ½ **Abhaath (USA)**[10] 7205 2-9-4 **72** (p) MartinLane 2 61
(Saeed Bin Suroor) *wl in tch in midfield: rdn over 2f out: nt qckn and outpcd over 1f out: wknd 1f out* **5/1**[2]
0001 **7** *2* **Atlantis Crossing (IRE)**[8] 7251 2-7-7 **52** 6ex (b) NathanAlison(5) 9 36
(Jim Boyle) *dwlt: t.k.h: hld up in tch: hdwy on outer to chse ldrs 4f out: rdn and unable qck 2f out: wknd over 1f out: fdd fnl f* **13/2**[3]
0120 **8** *3 ¼* **Crowning Star (IRE)**[34] 6699 2-9-5 **73** (t) LukeMorris 5 48
(J S Moore) *in tch: rdn and dropped to rr over 2f out: last and edgd lft u.p wl over 1f out: sn wknd and wl btn* **15/2**
1640 **9** *9* **Dishy Guru**[25] 6921 2-9-5 **73** SteveDrowne 4 25
(Michael Blanshard) *t.k.h: hld up wl in tch in midfield: rdn and wknd qckly wl over 1f out: wl bhd fnl f* **16/1**

1m 26.02s (1.22) **Going Correction** +0.125s/f (Slow) **9** Ran SP% **113.7**
Speed ratings (Par 96): **98,94,94,91,89 89,86,83,72**
toteswingers:1&2:£7.10, 2&3:£36.40, 1&3:£10.50 CSF £28.27 CT £406.12 TOTE £2.90: £1.90, £3.60, £9.20; EX 33.90.
Owner Godolphin **Bred** Tullpark Ltd **Trained** Newmarket, Suffolk

FOCUS
A fair nursery, but the early pace wasn't strong and that certainly helped the winner. A step up from the winner.

NOTEBOOK
Asifa(IRE) is already due to go up 4lb after his Warwick victim Intuition scored at Kempton the previous week and he made the most of apparently being well in. Soon in front, he dictated matters throughout and, though he hung away to his right into the centre of the track once into the straight, that is usually no bad thing here. The application of cheekpieces is helping him to recoup some of his 110,000euros purchase price and he still looks capable of a bit more. (op 2-1)
Not Bad For A Boy(IRE), disappointing since finishing runner-up twice in July, was making his AW/nursery debut and returned to form with a solid effort, holding every chance and keeping on under pressure. He lacks the scope of the winner, but can win one of these. (op 11-1)
All Nighter(IRE) was making his AW/nursery debut after showing some ability in three turf maidens at Grade 1 tracks, but may not have been in the ideal position at the back of the field in a moderately run race. He also made his effort close to the inside rail once in line for home, which again may not have been in his favour, and it's likely the best of him is still to be seen. (op 25-1)
Cresta Star, making her nursery debut after winning her maiden over this trip at Kempton, had her chance but proved one-paced and may need a greater test of stamina than this proved to be. (op 15-2 tchd 7-1)
Rocky Reef, making his nursery debut after finishing runner-up in a weak Wolverhampton maiden, failed to pick up. (op 8-1 tchd 17-2)
Abhaath(USA) was one of the first off the bridle and is looking very expensive at $400,000. Official explanation: jockey said colt suffered interference in running (op 9-2 tchd 4-1)
Atlantis Crossing(IRE) Official explanation: jockey said colt ran too free
Crowning Star(IRE) Official explanation: jockey said gelding suffered interference in runing
Dishy Guru Official explanation: jockey said colt suffered interference in running

7359 BRITISH STALLION STUDS EBF/SINGAPORE TURF CLUB MAIDEN STKS — 5f (P)
1:25 (1:26) (Class 5) 2-Y-0 — £3,340 (£986; £493) Stalls High

Form RPR
0 **1** **Intransigent**[32] 6743 2-9-3 0 LiamKeniry 3 84+
(Andrew Balding) *hld up in tch in midfield: gd hdwy to press ldr 2f out: pushed ahd over 1f out: sn qcknd clr and pushed out fnl f: comf* **4/1**[3]
5 **2** *3 ¼* **Lost City (IRE)**[236] 921 2-9-3 0 JimmyQuinn 4 71+
(Richard Fahey) *s.i.s: t.k.h: hld up in last pair: rdn and effrt over 1f out: r.o to chse clr wnr fnl 100yds: nvr a threat* **15/2**
3222 **3** ¾ **Lupo D'Oro (IRE)**[35] 6673 2-9-3 **78** SteveDrowne 2 71
(John Best) *t.k.h: hld up wl in tch: rdn and effrt wl over 1f out: no ch w wnr and styd on same pce fnl f* **85/40**[2]
2 **4** *1 ¾* **More Than Words (IRE)**[29] 6820 2-8-12 0 JimCrowley 5 57
(Richard Hannon) *restless in stalls: fly-jmpd leaving stalls: sn rcvrd and upsides ldr: led 2f out: sn rdn and hdd: drvn and nt pce of wnr 1f out: wknd fnl 150yds* **11/10**[1]
5 *2* **Pucon** 2-8-9 0 JohnFahy(3) 1 50
(Roger Teal) *s.i.s: in tch in last pair: rdn and sme hdwy whn swtchd rt over 1f out: no imp and wl hld fnl f* **66/1**
3000 **6** *6* **Joe M**[37] 6625 2-9-3 **45** (e[1]) ShaneKelly 8 34
(Simon Dow) *pressed ldrs on outer: rdn and wknd qckly 2f out: sn bhd* **100/1**
2500 **7** *2 ¼* **Launch On Line**[11] 7194 2-8-5 **70** JakePayne(7) 7 20
(Bill Turner) *led tl rdn and hdd 2f out: wknd qckly over 1f out: fdd fnl f* **66/1**

59.18 secs (0.38) **Going Correction** +0.125s/f (Slow) **7** Ran SP% **115.4**
Speed ratings (Par 96): **101,95,94,91,88 79,75**
toteswingers:1&2:£2.30, 2&3:£2.30, 1&3:£2.10 CSF £32.83 TOTE £6.50: £4.40, £1.90; EX 27.60.
Owner Kingsclere Racing CLub **Bred** Kingsclere Stud **Trained** Kingsclere, Hants

FOCUS
A modest maiden, dominated by the two market springers. The winner is rated up 20lb from his debut run.

NOTEBOOK
Intransigent was a disappointing second-favourite on his Salisbury debut last month, but obviously better was expected from him there and this effort shows why, as he was running all over his rivals rounding the home bend and produced a decent turn of foot to lead over a furlong out. His half-brother Border Music was a much better horse on sand than on turf, winning seven times on Polytrack including in Listed company, so it will be interesting to see if he follows suit. (op 8-1)
Lost City(IRE) hadn't been seen since finishing last of five when odds-on for his Curragh debut in March and has been gelded in the meantime. He again gave away ground at the start, but showed ability in the second half of the contest and looks by no means a lost cause. (op 12-1)
Lupo D'Oro(IRE) set the standard with a mark of 78, but he could only stay on at one pace for a modest third. The only time he has failed to place in his last eight starts was in the Windsor Castle, but he isn't progressing and is running out of excuses. (op 9-4 tchd 11-4)
More Than Words(IRE) was narrowly beaten over 6f on her Kempton debut last month, causing Richard Hughes to briefly relinquish his licence after being deemed to have hit the filly six times in the last furlong and receiving a ten-day ban. Despite getting edgy in the stalls and fly-jumping exiting the gate, she was soon up with the pace and had her chance, but the winner waltzed past her before the furlong pole and there was nothing left. The drop in trip may not have helped, but she now has a bit to prove. (op 4-5 tchd 8-11)
Pucon, a 6,500gns half-sister to a couple of winners at up to 1m, comes from a yard going through a quiet spell, but she wasn't totally disgraced on this debut. (op 100-1)

7360 FRP ADVISORY ABL MAIDEN STKS — 1m 4f (P)
2:00 (2:00) (Class 5) 3-Y-0+ — £2,385 (£704; £352) Stalls Low

Form RPR
6 **1** **Sky Crystal (GER)**[46] 6404 3-8-12 0 WilliamBuick 1 76+
(John Gosden) *chsd ldrs: rdn and rn green over 2f out: unable qck and looked hld over 1f out: styd on 1f out: led fnl 100yds: rdn out* **9/2**[3]
63 **2** *nk* **Agadir Summer**[50] 6286 3-8-12 0 MartinLane 7 75
(David Simcock) *hld up in last pair: chsd ldng quartet and rdn over 2f out: no imp tl styd on u.p 1f out: chal fnl 75yds: kpt on* **9/4**[1]
032 **3** *1 ¼* **Martine's Spirit (IRE)**[13] 7179 3-8-12 **70** ShaneKelly 6 73
(William Haggas) *chsd ldr 10f out tl led over 4f out: rdn and edgted rt over 1f out: hdd 1f out: stl ev ch tl no ex fnl 100yds: wknd towards fin* **7/2**[2]

3230 **4** *nk* **Ecossaise**[20] 7033 3-8-12 71.. AdamKirby 4 73
(Mark Johnston) *chsd ldr tl 10f out: styd chsng ldrs tl wnt 2nd again over 2f out: ev ch u.p 2f out: led narrowly 1f out: hdd fnl 100yds: wknd towards fin* **6/1**

6520 **5** *1 1/4* **Balandra**[10] 7204 3-8-12 79.. JimCrowley 2 71
(Luca Cumani) *hld up in tch in last pair: hdwy to chse ldng pair over 3f out: rdn and swtchd lft 1f out: sn drvn and fnd little: wknd fnl 75yds* **5/1**

0/0 **6** *28* **Sioux City Sue**[23] 6947 5-9-4 0.. StephenCraine 5 26
(Jim Boyle) *hld up in tch: rdn and lost tch over 3f out: t.o over 2f out* **100/1**

20 **7** *18* **Astragal**[29] 6810 3-8-12 0.. LiamKeniry 3 —
(Andrew Balding) *led tl over 4f out: sn rdn and struggling: wknd and bhd over 3f out: lost tch and t.o over 2f out* **16/1**

2m 32.61s (-0.39) **Going Correction** +0.125s/f (Slow)
WFA 3 from 5yo 6lb **7 Ran SP% 109.0**
Speed ratings (Par 103): **106,105,104,104,103 85,73**
toteswingers:1&2:£2.30, 1&3:£3.40, 2&3:£2.30 CSF £13.60 TOTE £5.00: £1.40, £1.90; EX 15.40.
Owner Lord Lloyd-Webber **Bred** Watership Down Stud **Trained** Newmarket, Suffolk

FOCUS
Seven fillies and mares lined up for this modest maiden, despite the race being open to both sexes. The early pace was far from strong and not much covered the first five at the finish, suggesting this is ordinary form.

7361 SINGAPORE TURF CLUB/BRITISH STALLION STUDS EBF FILLIES' H'CAP 1m 2f (P)
2:35 (2:35) (Class 3) (0-90,90) 3-Y-O **£6,792** (£2,021; £1,010; £505) **Stalls** High

Form RPR

60-5 **1** **Simayill**[13] 7171 3-8-10 79.. J-PGuillambert 4 85+
(Clive Brittain) *stdd s: hld up in tch: lft 3rd 5f out: gng best over 3f out: pushed along and rn green wl over 1f out: effrt between horses to ld 1f out: rdn and kpt on fnl f* **3/1**[2]

6000 **2** *1 1/4* **Emma's Gift (IRE)**[37] 6632 3-8-7 76..(b[1]) JimmyQuinn 3 77
(Julia Feilden) *hld up in tch in last: rdn over 2f out: hdwy on inner over 1f out: drvn and kpt on ins fnl f to go 2nd cl home: nt pce to threaten wnr* **11/1**

3254 **3** *hd* **Birdolini**[15] 7130 3-8-7 76 oh4.. FergusSweeney 1 77
(Alan King) *hld up in tch: hmpd and lft 4th 5f out: rdn and effrt over 2f out: pressed ldrs and drvn 1f out: edgd lft u.p and chsd wnr jst ins fnl f: no imp: lost 2nd cl home* **11/4**[1]

6600 **4** *3* **Cloud Illusions (USA)**[88] 5113 3-8-10 79..(v[1]) LiamKeniry 5 74
(Heather Main) *chsd ldr after 2f: rdn and ev ch 2f out: no ex and btn 1f out: wknd ins fnl f* **20/1**

04 **5** *1/2* **Fugnina**[31] 6770 3-9-7 90.. AdamKirby 6 84
(Marco Botti) *led: rdn ent fnl 2f: drvn and hdd 1f out: wknd fnl 150yds* **10/3**[3]

4063 **P** **Musharakaat (IRE)**[31] 6770 3-9-6 89.. WilliamBuick 2 —
(Ed Dunlop) *chsd ldr for 2f: chsd ldng pair after tl lost action and p.u 5f out: dismntd* **7/2**

2m 7.25s (0.65) **Going Correction** +0.125s/f (Slow) **6 Ran SP% 110.1**
Speed ratings (Par 103): **102,101,100,98,98** —
toteswingers:1&2:£5.40, 1&3:£2.40, 2&3:£4.20 CSF £31.70 TOTE £4.30: £1.10, £9.00; EX 31.40.
Owner Saeed Manana **Bred** Laundry Cottage Stud Farm **Trained** Newmarket, Suffolk
■ Stewards' Enquiry : Jimmy Quinn two-day ban: used whip with excessive frequency (Nov 25-26)
Fergus Sweeney two-day ban: used whip with excessive freaquency (Nov 25-26)

FOCUS
A decent prize for this fillies' handicap, but not the most competitive of races and weakened further when Musharakaat was pulled up at halfway. Potentially unreliable form with the bare form limited, although the winner should do better.

NOTEBOOK
Simayill was making her AW debut after finishing unplaced in four starts on turf, though she ran well following an absence of over a year at Newmarket 13 days earlier. There was a chance that she might 'bounce', but there was no sign of it and she was travelling like a winner on the turn for home. She found plenty when asked to go and win her race, despite looking green and carrying her head at an awkward angle, and she looks capable of winning something rather better than this. Official explanation: trainer's rep said, regarding apparent improvement in form, that the filly had matured and strengthened up since last year. (op 10-3)
Emma's Gift(IRE), disappointing since winning an Ascot conditions event in April, was tried in blinkers. She was one of the first off the bridle, but eventually consented to run on and just snatched second. She may reappear in another fillies-only race over 1m back here next week, but the question will be whether the headgear will continue to work. (op 12-1)
Birdolini also ran on after coming under pressure a fair way out and this was a creditable effort, especially as she was slightly hampered when Musharakaat was pulled up at halfway, but being 4lb wrong may have been a bigger problem. (tchd 5-2)
Cloud Illusions(USA) had been very disappointing since making a successful reappearance at Newmarket in May and was tried in a visor on this first attempt beyond 1m, but although she held every chance she had been keen enough earlier in the contest and that told against her late on. (op 16-1)
Fugnina, quiet in her first two starts in this country, tried to make all but she was easily picked off from over a furlong out. The trip shouldn't have been a problem as she has won over it in Italy. (op 9-2)
Musharakaat(IRE) Official explanation: vet said filly pulled up lame behind

7362 CHRISTMAS PARTIES AT LINGFIELD PARK H'CAP 1m (P)
3:10 (3:10) (Class 5) (0-75,75) 3-Y-O+ **£2,385** (£704; £352) **Stalls** High

Form RPR

060 **1** **Aquilifer (IRE)**[65] 5828 3-9-0 70.. ShaneKelly 4 79
(Mrs K Burke) *t.k.h: chsd ldrs: effrt to press ldr over 1f out: drvn to ld fnl 75yds: jst hld on* **15/2**

3406 **2** *shd* **Hereford Boy**[10] 7208 7-9-0 68..(b) AdamKirby 6 77
(Dean Ivory) *stdd after s: t.k.h: hld up in tch in last trio: effrt 2f out: rdn and hdwy over 1f out: wnt 3rd ins fnl f: str run fnl 100yds: clsng qckly after but nvr quite getting to wnr* **5/1**[2]

3046 **3** *1/2* **Mazamorra (USA)**[23] 6949 4-9-7 75.. WilliamBuick 7 82
(Marco Botti) *led: rdn and qcknd wl over 1f out: pressed and drvn over 1f out: hdd fnl 75yds: no ex and one pce cl home* **3/1**[1]

0400 **4** *2 1/2* **Mister Green (FR)**[10] 7208 5-9-1 69..(t) JimmyQuinn 3 71
(David Flood) *t.k.h: hld up in tch in mdfield: rdn over 2f out: hdwy u.p to chse ldrs 1f out: styd on same pce fnl f* **14/1**

0150 **5** *3/4* **Catchanova (IRE)**[9] 7227 4-9-6 74.. FergusSweeney 11 74
(Eve Johnson Houghton) *hld up in last pair: rdn 2f out: swtchd lft and hdwy over 1f out: styd on same pce fnl f: nvr trbld ldrs* **5/1**[2]

4031 **6** *hd* **Cativo Cavallino**[24] 6939 8-8-13 70.. NataliaGemelova[(3)] 9 70
(John E Long) *dwlt: t.k.h: hdwy to chse ldr after 2f: upsides 3f out tl rdn and unable qck 2f out: wknd ent fnl f* **7/1**

0065 **7** *1* **L'Hirondelle (IRE)**[30] 6797 7-9-3 71.. J-PGuillambert 2 68
(Michael Attwater) *t.k.h: chsd ldrs: rdn and unable qck jst over 2f out: wknd ent fnl f* **6/1**[3]

0006 **8** *1/2* **King's Colour**[11] 6239 6-9-1 72.. KierenFox[(3)] 10 68
(Brett Johnson) *s.i.s: a in rr: rdn and no imp jst over 2f out: styd on same pce after: nvr trbld ldrs* **16/1**

0000 **9** *2 1/4* **Rezwaan**[16] 7098 4-9-3 71..(b) FrankieMcDonald 1 62
(Murty McGrath) *t.k.h: hld up in midfield: rdn and lost pl ent fnl 2f: wknd over 1f out* **66/1**

1m 39.1s (0.90) **Going Correction** +0.125s/f (Slow)
WFA 3 from 4yo+ 2lb **9 Ran SP% 110.9**
Speed ratings (Par 103): **100,99,99,96,96 95,94,94,92**
toteswingers:1&2:£7.20, 1&3:£4.40, 2&3:£3.40 CSF £42.13 CT £131.70 TOTE £8.50: £2.60, £2.10, £1.50; EX 48.90.
Owner John Kelsey-Fry **Bred** Miss L Magnier **Trained** Middleham Moor, North Yorks

FOCUS
A modest but quite competitive handicap, despite the three non-runners. The early pace wasn't strong and it was an advantage to race handily. The winner rates back to his best.

7363 ASHURST WOOD APPRENTICE H'CAP 1m 5f (P)
3:45 (3:45) (Class 5) (0-70,70) 3-Y-O+ **£2,385** (£704; £352) **Stalls** Low

Form RPR

556 **1** **Appeal (IRE)**[30] 6804 3-8-5 63.. TimClark[(7)] 6 70+
(Sir Mark Prescott Bt) *chsd ldrs: chsd ldr over 3f out: led over 2f out: rdn and clr over 1f out: kpt on wl: rdn out* **7/4**[1]

0304 **2** *1 1/4* **Formidable Guest**[103] 4578 7-8-5 56 oh3.. CharlotteJenner[(7)] 5 61
(Jamie Poulton) *stdd after s: hld up in last pair: hdwy over 2f out: rdn and hdwy to chse ldrs over 1f out: wnt 2nd ins fnl f: kpt on* **16/1**

2441 **3** *2 1/4* **Zafranagar (IRE)**[165] 2567 6-9-11 69.. GeorgeDowning 2 71
(Tony Carroll) *t.k.h: chsd ldr tl led 5f out: hdd and rdn over 2f out: unable qck over 1f out: outpcd fnl f* **13/2**[2]

6000 **4** *2* **Kiss A Prince**[15] 7130 5-9-5 70..(p) PaulBooth[(7)] 4 69
(Dean Ivory) *stdd s: t.k.h: hld up in rr: hdwy on outer 7f out: jnd ldrs over 3f out: rdn and chsd wnr 2f out: no ex over 1f out: edgd lft and wknd ins fnl f* **17/2**

045 **5** *3 1/4* **Naheell**[15] 7122 5-8-7 58.. RichardOld[(7)] 7 52
(George Prodromou) *in tch in midfield: rdn and unable qck 2f out: wknd over 1f out* **16/1**

0364 **6** *1/2* **Soundbyte**[8] 7254 6-9-5 66.. IanBurns[(3)] 8 59
(John Gallagher) *in tch towards rr: reminder 6f out: nvr gng wl after: u.p and struggling 4f out: sn outpcd and no threat to ldrs fnl 3f* **20/1**

3563 **7** *3 1/4* **Nutshell**[24] 6926 3-8-4 58.. DannyBrock[(3)] 9 47
(Harry Dunlop) *led tl 5f out: rdn and outpcd 3f out: wknd over 2f out* **13/2**[2]

2216 **8** *3/4* **Rowan Ridge**[20] 6790 3-8-8 66..(v) DanielCremin[(7)] 1 53
(Jim Boyle) *in tch: rdn and losing pl whn hit rail over 2f out: sn wknd* **7/1**[3]

4340 **9** *2* **Broughtons Swinger**[30] 6790 4-8-13 64.. ShannonEdmondson[(7)] 3 48
(Willie Musson) *in tch towards rr: dropped to last 6f out: n.d after and wl btn fnl 2f* **7/1**[3]

2m 48.34s (2.34) **Going Correction** +0.125s/f (Slow)
WFA 3 from 4yo+ 7lb **9 Ran SP% 115.1**
Speed ratings (Par 103): **97,96,94,93,91 91,89,88,87**
toteswingers:1&2:£8.80, 1&3:£3.70, 2&3:£9.40 CSF £33.35 CT £151.73 TOTE £2.10: £1.02, £5.70, £3.60; EX 41.40.
Owner Denford Stud **Bred** Norelands Stallions **Trained** Newmarket, Suffolk
■ Tim Clark's first winner.
■ Stewards' Enquiry : Shannon Edmondson 14-day ban: failed to take all reasonable and permissable measures to obtain best possible placing (Nov 25-26,Nov 28-Dec 3,5-10)
Daniel Cremin seven-day ban: used whip when out of contention (Nov 25-26,Nov 28-Dec 2)

FOCUS
A modest apprentice handicap in which they crawled early and the tempo didn't quicken until well past halfway. Weak form, but the winner is up 8lb on her maiden efforts.
Appeal(IRE) Official explanation: trainer's rep said, regarding apparent improvement in form, that the filly has improved over its last three races with an increase in trip each time and has now reached its optimum distance.
Broughtons Swinger Official explanation: jockey said, regarding running and riding, that she was unhappy with her position in detached last with about half mile to run and she admitted she should have pushed more.
T/Plt: £447.60 to a £1 stake. Pool:£45,419.92 - 74.06 winning tickets T/Qpdt: £30.60 to a £1 stake. Pool:£4,723.41 - 113.90 winning tickets SP

7265 WOLVERHAMPTON (A.W) (L-H)
Friday, November 11

OFFICIAL GOING: Standard
Wind: Fresh across Weather: Overcast

7364 GRAND SLAM DARTS AT WOLVES CIVIC NURSERY 5f 20y(P)
4:15 (4:15) (Class 5) (0-75,75) 2-Y-O **£2,264** (£673; £336; £168) **Stalls** Low

Form RPR

0406 **1** **Profile Star (IRE)**[16] 7103 2-9-5 73.. GrahamGibbons 1 78
(David Barron) *led 1f: chsd ldr: shkn up over 1f out: rdn to ld ins fnl f: edgd lft: jst hld on* **6/1**

1001 **2** *nk* **Worth**[28] 6843 2-9-6 74..(b) EddieAhern 5 78
(Brian Meehan) *in rr: pushed along 3f out: hdwy over 1f out: rdn ins fnl f: r.o wl* **7/1**

6141 **3** *nk* **Uncle Timmy**[9] 7231 2-8-4 58 6ex.. JoeFanning 4 61
(John Quinn) *prom: pushed along over 3f out: rdn ins fnl f: r.o* **15/8**[1]

61 **4** *3/4* **Little China**[43] 6492 2-9-7 75.. WilliamCarson 3 75
(William Muir) *chsd ldrs: rdn ins fnl f: r.o* **7/2**[2]

3121 **5** *1* **Blodwen Abbey**[14] 7140 2-9-6 74.. TomEaves 7 71
(James Unett) *led 4f out: clr 1/2-way: rdn and hdd ins fnl f: no ex* **9/2**[3]

1300 **6** *1 1/4* **Compton Target (IRE)**[25] 6921 2-8-8 69..(t) NicoleNordblad[(7)] 6 61
(Hans Adielsson) *chsd ldrs: pushed along over 1f out: styd on same pce* **11/1**

0005 **7** *3 3/4* **Musical Strike**[7] 7267 2-7-12 52 oh7.. JamieMackay 2 31
(Shaun Harris) *prom: hmpd and lost pl 4f out: n.d after* **33/1**

62.61 secs (0.31) **Going Correction** +0.05s/f (Slow) **7 Ran SP% 113.2**
Speed ratings (Par 96): **99,98,98,96,95 93,87**
toteswingers:1&2:£8.90, 1&3:£2.00, 2&3:£1.90 CSF £45.40 TOTE £6.00: £2.40, £5.90; EX 66.70.
Owner Profile Storage Ltd **Bred** Knocklong House Stud **Trained** Maunby, N Yorks
■ Stewards' Enquiry : Eddie Ahern caution: careless riding.

FOCUS
Four last-time-out winners lined-up in this nursery. It was fast and furious and there was a tight three-way finish. The form has a sound feel to it.

NOTEBOOK
Profile Star(IRE) had not really gone on since winning a Thirsk maiden in April but he attracted plenty of support throughout the day and put in a battling performance to cash in on a sliding mark on AW debut. He has scope for further improvement on Polytrack and is fresh after just two runs back from three months off. (op 15-2)
Worth has been a bit hit and miss at times but this tactically versatile filly reeled in Blodwen Abbey close home in a C&D nursery last time and finished well in a close call off 4lb higher. She has form figures of 112 in nurseries on Polytrack and would be of strong interest in a similar race next time. (op 13-2 tchd 6-1)
Uncle Timmy was a clear-cut winner of a 5f soft-ground nursery at Nottingham last week. He was officially 4lb well in under a penalty and gave it a good try on AW debut but was just held. (tchd 7-4)
Little China left her debut form well behind when an emphatic 16-1 winner of a C&D maiden in September. She was prominent in the market for nursery debut, but couldn't quite get to grips with the front three. (op 11-4)
Blodwen Abbey made all when beating a 78-rated odds-on rival in a 7f novice event here last time. This free-going filly was run down dropped back to 5f in nursery company but she deserves credit for not being beaten far after setting a fast pace. (tchd 4-1)

7365 32RED CASINO CLAIMING STKS 5f 20y(P)
4:45 (4:45) (Class 6) 2-Y-O **£1,704** (£503; £251) **Stalls** Low

Form RPR
0131 **1** **Mr Knightley (IRE)**[30] 6786 2-8-12 **80**.....................(b) MatthewDavies 3 73+
(Jim Boyle) *led early: chsd ldr tl led 2f out: shkn up ins fnl f: styd on* **2/9**[1]
00 **2** *1 ¼* **Multi Blessing**[30] 6786 2-8-7 **72**................................ RichardKingscote 1 64+
(Alan Jarvis) *chsd ldrs: rdn to chse wnr fnl f: r.o* **4/1**[2]
0060 **3** *2 ¾* **Burnwynd Spirit (IRE)**[14] 7143 2-8-7 **52**............................ TomEaves 4 51
(Ian Semple) *sn led: hdd 2f out: rdn over 1f out: no ex fnl f* **20/1**[3]
62.83 secs (0.53) **Going Correction** +0.05s/f (Slow) **3** Ran SP% **106.6**
Speed ratings (Par 94): **97,95,90**
CSF £1.43 TOTE £1.20; EX 1.40.
Owner M Khan X2 **Bred** Miss Deirdre Cogan **Trained** Epsom, Surrey

FOCUS
The hot favourite scored with something in hand in this small-field claimer. The race was run at a steady tempo and the third limits the form.

NOTEBOOK
Mr Knightley(IRE) proved a revelation in first-time blinkers when off the mark with a runaway win in a 7f Kempton claimer on AW debut in September and justified favouritism when holding off an 80-rated rival over 6f at the same track last time on his final run for Richard Hannon. He had strong claims on adjusted figures on debut for a new yard and did the job in smooth style back at 5f to make it 3-3 in claimers. His current mark of 80 looks fairly tough for handicaps but he could continue to progress in headgear on Polytrack and looks a genuine and versatile type. (op 2-7)
Multi Blessing, tailed off in just two runs since a decisive surprise win in a 5f AW maiden in May, bounced back with a decent run behind a progressive rival. He has looked temperamental and was withdrawn twice in the summer after proving a handful in the preliminaries, but he has ability and is fairly treated off a current mark of 72 relative to his peak form. (op 10-3)
Burnwynd Spirit(IRE) is a nine-race maiden with an unconvincing profile but he ran well to finish not far behind a rival with a 28lb higher official rating.

7366 £32 FREE AT 32RED.COM H'CAP 5f 20y(P)
5:15 (5:16) (Class 6) (0-55,55) 3-Y-O+ **£1,908** (£563; £281) **Stalls** Low

Form RPR
0545 **1** **Yungaburra (IRE)**[9] 7224 7-8-13 **52** ow2....................(tp) SteveDrowne 9 60
(David C Griffiths) *hld up: hdwy over 1f out: rdn ins fnl f: r.o to ld nr fin* **10/1**
4023 **2** *½* **Cliffords Reprieve**[23] 6943 3-9-2 **55**................................ SebSanders 7 63
(Eric Wheeler) *chsd ldrs: rdn and hung lft fr over 1f out: led ins fnl f: hdd nr fin* **4/1**[2]
6540 **3** *1 ½* **Mosa Mine**[260] 664 4-9-0 **53**.. EddieAhern 11 56
(Bryn Palling) *hld up in tch: shkn up ins fnl f: styd on* **22/1**
132 **4** *shd* **Rightcar**[7] 7266 4-8-13 **52**.................................... RobbieFitzpatrick 10 54+
(Peter Grayson) *half-rrd s: bhd: hdwy and nt clr run over 1f out: swtchd rt: r.o: nt rch ldrs* **6/1**[3]
05 **5** *hd* **Brian Sprout**[23] 6943 3-8-8 **47**.. LukeMorris 2 49
(John Weymes) *led: rdn over 1f out: hdd and unable qck ins fnl f* **16/1**
0204 **6** *½* **Sandwith**[16] 7100 8-8-13 **55**..(p) GaryBartley(3) 12 55
(George Foster) *prom: rdn and hung lft over 1f out: styd on* **20/1**
0-40 **7** *½* **Monte Cassino (IRE)**[47] 6386 6-8-9 **48**........................... TomEaves 1 46
(Bryan Smart) *sn outpcd: hung lft over 1f out: r.o ins fnl f: nvr nrr* **16/1**
545 **8** *hd* **London Avenue (IRE)**[16] 7093 3-8-13 **52**........................ PaddyAspell 5 49
(Dominic Ffrench Davis) *chsd ldrs: rdn and ev ch over 1f out: no ex ins fnl f* **17/2**
4524 **9** *½* **Circuitous**[7] 7266 3-9-0 **53**..(b) JoeFanning 8 48
(Keith Dalgleish) *dwlt: hld up: nvr nr to chal* **9/4**[1]
2340 **10** *2* **Canadian Danehill (IRE)**[23] 6943 9-8-11 **50**..........(p) GrahamGibbons 6 38
(Robert Cowell) *chsd ldrs: ev ch 2f out: hmpd over 1f out: wknd ins fnl f* **11/1**
6000 **11** *nse* **Bertbrand**[9] 7230 6-8-9 **48**..(b) KirstyMilczarek 4 36
(Ian McInnes) *chsd ldrs: pushed along 1/2-way: btn whn hmpd 1f out* **33/1**
5U64 **12** *7* **Chester Deelyte (IRE)**[21] 6999 3-8-9 **48**..................(v) FrederikTylicki 13 11
(Lisa Williamson) *chsd ldrs tl wknd over 1f out* **12/1**
62.48 secs (0.18) **Going Correction** +0.05s/f (Slow) **12** Ran SP% **124.5**
Speed ratings (Par 101): **100,99,96,96,96 95,94,94,93,90 90,79**
toteswingers:1&2:£7.60, 1&3:£52.30, 2&3:£23.70 CSF £51.18 CT £895.01 TOTE £16.40: £4.90, £2.50, £9.20; EX 80.70.
Owner D W Noble **Bred** Newlands House Stud **Trained** Bawtry, S Yorks
■ Stewards' Enquiry : Graham Gibbons caution: careless riding.
Steve Drowne three-day ban: weighed in 2lb heavy (Nov 25,26,28)

FOCUS
An ordinary handicap run at a fair pace. The winner is rated in line wih his 2010 form.

7367 32REDBET.COM MAIDEN STKS (DIV I) 7f 32y(P)
5:45 (5:47) (Class 5) 2-Y-O **£2,264** (£673; £336; £168) **Stalls** High

Form RPR
2 **1** **Third Half**[18] 7066 2-9-3 0.. RichardKingscote 8 75+
(Tom Dascombe) *chsd ldrs: led over 2f out: rdn ins fnl f: styd on* **11/2**[3]
3 **2** *½* **Cappielow Park**[24] 6935 2-9-3 0.................................... SteveDrowne 11 73+
(William Jarvis) *dwlt: hdwy over 2f out: chsd wnr over 1f out: sn rdn: hung lft ins fnl f: styd on* **4/1**[2]
62 **3** *4* **Fourth Of June (IRE)**[31] 6768 2-9-3 0............................... PhillipMakin 3 61
(Ed Dunlop) *chsd ldrs: rdn and ev ch over 1f out: no ex ins fnl f* **4/7**[1]
0 **4** *hd* **Silent Energy (IRE)**[7] 7258 2-9-3 0.................................. LukeMorris 10 60
(Ronald Harris) *hld up in tch: rdn and hung lft fr over 1f out: styd on same pce* **66/1**
0 **5** *2 ½* **Dubai Sunshine (IRE)**[30] 6795 2-9-3 0........................ StevieDonohoe 9 54
(Michael Bell) *mid-div: hdwy over 4f out: rdn over 2f out: wknd over 1f out* **20/1**
6 *5* **Lhotse Sherpa** 2-9-3 0.. RussKennemore 1 42
(John Holt) *sn pushed along in rr: hdwy u.p over 1f out: wknd fnl f* **50/1**
44 **7** *1 ¼* **Clon Brulee (IRE)**[16] 7101 2-9-3 0............................ GrahamGibbons 6 39
(David Barron) *a in rr* **7/1**
00 **8** *¾* **Tallula (IRE)**[119] 4073 2-8-12 0....................................... FrederikTylicki 7 32
(Micky Hammond) *chsd ldr tl led 1/2-way: hdd over 2f out: wknd over 1f out* **100/1**
9 *1 ¼* **Kuwait Star** 2-9-3 0.. PaddyAspell 2 34
(Alan McCabe) *prom: lost pl 4f out: wknd over 2f out* **80/1**
10 *1* **Lady Author** 2-8-12 0.. TonyHamilton 4 27
(Richard Fahey) *sn pushed along towards rr: bhd fr 1/2-way* **28/1**
00 **11** *18* **Mrs Awkward**[11] 7197 2-8-9 0.. RyanClark(3) 5 —
(Mark Brisbourne) *led to 1/2-way: wknd 2f out: t.o* **200/1**
1m 31.0s (1.40) **Going Correction** +0.05s/f (Slow) **11** Ran SP% **125.9**
Speed ratings (Par 96): **94,93,88,88,85 80,78,77,76,75 54**
toteswingers:1&2:£3.00, 1&3:£1.80, 2&3:£1.90 CSF £29.07 TOTE £3.90: £1.10, £1.90, £1.10; EX 21.30.
Owner Owen Promotions Limited **Bred** Owen Promotions Ltd **Trained** Malpas, Cheshire

FOCUS
The odds-on favourite was well held in a maiden where the front two finished clear. They are rated as better than the facts in this steadily-run race.

NOTEBOOK
Third Half, a promising 8l second in a 1m Southwell maiden on debut, travelled well out wide and showed plenty of determination to hold off a persistent late challenger. He has already been gelded and is not as physically imposing as his high-class half-brother Brown Panther but he has plenty of ability and scope for further improvement as he goes up in trip. (op 6-1)
Cappielow Park was a 25-1 third behind a potentially useful Roger Varian-trained newcomer in a Yarmouth maiden on debut. Things didn't look promising after he lost around 5l with a slow start on AW debut but he did really well to give the winner a scare. An Exceed And Excel half-brother to ten winners including 1m3f Listed US winner Mabadi, he is open to further progress and should be able to win races. (op 7-2)
Fourth Of June(IRE) stepped up on his Newbury debut sixth when a staying-on second in a 7f Leicester maiden last month. He had leading form claims and was sent off at odds-on but he didn't really pick up when pressure was applied and was left behind by the first two. (op 8-13 tchd 4-6 in places)
Silent Energy(IRE) showed ability at a big price on his second run.
Dubai Sunshine(IRE) was never involved when 25-1 in a 7f Lingfield AW maiden on debut and is was a similar story here but this Dubawi colt who is out of a 11.7f French winner did show a bit of promise. (tchd 25-1)

7368 32REDBET.COM MAIDEN STKS (DIV II) 7f 32y(P)
6:15 (6:17) (Class 5) 2-Y-O **£2,264** (£673; £336; £168) **Stalls** High

Form RPR
4 **1** **Press Baron**[14] 7133 2-9-3 0... EddieAhern 10 77+
(J W Hills) *a.p: pushed along to chse ldr over 1f out: r.o to ld wl ins fnl f: readily* **11/8**[2]
6 **2** *2* **Restaurateur (IRE)**[14] 7134 2-9-3 0.................................. LiamKeniry 9 70+
(Andrew Balding) *a.p: chsd ldr 1/2-way: shkn up to ld over 2f out: hung lft over 1f out: rdn and hdd wl ins fnl f: styd on same pce* **11/10**[1]
00 **3** *3 ¾* **Eastlands Lad (IRE)**[28] 6828 2-9-3 0............................. FrederikTylicki 4 61+
(Micky Hammond) *hld up: racd keenly: hdwy over 2f out: styd on to go 3rd nr fin: nvr nrr* **50/1**
2050 **4** *1 ¼* **Lady Tycoon**[73] 5597 2-8-12 **52**.................................... GrahamGibbons 6 53
(Mark Brisbourne) *chsd ldr to 1/2-way: rdn over 1f out: styd on same pce: lost 3rd nr fin* **25/1**
0 **5** *5* **Gabrial's King (IRE)**[16] 7109 2-9-3 0............................ StevieDonohoe 2 46
(Ian Williams) *hld up: shkn up over 2f out: hung lft ins fnl f: nvr nr to chal* **16/1**
6 *3 ½* **Kuwait Moon** 2-9-3 0.. AndrewMullen 1 37
(Alan McCabe) *prom: pushed along over 2f out: wknd over 1f out* **66/1**
05 **7** *2 ¾* **Ypres**[14] 7142 2-9-3 0... TomEaves 3 30
(Jason Ward) *hld up in tch: rdn and wknd over 1f out* **50/1**
8 *2 ¾* **Baldassarre (IRE)** 2-9-3 0... TonyHamilton 5 24
(Richard Fahey) *dwlt: in rr: pushed along 4f out: lost tch fnl 3f* **7/1**[3]
00 **9** *5* **Shining Grace**[26] 6890 2-8-12 0....................................... NeilChalmers 7 6
(Bryn Palling) *led over 4f: wknd over 1f out* **80/1**
10 *4 ½* **Classy Lass** 2-8-12 0... RobbieFitzpatrick 8 —
(Derek Shaw) *s.s: outpcd* **100/1**
00 **11** *5* **Critical Point**[11] 7197 2-9-3 0.. SebSanders 11 —
(Sir Mark Prescott Bt) *s.s: outpcd* **33/1**
1m 30.73s (1.13) **Going Correction** +0.05s/f (Slow) **11** Ran SP% **122.5**
Speed ratings (Par 96): **95,92,88,87,81 77,74,71,65,60 54**
toteswingers:1&2:£1.30, 1&3:£23.50, 2&3:£13.10 CSF £3.26 TOTE £1.70: £1.10, £1.10, £10.60; EX 3.50.
Owner John M Cole **Bred** D R Tucker **Trained** Upper Lambourn, Berks

FOCUS
The two clear market leaders finished a long way ahead of the rest in this maiden. The winner did not need to match his debut effort, with a step up from the second.

NOTEBOOK
Press Baron had leading claims on his strong finishing fourth at 66-1 in 7f Newmarket maiden on debut last month and found a good change of gear to run down his main market rival. The form is hard to weigh up but he did the job in determined style and this King's Best half-brother to four winners at 6f-1m4f should go on to better things. (tchd 5-4)
Restaurateur(IRE) showed promise when a 4-1 sixth of 11 after a very slow start in a 7f Newmarket maiden on debut late last month. He broke much better this time and put in a decent effort but couldn't find a response to a stronger finishing rival. A half-brother to six winner, he has scope for further improvement and his pedigree suggests he may prove best at up to 1m. (op 6-5 tchd 11-8)
Eastlands Lad(IRE) showed little at big prices in two previous runs but there was some sign of ability in a staying-on third on AW debut. (op 40-1)
Lady Tycoon, beaten 15l or more in three runs since a second over C&D on debut, recaptured some form back on Polytrack, but this 52-rated filly holds the form down. (op 33-1)
Gabrial's King(IRE), well beaten in 1m maidens for two different yards, did a bit of late work from a long way back on his third run. A Hurricane Run colt, he should do better when sent handicapping over further. (tchd 14-1)

Ypres Official explanation: jockey said bit slipped through gelding's mouth

7369 32RED.COM MAIDEN STKS 1m 141y(P)
6:45 (6:47) (Class 5) 2-Y-O £2,522 (£750; £375; £187) Stalls Low

Form				RPR
	1		**Shihab (IRE)** 2-9-3 0 SebSanders 6 (Saeed Bin Suroor) a.p: rdn to ld over 1f out: r.o 2/1[2]	71+
00	2	1 1/4	**Harry Buckle**[41] 6529 2-9-3 0 StevieDonohoe 2 (Philip McBride) hld up: nt clr run over 2f out: hdwy over 1f out: chsd wnr ins fnl f: r.o 8/1[3]	68+
	3	2 3/4	**Aird Snout (USA)** 2-9-3 0 JoeFanning 9 (David Simcock) hld up: hdwy 1/2-way: shkn up over 2f out: styd on to go 3rd wl ins fnl f 9/1	66+
00	4	nk	**Frederickthegreat**[21] 6993 2-9-3 0 (t) RichardKingscote 7 (Hughie Morrison) mid-div: hdwy over 2f out: nt clr run ins fnl f: styd on to go 4th post: nt rch ldrs 25/1	61+
6	5	hd	**Great Nicanor (IRE)**[91] 5003 2-9-3 0 TomEaves 4 (Ian Semple) s.i.s: hdwy over 6f out: rdn and ev ch over 1f out: no ex ins fnl f 66/1	61
	6	nk	**Almuder** 2-9-3 0 SteveDrowne 3 (Ed Dunlop) s.i.s: hld up: hdwy over 2f out: hung lft ins fnl f: styd on 12/1	60+
63	7	1/2	**Poetic Power (IRE)**[9] 7233 2-9-3 0 LiamKeniry 13 (David Elsworth) prom: led over 6f out: rdn and hdd over 1f out: no ex ins fnl f 11/8[1]	59
05	8	hd	**Flashman**[18] 7060 2-9-3 0 TonyHamilton 1 (Richard Fahey) hld up: rdn over 1f out: r.o ins fnl f: nvr nrr 50/1	61+
	9	1/2	**Sir Dylan** 2-9-3 0 LukeMorris 10 (Ronald Harris) trckd ldrs: rdn and ev ch over 1f out: sn hung lft and wknd 50/1	57
0	10	2 1/2	**Kittens**[20] 7030 2-8-12 0 WilliamCarson 12 (William Muir) chsd ldrs: rdn over 3f out: wknd over 1f out 20/1	46
0	11	nk	**Tis Rock 'N' Roll (USA)**[17] 7083 2-9-3 0 EddieAhern 5 (David Lanigan) hld up: a in rr: bhd whn hmpd 1f out 25/1	55+
00	12	2	**Gabrial The Prince (IRE)**[17] 7082 2-9-3 0 AndreaAtzeni 8 (David Simcock) hld up: a in rr: bhd whn rdn and hung lft 1f out 66/1	46
00	13	35	**Silver Native (IRE)**[16] 7094 2-9-3 0 MartinLane 11 (Mike Murphy) sn led: hdd over 6f out: chsd ldrs: rdn over 3f out: wknd over 2f out: t.o 100/1	—

1m 51.68s (1.18) **Going Correction** +0.05s/f (Slow) **13** Ran SP% **124.6**
Speed ratings (Par 96): **96,94,92,92,92 91,91,91,90,88 88,86,55**
toteswingers:1&2:£3.70, 1&3:£3.60, 2&3:£9.90 CSF £18.18 TOTE £3.70: £1.60, £1.10, £1.90; EX 21.00.
Owner Godolphin **Bred** Darley **Trained** Newmarket, Suffolk

FOCUS

A well-backed Godolphin newcomer looked inexperienced but showed a good attitude to score. It was steadily run and the field was compressed, so the form is limited.

NOTEBOOK

Shihab(IRE) looked in trouble before the final turn but he knuckled down well and powered through against the far rail to eventually win with plenty in hand. This was a very promising start by a half-brother to six winners, including Group 3 1m 2yo winner Birthstone, and the style suggests he could improve significantly for the run. (op 9-4)

Harry Buckle finished well after finding some trouble. A half-brother to a 1m2f 3yo winner and out of a French middle-distance winner, he has improved with each of three maiden runs and should be suited by a stiffer test in handicaps. (op 10-1 tchd 15-2)

Aird Snout(USA) ran green before gradually getting the hang of things in a promising debut run. He is a Derby-entered $100,000 half-brother to 1,000 Guineas runner-up Arch Swing, and looks a sure-fire improver next time.

Frederickthegreat showed ability staying on late on his third run. He is a half-brother to 7f/1m3f winners and should have scope for progress when sent handicapping. (op 33-1)

Great Nicanor(IRE) trailed home in a heavy-ground maiden on debut but this was encouraging from a gelded son of Bertolini, who cost £15,000 at the breeze-up sales in April. (op 80-1)

Almuder, an Intikhab colt who is out of a 1m2f winner and from a prolific family, shaped with promise on debut and should improve for the experience. (op 9-1)

Poetic Power(IRE) took a big step forward when third behind a a filly with significant potential in a Nottingham maiden last time. He set a decent standard but was a bit keen after using energy up to get to the front from a wide draw and his effort flattened out early in the straight.

7370 32RED CLASSIFIED STKS 1m 1f 103y(P)
7:15 (7:15) (Class 6) 3-Y-O+ £1,704 (£503; £251) Stalls Low

Form				RPR
003	1		**Royal Alcor (IRE)**[39] 6589 4-9-1 52 (b) FrankieMcDonald 2 (Alastair Lidderdale) s.i.s: outpcd: hdwy over 2f out: rdn to ld ins fnl f: edgd lft: r.o 10/1	62
0413	2	1 1/4	**Beauchamp Xiara**[10] 7206 5-8-8 53 NicoleNordblad(7) 11 (Hans Adielsson) hld up: hdwy over 3f out: shkn up ins fnl f: styd on 11/2	59
0050	3	1 1/2	**Azurinta (IRE)**[44] 6446 3-8-12 51 StevieDonohoe 7 (Michael Bell) a.p: rdn to ld over 1f out: hdd and unable qck ins fnl f 10/1	56
440-	4	1 1/2	**Apache Kid (IRE)**[437] 5625 4-8-12 55 RyanClark(3) 13 (Ian Williams) trckd ldr: racd keenly: rdn and ev ch over 1f out: no ex ins fnl f 4/1[1]	53
5233	5	3	**Eastward Ho**[14] 7144 3-8-12 54 FrederikTylicki 9 (Jason Ward) led: rdn and hdd over 1f out: wknd ins fnl f 5/1[3]	46
0662	6	3 3/4	**Excellent Vision**[7] 7270 4-9-1 51 (t) RichardKingscote 4 (Milton Bradley) s.i.s: hld up: hdwy over 2f out: rdn over 1f out: wknd ins fnl f 9/2[2]	39
0660	7	16	**Tortilla (IRE)**[118] 4086 3-8-12 54 AndreaAtzeni 8 (Des Donovan) s.i.s: sn pushed along and a bhd 25/1	—
5510	8	1 1/4	**Mister Fantastic**[22] 6411 5-9-1 52 KellyHarrison 12 (Dai Burchell) hld up in tch: rdn over 3f out: wknd over 2f out 7/1	—
4205	9	1 3/4	**Eilean Eeve**[45] 6428 5-8-12 53 (p) GaryBartley(3) 5 (George Foster) prom: rdn over 3f out: wknd over 2f out 25/1	—
0053	10	18	**Lucky Dime**[21] 7004 3-8-12 52 MartinLane 1 (Noel Quinlan) prom tl wknd and eased over 2f out: t.o 8/1	—
5-60	11	15	**Number One Guy**[16] 7099 4-8-12 54 (b1) PaulPickard(3) 10 (Philip Kirby) prom: rdn 1/2-way: wknd over 3f out: t.o 25/1	—

2m 1.70s **Going Correction** +0.05s/f (Slow)
WFA 3 from 4yo+ 3lb **11** Ran SP% **123.6**
Speed ratings (Par 101): **102,100,99,98,95 92,78,76,75,59 46**
toteswingers:1&2:£6.30, 1&3:£22.50, 2&3:£13.20 CSF £66.06 TOTE £14.50: £3.30, £2.50, £2.90; EX 111.10.
Owner Royal Windsor Racing Club **Bred** John Hayes **Trained** Eastbury, Berks

FOCUS

The winner took a long time to find his rhythm but eventually scored with something in hand in this low-grade classified event. Limited form, but sound, with the winner improving again.

Azurinta(IRE) Official explanation: jockey said filly hung left

Tortilla(IRE) Official explanation: jockey said filly never travelled

Lucky Dime Official explanation: jockey said filly lost its action but returned sound

Number One Guy Official explanation: jockey said gelding hung left

7371 32REDPOKER.COM H'CAP 5f 216y(P)
7:45 (7:45) (Class 6) (0-55,55) 3-Y-O+ £1,908 (£563; £281) Stalls Low

Form				RPR
4063	1		**Memphis Man**[9] 7224 8-8-8 52 MatthewCosham(5) 11 (David Evans) hld up: hdwy over 1f out: rdn and hung lft ins fnl f: r.o to ld towards fin: comf 7/1[3]	62
000	2	1 1/2	**Namir (IRE)**[9] 7224 9-9-2 55 (vt) SebSanders 2 (James Evans) a.p: rdn to ld ins fnl f: hdd towards fin 25/1	60
4052	3	nk	**Fluctuation (IRE)**[18] 7071 3-8-10 52 (p) RyanClark(3) 9 (Ian Williams) hld up: hdwy over 1f out: rdn and hmpd ins fnl f: r.o 3/1[1]	57+
5246	4	1	**Ad Vitam (IRE)**[9] 7229 3-8-6 52 (vt) ClaireMurray(7) 10 (David C Griffiths) dwlt: hld up and bhd: swtchd lft over 1f out: running on wl on bit whn hmpd ins fnl f: nvr nr to chal 10/1	59+
005	5	3/4	**Wandering Lad**[21] 6999 3-8-7 53 JasonHart(7) 5 (Declan Carroll) sn led: rdn and hung lft over 1f out: hung rt: hdd and no ex ins fnl f 8/1	51
0066	6	shd	**Young Simon**[9] 7224 4-9-0 53 (v) LukeMorris 8 (George Margarson) hld up: hdwy over 2f out: rdn whn hmpd ins fnl f: styd on 7/1[3]	51
3526	7	4	**Weetentherty**[97] 4780 4-8-13 52 (p) TomEaves 4 (Linda Perratt) a.p: rdn over 2f out: looked hld whn hmpd ins fnl f 7/1[3]	45+
0/00	8	3/4	**Bridge Valley**[28] 6844 4-9-2 55 FrederikTylicki 6 (Jason Ward) hld up: pushed along 1/2-way: hdwy over 1f out: styng on whn hmpd ins fnl f: nt rcvr 9/1	53+
0202	9	2	**Dingaan (IRE)**[9] 7229 8-9-0 53 RobbieFitzpatrick 1 (Peter Grayson) s.i.s: in rr: hmpd 1f out: nvr on terms 13/2[2]	29
3000	10	3 1/4	**Quadra Hop (IRE)**[9] 7230 3-9-0 53 (t) RichardKingscote 3 (Bryn Palling) sn chsng ldr: rdn and ev ch over 2f out: wknd fnl f 33/1	19
3206	11	4 1/2	**Poppet's Joy**[22] 6981 3-8-12 51 GrahamGibbons 13 (Reg Hollinshead) chsd ldrs: rdn over 1f out: sn wknd 9/1	—

1m 15.64s (0.64) **Going Correction** +0.05s/f (Slow) **11** Ran SP% **122.8**
Speed ratings (Par 101): **97,95,94,93,92 92,86,85,83,78 72**
toteswingers:1&2:£12.50, 1&3:£4.80, 2&3:£22.20 CSF £173.11 CT £656.77 TOTE £8.80: £2.90, £9.60, £1.70; EX 95.70.
Owner Mrs I M Folkes **Bred** R T And Mrs Watson **Trained** Pandy, Monmouths
■ Stewards' Enquiry : Jason Hart two-day ban: careless riding (Nov 25-26)

FOCUS

Things got very messy in the closing stages off this modest handicap. The race is rated around the winner's turf form.

Ad Vitam(IRE) ◆ Official explanation: jockey said gelding was denied a clear run

Wandering Lad Official explanation: jockey said gelding hung right

Bridge Valley Official explanation: jockey said gelding hung right

T/Plt: £83.50 to a £1 stake. Pool:£50,995.14 - 445.39 winning tickets T/Qpdt: £12.00 to a £1 stake. Pool:£10,300.30 - 630.68 winning tickets CR

7372 - 7377a, 7379 - 7385a (Foreign Racing) - See Raceform Interactive

7273 DUNDALK (A.W) (L-H)
Friday, November 11

OFFICIAL GOING: Standard

7378a BOOKINGS@DUNDALKSTADIUM.COM RATED RACE 1m 4f (P)
9:15 (9:27) 3-Y-O+ £5,948 (£1,379; £603; £344)

			RPR
1		**Strandfield Lady (IRE)**[5] 7321 6-9-3 74 (b) CDHayes 9 (H Rogers, Ire) hld up towards rr: hdwy in 8th 2f out: rdn to ld 1f out: kpt on wl fnl f 16/1	81+
2	2 1/4	**Dazzling Light (UAE)**[16] 7102 6-9-3 74 FergalLynch 6 (Jim Goldie) mid-div early: towards rr 1/2-way: hdwy into 7th 2f out: rdn into 3rd 1f out: kpt on same pce fnl f to 2nd cl home 9/2[2]	77
3	hd	**Anshan Dreams**[57] 6109 7-9-6 68 SeamieHeffernan 12 (Adrian Maguire, Ire) in rr of mid-div early: impr to 7th 1/2-way: hdwy into 3rd 4f out: rdn to ld 1 1/2f out: hdd 1f out: no ex ins fnl f: kpt on same pce and lost 2nd cl home 14/1	80
4	hd	**Avanti Albert (IRE)**[7] 7278 7-9-6 74 (t) GFCarroll 11 (A J Martin, Ire) hld up towards rr: 10th travelling wl 2f out: rdn in 6th 1f out: kpt on wl fnl f 12/1	79+
5	1 1/2	**Cloudgazer (IRE)**[12] 7190 3-9-0 74 PJSmullen 5 (Noel Meade, Ire) mid-div: 8th 1/2-way: rdn 2f out: styd on into 4th 1f out: no ex ins fnl f: kpt on same pce 7/2[1]	77
6	1/2	**Mojita (IRE)**[23] 6965 3-9-0 77 (p) ShaneFoley 8 (K J Condon, Ire) mid-div: 11th 1/2-way: hdwy into 6th 2f out: rdn in 5th and no imp 1f out: kpt on same pce 9/2[2]	76
7	4 1/2	**Isabellareine (GER)**[23] 6966 8-8-10 67 SAGray(7) 13 (Mervyn Torrens, Ire) chsd ldrs: 4th 1/2-way: hdwy into 2nd 4f out: rdn to chal 2f out: no ex over 1f out 16/1	66
8	nk	**Blue Ridge Lane (IRE)**[12] 7190 5-8-13 71 (bt) DJBenson(7) 10 (John C McConnell, Ire) hld up towards rr: sme late hdwy into 8th 1f out: kpt on one pce 16/1	68
9	2 3/4	**Dearest Girl (IRE)**[23] 6966 4-9-3 70 WMLordan 2 (Charles O'Brien, Ire) chsd ldrs early: mid-div 1/2-way: rdn and no imp over 3f out 20/1	61
10	3	**Leaves You Baby (IRE)**[35] 6683 4-8-13 72 (p) MMMonaghan(7) 3 (M Halford, Ire) chsd ldrs: 5th 1/2-way: rdn 2f out: sn no ex and wknd 11/2[3]	59
11	4 3/4	**The Pier (IRE)**[7] 7278 5-9-1 74 (b) LFRoche(5) 7 (Joseph G Murphy, Ire) prom: led and disp after 4f: rdn and hdd 1 1/2f out: no ex over 1f out and wknd 7/1	52
12	1 1/4	**Table Forty Six (IRE)**[51] 3971 5-8-13 74 (t) RossCoakley(7) 1 (K J Condon, Ire) chsd ldrs: 6th 1/2-way: rdn and no ex over 2f out: wknd 33/1	50
13	6	**Custodian (IRE)**[14] 4051 9-8-10 67 CMWalsh(10) 14 (James M Barrett, Ire) chsd ldrs: 3rd 1/2-way: rdn and wknd 3f out 25/1	40
14	33	**Spinning Wings (IRE)**[23] 6966 5-9-3 70 (p) BACurtis 4 (T Hogan, Ire) led: disp after 4f: wknd over 4f out: t.o 25/1	—

2m 30.3s (150.30)
WFA 3 from 4yo+ 6lb **14** Ran SP% **133.9**
Daily Double: Not won CSF £92.64 TOTE £27.20: £6.70, £2.10, £3.70; DF 221.70.
Owner J Joseph Byrne **Bred** James Moynihan **Trained** Ardee, Co. Louth

FOCUS

The handicapper has been generous to Strandfield Lady with her winter reassessment leading to a 12lb drop. She did the job well here.

NOTEBOOK
Strandfield Lady(IRE) quickened up from off the pace and sustained her effort once getting to the front inside the final furlong. It was a good effort and she's the kind of mare who can put two or three decent efforts together. (op 14/1)
Dazzling Light(UAE) was held up behind horses and, although she couldn't really make any real progress when it was needed, she finished her race to good effect. Expect to see her returning over the coming months. (op 4/1)
Anshan Dreams ran a fair race and this should augur well for whatever he'll be doing over the winter. He made nice progress in the centre of the track to have every chance early in the straight and he kept going without having the pace of those horses who ended up challenging him. He was not good enough on the night, but there was nothing wrong with this effort.
Avanti Albert(IRE) was given a very confident ride and his rider was swinging along early in the straight. Others got first run and he may not have picked up to the degree that he threatened. (op 10/1)
Cloudgazer(IRE) made some late headway but never looked likely to get involved. (op 3/1)
T/Jkpt: Not won. T/Plt: @254.00. Pool of @24,769.44 - 73 winning units. II

6470 TOULOUSE
Friday, November 11

OFFICIAL GOING: Turf: soft

7386a PRIX FILLE DE L'AIR (GROUP 3) (F&M) TURF 1m 2f 110y
1:50 (12:00) 3-Y-O+ £34,482 (£13,793; £10,344; £6,896; £3,448)

RPR

1 **Skia (FR)**[49] 4-8-11 0 AnthonyCrastus 11 102
(C Laffon-Parias, France) *w.w: gd prog ent fnl f: short of room: swtchd towards rail: fnd opening between horses: fin strly to get up fnl strides* 25/1
2 nk **Skallet (FR)**[35] 6686 3-8-8 0 (b) StephanePasquier 2 103
(S Wattel, France) *racd 4th on rail: wnt 3rd bef st: u.p over 1f out: grabbed ld 100yds out: hdd fnl strides* 11/2[3]
3 nk **Casaca** 5-8-11 0 JeremyCrocquevieille 3 101
(J-M Osorio, Spain) *w.w: n.m.r in st: fin wl fnl f whn finding daylight: clst at fin* 28/1
4 hd **Intarsia (GER)**[68] 4-8-11 0 MickaelBarzalona 1 100
(A Fabre, France) *prom bhd ldrs: swtchd towards rail 1 1/2f out: r.o wl: wnt 2nd 100yds out: lost two pls cl home* 17/1
5 hd **Splendido (FR)**[37] 6642 3-8-8 0 FranckBlondel 4 102
(F Rossi, France) *prom bhd ldrs: ev ch 1 1/2f out: no ex fnl 100yds* 11/2[3]
6 1 1/4 **Night Serenade (IRE)**[26] 4-8-11 0 (p) FabriceVeron 9 98
(H-A Pantall, France) *racd towards rr: ev ch 1 1/2f out: no ex fnl f* 44/1
7 shd **Cat Nova (FR)**[22] 7114 3-8-8 0 DavyBonilla 7 99
(Y Barberot, France) *w.w: proged along rail in st: rdn but no ex fnl f* 10/1
8 hd **Don't Hurry Me (IRE)**[35] 6686 3-9-1 0 ChristopheSoumillon 5 106
(J-C Rouget, France) *tk ld after 1 1/2f and stl in front 1 1/2f out: hdd 1f out: rdn but no ex: wknd* 7/2[2]
9 nk **Garmerita (FR)**[26] 7-8-11 0 FabienLefebvre 14 96
(D Sepulchre, France) *racd towards rr: r.o in st wout threatening ldrs fnl f* 16/1
10 1 1/2 **Karsabruni (FR)**[17] 7090 3-9-1 0 MaximeGuyon 13 103
(H-A Pantall, France) *racd towards rr: rdn 1 1/2f out in centre of trck: no ex* 17/1
0 **Bellaside (IRE)**[33] 4-8-11 0 Roberto-CarlosMontenegro 8 —
(E Leon Penate, Spain) *a towards rr: no ex in st* 44/1
0 **Vertana (IRE)**[17] 7090 4-8-11 0 (b) SebastienCastellier 10 —
(H-A Pantall, France) *backmarker for much of r: nvr a factor in st* 64/1
0 **Toi Et Moi (IRE)**[33] 6739 4-8-11 0 ThierryThulliez 12 —
(P Bary, France) *racd 2nd wd of ldr: threatened briefly early in st: sn wknd* 3/1[1]
0 **Polarena (FR)**[35] 6686 3-8-8 0 TonyPiccone 6 —
(X Betron, France) *racd bhd ldrs: rdn but no ex fnl f over 1 1/2f out: fdd qckly* 47/1

2m 11.83s (131.83)
WFA 3 from 4yo+ 4lb 14 Ran SP% **119.4**
WIN (incl. 1 euro stake): 26.30. PLACES: 6.30, 2.70, 7.20. DF: 55.70. SF: 155.30.
Owner Leonidas Marinopoulos **Bred** Stilvi Compania Financiera S.A. **Trained** Chantilly, France

NOTEBOOK
Skia(FR) heads to the paddocks now.

7358 LINGFIELD (L-H)
Saturday, November 12

OFFICIAL GOING: Standard
Wind: Very light, across. Weather: sunny spells, mild

7387 PLAY RAINBOW RICHES AT BLUESQ.COM H'CAP (DIV I) 1m 2f (P)
12:00 (12:02) (Class 6) (0-60,60) 3-Y-O+ £1,704 (£503; £251) Stalls Low

Form RPR

00-0 1 **Hurricane Hymnbook (USA)**[25] 6938 6-9-10 **60** StevieDonohoe 7 78
(Willie Musson) *chsd ldrs: rdn and drew clr w runner-up 2f out: led jst ins fnl f: edgd rt but forged ahd fnl 50yds* 3/1[1]
0606 2 1/2 **Lord Lansing (IRE)**[91] 5036 4-9-8 **58** LukeMorris 9 75
(Mrs K Burke) *t.k.h: hld up in midfield: rdn and hdwy to ld jst over 2f out: sn clr w wnr: hdd jst ins fnl f: carried rt and no ex wl ins fnl f* 9/2[2]
4453 3 6 **Entrance**[17] 7113 3-9-4 **58** JimmyQuinn 12 65+
(Julia Feilden) *towards rr and niggled along early: effrt whn nt clr run 2f out tl swtchd rt over 1f out: styd on fnl f to go 3rd fnl 50yds: no ch w ldng pair* 12/1
4533 4 1/2 **Prince Of Thebes (IRE)**[23] 6969 10-8-11 **52** MarkCoumbe[(5)] 8 56
(Michael Attwater) *s.i.s: bhd and rdn along early: hdwy u.p over 1f out: styd on fnl f: no ch w ldng pair* 14/1
5460 5 nk **Rodrigo De Freitas (IRE)**[16] 7122 4-9-0 **57** (v) DanielCremin[(7)] 1 60
(Jim Boyle) *hld up towards rr: hdwy on inner over 1f out: kpt on ins fnl f: no threat to ldrs* 16/1
060 6 1/2 **Gay Gallivanter**[8] 7270 3-8-10 **50** MartinLane 13 52
(Michael Quinn) *chsd ldrs and pushed along early: rdn over 2f out: outpcd 2f out and no ch w ldrs after: plugged on same pce u.p* 20/1
00-U 7 1/2 **Whodunit (UAE)**[11] 7202 7-9-5 **58** (b) RyanClark[(3)] 6 59
(Peter Hiatt) *chsd ldrs: rdn and outpcd by ldng pair 2f out: 3rd and wl hld 1f out: one pce and lost 4 pls ins fnl f* 16/1
0000 8 4 1/2 **Inquisitress**[16] 7131 7-8-7 **46** oh1 KieranO'Neill[(3)] 10 38
(John Bridger) *hld up towards rr: hdwy over 3f out: rdn and no prog jst over 2f out: sn wknd* 22/1
054 9 1 3/4 **Days In May (IRE)**[39] 6608 3-9-3 **57** ShaneKelly 5 46
(Edward Vaughan) *in tch: rdn and fnd little ent fnl 2f: sn wknd* 9/1
000 10 hd **Hursley Hope (IRE)**[156] 2840 3-9-4 **58** WilliamBuick 4 47
(David Elsworth) *chsd ldr tl led 3f out: hdd and rdn jst over 2f out: sn wknd* 11/2[3]
3310 11 15 **If What And Maybe**[15] 7144 3-9-6 **60** (v) AdamKirby 2 19
(John Ryan) *s.i.s: sn rdn along in midfield: rdn and lost pl 3f out: wknd over 2f out: wl bhd and eased ins fnl f* 15/2
000 12 15 **Henry's Hero**[26] 6920 5-9-0 **50** (b) AndreaAtzeni 11 —
(Chris Dwyer) *led and set gd gallop: hdd and rdn 3f out: lost pl rapidly over 2f out: t.o and eased ins fnl f* 40/1
3000 13 107 **Trust Me Boy**[17] 7091 3-8-6 **46** oh1 (v) KirstyMilczarek 3 —
(John E Long) *sn rdn along in midfield: dropped to last over 4f out: sn lost tch and virtually p.u fnl 3f* 50/1

2m 4.88s (-1.72) **Going Correction** +0.025s/f (Slow)
WFA 3 from 4yo+ 4lb 13 Ran SP% **120.0**
Speed ratings (Par 101): **107,106,101,101,101 100,100,96,95,95 83,71,—**
Tote Swingers:1&2:£3.80, 2&3:£11.10, 1&3:£10.00 CSF £14.99 CT £144.83 TOTE £2.90: £1.10, £2.40, £3.40; EX 20.00.
Owner Python Partners **Bred** Respite Farm Inc **Trained** Newmarket, Suffolk

FOCUS
A moderate handicap that wouldn't have been noteworthy had a gamble not been landed. The early pace was strong and the time was good for the grade. The winner cashed in on a career-low mark.
Hursley Hope(IRE) Official explanation: jockey said filly stopped quickly

7388 DOWNLOAD THE BLUE SQUARE BET APP CLAIMING STKS 1m (P)
12:30 (12:31) (Class 6) 3-Y-O £1,704 (£503; £251) Stalls High

Form RPR

U55 1 **Daruband**[14] 7179 3-9-5 69 (v[1]) ShaneKelly 3 77
(Alan McCabe) *chsd ldr: rdn to ld 2f out: drvn and kpt on ins fnl f: drvn out* 17/2
4032 2 1 3/4 **Beautiful Day**[18] 7084 3-9-0 64 PhillipMakin 7 68
(Kevin Ryan) *t.k.h: chsd ldng pair: rdn and effrt 2f out: styd on u.p ins fnl f: wnt 2nd fnl 50yds: nvr looked a threat to wnr* 6/1[3]
4050 3 3/4 **Sky Diamond (IRE)**[10] 7235 3-8-12 65 (b) FrederikTylicki 5 64
(James Given) *broke fast: led and sn clr: rdn and hdd 2f out: no ex and btn ins fnl f: lost 2nd fnl 50yds* 7/2[2]
2032 4 1 3/4 **Cootehill Lass (IRE)**[19] 7055 3-8-7 68 (p) AndreaAtzeni 6 55
(David Evans) *hld up in midfield: rdn and effrt ent fnl 2f: chsd ldng trio over 1f out: no imp ins fnl f* 15/8[1]
4220 5 1/2 **Finefrenzyrolling (IRE)**[89] 5100 3-8-8 65 LukeMorris 10 55
(Mrs K Burke) *t.k.h: hld up in tch: rdn and styd on same pce fr over 1f out* 13/2
0043 6 4 1/2 **Elfine (IRE)**[61] 6004 3-8-5 62 (e[1]) MartinLane 8 42
(Rae Guest) *towards rr: rdn 4f out: outpcd and btn ent fnl 2f: no ch but styd on again fnl f* 14/1
0600 7 4 1/2 **Russian Storm**[25] 6929 3-8-0 0 (e[1]) JemmaMarshall[(5)] 4 31
(Pat Phelan) *stdd s: hld up in last pair: pushed along and outpcd over 2f out: no ch after but styd on ins fnl f* 50/1
5506 8 1 3/4 **Jackie Love (IRE)**[8] 7268 3-8-2 47 (b) JimmyQuinn 2 24
(Olivia Maylam) *t.k.h: hld up in midfield: rdn and unable qck over 2f out: wknd over 1f out: fdd 1f out* 25/1
5650 9 4 1/2 **Midnight Trader (IRE)**[56] 6179 3-8-9 60 ow1 (tp) TonyCulhane 11 21
(David Flood) *stdd after s: hld up in last trio: pushed along and sme hdwy jst over 2f out: wknd 2f out* 12/1
4230 10 3 **Cookieshake**[36] 6669 3-8-6 67 (b[1]) ChrisDCogan[(5)] 9 16
(Nick Littmoden) *s.i.s: pushed along and sn rcvrd and in tch: rdn and wknd over 2f out* 33/1
0500 11 7 **Zoriana**[39] 6608 3-8-7 0 (e[1]) AdrianNicholls 1 —
(Christine Dunnett) *s.i.s: a in rr: rdn wl over 3f out: losing tch whn hung rt bnd 2f out* 150/1

1m 37.7s (-0.50) **Going Correction** +0.025s/f (Slow) 11 Ran SP% **118.9**
Speed ratings (Par 98): **103,101,100,98,98 93,89,87,83,80 73**
Tote Swingers:1&2:£7.90, 2&3:£4.80, 1&3:£7.80 CSF £58.20 TOTE £13.50: £3.10, £2.20, £1.50; EX 62.30.
Owner Mrs June Bownes **Bred** Mickley Stud **Trained** Averham Park, Notts

FOCUS
A poor claimer with nine of the 11 runners sporting some sort of headgear. The early pace was solid, but it paid to race handily. The winner rates a personal best.

7389 BLUE SQUARE SPRINT SERIES RETURNS JANUARY MEDIAN AUCTION MAIDEN STKS 6f (P)
1:05 (1:05) (Class 6) 3-5-Y-O £1,704 (£503; £251) Stalls Low

Form RPR

3222 1 **Cheherazad (IRE)**[17] 7093 3-8-12 60 StevieDonohoe 2 62
(Paul Cole) *chsd ldng pair: rdn and effrt over 1f out: led 1f out: styd on wl: rdn out* 13/8[1]
2500 2 1 1/2 **Court Applause (IRE)**[2] 7349 3-9-3 63 SteveDrowne 12 62
(William Muir) *hld up in tch towards rr: rdn and hdwy on inner over 1f out: chsd wnr jst ins fnl f: kpt on but no imp fnl 75yds* 8/1
3 3/4 **Sketchy Evidence (USA)** 3-9-3 0 LukeMorris 8 59
(John Best) *s.i.s and swtchd lft after s: pushed along towards rr early: hdwy to chse ldrs jst over 2f out: n.m.r over 1f out: chsd ldng pair and drvn jst ins fnl f: kpt on* 13/2
0002 4 3 1/4 **Dusty Bluebells (IRE)**[25] 6929 3-8-7 55 (b) RyanPowell[(5)] 1 44
(J S Moore) *led and sn pushed along: hdd over 2f out: rdn to ld again over 1f out tl 1f out: wknd fnl f* 5/1[3]
4460 5 nk **Miakora**[18] 7086 3-8-12 46 ShaneKelly 4 43
(Michael Quinn) *in tch: hemmed in and nt clr run jst over 2f out: lost pl and swtchd rt over 1f out: styd on fnl f but no threat to ldrs* 80/1
0000 6 nse **My Best Man**[39] 6610 5-9-3 43 AdamKirby 5 48
(Tony Carroll) *hld up in tch: hdwy and nt clr run over 1f out: rdn and fnd little 1f out: wknd ins fnl f* 22/1
000 7 1/2 **Our Princess Ellie (USA)**[68] 5793 3-8-7 37 MarkCoumbe[(5)] 11 41
(Derek Shaw) *taken down early: a towards rr: rdn over 2f out: plugged on ins fnl f: n.d* 66/1
6-04 8 1 **Yashila (IRE)**[8] 7260 3-8-12 65 LiamKeniry 7 38
(J S Moore) *in tch: rdn and fnd little over 1f out: sn wknd* 9/2[2]
2300 9 6 **Abadejo**[58] 6090 3-9-3 61 JimCrowley 9 24
(J R Jenkins) *w ldr tl led jst over 2f out: hdd and rdn over 1f out: sn btn: fdd qckly 1f out: eased wl ins fnl f* 12/1
10 4 **Pill Boy** 3-9-3 0 SamHitchcott 3 11
(Dai Burchell) *s.i.s: a outpcd in rr: lost tch 1/2-way* 50/1

0000 **11** 1 1/4 **Lady Royal Oak (IRE)**[11] 7201 4-8-12 57.................. KirstyMilczarek 10 —
(Olivia Maylam) *taken down early and led rdrless to s: stdd s: plld hrd: hld up in rr: hdwy into midfield 1/2-way: wknd qckly jst over 2f out: wl bhd and eased ins fnl f* **33/1**

1m 12.34s (0.44) **Going Correction** +0.025s/f (Slow) **11** Ran SP% **117.1**
Speed ratings (Par 101): **98,96,95,90,90 90,89,88,80,74 73**
Tote Swingers:1&2:£3.40, 2&3:£8.90, 1&3:£4.00 CSF £14.99 TOTE £3.10: £1.20, £1.40, £2.30; EX 15.10.
Owner K Dhunjibhoy **Bred** John And Leslie Young **Trained** Whatcombe, Oxon

FOCUS
Older-horse maidens at this time of year are generally moderate affairs and this was no exception. The winner did not need to match her latest effort.

7390 E B F JEREMY CHAPMAN STILL SWINGING AT 70 NOVICE STKS 1m (P)
1:40 (1:41) (Class 4) 2-Y-O **£4,560** (£1,357; £678; £339) **Stalls** High

Form RPR
1 **1** **Asatir (USA)**[118] 4122 2-9-5 83.. WilliamBuick 4 89+
(Saeed Bin Suroor) *hld up in tch: shkn up and hdwy to press ldrs 3f out: rdn and sltly outpcd 2f out: rallied and ev ch whn carried rt 1f out: r.o wl under hands and heels riding fnl 100yds to ld last strides* **7/4**[1]

51 **2** hd **Gloriam (USA)**[15] 7142 2-9-2 85.. MartinLane 2 86
(David Simcock) *chsd ldr tl led 3f out: rdn and qcknd 2f out: edgd rt u.p over 1f out: r.o u.p tl hdd and no ex last strides* **7/2**[3]

311 **3** hd **Frog Hollow**[45] 6464 2-9-7 89... JimCrowley 1 90+
(Ralph Beckett) *hld up in tch: effrt and n.m.r jst over 2f out: chalng between horses and carried rt over 1f out: kpt on wl u.p ins fnl f* **2/1**[2]

3012 **4** 4 **Tidy Affair (IRE)**[48] 6372 2-8-13 82.......................... KieranO'Neill(3) 3 76
(Richard Hannon) *led at stdy gallop: hdd 3f out: rdn and unable qck 2f out: tried to rally on inner over 1f out: wknd ins fnl f* **11/2**

4300 **5** 6 **Faraway**[23] 6972 2-9-0 70..(v) AdamKirby 5 60
(David Evans) *stdd s: t.k.h: hld up in last: rdn and short-lived effrt 2f out: wknd over 1f out* **100/1**

1m 41.07s (2.87) **Going Correction** +0.025s/f (Slow) **5** Ran SP% **108.3**
Speed ratings (Par 98): **86,85,85,81,75**
CSF £7.91 TOTE £2.70: £2.10, £1.10; EX 7.20.
Owner Godolphin **Bred** Robert Raphaelson **Trained** Newmarket, Suffolk

FOCUS
They went no pace early in this novice event, but it produced a thrilling finish between the front three and the trio should all make nice 3yos. The winner gave the impression he can do significantly better.

NOTEBOOK
Asatir(USA) hadn't been seen since beating three subsequent winners on his Redcar debut in July and he still displayed signs of greenness on this second start, being niggled along over 3f out, not taking the home bend at all well, and taking time to get organised once in line for home. Despite all of that and the narrow margin of victory, he won this a shade cosily - his rider relied on hands and heels in the closing stages and always gave the impression that he was going to get there. His pedigree suggest that this sort of trip will prove his optimum and he seems likely to go on to much better things. (op 13-8 tchd 6-4)
Gloriam(USA) made no mistake when bolting up at odds of 4-9 in a Wolverhampton maiden on his second start and looked likely to follow up when sent past the leader running to the home bend, but despite keeping on strongly he hung away to his right in the straight and was run down almost on the line. Like the winner, he has the pedigree of a miler and there should be some decent prizes in him next year. (tchd 4-1)
Frog Hollow, a progressive juvenile on turf, promised to be suited by this step up to 1m, so could probably have done with a stronger all-round gallop. He tried hard to get involved from the final bend and put in a strong challenge between the front pair, but could never quite get there. This was a good effort conceding weight to his rivals and there are more races to be won with him. (tchd 15-8)
Tidy Affair(IRE) had shown useful form on turf, but was up against some unexposed sorts here. He had the run of the race out in front and rallied against the inside rail after being headed over 2f out, but was eventually put in his place. (op 6-1 tchd 8-1)

7391 BLUE SQUARE CHURCHILL STKS (LISTED RACE) 1m 2f (P)
2:15 (2:15) (Class 1) 3-Y-O+
£17,013 (£6,450; £3,228; £1,608; £807; £405) **Stalls** Low

Form RPR
1361 **1** **Hunter's Light (IRE)**[52] 6247 3-9-0 110............................ WilliamBuick 7 109+
(Saeed Bin Suroor) *hld up in tch: hdwy to join ldrs over 2f out: led over 1f out: sn rdn: kpt on u.p: veered lft wl ins fnl f: hld on cl home* **8/11**[1]

1646 **2** shd **Circumvent**[21] 7029 4-9-2 99.. ShaneKelly 3 107
(Paul Cole) *hld up wl in tch: effrt: nt clr run and swtchd lft over 1f out: str chal and drvn fnl 100yds: jst hld* **8/1**[3]

1202 **3** 1 3/4 **Suits Me**[51] 6277 8-9-2 101.. MickyFenton 4 106+
(David Barron) *led: rdn and qcknd ent fnl 2f: hdd over 1f out: kpt on wl u.p: cl 3rd but styng on same pce whn squeezed for room and snatched up wl ins fnl f* **6/1**[2]

4003 **4** 1 **Maali (IRE)**[14] 7166 3-8-12 97.......................................(bt) SebSanders 10 101
(Clive Brittain) *dwlt: hld up in tch: hdwy to chse ldrs jst over 2f out: kpt on same pce u.p fnl f* **10/1**

5000 **5** 2 **Nice Style (IRE)**[22] 6989 6-9-2 94................................(bt[1]) AdamKirby 1 97
(Jeremy Gask) *stdd after s: hld up in tch: rdn and effrt wl over 1f out: drvn and kpt on same pce fnl f* **20/1**

2210 **6** 2 **Satwa Pearl**[7] 7296 5-8-11 82.. SteveDrowne 6 88+
(Ed Dunlop) *s.i.s: hld up in tch in rr: rdn and effrt over 1f out: no imp and styd on same pce fnl f* **25/1**

3111 **7** 1/2 **Proud Chieftain**[11] 7204 3-8-12 81................................... JimCrowley 8 92
(Clifford Lines) *stdd after s: hld up in last pair: rdn and effrt jst over 2f out: c wd and no imp fr over 1f out* **16/1**

3250 **8** 1 **Classic Colori (IRE)**[21] 7029 4-9-2 91........................... DanielTudhope 5 90
(David O'Meara) *chsd ldr: rdn and unable qck whn short of room 2f out: wknd over 1f out* **25/1**

0002 **9** 2 1/2 **Night Lily (IRE)**[8] 7277 5-8-11 99.................................... LukeMorris 2 80
(Paul D'Arcy) *chsd ldrs: rdn and losing pl over 2f out: wknd over 1f out* **16/1**

2m 3.34s (-3.26) **Going Correction** +0.025s/f (Slow)
WFA 3 from 4yo+ 4lb **9** Ran SP% **116.6**
Speed ratings (Par 111): **114,113,112,111,110 108,108,107,105**
Tote Swingers:1&2:£2.70, 2&3:£3.70, 1&3:£2.40 CSF £7.01 TOTE £1.60: £1.10, £2.10, £1.50; EX 8.60 Trifecta £15.90 Pool £887.01 - 41.15 winning units..
Owner Godolphin **Bred** Darley **Trained** Newmarket, Suffolk

FOCUS
The last two winners of this race went on to win the Winter Derby. However, the early pace was modest and it developed into something of a sprint. The winner apart it was not a strong race for the grade, and he was not at his best.

NOTEBOOK
Hunter's Light(IRE), best in at the weights and winner of two Listed races on turf this year, seemed to handle the Polytrack when runner-up on his racecourse debut at Kempton and his sire Dubawi has a 23% strike-rate with his runners around here. Always travelling well behind the leaders on the outside, he was asked to go and win his race off the home turn, but had to battle hard. He looked to have the race under control when veering sharply to his left around 20yds from the line, badly hampering the third, but he was the best horse on merit and the stewards allowed the result to stand. (op 11-10, tchd 5-4 in places)
Circumvent hadn't run on sand since showing good form in his first two starts as a 2yo, but ran a blinder here especially as he was stuck in a pocket when still travelling well and was forced to switch to make his effort towards the inside of the track. The fact that he got so close is testament to his ability and he is well worth another try in a Pattern race around here. (tchd 9-1)
Suits Me, having his 14th start over C&D, finished third in this race for the third consecutive year. He was allowed the luxury of an uncontested lead and rallied gamely after being headed by the winner, but was held when badly hampered by him in the very closing stages. (op 5-1 tchd 13-2)
Maali(IRE), from the yard responsible for two of the last three winners of this race, ran on well down the outside of the track to finish a respectable fourth, but is still a maiden having faced some very stiff tasks. (tchd 11-1)
Nice Style(IRE) disappointed when sent of third-favourite for the Winter Derby, having pulled too hard, and was tried in first-time blinkers. However, he surely needs a stronger pace than he got here and could make little impression. (op 16-1)
Satwa Pearl had plenty to find on these terms and was another to make limited late progress from the back of the field. (op 20-1)
Proud Chieftain is a progressive handicapper and was bidding for a four-timer, but he also had a mountain to climb on these terms and wasn't up to it. (op 12-1 tchd 20-1)
Classic Colori(IRE) is on long losing run and was ridden close to the pace, but didn't stay.
Night Lily(IRE), a four-time winner on Polytrack, has now finished unplaced in all six starts over this trip or further. (op 14-1)

7392 BLUE SQUARE GOLDEN ROSE STKS (LISTED RACE) 6f (P)
2:50 (2:52) (Class 1) 3-Y-O+
£17,013 (£6,450; £3,228; £1,608; £807; £405) **Stalls** Low

Form RPR
0002 **1** **Docofthebay (IRE)**[7] 7295 7-9-2 103..........................(b) FrederikTylicki 2 106
(David Nicholls) *in tch: swtchd lft and gd hdwy towards inner over 1f out: rdn and chal ins fnl f: r.o to ld last strides* **8/1**

6020 **2** hd **Secret Witness**[7] 7298 5-9-2 94.......................................(b) JoeFanning 3 105
(Ronald Harris) *in tch: n.m.r wl over 1f out: rdn and effrt to ld 1f out: kpt on wl u.p tl hdd last strides* **11/1**

000 **3** shd **Global City (IRE)**[64] 5879 5-9-2 100..............................(t) WilliamBuick 4 105+
(Saeed Bin Suroor) *hld up in last trio: c wd and hdwy over 1f out: str run and edgd lft ins fnl f: gng on strly fin: nt quite get up* **6/1**[2]

0630 **4** 1/2 **Cochabamba (IRE)**[42] 6531 3-8-11 94.................................. JohnFahy 6 98
(Roger Teal) *in tch towards rr: rdn and effrt jst over 1f out: kpt on wl u.p fnl 100yds: nt quite rch ldrs* **16/1**

0025 **5** 1/2 **Elshabakiya (IRE)**[35] 6687 3-8-12 102 ow1....................... SebSanders 5 97
(Clive Brittain) *hld up in last trio: rdn and gd hdwy on inner over 1f out: kpt on but no imp fnl 75yds* **15/2**[3]

0124 **6** 1 **Secret Asset (IRE)**[11] 7221 6-9-2 114............................... LukeMorris 12 98
(Jane Chapple-Hyam) *chsd ldrs: rdn and effrt over 1f out: drvn and styd on same pce ins fnl f* **5/1**[1]

0333 **7** 3/4 **Five Star Junior (USA)**[15] 7149 5-9-2 97.......................... ShaneKelly 7 96
(Linda Stubbs) *in tch towards rr: hdwy on outer over 1f out: chsng ldrs and keeping on same pce whn squeezed for room ins fnl f: no imp after* **12/1**

0002 **8** 1/2 **Breathless Kiss (USA)**[22] 7012 4-8-11 98........................ TomEaves 10 89
(Kevin Ryan) *bhd: rdn and racing awkardly over 2f out: hdwy and edging lft 1f out: styd on wl: nvr trbld ldrs* **25/1**

0-60 **9** nk **Total Gallery (IRE)**[11] 7221 5-9-2 103............................... EddieAhern 8 95+
(Henry Candy) *stdd after s: hld up in midfield: rdn and effrt over 1f out: chsng ldrs and keeping on same pce whn squeezed for room and hmpd ins fnl f: n.d and eased after* **6/1**[2]

0060 **10** 1 1/2 **Silaah**[87] 5180 7-9-2 102..(p) AdrianNicholls 9 88
(David Nicholls) *racd freely: pressed ldr: rdn to ld wl over 1f out: hdd 1f out: wknd* **14/1**

0446 **11** 4 **Norville (IRE)**[78] 5430 4-9-2 97.......................................(b) AdamKirby 11 76
(David Evans) *chsd ldrs: rdn ent fnl 2f: wknd jst over 1f out* **20/1**

3001 **12** 1 3/4 **Bajan Tryst (USA)**[15] 7149 5-9-2 98................................ PhillipMakin 1 70
(Kevin Ryan) *led tl rdn and hdd wl over 1f out: wknd qckly jst over 1f out* **8/1**

1m 10.89s (-1.01) **Going Correction** +0.025s/f (Slow) **12** Ran SP% **116.4**
Speed ratings (Par 111): **107,106,106,105,105 103,102,102,101,99 94,92**
Tote Swingers:1&2:£18.50, 2&3:£13.70, 1&3:£7.00 CSF £91.25 TOTE £7.80: £2.40, £5.20, £1.90; EX 122.70 Trifecta £760.90 Part won. Pool £1,028.36 - 0.40 winning units..
Owner Paul J Dixon **Bred** G And Mrs Middlebrook **Trained** Sessay, N Yorks
■ Stewards' Enquiry : William Buick two-day ban: careless riding (Nov 26,28)

FOCUS
An extraordinary Listed sprint, run at a solid early pace thanks to a three-way battle for the early lead involving Bajan Tryst, Silaah and Norville, but they merely set it up for the closers. Tyoical form to assess, the winner stepping up on his latest turf effort and a personal best for the second.

NOTEBOOK
Docofthebay(IRE), on a losing run of 17, seemed likely to find this 6f trip too short and he doesn't run over it very often these days, but he was only 2l behind Hoof It when fourth of 20 over this distance at York in May and a strongly run race has always brought out the best in him. He travelled particularly well in mid-division before moving up rounding the home turn as the leaders started to fall in a hole, and maintained his effort to hit the front in the last couple of strides. He still has what it takes at the age of seven.
Secret Witness, a winner over C&D last December, had a bit to find on these terms, so ran a cracker. Having been handy from the off, he was in front a furlong out until the last couple of strides, but you have to worry about his handicap mark after this. (op 16-1)
Global City(IRE), unbeaten in two previous starts over C&D, he hadn't had much luck in a light campaign this year and again circumstances conspired against him. Unable to hold a position from his good draw, he soon found himself in last place and had to circle the entire field on the home bend in order to get a run. He flew home, despite hanging away to his left, but the post was always going to beat him. (op 9-1 tchd 11-2)
Cochabamba(IRE), successful over C&D on her racecourse debut (only previous try on sand), had failed to add to that win on turf since then, but the return here resulted in a decent effort and she was finishing in good style.
Elshabakiya(IRE), 0-10 and carrying 1lb overweight, was beaten just a head by Dubawi Gold in the Listed Spring Cup over 7f here in March (her only previous try on sand). She stayed on late against the inside rail, which isn't usually the best place to be, but it's likely that the drop back to this trip was a bigger problem. (op 8-1)
Secret Asset(IRE) had upwards of 11lb in hand of these rivals at the weights after his narrow defeat in the Abbaye and he has winning form over C&D, but the outside stall was a major problem and though he had his chance, the energy he had to expend in order to take a handy position from his draw must have counted against him. (op 9-2)

Five Star Junior(USA), just behind Bajan Tryst at Dundalk last time, is a triple winner over C&D and ran better than his final position as, like the third horse, he was forced very wide on the home bend. (op 11-1 tchd 14-1)
Breathless Kiss(USA) has gained all five wins over the minimum trip and was badly drawn here, so she also ran better than it might have appeared as she was just about last with plenty of ground to make up starting up the home straight. (op 16-1)

7393 THOUSANDS OF SPORTS EXPERIENCES AT BLUESQ.COM H'CAP 1m (P)
3:20 (3:22) (Class 2) (0-100,99) 3-Y-0+ **£11,320** (£3,368; £1,683; £841) **Stalls** High

Form RPR
0600 **1** **Riggins (IRE)**[36] 6672 7-9-2 **94** J-PGuillambert 8 105+
(Ed Walker) *chsd ldrs: pushed along to press ldrs 2f out: rdn and ev ch over 1f out: led fnl 100yds: r.o wl: rdn out* **9/2**[2]
0-05 **2** 3/4 **Mull Of Killough (IRE)**[14] 7168 5-9-0 **92** TonyHamilton 2 101
(Richard Fahey) *broke fast and led early: sn stdd and in tch: trckd ldrs and n.m.r 2f out: rdn and led over 1f out: hdd jst ins fnl f: kpt on same pce u.p fnl 100yds* **7/2**[1]
0011 **3** *shd* **Loyalty**[24] 6949 4-9-1 **93** (v) JoeFanning 6 103+
(Derek Shaw) *in tch towards rr: effrt and nt clr run ent fnl f: swtchd lft and hdwy 1f out: r.o strly fnl 100yds: nt rch ldrs* **6/1**[3]
0201 **4** *nk* **Mia's Boy**[21] 7023 7-9-5 **97** AndreaAtzeni 4 105
(Chris Dwyer) *hld up in tch in rr: shkn up 2f out: dream run on inner to chal 1f out: rdn to ld jst ins fnl f: hdd fnl 100yds: no ex and lost 2 pls cl home* **7/1**
3110 **5** 1/2 **Blue Moon**[8] 7277 4-9-2 **94** PhillipMakin 5 101
(Kevin Ryan) *broke wl: stdd and in tch in midfield: swtchd rt off of rail over 2f out: hdwy u.p and ev ch jst over 1f out: no ex and btn fnl 75yds* **10/1**
5363 **6** 3 1/2 **Chapter And Verse (IRE)**[17] 7110 5-9-0 **92** TonyCulhane 11 91
(Mike Murphy) *dwlt and bustled along early: in tch in midfield on outer: rdn and outpcd bnd 2f out: no threat to ldrs and plugged on same pce fr over 1f out* **10/1**
1000 **7** *nk* **Sinfonico (IRE)**[49] 6335 3-8-4 **87** KieranO'Neill(3) 7 85
(Richard Hannon) *pressed ldr: ev ch and rdn 2f out tl over 1f out: wknd ent fnl f* **20/1**
0615 **8** 2 **Nazreef**[17] 7110 4-9-7 **99** (bt) JimCrowley 1 93
(Hughie Morrison) *sn led: rdn 2f out: hdd over 1f out: sn wknd* **10/1**
3601 **9** *hd* **Fantasy Gladiator**[17] 7110 5-8-6 **87** (p) JohnFahy(3) 3 80
(Robert Cowell) *dropped to rr after 1f: rdn and no prog over 2f out: nvr trbld ldrs* **14/1**
2105 **10** *nk* **Hazzard County (USA)**[16] 7127 7-8-11 **94** LauraPike(5) 10 86
(David Simcock) *hld up in tch: rdn and unable qck over 1f out: wknd ins fnl f* **16/1**
4006 **11** 1 3/4 **Taajub (IRE)**[119] 4104 4-8-12 **90** SebSanders 9 78
(Peter Crate) *hld up in tch in last trio: rdn and no hdwy over 1f out: n.d* **40/1**
-004 **12** 19 **Zacynthus (IRE)**[21] 7023 3-8-8 **88** (p) ShaneKelly 12 33
(Alan McCabe) *chsd ldrs tl lost pl qckly over 2f out: wl bhd and eased fnl f* **14/1**

1m 36.3s (-1.90) **Going Correction** +0.025s/f (Slow) course record
WFA 3 from 4yo+ 2lb 12 Ran SP% **120.9**
Speed ratings (Par 109): **110,109,109,108,108 104,104,102,102,102 100,81**
Tote Swingers:1&2:£5.00, 2&3:£3.10, 1&3:£7.10 CSF £21.04 CT £99.37 TOTE £6.50: £2.00, £2.00, £1.80; EX 26.50.
Owner Dubai Thoroughbred Racing **Bred** Compagnia Generale S R L **Trained** Newmarket, Suffolk

FOCUS
A hot handicap, but the early pace wasn't that strong despite a disputed lead between Nazreef and Sinfonico. The winner is rated up a length on this year's turf form and this is a race to take fairly positively.

NOTEBOOK
Riggins(IRE) had been below form on turf this year, but was 3-3 on Polytrack coming into this, including a success in Listed company. Always close to the pace, he briefly looked held starting up the home straight, but never stopped trying and forged his way to the front inside the last half-furlong. He didn't run very well in one try at Meydan earlier this year and it will be interesting to see if he returns there in the new year. (op 7-1)
Mull Of Killough(IRE) ◆, making his all-weather debut, was sent off well-backed and had every chance having always been handy. Having taken well enough to the surface, he could be the ideal type for the Lincoln Trial at Wolverhampton next March, and perhaps another crack at the Lincoln itself in which he finished third last year. (op 9-2)
Loyalty, bidding for a hat-trick off a 9lb higher mark, was having his first try on the Polytrack at this venue, but didn't find his stride until it was too late and may prefer a more galloping track than this. (op 11-2)
Mia's Boy has winning form over C&D from his younger days and looked the one to beat when enjoying a dream run up the inside rounding the home bend to hit the front over a furlong out, but he probably got there too soon as he seemed to think he had done enough and was run right out of the places. (op 6-1)
Blue Moon was out of her depth in Listed company at Dundalk last time and performed better back in this grade, staying on well down the outside of the track, but she was 9lb higher than when winning a handicap at the same venue before that and may be in the handicapper's grip now. (op 8-1)
Chapter And Verse(IRE), winner of just one of his previous 25 starts, has plenty of form on Polytrack but this was his first try here and he could make little impression after racing keenly early. He may be happier back at Kempton.
Hazzard County(USA), reunited with Laura Pike under whom he had gained his last three wins, caught the eye on his return from 229 days off here last month but didn't get the strong pace he needs. (op 12-1)
Zacynthus(IRE)'s rider reported that the colt lost his action Official explanation: jockey said colt lost its action

7394 PLAY RAINBOW RICHES AT BLUESQ.COM H'CAP (DIV II) 1m 2f (P)
3:55 (3:55) (Class 6) (0-60,59) 3-Y-0+ **£1,704** (£503; £251) **Stalls** Low

Form RPR
0143 **1** **Woop Woop (IRE)**[26] 6923 3-9-1 **59** RyanPowell(5) 9 67
(Ian Williams) *in tch in midfield: nt clr run 2f out: outpcd and swtchd lft wl over 1f out: rallied u.p ins fnl f: r.o strly to ld towards fin* **9/1**
0005 **2** 1/2 **Indian Violet (IRE)**[16] 7131 5-9-2 **58** LukeRowe(7) 11 65
(Ralph Smith) *t.k.h: hld up in tch in midfield: hdwy over 2f out: rdn to chse ldng pair 1f out: edgd lft u.p but styd on to ld wl ins fnl f: sn hdd and no ex* **8/1**
0342 **3** 1/2 **Warden Bond**[17] 7092 3-8-7 **51** (p) LauraPike(5) 12 57
(William Stone) *chsd ldr tl led over 3f out: rdn and forged ahd wl over 1f out: hdd wl ins fnl f: no ex* **7/1**[3]
3200 **4** *nk* **Kai Mook**[16] 7131 4-9-1 **57** HarryPoulton(7) 8 62
(Roger Ingram) *hld up in last trio: rdn and effrt on outer over 1f out: r.o strly ins fnl f: nt rch ldrs* **14/1**
3504 **5** 1/2 **Miss Bounty**[16] 7121 6-9-5 **54** MatthewDavies 5 58
(Jim Boyle) *hld up in tch: hdwy over 2f out: nt clr run 2f out: swtchd rt and effrt over 1f out: styd on wl ins fnl f* **10/1**
0421 **6** 3/4 **Beggers Belief**[17] 7092 3-9-3 **56** (b) SebSanders 4 59
(Eric Wheeler) *chsd ldrs: wnt 2nd over 3f out: rdn and pressing ldr ent fnl 2f: wknd jst ins fnl f* **15/8**[1]
3102 **7** 1/2 **Abigails Angel**[11] 7202 4-9-9 **58** AdamKirby 2 61
(Brett Johnson) *t.k.h: chsd ldrs: wnt 3rd and rdn 2f out: styng on whn nt clr run and swtchd rt ins fnl f: nt clr run again and nt pushed after: unable to chal* **5/1**[2]
3102 **8** 3/4 **Tinkerbell Will**[16] 7119 4-8-12 **50** NataliaGemelova(3) 10 50
(John E Long) *s.i.s: hdwy on outer 3f out: rdn and no imp over 1f out: styd on same pce fnl f* **16/1**
0600 **9** 2 1/2 **Beckfield Dancer**[16] 7122 3-8-9 **48** SaleemGolam 3 43
(Stuart Williams) *chsd ldrs: rdn over 2f out: wknd over 1f out* **25/1**
6030 **10** 3 3/4 **Escape Artist**[10] 7228 4-9-2 **54** (t) KieranO'Neill(3) 7 42
(John Bridger) *a bhd: rdn and no prog over 2f out* **25/1**
0660 **11** 15 **Under Fire (IRE)**[17] 7091 8-8-10 **45** MartinLane 1 —
(Tony Carroll) *dwlt: sn bustled along and rcvrd to ld: hdd and rdn over 3f out: sn dropped out: wl bhd fnl 2f* **50/1**
4550 **F** **Ocean Of Peace (FR)**[11] 7202 8-9-7 **56** LukeMorris 6 —
(Martin Bosley) *in tch in midfield tl lost action: collapsed and fell 6f out: fatally injured* **20/1**

2m 6.46s (-0.14) **Going Correction** +0.025s/f (Slow)
WFA 3 from 4yo+ 4lb 12 Ran SP% **121.1**
Speed ratings (Par 101): **101,100,100,99,99 98,98,97,95,92 80,—**
Tote Swingers:1&2:£11.80, 2&3:£11.20, 1&3:£4.10 CSF £77.37 CT £544.12 TOTE £7.00: £2.40, £5.30, £2.40; EX 64.50.
Owner Lee Westwood & Chubby Chandler **Bred** C Amerian **Trained** Portway, Worcs

FOCUS
A moderate contest in which little covered the front eight at the line. The early pace was ordinary and the winning time was 1.58 seconds slower than the first division.A bunch finish and modest form.
Abigails Angel Official explanation: jockey said filly was denied a clear run
T/Plt: £67.40 to a £1 stake. Pool £48,414.59. 524.36 winning tickets T/Qpdt: £18.10 to a £1 stake. Pool £4,664.96. 190.66 winning tickets SP

7364 WOLVERHAMPTON (A.W) (L-H)
Saturday, November 12

OFFICIAL GOING: Standard
Wind: Light across Weather: Overcast

7395 32RED H'CAP 5f 20y(P)
6:20 (6:21) (Class 5) (0-70,71) 3-Y-0+ **£2,264** (£673; £336; £168) **Stalls** Low

Form RPR
0021 **1** **Prince James**[21] 7040 4-8-9 **65** DavidSimmonson(7) 2 76
(Michael Easterby) *a.p: rdn to ld ins fnl f: r.o* **11/2**[3]
0042 **2** 3/4 **Blown It (USA)**[14] 7173 5-9-0 **63** JoeFanning 12 71
(Keith Dalgleish) *mid-div: hdwy over 1f out: rdn and ev ch ins fnl f: styd on* **9/2**[2]
2400 **3** 1/2 **Atlantic Beach**[16] 7116 6-9-2 **65** (b) LiamKeniry 11 72
(Milton Bradley) *hld up: r.o ins fnl f: nt rch ldrs* **20/1**
6430 **4** *nse* **Atlantic Cycle (IRE)**[17] 7106 4-9-2 **65** RichardKingscote 6 71
(Milton Bradley) *a.p: rdn over 1f out: r.o* **16/1**
0102 **5** 1/2 **Haadeeth**[8] 7265 4-9-1 **71** (b) GeorgeChaloner(7) 1 76
(Richard Fahey) *chsd ldrs: led over 1f out: hdd and unable qck ins fnl f* **7/2**[1]
4000 **6** 2 1/4 **Cruise Tothelimit (IRE)**[17] 7106 3-9-4 **67** GrahamGibbons 4 63
(Mark Brisbourne) *chsd ldr: rdn and ev ch over 1f out: no ex ins fnl f* **7/1**
5300 **7** *nse* **Chjimes (IRE)**[14] 7172 7-9-4 **67** (b) KirstyMilczarek 7 63
(Conor Dore) *s.i.s and hmpd s: sn pushed along in rr: edgd lft and r.o ins fnl f: nvr nrr* **28/1**
2520 **8** 1 1/2 **Sharp Shoes**[37] 6655 4-9-2 **65** (p) FrederikTylicki 10 56
(Ann Duffield) *chsd ldrs: rdn over 1f out: wknd ins fnl f* **11/1**
0614 **9** *nk* **Bond Blade**[19] 7064 3-8-11 **63** DaleSwift(3) 8 53
(Geoffrey Oldroyd) *prom: rdn over 1f out: styd on same pce* **7/1**
0000 **10** *nk* **Skylla**[25] 6932 4-9-2 **70** MarkCoumbe(5) 13 59
(Derek Shaw) *hld up: a in rr* **33/1**
1230 **11** 1 1/4 **Grudge**[57] 6119 6-8-13 **67** (b) JustinNewman(5) 9 51
(Conor Dore) *sn pushed along in rr: nvr on terms* **12/1**
0560 **12** 1 3/4 **Overwhelm**[14] 7172 3-9-1 **64** (p) LiamJones 3 42
(Andrew Reid) *led: rdn and hdd over 1f out: wknd ins fnl f* **25/1**
1003 **13** 1 1/2 **Crimson Queen**[11] 7201 4-9-0 **63** TomEaves 5 35
(Roy Brotherton) *s.i.s: sn rcvrd to be mid-div: pushed along 3f out: wknd over 1f out* **10/1**

61.63 secs (-0.67) **Going Correction** -0.075s/f (Stan) 13 Ran SP% **126.8**
Speed ratings (Par 103): **102,100,100,99,99 95,95,93,92,92 90,87,84**
Tote Swingers: 1&2:£2.80, 2&3:£16.70, 1&3:£31.30 CSF £31.07 CT £497.49 TOTE £7.80: £2.70, £1.10, £8.70; EX 21.40.
Owner A Saha **Bred** A C M Spalding **Trained** Sheriff Hutton, N Yorks

FOCUS
A competitive race, with just two lengths covering the first five. A small personal best from the winner.
Bond Blade Official explanation: vet said gelding finished lame

7396 EBF "OVERBURY" MAIDEN FILLIES' STKS 7f 32y(P)
6:50 (6:51) (Class 5) 2-Y-0 **£3,234** (£962; £481; £240) **Stalls** High

Form RPR
65 **1** **Shabora (IRE)**[16] 7124 2-9-0 0 AndreaAtzeni 9 80
(Roger Varian) *a.p: chsd ldr 3f out: sn pushed along: rdn ins fnl f: r.o to ld nr fin* **8/1**
2 *nk* **Disposition** 2-9-0 0 WilliamBuick 7 79+
(John Gosden) *prom: rdn over 1f out: ev ch wl ins fnl f: r.o* **9/2**[3]
32 **3** 3/4 **Eluding**[16] 7118 2-9-0 0 JimCrowley 10 77
(Mahmood Al Zarooni) *w ldr tl led 5f out: pushed along and edgd rt fr over 1f out: rdn ins fnl f: hdd nr fin* **5/6**[1]
6 **4** 11 **Forever Janey**[18] 7072 2-8-9 0 MatthewLawson(5) 2 50
(Paul Green) *prom: rdn over 2f out: sn wknd* **66/1**
5 2 3/4 **Chignon (IRE)** 2-9-0 0 EddieAhern 4 43+
(Sir Henry Cecil) *s.i.s: hld up: nvr nrr* **3/1**[2]
05 **6** 1/2 **Beauchamp Orange**[12] 7197 2-8-7 0 NicoleNordblad(7) 5 42
(Hans Adielsson) *hld up: nvr on terms* **25/1**
0 **7** 1 3/4 **Pink Belini**[18] 7080 2-9-0 0 GrahamGibbons 1 38
(Alan McCabe) *led 2f: chsd ldr tl pushed along 3f out: wknd 2f out* **80/1**

 The Form Book, Raceform Ltd, Compton, RG20 6NL

8 4 ½ **L'Arlesienne** 2-9-0 0 .... LiamKeniry 6 27
(Sylvester Kirk) *s.i.s: pushed along over 2f out: n.d* **33/1**

0 9 2 ½ **Bonnie Blade**^{15} 7142 2-9-0 0 .... LiamJones 12 21
(James Unett) *a in rr* **100/1**

00 10 2 ¼ **Chateau Lola**^{7} 7293 2-8-9 0 ....(v) MarkCoumbe$^{(5)}$ 8 15
(Derek Shaw) *chsd ldrs tl wknd over 2f out* **100/1**

1m 29.2s (-0.40) **Going Correction** -0.075s/f (Stan) **10** Ran SP% **120.3**
Speed ratings (Par 93): **99,98,97,85,82 81,79,74,71,68**
Tote Swingers: 1&2:£6.50, 2&3:£2.00, 1&3:£1.70 CSF £43.52 TOTE £13.50: £2.80, £2.80, £1.02; EX 49.20.
Owner Sheikh Ahmed Al Maktoum **Bred** Darley **Trained** Newmarket, Suffolk

FOCUS
The first three, all relatively unexposed and from good stables, finished well clear, so the form of the placed horses looks sound. The time was quick too.

NOTEBOOK
Shabora(IRE) broke better this time, finally showing what she can do in beating two fair sorts at this level. She has some way to go to prove anything out of the ordinary, but she does have potential at a realistic level and should improve again. (op 10-1 tchd 15-2)
Disposition, a Selkirk debutante out of a respectably related maiden, made a promising debut. She looks up to typical maiden-winning level on Polytrack. (op 11-2 tchd 6-1)
Eluding sets the standard in this race, having been placed in her only two previous attempts. She continues to be caught in the closing stages, but she ought to win her maiden. (op 8-13)
Forever Janey, beaten a fair way on her debut (on turf), finished even further behind the winner this time but did better than her price suggested. She is more likely to be competitive when handicapped.
Chignon(IRE), who changed hands for 45,000euros this year, needed the experience. Though beaten some way, she should be capable of better next time and is worth monitoring with the longer term in mind. (op 4-1)
Beauchamp Orange now receives a handicap mark, and that will bring her more into the equation, particularly at 1m-plus.

7397 DICKIE BARTON'S TYING THE KNOT H'CAP 1m 1f 103y(P)
7:20 (7:20) (Class 4) (0-80,78) 3-Y-0+ **£4,431** (£1,308; £654) **Stalls** Low

Form RPR

0004 1 **Chosen Forever**^{22} 6990 6-9-3 **77** .... DaleSwift$^{(3)}$ 13 86
(Geoffrey Oldroyd) *led 8f out: rdn over 1f out: styd on u.p: all out* **10/1**

0000 2 nk **Snow Dancer (IRE)**^{12} 7199 7-9-6 **77** .... FrederikTylicki 3 85+
(Hugh McWilliams) *hld up: hdwy over 1f out: rdn and r.o wl* **8/1**^{3}

0503 3 ½ **Munsarim (IRE)**^{12} 7199 4-9-7 **78** .... JoeFanning 4 85
(Keith Dalgleish) *a.p: chsd wnr over 3f out: rdn over 1f out: styd on* **5/2**^{1}

-050 4 shd **Full Toss**^{14} 7161 5-9-2 **73** .... DanielTudhope 2 80
(Jim Goldie) *hld up: hdwy over 2f out: rdn over 1f out: r.o* **20/1**

5000 5 2 ¼ **Follow The Flag (IRE)**^{3} 7339 7-9-1 **75** ....(v) JohnFahy$^{(3)}$ 12 77
(Alan McCabe) *sn pushed along and prom: rdn over 2f out: styd on* **16/1**

3260 6 ¾ **Buzz Law (IRE)**^{36} 6674 3-9-1 **75** .... LukeMorris 1 75
(Mrs K Burke) *hld up: rdn over 2f out: hdwy and nt clr run over 1f out: r.o: nt rch ldrs* **14/1**

-000 7 2 ¾ **Flag Of Glory**^{16} 7130 4-8-13 **70** .... JimCrowley 6 65
(Peter Hiatt) *chsd ldrs: rdn over 1f out: wknd ins fnl f* **22/1**

026 8 hd **Strike Force**^{21} 7032 7-9-0 **71** ....(t) TomEaves 9 65
(Clifford Lines) *hld up: rdn over 1f out: nvr nrr* **10/1**

0243 9 ¾ **Triple Eight (IRE)**^{14} 7160 3-9-0 **77** ....(p) MichaelO'Connell$^{(3)}$ 10 70
(Philip Kirby) *led: hdd 8f out: chsd ldr tl pushed along over 3f out: wknd over 1f out* **33/1**

1600 10 4 **Black Coffee**^{11} 7215 6-9-1 **72** ....(b) ShaneKelly 5 56
(Mark Brisbourne) *s.i.s: a in rr* **20/1**

6045 11 1 **Kidlat**^{3} 7328 6-9-5 **76** .... WilliamBuick 7 58
(Alan Bailey) *s.i.s: hld up: hdwy over 4f out: wknd over 2f out* **7/2**^{2}

5361 12 2 **Elspeth's Boy (USA)**^{11} 7211 4-9-4 **75** .... AdamKirby 11 53
(Philip Kirby) *hld up: racd keenly: wknd over 2f out: eased over 1f out* **8/1**^{3}

2300 13 5 **Wild Desert (FR)**^{16} 7120 6-9-6 **77** .... LiamKeniry 8 45
(Charlie Longsdon) *chsd ldrs tl rdn and wknd over 2f out* **20/1**

1m 59.83s (-1.87) **Going Correction** -0.075s/f (Stan)
WFA 3 from 4yo+ 3lb **13** Ran SP% **125.3**
Speed ratings (Par 105): **105,104,104,104,102 101,99,98,98,94 93,92,87**
Tote Swingers:1&2:£11.00, 2&3:£5.00, 1&3:£11.00 CSF £91.00 CT £[illegible] TOTE £13.20: £4.30, £3.20, £1.10; EX 110.20.
Owner R C Bond **Bred** R C Bond **Trained** Brawby, N Yorks
■ Stewards' Enquiry : Dale Swift two-day ban: used whip with excessive frequency (Nov 26,28)

FOCUS
A number of these have been running on turf, but are at their best on AW tracks. The winner rates close to his old C&D form.
Kidlat Official explanation: jockey said gelding hit the gates before leaving stalls

7398 EBF 32RED.COM MAIDEN STKS 1m 1f 103y(P)
7:50 (7:52) (Class 5) 2-Y-0 **£3,234** (£962; £481; £240) **Stalls** Low

Form RPR

32 1 **Rebel Song (IRE)**^{31} 6805 2-9-3 0 .... JimCrowley 5 81+
(Mahmood Al Zarooni) *led over 8f out: rdn clr over 1f out: in command whn edgd rt towards fin* **2/1**^{1}

2 4 ½ **King Of Dudes** 2-9-3 0 .... EddieAhern 9 72+
(Sir Henry Cecil) *sn prom: pushed along over 2f out: wnt 2nd ins fnl f: no imp on wnr* **4/1**^{3}

3 1 **Cotton Trader (USA)** 2-9-3 0 .... WilliamBuick 7 71+
(John Gosden) *sn prom: chsd wnr over 4f out: rdn over 2f out: no ex and lost 2nd ins fnl f* **5/2**^{2}

4 8 **Rosselli (IRE)** 2-9-3 0 .... LukeMorris 12 55
(Mrs K Burke) *hld up: hdwy and hung lft over 1f out: r.o: nrst fin* **66/1**

6 5 ¾ **San Mambo**^{24} 6956 2-9-3 0 .... AdamKirby 4 54
(Marco Botti) *hld up: hdwy over 2f out: wknd over 1f out* **9/1**

6 shd **Bute Hall** 2-9-3 0 .... JoeFanning 8 54
(Mark Johnston) *s.i.s: hld up: r.o ins fnl f: nrst fin* **16/1**

0 7 1 ½ **Tundridge**^{22} 6993 2-9-3 0 ....(t) LiamKeniry 10 51+
(Sylvester Kirk) *s.i.s: hld up: hdwy over 3f out: wknd over 2f out* **100/1**

8 ¾ **Mutarjim (USA)** 2-9-3 0 .... TomEaves 1 49
(Saeed Bin Suroor) *s.s: hld up: rdn over 4f out: n.d* **9/1**

9 ¾ **Beauchamp Castle** 2-8-9 0 .... SophieDoyle$^{(3)}$ 3 43
(Hans Adielsson) *led 1f: chsd ldr tl over 4f out: wknd over 2f out* **100/1**

55 10 8 **No Time To Cry**^{17} 7101 2-8-12 0 .... GrahamGibbons 13 28
(Ann Duffield) *hld up: n.d* **33/1**

6 11 3 **Muhamee (IRE)**^{25} 6928 2-9-3 0 ....(p) FrederikTylicki 2 27
(Saeed Bin Suroor) *prom: pushed along 1/2-way: wknd 3f out* **12/1**

12 hd **Beauchamp Best** 2-8-5 0 .... NicoleNordblad$^{(7)}$ 6 22
(Hans Adielsson) *chsd ldrs tl wknd over 3f out* **100/1**

0 13 36 **Dancing Lancer**^{17} 7109 2-9-0 0 .... MichaelO'Connell$^{(3)}$ 11 —
(Kate Walton) *sn pushed along and a in rr: bhd fnl 3f: t.o* **100/1**

2m 0.96s (-0.74) **Going Correction** -0.075s/f (Stan) **13** Ran SP% **123.9**
Speed ratings (Par 96): **100,96,95,88,87 87,85,85,84,77 74,74,42**
Tote Swingers:1&2:£3.20, 2&3:£3.00, 1&3:£1.90 CSF £10.72 TOTE £3.50: £1.60, £1.10, £1.80; EX 14.40.
Owner Godolphin **Bred** Darley **Trained** Newmarket, Suffolk

FOCUS
A long trip for juveniles suggests these are not the speediest, but there were still some decent performances, from the first three in particular. Not much to hang the form on bar the winner, who probably took a step up.

NOTEBOOK
Rebel Song(IRE), placed in his two turf maidens, made a successful AW debut by a convincing margin. One of three Godolphin runners, but carrying the first colours, he looks a decent recruit to Polytrack and can be expected to go on from here. (op 9-4 tchd 5-2)
King Of Dudes, a 120,000gns Dansili colt out of a half-sister to the high-class Light Shift and Shiva, made a promising debut, if no match for the winner. This Derby entrant has some way to go to fulfil those ambitions, but there should be plenty more to come.
Cotton Trader(USA), related to many good winners from 6f-1m4f and out of a classy 7f-1m juvenile winner, ought to win races on breeding. This was a creditable start, and it would be no surprise to see him score at the second time of asking. (tchd 9-4 and 11-4)
Rosselli(IRE), half-brother to a bumper winner, looks likely to need some time compared with the first three. Though finishing some way behind them, it wasn't a bad first effort.
San Mambo didn't improve on his only previous race, on turf, but handicaps will see him in a better light after one more run. (op 8-1)
Bute Hall, a 22,000gns Halling half-brother to three winners from 7f-1m4f, is out of a 1m4f winner and this is likely to be his minimum trip. He looked better the longer the race went on and can improve as he matures.

7399 32RED CASINO H'CAP (DIV I) 1m 141y(P)
8:20 (8:20) (Class 6) (0-60,60) 3-Y-0+ **£1,704** (£503; £251) **Stalls** Low

Form RPR

4421 1 **Miss Villefranche**^{8} 7270 3-9-0 **56** ....(v) StevieDonohoe 3 66
(Michael Bell) *hld up in tch: chsd ldr over 1f out: r.o u.p to ld wl ins fnl f* **4/1**^{1}

5644 2 ½ **Wigram's Turn (USA)**^{94} 4918 6-9-4 **57** ....(t) GrahamGibbons 9 66
(Michael Easterby) *chsd ldr tl led 2f out: rdn over 1f out: hdd wl ins fnl f* **6/1**^{3}

3 2 **Waterloo Sunrise (IRE)**^{69} 5769 6-9-2 **55** .... GFCarroll 11 59
(S M Duffy, Ire) *hld up in tch: rdn over 1f out: styd on* **10/1**

0404 4 ¾ **Wishformore (IRE)**^{21} 7034 4-9-2 **60** ....(p) RyanPowell$^{(5)}$ 10 62
(J S Moore) *chsd ldrs: rdn over 1f out: styd on* **9/1**

5636 5 ¾ **Little Book**^{14} 7159 3-8-4 **46** .... AndreaAtzeni 4 47
(Jim Goldie) *hld up: r.o u.p ins fnl f: nrst fin* **9/1**

4123 6 2 ½ **Princess Gail**^{12} 7198 3-9-1 **57** .... ShaneKelly 13 52
(Mark Brisbourne) *s.i.s: hld up: hdwy over 2f out: rdn over 1f out: no ex fnl f* **9/2**^{2}

4610 7 1 ½ **Emeralds Spirit (IRE)**^{19} 7068 4-9-1 **59** .... JustinNewman$^{(5)}$ 5 50
(John Weymes) *sn led: rdn and hdd 2f out: wknd ins fnl f* **8/1**

5004 8 shd **Shunkawakhan (IRE)**^{22} 7006 8-8-8 **47** oh1 ow1........(tp) TomEaves 7 38
(Linda Perratt) *mid-div: hdwy over 2f out: rdn and wknd over 1f out* **20/1**

000 9 1 **Cottam Stella**^{11} 7213 3-8-7 **49** ....(vt^{1}) DuranFentiman 1 38
(Mel Brittain) *chsd ldrs: pushed along 1/2-way: rdn over 2f out: wknd fnl f* **50/1**

0010 10 4 ½ **El Libertador (USA)**^{22} 7003 5-9-2 **55** ....(b) LiamKeniry 6 33
(Eric Wheeler) *hld up: pushed along over 3f out: a in rr* **8/1**

0303 11 ½ **Social Rhythm**^{28} 6878 7-9-2 **58** .... DaleSwift$^{(3)}$ 12 35
(Alistair Whillans) *s.i.s: hld up: hdwy over 2f out: wknd over 1f out* **11/1**

4060 12 ¾ **Raghdaan**^{9} 7247 4-8-9 **48** .... LukeMorris 2 24
(Peter Hiatt) *sn pushed along in rr: hdwy into mid-div over 5f out: wknd over 2f out* **12/1**

4000 13 1 ¼ **Carnival Dream**^{57} 6134 6-8-7 **46** oh1........ MartinLane 8 19
(Hugh McWilliams) *hld up: a in rr: wknd over 2f out* **40/1**

1m 49.39s (-1.11) **Going Correction** -0.075s/f (Stan)
WFA 3 from 4yo+ 3lb **13** Ran SP% **129.0**
Speed ratings (Par 101): **101,100,98,98,97 95,93,93,92,88 88,87,86**
Tote Swingers:1&2:£1.00, 2&3:£[illegible], 1&3:£10.40 CSF £25.81 CT £244.84 TOTE £4.70: £3.00, £1.10, £5.90; EX 20.80.
Owner J L C Pearce **Bred** J L C Pearce **Trained** Newmarket, Suffolk

FOCUS
A modest race featuring largely infrequent winners, though the winner deserves credit for her recent surge in form on Polytrack. It was faster than division II and the form looks sound.

7400 32RED CASINO H'CAP (DIV II) 1m 141y(P)
8:50 (8:50) (Class 6) (0-60,62) 3-Y-0+ **£1,704** (£503; £251) **Stalls** Low

Form RPR

430 1 **Nina Rose**^{11} 7203 4-9-3 **56** ....(b^{1}) AdamKirby 1 65
(Clive Cox) *chsd ldrs: pushed along 3f out: rdn to chse ldr over 1f out: styd on u.p to ld nr fin* **11/4**^{1}

0066 2 ¾ **Justcallmehandsome**^{28} 6878 9-8-12 **58** ....(v) JoshBaudains$^{(7)}$ 11 65
(Dominic Ffrench Davis) *hld up: hdwy over 3f out: led over 2f out: edgd lft over 1f out: hdd nr fin* **8/1**

4002 3 1 ¼ **McCool Bannanas**^{12} 7198 3-9-6 **62** .... LiamJones 12 66
(James Unett) *hld up: hdwy over 1f out: sn rdn: r.o: nt rch ldrs* **9/2**^{3}

0050 4 1 ¾ **Hi Spec (IRE)**^{16} 7119 8-8-7 **46** oh1........(tp) JimmyQuinn 9 46
(Mandy Rowland) *s.s: hld up: hdwy over 1f out: r.o: nt trble ldrs* **14/1**

0253 5 nse **Gazboolou**^{10} 7228 7-9-4 **57** .... LukeMorris 4 57
(David Pinder) *prom: rdn over 2f out: styd on u.p* **4/1**^{2}

006 6 3 ¼ **Luv U Noo**^{59} 6050 4-8-7 **46** oh1........ RichardKingscote 3 39
(Brian Baugh) *hld up: sme hdwy over 1f out: nvr on terms* **16/1**

0-55 7 ½ **Northgate Lodge (USA)**^{29} 6839 6-8-11 **50** .... DuranFentiman 7 42
(Mel Brittain) *led: hdd over 2f out: wknd fnl f* **20/1**

4000 8 1 ¾ **The Right Time**^{29} 6845 3-8-6 **48** .... MartinLane 6 36
(Tony Carroll) *prom: pushed along 4f out: wknd fnl f* **16/1**

0000 9 ¾ **Barton Bounty**^{14} 7178 4-9-2 **55** .... TomEaves 10 41
(Peter Niven) *prom: rdn over 2f out: wknd over 1f out* **11/1**

4256 10 9 **Machir Bay**^{46} 5822 4-8-7 **46** oh1........(v^{1}) JoeFanning 13 —
(Keith Dalgleish) *chsd ldr tl rdn over 2f out: wknd wl over 1f out* **7/1**

0040 11 9 **Talkin Italian**^{232} 967 3-7-13 **46** oh1........ RyanPowell$^{(5)}$ 5 —
(Ian Williams) *sn pushed along in rr: bhd fnl 4f* **20/1**

1m 49.9s (-0.60) **Going Correction** -0.075s/f (Stan)
WFA 3 from 4yo+ 3lb **11** Ran SP% **124.7**
Speed ratings (Par 101): **99,98,97,95,95 92,92,90,90,82 74**
Tote Swingers:1&2:£6.60, 2&3:£5.70, 1&3:£3.60 CSF £27.36 CT £100.09 TOTE £2.20: £1.02, £3.70, £3.30; EX 26.30.
Owner Martin C Oliver **Bred** Red House Stud **Trained** Lambourn, Berks

FOCUS
Like the first division, a routine 46-60 for the track, run about half a second slower. The form is rated around the third.
The Right Time Official explanation: jockey said filly hung badly right

7401 £32 FREE AT 32RED.COM MAIDEN STKS 1m 141y(P)
9:20 (9:20) (Class 5) 3-Y-O+ **£2,264** (£673; £336; £168) **Stalls** Low

Form				RPR
36	1		**Night And Dance (IRE)**[64] 5877 3-8-9 0 .... JohnFahy(3) 9 (Clive Cox) *hld up in tch: shkn up to chse ldr over 1f out: r.o to ld nr fin* **6/1**	83
4	2	*1*	**Aqua Aura (USA)**[9] 7250 3-8-12 0 .... FrederikTylicki 3 (Saeed Bin Suroor) *led over 6f out: rdn over 1f out: hdd nr fin* **5/2**[2]	80
3	3	*6*	**Bravestofthebrave (USA)**[17] 7111 3-9-3 0 .... WilliamBuick 4 (John Gosden) *led: hdd over 6f out: chsd ldr to over 2f out: sn rdn: styd on same pce: wnt 3rd post* **13/8**[1]	72
34-3	4	*nk*	**Red Lover**[9] 7249 3-9-3 75 .... AdamKirby 7 (Ed Dunlop) *prom: chsd ldr over 2f out tl rdn over 1f out: no ex fnl f: lost 3rd post* **5/1**[3]	71
50	5	*9*	**Strategic Bid**[127] 3824 3-9-3 0 .... MartinLane 2 (David Simcock) *s.i.s: a in rr: bhd fnl 5f* **15/2**	50+
	6	*1 1/2*	**Lady Lyrath (IRE)**[34] 6735 4-9-1 0 .... GFCarroll 1 (S M Duffy, Ire) *hld up: a in rr: bhd fnl 5f* **50/1**	42
0	7	*1/2*	**Ivan The Terrible (IRE)**[32] 6781 3-9-0 0 .... RobertLButler(3) 5 (Richard Guest) *s.i.s: a in rr: bhd fnl 5f* **50/1**	46
0	8	*nk*	**Mataajir (USA)**[9] 7249 3-8-12 0 .... MarkCoumbe(5) 8 (Derek Shaw) *chsd ldrs tl wknd over 3f out* **66/1**	45

1m 50.05s (-0.45) **Going Correction** -0.075s/f (Stan)
WFA 3 from 4yo 3lb 8 Ran SP% **114.8**
Speed ratings (Par 103): **99,98,92,92,84 83,82,82**
Tote Swingers:1&2:£3.70, 2&3:£1.40, 1&3:£2.80 CSF £21.46 TOTE £4.60: £1.20, £1.30, £1.10; EX 27.50.
Owner H E Sheikh Sultan Bin Khalifa Al Nahyan **Bred** Round Hill Stud **Trained** Lambourn, Berks

FOCUS
These were mainly late-developing types, with the first three having had only four previous races between them. The first pair finished clear and the form is rated on the positive side.
T/Plt: £10.90 to a £1 stake. Pool £95,098.54 - 6,311.65 winning tickets. T/Qpdt: £4.80 to a £1 stake. Pool £7,393.79 - 1,127.99 winning tickets. CR

7402 - 7403a (Foreign Racing) - See Raceform Interactive

MARSEILLE BORELY (L-H)
Saturday, November 12
OFFICIAL GOING: Turf: very heavy

7404a GRAND PRIX DE MARSEILLE - PRIX LOUIS BRUNET (LISTED RACE) (3YO+) (TURF) 1m 2f
1:10 (12:00) 3-Y-O+ **£25,862** (£10,344; £7,758; £5,172; £2,586)

			RPR
1		**Military Bowl (USA)**[83] 3-8-10 0 .... Francois-XavierBertras 4 (F Rohaut, France) **9/1**	109
2	*1*	**Fadela Style (FR)**[91] 5075 4-8-10 0 .... (p) DavyBonilla 3 (F Rossi, France) **13/2**	103
3	*3/4*	**Tip Toe (FR)**[16] 4-9-0 0 .... SebastienMaillot 2 (F Doumen, France) **4/1**[3]	106
4	*1*	**Arizona Run (FR)**[64] 5910 3-9-3 0 .... FranckBlondel 9 (F Rossi, France) **14/5**[1]	111
5	*nk*	**Don Bosco (FR)**[55] 6206 4-9-0 0 .... AnthonyCrastus 5 (D Smaga, France) **3/1**[2]	103
6	*4*	**Mantoba**[24] 6955 3-8-10 0 .... (b) ThomasHenderson 7 (Brian Meehan) *a towards rr: u.p at end of bk st: dropped bk to last ent st: styd on u.p fnl 2f but no threat to ldrs* **27/1**	95
7	*dist*	**Tagar Bere (FR)**[36] 6686 4-9-0 0 .... Jean-BernardEyquem 6 (M Pimbonnet, France) **13/1**	—
8	*15*	**Belle Masquee (IRE)**[32] 4-8-10 0 .... (b) FlavienPrat 8 (D Smaga, France) **29/1**	—
9	*hd*	**Kilea (FR)**[56] 4-8-10 0 .... TonyPiccone 1 (Y Barberot, France) **10/1**	—

2m 12.25s (132.25)
WFA 3 from 4yo 4lb 9 Ran SP% **117.8**
WIN (incl. 1 euro stake):10.00. PLACES: 2.50, 2.00, 2.10. DF: 20.80. SF: 57.10.
Owner Berend Van Dalfsen **Bred** Berend Van Dalfsen **Trained** Sauvagnon, France

7256 SAINT-CLOUD (L-H)
Saturday, November 12
OFFICIAL GOING: Turf: heavy

7405a CRITERIUM DE SAINT-CLOUD (GROUP 1) (2YO COLTS & FILLIES) (TURF) 1m 2f
12:55 (12:00) 2-Y-O **£123,146** (£49,267; £24,633; £12,306; £6,163)

			RPR
1		**Mandaean**[27] 2-9-0 0 .... MaximeGuyon 7 (A Fabre, France) *racd in 2nd: rdn to ld 2f out: wnt clr: wandered lft and rt thrght fnl f but hung on wl: nvr threatened* **3/5**[1]	113+
2	*2 1/2*	**Brocottes (FR)**[20] 2-8-10 0 .... GregoryBenoist 2 (N Clement, France) *racd bhd ldrs: wnt 3rd bef st: u.p over 1 1/2f out: styd on wl fnl f to go 2nd fnl 50yds* **15/2**[3]	105+
3	*3/4*	**Tai Chi (GER)**[27] 6901 2-9-0 0 .... ThierryThulliez 5 (W Baltromei, Germany) *racd in 3rd for first 2f: swtchd to wd outside ent bk st: tk ld: stl in front ent st: hdd 2f out: styd on u.p fnl f: lost 2nd cl home* **14/5**[2]	107
4	*nk*	**Mirandola (FR)**[11] 2-8-10 0 .... Pierre-CharlesBoudot 8 (Y De Nicolay, France) *sn led: dropped bk to 3rd ent bk st: u.p 2f out: styd on fnl f: jst hld 4th* **23/1**	103
5	*nse*	**Tifongo (FR)**[27] 6902 2-9-0 0 .... FabriceVeron 3 (H-A Pantall, France) *towards rr tl st: u.p 2f out: r.o fnl f: narrowly missed 4th* **33/1**	107
6	*1 3/4*	**Betpak Dala**[27] 6902 2-9-0 0 .... ThierryJarnet 1 (A Savujev, Czech Republic) *racd towards rr: rdn but no ex ent st: styd on one pce fnl 2f* **38/1**	103
7	*1 3/4*	**Letsgoroundagain (IRE)**[26] 6914 2-9-0 0 .... WilliamCarson 4 (Charles Hills) *a towards rr: rdn early in st: nt qckn: styd on one pce fnl 2f* **13/1**	100
8	*10*	**Madam Blanche (IRE)**[20] 2-8-10 0 .... PJSmullen 6 (E J O'Neill, France) *a towards rr: rdn early in st: no ex: nvr figured* **47/1**	78

2m 20.2s (4.20) **Going Correction** +0.675s/f (Yiel) **8** Ran SP% **119.5**
Speed ratings: **110,108,107,107,107 105,104,96**
WIN (incl. 1 euro stake): 1.60. PLACES: 1.10, 1.20, 1.10. DF: 5.70. SF: 6.10.
Owner Godolphin SNC **Bred** Darley Stud Management **Trained** Chantilly, France

FOCUS
Testing ground and those that raced handily were at an advantage.

NOTEBOOK
Mandaean, taking a big step up in class after winning a newcomers' race at Longchamp last month, was always in the ideal position as things turned out and, as on his debut, showed good acceleration to move into the lead and pull clear. However, this much softer ground then started to take its toll on him and he wandered about all over the track, but never looked like conceding the advantage. He looks a very nice prospect and is currently a top-priced 25-1 to give his trainer back-to-back victories in the Epsom Derby.
Letsgoroundagain(IRE) could never get in a blow, as was the case with all those held up. His trainer described his effort as "flat" and "lethargic".

7406a PRIX DENISY (LISTED RACE) (3YO+) (TURF) 1m 7f 110y
1:30 (12:00) 3-Y-O+ **£22,413** (£8,965; £6,724; £4,482; £2,241)

			RPR
1		**Tac De Boistron (FR)**[20] 7049 4-9-1 0 .... ChristopheSoumillon 8 (A Lyon, France) **8/5**[1]	110
2	*3*	**Silver Valny (FR)**[20] 7049 5-9-1 0 .... ThomasMessina 7 (Mlle M-L Mortier, France) **10/1**[3]	107
3	*2*	**Hot Blood (IRE)**[71] 5694 3-8-4 0 .... MaximeGuyon 6 (A Fabre, France) **15/1**	103
4	*shd*	**Terre Du Vent (FR)**[41] 6562 5-9-1 0 .... Pierre-CharlesBoudot 2 (Y De Nicolay, France) **40/1**	105
5	*2 1/2*	**Western Pearl**[16] 7129 4-8-11 0 .... TheoBachelot 5 (William Knight) *racd towards rr: u.p and styd on wl in st but no threat to ldrs* **87/1**	98
6	*snk*	**Green Tango (FR)**[20] 8-9-1 0 .... (p) RonanThomas 4 (P Van De Poele, France) **19/1**	102
7	*3/4*	**Milago (GER)** 4-9-1 0 .... SoufyaneMoulin 10 (W Kujath, Germany) **39/1**	101
8	*nse*	**Ashbrittle**[35] 6690 4-9-1 0 .... (b) PJSmullen 13 (Ralph Beckett) *racd towards rr tl bk st: mde gd prog on wd outside: rdn but no ex in st: styd on fnl 1 1/2f* **58/1**	101
9	*1 1/4*	**Dawn Twister (GER)**[35] 6710 4-9-1 0 .... GaetanMasure 15 (J Hirschberger, Germany) **33/1**	100
10	*snk*	**Dayia (IRE)**[6] 7322 7-8-11 0 .... (b) AlexandreRoussel 1 (Lydia Pearce) *racd towards rr: mde gd prog along rail at end of bk st: sn rdn in st: no ex: sn wknd* **22/1**	95
0		**Winter Dream (IRE)**[364] 7457 7-9-1 0 .... GregoryBenoist 16 (Robert Collet, France) **46/1**	—
0		**Shahwardi (FR)**[20] 5-9-1 0 .... ThierryJarnet 12 (A De Royer-Dupre, France) **10/1**[3]	—
0		**Gaselee (USA)**[18] 7075 5-8-11 0 .... WilliamCarson 9 (Rae Guest) *sn led: stl in front ent st but sn u.p and hdd: grad fdd* **41/1**	—
0		**Ivory Land (FR)**[27] 6903 4-9-7 0 .... StephanePasquier 14 (A De Royer-Dupre, France) **172/1**	—
0		**All My Heart**[29] 6832 3-8-5 0 ow1 .... ThierryThulliez 3 (Sir Mark Prescott Bt) *racd in 2nd fr s: dropped bk to 4th bef st: rdn but no ex and sn wknd: eased fnl 1 1/2f* **43/10**[2]	—

3m 39.4s (0.70)
WFA 3 from 4yo+ 8lb **15** Ran SP% **106.9**
WIN (incl. 1 euro stake): 2.60. PLACES: 1.40, 2.80, 3.60. DF: 12.40. SF: 13.20.
Owner A Lyon **Bred** Mme J-P Reverseau **Trained** France

SANDOWN (AUS) (L-H)
Saturday, November 12
OFFICIAL GOING: Turf: good to soft

7407a ZIPPING CLASSIC (GROUP 2) (3YO+) (TURF) 1m 4f
4:30 (12:00) 3-Y-O+ **£137,908** (£41,176; £20,588; £10,294; £5,718)

			RPR
1		**Americain (USA)**[11] 7218 6-9-4 0 .... GeraldMosse 5 (A De Royer-Dupre, France) *settled 4th in tch: hdwy on outside under 2f out: qcknd to ld 110yds out: comf* **11/20**[1]	121+
2	*3/4*	**Manighar (FR)**[11] 7218 5-9-4 0 .... (b) DwayneDunn 2 (Luca Cumani) *a.p: chal ldr over 1f out: kpt on u.p to take 2nd fnl 50yds* **12/1**	118
3	*shd*	**Mourayan (IRE)**[14] 7182 5-9-4 0 .... (b) HughBowman 3 (Robert Hickmott, Australia) *trckd ldr: led at ordinary gallop after 1f: qcknd over 3f out: hdd appr 2f out: rallied to ld again over 1f out: hdd 110yds out: lost 2nd fnl 50yds* **19/5**[2]	118
4	*4*	**Lamasery (AUS)**[42] 5-9-4 0 .... BrentonAvdulla 4 (David Vandyke, Australia) *hld up last in tch: rdn and no imp over 2f out: kpt on ins fnl f: nt chal ldrs* **8/1**[3]	111
5	*1 3/4*	**Saptapadi (IRE)**[11] 7218 5-9-4 0 .... (b[1]) DannyNikolic 1 (Brian Ellison) *led: hdd after 1f: qcknd to ld appr 2f out: rdn and hdd over 1f out: wknd ins fnl f* **60/1**	109

2m 37.87s (157.87) **5** Ran SP% **105.8**
PARI-MUTUEL (NSW TAB - all including au$1 stakes): WIN 1.50 PLACE 1.20, 3.10; DF 4.70; SF 4.80.
Owner G T Ryan, K L Bamford, & Mrs C O Bamford **Bred** Wertheimer Et Frere **Trained** Chantilly, France

NOTEBOOK
Americain(USA) was an emphatic winner and may go for the Hong Kong Vase now.
Manighar(FR) ran a brave race in defeat and fought back well to edge second place.

7323 CAPANNELLE (R-H)
Sunday, November 13

OFFICIAL GOING: Turf: good to soft

7408a PREMIO CARLO & FRANCESCO ALOISI (GROUP 3) (2YO+) (TURF) 6f
3:10 (12:00) 2-Y-O+ **£34,482** (£15,172; £8,275; £4,137)

RPR
1 **Overdose**152 3010 6-9-8 0 .... FrankieDettori 8 111
(Jozef Roszival, Hungary) *sn led: hdd 1 1/2f out: rdn and rallied to ld again ins fnl f: r.o wl* **3/5**1
2 *1/2* **Dagda Mor (ITY)**28 6906 4-9-12 0 .... FabioBranca 4 113
(S Botti, Italy) *broke wl: trckd ldrs: pressed wnr 1/2-way: rdn to ld 1 1/2f out: hdd ins fnl f: r.o wl* **7/3**2
3 *2 1/2* **Rosendhal (IRE)**190 1919 4-9-8 0 ....(b) MarcoMonteriso 2 101
(M Narduzzi, Italy) *settled towards rr: hrd rdn and hdwy 2f out: styd on u.p on stands' rail fnl f: tk 3rd fnl 75yds: nvr on terms w first two* **219/10**
4 *1 1/2* **Questi Amori (IRE)**182 4-9-8 0 .... SSulas 12 96
(M Guarnieri, Italy) *prom on outside early: settled bhd ldng gp: rdn 2f out: kpt on u.p fnl f: nt pce to chal* **234/10**
5 *nk* **Traditional Chic (IRE)**28 6906 3-9-8 0 .... CristianDemuro 11 95
(L Riccardi, Italy) *w ldrs towards outside: rdn and nt qckn ins fnl 1 1/2f* **25/1**
6 *nse* **Back Hunting (USA)**28 6906 4-9-8 0 .... MEsposito 7 95
(A Renzoni, Italy) *hld up towards rr: rdn and prog 2f out: styd on fnl f: nrest at fin* **47/1**
7 *3* **Samysilver (USA)**121 3-9-8 0 .... GBietolini 10 85
(Gianluca Bietolini, Italy) *chsd ldrs: rdn and one pce over 1 1/2f out: wknd ins fnl f* **81/10**3
8 *3* **Morgan Drive (IRE)**364 7459 6-9-8 0 .... DarioVargiu 6 76
(M Gasparini, Italy) *midfield: rdn and no imp over 1 1/2f out: eased fnl 150yds* **124/10**
9 *shd* **Shabi**273 5-9-8 0 .... UmbertoRispoli 3 76
(A Di Dio, Italy) *prom early: grad dropped away fr 1/2-way* **45/1**
10 *3/4* **Black Mambazo (IRE)**364 7459 6-9-8 0 .... GMarcelli 1 73
(L Riccardi, Italy) *dwlt: in rr: rdn and nt qckn ins fnl 2f: nvr in contention* **34/1**
11 *1 1/2* **Malikayah (IRE)**121 3-9-5 0 .... PierantonioConvertino 5 65
(D Camuffo, Italy) *chsd ldng gp: rdn and wknd over 1 1/2f out: eased ins fnl f* **68/1**
12 *2* **Rebecca Rolfe**28 6906 5-9-5 0 .... MKolmarkaj 9 59
(M Gasparini, Italy) *chsd ldrs: rdn and lost pl 2f out: eased fnl f* **10/1**

68.40 secs (-1.90) **12 Ran SP% 140.9**
WIN (incl. 1 euro stake): 1.59. PLACES: 1.13, 1.24, 2.01. DF: 2.16.
Owner Miko Racing & Trading Kft **Bred** G And Mrs Robinson **Trained** Hungary

NOTEBOOK
Overdose, the 2008 winner, responded gamely to lead again inside the final furlong and ran on well to the line. Frankie Dettori described his mount as "a little rusty, but a top-class horse."

1739 FRANKFURT (L-H)
Sunday, November 13

OFFICIAL GOING: Turf: good

7409a HESSEN-POKAL (GROUP 3) (3YO+) (TURF) 1m 2f
[illegible] 3-Y-O+
£27,586 (£9,482; £4,741; £2,586; £1,724; £1,293)

RPR
1 **King's Hall**371 7375 3-8-10 0 .... EPedroza 10 106
(A Wohler, Germany) *hld up in midfield: gng wl: r.o wl in st: qcknd wl ins fnl f to get up in fnl strides* **107/10**
2 *1/2* **Neatico (GER)**21 7048 4-9-2 0 .... ASuborics 2 107
(P Schiergen, Germany) *settled midfield: proged towards end of bk st: r.o wl in st: tk ld 50yds out: ct in fnl strides* **16/1**
3 *1/2* **Poet**57 6149 6-9-2 0 .... AdamKirby 4 106
(Clive Cox) *sent st to ld: set str pce: r.o wl down centre of trck: ct and hdd fnl 50yds* **1/1**1
4 *2 1/2* **Liang Kay (GER)**14 7193 6-9-0 0 .... StephanePasquier 9 99
(A De Royer-Dupre, France) *hld up towards rr: r.o wl in st: rdn to chal ldr on wd outside fnl f: unable qck fnl 50yds* **58/10**3
5 *2* **Keep Cool**36 6710 4-9-0 0 .... AHelfenbein 8 95
(Andreas Lowe, Germany) *settled bhd ldng gp: rdn early in st: r.o wl wout threatening ldrs* **166/10**
6 *3* **Pain Perdu (FR)**17 4-9-0 0 .... KKerekes 7 89
(W Figge, Germany) *settled bhd ldr fr s: rdn to chal turning for home: unable qck: r.o one pce* **33/1**
7 *2* **Not For Sale (GER)**21 7047 4-8-13 0 .... EFrank 5 84
(T Mundry, Germany) *settled midfield: threatened briefly in st but unable qck: styd on one pce* **129/10**
8 *4 1/2* **Sindaco (GER)**36 6709 3-8-10 0 .... AndreBest 3 76
(W Hickst, Germany) *racd towards rr: proged down bk st but produced no ex in st* **44/1**
9 *hd* **Elle Shadow (IRE)**21 7047 4-9-1 0 .... FilipMinarik 1 77
(P Schiergen, Germany) *prom in 3rd fr s: rdn early in st but failed to qckn and fdd* **17/5**2
10 *1/2* **Auvano (GER)**21 7048 7-9-2 0 .... APietsch 12 77
(R Dzubasz, Germany) *settled 5th: flattered briefly early in st: sn wknd* **145/10**
11 *1 1/4* **Shoshoni (GER)** 4-9-0 0 .... ChristianHanotel 14 72
(A Kleinkorres, Germany) *bkmarker fr s: nvr figured* **82/1**
12 *12* **Ideology**32 5-9-0 0 .... THellier 13 48
(Mario Hofer, Germany) *settled midfield: r.o wl early in st but sn wknd* **49/1**
13 *2 1/2* **Perfect Son** 4-9-2 0 .... JBojko 6 45
(C Zeitz, Germany) *settled 4th: threatened briefly early in st but sn wknd* **48/1**
14 *11* **Integral (GER)**189 7-9-0 0 .... StefanieHofer 11 21
(Stanislav Otruba, Germany) *a towards rr: nvr figured* **58/1**

2m 11.26s (2.69)
WFA 3 from 4yo+ 4lb **14 Ran SP% 133.3**
WIN (incl. 10 euro stake): 117. PLACES: 20, 37, 12. SF: 1,331.
Owner Stall Route 66 **Bred** Gestut Elsetal **Trained** Germany

NOTEBOOK
King's Hall continues to improve.
Poet looked the winner coming into the home straight, when he began to drift to his right. He fought off the challenge of French raider Liang Kay but had nothing left to repel the first pair. He could have done with softer ground.

KYOTO (R-H)
Sunday, November 13

OFFICIAL GOING: Turf: firm

7410a QUEEN ELIZABETH II COMMEMORATIVE CUP (GRADE 1) (3YO+ FILLIES & MARES) (TURF) 1m 3f
6:40 (12:00) 3-Y-O+ **£741,616** (£293,084; £186,012; £110,514; £71,045)

RPR
1 **Snow Fairy (IRE)**29 6861 4-8-11 0 .... RyanMoore 18 114+
(Ed Dunlop) *hld up towards rr on outside: sn swtchd to ins: hdwy on rail 2 1/2f out: r.o wl ins fnl 1 1/2f to ld fnl 50yds* **17/10**1
2 *nk* **Aventura (JPN)**28 3-8-7 0 .... YasunariIwata 1 115
(Katsuhiko Sumii, Japan) *midfield on ins: tk clsr order 3f out: styd on fr 2f out: r.o fnl f to take 2nd cl home* **19/5**2
3 *1* **Apapane (JPN)**28 4-8-11 0 .... MasayoshiEbina 4 112
(Sakae Kunieda, Japan) *prom in main gp: 3rd and rdn 2f out: styd on u.p fnl f* **9/1**
4 *1 1/2* **Whale Capture (JPN)**28 3-8-7 0 .... KenichiIkezoe 3 110
(Kiyotaka Tanaka, Japan) *led main gp bhd clr ldr: grad reeled in ldr fr over 2f out: led over 110yds out: hdd fnl 50yds: no ex: lost two pls cl home* **104/10**
5 *1* **Rainbow Dahlia (JPN)**204 4-8-11 0 .... YugaKawada 9 107
(Yoshitaka Ninomiya, Japan) *midfield: effrt towards ins 2f out: 5th and styng on u.p fnl f: run flattened out fnl 100yds* **240/1**
6 *1 1/4* **Walkure (JPN)**105 7-8-11 0 .... RyujiWada 5 105
(Masaru Sayama, Japan) *midfield: effrt 3f out: 7th and styng on u.p 2f out: wknd ins fnl f* **104/1**
7 *nk* **Shimmei Fuji (JPN)**204 4-8-11 0 .... YuichiKitamura 12 104
(Takayuki Yasuda, Japan) *led: sn 10 l clr: rdn and 5 l clr ins fnl 2f: wkng qckly fnl f: hdd over 110yds out* **350/1**
8 *nk* **Fumino Imagine (JPN)**28 5-8-11 0 .... KeisukeDazai 10 104
(Masaru Honda, Japan) *hld up towards rr: hdwy on outside under 2f out: kpt on wl fnl f: nvr on terms* **188/10**
9 *1 1/2* **Italian Red (JPN)**28 5-8-11 0 .... SuguruHamanaka 2 101
(Sei Ishizaka, Japan) *midfield: rdn and nt qckn fr 2 1/2f out* **19/2**
10 *1 1/4* **Broad Street (JPN)**28 5-8-11 0 .... ShinjiFujita 11 99
(Hideaki Fujiwara, Japan) *racd in midfield: no imp u.p fr over 2f out* **100/1**
11 *nk* **Reve D'Essor (JPN)**253 3-8-7 0 .... YuichiFukunaga 8 99
(Hiroyoshi Matsuda, Japan) *midfield: rdn and no imp on outside fnl 2 1/2f* **63/10**3
12 *nse* **Erin Court (JPN)**28 3-8-7 0 .... HirokiGoto 15 99
(Kazuhide Sasada, Japan) *settled towards rr: no imp fr 2f out* **98/1**
13 *nse* **Animate Bio (JPN)**28 4-8-11 0 .... HironobuTanabe 7 98
(Koji Maki, Japan) *prom in main gp: rdn and nt qckn 2f out: wknd fnl f* **248/10**
14 *3/4* **Gullveig (JPN)**175 3-8-7 0 .... HirofumiShii 16 98
(Katsuhiko Sumii, Japan) *trckd ldrs in main gp: rdn and nt qckn over 2f out: sn wknd* **56/1**
15 *nk* **All That Jazz (JPN)** 3-8-7 0 .... FutoshiKomaki 13 97
(Katsuhiko Sumii, Japan) *last and wl bhd: nvr in contention* **190/1**
16 *1 3/4* **Dancing Rain (IRE)**29 6859 3-8-7 0 .... JMurtagh 14 94
(William Haggas) *dwlt: hld up towards rr: hdwy on wd outside over 3f out: c wd fnl bnd: sn rdn and btn* **107/10**
17 *3* **Lady Alba Rosa (JPN)**28 4-8-11 0 .... YutakaTake 17 88
(Kazuhide Sasada, Japan) *settled midfield towards outside: rdn and no imp 2 1/2f out: sn wknd* **67/1**
18 *1/2* **Saint Emilion (JPN)**28 4-8-11 0 .... MircoDemuro 6 87
(Masaaki Koga, Japan) *a bhd: nvr a factor* **85/1**

2m 11.6s (131.60)
WFA 3 from 4yo+ 5lb **18 Ran SP% 125.9**
PARI-MUTUEL (all including 100 ypj stake): WIN 270 SHOW 140, 150, 280 DF 700 SF 1160.
Owner Anamoine Limited **Bred** Windflower Overseas Holdings Inc **Trained** Newmarket, Suffolk

NOTEBOOK
Snow Fairy(IRE) completed back-to-back victories in this with a breathtaking performance under a truly brilliant ride. Drawn in the outside gate in an 18-runner field, she looked to have no chance as they turned for home before bursting through horses to get up, showing an amazing turn of foot. She is likely to head to Sha Tin for next month's Hong Kong International meeting, where she will run in either the Cup, a race she won last year, or the Vase. In the latter race she would meet her stablemate Red Cadeaux, the Melbourne Cup second. She will race on next year.
Dancing Rain(IRE) was never a factor and beat only two home.

7395 WOLVERHAMPTON (A.W) (L-H)
Monday, November 14

OFFICIAL GOING: Standard
Wind: Light across Weather: Overcast

7411 32RED CASINO MAIDEN FILLIES' STKS 7f 32y(P)
2:10 (2:10) (Class 5) 3-Y-O+ **£2,264** (£673; £336; £168) **Stalls** High

Form RPR
3 1 **Haamaat (IRE)**41 6608 3-8-12 0 .... LiamJones 6 75+
(William Haggas) *s.i.s: sn prom: chsd ldr 2f out: led 1f out: rdn and edgd lft ins fnl f: r.o wl* **5/6**1
-305 2 *3* **Les Verguettes (IRE)**138 3513 3-8-12 69 .... GrahamGibbons 5 67
(Chris Wall) *led: shkn up and hdd 1f out: styd on same pce* **11/2**3
/0- 3 *nk* **Amba**496 3766 5-8-13 0 .... MartinHarley 4 66
(Des Donovan) *chsd ldr tl pushed along 2f out: styd on same pce fr over 1f out* **125/1**

2 **4** *3 ¼* **True Satire**[21] 7063 3-8-12 0.. LukeMorris 2 57
(Jane Chapple-Hyam) *s.i.s: hld up: rdn over 2f out: edgd lft over 1f out: n.d* **2/1**[2]

0-0 **5** *8* **Da'Quonde (IRE)**[130] 3756 3-8-12 0.................................... TomEaves 3 36
(Bryan Smart) *chsd ldrs: rdn over 2f out: sn wknd* **25/1**

6000 **6** *6* **Colamandis**[54] 6266 4-8-13 46...(b[1]) DavidAllan 1 20
(Hugh McWilliams) *trckd ldrs: racd keenly: pushed along 1/2-way: wknd 2f out* **80/1**

-0 **7** *18* **Bowmans Well (IRE)**[151] 3090 6-8-13 0........................ NeilChalmers 7 —
(Peter Purdy) *hld up: pushed along and wknd 1/2-way: t.o* **200/1**

1m 28.06s (-1.54) **Going Correction** -0.075s/f (Stan)
WFA 3 from 4yo+ 1lb 7 Ran SP% **109.6**
Speed ratings (Par 100): **105,101,101,97,88 81,60**
toteswingers:1&2:£1.50, 1&3:£11.00, 2&3:£17.30 CSF £5.51 TOTE £2.10: £1.40, £2.70; EX 6.60.
Owner Hamdan Al Maktoum **Bred** Hunscote House Farm Stud **Trained** Newmarket, Suffolk

FOCUS
A weak maiden for fillies, but the time was marginally the quickest of four races at the distance. The form makes sense on paper if the second retains her ability.

7412 32REDPOKER.COM (S) STKS 7f 32y(P)
2:40 (2:41) (Class 6) 3-Y-O+ £1,704 (£503; £251) Stalls High

Form RPR

4352 **1** **Faithful Ruler (USA)**[188] 1976 7-9-7 73..........................(p) LukeMorris 2 74
(Ronald Harris) *chsd ldrs: led 1f out: rdn and edgd lft ins fnl f: r.o* **11/1**

0000 **2** *1 ¾* **One Way Or Another (AUS)**[11] 7243 8-8-8 67........(bt) RaulDaSilva(7) 8 63
(Jeremy Gask) *s.i.s: sn prom: led over 1f out: sn hdd: styd on same pce* **13/2**

510 **3** *hd* **Stevie Gee (IRE)**[28] 6920 7-9-4 71................................. RyanClark(3) 12 69
(Ian Williams) *hld up: hdwy over 2f out: rdn over 1f out: r.o* **6/1**[3]

0060 **4** *½* **Fault**[10] 7269 5-9-2 58.. AmyScott(5) 6 67?
(Alastair Lidderdale) *hld up in tch: shkn up over 1f out: r.o* **40/1**

0000 **5** *1 ¾* **Vitznau (IRE)**[14] 7199 7-8-12 69.....................................(v[1]) JohnFahy(3) 3 57
(Robert Cowell) *s.i.s: hld up: styd on u.p fr over 1f out: nt trble ldrs* **9/2**[2]

2141 **6** *1 ¼* **Opus Maximus (IRE)**[23] 7034 6-9-4 67...................(p) SophieDoyle(3) 11 59
(Jennie Candlish) *s.i.s: hld up: styng on whn nt clr run ins fnl f: nvr trbld ldrs* **9/2**[2]

5000 **7** *½* **Let It Rock (IRE)**[9] 7315 4-8-10 0................................. MartinHarley 10 47
(Mrs K Burke) *prom: chsd ldr over 4f out: rdn and ev ch over 1f out: wknd ins fnl f* **20/1**

5600 **8** *¾* **Bachelor Knight (IRE)**[13] 7213 3-9-0 56...................(t) DuranFentiman 4 50
(Suzzanne France) *led: rdn and hdd over 1f out: wknd ins fnl f* **80/1**

3000 **9** *¾* **Hand Painted**[21] 7057 5-8-12 59.....................................(p) AmyBaker(3) 9 48
(Anthony Middleton) *s.i.s: hld up: rdn over 2f out: n.d* **40/1**

2606 **10** *5* **Apache Ridge (IRE)**[11] 7253 5-9-7 73...........................(p) JoeFanning 7 40
(Keith Dalgleish) *hld up: pushed along over 2f out: rdn over 1f out: wknd fnl f* **7/2**[1]

444 **11** *24* **Khaki (IRE)**[10] 7270 3-8-9 54....................................(v[1]) GrahamGibbons 1 —
(David Evans) *chsd ldr tl over 4f out: pushed along 1/2-way: wknd over 2f out: eased: t.o* **10/1**

1m 28.74s (-0.86) **Going Correction** -0.075s/f (Stan)
WFA 3 from 4yo+ 1lb 11 Ran SP% **114.5**
Speed ratings (Par 101): **101,99,98,98,96 94,94,93,92,86 59**
toteswingers:1&2:£8.70, 1&3:£7.90, 2&3:£8.20 CSF £76.26 TOTE £6.70: £2.20, £3.20, £2.50; EX 96.30 Trifecta £324.90 Part won. Pool £439.15 - 0.43 winning units..There was no bid for the winner.
Owner Ridge House Stables Ltd **Bred** WinStar Farm LLC **Trained** Earlswood, Monmouths

FOCUS
A modest seller best rated through the fourth.

7413 32RED H'CAP 1m 4f 50y(P)
3:10 (3:10) (Class 5) (0-75,75) 3-Y-O+ £2,264 (£673; £336; £168) Stalls Low

Form RPR

0554 **1** **Dark Dune (IRE)**[11] 7255 3-8-12 **69**.................................... DavidAllan 1 83+
(Tim Easterby) *hld up: hdwy over 4f out: trckd ldr over 2f out: led on bit over 1f out: easily* **4/1**[3]

2402 **2** *2* **Sand Skier**[4] 7346 4-8-12 **70**.. NicoleNordblad(7) 4 81+
(Hans Adielsson) *led 1f: chsd ldr to over 8f out: remained handy tl nt clr run and lost pl over 3f out: nt clr run over 2f out: hdwy over 1f out: r.o to go 2nd ins fnl f: no ch w wnr* **3/1**[1]

1030 **3** *3 ¼* **Stand Guard**[38] 6666 7-9-8 **73**.. StevieDonohoe 5 76
(Noel Quinlan) *hld up: rdn over 1f out: r.o ins fnl f: nrst fin* **14/1**

060/ **4** *1 ¾* **Royal Entourage**[361] 6676 6-9-7 **75**.......................... MichaelO'Connell(3) 2 75
(Philip Kirby) *hld up: hdwy over 2f out: rdn over 1f out: hung lft ins fnl f: styd on same pce* **66/1**

5011 **5** *shd* **Castlemorris King**[37] 6701 3-8-5 **67** ow1................. MarkCoumbe(5) 10 67
(Michael Attwater) *a.p: chsd ldr over 3f out: led over 2f out: rdn and hdd over 1f out: wknd ins fnl f* **10/3**[2]

4443 **6** *2 ½* **Perilously (USA)**[11] 7255 3-8-9 **66**...................................(p) ShaneKelly 7 62
(Jeremy Noseda) *prom: chsd ldr over 8f out: led 4f out: rdn and hdd over 2f out: wknd over 1f out* **6/1**

3020 **7** *6* **Sharp Sovereign (USA)**[28] 6918 5-8-13 **67**.................. PaulPickard(3) 3 53
(Ian McInnes) *prom: pushed along over 6f out: wknd over 3f out* **33/1**

6502 **8** *½* **Hallstatt (IRE)**[23] 7036 5-9-3 **68**................................(t) GrahamGibbons 6 53
(John Mackie) *chsd ldrs: rdn over 2f out: wknd over 1f out* **20/1**

4042 **9** *2 ¼* **Ice Nelly (IRE)**[19] 7112 3-8-9 **66**..................................... RobertHavlin 9 48
(Hughie Morrison) *dwlt: hld up: effrt over 3f out: wknd over 2f out* **10/1**

0220 **10** *4 ½* **Amazing Blue Sky**[12] 7237 5-9-0 **65**................................. TomEaves 8 40
(Ruth Carr) *led after 1f: hdd 4f out: sn pushed along: wknd over 2f out* **14/1**

2m 37.48s (-3.62) **Going Correction** -0.075s/f (Stan)
WFA 3 from 4yo+ 6lb 10 Ran SP% **114.0**
Speed ratings (Par 103): **109,107,105,104,104 102,98,98,96,93**
toteswingers:1&2:£5.20, 1&3:£7.20, 2&3:£11.40 CSF £15.69 CT £149.63 TOTE £5.40: £1.80, £1.10, £5.50; EX 18.60 Trifecta £220.30 Part won. Pool £297.76 - 0.70 winning units..
Owner Miss Betty Duxbury **Bred** P Turley **Trained** Great Habton, N Yorks

FOCUS
An interesting handicap run at a sound pace and decent form for the grade, rated around the placed horses.

Stand Guard Official explanation: jockey said, regarding running and riding, that his orders were to setle the gelding early stages before making the best of his way home, he was unable to ride to the instructions as it hung to the right, is moderate and suffers from bad joints and may benefit in future to being dropped back to selling class.

7414 £32 FREE AT 32RED.COM CLAIMING STKS 1m 141y(P)
3:40 (3:40) (Class 5) 2-Y-O £2,385 (£704; £352) Stalls Low

Form RPR

2034 **1** **Let Your Love Flow (IRE)**[26] 6956 2-8-2 69.............. SophieDoyle(3) 9 64
(Sylvester Kirk) *chsd ldrs: pushed along over 2f out: rdn to ld ins fnl f: edgted lft: r.o* **11/4**[2]

4332 **2** *hd* **Final Delivery**[31] 6837 2-9-1 73...................................... AndreaAtzeni 8 75+
(Marco Botti) *chsd ldrs: nt clr run wl over 1f out: swtchd rt ins fnl f: sn rdn: r.o wl* **85/40**[1]

02 **3** *hd* **Barn Dance (FR)**[35] 6763 2-9-1 0................................... StephenCraine 2 73
(Jonathan Portman) *chsd ldr tl led over 2f out: rdn and hdd ins fnl f: r.o* **7/1**

002 **4** *2 ½* **Captain Cardington (IRE)**[10] 7259 2-8-13 68.............. TonyCulhane 4 66
(Mick Channon) *hld up: hdwy over 1f out: rdn and hung lft ins fnl f: styd on same pce* **10/3**[3]

6015 **5** *1 ¼* **Camrock Star (IRE)**[12] 7222 2-8-2 60................................ LukeMorris 1 52
(David Evans) *unruly in stalls: prom: rdn over 1f out: no ex ins fnl f* **12/1**

3003 **6** *2* **Angel Cake (IRE)**[19] 7108 2-7-13 55.......................(b[1]) KieranO'Neill(3) 6 48
(Amy Weaver) *hld up: rdn over 2f out: nvr trbld ldrs* **14/1**

0 **7** *2* **Aloysia**[32] 6819 2-8-1 0.. FrankieMcDonald 3 43
(Sylvester Kirk) *s.i.s: a in rr* **66/1**

0500 **8** *2 ¼* **Phoenician Blaze**[11] 7242 2-8-1 47.................................. JimmyQuinn 5 38
(Tim Etherington) *s.i.s: a in rr* **40/1**

00 **9** *4 ½* **Salaaheb (IRE)**[10] 7267 2-8-1 0............................... JemmaMarshall(5) 7 34
(Alastair Lidderdale) *led: pushed along and hdd over 2f out: wknd over 1f out* **25/1**

1m 50.7s (0.20) **Going Correction** -0.075s/f (Stan) 9 Ran SP% **116.4**
Speed ratings (Par 96): **96,95,95,93,92 90,88,86,82**
toteswingers:1&2:£3.10, 1&3:£4.40, 2&3:£3.60 CSF £8.98 TOTE £3.30: £1.10, £1.70, £1.90; EX 9.40 Trifecta £52.00 Pool £287.88 - 4.09 winning units..Final Delivery was claimed by Mustafa Khan for £14,000.
Owner Mrs K Devlin **Bred** E Tynan **Trained** Upper Lambourn, Berks
■ Stewards' Enquiry : Sophie Doyle ten-day ban: used whip with excessive frequency (Nov 28-Dec 3,5-8)

FOCUS
A modest claimer run at an ordinary pace. Straightforward form, the second and third running at least as well as their pre-race marks.

NOTEBOOK
Let Your Love Flow(IRE) was always well placed and made the most of the runner-up's troubled trip. She's a bit flattered and it's questionable whether she ran to her official mark of 69. (op 5-2)
Final Delivery was clearly travelling best entering the straight, but Andrea Atzeni continually failed to find a clear run until inside the final furlong and the gelding ran out of time. Considering he had 6lb to find with the winner at the weights, he may well be better than his official mark of 73. He was claimed for £14,000. (op 11-4)
Barn Dance(FR) was well enough positioned but wasn't good enough. He can now switch to handicaps. (tchd 15-2)
Captain Cardington(IRE) had a bit to find with the winner and runner-up at the weights and got too far back off the modest pace. (op 4-1)
Phoenician Blaze Official explanation: jockey said filly suffered interference at start

7415 GREAT OFFERS AT WOLVERHAMPTON-RACECOURSE.CO.UK H'CAP 2m 119y(P)
4:10 (4:10) (Class 5) (0-70,68) 3-Y-O+ £2,264 (£673; £336; £168) Stalls Low

Form RPR

3135 **1** **Hit The Switch**[14] 7200 5-9-9 **63**.......................................(p) JoeFanning 2 72
(Jennie Candlish) *mde all: set stdy pce tl qcknd over 3f out: rdn over 1f out: styd on gamely* **7/1**

1466 **2** *nk* **Resplendent Ace (IRE)**[21] 7070 7-9-10 **64**...................... JimmyQuinn 6 72
(Karen Tutty) *a.p: chsd wnr over 1f out: sn rdn: ev ch ins fnl f: styd on* **12/1**

0063 **3** *1 ¼* **Suzi's A Class Act**[52] 6306 3-9-2 **65**...............................(p) LukeMorris 8 72
(James Eustace) *hld up: hdwy over 3f out: rdn over 1f out: styd on* **11/2**[3]

0025 **4** *1 ¼* **Phonic (IRE)**[18] 7120 4-9-9 **63**.. EddieAhern 5 69
(John Dunlop) *a.p: chsd wnr over 4f out tl rdn over 1f out: styd on same pce fnl f* **6/4**[1]

2203 **5** *2 ¾* **Dr Finley (IRE)**[28] 6915 4-10-0 **68**..................................... DaneO'Neill 4 70
(Lydia Pearce) *hld up: rdn over 2f out: nvr trbld ldrs* **7/1**

11 **6** *7* **Strikemaster (IRE)**[19] 7105 5-9-0 **54**..........................(t) DuranFentiman 1 48
(Lee James) *hld up: rdn over 2f out: sn wknd* **5/1**[2]

2460 **7** *¾* **Dart**[209] 1470 7-9-13 **67**... GrahamGibbons 7 60
(John Mackie) *hld up: rdn over 2f out: sn wknd* **11/1**

6000 **8** *26* **Elegant Dancer (IRE)**[41] 6609 4-8-4 **49** oh4.......... MatthewLawson(5) 3 —
(Paul Green) *chsd wnr tl pushed along over 4f out: wknd 3f out: t.o* **50/1**

3m 41.36s (-0.44) **Going Correction** -0.075s/f (Stan)
WFA 3 from 4yo+ 9lb 8 Ran SP% **115.0**
Speed ratings (Par 103): **98,97,97,96,95 92,91,79**
toteswingers:1&2:£9.90, 1&3:£4.90, 2&3:£10.80 CSF £85.50 CT £495.80 TOTE £7.80: £3.00, £4.10, £2.70; EX 78.40 Trifecta £378.60 Pool £542.46 - 1.06 winning units..
Owner M M Allen **Bred** Mrs M T Dawson **Trained** Basford Green, Staffs

FOCUS
A modest staying handicap and they didn't go that quick. The form looks straightforward, with the placed horses the best guides.

7416 32RED.COM H'CAP (DIV I) 7f 32y(P)
4:40 (4:41) (Class 5) (0-75,75) 3-Y-O+ £2,264 (£673; £336; £168) Stalls High

Form RPR

0416 **1** **Frequency**[10] 7265 4-9-8 **75**...(b) JoeFanning 7 86
(Keith Dalgleish) *hld up: hdwy over 2f out: led ins fnl f: r.o* **11/2**[3]

0661 **2** *1* **Ryedane (IRE)**[10] 7265 9-8-10 **68**.................................(b) AdamCarter(5) 4 76
(Tim Easterby) *s.i.s: hld up: hdwy over 1f out: r.o wl* **20/1**

0051 **3** *shd* **Bavarian Princess (USA)**[16] 7176 3-9-0 **68**................. MartinHarley 11 76
(Mrs K Burke) *chsd ldrs: led over 1f out: rdn and hdd ins fnl f: styd on* **9/2**[2]

5014 **4** *2* **Glenridding**[16] 7175 7-9-4 **71**.. FrederikTylicki 8 74
(James Given) *chsd ldrs: rdn and ev ch over 1f out: styd on same pce fnl f* **4/1**[1]

1503 **5** *½* **Darcey**[23] 7040 5-9-3 **73**.. JohnFahy(3) 5 74
(Amy Weaver) *broke wl: sn lost pl: hdwy over 2f out: rdn and swtchd lft ins fnl f: styd on same pce* **11/2**[3]

3000 **6** ½ **Smalljohn**[25] [6980] 5-9-6 **73**....(v) TomEaves 3 73
(Bryan Smart) *chsd ldr tl led 3f out: rdn and hdd over 1f out: no ex ins fnl f* **10/1**

3053 **7** 1¼ **Methaaly (IRE)**[10] [7265] 8-9-3 **70**....(be) JimmyQuinn 9 67
(Michael Mullineaux) *hood removed sltly late: s.i.s: hld up: rdn over 1f out: nt trble ldrs* **14/1**

4-40 **8** 1¼ **Postscript (IRE)**[31] [6830] 3-9-2 **70**.... StevieDonohoe 10 63
(Ian Williams) *hld up: pushed along 3f out: nvr on terms* **12/1**

-000 **9** 4 **Hatta Stream (IRE)**[26] [6949] 5-9-8 **75**.... MickyFenton 1 57
(Lydia Pearce) *broke wl: sn lost pl: hdwy over 2f out: rdn over 1f out: wknd ins fnl f* **7/1**

0240 **10** 2¾ **Spin Again (IRE)**[186] [2016] 6-9-5 **72**.... RichardKingscote 6 47
(Mark Wellings) *led 4f: wknd over 1f out* **25/1**

3-50 **11** 7 **Seamster**[125] [3952] 4-8-12 **65**....(p) J-PGuillambert 12 21
(Richard Ford) *chsd ldrs: rdn over 2f out: wknd and eased over 1f out* **50/1**

1m 28.14s (-1.46) **Going Correction** -0.075s/f (Stan)
WFA 3 from 4yo+ 1lb **11** Ran SP% **115.5**
Speed ratings (Par 103): **105,103,103,101,100 100,98,97,92,89 81**
toteswingers:1&2:£20.20, 1&3:£2.10, 2&3:£7.10 CSF £110.11 CT £546.49 TOTE £8.10: £2.30, £5.70, £3.00; EX 82.50 Trifecta £406.90 Part won. Pool £549.90 - 0.10 winning units..
Owner Mrs Francesca Mitchell **Bred** Manor Farm Stud (rutland) **Trained** Carluke, South Lanarkshire

FOCUS
A modest handicap run at a good pace, and the time was 1.76 seconds faster than the next leg. The form is best rated around the placed horses.
Methaaly(IRE) Official explanation: jockey said blindfold had become stuck underneath eye-shield and gelding was slowly away

7417 32RED.COM H'CAP (DIV II) 7f 32y(P)
5:10 (5:11) (Class 5) (0-75,75) 3-Y-O+ **£2,264** (£673; £252; £252) **Stalls** High

Form RPR

3424 **1** **Bahamian Lad**[10] [7265] 6-8-12 **65**....(p) TonyCulhane 11 73
(Reg Hollinshead) *a.p: chsd ldr 1/2-way: shkn up to ld over 1f out: rdn ins fnl f: jst hld on* **20/1**

1502 **2** ½ **Woolfall Sovereign (IRE)**[16] [7175] 5-9-7 **74**.... ShaneKelly 2 81
(George Margarson) *a.p: rdn over 1f out: r.o wl* **7/1**

0020 **3** ¾ **Scottish Glen**[88] [5201] 5-9-4 **71**.... LiamKeniry 10 76+
(Patrick Chamings) *hld up: r.o ins fnl f: nrst fin* **12/1**

3402 **3** dht **Justbookie Dot Com (IRE)**[4] [7348] 3-9-2 **73**....(v) RichardEvans(3) 5 78
(David Evans) *led: rdn and hdd over 1f out: styd on same pce ins fnl f* **5/2**[1]

2014 **5** hd **Khajaaly (IRE)**[25] [6979] 4-9-6 **73**.... JimmyQuinn 12 77
(Julia Feilden) *hld up: racd keenly: nt clr run over 2f out: hdwy over 1f out: rdn ins fnl f: styd on same pce towards fin* **8/1**

0223 **6** 2½ **Roman Strait**[16] [7173] 3-9-0 **68**.... DaneO'Neill 6 66
(Michael Blanshard) *plld hrd and prom: rdn over 1f out: no ex ins fnl f* **4/1**[2]

020 **7** nk **Needwood Ridge**[16] [7175] 4-9-2 **69**....(bt) LukeMorris 7 66
(Frank Sheridan) *hld up: rdn 1/2-way: nvr trbld ldrs* **13/2**[3]

5660 **8** 5 **Lucky Dan (IRE)**[53] [6276] 5-9-8 **75**.... EddieAhern 3 58
(Paul Green) *racd keenly: trckd ldr to 1/2-way: rdn over 2f out: wknd fnl f* **14/1**

4030 **9** 1½ **Diapason (IRE)**[16] [7173] 5-9-4 **71**....(t) StephenCraine 9 50
(Tom Dascombe) *s.i.s: hld up: a in rr* **20/1**

1m 29.9s (0.30) **Going Correction** -0.075s/f (Stan)
WFA 3 from 4yo+ 1lb **9** Ran SP% **109.4**
Speed ratings (Par 103): **95,94,93,93,93 90,90,84,82**PL: Scottish Glen £1.90, Just Bookie Com £0.80, T/C: BL/WS/JBC £221.85, BL/WS/SG £819.51. Trif: BL/WS/SG £256.70, BL/WS/JBC £242.20. toteswinger: BL&WS £16.40, WS&JBC £2.00, WS&SG £7.30, BL&JBC £4.40, BL&SG £9.10 CSF £140.43 TOTE £21.10: £3.90, £2.60; EX 10727 Trifecta £0Owner Graham Brothers Racing Partnership Bred.

FOCUS
The pace seemed modest and that's a view supported by the clock. The time was 1.76 seconds off the first division and the slowest of four races at the distance but the form is straightforward rated around the second and third.

7418 32REDBET.COM H'CAP 1m 141y(P)
5:40 (5:40) (Class 6) (0-65,67) 3-Y-O+ **£1,704** (£503; £251) **Stalls** Low

Form RPR

4145 **1** **Ajdaad (USA)**[23] [7034] 4-9-3 **65**.... GrahamGibbons 12 75
(Alan McCabe) *hld up: nt clr run over 2f out: hdwy and swtchd rt over 1f out: rdn to ld ins fnl f: r.o* **11/1**

2412 **2** 1 **Know No Fear**[10] [7269] 6-9-3 **65**....(p) FergusSweeney 4 72
(Alastair Lidderdale) *hld up: nt clr run over 1f out: rdn and r.o wl ins fnl f: nt rch wnr* **4/1**[2]

5400 **3** 1½ **Fleetwoodsands (IRE)**[16] [7178] 4-9-0 **62**....(t) RichardKingscote 3 66
(Milton Bradley) *led for 1f: chsd ldr: rdn to ld over 1f out: hdd and unable qck ins fnl f* **10/1**

305 **4** ½ **Darsan (IRE)**[21] [7063] 3-9-0 **65**.... ShaneKelly 5 67
(Chris Wall) *hld up in tch: rdn and ev ch over 1f out: styd on same pce ins fnl f* **9/4**[1]

2423 **5** hd **Dream Of Fortune (IRE)**[16] [7178] 7-9-2 **67** ow2....(bt) RichardEvans(3) 2 69
(David Evans) *hld up: hdwy over 1f out: sn rdn: styd on same pce ins fnl f* **9/1**

0335 **6** ½ **Carcinetto (IRE)**[17] [7146] 9-8-10 **65**.... KevinLundie(7) 10 66
(David Evans) *prom: outpcd over 3f out: hdwy over 2f out: styd on same pce fnl f* **20/1**

3036 **7** 1¾ **Mr Chocolate Drop (IRE)**[27] [6938] 7-9-2 **64**....(t) JimmyQuinn 11 61
(Mandy Rowland) *hld up: hdwy over 2f out: nt clr run over 1f out: swtchd lft: no ex ins fnl f* **33/1**

5540 **8** hd **Cyflymder (IRE)**[24] [6990] 5-9-0 **62**.... SteveDrowne 9 58
(David C Griffiths) *plld hrd and prom: lost pl over 7f out: hdwy over 1f out: sn rdn: wknd ins fnl f* **20/1**

2045 **9** shd **Lion Court (IRE)**[31] [6831] 3-9-0 **65**....(p) LiamKeniry 6 61
(John Stimpson) *s.i.s: hdwy to chse ldr over 6f out: led over 2f out: rdn and hdd over 1f out: wknd ins fnl f* **16/1**

3012 **10** 3¾ **Wood Fairy**[23] [7033] 5-8-9 **64**.... LauraBarry(7) 7 51
(Richard Fahey) *sn prom: pushed along to chse ldr over 2f out: wknd ins fnl f* **11/2**[3]

5002 **11** nse **Dazakhee**[17] [6878] 4-9-2 **64**.... TonyCulhane 1 51
(David Flood) *s.s: hld up: pushed along 3f out: n.d* **28/1**

310- **12** 6 **Flotation (USA)**[91] 4-9-1 **63**.... TomEaves 8 37
(Roy Brotherton) *sn pushed along in mid-div: hdwy over 2f out: sn wknd* **66/1**

0001 **13** 20 **Ensnare**[132] [3720] 6-9-1 **63**.... StevieDonohoe 13 —
(Noel Quinlan) *led over 7f out: rdn and hdd over 2f out: sn wknd* **9/1**

1m 49.9s (-0.60) **Going Correction** -0.075s/f (Stan)
WFA 3 from 4yo+ 3lb **13** Ran SP% **126.9**
Speed ratings (Par 101): **99,98,96,96,96 95,94,93,93,90 90,85,67**
toteswingers:1&2:£15.90, 1&3:£23.50, 2&3:£13.20 CSF £55.02 CT £491.39 TOTE £15.40: £4.80, £3.20, £3.40; EX 97.70 Trifecta £366.20 Pool £494.97 - 1.00 winning units..
Owner Mrs Z Wentworth **Bred** Pontchartain **Trained** Averham Park, Notts
■ Stewards' Enquiry : Kevin Lundie two-day ban: careless riding (Nov 28-29)

FOCUS
A moderate but competitive handicap nd fair enough rated around the first two.
T/Jkpt: Not won. T/Plt: £120.90 to a £1 stake. Pool:£79,518.78 - 479.89 winning tickets T/Qpdt: £37.30 to a £1 stake. Pool:£6,119.34 - 121.20 winning tickets CR

7350 SOUTHWELL (L-H)
Tuesday, November 15

OFFICIAL GOING: Standard
Wind: Light, across. Weather: Fine and dry

7419 TVBRACKETSSALES.CO.UK H'CAP (DIV I) 6f (F)
12:20 (12:20) (Class 6) (0-65,65) 3-Y-O+ **£1,704** (£503; £251) **Stalls** Low

Form RPR

1 **1** **Take Cover**[22] [7069] 4-9-7 **65**.... SebSanders 10 82
(George Margarson) *chsd ldrs: hdwy 1/2-way: rdn to chse ldr over 1f out: led jst ins fnl f: styd on wl* **11/4**[1]

2434 **2** 2¼ **St Oswald**[35] [6777] 3-8-10 **59**....(b[1]) AshleyMorgan(5) 4 69
(David O'Meara) *midfield and rdn along 1/2-way: styd on u.p fr wl over 1f out: nrst fin* **13/2**[3]

0000 **3** ½ **Ace Of Spies (IRE)**[17] [7173] 6-9-4 **62**....(b) KirstyMilczarek 8 70
(Conor Dore) *led: rdn clr wl over 1f out: hdd jst ins fnl f: one pce* **16/1**

0053 **4** 1¼ **Transmit (IRE)**[14] [7216] 4-9-3 **61**....(b) DuranFentiman 7 65
(Tim Easterby) *towards rr: hdwy into midfield 1/2-way: rdn 2f out: styd on appr fnl f: nrst fin* **9/1**

5033 **5** 1 **Suddenly Susan (IRE)**[21] [7079] 3-8-9 **60**....(b) LeonnaMayor(7) 2 61
(David Nicholls) *trckd ldr: swtchd rt and hdwy 2f out: rdn wl over 1f out: fdd ent fnl f* **15/2**

0600 **6** nk **Takajan (IRE)**[5] [7351] 4-8-9 **60**.... RachealKneller(7) 13 60
(Mark Brisbourne) *in rr: hdwy and wd st: sn rdn: styd on fnl f: nrst fin* **12/1**

2460 **7** 3¼ **Arrivaderci**[6] [7341] 3-9-2 **63**....(e) RobertLButler(3) 12 53
(Richard Guest) *nvr bttr than midfield* **50/1**

5023 **8** ¾ **Lethal**[22] [7071] 8-8-7 **51** oh1....(p) LukeMorris 9 38
(Richard Price) *chsd ldng pair: rdn along over 2f out: grad wknd* **20/1**

4063 **9** ¾ **Tro Nesa (IRE)**[22] [7055] 3-9-7 **65**.... TomEaves 6 50
(Ann Duffield) *chsd ldrs: rdn over 2f out: sn wknd* **16/1**

0632 **10** 1¾ **Belinsky (IRE)**[19] [7123] 4-9-2 **60**.... JoeFanning 3 39
(Mark Campion) *chsd ldrs: rdn over 2f out: sn wknd* **5/1**[2]

2600 **11** ½ **Bonnie Prince Blue**[11] [7268] 8-8-11 **58**....(b) PaulPickard(3) 14 36
(Ian McInnes) *in rr: rdn over 2f out: sn swtchd to stands' rail and sme late hdwy* **16/1**

0000 **12** 2¼ **Beating Harmony**[12] [7245] 3-8-1 **52** oh3 ow1.... JackDuern(7) 1 22
(Michael Appleby) *rrd and s.i.s: a bhd* **200/1**

0201 **13** 3¼ **Fair Bunny**[13] [7230] 4-8-7 **51**....(b) AndrewMullen 11 —
(Alan Brown) *dwlt: a towards rr* **25/1**

1m 16.13s (-0.37) **Going Correction** +0.05s/f (Slow) **13** Ran SP% **114.8**
Speed ratings (Par 101): **104,100,100,98,97 96,92,91,90,87 87,84,79**
Tote Swingers:1&2:£11.60, 2&3:£28.00, 1&3:£11.60 CSF £18.36 CT £239.03 TOTE £3.40: £1.90, £2.40, £4.60; EX 21.00 TRIFECTA Not won..
Owner Norcroft Park Stud **Bred** Norcroft Park Stud **Trained** Newmarket, Suffolk

FOCUS
A moderate sprint handicap. The winer was unexposed and showed biggish improvement. It was the faster division by 0.61 seconds and the runner-up sets the standard, being rated close to his turf best.
Belinsky(IRE) Official explanation: jockey said gelding hung right in straight

7420 TVBRACKETSSALES.CO.UK H'CAP (DIV II) 6f (F)
12:50 (12:50) (Class 6) (0-65,65) 3-Y-O+ **£1,704** (£503; £251) **Stalls** Low

Form RPR

6060 **1** **Elhamri**[11] [7265] 7-9-2 **60**.... KirstyMilczarek 13 71
(Conor Dore) *prom on outer: hdwy to chse ldr 2f out: rdn to ld ent fnl f: styd on* **15/2**[2]

0416 **2** 1¼ **Brio**[5] [7352] 3-9-4 **62**....(v) ShaneKelly 6 69
(Alan McCabe) *cl up: led over 3f out: rdn wl over 1f out: hdd ent fnl f: one pce* **11/4**[1]

4440 **3** 2 **Gracie's Gift (IRE)**[13] [7229] 9-8-7 **54** oh1 ow3....(v) JohnFahy(3) 12 55
(Richard Guest) *midfield: hdwy over 2f out: rdn to chse ldrs and n.m.r over 1f out: kpt on ins fnl f* **16/1**

6000 **4** nse **Bookiesindex Boy**[5] [7356] 7-9-6 **64**....(b) StephenCraine 7 64
(J R Jenkins) *trckd ldrs: smooth hdwy to trck ldng pair 2f out: swtchd rt and shkn up over 1f out: sn one pce* **16/1**

0020 **5** 1¼ **Greenhead High**[14] [7216] 3-9-2 **60**.... AdrianNicholls 3 56
(David Nicholls) *chsd ldrs on inner: hdwy over 2f out: sn rdn and one pce appr fnl f* **9/1**

2500 **6** 1½ **Rio's Girl**[43] [6580] 4-8-8 **55**.... AmyRyan(3) 8 47
(Tony Coyle) *towards rr tl sme late hdwy* **8/1**[3]

0631 **7** 2¾ **Memphis Man**[4] [7371] 8-8-9 **58** 6ex.... MatthewCosham(5) 5 41
(David Evans) *towards rr and rdn along bef 1/2-way: n.d* **11/1**

1305 **8** 2 **Twennyshortkid**[77] [5601] 3-8-7 **51**....(v) JimmyQuinn 2 27
(Paul Midgley) *midfield: hdwy on inner over 2f out: rdn wl over 1f out: sn no imp* **10/1**

2451 **9** 1¼ **Half A Crown (IRE)**[14] [7216] 6-9-3 **61**.... AndrewMullen 9 33
(Peter Salmon) *prom: rdn along wl over 2f out: sn wknd* **11/1**

225 **10** ½ **Coastal Passage**[12] [7245] 3-9-2 **60**.... TonyCulhane 4 31
(John Balding) *hld up: a in rr* **17/2**

1500 **11** ¾ **Frognal (IRE)**[11] [7262] 5-9-4 **65**....(t) RobertLButler(3) 11 33
(Richard Guest) *bmpd s: a in rr* **25/1**

0060 **12** 9 **Maharanee (USA)**[38] [6696] 3-8-7 **51** oh4....(b[1]) DuranFentiman 10 —
(Ann Duffield) *dwlt and wnt rt s: a bhd* **50/1**

0000 **13** 8 **Eshoog (IRE)**[5] [7351] 3-8-9 **60**....(bt) LeonnaMayor(7) 1 —
(Phil McEntee) *led: pushed along and hdd over 3f out: rdn wl over 2f out and sn wknd* **50/1**

1m 16.74s (0.24) **Going Correction** +0.05s/f (Slow) **13** Ran SP% **115.4**
Speed ratings (Par 101): **100,98,95,95,93 91,88,85,83,83 82,70,59**
Tote Swingers:1&2:£5.30, 2&3:£13.30, 1&3:£35.20 CSF £26.85 CT £332.80 TOTE £11.80: £3.00, £1.10, £5.40; EX 32.90 TRIFECTA Not won..
Owner Chris Marsh **Bred** Highfield Stud Ltd **Trained** Cowbit, Lincs

FOCUS
The winning time was 0.61 seconds slower than the first division. The third and fourth are rated to their recent marks.

7421 32REDBET.COM NURSERY 6f (F)
1:20 (1:20) (Class 6) (0-60,61) 2-Y-O £1,704 (£503; £251) Stalls Low

Form RPR
6261 1 **Sonsie Lass**[12] 7252 2-9-3 **56**.......... JoeFanning 6 65+
(Keith Dalgleish) *mde all: rdn clr over 1f out: hung rt to stands' rail ins fnl f: kpt on* **11/2**
3422 2 2 ¼ **Mount McLeod (IRE)**[6] 7337 2-9-3 **56**.......... FergusSweeney 9 58
(Jamie Osborne) *trckd ldrs: smooth hdwy over 2f out: rdn to chse wnr over 1f out: no imp fnl f* **7/2**[2]
5005 3 ¾ **Allegri (IRE)**[38] 6695 2-9-7 **60**..........(p) TomEaves 5 60
(Ann Duffield) *chsd ldrs: hdwy 2f out: rdn wl over 1f out: kpt on fnl f* **9/1**
6003 4 nk **Bountiful Catch**[6] 7337 2-8-10 **49**.......... JimmyQuinn 7 48
(Pam Sly) *midfield: hdwy wl over 2f out: rdn wl over 1f out: styd on fnl f: nrst fin* **9/2**[3]
2031 5 1 **Make Up**[5] 7353 2-9-5 **61** 6ex.......... MichaelO'Connell(3) 12 57
(Noel Wilson) *prom: effrt to chse wnr over 2f out: rdn wl over 1f out: sn edgd rt and grad wknd fnl f* **15/8**[1]
5000 6 nse **Point At Issue (IRE)**[6] 7337 2-9-0 **53**..........(b[1]) AdrianNicholls 2 49
(David Nicholls) *in rr: pushed along after 2f: rdn 2f out: styd on wl appr fnl f: nrst fin* **50/1**
0000 7 8 **Medam**[10] 7293 2-8-13 **52**..........(t) RobbieFitzpatrick 4 24
(Shaun Harris) *dwlt: a towards rr* **25/1**
0000 8 ¾ **Fouracres**[13] 7231 2-8-7 **46** ow1..........(e[1]) NeilChalmers 1 16
(Michael Appleby) *a towards rr* **125/1**
000 9 ½ **The Games Gone (IRE)**[36] 6751 2-8-11 **50**.......... AndreaAtzeni 8 18
(David Evans) *a towards rr* **66/1**
006 10 3 ½ **Rivington**[15] 7194 2-8-9 **48**..........(b[1]) TonyHamilton 10 —
(Richard Fahey) *cl up: rdn along over 2f out: sn wknd* **16/1**
0500 11 2 ½ **Meet Joe Black (IRE)**[13] 7225 2-8-6 **45**..........(v[1]) LukeMorris 3 —
(David Evans) *dwlt: a in rr* **28/1**
5454 12 3 **Get The Trip**[29] 6919 2-9-0 **53**..........(t) WilliamCarson 13 —
(Giles Bravery) *chsd ldrs: rdn along wl over 2f out: sn wknd* **25/1**

1m 17.4s (0.90) **Going Correction** +0.05s/f (Slow) **12** Ran SP% **121.8**
Speed ratings (Par 94): **96,93,92,91,90 90,79,78,77,73 69,65**
Tote Swingers:1&2:£3.40, 2&3:£5.50, 1&3:£8.00 CSF £24.61 CT £176.57 TOTE £4.50: £1.20, £1.80, £3.30; EX 20.60 Trifecta £74.00 Pool £325.31 - 3.25 winning units..
Owner J S Morrison **Bred** Baldernock Bloodstock Ltd **Trained** Carluke, South Lanarkshire

FOCUS
A low-grade nursery but the fortm makes sense. The winner is progressing well and the third, fourth and fifth help establish the level.

NOTEBOOK
Sonsie Lass was put up 4lb for her Wolverhampton success earlier this month and was on Fibresand for the first time, but her sire has a smart record with his runners around here and she took to it like a duck to water. Soon in front, she hung over to the stands' rail under pressure over a furlong out, but never looked like getting caught. This opens up plenty more options for her. (op 4-1)
Mount McLeod(IRE) was racing off a 3lb higher mark and therefore 1lb better off with Sonsie Lass for a neck defeat by her at Wolverhampton. She had every chance in the home straight and didn't seem to do much wrong, but she is now 0-10 and this was yet another placing, her fifth in her last six outings. (tchd 3-1)
Allegri(IRE), tried in cheekpieces on this Fibresand debut, did well to keep on for third considering he was off the bridle at halfway and he is progressing slowly at a modest level.
Bountiful Catch, closely matched with Mount McLeod on C&D running six days earlier, attracted market support but his finishing effort was too little too late. (op 6-1)
Make Up was carrying a 6lb penalty for her win in a C&D seller five days earlier and was soon in a handy position from her wide draw, but she got tired from the furlong pole and found the task beyond her. (op 5-2)
Point At Issue(IRE), well beaten all four previous starts including here, ran better in the first-time blinkers and made plenty of late progress up the far rail after being behind early, but it would be wrong to get too carried away. (op 33-1)
The Games Gone(IRE) Official explanation: jockey said filly never travelled

7422 32REDBINGO.COM MEDIAN AUCTION MAIDEN STKS 1m (F)
1:50 (1:52) (Class 5) 2-Y-O £2,264 (£673; £336; £168) Stalls Low

Form RPR
3 1 **Hurler And Farmer (IRE)**[18] 7142 2-9-3 0.......... TonyHamilton 7 77+
(Richard Fahey) *prom: cl up 1/2-way: led over 2f out and sn jnd: rdn wl over 1f out: kpt on wl u.p fnl f* **6/1**
3 2 2 ¼ **Don Libre**[12] 7240 2-9-3 0..........(t) DaneO'Neill 9 72
(Paul Cole) *trckd ldrs: hdwy over 3f out: rdn to chal 2f out and ev ch tl one pce ins fnl f* **9/2**[3]
4 3 5 **Dora's Gift**[11] 7258 2-8-12 0.......... RobertHavlin 2 56+
(Hughie Morrison) *v s.i.s and bhd: swtchd wd after 1f: hdwy over 2f out: rdn and styd on fr over 1f out: tk 3rd ins fnl f* **9/4**[2]
02 4 1 ¼ **Shot In The Dark (IRE)**[68] 5841 2-9-3 0.......... LiamKeniry 4 58
(Andrew Balding) *cl up on inner: effrt 3f out: ev ch over 2f out: sn rdn and wknd over 1f out: lost 3rd ins fnl f* **13/8**[1]
06 5 2 ¼ **Miss Ella Jade**[80] 5487 2-8-9 0.......... AmyRyan(3) 5 47+
(Richard Whitaker) *chsd ldrs: rdn along over 3f out: sn one pce* **100/1**
00 6 2 ¼ **Cool Fantasy (IRE)**[46] 6506 2-9-3 0..........(b) LukeMorris 6 47
(Paul D'Arcy) *led: rdn along 3f out: hdd over 2f out and grad wknd* **14/1**
7 7 **Fleeting Fashion** 2-8-12 0.......... RobbieFitzpatrick 3 26
(Michael Appleby) *dwlt: a towards rr* **66/1**
00 8 nse **Johnny Cavagin**[189] 1966 2-9-3 0.......... TomEaves 8 31
(Richard Guest) *trckd ldrs: hdwy over 3f out: rdn wl over 2f out and sn wknd* **66/1**
00 9 29 **Willy McBay**[14] 7209 2-9-3 0.......... AndrewMullen 1 —
(George Moore) *pushed along and outpcd after 2f: bhd fr 1/2-way* **100/1**

1m 44.55s (0.85) **Going Correction** +0.05s/f (Slow) **9** Ran SP% **113.0**
Speed ratings (Par 96): **97,94,89,88,86 84,77,76,47**
Tote Swingers:1&2:£2.70, 2&3:£2.60, 1&3:£2.90 CSF £32.05 TOTE £8.10: £1.90, £1.60, £1.10; EX 20.50 Trifecta £107.70 Pool £714.81 - 4.91 winning units..
Owner G Devlin **Bred** G Devlin **Trained** Musley Bank, N Yorks

FOCUS
An uncompetitive maiden in which only half the field counted. The first pair disappointed and this is just fair form and a little fluid for the moment.

NOTEBOOK
Hurler And Farmer(IRE) finished an encouraging third of nine behind a nice sort on his Wolverhampton debut and showed the benefit of the experience on this different surface. He saw his race out well after drawing clear with his main rival over the last 2f and there should be further improvement in him. (op 13-2 tchd 7-1)
Don Libre, a fair third of seven on his debut over 7f here earlier this month, had every chance over the last 2f and, though the winner proved too strong, he pulled right away from the others. A modest maiden should come his way. (op 5-1)
Dora's Gift, an encouraging fourth on her Ffos Las debut, is a half-sister to a pair of AW winners, including one on this surface, so the Fibresand was likely to suit, but a lethargic break is the last thing you need around here and third place was probably the best that could be hoped for. The yard has a great record here and she can do better. (op 2-1)
Shot In The Dark(IRE) showed plenty of ability on his second start on turf and his sire has a decent record here, but he never looked that happy and found little off the bridle. (op 6-4 tchd 11-8)

7423 GOLF AND RACING AT SOUTHWELL (S) STKS 7f (F)
2:20 (2:20) (Class 6) 2-Y-O £1,704 (£503; £251) Stalls Low

Form RPR
2040 1 **Flying Pickets (IRE)**[32] 6846 2-9-0 61.......... JohnFahy(3) 6 70
(Alan McCabe) *dwlt: sn trcking ldrs on outer: led 4f out: pushed clr 2f out: easily* **5/6**[1]
365 2 8 **Raspberry Fizz**[11] 7259 2-8-7 52..........(b) JimmyQuinn 4 39
(Eve Johnson Houghton) *in rr: hdwy 3f out: rdn wl over 1f out: styd on appr fnl f: tk 2nd nr fin* **11/1**
64 3 nk **Can Do Les (IRE)**[15] 7196 2-8-12 0.......... JoeFanning 1 43
(Keith Dalgleish) *in tch: rdn along 1/2-way: styd on same pce fnl 2f: no imp towards fin* **3/1**[2]
3500 4 nk **Miserere Mei (IRE)**[5] 7353 2-8-9 62..........(e) RobertLButler(3) 5 42
(Richard Guest) *led 3f: cl up tl rdn 2f out and sn outpcd by wnr: wknd and lost 2nd towards fin* **20/1**
5450 5 6 **Complex**[24] 7035 2-8-7 56.......... LukeMorris 3 22
(David Evans) *in tch: reminders after 2f: outpcd fr: 1/2-way* **16/1**
5544 6 10 **Jaci Uzzi (IRE)**[20] 7108 2-8-7 49..........(v) AndreaAtzeni 2 —
(David Evans) *chsd ldrs on inner: rdn along 1/2-way: sn outpcd and bhd* **7/1**[3]
4040 7 14 **Fortune Star (IRE)**[108] 4538 2-8-12 48.......... TonyHamilton 7 —
(Noel Wilson) *chsd ldng pair: rdn along over 3f out: sn wknd* **66/1**

1m 31.52s (1.22) **Going Correction** +0.05s/f (Slow) **7** Ran SP% **112.5**
Speed ratings (Par 94): **95,85,85,85,78 66,50**
Tote Swingers:1&2:£2.20, 2&3:£3.90, 1&3:£1.40 CSF £11.33 TOTE £2.10: £1.80, £4.20; EX 9.80.The winner was bought in for 5,500gns.
Owner Mrs M J McCabe **Bred** Richard Frayne **Trained** Averham Park, Notts

FOCUS
A poor race, even for a seller, and as uncompetitive as you can get. The comprehensive winner could be worth 7lb more, with this form rated to the best reading of previous efforts.

NOTEBOOK
Flying Pickets(IRE) was penalised for winning a Redcar seller in June and had already proved effective on this surface. Despite a slow break, he was in front before halfway and gradually pulled further and further clear. However, this was a bad race and as he was by no means best in at the weights, it will be interesting to see how the handicapper reacts. He was bought in for 5,500gns at the auction. (op 5-4)
Raspberry Fizz, dropped in grade for this Fibresand debut, made up a lot of late ground to grab second, but was never in the same parish as the winner. (op 17-2 tchd 8-1)
Can Do Les(IRE), another trying Fibresand for the first time, also made up some late ground but will need to progress again to win a race. (op 11-4 tchd 7-2)
Miserere Mei(IRE), penalised for winning a Polytrack seller in August, has become disappointing in recent starts and dropped away after trying to mix it with the favourite early. (op 14-1)

7424 32REDPOKER.COM (S) STKS 1m (F)
2:50 (2:51) (Class 6) 3-Y-O+ £1,704 (£503; £251) Stalls Low

Form RPR
5040 1 **Mcconnell (USA)**[20] 7098 6-9-6 70..........(b) FergusSweeney 3 76+
(Gary Moore) *t.k.h: trckd ldrs: hdwy to chal 2f out: rdn to ld over 1f out: clr whn hung bdly rt ins fnl f: kpt on* **11/4**[1]
300/ 2 1 **King Pin**[803] 5601 6-9-0 55.......... TomEaves 14 65
(Tracy Waggott) *chsd ldrs on outer and sn cl up: effrt 3f out: chal 2f out and ev ch tl rdn over 1f out and kpt on same pce fnl f* **20/1**
4060 3 1 **Double Duchess**[22] 7068 3-8-13 60.......... WilliamCarson 5 64
(Paul D'Arcy) *led 2f: cl up tl led again 3f out: rdn over 2f out: hdd appr fnl f: kpt on same pce* **14/1**
4003 4 2 ¼ **Hits Only Jude (IRE)**[5] 7352 8-8-13 71..........(v) JasonHart(7) 7 64
(Declan Carroll) *towards rr: pushed along over 3f out: rdn and hdwy 2f out: swtchd rt over 1f out: kpt on fnl f: nrst fin* **12/1**
3-64 5 ½ **Dear Maurice**[25] 5200 7-9-0 69..........(t[1]) StevieDonohoe 2 57
(Tobias B P Coles) *chsd ldrs on inner: rdn along over 2f out: kpt on same pce appr fnl f* **25/1**
2500 6 1 **Golden Creek (USA)**[5] 7352 3-9-4 70.......... LukeMorris 9 60
(Mrs K Burke) *prom: cl up 3f out: rdn 2f out and grad wknd appr fnl f* **5/1**[3]
1406 7 ¾ **Charlie Cool**[24] 7034 8-9-6 84..........(b) FrederikTylicki 13 59
(Ruth Carr) *chsd ldrs: rdn along wl over 2f out: no hdwy* **7/2**[2]
0000 8 5 **Ours (IRE)**[32] 6831 8-9-6 85..........(p) SebSanders 10 47
(John Harris) *dwlt: a towards rr* **5/1**[3]
0324 9 ¾ **Flying Applause**[22] 7057 6-9-6 56..........(bt) RussKennemore 11 45
(Roy Bowring) *a towards rr* **16/1**
2240 10 12 **Jay Jays Joy**[112] 4409 3-9-4 63..........(b) MickyFenton 12 18
(Paul Midgley) *chsd ldrs: led after 2f: rdn along and hdd 3f out: sn wknd* **33/1**
3046 11 1 ¼ **Spin A Wish**[38] 6694 3-8-4 47..........(v) AmyRyan(3) 1 —
(Richard Whitaker) *in tch on inner: rdn along wl over 3f out: sn wknd* **66/1**
0040 12 ¾ **Freda's Rose (IRE)**[11] 7270 7-9-1 51.......... StephenCraine 8 —
(Owen Brennan) *v s.i.s: a bhd* **100/1**
0 13 57 **Bold Ambition (IRE)**[12] 7250 3-8-7 0.......... AndrewMullen 4 —
(Ruth Carr) *dwlt: a in rr: bhd fr over 3f out: t.o and eased fnl 2f* **100/1**
20P0 P **Old English (IRE)**[69] 5821 3-9-4 60.......... TonyHamilton 6 —
(Noel Wilson) *towards rr: sn outpcd and bhd whn p.u bef 1/2-way* **80/1**

1m 44.69s (0.99) **Going Correction** +0.05s/f (Slow)
WFA 3 from 6yo+ 2lb **14** Ran SP% **118.7**
Speed ratings (Par 101): **97,96,95,92,92 91,90,85,84,72 71,70,13,—**
Tote Swingers:1&2:£16.10, 2&3:£21.50, 1&3:£13.20 CSF £64.21 TOTE £3.20: £1.10, £6.40, £6.60; EX 63.10 TRIFECTA Not won..There was no bid for the winner.
Owner B Siddle & B D Haynes **Bred** Hall Et Al Farm **Trained** Lower Beeding, W Sussex

FOCUS
Quite a competitive seller but the winner and third have good records here and the fourth is rated close to his latest form.

Old English(IRE) Official explanation: jockey said gelding lost its action

7425 ROCKET RON RAPLEY 70TH BIRTHDAY H'CAP — 1m (F)
3:20 (3:21) (Class 5) (0-70,70) 3-Y-O+ — **£2,385** (£704; £352) **Stalls** Low

Form			Horse	RPR
0630	**1**		**William Haigh (IRE)**[34] 6116 3-9-0 **70**........................ GarryWhillans(5) 9	84
			(Alan Swinbank) *in rr: pushed along over 3f out: swtchd towards inner and gd hdwy over 1f out: sn rdn and str run to ld ins fnl f: won gng away* **6/1**[2]	
1000	**2**	2½	**Sofias Number One (USA)**[22] 7057 3-8-12 **63**..........(tp) AndreaAtzeni 4	71
			(Roy Bowring) *towards rr: pushed along after 3f: hdwy on inner wl over 1f out: sn rdn and styd on to chal ent fnl f: kpt on: no ch w wnr* **16/1**	
1644	**3**	3½	**Witchry**[79] 5513 9-9-2 **65**.................................... FergusSweeney 8	65
			(Tony Newcombe) *trckd ldrs: hdwy 3f out: chal 2f out: rdn to ld over 1f out: hdd and one pce ins fnl f* **20/1**	
1100	**4**	nk	**Bolodenka (IRE)**[24] 7034 9-9-0 **70**......................(p) GeorgeChaloner(7) 13	69
			(Richard Fahey) *s.i.s and in rr: hdwy on inner over 2f out: rdn to chse ldrs over 1f out: sn chal and ev ch tl one pce ins fnl f* **10/1**	
0006	**5**	shd	**Councellor (FR)**[12] 7243 9-9-2 **65**..........................(t) RobbieFitzpatrick 12	64
			(Derek Shaw) *chsd ldrs on outer: wd st: rdn to chal wl over 1f out and ev ch tl edgd lft and one pce ent fnl f* **20/1**	
5000	**6**	2½	**Hydrant**[14] 7215 5-9-1 **64**.................................... AndrewMullen 14	57
			(Peter Salmon) *chsd ldrs: effrt over 2f out: rdn wl over 1f out and ch tl wknd appr fnl f* **14/1**	
0341	**7**	¾	**On The Cusp (IRE)**[11] 7263 4-9-5 **68**..........................(p) MartinHarley 11	60
			(Richard Guest) *chsd ldrs: hdwy on outer 3f out: rdn 2f out and ev ch tl wknd appr fnl f* **3/1**[1]	
1300	**8**	1½	**Horatio Carter**[25] 6990 6-9-0 **68**..............................(b1) AshleyMorgan(5) 3	56
			(David O'Meara) *cl up: led over 3f out: rdn and hdd 2f out: grad wknd* **25/1**	
0600	**9**	6	**Just Five (IRE)**[20] 7099 5-9-5 **68**.................................... TomEaves 6	42
			(John Weymes) *a towards rr* **66/1**	
2506	**10**	hd	**San Antonio**[22] 7068 11-9-4 **67**...................................(b) MickyFenton 7	41
			(Pam Sly) *chsd ldrs: cl up 3f out: rdn to ld briefly 2f out: sn hdd & wknd wl over 1f out* **22/1**	
3163	**11**	2¼	**No Larking (IRE)**[22] 7057 3-8-11 **67**.................................. AmyScott(5) 1	36
			(Henry Candy) *led 1f: prom tl rdn along 1/2-way and sn wknd* **15/2**	
5566	**12**	4	**Fibs And Flannel**[48] 6453 4-8-13 **62**................................ TonyCulhane 2	21
			(Tony Coyle) *cl up: led after 1f: rdn along and hdd 3f out: sn wknd* **17/2**	
0000	**13**	2¼	**Fantasy Fry**[12] 7243 3-9-5 **70**..............................(t) RichardKingscote 10	24
			(Tom Dascombe) *midfield: outpcd and towards rr fr 1/2-way* **33/1**	
0002	**14**	¾	**Uncle Dermot (IRE)**[13] 7235 3-9-0 **65**................................ DaneO'Neill 5	18
			(Brendan Powell) *v s.i.s: hdwy and in tch on inner after 2f: rdn along wl over 3f out: sn wknd* **7/1**[3]	

1m 43.65s (-0.05) **Going Correction** +0.05s/f (Slow)
WFA 3 from 4yo+ 2lb — **14** Ran SP% **117.9**
Speed ratings (Par 103): **102,99,96,95,95 93,92,90,84,84 82,78,76,75**
Tote Swingers:1&2:£28.10, 2&3:£56.30, 1&3:£26.80 CSF £85.58 CT £1805.08 TOTE £5.20: £1.80, £5.50, £5.50; EX 111.60 TRIFECTA Not won..
Owner Shropshire Wolves II **Bred** Mrs C L Weld **Trained** Melsonby, N Yorks

FOCUS

An ordinary handicap in which the leaders went off far too quick and the front pair, who came from well back, picked up the pieces. The form is a bit fluid.
Just Five(IRE) Official explanation: jockey said gelding hung right
San Antonio Official explanation: jockey said gelding had no more to give

7426 £32 FREE AT 32RED.COM H'CAP — 1m 4f (F)
3:50 (3:50) (Class 6) (0-55,60) 3-Y-O+ — **£1,704** (£503; £251) **Stalls** Low

Form			Horse	RPR
01	**1**		**Sky High Diver (IRE)**[35] 6781 3-8-12 **53**............................ JoeFanning 8	62
			(Alan Swinbank) *hld up towards rr: hdwy over 3f out: effrt to chse ldrs over 1f out: sn rdn and styd on to ld ins fnl f* **8/1**	
0503	**2**	1¼	**Spahi (FR)**[12] 7246 5-8-13 **48**.................................... DanielTudhope 4	55
			(David O'Meara) *hld up towards rr: hdwy over 3f out: effrt on bit on inner 2f out and sn ev ch: rdn to ld jst over 1f out: hdd ins fnl f and kpt on same pce* **5/1**[2]	
0653	**3**	½	**Marina Ballerina**[12] 7247 3-8-6 **47**.................................... JimmyQuinn 5	58
			(Roy Bowring) *a.p: led 3f out: rdn wl over 1f out: hdd appr fnl f: kpt on* **5/1**[2]	
6055	**4**	1¾	**Carnac (IRE)**[15] 7195 5-9-2 **51**...................................(p) ShaneKelly 6	54
			(Alan McCabe) *led: pushed along and hdd 3f out: rdn 2f out: one pce appr fnl f* **6/1**[3]	
0005	**5**	shd	**Valdan (IRE)**[31] 6873 7-9-0 **49**.................................... AndreaAtzeni 12	52
			(David Evans) *trckd ldrs: hdwy 3f out: rdn wl over 1f out and ev ch tl one pce appr fnl f* **10/1**	
6000	**6**	3	**Ballinargh Boy**[68] 5864 3-8-5 **46**.................................... LukeMorris 9	44
			(Robert Wylie) *chsd ldrs: rdn along over 2f out: sn edgd lft and kpt on same pce* **28/1**	
0006	**7**	3½	**Applaude**[11] 7078 6-8-10 **45**...................................(b) MichaelStainton 10	38
			(Jason Ward) *trckd ldrs: hdwy over 4f out: rdn along 3f out: one pce fr wl over 1f out* **66/1**	
0060	**8**	4	**Circus Polka (USA)**[21] 7077 7-8-10 **45**.......................... RussKennemore 3	31
			(Owen Brennan) *chsd ldrs: rdn along 4f out: sn wknd* **66/1**	
1004	**9**	1½	**Harare**[20] 7113 10-9-3 **52**...(v) StephenCraine 1	36
			(Karen Tutty) *towards rr: gd hdwy on inner to trck ldrs 1/2-way: cl up over 4f out: rdn along over 3f out: sn wknd* **33/1**	
1-61	**10**	nk	**Gosforth Park**[5] 7357 5-9-11 **60** 6ex............................ DuranFentiman 14	44
			(Mel Brittain) *in tch on outer: pushed along over 3f out: rdn wl over 2f out: sn btn* **2/1**[1]	
4100	**11**	4	**Jackie Kiely**[42] 6613 10-9-3 **52**...................................(tp) TomEaves 2	29
			(Roy Brotherton) *in tch: hdwy 4f out: rdn along 3f out: sn wknd* **28/1**	
0040	**12**	nk	**Sister Sioux (IRE)**[59] 6153 3-7-13 **45**.......................... RyanPowell(5) 13	22
			(Robin Bastiman) *cl up: rdn along over 3f out: wknd over 2f out* **66/1**	
4000	**13**	29	**Quaestor (IRE)**[17] 7075 4-8-11 **46**..............................(p) AndrewMullen 7	—
			(Andrew Crook) *a towards rr: bhd fnl 3f* **66/1**	
00	**14**	23	**Orpen Bid (IRE)**[53] 6295 6-8-3 **45**..............................(be) NoelGarbutt(7) 11	—
			(Michael Mullineaux) *a in rr: bhd fr 1/2-way: t.o fnl 3f* **66/1**	

2m 42.42s (1.42) **Going Correction** +0.05s/f (Slow)
WFA 3 from 4yo+ 6lb — **14** Ran SP% **118.5**
Speed ratings (Par 101): **97,96,95,94,94 92,90,87,86,86 83,83,64,48**
Tote Swingers:1&2:£5.40, 2&3:£6.40, 1&3:£8.50 CSF £44.84 CT £219.72 TOTE £9.80: £2.50, £1.70, £1.60; EX 44.70 Trifecta £461.10 Part won. Pool £623.14 - 0.90 winning units..
Owner Mrs M C Keogh **Bred** Michael Downey & Roalso Ltd **Trained** Melsonby, N Yorks

FOCUS

A moderate middle-distance handicap in which the form is ordinary but sound.
Gosforth Park Official explanation: jockey said gelding ran flat
Orpen Bid(IRE) Official explanation: jockey said mare never travelled

T/Jkpt: £13,927.10 to a £1 stake. Pool £127,502.23. 6.50 winning tickets T/Plt: £104.50 to a £1 stake. Pool £74,472.28. 520.05 winning tickets T/Qpdt: £16.70 to a £1 stake. Pool £6,239.11. 275.60 winning tickets JR

7342 KEMPTON (A.W) (R-H)

Wednesday, November 16

OFFICIAL GOING: Standard

Wind: Light, half behind Weather: Gloomy

7427 FREE ENTRY FOR BETDAQ MEMBERS APPRENTICE CLASSIFIED CLAIMING STKS — 1m 2f (P)
4:10 (4:11) (Class 6) 3-Y-O — **£1,617** (£481; £240; £120) **Stalls** Low

Form			Horse	RPR
3235	**1**		**Encore Un Fois**[30] 6924 3-9-4 69.................................... DavidKenny(3) 1	69+
			(George Baker) *hld up in 4th: clsd fr 3f out: shkn up 2f out: led 1f out: rdn clr* **5/4**[1]	
-300	**2**	1¾	**Ice Cold Bex**[19] 7137 3-9-0 70.................................... MatthewCosham 2	58
			(Philip McBride) *led: set mod pce to 1/2-way: jnd 3f out: hdd and one pce 1f out* **7/4**[2]	
0025	**3**	1¼	**Roman Flame**[12] 7271 3-8-12 58.................................... MatthewLawson 5	54
			(Michael Quinn) *trckd ldr: moved up to chal 3f out: stl upsides over 1f out: nt qckn* **10/1**	
3000	**4**	¾	**Spade**[29] 6939 3-8-4 60.................................... JordanTaylor(7) 4	51
			(Tim Pitt) *stdd s and also awkward: t.k.h and hld up in last: gng wl 2f out: bmpd along and nvr chal* **20/1**	
0436	**5**	4½	**Elfine (IRE)**[4] 7388 3-8-7 62..(e) NoelGarbutt(5) 3	43
			(Rae Guest) *trckd ldng pair to over 1f out: wknd* **8/1**[3]	

2m 10.75s (2.75) **Going Correction** -0.05s/f (Stan) — **5** Ran SP% **105.8**
Speed ratings (Par 98): **87,85,84,84,80**
CSF £3.32 TOTE £1.50: £1.10, £2.10; EX 3.40.
Owner M Khan X2 **Bred** London Thoroughbred Services Ltd **Trained** Whitsbury, Hants
■ Stewards' Enquiry : Matthew Cosham two-day ban: used whip with excessive frequency (Nov 30-Dec 1)

FOCUS

A weak opener which was run over 6 secs slower that RP standard. None of the quintet had won a race before (from a combined total of 49 outingss) but that had to change for one of them. The pace was slow and the form is rated negatively.

7428 BETDAQ MULTIPLES H'CAP — 5f (P)
4:40 (4:42) (Class 5) (0-75,75) 3-Y-O+ — **£2,264** (£673; £336; £168) **Stalls** Low

Form			Horse	RPR
5001	**1**		**Estonia**[15] 7201 4-9-0 **68**.................................... AdamKirby 2	82
			(Michael Squance) *trckd ldng trio on inner: decisive move to ld 1f out: rdn and styd on wl* **8/1**	
0026	**2**	¾	**Triple Dream**[31] 6895 6-9-0 **68**..............................(tp) RichardKingscote 9	79
			(Milton Bradley) *pressed ldr: upsides over 1f out: nt qckn: chsd wnr fnl f and styd on: a hld* **16/1**	
001	**3**	1¾	**Nially Noo**[13] 7245 3-8-6 **65**.................................... MarkCoumbe(5) 3	70
			(Derek Shaw) *mde most to 1f out: fdd ins fnl f: jst hld on for 3rd* **11/2**[2]	
5041	**4**	nk	**Absa Lutte (IRE)**[29] 6932 8-9-4 **72**.................................... JimmyQuinn 4	76
			(Michael Mullineaux) *dwlt: settled in 8th: effrt over 1f out: styd on same pce fnl f: nvr able to chal* **14/1**	
1200	**5**	½	**Six Wives**[6] 7355 4-9-2 **73**.................................... BillyCray(3) 10	75
			(David Nicholls) *w ldng pair but forced to r wd: nt qckn over 1f out: fdd fnl f* **16/1**	
5000	**6**	hd	**Rocket Rob (IRE)**[18] 7171 5-9-7 **75**..........................(b1) StevieDonohoe 1	76
			(Willie Musson) *settled in last pair on inner: effrt over 1f out: kpt on fnl f: n.d* **7/2**[1]	
3045	**7**	½	**Welsh Inlet (IRE)**[67] 5939 3-8-13 **67**.................................... NeilChalmers 5	66
			(John Bridger) *pressed ldrs: nt qckn over 1f out: wknd ins fnl f* **40/1**	
3420	**8**	nk	**Wooden King (IRE)**[31] 6895 6-9-6 **74**.................................... LukeMorris 11	72
			(Malcolm Saunders) *sltly awkward s: in tch in midfield: nt qckn wl over 1f out: kpt on ins fnl f: n.d* **8/1**	
1023	**9**	¾	**Dancing Freddy (IRE)**[6] 7355 4-9-4 **75**..................(tp) RobertLButler(3) 6	71
			(Richard Guest) *trckd ldrs in 6th: shkn up and nt qckn over 1f out: wknd ins fnl f* **15/2**[3]	
1233	**10**	½	**Crew Cut (IRE)**[31] 6895 3-8-10 **71**.................................... RaulDaSilva(7) 7	65
			(Jeremy Gask) *s.i.s: wl in rr: keeping on one pce in 10th and nt ch of much bttr whn short of room last 50yds* **7/2**[1]	
0000	**11**	4	**Not My Choice (IRE)**[13] 7243 6-8-13 **67**..................(t) MichaelStainton 12	46
			(David C Griffiths) *dwlt and rousted along: forced to r wd and nvr on terms w ldrs: wknd 2f out* **66/1**	
1/0-	**12**	1¼	**Wishbone (IRE)**[557] 1917 4-9-6 **74**.................................... TonyCulhane 8	49
			(David Flood) *s.s: racd wd bnd over 3f out: a in last pair: bhd fnl 2f* **50/1**	

59.26 secs (-1.24) **Going Correction** -0.05s/f (Stan) — **12** Ran SP% **118.1**
Speed ratings (Par 103): **107,105,103,102,101 101,100,100,98,98 91,89**
toteswingers: 1&2 £24.40, 1&3 £7.30, 2&3 £14.50 CSF £126.96 CT £779.18 TOTE £13.20: £3.60, £5.40, £1.50; EX 153.40.
Owner Miss K Squance **Bred** Millsec Limited **Trained** Newmarket, Suffolk

FOCUS

A competitive sprint handicap run at a solid pace, and the overall time was only a fraction above standard. The form looks solid rated around the first three.
Rocket Rob(IRE) Official explanation: jockey said, regarding running and riding, that his orders were to drop the gelding out, get it running and make an effort in home straight, the race was run at a fast pace, and although it responded to the whip, it did not get the best of runs.

7429 BACK OR LAY AT BETDAQ.COM H'CAP — 5f (P)
5:10 (5:14) (Class 7) (0-50,55) 3-Y-O+ — **£1,455** (£433; £216; £108) **Stalls** Low

Form			Horse	RPR
00-4	**1**		**Lucky Royale**[32] 6874 3-9-0 **47**.................................... AdamKirby 2	55+
			(Jeremy Gask) *hld up in midfield on inner: prog over 1f out: drvn and r.o to ld narrowly last 50yds* **13/2**[3]	
055	**2**	hd	**Brian Sprout**[5] 7366 3-8-11 **49** ow2.......................... JustinNewman(5) 11	57+
			(John Weymes) *chsd ldrs but forced to r wd and pushed along: effrt over 1f out: c to chal last 100yds: jst hld* **9/2**[2]	
0240	**3**	hd	**Wrenigham**[22] 7086 6-9-0 **50**.................................... RyanClark(3) 5	57
			(Pat Eddery) *led: rdn 2f out: clung on to the ld tl collared last 50yds* **7/1**	
-050	**4**	¾	**Thalia Grace**[35] 6791 4-9-1 **48**..(t) LukeMorris 1	52
			(Les Hall) *cl up on inner: drvn over 1f out: styd on same pce fnl f: nvr able to chal* **20/1**	
0050	**5**	¾	**Replicator**[14] 7230 6-9-0 **50**..(e) DominicFox(3) 8	52
			(Patrick Gilligan) *disp 2nd pl: gng strly over 1f out: sn shkn up and nt qckn: one pce fnl f* **12/1**	

-000 **6** 3/4 **Emerald Royal**[21] 7096 3-9-0 **47**......(t) MarcHalford 6 46
(Edward Creighton) *awkward s: hld up in last trio: rdn over 1f out: styd on ins fnl f: nrst fin* **66/1**

5451 **7** *nk* **Yungaburra (IRE)**[5] 7366 7-9-8 **55** 6ex......(tp) SteveDrowne 9 53
(David C Griffiths) *racd on outer in midfield: shkn up over 1f out: kpt on fnl f: nvr nr to chal* **3/1**[1]

0503 **8** 1/2 **Clerical (USA)**[42] 6619 5-9-0 **47**......(p) ShaneKelly 10 43
(Robert Cowell) *racd wd in last trio: shkn up and last over 1f out: kpt on late: no ch* **8/1**

4350 **9** *hd* **Instructress**[47] 6501 3-9-3 **50**...... EddieAhern 7 45
(Robert Cowell) *s.i.s: nvr bttr than midfield: nt qckn over 1f out: fdd fnl f* **25/1**

-350 **10** 3/4 **Force To Spend**[285] 421 4-9-0 **47**...... MartinHarley 12 40
(Des Donovan) *dropped in fr wd draw and hld up in last trio: shkn up and no prog over 1f out* **14/1**

0600 **11** 1 1/4 **Future Impact (IRE)**[26] 6999 3-8-13 **49**......(b) JohnFahy(3) 4 37
(Ed de Giles) *disp 2nd pl to over 1f out: wknd qckly* **8/1**

60.09 secs (-0.41) **Going Correction** -0.05s/f (Stan) **11** Ran SP% **115.7**
Speed ratings (Par 97): **101,100,100,99,97 96,96,95,95,93 91**
toteswingers: 1&2 £3.50, 1&3 £10.70, 2&3 £6.80 CSF £34.51 CT £215.10 TOTE £10.50: £4.30, £1.10, £3.60; EX 39.90.
Owner Gracelands Stud Partnership **Bred** Gracelands Stud **Trained** Sutton Veny, Wilts

FOCUS
Handicaps don't come much weaker than this and it is best rated through the third to this year's best.

7430 BETDAQ MOBILE APPS CLAIMING STKS 1m 4f (P)
5:40 (5:40) (Class 6) 3-Y-O+ **£1,617** (£481; £240; £120) **Stalls** Centre

Form RPR

1000 **1** **Dr Livingstone (IRE)**[47] 6499 6-9-11 82...... SteveDrowne 2 85
(Charles Egerton) *stdd s: hld up in last pair: prog over 2f out: rdn to ld over 1f out: steadily drew clr* **2/1**[2]

0506 **2** 2 3/4 **Scamperdale**[25] 7036 9-9-6 87...... RyanPowell(5) 1 81
(Brian Baugh) *led at pedestrian pce for 5f: sn dropped to 3rd: rdn to chal 2f out: nt qckn over 1f out: wl hld after* **6/1**

5454 **3** 1/2 **Foxhaven**[49] 6445 9-9-9 77......(v) LiamKeniry 3 78
(Patrick Chamings) *w ldr: led after 5f and set even slower pce: fnlly kicked on 4f out: hdd and nt qckn over 1f out* **9/4**[3]

10 **4** *14* **Balajo (FR)**[102] 4775 5-9-5 85...... FergusSweeney 4 52
(Alison Batchelor) *stdd s: hld up in last: wnt 2nd 1/2-way: upsides over 3f out: wknd rapidly jst over 2f out* **15/8**[1]

2m 45.83s (11.33) **Going Correction** -0.05s/f (Stan) **4** Ran SP% **113.2**
Speed ratings (Par 101): **60,58,57,48**
CSF £12.95 TOTE £2.00; EX 16.60.
Owner Longmoor Holdings Ltd **Bred** Stone Ridge Farm **Trained** Chaddleworth, Berks

FOCUS
A messy race in which nothing wanted to make the running and not form to get excited about. The third looks the best guide to the level.

7431 TFM NETWORKS/BRITISH STALLION STUDS E B F MAIDEN STKS 7f (P)
6:10 (6:11) (Class 5) 2-Y-O **£3,234** (£962; £481; £240) **Stalls** Low

Form RPR

1 **Solar Deity (IRE)** 2-9-3 0...... AdamKirby 4 85+
(Marco Botti) *trckd ldrs: shkn up in 3rd 2f out: rdn and r.o to chse ldr fnl f: styd on wl to ld last strides* **8/1**

2 **2** *nk* **Galician**[15] 7209 2-8-12 0...... JoeFanning 13 77+
(Mark Johnston) *led after 2f: pressed but gng strly over 2f out: fought off rival jst over 1f out: rdn and edgd lft fnl f: hdd last strides* **6/4**[1]

42 **3** *3* **Safari Sunseeker (IRE)**[19] 7142 2-9-3 0...... JamieSpencer 1 74
(William Knight) *led 2f: settled into 3rd: chal and upsides over 2f out to over 1f out: wknd last 100yds* **8/1**

523 **4** *4* **Obliteright (IRE)**[35] 6795 2-9-3 76...... ShaneKelly 8 64
(William Knight) *trckd ldrs: rdn and outpcd jst over 2f out: kpt on same pce fr over 1f out* **7/2**[3]

0 **5** 2 1/4 **Saaboog**[18] 7164 2-8-12 0...... TedDurcan 5 53
(David Lanigan) *trckd ldrs in 7th and gng wl: shkn up and outpcd over 2f out: no ch after: kpt on* **11/4**[2]

6 3/4 **Royal Dutch** 2-9-0 0...... JohnFahy(3) 11 56
(Denis Coakley) *dwlt: rn v green and sn pumped along in rr: nvr on terms but styd on in encouraging style fr over 1f out* **33/1**

00 **7** 1 3/4 **Panettone (IRE)**[29] 6933 2-8-5 0...... JeanVanOvermeire(7) 12 46
(Roger Varian) *s.i.s: racd wd and in tch towards rr: outpcd over 2f out: kpt on* **33/1**

8 2 3/4 **Mariannes** 2-8-12 0...... EddieAhern 7 39
(John Dunlop) *t.o in last after 1f: steadily ct up w those in rr by 1/2-way: jst pushed along and kpt on pleasingly fnl 2f* **33/1**

0 **9** 1 1/4 **Strategic Action (IRE)**[30] 6919 2-9-3 0...... FrankieMcDonald 3 41
(Linda Jewell) *plld hrd: pressed ldr after 2f to over 2f out: wknd qckly* **100/1**

0 **10** *9* **Vagabond King**[21] 7094 2-9-3 0...... MarcHalford 6 18
(Edward Creighton) *chsd ldrs but racd wd: rdn 3f out: sn wknd* **100/1**

000 **11** *8* **Critical Point**[5] 7368 2-9-3 0...... SebSanders 2 —
(Sir Mark Prescott Bt) *urged along in rr early: stl in rr whn reminder 1/2-way: wknd: t.o* **66/1**

12 *13* **Royal Gig** 2-8-12 0...... JimmyQuinn 14 —
(Tim Etherington) *dwlt: a in rr: dropped to last sn after 1/2-way: wl t.o* **100/1**

1m 25.64s (-0.36) **Going Correction** -0.05s/f (Stan) **12** Ran SP% **124.4**
Speed ratings (Par 96): **100,99,96,91,89 88,86,83,81,71 62,47**
toteswingers: 1&2 £5.70, 1&3 £8.00, 2&3 £2.60 CSF £21.15 TOTE £11.60: £1.80, £1.40, £2.70; EX 27.60.
Owner Andrew Tinkler **Bred** Castlemartin Stud And Skymarc Farm **Trained** Newmarket, Suffolk

FOCUS
An interesting maiden in which those with form set quite a high standard so it would have needed an above average newcomer to win this. Solar Deity fitted the bill and the field was spaced out in a good time. The form looks pretty strong and reliable.

NOTEBOOK
Solar Deity(IRE) looks a colt of great potential. Bred to relish this surface being by Exceed And Excel, he was supported in the market, so carried some confidence from connections, and he finished strongly to run down the second. With the fourth-placed horse rated 76 and appearing to run his race, this form looks decent, and he could be anything at this stage. (op 12-1)
Galician has now run two excellent races and surely won't be long in going one better. She looks useful. (op 13-8 tchd 7-4)
Safari Sunseeker(IRE), having his first run for William Knight, was left behind by the front two in the final furlong but ran well, finishing ahead of his 76-rated stablemate. He looks up to wining in maiden company. (op 13-2)
Obliteright(IRE), a stablemate of the third, looks up to wining in maiden company, although his form might be levelling out now. (op 9-2 tchd 5-1)
Saaboog was well backed, suggesting she had come on plent for her encouraging debut at Newmarket, but she could never get in a blow and was a bit disappointing. (op 3-1 tchd 10-3)
Strategic Action(IRE) Official explanation: jockey said colt ran too free

7432 HAPPY RETIREMENT MICHAEL ELLIOTT NURSERY 1m (P)
6:40 (6:41) (Class 6) (0-60,60) 2-Y-O **£1,617** (£481; £240; £120) **Stalls** Low

Form RPR

0060 **1** **Compton Bird**[86] 5316 2-8-8 **54**......(t) NicoleNordblad(7) 11 60+
(Hans Adielsson) *broke wl but heavily restrained into last pair: stl there 3f out: str prog on outer 2f out: swept into ld jst ins fnl f: sn clr and in n.d* **20/1**

000 **2** 1 1/4 **Astroscarlet**[35] 6795 2-8-8 **47**...... JimmyQuinn 1 47+
(Mark H Tompkins) *hld up wl in rr: drvn over 2f out: prog over 1f out: r.o wl fnl f to take 2nd last 75yds: clsd on wnr but no ch* **25/1**

4455 **3** 1 3/4 **Chrissycross (IRE)**[14] 7223 2-9-4 **60**......(p[1]) JohnFahy(3) 8 56
(Roger Teal) *prom: u.p over 3f out: responded to chse ldr over 2f out to over 1f out: one pce after* **16/1**

0104 **4** *shd* **Coach Montana (IRE)**[14] 7223 2-9-4 **57**...... LukeMorris 4 53
(Jane Chapple-Hyam) *trckd ldrs: rdn over 2f out: disp 2nd briefly over 1f out: one pce after* **8/1**[3]

0450 **5** *hd* **Stag Hill (IRE)**[14] 7223 2-9-7 **60**...... StephenCraine 12 55
(Sylvester Kirk) *led at decent pce: kicked on 3f out: jinked lft over 2f out: hdd and fdd jst ins fnl f* **16/1**

630 **6** *1* **Lady Heartbeat**[89] 5232 2-9-1 **54**...... FrankieMcDonald 9 47
(Michael Blanshard) *hld up in 9th: nt clr run over 2f out: swtchd lft and stl nt clr run: prog over 1f out: styng on w ch of a pl whn no room last 100yds* **66/1**

0500 **7** 1 1/4 **Sandbanks**[34] 6818 2-8-3 **45**...... SophieDoyle(3) 10 35
(Sylvester Kirk) *sn hld up in last: rdn over 2f out: kpt on fr over 1f out on outer: n.d* **66/1**

0400 **8** 2 1/4 **Hollywood All Star (IRE)**[25] 7035 2-8-6 **45**...... AndreaAtzeni 3 30
(William Muir) *s.s: wl in rr: rdn over 2f out: nvr on terms* **14/1**

0006 **9** *nse* **Cool Light**[27] 6973 2-8-9 **48**...... MartinLane 2 33
(Alan Jarvis) *sn rdn to hold midfield pl on inner: nvr able to get competitive: wknd over 1f out* **12/1**

0400 **10** *2* **Authora (IRE)**[23] 7051 2-9-7 **60**...... DaneO'Neill 7 40
(Richard Hannon) *hld up in 8th: rdn over 2f out: no prog and wl btn over 1f out* **8/1**[3]

0002 **11** *5* **Auntie Kathryn (IRE)**[6] 7342 2-8-9 **48**......(v) WilliamCarson 5 17
(Stuart Williams) *prom: drvn to dispute 2nd briefly over 2f out: sn wknd: t.o* **11/8**[1]

0004 **12** *6* **Dickens Rules (IRE)**[14] 7222 2-9-6 **59**...... LiamKeniry 6 14
(Sylvester Kirk) *prom tl wknd rapidly over 2f out: t.o* **7/2**[2]

406U **13** 2 1/4 **Joli Colourful (IRE)**[64] 6021 2-8-6 **45**...... SamHitchcott 13 —
(Tony Newcombe) *t.k.h: w ldr tl wknd rapidly wl over 2f out: t.o* **66/1**

1m 40.41s (0.61) **Going Correction** -0.05s/f (Stan) **13** Ran SP% **125.8**
Speed ratings (Par 94): **94,92,91,90,90 89,88,86,86,84 79,73,70**
toteswingers: 1&2 £92.30, 1&3 £8.80, 2&3 £70.10 CSF £443.42 CT £8204.88 TOTE £20.50: £8.90, £18.00, £7.60; EX 763.20.
Owner Erik Penser **Bred** Whitsbury Manor Stud **Trained** Kingston Lisle, Oxon
■ Stewards' Enquiry : Jimmy Quinn one-day ban: careless riding (Nov 30)

FOCUS
A moderate nursery in which the gallop looked even enough. The first two can do better.

NOTEBOOK
Compton Bird moved through smoothly in the straight to take over in impressive style. She has been racing over shorter trips prior to this but, as a daughter of Motivator, the step up to 1m was always going to suit and she left previous form miles behind. A tongue tied was fitted for the first time too. She looks to have begun handicap life on a very lenient mark. Official explanation: trainer said, regarding apparent improvement in form, that the filly had had muscle problems, had benefited from having a break, and was suited by the longer trip.
Astroscarlet has shown very little in three maidens but she left those efforts behind on first try in handicaps. She is rated just 47 but looks capable of winning races and is still open to more improvement.
Chrissycross(IRE) was always front rank and kept on well in the first-time cheekpieces and hood. (op 14-1)
Auntie Kathryn(IRE) dominated the market, but she stopped quickly in the straight and clearly didn't show her form. (op 13-8)
Dickens Rules(IRE) dropped away quickly in the straight. (op 9-2 tchd 5-1)
Joli Colourful(IRE) Official explanation: jockey said colt ran too free

7433 RACING@SKYSPORTS.COM CONDITIONS STKS 7f (P)
7:10 (7:10) (Class 4) 3-Y-O+ **£4,075** (£1,212; £606; £303) **Stalls** Low

Form RPR

1422 **1** **Primaeval**[32] 6862 5-8-11 99......(v) JamieSpencer 5 107
(James Fanshawe) *hld up off the pce: shkn up and prog over 2f out: clsd to ld jst ins fnl f: drvn out* **13/8**[1]

0004 **2** 1 3/4 **Oasis Dancer**[37] 6747 4-8-11 92...... SebSanders 4 102
(Ralph Beckett) *prom: chsd ldr 3f out: clsd to ld wl over 1f out: hdd and one pce jst ins fnl f* **11/1**

0060 **3** 1/2 **Capone (IRE)**[26] 6987 6-8-11 92...... ShaneKelly 3 101
(David Nicholls) *settled in 7th: rdn and prog over 2f out: chsd ldng pair over 1f out: styd on* **12/1**

0561 **4** 1 1/2 **Citrus Star (USA)**[20] 7127 4-8-11 97...... TedDurcan 8 97
(Chris Wall) *settled in last: shkn up 1/2-way and struggling: kpt on past wkng rivals fnl 2f* **3/1**[2]

0200 **5** 1 1/4 **Bravo Echo**[95] 5043 5-9-3 103...... J-PGuillambert 6 99
(Michael Attwater) *t.k.h: chsd ldr to 3f out: rdn over 2f out: btn whn sltly impeded over 1f out: one pce* **33/1**

0000 **6** 3 1/2 **Thunderball**[32] 6862 5-8-4 90......(b) LeonnaMayor(7) 2 84
(David Nicholls) *led: stretched field after 3f: hung lft and hdd wl over 1f out: wknd* **20/1**

100- **7** 2 1/2 **Treadwell (IRE)**[453] 5275 4-8-11 100...... FergusSweeney 1 77
(Jamie Osborne) *trckd ldrs: gng strly 1/2-way: drvn and no rspnse wl over 2f out: steadily wknd* **20/1**

2002 **8** *15* **Kakatosi**[124] 4049 4-8-11 102...... WilliamBuick 7 37
(Andrew Balding) *t.k.h: racd wd: chsd ldrs to 1/2-way: wknd rapidly over 2f out: t.o* **4/1**[3]

1m 23.29s (-2.71) **Going Correction** -0.05s/f (Stan) course record **8** Ran SP% **111.6**
Speed ratings (Par 105): **113,111,110,108,107 103,100,83**
toteswingers: 1&2 £3.70, 1&3 £4.80, 2&3 £9.20 CSF £19.59 TOTE £2.00: £1.10, £3.30, £2.50; EX 22.10.
Owner The Foncey Syndicate **Bred** Stowell Park Stud **Trained** Newmarket, Suffolk
■ Stewards' Enquiry : Leonna Mayor two-day ban: careless riding (Nov 30-Dec 1)

FOCUS
A good-quality conditions event and the form looks pretty sound.

Kakatosi Official explanation: jockey said gelding lost its action
T/Plt: £939.70 to a £1 stake. Pool: £61,790.26. 48.00 winning tickets. T/Qpdt: £293.90 to a £1 stake. Pool: £8,381.34. 21.10 winning tickets. JN

7387 LINGFIELD (L-H)

Wednesday, November 16

OFFICIAL GOING: Standard
Wind: Very light, half behind Weather: Overcast, chilly

7434 CHRISTMAS PARTIES AT LINGFIELD PARK CLAIMING STKS — 7f (P)

12:20 (12:20) (Class 6) 2-Y-O — **£1,704** (£503; £251) **Stalls** Low

Form — RPR

6442 **1** — **Le King Beau (USA)**[16] 7196 2-8-4 63 .... WilliamCarson 1 — 56+
(William Muir) *mde all: set v slow gallop tl rdn and qcknd over 2f out: kpt on wl fnl f* — **3/1**[2]

0351 **2** *hd* **Young Prince (IRE)**[15] 7205 2-9-7 78 .... EddieAhern 3 — 73+
(Robert Mills) *w ldr: rdn and styd upsides wnr fr over 2f out: r.o but a jst hld fnl f* — **30/100**[1]

0600 **3** *1 ¾* **Liquid Sunshine**[13] 7251 2-7-12 50 .... NickyMackay 2 — 45
(Sylvester Kirk) *hld up in 3rd: rdn over 2f out: drvn and no imp ins fnl f* — **20/1**[3]

1m 37.16s (12.36) **Going Correction** +0.10s/f (Slow) — **3** Ran SP% **106.7**
Speed ratings (Par 94): **33,32,30**
CSF £4.53 TOTE £3.60; EX 6.70.
Owner Sills Racing **Bred** Haras Demeautry **Trained** Lambourn, Berks

FOCUS
A farce of a race, run at a dawdle until past halfway, and the unmistakable smell of burnt fingers on those who went in hard on the odds-on favourite, but the trio finished in the order that adjusted BHA rating suggested they should. Not form to take seriously.

NOTEBOOK
Le King Beau(USA) made sure the favourite had to come wider in order to get past him, something he was unable to do. Picked up by current connections after finishing runner-up in a Wolverhampton seller last time (ahead of a subsequent winner), he had 2lb in hand of the favourite on these terms so this wasn't quite the shock that it might have seemed.
Young Prince(IRE), the comfortable winner of a Kempton nursery off 72 earlier this month, was having his first start left-handed and seemed to travel well enough on the shoulder of the winner, but in what became a sprint from the start of the home bend he could never quite get to his rival, despite trying hard. Despite this defeat, he remains capable of winning back in nursery company in a truly run race. (op 1-3 tchd 4-11 in place)
Liquid Sunshine, unplaced in her first four starts, would have been better off with her two rivals in a handicap, but the way the race was run gave her a brief chance towards the inside a furlong out before getting outpaced. (tchd 16-1)

7435 BRITISH STALLION STUDS SUPPORTING BRITISH RACING E B F MAIDEN STKS — 6f (P)

12:50 (12:50) (Class 5) 2-Y-O — **£3,340** (£986; £493) **Stalls** Low

Form — RPR

04 **1** — **Miriam's Song**[23] 7056 2-8-12 0 .... FergusSweeney 11 — 66
(Stuart Kittow) *t.k.h: chsd ldr tl led over 2f out: rdn 2f out: hld on wl cl home* — **11/2**[3]

0 **2** *nse* **Chorister Sport (IRE)**[124] 4073 2-9-3 0 .... JoeFanning 10 — 71
(William Jarvis) *in tch: rdn and effrt to chse ldr over 1f out: sustained chal and ev ch ins fnl f: jst hld* — **4/1**[1]

3 *hd* **Vale Of Lingfield (IRE)** 2-9-3 0 .... LukeMorris 12 — 70
(John Best) *in tch in midfield: rdn and effrt 2f out: chal and ev ch ins fnl f: r.o* — **16/1**

4 *½* **Norlander** 2-8-12 0 .... StevieDonohoe 6 — 64+
(Ralph Beckett) *hld up in tch in midfield: hdwy over 1f out: swtchd lft and hdwy to chse ldrs ins fnl f: kpt on* — **9/2**[2]

63 **5** *2 ½* **Betty Brook (IRE)**[12] 7267 2-8-12 0 .... TomMcLaughlin 1 — 56
(Nick Littmoden) *in tch: rdn and effrt on inner wl over 1f out: drvn and styd on same pce ins fnl f* — **9/2**[2]

00 **6** *hd* **Here Comes Jeanie**[34] 6812 2-8-12 0 .... JamieGoldstein 5 — 55
(Michael Madgwick) *chsd ldrs: rdn and unable qck wl over 1f out: styd on same pce fnl f* — **250/1**

6 **7** *shd* **Nicholascopernicus (IRE)**[14] 7225 2-9-3 0 .... J-PGuillambert 2 — 60
(Ed Walker) *dwlt: hld up in tch towards rr: rdn and effrt over 1f out: kpt on ins fnl f: nvr gng pce to threaten ldrs* — **4/1**[1]

8 *1 ½* **Mrs Cash (IRE)** 2-8-12 0 .... LiamKeniry 4 — 51
(Sylvester Kirk) *t.k.h: stdd after s: hld up in last pair: hdwy on inner but hanging lft over 1f out: styng on whn nt clr run and swtchd rt ins fnl f: nvr able to chal* — **9/1**

00 **9** *nk* **Lana Mae**[18] 7174 2-8-5 0 .... RaulDaSilva(7) 3 — 50
(Jeremy Gask) *sn pushed along to ld: hdd over 2f out and rdn: wknd ent fnl f* — **66/1**

10 *2 ¾* **Kingshill Lad (IRE)** 2-9-3 0 .... MarcHalford 9 — 46
(Terry Clement) *s.i.s: t.k.h: hdwy on outer to chse ldrs 4f out: rdn and unable qck 2f out: wknd qckly over 1f out* — **50/1**

11 *2 ¼* **Lotarespect** 2-8-12 0 .... SteveDrowne 7 — 35
(John Best) *s.i.s: racd wd and a in rr* — **25/1**

0006 **12** *20* **Skyblue**[13] 7248 2-8-12 0 ....(t) MartinLane 8 — —
(Tobias B P Coles) *taken down early and led to post: in tch towards rr tl wknd qckly over 2f out: lost tch over 1f out* — **200/1**

1m 13.84s (1.94) **Going Correction** +0.10s/f (Slow) — **12** Ran SP% **115.8**
Speed ratings (Par 96): **91,90,90,90,86 86,86,84,83,80 77,50**
toteswingers: 1&2 £6.20, 1&3 £13.50, 2&3 £12.10 CSF £26.75 TOTE £7.70: £1.80, £2.20, £4.20; EX 37.80 TRIFECTA Not won..
Owner D R Tucker **Bred** D R Tucker **Trained** Blackborough, Devon

FOCUS
An ordinary maiden, though a couple of interesting performances in behind. The form looks modest and rather fluid.

NOTEBOOK
Miriam's Song had hinted at ability on her second start on turf and took another step forward on this all-weather debut. Always in a good position, she took up the running on the home turn and proved game in a driving finish. She should have a future in handicaps. (op 5-1)
Chorister Sport(IRE) hadn't been seen since finishing well beaten on his debut for another yard in July, and was a different proposition this time. Another to race handily, he kept on right to the line and should be up to winning an ordinary Polytrack maiden. (tchd 9-2)
Vale Of Lingfield(IRE) finished well down the outside to fare best of the newcomers and this half-brother to three winners, including the prolific Whispering Spirit, should give his owners plenty of fun around here in the coming months. (op 14-1 tchd 12-1)
Norlander also finished to good effect once switched inside. Retained for just £1,100 as a 2yo, she is out of a half-sister to the high-class Captain Rio and looks to have a future. (op 6-1)
Betty Brook(IRE), a staying-on third of nine in a 5f Wolverhampton maiden last time, finished well after getting outpaced on the home turn and now qualifies for a mark.
Here Comes Jeanie, beaten a very long way in her first two starts on turf, ran better here and can also now be handicapped. (op 200-1)
Nicholascopernicus(IRE) again found this trip too sharp, but remains one to be interested in when put over further. (op 3-1)
Mrs Cash(IRE) ◆, for whom there was money beforehand, was the eyecatcher. Soon restrained out the back, she raced keenly and was still on the bridle turning for home, but didn't see much daylight and was by no means given a hard time. A 20,000gns half-sister to a winner in Japan, her sire has a decent record with his runners on Polytrack, particularly here, so she is one to watch. Her rider reported that the filly hung left. Official explanation: jockey said filly hung left (op 20-1)
Lotarespect Official explanation: jockey said filly hung right

7436 JUSTBOOKIES.COM NURSERY — 1m (P)

1:20 (1:20) (Class 5) (0-75,75) 2-Y-O — **£2,385** (£704; £352) **Stalls** High

Form — RPR

0216 **1** — **Emmuska**[53] 6340 2-9-5 73 .... SteveDrowne 4 — 77
(Richard Hannon) *sn pushed along to chse ldrs: wnt 2nd over 5f out: led 2f out: drvn and kpt on wl fnl f* — **9/2**[2]

1 **2** *½* **Koko Loca (IRE)**[35] 6792 2-9-4 72 .... MartinHarley 3 — 75
(Marco Botti) *chsd ldrs: rdn and effrt over 1f out: ev ch ins fnl f: kpt on* — **5/2**[1]

4054 **3** *nk* **Flying Trader (USA)**[37] 6757 2-8-13 67 .... LukeMorris 7 — 69+
(Jane Chapple-Hyam) *s.i.s: in tch in rr: pushed along 4f out: hdwy u.p over 1f out: styd on u.p fnl f: nt clr run and swtchd rt towards fin* — **13/2**[3]

1022 **4** *nk* **Inniscastle Boy**[14] 7222 2-8-12 66 .... WilliamCarson 5 — 67
(William Muir) *in tch: rdn and effrt 2f out: drvn and chsd ldrs 1f out: styd on same pce fnl 100yds* — **20/1**

4152 **5** *hd* **Shannon Spree**[15] 7205 2-9-3 71 .... DaneO'Neill 2 — 72
(Richard Hannon) *in tch towards rr: rdn and hdwy u.p over 1f out: no ex and styd on same pce fnl 100yds* — **9/2**[2]

0343 **6** *2* **Really Lovely (IRE)**[37] 6753 2-9-5 73 .... WilliamBuick 6 — 70
(Jeremy Noseda) *in tch: hdwy to ld 6f out: hdd and rdn 2f out: unable qck over 1f out: styng on same pce and looked btn whn squeezed for room ins fnl f* — **15/2**

0400 **7** *3 ¼* **Whinging Willie (IRE)**[15] 7205 2-9-2 70 .... FergusSweeney 9 — 59
(Gary Moore) *in tch: hdwy to chse ldrs over 3f out: rdn and unable qck jst over 2f: wknd over 1f out* — **14/1**

044 **8** *8* **Good Luck Charm**[19] 7142 2-9-1 69 .... SebSanders 8 — 40
(Gary Moore) *in tch on outer: rdn and effrt ent fnl 2f: wknd qckly over 1f out* — **12/1**

4510 **9** *10* **Vociferous (USA)**[37] 6760 2-9-7 75 .... JoeFanning 1 — 23
(Mark Johnston) *led for 2f: chsd ldrs after tl rdn and lost pl qckly over 2f out: bhd fnl 2f* — **16/1**

1m 37.84s (-0.36) **Going Correction** +0.10s/f (Slow) — **9** Ran SP% **115.0**
Speed ratings (Par 96): **105,104,104,103,103 101,98,90,80**
toteswingers: 1&2 £2.20, 1&3 £7.40, 2&3 £4.90 CSF £16.09 CT £72.53 TOTE £5.10: £1.50, £1.70, £3.30; EX 18.40 Trifecta £153.20 Pool: £350.04 - 1.69 winning units..
Owner Martin A Collins **Bred** Martin A Collins **Trained** East Everleigh, Wilts

FOCUS
A routine nursery and the form should work out at a similar level.

NOTEBOOK
Emmuska was back up to the distance of her Sandown maiden success two starts previously and was well-backed for this. Always in a handy position, she battled on well after leading over a furlong from home and has more to offer on Polytrack over this sort of trip. (op 5-1)
Koko Loca(IRE), winner of a C&D maiden on her debut last month (third has won since), had every chance and kept battling to the line, but found the winner too determined. It's still early days with her and she can get better still. (op 9-4)
Flying Trader(USA) had looked exposed, but still deserves credit for finishing where he did as he gave away ground at the start and was then inclined to race in snatches at the back of the field. He may be worth a try over further. (op 12-1)
Inniscastle Boy, proven on Polytrack but up another 3lb, moved up to hold every chance on the outside in the home straight, but lacked a decisive turn of foot. He may prefer going right-handed at Kempton. (op 16-1 tchd 22-1)
Shannon Spree ran on well from off the pace once in line for home, but was making her effort tight against the inside rail, which may not have been in her favour. She had run her two best previous races at Kempton, so is another who may be better off back there. (op 4-1 tchd 9-2 in places)
Really Lovely(IRE) made much of the running on this all-weather debut before being swamped over a furlong from home. She has looked a hard ride and isn't progressing. (tchd 7-1 and 8-1)

7437 LINGFIELD MARRIOTT HOTEL & COUNTRY CLUB H'CAP — 1m (P)

1:50 (1:50) (Class 6) (0-55,55) 3-Y-O+ — **£1,704** (£503; £251) **Stalls** High

Form — RPR

0053 **1** — **Gallantry**[15] 7202 9-9-2 55 .... TomMcLaughlin 2 — 62
(Paul Howling) *chsd ldr: rdn and clsd over 2f out: led over 1f out: kpt on wl fnl f* — **7/2**[1]

1003 **2** *½* **Gee Major**[21] 7092 4-8-11 50 ....(p) LukeMorris 5 — 56
(Nicky Vaughan) *chsd ldr: rdn and clsd over 2f out: ev ch and drvn over 1f out: kpt on same pce and hld fnl 100yds* — **11/2**[3]

0005 **3** *½* **Querido (GER)**[26] 7005 7-8-9 51 ....(tp) RobertLButler(3) 10 — 56+
(Paddy Butler) *stdd after s: hld up in rr: hdwy towards inner over 1f out: drvn and chsd ldrs ins fnl f: kpt on* — **16/1**

6140 **4** *¾* **Love Nest**[21] 7096 3-9-0 55 .... EddieAhern 11 — 58
(John Dunlop) *hld up in last quartet: rdn and hdwy on inner over 1f out: chsd ldrs 1f out: styd on same pce and no imp fnl 100yds* — **9/2**[2]

3306 **5** *½* **Qaraqum (USA)**[21] 7096 4-9-0 53 .... ShaneKelly 7 — 55
(Denis Coakley) *w.w in midfield: rdn and effrt 2f out: unable qck over 1f out: kpt on again ins fnl f* — **9/2**[2]

4500 **6** *nk* **Harvest Mist (IRE)**[21] 7096 3-8-11 52 .... NeilChalmers 4 — 53
(Michael Blanshard) *chsd ldrs: rdn and unable qck 2f out: styd on again ins fnl f* — **12/1**

4000 **7** *2* **Chez Vrony**[90] 5214 5-8-11 50 .... MartinLane 12 — 47
(Dave Morris) *stdd after s: hld up in last quartet: effrt and wd bnd 2f out: kpt on but nvr a threat to ldrs* — **16/1**

0000 **8** *1* **Heading To First**[151] 3176 4-8-9 48 ....(p) MartinHarley 1 — 42
(Paddy Butler) *led and sn clr: rdn jst over 2f out: hdd over 1f out: wknd ins fnl f* — **28/1**

03-4 **9** *1 ¼* **Resplendent Alpha**[315] 56 7-8-8 54 ....(p) LeonnaMayor(7) 3 — 46
(Alastair Lidderdale) *v.s.a: a in rr: nvr trbld ldrs* — **12/1**

0000 **10** *8* **Carpentras**[64] 6033 3-8-12 53 .... JoeFanning 9 — 26
(Dr Jon Scargill) *in tch in midfield: rdn and wknd 2f out: wl btn and eased ins fnl f* — **12/1**

0600 **11** *19* **Dolly Parton (IRE)**[15] 7201 3-8-13 54 ....[1] DaneO'Neill 6 — —
(John Bridger) *in tch in midfield: rdn and struggling 3f out: bhd fnl 2f* — **50/1**

1m 38.12s (-0.08) **Going Correction** +0.10s/f (Slow)
WFA 3 from 4yo+ 2lb — **11** Ran SP% **114.2**
Speed ratings (Par 101): **104,103,103,102,101 101,99,98,97,89 70**
toteswingers: 1&2 £3.20, 1&3 £10.40, 2&3 £12.50 CSF £21.73 CT £273.45 TOTE £5.40: £2.50, £1.10, £7.10; EX 20.40 Trifecta £197.70 Pool: £267.21 - 0.63 winning units..

Owner J Wright D Patrick P D Woodward **Bred** Cheveley Park Stud Ltd **Trained** Bramshill, Hants
■ Stewards' Enquiry : Shane Kelly two-day ban: careless riding (Nov 30-Dec 1)

FOCUS

Handicaps don't come much worse than this 0-55 event, but at least the pace was sound with Heading To First pinging the gates and soon establishing a clear advantage. The form is weak with the runner-up pretty much to form.

7438 LINGFIELDPARK.CO.UK H'CAP (DIV I) 7f (P)

2:20 (2:20) (Class 4) (0-85,85) 3-Y-O+ £4,204 (£1,251; £625; £312) Stalls Low

Form				RPR
0002	1		**Seek The Fair Land**[20] 7127 5-9-7 **85**....(b) EddieAhern 5 *(Jim Boyle) chsd ldrs: rdn and effrt to ld 1f out: r.o wl: in command and eased towards fin* **9/2**[2]	96
2104	2	2	**Wilfred Pickles (IRE)**[126] 3982 5-9-5 **83**.... DaneO'Neill 4 *(Jo Crowley) in tch in midfield: rdn and hdwy jst over 1f out: chsd wnr fnl 100yds: r.o but no threat to wnr* **17/2**	89
5036	3	3/4	**Requisite**[11] 7298 6-8-11 **75**....(b) JoeFanning 3 *(Ian Wood) t.k.h: stdd after s: hld up in midfield: rdn and hdwy on inner over 1f out: chsd wnr ins fnl f: no ex and lost 2nd fnl 100yds* **11/1**	79
6006	4	1	**Judd Street**[20] 7127 9-9-4 **82**....(vt) SebSanders 6 *(Eve Johnson Houghton) chsd ldr: rdn to ld jst over 2f out: hdd 1f out: no ex and wknd fnl 75yds* **20/1**	83
/605	5	1/2	**Sos Brillante (CHI)**[11] 7298 6-9-2 **80**.... LukeMorris 12 *(Terry Clement) hld up in last trio: bhd a wall of horses 2f out: rdn and hdwy over 1f out: styd on fnl f: nvr trbld ldrs* **11/1**	80
313	6	hd	**Santefisio**[28] 6948 5-9-7 **85**....(p) WilliamBuick 1 *(Peter Makin) stdd after s: hld up in last trio: rdn and gd hdwy on inner over 1f out: chsd ldrs and drvn ent fnl f: no imp: wknd fnl 100yds* **4/1**[1]	84
0002	7	hd	**Ivory Silk**[13] 7253 6-9-0 **78**.... AdamKirby 7 *(Jeremy Gask) stdd s: hld up in rr: switching to outer and hdwy 2f out: edgd lft but styd on ins fnl f: nvr rchd ldrs* **10/1**	76
1010	8	shd	**Main Beach**[37] 6762 4-9-0 **78**....(t) StevieDonohoe 8 *(Tobias B P Coles) in tch in midfield: rdn and unable qck wl over 1f out: plugged on u.p ins fnl f: nt pce to chal ldrs* **25/1**	76
6056	9	shd	**Dubaianswer**[118] 4234 3-8-12 **77**.... AndreaAtzeni 10 *(Marco Botti) in tch: rdn and unable qck wl over 1f out: wknd u.p over 1f out* **10/1**	75
5-60	10	3 1/2	**Regeneration (IRE)**[22] 7076 5-8-12 **76**....(t) JamieSpencer 11 *(Michael Bell) chsd ldrs: rdn and unable qck 2f out: wknd over 1f out* **5/1**[3]	64
6400	11	3/4	**Ghostwing**[139] 3536 4-9-5 **83**.... FergusSweeney 2 *(James Evans) led tl jst over 2f out: stl pressing ldrs tl ent fnl f: fdd* **50/1**	69
4/	12	9	**Smoky Cloud (IRE)**[51] 6421 4-9-1 **79**.... TomMcLaughlin 9 *(Amy Weaver) in tch on outer: rdn and struggling whn wd bnd 2f out: sn wknd: wl bhd and eased ins fnl f* **33/1**	41

1m 24.02s (-0.78) **Going Correction** +0.10s/f (Slow)
WFA 3 from 4yo+ 1lb 12 Ran SP% 113.7
Speed ratings (Par 105): **108,105,104,103,103 102,102,102,102,98 97,87**
toteswingers: 1&2 £6.70, 1&3 £13.90, 2&3 £14.80 CSF £38.74 CT £393.21 TOTE £5.80: £2.10, £2.20, £2.90; EX 41.60 Trifecta £197.90 Pool: £355.70 - 1.33 winning units..
Owner Chris Watkins And David N Reynolds **Bred** Raimon Bloodstock **Trained** Epsom, Surrey

FOCUS

A competitive handicap, run at a solid pace and the form is rated back to his best.

7439 LINGFIELDPARK.CO.UK H'CAP (DIV II) 7f (P)

2:50 (2:57) (Class 4) (0-85,85) 3-Y-O+ £4,204 (£1,251; £625; £312) Stalls Low

Form				RPR
6003	1		**Amitola (IRE)**[18] 7171 4-9-4 **82**.... JamieSpencer 8 *(David Barron) mde all: drvn over 1f out: styd on wl ins fnl f* **4/1**[1]	92
3000	2	1 1/4	**Novellen Lad (IRE)**[38] 6723 6-9-7 **85**.... StevieDonohoe 3 *(Willie Musson) hld up in tch: rdn and effrt over 1f out: styd on wl ins fnl f: wnt 2nd wl ins fnl f: no threat to wnr* **16/1**	92
0305	3	1	**Dominium (USA)**[13] 7253 4-8-12 **76**....(b) SteveDrowne 1 *(Jeremy Gask) in tch: rdn and effrt to chal over 1f out: drvn 1f out: no ex and wknd fnl 100yds* **14/1**	80
2050	4	1 1/4	**Prince Of Burma (IRE)**[18] 7171 3-8-12 **77**.... J-PGuillambert 6 *(Jeremy Gask) sn niggled along in last pair: hdwy over 1f out: styng on and swtchd rt ins fnl f: r.o: nvr trbld ldrs* **8/1**	78+
0061	5	1/2	**Everymanforhimself (IRE)**[7] 7339 7-9-2 **83** 6ex....(b) AmyRyan(3) 2 *(Kevin Ryan) in tch towards rr: rdn and hdwy towards inner over 1f out: no imp ins fnl f: wknd fnl 100yds* **5/1**[2]	82
6225	6	nk	**Ree's Rascal (IRE)**[28] 6948 3-9-1 **80**.... StephenCraine 10 *(Jim Boyle) chsd ldrs: rdn and unable qck ent fnl 2f: wknd 1f out* **14/1**	78
111-	7	nk	**Podgies Boy (IRE)**[346] 7718 3-8-12 **77**.... FrederikTylicki 4 *(Richard Fahey) in tch: rdn and effrt on outer 2f out: wknd u.p 1f out* **14/1**	75
3304	8	hd	**Showboating (IRE)**[25] 7024 3-8-9 **74**....(tp) MartinHarley 7 *(Alan McCabe) dwlt: pushed along in rr early: gd hdwy on inner 2f out: drvn to press ldrs over 1f out: wknd ins fnl f* **15/2**[3]	71
1200	9	2 1/4	**Dasho**[18] 7171 3-9-0 **79**.... KirstyMilczarek 11 *(Olivia Maylam) taken down early: t.k.h: chsd ldrs: wnt 2nd 4f out tl over 1f out: sn wknd* **14/1**	70
6000	10	4 1/2	**Titan Triumph**[16] 7199 7-9-0 **78**.... ShaneKelly 5 *(William Knight) chsd wnr tl 4f out: rdn and struggling 2f out: sn wknd* **33/1**	57
2600	11	dist	**Quasi Congaree (GER)**[38] 6723 5-9-6 **84**....(t) JoeFanning 12 *(Ian Wood) in tch in midfield on outer: rein broke and plld wd 4f out: virtually p.u after* **20/1**	—

1m 24.2s (-0.60) **Going Correction** +0.10s/f (Slow)
WFA 3 from 4yo+ 1lb 11 Ran SP% 99.8
Speed ratings (Par 105): **107,105,104,103,102 102,101,101,98,93** —
toteswingers: 1&2 £10.60, 1&3 £5.90, 2&3 £23.80 CSF £49.88 CT £501.55 TOTE £3.80: £1.30, £4.00, £3.50; EX 36.80 Trifecta £206.40 Pool: £278.99 - 0.86 winning units..
Owner J Browne **Bred** Patrick J Monahan **Trained** Maunby, N Yorks

FOCUS

The second division of his handicap was weakened by the late withdrawal of George Guru after he got under the stalls, and by Quasi Congaree virtually running out on the first bend. The winning time was 0.18 seconds slower than the first leg and the runner-up looks the best guide, being rated close to this year's form.
Quasi Congaree(GER) Official explanation: jockey said reins broke

7440 LADBROKES MAIDEN STKS 1m 2f (P)

3:20 (3:25) (Class 5) 3-Y-O+ £2,385 (£704; £352) Stalls Low

Form				RPR
2630	1		**Heatherbird**[20] 7130 3-8-12 73.... EddieAhern 4 *(William Jarvis) taken down early: t.k.h: hld up wl in tch: hdwy to join ldrs on bit over 1f out: shkn up to ld ins fnl f: pushed out: cleverly* **9/2**[3]	74
352	2	1/2	**Shieldmaiden (USA)**[13] 7250 3-8-12 80.... JoeFanning 8 *(Mark Johnston) led at stdy gallop: rdn and qcknd jst over 2f out: hdd ins fnl f: kpt on same pce* **1/1**[1]	73
5	3	nk	**Stars In Your Eyes**[13] 7250 3-8-12 0.... WilliamBuick 7 *(John Gosden) chsd ldr tl 8f out: styd chsng ldrs: rdn and ev ch over 1f out: styd on same pce ins fnl f* **2/1**[2]	72
-50	4	1/2	**Archelao (IRE)**[21] 7111 3-9-3 0.... DaneO'Neill 1 *(Marcus Tregoning) chsd ldrs: lost pl but stl in tch in last trio 5f out: swtchd rt and rdn over 1f out: kpt on* **20/1**	76
6	5	2	**Nonaynever**[21] 7111 3-9-3 0.... ShaneKelly 2 *(Jeremy Noseda) in tch in last trio: hdwy to chse ldr 8f out: rdn and unable qck over 1f out: wknd ins fnl f* **10/1**	72
00	6	16	**Empyrean (USA)**[89] 5247 3-8-12 0.... SebSanders 5 *(Sir Mark Prescott Bt) in tch in last pair: rdn and struggling over 2f out: wknd 2f out* **66/1**	35
0	7	8	**Mon Petit Bijou**[21] 7111 3-8-12 0.... SaleemGolam 6 *(Lydia Pearce) t.k.h: hld up in last pair: wknd over 2f out: sn lost tch* **100/1**	19

2m 8.40s (1.80) **Going Correction** +0.10s/f (Slow) 7 Ran SP% 117.9
Speed ratings (Par 103): **96,95,95,94,93 80,74**
toteswingers: 1&2 £1.80, 1&3 £2.00, 2&3 £1.40 CSF £9.87 TOTE £3.50: £1.10, £1.70; EX 11.20 Trifecta £29.20 Pool: £836.00 - 21.13 winning units..
Owner Abdullah Saeed Belhab **Bred** Rabbah Bloodstock Limited **Trained** Newmarket, Suffolk

FOCUS

A modest maiden for older horses and the form looks shaky.

7441 LADBROKES GAME ON! AMATEUR RIDERS' H'CAP 1m 4f (P)

3:50 (3:52) (Class 6) (0-65,64) 3-Y-O+ £2,305 (£709; £177; £177) Stalls Low

Form				RPR
30/6	1		**Baan (USA)**[21] 7113 8-10-4 **61**.... MissCAMadgin(7) 12 *(James Eustace) bhd: pushed along and hdwy 3f out: styd on to ld jst ins fnl f: hld on cl home* **10/1**	66
3505	2	nse	**Laconicos (IRE)**[15] 7206 9-9-11 **54**....(t) MissCScott(7) 9 *(William Stone) dwlt: sn rcvrd and in tch: lost pl 6f out: hdwy over 2f out: chsd ldrs and swtchd lft over 1f out: str chal ins fnl f: jst failed* **6/1**[2]	59
0424	3	3/4	**Squad**[35] 6798 5-10-6 **61**....(be[1]) MrJCoffill-Brown(5) 10 *(Simon Dow) bhd and pushed along 8f out: stl plenty to do and swtchd rt wl over 1f out: hdwy u.p ent fnl f: r.o strly: nt rch ldrs* **9/2**[1]	65+
0-00	3	dht	**Honoured (IRE)**[25] 7032 4-9-10 **53**.... MissCHenderson(7) 13 *(Nicky Henderson) racd wd thrght: chsd ldrs: lost pl bnd 2f out: rallied and hanging lft 1f out: styd on wl ins fnl f* **14/1**	57
5656	5	1 3/4	**Novel Dancer**[15] 7202 3-10-6 **62**....(p) MrSWalker 7 *(Lydia Richards) in tch: rdn and chsd ldrs 2f out: styd on same pce fnl f* **8/1**	63
1100	6	1 1/4	**Camera Shy (IRE)**[114] 4396 7-10-6 **61**.... MrFMitchell(5) 4 *(Kevin Morgan) chsd ldr tl led over 2f out: edgd lft and forged ahd over 1f out: hdd ins fnl f: wknd fnl 100yds* **7/1**[3]	60
0000	7	1 1/4	**Cragganmore Creek**[90] 5209 8-9-9 **50** oh5.... MrBMMorris(5) 1 *(Dave Morris) bhd: dropped to last over 5f out: rallied and hdwy over 3f out: no imp fnl 2f* **150/1**	47?
3640	8	3/4	**Carlton Scroop (FR)**[42] 6622 8-10-5 **60**....(b) MissMBryant(5) 11 *(Paddy Butler) sn led: hdd over 2f out: no ex and rdn over 1f out: wknd fnl f* **25/1**	57
5060	9	hd	**Sunset Boulevard (IRE)**[15] 7206 8-10-3 **53**....(b) MissSBrotherton 5 *(Paddy Butler) chsd ldrs: upsides ldr and rdn ent fnl 2f: no ex and btn over 1f out: wknd fnl f* **12/1**	48
4300	10	1	**Transfer**[12] 7264 6-10-11 **64**.... MrMPrice(3) 14 *(Richard Price) stdd s: hld up in rr: sme hdwy on outer over 4f out: rdn and wknd 3f out* **8/1**	58
0350	11	3 1/2	**Granny Anne (IRE)**[21] 7113 3-9-8 **57**.... MrsRWilson(7) 6 *(Paul D'Arcy) chsd ldrs tl wknd over 3f out: bhd fnl 2f* **22/1**	45
0450	12	2 1/4	**Mustajed**[13] 7254 10-10-2 **57**....(b) MrPMillman(5) 8 *(Rod Millman) in tch tl wknd over 3f out* **16/1**	42
3100	13	4	**If What And Maybe**[4] 7387 3-9-11 **60**....(b) MissHMTurner(7) 2 *(John Ryan) dwlt: sn rcvrd and chsd ldrs: wknd qckly 3f out* **11/1**	38

2m 33.89s (0.89) **Going Correction** +0.10s/f (Slow)
WFA 3 from 4yo+ 6lb 13 Ran SP% 113.7
Speed ratings (Par 101): **101,100,100,100,99 98,97,97,97,96 94,92,89**PL: Squad 0.70, Honoured £3.60. toteswingers: 1&2 £11.80, 1&3 (S) £3.80, 1&3 (H) £15.60, 2&3 (S) £2.40, 2&3 (H) £9.70. TRIFECTA: 2-8-3: £105.50, 2-8-12: Not won. TRICAST: B/L/S £154.60 B/L/H £420.62 CSF £64.39 TOTE £8.00: £2.30, £1.70; EX 80.70 TRIFECTA27 Owner.

FOCUS

A competitive race, but varying qualities of jockeyship and the form should be taken with a pinch of salt, with the third probably the best guide.
T/Plt: £107.60 to a £1 stake. Pool: £46,858.96. 317.82 winning tickets. T/Qpdt: £10.70 to a £1 stake. Pool: £5,950.16. 409.10 winning tickets. SP

7427 KEMPTON (A.W) (R-H)

Thursday, November 17

OFFICIAL GOING: Standard

Wind: Viirtually nil

7442 STUDY LINK INTERNATIONAL H'CAP 7f (P)

4:20 (4:20) (Class 7) (0-50,50) 3-Y-O+ £1,455 (£433; £216; £108) Stalls Low

Form				RPR
500-	1		**Trip Switch**[414] 6456 5-9-2 **50**.... JamieSpencer 9 *(George Prodromou) hld up in rr: hdwy on outside fr 2f out: drvn to ld fnl 75yds: won gng away* **13/2**	60
2600	2	1 3/4	**Daniel Thomas (IRE)**[14] 7246 9-8-13 **50**....(tp) RobertLButler(3) 12 *(Richard Guest) chsd ldrs: drvn to dispute 2nd fr jst ins fnl f: chsd wnr fnl 30yds but nvr any ch* **16/1**	55
6403	3	3/4	**Ereka (IRE)**[34] 6848 3-9-0 **49**.... LukeMorris 6 *(John Best) chsd ldr: drvn and stl disputing 2nd ins fnl f: outpcd fnl 50yds* **4/1**[1]	52
1030	4	1/2	**Ocean Countess (IRE)**[45] 6586 5-8-13 **50**....(v) MichaelO'Connell(3) 8 *(Tony Carroll) s.i.s: in rr: hdwy fr 2f out: styd on wl fnl f: nt rch ldrs* **11/2**[3]	52
0501	5	nk	**Microlight**[76] 5670 3-9-0 **49**....(b) KirstyMilczarek 4 *(John E Long) led: rdn over 2f out: hdd fnl 75yds: sn wknd* **12/1**	50
0016	6	3/4	**Teen Ager (FR)**[183] 2201 7-8-13 **50**.... JohnFahy(3) 5 *(Paul Burgoyne) t.k.h towards rr: hdwy on ins over 1f out: kpt on fnl f but nvr gng pce to chal* **5/1**[2]	49
0643	7	hd	**Norcroft**[7] 7351 9-9-1 **49**....(p) SebSanders 3 *(Christine Dunnett) chsd ldrs: drvn over 2f out: outpcd fnl f* **8/1**	48

0000 **8** ¾ **Pastoral Jet**[78] 5633 3-8-8 **50** .... LukeRowe[(7)] 1 47
(Richard Rowe) *in rr tl styd on ins fnl f* **10/1**

0450 **9** ¾ **Titan Diamond (IRE)**[28] 6982 3-8-7 **49** .... RachealKneller[(7)] 10 43
(Mark Usher) *chsd ldrs tl wknd over 1f out* **7/1**

0000 **10** *nk* **Rileys Crane**[36] 6791 4-8-8 **49** .... DanielHarris[(7)] 7 43
(Christine Dunnett) *t.k.h: chsd ldrs tl dropped to rr over 2f out: styd on again cl home* **40/1**

1m 26.59s (0.59) **Going Correction** -0.025s/f (Stan)
WFA 3 from 4yo+ 1lb **10** Ran SP% **114.1**
Speed ratings (Par 97): **95,93,92,91,91 90,90,89,88,88**
Tote Swingers: 1&2 £19.30, 1&3 £7.20, 2&3 £5.10 CSF £101.97 CT £478.15 TOTE £9.50: £3.50, £4.90, £2.00; EX 167.40.
Owner George Prodromou **Bred** A Saccomando **Trained** East Harling, Norfolk

FOCUS
A low-grade handicap featuring horses rated 49 and 50. The gallop was an ordinary one and the winner came down the centre in the straight. The form is limited and best rated around the first two.
Pastoral Jet Official explanation: jockey said, regarding running and riding, that his orders were to make sure the colt got the trip by covering it up and coming with a late run, it jumperd slowly, became unbalanced on the bend, failed to get a clear run in the home straight and ran on to the heels of others.

7443 CME GROUP MEDIAN AUCTION MAIDEN STKS 7f (P)
4:50 (4:51) (Class 6) 3-5-Y-O **£1,617** (£481; £240; £120) **Stalls** Low

Form RPR

3-0 **1** **Ocean Bay**[19] 7166 3-9-3 95 .... AdamKirby 1 86+
(John Ryan) *trckd ldrs: led 2f out: c clr fnl f: v easily* **4/7**[1]

2040 **2** 2½ **Perfect Mission**[132] 3798 3-9-3 72 .... LiamKeniry 5 74
(Andrew Balding) *chsd ldrs in 3rd tl styd on to chse wnr ins fnl 2f but nvr any ch* **3/1**[2]

3 6 **Tribouley** 3-8-12 0 .... ShaneKelly 3 53
(Dean Ivory) *stdd in rr: hdwy on ins over 2f out: wnt mod 3rd wl over 1f out: edgd lft ins fnl f* **20/1**

6005 **4** 4½ **Chillie Peppar**[66] 6004 3-9-3 43 ....(p) KirstyMilczarek 2 46
(George Prodromou) *chsd ldr tl over 2f out: sn wknd* **66/1**

6000 **5** 2 **Russian Winter**[120] 4207 3-9-0 52 .... MichaelO'Connell[(3)] 4 40
(Tim Etherington) *t.k.h towards rr: pushed along and wknd ins fnl 3f* **50/1**

5 **6** 2¾ **Ready When You Are (IRE)**[13] 7260 3-8-12 65 ..(b) RichardKingscote 6 28
(Ralph Beckett) *sn led: hdd & wknd qckly 2f out* **8/1**[3]

3 **7** 7 **Chasin' Rainbows**[16] 7207 3-8-12 0 .... StephenCraine 7 —
(Sylvester Kirk) *s.i.s: in rr: sme hdwy 4f out: wknd 3f out* **16/1**

1m 25.69s (-0.31) **Going Correction** -0.025s/f (Stan) **7** Ran SP% **113.9**
Speed ratings (Par 101): **100,97,90,85,82 79,71**
Tote Swingers: 1&2 £1.10, 1&3 £4.10, 2&3 £4.50 CSF £2.46 TOTE £1.50: £1.10, £2.70; EX 3.20.
Owner W McLuskey **Bred** R G Levin **Trained** Newmarket, Suffolk

FOCUS
An uncompetitive maiden in which the proximity of the 43-rated fourth means the form can't really be taken at face value. The gallop was an ordinary one to the intersection and the winner came down the centre. The form looks weak and far from solid, with the runner-up and fourth the best guides.

7444 CHART PLAN NURSERY 7f (P)
5:20 (5:20) (Class 6) (0-65,65) 2-Y-O **£1,617** (£481; £240; £120) **Stalls** Low

Form RPR

0041 **1** **Night Flash (GER)**[15] 7222 2-9-7 **65** .... FrederikTylicki 4 75+
(James Given) *in tch: hdwy on outside fr 2f out to ld appr fnl f: pushed clr fnl f: easily* **7/2**[1]

0305 **2** 3¼ **Karma Chameleon**[51] 6424 2-8-9 **53** .... ShaneKelly 9 54
(John Berry) *chsd ldrs: drvn and kpt on fnl f to take 2nd fnl 50yds but no ch w easy wnr* **12/1**

042 **3** *nse* **La Romantique (IRE)**[30] 6927 2-9-7 **65** ....(b[1]) JamieSpencer 7 65
(Marco Botti) *in rr: hdwy on outside fr 2f out: styd on to dispute 2nd fnl 150yds but nvr any ch w easy wnr: dropped to 3rd last stride* **4/1**[2]

6003 **4** 1¾ **Liquid Sunshine**[1] 7434 2-8-6 **50** .... FrankieMcDonald 10 46
(Sylvester Kirk) *stdd s and swtchd rt to ins rail: hdwy over 2f out: nt clr run and swtchd rt wl over 1f out: kpt on fnl f: nvr a threat* **40/1**

0520 **5** ½ **King's Future**[14] 7252 2-9-7 **65** ....(p) LukeMorris 3 60
(John Akehurst) *chsd ldrs: wnt 2nd over 2f out: slt ld over 1f out: sn hdd: wknd fnl 100yds* **16/1**

500 **6** 1½ **Rock On Candy**[64] 6048 2-9-7 **65** .... StephenCraine 2 56
(Sylvester Kirk) *chsd ldrs: rdn over 2f out: wknd fnl f* **20/1**

0416 **7** *hd* **Littlecote Lady**[35] 6821 2-8-12 **56** .... DaneO'Neill 1 46
(Mark Usher) *in rr: pushed along 2f out: mod prog fnl f* **14/1**

0040 **8** ¾ **Street Angel (IRE)**[21] 7125 2-9-0 **61** ....(b) DominicFox[(3)] 6 49
(Alan Bailey) *in rr: mod prog clsng stages* **25/1**

6406 **9** 1½ **Stepharlie**[14] 7251 2-8-13 **57** .... WilliamBuick 5 41
(Bryan Smart) *sn led: riddn over 2f out: hdd & wknd over 1f out* **15/2**

503 **10** ¾ **Royale Ransom**[29] 6946 2-9-7 **65** .... AdamKirby 12 47
(Clive Cox) *racd towards outside: a outpcd* **5/1**[3]

006 **11** 1 **Jericho (IRE)**[19] 7177 2-9-7 **65** .... FergusSweeney 13 45
(Jamie Osborne) *chsd ldr 4f out to 2f out: wknd fnl f* **8/1**

1m 26.41s (0.41) **Going Correction** -0.025s/f (Stan) **11** Ran SP% **113.1**
Speed ratings (Par 94): **96,92,92,90,89 87,87,86,85,84 83**
Tote Swingers: 1&2 £8.70, 1&3 £2.40, 2&3 £6.30 CSF £43.10 CT £172.73 TOTE £4.10: £2.60, £6.20, £1.10; EX 43.40.
Owner Danethorpe Racing Partnership **Bred** Gestut Etzean **Trained** Willoughton, Lincs

FOCUS
A couple of unexposed sorts in a modest nursery and the winner is very much on the upgrade. The early gallop was only fair and the winner raced down the centre in the straight. The form is modest but sound and the winner is progressing.

NOTEBOOK
Night Flash(GER) ◆ is a scopey and progressive sort who took a bit of stoking up over this shorter trip, but galloped on relentlessly to win with plenty in hand and defy a 7lb rise in the weights. He'll be suited by the return to 1m and, although life will be tougher after reassessment, he's the type to win again on Polytrack. (tchd 10-3)
Karma Chameleon, who ran creditably in testing ground at Ayr on his previous start, was no match for the progressive winner but ran creditably on this all-weather debut on this first run for his new yard. The return to 1m won't inconvenience and there's a small race to be picked up this winter.
La Romantique(IRE), who progressed steadily in maidens, was far from disgraced on this nursery debut in the first-time blinkers. She won't be troubled by the return to 1m and she's lightly raced enough to be open to further improvement. (op 7-2)
Liquid Sunshine, turned out quickly, again showed ability at an ordinary level after being set plenty to do but she has yet to win and her record suggests she wouldn't be guaranteed to build on this next time.
King's Future had the run of the race but didn't get home as well as the principals after failing to settle early on. The return to 6f may suit at this stage but he needs to improve to win from his current mark.
Rock On Candy wasn't disgraced on this nursery and all-weather debut but who has still to reproduce the form of her debut run at Newbury in June, in a race that threw up winners.

7445 FRIENDS LIFE NURSERY 6f (P)
5:50 (5:50) (Class 4) (0-85,85) 2-Y-O **£3,428** (£1,020; £509; £254) **Stalls** Low

Form RPR

0310 **1** **Kune Kune**[61] 6146 2-9-7 **85** .... MartinHarley 5 91+
(Marco Botti) *trckd ldrs: led ins fnl 2f: sn drvn: styd on wl fnl f* **13/2**[3]

431 **2** 1¼ **Colorful Notion (IRE)**[146] 3342 2-9-0 **78** .... AdamKirby 8 80+
(Marco Botti) *bmpd s: in rr: hdwy on ins fr 3f out: chsd ldrs fr 2f out: wnt 2nd ins fnl 2f but no imp on wnr* **12/1**

51 **3** 1 **Dissent (IRE)**[36] 6787 2-9-4 **82** .... SebSanders 3 81
(Gerard Butler) *t.k.h: early trckd ldrs: pushed along and qckned ins fnl 2f: wnt 3rd ins fnl f: styd on same pce* **9/4**[1]

6262 **4** 1½ **Sunrise Dance**[43] 6620 2-8-13 **77** .... MartinLane 4 72
(Alan Jarvis) *sn led: hdd ins fnl 2f: styd on same pce fnl f: wknd clsng stages* **20/1**

3460 **5** 2½ **Safari Storm (USA)**[31] 6921 2-8-9 **73** ....(t) JamieSpencer 2 60
(Brian Meehan) *hld up in rr: hdwy over 1f out: kpt on fnl f: nvr gng pce to trble ldrs* **10/1**

1243 **6** 1½ **Sonko (IRE)**[45] 6590 2-8-5 **69** .... LukeMorris 1 52
(Tim Pitt) *chsd ldrs on ins: rdn 2f out: wknd fnl f* **25/1**

6501 **7** 2½ **Larwood (IRE)**[32] 6890 2-8-4 **68** .... FrankieMcDonald 6 43
(Henry Candy) *tk keen hoold: stdd towards rr: hdwy over 2f out: sn rdn and no imp* **11/1**

6105 **8** 2 **Main Focus (USA)**[13] 7261 2-9-1 **79** .... WilliamBuick 11 48
(John Gosden) *racd on outside: chsd ldrs: pushed along over 2f out: sn btn* **5/1**[2]

4204 **9** ½ **Key Ambition**[34] 6827 2-8-10 **79** .... JustinNewman[(5)] 10 47
(Bryan Smart) *wnt rt s: racd towards outside and chsd ldrs tl wknd over 2f out* **14/1**

0536 **10** *nk* **Piranha (IRE)**[43] 6625 2-9-1 **79** .... ChrisCatlin 9 46
(Ed Dunlop) *bmpd s: t.k.h: a towards rr* **33/1**

061 **11** 9 **Sandfrankskipsgo**[31] 6919 2-9-1 **79** ....(t) ShaneKelly 7 24
(Brett Johnson) *plld hrd: chsd ldrs: wknd ins fnl 2f: eased whn no ch fnl f* **8/1**

1m 11.89s (-1.21) **Going Correction** -0.025s/f (Stan) **11** Ran SP% **115.2**
Speed ratings (Par 98): **107,105,104,102,98 96,93,90,90,89 77**
Tote Swingers: 1&2 £13.70, 1&3 £4.20, 2&3 £7.80 CSF £77.73 TOTE £9.20: £2.70, £1.80, £1.80; EX 71.50.
Owner Mrs Anita Nicol **Bred** Miss S E Hall **Trained** Newmarket, Suffolk

FOCUS
A useful nursery run at an ordinary gallop to the intersection. The first four, who pulled a few lengths clear of the rest, raced down the centre. The third helps set the level and the form should prove fairly reliable.

NOTEBOOK
Kune Kune, bogged down in soft ground in Listed company at Ayr on her previous start, had the run of the race and posted her best effort on this nursery and all-weather debut. Things went her way but she's open to further progress on this surface. (op 6-1)
Colorful Notion(IRE) ◆ has improved with every run and posted her best effort on this first run for almost five months to fare the best of those held up on this nursery debut returned to Polytrack. She looks worth a try over 7f and is capable of picking up a similar event on this surface.
Dissent(IRE) was well supported for this nursery debut on the back of her fluent C&D maiden win, but he pulled far too hard to do himself full justice and wasn't disgraced in the circumstances. He'll be worth another chance from this mark when a stronger gallop looks on the cards. (op 2-1)
Sunrise Dance wasn't disgraced after being allowed the rub of things but her all-weather form has still to match the pick of her turf form, and she'll have to raise her game to win off 77 in competitive handicap company.
Safari Storm(USA), again tongue-tied, wasn't disgraced on this all-weather debut in a race where those held up weren't seen to best advantage. He may be of more interest in a more strongly run race returned to 5f. (op 12-1)
Sonko(IRE) had been running consistently well but she wasn't at her best, despite enjoying the run of the race returned to Polytrack. The return to 5f may be more to her liking and there will be easier opportunities on this surface than this one. (op 20-1)
Larwood(IRE) reportedly had a breathing problem. Official explanation: trainer said colt had a breathing problem (op 16-1)
Main Focus(USA) raced wide from his draw but was again a fair way below his best since winning at this course in June. He has plenty to prove. (op 6-1)
Sandfrankskipsgo's run of progressive turf efforts came to a halt in the first-time tongue-tie on this nursery and all-weather debut and he will have to settle better if he is to win races on this surface. Official explanation: jockey said colt ran too free (op 15-2)

7446 PCA 903 CLUB CLAIMING STKS 1m 4f (P)
6:20 (6:20) (Class 6) 3-Y-O **£1,617** (£481; £240; £120) **Stalls** Centre

Form RPR

5130 **1** **Junoob**[48] 6497 3-8-13 84 ....(b[1]) JohnFahy[(3)] 5 80
(Amy Weaver) *trckd ldrs in 4th: hdwy into 3rd 2f out: hdwy: nt clr run and swtchd rt appr fnl f: sn pressing ldr: slt ld fnl 120yds: drvn out* **3/1**[3]

0-3 **2** ¾ **Beat Of The Blues**[103] 4800 3-8-10 0 .... LiamKeniry 2 72
(Andrew Balding) *sn led: drvn over 1f out: jnd ins fnl f: hdd fnl 120yds: no ex u.p clsng stages* **15/8**[1]

1425 **3** 2½ **Zamina (IRE)**[32] 6893 3-9-0 76 .... JamieSpencer 6 72
(George Baker) *chsd ldr: rdn and one pce into 3rd appr fnl f: sn outpcd by ldng duo: hld on for 3rd cl home* **11/4**[2]

P353 **4** *nk* **Little Jazz**[14] 7254 3-8-12 66 ....(b[1]) LukeMorris 4 70
(Paul D'Arcy) *racd in 5th: drvn: swtchd lft to outer and hdwy over 1f out: styd on to cl on 3rd wl ins fnl f but no ch w ldng duo* **12/1**

4-0 **5** 9 **Baraaya (IRE)**[36] 6804 3-8-3 0 .... KellyHarrison 1 51
(William Haggas) *racd in cl 3rd: ins fnl 3f: wknd ins fnl 2f* **5/1**

2m 36.59s (2.09) **Going Correction** -0.025s/f (Stan) **5** Ran SP% **110.8**
Speed ratings (Par 98): **92,91,89,89,83**
CSF £9.13 TOTE £2.30: £1.10, £2.00; EX 7.40.Beat of The Blues was claimed by Mr T. R. Pearson for £8,000.
Owner Michael Bringloe **Bred** Shadwell Estate Company Limited **Trained** Newmarket, Suffolk

FOCUS
An uncompetitive claimer in which the steady pace means this bare form isn't entirely reliable, with the proximity of the fourth raising doubts. The field came down the centre.

Zamina(IRE) Official explanation: jockey said filly hung right

7447 PCA BENEVOLENT FUND H'CAP 1m (P)
6:50 (6:51) (Class 5) (0-75,74) 3-Y-0+ **£2,264** (£673; £336; £168) **Stalls** Low

Form RPR
4202 **1** **Sweet Secret**[20] 7146 4-9-0 **67** (b) JamieSpencer 11 76
(Jeremy Gask) *mde all: drvn along over 1f out: hld on wl thrght fnl f* **10/1**
2116 **2** 3/4 **Larkrise Star**[31] 6924 4-9-0 **67** ShaneKelly 8 74
(Dean Ivory) *in tch: hdwy on ins over 2f out: styd on to chse wnr wl over 1f out: styd on clsng stages whn n.m.r but a hld* **7/1**
2245 **3** *hd* **Lockantanks**[17] 7199 4-9-7 **74** WilliamBuick 10 81+
(Michael Appleby) *hld up in rr: stl plenty to do 2f out: hdwy on outside over 1f out: drvn and rapid hdwy ins fnl f: edgd rt: fin strly: gng on clsng stages: nt quite rch ldng duo* **13/2**[3]
4032 **4** *4* **Daffydowndilly**[28] 6971 3-8-12 **67** (t) LiamKeniry 2 64
(Hughie Morrison) *in rr: hdwy fr 2f out: styd on to take 4th fnl 100yds: nt trble ldng trio* **14/1**
6601 **5** *1 1/2* **Al Aqabah (IRE)**[22] 7097 6-9-6 **73** (b) LukeMorris 1 67
(Brian Gubby) *sn chsng ldrs: wnt 2nd wl over 2f out but no imp on wnr: wknd fnl f* **11/2**[2]
0303 **6** *nk* **Cool Hand Jake**[16] 7208 5-9-3 **70** SteveDrowne 7 63
(Peter Makin) *in rr: drvn along over 2f out: styd on fnl f: nvr a threat* **11/2**[2]
1505 **7** *1* **Catchanova (IRE)**[6] 7362 4-9-6 **73** FergusSweeney 5 64
(Eve Johnson Houghton) *chsd ldrs: rdn over 2f out: wknd appr fnl f* **8/1**
2100 **8** *nse* **Whodathought (IRE)**[29] 6944 3-9-3 **72** (b) AdamKirby 3 63
(Paul Rich) *chsd ldrs: rdn over 3f out: wknd ins fnl 2f* **25/1**
0014 **9** *4* **The Which Doctor**[16] 7202 6-8-13 **69** (e) RobertLButler(3) 9 51
(Richard Guest) *in rr: hdwy into mid-div ins fnl 3f: nvr nr ldrs and wknd ins fnl 2f* **16/1**
2062 **10** *6* **Ede's Dot Com (IRE)**[60] 5491 7-8-4 **62** JemmaMarshall(5) 4 30
(Pat Phelan) *s.i.s: t.k.h: shkn up ins fnl 3f a bhd* **50/1**
0001 **11** *1/2* **Mountrath**[15] 7228 4-8-12 **68** (v) JohnFahy(3) 6 35
(Gary Moore) *chsd ldrs: drvn over 2f out: wknd qckly over 1f out* **7/2**[1]

1m 38.36s (-1.44) **Going Correction** -0.025s/f (Stan)
WFA 3 from 4yo+ 2lb **11** Ran SP% **117.4**
Speed ratings (Par 103): **106,105,105,101,99 99,98,98,94,88 87**
Tote Swingers: 1&2 £7.90, 1&3 £7.80, 2&3 £6.50 CSF £78.19 CT £381.48 TOTE £14.20: £4.40, £2.10, £1.60; EX 98.10.
Owner 140 Characters **Bred** Carmel Stud **Trained** Sutton Veny, Wilts

FOCUS
Mainly exposed performers in an ordinary handicap. The gallop was an even one and the winner edged towards the far rail in the closing stages. The first three finished clear and the third looks the best guide to the level.

7448 JLT H'CAP 7f (P)
7:20 (3:21) (Class 5) (0-70,70) 3-Y-0+ **£2,264** (£673; £336; £168) **Stalls** Low

Form RPR
4102 **1** **Russian Ice**[29] 6944 3-9-2 **66** (b) ShaneKelly 12 76
(Dean Ivory) *n.m.r s and bhd: gd hdwy over 1f out: str run ins fnl f to ld fnl 30yds: won gng away* **6/1**[2]
3530 **2** *1* **Tislaam (IRE)**[22] 7106 4-9-6 **69** (p) MartinHarley 14 76
(Alan McCabe) *led after 2f: rdn and 3 l clr over 1f out: hdd and outpcd fnl 30yds* **12/1**
3121 **3** *1* **Trojan Rocket (IRE)**[13] 7269 3-9-2 **66** AdamKirby 1 70
(George Prodromou) *chsd ldrs: drvn over 2f out: styd on to take 3rd jst ins fnl f: no imp on ldng duo fnl 120yds* **3/1**[1]
3055 **4** *hd* **Leadenhall Lass (IRE)**[49] 6479 5-9-1 **69** JemmaMarshall(5) 4 73
(Pat Phelan) *chsd ldrs: drvn and styd on over 1f out: kpt on to press for 3rd clsng stages but no ch w ldng duo* **20/1**
1044 **5** *1 1/4* **Saturn Way (GR)**[81] 5511 5-9-2 **65** LiamKeniry 3 65
(Patrick Chamings) *towards rr: drvn and hdwy fr 2f out: styd on fnl f: nt pce to rch ldrs* **7/1**[3]
65-0 **6** *hd* **Mack's Sister**[38] 6752 4-8-12 **61** LukeMorris 8 61
(Dean Ivory) *chsd ldrs: rdn 2f out: wknd jst ins fnl f* **20/1**
6004 **7** *1 3/4* **Dead Cool**[19] 7173 3-9-4 **68** (t) RichardKingscote 5 63
(Hughie Morrison) *chsd ldrs: rdn 2f out: wknd 1f out* **8/1**
0061 **8** *1 1/4* **Mambo Spirit (IRE)**[21] 7123 7-9-3 **66** DaneO'Neill 10 58
(Tony Newcombe) *in rr: pushed along and hdwy towards outside over 1f out: kpt on clsng stages but nvr any ch* **7/1**[3]
000 **9** *nk* **Cristaliyev**[20] 7137 3-8-8 **58** FergusSweeney 6 49
(Jim Boyle) *in rr: sme prog fnl f* **40/1**
1030 **10** *3/4* **Grand Piano (IRE)**[71] 5836 4-8-11 **67** ThomasBrown(7) 9 56
(Andrew Balding) *chsd ldrs: rdn 2f out and sn wknd* **25/1**
3514 **11** *1 1/4* **Katmai River (IRE)**[80] 5539 4-9-0 **63** SteveDrowne 13 49
(Mark Usher) *a towards rr* **12/1**
0000 **12** *3/4* **Sir Mozart (IRE)**[22] 7097 8-9-2 **65** MickyFenton 2 49
(Barney Curley) *nt clr run on ins bnd over 3f out and over 2f out: a towards rr* **33/1**
-240 **13** *1* **Always Like This (IRE)**[36] 6796 3-9-6 **70** JamieSpencer 11 51
(Marco Botti) *sn led: hdd after 2f: wknd ins fnl 2f* **14/1**

1m 26.06s (0.06) **Going Correction** -0.025s/f (Stan)
WFA 3 from 4yo+ 1lb **13** Ran SP% **116.2**
Speed ratings (Par 103): **98,96,95,95,94 93,91,90,90,89 87,86,85**
Tote Swingers: 1&2 £17.20, 1&3 £4.50, 2&3 £12.60 CSF £67.78 CT £265.84 TOTE £8.10: £2.40, £4.50, £1.80; EX 94.30.
Owner Roger Beadle & Ben Bennett **Bred** Kingwood Bloodstock & Mrs M Gutkin **Trained** Radlett, Herts

FOCUS
An ordinary handicap in which the early gallop was no more than fair. The winner raced against the inside rail in the closing stages and the runner-up looks the key to the form.
T/Jkpt: Not won. T/Plt: £63.60 to a £1 stake. Pool: £75,365.38 - 864.35 winning tickets. T/Qpdt: £29.10 to a £1 stake. Pool: £8,991.17 - 227.90 winning tickets. ST

7405 SAINT-CLOUD (L-H)
Thursday, November 17

OFFICIAL GOING: Turf: very soft

7449a PRIX DE BOIS D'ARCY (CLAIMER) (2YO) (TURF) 1m
12:30 (12:00) 2-Y-0 **£9,051** (£3,620; £2,715; £1,810; £905)

RPR
1 **Becebege (FR)**[28] 2-8-3 0 (b) AntoineCoutier(5) 7 77
(A Bonin, France) **118/10**
2 *2 1/2* **Gentleshaw (FR)** 2-8-5 0 AnthonyCaramanolis(3) 20 72
(J Van Handenhove, France) **33/1**
3 *2 1/2* **Louvigny (FR)**[20] 2-9-2 0 (b) GregoryBenoist 3 74
(C Lerner, France) **6/1**[2]
4 *hd* **Dragon Ball (FR)**[31] 6925 2-8-11 0 JohanVictoire 7 69
(J Van Handenhove, France) **10/1**
5 *hd* **Soir D'Ete (FR)**[9] 2-8-8 0 SylvainRuis 13 65
(J-P Delaporte, France) **99/1**
6 *shd* **Litura (IRE)**[20] 2-8-13 0 (b) AllanBonnefoy 14 70
(J-V Toux, France) **22/1**
7 *nse* **Esquinade (FR)**[28] 2-8-10 0 CesarPasserat(6) 4 73
(A Bonin, France) **26/1**
8 *hd* **Marquis Du Nonan (FR)**[34] 2-9-1 0 ThierryThulliez 12 71
(G Collet, France) **38/1**
9 *nk* **Milyas (FR)**[25] 2-9-4 0 ChristopheSoumillon 16 74
(C Laffon-Parias, France) **2/1**[1]
10 *1 1/4* **Snowed In (IRE)**[21] 7117 2-9-6 0 MickaelBarzalona 15 73
(J S Moore) *prom bhd ldrs: shkn up 2f out on outside and r.o wl: u.p 1f out: no ex fnl 100yds* **9/1**
0 **White Burgundy (IRE)**[58] 2-8-2 0 (p) BenjaminBoutin(6) 1 —
(C Boutin, France) **82/1**
0 **Spidermania (FR)**[9] 2-8-11 0 (p) SebastienMaillot 19 —
(Robert Collet, France) **24/1**
0 **Muhta Speed (FR)**[146] 2-8-4 0 MathieuTavaresDaSilva(7) 10 —
(A Lyon, France) **70/1**
0 **Belle Trolette (FR)**[34] 2-8-5 0 AntoineHamelin(3) 2 —
(J Van Handenhove, France) **21/1**
0 **Feu De Glace (FR)**[29] 2-8-11 0 TheoBachelot 8 —
(C Boutin, France) **106/1**
0 **Coeur De Perle (FR)**[83] 2-8-4 0 PierreTomas(7) 6 —
(Y De Nicolay, France) **52/1**
0 **Royal Sharp**[18] 2-9-1 0 StephanePasquier 11 —
(G Botti, Italy) **69/1**
0 **Larga Charla (IRE)** 2-9-1 0 Pierre-CharlesBoudot 18 —
(G Botti, Italy) **93/1**
0 **Rinko (FR)** 2-8-11 0 SoufyaneMoulin(7) 5 —
(C Boutin, France) **73/1**
0 **French Rules (FR)** 2-8-11 0 MaximeGuyon 9 —
(H-A Pantall, France) **44/5**[3]

1m 51.08s (3.58) **20** Ran SP% **117.1**
WIN (incl. 1 euro stake): 12.80. PLACES: 4.50, 7.40, 2.50. DF: 156.80. SF: 612.60.
Owner Marcel Chaouat **Bred** F Bayrou **Trained** France

7442 KEMPTON (A.W) (R-H)
Friday, November 18

OFFICIAL GOING: Standard
Wind: Moderate, behind. Weather: Sunny getting dark

7451 COMBINED SERVICE PROVIDER MAIDEN AUCTION STKS 5f (P)
2:20 (2:20) (Class 6) 2-Y-O **£1,811** (£539; £269; £134) **Stalls** Low

Form RPR
1 **Nini Ok (IRE)**[143] 3497 2-8-3 0 (b[1]) JohnFahy(3) 2 79
(John Joseph Murphy, Ire) *in 4th tl smooth hdwy on rails to ld bnd 2f out: drvn and styd on strly fnl f* **10/3**[3]
432 **2** *3 1/4* **Kyleakin Lass**[25] 7052 2-8-8 72 ChrisCatlin 3 69
(Ian Wood) *disp ld tl carried wd bnd appr fnl 2f: rallied to chse wnr over 1f out but no imp* **11/8**[1]
3042 **3** *2 1/4* **Lady Gibraltar**[16] 7225 2-8-6 74 MartinLane 1 59
(Alan Jarvis) *disp ld tl rn wd bnd appr fnl 2f: wknd fnl f* **13/8**[2]
3300 **4** *10* **Red Socks (IRE)**[14] 7267 2-9-1 62 RobertWinston 4 32
(Gay Kelleway) *chsd ldrs in 3rd tl wknd ins fnl 2f* **20/1**

59.19 secs (-1.31) **Going Correction** -0.15s/f (Stan) **4** Ran SP% **108.0**
Speed ratings (Par 94): **104,98,95,79**
CSF £8.32 TOTE £4.60; EX 7.90.
Owner Mrs Mairead O'Keeffe **Bred** Sean O'Keeffe **Trained** Upton, Co. Cork

FOCUS
An eventful opening 2-y-o maiden auction event.

NOTEBOOK
Nini Ok(IRE), down in trip and with first-time blinkers, was rather handed this on a plate. Last away and soon outpaced when the leader carried the runner-up very wide on the turn in, she shot through up the inner and was always in command thereafter. She had luck on her side, but the trip and the headgear suited her. (op 3-1)
Kyleakin Lass, who turned in an improved effort on her third start when beaten a head over 6f at Leicester, was drawn on the outside of the errant leader. Matching strides, she was being forced wide starting the turn for home. Carried very wide off the final bend, she stuck to her guns but the winner was gone beyond recall. She deserves to break her duck. (op 5-4 tchd 6-4)
Lady Gibraltar, headed close home over 6f here, ran without a visor this time. Drawn one, she was hanging left away from the rail from the off. She veered very wide off the home turn, carrying the runner-up very wide. Rated 74, she can surely open her account round left-handed Lingfield or Wolverhampton. (op 7-4 tchd 15-8)
Red Socks(IRE), rated just 62, was having his second start after a five-month summer break. He set off in fair form, but has regressed and this was his third moderate effort in succession. (op 16-1)

7452 GOTOCSP.COM NURSERY 5f (P)
2:55 (2:55) (Class 6) (0-65,65) 2-Y-O **£1,811** (£539; £269; £134) **Stalls** Low

Form RPR
064 **1** **I See You**[14] 7267 2-9-0 **58** LukeMorris 6 65
(George Margarson) *chsd ldrs: wnt 2nd over 1f out: rdn and styd on wl to ld fnl 50yds: drvn out* **13/2**
6351 **2** *1* **Bookiesindexdotnet**[44] 6620 2-9-7 **65** KierenFallon 1 68
(J R Jenkins) *led: rdn along 2f out: kpt on wl tl hdd and outpcd fnl 50yds* **7/2**[1]
0656 **3** *1 3/4* **Chicarito**[25] 7059 2-9-0 **61** (p) JohnFahy(3) 3 58
(John Gallagher) *chsd ldrs: wnt 2nd 2f out: no imp and dropped to 3rd over 1f out: sn outpcd* **15/2**
350 **4** *1* **Princess Alessia**[46] 6590 2-9-4 **62** MarcHalford 9 56+
(Terry Clement) *towards rr: drvn and hdwy over 1f out: styd on fnl f but nt rch ldrs* **16/1**
030 **5** *nk* **Wrapped Up**[36] 6817 2-8-5 **56** JakePayne(7) 11 48
(Heather Main) *in tch: hdwy on outside to chse ldrs 2f out: styd on fnl f: nt rch ldrs* **33/1**

4400 **6** *nk* **Copper Falls**[21] 7143 2-8-5 **56** BrendanPowell(7) 4 47
(Brendan Powell) *chsd ldrs: rdn 2f out: wknd ins fnl f* **33/1**
6002 **7** *1 1/4* **Tangtastic (IRE)**[16] 7231 2-8-7 **51** JimmyQuinn 8 38
(Edward Creighton) *in rr: pushed along 1/2-way: sme prog fnl f* **12/1**
3305 **8** *nk* **Finalist**[30] 6942 2-9-0 **58** WilliamBuick 10 44
(Dean Ivory) *s.i.s: in rr: racd towards outside: pushed along over 1f out: r.o clsng stages but nvr a threat* **9/2**[2]
4030 **9** *2* **Claretintheblood (IRE)**[13] 7294 2-8-11 **55** FrederikTylicki 5 34
(Richard Fahey) *early spd: outpcd fr 1/2-way* **13/2**
5234 **10** *3/4* **Shout For Joy (IRE)**[79] 5613 2-9-1 **62** KieranO'Neill(3) 7 38
(Richard Hannon) *slowly away: outpcd* **7/1**
4551 **11** *1/2* **Mr Hendrix**[30] 6942 2-8-11 **58** KierenFox(3) 2 32
(Brett Johnson) *chsd ldrs 3f* **6/1**[3]

60.19 secs (-0.31) **Going Correction** -0.15s/f (Stan) **11** Ran SP% **125.1**
Speed ratings (Par 94): **96,94,91,90,89 89,87,86,83,82 81**
Tote Swingers:1&2:£6.70, 2&3:£6.70, 1&3:£10.70 CSF £31.51 CT £184.15 TOTE £9.30: £2.80, £1.40, £4.40; EX 47.70 Trifecta £310.00 Pool £439.96 - 1.05 winning units..
Owner Mrs C C Regalado-Gonzalez **Bred** Lilac Bloodstock & Redmyre Bloodstock **Trained** Newmarket, Suffolk

FOCUS
A modest nursery with just three in serious contention once in line for home.

NOTEBOOK
I See You, making her nursery debut from a mark of just 58, came out on top after a sustained battle with the runner-up. A likeable type, she will be even better suited by a return to 6f now she has learnt to settle and she can turn out over that trip under a penalty here next Thursday. (op 7-1)
Bookiesindexdotnet had shown much improved form to get off the mark at the fifth attempt in maiden company over this C&D. She looked potentially very well treated on a mark of just 65 and had the plum draw. Kieren Fallon rode a tactical race from the front, but in the end she was very much second best. (tchd 10-3)
Chicarito, with the cheekpieces retained on his second try in nursery company, had an inside draw on his all-weather debut. (op 8-1)
Princess Alessia, drawn wide and unable to go the pace, appeared very late on the scene. This was just her second start in nursery company and her best effort since finishing third on her second start three outings ago. She will be much better suited by a step up to six.
Wrapped Up, who ran over 7f on her previous start, did well considering she had the worst of the draw.
Mr Hendrix was reportedly never travelling. Official explanation: jockey said gelding was never travelling (op 5-1)

7453 CSP TRAFFIC MANAGEMENT H'CAP — 1m 2f (P)
3:30 (3:30) (Class 5) (0-75,75) 3-Y-O **£2,522** (£750; £375; £187) **Stalls** Low

Form RPR
1503 **1** **Spanish Plume**[29] 6978 3-9-5 **73** ChrisCatlin 11 81
(Reg Hollinshead) *sn trcking ldr: led wl over 2f out: drvn and styd on fr over 1f out: a holding on clsng stages* **10/1**
3621 **2** *1/2* **Love Your Looks**[21] 7144 3-8-11 **65** TonyCulhane 3 72
(Mike Murphy) *t.k.h: led 1f: styd chsng ldrs: wnt 2nd 2f out: rdn wl over 1f out: kpt on to cl on wnr fnl 50yds: a hld and hrd pressed for 2nd last strides* **5/2**[1]
6352 **3** *shd* **Conducting**[21] 7137 3-8-13 **67** RobertWinston 4 74
(Gay Kelleway) *t.k.h and hld up towards rr: hdwy and rdn over 1f out: styd on wl clsng stages to cl on 2nd last strides but nt rch wnr* **7/1**
341 **4** *3/4* **Full Bloom**[17] 7208 3-9-4 **75** (p) KieranO'Neill(3) 1 80
(Gerard Butler) *in tch: hdwy on ins over 1f out: styd on ins fnl f: one pce clsng stages* **13/2**[3]
0000 **5** *1/2* **Rasheed**[37] 6797 3-9-2 **70** WilliamBuick 6 74
(John Gosden) *chsd ldrs: drvn 2f out: outpcd appr fnl f* **11/2**[2]
2-05 **6** *5* **Barwick**[39] 6755 3-9-6 **74** KierenFallon 9 68
(Mark H Tompkins) *racd on outside: sn towards rr but in tch: hdwy on outer and rdn 3f out: nvr quite on terms and wknd appr fnl f* **5/2**[1]
0400 **7** *1 1/4* **Mafeteng**[16] 7236 3-8-12 **66** EddieAhern 10 58
(John Dunlop) *in rr and racd wd thrght: rdn 3f out and nvr in contention* **25/1**
0405 **8** *3/4* **Goldenveil (IRE)**[20] 7160 3-8-13 **74** GeorgeChaloner(7) 2 64
(Richard Fahey) *in tch whn hmpd and dropped to rr 6f out: rdn and stl in rr whn wd into st 2f out* **14/1**
0216 **9** *13* **High On The Hog (IRE)**[77] 5669 3-9-5 **73** TomMcLaughlin 8 37
(Paul Howling) *led after 1f: hdd wl over 2f out and sn btn* **33/1**

2m 6.31s (-1.69) **Going Correction** -0.15s/f (Stan) **9** Ran SP% **120.9**
Speed ratings (Par 102): **100,99,99,98,98 94,93,92,82**
Tote Swingers:1&2:£5.80, 2&3:£3.70, 1&3:£9.40 CSF £37.03 CT £195.98 TOTE £16.00: £3.70, £1.10, £2.80; EX 44.00 Trifecta £158.80 Pool £442.17 - 2.06 winning units..
Owner The Three R'S **Bred** Mrs J A Prescott **Trained** Upper Longdon, Staffs

FOCUS
A fair handicap in which the first two raced in the first three throughout. The first five are rated close to their marks.

7454 CSP CLEANING MAIDEN AUCTION STKS — 1m (P)
4:05 (4:05) (Class 6) 2-Y-O **£1,811** (£539; £269; £134) **Stalls** Low

Form RPR
020 **1** **Ocean Tempest**[20] 7167 2-8-10 78 KirstyMilczarek 5 78
(John Ryan) *sn led: jnd after 2f: narrowly hdd over 4f out: styd trcking ldrs: led again 2f out: sn hdd: styd chsng ldrs and kpt on wl fnl f to ld nr fin* **6/1**
533 **2** *1/2* **Cockney Rhyme**[20] 7164 2-7-11 78 NicoleNordblad(7) 3 71
(Heather Main) *trckd ldrs: hdwy on ins fr 3f out to ld ins fnl 2f: styd on wl fnl f: hdd and no ex nr fin* **11/4**[2]
62 **3** *1 1/4* **Hallmark Star**[20] 7177 2-8-13 0 DaneO'Neill 14 77
(Gerard Butler) *in rr: hdwy over 2f out: drvn and styd on to take 3rd 1f out: styd on but nt rch ldng duo clsng stages* **13/2**
0 **4** *2 1/4* **It's A Girl Thing (IRE)**[36] 6820 2-8-8 0 KierenFallon 7 67
(George Baker) *in tch: drvn and hdwy 3f out: chsd ldrs 2f out: styd on same pce* **20/1**
0 **5** *1/2* **Lady Sylvia**[51] 6462 2-8-5 0 LukeMorris 4 63+
(Joseph Tuite) *in rr: hdwy on outside over 2f out: chsd ldrs and styd on same pce fr over 1f out* **50/1**
6 *4* **Oratorian (IRE)** 2-8-10 0 ChrisCatlin 11 58
(Sylvester Kirk) *in rr: drvn along over 2f out: styd on ins fnl f but nvr any ch* **50/1**
7 *1 3/4* **Frock (IRE)** 2-8-5 0 NickyMackay 6 49
(Sylvester Kirk) *s.i.s: in rr: pushed along and styd on fr over 1f out: nvr any ch* **50/1**
033 **8** *1 3/4* **It's A Privilege**[31] 6928 2-8-13 77 MartinLane 10 53
(Ralph Beckett) *chsd ldrs: led over 4f out: hdd 2f out: wknd wl over 1f out* **9/2**[3]
44 **9** *5* **Engrossing**[30] 6954 2-8-13 0 WilliamBuick 9 42
(David Elsworth) *racd wd and w ldrs tl slt ld after 2f: hdd over 4f out: styd pressing ldr tl rdn 2f out: sn wknd: eased whn no ch ins fnl f* **5/2**[1]
10 *1* **Feb Thirtyfirst** 2-8-9 0 SamHitchcott 2 36
(Sheena West) *s.i.s: sn in tch: wknd ins fnl 3f* **33/1**
11 *1 1/4* **Rock Magic (IRE)**[69] 5949 2-8-5 0 JohnFahy(3) 8 32
(John Joseph Murphy, Ire) *chsd ldrs tl wknd qckly over 2f out* **16/1**
50 **12** *1 1/2* **Shredding (IRE)**[30] 6956 2-8-12 0 TonyCulhane 12 32
(Edward Vaughan) *s.i.s: a in rr* **33/1**

1m 39.24s (-0.56) **Going Correction** -0.15s/f (Stan) **12** Ran SP% **123.4**
Speed ratings (Par 94): **96,95,94,92,91 87,85,84,79,78 76,75**
Tote Swingers:1&2:£5.60, 2&3:£5.40, 1&3:£7.60 CSF £22.66 TOTE £8.10: £2.40, £1.10, £2.80; EX 33.10 Trifecta £232.50 Pool £392.76 - 1.25 winning units..
Owner W McLuskey & C Little **Bred** Old Mill Stud Ltd And Oomswell Ltd **Trained** Newmarket, Suffolk

FOCUS
A better-than-average maiden auction race for the time of the year.

NOTEBOOK
Ocean Tempest, who has plenty of size and scope, was absent for three months due to sore shins after finishing runner-up on his second start at Yarmouth in July. After breaking first, he was happy to accept a lead and, battling back in game fashion, put his head in front for a third time near the line. He will be suited by a return to 1m2f and there will be better to come at four.
Cockney Rhyme, rated 78, was a relatively cheap purchase and looked very well treated under bottom weight. Her promising 7lb claimer had to sit and suffer for a few strides when short of room once in line for home. Switched inside, she took a narrow advantage only to be worried out of it near the line. She can surely go one better. (op 3-1 tchd 5-2)
Hallmark Star, runner-up at Wolverhampton on his second start, had to bide his time from the worst of the draw. He stayed on in good style and this opens up the handicap route. (op 6-1 tchd 7-1)
It's A Girl Thing(IRE), up in trip on just her second start, still looked very inexperienced. She was pushed wide off the home turn and will improve again.
Lady Sylvia, far too keen on her only previous start on turf, settled better and showed ability, staying on steadily down the wide outside. (op 33-1)
Engrossing, on his toes beforehand on his third career start and all-weather debut, had to do too much running early on down the wide outside to contest the lead ahead of the winner. He stopped to nothing 2f out (which was later confirmed by the rider) and in the end was heavily eased. This may be best overlooked. Official explanation: jockey said colt stopped quickly (op 3-1)

7455 CSP VALET PARKING H'CAP — 1m (P)
4:35 (4:35) (Class 6) (0-65,65) 3-Y-O+ **£1,811** (£539; £269; £134) **Stalls** Low

Form RPR
1030 **1** **Spinning Ridge (IRE)**[20] 7175 6-9-3 **62** (v) LukeMorris 4 71
(Ronald Harris) *towards rr: hdwy and nt clr run over 2f out: drvn and qcknd to press ldr wl over 1f out: kpt on to chal jst ins fnl f and hung lft: sn led: drvn out* **16/1**
4025 **2** *1* **Woolston Ferry (IRE)**[16] 7228 5-9-6 **65** KierenFallon 11 72
(David Pinder) *in tch: hdwy on outside over 2f out to take slt ld wl over 1f out: jnd and bmpd jst ins fnl f: nt pce of wnr fnl 120yds* **5/1**[2]
6354 **3** *3/4* **Eastern Gift**[46] 6587 6-9-1 **60** RobertWinston 12 65
(Gay Kelleway) *in rr: rdn 2f out: hdwy wl over 1f out: styd on fnl f to take 3rd fnl 50yds: nt rch ldrs clsng stages* **8/1**
4122 **4** *1/2* **Know No Fear**[4] 7418 6-8-13 **65** (p) LeonnaMayor(7) 2 69
(Alastair Lidderdale) *t.k.h: in tch: hdwy and nt clr run over 1f out: styd on ins fnl f: gng on clsng stages* **7/2**[1]
3035 **5** *1/2* **Sarangoo**[42] 6664 3-9-4 **65** DaneO'Neill 8 68
(Malcolm Saunders) *s.i.s: in rr: hdwy on outside wl over 1f out: kpt on clsng stages nt rch ldrs* **16/1**
0316 **6** *3/4* **Dichoh**[37] 6784 8-9-0 **59** (p) ChrisCatlin 1 60
(Michael Madgwick) *led 1f: styd chsng ldrs: rdn over 2f out: one pce fnl f* **14/1**
5400 **7** *hd* **Cyflymder (IRE)**[4] 7418 5-9-3 **62** SteveDrowne 13 63
(David C Griffiths) *chsd ldrs: slt ld appr fnl 2f: hdd wl over 1f out: wknd fnl f* **14/1**
4003 **8** *1 3/4* **Fleetwoodsands (IRE)**[4] 7418 4-9-0 **62** (t) JohnFahy(3) 7 59
(Milton Bradley) *chsd ldrs: chal fr over 2f out tl over 1f out: wknd ins fnl f* **13/2**[3]
0065 **9** *1/2* **Councellor (FR)**[3] 7425 9-9-6 **65** (t) RobbieFitzpatrick 6 61
(Derek Shaw) *in tch 1/2-way: pushed along over 2f out: styd on same pce fr over 1f out* **16/1**
2000 **10** *3/4* **Blue Deer (IRE)**[17] 7208 3-9-3 **64** EddieAhern 10 58
(John Akehurst) *s.i.s: in rr: pushed along fr 2f out: nvr gng pce to get into contention* **15/2**
1630 **11** *5* **Hecton Lad (USA)**[141] 3568 4-9-5 **64** (b) FrederikTylicki 5 46
(John Best) *pushed along and hdwy to ld after 1f: hdd appr fnl 2f: sn wknd* **8/1**
12 *1* **Raise The Rafters (IRE)**[143] 3502 6-9-0 **62** KieranO'Neill(3) 9 42
(Pat Murphy) *bhd most of way* **66/1**
0060 **13** *1 3/4* **Come On Safari (IRE)**[21] 7146 4-9-4 **63** (v1) MartinHarley 14 39
(Joseph Tuite) *chsd ldrs until wknd over 2f out* **25/1**
-006 **14** *18* **Green Pearl (IRE)**[147] 3363 3-9-4 **65** MartinLane 3 —
(Ralph Beckett) *s.i.s: sn in tch and chsd ldrs over 3f out: wknd fr 2f out: eased whn no ch fnl f* **20/1**

1m 38.84s (-0.96) **Going Correction** -0.15s/f (Stan)
WFA 3 from 4yo+ 2lb **14** Ran SP% **127.3**
Speed ratings (Par 101): **98,97,96,95,95 94,94,92,92,91 86,85,83,65**
Tote Swingers:1&2:£24.30, 2&3:£5.90, 1&3:£22.70 CSF £97.89 CT £733.93 TOTE £23.90: £4.90, £2.70, £2.60; EX 74.50 TRIFECTA Not won..
Owner Robert & Nina Bailey **Bred** Eddie O'Leary **Trained** Earlswood, Monmouths

FOCUS
A modest handicap run at a strong pace and the first three home came from off the pace. The third and fourth are rated close to their recent marks.

7456 CSP SECURITY AND STEWARDING H'CAP (DIV I) — 6f (P)
5:05 (5:06) (Class 4) (0-85,85) 3-Y-O+ **£4,204** (£1,251; £625; £312) **Stalls** Low

Form RPR
0100 **1** **Main Beach**[2] 7438 4-9-0 **78** (t) MickyFenton 5 90
(Tobias B P Coles) *stdd s: in rr and hld up: looking for a gap over 2f out: gd hdwy on ins wl over 1f out: str run to ld fnl 150yds: edgd lft: readily* **8/1**
2040 **2** *1 1/4* **Mac Gille Eoin**[22] 7127 7-9-4 **85** JohnFahy(3) 4 93
(John Gallagher) *sn led: rdn over 1f out: edgd lft and rdn fnl 150yds: one pce* **5/1**[2]
2360 **3** *1 1/2* **Night Trade (IRE)**[14] 7262 4-9-1 **79** LukeMorris 3 82
(Ronald Harris) *chsd ldrs: wnt 2nd over 1f out but no imp: one pce and hung lft ins fnl f* **8/1**

2611 **4** 1/2 **Silenzio**[58] 6246 3-8-13 **77** .... DaneO'Neill 12 78
(Richard Hannon) *hld up in rr: drvn and hdwy over 1f out: nt qckn ins fnl f* **9/2**[1]

0060 **5** 1 **Gap Princess (IRE)**[24] 7074 7-8-12 **76** .... RobertWinston 1 74
(Geoffrey Harker) *chsd ldrs: rdn 2f out: wknd fnl f* **10/1**

5-50 **6** nk **Ventura Cove (IRE)**[27] 7039 4-8-7 **71** oh1 ....(b[1]) FrederikTylicki 6 68
(Richard Fahey) *in rr: hdwy towards ins 2f out: nvr rchd ldrs and one pce fr over 1f out* **20/1**

3504 **7** 2 1/4 **Cardinal**[39] 6762 6-8-8 **72** .... EddieAhern 7 62
(Robert Cowell) *s.i.s: in rr: sme hdwy 2f out and sn in bhd ldrs: no further prog and no ch fnl f* **15/2**

0464 **8** 1 1/4 **Sand Owl**[32] 6913 3-9-0 **78** ....(p) WilliamBuick 9 64
(Peter Chapple-Hyam) *sn trcking ldr: pushed along 2f out: wknd fnl f* **13/2**[3]

1600 **9** 1/2 **Serena's Pride**[29] 6974 3-8-11 **75** .... MartinLane 2 59
(Alan Jarvis) *plld hrd: chsd ldrs tl wknd over 1f out* **20/1**

3110 **10** 1 **Shifting Star (IRE)**[29] 6974 6-9-2 **83** .... KieranO'Neill(3) 11 64
(John Bridger) *in tch: sme hdwy towards outside over 2f out: nvr rchd ldrs and wknd over 1f out* **7/1**

5-06 **11** 4 1/2 **Barbieri (IRE)**[200] 1758 3-9-2 **80** ....(t) SteveDrowne 8 47
(Jeremy Gask) *in tch tl wknd over 2f out* **12/1**

1m 11.66s (-1.44) **Going Correction** -0.15s/f (Stan) **11** Ran SP% **121.0**
Speed ratings (Par 105): **103,101,99,98,97 96,93,92,91,90 84**
Tote Swingers:1&2:£8.30, 2&3:£8.10, 1&3:£15.80 CSF £49.22 CT £334.04 TOTE £10.40: £3.80, £2.50, £2.80; EX 67.20 Trifecta £284.00 Pool £433.73 - 1.13 winning units..
Owner Mrs R Coles **Bred** Miss J Chaplin **Trained** Newmarket, Suffolk

FOCUS
Part one of a competitive 71-85 sprint handicap. The placed horses set the level.
Serena's Pride Official explanation: jockey said filly ran too freely

7457 CSP SECURITY AND STEWARDING H'CAP (DIV II) 6f (P)
5:35 (5:35) (Class 4) (0-85,85) 3-Y-O+ **£4,204** (£1,251; £625; £312) **Stalls** Low

Form RPR

00 **1** **Googlette (IRE)**[104] 4779 3-9-6 **84** .... KierenFallon 9 93
(Edward Vaughan) *plld hrd: chsd ldrs: wnt 2nd over 3f out: led over 1f out: strly chal fr ins fnl f: drvn and a jst doing enough fnl 100yds* **8/1**

4055 **2** hd **New Leyf (IRE)**[29] 6974 5-9-7 **85** .... SteveDrowne 1 93
(Ed Walker) *t.k.h: chsd ldrs: wnt 2nd over 1f out and str chal fr ins fnl f: kpt on wl fnl 100yds but a jst hld* **5/1**[3]

6350 **3** 1 3/4 **Lujeanie**[41] 6703 5-9-3 **81** ....(p) MartinLane 8 83+
(Dean Ivory) *in rr: drvn and hdwy over 1f out to take 3rd ins fnl f: kpt on but no imp on ldng duo* **14/1**

261 **4** nk **Scarlet Rocks (IRE)**[32] 6920 3-8-7 **71** ....(tp) NickyMackay 10 72
(George Baker) *plld hrd: led: rdn and hdd over 1f out: lost 3rd ins fnl f: kpt on clsng stages* **25/1**

5110 **5** 1/2 **Emiratesdotcom**[29] 6974 5-9-0 **78** .... ChrisCatlin 3 78
(Milton Bradley) *in tch: rdn over 2f out: kpt on ins fnl f: gng on cl home* **14/1**

2621 **6** 1/2 **Aristeia**[99] 4973 3-9-0 **78** .... DaneO'Neill 5 76
(Richard Hannon) *s.i.s and hmpd s: hdwy on ins 2f out: kpt on fnl f: nt rch ldrs* **14/1**

1506 **7** hd **Italian Tom (IRE)**[32] 6913 4-8-12 **76** .... LukeMorris 2 74
(Ronald Harris) *chsd ldrs: drvn 2f out: styd on ins fnl f* **12/1**

0424 **8** 1/2 **Psychic's Dream**[29] 6974 3-9-0 **78** .... JimmyQuinn 4 74
(Marco Botti) *in tch: drvn and styd on same pce fr over 1f out* **13/2**

3460 **9** 1 1/4 **Arctic Lynx (IRE)**[20] 7171 4-8-8 **75** .... JohnFahy(3) 6 67
(John Best) *plld hrd: rdr: a outpcd* **4/1**[2]

10 **10** 2 **Intercept (IRE)**[20] 7171 3-9-2 **80** .... WilliamBuick 7 66
(John Gosden) *t.k.h: chsd ldrs: drvn 2f out: wknd over 1f out* **3/1**[1]

1m 12.15s (-0.95) **Going Correction** -0.15s/f (Stan) **10** Ran SP% **117.6**
Speed ratings (Par 105): **100,99,97,97,96 95,95,94,93,90**
Tote Swingers:1&2:£3.90, 2&3:£13.50, 1&3:£23.70 CSF £48.22 CT £572.04 TOTE £10.40: £3.00, £1.80, £4.30; EX 55.00 Trifecta £338.10 Part won. Pool £457.01 - 0.50 winning units..
Owner Pearl Bloodstock Ltd **Bred** Ged O'Leary **Trained** Newmarket, Suffolk

FOCUS
Part two and equally competitive, though the time was noticeably slower. The runner-up sets the level.

7458 CSP CSAS H'CAP 1m 3f (P)
6:05 (6:05) (Class 5) (0-75,73) 3-Y-O+ **£2,522** (£750; £375; £187) **Stalls** Low

Form RPR

0044 **1** **Beat Route**[8] 7346 4-8-12 **64** .... JohnFahy(3) 6 74+
(Michael Attwater) *mid-div: hdwy 3f out: drvn to ld appr fnl f: r.o strly clsng stages* **4/1**[1]

0314 **2** 1/2 **Brigadoon**[16] 7237 4-9-10 **73** .... DaneO'Neill 7 81
(William Jarvis) *in rr: hdwy 2f out: drvn and r.o wl to chse wnr fnl 75yds: kpt on cl home but a hld* **6/1**[2]

4366 **3** 1 1/4 **Ay Tay Tate (IRE)**[16] 7237 5-9-0 **63** ....(p) TonyCulhane 4 69
(David C Griffiths) *chsd ldrs: ev ch fr 2f out: chsd wnr ins fnl f but no imp: one pce into 3rd fnl 75yds* **14/1**

01 **4** 1/2 **Winning Spark (USA)**[30] 6947 4-9-9 **72** .... FergusSweeney 9 77
(Gary Moore) *in rr: gd hdwy on ins over 2f out: drvn to chal appr fnl f: wknd fnl 75yds* **7/1**

0456 **5** 2 1/4 **Choral Festival**[8] 7347 5-9-5 **68** .... NeilChalmers 5 69
(John Bridger) *chsd ldrs: rdn over 2f out: ev ch over 1f out: wknd ins fnl f* **20/1**

1201 **6** hd **Tegan (IRE)**[33] 6894 3-9-0 **71** .... KieranO'Neill(3) 13 72
(Richard Hannon) *chsd ldr: led 3f out: rdn and kpt slt advantage fr over 2f out tl hdd & wknd appr fnl f* **6/1**[2]

2132 **7** 1 **Hygrove Welshlady (IRE)**[15] 7255 3-8-8 **69** .... BrendanPowell(7) 1 68
(J W Hills) *chsd ldrs: rdn over 2f out: ev ch over 1f out: wknd fnl f* **13/2**[3]

-404 **8** 2 1/4 **Spey Song (IRE)**[39] 6756 3-9-2 **70** ....(p) WilliamBuick 3 65
(James Bethell) *s.i.s: in rr: pushed along and sme hdwy fr 2f out: nvr rchd ldrs and one pce fnl f* **7/1**

0433 **9** 6 **Zenarinda**[17] 7215 4-9-1 **64** .... KierenFallon 2 48
(Mark H Tompkins) *chsd ldrs: rdn 3f out: wknd appr fnl 2f* **7/1**

0000 **10** 3/4 **Time Square (FR)**[15] 7254 4-9-1 **64** .... LukeMorris 10 47
(Tony Carroll) *s.i.s: in rr: sme hdwy on ins over 2f out: nvr nr ldrs* **33/1**

0323 **11** 3/4 **Potentiale (IRE)**[27] 7036 7-9-1 **71** .... Leah-AnneAvery(7) 14 52
(J W Hills) *racd on outside: nvr beyond mid-div* **25/1**

6306 **12** hd **Tiny Temper (IRE)**[46] 6577 3-8-12 **66** .... FrederikTylicki 8 47
(Richard Fahey) *mid-div: rdn 3f out and no imp on ldrs: wknd over 2f out* **20/1**

0000 **13** 18 **Flag Of Glory**[6] 7397 4-9-7 **70** .... ChrisCatlin 12 18
(Peter Hiatt) *chsd ldrs 7f: eased whn no ch fnl f* **33/1**

1200 **14** 3/4 **Allanit (GER)**[120] 4253 7-9-1 **64** .... MickyFenton 11 11
(Barney Curley) *led: clr 7f out: hdd 3f out and sn btn* **20/1**

2m 18.69s (-3.21) **Going Correction** -0.15s/f (Stan)
WFA 3 from 4yo+ 5lb **14** Ran SP% **130.1**
Speed ratings (Par 103): **105,104,103,103,101 101,100,99,94,94 93,93,80,79**
Tote Swingers:1&2:£5.70, 2&3:£19.40, 1&3:£13.70 CSF £26.91 CT £322.67 TOTE £4.40: £1.50, £2.30, £5.60; EX 34.30 Trifecta £230.20 Part won. Pool £311.12 - 0.63 winning units..
Owner Canisbay Bloodstock **Bred** Canisbay Bloodstock Ltd **Trained** Epsom, Surrey

FOCUS
A modest handicap run at a furious pace. The clear leader went much too fast and finished tailed off in the end. There were five almost in a line a furlong from home but the pace was sound and the form looks pretty solid.
Beat Route Official explanation: two-day ban: used whip with excessive frequency (Dec 2-3)
T/Jkpt: Not won. T/Plt: £1,168.20 to a £1 stake. Pool £48,314.19. 30.19 winning tickets. T/Qpdt: £54.10 to a £1 stake. Pool £4,624.26. 63.15 winning tickets. ST

7411 WOLVERHAMPTON (A.W) (L-H)
Friday, November 18

OFFICIAL GOING: Standard
Wind: Fresh behind Weather: Overcast

7459 32REDBET.COM APPRENTICE H'CAP 5f 216y(P)
4:15 (4:15) (Class 6) (0-52,58) 3-Y-O+ **£1,704** (£503; £251) **Stalls** Low

Form RPR

U640 **1** **Chester Deelyte (IRE)**[7] 7366 3-8-7 **48** ....(v) ShirleyTeasdale(5) 6 59
(Lisa Williamson) *a.p: led ins fnl f: r.o* **33/1**

0666 **2** 1 1/2 **Young Simon**[7] 7371 4-8-9 **52** ....(v) RichardOld(7) 12 58
(George Margarson) *hld up: hdwy over 1f out: sn rdn: r.o to go 2nd post: nt rch wnr* **5/1**[3]

4342 **3** nk **Little Perisher**[41] 6696 4-9-2 **52** ow2 ....(b) MichaelJMurphy 9 57
(Graeme McPherson) *a.p: rdn over 1f out: r.o* **11/4**[1]

0523 **4** 1 3/4 **Metropolitan Chief**[199] 1787 7-9-0 **50** .... NatashaEaton 5 49
(Paul Burgoyne) *chsd ldrs: led 2f out: rdn and hdd ins fnl f: styd on same pce* **12/1**

2464 **5** 1 1/4 **Ad Vitam (IRE)**[7] 7371 3-8-9 **52** ....(v) ClaireMurray(7) 13 47
(David C Griffiths) *hld up: edgd lft and r.o ins fnl f: nvr nrr* **9/2**[2]

5/04 **6** hd **Perfect Honour (IRE)**[67] 5996 5-9-2 **52** .... ThomasBrown 7 47
(Des Donovan) *hld up: hdwy over 1f out: hung lft ins fnl f: styd on: nt rch ldrs* **16/1**

5300 **7** 1 **Whats For Pudding (IRE)**[14] 7268 3-8-13 **49** .... JasonHart 1 41
(Declan Carroll) *led: pushed along and hdd 2f out: sn rdn: wknd ins fnl f* **7/1**

6310 **8** 3/4 **Memphis Man**[3] 7420 8-9-3 **58** 6ex .... KevinLundie(5) 3 47
(David Evans) *hld up: racd keenly: shkn up over 2f out: styd on ins fnl f* **13/2**

2060 **9** 1 1/4 **Poppet's Joy**[7] 7371 3-9-1 **51** .... JackDuern 2 36
(Reg Hollinshead) *chsd ldrs: rdn over 1f out: wknd fnl f* **16/1**

0040 **10** 1 1/4 **Porthgwidden Beach (USA)**[16] 7224 3-9-2 **52** ....(t) NoelGarbutt 4 33
(Anthony Middleton) *chsd ldr: ev ch 2f out: wknd over 1f out* **20/1**

0000 **11** 11 **Bertbrand**[7] 7366 6-8-12 **48** ....(b) GeorgeDowning 11 —
(Ian McInnes) *dwlt: a in rr: wknd 1/2-way* **50/1**

1m 15.23s (0.23) **Going Correction** -0.025s/f (Stan) **11** Ran SP% **116.5**
Speed ratings (Par 101): **97,95,94,92,90 90,89,88,86,84 70**
Tote Swingers:1&2:£45.70, 2&3:£3.90, 1&3:£27.20 CSF £187.19 CT £618.80 TOTE £67.10: £12.80, £2.50, £1.70; EX 576.20.
Owner Hindford Oak Racing **Bred** Yeomanstown Stud **Trained** Saighton, Cheshire

FOCUS
A poor race won by one of the two bottom weights. The winner is rated back to his summer turf best, with the runner-up slightly better than his recent C&D form.
Chester Deelyte(IRE) Official explanation: trainer said, regarding the apparent improvement in form shown, filly benefited from a more patient ride and a better draw

7460 £32 FREE AT 32RED.COM MAIDEN STKS 5f 216y(P)
4:45 (4:46) (Class 5) 3-4-Y-O **£2,264** (£673; £336; £168) **Stalls** Low

Form RPR

-302 **1** **Excellent Aim**[15] 7245 4-9-3 61 ....(t) JamieSpencer 8 67
(George Margarson) *led 1f: chsd ldr tl led over 1f out: sn rdn and edgd lft: r.o* **6/4**[1]

0002 **2** 4 1/2 **Welsh Dancer**[14] 7260 3-9-3 55 .... WilliamCarson 3 53
(Ronald Harris) *sn pushed along towwards rr: hdwy u.p over 1f out: styd on to go 2nd wl ins fnl f: no ch w wnr* **15/2**[3]

-604 **3** 1/2 **Good Timin'**[15] 7245 3-9-3 52 ....(v) GrahamGibbons 4 51
(David Brown) *chsd ldrs: hmpd 5f out: rdn over 1f out: styd on same pce fnl f* **8/1**

4400 **4** 3/4 **Hootys Agogo**[41] 6694 3-8-10 46 ....(p) JasonHart(7) 7 49
(Declan Carroll) *mid-div: rdn over 1f out: styd on same pce* **22/1**

0000 **5** hd **Dililah**[29] 6982 3-8-12 47 .... ShaneKelly 9 43
(Linda Stubbs) *prom: rdn over 1f out: styd on same pce* **33/1**

6 **6** 2 1/4 **Cri Na Mara (IRE)**[84] 5433 3-8-8 40 ow1 ....(t) LMcNiff(5) 11 37
(Mark Michael McNiff, Ire) *led 5f out: rdn and hdd over 1f out: edgd lft and wknd fnl f* **20/1**

064/ **7** 1 1/2 **Sovereign Secure (IRE)**[21] 7148 4-8-12 58 .... StephenCraine 5 31
(Peter McCreery, Ire) *chsd ldrs: rdn over 2f out: wknd fnl f* **5/2**[2]

6600 **8** nk **Running Water**[62] 6175 3-8-12 42 .... PaddyAspell 6 30
(Hugh McWilliams) *s.s: a in rr* **66/1**

000- **9** 10 **Fire Commander**[349] 7700 3-9-3 0 .... J-PGuillambert 2 —
(Brian Baugh) *s.i.s: a in rr: lost tch 1/2-way* **40/1**

0 **10** hd **Powerball (IRE)**[23] 7093 3-8-9 0 .... RobertLButler(3) 1 —
(Lisa Williamson) *s.i.s: a in rr: bhd fr 1/2-way* **100/1**

11 4 1/2 **Tunza The Lion** 4-9-3 0 .... LiamJones 10 —
(Bruce Hellier) *plld hrd and prom: wknd wl over 1f out* **20/1**

1m 15.4s (0.40) **Going Correction** -0.025s/f (Stan) **11** Ran SP% **113.2**
Speed ratings (Par 103): **96,90,89,88,88 85,83,82,69,69 63**
Tote Swingers:1&2:£2.30, 2&3:£4.00, 1&3:£3.40 CSF £11.66 TOTE £2.40: £1.30, £2.50, £2.20; EX 9.90.
Owner Norcroft Park Stud **Bred** Norcroft Park Stud **Trained** Newmarket, Suffolk
■ Stewards' Enquiry : Stephen Craine two-day ban: careless riding (Dec 2-3)

FOCUS
This was never going to take much winning. The form looks messy with the winner not needing to improve on recent form to score.
Good Timin' Official explanation: jockey said gelding ran too free in the early stages

The Form Book, Raceform Ltd, Compton, RG20 6NL

Fire Commander Official explanation: jockey said gelding did not face the kick-back

7461 32RED.COM H'CAP 1m 5f 194y(P)
5:15 (5:16) (Class 5) (0-75,74) 3-Y-O+ **£2,264** (£673; £336; £168) **Stalls** Low

Form RPR
5561 **1** **Appeal (IRE)**[7] 7363 3-8-9 **63** StevieDonohoe 2 75+
(Sir Mark Prescott Bt) *a.p: chsd ldr over 1f out: rdn to ld ins fnl f: edgd lft: styd on* **13/8**[1]
0611 **2** *1 ¼* **Vittachi**[24] 7078 4-9-0 **60** JamieSpencer 6 70
(Alistair Whillans) *hld up: hdwy to ld 3f out: rdn and hung lft over 1f out: hdd and unable qck ins fnl f* **6/1**[2]
0221 **3** *1* **Body Language (IRE)**[25] 7062 3-9-5 **73** (p) DavidNolan 4 82
(Ann Duffield) *chsd ldrs: pushed along 3f out: rdn over 1f out: styd on same pce ins fnl f* **8/1**[3]
4663 **4** *8* **Dazzling Valentine**[16] 7237 3-9-3 **74** DominicFox(3) 8 72
(Alan Bailey) *hld up: hdwy over 2f out: wknd over 1f out* **10/1**
-263 **5** *5* **Jezza**[10] 872 5-9-13 **73** (p) ShaneKelly 3 64
(Victor Dartnall) *s.s: hld up: pushed along 1/2-way: hung lft ins fnl f: nvr on terms* **6/1**[2]
5500 **6** *nk* **Pelham Crescent (IRE)**[28] 7002 8-9-7 **74** ThomasBrown(7) 5 64
(Bryn Palling) *s.i.s: hld up: rdn 3f out: wknd over 2f out* **22/1**
0421 **7** *2 ½* **Ninfea (IRE)**[22] 7122 3-8-9 **63** (p) LiamKeniry 1 50
(Sylvester Kirk) *chsd ldrs tl rdn and wknd over 2f out* **8/1**[3]
0 **8** *4* **Rosenblatt (GER)**[119] 4273 9-8-9 **55** oh6 WilliamCarson 7 36
(John Spearing) *hld up: wknd over 2f out* **33/1**
4504 **9** *1 ¾* **Cloudy Start**[38] 6769 5-9-8 **71** (p) SophieDoyle(3) 9 50
(Jamie Osborne) *led: rdn and hdd 3f out: wknd over 2f out* **25/1**
0543 **10** *51* **Treacle Tart**[79] 5628 6-9-8 **68** AdamKirby 10 —
(James Ewart) *sn chsng ldr: rdn 5f out: wknd 3f out: eased: t.o* **20/1**

3m 3.28s (-2.72) **Going Correction** -0.025s/f (Stan)
WFA 3 from 4yo+ 8lb **10** Ran SP% **113.9**
Speed ratings (Par 103): **106,105,104,100,97 97,95,93,92,63**
Tote Swingers:1&2:£2.90, 2&3:£6.40, 1&3:£3.20 CSF £10.24 CT £59.42 TOTE £1.50: £1.02, £3.10, £2.60; EX 9.20.
Owner Denford Stud **Bred** Norelands Stallions **Trained** Newmarket, Suffolk

FOCUS
Not a bad little handicap as it featured several in-form horses. The form looks fair for the grade.
Ninfea(IRE) Official explanation: jockey said filly hung left in the straight
Treacle Tart Official explanation: jockey said mare hung right throughout

7462 32RED CASINO H'CAP (DIV I) 7f 32y(P)
5:45 (5:46) (Class 6) (0-60,60) 3-Y-O+ **£1,704** (£503; £251) **Stalls** High

Form RPR
5516 **1** **Silver Wind**[35] 6841 6-9-7 **60** (b) ShaneKelly 9 72
(Alan McCabe) *hld up: hdwy 1/2-way: chsd ldr 2f out: rdn to ld 1f out: r.o* **5/1**[3]
0112 **2** *2* **Michael's Nook**[14] 7268 4-9-0 **58** LMcNiff(5) 10 65+
(David Barron) *led 6f out: clr over 2f out: rdn and hdd 1f out: styd on same pce* **11/10**[1]
0604 **3** *¾* **Fault**[4] 7412 5-9-0 **58** AmyScott(5) 5 63+
(Alastair Lidderdale) *trckd ldrs: nt clr run over 2f out: shkn up over 1f out: styd on* **9/2**[2]
0000 **4** *¾* **Cabal**[34] 6871 4-8-9 **48** (p) AndrewMullen 7 51
(Andrew Crook) *s.i.s: hdwy over 4f out: chsd wnr over 2f out: sn rdn: styd on same pce fr over 1f out* **25/1**
1440 **5** *3 ¼* **Ace Master**[173] 2524 3-9-5 **59** RussKennemore 6 53
(Roy Bowring) *hld up: styd on fr over 1f out: nvr trbld ldrs* **22/1**
0204 **6** *1 ¾* **The Name Is Frank**[22] 7123 6-9-5 **58** (p) AdamKirby 4 47
(Mark Gillard) *led 1f: chsd ldrs: rdn over 2f out: wknd over 1f out* **14/1**
0-20 **7** *¾* **Cheers**[28] 7001 3-9-2 **56** FrankieMcDonald 3 43
(Oliver Sherwood) *hld up: n.d* **20/1**
0304 **8** *3* **Violet's Gift (IRE)**[24] 7084 3-9-1 **55** StevieDonohoe 2 34
(James Fanshawe) *prom: pushed along 1/2-way: wknd over 2f out* **15/2**
0006 **9** *10* **Colamandis**[4] 7411 4-8-1 **47** ow1 (t) VictorSantos(7) 12 —
(Hugh McWilliams) *s.i.s: hdwy to chse ldr over 5f out tl rdn over 2f out: sn wknd* **100/1**

1m 29.05s (-0.55) **Going Correction** -0.025s/f (Stan)
WFA 3 from 4yo+ 1lb **9** Ran SP% **114.8**
Speed ratings (Par 101): **102,99,98,98,94 92,91,88,76**
Tote Swingers:1&2:£2.20, 2&3:£2.30, 1&3:£4.40 CSF £10.41 CT £26.21 TOTE £6.50: £2.20, £1.10, £1.40; EX 13.80.
Owner Derek Buckley **Bred** W H R John And Partners **Trained** Averham Park, Notts

FOCUS
The right horses came to the fore here and the form looks solid enough for the level, rated around the winner and third.
Ace Master Official explanation: jockey said gelding fly leapt out of the stalls
The Name Is Frank Official explanation: jockey said gelding ran too free to the start
Violet's Gift(IRE) Official explanation: jockey said filly hung left and did not face the kick-back

7463 32RED CASINO H'CAP (DIV II) 7f 32y(P)
6:15 (6:15) (Class 6) (0-60,60) 3-Y-O+ **£1,704** (£503; £251) **Stalls** High

Form RPR
6033 **1** **Aerodynamic (IRE)**[20] 7159 4-9-7 **60** PaddyAspell 1 74
(Clive Mulhall) *a.p: led over 1f out: sn rdn: jst hld on* **6/4**[1]
0045 **2** *hd* **Pipers Piping (IRE)**[14] 7268 5-9-1 **59** (p) AmyScott(5) 8 72
(Alastair Lidderdale) *hld up: hdwy over 1f out: rdn to chse wnr fnl f: r.o* **7/2**[2]
0523 **3** *3 ½* **Fluctuation (IRE)**[7] 7371 3-8-9 **52** (p) RyanClark(3) 7 56
(Ian Williams) *hld up: hdwy over 2f out: rdn over 1f out: hung lft and no ex ins fnl f* **8/1**
2206 **4** *3 ½* **Fortunate Bid (IRE)**[70] 5902 5-9-3 **59** (p) MichaelO'Connell(3) 3 53
(Linda Stubbs) *hld up in tch: rdn and wknd fnl f* **9/1**
-500 **5** *4 ½* **Lady Deanie (IRE)**[18] 7198 3-8-4 **49** CharlesBishop(5) 9 31
(Bryn Palling) *hld up: plld hrd: outpcd over 2f out: styd on ins fnl f: n.d* **80/1**
0006 **6** *shd* **Meydan Style (USA)**[28] 7006 5-8-7 **46** LiamJones 5 28
(Bruce Hellier) *led: rdn and hdd over 1f out: sn wknd* **16/1**
0630 **7** *¾* **Tawseef (IRE)**[21] 7144 3-9-1 **55** ShaneKelly 2 35
(Roy Brotherton) *hld up: hdwy over 2f out: nt clr run and wknd over 1f out* **40/1**
0600 **8** *nk* **Carrie's Magic**[17] 7216 4-9-0 **58** (b) GarryWhillans(5) 4 37
(Alistair Whillans) *chsd ldrs: rdn over 2f out: wknd over 1f out* **28/1**
0506 **9** *3* **Silly Billy (IRE)**[20] 7176 3-9-0 **59** JemmaMarshall(5) 11 30
(Sylvester Kirk) *sn bhd* **20/1**
2452 **10** *23* **Yanbu (USA)**[119] 4278 6-9-3 **56** AndreaAtzeni 6 —
(Tobias B P Coles) *chsd ldr tl pushed along 1/2-way: wknd over 2f out: t.o* **9/2**[3]

1m 28.74s (-0.86) **Going Correction** -0.025s/f (Stan)
WFA 3 from 4yo+ 1lb **10** Ran SP% **119.3**
Speed ratings (Par 101): **103,102,98,94,89 89,88,88,84,58**
Tote Swingers:1&2:£2.70, 2&3:£3.10, 1&3:£3.70 CSF £6.62 CT £32.89 TOTE £2.70: £1.50, £1.10, £2.70; EX 11.40.
Owner Mrs C M Mulhall **Bred** Swettenham, Carradale, S Cosgrove & T Stack **Trained** Scarcroft, W Yorks

■ Stewards' Enquiry : Amy Scott seven-day ban: used whip with excessive frequency (Dec 2,3,5-9)

FOCUS
Marginally the quicker of the two divisions and the form looks solid.

7464 32REDPOKER.COM MAIDEN AUCTION STKS 7f 32y(P)
6:45 (6:46) (Class 6) 2-Y-O **£1,617** (£481; £240; £120) **Stalls** High

Form RPR
5006 **1** **The Name Is Don (IRE)**[15] 7242 2-8-9 57 LiamKeniry 8 72
(Mark Gillard) *mde all: rdn over 1f out: styd on* **40/1**
0423 **2** *1 ½* **Remix (IRE)**[31] 6927 2-8-6 67 LiamJones 7 66
(J W Hills) *prom: pushed along 1/2-way: rdn over 1f out: r.o to go 2nd ins fnl f: nt rch wnr* **7/2**[3]
025 **3** *2 ¼* **Flamborough Breeze**[84] 5424 2-8-6 76 WilliamCarson 3 60
(Edward Vaughan) *chsd wnr: rdn over 1f out: styd on same pce ins fnl f* **3/1**[2]
6330 **4** *1 ¾* **Millibar (IRE)**[27] 7028 2-7-13 79 RichardOld(7) 2 56
(Nick Littmoden) *hld up: hdwy over 1f out: rdn to go 4th wl ins fnl f: too much to do* **9/4**[1]
05 **5** *½* **One More Roman (IRE)**[27] 7038 2-8-10 0 ow1 (bt) JamieSpencer 6 58
(J S Moore) *prom: shkn up and hung lft over 1f out: no ex* **5/1**
0 **6** *9* **Rhyme Royal**[17] 7210 2-8-4 0 KellyHarrison 4 32+
(James Given) *chsd ldrs tl wknd over 2f out* **50/1**
7 *¾* **Lady Lyricist** 2-8-4 0 AndreaAtzeni 5 29+
(Reg Hollinshead) *s.s: a in rr: lost tch fnl 3f* **25/1**
8 *5* **Applaudere** 2-8-5 0 SophieDoyle(3) 1 20+
(Jamie Osborne) *s.s: a in rr: bhd fnl 3f* **12/1**

1m 30.29s (0.69) **Going Correction** -0.025s/f (Stan) **8** Ran SP% **110.6**
Speed ratings (Par 94): **95,93,90,88,88 77,77,71**
Tote Swingers:1&2:£16.30, 2&3:£2.60, 1&3:£16.90 CSF £164.58 TOTE £76.90: £12.00, £1.60, £1.10; EX 207.20.
Owner Don Hazzard **Bred** C M Farrell **Trained** Holwell, Dorset

FOCUS
No-one wanted to go on in this maiden and Liam Keniry took full advantage.

NOTEBOOK
The Name Is Don(IRE) was sent on as nothing else wanted to lead, and soon built up a clear advantage. He slowed things down at the end of the back straight, but then kicked again on the turn and soon had the rest in trouble. While the form might be unreliable (time was slower than both divisions of the 0-60 handicap earlier on the card), he clearly acts well on this surface and should be able to find a little handicap if the assessor doesn't take this form literally. Official explanation: trainer's rep said, regarding the apparent improvement in form shown, gelding benefited from a more positive ride (op 50-1)
Remix(IRE), who would have been 13lb worse off with the winner had this been a handicap, got a little outpaced leaving the back straight before finishing her race off well. She could have done with a more even gallop. (op 4-1 tchd 9-2)
Flamborough Breeze, a little keen in pursuit of the winner, was left behind from the turn in and may have needed this following almost three months off. (op 9-4)
Millibar(IRE) was staying on all too late under her inexperienced rider and is another who would have benefited from a stronger all-round gallop. (op 2-1)
One More Roman(IRE), whose rider put up 1lb overweight, found disappointingly little under pressure. Handicaps are now an option, though. (op 11-2 tchd 9-2)

7465 32RED H'CAP 1m 141y(P)
7:15 (7:15) (Class 5) (0-75,75) 3-Y-O+ **£2,587** (£770; £384; £192) **Stalls** Low

Form RPR
2055 **1** **Epernay**[33] 6888 4-8-11 **68** (bt[1]) MichaelO'Connell(3) 9 78
(Ian Williams) *s.i.s: hld up: hdwy over 3f out: chsd ldr over 2f out: rdn to ld and hung lft ins fnl f: r.o* **7/1**[3]
1306 **2** *1 ½* **I Confess**[107] 4679 6-9-3 **71** (b) AndrewMullen 10 78
(Geoffrey Harker) *sn led: hdd 7f out: chsd ldr tl led again over 3f out: rdn over 1f out: hdd and unable qck ins fnl f* **33/1**
0520 **3** *1 ¾* **Mighty Clarets (IRE)**[32] 6916 4-9-5 **73** DavidNolan 8 76
(Richard Fahey) *a.p: rdn over 1f out: styd on* **16/1**
1451 **4** *hd* **Ajdaad (USA)**[4] 7418 4-9-3 **71** 6ex GrahamGibbons 12 74+
(Alan McCabe) *s.i.s: hld up: hdwy and swtchd rt over 1f out: sn rdn: r.o: nt rch ldrs* **9/2**[2]
0463 **5** *hd* **Mazamorra (USA)**[7] 7362 4-9-7 **75** AndreaAtzeni 6 77
(Marco Botti) *prom: nt clr run and lost pl wl over 2f out: hdwy over 1f out: rdn and hung lft ins fnl f: styd on* **4/1**[1]
3356 **6** *nk* **Carcinetto (IRE)**[4] 7418 9-8-6 **65** MatthewCosham(5) 7 66
(David Evans) *hld up: rdn and r.o ins fnl f: nvr nrr* **14/1**
4034 **7** *2 ½* **Xpres Maite**[39] 6764 8-9-7 **75** (b) RussKennemore 11 71
(Roy Bowring) *led 7f out: pushed along and hdd over 3f out: wknd over 1f out* **16/1**
4235 **8** *nk* **Dream Of Fortune (IRE)**[4] 7418 7-8-11 **65** (bt) TomMcLaughlin 3 60
(David Evans) *hld up: pushed along over 2f out: styd on ins fnl f: nt trble ldrs* **11/1**
0332 **9** *3 ¼* **Choral**[9] 7334 3-9-2 **73** AdamKirby 1 60
(Richard Hannon) *chsd ldrs: rdn and hung lft over 1f out: wknd fnl f* **4/1**[1]
2114 **10** *4 ½* **John Potts**[232] 1066 6-9-2 **70** KellyHarrison 4 47
(Brian Baugh) *hld up: hmpd over 2f out: n.d* **16/1**
1000 **11** *2 ½* **Strong Vigilance (IRE)**[80] 5608 4-9-4 **72** JamieSpencer 5 43
(Michael Bell) *s.i.s: hld up: hdwy over 3f out: wknd 2f out* **10/1**

1m 49.7s (-0.80) **Going Correction** -0.025s/f (Stan)
WFA 3 from 4yo+ 3lb **11** Ran SP% **115.4**
Speed ratings (Par 103): **102,100,99,98,98 98,96,96,93,89 86**
Tote Swingers:1&2:£50.60, 2&3:£34.80, 1&3:£23.70 CSF £205.88 CT £3512.13 TOTE £7.50: £2.60, £6.30, £5.90; EX 342.40.
Owner Mr & Mrs G Middlebrook **Bred** Mr & Mrs G Middlebrook **Trained** Portway, Worcs

■ Stewards' Enquiry : Michael O'Connell caution: careless riding

FOCUS
A competitive heat and a good ride from Michael O'Connell. The form looks sound, although not rated as positively as it might have been.

7466 CELEBRATE CHRISTMAS AT WOLVERHAMPTON RACECOURSE H'CAP 1m 1f 103y(P)
7:45 (7:45) (Class 7) (0-50,51) 3-Y-O+ £1,704 (£503; £251) Stalls Low

Form RPR
3265 1 **Queenie's Star (IRE)**[22] 7119 4-8-8 47 MarkCoumbe(5) 6 55
(Michael Attwater) *s.i.s: hld up: hdwy over 2f out: rdn to ld over 1f out: r.o* 7/1³
2440 2 1 **Idol Deputy (FR)**[181] 2308 5-8-7 48 RachealKneller(7) 3 56+
(Mark Usher) *prom: nt clr run and lost pl over 2f out: hdwy over 1f out: rdn and hung lft ins fnl f: r.o* 13/2²
5000 3 1 **Love In The Park**[99] 4953 6-8-13 47 ShaneKelly 11 51
(Roy Brotherton) *hld up: hdwy 2f out: rdn over 1f out: r.o: nt rch ldrs* 7/1³
0606 4 1 3/4 **Gay Gallivanter**[6] 7387 3-8-13 50 (p) TomMcLaughlin 8 50
(Michael Quinn) *a.p: rdn and ev ch on outer fr over 2f out tl no ex fnl f* 11/1
/03- 5 3 **Time To Play**[602] 995 6-9-2 50 LiamKeniry 13 44
(Gary Brown) *chsd ldrs: led over 2f out: rdn and hdd over 1f out: wknd ins fnl f* 7/1³
404 6 2 1/4 **Baltimore Jack (IRE)**[50] 6494 7-9-2 50 GrahamGibbons 4 39
(G P Kelly) *led: hdd over 5f out: rdn and ev ch over 2f out: wknd fnl f* 9/4¹
04 7 1/2 **Zagarock**[135] 3726 4-8-10 49 (p) CharlesBishop(5) 2 37
(Bryn Palling) *chsd ldrs: rdn over 3f out: wknd over 1f out* 12/1
0430 8 7 **Hathaway (IRE)**[50] 6494 4-8-12 49 RyanClark(3) 12 22
(Mark Brisbourne) *hung rt almost thrght: hld up: plld hrd: hdwy to chse ldr over 6f out: led over 5f out: hdd over 2f out: sn wknd* 9/1
0-05 9 8 **Sunshine Buddy**[30] 6947 4-9-0 48 JamesMillman 5 —
(Rod Millman) *hld up: bhd fnl 5f* 25/1
00 10 6 **Ohwhataladу (IRE)**[24] 7085 3-9-0 51 ow1 (bt¹) AdamKirby 9 —
(Noel Quinlan) *chsd ldrs: pushed along over 3f out: wknd over 1f out* 33/1

2m 1.75s (0.05) **Going Correction** -0.025s/f (Stan)
WFA 3 from 4yo+ 3lb 10 Ran SP% 114.4
Speed ratings (Par 97): **98,97,96,94,92 90,89,83,76,70**
Tote Swingers:1&2:£8.10, 2&3:£5.90, 1&3:£5.00 CSF £50.94 CT £330.61 TOTE £9.30: £2.00, £1.80, £3.00; EX 43.70.
Owner The Attwater Partnership **Bred** Noel And Michael Buckley **Trained** Epsom, Surrey

FOCUS
An ordinary race rated around the first two.
Hathaway(IRE) Official explanation: jockey said filly hung right-handed
Sunshine Buddy Official explanation: jockey said filly was never travelling
T/Plt: £7.20 to a £1 stake. Pool £56,158.60 - 5,682.88 winning units. T/Qpdt: £3.50 to a £1 stake. Pool £7,207.34 - 1,509.92 winning units. CR

7372 DUNDALK (A.W) (L-H)
Friday, November 18

OFFICIAL GOING: Standard

7468a WWW.DUNDALKSTADIUM.COM H'CAP 6f (P)
6:55 (6:58) 3-Y-O+ £7,732 (£1,793; £784; £448)

RPR
1 **Gordon Lord Byron (IRE)**[21] 7148 3-8-7 78 WMLordan 13 86
(T Hogan, Ire) *mid-div: 9th 2f out: hdwy in 3rd and veered lft 1f out: rdn to ld ins fnl f: pressed cl home* 7/1³
2 nk **Tell The Wind (IRE)**[96] 5086 3-8-8 79 (t) CDHayes 8 86
(Kevin Prendergast, Ire) *mid-div: swtchd to outer over 1f out: rdn in 9th 1f out: r.o wl fnl f: pressed wnr cl home* 33/1
3 nk **Solent Ridge (IRE)**[55] 6364 6-8-2 83 MeganCarberry(10) 5 89
(G M Lyons, Ire) *hld up towards rr: wd st: rdn in 11th 1f out: r.o wl fnl f* 12/1
4 hd **Duff (IRE)**[28] 7010 8-9-10 95 KJManning 6 101
(Edward Lynam, Ire) *chsd ldrs: 5th 1/2-way: 3rd 2f out: rdn into 2nd 1f out: disp ins fnl f: no ex cl home* 7/2¹
5 1/2 **Queenie Keen (IRE)**[28] 7010 4-8-3 79 CPHoban(5) 9 83
(M Halford, Ire) *led: rdn and hdd ins fnl f: no ex and kpt on same pce* 7/1³
6 1 **Foot Perfect (IRE)**[35] 6854 3-8-8 79 ShaneFoley 3 80
(David Marnane, Ire) *in rr of mid-div: hdwy into 8th 2f out: rdn in 7th 1f out: no ex ins fnl f: kpt on same pce* 9/2²
7 nk **He's Got Rhythm (IRE)**[28] 7010 6-8-6 77 (b) WJSupple 1 77
(David Marnane, Ire) *chsd ldrs: 4th 1/2-way: rdn 2f out: no ex over 1f out: kpt on same pce fnl f* 18/1
8 1/2 **Billyford (IRE)**[42] 6677 6-8-7 78 (t) FergalLynch 7 76
(Liam Roche, Ire) *hld up towards rr: no imp in 10th 1f out: kpt on same pce fnl f* 20/1
9 1 **Maundy Money**[19] 7189 8-8-1 82 DHBergin(10) 4 77
(David Marnane, Ire) *hld up towards rr: rdn and no imp over 1f out: kpt on one pce* 14/1
10 hd **Knock Stars (IRE)**[21] 7149 3-9-1 86 (tp) PShanahan 11 80
(Patrick Martin, Ire) *mid-div: 7th 1/2-way: rdn 2f out: 5th 1f out: wknd fnl f* 16/1
11 2 **Madeira Man (IRE)**[371] 7431 3-8-11 82 GFCarroll 2 70
(J A Nash, Ire) *towards rr for most: nvr a factor* 14/1
12 hd **My Girl Anna (IRE)**[21] 7149 4-8-4 82 SAGray(7) 14 69
(Muredach Kelly, Ire) *chsd ldrs: 6th 1/2-way: rdn 2f out: no ex 1f out: wknd fnl f* 12/1
13 1 **Jembatt (IRE)**[75] 5762 4-8-7 78 (t) NGMcCullagh 12 62
(Michael Mulvany, Ire) *chsd ldr in 2nd: rdn 2f out: no ex in 4th 1f out: wknd fnl f* 14/1
14 8 **Love Delta (USA)**[139] 3627 4-9-8 93 PJSmullen 10 52
(Kevin Ryan) *chsd ldrs: 3rd 1/2-way: rdn in 5th 2f out: sn no ex and wknd* 7/1³

1m 11.3s (71.30) 14 Ran SP% 132.1
CSF £237.19 CT £2852.87 TOTE £8.40: £2.20, £5.30, £2.80; DF 423.00.
Owner Morgan J Cahalan **Bred** Roland H Alder **Trained** Nenagh, Co Tipperary

FOCUS
The fourth, fifth and sixth have been rated close to their recent best.

NOTEBOOK
Gordon Lord Byron(IRE) opened his account at the seventh time of asking when beating an irresolute sort last time but was originally given a 12lb hike for doing so. However, that effort was reassessed and the penalty was halved which made all the difference here. Drawn in the second worst stall, his rider had no option but to travel on the outside throughout, which made his performance all the more admirable. He came with a sustained challenge down the middle of the track in the home straight and hit the front inside the final furlong before holding off the challenge of the fast-finishing runner-up. Official explanation: jockey said gelding dived inwards while making a challenge and caused slight interference (op 15/2)
Tell The Wind(IRE) looked to have gone off the boil when last seen almost three months ago, but the break seemed to rekindle her enthusiasm as she was finishing fastest of all down the outside and would have been in front in another stride.
Solent Ridge(IRE) stayed on well after being held up in the early stages and gave the impression that another furlong or two would bring about improvement. (op 10/1)
Duff(IRE) may be advancing in years but he seems to retain plenty of ability and this was a cracking effort under top weight. He travelled with his usual zest and looked the likeliest winner when hitting the front 1f out, but his hefty burden told close home. (op 9/2)
Queenie Keen(IRE) showed plenty of speed but her brave attempt from the front came unstuck inside the final furlong.
Foot Perfect(IRE) was one of the first to come under pressure and, despite not being beaten far, she never looked like winning. (op 5/1)
Knock Stars(IRE) Official explanation: jockey said filly received slight interference in the straight

7467a, 7469 - 7480a (Foreign Racing) - See Raceform Interactive

7434 LINGFIELD (L-H)
Saturday, November 19

OFFICIAL GOING: Standard
Wind: Moderate, across. Weather: Overcast

7481 CHRISTMAS HOSPITALITY AT LINGFIELD PARK (S) STKS 1m (P)
11:40 (11:42) (Class 6) 2-Y-O £1,704 (£503; £251) Stalls High

Form RPR
2060 1 **Masters Club**[68] 5998 2-8-11 56 KirstyMilczarek 11 63
(John Ryan) *chsd ldrs: chal over 2f out: sn led: drvn clr ins fnl f: readily* 25/1
0504 2 3 **Rafaella**[23] 7117 2-8-6 58 (p) JoeFanning 9 51
(Harry Dunlop) *in tch: hdwy to chse ldng duo 2f out: styd on u.p to take 2nd fnl 120yds but no ch w wnr* 13/2
00 3 1 **Seemples (IRE)**[84] 5475 2-8-11 0 RyanMoore 3 54
(Richard Hannon) *led 1f: led again appr fnl 4f: jnd over 2f out and sn hdd: outpcd by wnr over 1f out: one pce and lost 2nd fnl 120yds* 5/2¹
0332 4 1 **Emerald Smile (IRE)**[24] 7108 2-8-6 53 LukeMorris 1 47
(J S Moore) *chsd ldrs: rdn over 2f out: styd on same pce fr over 1f out* 5/1²
000 5 3/4 **Pack Of Cards (IRE)**[65] 6100 2-8-11 42 MarcHalford 8 50
(Terry Clement) *in rr: hdwy on outside 2f out: styd on same pce fr over 1f out* 100/1
000 6 nse **You Got The Love**[9] 7344 2-7-13 40 (b¹) RaulDaSilva(7) 10 45
(Jeremy Gask) *in rr: hdwy towards outside and edgd lft wl over 1f out: styd on clsng stages: nvr a threat* 40/1
3660 7 1 1/2 **Kyllasie**[17] 7222 2-8-3 63 KieranO'Neill(3) 7 41
(Richard Hannon) *chsd ldrs: rdn over 2f out: wknd appr fnl f* 6/1³
2000 8 hd **Accustomed**[40] 6753 2-8-6 67 ChrisCatlin 6 41
(Sylvester Kirk) *in rr: pushed along and mod prog fnl f* 5/2¹
006 9 7 **Electric Daydream (IRE)**[45] 6620 2-8-6 38 AndreaAtzeni 4 25
(J S Moore) *t.k.h: chsd ldrs 4f* 16/1
00 10 7 **My Lady Picolla**[10] 7330 2-8-3 0 KierenFox(3) 12 9
(Dr Jon Scargill) *s.i.s: pushed along and hdwy to ld after 1f: hdd appr fnl 4f: sn wknd* 100/1
00 11 12 **Vagabond King**[3] 7431 2-8-11 0 FrankieMcDonald 2 —
(Edward Creighton) *a bhd: t.o fnl 3f* 100/1

1m 38.8s (0.60) **Going Correction** -0.025s/f (Stan) 11 Ran SP% 116.6
Speed ratings (Par 94): **96,93,92,91,90 90,88,88,81,74 62**
Tote Swingers:1&2:£7.40, 2&3:£4.30, 1&3:£13.70 CSF £176.06 TOTE £29.40: £6.90, £2.80, £1.10; EX 109.50 TRIFECTA Not won..There was no bid for the winner.
Owner Masters Stud & Partner **Bred** Bubble Media **Trained** Newmarket, Suffolk

FOCUS
A weak race.

NOTEBOOK
Masters Club, who had been gelded since he last ran in September, posted an improved effort. Never far away from the lead, he won with a bit in hand and may have more to offer now his problems appear to be behind him. (op 22-1 tchd 33-1)
Rafaella settled better and ran a sound race down in distance with cheekpieces applied. (tchd 7-1)
Seemples(IRE) was a shade disappointing, finding only the one pace under pressure in the straight. (op 7-2)
Emerald Smile(IRE) might not have been at an advantage in sticking to the inside. (op 7-2 tchd 10-3)
Pack Of Cards(IRE) ran his best race to date on this drop in class, but that's not saying a great deal.
Kyllasie didn't get home and needs dropping back in distance. (op 13-2 tchd 15-2)
Accustomed, a market drifter, never got involved and was disappointing considering he was best in at the weights. (tchd 11-4)

7482 LADBROKES.COM/BRITISH STALLION STUDS E B F MAIDEN STKS 5f (P)
12:10 (12:10) (Class 5) 2-Y-O £3,234 (£962; £481; £240) Stalls High

Form RPR
425 1 **Tango Sky (IRE)**[14] 7292 2-9-3 75 JimCrowley 1 76
(Ralph Beckett) *trckd ldrs: wnt narrow 2nd ins fnl 2f: pushed along and str chal fr jst ins fnl f: asserted cl home* 13/8²
5222 2 nk **Blanc De Chine (IRE)**[33] 6919 2-8-12 71 FergusSweeney 6 70
(Peter Makin) *w ld tl slt ld 3f out: drvn and jnd fr jst ins fnl f: fnd no ex u.p and hdd cl home* 11/10¹
04 3 1 1/2 **Love Island**[67] 6026 2-8-9 0 AmyRyan(3) 5 65
(Richard Whitaker) *led 2f: hdd 3f out: narrowly lost 2nd ins fnl 2f: rallied ins fnl f but nvr quite gng pce to chal again: wknd fnl 100yds* 5/1³
4004 4 2 **Arabian Flight**[77] 5737 2-8-9 59 KieranO'Neill(3) 3 57
(John Bridger) *chsd ldrs in cl 4th: rdn over 2f out: outpcd appr fnl f* 25/1
0 5 7 **Lotarespect**[3] 7435 2-8-12 0 SteveDrowne 7 32
(John Best) *s.i.s: racd in last pl tl styd on fnl 120yds to take mod 5th clsng stages* 66/1

0 6 1 1/4 **I B A Gee Gee**41 6725 2-9-3 0 DaneO'Neill 4 33
(Tony Newcombe) *s.i.s: racd in mod 5th tl dropped to last pl clsng stages* **100/1**

59.00 secs (0.20) **Going Correction** -0.025s/f (Stan) **6** Ran SP% **108.7**
Speed ratings (Par 96): **97,96,94,90,79 77**
Tote Swingers:1&2:£1.20, 2&3:£1.30, 1&3:£1.50 CSF £3.48 TOTE £2.50: £1.40, £1.60; EX 4.30 Trifecta £9.60 Pool 280.71 - 21.56 winning units..
Owner A W A Partnership **Bred** L Mulryan **Trained** Kimpton, Hants

FOCUS
A modest maiden.

NOTEBOOK
Tango Sky(IRE) didn't travel as strongly as the runner-up into the straight, but found that bit more under pressure. He stays 6f so always had a chance while the filly was in sight. (tchd 7-4)
Blanc De Chine(IRE) was finishing second for the fifth time in her career and for the fourth time having led inside the last. She might still win a weak maiden round here as she's not short of speed, but she doesn't tend to find a great deal off the bridle. (op 5-4)
Love Island, back from a two-month break, struggled to match strides with the leader early but kept on well having been beaten off. She could do alright in handicaps. (op 9-2)
Arabian Flight, debuting for a new trainer, had a bit to find on the book and ran about as well as could be expected. (tchd 20-1)

7483 LINGFIELD PARK OWNERS CLUB II CONDITIONS STKS 7f (P)
12:45 (12:46) (Class 3) 2-Y-O £6,792 (£2,021; £1,010; £505) Stalls Low

Form RPR
1105 1 **Storming Bernard (USA)**38 6788 2-9-6 95 RyanMoore 1 92
(Alan Bailey) *mde virtually all: drvn out fnl f* **5/4**1
31 2 1 1/2 **Jake's Destiny (IRE)**36 6842 2-9-0 80 KierenFallon 5 82
(George Baker) *trckd ldrs in 4th: pushed along to take 3rd over 2f out: styd on to dispute 2nd fr over 1f out: edgd lft and kpt on to chse wnr fnl 120yds but nvr any ch* **11/4**3
3004 3 3/4 **Hidden Passion (USA)**22 7135 2-8-12 90 (t) JamieSpencer 4 79
(Brian Meehan) *ponied to s: chsd wnr: drvn and no imp fr 2f out: lost wl hld 2nd fnl 120yds* **9/4**2
0130 4 5 **Singalat**65 6102 2-9-3 79 FrederikTylicki 3 70
(James Given) *racd in last: drvn along wl over 2f out: tk mod 4th fnl f* **20/1**
050 5 7 **Tectonic (IRE)**29 6993 2-9-0 0 AndreaAtzeni 2 49
(Chris Dwyer) *bmpd s: racd in 3rd: rdn wl over 2f out: sn btn: lost mod 4th fnl f* **100/1**

1m 24.14s (-0.66) **Going Correction** -0.025s/f (Stan) **5** Ran SP% **107.6**
Speed ratings (Par 100): **102,100,99,93,85**
CSF £4.77 TOTE £2.00: £1.10, £1.50; EX 4.90.
Owner John Stocker **Bred** Hill 'N' Dale Equine Holdings Inc & Netp **Trained** Newmarket, Suffolk

FOCUS
Effectively a three-horse race.

NOTEBOOK
Storming Bernard(USA) put up a nice performance, making just about all the running and quickening off the turn to win tidily. He ought not to go up much, if at all, for this, but his mark still doesn't make placing him particularly easy. (op 11-8 tchd 6-4)
Jake's Destiny(IRE) had quite a bit to find with the winner and third strictly on ratings, but it was interesting that connections were prepared to risk a hike in the weights in defeat here rather than go the easier handicap route. He ran well and, while the gamble didn't come off, he's lightly raced and entitled to improve further. Official explanation: jockey said gelding hung left (op 5-2)
Hidden Passion(USA) was going well enough running down the hill but she couldn't make any inroads into the winner's advantage in the straight. This trip is probably a little beyond her optimum and she disappointed on her previous run here. (op 5-2)
Singalat, under pressure from some way out, struggled to get competitive. He faced a tough task at the weights. (op 16-1 tchd 22-1)

7484 PHILPOTTS AT LINGFIELD H'CAP (DIV I) 7f (P)
1:15 (1:18) (Class 6) (0-65,74) 3-Y-O+ £1,704 (£503; £251) Stalls Low

Form RPR
01 1 **Shelagh (IRE)**240 953 3-9-6 65 DaneO'Neill 1 73
(Jo Crowley) *chsd ldrs on ins: led appr fnl f: drvn and styd on strly fnl f* **10/1**
6361 2 1 **Lutine Charlie (IRE)**10 7332 4-9-13 74 (p) KierenFox(3) 14 79
(Ronald Harris) *in rr tl gd hdwy on inner wl over 1f out: kpt on to chse wnr fnl 75yds but no imp* **6/1**2
3404 3 hd **Fenella Fudge**18 7213 3-9-5 64 (b) FrederikTylicki 3 68
(James Given) *rrd s: sn prom: rdn: awkward and lost position bnd fr 2f out: rallied ins fnl f and r.o clsng stages to take 3rd cl home and gaining on 2nd: no imp on wnr* **13/2**3
0005 4 3/4 **Wotatomboy**9 7351 5-8-4 51 oh5 (v) AmyRyan(3) 6 53
(Richard Whitaker) *led: hdd appr fnl f: one pce fnl 120yds and lost 2 pls fnl 75yds* **33/1**
5321 5 hd **Poppy**24 7093 3-9-2 61 RyanMoore 9 63
(Richard Hannon) *chsd ldrs: rdn and hung lft after bnd into home st and lost position: hdwy fnl f: r.o wl clsng stages: nt rch ldrs* **7/2**1
3460 6 1 **Saucy Buck (IRE)**31 6944 3-8-12 62 JustinNewman(5) 10 61
(Ralph Smith) *chsd ldrs on outside: wd into st and lost position: r.o again ins fnl f* **10/1**
3-04 7 nk **Menha**16 7249 3-9-1 60 LukeMorris 2 58
(John Gallagher) *disp 2nd tl appr fnl f: wknd fnl 100yds* **16/1**
5000 8 1/2 **Frognal (IRE)**4 7420 5-9-4 65 (bt) RobertLButler(3) 13 62
(Richard Guest) *pushed rt s: racd on outer and wd into st: styd on clsng stages but nvr any ch* **25/1**
0050 9 nk **Buxton**37 6814 7-9-4 62 (t) MartinLane 7 58
(Roger Ingram) *stdd and swtchd lft to ins sn after s: hdwy on inner wl over 1f out but nvr quite rchd ldrs: wknd ins fnl f* **10/1**
5014 10 1/2 **Demoiselle Bond**9 7348 3-8-13 58 SteveDrowne 12 53
(Lydia Richards) *wnt rt s: sn disputing 2nd: rdn over 1f out: wknd fnl f* **16/1**
000- 11 shd **Toga Tiger (IRE)**399 6935 4-9-0 58 TonyCulhane 8 53
(Jeremy Gask) *a towards rr but kpt on clsng stages* **16/1**
0-40 12 20 **Mrs Boss**243 928 4-9-4 62 JamesMillman 5 —
(Rod Millman) *a in rr: wl behnd fnl 2f* **25/1**

1m 24.4s (-0.40) **Going Correction** -0.025s/f (Stan)
WFA 3 from 4yo+ 1lb **12** Ran SP% **105.4**
Speed ratings (Par 101): **101,99,99,98,98 97,97,96,96,95 95,72**
Swingers:1&2:£9.80, 2&3:£7.10, 1&3:£11.30 CSF £54.13 CT £315.92 TOTE £12.30: £2.40, £2.80, £2.10; EX 68.80 Trifecta £139.70 Part won. Pool 188.84 - 0.20 winning units..
Owner Kilstone Limited **Bred** Levent Zumreoglu **Trained** Whitcombe, Dorset

FOCUS
The majority of these looked pretty exposed, but one of the exceptions was the winner. The form appears sound rated around the placed horses but limited by the fourth.

7485 PHILPOTTS AT LINGFIELD H'CAP (DIV II) 7f (P)
1:50 (1:50) (Class 6) (0-65,66) 3-Y-O+ £1,704 (£503; £251) Stalls Low

Form RPR
3220 1 **Bold Ring**23 7131 5-9-0 58 JimmyQuinn 4 67
(Edward Creighton) *trckd ldrs: wnt 2nd and rdn 1f out: styd on wl fnl 120yds: sn swtchd rt: led last strides* **40/1**
0531 2 nk **Rio Royale (IRE)**23 7131 5-8-11 62 (b) LukeRowe(7) 13 70
(Amanda Perrett) *sn chsng ldr: led ins fnl 2f: drvn and edgd lft ins fnl f: hdd last strides* **7/1**3
0003 3 3/4 **Cut The Cackle (IRE)**38 6791 5-8-10 54 (bt) MartinHarley 3 60
(Richard Guest) *t.k.h: in rr but in tch: hdwy over 1f out: styd on ins fnl f: tk 3rd last strides but nt rch ldng duo* **16/1**
0565 4 hd **Eager To Bow (IRE)**30 6971 5-9-5 63 JimCrowley 5 68
(Patrick Chamings) *in rr tl gd hdwy over 1f out: disp 3rd ins fnl f: kpt on wl clsng stages* **9/1**
5360 5 2 **Pose (IRE)**21 7173 4-8-11 60 (t) MarkCoumbe(5) 12 60
(Roger Ingram) *in rr: racd on outside and wd into st: gd hdwy 1f out: fin wl clsng stages* **50/1**
0330 6 1 **Speak The Truth (IRE)**24 7097 5-9-4 62 MatthewDavies 7 59
(Jim Boyle) *in rr: racd on outside and wd into st: hdwy and hung lft fnl f: one pce fnl 50yds* **14/1**
0022 7 1/2 **Forks**32 6939 4-9-5 63 LukeMorris 2 59
(Jane Chapple-Hyam) *mid-div: hdwy towards ins over 1f out: kpt on fnl f but nvr gng pce to rch ldrs* **7/1**3
0000 8 1/2 **Our Princess Ellie (USA)**7 7389 3-8-6 51 oh6 JoeFanning 6 46
(Derek Shaw) *chsd ldrs: pushed along ins fnl 2f: wknd fnl f* **40/1**
0002 9 3/4 **Lastkingofscotland (IRE)**9 7349 5-9-1 66 (b) NoelGarbutt(7) 11 59
(Conor Dore) *stdd s and swtchd lft towards ins: hdwy to chse ldrs over 1f out: wknd ins fnl f* **8/1**
0530 10 2 1/2 **Rapid Water**164 2816 5-9-7 65 RyanMoore 8 51
(Gary Moore) *chsd ldrs and racd towards outside: wd into st and sn btn* **9/4**1
0342 11 1 **For Life (IRE)**38 6794 9-9-4 65 NataliaGemelova(3) 14 48
(John E Long) *sn led fr wd draw: hdd ins fnl 2f: wknd qckly appr fnl f* **25/1**
0153 12 1/2 **Diamond Run**15 7269 3-9-1 60 SebSanders 10 42
(J W Hills) *chsd ldrs on outside: wknd 2f out* **6/1**2
0432 13 1 1/2 **Silvee**45 6626 4-8-10 57 KieranO'Neill(3) 1 35
(John Bridger) *chsd ldrs on ins: wknd ins fnl 2f* **25/1**

1m 24.34s (-0.46) **Going Correction** -0.025s/f (Stan)
WFA 3 from 4yo+ 1lb **13** Ran SP% **118.2**
Speed ratings (Par 101): **101,100,99,99,97 96,95,95,94,91 90,89,87**
Tote Swingers:1&2:£21.10, 2&3:£33.70, 1&3:£32.70 CSF £289.24 CT £4829.35 TOTE £37.00: £8.00, £2.60, £6.00; EX 282.30 TRIFECTA Not won..
Owner Daniel Creighton **Bred** J A Pickering & T Pears **Trained** Wormshill, Kent
■ Stewards' Enquiry : Luke Rowe two-day ban: careless riding (Dec 3, 5)

FOCUS
The winning time was almost identical to the first division and the form looks sound.
Speak The Truth(IRE) Official explanation: jockey said gelding was slowly away
Forks Official explanation: jockey said gelding suffered interference in running

7486 BRITISH STALLION STUDS SUPPORTING BRITISH RACING EBF FILLIES' H'CAP 1m (P)
2:25 (2:26) (Class 4) (0-85,84) 3-Y-O+ £5,822 (£1,732; £865; £432) Stalls High

Form RPR
5530 1 **Young Dottie**10 7328 5-8-7 75 JemmaMarshall(5) 10 82
(Pat Phelan) *towards rr but in tch: hdwy ins fnl 2f: drvn to ld fnl 120yds: hld on wl clsng stages* **14/1**
0002 2 1/2 **Emma's Gift (IRE)**8 7361 3-8-11 76 (b) JimmyQuinn 8 82+
(Julia Feilden) *in tch: hdwy on ins over 1f out: n.m.r: lost position and swtchd rt ins fnl f: rallied and r.o strly to take 2nd last strides but nt rch wnr* **16/1**
5430 3 hd **Chevise (IRE)**41 6728 3-8-13 78 MatthewDavies 12 83
(Steve Woodman) *chsd ldrs: disp ld 3f out tl chsd ldr over 2f out tl 1f out: kpt on clsng stages and jst lost 2nd last strides* **12/1**
2110 4 nk **Zafeen's Pearl**14 7299 4-8-12 75 ShaneKelly 9 79+
(Dean Ivory) *plld hrd early and racd on outside: wd into st and plenty to do: hdwy ins fnl f: kpt on clsng stages: nt rch ldrs* **4/1**2
1040 5 1/2 **Queen Of Cash (IRE)**17 7227 3-9-4 83 RobertWinston 11 86
(Hughie Morrison) *chsd ldrs: led over 2f out: rdn over 1f out: hdd fnl 120yds: one pce and lost 3 pls cl home* **15/2**
1010 6 1/2 **Supreme Spirit (IRE)**16 7243 4-9-1 78 (b) DaneO'Neill 2 80
(George Margarson) *trckd ldrs: hdwy on ins fr 2f out: drvn to chal 1f out: wknd clsng stages* **14/1**
6004 7 3/4 **Cloud Illusions (USA)**8 7361 3-8-12 77 (v) KierenFallon 7 77
(Heather Main) *s.i.s: in rr: wd into st and plenty to do: styd on ins fnl f but nt rch ldrs* **20/1**
0600 8 1/2 **Avonrose**19 7199 4-8-7 75 MarkCoumbe(5) 6 74
(Derek Shaw) *towards rr: pushed along and effrt over 1f out but nvr gng pce to get into contention* **33/1**
3100 9 1/2 **Fabulouslyspirited**10 7339 3-9-1 80 JimCrowley 3 78
(Ralph Beckett) *dropped towards rr after 3f: rdn 2f out: styd on same pce fnl f* **20/1**
-020 10 6 **Call To Reason (IRE)**23 7127 4-9-7 84 RyanMoore 4 68
(Jeremy Noseda) *chsd ldrs: rdn over 2f out: wknd and hung lft ins fnl 2f* **9/4**1
522 11 5 **Shieldmaiden (USA)**3 7440 3-9-1 80 JoeFanning 5 53
(Mark Johnston) *sn led: hdd over 2f out: sn btn* **13/2**3

1m 37.89s (-0.31) **Going Correction** -0.025s/f (Stan)
WFA 3 from 4yo+ 2lb **11** Ran SP% **115.2**
Speed ratings (Par 102): **100,99,99,99,98 98,97,96,96,90 85**
Tote Swingers:1&2:£14.40, 2&3:£28.90, 1&3:£17.30 CSF £206.91 CT £2746.81 TOTE £21.40: £6.60, £6.60, £4.20; EX 148.40 Trifecta £493.90 Part won. Pool 667.45 - 0.63 winning units..
Owner Tony Smith **Bred** Tony J Smith **Trained** Epsom, Surrey

FOCUS
There was a bit of a bunch finish to this fillies' handicap and the form looks ordinary.
Zafeen's Pearl Official explanation: jockey said filly hung right

Cloud Illusions(USA) Official explanation: vet said filly was stiff post race

7487 MAYFLOWER WASHROOMS SOLUTIONS 10TH ANNIVERSARY H'CAP 5f (P)

3:00 (3:00) (Class 4) (0-85,83) 3-Y-0+ **£4,204** (£1,251; £625; £312) **Stalls** High

Form RPR

2510 **1** **Sugar Beet**[33] 6917 3-9-4 **81** ... LukeMorris 2 92
(Ronald Harris) *in tch: rdn and hdwy over 1f out to chse ldr ins fnl f: kep on wl u.p to ld fnl 30yds: hld on all out* **8/1**

0502 **2** *nk* **Lenny Bee**[9] 7355 5-9-0 **80** ... (t) JohnFahy(3) 9 90
(Deborah Sanderson) *towards rr: drvn and hdwy over 1f out: swtchd rt and styd on wl fnl 50yds: tk 2nd clsng stages but nt quite rch wnr* **11/4**[2]

3065 **3** *1 ¼* **Island Legend (IRE)**[9] 7355 5-9-3 **80** ... (p) RichardKingscote 5 85
(Milton Bradley) *pressed ldr tl led ins fnl 3f: drvn over 1f out: kpt on tl hdd and no ex fnl 30yds: lost 2nd clsng stages* **11/2**[3]

5423 **4** *½* **Billy Red**[37] 6815 7-9-3 **80** ... (b) FergusSweeney 4 84
(J R Jenkins) *in rr but in tch: hdwy towards outside over 1f out: styng on whn checked fnl 50yds: keeping on again cl home* **12/1**

2404 **5** *1* **Flash City (ITY)**[42] 6703 3-9-1 **83** ... (v) JustinNewman(5) 7 83
(Bryan Smart) *chsd ldrs: wnt 2nd 2f out: no imp over 1f out: wknd ins fnl f* **9/4**[1]

0100 **6** *2 ¾* **Deerslayer (USA)**[30] 6974 5-9-5 **82** ... (p) JimCrowley 10 72
(Amy Weaver) *in rr and racd towards outer: drvn and hung lft over 1f out: sme prog clsng stages* **14/1**

4210 **7** *2 ½* **Lucky Art (USA)**[9] 7356 5-9-1 **78** ... KirstyMilczarek 3 59
(Conor Dore) *led tl hdd ins fnl 3f: wknd wl over 1f out* **9/1**

000 **8** *2 ¾* **Waabel**[30] 6974 4-8-12 **78** ... (p) RobertLButler(3) 1 49
(Richard Guest) *early spd: sn bhd* **20/1**

58.26 secs (-0.54) **Going Correction** -0.025s/f (Stan) **8** Ran SP% **113.1**
Speed ratings (Par 105): **103,102,100,99,98 93,89,85**
Tote Swingers:1&2:£5.80, 2&3:£2.90, 1&3:£6.50 CSF £29.62 CT £132.63 TOTE £9.00: £2.60, £1.40, £2.10; EX 39.90 Trifecta £263.70 Pool 555.96 - 1.56 winning units..
Owner Ridge House Stables Ltd **Bred** Coln Valley Stud **Trained** Earlswood, Monmouths

FOCUS
There was a fair pace on here and things set up nicely for the winner. The winner seconded a slight personal best.
Lucky Art(USA) Official explanation: trainer said gelding was unsuited by the track

7488 BET IN PLAY AT LADBROKES.COM H'CAP 6f (P)

3:35 (3:35) (Class 6) (0-60,61) 3-Y-0+ **£1,704** (£503; £251) **Stalls** Low

Form RPR

4330 **1** **Catalinas Diamond (IRE)**[23] 7123 3-9-4 **59** ... (t) SteveDrowne 6 67
(Pat Murphy) *prom and racd towards outside: hdwy appr fnl f: styd on strly to ld fnl 30yds: drvn out* **11/1**

5600 **2** *hd* **Amber Heights**[83] 5511 3-9-3 **58** ... FergusSweeney 5 65+
(David Pinder) *in rr: drvn along and str run ins fnl f: chal fnl 30yds: no ex last strides* **8/1**

3505 **3** *nk* **Dualagi**[52] 6444 7-9-4 **59** ... LiamKeniry 12 65
(Martin Bosley) *sn trcking ldr: led appr fnl f: sn strly chal: hdd: nt qckn and one pce into 3rd fnl 30yds* **20/1**

0464 **4** *1* **Fantasy Fighter (IRE)**[32] 6930 6-9-2 **57** ... (p) DaneO'Neill 10 60
(John E Long) *chsd ldrs: drvn and ev ch fr 1f out: one pce fnl 120yds* **13/2**[2]

6305 **5** *½* **Towy Boy (IRE)**[32] 6930 6-9-5 **60** ... (bt) RobertWinston 3 62
(Ian Wood) *towards rr but in tch: hdwy on ins appr fnl f: kpt on clsng stages but nt pce to rch ldrs* **11/2**[1]

0153 **6** *hd* **One Cool Chick**[9] 7348 3-9-4 **59** ... NeilChalmers 11 60
(John Bridger) *in rr and racd towards outside: stl in rr whn hung lft over 1f out: kpt on clsng stages: nt rch ldrs* **13/2**[2]

2000 **7** *nse* **Bilko Pak (IRE)**[50] 6505 3-9-0 **60** ... (v[1]) MarkCoumbe(5) 7 61
(Derek Shaw) *s.i.s: in rr and racd towards outside: hdwy u.p fnl f: nt rch ldrs* **11/2**[1]

0062 **8** *hd* **Make My Dream**[25] 7086 8-9-5 **60** ... MartinLane 4 60
(John Gallagher) *chsd ldrs: rdn 2f out: wknd ins fnl f* **12/1**

0216 **9** *1* **Seneschal**[23] 7131 10-9-1 **61** ow1 ... LucyKBarry(5) 1 58
(Adrian Chamberlain) *chsd ldrs: rdn and ev ch on ins 1f out: wknd fnl 100yds* **11/2**[1]

6600 **10** *1 ¼* **Whoateallthepius (IRE)**[25] 7086 3-9-0 **55** ... JimCrowley 8 48
(Dean Ivory) *led tl hdd appr fnl f: wknd fnl 120yds* **7/1**[3]

1m 12.0s (0.10) **Going Correction** -0.025s/f (Stan) **10** Ran SP% **117.2**
Speed ratings (Par 101): **98,97,97,96,95 95,95,94,93,91**
Tote Swingers:1&2:£16.80, 2&3:£27.20, 1&3:£20.60 CSF £96.38 CT £1782.17 TOTE £13.70: £2.90, £2.40, £6.50; EX 133.80 TRIFECTA Not won..
Owner Briton International **Bred** Sean Gorman **Trained** East Garston, Berks

FOCUS
The early pace didn't look that strong but the first two came from behind. The form looks sound with the third the best guide.
T/Plt: £263.70 to a 1 stake. Pool £46,834.38. 129.65 winning tickets T/Qpdt: £87.80 to a 1 stake. Pool £3,752.41. 31.60 winning tickets ST

7459 WOLVERHAMPTON (A.W) (L-H)

Saturday, November 19

OFFICIAL GOING: Standard
Wind: Light, across. Weather: Overcast

7489 32RED H'CAP 5f 216y(P)

5:50 (5:51) (Class 3) (0-90,90) 3-Y-0+ **£7,157** (£2,113; £1,057) **Stalls** Low

Form RPR

0106 **1** **Elna Bright**[41] 6723 6-9-7 **90** ... JimmyQuinn 12 99
(Peter Crate) *s.i.s: hld up: hdwy over 1f out: rdn ins fnl f: edgd rt: r.o to ld towards fin* **12/1**

0024 **2** *¾* **Defence Council (IRE)**[138] 3682 3-8-8 **77** ... GrahamGibbons 5 84
(Mel Brittain) *mid-div: hdwy over 2f out: rdn to ld and hung lft over 1f out: hung rt ins fnl f: hdd towards fin* **16/1**

0000 **3** *3 ¼* **Sir Geoffrey (IRE)**[73] 5831 5-8-13 **85** ... (b) MichaelO'Connell(3) 9 81
(David Nicholls) *prom: rdn over 1f out: styd on same pce* **40/1**

0240 **4** *1 ½* **Sutton Veny (IRE)**[41] 6723 5-9-4 **87** ... AdamKirby 7 78
(Jeremy Gask) *broke wl: sn stdd and lost pl: hdwy over 1f out: r.o: nt rch ldrs* **9/2**[2]

0050 **5** *shd* **Whozthecat (IRE)**[33] 6917 4-8-5 **81** ... (v) JasonHart(7) 13 72
(Declan Carroll) *chsd ldrs: led over 2f out: rdn and hdd over 1f out: wknd ins fnl f* **8/1**

0010 **6** *1 ¼* **Summerinthecity (IRE)**[14] 7295 4-9-5 **88** ... TomQueally 11 75
(Ed de Giles) *s.i.s: sn pushed along in rr: r.o ins fnl f: nvr nrr* **10/1**

5300 **7** *1 ½* **Star Rover (IRE)**[23] 7127 4-8-13 **89** ... KevinLundie(7) 1 71
(David Evans) *hld up: nvr on terms* **22/1**

6200 **8** *3 ¼* **Even Stevens**[64] 6112 3-9-3 **89** ... BillyCray(3) 8 61
(David Nicholls) *led: hdd over 4f out: remained w ldrs: rdn and ev ch over 2f out: wknd over 1f out* **16/1**

1334 **9** *1 ½* **Palais Glide**[99] 5000 3-8-7 **79** ... KieranO'Neill(3) 3 46
(Richard Hannon) *s.i.s: outpcd* **17/2**

0054 **10** *hd* **What About You (IRE)**[22] 7149 3-9-1 **84** ... (b) FrederikTylicki 6 50
(Richard Fahey) *prom: rdn over 2f out: wknd over 1f out* **5/2**[1]

1002 **11** *12* **Le Toreador**[42] 6703 6-9-5 **88** ... (tp) JamieSpencer 4 16
(Kevin Ryan) *led over 4f out: pushed along and hdd over 2f out: hung lft and wknd over 1f out* **7/1**[3]

1m 13.23s (-1.77) **Going Correction** -0.10s/f (Stan) **11** Ran SP% **116.2**
Speed ratings (Par 107): **107,106,101,99,99 97,95,91,89,89 73**
Tote Swingers:1&2:£33.40, 2&3:£110.80, 1&3:£42.70 CSF £186.38 CT £7364.40 TOTE £15.20: £4.00, £5.70, £6.00; EX 130.90.
Owner Peter Crate **Bred** D R Tucker **Trained** Newdigate, Surrey

FOCUS
A decent sprint handicap. Unsurprisingly there was no hanging about, which set it up for the closers, and there was an awful lot of kickback off the surface through the race. The winner is rated to last winter's best form.

NOTEBOOK
Elna Bright, set a lot to do on this debut for a new yard, cruised into the home straight and found plenty when asked to win the race from the furlong marker. He can be in and out, but this was his fourth Polytrack success and it's made more meritorious as he carried top weight. (op 11-1 tchd 10-1)
Defence Council(IRE) goes well fresh and very nearly made light of a 138-day break. He was a sitting duck for the winner late on, but finished nicely clear in second and this was his first taste of Polytrack. (op 18-1 tchd 20-1)
Sir Geoffrey(IRE) improved off the home turn and had his chance, but lacked the pace of the first pair. He should improve on this first outing for 73 days. (op 50-1)
Sutton Veny(IRE) broke smartly but was immediately steadied back and may have benefited from a more positive ride. She was previously 3-3 on Polytrack for her rider, but all those wins came at Kempton. (op 5-1 tchd 4-1)
Whozthecat(IRE) was not disgraced considering he raced from the outside stall and fared best of those up with the pace. He's worth persevering with on this surface and a drop back to 5f could do the trick. (op 11-1)
What About You(IRE), keen to post, turned in a laboured effort under pressure and disappointed. (op 3-1)
Le Toreador Official explanation: jockey said gelding had no more to give

7490 32REDBET.COM (S) STKS 5f 216y(P)

6:20 (6:21) (Class 6) 2-Y-0 **£1,704** (£503; £251) **Stalls** Low

Form RPR

1 **Just Breathe (IRE)** 2-8-7 0 ... AndreaAtzeni 5 62+
(Chris Down) *led 1f: chsd ldrs: rdn to ld and hung lft 1f out: r.o* **9/4**[1]

1401 **2** *nk* **Adranian (IRE)**[19] 7196 2-9-3 70 ... (v) AdamKirby 1 71
(David Evans) *a.p: pushed along and hmpd over 1f out: rdn and ev ch ins fnl f: r.o* **11/4**[2]

3553 **3** *7* **The Dancing Lord**[9] 7353 2-8-10 65 ... RyanWhile(7) 7 50
(Bill Turner) *chsd ldrs: led 5f out: rdn and hung lft over 1f out: sn hdd and no ex* **8/1**

000 **4** *1 ½* **Gone To Ground**[39] 6768 2-8-5 30 ... (b[1]) RaulDaSilva(7) 4 41
(Jeremy Gask) *plld hrd and prom: rdn over 2f out: sn wknd* **66/1**

0400 **5** *nk* **Street Angel (IRE)**[7] 7444 2-8-4 61 ... (b) DominicFox(3) 2 35
(Alan Bailey) *s.i.s: outpcd: nvr nrr* **17/2**

002 **6** *3 ½* **Multi Blessing**[8] 7365 2-9-3 70 ... (v[1]) MartinLane 8 34
(Alan Jarvis) *sn drvn along and prom: chsd ldr 4f out: rdn over 2f out: wknd wl over 1f out* **14/1**

7 *¾* **Englishgreek (IRE)** 2-8-12 0 ... JamieMackay 3 27
(George Prodromou) *s.s: outpcd* **16/1**

2305 **8** *½* **Regal Lady**[24] 7103 2-8-7 63 ... GrahamGibbons 6 20
(David Brown) *chsd ldrs tl wknd 2f out: eased* **9/2**[3]

1m 14.8s (-0.20) **Going Correction** -0.10s/f (Stan) **8** Ran SP% **111.3**
Speed ratings (Par 94): **97,96,87,85,84 80,79,78**
Tote Swingers:1&2:£1.70, 2&3:£2.60, 1&3:£3.70 CSF £8.04 TOTE £2.90: £1.10, £1.40, £2.20; EX 9.70.There was no bid for the winner.
Owner C J Down **Bred** Brendan Corbett **Trained** Mutterton, Devon
■ Stewards' Enquiry : Ryan While one-day ban: careless riding (Dec 3)
Andrea Atzeni caution: careless riding

FOCUS
The first pair came right away in this weak juvenile seller.

NOTEBOOK
Just Breathe(IRE), despite hailing from a yard that was previously 0-7 with juveniles in the past five seasons, was very well backed throughout the day and certainly knew her job as she broke smartly. Her rider delayed her challenge off the home turn, but was forced wide in the process and she did well to out-battle the more-experienced runner-up. It will be interesting to see if she builds on this. (op 2-1 tchd 15-8 and 11-4)
Adranian(IRE) landed his second success over 7f here last time out. He was faced with a solid pace down in trip and held every chance last time out. He was faced with a solid pace down in trip and held every chance despite having to wait for his challenge rounding the home turn. He was always just being held late on and is probably best over another furlong, but rates a solid benchmark here. (tchd 5-2 and 3-1)
The Dancing Lord did plenty through the early parts and paid from the furlong marker. He too helps to set the level. (tchd 15-2)
Gone To Ground raced in first-time blinkers but was still well beaten off. (op 50-1)
Regal Lady posted a tame effort. (op 6-1 tchd 4-1)

7491 32RED.COM NURSERY 7f 32y(P)

6:50 (6:52) (Class 4) (0-85,83) 2-Y-0 **£4,204** (£1,251; £625; £312) **Stalls** High

Form RPR

3231 **1** **Tones (IRE)**[121] 4240 2-9-0 **76** ... JimmyFortune 2 79
(Richard Hannon) *mde all: rdn and edgd rt over 1f out: drvn out* **11/4**[1]

2300 **2** *nk* **Leenavesta (USA)**[14] 7294 2-8-1 **66** ... KieranO'Neill(3) 1 68
(Richard Hannon) *chsd ldrs: rdn and ev ch ins fnl f: r.o* **13/2**

6120 **3** *½* **Amoure Medici**[29] 6995 2-8-13 **75** ... MartinLane 7 77
(Noel Quinlan) *s.i.s: hld up: hdwy over 1f out: sn rdn: r.o* **3/1**[2]

044 **4** *1* **Elite**[51] 6492 2-8-5 **67** ... ChrisCatlin 4 65
(Mick Channon) *trckd ldrs: nt clr run over 1f out: sn rdn: r.o* **16/1**

4221 **5** *nse* **Quite A Thing**[26] 7067 2-9-7 **83** ... SebSanders 9 81
(Sir Mark Prescott Bt) *a.p: rdn over 1f out: styd on* **11/2**[3]

1 **6** *1 ¾* **For Shia And Lula (IRE)**[58] 6281 2-9-0 **76** ... ShaneKelly 3 70
(Daniel Mark Loughnane, Ire) *hld up: hdwy over 1f out: sn rdn and hung lft: no ex ins fnl f* **17/2**

 The Form Book, Raceform Ltd, Compton, RG20 6NL

0150 **7** *1* **Bartley**[28] 7021 2-8-13 **75**....(p) JoeFanning 5 67
(Bryan Smart) *prom: chsd ldr over 5f out: rdn whn hmpd over 1f out: no ex* **16/1**
2301 **8** *shd* **Forest Edge (IRE)**[28] 7038 2-9-1 **77**.... AdamKirby 8 68
(David Evans) *hld up: pushed along over 3f out: nvr on terms* **12/1**
14 **9** *15* **Spiders Of Spring (IRE)**[188] 2121 2-8-4 **66**.... JimmyQuinn 6 20
(Richard Fahey) *sn pushed along in rr: lost tch fnl 3f* **40/1**

1m 29.41s (-0.19) **Going Correction** -0.10s/f (Stan) **9** Ran SP% **112.8**
Speed ratings (Par 98): **97,96,96,94,94 92,91,91,74**
Tote Swingers:1&2:£5.90, 2&3:£3.90, 1&3:£1.80 CSF £20.47 CT £55.60 TOTE £4.30: £1.50, £2.60, £1.10; EX 27.40.
Owner Global Commodity Imports Ltd **Bred** Whisperview Trading Ltd **Trained** East Everleigh, Wilts
■ Stewards' Enquiry : Kieran O'Neill two-day ban: excessive use of the whip (Dec 3, 5)

FOCUS
Not a bad nursery, featuring four last-time-out winners. There was something of an uneven pace on and it saw a 1-2 for top juvenile trainer Richard Hannon.

NOTEBOOK
Tones(IRE) was last seen making all to shed his maiden tag at the fourth attempt at Epsom four months earlier and was making his AW/handicap debut. He was able to dictate pretty much from the front and displayed a decent attitude when pressed in the home straight. He's open to further progress, especially over this trip. (op 3-1)
Leenavesta(USA), another AW debutante, held every chance and went down fighting. This was a return to something like her best and she deserves to go one better. (op 10-1)
Amoure Medici's previous C&D form figures read 12 and he was well backed. Once again he hampered his cause with a sloppy start, though, and just shaped as though he could be worth trying over an extra furlong now. (op 7-2 tchd 4-1)
Elite was making her handicap debut for a new trainer and didn't get the best of runs late on. She can win a weak maiden this winter. (op 10-1)
Quite A Thing is not obviously bred for this trip, but shaped as though she may be ready for it when winning at Southwell last time out and this was her nursery debut. She wasn't helped by the outside stall, however, and after being rushed up to race handily, her stamina petered out inside the final furlong. (op 9-2)
For Shia And Lula(IRE), a short-head winner of a 6f maiden here 58 days earlier, looked a player out wide turning for home. However, he hung throughout the final furlong and has something to prove with his attitude. Official explanation: jockey said colt hung left (op 15-2)

7492 32REDPOKER.COM CLAIMING STKS 1m 141y(P)
7:20 (7:22) (Class 6) 3-Y-O+ **£1,704** (£503; £251) **Stalls** Low

Form RPR
435 **1** **Standpoint**[44] 6658 5-9-3 77....(p) GrahamGibbons 6 83
(Reg Hollinshead) *mde all: rdn and hung lft fnl f: jst hld on* **6/1**[3]
1416 **2** *hd* **Opus Maximus (IRE)**[5] 7412 6-8-11 67....(p) JoeFanning 2 77
(Jennie Candlish) *a.p: chsd wnr over 2f out: rdn over 1f out: r.o* **12/1**
0045 **3** *1¾* **Lovelace**[9] 7352 7-8-11 80.... WilliamCarson 10 73
(Richard Fahey) *chsd ldrs: rdn over 1f out: sn hung lft: styd on same pce ins fnl f* **10/1**
4400 **4** *1¾* **Pendragon (USA)**[56] 6339 8-9-9 89.... JamieSpencer 5 80
(Brian Ellison) *hld up: hdwy over 1f out: nt rch ldrs* **13/8**[1]
5231 **5** *½* **Dialogue**[49] 6541 5-9-6 88.... MichaelO'Connell(3) 1 79+
(Ollie Pears) *hld up: swtchd rt wl over 1f out: rdn and r.o ins fnl f: nvr nrr* **5/2**[2]
0450 **6** *hd* **Kidlat**[7] 7397 6-8-12 75.... DominicFox(3) 9 71
(Alan Bailey) *s.i.s: sn pushed along to chse wnr over 7f out tl rdn over 2f out: styd on same pce appr fnl f* **12/1**
0050 **7** *3* **Moynahan (USA)**[31] 6948 6-9-9 80.... StevieDonohoe 7 72
(Paul Cole) *hld up: hmpd wl over 1f out: n.d* **12/1**
00 **8** *22* **Mufasa Rules (USA)**[46] 6608 3-8-9 0....(t) LiamKeniry 8 10
(Sylvester Kirk) *s.i.s: hld up: rdn and wknd over 1f out* **100/1**

1m 49.27s (-1.23) **Going Correction** -0.10s/f (Stan)
WFA 3 from 5yo+ 3lb **8** Ran SP% **114.1**
Speed ratings (Par 101): **101,100,99,97,97 97,94,74**
Tote Swingers:1&2:£5.40, 2&3:£13.60, 1&3:£5.30 CSF £73.03 TOTE £10.20: £2.30, £2.20, £2.80; EX 67.80.Opus Maximus was claimed by Conor Dore for £6,000.
Owner Moores Metals Ltd **Bred** Juddmonte Farms Ltd **Trained** Upper Longdon, Staffs
■ Stewards' Enquiry : Graham Gibbons caution: careless riding

FOCUS
A decent claimer rated around the first three.
Dialogue Official explanation: vet said gelding bled from the nose

7493 EBF MIRROR PUNTERS CLUB MAIDEN STKS (DIV I) 1m 141y(P)
7:50 (7:52) (Class 5) 2-Y-O **£3,234** (£962; £481; £240) **Stalls** Low

Form RPR
34 **1** **Prince Alzain (USA)**[47] 6588 2-9-3 0.... SebSanders 13 81+
(Gerard Butler) *hld up: hdwy over 2f out: led ins fnl f: pushed out* **11/4**[2]
0 **2** *2* **California English (IRE)**[106] 4762 2-9-3 0.... ChrisCatlin 3 77
(Marco Botti) *led: rdn over 1f out: hdd and unable qck ins fnl f* **16/1**
3 **3** *1* **Sparkling Portrait**[24] 7101 2-9-3 0.... FrederikTylicki 11 75
(Richard Fahey) *a.p: rdn over 1f out: styd on same pce fnl f* **9/2**[3]
00 **4** *5* **Watheeq (USA)**[39] 6772 2-9-3 0.... AndreaAtzeni 4 64
(Roger Varian) *prom: chsd ldr 2f out: sn rdn: wknd ins fnl f* **9/2**[3]
5 *2* **Dartford (USA)** 2-9-3 0.... WilliamBuick 12 60+
(John Gosden) *hld up: pushed along over 2f out: nvr trbld ldrs* **9/4**[1]
0 **6** *¾* **So Cheeky**[23] 7124 2-8-12 0.... DaneO'Neill 9 53
(Richard Hannon) *chsd ldr tl rdn 2f out: wknd over 1f out* **25/1**
50 **7** *2½* **Gabrial's Layla (IRE)**[29] 6985 2-8-12 0.... JoeFanning 8 48
(Mark Johnston) *chsd ldrs tl rdn and wknd over 1f out* **22/1**
8 *5* **Lord Nandi** 2-9-3 0.... TomQueally 6 43
(Sir Henry Cecil) *s.i.s: outpcd* **12/1**
0 **9** *¾* **Discern**[9] 7344 2-8-12 0.... JamieSpencer 1 40+
(James Fanshawe) *hld up in tch: wknd over 2f out* **33/1**
00 **10** *½* **Fine Finale**[39] 6772 2-9-3 0.... AdamKirby 5 40
(Jeremy Gask) *hld up: pushed along 1/2-way: a in rr* **200/1**
0 **11** *½* **Zarosa (IRE)**[31] 6956 2-8-12 0.... JimmyQuinn 2 34
(John Berry) *s.i.s: outpcd* **100/1**
00 **12** *1½* **Letham Cottage**[15] 7258 2-9-3 0.... TomMcLaughlin 10 36
(David Evans) *chsd ldrs: hung rt fr over 2f out: eased over 1f out* **100/1**
13 *2½* **Young Lou** 2-8-12 0.... MartinLane 7 26
(Robin Dickin) *hmpd over 7f out: sn pushed along in rr: bhd fnl 3f* **100/1**

1m 49.56s (-0.94) **Going Correction** -0.10s/f (Stan) **13** Ran SP% **122.0**
Speed ratings (Par 96): **100,98,97,92,91 90,88,83,83,82 82,80,78**
Tote Swingers:1&2:£12.70, 2&3:£64.00, 1&3:£3.10 CSF £45.23 TOTE £4.30: £1.40, £4.10, £2.30; EX 56.30.
Owner Asaad Al Banwan **Bred** Dermot Cantillon & Patrick Hayes **Trained** Newmarket, Suffolk

NOTEBOOK
Prince Alzain(USA) deservedly made it third time lucky and won readily. He had a horrible draw, but was the most talented runner in attendance and got a positive ride. This was his trainer's fourth 2-y-o success from ten runners at the track since 2007, and he should make a useful middle-distance handicapper in due course. (op 3-1 tchd 10-3)
California English(IRE) finished out the back on his debut, but that came in a better maiden at Newmarket back in August. He ran a solid race from the front, improving plenty, and should be winning one of these if kept on the go this winter. (tchd 20-1)
Sparkling Portrait wasn't helped by his draw, but had shaped as though he would improve when third on his debut at Musselburgh last month and ran a decent race in defeat. He too can win one of these. (op 5-1)
Watheeq(USA) was making his AW after two modest runs on turf. He got the run of the race and looked a big player turning for home, but lacked any sort of gear change. He wants a stiffer test and is now eligible for handicaps. (op 5-1 tchd 6-1)
Dartford(USA) is from a leading yard whose juveniles must always be respected around here and was very well backed to make a winning debut. Covered up early from the outside draw, he had his chance but ultimately the run looked needed. His trainer knows all about his breeding, he has scope and can better this next time. (op 5-2 tchd 11-4 in a place)
Letham Cottage Official explanation: jockey said colt hung badly right

7494 EBF MIRROR PUNTERS CLUB MAIDEN STKS (DIV II) 1m 141y(P)
8:20 (8:23) (Class 5) 2-Y-O **£3,234** (£962; £481; £240) **Stalls** Low

Form RPR
2 **1** **Lycidas (GER)**[15] 7257 2-9-3 0.... StevieDonohoe 9 75+
(Tobias B P Coles) *a.p: chsd ldr over 2f out: rdn to ld over 1f out: r.o: readily* **13/2**
0 **2** *2½* **Ace Of Valhalla**[24] 7109 2-9-3 0.... TomQueally 10 70
(Sir Henry Cecil) *a.p: rdn to go 2nd wl ins fnl f: nt rch wnr* **11/4**[2]
05 **3** *1½* **Confirmed**[57] 6300 2-9-3 0....(t) AdamKirby 2 67
(Marco Botti) *sn led: rdn and hdd over 1f out: no ex ins fnl f* **5/2**[1]
0 **4** *½* **Nordic Quest (IRE)**[25] 7082 2-9-3 0.... SebSanders 7 66
(Gerard Butler) *mid-div: hdwy over 2f out: rdn over 1f out: styd on* **18/1**
5 *1* **To The Sea (USA)** 2-8-12 0.... JoeFanning 6 58+
(Mark Johnston) *s.s: in rr: hdwy over 1f out: hung lft ins fnl f: styd on: nt rch ldrs* **11/1**
0453 **6** *3½* **I'm Harry**[21] 7157 2-9-3 71....(b[1]) RobertWinston 4 56
(Charles Hills) *chsd ldr tl rdn over 2f out: wknd fnl f* **13/2**
7 *¾* **Trove (IRE)** 2-9-3 0.... WilliamBuick 3 55
(John Gosden) *dwlt: sn mid-div: pushed along over 3f out: n.d* **6/1**[3]
00 **8** *3¼* **Cash Injection**[87] 5375 2-9-3 0.... TomMcLaughlin 1 48
(Karen George) *chsd ldrs: pushed along over 3f out: wknd over 1f out* **100/1**
9 *½* **Lady Burlesque (IRE)** 2-8-12 0.... TonyCulhane 8 42
(Mick Channon) *hld up: a in rr* **40/1**
10 *2¼* **Marshall Art** 2-9-0 0.... MichaelO'Connell(3) 11 42
(John Quinn) *s.s: in rr: hdwy over 2f out: sn wknd* **25/1**
11 *10* **Dorrit** 2-8-12 0.... SteveDrowne 5 16
(Roger Charlton) *prom: lost pl 5f out: bhd fnl 3f* **16/1**

1m 50.38s (-0.12) **Going Correction** -0.10s/f (Stan) **11** Ran SP% **122.9**
Speed ratings (Par 96): **96,93,92,92,91 88,87,84,84,82 73**
Tote Swingers:1&2:£8.50, 2&3:£4.90, 1&3:£7.90 CSF £25.66 TOTE £9.90: £3.20, £1.90, £1.20; EX 30.00.
Owner T Coles,Graf & Grafin von Stauffenberg **Bred** Graf And Grafin Von Stauffenberg **Trained** Newmarket, Suffolk

FOCUS
This second division of the juvenile maiden was run at a decent pace and the form should work out.

NOTEBOOK
Lycidas(GER) confirmed the promise of his debut second behind a useful winner at Ffos Las and ran out a taking winner. He moved sweetly through the race and wasn't in any serious danger after taking it up in the home straight. A juvenile with some size about him, he could make into a decent handicapper next year. (op 9-2)
Ace Of Valhalla was expected to improve on his debut effort last month and duly did so, but would have fared even better had he not been drawn wide. He still looked green under pressure and ought to take the beating next time out. (op 7-2 tchd 9-2)
Confirmed ran an encouraging race in defeat considering he did so much out in front on his first outing over this far. Handicaps are now an option for him. (op 7-2)
Nordic Quest(IRE), whose yard won the first division, ran well considering he was wide for most of the contest and this was a big improvement on his Yarmouth debut last month. (op 16-1)
To The Sea(USA) was bidding to give her yard a fifth winner from as many runners in this event, but proved easy to back. She fell out of the gates and so showed a nice deal of ability and it wouldn't surprise to see her winning next time out. (op 9-1)
Dorrit Official explanation: jockey said filly hung left

7495 32REDCASINO.COM H'CAP (DIV I) 1m 4f 50y(P)
8:50 (8:50) (Class 6) (0-60,60) 3-Y-O+ **£1,704** (£503; £251) **Stalls** Low

Form RPR
0031 **1** **Royal Alcor (IRE)**[8] 7370 4-9-7 **57**....(b) FrankieMcDonald 6 74+
(Alastair Lidderdale) *s.i.s: hld up: hdwy to chse ldr over 3f out: led over 2f out: rdn clr and hung lft over 1f out: styd on* **5/2**[1]
0531 **2** *3* **Art Thief**[77] 5739 3-8-13 **55**.... NeilChalmers 5 65
(Michael Appleby) *hld up: hdwy over 2f out: rdn to chse wnr over 1f out: no imp* **6/1**
3424 **3** *4½* **Royal Bonsai**[24] 6600 3-9-1 **60**.... MichaelO'Connell(3) 9 63
(John Quinn) *prom: rdn over 3f out: styd on same pce fnl 2f* **10/3**[2]
5303 **4** *5* **Dream Catcher (SWE)**[87] 5379 8-9-9 **59**....(p) RichardKingscote 1 54
(Jonjo O'Neill) *prom: chsd ldr over 6f out: tl pushed along over 3f out: rdn and wknd over 2f out* **7/1**
3132 **5** *9* **Fifty Cents**[23] 7122 7-9-1 **58**....(p) BrendanPowell(7) 3 38
(Brendan Powell) *led: hdd over 2f out: wknd wl over 1f out* **7/2**[3]
4040 **6** *27* **Graycliffe (IRE)**[19] 7195 5-9-5 **55**....(p) JoeFanning 2 —
(Jennie Candlish) *prom: pushed along over 3f out: sn wknd: t.o* **12/1**
0/00 **7** *16* **Crafty George (IRE)**[35] 6876 6-8-10 **46** oh1.... AndreaAtzeni 10 —
(Daniel Mark Loughnane, Ire) *chsd ldr over 5f: pushed along 5f out: rdn and wknd 4f out: t.o* **22/1**

2m 40.02s (-1.08) **Going Correction** -0.10s/f (Stan)
WFA 3 from 4yo+ 6lb **7** Ran SP% **112.7**
Speed ratings (Par 101): **99,97,94,90,84 66,56**
Tote Swingers:1&2:£3.80, 2&3:£4.00, 1&3:£2.40 CSF £17.40 CT £49.11 TOTE £4.30: £2.40, £2.00; EX 22.60.
Owner Royal Windsor Racing Club **Bred** John Hayes **Trained** Eastbury, Berks

FOCUS
A moderate handicap, run at a strong pace and fair form for the grade.

Fifty Cents Official explanation: trainer said gelding was unsuited by going left-handed

7496 32REDCASINO.COM H'CAP (DIV II) 1m 4f 50y(P)
9:20 (9:20) (Class 6) (0-60,59) 3-Y-O+ **£1,704** (£503; £251) **Stalls** Low

Form RPR

6013 **1** **Mazij**[16] 7241 3-9-4 **59** WilliamCarson 1 74
(Peter Hiatt) *mde all: rdn clr over 2f out: hung rt over 1f out: unchal* **13/2**

3565 **2** *8* **Cathcart Castle**[25] 7085 3-9-1 **56** TonyCulhane 4 58
(Mick Channon) *hld up: hdwy over 2f out: rdn to go 2nd ins fnl f: no ch w wnr* **5/1**[3]

4005 **3** *3/4* **Rasteau (IRE)**[10] 7327 3-8-6 **47** JimmyQuinn 10 48
(Tom Keddy) *hld up: hdwy whn hmpd over 2f out: styd on to go 3rd wl ins fnl f: nvr nrr* **16/1**

4132 **4** *1* **Beauchamp Xiara**[8] 7370 5-8-12 **54** NicoleNordblad(7) 2 53
(Hans Adielsson) *chsd wnr over 6f: wnt 2nd again over 2f out: rdn over 1f out: wknd fnl f* **9/4**[1]

0543 **5** *8* **Sir Randolf (IRE)**[10] 7333 3-8-10 **51** (t) LiamKeniry 6 38
(Sylvester Kirk) *prom: pushed along over 3f out: wknd over 2f out* **7/1**

0000 **6** *2* **Swords**[67] 6029 9-8-10 **45** (be1) StevieDonohoe 7 28
(Ray Peacock) *hld up: racd keenly: rdn and wknd over 2f out* **20/1**

455 **7** *2* **Naheell**[8] 7363 5-9-8 **57** JamieMackay 5 37
(George Prodromou) *chsd ldrs: rdn over 4f out: wknd wl over 2f out* **10/1**

00 **8** *1/2* **Green To Gold (IRE)**[23] 7122 6-9-10 **59** (b) JamieSpencer 9 38
(Don Cantillon) *stdd s: hld up: plld hrd: hdwy 8f out: chsd ldr over 5f out: rdn over 3f out: wknd wl over 1f out* **4/1**[2]

2m 42.29s (1.19) **Going Correction** -0.10s/f (Stan)
WFA 3 from 5yo+ 6lb **8** Ran SP% **113.0**
Speed ratings (Par 101): **92,86,86,85,80 78,77,77**
Tote Swingers:1&2:£8.70, 2&3:£8.90, 1&3:£19.10 CSF £37.87 CT £494.67 TOTE £10.30: £2.90, £2.10, £5.50; EX 45.50.
Owner P W Hiatt **Bred** The Hill Stud **Trained** Hook Norton, Oxon

FOCUS
The second division of the 1m4f handicap and it was run at a fair pace. The winner has improved but this was a weak race.
T/Plt: £660.80 to a £1 stake. Pool: £98,406.12. 108.71 winning tickets T/Qpdt: £37.40 to a £1 stake. Pool: £10,808.12. 213.30 winning tickets CR

7497 - 7499a (Foreign Racing) - See Raceform Interactive

7419 SOUTHWELL (L-H)
Tuesday, November 22

OFFICIAL GOING: Standard
Wind: Nil Weather: Murky

7500 32RED H'CAP (DIV I) 6f (F)
12:10 (12:11) (Class 4) (0-80,80) 3-Y-O+ **£4,431** (£1,308; £654) **Stalls** Low

Form RPR

1322 **1** **Mount Hollow**[37] 6895 6-8-6 **72** (e1) JackDuern(7) 10 82
(Reg Hollinshead) *stdd s and hld up in rr: smooth hdwy over 2f out: chal over 1f out: led ins fnl f: comf* **9/1**

3004 **2** *1 1/2* **Sleepy Blue Ocean**[13] 7341 5-9-1 **74** (p) LukeMorris 4 79
(John Balding) *a.p: hdwy to ld 2f out: sn rdn: hdd ins fnl f: kpt on same pce* **6/1**[3]

01 **3** *hd* **Il Battista**[49] 6616 3-8-13 **72** ow1 (be) SebSanders 6 76
(Alan McCabe) *chsd ldrs on inner: rdn along and outpcd 1/2-way: hdwy wl over 1f out: styd on ins fnl f: nrst fin* **5/1**[2]

0004 **4** *1/2* **Oldjoesaid**[13] 7332 7-9-1 **74** StephenCraine 7 77
(Kevin Ryan) *trckd ldrs: effrt and n.m.r wl over 1f out: sn rdn: swtchd rt ent fnl f: kpt on* **16/1**

1116 **5** *nk* **Captain Scooby**[12] 7355 5-9-3 **79** (e) RobertLButler(3) 8 81
(Richard Guest) *towards rr: rdn along 1/2-way: swtchd rt wl over 1f out: styd on fnl f: nrst fin* **28/1**

5414 **6** *3 1/4* **Tourist**[24] 7176 6-8-10 **69** StevieDonohoe 3 60
(Ian Williams) *in rr and sn pushed along: rdn 2f out: styd on appr fnl f: nrst fin* **11/1**

6400 **7** *hd* **Prince Of Vasa (IRE)**[12] 7355 4-8-7 **66** oh6 AdrianNicholls 2 57
(Michael Smith) *prom: cl up over 2f out: sn rdn and wknd wl over 1f out* **20/1**

0012 **8** *3/4* **Rowan Spirit (IRE)**[13] 7341 3-9-2 **75** GrahamGibbons 9 63
(Mark Brisbourne) *trckd ldrs: hdwy over 2f out: rdn wl over 1f out and grad wknd* **10/3**[1]

-110 **9** *1* **Sir Louis**[294] 377 4-8-8 **67** BarryMcHugh 1 52
(Richard Fahey) *cl up on inner: rdn along over 2f out: sn wknd* **16/1**

040 **10** *1 1/4* **Bravo King (IRE)**[18] 7262 3-9-7 **80** (t1) MartinHarley 11 61
(Richard Guest) *sn led: rdn along 1/2-way: hdd 2f out: sn wknd* **14/1**

2211 **11** *1* **Where's Reiley (USA)**[252] 853 5-9-6 **79** LeeNewman 12 57
(David Barron) *in tch on outer: rdn along 1/2-way and wd st: sn edgd rt and wknd* **5/1**[2]

1m 16.09s (-0.41) **Going Correction** 0.0s/f (Stan) **11** Ran SP% **115.7**
Speed ratings (Par 105): **102,100,99,99,98 94,94,93,91,90 88**
toteswingers:1&2:£9.10, 2&3:£7.70, 1&3:£12.10 CSF £61.13 CT £307.73 TOTE £10.00: £3.50, £2.90, £2.30; EX 64.20 TRIFECTA Not won..
Owner R Hollinshead **Bred** G Robinson **Trained** Upper Longdon, Staffs

FOCUS
A fair sprint handicap run in a time 0.42 seconds slower than the second division. The form looks pretty ordinary with the runner-up rated to his 5f form.

7501 ROB POPE IS THE BEST NOVICE STKS 1m (F)
12:40 (12:40) (Class 5) 2-Y-O **£2,264** (£673; £336; £168) **Stalls** Low

Form RPR

3031 **1** **Finbar**[13] 7336 2-9-2 75 FrederikTylicki 3 77+
(James Given) *trckd ldng pair: hdwy and cl up over 2f out: shkn up to ld over 1f out: sn clr: pushed out* **1/3**[1]

512 **2** *7* **Purple 'n Gold (IRE)**[25] 7140 2-9-2 76 (p) JoeFanning 2 60
(George Baker) *led to 1/2-way: cl up: rdn along to ld 2f out: edgd rt and hdd appr fnl f: sn one pce* **5/2**[2]

0 **3** *2 1/4* **Our Ivor**[20] 7232 2-9-0 NeilChalmers 4 53
(Michael Appleby) *cl up on outer: led 1/2-way: rdn along and hdd 2f out: hld whn sltly hmpd appr fnl f: sn one pce* **100/1**

00 **4** *4* **Dylans Verse (IRE)**[20] 7233 2-9-0 0 ChrisCatlin 1 44
(Reg Hollinshead) *chsd ldrs: rdn along 1/2-way: sn outpcd and bhd* **40/1**[3]

1m 43.37s (-0.33) **Going Correction** 0.0s/f (Stan) **4** Ran SP% **107.0**
Speed ratings (Par 96): **101,94,91,87**
CSF £1.39 TOTE £1.70; EX 1.40.
Owner Elite Racing Club **Bred** Elite Racing Club **Trained** Willoughton, Lincs

FOCUS
It would be unwise to take the bare form literally, with the disappointing Purple 'N Gold probably not running to his official mark of 76, but there was a useful winner. The third and fourth help to set the level.

NOTEBOOK
Finbar rather ran in snatches, still looking a bit green and probably not appreciating the kickback, but he came back on the bridle once in the clear in the straight before drawing away when asked. He'll surely face tougher tasks when back on turf next year, but he had also impressed when winning a C&D nursery off 67 last time and is progressing into a decent sort.
Purple 'n Gold(IRE) hasn't progressed as expected since winning a 6f Wolverhampton maiden. He disappointed when upped to 7f in a weak race at the same venue next time and didn't fare any better under these different conditions with cheekpieces tried. Facing competition for the lead from around halfway wasn't the issue. (tchd 11-4)
Our Ivor showed ability on his debut at Nottingham and did so again. (op 80-1)
Dylans Verse(IRE) seemingly needs more time.

7502 32RED H'CAP (DIV II) 6f (F)
1:10 (1:11) (Class 4) (0-80,80) 3-Y-O+ **£4,431** (£1,308; £654) **Stalls** Low

Form RPR

5012 **1** **Mottley Crewe**[12] 7356 4-8-11 **70** (b) MartinHarley 2 86+
(Richard Guest) *trckd ldrs on inner: smooth hdwy and cl up 2f out: led on bit appr fnl f: sn qcknd clr: easily* **9/2**[3]

2002 **2** *3 1/4* **Dorback**[13] 7332 4-9-2 **75** FergusSweeney 4 81
(Noel Wilson) *hld up: hdwy 1/2-way: swtchd wd wl over 1f out and sn rdn: styd on fnl f: no ch w wnr* **14/1**

0524 **3** *hd* **J R Hartley**[19] 7243 3-9-2 **75** (e1) TomEaves 7 80
(Bryan Smart) *led: rdn along 2f out: hdd appr fnl f: kpt on same pce: lost 2nd nr fin* **10/1**

6033 **4** *1 3/4* **Spitfire**[13] 7341 6-8-10 **69** FrederikTylicki 8 68
(J R Jenkins) *cl up: effrt 2f out: sn rdn and ev ch tl wknd appr fnl f* **4/1**[2]

5066 **5** *1 1/4* **Dickie Le Davoir**[12] 7356 7-8-9 **68** (be) JohnFahy 11 63
(Richard Guest) *dwlt and in rr: hdwy on inner wl over 1f out: sn rdn and kpt on: nrst fin* **25/1**

-245 **6** *shd* **Trade Secret**[12] 7356 4-9-0 **73** RobertWinston 1 68
(Mel Brittain) *chsd ldrs: rdn over 2f out: sn no imp* **12/1**

6225 **7** *1 1/4* **Ingleby Arch (USA)**[42] 6778 8-9-2 **80** LMcNiff(5) 3 71
(David Barron) *dwlt and towards rr on outer: hdwy and wd st: sn rdn and nvr nr ldrs* **10/1**

1524 **8** *1 3/4* **Ezra Church (IRE)**[197] 1942 4-9-1 **74** GrahamGibbons 5 59
(David Barron) *chsd ldrs: rdn along 1/2-way: sn wknd* **7/2**[1]

3603 **9** *2 1/2* **Night Trade (IRE)**[4] 7456 4-9-6 **79** (p) LukeMorris 10 56
(Ronald Harris) *a towards rr* **8/1**

1631 **10** *7* **Cape Of Storms**[217] 1463 8-8-7 **66** (b) JoeFanning 9 21
(Roy Brotherton) *cl up on outer: rdn along 1/2-way: wknd over 2f out* **16/1**

1m 15.67s (-0.83) **Going Correction** 0.0s/f (Stan) **10** Ran SP% **113.8**
Speed ratings (Par 105): **105,100,100,98,96 96,94,92,88,79**
toteswingers:1&2:£16.70, 2&3:£16.30, 1&3:£8.00 CSF £63.77 CT £594.56 TOTE £7.50: £2.00, £1.60, £3.00; EX 83.20 Trifecta £229.90 Pool: £372.83 - 1.20 winning units..
Owner Rakebackmypoker.com **Bred** Longdon Stud Ltd **Trained** Stainforth, S Yorks

FOCUS
The time was 0.42 seconds faster than the first leg, but 0.10 slower than the improving Take Cover managed later on the card. The third looks the best guide to the level.

7503 MARGARET RICE MEMORIAL MAIDEN STKS 1m 4f (F)
1:40 (1:40) (Class 5) 3-Y-O+ **£2,385** (£704; £352) **Stalls** Low

Form RPR

0-36 **1** **Mount Crystal (IRE)**[40] 6810 3-8-12 65 MichaelHills 6 72
(Charles Hills) *mde all: pushed along wl over 2f out: rdn wl over 1f out: edgd rt ent fnl f: kpt on gamely fnl f* **9/1**

- **2** *1 1/4* **Priceless Art (IRE)**[46] 6-9-9 0 DaneO'Neill 4 75
(Alan Swinbank) *hld up: hdwy 1/2-way: cl up 4f out: pushed along 3f out: rdn to chal 2f out and ev ch tl one pce fnl f* **2/1**[1]

3334 **3** *3 1/2* **Bow River Arch (USA)**[50] 6584 3-8-12 72 (p) JohnFahy 10 64
(Jeremy Noseda) *chsd ldrs: rdn along over 3f out: kpt on same pce fnl 2f* **3/1**[3]

0600 **4** *10* **Raghdaan**[10] 7399 4-9-4 45 LauraPike(5) 11 53
(Peter Hiatt) *hld up towards rr: hdwy over 3f out: kpt on fnl 2f: nrst fin* **40/1**

5 *2 1/2* **Saleem (IRE)** 3-8-12 0 JoeFanning 9 44
(Mark Johnston) *s.i.s and bhd: hdwy over 3f out: kpt on fnl 2f: nvr a factor* **8/1**

-006 **6** *shd* **Star Rebel**[36] 6923 3-9-3 63 (b1) BarryMcHugh 12 49
(George Margarson) *trckd ldrs: hdwy over 4f out: rdn 3f out: grad wknd* **20/1**

5004 **7** *1 1/2* **Northumberland**[18] 7271 5-9-4 51 LMcNiff(5) 8 47
(Owen Brennan) *prom: rdn along over 4f out: sn wknd* **100/1**

0253 **8** *7* **Midnight Waltz**[19] 7244 3-8-12 68 SebSanders 1 31
(Sir Mark Prescott Bt) *prom: rdn along 5f out: sn wknd* **11/4**[2]

0-00 **9** *2* **Nella Sofia**[42] 6781 3-8-12 39 KellyHarrison 2 27
(James Given) *chsd ldrs: rdn along 4f out: sn wknd* **100/1**

0-05 **10** *45* **The Mighty Mod (USA)**[8] 6575 4-9-2 34 NoelGarbutt(7) 3 —
(Michael Chapman) *a in rr: bhd fnl 4f* **100/1**

046- **11** *1* **Rio Caribe (IRE)**[493] 4155 4-9-9 57 RobbieFitzpatrick 7 —
(David Thompson) *midfield: rdn along 1/2-way: sn wknd* **100/1**

00 **12** *27* **Eyeforglory**[29] 7061 5-9-4 0 (t) DuranFentiman 5 —
(Suzzanne France) *a towards rr: bhd fnl 4f* **100/1**

2m 40.35s (-0.65) **Going Correction** 0.0s/f (Stan)
WFA 3 from 4yo+ 6lb **12** Ran SP% **118.3**
Speed ratings (Par 103): **102,101,98,92,90 90,89,84,83,53 52,34**
toteswingers:1&2:£5.70, 2&3:£2.30, 1&3:£6.30 CSF £26.97 TOTE £10.70: £3.30, £1.20, £1.50; EX 37.50 Trifecta £69.60 Pool: £413.20 - 4.39 winning units..
Owner Triermore Stud **Bred** Mrs U Schwarzenbach **Trained** Lambourn, Berks

FOCUS
Not a bad maiden, although plenty of these are hard to win with. The time was 0.36 seconds faster than the later modestly run Class 5 handicap. The runner-up is rated in line with his bumper form, while the fourth and seventh limit things.

7504 32RED.COM H'CAP 6f (F)
2:10 (2:11) (Class 6) (0-65,71) 3-Y-O+ **£1,704** (£503; £251) **Stalls** Low

Form RPR

11 **1** **Take Cover**[7] 7419 4-9-11 **71** 6ex SebSanders 9 86+
(George Margarson) *trckd ldng pair: hdwy to chal 2f out: rdn to ld appr fnl f: kpt on* **8/11**[1]

4000 **2** *1 1/2* **Soopacal (IRE)**[12] 7355 6-8-13 **64** JustinNewman(5) 2 74
(Michael Herrington) *cl up: led 2f out: sn rdn: hdd appr fnl f: kpt on same pce* **17/2**[2]

The Form Book, Raceform Ltd, Compton, RG20 6NL

0601 **3** *2* **Elhamri**[7] 7420 7-9-6 **66** 6ex.. BarryMcHugh 6 70
(Conor Dore) *chsd ldrs: rdn 2f out: kpt on fnl f* **10/1**

5020 **4** *1 1/4* **Caramelita**[35] 6939 4-9-1 **61**.......................... StephenCraine 3 61
(J R Jenkins) *chsd ldrs: rdn 2f out: one pce appr fnl f* **20/1**

0003 **5** *1 1/4* **Ace Of Spies (IRE)**[7] 7419 6-9-2 **62**..............................(b) DaneO'Neill 1 58
(Conor Dore) *led: rdn along 1/2-way: hdd 2f out: wknd over 1f out* **9/1**[3]

6202 **6** *5* **Deliberation (IRE)**[17] 7299 3-9-2 **65**.......................... JulieBurke(3) 11 45
(Kevin Ryan) *chsd ldrs: rdn over 2f out: sn wknd* **9/1**[3]

2006 **7** *1 3/4* **Diamond Vine (IRE)**[12] 7349 3-9-3 **63**............................(p) LukeMorris 7 37
(Ronald Harris) *nvr nr ldrs* **20/1**

6500 **8** *2* **Mazovian (USA)**[29] 7057 3-8-12 **65**.......................... NoelGarbutt(7) 12 33
(Michael Chapman) *nvr bttr than midfield* **33/1**

4500 **9** *nk* **Dunseverick (IRE)**[13] 7341 3-9-5 **65**.............................. TonyCulhane 5 32
(David Flood) *a in rr* **25/1**

4036 **10** *2 1/4* **Dunmore Boy (IRE)**[222] 1323 3-8-11 **64**............(p) GeorgeChaloner(7) 10 23
(Richard Fahey) *midfield: rdn along 1/2-way: sn wknd* **28/1**

-000 **11** *1 1/2* **Nacho Libre**[248] 915 6-9-0 **60**......................................(b) PaddyAspell 13 15
(Michael Easterby) *dwlt: a in rr* **50/1**

1m 15.57s (-0.93) **Going Correction** 0.0s/f (Stan) **11** Ran SP% **119.2**
Speed ratings (Par 101): **106,104,101,99,98 91,89,86,85,82 80**
toteswingers:1&2:£2.50, 2&3:£10.60, 1&3:£2.90 CSF £6.48 CT £40.60 TOTE £1.70: £1.10, £1.50, £2.40; EX 9.80 Trifecta £61.50 Pool: £539.29 - 6.48 winning units..
Owner Norcroft Park Stud **Bred** Norcroft Park Stud **Trained** Newmarket, Suffolk

FOCUS
The time was quicker than both divisions of the Class 4 handicap. The third is rated to recent course form.

7505 32RED CASINO CLAIMING STKS 7f (F)
2:40 (2:40) (Class 6) 2-Y-O **£1,704** (£503; £251) **Stalls** Low

Form RPR

0006 **1** **Point At Issue (IRE)**[7] 7421 2-8-11 49........................(b) AdrianNicholls 1 59
(David Nicholls) *mde all: jnd and rdn over 2f out: edgd lft over 1f out: sn clr: rdn out* **5/1**[3]

4421 **2** *6* **Le King Beau (USA)**[6] 7434 2-9-1 63.......................... WilliamCarson 3 48
(William Muir) *trckd wnr: hdwy on inner and cl up over 2f out: sn rdn and hung bdly rt over 1f out: sn one pce: jst hld on for 2nd* **10/11**[1]

3 *hd* **Siouxies Dream** 2-9-0 0.. NeilChalmers 5 47+
(Michael Appleby) *dwlt: sn chsng ldng pair: rdn: green and outpcd 2f out: styd on ins fnl f* **20/1**

5260 **4** *5* **Artists Corner**[12] 7353 2-8-2 55......................................(p) JimmyQuinn 2 22
(Richard Fahey) *dwlt: in tch: effrt 3f out: sn rdn and outpcd* **3/1**[2]

6 **5** *hd* **Ficelle (IRE)**[12] 7353 2-8-10 0.. MartinHarley 4 30
(Mrs K Burke) *chsd ldrs: rdn along 3f out: sn outpcd* **8/1**

1m 31.39s (1.09) **Going Correction** 0.0s/f (Stan) **5** Ran SP% **109.9**
Speed ratings (Par 94): **93,86,85,80,79**
CSF £10.11 TOTE £5.20: £2.10, £1.10; EX 10.80.
Owner David Fish **Bred** Lynn Lodge Stud **Trained** Sessay, N Yorks

FOCUS
A weak claimer. The winner has been afforded some improvement on his previous best but the second was well below form.

NOTEBOOK
Point At Issue(IRE) would have been 10lb worse off with Le King Beau in a handicap and surely the runner-up failed to run to his mark. That said, the winner was help by a step up in trip. (tchd 6-1)
Le King Beau(USA) was a winner over this distance on Polytrack last time, but didn't prove as effective back on Fibresand and failed to run up to his mark. (op Evens tchd 5-6 and 11-10 in places)
Siouxies Dream showed a bit of ability on this racecourse debut and could win a minor race. (op 16-1)
Artists Corner, who had cheekpieces on instead of a visor, remains unproven on the surface. (op 11-4 tchd 10-3)
Ficelle(IRE) Official explanation: jockey said filly hung left

7506 KRIS & HELEN CLARK'S 5TH WEDDING ANNIVERSARY H'CAP 1m 4f (F)
[illegible] **Stalls** Low

Form RPR

5302 **1** **Brockfield**[20] 7237 5-9-0 **65**... RobertWinston 4 73
(Mel Brittain) *mde all: set stdy pce: qcknd 3f out: rdn wl over 1f out: kpt on wl ins fnl f* **5/1**

3513 **2** *1* **Waahej**[12] 7346 5-9-5 **75**.. LauraPike(5) 6 81
(Peter Hiatt) *hld up in rr: hdwy 4f out: chsd wnr over 2f out: rdn wl over 1f out: no imp fnl f* **5/2**[1]

0052 **3** *7* **Calculating (IRE)**[19] 7244 7-9-2 **72**................................ LeeNewnes(5) 2 67
(Mark Usher) *chsd ldrs: cl up on inner 4f out: rdn 3f out: kpt on one pce fnl 2f* **12/1**

3/0- **4** *15* **Ibrox (IRE)**[448] 5646 6-9-1 **66**... AndrewMullen 5 37
(Alan Brown) *chsd ldrs: rdn along over 3f out: sn wknd* **20/1**

-000 **5** *3 3/4* **Effervesce (IRE)**[18] 7272 4-9-0 **65**.................................... DaneO'Neill 1 30
(David Pipe) *s.i.s: a in rr* **11/1**

1006 **6** *3 1/4* **Daaweitza**[52] 6538 8-9-10 **75**..(be) JoeFanning 7 35
(Brian Ellison) *chsd wnr: rdn along over 3f out: grad wknd fr over 2f out* **11/4**[2]

541 **P** **C P Joe (IRE)**[18] 7264 3-8-6 **63**..(v) LukeMorris 3 —
(Paul Green) *prom whn stmbld and lost pl over 4f out: sn in rr and bhd: lost action and p.u over 2f out: dismntd* **4/1**[3]

2m 40.71s (-0.29) **Going Correction** 0.0s/f (Stan)
WFA 3 from 4yo+ 6lb **7** Ran SP% **112.7**
Speed ratings (Par 103): **100,99,94,84,82 80,—**
toteswingers:1&2:£2.30, 2&3:£4.10, 1&3:£4.20 CSF £17.38 TOTE £5.40: £2.10, £2.60; EX 22.30.
Owner Mel Brittain **Bred** Cheveley Park Stud Ltd **Trained** Warthill, N Yorks
■ Stewards' Enquiry : Laura Pike two-day ban: used whip with excessive frequency (Dec 6-7)

FOCUS
A modest handicap in which the winner was allowed an uncontested lead and recorded a time 0.36 seconds slower than the earlier maiden. The winner is rated to his turf form with the second to his recent Polytrack mark.
C P Joe(IRE) Official explanation: jockey said gelding stumbled badly and pulled up

7507 £32 FREE AT 32RED.COM AMATEUR RIDERS' H'CAP 1m (F)
3:40 (3:43) (Class 6) (0-60,60) 3-Y-O+ **£1,646** (£506; £253) **Stalls** Low

Form RPR

0401 **1** **Minortransgression (USA)**[19] 7247 4-10-10 **59** MissSallyRandell(3) 14 69
(Paul Rich) *in tch on outer: stdy hdwy over 2f out: led 1 1/2f out: rdn ent fnl f: edgd rt: kpt on* **5/1**[2]

0201 **2** *1 1/4* **Lujano**[12] 7351 6-10-11 **57**... MrSWalker 1 64
(Ollie Pears) *chsd ldrs on inner: rdn along 1/2-way: hdwy 2f out: sn swtchd rt and rdn: styd on to chse wnr appr fnl f: no imp whn n.m.r towards fin* **15/2**[3]

2000 **3** *hd* **General Tufto**[35] 6938 6-10-10 **56**..................................(b) MissEJJones 2 63
(Charles Smith) *bhd on inner: swtchd rt to outer and hdwy 2f out: rdn over 1f out: styd on ins fnl f* **14/1**

0056 **4** *2* **Avalon Bay**[74] 5901 3-10-3 **56**....................................... MrMTStanley(5) 11 58
(Pat Eddery) *chsd ldrs: hdwy over 2f out: rdn over 1f out: kpt on same pce* **20/1**

2124 **5** *1/2* **Scarborough Lily**[12] 7351 3-10-12 **60**...................(b) MissSBrotherton 10 61
(Edward Vaughan) *hld up towards rr: hdwy 2f out: swtchd lft and rdn over 1f out: kpt on ins fnl f: nrst fin* **9/2**[1]

3500 **6** *nse* **Granny Anne (IRE)**[6] 7441 3-10-2 **57**.......................(b[1]) MrsRWilson(7) 3 58
(Paul D'Arcy) *bhd: hdwy on outer wl over 2f out: sn rdn: styd on appr fnl f: nrst fin* **20/1**

5000 **7** *1 1/4* **Kipchak (IRE)**[18] 7265 6-11-0 **60**................................(b) MissGAndrews 4 58
(Conor Dore) *led 3f: cl up tl rdn 2f out and grad wknd* **17/2**

6043 **8** *1* **Fault**[4] 7462 5-10-7 **58**...(vt) MrFTett(5) 9 54
(Alastair Lidderdale) *chsd ldrs: hdwy to ld after 3f: rdn over 2f out: hdd 1 1/2f out and sn wknd* **8/1**

2006 **9** *1 1/2* **Jonnie Skull (IRE)**[12] 7351 5-10-5 **58**....................(vt) MissJSohanta(7) 5 50
(Phil McEntee) *prom: rdn along 3f out: wknd wl over 1f out: sltly hmpd appr fnl f* **16/1**

1206 **10** *1* **Zarius**[49] 6616 4-10-8 **59**... MrFrazerWilliams(5) 8 49
(Chris Wall) *in rr and swtchd wd after 2f: sn bhd tl styd on u.p on inner fnl 2f: n.d* **8/1**

3650 **11** *3/4* **Merrjanah**[29] 7057 3-10-5 **60**.. MrAFrench(7) 13 48
(John Wainwright) *dwlt: a in rr* **66/1**

1005 **12** *1 1/2* **Zaheeb**[35] 6938 3-10-4 **57**.......................................(p) MrBMMorris(5) 12 42
(Dave Morris) *dwlt: sn pushed along into midfield after 2f: rdn over 3f out and sn wknd* **25/1**

4444 **13** *2 1/4* **Galloping Minister (IRE)**[32] 7001 3-10-4 **59**.......... MissALMurphy(7) 7 38
(Tom Dascombe) *midfield: rdn along wl over 3f out: sn wknd* **11/1**

0040 **14** *1/2* **Watch Chain (IRE)**[12] 7352 4-10-11 **57**......................(p) MrPCollington 6 35
(Alan McCabe) *prom: effrt and cl up over 2f out: sn rdn and wknd qckly wl over 1f out* **16/1**

1m 46.3s (2.60) **Going Correction** 0.0s/f (Stan)
WFA 3 from 4yo+ 2lb **14** Ran SP% **121.0**
Speed ratings (Par 101): **87,85,85,83,83 83,81,80,79,78 77,76,73,73**
toteswingers:1&2:£4.90, 2&3:£14.70, 1&3:£16.00 CSF £40.59 CT £516.47 TOTE £6.50: £2.30, £2.50, £4.30; EX 40.80 Trifecta £430.70 Pool: £745.03 - 1.28 winning units..
Owner G A Morgan **Bred** Padua Stables **Trained** Newport, Gwent
■ Stewards' Enquiry : Mr Frazer Williams five-day ban: used whip with excessive frequency (Dec 19,others tbn)

FOCUS
A moderate but competitive amateur riders' handicap. The form is rated around the first two.
T/Plt: £19.70 to a £1 stake. Pool of £52,971.76 - 1,961.79 winning tickets. T/Qpdt: £4.90 to a £1 stake. Pool of £4,558.16 - 687.40 winning tickets. JR

7449 SAINT-CLOUD (L-H)
Tuesday, November 22

OFFICIAL GOING: Turf: heavy

7508a PRIX ISONOMY (LISTED RACE) (2YO) (TURF) 1m
1:20 (12:00) 2-Y-O **£23,706** (£9,482; £7,112; £4,741; £2,370)

RPR

1 **All Shamar** 2-8-11 0.. ASuborics 8 98
(W Hickst, Germany) **76/10**

2 *1 1/2* **Hippolyte (FR)**[12] 2-8-11 0.. FlavienPrat 10 95
(T Clout, France) **6/4**[1]

3 *shd* **Got Happy (IRE)**[178] [illegible] MaximeGuyon [illegible]
(Mme Pia Brandt, France) **13/1**

4 *3/4* **Electrelane**[56] 6432 2-8-8 0.. JimCrowley 2 90
(Ralph Beckett) *racd towards rr on ins: qcknd wl early in st to cl on ldrs: r.o u.p fnl f wout threatening ldrs* **23/1**

5 *hd* **Unex Michelangelo (IRE)**[80] 5727 2-8-11 0................... WilliamBuick 1 93
(John Gosden) *racd in 3rd on ins: wnt 2nd bef st: rdn over 2f out: no ex: styd on fnl 1 1/2f* **11/1**

6 *1 1/2* **Sisyphe (FR)**[11] 7385 2-8-11 0.. ThierryThulliez 4 89
(P Demercastel, France) **11/1**

7 *nse* **Tycoon's Garden (FR)**[42] 6782 2-8-11 0...................... GregoryBenoist 7 89
(E Lellouche, France) **73/10**[3]

8 *1 3/4* **Ameriling (FR)** 2-8-8 0.. ThierryJarnet 3 82
(Mlle S-V Tarrou, France) **27/1**

9 *1* **Bling King**[52] 6535 2-8-11 0... JohanVictoire 5 83
(F Vermeulen, France) **37/1**

10 *3/4* **Paraggi**[25] 2-8-11 0.. OlivierPeslier 6 82
(M Delzangles, France) **4/1**[2]

1m 51.9s (4.40) **10** Ran SP% **117.9**
WIN (incl. 1 euro stake): 8.60. PLACES: 2.90. 1.30, 2.90. DF: 11.60. SF: 20.50.
Owner Stall Pregel **Bred** D R Tucker **Trained** Germany

NOTEBOOK
Electrelane ran a nice race and her rider considers her to have improved. He believes that she can be a nice filly next year.

7509a PRIX CERES (LISTED RACE) (3YO FILLIES) (TURF) 7f
1:50 (12:00) 3-Y-O **£23,706** (£9,482; £7,112; £4,741; £2,370)

RPR

1 **Lady Meydan (FR)**[41] 6809 3-8-11 0........................... GregoryBenoist 11 104
(F Rohaut, France) **77/10**

2 *hd* **Seeharn (IRE)**[16] 7318 3-9-1 0..................................... DPMcDonogh 8 107
(Kevin Prendergast, Ire) *racd freely on outside in 5th: gd prog bef st: qcknd wl 2f out whn field swtchd to stands' rail: tk ld over 1 1/2f out: r.o wl fnl f: ct fnl strides* **53/10**[2]

3 *3/4* **Waitress (USA)** 3-8-11 0.. FabriceVeron 6 101
(H-A Pantall, France) **14/1**

4 *1/2* **Paperchain**[88] 3-8-11 0... MaximeGuyon 1 100
(A Fabre, France) **4/1**[1]

5 *3* **Sweetie Time**[41] 6809 3-8-11 0.. OlivierPeslier 5 92
(Michael Bell) *racd promly bhd ldrs: wnt 3rd bef st: rdn and r.o fr 2f out: no ex ins fnl f* **15/1**

6 2 **Present Danger**[13] 7334 3-8-11 0 RichardKingscote 7 86
(Tom Dascombe) *racd in midfield: prom early in st: rdn but no ex fr over 1 1/2f out: styd on fnl f* **31/1**

7 2 **Katerini (FR)**[84] 3-8-11 0 AurelienLemaitre 9 81
(F Head, France) **17/1**

8 3/4 **Storming Honor (SPA)**[33] 3-8-11 0 JohanVictoire 2 79
(L A Urbano-Grajales, France) **19/1**

9 1/2 **Realisatrice (FR)**[20] 7239 3-8-11 0 (b[1]) AlexisBadel 3 77
(Mme M Bollack-Badel, France) **13/1**

10 3/4 **Blue Blue Sea**[41] 6809 3-8-11 0 Pierre-CharlesBoudot 13 75
(Y De Nicolay, France) **14/1**

0 **Whip And Win (FR)**[20] 7239 3-9-1 0 SebastienMaillot 12 —
(Robert Collet, France) **58/10**[3]

0 **Hail Holy Queen (IRE)**[147] 3-8-11 0 ThierryJarnet 4 —
(J E Hammond, France) **10/1**

0 **Reine Vite (GER)**[37] 3-9-1 0 ASuborics 10 —
(Uwe Ostmann, Germany) **20/1**

1m 31.1s (-1.10) **13** Ran SP% **116.3**
WIN (incl. 1 euro stake): 8.70. PLACES: 2.70, 2.30, 3.00. DF: 20.40. SF: 31.10.
Owner Gerard Augustin-Normand **Bred** M Scemama & Sarl Euro Normandy **Trained** Sauvagnon, France

NOTEBOOK
Sweetie Time's rider believed that she may not have got home in the ground.

7510a PRIX SOLITUDE (LISTED RACE) (3YO FILLIES) (TURF) 1m 2f
2:20 (12:00) 3-Y-O **£23,706** (£9,482; £7,112; £4,741; £2,370)

RPR

1 **Dealbata (IRE)**[29] 3-8-11 0 ThomasHuet 2 103
(M Delzangles, France) **84/10**

2 1/2 **Haya Landa (FR)**[51] 6568 3-9-2 0 FranckBlondel 15 107
(Mme L Audon, France) **33/10**[1]

3 1 1/4 **Private Eye (FR)**[25] 7156 3-8-11 0 ThierryThulliez 7 99
(E Libaud, France) **11/2**[3]

4 1 1/2 **Aquamarine (JPN)**[81] 5694 3-8-11 0 StephanePasquier 11 96
(M Delzangles, France) **11/1**

5 3/4 **La Folie (IRE)**[161] 3-8-11 0 (p) GregoryBenoist 12 95
(E Lellouche, France) **13/1**

6 snk **Angalia (IRE)**[53] 6517 3-8-11 0 (p) Pierre-CharlesBoudot 5 94
(E Lellouche, France) **22/1**

7 snk **Our Gal**[58] 6374 3-8-11 0 AlexandreRoussel 10 94?
(Noel Quinlan) *in rr fr s: mde gd prog u.p on inner fr 2f out: r.o fnl f: clst at fin* **45/1**

8 1 1/4 **Luna Tune (FR)**[25] 3-8-11 0 OlivierPeslier 3 91
(D De Watrigant, France) **43/10**[2]

9 1/2 **Fiammella (IRE)**[10] 3-8-11 0 (b) RonanThomas 9 90
(A Bonin, France) **22/1**

10 2 **Psireve (FR)**[25] 7156 3-8-11 0 GaetanMasure 4 86
(J-M Capitte, France) **57/1**

0 **Lyrique (IRE)**[73] 5958 3-8-11 0 MaximeGuyon 13 —
(A Fabre, France) **16/1**

0 **Miss Aix**[32] 6996 3-8-11 0 DavyBonilla 8 —
(Michael Bell) *racd freely in 5th: rdn early in st: no ex: eased fr over 1f out* **37/1**

0 **Un Jour (FR)**[17] 7313 3-8-11 0 SebastienMaillot 6 —
(Mlle Valerie Boussin, France) **11/1**

0 **Alkhana (IRE)**[23] 3-9-2 0 FilipMinarik 1 —
(P Schiergen, Germany) **34/1**

2m 20.1s (4.10) **14** Ran SP% **115.9**
WIN (incl. 1 euro stake): 9.40. PLACES: 2.70, 1.90, 2.10. DF: 26.40. SF: 43.20.
Owner Marquesa De Moratalla **Bred** Dr Fernand Krief **Trained** France

7451 KEMPTON (A.W) (R-H)
Wednesday, November 23

OFFICIAL GOING: Standard
Wind: Almost nil Weather: Cloudy

7511 FREE ENTRY FOR BETDAQ MEMBERS MEDIAN AUCTION MAIDEN STKS 5f (P)
4:05 (4:05) (Class 6) 3-5-Y-O **£1,617** (£481; £240; £120) **Stalls Low**

Form RPR

5223 1 **Bailadeira**[20] 7245 3-8-9 55 MichaelO'Connell(3) 8 53
(Tim Etherington) *sweating: mde most: set mod pce tl kicked on 2f out: drvn and hld on fnl f* **7/2**[2]

0232 2 3/4 **Cliffords Reprieve**[12] 7366 3-9-3 58 SebSanders 3 56
(Eric Wheeler) *hld up bhd ldrs: pushed along and prog to take 2nd 1f out: rdn and fnd nil ins fnl f* **5/6**[1]

4600 3 hd **Dolly Bay**[36] 6940 3-8-9 43 AdamBeschizza(3) 4 50
(Julia Feilden) *sn hld up on inner: effrt wl over 1f out: kpt on fnl f: nrly snatched 2nd but nvr able to chal* **33/1**

0006 4 2 1/4 **My Best Man**[11] 7389 5-9-3 46 LukeMorris 6 47
(Tony Carroll) *w wnr: led briefly 3f out: nt qckn 2f out: lost 2nd and wknd 1f out* **12/1**

-530 5 1 1/2 **Itum**[19] 7266 4-9-3 55 IanMongan 7 42
(Christine Dunnett) *stdd s: t.k.h: cl up tl wknd over 1f out* **13/2**[3]

4605 6 1 1/2 **Miakora**[11] 7389 3-8-12 46 WilliamCarson 1 31
(Michael Quinn) *in tch: rdn 1/2-way: wknd wl over 1f out* **14/1**

0 7 2 **Tunza The Lion**[5] 7460 4-9-3 0 NeilChalmers 9 29
(Bruce Hellier) *dwlt: t.k.h and racd wd: wl in tch tl wd bnd 2f out: sn wknd* **66/1**

60.99 secs (0.49) **Going Correction** -0.075s/f (Stan) **7** Ran SP% **108.9**
Speed ratings (Par 101): **93,91,91,87,85 83,79**
toteswingers: 1&2 £1.50, 1&3 £6.30, 2&3 £6.00 CSF £6.08 TOTE £4.40: £2.30, £1.10; EX 6.80 Trifecta £64.40 Pool: £469.12 - 5.39 winning units..
Owner World Wide Racing Partners **Bred** Summerville Bloodstock Associates Llp **Trained** Norton, N Yorks

FOCUS
A weak gallop for a 5f sprint until the winner kicked for home off the bend. The form looks shaky and is best rated around the second and fourth for now.

7512 BETDAQ MULTIPLES H'CAP 5f (P)
4:35 (4:36) (Class 5) (0-75,74) 3-Y-0+ **£2,264** (£673; £336; £168) **Stalls Low**

Form RPR

6100 1 **The Strig**[22] 7201 4-8-13 64 (v) WilliamCarson 12 71
(Stuart Williams) *chsd ldrs in 5th but off the pce: rdn 2f out: clsd fnl f: drvn to dispute ld last 50yds: jst prevailed* **14/1**

1356 2 shd **Griffin Point (IRE)**[22] 7201 4-8-10 61 MartinHarley 8 68
(William Muir) *chsd clr ldng pair: rdn fr 1/2-way: clsd over 1f out: drvn to dispute ld last 50yds: jst pipped* **8/1**

2300 3 nk **Grudge**[11] 7395 6-9-1 66 (b) TomQueally 1 72
(Conor Dore) *fast away: led and spreadeagled field: drvn and pressed over 1f out: hld on tl hdd and no ex last 50yds* **20/1**

4500 4 1/2 **Danzoe (IRE)**[42] 6802 4-9-0 65 IanMongan 2 69+
(Christine Dunnett) *hld up in last and wl off the pce: effrt 2f out: stl only 9th and rdn ent fnl f: r.o strly nr fin* **12/1**

2400 5 3/4 **Sherjawy (IRE)**[62] 6282 7-9-0 65 SamHitchcott 5 66
(Zoe Davison) *sn off the pce in midfield: rdn to cl over 1f out: kpt on thrght fnl f but nvr able to chal* **25/1**

614 6 nse **Scarlet Rocks (IRE)**[5] 7457 3-9-6 71 (tp) NickyMackay 4 72
(George Baker) *dwlt: hld up in rr and wl off the pce: swtchd lft over 1f out: rdn and styd on: nt pce to chal* **4/1**[2]

0013 7 hd **Nially Noo**[7] 7428 3-8-9 65 MarkCoumbe(5) 6 65
(Derek Shaw) *chsd clr ldng pair: clsd to take 2nd jst over 1f out tl ins fnl f: fdd* **11/4**[1]

0414 8 nk **Absa Lutte (IRE)**[7] 7428 8-9-7 72 JimmyQuinn 3 71
(Michael Mullineaux) *dwlt: hld up in last pair and wl off the pce: effrt against rail wl over 1f out: styd on: nvr gng pce to chal* **11/2**[3]

4304 9 1 **Atlantic Cycle (IRE)**[11] 7395 4-9-0 65 RichardKingscote 10 61
(Milton Bradley) *chsd ldr and clr of rest: rdn over 1f out: sn lost 2nd: wknd last 150yds* **15/2**

1060 10 2 1/4 **Commandingpresence (USA)**[34] 6974 5-9-0 68 KieranO'Neill(3) 11 56
(John Bridger) *dwlt: wl in rr on outer: rdn over 2f out: struggling whn bmpd over 1f out: no ch after* **25/1**

6300 11 1 1/4 **Athwaab**[36] 6932 4-8-9 65 MatthewLawson(5) 7 48
(Noel Chance) *sn rdn and racd wd in midfield: btn whn veered lft over 1f out* **20/1**

59.51 secs (-0.99) **Going Correction** -0.075s/f (Stan) **11** Ran SP% **116.5**
Speed ratings (Par 103): **104,103,103,102,101 101,100,100,98,95 93**
toteswingers: 1&2 £21.10, 1&3 £53.40, 2&3 £28.20 CSF £113.19 CT £2264.45 TOTE £22.10: £6.20, £1.30, £5.90; EX 195.50 TRIFECTA Not won..
Owner Brian Piper & David Cobill **Bred** Old Mill Stud **Trained** Newmarket, Suffolk

FOCUS
This was run at a much better gallop than the first race. The form is rated through the front-running third backed up by the runner-up.

7513 BACK OR LAY AT BETDAQ.COM H'CAP 1m 2f (P)
5:05 (5:05) (Class 5) (0-75,75) 3-Y-0+ **£2,264** (£673; £336; £168) **Stalls Low**

Form RPR

0063 1 **Hurricane Spirit (IRE)**[27] 7130 7-9-4 72 (b) SteveDrowne 1 80
(Terry Clement) *dwlt: hld up in 5th: effrt on inner wl over 1f out: rdn and r.o wl fnl f to ld last 75yds* **10/1**

2066 2 3/4 **Understory (USA)**[27] 7130 4-9-5 73 LukeMorris 3 79
(Tim McCarthy) *trckd ldr: clsd to ld over 1f out: drvn fnl f: hdd and one pce last 75yds* **12/1**

0001 3 nk **Lisahane Bog**[22] 7202 4-9-5 73 (b) JohnFahy 2 78
(Peter Hedger) *chsd clr ldng pair: rdn and nt qckn over 1f out: styd on same pce fnl f* **5/1**[2]

0345 4 shd **Sakhee's Pearl**[28] 7097 5-9-6 74 IanMongan 7 79
(Jo Crowley) *hld up in 7th: effrt and looking for room wl over 1f out: styd on wl fnl f: nvr able to chal* **7/1**

4022 5 nk **Sand Skier**[9] 7413 4-8-11 72 NicoleNordblad(7) 8 77
(Hans Adielsson) *hld up in 4th: clsd on ldrs over 2f out: wd bnd sn after: rdn and nt qckn over 1f out: kpt on* **7/4**[1]

0010 6 1 3/4 **Megalala (IRE)**[13] 7346 10-8-11 68 KieranO'Neill(3) 6 69
(John Bridger) *led at decent pce: drvn over 2f out: hdd over 1f out: wknd fnl f* **12/1**

0420 7 2 3/4 **Classically (IRE)**[54] 6507 5-9-2 75 DavidKenny(5) 5 71
(Peter Hedger) *stdd s: hld up in last: brought wd bnd 2f out: jst pushed along over 1f out: nvr remotely involved* **8/1**

6261 8 7 **Ela Gonda Mou**[19] 7271 4-9-2 70 RobertWinston 4 52
(Peter Charalambous) *hld up in 6th: rdn and wknd over 2f out: t.o* **6/1**[3]

2m 5.02s (-2.98) **Going Correction** -0.075s/f (Stan) **8** Ran SP% **115.4**
Speed ratings (Par 103): **108,107,107,107,106 105,103,97**
toteswingers: 1&2 £21.90, 1&3 £3.90, 2&3 £13.80 CSF £120.57 CT £673.60 TOTE £11.00: £3.00, £3.90, £1.50; EX 144.10 Trifecta £718.40 Pool: £8,825.54 - 9.09 winning units..
Owner The Little House Partnership **Bred** Knocktoran Stud **Trained** Newmarket, Suffolk

FOCUS
There was a solid gallop, set by a perennial front-runner, though it relaxed a little in the back straight. The placed horses are the best guide with the winner close to this year's best.

7514 BETDAQ MOBILE APPS NURSERY 7f (P)
5:35 (5:35) (Class 6) (0-65,65) 2-Y-O **£1,617** (£481; £240; £120) **Stalls Low**

Form RPR

0061 1 **Elegant Flight**[41] 6821 2-9-3 61 (v) JimCrowley 8 68
(Alan Jarvis) *trckd ldrs: prog to ld over 1f out: rdn clr fnl f* **7/1**[3]

0601 2 2 **Compton Bird**[7] 7432 2-8-9 60 6ex (t) NicoleNordblad(7) 6 62
(Hans Adielsson) *t.k.h: hld up in midfield: swtchd ins and prog over 2f out: chal over 1f out: no match for wnr after: wkng nr fin* **7/2**[1]

046 3 hd **Lady Arabella (IRE)**[13] 7345 2-9-2 60 SteveDrowne 11 61
(Alastair Lidderdale) *hld up in 7th: shkn up and no prog over 2f out: hdwy jst over 1f out: styd on wl to take 3rd and cl on runner-up at fin* **9/1**

3000 4 1 **Ice Loch**[23] 7196 2-8-9 53 (b) JimmyQuinn 1 52
(Michael Blanshard) *reminder sn after s: hld up in last trio: prog 2f out to chse ldrs over 1f out: styd on same pce* **25/1**

444 5 nse **Hey Fiddle Fiddle (IRE)**[23] 7197 2-8-13 62 MatthewLawson(5) 7 61
(Charles Hills) *led to over 1f out: wknd fnl f* **4/1**[2]

4030 6 1 **Purley Queen (IRE)**[53] 6524 2-9-7 65 LiamKeniry 4 61
(Sylvester Kirk) *hld up in last trio: looking for room over 2f out: prog jst over 1f out: styd on: nrst fin* **16/1**

0060 7 hd **Big Time Charlie (IRE)**[56] 6443 2-8-9 56 KieranO'Neill(3) 9 52
(Richard Hannon) *chsd ldr to 2f out: steadily wknd* **16/1**

0034 **8** 2 1/4 **Liquid Sunshine**[6] 7444 2-8-6 **50**.................................. NickyMackay 10 40
(Sylvester Kirk) *hld up in 8th: rdn and prog 2f out: no hdwy over 1f out: fdd* **10/1**

5646 **9** *shd* **Talya's Storm**[20] 7252 2-8-13 **57**.................................. FergusSweeney 3 47
(Jeremy Gask) *hld up in last trio: sme prog on outer over 1f out: nvr a factor* **7/1**[3]

053 **10** *8* **Hesperides**[41] 6819 2-9-4 **62**.. JohnFahy 12 31
(Harry Dunlop) *chsd ldrs tl wknd over 2f out: t.o* **8/1**

000 **11** *8* **Brian's Best**[53] 6540 2-7-8 **45**.. NoelGarbutt(7) 2 —
(Bruce Hellier) *t.k.h: chsd ldng pair to 3f out: bmpd along and wknd qckly: t.o* **100/1**

1m 26.04s (0.04) **Going Correction** -0.075s/f (Stan) 11 Ran SP% **114.0**
Speed ratings (Par 94): **96,93,93,92,92 91,90,88,88,79 69**
toteswingers: 1&2 £10.10, 1&3 £9.10, 2&3 £6.40 CSF £30.63 CT £227.96 TOTE £5.70: £2.20, £2.70, £4.00; EX 27.10 Trifecta £262.80 Pool: £4,596.79 - 12.94 winning units..
Owner Grant & Bowman Limited **Bred** Mrs Ann Jarvis **Trained** Twyford, Bucks

FOCUS
A ordinary nursery, but it was run at a decent gallop.

NOTEBOOK
Elegant Flight, trying 7f for the first time, travelled well and finished the job off in the style of an improving sort. She has responded well to the visor and there should be more to come at this trip, with 1m likely to suit as she matures. (op 11-2)
Compton Bird, attempting to follow up the previous week's win at 1m, ran well in defeat. However, her fate was sealed by the combination of the drop in trip, the 6lb penalty, and the presence of an improving winner. (tchd 4-1)
Lady Arabella(IRE) ◆ made a good nursery debut from a hard draw. This was only her fourth race, and she is one to note next time. (op 10-1 tchd 11-1)
Ice Loch ran his best race on Polytrack in second-time blinkers, which may be having some effect. He is not without hope but will probably have to be dropped in grade to win. (op 33-1)
Hey Fiddle Fiddle(IRE), arriving in handicaps on testing mark, produced a creditable run which suggests she can win a race if dropped a few pounds. (tchd 9-2)
Purley Queen(IRE) looks a bit too high in the weights, but she is a fair recruit for the AW scene and will be worth considering if the handicapper gives her a better chance.
Big Time Charlie(IRE) ran better than on his handicap debut and does seem to be making some progress. (op 20-1)
Liquid Sunshine has some ability, but she is finding a mark of 50 too high so a drop back in grade may be necessary. (op 9-1)
Talya's Storm, trying an extra furlong, has not yet established her best trip, but she is showing enough to suggest she she could find a little race. (op 13-2)

7515 REINDEER RACING CHRISTMAS PARTIES AT KEMPTON H'CAP 1m 4f (P)
6:05 (6:05) (Class 6) (0-65,65) 3-Y-O **£1,617** (£481; £240; £120) **Stalls** Centre

Form RPR

1431 **1** **Woop Woop (IRE)**[11] 7394 3-8-13 **62**.............................. RyanPowell(5) 6 71
(Ian Williams) *hld up in rr: looking for room wl over 2f out: gd prog sn after to ld over 1f out: clr fnl f: rdn out* **5/1**[2]

000 **2** 2 3/4 **Who Loves Ya Baby**[194] 2068 3-8-2 **51** oh3............... RosieJessop(5) 5 56
(Peter Charalambous) *trckd ldr after 1f: led over 3f out: hung lft jst over 2f out: hdd over 1f out and outpcd: kpt on fnl f* **20/1**

1035 **3** 3/4 **History Repeating**[20] 7255 3-8-11 **62**.................... RachealKneller(7) 8 65
(Mark Usher) *dwlt and stdd s: hld up detached fr main gp: effrt and brought wd in st: prog over 2f out: wnt 3rd over 1f out: styd on same pce after* **13/2**[3]

0146 **4** 2 1/4 **Guards Chapel**[21] 6052 3-9-3 **61**..............................(v) FergusSweeney 10 61
(Gary Moore) *hld up in rr: rdn and prog jst over 2f out to go 3rd briefly over 1f out: one pce after* **9/1**

5230 **5** *10* **Ultimate Best**[14] 7340 3-8-13 **57**.. JimmyQuinn 3 41
(Michael Mullineaux) *trckd ldrs: rdn over 2f out: sn outpcd: wknd qckly over 1f out* **16/1**

0502 **6** 1 1/2 **Layla's King**[142] 3681 3-9-3 **61**.................................. SebSanders 9 42
(George Margarson) *hld up in tch in rr: rdn over 2f out: no prog and sn btn: wknd over 1f out* **4/1**[1]

540 **7** 1 1/2 **Our Play (IRE)**[13] 7346 3-9-7 **65**..............................(b[1]) SteveDrowne 7 44
(Lydia Richards) *trckd ldrs: rdn over 2f out: wknd qckly wl over 1f out* **9/1**

0653 **8** *5* **Labroc (IRE)**[14] 7340 3-8-10 **57**............................ AdamBeschizza(3) 4 28
(William Haggas) *led to over 3f out: hrd rdn and wknd qckly over 1f out* **5/1**[2]

5330 **9** *1* **Drumadoon (IRE)**[49] 6621 3-8-11 **55**...............................(p) LiamKeniry 1 24
(Liam Corcoran) *chsd ldr 1f: styd prom tl wknd over 2f out* **20/1**

5353 **10** *53* **Black Iceman**[23] 7195 3-8-4 **51** oh1.......................... SimonPearce(3) 2 —
(Lydia Pearce) *hld up: hung violently lft after 2f and ended against nr side rail: continued t.o and running against outer rail thrght* **5/1**[2]

2m 33.93s (-0.57) **Going Correction** -0.075s/f (Stan) 10 Ran SP% **118.7**
Speed ratings (Par 98): **98,96,95,94,87 86,85,82,81,46**
toteswingers: 1&2 £30.90, 1&3 £10.80, 2&3 £31.20 CSF £100.44 CT £653.43 TOTE £3.10: £1.10, £9.10, £3.00; EX 70.00 Trifecta £335.50 Pool: £2,448.43 - 5.40 winning units..
Owner Lee Westwood & Chubby Chandler **Bred** C Amerian **Trained** Portway, Worcs
■ Stewards' Enquiry : Rosie Jessop five-day ban: used whip with excessive frequency (Dec 7-11)

FOCUS
A decent gallop set this up perfectly for the progressive winner. The winner is rated as having recorded a slight personal best, while the third helps set the standard.
Black Iceman Official explanation: jockey said gelding hung badly left throughout

7516 COME TO KEMPTON ON BOXING DAY HYDE STKS (LISTED RACE) 1m (P)
6:35 (6:35) (Class 1) 3-Y-O+
£17,013 (£6,450; £3,228; £1,608; £807; £405) **Stalls** Low

Form RPR

0001 **1** **Edinburgh Knight (IRE)**[39] 6862 4-9-2 98........................ JimCrowley 4 106+
(Paul D'Arcy) *hld up in 9th: gng strly over 2f out: smooth prog wl over 1f out: rdn to ld ins fnl f: hld on wl* **7/1**

1036 **2** *nk* **The Shrew**[27] 7128 3-8-9 94.. WilliamBuick 7 100
(John Gosden) *trckd ldng pair: effrt on inner to chal wl over 1f out: led briefly 1f out: fought on wl nr fin: a jst hld* **8/1**

0111 **3** 1 1/2 **Clinical**[19] 7277 3-8-11 103... SebSanders 8 99
(Sir Mark Prescott Bt) *disp ld: rdn and def advantage 2f out: hdd and one pce 1f out* **3/1**[1]

500 **4** *shd* **Mac Love**[25] 7166 10-9-2 98... SteveDrowne 3 101
(Roger Charlton) *t.k.h early: hld up disputing 7th: effrt 2f out: styd on fnl f: nrly grabbed 3rd* **25/1**

6001 **5** *1* **Riggins (IRE)**[11] 7393 7-9-2 98..................................... J-PGuillambert 12 99
(Ed Walker) *chsd ldng pair: rdn over 2f out: nt qckn wl over 1f out: styd on same pce after* **9/2**[2]

0013 **6** *hd* **Steed**[27] 7127 4-9-2 93..(b) FergusSweeney 5 99
(Tim Vaughan) *sn restrained into last: effrt on inner 2f out: styd on after: nrst fin but no ch to threaten* **33/1**

0113 **7** 3/4 **Loyalty**[11] 7393 4-9-2 95..(v) JoeFanning 1 97
(Derek Shaw) *chsd ldng quartet: rdn over 2f out: kpt chsng but nvr gng pce to threaten* **5/1**[3]

0050 **8** 1/2 **Spirit Of Sharjah (IRE)**[159] 3134 6-9-2 105.................... JimmyQuinn 9 96
(Julia Feilden) *sn restrained into last trio: prog 2f out: styd on fr over 1f out: nvr gng to threaten ldrs* **11/1**

2005 **9** 3 1/2 **Bravo Echo**[7] 7433 5-9-2 103... LukeMorris 14 88
(Michael Attwater) *t.k.h: disp ld to jst over 2f out: wknd over 1f out* **25/1**

-000 **10** 1/2 **Face Reality (USA)**[19] 7277 3-8-9 98......................... RobertWinston 2 81
(David Marnane, Ire) *hld up in midfield disputing 7th: urged along and no prog 2f out: steadily wknd* **20/1**

6055 **11** *1* **Sos Brillante (CHI)**[7] 7438 6-8-11 80.......................... MarkCoumbe 10 79
(Terry Clement) *a abt same pl: rdn and no prog over 2f out* **66/1**

5214 **12** *1* **Avon Lady**[27] 7128 4-8-11 94.. EddieAhern 11 77
(James Fanshawe) *chsd ldng quartet: rdn wl over 2f out: sn wknd* **20/1**

-006 **13** *13* **Karam Albaari (IRE)**[61] 6298 3-9-0 98.......................... TomQueally 13 52
(J R Jenkins) *sn restrained in rr and racd wd: wknd rapidly over 2f out: t.o* **16/1**

1m 36.8s (-3.00) **Going Correction** -0.075s/f (Stan)
WFA 3 from 4yo+ 2lb 13 Ran SP% **119.3**
Speed ratings (Par 111): **112,111,110,110,109 108,108,107,104,103 102,101,88**
toteswingers: 1&2 £9.90, 1&3 £6.50, 2&3 £7.80 CSF £56.03 TOTE £8.30: £2.00, £3.90, £1.20; EX 82.70 Trifecta £1847.80 Part won. Pool: £2,497.02 - 0.62 winning units..
Owner Knights Racing **Bred** New England Stud Myriad Norelands **Trained** Newmarket, Suffolk

FOCUS
A valuable contest, but a disappointingly modest gallop for a race of this class. The winner rated as having run a personal best with the runner-up close to his best mark.

NOTEBOOK
Edinburgh Knight(IRE), winner of two good turf handicaps at 6f and 7f this year, proved his questionable stamina with a stylish win. He cut through the field with impressive ease under a fine ride, but AW opportunities for a horse of his ability are limited, so connections may well wait for the Lincoln. (op 15-2 tchd 8-1)
The Shrew, having only her fifth race of the year, ran a solid race over a trip that suits her well. She is still improving and could be one for Dubai early next year.
Clinical had won her three previous races, all at this grade in fillies and mares-only events. Officially the pick of the weights, she made a bold bid for glory but this was a competitive event. (tchd 7-2)
Mac Love hasn't had a great year but this fine effort provided a reminder of what a grand performer he was at his peak. On this evidence, he isn't quite finished yet, though it won't be easy finding a winning opportunity for him at this level.
Riggins(IRE), more effective on Polytrack than turf, had a nice warm-up for this at Lingfield and had plenty in his favour. He ran with credit but wasn't quite at his best. (op 5-1 tchd 4-1)
Steed had a bit to find against these opponents and ran at least as well as could have been expected. (op 40-1)
Loyalty, a smart handicapper on this surface, held his own against stronger opponents than usual. (op 11-2 tchd 7-1 in places)
Spirit Of Sharjah(IRE) has not reached the first four all year, but he continues to show ability in good company like this.

7517 BOOK YOUR BOXING DAY TICKETS NOW H'CAP 7f (P)
7:05 (7:05) (Class 5) (0-75,74) 3-Y-O+ **£2,264** (£673; £336; £168) **Stalls** Low

Form RPR

6000 **1** **Ocean Legend (IRE)**[34] 6979 6-9-2 **72**................. MichaelO'Connell(3) 2 82
(Tony Carroll) *trckd ldng pair: wnt 2nd 3f out: chal 2f out: hrd rdn and edgd lft over 1f out: narrow ld fnl f: asserted last 75yds* **7/2**[1]

5302 **2** 1 1/4 **Tislaam (IRE)**[6] 7448 4-9-2 **69**...(p) MartinHarley 6 76
(Alan McCabe) *led: edgd lft fr 2f out: drvn over 1f out: narrowly hdd fnl f: no ex last 75yds* **9/2**[2]

2002 **3** 1/2 **Sermons Mount (USA)**[28] 7097 5-9-7 **74**.......................... JohnFahy 3 80
(Peter Hedger) *hld up in midfield: prog to chse clr ldng pair wl over 1f out: drvn and grad clsd: nvr able to chal* **6/1**

0560 **4** 2 1/4 **Garstang**[21] 7230 8-9-0 **67**.. JoeFanning 4 67
(Bruce Hellier) *hld up last of main gp: drvn over 2f out: styd on fr over 1f out: tk 4th ins fnl f: nrst fin* **40/1**

1410 **5** *2* **West Leake (IRE)**[189] 2207 5-9-1 **68**................................. LiamKeniry 1 62
(Paul Burgoyne) *t.k.h: hld up in rr: outpcd over 2f out: one pce and n.d fnl 2f* **20/1**

0064 **6** *hd* **Avertis**[30] 7050 6-9-6 **73**..(tp) SteveDrowne 9 67
(Alastair Lidderdale) *pressed ldr to 3f out: nt qckn and sn lost pl: n.d over 1f out* **11/1**

40-0 **7** 1 3/4 **Royal Intruder**[24] 7189 6-9-4 **71**...................................... TomQueally 11 60
(S Donohoe, Ire) *t.k.h: trckd ldrs: outpcd over 2f out: rdn and no prog wl over 1f out* **25/1**

4050 **8** 1 1/2 **Valentino Swing (IRE)**[86] 5539 8-8-0 **60** oh15............(p) JackDuern(7) 5 45
(Michael Appleby) *hld up in rr: brief prog 2f out: sn wknd* **100/1**

6015 **9** 1/2 **Al Aqabah (IRE)**[6] 7447 6-9-6 **73**...................................(b) LukeMorris 10 57
(Brian Gubby) *plld hrd: trckd ldrs: rdn and edgd lft over 2f out: sn btn* **5/1**[3]

3301 **10** *14* **Abriachan**[103] 5014 4-9-0 **67**.. RobertWinston 7 13
(Noel Quinlan) *hld up last: rn v wd bnd 3f out: wl bhd after: t.o* **14/1**

1/01 **U** **Regency Art (IRE)**[30] 7055 4-9-5 **72**........................ RichardKingscote 8 —
(Milton Bradley) *propped as stalls opened and uns rdr* **5/1**[3]

1m 25.29s (-0.71) **Going Correction** -0.075s/f (Stan) 11 Ran SP% **115.1**
Speed ratings (Par 103): **101,99,99,96,94 93,91,90,89,73 —**
toteswingers: 1&2 £4.70, 1&3 £7.80, 2&3 £4.20 CSF £17.86 CT £90.68 TOTE £4.70: £2.60, £1.90, £1.90; EX 21.10 Trifecta £120.10 Pool: £2,307.12 - 14.21 winning units..
Owner W McLuskey **Bred** Mark Commins **Trained** Cropthorne, Worcs

FOCUS
The gallop was just a medium one, but they were well stretched out by the finish. The form is straightforward rated through the runner-up to his latest C&D form.
Abriachan Official explanation: jockey said gelding suffered interference at start and hung badly left

T/Plt: £371.70 to a £1 stake. Pool: £59,654.11. 117.15 winning tickets. T/Qpdt: £24.80 to a £1 stake. Pool: £8,564.45. 255.10 winning tickets. JN

7481 LINGFIELD (L-H)

Wednesday, November 23

OFFICIAL GOING: Standard

Wind: nil Weather: fog

7518 CHRISTMAS PARTIES AT LINGFIELDPARK.CO.UK CLAIMING STKS 7f (P)

12:35 (12:35) (Class 6) 3-Y-0+ **£1,704** (£503; £251) **Stalls** Low

Form RPR

0000 **1** **City Legend**[13] 7348 3-8-8 63................................(vt) KieranO'Neill(3) 4 71
(Alan McCabe) *chsd ldrs tl led over 2f out: rdn and qcknd clr wl over 1f out: tiring fnl 100yds but a holding on* **25/1**

0100 **2** *1 ¼* **Golden Desert (IRE)**[39] 6862 7-9-6 93................................ IanMongan 2 75
(Simon Dow) *in tch: nt clr run and shuffled bk over 3f out: swtchd rt and effrt over 1f out: chsd wnr ins fnl f: kpt on but nvr gng to rch wnr* **11/8**[1]

0000 **3** *½* **Cristaliyev**[6] 7448 3-8-10 58................................(b[1]) EddieAhern 9 65
(Jim Boyle) *dwlt: t.k.h: sn in tch in midfield: rdn and nt gng pce of wnr wl over 1f out: kpt on ins fnl f* **33/1**

5000 **4** *½* **Tiradito (USA)**[23] 7199 4-9-1 76................................(p) MarkCoumbe(5) 6 73
(Michael Attwater) *dwlt: hld up in tch in last trio: rdn and effrt 2f out: kpt on wl ins fnl f: no threat to wnr* **10/1**

3521 **5** *hd* **Faithful Ruler (USA)**[9] 7412 7-8-13 73................................(p) LukeMorris 11 65
(Ronald Harris) *hld up in tch in last trio: hdwy over 3f out: chsd wnr 2f out but immediately outpcd: plugged on same pce fnl f* **4/1**[3]

3030 **6** *¾* **Mahadee (IRE)**[28] 7110 6-9-1 93................................(b) TomQueally 1 65
(Ed de Giles) *dwlt: bhd: rdn along over 3f out: hdwy on outer over 3f out: no imp 2f out tl kpt on ins fnl f: nvr trbld ldrs* **11/4**[2]

302- **7** *13* **Child Bride**[403] 6920 3-8-4 70................................ ChrisCatlin 7 20
(Paul Cole) *taken down early and led to post: led tl over 2f out: wknd qckly over 1f out* **14/1**

0600 **8** *¾* **Dream Express (IRE)**[38] 6889 6-8-3 42........................ JakePayne(7) 10 23
(Bill Turner) *in tch: hung rt over 2f out: wknd 2f out* **100/1**

3-20 **9** *2* **Majestical (IRE)**[37] 6920 9-8-10 37................................(p) JimCrowley 3 18
(Peter Hedger) *t.k.h: chsd ldr tl over 2f out: sn struggling and wknd qckly 2f out* **66/1**

1m 23.42s (-1.38) **Going Correction** -0.025s/f (Stan)

WFA 3 from 4yo+ 1lb **9** Ran SP% **113.8**

Speed ratings (Par 101): **106,104,104,103,103 102,87,86,84**

toteswingers:1&2:£10.70, 2&3:£15.20, 1&3:£32.30 CSF £58.69 TOTE £45.40: £6.80, £1.10, £8.60; EX 104.70 TRIFECTA Not won..

Owner Contango Syndicate **Bred** Contango Bloodstock Ltd **Trained** Averham Park, Notts

FOCUS

A modest claimer in which official ratings were turned on their head. The form is muddling and shaky, with the form trio disappointing to various degrees.

City Legend Official explanation: trainer had no explanation for the apparent improvement in form

Dream Express(IRE) Official explanation: jockey said gelding hung badly right

7519 JUMPING AT LINGFIELD 10TH DECEMBER H'CAP 6f (P)

1:05 (1:05) (Class 5) (0-75,74) 3-Y-0+ **£2,385** (£704; £352) **Stalls** Low

Form RPR

551 **1** **Triple Charm**[51] 6591 3-9-5 **72**................................ JimmyFortune 2 82+
(Jeremy Noseda) *dwlt: pushed along leaving stalls and sn in tch in midfield: rdn and effrt to chse ldr jst over 1f out: drvn and styd on wl to ld towards fin* **1/1**[1]

0001 **2** *½* **Ice Trooper**[36] 6929 3-9-5 **72**................................(p) TomEaves 9 80
(Linda Stubbs) *taken down early: led: rdn over 1f out: drvn and kpt on fnl f: hdd and no ex towards fin* **11/2**[3]

0604 **3** *1 ¼* **Loyal Royal (IRE)**[25] 7172 8-9-0 **67**......................(bt) RichardKingscote 7 71
(Milton Bradley) *stdd s: t.k.h: hld up in last trio: hdwy u.p ent fnl f: r.o wl ins fnl f: nvr threatened ldrs* **14/1**

0530 **4** *1* **Methaaly (IRE)**[9] 7416 8-9-3 **70**................................(be) JimmyQuinn 4 71
(Michael Mullineaux) *awkward leaving stalls and slowly away: hld up in last trio: pushed and hdwy towards inner over 1f out: styd on same pce u.p ins fnl f* **11/1**

0000 **5** *1* **Dream Catcher (FR)**[19] 7265 3-8-13 **66**.................. FergusSweeney 10 64
(David Pinder) *chsd ldr: rdn and unable qck and outpcd over 1f out: plugged on same pce and no threat to ldrs fnl f* **20/1**

3040 **6** *1 ¼* **Showboating (IRE)**[7] 7439 3-9-7 **74**................................(p) SebSanders 6 68
(Alan McCabe) *chsd ldrs on outer: rdn and unable qck ent fnl 2f: one pce and no threat to ldrs fnl f* **4/1**[2]

0000 **7** *¾* **Mi Regalo**[13] 7352 3-9-0 **67**................................ KirstyMilczarek 11 58
(Phil McEntee) *chsd ldrs: rdn and unable qck over 2f out: outpcd over 1f out and btn 1f out* **33/1**

0006 **8** *hd* **Strictly Pink (IRE)**[13] 7348 3-8-12 **68**................................ DominicFox(3) 1 59
(Alan Bailey) *chsd ldrs: rdn and unable qck over 2f out: wknd over 1f out* **10/1**

1650 **9** *1 ¼* **Muhandis (IRE)**[26] 7137 3-9-4 **71**................................(p) TomQueally 8 58
(Nick Littmoden) *bmpd s: a towards rr: wknd 2f out* **66/1**

0556 **10** *2 ¼* **Belle Bayardo (IRE)**[29] 7073 3-9-4 **71**................................ LukeMorris 3 50
(Ronald Harris) *hld up in tch: rn wd and lost pl bnd jst over 2f out: bhd fnl f* **8/1**

1m 11.21s (-0.69) **Going Correction** -0.025s/f (Stan) **10** Ran SP% **129.8**

Speed ratings (Par 103): **103,102,100,99,98 96,95,95,93,90**

toteswingers:1&2:£2.80, 2&3:£5.00, 1&3:£5.10 CSF £8.07 CT £60.79 TOTE £2.20: £1.10, £1.90, £2.90; EX 11.80 Trifecta £22.80 Pool: £223.14 - 7.24 winning units..

Owner Bluehills Racing Limited **Bred** Hesmonds Stud Ltd **Trained** Newmarket, Suffolk

FOCUS

An ordinary sprint handicap with the third rated to form.

Belle Bayardo(IRE) Official explanation: jockey said gelding hung right throughout

7520 BRITISH STALLION STUDS SUPPORTING BRITISH RACING E B F MAIDEN STKS (DIV I) 1m (P)

1:40 (1:41) (Class 5) 2-Y-0 **£3,169** (£943; £471; £235) **Stalls** High

Form RPR

1 **Zimira (IRE)** 2-8-12 0................................ RyanMoore 7 69+
(Ed Dunlop) *sn led: rdn ent fnl 2f: hdd ins fnl f: kpt on wl to ld again towards fin* **13/2**[3]

2 *½* **Widyaan (IRE)** 2-9-3 0................................ WilliamBuick 11 73+
(John Gosden) *v.s.a: sn rcvrd and jnd ldrs whn sltly hmpd 5f out: rdn and rn green over 1f out: drvn to ld ins fnl f: hdd and no ex towards fin* **4/1**[2]

3 *½* **Paddyfrommenlo (IRE)** 2-9-3 0................................ SebSanders 12 72+
(J W Hills) *in tch: rdn 2f out: hdwy and nt clr run ins fnl f: swtchd rt fnl 100yds: r.o wl towards fin* **20/1**

0 **4** *hd* **Northern Outlook**[35] 6953 2-9-3 0................................ JimmyFortune 3 71+
(Andrew Balding) *in tch: rdn and effrt to join ldrs over 1f out: rn green u.p ent fnl f: unable qck ins fnl f* **11/4**[1]

0 **5** *hd* **Superciliary**[33] 6993 2-9-3 0................................ JimCrowley 9 71
(Ralph Beckett) *in tch towards rr: effrt and rn green over 1f out: kpt on u.p ins fnl f* **10/1**

0 **6** *1 ¼* **Santadelacruze**[45] 6725 2-9-3 0................................ AmirQuinn 8 68
(Gary Moore) *t.k.h: trckd ldrs: sltly hmpd 5f out: rdn and effrt 2f out: no ex and one pce ins fnl f* **100/1**

0 **7** *1 ¼* **Little Red Minx (IRE)**[29] 7082 2-8-12 0................................ RobertHavlin 6 60
(Peter Chapple-Hyam) *w ldr: ev ch 3f out tl unable qck over 1f out: wknd ins fnl f* **25/1**

0 **8** *½* **Hidden Justice (IRE)**[131] 4054 2-9-3 0................................ EddieAhern 1 67+
(Amanda Perrett) *in tch towards rr: rdn and effrt wl over 1f out: hdwy and styng on whn nt clr run ins fnl f: unable to chal* **14/1**

9 *1 ½* **Lancaster Gate** 2-9-3 0................................ TomQueally 5 60+
(Amanda Perrett) *v.s.a: rcvrd and in tch in last pair: pushed along over 4f out: rdn and outpcd 2f out: styd on same pce fr over 1f out* **10/1**

004 **10** *shd* **Bareback (IRE)**[21] 7225 2-9-3 76................................ LukeMorris 2 60
(John Best) *trckd ldrs on inner: rdn over 2f out: drvn over 1f out: no imp and wknd ins fnl f* **7/1**

11 *10* **Dansable (IRE)** 2-8-12 0................................ ChrisCatlin 10 32
(Paul Cole) *chsd ldrs: sltly hmpd 5f out: ev ch 3f out tl rn wd and lost pl bnd 2f out: sn wknd and bhd* **16/1**

0 **12** *1* **Luna Vale**[18] 7293 2-8-12 0................................ AndreaAtzeni 4 30
(Robert Eddery) *in tch in last pair: rdn over 4f out: wknd over 2f out* **66/1**

1m 39.88s (1.68) **Going Correction** -0.025s/f (Stan) **12** Ran SP% **114.3**

Speed ratings (Par 96): **90,89,89,88,88 87,86,85,84,84 74,73**

toteswingers:1&2:£3.50, 2&3:£6.80, 1&3:£11.10 CSF £30.44 TOTE £9.00: £2.60, £1.40, £5.40; EX 23.40 Trifecta £199.50 Part won. Pool: £269.68 - 0.86 winning units..

Owner Nurlan Bizakov **Bred** Barouche Stud Ireland Ltd **Trained** Newmarket, Suffolk

FOCUS

An interesting maiden, but the early pace was pedestrian and nine of 12 runners were still within a couple of lengths of each other entering the last furlong. That said, a couple caught the eye.

NOTEBOOK

Zimira(IRE) put up a brave performance to make a winning debut as, after making much of the running, she was briefly headed by the runner-up inside the last furlong, but soon fought her way back to the front and stayed on strongly. Retained for 350,000gns as a yearling, she is a half-sister to four winners at up to 1m6f and looks to have a future. (op 6-1 tchd 15-2)

Widyaan(IRE), a 300,000gns yearling out of a Weatherbys Super Sprint winner, proved weak in the market and blew the start, but the slow pace meant that he was up amongst the leaders after a couple of furlongs. He looked to have been produced at just the right moment to lead entering the last furlong, but the filly bullied him out of it. He appeared to need this experience and can do better. (op 9-4 tchd 2-1)

Paddyfrommenlo(IRE) was staying on well from off the pace when his jockey had to stop riding for a stride or two inside the last furlong, but it didn't affect his finishing position. This Derby entry is bred to stay further and this performance appeared to confirm that. (op 25-1 tchd 33-1)

Northern Outlook, not knocked about on his Newmarket debut last month, was well backed to do much better here, but having been delivered with his effort towards the inside over a furlong out he appeared to run green and he my just have need this experience too. (op 11-2)

Superciliary was beaten a very long way on his Newbury debut last month, but was sent off third-favourite there so was obviously thought to possess ability. He stayed on well down the outside of the field and may be one for handicaps after one more run. (op 8-1 tchd 12-1)

Santadelacruze was never far away and fared much better than when beaten a long way on his Goodwood debut last month. He too looks one for handicaps. (tchd 66-1)

Little Red Minx(IRE), well beaten on her Yarmouth debut last month, fared better here having been up with the pace from the start. (op 20-1)

Hidden Justice(IRE), not seen since finishing seventh of nine on his Newbury debut in July, was possibly the main eye-catcher. Having travelled well, he was staying on under hands-and-heels riding when running into a cul-de-sac inside the last furlong and his rider soon eased off. He is one to keep onside. (tchd 16-1)

Lancaster Gate proved far too green to do himself justice on this debut. (op 8-1)

7521 BRITISH STALLION STUDS SUPPORTING BRITISH RACING E B F MAIDEN STKS (DIV II) 1m (P)

2:10 (2:12) (Class 5) 2-Y-0 **£3,169** (£943; £471; £235) **Stalls** High

Form RPR

62 **1** **Restaurateur (IRE)**[12] 7368 2-9-3 0................................ JimmyFortune 12 77
(Andrew Balding) *t.k.h: chsd ldrs: rdn and effrt towards inner over 1f out: led ins fnl f: kpt on wl* **7/2**[3]

2 *nk* **Hurricane In Dubai (IRE)** 2-9-3 0................................ JohnFahy 3 76
(Denis Coakley) *chsd ldrs: rdn and effrt on inner over 1f out: pressed wnr fnl 100yds: kpt on wl* **80/1**

3 **3** *shd* **Cotton Trader (USA)**[11] 7398 2-9-3 0................................ WilliamBuick 6 76
(John Gosden) *in tch in midfield: rdn and effrt wl over 1f out: str run fnl 100yds: nt quite rch ldrs* **2/1**[1]

35 **4** *nk* **Isthmus**[27] 7126 2-9-3 0................................ IanMongan 2 75
(Amanda Perrett) *led early: styd w ldr: rdn over 2f out: drvn and stl ev ch over 1f out: no ex and one pce fnl 100yds* **10/1**

002 **5** *½* **Royal Prospector**[14] 7329 2-9-3 74................................ RyanMoore 1 74
(Richard Hannon) *sn pushed along to ld: rdn wl over 1f out: drvn 1f out: hdd ins fnl f: one pce fnl 100yds* **5/1**

6 *½* **All That Rules** 2-9-3 0................................ TomQueally 9 74+
(Sir Henry Cecil) *in tch in midfield: pushed along and no imp wl over 1f out: 6th and looked wl hld 1f out: styd on and edgd lft ins fnl f: n.m.r fnl 75yds: gng on fin but nvr looked like rching ldrs* **10/3**[2]

00 **7** *6* **Tis Rock 'N' Roll (USA)**[12] 7369 2-9-3 0................................ ChrisCatlin 10 59
(David Lanigan) *dwlt: in tch in last pair: rdn and struggling over 2f out: outpcd and no threat to ldrs fr over 1f out* **100/1**

00 **8** *1* **Ben Croy**[26] 7134 2-9-3 0................................ EddieAhern 8 57
(Brian Meehan) *hld up in last quartet: rdn and outpcd wl over 1f out: no threat to ldrs after* **80/1**

9 *1 ½* **Astra Hall** 2-8-12 0................................ JimCrowley 11 49
(Ralph Beckett) *chsd ldrs on outer: rdn over 3f out: wknd 2f out* **50/1**

06 **10** *4 ½* **Tazweed (IRE)**[28] 7094 2-9-3 0................................ AndreaAtzeni 7 43
(Roger Varian) *in tch in last quartet: rdn and outpcd ent fnl 2f: wknd wl over 1f out* **28/1**

00 **11** *shd* **Graylyn Olivaa**[18] 7292 2-9-0 0................................ AdamBeschizza(3) 5 43
(Robert Eddery) *a in rr: rdn 4f out: wknd over 2f out* **200/1**

1m 39.73s (1.53) **Going Correction** -0.025s/f (Stan) **11** Ran SP% **113.8**

Speed ratings (Par 96): **91,90,90,90,89 89,83,82,80,76 76**

toteswingers:1&2:£30.70, 2&3:£26.10, 1&3:£2.20 CSF £254.07 TOTE £5.10: £1.60, £11.30, £1.40; EX 199.80 TRIFECTA Not won..

Owner Brook Farm Bloodstock **Bred** Glashare House Stud **Trained** Kingsclere, Hants

FOCUS

Again they didn't seem to go much of a pace early and only a couple of lengths separated the first six at the line. The winning time was 0.15 seconds faster than the first division.

NOTEBOOK

Restaurateur(IRE) finished clear of the rest when runner-up at Wolverhampton last time and was well backed to go one better. Never far away, he put in a sustained effort under pressure inside the last furlong and the extra furlong proved no problem at all. He should have a future in handicaps. (op 5-1)

Hurricane In Dubai(IRE) ran a huge race at a massive price on this debut, always racing close to the pace and sticking on really well against the inside rail. Out of a winning miler, he should be winning races in due course. (tchd 100-1)

Cotton Trader(USA) showed ability when third on his Wolverhampton debut, but this drop in trip on a quicker track may not have been ideal and he didn't engage the afterburner until it was far too late. A return to further should see him off the mark. (op 5-2 tchd 11-4)

Isthmus, up a furlong after showing promise in his first two starts, raced alongside Royal Prospector from the start and there was never much between them until the closing stages, but he lacked a turn of foot where it mattered. He now gets a mark, but doesn't seem to be progressing. (op 12-1)

Royal Prospector set the standard with a mark of 74 and took well to Polytrack when narrowly beaten at Kempton on his third start, but after make much of the running he didn't seem to see out the extra furlong. (op 13-2 tchd 7-1)

All That Rules, retained for 90,000euros as a yearling, is a half-brother to three winners at up to 2m and the market vibes were positive about him throughout the day, but he proved weak on track especially as he proved noisy in the paddock and was on his toes. Once under way, he travelled well enough but took an age to realise what was required after turning in and by the time he clicked into gear, it was far too late. He looked fit enough, but may have needed this mentally and is capable of better. (op 7-4 tchd 7-2)

7522 LINGFIELD MARRIOTT HOTEL & COUNTRY CLUB H'CAP 1m 2f (P)

2:45 (2:45) (Class 6) (0-65,65) 3-Y-O+ **£1,575** (£471; £235; £118; £58) **Stalls** Low

Form RPR

0033 **1** **Signora Frasi (IRE)**[36] 6938 6-9-3 **58**.................... DaneO'Neill 12 67
(Tony Newcombe) *s.i.s: hld up in tch in rr: stl plenty to do jst over 2f out: gd hdwy to chse ldrs and swtchd lft 1f out: r.o wl to ld cl home* **14/1**

6062 **2** *shd* **Lord Lansing (IRE)**[11] 7387 4-9-9 **64**.................... LukeMorris 13 73
(Mrs K Burke) *in tch towards rr: hdwy over 3f out: rdn to chse ldrs 2f out: drvn and ev ch 1f out: led ins fnl f: r.o wl tl hdd and no ex cl home* **13/8**[1]

250- **3** *2¼* **Land Hawk (IRE)**[523] 3168 5-9-2 **60**.................... SimonPearce(3) 9 64
(Lydia Pearce) *in tch in midfield: hdwy on ins to chse ldrs 2f out: pressing ldrs and rdn jst over 1f out: no ex and outpcd by ldng pair fnl 100yds* **25/1**

006 **4** *¾* **Archie Rice (USA)**[13] 7346 5-9-9 **64**.................... JimmyQuinn 2 67
(Tom Keddy) *chsd ldrs: wnt 2nd over 3f out: rdn to ld over 1f out: hdd ins fnl f: wknd fnl 100yds* **10/1**[3]

5334 **5** *3* **Prince Of Thebes (IRE)**[11] 7387 10-8-5 **51**..........(p) MarkCoumbe(5) 10 49
(Michael Attwater) *dwlt: in tch: hdwy to outer over 3f out: hmpd bnd 2f out: rdn and kpt on fr over 1f out: nvr trbld ldrs* **16/1**

4004 **6** *¾* **Mister Green (FR)**[12] 7362 5-9-10 **65**....................(t) TonyCulhane 14 60
(David Flood) *stdd s: hld up in tch in rr: nt clr run and switching wd over 2f out: kpt on fnl f but nvr trbld ldrs* **12/1**

2004 **7** *nk* **Kai Mook**[11] 7394 4-8-9 **57**.................... HarryPoulton(7) 11 52
(Roger Ingram) *hld up in tch in last quartet: rdn and styd on fr over 1f out: nvr trbld ldrs* **14/1**

0-U0 **8** *¾* **Whodunit (UAE)**[11] 7387 7-9-1 **56**....................(b) WilliamCarson 1 49
(Peter Hiatt) *sn led: rdn over 2f out: hdd over 1f out: fdd ins fnl f* **18/1**

4600 **9** *3¾* **Green Earth (IRE)**[13] 7346 4-9-8 **63**.................... IanMongan 3 49
(Pat Phelan) *chsd ldrs: rdn and unable qck 3f out: wknd 2f out* **14/1**

6420 **10** *½* **Ride The Wind**[68] 6134 3-9-4 **63**.................... ChrisCatlin 7 48
(Chris Wall) *in tch in midfield: nt clr run and shuffled bk over 2f out: n.d after* **10/1**[3]

0060 **11** *1* **Loch Fleet (IRE)**[78] 5815 3-9-3 **62**.................... AmirQuinn 4 45
(Gary Moore) *chsd ldrs: rdn and unable qck over 2f out: wknd 2f out* **40/1**

0040 **12** *4½* **Montegonian (USA)**[13] 7346 3-9-3 **62**....................(p) SebSanders 5 36
(Marcus Tregoning) *in tch in midfield: rdn and no rspnse 3f out: wknd over 2f out* **6/1**[2]

010 **13** *2¾* **Phluke**[22] 7203 10-9-2 **57**.................... FergusSweeney 8 25
(Eve Johnson Houghton) *chsd ldr tl over 3f out: rdn and losing pl qckly whn hmpd over 2f out: sn bhd* **25/1**

2m 4.02s (-1.30) **Going Correction** -0.025s/f (Stan)
WFA 3 from 4yo+ 4lb **13** Ran SP% **119.5**
Speed ratings (Par 101): **106,105,104,103,101 100,100,99,96,96 95,91,89**
toteswingers:1&2:£7.40, 2&3:£15.60, 1&3:£36.50 CSF £36.22 CT £603.37 TOTE £14.20: £3.50, £1.40, £9.70; EX 41.40 Trifecta £378.30 Part won. Pool of £511.25 - 0.64 winning units..
Owner Kenneth Eastup **Bred** Mrs Clodagh McStay **Trained** Yarnscombe, Devon

FOCUS

They appeared to go a decent enough pace in this moderate handicap. The form is rated around the first two and close to their previous C&D marks.

Prince Of Thebes(IRE) Official explanation: jockey said gelding was hampered on final bend

7523 BET IN PLAY AT LADBROKES.COM H'CAP 1m 2f (P)

3:15 (3:16) (Class 2) (0-100,94) 3-Y-O+ **£10,350** (£3,080; £1,539; £769) **Stalls** Low

Form RPR

0000 **1** **Tinshu (IRE)**[14] 7328 5-8-10 **80**....................(p) FergusSweeney 3 90
(Derek Haydn Jones) *hld up in tch: travelling wl but nt clr run ent fnl 2f: hdwy to chal 1f out: sn led and qcknd clr u.p: in command after* **16/1**

-100 **2** *1¼* **Alakhan (IRE)**[25] 7168 5-9-1 **85**.................... TomEaves 10 92
(Ian Williams) *t.k.h: hld up in tch in rr: effrt on outer bnd 2f out: edgd lft but kpt on wl ins fnl f* **6/1**[3]

-052 **3** *¾* **Mull Of Killough (IRE)**[11] 7393 5-9-10 **94**.................... TonyHamilton 5 100
(Richard Fahey) *in tch in midfield: rdn and effrt to chse ldrs 2f out: drvn over 1f out: kpt on same pce ins fnl f* **4/1**[1]

2061 **4** *nk* **Mountain Range (IRE)**[14] 7328 3-8-13 **87**.................... EddieAhern 2 92
(John Dunlop) *hld up in tch in last quartet: pushed along and nt clr run jst over 2f out: kpt on wl ins fnl f: nvr trbld ldrs* **7/1**

2102 **5** *1¾* **New Hampshire (USA)**[22] 7204 3-9-1 **89**.................... WilliamBuick 7 90
(John Gosden) *dwlt: sn rcvrd and chsd ldr tl 6f out: styd handy: drvn and effrt to chse ldr jst over 1f out tl ins fnl f: wknd fnl 100yds* **5/1**[2]

2-00 **6** *¾* **Mawaakef (IRE)**[77] 5830 3-9-0 **88**.................... JoeFanning 8 88
(J R Jenkins) *led: rdn jst over 2f out: hdd jst ins fnl f: wknd ins fnl f* **16/1**

0600 **7** *1¾* **Beaubrav**[51] 6592 5-9-7 **91**....................(t) JimCrowley 4 87
(Michael Madgwick) *s.i.s: pushed along in rr: switching rt and hdwy over 1f out: kpt on but nvr trbld ldrs* **16/1**

0013 **8** *½* **Byrony (IRE)**[35] 6949 3-8-13 **87**.................... RyanMoore 1 82
(Richard Hannon) *chsd ldng trio: rdn and unable qck ent fnl 2f: wknd 1f out* **7/1**

0005 **9** *1¼* **Nice Style (IRE)**[11] 7391 6-9-10 **94**....................(bt) TomQueally 9 87
(Jeremy Gask) *dwlt: pushed along early: chsd ldrs on outer 8f out: wnt 2nd 6f out tl over 1f out: wknd* **10/1**

0-04 **10** *12* **Hanoverian Baron**[18] 7297 6-9-7 **91**.................... DaneO'Neill 6 60
(Tony Newcombe) *in tch: hmpd after 1f out: rdn and wknd 2f out: wl btn and eased ins fnl f* **4/1**[1]

0231 **11** *24* **Hidden Glory**[21] 7237 4-9-0 **84**....................(b) MickyFenton 11 —
(James Given) *in tch in last trio: struggling over 2f out: lost tch 2f out: wl bhd and eased ins fnl f* **25/1**

2m 3.42s (-3.18) **Going Correction** -0.025s/f (Stan)
WFA 3 from 4yo+ 4lb **11** Ran SP% **126.5**
Speed ratings (Par 109): **111,110,109,109,107 107,105,105,104,94 75**
CSF £117.31 CT £475.93 TOTE £27.80: £7.80, £2.40, £2.60; EX 228.00 TRIFECTA Not won..
Owner Llewelyn, Runeckles **Bred** Mrs M L Parry & P M Steele-Mortimer **Trained** Efail Isaf, Rhondda C Taff

FOCUS

A decent quality handicap for a midweek meeting here. Al though the early pace was only ordinary the final time was solid for the grade. The placed horses are rated close to their marks backed up by the fourth.

NOTEBOOK

Tinshu(IRE)'s recent efforts on turf had been poor, but she had become well handicapped considering she has twice won off higher marks than this on Polytrack in the past, including one over this C&D. Having travelled powerfully in midfield throughout, she took off once into the straight to hit the front inside the last furlong and won this hot race with a degree of comfort. Now that she has returned to winning form, she could well go in again. (op 14-1)

Alakhan(IRE) was a real eye-catcher when eighth at Newmarket last time (Mull Of Killough second), but was disappointing in his only previous try on Polytrack. This was much more like it, however, and having been forced wide into the home straight he stayed on all the way to the line. He doesn't have that many miles on the clock for a horse of his age and looks to have a nice prize in him. (op 9-1)

Mull Of Killough(IRE) has been running well in defeat lately and looked to have been delivered with this effort at the right time, but he didn't find as much off the bridle as had seemed likely. He was well beaten in his only previous try over this far, so the conclusion may be that he doesn't stay. (op 7-2 tchd 9-2)

Mountain Range(IRE), raised 5lb for his Kempton success, finished well but all too late and perhaps he needs to go right-handed. (op 13-2 tchd 6-1)

New Hampshire(USA) was put up 5lb after finishing second at Kempton last time though that form hasn't worked out. He had a problem getting out of a pocket running towards the home turn, but had every chance towards the inside of the track once into the straight had he been good enough. He didn't see the racecourse until April, so may still have a been more improvement left. (op 15-2)

Mawaakef(IRE), ex Kevin Prendergast, showed little on his debut for the yard last time but ran better on this all-weather debut, lasting longer in front than might have been expected. (tchd 14-1, 20-1 and 25-1 in a place)

Beaubrav was unsuited by an ordinary gallop over a sharp 1m2f. (tchd 14-1 and 20-1)

Byrony(IRE) was the subject of a late plunge, bit this was her first try beyond 1m and she didn't get home. (op 16-1 tchd 20-1 and 6-1 in a place)

Hanoverian Baron was never going to be suited by an ordinary gallop over a sharp 1m2f around here but it was disconcerting to see him drop out so tamely, though it transpired that he had pulled a muscle. (op 5-1)

7524 LADBROKES GAME ON! ALL-WEATHER "HANDS & HEELS" APPRENTICE SERIES H'CAP (RACING EXCELLENCE INITATIVE) 7f (P)

3:45 (3:45) (Class 6) (0-58,64) 3-Y-O+ **£1,704** (£503; £251) **Stalls** Low

Form RPR

2201 **1** **Bold Ring**[4] 7485 5-9-4 **64** 6ex.................... JoshCrane(7) 5 71
(Edward Creighton) *hld up towards rr of main gp: rdn and hdwy over 1f out: chal ins fnl f: kpt on wl to ld on post* **5/1**[2]

2535 **2** *nse* **Gazboolou**[11] 7400 7-9-4 **57**.................... JakePayne 2 63
(David Pinder) *broke v fast: chsd ldrs: rdn and ev ch 2f out: led wl ins fnl f: hdd on post* **10/1**

5000 **3** *½* **Blueberry Fizz (IRE)**[29] 7084 3-8-0 **47**.................... BradleyBosley(7) 8 52
(John Ryan) *chsd ldr: ev ch and rdn over 1f out: kpt on same pce fnl 100yds* **33/1**

0464 **4** *nk* **Paperetto**[94] 5300 3-8-11 **58**.................... DanielCremin(7) 12 62
(Robert Mills) *sn pushed along to ld and crossed to rail: rdn over 1f out: hdd and no ex wl ins fnl f* **11/1**

5030 **5** *½* **Storm Runner (IRE)**[20] 7246 3-8-3 **50**.................... RichardOld(7) 7 53
(George Margarson) *t.k.h: hld up in tch in midfield: rdn and effrt over 1f out: swtchd lft 1f out: kpt on wl fnl 75yds* **25/1**

4521 **6** *nse* **Yakama (IRE)**[21] 7229 6-8-12 **56**....................(p) DanielHarris(5) 10 59
(Christine Dunnett) *in tch towards rr of main gp: effrt on outer 2f out: kpt on ins fnl f* **9/1**[3]

0164 **7** *hd* **Princess Lexi (IRE)**[21] 7228 4-9-5 **58**.................... MichaelJMurphy 6 60+
(William Knight) *hld up in rr of main gp: stl plenty to do 2f out: hdwy towards inner over 1f out: running on whn n.m.r ins fnl f: kpt on but nvr able to chal* **7/4**[1]

0000 **8** *1½* **Super Frank (IRE)**[21] 7224 8-8-13 **52**....................(b) GeorgeDowning 4 50
(Zoe Davison) *chsd ldrs: rdn and effrt wl over 1f out: nt qckn ent fnl f: one pce after* **20/1**

4500 **9** *1¾* **Titan Diamond (IRE)**[6] 7442 3-8-2 **49**.................... RobertSpencer(7) 3 42
(Mark Usher) *in tch in midfield: rdn and effrt on inner over 2f out: plugged on but no threat to ldrs* **14/1**

6003 **10** *nk* **Ghost Dancer**[38] 6889 7-8-5 **47**....................(p) DannyBrock(3) 9 39
(Milton Bradley) *t.k.h: hld up in tch in midfield: rdn unable qck over 1f out: one pce and btn ins fnl f* **10/1**

0602 **11** *2½* **Chicamia**[50] 6610 7-8-7 **46**....................[1] NoelGarbutt 13 32
(Michael Mullineaux) *s.i.s: rdn along in rr thrght: styd on fnl f: n.d* **16/1**

0064 **12** *5* **Scruffy Skip (IRE)**[20] 7247 6-8-7 **46**....................(p) JackDuern 14 18
(Christine Dunnett) *a in rr: nvr on terms* **14/1**

-300 **13** *17* **Bianco Boy (USA)**[36] 6940 4-8-10 **52**.................... IanBurns(3) 11 —
(John Best) *towards rr on outer: rdn and toiling over 2f out: wl bhd fnl 2f* **50/1**

1m 25.26s (0.46) **Going Correction** -0.025s/f (Stan)
WFA 3 from 4yo+ 1lb **13** Ran SP% **122.3**
Speed ratings (Par 101): **96,95,95,95,94 94,94,92,90,90 87,81,62**
toteswingers:1&2:£11.10, 2&3:£48.00, 1&3:£28.50 CSF £53.48 CT £1560.91 TOTE £7.80: £2.50, £3.60, £13.80; EX 46.20 TRIFECTA Not won..
Owner Daniel Creighton **Bred** J A Pickering & T Pears **Trained** Wormshill, Kent

FOCUS

They appeared to go a decent pace in this moderate "hands and heels" apprentice handicap, but there were still only a couple of lengths separating the front seven at the line. The form is rated around the three in the frame behind the winner.

T/Jkpt: Not won. T/Plt: £65.00 to a £1 stake. Pool of £64,157.48 - 720.46 winning tickets. T/Qpdt: £12.80 to a £1 stake. Pool of £5,062.19 - 290.70 winning tickets. SP

[7511] KEMPTON (A.W) (R-H)

Thursday, November 24

OFFICIAL GOING: Standard

Wind: Light, behind Weather: Fine

7525 ENHANCED SP'S AT BLUESQ.COM MEDIAN AUCTION MAIDEN STKS 6f (P)

4:10 (4:10) (Class 6) 3-5-Y-O £1,617 (£481; £240; £120) Stalls Low

Form RPR

4652 **1** **Royal Selection (IRE)**[23] 7207 3-8-12 65 TomMcLaughlin 1 52
(Karen George) *trckd ldng pair: led on inner 2f out: rdn and briefly pressed jst over 1f out: styd on to assert fnl f* **4/5[1]**

0064 **2** 2 **My Best Man**[1] 7511 5-9-3 46 LukeMorris 7 51
(Tony Carroll) *hld up in last trio: prog over 3f out: rdn to chse wnr over 1f out: nt qckn and wl hld fnl f* **8/1[3]**

4230 **3** 2 **Lovat Lane**[233] 1149 3-8-12 49 (b) ChrisCatlin 6 40
(Eve Johnson Houghton) *pressed ldr: chal and upsides 2f out: chsd wnr to over 1f out: one pce* **10/1**

2006 **4** 3 ½ **Mucky Molly**[20] 7269 3-8-12 53 IanMongan 5 28
(Olivia Maylam) *t.k.h: hld up in midfield: outpcd whn effrt over 2f out: no imp after* **7/2[2]**

0 **5** ½ **Whats Your Story**[29] 7093 3-9-3 0 FrankieMcDonald 4 32
(Murty McGrath) *stdd s: hld up in last pair: rdn in last wl over 2f out: styd on fr over 1f out* **100/1**

6 3 ¼ **Sid** 3-9-3 0 JamieGoldstein 2 21
(Zoe Davison) *dropped to rr and rdn over 3f out: nvr on terms after* **20/1**

000 **7** 1 **Lady Ellice**[40] 6874 3-8-9 46 (v[1]) AdamBeschizza(3) 8 13
(Phil McEntee) *nvr bttr than midfield: rdn and struggling over 2f out: wknd* **33/1**

0054 **8** 3 **Chillie Peppar**[7] 7443 3-9-3 43 (b[1]) KirstyMilczarek 3 —
(George Prodromou) *led to 2f out: wknd rapidly* **12/1**

600 **9** 8 **Grayfriars**[21] 7245 3-9-3 42 FergusSweeney 9 —
(J R Jenkins) *s.i.s: a in last trio: wknd over 2f out: t.o* **50/1**

1m 13.71s (0.61) **Going Correction** -0.05s/f (Stan) **9** Ran SP% **116.3**

Speed ratings (Par 101): **93,90,87,83,82 78,76,72,62**

Tote Swingers: 1&2 £2.80, 1&3 £2.20, 2&3 £3.90 CSF £7.97 TOTE £2.20: £1.20, £1.50, £1.10; EX 8.40.

Owner Athole Still **Bred** Leinster Stud **Trained** Higher Eastington, Devon

FOCUS

A low-grade maiden and the form looks weak rated around the runner-up. The gallop was a reasonable one and the winner came down the centre in the last furlong.

7526 BLUE SQUARE/BRITISH STALLION STUDS E B F MAIDEN STKS 6f (P)

4:40 (4:41) (Class 5) 2-Y-O £3,234 (£962; £481; £240) Stalls Low

Form RPR

22 **1** **Galician**[8] 7431 2-8-12 0 JoeFanning 11 79+
(Mark Johnston) *trckd ldr: led wl over 1f out: pushed along and a holding rivals fnl f* **5/4[1]**

2 1 **Gabbiano** 2-9-3 0 TonyCulhane 2 81+
(Jeremy Gask) *dwlt: t.k.h and sn in 6th: outpcd 3f out: rousted along and prog fr over 2f out: styd on thrght fnl 2f to take 2nd last strides* **4/1[2]**

620 **3** nk **Jwala**[27] 7135 2-8-12 80 DaneO'Neill 5 75
(Robert Cowell) *chsd ldng pair: rdn to chse wnr over 1f out: styd on but no imp fnl f: lost 2nd last strides* **4/1[2]**

030 **4** 2 ¾ **Red Bay**[19] 7293 2-9-3 65 LukeMorris 3 72
(Jane Chapple-Hyam) *chsd ldng pair: rdn and outpcd fr 2f out: tried to rally over 1f out: sn one pce* **16/1**

5 3 ¼ **Boudoir (IRE)** 2-8-9 0 KieranO'Neill(3) 1 57+
(Richard Hannon) *racd freely: led: clr w three others 3f out: hdd & wknd wl over 1f out* **14/1**

6 ½ **Kickingthelilly** 2-8-12 0 SteveDrowne 10 56+
(Rae Guest) *hld up in last trio: pushed along over 2f out: sme prog over 1f out: fin quite wl* **66/1**

7 nk **Boots And Spurs** 2-9-3 0 MartinHarley 4 60
(Mrs K Burke) *dwlt: wl off the pce towards rr: no ch fr 3f out: pushed along firmly and styd on fr over 1f out* **25/1**

06 **8** 1 ½ **Justbookies Dotnet**[79] 5812 2-9-3 0 FrankieMcDonald 12 55
(Louise Best) *plld hrd: hld up wl in rr and off the pce: no ch 3f out: kpt on fr over 1f out* **66/1**

3 **9** ¾ **Take A Note**[36] 6945 2-9-3 0 JimCrowley 8 53
(Patrick Chamings) *dwlt: taken patiently in last trio and wl off the pce: brought wd bnd 3f out: pushed along and kpt on steadily fnl 2f* **12/1[3]**

00 **10** 4 ½ **Johnny Splash (IRE)**[14] 7345 2-9-3 0 JohnFahy 9 39
(Roger Teal) *chsd ldng quartet: lft bhd fr 3f out: sn hrd rdn and wknd* **66/1**

00 **11** 3 ½ **Castalian Spring (IRE)**[45] 6744 2-8-12 0 AndreaAtzeni 6 24
(Robert Eddery) *a in last trio: wl bhd over 2f out: no prog* **100/1**

00 **12** 14 **Peters Pleasure**[54] 6539 2-8-9 0 AdamBeschizza(3) 7 —
(Robert Cowell) *nvr beyond midfield: wknd 3f out: t.o* **100/1**

1m 12.4s (-0.70) **Going Correction** -0.05s/f (Stan) **12** Ran SP% **115.0**

Speed ratings (Par 96): **102,100,100,96,92 91,91,89,88,82 77,58**

Tote Swingers: 1&2 £2.80, 1&3 £2.00, 2&3 £4.00 CSF £5.73 TOTE £2.60: £1.10, £1.20, £1.70; EX 9.80.

Owner Sheikh Hamdan Bin Mohammed Al Maktoum **Bred** Darley **Trained** Middleham Moor, N Yorks

FOCUS

Not the most competitive of maidens but fair form from the first three, who pulled a few lengths clear of the 65-rated fourth. The gallop was fair and the winner edged from the centre towards the far rail the in the closing stages. The third is rated to form and helps set the level.

NOTEBOOK

Galician, dropped in trip, is a steadily progressive sort who turned in her best effort to get off the mark. She won't be troubled by the return to 7f, she is in good hands and she may do better in handicaps. (tchd 11-8)

Gabbiano ◆ shaped with promise, despite his apparent greenness, on this racecourse debut. This brother to fair 6f winner Fayre Bella and half-brother to fair sprinter Miss Hollybell should come on a fair bit for this and is sure to pick up a similar event. (op 9-2)

Jwala may not be as good as her official mark of 80 suggests, but she again showed enough after enjoying the run of the race to indicate she should be able to pick up a similar event over this trip in the coming months. (op 7-2)

Red Bay had a bit to find at these weights judging on his turf form but he was far from disgraced on this all-weather debut. He may be seen to better effect in ordinary handicaps returned to a bit further. (op 14-1)

Boudoir(IRE), a half-sister to 1m2f Listed winner Forest Magic and to a juvenile 1m winner in France, was easy to back but showed ability at an ordinary level after racing with the choke out. She should do better in due course.

Kickingthelilly, who has several sprint winners in her pedigree, caught the eye after running green. Her trainer does well with fillies and she should win a small event at some point.

7527 DOWNLOAD THE BLUE SQUARE BET APP H'CAP (DIV I) 1m 4f (P)

5:10 (5:10) (Class 6) (0-60,60) 3-Y-0+ £1,617 (£481; £240; £120) Stalls Centre

Form RPR

0055 **1** **Valdan (IRE)**[9] 7426 7-8-8 49 MatthewCosham(5) 4 58
(David Evans) *dwlt: hld up in midfield: prog gng strly over 2f out: chsd ldr over 1f out: rdn to ld last 150yds: r.o and grad asserted* **6/1[3]**

0526 **2** 1 **Sail Home**[29] 7112 4-9-7 60 AdamBeschizza(3) 6 67
(Julia Feilden) *hld up in midfield: prog on outer over 3f out to ld 2f out: rdn over 1f out: hdd last 150yds: styd on* **15/2**

0100 **3** 2 ½ **El Libertador (USA)**[12] 7399 5-9-4 54 (b) SebSanders 3 57
(Eric Wheeler) *hld up bhd ldrs in 5th: effrt and prog over 2f out: rdn and nt pce to chal over 1f out: rdn on to take 3rd ins fnl f* **25/1**

0031 **4** 1 ¼ **Honourable Knight (IRE)**[15] 7333 3-9-2 58 (be) SteveDrowne 8 59
(Mark Usher) *trckd ldr: drvn over 2f out: outpcd by ldng pair over 1f out: lost 3rd ins fnl f* **11/4[1]**

5064 **5** 4 ½ **Mister Frosty (IRE)**[16] 7087 5-9-3 53 KirstyMilczarek 11 47
(George Prodromou) *led: rdn and hdd 2f out: steadily wknd* **12/1**

/06- **6** 1 ¼ **Red Lancer**[50] 4683 10-9-8 58 (b) LukeMorris 9 50
(Jonathen de Giles) *hld up in last trio: rdn and sme prog over 2f out: sn outpcd: kpt on same pce* **40/1**

0663 **7** 1 ¾ **Famagusta**[30] 7087 4-8-10 46 RobertWinston 5 35
(Peter Charalambous) *chsd ldng trio: rdn and immediately outpcd over 2f out: nvr on terms after* **8/1**

-000 **8** 5 **Shirataki (IRE)**[163] 3018 3-8-5 47 ChrisCatlin 2 28
(Peter Hiatt) *t.k.h: trckd ldr to over 2f out: wknd qckly over 1f out* **16/1**

5035 **9** ½ **Cardi King**[20] 7263 3-9-1 57 JimCrowley 7 37
(Ian Wood) *hld up in last trio: drvn in last over 2f out: no ch after* **15/2**

220 **10** 3 ¼ **Saloon (USA)**[56] 6493 7-9-5 55 (p) IvaMilickova 10 30
(Jane Chapple-Hyam) *hld up last: urged along over 3f out: no real prog over 2f out* **12/1**

6-50 **11** 13 **Lucas Pitt**[20] 7264 4-8-12 53 DavidKenny(5) 1 —
(Michael Scudamore) *settled in midfield: pushed along over 5f out: rdn and wknd over 2f out: t.o* **5/1[2]**

2m 34.71s (0.21) **Going Correction** -0.05s/f (Stan)

WFA 3 from 4yo+ 6lb **11** Ran SP% **119.8**

Speed ratings (Par 101): **97,96,94,93,90 90,88,85,85,83 74**

Tote Swingers: 1&2 £6.70, 1&3 £35.80, 2&3 £40.00 CSF £51.60 CT £1061.20 TOTE £9.30: £2.50, £2.90, £11.10; EX 61.70.

Owner Diamond Racing Ltd **Bred** Herbertstown Stud Ltd **Trained** Pandy, Monmouths

FOCUS

A moderate handicap in which an ordinary gallop soon steadied before picking up again approaching the intersection. The first two, who pulled a few lengths clear, came down the centre. The form is rated through the runner-up to recent turf form, backed up by the third and fourth to their marks.

7528 DOWNLOAD THE BLUE SQUARE BET APP H'CAP (DIV II) 1m 4f (P)

5:40 (5:40) (Class 6) (0-60,59) 3-Y-0+ £1,617 (£481; £240; £120) Stalls Centre

Form RPR

2440 **1** **Rose Aurora**[40] 6876 4-8-10 45 (vt) DaneO'Neill 7 58
(Marcus Tregoning) *trckd ldrs: prog to go 2nd 3f out: clsd to ld wl over 1f out: forged clr fnl f* **16/1**

0242 **2** 6 **Colinca's Lad (IRE)**[23] 7203 9-9-10 59 RobertWinston 6 62
(Peter Charalambous) *prog to ld after 3f: stdd pce 1/2-way: kicked on wl over 3f out: rdn and hdd wl over 1f out: no ch w wnr after: kpt on* **11/4[1]**

5045 **3** 2 **Miss Bounty**[12] 7394 6-9-5 54 MatthewDavies 8 54
(Jim Boyle) *hld up towards rr: prog over 3f out: tried to cl on ldrs over 1f out: styd on same pce fnl f* **14/1**

2054 **4** ¾ **Croix Rouge (USA)**[23] 7206 9-9-4 53 JamieGoldstein 3 52
(Ralph Smith) *led 3f: chsd ldr to 3f out: readily outpcd fnl 2f* **10/1**

5312 **5** 2 **Art Thief**[5] 7495 3-8-7 55 JackDuern(7) 1 51
(Michael Appleby) *prom: rdn over 5f out and lost pl: struggling bdly after: plugged on again over 1f out* **3/1[2]**

00/6 **6** 2 ¼ **Now**[246] 944 5-9-3 52 JamesMillman 9 44
(Rod Millman) *stdd s: hld up in last pair: plenty to do after pce lifted over 3f out: pushed along and passed a few rivals fnl 2f: nvr remotely involved* **14/1**

0333 **7** 1 ½ **Bold Adventure**[198] 1973 7-9-4 53 TonyCulhane 5 43
(Willie Musson) *hld up in last pair: plenty to do after pce lifted over 3f out: pushed along and plugged on: nvr involved* **20/1**

0-06 **8** 1 ¾ **Princess Runner**[21] 7254 4-8-10 45 MartinHarley 2 32
(Des Donovan) *settled in midfield: pushed along over 4f out: sn lost pl: struggling in rr over 2f out* **33/1**

1325 **9** 8 **Fifty Cents**[5] 7495 7-9-9 58 (p) FergusSweeney 4 32
(Brendan Powell) *cl up: rdn over 3f out: sn wknd rapidly: t.o* **11/2[3]**

40-4 **10** 74 **Apache Kid (IRE)**[13] 7370 4-9-5 54 StevieDonohoe 10 —
(Ian Williams) *in tch: drvn wl over 3f out: sn wknd qckly: virtually p.u over 1f out* **6/1**

2m 34.65s (0.15) **Going Correction** -0.05s/f (Stan)

WFA 3 from 4yo+ 6lb **10** Ran SP% **117.3**

Speed ratings (Par 101): **97,93,91,91,89 88,87,86,80,31**

Tote Swingers: 1&2 £9.00, 1&3 £34.90, 2&3 £10.90 CSF £60.34 CT £654.69 TOTE £17.40: £4.70, £1.10, £5.80; EX 81.50.

Owner Kingwood House Racing **Bred** Heather Raw **Trained** Lambourn, Berks

FOCUS

A moderate handicap in which a couple of the market leaders underperformed. The gallop soon steadied and the ready winner came down the centre in the straight. The runner-up is rated to the general level of his AW form.

Bold Adventure Official explanation: jockey said gelding hung right

Apache Kid(IRE) Official explanation: jockey said gelding stopped quickly

7529 WIN THOUSANDS OF SPORTS TICKETS AT BLUESQ.COM CLAIMING STKS 6f (P)

6:10 (6:10) (Class 6) 3-Y-0+ £1,617 (£481; £240; £120) Stalls Low

Form RPR

2402 **1** **Aye Aye Digby (IRE)**[38] 6920 6-9-11 79 JimCrowley 5 88
(Patrick Chamings) *trckd ldng trio: shkn up and prog to ld wl over 1f out: styd on fnl f: a holding on* **11/2[3]**

0-00 **2** 1 **Royal Intruder**[1] 7517 6-8-13 71 TomQueally 10 73
(S Donohoe, Ire) *hld up in last pair: prog over 2f out: rdn and r.o fnl f to take 2nd last stride* **10/1**

4530 **3** hd **Sarah's Art (IRE)**[15] 7341 8-8-5 67 (t) NickyMackay 3 64
(Derek Shaw) *trckd ldrs: effrt on inner to chal 2f out: chsd wnr fnl f: kpt on but a hld: lost 2nd post* **14/1**

3060 **4** *3/4* **Dvinsky (USA)**[14] 7349 10-8-5 62.................................(b) JimmyQuinn 2 62
(Paul Howling) *rousted along leaving stalls but unable to ld: chsd ldng pair: wnt 2nd 1/2-way: drvn to ld briefly 2f out: kpt on same pce fnl f* **25/1**

5602 **5** *2* **Perfect Act**[244] 960 6-9-2 83.................................. JimmyFortune 8 67
(Andrew Balding) *t.k.h: hld up in midfield: prog 2f out: tried to cl on ldng trio 1f out: fdd last 100yds* **5/2[1]**

1501 **6** *3/4* **Desert Icon (IRE)**[21] 7253 5-8-11 75.......................(bt) TonyCulhane 1 59
(David Flood) *c out of the stalls slowly: hld up last: shkn up and limited prog 2f out: no ch after: styng on at fin* **13/2**

3612 **7** *1 1/2* **Lutine Charlie (IRE)**[5] 7484 4-9-0 74......................(p) KierenFox(3) 6 60
(Ronald Harris) *racd wd in midfield: lost grnd bnd 3f out: nt on terms 2f out: n.d after* **10/3[2]**

3100 **8** *1* **Memphis Man**[6] 7459 8-8-8 57.............................. MatthewCosham(5) 9 53
(David Evans) *taken down early: racd wd: hld up: rdn and no prog over 2f out: n.d after* **66/1**

000 **9** *2 1/4* **Waabel**[5] 7487 4-9-0 78..(tp) RobertLButler(3) 7 50
(Richard Guest) *led to 2f out: sn wknd* **20/1**

403 **10** *1/2* **Mawjoodah**[48] 6665 3-8-12 71...................................... BarryMcHugh 12 43
(Brian Ellison) *chsd ldrs on outer: rdn and nt qckn over 2f out: sn btn* **9/1**

4206 **11** *7* **C'Mon You Irons (IRE)**[110] 4795 6-8-8 62 ow1............ RobertHavlin 11 17
(Mark Hoad) *chsd ldr to 1/2-way: wknd qckly: t.o* **20/1**

1m 12.4s (-0.70) **Going Correction** -0.05s/f (Stan) **11** Ran SP% **121.0**
Speed ratings (Par 101): **102,100,100,99,96 95,93,92,89,88 79**
Tote Swingers: 1&2 £10.20, 1&3 £12.40, 2&3 £22.30 CSF £57.99 TOTE £1.60: £1.02, £5.80, £3.10; EX 91.10.Desert Icon (IRE) claimed by Mr J. Babb for £5,000. Royal Intruder claimed by Mr S. Arnold for £6,000. Sarah's Art (IRE) claimed by Mr Gary Harrison for £2,000.
Owner Trolley Action **Bred** G J King **Trained** Baughurst, Hants

FOCUS
A fair claimer in which the gallop was soon sound. The winner came down the centre in the straight and the fourth sets the level rated to recent form.
Lutine Charlie(IRE) Official explanation: jockey said gelding hung left

7530 PLAY RAINBOW RICHES AT BLUESQ.COM NURSERY 6f (P)
6:40 (6:41) (Class 6) (0-65,65) 2-Y-O **£1,617** (£481; £240; £120) **Stalls** Low

Form RPR

0355 **1** **Intomist (IRE)**[15] 7337 2-8-13 57.................................... StephenCraine 3 62
(Jim Boyle) *trckd ldrs: cl up 2f out: rdn over 1f out: clsd to ld ins fnl f: styd on strly* **8/1**

3050 **2** *1* **Finalist**[6] 7452 2-9-0 58...(b[1]) JimmyQuinn 10 60
(Dean Ivory) *hld up in rr: prog over 2f out: effrt on inner over 1f out: rdn to chal and upsides ins fnl f: styd on but outpcd* **5/1[3]**

4006 **3** *3/4* **Copper Falls**[6] 7452 2-8-12 56.................................... KirstyMilczarek 2 56
(Brendan Powell) *t.k.h: pressed ldr: rdn to ld over 1f out: hdd and one pce ins fnl f* **25/1**

0406 **4** *2 1/2* **Illustrious Lad (IRE)**[113] 4661 2-9-6 64............................ TomQueally 4 56
(Jim Boyle) *led: rdn and hdd over 1f out: fdd* **16/1**

4222 **5** *hd* **Mount McLeod (IRE)**[9] 7421 2-8-12 56...................... FergusSweeney 8 48
(Jamie Osborne) *slowest away: hld up in rr: prog 2f out: tried to cl on ldrs over 1f out: kpt on same pce* **4/1[2]**

1604 **6** *nse* **Sweet Ovation**[21] 7252 2-8-12 56...................................... RobertHavlin 1 48
(Mark Usher) *trckd ldrs: effrt on inner over 2f out: cl enough over 1f out: fdd fnl f* **6/1**

5205 **7** *3 1/2* **King's Future**[7] 7444 2-9-7 65...(p) LukeMorris 5 46
(John Akehurst) *t.k.h: chsd ldr to over 2f out: nt qckn and lost pl: n.d over 1f out* **9/1**

400 **8** *1/2* **Marah Music**[36] 6956 2-9-7 65...................................... SteveDrowne 7 45
(Peter Makin) *hld up towards rr on inner: pushed along over 2f out: rdn and no prog over 1f out: wl hld after* **7/2[1]**

0060 **9** *hd* **Colourful Event (IRE)**[23] 7205 2-8-1 48...................(v) SophieDoyle(3) 6 27
(David Arbuthnot) *hld up last: pushed along 1/2-way: reminder 2f out: no ch but styng on at fin* **25/1**

0050 **10** *3 3/4* **Musical Strike**[13] 7364 2-8-8 52..................................... JamieMackay 11 20
(Shaun Harris) *racd wd: chsd ldrs: lost grnd bnd 3f out: struggling after* **66/1**

060 **11** *1 1/2* **Sarah Berry**[15] 7329 2-9-2 60 AndreaAtzeni 9 23
(Chris Dwyer) *chsd ldrs: rdn and wknd over 2f out* **33/1**

0034 **12** *2 1/2* **Bountiful Catch**[9] 7421 2-8-9 53.................................... MickyFenton 12 9
(Pam Sly) *racd v wd: a towards rr: bhd over 2f out* **12/1**

1m 13.43s (0.33) **Going Correction** -0.05s/f (Stan) **12** Ran SP% **120.0**
Speed ratings (Par 94): **95,93,92,89,89 89,84,83,83,78 76,73**
Tote Swingers: 1&2 £10.20, 1&3 £21.10, 2&3 £32.80 CSF £46.82 CT £990.55 TOTE £8.20: £2.60, £2.00, £7.70; EX 65.20.
Owner The Clueless Syndicate **Bred** Philip Guerin **Trained** Epsom, Surrey

FOCUS
A modest nusery in which the gallop to halfway was just an ordinary one. The winner raced centre-to-far side in the closing stages and is rated a slight improver on his turf form, while the runner-up is rated back to form in the first-time headgear.

NOTEBOOK
Intomist(IRE), with the blinkers left off for this switch back to Polytrack (reportedly stopped quickly on Fibresand), had the run of the race and turned in his best effort to get off the mark. He'll be equally effective over 7f and may do better.
Finalist had disappointed on her previous start but she isn't fully exposed, and showed enough (best of those held up) in first-time blinkers returned to this more suitable trip to suggest a similar event can be found. (op 4-1)
Copper Falls had the run of the race and ran creditably returned to this longer trip but she has yet to win and her record suggests she wouldn't be guaranteed to build on this next time.
Illustrious Lad(IRE), having his first run since August and his first since being gelded, had the run of the race and wasn't disgraced. His dam won the Lancashire Oaks and he left the impression here that he could benefit from a stiffer test of stamina. (op 20-1)
Mount McLeod(IRE) has been running consistently well but wasn't at her very best after losing ground at the start and after racing keenly. She's not one to be taking too short a price about. Official explanation: jockey said filly was slowly away (op 7-2)

7531 BET AT BLUESQ.COM H'CAP 7f (P)
7:10 (7:12) (Class 4) (0-85,85) 3-Y-0+ **£4,075** (£1,212; £606; £303) **Stalls** Low

Form RPR

3511 **1** **Iron Step**[31] 7054 3-9-4 83..(t) LukeMorris 6 94
(Nicky Vaughan) *trckd clr ldng pair: wnt 2nd over 2f out: clsd to ld over 1f out: drvn and hld on wl fnl f* **15/2[3]**

3011 **2** *1/2* **Numeral (IRE)**[14] 7348 3-8-13 78.................................. JimCrowley 3 88
(Richard Hannon) *chsd ldrs: prog over 2f out: drvn over 1f out: styd on fnl f to take 2nd last stride* **5/2[1]**

0552 **3** *nse* **New Leyf (IRE)**[6] 7457 5-9-7 85................................... SteveDrowne 8 94
(Ed Walker) *trckd ldrs on inner: prog over 2f out: rdn to chal over 1f out: pressed wnr fnl f: a hld and lost 2nd last stride* **11/2[2]**

0043 **4** *1* **Marajaa (IRE)**[46] 6728 9-9-0 78....................................... JamieMackay 12 85
(Willie Musson) *stdd s: hld up in last: pushed along over 2f out: eye-catching prog over 1f out: fin strly: too much to do* **28/1**

363 **5** *2 1/2* **Requisite**[8] 7438 6-8-11 75...(b) DaneO'Neill 5 75
(Ian Wood) *hld up towards rr: prog over 2f out: rdn and styd on fr over 1f out: nt pce to threaten* **14/1**

0060 **6** *1/2* **Taajub (IRE)**[12] 7393 4-9-7 85... SebSanders 4 84
(Peter Crate) *shuffled bk to last trio after 1f: effrt over 2f out: styd on same pce fr over 1f out: n.d* **14/1**

-140 **7** *1 1/4* **Rossetti**[26] 7171 3-9-1 80... StevieDonohoe 13 75
(James Fanshawe) *hld up wl in rr: rdn over 2f out: styd on same pce fnl 2f: no threat to ldrs* **12/1**

4110 **8** *1/2* **Roninski (IRE)**[78] 5830 3-9-1 85..............................(t) JustinNewman(5) 2 79
(Bryan Smart) *rousted along early: wl in rr: effrt on inner over 2f out: no prog over 1f out* **8/1**

111 **9** *1 3/4* **Reachforthebucks**[273] 668 3-9-1 80..................................... AWhelan 14 69
(Rae Guest) *pressed ldr at str pce: led 3f out and kicked on: hdd & wknd rapidly over 1f out* **20/1**

0-05 **10** *3 1/2* **My Best Bet**[15] 7332 5-8-5 74................................... MarkCoumbe(5) 9 54
(Derek Shaw) *chsd ldrs: rdn over 2f out: wknd qckly wl over 1f out* **20/1**

0100 **11** *7* **Reposer (IRE)**[36] 6949 3-9-2 81.................................. RobertWinston 1 42
(Noel Quinlan) *led at str pce: hdd & wknd qckly 3f out* **20/1**

4023 **12** *1* **Justbookie Dot Com (IRE)**[10] 7417 3-8-3 73...(v) MatthewCosham(5) 7 31
(David Evans) *a in last trio: toiling over 2f out* **14/1**

6561 **13** *3 1/4* **Jobe (USA)**[14] 7352 5-9-6 84...(p) JoeFanning 10 33
(Kevin Ryan) *s.i.s: sn rcvrd to chse ldng trio: wknd qckly over 2f out* **14/1**

0106 **14** *11* **Kakapuka**[22] 7227 4-9-2 80.. TomQueally 11 —
(Anabel K Murphy) *restless in stalls: a wl in rr: wknd and eased over 2f out: t.o* **25/1**

1m 24.43s (-1.57) **Going Correction** -0.05s/f (Stan)
WFA 3 from 4yo+ 1lb **14** Ran SP% **122.8**
Speed ratings (Par 105): **106,105,105,104,101 100,99,98,96,92 84,83,79,67**
Tote Swingers: 1&2 £5.90, 1&3 £11.10, 2&3 £2.30 CSF £24.73 CT £117.35 TOTE £7.20: £2.00, £2.30, £1.70; EX 35.80.
Owner Andrew Tinkler **Bred** Brook Stud Bloodstock Ltd **Trained** Helshaw Grange, Shropshire

FOCUS
A useful handicap run at a decent gallop in which the market leaders came to the fore and this race should be a reliable form guide. The first four finished clear and the winner raced centre-to-far side in the straight. The third looks a good guide to the level.
Justbookie Dot Com(IRE) Official explanation: jockey said gelding suffered interference at start
Kakapuka Official explanation: trainer said gelding was struck into

7532 BET AT BLUESQ.COM ON YOUR MOBILE H'CAP 1m (P)
7:40 (7:43) (Class 5) (0-75,75) 3-Y-0+ **£2,264** (£673; £336; £168) **Stalls** Low

Form RPR

2453 **1** **Lockantanks**[7] 7447 4-9-6 74.. LukeMorris 2 88
(Michael Appleby) *hld up in 9th: cruised through over 2f out: led on bit over 1f out: drvn and flashed clr fnl f: impressive* **7/2[1]**

-403 **2** *4* **Peponi**[29] 7098 5-9-7 75.. SteveDrowne 4 80
(Peter Makin) *sn hld up wl in rr: styd on inner and prog over 2f out: clsd on ldrs over 1f out: chsd wnr fnl f but no ch* **13/2[3]**

0403 **3** *1* **Caldercruix (USA)**[19] 7299 4-9-3 71................................(v) JimCrowley 7 74
(James Evans) *hld up in rr: prog 2f out: rdn over 1f out: styd on to take 3rd ins fnl f* **12/1**

422 **4** *2 1/4* **Tadabeer**[66] 6210 3-9-4 74.. StevieDonohoe 14 72+
(Ian Williams) *pressed ldng trio on outer: rdn over 2f out: nt qckn w ldrs sn after: styd on* **6/1[2]**

2215 **5** *3/4* **Good Authority (IRE)**[22] 7227 4-9-7 75...................... TomMcLaughlin 1 71
(Karen George) *hld up in midfield on inner: prog over 2f out: rdn to ld briefly wl over 1f out: wknd fnl f* **13/2[3]**

1240 **6** *2 3/4* **The Happy Hammer (IRE)**[194] 2111 5-9-1 72............... RyanClark(3) 5 61
(Eugene Stanford) *hld up in last pair: gng wl enough 3f out: effrt and sme prog 2f out: one pce and no imp over 1f out* **20/1**

5456 **7** *1 3/4* **Huzzah (IRE)**[89] 5495 6-9-7 75.............................. MichaelStainton 9 60
(Paul Howling) *led to jst over 2f out: sn wknd* **25/1**

0140 **8** *nk* **The Which Doctor**[7] 7447 6-8-12 69.......................(p) RobertLButler(3) 13 54
(Richard Guest) [illegible] *outer over 1f out: no threat* **20/1**

551 **9** *1* **Daruband**[12] 7388 3-9-3 73...(v) SebSanders 8 55
(Alan McCabe) *racd wd: in tch: rdn and fnd nil over 2f out: sn btn* **7/1**

6205 **10** *1* **Sasheen**[23] 7208 4-8-13 67...(p) FergusSweeney 3 47
(Jeremy Gask) *pressed ldng pair: led jst over 2f out to wl over 1f out: wknd qckly* **16/1**

340 **11** *1/2* **Isingy Red (FR)**[15] 7334 3-8-11 67.................................. DaneO'Neill 10 46
(Jim Boyle) *chsd ldrs: rdn over 2f out: sn wknd* **14/1**

0000 **12** *1* **Rezwaan**[13] 7362 4-8-13 67.......................................(b) FrankieMcDonald 12 44
(Murty McGrath) *sn pushed along in last trio: nvr a factor* **100/1**

0003 **13** *hd* **Afkar (IRE)**[14] 7354 3-9-4 74..(b) TomQueally 11 50
(Clive Brittain) *pressed ldr to over 2f out: wknd qckly* **12/1**

621 **14** *8* **Mad Ginger Alice**[23] 7207 3-8-11 67............................... KirstyMilczarek 6 25
(Olivia Maylam) *dwlt: wl in rr: brief effrt 1/2-way: sn btn: t.o* **20/1**

1m 38.59s (-1.21) **Going Correction** -0.05s/f (Stan)
WFA 3 from 4yo+ 2lb **14** Ran SP% **122.7**
Speed ratings (Par 103): **104,100,99,96,96 93,91,91,90,89 88,87,87,79**
Tote Swingers: 1&2 £5.10, 1&3 £12.50, 2&3 £21.30 CSF £23.84 CT £254.96 TOTE £3.30: £1.10, £2.40, £4.50; EX 25.70.
Owner Dallas Racing **Bred** Jeremy Green And Sons **Trained** Danethorpe, Notts

FOCUS
Exposed performers in just a fair handicap. The gallop was an ordinary one and the winner raced towards the far rail in the closing stages. The form is rated at face value around the placed horses.
T/Plt: £556.10 to a £1 stake. Pool: £70,818.08 - 92.96 winning tickets. T/Qpdt: £578.40 to a £1 stake Pool: £8,677.17 - 11.10 w. tckts JN

7533a - (Foreign Racing) - See Raceform Int.

[1122]FONTAINEBLEAU
Thursday, November 24
OFFICIAL GOING: Turf: very soft

7534a PRIX CONTESSINA (LISTED RACE) (3YO+) (TURF) 6f
1:20 (12:00) 3-Y-0+ **£22,413** (£8,965; £6,724; £4,482; £2,241)

RPR

1 **Eton Rifles (IRE)**[19] 7298 6-9-2 0................................ WilliamCarson 14 113
(Stuart Williams) *broke wl on stands' rail: sn disputing ld: led 1/2-way: qcknd clr ent fnl f: comf* **31/5[2]**

2 2 Fred Lalloupet[23] 7221 4-9-2 0.. OlivierPeslier 9 106
(D Smaga, France) **83/10**
3 2 Personified (GER)[173] 2744 4-8-8 0....(p) Roberto-CarlosMontenegro 18 92
(Mme J Bidgood, France) **17/1**
4 nk Vianello (IRE)[47] 4-8-11 0................................(b) ChristopheSoumillon 7 94
(D Rabhi, France) **3/1**[1]
5 nk Myasun (FR)[23] 4-8-11 0.. JohanVictoire 3 93
(C Baillet, France) **15/1**
6 nk Green Dandy (IRE)[50] 6643 4-8-8 0...................... StephanePasquier 13 89
(E J O'Neill, France) **31/1**
7 snk Definightly[23] 7221 5-9-2 0..(b) ThierryThulliez 4 97
(Roger Charlton) *settled towards rr: hdwy 1/2-way: 4th and rdn over 1f out: nt qckn fnl f* **13/2**[3]
8 ¾ Reine Heureuse (GER)[25] 4-8-8 0................................ FilipMinarik 15 86
(Uwe Ostmann, Germany) **31/1**
9 ½ Le Valentin (FR)[74] 5985 5-9-2 0...................... Pierre-CharlesBoudot 11 93
(Y De Nicolay, France) **14/1**
10 ½ Captain Chop (FR)[210] 1646 3-8-11 0.. FlavienPrat 16 86
(D Guillemin, France) **17/1**
0 Mariol (FR)[23] 7221 8-9-2 0.. SebastienMaillot 10 —
(Robert Collet, France) **29/1**
0 Cadeau For Maggi[23] 6-9-2 0.. FabriceVeron 12 —
(H-A Pantall, France) **34/1**
0 Anco Marzio[47] 5-8-11 0.. ThomasMessina 1 —
(B Goudot, France) **26/1**
0 Glad Sky[25] 7193 5-9-2 0..(p) ThierryJarnet 5 —
(J-L Pelletan, France) **62/1**
0 Clairvoyance (IRE)[23] 7221 4-9-3 0............................... FranckBlondel 6 —
(H-A Pantall, France) **24/1**
0 Its You Again[47] 3-8-11 0...(b) SylvainRuis 17 —
(Braem Horse Racing Sprl, Belgium) **70/1**
0 Glady Romana (GER)[22] 7239 4-8-13 0...................... GaetanMasure 2 —
(W Baltromei, Germany) **90/1**
0 Etive (USA)[25] 3-8-13 0.. MaximeGuyon 8 —
(H-A Pantall, France) **15/1**

68.80 secs (68.80) **18** Ran SP% **117.5**
PARI-MUTUEL (all including 1 euro stakes): WIN 7.20; PLACE 2.80, 3.20, 4.10; DF 28.10; SF 42.50.
Owner The Eton Riflemen **Bred** Grangecon Stud **Trained** Newmarket, Suffolk

NOTEBOOK
Eton Rifles(IRE) had the ground in his favour and made no mistake. He is finished for the year now and won't be going to Dubai, but his trainer hasn't ruled out the gelding returning to France next year.

7489 WOLVERHAMPTON (A.W) (L-H)
Friday, November 25

OFFICIAL GOING: Standard
Wind: Fresh behind Weather: Overcast

7535 32RED CASINO H'CAP 5f 20y(P)
4:00 (4:00) (Class 5) (0-75,75) 3-Y-O+ **£2,587** (£770; £384; £192) **Stalls** Low

Form RPR
0550 1 Red Cape (FR)[22] 7253 8-9-2 **70**..............................(b) JamesSullivan 10 81
(Ruth Carr) *a.p: rdn to ld ins fnl f: edgd lft: r.o* **20/1**
4200 2 2 Wooden King (IRE)[9] 7428 6-6-9 **74**................................ DaneO'Neill 1 78
(Malcolm Saunders) *chsd ldrs: rdn over 1f out: led ins fnl f: sn hdd and unable qck* **7/2**[1]
1140 3 ½ Riflessione[27] 7173 5-8-12 **66**..(v) LukeMorris 3 68
(Ronald Harris) *broke wl and led early: sn lost pl: hmpd over 3f out: sn drvn along in rr: hung rt over 1f out: rdn and r.o ins fnl f* **5/1**[2]
6600 4 1¼ Lucky Dan (IRE)[11] 7417 5-9-7 **75**.................................... FrannyNorton 4 73
(Paul Green) *s.i.s: in rr: r.o ins fnl f: nt rch ldrs* **12/1**
0000 5 hd Desert Strike[22] 7253 5-9-7 **75**.......................................(p) PaddyAspell 6 72
(Alan McCabe) *hld up: r.o u.p ins fnl f: nrst fin* **10/1**
0000 6 1 Skylla[13] 7395 4-8-8 **67**.. MarkCoumbe[(5)] 7 60
(Derek Shaw) *chsd ldrs: led 1/2-way: rdn and hdd ins fnl f: no ex* **14/1**
0000 7 2 Incomparable[44] 6802 6-9-2 **70**.....................................(bt) IanMongan 5 56
(David Nicholls) *mid-div: rdn over 1f out: nvr trbld ldrs* **7/1**
6040 8 1 La Capriosa[262] 794 5-9-1 **69**.. TomQueally 11 52
(David Nicholls) *chsd ldrs: rdn over 1f out: wknd fnl f* **20/1**
0631 9 1¼ Punching[16] 7341 7-9-4 **72**.. KirstyMilczarek 9 50
(Conor Dore) *sn led: hdd 1/2-way: wknd fnl f* **12/1**
0211 10 nk Prince James[13] 7395 4-9-2 **70**................................ GrahamGibbons 13 47
(Michael Easterby) *s.i.s: sn pushed along and a in rr* **11/2**[3]
6000 11 1 On The High Tops (IRE)[15] 7355 3-9-2 **70**..............(b) AndrewMullen 8 43
(Ruth Carr) *chsd ldrs: rdn over 1f out: wknd fnl f* **33/1**
0000 12 1½ Lucky Mellor[15] 7355 4-9-2 **70**.......................................(b) ShaneKelly 2 38
(Barry Murtagh) *hld up: hdwy over 1f out: wknd fnl f* **20/1**

61.27 secs (-1.03) **Going Correction** -0.025s/f (Stan) **12** Ran SP% **115.1**
Speed ratings (Par 103): **107,103,103,101,100 99,95,94,92,91 90,87**
toteswingers:1&2:£16.30, 2&3:£3.90, 1&3:£15.70 CSF £82.76 CT £420.85 TOTE £32.10: £6.70, £1.20, £2.10; EX 110.40.
Owner Middleham Park Racing LVI **Bred** Gilles And Mrs Forien **Trained** Huby, N Yorks

FOCUS
They went a fast pace in the sprint handicap and the 20-1 winner burst back to form in emphatic style. The winner is rated in line with this year's turf form, with the runner-up close to his best.
Prince James Official explanation: trainer's rep said gelding appeared to resent the kick-back.

7536 32RED.COM MAIDEN STKS 1m 5f 194y(P)
4:30 (4:31) (Class 5) 3-Y-O+ **£2,264** (£673; £336; £168) **Stalls** Low

Form RPR
525- 1 Priors Gold[12] 6640 4-9-11 70.. TomQueally 1 64+
(Gordon Elliott, Ire) *hld up: hdwy over 2f out: led on bit ins fnl f: canter* **4/9**[1]
04 2 2¾ Barachiel[46] 6754 3-9-3 0.. LukeMorris 3 60
(Ronald Harris) *set stdy pce tl hdd over 4f out: led again over 3f out: rdn over 1f out: hdd and unable qck ins fnl f* **8/1**[3]
3 2¾ Maggie Aron[16] 5-9-6 0.. IanMongan 2 51
(Tim Vaughan) *s.s: hld up: hdwy to chse ldr over 6f out: led over 4f out: hdd over 3f out: sn rdn: styd on same pce fr over 1f out* **14/1**
4 4½ Uncut Stone (IRE)[147] 3604 3-9-3 67.................................... TomEaves 4 50
(Peter Niven) *trckd ldr over 7f: rdn over 3f out: wknd over 2f out* **5/1**[2]
5 1 Bollistick[15] 5-9-4 0.. NoelGarbutt[(7)] 6 48
(Michael Mullineaux) *hld up: nvr on terms* **80/1**
064- 6 ½ Rock Relief (IRE)[381] 3524 5-9-11 54.......................... RobbieFitzpatrick 5 48
(David Thompson) *chsd ldrs tl rdn and wknd over 2f out* **66/1**
4/4- 7 47 Lileo (IRE)[553] 2281 4-9-11 0.. KirstyMilczarek 7 —
(Nikki Evans) *prom: rdn over 3f out: sn wknd: t.o* **33/1**

3m 15.09s (9.09) **Going Correction** -0.025s/f (Stan)
WFA 3 from 4yo+ 8lb **7** Ran SP% **109.4**
Speed ratings (Par 103): **73,71,69,67,66 66,39**
toteswingers:1&2:£1.50, 2&3:£5.30, 1&3:£2.90 CSF £4.14 TOTE £1.60: £1.80, £3.80; EX 5.00.
Owner Sean F Gallagher **Bred** The Complimentary Pass Partnership **Trained** Trim, Co Meath

FOCUS
The odds-on favourite scored in very smooth style in this modest maiden which was run at a steady pace. The form is rated loosely through the second while the third is in line with his bumper form.

7537 £32 FREE AT 32RED.COM H'CAP (DIV I) 1m 141y(P)
5:05 (5:05) (Class 6) (0-65,71) 3-Y-O+ **£1,704** (£503; £251) **Stalls** Low

Form RPR
0452 1 Pipers Piping (IRE)[7] 7463 5-9-1 **59**..............................(p) TomQueally 10 72
(Alastair Lidderdale) *trckd ldrs: rdn and hung lft ins fnl f: r.o to ld towards fin* **9/2**[2]
0331 2 hd Aerodynamic (IRE)[7] 7463 4-9-8 **66** 6ex.......................... PaddyAspell 5 79
(Clive Mulhall) *led: hdd 7f out: chsd ldrs: wnt 2nd over 2f out: rdn to ld and edgd lft ins fnl f: hdd towards fin* **5/2**[1]
0451 3 2½ Stylistickhill (IRE)[25] 7198 3-8-9 **59**................................(t) BillyCray[(3)] 6 66+
(David Nicholls) *hld up: plld hrd: hmpd 7f out: rdn and r.o ins fnl f: nt rch ldrs* **12/1**
433 4 1 Hierarch (IRE)[44] 6784 4-8-8 **57**.. LauraPike[(5)] 2 62
(David Simcock) *a.p: rdn and swtchd lft over 1f out: styd on same pce fnl f* **8/1**
4211 5 1¼ Miss Villefranche[13] 7399 3-9-0 **61**..........................(v) StevieDonohoe 7 63
(Michael Bell) *led 7f out: rdn over 2f out: hdd and no ex ins fnl f* **5/1**[3]
0004 6 2 Cabal[7] 7462 4-8-7 **51** oh3..(b[1]) AndrewMullen 3 48
(Andrew Crook) *hld up: hdwy over 3f out: rdn over 1f out: wknd fnl f* **40/1**
4514 7 ½ Ajdaad (USA)[7] 7465 4-9-8 **71** 6ex............................ RosieJessop[(5)] 11 67
(Alan McCabe) *dwlt: hld up: nt clr run over 2f out: nvr nrr* **9/1**
00-0 8 1¼ Laser Blazer[22] 7249 3-8-10 **57**.. LukeMorris 1 50
(Jeremy Gask) *hld up: rdn over 2f out: n.d* **40/1**
0002 9 nk Sofias Number One (USA)[10] 7425 3-9-2 **63**..........(tp) AndreaAtzeni 13 56
(Roy Bowring) *chsd ldrs: rdn over 2f out: wknd over 1f out* **16/1**
0355 10 nk Sarangoo[7] 7455 3-9-4 **65**.. DaneO'Neill 12 57
(Malcolm Saunders) *s.s: hdwy over 6f out: rdn over 2f out: sn wknd* **16/1**
3410 11 6 Belle Park[24] 7208 4-8-13 **57** ow1................................ TomMcLaughlin 9 35
(Karen George) *mid-div: lost pl 4f out: bhd fnl 3f* **33/1**
6000 12 5 Forward Feline (IRE)[28] 7146 5-9-1 **64**.................. CharlesBishop[(5)] 4 31
(Bryn Palling) *hld up: plld hrd: rdn and wknd over 2f out* **40/1**

1m 51.1s (0.60) **Going Correction** -0.025s/f (Stan)
WFA 3 from 4yo+ 3lb **12** Ran SP% **114.2**
Speed ratings (Par 101): **96,95,93,92,91 89,89,88,88,87 82,77**
toteswingers:1&2:£4.00, 2&3:£8.70, 1&3:£7.60 CSF £15.00 CT £122.08 TOTE £5.10: £1.80, £1.10, £3.30; EX 17.10.
Owner C S J Beek **Bred** Drumhass Stud **Trained** Eastbury, Berks

FOCUS
A strong handicap for the grade. The pace was decent and the two market leaders were involved in a tight finish. The first two improved on their recent meeting with the fourth rated to his mark.
Miss Villefranche ◆ Official explanation: jockey said filly lost its action

7538 £32 FREE AT 32RED.COM H'CAP (DIV II) 1m 141y(P)
5:35 (5:36) (Class 6) (0-65,68) 3-Y-O+ **£1,704** (£503; £251) **Stalls** Low

Form RPR
0450 1 Winged Valkyrie (IRE)[63] 6311 3-9-1 **62**..................(b[1]) PaulHanagan 11 70
(Charles Hills) *chsd ldr tl led over 3f out: rdn and hdd over 1f out: rallied to ld nr fin* **16/1**
0301 2 ½ Spinning Ridge (IRE)[7] 7455 6-9-10 **68** 6ex..................(v) LukeMorris 4 75
(Ronald Harris) *hld up in tch: led over 1f out: rdn ins fnl f: hdd nr fin* **4/1**[1]
0000 3 ½ Jibouti (IRE)[15] 7352 3-8-5 **52**..............................(b) KirstyMilczarek 3 58
(Clive Brittain) *s.s: hld up: hdwy over 2f out: rdn and hung lft ins fnl f: r.o* **11/1**
6600 4 1 Indian Emperor (IRE)[69] 6179 3-8-13 **60**............................ TomEaves 5 63
(Peter Niven) *chsd ldrs: rdn over 1f out: styd on* **50/1**
0020 5 nk Dazakhee[11] 7418 4-9-6 **64**.. TonyCulhane 2 67
(David Flood) *hld up: hdwy over 1f out: sn rdn: styd on* **9/1**
5362 6 5 Bidable[59] 6435 7-9-2 **60**.. RichardKingscote 1 51
(Bryn Palling) *hld up: rdn over 1f out: n.d* **15/2**[3]
0662 7 ½ Justcallmehandsome[13] 7400 9-8-9 **60**..................(v) JoshBaudains[(7)] 9 50
(Dominic Ffrench Davis) *s.s: bhd: nvr nrr* **9/2**[2]
5040 8 1 Amazing Win (IRE)[31] 7084 3-8-6 **58**........................ CharlesBishop[(5)] 10 46
(Mick Channon) *hld up: plld hrd: hdwy 2f out: wknd fnl f* **14/1**
6660 9 7 Join Up[179] 2561 5-8-5 **56**.. RachealKneller[(7)] 12 28
(Mark Brisbourne) *hld up: effrt over 2f out: wknd wl over 1f out* **20/1**
0000 10 2½ Bertie Blu Boy[55] 6543 3-9-4 **65**.. TomQueally 7 31
(Paul Green) *chsd ldrs tl rdn and wknd wl over 1f out* **11/1**
0023 11 1 McCool Bannanas[13] 7400 3-8-12 **62**........................ AdamBeschizza[(3)] 8 26
(James Unett) *hld up: rdn and wknd wl over 1f out* **9/2**[2]
0400 12 2 Very Well Red[40] 6888 8-8-13 **57**.. WilliamCarson 6 16
(Peter Hiatt) *led: pushed along and hdd over 3f out: cl up whn hmpd and eased 2f out* **14/1**

1m 50.61s (0.11) **Going Correction** -0.025s/f (Stan)
WFA 3 from 4yo+ 3lb **40** Ran SP% **120.7**
Speed ratings (Par 101): **98,97,97,96,95 91,91,90,83,81 80,79**
toteswingers:1&2:£16.70, 2&3:£9.50, 1&3:£40.00 CSF £80.47 CT £769.28 TOTE £23.30: £5.80, £1.40, £5.70; EX 124.10.
Owner Triermore Stud **Bred** C O P Hanbury **Trained** Lambourn, Berks

FOCUS
This didn't look as strong as the first division but it was run at a good pace and the revitalised winner put in a gutsy effort. The form is a bit muddling with the runner-up the best guide rated to his former best.

7539 ALAN FRENCH 80TH BIRTHDAY CELEBRATION CLAIMING STKS 5f 216y(P)
6:10 (6:10) (Class 6) 2-Y-O **£1,704** (£503; £251) **Stalls** Low

Form RPR
4012 1 Adranian (IRE)[6] 7490 2-8-7 70..(v) PaulHanagan 1 64+
(David Evans) *chsd ldrs: rdn to ld ins fnl f: edgd lft: r.o* **11/10**[1]

00 **2** *1 1/2* **Jay Peas Jacko**[28] [7142] 2-9-0 0................................. TomMcLaughlin 5 67
(Lucinda Featherstone) *trckd keenly: led over 4f out: sn hdd: rdn and ev ch ins fnl f: styd on same pce* **150/1**
3020 **3** *1 3/4* **Class Monitor**[21] [7275] 2-8-3 62... LukeMorris 3 53
(Mrs K Burke) *stirrup leather broke leaving stalls: sn prom: led over 4f out: rdn over 1f out: hdd and no ex ins fnl f* **7/1**[3]
3333 **4** *nk* **Poker Hospital**[23] [7225] 2-8-2 74..................................(p) NickyMackay 4 48
(George Baker) *led: hdd over 4f out: piushed along 1/2-way: rdn over 1f out: styd on* **11/8**[2]
005 **5** *3/4* **Princess Kaiulani (IRE)**[25] [7194] 2-8-3 50.................... WilliamCarson 2 47
(William Muir) *sn pushed along in rr: rdn over 1f out: styd on ins fnl f: nvr trbld ldrs* **33/1**

1m 15.73s (0.73) **Going Correction** -0.025s/f (Stan) **5** Ran SP% **105.8**
Speed ratings (Par 94): **94,92,89,89,88**
CSF £51.69 TOTE £1.70: £1.10, £5.10; EX 44.00.Adranian was claimed by D. Griffiths for £6,000.
Owner Cos We Can Partnership **Bred** Hugh O'Brien **Trained** Pandy, Monmouths

FOCUS
The 70-rated favourite finished well to land this claimer, but the form looks suspect because it was run at a stop-start pace and there was not much separating the five runners at the end. The winner did not need to run to his recent best while the fifth is rated to her mark.

NOTEBOOK
Adranian(IRE) had won twice in 7f selling/claiming company since September and was just held by a gambled-on newcomer when a clear second over C&D last week. Well backed, he made his move halfway up the straight and found a sustained burst to win with something in hand.
Jay Peas Jacko, beaten a total of 70l in two maidens last month, showed a big turnaround in form switched to sprinting in a claimer.
Class Monitor had a bit to find at the weights but she ran well, particularly as her rider had to navigate his way round with his right foot out of the iron after the stirrup leather broke leaving the stalls. Official explanation: jockey said off-side stirrup leather buckle became unfastened. (tchd 13-2)
Poker Hospital set the standard on her close third off a mark of 74 in a Windsor nursery two runs back, but she was held as favourite back in a maiden on her AW debut last time and was a bit laboured switched to claiming company. (tchd 6-4 in places)
Princess Kaiulani(IRE) didn't show a great deal in three sprint maidens at this track, but this 50-rated filly did well to be not beaten far behind some rivals with much higher marks.

7540 32RED MEDIAN AUCTION MAIDEN STKS 5f 216y(P)
6:40 (6:42) (Class 6) 2-Y-O **£1,704** (£503; £251) **Stalls** Low

Form RPR
52 **1** **Decision By One**[27] [7174] 2-9-3 0............................ RichardKingscote 8 80
(Tom Dascombe) *w ldr tl led 5f out: rdn over 1f out: r.o* **1/1**[1]
2 *1 1/4* **Al Freej (IRE)** 2-8-12 0.. AndreaAtzeni 7 71+
(Roger Varian) *mid-div: hdwy over 2f out: chsd wnr ins fnl f: r.o* **5/2**[2]
3 *2 1/2* **Baccarat (IRE)** 2-9-3 0... PaulHanagan 11 69+
(Richard Fahey) *s.i.s: hdwy over 2f out: rdn ins fnl f: r.o* **13/2**[3]
04 **4** *1 3/4* **Naughtical**[27] [7174] 2-8-12 0... EddieAhern 10 59
(J W Hills) *a.p: chsd wnr over 1f out: sn rdn: no ex fnl f* **20/1**
50 **5** *4 1/2* **Kathleensluckylad (IRE)**[20] [7292] 2-9-3 0...................... JoeFanning 12 50
(Kevin Ryan) *hld up: pushed along 1/2-way: styd on fr over 1f out: nvr nrr* **16/1**
02 **6** *nk* **Sweetnessandlight**[32] [7058] 2-8-12 0........................ MichaelStainton 3 44
(Jason Ward) *chsd ldrs: pushed along 1/2-way: wknd over 1f out* **20/1**
7 *nk* **Maria Montez** 2-8-12 0.. DaneO'Neill 5 43
(J W Hills) *sn outpcd: styd on fnl f: n.d* **50/1**
0 **8** *2 1/2* **Bella Ophelia (IRE)**[15] [7345] 2-8-12 0............................ NickyMackay 4 36
(Hughie Morrison) *prom: chsd wnr 4f out: rdn over 2f out: wknd over 1f out* **33/1**
9 *5* **Poontoon (IRE)** 2-9-3 0.. TonyHamilton 1 26
(Richard Fahey) *prom: pushed along 1/2-way: wknd over 2f out* **33/1**
0 **10** *4* **Classy Lass**[14] [7368] 2-8-7 0....................................... MarkCoumbe(5) 9 9
(Derek Shaw) *sn pushed along in rr: bhd fr 1/2-way* **200/1**
00 **11** *6* **Jenndale**[92] [5410] 2-9-3 0... FrannyNorton 6 —
(Chris Dwyer) *a in rr: wknd 1/2-way* **250/1**
0 **12** *5* **Italian Ice**[32] [7058] 2-8-12 0.. TomEaves 2 —
(D[illegible]) [illegible] **[illegible]**

1m 13.86s (-1.14) **Going Correction** -0.025s/f (Stan) **12** Ran SP% **117.5**
Speed ratings (Par 94): **106,104,101,98,92 92,91,88,81,76 68,61**
Tote Swingers: 1&2 £1.80, 1&3 £2.30, 2&3 £4.20 CSF £3.11 TOTE £2.20: £1.90, £1.02, £2.10; EX 5.00.
Owner The Half A Third Partnership **Bred** G E Amey **Trained** Malpas, Cheshire

FOCUS
The favourite put in a professional front-running display and was chased home by two promising newcomers in a fair maiden. He is rated to his mark.

NOTEBOOK
Decision By One had leading claims on his runner-up effort behind an odds-on rival in a C&D maiden on his second start. He set a decent pace and stayed on well to win with something in hand. A Bahamian Bounty half-brother to prolific sprint winner Taurus Twins, he looks a willing and uncomplicated type who should continue to progress. (op 6-4 tchd 7-4)
Al Freej(IRE) ♦ took a while to get the hang of things but this well-backed filly stayed on strongly in an encouraging debut. She could improve significantly next time and is a 40,000gns Iffraaj half-sister to two 5f winners, out of a dual sprint winner. (tchd 2-1 and 11-4)
Baccarat(IRE), a 180,000euros Dutch Art first foal of a Group-placed winning half-sister to several useful winners, was slowly away from a tough draw but did well to work his way into third in a promising debut run. A scopey colt, he should have learned quite a bit and should progress from this. (op 5-1 tchd 9-2 and 7-1)
Naughtical was beaten a bit further by Decision By One than she was over C&D last time.
Kathleensluckylad(IRE) showed a minor hint of promise staying on late on his third start. He was beaten quite a long way but is closely related to a couple of multiple winners at up to 8.6f and should do better handicapping over further.
Bella Ophelia(IRE) Official explanation: vet said filly had been struck into

7541 32REDPOKER.COM NURSERY 5f 20y(P)
7:10 (7:10) (Class 6) (0-60,64) 2-Y-O **£1,704** (£503; £251) **Stalls** Low

Form RPR
554 **1** **Gin Twist**[22] [7251] 2-9-7 60......................................(b[1]) RichardKingscote 7 68+
(Tom Dascombe) *hld up in tch: plld hrd: trckd ldr over 1f out: led ins fnl f: sn rdn clr and edgd lft* **7/1**[3]
2225 **2** *1 3/4* **Mount McLeod (IRE)**[1] [7530] 2-9-0 56..........................(p) SophieDoyle(3) 6 58
(Jamie Osborne) *hld up: hdwy over 1f out: r.o to go 2nd towards fin: nt rch wnr* **7/2**[2]
5003 **3** *1/2* **Monty Fay (IRE)**[22] [7252] 2-9-3 56..................................... DaneO'Neill 5 56
(Derek Haydn Jones) *w ldr tl led 2f out: rdn and hdd ins fnl f: styd on same pce* **9/2**[3]
522 **4** *2 1/4* **M J Woodward**[22] [7251] 2-9-0 53..................................(v[1]) StevieDonohoe 11 45
(Paul Green) *chsd ldrs: pushed along 1/2-way: no ex fnl f* **6/1**
0006 **5** *1 1/2* **Joe M**[14] [7359] 2-8-6 45..(e) ChrisCatlin 2 31
(Simon Dow) *sn outpcd: r.o ins fnl f: nvr nrr* **50/1**
2611 **6** *1 1/4* **Sonsie Lass**[10] [7421] 2-9-9 62 6ex.. JoeFanning 1 44
(Keith Dalgleish) *led 3f: sn rdn: wknd fnl f* **2/1**[1]
0000 **7** *nk* **Bolshoi Melody**[28] [7143] 2-8-10 49..................................(p) RobertHavlin 4 30
(Jeremy Gask) *chsd ldrs: rdn over 1f out: wknd fnl f* **40/1**
0100 **8** *1 1/4* **True Bond**[20] [7294] 2-9-4 60...(v[1]) DaleSwift(3) 3 36
(Geoffrey Oldroyd) *sn outpcd: no ch whn rdn over 1f out* **12/1**
000 **9** *7* **Chateau Lola**[13] [7396] 2-8-6 45.....................................(v) NickyMackay 10 —
(Derek Shaw) *sn outpcd* **100/1**
460 **10** *18* **Perfecto Tiempo (IRE)**[86] [5613] 2-8-10 52........................ RyanClark(3) 8 —
(Ronald Harris) *dwlt: outpcd* **33/1**

62.10 secs (-0.20) **Going Correction** -0.025s/f (Stan) **10** Ran SP% **116.5**
Speed ratings (Par 94): **100,97,96,92,90 88,87,85,74,45**
Tote Swingers: 1&2 £7.50, 1&3 £6.10, 2&3 £3.10 CSF £31.28 CT £124.05 TOTE £10.00: £2.90, £1.90, £2.00; EX 46.80.
Owner Manor House Stables LLP **Bred** Highclere Stud **Trained** Malpas, Cheshire

FOCUS
A low-grade nursery. The pace was strong and the winner scored with quite a bit in hand. The form looks solid but limited.

NOTEBOOK
Gin Twist had been consistent without winning in ten previous starts but first-time blinkers and a drop back to 5f worked and she put in a smooth display to get off the mark in good style. Her rating will move back up into the mid-60s after this but she has a good cruising speed at this level and is open to further improvement in headgear. (op 13-2 tchd 15-2)
Mount McLeod(IRE) was never dangerous in a Kempton handicap 24 hours earlier she finished runner-up in his three nurseries before that and gave it a good shot turned out quickly in first-time cheekpieces. She has yet to strike in 12 attempts but is a reliable type who is equally effective on both AW surfaces. (tchd 4-1)
Monty Fay(IRE) is still chasing a first win after seven starts but he ran well dropped back in trip and the run can be marked up because he set a strong pace and had competition for the lead.
M J Woodward has finished in the frame in sprint nurseries at this track with and without a visor on his last three runs. (op 7-1)
Joe M, beaten 13l+ in five previous starts, showed a hint of promise staying-on when it was all over on nursery debut. (op 66-1)
Sonsie Lass found plenty of progress when winning 6f handicaps here and at Southwell on her last two starts, but she got involved in a destructive battle up front and couldn't sustain her effort under a penalty dropped back to 5f. (op 11-4)

7542 32REDBET.COM H'CAP 1m 141y(P)
7:40 (7:42) (Class 4) (0-85,82) 3-Y-O+ **£4,204** (£1,251; £625; £312) **Stalls** Low

Form RPR
1512 **1** **Tarooq (USA)**[37] [6949] 5-9-7 82.. PaulHanagan 5 90
(Richard Fahey) *racd keenly: sn trcking ldr: led wl over 5f out: shkn up over 1f out: rdn ins fnl f: jst hld on* **5/2**[1]
4322 **2** *hd* **Change The Subject (USA)**[30] [7098] 3-8-7 76............... LauraPike(5) 6 84
(David Simcock) *s.i.s: hld up: hdwy over 1f out: r.o wl: jst failed* **6/1**[3]
500 **3** *1/2* **Star Links (USA)**[26] [7189] 5-9-6 81................................(b) ShaneKelly 10 88
(S Donohoe, Ire) *hld up: hdwy 1/2-way: rdn over 1f out: r.o* **9/1**
5033 **4** *1/2* **Munsarim (IRE)**[13] [7397] 4-9-3 78...................................... JoeFanning 4 84
(Keith Dalgleish) *sn led: hdd wl over 5f out: remained handy: chsd wnr over 1f out: sn rdn: no ex nr fin* **7/2**[2]
1006 **5** *nk* **Totally Ours**[16] [7328] 4-9-7 82... FrannyNorton 8 87
(William Muir) *prom: chsd ldr over 4f out tl rdn over 1f out: styd on: n.m.r towards fin* **7/1**
0400 **6** *1 1/4* **She Ain't A Saint**[76] [5948] 3-9-0 78...................................... LukeMorris 7 80
(Jane Chapple-Hyam) *prom: rdn over 2f out: styd on same pce ins fnl f* **25/1**
054 **7** *2 3/4* **Islesman**[23] [7227] 3-9-2 80.. RichardKingscote 1 76
(Heather Main) *chsd ldrs: rdn over 1f out: no ex fnl f* **7/1**
563 **8** *1 1/4* **Bakoura**[32] [7054] 3-8-12 76.. EddieAhern 11 69
(John Dunlop) *s.i.s: hld up: hdwy 2f out: sn rdn: styd on same pce* **10/1**
0000 **9** *3/4* **My Kingdom (IRE)**[32] [7050] 5-9-2 77.............................. StevieDonohoe 9 68
(Ian Williams) *hld up: rdn over 2f out: n.d* **33/1**
0005 **10** *nse* **Follow The Flag (IRE)**[13] [7397] 7-8-12 73.......................(v) JohnFahy 2 64
(Alan McCabe) *hld up: a in rr* **12/1**
0050 **11** *0* **[illegible] (IRE)**[35] [illegible] [illegible].. [illegible] 49
(Clive Brittain) *hld up: rdn over 3f out: sn lost tch* **66/1**

1m 49.62s (-0.88) **Going Correction** -0.025s/f (Stan)
WFA 3 from 4yo+ 3lb **11** Ran SP% **125.1**
Speed ratings (Par 105): **102,101,101,100,100 99,97,96,95,95 89**
Tote Swingers: 1&2 £3.60, 1&3 £8.70, 2&3 £9.00 CSF £19.01 CT £126.61 TOTE £5.30: £2.20, £1.90, £2.20; EX 32.90.
Owner Y Nasib **Bred** Kirsten Rausing **Trained** Musley Bank, N Yorks

FOCUS
A decent handicap. The pace was not very strong and the first five finished in a bunch but the winner is a progressive and likeable type. The third and fourth set the standard.
T/Plt: £24.80 to a £1 stake. Pool of £70,770.06 - 2,076.44 winning tickets. T/Qpdt: £10.80 to a £1 stake. Pool of £9,860.93 - 674.04 winning tickets. CR

7543a, 7545 - 7547a - (Foreign Racing) - See Raceform Interactive

[7467] DUNDALK (A.W) (L-H)
Friday, November 25

OFFICIAL GOING: Standard

7544a WINTER RACING AT DUNDALK H'CAP 2m (P)
6:55 (6:58) (60-90,89) 3-Y-O+ **£7,732** (£1,793; £784; £448)

RPR
1 **Fantasy King**[49] [6683] 5-9-4 79...(t) JMurtagh 9 87+
(Charles O'Brien, Ire) *settled in mid-div: 5th 1/2-way: swtchd rt early st: rdn to chal 1f out: led ins fnl f and kpt on wl u.p* **9/4**[1]
2 *1 1/4* **Talenti (IRE)**[12] [127] 8-8-4 65 oh1.................................(bt[1]) CDHayes 3 72
(P J McKenna, Ire) *trckd ldrs on inner: 3rd 1/2-way: hdwy to dispute early st: sn rdn and hdd ins fnl f: no imp on wnr* **20/1**
3 *hd* **Anshan Dreams**[14] [7378] 7-8-13 74.................................... KJManning 2 81
(Adrian Maguire, Ire) *mid-div on inner: t.k.h: briefly nt clr run early st: hdwy into 4th over 1f out: kpt on u.p ins fnl f wout rching wnr* **9/2**[3]
4 *1/2* **Gordonsville**[22] [7102] 8-9-8 83.. FergalLynch 7 89
(Jim Goldie) *mid-div: 6th 1/2-way: hdwy into 4th after 1/2-way: prog to chal and dispute early st: hdd early fnl f: no ex* **6/1**
5 *1 3/4* **Bravely Fought (IRE)**[134] [4034] 6-10-0 89............................ GFCarroll 4 93
(Sabrina J Harty, Ire) *hld up in rr: drvn along early st: kpt on same pce wout troubling ldrs* **16/1**

6 *nk* **Mutiska (IRE)**[26] 7190 4-8-4 65 oh1 .... ShaneFoley 5 69
(J C Hayden, Ire) *trckd ldrs: 4th 1/2-way: pushed along and dropped to 6th appr st: no imp fr over 1f out* **10/1**

7 *1 3/4* **Deutschland (USA)**[19] 7322 8-9-5 80 .... (t) PJSmullen 6 82
(W P Mullins, Ire) *settled towards rr: 9th 1/2-way: rdn ent st: no imp fr wl over 1f out* **4/1**[2]

8 *1/2* **Asiya (IRE)**[33] 7046 5-8-13 84 ow1 .... KCSexton(10) 10 86
(Norman Cassidy, Ire) *settled towards rr: sme hdwy on outer fr 1/2-way: 7th appr st: sn rdn and no imp fr 1 1/2f out* **12/1**

9 *2 1/2* **Isabellareine (GER)**[14] 7378 8-8-4 65 .... NGMcCullagh 1 64
(Mervyn Torrens, Ire) *led: strly pressed and hdd 2f out: sn no ex: wknd* **8/1**

10 *13* **Custodian (IRE)**[14] 7378 9-8-5 66 oh5 ow1 .... DavidMcCabe 8 50
(James M Barrett, Ire) *prom: 2nd 1/2-way: rdn appr st: no ex fr early st: eased whn btn fnl f* **20/1**

3m 27.2s (207.20) **10** Ran SP% **126.5**
CSF £58.95 CT £198.54 TOTE £2.70: £1.40, £5.40, £1.20; DF 120.80.
Owner Paul J McMahon **Bred** D R Tucker **Trained** Straffan, Co Kildare
■ Stewards' Enquiry : C D Hayes severe caution: used whip with excessive force

FOCUS
Ultimately a cosy win for Fantasy King, who looked one of the few here with a degree of potential off his mark. The fourth has been rated to his recent level.

NOTEBOOK
Fantasy King, unlucky here last time, travelled particularly strongly and the main danger was a similarly unfortunate occurrence. His rider gathered him when in the clear and he won like a horse who had a bit in hand. He cannot get too severe a hike either and should remain of interest next time as he is still unexposed. Gerry Abbott, representing Charles O'Brien, said: "He was very unlucky here last time - he got murdered when travelling well. He had a bit in hand and Johnny gave him a great ride." (op 9/4 tchd 15/8)
Talenti(IRE) was always prominent and ran a nice race, holding on gamely for second. He has proven his wellbeing and should remain competitive as he likes the AW.
Anshan Dreams was a bit free early, got shuffled back towards the rear and was slightly hampered when making his run. He should have finished at least second and there was notable market confidence behind him. (op 13/2 tchd 7/1)
Gordonsville was easy to back and might just be in the grip of the handicapper. He ran his usual game race but was outpaced when it mattered. (op 9/2)
Bravely Fought(IRE) came from the rear and never looked like winning but this was encouraging and he would be of interest next time, perhaps over a shorter trip. (op 14/1)
Deutschland(USA) could not get involved, which is disappointing given his trainer's form, and he seems out of sorts. (op 7/2)

7548a CHRISTMAS PARTIES AT DUNDALK H'CAP 1m 2f 150y(P)
8:50 (8:54) (55-75,74) 3-Y-O+ **£4,758** (£1,103; £482; £275)

RPR

1 **Key Breeze**[24] 7214 4-9-8 68 .... (t) PJSmullen 1 72
(Kevin Ryan) *trckd ldrs on inner: 5th 1/2-way: hdwy into 3rd early st: led 1f out: edgd rt and kpt on u.p ins fnl f* **4/1**[2]

2 *1/2* **Prince Of Fashion (IRE)**[51] 6640 4-9-10 70 .... (t) NGMcCullagh 13 73
(John Geoghegan, Ire) *mid-div on outer: 8th 1/2-way: rdn and hdwy into 3rd 1f out: kpt on u.p wout rching wnr* **10/1**

3 *3/4* **Pivotal Rock (IRE)**[60] 6421 4-9-10 70 .... KJManning 6 72
(T Stack, Ire) *trckd ldrs: 6th 1/2-way: 5th ent st: rdn in 4th 1f out: kpt on u.p and short of room wl ins fnl f* **10/1**

4 *shd* **Melodie D'Amour (IRE)**[28] 7153 4-9-1 66 .... CPHoban(5) 5 67
(M Halford, Ire) *led: strly pressed and hdd 1f out: no ex ins fnl f* **8/1**

5 *1/2* **Leaves You Baby (IRE)**[14] 7378 4-9-3 70 .... (tp) MMMonaghan(7) 4 70
(M Halford, Ire) *chsd ldrs: 7th 1/2-way: rdn early st: no imp in 6th over 1f out: kpt on u.p ins fnl f* **16/1**

6 *1 1/4* **Flavia Tatiana (IRE)**[21] 7278 3-9-10 74 .... JPO'Brien 7 73
(A P O'Brien, Ire) *mid-div: 9th 1/2-way: rdn and kpt on one pce in st: nt trble ldrs* **7/2**[1]

7 *nk* **Total Excitement (IRE)**[28] 7152 9-9-6 66 .... (p) CDHayes 10 63
(Thomas Cooper, Ire) *in rr of mid-div: 10th 1/2-way: kpt on one pce in st wout threatening* **12/1**

8 *1/2* **Avanti Albert (IRE)**[14] 7378 7-10-0 74 .... (t) GFCarroll 12 70
(A J Martin, Ire) *settled in rr of mid-div: 12th ent st: travelled wl and sme hdwy into 9th 1f out: kpt on* **6/1**[3]

9 *nk* **Blue Ridge Lane (IRE)**[14] 7378 5-9-3 70 .... (bt) CTKeane(7) 8 66
(John C McConnell, Ire) *slowly away and in rr: nvr a factor: kpt on one pce in st* **16/1**

10 *hd* **Saint By Day (IRE)**[35] 7014 5-9-6 66 .... (p) ShaneFoley 9 61
(M Halford, Ire) *hld up in rr: nvr a factor: kpt on one pce in st* **14/1**

11 *1* **Black N Brew (USA)**[120] 4480 5-9-10 70 .... MCHussey 3 63
(John C McConnell, Ire) *trckd ldr on inner in 2nd: rdn early st: no ex under 2f out: wknd* **50/1**

12 *4 3/4* **Slade (IRE)**[168] 2898 4-9-1 68 .... (t) SAGray(7) 11 52
(Andrew Heffernan, Ire) *trckd ldrs in 3rd: rdn appr st: no ex 2f out: sn wknd* **25/1**

13 *5 1/2* **Mount Abora (IRE)**[49] 6682 4-9-7 67 .... JMurtagh 2 40
(Charles O'Brien, Ire) *a towards rr* **14/1**

14 *2* **Norther Bay (FR)**[62] 4465 8-9-11 71 .... DJCasey 14 41
(Eoin Griffin, Ire) *trckd ldrs on outer: 4th 1/2-way: no ex ent st: wknd* **25/1**

2m 13.0s (133.00)
WFA 3 from 4yo+ 5lb **14** Ran SP% **128.2**
CSF £46.48 CT £394.11 TOTE £3.30: £1.02, £4.30, £4.00; DF 85.00.
Owner Allan Kerr Peter McGivney **Bred** Farmers Hill Stud **Trained** Hambleton, N Yorks

FOCUS
A game success in this decent handicap for Key Breeze, who enhanced his trainer's fine record in Ireland. The runner-up and third have been rated to their marks.

NOTEBOOK
Key Breeze, well placed throughout, was sent to the front early enough and was always holding on, despite drifting steadily right in the final furlong. In Pat Smullen's defence, he used the corrective measure of the whip in his right hand to no avail. Key Breeze likes the AW and is a consistent sort. Given the prize-money on offer, his connections unsurprisingly said he would likely run here again. (op 7/2)
Prince Of Fashion(IRE) ◆ was a bit unlucky as he was coming with a sustained run when carried into the centre of the track. He would likely not have won but keep him in mind next time. (op 14/1)
Pivotal Rock(IRE) ◆ was the meat in the proverbial sandwich when the winner started to drift right. He is totally unexposed over this trip and will certainly be of interest when he runs again.
Melodie D'Amour(IRE) went a good even pace and kept on battling when headed. She is a reliable filly.
Leaves You Baby(IRE) seemed to bounce back to form to some degree but she may have done enough for the year. (op 14/1)
Avanti Albert(IRE)'s run took the eye, with the stewards calling in trainer Tony Martin. He is probably a horse with his share of problems but he was ridden like a piece of work here, having been shuffled back in the first half of the race before staying on under tender handling. Official explanation: jockey said, regarding running and riding, that his orders were to jump smart, try to settle in mid-division, hold on to gelding as long as possible and challenge late. he added they went a good gallop, but he was trying to get it to drop the bridle and settle; it travelled well and he tried to coax it along without putting the gun to its head; when put it into the race late on, he did not have the clearest of runs and, in hindsight, he felt he should not have taken it back after the first bend as the field did not come back as he had hoped; trainer confirmed instructions and said that gelding's throat was inflamed; vet said gelding was found to be ciughing post-racw possibly as a result of swallowing kick-back. (op 6/1 tchd 13/2)
Slade(IRE) Official explanation: trainer said gelding made a respiratory noise in running

7549a WWW.DUNDALKSTADIUM.COM H'CAP 1m 4f (P)
9:15 (9:20) 3-Y-O+ **£7,732** (£1,793; £784; £448)

RPR

1 **Elizabeth Coffee (IRE)**[7] 7473 3-8-6 74 .... ShaneFoley 1 80
(M Halford, Ire) *trckd ldrs: 4th 1/2-way: wnt 3rd ent st: rdn to ld ins fnl f: kpt on u.p: hld on* **7/2**[2]

2 *hd* **Denny Crane**[35] 7013 5-9-10 86 .... PJSmullen 10 92
(Edward Lynam, Ire) *trckd ldrs on inner: 6th 1/2-way: 5th early st: hdwy between horses ins fnl f: kpt on wl u.p: jst failed* **11/4**[1]

3 *3/4* **Little Arrows (IRE)**[119] 4520 5-8-3 72 .... RossCoakley(7) 8 77
(K J Condon, Ire) *prom racing keenly: 2nd 1/2-way: disp early st: led narrowly over 1f out: hdd u.p ins fnl f: no ex* **25/1**

4 *nk* **Full Toss**[13] 7397 5-8-11 73 .... FergalLynch 7 77
(Jim Goldie) *trckd ldr racing keenly: led bef 1/2-way: jnd early st: hdd u.p over 1f out: no ex ins fnl f* **6/1**

5 *1* **Elusive Ridge (IRE)**[35] 7013 5-9-10 86 .... (p) KJManning 4 89
(H Rogers, Ire) *led early at stdy pce: hdd bef 1/2-way: 4th ent st: sn rdn and no imp ins fnl f* **7/1**

6 *shd* **Strandfield Lady (IRE)**[14] 7378 6-9-2 78 .... (b) CDHayes 11 81
(H Rogers, Ire) *hld up in rr: sme hdwy in 7th on outer appr st: no imp in 6th 1f out: kpt on one pce* **7/1**

7 *shd* **Un Hinged (IRE)**[19] 7321 11-8-12 81 .... (t) CTKeane(7) 3 83
(John J Coleman, Ire) *hld up towards rr: in tch 2f out: no imp in 7th 1f out: kpt on one pce* **12/1**

8 *2 3/4* **Buccaneer Bob (IRE)**[35] 7013 3-8-5 80 .... GJPhillips(7) 6 78
(G M Lyons, Ire) *towards rr: 8th 1/2-way: no ex fr 2f out: kpt on one pce* **9/2**[3]

9 *2 3/4* **Sun Disc (IRE)**[13] 7190 4-8-6 68 .... NGMcCullagh 5 62
(D T Hughes, Ire) *trckd ldrs: 5th 1/2-way: rdn early st: sn no ex* **12/1**

10 *2 3/4* **Hamalka (IRE)**[28] 7145 6-7-11 66 oh17 .... MMMonaghan(7) 9 55
(P Cluskey, Ire) *in rr of mid-div: 7th 1/2-way: no threat in st* **66/1**

2m 41.9s (161.90)
WFA 3 from 4yo+ 6lb **10** Ran SP% **127.1**
Daily Double: Not won CSF £15.01 CT £222.57 TOTE £4.30: £1.90, £1.90, £5.10; DF 18.40.
Owner David Carey **Bred** David Carey **Trained** Doneany, Co Kildare

FOCUS
This was run at a farcical pace and they predictably finished in a heap. That said, the form horses filled the first two places. The third has been rated to his recent best.

NOTEBOOK
Elizabeth Coffee(IRE), a good winner here last time, has become a really likeable performer and held on grimly. In truth, she got first run on the runner-up, but she had to battle, and the way the race was run was not exactly in her favour. She continues to progress, is ground-versatile and can only incur a negligible rise for this. She has a fine attitude. (op 9/2)
Denny Crane is a dream of a horse to be involved in as he settles, travels and battles. He did not pull like many of his rivals but the slow pace was still a negative for him and he just failed to win the sprint that ensued. He remains feasibly weighted. (op 11/4 tchd 7/2)
Little Arrows(IRE) barely gets this trip so the dawdle was more a help than a hindrance, though he ran keenly. He had every chance.
Full Toss had the run of things and just failed to reward each-way support. He had no obvious excuses on his favoured surface. (op 6/1 tchd 7/1)
Elusive Ridge(IRE)'s rider was intent on making this a tactical race from the front but the gallop was so slow that it invited others to do the same. He remains in good heart but seems in the handicapper's grip. (op 8/1)
T/Jkpt: @179.90 to a @1 stake. Pool: @9,280.00. T/Plt: @37.00 to a @1 stake. Pool of @24,480.00 - 399.00 winning tickets. II

7550 - 7554a (Foreign Racing) - See Raceform Interactive

7535 WOLVERHAMPTON (A.W) (L-H)
Saturday, November 26

OFFICIAL GOING: Standard
Wind: Strong behind Weather: Overcast

7555 STAY AT THE WOLVERHAMPTON HOLIDAY INN MAIDEN STKS 5f 20y(P)
6:20 (6:20) (Class 5) 2-Y-O **£2,264** (£673; £336; £168) **Stalls** Low

Form RPR

5 1 **Twilight Allure**[33] 7058 2-8-9 0 .... (t) AmyRyan(3) 1 67+
(Kevin Ryan) *mde all: rdn over 1f out: r.o* **8/1**

3 2 *3* **Ambitious Icarus**[17] 7335 2-9-0 0 .... RobertLButler(3) 7 61
(Richard Guest) *chsd ldrs: pushed along 1/2-way: sn outpcd: rdn over 1f out: styd on to go 2nd nr fin: nt trble wnr* **33/1**

3 3 *1/2* **Wild Sauce**[187] 2346 2-8-12 0 .... TomEaves 6 54
(Bryan Smart) *chsd wnr: rdn and edgd rt over 1f out: no ex ins fnl f: lost 2nd nr fin* **3/1**[1]

4 *1 1/4* **Availed Speaker (IRE)** 2-9-3 0 .... PaulHanagan 3 55
(Richard Fahey) *s.i.s: in rr: r.o ins fnl f: nrst fin* **9/2**[2]

52 5 *2 1/4* **Littlesuzie**[26] 7194 2-8-5 0 .... (t) NicoleNordblad(7) 9 42
(Hans Adielsson) *chsd ldrs: hung rt 1/2-way: wknd over 1f out* **9/2**[2]

344 6 *1 1/4* **Lana (IRE)**[71] 6118 2-8-7 62 .... MatthewCosham(5) 5 37
(David Evans) *chsd ldrs: rdn 1/2-way: wknd over 1f out: rdr dropped whip ins fnl f* **7/1**

7 *1 1/2* **Too Ambitious** 2-8-12 0 .... RussKennemore 2 32
(Reg Hollinshead) *s.i.s: outpcd* **18/1**

8 *1/2* **Prim By Night** 2-8-5 0 .... GeorgeChaloner(7) 10 30
(Richard Fahey) *s.i.s: outpcd* **40/1**

502 9 *10* **Bengaline**[17] 7335 2-9-0 68 .... BillyCray(3) 4 —
(David Nicholls) *prom: pushed along over 3f out: wknd 1/2-way* **11/2**[3]

62.30 secs **Going Correction** +0.05s/f (Slow) **9** Ran SP% **111.0**
Speed ratings (Par 96): **102,97,96,94,90 88,86,85,69**
toteswingers:1&2:£19.40, 2&3:£12.10, 1&3:£5.80 CSF £212.95 TOTE £8.00: £1.90, £8.90, £1.10; EX 108.70.
Owner Mrs T Marnane **Bred** Executive Bloodlines **Trained** Hambleton, N Yorks

 The Form Book, Raceform Ltd, Compton, RG20 6NL

FOCUS
There was an open market for this ordinary maiden and a gamble was landed. A tricky race to pin down but the runner-up is probably the best guide.

NOTEBOOK
Twilight Allure ◆ didn't show much in the French provinces and was well beaten at a big price on debut for her current yard last month, but she was a big market mover in the morning (backed from 33-1 into 7-1) and put in a strong front-running display to win with plenty in hand. The form is not strong but a tongue-tie and drop to 5f on Polytrack seem to have sparked this much improved form, and she could go on from this.
Ambitious Icarus, a £1,200 yearling who is out of a half-sister to three winners at up to 1m2f (one also scored over hurdles), has shown some ability in two maidens on both AW surfaces and shapes like a step up in trip will suit. (op 28-1)
Wild Sauce showed promise when third in a 5f Carlisle maiden on debut in May. The market vibes were positive on her return from six months off, and this Exceed And Excel filly showed plenty of speed but couldn't hang in there with the winner. Official explanation: jockey said filly hung right (op 11-4 tchd 5-2)
Availed Speaker(IRE), a 15,000euros gelded son of Iffraaj and a half-brother to four winners in North America, ran green before staying on steadily on this debut. (op 13-2)
Littlesuzie had decent claims on her improved second in a C&D maiden last month but she was forced wide for most of the way and couldn't make an impact with a tongue-tie tried. (op 4-1 tchd 5-1)
Bengaline is a fairly exposed 68-rated colt who had claims on a couple of runner-up efforts in sprint maidens at Southwell, but he was always outpaced and may not have handled Polytrack. (op 13-2)

7556 GREAT OFFERS AT WOLVERHAMPTON-RACECOURSE.CO.UK H'CAP 1m 4f 50y(P)
6:50 (6:51) (Class 5) (0-70,70) 3-Y-O+ **£2,264** (£673; £336; £168) **Stalls** Low

Form RPR
0131 **1** **Mazij**[7] 7496 3-9-4 **70** .... WilliamCarson 8 78
(Peter Hiatt) *chsd ldr tl led 5f out: rdn over 2f out: styd on u.p* **9/2**[2]
3215 **2** ½ **Boa**[50] 6666 6-9-2 **69** .... JackDuern(7) 10 76
(Reg Hollinshead) *a.p: chsd wnr over 3f out: rdn and ev ch ins fnl f: styd on* **6/1**[3]
6230 **3** ½ **Alubari**[170] 2830 4-9-7 **67** .... LiamKeniry 9 73
(Gordon Elliott, Ire) *hld up: pushed along 3f out: hdwy over 1f out: sn rdn: styd on: nt rch ldrs* **6/1**[3]
6323 **4** 1 ½ **The Winged Assasin (USA)**[123] 1874 5-9-3 **68** ....(t) LucyKBarry(5) 1 72
(Shaun Lycett) *chsd ldrs: rdn over 1f out: styd on* **10/1**
2636 **5** *nk* **Broughtons Paradis (IRE)**[22] 7272 5-9-7 **67** .... StevieDonohoe 3 70
(Willie Musson) *hld up: hdwy over 5f out: rdn over 1f out: styd on* **4/1**[1]
0450 **6** *nk* **Kames Park (IRE)**[32] 7087 9-9-1 **64** .... RobertLButler(3) 6 67
(Richard Guest) *hld up: rdn over 1f out: r.o ins fnl f: nt rch ldrs* **11/1**
6000 **7** 3 **Black Coffee**[14] 7397 6-9-10 **70** ....(b) ShaneKelly 11 68
(Mark Brisbourne) *s.i.s: hld up: hdwy over 2f out: rdn over 1f out: styd on same pce* **25/1**
0062 **8** 10 **Global**[18] 6546 5-9-1 **61** .... BarryMcHugh 7 43
(Brian Ellison) *hld up: hdwy 3f out: sn rdn: wknd wl over 1f out* **7/1**
6220 **9** ¾ **Ghufa (IRE)**[26] 7200 7-9-4 **67** .... SimonPearce(3) 4 48
(Lydia Pearce) *s.i.s: hld up: a in rr: wknd 3f out* **9/1**
10-0 **10** 11 **Flotation (USA)**[12] 7418 4-9-0 **60** .... TomEaves 2 23
(Roy Brotherton) *prom tl rdn and wknd 3f out* **100/1**
5666 **11** 3 ½ **Bentley**[100] 5208 7-9-1 **66** .... RyanPowell(5) 5 24
(Brian Baugh) *led 7f: sn rdn: wknd 3f out* **66/1**

2m 41.39s (0.29) **Going Correction** +0.05s/f (Slow)
WFA 3 from 4yo+ 6lb **11** Ran **SP% 113.0**
Speed ratings (Par 103): **101,100,100,99,99 98,96,90,89,82 80**
toteswingers:1&2:£6.00, 2&3:£6.80, 1&3:£7.00 CSF £30.03 CT £161.08 TOTE £4.80: £1.90, £2.50, £3.40; EX 35.20.
Owner P W Hiatt **Bred** The Hill Stud **Trained** Hook Norton, Oxon

FOCUS
A progressive 3-y-o put in a determined effort to complete a quick-fire C&D double in this steadily run handicap. The form makes sense, with the runner-up solid and the next three home close to their marks.

7557 ENJOY THE RINGSIDE ENTERTAINMENT AFTER RACING (S) STKS 1m 1f 103y(P)
7:20 (7:21) (Class 6) 3-Y-O+ **£1,704** (£503; £251) **Stalls** Low

Form RPR
012 **1** **True To Form (IRE)**[33] 7061 4-9-2 74........(p) DavidKenny(5) 9 89+
(George Baker) *hld up: hdwy over 2f out: led wl over 1f out: pushed clr fnl f* **11/4**[1]
5203 **2** 6 **Mighty Clarets (IRE)**[8] 7465 4-9-7 71........ PaulHanagan 6 76
(Richard Fahey) *chsd ldrs: nt clr run wl over 1f out: sn rdn: styd on same pce* **3/1**[2]
4506 **3** 1 ¼ **Kidlat**[7] 7492 6-9-0 74........(t) NatashaEaton(7) 10 74
(Alan Bailey) *sn pushed along and prom: led over 7f out: clr over 5f out: rdn and hdd wl over 1f out: no ex fnl f* **13/2**
0024 **4** 6 **Ravi River (IRE)**[42] 6868 7-9-7 73........ BarryMcHugh 1 61
(Brian Ellison) *prom: rdn over 3f out: wknd 2f out* **14/1**
6626 **5** 2 ½ **Alhaban (IRE)**[26] 7200 5-9-3 64........(v[1]) LukeMorris 5 52
(Ronald Harris) *chsd ldrs: wnt 2nd over 3f out tl rdn over 2f out: wknd over 1f out* **10/1**
1000 **6** 3 ½ **Whodathought (IRE)**[9] 7447 3-9-4 70........(tp) AdamKirby 7 49
(Paul Rich) *mid-div: rdn over 4f out: wknd over 2f out* **16/1**
030 **7** 3 ¾ **Ahlawy (IRE)**[35] 7036 8-9-0 68........(bt) LiviaMachalikova(7) 3 41
(Frank Sheridan) *s.s: a bhd* **33/1**
4000 **8** 11 **Neat Sweep (IRE)**[33] 7068 3-8-6 62........ SophieDoyle(3) 8 —
(Alan McCabe) *sn led: hdd over 7f out: chsd ldr tl over 3f out: wknd over 2f out: t.o* **66/1**
0300 **9** 12 **Back For Tea (IRE)**[23] 7246 3-9-0 45........(t) MickyFenton 13 —
(K F Clutterbuck) *hld up: a in rr: bhd fnl 3f: t.o* **150/1**
621/ **10** 11 **Bengal Tiger**[801] 5987 5-9-0 74........ MichaelO'Connell(3) 4 —
(Tony Carroll) *s.i.s: hld up: a in rr: bhd fnl 3f: t.o* **7/2**[3]
340 **11** 18 **Arctic Cat (IRE)**[63] 6357 3-9-0 57........ RobertWinston 12 —
(Geoffrey Harker) *hld up: a in rr: bhd fnl 3f: t.o* **33/1**
00 **12** 24 **Mon Petit Bijou**[10] 7440 3-8-6 0........ SimonPearce(3) 2 —
(Lydia Pearce) *sn pushed along in rr: bhd fnl 4f: t.o* **150/1**

1m 59.54s (-2.16) **Going Correction** +0.05s/f (Slow)
WFA 3 from 4yo+ 3lb **12** Ran **SP% 117.6**
Speed ratings (Par 101): **111,105,104,99,97 93,90,80,70,60 44,23**
CSF £10.81 TOTE £4.80: £1.80, £1.50, £1.80; EX 13.50.The winner was sold to Ron Harris for 12,000gns.
Owner Iraj Parvizi **Bred** Sir E J Loder **Trained** Whitsbury, Hants

FOCUS
This seller was run at a fast pace. They were well strung out at a relatively early stage and the favourite scored in smooth style from his main market rival. A personal best from the winner and the runner-up is rated to his latest mark.
Bengal Tiger Official explanation: jockey said gelding never travelled
Arctic Cat(IRE) Official explanation: jockey said gelding hung badly left

7558 BOOKIEFREEBIES.COM H'CAP 1m 1f 103y(P)
7:50 (7:50) (Class 4) (0-85,85) 3-Y-O+ **£4,204** (£1,251; £625; £312) **Stalls** Low

Form RPR
6301 **1** **William Haigh (IRE)**[11] 7425 3-8-10 **77** .... JimCrowley 5 89
(Alan Swinbank) *chsd ldrs: rdn over 2f out: styd on to ld nr fin* **14/1**
4351 **2** ¾ **Standpoint**[7] 7492 5-8-13 **77** ....(p) GrahamGibbons 2 87
(Reg Hollinshead) *led: hdd over 7f out: remained handy: chsd ldr over 1f out: rdn to ld ins fnl f: hdd nr fin* **13/2**[3]
6153 **3** 1 ¾ **Voodoo Prince**[148] 3585 3-9-4 **85** .... TomMcLaughlin 4 91
(Ed Dunlop) *hld up: hdwy over 2f out: rdn over 1f out: edgd lft ins fnl f: r.o* **7/2**[2]
0002 **4** ¾ **Snow Dancer (IRE)**[14] 7397 7-9-0 **78** .... PaddyAspell 12 83
(Hugh McWilliams) *hld up: hdwy over 1f out: r.o: nt rch ldrs* **12/1**
0041 **5** *nk* **Chosen Forever**[14] 7397 6-9-1 **79** .... RobertWinston 8 83
(Geoffrey Oldroyd) *a.p: chsd ldr over 5f out: pushed along to ld 2f out: sn rdn: hdd and unable qck ins fnl f* **9/1**
2000 **6** 7 **Thunderstruck**[40] 6918 6-9-2 **83** ....(p) MichaelO'Connell(3) 1 72
(David Nicholls) *chsd ldrs: rdn over 2f out: wknd over 1f out* **28/1**
0040 **7** 2 **Cloud Illusions (USA)**[7] 7486 3-8-9 **76** ....(v) LiamKeniry 9 61
(Heather Main) *mid-div: drvn along over 3f out: wknd over 2f out* **25/1**
0013 **8** 2 **Veroon (IRE)**[24] 7227 5-9-5 **83** ....(p) PaulHanagan 13 64
(James Given) *hld up: hmpd wl over 2f out: n.d* **9/1**
5250 **9** ½ **Guest Book (IRE)**[45] 6803 4-9-2 **85** .... DavidKenny(5) 6 65
(Michael Scudamore) *hld up: rdn over 3f out: a in rr* **28/1**
1511 **10** 1 ¼ **So Wise (USA)**[28] 7178 3-9-0 **81** .... JoeFanning 7 58
(Keith Dalgleish) *w ldr tl led over 7f out: rdn and hdd 2f out: wknd fnl f* **5/2**[1]
4540 **11** *nse* **The Lock Master (IRE)**[126] 4326 4-8-13 **77** .... NeilChalmers 11 54
(Michael Appleby) *prom: rdn over 3f out: wknd over 2f out* **50/1**
0501 **12** 3 **European Dream (IRE)**[14] 7161 8-9-1 **82** ....(p) RobertLButler(3) 10 53
(Richard Guest) *s.i.s: hld up: a in rr: wknd over 2f out* **25/1**

1m 59.72s (-1.98) **Going Correction** +0.05s/f (Slow)
WFA 3 from 4yo+ 3lb **12** Ran **SP% 115.0**
Speed ratings (Par 105): **110,109,107,107,106 100,98,97,96,95 95,92**
toteswingers:1&2:£27.30, 2&3:£3.60, 1&3:£23.10 CSF £93.36 CT £393.43 TOTE £20.60: £4.50, £2.60, £1.10; EX 125.70.
Owner Shropshire Wolves II **Bred** Mrs C L Weld **Trained** Melsonby, N Yorks

FOCUS
A decent handicap, involving five last-time-out winners. The favourite was disappointing but the first five pulled clear and the form looks solid rated through the second.

7559 ENJOY THE PARTY PACK GROUP OFFER MAIDEN STKS 7f 32y(P)
8:20 (8:23) (Class 5) 2-Y-O **£2,264** (£673; £336; £168) **Stalls** High

Form RPR
2 **1** **Haaf A Sixpence**[17] 7330 2-9-3 0 .... JimCrowley 1 71+
(Ralph Beckett) *chsd ldrs: rdn to ld over 1f out: r.o* **8/13**[1]
6 **2** 1 **Fistful Of Dollars (IRE)**[26] 7197 2-9-0 0 .... SophieDoyle(3) 7 67
(Jamie Osborne) *s.i.s: hld up: hdwy over 2f out: rdn to chse wnr ins fnl f: r.o* **14/1**
3 1 ½ **Sujet Bellagio** 2-9-3 0 .... ShaneKelly 10 65+
(Brian Meehan) *hld up: hdwy over 1f out: r.o: nt rch ldrs* **6/1**[2]
0 **4** *nk* **Sir Dylan**[15] 7369 2-9-3 0 .... LukeMorris 5 62
(Ronald Harris) *led: rdn and hdd over 1f out: styd on same pce ins fnl f* **7/1**[3]
0 **5** ¾ **Foursquare Funtime**[26] 7197 2-9-3 0 .... RussKennemore 8 60
(Reg Hollinshead) *hld up: racd keenly: hdwy 3f out: rdn over 1f out: r.o* **100/1**
0 **6** *shd* **Choccywoccydoodah**[21] 7293 2-8-12 0 .... JamesSullivan 9 55
(James Given) *prom: rdn over 2f out: hung lft over 1f out: styd on same pce fnl f* **40/1**
00 **7** 1 ½ **Welsh Bard (IRE)**[17] 7330 2-9-3 0 .... SebSanders 6 56
(Sir Mark Prescott Bt) *hld up: pushed along over 2f out: n.d* **40/1**
8 1 ¼ **Westward Hope (USA)** 2-9-3 0 .... LiamKeniry 11 53
(J W Hills) *hld up: nvr on terms* **12/1**
00 **9** *shd* **Princess Tamina (IRE)**[95] 5337 2-8-12 0 .... GrahamGibbons 2 48
(Mark Brisbourne) *chsd ldrs tl rdn and wknd over 1f out* **100/1**
10 1 ¾ **Diva Donkey (IRE)** 2-8-12 0 .... TomEaves 4 44
(Bryan Smart) *hld up: effrt over 2f out: sn wknd* **16/1**
64 **11** ¾ **Forever Janey**[14] 7396 2-8-7 0 .... MatthewLawson(5) 3 42
(Paul Green) *chsd ldr 6f out: rdn and ev ch 2f out: wknd over 1f out* **40/1**
12 15 **The Young Master** 2-9-3 0 .... AdamKirby 12 10
(Neil Mulholland) *dwlt: a in rr* **100/1**

1m 31.19s (1.59) **Going Correction** +0.05s/f (Slow) **12** Ran **SP% 119.2**
Speed ratings (Par 96): **92,90,89,88,87 87,86,84,84,82 81,64**
toteswingers:1&2:£3.40, 2&3:£13.20, 1&3:£2.10 CSF £11.22 TOTE £1.60: £1.10, £3.90, £2.10; EX 14.70.
Owner Melody Racing **Bred** Melody Bloodstock **Trained** Kimpton, Hants

FOCUS
There didn't seem to be much strength in depth in this maiden but the odds-on favourite delivered with a bit in hand. The form is weak in terms of depth, although the winner scored in fair style and the third caught the eye.

NOTEBOOK
Haaf A Sixpence set the standard on his 7l second behind useful odds-on Godolphin newcomer Rassam in a 7f maiden on his recent debut. Sent off a hot favourite, he was always well positioned and delivered in professional style. He was unsold at just £400 in January but has a fair amount of ability and is out of an unplaced half-sister to three winners at 5f-8.6f. (op 4-6)
Fistful Of Dollars(IRE) showed plenty of improvement on his debut 12l sixth over C&D last month. A gelded son of Holy Roman Emperor, he is related to five winners and should continue to progress.
Sujet Bellagio, a £38,000 gelded Acclamation half-brother to 7f 2yo/multiple 6f AW winner Perfect Art, showed signs of inexperience but put in a promising staying-on effort on this debut. (tchd 7-1)
Sir Dylan, a gelded son of Dylan Thomas out of a half-sister to high-class 1m2f-2m (Queen's Vase) winner Mahler, gave it a decent try under a front-running ride on his second start. (op 15-2 tchd 13-2)
Foursquare Funtime was always outpaced when 50-1 in a similar C&D maiden on recent debut but he showed much-improved form staying on steadily out wide. Official explanation: jockey said gelding hung right

Choccywoccydoodah showed ability stepped up in trip and switched to Polytrack on her second run. (op 33-1)

7560 DINE IN HORIZONS RESTAURANT H'CAP (DIV I) 7f 32y(P)
8:50 (8:50) (Class 6) (0-55,55) 3-Y-0+ **£1,704** (£503; £251) **Stalls** High

Form RPR

-043 **1** **Dashing Eddie (IRE)**[22] 7270 3-8-11 **51**....................(p) PaulHanagan 6 58
(Kevin Ryan) *chsd ldrs: rdn over 1f out: r.o to ld towards fin* **9/4**[1]

5000 **2** ½ **Stamp Duty (IRE)**[33] 7057 3-9-1 **55**............................ DuranFentiman 5 60
(Suzzanne France) *chsd ldrs: lost pl over 5f out: rdn over 2f out: hdwy over 1f out: r.o* **25/1**

0000 **3** *shd* **Beating Harmony**[11] 7419 3-8-8 **48**.................................. NeilChalmers 8 53
(Michael Appleby) *pushed along in rr early: hdwy over 1f out: r.o* **25/1**

0022 **4** *1* **Welsh Dancer**[8] 7460 3-8-12 **52**... LukeMorris 4 54
(Ronald Harris) *a.p: chsd ldr 3f out: rdn to ld ins fnl f: hung lft: hdd and no ex towards fin* **11/2**

1666 **5** *1* **Sopran Nad (ITY)**[36] 7001 7-9-2 **55**...........................(b) AndreaAtzeni 11 55
(Frank Sheridan) *sn led: rdn over 1f out: hdd ins fnl f: styd on same pce* **11/2**

3423 **6** ½ **Little Perisher**[8] 7459 4-8-11 **50**.............................(b) MichaelStainton 2 48
(Graeme McPherson) *sn prom: rdn over 2f out: styd on* **9/2**[3]

5240 **7** *15* **Circuitous**[15] 7366 3-8-12 **52**..(b) JoeFanning 1 —
(Keith Dalgleish) *chsd ldr tl pushed along 3f out: wknd 2f out* **7/2**[2]

66-0 **8** *5* **Tagena (IRE)**[31] 7111 3-8-10 **55**.................................... DavidKenny(5) 7 —
(Richard Price) *hld up: a in rr: bhd fnl 3f* **50/1**

1m 31.07s (1.47) **Going Correction** +0.05s/f (Slow)
WFA 3 from 4yo+ 1lb **8** Ran SP% **111.6**
Speed ratings (Par 101): **93,92,92,91,90 89,72,66**
toteswingers:1&2:£57.10, 2&3:£11.30, 1&3:£15.00 CSF £59.55 CT £1081.50 TOTE £3.30: £1.80, £6.60, £7.00; EX 74.20.
Owner T A Rahman **Bred** Scuderia San Pancrazio Sas **Trained** Hambleton, N Yorks

FOCUS
A low-grade handicap. The pace was not very strong and there was a tight finish. The winner and the fourth help set the level but the form of the placed horses is shaky.

7561 DINE IN HORIZONS RESTAURANT H'CAP (DIV II) 7f 32y(P)
9:20 (9:20) (Class 6) (0-55,55) 3-Y-0+ **£1,704** (£503; £251) **Stalls** High

Form RPR

0435 **1** **Monsieur Pontaven**[70] 6159 4-8-11 **50**..........................(b) LiamKeniry 3 61
(Robin Bastiman) *chsd ldrs: rdn to ld ins fnl f: r.o* **7/2**[1]

4033 **2** 2¾ **Ereka (IRE)**[9] 7442 3-8-9 **49**.. LukeMorris 1 53
(John Best) *chsd ldrs: led over 2f out: rdn over 1f out: hdd and unable qck ins fnl f* **9/2**[3]

4002 **3** 1¾ **Lennoxwood (IRE)**[30] 7131 3-8-1 **48**...................(be) RachealKneller(7) 6 47
(Mark Usher) *a.p: rdn over 1f out: edgd lft and styd on same pce fnl f* **4/1**[2]

/000 **4** *1* **Bridge Valley**[15] 7371 4-9-2 **55**.. MichaelStainton 9 51
(Jason Ward) *hld up: hdwy u.p over 1f out: nt rch ldrs* **12/1**

0005 **5** 1¼ **Russian Winter**[9] 7443 3-8-9 **49**.................................... JamesSullivan 12 42
(Tim Etherington) *hld up: rdn over 2f out: nt trble ldrs* **25/1**

000 **6** ¾ **Serial Sinner (IRE)**[108] 4911 3-9-0 **54**.............................. StevieDonohoe 2 45
(Paul Cole) *prom: rdn over 2f out: styd on same pce fr over 1f out* **13/2**

2005 **7** *1* **Cawdor (IRE)**[105] 5034 5-8-8 **54**................................ KristinStubbs(7) 11 42
(Linda Stubbs) *s.i.s: sn pushed along in rr: n.d* **9/1**

000 **8** *10* **Moonlark**[53] 6608 3-8-10 **50** ow3.................................... GrahamGibbons 8 11
(John Holt) *s.i.s: hdwy to chse ldr over 5f out: led over 3f out: sn hung rt: hdd over 2f out: wknd over 1f out* **12/1**

0230 **9** *76* **Lethal**[11] 7419 8-8-6 **50**..(p) DavidKenny(5) 4 —
(Richard Price) *hung rt thrght: led: racd alone far side fr 6f out: hdd & wknd over 3f out: t.o* **8/1**

1m 30.92s (1.32) **Going Correction** +0.05s/f (Slow)
WFA 3 from 4yo+ 1lb **9** Ran SP% **114.1**
Speed ratings (Par 101): **94,90,88,87,86 85,84,72,—**
toteswingers:1&2:£2.20, 2&3:£2.60, 1&3:£3.80 CSF £19.01 CT £64.73 TOTE £3.10: £1.10, £2.10, £2.00; EX 18.70.
Owner Ms M Austerfield **Bred** Whitsbury Manor Stud **Trained** Cowthorpe, N Yorks

FOCUS
They finished quite well strung out in the second division of this ordinary handicap and the three market leaders filled the first three positions. The winner recorded a slight personal best with the runner-up basically to his mark.
Moonlark Official explanation: jockey said filly hung right throughout
Lethal Official explanation: jockey said gelding hung badly right
T/Plt: £44.20 to a £1 stake. Pool of £108,426.38 - 1,787.66 winning tickets. T/Qpdt: £8.70 to a £1 stake. Pool of £10,422.93 - 885.49 winning tickets. CR

3652 HOLLYWOOD PARK (L-H)
Friday, November 25

OFFICIAL GOING: Turf: firm

7562a MIESQUE STKS (GRADE 3) (2YO FILLIES) (TURF) 1m (T)
10:32 (10:36) 2-Y-0 **£38,461** (£12,820; £7,692; £3,846; £1,282)

RPR

1 **More Than Love (USA)** 2-8-6 0.................................. RADominguez 7 100
(John Terranova II, U.S.A) **1/1**[1]

2 *nse* **Starship Flare (USA)** 2-8-4 0.. VEspinoza 3 98
(Kristin Mulhall, U.S.A) **30/1**

3 3½ **Island Paradise (IRE)**[84] 5691 2-8-5 0 ow1.......................... JRosario 1 91
(Charles Hills) **27/10**[2]

4 *nse* **Your Special Day (USA)** 2-8-6 0 ow2................................ MESmith 2 92
(James Cassidy, U.S.A) **23/5**[3]

5 1½ **Regal Betty (USA)**[12] 2-8-6 0... JTalamo 4 88
(John W Sadler, U.S.A) **128/10**

6 3½ **Katie's Ten (USA)** 2-8-5 0 ow3..................................(b) AQuinonez 5 79
(John W Sadler, U.S.A) **93/10**

7 *4* **Raesunbridledfaith (USA)**[27] 2-8-4 0........................... MGarcia 8 69
(Craig A Lewis, U.S.A) **187/10**

1m 36.32s (1.53) **7** Ran SP% **120.1**
PARI-MUTUEL (all including $2 stakes): WIN 4.00; PLACE (1-2) 3.20, 15.20; SHOW (1-2-3) 2.20, 6.20, 2.80; DF 72.40; SF 71.40.
Owner Newtown Anner Stud **Bred** Loft Hall Stud, Galleria Bloodstock & Samac **Trained** USA

7191 TOKYO (L-H)
Sunday, November 27

OFFICIAL GOING: Turf: firm

7563a JAPAN CUP (GRADE 1) (3YO+) (TURF) 1m 4f
6:20 (12:00) 3-Y-0**£2,000,663** (£797,158; £501,199; £299,968; £197,347)

RPR

1 **Buena Vista (JPN)**[28] 7191 5-8-9 0.................................. YasunariIwata 2 122
(Hiroyoshi Matsuda, Japan) *midfield on inner: rdn over 2f out: str chal over 1f out: led ins fnl 100yds: kpt on wl* **12/5**[2]

2 *nk* **Tosen Jordan (JPN)**[28] 7191 5-9-0 0.......................... CraigAWilliams 16 126
(Yasutoshi Ikee, Japan) *chsd clr ldr: 3rd and rdn over 3f out: led over 1f out: hdd fnl 100yds: kpt on* **131/10**

3 1¾ **Jaguar Mail (JPN)**[28] 7191 7-9-0 0.................................... HirofumiShii 1 123
(Noriyuki Hori, Japan) *hld up on inner: stdy prog on rail over 3f out: rdn over 2f out: r.o wl fnl 1f but nt pce of ldng duo* **106/1**

4 ½ **Trailblazer (JPN)**[21] 4-9-0 0.. YutakaTake 5 122
(Yasutoshi Ikee, Japan) *front rnk of main gp: rdn to chal over 2f out: kpt on same pce* **43/1**

5 ¾ **Win Variation (JPN)**[35] 3-8-9 0..................................... KatsumiAndo 12 122
(Masahiro Matsunaga, Japan) *hld up in last gp: rapid move on outer 5f out: 2nd and chal over 4f out: slt ld over 2f out: hdd over 1f out: no ex* **137/10**

6 *nk* **Danedream (GER)**[56] 6567 3-8-5 0... AStarke 13 118+
(P Schiergen, Germany) *hld up: rdn over 3f out: run on outer over 2f out: r.o fnl 1f: nvr able to chal* **23/10**[1]

7 1¼ **Shareta (IRE)**[56] 6567 3-8-5 0.................. Christophe-PatriceLemaire 14 117+
(A De Royer-Dupre, France) *midfield on outer: rdn over 3f out: outpcd over 2f out: r.o fnl 1f: nrst fin* **35/1**

8 *nk* **Eishin Flash (JPN)**[28] 7191 4-9-0 0.................................... KenichiIkezoe 15 118
(Hideaki Fujiwara, Japan) *midfield: swtchd to outer over 2f out: hrd rdn over 1f out: fdd fnl 100yds* **103/10**

9 ¾ **Rose Kingdom (JPN)**[28] 7191 4-9-0 0........................ IoritzMendizabal 3 117
(Kojiro Hashiguchi, Japan) *midfield: rdn over 2f out: outpcd over 1f out: kpt on* **21/1**

10 *hd* **Oken Bruce Lee (JPN)**[21] 6-9-0 0............................ MasayoshiEbina 4 117
(Hidetaka Otonashi, Japan) *hld up in last gp: last over 3f out: rdn over 2f out: kpt on fnl f: nvr able to chal* **45/1**

11 *nse* **To The Glory (JPN)**[28] 7191 4-9-0 0.............................. YuichiFukunaga 6 117
(Yasutoshi Ikee, Japan) *t.k.h in front rnk of main gp: rdn 2f out: chal over 1f out: wknd fnl 100yds* **153/10**

12 *nk* **Sarah Lynx (IRE)**[42] 6910 4-8-9 0.......................... ChristopheSoumillon 9 112
(J E Hammond, France) *hld up on inner: rdn over 2f out: outpcd over 1f out* **94/1**

13 *4* **Victoire Pisa (JPN)**[246] 1002 4-9-0 0.................................. MircoDemuro 8 110
(Katsuhiko Sumii, Japan) *hld up in last: rdn on outer over 2f out: outpcd over 1f out: wknd* **99/10**

14 ¾ **Mission Approved (USA)**[57] 6548 7-9-0 0............................ JLEspinoza 11 109
(Naipaul Chatterpaul, U.S.A) *led: hrd pressed over 3f out: hdd over 2f out: wknd* **168/1**

15 3½ **King Top Gun (JPN)**[21] 8-9-0 0.. KeitaTosaki 10 103
(Ippo Sameshima, Japan) *midfield: rdn over 2f out: wknd wl over 1f out* **239/1**

16 1¼ **Pelusa (JPN)**[28] 7191 4-9-0 0...................................... NorihiroYokoyama 7 101
(Kazuo Fujisawa, Japan) *hld up: rdn over 2f out: wknd and eased fnl f* **13/2**[3]

2m 24.2s (-1.30)
WFA 3 from 4yo+ 6lb **16** Ran SP% **125.9**
PARI-MUTUEL (all including 100 ypj stake): WIN 340 SHOW 140, 430, 1660 DF 2300 SF 4180.
Owner Sunday Racing Co Ltd **Bred** Northern Racing **Trained** Japan

FOCUS
The 31st Japan Cup produced a high-class field with the one-two from this season's Arc, the 2011 Dubai World Cup winner and seven of the first eight home in last year's race.

NOTEBOOK
Buena Vista(JPN) avenged last year's controversial demotion to run out a deserving winner. Jockey Yasunari Iwata settled the 5-y-o mare just behind the leaders and hugged the rail throughout. He asked for her effort turning into the straight and engineered a gap between rivals to challenge the runner-up 2f out. Despite a tussle between the two inside the final furlong, it was the wonder mare who stayed on strongest. The 2010 Japanese horse of the year has now won six Grade 1 contests and this was her first victory since 'winning' this race last season. She will have one final race before retirement, the Arima Kinen next month.
Tosen Jordan(JPN) ran a mighty race in defeat. Craig Williams deserves credit for getting him into a prominent position from the wide draw. The horse came under strong pressure around the final bend but responded admirably. He fended off all challengers in the straight but finally succumbed to the persistent winner after a tenacious fight. Winner of the Tenno Sho, this effort cements a progressive profile and he could be a live contender for this next year.
Jaguar Mail(JPN), fourth last year, followed the winner's run into the straight and stayed on strongly for third. A Grade 1 winner over 2m, he just lacked the pace to challenge the front pair but remains of interest at this level, especially when there's a strong pace.
Trailblazer(JPN), winner of the Grade 2 Copa Republica Argentina, sat in midfield before challenging the leaders with 2f left but did not have the finishing kick when it mattered.
Win Variation(JPN)'s jockey may regret urging his mount so early when sweeping to the outside and challenging for the lead 5f out. He was keen early but even so this move definitely hindered the horse's chance of lasting home and he finished tired.
Danedream(GER), the impressive Arc winner (record time) was bumped early and could never get into a handy position from her wide draw. She was forced wide into the homestretch and just stayed on past beaten horses. It may have been a combination of the fast ground, bad draw and wide trip that resulted in a disappointed run and she should be given another chance to confirm her brilliant Longchamp victory.
Shareta(IRE) could not get into a challenging position, having been outpaced before staying on takingly for pressure in the straight. She will continue to race on next season.
Eishin Flash(JPN), who won last season's Japanese Derby over course and distance, was far too keen and paid for it at the business end.
Rose Kingdom(JPN) could not repeat last year's 'victory' as traffic problems in the straight ended his chance.
To The Glory(JPN), aside from the winner, travelled like the best horse in the race but found little when asked for an effort. Perhaps a drop in trip would be the key.
Victoire Pisa(JPN), winner of the Dubai World Cup, sat last under exaggerated hold-up tactics and never got into the race. It was his first run back from injury.
Mission Approved(USA) set a brisk pace from the start and didn't last home.
Pelusa(JPN) was eased as if something was amiss.

The Form Book, Raceform Ltd, Compton, RG20 6NL

[7555]WOLVERHAMPTON (A.W) (L-H)

Monday, November 28

OFFICIAL GOING: Standard

Wind: Fresh behind Weather: Overcast

7564 32RED H'CAP (FOR AMATEUR RIDERS) 1m 5f 194y(P)

2:10 (2:11) (Class 6) (0-65,65) 3-Y-O+ £1,646 (£506; £253) Stalls Low

Form RPR

4243 1 **Squad**[12] 7441 5-10-5 **61**....................(be) MrJCoffill-Brown(5) 5 70
(Simon Dow) *dwlt: hld up: hdwy over 5f out: pushed along fnl f: styd on to ld post* **6/1**[2]

541P 2 *shd* **C P Joe (IRE)**[6] 7506 3-10-4 **63**....................(v) MrSWalker 2 71
(Paul Green) *hld up: hdwy 5f out: rdn to ld over 1f out: edgd lft ins fnl f: hdd post* **9/2**[1]

0503 3 *nse* **Turjuman (USA)**[59] 6503 6-10-0 **58**....................(p) MissAlexOwen(7) 12 66
(Alan Bailey) *hld up: plld hrd: hdwy 8f out: shkn up over 1f out: styd on wl* **10/1**

4662 4 *5* **Resplendent Ace (IRE)**[14] 7415 7-10-9 **65**.......... MissPhillipaTutty(5) 1 66
(Karen Tutty) *trckd ldr: plld hrd: led 1/2-way: pushed along and hdd over 1f out: wknd ins fnl f* **10/1**

-003 5 *nk* **Honoured (IRE)**[12] 7441 4-9-9 **53**.................... MissCHenderson(7) 6 54
(Nicky Henderson) *plld hrd and prom: ev ch wl over 1f out: wknd ins fnl f* **8/1**[3]

3350 6 *nk* **Redhotdoc**[173] 2815 7-10-9 **65**.................... MrBJPoste(5) 8 66
(Bill Moore) *hld up: hdwy over 2f out: rdn and nt clr run over 1f out: styd on same pce* **20/1**

5366 7 *nse* **Leyte Gulf (USA)**[172] 2846 8-10-4 **60**.................... MrMTStanley(5) 3 61
(Chris Bealby) *s.i.s: hld up: rdn over 1f out: styd on ins fnl f: nt rch ldrs* **16/1**

0/61 8 *1 1/4* **Baan (USA)**[12] 7441 8-10-7 **63**.................... MissCAMadgin(5) 13 62
(James Eustace) *chsd ldrs: pushed along over 3f out: styd on same pce fnl 2f* **10/1**

0505 9 *nk* **Storm Hawk (IRE)**[59] 6503 4-10-4 **62** ow1.............(p) MissELOwen(7) 11 60
(Pat Eddery) *prom: racd keenly: ev ch over 2f out: edgd lft over 1f out: wknd fnl f* **10/1**

244- 10 *1* **Caracal**[4] 6855 4-9-13 **55**....................(b) MrKEdgar(5) 10 52
(Gordon Elliott, Ire) *s.i.s: hld up: nvr on terms* **12/1**

4500 11 *2 3/4* **Mustajed**[12] 7441 10-9-11 **53**....................(p) MrPMillman(5) 4 46
(Rod Millman) *hld up: n.d* **33/1**

005 12 *4 1/2* **Harrys Yer Man**[37] 7036 7-10-1 **57**.................. MissBeckyBrisbourne(5) 7 44
(Mark Brisbourne) *plld hrd and prom: wknd over 2f out* **10/1**

0000 13 *21* **Flag Of Glory**[10] 7458 4-10-6 **64**.................... MissMEdden(7) 9 21
(Peter Hiatt) *racd wd: led to 1/2-way: wknd over 2f out: t.o* **12/1**

3m 8.14s (2.14) **Going Correction** -0.025s/f (Stan)
WFA 3 from 4yo+ 8lb 13 Ran SP% **118.0**
Speed ratings (Par 101): **92,91,91,89,88 88,88,87,87,87 85,83,71**
toteswingers:1&2:£4.80, 2&3:£10.80, 1&3:£9.70 CSF £32.63 CT £269.54 TOTE £7.00: £2.20, £1.30, £3.80; EX 40.60 Trifecta £184.10 Part won. Pool: £248.83 - 0.30 winning units..
Owner Sarah Snell & Anne Devine **Bred** Juddmonte Farms Ltd **Trained** Epsom, Surrey
■ Stewards' Enquiry : Miss Becky Brisbourne five-day ban: used whip when out of contention (Dec 19, tbn)

FOCUS
A modest event for amateur riders and no reason to think it was a particularly strong contest for the level. There were no major hard-luck stories, though the gallop was on the steady side for much of the way and it didn't pay to sit too far back. The winner rates close to last winter's form and the second built on his latest turf win.

7565 WOLVERHAMPTON-RACECOURSE.CO.UK (S) STKS 7f 32y(P)

2:45 (2:45) (Class 6) 3-Y-O+ £1,704 (£503; £251) Stalls High

Form RPR

0002 1 **One Way Or Another (AUS)**[14] 7412 8-8-11 65......(bt) RaulDaSilva(7) 4 74
(Jeremy Gask) *trckd ldrs: racd keenly: nt clr run over 1f out: r.o to ld wl ins fnl f* **3/1**[2]

-000 2 *1* **Autumn Blades (IRE)**[18] 7352 6-9-4 88....................(b) JamesSullivan 6 72
(Ruth Carr) *hld up: hdwy over 2f out: led ins fnl f: sn rdn and hdd styd on same pce* **7/1**

0453 3 *shd* **Lovelace**[9] 7492 7-9-4 75....................(p) WilliamCarson 8 71
(Richard Fahey) *s.i.s: hdwy and nt clr run over 2f out: swtchd lft over 1f out: sn rdn: styd on* **13/8**[1]

5030 4 *2* **Desert Auction (IRE)**[24] 7269 4-8-13 60....................(b) GarryWhillans(5) 7 66
(Ian Semple) *chsd ldrs: led over 1f out: rdn and hdd ins fnl f: no ex* **16/1**

6060 5 *5* **Apache Ridge (IRE)**[14] 7412 5-9-10 71....................(p) JoeFanning 1 59
(Keith Dalgleish) *led 1f: chsd ldr: ev ch over 1f out: wknd ins fnl f* **15/2**

0324 6 *3 1/2* **Cootehill Lass (IRE)**[16] 7388 3-8-13 67..........(v[1]) MatthewCosham(5) 9 44
(David Evans) *hld up: rdn over 1f out: n.d* **5/1**[3]

6000 7 *1/2* **Bachelor Knight (IRE)**[14] 7412 3-9-3 56....................(t) DuranFentiman 5 42
(Suzzanne France) *led 6f out: rdn and hdd over 1f out: wknd fnl f* **40/1**

-600 8 *3* **Deveze (IRE)**[195] 2177 3-8-12 45....................(p) RichardKingscote 2 29
(Milton Bradley) *chsd ldrs: rdn over 2f out: sn wknd* **80/1**

9 *12* **Colonial Harry**[26] 4-9-4 0....................(p) AdamKirby 3 —
(Neil Mulholland) *s.i.s: sn pushed along in rr: rdn 4f out: wknd wl over 2f out* **66/1**

/00- 10 *15* **Square Of Gold (FR)**[507] 3853 5-9-4 41....................(t) ChrisCatlin 10 —
(Milton Bradley) *hld up: rdn and wknd over 2f out: t.o* **80/1**

1m 29.61s (0.01) **Going Correction** -0.025s/f (Stan)
WFA 3 from 4yo+ 1lb 10 Ran SP% **116.3**
Speed ratings (Par 101): **98,96,96,94,88 84,84,80,67,49**
toteswingers:1&2:£5.40, 2&3:£4.00, 1&3:£2.20 CSF £24.04 TOTE £3.00: £1.10, £2.90, £1.60; EX 27.10 Trifecta £89.20 Pool: £552.29 - 4.58 winning units..The winner was bought by J Babb for 5000gns.
Owner Rowley & The Sectionals **Bred** Segenho Stud **Trained** Sutton Veny, Wilts

FOCUS
A seller which was dominated by a trio who were very useful in their prime. It's hard to know quite what they are up to these days, and the level of the form is shaky.

7566 32RED.COM H'CAP (DIV I) 5f 20y(P)

3:20 (3:20) (Class 6) (0-65,65) 3-Y-O+ £1,704 (£503; £251) Stalls Low

Form RPR

4003 1 **Atlantic Beach**[16] 7395 6-9-7 **65**....................(b) LiamKeniry 1 75
(Milton Bradley) *chsd ldrs: n.m.r 1f out: rdn to ld wl ins fnl f* **5/1**[2]

2231 2 *3/4* **Bailadeira**[5] 7511 3-9-0 **61** 6ex.................... MichaelO'Connell(3) 10 68
(Tim Etherington) *led: rdn and hung lft over 1f out: hdd wl ins fnl f* **16/1**

4635 3 *1/2* **Novabridge**[87] 5675 3-9-2 **60**....................(p) AdamKirby 6 65
(Neil Mulholland) *chsd ldrs: rdn and hung lft ins fnl f: r.o* **16/1**

0422 4 *1/2* **Blown It (USA)**[16] 7395 5-9-7 **65**.................... JoeFanning 5 73+
(Keith Dalgleish) *sn pushed along in rr: hdwy 1/2-way: hmpd 1f out: r.o: nvr able to chal* **2/1**[1]

1400 5 *nse* **Divertimenti (IRE)**[35] 7057 7-9-0 **58**....................(b) RussKennemore 2 61
(Roy Bowring) *w ldr: rdn over 1f out: no ex towards fin* **9/1**

5115 6 *shd* **Vhujon (IRE)**[32] 7123 6-8-13 **57**.................... RobbieFitzpatrick 7 60
(Peter Grayson) *sn pushed along in rr: hdwy over 1f out: r.o* **33/1**

2034 7 *nk* **Pitkin**[108] 5009 3-9-5 **63**.................... PaddyAspell 9 65+
(Michael Easterby) *hld up: racd keenly: r.o ins fnl f: nt rch ldrs* **11/2**[3]

1016 8 *1/2* **Here Now And Why (IRE)**[24] 7266 4-9-0 **58**..........(p) RobertWinston 11 58
(Ian Semple) *hld up: r.o ins fnl f: nvr nrr* **10/1**

2212 9 *1 1/4* **Bateleur**[26] 7224 7-8-10 **59**.................... CharlesBishop(5) 13 54
(Mick Channon) *chsd ldrs: rdn over 1f out: styd on same pce* **17/2**

0006 10 *1 1/4* **Cruise Tothelimit (IRE)**[16] 7395 3-9-7 **65**.................... GrahamGibbons 8 56
(Mark Brisbourne) *plld hrd and prom: rdn over 1f out: wknd fnl f* **9/1**

0000 11 *11* **Bilko Pak (IRE)**[9] 7488 3-8-10 **59**....................(v) MarkCoumbe(5) 3 10
(Derek Shaw) *s.v.s: a wl bhd* **14/1**

61.96 secs (-0.34) **Going Correction** -0.025s/f (Stan) 11 Ran SP% **126.4**
Speed ratings (Par 101): **101,99,99,98,98 97,97,96,94,92 75**
toteswingers:1&2:£15.60, 2&3:£39.20, 1&3:£33.70 CSF £88.55 CT £1244.23 TOTE £6.20: £1.60, £3.60, £5.70; EX 93.60 Trifecta £289.30 Part won. Pool: £390.95 - 0.10 winning units..
Owner E A Hayward **Bred** D R Brotherton **Trained** Sedbury, Gloucs
■ Stewards' Enquiry : Michael O'Connell one-day ban: careless riding (Dec 12)

FOCUS
A run-of-the-mill sprint. It was sound run and the faster division. The winner built on his C&D latest to reverse form with the possibly unlucky favourite, and the second ran well under a penalty.
Here Now And Why(IRE) Official explanation: vet said gelding lost its near-fore shoe
Bilko Pak(IRE) Official explanation: trainer said gelding finished distressed

7567 32RED.COM H'CAP (DIV II) 5f 20y(P)

3:50 (3:50) (Class 6) (0-65,65) 3-Y-O+ £1,704 (£503; £251) Stalls Low

Form RPR

0051 1 **Perlachy**[24] 7266 7-9-2 **60**....................(v) LukeMorris 13 71
(Ronald Harris) *hld up: hdwy 2f out: rdn to ld 1f out: r.o* **18/1**

4510 2 *1 1/4* **Yungaburra (IRE)**[12] 7429 7-8-13 **57**....................(tp) FrannyNorton 12 64
(David C Griffiths) *s.i.s: hdwy over 1f out: nt clr run and swtchd rt ins fnl f: edgd lft: r.o wl* **20/1**

0335 3 *3/4* **Suddenly Susan (IRE)**[13] 7419 3-8-11 **58**....................(b) BillyCray(3) 7 63
(David Nicholls) *hld up in tch: rdn over 1f out: r.o* **13/2**

4-26 4 *nk* **Ability N Delivery**[45] 6849 6-9-5 **63**....................(p) ShaneKelly 2 67+
(Michael J Browne, Ire) *led 4f out: rdn and hdd 1f out: styd on same pce* **4/1**[2]

3562 5 *1 3/4* **Griffin Point (IRE)**[5] 7512 4-9-3 **61**.................... MartinHarley 4 59+
(William Muir) *led 1f: chsd ldrs: rdn over 1f out: no ex ins fnl f* **7/2**[1]

0154 6 *shd* **Howyadoingnotsobad (IRE)**[27] 7201 3-9-0 **58**........ TomMcLaughlin 1 56+
(Karen George) *chsd ldrs: hmpd and lost pl 1/2-way: n.d after* **5/1**[3]

3040 7 *2* **Atlantic Cycle (IRE)**[5] 7512 4-9-7 **65**.................... RichardKingscote 10 56
(Milton Bradley) *prom: hmpd wl over 1f out: wknd fnl f* **12/1**

000 8 *nk* **Almaty Express**[45] 6841 9-8-11 **60**....................(b) JustinNewman(5) 8 50
(John Weymes) *mid-div: hdwy 1/2-way: rdn over 1f out: wknd fnl f* **20/1**

3510 9 *1* **Cape Royal**[33] 7106 11-8-12 **56**....................(tp) DavidProbert 5 43
(Milton Bradley) *chsd ldrs: edgd rt wl over 1f out: wknd ins fnl f* **12/1**

6140 10 *1/2* **Bond Blade**[16] 7395 3-9-4 **62**.................... RobertWinston 9 48
(Geoffrey Oldroyd) *s.i.s: a in rr* **8/1**

0-60 11 *3 1/4* **Lady Brookie**[314] 198 3-9-1 **59**.................... RobbieFitzpatrick 6 34
(Peter Grayson) *s.i.s: a in rr* **100/1**

0155 12 *30* **Imogen Louise (IRE)**[297] 423 3-9-4 **65**.................... RobertLButler(3) 3 —
(Richard Guest) *chsd ldrs: rdn 1/2-way: sn wknd and eased: t.o* **50/1**

62.30 secs **Going Correction** -0.025s/f (Stan) 12 Ran SP% **116.5**
Speed ratings (Par 101): **99,97,95,95,92 92,89,88,87,86 81,33**
toteswingers:1&2:£11.80, 2&3:£18.00, 1&3:£18.30 CSF £333.73 CT £2610.38 TOTE £16.00: £4.50, £5.90, £2.20; EX 132.00 Trifecta £400.50 Part won. Pool: £541.35 - 0.50 winning units..
Owner Mrs N Macauley **Bred** J James **Trained** Earlswood, Monmouths
■ Stewards' Enquiry : Franny Norton one-day ban: careless riding (Dec 12)

FOCUS
The second division of this low-grade sprint. The pace was once again sound but the time was slower than division I. The first two came from the rear and the winner showed his best form of the past year.

7568 32RED CASINO (S) STKS 1m 1f 103y(P)

4:20 (4:20) (Class 6) 2-Y-O £1,704 (£503; £251) Stalls Low

Form RPR

0601 1 **Masters Club**[9] 7481 2-9-3 66.................... KirstyMilczarek 5 64
(John Ryan) *sn led: hdd over 7f out: chsd ldrs: led and edgd lft 2f out: rdn and hung lft ins fnl f: styd on* **3/1**[2]

004 2 *shd* **Dylans Verse (IRE)**[6] 7501 2-8-12 0....................(p) ChrisCatlin 3 60
(Reg Hollinshead) *chsd ldrs: pushed along and ev ch whn hmpd 2f out: rallied u.p and ev ch ins fnl f: styd on* **13/2**

643 3 *3 1/4* **Can Do Les (IRE)**[13] 7423 2-8-12 0.................... JoeFanning 6 53
(Keith Dalgleish) *edgd rt s: sn prom: rdn over 1f out: edgd lft: styd on same pce* **9/2**[3]

5446 4 *nse* **Jaci Uzzi (IRE)**[13] 7423 2-8-7 49....................(b[1]) AndreaAtzeni 7 48
(David Evans) *hmpd s: sn prom: led over 7f out: rdn: hdd and edgd rt 2f out: no ex ins fnl f* **20/1**

6 5 *nk* **Spartilla**[18] 7350 2-8-12 0.................... JamesSullivan 1 52
(James Given) *s.i.s: hdwy over 6f out: rdn over 3f out: styd on* **28/1**

0036 6 *2 1/4* **Angel Cake (IRE)**[14] 7414 2-8-7 54....................(b) MartinLane 8 43
(Amy Weaver) *hmpd s: hld up: rdn over 1f out: nvr trbld ldrs* **10/1**

003 7 *nse* **Seemples (IRE)**[9] 7481 2-8-9 58.................... KieranO'Neill(3) 2 48
(Richard Hannon) *chsd ldrs: rdn 3f out: wknd ins fnl f* **11/4**[1]

016 8 *11* **Artlana**[19] 7336 2-8-9 55.................... JulieBurke(3) 9 27
(Julie Camacho) *hmpd s: hld up: a in rr: bhd fnl 3f* **17/2**

5450 9 *7* **Ciara Boo (IRE)**[18] 7342 2-8-7 48....................(v) LukeMorris 10 8
(David Evans) *in rr and drvn along 7f out: bhd fnl 3f* **25/1**

2m 2.59s (0.89) **Going Correction** -0.025s/f (Stan) 9 Ran SP% **114.9**
Speed ratings (Par 94): **95,94,92,91,91 89,89,79,73**
CSF £22.01 TOTE £3.70: £1.90, £1.70, £1.90; EX 20.10 Trifecta £210.90 Pool: £598.70 - 2.10 winning units..There was no bid for the winner.
Owner Masters Stud & Partner **Bred** Bubble Media **Trained** Newmarket, Suffolk
■ Stewards' Enquiry : Kirsty Milczarek two-day ban: used whip with excessive frequency (Dec 12-13)
Chris Catlin four-day ban: used whip with excessive frequency (Dec 12-15)

FOCUS
Just modest form in this seller.

NOTEBOOK
Masters Club probably didn't have to improve to follow up his recent Lingfield win at this level, pulling out a bit more just when it looked as though the runner-up would swamp him late on. He's no pretensions to do much better but is clearly capable at a low level on Polytrack. (op 9-4)
Dylans Verse(IRE) had cheekpieces on and stepped up a little on his previous efforts dropped into a seller, rallying after getting outpaced, the longer trip clearly in his favour. He'll stay further still. (op 9-1)
Can Do Les(IRE) has now made the frame on all three starts at this level since coming over from Ireland buth there's no sign he's capable of much better, the longer trip not bringing about any improvement. (op 4-1)
Jaci Uzzi(IRE) ran one of her better races with blinkers on for the first time, but has had plenty of chances at this level now. (tchd 22-1)
Spartilla was quickly dropped in grade and at least showed a bit of ability this time. He's only had the two starts so it's clearly not out of the question there'll be a bit more to come. (op 33-1)
Seemples(IRE) seems very much one of his yard's lesser lights, beaten further by Masters Club than at Lingfield despite meeting him on 5lb better terms. (op 4-1)

7569 £32 FREE AT 32RED.COM NURSERY — 1m 141y(P)
4:50 (4:50) (Class 6) (0-65,65) 2-Y-O — **£1,704** (£503; £251) **Stalls** Low

Form / RPR

053 **1** **Maybeagrey**[27] 7210 2-9-2 **60** DuranFentiman 12 67+
(Tim Easterby) *a.p: led over 2f out: styd on wl* **10/1**[3]

004 **2** *2* **Frederickthegreat**[17] 7369 2-9-6 **64** (t) RichardKingscote 7 67+
(Hughie Morrison) *prom: lost pl over 6f out: hdwy over 2f out: sn rdn: styd on to go 2nd wl ins fnl f: no ch w wnr* **15/8**[1]

4002 **3** *1* **Dutchman's Field**[19] 7338 2-8-8 **52** GrahamGibbons 11 52
(David Nicholls) *sn led: rdn and hdd over 2f out: hung lft over 1f out: styd on same pce fnl f* **14/1**

134 **4** *hd* **Anginola (IRE)**[27] 7205 2-9-7 **65** PhillipMakin 1 64
(Joseph Tuite) *chsd ldrs: rdn over 2f out: styd on same pce fnl f* **11/4**[2]

6306 **5** *1* **Lady Heartbeat**[12] 7432 2-8-9 **53** FrankieMcDonald 2 50+
(Michael Blanshard) *hld up: hdwy over 2f out: rdn over 1f out: edgd rt ins fnl f: nt rch ldrs* **12/1**

0040 **6** *3 1/4* **Quixote**[18] 7342 2-8-13 **57** MartinLane 9 48
(Clive Brittain) *sn pushed along in rr: edgd lft and r.o ins fnl f: nrst fin* **28/1**

6160 **7** *1 1/4* **Enjoying (IRE)**[47] 6806 2-9-1 **62** (b) KieranO'Neill(3) 4 50
(Richard Hannon) *hld up: plld hrd: effrt over 2f out: nvr on terms* **16/1**

4000 **8** *3 1/2* **Rapid Heat Lad (IRE)**[60] 6487 2-9-1 **62** (t) PaulPickard(3) 8 43
(Reg Hollinshead) *hld up: rdn over 3f out: n.d* **16/1**

5006 **9** *1 1/4* **Rock On Candy**[11] 7444 2-9-5 **63** LiamKeniry 3 41
(Sylvester Kirk) *prom: rdn over 2f out: wknd over 1f out* **33/1**

6004 **10** *1/2* **Disco Sensation**[55] 6611 2-8-8 **55** BillyCray(3) 13 32
(David Nicholls) *s.i.s: hld up: rdn over 3f out: sn wknd* **40/1**

000 **11** *3/4* **Awesome Rock (IRE)**[48] 6768 2-8-7 **51** ChrisCatlin 5 26
(Louise Best) *chsd ldr tl rdn over 2f out: wknd wl over 1f out* **50/1**

6544 **12** *1 3/4* **Bogey Hole (IRE)**[30] 7177 2-9-2 **60** AndreaAtzeni 6 32
(Nikki Evans) *hld up: rdn over 2f out: sn wknd* **22/1**

000 **13** *18* **Ventus D'Or**[113] 4823 2-8-5 **49** NickyMackay 10 —
(Derek Shaw) *hld up: hdwy over 5f out: rdn and wknd over 2f out: t.o* **25/1**

1m 50.83s (0.33) **Going Correction** -0.025s/f (Stan) **13** Ran SP% **115.6**
Speed ratings (Par 94): **97,95,94,94,93 90,89,86,85,84 83,82,66**
toteswingers:1&2:£6.40, 2&3:£8.60, 1&3:£9.40 CSF £26.06 CT £271.03 TOTE £8.40: £3.10, £1.20, £3.80; EX 37.50 Trifecta £349.60 Pool: £472.55 - 1.00 winning units..
Owner Habton Farms **Bred** J K Beckitt And Son **Trained** Great Habton, N Yorks

FOCUS
Ordinary fare, though at least a couple of unexposed sorts came to the fore. The pace steadied in the back straight and it didn't pay to sit too far back, with the runner-up rated a shade better than the result in that regard.

NOTEBOOK
Maybeagrey got a bit better with each start in maidens and duly pulled out a bit more switched to a nursery. She was well placed the way things developed but saw it out well after her rider made his move on the turn and it'll be a surprise if there's not more to come. (op 9-1)
Frederickthegreat ran well on his first start try in a nursery and it'll be a surprise if he's not winning from this sort of mark before long, staying on nicely after ending up a little further back than ideal. (op 9-4 tchd 5-2)
Dutchman's Field ran his race after getting across from his wide stall to lead, but has had a few chances now and will always be vulnerable to less-exposed types in these events. (op 16-1)
Anginola(IRE) is consistent and made the frame again but her efforts since her Kempton success suggests the handicapper has her about right for now. (op 5-2)
Lady Heartbeat stayed on quite nicely at the finish and is one to bear in mind at a similar level as she's been a shade better than the result on both starts in nurseries now. (op 9-1)
Quixote has shown only a little ability so far, but had little chance of getting seriously involved given how far back he was entering the straight. (op 33-1)
Bogey Hole(IRE) Official explanation: trainer said filly pulled a tooth out prior to race

7570 CONNOLLY'S RED MILLS "PURE NUTRITION" H'CAP — 2m 119y(P)
5:20 (5:20) (Class 5) (0-75,76) 3-Y-O+ — **£2,264** (£673; £336; £168) **Stalls** Low

Form / RPR

3000 **1** **Wild Desert (FR)**[16] 7397 6-10-0 **75** AdamKirby 6 87
(Charlie Longsdon) *chsd ldr tl led over 5f out: rdn clr over 2f out: styd on u.p* **16/1**

25-1 **2** *3 1/2* **Priors Gold**[3] 7536 4-9-8 **76** 6ex BrendanPowell(7) 10 84
(Gordon Elliott, Ire) *hld up: nt clr run and swtchd rt over 3f out: hdwy over 2f out: styd on to go 2nd nr fin: nt rch wnr* **5/4**[1]

0633 **3** *hd* **Suzi's A Class Act**[14] 7415 3-8-9 **65** (p) LukeMorris 3 73
(James Eustace) *a.p: chsd wnr over 3f out: sn rdn: styd on: lost 2nd nr fin* **4/1**[3]

0004 **4** *8* **Admirable Duque (IRE)**[24] 7264 5-9-5 **73** (be) HarryPoulton(7) 8 71
(Dominic Ffrench Davis) *hld up: hdwy over 4f out: rdn: edgd lft and wknd over 1f out* **33/1**

-100 **5** *5* **Jasmeno**[32] 7120 4-9-9 **70** (t) RobertHavlin 9 62
(Hughie Morrison) *hld up: hdwy over 3f out: rdn and wknd 2f out* **8/1**

6003 **6** *3 1/2* **Lady of Burgundy**[39] 6976 5-9-6 **72** LeeNewnes(5) 11 60
(Mark Usher) *s.i.s: hld up and bhd: nvr nrr* **11/1**

2152 **7** *hd* **Boa**[2] 7556 6-9-1 **69** JackDuern(7) 7 57
(Reg Hollinshead) *chsd ldrs tl rdn and wknd 2f out* **5/2**[2]

5020 **8** *nk* **Hallstatt (IRE)**[14] 7413 5-9-2 **66** (t) MichaelO'Connell(3) 2 54
(John Mackie) *chsd ldrs: rdn over 3f out: wknd over 2f out* **33/1**

4600 **9** *10* **Dart**[14] 7415 7-9-4 **65** GrahamGibbons 12 41
(John Mackie) *stdd s: hld up and bhd: rdn over 4f out: sn wknd: t.o* **16/1**

0052 **10** *1/2* **Mecox Bay (IRE)**[19] 7340 4-8-9 **56** oh1 LiamJones 5 31
(Michael Appleby) *led 11f: chsd wnr tl rdn and wknd over 3f out: t.o* **7/1**

450- **11** *13* **Sounds Of Thunder**[16] 7402 4-8-13 **60** LiamKeniry 1 19
(Gordon Elliott, Ire) *hld up: rdn over 3f out: sn wknd: t.o* **8/1**

0026 **12** *7* **Dubara Reef (IRE)**[24] 7264 4-8-9 **56** oh2 (v) ChrisCatlin 4 —
(Paul Green) *prom: drvn along over 7f out: wknd over 6f out: t.o* **40/1**

3m 38.09s (-3.71) **Going Correction** -0.025s/f (Stan)
WFA 3 from 4yo+ 9lb **12** Ran SP% **156.2**
Speed ratings (Par 103): **107,105,105,101,99 97,97,97,92,92 86,82**
toteswingers:1&2:£11.20, 2&3:£3.00, 1&3:£14.10 CSF £47.52 CT £124.66 TOTE £21.20: £5.70, £1.50, £1.80; EX 88.80 Trifecta £317.60 Pool: £545.12 - 1.27 winning units..
Owner Whites Of Coventry & Stephen Dunn **Bred** Wertheimer Et Frere **Trained** Over Norton, Oxon

FOCUS
A staying event in which few really threatened to get competitive, with a few apparent gambles well wide of the mark. It was well run and the time was good for the grade. The winner's best form in Britain, and the second's best on the Flat.

7571 32REDBET.COM H'CAP — 1m 1f 103y(P)
5:50 (5:52) (Class 6) (0-55,55) 3-Y-O+ — **£1,704** (£503; £251) **Stalls** Low

Form / RPR

0000 **1** **Barton Bounty**[16] 7400 4-9-0 **53** TomEaves 11 62+
(Peter Niven) *mid-div: hdwy over 2f out: rdn to ld and edgd lft wl ins fnl f: r.o* **16/1**

3240 **2** *1 3/4* **Flying Applause**[13] 7424 6-9-1 **54** (bt) RussKennemore 13 59
(Roy Bowring) *led: rdn and hdd over 2f out: styd on u.p* **8/1**

4402 **3** *nk* **Idol Deputy (FR)**[10] 7466 5-8-4 **50** RachealKneller(7) 10 54
(Mark Usher) *a.p: chsd ldr 6f out: led over 2f out: rdn and hdd wl ins fnl f* **11/2**[3]

5653 **4** *1 1/4* **Baby Driver**[24] 7271 3-8-10 **52** (t) RichardKingscote 7 54
(Tom Dascombe) *hld up: hdwy over 2f out: rdn over 1f out: nt rch ldrs* **9/1**

450 **5** *1* **Think**[35] 7063 4-8-13 **52** PaddyAspell 4 52
(Clive Mulhall) *prom: rdn over 2f out: sn outpcd: styd on u.p fnl f* **22/1**

2651 **6** *3/4* **Queenie's Star (IRE)**[10] 7466 4-8-7 **51** MarkCoumbe(5) 2 49
(Michael Attwater) *hld up: hdwy u.p over 1f out: nt trble ldrs* **9/1**

3030 **7** *1* **Corrib (IRE)**[24] 7263 8-9-2 **55** (p) LukeMorris 1 51
(Bryn Palling) *hld up: hdwy u.p over 1f out: nt trble ldrs* **16/1**

6626 **8** *1/2* **Excellent Vision**[17] 7370 4-9-2 **55** (t) LiamKeniry 8 50
(Milton Bradley) *hld up: rdn over 1f out: edgd lft: nvr trbld ldrs* **20/1**

0003 **9** *3 3/4* **Jibouti (IRE)**[3] 7538 3-8-10 **52** (b) MartinLane 9 39
(Clive Brittain) *chsd ldrs: rdn over 2f out: wknd fnl f* **5/1**[2]

435 **10** *8* **Yellow Printer**[33] 7096 5-9-1 **54** (b) AdamKirby 3 24
(Mark Gillard) *prom: pushed along 1/2-way: nt clr run and lost pl over 3f out: wknd over 2f out* **7/2**[1]

3500 **11** *11* **Duneen Dream (USA)**[38] 7003 6-9-0 **53** AndreaAtzeni 6 —
(Nikki Evans) *chsd ldrs tl rdn and wknd 2f out* **20/1**

0000 **12** *19* **Ruler's Honour (IRE)**[72] 6156 4-8-10 **52** ow2 (p) MichaelO'Connell(3) 12 —
(Tim Etherington) *s.s: a in rr: t.o* **50/1**

0040 **13** *5* **Lady Morganna (IRE)**[140] 3926 3-8-12 **54** KirstyMilczarek 5 —
(Olivia Maylam) *pushed along and prom: rdn over 3f out: sn wknd: t.o* **40/1**

2m 1.26s (-0.44) **Going Correction** -0.025s/f (Stan)
WFA 3 from 4yo+ 3lb **13** Ran SP% **115.4**
Speed ratings (Par 101): **100,98,98,97,96 95,94,94,90,83 73,57,52**
toteswingers:1&2:£36.10, 2&3:£8.50, 1&3:£22.90 CSF £124.85 CT £802.18 TOTE £23.40: £6.10, £2.80, £2.20; EX 235.40 TRIFECTA Not won..
Owner Francis Green Racing Ltd **Bred** Mrs M L Parry **Trained** Barton-le-Street, N Yorks

FOCUS
Another modest handicap, though it was at least well run. The winner rates back to his spring form.
Queenie's Star(IRE) Official explanation: jockey said filly never travelled
Yellow Printer Official explanation: jockey said gelding stopped quickly
T/Jkpt: Not won. T/Plt: £350.70 to a £1 stake. Pool of £95,249.39 - 198.22 winning tickets. T/Qpdt: £120.50 to a £1 stake. Pool of £6,782.31 - 41.64 winning tickets. CR

7562 HOLLYWOOD PARK (L-H)
Monday, November 28
OFFICIAL GOING: Turf: firm

7572a HOLLYWOOD DERBY (GRADE 1) (3YO) (TURF) — 1m 2f
12:37 (12:00) 3-Y-O — **£96,153** (£32,051; £19,230; £9,615; £3,205)

RPR

1 **Ultimate Eagle (USA)**[43] 3-8-10 0 (b) MPedroza 11 117
(Michael Pender, U.S.A) *mde all: qcknd whn chal over 2f out: r.o wl fnl f* **147/10**

2 *3/4* **Imagining (USA)** 3-8-10 0 JJCastellano 2 115
(Claude McGaughey III, U.S.A) *plld early: trckd ldr: tried to chal over 2f out: sn rdn: r.o fnl f: a hld by wnr* **135/10**

3 *1/2* **Western Aristocrat (USA)**[51] 6716 3-8-10 0 CNakatani 4 114
(Jeremy Noseda) *w.w in midfield: rdn and effrt outside rivals ins fnl 2f: r.o between horses fnl f: tk 3rd cl home* **97/10**[3]

4 *nk* **Slumber**[30] 7170 3-8-10 0 GKGomez 3 113+
(Charles Hills) *hld up towards rr: hdwy over 2 1/2f out: c wd into st: r.o wl fnl f: nrest at fin* **39/10**[2]

5 *1* **Venomous**[43] 3-8-10 0 JRosario 6 111
(Leonard Powell, U.S.A) *settled towards rr hdwy on ins to go 3rd ins fnl 2f: kpt on wout able to qckn fnl 100yds: lost two pls cl home* **17/5**[1]

6 *hd* **Casino Host (USA)**[51] 6716 3-8-10 0 JTalamo 5 111
(Chad C Brown, U.S.A) *hld up in midfield: rdn over 2f out: kpt on fnl f: nt pce to chal* **163/10**

7 *nse* **Cozy Kitten (USA)**[43] 3-8-10 0 (b) AQuinonez 10 111
(Wesley A Ward, U.S.A) *racd in midfield: 6th and scrubbed along over 3f out: sn rdn: nt qckn fnl 1 1/2f* **12/1**

8 *2 1/4* **Willcox Inn (USA)**[44] 3-8-10 0 (b) RAlbarado 12 106
(Michael Stidham, U.S.A) *hld up towards rr: shortlived effrt on outside 2f out: sn rdn and no imp* **17/5**[1]

9 *3/4* **Irish Art (USA)** 3-8-10 0 RBejarano 9 105
(Carla Gaines, U.S.A) *chsd ldrs: rdn and wknd ins fnl 2 1/2f* **125/10**

10 *26* **Surrey Star (IRE)**[43] 3-8-10 0 ChantalSutherland 7 53
(James Cassidy, U.S.A) *chsd ldr: wknd u.p ent fnl 2f: eased last f: fin lame* **54/1**

P **Cloud Man (USA)**[43] 3-8-10 0 MESmith 1 —
(John Shirreffs, U.S.A) *midfield: p.u lame 3f out* **11/1**

2m 1.43s (121.43) **11** Ran SP% **119.5**
PARI-MUTUEL (all including $2 stakes): WIN 31.40; PLACE (1-2) 13.00, 14.60; SHOW (1-2-3) 7.60, 10.80, 8.20; DF 261.00; SF 556.00.
Owner B J Wright **Bred** B P Walden & D Hanley **Trained** North America

The Form Book, Raceform Ltd, Compton, RG20 6NL

[7518]LINGFIELD (L-H)

Tuesday, November 29

OFFICIAL GOING: Standard

Wind: Very strong, behind Weather: Overcast

7573 TANDRIDGE AMATEUR RIDERS' H'CAP (DIV I) 2m (P)
12:10 (12:10) (Class 6) (0-60,60) 3-Y-O+ **£1,646** (£506; £253) **Stalls** Low

Form RPR

313/ **1** **Participation**[188] 3488 8-10-9 **55** .... MrSWalker 4 64
(Laura Young) *hld up wl in tch: prog to go 2nd over 3f out w rdr looking arnd: led over 2f out and kicked on: drvn out to hold on fnl f* **12/1**

3300 **2** *3/4* **Holden Eagle**[28] 7206 6-10-6 **52** .... MissSBrotherton 5 60
(Tony Newcombe) *stdd s: hld up in rr but wl in tch: prog over 3f out: chsd wnr 2f out: clsd fnl f: nvr quite got there* **2/1**[1]

0554 **3** *6* **Carnac (IRE)**[14] 7426 5-9-12 **51** .... (p) MissDLenge(7) 2 52
(Alan McCabe) *cl up: led 7f out to over 2f out: sn outpcd* **3/1**[2]

6400 **4** *3* **Carlton Scroop (FR)**[13] 7441 8-10-6 **57** .... (b) MissMBryant(5) 9 54
(Paddy Butler) *t.k.h: led at modest pce for 3f: shuffled bk in rr after 7f: effrt on outer over 3f out: disp 2nd and wd bnd 2f out: sn btn* **12/1**

0-00 **5** *6* **Dazzling Begum**[19] 7357 6-9-11 **48** .... (bt) MrOGarner(5) 3 38
(Des Donovan) *cl up on inner: pushed along over 3f out: sn outpcd: no ch over 2f out* **16/1**

0030 **6** *6* **Chantilly Dancer (IRE)**[28] 7206 5-9-9 **46** oh1 .... MissJoeyEllis(5) 10 29
(Michael Quinn) *led after 3f to 7f out: wknd 3f out* **25/1**

0000 **7** *11* **Cragganmore Creek**[13] 7441 8-9-9 **46** oh1 .... (p) MrBMMorris(5) 6 16
(Dave Morris) *prog on outer to go prom after 6f: pushed along and wknd over 5f out: t.o* **25/1**

1200 **8** *6* **Herrera (IRE)**[49] 6780 6-10-7 **60** .... MrSAHuggan(7) 1 22
(Richard Fahey) *trckd ldrs: pushed along and wknd 4f out: t.o* **4/1**[3]

3m 30.68s (4.98) **Going Correction** +0.075s/f (Slow) **8** Ran SP% **107.3**

Speed ratings (Par 101): **90,89,86,85,82 79,73,70**

toteswingers:1&2:£6.70, 2&3:£1.40, 1&3:£4.30 CSF £31.94 CT £78.80 TOTE £11.90: £3.50, £1.30, £1.20; EX 48.20 Trifecta £195.20 Pool: £411.55 - 1.56 winning units..

Owner Mrs Laura Young **Bred** Juddmonte Farms Ltd **Trained** Broomfield, Somerset

■ Celtic Charlie was withdrawn after proving unruly in the stalls (14/1, deduct 5p in the £ under R4).

FOCUS

A dreadful contest in terms of quality, but another chance for jockeyship to shine and the finish was dominated by the two most successful riders in the race. They went no pace at all early and the form looks weak, rated around the runner-up.

7574 TANDRIDGE AMATEUR RIDERS' H'CAP (DIV II) 2m (P)
12:40 (12:41) (Class 6) (0-60,59) 3-Y-O+ **£1,646** (£506; £253) **Stalls** Low

Form RPR

0033 **1** **Galiotto (IRE)**[20] 7331 5-10-4 **54** .... (v) MissHayleyMoore(5) 8 64
(Gary Moore) *hld up: prog to trck ldng pair 6f out: clr of rest 4f out: wnt 2nd over 2f out: plld out and led over 1f out: drvn clr* **9/4**[1]

3014 **2** *7* **Henry Holmes**[20] 7331 8-10-5 **50** .... MrSWalker 9 52
(Lydia Richards) *trckd ldrs: led over 6f out: rdn and hdd over 1f out: no ch w wnr after* **5/2**[2]

2/50 **3** *4 1/2* **Bring It On Home**[61] 6486 7-10-0 **52** .... (b) MissSKerswell(7) 5 48
(Brendan Powell) *prom bhd clr ldr: lost pl 6f out: outpcd 4f out: n.d after: styd on to take 3rd fnl 100yds* **16/1**

4 *2 1/4* **Marching Orders (IRE)**[85] 3332 4-9-9 **45** .... MrFTett(5) 7 39
(Natalie Lloyd-Beavis) *in tch: outpcd by ldng trio 4f out: n.d after: plugged on fnl f* **11/1**

0006 **5** *1/2* **William's Way**[66] 6356 9-10-9 **57** .... (t) MrCMartin(3) 3 50
(Ian Wood) *hld up: prog to press ldr 6f out: rdn 4f out: styd cl up tl wknd qckly 2f out: lost 2 pls fnl 100yds* **3/1**[3]

0050 **6** *1 3/4* **Warrior Nation (FR)**[38] 5785 5-9-11 **45** .... MissLMasterton(3) 6 36
(Adrian Chamberlain) *wl in tch: outpcd by ldng trio 4f out: nvr on terms after* **100/1**

0000 **7** *60* **Ourlaugh Mountain**[40] 6968 7-9-10 **46** ow1 .... MissMBryant(5) 2 —
(Paddy Butler) *chsd ldr to over 6f out: lost pl qckly: wl t.o* **50/1**

0/06 **8** *12* **Sioux City Sue**[18] 7360 5-10-0 **45** .... (p) MissEJJones 10 —
(Jim Boyle) *t.k.h: led and sn clr: 15 l up after 6f: wknd and hdd over 6f out: wl t.o* **25/1**

3m 29.44s (3.74) **Going Correction** +0.075s/f (Slow)

WFA 3 from 4yo+ 9lb **8** Ran SP% **105.4**

Speed ratings (Par 101): **93,89,87,86,85 85,56,50**

toteswingers:1&2:£1.40, 2&3:£5.40, 1&3:£4.90 CSF £6.68 CT £49.76 TOTE £3.30: £1.20, £1.30, £4.00; EX 6.60 Trifecta £51.20 Pool: £439.03 - 6.34 winning units..

Owner Andrew Bradmore **Bred** Ballintaggart Syndicate **Trained** Lower Beeding, W Sussex

FOCUS

Probably an even worse line-up than the first division with half the field officially rated less than 45, so effectively out of the handicap. However, this was run at a much faster tempo thanks to Sioux City Sue bolting into a clear advantage, and the winning time was 1.24 seconds faster. The form is best rated around the first two.

7575 MARSH GREEN CLAIMING STKS 5f (P)
1:10 (1:10) (Class 6) 3-Y-O+ **£1,704** (£503; £251) **Stalls** High

Form RPR

1006 **1** **Deerslayer (USA)**[10] 7487 5-8-9 80 .... (p) MartinHarley 1 85
(Amy Weaver) *fast away fr ins draw: mde all: drvn and edgd rt fr over 1f out: hld on* **5/1**

0020 **2** *nk* **Le Toreador**[10] 7489 6-9-0 88 .... (bt) PhillipMakin 7 89
(Kevin Ryan) *racd on outer: pressed ldrs: wnt 2nd wl over 1f out: chal and carried sltly rt fnl f: nt qckn last 50yds* **5/2**[1]

4035 **3** *1* **Drawnfromthepast (IRE)**[45] 6875 6-9-1 92 .... FrannyNorton 5 86
(Jamie Osborne) *chsd ldng trio: rdn 2f out: tried to cl fnl f: nt qckn last 150yds: b.b.v* **3/1**[2]

5043 **4** *1* **Forty Proof (IRE)**[50] 6752 3-8-3 78 .... (p) KieranO'Neill(3) 3 74
(Alan McCabe) *chsd ldrs disputing 5th: effrt on inner wl over 1f out: kpt on same pce* **8/1**

6562 **5** *1 1/4* **Osiris Way**[33] 7116 9-8-9 77 .... JimCrowley 8 72
(Patrick Chamings) *dwlt fr wdst stall: chsd ldng quartet: reminder over 1f out: styd on same pce: nvr chal* **7/2**[3]

0005 **6** *1* **Vitznau (IRE)**[15] 7412 7-8-1 67 .... JemmaMarshall(5) 2 66
(Alastair Lidderdale) *dwlt: outpcd in last: styd on fr over 1f out: nrst fin* **25/1**

0000 **7** *1 1/2* **Lesley's Choice**[19] 7352 5-8-11 67 .... (p) ChrisCatlin 6 65
(Paul Rich) *chsd wnr to wl over 1f out: wknd* **50/1**

0006 **8** *6* **Emerald Royal**[13] 7429 3-8-5 46 .... (t) JimmyQuinn 4 38
(Edward Creighton) *s.i.s: outpcd in last pair: a bhd* **100/1**

57.79 secs (-1.01) **Going Correction** +0.075s/f (Slow) **8** Ran SP% **110.4**

Speed ratings (Par 101): **111,110,108,107,105 103,101,91**

toteswingers:1&2:£3.10, 2&3:£2.00, 1&3:£3.20 CSF £16.59 TOTE £3.90: £1.10, £2.10, £1.80; EX 19.00 Trifecta £50.50 Pool: £406.43 - 5.95 winning units..

Owner Wildcard Racing Syndicate **Bred** Bjorn Nielsen **Trained** Newmarket, Suffolk

FOCUS

Probably not a bad claimer with the top weight officially rated 92 and the pace was always going to be decent. With doubts over one or two the form is rated cautiously through the winner.

7576 MIRROR PUNTERS CLUB NURSERY 1m (P)
1:45 (1:45) (Class 4) (0-85,80) 2-Y-O **£4,204** (£1,251; £625; £312) **Stalls** High

Form RPR

2161 **1** **Emmuska**[13] 7436 2-9-0 **76** .... KieranO'Neill(3) 4 81
(Richard Hannon) *mde all: dictated mod pce to 1/2-way: kicked on and pressed over 2f out: rdn 2 l clr 1f out: styd on* **13/8**[1]

2311 **2** *3/4* **Tones (IRE)**[10] 7491 2-9-6 **79** .... JimmyFortune 1 82
(Richard Hannon) *trckd ldrs: effrt 2f out: drvn to take 2nd 1f out: styd on but nvr getting to wnr* **11/4**[2]

0201 **3** *2 1/4* **Ocean Tempest**[11] 7454 2-9-7 **80** .... KirstyMilczarek 6 78
(John Ryan) *trckd wnr to 1/2-way: rdn and nt qckn 2f out: kpt on one pce after* **7/2**[3]

5034 **4** *1 3/4* **Abshir Zain (IRE)**[20] 7337 2-8-5 **64** .... (bt) MartinLane 3 58
(Clive Brittain) *cl up: prog to chse wnr 1/2-way: rdn to chal over 2f out: nt qckn over 1f out: sn lost 2nd and wknd* **9/1**

1304 **5** *1 3/4* **Singalat**[10] 7483 2-9-5 **78** .... TomQueally 2 68
(James Given) *hld up in last: rdn sn after 1/2-way: lost tch and wl bhd over 2f out: keeping on at fin* **9/1**

1m 38.96s (0.76) **Going Correction** +0.075s/f (Slow) **5** Ran SP% **107.0**

Speed ratings (Par 98): **99,98,96,94,92**

CSF £5.90 TOTE £2.40: £1.10, £1.10; EX 4.30.

Owner Martin A Collins **Bred** Martin A Collins **Trained** East Everleigh, Wilts

FOCUS

A fair nursery, though the early pace was ordinary. It resulted in a 1-2 for Richard Hannon.

NOTEBOOK

Emmuska was 3lb higher than for her game success over C&D 13 days earlier, but she had the run of the race out in front and quickened up smartly to clear away from her rivals inside the last furlong. She had more in hand over her stable-companion than the winning margin would suggest and is a filly on the up. (tchd 6-4 and 7-4)

Tones(IRE), bidding for a hat-trick off a 3lb higher mark, was trying this trip for the first time though this wouldn't have tested his stamina thoroughly. Making headway against the inside rail over a furlong out, he stayed on under pressure when switched to his right but is flattered by the winning margin. (op 5-2)

Ocean Tempest, making his nursery debut after narrowly winning a Kempton maiden over this trip, proved a bit of a handful in the preliminaries but had every chance in the race itself and failed to quicken for pressure. (op 4-1)

Abshir Zain(IRE) found the drop to 6f against him last time, but although right alongside the winner in the middle part of the contest he didn't get home. A return to 7f may help, but he isn't progressing. (op 14-1)

Singalat, another trying this trip for the first time, was beaten a long way from home. (op 8-1)

7577 HINDLEAP H'CAP 1m 4f (P)
2:15 (2:15) (Class 4) (0-80,80) 3-Y-O+ **£4,204** (£1,251; £625; £312) **Stalls** Low

Form RPR

3104 **1** **Where's Susie**[33] 7120 6-9-5 **75** .... DaneO'Neill 9 82
(Michael Madgwick) *hld up towards rr: prog on outer over 2f out: drvn and r.o fr over 1f out: led last 50yds* **10/1**

2423 **2** *nk* **Reem Star**[39] 7002 3-9-1 **77** .... PhillipMakin 1 83
(Kevin Ryan) *trckd ldr 4f: styd prom: rdn 3f out: styd on over 1f out: tk 2nd nr fin* **11/2**[3]

0002 **3** *hd* **Pittodrie Star (IRE)**[44] 6893 4-9-9 **79** .... (v1) DavidProbert 7 85
(Andrew Balding) *led at mod pce: fnlly kicked on over 2f out: styd on inner in st: hdd and no ex last 50yds* **5/1**[2]

0260 **4** *nk* **Strike Force**[17] 7397 7-8-10 **69** .... (t) AdamBeschizza(3) 8 75
(Clifford Lines) *hld up in last pair: plenty to do whn pce lifted over 2f out: wl over 1f out: styd on fnl f: gaining at fin* **25/1**

0441 **5** *1/2* **Beat Route**[11] 7458 4-8-8 **69** .... JemmaMarshall(5) 3 74
(Michael Attwater) *t.k.h: trckd ldr after 4f: rdn to chal over 2f out: upsides over 1f out: nt qckn and lost pl fnl f* **10/1**

6411 **6** *nse* **Green Wadi**[33] 7130 6-9-8 **78** .... (p) TomQueally 10 83
(Gary Moore) *hld up in last pair: plenty to do whn pce qcknd over 2f out: effrt on inner over 1f out: styd on but nvr cl enough to chal* **6/1**

3141 **7** *1/2* **Alshazah**[26] 7255 3-9-4 **80** .... JamesMillman 4 84
(Rod Millman) *hld up in midfield: rdn and nt qckn over 2f out: one pce and no imp over 1f out* **5/2**[1]

1-50 **8** *shd* **Dubai Bounty**[62] 6439 4-9-7 **80** .... (tp) KieranO'Neill(3) 6 84
(Gerard Butler) *t.k.h early: trckd ldrs: rdn over 2f out: nt qckn wl over 1f out: kpt on same pce after* **11/1**

6634 **9** *hd* **Dazzling Valentine**[11] 7461 3-8-9 **74** .... AmyBaker(3) 5 77
(Alan Bailey) *hld up in rr: prog fr 1/2-way to go prom 4f out: rdn to chal in cl 3rd 2f out: nt qckn over 1f out: lost pl sn after* **16/1**

0151 **10** *19* **Bennelong**[19] 7346 5-9-0 **70** .... AmirQuinn 11 43
(Richard Rowe) *trckd ldrs: lost pl over 3f out: wknd over 2f out: t.o* **14/1**

2m 33.78s (0.78) **Going Correction** +0.075s/f (Slow)

WFA 3 from 4yo+ 6lb **10** Ran SP% **117.8**

Speed ratings (Par 105): **100,99,99,99,99 99,98,98,98,85**

toteswingers:1&2:£10.00, 2&3:£5.20, 1&3:£11.40 CSF £64.84 CT £313.28 TOTE £15.20: £4.50, £2.50, £2.10; EX 78.40 Trifecta £410.50 Part won. Pool: £554.84 - 0.20 winning units..

Owner Recycled Products Limited **Bred** Mrs L R Burrage **Trained** Denmead, Hants

FOCUS

They didn't go much of a pace early on here and it resulted in nine of the ten runners finishing within about 3l of each other at the line. Strangely though, the first three home had all proved themselves over further. The form is muddling with the placed horses the best guides.

7578 FELBRIDGE H'CAP 6f (P)
2:50 (2:50) (Class 2) (0-100,100) 3-Y-O+ **£10,350** (£3,080; £1,539; £769) **Stalls** Low

Form RPR

0603 **1** **Capone (IRE)**[13] 7433 6-8-13 **92** .... ShaneKelly 3 101+
(David Nicholls) *hld up in last trio: plenty to do 2f out: nt clr run over 1f out: eased rt and shkn up jst ins fnl f: r.o strly to ld last strides* **9/2**[1]

1020 **2** *hd* **Dickie's Lad (IRE)**[51] 6723 3-8-9 **88** .... (t) TonyHamilton 11 96
(Kevin Ryan) *led: rdn over 1f out: kpt on wl fnl f: hdd last strides* **15/2**

0540 **3** *1 1/4* **What About You (IRE)**[10] 7489 3-8-7 **86** oh3 .... BarryMcHugh 6 90
(Richard Fahey) *chsd ldng pair: rdn to chse wnr fnl f: no imp: lost 2nd nr fin* **16/1**

0006 **4** *1* **Thunderball**[13] 7433 5-8-9 **88**......(b) LukeMorris 7 89
(David Nicholls) *chsd ldng trio: hrd rdn over 1f out: styd on same pce fnl f* **14/1**

0202 **5** *nse* **Secret Witness**[17] 7392 5-9-7 **100**......(b) JoeFanning 1 101
(Ronald Harris) *chsd ldng quartet: effrt towards inner over 1f out: styd on: nt gng pce to chal* **6/1**[2]

4460 **6** *hd* **Norville (IRE)**[17] 7392 4-8-11 **95**......(b) MatthewCosham(5) 10 95
(David Evans) *sn chsd ldr: drvn and nt qckn over 1f out: sn lost pl and btn* **12/1**

1061 **7** *3/4* **Elna Bright**[10] 7489 6-9-2 **95**...... JimmyQuinn 4 93
(Peter Crate) *hld up in midfield: disputing 6th over 2f out: shkn up over 1f out: carried sltly rt ins fnl f: styd on last 100yds: no ch to threaten* **15/2**

6304 **8** *nk* **Cochabamba (IRE)**[17] 7392 3-9-1 **94**...... JohnFahy 2 91
(Roger Teal) *urged along leaving stalls: towards rr: 8th 1/2-way: drvn and one pce fnl 2f* **13/2**[3]

3330 **9** *hd* **Five Star Junior (USA)**[17] 7392 5-9-4 **97**...... JamesSullivan 8 93
(Linda Stubbs) *sn towards rr: 9th 1/2-way: effrt over 1f out: carried sltly rt ins fnl f: kpt on: n.d* **14/1**

000 **10** *nse* **Piscean (USA)**[38] 7018 6-9-1 **94**...... JimmyFortune 5 90
(Tom Keddy) *hld up in last trio: effrt 2f out and c to outer early in st: carried sltly rt ins fnl f: kpt on one pce* **10/1**

0250 **11** *4 1/2* **Arganil (USA)**[74] 6112 6-9-4 **97**......(p) PhillipMakin 12 79
(Kevin Ryan) *hld up in last trio: urged along on outer over 2f out: no prog and sn btn* **20/1**

-200 **12** *nk* **Dozy Joe**[144] 3820 3-8-9 **88**......(bt[1]) DaneO'Neill 9 69
(Ian Wood) *nvr bttr than midfield: rdn and wknd wl over 1f out* **14/1**

1m 10.15s (-1.75) **Going Correction** +0.075s/f (Slow) course record**12** Ran SP% **116.8**
Speed ratings (Par 109): **114,113,112,110,110 110,109,109,108,108 102,102**
toteswingers:1&2:£7.70, 2&3:£25.30, 1&3:£13.00 CSF £36.80 CT £503.87 TOTE £3.80: £1.40, £3.00, £5.90; EX 41.70 TRIFECTA Not won..
Owner Brooklands Racing **Bred** S J Macdonald **Trained** Sessay, N Yorks

FOCUS
A hot sprint handicap, run at a strong pace. Although most of the principals raced handily from the start, the winner came from well back. The form looks sound with the winner rated to his old best and the runner-up to his turf form.

NOTEBOOK
Capone(IRE) ran well against higher-rated rivals in a 7f conditions event at Kempton last time, but this is his best trip. Ridden with plenty of confidence, he still had plenty to do starting up the home straight, but once switched right for his effort he flew home as though his rivals were standing still. He was the only one to make any impact at all from off the pace so this effort can be marked up. (op 5-1)
Dickie's Lad(IRE), making his all-weather debut, tried to make every yard from his wide draw and looked like doing so until the winner swamped him close to the line. He remains lightly raced and had no problem with the surface, so compensation surely awaits. (op 10-1)
What About You(IRE), beaten a long way when favourite for Elna Bright's race at Wolverhampton last time, had it to do from 3lb out of the weights but proved that last effort to be all wrong. Never far off the pace, he kept on going close to the inside rail all the way to the line and the removal of the blinkers didn't do him any harm. A stiffer 6f may suit him better, however. (op 20-1 tchd 14-1)
Thunderball loves Polytrack, but has found life tough in recent months. He finished well behind Capone at Kempton last time, but this was much better having always been in about the same place. (tchd 16-1)
Secret Witness ran a cracker when beaten a head in a Listed event over C&D last time (three of these behind), but was rewarded with a 6lb rise in his mark, making him 10lb higher than when last successful in a handicap. He was always in about the same place, but couldn't quicken and may not be easy to place now.
Norville(IRE), in cracking form over C&D at the start of the year and most progressive on turf since, beat only one home in that Listed event here last time, but performed much better back in handicap company and was only shaken off well inside the last furlong. He is 27lb higher than for his last win here, but you wouldn't bet against him defying this sort of mark. (op 16-1)
Elna Bright, 5lb higher than when making a winning debut for the yard at Wolverhampton last time, could only stay on at one pace and may need a stiffer 6f than this. (op 6-1)
Cochabamba(IRE) didn't run as well as she did in that Listed race here last time and remains winless since her racecourse debut. (tchd 6-1 and 7-1)

7579 GOAT CROSS H'CAP — 7f (P)
3:20 (3:20) (Class 5) (0-70,71) 3-Y-O+ **£2,385** (£704; £352) **Stalls** Low

Form RPR

0220 **1** **Forks**[10] 7485 4-9-0 **63**...... LukeMorris 7 74
(Jane Chapple-Hyam) *hld up in midfield on outer: rdn 3f out: prog over 2f out: drvn and r.o to ld jst ins fnl f: styd on* **10/1**

3231 **2** *1/2* **Chokidar (IRE)**[26] 7249 3-9-6 **70**......(b) TomQueally 3 80
(David Nicholls) *sn trckd ldng pair: clsd to ld over 1f out: edgd rt and hdd jst ins fnl f: nt qckn* **4/1**[1]

6032 **3** *1 1/4* **My Learned Friend (IRE)**[65] 6378 7-9-5 **68**...... DavidProbert 2 74
(Andrew Balding) *wl in tch bhd ldrs: cl up 2f out: rdn over 1f out: styd on to take 3rd ins fnl f: unable to chal* **12/1**

5654 **4** *shd* **Eager To Bow (IRE)**[10] 7485 5-9-0 **63**...... JimCrowley 14 69
(Patrick Chamings) *stdd s: dropped in fr wdst draw and hld up wl in rr: effrt over 2f out: styd on fr over 1f out: nrst fin* **9/1**

2011 **5** *1/2* **Bold Ring**[6] 7524 5-8-12 **61**...... JimmyQuinn 6 66
(Edward Creighton) *hld up in midfield on inner: prog 2f out: tried to chal 1f out: one pce* **7/1**[2]

4521 **6** *1 3/4* **Pipers Piping (IRE)**[4] 7537 5-9-8 **71** 6ex......(p) JimmyFortune 11 71
(Alastair Lidderdale) *plld hrd: hld up wl in rr: effrt and hanging 2f out: kpt on fnl f: n.d* **15/2**[3]

011 **7** *nk* **Shelagh (IRE)**[10] 7484 3-9-4 **68**...... DaneO'Neill 9 67
(Jo Crowley) *hld up in rr: effrt 2f out: rdn and kpt on fr over 1f out: nt gng pce to threaten* **4/1**[1]

0010 **8** *nse* **Mountrath**[12] 7447 4-9-5 **68**......(v) AdamKirby 5 67
(Gary Moore) *towards rr: rdn on inner 3f out: tried to chal over 1f out: nt gng pce to threaten* **16/1**

4400 **9** *3* **Anjomarba (IRE)**[19] 7349 4-8-13 **62**...... KirstyMilczarek 8 53
(Conor Dore) *prom: rdn and cl up 2f out: wknd fnl f* **40/1**

-506 **10** *1* **Ventura Cove (IRE)**[11] 7456 4-9-5 **68**......(b) TonyHamilton 10 56
(Richard Fahey) *settled towards rr: shkn up over 3f out on outer: no prog over 1f out: n.d after* **25/1**

11 *1 1/4* **Indus Valley (IRE)**[60] 6510 4-8-12 **61**...... MartinHarley 1 46
(Des Donovan) *led at str pce but pressed: hdd over 1f out: wknd qckly fnl f* **11/1**

1600 **12** *2 1/4* **Mary's Pet**[19] 7349 4-8-13 **62**...... StevieDonohoe 4 41
(John Akehurst) *t.k.h: hld up wl in rr: rdn over 2f out: no prog* **100/1**

1640 **13** *3/4* **Pytheas (USA)**[25] 7268 4-8-5 **59**......(p) MarkCoumbe(5) 12 36
(Michael Attwater) *pressed ldr at str pce to wl over 1f out: wknd qckly* **25/1**

0225 **14** *3 1/4* **Timpanist (USA)**[47] 6814 4-8-12 **61**......(be) SebSanders 13 29
(Simon Dow) *a wl in rr: rdn 1/2-way: sn bhd* **40/1**

1m 23.9s (-0.90) **Going Correction** +0.075s/f (Slow)
WFA 3 from 4yo+ 1lb **14** Ran SP% **118.8**
Speed ratings (Par 103): **108,107,106,105,105 103,102,102,99,98 96,94,93,89**
toteswingers:1&2:£10.20, 2&3:£11.50, 1&3:£11.00 CSF £47.09 CT £497.62 TOTE £12.90: £4.10, £1.80, £3.90; EX 72.70 Trifecta £453.40 Part won. Pool: £612.71 - 0.10 winning units..
Owner Mrs Julie Martin **Bred** Julie Routledge-Martin **Trained** Dalham, Suffolk

FOCUS
A modest handicap, but a competitive one and the pace was good with a contested lead. The reliable fourth sets the standard on recent form.
T/Jkpt: £144,033.00 to a £1 stake. Pool of £405,727.03 - 2.00 winning tickets. T/Plt: £37.90 to a £1 stake. Pool of £84,790.10 - 1,631.31 winning tickets. T/Qpdt: £21.40 to a £1 stake. Pool of £7,091.94 - 245.00 winning tickets. JN

7533 FONTAINEBLEAU
Tuesday, November 29

OFFICIAL GOING: Turf: very soft

7580a PRIX BELLE DE NUIT (LISTED RACE) (3YO+ FILLIES & MARES) (TURF) — 1m 4f 110y
12:50 (12:00) 3-Y-O+ **£22,413** (£8,965; £5,603; £2,241)

RPR

1 **Racemate**[17] 3-8-8 0...... ThierryThulliez 6 100
(S Wattel, France) **56/10**[1]

2 *nk* **Molly Malone (FR)** 3-8-8 0...... SebastienMaillot 1 100
(M Delzangles, France) **24/1**

3 *1/2* **Western Pearl**[17] 7406 4-9-0 0...... Francois-XavierBertras 5 98
(William Knight) *racd freely in midfield on rail: rdn early in st: qcknd wl to join ldrs 1 1/2f out: r.o wl: wnt 2nd 1f out: nt qckn fnl 100yds: lost 2nd cl home* **23/1**

3 *dht* **Roche Ambeau (FR)**[35] 4-9-0 0...... TonyPiccone 2 98
(E Lellouche, France) **14/1**

5 *1 1/2* **Jehannedarc (IRE)**[36] 3-8-8 0...... ThierryJarnet 4 97
(A De Royer-Dupre, France) **17/1**

6 *3* **Brasileira**[35] 7089 3-8-8 0...... AlexisBadel 18 92
(J-M Beguigne, France) **13/2**[2]

7 *1 1/4* **Fleur Enchantee (FR)**[35] 7090 7-9-0 0......(p) RonanThomas 14 89
(P Van De Poele, France) **10/1**

8 *snk* **Tidespring (IRE)**[30] 3-8-8 0...... MickaelBarzalona 9 88
(H-A Pantall, France) **21/1**

9 *3/4* **Foundation Filly**[35] 7089 4-9-0 0...... ThomasHuet 15 86
(F Doumen, France) **35/1**

10 **Sallen (IRE)**[40] 7114 3-8-8 0...... GregoryBenoist 7 —
(S Wattel, France) **9/1**

0 **Highest**[33] 7129 3-8-8 0...... WilliamBuick 11 —
(John Gosden) *racd in midfield towards outside: rdn early in st: no ex u.p fr over 1 1/2f out: eased ins fnl f* **24/1**

0 **Zillione Beauty (FR)**[30] 5-9-0 0......(p) AlexandreRoussel 10 —
(Mme P Butel, France) **50/1**

0 **Tameen**[24] 7296 3-8-8 0...... FranckBlondel 12 —
(John Dunlop) *a towards rr: u.p over 2f out: styd on fnl f: nvr threatened* **26/1**

0 **Floating World (IRE)**[21] 3-8-8 0...... Pierre-CharlesBoudot 17 —
(A Fabre, France) **83/10**

0 **Mourasana**[37] 3-8-10 0 ow1...... ChristopheSoumillon 13 —
(C Lerner, France) **13/1**

0 **Hot Blood (IRE)**[17] 7406 3-8-8 0...... MaximeGuyon 3 —
(A Fabre, France) **78/10**[3]

0 **Paulaya (GER)**[135] 3-8-8 0...... FilipMinarik 16 —
(P Schiergen, Germany) **45/1**

D *1 1/4* **All Annalena (IRE)**[39] 6989 5-9-0 0...... JohanVictoire 8 87
(Lucy Wadham) *sn led on ins: stl in front ent long st: r.o wl: ev ch 1 1/2f out: began to weaken 1f out: eased fnl 100yds: fin 8th: disqualified - jockey failed to weigh-in* **59/1**

2m 47.0s (167.00)
WFA 3 from 4yo+ 6lb **18** Ran SP% **118.1**
WIN (incl. 1 euro stake): 6.60. PLACES: 2.80, 6.30, 3.60 (Western Pearl), 2.50 (Roche Ambeau). DF: 106.70. SF: 180.20.
Owner L Haegel **Bred** Haras De La Perelle **Trained** France

NOTEBOOK
Western Pearl would have been well suited by this stamina test (only previous win gained under similar conditions) and ran a fine race, despite being keener than ideal. She just held on to a share of third and picked up some more black type.
Highest hasn't progressed as expected and failed to take to the bad ground.
Tameen had conditions to suit and appeared progressive, so much better was expected. Seemingly she's had enough for the year.
All Annalena(IRE) had the ground to suit but stamina to prove. She ran creditably under a positive ride, but didn't really see her race out. She lost eighth place after her rider failed to weigh in.

7525 KEMPTON (A.W) (R-H)
Wednesday, November 30

OFFICIAL GOING: Standard
Wind: Fresh, half behind Weather: Cloudy

7581 BETDAQ MULTIPLES AW "HANDS AND HEELS" APPRENTICE SERIES H'CAP (RACING EXCELLENCE INITIATIVE) — 1m (P)
4:00 (4:00) (Class 7) (0-50,50) 3-Y-O+ **£1,533** (£452; £226) **Stalls** Low

Form RPR

0305 **1** **Storm Runner (IRE)**[7] 7524 3-8-7 **50**...... RichardOld(5) 13 61
(George Margarson) *hld up in midfield: styd on inner and prog 3f out: c to chal whn n.m.r over 2f out: rallied over 1f out: sustained duel w runner-up fnl f and edgd lft: jst prevailed* **12/1**

022 **2** *nse* **Shaunas Spirit (IRE)**[76] 6083 3-8-4 **47**...... PaulBooth(5) 14 58
(Dean Ivory) *t.k.h: hld up in midfield: prog over 2f out: c to chal over 1f out: duelled w wnr fnl f and pair drew rt away: jst failed* **7/1**[2]

6430 **3** *8* **Norcroft**[13] 7442 9-8-10 **49**......(p) DanielHarris(3) 5 41
(Christine Dunnett) *mostly in ldng trio: pushed along to chal over 1f out: upsides sn after: wknd ins fnl f* **16/1**

5346 **4** 2 ½ **Kyncraighe (IRE)**[231] 1303 3-8-11 **49**........................... ThomasBrown 2 36
(Joseph Tuite) *led after 2f: hrd pressed over 2f out: hdd & wknd 1f out* **12/1**

0/40 **5** 1 ¾ **The Ducking Stool**[105] 5168 4-8-6 **45**........................(p) HannahNunn(3) 3 28
(Julia Feilden) *w ldrs: hung lft after 2f: pressed ldr 4f out to over 2f out: fdd* **7/1**[2]

0304 **6** ¾ **Ocean Countess (IRE)**[13] 7442 5-8-13 **49**............(v) GeorgeDowning 10 30
(Tony Carroll) *slowest away: detached in last trio: prog over 2f out to dispute modest 5th 1f out: no hdwy after* **8/1**[3]

4066 **7** 1 ½ **My Jeanie (IRE)**[90] 5653 7-8-9 **45**............................... GeorgeChaloner 4 23
(Jimmy Fox) *led 2f: lost pl over 3f out: outpcd fr 2f out* **14/1**

0000 **8** ½ **Satwa Ballerina**[15] 4928 3-8-7 **48**.................................. DannyBrock(3) 8 24
(Mark Rimmer) *pushed along firmly towards rr after 3f: nvr on terms w ldrs* **100/1**

0-46 **9** 1 ¼ **Brave Enough (USA)**[104] 2659 4-8-9 **50**.......................(p) NedCurtis(5) 1 24
(Roger Curtis) *rn wout declared tongue-strap: wl in rr: pushed along and detached in last trio 1/2-way: nvr a factor: styd on fnl f* **18/1**

4360 **10** 1 ¾ **Grand Honour (IRE)**[252] 950 5-8-12 **48**............................ JakePayne 9 17
(Paul Howling) *s.i.s: hld up in rr: effrt over 2f out: sn no prog and btn* **10/1**

2040 **11** 1 ½ **Kenswick**[57] 6609 4-8-5 **46**.......................................(v) DavidWarren(5) 12 12
(Pat Eddery) *chsd ldrs: wd bnd 3f out and lost grnd: n.d fnl 2f* **17/2**

0003 **12** 4 ½ **Blueberry Fizz (IRE)**[7] 7524 3-8-9 **47**........................ NatashaEaton 6 —
(John Ryan) *trckd ldrs: effrt over 3f out: wknd over 2f out* **11/2**[1]

-003 **13** nse **Fayre Bella**[34] 7119 4-8-11 **47**.. NoelGarbutt 11 3
(John Gallagher) *s.i.s: sn in midfield on outer: wdst of all bnd 3f out: sn lost pl and btn* **12/1**

0/06 **14** 5 **Bertie Boo**[26] 7270 6-8-9 **45**.. JackDuern 7 —
(Michael Appleby) *sn dropped to rr: pushed along and detached in last trio bef 1/2-way: t.o* **12/1**

1m 42.15s (2.35) **Going Correction** +0.05s/f (Slow)
WFA 3 from 4yo+ 2lb **14** Ran SP% **120.7**
Speed ratings (Par 97): **90,89,81,79,77 76,75,74,73,71 70,65,65,60**
toteswingers: 1&2 £14.20, 1&3 £17.10, 2&3 £14.70. CSF £93.86 CT £1403.73 TOTE £19.70: £4.60, £2.40, £4.30; EX 82.80 Trifecta £215.90 Part won. Pool: £291.80 - 0.43 winning units..
Owner Pitfield Partnership **Bred** Kevin Foley **Trained** Newmarket, Suffolk
■ Richard Old's first winner.
■ Stewards' Enquiry : Richard Old two-day ban: careless riding (Dec 14-15)

FOCUS
A low-grade handicap in which the pace was an ordinary one. The winner drifted towards the centre late on and the first two pulled clear. The time was modest and the form is weak.
Blueberry Fizz(IRE) Official explanation: trainer said filly was in season

7582 FREE ENTRY FOR BETDAQ MEMBERS CLAIMING STKS 1m (P)
4:30 (4:32) (Class 6) 2-Y-O **£1,617** (£481; £240; £120) **Stalls** Low

Form RPR

4120 **1** **Snowed In (IRE)**[13] 7449 2-8-9 68.. LukeMorris 2 73
(J S Moore) *hld up in last pair: prog over 2f out: drvn to ld over 1f out: styd on wl* **3/1**[3]

251 **2** 1 ¾ **Cristal Gem**[43] 6927 2-8-5 77... KieranO'Neill(3) 7 68
(Richard Hannon) *t.k.h: hld up bhd ldrs: prog to go 2nd over 2f out: led briefly wl over 1f out: chsd wnr after: one pce* **11/8**[1]

3 **3** 1 ¾ **Siouxies Dream**[8] 7505 2-8-5 0 ow1............................... NeilChalmers 1 61
(Michael Appleby) *hld up in last: prog over 2f out: chsd ldng pair over 1f out: styd on but no real imp* **20/1**

1344 **4** 4 **Anginola (IRE)**[2] 7569 2-8-6 65.. WilliamCarson 5 53
(Joseph Tuite) *sn pressed ldr: led over 3f out: hung bdly lft over 2f out: ended against nr side rail and hdd wl over 1f out: threw away any ch* **9/4**[2]

0600 **5** 1 ½ **Big Time Charlie (IRE)**[7] 7514 2-8-0 56........................ RyanPowell(5) 4 48
(Richard Hannon) *chsd ldrs: rdn wl over 2f out: sn outpcd: fdd over 1f out* **22/1**

0 **6** 14 **Green Mountain (IRE)**[43] 6934 2-8-3 0................(t) AdamBeschizza(3) 6 17
(Philip McBride) *dwlt: rousted along and sn chsd ldrs: wknd qckly wl over 2f out: t.o* **50/1**

0060 **7** 5 **Cool Light**[14] 7432 2-8-6 46...(v[1]) DavidProbert 8 6
(Alan Jarvis) *racd freely: led to over 3f out: wknd rapidly over 2f out: t.o* **100/1**

1m 41.07s (1.27) **Going Correction** +0.05s/f (Slow) 7 Ran SP% **109.9**
Speed ratings (Par 94): **95,93,91,87,86 72,67**
toteswingers: 1&2 £1.70, 1&3 £3.10, 2&3 £3.00. CSF £6.90 TOTE £3.30: £1.40, £1.10; EX 7.70 Trifecta £42.70 Pool: £890.13 - 15.42 winning units..Cristal Gem was claimed by A S Reid for £12,000. Snowed In was claimed by Jennie Candish for £8,000.
Owner Norton Common Farm Racing **Bred** T Cahalan & D Cahalan **Trained** Upper Lambourn, Berks

FOCUS
A modest and uncompetitive claimer in which an ordinary gallop only picked up on the approach to the intersection. The winner raced towards the inside rail in the closing stages.

NOTEBOOK
Snowed In(IRE) is a reliable sort for this grade who had a decent chance at the weights and he showed a decent attitude to notch his fourth win on Polytrack. He's capable of adding to his tally in this type of event, especially when the gallop is a truer one. He now joins Jennie Candlish. (op 7-2 tchd 11-4)
Cristal Gem was the clear form-choice at these weights but she spoilt her chance by taking a good hold to post and by refusing to settle in the race on this first start over 1m. It's too soon to write her off but she'll have to settle better if she is to progress. (op Evens)
Siouxies Dream bettered the form she showed on her debut at Southwell but she'll be of more interest granted a stiffer test of stamina once qualified for a handicap mark.
Anginola(IRE) looked to have decent claims on these terms turned out quickly but she didn't impress with the way she hung left once pressure was applied and she proved disappointing. She will be one to watch next time. (op 5-2 tchd 11-4)

7583 BETDAQ MOBILE APPS/BRITISH STALLION STUDS E B F MAIDEN FILLIES' STKS 6f (P)
5:00 (5:02) (Class 5) 2-Y-O **£3,169** (£943; £471; £235) **Stalls** Low

Form RPR

3 **1** **Topflight Princess**[20] 7345 2-9-0 0............................ FergusSweeney 6 72+
(Jeremy Gask) *slowly away: rcvrd to chse ldrs after 2f: prog on inner to ld over 1f out: rdn and styd on wl* **9/4**[1]

5 **2** 1 ¼ **Pucon**[19] 7359 2-9-0 0.. JohnFahy 2 68+
(Roger Teal) *dwlt and sltly hmpd s: rn green in last pair: gd prog over 2f out: sustained effrt to go 2nd ins fnl f: styd on but unable to rch wnr* **13/2**

3 1 **Dahab Gold (IRE)** 2-9-0 0.. LukeMorris 12 65+
(Jane Chapple-Hyam) *led: rdn and hdd over 1f out: styd on same pce after* **11/2**[3]

63 **4** 2 ¼ **Wiltshire Life (IRE)**[20] 7345 2-9-0 0............................ SteveDrowne 1 61
(Jeremy Gask) *awkward s and rdr lost iron briefly: towards rr: pushed along over 2f out: styd on and reminder ins fnl f to take nvr nrr 4th* **7/2**[2]

05 **5** 1 ¾ **Cincinnati Kit**[62] 6480 2-9-0 0.......................................(t) WilliamCarson 10 53
(Stuart Williams) *chsd ldng pair: nt qckn 2f out: drvn and fdd over 1f out* **9/1**

6 ¾ **Place That Face** 2-9-0 0.. JimmyFortune 9 51
(Hughie Morrison) *slowly away: rcvrd to chse ldrs on outer: shkn up and nt qckn 2f out: fdd* **6/1**

0 **7** nk **Make A Fuss**[20] 7345 2-9-0 0... DaneO'Neill 5 50
(Sylvester Kirk) *t.k.h: pressed ldr: upsides 2f out: wknd over 1f out* **25/1**

8 ½ **Silky Bleu** 2-9-0 0.. MarcHalford 11 49
(Terry Clement) *racd wd towards rr: no prog over 2f out: sn btn* **25/1**

9 ½ **Rainbow Riches (IRE)** 2-8-7 0.. NedCurtis(7) 4 47
(Roger Curtis) *sn wl in rr: appeared to hit rail over 2f out: stl last and bmpd along 1f out: fin wl last 50yds* **100/1**

00 **10** hd **Pink Belini**[18] 7396 2-9-0 0.. LiamKeniry 8 47
(Alan McCabe) *chsd ldrs over 2f: sn lost pl: struggling over 2f out* **66/1**

1m 14.27s (1.17) **Going Correction** +0.05s/f (Slow) **10** Ran SP% **116.2**
Speed ratings (Par 93): **94,92,91,88,85 84,84,83,82,82**
toteswingers: 1&2 £4.00, 1&3 £3.80, 2&3 £6.60. CSF £16.95 TOTE £3.90: £1.50, £2.30, £2.80; EX 23.80 Trifecta £139.30 Pool: £8,750.88 - 46.48 winning units..
Owner P Bamford **Bred** Dandy's Farm **Trained** Sutton Veny, Wilts

FOCUS
A modest and uncompetitive fillies maiden run at just an ordinary gallop. The winner raced close to the inside rail until edging left in the closing stages.

NOTEBOOK
Topflight Princess duly stepped up on her debut effort over this course-and-distance to get off the mark at the second attempt. A mark somewhere in the mid-60s looks a likely scenario and she could well improve again in handicaps. (tchd 11-4)

Pucon, from a yard that has struggled for winners, bettered the (very moderate) form she showed on her debut at Lingfield earlier in the month. She'll be of more interest once qualified for a handicap mark. (op 8-1)

Dahab Gold(IRE), a 22,000gns half-sister to winners from 5f-1m, had the run of the race and showed ability at a moderate level on this racecourse debut. She is entitled to improve for this experience. (tchd 5-1 and 6-1)

Wiltshire Life(IRE) finished alongside this winner at this course on her previous run (second start) but failed to match that run after her rider lost an iron briefly at the start. Nevertheless she showed enough to suggest she'll be worth a second look in ordinary handicaps. Official explanation: jockey said he lost an iron coming out of stalls (op 4-1 tchd 9-2)

Cincinnati Kit wasn't disgraced dropped in trip and returned to Polytrack. Moderate handicaps will be the way forward with her and, as usual with runners from this yard, she'll be of most interest once the market speaks in her favour. (op 8-1)

Place That Face, a half-sister to 5f Listed scorer Tropical Treat and who is out of a 5f winner, wasn't totally disgraced on this racecourse debut but, although she should improve for this run, her short-term future lies in very ordinary handicaps. (tchd 11-2 and 13-2)

7584 BACK OR LAY AT BETDAQ.COM WILD FLOWER STKS (LISTED RACE) 1m 4f (P)
5:30 (5:30) (Class 1) 3-Y-0+
£17,013 (£6,450; £3,228; £1,608; £807; £405) **Stalls** Centre

Form RPR

1113 **1** **Barbican**[39] 7027 3-9-2 106... RyanMoore 3 116+
(Alan Bailey) *t.k.h: trckd ldng pair: prog to ld 2f out: drvn and edgd lft over 1f out: styd on strly* **1/1**[1]

63 **2** 5 **Ceilidh House**[25] 7296 4-9-1 102.....................................(t) JimCrowley 5 101
(Ralph Beckett) *hld up in last pair: prog 3f out: chsd wnr over 1f out and looked dangerous: one pce and lft bhd ins fnl f* **5/1**[3]

/500 **3** 7 **Bolivia (GER)**[25] 7296 5-9-1 88.. LukeMorris 7 90
(Lucy Wadham) *trckd ldng pair: rdn over 4f out: dropped to last pair and btn 3f out: plugged on to claim modest 3rd last strides* **40/1**

5403 **4** 1 **Laaheb**[28] 7226 5-9-6 110... RichardHills 4 93
(Roger Varian) *pressed ldr: led over 3f out: rdn and hdd 2f out: wknd qckly over 1f out: lost 3rd last strides* **11/4**[2]

0064 **5** ½ **Precision Break (USA)**[28] 7226 6-9-6 94.......................... MartinLane 1 92
(David Simcock) *led: rdn and hdd over 3f out: wknd over 2f out* **20/1**

0015 **6** 34 **Askaud (IRE)**[25] 7296 3-8-9 99.................................(p) GrahamGibbons 2 33
(David Nicholls) *a in last pair: rdn and wknd 4f out: wl t.o* **11/1**

2m 30.0s (-4.50) **Going Correction** +0.05s/f (Slow)
WFA 3 from 4yo+ 6lb **6** Ran SP% **108.9**
Speed ratings (Par 111): **117,113,109,108,108 85**
toteswingers: 1&2 £1.60, 1&3 £7.40, 2&3 £25.40. CSF £6.03 TOTE £2.20: £1.50, £2.30; EX 7.70.
Owner John Stocker **Bred** Hascombe And Valiant Studs **Trained** Newmarket, Suffolk

FOCUS
The fifth running of a Listed event taken in the past by smart performers Dansant (twice), Les Fazzani and Cheetah and, although this race lacked any depth, this year's progressive winner looks well up to that standard. The gallop was a modest one to the home turn and the winner came down the centre in the straight. The runner-up to form sets the level.

NOTEBOOK
Barbican ◆ has made up into a smart sort up to 1m6f and, although his main market rival disappointed, he ran up to his best to account for another smart type after racing with the choke out and to maintain his unbeaten record on synthetics. A stronger overall pace would have suited and he should be able to hold his own in minor Group company next season. He reportedly goes to Dubai and will be interesting over this trip and beyond. (op 5-4)

Ceilidh House, back up in trip and having her first run on an artificial surface, ran as well as she has done all year, especially as she gave start in a muddling race to a smart rival who has progressed well this season. She's capable of picking up a similarly uncompetitive event either on turf or on this surface if she stays in training. (op 4-1)

Bolivia(GER)'s form for current connections has been patchy but she wasn't disgraced (probably flattered in muddling event) in the face of a stiff task returned to Polytrack. A stronger overall gallop would have suited better but she may not be the easiest to place successfully either in this company or from her 88 mark back in handicaps.

Laaheb again failed to get home at this course and was again a long way below the form shown when winning last year's Group 3 September Stakes over this course-and-distance. He may do better after a break on turf next year but looks one to tread carefully with from a punting perspective. (op 9-4)

Precision Break(USA), who had a stiff task at the weights, finished a couple of lengths closer to a below-par Laaheb than at this course on his previous start and wasn't totally disgraced but he's likely to remain vulnerable against the better types in this grade. (op 25-1 tchd 18-1)

Askaud(IRE) has developed into a very useful sort on turf in cheekpieces this year but, although she had something to find at the weights, she was beaten before stamina should have been an issue. She'll have to raise her game to win in Listed company or a competitive handicap from her current mark (99). (op 12-1)

7585 RACING@SKYSPORTS.COM MEDIAN AUCTION MAIDEN STKS 7f (P)
6:00 (6:00) (Class 6) 3-5-Y-O **£1,617** (£481; £240; £120) **Stalls** Low

Form RPR

40 **1** **Yashila (IRE)**[18] 7389 3-8-7 62..............................(p) RyanPowell(5) 11 61
(J S Moore) *chsd ldr: outpcd over 2f out: clsd to ld jst over 1f out: styd on* **20/1**

360- **2** 1 ¼ **Hooligan Sean**[442] 6056 4-8-13 68.............................. AmyScott(5) 2 63
(Henry Candy) *trckd ldng pair: nt qckn over 2f out: styd on fr over 1f out to take 2nd ins fnl f: no imp on wnr nr fin* **13/2**[3]

0-40 **3** nk **Cerejeira (IRE)**[27] 7245 3-8-12 46..............................(b[1]) GrahamGibbons 12 57
(Eric Alston) *chsd ldng trio: outpcd over 2f out: styd on fr over 1f out to take 3rd nr fin* **40/1**

-530 **4** ¾ **Perfect Cracker**[112] 4914 3-9-3 74.............................. AdamKirby 3 60
(Clive Cox) *led: drvn for home wl over 2f out: hdd & wknd jst over 1f out* **2/1**[1]

5 nse **Great Expectations** 3-9-3 0.............................. JimCrowley 8 60+
(J R Jenkins) *s.s: last early and wl off the pce: prog after 3f: rdn wl over 2f out: wnt 5th over 1f out but nt on terms: styd on thrght fnl f: nrst fin* **11/4**[2]

0 **6** 7 **Hot Tub**[135] 4163 3-9-3 0.............................. IanMongan 4 41
(Christine Dunnett) *dwlt: chsd ldng quartet but nt on terms w them after 3f: no imp over 2f out: wknd over 1f out* **100/1**

0 **7** 4 ½ **Sondray**[35] 7111 3-8-12 0..............................(t) ChrisCatlin 1 24
(Jo Crowley) *dwlt: racd in 6th and nowhere nr ldrs: wknd 2f out* **20/1**

5-5 **8** 6 **Sawahill**[152] 3575 3-8-12 0.............................. RyanMoore 5 —
(Clive Brittain) *a in last quartet: wl bhd in last trio 1/2-way: t.o* **7/1**

0 **9** 4 **Clear Spring (IRE)**[26] 7260 3-9-3 0.............................. WilliamCarson 7 —
(John Spearing) *a wl off the pce: bhd in last trio fr 1/2-way: t.o* **20/1**

0-6 **10** 2 ½ **Harlequin Girl**[29] 7207 3-8-9 0.............................. DominicFox(3) 9 —
(Terry Clement) *a in last quartet: wl bhd in last trio 1/2-way: t.o* **100/1**

4 **U** **Community (USA)**[20] 7354 3-8-12 0.............................. KirstyMilczarek 10 —
(Phil McEntee) *stmbld and uns rdr sn after s* **15/2**

1m 26.43s (0.43) **Going Correction** +0.05s/f (Slow)
WFA 3 from 4yo+ 1lb **11** Ran SP% **116.3**
Speed ratings (Par 101): **99,97,97,96,96 88,83,76,71,68** —
toteswingers: 1&2 £13.70, 1&3 £32.10, 2&3 £34.10. CSF £134.89 TOTE £17.30: £3.40, £3.00, £7.40; EX 132.30 Trifecta £2655.80 Part won. Pool: £3,589.01 - 0.20 winning units..
Owner J S Moore **Bred** Waterford Hall Stud **Trained** Upper Lambourn, Berks

FOCUS
A moderate maiden in which the proximity of the 46-rated third casts a big doubt over the worth of the form. The gallop was an ordinary one and the winner came down the centre. The form is rated on the negative side.

7586 SKYSPORTS.COM RACING H'CAP 6f (P)
6:30 (6:30) (Class 4) (0-85,86) 3-Y-O+ **£4,075** (£1,212; £606; £303) **Stalls** Low

Form RPR

635 **1** **Requisite**[6] 7531 6-8-12 75..............................(b) DaneO'Neill 7 82
(Ian Wood) *dwlt: hld up in last pair: looking for room 2f out tl gaps appeared jst over 1f out: r.o wl through rivals to ld last strides* **9/1**

6114 **2** shd **Silenzio**[12] 7456 3-9-0 77.............................. RyanMoore 4 84
(Richard Hannon) *trckd ldng pair: pushed along 1/2-way: effrt u.p 2f out: chal ins fnl f: jst denied* **3/1**[1]

0000 **3** nse **Levitate**[51] 6761 3-9-3 80..............................(b[1]) GrahamGibbons 10 87
(Alan McCabe) *mde most to 2f out: u.p and looked like dropping away over 1f out: kpt on wl fnl f* **15/2**

0121 **4** nse **Mottley Crewe**[8] 7502 4-8-13 76 6ex..............................(b) MartinHarley 3 82
(Richard Guest) *w ldr: led 2f out: fended off rivals tl hdd and lost pls last strides* **9/2**[2]

1001 **5** ½ **Main Beach**[12] 7456 4-9-7 84..............................(t) MartinLane 11 89
(Tobias B P Coles) *dwlt: dropped in fr wd draw and hld up in last: effrt on inner 2f out: hrd rdn and styd on fr over 1f out: nrst fin but jst unable to chal* **6/1**[3]

1100 **6** nk **Shifting Star (IRE)**[12] 7456 6-9-5 82.............................. IanMongan 9 86
(John Bridger) *sn in 7th: drvn and no prog over 2f out: clsd u.p jst over 1f out: styd on nr fin: nvr quite getting there* **33/1**

5101 **7** ¾ **Sugar Beet**[11] 7487 3-9-7 84.............................. LukeMorris 6 85
(Ronald Harris) *restless in stalls: n.m.r after 1f and sn shuffled bk to 8th: rdn 2f out: clsd on ldrs over 1f out: ch ins fnl f: no ex* **12/1**

0230 **8** nk **Bandstand**[119] 4670 5-9-0 77.............................. TomEaves 2 77
(Bryan Smart) *trckd ldng pair: effrt over 2f out: chal over 1f out: stl pressing jst ins fnl f: wknd last 100yds* **16/1**

6025 **9** 4 **Perfect Act**[6] 7529 6-9-6 83.............................. DavidProbert 1 71
(Andrew Balding) *trckd ldrs: rdn and cl up over 1f out: sn wknd* **9/1**

0050 **10** 1 **Masked Dance (IRE)**[25] 7295 4-9-3 80..............................(b) TomQueally 5 64
(David Nicholls) *racd wd: chsd ldrs: rdn over 2f out: wknd wl over 1f out* **9/1**

1m 12.45s (-0.65) **Going Correction** +0.05s/f (Slow) **10** Ran SP% **115.7**
Speed ratings (Par 105): **106,105,105,105,105 104,103,103,97,96**
toteswingers: 1&2 £7.20, 1&3 £13.10, 2&3 £9.10. CSF £35.90 CT £221.06 TOTE £11.90: £3.40, £1.50, £4.10; EX 57.10 Trifecta £357.60 Pool: £3,702.52 - 7.66 winning units..
Owner Paddy Barrett **Bred** Darley **Trained** Upper Lambourn, Berks
■ Stewards' Enquiry : Graham Gibbons five-day ban: used whip with excessive frequency (Dec 14-18)

FOCUS
A useful handicap run at a reasonable pace and a triumph for the handicapper, given the first eight home finished in a heap. The form seems sound but ordinary for the grade. The winner raced centre-to-far-side in the closing stages.

7587 BOOK NOW FOR WHWF H'CAP (DIV I) 6f (P)
7:00 (7:00) (Class 6) (0-65,65) 3-Y-O+ **£1,617** (£481; £240; £120) **Stalls** Low

Form RPR

1 **1** **Rivas Rhapsody (IRE)**[26] 7260 3-9-3 62.............................. DaneO'Neill 2 72
(Ian Wood) *sltly awkward s: settled in last pair: plld out wd and plenty to do wl over 1f out: gd prog fnl f: r.o to ld last strides* **9/2**[3]

3306 **2** hd **Speak The Truth (IRE)**[11] 7485 5-9-1 60..............................(p) JimCrowley 6 69
(Jim Boyle) *trckd ldrs in 5th: cajoled along to cl over 1f out: produced to ld last 110yds: styd on but hdd fnl strides* **7/1**

3021 **3** 2 **Excellent Aim**[12] 7460 4-9-3 62..............................(t) SebSanders 3 65
(George Margarson) *t.k.h: trckd ldng pair: wnt 2nd 2f out: clsd to ld jst over 1f out: hdd and outpcd last 110yds* **7/2**[1]

4043 **4** 1 **Fenella Fudge**[11] 7484 3-9-5 64..............................(b) TomQueally 1 63
(James Given) *led: rdn 2f out: hdd and nt qckn jst over 1f out: fdd* **13/2**

0060 **5** shd **Diamond Vine (IRE)**[8] 7504 3-9-4 63..............................(v[1]) LukeMorris 5 62
(Ronald Harris) *in tch in 6th: effrt over 2f out: tried to cl on inner 1f out: n.m.r and sn outpcd* **33/1**

4005 **6** 3 ½ **Sherjawy (IRE)**[7] 7512 7-9-6 65.............................. SamHitchcott 11 53
(Zoe Davison) *pressed ldr to 2f out: steadily wknd* **20/1**

5300 **7** shd **Rapid Water**[11] 7485 5-9-4 63..............................(b) RyanMoore 10 51
(Gary Moore) *chsd ldrs on outer: drvn over 2f out: steadily wknd* **4/1**[2]

6400 **8** 2 **Super Duplex**[28] 7228 4-9-3 62.............................. IanMongan 12 43
(Pat Phelan) *a in last pair: lost tch 2f out: no ch after* **10/1**

6320 **P** **Belinsky (IRE)**[15] 7419 4-8-8 60.............................. GeorgeChaloner(7) 9 —
(Mark Campion) *rrd s: rdr lost irons and p.u* **10/1**

1m 12.89s (-0.21) **Going Correction** +0.05s/f (Slow) **9** Ran SP% **112.1**
Speed ratings (Par 101): **103,102,100,98,98 93,93,91,**—
toteswingers: 1&2 £4.50, 1&3 £5.00, 2&3 £9.10. CSF £34.51 CT £120.45 TOTE £4.60: £1.60, £2.30, £1.60; EX 19.20 Trifecta £164.90 Pool: £3,903.07 - 17.51 winning units..
Owner D Hefin Jones **Bred** D Hefin Jones **Trained** Upper Lambourn, Berks

FOCUS
The first division of a modest handicap. The pace was fair and the unexposed winner came down the centre, while the placed horses help set the level of the form.
Belinsky(IRE) Official explanation: jockey said saddle slipped

7588 BOOK NOW FOR WHWF H'CAP (DIV II) 6f (P)
7:30 (7:30) (Class 6) (0-65,71) 3-Y-O+ **£1,617** (£481; £240; £120) **Stalls** Low

Form RPR

5-06 **1** **Mack's Sister**[13] 7448 4-9-1 60.............................. LukeMorris 2 68
(Dean Ivory) *pressed ldr: drvn ahd over 1f out: hrd pressed fnl f: hld on wl* **9/2**[2]

0604 **2** nk **Dvinsky (USA)**[6] 7529 10-9-3 62..............................(b) TomMcLaughlin 8 69
(Paul Howling) *led: drvn and hdd over 1f out: battled bk wl fnl f: jst hld* **20/1**

3215 **3** 1 **Poppy**[11] 7484 3-9-2 61.............................. RyanMoore 7 65+
(Richard Hannon) *stdd s: hld up in last: shkn up over 2f out: tk long time to pick up and stl in last pair jst over 1f out: r.o to take 3rd fnl strides* **7/2**[1]

5004 **4** nk **Danzoe (IRE)**[7] 7512 4-9-6 65.............................. IanMongan 6 68
(Christine Dunnett) *hld up in last trio: prog 2f out: clsd on ldrs and hrd rdn jst over 1f out: nt qckn and styd on same pce after* **13/2**[3]

0000 **5** hd **Frognal (IRE)**[11] 7484 5-9-1 63..............................(bt) RobertLButler(3) 10 65
(Richard Guest) *racd wd in midfield: gng strly but hanging over 2f out: clsd over 1f out: nt qckn fnl f* **25/1**

3201 **6** nse **Doctor Hilary**[28] 7224 9-9-1 60..............................(v) RobertHavlin 1 62
(Mark Hoad) *pressed ldng pair: tried to chal fr 2f out: cl enough ins fnl f: nt qckn* **15/2**

0031 **7** 1 ¼ **Atlantic Beach**[2] 7566 6-9-12 71 6ex..............................(b) LiamKeniry 5 69
(Milton Bradley) *trckd ldng pair: rdn over 2f out: fdd and lost pl fr over 1f out* **8/1**

1206 **8** hd **Efistorm**[32] 7173 10-9-4 63.............................. KirstyMilczarek 9 60
(Conor Dore) *towards rr: rdn over 2f out: no prog after tl styd on last 100yds: nrst fin* **20/1**

0003 **9** ½ **Custom House (IRE)**[20] 7349 3-9-3 65..............(b) NataliaGemelova(3) 3 61
(John E Long) *wl in tch in midfield: effrt on inner 2f out: no imp on ldrs 1f out: grad fdd* **11/1**

5140 **10** ½ **Katmai River (IRE)**[13] 7448 4-9-3 62.............................. SteveDrowne 4 56
(Mark Usher) *trckd ldrs: nt qckn 2f out: steadily lost pl fnl f* **9/1**

02P **11** nk **Torres Del Paine**[47] 6841 4-9-2 64.............................. KieranO'Neill(3) 11 57
(Jimmy Fox) *stdd s: racd wd in midfield: effrt 2f out: no imp 1f out: wknd last 150yds* **16/1**

1536 **12** 1 **One Cool Chick**[11] 7488 3-9-0 59.............................. NeilChalmers 12 49
(John Bridger) *awkward s: hld up in last pair: shkn up and no prog over 1f out: nvr involved* **25/1**

1m 13.43s (0.33) **Going Correction** +0.05s/f (Slow) **12** Ran SP% **118.0**
Speed ratings (Par 101): **99,98,97,96,96 96,94,94,93,93 92,91**
toteswingers: 1&2 £16.50, 1&3 £5.40, 2&3 £13.40. CSF £96.08 CT £354.25 TOTE £5.70: £2.30, £3.50, £1.40; EX 110.70 Trifecta £248.20 Pool: £942.85 - 2.81 winning units..
Owner Recycled Products Limited **Bred** Mrs L R Burrage **Trained** Radlett, Herts
■ Stewards' Enquiry : Natalia Gemelova two-day ban: used whip with excessive frequency (Dec 14-15)

FOCUS
Another modest handicap but, although the gallop seemed reasonable, those held up seemed at a disadvantage. The runner-up to his recent best looks the guide to the form.
T/Plt: £1,614.40 to a £1 stake. Pool of £67,896.78 - 30.70 winning tickets. T/Qpdt: £138.80 to a £1 stake. Pool of £8,602.12 - 45.83 winning tickets. JN

7564 WOLVERHAMPTON (A.W) (L-H)
Thursday, December 1

OFFICIAL GOING: Standard
Wind: Light, half behind Weather: Cloudy

7589 TOTEPLACEPOT APPRENTICE H'CAP 1m 141y(P)
4:00 (4:00) (Class 5) (0-70,70) 3-Y-O+ **£2,264** (£673; £336; £168) **Stalls** Low

Form RPR

3602 **1** **Greyfriarschorista**[107] 5151 4-9-6 69.............................. JohnFahy 8 85+
(Brian Ellison) *racd keenly: mde all: rdn whn in command over 1f out: r.o wl: eased cl home* **2/1**[1]

4162 **2** ½ **Opus Maximus (IRE)**[12] 7492 6-9-4 70..............................(p) DavidKenny(3) 3 82+
(Conor Dore) *hld up: hdwy over 2f out: rdn over 1f out: styd on to take 2nd wl ins fnl f: clsd on wnr nr fin: flattered* **15/2**

2325 **3** 2 ¼ **Burning Stone (USA)**[50] 6793 4-9-5 68.............................. MichaelO'Connell 2 75
(Gay Kelleway) *a.p: chsd wnr over 2f out: edgd rt ent fnl f: no imp on wnr: styd on same pce and lost 2nd wl ins fnl f* **7/2**[2]

6620 **4** 3 ¾ **Justcallmehandsome**[6] 7538 9-8-4 60..............................(be) JoshBaudains(7) 6 58
(Dominic Ffrench Davis) *s.v.s: wl bhd tl 6f out: hdwy on outer over 4f out: chsd ldrs over 3f out: rdn over 1f out: one pce fnl f* **10/1**

0203 **5** shd **Tobrata**[38] 7068 5-8-4 58.............................. JasonHart(5) 7 56
(Mel Brittain) *midfield: pushed along over 3f out: nt clr run 2f out: one pce and no imp on ldrs over 1f out* **11/2**[3]

0010 **6** 4 ½ **Shelovestobouggie**[31] 7198 3-8-12 63..............................(t) MartinHarley 4 51
(Marco Botti) *chsd ldrs: rdn 2f out: wknd wl over 1f out* **9/1**

2060 **7** 3 **Master Leon**[22] 7339 4-9-2 70..............................(p) JustinNewman(5) 1 51
(Bryan Smart) *in rr: drvn and outpcd 3f out: nvr a threat* **16/1**

0000 **8** 5 **Douze Points (IRE)**[22] 7339 5-9-4 67.............................. SimonPearce 9 36
(Pat Murphy) *hld up: pushed along towards rr over 3f out: wl outpcd fnl 2f* **9/1**

0360 **9** 5 **Royal Premium**[47] 6878 5-8-2 **56** oh11 NoelGarbutt(5) 5 —
(Bruce Hellier) *racd keenly: chsd wnr after 1f tl over 2f out: wknd wl over 1f out* **100/1**

1m 49.35s (-1.15) **Going Correction** -0.075s/f (Stan)
WFA 3 from 4yo+ 2lb **9** Ran SP% **118.7**
Speed ratings (Par 103): **102,101,99,96,96 92,89,85,80**
CSF £18.56 CT £51.30 TOTE £3.40: £2.10, £1.10, £1.10; EX 13.40.
Owner Koo's Racing Club **Bred** Castlemartin Stud And Skymarc Farm **Trained** Norton, N Yorks

FOCUS
A modest handicap in which the winner made all at a steady pace. The placed horses set the level.

7590 STAY AT THE WOLVERHAMPTON HOLIDAY INN (S) STKS 1m 141y(P)
4:30 (4:30) (Class 6) 2-Y-O **£1,704** (£503; £251) **Stalls** Low

Form RPR

1 **1** **Mr Red Clubs (IRE)**[13] 7471 2-9-3 0 JimmyFortune 1 66+
(Paul W Flynn, Ire) *mde all: rdn whn edgd rt over 1f out: edgd lft wl ins fnl f: a doing enough whn pressed* **1/3**[1]

5042 **2** 3/4 **Rafaella**[12] 7481 2-8-7 56 (p) JoeFanning 5 53
(Harry Dunlop) *racd keenly: in tch: effrt to take 2nd 2f out: swtchd lft jst over 1f out: chalng wl ins fnl f: a hld* **7/2**[2]

4505 **3** 4 **Complex**[16] 7423 2-8-7 53 AndreaAtzeni 3 45
(David Evans) *chsd wnr to 2f out: plugged on at one pce u.p ins fnl f: no ch w front two fnl 150yds* **25/1**

0 **4** 1 3/4 **Vicgernic**[34] 7132 2-8-12 0 (p) FergusSweeney 6 46
(Gary Moore) *s.i.s: in rr: rdn and outpcd over 2f out: kpt on modly ins fnl f: nvr able to get on terms w ldrs* **20/1**[3]

0 **5** 3/4 **Kuwait Star**[20] 7367 2-8-12 0 MartinHarley 4 44
(Alan McCabe) *in tch: rdn 3f out: wknd over 2f out* **25/1**

535 **6** 3/4 **Brackendale**[111] 4983 2-8-12 45 LukeMorris 7 43
(John Weymes) *in tch: u.p 3f out: rdn and wknd over 2f out* **80/1**

7 17 **Princeofperfection** 2-8-12 0 LeeNewman 2 7
(Bruce Hellier) *chsd ldrs: niggled along most of way: wkng whn hung rt wl over 2f out* **100/1**

1m 52.29s (1.79) **Going Correction** -0.075s/f (Stan) **7** Ran SP% **111.9**
Speed ratings (Par 94): **89,88,84,83,82 81,66**
toteswingers:1&2:£1.20, 2&3:£4.10, 1&3:£2.90 CSF £1.53 TOTE £1.20: £1.10, £1.60; EX 1.90.There was no bid for the winner.
Owner Miss C Howes **Bred** Tally-Ho Stud **Trained** Colehill, Co Longford

FOCUS
Not a great contest even by selling standards. The runner-up looks the best guide.

NOTEBOOK
Mr Red Clubs(IRE) probably didn't even have to match the pick of his Irish form to land the odds, wandering about under pressure but essentially always leaving the impression he had matters under control. He's now 2-2 in sellers/claimers. (op 4-9)
Rafaella's Lingfield conqueror Masters Club had boosted that form since and she certainly kept the winner honest here. She's only modest but a similar event will probably come her way at some stage. (op 10-3 tchd 4-1)
Complex was well held back in third and this doesn't represent any improvement on her previous efforts. (op 20-1)
Vicgernic was quickly dropped in grade and showed a glimmer of ability in first-time cheekpieces. He's in decent hands so may have a bit more to offer. (tchd 25-1)
Kuwait Star fared only a little better than on his debut.
Brackendale looks very limited at this stage. (op 66-1)

7591 TOTEQUADPOT H'CAP 7f 32y(P)
5:00 (5:00) (Class 6) (0-65,65) 3-Y-O+ **£1,704** (£503; £251) **Stalls** High

Form RPR

5531 **1** **Berbice (IRE)**[27] 7268 6-8-13 **63** JulieBurke(3) 7 72+
(Linda Perratt) *hld up: smooth hdwy over 1f out: travelling on bit ins fnl f: rdn to ld fnl 50yds: in command cl home* **6/1**

5161 **2** 1/2 **Silver Wind**[13] 7462 6-9-3 **64** (b) RobertWinston 12 72
(Alan McCabe) *in tch: effrt to chal 3 wd 2f out: ev ch thrght fnl f: styd on but hld cl home* **11/4**[1]

0115 **3** 1/2 **Bold Ring**[2] 7579 5-9-0 **61** JimmyQuinn 8 68
(Edward Creighton) *hld up: hdwy 3f out: effrt to chse ldrs over 1f out: chalng wl ins fnl f: styd on but nt quite gng pce of first two* **5/1**[3]

4000 **4** 1/2 **Anjomarba (IRE)**[2] 7579 4-9-1 **62** KirstyMilczarek 9 67
(Conor Dore) *led: rdn and hdd narrowly over 1f out: led again jst ins fnl f: hdd fnl 50yds: no ex cl home* **16/1**

0365 **5** 1 **Lady Gar Gar**[31] 7198 3-8-13 **63** (v) DaleSwift(3) 5 66
(Geoffrey Oldroyd) *in tch: effrt to chse ldrs 2f out: styd on same pce ins fnl f* **7/2**[2]

3550 **6** 1 1/2 **Sarangoo**[6] 7537 3-9-3 **64** TomMcLaughlin 3 63
(Malcolm Saunders) *racd keenly: w ldr: rdn to take advantage over 1f out: hdd jst ins fnl f: fdd fnl 50yds* **8/1**

44-0 **7** 1/2 **Indian Arrow**[30] 7213 3-9-1 **65** MichaelO'Connell(3) 11 62
(John Quinn) *hld up: hrd at work over 3f out: kpt on fnl f: nt gng pce to trble ldrs* **33/1**

0000 **8** 1/2 **Fantasy Fry**[16] 7425 3-9-3 **64** (t) RichardKingscote 10 60
(Tom Dascombe) *hld up: u.p over 1f out: kpt on fnl f: no imp* **20/1**

-400 **9** 5 **Mac Tiernan (IRE)**[22] 7341 4-9-1 **62** AdamKirby 4 44
(Pat Murphy) *trckd ldrs tl wknd under 2f out* **9/1**

1m 29.38s (-0.22) **Going Correction** -0.075s/f (Stan) **9** Ran SP% **114.5**
Speed ratings (Par 101): **98,97,96,96,95 93,92,92,86**
CSF £22.66 CT £89.05 TOTE £5.50: £1.60, £1.30, £2.20; EX 19.60.
Owner Ken McGarrity **Bred** William Flynn **Trained** East Kilbride, S Lanarks

FOCUS
Just a run-of-the-mill contest but the form is straightforward and seems sound enough.
Mac Tiernan(IRE) Official explanation: jockey said gelding hung right from 2 1/2f out

7592 WOLVERHAMPTON-RACECOURSE.CO.UK NURSERY 5f 216y(P)
5:30 (5:31) (Class 6) (0-65,65) 2-Y-O **£1,704** (£503; £251) **Stalls** Low

Form RPR

3366 **1** **Sunny Side Up (IRE)**[112] 4943 2-9-2 **60** TonyHamilton 6 64
(Richard Fahey) *racd keenly: trckd ldrs: led wl over 1f out: rdn ins fnl f: hld on wl towards fin* **9/2**[2]

0005 **2** hd **Songbird Blues**[28] 7251 2-8-4 **48** DavidProbert 13 51
(Mark Usher) *hld up: hdwy 2f out: wnt 2nd ins ins fnl f: pressed wnr towards fin: jst hld* **9/1**

2001 **3** nk **Berlusca (IRE)**[54] 6695 2-9-7 **65** WilliamCarson 12 67
(William Jarvis) *midfield: hdwy on outer to chse ldrs over 2f out: rdn and nt qckn over 1f out: styd on towards fin: nt quite gng pce of first two* **11/4**[1]

53 **4** 2 **Heidi's Delight (IRE)**[28] 7251 2-8-3 **47** DuranFentiman 1 43
(Ann Duffield) *trckd ldrs: rdn 2f out: styd on same pce fnl 75yds* **11/1**

5224 **5** 3/4 **M J Woodward**[6] 7541 2-8-9 **53** StevieDonohoe 8 47
(Paul Green) *hld up: pushed along over 1f out: styd on ins fnl f: nrst fin* **9/2**[2]

0600 **6** 1 1/4 **Colourful Event (IRE)**[7] 7530 2-8-4 **48** (v) JoeFanning 10 38
(David Arbuthnot) *bhd: pushed along thrght: styd on ins fnl f: nt pce to rch ldrs* **20/1**

005 **7** 3/4 **Villa Reigns**[37] 7072 2-8-10 **54** (b[1]) LukeMorris 5 42
(John Weymes) *sn led: rdn and hung lft whn hdd wl over 1f out: wknd fnl 100yds* **22/1**

000 **8** hd **Lana Mae**[15] 7435 2-8-4 **55** RaulDaSilva(7) 4 42
(Jeremy Gask) *racd keenly in midfield: u.p over 1f out: no imp* **40/1**

6130 **9** 1 1/2 **Dansili Dutch (IRE)**[74] 6186 2-9-3 **61** LeeNewman 7 44
(David Barron) *midfield: pushed along and outpcd over 2f out: n.d* **11/2**[3]

0020 **10** 1 1/2 **Tangtastic (IRE)**[13] 7452 2-8-7 **51** MarcHalford 11 29
(Edward Creighton) *led early: prom tl rdn and wknd over 1f out* **16/1**

1m 15.34s (0.34) **Going Correction** -0.075s/f (Stan) **10** Ran SP% **114.2**
Speed ratings (Par 94): **94,93,93,90,89 88,87,86,84,82**
toteswingers:1&2:£5.80, 2&3:£5.80, 1&3:£3.80 CSF £42.27 CT £134.05 TOTE £6.70: £2.30, £2.20, £1.50; EX 40.70.
Owner Jim McGrath, Roger & Dianne Trevitt **Bred** Jim McGrath & Reg Griffin **Trained** Musley Bank, N Yorks

FOCUS
Just a modest nursery, though it was at least run at a sound pace. The form looks pretty weak but straightforward.

NOTEBOOK
Sunny Side Up(IRE) hadn't got home in the mud over 7.5f at Beverley back in August and it was no surprise to see her fare better dropped back in trip on her return from a break. She was all out in the end but impressed with the way she got to the front on the bridle over 1f out and the likely smallish rise in the weights isn't going to stop her being of interest next time. The way she travels, 5f could suit her just as well at this stage. (op 4-1 tchd 5-1)
Songbird Blues had come down another 4lb and finally made an impact in this sphere, staying on well and suggesting a return to 7f may suit ideally.
Berlusca(IRE), a C&D winner in October, ran just as well in defeat off his revised mark, particularly as he was always caught a bit wide from the 12 stall. (op 3-1)
Heidi's Delight(IRE) turned round last month's C&D form with M J Woodward. She doesn't look any better than modest at this stage but is worth a try over 7f at some point. (op 8-1)
M J Woodward had the visor left off this time but was again a bit below the form he showed when twice runner-up here this autumn. (op 11-2)
Villa Reigns Official explanation: jockey said gelding hung left-handed
Dansili Dutch(IRE), given a break since disappointing in the mud at Hamilton in September, wasn't at her best trying Polytrack for the first time on her return. (tchd 6-1)

7593 NAME A RACE TO ENHANCE YOUR BRAND MAIDEN STKS 5f 216y(P)
6:00 (6:02) (Class 5) 2-Y-O **£2,264** (£673; £336; £168) **Stalls** Low

Form RPR

2 **1** **Mezzotint (IRE)**[44] 6935 2-9-3 0 AdamKirby 8 80+
(Marco Botti) *racd keenly: a.p: wnt 2nd 2f out: led over 1f out: rdn ins fnl f: r.o: in control cl home* **2/1**[1]

2 3/4 **Hurry Up George** 2-9-3 0 JimCrowley 2 78+
(Ralph Beckett) *s.i.s: in rr: hdwy 2f out: swtchd lft over 1f out: prog to take 2nd fnl 110yds: r.o but a looked hld* **11/4**[2]

5 **3** 1 **Sky Crossing**[30] 7209 2-9-3 0 JamesSullivan 3 75
(James Given) *racd keenly: led: rdn and hdd whn carried hd fairly high over 1f out: lost 2nd fnl 110yds: styd on same pce towards fin: stl green* **16/1**

024 **4** 3 3/4 **Chapellerie (IRE)**[96] 5480 2-8-12 73 JimmyFortune 6 60
(Brian Meehan) *midfield: hdwy over 1f out: no imp on ldrs: one pce fnl f* **10/3**[3]

3304 **5** 2 1/4 **Millibar (IRE)**[13] 7464 2-8-12 73 TomMcLaughlin 4 52
(Nick Littmoden) *hld up in rr: hdwy 2f out: racd on outer wl over 1f out ent st: no imp on ldrs and one pce fnl f* **8/1**

06 **6** 1 **Kingscombe (USA)**[94] 5536 2-9-3 0 DaneO'Neill 9 54
(Pat Eddery) *chsd ldr to 2f out: rdn over 1f out: wknd ins fnl f* **50/1**

00 **7** 3 1/4 **My Name Is Sam**[57] 6620 2-9-3 0 LukeMorris 1 44
(Ronald Harris) *in tch: rdn and wknd over 1f out* **80/1**

00 **8** 7 **Jeremy Sue**[56] 6654 2-8-12 0 FergusSweeney 5 18
(Derek Haydn Jones) *hld up: pushed along over 1f out: nvr a danger* **100/1**

00 **9** 1 3/4 **Chart**[26] 7292 2-9-3 0 LeeNewman 10 18
(William Jarvis) *midfield: u.p over 2f out: sn wknd* **16/1**

1m 14.05s (-0.95) **Going Correction** -0.075s/f (Stan) **9** Ran SP% **110.1**
Speed ratings (Par 96): **103,102,100,95,92 91,87,77,75**
toteswingers:1&2:£2.40, 2&3:£12.70, 1&3:£8.10 CSF £6.94 TOTE £3.10: £1.10, £1.40, £3.40; EX 8.30.
Owner Miss A Bonito **Bred** David Barry **Trained** Newmarket, Suffolk

FOCUS
Fair form from the principals in this maiden with the time good and the form should prove sound.

NOTEBOOK
Mezzotint(IRE), who'd been sold out of Luca Cumani's stable since his debut second at Yarmouth in October, probably didn't have to improve on that form to go one better here. He didn't have much to spare come the finish but is entitled go on after just two starts. (op 7-4)
Hurry Up George, a gelded son of Intikhab, made a promising start and will be tough to beat in a similar event next time, travelling comfortably under restraint for a long way and keeping on well in the straight. (tchd 5-2)
Sky Crossing stepped up on the form of last month's debut, setting the pace and sticking to his task once headed. He could be the type to progress with racing. (tchd 14-1)
Chapellerie(IRE) had made the frame in a couple of turf maidens at the big tracks in August so might have been expected to do better switched to Polytrack after a break, not having any apparent excuses. (op 7-2 tchd 4-1)
Millibar(IRE) was well below her best and has now been disappointing on her last two starts, while none of the others offered any obvious encouragement, though this does at least open up the handicap route for a few of them.

7594 TOTEEXACTA H'CAP 5f 20y(P)
6:30 (6:30) (Class 5) (0-75,76) 3-Y-O+ **£2,264** (£673; £336; £168) **Stalls** Low

Form RPR

0516 **1** **No Mean Trick (USA)**[111] 5019 5-8-7 **61** BarryMcHugh 11 70+
(Paul Midgley) *chsd ldrs: rdn to ld over 1f out: all out cl home* **66/1**

5501 **2** hd **Red Cape (FR)**[6] 7535 8-9-8 **76** 6ex (b) JamesSullivan 3 84
(Ruth Carr) *hld up in midfield: nt clr run wl over 1f out: hdwy on inner appr fnl f: r.o and pressed wnr towards fin: jst denied* **11/2**[3]

0005 **3** nk **Desert Strike**[6] 7535 5-9-7 **75** (p) RobertWinston 2 82
(Alan McCabe) *in rr div: hdwy over 1f out: r.o for press ins fnl f: gng on at fin* **8/1**

0262 **4** *1* **Triple Dream**[15] 7428 6-9-3 **71**..........................(tp) RichardKingscote 10 75
(Milton Bradley) *midfield: rdn and hdwy over 1f out: styd on ins fnl f: nt quite gng pce of ldrs* **15/2**
0300 **5** *2 1/2* **Royal Bajan (USA)**[64] 6456 3-8-9 **66**.............................. DaleSwift(3) 6 62
(James Given) *prom: led after 1f: rdn and hdd over 1f out: no ex fnl 50yds* **9/2**[2]
2002 **6** *hd* **Wooden King (IRE)**[6] 7535 6-9-5 **73**.......................... TomMcLaughlin 5 68
(Malcolm Saunders) *w ldr to over 2f out: rdn over 1f out: sn outpcd: no imp after* **7/2**[1]
0011 **7** *1/2* **Estonia**[15] 7428 4-9-6 **74**.. AdamKirby 9 68
(Michael Squance) *midfield: effrt over 1f out: no imp on ldrs* **15/2**
4140 **8** *1* **Absa Lutte (IRE)**[8] 7512 8-9-4 **72**.................................... JimmyQuinn 7 62
(Michael Mullineaux) *missed break: bhd: nvr able to get on terms: eased whn no imp on ldrs ins fnl f* **14/1**
5200 **9** *1 3/4* **Sharp Shoes**[19] 7395 4-8-9 **63**....................................(p) TonyHamilton 4 48
(Ann Duffield) *led for 1f: chsd ldr tl wl over 1f out: wknd ins fnl f* **16/1**
3000 **10** *1 1/4* **Chjimes (IRE)**[19] 7395 7-8-11 **65**..............................(b) KirstyMilczarek 1 46
(Conor Dore) *a bhd: nvr able to get on terms* **16/1**
1220 **11** *27* **Shawkantango**[156] 3493 4-8-10 **69**..............................(v) MarkCoumbe(5) 8 —
(Derek Shaw) *missed break: a outpcd and wl bhd* **40/1**

61.09 secs (-1.21) **Going Correction** -0.075s/f (Stan) **11** Ran SP% **112.8**
Speed ratings (Par 103): **106,105,105,103,99 99,98,96,94,92 48**
toteswingers:1&2:£30.10, 2&3:£6.50, 1&3:£42.70 CSF £387.71 CT £3314.61 TOTE £63.00: £17.80, £3.30, £4.10; EX 521.60.
Owner John Allan Milburn **Bred** Larry Byer **Trained** Westow, N Yorks

FOCUS
A fair sprint and no reason why the form won't hold up. The form is sound enough with the runner-up to this year's turf best.

7595 TOTEPOOL H'CAP (DIV I) 5f 216y(P)
7:00 (7:00) (Class 5) (0-75,79) 3-Y-O+ **£2,264** (£673; £336; £168) **Stalls** Low

Form RPR
1240 **1** **Libys Dream (IRE)**[34] 7141 3-8-12 **66**.................. RichardKingscote 11 78
(Tom Dascombe) *chsd ldr after 1f: rdn to chal over 1f out: r.o to ld fnl 75yds: in control cl home* **11/2**[2]
2330 **2** *1/2* **Crew Cut (IRE)**[15] 7428 3-8-9 **70**.................................. RaulDaSilva(7) 9 80
(Jeremy Gask) *a.p: rdn on inner over 1f out: led jst ins fnl f: hdd fnl 75yds: hld cl home* **6/1**[3]
2456 **3** *1 3/4* **Trade Secret**[9] 7502 4-9-5 **73**..................................... RobertWinston 8 78
(Mel Brittain) *fly-jmpd leaving stalls: racd keenly in midfield: hdwy over 1f out: styd on ins fnl f: nt gng pce of front two and no imp fnl 50yds* **15/2**
6612 **4** *1 1/2* **Ryedane (IRE)**[17] 7416 9-8-11 **70**..............................(b) AdamCarter(5) 7 70+
(Tim Easterby) *s.i.s: hld up: pushed along 3f out: hdwy over 1f out: styd on ins fnl f: nt gng pce to rch ldrs* **9/1**
3221 **5** *shd* **Mount Hollow**[9] 7500 6-9-4 **79** 7ex..............................(p) JackDuern(7) 12 79+
(Reg Hollinshead) *bhd: hdwy over 1f out: styd on ins fnl f: nt gng pce to chal* **13/2**
5035 **6** *1/2* **Darcey**[17] 7416 5-9-4 **72**... MartinHarley 2 70
(Amy Weaver) *led early: in tch: rdn over 1f out: kpt on ins fnl f: one pce fnl 50yds* **15/2**
0340 **7** *1* **Devil You Know (IRE)**[169] 3036 5-8-12 **66**................(t) JamesSullivan 6 61
(Michael Easterby) *racd keenly: sn led: rdn over 1f out: hdd jst ins fnl f: wknd fnl 50yds* **25/1**
0665 **8** *hd* **Dickie Le Davoir**[9] 7502 7-8-11 **68**........................(b) RobertLButler(3) 1 62
(Richard Guest) *hld up: styd on ins fnl f: unable to rch ldrs* **22/1**
6004 **9** *1 1/2* **Lucky Dan (IRE)**[6] 7535 5-9-5 **73**..................................... FrannyNorton 5 62+
(Paul Green) *in tch: effrt 2f out: wknd ins fnl f* **5/1**[1]
5304 **10** *3/4* **Methaaly (IRE)**[8] 7519 8-9-2 **70**..............................(be) JimmyQuinn 13 57
(Michael Mullineaux) *hld up: rdn over 1f out: nvr a threat* **16/1**
2110 **11** *shd* **Istiqdaam**[61] 6544 6-9-7 **75**.....................................(b) KirstyMilczarek 4 62
(Conor Dore) *in tch: rdn over 1f out: sn wknd* **20/1**
5444 **12** *1 1/2* **Whipphound**[121] 4643 3-9-6 **74**................................ TomMcLaughlin 10 56
(Mark Brisbourne) *midfield: pushed along 2f out: wknd over 1f out* **25/1**

1m 14.05s (-0.95) **Going Correction** -0.075s/f (Stan) **12** Ran SP% **115.9**
Speed ratings (Par 103): **103,102,100,98,97 97,95,95,93,92 92,90**
toteswingers:1&2:£7.30, 2&3:£7.70, 1&3:£12.70 CSF £35.30 CT £245.07 TOTE £6.80: £1.70, £3.30, £3.30.
Owner Ms A Quinn **Bred** Irish National Stud **Trained** Malpas, Cheshire

FOCUS
They didn't go as frantic a pace as is sometimes the case in races of this nature and it didn't pay to sit too far back with the first two home both handy throughout. The third is the guide rated to his best form at the trip.
Lucky Dan(IRE) Official explanation: jockey said gelding ran too freely

7596 TOTEPOOL H'CAP (DIV II) 5f 216y(P)
7:30 (7:32) (Class 5) (0-75,75) 3-Y-O+ **£2,264** (£673; £336; £168) **Stalls** Low

Form RPR
0000 **1** **Restless Bay (IRE)**[63] 6491 3-9-5 **73**..........................(e1) AdamKirby 10 83
(Reg Hollinshead) *hld up: hdwy over 1f out: swtchd rt ent fnl f: r.o to ld towards fin* **7/1**[3]
0610 **2** *3/4* **Mambo Spirit (IRE)**[14] 7448 7-8-12 **66**............................ DaneO'Neill 7 73
(Tony Newcombe) *chsd ldr after 1f: rdn to ld over 1f out: hdd and hld towards fin* **14/1**
1042 **3** *shd* **Bond Fastrac**[51] 6779 4-9-3 **74**...................................... DaleSwift(3) 9 81
(Geoffrey Oldroyd) *hld up: hdwy on outer over 1f out: r.o ins fnl f: gng on at fin* **5/1**[2]
0020 **4** *3/4* **Lastkingofscotland (IRE)**[12] 7485 5-8-12 **66**..........(b) KirstyMilczarek 1 71
(Conor Dore) *midfield: rdn over 2f out: prog ins fnl f: styd on for press: nt quite pce of ldrs* **16/1**
0654 **5** *nk* **Above The Stars**[21] 7355 3-9-2 **70**............................... TonyHamilton 12 74
(Richard Fahey) *in tch: rdn over 1f out: styd on same pce ins fnl f* **9/1**
5060 **6** *1/2* **Italian Tom (IRE)**[13] 7457 4-9-7 **75**................................... LukeMorris 3 77
(Ronald Harris) *midfield: rdn and hdwy over 1f out: styd on same pce ins fnl f* **12/1**
1434 **7** *shd* **Two Turtle Doves (IRE)**[21] 7349 5-8-10 **64**..................... JimmyQuinn 5 66
(Michael Mullineaux) *chsd ldrs: rdn over 1f out: kpt on u.p ins fnl f: no ex fnl 50yds* **18/1**
5040 **8** *3/4* **Cardinal**[13] 7456 6-9-2 **70**... JimCrowley 6 69
(Robert Cowell) *hld up: pushed along after 2f: hdwy on inner over 1f out: kpt on ins fnl f: nt pce to chal* **17/2**
0503 **9** *nk* **Steelcut**[35] 7116 7-8-13 **67**.......................................(p) TomMcLaughlin 4 65
(David Evans) *hld up: kpt on ins fnl f: nvr a threat* **16/1**
0012 **10** *2 1/2* **Ice Trooper**[8] 7519 3-9-4 **72**..(p) TomEaves 2 62
(Linda Stubbs) *led: rdn and hdd over 1f out: wknd wl ins fnl f* **4/1**[1]
-002 **11** *1/2* **Royal Intruder**[7] 7529 6-9-3 **71**.. MartinHarley 13 60
(Richard Guest) *hld up: pushed along over 1f out: nvr a threat* **14/1**
310 **12** *3/4* **Polemica (IRE)**[68] 6354 5-9-0 **68**..................................(bt) LiamKeniry 8 54
(Frank Sheridan) *racd keenly in midfield: u.p and wknd over 1f out* **28/1**
0605 **13** *5* **Gap Princess (IRE)**[13] 7456 7-9-6 **74**............................ RobertWinston 11 44
(Geoffrey Harker) *chsd ldrs tl rdn and wknd under 2f out* **16/1**

1m 13.94s (-1.06) **Going Correction** -0.075s/f (Stan) **13** Ran SP% **117.1**
Speed ratings (Par 103): **104,103,102,101,101 100,100,99,99,95 95,94,87**
toteswingers:1&2:£16.20, 2&3:£11.60, 1&3:£7.50 CSF £99.15 CT £536.67 TOTE £9.50: £3.70, £2.50, £1.30; EX 114.40.
Owner John L Marriott **Bred** Grangemore Stud **Trained** Upper Longdon, Staffs

FOCUS
In contrast to the first division they went a good pace. The form is rated around the third, fourth, fifth and seventh and looks pretty solid.
Gap Princess(IRE) Official explanation: jockey said mare hung left-handed
T/Plt: £12.40 to a £1 stake. Pool of £75,850.98 - 4,440.73 winning units. T/Qpdt: £9.40 to a £1 stake. Pool of £9,027.64 - 706.99 winning units. DO

7573 LINGFIELD (L-H)
Friday, December 2

OFFICIAL GOING: Standard
Wind: Virtually nil Weather: Sunny and chilly

7597 FRED GIBSON MEMORIAL NURSERY 6f (P)
12:10 (12:10) (Class 5) (0-75,72) 2-Y-O **£2,385** (£704; £352) **Stalls** Low

Form RPR
0423 **1** **Lady Gibraltar**[14] 7451 2-9-6 **71**..(v) JimCrowley 4 76
(Alan Jarvis) *mde all: rdn wl over 1f out: styd on strly ins fnl f* **11/1**
6400 **2** *2 1/4* **Dishy Guru**[21] 7358 2-9-5 **70**.. LukeMorris 1 68
(Michael Blanshard) *chsd ldng pair: rdn to chse wnr 2f out: drvn and no imp ins fnl f* **14/1**
0044 **3** *3/4* **Arabian Flight**[13] 7482 2-8-6 **60**.................................... KieranO'Neill(3) 5 56
(John Bridger) *taken down early: t.k.h: hld up in last trio: effrt on inner 2f out: kpt on wl ins fnl f: no threat to wnr* **50/1**
1230 **4** *nse* **Guava**[27] 7294 2-9-3 **68**.. RyanMoore 3 64
(Richard Hannon) *in tch: rdn and chsd ldng trio 2f out: drvn and styd on same pce fr 1f out* **5/1**[3]
4322 **5** *6* **Kyleakin Lass**[14] 7451 2-9-7 **72**.. TomQueally 8 50
(Ian Wood) *stdd s: t.k.h and hld up in rr for 1f: sn pushed along and nvr travelling after: c wd bnd 2f out: plugged on but n.d* **9/2**[2]
4064 **6** *1* **Illustrious Lad (IRE)**[8] 7530 2-8-13 **64**....................... JimmyFortune 7 39
(Jim Boyle) *chsd wnr tl 2f out: wknd qckly over 1f out* **9/1**
4605 **7** *3/4* **Safari Storm (USA)**[15] 7445 2-9-4 **69**..............................(t) EddieAhern 9 42
(Brian Meehan) *in tch in midfield: rdn and unable qck ent fnl 2f: wknd qckly over 1f out* **11/2**
505 **8** *3/4* **Star Kingdom (IRE)**[77] 6127 2-9-5 **70**......................... StevieDonohoe 2 40
(Robert Mills) *in tch in midfield: rdn and struggling whn sltly hmpd and lost pl ent fnl 2f: no imp u.p 1f out* **5/2**[1]
5533 **9** *2 1/2* **Art Show**[46] 6919 2-9-0 **65**.. TomMcLaughlin 6 28
(Ed Dunlop) *hld up in tch: hung rt bnd over 4f out: cocked jaw and hung rt bnd ent fnl 2f: lost pl and bhd after* **14/1**

1m 11.35s (-0.55) **Going Correction** -0.125s/f (Stan) 2y crse rec **9** Ran SP% **112.4**
Speed ratings (Par 96): **98,95,94,93,85 84,83,82,79**
toteswingers: 1&2 £24.30, 1&3 £28.90, 2&3 £30.60 CSF £147.01 CT £7139.07 TOTE £12.50: £3.40, £5.40, £6.80; EX 92.80 Trifecta £226.90 Part won. Pool: £306.70 - 0.43 winning units..
Owner Buckingham Flooring **Bred** Netherfield House Stud **Trained** Twyford, Bucks

FOCUS
Just a modest nursery with the placed horses close to their marks in a straightforward race.

NOTEBOOK
Lady Gibraltar, who has hung badly left in the past, including at Kempton last time, appreciated hugging the rail all the way into the straight and, once in line for home up the middle of the track, saw off her pursuers with ease. She might have more to offer around here or at Wolverhampton, but is apparently now going to be given a break. (op 10-1 tchd 12-1)
Dishy Guru settled better than on his previous two starts and put in a better effort as a result. (op 16-1 tchd 12-1)
Arabian Flight, who was held up early, raced a shade keenly. Nipping through on the inside turning in, she seemed to get this longer trip well enough. (op 40-1)
Guava got a little outpaced running down the hill but kept on for pressure. (op 11-2 tchd 9-2)
Kyleakin Lass, held up for a change, got detached early, swung widest off the bend and could never land a blow. Perhaps she is happiest when ridden more prominently. (op 3-1)
Illustrious Lad(IRE) Official explanation: jockey said gelding ran wide on bend
Star Kingdom(IRE), returning from an 11-week absence, was a well-backed favourite but never really threatened to get involved. His pedigree suggests a longer trip may be needed. (op 100-30)
Art Show Official explanation: jockey said filly did not turn

7598 RON GIBSON BRITISH STALLION STUDS EBF MAIDEN FILLIES' STKS (DIV I) 1m (P)
12:40 (12:41) (Class 5) 2-Y-O **£3,234** (£962; £481; £240) **Stalls** High

Form RPR
54 **1** **Strathnaver**[36] 7124 2-9-0 0... JimmyFortune 1 74+
(Ed Dunlop) *sn led: hdd 6f out: chsd ldr after tl led again 2f out: drvn and edgd rt 1f out: kpt on u.p fnl 100yds* **7/4**[1]
423 **2** *3/4* **Miss Astragal (IRE)**[22] 7344 2-9-0 72.............................. RyanMoore 3 72
(Richard Hannon) *chsd ldrs: rdn and effrt to press ldrs 2f out: drvn and wnt 2nd 1f out tl jst ins fnl f: styd on same pce and wnt 2nd again towards fin* **2/1**[2]
3 *1/2* **Between Us** 2-9-0 0... SebSanders 2 73+
(Sir Mark Prescott Bt) *dwlt: sn rcvrd and chsng ldrs: rdn and effrt wl over 1f out: swtchd to inner 1f out: sn pressing wnr: sltly short of room fnl 100yds: eased and swtchd rt fnl 75yds* **5/1**[3]
0 **4** *1 1/2* **Frock (IRE)**[14] 7454 2-9-0 0... LiamKeniry 4 67+
(Sylvester Kirk) *in tch in midfield: rdn and effrt ent fnl 2f: styd on same pce fnl f* **20/1**
5 *4 1/2* **Vickers Vimy** 2-9-0 0... JimCrowley 10 57
(Ralph Beckett) *t.k.h: racd wd for 2f: hdwy to ld and crossed to rail 6f out: hdd 2f out: sn rdn: wknd ent fnl f* **13/2**
0 **6** *8* **La Passionata**[92] 5655 2-9-0 0..................................... StevieDonohoe 8 39
(Robert Mills) *stdd s: t.k.h: hld up in last trio: outpcd over 3f out: n.d fnl 3f* **40/1**
0 **7** *7* **Dorrit**[13] 7494 2-9-0 0.. SteveDrowne 6 23
(Roger Charlton) *stdd s: hld up in last trio: pushed along over 4f out: lost tch and bhd fnl 3f* **33/1**

0 **8** *6* **Asparella**[36] 7118 2-9-0 0 DaneO'Neill 5 9
(Raymond York) *hld up in last trio: rdn and lost tch over 3f out: sn wl bhd* **100/1**

1m 39.13s (0.93) **Going Correction** -0.125s/f (Stan) **8** Ran SP% **110.8**
Speed ratings (Par 93): **90,89,88,87,82 74,67,61**
toteswingers: 1&2 £1.40, 1&3 £2.50, 2&3 £2.40 CSF £5.03 TOTE £3.20: £1.50, £1.02, £2.40; EX 4.90 Trifecta £12.00 Pool: £379.32 - 23.31 winning units..
Owner St Albans Bloodstock LLP **Bred** Mrs C R Philipson & Mrs H G Lascelles **Trained** Newmarket, Suffolk

FOCUS
An ordinary fillies' maiden with the winner improving and the runner-up setting the level, although the form is limited by the modest time.

NOTEBOOK
Strathnaver found the step up to 1m proving the key, getting off the mark at the third attempt, and it also helped that, as her rider was using his whip with his right hand and the filly edged towards the inside rail in the closing stages. (tchd 2-1)
Miss Astragal(IRE) is pretty exposed now but she runs to a predictable level and is a good guide for rating the form. (op 15-8 tchd 13-8)
Between Us ◆ travelled well to the turn in and, after getting caught a little flat-footed, was staying on strongly at the finish, but switching to challenge to the winner's inner was a big mistake and she got stopped in her run when that filly edged left, towards the rail, in front of her. A half-sister to five winners including French Oaks winner Confidential Lady, she'll have no trouble winning her maiden. (op 6-1)
Frock(IRE) improved on her debut effort and will be of interest once she's eligible for a mark. (tchd 25-1)
Vickers Vimy pulled hard early and didn't see her race out as a result, but she's well bred by Montjeu out of a half-sister to high-class 6f-7f performer Diffident, and she should improve for this debut effort. Official explanation: jockey said filly ran too free (tchd 6-1)

7599 RON GIBSON BRITISH STALLION STUDS EBF MAIDEN FILLIES' STKS (DIV II) 1m (P)
1:10 (1:10) (Class 5) 2-Y-O **£3,234** (£962; £481; £240) **Stalls** High

Form RPR
6463 **1** **Tina's Spirit (IRE)**[22] 7343 2-9-0 75 (b) AdamKirby 8 72
(Clive Cox) *chsd ldr tl led over 2f out: shkn up and sn clr: reminder wl over 1f out: in command after: eased towards fin* **15/8**[1]
2 *¾* **Zaina (IRE)** 2-9-0 0 DaneO'Neill 5 67+
(Gerard Butler) *hld up in tch: swtchd rt and effrt bnd 2f out: gd hdwy to chse clr ldng pair jst over 1f out: styd on wl to chse wnr fnl 75yds: clsng on eased wnr at fin* **10/1**
0 **3** *1* **Cape Safari (IRE)**[45] 6934 2-9-0 0 JoeFanning 1 65+
(James Tate) *led: hdd and rdn along over 2f out: sn outpcd by wnr: kpt on: lost 2nd fnl 75yds* **15/2**
0 **4** *1 ½* **Anabedweyah (IRE)**[45] 6934 2-9-0 0 JimmyFortune 10 62
(Clive Brittain) *hld up in rr: hdwy 2f out: rn green but styd on steadily fnl f: nt rch ldrs* **20/1**
04 **5** *2 ¾* **It's A Girl Thing (IRE)**[14] 7454 2-9-0 0 RyanMoore 4 55
(George Baker) *in tch: rdn and outpcd over 2f out: no threat to ldrs but plugged on past btn horses fnl f* **7/2**[2]
05 **6** *hd* **Isobella**[28] 7257 2-9-0 0 JimCrowley 9 55
(Hughie Morrison) *dwlt: in tch in last pair: outpcd over 2f out: styd on past btn horses fnl f: no threat to ldrs* **66/1**
00 **7** *hd* **Synfonica**[50] 6819 2-8-11 0 KieranO'Neill(3) 3 54
(Richard Hannon) *t.k.h: chsd ldrs: rdn and outpcd over 2f out: btn over 1f out: wknd 1f out* **66/1**
8 *1* **News Desk** 2-9-0 0 RobertHavlin 2 52
(John Gosden) *dwlt: sn bustled along and rcvrd to chse ldrs after 1f: rdn and outpcd over 2f out: wknd over 1f out* **7/1**
5 **9** *1* **Chignon (IRE)**[20] 7396 2-9-0 0 TomQueally 7 50
(Sir Henry Cecil) *chsd ldrs: 3rd and outpcd jst over 2f out: lost 3rd jst over 1f out: fdd ins fnl f* **13/2**[3]
0 **10** *2 ½* **L'Arlesienne**[20] 7396 2-9-0 0 LiamKeniry 6 44
(Sylvester Kirk) *in tch in last trio: rdn and struggling over 2f out: bhd fnl 2f* **66/1**

1m 38.21s (0.01) **Going Correction** -0.125s/f (Stan) **10** Ran SP% **112.9**
Speed ratings (Par 93): **94 93 92 90 88 87 87 86 85 83**
toteswingers: 1&2 £3.70, 1&3 £5.00, 2&3 £15.00 CSF £20.78 TOTE £3.00: £1.40, £3.70, £2.80; EX 18.30 Trifecta £162.80 Part won. Pool: £220.05 - 0.30 winning units..
Owner S R Hope And S W Barrow **Bred** Mrs Chris Harrington **Trained** Lambourn, Berks

FOCUS
The quicker of the two divisions by 0.92sec and the winner sets the standard.

NOTEBOOK
Tina's Spirit(IRE) made the most of her easiest task to date and finally got off the mark at the 11th attempt, but on only her second start for this stable. Prominent from the outset, she kicked on running down the hill and the advantage she gained allowed her to be eased down close home. Moving back into handicaps will prove more difficult. (op 3-1)
Zaina(IRE) ◆, a half-sister to four winners, is bred to be a middle-distance filly next year. The winner got first run on her heading to the turn and the race was lost, but the ground she made up once in line for home was eyecatching, and she should be able to go one better soon, before stepping up in trip next season. (op 11-2 tchd 11-1)
Cape Safari(IRE) disputed the lead early and kept battling away once the winner kicked clear. (op 14-1)
Anabedweyah(IRE) was given plenty to do. Held up at the back, she ran into traffic on the turn and then ran green when asked to pick up in the straight. This daughter of Authorized looks capable of doing better with more experience. (op 16-1)
It's A Girl Thing(IRE) didn't run up to the form of her latest Kempton effort, but handicaps are now open to her. (op 3-1)

7600 LIMPIO STORAGE SOLUTIONS CLAIMING STKS 1m 2f (P)
1:45 (1:45) (Class 6) 3-Y-O+ **£1,704** (£503; £251) **Stalls** Low

Form RPR
1301 **1** **Junoob**[15] 7446 3-9-5 84 (b) RyanMoore 2 94
(Amy Weaver) *in tch: hdwy to trck ldr 2f out: pushed along to ld 1f out: sn rdn clr and r.o strly: eased towards fin* **5/4**[1]
0520 **2** *7* **Marvo**[24] 5728 7-8-10 66 (b) EddieAhern 5 68
(Mark H Tompkins) *chsd ldrs: hdwy to ld traveling wl jst over 2f out: rdn and edgd rt u.p jst over 1f out: hdd 1f out: sn outpcd and no ch w wnr* **20/1**
0001 **3** *2* **Dr Livingstone (IRE)**[16] 7430 6-9-8 82 SteveDrowne 6 76
(Charles Egerton) *dwlt: racd in last pair: rdn over 3f out: styd on to chse ldng pair jst ins fnl f: kpt on but nvr nr ldrs* **7/2**[2]
2160 **4** *5* **Rowan Ridge**[21] 7363 3-8-7 65 (v) NickyMackay 3 54
(Jim Boyle) *chsd ldrs tl wnt 2nd 4f out: rdn and ev ch over 2f out: struggling u.p 2f out: 4th and wl btn after* **10/1**[3]
0-32 **5** *4 ½* **Beat Of The Blues**[15] 7446 3-8-10 77 KieranO'Neill(3) 7 51
(Alan McCabe) *chsd ldr tl 4f out: lost pl u.p over 2f out: wl btn over 1f out* **7/2**[2]
3002 **6** *2* **Ice Cold Bex**[16] 7427 3-8-2 65 (b[1]) MatthewCosham(5) 4 41
(Philip McBride) *led tl hdd and rdn jst over 2f out: sn struggling: wknd and wl btn over 1f out* **12/1**
060/ **7** *4 ½* **Keep A Welcome**[1656] 1895 8-8-7 29 SimonPearce(3) 1 32
(Gerry Enright) *a bhd: lost tch 3f out* **200/1**

2m 2.82s (-3.78) **Going Correction** -0.125s/f (Stan)
WFA 3 from 6yo+ 3lb **7** Ran SP% **110.9**
Speed ratings (Par 101): **110,104,102,98,95 93,90**
toteswingers: 1&2 £4.40, 1&3 £1.80, 2&3 £6.80 CSF £28.21 TOTE £2.10: £1.60, £7.30; EX 20.60.Junoob was claimed by Tom Dascombe for £12,000.
Owner Michael Bringloe **Bred** Shadwell Estate Company Limited **Trained** Newmarket, Suffolk

FOCUS
Not a bad claimer run in a time 2.39 seconds faster than the following handicap. The winner was helped by the third and fifth running below their marks but could be rated higher at face value.

7601 JENNY CUTTING MEMORIAL H'CAP 1m 2f (P)
2:20 (2:20) (Class 5) (0-75,78) 3-Y-O+ **£2,385** (£704; £352) **Stalls** Low

Form RPR
4565 **1** **Choral Festival**[14] 7458 5-8-10 **67** KieranO'Neill(3) 4 76
(John Bridger) *led early: sn hdd and chsd ldrs: effrt and ev ch wl over 1f out: led 1f out: r.o wl u.p* **25/1**
014 **2** *1 ¼* **Winning Spark (USA)**[14] 7458 4-9-5 **73** RyanMoore 10 80
(Gary Moore) *chsd ldng trio: rdn and effrt ent fnl 2f: ev ch over 1f out: styd on same pce u.p ins fnl f* **5/1**[2]
3000 **3** *shd* **Buxfizz (USA)**[31] 7204 3-9-4 **75** (p) JimCrowley 12 81
(Robert Mills) *bustled along leaving stalls and sn chsng ldr: led over 2f out: drvn and hrd pressed over 1f out: hdd 1f out: styd on same pce after* **50/1**
2005 **4** *2 ¼* **If You Whisper (IRE)**[31] 7204 3-9-1 **72** (b[1]) TonyCulhane 11 74+
(Mike Murphy) *stdd s: t.k.h: hld up in last pair: pushed along and hdwy on outer bnd 2f out: edgd lft and styd on fnl f: nvr threatened ldrs* **16/1**
2604 **5** *½* **Strike Force**[3] 7577 7-8-10 **69** (t) MatthewCosham(5) 6 70+
(Clifford Lines) *in tch in midfield: rdn and effrt whn n.m.r wl over 1f out: styd on ins fnl f: nvr trbld ldrs* **14/1**
4 **6** *nse* **Daring Indian**[34] 7179 3-9-1 **72** DavidProbert 2 73
(Ian Williams) *in tch: rdn and unable qck ent fnl 2f: styd on same pce u.p fr over 1f out* **4/1**[1]
3013 **7** *hd* **Focail Maith**[30] 7236 3-9-2 **73** JimmyFortune 13 73
(John Ryan) *in tch: rdn and unable qck over 2f out: kpt on same pce u.p fnl 2f* **8/1**[3]
0-01 **8** *½* **Hurricane Hymnbook (USA)**[20] 7387 6-9-0 **68** StevieDonohoe 1 67+
(Willie Musson) *in tch in midfield: shuffled bk and swtchd arnd wkng rival over 2f out: rallied u.p over 1f out: kpt on but nvr a threat to ldrs* **4/1**[1]
0631 **9** *nk* **Hurricane Spirit (IRE)**[9] 7513 7-9-10 **78** 6ex (b) SteveDrowne 9 77+
(Terry Clement) *hld up in tch in last trio: shkn up and effrt 2f out: no prog and wl hld whn nt clr run jst over 1f out: kpt on but n.d fnl f* **16/1**
032P **10** *1 ¼* **Nibani (IRE)**[34] 7178 4-9-5 **73** (p) TomQueally 7 69
(Alastair Lidderdale) *in tch: rdn and nt qckn whn c wd bnd 2f out: wknd wl over 1f out* **8/1**[3]
0013 **11** *1 ½* **Lisahane Bog**[9] 7513 4-9-5 **73** (b) DaneO'Neill 5 66
(Peter Hedger) *dwlt and bustled along early: in tch in midfield: shuffled bk and towards rr whn rdn over 2f out: no imp fnl 2f* **10/1**
1140 **12** *1 ¼* **Count Ceprano (IRE)**[30] 7237 7-8-7 **64** SimonPearce(3) 8 55
(Lydia Pearce) *hld up in tch in rr: rdn and no prog wl over 1f out: n.d* **50/1**
0000 **13** *5* **Strong Vigilance (IRE)**[14] 7465 4-9-1 **69** MartinLane 14 50
(Michael Bell) *stdd s: hld up in tch in rr: rdn 2f out: sn wknd and bhd 1f out* **66/1**
2160 **14** *18* **High On The Hog (IRE)**[14] 7453 3-9-1 **72** TomMcLaughlin 3 —
(Paul Howling) *bustled along leaving stalls: sn led and t.k.h: rdn and hdd over 2f out: sn dropped out: wl bhd and eased ins fnl f* **150/1**

2m 5.21s (-1.39) **Going Correction** -0.125s/f (Stan)
WFA 3 from 4yo+ 2lb **14** Ran SP% **116.2**
Speed ratings (Par 103): **100,99,98,97,96 96,96,96,95,94 93,92,88,74**
toteswingers: 1&2 £20.80, 1&3 £89.50, 2&3 £31.90 CSF £139.78 CT £6153.50 TOTE £34.00: £7.00, £1.50, £7.10; EX 165.20 TRIFECTA Not won..
Owner Mrs Liz Gardner **Bred** Cheveley Park Stud Ltd **Trained** Liphook, Hants

FOCUS
It paid to race prominently here but the form looks reasonable, with the winner the best guide.

7602 FRED & RON GIBSON MEMORIAL H'CAP 6f (P)
2:55 (2:55) (Class 4) (0-85,84) 3-Y-O+ **£4,204** (£1,251; £625; £312) **Stalls** Low

Form RPR
3503 **1** **Lujeanie**[14] 7457 5-9-4 **81** (p) MartinLane 5 92
(Dean Ivory) *hld up in tch in last quartet: rdn and hdwy 2f out: swtchd rt over 1f out: led 1f out: r.o wl* **11/4**[1]
2300 **2** *¾* **Admirable Spirit**[71] 6272 3-9-3 **80** RyanMoore 12 89
(Richard Hannon) *stdd and dropped in bhd after s: rdn and hdwy over 1f out: swtchd rt 1f out: chsd wnr fnl 100yds: r.o but a hld* **7/1**[3]
0064 **3** *3* **Judd Street**[16] 7438 9-9-5 **82** (vt) DaneO'Neill 1 83+
(Eve Johnson Houghton) *dwlt and stuck towards rr on inner: hdwy into midfield 1/2-way: n.m.r 2f out tl hdwy to chse ldrs 1f out: kpt on to go 3rd fnl 75yds* **10/3**[2]
3140 **4** *½* **Close To The Edge (IRE)**[63] 6495 3-9-1 **81** KieranO'Neill(3) 10 79
(Alan McCabe) *dwlt and bustled along early: in tch: effrt and rdn to chse ldr 2f out: drvn and unable qck over 1f out: wknd fnl 100yds* **8/1**
6216 **5** *1* **Aristeia**[14] 7457 3-9-1 **78** SteveDrowne 11 73
(Richard Hannon) *hld up in rr: effrt but stl plenty to do whn nt clr run and swtchd rt over 1f out: r.o wl ins fnl f: n.d* **16/1**
6000 **6** *nk* **Quasi Congaree (GER)**[16] 7439 5-9-7 **84** (t) TomQueally 7 78
(Ian Wood) *hld up towards rr: effrt on outer bnd 2f out: drvn and styd on same pce fnl f* **11/1**
0000 **7** *3* **Cadeaux Pearl**[22] 7356 3-8-11 **77** (b) BillyCray(3) 4 61
(David Nicholls) *led: rdn 2f out: hdd 1f out: sn wknd* **25/1**
4234 **8** *2 ¼* **Billy Red**[13] 7487 7-9-2 **79** (b) FergusSweeney 9 56
(J R Jenkins) *chsd ldr tl 2f out: wkng whn sltly hmpd over 1f out: fdd ins fnl f* **9/1**
0003 **9** *nk* **Sir Geoffrey (IRE)**[13] 7489 5-9-7 **84** (b) IanMongan 2 60
(David Nicholls) *chsd ldrs: rdn and unable qck wl over 1f out: wknd 1f out: fdd ins fnl f* **8/1**

4/0 **10** *6* **Smoky Cloud (IRE)**[16] 7438 4-9-0 **77**.......................... TomMcLaughlin 6 34
(Amy Weaver) *chsd ldrs: rdn and losing pl whn sltly hmpd ent fnl 2f: bhd over 1f out* **20/1**

1m 10.24s (-1.66) **Going Correction** -0.125s/f (Stan) course record **10** Ran SP% **117.3**
Speed ratings (Par 105): **106,105,101,100,99 98,94,91,91,83**
toteswingers: 1&2 £6.70, 1&3 £3.20, 2&3 £4.60 CSF £22.62 CT £68.16 TOTE £3.70: £1.30, £2.30, £1.30; EX 27.30 Trifecta £58.60 Pool: £484.32 - 6.11 winning units..
Owner K T Ivory **Bred** K T Ivory **Trained** Radlett, Herts

FOCUS
There was a good gallop on this time and those held up had the race set up for them. The winner is rated back to last year's form with the runner-up to her best.

7603 LIMPIO FACILITIES MANAGEMENT H'CAP — 1m 4f (P)
3:30 (3:30) (Class 6) (0-65,65) 3-Y-O+ — £1,704 (£503; £251) **Stalls** Low

Form — RPR

4210 **1** **Ninfea (IRE)**[14] 7461 3-9-4 **64**...............................(p) LiamKeniry 10 72
(Sylvester Kirk) *hld up in tch: pushed along 4f out and hdwy on outer to chse ldrs 3f out: rdn 2f out: ev ch ins fnl f: edgd lft and led wl ins fnl f: r.o* **12/1**

4605 **2** *nk* **Rodrigo De Freitas (IRE)**[20] 7387 4-9-0 **55**..................(v) EddieAhern 6 62
(Jim Boyle) *hld up in tch: rdn and effrt on inner 2f out: drvn to chal 1f out: led ins fnl f: hdd and no ex wl ins fnl f* **13/2**

3042 **3** *1* **Formidable Guest**[21] 7363 7-9-4 **59**.......................... RobertHavlin 7 65+
(Jamie Poulton) *stdd s: hld up in tch in last pair: hdwy and pushed along ent fnl 2f: chsd ldrs and drvn 1f out: kpt on fnl 100yds* **3/1**[1]

5245 **4** *½* **Rosco Flyer (IRE)**[22] 7346 5-9-9 **64**...............................(b) JimmyFortune 2 70
(Roger Teal) *bustled along leaving stalls: sn led: rdn and hrd pressed 2f out: edgd rt u.p jst over 1f out: hdd ins fnl f: keeping on same pce and hld whn nt clr run and hmpd towards fin* **9/2**[2]

1350 **5** *½* **Prince Blue**[36] 7121 4-8-10 **51**.. SamHitchcott 9 55
(John E Long) *in tch: chsd ldr over 2f out: ev ch and rdn 2f out: carried rt jst over 1f out: no ex and plugged on same pce fnl 100yds* **20/1**

5040 **6** *shd* **Cloudy Start**[14] 7461 5-9-10 **65**...............................(b) FergusSweeney 8 69
(Jamie Osborne) *chsd ldrs: rdn and unable qck whn squeezed for room and lost pl jst over 2f out: swtchd lft and rallied ins fnl f: kpt on* **14/1**

3400 **7** *¾* **Broughtons Swinger**[21] 7363 4-9-9 **64**.................. StevieDonohoe 5 67
(Willie Musson) *hld up in tch in rr: rdn and effrt 2f out: styd on ins fnl f: nvr able to chal* **14/1**

6S23 **8** *½* **Aine's Delight (IRE)**[22] 3690 5-9-1 **56**........................ DaneO'Neill 4 60+
(Andy Turnell) *t.k.h: chsd ldrs: edgd out rt and effrt u.p wl over 1f out: stl pressing ldrs and keeping on whn squeezed for room and snatched up ins fnl f: nt rcvr* **11/2**[3]

640 **9** *6* **Swaninstockwell (IRE)**[46] 6923 3-8-13 **59**...................... IanMongan 3 51
(Pat Phelan) *t.k.h: chsd ldr tl rdn and struggling over 2f out: wknd over 1f out* **7/1**

0040 **10** *19* **Circle Of Angels**[29] 7255 3-9-2 **62**................................ MartinLane 11 24
(Ian Williams) *chsd ldrs tl rdn and lost pl 5f out: bhd 3f out: lost tch 2f out* **16/1**

2m 31.09s (-1.91) **Going Correction** -0.125s/f (Stan)
WFA 3 from 4yo+ 5lb **10** Ran SP% **116.1**
Speed ratings (Par 101): **101,100,100,99,99 99,98,98,94,81**
toteswingers: 1&2 £13.70, 1&3 £8.80, 2&3 £5.50 CSF £87.44 CT £297.88 TOTE £14.20: £4.60, £2.50, £2.20; EX 83.80 TRIFECTA Not won..
Owner Miss A Jones **Bred** Kilco Builders **Trained** Upper Lambourn, Berks
■ Stewards' Enquiry : Jimmy Fortune two-day ban: careless riding (Dec 16-17)
Liam Keniry two-day ban: used whip with excessive frequency (Dec 16-17)

FOCUS
They didn't go much of an early pace here but the overall time was reasonable for the grade, and the form looks sound enough, with the runner-up to his Polytrack best.
T/Plt: £564.00 to a £1 stake. Pool: £49,949.07. 64.65 winning tickets. T/Qpdt: £79.50 to a £1 stake. Pool: £5,964.16. 55.50 winning tickets. SP

7589 WOLVERHAMPTON (A.W) (L-H)
Friday, December 2

OFFICIAL GOING: Standard
Wind: Fresh, behind Weather: Overcast

7604 TOTEPLACEPOT APPRENTICE H'CAP — 1m 1f 103y(P)
4:00 (4:00) (Class 6) (0-65,65) 3-Y-O+ — £1,704 (£503; £251) **Stalls** Low

Form — RPR

0064 **1** **Archie Rice (USA)**[9] 7522 5-9-3 **64**...................... MichaelJMurphy(3) 11 73
(Tom Keddy) *a.p: edgd lft over 7f out: led over 2f out: rdn out* **13/2**[2]

4130 **2** *1* **Knowe Head (NZ)**[39] 7068 4-9-6 **64**............................... NathanAlison 8 72+
(James Unett) *a.p: nt clr run and swtchd lft over 1f out: r.o* **5/1**[1]

0006 **3** *1½* **Hydrant**[17] 7425 5-8-12 **61**.................................... HannahNunn(5) 10 65+
(Peter Salmon) *hld up: nt clr run over 2f out: hdwy over 1f out: r.o* **17/2**

2301 **4** *¾* **Master Of Song**[59] 6613 4-9-5 **63**...............................(p) LucyKBarry 7 65
(Roy Bowring) *mid-div: hmpd over 6f out: hdwy over 1f out: sn rdn: r.o* **5/1**[1]

0506 **5** *½* **Isdaal**[30] 7228 4-9-2 **60**...(p) CharlesBishop 12 61
(Kevin Morgan) *hld up: nt clr run over 1f out: r.o ins fnl f: nt rch ldrs* **8/1**

3566 **6** *¾* **Carcinetto (IRE)**[14] 7465 9-9-1 **64**..........................(v) KevinLundie(5) 3 63
(David Evans) *chsd ldrs: rdn over 2f out: hmpd over 1f out: styd on same pce* **10/1**

/003 **7** *½* **Miss Beat (IRE)**[32] 7200 5-9-3 **64**................................ JasonHart(3) 13 62
(Declan Carroll) *s.i.s: sn chsng ldr: rdn and ev ch over 2f out: no ex fnl f* **15/2**[3]

8 *2¼* **The Fox Tully (IRE)**[14] 7472 6-9-0 **61**..................... ThomasBrown(3) 5 55
(Gerard Keane, Ire) *chsd ldrs: rdn over 2f out: wknd over 1f out* **8/1**

4300 **9** *shd* **Hathaway (IRE)**[14] 7466 4-8-7 **51** oh3.......................... RachealKneller 4 44
(Mark Brisbourne) *hld up: pushed along 3f out: nvr on terms* **33/1**

0066 **10** *2* **Luv U Noo**[20] 7400 4-8-2 **51** oh6.............................. DannyBrock(5) 2 40
(Brian Baugh) *s.s: hld up: n.d* **66/1**

5204 **11** *nse* **Retreat Content (IRE)**[34] 7160 3-9-5 **65**..................... GarryWhillans 9 54
(Linda Perratt) *chsd ldrs: hmpd and lost pl over 7f out: wknd over 1f out* **20/1**

3400 **12** *1¼* **Nicola's Dream**[32] 7198 3-8-11 **60**.....................(v[1]) GeorgeChaloner(3) 6 46
(Richard Fahey) *led: hdd over 2f out: wknd over 1f out* **16/1**

2m 0.27s (-1.43) **Going Correction** -0.10s/f (Stan)
WFA 3 from 4yo+ 2lb **12** Ran SP% **115.3**
Speed ratings (Par 101): **102,101,99,99,98 98,97,95,95,93 93,92**
toteswingers: 1&2 £, 1&3 £, 2&3 £ CSF £37.17 CT £279.46 TOTE £4.50: £1.50, £2.10, £3.30; EX 28.60.
Owner Andrew Duffield **Bred** Baltusrol Thoughbreds Llc Et Al **Trained** Newmarket, Suffolk
■ Stewards' Enquiry : Michael J Murphy two-day ban: careless riding (Dec 16-17)

FOCUS
A modest handicap run at an ordinary gallop. The winner raced centre-to-far side in the straight and is rated to this year's best, while the runner-up is rated better than the bare form.

7605 SPIFFING CRABBIE'S ALCOHOLIC GINGER BEER CLASSIFIED CLAIMING STKS — 1m 141y(P)
4:30 (4:30) (Class 5) 3-Y-O+ — £2,264 (£673; £336; £168) **Stalls** Low

Form — RPR

1622 **1** **Opus Maximus (IRE)**[1] 7589 6-8-8 **70**...............(p) KirstyMilczarek 11 72+
(Conor Dore) *hld up: plld hrd: hdwy over 1f out: rdn and hung lft ins fnl f: r.o to ld nr fin* **7/2**[2]

3012 **2** *½* **Spinning Ridge (IRE)**[7] 7538 6-8-12 **66**.........................(v) LukeMorris 3 75
(Ronald Harris) *a.p: rdn to ld wl ins fnl f: hdd nr fin* **13/2**[3]

0- **3** *½* **Brown Pete (IRE)**[14] 7470 3-8-0 **62**...............................(b) JimmyQuinn 4 64
(Paul W Flynn, Ire) *w ldr tl led 6f out: rdn and hdd wl ins fnl f* **33/1**

0413 **4** *½* **Saharia (IRE)**[35] 7146 4-8-12 **67**..................................(v) ShaneKelly 2 73+
(Michael Attwater) *hld up: hdwy and nt clr run fr over 1f out: r.o: nvr able to chal* **7/1**

5140 **5** *1¼* **Ajdaad (USA)**[7] 7537 4-8-9 **69** ow1............................... GrahamGibbons 7 67+
(Alan McCabe) *hld up: hdwy over 1f out: nt clr run ins fnl f: styd on* **3/1**[1]

0503 **6** *¾* **Sky Diamond (IRE)**[20] 7388 3-8-2 **64**.........................(b) JamesSullivan 9 60
(James Given) *led: hdd 6f out: chsd ldr: rdn over 1f out: no ex ins fnl f* **11/1**

2350 **7** *nse* **Dream Of Fortune (IRE)**[14] 7465 7-8-2 **65**.................(bt) AndreaAtzeni 1 58
(David Evans) *hld up: hdwy over 1f out: styd on* **15/2**

1400 **8** *¾* **The Which Doctor**[8] 7532 6-8-8 **68**...............................(e) MartinHarley 6 62
(Richard Guest) *chsd ldrs: rdn and hung lft over 1f out: no ex fnl f* **18/1**

200 **9** *2¾* **Needwood Ridge**[18] 7417 4-8-8 **68**..............................(bt) TomEaves 10 56
(Frank Sheridan) *mid-div: rdn over 2f out: wknd over 1f out* **12/1**

300 **10** *¾* **Ahlawy (IRE)**[6] 7557 8-8-4 **68**.................................(bt) FrannyNorton 8 50
(Frank Sheridan) *s.i.s: a in rr* **25/1**

1m 49.7s (-0.80) **Going Correction** -0.10s/f (Stan)
WFA 3 from 4yo+ 2lb **10** Ran SP% **112.9**
Speed ratings (Par 103): **99,98,98,97,96 95,95,95,92,92**
toteswingers: 1&2 £3.20, 1&3 £18.60, 2&3 £22.40 CSF £25.65 TOTE £4.60: £2.30, £1.10, £6.80; EX 18.90.Brown Pete was claimed by Mr S. Arnold for £5,000. Sky Diamond was claimed by Mr J. Mackie for £6,000.
Owner Mrs Louise Marsh **Bred** Mrs Anne Marie Burns **Trained** Cowbit, Lincs

FOCUS
A modest but tightly knit race of its type. The gallop was a steady one to the home turn and the winner came down the centre (edged left late on) in the straight. The form is rated through the runner-up to his latest C&D mark.
Saharia(IRE) Official explanation: jockey said gelding was denied a clear run final furlong

7606 TOTEQUADPOT CONDITIONS STKS — 1m 141y(P)
5:00 (5:00) (Class 4) 3-Y-O+ — £4,204 (£1,251; £625; £312) **Stalls** Low

Form — RPR

1130 **1** **Loyalty**[9] 7516 4-8-11 **95**...(v) JoeFanning 6 95
(Derek Shaw) *hld up: hdwy over 2f out: led and edgd lft ins fnl f: jst hld on* **5/2**[2]

6 **2** *nk* **Famusa**[27] 7296 4-9-1 **97**.. AdamBeschizza(3) 8 101+
(Marco Botti) *chsd ldrs: rdn and outpcd over 2f out: rallied ins fnl f: r.o wl* **4/1**[3]

1105 **3** *½* **Blue Moon**[20] 7393 4-8-6 **94**.. FrannyNorton 4 88
(Kevin Ryan) *trckd ldrs: racd keenly: led wl over 1f out: rdn: edgd rt and hdd ins fnl f: unable qck nr fin* **9/4**[1]

0024 **4** *1¼* **Snow Dancer (IRE)**[6] 7558 7-8-6 **78**............................. JamesSullivan 3 85
(Hugh McWilliams) *hld up: hdwy over 1f out: r.o* **22/1**

0020 **5** *2* **Night Lily (IRE)**[20] 7391 5-8-6 **99**.. LukeMorris 1 80
(Paul D'Arcy) *sn led at stdy pce: qcknd over 2f out: hdd wl over 1f out: sn rdn and edgd lft: no ex ins fnl f* **5/1**

-01 **6** *2* **Ocean Bay**[15] 7443 3-8-4 **95**.. RyanPowell(5) 2 81
(John Ryan) *chsd ldr tl rdn over 2f out: wknd ins fnl f* **10/1**

-00 **7** *37* **Bowmans Well (IRE)**[18] 7411 6-8-6 **0**.......................... NeilChalmers 5 —
(Peter Purdy) *dwlt: hld up: rdn 4f out: sn lost tch: t.o* **200/1**

1m 50.18s (-0.32) **Going Correction** -0.10s/f (Stan)
WFA 3 from 4yo+ 2lb **7** Ran SP% **109.9**
Speed ratings (Par 105): **97,96,96,95,93 91,58**
toteswingers: 1&2 £2.80, 1&3 £1.80, 2&3 £2.60 CSF £11.87 TOTE £2.50: £1.10, £4.60; EX 11.80.
Owner Brian Johnson (Northamptonshire) **Bred** Ecoutila Partnership **Trained** Sproxton, Leics

FOCUS
A very useful conditions event but a steady pace to the home straight means this bare form isn't entirely reliable. The winner came down the centre but the form is limited by the proximity of the fourth.

7607 MTB MIDLANDS MEDIAN AUCTION MAIDEN FILLIES' STKS — 5f 20y(P)
5:35 (5:35) (Class 6) 2-Y-O — £2,264 (£673; £336; £168) **Stalls** Low

Form — RPR

2222 **1** **Blanc De Chine (IRE)**[13] 7482 2-9-0 **70**.......................... LukeMorris 6 62
(Peter Makin) *chsd ldr: shkn up over 1f out: rdn to ld wl ins fnl f: r.o* **2/9**[1]

2 *1¾* **Like The Night** 2-9-0 **0**.. AndreaAtzeni 4 56+
(Marco Botti) *sn pushed along in rr: hdwy to go 3rd over 1f out: rdn and edgd lft ins fnl f: r.o to go 2nd post: no ch w wnr* **11/2**[2]

3050 **3** *hd* **Regal Lady**[13] 7490 2-9-0 **58**.....................................(v[1]) MichaelStainton 2 55
(David Brown) *led: rdn over 1f out: hdd and no ex wl ins fnl f* **16/1**[3]

00 **4** *7* **Italian Ice**[7] 7540 2-9-0 **0**.. TomEaves 1 30
(Bryan Smart) *chsd ldrs: rdn 1/2-way: wknd fnl f* **50/1**

62.44 secs (0.14) **Going Correction** -0.10s/f (Stan) **4** Ran SP% **105.1**
Speed ratings (Par 91): **94,91,90,79**
toteswingers: 1&2 £1.60 CSF £1.62 TOTE £1.20; EX 1.40.
Owner R P Marchant & Mrs E Lee **Bred** Newlands House Stud **Trained** Ogbourne Maisey, Wilts

FOCUS
A most uncompetitive fillies' maiden in which the gallop was a reasonable one and the winner came down the centre. The time was slow though and this looks form to be against.

NOTEBOOK
Blanc De Chine(IRE) has proved expensive to follow and she didn't have to improve to get off the mark in an uncompetitive event in workmanlike fashion. She wouldn't be an obvious one to follow up. (tchd 1-5 and 1-4)
Like The Night, an £8,000 first foal of a modest 6f fast-ground winner, showed ability at a modest level, despite her inexperience, on this racecourse debut. She should improve for this experience but is likely to remain vulnerable against the better types in this grade. (op 5-1)
Regal Lady returned to form back in trip in the first-time visor and she's probably the best guide to this form. Low-grade handicaps will be the way forward with her but she doesn't appeal as a winner waiting to happen. (op 14-1 tchd 20-1)

Italian Ice is now qualified for a handicap mark and may do better in that type of event but she'll have to show a good deal more before she's a solid betting proposition. (op 40-1)

7608 PLAY THE LIFE CHANGING TOTESCOOP6 TOMORROW H'CAP 1m 4f 50y(P)
6:10 (6:10) (Class 6) (0-60,58) 3-Y-O £1,704 (£503; £251) Stalls Low

Form RPR
3030 **1** **Cadgers Brig**[48] 6870 3-9-5 **56**..........(v) JoeFanning 8 73+
(Keith Dalgleish) *chsd ldr: led over 2f out: sn clr: easily* **6/1**
0010 **2** *9* **Imperial Fong**[17] 6823 3-9-1 **52**.......... FrannyNorton 4 50
(Chris Dwyer) *hld up: hdwy over 2f out: styd on to go 2nd ins fnl f: no ch w wnr* **50/1**
4560 **3** *1 1/2* **Madam Tessa (IRE)**[28] 7264 3-9-4 **55**.......... NeilChalmers 9 51
(Bryn Palling) *hld up: hdwy over 3f out: rdn over 2f out: no imp* **33/1**
1 **4** *nk* **The Drunken Dr (IRE)**[32] 7195 3-9-6 **57**..........(b) ChrisCatlin 11 52
(Niall Moran, Ire) *hld up: rdn over 5f out: hdwy over 2f out: nvr trbld ldrs* **5/1**[3]
6533 **5** *2* **Marina Ballerina**[17] 7426 3-8-12 **49**.......... JimmyQuinn 6 41
(Roy Bowring) *hld up: rdn over 3f out: n.d* **9/2**[2]
0006 **6** *nse* **Ballinargh Boy**[17] 7426 3-8-8 **45**.......... LukeMorris 2 37
(Robert Wylie) *led: rdn and hdd over 2f out: wknd over 1f out* **11/1**
4533 **7** *7* **Entrance**[20] 7387 3-9-4 **58**.......... AdamBeschizza(3) 7 39
(Julia Feilden) *s.s: reminders whn eventually sed: n.d* **8/1**
6600 **8** *1 1/2* **Tortilla (IRE)**[21] 7370 3-9-0 **51**.......... MartinHarley 10 29
(Des Donovan) *hld up: hdwy over 4f out: rdn over 3f out: wknd 2f out* **20/1**
0053 **9** *3* **Rasteau (IRE)**[13] 7496 3-8-6 **48** ow1.......... DavidKenny(5) 3 21
(Tom Keddy) *hld up: rdn over 3f out: a in rr* **22/1**
0503 **10** *nk* **Azurinta (IRE)**[21] 7370 3-9-0 **51**..........(b[1]) AdamKirby 1 24
(Michael Bell) *chsd ldrs: rdn over 3f out: wknd over 2f out* **11/2**
3200 **11** *30* **Srimenanti**[39] 7062 3-9-4 **55**..........(p) PaddyAspell 5 —
(Brian Rothwell) *chsd ldrs: rdn and lost pl over 5f out: bhd fnl 4f: t.o* **50/1**
12 *11* **Ma Browne (IRE)**[149] 3752 3-8-8 **45**..........(b[1]) TomEaves 12 —
(Tony Coyle) *hld up in tch: rdn and wknd 4f out: t.o* **4/1**[1]

2m 38.79s (-2.31) **Going Correction** -0.10s/f (Stan) **12** Ran SP% **119.9**
Speed ratings (Par 98): **103,97,96,95,94 94,89,88,86,86 66,59**
toteswingers: 1&2 £58.80, 1&3 £24.00, 2&3 £63.10 CSF £290.44 CT £8799.25 TOTE £8.80: £2.80, £9.70, £7.40; EX 252.80.
Owner John F Allan **Bred** Jock Allan **Trained** Carluke, South Lanarkshire

FOCUS
A moderate maiden but one turned into a procession by the wide-margin winner, who raced close to the inside rail throughout. The gallop was an ordinary one and, although the winner was a big improver there were few solid in behind.
Cadgers Brig Official explanation: trainer's rep said, regarding apparent improvement in form, that the gelding appeared to benfit from a return to the Polytrack surface.
Azurinta(IRE) Official explanation: jockey said filly stopped quickly
Ma Browne(IRE) Official explanation: vet said filly returned jarred up

7609 WOLVERHAMPTON HOLIDAY INN MEDIAN AUCTION MAIDEN STKS 1m 1f 103y(P)
6:40 (6:42) (Class 6) 3-4-Y-O £1,704 (£503; £251) Stalls Low

Form RPR
322 **1** **Double Trouble**[42] 7004 3-8-12 **65**.......... AdamKirby 2 61
(Marco Botti) *mde all: rdn over 1f out: edgd lft: styd on* **2/5**[1]
0 **2** *1 3/4* **Ripristini (IRE)**[39] 7063 3-9-3 **0**.......... DuranFentiman 4 62
(Patrick Holmes) *a.p: rdn to chse wnr over 1f out: styd on* **33/1**
0530 **3** *6* **Lucky Dime**[21] 7370 3-8-12 **52**..........(b[1]) ChrisCatlin 3 45
(Noel Quinlan) *trckd ldr tl rdn over 1f out: edgd lft: wknd ins fnl f* **14/1**[3]
-422 **4** *1 3/4* **Bull Five**[310] 309 4-9-5 **67**.......... LukeMorris 7 46
(Nick Littmoden) *hld up: hdwy over 3f out: rdn over 2f out: wknd over 1f out* **4/1**[2]
00 **5** *1 1/2* **Ivan The Terrible (IRE)**[20] 7401 3-9-0 **0**.......... RobertLButler(3) 6 43
(Richard Guest) *s.s: in rr: drvn along over 3f out: sn outpcd: styd on ins fnl f* **40/1**
6 *1 3/4* **Pastures New** 3-9-3 **0**.......... MartinHarley 8 39
(Des Donovan) *prom: pushed along 6f out: rdn and wknd over 2f out* **25/1**
600- **7** *20* **Knowledgeable**[456] 5700 4-8-12 **34**.......... ThomasBrown(7) 1 —
(Bryn Palling) *chsd ldrs tl rdn and wknd over 3f out* **80/1**

2m 1.00s (0.00) **Going Correction** 0.10s/f (Stan)
WFA 3 from 4yo 2lb **7** Ran SP% **108.6**
Speed ratings (Par 101): **97,95,90,88,87 85,67**
toteswingers: 1&2 £4.80, 1&3 £2.20, 2&3 £11.30 CSF £20.17 TOTE £1.20: £1.02, £14.30; EX 19.30.
Owner Dachel Stud **Bred** Dachel Stud **Trained** Newmarket, Suffolk
■ Stewards' Enquiry : Luke Morris caution: careless riding.

FOCUS
Another modest and uncompetitive maiden and one in which took less winning than seemed likely with the second favourite disappointing and with Call Me April being withdrawn at the start. The gallop was an ordinary one and the winner raced towards the far rail in the straight. The form looks weak with the pace modest and the winner not needing to match earlier efforts to score.

7610 TOTEPOOL H'CAP 1m 1f 103y(P)
7:10 (7:10) (Class 6) (0-60,60) 3-Y-O £1,704 (£503; £251) Stalls Low

Form RPR
6550 **1** **Maven**[31] 7213 3-9-5 **58**.......... DavidAllan 4 72+
(Tim Easterby) *a.p: rdn over 2f out: led over 1f out: edgd lft: styd on* **8/1**
6400 **2** *3/4* **Edgware Road**[31] 7216 3-9-5 **58**.......... AdamKirby 8 70
(Paul Rich) *hld up: hdwy over 2f out: rdn to chse wnr fnl f: r.o* **4/1**[2]
6534 **3** *6* **Baby Driver**[4] 7571 3-8-13 **52**..........(t) RichardKingscote 12 51
(Tom Dascombe) *sn led: rdn and hdd over 1f out: wknd ins fnl f* **7/2**[1]
3004 **4** *2 3/4* **Polar Auroras**[31] 7208 3-9-7 **60**.......... LukeMorris 3 54
(Tony Carroll) *mid-div: hdwy over 4f out: rdn and wknd over 1f out* **7/1**[3]
4405 **5** *2 1/4* **Ace Master**[14] 7462 3-9-5 **58**.......... RussKennemore 13 47
(Roy Bowring) *prom: racd keenly: rdn over 2f out: wknd fnl f* **11/1**
6500 **6** *1 1/4* **Merrjanah**[10] 7507 3-9-7 **60**.......... PaddyAspell 6 46
(John Wainwright) *s.i.s: hld up: rdn over 2f out: n.d* **33/1**
6004 **7** *2* **Indian Emperor (IRE)**[7] 7538 3-9-7 **60**.......... TomEaves 10 42
(Peter Niven) *hld up in tch: rdn over 2f out: wknd wl over 1f out* **9/1**
1236 **8** *1 3/4* **Princess Gail**[20] 7399 3-9-3 **56**.......... ShaneKelly 7 34
(Mark Brisbourne) *s.i.s: hld up: nvr nrr* **4/1**[2]
6000 **9** *7* **Excellence (IRE)**[192] 2384 3-8-0 **46**.......... JulieCumine(7) 5 —
(Karen George) *s.i.s: hld up: plld hrd: no ch whn rdn over 1f out* **80/1**
050- **10** *5* **Joyously**[351] 7888 3-9-6 **59**.......... MartinHarley 11 —
(Richard Guest) *s.i.s: rdn 1/2-way: a in rr* **25/1**
-366 **11** *9* **Littleportnbrandy (IRE)**[295] 494 3-8-12 **54**..........(p) RobertLButler(3) 1 —
(Richard Guest) *chsd ldrs tl rdn and wknd wl over 2f out: t.o* **50/1**
-600 **12** *3* **Cairanne**[22] 7354 3-8-7 **46** oh1.......... JimmyQuinn 9 —
(Tom Keddy) *prom: racd keenly: wknd wl over 2f out: t.o* **25/1**
5000 **13** *10* **Illawalla**[32] 7198 3-8-7 **46** oh1..........(p) JamesSullivan 2 —
(Hugh McWilliams) *hld up: rdn 1/2-way: wknd over 3f out: t.o* **100/1**

1m 59.85s (-1.85) **Going Correction** -0.10s/f (Stan) **13** Ran SP% **119.0**
Speed ratings (Par 98): **104,103,98,95,93 92,90,89,82,78 70,67,58**
toteswingers: 1&2 £9.10, 1&3 £9.90, 2&3 £5.20 CSF £38.05 CT £135.53 TOTE £11.40: £3.70, £1.80, £2.10; EX 50.70.
Owner Habton Farms **Bred** Habton Farms **Trained** Great Habton, N Yorks
■ Stewards' Enquiry : Julie Cumine five-day ban: used whip when out of contention (Dec 16-20)

FOCUS
A moderate handicap run at just a fair pace and one in which those held up were at a disadvantage. The winner edged towards the far rail in the straight and the first two did well to pull clear. Not form to get carried away with but the runner-up is rated to his maiden form, with the winner an improver.
Maven ◆ Official explanation: trainer's rep said, regarding apparent improvement in form, that the filly was better suited by the longer distance.
Cairanne Official explanation: jockey said filly ran too freely
T/Plt: £254.20 to a £1 stake. Pool: £73,098.29. 209.88 winning tickets. T/Qpdt: £51.00 to a £1 stake. Pool: £8,569.72. 124.20 winning tickets. CR

7611 - 7617a, 7619 - 7624a (Foreign Racing) - See Raceform Interactive

7543 DUNDALK (A.W) (L-H)
Friday, December 2

OFFICIAL GOING: Standard

7618a WWW.DUNDALKSTADIUM.COM H'CAP 1m 2f 150y(P)
9:25 (9:33) 3-Y-O+ £7,732 (£1,793; £784; £448)

RPR
1 **Maggie Neary (IRE)**[7] 7547 3-8-0 79.......... CPHoban(5) 13 84
(C F Swan, Ire) *chsd ldr in 2nd: rdn 2f out: u.p in cl 3rd 1f out: kpt on to ld cl home: all out* **10/1**
2 *hd* **Ultra Cool (IRE)**[26] 7321 4-8-11 82.......... NGMcCullagh 14 86
(Adrian McGuinness, Ire) *chsd ldrs: 4th 1/2-way: rdn 2f out: styd on to chal in 2nd 1f out: ev ch cl home: jst hld* **28/1**
3 *1 1/4* **Elusive Ridge (IRE)**[7] 7549 5-9-0 85..........(p) KJManning 9 87
(H Rogers, Ire) *attempted to make all: rdn and strly pressed 1f out: hdd cl home* **9/1**[3]
4 *1/2* **Denny Crane**[7] 7549 5-9-3 88.......... PJSmullen 6 89
(Edward Lynam, Ire) *chsd ldrs: 7th 1/2-way: rdn in 6th 2f out: no imp in 5th 1f out: kpt on same pce fnl f* **6/4**[1]
5 *1/2* **Bravely Fought (IRE)**[7] 7544 6-8-13 89.......... RPWhelan(5) 5 89
(Sabrina J Harty, Ire) *chsd ldrs: 3rd 1/2-way: rdn 2f out: no ex in 4th 1f out: kpt on same pce* **10/1**
6 *1/2* **If Per Chance (IRE)**[21] 7375 6-8-9 80..........(p) ShaneFoley 8 79
(M Halford, Ire) *mid-div early: 6th 1/2-way: rdn in 5th 2f out: no ex over 1f out: kpt on same pce* **8/1**[2]
7 *1* **Westtower Boy (IRE)**[42] 7013 5-8-9 80..........(t) RPCleary 12 77
(Edward Lynam, Ire) *mid-div: rdn in 8th 2f out: no imp in 7th 1f out: kpt on one pce* **11/1**
8 *1 1/4* **Monteriggioni (IRE)**[42] 7013 9-8-3 81.......... RossCoakley(7) 1 75
(John Geoghegan, Ire) *mid-div: 8th 1/2-way: rdn in 9th 2f out: no imp and kpt on one pce* **25/1**
9 *1* **Mid Mon Lady (IRE)**[21] 7376 6-9-6 98..........(b) DJBenson(7) 11 90
(H Rogers, Ire) *towards rr for most: sme late hdwy fnl f* **8/1**[2]
10 *1* **Dhaular Dhar (IRE)**[25] 6989 9-9-0 85.......... FergalLynch 7 75
(Jim Goldie) *in rr of mid-div: rdn in 10th 2f out: no imp and kpt on one pce* **14/1**
11 *1 1/4* **Solo Performer (IRE)**[26] 7322 6-9-0 85..........(b) CDHayes 3 73
(H Rogers, Ire) *towards rr for most: nvr a factor* **8/1**[2]
12 *1 1/4* **Mister Carter (IRE)**[209] 2948 4-9-2 87.......... SeamieHeffernan 4 72
(T Stack, Ire) *chsd ldrs: 5th 1/2-way: rdn in 7th 2f out: no ex and wknd* **16/1**
13 *3 1/2* **Trans City (IRE)**[16] 4937 3-8-7 81.......... WJSupple 10 61
(J A Nash, Ire) *hld up towards rr: hdwy into 5th 4f out: rdn and wknd ent st* **25/1**
14 *shd* **Syrian**[210] 1849 4-9-3 88.......... GFCarroll 2 66
(S M Duffy, Ire) *a towards rr* **33/1**

2m 18.0s (138.00)
WFA 3 from 4yo+ 4lb **14** Ran SP% **136.5**
Daily Double: Not won. Pool of 60 euros carried over to Fairyhouse Saturday 3rd December. CSF £290.61 CT £2662.93 TOTE £10.70: £4.00, £4.50, £2.50; DF 349.50.
Owner Simon Graham **Bred** Padraig Connolly **Trained** Cloughjordan, Co Tipperary

NOTEBOOK
Maggie Neary(IRE) showed plenty of resolution here. Taking close enough order and getting over from her outside draw, she sustained her effort all the way up the straight and battled on strongly between horses to have her head in front where it counted. She seems likely to be a good dual-purpose mare as she reportedly jumps well, but there could be another Flat handicap to be won with her as well. (op 9/1)
Ultra Cool(IRE) came back to just about her best. Racing just off the pace, she challenged over a furlong out and had her head in front inside the last but just couldn't see off the determined winner. There was no disgrace in that and a drop in the handicap will have to wait a while yet. (op 25/1)
Elusive Ridge(IRE) received a fine front-running tactical ride from Kevin Manning. He managed to keep a bit in the tank, which enabled him to kick again over a furlong out but in the end he was unable to stretch them quite enough. It was still a very decent effort. (op 10/1)
Denny Crane was held up off the pace but appeared to take a keen enough hold. He also ran into some slight traffic issues in the straight but ultimately he wasn't quite good enough on the night. (op 6/4 tchd 11/8)
Bravely Fought(IRE) raced fairly prominently and realistically had every chance on the inner turning in but gradually ran out of steam. (op 9/1)
T/Jkpt: Not won. T/Plt: @49.40. Pool: @26,681.44. 405 winning units. II

7604 WOLVERHAMPTON (A.W) (L-H)
Saturday, December 3

OFFICIAL GOING: Standard
Wind: Fresh, behind. Weather: Cloudy

7625 TOTEPLACEPOT H'CAP 7f 32y(P)
5:50 (5:50) (Class 5) (0-75,74) 3-Y-O+ £2,264 (£673; £336; £168) Stalls High

Form RPR
2312 **1** **Chokidar (IRE)**[4] 7579 3-8-11 **70**..........(v[1]) BillyCray(3) 3 79+
(David Nicholls) *s.i.s: pushed along early in rr: nt clr run over 2f out: hdwy over 1f out: led ins fnl f: r.o* **6/4**[1]

2430 **2** *¾* **Triple Eight (IRE)**[21] 7397 3-8-11 **72**......................(p) JustinNewman(5) 2 79
(Philip Kirby) *chsd ldrs: pushed along over 2f out: led over 1f out: sn rdn and edgd rt: hdd ins fnl f: styd on* **33/1**

3062 **3** *hd* **I Confess**[15] 7465 6-9-2 **72**..(b) RobertWinston 1 78
(Geoffrey Harker) *a.p: rdn over 1f out: r.o* **12/1**

5153 **4** *1 ¼* **Bianca De Medici**[30] 7243 4-9-4 **74**............................(b[1]) JimmyFortune 7 77
(Hughie Morrison) *s.i.s: hld up: rdn and r.o wl ins fnl f: nt rch ldrs* **6/1**[2]

6000 **5** *shd* **Avonrose**[14] 7486 4-9-4 **74**.. AdamKirby 6 78+
(Derek Shaw) *hld up: hdwy over 1f out: cl up whn nt clr run ins fnl f: nvr able to chal* **16/1**

0000 **6** *nk* **Hatta Stream (IRE)**[19] 7416 5-9-2 **72**............................. RobertHavlin 5 74
(Lydia Pearce) *led: rdn: edgd rt and hdd over 1f out: styd on same pce ins fnl f* **40/1**

0006 **7** *2 ¼* **Smalljohn**[19] 7416 5-9-1 **71**..(v) TomEaves 9 66
(Bryan Smart) *chsd ldrs: rdn over 1f out: no ins ex fnl f* **16/1**

-600 **8** *½* **Regeneration (IRE)**[17] 7438 5-9-3 **73**...........................(vt[1]) StevieDonohoe 4 67
(Michael Bell) *s.i.s: sn pushed along in rr: styd on ins fnl f: nvr nrr* **10/1**

1432 **9** *2 ¼* **Master Of Dance (IRE)**[32] 7211 4-9-1 **71**....................(p) JoeFanning 10 59
(Keith Dalgleish) *prom: rdn over 2f out: wknd over 1f out* **9/1**

/01U **10** *5* **Regency Art (IRE)**[10] 7517 4-9-2 **72**.................. RichardKingscote 11 47
(Milton Bradley) *s.i.s: hld up: rdn over 1f out: n.d* **17/2**[3]

0144 **11** *hd* **Glenridding**[19] 7416 7-8-11 **70**... DaleSwift(3) 8 44
(James Given) *prom: lost pl after 1f: sn pushed along: wknd over 1f out* **12/1**

2400 **12** *9* **Spin Again (IRE)**[19] 7416 6-9-0 **70**.................................... LiamJones 12 20
(Mark Wellings) *chsd ldr over 5f out tl rdn over 2f out: wknd over 1f out* **100/1**

1m 27.97s (-1.63) **Going Correction** -0.10s/f (Stan) **12** Ran SP% **117.4**
Speed ratings (Par 103): **105,104,103,102,102 102,99,98,96,90 90,80**
Tote Swingers:1&2:£15.40, 2&3:£20.70, 1&3:£6.10 CSF £66.65 CT £420.80 TOTE £3.00: £1.50, £8.60, £2.10; EX 68.50.

Owner Paul J Dixon **Bred** Jeremy Gompertz **Trained** Sessay, N Yorks

■ Stewards' Enquiry : Robert Winston two-day ban: excessive use of the whip (Dec 17-18)

FOCUS
A routine handicap, but competitive enough, with six holding a chance in the last furlong. The form looks sound rated through the third.

7626 BRITISH STALLION STUDS SUPPORTING BRITISH RACING E B F MAIDEN STKS (DIV I) — 7f 32y(P)

6:20 (6:21) (Class 5) 2-Y-0 **£3,234** (£962; £481; £240) **Stalls** High

Form RPR

0632 **1** **Rio Grande**[43] 7000 2-9-3 71..(p) TomEaves 3 78+
(Ann Duffield) *mde all: shkn up fnl f: styd on wl* **9/4**[1]

052 **2** *3* **Andalieb**[33] 7197 2-9-3 72.. MartinLane 9 71+
(David Simcock) *a.p: chsd wnr 2f out: sn rdn: edgd lft and no imp ins fnl f* **9/4**[1]

00 **3** *9* **Holy Empress (IRE)**[135] 4232 2-8-5 0.................. ThomasHemsley(7) 8 44
(Michael Bell) *s.i.s: hdwy over 4f out: rdn over 2f out: wknd over 1f out* **33/1**

0004 **4** *1 ½* **Gone To Ground**[14] 7490 2-8-10 44...........................(b) RaulDaSilva(7) 7 45
(Jeremy Gask) *chsd wnr tl rdn 2f out: wknd over 1f out* **100/1**

5 *1 ¼* **First Glance** 2-9-3 0.. LiamJones 10 42
(Michael Appleby) *chsd ldrs: rdn 1/2-way: wknd over 2f out* **50/1**

6 *1 ¼* **Neige D'Antan** 2-8-12 0.. SebSanders 2 34+
(Sir Mark Prescott Bt) *s.i.s: sn pushed along and a in rr* **6/1**[3]

6 **7** *shd* **Kuwait Moon**[22] 7368 2-9-3 0.. AndrewMullen 11 39
(Alan McCabe) *hld up: hdwy over 4f out: rdn and wknd wl over 2f out* **40/1**

8 *28* **National Hero (IRE)** 2-9-3 0... JoeFanning 1 —
(Mark Johnston) *s.i.s and unruly early on: sn t.o* **11/4**[2]

1m 28.97s (-0.63) **Going Correction** -0.10s/f (Stan) **8** Ran SP% **110.8**
Speed ratings (Par 96): **99,95,85,83,82 80,80,48**
Tote Swingers:1&2:£1.50, 2&3:£8.10, 1&3:£10.70 CSF £7.01 TOTE £4.20: £1.40, £1.10, £10.50; EX 9.00.

Owner Sir Robert Ogden **Bred** Haras Du Mezeray & Ronchalon Racing **Trained** Constable Burton, N Yorks

FOCUS
Though the winner was rated 71, this didn't look a great maiden. A step up from the winner and the runner-up can also do better.

NOTEBOOK
Rio Grande is not straightforward, but the combination of first-time cheekpieces and front-running over this longer trip brought out the best in her. She will need to keep responding to the headgear when switching to handicaps, but the ability is there. (tchd 15-8 and 5-2)

Andalieb has now run two creditable races over this C&D since switching to Polytrack. He is good enough to win an AW maiden. (op 15-8)

Holy Empress(IRE) had not set the world alight on turf, but this was more encouraging. On the basis of her three races, she is likely to get a working handicap mark now she is qualified, but her sights will need to be kept low. (op 28-1)

Gone To Ground has run better since being equipped with blinkers, but he isn't quite getting home at either 6f or 7f. Though beaten in a seller last time, that grade does look more suitable than maidens.

First Glance, out of an unsuccessful dual-purpose mare who is nonetheless related to winners on the Flat and over hurdles, is likely to need 1m-plus in the long term, so this was a respectable debut.

Neige D'Antan, half-sister to a winning juvenile sprinter and two middle-distance winners, was too green to do herself justice. (op 7-1)

National Hero(IRE) is the first foal of a mare who won over 1m2f and who is a half-sister to six other winners. However, he needs to show a more professional attitude before he can follow in their footsteps. (op 3-1)

7627 BRITISH STALLION STUDS SUPPORTING BRITISH RACING E B F MAIDEN STKS (DIV II) — 7f 32y(P)

6:50 (6:51) (Class 5) 2-Y-0 **£3,234** (£962; £481; £240) **Stalls** High

Form RPR

4 **1** **Delft**[51] 6820 2-8-12 0.. JimmyFortune 8 75+
(Jeremy Noseda) *mde all: clr fr over 1f out: easily* **6/5**[1]

6 **2** *4 ½* **Going Grey (IRE)**[50] 6837 2-9-3 0................................. BarryMcHugh 4 64
(Richard Fahey) *trckd wnr: plld hrd: rdn over 2f out: outpcd fr over 1f out* **10/1**

3 *¾* **Gold Falcon (IRE)** 2-9-3 0.. MartinLane 9 62+
(David Simcock) *s.i.s: hld up: hdwy over 1f out: styd on: nvr nr ldrs* **12/1**

4 *shd* **Josam (IRE)** 2-9-3 0.. DaneO'Neill 7 62+
(Richard Hannon) *s.i.s: hld up: r.o ins fnl f: nrst fin* **5/1**[3]

0 **5** *shd* **Lady Lyricist**[15] 7464 2-8-12 0....................................... GrahamGibbons 11 57
(Reg Hollinshead) *prom: rdn over 2f out: styd on same pce* **50/1**

60 **6** *¾* **Nicholascopernicus (IRE)**[17] 7435 2-9-3 0........... RichardKingscote 6 60
(Ed Walker) *hld up: shkn up over 1f out: nvr nr to chal* **3/1**[2]

7 *3 ¾* **Vermeyen** 2-9-3 0.. TomEaves 1 51
(Ann Duffield) *chsd ldrs: rdn over 2f out: wknd over 1f out* **18/1**

8 *1* **Abdul Malik** 2-9-3 0... LiamKeniry 3 48
(David Simcock) *hld up: shkn up over 1f out: nvr on terms* **28/1**

00 **9** *6* **Hardy Plume**[24] 7329 2-9-3 0.. ShaneKelly 10 33
(Denis Coakley) *hld up: shkn up over 2f out: no ch whn hmpd wl over 1f out* **50/1**

10 *½* **Pull The Pin (IRE)** 2-9-0 0.. SimonPearce(3) 5 32
(Lydia Pearce) *prom: rdn over 2f out: wknd wl over 1f out* **66/1**

1m 30.3s (0.70) **Going Correction** -0.10s/f (Stan) **10** Ran SP% **118.0**
Speed ratings (Par 96): **92,86,86,85,85 84,80,79,72,72**
Tote Swingers:1&2:£4.00, 2&3:£13.10, 1&3:£4.90 CSF £15.06 TOTE £2.00: £1.10, £3.90, £6.10; EX 18.30.

Owner Cheveley Park Stud **Bred** Cheveley Park Stud Ltd **Trained** Newmarket, Suffolk

■ Stewards' Enquiry : Jimmy Fortune two-day ban: careless riding (Dec 18-19)

FOCUS
Overall, this second division of the maiden wasn't significantly different from the first, but the debutants showed more promise and the winner was a class above the rest. The winner sets the level but the time was modest and the level is slightly guessy.

NOTEBOOK
Delft stepped up on her debut with an authoritative performance from the front. There is plenty of speed in her pedigree so, while she could well stay 1m on this evidence, 7f looks ideal at present. (op 5-4 tchd 11-8)

Going Grey(IRE) made a satisfactory AW debut, albeit not in the same league as the winner. This is probably his right trip, and he could win a Polytrack maiden if continuing to progress. (tchd 11-1)

Gold Falcon(IRE), out of a winning 6f juvenile who is closely related to five winners from 6f-1m2f on the Flat, and 2m over hurdles, did pretty well after taking time to warm up. He looks likely to improve. (op 11-1)

Josam(IRE) ◆, a 20,000gns Montjeu colt out of a 1m4f winner, is a half-brother to winners at 6f and 7f. There was plenty to like about the way he picked up after a slow start, so he is one to consider next time. (op 11-2 tchd 9-2)

Lady Lyricist improved hugely on her debut, which can now be safely forgotten. More is needed to win a maiden, but she does seem to be learning from her experiences.

Nicholascopernicus(IRE) has shown ability in three maidens and should be an interesting contender when switching to handicaps. (op 7-2)

7628 DID THE LIFE CHANGING TOTESCOOP6 ROLLOVER H'CAP — 7f 32y(P)

7:20 (7:21) (Class 3) (0-95,94) 3-Y-0+ **£6,616** (£1,980; £990; £495; £246) **Stalls** Low

Form RPR

0010 **1** **Clockmaker (IRE)**[28] 7295 5-9-3 **90**................................ DuranFentiman 8 101
(Tim Easterby) *chsd ldr tl led over 2f out: rdn out* **11/1**

4531 **2** *2 ¼* **Lockantanks**[9] 7532 4-8-9 **82**... LukeMorris 10 87+
(Michael Appleby) *prom: rdn over 2f out: nt clr run over 1f out: r.o u.p to go 2nd wl ins fnl f: nt rch wnr* **5/1**[3]

0000 **3** *½* **Mr Willis**[37] 7127 5-9-0 **87**.. MarcHalford 3 91+
(Terry Clement) *prom: nt clr run over 2f out: rdn and hmpd 1f out: r.o* **33/1**

1100 **4** *¾* **Roninski (IRE)**[9] 7531 3-8-11 **84**.......................................(t) TomEaves 11 86
(Bryan Smart) *chsd ldrs: rdn and hung lft fr over 1f out: no ex wl ins fnl f* **16/1**

0-40 **5** *shd* **Ceremonial Jade (UAE)**[112] 5046 8-8-13 **93**.........(t) GemmaNellist(7) 7 94
(Marco Botti) *sn outpcd: r.o ins fnl f: nt rch ldrs* **25/1**

4160 **6** *1 ¾* **Justonefortheroad**[35] 7168 5-9-0 **94**.................... GeorgeChaloner(7) 9 91
(Richard Fahey) *mid-div: pushed along 1/2-way: hdwy over 2f out: sn rdn: styd on same pce fnl f* **12/1**

0015 **7** *nk* **Main Beach**[3] 7586 4-8-11 **84**..(t) StevieDonohoe 5 80
(Tobias B P Coles) *sn outpcd: r.o ins fnl f: nvr nrr* **15/2**

0021 **8** *1 ½* **Seek The Fair Land**[17] 7438 5-9-3 **90**..............................(b) EddieAhern 1 82
(Jim Boyle) *chsd ldrs: rdn whn hmpd 1f out: no ex* **11/4**[1]

0610 **9** *5* **Rulesn'regulations**[49] 6862 5-9-1 **88**..............................(b) AdamKirby 2 66
(Matthew Salaman) *sn led: hdd over 2f out: rdn whn hmpd 1f out: sn wknd* **8/1**

3000 **10** *4 ½* **Star Rover (IRE)**[14] 7489 4-9-0 **87**..........................(v) TomMcLaughlin 12 53
(David Evans) *hld up: n.d* **50/1**

0115 **11** *nk* **Greensward**[42] 7023 5-9-4 **91**.. JimmyFortune 4 95+
(Mike Murphy) *s.i.s: hld up: hdwy whn hmpd 1f out: eased* **4/1**[2]

5640 **12** *3 ½* **Spectait**[25] 6124 9-9-1 **88**... RichardKingscote 6 44
(Jonjo O'Neill) *s.i.s: outpcd* **33/1**

1m 27.22s (-2.38) **Going Correction** -0.10s/f (Stan) **12** Ran SP% **119.8**
Speed ratings (Par 107): **109,106,105,105,104 102,102,100,95,89 89,85**
Tote Swingers:1&2:£12.20, 2&3:£35.60, 1&3:£52.90 CSF £64.03 CT £1807.76 TOTE £15.40: £5.30, £2.20, £6.60; EX 82.60.

Owner Middleham Park Racing XI & Partners **Bred** Lemongrove Stud & Brendan Arthur **Trained** Great Habton, N Yorks

■ Stewards' Enquiry : Eddie Ahern one-day ban: careless riding (Dec 17)

FOCUS
This attracted a good turnout for an above-average AW contest and the form looks solid, with the winner recording a personal best.

NOTEBOOK
Clockmaker(IRE) returned to the AW on a stiff-looking mark but shrugged it off without having to seriously exert himself. He handles Polytrack well, but he will go up again for this and that will make races in the near future something of a challenge. (op 10-1)

Lockantanks, racing more handily over this shorter trip, did well from an 8lb higher mark than last time. Though he handled this 7f well enough, he is probably best at 1m. (op 11-2)

Mr Willis seems to be on the way back and, although he is till 3lb above his highest winning mark, it may not be beyond him. All his five wins have been at Lingfield, so a return to his favourite track should be noted.

Roninski(IRE) was close to his best again, but he seems to be finding this higher mark just a few pounds too much. (op 20-1)

Ceremonial Jade(UAE) has not won since March 2009 but still has plenty of ability. This was a likeable effort under a 7lb claimer, who appeared to get on well with him. (op 22-1)

Justonefortheroad, a smart turf handicapper, runs rarely on sand, but this was a solid effort. (tchd 14-1)

Main Beach, up 6lb since winning last month, is still seeing his races out well and this trip appears to be well within his range these days. Official explanation: jockey said gelding lost a shoe (op 7-1)

Seek The Fair Land, who looked to be bang in form over this trip at Lingfield last time, was disappointing off a 5lb higher mark.

Greensward was blocked as he began his move on the inside rail in the straight. Though he would not have won, he still had a bit to give and might have made it into the battle for the places. (tchd 7-2)

7629 STAY AT THE WOLVERHAMPTON HOLIDAY INN (S) STKS 5f 216y(P)
7:50 (7:53) (Class 6) 3-Y-0+ **£1,704** (£503; £251) **Stalls** Low

Form RPR
0200 **1** **Tombi (USA)**[30] [7253] 7-9-0 75 ... JimmyFortune 7 73
(Ollie Pears) *hld up: rdn ins fnl f: edgd lft and str burst to ld nr fin* **5/1**[2]
6153 **2** ¾ **Hinton Admiral**[49] [6875] 7-9-6 82 ... JoeFanning 12 76
(Keith Dalgleish) *chsd ldrs: led over 1f out: rdn ins fnl f: hdd nr fin* **6/1**[3]
3055 **3** ¾ **Towy Boy (IRE)**[14] [7488] 6-8-7 59 ...(bt) JackDuern(7) 5 68
(Ian Wood) *hld up in tch: pushed along and n.m.r over 2f out: rdn ins fnl f: styd on* **25/1**
0434 **4** nk **Forty Proof (IRE)**[4] [7575] 3-9-0 78 ...(p) ShaneKelly 4 67
(Alan McCabe) *rn wout declared tongue strap: a.p: rdn and ev ch ins fnl f: styd on same pce* **7/2**[1]
0110 **5** hd **Princess Dayna**[29] [7268] 3-9-1 67 ... RichardKingscote 13 67
(Tom Dascombe) *hld up in tch: rdn over 1f out: styd on* **10/1**
030 **6** nse **Mawjoodah**[9] [7529] 3-9-1 71 ...(b[1]) BarryMcHugh 1 67
(Brian Ellison) *a.p: rdn and ev ch ins fnl f: styd on same pce* **10/1**
5016 **7** nse **Desert Icon (IRE)**[9] [7529] 5-9-6 74 ...(tp) GrahamGibbons 3 72
(Alan McCabe) *s.i.s: hld up: plld hrd: r.o ins fnl f: nt rch ldrs* **7/1**
5303 **8** nk **Sarah's Art (IRE)**[9] [7529] 8-9-0 67 ...(t) ChrisCatlin 6 65
(Gary Harrison) *hld up: rdn over 1f out: r.o ins fnl f: nvr nrr* **16/1**
3400 **9** nse **Devil You Know (IRE)**[2] [7595] 5-9-0 66 ...(t) JamesSullivan 10 65
(Michael Easterby) *s.i.s: hld up: r.o ins fnl f: nrst fin* **12/1**
4203 **10** 1¾ **Silver Turn**[24] [7332] 3-8-8 69 ... RaulDaSilva(7) 9 60
(Jeremy Gask) *led: rdn and hdd over 1f out: no ex ins fnl f* **11/1**
3650 **11** 1 **Athaakeel (IRE)**[35] [7172] 5-9-1 62 ...(b) KirstyMilczarek 11 57
(Ronald Harris) *sn pushed along in rr: rdn over 2f out: n.d* **33/1**
3066 **12** 1¼ **My Lord**[24] [7332] 3-9-6 72 ... LukeMorris 8 58
(Ronald Harris) *prom: rdn over 1f out: wknd fnl f* **12/1**
2000 **13** 3¾ **Lake Chini (IRE)**[173] [2987] 9-9-0 58 ...(b) PaddyAspell 2 40
(Michael Easterby) *chsd ldr: rdn and ev ch over 2f out: wknd over 1f out* **66/1**

1m 14.41s (-0.59) **Going Correction** -0.10s/f (Stan) **13** Ran SP% **121.7**
Speed ratings (Par 101): **99,98,97,96,96 96,96,95,95,93 92,90,85**
Tote Swingers:1&2:£7.20, 2&3:£52.30, 1&3:£44.30 CSF £35.35 TOTE £8.30: £3.40, £1.70, £6.70; EX 47.90.There was no bid for the winner.
Owner An Englishman, Irishman & Scotsman **Bred** Sun Valley Farm **Trained** Norton, N Yorks
FOCUS
Many were still in contention late on in this competitive seller. The proximity of the third casts doubts over the form but he sets the level rated to his best.
Devil You Know(IRE) Official explanation: jockey said gelding missed the break

7630 TOTEEXACTA MAIDEN STKS 1m 4f 50y(P)
8:20 (8:20) (Class 5) 3-Y-0+ **£2,264** (£673; £336; £168) **Stalls** Low

Form RPR
0323 **1** **Martine's Spirit (IRE)**[22] [7360] 3-8-12 72 ... ShaneKelly 11 77+
(William Haggas) *a.p: chsd ldr over 5f out: led over 2f out: sn clr: easily* **3/1**[2]
2240 **2** 6 **Echos Of Motivator**[54] [6756] 3-9-0 67 ... RyanClark(3) 4 69
(Ronald Harris) *hld up: hdwy over 3f out: rdn to chse wnr and hung lft over 1f out: styd on same pce* **10/1**
6 **3** 1¼ **Cloudy Spirit**[12] [7053] 6-9-3 0 ... TonyCulhane 1 62+
(Reg Hollinshead) *led 1f: sn lost pl: pushed along over 2f: hmpd sn after: styd on to go 3rd ins fnl f: nt trble ldrs* **7/1**
4 1¾ **Scribe (IRE)**[188] [2537] 3-9-3 0 ... AdamKirby 3 65
(David Evans) *hld up: hdwy over 2f out: hmpd over 1f out: wknd fnl f* **5/1**[3]
03 **5** 2¾ **Silver Blossom (IRE)**[35] [7179] 3-8-12 0 ... JimmyFortune 5 55
(Andrew Balding) *chsd ldrs: pushed along over 2f out: wkng whn bmpd over 1f out* **7/4**[1]
042 **6** nk **Barachiel**[8] [7536] 3-9-3 65 ... LukeMorris 6 60
(Ronald Harris) *led after 1f: rdn and hdd over 2f out: wknd over 1f out* **17/2**
7 81 **Fish Called Peppa (IRE)**[30] 4-9-3 0 ... LiamKeniry 7 —
(Peter Fahey, Ire) *sn chsng ldr tl rdn and lost pl over 5f out: bhd fnl 4f: t.o* **50/1**

2m 39.61s (-1.49) **Going Correction** -0.10s/f (Stan)
WFA 3 from 4yo+ 5lb **7** Ran SP% **112.1**
Speed ratings (Par 103): **100,96,95,94,92 91,37**
Tote Swingers:1&2:£8.60, 2&3:£14.30, 1&3:£4.10 CSF £30.65 TOTE £4.30: £2.00, £4.60; EX 39.20.
Owner Miss Pat O'Kelly **Bred** Kilcarn Stud **Trained** Newmarket, Suffolk
FOCUS
This was an unremarkable maiden although the winner is value for more than the official margin. They went a fair tempo for 1m4f, but only one of them was still galloping in the home straight.
Silver Blossom(IRE) Official explanation: jockey said filly never travelled

7631 HUK-VALVES.CO.UK H'CAP 2m 119y(P)
8:50 (8:51) (Class 6) (0-65,58) 3-Y-0+ **£1,704** (£503; £251) **Stalls** Low

Form RPR
1 **Limpopo Tom (IRE)**[41] [7046] 4-9-13 57 ... JimmyFortune 5 74+
(Paul W Flynn, Ire) *a.p: led wl over 3f out: hrd rdn ins fnl f: styd on wl* **9/4**[1]
1625 **2** 6 **Red Current**[24] [7331] 7-9-8 57 ... DavidKenny(5) 13 67
(Michael Scudamore) *hld up: hdwy over 2f out: chsd wnr over 1f out: eased whn hld ins fnl f* **16/1**
0- **3** 3¾ **Sughera (IRE)**[15] [7472] 4-9-2 46 ... EddieAhern 9 51
(A J Martin, Ire) *hld up: hdwy over 5f out: rdn over 1f out: styd on same pce* **11/2**[3]
2124 **4** 2 **Spice Bar**[8] [6780] 7-9-7 58 ...(b) JasonHart(7) 11 60
(Declan Carroll) *s.i.s: hld up: racd keenly: hdwy 11f out: rdn over 1f out: styd on same pce* **8/1**
311- **5** 4½ **Mutadarrej (IRE)**[15] [7472] 7-9-12 56 ...(p) TomEaves 3 53
(Mrs Y Dunleavy, Ire) *chsd ldrs: rdn over 2f out: wknd over 1f out* **22/1**
561/ **6** 5 **Monahullan Prince**[17] [5909] 10-9-3 54 ...(tp) CTKeane(7) 10 45
(Gerard Keane, Ire) *hld up: hdwy over 4f out: rdn and wknd over 1f out* **9/1**
14 **7** 9 **The Drunken Dr (IRE)**[1] [7608] 3-9-5 57 ...(b) MartinHarley 12 37
(Niall Moran, Ire) *hld up: rdn over 3f out: sn wknd: t.o* **3/1**[2]
006 **8** 6 **Empyrean (USA)**[17] [7440] 3-8-7 45 ... LukeMorris 8 18
(Sir Mark Prescott Bt) *led: rdn over 4f out: hdd wl over 3f out: sn wknd: t.o* **10/1**
05 **9** 1¼ **Tinas Exhibition (IRE)**[163] [3332] 4-9-13 57 ...(p) LiamKeniry 7 29
(Seamus Fahey, Ire) *chsd ldrs tl rdn and wknd over 2f out: t.o* **20/1**
0400 **10** 4 **Talkin Italian**[21] [7400] 3-8-7 45 ... MartinLane 6 12
(Ian Williams) *hld up: rdn over 6f out: wknd 4f out: t.o* **40/1**
5500 **11** 8 **Court Wing (IRE)**[170] [3095] 5-9-3 50 ... DaleSwift(3) 2 —
(Richard Price) *chsd ldrs: rdn over 4f out: sn wknd: t.o* **28/1**

3m 40.78s (-1.02) **Going Correction** -0.10s/f (Stan)
WFA 3 from 4yo+ 8lb **11** Ran SP% **122.2**
Speed ratings (Par 101): **98,95,93,92,90 88,83,80,80,78 74**
Tote Swingers:1&2:£9.80, 2&3:£13.30, 1&3:£5.60 CSF £40.75 CT £188.03 TOTE £3.80: £1.50, £2.50, £2.30; EX 69.70.
Owner MML Syndicate **Bred** John McEnery **Trained** Colehill, Co Longford
FOCUS
The pace was ordinary for the first circuit in this weak race, but it wound up significantly at halfway and provided a good test of stamina. The winner was a big improver but the runner-up is rated to his best and the form looks sound.
Limpopo Tom(IRE) Official explanation: trainer said, regarding apparent improvemenmt in form, that the gelding had benefited from running on the all-weather and in handicap company.

7632 TOTEPOOL H'CAP 1m 141y(P)
9:20 (9:20) (Class 6) (0-60,60) 3-Y-0+ **£1,704** (£503; £251) **Stalls** Low

Form RPR
6204 **1** **Justcallmehandsome**[2] [7589] 9-9-0 60 ...(be) JoshBaudains(7) 12 69
(Dominic Ffrench Davis) *hld up: hdwy over 2f out: led over 1f out: hung lft fnl f: styd on* **10/1**
4513 **2** 1¾ **Stylistickhill (IRE)**[8] [7537] 3-9-5 60 ...(t) MartinLane 2 65+
(David Nicholls) *hld up: nt clr run fr over 2f out tl r.o wl ins fnl f: nt rch wnr* **3/1**[1]
5030 **3** 1¾ **Rock Anthem (IRE)**[38] [7098] 7-9-7 60 ... AndreaAtzeni 1 61
(Mike Murphy) *a.p: rdn over 1f out: styd on* **9/1**
2050 **4** ½ **Aviso (GER)**[12] [7268] 7-9-4 60 ... RichardEvans(3) 9 60
(David Evans) *chsd ldrs: rdn over 1f out: styd on* **25/1**
1-0 **5** 1 **Sports Casual**[15] [7470] 8-9-5 58 ...(vt[1]) TomEaves 4 56
(Mrs Y Dunleavy, Ire) *prom: hmpd and lost pl 7f out: hdwy over 2f out: styd on same pce fnl f* **16/1**
-500 **6** ¾ **Seamster**[19] [7416] 4-9-0 58 ...(vt[1]) LucyKBarry(5) 7 54
(Richard Ford) *led: rdn and hdd over 1f out: no ex fnl f* **50/1**
6442 **7** 2½ **Wigram's Turn (USA)**[21] [7399] 6-9-7 60 ...(t) GrahamGibbons 11 50
(Michael Easterby) *prom: edgd lft and chsd ldr 7f out: rdn over 1f out: wknd fnl f* **9/2**[2]
4301 **8** 1¾ **Nina Rose**[21] [7400] 4-9-7 60 ...(b) AdamKirby 6 46
(Clive Cox) *prom: hmpd and lost pl 7f out: rdn and hung rt over 2f out: nvr trbld ldrs* **9/2**[2]
-400 **9** ½ **Penbryn (USA)**[278] [712] 4-9-4 57 ... JimmyFortune 10 42
(Nick Littmoden) *s.i.s: n.d* **20/1**
3543 **10** 1¾ **Eastern Gift**[15] [7455] 6-9-7 60 ... RobertWinston 8 41
(Gay Kelleway) *hld up: nvr on terms* **7/1**[3]
-000 **11** 10 **Sir Ike (IRE)**[114] [4948] 6-9-0 53 ...(tp) LukeMorris 3 —
(Michael Appleby) *prom: hmpd 7f out: rdn over 3f out: wknd 2f out* **50/1**
20-5 **12** 3¾ **Marksbury**[314] [273] 4-9-6 59 ... TomMcLaughlin 5 —
(Mark Brisbourne) *s.i.s: hld up: a in rr* **40/1**
0050 **13** 2 **Qeethaara (USA)**[36] [7146] 7-9-7 60 ...(p) ShaneKelly 13 5
(Mark Brisbourne) *trckd ldrs: racd keenly: wknd over 1f out* **28/1**

1m 49.11s (-1.39) **Going Correction** -0.10s/f (Stan)
WFA 3 from 4yo+ 2lb **13** Ran SP% **117.3**
Speed ratings (Par 101): **102,100,98,98,97 96,94,93,92,91 82,78,77**
Tote Swingers:1&2:£9.70, 2&3:£8.90, 1&3:£13.60 CSF £36.70 CT £294.84 TOTE £12.40: £3.60, £1.50, £2.80; EX 50.60.
Owner Mrs J E Taylor **Bred** Mrs J E Taylor **Trained** Lambourn, Berks
FOCUS
A modest handicap, in which only a few were in form beforehand, turned into a one-horse race. The winner ran his best race since last winter.
Stylistickhill(IRE) Official explanation: jockey said filly suffered interference in running
Nina Rose Official explanation: jockey said filly suffered interference in running
T/Plt: £64.80 to a £1 stake. Pool £108,668.71. 1,222.77 winning tickets T/Qpdt: £32.50 to a £1 stake. Pool £8,486.56. 192.80 winning tickets CR

7633 - (Foreign Racing) - See Raceform Interactive

7597 LINGFIELD (L-H)
Monday, December 5

OFFICIAL GOING: Standard
Wind: Strong, half behind Weather: Fine, cold

7634 CROWHURST MEDIAN AUCTION MAIDEN STKS 1m (P)
12:30 (12:31) (Class 6) 2-Y-0 **£1,704** (£503; £251) **Stalls** High

Form RPR
4 **1** **Instrumentalist (IRE)**[54] [6795] 2-9-3 0 ... LukeMorris 6 73
(John Best) *pressed ldr: rdn to ld narrowly 1f out: styd on wl fnl f* **7/2**[2]
4 **2** 1¼ **Dark Falcon (IRE)**[103] [5393] 2-9-3 0 ... JoeFanning 3 70
(James Tate) *led: shkn up over 2f out: narrowly hdd 1f out: styd on same pce* **7/2**[2]
03 **3** shd **Villa Royale**[31] [7258] 2-8-12 0 ... EddieAhern 12 65
(Harry Dunlop) *trckd ldng trio: pushed along firmly over 3f out: wnt 3rd over 2f out: hanging lft fnl f and jst nudged along nr fin* **8/1**[3]
4 1¾ **Pallasator** 2-9-3 0 ... SebSanders 8 66+
(Sir Mark Prescott Bt) *dwlt: rn green in last pair: sme prog over 2f out: pushed along and styd on wl fnl f: nrst fin* **20/1**
6 **5** ½ **Hill Of Dreams (IRE)**[38] [7142] 2-8-12 0 ... ShaneKelly 10 60
(Dean Ivory) *hld up in 6th: effrt on outer 3f out: no imp over 2f out: kpt on one pce after* **66/1**
0 **6** nk **Man Of Ice**[47] [6951] 2-9-3 0 ... AdamKirby 2 64
(Jane Chapple-Hyam) *chsd ldng pair to over 2f out: wknd fnl f* **20/1**
7 ¾ **Duke Of Clarence (IRE)** 2-9-3 0 ... JimmyFortune 7 62+
(Richard Hannon) *slowly away: towards rr: effrt into midfield 3f out but sn outpcd: pushed along and one pce over 1f out* **11/8**[1]
8 2¾ **Jennifer J** 2-8-12 0 ... JimmyQuinn 1 51
(Mark H Tompkins) *restless in stalls and slowest away: mostly in last pair: sme prog over 1f out: nvr a factor* **100/1**
9 2¾ **Masters Blazing** 2-8-12 0 ... RyanPowell(5) 11 50
(John Ryan) *dwlt: a in rr: rdn on outer 3f out: no prog* **100/1**
10 shd **Equation Of Time** 2-9-3 0 ... TonyCulhane 5 49
(David Flood) *t.k.h: hld up in midfield: dropped in rr over 2f out: wl btn after* **100/1**
0 **11** ¾ **Green Legacy (USA)**[54] [6795] 2-9-3 0 ... JimCrowley 4 48
(Amanda Perrett) *slowly away: in tch in midfield: lost pl over 3f out: struggling in rr after* **25/1**

0 **12** *nk* **Applaudere**[17] 7464 2-8-12 0.. FergusSweeney 9 42
(Jamie Osborne) *in tch in midfield tl wknd over 2f out* **100/1**

1m 39.06s (0.86) **Going Correction** -0.025s/f (Stan) **12** Ran SP% **116.5**
Speed ratings (Par 94): **94,92,92,90,90 90,89,86,83,83 83,82**
toteswingers:1&2:£3.10, 2&3:£3.80, 1&3:£3.60 CSF £14.89 TOTE £6.00: £1.40, £1.30, £2.40; EX 20.20 Trifecta £39.20 Pool: £216.75 - 4.09 winning units..
Owner Kingsgate Racing 4 **Bred** Pheroze Sorabjee **Trained** Hucking, Kent

FOCUS
This looked no more than a fair maiden and they seemed to go an even pace.

NOTEBOOK
Instrumentalist(IRE) improved on the form he showed when fourth over 7f here on his debut in October. His task was made easier by the third-placed finisher hanging badly under pressure, but he's a colt with a lot of scope and can progress to a useful level. (op 9-2)
Dark Falcon(IRE), fourth over 7f at Wolverhampton in August when trained by Ed Dunlop, tried to make all but was run out of it. He's entitled to come on for this. (op 11-4)
Villa Royale hung badly left under pressure and consequently wasn't ridden out with anything like maximum force. She otherwise would have been at least second and arguably would have won. Eddie Ahern officially reported the filly hung left. Official explanation: jockey said filly hung badly left (op 7-1)
Pallasator, a 32,000gns purchase out of a Lancashire Oaks winner, has already been gelded. He ran on from well off the pace, showing enough to suggest he can win a similarly ordinary race granted normal improvement, but we surely won't see the best of him until he goes up to middle-distances. (tchd 16-1)
Hill Of Dreams(IRE) hinted at ability on her debut at Wolverhampton and did so again. (op 40-1)
Duke Of Clarence(IRE) was well backed, but this 45,000gns yearling ran green throughout. A half-brother to smart French 7f-1m2f performer (including Group 2 winner) Special Kaldoun, he's presumably thought capable of a lot better. (op 7-4 tchd 15-8 and 5-4 and 2-1 in a place)
Equation Of Time Official explanation: jockey said colt ran too keen

7635 COWDEN (S) STKS 6f (P)
1:00 (1:00) (Class 6) 2-Y-O **£1,704** (£503; £251) **Stalls** Low

Form RPR
055 **1** **One More Roman (IRE)**[17] 7464 2-8-11 66..................(bt) LiamKeniry 4 60+
(J S Moore) *mde all and nvr seriously pressed: kicked on over 2f out: rdn and in command fnl f* **11/4**[1]
5533 **2** *1* **The Dancing Lord**[16] 7490 2-8-9 62................................ RyanWhile(7) 3 62+
(Bill Turner) *hld up in 5th: stl gng strly over 2f out: prog on inner over 1f out: urged along and styd on to take 2nd last 100yds: unable to chal* **4/1**[2]
0604 **3** *1* **House Limit (IRE)**[25] 7342 2-8-11 49............................(b) EddieAhern 1 54
(Harry Dunlop) *trckd ldng trio: rdn over 2f out: effrt to chse wnr jst over 1f out: wl hld and lost 2nd last 100yds* **15/2**
0026 **4** *3 3/4* **Multi Blessing**[16] 7490 2-9-2 64.. JimCrowley 7 48
(Alan Jarvis) *chsd wnr: rdn over 2f out: nt qckn over 1f out: sn lost 2nd and wknd* **5/1**[3]
5 **5** *1/2* **Red Hermes (IRE)**[25] 7350 2-8-6 0.................................. JimmyQuinn 6 36
(Mark H Tompkins) *dwlt: rn green in last pair: no prog 2f out: styd on ins fnl f: no ch* **13/2**
0060 **6** *1/2* **J Cunningham**[47] 6942 2-8-6 42...................................... DavidProbert 9 35
(Mark Usher) *towards rr: rdn and no prog over 2f out: nvr on terms* **66/1**
2340 **7** *3/4* **Shout For Joy (IRE)**[17] 7452 2-8-1 62.......................... RyanPowell(5) 8 33
(Richard Hannon) *mostly chsd ldng pair: rdn over 2f out: wknd qckly over 1f out* **13/2**
0500 **8** *nse* **Lady Nickandy (IRE)**[53] 6821 2-8-12 53 ow1............. StevieDonohoe 2 38
(Alan McCabe) *s.i.s: urged along in last pair and nvr gng wl: nvr a factor* **12/1**

1m 12.24s (0.34) **Going Correction** -0.025s/f (Stan) **8** Ran SP% **110.9**
Speed ratings (Par 94): **96,94,93,88,87 87,86,85**
toteswingers:1&2:£2.60, 2&3:£5.00, 1&3:£5.00 CSF £12.85 TOTE £3.80: £1.70, £1.20, £2.20; EX 15.60 Trifecta £61.10 Pool: £268.37 - 3.25 winning units..There was no bid for the winner.
Owner Mrs Fitri Hay **Bred** Mrs Fitriani Hay **Trained** Upper Lambourn, Berks

FOCUS
A moderate seller

NOTEBOOK
One More Roman(IRE) didn't have to run to his official mark of 66 to gain his first win at the fourth attempt. He would have been 9lb worse off with the runner-up in a handicap and 17lb worse off with the third. (op 3-1 tchd 7-2)
The Dancing Lord simply found the winner too good. (op 5-1 tchd 11-2)
House Limit(IRE) seems to have run a bit above his official rating of 49. (op 6-1)
Multi Blessing was held by The Dancing Lord on a couple of recent meetings. (op 6-1 tchd 13-2)
Red Hermes(IRE) never threatened after a slow start. (op 5-1)

7636 TOTEQUADPOT CLAIMING STKS 7f (P)
1:30 (1:30) (Class 6) 3-Y-0+ **£1,704** (£503; £251) **Stalls** Low

Form RPR
0021 **1** **One Way Or Another (AUS)**[7] 7565 8-8-12 65...........(bt) LukeMorris 5 74
(David Evans) *hld up towards rr: stdy prog on outer 2f out: asked for effrt jst over 1f out: led ins fnl f: r.o* **5/1**[2]
6210 **2** *3/4* **Fishforcompliments**[38] 7150 7-8-6 77................(v) GeorgeChaloner(7) 4 73
(Richard Fahey) *rrd s: hld up: last 3f out: prog wl over 1f out: shkn up and r.o to take 2nd nr fin: no ch to chal* **5/1**[2]
0004 **3** *nk* **Tiradito (USA)**[12] 7518 4-8-11 74.............................(p) MarkCoumbe(5) 6 76
(Michael Attwater) *t.k.h: hld up in 3rd: clsd on ldrs over 1f out: rdn to dispute ld jst ins fnl f: nt qckn* **7/1**[3]
1002 **4** *nk* **Golden Desert (IRE)**[12] 7518 7-9-5 88............................. EddieAhern 1 78
(Simon Dow) *hld up in 4th: crowded for room 2f out and swtchd ins over 1f out: drvn to chal ins fnl f: nt qckn last 100yds* **4/5**[1]
3420 **5** *2 1/2* **For Life (IRE)**[16] 7485 9-8-7 62............................... NataliaGemelova(3) 8 62
(John E Long) *sn led and clr: stl 4 l up 2f out: wknd and hdd jst ins fnl f* **33/1**
5103 **6** *1 1/2* **Stevie Gee (IRE)**[21] 7412 7-8-9 71.................................... RyanClark(3) 2 60
(Ian Williams) *hld up towards rr: shkn up on inner wl over 1f out: nvr on terms* **9/1**
-200 **7** *3 3/4* **Majestical (IRE)**[12] 7518 9-8-4 37.........................(e) JemmaMarshall(5) 3 47?
(Peter Hedger) *broke wl: t.k.h and sn restrained bhd clr ldr: wknd 2f out* **100/1**
4-6 **8** *3* **Vivre La Secret**[221] 1629 3-8-0 0....................................... JakePayne(7) 9 37
(Bill Turner) *a in rr: lost tch over 2f out* **100/1**

1m 24.19s (-0.61) **Going Correction** -0.025s/f (Stan) **8** Ran SP% **116.3**
Speed ratings (Par 101): **102,101,100,100,97 95,91,88**
toteswingers:1&2:£3.10, 2&3:£3.80, 1&3:£3.60 CSF £30.39 TOTE £3.80: £1.50, £1.30, £1.90; EX 33.30 Trifecta £106.20 Pool: £484.04 - 3.37 winning units..
Owner Mrs E Evans **Bred** Segenho Stud **Trained** Pandy, Monmouths

FOCUS
A fair claimer. The pace seemed modest early, but gradually increased with For Life going off in a clear lead. The form is rated around the fourth and may not be entirely solid.

7637 TOTEEXACTA H'CAP 1m (P)
2:00 (2:08) (Class 5) (0-75,75) 3-Y-0+ **£2,726** (£805; £402) **Stalls** High

Form RPR
4635 **1** **Mazamorra (USA)**[17] 7465 4-9-6 75.................................. AndreaAtzeni 5 84
(Marco Botti) *trckd ldng pair: rdn over 2f out: clsd to ld jst over 1f out: hrd pressed ins fnl f: hld on* **10/1**
4062 **2** *hd* **Hereford Boy**[24] 7362 7-9-1 70.......................................(b) AdamKirby 11 79
(Dean Ivory) *hld up wl in rr: stdy prog over 2f out: weaved through over 1f out: drvn to chal ins fnl f and upsides: nt go by* **8/1**
4033 **3** *2* **Caldercruix (USA)**[11] 7532 4-8-8 70.........................(p) RaulDaSilva(7) 12 74
(James Evans) *pressed ldr: rdn to ld 2f out: hdd and one pce jst over 1f out* **10/1**
0316 **4** *1 1/4* **Cativo Cavallino**[24] 7362 8-8-11 69....................... NataliaGemelova(3) 1 70
(John E Long) *slowly away: hld up in last trio: last and pushed along whn wd bnd 2f out: styd on wl fnl f: nrst fin* **25/1**
4032 **5** *1/2* **Peponi**[11] 7532 5-9-6 75... SteveDrowne 4 75
(Peter Makin) *chsd ldrs: pushed along and outpcd over 2f out: kpt on same pce fr over 1f out* **13/2**[3]
0050 **6** *hd* **Follow The Flag (IRE)**[10] 7542 7-9-2 71..................(v) RobertWinston 7 70
(Alan McCabe) *mostly in midfield: u.p sn after 1/2-way: plugged on but nvr gng pce to threaten* **10/1**
-000 **7** *1/2* **King Of Windsor (IRE)**[40] 7110 4-9-5 74.......................(b) JimCrowley 2 72
(Ralph Beckett) *hld up in last trio: pushed along over 2f out: angled out over 1f out: styd on one pce: nvr involved* **5/1**[2]
0601 **8** *1 1/4* **Aquilifer (IRE)**[24] 7362 3-9-3 73.. ShaneKelly 8 68
(Mrs K Burke) *nvr bttr than midfield: outpcd by ldrs over 2f out: no prog after* **13/2**[3]
5003 **9** *1* **The Holyman (IRE)**[54] 6799 3-9-0 70.............................. DaneO'Neill 10 63
(Jo Crowley) *dwlt: sn chsd ldrs on outer: outpcd over 2f out: wknd over 1f out* **9/2**[1]
4560 **10** *3 1/2* **Huzzah (IRE)**[11] 7532 6-9-4 73..................................... MichaelStainton 3 58
(Paul Howling) *sn in rr: rdn in last trio and struggling over 2f out: no prog* **33/1**
510 **11** *nk* **Daruband**[11] 7532 3-9-3 73...(b[1]) SebSanders 6 57
(Alan McCabe) *s.i.s but pushed up to press ldrs: rdn and wnt wd bnd 2f out: wknd tamely* **10/1**
2021 **12** *1/2* **Sweet Secret**[18] 7447 4-9-3 72..................................(b) FergusSweeney 9 55
(Jeremy Gask) *sn led fr wd draw: hdd & wknd qckly 2f out* **12/1**

1m 36.05s (-2.15) **Going Correction** -0.025s/f (Stan) course record
WFA 3 from 4yo+ 1lb **12** Ran SP% **123.5**
Speed ratings (Par 103): **109,108,106,105,105 104,104,103,102,98 98,97**
toteswingers:1&2:£12.80, 2&3:£20.10, 1&3:£25.90 CSF £91.47 CT £851.30 TOTE £7.20: £4.20, £3.00, £3.60; EX 66.60 TRIFECTA Not won..
Owner J Barton & C Pizarro **Bred** Sarah S Farish **Trained** Newmarket, Suffolk

FOCUS
A fair handicap which was sound run, and the form is solid enough.
Huzzah(IRE) Official explanation: jockey said blindfold became stuck

7638 TOTETRIFECTA H'CAP 1m 4f (P)
2:30 (2:35) (Class 5) (0-75,72) 3-Y-0 **£2,385** (£704; £352) **Stalls** Low

Form RPR
4311 **1** **Woop Woop (IRE)**[12] 7515 3-8-12 68............................ RyanPowell(5) 3 75
(Ian Williams) *prom: disp 2nd pl after 4f: brought wd in st: drvn and clsd to ld last 100yds: sn in command* **3/1**[2]
0115 **2** *1 1/4* **Castlemorris King**[21] 7413 3-8-10 66......................... MarkCoumbe(5) 1 71
(Michael Attwater) *hld up tl swift move to ld after 4f: kicked on 3f out: over 2 l ahd over 1f out: hdd and outpcd last 100yds* **9/4**[1]
3030 **3** *3/4* **Trend Line (IRE)**[77] 6226 3-9-7 72.................................... RobertHavlin 2 76
(Peter Chapple-Hyam) *led tl: stdd: lost pl over 3f out: last 2f out but stl gng wl: drvn and r.o to take 3rd ins fnl f: clsng on runner-up at fin: too much to do* **9/2**[3]
0253 **4** *1 3/4* **Roman Flame**[19] 7427 3-8-6 57... FrannyNorton 5 58
(Michael Quinn) *t.k.h: hld up in tch: rdn over 2f out: nt qckn over 1f out whn disputing 3rd: fdd nr fin* **16/1**
2351 **5** *1/2* **Encore Un Fois**[19] 7427 3-9-0 70.................................. DavidKenny(5) 6 70
(George Baker) *taken down early: loaded in stalls wout jockey: stdd s: hld up last: effrt on outer over 2f out: nt qckn and btn over 1f out* **11/2**
2016 **6** *3* **Tegan (IRE)**[17] 7458 3-9-6 71.. JimmyFortune 4 67
(Richard Hannon) *led after 1f tl after 4f: disp 2nd pl tl wknd over 2f out* **5/1**

2m 34.85s (1.85) **Going Correction** -0.025s/f (Stan) **6** Ran SP% **111.9**
Speed ratings (Par 102): **92,91,90,89,89 87**
CSF £10.12 TOTE £3.00: £1.70, £1.60; EX 10.00.
Owner Lee Westwood & Chubby Chandler **Bred** C Amerian **Trained** Portway, Worcs

FOCUS
A modest handicap run at a steady early pace. Sound if ordinary form, the winner continuing to progress.
Tegan(IRE) Official explanation: trainer said filly ran flat

7639 TOTEPOOL H'CAP (DIV I) 1m 2f (P)
3:00 (3:01) (Class 6) (0-52,52) 3-Y-0+ **£2,045** (£603; £302) **Stalls** Low

Form RPR
641- **1** **Sovento (GER)**[160] 3502 7-9-3 52.................................... MartinHarley 14 61+
(Shaun Harley, Ire) *hld up in last pair: prog into midfield over 2f out and looking for room: drvn and hdwy over 1f out: r.o to ld last 75yds* **15/8**[1]
034 **2** *nk* **Avon Supreme**[26] 7333 3-9-0 52.................................... StevieDonohoe 3 61
(Gay Kelleway) *trckd ldrs: prog and squeezed through to chse ldr over 1f out: drvn ahd ins fnl f: hdd last 75yds: styd on* **12/1**
3423 **3** *3/4* **Warden Bond**[23] 7394 3-8-13 51.......................................(p) MartinLane 7 58
(William Stone) *prom: chsd ldr over 3f out: led over 2f out: hdd ins fnl f: styd on* **7/1**[3]
6 **4** *2 3/4* **The Catenian (IRE)**[26] 7333 3-8-8 46 oh1..................... JimmyQuinn 13 48
(Eoin Doyle, Ire) *racd wd: trckd ldrs: cl enough jst over 2f out: nt qckn then reminders over 1f out: styd on ins fnl f* **16/1**
2026 **5** *nk* **Holyfield Warrior (IRE)**[240] 1233 7-8-10 50.............. MarkCoumbe(5) 8 51
(Michael Attwater) *t.k.h: hld up in rr: prog into midfield over 2f out gng strly: rdn and fnd nil over 1f out* **16/1**
0053 **6** *nk* **Querido (GER)**[19] 7437 7-8-13 51...............................(t) RobertLButler(3) 6 51
(Paddy Butler) *trckd ldrs: prog and cl enough jst over 2f out: n.m.r and nt qckn over 1f out: one pce after* **16/1**

6000 **7** *shd* **Tortilla (IRE)**[3] 7608 3-8-10 **51**..............................(v[1]) AdamBeschizza(3) 9 51
(Des Donovan) *rousted along early to rch midfield: rdn over 2f out: nvr gng pce to threaten but kpt on u.p* **33/1**

3300 **8** *6* **Drumadoon (IRE)**[12] 7515 3-9-0 **52**..............................(p) LiamKeniry 5 40
(Liam Corcoran) *t.k.h: hld up towards rr: rdn over 2f out: wknd* **40/1**

6 **9** *1* **Oxford Gold (IRE)**[32] 7246 4-8-11 **46** oh1....................(bt) ShaneKelly 12 32
(Edward Vaughan) *stdd s: hld up in last pair: rdn and no prog over 2f out: n.d after* **11/4**[2]

0200 **10** *nk* **Aurora Lights**[255] 969 4-8-5 **47**............................ GeorgeChaloner(7) 10 33
(Richard Fahey) *racd wd: prom: cl enough over 2f out: sn wknd* **33/1**

5-40 **11** *nse* **Sommersturm (GER)**[27] 3047 7-9-2 **51**.......................... MickyFenton 2 36
(Barney Curley) *led to over 2f out: wknd rapidly* **50/1**

040- **12** *2* **Expensive Legacy**[446] 6080 4-8-12 **50**....................... RossAtkinson(3) 1 31
(Tor Sturgis) *mostly chsd ldr to over 3f out: sn wknd* **100/1**

6064 **13** *3* **Gay Gallivanter**[17] 7466 3-8-9 **47**................................. FrannyNorton 11 22
(Michael Quinn) *racd wd in rr: no prog over 2f out: sn wknd* **14/1**

2m 7.13s (0.53) **Going Correction** -0.025s/f (Stan)
WFA 3 from 4yo+ 3lb **13** Ran SP% **117.2**
Speed ratings (Par 101): **96,95,95,92,92 92,92,87,86,86 86,84,82**
toteswingers:1&2:£7.00, 2&3:£5.20, 1&3:£4.40 CSF £24.87 CT £134.04 TOTE £3.20: £1.30, £3.50, £2.20; EX 29.10 Trifecta £120.20 Pool: £445.22 - 2.74 winning units..
Owner Lough Derg Syndicate **Bred** A Stahn **Trained** Letterkenny, Co Donegal

FOCUS
The time was 1.59 seconds slower than the strongly run second division. A steady pace compressed the distances, but the well-handicapped Sovento always looked likely to get up under a well-judged ride. He rates better than the bare form, with a 3lb personal best from the second.

7640 TOTEPOOL H'CAP (DIV II) 1m 2f (P)
3:30 (3:30) (Class 6) (0-52,52) 3-Y-O+ **£2,045** (£603; £302) **Stalls** Low

Form RPR

0000 **1** **Shirataki (IRE)**[11] 7527 3-8-8 **46** oh1................................ ChrisCatlin 14 54
(Peter Hiatt) *hld up wl in rr fr wdst draw: prog over 3f out: chsd ldrs over 2f out: wnt 2nd over 1f out: looked hld tl drvn ahd last 50yds: jst hld on* **40/1**

3345 **2** *shd* **Prince Of Thebes (IRE)**[12] 7522 10-8-11 **51**........(p) MarkCoumbe(5) 13 59
(Michael Attwater) *slowly away: hld up wl in rr and wl off the pce: prog on outer over 3f out: chsd ldrs over 1f out: styd on to take 2nd last strides: jst failed* **14/1**

6002 **3** *½* **Daniel Thomas (IRE)**[18] 7442 9-8-13 **51**..............(tp) RobertLButler(3) 10 58
(Richard Guest) *hld up in 7th: smooth prog to ld 3f out: kpt on fr over 1f out: looked like holding on tl hdd last 50yds* **25/1**

0003 **4** *1* **Love In The Park**[17] 7466 6-8-12 **47**.................................. ShaneKelly 2 52
(Roy Brotherton) *hld up in midfield: prog over 3f out: chsd ldng pair briefly over 2f out: kpt on fr over 1f out: a hld* **9/1**

222 **5** *1 ¼* **Shaunas Spirit (IRE)**[5] 7581 3-8-9 **47**............................. JimmyQuinn 8 50
(Dean Ivory) *prom and gng best of ldrs fr 1/2-way: clsd to ld briefly over 3f out: chsd new ldr after: rdn 2f out: fdd fnl f* **10/3**[1]

0050 **6** *½* **Regal Rave (USA)**[34] 7206 4-9-1 **50**...............................(e) JohnFahy 6 52
(Peter Hedger) *hld up in last trio and wl off the pce: prog on inner over 3f out: hrd rdn over 1f out: kpt on but nt gng pce to chal* **12/1**

0004 **7** *2 ½* **Alfraamsey**[38] 2805 3-8-7 **52**.................................... MartinLeonard(7) 5 49+
(Sheena West) *hld up in rr: no prog whn r unfolded 3f out and no ch after: nudged along and styd on fr over 1f out* **7/2**[2]

6000 **8** *1 ¼* **Russian Storm**[23] 7388 3-8-3 **46**.............................. JemmaMarshall(5) 9 40
(Pat Phelan) *hld up in last trio: taken to wd outside over 3f out: modest prog 2f out: reminder fnl f: kpt on but nvr remotely involved* **10/1**

1020 **9** *½* **Tinkerbell Will**[23] 7394 4-9-1 **50**..................................... SamHitchcott 11 43
(John E Long) *chsd ldrs: u.p over 4f out: struggling over 2f out: steadily fdd* **25/1**

0032 **10** *6* **Gee Major**[19] 7437 4-9-2 **51**..(p) LukeMorris 1 32
(Nicky Vaughan) *chsd clr ldr 2f: styd prom: drvn over 4f out: wknd over 3f out* **5/1**[3]

3544 **11** *3 ½* **Olimamu (IRE)**[84] 5994 4-8-10 **48**...............................(t) SimonPearce(3) 7 22
(Lydia Pearce) *s.i.s: wl in rr: pushed along over 3f out: sn btn* **16/1**

0550 **12** *12* **Warbond**[40] 7092 3-9-0 **52**...(v) DaneO'Neill 12 —
(Michael Madgwick) *nt that wl away but rousted along and prog to go 2nd after 2f: wknd 3f out: t.o* **20/1**

3000 **13** *10* **Tous Les Deux**[271] 809 8-8-9 **49**.......................... MatthewCosham(5) 4 —
(Dr Jeremy Naylor) *prom: drvn over 4f out: wknd over 3f out: t.o* **40/1**

000 **14** *2 ½* **Heading To First**[19] 7437 4-8-11 **46**............................(vt[1]) MartinHarley 3 —
(Paddy Butler) *blasted off in front and sn clr: wknd rapidly and hdd over 3f out: t.o* **16/1**

2m 5.54s (-1.06) **Going Correction** -0.025s/f (Stan)
WFA 3 from 4yo+ 3lb **14** Ran SP% **124.5**
Speed ratings (Par 101): **103,102,102,101,100 100,98,97,96,92 89,79,71,69**
toteswingers:1&2:£83.10, 2&3:£51.50, 1&3:£101.30 CSF £518.24 CT £13438.36 TOTE £40.90: £14.40, £4.90, £6.90; EX 300.10 Trifecta £378.30 Part won. Pool: £511.27 - 0.64 winning units..
Owner P W Hiatt **Bred** Deerfield Farm **Trained** Hook Norton, Oxon
■ Stewards' Enquiry : Jemma Marshall ten-day ban: failed to obtain best possible placing (Dec 19-22,26-31)

FOCUS
The pace was much too strong with Heading To First racing off in a clear lead before inevitably fading, and the time was 1.59 seconds faster than the first division. The form is still pretty ordinary.
Shirataki(IRE) Official explanation: trainer said, regarding apparent improvement in form, that the gelding had benefited from a drop in trip and settling.
Russian Storm Official explanation: jockey said, regarding runing and riding, that her orders were to jump out, keep the filly out of the kickback and enjoy itself; vet said filly finished one-fifth lame and had some nasal discharge.
T/Jkpt: Not won. T/Plt: £64.00 to a £1 stake. Pool of £61,771.26 - 703.65 winning tickets. T/Qpdt: £26.50 to a £1 stake. Pool of £5,139.93 - 143.00 winning tickets. JN

7500 SOUTHWELL (L-H)
Tuesday, December 6

OFFICIAL GOING: Standard
Wind: light half behind until virtually nil after Race 3 Weather: Fine and dry

7641 PLAY THE BIG MONEY TOTEJACKPOT TODAY H'CAP 6f (F)
12:00 (12:03) (Class 6) (0-60,60) 3-Y-O+ **£1,704** (£503; £251) **Stalls** Low

Form RPR

3353 **1** **Suddenly Susan (IRE)**[8] 7567 3-9-5 **58**...................(b) GrahamGibbons 2 73
(David Nicholls) *qckly away and sn clr: mde all: styd on wl fnl f* **7/1**

0205 **2** *5* **Greenhead High**[21] 7420 3-9-5 **58**.................................. AndrewMullen 5 57
(David Nicholls) *prom: chsd wnr 1/2-way: rdn over 2f out: drvn wl over 1f out: no imp* **16/1**

4000 **3** *½* **Prince Of Vasa (IRE)**[14] 7500 4-9-7 **60**............................. SebSanders 6 57
(Michael Smith) *towards rr: pushed along 1/2-way: rdn wl over 1f out: styd on fnl f: tk 3rd nr fin* **13/2**[3]

055 **4** *hd* **Wandering Lad**[25] 7371 3-9-0 **53**.................................. DanielTudhope 3 50
(Declan Carroll) *chsd wnr: rdn along over 2f out: sn drvn and kpt on same pce: lost 3rd nr fin* **20/1**

0340 **5** *1 ¼* **Unwrapit (USA)**[46] 7001 3-9-4 **57**..................................(tp) TomEaves 10 50
(Bryan Smart) *in rr whn n.m.r and sltly hmpd after 1 1/2f: hdwy 2f out and sn rdn: swtchd rt appr fnl f: kpt on: nrst fin* **25/1**

4006 **6** *hd* **Sands Of Dee (USA)**[27] 7341 4-9-7 **60**......................(b) RobertWinston 1 52
(David Nicholls) *towards rr: rdn along on inner 1/2-way: kpt on appr fnl f: nrst fin* **16/1**

211/ **7** *1* **Wellmarked (IRE)**[32] 7274 4-9-3 **56**..............................(tp) LiamKeniry 14 45
(P G Fahey, Ire) *dwlt and in rr: wd st: sn rdn and kpt on fnl 2f: nvr nr ldrs* **6/1**[2]

0/2- **8** *hd* **Always Gunner**[417] 6896 5-9-4 **57**.................................. MickyFenton 11 45
(Paul Midgley) *in tch: hdwy wl over 2f out: sn rdn along and n.d* **25/1**

5660 **9** *¾* **Fibs And Flannel**[21] 7425 4-9-7 **60**......................... RobbieFitzpatrick 9 46
(Tony Coyle) *dwlt and sn rdn along in rr: wd st: n.d* **25/1**

05-0 **10** *hd* **Footstepsofspring (FR)**[244] 1177 4-9-3 **56**................. TonyCulhane 12 41
(Willie Musson) *in rr and pushed along whn hmpd after 1 1/2f: bhd and rdn 1/2-way: sme late hdwy* **11/4**[1]

4600 **11** *shd* **Arrivaderci**[21] 7419 3-9-4 **60**....................................(e) RobertLButler(3) 13 45
(Richard Guest) *in tch: rdn along over 2f out: sn edgd lft and wknd* **40/1**

0040 **12** *1* **Steel City Boy (IRE)**[48] 6943 8-9-1 **54**........................... JimmyQuinn 8 36
(Garry Woodward) *chsd ldrs: rdn along wl over 2f out: sn wknd* **50/1**

6006 **13** *hd* **Takajan (IRE)**[21] 7419 4-9-4 **57**.............................. SilvestreDeSousa 7 38
(Mark Brisbourne) *midfield: n.m.r after 2f: rdn along 1/2-way: wd st: sn wknd* **7/1**

0553 **14** *nk* **Yours**[195] 2396 3-9-0 **53**.. PhillipMakin 4 33
(Kevin Ryan) *chsd ldrs: rdn along 1/2-way: sn wknd* **16/1**

1m 15.07s (-1.43) **Going Correction** -0.25s/f (Stan) **14** Ran SP% **117.6**
Speed ratings (Par 101): **99,92,91,91,89 89,88,87,86,86 86,85,84,84**
toteswingers:1&2:£19.70, 2&3:£23.00, 1&3:£9.70 CSF £100.18 CT £766.62 TOTE £8.60: £2.60, £5.10, £2.50; EX 78.30 Trifecta £202.90 Part won. Pool: £274.30 - 0.30 winning units..
Owner Paul J Dixon **Bred** L Mulryan **Trained** Sessay, N Yorks

FOCUS
A moderate handicap and very few ever figured. It resulted in a 1-2 for David Nicholls and the first four home came from the six lowest stalls. The time was good and the winner is rated back to his 2yo best.

7642 TOTEEXACTA NURSERY 5f (F)
12:30 (12:30) (Class 5) (0-75,69) 2-Y-O **£2,264** (£673; £336; £168) **Stalls** High

Form RPR

0354 **1** **Whisky Bravo**[31] 7294 2-9-1 **63**.. SteveDrowne 2 72+
(David Brown) *chsd ldrs: pushed along 1/2-way: sltly outpcd and rdn 2f out: styd on to ld ins fnl f: kpt on strly* **6/5**[1]

3512 **2** *1 ¾* **Bookiesindexdotnet**[18] 7452 2-9-7 **69**.............................. JoeFanning 4 72
(J R Jenkins) *cl up: led after 1f: hdd 3f out: led again wl over 1f out and sn rdn: hdd and one pce ins fnl f* **4/1**[2]

021 **3** *2* **Wicked Wench**[27] 7335 2-9-0 **69**................................ JoshBaudains(7) 1 65
(Jo Hughes) *s.i.s: sn trcking ldrs: effrt to chse ldng pair over 2f out: rdn wl over 1f out: kpt on same pce* **5/1**[3]

4304 **4** *1 ¼* **Thorpe Bay**[26] 7353 2-8-9 **60**................................(b) AdamBeschizza(3) 7 51
(Mark Rimmer) *cl up nr stands' rail: led after 1f: hdd 3f out: cl up and rdn 2f out: sn edgd lft and wknd* **7/1**

3533 **5** *3 ½* **First Bid**[79] 6186 2-9-2 **67**... DaleSwift(3) 3 46
(James Given) *a in rr: outpcd and bhd fr 1/2-way* **11/1**

020 **6** *6* **Bengaline**[10] 7555 2-9-6 **68**...(p) RobertWinston 5 34
(David Nicholls) *led 1f: cl up: rdn along 1/2-way: sn swtchd lft and wknd* **20/1**

59.29 secs (-0.41) **Going Correction** -0.175s/f (Stan) **6** Ran SP% **107.7**
Speed ratings (Par 96): **96,93,90,88,82 72**
toteswingers:1&2:£1.90, 2&3:£1.10, 1&3:£2.00 CSF £5.58 TOTE £2.10: £1.30, £1.70; EX 5.80.
Owner S Rolland & C Watson **Bred** Peter Onslow **Trained** Averham Park, Notts

FOCUS
An ordinary sprint nursery. The winner showed a good attitude.

NOTEBOOK
Whisky Bravo was sent off the well-backed favourite and justified the support in style. Having come into this 1-1 at the track after gaining his only previous success in a C&D maiden in August, there was one anxious moment when he became outpaced before halfway, but he came home strongly and was well in control once leading inside the last furlong. He will always have to be feared when returned here. (op 6-4 tchd 7-4)
Bookiesindexdotnet, proven on Polytrack, was trying this surface for the first time but her breeding gave plenty of encouragement she would handle it. Quickly away, she did little wrong but was firmly put in her place by the winner late on. (op 3-1 tchd 11-4)
Wicked Wench was making her nursery debut after making all to win a four-runner maiden over C&D last month. She wasn't best away and was up against another fast starter, which meant the same tactics couldn't be utilised, but she still had every chance coming to the last furlong and wasn't disgraced. (tchd 9-2)
Thorpe Bay may not have been helped by racing alone next to the stands' rail and is now 0-11. (op 6-1)
First Bid, making his debut for the yard and all-weather debut, barely went a yard. (op 12-1)
Bengaline should have comfortably reversed last month's C&D running with Wicked Wench on 10lb better terms, but he dropped out tamely at halfway. (tchd 22-1)

7643 TOTEQUADPOT H'CAP (DIV I) 5f (F)
1:00 (1:04) (Class 4) (0-85,85) 3-Y-O+ **£4,204** (£1,251; £625; £312) **Stalls** High

Form RPR

2000 **1** **Even Stevens**[17] 7489 3-9-7 **85**................................. GrahamGibbons 10 97+
(David Nicholls) *cl up: rdn to ld over 1f out: kpt on wl* **7/2**[3]

1U01 **2** *1 ¾* **Monsieur Jamie**[26] 7355 3-9-3 **81**..................................... JoeFanning 2 86
(J R Jenkins) *prom: effrt and ev ch wl over 1f out: sn rdn and one pce ins fnl f* **3/1**[2]

0505 **3** *nse* **Whozthecat (IRE)**[17] 7489 4-9-1 **79**...........................(v) DanielTudhope 1 84
(Declan Carroll) *chsd ldrs: rdn along and sltly outpcd over 2f out: styd on u.p fnl f* **5/2**[1]

0230 **4** *nk* **Dancing Freddy (IRE)**[20] 7428 4-8-10 **74**.................(tp) MartinHarley 7 78
(Richard Guest) *trckd ldrs: hdwy 2f out: swtchd rt and rdn over 1f out: kpt on u.p fnl f* **14/1**

6300 **5** *1* **Dancing Maite**[31] 7299 6-8-12 **76**...........................(p) AndreaAtzeni 6 76
(Roy Bowring) *chsd ldrs: rdn along 2f out: kpt on same pce appr fnl f* **16/1**

400 **6** 1 ¼ **Bravo King (IRE)**[14] 7500 3-8-11 **78**........................(t) RobertLButler(3) 5 74
(Richard Guest) *dwlt: a in rr* **33/1**
4341 **7** 6 **Crimson Cloud**[26] 7356 3-8-10 **74**..............................(b) TonyHamilton 3 48
(Richard Fahey) *led: rdn along 2f out: hdd over 1f out: wknd qckly and eased ins fnl f: b.b.v* **4/1**
58.53 secs (-1.17) **Going Correction** -0.175s/f (Stan) **7** Ran SP% **111.3**
Speed ratings (Par 105): **102,99,99,98,97 95,85**
toteswingers:1&2:£2.00, 2&3:£1.80, 1&3:£2.00 CSF £13.61 CT £28.47 TOTE £4.00: £3.10, £2.20; EX 15.00 Trifecta £38.80 Pool: £373.41 - 7.11 winning units..
Owner Paul J Dixon **Bred** Mrs Yvette Dixon **Trained** Sessay, N Yorks

FOCUS
Three non-runners, including Hotham, who was withdrawn at the start, but this is still solid form. The winner improved his fine record here. The time was 0.10 seconds quicker than the second division.
Crimson Cloud Official explanation: trainer's rep said filly bled from the nose

7644 TOTEQUADPOT H'CAP (DIV II) 5f (F)
1:30 (1:30) (Class 4) (0-85,82) 3-Y-0+ **£4,204** (£1,251; £625; £312) **Stalls** High

Form RPR
0042 **1** **Sleepy Blue Ocean**[14] 7500 5-8-13 **74**..........................(p) LukeMorris 4 85
(John Balding) *towards rr: rdn along 1/2-way: hdwy wl over 1f out: styd on to ld last 75yds* **4/1**[2]
1214 **2** *hd* **Mottley Crewe**[6] 7586 4-9-3 **78**..........................(b) MartinHarley 7 88
(Richard Guest) *trckd ldrs: hdwy wl over 1f out: rdn to ld jst ins fnl f: hdd and nt qckn last 75yds* **4/1**[2]
1165 **3** 1 ¼ **Captain Scooby**[14] 7500 5-8-13 **77**.............................. RobertLButler(3) 2 83
(Richard Guest) *trckd ldrs: hdwy wl over 1f out: swtchd rt and rdn whn n.m.r jst ins fnl f: kpt on* **20/1**
5022 **4** 1 ¼ **Lenny Bee**[17] 7487 5-9-7 **82**..................................(t) SilvestreDeSousa 3 83
(Deborah Sanderson) *cl up: effrt to chalr 2f out: sn rdn and ev ch tl edgd rt ent fnl f: sn one pce* **3/1**[1]
0653 **5** ½ **Island Legend (IRE)**[17] 7487 5-9-5 **80**................(p) RichardKingscote 6 79
(Milton Bradley) *led: rdn wl over 1f out: hdd jst ins fnl f: sn wknd* **12/1**
0044 **6** 1 ½ **Oldjoesaid**[14] 7500 7-8-12 **73**..(b) PhillipMakin 5 67
(Kevin Ryan) *dwlt: sn trcking ldrs: rdn wl over 1f out: kpt on same pce* **9/1**
4560 **7** 1 ½ **Luscivious**[112] 5148 7-9-3 **78**....................................(b) GrahamGibbons 1 67
(David Nicholls) *dwlt: sn cl up on outer: rdn along 2f out: wknd appr fnl f* **12/1**
5012 **8** 2 **Red Cape (FR)**[5] 7594 8-9-1 **76**..................................(b) JamesSullivan 9 57
(Ruth Carr) *a towards rr* **16/1**
0242 **9** 3 **Defence Council (IRE)**[17] 7489 3-9-5 **80**.................... RobertWinston 10 51
(Mel Brittain) *cl up: rdn along over 2f out: sn wknd* **8/1**[3]
0000 **10** *hd* **Waabel**[12] 7529 4-8-11 **72**..(bt1) WilliamCarson 8 42
(Richard Guest) *a in rr* **50/1**
58.63 secs (-1.07) **Going Correction** -0.175s/f (Stan) **10** Ran SP% **114.1**
Speed ratings (Par 105): **101,100,98,96,95 93,91,87,83,82**
toteswingers:1&2:£3.80, 2&3:£18.80, 1&3:£18.60 CSF £19.91 CT £286.94 TOTE £5.40: £2.10, £1.80, £5.60; EX 20.00 Trifecta £237.80 Part won. Pool: £321.43 - 0.60 winning units..
Owner Tykes And Terriers Racing Club **Bred** Exors Of The Late N Ahamad & P C Scott **Trained** Scrooby, Notts

FOCUS
They went a decent pace with a three-way battle for the early lead, though the winning time was 0.1 seconds slower than the first division. Sound form.

7645 TOTEPOOL H'CAP 1m 6f (F)
2:00 (2:00) (Class 6) (0-60,59) 3-Y-0+ **£1,704** (£503; £251) **Stalls** Low

Form RPR
0552 **1** **Decana**[54] 6823 3-9-3 **57**.. JimmyFortune 5 67
(Hughie Morrison) *hld up in tch: smooth hdwy over 4f out: led 3f out: rdn and edgd rt wl over 1f out: drvn and hung bdly rt ins fnl f: kpt on* **11/4**[1]
5543 **2** ½ **Carnac (IRE)**[7] 7573 5-9-4 **51**..(p) ShaneKelly 1 60
(Alan McCabe) *a.p: cl up 4f out: rdn along 3f out: styd on wl u.p fnl f* **4/1**[2]
-066 **3** 1 **Seawood**[33] 7241 5-8-12 **45**.. RussKennemore 4 53
(Roy Bowring) *hld up: gd hdwy over 6f out: trckd ldrs 4f out: effrt 3f out and sn ev ch: sn rdn and kpt on same pce fnl f* **25/1**
5443 **4** 8 **Maslak (IRE)**[26] 7357 7-9-10 **57**...................................... ChrisCatlin 6 53
(Peter Hiatt) *in tch: pushed along and outpcd over 5f out: rdn and hdwy 3f out: styd on same pce fnl 2f* **13/2**[3]
0520 **5** *nk* **Mecox Bay (IRE)**[8] 7570 4-8-13 **53**...........................(p) JackDuern(7) 2 49
(Michael Appleby) *led 2f: prom tl led again after 6f: rdn along and hdd 3f out: grad wknd* **9/1**
0404 **6** 6 **Simple Jim (FR)**[41] 7107 7-9-6 **53**............................ SilvestreDeSousa 7 41
(David O'Meara) *in tch on inner: pushed along over 4f out: sn rdn along and wknd over 3f out* **11/4**[1]
25-0 **7** 42 **Tilos Gem (IRE)**[236] 1324 5-9-9 **59**.................................... DaleSwift(3) 3 —
(Brian Ellison) *chsd ldrs: rdn along over 5f out: sn lost pl and bhd* **9/1**
3350 **P** **They All Laughed**[42] 7077 8-9-0 **47**..........................(p) PhillipMakin 8 —
(Marjorie Fife) *a in rr: pushed along and outpcd 1/2-way: sn wl bhd and p.u 3f out* **28/1**
3m 6.07s (-2.23) **Going Correction** -0.25s/f (Stan)
WFA 3 from 4yo+ 7lb **8** Ran SP% **114.0**
Speed ratings (Par 101): **96,95,95,90,90 86,62,—**
toteswingers:1&2:£3.60, 2&3:£13.80, 1&3:£14.00 CSF £13.79 CT £220.36 TOTE £3.60: £1.10, £1.70, £7.00; EX 16.50 TRIFECTA Not won..
Owner R M, S R & P J Payne **Bred** Frazer Hines & John James **Trained** East Ilsley, Berks
■ Stewards' Enquiry : Jack Duern two-day ban: used whip with excessive frequency (Dec 20-21)

FOCUS
As with most staying events around here, this was exhausting to watch as much as to take part in. This was sound run, but the form is moderate.
They All Laughed Official explanation: trainer said gelding finished distressed

7646 MEMBERSHIP AT SOUTHWELL GOLF CLUB CLASSIFIED CLAIMING STKS 6f (F)
2:30 (2:32) (Class 6) 3-Y-0+ **£1,704** (£503; £251) **Stalls** Low

Form RPR
0513 **1** **Global Village (IRE)**[38] 7175 6-8-7 66............................ BarryMcHugh 3 83
(Brian Ellison) *midfield: hdwy on inner wl over 2f out: rdn over 1f out: styd on wl to ld ins fnl f* **9/2**[3]
0002 **2** 2 **Soopacal (IRE)**[14] 7504 6-8-2 67.................................. JamesSullivan 2 72
(Michael Herrington) *cl up: led over 3f out: rdn 2f out: drvn and hdd ins fnl f: one pce* **7/4**[1]
2464 **3** 3 ¼ **Boy The Bell**[26] 7352 4-8-3 70...................................... FrannyNorton 4 63
(Ollie Pears) *midfield: hdwy on inner 1/2-way: sn rdn: styd on appr fnl f: tk 3rd nr fin* **7/2**[2]
0000 **4** *nse* **Incomparable**[11] 7535 6-8-2 68..................................(b) DuranFentiman 14 61
(David Nicholls) *chsd ldrs on outer: rdn along over 2f out: sn drvn and kpt on same pce* **25/1**
6310 **5** ½ **Cape Of Storms**[14] 7502 8-8-8 65 ow1...........................(b) TomEaves 8 66
(Roy Brotherton) *led: hdd over 3f out: rdn over 2f out: grad wknd fr wl over 1f out* **28/1**
3000 **6** 1 **Horatio Carter**[21] 7425 6-8-3 67.............................(b) SilvestreDeSousa 6 58
(David O'Meara) *dwlt and in rr: hdwy over 2f out: swtchd rt and rdn over 1f out: kpt on: nrst fin* **8/1**
162 **7** 1 **Brio**[21] 7420 3-8-3 65..(v) LukeMorris 5 54
(Alan McCabe) *chsd ldrs: rdn along over 2f out: sn one pce* **6/1**
5000 **8** 1 ½ **Mazovian (USA)**[14] 7504 3-8-6 63........................... AdamBeschizza(3) 7 56
(Michael Chapman) *towards rr: rdn along over 2f out and sme late hdwy* **50/1**
4000 **9** 3 ¼ **Nadeen (IRE)**[26] 7356 4-8-6 67....................................... AndrewMullen 9 42
(Michael Smith) *dwlt: a in rr* **14/1**
2026 **10** 1 ¾ **Deliberation (IRE)**[14] 7504 3-7-12 62............................ PaulMcGiff(7) 12 36
(Kevin Ryan) *chsd ldng pair: rdn along wl over 2f out: sn wknd* **33/1**
5006 **11** *nk* **Rio's Girl**[21] 7420 4-8-1 52 ow1.. AmyRyan(3) 11 34
(Tony Coyle) *a towards rr* **66/1**
0340 **12** 3 ¼ **Logans Legend (IRE)**[71] 6414 3-8-3 68 ow3............. AdamCarter(5) 10 27
(Lawrence Mullaney) *a in rr* **66/1**
4300 **13** 3 ¾ **Sophie's Beau (USA)**[43] 7055 4-8-3 47........................(p) AndreaAtzeni 1 10
(Michael Chapman) *s.i.s: a bhd* **150/1**
1m 14.41s (-2.09) **Going Correction** -0.25s/f (Stan) **13** Ran SP% **124.7**
Speed ratings (Par 101): **103,100,96,95,95 93,92,90,86,83 83,79,74**
toteswingers:1&2:£4.00, 2&3:£3.10, 1&3:£3.80 CSF £12.88 TOTE £4.60: £1.20, £1.80, £1.70; EX 21.10 Trifecta £48.50 Pool: £469.99 - 7.16 winning units..Soopacal was claimed by Mustafa Khan for £5000.
Owner Jack Racing Melksham **Bred** Kilfrush Stud **Trained** Norton, N Yorks
■ Stewards' Enquiry : Franny Norton two-day ban: used whip with excessive frequency (Dec 20-21)

FOCUS
A routine claimer, run at a decent pace in a fair time. The winner was seemingly back to his old best.
Sophie's Beau(USA) Official explanation: jockey said gelding was slowly away

7647 GOLF AND RACING AT SOUTHWELL H'CAP 1m 3f (F)
3:00 (3:00) (Class 6) (0-65,65) 3-Y-0+ **£1,704** (£503; £251) **Stalls** Low

Form RPR
2001 **1** **Mediterranean Sea (IRE)**[27] 7340 5-9-10 **65**............... StephenCraine 1 74
(J R Jenkins) *hld up in tch: smooth hdwy 4f out: effrt over 2f out: led 1 1/2f out: sn rdn: kpt on wl u.p fnl f* **6/1**
2035 **2** *hd* **Tobrata**[5] 7589 5-9-3 **58**... RobertWinston 5 66
(Mel Brittain) *prom: hdwy to ld 3f out: rdn and hdd 1 1/2f out: drvn and rallied ins fnl f: ev ch tl edgd rt and no ex towards fin* **7/1**
5032 **3** 2 **Spahi (FR)**[21] 7426 5-8-10 **51**.................................... SilvestreDeSousa 7 56
(David O'Meara) *hld up in tch: hdwy 4f out: chsd ldng pair 2f out: rdn and edgd lft over 1f out: kpt on same pce* **10/3**[1]
302 **4** 3 **Locum**[26] 7357 6-9-4 **59**.. JimmyQuinn 4 58
(Mark H Tompkins) *trckd ldrs: effrt 4f out: rdn along over 3f out: kpt on same pce fnl 2f* **9/2**[2]
0000 **5** 1 ½ **Kipchak (IRE)**[14] 7507 6-9-4 **59**..............................(b) KirstyMilczarek 3 56
(Conor Dore) *led and sn clr at gd pce: rdn along 4f out: hdd 3f out: grad wknd fnl 2f* **16/1**
3663 **6** 2 ½ **Ay Tay Tate (IRE)**[18] 7458 5-9-10 **65**........................(p) FrannyNorton 11 57
(David C Griffiths) *chsd clr ldr: hdwy 4f out: cl up 3f out: rdn over 2f out: sn drvn and wknd* **5/1**[3]
0000 **7** 2 ½ **Nha Trang (IRE)**[33] 7247 4-8-3 **51** oh6............................. JackDuern(7) 8 39
(Michael Appleby) *a in rr* **66/1**
0000 **8** 17 **Addikt (IRE)**[26] 7346 6-9-5 **65**.. DavidKenny(5) 2 22
(Michael Scudamore) *s.i.s: a bhd* **33/1**
0020 **9** 8 **Sofias Number One (USA)**[11] 7537 3-9-5 **64**............(tp) AndreaAtzeni 6 —
(Roy Bowring) *trckd ldrs on inner: pushed along 5f out: rdn 4f out and sn wknd* **5/1**[3]
2m 24.49s (-3.51) **Going Correction** -0.25s/f (Stan)
WFA 3 from 4yo+ 4lb **9** Ran SP% **111.7**
Speed ratings (Par 101): **102,101,100,98,97 95,93,81,75**
toteswingers:1&2:£8.00, 2&3:£6.00, 1&3:£5.20 CSF £45.23 CT £159.48 TOTE £10.00: £2.50, £3.40, £1.50; EX 54.50 Trifecta £258.90 Part won. Pool: £349.93 - 0.72 winning units..
Owner Mrs Wendy Jenkins **Bred** D H W Dobson **Trained** Royston, Herts

FOCUS
A moderate handicap, but run at a solid pace thanks to Kipchak. The form looks solid too.
Addikt(IRE) Official explanation: jockey said horse hung left throughout

7648 BOOK YOUR TICKETS ON LINE AT SOUTHWELL-RACECOURSE.CO.UK H'CAP 7f (F)
3:30 (3:34) (Class 6) (0-60,60) 3-Y-0+ **£1,704** (£503; £251) **Stalls** Low

Form RPR
4342 **1** **St Oswald**[21] 7419 3-9-7 **60**..................................(b) SilvestreDeSousa 10 71
(David O'Meara) *chsd ldrs on outer: hdwy over 2f out: rdn to chal wl over 1f out: styd on to ld ins fnl f: rdn out* **7/4**[1]
4000 **2** 1 **Cyflymder (IRE)**[18] 7455 5-9-7 **60**..................................... SteveDrowne 2 68
(David C Griffiths) *cl up: led after 2f: qcknd 2f out: rdn over 1f out: hdd ins fnl f: no ex last 100yds* **8/1**[2]
0534 **3** 1 ½ **Transmit (IRE)**[21] 7419 4-9-7 **60**..............................(b) DuranFentiman 1 64
(Tim Easterby) *in tch on inner: rdn along and hdwy to chse ldrs wl over 1f out: styd on u.p fnl f* **11/1**
0060 **4** 1 ½ **Jonnie Skull (IRE)**[14] 7507 5-9-3 **56**...............................(vt) LukeMorris 3 56
(Phil McEntee) *led 2f: prom: rdn over 2f out: kpt on same pce appr fnl f* **20/1**
4200 **5** 1 **Andiamo Via**[43] 7063 4-9-5 **58**... SebSanders 5 55
(Michael Smith) *midfield: hdwy 2f out: sn rdn: kpt on same pce appr fnl f* **8/1**[2]
3325 **6** ½ **Elusive Warrior (USA)**[33] 7243 8-9-5 **58**................(p) MartinHarley 12 54
(Alan McCabe) *prom: cl up 1/2-way: rdn wl over 2f out: grad wknd* **16/1**
2012 **7** 3 ¼ **Lujano**[14] 7507 6-9-3 **59**.. DaleSwift(3) 13 46
(Ollie Pears) *in tch: pushed along 3f out: swtchd rt and rdn 2f out: sn no imp* **9/1**[3]
1060 **8** *nk* **This Ones For Eddy**[32] 7268 6-9-7 **60**.................... GrahamGibbons 14 46
(John Balding) *a towards rr* **10/1**
6665 **9** 2 ½ **Sopran Nad (ITY)**[10] 7560 7-9-1 **54**...............................(bt) AndreaAtzeni 9 34
(Frank Sheridan) *prom: cl up 3f out: rdn over 2f out: sn wknd* **10/1**
0 **10** 1 ½ **Raise The Rafters (IRE)**[18] 7455 6-9-4 **57**..................... RobertHavlin 4 32
(Pat Murphy) *nvr bttr than midfield* **66/1**

0-30 **11** *4 1/2* **Avoncharm**[53] 6834 3-8-11 **50**.......................................(b[1]) JimmyQuinn 6 13
(Mel Brittain) *chsd ldrs: rdn along 1/2-way: sn wknd* **66/1**

3026 **12** *28* **Misere**[204] 2163 3-9-7 **60**.. PhillipMakin 7 —
(Kevin Ryan) *chsd ldrs: rdn along over 3f out: sn wknd* **22/1**

2250 **13** *1/2* **Coastal Passage**[21] 7420 3-9-4 **57**.................................. TonyCulhane 8 —
(John Balding) *sn outpcd and wl bhd fr 1/2-way* **33/1**

1m 29.19s (-1.11) **Going Correction** -0.25s/f (Stan) **13** Ran SP% **116.0**
Speed ratings (Par 101): **96,94,93,91,90 89,86,85,82,81 75,43,43**
toteswingers:1&2:£5.10, 2&3:£18.60, 1&3:£5.80 CSF £13.94 CT £121.87 TOTE £2.40: £1.10, £5.00, £4.20; EX 21.30 Trifecta £107.20 Pool: £547.64 - 3.78 winning units..
Owner Richard Jeffrey **Bred** Paul Hearson Bloodstock **Trained** Nawton, N Yorks

FOCUS
Not much to get excited about here and another race dominated by those that raced handily. Slight improvement from the winner.
T/Jkpt: Part won. Pool of £56495.56 - 0.50 winning units. T/Plt: £52.70 to a £1 stake. Pool of £63,197.78 - 875.23 winning tickets. T/Qpdt: £14.30 to a £1 stake. Pool of £5,855.90 - 303.00 winning tickets. JR

7581 KEMPTON (A.W) (R-H)

Wednesday, December 7

OFFICIAL GOING: Standard
Wind: Strong, across (away from stands) Weather: Fine, cold

7649 FREE ENTRY FOR BETDAQ MEMBERS H'CAP 5f (P)
3:50 (3:54) (Class 6) (0-65,66) 3-Y-O+ **£1,617** (£481; £240; £120) **Stalls** Low

Form RPR

0200 **1** **Black Baccara**[28] 7341 4-8-13 **60**...................................(be) RyanClark(3) 1 71
(Phil McEntee) *hld up in midfield: prog gng wl fr 2f out: shkn up to ld jst ins fnl f: sn clr* **8/1**[3]

0511 **2** *2 1/4* **Perlachy**[9] 7567 7-9-8 **66** 6ex..................................(v) LukeMorris 5 69
(Ronald Harris) *scrubbed along early to rch midfield: prog over 1f out: styd on to take 2nd last 50yds: no ch w wnr* **8/1**[3]

0004 **3** *nk* **Bookiesindex Boy**[22] 7420 7-9-4 **62**...........................(b) TonyCulhane 10 64
(J R Jenkins) *hld up in last trio fr wd draw: effrt over 1f out: gd prog fnl f: styd on to take 3rd last strides* **16/1**

2322 **4** *1/2* **Cliffords Reprieve**[14] 7511 3-9-0 **58**................................. SebSanders 4 58
(Eric Wheeler) *reluctant to go to post: reluctant to enter stalls: chsd ldr wl over 3f out: led over 1f out: hdd and no rspnse jst ins fnl f: lost 2 pls nr fin* **9/2**[1]

0044 **5** *1/2* **Danzoe (IRE)**[7] 7588 4-9-7 **65**...................................... WilliamCarson 11 63+
(Christine Dunnett) *s.s: detached in last pair: effrt on inner 2f out: nt clr run 1f out: styd on wl after: nrst fin* **8/1**[3]

0450 **6** *1/2* **Welsh Inlet (IRE)**[21] 7428 3-9-4 **65**.............................. KieranO'Neill(3) 6 63+
(John Bridger) *chsd ldrs: rdn over 1f out: kpt on same pce after: no threat* **11/2**[2]

0056 **7** *1/2* **Sherjawy (IRE)**[7] 7587 7-9-6 **64**..................................... SamHitchcott 12 59
(Zoe Davison) *forced to r wd and pushed along to stay in tch in midfield: nvr on terms: kpt on ins fnl f* **25/1**

0030 **8** *1 1/4* **Crimson Queen**[25] 7395 4-9-5 **63**.. AdamKirby 7 53
(Roy Brotherton) *chsd ldrs: rdn 2f out: steadily wknd fnl f* **14/1**

0000 **9** *1 3/4* **Mi Regalo**[14] 7519 3-9-6 **64**.......................................(b[1]) TomMcLaughlin 8 48
(Phil McEntee) *sn scrubbed along and detached in last pair: nvr a factor* **20/1**

0006 **10** *shd* **Skylla**[12] 7535 4-9-2 **65**.. MarkCoumbe(5) 2 48
(Derek Shaw) *chsd ldrs: nt qckn wl over 1f out: wknd fnl f* **11/2**[2]

0400 **11** *nse* **Atlantic Cycle (IRE)**[9] 7567 4-9-6 **64**.......................... RichardKingscote 3 47
(Milton Bradley) *led to over 1f out: wknd qckly fnl f* **8/1**[3]

0160 **12** *2* **Too Many Questions (IRE)**[63] 6634 3-9-5 **63**.......(p) GrahamGibbons 9 39
(David Evans) *chsng ldr whn rn v wd bnd wl over 3f out: wknd over 1f out* **33/1**

59.71 secs (-0.79) **Going Correction** -0.025s/f (Stan) **12** Ran SP% **117.5**
Speed ratings (Par 101): **105,101,100,100,99 98,97,95,92,92 92,89**
toteswingers:1&2:£8.70, 2&3:£15.30, 1&3:£29.50 CSF £68.23 CT £1020.01 TOTE £14.90: £4.00, £2.80, £6.80; EX 63.10.
Owner Eventmaker Racehorses **Bred** Peter Balding **Trained** Newmarket, Suffolk

FOCUS
There was a strong wind on a cold night. They went a fair pace in this minor sprint handicap and there was a decisive winner who is rated in line with his best form.

7650 BETDAQ MULTIPLES MAIDEN AUCTION STKS 1m 2f (P)
4:20 (4:21) (Class 6) 2-Y-O **£1,617** (£481; £240; £120) **Stalls** Low

Form RPR

022 **1** **Quizzed**[49] 6956 2-8-8 75.. ShaneKelly 7 74
(Edward Vaughan) *led after 1f: mde rest: pushed along 2f out: rdn to assert fnl f* **1/1**[1]

6533 **2** *2 1/4* **Haafhd Handsome**[49] 6956 2-8-7 73................................ KieranO'Neill(3) 9 72
(Richard Hannon) *trckd wnr after 1f: rdn 3f out and hd high: nt qckn over 1f out: kpt on* **2/1**[2]

0 **3** *nk* **Totom Chief**[35] 7232 2-8-11 0.. RobertWinston 1 72
(Gay Kelleway) *hld up towards rr: chsd ldng quartet 3f out: prog on inner and hanging over 1f out: disp 2nd ins fnl f: kpt on* **50/1**

65 **4** *3/4* **San Mambo**[25] 7398 2-8-13 0.. AdamKirby 2 73
(Marco Botti) *trckd ldng pair after 1f: rdn over 2f out: disp 2nd over 1f out: no ex ins fnl f* **5/1**[3]

40 **5** *4 1/2* **Fleur De La Vie (IRE)**[27] 7343 2-8-4 0................................ MartinLane 8 55
(Ralph Beckett) *dwlt: prog fr rr to chse ldrs 1/2-way: cl up over 2f out: wknd over 1f out* **14/1**

0005 **6** *8* **Pack Of Cards (IRE)**[18] 7481 2-8-10 54........................... MarcHalford 4 46
(Terry Clement) *led 1f: restrained: dropped to rr 1/2-way: wknd over 2f out* **66/1**

0 **7** *7* **Feb Thirtyfirst**[19] 7454 2-8-9 0.. SamHitchcott 3 32
(Sheena West) *settled in last: urged along 4f out: sn lft bhd: t.o* **33/1**

04 **8** *50* **Silent Energy (IRE)**[26] 7367 2-8-13 0................................. LukeMorris 6 —
(Ronald Harris) *chsd ldrs: rdn bef 1/2-way: wknd rapidly over 3f out: wl t.o* **16/1**

P **King's Wharf (IRE)** 2-8-10 0... GrahamGibbons 5 —
(David Evans) *awkward s: hanging bdly and p.u after 2f* **50/1**

2m 9.12s (1.12) **Going Correction** -0.025s/f (Stan) **9** Ran SP% **120.9**
Speed ratings (Par 94): **94,92,91,91,87 81,75,35,—**
toteswingers:1&2:£1.30, 1&3:£18.80, 2&3:£26.80 CSF £3.31 TOTE £2.10: £1.10, £1.40, £15.80; EX 3.90.
Owner Owen G Glenn **Bred** Hascombe And Valiant Studs **Trained** Newmarket, Suffolk

FOCUS
There didn't seem to be much strength in depth in this maiden. The favourite won with quite a bit in hand and the next three were clear of the rest.

NOTEBOOK
Quizzed was not far behind subsequent Group 1 Fillies' Mile winner Lyric Of Light on debut at Newmarket in August and had finished runner-up in pair of AW/turf maidens at around 1m since. She had leading form claims and travelled comfortably in the lead before knuckling down well to get off the mark stepped up in trip. A current handicap mark of 75 looks fair and this half-sister to 1m2f Listed winner Primevere has scope for further progress at this trip. (op 10-11 tchd 5-6)
Haafhd Handsome gave it a fair try stepped up in trip but couldn't reverse latest Newmarket form with Quizzed. His head carriage was a bit high and he looked a bit awkward, but he seems willing enough and is closely related to useful 1m1f-1m6f winner Linas Selection, so could have more to offer at this trip and beyond. (op 11-4)
Totom Chief was always in rear when last of 17 at 100-1 in 1m Nottingham maiden on debut last month, but he showed plenty of promise up in trip on his second run. A half-brother to seven winners, notably decent dual-purpose performer Buster Hyvonen, he should continue to progress with time and distance.
San Mambo showed mixed form in his first two runs but he shaped quite well before his effort flattened out in the final furlong here. A Singspiel colt, he is related to four winners at up to 1m1f and handicaps look the way forward after this. (op 9-2)
Fleur De La Vie(IRE) failed to build on her debut fourth last time and she looked awkward around the final turn and was left behind by the front four here. (tchd 12-1)
King's Wharf(IRE) Official explanation: jockey said gelding hung badly left

7651 BACK OR LAY AT BETDAQ.COM H'CAP 1m 2f (P)
4:50 (4:51) (Class 4) (0-85,85) 3-Y-O+ **£4,075** (£1,212; £606; £303) **Stalls** Low

Form RPR

0121 **1** **True To Form (IRE)**[11] 7557 4-9-6 **84**...............................(p) LukeMorris 4 94+
(Ronald Harris) *trckd ldng quartet: wnt 3rd over 2f out gng strly: rdn to ld briefly jst over 1f out: drvn to ld again narrowly last 75yds: r.o wl* **11/2**[2]

0052 **2** *hd* **Emerald Wilderness (IRE)**[28] 7328 7-9-5 **83**.............(p) JimCrowley 14 93
(Robert Cowell) *hld up in last trio fr wdst draw: prog arnd wd outside bnd over 2f out: sustained hdwy despite awkward hd carriage to ld 1f out: edgd rt and hdd last 75yds: r.o but hld nr fin* **8/1**

4003 **3** *2 1/2* **Ellemujie**[28] 7328 6-9-6 **84**..(p) AdamKirby 2 90+
(Dean Ivory) *hld up in midfield on inner: prog 2f out: chsd ldrs but nowhere to go over 1f out: styd on wl fnl f but nt on terms w ldng pair* **3/1**[1]

1000 **4** *hd* **Zebrano**[47] 6989 5-9-7 **85**..(b) StevieDonohoe 12 90
(Emma Lavelle) *s.i.s: hld up in last trio fr wd draw: trying to make prog on inner whn nowhere to go 2f out: gd hdwy over 1f out: styd on fnl f: nt on terms w ldng pair* **20/1**

0130 **5** *2* **Veroon (IRE)**[11] 7558 5-9-5 **83**.......................................(p) TomQueally 7 84
(James Given) *hld up towards rr: gng bttr than many over 2f out: prog on inner and rdn over 1f out: kpt on same pce* **12/1**

510 **6** *1* **Uphold**[34] 7241 4-9-6 **84**..(vt) RobertWinston 8 83
(Gay Kelleway) *trckd ldng pair: cl enough and rdn over 1f out: fnd nil: hmpd and wknd jst ins fnl f* **25/1**

-060 **7** *3 1/2* **Lyric Poet (USA)**[57] 6773 4-8-9 **73**................................ WilliamCarson 5 65
(Anthony Carson) *dwlt: hld up in last: rdn fr 1/2-way: struggling and n.d after: passed wkng rivals fr over 1f out* **20/1**

0261 **8** *hd* **Songburst**[35] 7227 3-8-8 **78**... KieranO'Neill(3) 9 69
(Richard Hannon) *racd on outer in midfield: drvn 3f out: struggling wl over 1f out: wknd* **11/2**[2]

0600 **9** *1/2* **Big Bay (USA)**[49] 6948 5-8-11 **75**...................................... ChrisCatlin 13 65
(Jane Chapple-Hyam) *wl in rr fr wd draw: drvn on outer and no real prog over 2f out: no ch over 1f out* **50/1**

0551 **10** *nk* **Epernay**[19] 7465 4-8-8 **72**..(bt) MartinLane 11 62
(Ian Williams) *nvr bttr than midfield: rdn 3f out: sn lost pl and btn* **15/2**[3]

2310 **11** *4* **Hidden Glory**[14] 7523 4-9-3 **81**.......................................(b) SebSanders 3 63
(James Given) *pressed ldr: rdn to ld 2f out: hdd jst over 1f out: wknd v rapidly* **25/1**

4200 **12** *1 1/2* **Classically (IRE)**[14] 7513 5-8-9 **73**.....................................(e) LiamKeniry 6 52
(Peter Hedger) *led: rdn and hdd 2f out: wknd qckly over 1f out* **14/1**

5062 **13** *6* **Scamperdale**[21] 7430 9-9-4 **82**.. JimmyFortune 1 49
(Brian Baugh) *trckd ldrs on inner: appeared nt to have much room 3f out and eased bk: n.d over 1f out: wknd rapidly fnl f* **20/1**

21/0 **14** *6* **Bengal Tiger**[11] 7557 5-8-8 **72**...................................... DavidProbert 10 27
(Tony Carroll) *nvr bttr than midfield: drvn over 3f out: wknd over 2f out: t.o* **33/1**

2m 5.81s (-2.19) **Going Correction** -0.025s/f (Stan)
WFA 3 from 4yo+ 3lb **14** Ran SP% **119.9**
Speed ratings (Par 105): **107,106,104,104,103 102,99,99,98,98 95,94,89,84**
toteswingers:1&2:£10.60, 1&3:£4.70, 2&3:£5.50 CSF £43.76 CT £158.80 TOTE £8.70: £2.30, £4.00, £1.10; EX 40.60.
Owner David & Gwyn Joseph **Bred** Sir E J Loder **Trained** Earlswood, Monmouths

FOCUS
The first two pulled clear in this decent handicap and the placed favourite didn't get much luck. The form is rated around the second and third.

7652 BETDAQ MOBILE APPS MAIDEN STKS 6f (P)
5:20 (5:22) (Class 5) 3-Y-O+ **£2,264** (£673; £336; £168) **Stalls** Low

Form RPR

3 **1** **Sketchy Evidence (USA)**[25] 7389 3-9-3 0.............................. LukeMorris 6 71
(John Best) *sat off str pce set by ldng trio: clsd to ld 2f out: rn green in front and jnd over 1f out: drvn and narrow ld fnl f: edgd lft but clung on* **1/1**[1]

6002 **2** *hd* **Amber Heights**[18] 7488 3-8-12 60.................................... FergusSweeney 7 65
(David Pinder) *saty off str pce set by ldng trio: clsd fr 3f out: rdn to chal and w wnr over 1f out: nt qckn sn after: kpt on nr fin: jst hld* **9/4**[2]

006 **3** *5* **Serial Sinner (IRE)**[11] 7561 3-8-12 50..........................(t) StevieDonohoe 4 49
(Paul Cole) *awkward s: wl off the pce in last pair: kpt on fr over 2f out: rdn to take modest 3rd ins fnl f: n.d* **14/1**

2303 **4** *nk* **Lovat Lane**[13] 7525 3-8-12 49..(b) ChrisCatlin 3 48
(Eve Johnson Houghton) *duelled for ld at str pce: led over 2f out to 2f out: sn wknd* **16/1**

5 *7* **Queen Of Heaven (USA)** 3-8-12 0.................................... JimCrowley 5 26
(Peter Makin) *s.s: rn green and outpcd in last pair: nvr on terms* **5/1**[3]

000 **6** *5* **Abadejo**[25] 7389 3-9-3 59... EddieAhern 8 15
(J R Jenkins) *racd on outer of ldng trio at str pce: wknd qckly wl over 2f out: t.o* **14/1**

6056 **7** *3 1/4* **Miakora**[14] 7511 3-8-12 46.. ShaneKelly 1 —
(Michael Quinn) *racd on inner of ldng trio at str pce: hdd & wknd qckly over 2f out: t.o* **40/1**

1m 13.96s (0.86) **Going Correction** -0.025s/f (Stan) **7** Ran SP% **119.1**
Speed ratings (Par 103): **93,92,86,85,76 69,65**
toteswingers:1&2:£1.20, 1&3:£3.80, 2&3:£4.30 CSF £3.71 TOTE £2.20: £1.70, £1.60; EX 3.60.
Owner Splinter Group **Bred** Stoneway Farm **Trained** Hucking, Kent

FOCUS
The two market leaders both came from off the strong pace and finished a long way clear in this weak maiden. The winner improved and the next two ran to form.

7653 RACING@SKYSPORTS.COM NURSERY 1m (P)
5:50 (5:51) (Class 5) (0-75,75) 2-Y-O £2,264 (£673; £336; £168) Stalls Low

Form RPR

5 **1** **Cockney Rocker**[84] 6064 2-9-0 **68**.................... AdamKirby 5 75+
(Jane Chapple-Hyam) *hld up last: stylish prog fr 2f out: clsd and two sharp reminders to ld ins fnl f: sn clr* **9/2**[3]

0440 **2** *1 3/4* **Good Luck Charm**[21] 7436 2-8-13 **67**.................... TomQueally 7 69
(Gary Moore) *trckd ldr: drvn ahd over 1f out: hdd and outpcd ins fnl f* **20/1**

2052 **3** *1* **Not Bad For A Boy (IRE)**[26] 7358 2-9-2 **70**.................... JimmyFortune 3 70
(Richard Hannon) *trckd ldng pair: rdn 2f out: wnt 2nd briefly 1f out: sn outpcd* **5/1**

4631 **4** *shd* **Next Cry (USA)**[35] 7223 2-8-13 **70**.................... KieranO'Neill(3) 1 69
(Richard Hannon) *led: kicked on over 3f out: hdd over 1f out: outpcd after* **7/4**[1]

0411 **5** *1 3/4* **Night Flash (GER)**[20] 7444 2-9-7 **75**.................... JimCrowley 8 70
(James Given) *trckd ldng pair: rdn 3f out: nt qckn and struggling over 2f out: wl btn over 1f out* **3/1**[2]

006 **6** *nk* **Excellent News (IRE)**[27] 7344 2-8-12 **66**.................... SebSanders 4 61
(J W Hills) *trckd ldrs: rdn and nt qckn wl over 2f out: btn after* **12/1**

000 **7** *8* **Weood (IRE)**[61] 6673 2-8-4 **58**....................(b[1]) ChrisCatlin 2 34
(Clive Brittain) *t.k.h: hld up in last pair: rdn over 2f out: sn wknd* **16/1**

1m 40.29s (0.49) **Going Correction** -0.025s/f (Stan) 7 Ran SP% **114.5**
Speed ratings (Par 96): **96,94,93,93,91 91,83**
toteswingers:1&2:£10.50, 2&3:£6.80, 1&3:£3.00 CSF £80.93 CT £465.42 TOTE £7.70: £3.20, £9.20; EX 133.40.
Owner Chris Fahy & Lee Jordan **Bred** Mette Campbell-Andenaes **Trained** Dalham, Suffolk

FOCUS
The winner was a big market springer in the morning and did the job in good style from off a steady pace in this nursery.

NOTEBOOK
Cockney Rocker had not really gone on from his encouraging debut third at York in May, but a step up in trip and switch to AW helped spark a more dynamic effort as he came from last to first to land a gamble with quite a bit in hand on nursery debut. This big upturn in form can be marked up because the next three home all raced near the pace. He has a useful and speedy pedigree, so should have more to offer and could prove as potent in a strongly run 7f handicap. (op 5-1)
Good Luck Charm dropped right out on nursery debut over the same trip last time but this half-brother to dual 1m winner The Shuffler bounced back with a good effort.
Not Bad For A Boy(IRE) posted a second solid nursery effort and seemed to stay the trip fairly well. He has a fair cruising speed and should continue to run well but the problem is that he is not look particularly well handicapped on the balance of his form. (tchd 11-2)
Next Cry(USA) improved for the step up to 1m and switch back to Polytrack when staying on well to get off the mark in a C&D nursery last month. Well backed, he got a comfortable lead in a steadily run race, but couldn't repel the finishers off 5lb higher. (op 2-1)
Night Flash(GER) left his modest turf maiden form well behind when winning a pair of 7f/1m handicaps in good style here last month. Racing off 10lb higher from a tricky draw, he was weak in the market and went a bit in snatches in a disappointing bid to make it 3-3 on Polytrack. (op 9-4)

7654 IS GO BURN GREY OUTPACED H'CAP 1m 4f (P)
6:20 (6:21) (Class 6) (0-55,58) 3-Y-0+ £1,617 (£481; £240; £120) Stalls Centre

Form RPR

2600 **1** **Jamarjo (IRE)**[93] 5788 4-8-12 **48**.................... RobertWinston 11 58
(Steve Gollings) *hld up in last pair: prog fr 3f out but lot to do: cajoled along w little recrse to whip and styd on wl fr 2f out: led last 50yds* **33/1**

41-1 **2** *nk* **Sovento (GER)**[2] 7639 7-9-8 **58** 6ex.................... MartinHarley 3 68
(Shaun Harley, Ire) *hld up in 8th: prog 3f out: hrd rdn 2f out: styd on to take 2nd jst over 1f out: clsd on tiring ldr: got upsides 50yds out as wnr wnt past* **5/4**[1]

-U00 **3** *1* **Whodunit (UAE)**[14] 7522 7-9-4 **54**....................(b) ChrisCatlin 2 62
(Peter Hiatt) *racd freely: mde most: drew away fr 5f out: abt 8 l clr over 2f out: hrd rdn and tiring over 1f out: collared last 50yds* **8/1**[3]

0551 **4** *2 3/4* **Valdan (IRE)**[13] 7527 7-9-0 **55**.................... MatthewCosham(5) 6 59
(David Evans) *hld up in 5th: prog over 3f out: chsd clr ldr over 2f out: no real imp: lost 2nd jst over 1f out: one pce* **5/1**[2]

03-5 **5** *1 1/4* **Time To Play**[19] 7466 6-9-0 **50**.................... LiamKeniry 13 52
(Gary Brown) *hld up last: rdn 3f out: styd on u.p fr over 2f out: nvr rchd ldrs* **33/1**

4003 **6** *1/2* **It's Dubai Dolly**[42] 7091 5-9-0 **50**....................(b) DaneO'Neill 9 51
(Alastair Lidderdale) *hld up in 4th: prog to chse clr ldr 3f out to over 2f out: fdd over 1f out* **10/1**

0544 **7** *9* **Croix Rouge (USA)**[13] 7528 9-9-3 **53**.................... JamieGoldstein 7 40
(Ralph Smith) *hld up in 7th: rdn and no prog wl over 2f out: sn wknd* **16/1**

1003 **8** *1 3/4* **El Libertador (USA)**[13] 7527 5-9-5 **55**.................... SebSanders 10 39
(Eric Wheeler) *hld up in 6th: effrt over 3f out: rdn and no prog over 2f out: sn wknd* **14/1**

-500 **9** *1 1/2* **Lucas Pitt**[13] 7527 4-8-11 **52**....................(p) DavidKenny(5) 14 34
(Michael Scudamore) *chsd ldr: lft bhd fr 5f out: lost 2nd 3f out: sn wknd* **33/1**

0/66 **10** *1 3/4* **Now**[13] 7528 5-9-0 **50**.................... JamesMillman 5 29
(Rod Millman) *hld up in 9th: rdn and no prog 3f out: wl btn after* **20/1**

060 **11** *8* **Robby Bobby**[28] 7331 6-9-5 **55**.................... FergusSweeney 8 21
(Laura Mongan) *hld up in 10th: effrt over 3f out: no prog over 2f out: sn wknd: t.o* **20/1**

4404 **12** *16* **Laura Land**[212] 1959 5-8-13 **49**.................... GrahamGibbons 4 —
(Mark Brisbourne) *chsd ldng pair: wknd rapidly wl over 3f out: t.o* **20/1**

2m 33.79s (-0.71) **Going Correction** -0.025s/f (Stan) 12 Ran SP% **117.0**
Speed ratings (Par 101): **101,100,100,98,97 97,91,89,88,87 82,71**
toteswingers:1&2:£11.40, 2&3:£2.70, 1&3:£31.80 CSF £69.06 CT £386.37 TOTE £55.00: £8.70, £1.10, £2.80; EX 134.50.
Owner Northern Bloodstock Racing **Bred** Frank Dunne **Trained** Scamblesby, Lincs

FOCUS
A low-grade handicap. The pace was strong and a surpise winner beat the hot favourite in a tight three-way-finish. The first two are rated to the best view of their past form.

7655 BOOK WINTER FESTIVAL TICKETS NOW H'CAP (DIV I) 7f (P)
6:50 (6:52) (Class 6) (0-55,55) 3-Y-0+ £1,617 (£481; £240; £120) Stalls Low

Form RPR

3051 **1** **Storm Runner (IRE)**[7] 7581 3-8-5 **49**.................... RyanPowell(5) 3 58
(George Margarson) *settled in midfield: pushed along in 8th 3f out: looked in trble over 2f out: prog over 1f out to take 2nd fnl f: styd on wl to ld nr fin* **10/3**[1]

0332 **2** *3/4* **Ereka (IRE)**[11] 7561 3-8-10 **49**.................... LukeMorris 10 56
(John Best) *pressed ldr: rdn to ld 2f out and wnt for home: 2 l up ins fnl f: tired and hdd nr fin* **12/1**

5060 **3** *1* **Jackie Love (IRE)**[25] 7388 3-8-0 **46**....................(b) JenniferFerguson(7) 14 53+
(Olivia Maylam) *s.s fr wdst draw: hld up in last pair: tried to make prog on inner 2f out: nowhere to go over 1f out and repeatedly swtchd lft: stl only 8th 100yds out: flashed home to snatch 3rd nr fin* **66/1**

5233 **4** *nk* **Fluctuation (IRE)**[19] 7463 3-8-10 **52**....................(v) RyanClark(3) 13 55
(Ian Williams) *stdd s: hld up in last pair: stl there 2f out: rdn and effrt wl over 1f out: styd on wl fnl f but nvr qckly enough to chal* **4/1**[2]

033 **5** *nse* **Cut The Cackle (IRE)**[18] 7485 5-8-12 **54**....................(bt) RobertLButler(3) 12 57
(Richard Guest) *trckd ldng pair: rdn and nt qckn 2f out: no imp over 1f out: kpt on ins fnl f* **9/2**[3]

5006 **6** *hd* **Granny Anne (IRE)**[15] 7507 3-9-2 **55**....................(b) JimCrowley 9 58
(Paul D'Arcy) *hld up in last quartet: shkn up and effrt over 2f out: styd on fr wl over 1f out but nt as qckly as others* **12/1**

0023 **7** *3/4* **Lennoxwood (IRE)**[11] 7561 3-8-9 **48**....................(be) DavidProbert 7 49
(Mark Usher) *prom: rdn to chse ldr wl over 1f out tl last 130yds: wknd* **16/1**

1404 **8** *1* **Love Nest**[21] 7437 3-9-2 **55**.................... EddieAhern 6 53
(John Dunlop) *racd wd in midfield: drvn over 2f out: nt qckn wl over 1f out: one pce after* **11/2**

5030 **9** *1* **Clerical (USA)**[21] 7429 5-8-7 **46**....................(p) JohnFahy 11 41
(Robert Cowell) *racd in last quartet: rdn on outer wl over 2f out: nt qckn and no real prog: one pce* **33/1**

0000 **10** *2 1/2* **Rileys Crane**[20] 7442 4-8-10 **47** ow2.................... GrahamGibbons 8 38
(Christine Dunnett) *led to 2f out: wknd over 1f out* **33/1**

2220 **11** *1 1/2* **Do More Business (IRE)**[113] 5138 4-8-8 **52**.................... JemmaMarshall(5) 5 37
(Pat Phelan) *trckd ldrs on inner: rdn over 2f out: wknd over 1f out* **25/1**

002 **12** *shd* **Bint Elnadim (IRE)**[34] 7249 3-9-2 **55**.................... JimmyQuinn 2 39
(Derek Shaw) *hld up in midfield on inner: gng wl enough over 2f out: rdn and nt qckn sn after: wknd over 1f out* **10/1**

6040 **13** *3 3/4* **Figaro Flyer (IRE)**[205] 2162 8-8-12 **51**.................... MichaelStainton 4 25
(Paul Howling) *hld up in midfield: rdn over 2f out: sn wknd* **50/1**

1m 26.33s (0.33) **Going Correction** -0.025s/f (Stan) 13 Ran SP% **120.2**
Speed ratings (Par 101): **97,96,95,94,94 94,93,92,91,88 86,86,82**
toteswingers:1&2:£11.40, 2&3:£40.50, 1&3:£43.40 CSF £43.27 CT £2310.04 TOTE £5.00: £1.30, £3.10, £15.60; EX 32.10.
Owner Pitfield Partnership **Bred** Kevin Foley **Trained** Newmarket, Suffolk
■ Stewards' Enquiry : Eddie Ahern two day ban; excessive use of whip (21st-22nd Dec)

FOCUS
An ordinary handicap, but the well-treated favourite reeled in an in-form rival and the form looks solid. The winner rates a length off last week's form.
Fluctuation(IRE) Official explanation: jockey said gelding hung right handed

7656 BOOK WINTER FESTIVAL TICKETS NOW H'CAP (DIV II) 7f (P)
7:20 (7:20) (Class 6) (0-55,55) 3-Y-0+ £1,617 (£481; £240; £120) Stalls Low

Form RPR

4003 **1** **Cut And Thrust (IRE)**[35] 7229 5-9-2 **55**.................... AdamKirby 8 66
(Mark Wellings) *hld up in last trio: prog towards inner fr jst over 2f out: sustained effrt to go 2nd ins fnl f: clsd to ld last strides* **9/2**[1]

000 **2** *1/2* **Peace Seeker**[60] 6700 3-8-13 **52**.................... WilliamCarson 13 62+
(Anthony Carson) *wnt lft s: trckd ldrs: prog to ld over 2f out: drvn over 1f out: looked like holding on tl hdd last strides* **15/2**

6042 **3** *1 3/4* **Having A Ball**[35] 7228 7-9-2 **55**.................... ChrisCatlin 5 60
(Jonathan Portman) *trckd ldrs: u.p and nt qckn over 2f out: rallied over 1f out to chse ldr: one pce and lost 2nd ins fnl f* **15/2**

243 **4** *1 1/2* **Royal Envoy (IRE)**[259] 950 8-8-8 **47**.................... MichaelStainton 2 48
(Paul Howling) *trckd ldrs: rdn over 2f out: disp 2nd over 1f out: fdd ins fnl f* **12/1**

4303 **5** *hd* **Norcroft**[7] 7581 9-8-3 **49**....................(p) DanielHarris(7) 11 49
(Christine Dunnett) *in tch in midfield: rdn and nt qckn over 2f out: renewed effrt over 1f out: one pce fnl f* **20/1**

0030 **6** *hd* **Ghost Dancer**[14] 7524 7-8-8 **47**....................(p) RichardKingscote 10 47
(Milton Bradley) *stdd s: hld up in last trio: prog alongside wnr fr jst over 2f out tl nt sustain effrt jst over 1f out* **12/1**

5006 **7** *2 3/4* **Harvest Mist (IRE)**[21] 7437 3-8-11 **50**.................... DaneO'Neill 14 42
(Michael Blanshard) *bmpd s: racd on outer in midfield: shkn up and no prog over 2f out: n.d after* **8/1**

0564 **8** *1 3/4* **Avalon Bay**[15] 7507 3-8-13 **55**....................(p) RyanClark(3) 12 43
(Pat Eddery) *mde most to over 2f out: sn btn: wknd over 1f out* **7/1**[3]

6662 **9** *3/4* **Young Simon**[19] 7459 4-8-8 **52**....................(v) RyanPowell(5) 1 38
(George Margarson) *trckd ldng pair: cl enough over 2f out: sn nt qckn: wknd over 1f out* **5/1**[2]

0003 **10** *1 1/2* **Beating Harmony**[11] 7560 3-8-10 **49**.................... NeilChalmers 4 31
(Michael Appleby) *a towards rr: rdn and no prog over 2f out* **16/1**

4665 **11** *1 1/4* **White Shift (IRE)**[237] 1336 5-8-10 **52**.................... KierenFox(3) 6 30
(Paul Howling) *hld up in last trio: shuffled along on outer over 2f out: nvr remotely involved* **16/1**

0640 **12** *2 3/4* **Scruffy Skip (IRE)**[14] 7524 6-8-4 **46** oh1....................(tp) AdamBeschizza(3) 3 17
(Christine Dunnett) *sn pushed along in midfield: struggling over 2f out: wknd over 1f out* **25/1**

0060 **13** *30* **Emerald Royal**[8] 7575 3-8-7 **46**....................(t) MarcHalford 9 —
(Edward Creighton) *racd freely: w ldr to 1/2-way: wknd rapidly: eased and t.o* **50/1**

1m 25.87s (-0.13) **Going Correction** -0.025s/f (Stan) 13 Ran SP% **119.7**
Speed ratings (Par 101): **99,98,96,94,94 94,91,89,88,86 85,81,47**
toteswingers:1&2:£6.30, 2&3:£9.90, 1&3:£5.60 CSF £37.11 CT £260.35 TOTE £3.50: £1.10, £3.00, £3.60; EX 39.00.
Owner Nicholls Family **Bred** Bloomsbury Stud **Trained** Six Ashes, Shropshire
■ Stewards' Enquiry : Chris Catlin six day ban; excessive use of whip (21st, 22nd, 26th ,27th, 29th, 30th Dec)

FOCUS
There was an exciting finish in this strongly-run second division of a minor handicap. It was faster than division I and this looks fair form for the grade, the winner not far off last season's form.
White Shift(IRE) Official explanation: jockey said saddle slipped

T/Jkpt: Not won. T/Plt: £196.10 to a £1 stake. Pool of £72,692.45 - 270.47 winning tickets. T/Qpdt: £54.30 to a £1 stake. Pool of £8,680.74 - 118.26 winning tickets. JN

7634 LINGFIELD (L-H)
Wednesday, December 7

OFFICIAL GOING: Standard
Wind: fresh, across Weather: bright and breezy

7657 TOTEPLACEPOT CLAIMING STKS — 7f (P)
12:40 (12:40) (Class 6) 2-Y-O — **£1,704** (£503; £251) **Stalls** Low

Form — RPR
0061 **1** **The Name Is Don (IRE)**[19] 7464 2-9-7 76........................ LiamKeniry 4 67+
(Mark Gillard) *mde all: hung rt bnd 2f out: drvn and a holding runner-up ins fnl f* **7/2**[2]
512 **2** *nk* **Cristal Gem**[7] 7582 2-8-13 77........................ KieranO'Neill(3) 2 61+
(Andrew Reid) *chsd ldng pair: rdn to chse wnr 2f out: ev ch and drvn 1f out: kpt on but a hld* **2/5**[1]
0 **3** *1 1/2* **Sea Anemone**[41] 7118 2-8-9 0........................ DavidProbert 6 50
(Andrew Balding) *dwlt: in tch in last pair: hdwy to chse ldrs and rdn over 1f out: kpt on same pce fnl f* **14/1**[3]
0055 **4** *hd* **Princess Kaiulani (IRE)**[12] 7539 2-8-8 50........................ WilliamCarson 5 49
(William Muir) *chsd wnr tl 2f out: styd on same pce u.p fnl f* **25/1**
0065 **5** *3 1/4* **Joe M**[12] 7541 2-8-11 44........................(e) ChrisCatlin 1 43
(Simon Dow) *hld up in last pair: effrt and rn wd bnd 2f out: no imp* **66/1**
140 **6** *2* **Spiders Of Spring (IRE)**[18] 7491 2-8-11 60........................ TonyHamilton 3 38
(Richard Fahey) *in tch: rdn and lost pl wl over 2f out: bhd and wl btn over 1f out* **40/1**

1m 26.09s (1.29) **Going Correction** -0.025s/f (Stan) **6** Ran SP% **108.1**
Speed ratings (Par 94): **91,90,88,88,85 82**
toteswingers:1&2:£1.10, 1&3:£1.30, 2&3:£1.80 CSF £4.90 TOTE £3.90: £1.90, £1.02; EX 5.70.
Owner Don Hazzard **Bred** C M Farrell **Trained** Holwell, Dorset

FOCUS
A weak claimer in which odd-on favourite Cristal Gem again didn't run to her official mark of 77 - she would have been 6lb worse off with the winner in a handicap. The winner did not need to match her maiden victory.

NOTEBOOK
The Name Is Don(IRE) made all in a Wolverhampton maiden last time and positive tactics did the trick again, the gelding able to set fractions to suit and showing a good attitude when strongly challenged all the way up the straight. The bare form probably shouldn't be taken literally, though, and it's doubtful he had to run above his official rating of 76. (op 10-3 tchd 3-1)
Cristal Gem won a maiden over C&D two starts ago, but she was below form in a similar race to this at Kempton last time (claimed out of Richard Hannon's yard for £12,000 afterwards) and is not progressing. (op 4-9, tchd 1-2 in a place)
Sea Anemone showed nothing on her debut over 1m at Kempton, but this was better. She plugged on dourly, looking as though she's inherited stamina from her sire Phoenix Reach, and might appreciate going back up in distance. (op 12-1)
Princess Kaiulani(IRE) had plenty to find at the weights, but even so this sprint-bred filly ran like a non-stayer. Admittedly, she's yet to look sharp enough at shorter distances, but perhaps headgear will help. (op 22-1 tchd 33-1)
Joe M Official explanation: jockey said gelding hung right

7658 TOTEEXACTA (S) STKS — 7f (P)
1:10 (1:10) (Class 6) 3-Y-O+ — **£1,704** (£503; £251) **Stalls** Low

Form — RPR
5240 **1** **Ezra Church (IRE)**[15] 7502 4-9-4 72........................ JamieSpencer 4 66
(David Barron) *led for 1f: chsd ldrs after tl rdn to ld over 1f out: idling and drvn ins fnl f: a gng to hold on* **7/4**[1]
1036 **2** *hd* **Stevie Gee (IRE)**[2] 7636 7-9-1 71........................ RyanClark(3) 2 65
(Ian Williams) *hld up wl in tch: swtchd rt and effrt over 1f out: drvn to chse wnr jst ins fnl f: kpt on u.p but nvr quite getting to wnr* **9/2**[3]
205 **3** *1/2* **Finefrenzyrolling (IRE)**[25] 7388 3-8-7 63........................(p) LukeMorris 1 53
(Mrs K Burke) *hld up wl in tch: hdwy on inner and swtchd rt jst over 1f out: chsd ldrs 1f out: kpt on u.p* **9/2**[3]
5216 **4** *3/4* **Pipers Piping (IRE)**[8] 7579 5-8-13 66........................(p) JemmaMarshall(5) 7 62
(Alastair Lidderdale) *in tch: rdn and effrt over 1f out: kpt edging lft u.p: kpt on fnl 100yds but nvr gng pce to chal wnr* **3/1**[2]
2000 **5** *3* **Majestical (IRE)**[2] 7636 9-8-12 37........................(p) MartinLane 6 48
(Peter Hedger) *s.i.s: in tch in rr: rdn and c v wd bnd 2f out: styd on past btn horses fnl f: nvr threatened ldrs* **100/1**
6042 **6** *3/4* **Dvinsky (USA)**[7] 7588 10-9-4 62........................(b) TomMcLaughlin 8 52
(Paul Howling) *awkward s and nt best away: sn rdn along and hdwy to ld after 1f: rdn and hdd over 1f out: wknd fnl f* **14/1**
4500 **7** *2 1/4* **Stoppers (IRE)**[257] 968 4-8-5 58........................ DanielCremin(7) 5 40
(Robert Mills) *chsd ldrs: wnt 2nd over 5f out tl 2f out: sn wknd* **40/1**
2250 **8** *4 1/2* **Timpanist (USA)**[8] 7579 4-8-7 61........................(b) ChrisCatlin 3 23
(Simon Dow) *sn bustled along to chse ldrs: rdn and struggling whn rn wd bnd 2f out: sn wknd* **16/1**

1m 23.9s (-0.90) **Going Correction** -0.025s/f (Stan) **8** Ran SP% **113.7**
Speed ratings (Par 101): **104,103,103,102,98 98,95,90**
toteswingers:1&2:£2.70, 1&3:£2.20, 2&3:£3.80 CSF £9.92 TOTE £2.10: £1.30, £1.70, £1.20; EX 9.90 Trifecta £82.00 Pool: £394.91 - 3.56 winning units..There was no bid for the winner.
Owner Clive Washbourn **Bred** Mrs E Byrne **Trained** Maunby, N Yorks

FOCUS
Jamie Spencer made the difference in this modest seller. The time was reasonable, but given the doubts over the field the form is rated cautiously.
Stoppers(IRE) Official explanation: trainer said gelding lost right hind shoe

7659 TOTEQUADPOT (S) STKS — 5f (P)
1:40 (1:40) (Class 6) 3-Y-O+ — **£1,704** (£503; £251) **Stalls** High

Form — RPR
2110 **1** **Where's Reiley (USA)**[15] 7500 5-9-4 79........................(b) JamieSpencer 3 82+
(David Barron) *chsd ldr tl pushed along to ld ent fnl f: in command fnl 150yds: easily* **4/7**[1]
3003 **2** *3 3/4* **Grudge**[14] 7512 6-9-4 67........................(b) TomQueally 4 68
(Conor Dore) *sn led: rdn and hdd ent fnl f: no ch w wnr fnl 150yds* **15/8**[2]
00 **3** *2 1/2* **Evening Pinot**[42] 7093 3-8-7 0........................(e[1]) ChrisCatlin 2 48?
(Simon Dow) *s.i.s: sn niggled along and chsd ldng pair: rdn and dropped to last wl over 1f out: n.d after: wnt 3rd again ins fnl f* **25/1**
0000 **4** *3 1/4* **Lady Royal Oak (IRE)**[25] 7389 4-8-0 52........................ JenniferFerguson(7) 1 36
(Olivia Maylam) *lost many l s: racd freely: grad clsd and chsd ldng pair ent fnl 2f: rdn and wknd over 1f out: fdd ins fnl f* **22/1**[3]

58.41 secs (-0.39) **Going Correction** -0.025s/f (Stan) **4** Ran SP% **106.6**
Speed ratings (Par 101): **102,96,92,86**
CSF £1.81 TOTE £1.50; EX 1.30.The winner was sold to Alastair Lidderdale for 5,400gns.
Owner Dovebrace Ltd Air-Conditioning-Projects **Bred** Overbrook Farm **Trained** Maunby, N Yorks

FOCUS
An uncompetitive seller and essentially a match race. Not easy form to assess with the winner much better at Southwell in the past.

7660 TOTEPOOL H'CAP — 7f (P)
2:10 (2:11) (Class 4) (0-85,85) 3-Y-O+ — **£4,204** (£1,251; £625; £312) **Stalls** Low

Form — RPR
0112 **1** **Numeral (IRE)**[13] 7531 3-9-0 81........................ KieranO'Neill(3) 8 91
(Richard Hannon) *in tch: rdn and effrt to chal over 1f out: r.o wl to ld wl ins fnl f* **4/1**[2]
0031 **2** *1/2* **Amitola (IRE)**[21] 7439 4-9-7 85........................ JamieSpencer 5 94
(David Barron) *led: rdn 2f out: drvn over 1f out: hdd and no ex wl ins fnl f* **2/1**[1]
0340 **3** *hd* **Chilli Green**[134] 4415 4-9-2 80........................ SebSanders 6 88
(John Akehurst) *w ldr: ev ch and rdn 2f out: no ex wl ins fnl f* **16/1**
0000 **4** *1* **Titan Triumph**[21] 7439 7-8-12 76........................(t) JimCrowley 14 82+
(William Knight) *stdd and dropped in bhd after s: hld up in last trio: hdwy and wd bnd 2f out: kpt on wl u.p fnl f: nt rch ldrs* **33/1**
4303 **5** *1/2* **Chevise (IRE)**[18] 7486 3-9-1 79........................ MatthewDavies 12 83
(Steve Woodman) *bmpd s: sn rcvrd and in tch: rdn and effrt 2f out: kpt on u.p ins fnl f* **22/1**
5301 **6** *shd* **Young Dottie**[18] 7486 5-8-9 78........................ JemmaMarshall(5) 9 82
(Pat Phelan) *chsd ldrs: rdn over 1f out: styd on same pce ins fnl f* **28/1**
0504 **7** *shd* **Prince Of Burma (IRE)**[21] 7439 3-8-12 76........................ RobertWinston 7 80
(Jeremy Gask) *hld up in tch towards rr: hdwy into midfield over 2f out: drvn and chsd ldrs 1f out: kpt on same pce after* **5/1**[3]
1042 **8** *3/4* **Wilfred Pickles (IRE)**[21] 7438 5-9-5 83........................ DaneO'Neill 4 85
(Jo Crowley) *hld up in tch towards rr: rdn and hdwy on inner over 1f out: no ex jst ins fnl f: wknd fnl 75yds* **13/2**
0643 **9** *1 1/2* **Judd Street**[5] 7602 9-9-4 82........................(vt) TomQueally 11 80
(Eve Johnson Houghton) *in tch in midfield: rdn and effrt wl over 1f out: styd on same pce and no imp after* **16/1**
0300 **10** *1/2* **Viva Ronaldo (IRE)**[88] 5920 5-9-1 79........................ TonyHamilton 10 75
(Richard Fahey) *towards rr: hdwy on outer and chsd ldrs 3f out: rdn and unable qck ent fnl 2f: wknd ent fnl f* **25/1**
1250 **11** *1 1/4* **Time Medicean**[51] 6917 5-8-13 77........................ DavidProbert 13 70
(Tony Carroll) *wnt lft s: sn chsng ldrs: rdn and unable qck jst over 2f out: wknd jst over 1f out* **28/1**
4000 **12** *1/2* **Ghostwing**[21] 7438 4-9-2 80........................ FergusSweeney 3 72
(James Evans) *stdd s: hld up in rr: c wd and effrt 2f out: no real prog: n.d* **33/1**
1000 **13** *hd* **Reposer (IRE)**[13] 7531 3-9-1 79........................ MartinLane 1 70
(Noel Quinlan) *hld up in last trio: rdn and no hdwy 2f out: wknd over 1f out* **50/1**
0020 **14** *2 1/4* **Ivory Silk**[21] 7438 6-9-0 78........................(b) AdamKirby 2 63
(Jeremy Gask) *towards rr: pushed along and sltly hmpd bnd 2f out: no prog over 1f out: wknd fnl f* **16/1**

1m 23.21s (-1.59) **Going Correction** -0.025s/f (Stan) **14** Ran SP% **123.9**
Speed ratings (Par 105): **108,107,107,106,105 105,105,104,102,102 100,100,99,97**
toteswingers:1&2:£3.40, 1&3:£10.70, 2&3:£9.30 CSF £11.73 CT £121.76 TOTE £5.40: £1.50, £1.40, £4.90; EX 17.70 Trifecta £89.90 Pool: £537.55 - 4.42 winning units..
Owner Highclere Thoroughbred Racing-Flying Fox **Bred** Tinnakill Bloodstock & Forenaghts Stud **Trained** East Everleigh, Wilts

FOCUS
The pace was modest through the opening stages, but gradually increased. The form seems sound enough.

7661 RAY MORRIS 70TH BIRTHDAY H'CAP — 1m 4f (P)
2:40 (2:40) (Class 5) (0-75,75) 3-Y-O+ — **£2,385** (£704; £352) **Stalls** Low

Form — RPR
1352 **1** **Tornado Force (IRE)**[48] 6978 3-9-1 71........................ JimmyFortune 2 79+
(Jeremy Noseda) *chsd ldrs: swtchd rt and hdwy to press ldr gng wl 2f [illegible] fnl 75yds: [illegible] holding on* **3/1**[1]
4415 **2** *1/2* **Beat Route**[8] 7577 4-9-4 69........................ JohnFahy 8 75
(Michael Attwater) *in tch in midfield: rdn and effrt over 1f out: swtchd rt 1f out: sn drvn: chsd wnr wl ins fnl f: kpt on wl* **11/2**
0225 **3** *1/2* **Sand Skier**[14] 7513 4-9-1 73........................ NicoleNordblad(7) 4 78
(Hans Adielsson) *led: rdn 2f out: hdd ent fnl f: kpt on same pce ins fnl f* **5/1**[3]
4506 **4** *1* **Kames Park (IRE)**[11] 7556 9-8-9 63........................ RobertLButler(3) 3 67
(Richard Guest) *stdd s: hld up in rr: stl plenty to do in last pair 2f: rdn and hdwy over 1f out: kpt on wl ins fnl f: nt rch ldrs* **25/1**
0004 **5** *nk* **Kiss A Prince**[26] 7363 5-9-4 69........................(b) ShaneKelly 9 72
(Dean Ivory) *stdd s: hld up in last quartet: hdwy over 3f out: chsd ldrs and rdn 1f out: styd on same pce and no imp fnl 100yds* **6/1**
6-52 **6** *1 3/4* **Sircozy (IRE)**[13] 7032 5-9-8 73........................(b) TomQueally 10 73
(Gary Moore) *in tch in midfield: rdn and effrt over 2f out: nt qckn and outpcd over 1f out: styd on same pce ins fnl f* **16/1**
0044 **7** *3* **Admirable Duque (IRE)**[9] 7570 5-9-1 73........................(be) HarryPoulton(7) 6 69
(Dominic Ffrench Davis) *in tch towards rr: shkn up 3f out: rdn and no imp jst over 2f out: no threat to ldrs fr wl over 1f out* **33/1**
0311 **8** *2 1/2* **Royal Alcor (IRE)**[18] 7495 4-9-0 65........................(b) FergusSweeney 7 57
(Alastair Lidderdale) *stdd s: t.k.h: hld up in last trio: rdn and no prog over 2f out: no threat to ldrs fr wl over 1f out* **9/2**[2]
2304 **9** *nk* **Ecossaise**[26] 7360 3-9-1 71........................ JoeFanning 5 62
(Mark Johnston) *chsd ldr tl 2f out: sn wknd u.p: fdd ins fnl f* **11/1**
0003 **10** *2* **Buxfizz (USA)**[5] 7601 3-9-5 75........................(p) JimCrowley 1 63
(Robert Mills) *chsd ldrs: rdn over 3f out: wknd u.p wl over 1f out: bhd ins fnl f* **16/1**

2m 31.79s (-1.21) **Going Correction** -0.025s/f (Stan)
WFA 3 from 4yo+ 5lb **10** Ran SP% **116.4**
Speed ratings (Par 103): **103,102,102,101,101 100,98,96,96,95**
toteswingers:1&2:£4.70, 1&3:£5.10, 2&3:£5.80 CSF £19.43 CT £79.98 TOTE £3.40: £1.70, £1.30, £2.20; EX 28.80 Trifecta £48.70 Pool: £605.19 - 9.19 winning units..
Owner Faisal Alsheikh **Bred** Haras Du Mezeray & Ronchalon Racing **Trained** Newmarket, Suffolk

FOCUS
The pace was modest and those held up were at a disadvantage. The winner probably didn't improve much here but has more to offer.

Royal Alcor(IRE) Official explanation: trainer said gelding ran flat

7662 FELBRIDGE MEDIAN AUCTION MAIDEN STKS — 1m 2f (P)
3:10 (3:11) (Class 6) 3-5-Y-O — £1,704 (£503; £251) Stalls Low

Form — RPR

1 **Calypso Cay** 3-9-3 0 .... JoeFanning 1 — 64+
(Mark Johnston) *mde all: rdn and flashed tail 2f out: flashed tail again u.p ins fnl f: pressed but looked to be holding rival whn veered bdly rt fnl 75yds* — **8/13**[1]

2003 2 ¾ **Grand Theft Equine**[28] 7327 3-9-3 67 .... StephenCraine 3 — 63
(Jim Boyle) *chsd ldrs: wnt 2nd 2f out: drvn over 1f out: pressing wnr but keeping on same pce whn pushed bdly rt fnl 75yds: nt rcvr* — **7/2**[2]

3 2 **Vertibes** 3-9-3 0 .... DaneO'Neill 5 — 58+
(Marcus Tregoning) *rn green in last pair: swtchd rt and effrt ent fnl 2f: hdwy over 1f out: swtchd lft and kpt on wl ins fnl f* — **6/1**[3]

0 4 1 ½ **Jumeirah Liberty**[117] 4991 3-9-3 0 .... JamieGoldstein 6 — 55
(Zoe Davison) *in tch: chsd ldrs and rdn 2f out: unable qck over 1f out: wknd ins fnl f* — **33/1**

4U 5 nk **Community (USA)**[7] 7585 3-8-12 0 .... ChrisCatlin 7 — 49
(Phil McEntee) *chsd ldr tl 2f out: wknd u.p 1f out* — **12/1**

00 6 6 **Four Steps Back**[49] 6947 4-9-6 0 .... DavidProbert 2 — 42
(Mark Usher) *chsd ldrs: rdn and struggling over 2f out: wknd wl over 1f out* — **66/1**

7 10 **Onwards'N'Upwards**[29] 3-9-3 0 .... JamieMackay 4 — 22
(Christine Dunnett) *s.i.s: in last pair tl hdwy on outer to chse ldrs 6f out: u.p and struggling 3f out: wknd 2f out* — **250/1**

2m 7.57s (0.97) **Going Correction** -0.025s/f (Stan)
WFA 3 from 4yo 3lb — **7** Ran SP% **111.0**
Speed ratings (Par 101): **95,94,92,91,91 86,78**
toteswingers:1&2:£1.70, 1&3:£1.90, 2&3:£2.30 CSF £2.80 TOTE £1.90: £2.20, £1.10; EX 4.10.
Owner Sheikh Hamdan Bin Mohammed Al Maktoum **Bred** Darley **Trained** Middleham Moor, N Yorks

FOCUS
A weak maiden in which the heavily supported newcomer Calypso Cay made a winning debut, despite being hassled for the lead, albeit while going an ordinary pace (time over five seconds above standard). There is some doubt over what the form is worth.

7663 TANDRIDGE APPRENTICE H'CAP — 1m (P)
3:40 (3:40) (Class 6) (0-62,62) 3-Y-O+ — £1,704 (£503; £251) Stalls High

Form — RPR

0000 1 **Blue Deer (IRE)**[19] 7455 3-8-12 **61** ....(p) CharlesBishop(3) 8 — 69
(John Akehurst) *w ldr tl led 4f out: mde rest: drvn clr over 1f out: a gng to hold on: drvn out* — **9/2**[1]

00-1 2 ½ **Trip Switch**[20] 7442 5-8-10 **55** .... DavidKenny 3 — 62+
(George Prodromou) *s.i.s: hld up in last quartet: c wd and hdwy over 1f out: r.o wl u.p fnl f: wnt 2nd and clsng on wnr fnl 75yds* — **9/2**[1]

3166 3 1 ¼ **Dichoh**[19] 7455 8-8-13 **58** ....(p) RyanPowell 10 — 62+
(Michael Madgwick) *hld up in last quartet: stl plenty to do over 1f out: r.o strly ins fnl f: wnt 3rd towards fin: nt rch wnr* — **8/1**[3]

0531 4 nk **Gallantry**[21] 7437 9-8-13 **58** .... MatthewCosham 9 — 61
(Paul Howling) *in tch in midfield: rdn and outpcd jst over 2f out: rallied and styd on wl ins fnl f* — **8/1**[3]

5216 5 hd **Yakama (IRE)**[14] 7524 6-8-6 **56** ....(p) DanielHarris(5) 7 — 59
(Christine Dunnett) *chsd ldrs: wnt 2nd and pressed wnr over 2f out: unable qck over 1f out: plugged on same pce and lost 3 pls fnl 75yds* — **10/1**

3-40 6 shd **Resplendent Alpha**[21] 7437 7-8-2 **54** ow1 .... NedCurtis(7) 2 — 57
(Alastair Lidderdale) *in tch in midfield: pushed along and outpcd 2f out: swtchd rt and kpt on ins fnl f: nt pce to chal wnr* — **25/1**

5352 7 ¾ **Gazboolou**[14] 7524 7-8-13 **58** .... JamesRogers 4 — 59
(David Pinder) *led tl 4f out: rdn and unable qck over 2f out: 4th and btn 1f out: one pce and hld after* — **9/1**

5313 8 ½ **Fitz**[32] 7314 5-9-0 **62** .... LucyKBarry(3) 12 — 62
(Matthew Salaman) *hld up in rr: c wd and rdn wl over 1f out: styd on ins fnl f: nvr trbld ldrs* — **6/1**[2]

0030 9 nk **Blueberry Fizz (IRE)**[7] 7581 3-7-12 **51** oh4 ....(p) BradleyBosley(7) 1 — 50
(John Ryan) *chsd ldrs after 1f: 3rd and unable qck whn rdn 2f out: wknd ins fnl f* — **16/1**

0500 10 shd **Buxton**[18] 7484 7-8-8 **60** ....(t) DanielCremin(7) 11 — 59
(Roger Ingram) *hld up in last quartet: rdn and effrt wl over 1f out: kpt on but nvr gng pce to chal ldrs* — **33/1**

0430 11 2 **Fault**[15] 7507 5-8-8 **58** ....(t) NicoleNordblad(5) 5 — 52
(Alastair Lidderdale) *in tch: rdn and unable qck over 2f out: wknd over 1f out* — **8/1**[3]

1m 38.44s (0.24) **Going Correction** -0.025s/f (Stan)
WFA 3 from 4yo+ 1lb — **11** Ran SP% **115.7**
Speed ratings (Par 101): **97,96,95,94,94 94,93,93,93,93 91**
toteswingers:1&2:£6.30, 1&3:£9.70, 2&3:£10.20 CSF £23.31 CT £160.32 TOTE £4.40: £1.40, £1.70, £3.50; EX 29.50 Trifecta £374.90 Part won. Pool: £506.70 - 0.82 winning units..
Owner Mrs I Marshall **Bred** Pier House Stud **Trained** Epsom, Surrey

FOCUS
A moderate handicap. The winner is rated close to his summer best.
T/Plt: £7.00 to a £1 stake. Pool:£48,851.58 - 5,069.93 winning tickets T/Qpdt: £4.10 to a £1 stake. Pool:£3,446.45 - 610.33 winning tickets SP

7114 DEAUVILLE (R-H)
Wednesday, December 7

OFFICIAL GOING: Fibresand: standard

7664a PRIX DU PONT DE LA PIERRE (MAIDEN) (2YO COLTS & GELDINGS) (FIBRESAND) — 1m 1f 110y
9:20 (12:00) 2-Y-O — £10,344 (£4,137; £3,103; £2,068; £1,034)

RPR

1 **Telstar (GER)** 2-9-2 0 .... ThierryThulliez 8 — —
(A Kleinkorres, Germany) — **16/1**

2 4 **Cotton Trader (USA)**[14] 7521 2-9-2 0 .... ChristopheSoumillon 14 — —
(John Gosden) *broke wl: sn led: set mod pce: briefly hdd bef st: shkn up to regain ld 2f out: r.o: hdd over 1f out: styd on* — **9/10**[1]

3 ½ **Pigeon Catcher (IRE)**[75] 2-9-2 0 .... GregoryBenoist 5 — —
(Mme Pia Brandt, France) — **73/10**[2]

4 ½ **At A Premium (FR)** 2-9-2 0 .... Roberto-CarlosMontenegro 10 — —
(X Thomas-Demeaulte, France) — **26/1**

5 1 **Quilmes (IRE)** 2-8-10 0 .... MarcLerner(6) 12 — —
(C Lerner, France) — **25/1**

6 snk **Droit Au Reve (FR)** 2-9-2 0 ....(p) Francois-XavierBertras 16 — —
(D De Watrigant, France) — **8/1**[3]

7 6 **Victorious Venture (FR)** 2-9-2 0 .... ArnaudBourgeais 1 — —
(E Leenders, France) — **40/1**

8 1 ¾ **Diamant Rouge (FR)** 2-8-8 0 .... NicolasGauffenic(8) 13 — —
(C Boutin, France) — **89/1**

9 snk **Happy March (FR)** 2-9-2 0 .... ThomasMessina 7 — —
(D Allard, France) — **57/1**

10 3 **Tiger Best (FR)** 2-9-2 0 .... AlexandreRoussel 4 — —
(P Monfort, France) — **27/1**

0 **Colonel Whitmore (IRE)**[60] 2-9-2 0 .... FranckBlondel 15 — —
(E J O'Neill, France) — **37/1**

0 **Picking Apples (FR)**[29] 2-8-10 0 .... AntoineCoutier(6) 2 — —
(Mlle C Cardenne, France) — **16/1**

0 **Barclay Jelois (FR)**[25] 2-9-2 0 .... LouisBeuzelin 11 — —
(Robert Collet, France) — **106/1**

0 **Tandakayou (FR)** 2-9-2 0 .... JohanVictoire 6 — —
(J Boisnard, France) — **11/1**

0 **New Delight (FR)** 2-9-2 0 .... FabriceVeron 9 — —
(S Morineau, France) — **77/1**

2m 3.10s (123.10) — **15** Ran SP% **117.1**
WIN (incl. 1 euro stake): 17.00. PLACES: 2.90, 1.30, 1.90. DF: 16.20. SF: 81.00.
Owner Stall Unia **Bred** Gestut Schattauer & Stall Granum **Trained** Germany

NOTEBOOK
Cotton Trader(USA) was sent off the 9-10 favourite under Christophe Soumillon, but had to settle for second behind the German raider. The son of Hard Spun was quickly into stride and led the field turning for home, but had no answer to the winner's challenge inside the final 2f.

7665a PRIX DE BOIS CARROUGES (DIV 2) (MAIDEN) (2YO) (FIBRESAND) — 6f 110y
10:20 (12:00) 2-Y-O — £10,344 (£4,137; £3,103; £2,068; £1,034)

RPR

1 **Al Malek (FR)** 2-9-2 0 .... AndreBest 5 — —
(Mario Hofer, Germany) — **19/5**[2]

2 3 ½ **Small Frida (FR)**[35] 7238 2-8-13 0 ....(p) GregoryBenoist 10 — —
(Mme Pia Brandt, France) — **7/2**[1]

3 1 **Derivatives (IRE)**[27] 7344 2-8-13 0 .... ChristopheSoumillon 14 — —
(John Gosden) *broke smartly on outside: sn tk clr ld: led into st: swtchd towards stands' rail: sn u.p: hdd over 1 1/2f out: styd on fnl f: rallied cl home to take 3rd on line* — **63/10**[3]

4 nse **Willibr (IRE)**[29] 2-9-2 0 .... FabienLefebvre 12 — —
(P Costes, France) — **11/1**

5 hd **American Saga (FR)**[114] 2-8-13 0 .... ThomasHuet 7 — —
(M Delzangles, France) — **13/2**

6 ½ **Sonik (FR)**[109] 2-8-10 0 .... RomainAuray(6) 9 — —
(J Helouty, France) — **14/1**

7 1 ¼ **Away My Love** 2-8-13 0 .... RonanThomas 4 — —
(R Pritchard-Gordon, France) — **47/1**

8 nk **Monday Night (SWI)** 2-8-13 0 .... FabriceVeron 13 — —
(H-A Pantall, France) — **12/1**

9 snk **Princess Vati (FR)**[48] 2-8-13 0 .... JeromeCabre 3 — —
(S Wattel, France) — **20/1**

10 shd **Mr Splendid (FR)** 2-8-13 0 .... TristanNormand(3) 1 — —
(G Doleuze, France) — **47/1**

0 **Finisteria (FR)**[30] 7326 2-8-13 0 ....(b[1]) FranckBlondel 8 — —
(Mme C Barande-Barbe, France) — **41/1**

0 **Break Free (FR)**[127] 4652 2-9-2 0 .... Pierre-CharlesBoudot 15 — —
(Y De Nicolay, France) — **27/1**

0 **Dorlion (IRE)** 2-9-2 0 .... WilliamsSaraiva 11 — —
(Mme J Bidgood, France) — **26/1**

0 **Fiefs Dolois (FR)** 2-8-10 0 .... AntoineCoutier(6) 6 — —
(A Bonin, France) — **31/1**

0 **Le Danu (FR)** 2-9-2 0 .... ThierryThulliez 2 — —
(E Libaud, France) — **35/1**

1m 20.0s (80.00) — **15** Ran SP% **117.3**
WIN (incl. 1 euro stake): 4.80. PLACES: 2.00, 1.70, 2.60. DF: 13.80. SF: 30.20.
Owner Stall Mabrouk **Bred** Haras De Quesnay **Trained** Germany

NOTEBOOK
Derivatives(IRE)' rider took the bull by the horns, rushing the Dansili colt into the lead from a wide draw and then heading for the stands' side rail in the straight. However, he could not hold off the German challenger, who emerged from the pack, despite running on all the way to the line.

7666a PRIX DE MONTEILLERIE (CLAIMER) (2YO) (FIBRESAND) — 6f 110y
10:50 (12:00) 2-Y-O — £7,327 (£2,931; £2,198; £1,465; £732)

RPR

1 **Souslecieldeparis (USA)**[45] 2-8-11 0 .... JeromeCabre 10 — —
(Y Barberot, France) — **136/10**

2 1 ½ **Shanjia (GER)**[117] 2-8-8 0 ....(b) AndreBest 11 — —
(Mario Hofer, Germany) — **14/1**

3 ¾ **Lord Ali McJones**[84] 6043 2-8-11 0 .... DPorcu 16 — —
(S Smrczek, Germany) — **64/1**

4 1 ¼ **Full Support (IRE)**[71] 6431 2-9-8 0 .... JohanVictoire 8 — —
(F Vermeulen, France) — **9/1**[3]

5 shd **Mystical Power (FR)**[99] 2-8-7 0 .... MlleLaurieFoulard(8) 4 — —
(D Windrif, France) — **41/1**

6 nk **Litura (IRE)**[20] 7449 2-9-3 0 ....(b) AllanBonnefoy 13 — —
(J-V Toux, France) — **11/1**

7 1 **Obsidienne (FR)**[54] 2-8-5 0 ....(b) AntoineHamelin(3) 7 — —
(C Gourdain, France) — **15/2**[2]

8 shd **Wrapped Up**[19] 7452 2-8-8 0 .... Francois-XavierBertras 3 — —
(Heather Main) *racd midfield: mde prog into 6th early in st: u.p 1 1/2f out: nt qckn: styd on one pce* — **13/1**

9 ½ **Sandra Mia (FR)**[54] 2-8-8 0 .... AlexisBadel 9 — —
(F-X De Chevigny, France) — **14/1**

10 3 ½ **Hamamba (USA)** 2-8-11 0 .... WilliamsSaraiva 12 — —
(Mme J Bidgood, France) — **30/1**

0 **Inbaileysfootsteps (IRE)**[200] 2-9-1 0 .... ChristopheSoumillon 2 — —
(E J O'Neill, France) — **9/5**[1]

0 **Countrystar (FR)**[35] 7238 2-9-4 0 .... ThierryThulliez 14 — —
(C Boutin, France) — **25/1**

0 **Lady Rocket (FR)**[35] 7238 2-8-0 0 .... SoufyaneMoulin(8) 15 — —
(C Boutin, France) — **57/1**

0 **Mocca Mare**[49] 2-9-1 0 (p) EPedroza 1 —
(Manfred Hofer, Germany) **9/1**[3]
0 **Mille Secrets (FR)** 2-8-9 0 AntoineCoutier(6) 5 —
(A Bonin, France) **58/1**
0 **Minaudiere (IRE)** 2-8-4 0 CesarPasserat(4) 6 —
(Remy Nerbonne, France) **92/1**
1m 20.6s (80.60) **16** Ran SP% **118.6**
WIN (incl. 1 euro stake): 14.60. PLACES: 4.90, 4.60, 16.90. DF: 101.30. SF: 302.10.
Owner Maurice Lagasse **Bred** Pontchartrain Stud **Trained** France

7667a PRIX DE BREHAL (CLAIMER) (3YO) (FIBRESAND) 6f 110y
12:00 (12:00) 3-Y-O **£8,620** (£3,448; £2,586; £1,724; £862)

RPR
1 **Dschahan (GER)**[30] 3-8-11 0 AndreBest 2 75
(Mario Hofer, Germany) **176/10**
2 2 **Upside Down Cake**[50] 3-8-8 0 FabienLefebvre 10 66
(J E Hammond, France) **22/1**
3 *nk* **Heidikly (FR)**[30] 3-8-13 0 Francois-XavierBertras 16 70
(B De Montzey, France) **9/2**[3]
4 *nk* **Jag War (FR)**[48] 3-9-6 0 FabriceVeron 5 76
(H-A Pantall, France) **33/10**[1]
5 *3/4* **Beautiful Lando (FR)**[58] 6746 3-9-2 0 (b) AlexandreRoussel 14 70
(Heather Main) *broke wl on outside: racd 2nd: r.o wl in st in centre of trck: rdn but nt qckn ent fnl f: lost 2nd fnl 50yds* **10/1**
6 *snk* **Dance In The Dark (FR)**[30] 3-8-8 0 JeromeCabre 6 61
(S Wattel, France) **21/1**
7 *1 1/2* **Droit Devant (FR)**[30] 3-8-8 0 ThomasHuet 9 57
(S Morineau, France) **32/1**
8 *3/4* **Maria Grazie (IRE)**[34] 3-8-8 0 (b) FranckBlondel 13 55
(Mlle C Cardenne, France) **10/1**
9 *1* **Emperor's Princess (FR)**[434] 6468 3-8-3 0 JimmyTastayre(5) 4 52
(J E Hammond, France) **46/1**
10 *1/2* **Imperiale Noire (FR)**[65] 3-8-8 0 (b) BriceRaballand 7 51
(R Laplanche, France) **67/1**
0 **Trille Divine**[56] 3-8-9 0 (b) StephaneLaurent(6) 8 —
(Mme C De La Soudiere-Niault, France) **60/1**
0 **Good News (FR)**[20] 3-8-13 0 ChristopheSoumillon 12 —
(C Laffon-Parias, France) **43/10**[2]
0 **Gone Fighting (FR)**[50] 3-8-8 0 (p) AlexisBadel 11 —
(Y De Nicolay, France) **33/1**
0 **Kialoskar (IRE)**[48] 3-8-13 0 SylvainRuis 15 —
(T Lemer, France) **13/1**
0 **I Bloody Do (FR)**[30] 3-8-8 0 ThierryThulliez 1 —
(Rod Collet, France) **15/1**
1m 17.6s (77.60) **15** Ran SP% **117.4**
WIN (incl. 1 euro stake): 18.60. PLACES: 5.00, 5.70, 2.40. DF: 119.50. SF: 100.20.
Owner WH Sport International **Bred** Gestut Fahrhof **Trained** Germany

7669a PRIX DE PRECOLETTE (CONDITIONS) (3YO COLTS & GELDINGS) (APPRENTICE RIDERS) (FIBRESAND) 7f 110y
2:35 (12:00) 3-Y-O **£10,344** (£4,137; £3,103; £2,068; £1,034)

RPR
1 **Gammarth (FR)**[27] 3-8-4 0 FabriceNicoleau(7) 14 98
(H-A Pantall, France) **58/10**[3]
2 *6* **Lord Shuffle (GER)** 3-8-6 0 (p) SoufyaneMoulin(5) 12 83
(H Blume, Germany) **15/2**
3 *nk* **Lion King (FR)**[56] 3-8-6 0 AnthonyCaramanolis(5) 10 82
(N Clement, France) **48/10**[2]
4 *shd* **Heraclius**[27] 3-8-8 0 AlexandreChampenois(3) 1 82
(J-M Beguigne, France) **23/10**[1]
5 *3/4* **Mubaarez**[160] 3-8-6 0 CesarPasserat(5) 7 80
(F Vermeulen, France) **12/1**
6 *2* **El Caballito (FR)**[27] 3-8-6 0 RomainAuray(5) 3 75
(J Heloury, France) **20/1**
7 *shd* **Lewis De La Vis (FR)**[124] 3-8-4 0 MlleLaurieFoulard(7) 8 75
(D Windrif, France) **62/1**
8 *3 1/2* **Altamir One** 3-8-8 0 MatthieuAutier(3) 13 66
(Mme B Valenti, Spain) **34/1**
9 *1 1/2* **Panipro (FR)**[117] 3-8-8 0 (p) EddyHardouin(3) 6 62
(F Lemercier, France) **49/1**
10 *snk* **Iron Green (FR)**[81] 6181 3-8-8 0 TristanNormand(3) 5 62
(Heather Main) *s.i.s: a towards rr: hrd rdn bef st: no ex: nvr a factor* **39/1**
0 **Valerius Maximus**[40] 3-8-8 0 MlleEmilieLalaouna(8) 11 —
(M Boutin, France) **39/1**
0 **King David (FR)**[187] 3-8-10 0 ElliotCanal(6) 4 —
(M Boutin, France) **11/1**
0 **Universal Law (FR)**[124] 3-8-13 0 AntoineHamelin(3) 9 —
(E Danel, France) **17/2**
1m 30.0s (90.00) **13** Ran SP% **116.8**
WIN (incl. 1 euro stake): 6.80. PLACES: 2.30, 2.80, 2.30. DF: 25.20. SF: 58.50.
Owner G Mimouni **Bred** Mme M-T Mimouni **Trained** France

7668a (Foreign Racing) - See RI

7649 KEMPTON (A.W) (R-H)
Thursday, December 8

OFFICIAL GOING: Standard
Wind: Strong, half behind Weather: Windy, showers

7670 BET AT BLUESQ.COM CLAIMING STKS 5f (P)
4:00 (4:00) (Class 6) 2-Y-O **£1,617** (£481; £240; £120) **Stalls** Low

Form RPR
2436 1 **Sonko (IRE)**[21] 7445 2-8-9 67 ow1 (p) GrahamGibbons 4 68
(Tim Pitt) *mde all: rdn over 1f out: clr and in command fnl f: eased towards fin* **11/8**[2]
1311 2 *3/4* **Mr Knightley (IRE)**[27] 7365 2-9-7 80 (b) MatthewDavies 5 75
(Jim Boyle) *chsd wnr: rdn and unable qck over 1f out: wl hld ins fnl f: clsd on eased wnr towards fin* **8/11**[1]
5250 3 *2* **Marie's Fantasy**[63] 6652 2-8-8 56 ow2 JamieGoldstein 3 54
(Zoe Davison) *chsd ldrs: rdn and outpcd 1/2-way: wl hld over 1f out: clsd on eased wnr towards fin* **25/1**[3]
06 4 *20* **I B A Gee Gee**[19] 7482 2-8-8 0 FergusSweeney 2 —
(Tony Newcombe) *chsd ldrs: rdn and struggling 1/2-way: sn wknd and bhd fnl 2f* **66/1**
0 5 *6* **Englishgreek (IRE)**[19] 7490 2-7-13 0 RichardOld(7) 1 —
(George Prodromou) *a in last: rn green and lost tch 1/2-way: sddle slipped and almost uns rdr 2f out: rdr looking down and eased after* **33/1**
61.04 secs (0.54) **Going Correction** +0.05s/f (Slow) **5** Ran SP% **108.3**
Speed ratings (Par 94): **97,95,92,60,51**
CSF £2.59 TOTE £2.10: £1.20, £1.10; EX 2.70.
Owner Saintly Racing **Bred** Tally-Ho Stud **Trained** Newmarket, Suffolk
■ Tim Pitt's first winner since relocating to Newmarket.

FOCUS
An uncompetitive claimer in which the two market leaders dominated. The gallop was an ordinary one and the winner raced against the inside rail throughout.

NOTEBOOK
Sonko(IRE), who had a good chance at the weights with cheekpieces refitted, had the run of the race and showed too much foot for one that has shown his best form over further. She won with more in hand than the winning margin suggested and can score again in this grade when allowed the same rope in front. (op 6-4 tchd 13-8)
Mr Knightley(IRE), the pick of the weights, ran creditably over a trip that is an absolute minimum and he was done by one that had too much pace. The return to 6f or 7f will be more to his liking and he's the type to win again in this grade. (op 4-6 tchd 8-13)
Marie's Fantasy, dropped in trip, ran as well as could be expected on these unfavourable terms (also carried 2lb overweight). A switch to low-grade handicaps and a step up to 6f will see her in a more favourable light.
Englishgreek(IRE) Official explanation: jockey said saddle slipped

7671 BLUE SQUARE H'CAP 1m 2f (P)
4:30 (4:30) (Class 5) (0-70,70) 3-Y-O+ **£2,264** (£673; £336; £168) **Stalls** Low

Form RPR
0106 1 **Megalala (IRE)**[15] 7513 10-9-1 **67** KieranO'Neill(3) 12 82
(John Bridger) *chsd ldr tl led over 3f out: clr and rdn 2f out: styd on wl and in n.d fnl f: eased towards fin* **12/1**
3-53 2 *4 1/2* **Opera Prince**[246] 1174 6-8-12 **61** JimCrowley 11 67
(Simon Earle) *in tch: effrt to chse ldrs 3f out: chsd clr wnr u.p over 1f out: no imp* **16/1**
0622 3 *2 3/4* **Lord Lansing (IRE)**[15] 7522 4-9-4 **67** MartinHarley 4 68
(Mrs K Burke) *hld up in midfield: hdwy 3f out: drvn and wnt modest 3rd over 1f out: kpt on but no real imp after* **3/1**[1]
1162 4 *6* **Larkrise Star**[21] 7447 4-9-6 **69** ShaneKelly 8 58
(Dean Ivory) *t.k.h: chsd ldrs: rdn and outpcd whn hung rt wl over 1f out: wl hld whn swtchd lft ent fnl f: no ch but plugged on to take 4th last strides* **9/2**[2]
3130 5 *hd* **Scary Movie (IRE)**[76] 6317 6-9-6 **69** (p) LukeMorris 3 57
(Emmet Michael Butterly, Ire) *chsd ldrs: wnt 2nd and rdn over 2f out tl drvn and no hdwy over 1f out: sn lost 2nd and wknd* **6/1**[3]
0000 6 *9* **Rezwaan**[14] 7532 4-9-0 **63** (b) LiamKeniry 14 33
(Murty McGrath) *stdd s: t.k.h: hld up in last quartet: outpcd by ldrs and wl btn over 2f out: no ch but styd on past btn horses fnl f* **66/1**
0331 7 *shd* **Signora Frasi (IRE)**[15] 7522 6-9-0 **63** ow1 DaneO'Neill 9 33
(Tony Newcombe) *s.i.s: hld up in last quartet: outpcd by ldrs and wl btn over 2f out: no ch but plugged on fnl f* **8/1**
-630 8 *1 3/4* **Perfect Vision**[195] 2459 4-9-0 **63** AdamKirby 7 29
(Charlie Longsdon) *s.i.s: hld up in last quartet: outpcd by ldrs and no ch whn nt clr run ent fnl 2f: nvr on terms* **7/1**
2000 9 *2* **Allanit (GER)**[20] 7458 7-9-0 **63** TomQueally 10 25
(Barney Curley) *taken down early: led tl over 3f out: 6th and wkng qckly 2f out: fdd over 1f out* **33/1**
10-2 10 *3/4* **Khun John (IRE)**[337] 54 8-9-1 **64** StevieDonohoe 5 25
(Willie Musson) *s.i.s: hld up in rr: lost tch w ldrs over 2f out: n.d* **12/1**
200 11 *3/4* **Astragal**[27] 7360 3-8-12 **64** (v[1]) DavidProbert 1 23
(Andrew Balding) *in tch in midfield: rdn and fnd nil 3f out: sn wknd* **33/1**
0046 12 *4 1/2* **Mister Green (FR)**[15] 7522 5-8-10 **64** (bt) MatthewCosham(5) 2 14
(David Flood) *hld up in midfield: rdn and lost pl 3f out: wl bhd fnl f* **12/1**
2m 5.30s (-2.70) **Going Correction** +0.05s/f (Slow)
WFA 3 from 4yo+ 3lb **12** Ran SP% **117.4**
Speed ratings (Par 103): **112,108,106,101,101 94,93,92,90,90 89,86**
toteswingers: 1&2 £20.60, 1&3 £7.00, 2&3 £11.10 CSF £184.94 CT £728.48 TOTE £11.50: £4.10, £4.80, £1.80; EX 152.30.
Owner Tommy Ware **Bred** Joseph Gallagher **Trained** Liphook, Hants

FOCUS
A modest handicap run in a fast time for the grade. Those held-up were able to make little impact and the winner raced close to the inside rail throughout. He rates a personal best.

7672 BET AT BLUESQ.COM ON YOUR MOBILE MEDIAN AUCTION MAIDEN STKS 7f (P)
5:00 (5:01) (Class 6) 2-Y-O **£1,617** (£481; £240; £120) **Stalls** Low

Form RPR
1 **Moderator** 2-9-3 0 TomQueally 1 74+
(Gary Moore) *in tch in last trio: nt clr run over 2f out: stl last and rdn 2f out: swtchd rt and gd hdwy over 1f out: str run fnl f to ld nr fin* **4/1**[3]
0253 2 *1/2* **Flamborough Breeze**[20] 7464 2-8-9 73 RyanClark(3) 2 68
(Edward Vaughan) *led: rdn wl over 1f out: battled on gamely u.p fnl f tl hdd and no ex nr fin* **9/1**
5 3 *nk* **Kalokagathia (IRE)**[29] 7330 2-9-3 0 DaneO'Neill 10 72+
(Jo Crowley) *in tch: rdn and effrt 2f out: hdwy u.p 1f out: kpt on wl* **10/3**[2]
423 4 *nse* **Safari Sunseeker (IRE)**[22] 7431 2-9-3 76 JimCrowley 14 72
(William Knight) *chsd ldr: rdn and ev ch 2f out: kpt on u.p tl no ex wl ins fnl f* **9/4**[1]
5 *3/4* **King Vahe (IRE)** 2-9-3 0 DavidProbert 4 70
(Alan Jarvis) *in tch in midfield: rdn and effrt 2f out: hdwy and rdn to chse ldrs over 1f out: no ex and one pce fnl 100yds* **33/1**
6 *2 1/4* **Sareeah (IRE)** 2-8-12 0 SebSanders 8 59+
(Clive Brittain) *s.i.s: rn green and detached in last early: clsd and in tch 1/2-way: hdwy on outer wl over 1f out: kpt on but no imp fnl 100yds* **11/1**
0 7 *shd* **Graylyn Valentino**[36] 7225 2-9-3 0 StevieDonohoe 6 64
(Robin Dickin) *chsd ldrs: cl 3rd and rdn ent fnl 2f: drvn and no ex 1f out: outpcd fnl 150yds* **66/1**
8 *nk* **Boris The Bold** 2-9-3 0 LukeMorris 3 63
(John Best) *s.i.s: in tch towards rr: hdwy wl over 1f out: drvn and no imp ins fnl f* **12/1**
00 9 *4 1/2* **Strategic Action (IRE)**[22] 7431 2-9-3 0 FergusSweeney 7 51
(Linda Jewell) *chsd ldrs: rdn and unable qck whn short of room jst over 2f out: wknd over 1f out* **66/1**

5 **10** ½ **Jane Lachatte (IRE)**[93] 5812 2-8-12 0 WilliamCarson 11 45
(Stuart Williams) *mounted on crse: s.i.s: in tch towards rr: rdn and effrt over 2f out: no prog and no threat to ldrs fnl 2f* **14/1**

11 *1* **Yalding Dancer** 2-8-12 0 LiamJones 5 42
(John Best) *t.k.h: hld up in midfield: rdn and effrt jst over 2f out: wknd over 1f out* **66/1**

0 **12** 1 ¼ **Mariannes**[22] 7431 2-8-12 0 EddieAhern 9 39
(John Dunlop) *in tch towards rr: nt clr run on inner over 2f out: rdn and effrt 2f out: wknd u.p over 1f out* **25/1**

1m 27.07s (1.07) **Going Correction** +0.05s/f (Slow) **12** Ran SP% **117.8**
Speed ratings (Par 94): **95,94,94,94,93 90,90,90,85,84 83,81**
toteswingers: 1&2 £4.80, 1&3 £4.20, 2&3 £7.40 CSF £38.18 TOTE £4.20: £1.10, £2.90, £1.20; EX 45.60.

Owner D J Deer **Bred** D J And Mrs Deer **Trained** Lower Beeding, W Sussex

FOCUS
No more than a fair maiden. The gallop was an ordinary one and the winner raced just off the inside rail in the straight.

NOTEBOOK
Moderator ◆, a half-brother to useful flat stayer and winning hurdler Whenever, created a good impression after missing the break and running green on this racecourse debut, faring easily the best of those held up. He should be able to build on this if granted a stiffer test of stamina. (op 5-1)
Flamborough Breeze returned to form from the front. She's capable of picking up an uncompetitive race on Polytrack, but is likely to remain vulnerable to the better types in this grade. (op 5-1)
Kalokagathia(IRE) stepped up on the form shown over this C&D on his debut in November. He should be better suited by 1m and run-of-the-mill handicaps will be the way forward with him. (op 7-2 tchd 3-1)
Safari Sunseeker(IRE)'s run of steadily progressive form came to a halt, though he was far from disgraced after racing wide throughout. He should be able to pick up a small race on this surface, though he'll have to improve to win from his current mark of 76. Official explanation: jockey said gelding hung left (op 5-2 tchd 11-4 in a place)
King Vahe(IRE), a half-brother to several winners from 1m-1m2f, showed ability at a modest level on this racecourse debut. He is entitled to improve for this experience and should be suited by 1m in due course. (op 40-1)
Sareeah(IRE) ◆, a half-sister to one-time smart 6f-7f performer Golden Desert, who showed ability after missing the break, after running green and after racing widest of all. She is entitled to improve a fair bit for this experience. (op 12-1)

7673 BOOK YOUR NEXT MEETING AT KEMPTON PARK MAIDEN AUCTION STKS 1m (P)
5:30 (5:31) (Class 6) 2-Y-O **£1,617** (£481; £240; £120) **Stalls** Low

Form RPR

1 **Kingsdesire (IRE)** 2-9-1 0 (t) AdamKirby 6 79+
(Marco Botti) *s.i.s: pushed along early: in tch in rr: smooth hdwy to join ldrs 2f out: pushed ahd over 1f out: in command fnl f: eased towards fin: v easily* **2/5**[1]

2 *2* **Macy Anne (IRE)** 2-8-10 0 JimCrowley 4 63
(Robert Mills) *in tch: cl 4th and pushed along 2f out: no threat to wnr but kpt on ins fnl f to snatch 2nd last stride* **16/1**

6 **3** *shd* **Oratorian (IRE)**[20] 7454 2-8-10 0 LiamKeniry 7 63
(Sylvester Kirk) *led tl 6f out: chsd ldrs after: rdn to ld 2f out: sn drvn and hdd: no ch w wnr but plugged on fnl f: lost 2nd last stride* **8/1**[3]

33 **4** ½ **Bursting Bubbles (IRE)**[40] 7177 2-8-4 0 ChrisCatlin 2 56
(Ed Dunlop) *in tch: pushed along and dropped to last pair 4f out: hdwy on inner to press ldrs 2f out: drvn and outpcd over 1f out: no threat to wnr and one pce fnl f* **9/2**[2]

4000 **5** *10* **Hollywood All Star (IRE)**[22] 7432 2-8-10 43 WilliamCarson 8 39
(William Muir) *chsd ldr tl led 5f out: drvn and hdd 2f out: sn wknd* **100/1**

6 *24* **Midnite Motivation** 2-8-5 0 LukeMorris 3 —
(Derek Shaw) *t.k.h: hld up in tch tl hdwy to ld 6f out: rn green after: hdd and rdn 3f out: wknd qckly over 2f out: eased fnl f: t.o* **25/1**

1m 42.61s (2.81) **Going Correction** +0.05s/f (Slow) **6** Ran SP% **111.4**
Speed ratings (Par 94): **87,85,84,84,74 50**
toteswingers: 1&2 £1.40, 1&3 £1.40, 2&3 £6.00 CSF £8.72 TOTE £1.30: £1.10, £5.00; EX 13.40.

Owner Giuliano Manfredini **Bred** Mrs Cherry Faeste **Trained** Newmarket, Suffolk

FOCUS
A modest and uncompetitive maiden in which the gallop was a steady one, resulting in a time nearly six seconds above the Racing Post standard. The winner raced towards the centre in the straight.

NOTEBOOK
Kingsdesire(IRE) ◆, a 22,000euro first foal of a half-sister to multiple Group winner (from 1m-1m2f) Special Kaldoun, was well supported at prohibitive odds and didn't have to show anything other than modest form after missing the break to win an uncompetitive event with more in hand than the official margin suggested. He has scope and it'll be a surprise if he can't step up on this. (op 8-13)
Macy Anne(IRE), a 20,000gns sister to useful dual 1m winner Night Of Joy and half-sister to three other winners on the Flat and over hurdles, showed ability at an ordinary level on this racecourse debut. A stiffer test of stamina would have suited and she is open to improvement.
Oratorian(IRE) probably ran to a similar level as on his debut over this track and trip. He'll be seen to better effect in moderate handicaps in due course.
Bursting Bubbles(IRE) had run well over 1m at Wolverhampton on her previous start but failed to build on that in this muddling event over this shorter trip. A stiffer test of stamina should suit. (op 10-3)

7674 BOXINGDAYRACES.CO.UK H'CAP 2m (P)
6:00 (6:01) (Class 5) (0-75,81) 3-Y-O+ **£2,264** (£673; £336; £168) **Stalls** Low

Form RPR

4013 **1** **Epsom Salts**[48] 6998 6-9-7 73 JemmaMarshall(5) 3 81
(Pat Phelan) *stdd s: t.k.h: in tch: chsd ldr 8f out: rdn and clr of field 3f out: looked hld over 1f out: styd on ins fnl f to ld fnl 50yds* **9/2**[3]

0001 **2** *1* **Wild Desert (FR)**[10] 7570 6-10-6 81 6ex AdamKirby 4 88
(Charlie Longsdon) *led and set stdy gallop: grad qcknd pce and clr w wnr 3f out: rdr looking arnd and looked in command over 1f out: rdn ins fnl f: hdd fnl 75yds: sn btn* **6/4**[1]

2431 **3** *9* **Squad**[10] 7564 5-9-6 67 6ex (b) EddieAhern 5 63
(Simon Dow) *hld up in last pair: outpcd and lost tch w ldng pair over 3f out: rdn and hdwy to go modest 3rd over 2f out: no imp* **6/1**

2000 **4** *5* **Blackmore**[52] 6915 4-9-6 70 AdamBeschizza(3) 1 60
(Julia Feilden) *dwlt: hld up in tch: hdwy to chse ldr 12f out tl 8f out: rdn and outpcd over 3f out: wl btn over 2f out* **7/2**[2]

2035 **5** 1 ¼ **Dr Finley (IRE)**[24] 7415 4-9-3 67 SimonPearce(3) 2 56
(Lydia Pearce) *chsd ldr tl 12f out: in tch in last pair after: rdn over 4f out: outpcd over 3f out and wl btn fnl 3f* **8/1**

0523 **6** *8* **Calculating (IRE)**[16] 7506 7-9-5 71 LeeNewnes(5) 6 50
(Mark Usher) *chsd ldrs: rdn 4f out: outpcd by ldng pair over 3f out: wl bhd over 2f out* **14/1**

3m 34.3s (4.20) **Going Correction** +0.05s/f (Slow) **6** Ran SP% **112.5**
Speed ratings (Par 103): **91,90,86,83,82 78**
toteswingers: 1&2 £1.10, 1&3 £4.20, 2&3 £2.50 CSF £11.79 TOTE £8.00: £5.90, £1.10; EX 15.60.

Owner The Epsom Racegoers **Bred** Heatherwold Stud **Trained** Epsom, Surrey

FOCUS
A fair handicap in which the first two pulled clear but a pedestrian gallop to the home turn confirms this bare form isn't entirely reliable. The winner raced just off the inside rail in the closing stages and rates his best form since the summer of 2010.
Calculating(IRE) Official explanation: jockey said gelding had a breathing problem

7675 BOOK TICKETS ON 0844 579 3008 H'CAP 6f (P)
6:30 (6:30) (Class 4) (0-85,85) 3-Y-O+ **£4,075** (£1,212; £606; £303) **Stalls** Low

Form RPR

2000 **1** **Dasho**[22] 7439 3-9-0 78 KirstyMilczarek 2 86
(Olivia Maylam) *hld up in tch: effrt on inner 2f out: chal ent fnl f: drvn ahd jst ins fnl f: r.o wl* **12/1**

4600 **2** ½ **Arctic Lynx (IRE)**[20] 7457 4-8-9 73 LiamJones 3 79
(John Best) *hld up in tch: rdn and effrt 2f out: chsd ldrs and swtchd lft jst ins fnl f: r.o wl and pressing wnr cl home* **13/2**

6351 **3** ¾ **Requisite**[8] 7586 6-9-2 80 6ex (b) DaneO'Neill 12 84+
(Ian Wood) *s.i.s: hld up in rr: swtchd lft and hdwy over 1f out: pushed lft jst ins fnl f: r.o wl to snatch 3rd cl home: nt rch ldrs* **16/1**

2404 **4** *nk* **Sutton Veny (IRE)**[19] 7489 5-9-7 85 AdamKirby 6 88
(Jeremy Gask) *chsd ldr tl over 4f out: styd chsng ldrs: rdn to ld over 1f out: hdd jst ins fnl f: no ex and lost 2 pls wl ins fnl f* **4/1**[1]

0606 **5** *shd* **Taajub (IRE)**[14] 7531 4-9-5 83 SebSanders 1 86
(Peter Crate) *hld up in tch towards rr: nt clr run over 2f out: hdwy and nt clr run ent fnl f: swtchd sharply lft and bmpd rivals jst ins fnl f: r.o wl: nt rch ldrs* **9/2**[2]

4500 **6** ½ **Clear Praise (USA)**[100] 5578 4-9-4 82 EddieAhern 11 83
(Simon Dow) *stdd and dropped in bhd after s: hld up in rr: swtchd rt and effrt on inner 2f out: hdwy and chsd ldrs 1f out: kpt on* **16/1**

0003 **7** *1* **Levitate**[8] 7586 3-9-2 80 (b) GrahamGibbons 9 78
(Alan McCabe) *led and grad crossed to inner: rdn and hdd over 1f out: wknd ins fnl f* **7/1**

1204 **8** 1 ½ **Highland Harvest**[87] 5997 7-8-13 77 RobertHavlin 10 73
(Jamie Poulton) *t.k.h: hld up in tch towards rr: rdn and effrt wl over 1f out: keeping on but stl plenty to do whn squeezed and bdly hmpd jst ins fnl f: styd on same pce after* **40/1**

1142 **9** ¾ **Silenzio**[8] 7586 3-8-10 77 (b[1]) KieranO'Neill(3) 5 68
(Richard Hannon) *in tch: effrt u.p to chse ldrs 2f out: wknd jst ins fnl f* **5/1**[3]

0022 **10** *3* **Dorback**[16] 7502 4-8-11 75 FergusSweeney 8 56
(Noel Wilson) *racd keenly: chsd ldrs tl wnt 2nd over 4f out tl wl over 1f out: wknd ent fnl f* **10/1**

4426 **11** *8* **Local Singer (IRE)**[108] 5322 3-9-5 83 TomMcLaughlin 7 39
(Paul Howling) *in tch in midfield: rdn and struggling over 3f out: wknd 2f out* **20/1**

0606 **12** *5* **Finn's Rainbow**[155] 3731 3-8-9 73 LukeMorris 4 13
(John Weymes) *chsd ldrs: rdn and wkng over 2f out: wl bhd over 1f out* **100/1**

1m 12.2s (-0.90) **Going Correction** +0.05s/f (Slow) **12** Ran SP% **117.4**
Speed ratings (Par 105): **108,107,106,105,105 105,103,101,100,96 86,79**
toteswingers: 1&2 £21.00, 1&3 £26.00, 2&3 £23.50 CSF £86.01 CT £1284.05 TOTE £13.70: £6.00, £2.70, £5.30; EX 53.80.

Owner Mrs P A Clark **Bred** Mrs P A Clark **Trained** Epsom, Surrey
■ Stewards' Enquiry : Seb Sanders three-day ban: careless riding (Dec 22,26-27)

FOCUS
Exposed performers in a useful handicap. The gallop was reasonable but several finished in a heap. The winner raced close to the inside rail throughout. Sound form is unexceptional for the grade.

7676 BOOK YOUR NEXT EVENT HERE APPRENTICE H'CAP 6f (P)
7:00 (7:01) (Class 7) (0-50,50) 3-Y-O+ **£1,533** (£452; £226) **Stalls** Low

Form RPR

0-41 **1** **Lucky Royale**[22] 7429 3-8-13 49 RaulDaSilva 5 62+
(Jeremy Gask) *hld up in tch: trcking ldrs and gng wl whn nt clr run jst over 1f out: swtchd lft jst ins fnl f: r.o wl to ld cl home* **11/4**[1]

0505 **2** ½ **Replicator**[22] 7429 6-8-13 49 (e) LukeRowe 4 56
(Patrick Gilligan) *t.k.h: chsd ldrs: rdn to ld over 1f out: hrd pressed ins fnl f: hdd and no ex cl home* **4/1**[2]

0604 **3** ¾ **Slatey Hen (IRE)**[89] 5941 3-8-7 50 (p) RobertSpencer(7) 1 55
(Richard Guest) *hld up in rr: swtchd rt and hdwy on inner wl over 1f out: ev ch ins fnl f: no ex fnl 50yds* **8/1**

006 **4** 2 ¾ **First Class**[28] 7354 3-8-8 47 NoelGarbutt(3) 12 43
(Rae Guest) *t.k.h: chsd ldrs: rdn and effrt 2f out: unable qck over 1f out: outpcd by ldng trio ins fnl f* **5/1**

4040 **5** ¾ **Jemimaville (IRE)**[64] 6619 4-8-8 47 JackDuern(3) 3 40
(Giles Bravery) *hld up in tch towards rr: rdn and effrt wl over 1f out: kpt on ins fnl f: nvr able to chal* **10/1**

0600 **6** *1* **Emerald Royal**[1] 7656 3-8-9 48 ow2 (t) ThomasBrown(3) 8 36
(Edward Creighton) *hld up in tch towards rr: rdn and hdwy wl over 1f out: styng on but no threat to ldrs whn nt clr run ins fnl f: no imp fnl 100yds* **33/1**

0642 **7** ½ **My Best Man**[14] 7525 5-8-11 50 GeorgeDowning(3) 9 39
(Tony Carroll) *t.k.h: hld up in tch in midfield: rdn and unable qck 2f out: wknd ent fnl f* **8/1**

0552 **8** 1 ¾ **Brian Sprout**[22] 7429 3-9-0 50 JustinNewman 10 33
(John Weymes) *taken down early: racd keenly: led tl rdn and hdd over 1f out: wknd fnl f* **9/2**[3]

3640 **9** 1 ¾ **Thoughtsofstardom**[229] 1523 8-8-12 48 LucyKBarry 11 25
(Phil McEntee) *pressed ldr tl over 2f out: wknd over 1f out* **20/1**

0540 **10** *1* **Chillie Peppar**[14] 7525 3-8-8 49 RichardOld(5) 2 23
(George Prodromou) *in tch: pushed along and no prog over 2f out: wknd wl over 1f out* **25/1**

0000 **11** *29* **Super Frank (IRE)**[15] 7524 8-8-11 50 (b) JakePayne(3) 6 —
(Zoe Davison) *virtually ref to r and v.s.a: t.o thrght* **16/1**

1m 13.84s (0.74) **Going Correction** +0.05s/f (Slow) **11** Ran SP% **130.3**
Speed ratings (Par 97): **97,96,95,91,90 89,88,86,84,82 44**
toteswingers: 1&2 £5.50, 1&3 £13.30, 2&3 £8.80 CSF £15.00 CT £86.10 TOTE £3.70: £1.10, £1.60, £4.70; EX 29.20.

Owner Gracelands Stud Partnership **Bred** Gracelands Stud **Trained** Sutton Veny, Wilts
■ Stewards' Enquiry : Thomas Brown two-day ban: weighed in 2lb heavy (Dec 22,26)

FOCUS
A low-grade handicap in which the pace was sound. The winner came down the centre in the straight and the first three finished clear. Sound form, and the winner has more to offer.
T/Plt: £95.50 to a £1 stake. Pool: £72,359.04. 553.02 winning tickets. T/Qpdt: £28.40 to a £1 stake. Pool: £8,027.96. 209.10 winning tickets. SP

7664 DEAUVILLE (R-H)
Thursday, December 8

OFFICIAL GOING: Fibresand: standard

7677a PRIX DE BURSARD (CONDITIONS) (3YO) (FIBRESAND) 1m 4f
12:00 (12:00) 3-Y-O **£12,500** (£5,000; £3,750; £2,500; £1,250)

RPR
1 **Technokrat (IRE)** 3-9-4 0 ....(b) APietsch 6 91
(W Hickst, Germany) **21/10**[2]
2 *hd* **Korgon**[77] 3-8-11 0 ....(p) AntoineHamelin(4) 4 88
(J-L Guillochon, France) **10/1**
3 *nk* **Val De Majorque (FR)**[43] 3-9-4 0 ....(b) FabienLefebvre 5 90
(D Sepulchre, France) **14/5**[3]
4 *2* **Achalas (IRE)**[47] 7022 3-9-1 0 .... ChristopheSoumillon 7 84
(Heather Main) *racd 3rd on settling: bhd v slow pce: wnt 2nd end of bk st: tk ld u.p 2f out: hdd 1 1/2f out: r.o but no ex ins fnl f* **2/1**[1]
5 *1* **Kassyield (FR)**[45] 3-9-4 0 ....(p) ArnaudBourgeais 3 85
(H Paysan, France) **9/1**
6 *5* **Saga D'Oree (FR)** 3-8-8 0 .... SebastienMaillot 1 67
(Mlle Valerie Boussin, France) **15/1**
2m 43.7s (163.70) **6** Ran SP% **117.2**
WIN (incl. 1 euro stake): 3.10. PLACES: 2.10, 3.80. SF: 22.60.
Owner Stall Grafenberg **Bred** Gestut Wittekindshof **Trained** Germany

7678a PRIX LUTHIER (LISTED RACE) (3YO+) (FIBRESAND) 7f 110y
2:05 (12:00) 3-Y-0+ **£22,413** (£8,965; £6,724; £4,482; £2,241)

RPR
1 **Ariete Arrollador**[60] 4-8-11 0 .... Jean-BaptisteHamel 11 106
(G Arizkorreta Elosegui, Spain) **119/10**
2 *hd* **So Long Malpic (FR)**[54] 6643 4-8-8 0 .... FabriceVeron 13 102
(T Lemer, France) **12/1**
3 *1* **Sulle Orme (FR)**[58] 6783 3-9-1 0 .... PhilippeSogorb 4 108
(C Ferland, France) **7/1**[2]
4 *snk* **Nova Step**[95] 5772 3-8-11 0 .... RaphaelMarchelli 8 103
(F Rohaut, France) **20/1**
5 *nk* **Myasun (FR)**[14] 7534 4-8-11 0 .... JohanVictoire 5 101
(C Baillet, France) **9/1**
6 *3/4* **Rosa Bonheur (USA)**[77] 6288 3-8-10 0 ow2.... ChristopheSoumillon 6 100
(E Lellouche, France) **11/1**
7 *nk* **Volcanico (IRE)**[21] 7450 3-8-11 0 .... SebastienMaillot 2 100
(F Rodriguez Puertas, Spain) **61/1**
8 *1/2* **Konig Concorde (GER)**[33] 7311 6-9-4 0 .... FilipMinarik 7 105
(C Sprengel, Germany) **14/1**
9 *1 1/2* **Baroness (FR)**[75] 6397 4-8-8 0 .... AlexandreRoussel 12 91
(F Monnier, France) **88/1**
10 *1* **Surfrider (IRE)**[67] 6566 3-9-4 0 .... ThierryThulliez 14 99
(S Wattel, France) **3/1**[1]
0 **The Shrew**[15] 7516 3-8-8 0 .... Pierre-CharlesBoudot 15 —
(John Gosden) *settled midfield wdst of all: rdn and swtchd towards stands' rail early in st: no ex: fdd* **78/10**[3]
0 **Konig Bernard (FR)**[58] 6783 5-8-11 0 .... FlavienPrat 9 —
(W Baltromei, Germany) **18/1**
0 **Western Mystic (GER)**[39] 4-8-9 0 ow1 .... APietsch 3 —
(W Hickst, Germany) **49/1**
0 **Pas Perdus**[21] 7450 3-8-11 0 .... GregoryBenoist 1 —
(M Delzangles, France) **10/1**
0 **Elke's Friend's**[21] 7450 4-8-8 0 .... SylvainRuis 16 —
(W Hickst, Germany) **48/1**
0 **Valle (USA)** 3-8-11 0 .... Jean-BernardEyquem 10 —
(M Delcher-Sanchez, Spain) **28/1**
1m 29.0s (89.00) **16** Ran SP% **118.6**
WIN (incl. 1 euro stake): 12.90. PLACES: 3.60, 3.10, 2.60. DF: 43.10. SF: 89.20.
Owner Juan Benjumea Alarcon **Bred** Loughtown Stud Ltd **Trained** Spain

NOTEBOOK
The Shrew failed to follow up her recent second in this grade at Kempton, racing wide and never landing a blow when swithced in the straight.

7641 SOUTHWELL (L-H)
Friday, December 9

OFFICIAL GOING: Standard
Wind: Moderate behind Weather: Fine and dry

7684 PLAY THE BIG MONEY TOTEJACKPOT TODAY CLAIMING STKS 1m (F)
11:10 (11:10) (Class 6) 2-Y-O **£1,704** (£503; £251) **Stalls** Low

Form RPR
023 1 **Barn Dance (FR)**[25] 7414 2-8-12 77 .... LeeNewman 3 69+
(Jonathan Portman) *trckd ldrs: hdwy 1/2-way: chsd clr ldr over 2f out: rdn and styd on to ld ent fnl f: kpt on wl* **13/8**[1]
0061 2 *2 1/4* **Point At Issue (IRE)**[17] 7505 2-8-9 60 ....(b) AdrianNicholls 5 59
(David Nicholls) *sn led: pushed clr 3f out: rdn wl over 1f out: hdd ent fnl f: one pce* **13/8**[1]
652 3 *1* **Raspberry Fizz**[24] 7423 2-8-2 49 ....(b) JimmyQuinn 4 50+
(Eve Johnson Houghton) *dwlt: sn outpcd and rdn along in rr: bhd 1/2-way: hdwy u.p over 2f out: styd on appr fnl f: nrst fin* **25/1**
0366 4 *3 1/2* **Angel Cake (IRE)**[11] 7568 2-7-12 54 ....[1] KieranO'Neill(3) 6 41
(Amy Weaver) *trckd ldrs: effrt to chse ldng pair 3f out: rdn along 2f out: sn one pce* **16/1**
33 5 *10* **Siouxies Dream**[9] 7582 2-8-6 0 .... LukeMorris 2 24
(Michael Appleby) *cl up: rdn along over 3f out: sn wknd* **7/1**[2]
6433 6 *9* **Can Do Les (IRE)**[11] 7568 2-8-6 0 ....(p) JoeFanning 1 4
(Keith Dalgleish) *cl up: rdn along over 3f out: sn wknd* **8/1**[3]
1m 43.28s (-0.42) **Going Correction** -0.175s/f (Stan) **6** Ran SP% **109.5**
Speed ratings (Par 94): **95,92,91,88,78 69**
toteswingers:1&2:£1.40, 1&3:£8.30, 2&3:£5.70 CSF £4.02 TOTE £2.50: £1.10, £1.10; EX 4.20.Barn Dance was claimed by Claes Bjorling for £11,000.
Owner Jaliza Partnership **Bred** Mme Heather Murat Beauchene **Trained** Compton, Berks

FOCUS
Varying levels of ability in this juvenile claimer, but the race only featured the joint favourites in the straight. The winner deserved it and the second may not be as good as rated.

NOTEBOOK
Barn Dance(FR), proven at the trip but not on the surface, was clear top on official ratings. He looked in trouble when his market rival kicked clear off the bend, but his stamina came in to play in the last quarter-mile and he got on top entering the last furlong to win comfortably. He can go in again. (op 6-4 tchd 15-8)
Point At Issue(IRE), who made all to win a similar contest over 7f here last time, adopted identical tactics and looked the most likely winner when kicking for home around 3f out. However, he edged right under pressure and had no answer to the winner's challenge. A drop back in trip can be expected after this. (op 7-4 tchd 6-4)
Raspberry Fizz, as she did last time over 7f here, finished well to close down the principals, having missed the break and looking set to finish last leaving the back straight. She can win a seller here at this trip. (op 33-1)
Angel Cake(IRE), wearing a hood instead of blinkers and having her first try on the surface, was struggling from the home turn. (tchd 20-1)
Siouxies Dream failed to run up to her debut form with today's second. (op 6-1 tchd 11-2)

7685 BRITISH STALLION STUDS SUPPORTING BRITISH RACING EBF MAIDEN STKS 7f (F)
11:40 (11:42) (Class 5) 2-Y-O **£3,408** (£1,006; £503) **Stalls** Low

Form RPR
62 1 **Fistful Of Dollars (IRE)**[13] 7559 2-9-3 0 .... FergusSweeney 4 68
(Jamie Osborne) *cl up: led after 2f: rdn wl over 1f out: kpt on u.p fnl f* **8/11**[1]
00 2 *1 3/4* **Duke Liam (IRE)**[38] 7209 2-9-3 0 .... AdrianNicholls 7 63
(David Nicholls) *chsd ldrs: wd in st: hdwy wl over 1f out: sn rdn and styd on fnl f* **22/1**
5 3 *nk* **To The Sea (USA)**[20] 7494 2-8-12 0 .... JoeFanning 2 58+
(Mark Johnston) *led 2f: cl up: pushed along and sltly outpcd over 3f out: hdwy on inner 2f out: sn rdn and ev ch: kpt on same pce fnl f* **13/8**[2]
0 4 *1 3/4* **Sweet Grace**[46] 7060 2-8-12 0 ....(t) MichaelStainton 5 53
(David Brown) *trckd ldrs: effrt and cl up 3f out: ev ch 2f out: sn rdn: edgd lft and one pce ent fnl f* **25/1**
0 5 *5* **Diva Donkey (IRE)**[13] 7559 2-8-12 0 .... TomEaves 6 40
(Bryan Smart) *dwlt: sn prom: effrt and cl up 1/2-way: rdn along wl over 2f out: sn wknd* **16/1**[3]
0 6 *8* **Lady Author**[28] 7367 2-8-12 0 .... TonyHamilton 1 19
(Richard Fahey) *sn pushed along on inner: in tch: rdn along and outpcd fr 1/2-way* **50/1**
00 7 *30* **Blue Pencil**[37] 7232 2-9-3 0 ....(b[1]) LiamKeniry 8 —
(Paul Fitzsimons) *dwlt: hdwy and in tch 1/2-way: sn rdn and wknd* **66/1**
1m 30.13s (-0.17) **Going Correction** -0.175s/f (Stan) **7** Ran SP% **113.5**
Speed ratings (Par 96): **93,91,90,88,82 73,39**
toteswingers:1&2:£3.30, 1&3:£1.10, 2&3:£3.50 CSF £21.63 TOTE £1.60: £1.10, £7.40; EX 15.30 Trifecta £42.20 Pool: £429.95 - 7.53 winning units..
Owner J Stunt, D Dixon, S Bukhari **Bred** Swettenham Stud **Trained** Upper Lambourn, Berks
■ Stewards' Enquiry : Adrian Nicholls two-day ban: used whip with excessive frequency (Dec 26-27)

FOCUS
A modest juvenile maiden in which none of the runners had previous experience of the surface. It was a match according to the market, but it proved more competitive than that. The form could be rated slightly higher.

NOTEBOOK
Fistful Of Dollars(IRE) was sent off at odds-on to build on his promising effort over this trip at Wolverhampton at the end of last month. He made much of the running, but had to work pretty hard to hold off several challenges. Much depends on what mark he gets as regards his future prospects. (op 5-6)
Duke Liam(IRE), well beaten in two maidens on good ground, ran much better on this surface, staying on well under pressure in the straight. He should be up to winning a similar contest, although he now also qualifies for a mark. (op 18-1)
To The Sea(USA), who looked in need of the experience on her debut last time, was backed against the favourite and had every chance in the straight. She is well related and can do better. (tchd 15-8)
Sweet Grace, who reared over backwards at the start before showing ability on her debut at Redcar, had a tongue tie fitted and only weakened late on. (op 33-1)

7686 TOTEQUADPOT NURSERY 6f (F)
12:15 (12:15) (Class 5) (0-75,72) 2-Y-O **£2,264** (£673; £336; £168) **Stalls** Low

Form RPR
3541 1 **Whisky Bravo**[3] 7642 2-9-4 69 6ex .... MichaelStainton 5 76+
(David Brown) *cl up: effrt to ld wl over 1f out: rdn and kpt on wl fnl f* **5/6**[1]
0121 2 *1 3/4* **Adranian (IRE)**[14] 7539 2-9-5 70 ....(v) LukeMorris 4 72
(David C Griffiths) *cl up on outer: effrt over 2f out: sn rdn: styd on same pce* **9/2**[3]
6116 3 *4* **Sonsie Lass**[14] 7541 2-8-12 63 .... JoeFanning 3 53
(Keith Dalgleish) *led: jnd and rdn over 2f out: hdd wl over 1f out: wknd appr fnl f* **11/4**[2]
1500 4 *3* **Bartley**[20] 7491 2-9-7 72 ....(p) TomEaves 1 53
(Bryan Smart) *chsd ldrs: rdn along 1/2-way: wknd over 2f out* **12/1**
1m 14.85s (-1.65) **Going Correction** -0.175s/f (Stan) **4** Ran SP% **107.1**
Speed ratings (Par 96): **104,101,96,92**
CSF £4.79 TOTE £1.60; EX 5.40.
Owner S Bolland & C Watson **Bred** Peter Onslow **Trained** Averham Park, Notts

FOCUS
Quite a competitive nursery on paper, despite the small field, but in the end an authoritative success. The winner is 3/3 here and the second posted a personal best.

NOTEBOOK
Whisky Bravo, a strong-finishing winner over 5f here earlier in the week, he was able to lie closer to the pace over this longer trip and took over before the last furlong to win with something in hand. There looks to be more to come, although the trainer indicated that he might give the gelding a bit of time. (op 10-11 tchd Evens)
Adranian(IRE), a three-time winner in sellers and claimers for David Evans, was claimed by current connections for £6,000 and stuck to his task really well on his first try on this surface. This gives his trainer more options. (tchd 7-2)

Sonsie Lass, a C&D winner who is well suited by making the running, set the pace but the winner was always close to her and she could not respond when he asserted. (op 5-2 tchd 9-4)

7687 PLAY THE LIFE CHANGING TOTESCOOP6 TOMORROW H'CAP 1m (F)
12:50 (12:50) (Class 5) (0-70,69) 3-Y-O+ **£2,264** (£673; £336; £168) **Stalls** Low

Form RPR
6021 **1** **Greyfriarschorista**[8] 7589 4-9-7 **69** BarryMcHugh 3 88
(Brian Ellison) *in tch: trckd ldrs 1/2-way: effrt on outer 3f out: led over 2f out: sn clr: easily* **8/11**[1]
2-40 **2** *10* **Hilbre Court (USA)**[49] 7005 6-8-7 **55** oh2 (p) WilliamCarson 7 51
(Brian Baugh) *sn pushed along to chse ldrs: hdwy on outer to ld 3f: sn rdn and hdd over 2f out: kpt on: no ch w wnr* **8/1**
3410 **3** *7* **On The Cusp (IRE)**[24] 7425 4-9-6 **68** (p) MartinHarley 4 48
(Richard Guest) *sn led: rdn along and hdd 3f out: sn drvn and wknd* **4/1**[2]
0010 **4** *3 ¾* **Putin (IRE)**[29] 7351 3-8-8 **57** (p) LukeMorris 5 28
(Phil McEntee) *cl up: rdn along 3f out: sn wknd* **15/2**[3]
5060 **5** *4 ½* **San Antonio**[24] 7425 11-9-2 **64** (b) MickyFenton 1 25
(Pam Sly) *cl up on inner: rdn along wl over 3f out: sn wknd* **14/1**
0040 **6** *1 ¼* **Indian Emperor (IRE)**[7] 7610 3-8-10 **59** TomEaves 2 17
(Peter Niven) *dwlt: a in rr* **22/1**

1m 41.19s (-2.51) **Going Correction** -0.175s/f (Stan)
WFA 3 from 4yo+ 1lb 6 Ran SP% **111.8**
Speed ratings (Par 103): **105,95,88,84,79 78**
toteswingers:1&2:£2.00, 1&3:£1.60, 2&3:£1.90 CSF £7.34 TOTE £1.50: £1.20, £2.80; EX 4.80.
Owner Koo's Racing Club **Bred** Castlemartin Stud And Skymarc Farm **Trained** Norton, N Yorks
■ Cottam Donny (10/1) was withdrawn on vet's advice. Deduct 5p in the £ under R4.

FOCUS
A modest handicap but there was a strong early pace as three battled for the lead, which played into the hands of the winner. It's hard to know quite what he achieved.

7688 TOTEPOOL H'CAP 2m (F)
1:25 (1:25) (Class 6) (0-60,53) 3-Y-O+ **£1,704** (£503; £251) **Stalls** Low

Form RPR
5432 **1** **Carnac (IRE)**[3] 7645 5-9-10 **51** (p) ShaneKelly 3 61
(Alan McCabe) *pushed along early to go prom: led after 2f: hdd after 5f: cl up: rdn along over 4f out: led 3f out: drvn and kpt on gamely fnl 2f* **15/8**[2]
2 *3 ½* **The Ice Factor**[42] 5769 3-8-10 **45** (b) LiamKeniry 7 51
(Gordon Elliott, Ire) *rn in snatches: in tch: pushed along after 4f: rdn and lost pl after 6f: hdwy 1/2-way: cl up on bridle 5f out: rdn to chse wnr wl over 2f out: sn drvn and no imp* **6/5**[1]
6630 **3** *3 ¾* **Famagusta**[15] 7527 4-9-4 **45** (v) RobertWinston 2 46
(Peter Charalambous) *led 2f: prom: rdn along and outpcd 4f out: plugged on fnl 2f* **10/1**
5205 **4** *3 ¾* **Mecox Bay (IRE)**[3] 7645 4-9-12 **53** LukeMorris 4 50
(Michael Appleby) *prom: led after 5f: rdn along 4f out: hdd 3f out: sn drvn and wknd fnl 2f* **7/1**[3]
0500 **5** *8* **In The Long Grass (IRE)**[52] 6926 3-8-7 **47** (b[1]) NathanAlison(5) 6 34
(Jim Boyle) *prom on inner: rdn along 4f out: drvn 3f out: sn wknd* **16/1**
-000 **6** *16* **Nella Sofia**[17] 7503 3-8-10 **45** JamesSullivan 1 13
(James Given) *in rr: rdn along 5f out: sn outpcd and bhd fnl 2f* **50/1**

3m 48.97s (3.47) **Going Correction** -0.175s/f (Stan)
WFA 3 from 4yo+ 8lb 6 Ran SP% **109.7**
Speed ratings (Par 101): **84,82,80,78,74 66**
toteswingers:1&2:£1.20, 1&3:£2.60, 2&3:£2.20 CSF £4.23 TOTE £3.20: £2.50, £1.10; EX 5.20.
Owner A J McCabe & Charles Wentworth **Bred** Kilfrush Stud **Trained** Averham Park, Notts

FOCUS
A very moderate staying handicap and not a race that is likely to have much bearing on the future. It was a real war of attrition, with most of the field off the bridle before leaving the back straight. It's doubtful this took much winning.

7689 MEMBERSHIP AT SOUTHWELL GOLF CLUB H'CAP 1m 4f (F)
2:00 (2:00) (Class 6) (0-65,65) 3-Y-O+ **£1,704** (£503; £251) **Stalls** Low

Form RPR
41P2 **1** **C P Joe (IRE)**[11] 7564 3-9-3 **63** (v) FrannyNorton 3 73+
(Paul Green) *t.k.h: trckd ldrs: hdwy wl over 3f out: chsd ldr over 2f out: rdn to chal over 1f out: led jst ins fnl f: kpt on* **3/1**[2]
6636 **2** *2* **Ay Tay Tate (IRE)**[3] 7647 5-9-5 **65** (p) JustinNewman(5) 5 72
(David C Griffiths) *led and sn clr: pushed along over 3f out: rdn 2f out: hdd ins fnl f: no ex* **9/2**
0064 **3** *1 ¼* **Irish Jugger (USA)**[39] 7200 4-9-9 **64** JamesMillman 6 69+
(Rod Millman) *hld up and bhd: hdwy 4f out: effrt on outer 3f out: rdn to chse ldng pair wl over 1f out: kpt on same pce* **5/2**[1]
-610 **4** *nk* **Gosforth Park**[24] 7426 5-9-3 **58** RobertWinston 4 63
(Mel Brittain) *trckd ldrs: effrt on outer 4f out: rdn along 3f out: drvn and one pce fr wl over 1f out* **7/2**[3]
4 **5** *shd* **Uncut Stone (IRE)**[14] 7536 3-9-4 **64** TomEaves 7 68
(Peter Niven) *chsd clr ldr: rdn along 4f out: outpcd and lost pl over 3f out: styd on fnl 2f: nrst fin* **25/1**
3045 **6** *8* **Bavarian Nordic (USA)**[27] 7077 6-9-6 **61** JoeFanning 2 53
(Richard Whitaker) *prom: chsd clr ldr 1/2-way: rdn 3f out: sn wknd* **16/1**
0030 **7** *5* **Miss Beat (IRE)**[7] 7604 5-9-2 **64** JasonHart(7) 1 48
(Declan Carroll) *hld up: hdwy and in tch over 4f out: rdn along over 3f out and sn wknd* **12/1**

2m 38.44s (-2.56) **Going Correction** -0.175s/f (Stan)
WFA 3 from 4yo+ 5lb 7 Ran SP% **111.4**
Speed ratings (Par 101): **101,99,98,98,98 93,89**
toteswingers:1&2:£1.20, 1&3:£2.60, 2&3:£2.20 CSF £15.93 CT £35.98 TOTE £3.40: £1.70, £2.70; EX 17.60 Trifecta £30.90 Pool: £387.76 - 9.26 winning units..
Owner Gary Williams **Bred** David And Elizabeth Kennedy **Trained** Lydiate, Merseyside

FOCUS
Another quite competitive handicap judged on official ratings, although the race was weakened by the absence of the likely favourite. It wasn't strong run. The winner took another step forward.
Irish Jugger(USA) Official explanation: jockey said gelding lost a front shoe

7690 SOUTHWELL-RACECOURSE.CO.UK APPRENTICE H'CAP (DIV I) 5f (F)
2:35 (2:35) (Class 6) (0-55,55) 3-Y-O+ **£1,704** (£503; £251) **Stalls** High

Form RPR
0400 **1** **Steel City Boy (IRE)**[3] 7641 8-8-10 **54** GeorgeChaloner(5) 4 65
(Garry Woodward) *cl up: led after 2f: rdn over 1f out: kpt on strly* **13/2**[3]
5405 **2** *2 ¼* **Gorgeous Goblin (IRE)**[177] 3049 4-8-7 **49** (vt) CharlesBishop(3) 10 52
(David C Griffiths) *chsd ldrs: hdwy 2f out: rdn wl over 1f out: kpt on same pce fnl f* **9/2**[2]
421 **3** *1 ¼* **Cheyenne Red (IRE)**[64] 6646 5-8-10 **52** JustinNewman(3) 8 50
(Michael Herrington) *led 2f: cl up: rdn over 2f out: kpt on same pce* **10/3**[1]
0034 **4** *½* **The Jailer**[37] 7224 8-9-2 **55** (p) RyanPowell 1 52
(John O'Shea) *cl up on outer: rdn along wl over 1f out: kpt on same pce* **15/2**
0400 **5** *nk* **Porthgwidden Beach (USA)**[21] 7459 3-8-7 **51** (t) NoelGarbutt(5) 9 47
(Anthony Middleton) *chsd ldrs: rdn 2f out: no imp appr fnl f* **20/1**
006 **6** *2 ½* **Georgian Silver**[55] 6874 3-8-4 **46** oh1 (b) NathanAlison(3) 5 33
(George Foster) *trckd ldrs: rdn and hung lft wl over 1f out: sn wknd* **16/1**
0000 **7** *1 ½* **Ronnie Howe**[37] 7230 7-8-7 **46** oh1 (bt) DavidKenny 11 27
(Roy Bowring) *chsd ldrs nr stands' rail: rdn along over 2f out: sn wknd* **50/1**
4004 **8** *nse* **Hootys Agogo**[21] 7460 3-8-1 **47** (p) MichaelKenny(7) 3 28
(Declan Carroll) *in tch: rdn along 1/2-way: sn wknd* **8/1**
0064 **9** *1* **Mucky Molly**[15] 7525 3-8-6 **50** JenniferFerguson(5) 2 27
(Olivia Maylam) *a in rr: rdn along and outpcd fr 1/2-way* **7/1**
2400 **10** *5* **Circuitous**[13] 7560 3-8-11 **50** (b) MatthewLawson 7 9
(Keith Dalgleish) *dwlt: sn rdn along in rr: bhd fr 1/2-way* **15/2**

57.97 secs (-1.73) **Going Correction** -0.35s/f (Stan) **10** Ran SP% **114.3**
Speed ratings (Par 101): **99,95,93,92,92 88,85,85,84,76**
toteswingers:1&2:£6.10, 1&3:£4.90, 2&3:£3.50 CSF £35.11 CT £116.79 TOTE £7.30: £1.90, £1.50, £1.50; EX 36.40 TRIFECTA Not won..
Owner J Medley **Bred** Mrs A B McDonnell **Trained** Maltby, S Yorks

FOCUS
The first leg of this moderate sprint handicap and a decisive success for Steel City Boy, who looks the best guide. It was the slower division but still a fair time for the grade.
Steel City Boy(IRE) Official explanation: trainer said, regarding apparent improvement in form, that the gelding appreciated the drop back in trip to 5f

7691 SOUTHWELL-RACECOURSE.CO.UK APPRENTICE H'CAP (DIV II) 5f (F)
3:10 (3:10) (Class 6) (0-55,55) 3-Y-O+ **£1,704** (£503; £251) **Stalls** High

Form RPR
2403 **1** **Wreningham**[23] 7429 6-8-8 **50** CharlesBishop(3) 11 64
(Pat Eddery) *racd nr stands' rail: trckd ldrs: cl up 1/2-way: sn led: rdn clr and edgd lft over 1f out: kpt on strly* **4/1**[1]
2046 **2** *2 ¾* **Sandwith**[28] 7366 8-9-1 **54** (p) LMcNiff 3 58
(George Foster) *chsd ldrs: hdwy 2f out: rdn over 1f out: edgd lft and kpt on fnl f* **7/1**[3]
0060 **3** *1 ½* **Lujiana**[46] 7071 6-8-3 **47** ShirleyTeasdale(5) 2 46
(Mel Brittain) *prom: effrt on outer 2f out: sn rdn: edgd lft and kpt on same pce fnl f* **6/1**[2]
4630 **4** *1 ¾* **Madam Isshe**[54] 6889 4-8-10 **52** NathanAlison(3) 1 44
(Mandy Rowland) *chsd ldrs: rdn along and outpcd bef 1/2-way: styd on u.p fr wl over 1f out* **6/1**[2]
-000 **5** *shd* **The Magic Of Rio**[262] 941 5-8-7 **46** oh1 AdamCarter 10 38
(John Balding) *led: rdn and hdd over 2f out: grad wknd appr fnl f* **14/1**
3400 **6** *¾* **Canadian Danehill (IRE)**[28] 7366 9-8-5 **49** (p) JakePayne(5) 4 38
(Robert Cowell) *prom: rdn along over 2f out: grad wknd* **7/1**[3]
0000 **7** *1* **Bird Dog**[46] 7071 5-8-2 **46** oh1 (v) DannyBrock(5) 7 32
(Phil McEntee) *dwlt: sn swtchd lft and in tch: rdn along over 2f out: sn wknd* **66/1**
00 **8** *4* **Simple Rhythm**[45] 7086 5-9-2 **55** (p) RyanPowell 6 26
(John Ryan) *a towards rr* **8/1**
0160 **9** *½* **Bathwick Xaara**[35] 7269 4-9-0 **53** MatthewLawson 8 23
(Jonathan Portman) *a towards rr* **9/1**
6000 **10** *1* **Hereselle (IRE)**[66] 6615 3-8-6 **50** GeorgeDowning(5) 5 16
(Michael Chapman) *a towards rr* **33/1**
11 *1 ¼* **Rise To Glory (IRE)**[55] 6885 3-8-7 **46** oh1 DavidKenny 9 —
(Denis P Quinn, Ire) *hld up: a towards rr* **7/1**[3]

57.63 secs (-2.07) **Going Correction** -0.35s/f (Stan) **11** Ran SP% **118.3**
Speed ratings (Par 101): **102,97,95,92,92 91,89,83,82,80 78**
toteswingers:1&2:£4.20, 1&3:£4.70, 2&3:£8.20 CSF £32.05 CT £170.87 TOTE £4.70: £2.40, £1.50, £2.60; EX 28.60 Trifecta £58.50 Pool: £355.25 - 4.49 winning units..
Owner Miss Emma L Owen **Bred** Executive Bloodlines Ltd **Trained** Nether Winchendon, Bucks

FOCUS
The second leg of this moderate sprint was run 0.34secs faster than the first in a good time for the grade. The winner rates back to something like his 2010 best.
T/Plt: £11.20 to a £1 stake. Pool:£27,612.04 - 1,790.94 winning tickets T/Qpdt: £8.70 to a £1 stake. Pool:£3,710.00 - 314.55 winning tickets JR

7625 WOLVERHAMPTON (A.W) (L-H)
Friday, December 9

OFFICIAL GOING: Standard
Wind: Fresh behind Weather: Cloudy

7692 TOTEPLACEPOT NURSERY 5f 20y(P)
3:40 (3:40) (Class 6) (0-65,62) 2-Y-O **£1,704** (£377; £377) **Stalls** Low

Form RPR
5630 **1** **Russian Bullet**[102] 5535 2-8-9 **50** FergusSweeney 2 55
(Jamie Osborne) *hld up: hdwy over 1f out: rdn to ld ins fnl f: edgd lft: r.o* **6/1**
4000 **2** *¾* **Alnair (IRE)**[34] 7294 2-9-2 **57** DanielTudhope 7 59
(Declan Carroll) *led: rdn over 1f out: hdd ins fnl f: styd on* **3/1**[1]
060 **2** *dht* **Look At Me Now**[91] 5889 2-9-4 **59** (v[1]) StephenCraine 3 61
(Jim Boyle) *chsd ldr: rdn and ev ch fr over 1f out: styd on* **3/1**[1]
060 **4** *2 ¾* **Justbookies Dotnet**[15] 7526 2-9-7 **62** ChrisCatlin 5 54
(Louise Best) *prom: pushed along over 3f out: rdn over 1f out: styd on same pce* **11/2**[3]
0503 **5** *hd* **Regal Lady**[7] 7607 2-9-3 **58** (v) MichaelStainton 1 50
(David Brown) *chsd ldrs: rdn over 1f out: styd on same pce* **6/1**
0300 **6** *2* **Claretintheblood (IRE)**[21] 7452 2-8-13 **54** TonyHamilton 4 38
(Richard Fahey) *rrd s: sn pushed along in rr: rdn over 1f out: n.d* **5/1**[2]
000 **7** *12* **Castalian Spring (IRE)**[15] 7526 2-8-11 **52** (p) AndreaAtzeni 6 —
(Robert Eddery) *chsd ldrs tl rdn 1/2-way: sn wknd* **25/1**

63.17 secs (0.87) **Going Correction** +0.075s/f (Slow) 7 Ran SP% **114.5**
Speed ratings (Par 94): **96,94,94,90,90 86,67**
toteswingers: 1& Look at Me Now £5.10, 1& Alnair £3.30, Look At Me Now & Alnair £3.00. TOTE £9.90: £5.10 Places: LAMN £1.20, Alnair £0.90. EXACTA: RB & LAMN £13.60, RB & A £13.10. CSF: RB & LAMN £12.18, RB & A £12.18..
Owner Martyn and Elaine Booth **Bred** Cranford Bloodstock Uk Ltd **Trained** Upper Lambourn, Berks

FOCUS
A weak nursery. It was run at a good pace and the first three pulled clear. The winner rates back to his early AW form.

NOTEBOOK

Russian Bullet looked a bit short of tactical speed in 5f nurseries on his last two starts in August, but he travelled more fluently with blinkers removed back from 102 days off and found a strong finishing effort out wide to get off the mark on the ninth attempt. He may be able to go from this improved effort and a step back up to 6f should suit. (op 11-2)

Alnair(IRE) showed very little in his first three nursery runs at 6f on slow turf but he was well-backed on this switch to 5f on Polytrack and gave it a good shot under an attacking ride but was worn down. He should be able to hold on over this trip, and is a half-brother to five winning sprinters, notably one-time smart performer Whitbarrow. (tchd 11-4)

Look At Me Now didn't do a great deal in three maidens but he showed improvement and fighting spirit to go close with a visor applied on AW/nursery debut. (tchd 11-4)

Justbookies Dotnet, well held at 66-1 or bigger in three 6f maidens, ran respectably on nursery debut. He looks on a stiff mark on what he has achieved, but is a half-brother to five Flat/hurdle winners and could be a late-developing type.

Regal Lady has a record of 232335 over this C&D but she has not really progressed with and without headgear and is 0-9. (op 5-1)

Claretintheblood(IRE) was always fighting a losing battle after rearing at the start.

7693 THE BLACK COUNTRY'S ONLY RACECOURSE MEDIAN AUCTION MAIDEN STKS — 5f 20y(P)

4:10 (4:11) (Class 6) 3-5-Y-O — **£1,704** (£503; £251) **Stalls** Low

Form — RPR

66 **1** — **Cri Na Mara (IRE)**[21] 7460 3-8-12 44 ....(t) MartinHarley 2 — 57
(Mark Michael McNiff, Ire) *a.p: chsd ldr wl over 1f out: rdn to ld ins fnl f: r.o* **12/1**

6000 **2** *3 1/2* **Deveze (IRE)**[11] 7565 3-8-12 45 ....(b[1]) RichardKingscote 10 — 44
(Milton Bradley) *s.i.s: swtchd lft sn after s: hdwy over 1f out: r.o to go 2nd towards fin: no ch w wnr* **16/1**

6043 **3** *1 1/4* **Good Timin'**[21] 7460 3-9-3 50 ....(v) MichaelStainton 12 — 45
(David Brown) *chsd ldr tl led 3f out: rdn and edgd rt fr over 1f out: hdd and no ex ins fnl f: lost 2nd towards fin* **10/3**[1]

6000 **4** *1 1/4* **Running Water**[21] 7460 3-8-13 42 ow1 .... PaddyAspell 4 — 36
(Hugh McWilliams) *hld up: hdwy over 1f out: r.o: nt trble ldrs* **40/1**

-430 **5** *1/2* **Lisselton Cross**[156] 3721 3-9-3 53 .... LukeMorris 8 — 38
(Martin Bosley) *mid-div: hdwy 1/2-way: rdn over 1f out: no ex fnl f* **7/2**[2]

0000 **6** *1 3/4* **Our Princess Ellie (USA)**[20] 7485 3-8-7 45 .... MarkCoumbe[(5)] 7 — 27
(Derek Shaw) *sn pushed along in rr: nvr nrr* **11/2**

0060 **7** *3/4* **Stoneacre Joe Joe**[90] 5941 3-9-3 37 .... RobbieFitzpatrick 13 — 29
(Peter Grayson) *dwlt: outpcd: nvr nrr* **100/1**

3060 **8** *3/4* **Cara Carmela**[62] 6694 3-8-9 45 ....(t) RyanClark[(3)] 6 — 22
(Stuart Williams) *chsd ldrs tl rdn and wknd over 1f out* **6/1**

6003 **9** *1/2* **Dolly Bay**[16] 7511 3-8-9 50 .... AdamBeschizza[(3)] 1 — 20
(Julia Feilden) *led 2f: rdn 1/2-way: wknd fnl f* **4/1**[3]

3500 **10** *3 1/4* **Una Vita Pius (IRE)**[181] 2918 3-8-12 47 .... FergusSweeney 5 — —
(Patrick Gilligan) *sn outpcd* **20/1**

00 **11** *6* **Tunza The Lion**[16] 7511 4-9-3 0 .... NeilChalmers 3 — —
(Bruce Hellier) *prom tl wknd wl over 1f out* **100/1**

62.47 secs (0.17) **Going Correction** +0.075s/f (Slow) — **11** Ran SP% **117.7**
Speed ratings (Par 101): **101,95,93,91,90 87,86,85,84,79 69**
toteswingers: 1&2 £18.20, 1&3 £8.20, 2&3 £11.20. CSF £181.15 TOTE £16.40: £5.30, £7.30, £1.10; EX 117.60.
Owner Terry McGowan **Bred** Patrick Mulligan **Trained** Sligo, Co. Sligo

FOCUS

There was an open market for this very modest maiden which was won by a 44-rated filly who was much improved.

7694 TOTEQUADPOT CLAIMING STKS — 5f 216y(P)

4:40 (4:40) (Class 5) 2-Y-O — **£2,264** (£673; £336; £168) **Stalls** Low

Form — RPR

3005 **1** — **Faraway**[27] 7390 2-8-3 70 ....(v) LukeMorris 4 — 69
(David Evans) *hld up: nt clr run over 2f out: hdwy sn after: led over 1f out: rdn clr* **2/5**[1]

0440 **2** *7* **I'm Still The Man (IRE)**[102] 5562 2-8-11 67 .... WilliamCarson 1 — 56
(Bill Turner) *trckd ldrs: racd keenly: rdn and ev ch over 1f out: hung rt and wknd ins fnl f* **11/4**[2]

0450 **3** *1 1/4* **Well Wishes**[119] 5005 2-7-9 45 .... KieranO'Neill[(3)] 5 — 39
(Bryan Smart) *led early: chsd ldr and sn pushed along: hung lft 4f out: rdn over 1f out: wknd ins fnl f* **14/1**

0000 **4** *1 1/2* **Chateau Lola**[14] 7541 2-8-2 37 ....(v) JimmyQuinn 6 — 39
(Derek Shaw) *hld up: pushed along over 3f out: rdn over 2f out: wknd wl over 1f out* **100/1**

004 **5** *4* **Red Socks (IRE)**[21] 7451 2-8-0 59 ....(v[1]) NataliaGemelova[(3)] 3 — 28
(Gay Kelleway) *sn led: rdn and hdd over 1f out: wknd fnl f* **9/1**[3]

1m 16.25s (1.25) **Going Correction** +0.075s/f (Slow) — **5** Ran SP% **115.8**
Speed ratings (Par 96): **94,84,83,81,75**
toteswinger: 1&2 £1.90. CSF £2.03 TOTE £1.10: £1.02, £1.50; EX 2.30.Faraway was claimed by Ron Harris for £5,000.
Owner Nick Shutts **Bred** Stourbank Stud **Trained** Pandy, Monmouths

FOCUS

The 70-rated odds-on favourite powered clear in this uncompetitive claimer. A weak race, rated around the winner and third.

NOTEBOOK

Faraway won 6f sellers at Haydock in June and over C&D in September. His stamina had not looked entirely convincing at 7f/1m in varied company on his last four starts, but he had leading form claims back in a 6f claimer and negotiated his through some potential traffic problems before surging clear to improve his record to 3-15. (tchd 1-2)

I'm Still The Man(IRE) struggled in four runs in varied company after powering to a 25-1 success against the far rail at Sandown on debut in June. He was not disgraced conceding weight to a higher rated rival on this return from 102 days off, but he didn't finish far ahead of a 45-rated rival and still has quite a bit to prove. (op 4-1)

Well Wishes ran as well as could be expected with plenty to find on official figures on return from 119 days off. (op 12-1)

Chateau Lola showed nothing in three maidens and a nursery but there was a minor glimmer of ability, plugging on late at a big price in this claimer.

Red Socks(IRE) was well below form in two 5f AW maidens since returning from four months off and it was a similar story in a first-time visor on this switch to claiming company. (tchd 8-1)

7695 ENJOY THE PARTY PACK GROUP OFFER H'CAP (DIV I) — 7f 32y(P)

5:10 (5:11) (Class 6) (0-65,77) 3-Y-O+ — **£1,704** (£503; £251) **Stalls** High

Form — RPR

3405 **1** — **Orpens Peach (IRE)**[42] 7141 4-9-3 61 .... MartinHarley 7 — 73
(Seamus Fahey, Ire) *hld up: hdwy 2f out: rdn to ld ins fnl f: r.o* **9/1**

0600 **2** *1* **Moral Issue**[55] 6867 3-9-3 64 .... DaleSwift[(3)] 10 — 73
(Ian McInnes) *chsd ldrs: rdn and ev ch ins fnl f: styd on same pce* **28/1**

0211 **3** *2* **One Way Or Another (AUS)**[4] 7636 8-10-0 77 12ex(b) MatthewCosham[(5)] 6 — 81
(David Evans) *rn wout declared tongue strap: s.i.s: hld up: hdwy on outer over 2f out: rdn over 1f out: styd on: wnt 3rd nr fin: nt rch ldrs* **11/4**[1]

0004 **4** *1/2* **Anjomarba (IRE)**[8] 7591 4-9-4 62 .... KirstyMilczarek 12 — 64
(Conor Dore) *led: rdn over 1f out: hdd and no ex ins fnl f* **14/1**

5030 **5** *1 1/4* **Music Festival (USA)**[55] 6869 4-9-7 65 .... DanielTudhope 1 — 64
(Jim Goldie) *hld up: rdn over 1f out: styd on: nt trble ldrs* **9/2**

5343 **6** *1 1/2* **Transmit (IRE)**[3] 7648 4-9-2 60 ....(b) DuranFentiman 4 — 55
(Tim Easterby) *hld up: hdwy u.p over 1f out: no ex fnl f* **3/1**[2]

/405 **7** *1 1/2* **The Ducking Stool**[9] 7581 4-8-4 51 oh6 ....(p) AdamBeschizza[(3)] 3 — 42
(Julia Feilden) *s.i.s: sn pushed along in rr: nvr nrr* **33/1**

0066 **8** *2 1/2* **Meydan Style (USA)**[21] 7463 5-8-7 51 oh6 .... JoeFanning 5 — 35
(Bruce Hellier) *chsd ldr tl rdn over 1f out: wknd fnl f* **25/1**

2334 **9** *3/4* **Fluctuation (IRE)**[2] 7655 3-8-7 54 ow2 ....(v) RyanClark[(3)] 8 — 36
(Ian Williams) *s.s: hld up: rdn over 1f out: sn wknd* **4/1**[3]

0000 **10** *1* **Lake Chini (IRE)**[6] 7629 9-9-0 58 ....(b) JamesSullivan 2 — 37
(Michael Easterby) *chsd ldrs: rdn over 2f out: wknd over 1f out* **50/1**

0000 **11** *10* **Let It Rock (IRE)**[25] 7412 4-8-9 53 .... MartinLane 11 — —
(Mrs K Burke) *chsd ldr: rdn over 2f out: sn wknd* **33/1**

1m 29.33s (-0.27) **Going Correction** +0.075s/f (Slow) — **11** Ran SP% **121.7**
Speed ratings (Par 101): **104,102,100,100,98 96,95,92,91,90 78**
toteswingers: 1&2 £21.30, 1&3 £5.90, 2&3 £14.90. CSF £240.73 CT £884.57 TOTE £16.30: £5.30, £13.30, £1.10; EX 260.60.
Owner Mrs V Maxwell **Bred** R Grehan & H Maxwell **Trained** Monasterevin, Co. Kildare

FOCUS

A minor handicap run at a fair pace and 1.06 seconds quicker than the second division. A clear personal best from the generally progressive winner.

7696 ENJOY THE PARTY PACK GROUP OFFER H'CAP (DIV II) — 7f 32y(P)

5:40 (5:40) (Class 6) (0-65,69) 3-Y-O+ — **£1,704** (£503; £251) **Stalls** High

Form — RPR

4420 **1** — **Wigram's Turn (USA)**[6] 7632 6-9-2 60 ....(t) PaddyAspell 1 — 72
(Michael Easterby) *chsd ldrs: nt clr run and swtchd lft over 1f out: rdn to ld ins fnl f: r.o* **11/2**[3]

0431 **2** *2 1/4* **Dashing Eddie (IRE)**[13] 7560 3-8-10 54 ....(p) TonyHamilton 2 — 60
(Kevin Ryan) *sn led: hdd over 5f out: led again over 2f out: rdn and hdd ins fnl f: styd on same pce* **7/2**[2]

0000 **3** *nk* **Cwmni**[66] 6609 5-8-7 51 oh4 .... LukeMorris 9 — 56+
(Bryn Palling) *hld up: hdwy u.p over 1f out: r.o: nrst fin* **33/1**

5311 **4** *1* **Berbice (IRE)**[8] 7591 6-9-8 69 6ex .... JulieBurke[(3)] 6 — 71
(Linda Perratt) *s.s: hld up: hdwy over 2f out: rdn ins fnl f: styd on same pce* **3/1**[1]

5604 **5** *3/4* **Garstang**[16] 7517 8-9-7 65 .... JoeFanning 12 — 65
(Bruce Hellier) *plld hrd and prom: rdn and hung lft fr over 1f out: styd on* **11/1**

0030 **6** *hd* **Fleetwoodsands (IRE)**[21] 7455 4-9-3 61 ....(t) RichardKingscote 5 — 61
(Milton Bradley) *trckd ldrs: plld hrd: wnt 2nd over 2f out: rdn over 1f out: hung lft and no ex fnl f* **3/1**[1]

2060 **7** *1 1/2* **Efistorm**[9] 7588 10-9-5 63 .... KirstyMilczarek 11 — 59
(Conor Dore) *hld up: r.o ins fnl f: nvr trbld ldrs* **14/1**

0630 **8** *4 1/2* **Tro Nesa (IRE)**[24] 7419 3-9-4 62 ....(p) TomEaves 4 — 46
(Ann Duffield) *prom: pushed along 1/2-way: wknd over 1f out* **12/1**

000 **9** *3 3/4* **Chambers (IRE)**[49] 6999 5-8-8 52 .... NeilChalmers 7 — 26
(Bruce Hellier) *hld up: rdn over 2f out: wknd wl over 1f out* **80/1**

0060 **10** *2 1/2* **Colamandis**[21] 7462 4-8-0 51 oh6 .... VictorSantos[(7)] 8 — 18
(Hugh McWilliams) *prom: led over 5f out: hung rt and hdd over 2f out: wknd over 1f out* **100/1**

00-0 **11** *13* **Fire Commander**[21] 7460 3-8-7 51 oh6 .... ChrisCatlin 3 — —
(Brian Baugh) *hld up: a in rr: bhd fnl 3f* **150/1**

1m 30.39s (0.79) **Going Correction** +0.075s/f (Slow) — **11** Ran SP% **116.1**
Speed ratings (Par 101): **98,95,95,93,93 92,91,86,81,78 64**
toteswingers: 1&2 £4.80, 1&3 £16.40, 2&3 £17.30. CSF £24.65 CT £594.91 TOTE £5.20: £1.40, £1.60, £7.10; EX 30.40.
Owner Steve Hull **Bred** Lone Cedar Thoroughbred Holdings, Llc **Trained** Sheriff Hutton, N Yorks

FOCUS

There was a decisive winner in this steadily-run second division of a minor handicap, finally taking advantage of a reduced mark. It was the slower division by 1.06 seconds.

7697 TOTEEXACTA NURSERY — 1m 141y(P)

6:10 (6:12) (Class 6) (0-60,66) 2-Y-O — **£1,704** (£503; £251) **Stalls** Low

Form — RPR

0531 **1** — **Maybeagrey**[11] 7569 2-9-13 66 6ex .... DuranFentiman 13 — 71
(Tim Easterby) *chsd ldrs: rdn to ld ins fnl f: jst hld on* **1/1**[1]

0406 **2** *shd* **Quixote**[11] 7569 2-9-4 57 ....(b[1]) TomQueally 8 — 62
(Clive Brittain) *sn pushed along in rr: hdwy over 3f out: rdn over 1f out: ev ch ins fnl f: styd on* **11/2**[3]

4505 **3** *1 1/2* **Stag Hill (IRE)**[23] 7432 2-9-6 59 .... LiamKeniry 1 — 61
(Sylvester Kirk) *led over 7f out: rdn and edgd rt over 1f out: hdd and unable qck ins fnl f* **4/1**[2]

0060 **4** *7* **Cat Queen**[65] 6628 2-8-13 55 .... NataliaGemelova[(3)] 5 — 42
(Gay Kelleway) *chsd ldrs: rdn over 2f out: wknd over 1f out* **16/1**

5000 **5** *7* **Meet Joe Black (IRE)**[24] 7421 2-8-6 45 ....(v) LukeMorris 7 — 18
(David Evans) *mid-div: drvn along over 4f out: wknd 2f out* **66/1**

5650 **6** *1 1/4* **Chorister Girl**[65] 6627 2-8-11 50 .... TonyHamilton 2 — 20
(Richard Ford) *led 1f: chsd ldr: rdn over 2f out: wknd over 1f out* **16/1**

0000 **7** *3 1/4* **Awesome Rock (IRE)**[11] 7569 2-8-12 51 .... ChrisCatlin 12 — 14
(Louise Best) *hld up: hdwy over 3f out: rdn and wknd over 2f out* **66/1**

000 **8** *1/2* **Princess Tamina (IRE)**[13] 7559 2-9-0 53 .... GrahamGibbons 6 — 15
(Mark Brisbourne) *chsd ldrs: rdn over 3f out: sn wknd* **18/1**

0000 **9** *1 1/4* **My New Angel (IRE)**[93] 5817 2-8-7 46 .... JamesSullivan 10 — 5
(Paul Green) *hmpd sn after s: n.d* **50/1**

000 **10** *1* **Pre Catalan**[45] 7082 2-9-0 53 ....(v[1]) TomMcLaughlin 4 — 10
(Ed Dunlop) *s.i.s: sn pushed along in rr: bhd fnl 3f* **12/1**

0000 **11** *14* **The Games Gone (IRE)**[24] 7421 2-8-3 45 .... KieranO'Neill[(3)] 3 — —
(David Evans) *s.i.s: sn prom: rdn 1/2-way: sn wknd* **66/1**

000 **12** *2 1/2* **Fine Finale**[20] 7493 2-7-13 45 ....(b[1]) RaulDaSilva[(7)] 9 — —
(Jeremy Gask) *hld up: bhd fnl 6f* **28/1**

1m 51.72s (1.22) **Going Correction** +0.075s/f (Slow) — **12** Ran SP% **120.0**
Speed ratings (Par 94): **97,96,95,89,83 82,79,78,77,76 64,62**
toteswingers: 1&2 £2.70, 1&3 £2.30, 2&3 £3.40. CSF £6.64 CT £16.61 TOTE £2.50: £1.30, £2.20, £1.10; EX 8.30.
Owner Habton Farms **Bred** J K Beckitt And Son **Trained** Great Habton, N Yorks
■ Stewards' Enquiry : Liam Keniry caution: careless riding.

FOCUS

The three market leaders pulled a long way clear in this nursery and the form looks solid. The race lacked depth.

NOTEBOOK

Maybeagrey found plenty of improvement on nursery debut when beating a well-backed, similarly unexposed rival over C&D last Monday. She had to work hard to defy a penalty and complete a double, but she showed a good attitude to just hold on. A 20,000gns half-sister to 1m-1m3f Flat/2m-2m2f hurdle/chase winner River Logic, she could continue to progress and should stay quite a bit further than this in time. (op 5-6)

Quixote was over 7l behind Maybeagrey here last time, but he responded well to blinkers and nearly reversed the form. This was a much-improved effort by a lightly raced Singspiel gelding who could be suited by going up in trip. (op 8-1)

Stag Hill(IRE) is basically exposed but he has not been beaten far under forcing tactics in AW nurseries on his last two starts. (op 5-1)

Cat Queen has a very patchy six-race profile, but she has looked short of speed over 6f-7f and this half-sister to four winners at up to 1m3f, shaped with a bit of promise stepped up in trip.

Meet Joe Black(IRE) couldn't find any improvement stepped up in trip with a visor applied and has been beaten 11l+ at big prices in all of his six starts.

My New Angel(IRE) Official explanation: jockey said filly was hampered at start

7698 TIPSTERSUITE.COM TIPSTER AUTOMATION SOFTWARE H'CAP 1m 1f 103y(P)
6:40 (6:40) (Class 6) (0-60,64) 3-Y-O+ **£1,704** (£503; £251) **Stalls** Low

Form				RPR
5501	1		**Maven**[7] 7610 3-9-9 **64** 6ex. DuranFentiman 6	73+
			(Tim Easterby) *plld hrd: led over 8f out: hdd 2f out: rallied to ld nr fin* **4/1**[2]	
4002	2	hd	**Edgware Road**[7] 7610 3-9-3 **58**. (b[1]) AdamKirby 7	66+
			(Paul Rich) *trckd ldrs: plld hrd: led 2f out: rdn ins fnl f: hdd nr fin* **15/8**[1]	
0300	3	2	**Corrib (IRE)**[11] 7571 8-9-2 **55**. (p) DavidProbert 5	59
			(Bryn Palling) *hld up: rdn over 2f out: swtchd lft and r.o ins fnl f: nt rch ldrs* **40/1**	
25	4	hd	**Senor Tommie (IRE)**[66] 1665 5-8-12 **51**. (t) MartinHarley 8	55
			(Seamus Fahey, Ire) *prom: rdn over 1f out: styd on* **14/1**	
0025	5	hd	**Celtic Step**[41] 7178 7-9-2 **58**. DaleSwift(3) 13	61
			(Peter Niven) *led 1f: chsd wnr tl rdn over 2f out: hung lft ins fnl f: styd on* **20/1**	
0-00	6	1 1/4	**Laser Blazer**[14] 7537 3-8-13 **54**. FergusSweeney 9	55
			(Jeremy Gask) *stdd s: hld up: r.o ins fnl f: nrst fin* **16/1**	
3626	7	1/2	**Bidable**[14] 7538 7-9-4 **57**. LukeMorris 4	56
			(Bryn Palling) *hld up: rdn over 2f out: r.o ins fnl f: nrst fin* **20/1**	
0001	8	hd	**Barton Bounty**[11] 7571 4-9-6 **59** 6ex. TomEaves 12	58
			(Peter Niven) *hld up: pushed along 3f out: rdn and swtchd rt over 1f out: r.o ins fnl f: nrst fin* **10/1**	
0506	9	1 3/4	**Diplomasi**[45] 7085 3-9-4 **59**. TomQueally 2	54
			(Clive Brittain) *chsd ldrs: rdn over 2f out: wknd fnl f* **15/2**[3]	
0040	10	3/4	**Kai Mook**[16] 7522 4-8-12 **56**. MarkCoumbe(5) 3	50
			(Roger Ingram) *prom: rdn over 2f out: wknd over 1f out* **14/1**	
000	11	5	**Monsieur Broughton**[91] 5900 3-9-0 **58**. AdamBeschizza(3) 11	41
			(Willie Musson) *hld up: pushed along and hdwy over 3f out: wknd over 1f out* **33/1**	
5041	12	19	**Valley Tiger**[49] 7005 3-9-4 **59**. TonyHamilton 10	—
			(Richard Fahey) *hld up in tch: plld hrd: rdn and wknd over 2f out* **8/1**	

2m 3.00s (1.30) **Going Correction** +0.075s/f (Slow)
WFA 3 from 4yo+ 2lb **12** Ran **SP% 120.9**
Speed ratings (Par 101): **97,96,95,94,94 93,93,92,91,90 86,69**
toteswingers: 1&2 £3.20, 1&3 £40.20, 2&3 £20.70. CSF £11.52 CT £268.70 TOTE £7.40: £2.30, £1.10, £14.00; EX 10.60.

Owner Habton Farms **Bred** Habton Farms **Trained** Great Habton, N Yorks

FOCUS

A competitive handicap, involving three last-time-out winners. The pace was steady but there was tight finish between the two market leaders, who can probably do a bit better yet. The winner confirmed latest C&D form with the second.

7699 TOTETRIFECTA H'CAP 1m 4f 50y(P)
7:10 (7:11) (Class 4) (0-85,85) 3-Y-O+ **£4,204** (£1,251; £625; £312) **Stalls** Low

Form				RPR
3011	1		**William Haigh (IRE)**[13] 7558 3-9-3 **83**. JimCrowley 9	91+
			(Alan Swinbank) *hld up: hdwy over 2f out: rdn over 1f out: styd on to ld nr fin* **3/1**[1]	
0511	2	3/4	**Raucous Behaviour (USA)**[35] 7272 3-9-1 **81**. DavidProbert 3	88
			(George Prodromou) *a.p: chsd ldr over 3f out: led 2f out: sn rdn: hdd nr fin* **6/1**	
2144	3	1/2	**Pertemps Networks**[41] 7162 7-9-1 **76**. PaddyAspell 12	82
			(Michael Easterby) *chsd ldr tl led over 3f out: hdd 2f out: rdn and ev ch ins fnl f: no ex nr fin* **22/1**	
5514	4	4 1/2	**Art Scholar (IRE)**[35] 7272 4-9-4 **79**. LukeMorris 1	78
			(Michael Appleby) *hld up: hdwy over 2f out: sn rdn: styd on same pce fr over 1f out* **9/2**[3]	
5541	5	1/2	**Dark Dune (IRE)**[25] 7413 3-8-13 **79**. DuranFentiman 4	77+
			(Tim Easterby) *hld up: hdwy over 1f out: nvr trbld ldrs* **7/2**[2]	
1502	6	2 3/4	**Brouhaha**[35] 7272 7-9-3 **81**. RossAtkinson(3) 2	75
			(Tom Dascombe) *chsd ldrs: rdn over 2f out: wknd over 1f out* **14/1**	
0-00	7	3 1/2	**Nezhenka**[48] 7017 4-9-7 **82**. JoeFanning 5	70
			(Mark Johnston) *hld up: rdn over 2f out: nvr nrr* **13/2**	
2500	8	1/2	**Guest Book (IRE)**[13] 7558 4-9-3 **83**. DavidKenny(5) 6	70
			(Michael Scudamore) *s.i.s: hld up: rdn over 3f out: nvr on terms* **40/1**	
5400	9	9	**The Lock Master (IRE)**[13] 7558 4-9-1 **76**. NeilChalmers 11	49
			(Michael Appleby) *hld up: rdn over 3f out: sn wknd* **33/1**	
2305	10	11	**Sir Boss (IRE)**[29] 7347 6-9-10 **85**. TomEaves 10	40
			(Michael Mullineaux) *s.i.s: sn prom: rdn and wknd over 2f out* **33/1**	
1060	11	3 3/4	**Jeer (IRE)**[141] 4237 7-8-5 **73**. (b) DavidSimmonson(7) 7	22
			(Michael Easterby) *set stdy pce tl hdd over 3f out: wknd over 2f out* **66/1**	

2m 40.45s (-0.65) **Going Correction** +0.075s/f (Slow)
WFA 3 from 4yo+ 5lb **11** Ran **SP% 113.9**
Speed ratings (Par 105): **105,104,104,101,100 99,96,96,90,83 80**
toteswingers: 1&2 £4.60, 1&3 £15.30, 2&3 £18.20. CSF £19.43 CT £328.78 TOTE £3.20: £1.50, £2.30, £9.00; EX 24.30 Trifecta £198.70 Pool: £510.19 - 1.90 winning units..

Owner Shropshire Wolves II **Bred** Mrs C L Weld **Trained** Melsonby, N Yorks

FOCUS

They went a steady pace in this decent handicap and the progressive winner did well to reel in the breakaway front pair who finished clear of the rest. The bare form is set around the third, with another step forward from the winner.

T/Plt: £42.40 to a £1 stake. Pool:£74,929.81 - 1,287.55 winning tickets T/Qpdt: £6.60to a £1 stake. Pool:£9,815.55 - 1,095.69 winning tickets CR

7700 - 7707a (Foreign Racing) - See Raceform Interactive

7684 SOUTHWELL (L-H)
Saturday, December 10

OFFICIAL GOING: Standard

Wind: Light across Weather: Cloudy and dry

7708 BETFRED BUNDLES NURSERY 1m (F)
12:05 (12:05) (Class 6) (0-65,64) 2-Y-O **£1,704** (£503; £251) **Stalls** Low

Form				RPR
4553	1		**Chrissycross (IRE)**[24] 7432 2-9-2 **59**. (b[1]) AdamKirby 8	70+
			(Roger Teal) *cl up: led wl over 2f out: rdn clr over 1f out: styd on strly* **6/1**[3]	
500	2	12	**Shredding (IRE)**[22] 7454 2-8-11 **54**. (b[1]) JoeFanning 10	37
			(Edward Vaughan) *trckd ldrs: effrt over 2f out: sn rdn and sltly outpcd: styd on wl fnl f: no ch w wnr* **7/1**	
0002	3	1/2	**Astroscarlet**[24] 7432 2-8-6 **49**. JimmyQuinn 4	31
			(Mark H Tompkins) *in tch: pushed along 1/2-way: rdn wl over 2f out: plugged on u.p appr fnl f* **3/1**[2]	
0202	4	shd	**Man Of My Word**[37] 7242 2-9-6 **63**. (p) GrahamGibbons 6	45
			(David Nicholls) *led: pushed along 3f out: sn hdd and rdn: wknd over 1f out* **10/11**[1]	
065	5	4 1/2	**Miss Ella Jade**[25] 7422 2-8-12 **58**. AmyRyan(3) 3	30
			(Richard Whitaker) *in tch: rdn along wl over 3f out: sn outpcd* **14/1**	
0500	6	41	**Bit A Craic**[45] 7108 2-7-9 **45**. (t) BradleyBosley(7) 9	—
			(John Ryan) *dwlt: sn outpcd and a bhd* **50/1**	

1m 42.4s (-1.30) **Going Correction** -0.125s/f (Stan) **6** Ran **SP% 112.8**
Speed ratings (Par 94): **101,89,88,88,83 42**
Tote Swingers: 1&2 £3.30, 1&3 £2.00, 2&3 £3.10 CSF £45.36 CT £149.10 TOTE £7.10: £2.30, £3.50; EX 35.80 Trifecta £155.30 Part won. Pool: 209.95 - 0.74 winning units..

Owner John Morton **Bred** David Watson & Shane Horan **Trained** Ashtead, Surrey

FOCUS

An uncompetitive nursery, but a decent performance in the context of the grade from the wide-margin winner. According to hand times, she recorded the quickest time of four races at the trip, including going around half a second faster than the later Class 6 handicap for older horses.

NOTEBOOK

Chrissycross(IRE) ◆ evidently took extremely well to the Fibresand at the first attempt. The fitting of blinkers, in place of the cheekpieces/hood combination, also seemingly helped and she is one to keep on side at this track. She will, though, have to prove she can be as effective elsewhere. (op 4-1)

Shredding(IRE) raced enthusiastically in first-time blinkers but was no match at all for the winner and just plugged on for a distant second. He won't always run into such an improved type at this level. (tchd 9-1)

Astroscarlet, 2lb higher than when runner-up over this trip on Polytrack last time, was never really travelling on this switch to Fibresand. She's a half-sister a winner on the surface, but her sire is now 0-24 here. (op 7-2)

Man Of My Word, 3lb higher than when runner-up over 7f here last time and fitted with cheekpieces for the first time, didn't travel all that strongly and was beaten before the straight. He might not get 1m, but wouldn't have won at any trip on this occasion. (op 5-4)

7709 E B F MIRROR PUNTERS CLUB MAIDEN STKS 1m (F)
12:40 (12:40) (Class 5) 2-Y-O **£3,234** (£962; £481; £240) **Stalls** Low

Form				RPR
33	1		**Sparkling Portrait**[21] 7493 2-9-3 0. TonyHamilton 6	80+
			(Richard Fahey) *prom: hdwy to ld wl over 2f out: sn pushed clr: easily* **6/4**[1]	
0	2	12	**Chankillo**[43] 7133 2-9-3 0. EddieAhern 7	50
			(Mark H Tompkins) *hld up and bhd: hdwy over 3f out: rdn 2f out: styd on appr fnl f: no ch w wnr* **33/1**	
	3	3	**Saslong** 2-9-3 0. JoeFanning 1	44
			(Mark Johnston) *cl up on inner: led over 4f out: rdn and hdd wl over 2f out: outpcd by wnr wl over 1f out: lost 2nd ins fnl f* **11/4**[2]	
03	4	4 1/2	**Our Ivor**[18] 7501 2-9-3 0. NeilChalmers 2	33
			(Michael Appleby) *led 3f: cl up: rdn along 3f out: grad wknd* **25/1**	
33	5	1	**Yours Ever**[60] 6776 2-8-12 0. SebSanders 3	26
			(Sir Mark Prescott Bt) *sn rdn along and in tch: drvn over 3f out: sn outpcd and bhd* **3/1**[3]	
0	6	5	**Marshall Art**[21] 7494 2-9-0 0. MichaelO'Connell(3) 4	19
			(John Quinn) *chsd ldrs: rdn along over 3f out: sn wknd* **100/1**	
	7	16	**Gabrial's Hope (FR)** 2-9-3 0. AdamKirby 5	—
			(Mark Johnston) *chsd ldrs: rdn along 1/2-way: sn wknd* **7/1**	

1m 43.36s (-0.34) **Going Correction** -0.125s/f (Stan) **7** Ran **SP% 111.9**
Speed ratings (Par 96): **96,84,81,76,75 70,54**
Tote Swingers: 1&2 £8.60, 1&3 £2.20, 2&3 £11.10 CSF £50.94 TOTE £2.30: £1.20, £9.00; EX 37.60.

Owner Mike Browne **Bred** Dukes Stud & Overbury Stallions Ltd **Trained** Musley Bank, N Yorks

FOCUS

An uncompetitive maiden run in a time around a second slower than the earlier Class 6 nursery.

NOTEBOOK

Sparkling Portrait, trying Fibresand for the first time, didn't face much competition and won with quite a bit in hand to confirm the promise he'd shown on turf and Polytrack. While he didn't achieve much, he has scope and should make a fair enough handicapper. (op 15-8)

Chankillo's sire is now 1-67 here, so this performance might need upgrading. He didn't show much on his debut over 7f at Newmarket, but he's a half-brother to the stable's 1m4f Listed winner Brushing and is clearly not short of stamina. (op 28-1)

Saslong, a 19,000gns first foal of a 1m2f Listed winner, travelled well to a point but raced towards the inside from most of the way, which is rarely ideal, and gradually faded. He can improve. (op 5-2 tchd 3-1)

Our Ivor again showed some ability without seeing his race out. Handicaps are now an option. (tchd 20-1)

Yours Ever was beaten leaving the back straight and ran nowhere near her previous level on this first taste of Fibresand. (op 9-4)

7710 BETFRED WHEN BOTH TEAMS SCORE (S) STKS 1m (F)
1:15 (1:15) (Class 6) 3-Y-O+ **£1,704** (£503; £251) **Stalls** Low

Form				RPR
506	1		**River Ardeche**[32] 6309 6-9-1 53. JoeFanning 5	71
			(Tracy Waggott) *mde all: set stdy pce: qcknd wl over 2f out: rdn over 1f out: edgd rt and styd on wl fnl f* **20/1**	
5202	2	4	**Marvo**[8] 7600 7-9-1 66. (b) EddieAhern 4	62
			(Mark H Tompkins) *trckd ldrs: hdwy to chse wnr 3f out: rdn 2f out: drvn and no imp fnl f* **7/1**[3]	
662	3	nse	**Salerosa (IRE)**[30] 7352 6-8-10 72. (p) TomEaves 2	57
			(Ann Duffield) *hld up towards rr: hdwy on inner 3f out: rdn to chse ldng pair over 2f out: drvn over 1f out: kpt on same pce* **7/4**[2]	

0401 **4** 2 3/4 **Mcconnell (USA)**[25] 7424 6-9-7 73 (b) FergusSweeney 3 62
(Gary Moore) *hld up towards rr: hdwy 1/2-way: chsd ldrs over 2f out: sn rdn: edgd lft and btn wl over 1f out* **11/10**[1]

10 **5** 13 **Cheers Buddy (IRE)**[43] 7150 3-9-6 76 (b) TonyCulhane 7 32
(John Joseph Hanlon, Ire) *chsd wnr: rdn along 3f out: wknd over 2f out* **16/1**

6 16 **Russian Bay (IRE)**[76] 6393 5-9-1 0 (t) ChrisCatlin 6 —
(John Joseph Hanlon, Ire) *dwlt: in tch: rdn along wl over 3f out and sn wknd* **50/1**

0 **7** 13 **La Danse Champetre**[105] 5469 3-8-9 0 RobbieFitzpatrick 1 —
(Charles Smith) *chsd ldrs: rdn along and lost pl 1/2-way: sn bhd* **125/1**

1m 43.92s (0.22) **Going Correction** -0.125s/f (Stan)
WFA 3 from 5yo+ 1lb 7 Ran SP% **109.9**
Speed ratings (Par 101): **93,89,88,86,73 57,44**
Tote Swingers: 1&2 £5.00, 1&3 £4.20, 2&3 £2.10 CSF £137.42 TOTE £30.20: £5.50, £3.20; EX 94.30.No bid for the winner.
Owner Littlethorpe Park Racing **Bred** D R Tucker **Trained** Spennymoor, Co Durham

FOCUS
A modest seller and, typically for the grade, a few of these underperformed. The pace, set by the winner, seemed modest and the time was the slowest of four races at the trip, including two juvenile events. The form looks weak but the winner used to be a lot better than this and is rated to something like his latter 2010 form.

7711 BETFRED GOALS GALORE H'CAP 1m (F)
1:50 (1:50) (Class 6) (0-65,65) 3-Y-O+ £1,704 (£503; £251) Stalls Low

Form RPR

4011 **1** **Minortransgression (USA)**[18] 7507 4-9-7 65 SebSanders 8 74
(Paul Rich) *trckd ldrs: hdwy on outer and cl up 3f out: led over 2f out: rdn wl over 1f out: styd on wl fnl f* **11/4**[1]

5430 **2** 2 1/2 **Eastern Gift**[7] 7632 6-9-2 60 StevieDonohoe 3 63
(Gay Kelleway) *hld up towards rr: hdwy 2f out: rdn over 1f out: kpt on fnl f* **11/1**

0360 **3** nk **Mr Chocolate Drop (IRE)**[26] 7418 7-9-0 63 (t) NathanAlison(5) 6 66
(Mandy Rowland) *hld up in tch: hdwy over 2f out: rdn to chse wnr appr fnl f: kpt on same pce* **20/1**

00/2 **4** 3/4 **King Pin**[25] 7424 6-9-3 61 JoeFanning 2 62
(Tracy Waggott) *trckd ldrs on inner: hdwy over 2f out: rdn wl over 1f out: sn one pce* **4/1**[2]

332 **5** 2 **Pulsatilla**[30] 7354 3-9-0 59 TomEaves 5 55
(Bryan Smart) *led after 1f: rdn along and hdd over 2f out: grad wknd* **11/1**

0604 **6** 1 **Jonnie Skull (IRE)**[4] 7648 5-8-12 56 (bt) LukeMorris 7 50
(Phil McEntee) *led 1f: prom: rdn along wl over 2f out: grad wknd* **8/1**

5002 **7** 1 **Exopuntia**[53] 6938 5-8-11 55 TonyCulhane 4 47
(Julia Feilden) *chsd ldrs on outer: effrt 3f out: rdn over 2f out: sn wknd* **4/1**[2]

641 **8** 6 **Riczar**[30] 7354 3-9-1 60 RichardKingscote 9 38
(Tom Dascombe) *cl up: rdn along wl over 2f out: wknd wl over 1f out* **6/1**[3]

2400 **9** 8 **Jay Jays Joy**[25] 7424 3-9-1 60 (b) MickyFenton 1 19
(Paul Midgley) *s.i.s: a bhd* **40/1**

1m 42.99s (-0.71) **Going Correction** -0.125s/f (Stan)
WFA 3 from 4yo+ 1lb 9 Ran SP% **115.9**
Speed ratings (Par 101): **98,95,95,94,92 91,90,84,76**
Tote Swingers: 1&2 £5.30, 1&3 £10.90, 2&3 £21.20 CSF £34.82 CT £509.53 TOTE £3.90: £1.70, £2.60, £4.50; EX 44.50 Trifecta £406.00 Part won. Pool: £548.72 - 0.43 winning units..
Owner G A Morgan **Bred** Padua Stables **Trained** Newport, Gwent

FOCUS
A moderate handicap. The winner is rated back to his old bests.

7712 BETFRED 1350 SHOPS NATIONWIDE MAIDEN STKS 1m 4f (F)
2:25 (2:25) (Class 5) 3-4-Y-O £2,264 (£673; £336; £168) Stalls Low

Form RPR

220 **1** **Shieldmaiden (USA)**[21] 7486 3-8-12 77 JoeFanning 2 69+
(Mark Johnston) *prom on inner: hdwy 3f out: led over 2f out: rdn and hung rt over 1f out: drvn ins fnl f: edgd rt nr fin and jst hld on* **5/2**[2]

33 **2** shd **Bravestofthebrave (USA)**[28] 7401 3-9-3 0 WilliamBuick 9 74
(John Gosden) *bmpd sltly s: hld up in rr: pushed along bef 1/2-way: hdwy to chse ldrs 3f out: wd st and rdn wl over 1f out: styd on to chal ins fnl f and ev ch: n.m.r and no ex nr line* **10/11**[1]

4330 **3** 8 **Zenarinda**[22] 7458 4-9-3 63 EddieAhern 4 56
(Mark H Tompkins) *trckd ldrs: hdwy 4f out: chsd wnr wl over 1f out: sn rdn and one pce* **7/1**

3630 **4** 2 3/4 **Phoenix Flame**[49] 7037 3-8-12 48 (p) ShaneKelly 5 52
(Alan McCabe) *led: rdn along 4f out: hdd over 2f out and grad wknd* **33/1**

5 1 3/4 **Keltbray (IRE)** 3-9-3 0 RichardKingscote 6 54
(Robert Mills) *t.k.h: chsd ldrs: cl up after 4f: rdn along over 3f out: wknd 2f out* **13/2**[3]

4505 **6** 9 **Think**[12] 7571 4-9-8 50 PaddyAspell 1 40
(Clive Mulhall) *hld up towards rr: hdwy to chse ldrs 3f out: sn rdn and wknd* **25/1**

3000 **7** 35 **Back For Tea (IRE)**[14] 7557 3-9-3 43 (t) AdamKirby 7 —
(K F Clutterbuck) *chsd ldrs: rdn along over 4f out and sn wknd* **80/1**

0/ **8** 3 **Towneley Arms (IRE)**[865] 4396 4-9-5 0 MichaelO'Connell(3) 8 —
(Ollie Pears) *wnt rt s: hld up in rr: hdwy on outer to chse ldrs 1/2-way: rdn over 4f out and sn wknd* **25/1**

2m 39.28s (-1.72) **Going Correction** -0.125s/f (Stan)
WFA 3 from 4yo 5lb 8 Ran SP% **118.7**
Speed ratings (Par 103): **100,99,94,92,91 85,62,60**
Tote Swingers: 1&2 £1.60, 1&3 £2.80, 2&3 £2.30 CSF £5.21 TOTE £3.20: £1.70, £1.10, £1.80; EX 6.60 Trifecta £17.60 Pool: £529.72 - 22.17 winning units..
Owner Sheikh Hamdan Bin Mohammed Al Maktoum **Bred** W S Farish, Bcwt Ltd And Inwood Stable **Trained** Middleham Moor, N Yorks

FOCUS
Middle-distance maidens at this time of the year are rarely worth following and this looked no exception. It was s lowly run and the first two, who were clear, are probably a bit better than they were able to show.

7713 JO NEWBY'S HEN PARTY H'CAP 1m 3f (F)
2:55 (2:55) (Class 5) (0-75,75) 3-Y-O+ £2,264 (£673; £336; £168) Stalls Low

Form RPR

0506 **1** **Follow The Flag (IRE)**[5] 7637 7-9-6 71 (v) ShaneKelly 5 82
(Alan McCabe) *hld up towards rr: hdwy 3f out: trckd ldrs 2f out: swtchd ins over 1f out: rdn ent fnl f: styd on to ld last 50yds* **9/2**[3]

5040 **2** 3/4 **Royal Swain (IRE)**[49] 7017 5-9-10 75 JoeFanning 3 85
(Alan Swinbank) *trckd ldrs: hdwy 3f out: effrt wl over 1f out: rdn to ld ins fnl f: hdd and no ex last 50yds* **2/1**[1]

404- **3** 2 **Ostentation**[264] 7205 4-9-4 69 AdamKirby 4 75
(Roger Teal) *led: rdn along 3f out: drvn wl over 1f out: hdd ins fnl f: one pce* **9/1**

5262 **4** 2 1/2 **Sail Home**[16] 7527 4-8-10 64 AdamBeschizza(3) 6 66
(Julia Feilden) *cl up: rdn and ev ch 2f out: drvn over 1f out: wknd ent fnl f* **4/1**[2]

0034 **5** 2 **Hits Only Jude (IRE)**[11] 7424 8-8-11 69 (v) JasonHart(7) 1 67
(Declan Carroll) *trckd ldrs on inner: rdn along over 2f out: wknd over 1f out* **33/1**

1130 **6** 8 **Stanley Rigby**[36] 7272 5-9-0 72 LauraBarry(7) 7 56
(Richard Fahey) *hld up: hdwy to trck ldrs 1/2-way: rdn along over 3f out: sn wknd* **9/2**[3]

54/ **7** 5 **Rajamand (FR)**[288] 7612 5-9-10 75 FergusSweeney 8 50
(Gary Moore) *chsd ldrs on outer: rdn along 4f out: wknd over 3f out* **10/1**

0-06 **8** 1 3/4 **Magic Echo**[106] 5440 7-9-9 74 TomEaves 2 46
(Rose Dobbin) *a in rr* **25/1**

2m 26.68s (-1.32) **Going Correction** -0.125s/f (Stan) 8 Ran SP% **115.6**
Speed ratings (Par 103): **99,98,97,95,93 87,84,83**
Tote Swingers: 1&2 £2.40, 1&3 £4.80, 2&3 £4.70 CSF £14.11 CT £77.05 TOTE £6.90: £1.60, £1.50, £3.40; EX 11.20 Trifecta £182.10 Pool: £647.33 - 2.63 winning units..
Owner S Gillen **Bred** Martin Francis **Trained** Averham Park, Notts

FOCUS
An ordinary handicap and slightly mudling form, but the first two were on good marks and the form has been given a bit of a chance.

7714 ALF PARKIN IS 80 H'CAP 7f (F)
3:30 (3:30) (Class 6) (0-55,55) 3-Y-O+ £1,704 (£503; £251) Stalls Low

Form RPR

00 **1** **Mataajir (USA)**[28] 7401 3-8-7 46 oh1 LukeMorris 7 59+
(Derek Shaw) *in tch: rdn along 3f out: hdwy wl over 1f out: styd on strly appr fnl f to ld last 100yds* **20/1**

060- **2** 1 1/4 **Only Ten Per Cent (IRE)**[474] 5373 3-8-10 49 AdrianNicholls 4 59
(J R Jenkins) *cl up: led over 2f out: rdn and hung lft ent fnl f: hdd and no ex last 100yds* **13/2**[3]

4-32 **3** 1 **Fearless Poet (IRE)**[37] 7247 3-8-11 50 (p) TomEaves 2 57
(Bryan Smart) *trckd ldrs on inner: hdwy over 2f out: swtchd rt and rdn to chse ldr over 1f out: kpt on same pce fnl f* **9/4**[1]

5405 **4** 1 **St Ignatius**[130] 4651 4-8-10 49 (p) NeilChalmers 14 53
(Michael Appleby) *chsd ldrs on outer: rdn 2f out: kpt on same pce appr fnl f* **10/1**

3300 **5** 1/2 **Like A Boy**[31] 7333 3-8-4 50 JakePayne(7) 8 53
(Bill Turner) *towards rr: hdwy on inner over 2f out: sn rdn and kpt on: nrst fin* **7/1**

5235 **6** 3/4 **Spacecraft (IRE)**[37] 7247 4-8-7 46 oh1 (b) ChrisCatlin 6 47
(Christopher Kellett) *midfield: hdwy over 2f out: sn rdn and kpt on: nrst fin* **8/1**

0046 **7** 2 **Cabal**[15] 7537 4-8-8 47 (b) AndrewMullen 9 43
(Andrew Crook) *dwlt and towards rr: hdwy wl over 2f out: sn rdn and kpt on: nrst fin* **16/1**

3050 **8** 3 3/4 **Twennyshortkid**[25] 7420 3-8-9 48 (v) TonyHamilton 1 33
(Paul Midgley) *prom on inner: led over 4f out: rdn along and hdd over 2f out: sn drvn and wknd over 1f out* **18/1**

0000 **9** 3 3/4 **Norton Girl**[47] 7071 3-8-7 46 JoeFanning 12 21
(Tracy Waggott) *a towards rr* **20/1**

4351 **10** 1 **Monsieur Pontaven**[14] 7561 4-9-2 55 (b) LeeNewman 11 28
(Robin Bastiman) *dwlt: a towards rr* **5/1**[2]

2050 **11** 4 1/2 **Eilean Eeve**[29] 7370 5-8-10 49 (v[1]) RobertHavlin 3 —
(George Foster) *led over 2f: cl up: rdn along 3f out: sn wknd* **33/1**

000 **12** 4 **Lady Ellice**[16] 7525 3-8-7 46 oh1 KirstyMilczarek 13 —
(Phil McEntee) *a in rr* **80/1**

004 **13** 2 3/4 **Apassionforfashion**[47] 7069 3-8-7 46 oh1 (b[1]) JamesSullivan 5 —
(Bryan Smart) *t.k.h: chsd ldrs to 1/2-way: sn wknd* **40/1**

1m 28.12s (-2.18) **Going Correction** -0.125s/f (Stan) 13 Ran SP% **120.8**
Speed ratings (Par 101): **107,105,104,103,102 101,99,95,91,89 84,80,77**
Tote Swingers: 1&2 £25.70, 1&3 £14.90, 2&3 £4.90 CSF £140.65 CT £417.38 TOTE £31.10: £4.80, £2.10, £1.30; EX 240.90 TRIFECTA Not won..
Owner Derek Shaw **Bred** Shadwell Australia Ltd **Trained** Sproxton, Leics

FOCUS
A moderate handicap run at a fair pace. The first two were unexposed and this looks fair form for the grade.
Mataajir(USA) Official explanation: trainer's rep said, regarding apparent improvement in form, that the gelding was better suited by the fibresand and drop back to 7f.
Lady Ellice Official explanation: jockey said filly never travelled
T/Plt: £739.60 to a £1 stake. Pool: £55,092.22 - 54.37 winning tickets. T/Qpdt: £69.80 to a £1 stake. Pool: £4,678.57 - 49.60 winning tickets. JR

7692 WOLVERHAMPTON (A.W) (L-H)
Saturday, December 10

OFFICIAL GOING: Standard
Wind: Light, behind. Weather: Cloudy

7715 TOTEPLACEPOT H'CAP (DIV I) 7f 32y(P)
6:20 (6:21) (Class 5) (0-75,77) 3-Y-O+ £2,264 (£673; £336; £168) Stalls High

Form RPR

2401 **1** **Libys Dream (IRE)**[9] 7595 3-9-3 71 RichardKingscote 11 85+
(Tom Dascombe) *chsd ldr: pushed along 3f out: led over 1f out: edgd lft ins fnl f: rdn out* **6/1**[3]

6124 **2** 3 **Ryedane (IRE)**[9] 7595 9-8-11 70 (b) AdamCarter(5) 2 76
(Tim Easterby) *hld up in tch: plld hrd: pushed along over 2f out: edgd lft and r.o ins fnl f: wnt 2nd nr fin* **16/1**

0001 **3** nk **Restless Bay (IRE)**[9] 7596 3-9-9 77 (e) AdamKirby 3 83
(Reg Hollinshead) *hld up: hdwy over 1f out: sn rdn: r.o* **5/1**[2]

1612 **4** hd **Silver Wind**[9] 7591 6-8-11 65 (b) ShaneKelly 9 70
(Alan McCabe) *s.i.s: hdwy 1/2-way: rdn over 1f out: styd on same pce ins fnl f* **7/1**

0010 **5** 3/4 **Without Prejudice (USA)**[43] 7146 6-9-0 68 PaddyAspell 6 71
(Michael Easterby) *prom: rdn over 2f out: edgd lft and styd on same pce fnl f* **20/1**

3010 **6** 3/4 **Abriachan**[17] 7517 4-8-13 67 LiamKeniry 7 70+
(Noel Quinlan) *hld up: nt clr run ins fnl f: r.o: nvr nr to chal* **33/1**

0000 **7** 1/2 **Double Carpet (IRE)**[53] 6939 8-8-10 64 ow1 FergusSweeney 5 64
(Garry Woodward) *led: rdn and hdd over 1f out: no ex ins fnl f* **50/1**

1213 **8** *shd* **Trojan Rocket (IRE)**[23] [7448] 3-8-12 **66**............................ EddieAhern 8 65
(George Prodromou) *chsd ldrs: rdn over 2f out: edgd lft and no ex ins fnl f* **5/1**[2]

1400 **9** *nk* **Katmai River (IRE)**[10] [7588] 4-8-7 **61**............................... DavidProbert 4 60
(Mark Usher) *hld up: hdwy over 2f out: styd on same pce fr over 1f out* **17/2**

3114 **10** *½* **Berbice (IRE)**[1] [7696] 6-8-10 **67**....................................... DaleSwift(3) 12 64
(Linda Perratt) *s.i.s: hld up: nt clr run over 1f out: nvr trbld ldrs* **8/1**

0005 **11** *1* **Avonrose**[7] [7625] 4-9-6 **74**.. JoeFanning 1 73
(Derek Shaw) *prom: pushed along over 2f out: btn whn n.m.r and eased ins fnl f* **4/1**[1]

1100 **12** *12* **Istiqdaam**[9] [7595] 6-9-6 **74**..(b) KirstyMilczarek 10 36
(Conor Dore) *hld up: a in rr: rdn 1/2-way: sn lost tch* **40/1**

1m 28.67s (-0.93) **Going Correction** +0.075s/f (Slow) **12** Ran SP% **119.7**
Speed ratings (Par 103): **108,104,104,104,103 102,101,101,101,100 99,85**
Tote Swingers:1&2:£22.70, 2&3:£5.90, 1&3:£5.60 CSF £94.51 CT £527.61 TOTE £8.40: £2.20, £4.70, £1.70; EX 105.70.

Owner Ms A Quinn **Bred** Irish National Stud **Trained** Malpas, Cheshire

FOCUS
Quite a few of these came here in good form and the pace looked even enough, contributing to the best time performance of the three 7f races on the card, so this looks solid enough form, rated around the placed horses.

Abriachan Official explanation: jockey said gelding was denied a clear run
Avonrose Official explanation: trainer had no explanation for the poor form shown
Istiqdaam Official explanation: jockey said gelding never travelled

7716 TOTEPLACEPOT H'CAP (DIV II) 7f 32y(P)
6:50 (6:50) (Class 5) (0-75,75) 3-Y-O+ **£2,264** (£673; £336; £168) **Stalls** High

Form RPR

2045 **1** **Tamareen (IRE)**[79] [6283] 3-9-5 **73**.................................... TonyHamilton 2 82
(Richard Fahey) *hld up in tch: shkn up over 1f out: rdn to ld wl ins fnl f: r.o* **12/1**

3253 **2** *½* **Burning Stone (USA)**[9] [7589] 4-8-13 **67**.............................. MartinLane 3 75
(Gay Kelleway) *chsd ldrs: pushed along over 2f out: rdn to ld ins fnl f: sn hdd: styd on* **4/1**[2]

0204 **3** *1 ½* **Lastkingofscotland (IRE)**[9] [7596] 5-8-11 **65**............(b) KirstyMilczarek 9 69
(Conor Dore) *s.i.s: hld up: rdn over 1f out: r.o ins fnl f: wnt 3rd post: nt rch ldrs* **11/1**

3212 **4** *hd* **Ducal**[51] [6980] 3-9-7 **75**.. JohnFahy 12 78+
(Mike Murphy) *dwlt: hld up: racd keenly: hdwy over 2f out: rdn and ev ch ins fnl f: edgd lft: styd on same pce: lost 3rd post* **15/8**[1]

1605 **5** *nk* **Downhill Skier (IRE)**[51] [6979] 7-8-6 **67**.......................... JackDuern(7) 5 70
(Mark Brisbourne) *led: rdn over 1f out: edgd rt and hdd ins fnl f: styd on same pce* **33/1**

2406 **6** *2 ¼* **The Happy Hammer (IRE)**[16] [7532] 5-9-2 **70**............ WilliamCarson 10 67
(Eugene Stanford) *hld up: hdwy over 2f out: rdn over 1f out: hung lft ins fnl f: one pce* **12/1**

4146 **7** *1 ¼* **Tourist**[18] [7500] 6-8-13 **67**.. StevieDonohoe 8 62
(Ian Williams) *hld up: rdn over 2f out: styd on ins fnl f: nvr nrr* **12/1**

4241 **8** *¾* **Bahamian Lad**[26] [7417] 6-9-0 **68**..................................(p) TonyCulhane 11 59
(Reg Hollinshead) *prom: pushed along over 2f out: looked hld whn hmpd and no ex ins fnl f* **14/1**

0305 **9** *nk* **Music Festival (USA)**[1] [7695] 4-8-12 **66** ow1.............. DanielTudhope 7 56
(Jim Goldie) *hld up: rdn over 1f out: n.d* **7/1**[3]

0000 **10** *nk* **Bertie Blu Boy**[15] [7538] 3-8-8 **62**...................................... LukeMorris 6 52
(Paul Green) *prom: chsd ldr over 5f out: rdn over 2f out: wknd over 1f out* **33/1**

-300 **11** *1* **Monadreen Dancer**[134] [4522] 3-8-7 **61** oh2.................... AndreaAtzeni 1 48
(Daniel Mark Loughnane, Ire) *prom: racd keenly: rdn over 2f out: wknd fnl f* **100/1**

1460 **12** *25* **Above Standard (IRE)**[115] [5171] 3-9-6 **74**..................... JamesSullivan 4 —
(G P Kelly) *nt move wl to post: sn outpcd: t.o* **25/1**

1m 29.38s (-0.22) **Going Correction** +0.075s/f (Slow) **12** Ran SP% **116.1**
Speed ratings (Par 103): **104,103,101,101,101 98,97,96,95,95 94,65**
Tote Swingers:1&2:£11.70, 2&3:£10.90, 1&3:£30.40 CSF £56.83 CT £559.83 TOTE £17.60: £4.80, £1.20, £2.20; EX 63.60.

Owner Dr Marwan Koukash **Bred** Mcdonnell Cbs Bloodstock **Trained** Musley Bank, N Yorks
■ Stewards' Enquiry : Jack Duern two-day ban: careless riding (Dec 26-27)

FOCUS
Another even-looking gallop and there were plenty in with chances entering the final furlong. The form looks sound with the time reasonable and the three in the frame behind the winner setting the level.

7717 DID THE LIFECHANGING TOTESCOOP6 ROLLOVER MAIDEN STKS 7f 32y(P)
7:20 (7:25) (Class 5) 3-Y-O+ **£2,385** (£704; £352) **Stalls** High

Form RPR

1 **Prodigality**[176] 3-9-3 0.. LukeMorris 6 66+
(Ronald Harris) *hld up in tch: led on bit over 1f out: shkn up and r.o: readily* **9/2**[2]

6 **2** *1 ¼* **Aqua Ardens (GER)**[37] [7249] 3-9-3 0.............................. StephenCraine 9 57
(George Baker) *hld up: hdwy and edgd rt over 1f out: r.o to go 2nd post: no ch w wnr* **16/1**

60- **3** *hd* **Mystic Halo**[393] [7419] 8-8-12 0...................................... RobbieFitzpatrick 1 52
(Frank Sheridan) *prom: rdn over 1f out: r.o wl ins fnl f* **200/1**

24 **4** *1* **True Satire**[26] [7411] 3-8-12 0.. IvaMilickova 12 49
(Jane Chapple-Hyam) *chsd ldrs: led 2f out: rdn and hdd over 1f out: edgd lft ins fnl f: no ex towards fin* **5/1**[3]

0 **5** *½* **Fortunelini**[158] [3716] 6-8-12 0.. RussKennemore 8 48
(Frank Sheridan) *s.i.s: hld up: r.o ins fnl f: nrst fin* **100/1**

30- **6** *¾* **Too Late Jones (USA)**[368] [7732] 4-9-0 0.................. RobertLButler(3) 7 51
(Richard Guest) *hld up: hung lft fr over 2f out: hmpd wl over 1f out: r.o ins fnl f: nvr nr to chal* **12/1**

0 **7** *¾* **Tiger Royale**[133] [4559] 3-8-12 0..................................... DanielTudhope 5 44
(Michael Mullineaux) *prom: rdn 1/2-way: hung lft and styd on same pce fnl f* **50/1**

0 **8** *2 ¼* **Ragda**[208] [2151] 3-8-12 0.. MartinHarley 11 38
(Marco Botti) *chsd ldr over 5f out: led over 2f out: sn rdn and hdd: wknd ins fnl f* **15/8**[1]

9 *2* **Dubonny** 4-8-12 0...(t) AndreaAtzeni 4 32
(Frank Sheridan) *s.i.s: hld up: rdn over 1f out: n.d* **20/1**

0 **10** *6* **Fifth Auntie**[37] [7250] 4-8-12 0.. JoeFanning 2 16
(J R Jenkins) *chsd ldrs: rdn over 2f out: wknd over 1f out* **66/1**

0 **11** *4 ½* **Pill Boy**[28] [7389] 3-9-3 0.. SamHitchcott 10 —
(Dai Burchell) *sn led: hdd over 2f out: wknd over 1f out* **100/1**

1m 31.06s (1.46) **Going Correction** +0.075s/f (Slow) **11** Ran SP% **93.9**
Speed ratings (Par 103): **94,92,92,91,90 89,88,86,84,77 72**
Tote Swingers:1&2:£6.90, 2&3:£52.50, 1&3:£33.00 CSF £42.11 TOTE £4.50: £1.40, £3.40, £17.30; EX 47.50.

Owner Paul Moulton **Bred** Darley **Trained** Earlswood, Monmouths
■ Stewards' Enquiry : Daniel Tudhope two-day ban: careless riding (Dec 26-27)

FOCUS
With leading form contender Eljowzah a late withdrawal this looked quite a weak maiden on paper but it threw up an impressive winner. The form is dubious though and rated fairly negatively.

7718 SPIFFING CRABBIE'S ALCOHOLIC GINGER BEER CLAIMING STKS 1f 103y(P)
7:50 (7:50) (Class 5) 2-Y-O **£2,264** (£673; £336; £168) **Stalls** Low

Form RPR

2304 **1** **Guava**[8] [7597] 2-7-11 67.. KieranO'Neill(3) 7 57+
(Richard Hannon) *chsd ldrs: pushed along over 2f out: rdn to ld 1f out: styd on u.p* **6/4**[1]

0341 **2** *½* **Let Your Love Flow (IRE)**[26] [7414] 2-8-6 68............... SophieDoyle(3) 3 65
(Sylvester Kirk) *trckd ldrs: plld hrd: rdn and ev ch fnl f: styd on* **9/4**[2]

0000 **3** *1 ¾* **Rapid Heat Lad (IRE)**[12] [7569] 2-9-1 58....................(e[1]) TonyCulhane 1 66
(Reg Hollinshead) *led: rdn and hdd 1f out: styd on same pce* **33/1**

65 **4** *¾* **Spartilla**[12] [7568] 2-8-5 0... JamesSullivan 5 54
(James Given) *hld up: hdwy u.p over 2f out: styd on: nt rch ldrs* **16/1**

1250 **5** *1 ½* **King Kenobi (IRE)**[49] [7035] 2-8-8 60 ow1......................... LiamKeniry 9 54
(J S Moore) *chsd ldr: rdn over 1f out: no ex ins fnl f* **7/1**[3]

0606 **6** *¾* **Emma Jean Boy**[109] [5343] 2-8-5 50.................................(p) LukeMorris 4 50
(J S Moore) *hld up: rdn over 2f out: sn hung lft fr over 1f out: no ex fnl f* **25/1**

0023 **7** *2* **Dutchman's Field**[12] [7569] 2-8-5 52.................................... JoeFanning 2 46
(David Nicholls) *chsd ldrs: rdn 2f out: wknd ins fnl f* **7/1**[3]

0 **8** *6* **Lone Star State (IRE)**[248] [1185] 2-9-5 0....................... RussKennemore 8 48
(Frank Sheridan) *s.i.s: a in rr: rdn and wknd over 2f out* **80/1**

9 *½* **Dr Albert** 2-9-5 0.. RobbieFitzpatrick 6 47
(Frank Sheridan) *s.i.s: a in rr: rdn over 3f out: wknd over 2f out* **100/1**

503 **10** *1 ¾* **Notnowstanley**[31] [7338] 2-8-0 43..........................(b) RyanPowell(5) 10 30
(J S Moore) *hld up: rdn over 3f out: wknd over 2f out* **50/1**

2m 3.48s (1.78) **Going Correction** +0.075s/f (Slow) **10** Ran SP% **112.6**
Speed ratings (Par 96): **95,94,93,92,91 90,88,83,82,81**
Tote Swingers:1&2:£1.50, 2&3:£11.60, 1&3:£10.70 CSF £4.51 TOTE £2.50: £1.30, £1.10, £5.70; EX 5.80.Guava was claimed by Frank Sheridan for £5,000.

Owner Middleham Park Racing Vi **Bred** B R Marsden **Trained** East Everleigh, Wilts
■ Richard Hannon's 217th winner in 2011, breaking Mark Johnston's calendar year record. Hannon held the record previously.
■ Stewards' Enquiry : Sophie Doyle two-day ban: used whip with excessive frequency (Dec 26-27)

FOCUS
Not much depth here.

NOTEBOOK
Guava, who was by far the best treated at the weights, coped with the step up in trip to bag a second career win. She has been racing over 6-7f this year but there was encouragement in the dam's side of her pedigree about being able to see out this trip, and she was probably helped by the fact that the gallop wasn't overly strong, which explains the slow time. (tchd 7-4)

Let Your Love Flow(IRE) ◆ deserves real credit for sticking on so well having pulled so hard through the first half of the race. She will do better still when getting a stronger pace and is still open to improvement after just six starts. (op 2-1 tchd 15-8)

Rapid Heat Lad(IRE) had work to do on these terms, especially as the step up in trip wasn't sure to suit. He acquitted himself well but was allowed to set a steady gallop, so is probably slightly flattered. (op 50-1)

Spartilla finished well from off the pace but was unsuited by the way this panned out. His form hasn't been anything great so far but he shapes as if he'll be seen to better effect when getting a stronger pace to run down. (tchd 14-1)

King Kenobi(IRE) was up against it on these terms and he is probably better suited by slightly shorter. (op 15-2)

Emma Jean Boy Official explanation: jockey said gelding hung left-handed

7719 TOTETRIFECTA H'CAP 1m 141y(P)
8:20 (8:20) (Class 2) (0-100,98) 3-Y-O+ **£10,081** (£3,017; £1,508; £755; £376) **Stalls** Low

Form RPR

2014 **1** **Mia's Boy**[28] [7393] 7-9-7 **98**.. AndreaAtzeni 1 106
(Chris Dwyer) *hld up: r.o ins fnl f: rdn to ld post* **9/2**[3]

1301 **2** *nse* **Loyalty**[8] [7606] 4-9-4 **95**..(v) JoeFanning 11 103+
(Derek Shaw) *s.i.s: hld up: hdwy over 1f out: hung lft and led ins fnl f: hdd post* **4/1**[2]

1053 **3** *1 ½* **Blue Moon**[8] [7606] 4-9-2 **93**.. PhillipMakin 6 100+
(Kevin Ryan) *a.p: pushed along: nt clr run and swtchd rt over 1f out: nt clr run ins fnl f: r.o* **15/2**

0010 **4** *½* **Dhaular Dhar (IRE)**[8] [7618] 9-8-7 **84**................................. JohnFahy 5 87
(Jim Goldie) *hld up: hdwy over 1f out: rdn and edgd lft ins fnl f: r.o* **28/1**

0523 **5** *¾* **Mull Of Killough (IRE)**[17] [7523] 5-9-3 **94**....................(b[1]) ShaneKelly 10 96
(Richard Fahey) *trckd ldrs: racd keenly: led over 1f out: rdn and hdd ins fnl f: styd on same pce* **7/2**[1]

0136 **6** *nk* **Steed**[17] [7516] 4-9-6 **97**...(b) FergusSweeney 9 98
(Tim Vaughan) *hld up: rdn over 1f out: r.o: nt rch ldrs* **12/1**

1256 **7** *¾* **Calypso Magic (IRE)**[149] [4015] 3-8-8 **87**............................ LukeMorris 2 86
(Linda Jewell) *led: rdn and hdd over 1f out: no ex ins fnl f* **28/1**

30 **8** *1 ½* **Fattsota**[59] [6803] 3-9-1 **94**... MartinHarley 8 90
(Marco Botti) *chsd ldrs: rdn over 2f out: no ex fnl f* **9/2**[3]

1050 **9** *shd* **Hazzard County (USA)**[28] [7393] 7-8-9 **93**..................... AliceHaynes(7) 4 89
(David Simcock) *hld up: effrt over 1f out: nvr trbld ldrs* **28/1**

1606 **10** *2* **Justonefortheroad**[7] [7628] 5-9-2 **93**................................ TonyHamilton 3 84
(Richard Fahey) *trckd ldrs: rdn and ev ch over 1f out tl wknd ins fnl f* **14/1**

1m 50.05s (-0.45) **Going Correction** +0.075s/f (Slow)
WFA 3 from 4yo+ 2lb **10** Ran SP% **115.1**
Speed ratings (Par 109): **105,104,103,103,102 102,101,100,100,98**
Tote Swingers:1&2:£4.70, 2&3:£4.80, 1&3:£8.10 CSF £22.03 CT £131.63 TOTE £5.60: £2.20, £1.70, £1.50; EX 25.70 Trifecta £43.40 Pool 308.59 - 5.25 winning units..

Owner Mrs Shelley Dwyer **Bred** Sir Eric Parker **Trained** Burrough Green, Cambs
■ Stewards' Enquiry : Phillip Makin one-day ban: careless riding (Dec 26)

FOCUS
A strong race and, despite the gallop not looking overly strong, the finish was dominated by two horses held up out the back for the most part. The first three ran to similar marks as Lingfield last month.

NOTEBOOK

Mia's Boy ran well in a similarly competitive event at Lingfield last month but this was a cracking performance for he travelled noticeably well around the inside before finding plenty to nail the bang in-form runner-up right on the line. This is the first time Mia's Boy has won a handicap since 2008 but he's got stacks of good runs in the bank and he's clearly at the top of his game right now. He has now finished first or second on four of his five visits to Wolverhampton.

Loyalty is also at the top of his game and he went desperately close to a fourth all-weather win of the winter, showing a smart turn of foot out wide to hit the front in the final furlong before being run down close home. He is well suited by coming from off the pace, so the quicker they go, the better for him.

Blue Moon's performance needs upgrading because she was chopped for room at the top of the straight and had to be switched out. She picked up nicely but faced an uphill task from there. (op 7-1 tchd 13-2)

Dhaular Dhar(IRE) likes to come off a strong pace, so could have done with them going a bit quicker early but he ran as well as he has ever done on Polytrack. (op 33-1)

Mull Of Killough(IRE) had every chance but was done by speedier types in the closing stages. He was a bit keen early on, in the first-time blinkers, which wouldn't have helped his cause. (op 9-2)

Steed ran on late but is better suited by slightly shorter trips, where the pace is quicker.

7720 HORIZONS RESTAURANT H'CAP — 1m 4f 50y(P)
8:50 (8:51) (Class 6) (0-60,70) 3-Y-O+ — **£1,704** (£503; £251) **Stalls** Low

Form / RPR

0314 **1** **Honourable Knight (IRE)**[16] 7527 3-9-2 **57**.............(be) DavidProbert 9 66
(Mark Usher) *hld up in tch: rdn to ld over 1f out: edgd lft ins fnl f: styd on* **7/1**[3]

2140 **2** *1* **Thundering Home**[81] 6240 4-9-4 **59**...........................(t) DavidKenny(5) 7 66
(George Baker) *hld up: hdwy u.p over 2f out: r.o to go 2nd towards fin: nt rch wnr* **11/1**

0301 **3** *1 3/4* **Cadgers Brig**[8] 7608 3-10-1 **70**.....................................(v) JoeFanning 12 74
(Keith Dalgleish) *chsd ldr tl led 5f out: rdn and hdd over 1f out: styd on same pce ins fnl f* **11/10**[1]

0/ **4** *1/2* **Marlos Moment**[30] 5570 5-8-10 **46**.........................(bt) GrahamGibbons 4 49
(Mark Michael McNiff, Ire) *prom: chsd ldr over 3f out: rdn and hung lft over 1f out: styd on same pce ins fnl f* **10/1**

232 **4** *dht* **Dolly Colman (IRE)**[31] 7333 3-8-6 **47**................................ LukeMorris 3 50
(Michael Blake) *mid-div: hdwy over 3f out: sn rdn: styd on* **10/1**

0300 **6** *2* **Yossi (IRE)**[66] 6235 7-8-3 **46** oh1..........................(b) CharlesEddery(7) 11 46
(Richard Guest) *s.s: hld up: hdwy over 2f out: no ex fnl f* **50/1**

5033 **7** *nk* **Turjuman (USA)**[12] 7564 6-9-3 **60**.........................(p) NatashaEaton(7) 6 60
(Alan Bailey) *hld up: hdwy over 1f out: styd on: nt trble ldrs* **13/2**[2]

0050 **8** *2 3/4* **Harrys Yer Man**[12] 7564 7-9-4 **54**....................................... ShaneKelly 5 49
(Mark Brisbourne) *hld up: rdn over 1f out: nvr trbld ldrs* **33/1**

5064 **9** *5* **Abernethy (IRE)**[15] 7105 3-8-5 **46** oh1......................(t) JamesSullivan 10 33
(Linda Perratt) *s.i.s: hld up and bhd: nvr any ch* **33/1**

6660 **10** *11* **Bentley**[14] 7556 7-9-5 **60**.. RyanPowell(5) 2 30
(Brian Baugh) *led 7f: rdn and wknd over 2f out* **66/1**

21-4 **11** *15* **William Morgan (IRE)**[341] 17 4-9-7 **57**.................... WilliamCarson 1 —
(Mike Hammond) *chsd ldrs tl rdn and wknd over 3f out: t.o* **28/1**

2m 41.29s (0.19) **Going Correction** +0.075s/f (Slow)
WFA 3 from 4yo+ 5lb — **11 Ran SP% 112.8**
Speed ratings (Par 101): **102,101,100,99,99 98,98,96,93,85 75**
Tote Swingers:1&2:£3.20, 2&3:£4.40, 1&3:£2.60 CSF £73.14 CT £146.08 TOTE £10.20: £3.10, £3.40, £1.10; EX 95.30.
Owner Bryan Fry **Bred** Mohammed Al Sulaim **Trained** Upper Lambourn, Berks
■ Stewards' Enquiry : Joe Fanning one-day ban: careless riding (Dec 26)

FOCUS

A sound run hcap. The favourite was unable to defy a big rise for his previous C&D win, but probably ran every bit as well, while the winner was not far off his 2yo best.

7721 TOTEPOOL CONDITIONS STKS — 5f 216y(P)
9:20 (9:21) (Class 4) 3-Y-O+ — **£4,204** (£1,251; £625; £312) **Stalls** Low

Form / RPR

0042 **1** **Oasis Dancer**[24] 7433 4-8-11 92.. JimCrowley 3 103
(Ralph Beckett) *chsd ldrs: shkn up to ld over 1f out: r.o strly* **7/4**[1]

0000 **2** *4* **Piscean (USA)**[11] 7578 6-8-11 92................................ WilliamCarson 5 90
(Tom Keddy) *prom: rdn over 2f out: styd on to go 2nd wl ins fnl f: no ch w wnr* **16/1**

0010 **3** *1/2* **Bajan Tryst (USA)**[28] 7392 5-8-11 98.............................. PhillipMakin 2 89
(Kevin Ryan) *led: rdn and hdd over 1f out: no ex ins fnl f* **4/1**[3]

00-0 **4** *1/2* **Treadwell (IRE)**[24] 7433 4-8-11 98............................ FergusSweeney 1 87
(Jamie Osborne) *hld up: rdn over 2f out: nvr trbld ldrs* **15/2**

2025 **5** *shd* **Secret Witness**[11] 7578 5-8-11 100..................................(b) JoeFanning 7 87
(Ronald Harris) *chsd ldr tl rdn 2f out: no ex fnl f* **3/1**[2]

0-0U **6** *1 1/4* **Little Garcon (USA)**[168] 3410 4-8-11 95......................... AndreaAtzeni 4 83
(Marco Botti) *s.i.s: hld up: rdn over 2f out: n.d* **7/1**

1m 14.5s (-0.50) **Going Correction** +0.075s/f (Slow) — **6 Ran SP% 111.5**
Speed ratings (Par 105): **106,100,100,99,99 97**
Tote Swingers:1&2:£9.00, 2&3:£7.40, 1&3:£3.10 CSF £29.03 TOTE £2.70: £1.20, £4.30; EX 33.10.
Owner Mrs M E Slade **Bred** Whitsbury Manor Stud And Mrs M E Slade **Trained** Kimpton, Hants

FOCUS

A good quality conditions event on paper but it was turned into a rout by Oasis Dancer, who took another step forward. This form is arguably worth a bit more.

T/Plt: £216.40 to a 1 stake. Pool £113,795.64. 383.70 winning tickets. T/Qpdt: £33.60 to a 1 stake. Pool £9,450.16. 207.90 winning tickets. CR

7708 SOUTHWELL (L-H)
Sunday, December 11

OFFICIAL GOING: Standard

Wind: Light across Weather: Overcast

7722 TOTEPLACEPOT CLASSIFIED CLAIMING STKS — 1m 4f (F)
12:30 (12:30) (Class 6) 3-Y-O+ — **£1,617** (£481; £240; £120) **Stalls** Low

Form / RPR

124- **1** **Bivouac (UAE)**[348] 7130 7-8-13 73.................................... JoeFanning 6 73
(Alan Swinbank) *trckd ldrs: hdwy 4f out: led over 2f out: rdn over 1f out: styd on* **6/4**[1]

1400 **2** *1 3/4* **Lifetime (IRE)**[65] 6674 3-8-9 72...................................... BarryMcHugh 1 71
(Brian Ellison) *trckd ldrs: hdwy on inner 3f out: rdn 2f out: sn chsng wnr: no imp fnl f* **9/4**[2]

0050 **3** *2 1/2* **Magic Millie (IRE)**[61] 6769 4-8-0 43................................. RyanPowell(5) 5 58
(David O'Meara) *prom: led over 3f out: sn rdn and hdd over 2f out: sn drvn and one pce* **66/1**

0340 **4** *3* **Xpres Maite**[23] 7465 8-8-13 72.................................(p) RussKennemore 4 61
(Roy Bowring) *racd wd: mde most tl rdn and hdd over 3f out: wknd 2f out* **7/1**

2660 **5** *4* **Overrule (USA)**[65] 6676 7-8-6 70.. AmyRyan(3) 2 51
(Brian Ellison) *hld up in rr: effrt and wd st: sn rdn and n.d* **11/2**[3]

0620 **6** *dist* **Global**[15] 7556 5-8-5 60... JohnFahy 3 —
(Brian Ellison) *pushed along s to dispute ld: cl up on inner: rdn along 1/2-way: sn wknd: t.o whn virtually p.u wl over 2f out* **10/1**

2m 39.47s (-1.53) **Going Correction** -0.15s/f (Stan)
WFA 3 from 4yo+ 5lb — **6 Ran SP% 109.2**
Speed ratings (Par 101): **99,97,96,94,91** —
Tote Swingers: 1&2 £1.60, 1&3 £6.30, 2&3 £9.60 CSF £4.76 TOTE £2.00: £1.30, £1.10; EX 4.60.

Owner Mrs J M Penney **Bred** Darley **Trained** Melsonby, N Yorks

Global Official explanation: vet said gelding finished distressed

7723 TOTEPOOL H'CAP — 1m 4f (F)
1:00 (1:01) (Class 6) (0-60,59) 3-Y-O — **£2,045** (£603; £302) **Stalls** Low

Form / RPR

011 **1** **Sky High Diver (IRE)**[26] 7426 3-9-7 **59**.............................. JoeFanning 4 68+
(Alan Swinbank) *hld up: hdwy over 3f out: rdn to chal on inner wl over 1f out: drvn and styd on to ld ins fnl f* **15/8**[1]

5335 **2** *3/4* **Marina Ballerina**[9] 7608 3-8-11 **49**............................... JimmyQuinn 2 57
(Roy Bowring) *t.k.h: trckd ldr: hdwy 3f out: led wl over 1f out: sn rdn: drvn and hdd ins fnl f: no ex* **7/2**[3]

0362 **3** *3* **Sistine**[37] 7264 3-9-7 **59**... TomEaves 3 62
(Nicky Henderson) *hld up in rr: hdwy 3f out: effrt to chse ldrs 2f out: sn rdn and no imp* **85/40**[2]

0250 **4** *4 1/2* **Hal Of A Lover**[19] 7062 3-9-5 **57**................................. DanielTudhope 6 53
(David O'Meara) *led: rdn along over 3f out: jnd and drvn 2f out: hdd wl over 1f out and grad wknd* **25/1**

2-46 **5** *shd* **Fonnie (IRE)**[37] 7271 3-9-3 **55**.. MartinLane 5 51
(Rae Guest) *prom: rdn along 4f out: wknd 3f out* **50/1**

0010 **6** *1* **Thank You Joy**[26] 6823 3-9-6 **58**.................................(p) StephenCraine 7 52
(J R Jenkins) *in tch: rdn along over 3f out: sn wknd* **20/1**

3125 **7** *14* **Art Thief**[17] 7528 3-9-6 **58**.. LukeMorris 1 30
(Michael Appleby) *trckd ldrs on inner: rdn along over 4f out: sn wknd* **15/2**

2m 41.24s (0.24) **Going Correction** -0.15s/f (Stan) — **7 Ran SP% 111.3**
Speed ratings (Par 98): **93,92,90,87,87 86,77**
Tote Swingers: 1&2 £2.10, 1&3 £2.10, 2&3 £1.70 CSF £8.25 CT £13.33 TOTE £2.40: £1.30, £2.00; EX 9.20 Trifecta £18.90.
Owner Mrs M C Keogh **Bred** Michael Downey & Roalso Ltd **Trained** Melsonby, N Yorks

7724 TOTEQUADPOT MAIDEN STKS — 6f (F)
1:30 (1:30) (Class 5) 2-Y-O — **£2,264** (£673; £336; £168) **Stalls** Low

Form / RPR

53 **1** **Sky Crossing**[10] 7593 2-9-3 0....................................... JamesSullivan 3 75
(James Given) *t.k.h and carried hd high: led: qcknd clr 2f out: pushed out* **8/15**[1]

2 *1 1/4* **Bold Cuffs** 2-9-3 0.. SebSanders 6 70+
(Sir Mark Prescott Bt) *dwlt and in rr: hdwy on outer wl over 2f out: rdn to chse wnr wl over 1f out: styng on whn green and edgd lft ent fnl f: kpt on wl towards fin* **6/1**[3]

66 **3** *2 3/4* **Bond Style**[40] 7210 2-9-3 0... TomEaves 4 62
(Bryan Smart) *prom: rdn along and sltly outpcd 2f out: styd on appr fnl f* **14/1**

4 **4** *4 1/2* **Availed Speaker (IRE)**[15] 7555 2-9-3 0........................... TonyHamilton 7 49
(Richard Fahey) *chsd ldrs: rdn along to chse wnr 1/2-way: wknd wl over 1f out* **9/2**[2]

640 **5** *2 1/4* **Essexvale (IRE)**[64] 6695 2-8-12 60................................. PhillipMakin 1 37
(Alan Berry) *chsd ldrs: rdn over 2f out: sn wknd* **50/1**

0 **6** *2 3/4* **Prim By Night**[15] 7555 2-8-5 0................................ GeorgeChaloner(7) 5 29
(Richard Fahey) *dwlt: a towards rr: rdn and outpcd fr over 2f out* **40/1**

1m 16.42s (-0.08) **Going Correction** -0.15s/f (Stan) — **6 Ran SP% 108.8**
Speed ratings (Par 96): **94,92,88,82,79 76**
Tote Swingers: 1&2 £1.20, 1&3 £2.30, 2&3 £2.70 CSF £3.91 TOTE £1.80: £1.20, £2.70; EX 5.30.

Owner Bolton Grange **Bred** Bolton Grange **Trained** Willoughton, Lincs

NOTEBOOK

Sky Crossing made it third time lucky and landed some hefty bets. He shot clear when asked to win the race at the top of the home straight and was in no danger inside the final furlong. He still looked distinctly green, which allowed the runner-up to close late on, and so further improvement should really be forthcoming. (op 8-11 tchd 4-5)

Bold Cuffs ◆ was the obvious eye-catcher. He is really bred to appreciate a stiffer test, so it was not surprising to see him left behind as the winner went on. However, the penny was dropping throughout the final furlong and he did some promising late work. (op 13-2 tchd 5-1)

Bond Style posted his best effort to date on this AW debut but wasn't suited by the drop back a furlong. Handicaps are now an option. (op 9-1)

Availed Speaker(IRE) lacked anything like a gear change on this switch to Fibresand and step up in trip. He looks to need more time. (op 7-2)

7725 YVONNE AND BOB BARNES 40TH ANNIVERSARY NURSERY — 7f (F)
2:00 (2:02) (Class 5) (0-75,77) 2-Y-O — **£2,264** (£673; £336; £168) **Stalls** Low

Form / RPR

0401 **1** **Flying Pickets (IRE)**[26] 7423 2-8-13 **67**................................ JohnFahy 1 75
(Alan McCabe) *in tch: hdwy on inner 1/2-way: rdn to chal wl over 1f out: sn led: clr whn edgd lft ent fnl f: styd on wl* **4/1**[3]

6321 **2** *2 1/4* **Rio Grande**[8] 7626 2-9-6 **77**..(p) DaleSwift(3) 4 78
(Ann Duffield) *trckd ldng pair: hdwy to ld over 2f out: rdn: hung rt and hdd wl over 1f out: kpt on same pce* **13/8**[1]

3224 **3** *4 1/2* **Ishiamiracle**[31] 7350 2-8-6 **60**... LukeMorris 5 49
(Phil McEntee) *led 2f: cl up: rdn wl over 2f out: one pce fr wl over 1f out* **13/2**

5000 **4** *5* **Lady Nickandy (IRE)**[6] 7635 2-7-13 **53**...................(v[1]) AndrewMullen 8 29
(Alan McCabe) *dwlt: sn chsng ldrs and led after 2f: rdn along and hdd over 2f out: sn wknd* **33/1**

1212 **5** *3/4* **Adranian (IRE)**[2] 7686 2-9-2 **70**.................................(v) AdrianNicholls 6 45
(David C Griffiths) *prom: rdn along and cl up 3f out: wd st: wknd fnl 2f* **2/1**[2]

0000 **6** *6* **Fouracres**[26] 7421 2-7-9 **52** oh7...................................(e) DominicFox(3) 3 11
(Michael Appleby) *a towards rr* **100/1**

5006 **7** *7* **Bit A Craic**[1] 7708 2-7-5 **52** oh7................................(t) BradleyBosley(7) 7 —
(John Ryan) *a in rr: outpcd and bhd fr 1/2-way* **100/1**
0000 **8** *5* **Ventus D'Or**[13] 7569 2-7-13 **53** oh3 ow1........................ JimmyQuinn 2 —
(Derek Shaw) *a in rr: outpcd and bhd fr 1/2-way* **25/1**
1m 29.68s (-0.62) **Going Correction** -0.15s/f (Stan) **8** Ran SP% **113.5**
Speed ratings (Par 96): **97,94,89,83,82 75,67,62**
Tote Swingers: 1&2 £1.60, 1&3 £2.50, 2&3 £2.60 CSF £10.73 CT £39.64 TOTE £3.70: £1.10, £1.10, £2.70; EX 13.60 Trifecta £20.10.
Owner Tariq Al Nisf **Bred** Richard Frayne **Trained** Averham Park, Notts

FOCUS
A moderate nursery. It was run at a solid pace and the form looks sound enough.

NOTEBOOK
Flying Pickets(IRE) was the sole previous C&D winner but was easy to back. The way the race was run proved right up his street and his rider's patience paid off inside the final furlong. This was a career-best and he will always have to be respected around here. (op 3-1)
Rio Grande got off the mark at Wolverhampton eight days earlier and was well backed to follow up on his handicap debut. It was his first outing on the surface and the handicapper hiked him up 7lb for his maiden win, but for a long way he looked as though he would go in again. Ultimately the winner outpaced him, but he was a clear second-best and remains progressive. (op 2-1)
Ishiamiracle ran a solid race under a positive ride and deserves a change of luck, but does seem held by the handicapper. (tchd 7-1)
Lady Nickandy(IRE), reluctant to load up, did plenty from the front and paid the price after turning for home. (tchd 40-1)
Adranian(IRE) had good claims back up a furlong but made his debut here just two days earlier and the run did look to come that bit too soon. He helps to set the level. (op 15-8)

7726 TOTEEXACTA CLAIMING STKS 7f (F)
2:30 (2:31) (Class 6) 3-Y-0+ **£1,704** (£503; £251) **Stalls** Low

Form RPR
2250 **1** **Ingleby Arch (USA)**[19] 7502 8-8-9 77........................ GrahamGibbons 4 84
(David Barron) *chsd ldrs: rdn along 3f out: hdwy to chal 2f out: led 1 1/2f out: kpt on* **9/2**[3]
0002 **2** *1 1/4* **Autumn Blades (IRE)**[13] 7565 6-8-13 84...................(b) JamesSullivan 2 85
(Ruth Carr) *trckd ldrs: smooth hdwy over 2f out and sn ev ch: rdn to chse wnr over 1f out: no imp fnl f* **8/1**
5610 **3** *2 1/2* **Jobe (USA)**[17] 7531 5-8-13 84..(tp) PhillipMakin 8 78
(Kevin Ryan) *trckd ldng pair: hdwy to ld 3f out: rdn 2f out: hdd 1 1/2f out: kpt on same pce* **15/8**[1]
0360 **4** *6* **Bawaardi (IRE)**[51] 7010 5-8-11 82................................. LauraBarry(7) 6 67
(Richard Fahey) *in tch: hdwy to chse ldrs 3f out: sn rdn and n.d* **11/4**[2]
0000 **5** *6* **Waabel**[5] 7644 4-8-13 72...(bt) WilliamCarson 7 45
(Richard Guest) *cl up: rdn along 3f out: wknd over 2f out* **50/1**
1620 **6** *3 1/2* **Brio**[5] 7646 3-8-11 65...(v) ShaneKelly 5 34
(Alan McCabe) *dwlt: stdd and swtchd wd after s: sn wl bhd: tenderly rdn and sme late hdwy* **15/2**
0020 **7** *4 1/2* **Royal Intruder**[10] 7596 6-9-1 70...................................(p) MartinHarley 1 26
(Richard Guest) *led: rdn along and hdd 3f out: sn wknd* **16/1**
4006 **8** *1/2* **Bravo King (IRE)**[5] 7643 3-9-4 78...........................(t) RobertLButler(3) 3 31
(Richard Guest) *a in rr* **25/1**
1m 28.61s (-1.69) **Going Correction** -0.15s/f (Stan) **8** Ran SP% **114.2**
Speed ratings (Par 101): **103,101,98,91,85 81,75,75**
Tote Swingers: 1&2 £3.50, 1&3 £2.50, 2&3 £2.20 CSF £39.72 TOTE £6.10: £2.00, £2.70, £1.50; EX 24.90 Trifecta £108.70.
Owner Dave Scott **Bred** Alexander-Groves Thoroughbreds **Trained** Maunby, N Yorks

FOCUS
A fairly tight claimer and solid form.
Brio Official explanation: jockey said, regarding running and riding, that his orders were to jump and make the running, but the gelding anticipated the start and missed the break, after which it was reluctant to face the kickback.

7727 RICHARD WENTWORTH'S 80TH BIRTHDAY H'CAP 1m (F)
3:00 (3:00) (Class 5) (0-75,75) 3-Y-0 **£2,264** (£673; £336; £168) **Stalls** Low

Form RPR
0322 **1** **Beautiful Day**[29] 7388 3-8-7 **64**... AmyRyan(3) 3 79
(Kevin Ryan) *mde all: rdn 2f out: styd on strly fnl f* **3/1**[2]
013 **2** *2 3/4* **Il Battista**[19] 7500 3-9-4 **72**..(be) ShaneKelly 4 81
(Alan McCabe) *trckd ldrs: effrt to chse wnr 3f out: rdn wl over 1f out: no imp fnl f* **7/4**[1]
5100 **3** *1 1/4* **Patriotic (IRE)**[129] 4730 3-8-10 **64**................................. FrannyNorton 6 70
(Chris Dwyer) *trckd ldrs on outer: hdwy 3f out: rdn over 2f out and ev ch: edgd lft over 1f out: kpt on towards fin* **7/1**
060 **4** *16* **Absolute Princess**[174] 3228 3-9-3 **71**.......................... GrahamGibbons 2 40
(David Nicholls) *chsd wnr: rdn along and wkng whn n.m.r 3f out: sn outpcd* **9/1**
0500 **5** *4 1/2* **Beyeh (IRE)**[79] 6311 3-8-0 **61** oh1.. JackDuern(7) 1 20
(Michael Appleby) *dwlt: a outpcd and bhd* **33/1**
5100 **6** *1/2* **Daruband**[6] 7637 3-9-5 **73**..(v) JoeFanning 5 31
(Alan McCabe) *dwlt: sn chsng ldrs on inner: rdn along over 3f out: sn wknd* **7/2**[3]
1m 40.96s (-2.74) **Going Correction** -0.15s/f (Stan) **6** Ran SP% **109.0**
Speed ratings (Par 102): **107,104,103,87,82 82**
Tote Swingers: 1&2 £1.90, 1&3 £3.90, 2&3 £1.90 CSF £8.14 CT £27.35 TOTE £4.20: £2.50, £1.10; EX 10.00 Trifecta £18.50.
Owner Guy Reed **Bred** G Reed **Trained** Hambleton, N Yorks

FOCUS
A tight handicap. It was run at a good pace and the principals dominated.

7728 SPIFFING CRABBIE'S ALCOHOLIC GINGER BEER H'CAP 6f (F)
3:30 (3:31) (Class 6) (0-60,60) 3-Y-0+ **£1,704** (£503; £251) **Stalls** Low

Form RPR
-400 **1** **Monte Cassino (IRE)**[30] 7366 6-8-6 **47**............................ TomEaves 2 57
(Bryan Smart) *prom on inner: rdn 2f out: edgd rt and styd on ent fnl f to ld last 100yds* **40/1**
2052 **2** *3/4* **Greenhead High**[5] 7641 3-9-5 **58**................................. AdrianNicholls 4 66
(David Nicholls) *led: rdn 2f out: drvn ent fnl f: hdd and no ex last 100yds* **7/2**[2]
0204 **3** *1* **Caramelita**[19] 7504 4-9-7 **60**.....................................(v) StephenCraine 5 65
(J R Jenkins) *trckd ldrs: hdwy over 2f out: rdn to chse ldr over 1f out: kpt on same pce fnl f* **9/1**
4403 **4** *1 1/2* **Gracie's Gift (IRE)**[26] 7420 9-8-13 **52**............................(v) LukeMorris 3 52
(Richard Guest) *chsd ldrs: hdwy 2f out: rdn over 1f out: n.m.r ent fnl f: one pce* **7/1**[3]
1122 **5** *1/2* **Michael's Nook**[23] 7462 4-9-5 **58**................................... PhillipMakin 8 56
(David Barron) *dwlt and towards rr: hdwy over 2f out: sn rdn: styd on wl fnl f: nrst fin* **7/4**[1]

0060 **6** *1* **Takajan (IRE)**[5] 7641 4-8-11 **57**.............................. RachealKneller(7) 11 52
(Mark Brisbourne) *prom on outer: rdn 2f out and ch tl drvn and one pce appr fnl f* **14/1**
0360 **7** *3/4* **Dunmore Boy (IRE)**[19] 7504 3-9-0 **60**.................(p) GeorgeChaloner(7) 6 53
(Richard Fahey) *dwlt and towards rr: hdwy over 2f out: sn rdn and kpt on fnl f: nrst fin* **25/1**
4055 **8** *3/4* **Ace Master**[9] 7610 3-9-4 **57**... JimmyQuinn 13 47
(Roy Bowring) *midfield: hdwy 2f out: sn rdn and no imp fnl f* **7/1**[3]
0000 **9** *3/4* **Nacho Libre**[19] 7504 6-9-4 **57**....................................(b) JamesSullivan 1 45
(Michael Easterby) *in rr: hdwy on inner 2f out: sn rdn and nrst fin* **66/1**
0060 **10** *7* **Rio's Girl**[5] 7646 4-8-10 **52**...(b) AmyRyan(3) 9 18
(Tony Coyle) *cl up: rdn wl over 2f out: sn wknd* **22/1**
1412 **11** *6* **Ridgeway Hawk**[264] 936 3-9-6 **59**.............................(v) DavidProbert 10 —
(Mark Usher) *a towards rr* **9/1**
400 **12** *3/4* **Royal Blade (IRE)**[48] 7065 4-8-12 **58**.................. MatthewHopkins(7) 12 —
(Alan Berry) *chsd ldrs to 1/2-way: sn wknd* **80/1**
000 **13** *12* **Simple Rhythm**[2] 7691 5-8-11 **55**................................(p) RyanPowell(5) 14 —
(John Ryan) *chsd ldrs on wd outside: rdn along 1/2-way: sn wknd* **33/1**
1m 15.57s (-0.93) **Going Correction** -0.15s/f (Stan) **13** Ran SP% **126.6**
Speed ratings (Par 101): **100,99,97,95,95 93,92,91,90,81 73,72,56**
Tote Swingers: 1&2 £9.60, 1&3 £42.30, 2&3 £7.90 CSF £180.10 CT £1095.13 TOTE £39.00: £11.60, £2.10, £5.30; EX 241.40.
Owner Woodcock Electrical Limited **Bred** R N Auld **Trained** Hambleton, N Yorks

FOCUS
A competitive sprint handicap for the class. There was no hanging about early on and the form makes some sense.
T/Plt: £4.30 to a £1 level stake. Pool: £62,761.79. 10,592.40 winning units. T/Qpdt: £2.00 to a £1 level stake. Pool: £4,955.70. 1,828.80 winning units. JR

7497 SHA TIN (R-H)
Sunday, December 11
OFFICIAL GOING: Turf: good to firm

7729a CATHAY PACIFIC HONG KONG VASE (GROUP 1) (3YO+) (TURF) 1m 4f
6:00 (12:00) 3-Y-0+
£658,959 (£254,335; £90,834; £90,834; £37,985; £23,121)

RPR
1 **Dunaden (FR)**[40] 7218 5-9-0 0....................................... CraigAWilliams 3 121
(M Delzangles, France) *hld up in midfield: effrt and pushed along over 1f out: qcknd to ld fnl 100yds: kpt on strly* **56/10**
2 *3/4* **Thumbs Up (NZ)**[21] 7498 7-9-0 0.................................... BrettPrebble 1 120
(C Fownes, Hong Kong) *hld up towards rr: hdwy on outside over 2f out: sn rdn: led 1f out tl hdd fnl 100yds: kpt on same pce* **14/1**
3 *3/4* **Red Cadeaux**[40] 7218 5-9-0 0... RyanMoore 7 119
(Ed Dunlop) *hld up on ins: drvn over 2f out: hdwy and angled lft over 1f out: kpt on u.p fnl f: nt pce to chal* **15/1**
3 *dht* **Silver Pond (FR)**[70] 6567 4-9-0 0..................................(t) ThierryJarnet 2 119
(F Head, France) *hld up in tch on ins: nt clr run and lost pl over 3f out: hdwy whn short of room fr over 1f out: rdn and kpt on fnl 100yds: nrst fin* **43/10**[2]
5 *1 1/4* **Campanologist (USA)**[56] 6907 6-9-0 0........................... FrankieDettori 6 117
(Saeed Bin Suroor) *trckd ldrs gng wl: effrt and drvn over 1f out: kpt on same pce ins fnl f* **31/10**[1]
6 *2* **Trailblazer (JPN)**[14] 7563 4-9-0 0.................................... KatsumiAndo 8 114
(Yasutoshi Ikee, Japan) *dwlt: hld up: pushed along and plenty to do home bnd over 2f out: hdwy on outside over 1f out: kpt on: nvr able to chal* **74/10**
7 *1* **Jakkalberry (IRE)**[84] 6202 5-9-0 0..............................(t) FabioBranca 13 112
(Marco Botti) *pressed ldr: led and maintained ordinary gallop 1/2-way: rdn and qcknd 2f out: hdd 1f out: sn no ex: eased whn hld towards fin* **70/1**
8 *2* **Mighty High (FR)**[21] 7498 5-9-0 0.............................. DarrenBeadman 11 109
(J Moore, Hong Kong) *t.k.h: led at ordinary gallop to 1/2-way: cl up tl rdn and wknd over 1f out* **49/1**
9 *1/2* **Super Satin (NZ)**[21] 7498 6-9-0 0.. ODoleuze 9 108
(C Fownes, Hong Kong) *hld up last: effrt on wd outside over 2f out: sn rdn along no imp fr over 1f out* **55/1**
10 *2 1/4* **Vadamar (FR)**[56] 6903 3-8-9 0.................. Christophe-PatriceLemaire 10 104
(A De Royer-Dupre, France) *s.i.s: t.k.h early: hld up on outside: rdn and edgd rt over 2f out: nvr on terms* **22/5**[3]
11 *1/2* **Redwood**[56] 6910 5-9-0 0.. MichaelHills 12 104
(Charles Hills) *prom: effrt and drvn over 2f out: wknd over 1f out* **15/1**
12 *1 1/2* **Mr Medici (IRE)**[21] 7498 6-9-0 0...................................... GeraldMosse 5 101
(L Ho, Hong Kong) *trckd ldrs: nt clr run and rdn over 2f out: wknd over 1f out* **36/1**
13 *31* **Sarah Lynx (IRE)**[14] 7563 4-8-10 0..................(b) ChristopheSoumillon 4 97
(J E Hammond, France) *hld up in midfield on outside: stdy hdwy over 4f out: struggling over 3f out: eased whn btn ent st* **14/1**
2m 27.5s (-0.70)
WFA 3 from 4yo+ 5lb **13** Ran SP% **122.6**
PARI-MUTUEL (all including HK$10 stake): WIN 66.00; PLACE 20.50, 43.00, 3 DH (Silver Pond) 10.50, (Red Cadeaux) 24.50; DF 283.00.
Owner Pearl Bloodstock Ltd **Bred** Comte E Decazes **Trained** France

FOCUS
In the absence Snow Fairy, last year's Hong Kong Cup winner who was being aimed at the Vase until getting injured, the race was left wide open. It wasn't a strong contest but there was still a worthy winner in Melbourne Cup hero. The sectionals (set by the leader at each quarter) show the pace was just modest: 25.55, 24.58 (50.13), 25.23 (1.15.36), 24.05 (1.39.41), and 24.20 (2.03.61), with the last couple of furlongs covered in 23.89.

NOTEBOOK
Dunaden(FR) had the quickest closing sectional and it was his late surge that proved decisive, having initially taken a while to pick up. He was really strong at the line and has improved again to show himself a genuinely high-class middle-distance/stayer. Perhaps his connections will now be tempted by the Sheema Classic (1m4f, Group 1) at Meydan in March, as he hasn't been over-raced in recent months, but in the longer term the handicapper will doubtless ensure a repeat in the Melbourne Cup is unlikely.
Thumbs Up(NZ), only seventh in this in 2009 and sixth in last year's Mile, had his chance but was simply outstayed. He had subsequent Cup winner California Memory behind when taking a 1m2f Group 2 last time, but recorded just the fourth fastest final quarter over this longer trip.
Red Cadeaux came from further back than those who finished around him. He was 2lb worse off with Dunaden than when beaten a nose by that rival in the Melbourne Cup, and also had livelier ground to contend with, and Ryan Moore reportedly felt the gelding wouldn't fully let himself down. He's a possible for Dubai, but another trip to Australia is said to be the main aim.

Silver Pond(FR) ◆, extremely well backed locally, probably would have finished closer granted a clear run. This followed a highly respectable run in the Arc (little chance under hold-up ride) and he'll be interesting if kept in training. He's another who might be suited by a race like the Sheema Classic.
Campanologist(USA) was beautifully placed turning into the straight, but he couldn't pick up sufficiently. This was tougher than the back-to-back European Group 1s he landed this year.
Trailblazer(JPN) was set too much to do and found a bit of trouble, though he made late progress. His rider felt he wasn't handling the surface.
Jakkalberry(IRE) seemed to be hanging under pressure and was eased inside the final 50 yards.
Vadamar(FR) didn't build on his recent Longchamp Group 2 win and his rider felt the ground was too quick.
Redwood, last year's runner-up, was another to disappoint. He didn't stride out well in the straight.
Sarah Lynx(IRE) was set a lot to do and probably didn't appreciate the ground.

7730a CATHAY PACIFIC HONG KONG SPRINT (GROUP 1) (3YO+) (TURF) 6f

6:40 (12:00) 3-Y-0+

£658,959 (£184,971; £184,971; £66,061; £37,985; £23,121)

RPR

1 **Lucky Nine (IRE)**[70] 4-9-0 0 .... BrettPrebble 6 121
(C Fownes, Hong Kong) *dwlt: hld up towards rr: gd hdwy on outside over 2f out: sn rdn: edgd rt and chal ins fnl f: kpt on wl to ld cl home* **67/20**[2]

2 *hd* **Joy And Fun (NZ)**[21] 7497 8-9-0 0 ....(p) BrettDoyle 7 120
(D Cruz, Hong Kong) *hld up in midfield: hdwy on outside 2f out: sn rdn: edgd rt and disp ld fnl f: kpt on u.p: hld cl home* **81/1**

2 *dht* **Entrapment (AUS)**[21] 7497 5-9-0 0 .... DouglasWhyte 5 120
(J Size, Hong Kong) *t.k.h early: prom: hdwy against ins rail to ld over 1f out: hrd pressed fnl f: kpt on u.p: hdd nr fin* **51/10**[3]

4 *1 ¾* **Little Bridge (NZ)**[21] 7497 5-9-0 0 ....(t) GeraldMosse 3 114
(C S Shum, Hong Kong) *prom: drvn and outpcd 2f out: rallied u.p fnl f: nt pce to rch first three* **19/10**[1]

5 *¼* **Curren Chan (JPN)**[70] 4-8-10 0 .... KenichiIkezoe 11 110
(Takayuki Yasuda, Japan) *in tch: drvn and outpcd wl over 1f out: rallied fnl f: kpt on but nt pce to chal* **9/1**

6 *½* **Rich Unicorn (AUS)**[21] 7497 5-9-0 0 .... MarkDuPlessis 9 112
(J Size, Hong Kong) *sn bhd: rdn and hdwy on wd outside 2f out: kpt on fnl f: nrst fin* **15/1**

7 *½* **Admiration (AUS)**[21] 7497 4-9-0 0 ....(b[1]) DarrenBeadman 10 110
(J Moore, Hong Kong) *hld up towards rr: drvn along over 2f out: kpt on fnl 100yds: nvr rchd ldrs* **13/1**

8 *shd* **Bated Breath**[56] 6908 4-9-0 0 .... SteveDrowne 12 110
(Roger Charlton) *t.k.h: disp ld after 2f: rdn and led over 2f out to over 1f out: no ex fnl f* **106/1**

9 *1 ¼* **Sole Power**[70] 6563 4-9-0 0 .... KLatham 8 106
(Edward Lynam, Ire) *towards rr: drvn along over 2f out: hdwy fnl f: nvr able to chal* **181/1**

10 *½* **Sacred Kingdom (AUS)**[71] 8-9-0 0 ....(t) ZacPurton 14 104
(P F Yiu, Hong Kong) *s.i.s: t.k.h early in rr: rdn: effrt and hdwy wl over 1f out: no imp and btn ins fnl f* **10/1**

11 *½* **Green Birdie (NZ)**[70] 8-9-0 0 .... TyeAngland 4 103
(C Fownes, Hong Kong) *hld up on ins: rdn and shortlived effrt over 1f out: btn fnl f* **158/1**

12 *shd* **Rocket Man (AUS)**[30] 6-9-0 0 .... BVorster 13 103
(Patrick Shaw, Singapore) *disp ld on outside 2f: trckd ldrs: rdn over 2f out: wknd over 1f out* **76/10**

13 *¾* **Society Rock (IRE)**[57] 6858 4-9-0 0 .... JMurtagh 2 100
(James Fanshawe) *s.i.s: bhd and sn pushed along on ins: drvn over 2f out: nvr on terms* **148/1**

14 *6 ¼* **Pas De Trois (JPN)**[70] 4-9-0 0 .... KatsumiAndo 1 80
(Ippo Sameshima, Japan) *led at decent gallop against ins rail: hdd over 2f out: wknd qckly over 1f out* **53/1**

68.98 secs (68.98) **14** Ran SP% **123.8**
PARI-MUTUEL (all including HK$10 stake): WIN 43.50; PLACE 16.50, 2 DH (Entrapment) 21.00, (Joy And Fun) 118.00; DF (Lucky Nine & Entrapment) 94.50, (Lucky Nine & Joy And Fun) 1,127.00.
Owner Dr Chang Fuk To & Maria Chang Lee Ming Shum **Bred** Darley **Trained** Hong Kong

FOCUS

A sub-standard running of the Sprint and it was dominated by the locals, who were responsible for the first four finishers. The home team missed out last year, but this was their tenth success in 13 runnings. They went 23.61 for the first quarter and 22.33 (45.94) for the half, with the final couple of furlongs covered in 23.04.

NOTEBOOK

Lucky Nine(IRE) was only seventh in this last year, although it was a better run than the bare result suggested as 3yos have a 0-9 record in the race and he missed the break from stall 12 before producing the quickest closing sectional. On his most recent outing he looked unlucky not to finish second behind Curren Chan in the Sprinters Stakes in Japan and he built on that to record the second top-level win of his career. The other was gained over 1m. While the form doesn't amount to a great deal by Group 1 standards, he's better than he showed as he again missed a beat at the start and was then forced wider than ideal into the straight. His head was a touch high under pressure, but there was nothing wrong with his attitude under a forceful ride.
Entrapment(AUS) got a lovely split against the inside rail in the straight, saving more ground than his main rivals, and can have no excuses.
Joy And Fun(NZ), third in 2009 but well beaten last year, ran a terrific race, although his proximity limits the level.
Little Bridge(NZ) couldn't build up sufficient momentum when short of room in the straight and otherwise would probably have finished a bit closer. Interestingly, when commenting on the lack of room, Gerald Mosse also said the horse was "a bit timid, a bit shy".
Curren Chan(JPN) couldn't confirm Sprinters Stakes form with Lucky Nine, but she emerges with plenty of credit in defeat. Much like Little Bridge, she lost her place when having to wait for a run early in the straight, but she still fared best of those from a double-figure gate. She reportedly didn't have a good trip over and Japanese runners are now 0-13 in this with none placed, while fillies are 0-15. Clearly she was up against it.
Rich Unicorn(AUS) got too far behind and came just about widest of all into the straight, but only the winner finished quicker. He's very much going the right way and it wouldn't surprise if he is a more serious contender in 12 months' time.
Admiration(AUS) didn't step up as one might have hoped in first-time blinkers, but time is on his side.
Bated Breath was asked to dispute the lead from stall 12 and had little hope of sustaining his bid. Before the off British runners had a 0-28 record, and now they're 0-30. He stays in training.
Sole Power didn't run a bad race considering he'd never previously raced around a right-handed bend and has looked a 5f specialist.
Sacred Kingdom(AUS), winner of this in 2007 and 2009, as well as third last year, was dropped in from the widest gate, but he didn't have much room in the straight and was always struggling to make up the conceded ground.
Rocket Man(AUS) had a wide trip from an unfavourable draw, but he might not be one to make excuses for. He's been a terrific sprinter over the years, but there have been signs lately that he's no longer the force of old. Connections will hope he returns to something like his best after a much-needed break.
Society Rock(IRE) had a bit to find in this company, so it was game over when he lost a few lengths at the start.

7731a CATHAY PACIFIC HONG KONG MILE (GROUP 1) (3YO+) (TURF) 1m

7:50 (12:00) 3-Y-0+

£941,370 (£363,336; £165,152; £94,137; £54,500; £33,030)

RPR

1 **Able One (NZ)**[21] 7499 9-9-0 0 .... JeffLloyd 7 123
(J Moore, Hong Kong) *chsd clr ldr: shkn up to ld over 1f out: drvn and hld on wl fnl f* **66/1**

2 *nk* **Cityscape**[42] 7193 5-9-0 0 .... SteveDrowne 12 122
(Roger Charlton) *hld up in midfield on outside: effrt and drvn over 2f out: chsd wnr last 175yds: kpt on u.p towards fin* **32/1**

3 *nk* **Xtension (IRE)**[21] 7499 4-9-0 0 .... DarrenBeadman 5 121+
(J Moore, Hong Kong) *hld up on ins: effrt whn n.m.r and angled lft over 1f out: drvn and kpt on wl fnl f* **6/4**[1]

4 *nk* **Dubawi Gold**[57] 6860 3-8-13 0 .... RichardHughes 14 121
(Richard Hannon) *hld up: effrt and hdwy on wd outside 2f out: kpt on fnl f: hld towards fin* **102/1**

5 *1 ½* **Sichuan Success (AUS)**[42] 5-9-0 0 ....(t) DouglasWhyte 13 117
(J Size, Hong Kong) *t.k.h early: prom: hdwy to chse wnr over 1f out: edgd rt and lost 2nd last 175yds: one pce* **67/10**[2]

6 *shd* **Beauty Flash (NZ)**[21] 7499 6-9-0 0 ....(t) GeraldMosse 10 117
(A S Cruz, Hong Kong) *prom: drvn along over 2f out: kpt on same pce fnl f* **14/1**

7 *shd* **Rajsaman (FR)**[71] 6556 4-9-0 0 ....(b) ThierryJarnet 4 117
(F Head, France) *hld up: effrt and drvn on outside wl over 1f out: kpt on fnl f: nvr able to chal* **12/1**

8 *shd* **Sahpresa (USA)**[21] 6-8-10 0 ....(t) Christophe-PatriceLemaire 8 112
(Rod Collet, France) *towards rr: n.m.r and outpcd wl over 1f out: drvn and kpt on fnl f: no imp* **15/2**[3]

9 *½* **Jimmy Choux (NZ)**[36] 4-9-0 0 .... JonathanRiddell 2 115
(John Bary, New Zealand) *trckd ldrs: effrt and wnt 2nd briefly over 1f out: sn drvn: kpt on same pce fnl f* **8/1**

10 *shd* **Outdoor Pegasus**[7] 4-9-0 0 ....(t) JMurtagh 3 115
(P F Yiu, Hong Kong) *hld up on ins: rdn over 2f out: hdwy over 1f out: nvr able to chal* **90/1**

11 *1 ¼* **Fat Choy Oohlala**[56] 4-9-0 0 ....(b) MaximeGuyon 11 112
(C H Yip, Hong Kong) *s.i.s: bhd: pushed along over 2f out: sme late hdwy: nvr on terms* **36/1**

12 *1 ¼* **Destined For Glory (IRE)**[21] 7499 4-9-0 0 ....(t[1]) TimothyClark 1 109
(J Moore, Hong Kong) *midfield on ins: rdn over 2f out: edgd lft and wknd over 1f out* **9/1**

13 *3 ¾* **Apapane (JPN)**[28] 7410 4-8-10 0 .... MasayoshiEbina 9 97
(Sakae Kunieda, Japan) *prom: drvn along over 2f out: wknd over 1f out* **19/1**

14 *19 ½* **Flying Blue (AUS)**[21] 7499 5-9-0 0 .... ODoleuze 6 56
(J Size, Hong Kong) *led and 3 l clr: rdn and hdd over 1f out: sn wknd and eased* **12/1**

1m 33.98s (-0.72)
WFA 3 from 4yo+ 1lb **14** Ran SP% **122.2**
PARI-MUTUEL (all including HK$10 stake): WIN 668.50; PLACE 151.00, 67.50, 12.50; DF 6,747.50.
Owner Dr & Mrs Cornel Li Fook Kwan **Bred** Sir Partick & Lady Hogan **Trained** Hong Kong

FOCUS

Not a strong race and the form is misleading. The opening split was 24.02 and increased to a sound gallop by halfway, with the sectional at that point 22.39 (46.41). However, the leader soon slowed it down, going 23.70 (1.10.11) before coming home in 23.87.

NOTEBOOK

Able One(NZ) was second slowest through the third section, yet he was able to pinch a lead of over a length when taking up the running early in the straight and it proved decisive. Despite being just fifth quickest of the 14 runners in the final quarter, and getting noticeably tired when changing his legs near the line, he was able to hang on. He stole this under a finely judged ride.
Cityscape had a wide trip, including being five horse-widths out on the turn into the straight, and he did well to get so close. He usually avoids ground this quick but seemed to handle it fine.
Xtension(IRE) had to wait a long time for a clear run in the straight but couldn't quicken sufficiently when in the open. His jockey feels the horse is more of a 1m2f type.
Dubawi Gold ◆ made his move after Cityscape and wider than that rival, and his run flattened out near the line. Despite that, he produced the quickest closing sectional. He's had a long season, while 3yos are now only 1-22 in the Mile, so all things considered this was a huge effort.
Sichuan Success(AUS) wasn't good enough, while last year's winner \bBeauty Flash\p found disappointingly little for pressure.
Beauty Flash(NZ) found disappointingly little for pressure.
Rajsaman(FR), who dead-heated for fourth in this last season, was poorly placed after starting slowly but finished well.
Sahpresa(USA), last year's third, simply had an "off day" according to her rider.
Jimmy Choux(NZ) was better than placed than most turning into the straight and looked to have something to offer, but he didn't pick up for pressure. He was nowhere near the form he has shown in Australasia and perhaps a busy period, as well as the travelling, has taken its toll.

7732a CATHAY PACIFIC HONG KONG CUP (GROUP 1) (3YO+) (TURF) 1m 2f

8:30 (12:00) 3-Y-0+

£941,370 (£363,336; £165,152; £94,137; £54,500; £33,030)

RPR

1 **California Memory (USA)**[21] 7498 5-9-0 0 .... MChadwick 1 121
(A S Cruz, Hong Kong) *trckd ldrs: rdn along over 1f out: qcknd to ld last 100yds: kpt on strly* **69/20**[3]

2 *1* **Irian (GER)**[21] 7498 5-9-0 0 .... DarrenBeadman 10 119
(J Moore, Hong Kong) *stdd last off slow pce: rdn and hdwy on wd outside over 1f out: styd on strly to take 2nd nr fin: too much to do* **16/1**

3 *¼* **Zazou (GER)**[35] 7324 4-9-0 0 .... OlivierPeslier 8 119
(W Hickst, Germany) *trckd ldr: rdn to ld over 1f out: hdd last 100yds: kpt on same pce* **51/1**

4 *shd* **Ambitious Dragon (NZ)**[21] 7499 5-9-0 0 ....(b) DouglasWhyte 5 118
(A T Millard, Hong Kong) *dwlt: hld up in slowly run r: hdwy on outside over 2f out: rdn and ev ch ins fnl f: kpt on: hld towards fin* **11/10**[1]

5 *¾* **Cirrus Des Aigles (FR)**[57] 6861 5-9-0 0 .... ChristopheSoumillon 2 117
(Mme C Barande-Barbe, France) *hld up bhd ldng gp: stdy hdwy 3f out: hung rt and outpcd wl over 1f out: styd on strly under hands and heels riding fnl f: nrst fin* **12/5**[2]

6 ¾ **Byword**[36] 7307 5-9-0 0 MaximeGuyon 6 115
(A Fabre, France) *prom: effrt and drvn along over 2f out: kpt on same pce ins fnl f* **13/1**

7 ¼ **Pure Champion (IRE)**[21] 7498 4-9-0 0 (t) GeraldMosse 3 115
(A S Cruz, Hong Kong) *led at slow pce: rdn and hdd over 1f out: kpt on same pce fnl f* **17/1**

8 2 ¾ **Ransom Note**[57] 6861 4-9-0 0 MichaelHills 4 109
(Charles Hills) *midfield on ins: n.m.r briefly 2f out: sn rdn along and sn btn* **161/1**

9 ½ **Jacobee**[21] 7498 4-9-0 0 (t[1]) TimothyClark 9 108
(J Moore, Hong Kong) *hld up on ins in slowly run r: nt clr run over 2f out: sn swtchd lft and rdn: nvr on terms* **93/1**

10 5 **Durban Thunder (GER)**[71] 6558 5-9-0 0 AStarke 7 98
(T Mundry, Germany) *midfield on outside: drvn and outpcd 2f out: sn wknd* **169/1**

2m 4.57s (3.17) **10** Ran SP% **122.3**
PARI-MUTUEL (all including HK$10 stake): WIN 44.50; PLACE 14.50, 31.50, 74.50; DF 331.50.
Owner Howard Liang Yum Shing **Bred** F Seitz **Trained** Hong Kong

FOCUS
They went a slower pace through the first six furlongs of this contest than the runners in the Vase, but the final quarter was quickest split of all Group 1s on the card. The sectionals were: 27.38, 25.97 (53.35), 25.15 (1.18.47), 24.17 (1.42.64) before a rapid 21.93 for the last two furlongs.

NOTEBOOK
California Memory(USA) was ridden sensibly closer to the lead than is often the case and his jockey waited for a run towards the inside, rather than lose ground by switching. A gap eventually appeared and the horse quickened well. This isn't form to take literally, but he's evidently high class. He has a number of options, with Dubai and Singapore being considered.
Irian(GER) was runner-up in this last year when the race unfolded at a similarly slow pace, and clearly this scenario suits. He was last turning into the straight but produced the quickest closing sectional. On this evidence he'll be worth another try over shorter and maybe he'll be considered for the Duty Free at Meydan in March.
Zazou(GER), who won an Italian Group 1 last time, raced up with the slow pace but was outsprinted in the straight.
Ambitious Dragon(NZ) was further back and wider than ideal on the final bend, and couldn't keep on as well as some. Better could have been expected considering he was a winner over 7f as recently as October.
Cirrus Des Aigles(FR) didn't get much of a run in the straight and never had a chance to show his best. Being a gelding, he stays in training and British Champions Day is again likely to be on his agenda in 2012.
Byword didn't pick up well enough.
Ransom Note simply didn't fire.

7385 TOULOUSE
Sunday, December 11

OFFICIAL GOING: Turf: soft

7733a PRIX MAX SICARD (LISTED RACE) (3YO+) (TURF) 1m 4f
2:25 (12:00) 3-Y-O+ **£25,862** (£10,344; £7,758; £5,172; £2,586)

RPR

1 **Aizavoski (IRE)**[47] 7089 5-9-6 0 PhilippeSogorb 1 113
(E Lellouche, France) **11/5**[1]

2 nk **Tip Toe (FR)**[29] 7404 4-9-0 0 SebastienMaillot 2 107
(F Doumen, France) **10/1**

3 ½ **Zuider Zee (GER)**[36] 7297 4-9-0 0 RobertHavlin 4 106
(John Gosden) *broke wl: sn settled in 2nd bhd stdy pce: gng easily: rdn bef st: nt qckn: dropped bk to 5th: raillied u.p ent fnl f to go 3rd: styd on wl* **5/1**[2]

4 ½ **Aristote**[23] 7480 5-9-3 0 (b) RonanThomas 3 108
(P Van De Poele, France) **13/2**[3]

5 1 ½ **Ok Coral (FR)**[23] 7480 4-9-0 0 LaurentDoreau 9 103
(K Borgel, France) **52/1**

6 nse **Intarsia (GER)**[30] 7386 4-8-10 0 Pierre-CharlesBoudot 5 99
(A Fabre, France) **10/1**

7 nk **Domeside**[364] 7855 5-9-0 0 Jean-BernardEyquem 12 102
(C Delcher-Sanchez, Spain) **30/1**

8 hd **Night Serenade (IRE)**[30] 7386 4-9-0 0 (p) FabriceVeron 10 102
(H-A Pantall, France) **28/1**

9 nk **Silver Valny (FR)**[29] 7406 5-9-0 0 ThomasMessina 8 102
(Mlle M-L Mortier, France) **10/1**

10 1 ¼ **Griraz (FR)**[33] 6-9-0 0 Francois-XavierBertras 13 100
(J-L Dubord, France) **9/1**

0 **Da Capo (IRE)**[45] 5-9-0 0 SylvainRuis 11 —
(Mme Pia Brandt, France) **36/1**

0 **Angolaner (GER)**[23] 7480 4-9-0 0 GregoryBenoist 7 —
(X Nakkachdji, France) **13/1**

0 **Grand Akbar (FR)**[32] 4-9-0 0 CharlesNora 6 —
(Y-M Porzier, France) **49/1**

2m 31.94s (-0.36) **13** Ran SP% **118.9**
WIN (incl. 1 euro stake): 3.20. PLACES: 1.60, 2.50, 2.50. DF: 14.00. SF: 27.40.
Owner Ecurie Wildenstein **Bred** Dayton Investments Ltd **Trained** Lamorlaye, France

NOTEBOOK
Aizavoski(IRE), a consistent sort, will remain in training next year.
Zuider Zee(GER) ran a solid race. He was asked for a final effort early in the straight and took a little time to quicken but was catching the winner and runner-up inside the final furlong.

7715 WOLVERHAMPTON (A.W) (L-H)
Monday, December 12

OFFICIAL GOING: Standard
Wind: Fresh behind Weather: Fine

7734 ALL WEATHER "HANDS AND HEELS" APPRENTICE SERIES H'CAP (PART OF THE RACING EXCELLENCE INITIATIVE) 1m 1f 103y(P)
2:15 (2:15) (Class 5) (0-75,73) 3-Y-O+ **£2,264** (£673; £336; £168; £15; £Form) **Stalls** Low

0641 1 **Archie Rice (USA)**[10] 7604 5-9-0 69 DannyBrock(3) 8 80
(Tom Keddy) *chsd ldr tl led over 2f out: sn pushed clr: styd on wl* **9/2**[2]

6221 2 3 ¼ **Opus Maximus (IRE)**[10] 7605 6-9-7 73 (p) NoelGarbutt 9 77
(Conor Dore) *hld up: plld hrd: hdwy over 6f out: pushed along over 2f out: styd on same pce fr over 1f out: edgd lft ins fnl f: wnt 2nd nr fin* **6/1**

0130 3 hd **Focail Maith**[10] 7601 3-9-4 72 MichaelJMurphy 1 76
(John Ryan) *hld up: hdwy over 2f out: pushed along to chse wnr over 1f out: styd on same pce ins fnl f: lost 2nd nr fin* **5/1**[3]

4413 4 nk **Zafranagar (IRE)**[15] 7363 6-9-4 70 GeorgeDowning 2 73
(Tony Carroll) *prom: pushed along over 2f out: styng on whn nt clr run and swtchd rt ins fnl f* **13/2**

5063 5 1 ½ **Kidlat**[16] 7557 6-9-6 72 (t) NatashaEaton 7 72
(Alan Bailey) *sn pushed along: led after 1f: hdd over 2f out: no ex fnl f* **4/1**[1]

2041 6 2 ½ **Justcallmehandsome**[9] 7632 9-8-10 65 (be) JoshBaudains(3) 4 60
(Dominic Ffrench Davis) *s.i.s: hld up: hdwy over 2f out: wknd over 1f out* **5/1**[3]

1305 7 14 **Scary Movie (IRE)**[4] 7671 6-9-0 69 (p) RossCoakley(3) 6 34
(Emmet Michael Butterly, Ire) *dwlt: hld up: pushed along and wknd over 2f out* **11/1**

2033 8 5 **Bussa**[8] 4022 3-9-0 71 KevinLundie(3) 3 26
(David Evans) *led 1f: chsd ldrs: lost pl 5f out: wknd over 3f out* **28/1**

2m 0.21s (-1.49) **Going Correction** 0.0s/f (Stan)
WFA 3 from 5yo+ 2lb **8** Ran SP% **110.9**
Speed ratings (Par 103): **106,103,102,102,101 99,86,82**
toteswingers:1&2:£5.80, 2&3:£4.70, 1&3:£4.70 CSF £29.49 CT £132.62 TOTE £6.40: £2.00, £2.10, £1.40; EX 37.20 Trifecta £139.20 Pool: £590.87 - 3.14 winning units..
Owner Andrew Duffield **Bred** Baltusrol Thoroughbreds Llc Et Al **Trained** Newmarket, Suffolk
■ Stewards' Enquiry : Josh Baudains seven-day ban: used whip contrary to conditions (Dec 28, Jan 1,4,6,8,9,12)

FOCUS
Some in-form horses lined up for this apprentices' handicap. It was sound run and the winner is rated back to his best post-3yo form.

7735 WOLVERHAMPTON HOLIDAY INN (S) STKS 7f 32y(P)
2:45 (2:45) (Class 6) 2-Y-O **£1,704** (£503; £251) **Stalls** High

Form RPR

11 1 **Mr Red Clubs (IRE)**[11] 7590 2-9-3 0 JimmyFortune 2 70
(Des Donovan) *led: hdd over 5f out: chsd ldr: led over 1f out: sn rdn and edgd rt: r.o* **5/4**[1]

0422 2 2 **Rafaella**[11] 7590 2-8-7 56 (p) LukeMorris 1 55
(Harry Dunlop) *s.i.s: sn prom: rdn over 2f out: styd on to chse wnr ins fnl f: no imp* **9/2**[3]

0023 3 1 ¾ **Astraios (IRE)**[63] 6763 2-8-12 68 (b) ShaneKelly 3 56
(Brian Meehan) *hld up: pushed along 1/2-way: hdwy u.p over 1f out: no ex ins fnl f* **4/1**[2]

0315 4 2 ¼ **Make Up**[27] 7421 2-8-12 60 BarryMcHugh 6 50
(Noel Wilson) *chsd ldr tl led over 5f out: rdn and hdd over 1f out: wknd ins fnl f* **9/2**[3]

6003 5 11 **Rooknrasbryripple**[60] 6821 2-8-7 57 DavidKenny(5) 7 23
(Ralph Smith) *hld up: rdn over 2f out: sn wknd* **25/1**

000 6 3 ¾ **Lady Jane Grace (IRE)**[38] 7257 2-8-7 30 DavidProbert 4 9
(David Evans) *chsd ldrs tl pushed along 1/2-way: sn wknd* **80/1**

04 7 6 **Vicgernic**[11] 7590 2-8-12 0 (p) FergusSweeney 5 —
(Gary Moore) *s.i.s: plld hrd: hdwy over 5f out: rdn and wknd over 2f out* **25/1**

1m 30.08s (0.48) **Going Correction** 0.0s/f (Stan) **7** Ran SP% **109.7**
Speed ratings (Par 94): **97,94,92,90,77 73,66**
toteswingers:1&2:£1.70, 2&3:£2.30, 1&3:£1.90 CSF £6.50 TOTE £2.00: £1.20, £2.80; EX 6.00.There was no bid for the winner.
Owner W P Flynn **Bred** Tally-Ho Stud **Trained** Newmarket, Suffolk

FOCUS
An ordinary seller but a likeable effort from the winner who is a bit better than this grade.

NOTEBOOK
Mr Red Clubs(IRE) recorded a straightforward success. Despite appearing to be on the wrong leg around the turn into the straight, he ran on well once straightened up and won cosily on his debut for his new yard. He might be happier on a right-handed track so might be interesting in similar company at Kempton. (op Evens)
Rafaella, runner-up to Mr Red Clubs over the extended mile here last time, couldn't reverse the form over this shorter trip and was in fact beaten even further. (op 5-1 tchd 11-2)
Astraios(IRE) looked to find this shorter trip against her. (op 5-1)
Make Up, who had a bit to find with the winner at the weights, was up in distance and didn't get home after making the early running. (op 4-1)

7736 TOTEQUADPOT MAIDEN STKS 5f 20y(P)
3:15 (3:16) (Class 5) 2-Y-O **£2,264** (£673; £336; £168) **Stalls** Low

Form RPR

6203 1 **Jwala**[18] 7526 2-8-12 76 ShaneKelly 8 77
(Robert Cowell) *mde all: clr 1/2-way: comf* **9/4**[2]

2 2 ¾ **Pale Orchid (IRE)**[80] 6312 2-8-12 0 LukeMorris 5 67+
(David Evans) *plld hrd: trckd wnr tl over 3f out: wnt 2nd again over 2f out: sn rdn: styd on: nt trble wnr* **15/2**[3]

52 3 4 ½ **Lost City (IRE)**[31] 7359 2-9-3 0 TonyHamilton 4 54
(Richard Fahey) *s.i.s: hdwy over 1f out: nvr on terms* **10/11**[1]

40 4 6 **Flaming Ferrari (IRE)**[74] 6474 2-8-12 0 JimmyFortune 1 27
(Peter Chapple-Hyam) *prom: pushed along 1/2-way: wknd over 1f out* **10/1**

5 2 ¼ **Saint Boniface** 2-9-3 0 FergusSweeney 6 24
(Peter Makin) *s.i.s: outpcd* **33/1**

6 4 ½ **Jealous Hart** 2-8-12 0 FrannyNorton 2 3
(Ollie Pears) *s.i.s: sn outpcd* **40/1**

0 7 10 **Dubar Way (IRE)**[154] 3921 2-8-12 0 PhillipMakin 7 —
(Kevin Ryan) *plld hrd: trckd wnr over 3f out tl hung rt fr 1/2-way: sn wknd and eased* **50/1**

61.55 secs (-0.75) **Going Correction** 0.0s/f (Stan) **7** Ran SP% **111.3**
Speed ratings (Par 96): **106,101,94,84,81 74,58**
toteswingers:1&2:£2.10, 2&3:£2.00, 1&3:£1.20 CSF £17.74 TOTE £2.30: £1.10, £2.90; EX 16.40 Trifecta £18.00 Pool: £683.67 - 27.97 winning units..
Owner Manor Farm Stud & Miss S Hoare **Bred** Manor Farm Stud (rutland) **Trained** Six Mile Bottom, Cambs

FOCUS
A fair maiden. The winner made all and ran basically to form, the second made a fair debut but the favourite disappointed.

NOTEBOOK
Jwala, dropping down to the minimum trip for the first time, made just about all the running. As a half-sister to Airwave this success will have increased her value nicely, but she's due to stay in training at three, and looks the type who could do well in sprint handicaps. (op 2-1 tchd 5-2)
Pale Orchid(IRE) didn't settle early on this debut for her new trainer and in the circumstances she did quite well to stay on for second. She should come on for this first outing in 80 days. (op 8-1)
Lost City(IRE), once again a little slowly away, was disappointing, but this was his third run for a mark and he could be of more interest in handicaps. (op Evens tchd 5-6)

Flaming Ferrari(IRE) is out of a sprinting 2yo winner, but she's by Authorized and perhaps the drop back to 5f was too sharp for her. (op 8-1)
Dubar Way(IRE) Official explanation: jockey said filly hung right-handed

7737 DINE IN HORIZONS RESTAURANT H'CAP 5f 20y(P)
3:45 (3:45) (Class 6) (0-60,60) 3-Y-0+ £1,704 (£503; £251) Stalls Low

Form | RPR

2405 **1** **The Tatling (IRE)**[91] 5997 14-9-7 **60**........................ RichardKingscote 11 68
(Milton Bradley) *s.i.s: hld up: nt clr run and swtchd rt over 1f out: swtchd rt again ins fnl f: edgd lft and str burst to ld post* **16/1**

6353 **2** *shd* **Novabridge**[14] 7566 3-9-7 **60**..............................(b) AdamKirby 1 68
(Neil Mulholland) *a.p: rdn to chse ldr fnl f: r.o* **6/1**

0003 **3** *shd* **Grand Stitch (USA)**[38] 7266 5-9-5 **58**........................(v) DanielTudhope 8 66
(Declan Carroll) *led: clr 1/2-way: rdn ins fnl f: hdd post* **7/2**[1]

5403 **4** *1 ¼* **Mosa Mine**[31] 7366 4-9-0 **53**.............................. EddieAhern 3 56
(Bryn Palling) *chsd ldr tl rdn over 1f out: styd on same pce ins fnl f* **14/1**

3445 **5** *nk* **Dorothy's Dancing (IRE)**[41] 7201 3-9-5 **58**..................(p) ShaneKelly 7 60
(Gary Moore) *hld up in tch: rdn over 1f out: r.o* **9/2**[2]

0554 **6** *hd* **Wandering Lad**[6] 7641 3-8-7 **53**.............................. JasonHart(7) 2 54
(Declan Carroll) *prom: pushed along over 3f out: r.o* **5/1**[3]

0010 **7** *2* **Francis Albert**[38] 7266 5-9-5 **58**.............................. TomEaves 5 52
(Michael Mullineaux) *mid-div: plld hrd: hdwy over 1f out: sn rdn: edgd rt ins fnl f: styd on same pce* **20/1**

5102 **8** *nk* **Yungaburra (IRE)**[14] 7567 7-9-6 **59**..........................(tp) FrannyNorton 12 52
(David C Griffiths) *hld up: rdn over 1f out: nvr trbld ldrs* **10/1**

1000 **9** *1 ¼* **Memphis Man**[18] 7529 8-9-4 **60** ow3.......................... RichardEvans(3) 13 48
(David Evans) *sn pushed along in rr: nvr nrr* **40/1**

24 **10** *1 ½* **Rightcar**[31] 7366 4-9-0 **53**.............................. RobbieFitzpatrick 10 36
(Peter Grayson) *s.i.s: a in rr* **14/1**

002 **11** *½* **Namir (IRE)**[31] 7371 9-9-3 **56**..............................(vt) DaneO'Neill 4 37
(James Evans) *hld up: a in rr* **20/1**

0300 **12** *7* **Morermaloke**[38] 7266 3-9-4 **57**..............................(v[1]) BarryMcHugh 9 13
(Ian McInnes) *mid-div: rdn 1/2-way: sn wknd* **14/1**

0042 **13** *1* **Inde Country**[40] 7230 3-9-4 **57**..............................(t) LukeMorris 6 9
(Nicky Vaughan) *chsd ldrs: pushed along 1/2-way: wknd over 1f out: eased ins fnl f* **14/1**

62.52 secs (0.22) **Going Correction** 0.0s/f (Stan) **13** Ran SP% **125.0**
Speed ratings (Par 101): **98,97,97,95,95 94,91,91,89,86 86,74,73**
toteswingers:1&2:£19.30, 2&3:£8.70, 1&3:£19.90 CSF £111.66 CT £442.51 TOTE £23.20: £4.80, £2.80, £1.70; EX 159.70 Trifecta £345.00 Part won. Pool: £466.30 - 0.20 winning units..
Owner Darren Hudson-Wood **Bred** Patrick J Power **Trained** Sedbury, Gloucs

FOCUS
From a form perspective just a moderate sprint handicap, but a real racing highlight. Straightforward form.
Inde Country Official explanation: jockey said filly moved poorly

7738 TOTETRIFECTA H'CAP 1m 5f 194y(P)
4:15 (4:15) (Class 5) (0-75,75) 3-Y-0+ £2,264 (£673; £336; £168) Stalls Low

Form | RPR

0440 **1** **Admirable Duque (IRE)**[5] 7661 5-9-4 **72**.............(be) JoshBaudains(7) 5 85
(Dominic Ffrench Davis) *hld up: hdwy over 6f out: led 4f out: pushed clr over 1f out* **11/2**[3]

0101 **2** *7* **Quinsman**[39] 7254 5-9-6 **72**.............................. RyanPowell(5) 2 75
(J S Moore) *hld up: hdwy over 6f out: chsd wnr 3f out: sn rdn: styd on same pce fnl 2f* **4/1**[2]

1520 **3** *3* **Boa**[14] 7570 6-9-2 **70**..............................(e[1]) JackDuern(7) 6 69
(Reg Hollinshead) *trckd ldr: racd keenly: rdn over 3f out: wknd over 1f out* **8/1**

5006 **4** *5* **Pelham Crescent (IRE)**[24] 7461 8-9-11 **72**........................ LukeMorris 1 64
(Bryn Palling) *hld up: rdn over 3f out: wknd 2f out* **25/1**

2213 **5** *5* **Body Language (IRE)**[24] 7461 3-9-7 **75**........................(p) PhillipMakin 4 60
(Ann Duffield) *led 10f: sn rdn: wknd over 2f out* **13/8**[1]

0611 **P** **War Of The Roses (IRE)**[255] 1080 8-9-7 **68**........................ TomEaves 8 —
(Roy Brotherton) *hld up: in rr whn bdly hmpd 7f out: sn bhd: p.u over 3f out* **20/1**

461 **P** **Ashammar (FR)**[18] 7036 6-9-13 **74**..............................(t) StevieDonohoe 9 —
(Paul Webber) *prom: racd keenly: wnt 3rd 8f out: broke leg and p.u 7f out: fatally injured* **10/1**

5214 **B** **Blue Cossack (IRE)**[45] 7145 3-8-3 **57**........................(be) DavidProbert 3 —
(Mark Usher) *chsd ldrs: cl 4th whn b.d 7f out* **12/1**

3m 5.25s (-0.75) **Going Correction** 0.0s/f (Stan)
WFA 3 from 5yo+ 7lb **8** Ran SP% **110.0**
Speed ratings (Par 103): **102,98,96,93,90 —,—,—**
toteswingers:1&2:£4.40, 2&3:£6.20, 1&3:£6.70 CSF £25.55 CT £161.50 TOTE £6.30: £2.10, £1.20, £1.40; EX 30.10 Trifecta £173.10 Pool: £596.74 - 2.55 winning units..
Owner Exors of the Late Brian W Taylor **Bred** Airlie Stud And R N Clay **Trained** Lambourn, Berks

FOCUS
There was trouble on the bend heading out onto the final circuit when Blue Cossack was squeezed up on the rail, clipped heels and was brought down. War Of The Roses was badly hampered in the incident and so too was Pelham Crescent, although to a lesser extent. The favourite disappointed too, but the winner is still rated back to something like his best.
War Of The Roses(IRE) Official explanation: jockey said gelding lost its action

7739 TOTEEXACTA MEDIAN AUCTION MAIDEN STKS 1m 141y(P)
4:45 (4:45) (Class 6) 3-5-Y-0 £1,704 (£503; £251) Stalls Low

Form | RPR

0402 **1** **Perfect Mission**[25] 7443 3-9-3 70.............................. JimmyFortune 6 74
(Andrew Balding) *mde all: shkn up over 1f out: styd on wl* **2/5**[1]

32-3 **2** *4* **Frosty Friday**[216] 1974 3-8-12 64.............................. AdrianNicholls 5 59
(J R Jenkins) *a.p: chsd wnr over 2f out: sn rdn: styd on same pce fnl f* **9/2**[2]

4-00 **3** *1* **Indian Arrow**[11] 7591 3-9-0 62.............................. MichaelO'Connell(3) 4 62
(John Quinn) *chsd ldrs: rdn over 2f out: wknd ins fnl f:* **14/1**

60 **4** *1 ¾* **Excuse Me**[211] 2125 3-9-3 0.............................. PhillipMakin 7 58
(Kevin Ryan) *s.s: hld up: nt clr run 3f out: sn rdn: hdwy 2f out: hung lft and no ex fnl f over 1f out* **40/1**

5 *21* **Supastarqueen (USA)** 3-8-13 0 ow1.......................... J-PGuillambert 1 —
(Brian Baugh) *sn pushed along in rr: wknd over 3f out* **50/1**

5 **6** *6* **Debbie Doo**[66] 6668 3-8-12 0.............................. WilliamCarson 3 —
(Anthony Carson) *chsd wnr tl rdn over 2f out: sn wknd* **12/1**[3]

1m 51.31s (0.81) **Going Correction** 0.0s/f (Stan)
WFA 3 from 5yo 2lb **6** Ran SP% **108.4**
Speed ratings (Par 101): **96,92,91,90,71 66**
toteswingers:1&2:£1.30, 2&3:£2.90, 1&3:£1.80 CSF £2.26 TOTE £1.30: £1.10, £1.30; EX 1.70 Trifecta £6.00 Pool: £838.57 - 102.31 winning units..
Owner Mildmay Racing & D H Caslon **Bred** Mildmay Bloodstock **Trained** Kingsclere, Hants

FOCUS
A weak maiden and the winner only needed to match his latest form.

7740 DID BIG MONEY TOTEJACKPOT ROLLOVER TODAY H'CAP (DIV I) 1m 141y(P)
5:15 (5:15) (Class 6) (0-55,55) 3-Y-0+ £1,704 (£503; £251) Stalls Low

Form | RPR

6600 **1** **Join Up**[17] 7538 5-8-9 **55**.............................. RachealKneller(7) 7 65
(Mark Brisbourne) *chsd ldrs: led wl over 1f out: edgd lft ins fnl f: comf* **9/1**

2563 **2** *1 ¾* **Deslaya (IRE)**[52] 7006 3-8-12 **53**.............................. ShaneKelly 8 58
(Linda Stubbs) *hld up in tch: nt clr run over 2f out: sn rdn and ev ch: styd on same pce ins fnl f* **7/2**[3]

6260 **3** *nk* **Excellent Vision**[14] 7571 4-9-1 **54**..........................(t) RichardKingscote 3 58+
(Milton Bradley) *hld up: hdwy and nt clr run over 1f out: r.o wl ins fnl f: nvr able to chal* **5/1**

0/ **4** *1* **Lift The Gloom**[794] 6655 5-8-11 **50**..........................(t[1]) DaneO'Neill 5 52
(Noel Lawlor, Ire) *hld up: hdwy over 2f out: rdn and hung lft ins fnl f: styd on* **10/3**[2]

5 *2* **Bendzoldan (IRE)**[17] 7543 3-8-13 **54**.............................. RPCleary 9 51
(Thomas Cleary, Ire) *chsd ldr: rdn over 1f out: styd on same pce* **5/2**[1]

6020 **6** *4 ½* **Chicamia**[19] 7524 7-8-8 **47** ow1.............................. TomEaves 4 34
(Michael Mullineaux) *hld up: rdn over 1f out: nvr trbld ldrs* **22/1**

0000 **7** *6* **Carnival Dream**[30] 7399 6-8-7 **46** oh1.......................... JamesSullivan 2 19
(Hugh McWilliams) *chsd ldrs: rdn over 2f out: sn wknd* **16/1**

0/0- **8** *nk* **Blue Cross Boy (USA)**[15] 3653 6-8-7 **46** oh1..................(b) JohnFahy 10 19
(Adrian McGuinness, Ire) *led: rdn and hdd wl over 1f out: wknd fnl f* **20/1**

006 **9** *4* **Grand Sort**[33] 7327 3-8-5 **46** oh1.............................. KellyHarrison 11 —
(Tony Newcombe) *prom: chsd ldr over 5f out: rdn over 2f out: wknd over 1f out* **25/1**

/060 **10** *7* **Bertie Boo**[12] 7581 6-8-7 **46** oh1..............................(p) NeilChalmers 1 —
(Michael Appleby) *hld up: pushed along over 4f out: wknd 3f out* **25/1**

6-00 **11** *30* **Tagena (IRE)**[16] 7560 3-8-10 **51**.............................. LukeMorris 6 —
(Richard Price) *hld up: rdn 1/2-way: wknd 3f out: t.o* **50/1**

1m 51.08s (0.58) **Going Correction** 0.0s/f (Stan)
WFA 3 from 4yo+ 2lb **11** Ran SP% **125.2**
Speed ratings (Par 101): **97,95,95,94,92 88,83,82,79,73 46**
toteswingers:1&2:£8.10, 2&3:£4.40, 1&3:£7.20 CSF £40.67 CT £187.34 TOTE £12.90: £4.00, £1.30, £1.70; EX 36.60 Trifecta £218.10 Pool: £742.93 - 2.52 winning units..
Owner P R Kirk **Bred** A Reid **Trained** Great Ness, Shropshire

FOCUS
Just a moderate handicap and 0.61 sec slower than division II. The winner is rated back to his best but the form is limited.

7741 DID BIG MONEY TOTEJACKPOT ROLLOVER TODAY H'CAP (DIV II) 1m 141y(P)
5:45 (5:45) (Class 6) (0-55,55) 3-Y-0+ £1,704 (£503; £251) Stalls Low

Form | RPR

2335 **1** **Eastward Ho**[31] 7370 3-8-11 **52**.............................. MichaelStainton 6 62
(Jason Ward) *chsd ldr tl led over 2f out: rdn out* **5/1**[2]

0555 **2** *1 ¾* **Look For Love**[52] 7006 3-8-0 **48** ow2..........................(e[1]) JackDuern(7) 5 54
(Reg Hollinshead) *a.p: rdn to chse wnr over 1f out: styd on* **9/1**

4023 **3** *2 ¼* **Idol Deputy (FR)**[14] 7571 5-8-4 **50**.......................... RachealKneller(7) 11 51+
(Mark Usher) *hld up and bhd: hdwy and swtchd lft over 1f out: swtchd rt ins fnl f: r.o: too much to do* **6/4**[1]

4350 **4** *2* **Yellow Printer**[14] 7571 5-9-0 **53**..............................(b) LiamKeniry 2 49
(Mark Gillard) *led: rdn and hdd over 2f out: wknd ins fnl f* **8/1**

0000 **5** *hd* **Nha Trang (IRE)**[6] 7647 4-8-7 **46** oh1.......................... LukeMorris 10 42
(Michael Appleby) *hld up: rdn over 3f out: hung lft and styd on ins fnl f: nrst fin* **8/1**

0000 **6** *1 ¼* **Chez Vrony**[26] 7437 5-8-8 **47**.............................. MartinLane 8 40
(Dave Morris) *hld up: hdwy u.p over 2f out: styd on same pce fr over 1f out* **14/1**

0320 **7** *8* **Pursuing**[48] 7085 3-8-13 **54**.............................. TomEaves 1 28
(Nigel Tinkler) *chsd ldrs tl rdn and wknd 2f out* **15/2**[3]

0660 **8** *2 ¾* **Libre**[166] 3515 11-8-7 **46** oh1.............................. RichardKingscote 7 14
(Violet M Jordan) *chsd ldrs: rdn over 2f out: wknd over 1f out* **50/1**

4100 **9** *3 ½* **Belle Park**[17] 7537 4-8-9 **55**.............................. JulieCumine(7) 3 15
(Karen George) *s.i.s: a in rr* **16/1**

56-0 **10** *2 ¾* **Capacity (IRE)**[73] 6515 4-8-7 **46** oh1..........................(v) WilliamCarson 4 —
(T G McCourt, Ire) *hld up: rdn and wknd [illegible] out* **[illegible]**

1m 50.47s (-0.03) **Going Correction** 0.0s/f (Stan)
WFA 3 from 4yo+ 2lb **10** Ran SP% **121.0**
Speed ratings (Par 101): **100,98,96,94,94 93,86,83,80,78**
toteswingers:1&2:£8.40, 2&3:£4.00, 1&3:£2.20 CSF £51.51 CT £103.06 TOTE £4.50: £1.70, £2.60, £1.20; EX 73.80 Trifecta £54.20 Pool: £548.56 - 7.48 winning units..
Owner Miss Vivian Pratt **Bred** H & V Pratt **Trained** Middleham, North Yorkshire
■ A first training success for Jason Ward.

FOCUS
The time the quickest of three races at the trip, and 0.61sec faster than the first division, yet it paid to race handily. Limited form, the winner rated to his October turf level.
T/Jkpt: £15,202.60 to a £1 stake. Pool of £128,472.84 - 6.00 winning tickets. T/Plt: £35.80 to a £1 stake. Pool of £102,646.09 - 2,090.86 winning tickets. T/Qpdt: £11.20 to a £1 stake. Pool of £7,334.74 - 481.20 winning tickets. CR

7722 SOUTHWELL (L-H)
Tuesday, December 13

OFFICIAL GOING: Standard
Wind: Fresh across Weather: Fine

7742 TOTEPLACEPOT NURSERY 6f (F)
12:30 (12:30) (Class 6) (0-60,60) 2-Y-0 £1,704 (£503; £251) Stalls Low

Form | RPR

534 **1** **Heidi's Delight (IRE)**[12] 7592 2-8-7 **46**........................(b[1]) WilliamCarson 7 53
(Ann Duffield) *s.i.s: hdwy to ld 1/2-way: rdn over 1f out: readily* **7/1**[3]

5004 **2** *2 ½* **Miserere Mei (IRE)**[28] 7423 2-9-0 **56**........................(e) RobertLButler(3) 1 55
(Richard Guest) *w ldr tl led over 4f out: hdd 1/2-way: rdn over 1f out: styd on same pce fnl f* **14/1**

00 **3** *1* **Son Of May**[40] 7242 2-9-0 **53**..............................(b) StevieDonohoe 2 49
(Jo Hughes) *trckd ldrs: racd keenly: rdn over 2f out: styd on* **5/1**[2]

0004 **4** *1 ¼* **Lady Nickandy (IRE)**[2] 7725 2-8-11 **53**........................(v) KieranO'Neill(3) 9 45
(Alan McCabe) *hld up: hdwy 1/2-way: rdn over 1f out: no ex ins fnl f* **16/1**

4160 **5** *nk* **Littlecote Lady**[26] 7444 2-9-2 **55**.............................. JimmyFortune 8 47
(Mark Usher) *chsd ldrs: outpcd 1/2-way: rdn and hung lft over 1f out: styd on ins fnl f* **8/1**

5000 **6** *1 ½* **Gabrial's Princess (IRE)**[103] 5645 2-8-13 **52**..................(t) TomEaves 3 39
(Bryan Smart) *led: hdd over 4f out: rdn over 2f out: styd on same pce* **9/1**

0053 **7** ¾ **Allegri (IRE)**[28] 7421 2-9-4 **60**....................(p) DaleSwift(3) 5 45
(Ann Duffield) *prom: rdn 1/2-way: styd on same pce fnl 2f* **13/8**[1]

6006 **8** 2¼ **Colourful Event (IRE)**[12] 7592 2-8-6 **45**....................(v) JoeFanning 6 23
(David Arbuthnot) *sn pushed along in rr: rdn over 2f out: n.d* **9/1**

0606 **9** 5 **J Cunningham**[8] 7635 2-8-6 **45**.................... LukeMorris 10 8
(Mark Usher) *prom: rdn over 3f out: sn wknd* **33/1**

1m 16.05s (-0.45) **Going Correction** -0.15s/f (Stan) 9 Ran SP% **113.9**
Speed ratings (Par 94): **97,93,92,90,90 88,87,84,77**
toteswingers:1&2:£14.00, 2&3:£11.50, 1&3:£5.20 CSF £97.08 CT £536.76 TOTE £8.80: £1.90, £4.30, £2.30; EX 67.20 Trifecta £181.70 Part won. Pool: £245.64 - 0.10 winning units..
Owner David & Carole McMahon **Bred** Mountarmstrong Stud **Trained** Constable Burton, N Yorks

FOCUS
A weak contest but an interesting winner, who stepped up in the blinkers. It's form to treat with caution overall.

NOTEBOOK
Heidi's Delight(IRE) ◆ exhibited much more ability than one would expect for a horse officially rated just 46, recording her first success at the seventh attempt. She wasn't going at all well early on, but made rapid progress out wide to lead into the straight and, despite having used up plenty of energy to get there, maintained her advantage. It's unclear whether she improved for the blinkers and/or the switch to Fibresand, but there may be more to come. (op 13-2 tchd 15-2)
Miserere Mei(IRE) is well exposed and simply wasn't good enough. (op 10-1)
Son Of May attracted support and may yet do better. (op 11-2 tchd 6-1 in a place)
Lady Nickandy(IRE) raced tight against the inside rail in the straight, and that's rarely the place to be. (op 20-1)
Littlecote Lady is related to winners here, so better could have been expected. Official explanation: jockey said filly hung left (op 13-2)
Allegri(IRE) was a disappointment, not building on the form of his recent C&D third. (op 2-1)

7743 TOTEEXACTA CLAIMING STKS 1m 3f (F)
1:00 (1:00) (Class 6) 3-Y-O+ **£1,704** (£503; £251) **Stalls** Low

Form RPR

1453 **1** **West End Lad**[41] 7234 8-9-7 79....................(b) RussKennemore 10 84+
(Roy Bowring) *chsd ldrs: led over 2f out: sn clr: easily* **6/4**[1]

0345 **2** 5 **Hits Only Jude (IRE)**[3] 7713 8-8-2 69....................(v) JasonHart(7) 7 58
(Declan Carroll) *chsd ldr tl led over 3f out: rdn and hdd over 2f out: sn btn* **11/4**[2]

6400 **3** 2½ **Miereveld**[16] 6775 4-8-7 53....................(b) FrannyNorton 8 52
(Shaun Harris) *s.s: hld up: hdwy 1/2-way: rdn over 3f out: styd on to go 3rd fnl f: nvr trbld ldrs* **20/1**

6004 **4** 4½ **Raghdaan**[21] 7503 4-8-7 55.................... WilliamCarson 4 44
(Peter Hiatt) *led: rdn and hdd over 3f out: wknd over 2f out: lost 3rd fnl f* **11/2**

0000 **5** 1 **Cragganmore Creek**[14] 7573 8-8-7 43....................(b) LukeMorris 2 42
(Dave Morris) *s.i.s: sn drvn along in rr: hdwy 8f out: rdn and outpcd fr over 5f out* **28/1**

0056 **6** 13 **Kalahaag (IRE)**[33] 7357 3-7-12 52....................(b) JamieMackay 9 14
(David Nicholls) *s.i.s: plld hrd and sn prom: rdn and wknd over 4f out* **7/2**[3]

0-0 **7** 26 **Bahri Beat (IRE)**[33] 7352 3-8-9 0.................... PaddyAspell 5 —
(John Norton) *prom: lost pl over 8f out: bhd fr 1/2-way: t.o* **33/1**

000/ **8** 8 **Night Reveller (IRE)**[53] 4920 8-7-11 24.................... DanielleMcCreery(5) 3 —
(Michael Chapman) *sn wl bhd: t.o* **125/1**

3005 **9** 1½ **Kathindi (IRE)**[120] 5116 4-8-3 39 ow3.................... JackDuern(7) 6 —
(Michael Chapman) *hld up: bhd fr 1/2-way: t.o* **100/1**

2m 25.94s (-2.06) **Going Correction** -0.15s/f (Stan)
WFA 3 from 4yo+ 4lb 9 Ran SP% **117.2**
Speed ratings (Par 101): **101,97,95,92,91 82,63,57,56**
CSF £5.69 TOTE £3.10: £1.20, £1.20, £2.70; EX 8.20 Trifecta £42.70 Pool: £349.12 - 6.04 winning units..
Owner K Nicholls **Bred** Keith Nicholls **Trained** Edwinstowe, Notts

FOCUS
A modest claimer. the winner is rated to form, value for 8l, with the second below his best.

7744 TOTEQUADPOT H'CAP 6f (F)
1:30 (1:33) (Class 5) (0-70,72) 3-Y-O+ **£2,264** (£673; £336; £168) **Stalls** Low

Form RPR

5131 **1** **Global Village (IRE)**[7] 7646 6-9-8 **72** 6ex.................... BarryMcHugh 3 82
(Brian Ellison) *hld up: hdwy over 1f out: r.o to ld wl ins fnl f: readily* **13/8**[1]

0150 **2** nk **El Dececy (USA)**[42] 7216 7-9-3 **67**....................(t) MartinHarley 5 76
(Richard Guest) *led: rdn over 1f out: hdd wl ins fnl f* **33/1**

1403 **3** nk **Riflessione**[18] 7535 5-9-2 **66**....................(v) LukeMorris 6 74
(Ronald Harris) *prom: rdn over 2f out: styd on* **12/1**

0334 **4** 1¼ **Spitfire**[21] 7502 6-9-3 **67**....................(v) TonyCulhane 4 71
(J R Jenkins) *hld up: rdn 1/2-way: swtchd rt and hdwy over 1f out: styd on* **15/2**[3]

6650 **5** 1¾ **Dickie Le Davoir**[12] 7595 7-8-8 **65**....................(be) CharlesEddery(7) 14 63
(Richard Guest) *s.s: hld up: hdwy over 1f out: nt rch ldrs* **25/1**

0004 **6** 1¼ **Incomparable**[7] 7646 6-9-4 **68**....................(b) FrederikTylicki 12 62
(David Nicholls) *chsd ldrs: rdn 1/2-way: styd on same pce fnl f* **20/1**

140 **7** 1¾ **Twice Red**[157] 3853 3-9-6 **70**.................... JoeFanning 1 59
(Derek Shaw) *s.i.s: sn prom: pushed along over 2f out: wknd fnl f* **22/1**

6206 **8** 1½ **Brio**[2] 7726 3-8-12 **65**....................(v) KieranO'Neill(3) 2 49
(Alan McCabe) *sn outpcd: hdwy u.p over 1f out: wknd ins fnl f* **22/1**

3531 **9** 1¾ **Suddenly Susan (IRE)**[7] 7641 3-9-0 **64** 6ex....................(b) GrahamGibbons 9 42
(David Nicholls) *sn pushed along and prom: jnd ldrs wl over 3f out: pushed along over 2f out: wknd over 1f out* **7/2**[2]

6013 **10** hd **Elhamri**[21] 7504 7-9-2 **66**.................... ShaneKelly 7 44
(Conor Dore) *sn pushed along in rr: nvr on terms* **14/1**

3105 **11** 1 **Cape Of Storms**[7] 7646 8-9-1 **65**....................(b) TomEaves 8 40
(Roy Brotherton) *w ldr tl over 3f out: wknd wl over 1f out* **33/1**

1025 **12** 1½ **Haadeeth**[31] 7395 4-8-13 **70**....................(b) GeorgeChaloner(7) 11 40
(Richard Fahey) *prom: rdn over 2f out: wknd over 1f out* **25/1**

0000 **13** 1¾ **Lesley's Choice**[14] 7575 5-9-1 **65**....................(p) AdamKirby 10 29
(Paul Rich) *chsd ldrs to 1/2-way* **33/1**

14-0 **14** 10 **Efisio Princess**[34] 7341 8-9-3 **67**.................... SamHitchcott 13 —
(John E Long) *prom: rdn 1/2-way: sn wknd* **50/1**

1m 15.53s (-0.97) **Going Correction** -0.15s/f (Stan) 14 Ran SP% **118.4**
Speed ratings (Par 103): **100,99,99,97,95 93,91,89,86,86 85,83,80,67**
CSF £75.22 CT £513.17 TOTE £2.20: £1.50, £9.50, £2.70; EX 70.70 Trifecta £283.00 Part won. Pool: £382.55 - 0.10 winning units..
Owner Jack Racing Melksham **Bred** Kilfrush Stud **Trained** Norton, N Yorks

FOCUS
Just a modest sprint handicap, but it looked strong run. The winner was well in and pretty much matched his claiming win, while the runner-up has slipped to a good mark.

Efisio Princess Official explanation: jockey said mare never travelled

7745 TOTETRIFECTA FILLIES' H'CAP 1m (F)
2:00 (2:01) (Class 5) (0-75,75) 3-Y-O+ **£2,264** (£673; £336; £168) **Stalls** Low

Form RPR

0-23 **1** **Fakhuur**[40] 7250 3-9-4 **73**.................... SebSanders 5 83
(Clive Brittain) *sn chsng ldr: rdn over 2f out: hung lft over 1f out: led ins fnl f: styd on wl* **9/4**[2]

1534 **2** 2 **Bianca De Medici**[10] 7625 4-9-6 **74**....................(b) JimmyFortune 4 79
(Hughie Morrison) *led: shkn up 1f out: rdn and hdd ins fnl f: fnd nil* **5/4**[1]

14 **3** 13 **Full Bloom**[25] 7453 3-9-6 **75**....................(p) SteveDrowne 3 50
(Gerard Butler) *chsd ldrs: pushed along 1/2-way: wknd over 2f out* **9/2**[3]

0205 **4** 9 **Dazakhee**[18] 7538 4-8-10 **64** ow1.................... TonyCulhane 1 18
(Jo Hughes) *s.s: hdwy 1/2-way: rdn: edgd lft and wknd over 1f out* **8/1**

/46- **5** 19 **Athenian Garden (USA)**[594] 1619 4-8-11 **65**....................(t) MartinHarley 2 —
(Richard Guest) *hld up: wknd over 2f out: t.o* **22/1**

1m 41.96s (-1.74) **Going Correction** -0.15s/f (Stan)
WFA 3 from 4yo 1lb 5 Ran SP% **108.9**
Speed ratings (Par 100): **102,100,87,78,59**
CSF £5.33 TOTE £2.80: £1.20, £1.30; EX 5.10.
Owner Saeed Manana **Bred** Stowell Hill Ltd **Trained** Newmarket, Suffolk

FOCUS
Only five runners and a modest race, but the front two were well clear. The form is taken at face value.

7746 DINE IN THE PANTRY H'CAP 5f (F)
2:30 (2:31) (Class 5) (0-75,75) 3-Y-O+ **£2,264** (£673; £336; £168) **Stalls** High

Form RPR

2005 **1** **Six Wives**[27] 7428 4-9-4 **72**.................... GrahamGibbons 8 84+
(David Nicholls) *chsd ldr tl led 3f out: rdn over 1f out: r.o* **7/2**[1]

4513 **2** 1½ **Rambo Will**[128] 4819 3-9-2 **70**.................... JoeFanning 1 76
(J R Jenkins) *a.p: rdn 1/2-way: r.o to go 2nd wl ins fnl f: no ch w wnr* **12/1**

0160 **3** ¾ **Desert Icon (IRE)**[10] 7629 5-9-3 **74**....................(tp) KieranO'Neill(3) 7 77
(Alan McCabe) *s.i.s: outpcd: hdwy over 1f out: r.o to go 3rd nr fin: nt rch ldrs* **14/1**

0400 **4** 1 **La Capriosa**[18] 7535 5-8-13 **67**.................... FrederikTylicki 5 67
(David Nicholls) *a.p: chsd wnr 1/2-way: rdn over 1f out: no ex wl ins fnl f* **10/1**

2304 **5** nk **Dancing Freddy (IRE)**[7] 7643 4-9-3 **74**....................(tp) RobertLButler(3) 6 73
(Richard Guest) *sn pushed along and prom: rdn 1/2-way: styd on same pce fnl f* **6/1**[2]

0615 **6** shd **Equuleus Pictor**[34] 7341 7-9-7 **75**....................(p) AdamKirby 12 73
(John Spearing) *led: hdd over 3f out: rdn 1/2-way: edgd lft over 1f out: styd on same pce fnl f* **15/2**[3]

3130 **7** ½ **Upper Lambourn (IRE)**[110] 5419 3-9-3 **71**.................... FergusSweeney 2 67
(Jamie Osborne) *sn pushed along in rr: hdwy u.p over 1f out: nt trble ldrs* **12/1**

5330 **8** ¾ **Rylee Mooch**[85] 6212 3-8-11 **72**....................(e) CharlesEddery(7) 9 66
(Richard Guest) *s.i.s: sn drvn along in mid-div: nvr trbld ldrs* **14/1**

0606 **9** 1¼ **Italian Tom (IRE)**[12] 7596 4-9-6 **74**.................... LukeMorris 10 63
(Ronald Harris) *chsd ldrs: pushed along and edgd lft fr 1/2-way: no ex fr over 1f out* **8/1**

4344 **10** ¾ **Forty Proof (IRE)**[10] 7629 3-9-6 **74**....................(tp) ShaneKelly 3 61
(Alan McCabe) *sn pushed along in rr: n.d* **9/1**

1400 **11** 1¼ **Mandy's Hero**[164] 3628 3-9-4 **72**.................... SteveDrowne 4 54
(Olivia Maylam) *mid-div: pushed along 1/2-way: wknd ins fnl f* **33/1**

2200 **12** ¾ **Shawkantango**[12] 7594 4-8-10 **67**.................... DaleSwift(3) 11 46
(Derek Shaw) *s.i.s: outpcd* **20/1**

1100 **13** 1 **Sir Louis**[21] 7500 4-8-11 **65**.................... TonyHamilton 13 41
(Richard Fahey) *s.i.s: outpcd* **25/1**

0200 **14** 3¼ **Green Warrior**[62] 6801 3-8-11 **65**....................(e1) RobbieFitzpatrick 14 29
(Richard Guest) *s.i.s: outpcd* **66/1**

57.95 secs (-1.75) **Going Correction** -0.275s/f (Stan) 14 Ran SP% **120.2**
Speed ratings (Par 103): **103,100,99,97,97 97,96,95,93,91 89,88,87,81**
toteswingers:1&2:£6.40, 2&3:£22.00, 1&3:£15.60 CSF £44.92 CT £551.62 TOTE £3.40: £1.30, £3.50, £5.90; EX 46.90 TRIFECTA Not won..
Owner Sexy Six Partnership **Bred** Cheveley Park Stud Ltd **Trained** Sessay, N Yorks

FOCUS
An ordinary sprint handicap but a fair time for the grade. The winner has a good record here.

7747 PLAY GOLF BEFORE RACING AT SOUTHWELL MEDIAN AUCTION MAIDEN STKS 6f (F)
3:00 (3:01) (Class 6) 3-5-Y-O **£1,704** (£503; £251) **Stalls** Low

Form RPR

0000 **1** **Bird Dog**[4] 7691 5-8-10 30....................(v) DannyBrock(7) 1 55
(Phil McEntee) *mde all: rdn over 1f out: edgd rt fnl f: styd on* **50/1**

4052 **2** 2¼ **Gorgeous Goblin (IRE)**[4] 7690 4-8-12 49....................(vt) SteveDrowne 6 43
(David C Griffiths) *chsd wnr tl over 4f out: wnt 2nd again over 3f out: rdn over 1f out: no imp ins fnl f* **11/10**[1]

6420 **3** 1¾ **My Best Man**[5] 7676 5-9-3 50.................... LukeMorris 7 42
(Tony Carroll) *hld up in tch: rdn and edgd lft over 2f out: styd on to go 3rd ins fnl f: nt trble ldrs* **8/1**

0020 **4** ¾ **Bint Elnadim (IRE)**[6] 7655 3-8-12 55.................... JimmyQuinn 4 35
(Derek Shaw) *prom: rdn over 1f out: styd on same pce: lost 3rd ins fnl f* **5/1**[3]

6 **5** 3½ **Hubood**[81] 6307 3-8-12 0.................... SebSanders 5 24
(Clive Brittain) *s.i.s: sn prom: pushed along 1/2-way: wknd over 1f out* **7/2**[2]

3660 **6** 8 **Littleportnbrandy (IRE)**[11] 7610 3-8-12 52....................(b) MartinHarley 8 —
(Richard Guest) *prom and pushed along early: chsd wnr over 4f out to over 3f out: sn rdn: wknd over 2f out* **33/1**

0 **7** 2¼ **Field Finner**[33] 7354 3-8-12 0.................... GrahamGibbons 2 —
(David Nicholls) *s.i.s: hld up: plld hrd: bhd fr 1/2-way* **28/1**

6660 **8** 3¾ **Mrs Medley**[50] 7069 5-8-12 30....................(b1) FergusSweeney 3 —
(Garry Woodward) *hld up: plld hrd: wknd 1/2-way* **100/1**

9 3¼ **Rosa Luxemburg** 3-8-12 0.................... TomEaves 9 —
(Bryan Smart) *s.i.s: hdwy 4f out: wknd 1/2-way* **12/1**

1m 16.17s (-0.33) **Going Correction** -0.15s/f (Stan) 9 Ran SP% **114.7**
Speed ratings (Par 101): **96,93,90,89,85 74,71,66,62**
toteswingers:1&2:£17.20, 2&3:£2.60, 1&3:£24.70 CSF £104.92 TOTE £94.50: £12.20, £1.02, £3.10; EX 252.00 TRIFECTA Not won..
Owner Steve Shore **Bred** Caroline Shore **Trained** Newmarket, Suffolk

FOCUS
An extremely moderate maiden - the winner was officially rated just 30 and time was the slowest of three races at the trip. The form is far from solid and has been rateed cautiously.

7748 TICKETS ON LINE @ SOUTHWELL-RACECOURSE.CO.UK H'CAP 7f (F)
3:30 (3:34) (Class 6) (0-65,65) 3-Y-O+ **£1,617** (£481; £240; £120) **Stalls** Low

Form RPR
0324 **1** **Daffydowndilly**[26] 7447 3-9-7 **65**..............................(bt[1]) JimmyFortune 7 74
(Hughie Morrison) *prom: shkn up 1/2-way: rdn to ld ins fnl f: r.o* **4/1**[2]
0600 **2** ½ **This Ones For Eddy**[7] 7648 6-9-2 **60**.................... GrahamGibbons 9 68
(John Balding) *chsd ldrs: outpcd over 3f out: hdwy 2 out: rdn and ev ch fr over 1f out: r.o* **8/1**
0002 **3** *nk* **Cyflymder (IRE)**[7] 7648 5-9-2 **60**................................ SteveDrowne 1 67
(David C Griffiths) *chsd ldrs: led wl over 1f out: sn rdn: hdd and unable qck ins fnl f* **6/4**[1]
3405 **4** *8* **Unwrapit (USA)**[7] 7641 3-8-13 **57**..............................(tp) TomEaves 6 42
(Bryan Smart) *prom: chsd ldr over 4f out: rdn and ev ch 2f out: wknd fnl f* **7/1**[3]
0005 **5** *1¼* **Frognal (IRE)**[13] 7588 5-9-2 **63**..............................(bt) RobertLButler[(3)] 8 45
(Richard Guest) *hld up: hdwy 1/2-way: rdn over 1f out: wknd fnl f* **28/1**
3330 **6** *4½* **Gordy Bee (USA)**[188] 2828 5-8-1 **52**..........................(e) CharlesEddery[(7)] 3 22
(Richard Guest) *sn pushed along in rr: wknd over 2f out* **20/1**
0350 **7** *9* **Totally Trusted**[33] 7351 3-8-12 **56**..........................(b[1]) FrederikTylicki 4 —
(David Nicholls) *led: hdd & wknd wl over 1f out* **20/1**
1550 **8** *12* **Imogen Louise (IRE)**[15] 7567 3-9-4 **62**.......................... MartinHarley 5 —
(Richard Guest) *chsd ldrs: rdn and lost pl wl over 3f out: sn bhd: t.o* **80/1**

1m 29.21s (-1.09) **Going Correction** -0.15s/f (Stan) **8 Ran SP% 97.8**
Speed ratings (Par 101): **100,99,99,89,88 83,73,59**
toteswingers:1&2:£2.70, 2&3:£2.40, 1&3:£1.60 CSF £23.31 CT £40.60 TOTE £3.40: £1.30, £1.60, £1.10; EX 16.50 Trifecta £58.00 Pool: £279.93 - 3.57 winning units..
Owner Lady Blyth **Bred** D Curran **Trained** East Ilsley, Berks

FOCUS
Ahead of this moderate handicap, Elusive Warrior was unruly at the stalls, refused to enter and was withdrawn (11/2, deduct 15p in the £ under R4). This being the third occasion the gelding had been reported within the previous 12 months, the trainer was informed that, under Schedule (C)5 3.5, the horse would be prevented from having a stalls test for six months. A sound run race in which the first two were clear. Ordinary form.
Totally Trusted Official explanation: jockey said filly lost its action
T/Plt: £49.70 to a £1 stake. Pool of £54,356.14 - 798.09 winning tickets. T/Qpdt: £11.70 to a £1 stake. Pool of £5,673.49 - 357.50 winning tickets. CR

[7670]KEMPTON (A.W) (R-H)
Wednesday, December 14

OFFICIAL GOING: Standard
Wind: Fresh, across (away from stands) Weather: Cloudy, cold

7749 FREE ENTRY FOR BETDAQ MEMBERS MEDIAN AUCTION MAIDEN STKS 6f (P)
3:50 (3:51) (Class 6) 2-Y-O **£1,617** (£481; £240; £120) **Stalls** Low

Form RPR
2 **1** **Gabbiano**[20] 7526 2-9-3 0.. TonyCulhane 6 81+
(Jeremy Gask) *trckd ldr: pushed into ld over 1f out: in command whn swvd lft nr fin* **1/5**[1]
6 **2** *1¾* **Chaud Lapin**[69] 6654 2-9-3 0...................................... WilliamCarson 1 72
(Anthony Carson) *led: rdn over 2f out and edgd lft: hdd over 1f out: styd on but readily hld* **12/1**
6 **3** ½ **Place That Face**[14] 7583 2-8-12 0................................. JimmyFortune 4 66
(Hughie Morrison) *sltly awkward s: sn trckd ldrs in 5th: prog to try to chal wl over 1f out: rdn and styd on same pce* **10/1**[3]
0502 **4** *2¼* **Finalist**[20] 7530 2-8-12 60...(b) ShaneKelly 9 59
(Dean Ivory) *chsd ldrs in 6th: rdn wl over 2f out: wnt 4th over 1f out: nt pce to threaten* **9/2**[2]
5 *4½* **Spellmaker** 2-9-3 0.. DaneO'Neill 8 51
(Tony Newcombe) *s.s: detached in last: in danger of tailing off over 2f out: pushed along and styd on fnl f* **33/1**
6 ½ **Pettochside** 2-9-0 0.. RyanClark[(3)] 5 49
(Stuart Williams) *dwlt: in tch in last pair: effrt over 2f out: hanging and rn green: wknd over 1f out* **33/1**
006 **7** *1¼* **Here Comes Jeanie**[28] 7435 2-8-12 59...................... JamieGoldstein 3 40
(Michael Madgwick) *cl up: rdn over 2f out: wknd over 1f out* **33/1**
0 **8** *6* **Mrs Cash (IRE)**[28] 7435 2-8-12 0................................... LiamKeniry 7 22
(Sylvester Kirk) *t.k.h: pressed ldrs on outer: rdn over 2f out: sn wknd qckly* **25/1**

1m 14.37s (1.27) **Going Correction** 0.0s/f (Stan) **8 Ran SP% 131.0**
Speed ratings (Par 94): **91,88,88,85,79 78,76,68**
toteswingers:1&2:£3.10, 1&3:£1.90, 2&3:£5.30 CSF £5.90 TOTE £1.10: £1.02, £2.70, £2.40; EX 5.60.
Owner Tony Bloom **Bred** Mrs R J Gallagher **Trained** Sutton Veny, Wilts

FOCUS
An uncompetitive maiden in which a moderate gallop returned a time nearly three seconds outside Racing Post Standard. The winner came down the centre in the straight and did not quite match what he showed on his debut. The runner-up built on his debut effort.

NOTEBOOK
Gabbiano, who had created a pleasing debut impression (at this course) in a race that has already been franked, didn't have to improve to get off the mark in workmanlike fashion without his rider having to resort to the whip. He still has a bit of maturing to do but he's the type to progress again next year. (op 2-9 tchd 1-4 in a place)
Chaud Lapin showed ability at a moderate level on debut and he stepped up on that effort after enjoying the run of the race on this first run for his new trainer. His best chance of success will be in ordinary handicaps over further in due course.
Place That Face stepped up on her debut effort, despite taking on the boys this time. This isn't strong form but she's open to further improvement.
Finalist had run to her best in first-time blinkers in a course-and-distance nursery last time but had her limitations exposed back in this grade. A stronger gallop would have suited but she's likely to remain vulnerable against the better types in maidens. (op 4-1 tchd 5-1)

Spellmaker, a half-brother to one-time fair triple sprint winner Seafield Towers, hinted at ability after missing the break and running green on this racecourse debut (very easy in the market). He's open to improvement but ordinary handicaps will be the way forward with him.

7750 BACK AND LAY AT BETDAQ.COM MEDIAN AUCTION MAIDEN STKS 7f (P)
4:20 (4:21) (Class 6) 3-5-Y-O **£1,617** (£481; £240; £120) **Stalls** Low

Form RPR
5304 **1** **Perfect Cracker**[14] 7585 3-9-3 69.................................. AdamKirby 9 76
(Clive Cox) *trckd ldrs: smooth prog to ld wl over 1f out: pushed along and drew rt away* **5/4**[1]
60-2 **2** *10* **Hooligan Sean**[14] 7585 4-8-12 67.................................. AmyScott[(5)] 1 49
(Henry Candy) *hld up bhd ldrs: prog on inner to go 3rd 2f out but wnr sn drew clr: wnt 2nd over 1f out: lft further bhd fnl f* **15/8**[2]
6000 **3** *2¾* **Cairanne**[12] 7610 3-8-9 36.. RyanClark[(3)] 5 37
(Tom Keddy) *in tch: drvn over 2f out: sn outpcd: kpt on fr over 1f out to take 3rd nr fin* **50/1**
0000 **4** ¾ **Hursley Hope (IRE)**[32] 7387 3-8-12 56........................(t) NickyMackay 8 35
(David Elsworth) *led after 1f: rdn and hdd 2f out: no ch w wnr after: grad fdd* **7/1**[3]
06 **5** *7* **Hot Tub**[14] 7585 3-9-3 0.. SebSanders 2 21
(Christine Dunnett) *towards rr: rdn over 2f out: hanging and sn lft wl bhd: v modest prog fnl f* **33/1**
00 **6** ½ **Clear Spring (IRE)**[14] 7585 3-9-3 0............................ WilliamCarson 7 19
(John Spearing) *prog arnd wd outside over 4f out to chse ldr 3f out to over 2f out: wknd rapidly* **100/1**
6 **7** *nse* **Sid**[20] 7525 3-9-3 0.. JamieGoldstein 10 19
(Zoe Davison) *dwlt: hld up in last pair: effrt over 2f out but sn wl outpcd: wknd over 1f out* **66/1**
3 **8** *1* **Tribouley**[27] 7443 3-8-12 0.. ShaneKelly 3 11
(Dean Ivory) *led 1f: chsd ldr to 3f out: wknd over 2f out* **9/1**
05 **9** ¾ **Whats Your Story**[20] 7525 3-9-3 0.......................... FrankieMcDonald 4 14
(Murty McGrath) *dwlt: mostly in last: nvr on terms: no ch fnl 2f* **66/1**
5 **10** *12* **Bon Royale**[43] 7207 3-8-12 0.................................. TomMcLaughlin 6 —
(Phil McEntee) *t.k.h: prom tl wknd rapidly wl over 2f out: t.o* **50/1**

1m 26.03s (0.03) **Going Correction** 0.0s/f (Stan) **10 Ran SP% 112.6**
Speed ratings (Par 101): **99,87,84,83,75 75,74,73,72,59**
toteswingers:1&2:£1.60, 1&3:£18.30, 2&3:£25.20 CSF £3.43 TOTE £2.60: £1.30, £1.10, £9.40; EX 4.40.
Owner Mildmay Racing **Bred** Mildmay Bloodstock **Trained** Lambourn, Berks

FOCUS
A weak maiden and another uncompetitive race and, although the winner won with plenty in hand, the proximity of the 36-rated third holds the form down. The gallop was an ordinary one and the winner came down the centre. He reversed C&D form with the runner-up.

7751 BETDAQ MULTIPLES/BRITISH STALLION STUDS EBF MAIDEN STKS 1m (P)
4:50 (4:53) (Class 5) 2-Y-O **£3,169** (£943; £471; £235) **Stalls** Low

Form RPR
02 **1** **California English (IRE)**[25] 7493 2-9-3 0...................... AdamKirby 14 78+
(Marco Botti) *mde virtually all: pressed 2f out: drvn to assert over 1f out: clr fnl f: readily* **11/8**[1]
2 *3½* **Fortieth And Fifth (IRE)** 2-9-3 0.............................. StevieDonohoe 8 71+
(Michael Bell) *s.s: rn green and pushed along in detached last early: stl in last pair over 2f out: gd prog wl over 1f out: r.o strly fnl f: tk 2nd last strides* **33/1**
0 **3** ½ **Masters Blazing**[9] 7634 2-9-3 0.................................. KirstyMilczarek 6 68
(John Ryan) *prom: rdn over 2f out: styd on to chse wnr last 150yds: no imp: lost 2nd last strides* **100/1**
3 **4** *1* **Sujet Bellagio**[18] 7559 2-9-3 0...................................... ShaneKelly 7 66
(Brian Meehan) *chsd wnr to over 2f out: rdn and nt qckn: kpt on same pce over 1f out* **5/1**[3]
5 *3* **Cape Savannah** 2-9-3 0.. MartinLane 2 59
(David Simcock) *in tch in midfield: effrt to chse clr ldng quartet 2f out: no imp: kpt on* **50/1**
6 *hd* **Dark Castle** 2-9-3 0.. StephenCraine 5 58+
(Sylvester Kirk) *prom: rdn to chse wnr over 2f out: sn tried to chal: wl hld over 1f out: wknd qckly ins fnl f* **4/1**[2]
7 *nk* **Flash Crash** 2-9-3 0.. JohnFahy 10 57+
(Robert Cowell) *s.i.s: t.k.h: hld up wl in rr: pushed along over 2f out: styd on steadily fr over 1f out: nvr nrr* **66/1**
00 **8** ½ **Green Legacy (USA)**[9] 7634 2-9-3 0.............................. JimCrowley 1 56
(Amanda Perrett) *nvr bttr than midfield: rdn and no prog over 2f out: wl btn after: plugged on* **50/1**
9 *2¼* **Archina (IRE)** 2-8-12 0.. JimmyFortune 11 46
(Andrew Balding) *t.k.h and rn green in midfield: wknd wl over 1f out* **14/1**
3 **10** *1* **Aird Snout (USA)**[33] 7369 2-9-3 0.............................. JoeFanning 9 49
(David Simcock) *prom: rdn 3f out: wknd over 2f out* **4/1**[2]
11 *2½* **Phenomena** 2-9-3 0.. FergusSweeney 4 43+
(Jeremy Gask) *s.i.s: wl in rr: no ch whn effrt and nt clr run over 2f out: wknd over 1f out* **25/1**
63 **12** *1* **Godber (IRE)**[176] 3242 2-9-3 0.................................. JamieGoldstein 12 41+
(Ralph Smith) *t.k.h: hld up and sn last: brief effrt on inner over 2f out: sn wknd* **100/1**
0 **13** *1* **The Young Master**[18] 7559 2-9-3 0.............................. LiamKeniry 13 38+
(Neil Mulholland) *hld up wl in rr: shkn up over 2f out and no prog: wknd over 1f out* **200/1**
0 **14** *16* **Midnight Sequel**[112] 5375 2-8-12 0.............................. LukeMorris 3 —
(Michael Blake) *rdn in midfield after 3f: wknd over 2f out: t.o* **200/1**

1m 40.44s (0.64) **Going Correction** 0.0s/f (Stan) **14 Ran SP% 120.6**
Speed ratings (Par 96): **96,92,92,91,88 87,87,87,84,83 81,80,79,63**
toteswingers:1&2:£15.00, 1&3:£19.90, 2&3:£65.20 CSF £65.04 TOTE £3.30: £1.30, £10.80, £18.30; EX 54.20.
Owner California English Partnership **Bred** J G Davis **Trained** Newmarket, Suffolk

FOCUS
No more than a fair maiden run at an ordinary gallop and one in which the performance of the runner-up caught the eye. The winner came down the centre in the straight for a decisive success.

NOTEBOOK
California English(IRE) is a steadily progressive sort who had the run of the race (despite his wide draw) and he turned in his best effort to get off the mark. He may not be entirely straightforward (edgy before start and loaded with blanket) but didn't do much wrong in the race itself and he may do better in handicaps. (op 13-8)
Fortieth And Fifth(IRE) ◆ very much caught the eye after a tardy start to fare easily the best of those to come from behind on this racecourse debut. This 72,000gns second foal of an unraced half-sister to a useful Japanese middle distance performer will be suited by the step up to 1m2f and is sure to win a similar event at the very least. (op 28-1)

Masters Blazing hadn't shown much on his debut at Lingfield earlier in the month but he fared a good deal better this time after having the run of the race. He'll be vulnerable to the better types in this grade but should pick up a small event once handicapped.

Sujet Bellagio attracted support and probably ran to a similar level as he had done on his debut at Wolverhampton over 7f at the end of last month. He is another that may do better once qualified for a handicap mark. (op 11-2 tchd 9-2)

Cape Savannah, a 34,000gns yearling who is closely related to this year's fair 6f Fibresand maiden winner Formal Demand, was far from disgraced on this racecourse debut. He'll have to improve a fair bit to win a similar event but can be expected to step up on these bare facts.

Dark Castle attracted support but didn't get home after showing up well for much of the way on this racecourse debut. There is plenty of speed in his pedigree and it's a fair bet he'll better this form dropped in distance at some point. (op 6-1)

Archina(IRE) Official explanation: jockey said filly ran too freely

7752 BETDAQ MOBILE APPS H'CAP — 1m (P)
5:20 (5:21) (Class 5) (0-75,75) 2-Y-O — **£2,264** (£673; £336; £168) **Stalls** Low

Form — RPR

361 **1** — **Titus Star (IRE)**[103] 5672 2-9-0 **68** .... LukeMorris 3 — 74
(J S Moore) *trckd ldr: led jst over 2f out gng wl: drvn over 1f out: 2 l clr fnl f: styd on* **3/1[2]**

3045 **2** *1 ¾* **Singalat**[15] 7576 2-9-7 **75** .... TomQueally 6 — 77
(James Given) *restless stalls and slowly away: hld up in last pair: rdn on outer over 2f out: sme prog over 1f out: drvn and styd on fnl f to take 2nd last strides* **10/1**

0003 **3** *nk* **All Nighter (IRE)**[33] 7358 2-9-2 **70** .... ShaneKelly 9 — 71
(Brian Meehan) *trckd ldng pair: rdn 2f out: styd on to dispute 2nd ins fnl f: nvr able to chal* **11/4[1]**

0423 **4** *nk* **La Romantique (IRE)**[27] 7444 2-8-13 **67** ....(b) AndreaAtzeni 2 — 68
(Marco Botti) *trckd ldng pair: rdn to chse wnr over 1f out: kpt on but no imp fnl f: lost 2 pls nr fin* **11/2[3]**

003 **5** *3 ¼* **Fine Resolve**[40] 7257 2-9-4 **72** .... JimmyFortune 7 — 65
(Andrew Balding) *hld up in 6th: pushed along 2f out: no prog over 1f out: fdd ins fnl f* **11/2[3]**

3006 **6** *nk* **Compton Target (IRE)**[33] 7364 2-8-6 **67** ....(t) NicoleNordblad[(7)] 5 — 59
(Hans Adielsson) *hld up in 5th: effrt on inner and cl enough 2f out: no imp jst over 1f out: fdd* **8/1**

0024 **7** *5* **Captain Cardington (IRE)**[30] 7414 2-9-2 **70** .... TonyCulhane 4 — 51
(Mick Channon) *restrained after s: t.k.h and hld up in last pair: jst pushed along fnl 2f: nvr involved* **8/1**

0000 **8** *2* **Leading Star**[34] 7342 2-7-10 **55** oh6 ow3........ RyanPowell[(5)] 1 — 31
(Michael Madgwick) *led: set modest pce tl kicked on over 3f out: drvn and hdd jst over 2f out: wknd qckly over 1f out* **50/1**

1m 40.92s (1.12) **Going Correction** 0.0s/f (Stan) — **8** Ran SP% **115.7**
Speed ratings (Par 96): **94,92,91,91,88 88,83,81**
toteswingers:1&2:£7.10, 1&3:£2.60, 2&3:£6.90 CSF £33.14 CT £91.74 TOTE £5.00: £1.60, £3.60, £1.02; EX 41.10.

Owner Ray Styles & J S Moore **Bred** A M F Persse **Trained** Upper Lambourn, Berks

FOCUS
A fair nursery but one in which the pace was no more than fair. The winner came down the centre and the first four pulled a few lengths clear. Straightforward form, the winner to his turf mark.

NOTEBOOK
Titus Star(IRE) looked on a lenient mark for this nursery and AW debut on this first run after a break of over three months and he posted his best effort after being well placed in a moderately run race. Things went his way but he'll be interesting if turned out under a penalty at Wolverhampton tomorrow. (op 11-4 tchd 7-2)

Singalat hadn't been at his best on his two all-weather starts but he fared better after coming from off the pace, especially as this race was run to suit the prominent racers. A more truly run race would have suited but he has little margin for error from this mark. (op 9-1)

All Nighter(IRE) attracted support and ran creditably but he left the impression that he'd be at least as effective in a more truly run race returned to 7f. He's worth another chance. (op 4-1)

La Romantique(IRE), from an in-form yard and with the headgear again fitted, is a reliable sort who seemed to give it her best shot and she's a good guide to the worth of this form. She doesn't have much in hand of her current mark but she should continue to give a good account. (op 9-2)

Fine Resolve looked an interesting runner on this nursery debut but he wasn't seen to best effect in a race that wasn't run to suit. A better gallop over this trip or the step up to longer trip should suit and he should be able to pick up a similar event at some point. (op 5-1)

7753 RACING@SKYSPORTS.COM H'CAP — 2m (P)
5:50 (5:50) (Class 4) (0-85,84) 3-Y-0+ — **£4,075** (£1,212; £606; £303) **Stalls** Low

Form — RPR

2-20 **1** — **Right Stuff (FR)**[20] 2931 8-10-0 **84** .... TomQueally 4 — 94
(Gary Moore) *t.k.h: sn trckd ldng trio: smooth prog to dispute ld wl over 2f out: narrowly hdd over 1f out: edging rt but rallied to ld last 100yds* **11/2**

0223 **2** *½* **Dark Ranger**[31] 7139 5-9-0 **70** .... EddieAhern 7 — 79
(Tim Pitt) *hld up and last to 6f out: smooth prog on inner over 3f out: disp ld wl over 2f out: narrow advantage and edging lft over 1f out: hdd and nt qckn last 100yds* **4/1[2]**

0601 **3** *4 ½* **La Estrella (USA)**[41] 7241 8-10-0 **84** .... DaneO'Neill 3 — 88
(Don Cantillon) *hld up in last trio: wl in tch over 3f out: rdn and nt qckn wl over 2f out: kpt on to take 3rd over 1f out: no imp on ldng pair* **4/1[2]**

0004 **4** *6* **Blackmore**[6] 7674 4-9-0 **70** .... ShaneKelly 2 — 66
(Julia Feilden) *led: drvn over 3f out: hdd wl over 2f out: sn outpcd* **12/1**

4200 **5** *1 ¼* **Rosewood Lad**[48] 7120 4-9-2 **72** .... LukeMorris 8 — 67
(J S Moore) *chsd ldr 5f: rdn in 3rd bef 1/2-way: lost pl over 3f out: readily outpcd after* **8/1**

2230 **6** *10* **Quiz Mistress**[48] 7129 3-8-10 **77** ....(t) AmyRyan[(3)] 5 — 60
(Gerard Butler) *trckd ldr after 5f: rdn to dispute ld briefly 3f out: wknd over 2f out* **7/2[1]**

1012 **7** *11* **Quinsman**[2] 7738 5-9-2 **72** .... LiamKeniry 6 — 42
(J S Moore) *hld up in last trio: rdn 5f out: sn lost tch: t.o* **5/1[3]**

5236 **8** *½* **Calculating (IRE)**[6] 7674 7-8-10 **71** .... LeeNewnes[(5)] 1 — 40
(Mark Usher) *in tch: rdn and wknd 6f out: t.o* **40/1**

3m 26.89s (-3.21) **Going Correction** 0.0s/f (Stan)
WFA 3 from 4yo+ 8lb — **8** Ran SP% **115.5**
Speed ratings (Par 105): **108,107,105,102,101 96,91,91**
toteswingers:1&2:£3.20, 1&3:£3.70, 2&3:£5.50 CSF £28.06 CT £97.68 TOTE £4.80: £1.90, £1.20, £1.40; EX 15.50.

Owner The Ashden Partnership & Partners **Bred** N P Bloodstock Ltd **Trained** Lower Beeding, W Sussex

FOCUS
Exposed performers in a useful handicap. The gallop to the home turn was a moderate one and the first two pulled clear. The form appears solid.

7754 SKYSPORTS.COM RACING H'CAP — 7f (P)
6:20 (6:20) (Class 6) (0-65,64) 3-Y-0 — **£1,617** (£481; £240; £60; £60) **Stalls** Low

Form — RPR

0050 **1** — **Zaheeb**[22] 7507 3-8-12 **55** .... WilliamCarson 5 — 64
(Dave Morris) *pressed ldrs: led on inner 3f out: hung bdly lft over 2f out: drvn and kpt on wl fnl f* **16/1**

6 **2** *1 ½* **Automotive**[68] 6668 3-9-1 **58** .... ShaneKelly 9 — 63
(Julia Feilden) *hld up wl in rr and off the pce: prog over 2f out: hung lft over 1f out: chsd wnr fnl f: styd on same pce* **12/1**

0044 **3** *¾* **Polar Auroras**[12] 7610 3-9-1 **58** .... LukeMorris 3 — 61
(Tony Carroll) *chsd clr ldng quintet: pushed along 1/2-way: prog and hung lft 2f out: chsd wnr over 1f out: nt qckn and lost 2nd fnl f* **5/1[2]**

0140 **4** *2 ¼* **Demoiselle Bond**[25] 7484 3-9-0 **57** .... SteveDrowne 6 — 54
(Lydia Richards) *led at decent pce: hung lft and hdd 3f out: fdd over 1f out* **8/1**

5000 **4** *dht* **Dunseverick (IRE)**[22] 7504 3-9-5 **62** .... TonyCulhane 2 — 59
(Jo Hughes) *stdd s: hld up in last pair: stl last over 2f out: jst pushed along and styd on steadily fnl 2f: nrst fin* **8/1**

062- **6** *¾* **Dells Breezer**[375] 7691 3-9-2 **59** .... IanMongan 4 — 54
(Pat Phelan) *awkward s: hld up in last pair: effrt over 2f out: prog over 1f out but hd to one side: kpt on same pce* **8/1**

0000 **7** *1 ¾* **Mi Regalo**[7] 7649 3-9-7 **64** ....(p) TomMcLaughlin 12 — 54
(Phil McEntee) *chsd ldng quartet: rdn whn sltly hmpd 2f out: wknd over 1f out* **20/1**

0001 **8** *nk* **Blue Deer (IRE)**[7] 7663 3-8-13 **61** ....(p) CharlesBishop[(5)] 13 — 50
(John Akehurst) *pressed ldrs: rdn whn carried lft over 2f out: wknd over 1f out* **7/2[1]**

4644 **9** *5* **Paperetto**[21] 7524 3-9-1 **58** .... StevieDonohoe 8 — 34
(Robert Mills) *chsd ldr to 3f out: sing to weaken whn sltly hmpd 2f out* **11/2[3]**

5060 **10** *5* **Silly Billy (IRE)**[26] 7463 3-8-9 **57** .... JemmaMarshall[(5)] 7 — 19
(Sylvester Kirk) *nvr on terms u.p and struggling by 1/2-way: t.o* **20/1**

445- **11** *5* **Darwin Star**[419] 7040 3-9-3 **60** .... MartinLane 11 — —
(Dean Ivory) *a in rr: rdn and struggling 1/2-way: sn wknd: t.o* **14/1**

6000 **12** *6* **Koha (USA)**[50] 7086 3-8-7 **50** oh4........ SamHitchcott 1 — —
(Dean Ivory) *a in rr: rdn 1/2-way: no real prog over 2f out: wknd rapidly: t.o* **40/1**

1m 25.85s (-0.15) **Going Correction** 0.0s/f (Stan) — **12** Ran SP% **119.8**
Speed ratings (Par 98): **100,98,97,94,94 94,92,91,85,80 74,67**
toteswingers:1&2:£41.00, 1&3:£17.50, 2&3:£6.00 CSF £192.05 CT £1126.91 TOTE £15.40: £4.00, £4.70, £1.30; EX 318.10.

Owner Stuart Wood **Bred** Theakston Stud **Trained** Baxter's Green, Suffolk

FOCUS
A modest handicap in which the pace was sound. The winner drifted towards the stands rail passing the intersection before edging towards the centre late on. he's rated to his August Yarmouth form.

Polar Auroras Official explanation: jockey said filly hung left

Demoiselle Bond Official explanation: jockey said filly hung left

Dunseverick(IRE) Official explanation: jockey said, regarding running and riding, that his orders were to settle gelding as it is very free and unruly, however it took a keen hold, attempted to fly leap and threw its head up in the air, having got round the bend and into the straight, he was afraid to give it a longer rein and was concerned for his safety and that of the horses upsides.

Koha(USA) Official explanation: jockey said filly bled from the nose

7755 BOXINGDAYRACES.CO.UK CLASSIFIED STKS — 6f (P)
6:50 (6:50) (Class 6) 3-Y-0+ — **£1,617** (£481; £240; £120) **Stalls** Low

Form — RPR

0002 **1** — **Peace Seeker**[7] 7656 3-9-0 52 .... WilliamCarson 11 — 73+
(Anthony Carson) *fast away fr wd draw: mde all and sn crossed to inner: gng bttr than rest over 2f out: clr whn drifted lft over 1f out: eased last 50yds* **1/1[1]**

0400 **2** *2 ¾* **Amazing Win (IRE)**[19] 7538 3-9-0 55 .... TonyCulhane 4 — 61
(Mick Channon) *hld up towards rr on inner: prog over 2f out: rdn to chse wnr over 1f out: nvr any imp* **16/1**

6620 **3** *6* **Young Simon**[7] 7656 4-9-0 52 ....(v) IanMongan 1 — 42
(George Margarson) *t.k.h: prom: chsd wnr over 2f out to over 1f out: fdd fnl f* **9/2[2]**

6000 **4** *1 ¾* **Whoateallthepius (IRE)**[25] 7488 3-8-7 52 .... PaulBooth[(7)] 8 — 36
(Dean Ivory) *hld up and sn detached in last: urged along 2f out: styd on fr over 1f out: tk 4th wl ins fnl f* **14/1**

5305 **5** *2* **Itum**[21] 7511 4-9-0 52 .... SebSanders 7 — 30
(Christine Dunnett) *plld hrd early and hld up in rr: sme prog over 2f out: tk modest 4th jst over 1f out: wknd ins fnl f* **20/1**

0-00 **6** *nse* **Queens Troop**[211] 2177 3-9-0 54 .... ShaneKelly 3 — 30
(Dean Ivory) *wl in rr and off the pce: no real prog over 2f out: nvr a factor* **33/1**

065 **7** *hd* **Mustafeed (USA)**[41] 7249 3-9-0 54 .... JoeFanning 2 — 29
(Keith Dalgleish) *t.k.h: mostly chsd wnr to over 2f out: wknd* **9/2[2]**

0005 **8** *6* **Dililah**[26] 7460 3-9-0 46 .... JamesSullivan 6 — —
(Linda Stubbs) *chsd ldrs: rdn and wknd over 2f out* **66/1**

00-6 **9** *11* **Striking Willow**[288] 721 3-9-0 44 .... JamesMillman 10 — —
(Rod Millman) *chsd ldrs and racd v wd: wknd wl over 2f out: t.o* **80/1**

0024 **10** *½* **Dusty Bluebells (IRE)**[32] 7389 3-9-0 55 ....(b) LiamKeniry 9 — —
(J S Moore) *restless stalls: chsd ldrs and racd wd: wknd qckly over 2f out: t.o* **10/1[3]**

1m 12.42s (-0.68) **Going Correction** 0.0s/f (Stan) — **10** Ran SP% **118.4**
Speed ratings (Par 101): **104,100,92,90,87 87,87,79,64,63**
toteswingers:1&2:£5.30, 1&3:£1.90, 2&3:£9.50 CSF £20.44 TOTE £2.10: £1.10, £3.70, £1.10; EX 21.40.

Owner Neville Chamberlain Syndicate **Bred** C J Mills **Trained** Newmarket, Suffolk

■ The first winner as a trainer for Tony Carson, son of former jockey Willie and father of William who rode the horse.

FOCUS
A low-grade event but a ready winner and a reasonable gallop helped to ensure this was the best comparative time on the card. The winner ended up towards the centre. He was value for a bit further and posted a big figure for the grade, if anything rated conservatively.

T/Plt: £42.20 to a £1 stake. Pool:£68,278.68 - 1,178.79 winning tickets T/Qpdt: £22.30 to a £1 stake. Pool:£6,864.78 - 227.20 winning tickets JN

[7657]LINGFIELD (L-H)

Wednesday, December 14

OFFICIAL GOING: Standard

Wind: fresh, across Weather: dry

7756 TOTEPLACEPOT CLASSIFIED (S) STKS 1m 2f (P)

12:30 (12:30) (Class 6) 3-Y-O+ £1,704 (£503; £251) Stalls Low

Form RPR

0060 **1** **King's Colour**[33] 7362 6-9-3 68 .... AdamKirby 6 74
(Brett Johnson) *hld up in tch: hdwy on outer 3f out: rdn and qcknd to ld 1f out: sn clr: easily* **4/1**[2]

3230 **2** *4½* **Potentiale (IRE)**[26] 7458 7-9-3 70 .... (v[1]) SebSanders 8 65
(J W Hills) *in tch: rdn and effrt to press ldr 2f out: drvn and nt qckn ent fnl f: no ch w wnr but 2nd fnl 100yds* **5/2**[1]

4400 **3** *½* **Wisecraic**[18] 6401 4-9-3 62 .... LiamKeniry 4 64
(J S Moore) *chsd ldr tl led over 2f out: rdn over 1f out: hdd 1f out and sn no ch w wnr: lost 2nd fnl 100yds* **10/1**

4000 **4** *3* **Divine Rule (IRE)**[29] 7333 3-8-7 53 .... CharlotteJenner[(7)] 1 58
(Laura Mongan) *in tch in midfield: rdn and chsd ldrs 2f out: sn outpcd and wl hld whn hung rt ins fnl f* **40/1**

4000 **5** *¾* **The Which Doctor**[12] 7605 6-9-9 66 .... (b[1]) MartinHarley 9 63
(Richard Guest) *s.i.s: hld up in last pair: nt clr run and swtchd rt jst over 2f out: rdn and hdwy 2f out: no ex and btn 1f out: wknd fnl f* **9/1**[3]

0406 **6** *6* **Cloudy Start**[12] 7603 5-9-3 65 .... (b) FergusSweeney 3 45
(Jamie Osborne) *led tl rdn and hdd over 2f out: wknd over 1f out* **5/2**[1]

504 **7** *11* **Pacific Reach**[43] 7207 3-9-0 65 .... (t) RichardKingscote 5 23
(Brendan Powell) *hld up in last pair: rdn and no prog over 2f out: wknd wl over 1f out* **10/1**

0400 **8** *5* **Lady Morganna (IRE)**[16] 7571 3-8-7 51 .... (v[1]) JenniferFerguson[(7)] 7 13
(Olivia Maylam) *in tch: rdn and lost pl 3f out: wl bhd fnl 2f* **50/1**

2660 **9** *1¼* **Highly Regal (IRE)**[8] 2562 6-9-3 69 .... (bt) DaneO'Neill 2 —
(Chris Gordon) *chsd ldrs tl rdn and dropped out over 2f out: wl bhd fr over 1f out* **25/1**

2m 4.99s (-1.61) **Going Correction** -0.10s/f (Stan)
WFA 3 from 4yo+ 3lb **9** Ran SP% **113.6**
Speed ratings (Par 101): **102,98,98,95,95 90,81,77,76**
toteswingers:1&2:£3.20, 1&3:£6.60, 2&3:£5.80 CSF £13.95 TOTE £4.20: £1.60, £1.40, £2.30; EX 17.10 Trifecta £39.30 Pool: £243.09 - 4.57 winning units..There was no bid for the winner.
Owner Tann Racing **Bred** Cheveley Park Stud Ltd **Trained** Ashtead, Surrey

FOCUS

An ordinary claimer with doubts over most. The winner was still 10lb off last winter's best.

7757 BRITISH STALLION STUDS SUPPORTING BRITISH RACING EBF MAIDEN FILLIES' STKS 7f (P)

1:00 (1:00) (Class 5) 2-Y-O £3,340 (£986; £493) Stalls Low

Form RPR

1 **Apothecary** 2-9-0 0 .... NickyMackay 9 70+
(John Gosden) *s.i.s and bustled along early: clsd and hmpd 4f out: rdn and effrt 2f out: str run ent fnl f: led fnl 75yds: r.o wl* **8/1**

2 *hd* **Appealing (IRE)** 2-9-0 0 .... AdamKirby 7 70+
(Marco Botti) *dwlt: hld up in tch towards rr: effrt and nt clr run wl over 1f out: gd hdwy to press ldrs 1f out: led fnl 100yds: sn hdd: r.o wl but a jst hld* **17/2**

05 **3** *¾* **Shamardeliah (IRE)**[82] 6308 2-9-0 0 .... JoeFanning 4 68
(James Tate) *in tch on outer: hdwy to chse ldr over 2f out: rdn to ld ent fnl 2f: hdd fnl 100yds: flashed tail and no ex after* **7/2**[2]

0 **4** *½* **Sigurwana (USA)**[34] 7344 2-8-11 0 .... AdamBeschizza[(3)] 5 67
(William Haggas) *in tch in midfield: rdn and effrt to chse ldrs jst over 1f out: styd on same pce fnl 100yds* **8/1**

5 *2½* **Blaugrana (IRE)** 2-9-0 0 .... RobertHavlin 1 60+
(John Gosden) *chsd ldrs: rdn and edgd rt bnd wl over 1f out: drvn and unable qck jst over 1f out: wknd fnl 100yds* **13/2**[3]

400 **6** *hd* **Silver Marizah (IRE)**[63] 6795 2-9-0 68 .... TomQueally 3 60
(Gary Moore) *led for 2f: settled in tch after: swtchd rt and effrt jst over 2f [illegible] wknd fnl 100yds* **13/2**[3]

00 **7** *½* **Chambles**[54] 6991 2-8-11 0 .... KieranO'Neill[(3)] 6 58
(Andrew Reid) *chsd ldr tl over 2f out: rdn and unable qck over 1f out: wknd fnl f* **20/1**

8 *hd* **Alushta** 2-9-0 0 .... JimmyFortune 8 58
(Ed Dunlop) *hld up in tch towards rr: rdn and effrt wl over 1f out: no imp and btn over 1f out: nvr trbld ldrs* **3/1**[1]

00 **9** *8* **Applaudere**[9] 7634 2-9-0 0 .... FergusSweeney 2 37
(Jamie Osborne) *hld up in tch in last trio: rdn and effrt 2f out: drvn and wknd over 1f out* **200/1**

06 **10** *1½* **La Passionata**[12] 7598 2-9-0 0 .... StevieDonohoe 10 33
(Robert Mills) *taken down early: hdwy to ld 5f out: hdd over 2f out: edgd rt and fdd over 1f out* **40/1**

1m 24.41s (-0.39) **Going Correction** -0.10s/f (Stan) **10** Ran SP% **114.3**
Speed ratings (Par 93): **98,97,96,96,93 93,92,92,83,81**
toteswingers:1&2:£10.70, 1&3:£6.90, 2&3:£6.40 CSF £71.35 TOTE £10.60: £3.30, £2.80, £1.70; EX 86.30 Trifecta £181.20 Pool: £293.96 - 1.20 winning units..
Owner H R H Princess Haya Of Jordan **Bred** Cliveden Stud Ltd **Trained** Newmarket, Suffolk

FOCUS

No more than a fair maiden, but there were one or two interesting newcomers in the line-up and it was one of them who came out on top. The bare form is only ordinary.

NOTEBOOK

Apothecary was worst away from the stalls and dropped in at the back of the field. Still towards the rear turning in, she quickened up in really taking fashion once straightened up and split rivals to edge ahead close home. She's bred to improve for middle distances next year and could be interesting in handicaps as she can't be rated too highly on the back of this narrow win in a bunch finish involving a couple of rivals who'd shown only modest form previously. (tchd 7-1)

Appealing(IRE), in contrast to the winner, is unlikely to want much further than this next year. This was a pleasing debut effort and she should be up to winning something similar around here. (op 13-2 tchd 9-1)

Shamardeliah(IRE), debuting for her new stable having been with Ed Dunlop previously, ran her best race to date and, while handicaps are now an option, an ordinary winter maiden may prove easier to pick up. (op 9-2 tchd 10-3)

Sigurwana(USA) was keeping on well at the finish and stepped up on her debut effort. Her dam won round here and her sire Arch has a great record with his runners on both AW surfaces, including a 23% strike-rate at this track. (tchd 15-2 and 9-1)

Blaugrana(IRE), whose dam won a Group 3 over 1m4f and is a half-sister to Invincible Spirit, was keen early and that may have blunted her finishing effort. She's from a successful family and should come on for this. (op 5-1 tchd 7-1)

Silver Marizah(IRE), who was cut up going to the first bend and dropped back in the pack a little, got involved in the battle for the places early in the straight but, not for the first time, failed to see her race out. (op 6-1 tchd 7-1)

Alushta swung widest off the turn into the straight and failed to get into it. She's a sister to three winners, including two at pattern level, so it wouldn't be a surprise if she left this form behind in due course. (op 7-2 tchd 4-1)

7758 BRITISH STALLION STUDS SUPPORTING BRITISH RACING EBF MAIDEN STKS (C&G) 7f (P)

1:35 (1:36) (Class 5) 2-Y-O £3,340 (£986; £493) Stalls Low

Form RPR

00 **1** **Hidden Justice (IRE)**[21] 7520 2-9-0 0 .... EddieAhern 3 70+
(Amanda Perrett) *chsd ldng pair: hdwy to join ldr and qcknd clr over 2f out: drvn 1f out: flashed tail u.p but led wl ins fnl f: drvn out* **10/11**[1]

0 **2** *hd* **Boots And Spurs**[20] 7526 2-9-0 0 .... MartinHarley 1 69+
(Mrs K Burke) *w ldr tl led and qcknd clr w wnr over 2f out: rdn ins fnl f: hdd and no ex wl ins fnl f* **9/4**[2]

0 **3** *12* **Pearl Frost**[39] 7292 2-9-0 0 .... JimCrowley 6 41+
(Ralph Beckett) *s.i.s: in tch in last pair: rdn 4f out: lost tch w ldng pair over 2f out: carried rt bnd wl over 1f out: wnt poor 3rd nr fin* **9/2**[3]

4 *½* **Athletic** 2-8-11 0 .... KieranO'Neill[(3)] 2 37
(Andrew Reid) *s.i.s: rn green and rdn along thrght: veered rt after s: lost tch w ldng pair over 2f out: wnt poor 3rd and hung rt bnd wl over 1f out tl nr fin* **25/1**

5 *17* **Toss A Coin (IRE)** 2-8-7 0 .... HarryPoulton[(7)] 4 —
(Roger Teal) *led tl over 2f out: sn outpcd and btn: hung rt bnd wl over 1f out: sn last and t.o fnl f* **40/1**

1m 25.44s (0.64) **Going Correction** -0.10s/f (Stan) **5** Ran SP% **107.6**
Speed ratings (Par 96): **92,91,78,77,58**
CSF £3.00 TOTE £1.90: £1.10, £1.70; EX 3.30.
Owner George Materna **Bred** Ballylinch Stud **Trained** Pulborough, W Sussex

FOCUS

A weak maiden and a two-horse race from the turn in. The front pair are both improving and possibly under rated.

NOTEBOOK

Hidden Justice(IRE) had the advantage of being one off the inside rail but still took an age to get past the leader, and he flashed his tail when hit with the whip close home. That said, his pedigree suggests there should be improvement to come when stepped up in trip, especially when sent over middle distances next year. (op 5-4)

Boots And Spurs stuck to the rail all the way round and that was probably his undoing. While the winner will want further in time this looks about the right distance for him. (op 3-1)

Pearl Frost, outpaced running down the hill, swung widest off the bend and plugged on well enough to take a well-beaten third. He'll appreciate further in time and, as his two half-brothers who have run in this country have only ever won on the Fibresand at Southwell, he'll be of far more interest when he turns up there. (op 11-4)

7759 TOTEPOOL H'CAP 1m 2f (P)

2:10 (2:11) (Class 4) (0-85,84) 3-Y-O+ £4,204 (£1,251; £625; £312) Stalls Low

Form RPR

0522 **1** **Emerald Wilderness (IRE)**[7] 7651 7-9-6 **83** .... (p) EddieAhern 9 91+
(Robert Cowell) *dwlt: hld up in tch: hdwy to trck ldrs gng wl 2f out: rdn and qcknd to ld 1f out: drvn fnl 75yds: hld on towards fin* **5/2**[1]

2212 **2** *hd* **Opus Maximus (IRE)**[2] 7734 6-8-10 **73** .... (p) KirstyMilczarek 12 81
(Conor Dore) *t.k.h: hld up in last pair: rdn and hdwy on outer over 1f out: str run u.p ins fnl f: ev ch fnl 75yds: kpt on wl* **8/1**

0000 **3** *½* **King Of Windsor (IRE)**[9] 7637 4-8-11 **74** .... JimCrowley 8 81
(Ralph Beckett) *hld up in tch towards rr: rdn and effrt over 1f out: swtchd lft and gd hdwy ent fnl f: pressed wnr ins fnl f: styd on same pce towards fin* **10/3**[2]

0130 **4** *3* **Lisahane Bog**[12] 7601 4-8-10 **73** .... (v) JohnFahy 5 74
(Peter Hedger) *chsd ldrs: rdn and effrt 2f out: no ex u.p 1f out: outpcd and btn fnl 150yds* **10/1**

5651 **5** *hd* **Choral Festival**[12] 7601 5-8-4 **70** .... KieranO'Neill[(3)] 10 71
(John Bridger) *t.k.h: chsd ldrs: rdn and ev ch 2f out: unable qck over 1f out: outpcd and btn ins fnl f* **11/1**

4116 **6** *1* **Green Wadi**[15] 7577 6-9-1 **78** .... (p) TomQueally 11 77
(Gary Moore) [illegible] 1f out: hdd 1f out: wknd ins fnl f* **13/2**[3]

4006 **7** *¾* **She Ain't A Saint**[19] 7542 3-8-11 **77** .... LukeMorris 4 74
(Jane Chapple-Hyam) *chsd ldrs: rdn and effrt on inner to press ldrs over 1f out: no ex and btn 1f out: wknd fnl f* **8/1**

0460 **8** *nk* **Mister Green (FR)**[6] 7671 5-8-7 **70** oh6 .... (bt) JamieMackay 6 67
(David Flood) *t.k.h: hld up in midfield: stl gng wl enough ent fnl 2f: rdn and no prog over 1f out* **33/1**

010 **9** *3¼* **Silver Bullitt**[126] 4914 3-9-1 **81** .... JoeFanning 1 71
(Mark Johnston) *led tl 2f out: wknd over 1f out: fdd fnl f* **16/1**

0000 **10** *7* **Jawaab (IRE)**[27] 7272 7-8-13 **79** .... (e) RobertLButler[(3)] 7 55
(Richard Guest) *stdd after s: hld up in last pair: rdn and toiling over 3f out: lost tch over 2f out* **100/1**

2m 4.75s (-1.85) **Going Correction** -0.10s/f (Stan)
WFA 3 from 4yo+ 3lb **10** Ran SP% **114.4**
Speed ratings (Par 105): **103,102,102,100,99 99,98,98,95,90**
toteswingers:1&2:£3.70, 1&3:£3.20, 2&3:£6.30 CSF £22.75 CT £66.90 TOTE £2.70: £1.40, £2.70, £1.80; EX 17.20 Trifecta £44.20 Pool: £454.05 - 7.60 winning units..
Owner Mrs J Morley & Khalifa Dasmal **Bred** Mrs Joan Murphy **Trained** Six Mile Bottom, Cambs

FOCUS

They didn't go a great pace early here and it developed into a bit of a sprint in the straight, although the first three came from off the pace. The form is probably sound enough.

7760 TOTETRIFECTA H'CAP 6f (P)

2:40 (2:40) (Class 6) (0-55,55) 3-Y-O+ £1,704 (£503; £251) Stalls Low

Form RPR

5015 **1** **Microlight**[27] 7442 3-8-10 **49** .... (b) KirstyMilczarek 6 56
(John E Long) *mde all and sn crossed towards inner: rdn over 1f out: drvn fnl f: hld on wl towards fin: all out* **11/2**[3]

0000 **2** *¾* **Super Frank (IRE)**[6] 7676 8-8-11 **50** .... (b) SamHitchcott 8 55
(Zoe Davison) *awkward s and s.i.s: sn swtchd lft and in rr: hdwy jst over 2f out: swtchd rt and chsd wnr wl over 1f out: chal fnl 75yds: nt qckn and hld towards fin* **12/1**

0000 **3** *2* **Royal Acclamation (IRE)**[48] 7131 6-8-3 **47** oh1 ow1 .... (p) DavidKenny[(5)] 7 46
(Michael Scudamore) *chsd ldrs and outer: rdn and outpcd over 1f out: plugged on same pce u.p fnl f* **8/1**

3500 **4** *¾* **Force To Spend**[28] 7429 4-8-7 **46** .... JoeFanning 3 42
(Des Donovan) *stdd s: t.k.h: hld up in rr: hmpd over 4f out: rdn and effrt on inner to chse ldrs over 1f out: no ex and btn fnl 150yds* **15/2**

-000 **5** 1 1/4 **Suhayl Star (IRE)**[212] 2161 7-8-7 **46** oh1............................. JohnFahy 2 38
(Paul Burgoyne) *plld hrd: hld up in tch: hmpd and lost pl over 4f out: rdn and effrt on inner wl over 1f out: pressed ldrs wl over 1f out tl ins fnl f: wknd fnl 75yds* **16/1**
4236 **6** 4 1/2 **Little Perisher**[18] 7560 4-8-11 **50**..............................(b) MichaelStainton 5 28
(Paul Howling) *chsd ldrs on outer: carried wd and lost pl bnd wl over 1f out: no ch after* **5/2**[1]
6043 **7** 1/2 **Slatey Hen (IRE)**[6] 7676 3-8-11 **50**..............................(p) MartinHarley 4 26
(Richard Guest) *chsd ldrs: rdn over 2f out: carried rt and lost pl bnd wl over 1f out: no ch after* **7/2**[2]
12 **8** 1 **Dangerous Illusion (IRE)**[95] 5941 3-9-2 **55**.................. AndreaAtzeni 1 28
(Michael Quinn) *chsd ldr: hung rt bnd wl over 1f out: sn hmpd and lost pl: fdd bdly over 1f out* **6/1**

1m 11.74s (-0.16) **Going Correction** -0.10s/f (Stan) **8** Ran SP% **116.9**
Speed ratings (Par 101): **97,96,93,92,90 84,84,82**
toteswingers:1&2:£4.80, 1&3:£7.90, 2&3:£12.60 CSF £69.09 CT £411.50 TOTE £7.10: £2.60, £3.20, £2.90; EX 70.80 Trifecta £211.70 Part won. Pool: £286.11 - 0.65 winning units..
Owner R D John **Bred** Newsells Park Stud **Trained** Caterham, Surrey

FOCUS
A weak sprint handicap. The winner's first real form this year.

7761 TOTEEXACTA APPRENTICE H'CAP 1m 4f (P)
3:15 (3:15) (Class 5) (0-70,74) 3-Y-O+ **£2,385** (£704; £352) **Stalls** Low

Form RPR
5064 **1** **Kames Park (IRE)**[7] 7661 9-8-13 **63**.......................... CharlesEddery[(5)] 8 73
(Richard Guest) *stdd s: hld up in last pair: smooth hdwy to chse ldrs wl over 1f out: rdn to ld 1f out: styd on wl to draw clr fnl 100yds: pushed out* **6/1**
6045 **2** 2 **Strike Force**[12] 7601 7-9-10 **69**..............................(t) AdamBeschizza 10 76
(Clifford Lines) *in tch in midfield: rdn and qcknd to ld over 2f out: hdd 1f out: no ex and outpcd fnl 100yds* **12/1**
3111 **3** 2 1/4 **Woop Woop (IRE)**[9] 7638 3-9-7 **74** 6ex................... RyanPowell[(3)] 2 81+
(Ian Williams) *chsd ldr: nt clr run bhd wkng rival and dropped to rr over 2f out: swtchd rt and rallied but stl plenty to do over 1f out: swtchd lft 1f out and r.o wl fnl f: nvr able to chal* **5/2**[1]
1510 **4** 1/2 **Bennelong**[15] 7577 5-9-5 **69**.. LukeRowe[(5)] 7 71
(Richard Rowe) *stdd s: hld up in last pair: rdn and hdwy over 2f out: chsd ldrs over 1f out: no imp ins fnl f* **12/1**
0423 **5** 3/4 **Formidable Guest**[12] 7603 7-9-1 **60**.............................. KierenFox 5 61
(Jamie Poulton) *pushed along leaving stalls: rdn 4f out: hdwy to join ldr and qcknd ahd over 2f out: stl ev ch 1f out: wknd ins fnl f* **15/2**
6365 **6** 1 3/4 **Broughtons Paradis (IRE)**[18] 7556 5-9-2 **66**........ MichaelJMurphy[(5)] 1 64
(Willie Musson) *hld up in midfield: shuffled bk and dropped to rr over 2f out: rdn and effrt wl over 1f out: plugged on but no threat to ldrs* **4/1**[2]
2200 **7** 3 3/4 **Ghufa (IRE)**[18] 7556 7-9-6 **65**.............................. SimonPearce 4 57
(Lydia Pearce) *rdn along early: in tch: rdn over 3f out: wknd 2f out* **33/1**
6052 **8** 2 3/4 **Rodrigo De Freitas (IRE)**[12] 7603 4-8-5 **57**...........(v) DanielCremin[(7)] 9 45
(Jim Boyle) *in tch in midfield: rdn and hdwy on outer over 3f out: wknd u.p wl over 1f out* **9/1**
0-3 **9** 2 1/4 **Brown Pete (IRE)**[12] 7605 3-8-12 **62**..............................(b) MartinHarley 3 46
(Richard Guest) *led tl over 2f out: wknd qckly ent fnl 2f* **16/1**
4401 **10** 4 1/2 **Rose Aurora**[20] 7528 4-8-10 **55**..............................(vt) SophieDoyle 6 32
(Marcus Tregoning) *t.k.h: chsd ldrs tl rdn and wknd over 2f out: wl bhd over 1f out* **11/2**[3]

2m 30.18s (-2.82) **Going Correction** -0.10s/f (Stan)
WFA 3 from 4yo+ 5lb **10** Ran SP% **124.2**
Speed ratings (Par 103): **105,103,102,101,101 100,97,95,94,91**
toteswingers:1&2:£16.50, 1&3:£6.60, 2&3:£11.80 CSF £80.57 CT £231.80 TOTE £9.70: £2.80, £4.20, £1.30; EX 91.00 Trifecta £425.90 Part won. Pool: £575.55 - 0.75 winning units..
Owner Future Racing (Notts) Limited **Bred** Pat Beirne **Trained** Stainforth, S Yorks

FOCUS
There was a fair gallop on in this apprentices' handicap. The winner's best form since the spring, rated around the runner-up.
T/Plt: £78.60 to a £1 stake. Pool:£57,330.08 - 532.15 winning tickets T/Qpdt: £19.70 to a £1 stake. Pool:£5,316.80 - 198.80 winning tickets SP

7749 KEMPTON (A.W) (R-H)
Thursday, December 15

OFFICIAL GOING: Standard
Wind: Brisk across

7762 FREE ENTRY FOR BLUE SQUARE CUSTOMERS CLAIMING STKS 7f (P)
4:00 (4:01) (Class 6) 2-Y-O **£1,617** (£481; £240; £120) **Stalls** Low

Form RPR
4212 **1** **Le King Beau (USA)**[23] 7505 2-8-13 62........................... DaneO'Neill 4 68
(William Muir) *trckd ldrs in 3rd: hdwy to ld ins fnl 2f: pushed out fnl f: readily* **13/2**[3]
3512 **2** 2 1/2 **Young Prince (IRE)**[29] 7434 2-9-7 78.......................... StevieDonohoe 1 69
(Robert Mills) *trckd ldrs in 4th: drvn and hdwy to chse wnr over 1f out: rdn and no imp fnl 150yds* **1/2**[1]
6005 **3** 2 1/2 **Big Time Charlie (IRE)**[15] 7582 2-9-0 52.................... KieranO'Neill[(3)] 2 59
(Richard Hannon) *led 1f: styd chsng ldr: rdn 2f out: one pce into 3rd over 1f out* **16/1**
1200 **4** 9 **Crowning Star (IRE)**[34] 7358 2-8-8 70....................(bt[1]) RyanPowell[(3)] 5 31
(J S Moore) *s.i.s: t.k.h and sn led: 3 l clr 4f out: rdn: hdd & wknd ins fnl 2f* **4/1**[2]
05 **5** 6 **Lotarespect**[26] 7482 2-8-10 0.. SteveDrowne 3 13
(John Best) *a struggling in rr* **66/1**

1m 26.93s (0.93) **Going Correction** +0.001s/f **5** Ran SP% **107.4**
Speed ratings (Par 94): **94,91,88,78,71**
CSF £9.91 TOTE £5.30: £1.60, £1.10; EX 10.20.Le King Beau was the subject of a friendly claim.
Owner Sills Racing **Bred** Haras Demeautry **Trained** Lambourn, Berks

FOCUS
There was no hanging about in this 2-y-o claimer and the form is straightforward.

NOTEBOOK
Le King Beau(USA) was on 8lb worse terms than when just holding Young Prince on his penultimate outing in this class at Lingfield and proved very easy to back. However, his old rival again allowed him first run and he confirmed previous form with even greater authority. He's developed into a likeable sort on Polytrack and obviously doesn't need to dictate. (op 11-2 tchd 7-1)
Young Prince(IRE) was all the rage to resume winning ways on his return to the C&D he scored over two runs back. He got a confident ride, but it was clear half a furlong out his old rival again held his measure. He really looks to need more use made of him in a small field like this, but on recent evidence he's flattered by his official mark. (op 8-15 tchd 4-9)
Big Time Charlie(IRE) was up against it at the weights and ran close to his previous level, so looks a fair guide for the form. (op 25-1)
Crowning Star(IRE), in first-time blinkers, spread a plate and didn't bother with the parade ring. He shot to the front after half a furlong and made it a test, but was a sitting duck in the home straight and looks in decline. (op 7-2 tchd 9-2)

7763 DOWNLOAD THE BLUE SQUARE BET APP NURSERY 1m (P)
4:30 (4:30) (Class 6) (0-65,65) 2-Y-O **£1,617** (£481; £240; £120) **Stalls** Low

Form RPR
3052 **1** **Karma Chameleon**[28] 7444 2-8-11 **55**.............................. SebSanders 5 63
(John Berry) *trckd ldrs: drvn to ld 1f out: pushed out* **9/2**[2]
545 **2** 2 **Manomine**[36] 7336 2-9-4 **62**.. TomQueally 4 65
(Clive Brittain) *towards rr: hdwy over 2f out: drvn and styd on fnl f to chse wnr fnl 75yds but no imp* **4/1**[1]
5053 **3** 1 **Stag Hill (IRE)**[6] 7697 2-9-1 **59**...................................... LiamKeniry 6 60
(Sylvester Kirk) *chsd ldrs: led appr fnl 2f: sn rdn: hdd 1f out: one pce into 3rd fnl 75yds* **6/1**[3]
4336 **4** 1/2 **Can Do Les (IRE)**[6] 7684 2-8-12 **56**................................ JimCrowley 10 56
(Keith Dalgleish) *chsd ldrs: drvn over 1f out: styd on same pce ins fnl f* **20/1**
3065 **5** 2 3/4 **Lady Heartbeat**[17] 7569 2-8-7 **51**...................................... LukeMorris 11 44
(Michael Blanshard) *in tch: drvn over 2f out: styd on fnl f: nt pce to rch ldrs* **12/1**
6011 **6** 6 **Masters Club**[17] 7568 2-9-7 **65**...................................... StevieDonohoe 7 44
(John Ryan) *chsd ldrs: rdn over 2f out: wknd appr fnl f* **10/1**
1044 **7** nk **Coach Montana (IRE)**[29] 7432 2-8-12 **56**........................ IvaMilickova 2 35
(Jane Chapple-Hyam) *mid-div: rdn 3f out: sme hdwy on ins over 2f out: nvr rchd ldrs: wknd fnl f* **16/1**
056 **8** 1/2 **Beauchamp Orange**[33] 7396 2-8-7 **58**..................(b) NicoleNordblad[(7)] 9 36
(Hans Adielsson) *s.i.s: in rr: mod late prog towards outside* **12/1**
0155 **9** 1 1/2 **Camrock Star (IRE)**[31] 7414 2-9-0 **58**..............................(v[1]) AdamKirby 3 32
(David Evans) *led tl hdd appr fnl 2f: sn wknd* **16/1**
3050 **10** 1 3/4 **Foster's Road**[64] 6806 2-9-7 **65**...................................... TonyCulhane 13 35
(Mick Channon) *s.i.s: in rr: mod prog clsng stages* **25/1**
4340 **11** 2 3/4 **King's Ciel**[60] 6890 2-9-1 **64**..............................(p) DavidKenny[(5)] 8 28
(George Baker) *sn bhd* **33/1**
0260 **12** 3 1/4 **Al Jemailiya (IRE)**[105] 5645 2-9-6 **64**.......................... StephenCraine 12 20
(Kevin Ryan) *sn bhd* **14/1**
056 **13** 8 **Isobella**[13] 7599 2-9-0 **58**.. JimmyFortune 1 —
(Hughie Morrison) *chsd ldrs over 5f* **8/1**
0000 **14** 1 **Imperial Stargazer**[41] 7259 2-9-4 **62**............................ SamHitchcott 14 —
(Mick Channon) *s.i.s: a in rr* **33/1**

1m 39.77s (-0.03) **Going Correction** +0.001s/f **14** Ran SP% **121.0**
Speed ratings (Par 94): **100,98,97,96,93 87,87,86,85,83 80,77,69,68**
toteswingers:1&2:£4.10, 1&3:£4.90, 2&3:£6.00 CSF £21.84 CT £110.13 TOTE £5.30: £1.50, £1.70, £2.50; EX 23.90.
Owner EERC **Bred** D R Tucker **Trained** Newmarket, Suffolk

FOCUS
A wide-open nursery. There was an average pace on and the form makes sense.

NOTEBOOK
Karma Chameleon put up an honest performance and shed his maiden tag at the eighth time of asking. Things panned out nicely for him and, showing a willing attitude on the inside from a furlong out, he was comfortably on top at the finish. The extra furlong looked to make all the difference and there could be more to come.
Manomine returned to something like his best back on Polytrack. He probably needs more positive tactics and there is surely a race around here for him this winter. (op 5-1)
Stag Hill(IRE) was swamped by the winner at the furlong marker. He ran very close to his previous level and rates a sound benchmark. (op 5-1)
Can Do Les(IRE) moved nicely into contention and held every chance. He ultimately shaped as though he needs a stiffer test. (op 25-1)
Isobella Official explanation: jockey said filly had stopped quickly

7764 WIN THOUSANDS OF SPORTS EXPERIENCES AT BLUESQ.COM H'CAP 1m (P)
5:00 (5:00) (Class 5) (0-70,70) 3-Y-O+ **£2,264** (£673; £336; £168) **Stalls** Low

Form RPR
0200 **1** **Whitechapel**[77] 6477 4-9-4 **67**.. LiamKeniry 1 75
(Andrew Balding) *trckd ldrs: led appr fnl 2f: rdn ins fnl f: styd on strly* **6/1**
0100 **2** 1 **Mountrath**[16] 7579 4-9-4 **67**..............................(v) AdamKirby 3 73
(Gary Moore) *t.k.h: stdd in rr after 1f: hdwy appr fnl f: rdn and styd on wl to take 2nd clsng stages but no imp on wnr* **5/1**[3]
0252 **3** 1/2 **Woolston Ferry (IRE)**[27] 7455 5-8-13 **67**.................. JamesRogers[(5)] 2 72
(David Pinder) *s.i.s: in rr: hdwy on ins over 2f out: chsd wnr appr fnl f: no imp: one pce and lost 2nd clsng stages* **10/3**[1]
2324 **4** 3/4 **Shared Moment (IRE)**[253] 1183 5-8-12 **61**...............(v) StevieDonohoe 5 64
(John Gallagher) *stdd s: in rr: hdwy over 1f out: chsd ldrs ins fnl f: one pce fnl 120yds* **16/1**
0110 **5** 2 **Shelagh (IRE)**[16] 7579 3-9-4 **68**...................................... DaneO'Neill 9 67
(Jo Crowley) *in tch: hdwy over 1f out: chsd ldrs ins fnl f but no imp: wknd clsng stages* **7/2**[2]
2164 **6** 3/4 **Pipers Piping (IRE)**[8] 7658 5-9-0 **68**...................(b) JemmaMarshall[(5)] 7 65
(Alastair Lidderdale) *in rr: racd wd and hdwy over 1f out: styd on clsng stages: nvr a threat* **6/1**
3605 **7** 5 **Pose (IRE)**[26] 7485 4-8-5 **59**..............................(t) MarkCoumbe[(5)] 4 44
(Roger Ingram) *in tch 1/2-way and racd towards outside: rdn 2f out: no imp on ldrs over 1f out: hung rt and wknd ins fnl f* **20/1**
1600 **8** shd **High On The Hog (IRE)**[13] 7601 3-9-6 **70**................ TomMcLaughlin 8 55
(Paul Howling) *chsd ldr tl appr fnl 2f: wknd appr fnl f* **50/1**
/4-2 **9** nk **Kenton Street**[48] 7151 6-8-12 **61**...................................... LukeMorris 6 45
(Michael J Browne, Ire) *led tl hdd appr fnl 2f: wknd over 1f out* **9/1**

1m 41.08s (1.28) **Going Correction** +0.001s/f
WFA 3 from 4yo+ 1lb **9** Ran SP% **113.1**
Speed ratings (Par 103): **93,92,91,90,88 88,83,82,82**
toteswingers:1&2:£6.10, 1&3:£4.00, 2&3:£4.40 CSF £35.25 CT £109.41 TOTE £7.50: £1.90, £1.90, £1.50; EX 40.40.
Owner Mr & Mrs Middlebrook/Mr & Mrs Nicholson **Bred** Mr & Mrs G Middlebrook **Trained** Kingsclere, Hants

FOCUS
A moderate handicap which was steadily run. The form is rated through the third.

Pipers Piping(IRE) Official explanation: jockey said gelding hung left

7765 BET AT BLUESQ.COM ON YOUR MOBILE NURSERY 6f (P)
5:30 (5:30) (Class 4) (0-85,82) 2-Y-O **£3,428** (£1,020; £509; £254) **Stalls** Low

Form RPR

21 **1** **Mezzotint (IRE)**^{14} 7593 2-9-5 **80** .... AdamKirby 6 85+
(Marco Botti) *t.k.h: in tch: hdwy towards outside over 1f out: rdn and r.o to ld fnl 120yds: kpt on wl* **8/11**^{1}

1436 **2** *1* **Waseem Faris (IRE)**^{78} 6464 2-9-6 **81** .... TonyCulhane 5 83
(Mick Channon) *bmpd s: in rr: hdwy over 1f out: qcknd between horses fnl 120yds: styd on under hand driving to take 2nd last strides: nt pce of wnr* **20/1**

6215 **3** *nk* **Taffe**^{62} 6843 2-9-4 **79** .... FrederikTylicki 8 80
(James Given) *led: rdn over 1f out: hdd fnl 120yds: no ex and lost 2nd last strides* **10/1**

2624 **4** *2 1/4* **Sunrise Dance**^{28} 7445 2-8-13 **74** .... JimCrowley 2 68
(Alan Jarvis) *t.k.h: chsd ldrs: wnt 2nd 2f out: no imp and lost 2nd ins fnl f: wknd fnl 120yds* **13/2**^{3}

31 **5** *1/2* **Fortrose Academy (IRE)**^{35} 7345 2-9-3 **78** .... LiamKeniry 4 71
(Andrew Balding) *chsd ldrs: rdn over 1f out: wknd ins fnl f* **3/1**^{2}

4002 **6** *hd* **Dishy Guru**^{13} 7597 2-8-10 **71** .... LukeMorris 3 63
(Michael Blanshard) *sn chsng ldr: lost 2nd 2f out: styd on chsng ldrs: wknd fnl 120yds* **14/1**

5541 **7** *5* **Gin Twist**^{20} 7541 2-8-5 **66** ....(b) RichardKingscote 7 43
(Tom Dascombe) *plld hrd and stdd towards rr: hdwy 1/2-way: wknd qckly over 2f out* **11/1**

1m 13.03s (-0.07) **Going Correction** +0.001s/f **7** Ran SP% **125.1**
Speed ratings (Par 98): **100,98,98,95,94 94,87**
toteswingers:1&2:£5.70, 1&3:£2.70, 2&3:£17.20 CSF £22.61 CT £106.93 TOTE £1.70: £1.50, £8.50; EX 22.90.
Owner Miss A Bonito **Bred** David Barry **Trained** Newmarket, Suffolk

FOCUS
This interesting sprint nursery was run at an uneven pace and the principals came a little way clear of the remainder.

NOTEBOOK
Mezzotint(IRE), off a mark of 80, followed up his Wolverhampton maiden success and is now 2-2 for Marco Botti. He found the race run to suit and it was apparent half a furlong out as he hit full stride that he would collect. This lightly raced colt still has some growing to do and it wouldn't at all surprise to see him make into a very useful handicapper next year. (op 10-11 tchd Evens)
Waseem Faris(IRE) ◆, another handicap debutant, was dropping back in trip on this return from a 78-day break and got going too late in the day. It was a promising effort and he's well up to winning off this mark. (op 25-1)
Taffe, back up in trip, turned in a decent effort from the front and he too looks capable of success from his current official rating. (op 14-1)
Sunrise Dance probably ran right up to his previous level. (op 7-1 tchd 15-2)
Fortrose Academy(IRE) returned from injury to score in a C&D maiden last month. He was never looking that happy and found very little for pressure. Official explanation: jockey said colt suffered interference at start (op 7-2)

7766 MEDIFORCE INDEPENDENT AMBULANCE SERVICE MEDIAN AUCTION MAIDEN STKS 1m 4f (P)
6:00 (6:01) (Class 6) 3-5-Y-O **£1,617** (£481; £240; £120) **Stalls** Centre

Form RPR

02 **1** **Refractor (IRE)**^{36} 7327 3-9-3 0 .... MartinLane 1 66+
(James Fanshawe) *trcked ldrs: led travelling smoothly wl over 1f out: pushed along fnl f: kpt on strly clsng stages* **13/8**^{1}

2 *3/4* **Bert The Alert**^{49} 3-9-3 0 .... TomQueally 5 63+
(Gary Moore) *in tch: hdwy 4f out: drvn to chse wnr appr fnl f: styd on wl clsng stages but a readily hld* **20/1**

30 **3** *7* **The Snorer**^{215} 2114 3-9-3 0 .... RussKennemore 10 52
(John Holt) *in rr: hdwy fr 4f out: drvn and styd on fnl 2f to take wl-hld 3rd ins fnl f* **66/1**

0254 **4** *3/4* **Phonic (IRE)**^{31} 7415 4-9-8 63 .... EddieAhern 8 51
(John Dunlop) *chsd ldrs 7f out: wnt 2nd 5f out led over 2f out: sn rdn: hdd wl over 1f out: wknd into 4th ins fnl f* **2/1**^{2}

3 **5** *nk* **Vertibes**^{8} 7662 3-9-3 0 .... DaneO'Neill 6 51
(Marcus Tregoning) *in rr: hdwy 4f out: styd on fnl 2f: nvr gng pce to get into contention* **4/1**^{3}

00 **6** *1* **Turbulent Priest**^{36} 7327 3-9-3 0 ....(b^{1}) JamieGoldstein 4 49
(Zoe Davison) *chsd ldr to 5f out: rdn over 2f out: wknd over 1f out* **66/1**

7 *8* **Western Approaches**^{42} 4-9-3 0 .... SebSanders 2 31
(Nicky Henderson) *led tl hdd over 2f out: sn btn* **13/2**

8 *16* **Before Bruce**^{16} 4-9-8 0 ....(p) LiamKeniry 7 11
(Brendan Powell) *rdn after 3f: a in rr* **50/1**

00 **9** *12* **Bondie**^{36} 7327 3-9-0 0 .... KieranO'Neill$^{(3)}$ 9 —
(John Bridger) *a in rr: t.o* **66/1**

10 *47* **Give Or Take** 3-9-3 0 .... IanMongan 3 —
(Christine Dunnett) *prom to 1/2-way: sn bhd: t.o* **50/1**

2m 36.1s (1.60) **Going Correction** +0.001s/f **10** Ran SP% **117.9**
WFA 3 from 4yo 5lb
Speed ratings (Par 101): **94,93,88,88,88 87,82,71,63,32**
toteswingers:1&2:£5.70, 1&3:£2.70, 2&3:£17.20 CSF £38.54 TOTE £2.50: £1.10, £4.60, £9.90; EX 40.00.
Owner Mr & Mrs W J Williams **Bred** B Dolan **Trained** Newmarket, Suffolk

FOCUS
A weak maiden, run at an orinary pace. The first pair were clear but there was little depth with the favourite disappointing and the winner did not need to match his debut form.

7767 MEDIFORCE.ORG PRIVATE AMBULANCE PROVIDER H'CAP 7f (P)
6:30 (6:32) (Class 5) (0-75,75) 3-Y-O+ **£2,264** (£673; £336; £168) **Stalls** Low

Form RPR

11 **1** **Rivas Rhapsody (IRE)**^{15} 7587 3-8-12 **66** .... DaneO'Neill 8 78+
(Ian Wood) *in tch: swtchd rt and hdwy appr fnl 2f: drvn and qcknd to ld fnl 150yds:* **5/2**^{1}

3022 **2** *1 1/4* **Tislaam (IRE)**^{22} 7517 4-9-3 **71** ....(p) MartinHarley 9 79
(Alan McCabe) *chsd ldrs: led over 2f out: sn rdn and hrd pressed: hdd fnl 150yds: nt pce of wnr but hld on wl for 2nd* **7/1**^{3}

2201 **3** *nk* **Forks**^{16} 7579 4-9-1 **69** .... LukeMorris 2 77
(Jane Chapple-Hyam) *chsd ldrs: drvn to chal wl over 1f out: styd on to press for 2nd fnl 150yds: one pce into 3rd clsng stages* **4/1**^{2}

0613 **4** *hd* **Chookie Avon**^{41} 7268 4-9-0 **68** ....(p) JimmyFortune 12 75+
(Keith Dalgleish) *in rr: hdwy on outside over 1f out: styd on to press for 3rd clsng stages but no imp on wnr* **8/1**

0505 **5** *1 1/4* **Malpas Missile (IRE)**^{35} 7348 3-9-0 **68** .... RichardKingscote 3 72
(Tom Dascombe) *chsd ldrs: rdn over 1f out: one pce ins fnl f* **14/1**

0150 **6** *shd* **Al Aqabah (IRE)**^{22} 7517 6-9-1 **72** ....(b) AdamBeschizza$^{(3)}$ 13 77+
(Brian Gubby) *s.i.s: in rr: hdwy on ins whn hmpd appr fnl f: styd on ins fnl f: nt rch ldrs* **16/1**

0203 **7** *2 1/2* **Scottish Glen**^{31} 7417 5-9-3 **71** .... JimCrowley 5 68
(Patrick Chamings) *towards rr: hdwy on ins 2f out: sn rdn: chsd ldrs over 1f out: wknd ins fnl f* **8/1**

106 **8** *1 3/4* **Aldermoor (USA)**^{69} 6665 5-9-2 **70** ....(t) WilliamCarson 14 62
(Stuart Williams) *in rr: hdwy over 1f out: nvr gng pce to rch ldrs: wknd ins fnl f* **20/1**

0023 **9** *1 1/4* **Sermons Mount (USA)**^{22} 7517 5-9-6 **74** .... LiamKeniry 11 63
(Paul Howling) *chsd ldrs: rdn over 2f out: wknd over 1f out* **16/1**

6000 **10** *5* **Serena's Pride**^{27} 7456 3-8-12 **73** ....(v) JordanUys$^{(7)}$ 6 48
(Alan Jarvis) *w ldr after 2f tl ins fnl 4f: wknd ins fnl 3f: btn whn hung lft fnl f* **50/1**

01U0 **11** *hd* **Regency Art (IRE)**^{12} 7625 4-9-2 **70** .... AdamKirby 7 44
(Milton Bradley) *s.i.s: outpcd most of way* **20/1**

4/00 **12** *6* **Smoky Cloud (IRE)**^{13} 7602 4-9-5 **73** .... TomMcLaughlin 1 31
(Amy Weaver) *led tl hdd & wknd over 2f out* **25/1**

6000 **13** *1 3/4* **Mary's Pet**^{16} 7579 4-8-4 **61** .... SimonPearce$^{(3)}$ 10 15
(John Akehurst) *a in rr* **66/1**

1m 24.94s (-1.06) **Going Correction** +0.001s/f **13** Ran SP% **118.5**
Speed ratings (Par 103): **106,104,104,104,102 102,99,97,96,90 90,83,81**
toteswingers:1&2:£7.00, 1&3:£23.70, 2&3:£30.10 CSF £18.43 CT £72.03 TOTE £2.80: £1.70, £2.60, £1.90; EX 20.50.
Owner D Hefin Jones **Bred** D Hefin Jones **Trained** Upper Lambourn, Berks
■ Stewards' Enquiry : Dane O'Neill two-day ban: careless riding (Dec 29-30)

FOCUS
This modest handicap was run at a fair pace, but the field was still bunched at the two-furlong marker. The time was good and the form looks solid. The winner remains on the upgrade.

7768 MEDIFORCE EVENT MEDICAL COVER SPECIALISTS H'CAP 7f (P)
7:00 (7:02) (Class 7) (0-50,50) 3-Y-O+ **£1,533** (£452; £226) **Stalls** Low

Form RPR

0603 **1** **Jackie Love (IRE)**^{8} 7655 3-8-6 **46** ....(b) JenniferFerguson$^{(7)}$ 4 55
(Olivia Maylam) *s.i.s: in rr: gd hdwy fr 2f out: led ins fnl f: drvn out* **11/2**^{3}

0230 **2** *1* **Lennoxwood (IRE)**^{8} 7655 3-8-8 **48** ....(be) RachealKneller$^{(7)}$ 9 54
(Mark Usher) *chsd ldrs: shkn up and kpt on ins fnl f to take 2nd nr fin but a hld* **7/1**

0300 **3** *3/4* **Blueberry Fizz (IRE)**^{8} 7663 3-8-9 **47** ....(p) RyanPowell$^{(5)}$ 2 51
(John Ryan) *chsd ldrs: led over 1f out: hdd ins fnl f: nt pce of wnr: one pce into 3rd nr fin* **20/1**

0000 **4** *1* **Pastoral Jet**^{28} 7442 3-8-10 **50** .... LukeRowe$^{(7)}$ 11 51
(Richard Rowe) *chsd ldrs: drvn and styd on same pce in 4th ins fnl f* **9/2**^{2}

0306 **5** *2 1/4* **Ghost Dancer**^{8} 7656 7-9-1 **48** ....(p) RichardKingscote 8 43
(Milton Bradley) *in rr: hdwy fr 2f out: styd on fnl f: nvr gng pce to trble ldrs* **10/1**

3322 **6** *1/2* **Ereka (IRE)**^{8} 7655 3-9-2 **49** .... LukeMorris 13 43
(John Best) *in rr: drvn over 2f out: kpt on fnl f but nvr gng pce to rch ldrs* **3/1**^{1}

0030 **7** *nk* **Fayre Bella**^{15} 7581 4-8-13 **46** .... JohnFahy 5 39
(John Gallagher) *chsd ldrs: led appr fnl 2f: hdd over 1f out: wknd fnl f* **16/1**

3600 **8** *2 1/2* **Grand Honour (IRE)**^{15} 7581 5-8-13 **46** .... IanMongan 7 32
(Paul Howling) *chsd ldrs: rdn over 2f out: wknd ins fnl f* **12/1**

5303 **9** *2 3/4* **Lucky Dime**^{13} 7609 3-9-3 **50** ....(b) AdamKirby 14 29
(Noel Quinlan) *s.i.s: hdwy and wl in tch w ldrs on outside over 3f out: wknd over 2f out* **16/1**

3464 **10** *6* **Kyncraighe (IRE)**^{15} 7581 3-9-0 **47** .... TomQueally 10 10
(Joseph Tuite) *disputed 2nd to 3f out: wknd over 2f out* **16/1**

063 **11** *nk* **Serial Sinner (IRE)**^{8} 7652 3-9-3 **50** ....(tp) StevieDonohoe 3 12
(Paul Cole) *rdn fr s and bhd: sme hdwy 3f out but nvr any ch: sn bhd* **12/1**

0655 **12** *1 1/4* **Five Cool Kats (IRE)**^{178} 3226 3-8-12 **45** ....(b) EddieAhern 12 —
(Bill Turner) *bhd most of way* **25/1**

0000 **13** *4 1/2* **Sonny G (IRE)**^{62} 6847 4-8-12 **45** ....(b^{1}) SteveDrowne 1 —
(John Best) *led tl hdd appr fnl 2f: wknd qckly* **10/1**

1m 26.36s (0.36) **Going Correction** +0.001s/f **13** Ran SP% **130.9**
Speed ratings (Par 97): **97,95,95,93,91 90,90,87,84,77 77,75,70**
CSF £48.47 CT £777.38 TOTE £7.70: £2.30, £3.10, £6.70; EX 44.80.
Owner Miss Olivia Maylam **Bred** Bigwigs Bloodstock **Trained** Epsom, Surrey

FOCUS
A bottom-drawer handicap. It was run at a decent pace and that suited the closers. The form looks sound if limited.
Pastoral Jet Official explanation: jockey said colt ran too freely
Serial Sinner(IRE) Official explanation: jockey said filly missed the break
T/Plt: £11.80 to a £1 stake. Pool:£64,023.39 - 3,929.44 winning tickets T/Qpdt: £6.90 to a £1 stake. Pool:£6,929.98 - 739.74 winning tickets ST

7742 SOUTHWELL (L-H)
Thursday, December 15

OFFICIAL GOING: Standard
Wind: Moderate behind Weather: Fine and dry

7769 PLAY THE BIG MONEY TOTEJACKPOT TODAY MAIDEN AUCTION STKS 7f (F)
12:30 (12:31) (Class 6) 2-Y-O **£1,704** (£503; £251) **Stalls** Low

Form RPR

0604 **1** **Cat Queen**^{6} 7697 2-8-1 55 .... AmyRyan$^{(3)}$ 1 54
(Gay Kelleway) *mde all: rdn 2f out: styd on gamely fnl f* **9/1**^{3}

65 **2** *1 1/4* **Great Nicanor (IRE)**^{34} 7369 2-9-0 0 .... TomEaves 4 61
(Ian Semple) *trckd ldrs: effrt and nt clr run 2f out and again over 1f out: squeezed through and rdn to chal ent fnl f: ev ch tl sn hung lft and one pce towards fin* **3/1**^{2}

55 **3** *3/4* **Red Hermes (IRE)**^{10} 7635 2-8-2 0 .... FrankieMcDonald 3 47
(Mark H Tompkins) *prom: pushed along and sltly outpcd over 2f out: swtchd rt and rdn over 1f out: ev ch ent fnl f: sn one pce* **22/1**

06 **4** *1 3/4* **Green Mountain (IRE)**^{15} 7582 2-8-2 0 ....(t) AndreaAtzeni 2 42
(Philip McBride) *cl up on inner: effrt over 2f out and ev ch: hld whn n.m.r and wknd ins fnl f* **50/1**

002 **5** *2* **Duke Liam (IRE)**^{6} 7685 2-9-2 0 .... AdrianNicholls 6 51
(David Nicholls) *chsd ldrs on outer: rdn along over 2f out: drvn wl over 1f out and sn btn* **8/13**^{1}

0 **6** *15* **Kingshill Lad (IRE)**[29] 7435 2-8-5 0 .... RyanPowell(5) 5 6
(Terry Clement) *v.s.a and awkward s: a bhd* **18/1**

1m 29.79s (-0.51) **Going Correction** -0.275s/f (Stan) **6** Ran SP% **108.5**
Speed ratings (Par 94): **91,89,88,86,84 67**
toteswingers:1&2:£1.30, 1&3:£3.00, 2&3:£3.00 CSF £33.48 TOTE £8.40: £2.20, £1.80; EX 23.10.
Owner T & Z Racing Club **Bred** R Haim **Trained** Exning, Suffolk
■ Stewards' Enquiry : Tom Eaves caution: careless riding.

FOCUS
A weak maiden auction event.

NOTEBOOK
Cat Queen, officially rated just 55, opened her account at the seventh attempt. It was her third start on AW but her Fibresand debut. She returned with a nasty cut on a hind leg. (op 10-1 tchd 17-2)
Great Nicanor(IRE), given a patient ride, was short of room once in line for home. Upsides a furlong out he edged left and found the winner too determined. (tchd 11-4 and 7-2)
Red Hermes(IRE), fifth in a seller here on her second start, was another holding every chance a furlong from home. It marked a big improvement but her proximity almost certainly underlines what a poor maiden this was. (op 20-1 tchd 18-1 and 25-1)
Green Mountain(IRE) stepped up on her two previous efforts on her Fibresand debut though tiring markedly in the closing stages. (op 40-1)
Duke Liam(IRE), who seemed to show much improved form when runner-up behind an odds-on shot on his Fibresand debut over this C&D on his third start a week previously, gave problems going down and had to be led to the start. He was drawn wide and, hanging left once in line for home, he was soon making very hard work of it. He must be better than he showed here but there is a question mark over his temperament. (op 4-7)

7770 TOTEEXACTA NURSERY — 5f (F)
1:00 (1:00) (Class 6) (0-60,60) 2-Y-O — £1,704 (£503; £251) Stalls High

Form RPR

3006 **1** **Claretintheblood (IRE)**[6] 7692 2-9-1 **54** .... TonyHamilton 3 58
(Richard Fahey) *prom: effrt to chal wl over 1f out: rdn to ld appr fnl f: drvn out* **12/1**

6301 **2** *½* **Russian Bullet**[6] 7692 2-9-3 **56** 6ex .... FergusSweeney 7 58
(Jamie Osborne) *led: rdn wl over 1f out: hdd appr fnl f: ev ch whn edgd lft ins fnl f: kpt on* **5/1**[3]

0603 **3** *1 ¼* **Burnwynd Spirit (IRE)**[34] 7365 2-8-13 **52** .... TomEaves 2 50
(Ian Semple) *chsd ldrs on outer: hdwy wl over 1f out: rdn to chse ldng pair whn edgd rt ent fnl f: kpt on same pce* **16/1**

0033 **4** *3 ¼* **Monty Fay (IRE)**[20] 7541 2-9-3 **56** .... WilliamCarson 4 42
(Derek Haydn Jones) *prom: rdn along 2f out: one pce appr fnl f* **11/8**[1]

0104 **5** *1 ½* **Lord Buffhead**[107] 5591 2-9-1 **57** .... RobertLButler(3) 5 38
(Richard Guest) *cl up: rdn along 2f out: sn wknd* **25/1**

3044 **6** *7* **Thorpe Bay**[9] 7642 2-9-4 **60** ....(b) AdamBeschizza(3) 6 15
(Mark Rimmer) *rrd and lost many l s: a bhd* **4/1**[2]

0006 **7** *1* **Willow Beauty**[63] 6820 2-9-2 **55** .... JoeFanning 8 7
(J R Jenkins) *chsd ldrs: rdn along 1/2-way: sn outpcd and bhd* **6/1**

59.27 secs (-0.43) **Going Correction** -0.225s/f (Stan) **7** Ran SP% **110.5**
Speed ratings (Par 94): **94,93,91,86,83 72,70**
toteswingers:1&2:£4.00, 1&3:£10.30, 2&3:£5.50 CSF £65.18 CT £919.55 TOTE £15.70: £3.60, £2.40; EX 39.80 TRIFECTA Not won..
Owner The Matthewman Partnership **Bred** O McElroy **Trained** Musley Bank, N Yorks
■ Stewards' Enquiry : Fergus Sweeney five-day ban: used whip with excessive frequency (Dec 29-31,Jan 1-2)

FOCUS
A modest nursery and it paid to race up with the pace.

NOTEBOOK
Claretintheblood(IRE) put three modest efforts behind him on his Fibresand debut. He really stuck his head down and battled, and deserves credit for this. (tchd 16-1)
Russian Bullet, off the mark at Wolverhampton from a 6lb lower mark on his first start since being gelded, travelled supremely well towards the stands' side rail. In front at halfway, he tended to hang left and in the end found the winner the more determined. The quicker Polytrack surface probably suits his style of running better. (op 4-1 tchd 11-2)
Burnwynd Spirit(IRE), who seemed to run right up to his best when last of three in a claimer at Wolverhampton, confirmed that improvement and will be suited by a return to six. (op 12-1 tchd 18-1)
Monty Fay(IRE), who raced upsides towards the centre, showed plenty of toe but is another whose run style suggests Polytrack suits him better. (op 13-8 tchd 7-4 and 5-4)
Lord Buffhead was having his first start for over three months and should benefit from it. (op 18-1 tchd 16-1)
Thorpe Bay, a maiden after 11 previous attempts, lost all chance when rearing in the stalls, which was confirmed by his jockey. Official explanation: jockey said gelding reared as stalls opened (tchd 7-2)

7771 TOTEQUADPOT H'CAP — 1m (F)
1:30 (1:30) (Class 4) (0-80,81) 3-Y-O+ — £4,204 (£1,251; £625; £312) Stalls Low

Form RPR

132 **1** **Il Battista**[4] 7727 3-8-12 **72** ....(be) ShaneKelly 5 82
(Alan McCabe) *trckd ldrs: hdwy 2f out: rdn to ld over 1f out: drvn and kpt on gamely towards fin* **15/2**[2]

3512 **2** *½* **Standpoint**[19] 7558 5-9-0 **80** ....(e[1]) JackDuern(7) 9 89
(Reg Hollinshead) *trckd ldrs on inner: hdwy over 2f out: rdn over 1f out: styd on to chal ent fnl f: ev ch tl no ex last 75yds* **10/1**

0056 **3** *4* **Vitznau (IRE)**[16] 7575 7-8-4 **66** oh1 .... SophieDoyle(3) 2 66
(Alastair Lidderdale) *trckd ldng pair: hdwy to ld over 2f out: rdn wl over 1f out: hdd appr fnl f: kpt on same pce* **50/1**

0633 **4** *1* **Piceno (IRE)**[36] 7339 3-9-2 **76** ....(b) FrederikTylicki 1 74
(Scott Dixon) *led: rdn along over 2f out: sn hdd: kpt on same pce* **8/1**[3]

11-0 **5** *1* **Podgies Boy (IRE)**[29] 7439 3-9-3 **77** .... TonyHamilton 8 72
(Richard Fahey) *chsd ldrs: rdn along over 2f out: no imp appr fnl f* **25/1**

0211 **6** *½* **Greyfriarschorista**[6] 7687 4-9-8 **81** 6ex .... BarryMcHugh 7 75
(Brian Ellison) *hld up towards rr: hdwy over 3f out: chsd ldrs over 2f out: sn rdn and btn* **4/6**[1]

2542 **7** *4* **Carragold**[43] 7236 5-8-11 **70** .... DuranFentiman 3 55
(Mel Brittain) *sn rdn along and a towards rr* **16/1**

0054 **8** *4 ½* **If You Whisper (IRE)**[13] 7601 3-8-11 **71** ....(b) TonyCulhane 10 46
(Mike Murphy) *a towards rr* **20/1**

0020 **9** *12* **Christmas Carnival**[18] 5728 4-8-11 **70** .... JamesSullivan 6 17
(Michael Easterby) *in tch: rdn along 1/2-way: sn lost pl and bhd* **66/1**

0116 **P** **Eastern Hills**[36] 7339 6-9-6 **79** ....(p) MartinHarley 4 —
(Alan McCabe) *cl up: rdn along over 3f out: wknd qckly: p.u and dismntd 2f out* **16/1**

1m 40.68s (-3.02) **Going Correction** -0.275s/f (Stan)
WFA 3 from 4yo+ 1lb **10** Ran SP% **115.8**
Speed ratings (Par 105): **104,103,99,98,97 97,93,88,76,—**
toteswingers:1&2:£7.50, 1&3:£20.00, 2&3:£46.50 CSF £75.35 CT £3536.77 TOTE £10.50: £2.40, £2.20, £11.70; EX 61.70 TRIFECTA Not won..
Owner Alotincommon Partnership **Bred** Cheveley Park Stud Ltd **Trained** Averham Park, Notts

FOCUS
A strongly run good-class handicap. The winner got a bit closer to his early 3yo form.
Greyfriarschorista Official explanation: vet said gelding bled from the nose
Eastern Hills Official explanation: trainer said gelding finished distressed

7772 TOTETRIFECTA H'CAP — 1m 4f (F)
2:00 (2:00) (Class 5) (0-75,77) 3-Y-O+ — £2,264 (£673; £336; £168) Stalls Low

Form RPR

1311 **1** **Mazij**[19] 7556 3-9-2 **72** .... WilliamCarson 4 82
(Peter Hiatt) *trckd ldng pair: hdwy to chse ldr 3f out: led over 2f out: rdn clr wl over 1f out: edgd rt ins fnl f: kpt on wl towards fin* **9/2**[2]

5061 **2** *1* **Follow The Flag (IRE)**[5] 7713 7-9-12 **77** 6ex ....(v) ShaneKelly 1 85
(Alan McCabe) *hld up in rr: hdwy over 3f out: rdn to chse ldrs 2f out: drvn to chse wnr whn swtchd lft ins fnl f: kpt on* **6/1**

0402 **3** *2 ¼* **Royal Swain (IRE)**[5] 7713 5-9-10 **75** .... JoeFanning 6 79
(Alan Swinbank) *trckd ldrs: hdwy on inner to chse ldng pair 3f out: rdn over 2f out: drvn and one pce appr fnl f* **4/5**[1]

6362 **4** *nk* **Ay Tay Tate (IRE)**[6] 7689 5-8-11 **67** ow2 ....(p) JustinNewman(5) 5 71
(David C Griffiths) *led and sn clr: rdn along 3f out: hdd over 2f out: grad wknd* **11/2**[3]

3045 **5** *8* **John Forbes**[90] 6115 9-9-5 **70** .... BarryMcHugh 3 61
(Brian Ellison) *a in rr* **20/1**

6000 **6** *1 ¾* **Just Five (IRE)**[30] 7425 5-9-0 **65** .... TomEaves 2 53
(John Weymes) *chsd clr ldr: rdn along over 3f out: sn wknd* **66/1**

2m 37.03s (-3.97) **Going Correction** -0.275s/f (Stan)
WFA 3 from 5yo+ 5lb **6** Ran SP% **109.7**
Speed ratings (Par 103): **102,101,99,99,94 93**
toteswingers:1&2:£2.30, 1&3:£1.90, 2&3:£2.00 CSF £28.97 TOTE £4.20: £2.20, £1.90; EX 20.40.
Owner P W Hiatt **Bred** The Hill Stud **Trained** Hook Norton, Oxon

FOCUS
No hanging about here. The winenr continues on the upgrade and may do a bit better, but the favourite was disappointing.

7773 PLAY GOLF AT SOUTHWELL IN 2012 CLAIMING STKS — 1m (F)
2:30 (2:30) (Class 6) 3-4-Y-O — £1,704 (£503; £251) Stalls Low

Form RPR

4103 **1** **On The Cusp (IRE)**[6] 7687 4-8-12 68 ....(p) MartinHarley 4 75
(Richard Guest) *cl up: led on bit wl over 2f out: shkn up over 1f out: rdn and edgd lft ins fnl f: kpt on* **11/4**[2]

5006 **2** *3* **Golden Creek (USA)**[30] 7424 3-8-13 65 .... WilliamCarson 1 70
(Mrs K Burke) *chsd ldng pair: rdn along 3f out: outpcd over 2f out: styd on u.p to chse wnr ins fnl f: sn no imp* **7/2**[3]

0603 **3** *3* **Double Duchess**[30] 7424 3-8-0 60 .... AndreaAtzeni 3 50
(Paul D'Arcy) *led: rdn along 3f out: sn hdd & wknd fnl 2f* **10/11**[1]

0020 **4** *29* **Dimaire**[52] 7055 4-8-3 52 ....(p) FrankieMcDonald 5 —
(Derek Haydn Jones) *chsd ldrs: rdn along over 3f out: sn wknd* **16/1**

1m 40.71s (-2.99) **Going Correction** -0.275s/f (Stan)
WFA 3 from 4yo 1lb **4** Ran SP% **107.2**
Speed ratings (Par 101): **103,100,97,68**
CSF £11.68 TOTE £2.40; EX 7.70.
Owner Rakebackmypoker.com **Bred** J Stan Cosgrove **Trained** Stainforth, S Yorks

FOCUS
A weak claimer and a most disappointing favourite, but it was sound run. The winner rates back to his best.

7774 KEITH OLIVER HAPPY 50TH BIRTHDAY MAIDEN STKS — 1m 3f (F)
3:00 (3:00) (Class 5) 3-Y-O+ — £2,385 (£704; £352) Stalls Low

Form RPR

-2 **1** **Priceless Art (IRE)**[23] 7503 6-9-7 0 .... JoeFanning 4 78+
(Alan Swinbank) *mde all: pushed along 3f out: jnd and rdn 2f out: drvn and edgd lft ins fnl f: styd on wl towards fin* **4/6**[1]

32P0 **2** *1 ¾* **Nibani (IRE)**[13] 7601 4-9-2 72 ....(p) AmyScott(5) 1 76
(Alastair Lidderdale) *hld up in rr: gd hdwy over 3f out: chal wl over 1f out: sn rdn and ev ch tl edgd rt and one pce wl ins fnl f* **8/1**[3]

0652 **3** *2 ¾* **Kishanda**[6] 7241 3-8-12 60 .... AndreaAtzeni 2 65
(Gay Kelleway) *hld up in tch: hdwy 4f out: chsd ldrs 3f out: rdn over 2f out and ch tl one pce ent fnl f* **5/2**[2]

3303 **4** *1* **Zenarinda**[5] 7712 4-9-2 63 .... TomEaves 5 63
(Mark H Tompkins) *trckd ldrs on outer: hdwy and cl up 3f out: rdn to chal 2f out and ev ch tl hung lft and wknd ent fnl f* **16/1**

0-00 **5** *6* **Nippy Nikki**[50] 7113 3-8-12 39 .... PaddyAspell 7 52?
(John Norton) *chsd wnr: pushed along over 4f out: rdn over 3f out and sn wknd* **100/1**

3 **6** *11* **Maggie Aron**[20] 7536 5-9-2 0 .... FergusSweeney 6 33
(Tim Vaughan) *hld up towards rr: hdwy and in tch over 3f out: sn rdn and wknd* **25/1**

040- **7** *32* **Sposalizio (IRE)**[185] 4407 4-9-7 47 .... RobbieFitzpatrick 3 —
(Colin Teague) *chsd ldrs: lost pl over 4f out: sn bhd* **100/1**

2m 24.64s (-3.36) **Going Correction** -0.275s/f (Stan)
WFA 3 from 4yo+ 4lb **7** Ran SP% **111.4**
Speed ratings (Par 103): **101,99,97,97,92 84,61**
toteswingers:1&2:£1.70, 1&3:£1.50, 2&3:£2.30 CSF £6.67 TOTE £1.60: £1.10, £3.30; EX 5.90.
Owner Matthew Green & David Manasseh **Bred** Lady Bamford **Trained** Melsonby, N Yorks

FOCUS
No depth, but the first two set a superior standard to most maidens around here. The form makes sense.

7775 HOSPITALITY AT SOUTHWELL RACECOURSE H'CAP — 1m (F)
3:30 (3:32) (Class 6) (0-60,60) 3-Y-O+ — £1,704 (£503; £251) Stalls Low

Form RPR

2356 **1** **Spacecraft (IRE)**[5] 7714 4-8-7 **46** oh1 ....(b) JoeFanning 11 55
(Christopher Kellett) *trckd ldrs: hdwy over 2f out: rdn to chse ldr over 1f out: styd on ins fnl f to ld last 100yds* **7/2**[1]

-402 **2** *nk* **Hilbre Court (USA)**[6] 7687 6-9-0 **53** ....(p) J-PGuillambert 7 61
(Brian Baugh) *trckd ldng pair: hdwy to ld 3f out: rdn wl over 1f out: drvn ent fnl f: hdd and no ex last 100yds* **7/2**[1]

-406 **3** *2 ¾* **Resplendent Alpha**[6] 7663 7-9-0 **53** ....(p) FergusSweeney 12 55
(Alastair Lidderdale) *midfield: hdwy on outer over 2f out: rdn over 1f out: kpt on fnl f* **20/1**

0003 **4** *nk* **General Tufto**[23] 7507 6-9-5 **58** ....(b) RobbieFitzpatrick 4 59
(Charles Smith) *in tch on inner: hdwy 3f out: rdn to chse ldrs 2f out: one pce ent fnl f* **9/2**[2]

4302 **5** *2 ¼* **Eastern Gift**[5] 7711 6-9-7 **60** .... AndreaAtzeni 10 56
(Gay Kelleway) *trckd ldrs: hdwy wl over 2f out: rdn to chse ldng pair wl over 1f out: one pce ent fnl f* **7/2**[1]

6046 **6** *3/4* **Jonnie Skull (IRE)**[5] 7711 5-9-0 **56**..............................(vt) RyanClark(3) 1 50
(Phil McEntee) *led: rdn along and hdd 3f out: grad wknd* **9/1**[3]
30/0 **7** *7* **Dado Mush**[240] 1468 8-8-2 **48**..................................(p) JessicaSteven(7) 6 26
(Terry Clement) *nvr bttr than midfield* **33/1**
4000 **8** *hd* **Very Well Red**[20] 7538 8-8-11 **55**.............................. JustinNewman(5) 9 33
(Peter Hiatt) *chsd ldrs: rdn wl over 2f out: sn wknd* **10/1**
00/0 **9** *2 3/4* **Marina's Ocean**[42] 7246 7-8-7 **46** oh1..........................(t) KellyHarrison 8 17
(Roy Bowring) *a in rr* **100/1**
50-0 **10** *2 1/4* **Joyously**[13] 7610 3-9-0 **57**..(tp) RobertLButler(3) 5 23
(Richard Guest) *dwlt: a in rr* **33/1**
-300 **11** *3/4* **Avoncharm**[9] 7648 3-8-10 **50**......................................(b) DuranFentiman 3 14
(Mel Brittain) *cl up: rdn along over 3f out: sn wknd* **40/1**
1m 42.35s (-1.35) **Going Correction** -0.275s/f (Stan)
WFA 3 from 4yo+ 1lb **11** Ran SP% **118.0**
Speed ratings (Par 101): **95,94,91,91,89 88,81,81,78,76 75**
toteswingers:1&2:£3.30, 1&3:£7.10, 2&3:£10.00 CSF £14.97 CT £218.42 TOTE £5.10: £1.60, £1.30, £4.00; EX 20.30 Trifecta £326.80 Part won. Pool: £441.70 - 0.62 winning units..
Owner The Edwardsons **Bred** Epona Bloodstock Ltd **Trained** Appleby Magna, Derbys
■ Stewards' Enquiry : J-P Guillambert two-day ban: used whip with excessive frequency (Dec 29-30)

FOCUS
An open handicap but it was not as strong run as most and the form is modest. A 4lb personal best from the winner.
T/Plt: £325.60 to a £1 stake. Pool:£43,510.54 - 97.54 winning tickets T/Qpdt: £41.20 to a £1 stake. Pool:£4,898.02 - 87.95 winning tickets JR

7769 SOUTHWELL (L-H)
Friday, December 16

OFFICIAL GOING: Standard
Wind: Moderate behind Weather: Overcast

7776 PLAY THE BIG MONEY TOTEJACKPOT TODAY CLAIMING STKS 6f (F)
11:55 (11:55) (Class 6) 3-Y-0+ **£1,704** (£503; £251) **Stalls** Low

Form RPR
1220 **1** **Katy's Secret**[57] 6979 4-8-0 70.............................. RyanPowell(5) 1 79
(William Jarvis) *trckd ldrs on inner: gd hdwy over 2f out: rdn to ld ent fnl f: sn edgd rt and rdn out* **11/2**[3]
0362 **2** *1/2* **Stevie Gee (IRE)**[9] 7658 7-8-8 71...............................(v) FrannyNorton 2 80
(Ian Williams) *cl up: rdn and sltly outpcd wl over 1f out: swtchd rt appr fnl f: styd on u.p* **8/1**
6156 **3** *2 3/4* **Equuleus Pictor**[3] 7746 7-8-13 75 ow1..........................(p) AdamKirby 5 77
(John Spearing) *led: rdn and qcknd 21f out: hdd ent fnl f: sn one pce* **5/2**[1]
030 **4** *2 1/2* **Hotham**[36] 7356 8-8-12 79.. BarryMcHugh 8 68
(Noel Wilson) *t.k.h early: hld up towards rr: hdwy over 2f out: sn rdn and kpt on same pce* **22/1**
0022 **5** *3/4* **Autumn Blades (IRE)**[5] 7726 6-8-10 84....................(b) JamesSullivan 3 63
(Ruth Carr) *t.k.h: trckd ldrs: effrt over 2f out: sn rdn and wknd over 1f out* **11/4**[2]
0053 **6** *1 1/4* **Desert Strike**[15] 7594 5-8-10 75......................................(p) ShaneKelly 6 59
(Alan McCabe) *s.i.s and in rr: hdwy 2f out: sn rdn and kpt on: nvr nr ldrs* **9/1**
0460 **7** *2* **Trans Sonic**[209] 2320 8-9-3 87...................................... DanielTudhope 10 60
(David O'Meara) *chsd ldrs on outer: rdn along over 2f out: sn wknd* **14/1**
-004 **8** *2 1/4* **Stansonnit**[142] 4439 3-8-10 77.. JoeFanning 11 46
(Alan Swinbank) *dwlt: a towards rr* **14/1**
3440 **9** *1/2* **Forty Proof (IRE)**[3] 7746 3-8-2 74........................(tp) RobJFitzpatrick(7) 4 43
(Alan McCabe) *chsd ldrs: n.m.r after 2f: sn lost pl and towards rr fr 1/2-way* **20/1**
6060 **10** *10* **Finn's Rainbow**[8] 7675 3-8-7 73.................................. MartinLane 9 —
(John Weymes) *midfield: rdn along 1/2-way: sn wknd* **66/1**
1m 14.57s (-1.93) **Going Correction** -0.225s/f (Stan) **10** Ran SP% **115.7**
Speed ratings (Par 101): **103,102,98,95,94 92,90,87,86,73**
toteswingers.1&2.£3.30, 1&3.£4.10, 2&3.£6.10 CSF £47.00 TOTE £0.00. £2.10, £2.50, £1.90, EX 30.50 Trifecta £132.20 Part won. Pool: £178.75 - 0.10 winning units..Katy's Secret was the subject of a friendly claim.
Owner Miss S E Hall **Bred** Miss S E Hall **Trained** Newmarket, Suffolk

FOCUS
A fair claimer and the entire field were separated by just 11lb on official figures. They didn't seem to go that fast early on and those held up were disadvantaged. There is a chance the form is a bit better than rated.
Autumn Blades(IRE) Official explanation: jockey said gelding ran too free

7777 TOTEEXACTA FILLIES' MAIDEN STKS 1m (F)
12:25 (12:27) (Class 5) 2-Y-0 **£2,264** (£673; £336; £168) **Stalls** Low

Form RPR
3436 **1** **Really Lovely (IRE)**[30] 7436 2-9-0 72.............................. ShaneKelly 6 70
(Jeremy Noseda) *cl up: led after 1/2f: clr wl over 1f out: rdn and kpt on fnl f* **6/4**[1]
04 **2** *2 1/4* **Sweet Grace**[7] 7685 2-9-0 0.......................................(t) MichaelStainton 1 65
(David Brown) *led 1 1/2f: trckd ldrs on inner: hdwy to chse wnr wl over 1f out: sn rdn and kpt on same pce fnl f* **11/1**
06 **3** *4 1/2* **Rhyme Royal**[28] 7464 2-9-0 0.. FrederikTylicki 4 55
(James Given) *cl up: rdn along over 2f out: sn one pce* **100/1**
3664 **4** *1 1/4* **Angel Cake (IRE)**[7] 7684 2-9-0 54...................................(vt[1]) AdamKirby 10 52
(Phil McEntee) *chsd ldrs: hdwy to chse wnr wl over 2f out: sn rdn and wknd wl over 1f out* **33/1**
4 **5** *3/4* **Minnie Diva (IRE)**[83] 6329 2-9-0 0.................................. JoeFanning 5 50
(Kevin Ryan) *in rr and sn rdn along: hdwy 2f out: nvr nr ldrs* **9/4**[2]
43 **6** *3* **Dora's Gift**[31] 7422 2-9-0 0... PhillipMakin 8 43
(Hughie Morrison) *in rr tl sme late hdwy* **11/2**[3]
06 **7** *1 3/4* **Lady Author**[7] 7685 2-9-0 0... BarryMcHugh 3 39
(Richard Fahey) *a towards rr* **80/1**
8 *2 1/4* **Medlaur** 2-9-0 0.. JamesSullivan 7 34
(James Given) *dwlt: a in rr* **33/1**
0 **9** *1/2* **Fleeting Fashion**[31] 7422 2-9-0 0.................................... NeilChalmers 9 33
(Michael Appleby) *in tch: rdn along over 3f out: sn wknd* **100/1**
00 **10** *3/4* **Little Red Minx (IRE)**[23] 7520 2-9-0 0............................ FrannyNorton 11 31
(Peter Chapple-Hyam) *in tch: rdn along over 3f out: sn wknd* **9/1**
1m 43.7s **Going Correction** -0.225s/f (Stan) **10** Ran SP% **113.6**
Speed ratings (Par 93): **91,88,84,83,82 79,77,75,74,74**
toteswingers:1&2:£4.00, 1&3:£21.90, 2&3:£52.40 CSF £18.58 TOTE £2.40: £1.20, £2.90, £12.60; EX 20.50 Trifecta £187.90 Part won. Pool: £254.03 - 228.62 winning units..Lady Electra was withdrawn price at time of withdrawal 100/1. Rule 4 does not apply.
Owner Michael Tabor, Mrs John Magnier & Derrick Smith **Bred** Roncon, Wynatt & Chelston **Trained** Newmarket, Suffolk

FOCUS
Most of these were in trouble leaving the back straight and the form looks pretty modest.

NOTEBOOK
Really Lovely(IRE) travelled better than most and stayed on under strong pressure to record her first success at the sixth attempt. She's extremely well bred, being by Galileo out of a dual Group 1 winner (Fillies' Mile and Falmouth), so this victory will have increased her value as a broodmare prospect, and it's questionable whether we'll see much more of her on the race track. (op 7-4 tchd 15-8)
Sweet Grace was always held late on, but she might be a bit better than she showed as she did much of her racing around the inside and had to wait for a run on the turn into the straight. Handicaps are now an option. (op 12-1 tchd 10-1)
Rhyme Royal didn't see her race out after being handy, but she's another who can now switch to handicaps and there may be more to come in due course.
Angel Cake(IRE) had a tongue-tie and visor added, but it's doubtful she improved a great deal on her official mark of 54. (op 25-1)
Minnie Diva(IRE) was never going and failed to confirm the promise she showed first time out at Haydock in September. She'll be worth another chance elsewhere, however. (op 3-1 tchd 2-1)
Dora's Gift was another who didn't travel at any stage. She had run to a moderate level here last time as well and it seems the surface doesn't suit. Official explanation: jockey said filly was hampered at start (op 7-2 tchd 6-1)
Medlaur Official explanation: jockey said filly was hampered at start

7778 TOTEQUADPOT NURSERY 5f (F)
1:00 (1:00) (Class 5) (0-75,75) 2-Y-0 **£2,264** (£673; £336; £168) **Stalls** High

Form RPR
2245 **1** **M J Woodward**[15] 7592 2-7-12 **52** oh2.......................... JamesSullivan 3 58
(Paul Green) *trckd ldng pair: effrt to chse wnr wl over 1f out: rdn ent fnl f: kpt on to ld last 50yds* **5/1**[3]
0213 **2** *1/2* **Wicked Wench**[10] 7642 2-9-1 **69**.................................. TonyCulhane 1 73
(Jo Hughes) *cl up: led after 1f: rdn over 1f out: sn edgd rt and drvn: hdd and no ex last 50yds* **11/4**[2]
2536 **3** *3 3/4* **Superplex**[114] 5367 2-9-0 **68**.. TomEaves 4 59
(John Quinn) *chsd ldrs: rdn along and outpcd 1/2-way: kpt on fnl f* **6/1**
51 **4** *1 3/4* **Twilight Allure**[20] 7555 2-9-4 **75**.....................................(t) AmyRyan(3) 6 59
(Kevin Ryan) *led 1f: cl up: rdn 2f out and sn wknd* **6/5**[1]
050 **5** *hd* **Ypres**[35] 7368 2-8-8 **62**.. MichaelStainton 5 46
(Jason Ward) *dwlt: sn in tch: rdn along and edgd lft over 2f out: sn one pce* **20/1**
405 **6** *shd* **Essexvale (IRE)**[5] 7724 2-7-13 **60**.......................... MatthewHopkins(7) 2 43
(Alan Berry) *dwlt: a in rr* **40/1**
58.54 secs (-1.16) **Going Correction** -0.325s/f (Stan) **6** Ran SP% **110.3**
Speed ratings (Par 96): **96,95,89,86,86 85**
toteswingers:1&2:£1.70, 1&3:£2.00, 2&3:£2.60 CSF £18.37 TOTE £5.50: £2.40, £1.20; EX 18.50.
Owner E Sciarrillo **Bred** Paul Green **Trained** Lydiate, Merseyside

FOCUS
A modest nursery.

NOTEBOOK
M J Woodward took well to Fibresand, gaining his first success at the tenth attempt despite being 2lb out of the handicap. He could have more to offer on this surface. (op 6-1)
Wicked Wench didn't seem to have any excuses. She travelled well but found the winner too strong. (op 2-1 tchd 7-4 and 3-1)
Superplex, trying Fibresand for the first time after a 114-day break, didn't travel but kept on. It remains to be seen whether this surface is for him, but he can do better. (op 8-1 tchd 9-1)
Twilight Allure showed early pace but was in trouble by around halfway and couldn't follow up her Wolverhampton maiden win. Her sire has a good record here, so it might be unwise to assume she simply didn't take to the surface. (op 6-4)
Ypres Official explanation: jockey said gelding hung left throughout

7779 TOTETRIFECTA H'CAP 1m 3f (F)
1:35 (1:35) (Class 5) (0-70,68) 3-Y-0 **£2,385** (£704; £352) **Stalls** Low

Form RPR
0111 **1** **Sky High Diver (IRE)**[5] 7723 3-9-4 **65** 6ex.......................... JoeFanning 1 75+
(Alan Swinbank) [illegible] *styd on wl fnl f* **4/6**[1]
2402 **2** *1* **Echos Of Motivator**[13] 7630 3-9-3 **67**...........................(p) RyanClark(3) 5 75
(Ronald Harris) *trckd ldrs: pushed along over 3f out: rdn along and rdr dropped whip over 2f out: styd on to chal wl over 1f out and ev ch tl no ex ins fnl f* **11/2**[3]
3523 **3** *3* **Conducting**[28] 7453 3-9-4 **68**.. DaleSwift(3) 6 71
(Gay Kelleway) *dwlt: hld up in rr: hdwy 3f out: rdn 2f out: styd on same pce* **7/2**[2]
2405 **4** *3 1/4* **Toucan Tango (IRE)**[55] 7037 3-8-10 **57**.......................... FrannyNorton 2 54
(Michael Quinn) *led: rdn along 3f out: hdd 2f out: grad wknd* **28/1**
3205 **5** *3 3/4* **Philharmonic Hall**[15] 6192 3-8-13 **60**...........................(p) BarryMcHugh 4 50
(Richard Fahey) *chsd ldrr: rdn along over 3f out: wknd over 2f out* **10/1**
2m 27.91s (-0.09) **Going Correction** -0.225s/f (Stan) **5** Ran SP% **110.1**
Speed ratings (Par 102): **91,90,88,85,83**
CSF £4.86 TOTE £1.50: £1.10, £2.80; EX 4.50.
Owner Mrs M C Keogh **Bred** Michael Downey & Roalso Ltd **Trained** Melsonby, N Yorks

FOCUS
An uncompetitive handicap run at a modest pace. The form is a bit muddling but has been taken at face value.

7780 ARCHER ELECTRICAL 25TH ANNIVERSARY NURSERY 7f (F)
2:10 (2:12) (Class 6) (0-60,60) 2-Y-0 **£1,704** (£503; £251) **Stalls** Low

Form RPR
026 **1** **Sweetnessandlight**[21] 7540 2-9-7 **60**.......................... MichaelStainton 3 67
(Jason Ward) *midfield: hdwy on inner over 2f out: rdn over 1f out: styd on to ld nr fin* **16/1**
2243 **2** *hd* **Ishiamiracle**[5] 7725 2-9-0 **60**.. DannyBrock(7) 7 66
(Phil McEntee) *led: rdn 2f out: hung rt ent fnl f: hdd and no ex nr fin* **9/2**[3]
0400 **3** *1* **Doyouknowwhoiam**[82] 6384 2-9-2 **55**.................................. TomEaves 8 59
(Bryan Smart) *prom: effrt 2f out: chal wl over 1f out: sn rdn and ev ch tl drvn and nt qckn fnl 100yds* **10/1**
0000 **4** *1* **Ferdy (IRE)**[43] 7252 2-8-6 **45**.. JamesSullivan 4 46
(Paul Green) *chsd ldrs: rdn along 3f out: kpt on u.p fnl 2f* **40/1**
0052 **5** *hd* **Songbird Blues**[15] 7592 2-8-11 **50**.......................... RichardKingscote 9 51
(Mark Usher) *hld up towards rr: gd hdwy over 2f out: rdn to chse ldrs wl over 1f out: kpt on same pce fnl f* **4/1**[2]
0004 **6** *3* **Small Steps (IRE)**[88] 6222 2-9-1 **54**.................................. ShaneKelly 10 47
(Ed McMahon) *dwlt and towards rr: hdwy 3f out: rdn over 2f out: no imp appr fnl f* **7/4**[1]

0004 **7** *8* **Chateau Lola**[7] 7694 2-8-6 **45**..(v) JoeFanning 11 17
(Derek Shaw) *chsd ldrs on outer: rdn along 3f out: sn wknd* **33/1**

3033 **8** *shd* **Clarkson (IRE)**[135] 4658 2-9-0 **56**.............................. SophieDoyle(3) 2 28
(Jamie Osborne) *t.k.h: chsd ldrs on inner: rdn along over 2f out: sn wknd* **20/1**

0005 **9** *2 ½* **Singspiel Spirit**[73] 6611 2-8-9 **48**.................................. FrederikTylicki 6 13
(Clive Brittain) *sn rdn along and a in rr* **5/1**

1m 29.14s (-1.16) **Going Correction** -0.225s/f (Stan) **9** Ran SP% **116.3**
Speed ratings (Par 94): **97,96,95,94,94 90,81,81,78**
toteswingers:1&2:£7.50, 1&3:£13.60, 2&3:£9.10 CSF £85.43 CT £776.98 TOTE £16.40: £3.80, £2.00, £3.30; EX 51.30 Trifecta £499.30 Part won. Pool: £674.39 - 0.83 winning units..

Owner Mrs Jill Ward **Bred** Dxb Bloodstock Ltd **Trained** Middleham, North Yorkshire

FOCUS
The time was 0.41 seconds faster than the following older-horse Class 6 classified event, but this is still moderate form.

NOTEBOOK
Sweetnessandlight didn't offer much on her debut here, or at Wolverhampton last time, but this performance confirmed the promise she showed when runner-up on her second start, and clearly she started off in handicaps on a reasonable mark. The step up from 6f helped and she might be capable of better again as she didn't get the best of runs into the straight before being strong at the line. (op 8-1)

Ishiamiracle, ridden positively, went close to gaining her first success on her tenth start. She's probably due a rise in the weights now. (op 10-3 tchd 11-4)

Doyouknowwhoiam, without the cheekpieces this time, offered encouragement after an 82-day break. (op 9-1 tchd 12-1)

Ferdy(IRE), 5lb wrong, ran his best race since his debut. (op 33-1 tchd 50-1)

Songbird Blues found disappointingly little after appearing to travel okay. She has the ability to win, but is not proving easy to catch right. (tchd 9-2)

Small Steps(IRE), reported the filly was slowly away. This was a disappointing performance from the favourite, with her simply not picking up after looking to move okay early on. Official explanation: jockey said filly was slowly away (op 5-2)

7781 MEMBERSHIP OF SOUTHWELL GOLF CLUB CLASSIFIED STKS 7f (F)
2:45 (2:45) (Class 6) 3-Y-0+ **£1,617** (£481; £240; £120) **Stalls** Low

Form RPR

5006 **1** **Seamster**[13] 7632 4-9-0 **54**..(vt) FrederikTylicki 9 61
(Richard Ford) *mde all: rdn clr wl over 1f out: kpt on* **4/1**[3]

0500 **2** *2* **Twennyshortkid**[6] 7714 3-9-0 **48**...............................(b[1]) BarryMcHugh 1 56
(Paul Midgley) *trckd ldrs on inner: hdwy and swtchd rt over 2f out: rdn to chse wnr over 1f out: no imp ins fnl f* **20/1**

4062 **3** *1* **Billy Cadiz**[36] 7351 6-8-11 **51**.. DaleSwift(3) 10 53
(Julie Camacho) *in tch: hdwy on outer 3f out: rdn to chse ldrs 2f out: swtchd lft and drvn over 1f out: edgd lft to far rail and kpt on fnl f* **5/1**

-323 **4** *1 ½* **Fearless Poet (IRE)**[6] 7714 3-9-0 **50**................................(p) TomEaves 8 49
(Bryan Smart) *trckd ldr: effrt wl over 2f out: sn rdn and kpt on same pce fr wl over 1f out* **9/4**[1]

4312 **5** *1* **Dashing Eddie (IRE)**[7] 7696 3-9-0 **54**...........................(p) PhillipMakin 3 47+
(Kevin Ryan) *stmbld bdly and lost many l s: bhd tl styd on fnl 2f: nrst fin* **5/2**[2]

5463 **6** *1* **American Lover (FR)**[45] 7211 4-9-0 **55**........................... PaddyAspell 2 44
(John Wainwright) *chsd ldrs: rdn along wl over 2f out: sn btn* **10/1**

0303 **7** *1* **Spread Boy (IRE)**[48] 7158 4-8-7 **49**...................... MatthewHopkins(7) 7 41
(Alan Berry) *chsd ldrs: rdn along 3f out: sn wknd* **66/1**

000- **8** *18* **Auburn Lady**[7] 6891 3-9-0 **48**... AndrewMullen 4 —
(Alan Brown) *a towards rr: outpcd and bhd fr 1/2-way* **100/1**

1m 29.55s (-0.75) **Going Correction** -0.225s/f (Stan) **8** Ran SP% **112.3**
Speed ratings (Par 101): **95,92,91,89,88 87,86,65**
toteswingers:1&2:£8.00, 1&3:£4.50, 2&3:£6.30 CSF £69.57 TOTE £5.50: £1.90, £4.00, £2.30; EX 62.30 Trifecta £476.30 Part won. Pool: £643.72 - 0.45 winning units..

Owner Dave Watson & David Sibson **Bred** D G Hardisty Bloodstock **Trained** Butterton, Staffs

■ Stewards' Enquiry : Matthew Hopkins seven-day ban: used whip with excessive frequency (Dec 30-Jan 5)

FOCUS
A moderate classified event. The favourite disappointed and the second favourite blew the start. The winner's first form since he was a 3yo.

Dashing Eddie(IRE) Official explanation: jockey said colt was slowly away

7782 GOLF AND RACING AT SOUTHWELL H'CAP 1m (F)
3:20 (3:20) (Class 6) (0-65,70) 3-Y-0 **£1,617** (£481; £240; £120) **Stalls** Low

Form RPR

3221 **1** **Beautiful Day**[5] 7727 3-9-10 **70** 6ex.................................. AmyRyan(3) 7 86
(Kevin Ryan) *trckd ldrs: hdwy and cl up 1/2-way: led wl over 3f out: shkn up and clr wl over 1f out: easily* **10/11**[1]

3421 **2** *7* **St Oswald**[10] 7648 3-9-9 **66** 6ex..................................(b) DanielTudhope 4 67
(David O'Meara) *trckd ldrs: hdwy to chse wnr over 2f out: rdn and edgd lft over 1f out: sn one pce* **11/8**[2]

4054 **3** *5* **Unwrapit (USA)**[3] 7748 3-9-0 **57**......................................(p) TomEaves 6 46
(Bryan Smart) *dwlt: sn in tch: rdn wl over 2f out: styd on appr fnl f* **25/1**

0640 **4** *1 ¾* **Gay Gallivanter**[11] 7639 3-8-7 **50** oh3..........................(v[1]) FrannyNorton 1 34
(Michael Quinn) *dwlt: sn outpcd and bhd: rdn 3f out: styd on fnl 2f: nvr nr ldrs* **50/1**

410 **5** *nk* **Riczar**[6] 7711 3-9-3 **60**.. RichardKingscote 3 44
(Tom Dascombe) *prom: effrt on inner wl over 2f out: sn rdn and btn* **16/1**[3]

104 **6** *1 ¾* **Putin (IRE)**[7] 7687 3-8-7 **57**....................................(p) DannyBrock(7) 5 37
(Phil McEntee) *led: rdn along and hdd wl over 3f out: sn wknd* **25/1**

3655 **7** *4* **Lady Gar Gar**[15] 7591 3-9-2 **62**..(v) DaleSwift(3) 2 33
(Geoffrey Oldroyd) *a towards rr* **16/1**[3]

1m 41.11s (-2.59) **Going Correction** -0.225s/f (Stan) **7** Ran SP% **115.9**
Speed ratings (Par 98): **103,96,91,89,88 87,83**
toteswingers:1&2:£1.10, 1&3:£5.70, 2&3:£5.20 CSF £2.40 TOTE £2.10: £1.10, £1.10; EX 3.00.

Owner Guy Reed **Bred** G Reed **Trained** Hambleton, N Yorks

FOCUS
An ordinary handicap. Another step forward from the winner, who goes well here.

T/Plt: £121.50 to a £1 stake. Pool:£39,352.20 - 236.26 winning tickets T/Qpdt: £20.00 to a £1 stake. Pool:£4,280.72 - 158.15 winning tickets JR

7734 WOLVERHAMPTON (A.W) (L-H)
Friday, December 16

OFFICIAL GOING: Standard
Wind: Blustery, half behind Weather: Cloudy with Showers

7783 TOTEPLACEPOT MEDIAN AUCTION MAIDEN STKS 7f 32y(P)
3:50 (3:52) (Class 5) 2-Y-0 **£2,264** (£673; £336; £168) **Stalls** High

Form RPR

3 **1** **Baccarat (IRE)**[21] 7540 2-9-3 0.. TonyHamilton 4 74
(Richard Fahey) *midfield: hdwy 2f out: led jst over 1f out: r.o gamely and edgd rt ins fnl f whn pressed: plld out more towards fin* **1/3**[1]

4232 **2** *½* **Remix (IRE)**[28] 7464 2-8-12 70... DaneO'Neill 2 68
(J W Hills) *midfield: pushed along over 3f out: rdn and hdwy under 2f out: str chal fr over 1f out: nt qckn and hld towards fin* **7/2**[2]

3 *4 ½* **Mighty Motive** 2-9-0 0.. MichaelO'Connell(3) 3 62
(John Mackie) *chsd ldrs: effrt and hung rt 2f out: chalng over 1f out: styd on same pce and wl hld by ldrs fnl 100yds* **66/1**

P **4** *hd* **King's Wharf (IRE)**[9] 7650 2-8-12 0........................ MatthewCosham(5) 5 61
(David Evans) *led: rdn 2f out: hung lft u.p over 1f out: sn hdd: kpt on same pce ins fnl f* **200/1**

00 **5** *1 ½* **Bulldog Beasley (USA)**[49] 7133 2-9-3 0..........................(t) MartinLane 1 58
(Brian Meehan) *chsd ldrs: effrt on inner over 1f out: one pce ins fnl f* **40/1**

6 **6** *2 ¼* **Lhotse Sherpa**[35] 7367 2-9-3 0.................................. RussKennemore 9 52
(John Holt) *midfield: hdwy over 3f out: effrt to chal 4 wd over 2f out: outpcd wl over 1f out: no imp fnl f* **150/1**

6 **7** *½* **Neige D'Antan**[13] 7626 2-8-12 0.. SebSanders 11 46
(Sir Mark Prescott Bt) *s.i.s: in rr: outpcd 3f out: styd on fnl f: nt pce to trble ldrs* **33/1**

0 **8** *nk* **Poontoon (IRE)**[21] 7540 2-9-3 0................................... PatrickMathers 7 50
(Richard Fahey) *midfield: lost pl and pushed along wl over 3f out: kpt on fnl f: nt pce to threaten* **80/1**

00 **9** *nk* **Bonnie Blade**[34] 7396 2-8-12 0.. AndreaAtzeni 12 44
(James Unett) *chsd ldr: ev ch 2f out: rdn and wknd 1f out* **500/1**

00 **10** *19* **Classy Lass**[21] 7540 2-8-7 0....................................... MarkCoumbe(5) 6 —
(Derek Shaw) *hld up: hung rt and shkn up ent st wl over 1f out: nvr a danger* **500/1**

05 **11** *6* **Lady Lyricist**[13] 7627 2-8-12 0.. ChrisCatlin 10 —
(Reg Hollinshead) *in rr: wl outpcd over 3f out: nvr on terms* **28/1**[3]

1m 31.78s (2.18) **Going Correction** +0.10s/f (Slow) **11** Ran SP% **110.4**
Speed ratings (Par 96): **91,90,85,85,83 80,80,79,79,57 50**
toteswingers:1&2:£1.10, 1&3:£7.10, 2&3:£10.50 CSF £1.40 TOTE £1.30: £1.02, £1.10, £8.70; EX 1.60.

Owner Sir Robert Ogden **Bred** Twelve Oaks Stud **Trained** Musley Bank, N Yorks

FOCUS
There was little strength in depth in this maiden auction but the pace was strong and the hot favourite held off his 70-rated main market rival who was clear of the rest.

NOTEBOOK
Baccarat(IRE) showed plenty of promise when third of 12 in a 6f maiden here on debut last month. He had strong form claims stepped up in trip and quickened up well from just off the pace before battling to justify odds-on favouritism. The winning margin was narrow in the end but he still showed signs of inexperience and the second looks a solid marker for the form. A scopey, 180,000euros Dutch Art colt who is out of a Group-placed 7f 2yo winner, he looks a fair type who should go on to better things.

Remix(IRE) ran a solid race to give the favourite a scare. She is fairly exposed after six runs but is a consistent and willing sort who has been placed in Polytrack maidens on her last four starts. (op 4-1)

Mighty Motive looked inexperienced but shaped with some promise behind the two principals on debut. He should improve for the run and is an 11,000gns Motivator colt out of a fairly useful 7f fast-ground nursery winner.

King's Wharf(IRE) looked a very tricky ride when pulled up soon after the start at Kempton on debut earlier this month, but he was more tractable under front-running tactics and showed ability at a massive price dropped 3f in trip. Official explanation: jockey said gelding ran green

Bulldog Beasley(USA), beaten 15l+ at big prices in two 7f maidens at Newmarket in October, showed some improvement with a tongue-tie applied on the switch to AW. He is related to five 5f-1m winners and should do better in handicaps. (op 50-1)

Classy Lass Official explanation: jockey said filly hung right off bend

Lady Lyricist Official explanation: trainer said filly finished lame

7784 DINE IN HORIZONS MEDIAN AUCTION MAIDEN FILLIES' STKS 5f 216y(P)
4:20 (4:22) (Class 6) 2-Y-0 **£1,704** (£503; £251) **Stalls** Low

Form RPR

06 **1** **Choccywoccydoodah**[20] 7559 2-9-0 0.......................... JamesSullivan 5 64
(James Given) *chsd ldrs: hung lft whn effrt on outer to chal over 1f out: flashed tail ins fnl f: styd on to ld towards fin* **15/2**

2 **2** *½* **Like The Night**[14] 7607 2-9-0 0.. AndreaAtzeni 6 62
(Marco Botti) *broke wl: led early: remained w ldr: rdn whn chalng over 1f out: led ins fnl f: hdd towards fin* **7/2**[3]

6 **3** *1* **Kickingthelilly**[22] 7526 2-9-0 0.. SteveDrowne 3 59
(Rae Guest) *pushed along early to chse ldrs: effrt to chal over 1f out: kpt on same pce fnl 50yds* **9/4**[2]

4 *¾* **Chester'Slittlegem (IRE)** 2-9-0 0.. JohnFahy 4 57
(Ed de Giles) *s.i.s: hld up in rr: rdn and clsd to chse ldrs over 1f out: edgd rt ins fnlf urlong: unable to chal: green* **33/1**

3 **5** *nk* **Dahab Gold (IRE)**[16] 7583 2-9-0 0.. LukeMorris 2 56
(Jane Chapple-Hyam) *sn led: rdn whn pressed over 1f out: hdd ins fnl f: no ex fnl 50yds* **2/1**[1]

6 *6* **Pink Evie** 2-9-0 0... MartinLane 8 38
(Gay Kelleway) *s.s: a outpcd and bhd* **16/1**

0 **7** *4 ½* **Miss Bloom**[154] 4068 2-9-0 0.. KellyHarrison 7 24
(Garry Woodward) *chsd ldrs: pushed along and outpcd over 2f out: bhd fnl f* **250/1**

1m 16.62s (1.62) **Going Correction** +0.10s/f (Slow) **7** Ran SP% **107.3**
Speed ratings (Par 91): **93,92,91,90,89 81,75**
toteswingers:1&2:£3.00, 1&3:£2.30, 2&3:£2.10 CSF £29.64 TOTE £12.90: £5.50, £1.30; EX 33.50.

Owner Danethorpe Racing Partnership **Bred** Danethorpe Racing Partnership **Trained** Willoughton, Lincs

FOCUS
An ordinary fillies' maiden. The pace was fair but there was not much separating the first five in the end.

NOTEBOOK

Choccywoccydoodah was beaten just over 3l at 40-1 in a 7f maiden here on her second start. She had something to find with the leading form contenders but finished well out wide to get off the mark. Out of a 5f winner, she has improved significantly with each of her starts and could continue to progress in handicaps at this trip or a bit further. (op 8-1 tchd 9-1)

Like The Night showed promise when chasing home an odds-on 70-rated rival in a four-runner 5f maiden here on debut this month. There were still signs of inexperience on her second run but she looked suited by the move to 6f and battled and stayed on well in a close call. She is out of a 6f winning half-sister to four speedy winners and should continue to go the right way. (tchd 4-1)

Kickingthelilly ran green but caught the eye when sixth over 6f at Kempton on debut. Strong in the market, she was under pressure around the final turn but kept responding and shaped like a step up to 7f will suit. (op 5-2 tchd 7-4)

Chester'Slittlegem(IRE) cost just £800 in January and is out of a modest maiden but she showed quite a bit of promise staying on well at a biggish price on debut.

Dahab Gold(IRE) had leading claims on her 11-2 third in a 6f Kempton maiden on debut but she couldn't sustain her front-running effort and was vulnerable to finishers on both sides. (op 7-4)

7785 ENJOY THE PARTY PACK GROUP OFFER H'CAP 5f 20y(P)

4:50 (4:50) (Class 6) (0-52,52) 3-Y-O+ **£1,704** (£503; £251) **Stalls** Low

Form RPR

6401 **1** **Chester Deelyte (IRE)**[28] 7459 3-8-9 **52**..............(v) ShirleyTeasdale(7) 7 64
(Lisa Williamson) *midfield: rdn and hdwy over 1f out: r.o ins fnl f to ld towards fin* **18/1**

4031 **2** *1* **Wreningham**[7] 7691 6-8-9 **50**........................ CharlesBishop(5) 9 59
(Pat Eddery) *led: over 2 l clr 2f out: rdn and reduced advantage ins fnl f: hdd towards fin* **11/8**[1]

4006 **3** *nk* **Canadian Danehill (IRE)**[7] 7691 9-8-6 **49**..............(e[1]) JakePayne(7) 12 57
(Robert Cowell) *chsd ldr: over 2 l down 2f out: rdn over 1f out: styd on but lost 2nd wl ins fnl f: nt pce of wnr* **28/1**

661 **4** *1 1/2* **Cri Na Mara (IRE)**[7] 7693 3-8-10 **51** 6ex..........................(t) LMcNiff(5) 4 56+
(Mark Michael McNiff, Ire) *midfield: pushed along over 1f out: styd on ins fnl furlong: nvr able to chal* **3/1**[2]

224 **5** *1 3/4* **Welsh Dancer**[20] 7560 3-9-2 **52**........................ LukeMorris 5 48
(Ronald Harris) *chsd ldrs: pushed along over 3f out: one pce and no imp over 1f out* **9/2**[3]

5520 **6** *1/2* **Brian Sprout**[8] 7676 3-9-0 **50**........................ MartinLane 1 44
(John Weymes) *midfield: rdn and outpcd over 2f out: nvr able to chal* **15/2**

0002 **7** *nk* **Deveze (IRE)**[7] 7693 3-8-10 **46** oh1..........................(b) RussKennemore 8 39
(Milton Bradley) *hld up: rdn over 1f out: nvr able to trble ldrs* **28/1**

0004 **8** *2 1/4* **Lady Royal Oak (IRE)**[9] 7659 4-8-9 **52**.............. JenniferFerguson(7) 10 37
(Olivia Maylam) *s.i.s: plld hrd in rr: outpcd 2f out: nvr able to get on terms* **50/1**

0000 **9** *1 1/4* **Bertbrand**[28] 7459 6-8-10 **46**..........................(p) JamesSullivan 2 27
(Ian McInnes) *chsd ldrs: rdn over 2f out: wknd 1f out* **80/1**

6004 **10** *9* **Lois Lane**[158] 3920 3-8-11 **50**........................ SimonPearce(3) 11 —
(Ron Hodges) *s.i.s: hld up: pushed along and outpcd over 2f out: nvr on terms* **40/1**

62.31 secs (0.01) **Going Correction** +0.10s/f (Slow) **10** Ran SP% **114.8**
Speed ratings (Par 101): **103,101,100,98,95 94,94,90,88,74**
toteswingers:1&2:£6.80, 1&3:£14.70, 2&3:£8.60 CSF £41.79 CT £745.23 TOTE £15.30: £2.60, £1.10, £5.30; EX 56.20.

Owner Hindford Oak Racing **Bred** Yeomanstown Stud **Trained** Saighton, Cheshire

FOCUS

It was fast and furious in this sprint handicap and the unpenalised strong favourite was run down in the closing stages. The form is rated around the third.

Deveze(IRE) Official explanation: jockey said filly hung right-handed throughout

7786 PLAY THE LIFE CHANGING TOTESCOOP6 TOMORROW NURSERY 1m 141y(P)

5:20 (5:20) (Class 4) (0-85,79) 2-Y-O **£4,204** (£1,251; £625; £312) **Stalls** Low

Form RPR

0543 **1** **Flying Trader (USA)**[30] 7436 2-8-9 **67**........................ LukeMorris 2 72
(Jane Chapple-Hyam) *chsd ldrs: pushed along and wnt 2nd 2f out: [illegible] 1f out: r.o to ld ins fnl f: in command towards fin* **13/8**[1]

2013 **2** *3* **Ocean Tempest**[17] 7576 2-9-7 **79**........................ AdamKirby 4 78
(John Ryan) *led: rdn and hung rt ent st wl over 1f out: continued to hang rt: hdd ins fnl f: nt pce of wnr towards fin* **7/2**[3]

5221 **3** *1 1/4* **Chelsea Mick**[70] 6663 2-8-13 **74**........................ MichaelO'Connell(3) 3 70
(John Mackie) *racd keenly: chsd ldrs: effrt over 2f out: 3rd and jst over 2 l off the pce whn hmpd ent st wl over 1f out: kpt on same pce u.p ins fnl f* **12/1**

3611 **4** *8* **Titus Star (IRE)**[2] 7752 2-8-11 **74** 6ex........................ RyanPowell(5) 1 53
(J S Moore) *racd keenly: chsd ldr: chalng 3f out: rdn and lost 2nd 2f out: outpcd over 1f out: wl btn fnl 120yds* **2/1**[2]

630 **5** *1 3/4* **Ctappers**[72] 6630 2-8-5 **68**........................ CharlesBishop(5) 5 44
(Mick Channon) *sn bhd: nvr gng pce to get competitive* **18/1**

1m 51.96s (1.46) **Going Correction** +0.10s/f (Slow) **5** Ran SP% **106.6**
Speed ratings (Par 98): **97,94,93,86,84**
CSF £7.08 TOTE £2.60: £1.30, £1.10; EX 7.40.

Owner Greg Secker - Unlimited Racing **Bred** Hot Pepper Farm **Trained** Dalham, Suffolk

FOCUS

Things became very tactical in this small-field nursery, but the well-backed favourite eventually scored with plenty of authority.

NOTEBOOK

Flying Trader(USA) went close behind a subsequent winner after finding some trouble in a 1m Lingfield nursery last time. The steady pace here was not ideal for his closing style, but he kept battling and eventually forged clear near the stands' rail to get off the mark with quite a bit in hand on the ninth attempt. His profile has been consistent rather than progressive and this form does not look very strong, but a win should boost his confidence and a more strongly run race will play more to his strengths. (op 2-1)

Ocean Tempest had the run of things in a race where he dictated a stop-start gallop but he hung right under pressure and was ultimately well held. He has found life difficult in two nurseries since rallying to beat a 78-rated rival in a 1m Kempton maiden last month. (tchd 4-1)

Chelsea Mick made hard work of landing the odds odds-on in an ordinary 7f maiden here in October. That form had not worked out and he was vulnerable with quite a bit more to do on nursery debut for a new trainer after 70-days off. However, he was hampered at a crucial stage and rates a bit better than the form implies. (op 11-1 tchd 10-1)

Titus Star(IRE) won a Chepstow maiden auction in September before scoring comfortably back from a break on his nursery/AW debut at Kempton on Wednesday. This lightly raced and well-regarded type had a penalty to defy, but there was no spark this time and the race probably came too soon. Official explanation: jockey said gelding stopped quickly (op 7-4 tchd 6-4)

Ctappers, beaten 11l+ at 14-1 or bigger in three maidens, was always outpaced off a tough-looking mark on nursery debut. (op 20-1)

7787 TOTEEXACTA H'CAP 1m 141y(P)

5:50 (5:51) (Class 7) (0-50,52) 3-Y-O+ **£1,704** (£503; £251) **Stalls** Low

Form RPR

0233 **1** **Idol Deputy (FR)**[4] 7741 5-8-8 **50**........................ RachealKneller(7) 10 60+
(Mark Usher) *midfield: hdwy gng wl over 1f out: led 1f out: r.o wl and a in command ins fnl f* **9/4**[1]

-004 **2** *1 3/4* **Red Flash (IRE)**[128] 4917 4-8-12 **47**........................ TonyCulhane 11 53
(David Bridgwater) *in rr: rdn over 3f out: hdwy over 1f out: swtchd rt ins fnl f: styd on towards fin: nt rch wnr* **25/1**

0060 **3** *1 1/4* **Harvest Mist (IRE)**[9] 7656 3-8-13 **50**........................ NeilChalmers 5 53
(Michael Blanshard) *midfield: hdwy 2f out: chsd ldrs over 1f out: sn chalng: nt qckn fnl 75yds* **20/1**

404 **4** *3/4* **Brave Decision**[287] 773 4-8-11 **46**..........................(p) JohnFahy 13 47
(Robert Cowell) *in tch: clsd over 2f out: rdn to chal 1f out: no ex fnl 75yds* **12/1**

5552 **5** *nk* **Look For Love**[4] 7741 3-8-2 **46**..........................(e) JackDuern(7) 1 47
(Reg Hollinshead) *racd keenly: chsd ldrs: effrt to ld over 1f out: sn hdd: styd on same pce fnl 110yds* **11/2**[3]

0036 **6** *3/4* **It's Dubai Dolly**[9] 7654 5-9-1 **50**..........................(b) DaneO'Neill 12 49
(Alastair Lidderdale) *hld up: rdn over 1f out: no real imp on ldrs whn bmpd ins fnl f: kpt on towards fin* **9/1**

3000 **7** *nk* **Hathaway (IRE)**[14] 7604 4-8-9 **47**........................ RyanClark(3) 6 45
(Mark Brisbourne) *hld up: rdn 5f out: hdwy ent fnl f: styd on wout troubling ldrs* **16/1**

0030 **8** *1 3/4* **Beating Harmony**[9] 7656 3-8-12 **49**..........................(p) LukeMorris 9 43
(Michael Appleby) *in rr: pushed along over 2f out: sme hdwy ins fnl f: nvr able to trble ldrs* **25/1**

0000 **9** *4* **Zee Zee Dan (IRE)**[52] 7084 3-8-11 **48**..........................(b[1]) AdamKirby 4 33
(Noel Quinlan) *plld hrd: effrt and ev ch 2f out: hung rt ent st wl over 1f out: sn lost pl: hld whn hmpd ins fnl f* **4/1**[2]

01/0 **10** *3/4* **Key Decision (IRE)**[171] 3502 7-8-10 **45**..........................(t) SteveDrowne 8 28
(Jo Davis) *chsd ldr: led wl over 2f out: rdn and hdd over 1f out: wknd ins fnl f: eased* **8/1**

00 **11** *6* **Mujady Star (IRE)**[40] 7246 3-8-8 **45**..........................(t) JamesSullivan 3 14
(Kevin M Prendergast) *midfield tl wknd over 1f out* **40/1**

050P **12** *10* **Le Reveur**[21] 7352 9-8-3 **45**........................ CharlesEddery(7) 2 —
(Richard Guest) *led: hdd wl over 2f out: wknd wl over 1f out: eased ins fnl f* **100/1**

1m 52.08s (1.58) **Going Correction** +0.10s/f (Slow)
WFA 3 from 4yo+ 2lb **12** Ran SP% **116.7**
Speed ratings (Par 97): **96,94,93,92,92 91,91,89,86,85 80,71**
toteswingers:1&2:£7.40, 1&3:£8.10, 2&3:£30.60 CSF £71.42 CT £926.54 TOTE £3.30: £1.20, £10.10, £6.40; EX 85.80.

Owner Miss J C Blackwell **Bred** Sheikh Sultan Bin Khalifa Al Nayan **Trained** Upper Lambourn, Berks

FOCUS

A low-grade handicap run at a fair pace. There could be more to come from the winner and the second was back to his early maiden form.

Zee Zee Dan(IRE) Official explanation: jockey said gelding hung right from 2f out

7788 HOTEL & CONFERENCING AT WOLVERHAMPTON H'CAP 1m 1f 103y(P)

6:20 (6:20) (Class 6) (0-65,64) 3-Y-O+ **£1,704** (£503; £251) **Stalls** Low

Form RPR

2320 **1** **Yourinthewill (USA)**[62] 6872 3-9-5 **64**........................ StephenCraine 8 74
(Daniel Mark Loughnane, Ire) *hld up: hdwy on outer over 2f out: str chal ins fnl f: r.o to ld post* **10/1**

0230 **2** *shd* **McCool Bannanas**[21] 7538 3-9-2 **61**........................ AndreaAtzeni 3 70
(James Unett) *midfield: hdwy over 2f out: rdn to ld jst ins fnl f: sn hrd pressed: hdd post* **14/1**

0602 **3** *3* **Vanilla Rum**[69] 6698 4-8-8 **51**..........................(b) JoeFanning 6 54
(John Mackie) *prom: wnt 2nd over 6f out: led wl over 1f out: hdd jst ins fnl f: styd on same pce and wl hld by front pair fnl 75yds* **9/2**[2]

0621 **4** *3* **Arkaim**[69] 6698 3-9-2 **61**..........................(v) MickyFenton 9 58
(Pam Sly) *racd keenly: led: rdn and hdd wl over 1f out: no ex fnl 75yds* **3/1**[1]

0010 **5** *2 1/4* **Barton Bounty**[7] 7698 4-9-0 **57**........................ TomEaves 1 49
(Peter Niven) *in rr div: pushed along 6f out: hrd at work to chse ldrs 1f out: one pce and no imp ins fnl f* **8/1**[3]

0040 **6** *1* **Petomic (IRE)**[53] 7068 6-8-10 **56**..........................(p) RobertLButler(3) 5 46
(Richard Guest) *racd keenly: trckd ldrs: rdn 2f out: wknd ent fnl f* **20/1**

2402 **7** *shd* **Flying Applause**[18] 7571 6-8-11 **54**..........................(bt) RussKennemore 4 44
(Roy Bowring) *racd keenly: chsd ldr tl over 6f out: remained prom: rdn 3f out: wknd 2f out* **3/1**[1]

6062 **8** *3* **Final Tune (IRE)**[130] 4869 8-8-7 **55**........................ NathanAlison(5) 7 38
(Mandy Rowland) *hld up: rdn over 2f out: nvr on terms w ldrs* **14/1**

0000 **9** *17* **Douze Points (IRE)**[15] 7589 5-9-6 **63**..........................(p) AdamKirby 2 —
(Pat Murphy) *hld up in last pl: pushed along 3f out: lft bhd fnl 2f* **12/1**

2m 1.87s (0.17) **Going Correction** +0.10s/f (Slow)
WFA 3 from 4yo+ 2lb **9** Ran SP% **114.2**
Speed ratings (Par 101): **103,102,100,97,95 94,94,91,76**
toteswingers:1&2:£18.00, 1&3:£6.20, 2&3:£14.10 CSF £136.85 CT £717.89 TOTE £11.30: £3.00, £3.90, £2.00; EX 111.30.

Owner M V Kirby **Bred** Branch Equine Llc **Trained** Trim, Co Meath

FOCUS

There was a very tight finish in this sound run, modest handicap in which the front pair pulled clear. A length personal best from the winner.

7789 TOTETRIFECTA H'CAP 1m 4f 50y(P)

6:50 (6:50) (Class 6) (0-65,63) 3-Y-O+ **£1,704** (£503; £251) **Stalls** Low

Form RPR

6001 **1** **Jamarjo (IRE)**[9] 7654 4-9-1 **54** 6ex........................ LukeMorris 5 62+
(Steve Gollings) *hld up: hdwy 3f out: chsd ldrs 2f out: led over 1f out: edgd rt ins fnl f: r.o: in command towards fin* **17/2**

2655 **2** *2* **Straversjoy**[119] 5249 4-9-10 **63**........................ AdamKirby 4 67+
(Reg Hollinshead) *midfield: pushed along over 2f out: rdn and hdwy to chse ldrs over 1f out: styd on to take 2nd wl ins fnl f: nt pce of wnr* **6/1**[2]

3132 **3** *hd* **Pinotage**[49] 7144 3-9-4 **62**........................ TomEaves 8 66
(Peter Niven) *chsd ldrs: led over 2f out: rdn and flashed tail whn hdd over 1f out: continued to flash tail u.p ins fnl f: styd on same pce towards fin* **15/2**[3]

500 **4** *4 1/2* **Spartan King (IRE)**[55] 7037 3-8-9 **53** MartinLane 9 50
(Ian Williams) *completely missed break: hld up bhd: gd hdwy 4f out: led wl over 3f out: rdn and hdd over 2f out: stl ch wl over 1f out: one pce ins fnl f* **33/1**

0641 **5** *1 3/4* **Kames Park (IRE)**[2] 7761 9-9-3 **63** CharlesEddery(7) 2 57
(Richard Guest) *stdd s: hld up: hdwy to chse ldrs 3f out: no imp fnl 2f* **2/1**[1]

0353 **6** *5* **History Repeating**[23] 7515 3-8-11 **62** RachealKneller(7) 3 48
(Mark Usher) *hld up: outpcd 3f out: nvr a threat* **15/2**[3]

3014 **7** *16* **Master Of Song**[14] 7604 4-9-5 **63** (p) DavidKenny(5) 6 23
(Roy Bowring) *racd keenly: chsd ldrs: wnt 2nd after 2f: lost 2nd 4f out: wknd over 2f out* **8/1**

2504 **8** *10* **Hal Of A Lover**[5] 7723 3-8-10 **57** MichaelO'Connell(3) 7 —
(David O'Meara) *chsd ldr for 2f: remained handy tl rdn and wknd over 3f out* **25/1**

-532 **9** *3 1/2* **Opera Prince**[8] 7671 6-9-8 **61** SteveDrowne 1 —
(Simon Earle) *led: hdd wl over 3f out: rdn and wknd over 2f out* **6/1**[2]

2m 41.47s (0.37) **Going Correction** +0.10s/f (Slow)
WFA 3 from 4yo+ 5lb **9** Ran SP% **113.9**
Speed ratings (Par 101): **102,100,100,97,96 93,82,75,73**
toteswingers:1&2:£9.60, 1&3:£8.20, 2&3:£7.80 CSF £57.73 CT £400.58 TOTE £10.60: £3.40, £1.80, £1.50; EX 58.90 Trifecta £281.50.
Owner Northern Bloodstock Racing **Bred** Frank Dunne **Trained** Scamblesby, Lincs

FOCUS
This looked a competitive handicap, but several runners pulled hard off the steady pace and they finished quite well strung out. The winner clearly improved for the trick.
Master Of Song Official explanation: jockey said gelding suffered interference in running
Hal Of A Lover Official explanation: jockey said gelding stopped quickly
Opera Prince Official explanation: jockey said gelding had no more to give
T/Plt: £99.00 to a £1 stake. Pool:£74,656.80 - 550.24 winning tickets T/Qpdt: £36.60 to a £1 stake. Pool:£8,643.20 - 174.60 winning tickets DO

7700 DUNDALK (A.W) (L-H)
Friday, December 16

OFFICIAL GOING: Standard

7790a WWW.DUNDALKSTADIUM.COM H'CAP 6f (P)
6:00 (6:00) 3-Y-0+ **£7,732** (£1,793; £784; £448)

RPR

1 **Farmleigh House (IRE)**[7] 7700 4-7-13 74 oh5 CPHoban(5) 1 81
(W J Martin, Ire) *chsd ldrs: 6th 1/2-way: hdwy into 4th 2f out: swtchd and rdn into 2nd 1f out: kpt on to press ldr ins fnl f: led on line* **8/1**[3]

2 *nse* **Dickie's Lad (IRE)**[17] 7578 3-9-7 91 (t) PJSmullen 11 98
(Kevin Ryan) *attempted to make all: rdn over 1f out: strly pressed ins fnl f and hdd on line* **9/4**[1]

3 *3/4* **Gordon Lord Byron (IRE)**[14] 7612 3-9-4 88 JMurtagh 6 93
(T Hogan, Ire) *chsd ldrs: 5th 1/2-way: rdn into 3rd 1f out: kpt on same pce fnl f* **4/1**[2]

4 *1/2* **Mountain Coral (IRE)**[7] 7700 7-8-3 80 CTKeane(7) 2 83
(F Oakes, Ire) *hld up towards rr: 9th 1/2-way: hdwy into 7th 2f out: rdn into 5th 1f out: kpt on same pce fnl f* **8/1**[3]

5 *3/4* **Thats A Fret (IRE)**[7] 7700 5-7-11 74 oh5 (b) GJPhillips(7) 8 75
(Liam McAteer, Ire) *chsd ldr: 2nd 1/2-way: rdn 2f out: no ex in 4th 1f out: kpt on same pce fnl f* **20/1**

6 *hd* **Jamesie (IRE)**[104] 5746 3-9-10 94 ShaneFoley 9 94
(David Marnane, Ire) *mid-div: 7th 1/2-way: rdn in 6th 1f out: no imp fnl f: kpt on same pce* **4/1**[2]

7 *nse* **Copper Dock (IRE)**[7] 7700 7-8-4 74 CDHayes 3 74
(T G McCourt, Ire) *trckd ldrs: 4th 1/2-way: 6th bhd horses 2f out: rdn in 7th 1f out: no imp fnl f* **10/1**

8 *3/4* **Tornadodancer (IRE)**[14] 7612 8-8-5 80 ow2 (bt) SHJames(5) 10 77
(T G McCourt, Ire) *towards rr for most: nvr a factor* **14/1**

9 *1 1/4* **Winning Impact (IRE)**[20] 7189 4-8-8 78 NGMcCullagh 7 71
(J G Coogan, Ire) *towards rr for most: nvr a factor* **33/1**

10 *hd* **Duke Of Rutherford (USA)**[7] 7700 3-8-8 78 (b) MCHussey 4 71
(P D Deegan, Ire) *chsd ldrs: 3rd 1/2-way: rdn 2f out: no ex over 1f out* **20/1**

11 *1/2* **Enigma Code (UAE)**[164] 3713 6-7-11 74 oh7 (tp) MMMonaghan(7) 5 65
(James McAuley, Ire) *mid-div: 8th 1/2-way: rdn and no ex 2f out* **33/1**

1m 10.6s (70.60) **11** Ran SP% **124.2**
CSF £26.71 CT £88.17 TOTE £6.80: £1.30, £3.10, £1.40; DF 28.00.
Owner W J Martin **Bred** Mrs E Fitzsimons **Trained** Enniscorthy, Co Wexford

FOCUS
A useful-looking handicap.

NOTEBOOK
Farmleigh House(IRE) ♦, placed on two of his previous visits here, more recently when runner-up to Mountain Coral a week previously, was 5lb out of the handicap although that was negated somewhat by his rider's 5lb claim. Drawn next to the rail, he tracked the leaders into the straight and, after being switched off the rails to go second just over 1f out, he ran on to grab the verdict in virtually the last stride. (op 7/1 tchd 17/2)
Dickie's Lad(IRE), whose only win came in a maiden over this trip on good to firm at Nottingham in May, had lost narrowly over the distance at Lingfield on his previous start last month when he tried to make all. He had the worst of the draw, but broke well and was soon in front. He shook off all-comers in the straight only to be denied virtually on the line. (op 2/1 tchd 11/4)
Gordon Lord Byron(IRE), winner of a maiden and a handicap over the course and trip before finishing third again over the course and trip two weeks previously, went up 6lb for his handicap win and another 4lb for running third. He began his effort early in the straight and had every chance over 1f out, keeping on under pressure. Official explanation: trainer said gelding was struck into behind (op 9/2)
Mountain Coral(IRE), up 5lb for his win a week previously and seeking a fifth victory over the course and trip, missed the break before making steady headway and staying on from over 1f out.
Thats A Fret(IRE), third in the race in which Mountain Coral beat Farmleigh House a week previously, broke well and remained prominent although unable to raise any extra from 1f out.

7792a BOOKINGS@DUNDALKSTADIUM.COM RATED RACE 1m (P)
7:00 (7:01) 3-Y-0+ **£4,758** (£1,103; £482; £275)

RPR

1 **Billyford (IRE)**[14] 7615 6-9-1 75 JMurtagh 11 83
(Liam Roche, Ire) *chsd ldrs: 3rd 1/2-way: hdwy in 2nd 2f out: impr to ld 1 1/2f out: rdn and kpt on wl fnl f* **13/2**[3]

2 *1 3/4* **He's Got Rhythm (IRE)**[28] 7468 6-9-1 75 SeamieHeffernan 8 79
(David Marnane, Ire) *chsd ldrs: 6th 1/2-way: rdn 2f out: styd on into 4th 1f out: kpt on fnl f* **14/1**

3 *1/2* **Black N Brew (USA)**[14] 7615 5-9-1 69 MCHussey 14 78
(John C McConnell, Ire) *disp early: sn chsd ldr in 2nd: rdn in 3rd 2f out: kpt on same pce fr over 1f out* **20/1**

4 *hd* **Orpens Peach (IRE)**[7] 7695 4-8-9 66 ow2 RPWhelan(5) 3 76
(Seamus Fahey, Ire) *chsd ldrs early: mid-div in 8th 1/2-way: rdn 2f out: styd on into 5th 1f out: kpt on same pce fnl f* **10/1**

5 *1* **Fountain Of Honour (IRE)**[14] 7615 3-8-11 75 KJManning 12 72
(Noel Meade, Ire) *chsd ldrs: 5th 1/2-way: 4th 2f out: sn rdn: styd on into 2nd 1f out: no ex ins fnl f* **11/4**[2]

6 *shd* **Key Breeze**[21] 7548 4-9-1 73 (t) PJSmullen 4 75
(Kevin Ryan) *chsd ldrs: 4th 1/2-way: sltly hmpd 2f out: rdn and no ex over 1f out* **5/2**[1]

7 *shd* **Devonelli (IRE)**[7] 7701 3-8-6 72 CPHoban(5) 2 72
(M Halford, Ire) *hld up towards rr: late hdwy into 8th 1f out: rdn and kpt on same pce fnl f* **9/1**

8 *2 3/4* **Little Arrows (IRE)**[21] 7549 5-9-1 72 ShaneFoley 7 68
(K J Condon, Ire) *hld up towards rr: sme late hdwy fnl f: nvr a danger* **7/1**

9 *1 1/2* **Rambling Dancer (IRE)**[35] 7375 7-8-12 67 SMGorey(3) 5 65
(Mrs Valerie Keatley, Ire) *mid-div: 9th 1/2-way: rdn in 7th 2f out: no ex over 1f out* **20/1**

10 *1/2* **Money Trader (IRE)**[7] 7701 4-9-1 72 CDHayes 13 64
(J T Gorman, Ire) *mid-div: 7th 1/2-way: rdn and no ex over 2f out* **33/1**

11 *1 1/4* **Supercharged (IRE)**[14] 7612 3-8-4 71 MeganCarberry(10) 6 61
(G M Lyons, Ire) *a towards rr* **25/1**

12 *nk* **No Trimmings (IRE)**[14] 7615 5-8-5 72 (tp) CTKeane(7) 9 57
(Gerard Keane, Ire) *towards rr early: t.k.h and sn in rr of mid-div: no ex ent st* **14/1**

13 *2* **Solid Air**[155] 4033 6-9-1 66 WJLee 1 56
(Edward Lynam, Ire) *a towards rr* **33/1**

14 *1 1/2* **Princess Severus (IRE)**[14] 7614 3-8-11 75 (b) WJSupple 10 49
(Mrs John Harrington, Ire) *sn led: rdn and hdd 1 1/2f out: no ex and wknd* **14/1**

1m 36.5s (96.50)
WFA 3 from 4yo+ 1lb **14** Ran SP% **139.4**
CSF £102.66 TOTE £11.40: £3.60, £5.00, £7.30; DF 102.66.
Owner Mrs Sally Roche **Bred** J S Bolger **Trained** Brownstown, Co Meath

FOCUS
A fair contest. It paid to race handy.

NOTEBOOK
Billyford(IRE), once rated 106 and now down to 75, was having his fifth run here since returning from a three-year absence in September. Two of his four previous wins were achieved here and this was his first success since scoring over this course and trip in March 2008. He had shown signs of a return to form when fourth over the C&D two weeks previously and ran out a comfortable winner after tracking the leaders and going to the front well over 1f out. (op 11/2)
He's Got Rhythm(IRE), a four-time winner at up to 7f, ran his best race for some time. Sixth approaching the straight, he kept on quite well from over 1f out without causing the winner any problems.
Black N Brew(USA), third behind Fountain Of Honour over the course and distance two weeks previously, led early and remained prominent. Second into the straight, he kept on under pressure although the winner was well on top throughout the final furlong.
Orpens Peach(IRE), a winner off 61 over 7f at Wolverhampton a week previously, began to close over 1f out and kept on well inside the final furlong. (op 8/1)
Fountain Of Honour(IRE), winner of the race in which Billyford finished fourth here two weeks previously, was up 5lb. Fifth approaching the straight, she soon got into contention, but was under pressure in second over 1f out and found little. (op 5/1)
Key Breeze, down in trip following his win over just short of 1m3f here last month, tracked the leaders and kept on after appearing to run into a spot of trouble early in the straight. (op 3/1 tchd 7/2)

7793a WWW.DUNDALKSTADIUM.COM H'CAP 1m (P)
7:30 (7:31) 3-Y-0+ **£7,732** (£1,793; £784; £448)

RPR

1 **Elusive Ridge (IRE)**[7] 7701 5-9-2 91 (p) PJSmullen 6 98
(H Rogers, Ire) *led: hdd after 1f: led again 2f out: rdn and kpt on wl fr over 1f out* **6/1**[3]

2 *3/4* **Toufan Express**[7] 7701 9-8-0 80 (b) CPHoban(5) 2 85
(Adrian McGuinness, Ire) *chsd ldrs: 4th 1/2-way: rdn 2f out: styd on into 3rd 1f out: kpt on fnl f* **12/1**

3 *1/2* **Tarrsille (IRE)**[7] 7701 5-8-0 82 (t) GJPhillips(7) 5 86
(G M Lyons, Ire) *chsd ldrs: 3rd 1/2-way: rdn 2f out: 2nd over 1f out: no ex ins fnl f: kpt on same pce* **7/1**

4 *shd* **If Per Chance (IRE)**[14] 7618 6-8-5 80 (p) ShaneFoley 1 84
(M Halford, Ire) *mid-div: 7th 1/2-way: rdn in 6th 2f out: 4th 1f out: no ex ins fnl f: kpt on same pce* **10/1**

5 *3/4* **Iron Major (IRE)**[14] 7614 4-8-5 85 (p) SHJames(5) 13 87
(Edward Lynam, Ire) *hld up towards rr: hdwy 2f out: rdn into 6th 1f out: kpt on same pce fnl f* **12/1**

6 *1/2* **Tell The Wind (IRE)**[14] 7614 3-8-8 84 (t) CDHayes 14 85
(Kevin Prendergast, Ire) *hld up towards rr: hdwy 2f out: rdn in 7th 1f out: no ex fnl f: kpt on same pce* **10/1**

7 *nk* **Zabarajad (IRE)**[161] 3833 3-9-10 100 JMurtagh 12 100
(John M Oxx, Ire) *in rr of mid-div: hdwy into 7th 2f out: sn rdn and no imp: kpt on one pce fr over 1f out* **11/4**[1]

8 *2* **Napa Starr (FR)**[77] 6513 7-8-13 88 GFCarroll 4 84
(Eoin Griffin, Ire) *towards rr: rdn and no imp 2f out: kpt on one pce fr over 1f out* **20/1**

9 *1/2* **Sunset Beauty (IRE)**[42] 7277 4-8-11 86 (t) KJManning 8 81
(J S Bolger, Ire) *chsd ldrs: 5th 1/2-way: rdn 2f out: no ex over 1f out: wknd fnl f* **11/2**[2]

10 *1 3/4* **Casela Park (IRE)**[14] 7614 6-8-7 82 WJSupple 11 73
(Jaclyn Tyrrell, Ire) *led after 1f: rdn and hdd 2f out: sn no ex and wknd* **33/1**

11 *2* **Duff (IRE)**[14] 7612 8-9-1 95 RPWhelan(5) 10 81
(Edward Lynam, Ire) *mid-div: 8th 1/2-way: rdn and no ex 2f out* **9/1**

12 *3 1/4* **Arganil (USA)**[17] 7578 6-9-3 95 JulieBurke(3) 3 73
(Kevin Ryan) *chsd ldrs: 6th 1/2-way: rdn and wknd ent st* **18/1**

13 *2 1/2* **Headford View (IRE)**[187] 2970 7-9-5 94 (p) SeamieHeffernan 9 67
(James Halpin, Ire) *mid-div: 9th 1/2-way: rdn and wknd ent st* **33/1**

1m 35.8s (95.80)
WFA 3 from 4yo+ 1lb **13** Ran SP% **128.3**
CSF £80.50 CT £530.68 TOTE £5.40: £1.80, £3.10, £2.20; DF 57.30.
Owner Nap Racing Syndicate **Bred** Michael Harty **Trained** Ardee, Co. Louth

FOCUS
A useful handicap. The placers set a solid standard to their recent course best.

NOTEBOOK

Elusive Ridge(IRE) was successfully dropped to 7f here a week previously. He was 6lb higher here and, with winning form at up to 1m2f plus, he had plenty of use made of him, leading early on and kicking on again over 2f out. He kept on well and will be back here for a conditions event over the trip on Friday. (op 5/1)

Toufan Express took the runner-up spot on this occasion. Back up in trip here, he was prominent throughout and kept on for pressure

Tarrsille(IRE) had finished second on five of his six previous visits here this year and ran another solid race, having every chance and going second over 1f out before finding no extra late on. (op 15/2)

If Per Chance(IRE), a C&D winner last month before finishing a close up sixth over just short of 1m3f here two weeks ago, tried hard to get to the leaders from over 1f out and kept on under pressure. (op 9/1)

Iron Major(IRE), twice a winner over 7f here, was trying a new trip. He trailed the field early on before making steady progress in the straight and keeping on under pressure.

Zabarajad(IRE), a maiden when finishing sixth of eight in the Irish 2,000 Guineas, had been gelded since narrowly winning a 7f maiden at Gowran Park in July. This was his first run back and his first run in a handicap. He was well supported but never really threatened and, while he appeared to get a bit crowded early in the straight, that could hardly be put forward as much of an excuse. (op 4/1)

7791 - 7797a (Foreign Racing) - See Raceform Interactive

[7756]LINGFIELD (L-H)

Saturday, December 17

OFFICIAL GOING: Standard

Wind: Medium, across Weather: Bright, chilly

7798 BETFRED 1350 SHOPS NATIONWIDE CLAIMING STKS 6f (P)

12:20 (12:20) (Class 6) 2-Y-O **£1,704** (£503; £251) **Stalls** Low

Form RPR

2121 **1** **Le King Beau (USA)**[2] 7762 2-8-12 62................................ DaneO'Neill 4 68
(William Muir) *in tch: swtchd rt and effrt to chse ldr wl over 1f out: rdn to ld 1f out: in command whn idled fnl 100yds: rdn out* **11/4**[3]

3112 **2** *¾* **Mr Knightley (IRE)**[9] 7670 2-9-7 80..........................(b) StephenCraine 3 75
(Jim Boyle) *led: rdn and qcknd wl over 1f out: drvn and hdd 1f out: kpt on u.p but a hld fnl f* **9/4**[2]

0443 **3** *1 ¼* **Arabian Flight**[15] 7597 2-8-6 59.................................... KieranO'Neill(3) 7 59
(John Bridger) *stdd s: hld up in tch: rdn ent fnl 2f: hdwy on inner over 1f out: kpt on ins fnl f* **12/1**

0013 **4** *½* **Berlusca (IRE)**[16] 7592 2-9-2 66.................................... WilliamCarson 5 65
(William Jarvis) *pressed ldr tl rdn and unable qck ent fnl 2f: styd on same pce fr over 1f out* **7/4**[1]

0 **5** *¾* **Maria Montez**[22] 7540 2-8-13 0.. SebSanders 8 59
(J W Hills) *chsd ldrs: rdn and unable qck ent fnl 2f: one pce and no threat to ldrs fr over 1f out* **33/1**

4402 **6** *9* **I'm Still The Man (IRE)**[8] 7694 2-8-6 65......................... JakePayne(7) 6 32
(Bill Turner) *awkward leaving stalls: t.k.h: hld up in tch: rdn and struggling over 2f out: wknd over 1f out* **20/1**

1m 11.98s (0.08) **Going Correction** -0.10s/f (Stan) **6** Ran SP% **109.2**

Speed ratings (Par 94): **95,94,92,91,90 78**

toteswingers: 1&2 £1.70, 1&3 £4.40, 2&3 £6.30 CSF £8.81 TOTE £3.70: £1.60, £2.40; EX 8.40 Trifecta £21.90 Pool £95.46 - 3.22 winning units..The winner was claimed by Mr J. J. Bridger for £6,000.

Owner Sills Racing **Bred** Haras Demeautry **Trained** Lambourn, Berks

FOCUS

One or two in-form horses lined up for this claimer.

NOTEBOOK

Le King Beau(USA), successful at Kempton on Thursday, coped well with the drop back to 6f and saw his race out strongly. He didn't handle Fibresand two starts ago but is now unbeaten in his last three starts on Polytrack and has clearly never been better. He was claimed by John Bridger. (tchd 5-2 and 3-1)

Mr Knightley(IRE) was best in at the weights but very weak in the betting and, after making much of the running towards the inside, he was cosily seen off by the winner in the straight. (op 11-4)

Arabian Flight tracked the leader and stuck to the inside in the straight, posting a solid effort in the circumstances on this drop in class. On the negative side, he suffered a superficial cut on his near fore. (op 11-1 tchd 14-1)

Berlusca(IRE), backed into favouritism, raced a shade keenly early and came under pressure heading to the turn. He couldn't really pick up in the straight and was a bit disappointing. Official explanation: trainer said colt ran too freely (tchd 13-8 and 15-8)

Maria Montez had less to do in this company than on her debut in a maiden at Wolverhampton, and showed improved form. She won't be without hope dropped to a seller. Official explanation: vet said filly had been struck into right-hind (op 25-1)

7799 BETFRED WHEN BOTH TEAMS SCORE NOVICE STKS 7f (P)

12:50 (12:50) (Class 5) 2-Y-O **£2,726** (£805; £402) **Stalls** Low

Form RPR

0523 **1** **Not Bad For A Boy (IRE)**[10] 7653 2-8-11 70.............. KieranO'Neill(3) 3 76
(Richard Hannon) *chsd ldr tl led over 2f out: rdn and qcknd 2f out: hrd pressed ins fnl f: hld on wl* **9/1**[3]

41 **2** *nk* **Delft**[14] 7627 2-9-0 78.. JohnFahy 4 75
(Jeremy Noseda) *chsd ldrs: rdn and swtchd lft wl over 1f out: drvn and edgd rt 1f out: swtchd rt ins fnl f: styd on wl u.p to snatch 2nd last stride: nt quite rch wnr* **11/8**[2]

4312 **3** *shd* **Colorful Notion (IRE)**[30] 7445 2-9-0 82............................ AdamKirby 2 75
(Marco Botti) *chsd ldrs: rdn and effrt between horses to chse wnr ent fnl 2f: ev ch fnl f: a jst hld: lost 2nd last stride* **10/11**[1]

0 **4** *3 ¾* **Beauchamp Castle**[35] 7398 2-8-2 0......................... NicoleNordblad(7) 5 60
(Hans Adielsson) *stdd s: hld up in last: pushed along and rn wd bnd 2f out: edgd lft and hdwy over 1f out: styd on same pce ins fnl f* **100/1**

0 **5** *8* **Beauchamp Best**[35] 7398 2-8-6 0.............................. SophieDoyle(3) 1 39
(Hans Adielsson) *led tl rdn and hdd over 2f out: wknd over 1f out* **200/1**

1m 24.79s (-0.01) **Going Correction** -0.10s/f (Stan) **5** Ran SP% **106.0**

Speed ratings (Par 96): **96,95,95,91,82**

CSF £20.45 TOTE £5.80: £2.60, £1.70; EX 15.60.

Owner Middleham Park Racing Xxi **Bred** A Brosnan **Trained** East Everleigh, Wilts

■ Stewards' Enquiry : John Fahy four-day ban: used whip with excessive frequency (Dec 31-Jan 3) 2nd offence in 12mths.

FOCUS

A messy race but a good ride by Kieran O'Neill.

NOTEBOOK

Not Bad For A Boy(IRE) sat on the leader's outside early while the pace was steady, before taking a length out of the field kicking into the straight. Keeping a bit in reserve, he had enough to hold off his higher-rated rivals at the line. It would be unwise to take the form literally. (op 15-2)

Delft ◆ easily won her maiden at Wolverhampton from the front, but she was ridden with more patience this time, got caught out when the winner quickened up and was pushed wide on the bend as the favourite angled for room. Switched back inside, and then outside again, she finished best of all, but the line came too soon. This was not her rider's finest hour. (tchd 5-4 and 6-4)

Colorful Notion(IRE) was the one to beat on the ratings, but she got caught on the rail behind a weakening leader and, as the winner was kicking for home, struggled for racing room, didn't handle the bend into the straight well, and was then always being held inside the last. (tchd Evens tchd 5-4 in a place)

Beauchamp Castle, held up at the back of the field, swung very wide off the bend into the straight before staying on pleasingly in the closing stages. This was a big step up on her debut effort and she'll be of interest in handicaps after one more run.

7800 BETFRED GOALS GALORE H'CAP 1m 4f (P)

1:20 (1:20) (Class 6) (0-65,64) 3-Y-O **£1,704** (£503; £251) **Stalls** Low

Form RPR

1604 **1** **Rowan Ridge**[15] 7600 3-9-7 64...........................(b[1]) JimCrowley 6 72
(Jim Boyle) *t.k.h: chsd ldrs: rdn to chse ldr wl over 1f out: drvn and chal fnl 100yds: led wl ins fnl f: r.o wl* **10/1**

0000 **2** *¾* **Irons On Fire (USA)**[47] 7200 3-9-1 63.......................(p) DavidKenny(5) 2 69
(George Baker) *t.k.h early: chsd ldrs: rdn to ld wl over 1f out: hrd drvn ins fnl f: hdd and one pce wl ins fnl f* **6/4**[1]

5330 **3** *1 ½* **Entrance**[15] 7608 3-9-0 57.. ShaneKelly 9 61
(Julia Feilden) *stdd s: hld up in last pair: hdwy jst over 2f out: chsd ldrs and drvn 1f out: kpt on same pce ins fnl f* **9/1**

1464 **4** *nk* **Guards Chapel**[24] 7515 3-9-3 60.......................................(v) AdamKirby 4 64
(Gary Moore) *s.i.s: rdn along early: in tch: drvn and effrt on inner 2f out: kpt on u.p fnl f* **7/2**[3]

0002 **5** *2 ½* **Who Loves Ya Baby**[24] 7515 3-8-6 52......................... KieranO'Neill(3) 8 52
(Peter Charalambous) *awkward leaving stalls: sn rcvrd and led: hdd over 8f out: rdn to ld again over 2f out tl wl over 1f out: wknd fnl f* **3/1**[2]

2534 **6** *10* **Roman Flame**[12] 7638 3-8-13 56.. SebSanders 7 40
(Michael Quinn) *chsd ldr tl led over 8f out: rdn and hdd over 2f out: wknd qckly wl over 1f out* **16/1**

0530 **7** *8* **Rasteau (IRE)**[15] 7608 3-8-0 50 oh3.............................. DannyBrock(7) 3 21
(Tom Keddy) *chsd ldrs: rdn and lost pl over 2f out: sn bhd* **33/1**

2m 31.82s (-1.18) **Going Correction** -0.10s/f (Stan) **7** Ran SP% **115.1**

Speed ratings (Par 98): **99,98,97,97,95 88,83**

toteswingers: 1&2 £4.80, 1&3 £20.80, 2&3 £5.40 CSF £25.93 CT £145.23 TOTE £12.00: £3.20, £1.50; EX 45.90 Trifecta £117.80 Part won. Pool: £159.19 - 0.63 winning units..

Owner Rowan Stud Partnership 1 **Bred** Rowan Farm Stud **Trained** Epsom, Surrey

■ Stewards' Enquiry : Jim Crowley two-day ban: used whip with excessive frequency (Dec 31-Jan 1)

David Kenny 10-day ban: used whip with excessive frequency (Dec 31,Jan 1-9)

FOCUS

A sound run handicap with the winner improving a little for the blinkers.

7801 BETFRED DOUBLE DELIGHT CONDITIONS STKS 1m (P)

1:50 (1:50) (Class 3) 3-Y-O+ **£6,792** (£2,021; £1,010; £505) **Stalls** High

Form RPR

3012 **1** **Loyalty**[7] 7719 4-9-3 97...(v) JoeFanning 11 104+
(Derek Shaw) *stdd s: hld up off the pce in last quartet: rdn and hdwy over 1f out: str run to ins fnl f to ld cl home* **5/1**[2]

0205 **2** *nk* **Night Lily (IRE)**[15] 7606 5-8-7 95... JimCrowley 2 93
(Paul D'Arcy) *racd off the pce in midfield: rdn over 2f out: drvn and clsd on ldrs jst over 1f out: led wl ins fnl f: hdd and no ex cl home* **9/1**

0101 **3** *nk* **Clockmaker (IRE)**[14] 7628 5-8-12 96.............................. DuranFentiman 3 97
(Tim Easterby) *taken down early: sn led and clr of field w rival: rdn wl over 1f out: drvn 1f out: hdd and no ex wl ins fnl f* **7/2**[1]

0500 **4** *hd* **Spirit Of Sharjah (IRE)**[24] 7516 6-8-12 104........................ ShaneKelly 1 97
(Julia Feilden) *hld up off the pce in midfield: clsd on inner wl over 1f out: chsd ldrs and drvn 1f out: ev ch fnl 100yds: no ex towards fin* **5/1**[2]

0020 **5** *hd* **Kakatosi**[31] 7433 4-8-12 102... DavidProbert 10 96
(Andrew Balding) *chsd ldr and clr of field: rdn and ev ch over 2f out: drvn over 1f out: stl ev ch ins fnl f: no ex and btn fnl 50yds* **8/1**

0003 **6** *hd* **Mr Willis**[14] 7628 5-8-12 87... SteveDrowne 5 96
(Tony Clement) [illegible] in midfield: rdn and clsd wl over 1f out: *r.o and pressed ldrs ins fnl f: no imp towards fin* **14/1**

0050 **7** *2* **Bravo Echo**[24] 7516 5-9-3 100.. J-PGuillambert 7 96
(Michael Attwater) *t.k.h: chsd ldng pair: rdn over 2f out: unable qck u.p over 1f out: styd on same pce fnl f* **10/1**

0605 **8** *nse* **Mabait**[68] 6747 5-8-12 107... MartinLane 9 91
(David Simcock) *stdd s: hld up off the pce in last quartet: rdn and effrt wl over 1f out: swtchd rt 1f out: r.o but nvr gng pce to threaten ldrs* **6/1**[3]

0610 **9** *½* **Elna Bright**[18] 7578 6-8-12 95.. SebSanders 4 90
(Peter Crate) *stdd s: hld up in last quartet: rdn and effrt on inner over 1f out: kpt on but nvr gng pce to chal* **14/1**

6006 **10** *4* **Layline (IRE)**[85] 6302 4-9-5 90...................................... AndreaAtzeni 8 88
(Gay Kelleway) *taken down early: stdd s: hld up off the pce in last quartet: rdn effrt wl over 1f out: no imp: n.d* **33/1**

1m 35.87s (-2.33) **Going Correction** -0.10s/f (Stan) course record **10** Ran SP% **116.3**

Speed ratings (Par 107): **107,106,106,106,106 105,103,103,103,99**

toteswingers: 1&2 £2.20, 1&3 £2.70, 2&3 £8.50 CSF £49.31 TOTE £4.10: £1.30, £2.10, £2.20; EX 38.60 Trifecta £134.30 Pool: £450.11 - 2.48 winning units..

Owner Brian Johnson (Northamptonshire) **Bred** Ecoutila Partnership **Trained** Sproxton, Leics

FOCUS

The early gallop was too hot and the race set up for a closer. The race is rated cautiously and the winner is possibly a bit better than the bare form.

NOTEBOOK

Loyalty hasn't stopped improving. Held up as usual, he had the race run to suit and finished strongly between runners to hit the front close home. His trainer doesn't expect 1m2f to pose him any problems and the Winter Derby will be his target. (op 9-2)

Night Lily(IRE) made the running when well beaten by Loyalty at Wolverhampton last time, but her rider was more patient here and she was only narrowly denied. She's better ridden this way. (op 8-1 tchd 10-1 in places)

Clockmaker(IRE) ◆, up in trip, had plenty of use made of him and clung to the rail most of the way. In the circumstances he ran a mighty race, but his chance would have been enhanced had he taken a lead and raced off the inside. (op 4-1)

Spirit Of Sharjah(IRE) hugged the rail so, given that, put up a really good effort. He got the trip fine and will be of interest whenever he returns to Lingfield. (op 11-2 tchd 13-2)

Kakatosi, who lost his action at Kempton last time, returned to form, but perhaps found the extra furlong just stretching him a touch. (op 17-2 tchd 9-1)

Mr Willis, hampered when third to Clockmaker at Wolverhampton last time, had a clear run down the outside from off the pace here and finished well. His mark may now suffer as a result, though. (op 16-1)

Mabait, having his first start for a new stable, was best in at the weights but was weak in the betting and presumably needed the run. He's likely to be off to Dubai in the new year. (op 8-1)

7802 BETFRED QUEBEC STKS (LISTED RACE) 1m 2f (P)

2:20 (2:20) (Class 1) 3-Y-0+

£17,013 (£6,450; £3,228; £1,608; £807; £405) **Stalls** Low

Form				RPR
0001	**1**		**Tinshu (IRE)**[24] 7523 5-8-12 85 ....(p) DaneO'Neill 4 (Derek Haydn Jones) *hld up in tch in midfield hdwy and gng wl 2f out: rdn and effrt over 1f out: led ins fnl f: r.o wl* **16/1**	94
3011	**2**	*hd*	**Junoob**[15] 7600 3-9-0 90 ....(b) RichardKingscote 10 (Tom Dascombe) *hld up in tch towards rr: rdn: edging lft and gd hdwy jst over 1f out: r.o wl fnl 150yds: snatched 2nd on post: nt quite get up* **7/1**	99
-046	**3**	*nse*	**Mantoba**[35] 7404 3-9-0 96 ....(t) ShaneKelly 5 (Brian Meehan) *chsd ldrs: rdn and ev ch over 1f out: drvn ahd jst ins fnl f: sn hdd: kpt on wl: lost 2nd on post* **40/1**	99
P664	**4**	*¾*	**Trade Storm**[101] 5830 3-9-0 98 .... MartinLane 7 (David Simcock) *in tch in midfield: effrt u.p over 1f out: hdwy 1f out: r.o wl u.p* **12/1**	97
2023	**5**	*1 ¼*	**Suits Me**[35] 7391 8-9-3 100 .... MickyFenton 8 (David Barron) *led: edgd rt wl over 1f out: drvn and hdd jst ins fnl f: no ex and btn fnl 75yds* **6/1**[3]	95
632	**6**	*¾*	**Ceilidh House**[17] 7584 4-8-12 102 ....(t) JimCrowley 11 (Ralph Beckett) *in tch in midfield: lost pl 2f out: in tch but towards rr wl over 1f out: rallied ins fnl f and running on at fin* **9/4**[1]	88+
1066	**7**	*nk*	**Navajo Chief**[70] 6693 4-9-3 106 .... LukeMorris 9 (Alan Jarvis) *in tch: rdn and unable qck wl over 1f out: styd on same pce ins fnl f* **16/1**	92
4-40	**8**	*¾*	**Lyssio (GER)**[70] 6710 4-9-3 99 .... J-PGuillambert 1 (Michael Attwater) *hld up in tch: stl gng wl 2f out: rdn and unable qck over 1f out: drvn and styd on same pce after* **50/1**	91
	9	*nk*	**King's Trail (JPN)**[630] 9-9-3 108 .... SebSanders 2 (Takashi Kodama, Ire) *hld up in last pair: rdn and effrt on inner wl over 1f out: drvn and styd on same pce fnl f* **66/1**	90
6000	**10**	*nk*	**Beaubrav**[24] 7523 5-9-3 90 ....(tp) AdamKirby 6 (Michael Madgwick) *dwlt: in tch in rr: rdn and effrt over 1f out: kpt on ins fnl f: nvr trbld ldrs* **40/1**	90
-341	**11**	*nk*	**Whey Sauce (JPN)**[44] 7250 3-8-9 83 .... SteveDrowne 12 (Peter Chapple-Hyam) *chsd ldr: rdn and pressing ldrs whn pushed rt and hmpd wl over 1f out: lost pl and styd on same pce after* **22/1**	84
6462	**12**	*½*	**Circumvent**[35] 7391 4-9-3 100 .... StevieDonohoe 13 (Paul Cole) *chsd ldrs: rdn and unable qck whn sltly hmpd wl over 1f out: sn lost pl: styd on same pce and no imp fnl f* **4/1**[2]	88
0130	**13**	*2 ½*	**Status Symbol (IRE)**[42] 7297 6-9-3 99 ....(t) WilliamCarson 3 (Anthony Carson) *hmpd and lost pl sn after s: racd in last trio after: hdwy into midfield wl over 1f out: unable qck and short of room 1f out: no hdwy after: eased towards fin* **6/1**[3]	83

2m 2.67s (-3.93) **Going Correction** -0.10s/f (Stan)
WFA 3 from 4yo+ 3lb **13** Ran SP% **124.0**
Speed ratings (Par 111): **111,110,110,110,109 108,108,107,107,107 107,106,104**
toteswingers: 1&2 £5.10, 1&3 £45.20, 2&3 £37.00 CSF £124.41 TOTE £20.00: £4.60, £2.50, £11.00; EX 263.70 TRIFECTA Not won..
Owner Llewelyn, Runeckles **Bred** Mrs M L Parry & P M Steele-Mortimer **Trained** Efail Isaf, Rhondda C Taff
■ Stewards' Enquiry : Micky Fenton two-day ban: careless riding (Dec 31-Jan 1)
Dane O'Neill one-day ban: careless riding (Dec 31)

FOCUS
A competitive Listed race, but a surprise result and very ordinary form for the grade. There was a bunch finish and the form looks far from solid.

NOTEBOOK
Tinshu(IRE), who won a handicap off just 80 last time out, edged a three-way photo. She had a nice run through the race and quickened up well in the straight, and her trainer, who had said he thought she could win at this level after her last win, pointed the way to the Winter Derby. (op 12-1)
Junoob, wide-margin winner of a claimer over the C&D last time, was debuting for his new stable and finished well from the back of the pack, picking up a little over half his purchase price in the process. He hasn't had that much racing and remains open to further improvement. (op 15-2)
Mantoba, who had the tongue-tie back on but went without the blinkers, has yet to recapture his 2yo form, but this was a decent effort on his Polytrack debut, and he hasn't had much racing in total so could have more to offer. (op 33-1)
Trade Storm, running for a new stable, was stepping up in distance and had no trouble with it. This opens up new opportunities and he could be a candidate for Dubai.
Suits Me, runner-up in this race in 2008 and 2009, tried to make all but, despite edging off the rail in the straight, proved a sitting duck 1f out. (op 13-2 tchd 11-2)
Ceilidh House was keeping on all too late, and perhaps a stronger all-round pace would have suited her better. (op 10-3 tchd 7-2)
Circumvent was below his best. He got a couple of bumps approaching the final furlong, but wasn't really going anywhere at the time.
Status Symbol(IRE), debuting for a new yard, was well supported on this return to AW, but he struggled to pick up turning into the straight and was eased off. (op 11-1)

7803 BETFRED HAT TRICK HEAVEN H'CAP 1m 4f (P)

2:55 (2:55) (Class 4) (0-85,89) 3-Y-0+ **£4,204** (£1,251; £625; £312) **Stalls** Low

Form				RPR
4320	**1**		**George Adamson (IRE)**[44] 6279 5-9-1 **76** .... JimCrowley 9 (Alan Swinbank) *stdd s: hld up in rr: smooth hdwy over 2f out: rdn to chse ldr jst ins fnl f: led wl ins fnl f: pushed out towards fin* **10/1**	84+
2253	**2**	*1*	**Sand Skier**[10] 7661 4-8-5 **73** ....(b) NicoleNordblad(7) 10 (Hans Adielsson) *t.k.h: chsd ldrs: wnt 2nd 3f out: rdn to ld over 1f out: hdd and no ex wl ins fnl f* **8/1**[3]	79
3142	**3**	*hd*	**Brigadoon**[29] 7458 4-9-2 **77** .... LeeNewman 4 (William Jarvis) *chsd ldrs: rdn along over 4f out: chsd ldrs u.p over 1f out: kpt on same pce ins fnl f* **4/1**[1]	83
0303	**4**	*¾*	**Trend Line (IRE)**[12] 7638 3-8-6 **72** .... FrannyNorton 3 (Peter Chapple-Hyam) *awkward leaving stalls and s.i.s: racd in last trio: hdwy on inner 2f out: nt clr run and swtchd rt over 1f out: no ex u.p and one pce ins fnl f* **4/1**[1]	78+
1041	**5**	*1*	**Where's Susie**[18] 7577 6-9-2 **77** .... DaneO'Neill 1 (Michael Madgwick) *in tch in midfield: lost pl over 3f out: bhd and rdn over 2f out: styd on wl ins fnl f: unable to chal* **8/1**[3]	80
4152	**6**	*¾*	**Beat Route**[10] 7661 4-8-10 **71** oh1 .... JohnFahy 5 (Michael Attwater) *t.k.h: hld up in midfield: hdwy to chse ldrs and rdn 2f out: wknd ins fnl f* **11/2**[2]	73
030-	**7**	*¾*	**Brunston**[16] 7350 5-9-10 **85** ....(p) RichardKingscote 6 (Roger Charlton) *chsd ldr tl led over 3f out: rdn and hdd over 1f out: wknd ins fnl f* **16/1**	85
1211	**8**	*6*	**True To Form (IRE)**[10] 7651 4-10-0 **89** ....(p) LukeMorris 8 (Ronald Harris) *hld up in last trio: hdwy on outer over 3f out: drvn and unable qck bnd 2f out: wknd fnl f* **4/1**[1]	80
-100	**9**	*26*	**Battleoftrafalgar**[203] 2499 4-9-8 **83** ....(v[1]) J-PGuillambert 7 (Michael Attwater) *led: hdd and rdn over 3f out: bhd and lost tch 2f out: t.o and eased ins fnl f* **25/1**	32

2m 29.66s (-3.34) **Going Correction** -0.10s/f (Stan)
WFA 3 from 4yo+ 5lb **9** Ran SP% **116.4**
Speed ratings (Par 105): **107,106,106,105,105 104,104,100,82**
toteswingers: 1&2 £16.40, 1&3 £14.00, 2&3 £45.40 CSF £87.59 CT £376.62 TOTE £8.30: £2.50, £3.30, £1.90; EX 92.60 Trifecta £270.00 Pool: £383.24 - 1.05 winning units..
Owner Mrs S Sanbrook **Bred** Miss O O'Connor & Stephanie Von Schilcher **Trained** Melsonby, N Yorks

FOCUS
This looked quite open on paper. It was sound run and the winner did not really improve from his reappearance.
Trend Line(IRE) Official explanation: jockey said filly stumbled leaving stalls and was denied a clear run in straight

7804 C W SURFACING H'CAP 5f (P)

3:30 (3:30) (Class 5) (0-70,70) 3-Y-0+ **£2,385** (£704; £352) **Stalls** High

Form				RPR
2624	**1**		**Triple Dream**[16] 7594 6-9-7 **70** ....(tp) RichardKingscote 5 (Milton Bradley) *chsd ldr: rdn wl over 1f out: led over 1f out: clr and r.o wl fnl f* **6/1**[3]	80
05	**2**	*2*	**Picansort**[117] 5326 4-9-1 **64** .... ShaneKelly 3 (Peter Crate) *chsd ldrs: effrt on inner whn bdly hmpd and lost pl over 1f out: swtchd rt jst ins fnl f: rallied and r.o wl to go 2nd cl home* **3/1**[1]	72+
0310	**3**	*hd*	**Atlantic Beach**[17] 7588 6-9-6 **69** ....(b) LukeMorris 6 (Milton Bradley) *in tch in midfield: rdn and swtchd rt wl over 1f out: chsd clr wnr jst ins fnl f: kpt on: lost 2nd cl home* **13/2**	71
5625	**4**	*½*	**Griffin Point (IRE)**[19] 7567 4-9-0 **63** .... WilliamCarson 8 (William Muir) *chsd ldrs: rdn and effrt 2f out: styd on same pce u.p fr over 1f out* **9/1**	63
6454	**5**	*1*	**Even Bolder**[60] 6932 8-9-0 **66** .... KierenFox(3) 4 (Eric Wheeler) *hmpd and dropped to rr after 1f: rdn and effrt over 1f out: styd on wl fnl f* **15/2**	65+
0032	**6**	*shd*	**Grudge**[10] 7659 6-8-13 **67** ....(b) DavidKenny(5) 10 (Conor Dore) *led: hung lft and hdd over 1f out: wknd ins fnl f* **22/1**	63
46	**7**	*nk*	**Scarlet Rocks (IRE)**[24] 7512 3-9-7 **70** ....(tp) DaneO'Neill 1 (George Baker) *s.i.s and rdn along early: hdwy over 1f out: keeping on but stl plenty to do whn hmpd jst ins fnl f: no threat to wnr and nt pushed out fnl 100yds* **4/1**[2]	69+
1600	**8**	*½*	**Sulis Minerva (IRE)**[81] 6436 4-8-11 **67** .... RaulDaSilva(7) 7 (Jeremy Gask) *chsd ldrs: pushed rt and lost pl bnd wl over 1f out: pushed along and kpt on same pce fnl f* **16/1**	60
2001	**9**	*2*	**Black Baccara**[10] 7649 4-9-1 **67** ....(be) RyanClark(3) 9 (Phil McEntee) *v.s.a: a in rr* **7/1**	53

58.54 secs (-0.26) **Going Correction** -0.10s/f (Stan) **9** Ran SP% **117.1**
Speed ratings (Par 103): **98,94,94,93,92 91,91,90,87**
toteswingers: 1&2 £2.10, 1&3 £8.90, 2&3 £18.60 CSF £24.73 CT £122.48 TOTE £7.00: £2.00, £1.70, £3.10; EX 46.20 TRIFECTA Not won..
Owner J M Bradley **Bred** Hesmonds Stud Ltd **Trained** Sedbury, Gloucs
■ Stewards' Enquiry : Dane O'Neill caution: failed to take all reasonable and permissable measures to obtain best possible placing

FOCUS
The well-backed favourite looked unlucky here. An ordinary handicap run at a decent pace, and it's unlikely the winner improved.
Even Bolder Official explanation: jockey said gelding suffered interference leaving stalls
Grudge Official explanation: jockey said gelding hung left
Scarlet Rocks(IRE) Official explanation: jockey said filly was denied a clear run
Black Baccara Official explanation: jockey said filly anticipated start causing it to miss the break and become disappointed
T/Plt: £397.00 to a £1 stake. Pool: £53,400.99. 98.18 winning tickets. T/Qpdt: £98.10 to a £1 stake. Pool: £4,522.48. 34.10 winning tickets. SP

7762 KEMPTON (A.W) (R-H)

Sunday, December 18

OFFICIAL GOING: Standard
Wind: Almost nil. Weather: overcast, cold

7805 DOWNLOAD THE BLUE SQUARE BET APP H'CAP 1m 2f (P)

1:40 (1:41) (Class 6) (0-60,61) 3-Y-0+ **£1,617** (£481; £240; £120) **Stalls** Low

Form				RPR
U003	**1**		**Whodunit (UAE)**[11] 7654 7-9-4 **57** ....(b) ChrisCatlin 13 (Peter Hiatt) *pressed ldr for 2f: trckd ldr: rdn over 2f out: led over 1f out: styd on wl fnl f: rdn out* **9/2**[2]	68
0506	**2**	*2 ¾*	**Regal Rave (USA)**[13] 7640 4-8-10 **49** ....(v) JohnFahy 10 (Peter Hedger) *stdd s: bhd: hdwy fr over 4f out: rdn to chse ldrs over 2f out: styd on to chse wnr ins fnl f: a being hld* **8/1**	54
6600	**3**	*hd*	**Bubbly Braveheart (IRE)**[53] 7097 4-9-7 **60** .... IanMongan 3 (Pat Phelan) *trckd ldrs: rdn over 2f out: nt quite pce to chal: styd on fnl f* **6/1**	65
2422	**4**	*¾*	**Colinca's Lad (IRE)**[24] 7528 9-9-1 **61** ow1 .... JoshCrane(7) 7 (Peter Charalambous) *led: rdn 2f out: hdd over 1f out: kpt on but no ex fnl 120yds* **7/2**[1]	64
0400	**5**	*¾*	**Kai Mook**[9] 7698 4-8-11 **55** .... MarkCoumbe(5) 5 (Roger Ingram) *hld up towards rr: rdn and stdy prog fr over 2f out: styd on but nt pce to get on terms* **14/1**	57
050-	**6**	*2*	**Equine Science**[445] 6452 4-8-11 **50** .... AWhelan 11 (Jane Chapple-Hyam) *hld up towards rr: rdn and sme hdwy into midfield over 2f out: styd on same pce fr over 1f out* **33/1**	48
3025	**7**	*½*	**Fair Breeze**[44] 7270 4-8-12 **51** .... SteveDrowne 6 (Richard Phillips) *rdn over 2f out: a mid-div* **10/1**	48
0536	**8**	*1*	**Querido (GER)**[13] 7639 7-8-10 **52** ow1 ....(tp) RobertLButler(3) 12 (Paddy Butler) *hld up towards rr: sme prog on outer over 2f out: sn rdn: no further imp fr over 1f out* **20/1**	47
S230	**9**	*¾*	**Aine's Delight (IRE)**[16] 7603 5-9-3 **56** .... DaneO'Neill 9 (Andy Turnell) *mid-div: wnt 4th over 4f out: rdn over 2f out: sn one pce* **5/1**[3]	49
2000	**10**	*2 ½*	**Aurora Lights**[13] 7639 4-8-9 **48** oh1 ow2 .... TonyHamilton 2 (Richard Fahey) *mid-div: rdn over 2f out: wknd over 1f out* **33/1**	36
000-	**11**	*½*	**Good Buy Dubai (USA)**[349] 7315 5-8-8 **47** .... WilliamCarson 1 (Mark Hoad) *s.i.s: sn mid-div: pushed along over 5f out: sn in rr* **66/1**	34

The Form Book, Raceform Ltd, Compton, RG20 6NL

5-50 **12** ½ **Sawahill**[18] 7585 3-8-10 **55**.............................. KieranO'Neill(3) 4 41
(Clive Brittain) *rdn over 3f out: a towards rr* **20/1**
-310 **13** 9 **Ashgrove Nell (IRE)**[64] 6877 3-9-2 **58**.............................. StephenCraine 14 26
(Daniel Mark Loughnane, Ire) *mid-div: rdn over 2f out: sn wknd* **25/1**
100- **14** 24 **Moscow Oznick**[431] 6846 6-9-7 **60**.............................. DavidProbert 8 —
(Des Donovan) *chsd ldrs tl over 3f out: bhd fnl 2f* **25/1**
2m 6.88s (-1.12) **Going Correction** +0.05s/f (Slow)
WFA 3 from 4yo+ 3lb **14** Ran SP% **122.8**
Speed ratings (Par 101): **106,103,103,103,102 100,100,99,99,97 96,96,89,69**
toteswingers: 1&2: £8.60, 2&3: £19.70, 1&3: £10.00 CSF £37.62 CT £224.59 TOTE £7.00: £1.90, £2.90, £2.70; EX 43.30 Trifecta £178.40 Part won. Pool £241.10 - 0.63 winning units..
Owner Exors of the Late John Hedges **Bred** Darley **Trained** Hook Norton, Oxon

FOCUS
There was a good gallop on here and the form looks sound, if modest. The winner is rated back towards his best.

7806 WIN THOUSANDS OF SPORTS EXPERIENCES AT BLUESQ.COM H'CAP 1m 2f (P)
2:10 (2:10) (Class 4) (0-85,78) 3-Y-O **£4,075** (£1,212; £606; £303) **Stalls** Low

Form RPR
46 **1** **Daring Indian**[16] 7601 3-9-0 **71**.............................. StevieDonohoe 1 78
(Ian Williams) *trckd ldrs: rdn wl over 1f out: led ent fnl f: kpt on: rdn out* **9/2**[3]
0022 **2** 1 ¼ **Emma's Gift (IRE)**[29] 7486 3-9-4 **78**..............(b) AdamBeschizza(3) 6 85+
(Julia Feilden) *wnt lft s: hld up in last pair but wl in tch: trckd ldrs 3f out: nt best of runs and lost pl wl over 1f out: swtchd lft and r.o wl fnl f: wnt 2nd nring fin* **11/4**[2]
2201 **3** 1 **Shieldmaiden (USA)**[8] 7712 3-9-5 **76**..............(b[1]) JoeFanning 2 79
(Mark Johnston) *led at stdy pce tl increased tempo over 2f out: rdn and hdd ent fnl f: kpt on same pce: lost 2nd nring fin* **5/1**
2610 **4** ¾ **Songburst**[11] 7651 3-9-3 **77**.............................. KieranO'Neill(3) 9 78
(Richard Hannon) *sn w ldr: rdn over 2f out: kpt on same pce fnl f* **5/2**[1]
0032 **5** ½ **Grand Theft Equine**[11] 7662 3-8-10 **67**.............................. NickyMackay 5 67
(Jim Boyle) *t.k.h: trckd ldrs: rdn 2f out: kpt on same pce* **12/1**
3-4 **6** 1 ½ **Beginnings (USA)**[47] 7204 3-9-4 **75**.............................. SebSanders 7 72
(Lydia Pearce) *squeezed up s: hld up in last pair but wl in tch: rdn over 2f out: nt pce to get on terms* **8/1**
2m 9.69s (1.69) **Going Correction** +0.05s/f (Slow) **6** Ran SP% **108.9**
Speed ratings (Par 104): **95,94,93,92,92 91**
toteswingers: 1&2: £3.00, 2&3: £2.40, 1&3: £3.70 CSF £16.14 CT £55.71 TOTE £6.40: £2.40, £2.10; EX 21.90 Trifecta £253.70 Part won. Pool £342.97 - 0.65 winning units..
Owner Denarius Consulting Ltd **Bred** Juddmonte Farms Ltd **Trained** Portway, Worcs

FOCUS
The top-weight weighed in 7lb below the ceiling. It was a bit of a messy race as no-one wanted to go on early and it developed into a dash from the turn in. Dubious form.
Grand Theft Equine Official explanation: jockey said gelding ran too free

7807 EXCLUSIVE LIVE SHOWS AT BLUESQ.COM CLAIMING STKS 7f (P)
2:45 (2:45) (Class 6) 3-Y-0+ **£1,617** (£481; £240; £120) **Stalls** Low

Form RPR
0434 **1** **Marajaa (IRE)**[24] 7531 9-8-13 78.............................. JamieMackay 6 84+
(Willie Musson) *travelled wl in tch: smooth hdwy fr 2f out: led ins fnl f: qcknd clr: comf* **11/10**[1]
2102 **2** 3 **Fishforcompliments**[13] 7636 7-8-12 75..............(v) TonyHamilton 7 75
(Richard Fahey) *wnt lft s: trckd ldrs: rdn over 2f out: chal ent fnl f: kpt on to go 2nd fnl 140yds but no ch w wnr* **9/2**[3]
1101 **3** 1 **Where's Reiley (USA)**[11] 7659 5-8-8 80.............................. AmyScott(5) 2 73
(Alastair Lidderdale) *disp ld tl outrt ldr over 2f out: rdn and hrd pressed fr 2f out: hdd ins fnl f: kpt on but no ex* **5/1**
0001 **4** ¾ **City Legend**[25] 7518 3-8-9 69..............(bt) KieranO'Neill(3) 4 70
(Alan McCabe) *disp ld: nk down whn rdn over 2f out: ev ch ent fnl f: no ex fnl 120yds* **15/2**
6120 **5** 2 ¾ **Lutine Charlie (IRE)**[24] 7529 4-8-11 74..............(p) LukeMorris 1 62
(Ronald Harris) *chsd ldrs: rdn over 2f out: kpt on same pce* **4/1**[2]
5640 **6** nk **Avalon Bay**[11] 7656 3-8-11 54 ow1..............(p) DaneO'Neill 8 61
(Pat Eddery) *carried lft s: in tch: effrt 2f out: nt pce to threaten* **16/1**
-004 **7** 19 **Pharoh Jake**[241] 1504 3-8-5 46 CharlesBishop(5) 9
(John Bridger) *slowly away: t.k.h: sn trcking ldrs: rdn over 2f out: wknd over 1f out* **100/1**
8 dist **Stanwell** 3-9-0 0.............................. WilliamCarson 5 —
(H Edward Haynes) *s.i.s: sn outpcd: a bhd: t.o* **50/1**
1m 25.72s (-0.28) **Going Correction** +0.05s/f (Slow) **8** Ran SP% **123.1**
Speed ratings (Par 101): **103,99,98,97,94 94,72,—**
toteswingers: 1&2: £2.40, 2&3: £4.80, 1&3: £3.00 CSF £7.28 TOTE £2.10: £1.20, £1.70, £1.90; EX 8.60 Trifecta £24.90 Pool £381.30 - 11.29 winning units..
Owner W J Musson **Bred** Shadwell Estate Company Limited **Trained** Newmarket, Suffolk

FOCUS
Not a bad claimer run at a reasonable pace. The winner didn't need to improve on his latest effort.

7808 BET AT BLUESQ.COM ON YOUR MOBILE NURSERY 7f (P)
3:15 (3:16) (Class 5) (0-75,75) 2-Y-O **£2,264** (£673; £336; £168) **Stalls** Low

Form RPR
0304 **1** **Red Bay**[24] 7526 2-9-5 **73**.............................. LukeMorris 6 76
(Jane Chapple-Hyam) *trckd ldrs: rdn to chal over 1f out: v narrow advantage ins fnl f: asserted nring fin: drvn out* **7/2**[3]
3551 **2** nk **Intomist (IRE)**[24] 7530 2-8-3 **62**.............................. NathanAlison(5) 1 64
(Jim Boyle) *trckd ldr: rdn to ld over 1f out: sn hrd pressed: v narrowly hdd ins fnl f: kpt on: hld nring fin* **10/3**[2]
31 **3** 1 ¼ **Topflight Princess**[18] 7583 2-9-7 **75**.............................. AdamKirby 4 74
(Jeremy Gask) *hld up bhd ldrs: swtchd out to chal over 1f out: sn rdn: ev ch ent fnl f: no ex fnl 120yds* **4/1**
0066 **4** 2 ¼ **Compton Target (IRE)**[4] 7752 2-8-6 **67**..............(t) NicoleNordblad(7) 3 60
(Hans Adielsson) *racd keenly: trckd ldr: pushed along whn sltly hmpd 2f out: styd on same pce fnl f* **6/1**
4560 **5** 2 ¾ **Rock Canyon (IRE)**[103] 5809 2-9-0 **68**..............(p) JimCrowley 2 54
(Robert Mills) *led: rdn and drifted lft 2f out: sn hdd: fdd fnl f* **14/1**
0025 **6** 21 **Royal Prospector**[25] 7521 2-9-2 **73**.............................. KieranO'Neill(3) 5 4
(Richard Hannon) *nvr travelling in last but in tch: wknd over 2f out* **11/4**[1]
1m 29.73s (3.73) **Going Correction** +0.05s/f (Slow) **6** Ran SP% **112.9**
Speed ratings (Par 96): **80,79,78,75,72 48**
toteswingers: 1&2: £2.70, 2&3: £2.40, 1&3: £1.80 CSF £15.67 TOTE £4.90: £2.00, £2.20; EX 17.10.
Owner Mrs Julie Martin **Bred** Julie Routledge-Martin **Trained** Dalham, Suffolk

FOCUS
The early pace was steady and the race developed into a sprint from the cutaway. Strength from the saddle looked the difference in the end.

NOTEBOOK
Red Bay, fourth in a maiden that has worked out well last time out, was running in a handicap for the first time and appreciated the return to 7f. He responded well to hard driving and could have more to offer. (op 4-1 tchd 10-3)
Intomist(IRE), a winner over 6f here last time, was 5lb higher. He travelled well into contention, but when it came down to a final furlong duel the winner simply had the stronger jockey aboard. (op 4-1)
Topflight Princess challenged towards the inside but couldn't quite match the front two inside the last half furlong. It wasn't a bad effort off what looked a stiff enough opening mark, and she can probably do better again. (op 10-3 tchd 3-1)
Compton Target(IRE), a shade keen early, could have done with a stronger all-round gallop. It would be hasty to suggest he doesn't stay this trip. (op 7-1)
Rock Canyon(IRE) enjoyed the run of things out in front, but he wasn't anywhere near good enough to take advantage. (tchd 11-1)
Royal Prospector was never going at any stage and presumably something was amiss. Official explanation: jockey said colt never travelled; vet said colt was lame (tchd 7-2)

7809 BLUE SQUARE MAIDEN AUCTION STKS 1m (P)
3:45 (3:45) (Class 5) 2-Y-O **£2,264** (£673; £336; £168) **Stalls** Low

Form RPR
005 **1** **Island Melody (IRE)**[146] 4390 2-8-9 70.............................. LukeMorris 1 67
(J S Moore) *trckd ldrs: rdn 2f out: str chal ent fnl f: led fnl 100yds: hld on wl* **10/3**[2]
4 **2** nk **Josam (IRE)**[15] 7627 2-9-1 0.............................. DaneO'Neill 3 72
(Richard Hannon) *s.i.s: trckd ldrs: rdn 2f out: str chal ins fnl f: hld nring fin* **10/11**[1]
63 **3** ½ **Oratorian (IRE)**[10] 7673 2-8-10 0.............................. LiamKeniry 4 66
(Sylvester Kirk) *w ldr: rdn to ld over 2f out: jnd ent fnl f: kpt on but no ex whn hdd fnl 100yds* **5/1**[3]
30 **4** 4 ½ **Whipcrackaway (IRE)**[61] 6927 2-8-10 0.............................. JohnFahy 5 56
(Peter Hedger) *trckd ldrs early: dropped to last but in tch after 2f: rdn over 2f out: nt pce to threaten* **8/1**
0554 **5** 9 **Princess Kaiulani (IRE)**[11] 7657 2-8-9 50..............(p) WilliamCarson 2 34
(William Muir) *led: rdn over 2f out: sn hdd: wknd over 1f out* **25/1**
1m 41.16s (1.36) **Going Correction** +0.05s/f (Slow) **5** Ran SP% **107.1**
Speed ratings (Par 96): **95,94,94,89,80**
CSF £6.43 TOTE £4.00: £2.00, £1.10; EX 6.90.
Owner D Kerr & J S Moore **Bred** Coleman Bloodstock Limited **Trained** Upper Lambourn, Berks
■ Stewards' Enquiry : Dane O'Neill five-day ban: excessive use of the whip (Jan 1-5)

FOCUS
A pretty ordinary maiden.

NOTEBOOK
Island Melody(IRE) wasn't disgraced in the Chesham on his second start but hadn't been seen since running below that level in finishing fifth in a Yarmouth maiden in July. He has been gelded since then, and his trainer warned that he was not fully wound up and would probably benefit from a longer trip, and it certainly looked that way as he needed to be niggled along at various points. He took a good while to get rolling in the straight, too, and while he eventually saw it out best, it certainly looks as though his trainer is right in suggesting he'll improve for further in time. Apparently Deauville could be on the agenda for him. (op 11-2)
Josam(IRE), a running-on fourth on his debut at Wolverhampton, needed to improve on that to win this, but he didn't improve as much as those who sent him off at odds-on expected him to. His pedigree suggests he'll only come into his own once sent over middle distances next year. (op 4-5, tchd Evens in places)
Oratorian(IRE) travelled best through the race and went to the front looking the likely winner, but in the end he was outstayed. He'll be interesting back over 7f, and handicaps are now an option. (op 7-2)
Whipcrackaway(IRE)'s trainer suggested beforehand that he's a bit quirky and will probably need blinkers at some point. Now eligible for handicaps, he might improve for headgear in that sphere. (tchd 7-1)

7810 PLAY ROULETTE AT BLUESQ.COM/CASINO H'CAP 1m (P)
4:15 (4:15) (Class 6) (0-65,63) 3-Y-O+ **£1,617** (£481; £180; £180) **Stalls** High

Form RPR
6000 **1** **Green Earth (IRE)**[25] 7522 4-9-3 **60**.............................. IanMongan 8 70
(Pat Phelan) *mid-div: hdwy fr 2f out: rdn and edgd rt sn after: led jst over 1f out: r.o wl* [illegible]
6300 **2** 1 ¾ **Hecton Lad (USA)**[30] 7455 4-9-6 **63**..............(b) LukeMorris 4 69
(John Best) *trckd ldrs: rdn 2f out: ev ch ent fnl f: kpt on but sn hld by wnr* **8/1**
50-3 **3** 1 ¾ **Land Hawk (IRE)**[25] 7522 5-9-0 **60**.............................. SimonPearce(3) 3 62
(Lydia Pearce) *in tch: rdn 2f out: chal ent fnl f: kpt on but no ex* **9/2**[2]
5065 **3** dht **Isdaal**[16] 7604 4-9-1 **58**..............(p) JoeFanning 7 62+
(Kevin Morgan) *mid-div: hdwy 3f out: rdn to mount chal whn squeezed up wl over 1f out: kpt on ins fnl f* **9/2**[2]
5000 **5** 1 ¾ **Buxton**[11] 7663 7-9-1 **58**..............(t) SebSanders 2 56
(Roger Ingram) *mid-div: hdwy to chse ldrs 2f out: sn rdn: styd on same pce fnl f* **25/1**
3130 **6** ¾ **Fitz**[11] 7663 5-8-12 **60**.............................. LeeNewnes(5) 9 56
(Matthew Salaman) *s.i.s: towards rr: hdwy over 4f out: rdn over 2f out: sn one pce* **12/1**
3520 **7** ½ **Gazboolou**[11] 7663 7-9-0 **57**.............................. RichardKingscote 1 52
(David Pinder) *led: rdn over 2f out: hdd jst over 1f out: fdd* **7/1**[3]
0410 **8** nk **Valley Tiger**[9] 7698 3-9-1 **59**.............................. TonyHamilton 11 53
(Richard Fahey) *hld up bhd: sme hdwy over 2f out: sn rdn: no further imp* **14/1**
5314 **9** 3 ¼ **Gallantry**[11] 7663 9-9-1 **58**.............................. TomMcLaughlin 5 45
(Paul Howling) *chsd ldrs: rdn over 2f out: fdd fr over 1f out* **10/1**
300- **10** 2 ¾ **Cottonfields (USA)**[485] 5254 5-9-1 **58**.............................. TonyCulhane 6 38
(Heather Main) *t.k.h: a towards rr* **25/1**
1m 39.88s (0.08) **Going Correction** +0.05s/f (Slow)
WFA 3 from 4yo+ 1lb **10** Ran SP% **116.1**
Speed ratings (Par 101): **101,99,97,97,95 95,94,94,90,88**Pl: Land Hawk £0.90, Isdaal £0.70; Tricast: GE/HL/LH £53.19, GE/HL/I £52.10; Trifecta: GE/HL/LH £136.20. Pool £732.83 - 1.99 w/u. GE/HL/I £88.60. Pool £732.82 - 3.06 w/u; toteswingers: 1&2: £6.00, 2&3: £4.20, 1&3: £2.40, 2&3: £3.60, 1&3: £1.70 CSF £27.48 TOTE £27: £Owner, £P Wheatley, £Bred, £Woodcote Stud LtdTrained Epsom, Surrey.

FOCUS
The winner landed a gamble in this ordinary handicap and returned to his summer turf form.

7811 PLAY DA VINCI DIAMONDS AT BLUESQ.COM/GAMES H'CAP (DIV I) 6f (P)
4:45 (4:45) (Class 6) (0-60,61) 3-Y-O+ **£1,617** (£481; £240; £120) **Stalls** Low

Form RPR
0021 **1** **Peace Seeker**[4] 7755 3-9-8 **61** 6ex.............................. WilliamCarson 9 79+
(Anthony Carson) *sn swtchd to rails: mde all: clr over 1f out: readily* **4/11**[1]

3000 **2** *3* **Rapid Water**[18] 7587 5-9-7 **60** AdamKirby 6 65
(Gary Moore) *s.i.s: in last pair: hdwy fr 2f out: rdn over 1f out: wnt 2nd jst ins fnl f: no ch w easy wnr* **8/1**[2]
2020 **3** *3/4* **Dingaan (IRE)**[37] 7371 8-9-2 **55** DaneO'Neill 7 58
(Peter Grayson) *s.i.s: towards rr: swtchd lft 2f out: sn rdn and gd hdwy: r.o ins fnl f: nrst fin* **20/1**
1156 **4** *1 1/2* **Vhujon (IRE)**[20] 7566 6-9-4 **57** RobbieFitzpatrick 4 55
(Peter Grayson) *mid-div: hdwy 2f out: sn rdn: kpt on same pce fnl f* **16/1**
4320 **5** *1 1/2* **Silvee**[29] 7485 4-9-1 **57** KieranO'Neill(3) 2 50
(John Bridger) *chsd wnr: rdn over 2f out: no ex ins fnl f* **12/1**[3]
6650 **6** *1/2* **White Shift (IRE)**[11] 7656 5-8-9 **51** KierenFox(3) 5 42
(Paul Howling) *in tch: effrt 2f out: styd on same pce fr over 1f out* **25/1**
2016 **7** *hd* **Doctor Hilary**[18] 7588 9-9-7 **60** (v) JimCrowley 1 51
(Mark Hoad) *chsd ldrs: rdn over 2f out: fdd fnl f* **8/1**[2]
2120 **8** *6* **Bateleur**[20] 7566 7-9-0 **58** CharlesBishop(5) 8 30
(Mick Channon) *chsd ldrs: rdn 2f out: wknd over 1f out* **14/1**
0000 **9** *7* **Mirabile Visu**[61] 6930 3-8-13 **52** (be) TonyCulhane 10 —
(Heather Main) *chsd ldrs: c wd ent st: sn lost pl and rdn: wknd over 1f out* **50/1**

1m 12.56s (-0.54) **Going Correction** +0.05s/f (Slow) **9** Ran SP% **126.3**
Speed ratings (Par 101): **105,101,100,98,96 95,95,87,77**
toteswingers: 1&2: £2.20, 2&3: £16.90, 1&3: £4.00 CSF £4.92 CT £35.88 TOTE £1.30: £1.10, £1.80, £3.50; EX 5.80 Trifecta £35.90 Pool £716.43 - 14.74 winning units.
Owner Neville Chamberlain Syndicate **Bred** C J Mills **Trained** Newmarket, Suffolk

FOCUS
This proved very straightforward for the favourite, who is rated value for 4l and looks way ahead of his mark.

7812 PLAY DA VINCI DIAMONDS AT BLUESQ.COM/GAMES H'CAP (DIV II) 6f (P)
5:15 (5:15) (Class 6) (0-60,60) 3-Y-O+ **£1,617** (£481; £240; £120) **Stalls** Low

Form RPR
5004 **1** **Force To Spend**[4] 7760 4-8-7 **46** DavidProbert 7 54
(Des Donovan) *hld up but in tch: rdn and gd prog fr 2f out: r.o strly fnl f: led nring fin* **10/1**
4360 **2** *hd* **Liberal Lady**[39] 7332 3-9-4 **57** (e[1]) JamieGoldstein 4 64
(Ralph Smith) *led: rdn wl over 1f out: kpt on but no ex whn ct nring fin* **25/1**
0600 **3** *2* **A Pocketful Of Rye (IRE)**[297] 662 4-8-7 **45** MichaelStainton 3 47
(Paul Howling) *s.i.s: sn in tch: rdn 2f out: kpt on ins fnl f* **33/1**
-066 **4** *hd* **First In Command (IRE)**[87] 6283 6-9-4 **57** (t) StephenCraine 5 57
(Daniel Mark Loughnane, Ire) *chsd ldrs: rdn over 2f out: kpt on same pce fnl f* **7/1**
5053 **5** *3/4* **Dualagi**[29] 7488 7-9-7 **60** LiamKeniry 8 58
(Martin Bosley) *hld up bhd: rdn over 2f out: styd on fnl f: nvr trbld ldrs* **12/1**
0022 **6** *2* **Amber Heights**[11] 7652 3-9-7 **60** RichardKingscote 2 52
(David Pinder) *trckd ldrs: rdn over 2f out: wknd fnl f* **2/1**[1]
4300 **7** *1/2* **Fault**[11] 7663 5-8-12 **56** AmyScott(5) 1 46
(Alastair Lidderdale) *w ldr: rdn over 2f out: wknd fnl f* **9/2**[3]
0621 **8** *3* **Glastonberry**[67] 6791 3-9-2 **58** SophieDoyle(3) 9 38
(Geoffrey Deacon) *trckd ldrs: rdn over 2f out: wknd jst over 1f out* **10/3**[2]
-600 **9** *11* **Lady Brookie**[20] 7567 3-9-2 **55** RobbieFitzpatrick 6 —
(Peter Grayson) *rrd bdly leaving stalls: a detached: nvr rcvrd* **66/1**

1m 12.81s (-0.29) **Going Correction** +0.05s/f (Slow) **9** Ran SP% **112.2**
Speed ratings (Par 101): **103,102,100,99,98 96,95,91,76**
toteswingers: 1&2: £16.80, 2&3: £38.20, 1&3: £33.70 CSF £213.82 CT £7641.75 TOTE £11.50: £3.10, £6.10, £6.30; EX 157.80 Trifecta £479.00 Part won. Pool £647.37 - 0.20 winning units..
Owner River Racing **Bred** Theresa Fitsall **Trained** Newmarket, Suffolk
■ Stewards' Enquiry : Jamie Goldstein five-day ban: excessive use of the whip (Jan 1-5)

FOCUS
There was a disputed lead and that set things up for a closer. The winning time was 0.65sec slower than that recorded by Peace Seeker in the first division. The winner is rated to last winter's mark.
Glastonberry Official explanation: jockey said filly hung badly left
Lady Brookie Official explanation: jockey said filly reared in stalls and was slowly away
T/Jkpt: £16,666.60 to a £1 stake. Pool: £35,211.27. 1.50 winning units. T/Plt: £51.70 to a £1 stake. Pool: £81,620.23. 1,150.38 winning units. T/Qpdt: £9.00 to a £1 stake. Pool: £6,269.68. 515.10 winning units. TM

7677 DEAUVILLE (R-H)
Friday, December 16
OFFICIAL GOING: Fibresand: standard

7813a PRIX SANDEDTKI (CONDITIONS) (2YO FILLIES) (FIBRESAND) 7f 110y
9:30 (12:00) 2-Y-O **£12,500** (£5,000; £3,750; £2,500; £1,250)

RPR
1 **La Haye**[66] 2-9-2 0 GregoryBenoist 2 —
(J-C Rouget, France) **1/2**[1]
2 *1 1/4* **Saphira (GER)** 2-8-9 0 EPedroza 5 —
(A Wohler, Germany) **24/1**
3 *nk* **Britney (FR)**[36] 2-9-2 0 (p) OlivierPeslier 6 —
(Mario Hofer, Germany) **13/2**[3]
4 *hd* **Marasia (FR)**[69] 2-9-2 0 AlexisBadel 9 —
(Mme M-C Naim, France) **14/1**
5 *2* **Marble Game (FR)** 2-8-9 0 ThierryThulliez 7 —
(E Libaud, France) **14/1**
6 *1 1/2* **Miss Carmie (FR)**[43] 2-9-2 0 ThierryJarnet 4 —
(Mlle S-V Tarrou, France) **58/10**[2]
7 *4 1/2* **Baltic Fizz (IRE)**[69] 6699 2-8-9 0 MartinHarley 3 —
(Mrs K Burke) *bkmarker fr s: rdn and u.p early in st: no ex: nvr a factor* **76/1**
8 *3 1/2* **Imagine This**[96] 2-8-13 0 StephaneBreux 8 —
(E J O'Neill, France) **80/1**
9 *18* **Imazagan (FR)**[58] 2-9-2 0 JohanVictoire 1 —
(C Baillet, France) **31/1**

1m 31.91s (91.91) **9** Ran SP% **117.7**
WIN (incl. 1 euro stake): 1.50. PLACES: 1.10, 4.30, 1.40. DF: 10.60. SF: 56.30.
Owner Gerard Augustin-Normand **Bred** E Puerari & Oceanic Bloodstock **Trained** Pau, France

7814a PRIX DE L'EPEE (CLAIMER) (2YO) (FIBRESAND) 6f 110y
10:00 (12:00) 2-Y-O **£8,620** (£3,448; £2,586; £1,724; £862)

RPR
1 **Souslecieldeparis (USA)**[9] 7666 2-8-13 0 GregoryBenoist 1 —
(Y Barberot, France) **43/10**[2]
2 *2* **Class Monitor**[21] 7539 2-8-13 0 MartinHarley 2 —
(Mrs K Burke) *towards rr fr s: gd prog early in st: r.o wl to join ldrs 1f out: r.o wl fnl f: no ch w wnr but clr 2nd* **13/1**
3 *2* **Elusive Storm (FR)** 2-8-8 0 RaphaelMarchelli 14 —
(F Rohaut, France) **26/1**
4 *1 1/2* **Ma Victoryan (FR)** 2-8-8 0 AurelienLemaitre 7 —
(C Baillet, France) **31/1**
5 *nk* **Misedargent (FR)**[49] 7155 2-8-8 0 MickaelForest 12 —
(C Boutin, France) **31/1**
6 *snk* **Blanzac (FR)**[108] 2-8-6 0 MathieuTavaresDaSilva(5) 11 —
(T Lemer, France) **6/1**[3]
7 *hd* **Boulba D'Alben (FR)**[36] 2-8-8 0 FabriceVeron 9 —
(H-A Pantall, France) **15/1**
8 *1/2* **Yun (FR)** 2-9-1 0 (p) JohanVictoire 4 —
(C Baillet, France) **10/1**
9 *2 1/2* **Stronger (FR)**[36] 2-8-11 0 ThierryThulliez 13 —
(N Clement, France) **3/1**[1]
10 *hd* **Blues Dream (FR)** 2-8-8 0 (b) JeromeCabre 5 —
(E Danel, France) **27/1**
0 **Khanbaligh (FR)**[59] 2-8-3 0 (p) MarcLerner(5) 15 —
(C Lerner, France) **30/1**
0 **Finisterien (IRE)**[36] 2-8-11 0 FranckBlondel 6 —
(J-V Toux, France) **28/1**
0 **Farasha (FR)**[79] 2-8-8 0 SebastienMaillot 3 —
(M Boutin, France) **22/1**
0 **Dancinginmydreams (IRE)**[63] 2-8-8 0 (b) AlexisBadel 8 —
(U Suter, France) **9/1**
0 **Countrystar (FR)**[9] 7666 2-8-7 0 (p) SoufyaneMoulin(8) 10 —
(C Boutin, France) **69/1**
0 **Zen In Love (FR)**[63] 2-8-8 0 AlexandreChampenois(3) 16 —
(Mme J Bidgood, France) **81/1**

1m 20.6s (80.60) **16** Ran SP% **117.8**
WIN (incl. 1 euro stake): 5.30. PLACES: 2.40, 4.70, 7.80. DF: 33.10. SF: 53.70.
Owner Gerard Augustin-Normand **Bred** Pontchartrain Stud **Trained** France

7815 - (Foreign Racing) - See Raceform Interactive

7783 WOLVERHAMPTON (A.W) (L-H)
Monday, December 19
OFFICIAL GOING: Standard
Wind: Light across Weather: Light rain

7816 TOTEPLACEPOT AMATEUR RIDERS' H'CAP (DIV I) 1m 1f 103y(P)
1:50 (1:51) (Class 5) (0-70,70) 3-Y-O+ **£2,183** (£677; £338; £169) **Stalls** Low

Form RPR
5011 **1** **Maven**[10] 7698 3-10-7 **70** MrWEasterby(5) 10 75+
(Tim Easterby) *led after 1f: mde rest: rdn out* **9/4**[1]
1140 **2** *1* **John Potts**[31] 7465 6-11-0 **70** MissSBrotherton 7 73
(Brian Baugh) *hld up in tch: racd keenly: rdn over 1f out: styd on* **6/1**[3]
0045 **3** *1/2* **Kiss A Prince**[12] 7661 5-10-5 **68** MissECrossman(7) 13 70
(Dean Ivory) *hld up: hdwy over 3f out: rdn over 1f out: swtchd lft: r.o* **8/1**
4004 **4** *nk* **Carlton Scroop (FR)**[20] 7573 8-9-9 **56** oh1 (b) MissMBryant(5) 9 57
(Paddy Butler) *a.p: chsd wnr over 5f out tl rdn over 1f out: styd on* **40/1**
0563 **5** *nse* **Vitznau (IRE)**[4] 7771 7-10-6 **65** MissPernillaHermansson(3) 3 66
(Alastair Lidderdale) *hld up: hdwy over 2f out: shkn up over 1f out: edgd lft: styd on* **9/2**[2]
4115 **6** *1 1/4* **James Pollard (IRE)**[37] 6461 6-10-10 **69** (t) MrJWilliams(3) 12 68
(Bernard Llewellyn) *hld up: hdwy over 2f out: rdn over 1f out: nt trble ldrs* **16/1**
2600 **7** *1 3/4* **Moody Tunes**[47] 7236 8-10-2 **65** MissALMurphy(7) 2 60
(Tom Dascombe) *led 1f: chsd wnr tl over 5f out: remained handy: rdn over 1f out: one pce fnl f* **12/1**
3303 **8** *1 1/2* **Entrance**[2] 7800 3-9-8 **57** MissSBirkett(5) 5 49
(Julia Feilden) *hld up: styd on ins fnl f: nvr nrr* **11/1**
4260 **9** *3/4* **Maz**[54] 7112 3-9-10 **61** MissAlexOwen(7) 11 51
(Alan Bailey) *chsd ldrs: lost pl over 4f out: hdwy over 1f out: no ex fnl f* **14/1**
5666 **10** *1* **Carcinetto (IRE)**[17] 7604 9-9-13 **62** MissMLEvans(7) 6 50
(David Evans) *hld up: pushed along over 2f out: n.d* **25/1**

2m 3.31s (1.61) **Going Correction** +0.10s/f (Slow)
WFA 3 from 4yo+ 2lb **10** Ran SP% **109.2**
Speed ratings (Par 103): **96,95,94,94,94 93,91,90,89,88**
toteswingers:1&2:£3.20, 2&3:£8.70, 1&3:£6.50 CSF £13.96 CT £80.07 TOTE £2.70: £1.30, £2.50, £2.60; EX 16.20 Trifecta £125.20 Part won. Pool: £169.29 - 0.92 winning units..
Owner Habton Farms **Bred** Habton Farms **Trained** Great Habton, N Yorks

FOCUS
The time was 0.71 seconds slower than the second division, and Maven was allowed an uncontested lead, so those held up were at a disadvantage.

7817 TOTEPLACEPOT AMATEUR RIDERS' H'CAP (DIV II) 1m 1f 103y(P)
2:20 (2:23) (Class 5) (0-70,69) 3-Y-O+ **£2,183** (£677; £338; £169) **Stalls** Low

Form RPR
6411 **1** **Archie Rice (USA)**[7] 7734 5-11-0 **69** MrSWalker 8 77
(Tom Keddy) *hld up: hdwy 1/2-way: led over 1f out: rdn out* **10/11**[1]
-041 **2** *1* **Northern Spy (USA)**[180] 3293 7-10-3 **63** MrJCoffill-Brown(5) 7 69
(Simon Dow) *hld up: hdwy over 2f out: rdn over 1f out: styd on* **20/1**
5006 **3** *1/2* **Merrjanah**[17] 7610 3-9-5 **55** MrAFrench(7) 4 60
(John Wainwright) *hld up: hdwy over 2f out: styd on* **100/1**
0452 **4** *3/4* **Strike Force**[5] 7761 7-10-11 **69** (t) MissALHutchinson(3) 2 72+
(Clifford Lines) *chsd ldrs: lost pl over 3f out: swtchd rt over 2f out: hdwy over 1f out: styd on* **11/2**[2]
0330 **5** *1* **Turjuman (USA)**[9] 7720 6-9-12 **60** (p) MissAlexOwen(7) 6 61
(Alan Bailey) *hld up: r.o ins fnl f: nt rch ldrs* **25/1**
1215 **6** *4 1/2* **Royal Box**[83] 6436 4-10-0 **62** MissSLewis(7) 9 54
(Dai Burchell) *chsd ldr tl led over 3f out: hdd over 1f out: wknd ins fnl f* **28/1**

3012 **7** 3/4 **Taste The Wine (IRE)**[22] 7263 5-10-6 **64**................ MrRJWilliams(3) 11 54
(Bernard Llewellyn) *hld up: hdwy over 2f out: rdn over 1f out: wknd fnl f* **25/1**

3300 **8** *hd* **Ibiza Sunset (IRE)**[61] 6944 3-10-3 **67**...................... MissSKerswell(7) 12 57
(Brendan Powell) *s.i.s: hdwy over 5f out: rdn over 1f out: wknd ins fnl f* **18/1**

0006 **9** 1 1/2 **Whodathought (IRE)**[23] 7557 3-10-3 **67**..............(b) MissBHampson(7) 5 54
(Paul Rich) *trckd ldrs: racd keenly: nt clr run over 2f out: wknd over 1f out* **40/1**

3052 **10** 3/4 **Nolecce**[59] 6990 4-10-6 **68**..(p) MrsAGuest(7) 13 53
(Richard Guest) *s.i.s: hld up: nvr on terms* **14/1**

3110 **11** 2 **Royal Alcor (IRE)**[12] 7661 4-10-9 **64**..........................(b) MissZoeLilly 10 45
(Alastair Lidderdale) *prom: edgd lft over 2f out: rdn over 1f out: wknd fnl f* **6/1**[3]

0504 **12** 9 **Aviso (GER)**[11] 7632 7-10-3 **58**... MissEJJones 1 20
(David Evans) *led 6f: sn rdn: hmpd and wknd over 2f out* **33/1**

5514 **13** 12 **Valdan (IRE)**[12] 7654 7-10-0 **55**.. MrsEEvans 3 —
(David Evans) *hld up: rdn and wknd over 3f out: t.o* **20/1**

2m 2.60s (0.90) **Going Correction** +0.10s/f (Slow)
WFA 3 from 4yo+ 2lb **13** Ran SP% **121.0**
Speed ratings (Par 103): **100,99,98,98,97 93,92,92,90,90 88,80,69**
CSF £28.10 CT £1207.52 TOTE £1.90: £1.10, £4.40, £17.50; EX 24.30 Trifecta £263.90 Part won. Pool: £356.69 - 0.65 winning units..
Owner Andrew Duffield **Bred** Baltusrol Thoughbreds Llc Et Al **Trained** Newmarket, Suffolk

FOCUS
The time was 0.71 seconds faster than the first division.

7818 WOLVERHAMPTON-RACECOURSE.CO.UK (S) STKS 1m 4f 50y(P)
2:50 (2:50) (Class 6) 3-Y-O+ £1,704 (£503; £251) Stalls Low

Form RPR

000 **1** **Ahlawy (IRE)**[17] 7605 8-9-8 60.................................(t) RobbieFitzpatrick 3 66
(Frank Sheridan) *hld up: pushed along over 3f out: hdwy over 1f out: rdn to ld wl ins fnl f: r.o* **40/1**

4434 **2** 1 1/4 **Maslak (IRE)**[13] 7645 7-9-4 56.. ChrisCatlin 4 60
(Peter Hiatt) *led 3f: chsd ldr tl led again 2f out: sn rdn: hdd wl ins fnl f* **15/2**[2]

3424 **3** 1 1/2 **Dew Reward (IRE)**[98] 6004 3-9-3 58.................................. AdamKirby 2 62
(Bill Turner) *chsd ldrs: rdn over 2f out: styd on same pce ins fnl f* **20/1**

5-12 **4** 1/2 **Priors Gold**[21] 7570 4-9-8 78.. LiamKeniry 5 61
(Gordon Elliott, Ire) *hld up: hdwy 1/2-way: rdn over 1f out: sn hung lft: styd on same pce fnl f* **1/5**[1]

-060 **5** 1/2 **Herschel (IRE)**[53] 5857 5-9-4 66.. AmirQuinn 6 56
(Gary Moore) *s.i.s: sn chsng ldr: led 9f out: rdn and hdd 2f out: hung lft and no ex fnl f* **16/1**[3]

2m 43.92s (2.82) **Going Correction** +0.10s/f (Slow)
WFA 3 from 4yo+ 5lb **5** Ran SP% **108.2**
Speed ratings (Par 101): **94,93,92,91,91**
CSF £262.62 TOTE £26.90: £15.20, £2.20; EX 75.30.There was no bid for the winner. Priors Gold was claimed by O Pears for £6000.
Owner Frank Sheridan **Bred** Castlemartin Stud And Skymarc Farm **Trained** Wolverhampton, W Midlands

FOCUS
The odds-on favourite underperformed and this was just a moderate seller.
Priors Gold Official explanation: jockey said gelding hung left

7819 TOTEQUADPOT H'CAP 5f 216y(P)
3:20 (3:22) (Class 5) (0-70,70) 3-Y-O+ £2,264 (£673; £336; £168) Stalls Low

Form RPR

0333 **1** **Caldercruix (USA)**[14] 7637 4-8-12 **70**......................(v) RaulDaSilva(7) 11 82
(James Evans) *led early: remained handy: chsd ldr over 3f out: led over 2f out: rdn over 1f out: edgd lft ins fnl f: r.o* **6/1**[3]

6124 **2** 1 3/4 **Silver Wind**[9] 7715 6-9-0 **65**...................................(b) ShaneKelly 2 71
(Alan McCabe) *a.p: rdn to chse wnr fnl f: sn hung lft: styd on* **7/2**[1]

6055 **3** 2 **Downhill Skier (IRE)**[9] 7716 7-8-8 **66**........................... JackDuern(7) 8 66
(Mark Brisbourne) *mid-div: hdwy over 2f out: rdn over 1f out: styd on* **16/1**

6043 **4** 1 1/4 **Loyal Royal (IRE)**[26] 7519 8-9-2 **67**.....................(bt) RichardKingscote 5 63
(Milton Bradley) *s.i.s: hld up: hdwy over 1f out: r.o: nt rch ldrs* **8/1**

2130 **5** 3/4 **Trojan Rocket (IRE)**[9] 7715 3-9-1 **66**........................... DavidProbert 9 59
(George Prodromou) *hld up: hdwy over 1f out: sn rdn: styd on same pce fnl f* **5/1**[2]

100 **6** 3/4 **Polemica (IRE)**[18] 7596 5-9-1 **66**.........................(bt) RobbieFitzpatrick 6 57
(Frank Sheridan) *led 5f out: rdn and hdd over 2f out: wknd ins fnl f* **33/1**

041 **7** 1 3/4 **Qubuh (IRE)**[39] 7349 3-9-2 **67**.. TomEaves 13 52
(Linda Stubbs) *chsd ldrs: rdn over 1f out: wknd fnl f* **9/1**

0054 **8** *nk* **Johnstown Lad (IRE)**[58] 7039 7-9-5 **70**.....................(bt) StephenCraine 4 54
(Daniel Mark Loughnane, Ire) *hld up: nt clr run over 2f out: rdn over 1f out: nvr trbld ldrs* **10/1**

/0-0 **9** *nk* **Wishbone (IRE)**[33] 7428 4-9-4 **69**..................................... TonyCulhane 3 52
(Jo Hughes) *s.i.s: hld up: n.d* **66/1**

0040 **10** 2 3/4 **Lucky Dan (IRE)**[18] 7595 5-9-5 **70**............................... FrannyNorton 12 44
(Paul Green) *prom: racd keenly: rdn over 2f out: wknd over 1f out* **12/1**

4033 **11** 2 1/4 **Riflessione**[6] 7744 5-9-1 **66**.......................................(v) LukeMorris 10 33
(Ronald Harris) *sn pushed along in rr: nvr on terms* **5/1**[2]

4000 **12** 2 **Spin Again (IRE)**[16] 7625 6-9-2 **67**...................................... AdamKirby 1 28
(Mark Wellings) *sn pushed along to ld: hdd 5f out: rdn over 2f out: wknd over 1f out* **25/1**

1m 14.74s (-0.26) **Going Correction** +0.10s/f (Slow) **12** Ran SP% **121.9**
Speed ratings (Par 103): **105,102,100,98,97 96,94,93,93,89 86,83**
toteswingers:1&2:£4.90, 2&3:£15.40, 1&3:£22.90 CSF £27.70 CT £334.87 TOTE £7.80: £2.70, £1.80, £4.90; EX 34.50 Trifecta £392.30 Part won. Pool £530.26 - 0.63 winning units..
Owner David Mantle **Bred** Bjorn Nielsen **Trained** Broadwas, Worcs

FOCUS
A modest sprint handicap in which it proved difficult to make up significant ground.
Riflessione Official explanation: jockey said gelding hung right
Spin Again(IRE) Official explanation: jockey said gelding had no more to give

7820 DINE IN THE HORIZONS RESTAURANT H'CAP 7f 32y(P)
3:50 (3:50) (Class 6) (0-60,60) 3-Y-O+ £1,704 (£503; £251) Stalls High

Form RPR

0306 **1** **Fleetwoodsands (IRE)**[10] 7696 4-9-3 **60**..........................(t) LiamKeniry 2 71
(Milton Bradley) *hld up: hdwy over 2f out: led 1f out: r.o wl* **9/2**[2]

0044 **2** 2 **Anjomarba (IRE)**[10] 7695 4-8-12 **60**............................(p) DavidKenny(5) 7 66
(Conor Dore) *a.p: rdn over 1f out: styd on* **7/1**[3]

0000 **3** 3 1/2 **Fantasy Fry**[18] 7591 3-9-3 **60**...................................(t) RichardKingscote 4 56
(Tom Dascombe) *led early: chsd ldr: rdn over 2f out: ev ch 1f out: no ex ins fnl f* **14/1**

6002 **4** 2 1/4 **This Ones For Eddy**[6] 7748 6-9-2 **59**.................................. MartinLane 5 49
(John Balding) *mid-div: drvn along 1/2-way: nvr trbld ldrs* **3/1**[1]

4000 **5** 3/4 **Katmai River (IRE)**[9] 7715 4-9-2 **59**...............................(v) SteveDrowne 9 47
(Mark Usher) *s.i.s: sn pushed along in rr: rdn 3f out: nvr on terms* **3/1**[1]

-403 **6** *nk* **Cerejeira (IRE)**[19] 7585 3-9-2 **59**.......................................(b) ShaneKelly 1 46
(Eric Alston) *sn led: clr over 2f out: hdd & wknd 1f out* **16/1**

6100 **7** 1/2 **Emeralds Spirit (IRE)**[37] 7399 4-9-0 **57**............................. TomEaves 6 43
(John Weymes) *s.i.s: hdwy over 5f out: rdn over 2f out: wknd over 1f out* **16/1**

0260 **8** 2 1/4 **Misere**[13] 7648 3-8-12 **58**...(t) AmyRyan(3) 10 38
(Kevin Ryan) *sn pushed along and a in rr* **22/1**

0000 **9** *hd* **Bertie Blu Boy**[9] 7716 3-9-2 **59**.............................(v[1]) LukeMorris 8 38
(Paul Green) *s.i.s: hld up: hdwy over 5f out: rdn over 2f out: hung lft and wknd over 1f out* **10/1**

4000 **10** 2 1/2 **Mac Tiernan (IRE)**[18] 7591 4-9-1 **58**................................... AdamKirby 11 31
(Pat Murphy) *hld up: a in rr* **25/1**

1m 29.48s (-0.12) **Going Correction** +0.10s/f (Slow) **10** Ran SP% **116.4**
Speed ratings (Par 101): **104,101,97,95,94 93,93,90,90,87**
toteswingers:1&2:£6.80, 2&3:£13.80, 1&3:£14.40 CSF £36.02 CT £409.44 TOTE £5.90: £1.70, £2.30, £5.10; EX 39.70 TRIFECTA Not won..
Owner E R Griffiths **Bred** Gary O'Reilly **Trained** Sedbury, Gloucs

FOCUS
A modest handicap run at a good pace.
Katmai River(IRE) Official explanation: jockey said gelding never travelled

7821 TOTEEXACTA CLAIMING STKS 1m 141y(P)
4:20 (4:21) (Class 6) 2-Y-O £1,704 (£503; £251) Stalls Low

Form RPR

5053 **1** **Complex**[18] 7590 2-8-0 53.. LukeMorris 1 50
(David Evans) *chsd ldr: rdn to ld over 1f out: r.o* **16/1**

3412 **2** *nk* **Let Your Love Flow (IRE)**[9] 7718 2-8-4 68................ SophieDoyle(3) 4 56
(Sylvester Kirk) *trckd ldrs: rdn and ev ch ins fnl f: r.o* **5/6**[1]

0005 **3** 2 1/2 **Meet Joe Black (IRE)**[10] 7697 2-8-5 41............................ MartinLane 3 49
(David Evans) *prom: pushed along over 5f out: rdn over 1f out: styd on same pce ins fnl f* **66/1**

4234 **4** *shd* **La Romantique (IRE)**[5] 7752 2-8-10 67.............................. ChrisCatlin 2 54
(Marco Botti) *chsd ldrs: rdn and bmpd over 1f out: hung lft ins fnl f: styd on same pce* **2/1**[2]

00 **5** 1 1/4 **Lone Star State (IRE)**[9] 7718 2-9-5 0...................... RussKennemore 7 60
(Frank Sheridan) *hld up in tch: rdn over 2f out: no ex ins fnl f* **40/1**

6 3/4 **Redclue (IRE)** 2-8-13 0.. AndreaAtzeni 9 53
(Marco Botti) *s.i.s: outpcd: styd on ins fnl f: nvr nrr* **7/1**[3]

0 **7** 1 **Dr Albert**[9] 7718 2-9-5 0.. RobbieFitzpatrick 6 57
(Frank Sheridan) *hld up: rdn over 2f out: n.d* **66/1**

4464 **8** 1 **Jaci Uzzi (IRE)**[21] 7568 2-7-7 49................................(v) KevinLundie(7) 8 36
(David Evans) *sn led: rdn: edgd rt and hdd over 1f out: wkng whn hmpd ins fnl f* **25/1**

9 21 **Danafisiak (IRE)** 2-9-5 0.. LiamKeniry 5 10
(Frank Sheridan) *prom: stdd and lost pl after 1f: rdn 3f out: wknd over 2f out* **25/1**

1m 51.59s (1.09) **Going Correction** +0.10s/f (Slow) **9** Ran SP% **119.4**
Speed ratings (Par 94): **99,98,96,96,95 94,93,92,74**
toteswingers:1&2:£3.60, 2&3:£17.10, 1&3:£22.20 CSF £30.67 TOTE £15.30: £2.80, £1.10, £6.50; EX 56.50 Trifecta £516.00 Pool: £767.05 - 1.10 winning units..
Owner S Michael & A Stennett **Bred** Mickley Stud **Trained** Pandy, Monmouths
■ Stewards' Enquiry : Sophie Doyle 15-day ban: used whip with excessive frequency (Jan 2-16) 3rd offence in 12mths

FOCUS
It's hard to know the exact worth of the form as Complex had 7lb to find with Let Your Love Flow, yet had 17lb in hand of Meet Joe Black, but clearly it was just a moderate contest.

NOTEBOOK
Complex had been beaten in sellers on her last two outings, but she showed a good attitude to gain her first win on her seventh start. (op 20-1)
Let Your Love Flow(IRE) didn't run to her official mark of 68, but she was caught wide for some of the way and was pushed out even further by a wandering rival around the final turn. (op 10-11 tchd Evens)
Meet Joe Black(IRE), a stablemate of the winner, seemed to run a bit above his mark.
La Romantique(IRE) seemed to travel well but she found disappointingly little for pressure. She was a bit tight for room around the final bend and was another pushed wide, but she basically didn't pick up sufficiently. (op 15-8)
Redclue(IRE), an already gelded 15,000gns purchase, had been due to contest a seller in blinkers recently. He looked pretty limited on this racecourse debut, needing early pressure after missing the break, although he did plug on and should have learnt from the experience. Official explanation: jockey said gelding was slow away

7822 STAY AT THE WOLVERHAMPTON HOLIDAY INN MAIDEN STKS 1m 141y(P)
4:50 (4:50) (Class 5) 3-Y-O+ £2,264 (£673; £336; £168) Stalls Low

Form RPR

1 **Ariyfa (IRE)**[45] 7279 3-8-12 0.. AdamKirby 7 70+
(Noel Quinlan) *chsd ldr tl led over 2f out: rdn out* **4/7**[1]

0325 **2** 4 1/2 **Peponi**[14] 7637 5-9-5 75... SteveDrowne 8 65
(Peter Makin) *led 6f: no ex fnl f* **7/4**[2]

0300 **3** 5 **Wing N Prayer (IRE)**[81] 6494 4-9-0 46............................ PaddyAspell 1 48
(John Wainwright) *prom: rdn over 2f out: wnt 3rd fnl f: no ch w front pair* **40/1**

0-00 **4** 1 3/4 **Ponte Di Rosa**[224] 1949 3-8-12 60.................................... LukeMorris 5 44
(Michael Appleby) *chsd ldrs: rdn over 3f out: wknd over 1f out* **33/1**

30 **5** *nk* **Chasin' Rainbows**[32] 7443 3-8-12 0.................................. LiamKeniry 4 43
(Sylvester Kirk) *mid-div: rdn 3f out: sn outpcd* **16/1**[3]

0000 **6** *shd* **Northern Genes (AUS)**[12] 6844 5-8-12 42...............(be[1]) JackDuern(7) 2 48
(Michael Appleby) *chsd ldrs: rdn over 3f out: wknd over 1f out* **66/1**

05 **7** 1 3/4 **Fortunelini**[9] 7717 6-9-0 0.. RussKennemore 9 39
(Frank Sheridan) *hld up: racd keenly: nvr nr to chal* **16/1**[3]

0 **8** 13 **Dubonny**[9] 7717 4-9-0 0.......................................(t) RobbieFitzpatrick 3 —
(Frank Sheridan) *hld up: a in rr: rdn and wknd over 2f out* **33/1**

9 1 3/4 **Asleep In Penn**[16] 3-9-3 0.. TomEaves 6 —
(Peter Niven) *dwlt: hld up: a in rr: wknd over 2f out* **33/1**

1m 50.85s (0.35) **Going Correction** +0.10s/f (Slow)
WFA 3 from 4yo+ 2lb **9** Ran SP% **124.5**
Speed ratings (Par 103): **102,98,93,92,91 91,90,78,76**
toteswingers:1&2:£1.10, 2&3:£11.90, 1&3:£11.30 CSF £1.92 TOTE £1.50: £1.02, £1.40, £10.10; EX 2.00 Trifecta £26.90 Pool: £1079.67 - 29.68 winning units..
Owner Tommy Cummins **Bred** His Highness The Aga Khan's Studs S C **Trained** Newmarket, Suffolk

FOCUS
The time was 1.65 seconds slower than the following Class 5 handicap.

7823 TOTETRIFECTA H'CAP 1m 141y(P)
5:20 (5:21) (Class 5) (0-75,74) 3-Y-O+ £2,264 (£673; £336; £168) Stalls Low

Form RPR
3312 1 **Aerodynamic (IRE)**[24] 7537 4-9-5 72 PaddyAspell 9 81+
(Michael Easterby) *trckd ldrs: led over 1f out: rdn out* 9/4[1]
6340 2 ½ **Dazzling Valentine**[20] 7577 3-9-0 72 DominicFox(3) 11 80
(Alan Bailey) *hld up: pushed along over 3f out: rdn to chse wnr fnl f: styd on* 16/1
1302 3 2 **Knowe Head (NZ)**[17] 7604 4-9-0 67 (p) AndreaAtzeni 5 70+
(James Unett) *a.p: rdn over 2f out: styd on* 4/1[2]
0623 4 ½ **I Confess**[16] 7625 6-9-6 73 (b) AndrewMullen 4 75
(Geoffrey Harker) *led 1f: hmpd 7f out: chsd ldrs: rdn over 2f out: styd on same pce fnl f* 20/1
4134 5 ¾ **Saharia (IRE)**[17] 7605 4-9-2 69 (v) ShaneKelly 3 70
(Michael Attwater) *s.i.s: hld up: hdwy over 1f out: rdn and hung lft ins fnl f: no ex* 8/1[3]
0210 6 1½ **Sweet Secret**[14] 7637 4-8-12 72 (b) RaulDaSilva(7) 13 70
(Jeremy Gask) *chsd ldrs: led over 5f out: rdn and hdd over 1f out: eased whn btn ins fnl f* 20/1
0622 7 1½ **Hereford Boy**[14] 7637 7-9-6 73 (p) AdamKirby 1 67
(Dean Ivory) *hld up: rdn over 1f out: nvr trbld ldrs* 8/1[3]
0122 8 ¾ **Spinning Ridge (IRE)**[17] 7605 6-9-4 71 (v) LukeMorris 7 63
(Ronald Harris) *hld up: hdwy over 2f out: rdn over 1f out: wknd ins fnl f* 14/1
4302 9 8 **Triple Eight (IRE)**[16] 7625 3-9-2 74 (p) MichaelO'Connell(3) 8 48
(Philip Kirby) *chsd ldrs: hmpd 7f out: rdn over 2f out: wknd fnl f* 12/1
10 2½ **Lisselan Pleasure (USA)**[102] 4-9-2 69 MartinLane 12 37
(Bernard Llewellyn) *hld up: rdn over 2f out: n.d* 66/1
2532 11 13 **Burning Stone (USA)**[9] 7716 4-9-3 70 (b[1]) StevieDonohoe 10 —
(Gay Kelleway) *led over 7f out: hdd over 5f out: rdn and wknd over 2f out* 9/1

1m 49.2s (-1.30) **Going Correction** +0.10s/f (Slow)
WFA 3 from 4yo+ 2lb 11 Ran SP% **114.2**
Speed ratings (Par 103): **109,108,106,106,105 104,103,102,95,93 81**
toteswingers:1&2:£14.70, 2&3:£15.10, 1&3:£3.50 CSF £39.25 CT £139.93 TOTE £4.00: £1.80, £3.10, £1.70; EX 61.70 Trifecta £419.70 Part won. Pool: £567.18 - 0.20 winning units..
Owner M W Easterby **Bred** Swettenham, Carradale, S Cosgrove & T Stack **Trained** Sheriff Hutton, N Yorks
■ Stewards' Enquiry : Raul Da Silva two-day ban: careless riding (Jan 2-3)

FOCUS
The lead was contested and the pace looked strong.
T/Plt: £354.30 to a £1 stake. Pool of £71,673.04 - 147.64 winning tickets. T/Qpdt: £93.60 to a £1 stake. Pool of £4,896.55 - 38.70 winning tickets. CR

7805 KEMPTON (A.W) (R-H)
Tuesday, December 20

OFFICIAL GOING: Standard
Wind: Fresh, half against Weather: Cloudy

7829 DOWNLOAD THE BLUE SQUARE BET APP MEDIAN AUCTION MAIDEN STKS 5f (P)
1:40 (1:40) (Class 6) 3-5-Y-O £1,617 (£481; £240; £120) Stalls Low

Form RPR
3224 1 **Cliffords Reprieve**[13] 7649 3-9-3 57 (b[1]) SebSanders 2 66
(Eric Wheeler) *pressed ldr: led 2f out: sn rdn 3 l clr: in n.d fnl f* 4/7[1]
4305 2 3½ **Lisselton Cross**[11] 7693 3-9-3 52 (v[1]) LukeMorris 3 53
(Martin Bosley) *chsd ldng pair: rdn and nt qckn 2f out: wnt 2nd over 1f out: one pce and no imp on wnr* 6/1[2]
3034 3 1¼ **Lovat Lane**[13] 7652 3-8-12 48 (v[1]) ChrisCatlin 7 44
(Eve Johnson Houghton) *chsd ldng pair: rdn and nt qckn 2f out: kpt on to take 3rd jst ins fnl f* 7/1[3]
0-60 4 2 **Striking Willow**[6] 7755 3-9-3 44 (b[1]) JamesMillman 5 42
(Rod Millman) *chsd ldng quartet: pushed along 1/2-way: outpcd 2f out: plugged on to snatch 4th last strides* 25/1
5000 5 nk **Una Vita Pius (IRE)**[11] 7693 3-8-13 45 ow1 IanMongan 1 37
(Patrick Gilligan) *rousted along to ld: hdd 2f out: wknd over 1f out* 25/1
0600 6 2 **Cara Carmela**[11] 7693 3-8-9 43 RyanClark(3) 9 28
(Stuart Williams) *racd wd in midfield: outpcd and rdn 2f out: no prog after* 12/1
7 1¾ **Fancourt** 3-8-12 0 WilliamCarson 6 22
(William Muir) *settled in last trio: pushed along and outpcd 2f out: nvr on terms after* 7/1[3]
60 8 3 **Sid**[6] 7750 3-9-3 0 JamieGoldstein 8 16
(Zoe Davison) *dwlt: hld up in last trio: rdn and no prog 2f out: wknd fnl f* 66/1
0600 9 10 **Stoneacre Joe Joe**[11] 7693 3-9-3 35 RobbieFitzpatrick 4 —
(Peter Grayson) *s.i.s: a in last trio: wknd 1/2-way: t.o* 66/1

60.17 secs (-0.33) **Going Correction** -0.075s/f (Stan) 9 Ran SP% **121.3**
Speed ratings (Par 101): **99,93,91,88,87 84,81,76,60**
Tote Swingers: 1&2 £2.30, 1&3 £1.70, 2&3 £2.80 CSF £4.80 TOTE £1.60: £1.10, £1.70, £2.10; EX 4.00 Trifecta £12.90 Pool: £401.42 - 23.00 winning units..
Owner G W Witheford **Bred** D R Tucker **Trained** Whitchurch-on-Thames, Oxon

FOCUS
An extremely moderate sprint maiden.

7830 WIN THOUSANDS OF SPORTS EXPERIENCES AT BLUESQ.COM NURSERY 5f (P)
2:10 (2:10) (Class 6) (0-65,63) 2-Y-O £1,617 (£481; £240; £120) Stalls Low

Form RPR
3012 1 **Russian Bullet**[5] 7770 2-8-9 54 SophieDoyle(3) 4 61+
(Jamie Osborne) *w.w in 7th: cajoled along over 1f out and hanging rt: r.o wl fnl f to ld last 50yds: cleverly* 13/8[1]
525 2 ½ **Littlesuzie**[24] 7555 2-9-0 63 NicoleNordblad(7) 6 68
(Hans Adielsson) *led: pushed more than a l clr jst ins fnl f: styd on but collared last 50yds* 10/1
2503 3 1¾ **Marie's Fantasy**[12] 7670 2-8-13 55 JamieGoldstein 2 54
(Zoe Davison) *trckd ldrs in 6th on inner: shkn up wl over 1f out: styd on fnl f to take 3rd last strides* 16/1
5330 4 ½ **Art Show**[18] 7597 2-9-6 62 JimmyFortune 1 59
(Ed Dunlop) *s.i.s and forfeited gd draw: hld up in last pair: eased off rail over 1f out: only 8th ent fnl f: shkn up and r.o to take 4th last strides: no ch* 8/1[3]
0063 5 ¾ **Copper Falls**[26] 7530 2-9-0 56 HayleyTurner 9 50
(Brendan Powell) *chsd ldr: rdn and no imp over 1f: lost 2nd and wknd ins fnl f* 8/1[3]
0604 6 shd **Justbookies Dotnet**[11] 7692 2-9-4 60 (v[1]) ChrisCatlin 3 54
(Louise Best) *too fierce hold: disp 3rd: shkn up and fnd nil wl over 1f out: fdd* 14/1
0000 7 1½ **Lana Mae**[19] 7592 2-8-4 53 RaulDaSilva(7) 7 42
(Jeremy Gask) *mostly in last trio: shkn up over 2f out: nvr on terms* 40/1
055 8 1½ **Cincinnati Kit**[20] 7583 2-9-4 60 (t) WilliamCarson 5 43
(Stuart Williams) *disp 3rd: drvn 1/2-way: wknd wl over 1f out* 11/1
0646 9 1½ **Illustrious Lad (IRE)**[18] 7597 2-9-2 58 TomQueally 10 36
(Jim Boyle) *forced to r wd fr worst draw: mostly chsd ldng pair to wl over 1f out: wknd* 4/1[2]
0000 10 2½ **Castalian Spring (IRE)**[11] 7692 2-8-6 48 AndreaAtzeni 8 17
(Robert Eddery) *s.s: a in last pair: nvr a factor* 100/1

60.18 secs (-0.32) **Going Correction** -0.075s/f (Stan) 10 Ran SP% **113.7**
Speed ratings (Par 94): **99,98,95,94,93 93,90,88,86,82**
Tote Swingers: 1&2 £4.30, 1&3 £6.10, 2&3 £17.60 CSF £18.72 CT £190.88 TOTE £3.10: £1.50, £3.00, £4.90; EX 17.60 TRIFECTA Not won..
Owner Martyn and Elaine Booth **Bred** Cranford Bloodstock Uk Ltd **Trained** Upper Lambourn, Berks

FOCUS
Just a moderate nursery.

NOTEBOOK
Russian Bullet threatened to throw this away by hanging right under pressure, so full marks to Sophie Doyle for straightening the gelding up in sufficient time. The winner is seemingly not straightforward, but he's progressing well at this lowly level and was defying a mark 4lb higher than when successful at Wolverhampton two starts previously. (op 2-1 tchd 6-4)
Littlesuzie showed plenty of pace on this handicap debut and should be up to winning a similar race. (op 16-1)
Marie's Fantasy again shaped as though she may get another furlong. (op 14-1)
Art Show, who didn't seem to handle the bends at Lingfield last time (it was reported by her rider that she didn't turn), didn't help herself here, missing the break and then racing keenly. As a consequence she was left with enough to do and she failed to match the winner's late burst. Jimmy Fortune reported the filly did not handle the bend. Official explanation: jockey said filly did not handle the bend (op 7-1 tchd 13-2)
Illustrious Lad(IRE) had a tough trip from the widest draw and can be excused. (op 5-1 tchd 11-2)

7831 BET AND WATCH AT BLUESQ.COM H'CAP 1m 2f (P)
2:45 (2:45) (Class 5) (0-75,75) 3-Y-O+ £2,264 (£673; £336; £168) Stalls Low

Form RPR
3454 1 **Sakhee's Pearl**[27] 7513 5-9-6 74 IanMongan 12 83
(Jo Crowley) *trckd ldrs: prog over 2f out: rdn and styd on to ld jst over 1f out: hld on gamely* 6/1[2]
6515 2 ¾ **Choral Festival**[6] 7759 5-8-13 70 KieranO'Neill(3) 13 77
(John Bridger) *stdd s: t.k.h early: hld up in midfield: prog 2f out: rdn to chse wnr ins fnl f: kpt on but a hld* 16/1
2P02 3 nk **Nibani (IRE)**[5] 7774 4-8-13 72 (p) AmyScott(5) 6 78+
(Alastair Lidderdale) *stdd s: hld up and last to 1/2-way: prog and wdst of all bnd 2f out: r.o to take 3rd ins fnl f: clsng at fin: too much to do* 12/1
-010 4 2 **Hurricane Hymnbook (USA)**[18] 7601 6-9-1 69 StevieDonohoe 3 71
(Willie Musson) *settled towards rr: rdn and prog fr 2f out: styd on to take 4th nr fin: nt pce to threaten* 8/1
0662 5 1 **Understory (USA)**[27] 7513 4-9-6 74 LukeMorris 10 74
(Tim McCarthy) *pressed ldr 4f: wnt 2nd again over 2f out: rdn to ld briefly over 1f out: wknd ins fnl f* 8/1
2122 6 1 **Opus Maximus (IRE)**[6] 7759 6-9-5 73 (p) HayleyTurner 7 71
(Conor Dore) *hld up in 8th tl rapid prog on outer to join ldr 6f out: led 4f out: hdd over 1f out: wknd fnl f* 2/1[1]
6310 7 5 **Hurricane Spirit (IRE)**[18] 7601 7-9-7 75 (b) SteveDrowne 1 63
(Terry Clement) *trckd ldrs: cl 4th over 2f out: effrt wl over 1f out: sn rdn and no rspnse: wknd rapidly fnl f* 15/2
2000 8 1¾ **Classically (IRE)**[13] 7651 5-9-3 71 (e) ChrisCatlin 11 56
(Peter Hedger) *taken down early: trckd ldrs: wd bnd 2f out and wknd qckly* 16/1
6000 9 ½ **Bilidn**[61] 6978 3-8-10 67 MartinLane 5 51
(Noel Quinlan) *mostly in last trio: dropped to last and pushed along 1/2-way: struggling after* 33/1
6301 10 2¾ **Heatherbird**[34] 7440 3-9-2 73 EddieAhern 8 51
(William Jarvis) *taken down early: hld up in midfield on inner: gng wl enough whn tight for room briefly 2f out: wknd tamely* 7/1[3]
1/00 11 6 **Bengal Tiger**[13] 7651 5-9-0 68 DavidProbert 9 34
(Tony Carroll) *a towards rr: rdn and no prog over 2f out: wknd rapidly over 1f out* 40/1
0003 P **Buddy Holly**[54] 7121 6-8-11 65 AndreaAtzeni 2 —
(Robert Eddery) *led: jnd 6f out: hdd 4f out: lost 2nd over 2f out: wkng qckly whn p.u 100yds out: lame* 20/1

2m 5.87s (-2.13) **Going Correction** -0.075s/f (Stan)
WFA 3 from 4yo+ 3lb 12 Ran SP% **123.7**
Speed ratings (Par 103): **105,104,104,102,101 100,96,95,95,92 88,—**
Tote Swingers: 1&2 £16.60, 1&3 £11.60, 2&3 £29.60 CSF £100.05 CT £1139.01 TOTE £5.50: £1.50, £5.20, £4.40; EX 118.90 TRIFECTA Not won..
Owner The Peregrina Partnership **Bred** Andrea Wilkinson Gay Kelleway **Trained** Whitcombe, Dorset

FOCUS
The early paced seemed just modest, but Opus Maximus and Buddy Holly duelled for the lead down the back straight and neither had much chance of seeing it out.
Buddy Holly Official explanation: jockey said gelding pulled up lame

7832 BET AT BLUESQ.COM ON YOUR MOBILE H'CAP (DIV I) 5f (P)
3:15 (3:15) (Class 4) (0-85,85) 3-Y-O+ £4,075 (£1,212; £606; £303) Stalls Low

Form RPR
1010 1 **Sugar Beet**[20] 7586 3-9-5 83 LukeMorris 7 92
(Ronald Harris) *off the pce in midfield: rdn 1/2-way: clsd fr 2f out: drvn ahd last 150yds: hld on* 5/1[3]
6313 2 ¾ **Earlsmedic**[61] 6974 6-8-8 72 (v) WilliamCarson 5 78
(Stuart Williams) *slowly away: outpcd in last pair and sn urged along: wd bnd 2f out: prog after: styd on to take 2nd last 100yds: a hld* 8/1
1013 3 ¾ **Where's Reiley (USA)**[2] 7807 5-8-9 80 (b) LeonnaMayor(7) 4 84
(Alastair Lidderdale) *lost midfield pl after 2f: bmpd along in last trio over 1f out: styd on wl fnl f to take 3rd nr fin* 10/1

0202 **4** 3/4 **Le Toreador**[21] 7575 6-9-7 **85**........................(tp) PhillipMakin 2 86
(Kevin Ryan) *off the pce in midfield: effrt over 1f out: styd on to dispute 3rd ins fnl f: nvr cl enough to chal* **7/2**[1]

1653 **5** 1 **Captain Scooby**[14] 7644 5-8-6 **77**........................ CharlesEddery(7) 6 74
(Richard Guest) *settled in last pair and wl off the pce: styd on in taking style fr over 1f out wout coming under any great press: nrst fin* **10/1**

6535 **6** 1/2 **Island Legend (IRE)**[14] 7644 5-9-0 **78**..................(p) RichardKingscote 9 74+
(Milton Bradley) *awkward s: spd fr wd draw to press ldr and pair clr after 2f: led over 1f out: hdd & wknd last 150yds* **4/1**[2]

0150 **7** nk **Victorian Bounty**[109] 5683 6-9-5 **83**........................ DaneO'Neill 10 77
(Tony Newcombe) *urged along in last trio over 3f out: tried to cl over 1f out: fdd last 100yds* **16/1**

0060 **8** 1 3/4 **Bravo King (IRE)**[9] 7726 3-8-11 **75**........................ MartinHarley 8 63
(Richard Guest) *chsd ldrs but off the pce after 2f: no prog over 1f out: fdd* **33/1**

00 **9** 2 1/4 **Best Trip (IRE)**[104] 5831 4-8-13 **80**........................ RobertLButler(3) 3 60
(Richard Guest) *taken down early: mde most at furious pce and clr w one other after 2f: hdd & wknd over 1f out* **7/1**

4000 **10** 1 **Mandy's Hero**[7] 7746 3-8-1 **72**........................ JenniferFerguson(7) 1 48
(Olivia Maylam) *chsd clr ldng pair tl over 1f out: wkng whn short of room briefly ins fnl f* **25/1**

59.60 secs (-0.90) **Going Correction** -0.075s/f (Stan) **10** Ran SP% **113.4**
Speed ratings (Par 105): **104,102,101,100,98 98,97,94,91,89**
Tote Swingers: 1&2 £5.80, 1&3 £9.20, 2&3 £5.00 CSF £43.33 CT £381.94 TOTE £8.40: £2.60, £2.30, £2.40; EX 49.50 Trifecta £202.50 Part won. Pool: £273.68 - 0.65 winning units..

Owner Ridge House Stables Ltd **Bred** Coln Valley Stud **Trained** Earlswood, Monmouths

FOCUS
A fair sprint handicap run at an overly strong pace, with Best Trip hassled up front by Island Legend. Both are better than they showed.

7833 BET AT BLUESQ.COM ON YOUR MOBILE H'CAP (DIV II) 5f (P)
3:45 (3:52) (Class 4) (0-85,85) 3-Y-O+ **£4,075** (£1,212; £606; £303) **Stalls** Low

Form RPR

2105 **1** **Diamond Charlie (IRE)**[92] 6217 3-9-5 **83**........................ SebSanders 9 89
(Simon Dow) *v awkward s and slowest away: hld up in last pair: rdn 2f out: str burst fnl f to ld nr fin* **5/1**

5403 **2** nk **What About You (IRE)**[21] 7578 3-9-7 **85**..................(p) TonyHamilton 7 90
(Richard Fahey) *led after 100yds: hrd pressed fnl f: hld on tl hdd nr fin* **9/4**[1]

0010 **3** 1/2 **Black Baccara**[3] 7804 4-8-0 **71** oh4........................(be) DannyBrock(7) 4 74
(Phil McEntee) *s.s: sn chsd ldng trio: tried to cl fnl f: outpcd nr fin* **14/1**

1310 **4** 1 **Volcanic Dust (IRE)**[130] 5000 3-9-2 **80**........................ LiamKeniry 3 87+
(Milton Bradley) *hld up in 5th: looking for room over 1f out: gng wl but nowhere to go thrght fnl f: nt rcvr* **8/1**

0110 **5** shd **Estonia**[19] 7594 4-8-10 **74**........................ LukeMorris 5 73
(Michael Squance) *taken down early: t.k.h: led 100yds: sn restrained into 3rd: drvn over 1f out: disp 2nd ins fnl f: one pce* **9/2**[3]

3513 **6** hd **Requisite**[12] 7675 6-9-2 **80**........................(b) DaneO'Neill 10 79
(Ian Wood) *rrd s: mostly in last pair: rdn 2f out: styd on ins fnl f: nvr rchd ldrs* **5/1**

0536 **7** shd **Desert Strike**[4] 7776 5-8-11 **75**........................(p) ShaneKelly 6 75
(Alan McCabe) *taken down early: trckd ldr after 1f: drvn over 1f out: lost 2nd last 75yds and hmpd sn after* **3/1**[2]

59.69 secs (-0.81) **Going Correction** -0.075s/f (Stan) **7** Ran SP% **125.1**
Speed ratings (Par 105): **103,102,101,100,99 99,99**
Tote Swingers: 1&2 £2.80, 1&3 £10.30, 2&3 £7.20 CSF £18.69 CT £157.27 TOTE £9.50: £3.30, £2.60; EX 30.40 Trifecta £173.70 Part won. Pool: £234.83 - 0.10 winning units..

Owner David & Stanley Adams **Bred** John Malone **Trained** Epsom, Surrey

FOCUS
There was a false start after Mottley Crewe burst his stall open. That runner was subsequently withdrawn, and so too was Lucky Art, who couldn't be pulled up before he passed the winning post. Those who did take part had been pulled up sharply enough first time around. The time was only fractionally slower than the first division, but they went overly quick in that race. This was a messy contest with What About You setting a steady pace in an uncontested lead. The field finished in a bunch.

Black Baccara Official explanation: two-day ban: careless riding (Jan 3-4)

Volcanic Dust(IRE) ◆ Official explanation: jockey said filly was denied a clear run

7834 PLAY ROULETTE AT BLUESQ.COM/CASINO (S) STKS 6f (P)
4:15 (4:16) (Class 6) 3-Y-O+ **£1,617** (£481; £240; £120) **Stalls** Low

Form RPR

6102 **1** **Mambo Spirit (IRE)**[19] 7596 7-9-6 67........................ DaneO'Neill 1 76
(Tony Newcombe) *trckd ldng pair: poised to chal gng wl 2f out: rdn over 1f out: disp ld ins fnl f: edgd ahd nr fin* **4/1**[3]

0250 **2** nk **Perfect Act**[20] 7586 6-8-9 78........................ DavidProbert 3 64
(Andrew Balding) *restless stalls and rrd s: sn chsd ldrs in 5th: swtchd ins and prog 2f out: drvn into narrow ld jst ins fnl f: sn jnd: hdd and no ex nr fin* **5/2**[1]

0446 **3** 1 3/4 **Oldjoesaid**[14] 7644 7-9-6 73........................ PhillipMakin 5 69
(Kevin Ryan) *trckd ldr: led over 2f out: drvn and hdd jst ins fnl f: one pce* **6/1**

6545 **4** 1 **Above The Stars**[19] 7596 3-8-9 69........................ TonyHamilton 7 55
(Richard Fahey) *reluctant to enter stalls: t.k.h: hld up in last pair: shkn up over 2f out: kpt on one pce: n.d* **11/4**[2]

1205 **5** shd **Lutine Charlie (IRE)**[2] 7807 4-9-6 74........................(p) LukeMorris 6 66
(Ronald Harris) *trckd ldng trio: rdn and nt qckn over 2f out: one pce and no imp fr over 1f out* **11/2**

0556 **6** 1 3/4 **Bunkered Again**[46] 7260 4-8-2 41........................(bt[1]) RaulDaSilva(7) 4 49?
(Jeremy Gask) *t.k.h: hld up in last pair: effrt on inner 2f out: no real prog* **50/1**

2060 **7** 3 **C'Mon You Irons (IRE)**[26] 7529 6-8-11 60........................(b) KierenFox(3) 2 45
(Mark Hoad) *led to over 2f out: wknd over 1f out* **25/1**

1m 12.5s (-0.60) **Going Correction** -0.075s/f (Stan) **7** Ran SP% **110.7**
Speed ratings (Par 101): **101,100,98,96,96 94,90**
Tote Swingers: 1&2 £2.30, 1&3 £3.60, 2&3 £3.30 CSF £13.47 TOTE £4.60: £2.20, £1.60; EX 14.50.There was no bid for the winner.

Owner Nigel Hardy **Bred** R Warren **Trained** Yarnscombe, Devon

FOCUS
A muddling seller. The winner had plenty to find at the weights, and the sixth, who wasn't beaten far, came into this officially rated just 41.

7835 BLUE SQUARE MEDIAN AUCTION MAIDEN STKS 1m (P)
4:45 (4:48) (Class 6) 2-Y-O **£1,704** (£503; £251) **Stalls** Low

Form RPR

0 **1** **Lancaster Gate**[27] 7520 2-9-3 0........................ TomQueally 2 74
(Amanda Perrett) *s.i.s: in tch towards rr: 9th over 3f out: gd prog fr 2f out: sustained effrt and drvn ahd last 120yds* **13/2**[3]

66 **2** 3/4 **Spanish Wedding**[138] 4722 2-9-3 0........................ AndreaAtzeni 3 72
(Marco Botti) *trckd ldr: led 2f out: drvn and hdd last 120yds: styd on* **11/4**[2]

0 **3** 1 1/4 **Rei D'Oro (USA)**[73] 6697 2-9-3 0........................ ShaneKelly 9 69
(David Simcock) *slowest away: rcvrd into midfield: disp 7th over 3f out: nt clr run and swtchd lft 2f out: clsd on ldrs 1f out: rn green and styd on same pce after* **50/1**

0 **4** 2 1/4 **Abdul Malik**[17] 7627 2-9-3 0........................ MartinLane 4 64
(David Simcock) *dwlt: sn rcvrd to chse ldrs: disp 4th over 3f out: drvn over 2f out: kpt on same pce* **18/1**

0 **5** 2 **Duke Of Clarence (IRE)**[15] 7634 2-9-3 0........................ JimmyFortune 8 59
(Richard Hannon) *difficult to load into stall: towards rr: dropped to last after 3f: brought wd in st: styd on fnl 2f: nrst fin* **6/4**[1]

4402 **6** 1 **Good Luck Charm**[13] 7653 2-9-3 69........................ JamieGoldstein 5 57
(Gary Moore) *led to 2f out: wknd jst over 1f out* **9/1**

7 2 1/2 **Ashdown Lad** 2-9-3 0........................ LeeNewman 6 51
(William Jarvis) *pushed up to go prom and sn chsd ldng pair: rdn over 2f out: rn green and edgd lft: wknd jst over 1f out* **16/1**

06 **8** 1 3/4 **Santadelacruze**[27] 7520 2-9-3 0........................ AmirQuinn 1 47
(Gary Moore) *trckd ldrs on inner: rdn over 2f out: wknd over 1f out* **33/1**

03 **9** hd **Masters Blazing**[6] 7751 2-8-12 0........................ RyanPowell(5) 10 47
(John Ryan) *racd wd: trckd ldrs: rdn over 2f out: sn wknd* **33/1**

10 2 1/2 **Pink Delight (IRE)** 2-8-12 0........................ LiamKeniry 13 36
(J S Moore) *dwlt: a in rr: no real prog over 2f out* **40/1**

0 **11** 6 **Parque Atlantico**[166] 3779 2-9-3 0........................ DavidProbert 12 27
(Andrew Balding) *wl in rr: brief effrt over 2f out: sn wknd* **100/1**

5 **12** hd **King Vahe (IRE)**[12] 7672 2-9-3 0........................ JimCrowley 11 27
(Alan Jarvis) *racd wd in midfield: disp 7th over 3f out: wknd over 2f out* **15/2**

00 **13** 10 **Hearduthefirsttime (IRE)**[41] 7329 2-9-3 0........................ MickyFenton 7 —
(Barney Curley) *sn wl in rr: bhd in last over 3f out: t.o* **100/1**

1m 39.62s (-0.18) **Going Correction** -0.075s/f (Stan) **13** Ran SP% **125.2**
Speed ratings (Par 94): **97,96,95,92,90 89,87,85,85,82 76,76,66**
Tote Swingers: 1&2 £5.40, 1&3 £77.50, 2&3 £39.20 CSF £25.31 TOTE £8.70: £2.50, £1.50, £14.30; EX 29.10 TRIFECTA Not won..

Owner K Abdulla **Bred** Juddmonte Farms Ltd **Trained** Pulborough, W Sussex

FOCUS
Probably not a bad maiden for the time of year.

NOTEBOOK
Lancaster Gate was behind Santadelacruze on his debut at Lingfield, but clearly he'd learnt plenty. He was still green, coming off the bridle a fair way out, but he was nicely on top at the line and really should progress again. (tchd 6-1 and 7-1)

Spanish Wedding, having his first start since August, plugged on in a manner that suggests he'll get further, as his breeding suggests. He can now switch to handicaps if connections so choose. (op 4-1)

Rei D'Oro(USA) ran better than on his debut and gave the distinct impression there will be more to come, missing the break and running green under pressure. (op 66-1)

Abdul Malik stepped up on his debut running. He might find a weak maiden, but handicaps will be an option after one more run. (op 20-1 tchd 16-1)

Duke Of Clarence(IRE) was far too green to justify strong market support on his recent debut at Lingfield and it was the same story here, the colt again not applying himself despite having been well backed. He made late progress without being given a hard time, suggesting he'll know more in future, and he could be alright if going the right way, although he does have plenty of maturing to do. (tchd 2-1)

Good Luck Charm didn't run to his official mark of 69. (op 11-1)

7836 PLAY RAINBOW RICHES ON YOUR IPHONE H'CAP 1m 3f (P)
5:15 (5:15) (Class 6) (0-60,60) 3-Y-O **£1,617** (£481; £240; £120) **Stalls** Low

Form RPR

0001 **1** **Shirataki (IRE)**[15] 7640 3-8-9 **48**........................ ChrisCatlin 6 57
(Peter Hiatt) *t.k.h: trckd ldr after 3f: led over 2f out: rdn and hdd over 1f out: rallied to ld ins fnl f: styd on wl* **7/2**[2]

4216 **2** 1/2 **Beggers Belief**[38] 7394 3-9-3 **56**........................(b) SebSanders 5 64
(Eric Wheeler) *hld up bhd ldng pair: effrt over 2f out: rdn to ld over 1f out: hdd ins fnl f: nt qckn* **11/8**[1]

346 **3** 3 **Mayan Flight (IRE)**[73] 6701 3-8-0 **46**........................ RaulDaSilva(7) 1 49
(Tony Carroll) *led 1f: trckd ldng pair after 3f and t.k.h: cl enough wl over 1f out: outpcd after* **11/2**

5435 **4** 1 **Sir Randolf (IRE)**[31] 7496 3-8-11 **50**........................(p) LiamKeniry 4 51
(Sylvester Kirk) *hld up and sn in last pair: effrt on inner over 2f out: nt qckn over 1f out: one pce after* **12/1**

0004 **5** 1 **Spade**[34] 7427 3-9-4 **57**........................ ShaneKelly 2 56
(Tim Pitt) *stdd s: hld up in last pair: t.k.h after 5f: effrt and shkn up over 1f out: no great prog: fdd nr fin* **10/1**

324 **6** 4 1/2 **Dolly Colman (IRE)**[10] 7720 3-8-8 **47**........................ LukeMorris 7 38
(Michael Blake) *led after 1f and set modest pce: hdd over 2f out: wknd over 1f out* **5/1**[3]

2m 25.04s (3.14) **Going Correction** -0.075s/f (Stan) **6** Ran SP% **113.2**
Speed ratings (Par 98): **85,84,82,81,81 77**
Tote Swingers: 1&2 £1.80, 1&3 £2.80, 2&3 £2.70 CSF £8.91 TOTE £4.70: £2.10, £1.50; EX 7.60.

Owner P W Hiatt **Bred** Deerfield Farm **Trained** Hook Norton, Oxon

FOCUS
They went a steady pace and the time well above standard.

T/Plt: £49.40 to a £1 winning stake. Pool: £60,433.750 - 892.70 winning tickets. T/Qpdt: £24.80 to a £1 winning stake. Pool: £5,754.60 - 171.18 winning tickets. JN

[7829]KEMPTON (A.W) (R-H)

Wednesday, December 21

OFFICIAL GOING: Standard

Wind: Moderate, across (away from stands) Weather: Fine but cloudy

7837 FREE ENTRY FOR BETDAQ MEMBERS MEDIAN AUCTION MAIDEN STKS 6f (P)

4:15 (4:16) (Class 6) 2-Y-O **£1,617** (£481; £240; £120) **Stalls** Low

Form RPR

1 **Pearl Rebel** 2-9-3 0 WilliamCarson 6 66
(Stuart Williams) *dwlt: rcvrd arnd outer to trck ldrs over 3f out: pushed along 2f out: clsd to ld jst ins fnl f: styd on wl* **15/8**[2]

2 1 ½ **Aurens (IRE)** 2-9-0 0 AdamBeschizza(3) 1 62
(Michael Attwater) *in tch in rr: prog on inner fr 2f out: rdn to chal 1f out: styd on same pce* **66/1**

6046 3 1 ½ **Justbookies Dotnet**[1] 7830 2-9-3 60 (v) KierenFallon 4 57
(Louise Best) *led: drvn 2f out: hdd jst ins fnl f: sn outpcd: clung on for 3rd* **16/1**

00 4 ¾ **Graylyn Valentino**[13] 7672 2-9-3 0 StevieDonohoe 3 55
(Robin Dickin) *wl in tch: shkn up 2f out: nt qckn sn after: styd on ins fnl f* **25/1**

3 5 nk **Gold Falcon (IRE)**[18] 7627 2-9-3 0 MartinLane 5 54
(David Simcock) *dwlt: t.k.h: hld up in last pair: pushed along and no prog over 2f out: rdn over 1f out: styd on ins fnl f* **8/1**

02 6 1 ¼ **Chorister Sport (IRE)**[35] 7435 2-9-3 0 JoeFanning 2 50
(William Jarvis) *trckd ldr 2f: wnt 2nd again jst over 2f out: shkn up over 1f out: nt qckn and jockey looking down: sn wknd* **7/4**[1]

52 7 2 ¼ **Pucon**[21] 7583 2-8-12 0 DaneO'Neill 7 38
(Roger Teal) *t.k.h: trckd ldr after 2f to jst over 2f out: wknd tamely* **9/2**[3]

00 8 7 **Mariannes**[13] 7672 2-8-12 0 JimmyFortune 8 17
(John Dunlop) *wnt lft s: settled in last: outpcd fr over 2f out* **40/1**

1m 12.78s (-0.32) **Going Correction** -0.05s/f (Stan) **8 Ran SP% 114.1**
Speed ratings (Par 94): **100,98,96,95,94 92,89,80**
toteswingers:1&2:£16.60, 2&3:£30.60, 1&3:£8.70 CSF £118.82 TOTE £3.60: £1.20, £9.30, £3.50; EX 221.60.
Owner Pearl Bloodstock Ltd **Bred** Mrs T A Foreman **Trained** Newmarket, Suffolk

FOCUS
Not a strong maiden by any means, a point backed-up by the proximity of the third, and the pace, set by him, was only steady.

NOTEBOOK
Pearl Rebel's trainer is not normally noted for first-time out winners but this one had been supported throughout the day and the money proved well placed. Despite racing quite wide throughout, he had plenty left to come clear in the final furlong and win with more in hand than the official margin suggests. He will probably need further in due course. He finished only three lengths in front of a 60-rated runner in third. Because of that, he could be awarded a mark that underestimates his ability. (op 5-2 tchd 11-4)
Aurens(IRE) had no chance on his debut according to the market, and trainer Michael Attwater is 0-27 with 2-y-os in the last five seasons, but this already-gelded son of One Cool Cat shaped with promise. He travelled well around the inside before keeping on nicely for pressure in the straight. He ought to prove good enough to go one better in a similar heat. (op 80-1)
Justbookies Dotnet didn't set strong fractions out in front, which helps to explain how he managed to get into the frame. (op 25-1)
Graylyn Valentino was keeping on well when forced to switch to get a clear run. (op 20-1)
Chorister Sport(IRE) proved a disappointing favourite, but the Lingfield maiden in which he finished second last time was a weak affair and he wasn't up to this slightly stiffer company. (op 5-4)

7838 BETDAQ MULTIPLES MEDIAN AUCTION MAIDEN FILLIES' STKS 7f (P)

4:45 (4:45) (Class 6) 2-Y-O **£1,617** (£481; £240; £120) **Stalls** Low

Form RPR

1 **Slewtoo** 2-9-0 0 AdamKirby 11 68
(Marco Botti) *dwlt: hld up in last trio: prog on outer 2f out: reminder ins fnl f: r.o to ld last 75yds: readily* **9/2**

344 2 nk **By Invitation (USA)**[78] 6612 2-9-0 67 JimCrowley 7 67
(Ralph Beckett) *trckd ldr: upsides over 2f out: drvn to ld over 1f out but only narrowly: kpt on u.p: hdd and hld last 75yds* **4/1**[3]

5 3 ½ **Boudoir (IRE)**[27] 7526 2-8-11 0 KieranO'Neill(3) 1 66
(Richard Hannon) *settled in midfield: effrt on inner 2f out: clsd on ldrs 1f out: rdn and styd on: a jst hld* **5/2**[1]

0 4 1 ¼ **Nevaeh**[41] 7345 2-9-0 0 SamHitchcott 6 62
(Pat Eddery) *led: jnd over 2f out: narrowly hdd over 1f out: stuck on wl and upsides ins fnl f: no ex last 100yds* **20/1**

63 5 1 ¼ **Words Come Easy**[53] 7174 2-8-11 0 AdamBeschizza(3) 5 59
(Philip McBride) *trckd ldrs: rdn and cl enough 2f out: one pce over 1f out* **20/1**

605 6 2 ¼ **Princess Maya**[49] 7225 2-9-0 64 DaneO'Neill 4 53
(Jo Crowley) *trckd ldrs: rdn over 2f out: nt qckn wl over 1f out: steadily outpcd* **5/1**

20 7 ¾ **Diamond Finesse (IRE)**[147] 4427 2-9-0 0 (b[1]) JimmyFortune 2 51
(Ed Dunlop) *dwlt: hld up in last trio: prog over 2f out: drvn and no imp over 1f out: wknd fnl f* **7/2**[2]

8 1 **Cufflink** 2-9-0 0 SteveDrowne 10 49
(Rae Guest) *t.k.h: racd wd in midfield: steadily wknd over 2f out* **50/1**

60 9 ½ **Neige D'Antan**[5] 7783 2-9-0 0 SebSanders 8 48
(Sir Mark Prescott Bt) *dwlt: mostly in last: struggling to go the pce fr 1/2-way: nvr a factor* **40/1**

00 10 8 **L'Arlesienne**[19] 7599 2-9-0 0 StephenCraine 3 27
(Sylvester Kirk) *trckd ldrs tl wknd qckly over 2f out: t.o* **100/1**

1m 26.86s (0.86) **Going Correction** -0.05s/f (Stan) **10 Ran SP% 120.6**
Speed ratings (Par 91): **93,92,92,90,89 86,85,84,84,74**
toteswingers:1&2:£6.50, 2&3:£4.10, 1&3:£6.00 CSF £22.54 TOTE £8.50: £2.40, £1.20, £1.20; EX 18.70.
Owner Dachel Stud **Bred** Dachel Stud **Trained** Newmarket, Suffolk

FOCUS
Not a bad fillies' maiden for the time of year.

NOTEBOOK
Slewtoo ◆ looks to have a bright future after storming down the outside to make a winning debut. She had to sit at the back of the field after breaking a little slowly and raced a little free, but she picked up in taking style in the straight. She won't be hit hard by the handicapper, given the runner-up is rated 67 (although she is probably better than that) and she looks sure to win plenty of races. (op 6-1 tchd 7-1)
By Invitation(USA) is much better than she showed at Southwell last time and the switch to Polytrack proved that. She travelled strongly close to the speed and looked the most likely winner turning in, before just not finding the same sort of acceleration as the winner. She looks well up to going one better. (op 9-2 tchd 7-2)
Boudoir(IRE) pulled her chance away on debut but, held up down the inside, she settled much better this time and finished her race in much stronger style. She looks the type who will improve with experience and will be winning races before long. (op 3-1 tchd 10-3)
Nevaeh left her maiden run a long way behind, keeping on well having made the running. She is another who can win races if building on this.
Diamond Finesse(IRE) was the biggest disappointment and the combination of first-time blinkers and step up in trip didn't work for her. She was keen early and found nothing in the straight, so it is back to the drawing board with her. (op 10-3)

7839 BACK OR LAY AT BETDAQ.COM H'CAP 1m 4f (P)

5:15 (5:17) (Class 5) (0-75,72) 3-Y-O **£2,264** (£673; £336; £168) **Stalls** Centre

Form RPR

005 1 **Rasheed**[33] 7453 3-9-4 69 (b[1]) NickyMackay 9 77
(John Gosden) *trckd ldr: keen whn pce stdd 1/2-way and dropped to 3rd: rdn to chal 2f out: disp ld jst over 1f out: edgd ahd against rail nr fin* **10/3**[2]

-411 2 hd **Dance For Livvy (IRE)**[200] 1969 3-8-10 61 MartinLane 8 69
(Robin Dickin) *trckd ldrs: pushed along 4f out: effrt over 2f out: drvn to dispute ld jst over 1f out: styd on: jst hld nr fin* **20/1**

3141 3 shd **Honourable Knight (IRE)**[11] 7720 3-8-10 61 (be) DavidProbert 10 69
(Mark Usher) *hld up in last trio: rdn over 2f out: chsd ldng trio sn after: styd on grad fr over 1f out: clsd on ldng pair fin* **3/1**[1]

1152 4 3 ¼ **Castlemorris King**[16] 7638 3-8-11 67 MarkCoumbe(5) 1 70
(Michael Attwater) *prom: wnt 2nd 1/2-way: effrt to ld wl over 2f out: hdd jst over 1f out: wknd last 150yds* **7/2**[3]

4022 5 1 ¾ **Echos Of Motivator**[5] 7779 3-9-2 67 (p) LukeMorris 6 67
(Ronald Harris) *settled in last pair: urged along fr 7f out and nvr gng wl: plugged on into 5th 2f out: nvr gng pce to threaten* **4/1**

5005 6 7 **Beyeh (IRE)**[10] 7727 3-8-9 60 NeilChalmers 7 49
(Michael Appleby) *hld up last: shkn up and no real prog over 2f out: nvr on terms* **66/1**

0500 7 2 **Huwayit (IRE)**[26] 7542 3-9-2 67 SebSanders 4 53
(Clive Brittain) *trckd ldrs: pushed along wl over 3f out: wknd qckly 2f out* **16/1**

1 8 15 **Calypso Cay**[14] 7662 3-9-7 72 JoeFanning 2 34
(Mark Johnston) *led at gd pce: lots of tail swishing and jinked bnd 8f out: stdd pce 1/2-way: hdd wl over 2f out: immediately dropped out: t.o* **8/1**

2m 32.14s (-2.36) **Going Correction** -0.05s/f (Stan) **8 Ran SP% 113.5**
Speed ratings (Par 102): **105,104,104,102,101 96,95,85**
toteswingers:1&2:£10.00, 2&3:£6.80, 1&3:£2.70 CSF £63.45 CT £218.77 TOTE £5.40: £2.10, £4.80, £2.60; EX 37.00.
Owner Ms Rachel D S Hood **Bred** Miss K Rausing And Mrs S M Rogers **Trained** Newmarket, Suffolk
■ Stewards' Enquiry : Mark Coumbe nine-day ban: used whip with excessive frequency (4 - 12 Jan)

FOCUS
A fairly competitive handicap and although the pace looked a little stop-start, the overall time was quite strong.

7840 BETDAQ MOBILE APPS CLAIMING STKS 1m (P)

5:45 (5:47) (Class 6) 3-Y-O **£1,617** (£481; £240; £120) **Stalls** Low

Form RPR

3515 1 **Encore Un Fois**[16] 7638 3-8-13 70 DavidKenny(5) 2 68
(George Baker) *plenty of effrt taken to load into stalls: hld up last: prog to go 2nd 2f out: cajoled along to chal and upsides 1f out: led last 75yds* **5/6**[1]

0026 2 nk **Ice Cold Bex**[19] 7600 3-8-9 62 (b) LukeMorris 1 58
(Philip McBride) *led: set stdy pce to 1/2-way: rdn and jnd 1f out: kpt on wl hdd and hld last 75yds* **11/4**[2]

0-30 3 1 ¾ **Brown Pete (IRE)**[7] 7761 3-8-4 62 (b) CharlesEddery(7) 4 56
(Richard Guest) *trckd ldng pair: disp 2nd 2f out: rdn and nt qckn over 1f out: one pce after* **8/1**

0260 4 11 **Deliberation (IRE)**[15] 7646 3-8-11 57 KierenFallon 6 31
(Kevin Ryan) *t.k.h: trckd ldr to 2f out: wknd over 1f out: eased* **3/1**[3]

1m 39.87s (0.07) **Going Correction** -0.05s/f (Stan) **4 Ran SP% 117.3**
Speed ratings (Par 98): **97,96,94,83**
CSF £3.92 TOTE £2.00; EX 3.50.
Owner M Khan X2 **Bred** London Thoroughbred Services Ltd **Trained** Whitsbury, Hants
■ Stewards' Enquiry : David Kenny two-day ban: used whip with excessive frequency (10-11 Jan)

FOCUS
A weak claimer.

7841 CALVERTS CARPETS YORK LTD H'CAP 1m (P)

6:15 (6:15) (Class 4) (0-85,85) 3-Y-O+ **£4,075** (£1,212; £606; £303) **Stalls** Low

Form RPR

5312 1 **Lockantanks**[18] 7628 4-9-5 83 LukeMorris 4 95
(Michael Appleby) *trckd ldng pair: effrt 2f out: led 1f out: drvn clr: decisively* **11/2**[2]

5121 2 2 **Tarooq (USA)**[26] 7542 5-9-7 85 TonyHamilton 8 92
(Richard Fahey) *trckd ldr: led jst over 2f out gng easily: drvn and hdd 1f out: styd on but no match for wnr* **7/1**[3]

1130 3 1 ½ **Sunset Kitty (USA)**[165] 3840 4-9-6 84 AdamKirby 6 88
(Mike Murphy) *blindfold off late and lft 5 l: in tch at bk of field: rdn over 2f out: prog jst over 1f out: styd on wl to take 3rd nr fin* **16/1**

0-51 4 ½ **Simayill**[40] 7361 3-9-4 83 SebSanders 2 85
(Clive Brittain) *trckd ldrs in 5th: effrt 2f out: disp 3rd fnl f: one pce and no imp* **11/1**

136 5 hd **Santefisio**[35] 7438 5-9-7 85 (p) SteveDrowne 11 87
(Peter Makin) *t.k.h: hld up in 7th: gng wl 2f out: prog over 1f out: disp 3rd fnl f but no imp: one pce* **12/1**

1006 6 hd **Shifting Star (IRE)**[21] 7586 6-9-4 82 IanMongan 1 83
(John Bridger) *t.k.h and sn restrained into last trio: effrt 2f out: kpt on fr over 1f out: nt gng pce to threaten* **40/1**

5040 7 ½ **Prince Of Burma (IRE)**[14] 7660 3-8-4 76 RaulDaSilva(7) 10 76
(Jeremy Gask) *plld hrd: hld up in rr: rdn 2f out and hung lft towards nr side rail: nvr on terms* **8/1**

1400 8 nk **Rossetti**[27] 7531 3-9-0 79 StevieDonohoe 7 79
(James Fanshawe) *t.k.h: hld up in last trio: effrt over 2f out: one pce and no imp* **7/1**[3]

1110 9 1 ½ **Reachforthebucks**[27] 7531 3-8-13 78 KierenFallon 9 74
(Rae Guest) *t.k.h: hld up in 6th: rdn and nt qckn over 2f out: lost pl and btn over 1f out* **2/1**[1]

3403 **10** *1* **Chilli Green**[14] 7660 4-9-5 **83** .... DaneO'Neill 3 77
(John Akehurst) *trckd ldng pair: rdn and effrt on inner 2f out: wl hld over 1f out: wknd fnl f* **15/2**
4640 **11** *5* **Amethyst Dawn (IRE)**[46] 7296 5-9-1 **82** .... KieranO'Neill(3) 5 64
(Andrew Reid) *led to jst over 2f out: wknd qckly over 1f out* **33/1**
1m 38.93s (-0.87) **Going Correction** -0.05s/f (Stan)
WFA 3 from 4yo+ 1lb **11** Ran SP% **123.9**
Speed ratings (Par 105): **102,100,98,98,97 97,97,96,95,94 89**
toteswingers:1&2:£4.80, 2&3:£33.90, 1&3:£12.20 CSF £46.43 CT £598.33 TOTE £5.80: £1.90, £1.80, £6.90; EX 24.10.
Owner Dallas Racing **Bred** Jeremy Green And Sons **Trained** Danethorpe, Notts
FOCUS
A strong handicap which was packed with quality Polytrack performers, but the pace wasn't very strong and a few of these were quite keen early on. The form has a solid look to it.

7842 RACING AT SKYSPORTS.COM H'CAP 1m (P)
6:45 (6:45) (Class 5) (0-75,75) 3-Y-O **£2,264** (£673; £336; £168) **Stalls** Low

Form RPR
3041 **1** **Perfect Cracker**[7] 7750 3-9-7 **75** 6ex........ AdamKirby 7 91+
(Clive Cox) *hld up and mostly in 5th: smooth prog over 2f out to ld wl over 1f out: sn pushed clr: eased last 50yds* **13/8**[1]
501 **2** *5* **Cheylesmore (IRE)**[69] 6814 3-9-4 **72**........ WilliamCarson 3 72
(Stuart Williams) *led and clr w one rival to over 3f out: hdd wl over 1f out: boxed on but no ch w wnr* **12/1**
1021 **3** *1 ½* **Russian Ice**[34] 7448 3-9-0 **71**........ KieranO'Neill(3) 5 68
(Dean Ivory) *s.i.s: pushed along in detached in last pair 1/2-way: prog u.p over 2f out: wnt 3rd over 1f out: one pce and no hdwy after* **9/2**[3]
1 **4** *1 ¼* **Prodigality**[11] 7717 3-9-4 **72**........ LukeMorris 6 66
(Ronald Harris) *chsd clr ldng pair: clsd over 3f out: drvn over 2f out: wl outpcd fnl 2f* **5/2**[2]
1003 **5** *¾* **Patriotic (IRE)**[10] 7727 3-8-10 **64**........ AndreaAtzeni 1 56
(Chris Dwyer) *trckd clr ldrs: rdn and in tch over 2f out: sn wl outpcd* **8/1**
10 **6** *4 ½* **Casual Mover (IRE)**[251] 1344 3-9-7 **75**........ SteveDrowne 2 57
(John Best) *dropped to last pair after 3f and detached at 1/2-way: rdn over 2f out: no prog* **16/1**
0-06 **7** *9* **Jolah**[161] 3983 3-9-2 **70**........ SebSanders 4 31
(Clive Brittain) *pressed ldr and clr of rest to over 3f out: wknd qckly over 2f out: t.o* **20/1**
1m 38.69s (-1.11) **Going Correction** -0.05s/f (Stan) **7** Ran SP% **114.3**
Speed ratings (Par 102): **103,98,96,95,94 90,81**
toteswingers:1&2:£2.80, 2&3:£3.20, 1&3:£1.30 CSF £22.49 TOTE £2.40: £1.10, £5.30; EX 21.40.
Owner Mildmay Racing **Bred** Mildmay Bloodstock **Trained** Lambourn, Berks
■ Stewards' Enquiry : Kieran O'Neill £280 fine: failed to arrive in time to weigh out
FOCUS
Some progressive and unexposed types were on show and they went a good gallop.
Prodigality Official explanation: jockey said that the gelding hung left throughout

7843 CWB CONTROLS LTD ALL WEATHER "HANDS AND HEELS" APPRENTICE SERIES H'CAP (RACING EXCELLENCE) 1m (P)
7:15 (7:15) (Class 6) (0-65,61) 4-Y-O+ **£1,617** (£481; £240; £120) **Stalls** Low

Form RPR
334 **1** **Hierarch (IRE)**[26] 7537 4-9-0 **57**........ AliceHaynes(3) 3 66
(David Simcock) *hld up bhd ldrs: prog to go 2nd over 1f out: pushed into narrow ld jst ins fnl f: a holding on after* **5/2**[2]
0303 **2** *nk* **Rock Anthem (IRE)**[18] 7632 7-9-5 **59**........ DannyBrock 4 67
(Mike Murphy) *racd freely: mde most: rdn and narrowly hdd jst ins fnl f: styd on but a jst hld* **9/4**[1]
0400 **3** *2 ¼* **Kenswick**[21] 7581 4-8-7 **47** oh2........(b) GeorgeDowning 1 50
(Pat Eddery) *hld up in tch: effrt on inner 2f out: nt qckn over 1f out: kpt on same pce after* **20/1**
5200 **4** *nse* **Gazboolou**[3] 7810 7-9-3 **57**........ JakePayne 2 60
(David Pinder) *trckd ldrs: effrt 2f out: nt qckn over 1f out: kpt on one pce after* **8/1**
1020 **5** *1 ¼* **Abigails Angel**[39] 7394 4-8-12 **57**........ AccursioRomeo(5) 5 57
(Brett Johnson) *t.k.h: mostly trckd ldr: cl enough 2f out: urged along and nt qckn over 1f out: fdd* **11/2**[3]
0500 **6** *3* **Valentino Swing (IRE)**[28] 7517 8-8-7 **47** oh2........(p) NoelGarbutt 7 40
(Michael Appleby) [illegible] *over 2f out: no imp over 1f out: fdd fnl f* **40/1**
0600 **7** *2* **Come On Safari (IRE)**[33] 7455 4-9-7 **61**........(v) ThomasBrown 8 49
(Joseph Tuite) *hld up and sn last: shkn up over 2f out: no rspnse and wl btn after* **14/1**
2165 **8** *7* **Yakama (IRE)**[14] 7663 6-8-12 **55**........(p) DanielHarris(3) 6 27
(Christine Dunnett) *plld hrd: racd wd: in tch tl wknd qckly over 2f out* **13/2**
1m 39.6s (-0.20) **Going Correction** -0.05s/f (Stan) **8** Ran SP% **113.0**
Speed ratings (Par 101): **99,98,96,96,95 92,90,83**
toteswingers:1&2:£2.80, 2&3:£11.30, 1&3:£4.80 CSF £8.33 CT £84.77 TOTE £3.20: £1.90, £1.60, £4.60; EX 9.70.
Owner DM Partnership **Bred** Castlemartin Stud And Skymarc Farm **Trained** Newmarket, Suffolk
FOCUS
A hands-and-heels race for apprentices and just modest form, although the two market leaders fought out the finish and the pair came nicely clear.
T/Plt: £317.20 to a £1 stake. Pool of £60,127.49 - 138.37 winning units. T/Qpdt: £24.90 to a £1 stake. Pool of £9,045.34 - 268.10 winning units. JN

7816 WOLVERHAMPTON (A.W) (L-H)
Wednesday, December 21

OFFICIAL GOING: Standard
Wind: Light behind Weather: Overcast

7844 WOLVERHAMPTON-RACECOURSE.CO.UK H'CAP 5f 216y(P)
1:20 (1:20) (Class 6) (0-60,60) 3-Y-O+ **£1,704** (£503; £251) **Stalls** Low

Form RPR
0553 **1** **Towy Boy (IRE)**[18] 7629 6-8-9 **60**........(bt) RaulDaSilva(7) 3 70
(Ian Wood) *trckd ldrs: shkn up to ld ins fnl f: r.o* **6/1**[3]
2630 **2** *¾* **Meia Noite**[47] 7265 4-9-1 **59**........ IanMongan 6 67
(Chris Wall) *mid-div: hdwy over 2f out: rdn and hung lft ins fnl f: r.o* **9/2**[2]
0000 **3** *2 ¾* **Almaty Express**[23] 7567 9-9-0 **58**........(b) MartinLane 4 57
(John Weymes) *chsd ldr: rdn over 1f out: styd on same pce ins fnl f* **33/1**
3532 **4** *shd* **Novabridge**[9] 7737 3-9-2 **60**........(v[1]) LiamKeniry 13 59
(Neil Mulholland) *led: rdn over 1f out: hdd and no ex ins fnl f* **12/1**

0442 **5** *2* **Anjomarba (IRE)**[2] 7820 4-8-11 **60**........(p) DavidKenny(5) 5 52
(Conor Dore) *chsd ldrs: rdn over 2f out: edgd lft and styd on same pce fnl f* **7/2**[1]
0600 **6** *hd* **Efistorm**[12] 7696 10-9-2 **60**........ HayleyTurner 10 52
(Conor Dore) *hld up: r.o ins fnl f: nrst fin* **10/1**
100 **7** *½* **Welcome Approach**[66] 6889 8-9-1 **59**........ PhillipMakin 2 49
(John Weymes) *sn pushed along in rr: styd on ins fnl f: nvr nrr* **25/1**
6500 **8** *1* **Athaakeel (IRE)**[18] 7629 5-9-2 **60**........(b) LukeMorris 9 47
(Ronald Harris) *s.i.s: sn pushed along in rr: hmpd over 3f out: nvr nrr* **14/1**
503 **9** *nk* **Lindoro**[95] 6159 6-9-1 **59**........ BarryMcHugh 12 45
(Kevin M Prendergast) *hld up: rdn 1/2-way: n.d* **20/1**
0060 **10** *1 ¼* **Skylla**[14] 7649 4-9-2 **60**........ GrahamGibbons 8 42
(Derek Shaw) *hld up: hdwy over 2f out: rdn over 1f out: wknd fnl f* **16/1**
4005 **11** *shd* **Divertimenti (IRE)**[23] 7566 7-9-0 **58**........(b) RussKennemore 7 40
(Roy Bowring) *chsd ldrs: rdn over 2f out: wknd fnl f* **7/1**
4120 **12** *2 ¾* **Ridgeway Hawk**[10] 7728 3-8-10 **59**........(v) LeeNewnes(5) 1 32
(Mark Usher) *dwlt: sn pushed along and a in rr* **16/1**
1020 **13** *1 ¼* **Yungaburra (IRE)**[9] 7737 7-9-1 **59**........(tp) SteveDrowne 11 28
(David C Griffiths) *prom: rdn over 2f out: wknd over 1f out* **25/1**
1m 13.75s (-1.25) **Going Correction** -0.075s/f (Stan) **13** Ran SP% **117.8**
Speed ratings (Par 101): **105,104,100,100,97 97,96,95,94,93 93,89,87**
toteswingers:1&2:£5.30, 2&3:£42.80, 1&3:£26.90 CSF £30.94 CT £830.38 TOTE £5.90: £2.40, £1.70, £10.00; EX 31.40 TRIFECTA Not won..
Owner C R Lambourne **Bred** R W K Lewis **Trained** Upper Lambourn, Berks
FOCUS
A tight if moderate handicap, with just 2lb covering the 13 runners, and very few got into the race from off the pace.

7845 RINGSIDE ENTERTAINMENT MEDIAN AUCTION MAIDEN STKS 5f 216y(P)
1:50 (1:50) (Class 6) 3-4-Y-O **£1,617** (£481; £240; £120) **Stalls** Low

Form RPR
363 **1** **Gold Tobougg**[62] 6981 3-8-12 60........ MartinLane 8 60
(David Simcock) *hld up: hdwy over 2f out: rdn to ld wl ins fnl f: r.o* **6/5**[1]
5002 **2** *2 ½* **Court Applause (IRE)**[39] 7389 3-9-3 63........ SteveDrowne 9 57
(William Muir) *hld up: hdwy over 1f out: sn rdn: styd on* **5/2**[2]
006 **3** *1* **Skystream (IRE)**[54] 7144 3-8-12 46........ TomEaves 6 49
(Ian Semple) *chsd ldr tl lft in ld over 2f out: rdn over 1f out: hung lft and hdd wl ins fnl f* **22/1**
0004 **4** *4* **Running Water**[12] 7693 3-8-12 40........ PaddyAspell 3 36
(Hugh McWilliams) *prom: lost pl whn nt clr run 1/2-way: hdwy over 1f out: nt trble ldrs* **66/1**
0040 **5** *1 ¼* **Hootys Agogo**[12] 7690 3-8-10 47........(p) JasonHart(7) 7 37
(Declan Carroll) *trckd ldrs: racd keenly: rdn over 2f out: wknd over 1f out* **25/1**
0006 **6** *nk* **Our Princess Ellie (USA)**[12] 7693 3-8-12 45........ GrahamGibbons 2 31
(Derek Shaw) *s.i.s: nvr on terms* **22/1**
00-6 **7** *¾* **Karens Legacy (IRE)**[197] 2781 3-8-10 0 ow1........ DaleSwift(3) 4 30
(Ian McInnes) *chsd ldrs: rdn over 2f out: wknd fnl f* **50/1**
0522 **8** *nk* **Gorgeous Goblin (IRE)**[8] 7747 4-8-5 49........(bt) RachealKneller(7) 1 28
(David C Griffiths) *led: hung rt fr over 3f out: hdd over 2f out: wknd fnl f* **4/1**[3]
9 *11* **Fireball Express** 3-9-3 0........ J-PGuillambert 5 —
(Brian Baugh) *s.i.s: sn pushed along in rr: bhd fr 1/2-way* **14/1**
1m 14.56s (-0.44) **Going Correction** -0.075s/f (Stan) **9** Ran SP% **116.7**
Speed ratings (Par 101): **99,95,94,89,87 86,85,85,70**
toteswingers:1&2:£1.40, 2&3:£8.50, 1&3:£7.90 CSF £4.07 TOTE £2.70: £1.10, £1.40, £5.20; EX 5.90 Trifecta £36.30 Pool: £439.54 - 8.94 winning units..
Owner Jaber Abdullah **Bred** Red House Stud **Trained** Newmarket, Suffolk
FOCUS
As weak a sprint maiden as you are likely to see and the highest-rated horses filled the first two places.
Gorgeous Goblin(IRE) Official explanation: jockeu said that the filly hung right in the latter stages

7846 TOTEQUADPOT H'CAP (DIV I) 5f 216y(P)
2:25 (2:25) (Class 4) (0-85,85) 3-Y-O+ **£4,075** (£1,212; £606; £303) **Stalls** Low

Form RPR
[illegible] **1** **Woolfall Sovereign (IRE)**[37] 7417 5-8-12 **76**........ IanMongan 7 84
(George Margarson) *chsd ldrs: rdn to ld ins fnl f: r.o* **6/1**[2]
1404 **2** *nk* **Close To The Edge (IRE)**[19] 7602 3-9-2 **80**........ MartinHarley 4 87
(Alan McCabe) *chsd ldrs: rdn over 1f out: r.o* **8/1**[3]
5136 **3** *¾* **Requisite**[1] 7833 6-8-9 **80**........(b) RaulDaSilva(7) 8 85
(Ian Wood) *mid-div: rdn over 2f out: hdwy over 1f out: r.o* **10/1**
5031 **4** *½* **Lujeanie**[19] 7602 5-9-7 **85**........(p) ShaneKelly 10 88
(Dean Ivory) *hld up: hdwy over 1f out: sn rdn: r.o: nt rch ldrs* **7/2**[1]
2140 **5** *nk* **Master Of Disguise**[48] 7253 5-9-0 **78**........(t) FrederikTylicki 5 80
(Brian Baugh) *prom: racd keenly: hmpd wl over 3f out: rdn over 1f out: r.o* **9/1**
0001 **6** *½* **Dasho**[13] 7675 3-9-4 **82**........ HayleyTurner 2 82
(Olivia Maylam) *led 1f: chsd ldr tl led again over 1f out: rdn and hdd ins fnl f: styd on same pce* **7/2**[1]
0540 **7** *4* **Johnstown Lad (IRE)**[2] 7819 7-8-7 **71** oh1........(bt) JohnFahy 1 59
(Daniel Mark Loughnane, Ire) *s.s: bhd: rdn over 1f out: styd on ins fnl f: nvr nrr* **20/1**
0000 **8** *½* **Reposer (IRE)**[14] 7660 3-8-13 **77**........ RobbieFitzpatrick 3 63
(Noel Quinlan) *sn pushed along and a in rr* **16/1**
0200 **9** *1* **Ivory Silk**[14] 7660 6-8-11 **75**........(p) LukeMorris 11 58
(Jeremy Gask) *sn bhd* **14/1**
2420 **10** *½* **Defence Council (IRE)**[15] 7644 3-9-1 **79**........ DuranFentiman 9 60
(Mel Brittain) *chsd ldrs tl rdn and wknd over 1f out* **12/1**
0030 **11** *3* **Sir Geoffrey (IRE)**[19] 7602 5-9-4 **82**........(b) GrahamGibbons 6 54
(Scott Dixon) *led 5f out: rdn and hdd over 1f out: wknd ins fnl f* **20/1**
1m 13.44s (-1.56) **Going Correction** -0.075s/f (Stan) **11** Ran SP% **118.7**
Speed ratings (Par 105): **107,106,105,104,104 103,98,97,96,95 91**
toteswingers:1&2:£6.60, 2&3:£10.30, 1&3:£5.00 CSF £53.97 CT £470.12 TOTE £5.70: £1.80, £2.60, £2.80; EX 40.00 Trifecta £237.90 Pool: £462.99 - 1.44 winning units..
Owner Graham Lodge Partnership **Bred** Saud Bin Saad **Trained** Newmarket, Suffolk
FOCUS
A decent sprint handicap with a strong pace set by Sir Geoffrey, who merely ran himself into the ground.

7847 TOTEQUADPOT H'CAP (DIV II) 5f 216y(P)
3:00 (3:00) (Class 4) (0-85,83) 3-Y-O+ **£4,075** (£1,212; £606; £303) **Stalls** Low

Form RPR
0220 **1** **Dorback**[13] 7675 4-8-13 **75**........ BarryMcHugh 9 84
(Noel Wilson) *hld up: hdwy over 1f out: led ins fnl f: r.o: comf* **15/2**

0120 **2** *1* **Red Cape (FR)**[15] 7644 8-9-1 **77**................................(b) JamesSullivan 5 83
(Ruth Carr) *trckd ldrs: led over 1f out: rdn: hung lft and hdd ins fnl f: styd on same pce* **11/1**

6030 **3** *1 1/2* **Night Trade (IRE)**[29] 7502 4-9-2 **78**........................(p) GrahamGibbons 6 79
(Ronald Harris) *hld up: hdwy u.p over 1f out: r.o* **12/1**

0514 **4** *nk* **Forever's Girl**[41] 7356 5-9-1 **80**.. DaleSwift(3) 3 80
(Geoffrey Oldroyd) *chsd ldrs: pushed along over 2f out: rdn over 1f out: styd on* **8/1**

3611 **5** *nk* **Titus Gent**[75] 6665 6-8-13 **82**.. RaulDaSilva(7) 8 81
(Jeremy Gask) *w ldr tl led over 3f out: rdn and hdd over 1f out: styd on same pce ins fnl f* **5/1[3]**

0224 **6** *hd* **Lenny Bee**[15] 7644 5-9-5 **81**...(t) JohnFahy 4 80
(Deborah Sanderson) *hld up: rdn over 1f out: styd on: nt trble ldrs* **9/2[2]**

0000 **7** *3/4* **Star Rover (IRE)**[18] 7628 4-9-2 **83**......................(v) MatthewCosham(5) 1 79
(David Evans) *sn led: hdd over 3f out: rdn and ev ch over 1f out: no ex ins fnl f* **8/1**

1460 **8** *1 1/2* **Roodee Queen**[104] 5862 3-9-3 **79**........................ RichardKingscote 2 70
(Milton Bradley) *chsd ldrs: rdn over 1f out: no ex ins fnl f* **25/1**

3414 **9** *nse* **Dashwood**[102] 5948 4-8-11 **76**.. RyanClark(3) 7 67
(Anthony Carson) *hld up: rdn over 2f out: n.d* **7/2[1]**

1m 14.04s (-0.96) **Going Correction** -0.075s/f (Stan) 9 Ran SP% **110.9**
Speed ratings (Par 105): **103,101,99,99,98 98,97,95,95**
CSF £80.94 CT £944.82 TOTE £7.30: £3.10, £3.40, £4.60; EX 79.80 Trifecta £436.30 Part won. Pool: £589.71 - 0.10 winning units..
Owner Ms Sara Hattersley **Bred** Winterbeck Manor Stud **Trained** Sandhutton, N Yorks

FOCUS
The winning time was 0.6 seconds slower than the first division.

7848 TOTEPOOL H'CAP 1m 141y(P)
3:30 (3:30) (Class 6) (0-55,61) 3-Y-O+ **£1,704** (£503; £251) **Stalls** Low

Form RPR

3351 **1** **Eastward Ho**[9] 7741 3-9-4 **58** 6ex.............................. MichaelStainton 13 67
(Jason Ward) *led: hdd over 7f out: chsd ldr: rdn over 1f out: r.o to ld wl ins fnl f* **4/1[2]**

3 **2** *nk* **Waterloo Sunrise (IRE)**[39] 7399 6-9-3 **55**...................... ShaneKelly 11 63
(S M Duffy, Ire) *led over 7f out: rdn over 1f out: hdd wl ins fnl f* **7/1[3]**

0030 **3** *1 1/2* **Jibouti (IRE)**[23] 7571 3-8-13 **53**..............................(b) J-PGuillambert 8 58
(Clive Brittain) *chsd ldrs: rdn over 2f out: styd on* **20/1**

0023 **4** *1* **Daniel Thomas (IRE)**[16] 7640 9-8-13 **51**....................(tp) MartinHarley 7 53
(Richard Guest) *s.i.s: hld up: hdwy over 1f out: r.o: nt rch ldrs* **4/1[2]**

5050 **5** *1/2* **Karate (IRE)**[55] 7131 3-8-8 **55**..............................(t) NicoleNordblad(7) 2 56
(Hans Adielsson) *plld hrd and prom: lost pl over 3f out: hdwy over 1f out: r.o* **16/1**

2603 **6** *1/2* **Excellent Vision**[9] 7740 4-9-2 **54**......................(bt[1]) RichardKingscote 12 54
(Milton Bradley) *hld up: r.o ins fnl f: nvr nrr* **9/1**

6001 **7** *3/4* **Join Up**[9] 7740 5-9-2 **61** 6ex...................................... RachealKneller(7) 1 59
(Mark Brisbourne) *prom: shkn up over 2f out: swtchd rt over 1f out: no ex fnl f* **14/1**

0 **8** *3* **Sumbe (USA)**[64] 6938 5-9-3 **55**..(p) TomEaves 4 46
(Michael Wigham) *hld up: rdn over 1f out: nvr on terms* **10/3[1]**

0620 **9** *3 1/4* **Final Tune (IRE)**[5] 7788 8-8-12 **55**........................... NathanAlison(5) 5 39
(Mandy Rowland) *mid-div: hmpd over 7f out: rdn 3f out: n.d* **25/1**

4002 **10** *5* **Amazing Win (IRE)**[7] 7755 3-9-1 **55**.............................. TonyCulhane 3 27
(Mick Channon) *hld up: hdwy u.p over 2f out: wknd over 1f out* **16/1**

1-40 **11** *7* **William Morgan (IRE)**[11] 7720 4-8-9 **52**.................. CharlesBishop(5) 6 —
(Mike Hammond) *plld hrd and prom: hmpd over 7f out: wknd over 2f out* **33/1**

0204 **12** *1 1/2* **Bint Elnadim (IRE)**[8] 7747 3-9-1 **55**....................... RobbieFitzpatrick 9 —
(Derek Shaw) *hld up: a in rr* **50/1**

1m 50.06s (-0.44) **Going Correction** -0.075s/f (Stan)
WFA 3 from 4yo+ 2lb 12 Ran SP% **117.5**
Speed ratings (Par 101): **98,97,96,95,95 94,93,91,88,83 77,76**
toteswingers:1&2:£6.30, 2&3:£22.30, 1&3:£11.10 CSF £30.48 CT £503.26 TOTE £7.30: £2.20, £1.70, £4.30; EX 37.10 TRIFECTA Not won..
Owner Miss Vivian Pratt **Bred** H & V Pratt **Trained** Middleham, North Yorkshire
■ Stewards' Enquiry : Shane Kelly two-day ban: used whip with excessive frequency (4-5 Jan)

FOCUS
A modest handicap and they didn't go much of a pace, which helps explain why the first three horses home held the first three positions throughout.
Amazing Win(IRE) Official explanation: jocekey said that the filly hung left

7849 TOTEEXACTA NURSERY 1m 141y(P)
4:00 (4:00) (Class 5) (0-75,73) 2-Y-O **£2,264** (£673; £336; £168) **Stalls** Low

Form RPR

0521 **1** **Karma Chameleon**[6] 7763 2-9-0 **61** 6ex.............................. ShaneKelly 2 76
(John Berry) *chsd ldrs: led over 1f out: r.o wl* **9/4[1]**

4062 **2** *6* **Quixote**[12] 7697 2-8-13 **60**..(b) HayleyTurner 1 62
(Clive Brittain) *sn pushed along in mid-div: drvn 1/2-way: hdwy 3f out: rdn to chse wnr fnl f: edgd lft and styd on same pce* **11/4[2]**

4122 **3** *3* **Let Your Love Flow (IRE)**[2] 7821 2-9-4 **68**................ SophieDoyle(3) 3 64
(Sylvester Kirk) *hld up in tch: pushed along 3f out: effrt and nt clr run over 1f out: swtchd rt ins fnl f: nvr able to chal* **5/1[3]**

0340 **4** *3* **Orwellian**[75] 6667 2-8-12 **64**.. CharlesBishop(5) 8 53
(Brian Meehan) *s.i.s: sn pushed along to chse ldr: led over 3f out: rdn and hdd over 1f out: sn edgd lft: wknd fnl f* **10/1**

040 **5** *8* **Silent Energy (IRE)**[14] 7650 2-9-4 **65**........................ GrahamGibbons 7 38
(Ronald Harris) *prom: pushed along over 5f out: rdn over 2f out: sn wknd* **50/1**

4011 **6** *3* **Flying Pickets (IRE)**[10] 7725 2-9-7 **73** 6ex................(p) RyanPowell(5) 4 39
(Alan McCabe) *sn pushed along in rr: rdn over 3f out: wknd 2f out* **8/1**

0136 **7** *8* **Jimmy The Lollipop (IRE)**[76] 6652 2-9-6 **67**.................... LiamKeniry 6 17
(Neil Mulholland) *hld up: rdn over 3f out: sn wknd* **22/1**

040 **8** *3 3/4* **Aiaam Al Wafa (IRE)**[55] 7125 2-9-7 **68**........................ PhillipMakin 5 10
(James Tate) *sn led: rdn and hdd over 3f out: wknd 2f out* **10/1**

1m 49.08s (-1.42) **Going Correction** -0.075s/f (Stan) 8 Ran SP% **109.7**
Speed ratings (Par 96): **103,97,95,92,85 82,75,72**
toteswingers:1&2:£2.40, 2&3:£3.20, 1&3:£3.00 CSF £7.76 CT £23.56 TOTE £4.00: £2.00, £1.10, £1.50; EX 8.10 Trifecta £47.30 Pool: £856.95 - 13.40 winning units..
Owner EERC **Bred** D R Tucker **Trained** Newmarket, Suffolk

FOCUS
An ordinary nursery and they finished very well spread out.

NOTEBOOK
Karma Chameleon was carrying a 6lb penalty for his Kempton success six days earlier, but was always travelling like a winner here and his rider was looking around for dangers before taking over in front inside the last 2f. He absolutely bolted up and, although the handicapper will hit him for this, the change of yards has obviously done him little harm, so there may well be more to come. (op 7-4 tchd 5-2)
Quixote seemed to improve for the fitting of blinkers when narrowly beaten over C&D 12 days earlier, but looked hard work here, coming on and off the bridle at various stages and needing to be given some stiff reminders at halfway. To his credit he kept plugging on, but was very much second best. (op 4-1 tchd 5-2)
Let Your Love Flow(IRE), twice narrowly beaten here since winning a C&D claimer last month, was contesting her first nursery. She tried for a very optimistic gap up the inside rail soon after turning in which soon closed completely when the weakening Orwellian hung to his left and trapped her against the rail a furlong out. She would have finished closer otherwise, but would probably still have finished third. (tchd 9-2)
Orwellian Official explanation: one-day ban: careless riding (4 Jan)
Flying Pickets(IRE), bidding for a hat-trick under a 6lb penalty after two wins at Southwell, had cheekpieces on for the first time but never got into the race and this demonstrates the big difference between the two all-weather surfaces. His rider reported that he was never travelling. Official explanation: jockey said that the gelding was never travelling (op 11-2)

7850 HOTEL & CONFERENCING AT WOLVERHAMPTON H'CAP 2m 119y(P)
4:30 (4:30) (Class 6) (0-65,65) 3-Y-O+ **£1,704** (£503; £251) **Stalls** Low

Form RPR

3034 **1** **Dream Catcher (SWE)**[32] 7495 8-9-7 **58**..................(p) HayleyTurner 13 67
(Jonjo O'Neill) *chsd ldr tl led 10f out: rdn and edgd lft over 1f out: styd on wl* **9/2[1]**

5144 **2** *2 1/4* **Lucky Diva**[102] 5916 4-8-9 **53**..(p) JakePayne(7) 9 59
(Bill Turner) *hld up: hdwy over 3f out: rdn and nt clr run over 1f out: swtchd rt: chsd wnr ins fnl f: styd on* **12/1**

6000 **3** *2 3/4* **Dart**[23] 7570 7-9-8 **62**.. MichaelO'Connell(3) 2 65
(John Mackie) *mid-div: hdwy over 6f out: chsd wnr over 2f out tl rdn over 1f out: no ex fnl f* **13/2[2]**

3660 **4** *3 1/4* **Leyte Gulf (USA)**[23] 7564 8-9-8 **59**.................................. PhillipMakin 12 58
(Chris Bealby) *s.s: hld up: hdwy over 2f out: rdn over 1f out: no ex* **9/2[1]**

6300 **5** *2 1/4* **Perfect Vision**[13] 7671 4-9-11 **62**......................................(t) LiamKeniry 6 58
(Charlie Longsdon) *hld up: rdn over 3f out: r.o ins fnl f: n.d* **8/1[3]**

0260 **6** *1/2* **Dubara Reef (IRE)**[23] 7570 4-8-13 **50**........................(p) JamesSullivan 5 46
(Paul Green) *prom: rdn over 3f out: wknd over 1f out* **12/1**

-460 **7** *2 3/4* **Brave Enough (USA)**[21] 7581 4-8-6 **50** ow2.................(p) NedCurtis(7) 4 42
(Roger Curtis) *prom tl rdn and wknd over 2f out* **80/1**

2000 **8** *nk* **Herrera (IRE)**[22] 7573 6-9-1 **59**.. LauraBarry(7) 3 51
(Richard Fahey) *hld up: rdn over 2f out: sn wknd* **20/1**

/0-2 **9** *5* **Alaghiraar (IRE)**[219] 2159 7-10-0 **65**..........................(v) FrederikTylicki 7 51
(Richard Ford) *led over 6f: remained handy tl rdn and wknd over 2f out* **9/2[1]**

1244 **10** *15* **Spice Bar**[14] 7631 7-8-13 **57**..(p) JasonHart(7) 10 25
(Declan Carroll) *trckd ldrs: racd keenly: wnt 2nd 6f out: rdn over 2f out: sn wknd: t.o* **9/1**

531- **11** *75* **Calzaghe (IRE)**[276] 3819 7-9-9 **60**................................ J-PGuillambert 11 —
(Martin Hill) *hld up: rdn and wknd over 3f out: t.o* **16/1**

3m 41.05s (-0.75) **Going Correction** -0.075s/f (Stan)
WFA 3 from 4yo+ 8lb 11 Ran SP% **116.3**
Speed ratings (Par 101): **98,96,95,94,93 92,91,91,89,81 46**
toteswingers:1&2:£9.50, 2&3:£17.10, 1&3:£5.70 CSF £59.86 CT £351.22 TOTE £7.20: £2.70, £4.10, £2.90; EX 61.10 Trifecta £199.80 Pool: £440.25 - 1.63 winning units..
Owner Ms Mary Miles **Bred** Anna-Lena Smeds **Trained** Cheltenham, Gloucs

FOCUS
A moderate staying event run at an ordinary early pace, which wasn't to the satisfaction of Hayley Turner aboard Dream Catcher, who decided to take over in front with well over a circuit left.
Spice Bar Official explanation: jockey said that the gelding ran too free
Calzaghe(IRE) Official explanation: jockey said that the gelding lost action

7851 TOTETRIFECTA APPRENTICE H'CAP 1m 1f 103y(P)
5:00 (5:00) (Class 6) (0-60,60) 3-Y-O+ **£1,704** (£503; £251) **Stalls** Low

Form RPR

0-12 **1** **Trip Switch**[14] 7663 5-9-1 **59** ow2.......................... MichaelJMurphy(5) 11 66
(George Prodromou) *a.p: led 1f out: rdn out* **9/2[2]**

0000 **2** *1/2* **Hathaway (IRE)**[5] 7787 4-8-5 **47**.............................. RachealKneller(3) 7 53
(Mark Brisbourne) *hld up: hdwy over 1f out: r.o wl* **12/1**

0033 **3** *nk* **Poppy Golightly**[76] 6659 4-8-8 **52**.................................... JasonHart(5) 3 57
(Declan Carroll) *chsd ldr tl led over 2f out: rdn and hdd 1f out: styd on:* **12/1**

0056 **4** *nk* **Striding Edge (IRE)**[113] 5608 5-9-1 **59**................. NicoleNordblad(5) 8 64
(Hans Adielsson) *mid-div: hdwy over 2f out: rdn over 1f out: styd on* **5/2[1]**

0300 **5** *1/2* **Miss Beat (IRE)**[12] 7689 5-8-13 **59**......................(t) MichaelKenny(7) 1 63
(Declan Carroll) *s.s: hld up: hdwy over 1f out: r.o: nvr nrr* **12/1**

0660 **6** *3/4* **Luv U Noo**[19] 7604 4-8-7 **46** oh1.. JamesRogers 5 48
(Brian Baugh) *chsd ldrs: rdn over 1f out: styd on same pce ins fnl f* **33/1**

0034 **7** *1* **Love In The Park**[16] 7640 6-8-8 **47**.............................. MatthewCosham 2 47
(Roy Brotherton) *s.i.s: hld up: rdn over 1f out: r.o ins fnl f: nvr nrr* **9/2[2]**

0304 **8** *2* **Desert Auction (IRE)**[23] 7565 4-9-4 **60**..............(v) GarryWhillans(3) 12 56
(Ian Semple) *hld up: rdn over 1f out: r.o ins fnl f: nrst fin* **7/1[3]**

000 **9** *4* **Chillianwallah**[77] 5898 3-8-5 **46** oh1.................................. RyanPowell 4 33
(James Unett) *prom: rdn over 2f out: wknd over 1f out* **80/1**

000 **10** *1 1/4* **Fitzwarren**[98] 6050 10-8-4 **46** oh1............................(tp) CharlesBishop(5) 6 31
(Alan Brown) *plld hrd: led: rdn and hdd over 2f out: wknd over 1f out* **66/1**

03-3 **11** *4 1/2* **Forbidden (IRE)**[351] 30 8-9-4 **57**...............................(vt) AdamCarter 9 32
(Ian McInnes) *mid-div: rdn and wknd over 2f out* **16/1**

400- **12** *6* **Kirstys Lad**[635] 995 9-8-3 **47**.. RichardOld(5) 10 10
(Michael Mullineaux) *prom tl rdn and wknd over 2f out* **33/1**

2m 1.56s (-0.14) **Going Correction** -0.075s/f (Stan)
WFA 3 from 4yo+ 2lb 12 Ran SP% **115.0**
Speed ratings (Par 101): **97,96,96,96,95 94,94,92,88,87 83,78**
toteswingers:1&2:£14.40, 2&3:£18.10, 1&3:£6.80 CSF £54.32 CT £604.99 TOTE £5.20: £1.30, £3.90, £3.10; EX 71.60 Trifecta £189.80 Pool: £597.64 - 2.33 winning units..
Owner George Prodromou **Bred** A Saccomando **Trained** East Harling, Norfolk

FOCUS
A moderate apprentice handicap and the principals finished in a heap, suggesting the form is nothing to write home about.
T/Jkpt: £15,187.70 to a £1 stake. Pool of £96,260.14 - 4.50 winning tickets. T/Plt: £143.70 to a £1 stake. Pool of £72,282.07 - 367.13 winning tickets. T/Qpdt: £74.20 to a £1 stake. Pool of £5,675.62 - 56.60 winning tickets. CR

[7776]SOUTHWELL (L-H)

Thursday, December 22

OFFICIAL GOING: Standard

Wind: Light half behind Weather: Fine and dry

7852 TOTEPLACEPOT (S) STKS — 1m (F)

12:00 (12:01) (Class 6) 2-Y-O — **£1,704** (£503; £251) **Stalls** Low

Form — RPR

654 **1** — **Spartilla**[12] 7718 2-8-11 53 .... JamesSullivan 6 — 58
(James Given) *cl up on outer: led wl over 1f out: sn rdn and edgd lft: drvn and hung rt ins fnl f: kpt on* — **13/8**[1]

505 **2** *½* **Samasana (IRE)**[49] 7242 2-8-6 50 .... LukeMorris 4 — 52
(Ian Wood) *trckd ldrs: hdwy 3f out: n.m.r and swtchd rt wl over 1f out: rdn to chal appr fnl f and ev ch tl no ex last 50yds* — **11/4**[2]

6644 **3** *9* **Angel Cake (IRE)**[6] 7777 2-7-13 52 ....(bt) DannyBrock(7) 5 — 31
(Phil McEntee) *cl up: led over 3f out: rdn over 2f out: hdd wl over 1f out: wknd appr fnl f* — **9/2**[3]

0500 **4** *13* **Koalition (IRE)**[49] 7242 2-8-6 56 .... RyanPowell(5) 3 — —
(David O'Meara) *led: rdn along and hdd over 3f out: sn wknd* — **6/1**

0200 **P** — **No More Games**[70] 6817 2-8-11 57 .... TomEaves 2 — —
(Kevin Ryan) *trckd ldrs on inner: rdn along and lost pl after 3f: bhd whn lost action and p.u over 3f out* — **10/1**

1m 43.66s (-0.04) **Going Correction** -0.10s/f (Stan) — **5** Ran SP% **106.3**
Speed ratings (Par 94): **96,95,86,73,—**
CSF £5.79 TOTE £2.30: £1.10, £1.90; EX 5.20.There was no bid for the winner.
Owner Bolton Grange **Bred** J Ellis **Trained** Willoughton, Lincs

FOCUS
Just a moderate contest, but possibly a slightly better race than appeared the case beforehand. The front two finished clear, appearing to run a bit above their respective official marks, and the time was 0.68 seconds quicker than the later maiden for older fillies.

NOTEBOOK
Spartilla had been going the right way in similar company and took another step forward to gain his first success at the fourth attempt. A big colt with an awkward and high knee action, it was no surprise this surface suited. He's well bred (dam dual Group-race winner for these connections) and there could be more to come, although he won't want a fast surface. (op 6-4 tchd 7-4)
Samasana(IRE) raced in snatches but had her chance. She had been off for 49 days and was just worried out it by a rival with more scope, so this was not a bad effort, and she's up to winning. (op 4-1 tchd 5-2)
Angel Cake(IRE) ran poorly and looks one to avoid. (op 11-2)
No More Games, who was pulled up having lost his action, might have been affected by Kuwait Moon playing up in the stall next to him before that one was withdrawn. Official explanation: jockey said that the gelding lost action (op 11-2)

7853 TOTEEXACTA H'CAP (DIV I) — 5f (F)

12:30 (12:30) (Class 6) (0-60,60) 3-Y-O+ — **£1,704** (£503; £251) **Stalls** High

Form — RPR

0462 **1** — **Sandwith**[13] 7691 8-9-0 53 ....(p) LeeNewman 3 — 61
(George Foster) *prom: hdwy 2f out: rdn over 1f out: kpt on to ld ins fnl f* — **6/1**[3]

55 **2** *½* **Nafa (IRE)**[83] 6501 3-9-2 55 .... DanielTudhope 9 — 62
(Michael Mullineaux) *led 1 1/2f: cl up: rdn to ld again wl over 1f out: hdd and no ex ins fnl f* — **17/2**

3055 **3** *1* **Itum**[8] 7755 4-8-13 52 .... WilliamCarson 1 — 55
(Christine Dunnett) *prom: cl up 2f out: sn rdn and ev ch tl drvn and one pce fnl f* — **7/1**

2366 **4** *¾* **Little Perisher**[8] 7760 4-8-11 50 ....(p) KierenFallon 4 — 50
(Paul Howling) *sn outpcd and bhd after 1f: swtchd to far side and hdwy wl over 1f out: rdn and styd on ins fnl f: nrst fin* — **17/2**

2000 **5** *nk* **Sharp Shoes**[21] 7594 4-9-4 60 ....(p) DaleSwift(3) 6 — 59
(Ann Duffield) *dwlt: hdwy 1/2-way: rdn wl over 1f out: kpt on one pce fnl f* — **11/4**[1]

4213 **6** *shd* **Cheyenne Red (IRE)**[13] 7690 5-8-12 51 .... TonyHamilton 2 — 50
(Michael Herrington) *cl up: led 1/2-way: sn rdn: hdd and n.m.r wl over 1f out: grad wknd* — **9/2**[2]

6304 **7** *3¼* [illegible] ....(b1) NathanAlison(5) 10 — 37
(Mandy Rowland) *chsd ldrs: rdn along over 2f out: sn wknd* — **16/1**

45-0 **8** *½* **Darwin Star**[8] 7754 3-9-7 60 .... MartinLane 7 — 44
(Dean Ivory) *dwlt: hdwy and prom after 2f: sn rdn and wknd 2f out* — **33/1**

6400 **9** *1¾* **Thoughtsofstardom**[14] 7676 8-8-1 47 ....(be) DannyBrock(7) 8 — 25
(Phil McEntee) *cl up: led after 1 1/2f: hdd 1/2-way and sn wknd* — **14/1**

0433 **10** *6* **Good Timin'**[13] 7693 3-8-10 49 ....(be) MichaelStainton 11 — —
(David Brown) *prom on stands' rail: rdn along 1/2-way: sn wknd* — **10/1**

60.20 secs (0.50) **Going Correction** +0.05s/f (Slow) — **10** Ran SP% **117.3**
Speed ratings (Par 101): **98,97,95,94,93 93,88,87,84,74**
toteswingers:1&2:£10.30, 2&3:£14.80, 1&3:£8.80 CSF £56.46 CT £376.78 TOTE £5.80: £2.10, £3.60, £3.00; EX 34.00 TRIFECTA Not won..
Owner Stoneypath Racing Club **Bred** R R Whitton **Trained** Haddington, East Lothian
■ Stewards' Enquiry : Nathan Alison two-day ban: used whip with excessive frequency (Jan 5-6)

FOCUS
The time was 0.75 seconds slower than the second division.
Good Timin' Official explanation: trainer's representative said that the gelding bled

7854 TOTEQUADPOT H'CAP (DIV II) — 5f (F)

1:00 (1:01) (Class 6) (0-60,60) 3-Y-O+ — **£1,704** (£503; £251) **Stalls** High

Form — RPR

0312 **1** — **Wreningham**[6] 7785 6-9-1 57 .... RyanClark(3) 3 — 69
(Pat Eddery) *cl up: effrt to ld over 1f out: sn rdn clr: kpt on* — **5/2**[1]

6042 **2** *1¼* **Argentine (IRE)**[64] 6943 7-9-0 53 ....(b) TomEaves 7 — 60
(Ian Semple) *in tch: hdwy wl over 1f out: sn rdn: styd on to chse wnr ins fnl f: no imp towards fin* — **5/1**[3]

264 **3** *1¼* **Tancred Spirit**[120] 5368 3-8-8 47 ....(v) BarryMcHugh 5 — 50
(Paul Midgley) *in tch: hdwy to chse ldrs 2f out: sn rdn and kpt on fnl f* — **22/1**

4001 **4** *hd* **Steel City Boy (IRE)**[13] 7690 8-9-7 60 .... KellyHarrison 8 — 62
(Garry Woodward) *led 1 1/2f: chsd ldrs: rdn along 2f out: kpt on u.p fnl f* — **14/1**

4005 **5** *hd* **Porthgwidden Beach (USA)**[13] 7690 3-8-10 49 ....(t) LeeNewman 4 — 50
(Anthony Middleton) *prom: rdn along wl over 1f out: kpt on same pce* — **16/1**

1400 **6** *hd* **Bond Blade**[24] 7567 3-9-4 60 .... DaleSwift(3) 2 — 60
(Geoffrey Oldroyd) *dwlt: hdwy to chse ldrs 1/2-way: sn rdn and no imp appr fnl f* — **4/1**[2]

0001 **7** *2* **Bird Dog**[9] 7747 5-8-5 51 6ex ....(v) DannyBrock(7) 1 — 44
(Phil McEntee) *prom: effrt 2f out: sn rdn and wknd appr fnl f* — **10/1**

0040 **8** *hd* **Lady Royal Oak (IRE)**[6] 7785 4-8-3 49 .... JenniferFerguson(7) 9 — 41
(Olivia Maylam) *dwlt: rapid hdwy to ld after 1 1/2f: rdn and hdd over 1f out: sn wknd* — **50/1**

0004 **9** *4* **Whoateallthepius (IRE)**[8] 7755 3-8-13 52 .... ShaneKelly 6 — 30
(Dean Ivory) *a towards rr* — **20/1**

0650 **10** *7* **Mustafeed (USA)**[8] 7755 3-9-1 54 ....(b1) JimCrowley 11 — —
(Keith Dalgleish) *in tch: rdn along bef 1/2-way: sn outpcd* — **9/1**

5546 **11** *½* **Wandering Lad**[10] 7737 3-8-4 50 .... JasonHart(7) 10 — —
(Declan Carroll) *a towards rr* — **12/1**

59.45 secs (-0.25) **Going Correction** +0.05s/f (Slow) — **11** Ran SP% **115.6**
Speed ratings (Par 101): **104,102,100,99,99 99,95,95,89,77 77**
toteswingers:1&2:£3.20, 1&3:£10.50, 2&3:£10.90 CSF £14.01 CT £221.24 TOTE £3.60: £1.70, £2.20, £5.40; EX 8.80 Trifecta £64.30 Pool: £504.26 - 5.80 winning units..
Owner Miss Emma L Owen **Bred** Executive Bloodlines Ltd **Trained** Nether Winchendon, Bucks

FOCUS
The time was 0.75 seconds quicker than the first division.
Whoateallthepius(IRE) Official explanation: trainer's rep said the filly, who is moody, resented the kickback

7855 TOTEQUADPOT MAIDEN STKS — 7f (F)

1:30 (1:35) (Class 5) 2-Y-O — **£2,328** (£693; £346; £173) **Stalls** Low

Form — RPR

42 **1** — **Dark Falcon (IRE)**[17] 7634 2-9-3 0 .... KierenFallon 3 — 77
(James Tate) *trckd ldr: hdwy 2f out: rdn over 1f out: led jst ins fnl f: kpt on* — **3/1**[2]

2 **2** *1¼* **Bold Cuffs**[11] 7724 2-9-3 0 .... StevieDonohoe 2 — 74
(Sir Mark Prescott Bt) *s.i.s and in rr: pushed along and hdwy 1/2-way: rdn to chse ldrs over 2f out: kpt on fnl f: nrst fin* — **4/7**[1]

2432 **3** *½* **Ishiamiracle**[6] 7780 2-8-5 60 ....(p) LeonnaMayor(7) 5 — 67
(Phil McEntee) *led: clr 1/2-way: rdn wl over 1f out: hdd jst ins fnl f: kpt on same pce: lost 2nd nr fin* — **13/2**[3]

44 **4** *3* **Availed Speaker (IRE)**[11] 7724 2-9-3 0 .... TonyHamilton 6 — 65
(Richard Fahey) *chsd ldrs: rdn along wl over 2f out: sn one pce* — **25/1**

3 **5** *14* **Perla Du Ma (IRE)**[34] 7471 2-9-3 0 ....(vt1) MartinLane 1 — 28
(Tobias B P Coles) *chsd ldng pair: rdn along 3f out: wknd 2f out* — **14/1**

6 *¾* **Showsinger** 2-8-12 0 .... BarryMcHugh 8 — 21
(Richard Fahey) *dwlt: a in rr* — **40/1**

0 **7** *½* **Luctor Emergo (IRE)**[85] 6448 2-9-3 0 .... JimCrowley 4 — 25
(Keith Dalgleish) *a in rr* — **50/1**

0 **8** *20* **National Hero (IRE)**[19] 7626 2-9-3 0 .... JoeFanning 7 — —
(Mark Johnston) *in tch: rdn along over 3f out: sn wknd* — **20/1**

1m 29.62s (-0.68) **Going Correction** -0.10s/f (Stan) — **8** Ran SP% **121.7**
Speed ratings (Par 96): **99,97,97,93,77 76,76,53**
toteswingers:1&2:£1.60, 1&3:£1.60, 2&3:£2.00 CSF £5.28 TOTE £4.20: £1.40, £1.02, £1.60; EX 7.10 Trifecta £20.70 Pool: £903.26 - 32.17 winning units..
Owner Saeed Manana **Bred** Michael O'Mahony **Trained** Newmarket, Suffolk
■ A first winner for James Tate as a trainer.
■ Stewards' Enquiry : Stevie Donohoe two-day ban: used whip with excessive frequency (Jan 5-6)

FOCUS
The form is ordinary, but the front two both look reasonable types in the making.

NOTEBOOK
Dark Falcon(IRE) didn't quite see out 1m on Polytrack when debuting for this yard last time, although that was his first start after a break. Dropped in trip but on a more demanding track, he plugged on at the one pace and that proved good enough. The winner should be fine over further in due course and can make a fair handicapper. (tchd 11-4)
Bold Cuffs, runner-up on his debut over 6f here, was still in need of the experience and couldn't justify odds-on favouritism. This big horse compromised his chance with a slow start and took an age to pick up, displaying a giant stride and plenty of knee action. He's open to a deal of improvement and should stay further, with there being plenty of stamina on the dam's side of his pedigree. (op 4-6 tchd 8-11)
Ishiamiracle looked a thoroughly awkward character beforehand, continually playing up and proving tricky to handle. In the race itself she was allowed an uncontested lead, but she couldn't make the most of it. (op 7-1)
Availed Speaker(IRE) was stepped up in trip once again but still didn't have the required speed. Handicaps are now an option. (op 22-1)

7856 TOTEPOOL MAIDEN FILLIES' STKS — 1m (F)

2:00 (2:02) (Class 5) 3-Y-O+ — **£2,328** (£693; £346; £173) **Stalls** Low

Form — RPR

4U5 **1** — **Community (USA)**[15] 7662 3-8-7 0 .... LeonnaMayor(7) 8 — 65
(Phil McEntee) *mde all: clr over 2f out: rdn wl over 1f out: kpt on* — **11/2**[3]

3040 **2** *3¼* **Ecossaise**[15] 7661 3-9-0 70 .... JoeFanning 2 — 58
(Mark Johnston) *trckd wnr: hdwy over 2f out: rdn wl over 1f out: sn edgd lft and kpt on same pce fnl f* — **10/11**[1]

3 *2½* **Vehement**[22] 5-8-12 0 .... SimonPearce(3) 5 — 52
(Andy Turnell) *s.i.s and bhd: hdwy over 3f out: rdn over 2f out: kpt on: nrst fin* — **16/1**

-340 **4** *4* **Moon Over Water (IRE)**[49] 7250 3-9-0 63 .... JimCrowley 6 — 43
(Roger Varian) *chsd ldng pair: rdn along 3f out: sn one pce* — **2/1**[2]

5 *12* **Ravanchi**[139] 7-9-1 0 .... RussKennemore 1 — 15
(Frank Sheridan) *a towards rr* — **100/1**

0 **6** *13* **Rosa Luxemburg**[9] 7747 3-9-0 0 .... TomEaves 4 — —
(Bryan Smart) *in tch: rdn along 1/2-way: sn wknd* — **50/1**

7 *2¼* **Exeptional Girl**[139] 5-9-1 0 .... RobbieFitzpatrick 7 — —
(Frank Sheridan) *a towards rr: outpcd and bhd fnl 3f* — **40/1**

1m 44.34s (0.64) **Going Correction** -0.10s/f (Stan)
WFA 3 from 4yo+ 1lb — **7** Ran SP% **112.4**
Speed ratings (Par 100): **92,88,86,82,70 57,55**
toteswingers:1&2:£1.60, 1&3:£4.20, 2&3:£3.10 CSF £10.63 TOTE £7.20: £2.80, £1.10; EX 10.70 Trifecta £56.90 Pool: £808.65 - 10.50 winning units..
Owner S Jakes **Bred** Brereton C Jones **Trained** Newmarket, Suffolk
■ Stewards' Enquiry : Leonna Mayor two-day ban: used whip with excessive frequency (Jan 5-6)

FOCUS
The time was 0.68 seconds slower than the earlier juvenile seller, and the runner-up's official rating offers nothing like a reliable guide to the form. It was an uncompetitive, moderate contest.
Vehement Official explanation: jockey said mare was slowly away

7857 SOUTHWELL-RACECOURSE.CO.UK H'CAP — 7f (F)

2:30 (2:32) (Class 5) (0-70,70) 3-Y-O+ — **£2,393** (£712; £355; £177) **Stalls** Low

Form — RPR

2005 **1** — **Andiamo Via**[16] 7648 4-8-8 57 .... KierenFallon 10 — 66
(Michael Smith) *led: rdn 2f out: hdd over 1f out: rallied to ld again ins fnl f: jst hld on* — **8/1**[3]

6134	2	shd	**Chookie Avon**[7] 7767 4-9-5 **68**....(p) JimCrowley 1 (Keith Dalgleish) *in tch on inner: rdn along wl over 2f out: hdwy wl over 1f out: rdn to chal ins fnl f: ev ch tl nt qckn nr fin*	77
			11/4[1]	
0130	3	1 ½	**Elhamri**[9] 7744 7-9-3 **66**.... HayleyTurner 2 (Conor Dore) *cl up: rdn to ld wl over 1f out: hdd ins fnl f: one pce towards fin*	71
			14/1	
0006	4	1	**Horatio Carter**[16] 7646 6-9-1 **64**....(b) DanielTudhope 3 (David O'Meara) *hld up in rr: hdwy wl over 2f out: rdn to chse ldrs over 1f out: ev ch ent fnl f: kpt on same pce*	66
			10/1	
0000	5	1 ¾	**Mazovian (USA)**[16] 7646 3-8-10 **62**.... AdamBeschizza[(3)] 13 (Michael Chapman) *cl up: rdn along 3f out: wknd wl over 1f out* **40/1**	59
0003	6	½	**Prince Of Vasa (IRE)**[16] 7641 4-8-8 **57**.... AndrewMullen 9 (Michael Smith) *towards rr: rdn along 1/2-way: styd on fnl 2f: nrst fin* **12/1**	53
4643	7	1	**Boy The Bell**[16] 7646 4-9-4 **67**.... FrannyNorton 5 (Ollie Pears) *hld up in rr: hdwy over 2f out: sn rdn and kpt on: nrst fin* **7/1**[2]	60
1400	8	3	**Twice Red**[9] 7744 3-9-7 **70**.... JoeFanning 6 (Derek Shaw) *hld up: a towards rr* **14/1**	55
623	9	¾	**Salerosa (IRE)**[12] 7710 6-9-4 **70**....(p) DaleSwift[(3)] 7 (Ann Duffield) *in tch: hdwy to chse ldrs over 2f out: sn rdn and wknd over 1f out* **7/1**[2]	53
0060	10	½	**Smalljohn**[19] 7625 5-9-6 **69**....(v) TomEaves 11 (Bryan Smart) *chsd ldrs: rdn along over 2f out: sn wknd* **8/1**[3]	51
5600	11	nse	**Huzzah (IRE)**[17] 7637 6-9-7 **70**.... MichaelStainton 4 (Paul Howling) *hld up: a in rr* **18/1**	52
5113	12	2 ½	**Quite A Catch (IRE)**[55] 7137 3-9-6 **69**....(v) LeeNewman 12 (Jonathan Portman) *a towards rr* **11/1**	44
0005	13	17	**Waabel**[11] 7726 4-9-5 **68**.... WilliamCarson 14 (Richard Guest) *cl up: rdn along wl over 2f out: sn wknd* **66/1**	—

1m 29.45s (-0.85) **Going Correction** -0.10s/f (Stan) 13 Ran SP% **121.5**
Speed ratings (Par 103): **100,99,98,97,95 94,93,89,89,88 88,85,66**
toteswingers:1&2:£6.70, 1&3:£31.10, 2&3:£14.30 CSF £30.62 CT £326.40 TOTE £11.70: £3.40, £1.20, £4.50; EX 40.30 TRIFECTA Not won..
Owner Mrs H I S Calzini **Bred** Mrs H I S Calzini **Trained** Kirkheaton, Northumberland

FOCUS
A modest handicap.

7858 SOUTHWELL GOLF CLUB H'CAP — 1m 6f (F)

3:00 (3:00) (Class 6) (0-65,65) 3-Y-O+ — **£1,772** (£523; £261) Stalls Low

Form				RPR
5050	1		**Storm Hawk (IRE)**[24] 7564 4-9-6 **60**....(b[1]) RyanClark[(3)] 6 (Pat Eddery) *dwlt and rr: smooth hdwy 1/2-way: trckd ldng pair over 3f out: led wl over 2f out: sn clr* **8/1**	78+
4321	2	7	**Carnac (IRE)**[13] 7688 5-9-4 **55**....(p) ShaneKelly 5 (Alan McCabe) *trckd ldr: led over 4f out: rdn along and hdd wl over 2f out: kpt on u.p: no ch w wnr* **7/2**[1]	60
45	3	1 ¾	**Uncut Stone (IRE)**[13] 7689 3-9-4 **62**.... TomEaves 9 (Peter Niven) *trckd ldrs: hdwy and cl up 4f out: chsd ldr over 3f out: rdn wl over 2f out: kpt on same pce* **5/1**[3]	65
0060	4	11	**Empyrean (USA)**[19] 7631 3-8-2 **46** oh1.... LukeMorris 12 (Sir Mark Prescott Bt) *chsd ldrs: rdn along over 4f out: plugged on same pce fnl 3f* **20/1**	33
0060	5	1	**Motirani**[57] 7107 4-9-6 **60**....(t) SimonPearce[(3)] 8 (Lydia Pearce) *bhd tl sme hdwy fnl 3f: nvr a factor* **25/1**	46
0663	6	hd	**Seawood**[16] 7645 5-8-11 **48**.... RussKennemore 3 (Roy Bowring) *hld up towards rr: sme hdwy over 3f out: sn rdn along and n.d* **4/1**[2]	34
0/00	7	16	**Marina's Ocean**[7] 7775 7-8-9 **46** oh1....(t) KellyHarrison 7 (Roy Bowring) *hld up: a in rr* **66/1**	9
0-4	8	6	**Ibrox (IRE)**[16] 7506 6-9-12 **63**....(p) AndrewMullen 10 (Alan Brown) *chsd ldrs: rdn along 5f out: sn wknd* **25/1**	18
0000	9	13	**Sirgarfieldsobers (IRE)**[9] 7215 5-10-0 **65**.... DanielTudhope 4 (Declan Carroll) *led: rdn along 5f out: hdd over 4f out and sn wknd* **14/1**	—
-422	10	7	**Arizona High**[146] 2305 3-9-5 **63**....(t) JoeFanning 2 (Andrew Crook) *chsd ldrs: rdn along over 4f out: sn wknd* **25/1**	—
0306	11	4 ½	**Chantilly Dancer (IRE)**[23] 7573 5-8-9 **46** oh1.... FrannyNorton 11 (Michael Quinn) *dwlt: a in rr* **40/1**	—
0/4	12	2 ¼	**Marlos Moment**[12] 7720 5-8-9 **46**....(bt) GrahamGibbons 1 (Mark Michael McNiff, Ire) *trckd ldrs: rdn along over 4f out: sn wknd* **4/1**[2]	—

3m 6.53s (-1.77) **Going Correction** -0.10s/f (Stan)
WFA 3 from 4yo+ 7lb 12 Ran SP% **116.9**
Speed ratings (Par 101): **101,97,96,89,89 89,79,76,69,65 62,61**
toteswingers:1&2:£7.30, 1&3:£9.90, 2&3:£4.20 CSF £32.77 CT £157.12 TOTE £10.20: £2.50, £1.10, £2.00; EX 44.30 Trifecta £170.50 Pool: £472.53 - 2.05 winning units..
Owner Storm Hawk Partnership **Bred** Rodger O'Dwyer **Trained** Nether Winchendon, Bucks

FOCUS
A modest handicap, but an easy winner.
Uncut Stone(IRE) Official explanation: joceky said gelding hung left-handed throughout
Marlos Moment Official explanation: jockey said gelding hung badly left-handed from 3f out and had no more to give

7859 HAPPY CHRISTMAS H'CAP — 1m 4f (F)

3:30 (3:34) (Class 6) (0-60,58) 3-Y-O+ — **£1,704** (£503; £251) Stalls Low

Form				RPR
0323	1		**Spahi (FR)**[16] 7647 5-9-3 **51**.... DanielTudhope 12 (David O'Meara) *hld up in rr: smooth hdwy 4f out: wd st towards stands rail: chal on bit over 1f out: rdn to ld ins fnl f: kpt on* **5/2**[1]	60
-000	2	nk	**Newport Arch**[54] 7159 3-8-12 **54**.... MichaelO'Connell[(3)] 14 (John Quinn) *in tch on outer: hdwy over 4f out: cl up 3f out: wd st: rdn to ld 1 1/2f out: hdd ins fnl f: no ex towards fin* **20/1**	63
0503	3	2 ¾	**Magic Millie (IRE)**[11] 7722 4-8-6 **45**.... RyanPowell[(5)] 9 (David O'Meara) *hld up: hdwy over 3f out: swtchd wd to stands' rail over 2f out: str run to chal over 1f out: sn rdn and ev ch tl one pce ins fnl f* **14/1**	50
605-	4	4 ½	**Broughtons Bandit**[399] 7495 4-8-11 **45**.... StevieDonohoe 10 (Willie Musson) *towards rr: hdwy over 4f out: rdn to chse ldrs over 2f out: kpt on same pce appr fnl f* **25/1**	42
6304	5	½	**Phoenix Flame**[12] 7712 3-9-2 **55**....(v) ShaneKelly 13 (Alan McCabe) *trckd ldrs: effrt over 3f out: rdn over 2f out: drvn wl over 1f out and grad wknd* **25/1**	52
0005	6	hd	**Nha Trang (IRE)**[10] 7741 4-8-11 **45**.... LukeMorris 1 (Michael Appleby) *in tch: effrt over 3f out: rdn along over 2f out: kpt on same pce* **16/1**	41
3352	7	1 ¼	**Marina Ballerina**[11] 7723 3-8-6 **50** ow1.... DavidKenny[(5)] 11 (Roy Bowring) *hld up in rr: sme hdwy 3f out: n.d* **11/2**[3]	44
3024	8	1	**Locum**[16] 7647 6-9-10 **58**.... KierenFallon 8 (Mark H Tompkins) *trckd ldrs: cl up 4f out: led wl over 2f out: rdn and hdd 1 1/2f out: wknd ent fnl f* **7/2**[2]	51
0005	9	2 ¼	**Kipchak (IRE)**[16] 7647 6-9-10 **58**....(b) HayleyTurner 4 (Conor Dore) *led after 1f: rdn along 3f out: hdd over 2f out and sn wknd* **16/1**	47
0406	10	6	**Indian Emperor (IRE)**[13] 7687 3-9-4 **57**.... TomEaves 7 (Peter Niven) *a towards rr* **40/1**	36
4003	11	3 ¼	**Miereveld**[9] 7743 4-9-5 **53**....(b) FrannyNorton 2 (Shaun Harris) *dwlt: a towards rr* **28/1**	27
3006	12	17	**Yossi (IRE)**[12] 7720 7-8-4 **45**....(b) CharlesEddery[(7)] 3 (Richard Guest) *dwlt: sn chsng ldrs on inner: rdn along 4f out: wknd over 2f out* **20/1**	—
0044	13	1 ¼	**Raghdaan**[9] 7743 4-9-2 **55**....(b[1]) LauraPike[(5)] 6 (Peter Hiatt) *midfield: lost pl after 4f and sn in rr* **12/1**	—
650P	14	14	**Kingaroo (IRE)**[59] 7070 5-9-8 **56**.... GrahamGibbons 5 (Garry Woodward) *led 1f: cl up tl rdn along over 4f out and sn wknd* **12/1**	—

2m 39.69s (-1.31) **Going Correction** -0.10s/f (Stan)
WFA 3 from 4yo+ 5lb 14 Ran SP% **123.1**
Speed ratings (Par 101): **100,99,97,94,94 94,93,93,91,87 85,74,73,63**
CSF £63.30 CT £615.78 TOTE £2.80: £1.60, £8.10, £3.30; EX 95.00 TRIFECTA Not won..
Owner R G Fell **Bred** Snig Elevage **Trained** Nawton, N Yorks
■ Stewards' Enquiry : Kieren Fallon caution: entered wrong stall.

FOCUS
A moderate handicap run at a strong gallop.
Locum Official explanation: jockey said gelding had no more to give
T/Plt: £23.80 to a £1 stake. Pool:£49,924.87 - 1,527.03 winning tickets T/Qpdt: £4.00 to a £1 stake. Pool:£5,252.92 - 965.78 winning tickets JR

7860 - 7872a (Foreign Racing) - See Raceform Interactive

NAKAYAMA
Sunday, December 25

OFFICIAL GOING: Turf: firm

7873a ARIMA KINEN (THE GRAND PRIX) (GRADE 1) (3YO+) (TURF) — 1m 4f 110y

6:25 (12:00) 3-Y-O+ **£1,602,652** (£638,332; £398,105; £236,817; £157,878)

			RPR
1		**Orfevre (JPN)**[63] 3-8-9 0.... Kenichilkezoe 9 (Yasutoshi Ikee, Japan) **6/5**[1]	128+
2	¾	**Eishin Flash (JPN)**[28] 7563 4-9-0 0.... Christophe-PatriceLemaire 5 (Hideaki Fujiwara, Japan) **26/1**	124
3	nk	**To The Glory (JPN)**[28] 7563 4-9-0 0.... YuichiFukunaga 7 (Yasutoshi Ikee, Japan) **46/1**	124
4	¾	**Rulership (JPN)**[182] 4-9-0 0.... IoritzMendizabal 14 (Katsuhiko Sumii, Japan) **52/1**	122+
5	nk	**Tosen Jordan (JPN)**[28] 7563 5-9-0 0.... CraigAWilliams 10 (Yasutoshi Ikee, Japan) **41/5**[3]	122
6	¾	**Hiruno D'Amour (JPN)**[84] 6567 4-9-0 0.... ShinjiFujita 3 (Mitsugu Kon, Japan) **29/1**	121+
7	¾	**Buena Vista (JPN)**[28] 7563 5-8-9 0.... Yasunarilwata 1 (Hiroyoshi Matsuda, Japan) **11/5**[2]	115
8	nse	**Victoire Pisa (JPN)**[28] 7563 4-9-0 0.... MircoDemuro 2 (Katsuhiko Sumii, Japan) **92/10**	120
9	nk	**Red Davis (JPN)**[22] 3-8-9 0.... YutakaTake 13 (Hidetaka Otonashi, Japan) **172/10**	120
10	nk	**Earnestly (JPN)**[56] 7191 6-9-0 0.... TetsuzoSato 12 (Shozo Sasaki, Japan) **126/10**	119
11	1 ½	**Jaguar Mail (JPN)**[28] 7563 7-9-0 0....(b) HirofumiShii 11 (Noriyuki Hori, Japan) **76/1**	117
12	2	**Rose Kingdom (JPN)**[28] 7563 4-9-0 0.... HirokiGoto 8 (Kojiro Hashiguchi, Japan) **50/1**	114
13	1 ¾	**King Top Gun (JPN)**[28] 7563 8-9-0 0.... YoshitomiShibata 6 (Ippo Sameshima, Japan) **132/1**	111

2m 36.0s (156.00)
WFA 3 from 4yo+ 5lb 13 Ran SP% **125.3**
PARI-MUTUEL (all including 100 ypj stake): WIN 220 SHOW 140, 490, 740 DF 3170 SF 3650.
Owner Sunday Racing Co Ltd **Bred** Shadai Corporation Inc **Trained** Japan

7844 WOLVERHAMPTON (A.W) (L-H)
Monday, December 26

OFFICIAL GOING: Standard
Wind: Fresh, half behind Weather: Cloudy

7874 BRITISH STALLION STUDS SUPPORTING BRITISH RACING E B F MEDIAN AUCTION MAIDEN STKS — 5f 20y(P)

1:15 (1:15) (Class 5) 2-Y-O — **£3,234** (£962; £481; £240) Stalls Low

Form				RPR
4445	1		**Hey Fiddle Fiddle (IRE)**[33] 7514 2-8-12 **62**....(b[1]) WilliamCarson 1 (Charles Hills) *trckd ldrs: hdwy to ld over 1f out: rdn and edgd lft ins fnl f: kpt on wl* **15/8**[2]	63+
	2	2 ¾	**Magilini (IRE)** 2-8-12 0.... GrahamGibbons 4 (David Barron) *dwlt: sn prom on outside: swtchd lft and effrt over 2f out: chsd wnr ins fnl f: kpt on: no imp* **11/4**[3]	53
050	3	1	**Villa Reigns**[25] 7592 2-9-3 **52**....(b) LukeMorris 3 (John Weymes) *led: rdn: hung lft and hdd over 1f out: kpt on same pce fnl f* **11/1**	55
602	4	6	**Look At Me Now**[17] 7692 2-9-3 **60**....(v) RyanMoore 5 (Jim Boyle) *t.k.h: trckd ldr: rdn and outpcd whn hung lft bnd ent st: sn btn* **7/4**[1]	33

62.84 secs (0.54) **Going Correction** +0.075s/f (Slow) 4 Ran SP% **106.1**
Speed ratings (Par 96): **98,93,92,82**
CSF £6.94 TOTE £2.80; EX 6.50.
Owner Triermore Stud **Bred** C O P Hanbury **Trained** Lambourn, Berks

FOCUS
This was a pretty modest maiden but the winner did not need to improve much and could be capable of stepping up again.

NOTEBOOK
Hey Fiddle Fiddle(IRE) coped with the drop from 7f. The first-time blinkers seemed to help, but she'll surely find it tougher when attempting to follow up. (tchd 13-8 and 2-1)
Magilini(IRE) is a half-sister to winners at up to 7f, out of a successful sprinter. She showed ability on this racecourse debut and should have learnt from the experience. (op 9-4)
Villa Reigns would have been 15lb better off with the winner in a handicap. (op 8-1 tchd 15-2 and 12-1)

The Form Book, Raceform Ltd, Compton, RG20 6NL

Look At Me Now couldn't repeat the form he showed when dead-heating for second in a first-time here on his previous outing. He never looked happy, including not handling the bend as well as the others. He was reported to have hung right. Official explanation: jockey said colt hung right (op 9-4 tchd 13-8)

7875 BETFRED WHEN BOTH TEAMS SCORE NURSERY — 7f 32y(P)
1:50 (1:50) (Class 4) (0-85,78) 2-Y-O **£4,204** (£1,251; £625; £312) **Stalls** High

Form RPR

111 **1** **Mr Red Clubs (IRE)**[14] 7735 2-9-1 **72**................ ShaneKelly 1 76
(Tim Pitt) *in tch: effrt over 2f out: hdwy over 1f out: edgd lft and led ins fnl f: pushed out* **4/1**[2]

0344 **2** *1* **Abshir Zain (IRE)**[27] 7576 2-8-4 **61**................(bt) NickyMackay 5 63
(Clive Brittain) *pckd s: sn prom: led over 3f out: rdn: edgd lft and hdd ins fnl f: kpt on same pce* **12/1**

0533 **3** *1 1/2* **Stag Hill (IRE)**[11] 7763 2-8-1 **58**................ LukeMorris 6 56
(Sylvester Kirk) *dwlt: sn in tch on outside: rdn and outpcd over 2f out: rallied over 1f out: hung lft and kpt on fnl f: tk 3rd cl home* **7/4**[1]

5231 **4** *1/2* **Not Bad For A Boy (IRE)**[9] 7799 2-9-7 **78**................ RyanMoore 7 75
(Richard Hannon) *t.k.h early: cl up: rdn and effrt 2f out: edgd lft and kpt on same pce fnl f* **5/1**[3]

0340 **5** *1 1/4* **Clean Bowled (IRE)**[112] 5783 2-7-12 **62**................ NoraLooby(7) 2 57
(Alan McCabe) *hld up on ins: outpcd after 3f: hung lft and stdy hdwy fnl 2f: nrst fin* **22/1**

2213 **6** *1/2* **Chelsea Mick**[10] 7786 2-8-12 **72**................ DaleSwift(3) 3 65
(John Mackie) *trckd ldrs: drvn and outpcd over 2f out: no imp fnl f* **7/1**

315 **7** *4* **Fortrose Academy (IRE)**[11] 7765 2-9-7 **78**................ DavidProbert 4 61
(Andrew Balding) *led to over 3f out: rallied: rdn and wknd appr fnl f* **6/1**

10 **8** *4 1/2* **Jawking**[236] 1806 2-9-1 **72**................ AdamKirby 8 44
(David Evans) *t.k.h: hld up: racd wd 1f: rdn and outpcd 1/2-way: no ch after* **25/1**

1m 30.89s (1.29) **Going Correction** +0.075s/f (Slow) **8** Ran SP% **115.7**
Speed ratings (Par 98): **95,93,92,91,90 89,85,79**
toteswingers:1&2:£7.30, 2&3:£5.80, 1&3:£2.70 CSF £50.58 CT £113.07 TOTE £5.20: £1.60, £3.20, £1.40; EX 55.90 Trifecta £180.90 Pool: £332.58 - 1.36 winning units..
Owner Ferrybank Properties Limited **Bred** Tally-Ho Stud **Trained** Newmarket, Suffolk
■ Stewards' Enquiry : Nicky Mackay one-day ban: careless riding (Jan 9)

FOCUS
A fair nursery and it went to a bang in-form improver. The form looks straightforward, rated around the placed horses.

NOTEBOOK
Mr Red Clubs(IRE), making his debut for another new yard, coped with the rise in class to make it three wins from his last four starts. He did this quite well and is now unbeaten in three outings at Wolverhampton.
Abshir Zain(IRE) recovered from a slight stumble on leaving stalls and had his chance under a positive ride.
Stag Hill(IRE) didn't get the best of trips, including being forced wide on the bend into the straight, and he did well to finish so close. (op 11-4 tchd 3-1)
Not Bad For A Boy(IRE) found this tougher than the five-runner novice event he won at Lingfield last time. (op 9-2)
Clean Bowled(IRE) sported a visor and tongue-tie when last seen in September, but he has since been gelded. This was an eyecatching debut for his new yard, with him staying on from an unpromising position without being given a hard time, but it was disconcerting that he hung left. Official explanation: jockey said gelding hung left-handed throughout (op 28-1 tchd 20-1)

7876 BETFRED GOALS GALORE CLAIMING STKS — 7f 32y(P)
2:25 (2:25) (Class 6) 3-Y-O+ **£1,704** (£503; £251) **Stalls** High

Form RPR

3604 **1** **Bawaardi (IRE)**[15] 7726 5-8-13 80................ RyanMoore 2 89
(Richard Fahey) *trckd ldr: drvn along over 2f out: rallied to ld ent fnl f: kpt on wl u.p* **9/2**[2]

2113 **2** *hd* **One Way Or Another (AUS)**[17] 7695 8-8-9 76................(b) HayleyTurner 3 84
(David Evans) *t.k.h: stdd bhd ldrs: smooth hdwy over 1f out: rdn: edgd lft and ev ch ins fnl f: kpt on: hld nr fin* **3/1**[1]

2401 **3** *3/4* **Ezra Church (IRE)**[19] 7658 4-8-7 72................ BarryMcHugh 1 80
(David Barron) *led at stdy pce: rdn and edgd lft over 1f out: hdd ent fnl f: kpt on same pce* **8/1**

5215 **4** *1* **Faithful Ruler (USA)**[33] 7510 [illegible]................(p) LukeMorris 9 76
(Ronald Harris) *hld up on ins: effrt and cl up over 1f out: kpt on same pce fnl f* **15/2**

2365 **5** *nk* **Kingswinford (IRE)**[55] 7211 5-8-5 79................ WilliamCarson 4 75
(Brian Ellison) *prom: drvn and outpcd 1/2-way: rallied 2f out: kpt on same pce fnl f* **9/2**[2]

0105 **6** *1 3/4* **Without Prejudice (USA)**[16] 7715 6-8-5 67................ JamesSullivan 6 70
(Michael Easterby) *hld up: hdwy on outside over 2f out: sn drvn along: edgd lft and no imp over 1f out* **8/1**

1105 **7** *1 1/4* **Princess Dayna**[23] 7629 3-8-0 65................ NickyMackay 12 62
(Tom Dascombe) *t.k.h: hld up: rdn over 2f out: hdwy fnl f: nvr able to chal* **20/1**

3622 **8** *hd* **Stevie Gee (IRE)**[10] 7776 7-8-2 71................(v) RyanPowell(5) 5 68
(Ian Williams) *hld up in tch: effrt and rdn over 2f out: outpcd appr fnl f* **7/1**[3]

0200 **9** *nk* **Christmas Carnival**[11] 7771 4-8-2 68................ AmyRyan(3) 7 65
(Michael Easterby) *sn towards rr: rdn over 3f out: c wd st: sme late hdwy: nvr on terms* **40/1**

00 **10** *12* **Dubonny**[7] 7822 4-8-10 0................(t) RobbieFitzpatrick 11 38
(Frank Sheridan) *s.i.s: bhd: struggling over 3f out: sn btn* **80/1**

1m 30.01s (0.41) **Going Correction** +0.075s/f (Slow) **10** Ran SP% **116.3**
Speed ratings (Par 101): **100,99,98,97,97 95,94,93,93,79**
toteswingers:1&2:£3.50, 2&3:£6.10, 1&3:£6.50 CSF £18.08 TOTE £5.20: £1.80, £1.10, £4.10; EX 18.50 Trifecta £60.10 Pool: £313.51 - 3.86 winning units..Bawaardi was claimed by P. D. Evans for £9000. Kingswinford was claimed by J. E. Abbey for £5000.
Owner The Matthewman One Partnership **Bred** Millsec Limited **Trained** Musley Bank, N Yorks

FOCUS
A fair claimer.

7877 BETFRED DOUBLE DELIGHT H'CAP — 1m 1f 103y(P)
2:55 (2:55) (Class 4) (0-85,82) 3-Y-O+ **£4,204** (£1,251; £625; £312) **Stalls** Low

Form RPR

1226 **1** **Opus Maximus (IRE)**[6] 7831 6-9-0 **75**................ HayleyTurner 10 83
(Conor Dore) *confidently rdn: stdy hdwy on ins over 1f out: pushed along and led last 50yds: comf* **7/1**

0415 **2** *1* **Chosen Forever**[30] 7558 6-9-1 **79**................ DaleSwift(3) 8 85
(Geoffrey Oldroyd) *cl up: led 1/2-way: rdn over 3f out: hdd and no ex last 50yds* **15/2**

0612 **3** *1* **Follow The Flag (IRE)**[11] 7772 7-9-5 **80**................(v) ShaneKelly 9 84
(Alan McCabe) *hld up in midfield on outside: hdwy and cl up after 3f: rdn and edgd lft over 1f out: kpt on same pce fnl f* **20/1**

0-00 **4** *shd* **Honey Of A Kitten (USA)**[94] 6319 3-9-5 **82**................ AdamKirby 3 86
(David Evans) *t.k.h: midfield: drvn along over 3f out: rallied over 1f out: nrst fin* **25/1**

6011 **5** *1/2* **Gritstone**[56] 7199 4-9-6 **81**................ BarryMcHugh 6 84
(Richard Fahey) *t.k.h early: trckd ldrs: effrt over 1f out: kpt on same pce fnl f* **7/2**[2]

1316 **6** *3/4* **Jordaura**[63] 7050 5-9-2 **77**................ DavidProbert 1 78
(Gay Kelleway) *hld up: effrt over 2f out: kpt on fnl f: nvr able to chal* **16/1**

0244 **7** *nk* **Snow Dancer (IRE)**[24] 7606 7-9-4 **79**................ PaddyAspell 5 79
(Hugh McWilliams) *hld up: rdn over 2f out: kpt on fnl f: nrst fin* **15/2**

3100 **8** *3* **Hidden Glory**[19] 7651 4-9-4 **79**................ FrederikTylicki 7 73
(James Given) *hld up on outside: drvn along over 3f out: sn no imp* **20/1**

0000 **9** *3 1/4* **Jawaab (IRE)**[12] 7759 7-8-10 **74**................(e) RobertLButler(3) 11 61
(Richard Guest) *midfield on outside: struggling over 2f out: sn btn* **50/1**

0000 **10** *6* **Fastnet Storm (IRE)**[79] 6708 5-9-3 **78**................ GrahamGibbons 4 53
(David Barron) *led to 1/2-way: cl up tl rdn and wknd over 1f out* **13/2**[3]

-231 **11** *3 1/2* **Fakhuur**[13] 7745 3-9-0 **77**................ RyanMoore 2 44
(Clive Brittain) *trckd ldrs: drvn over 3f out: wknd 2f out: sn btn and eased* **11/4**[1]

2m 1.21s (-0.49) **Going Correction** +0.075s/f (Slow)
WFA 3 from 4yo+ 2lb **11** Ran SP% **119.5**
Speed ratings (Par 105): **105,104,103,103,102 102,101,99,96,90 87**
toteswingers:1&2:£8.70, 2&3:£18.10, 1&3:£16.60 CSF £56.56 CT £1014.22 TOTE £10.20: £3.00, £2.60, £5.90; EX 80.90 Trifecta £186.40 Part won. Pool: £251.99 - 0.62 winning units..
Owner Mrs Louise Marsh **Bred** Mrs Anne Marie Burns **Trained** Cowbit, Lincs
■ Stewards' Enquiry : Dale Swift four-day ban: used whip with excessive frequency (Jan 9-12)

FOCUS
A fair handicap and the gallop must have been pretty sound.
Fakhuur Official explanation: trainer's rep had no explanation for the poor form shown

7878 BETFRED HAT TRICK HEAVEN BOXING DAY H'CAP — 1m 4f 50y(P)
3:30 (3:30) (Class 5) (0-75,75) 3-Y-O+ **£2,264** (£673; £336; £168) **Stalls** Low

Form RPR

3521 **1** **Tornado Force (IRE)**[19] 7661 3-9-4 **74**................ RyanMoore 7 91
(Jeremy Noseda) *trckd ldrs: hdwy to ld wl over 1f out: pushed clr* **8/11**[1]

1113 **2** *6* **Woop Woop (IRE)**[12] 7761 3-8-12 **73**................ RyanPowell(5) 6 80
(Ian Williams) *hld up in tch: rdn and hdwy over 2f out: chsd (clr) wnr over 1f out: kpt on: no imp* **7/2**[2]

2-20 **3** *1/2* **Crunched**[13] 1325 4-9-10 **75**................(p) ShaneKelly 5 81
(Tim Pitt) *led 3f: cl up: led over 2f out to wl over 1f out: sn one pce* **20/1**

6415 **4** *1/2* **Kames Park (IRE)**[10] 7789 9-8-9 **67**................ CharlesEddery(7) 8 72
(Richard Guest) *hld up: rdn along over 2f out: rdn and no imp over 1f out* **10/1**

0064 **5** *3 1/4* **Pelham Crescent (IRE)**[14] 7738 8-9-5 **70**................ DavidProbert 2 70
(Bryn Palling) *hld up on ins: effrt over 2f out: sn no imp: btn fnl f* **16/1**

5203 **6** *5* **Boa**[14] 7738 6-9-4 **69**................(e) AdamKirby 3 61
(Reg Hollinshead) *trckd ldrs: drvn and outpcd over 2f out: btn over 1f out* **7/1**[3]

0060 **7** *10* **Yossi (IRE)**[4] 7859 7-8-3 **61** oh16................(b) ShirleyTeasdale(7) 4 37
(Richard Guest) *t.k.h: cl up: led after 3f to over 2f out: sn wknd* **25/1**

2m 40.5s (-0.60) **Going Correction** +0.075s/f (Slow)
WFA 3 from 4yo+ 5lb **7** Ran SP% **116.2**
Speed ratings (Par 103): **105,101,100,100,98 94,88**
toteswingers:1&2:£1.70, 2&3:£6.20, 1&3:£4.40 CSF £3.66 CT £25.43 TOTE £1.40: £1.10, £1.80; EX 4.80 Trifecta £32.50 Pool: £723.42 - 16.46 winning units..
Owner Faisal Alsheikh **Bred** Haras Du Mezeray & Ronchalon Racing **Trained** Newmarket, Suffolk

FOCUS
An ordinary handicap.

7879 BOXING DAY NOVICE STKS — 1m 141y(P)
4:05 (4:05) (Class 5) 2-Y-O **£2,264** (£673; £336) **Stalls** Low

Form RPR

341 **1** **Prince Alzain (USA)**[37] 7493 2-9-3 82................ SteveDrowne 1 89+
(Gerard Butler) *t.k.h: trckd ldr: effrt and drvn over 1f out: led ins fnl f: kpt on strly* **3/1**[2]

212 **2** *1 1/4* **Harvard N Yale (USA)**[101] 6126 2-9-3 91................ RyanMoore 3 86
(Jeremy Noseda) *led at stdy pce: rdn over 2f out: hdd ins fnl f: kpt on same pce towards fin* **1/4**[1]

00 **3** *20* **Dr Albert**[7] 7821 2-8-12 0................ RobbieFitzpatrick 2 39
(Frank Sheridan) *t.k.h: chsd ldrs tl lost tch fr 3f out* **50/1**[3]

1m 52.13s (1.63) **Going Correction** +0.075s/f (Slow) **3** Ran SP% **107.0**
Speed ratings (Par 96): **95,93,76**
CSF £4.40 TOTE £4.00; EX 3.90.
Owner Asaad Al Banwan **Bred** Dermot Cantillon & Patrick Hayes **Trained** Newmarket, Suffolk

FOCUS
It's difficult to establish the true worth of this form, but the front two are well regarded. It didn't go as the market expected, however, with the odds-on favourite beaten fair and square. The winner could be underestimated but the second did not look ideally suited by the track.

NOTEBOOK
Prince Alzain(USA)'s C&D maiden win is working out nicely (runner-up and third won next time) and he confirmed he's pretty useful. There's talk of him going to Dubai. (op 9-4)
Harvard N Yale(USA) was allowed to set a steady pace in an uncontested lead, but couldn't match the winner's speed in the straight. There was talk pre-race of him being trained for the Kentucky Derby, so clearly he's believed to be pretty smart, but he had also been beaten at odds on when last seen in the Haynes, Hanson & Clark conditions race and that form has not been working out. Only time will show what he achieved here, but he does have sufficient scope to believe he may one day make it a decent level. (op 4-11)
Dr Albert was totally outclassed, but he can now switch to handicaps. (op 33-1)
T/Plt: £230.40 to a £1 stake. Pool of £44,346.94 - 140.46 winning tickets. T/Qpdt: £32.40 to a £1 stake Pool of £2,546.07 -58.00 w. tckts RY

7880a (Foreign Racing) - See RI

[7852] SOUTHWELL (L-H)
Tuesday, December 27

OFFICIAL GOING: Standard
Wind: Light across Weather: Fine and dry

7881 PLAY BIG MONEY TOTEJACKPOT TODAY NURSERY — 6f (F)
12:10 (12:10) (Class 5) (0-75,74) 2-Y-O **£2,385** (£704; £352) **Stalls** Low

Form RPR

2024 **1** **Man Of My Word**[17] 7708 2-8-11 **64** ow1................(p) GrahamGibbons 3 71
(Scott Dixon) *mde all: rdn wl over 1f out: kpt on strly fnl f* **16/1**

3661 **2** 1 ¼ **Sunny Side Up (IRE)**[26] 7592 2-8-10 **63** BarryMcHugh 6 66
(Richard Fahey) *hld up in tch: hdwy on outer 1/2-way: rdn to chse ldrs wl over 1f out and sn edgd lft: styd on wl fnl f* **6/1**[3]

5411 **3** ½ **Whisky Bravo**[18] 7686 2-9-2 **74** RyanPowell(5) 5 76
(David Brown) *promnent: hdwy to chse wnr wl over 2f out: rdn wl over 1f out and ev ch tl drvn and one pce ins fnl f* **11/10**[1]

0051 **4** ¾ **Faraway**[18] 7694 2-9-3 **70** LukeMorris 2 69
(Ronald Harris) *trckd ldrs: hdwy 1/2-way: rdn along wl over 1f out: drvn and one pce ent fnl f* **22/1**

2451 **5** ½ **M J Woodward**[11] 7778 2-8-2 **55** JamesSullivan 8 53
(Paul Green) *s.i.s: hdwy 1/2-way: rdn 2f out: styd on to chse ldrs whn n.m.r ins fnl f: nrst fin* **5/1**[2]

0116 **6** 1 **Flying Pickets (IRE)**[6] 7849 2-8-13 **73** SAJackson(7) 7 71
(Alan McCabe) *s.i.s and bhd: hdwy 2f out: styng on whn n.m.r ent fnl f: nrst fin* **6/1**[3]

2125 **7** 1 **Adranian (IRE)**[16] 7725 2-9-3 **70** (v) AdamKirby 1 62
(David C Griffiths) *chsd wnr on inner: rdn along 2f out: wknd over 1f out* **11/1**

5335 **8** 11 **First Bid**[21] 7642 2-8-11 **64** FrederikTylicki 4 23
(James Given) *in tch: rdn along bef 1/2-way: wknd wl over 2f out* **25/1**

1m 15.85s (-0.65) **Going Correction** -0.175s/f (Stan) **8** Ran SP% **115.3**
Speed ratings (Par 96): **97,95,94,93,93 91,90,75**
toteswingers:1&2:£12.90, 2&3:£2.40, 1&3:£4.10 CSF £108.67 CT £195.56 TOTE £21.30: £3.90, £1.60, £1.10; EX 127.40 Trifecta £323.80 Pool: £603.86 - 1.38 winning units..
Owner P J Dixon & Partners **Bred** Mrs Yvette Dixon **Trained** Babworth, Notts
■ A first winner with his third runner for Scott Dixon. At 24 he is Britain's youngest trainer.

FOCUS
Several recent winners in a fair nursery. An ordinary gallop saw those held up at a disadvantage and the winner came down the centre. The form stacks up quite well but this is not a race to take too literally.

NOTEBOOK
Man Of My Word, down in trip and with the cheekpieces again fitted on this first run for his new trainer, was allowed an easy lead and did enough to get off the mark at the 11th attempt. Things went his way and he wouldn't be certain to build on this next time. (tchd 14-1)
Sunny Side Up(IRE) ◆, up 3lb for her Polytrack success and the sole filly in the race, ran creditably on this Fibresand debut against one that had an uncontested lead. She shaped as though a stiffer test over this trip or the step up to 7f would suit and she's sufficiently lightly raced to be open to improvement. (op 5-1)
Whisky Bravo, the well-backed market leader, had the run of the race but was found out from this higher mark in this more competitive event and lost his unbeaten record on the surface. Neverthless he was far from disgraced in terms of form and should continue to run well. (op 11-8 tchd Evens)
Faraway is exposed but was far from disgraced on this Fibresand debut and first run for his new yard, in the process shaping as though the return to 7f would suit better. (op 25-1 tchd 20-1)
M J Woodward wasn't disgraced after a tardy start in a race that suited those up with the pace and he'll be worth another chance away from progressive sorts. (op 7-1 tchd 8-1)
Flying Pickets(IRE) was another that wasn't seen to best effect after a slow start returned to this surface and dropped in distance. The return to 7f will suit and he is worth another chance. (op 9-2)

7882 TOTEPOOL MOBILE TEXT TOTE TO 89660 (S) STKS 5f (F)
12:45 (12:45) (Class 6) 2-Y-O **£1,704** (£503; £251) **Stalls** High

Form RPR
0044 **1** **Lady Nickandy (IRE)**[14] 7742 2-8-12 50 (v) AndrewMullen 2 54+
(Alan McCabe) *cl up: led 1/2-way: rdn and hung lft over 1f out: clr fnl f* **5/2**[2]

004 **2** 3 ½ **Italian Ice**[25] 7607 2-8-8 41 ow1 TomEaves 1 37
(Bryan Smart) *led: hdd 1/2-way and sn pushed along: swtchd rt and rdn over 1f out: kpt on one pce* **10/1**

1045 **3** 1 **Lord Buffhead**[12] 7770 2-9-0 53 RobertLButler(3) 3 42
(Richard Guest) *cl up: rdn along over 2f out: sn one pce* **7/1**

0460 **4** 2 ½ **Deduction (IRE)**[83] 6628 2-8-4 55 AdamBeschizza(3) 4 23
(Nigel Tinkler) *in tch nr stands' rail: rdn along over 2f out: sn edgd rt and one pce* **7/2**[3]

5035 **5** 2 **Regal Lady**[18] 7692 2-8-2 58 RyanPowell(5) 5 16
(David Brown) *slowly in stride: racd nr stands' rail: rdn along 1/2-way: a in rr* **7/4**[1]

60.47 secs (0.77) **Going Correction** -0.075s/f (Stan) **5** Ran SP% **108.7**
Speed ratings (Par 94): **90,84,82,78,75**
CSF £23.46 TOTE £3.70: £1.50, £5.70; EX 21.90.There was no bid for the winner.
Owner K N Lane **Bred** Martin Francis **Trained** Averham Park, Notts

FOCUS
A weak race, even by selling standards and one that took less winning than seemed likely with two of the market leaders disappointing. The pace was sound and the winner raced in the centre. The form could be rated 4lb out either way.

NOTEBOOK
Lady Nickandy(IRE), down in trip and in grade, returned to her best to win a weak event in which her main rivals disappointed. This looks her trip but she wouldn't be an obvious one to follow up. (op 4-1)
Italian Ice, who had a stiff task at the weights, confirms she possesses a little ability but she didn't show enough in this moderate event to suggest she would be one to go in head down for next time. (op 8-1 tchd 7-1)
Lord Buffhead, the only male in the field, had something to find conceding weight all round but, while he wasn't totally disgraced he's of little short-term interest. (tchd 8-1)
Deduction(IRE) had shown ability at a moderate level in maidens but proved disappointing after a break on this all-weather debut and first run for new connections. The return to further will suit better but she has plenty to prove. (op 10-3 tchd 3-1)
Regal Lady anticipated the start and was a long way below her best after racing away from the centre action for much of the way on this Fibresand debut. She will be worth another chance in similar company back on Polytrack but she is clearly limited. (op 6-4 tchd 2-1)

7883 TOTEQUADPOT CLAIMING STKS 5f (F)
1:15 (1:15) (Class 6) 3-Y-O+ **£1,704** (£503; £251) **Stalls** High

Form RPR
2024 **1** **Le Toreador**[7] 7832 6-9-9 85 (p) PhillipMakin 4 94
(Kevin Ryan) *mde most: rdn clr over 1f out: sn edgd lft: rdn out* **11/8**[2]

1603 **2** 3 ¼ **Desert Icon (IRE)**[14] 7746 5-8-0 74 (tp) RyanPowell(5) 2 64
(Alan McCabe) *v.s.a and bhd: hdwy 2f out: swtchd rt to stands' rail and rdn wl over 1f out: styd on strly fnl f: tk 2nd nr line* **5/4**[1]

0326 **3** ½ **Grudge**[10] 7804 6-8-5 66 (b) HayleyTurner 3 63
(Conor Dore) *cl up: rdn along and ev ch 2f out: sn hung lft to far rail: kpt on same pce: lost 2nd nr line* **9/2**[3]

0600 **4** 7 **Finn's Rainbow**[11] 7776 3-8-3 67 LukeMorris 5 35
(John Weymes) *dwlt: in tch: rdn along 1/2-way: sn wknd* **25/1**

58.72 secs (-0.98) **Going Correction** -0.075s/f (Stan) **4** Ran SP% **108.6**
Speed ratings (Par 101): **104,98,98,86**
CSF £3.47 TOTE £1.90; EX 3.50.Desert Icon was claimed by A. J. D. Lidderdale for £6000.
Owner Guy Reed **Bred** G Reed **Trained** Hambleton, N Yorks

FOCUS
An uncompetitive claimer in which only two of the four runners figured. The gallop was sound and the winner raced in the centre.

7884 BET TOTEPOOL TEXT TOTE TO 89660 H'CAP 1m 3f (F)
1:50 (1:50) (Class 5) (0-75,73) 3-Y-O+ **£2,385** (£704; £352) **Stalls** Low

Form RPR
3404 **1** **Xpres Maite**[16] 7722 8-9-4 68 (b) RussKennemore 1 77
(Roy Bowring) *sn led and clr after 2f: rdn along over 3f out: hdd wl over 2f out: cl up tl led again over 1f out: styd on gamely ins fnl f* **14/1**

4000 **2** 1 ¾ **The Lock Master (IRE)**[18] 7699 4-9-9 73 NeilChalmers 7 79
(Michael Appleby) *hld up: hdwy 4f out: rdn along to chse ldrs 3f out: effrt to chal on outer 2f out: sn rdn and ev ch tl one pce ins fnl f* **6/1**

4-1 **3** 2 **Bivouac (UAE)**[16] 7722 7-9-4 73 GarryWhillans(5) 3 75
(Alan Swinbank) *trckd ldrs: smooth hdwy and cl up over 3f out: led wl over 2f out: rdn and hdd over 1f out: one pce ins fnl f* **10/3**[2]

1P21 **4** ¾ **C P Joe (IRE)**[18] 7689 3-9-0 68 (v) FrannyNorton 4 69
(Paul Green) *trckd ldrs: pushed along wl over 3f out: rdn to chse ldrs 2f out: drvn and no imp appr fnl f* **85/40**[1]

04-3 **5** 10 **Ostentation**[17] 7713 4-9-5 69 AdamKirby 2 52
(Roger Teal) *chsd clr ldr: hdwy and cl up on inner 3f out: sn rdn and wknd fnl 2f* **4/1**[3]

056 **6** 6 **Rubi Dia**[96] 6279 4-9-3 67 BarryMcHugh 6 39
(Kevin M Prendergast) *a in rr* **7/1**

/02- **7** 7 **Black Jacari (IRE)**[517] 3402 6-9-6 73 MichaelO'Connell(3) 5 33
(Philip Kirby) *in tch: rdn along over 4f out: sn outpcd and bhd* **20/1**

2m 25.52s (-2.48) **Going Correction** -0.175s/f (Stan)
WFA 3 from 4yo+ 4lb **7** Ran SP% **113.3**
Speed ratings (Par 103): **102,100,99,98,91 87,82**
toteswingers:1&2:£9.60, 2&3:£5.50, 1&3:£5.70 CSF £91.53 TOTE £14.10: £5.90, £4.10; EX 63.90.
Owner Charterhouse Holdings Plc **Bred** S R Bowring **Trained** Edwinstowe, Notts

FOCUS
A fair handicap run at just an ordinary gallop. The winner continued the trend of racing down the centre.

7885 DUNCAN HIRD 60TH BIRTHDAY H'CAP 1m (F)
2:25 (2:25) (Class 6) (0-60,60) 3-Y-O+ **£1,704** (£503; £251) **Stalls** Low

Form RPR
0550 **1** **Ace Master**[16] 7728 3-9-1 55 RussKennemore 11 65
(Roy Bowring) *mde all: rdn wl over 1f out: styd on wl ins fnl f* **10/1**

6214 **2** 1 **Arkaim**[11] 7788 3-9-6 60 MickyFenton 1 68
(Pam Sly) *chsd wnr: rdn and sltly outpcd 2f out: styd on and ch ent fnl f: sn no ex* **11/2**

4000 **3** 4 ½ **Jay Jays Joy**[17] 7711 3-9-0 54 (v[1]) FrederikTylicki 12 51
(Paul Midgley) *in tch towards outer: hdwy 3f out: rdn to chse ldng pair 2f out: drvn and kpt on same pce appr fnl f* **25/1**

4504 **4** 1 ¾ **Corvette**[48] 7327 3-9-4 58 LukeMorris 6 51
(Michael Appleby) *in rr and rdn along on inner: swtchd rt and hdwy 2f out: styd on appr fnl f: nrst fin* **16/1**

4022 **5** ¾ **Hilbre Court (USA)**[12] 7775 6-9-3 56 (p) J-PGuillambert 4 48
(Brian Baugh) *midfield: pushed along 3f out: hdwy to chse ldrs 2f out: sn rdn and no imp fr over 1f out* **11/4**[1]

0020 **6** nk **Exopuntia**[17] 7711 5-9-2 55 HayleyTurner 8 46
(Julia Feilden) *trckd ldrs: hdwy 3f out: rdn wl over 1f out: sn no imp* **5/1**[3]

0120 **7** 3 ¾ **Lujano**[21] 7648 6-9-3 59 DaleSwift(3) 7 41
(Ollie Pears) *in rr: rdn along 3f out: swtchd wd and hdwy 2f out: drvn and no imp fr over 1f out* **7/1**

0/24 **8** 1 ½ **King Pin**[17] 7711 6-9-7 60 TomEaves 10 39
(Tracy Waggott) *dwlt: towards rr: hdwy on outer over 2f out: rdn to chse ldrs wl over 1f out: sn no imp* **9/2**[2]

5600 **9** 3 ¼ **Vogarth**[119] 5601 7-8-4 46 oh1 (b) AdamBeschizza(3) 5 17
(Michael Chapman) *prom: rdn along wl over 2f out: sn wknd* **66/1**

0000 **10** 3 ¾ **Ptolomeos**[62] 7113 8-8-1 47 oh1 ow1 (p) LeonnaMayor(7) 9 10
(Sean Regan) *s.i.s: a in rr* **50/1**

0002 **11** 8 **Stamp Duty (IRE)**[31] 7560 3-9-2 56 DuranFentiman 3 —
(Suzzanne France) *chsd ldrs: rdn along over 3f out: sn wknd* **16/1**

000- **12** dist **Portrush Storm**[465] 6213 6-8-7 46 oh1 WilliamCarson 2 —
(Ray Peacock) *chsd ldrs on inner: rdn along 1/2-way: sn wknd and eased whn bhd over 2f out* **50/1**

1m 42.75s (-0.95) **Going Correction** -0.175s/f (Stan)
WFA 3 from 4yo+ 1lb **12** Ran SP% **119.5**
Speed ratings (Par 101): **97,96,91,89,89 88,84,83,80,76 68,—**
toteswingers:1&2:£6.20, 2&3:£19.10, 1&3:£30.00 CSF £63.51 CT £1374.95 TOTE £16.60: £4.10, £1.80, £6.20; EX 81.10 TRIFECTA Not won..
Owner S R Bowring **Bred** S R Bowring **Trained** Edwinstowe, Notts

FOCUS
A moderate handicap run at a fair pace but another race on the card that suited those right up with the pace. The first two, who were first and second throughout and came down the centre, pulled clear in the straight.

7886 CO-OPERATIVE MOTOR GROUP, MANSFIELD MAIDEN STKS 6f (F)
3:00 (3:00) (Class 5) 3-Y-O+ **£2,385** (£704; £352) **Stalls** Low

Form RPR
0-05 **1** **Da'Quonde (IRE)**[43] 7411 3-8-12 45 TomEaves 8 56
(Bryan Smart) *qckly away and sn led: jnd and rdn wl over 1f out: kpt on gamely u.p fnl f* **14/1**

5220 **2** 1 ¼ **Gorgeous Goblin (IRE)**[6] 7845 4-8-12 49 (t) FrannyNorton 3 52
(David C Griffiths) *hld up in tch: hdwy to trck ldrs 1/2-way: swtchd lft 2f out and sn chsng ldng pair: rdn to chal over 1f out: drvn and ev ch ins fnl f: kpt on same pce: tk 2nd nr line* **9/2**[2]

60-2 **3** hd **Only Ten Per Cent (IRE)**[17] 7714 3-9-3 50 FrederikTylicki 2 56
(J R Jenkins) *trckd ldr: cl up and gng wl 1/2-way: effrt to chal wl over 1f out: sn rdn and ev ch tl drvn and one pce wl ins fnl f* **5/6**[1]

0343 **4** 10 **Lovat Lane**[7] 7829 3-8-12 48 (v) WilliamCarson 6 19
(Eve Johnson Houghton) *chsd ldrs: rdn along over 2f out: wknd wl over 1f out* **14/1**

245 **5** shd **Welsh Dancer**[11] 7785 3-9-3 51 LukeMorris 5 24
(Ronald Harris) *chsd ldrs: rdn along wl over 2f out: grad wknd* **6/1**[3]

3030 **6** ½ **Lucky Dime**[12] 7768 3-8-12 49 (b) HayleyTurner 7 17
(Noel Quinlan) *hld up: rapid hdwy on outer to join ldrs over 3f out: rdn over 2f out and sn wknd* **18/1**

7 5 **Coral Sands (IRE)** 3-8-12 0 GarryWhillans(5) 4 —
(Alan Swinbank) *dwlt: squeezed out and wnt rt s: a bhd* **8/1**

The Form Book, Raceform Ltd, Compton, RG20 6NL

00 **8** *16* **Irish Law**[54] 7245 3-9-0 0....................(t) RobertLButler(3) 1 —
(John Balding) *prom on inner: rdn along bef 1/2-way: sn wknd and bhd* **50/1**

1m 15.75s (-0.75) **Going Correction** -0.175s/f (Stan) **8** Ran SP% **118.7**
Speed ratings (Par 103): **98,96,96,82,82 81,75,53**
toteswingers:1&2:£8.30, 2&3:£2.50, 1&3:£5.40 CSF £78.49 TOTE £27.10: £5.40, £1.10, £1.10; EX 135.10 Trifecta £535.20 Part won. Pool: £723.35 - 0.10 winning units..
Owner The Barber Girls **Bred** Gestut Sohrenhof **Trained** Hambleton, N Yorks

FOCUS
A weak maiden. Another ordinary gallop and another race that went to one making all. The first three, who came down the centre, pulled a long way clear.

7887 SOUTHWELL-RACECOURSE.CO.UK H'CAP 1m (F)
3:35 (3:35) (Class 5) (0-75,75) 3-Y-O+ **£2,385** (£704; £352) **Stalls** Low

Form RPR
1031 **1** **On The Cusp (IRE)**[12] 7773 4-8-12 **66**....................(p) WilliamCarson 4 78
(Richard Guest) *mde all: rdn wl over 1f out: kpt on strly fnl f* **5/2**[1]
0111 **2** *4* **Minortransgression (USA)**[17] 7711 4-9-3 **71**.................... AdamKirby 8 74
(Paul Rich) *trckd ldrs: hdwy to chse wnr over 2f out: rdn wl over 1f out: drvn and no imp fnl f* **3/1**[2]
0005 **3** *4 ½* **Mazovian (USA)**[5] 7857 3-8-4 **62**.................... AdamBeschizza(3) 6 54
(Michael Chapman) *prom: rdn along over 2f out: kpt on same pce* **16/1**
2032 **4** *½* **Mighty Clarets (IRE)**[31] 7557 4-9-3 **71**.................... PatrickMathers 1 62
(Richard Fahey) *chsd ldrs on inner: hdwy wl over 2f out: rdn wl over 1f out: kpt on same pce* **11/2**[3]
0560 **5** *1* **Dubaianswer**[41] 7438 3-9-6 **75**.................... BarryMcHugh 2 64
(Tony Coyle) *in tch: hdwy to chse ldrs over 2f out: sn rdn and no imp* **10/1**
0646 **6** *3 ¼* **Avertis**[34] 7517 6-8-9 **70**....................(tp) LeonnaMayor(7) 10 52
(Alastair Lidderdale) *chsd ldrs on outer: rdn along wl over 2f out: sn btn* **15/2**
0006 **7** *4 ½* **Just Five (IRE)**[12] 7772 5-8-8 **62**.................... LukeMorris 5 33
(John Weymes) *dwlt: a in rr* **33/1**
0040 **8** *7* **Stansonnit**[11] 7776 3-8-11 **71** ow1.................... GarryWhillans(5) 3 26
(Alan Swinbank) *dwlt: a in rr* **16/1**
0604 **9** *13* **Absolute Princess**[16] 7727 3-8-13 **68**.................... FrederikTylicki 7 —
(Scott Dixon) *chsd wnr: rdn along wl over 3f out: sn wknd* **14/1**
0600 **10** *1 ½* **Master Leon**[26] 7589 4-8-13 **67**....................(p) TomEaves 9 —
(Bryan Smart) *sn rdn along in rr: bhd fr 1/2-way* **25/1**

1m 40.37s (-3.33) **Going Correction** -0.175s/f (Stan)
WFA 3 from 4yo+ 1lb **10** Ran SP% **115.0**
Speed ratings (Par 103): **109,105,100,100,99 95,91,84,71,69**
toteswingers:1&2:£2.50, 2&3:£8.50, 1&3:£7.00 CSF £9.74 CT £95.55 TOTE £3.40: £1.40, £1.10, £3.90; EX 8.00 Trifecta £186.20 Pool: £667.04 - 2.65 winning units..
Owner Rakebackmypoker.com **Bred** J Stan Cosgrove **Trained** Stainforth, S Yorks

FOCUS
A fair handicap in which the two market leaders dominated in the straight and the sixth race on the card that went to one that made all. The gallop was reasonable and the winner came down the centre.
T/Plt: £852.80 to a £1 stake. Pool of £52,572.68 - 45.00 winning tickets. T/Qpdt: £376.40 to a £1 stake. Pool of £3,968.03 - 7.80 winning tickets. JR

[7798] LINGFIELD (L-H)
Wednesday, December 28

OFFICIAL GOING: Standard
Wind: Strong, half behind Weather: Overcast with drizzle, clearing after race 5

7888 MIRROR PUNTERS CLUB APPRENTICE (S) STKS 1m (P)
12:10 (12:10) (Class 6) 3-Y-O+ **£1,704** (£503; £251) **Stalls** High

Form RPR
1405 **1** **Ajdaad (USA)**[26] 7605 4-9-0 68.................... SAJackson(7) 6 70
(Alan McCabe) *awkward s: hld up in last pair: prog on inner fr 2f out: wnt 2nd 1f out: edgd lft but std on to ld last 50yds* **11/10**
1040 **2** *nk* **Pipers Piping (IRE)**[13] 7764 5-9-7 67....................(p) LeonnaMayor 2 69
(Alastair Lidderdale) *t.k.h: trckd ldr: led 2f out: shkn up and hanging over 1f out: kpt on: hdd last 50yds* **5/2**[2]
5360 **3** *3* **Querido (GER)**[10] 7805 7-9-1 51....................(tp) NathanAlison 1 56
(Paddy Butler) *trckd ldng pair: effrt 2f out: nt qckn jst over 1f out: kpt on same pce* **8/1**[3]
4-60 **4** *2* **Vivre La Secret**[23] 7636 3-8-6 41.................... JakePayne(3) 3 46
(Bill Turner) *taken down early: led: set modest pce tl kicked on 5f out: hdd 2f out: wknd fnl f* **80/1**
5354 **5** *nk* **Batchworth Blaise**[118] 5653 8-9-1 52....................(b) RaulDaSilva 7 51
(Eric Wheeler) *t.k.h: hld up in last: pushed along and no prog 2f out: plugged on fnl f* **10/1**
0600 **6** *1 ¼* **Loch Fleet (IRE)**[35] 7522 3-8-13 57....................(be[1]) RyanDuthie(7) 4 54
(Gary Moore) *t.k.h: trckd ldng pair: pushed along 2f out: wknd over 1f out* **8/1**[3]
0000 **7** *1* **Majestueux (USA)**[15] 6969 4-8-12 48.................... DannyBrock(3) 5 46
(Mark Hoad) *t.k.h early: hld up in 5th: pushed along 1/2-way: struggling and no prog 2f out* **50/1**

1m 38.12s (-0.08) **Going Correction** 0.0s/f (Stan)
WFA 3 from 4yo+ 1lb **7** Ran SP% **110.7**
Speed ratings (Par 101): **100,99,96,94,94 93,92**
toteswingers:1&2:£1.30, 2&3:£4.30, 1&3:£3.00 CSF £3.66 TOTE £2.80: £2.10, £1.10; EX 4.40.There was no bid for the winner.
Owner Mrs Z Wentworth **Bred** Pontchartain **Trained** Averham Park, Notts
■ Sean Jackson's first winner.

FOCUS
A very moderate contest in which they basically finished in the order adjusted BHA ratings suggested they should. The two market leaders dominated in the end.

7889 BRITISH STALLION STUDS SUPPORTING BRITISH RACING E B F MAIDEN STKS 7f (P)
12:40 (12:40) (Class 5) 2-Y-O **£3,557** (£793; £793; £264) **Stalls** Low

Form RPR
342 **1** **Bronze Angel (IRE)**[134] 5133 2-9-3 83.................... HayleyTurner 2 80+
(Marcus Tregoning) *settled in abt 9th: eased off rail over 2f out but plenty to do: stl only 6th jst over 1f out: str run fnl f to ld nr fin* **10/11**[1]
34 **2** *½* **Sujet Bellagio**[14] 7751 2-9-3 0.................... ShaneKelly 10 78
(Brian Meehan) *led: kicked on over 2f out: hrd rdn over 1f out: hdd and outpcd nr fin* **13/2**[3]
2 *dht* **Discoverer (IRE)** 2-9-3 0.................... NickyMackay 14 78
(John Gosden) *prom: chsd ldr wl over 2f out: tried to cl fnl f: styd on but outpcd nr fin* **9/2**[2]
3045 **4** *1 ¼* **Millibar (IRE)**[27] 7593 2-8-12 70....................(p) TomMcLaughlin 4 70
(Nick Littmoden) *s.s: rcvrd to trck ldrs: effrt over 2f out: chsd ldng pair over 1f out: keeping on whn short of room last 75yds* **22/1**
0244 **5** *1 ½* **Chapellerie (IRE)**[27] 7593 2-8-12 70.................... LukeMorris 5 66
(Brian Meehan) *t.k.h: hld up towards rr: pushed along firmly over 2f out: prog over 1f out: kpt on but nt gng pce to threaten* **8/1**
6 *3 ½* **Nip And Tuck** 2-9-3 0.................... LiamKeniry 9 62
(William Jarvis) *t.k.h: trckd ldrs in 5th: effrt over 2f out: one pce over 1f out: wknd fnl f* **33/1**
04 **7** *1* **Beauchamp Castle**[11] 7799 2-8-5 0....................(t) NicoleNordblad(7) 8 54
(Hans Adielsson) *trckd ldrs: lost pl on inner over 2f out: shkn up over 1f out: fdd* **33/1**
0 **8** *1* **News Desk**[26] 7599 2-8-12 0.................... MarcHalford 3 52
(John Gosden) *s.s: mostly in last pair: nvr a factor but kpt on steadily fnl 2f* **20/1**
9 *6* **Norwood Lane** 2-9-3 0.................... FrannyNorton 11 41
(Peter Hedger) *chsd ldr to wl over 2f out: wknd over 1f out* **50/1**
06 **10** *2 ½* **So Cheeky**[39] 7493 2-8-12 0.................... SteveDrowne 6 30
(Richard Hannon) *a in rr: struggling fr 1/2-way* **16/1**
05 **11** *1* **Beauchamp Best**[11] 7799 2-8-9 0.................... SophieDoyle(3) 1 27
(Hans Adielsson) *nvr bttr than midfield: wknd over 2f out* **100/1**
0 **12** *½* **Ewenny Star**[54] 7258 2-8-12 0.................... DavidProbert 12 26
(Bryn Palling) *dwlt: a in last pair: struggling fr 1/2-way* **125/1**

1m 25.35s (0.55) **Going Correction** 0.0s/f (Stan) **12** Ran SP% **119.6**
Speed ratings (Par 96): **96,95,95,94,92 88,87,86,79,76 75,74**WIN 1.60 PL: 1.10, 1.60 (Discoverer), 2.20 (Sujet Bellagio); EX: 3.40 (D), 3.90 (SB); CSF: 2.33 (D), 3.38 (SB); Trifecta: 8.30 (D/SB), 8.70 (SB/D); toteswingers: 2.30 (BA/D), 1.80 (BA/SB), 5.60 (D/SB) TRIFECTA Pool: £330.27 Owner.

FOCUS
Probably not a bad maiden for the time of year with some big stables represented. The first five came clear.

NOTEBOOK
Bronze Angel(IRE) had made the frame in all five starts on turf and set the standard with a mark of 83, despite a 134-day absence. He wasn't in the best position early, tucked away amongst horses well off the pace, but his rider angled him to the outside before the home bend which gave him the chance of a clear run. He made the most of it too, producing an impressive turn of foot to grab the race near the line. He probably ran close to his mark, but his consistency should continue to stand him in good stead. (old market op 11-8 new market op evens)
Sujet Bellagio, in the frame in his first two starts on Polytrack, tried to steal the race from the front and very nearly succeeded. He now gets a mark. (old market op 6-1 new market op 13-2)
Discoverer(IRE), a half-brother to a UAE Oaks winner out of a dam who won the same race, was always close to the pace and kept on right to the line. He is no superstar, but should win races. (old market op 6-1 new market op 13-2)
Millibar(IRE), 8lb badly in with the winner and tried in cheekpieces, didn't fare badly as she blew the start and ran wide off the final bend, but she has already demonstrated her limits. (old market op 18-1 new market op 20-1)
Chapellerie(IRE) ran creditably, but this looks as good as she is. (old market op 8-1 new market op 7-1)
So Cheeky Official explanation: jockey said filly was unsuited by kickback
Beauchamp Best Official explanation: jockey said filly was unsuited by kickback
Ewenny Star Official explanation: jockey said filly was unsuited by kickback

7890 TOTEQUADPOT H'CAP 1m (P)
1:10 (1:10) (Class 6) (0-65,65) 3-Y-O **£1,704** (£503; £251) **Stalls** High

Form RPR
511 **1** **Storm Runner (IRE)**[21] 7655 3-8-5 **54**.................... RyanPowell(5) 6 62
(George Margarson) *hld up last: effrt and brought wd bnd 2f out: plent to do over 1f out: drvn and r.o fnl f to ld last 50yds* **15/8**[1]
501 **2** *½* **Zaheeb**[14] 7754 3-8-12 **59**.................... DaleSwift(3) 4 66
(Dave Morris) *trckd ldng pair: effrt over 2f out: drvn in front 1f out: styd on but hdd last 50yds* **11/4**[2]
3 *2* **Kucharova (IRE)**[70] 6964 3-8-13 **57**.................... LiamKeniry 1 59
(Seamus Mullins) [illegible] *prog on inner 2f out: cl up 1f out: one pce after* **33/1**
0262 **4** *½* **Ice Cold Bex**[7] 7840 3-9-4 **62**....................(b) LukeMorris 5 63
(Philip McBride) *t.k.h: hld up towards rr: rdn over 2f out: nt qckn wl over 1f out: styd on same pce after* **3/1**[3]
-303 **5** *½* **Brown Pete (IRE)**[7] 7840 3-9-2 **60**....................(b) DavidProbert 7 60
(Richard Guest) *s.i.s: rcvrd to join ldr over 5f out: disp after tl fdd 1f out* **7/1**
1046 **6** *2* **Putin (IRE)**[12] 7782 3-8-4 **55**....................[1] LeonnaMayor(7) 2 51
(Phil McEntee) *t.k.h: trckd ldr 2f: lost pl 1/2-way: struggling in last over 2f out* **16/1**
2000 **7** *nse* **Sottovoce**[76] 6813 3-9-7 **65**.................... HayleyTurner 3 60
(Simon Dow) *led: jnd over 5f out: duelled for ld after tl hdd & wknd 1f out* **16/1**

1m 37.46s (-0.74) **Going Correction** 0.0s/f (Stan) **7** Ran SP% **113.7**
Speed ratings (Par 98): **103,102,100,100,99 97,97**
toteswingers:1&2:£2.10, 2&3:£14.00, 1&3:£9.50 CSF £7.15 TOTE £2.80: £1.60, £1.50; EX 6.90.
Owner Pitfield Partnership **Bred** Kevin Foley **Trained** Newmarket, Suffolk

FOCUS
A modest handicap and the early pace didn't look that strong despite a contested lead between Sottovoce and Brown Pete.

7891 TOTEPOOL MOBILE TEXT TOTE TO 89660 H'CAP (DIV I) 1m 2f (P)
1:40 (1:40) (Class 6) (0-55,55) 3-Y-O+ **£1,704** (£503; £251) **Stalls** Low

Form RPR
4063 **1** **Resplendent Alpha**[13] 7775 7-8-8 **52**.................... LeonnaMayor(7) 2 59
(Alastair Lidderdale) *s.s: hld up in last pair: gd prog on inner fr 2f out: led jst ins fnl f: shkn up and sn in command* **11/1**
4000 **2** *1 ¼* **Penbryn (USA)**[25] 7632 4-9-3 **54**.................... SteveDrowne 3 59
(Nick Littmoden) *led 2f: a in ldng trio after: rdn over 2f out: led over 1f out tl jst ins fnl f: outpcd after and jst hld on for 2nd* **7/1**[3]
4005 **3** *nk* **Kai Mook**[10] 7805 4-8-13 **55**.................... MarkCoumbe(5) 6 59
(Roger Ingram) *hld up towards rr: effrt 2f out: nt clr run briefly over 1f out: styd on to take 3rd ins fnl f* **5/1**[2]
0042 **4** *½* **Red Flash (IRE)**[12] 7787 4-8-11 **48**.................... JimCrowley 8 51
(David Bridgwater) *hld up in last quartet: effrt 2f out on outer: styd on same pce fr over 1f out: n.d* **7/2**[1]
5052 **5** *¾* **Laconicos (IRE)**[42] 7441 9-9-4 **55**....................(t) FrannyNorton 12 56
(William Stone) *prog to ld after 2f: kicked on over 2f out but limited rspnse: hdd and fdd over 1f out* **5/1**[2]

0600 **6** ½ **Sunset Boulevard (IRE)**[42] 7441 8-8-8 **50**............(b) NathanAlison(5) 10 50
(Paddy Butler) *stdd s: hld up in last pair: effrt and taken wd bnd 2f out: no prog over 1f out: styd on last 150yds* **25/1**

6060 **7** *nk* **Farmers Hill**[49] 7333 3-8-1 **46** oh1.................................. RyanPowell(5) 1 46
(Mark Hoad) *t.k.h: hld up bhd ldrs on inner: rdn over 2f out: nt qckn over 1f out: fdd* **16/1**

0342 **8** 1 ¾ **Avon Supreme**[23] 7639 3-8-11 **54**...................................... DaleSwift(3) 9 50
(Gay Kelleway) *t.k.h: trckd ldrs: rdn and nt qckn 2f out: wknd fnl f* **7/2**[1]

0500 **9** 1 ½ **Vinces**[57] 7206 7-8-12 **49**...(p) HayleyTurner 5 42
(Tim McCarthy) *trckd ldrs: rdn and cl enough over 2f out: wknd over 1f out* **14/1**

6600 **10** 1 **Libre**[16] 7741 11-8-9 **46** oh1.. MarcHalford 7 37
(Violet M Jordan) *prom: chsd ldr over 4f out: hrd rdn and fnd nil 2f out: sn btn* **100/1**

2m 7.74s (1.14) **Going Correction** 0.0s/f (Stan)
WFA 3 from 4yo+ 3lb **10** Ran SP% **116.0**
Speed ratings (Par 101): **95,94,93,93,92 92,92,90,89,88**
toteswingers:1&2:£16.60, 2&3:£9.10, 1&3:£13.00 CSF £85.34 CT £437.85 TOTE £12.50: £3.00, £2.70, £2.30; EX 127.90 TRIFECTA Not won..
Owner C S J Beek **Bred** Sunley Stud **Trained** Eastbury, Berks

FOCUS
A poor handicap, but an extraordinary effort from the winner.

7892 TOTEPOOL MOBILE TEXT TOTE TO 89660 H'CAP (DIV II) 1m 2f (P)
2:10 (2:11) (Class 6) (0-55,55) 3-Y-0+ **£1,704** (£503; £251) **Stalls** Low

Form RPR

3452 **1** **Prince Of Thebes (IRE)**[23] 7640 10-8-10 **52**..........(p) MarkCoumbe(5) 6 59
(Michael Attwater) *hld up in last trio: prog on outer over 3f out to chse ldng pair over 2f out: drvn to ld jst ins fnl f: jst hld on* **13/2**

2331 **2** *hd* **Idol Deputy (FR)**[12] 7787 5-9-4 **55**.................................. HayleyTurner 5 62
(Mark Usher) *hld up towards rr: trapped bhd rivals fr 3f out: prog wl over 1f out: brought to chal and upsides last 75yds: nt qckn last strides* **5/2**[1]

5062 **3** 1 ¼ **Regal Rave (USA)**[10] 7805 4-8-12 **49**..............................(v) LiamKeniry 2 54
(Peter Hedger) *hld up in last trio: taken wdst of all and effrt bnd 2f out: styd on fr over 1f out: tk 3rd last 50yds* **5/1**[2]

3505 **4** 1 ¼ **Prince Blue**[26] 7603 4-9-0 **51**... SamHitchcott 4 53
(John E Long) *led or disp ld: wnt at it hrd fr 1/2-way: beat off other pcemaker 2f out: hdd and fdd jst ins fnl f* **6/1**[3]

-006 **5** 3 ¾ **Laser Blazer**[19] 7698 3-8-13 **53**.. JimCrowley 8 48
(Jeremy Gask) *t.k.h: hld up towards rr: gng wl enough on outer 3f out: rdn and nt qckn 2f out: one pce after* **5/1**[2]

3003 **6** ½ **Corrib (IRE)**[19] 7698 8-9-4 **55**.......................................(p) DavidProbert 10 49
(Bryn Palling) *hld up in midfield: effrt over 2f out: nt qckn wl over 1f out: btn after* **12/1**

000 **7** 1 ¼ **Heading To First**[23] 7640 4-8-4 **46**.................(p) NathanAlison(5) 11 37
(Paddy Butler) *disp ld: wnt at it hrd fr 1/2-way: cracked 2f out: steadily wknd* **28/1**

2200 **8** 1 ½ **Do More Business (IRE)**[21] 7655 4-9-0 **51**...................... IanMongan 1 39
(Pat Phelan) *chsd ldrs: u.p wl over 3f out: stl 4th over 2f out: wknd over 1f out* **14/1**

0060 **9** ½ **Suffolini**[49] 7333 3-8-1 **46** oh1... RyanPowell(5) 3 33
(William Stone) *prom: u.p over 4f out: lost pl and btn over 3f out* **100/1**

5300 **10** ¾ **Diamond Twister (USA)**[37] 3225 5-9-4 **55**......................... ShaneKelly 9 41
(Lisa Williamson) *chsd ldrs: u.p 4f out: wknd 2f out* **33/1**

-000 **11** 4 ½ **Nesnaas (USA)**[2] 7091 10-8-3 **47** oh1 ow1.............(tp) LeonnaMayor(7) 7 24
(Alastair Lidderdale) *v awkward s: a in last pair: nvr a factor* **40/1**

2m 6.00s (-0.60) **Going Correction** 0.0s/f (Stan)
WFA 3 from 4yo+ 3lb **11** Ran SP% **113.7**
Speed ratings (Par 101): **102,101,100,99,96 96,95,94,93,93 89**
toteswingers:1&2:£3.80, 2&3:£3.50, 1&3:£6.40 CSF £21.75 CT £87.77 TOTE £5.80: £1.10, £1.60, £2.30; EX 15.70 Trifecta £67.10 Pool: £781.56 - 8.60 winning units..
Owner Canisbay Bloodstock **Bred** Mrs A Rothschild & London Thoroughbred Services L **Trained** Epsom, Surrey
■ Stewards' Enquiry : Mark Coumbe two-day ban; excessive use of whip (13th-14th Jan)

FOCUS
Like in the first division, the winner was ending a very long losing run. The time was 1.74 seconds faster than the first leg.

7893 BET TOTEPOOL TEXT TOTE TO 89660 H'CAP 6f (P)
2:40 (2:43) (Class 5) (0-75,75) 3-Y-0+ **£3,234** (£962; £481; £240) **Stalls** Low

Form RPR

0006 **1** **Hatta Stream (IRE)**[25] 7625 5-9-3 **71**............................. SteveDrowne 9 80
(Lydia Pearce) *prom: rdn over 2f out: clsd to chal fnl f: led last 100yds: hld on* **11/2**[2]

6002 **2** ½ **Arctic Lynx (IRE)**[20] 7675 4-9-7 **75**.................................. JimCrowley 12 82
(John Best) *hld up in last fr wdst draw: stl there over 1f out and nt clr run sn after: gd prog ins fnl f: r.o to take 2nd last strides* **15/8**[1]

0230 **3** *nk* **Sermons Mount (USA)**[13] 7767 5-9-6 **74**.................. J-PGuillambert 10 80
(Paul Howling) *prom: chsd ldr over 3f out: rdn to chal 1f out: nt qckn last 150yds* **14/1**

6310 **4** *hd* **Punching**[33] 7535 7-9-4 **72**... HayleyTurner 11 77
(Conor Dore) *led at str pce: rdn over 1f out: hdd and no ex last 100yds* **33/1**

2236 **5** *shd* **Roman Strait**[44] 7417 3-8-13 **67**... LiamKeniry 4 72
(Michael Blanshard) *hld up in last trio: brought wd bnd 2f out: prog jst over 1f out: styd on: nvr able to chal* **6/1**[3]

2040 **6** ½ **Highland Harvest**[20] 7675 7-9-7 **75**..................................... IanMongan 8 78
(Jamie Poulton) *trckd ldrs: prog to chse ldng pair over 2f out: cl enough 1f out: nt qckn* **8/1**

5400 **7** *hd* **Johnstown Lad (IRE)**[7] 7846 7-9-2 **70**.....................(bt) SamHitchcott 1 73
(Daniel Mark Loughnane, Ire) *towards rr: rdn over 2f out: effrt over 1f out: styd on but nt gng pce to chal* **20/1**

0434 **8** ½ **Loyal Royal (IRE)**[9] 7819 8-8-13 **67**.........................(bt) DavidProbert 5 68
(Milton Bradley) *s.s: hld up in last pair: effrt over 2f out on inner: prog 1f out: nt rch ldrs and fdd nr fin* **16/1**

2000 **9** *nk* **Ivory Silk**[7] 7846 6-9-0 **75**.. RaulDaSilva(7) 2 75
(Jeremy Gask) *taken down early: dwlt: wl in rr: rdn in last trio over 1f out: styd on but no ch* **11/1**

4400 **10** ½ **Forty Proof (IRE)**[12] 7776 3-9-2 **70**.................................(vt) ShaneKelly 6 69
(Alan McCabe) *chsd ldrs: rdn on inner over 2f out: nt qckn over 1f out: tried to make prog fnl f: wknd last 75yds* **10/1**

200 **11** ¾ **Clear Ice (IRE)**[76] 6815 4-9-3 **74**............................ NataliaGemelova(3) 7 70
(Gay Kelleway) *chsd ldrs in 7th: rdn over 2f out: lost pl over 1f out: n.d fnl f* **33/1**

/000 **12** ½ **Smoky Cloud (IRE)**[13] 7767 4-9-0 **68**................................ MarcHalford 3 63
(Amy Weaver) *chsd ldr to over 3f out: styd in tch on inner: wknd fnl f* **40/1**

1m 11.03s (-0.87) **Going Correction** 0.0s/f (Stan) **12** Ran SP% **118.6**
Speed ratings (Par 103): **105,104,103,103,103 102,102,101,101,100 99,99**
toteswingers:1&2:£3.70, 2&3:£9.50, 1&3:£17.80 CSF £15.51 CT £136.53 TOTE £8.10: £2.70, £1.10, £4.90; EX 15.20 Trifecta £315.10 Pool: £468.51 - 1.10 winning units..
Owner Macniler Racing Partnership **Bred** T W Bloodstock Ltd **Trained** Newmarket, Suffolk
■ Stewards' Enquiry : Jim Crowley one-day ban; careless riding (11th Jan)

FOCUS
A typical Lingfield sprint handicap in which they finished in a heap.

7894 TOTEPOOL MAIDEN STKS 1m (P)
3:15 (3:16) (Class 5) 3-Y-0+ **£2,385** (£704; £352) **Stalls** High

Form RPR

3222 **1** **Change The Subject (USA)**[33] 7542 3-8-12 **78**............. LauraPike(5) 6 82
(David Simcock) *prom: trckd ldr over 4f out: upsides fr 3f out: rdn over 1f out: narrow ld ins fnl f: jst hld on* **4/6**[1]

5 **2** *shd* **Forceful Appeal (USA)**[172] 3-9-3 **84**............................ HayleyTurner 7 82
(Simon Dow) *led after 2f: jnd 3f out: shkn up over 1f out: narrowly hdd ins fnl f: jst denied* **11/2**[3]

3 7 **Rocky Elsom (USA)**[624] 1287 4-9-4 **0**............................ JimCrowley 4 65
(David Arbuthnot) *trckd ldrs: wnt 3rd over 2f out: sn wl outpcd by ldng pair* **10/3**[2]

04 **4** 4 ½ **Jumeirah Liberty**[21] 7662 3-9-3 **0**.............................. JamieGoldstein 5 54
(Zoe Davison) *led 2f: chsd ldrs tl easily outpcd over 2f out: wknd* **33/1**

00 **5** ½ **Ragda**[18] 7717 3-8-9 **0**.. AdamBeschizza(3) 8 48
(Marco Botti) *in tch: effrt to dispute 3rd wl over 2f out: sn outpcd: wknd* **12/1**

6 1 ¼ **Finlodex** 4-9-4 **0**.. ShaneKelly 3 50
(Murty McGrath) *dwlt: a in rr: lost tch fr 3f out* **66/1**

36 **7** 2 ½ **Maggie Aron**[13] 7774 5-8-13 **0**.. LiamKeniry 1 39
(Tim Vaughan) *s.s: hld up in rr: pushed along and lost tch 3f out* **22/1**

8 12 **Estee Will** 4-8-13 **0**.. SamHitchcott 2 10
(John E Long) *dwlt: rdn in last 1/2-way: t.o* **50/1**

1m 38.29s (0.09) **Going Correction** 0.0s/f (Stan)
WFA 3 from 4yo+ 1lb **8** Ran SP% **116.9**
Speed ratings (Par 103): **99,98,91,87,86 85,83,71**
toteswingers:1&2:£1.80, 2&3:£2.20, 1&3:£1.60 CSF £4.93 TOTE £1.80: £1.02, £1.30, £1.40; EX 5.10 Trifecta £12.60 Pool: £927.55 - 54.30 winning units..
Owner Si Bamber Jonathan Barnett Malcolm Caine **Bred** Forging Oaks Llc **Trained** Newmarket, Suffolk

FOCUS
An uncompetitive maiden, but made interesting by the presence of two foreign imports. The front pair had the race to themselves over the last couple of furlongs. The time was the slowest of the three races over the trip on the card.

7895 GALLAGHER GROUP H'CAP 7f (P)
3:45 (3:50) (Class 6) (0-65,65) 3-Y-0+ **£1,704** (£503; £251) **Stalls** Low

Form RPR

1460 **1** **Tourist**[18] 7716 6-9-2 **65**... RyanPowell(5) 4 73
(Ian Williams) *rrd s: hld up in last trio: stl there 2f out: rapid prog on inner jst over 1f out: r.o wl to ld post* **13/2**[3]

6544 **2** *hd* **Eager To Bow (IRE)**[29] 7579 5-9-6 **64**............................... JimCrowley 6 71
(Patrick Chamings) *hld up towards rr: looking for room and swtchd rt over 1f out: r.o wl last 100yds: jst failed* **7/2**[1]

0055 **3** *shd* **Frognal (IRE)**[15] 7748 5-9-4 **62**..................................(bt) DavidProbert 12 69
(Richard Guest) *most reluctant to enter stalls: racd freely: w ldrs: led 3f out and sn clr: 2 l up 100yds out: swamped last strides* **14/1**

1242 **4** *hd* **Silver Wind**[9] 7819 6-9-7 **65**..(b) ShaneKelly 9 71
(Alan McCabe) *prom: chsd ldr over 2f out: clsd u.p ins fnl f: jst outpcd nr fin* **5/1**[2]

6006 **5** ½ **Efistorm**[7] 7844 10-9-2 **60**... J-PGuillambert 7 65
(Conor Dore) *settled in rr: effrt on outer 2f out: no prog tl styd on wl fnl f: nrst fin* **50/1**

6000 **6** ½ **Sulis Minerva (IRE)**[11] 7804 4-9-0 **65**......................... RaulDaSilva(7) 10 68
(Jeremy Gask) *led 2f: styd prom: rdn in 3rd fnl f: kpt on but lost pls nr fin* **50/1**

3205 **7** *nse* **Silvee**[10] 7811 4-8-13 **57**.. SamHitchcott 8 60
(John Bridger) *racd wd in rr: pushed along 1/2-way: effrt over 1f out: styd on fnl f: nrst fin* **66/1**

0005 **8** ½ **Buxton**[10] 7810 7-9-0 **58**.......................................(vt[1]) FrannyNorton 3 60
(Roger Ingram) *hld up in last trio: effrt 2f out: styd on fnl f: nrst fin but no ch* **16/1**

3133 **9** ½ **Patavium Prince (IRE)**[117] 5669 8-9-3 **61**........................ IanMongan 11 62
(Jo Crowley) *chsd ldrs: no imp 2f out: wknd fnl f* **7/1**

2043 **10** 1 ¼ **Lastkingofscotland (IRE)**[18] 7716 5-9-7 **65**...............(b) HayleyTurner 5 62
(Conor Dore) *hld up towards rr: effrt whn nt clr run wl over 1f out: no ch after* **5/1**[2]

0000 **11** 2 **Mi Regalo**[14] 7754 3-8-9 **60**.......................................[1] LeonnaMayor(7) 1 52
(Phil McEntee) *hld up in last: effrt on inner 2f out: no prog over 1f out: no ch after* **33/1**

600 **12** ½ **Mister Green (FR)**[14] 7759 5-9-0 **63**...................(bt) MarkCoumbe(5) 13 54
(David Flood) *slowly away and reminder: sn chsd ldrs: wknd over 1f out* **28/1**

2050 **13** ¾ **Sasheen**[34] 7532 4-9-7 **65**..(b[1]) SteveDrowne 14 54
(Jeremy Gask) *rousted along fr wd draw to press ldr: led 5f out to 3f out: wknd 2f out* **7/1**

1153 **14** 3 ¼ **Bold Ring**[27] 7591 5-9-7 **65**... LiamKeniry 2 45
(Eric Wheeler) *chsd ldrs: lost pl over 2f out: wkng whn hmpd jst over 1f out* **12/1**

1m 24.31s (-0.49) **Going Correction** 0.0s/f (Stan) **14** Ran SP% **125.9**
Speed ratings (Par 101): **102,101,101,101,100 100,100,99,99,97 95,94,93,90**
toteswingers:1&2:£7.70, 2&3:£12.70, 1&3:£26.60 CSF £30.01 CT £332.82 TOTE £10.90: £3.80, £1.10, £6.40; EX 45.10 Trifecta £635.30 Pool: £1699.85 - 1.98 winning units..
Owner Stratford Bards Racing No 2 **Bred** Juddmonte Farms Ltd **Trained** Portway, Worcs
■ Stewards' Enquiry : Jim Crowley three-day ban; careless riding (Jan 12-14)
David Probert two-day ban; careless riding (Jan 11-12)

FOCUS
A moderate handicap, but a race of changing fortunes and another handicap in which the leaders finished in a heap.
Sasheen Official explanation: jockey said filly had no more to give
T/Plt: £30.40 to a £1 stake. Pool: £55,407.85 - 1,330.06 winning tickets T/Qpdt: £35.80 to a £1 stake. Pool:£4,196.47 - 86.60 winning tickets JN

7874 WOLVERHAMPTON (A.W) (L-H)

Wednesday, December 28

OFFICIAL GOING: Standard

Wind: fresh, behind Weather: breezy, dry

7896 TOTEPLACEPOT H'CAP (DIV I) 5f 20y(P)

3:50 (3:52) (Class 6) (0-65,69) 3-Y-0+ **£1,704** (£503; £251) **Stalls** Low

Form RPR

0211 **1** **Peace Seeker**[10] 7811 3-9-11 **69** 6ex .... WilliamCarson 9 83
(Anthony Carson) *mde all: rdn 2f out: edgd lft u.p ent fnl f: styd on strly* **5/4**[1]

0213 **2** *2* **Excellent Aim**[28] 7587 4-9-4 **62** ....(t) AdamKirby 3 69
(George Margarson) *chsd ldrs: rdn and effrt to chse wnr over 1f out: no imp ins fnl f: eased towards fin* **3/1**[2]

2000 **3** *1 ¼* **Shawkantango**[15] 7746 4-9-7 **65** ....(v) GrahamGibbons 11 68
(Derek Shaw) *dwlt: sn rcvrd and chsd ldrs on outer: rdn 2f out: drvn and styd on same pce fr over 1f out* **80/1**

0340 **4** *hd* **Pitkin**[30] 7566 3-9-4 **62** .... PaddyAspell 7 64
(Michael Easterby) *in tch in midfield: effrt u.p and swtchd lft over 1f out: styd on fnl f: nvr trbld ldrs* **6/1**[3]

0664 **5** *hd* **First In Command (IRE)**[10] 7812 6-8-13 **57** ....(tp) MartinHarley 4 58
(Daniel Mark Loughnane, Ire) *t.k.h: hld up in tch: rdn and effrt over 1f out: one pce and no imp ins fnl f* **12/1**

0300 **6** *1 ¼* **Crimson Queen**[21] 7649 4-9-4 **62** ....(b[1]) TomEaves 2 59
(Roy Brotherton) *hld up in rr: rdn wl over 1f out: kpt on ins fnl f: nvr trbld ldrs* **50/1**

5635 **7** *1 ½* **Vitznau (IRE)**[9] 7816 7-8-13 **64** .... RachealKneller(7) 6 55
(Alastair Lidderdale) *stdd after s: hld up in rr: rdn and hdwy jst over 1f out: edgd lft and kpt on fnl f: n.d* **14/1**

0043 **8** *1 ½* **Bookiesindex Boy**[21] 7649 7-9-4 **62** ....(b) StephenCraine 10 48
(J R Jenkins) *chsd wnr: shkn up and fnd little wl over 1f out: lost 2nd over 1f out: wknd fnl f* **28/1**

4340 **9** *½* **Two Turtle Doves (IRE)**[27] 7596 5-9-4 **62** .... DanielTudhope 1 46
(Michael Mullineaux) *a towards rr: rdn over 1f out: no prog and n.d* **14/1**

5460 **10** *nk* **Wandering Lad**[6] 7854 3-8-7 **51** .... KellyHarrison 8 34
(Declan Carroll) *s.i.s: hld up in tch in midfield: rdn and no prog over 1f out: sn wknd* **40/1**

2000 **11** *hd* **Green Warrior**[15] 7746 3-8-13 **60** ....(e) RobertLButler(3) 5 42
(Richard Guest) *in tch in midfield: rdn 1/2-way: wknd over 1f out* **100/1**

61.80 secs (-0.50) **Going Correction** 0.0s/f (Stan) **11** Ran SP% **114.8**
Speed ratings (Par 101): **104,100,98,98,98 96,93,91,90,90 89**
toteswingers:1&2:£1.50, 2&3:£30.50, 1&3:£20.30 CSF £4.52 CT £179.29 TOTE £1.90: £1.30, £1.10, £9.60; EX 5.40.

Owner Neville Chamberlain Syndicate **Bred** C J Mills **Trained** Newmarket, Suffolk

■ Stewards' Enquiry : Stephen Craine one-day ban; not keeping straight from the stalls (Jan 11)
William Carson one-day ban: not keep straight from stalls (Jan 11)

FOCUS

A routine handicap run at a decent gallop, but the winner is improving so fast he is likely to leave this company behind before long.

7897 TOTEPLACEPOT H'CAP (DIV II) 5f 20y(P)

4:20 (4:20) (Class 6) (0-65,65) 3-Y-0+ **£1,704** (£503; £251) **Stalls** Low

Form RPR

5030 **1** **Steelcut**[27] 7596 7-9-7 **65** ....(p) TomMcLaughlin 9 75
(David Evans) *dropped in bhd after s: rdn and hdwy on outer over 1f out: r.o wl fnl f to ld cl home* **9/2**[2]

6254 **2** *hd* **Griffin Point (IRE)**[11] 7804 4-9-4 **62** ....(p) WilliamCarson 4 71
(William Muir) *chsd ldrs: rdn to chse ldng pair 2f out: drvn to chal 1f out: led ins fnl f: r.o wl tl hdd and no ex cl home* **13/2**

5161 **3** *1 ¾* **No Mean Trick (USA)**[27] 7594 5-9-5 **63** .... BarryMcHugh 1 66
(Paul Midgley) *chsd ldr: rdn and unable qck over 1f out: kpt on u.p ins fnl f: wnt 3rd cl home* **15/8**[1]

6203 **4** *nse* **Young Simon**[14] 7755 4-8-4 **51** ....(v) SimonPearce(3) [illegible] [illegible]
([illegible]) *dwlt: sn bustled along in midfield: nt clr run 1/2-way: swtchd rt and effrt 2f out: kpt on ins fnl f: nt pce to rch ldrs* **10/1**

43-6 **5** *nk* **Mercers Row**[126] 5373 4-9-1 **62** .... MichaelO'Connell(3) 3 63
(Noel Wilson) *dwlt and squeezed for room s: effrt on inner jst over 1f out: kpt on wl u.p fnl f: nt rch ldrs* **20/1**

0033 **6** *¾* **Grand Stitch (USA)**[16] 7737 5-9-2 **60** ....(v) DanielTudhope 5 59
(Declan Carroll) *led: rdn wl over 1f out: hdd ins fnl f: wknd fnl 75yds* **6/1**[3]

0035 **7** *2 ½* **Ace Of Spies (IRE)**[36] 7504 6-8-13 **62** ....(b) DavidKenny(5) 10 52
(Conor Dore) *in tch in midfield on outer: rdn and lost pl wl over 2f out: one pce and no threat to ldrs fr over 1f out* **33/1**

/046 **8** *1 ¼* **Perfect Honour (IRE)**[40] 7459 5-8-9 **53** oh1 ow2............ MartinHarley 8 38
(Des Donovan) *in tch: rdn and unable qck wl over 1f out: wknd ent fnl f* **12/1**

5240 **9** *1 ½* **Decider (USA)**[175] 3721 8-9-6 **64** ....(p) GrahamGibbons 6 44
(Ronald Harris) *taken down early: chsd ldr tl over 1f out: wknd fnl f* **25/1**

0655 **10** *2 ½* **Olynard (IRE)**[120] 5604 5-9-3 **61** ....(be) TomEaves 7 32
(Michael Mullineaux) *sn rdn along and struggling to go pce: bhd fr 1/2-way* **22/1**

61.87 secs (-0.43) **Going Correction** 0.0s/f (Stan) **10** Ran SP% **113.3**
Speed ratings (Par 101): **103,102,99,99,99 98,94,92,89,85**
toteswingers:1&2:£6.80, 2&3:£3.20, 1&3:£3.00 CSF £30.73 CT £73.42 TOTE £7.10: £2.70, £1.20, £1.80; EX 43.20.

Owner Shropshire Wolves 3 **Bred** Mrs B Skinner **Trained** Pandy, Monmouths

FOCUS

This was run in a similar time to division 1, with a good pace set by two front-runners taking one another on.

7898 WOLVERHAMPTON-RACECOURSE.CO.UK MAIDEN AUCTION STKS 5f 216y(P)

4:50 (4:50) (Class 6) 2-Y-0 **£1,704** (£503; £251) **Stalls** Low

Form RPR

4 **1** **Chester'Slittlegem (IRE)**[12] 7784 2-8-1 0 .... AmyRyan(3) 1 66
(Ed de Giles) *mde all: rdn over 1f out: 2 l clr and drvn ins fnl f: hung rt fnl 100yds: hld on cl home* **7/2**[2]

5032 **2** *hd* **Tenbridge**[75] 6842 2-8-5 65 ....(p) FrankieMcDonald 3 66
(Derek Haydn Jones) *chsd ldrs: sn pushed along: rdn and hld hd high over 1f out: edgd lft u.p jst ins fnl f: styd on to press wnr and swtchd rt wl ins fnl f: clsng cl home but nvr quite getting up* **4/1**[3]

3 *1* **El McGlynn (IRE)**[40] 7467 2-8-4 0 .... LukeMorris 2 62
(John O'Shea) *chsd ldr: rdn jst over 2f out: drvn and no imp ent fnl f: kpt on fnl 100yds* **11/2**

0 **4** *4 ½* **Sleepy Lucy**[57] 7210 2-8-4 0 .... JamesSullivan 6 49
(Richard Guest) *s.i.s: sn outpcd in rr: rdn 1/2-way: nvr trbld ldrs* **40/1**

62 **5** *3* **Chaud Lapin**[14] 7749 2-8-9 0 .... WilliamCarson 4 45
(Anthony Carson) *s.i.s: nvr gng wl and sn niggled along: drvn and no prog over 2f out: wknd and wl btn over 1f out* **6/5**[1]

000 **6** *5* **Jeremy Sue**[27] 7593 2-8-2 0 .... SimonPearce(3) 5 26
(Derek Haydn Jones) *sn outpcd: wl bhd fr 1/2-way* **20/1**

1m 16.22s (1.22) **Going Correction** 0.0s/f (Stan) **6** Ran SP% **110.3**
Speed ratings (Par 94): **91,90,89,83,79 72**
toteswingers:1&2:£1.40, 2&3:£2.40, 1&3:£2.80 CSF £16.99 TOTE £6.00: £2.70, £2.30; EX 21.60.

Owner Chester Racing Club Ltd **Bred** Pat Todd **Trained** Ledbury, Herefordshire

■ Stewards' Enquiry : Amy Ryan caution; careless riding

FOCUS

A weak race, but run at a good gallop.

NOTEBOOK

Chester'Slittlegem(IRE) fulfilled the promise of his debut, this time from the front. Though she didn't beat much, and wandered right-handed in the straight, she went a decent pace all the way so she deserves credit for holding on. (op 4-1)

Tenbridge has looked more of a racehorse since switching to Polytrack. She has now run three good races here, and a similarly easy maiden may yet fall to her. (tchd 9-2)

El McGlynn(IRE), an ex-Irish filly having her first race for new connections, may be capable of winning a weak maiden at her best. However, she is pretty exposed and handicaps are likely to be her best option. (op 5-1)

Sleepy Lucy will be more effective over longer trips when receiving a handicap mark.

Chaud Lapin, the only colt in the field, was always up against it after fluffing the start but had shown at Kempton that he can do better than this. Official explanation: trainer was unable to give any explanation for colt's poor performance. (tchd 11-10 and 5-4)

Jeremy Sue is sprint-bred but will struggle to win over 5f or 6f. (op 33-1 tchd 18-1)

7899 GREAT OFFERS AT WOLVERHAMPTON-RACECOURSE.CO.UK H'CAP 7f 32y(P)

5:20 (5:21) (Class 7) (0-50,50) 3-Y-0+ **£1,704** (£503; £251) **Stalls** High

Form RPR

001 **1** **Mataajir (USA)**[18] 7714 3-9-3 **50** .... GrahamGibbons 1 59
(Derek Shaw) *t.k.h: chsd ldrs: rdn to chse ldr over 2f out: drvn and ev ch 1f out: kpt on to ld ins fnl f: forged ahd towards fin* **11/4**[1]

3003 **2** *¾* **Blueberry Fizz (IRE)**[13] 7768 3-8-13 **46** ....(v[1]) AdamKirby 8 53
(John Ryan) *sn bustled along to chse ldr: rdn to ld and qcknd 2 l clr wl over 2f out: drvn and hrd pressed 1f out: hdd ins fnl f: no ex towards fin* **12/1**

0000 **3** *1 ¼* **Pilgrim Dancer (IRE)**[142] 4869 4-9-0 **50** ....(b) AmyRyan(3) 4 54
(Tony Coyle) *t.k.h: hld up in tch in midfield: rdn and effrt on inner wl over 1f out: ev ch and drvn 1f out: no ex fnl 100yds: wknd towards fin* **7/2**[2]

4054 **4** *6* **St Ignatius**[18] 7714 4-9-1 **48** ....(p) NeilChalmers 7 35
(Michael Appleby) *t.k.h: chsd ldrs: rdn and chsd ldng pair over 2f out: outpcd and btn over 1f out: one pce and wl hld fnl f* **13/2**[3]

2302 **5** *1* **Lennoxwood (IRE)**[13] 7768 3-8-9 **49** ....(be) RachealKneller(7) 6 34
(Mark Usher) *hld up off the pce in last quartet: clsd and in tch 4f out: hdwy wl over 1f out: no imp u.p 1f out: wl hld fnl f* **8/1**

5525 **6** *nk* **Look For Love**[12] 7787 3-8-8 **48** ....(e) JackDuern(7) 10 32
(Reg Hollinshead) *s.i.s: hld up off the pce in last quartet: rdn and no imp over 2f out: no ch w ldrs but kpt on ins fnl f* **9/1**

2434 **7** *shd* **Royal Envoy (IRE)**[21] 7656 8-9-0 **47** .... MichaelStainton 5 31
(Paul Howling) *hld up in tch in midfield on outer: rdn and unable qck ent fnl 2f: wknd over 1f out* **7/1**

3065 **8** *1 ½* **Ghost Dancer**[13] 7768 7-8-13 **46** ....(b) RichardKingscote 12 26
(Milton Bradley) *stdd s: hld up off the pce in rr: clsd and in tch 4f out: outpcd over 2f out: rdn and effrt over 1f out: n.d* **14/1**

6031 **9** *2 ¼* **Jackie Love (IRE)**[13] 7768 3-8-10 **50** ....(b) JenniferFerguson(7) 11 [illegible]
(Olivia Maylam) [illegible] *hld up off the pce in last quartet: sme hdwy on outer 4f out: lost pl and bhd over 2f out: wl btn and hung lft over 1f out* **16/1**

00-0 **10** *½* **Kirstys Lad**[7] 7851 9-9-0 **47** .... KellyHarrison 2 19
(Michael Mullineaux) *in tch in midfield: rdn and lost pl ent fnl 2f: no ch over 1f out* **50/1**

0040 **11** *26* **Lois Lane**[12] 7785 3-8-10 **48** .... CharlesBishop(5) 3 —
(Ron Hodges) *led tl wl over 2f out: wknd qckly jst over 2f out: t.o fnl f* **100/1**

1m 29.92s (0.32) **Going Correction** 0.0s/f (Stan) **11** Ran SP% **119.0**
Speed ratings (Par 97): **98,97,95,88,87 87,87,85,82,82 52**
toteswingers:1&2:£7.40, 2&3:£14.20, 1&3:£4.20 CSF £38.13 CT £123.23 TOTE £4.00: £1.80, £3.60, £1.30; EX 40.30.

Owner Derek Shaw **Bred** Shadwell Australia Ltd **Trained** Sproxton, Leics

FOCUS

The gallop was testing in this selling-class handicap, and the form looks solid for the grade.

7900 TOTEPOOL H'CAP 2m 119y(P)

5:50 (5:50) (Class 4) (0-85,83) 3-Y-0+ **£4,204** (£1,251; £625; £312) **Stalls** Low

Form RPR

6013 **1** **La Estrella (USA)**[14] 7753 8-10-0 **83** .... AdamKirby 2 92
(Don Cantillon) *in tch: rdn to chse ldr over 2f out: drvn and ev ch over 1f out: led 1f out: sn hdd: edgd lft but led again wl ins fnl f: styd on wl and forged ahd towards fin* **4/1**[2]

5611 **2** *1 ¼* **Appeal (IRE)**[40] 7461 3-8-7 **70** .... LukeMorris 1 78
(Sir Mark Prescott Bt) *in tch: shuffled bk and swtchd rt over 3f out: rdn and rallied ent fnl 2f: ev ch 1f out: sn led: hdd and no ex wl ins fnl f* **5/4**[1]

3234 **3** *1 ½* **The Winged Assasin (USA)**[32] 7556 5-8-12 **67**....(t) RussKennemore 4 73
(Shaun Lycett) *chsd ldr: jnd ldr 1/2-way tl led wl over 3f out: drvn and hrd pressed over 1f out: hdd 1f out: wknd fnl 100yds* **18/1**

-21 **4** *2 ½* **Priceless Art (IRE)**[13] 7774 6-9-1 **75** .... GarryWhillans(5) 7 78
(Alan Swinbank) *chsd ldrs: rdn to chse ldr over 3f out tl over 2f out: outpcd and drvn over 1f out: edgd lft and plugged on same pce fnl f* **9/2**[3]

4401 **5** *½* **Admirable Duque (IRE)**[16] 7738 5-9-4 **80** ....(be) JackDuern(7) 6 82
(Dominic Ffrench Davis) *s.i.s: bhd and niggled along: rdn and struggling over 4f out: rallied 1f out: styd on wl ins fnl f: nvr trbld ldrs* **10/1**

4253 **6** *3 ½* **Zamina (IRE)**[26] 7446 3-8-8 **76** .... DavidKenny(5) 5 74
(George Baker) *hld up in tch: hdwy over 3f out: drvn and outpcd 2f out: wknd over 1f out* **25/1**

2532 **7** *12* **Sand Skier**[11] 7803 4-8-12 **74**.................................(b) NicoleNordblad(7) 3 58
(Hans Adielsson) *racd keenly: led tl wl over 3f out: sn struggling and lost pl: bhd over 1f out* **15/2**

3m 40.38s (-1.42) **Going Correction** 0.0s/f (Stan)
WFA 3 from 4yo+ 8lb **7** Ran SP% **112.6**
Speed ratings (Par 105): **103,102,101,100,100 98,93**
toteswingers:1&2:£1.50, 2&3:£5.80, 1&3:£5.30 CSF £9.11 TOTE £5.60: £2.00, £1.10; EX 10.70.
Owner Don Cantillon **Bred** Five Horses Ltd And Theatrical Syndicate **Trained** Newmarket, Suffolk
■ Stewards' Enquiry : Jack Duern four-day ban; excessive use of whip (11th-14th Jan)

FOCUS
There was a fair if unspectacular gallop for this stamina test featuring some decent AW sorts.

7901 STAY AT THE WOLVERHAMPTON HOLIDAY INN H'CAP 1m 1f 103y(P)
6:20 (6:20) (Class 5) (0-70,70) 3-Y-O+ **£2,264** (£673; £336; £168) **Stalls** Low

Form RPR
5400 **1** **Spes Nostra**[57] 7215 3-9-3 **68**.................................(b[1]) GrahamGibbons 5 81
(David Barron) *mde all: rdn and clr wl over 1f out: styd on wl fnl f* **4/1**[2]

3023 **2** *2 ¼* **Knowe Head (NZ)**[9] 7823 4-9-4 **67**.................................(p) AdamKirby 8 75
(James Unett) *bmpd s: hld up in tch: hdwy over 2f out: rdn to chse wnr wl over 1f out: no imp fnl f* **9/4**[1]

4524 **3** *1 ½* **Strike Force**[9] 7817 7-9-7 **70**.................................(t) TomEaves 2 75
(Clifford Lines) *chsd ldrs tl lft 2nd 7f out tl 5f out: rdn to chse wnr again over 2f out tl wl over 1f out: no imp and one pce after* **6/1**[3]

201 **4** *3 ½* **Yourinthewill (USA)**[12] 7788 3-9-4 **69**......................... StephenCraine 11 67
(Daniel Mark Loughnane, Ire) *stdd s: hld up in tch: rdn and outpcd over 2f out: kpt on but no threat to ldrs fnl f* **8/1**

1402 **5** *nk* **John Potts**[9] 7816 6-9-7 **70**.. KellyHarrison 9 67
(Brian Baugh) *t.k.h: stdd after s: hld up in tch: hdwy over 2f out: outpcd 2f out: swtchd rt over 1f out: kpt on but no threat to ldrs fnl f* **12/1**

0540 **6** *¾* **If You Whisper (IRE)**[13] 7771 3-9-4 **69**.........................(b) PhillipMakin 1 65
(Mike Murphy) *s.i.s: sn pushed along in rr: swtchd rt and effrt over 2f out: no prog: n.d* **11/1**

5036 **7** *1 ½* **Sky Diamond (IRE)**[26] 7605 3-8-11 **62**.......................(b) JamesSullivan 6 54
(John Mackie) *t.k.h: chsd ldrs: wnt 2nd 5f out tl over 2f out: wknd wl over 1f out* **22/1**

0-20 **8** *4 ½* **Khun John (IRE)**[20] 7671 8-8-13 **62**............................... StevieDonohoe 4 45
(Willie Musson) *s.i.s: nvr gng wl and sn pushed along in rr: n.d* **28/1**

3452 **9** *12* **Hits Only Jude (IRE)**[15] 7743 8-8-9 **65**.......................(v) JasonHart(7) 10 23
(Declan Carroll) *chsd ldrs on outer: rdn and struggling over 3f out: wknd and bhd fnl 2f* **40/1**

0 **10** *shd* **Indus Valley (IRE)**[29] 7579 4-8-11 **60**............................ MartinHarley 3 18
(Des Donovan) *stdd s: in tch in midfield: rdn and wknd 3f out: bhd fnl 2f* **15/2**

230- **P** **Zarazar**[7] 5675 3-9-0 **65**.. RobbieFitzpatrick 7 —
(Tim Vaughan) *plld v hrd: chsd ldr tl hung bdly rt bnd 7f out: sn dropped to rr: t.o and eased: p.u 4f out* **40/1**

1m 59.83s (-1.87) **Going Correction** 0.0s/f (Stan)
WFA 3 from 4yo+ 2lb **11** Ran SP% **116.6**
Speed ratings (Par 103): **108,106,104,101,101 100,99,95,84,84** —
toteswingers:1&2:£3.40, 2&3:£2.20, 1&3:£6.20 CSF £12.74 CT £52.11 TOTE £7.50: £2.20, £1.70, £1.30; EX 18.00.
Owner J Cringan & D Pryde **Bred** James A Cringan **Trained** Maunby, N Yorks

FOCUS
They went an average pace for the trip, enabling the winner to make all.
Zarazar Official explanation: jockey said gelding was unsteerable.

7902 TOTETRIFECTA H'CAP 1m 1f 103y(P)
6:50 (6:50) (Class 6) (0-60,60) 3-Y-O **£1,704** (£503; £251) **Stalls** Low

Form RPR
2162 **1** **Beggers Belief**[8] 7836 3-9-3 **56**.................................(b) WilliamCarson 3 63
(Eric Wheeler) *in tch: nt clr run over 2f out: hdwy to chse ldr wl over 1f out: led ent fnl f: drvn and kpt on fnl 150yds* **4/5**[1]

0063 **2** *1 ½* **Merrjanah**[9] 7817 3-9-2 **55**.. PaddyAspell 9 59
(John Wainwright) *in tch: rdn and effrt 2f out: kpt on same pce u.p fr over 1f out: wnt 2nd ins fnl f: no imp on wnr* **11/2**[2]

005 **3** *¾* **Ivan The Terrible (IRE)**[26] 7609 3-8-10 **52**............... RobertLButler(3) 5 54
(Richard Guest) *awkward leaving stalls and s.i.s: hld up in tch in rr: rdn and effrt on outer over 2f out: swtchd lft jst ins fnl f: styd on to go 3rd nr fin* **20/1**

0066 **4** *nk* **Ballinargh Boy**[26] 7608 3-8-7 **46** oh1............................ JamesSullivan 2 48?
(Robert Wylie) *racd keenly: led: rdn 2f out: hdd ent fnl f: no ex and lost 2 pls ins fnl f* **8/1**[3]

0000 **5** *1 ¼* **Tortilla (IRE)**[23] 7639 3-8-10 **49**..................................(b[1]) MartinHarley 8 48
(Des Donovan) *hld up in tch: nt clr run jst over 2f out: rdn and effrt u.p over 1f out: kpt on fnl f but nvr gng pce to threaten ldrs* **10/1**

6300 **6** *¾* **Tawseef (IRE)**[40] 7463 3-8-13 **52**..................................... TomEaves 4 50
(Roy Brotherton) *s.i.s: hld up in tch: nt clr run wl over 2f out: effrt u.p to chse ldrs over 1f out: no ex 1f out: wknd ins fnl f* **14/1**

3100 **7** *4 ½* **Ashgrove Nell (IRE)**[10] 7805 3-9-5 **58**.......................(p) StephenCraine 1 46
(Daniel Mark Loughnane, Ire) *chsd ldrs: rdn and unable qck over 1f out: wknd 1f out* **16/1**

2600 **8** *8* **Misere**[9] 7820 3-9-5 **58**.. PhillipMakin 6 29
(Kevin Ryan) *chsd ldr: rdn 3f out: stl pressing wnr 2f out: sn wknd: bhd and eased ins fnl f* **12/1**

2m 2.46s (0.76) **Going Correction** 0.0s/f (Stan) **8** Ran SP% **116.1**
Speed ratings (Par 98): **96,94,94,93,92 91,87,80**
toteswingers:1&2:£2.10, 2&3:£14.80, 1&3:£5.50 CSF £5.66 CT £49.88 TOTE £1.80: £1.10, £1.20, £5.20; EX 5.70 Trifecta £36.40 Pool £553.49 - 11.23 winning units.
Owner G W Witheford **Bred** Witheford Equine **Trained** Whitchurch-on-Thames, Oxon

FOCUS
The pace was modest, and so were the competitors.

7903 DID THE BIG MONEY TOTEJACKPOT ROLLOVER TODAY H'CAP 1m 4f 50y(P)
7:20 (7:21) (Class 6) (0-65,66) 3-Y-O+ **£1,704** (£503; £251) **Stalls** Low

Form RPR
1402 **1** **Thundering Home**[18] 7720 4-9-1 **61**...........................(t) DavidKenny(5) 11 70
(George Baker) *hld up towards rr: hdwy to chse ldrs 4f out: nt clr run and swtchd lft 2f out: chsd ldrs whn n.m.r and swtchd lft 1f out: r.o wl to ld fnl 50yds* **7/1**

3656 **2** *½* **Broughtons Paradis (IRE)**[14] 7761 5-9-10 **65**........... StevieDonohoe 2 73
(Willie Musson) *stdd s: hld up in rr: hdwy 4f out: chsd ldrs over 2f out: rdn and ev ch jst over 1f out: led ins fnl f: hdd and no ex fnl 50yds* **7/1**

004 **3** *1 ¾* **Spartan King (IRE)**[12] 7789 3-8-2 **53**................................ RyanPowell(5) 9 58
(Ian Williams) *v.s.a: in rr: gd hdwy on outer 4f out: rdn to press wnr 2f out: led jst over 1f out tl ins fnl f: one pce fnl 100yds* **15/2**

6552 **4** *2* **Straversjoy**[12] 7789 4-9-10 **65**.. AdamKirby 7 67
(Reg Hollinshead) *chsd ldrs: led 5f out: rdn and pressed 2f out: hdd jst over 1f out: wknd ins fnl f* **7/2**[2]

0011 **5** *nk* **Jamarjo (IRE)**[12] 7789 4-9-4 **59**.. LukeMorris 3 61
(Steve Gollings) *in tch: rdn to chse ldr 3f out tl 2f out: stl pressing ldrs but keeping on one pce whn squeezed and hmpd 1f out: nt rcvr and no threat to ldrs after: kpt on cl home* **11/4**[1]

1100 **6** *3* **Royal Alcor (IRE)**[9] 7817 4-9-8 **63**............................. FrankieMcDonald 1 60
(Alastair Lidderdale) *hld up in midfield: rdn and effrt over 2f out: 6th and no imp over 1f out* **11/2**[3]

1250 **7** *4 ½* **Art Thief**[17] 7723 3-8-10 **56**...(p) NeilChalmers 4 46
(Michael Appleby) *chsd ldrs: nt clr run and shuffled bk to rr 4f out: nt rcvr and n.d after* **16/1**

001 **8** *4 ½* **Ahlawy (IRE)**[9] 7818 8-9-11 **66** 6ex..........................(t) RobbieFitzpatrick 8 48
(Frank Sheridan) *hld up in rr: lost tch 3f out* **25/1**

000 **9** *28* **Orpen Bid (IRE)**[43] 7426 6-8-10 **51** oh6............................ KellyHarrison 6 —
(Michael Mullineaux) *chsd ldrs: rdn to chse ldr over 3f out tl 3f out: sn wknd: t.o fnl f* **80/1**

00-0 **10** *14* **Moscow Oznick**[10] 7805 6-9-5 **60**.................................(v) MartinHarley 10 —
(Des Donovan) *led tl 5f out: dropped out qckly 4f out: t.o over 2f out* **33/1**

-000 **11** *2* **Bowmans Well (IRE)**[26] 7606 6-8-5 **51** oh6..........(e[1]) CharlesBishop(5) 5 —
(Peter Purdy) *chsd ldr tl 5f out: dropped out qckly 4f out: t.o over 2f out* **100/1**

2m 41.64s (0.54) **Going Correction** 0.0s/f (Stan)
WFA 3 from 4yo+ 5lb **11** Ran SP% **115.9**
Speed ratings (Par 101): **98,97,96,95,94 92,89,86,68,58 57**
toteswingers:1&2:£6.80, 2&3:£11.10, 1&3:£5.00 CSF £53.26 CT £380.11 TOTE £9.70: £3.00, £2.70, £2.60; EX 52.90.
Owner George Baker **Bred** Rabbah Bloodstock Limited **Trained** Whitsbury, Hants

FOCUS
A slack early pace turned this into a 4f sprint, and things got messy in the home straight.
Jamarjo(IRE) Official explanation: jockey said gelding was denied a clear run.
Royal Alcor(IRE) Official explanation: jockey said gelding hung left handed
T/Plt: £20.40 to a £1 stake. Pool: £84,204.95 - 3,002.52 winning tickets T/Qpdt: £17.30 to a £1 stake. Pool: £8,845.04 - 377.50 winning tickets SP

7837 KEMPTON (A.W) (R-H)
Thursday, December 29

OFFICIAL GOING: Standard
Wind: Strong, across (away from stands) Weather: Cloudy, heavy rain race 5

7904 HOSPITALITY PACKAGES 2012 NOW AVAILABLE H'CAP 1m 2f (P)
3:50 (3:51) (Class 6) (0-65,63) 3-Y-O+ **£1,617** (£481; £240; £120) **Stalls** Low

Form RPR
-121 **1** **Trip Switch**[8] 7851 5-9-1 **57**.. AdamKirby 6 68
(George Prodromou) *sn trckd ldng trio: wnt 3rd 3f out: clsd on ldng pair over 1f out: rdn to ld last 150yds: sn in command: readily* **5/4**[1]

0022 **2** *¾* **Edgware Road**[20] 7698 3-8-13 **63**.................................(b) RyanPowell(5) 8 73
(Paul Rich) *trckd ldr: led over 5f out: hrd pressed 2f out: hdd and outpcd last 150yds* **11/4**[2]

0234 **3** *1 ¼* **Daniel Thomas (IRE)**[8] 7848 9-8-9 **51**.........................(tp) MartinHarley 4 58
(Richard Guest) *trckd ldng pair: wnt 2nd 4f out: rdn to chal and upsides 2f out: nt qckn over 1f out: one pce and lost 2nd sn after* **6/1**[3]

1640 **4** *1 ½* **Princess Lexi (IRE)**[36] 7524 4-9-1 **57**................................ JimCrowley 7 61
(William Knight) *dwlt: hld up in last trio: effrt over 2f out: styd on to take 4th over 1f out: nt pce to threaten* **7/1**

0653 **5** *½* **Isdaal**[11] 7810 4-8-9 **58**..(p) RaulDaSilva(7) 5 61
(Kevin Morgan) *hld up in last: rdn over 2f out: nvr on terms but styd on ins fnl f* **15/2**

0006 **6** *½* **Rezwaan**[21] 7671 4-9-5 **61**...(b) ShaneKelly 1 63
(Murty McGrath) *hld up in last trio: pushed along over 2f out: n.d after: rdn and kpt on fnl f* **20/1**

1400 **7** *1 ¾* **Count Ceprano (IRE)**[27] 7601 7-9-1 **60**.................. SimonPearce(3) 2 59
(Lydia Pearce) *trckd ldrs: pushed along over 3f out: sn lost pl and dropped to last pair: no ch whn no room against rail jst over 1f out* **33/1**

000- **8** *½* **Just Say Please**[37] 1495 4-8-7 **49** oh1............................ LukeMorris 3 47
(Martin Bosley) *had to be led to post and mounted at s: led to over 5f out: steadily lost pl fr 3f out* **80/1**

2m 8.56s (0.56) **Going Correction** +0.05s/f (Slow)
WFA 3 from 4yo+ 3lb **8** Ran SP% **118.6**
Speed ratings (Par 101): **99,98,97,96,95 95,94,93**
toteswingers:1&2:£1.60, 2&3:£2.60, 1&3:£3.20 CSF £4.97 CT £14.79 TOTE £2.70: £1.60, £1.60, £1.10; EX 6.20.
Owner George Prodromou **Bred** A Saccomando **Trained** East Harling, Norfolk

FOCUS
Runners were aided by a stiff tail-wind in the home straight. Racing began with a low-grade handicap, in which the top weight was rated just 61. The early pace was steady.
Count Ceprano(IRE) Official explanation: jockey said gelding was denied a clear run

7905 JANUARY 20% OFF SALES NOW LAUNCHED NURSERY 5f (P)
4:20 (4:20) (Class 5) (0-75,72) 2-Y-O **£2,264** (£673; £336; £168) **Stalls** Low

Form RPR
3225 **1** **Kyleakin Lass**[27] 7597 2-9-7 **72**.. LukeMorris 2 79
(Ian Wood) *t.k.h early: trckd ldng pair: wnt 2nd against rail 1f out: rdn to ld last 100yds: styd on wl* **11/4**[1]

4361 **2** *¾* **Sonko (IRE)**[21] 7670 2-9-4 **69**...(p) ShaneKelly 4 73
(Tim Pitt) *trckd ldr: shkn up to ld over 1f out: hdd and nt qckn last 100yds* **9/2**

5122 **3** *3 ¾* **Bookiesindexdotnet**[23] 7642 2-9-5 **70**............................ DavidProbert 5 61
(J R Jenkins) *led to over 1f out: wknd ins fnl f* **3/1**[2]

2132 **4** *1 ½* **Wicked Wench**[13] 7778 2-9-6 **71**.................................... StevieDonohoe 1 56
(Jo Hughes) *nt that wl away: racd in last pair: wnt 4th 2f out but sn wl outpcd: no ch after* **7/2**[3]

5510 **5** *2 ¼* **Mr Hendrix**[41] 7452 2-8-7 **58**.. WilliamCarson 6 35
(Brett Johnson) *awkward s and hanging lft: mostly in last: pushed along and wd bnd 2f out: bhd after* **11/1**

514 **6** *nk* **Twilight Allure**[13] 7778 2-8-13 **71**.................................(t) PaulMcGiff(7) 3 47
(Kevin Ryan) *chsd ldng trio: wd bnd over 3f out: lost 4th and wknd 2f out* **8/1**

60.19 secs (-0.31) **Going Correction** +0.05s/f (Slow) **6** Ran SP% **111.5**
Speed ratings (Par 96): **104,102,96,94,90 90**
toteswingers:1&2:£2.50, 2&3:£3.30, 1&3:£1.80 CSF £15.12 TOTE £3.70: £2.00, £3.70; EX 14.20.
Owner C R Lambourne, M Forbes, D Losse **Bred** West Dereham Abbey Stud **Trained** Upper Lambourn, Berks

The Form Book, Raceform Ltd, Compton, RG20 6NL

■ Stewards' Enquiry : Shane Kelly one-day ban: careless riding (Jan 12)

FOCUS

Just a run-of-the-mill nursery, but seemingly competitive.

NOTEBOOK

Kyleakin Lass, runner-up here off this mark two starts back, broke her duck under a fine ride. Always in the first three, she stuck closely to the inside rail and edged ahead in the final furlong. This win was registered without recourse to the whip. (op 5-2 tchd 7-2 in a place)

Sonko(IRE), winner of a claimer here three weeks previously, ran another cracker in this slightly better company. In the first two from the outset, she led 2f from home, but could not hold off the winner's late thrust on her inner. (op 6-1 tchd 13-2)

Bookiesindexdotnet, 1lb higher than when second last time out, set off in front and was still ahead on the home turn. She was no match for the first two, however, in the closings stages. (op 7-2)

Wicked Wench, 2lb higher than when second at Southwell last time, lost ground at the start and could never make a more serious impact. Official explanation: jockey said filly was slowly away (op 3-1)

Mr Hendrix failed to recover from a poor start. (op 12-1 tchd 14-1)

7906 BRITISH STALLION STUDS E B F MAIDEN STKS — 6f (P)

4:50 (4:50) (Class 5) 2-Y-O — **£3,234** (£962; £481; £240) **Stalls** Low

Form — RPR

2 **1** — **Hurry Up George**[28] 7593 2-9-3 0 .... JimCrowley 2 — 83+
(Ralph Beckett) *disp ld tl led 2f out: reminder over 1f out: pushed out fnl f and r.o wl* **4/6**[1]

2 **2** *1* **Pale Orchid (IRE)**[17] 7736 2-8-12 0 .... LukeMorris 7 — 75+
(David Evans) *t.k.h: hld up in 5th: nt clr run briefly on inner over 2f prog after: wnt 2nd 1f out: r.o but no threat to wnr* **10/1**

6543 **3** *5* **Derivatives (IRE)**[22] 7665 2-8-12 72 .... NickyMackay 1 — 59
(John Gosden) *disp ld to 2f out: lost 2nd 1f out: wl outpcd after* **7/2**[2]

4 *2 3/4* **Whispering Warrior (IRE)** 2-9-3 0 .... ShaneKelly 3 — 56
(Jeremy Noseda) *dwlt: hld up in last: outpcd whn swtchd rt over 1f out: kpt on to take 4th ins fnl f* **9/1**[3]

0 **5** *2* **Rainbow Riches (IRE)**[29] 7583 2-8-7 0 ow2 .... NedCurtis(7) 4 — 47
(Roger Curtis) *chsd ldrs: bmpd along and wknd 2f out* **100/1**

2630 **6** *2 3/4* **Lemon Rock**[89] 6526 2-9-0 78 ow2 .... (p) AdamKirby 5 — 39
(Noel Quinlan) *chsd ldrs tl wknd 2f out: lame* **10/1**

1m 13.66s (0.56) **Going Correction** +0.05s/f (Slow) — **6** Ran SP% **111.4**

Speed ratings (Par 96): **98,96,90,86,83 80**

toteswingers:1&2:£2.40, 2&3:£3.40, 1&3:£1.20 CSF £8.43 TOTE £1.80: £1.20, £3.30; EX 8.30.

Owner A E Frost **Bred** Digamist Bloodstock **Trained** Kimpton, Hants

FOCUS

An interesting juvenile maiden, featuring a quartet with fair form and a nicely-bred newcomer.

NOTEBOOK

Hurry Up George, second on his debut a month earlier, went one better with the minimum of fuss. Fast away, he disputed the lead from the start and grabbed a significant advantage 3f from home. He seemed to idle slightly late on, but was well on top nonetheless. (op 8-11)

Pale Orchid(IRE), second on her first start for this yard 17 days previously and officially rated 73, looks a decent guide to the form. Held up in midfield early on, she went fourth 3f out and was the only one to give the winner a race in the closing stages. (op 16-1)

Derivatives(IRE) has an official mark of 72, but seems flattered by that figure. She faded quite tamely in the home straight, having disputed the lead until the turn for home. This was not the first time she has finished weakly. (op 4-1)

Whispering Warrior(IRE), a newcomer who cost 100,000gns as a yearling, showed a little promise. Last early on, he plugged on gamely in the home straight and shaped as if he will stay longer trips. Official explanation: jockey said colt gelding hung right

Rainbow Riches(IRE), well beaten over C&D on her only previous run, appeared to improve on that effort. She needs one more run for a mark.

Lemon Rock, making her all-weather debut with an official mark of 78, drifted dramatically in the betting and ran poorly, dropping away late on after racing in third until approaching the 3f pole. Official explanation: vet said filly was found to be lame on its' off fore leg (op 13-2)

7907 SAVE YOUR 2012 REINDEER PARTY DATES CLAIMING STKS — 6f (P)

5:20 (5:20) (Class 6) 2-Y-O — **£1,617** (£481; £240; £120) **Stalls** Low

Form — RPR

1211 **1** — **Le King Beau (USA)**[12] 7798 2-8-10 69 .... KieranO'Neill(3) 4 — 71
(John Bridger) *sn settled bk into 3rd: led wl over 2f out: drvn over 1f out: hld on wl fnl f* **13/8**[1]

0514 **2** *hd* **Faraway**[2] 7881 2-8-13 70 .... LukeMorris 3 — 70
(Ronald Harris) *hld up in 4th* [illegible] *out: drvn over 1f out: grad clsd fnl f: a jst hld* **7/4**[2]

5605 **3** *5* **Rock Canyon (IRE)**[11] 7808 2-8-0 68 .... RaulDaSilva(7) 1 — 49
(Robert Mills) *hld up in last: chsd ldng pair 2f out: no imp after* **9/2**[3]

0551 **4** *2 3/4* **One More Roman (IRE)**[24] 7635 2-8-9 65 .... (bt) LiamKeniry 5 — 43
(J S Moore) *chsd ldr after 1f: nt qckn and lost pl over 2f out: n.d after* **6/1**

5 **5** *25* **Toss A Coin (IRE)**[15] 7758 2-8-7 0 .... (b1) WilliamCarson 7 — —
(Roger Teal) *sn led: hdd & wknd wl over 2f out: t.o* **40/1**

1m 14.11s (1.01) **Going Correction** +0.05s/f (Slow) — **5** Ran SP% **109.4**

Speed ratings (Par 94): **95,94,88,84,51**

toteswingers:1&2:£2.30 CSF £4.73 TOTE £2.50: £1.20, £2.10; EX 3.70.Rock Canyon was claimed by Miss L. A. Perratt for £4,000.

Owner P Cook **Bred** Haras Demeautry **Trained** Liphook, Hants

FOCUS

A competitive race of its type. The early pace was not that strong.

NOTEBOOK

Le King Beau(USA) lined up on a hat-trick after back-to-back claimer victories at Lingfield and kept up his winning sequence in a tight finish. Always in the first three, he led 2f out and battled on gamely when the runner-up drew alongside. He can score again at this level. (op 6-4 tchd 7-4)

Faraway, a solid nursery fourth last time out, was just touched off. Fourth at halfway, he went second 2f out and did everything right except pass the winner in the closing stages. (op 15-8)

Rock Canyon(IRE), dropped in trip after disappointing over 7f last time, ran a good deal better here. He was no match for the first two, however, despite plugging on gamely in the home straight. (op 13-2)

One More Roman(IRE), winner of a Lingfield seller on his most recent start, raced in the first three until halfway. He faded late on, though, and may be better off kept to basement contests. (op 5-1 tchd 9-2)

Toss A Coin(IRE), tailed off on his only previous outing, figured prominently until fading quickly in the closing stages.

7908 BOOK YOUR 2012 WEDDING AT KEMPTON PARK H'CAP — 1m 4f (P)

5:50 (5:52) (Class 4) (0-85,85) 3-Y-O+ — **£4,075** (£1,212; £606; £303) **Stalls** Centre

Form — RPR

41-0 **1** — **All The Winds (GER)**[14] 1402 6-9-0 80 .... RyanPowell(5) 11 — 88
(Shaun Lycett) *dwlt: hld up last: brought v wd bnd 3f out: rapid prog over 2f out to ld over 1f out: styd on* **20/1**

0415 **2** *1* **Where's Susie**[12] 7803 6-9-2 77 .... LukeMorris 7 — 83
(Michael Madgwick) *hld up in last trio: looking for room over 2f out: prog over 1f out: drvn and r.o to take 2nd last 100yds* **8/1**[3]

5144 **3** *3/4* **Art Scholar (IRE)**[20] 7699 4-9-3 78 .... NeilChalmers 3 — 83
(Michael Appleby) *hld up in midfield: looking for room over 2f out: prog wl over 1f out and looked a threat: rdn and styd on same pce fnl f* **12/1**

/002 **4** *shd* **First Avenue**[26] 6445 6-9-1 76 .... IanMongan 6 — 81
(Laura Mongan) *hld up in last trio: nt clr run on inner wl over 2f out: prog wl over 1f out: nt clr run again fnl f: styd on* **8/1**[3]

0033 **5** *hd* **Ellemujie**[22] 7651 6-9-9 84 .... (p) AdamKirby 2 — 89
(Dean Ivory) *sn settled in rr: looking for room over 2f out: prog wl over 1f out: drvn to chal for 2nd ins fnl f: one pce* **7/2**[2]

5112 **6** *nk* **Raucous Behaviour (USA)**[20] 7699 3-9-3 83 .... DavidProbert 4 — 87
(George Prodromou) *prom: wnt 2nd 2f out: led briefly on inner over 1f out: chsd wnr after tl lost pls last 100yds* **2/1**[1]

1423 **7** *3 1/2* **Brigadoon**[12] 7803 4-9-3 78 .... JimCrowley 12 — 76
(William Jarvis) *trckd ldrs: rdn over 2f out: nt qckn wl over 1f out but stl chsng ldrs: wknd fnl f* **8/1**[3]

-445 **8** *2 3/4* **Russian George (IRE)**[22] 1676 5-9-4 79 .... (t) MartinHarley 1 — 73
(Steve Gollings) *trckd ldrs: rdn and lost pl on inner over 3f out: tried to rally over 2f out: cl up but hld whn hmpd over 1f out: no ch after* **40/1**

1061 **9** *2 3/4* **Megalala (IRE)**[21] 7671 10-8-11 75 .... KieranO'Neill(3) 13 — 65
(John Bridger) *led at decent pce: hdd & wknd over 1f out* **14/1**

2600 **10** *1 1/2* **Plattsburgh (USA)**[77] 6822 3-8-11 77 .... FrannyNorton 8 — 64
(Mark Johnston) *chsd ldr to 2f out: wknd qckly* **14/1**

-500 **11** *2 1/2* **Dubai Bounty**[30] 7577 4-9-3 78 .... (t) NickyMackay 5 — 61
(Gerard Butler) *wl in tch in midfield tl wknd over 2f out* **20/1**

-104 **12** *2 1/4* **Taaresh (IRE)**[131] 803 6-9-3 85 .... RaulDaSilva(7) 10 — 65
(Kevin Morgan) *racd wd: in tch tl wknd 3f out* **33/1**

2m 34.03s (-0.47) **Going Correction** +0.05s/f (Slow)

WFA 3 from 4yo+ 5lb — **12** Ran SP% **124.8**

Speed ratings (Par 105): **103,102,101,101,101 101,99,97,95,94 92,91**

toteswingers:1&2:£25.50, 2&3:£18.90, 1&3:£15.90 CSF £174.33 CT £2041.41 TOTE £28.10: £7.70, £3.10, £4.50; EX 187.00.

Owner Nicholls Family **Bred** Stall Tralopp **Trained** Clapton-on-the-Hill, Gloucs

FOCUS

A competitive handicap, run in heavy rain, and in which few cold be confidently discounted. The pace was strong from the outset.

7909 SOCIAL OR BUSINESS BOOK YOUR SPONSORSHIP MEDIAN AUCTION MAIDEN FILLIES' STKS — 1m (P)

6:20 (6:20) (Class 6) 2-Y-O — **£1,617** (£481; £240; £120) **Stalls** Low

Form — RPR

65 **1** — **Hill Of Dreams (IRE)**[24] 7634 2-9-0 0 .... ShaneKelly 6 — 60
(Dean Ivory) *mde all: rdn 2f out: kpt on wl on inner fr over 1f out* **9/2**[2]

06 **2** *1 1/4* **Moment In The Sun**[77] 6817 2-9-0 55 .... WilliamCarson 3 — 57
(William Muir) *trckd ldrs: rdn to chse wnr wl over 1f out: kpt on but readily hld* **14/1**

40 **3** *1/2* **Canning Vale**[130] 5299 2-9-0 0 .... MartinHarley 9 — 56
(Julia Feilden) *racd wd: prom: rdn over 2f out: kpt on fr over 1f out to take 3rd last stride* **66/1**

232 **4** *shd* **Miss Astragal (IRE)**[27] 7598 2-8-11 72 .... KieranO'Neill(3) 7 — 56
(Richard Hannon) *t.k.h early: trckd ldrs: rdn to dispute 2nd 2f out but carried hd at awkward angle: fnd nil and hld over 1f out: lost 3rd last stride* **8/13**[1]

03 **5** *1 1/2* **Sea Anemone**[22] 7657 2-9-0 0 .... DavidProbert 10 — 52
(Andrew Balding) *mostly chsd wnr to wl over 1f out: fdd ins fnl f* **14/1**

6 *shd* **Palmyra (IRE)** 2-9-0 0 .... MartinLane 8 — 52
(David Simcock) *s.i.s: settled in last trio: pushed along over 3f out: sme prog into 6th over 1f out but nt on terms: styd on wl fnl f: nrst fin* **7/1**[3]

7 *5* **Play Street** 2-9-0 0 .... JimCrowley 1 — 40
(Jonathan Portman) *s.s: sn in tch in last: outpcd 3f out: nvr on terms after* **20/1**

0 **8** *nk* **Bellinda**[104] 6131 2-9-0 0 .... LukeMorris 4 — 40
(Martin Bosley) *a in last trio: no prog 3f out: nvr a factor* **40/1**

00 **9** *9* **Make A Fuss**[29] 7583 2-9-0 0 .... LiamKeniry 5 — 19
(Sylvester Kirk) *t.k.h: hld up in tch: outpcd and rdn over 3f out: wknd over 2f out* **40/1**

00 **10** *22* **Luna Vale**[illegible] 7520 2-8-11 0 .... AdamBeschizza(3) 2 — —
(Robert Eddery) *in tch tl wknd rapidly over 2f out: t.o* **33/1**

1m 43.51s (3.71) **Going Correction** +0.05s/f (Slow) — **10** Ran SP% **120.0**

Speed ratings (Par 91): **83,81,81,81,79 79,74,74,65,43**

toteswingers:1&2:£6.60, 2&3:£31.80, 1&3:£20.80 CSF £60.78 TOTE £4.70: £1.60, £3.20, £15.10; EX 76.80.

Owner I Gethin & R Gethin **Bred** Miss Breda Wright **Trained** Radlett, Herts

FOCUS

Little obvious strength in depth to this very ordinary fillies' median auction maiden.

NOTEBOOK

Hill Of Dreams(IRE), not beaten far when fifth at Lingfield last time, led throughout. She set only a fair gallop and, after accepting the easy lead, quickened in the home straight. She saw her race out well too. (op 5-1 tchd 4-1)

Moment In The Sun, having her seventh run and rated just 55, probably gives a good indication of the level of form achieved by the winner. She was always in the first four and plugged on gamely in the closing stages.

Canning Vale, tailed off on her two previous starts, is another whose proximity indicates the weakness of this event.

Miss Astragal(IRE), rated 72 but having her ninth crack at breaking her duck, was keen in the early stages and apparently reluctant to go through with her effort late on. Her head carriage and tendency to flash her tail suggested all was not right with her here. (tchd 4-6 in places)

Sea Anemone, third of six in a claimer on her more recent start, was second early on. She faded late, though, and may do better now she is eligible for handicaps. (op 12-1)

7910 WISHING YOU ALL HAPPY NEW YEAR H'CAP — 1m (P)

6:50 (6:50) (Class 6) (0-55,60) 3-Y-O+ — **£1,617** (£481; £240; £120) **Stalls** Low

Form — RPR

0505 **1** — **Karate (IRE)**[8] 7848 3-8-10 55 .... (t) NicoleNordblad(7) 8 — 64
(Hans Adielsson) *hld up towards rr: rchd midfield over 2f out: effrt over 1f out: shkn up and r.o fnl f to ld last strides* **10/1**

5500 **2** *nk* **Warbond**[24] 7640 3-8-12 50 .... (p) JamieGoldstein 10 — 58
(Michael Madgwick) *trckd ldrs: effrt to go 2nd 2f out: clsd on ldr over 1f out: led jst ins fnl f gng strly: idled and hdd last strides* **25/1**

2225 **3** *1* **Shaunas Spirit (IRE)**[24] 7640 3-8-12 50 .... ShaneKelly 11 — 56
(Dean Ivory) *led after 100yds: kicked clr over 2f out: drvn over 1f out: hdd and no ex jst ins fnl f* **15/8**[1]

0423 **4** *3/4* **Having A Ball**[22] 7656 7-8-13 55 .... RyanPowell(5) 14 — 59
(Jonathan Portman) *hld up towards rr: gd prog on outer over 2f out to chse ldng pair over 1f out: styd on same pce after* **7/1**[3]

0066 **5** 5 **Our Princess Ellie (USA)**[8] 7845 3-8-8 **46** oh1 .... MartinLane 4 39
(Derek Shaw) *snatched up sn after s and dropped to last: pushed along 1/2-way: brought wd and drvn over 2f out: kpt on to take 5th fnl f: nvr on terms* **40/1**

0004 **6** 2 3/4 **Divine Rule (IRE)**[15] 7756 3-9-1 **53** .... IanMongan 6 39
(Laura Mongan) *prom on inner: rdn to chse ldr briefly over 2f out: wknd over 1f out* **20/1**

0000 **7** hd **Very Well Red**[14] 7775 8-9-1 **52** .... WilliamCarson 9 38
(Peter Hiatt) *led 100yds: settled bhd ldrs: wnt 2nd over 3f out to over 2f out: wknd over 1f out* **16/1**

5632 **8** nk **Deslaya (IRE)**[17] 7740 3-8-12 **53** .... AmyRyan(3) 7 38
(Linda Stubbs) *wl in tch in midfield: rdn wl over 2f out: sn btn* **6/1**[2]

0265 **9** 5 **Holyfield Warrior (IRE)**[24] 7639 7-8-6 **48** .... MarkCoumbe(5) 12 22
(Michael Attwater) *racd on outer: chsd ldrs: rdn wl over 2f out: sn wknd* **9/1**

0540 **10** 4 1/2 **Days In May (IRE)**[47] 7387 3-9-3 **55** ....(b[1]) StevieDonohoe 5 18
(Edward Vaughan) *slowest away: a in rr: rdn and no prog 3f out* **10/1**

/6-0 **11** 3/4 **Confide In Me**[271] 656 7-9-0 **51** .... LukeMorris 3 13
(Mark Hoad) *rdn in rr bef 1/2-way: nvr a factor* **66/1**

3005 **12** nk **Like A Boy**[19] 7714 3-8-4 **49** .... JakePayne(7) 13 10
(Bill Turner) *chsd ldr after 1f to over 3f out: wknd u.p* **20/1**

0066 **13** 7 **Granny Anne (IRE)**[22] 7655 3-9-2 **54** ....(b) JimCrowley 2 —
(Paul D'Arcy) *rdn in midfield bef 1/2-way: sn struggling: t.o* **14/1**

1m 40.14s (0.34) **Going Correction** +0.05s/f (Slow) **13** Ran SP% **119.6**
WFA 3 from 7yo+ 1lb
Speed ratings (Par 101): **100,99,98,97,92 90,90,89,84,80 79,79,72**
toteswingers:1&2:£141.10, 2&3:£18.30, 1&3:£8.00 CSF £245.26 CT £675.92 TOTE £13.50: £4.50, £10.00, £1.10; EX 368.10.
Owner Erik Penser **Bred** C J Foy **Trained** Kingston Lisle, Oxon

FOCUS
A modest finale with the top weights rated only 55, but fiercely competitive on paper.
T/Plt: £178.40 to a £1 stake. Pool: £76,795.20. 314.08 winning tickets. T/Qpdt: £65.60 to a £1 stake. Pool: £8,284.01. 93.40 winning tickets. JN

7881 SOUTHWELL (L-H)

Thursday, December 29

OFFICIAL GOING: Standard
Wind: Fresh half behind Weather: Cloudy

7911 BIG MONEY TOTEJACKPOT PAYOUTS DAILY CLASSIFIED STKS 6f (F)
12:20 (12:21) (Class 6) 3-Y-0+ **£1,704** (£503; £251) **Stalls** Low

Form RPR

420 **1** **Beachwood Bay**[122] 5534 3-8-7 53 .... JoshBaudains(7) 5 60
(Jo Hughes) *prom: chsd clr ldr after 2f: rdn wl over 1f out: styd on to ld jst ins fnl f: kpt on* **8/1**[3]

3340 **2** nk **Fluctuation (IRE)**[20] 7695 3-9-0 51 ....(vp) StevieDonohoe 13 59
(Ian Williams) *towards rr: pushed along on outer 1/2-way: wd st and rdn: str run nr stands' rail fr over 1f out: kpt on* **4/1**[2]

0010 **3** 3 3/4 **Bird Dog**[7] 7854 5-8-7 55 ....(v) DannyBrock(7) 10 47
(Phil McEntee) *led: clr bef 1/2-way: rdn over 1f out: hdd jst ins fnl f: kpt on same pce* **8/1**[3]

3000 **4** 1 **Morermaloke**[17] 7737 3-8-11 55 .... DaleSwift(3) 9 44
(Ian McInnes) *trckd ldrs: hdwy 1/2-way: rdn 2f out: kpt on same pce* **25/1**

4001 **5** hd **Monte Cassino (IRE)**[18] 7728 6-9-0 51 .... TomEaves 3 43
(Bryan Smart) *chsd ldrs on inner: rdn along bef 1/2-way: drvn wl over 1f out and sn one pce* **15/8**[1]

2040 **6** 4 **Bint Elnadim (IRE)**[8] 7848 3-9-0 52 .... RobbieFitzpatrick 11 30
(Derek Shaw) *towards rr: sme hdwy wl over 1f out: nvr nr ldrs* **50/1**

0004 **7** nk **Bridge Valley**[33] 7561 4-9-0 53 .... MichaelStainton 7 29
(Jason Ward) *bhd and sn rdn along: sme hdwy 2f out: nvr nr ldrs* **8/1**[3]

2500 **8** 1 1/4 **Coastal Passage**[23] 7648 3-9-0 54 .... GrahamGibbons 12 25
(John Balding) *dwlt: sn chsng ldrs on outer: rdn along wl over 2f out: grad wknd* **9/1**

3040 **9** 3/4 **Madam Isshe**[7] 7853 4-9-0 51 .... TomMcLaughlin 1 23
(Mandy Rowland) *in tch: rdn along to chse ldrs 1/2-way: wknd fnl 2f* **28/1**

0000 **10** 1 **Douze Points (IRE)**[13] 7788 5-9-0 55 ....(p) JamieMackay 4 20
(Pat Murphy) *s.i.s: a bhd* **16/1**

100 **11** 2 1/2 **Odd Ball (IRE)**[227] 2164 4-9-0 55 .... JamesSullivan 6 12
(Lisa Williamson) *midfield: rdn along bef 1/2-way: sn wknd* **22/1**

1m 16.23s (-0.27) **Going Correction** -0.05s/f (Stan) **11** Ran SP% **117.6**
Speed ratings (Par 101): **99,98,93,92,92 86,86,84,83,82 78**
toteswingers:1&2:£6.00, 2&3:£4.60, 1&3:£7.20 CSF £38.48 TOTE £5.30: £1.20, £2.20, £2.40; EX 42.80 Trifecta £135.10 Pool: £266.69 - 1.46 winning units..
Owner Mrs Joanna Hughes **Bred** Bumble Bloodstock Ltd **Trained** Lambourn, Berks

FOCUS
A race full of disappointing sorts and non-winners. As was the case here two days earlier, it paid to race handily.

7912 TOTEQUICKPICK (S) H'CAP 1m 3f (F)
12:50 (12:53) (Class 6) (0-60,58) 3-Y-0+ **£1,704** (£503; £251) **Stalls** Low

Form RPR

0606 **1** **Dunaskin (IRE)**[86] 6613 11-8-4 **45** ....(b) CharlesEddery(7) 8 53
(Richard Guest) *chsd ldrs: rdn along 4f out: led 3f out: drvn and styd on gamely fnl f* **18/1**

4020 **2** 2 1/2 **Flying Applause**[13] 7788 6-9-6 **54** ....(bt) RussKennemore 3 57
(Roy Bowring) *led 3f: cl up: rdn over 2f out and ev ch tl drvn and no ex ins fnl f* **13/8**[1]

0050 **3** 1 **Kipchak (IRE)**[7] 7859 6-9-10 **58** ....(b) HayleyTurner 6 59
(Conor Dore) *cl up: led after 3f: rdn along and hdd 3f out: drvn wl over 1f out: kpt on same pce fnl f* **11/4**[2]

/000 **4** 2 **Marina's Ocean**[7] 7858 7-8-9 **46** ow1 ....(bt[1]) RyanClark(3) 1 44
(Roy Bowring) *in rr: stdy hdwy 1/2-way: cl up 3f out: rdn to chal and ev ch 2f out: drvn over 1f out: grad wknd* **14/1**

50P0 **5** 10 **Kingaroo (IRE)**[7] 7859 5-9-3 **56** ....(t) JustinNewman(5) 4 36
(Garry Woodward) *chsd ldrs: rdn along 5f out: wknd wl over 3f out* **4/1**[3]

656 **6** 18 **Prince Golan (IRE)**[108] 5994 7-9-0 **51** .... DaleSwift(3) 2 —
(Richard Price) *a towards rr: bhd fr 1/2-way* **7/1**

00-0 **7** 1 **Auburn Lady**[13] 7781 3-8-7 **45** .... AndrewMullen 5 —
(Alan Brown) *towards rr: bhd fr 1/2-way* **80/1**

2m 28.02s (0.02) **Going Correction** -0.05s/f (Stan)
WFA 3 from 5yo+ 4lb **7** Ran SP% **110.4**
Speed ratings (Par 101): **97,95,94,93,85 72,71**
toteswingers:1&2:£4.30, 2&3:£1.70, 1&3:£3.90 CSF £44.67 CT £103.66 TOTE £22.20: £7.40, £1.10; EX 45.60 Trifecta £76.90 Pool: £196.47 - 1.89 winning units..There was no bid for the winner.
Owner Mrs Alison Guest **Bred** J P And Miss M Mangan **Trained** Stainforth, S Yorks

FOCUS
A moderate selling handicap in which Kipchak and Flying Applause duelled for the lead and made sure this was run at a solid gallop. It's testament to the speed-favouring nature of the track that the pair managed to stay in the race for so long after being headed.

7913 TOTEQUADPOT MAIDEN STKS 7f (F)
1:25 (1:25) (Class 5) 3-Y-0+ **£2,587** (£770; £384; £192) **Stalls** Low

Form RPR

5 **1** **Great Expectations**[29] 7585 3-9-3 0 .... SteveDrowne 6 71+
(J R Jenkins) *trckd ldng pair: smooth hdwy to chal 2f out: shkn up to ld over 1f out: clr fnl f* **8/11**[1]

3325 **2** 3 **Pulsatilla**[19] 7711 3-8-12 57 .... TomEaves 2 58
(Bryan Smart) *led: jnd 2f out and sn rdn: hdd and drvn over 1f out: kpt on same pce* **3/1**[2]

0402 **3** 2 1/2 **Ecossaise**[7] 7856 3-8-12 70 ....(b[1]) FrannyNorton 5 51
(Mark Johnston) *chsd ldrs: rdn 2f out: sn edgd lft: kpt on appr fnl f* **7/2**[3]

30-6 **4** 7 **Too Late Jones (USA)**[19] 7717 4-9-0 0 .... RobertLButler(3) 4 37
(Richard Guest) *trckd ldr: effrt over 2f out: sn rdn and edgd lft: wknd wl over 1f out* **16/1**

5 22 **Darcy May** 3-8-12 0 .... GrahamGibbons 1 —
(Garry Woodward) *dwlt: swtchd to outer and in tch 1/2-way: sn rdn and wknd 3f out* **50/1**

6 23 **Myfourthboy** 4-8-10 0 .... VictorSantos(7) 3 —
(Alan Berry) *dwlt: a towards rr: outpcd and bhd fr 1/2-way* **100/1**

1m 29.15s (-1.15) **Going Correction** -0.05s/f (Stan) **6** Ran SP% **114.0**
Speed ratings (Par 103): **104,100,97,89,64 38**
toteswingers:1&2:£1.50, 2&3:£1.20, 1&3:£1.80 CSF £3.36 TOTE £1.80: £1.30, £1.40; EX 3.70.
Owner The Great Expectations Partnership **Bred** R B Hill **Trained** Royston, Herts

FOCUS
A weak and uncompetitive maiden, but the winner looks alright.
Too Late Jones(USA) Official explanation: vet said gelding was lame

7914 TOTETRIFECTA H'CAP 2m (F)
2:00 (2:00) (Class 5) (0-70,68) 3-Y-0+ **£2,264** (£673; £336; £168) **Stalls** Low

Form RPR

0501 **1** **Storm Hawk (IRE)**[7] 7858 4-9-9 **66** 6ex ....(b) RyanClark(3) 8 76
(Pat Eddery) *hld up in rr: smooth hdwy 6f out: trckd ldrs over 3f out: led 2f out: clr over 1f out: comf* **11/10**[1]

0044 **2** 2 1/2 **Blackmore**[15] 7753 4-9-13 **67** .... HayleyTurner 2 74
(Julia Feilden) *hld up: hdwy 4f out: chsd ldrs 3f out: rdn over 2f out: chsd wnr fnl f: no imp* **12/1**

3261 **3** 3/4 **First Rock (IRE)**[56] 7244 5-9-7 **66** .... GarryWhillans(5) 7 72
(Alan Swinbank) *hld up: hdwy to trck ldrs 6f out: led 3f out: sn rdn and hdd 2f out: drvn and one pce appr fnl f* **11/2**[2]

6151 **4** nse **River Dragon (IRE)**[3] 7163 6-9-11 **65** .... BarryMcHugh 4 71
(Tony Coyle) *trckd ldrs: hdwy over 4f out: rdn wl over 2f out: drvn and kpt on same pce appr fnl f* **7/1**[3]

2015 **5** 4 1/2 **Shifting Gold (IRE)**[33] 4941 5-9-11 **68** ....(bt) AmyRyan(3) 6 69
(Kevin Ryan) *s.i.s and reminders s: hdwy and cl up after 5f: rdn along 4f out: sn wknd* **12/1**

2360 **6** 10 **Calculating (IRE)**[15] 7753 7-9-9 **68** .... LeeNewnes(5) 5 57
(Mark Usher) *in tch: effrt over 4f out: sn rdn along and wknd over 3f out* **14/1**

3212 **7** 6 **Carnac (IRE)**[7] 7858 5-9-1 **55** ....(p) AndrewMullen 9 36
(Alan McCabe) *prom: led after 3f: reminders 1/2-way: hdd 3f out: sn drvn and wknd* **17/2**

2606 **8** 4 1/2 **Dubara Reef (IRE)**[8] 7850 4-8-10 **50** ....(v) JamesSullivan 3 26
(Paul Green) *led 3f: prom tl rdn along 6f out: sn wknd* **33/1**

3624 **9** 22 **Ay Tay Tate (IRE)**[14] 7772 5-9-8 **67** ....(p) JustinNewman(5) 1 17
(David C Griffiths) *prom: slt ld 1/2-way: hdd 6f out: cl up tl rdn along over 4f out and sn wknd* **18/1**

3m 40.44s (-5.06) **Going Correction** -0.05s/f (Stan) **9** Ran SP% **116.3**
Speed ratings (Par 103): **110,108,108,108,106 101,98,95,84**
toteswingers:1&2:£5.10, 2&3:£10.80, 1&3:£3.30 CSF £16.34 CT £54.94 TOTE £2.20: £1.30, £3.80, £1.70; EX 16.20 Trifecta £206.90 Pool: £819.23 - 2.93 winning units..
Owner Storm Hawk Partnership **Bred** Rodger O'Dwyer **Trained** Nether Winchendon, Bucks

FOCUS
One of the most severe stamina tests in racing.

7915 MIRROR PUNTERS CLUB NURSERY 1m (F)
2:35 (2:36) (Class 6) (0-65,66) 2-Y-O **£1,704** (£503; £251) **Stalls** Low

Form RPR

5211 **1** **Karma Chameleon**[8] 7849 2-9-8 **66** 6ex .... HayleyTurner 9 76+
(John Berry) *trckd ldrs: effrt on inner 2f out: rdn to ld 1 1/2f out: sn hung rt and clr: styd on* **13/8**[1]

0000 **2** 1 1/2 **Quiet Appeal (IRE)**[56] 7242 2-8-1 **45** .... MartinLane 7 52
(Mark Johnston) *in tch on outer: hdwy 2f out: sn rdn and styd on to chse wnr ins fnl f: no imp towards fin* **20/1**

0261 **3** 1 1/4 **Sweetnessandlight**[13] 7780 2-9-5 **63** .... MichaelStainton 4 67
(Jason Ward) *trckd ldrs on inner: hdwy whn hmpd 3f out: rdn and styd on wl appr fnl f: nrst fin* **7/1**[3]

5510 **4** 3 1/2 **Bitaphon (IRE)**[78] 6807 2-9-4 **65** .... DaleSwift(3) 3 61
(Deborah Sanderson) *cl up: led 3f out: rdn and hdd 1 1/2f out: sn sltly hmpd and swtchd lft: wknd ent fnl f* **2/1**[2]

0000 **5** nk **My New Angel (IRE)**[20] 7697 2-8-1 **45** .... JamieMackay 1 40+
(Paul Green) *s.i.s and towards rr tl styd on fnl 2f: nrst fin* **50/1**

042 **6** 4 **Sweet Grace**[13] 7777 2-9-6 **64** ....(t) SteveDrowne 8 50
(David Brown) *trckd ldrs: hdwy to chal over 2f out: sn rdn and ev ch tl wknd appr fnl f* **9/1**

4003 **7** 2 1/2 **Doyouknowwhoiam**[13] 7780 2-8-11 **55** .... TomEaves 10 35
(Bryan Smart) *prom: cl up 3f out: rdn over 2f out and sn wknd* **10/1**

000 **8** 2 3/4 **Classy Lass**[13] 7783 2-7-12 **45** .... DominicFox(3) 5 19
(Derek Shaw) *s.i.s: a towards rr* **100/1**

000 **9** 8 **Pink Belini**[29] 7583 2-8-7 **51** ....(t) AndrewMullen 11 6
(Alan McCabe) *chsd ldrs on outer: rdn along over 3f out: sn wknd* **33/1**

000 **10** 6 **Silver Native (IRE)**[48] 7369 2-8-3 **47** ow2 .... FrankieMcDonald 2 —
(Mike Murphy) *sn led: rdn along and hdd 3f out: sn wknd* **50/1**

1m 44.5s (0.80) **Going Correction** -0.05s/f (Stan) **10** Ran SP% **115.6**
Speed ratings (Par 94): **94,92,91,87,87 83,80,78,70,64**
toteswingers:1&2:£8.50, 2&3:£14.60, 1&3:£2.90 CSF £40.04 CT £186.01 TOTE £3.00: £1.10, £5.90, £2.10; EX 41.20 Trifecta £154.00 Pool: £792.28 - 3.81 winning units..
Owner EERC **Bred** D R Tucker **Trained** Newmarket, Suffolk

FOCUS
A modest nursery, but won by a progressive 2yo. The winner is clearly progressive and the form is rated around the third.

NOTEBOOK

Karma Chameleon was bidding for a hat-trick under a 6lb penalty, but was still 6lb well in compared to his revised mark. His sire's record on Fibresand suggested that the change in surface wouldn't be a problem and so it proved. He did edge away to his right once in front, but he still won this with plenty in hand so his new mark may not be beyond him. (tchd 6-4 and 7-4)

Quiet Appeal(IRE) had become bitterly disappointing since her promising racecourse debut, but this was a much better effort, especially as she struggled to go the early pace. The longer trip helped and she may be able to find a small race here off her basement handicap mark. (tchd 22-1)

Sweetnessandlight ◆, raised 3lb following her narrow success over 7f here earlier in the month, can have her performance marked up as she got stuck in behind the weakening Silver Native at a vital stage and lost significant ground in the process. (op 15-2 tchd 6-1)

Bitaphon(IRE), 4lb higher than when winning over 7f here in August, had every chance but again didn't seem to see out the extra furlong. (op 15-8)

My New Angel(IRE) had shown little ability to date and it's probably not worth getting carried away by this seemingly improved effort. (op 66-1)

Sweet Grace, making her nursery debut after running well in a couple of recent maidens here, seemed to have every chance when getting intimidated approaching the last furlong, but can't be counted unlucky. (op 8-1)

Classy Lass Official explanation: jockey said filly hung right

7916 SOUTHWELL MAIDEN AUCTION STKS — 5f (F)

3:10 (3:10) (Class 6) 2-Y-O — **£1,704** (£503; £251) **Stalls** High

Form — RPR

4323 **1** — **Ishiamiracle**[7] 7855 2-7-13 62....................(p) DannyBrock(7) 2 — 69
(Phil McEntee) *qckly away: mde all: rdn clr wl over 1f out: edgd rt and kpt on fnl f* **15/8**[1]

640 **2** *6* **Forever Janey**[33] 7559 2-8-5 52.................... JamesSullivan 7 — 46
(Paul Green) *chsd wnr: rdn along 2f out: edgd lft appr fnl f and kpt on same pce* **20/1**

32 **3** *3/4* **Ambitious Icarus**[33] 7555 2-8-3 0.................... CharlesEddery(7) 4 — 49
(Richard Guest) *chsd ldrs: rdn along 1/2-way: styd on same pce* **9/4**[2]

0566 **4** *3/4* **Gulf Storm (IRE)**[57] 7231 2-9-2 57.................... TomEaves 6 — 52
(Bryan Smart) *chsd ldrs: rdn along bef 1/2-way: sn outpcd and rr tl styd on fnl f* **13/2**

056 **5** *1* **Essexvale (IRE)**[13] 7778 2-8-4 57.................... JoshBaudains(7) 3 — 43
(Alan Berry) *chsd ldrs: rdn along 1/2-way: sn edgd lft and outpcd* **80/1**

2252 **R** — **Mount McLeod (IRE)**[34] 7541 2-8-4 57....................(p) NoraLooby(7) 5 — —
(Alan McCabe) *ref to r: tk no part* **3/1**[3]

58.17 secs (-1.53) **Going Correction** -0.40s/f (Stan) 2y crse rec — **6** Ran SP% **109.9**

Speed ratings (Par 94): **96,86,85,84,82** —

toteswingers:1&2:£6.50, 2&3:£4.40, 1&3:£1.20 CSF £34.57 TOTE £2.30: £1.10, £7.10; EX 24.10.

Owner S Jakes **Bred** M A L Evans **Trained** Newmarket, Suffolk

FOCUS

A weak maiden auction, made even more so when second-favourite Mount McLeod refused to exit the stalls.

NOTEBOOK

Ishiamiracle, with Mount McLeod out of the way, faced a straightforward task despite the big drop in trip. In the frame in all six previous starts here over 7f-1m, she was the one to beat on official ratings and as soon as she established an early advantage she was in no danger. Things will be harder back in handicaps, but this does widen her options somewhat. (op 7-4 tchd 13-8 and 2-1)

Forever Janey showed only limited ability in her first three starts and was very much second-best here, but she had 9lb to find with the winner so probably ran close to her mark. (op 28-1 tchd 18-1)

Ambitious Icarus had shown ability in his first two starts and was less exposed than his rivals, but again he looked very much in need of further. (op 7-2)

Gulf Storm(IRE) had a bit to find on official ratings and ran accordingly. (op 5-1 tchd 15-2)

Essexvale(IRE) has become very disappointing and tended to hang here. (op 100-1)

7917 PLAY GOLF AT SOUTHWELL RACECOURSE 2012 H'CAP — [illegible]

[illegible] 3-Y-O+ — **£2,264** (£673; £336; £168) **Stalls** High

Form — RPR

0000 **1** — **Cadeaux Pearl**[27] 7602 3-9-6 **74**....................(b) FrederikTylicki 3 — 85
(Scott Dixon) *mde most: rdn wl over 1f out: kpt on wl fnl f* **7/1**

0000 **2** *1* **Ghostwing**[22] 7660 4-9-7 **75**.................... SteveDrowne 9 — 82
(James Evans) *sn rdn along and outpcd in rr: hdwy on stands' rail over 1f out: styd on strly ins fnl f: nt rch wnr* **7/1**

3300 **3** *3/4* **Rylee Mooch**[16] 7746 3-8-9 **70**....................(e) CharlesEddery(7) 2 — 75
(Richard Guest) *a.p: effrt to chal wl over 1f out: sn rdn and ev ch tl drvn and one pce ins fnl f* **8/1**

6241 **4** *1/2* **Triple Dream**[12] 7804 6-9-7 **75**....................(tp) RichardKingscote 4 — 78
(Milton Bradley) *towards rr: hdwy 2f out: sn rdn and kpt on fnl f: nrst fin* **7/2**[1]

3045 **5** *nse* **Dancing Freddy (IRE)**[16] 7746 4-9-2 **73**....................(tp) RobertLButler(3) 5 — 76
(Richard Guest) *in tch: hdwy wl over 1f out: swtchd rt and sltly hmpd ent fnl f: kpt on same pce* **4/1**[2]

5600 **6** *2 1/4* **Luscivious**[23] 7644 7-9-7 **75**....................(b) GrahamGibbons 8 — 70
(Scott Dixon) *cl up: rdn along 2f out: hld whn swtchd lft and n.m.r ent fnl f* **9/2**[3]

0103 **7** *2* **Black Baccara**[9] 7833 4-8-6 **67**....................(be) DannyBrock(7) 7 — 54
(Phil McEntee) *s.i.s and swtchd lft s: gd hdwy on outer to join ldrs 1/2-way: rdn along wl over 1f out and sn wknd* **11/1**

3103 **8** *4 1/2* **Atlantic Beach**[12] 7804 6-9-1 **69**....................(b) HayleyTurner 6 — 40
(Milton Bradley) *chsd ldrs: rdn along 2f out: sn wknd* **8/1**

57.55 secs (-2.15) **Going Correction** -0.40s/f (Stan) — **8** Ran SP% **116.0**

Speed ratings (Par 103): **101,99,98,97,97 93,90,83**

toteswingers:1&2:£10.40, 2&3:£11.00, 1&3:£9.40 CSF £55.44 CT £405.51 TOTE £10.50: £3.10, £3.10, £3.10; EX 70.10 TRIFECTA Not won..

Owner Paul J Dixon **Bred** Catridge Farm Stud Ltd **Trained** Babworth, Notts

FOCUS

Just a fair sprint handicap.

T/Plt: £91.30 to a £1 stake. Pool: £50,174.97 - 401.07 winning tickets T/Qpdt: £10.00 to a £1 stake. Pool: £5,030.22 - 369.90 winning tickets JR

7888 LINGFIELD (L-H)

Friday, December 30

OFFICIAL GOING: Standard

Wind: medium, across Weather: rain threatening

7918 TOTEPLACEPOT NURSERY — 6f (P)

12:30 (12:30) (Class 4) (0-85,84) 2-Y-O — **£4,204** (£1,251; £625; £312) **Stalls** Low

Form — RPR

2153 **1** — **Taffe**[15] 7765 2-9-2 **79**.................... FrederikTylicki 3 — 82
(James Given) *mde virtually all: rdn and edgd rt 1f out: drvn and edgd lft u.p ins fnl f: wnt rt fnl 75yds: hld on cl home* **5/1**

4061 **2** *1/2* **Profile Star (IRE)**[49] 7364 2-9-0 **77**.................... GrahamGibbons 4 — 79
(David Barron) *in tch: effrt u.p and hanging lft over 1f out: swtchd rt and r.o wl ins fnl f: pressing wnr and pushed rt wl ins fnl f: r.o* **8/1**

2215 **3** *nk* **Quite A Thing**[41] 7491 2-9-5 **82**....................(b[1]) LukeMorris 1 — 83
(Sir Mark Prescott Bt) *dwlt and pushed along leaving stalls: in tch in last pair: rdn and effrt over 1f out: drvn and edgd lft 1f out: chsd wnr ins fnl f: one pce fnl 100yds* **3/1**[2]

1122 **4** *1* **Mr Knightley (IRE)**[13] 7798 2-9-1 **78**....................(b) StephenCraine 7 — 76
(Jim Boyle) *w ldr: rdn and sltly outpcd over 1f out: keeping on same pce whn n.m.r wl ins fnl f* **14/1**

4362 **5** *1 1/4* **Waseem Faris (IRE)**[15] 7765 2-9-0 **82**.................... CharlesBishop(5) 5 — 76
(Mick Channon) *stdd s: t.k.h: hld up in last pair: effrt and hung rt bnd 2f out: edgd lft and kpt on same pce ins fnl f: nt pce to rch ldrs* **9/4**[1]

5143 **6** *1/2* **Bubbly Ballerina**[56] 7261 2-9-4 **84**....................(p) DominicFox(3) 2 — 76
(Alan Bailey) *t.k.h: trckd ldng pair: rdn and unable qck over 1f out: edgd rt and no prog 1f out* **4/1**[3]

1m 11.44s (-0.46) **Going Correction** -0.05s/f (Stan) 2y crse rec — **6** Ran SP% **110.2**

Speed ratings (Par 98): **101,100,99,98,96 96**

toteswingers:1&2:£3.90, 1&3:£2.80, 2&3:£4.30 CSF £40.27 TOTE £7.10: £3.90, £6.70; EX 32.90.

Owner Ingram Racing **Bred** Graham Wilson **Trained** Willoughton, Lincs

FOCUS

Not a bad nursery, but they went steady early and it was a dash to the line from the turn in. There was a compressed finish and it's hard to believe the bare form is much better.

NOTEBOOK

Taffe dominated throughout and, kicking off the front and shrewdly angled to the centre of the track turning in, was always comfortably holding off his rivals from there. He shouldn't go up too much for this and ought to remain competitive. (op 9-2 tchd 4-1)

Profile Star(IRE) got the extra furlong perfectly well, albeit in a race not run at a strong gallop, but he didn't help himself by hanging left in the straight. (op 11-1 tchd 12-1)

Quite A Thing, blinkered for the first time, got outpaced before keeping on late and would have been better suited by a stronger all-round gallop. (op 4-1)

Mr Knightley(IRE) remains vulnerable in handicaps off his current mark. (op 11-1)

Waseem Faris(IRE), a neck in front of Taffe at Kempton last time, didn't settle off the steady early gallop and struggled to get involved. (op 5-2)

Bubbly Ballerina was very keen early, her saddle appeared to slip forward, she raced towards the inside in the straight and didn't get home. (op 3-1)

7919 LINGFIELD MARRIOTT HOTEL & COUNTRY CLUB (S) STKS — 6f (P)

1:00 (1:00) (Class 6) 3-Y-O+ — **£1,704** (£503; £251) **Stalls** Low

Form — RPR

6220 **1** — **Stevie Gee (IRE)**[4] 7876 7-9-6 71....................(b) FrederikTylicki 5 — 80
(Ian Williams) *trckd ldrs: travelling best 2f out: rdn to ld 1f out: sn clr and in command: comf* **7/2**[3]

1050 **2** *2 1/2* **Princess Dayna**[4] 7876 3-9-1 65.................... RichardKingscote 4 — 67
(Tom Dascombe) *racd in last pair: rdn and effrt ent fnl 2f: hdwy u.p 1f out: drvn and kpt on to go 2nd wl ins fnl f: no threat to wnr* **11/4**[2]

2055 **3** *1/2* **Lutine Charlie (IRE)**[10] 7834 4-9-6 74....................(b[1]) LukeMorris 3 — 70
(Ronald Harris) *in tch in midfield: rdn and effrt 2f out: kpt on u.p to chse wnr fnl 100yds: no imp and lost 2nd wl ins fnl f* **6/1**

460 **4** *1 1/2* **Scarlet Rocks (IRE)**[13] 7804 3-8-10 70....................(tp) DavidKenny(5) [illegible] — 61
([illegible]) [illegible] last pair: drvn and effrt 2f out: kpt on u.p ins fnl f: no threat to wnr* **9/4**[1]

4205 **5** *3 1/2* **For Life (IRE)**[25] 7636 9-8-11 61.................... NataliaGemelova(3) 8 — 48
(John E Long) *taken down early: led after 1f out: rdn wl over 1f out: hdd 1f out: sn btn: lost 2nd fnl 100yds: wknd* **17/2**

0240 **6** *2 3/4* **Dusty Bluebells (IRE)**[16] 7755 3-8-9 52....................(b) LiamKeniry 6 — 35
(J S Moore) *led for 1f: pressed ldr after: ev ch and rdn wl over 1f out: wknd ins fnl f* **25/1**

0340 **7** *2 1/4* **Waterloo Dock**[163] 4206 6-9-6 64.................... ChrisCatlin 1 — 38
(Michael Quinn) *rdn along thrght: chsd ldrs: wknd over 1f out* **40/1**

0041 **8** *1/2* **Force To Spend**[12] 7812 4-9-1 46.................... DavidProbert 7 — 32
(Des Donovan) *s.i.s: a in rr: wknd wl over 1f out* **16/1**

1m 10.74s (-1.16) **Going Correction** -0.05s/f (Stan) — **8** Ran SP% **116.6**

Speed ratings (Par 101): **105,101,101,99,94 90,87,87**

toteswingers:1&2:£3.40, 1&3:£4.30, 2&3:£4.40 CSF £13.91 TOTE £5.70: £2.00, £1.10, £1.80; EX 15.70 Trifecta £69.00 Pool: £752.06 - 8.06 winning units..There was no bid for the winner. Scarlet Rocks was claimed by P D Evans for £6,000.

Owner Steve Gray **Bred** Irish National Stud **Trained** Portway, Worcs

FOCUS

There was a decent gallop on here thanks to For Life and Dusty Bluebells, who kept him company.

7920 EAST GRINSTEAD CLAIMING STKS — 1m 2f (P)

1:35 (1:39) (Class 6) 3-4-Y-O — **£1,704** (£503; £251) **Stalls** Low

Form — RPR

P023 **1** — **Nibani (IRE)**[10] 7831 4-9-8 72....................(p) KierenFallon 7 — 81
(Alastair Lidderdale) *hld up in tch: hdwy to trck ldr jst over 2f out: rdn to ld jst ins fnl f: kpt on wl* **5/4**[1]

4003 **2** *2* **Wisecraic**[16] 7756 4-8-9 61 ow1.................... LiamKeniry 3 — 64
(J S Moore) *chsd ldr tl over 7f out: hdwy to ld wl over 2f out: drvn and clr w wnr over 1f out: hdd jst ins fnl f: no ex* **4/1**[3]

6404 **3** *6* **Gay Gallivanter**[14] 7782 3-8-0 46.................... NickyMackay 4 — 46
(Michael Quinn) *led tl hdd and rdn wl over 2f out: outpcd 2f out: 3rd and wl hld after* **22/1**

5151 **4** *1 1/2* **Encore Un Fois**[9] 7840 3-8-6 70.................... DavidKenny(5) 2 — 54
(George Baker) *v reluctant to go to post: in tch: rdn and little rspnse 2f out: 4th and wl hld over 1f out* **13/8**[2]

0030 **5** *2 1/2* **Miereveld**[8] 7859 4-8-7 52....................(p) ChrisCatlin 6 — 42
(Shaun Harris) *hld up in last pair: hdwy to press ldr over 7f out: rdn and lost pl qckly 3f out: bhd fnl 2f* **50/1**

6 shd **Broughton Place** 3-8-1 0 ..... JamieMackay 1 39
(Willie Musson) *s.i.s: t.k.h early: hld up in last pair: rdn and outpcd 2f out: n.d after* **14/1**

2m 6.61s (0.01) **Going Correction** -0.05s/f (Stan)
WFA 3 from 4yo 3lb — 6 Ran SP% **115.5**
Speed ratings (Par 101): **97,95,90,89,87 87**
toteswingers:1&2:£1.60, 1&3:£3.40, 2&3:£4.30 CSF £7.16 TOTE £2.00: £1.30, £2.70; EX 6.00.
Owner C S J Beek **Bred** Ballymacoll Stud Farm Ltd **Trained** Eastbury, Berks

FOCUS
A run-of-the-mill claimer.
Miereveld Official explanation: jockey said gelding failed to handle the downhill

7921 TOTEQUICKPICK MAIDEN STKS — 1m 2f (P)
2:10 (2:10) (Class 5) 3-Y-O — **£2,385** (£704; £352) **Stalls** Low

Form — RPR

224 1 **Tadabeer**[36] 7532 3-9-3 73 ..... FrederikTylicki 5 76
(Ian Williams) *chsd ldr: rdn and ev ch 2f out: led over 1f out: styd on strly and drew clr fnl f* **11/10**[1]

-504 2 4 ½ **Archelao (IRE)**[44] 7440 3-9-3 75 ..... HayleyTurner 4 67
(Marcus Tregoning) *led at stdy gallop: rdn ent fnl 2f: hdd over 1f out: nt pce of wnr and wl hld ins fnl f* **3/1**[2]

2 3 2 ¼ **Bert The Alert**[15] 7766 3-9-3 0 ..... AmirQuinn 1 63
(Gary Moore) *t.k.h: chsd ldng pair: rdn and effrt on inner to chal 2f out: sn unable qck and outpcd: wknd 1f out* **4/1**[3]

4 ½ **Broughton Sands**[16] 3-8-12 0 ..... JamieMackay 6 57
(Willie Musson) *hld up in last trio: rdn and effrt 2f out: wnt 4th jst ins fnl f: nudged along and kpt on fnl 150yds: eased nr fin* **50/1**

00 5 2 ¾ **Sondray**[30] 7585 3-9-0 0 ow2 ..... (t) IanMongan 8 53
(Jo Crowley) *in tch in midfield: rdn and unable qck ent fnl 2f: racd awkwardly and wknd over 1f out* **33/1**

6 1 **House Of Mirrors (USA)** 3-9-3 0 ..... (t) NickyMackay 3 54
(John Gosden) *s.i.s and pushed along leaving stalls: in tch in last trio: rdn over 2f out: drvn and wknd over 1f out* **6/1**

7 ½ **Hiscano** 3-9-3 0 ..... MarcHalford 9 53
(Terry Clement) *awkward leaving stalls and slowly away: in tch in rr: rdn and effrt ent fnl 2f: wknd over 1f out* **40/1**

6 8 8 **Pastures New**[28] 7609 3-9-3 0 ..... DavidProbert 2 37
(Des Donovan) *in tch in midfield: rdn over 3f out: wknd jst over 2f out: wl bhd over 1f out* **50/1**

2m 5.74s (-0.86) **Going Correction** -0.05s/f (Stan) — 8 Ran SP% **116.2**
Speed ratings (Par 102): **101,97,95,95,93 92,91,85**
toteswingers:1&2:£2.10, 1&3:£2.20, 2&3:£2.00 CSF £4.62 TOTE £1.90: £1.02, £1.70, £1.40; EX 4.50 Trifecta £18.20 Pool: £673.69 - 27.33 winning units..
Owner Sir Alex Ferguson & Sotirios Hassiakos **Bred** Shadwell Estate Co Ltd **Trained** Portway, Worcs

FOCUS
An ordinary maiden.

7922 TOTEEXACTA H'CAP — 1m (P)
2:45 (2:45) (Class 4) (0-85,89) 3-Y-O+ — **£4,204** (£1,251; £625; £312) **Stalls** High

Form — RPR

3121 1 **Lockantanks**[9] 7841 4-9-13 89 6ex ..... LukeMorris 3 98
(Michael Appleby) *trckd ldrs: effrt over 1f out: swtchd lft 1f out and qcknd to ld fnl 100yds: pushed out and in command after* **5/2**[1]

0004 2 1 **Titan Triumph**[23] 7660 7-9-1 77 ..... (t) JimCrowley 6 84
(William Knight) *stdd s: hld up in rr: rdn and effrt over 1f out: hdwy and swtchd lft ins fnl f: chsd wnr wl ins fnl f: no imp* **11/2**[3]

0420 3 ½ **Wilfred Pickles (IRE)**[23] 7660 5-9-7 83 ..... IanMongan 5 89
(Jo Crowley) *in tch: rdn and effrt on inner wl over 1f out: kpt on u.p ins fnl f* **15/2**

6351 4 nk **Mazamorra (USA)**[25] 7637 4-9-3 79 ..... ChrisCatlin 1 84
(Marco Botti) *sn led and set stdy gallop: rdn over 1f out: hdd fnl 100yds: no ex and lost 2 pls wl ins fnl f* **8/1**

1305 5 ½ **Veroon (IRE)**[23] 7651 5-9-6 82 ..... (p) FrederikTylicki 8 86
(James Given) *in tch in last pair: rdn and effrt over 1f out: styd on wl ins fnl f: unable to chal* **12/1**

1-05 6 1 **Podgies Boy (IRE)**[15] 7771 3-8-5 75 ..... LauraBarry(7) 7 76
(Richard Fahey) *chsd ldrs: hdwy to join ldr 5f out: rdn ent fnl 2f: unable qck over 1f out: wknd ins fnl f* **11/1**

545 7 1 ¼ **Focail Eile**[55] 7299 6-9-3 79 ..... KierenFallon 4 78
(John Ryan) *in tch in midfield: rdn and outpcd wl over 1f out: kpt on same pce and no threat to ldrs fnl f* **8/1**

6312 8 1 ¾ **Elijah Pepper (USA)**[60] 7199 6-9-2 78 ..... GrahamGibbons 2 73
(David Barron) *t.k.h: chsd ldr 3f out: styd chsng ldrs: rdn and unable qck 2f out: wknd ent fnl f* **4/1**[2]

1m 37.35s (-0.85) **Going Correction** -0.05s/f (Stan)
WFA 3 from 4yo+ 1lb — 8 Ran SP% **114.0**
Speed ratings (Par 105): **102,101,100,100,99 98,97,95**
toteswingers:1&2:£4.70, 1&3:£4.70, 2&3:£7.80 CSF £16.32 CT £88.99 TOTE £2.30: £1.10, £1.90, £2.80; EX 13.00 Trifecta £49.40 Pool: £716.05 - 10.71 winning units..
Owner Dallas Racing **Bred** Jeremy Green And Sons **Trained** Danethorpe, Notts

FOCUS
Some in-form horses lined up here.

7923 TOTETRIFECTA H'CAP (DIV I) — 7f (P)
3:20 (3:20) (Class 6) (0-55,55) 3-Y-O+ — **£1,704** (£503; £251) **Stalls** Low

Form — RPR

200 1 **Cheers**[42] 7462 3-9-1 54 ..... IanMongan 6 65
(Oliver Sherwood) *hld up in tch: rdn and ev ch ent fnl f: drvn 1f out: led fnl 75yds: r.o wl* **15/8**[1]

0003 2 ¾ **Royal Acclamation (IRE)**[16] 7760 6-8-7 46 oh1 ..... (p) SamHitchcott 4 55
(Michael Scudamore) *hld up in tch in midfield: rdn and qcknd to ld over 1f out: drew clr w wnr 1f out: hdd and no ex fnl 75yds* **5/1**[2]

0000 3 4 **Sir Ike (IRE)**[27] 7632 6-8-9 48 ..... (tp) LukeMorris 7 46
(Michael Appleby) *stdd and dropped in bhd after s: hld up in last pair: rdn and effrt over 1f out: r.o to go 3rd wl ins fnl f: no ch w ldrs* **8/1**

0005 4 ¾ **Suhayl Star (IRE)**[16] 7760 7-8-2 46 oh1 ..... CharlesBishop(5) 8 42
(Paul Burgoyne) *t.k.h: w ldr tl led 2f out: sn rdn and hdd over 1f out: outpcd and no ch w ldng pair ins fnl f: lost 3rd wl ins fnl f* **15/2**

6003 5 1 **A Pocketful Of Rye (IRE)**[12] 7812 4-8-7 46 oh1 ..... MichaelStainton 5 39
(Paul Howling) *in tch: rdn and unable qck wl over 1f out: outpcd and no ch w ldrs fr over 1f out* **15/2**

0466 6 ¾ **Putin (IRE)**[2] 7890 3-8-9 55 ..... DannyBrock(7) 3 46
(Phil McEntee) *led tl hdd and rdn 2f out: wknd jst over 1f out: fdd fnl f* **7/1**[3]

0050 7 1 ½ **Cavalry Guard (USA)**[64] 7131 7-8-4 46 oh1 ..... (b) AdamBeschizza(3) 2 33
(Tim McCarthy) *chsd ldrs: effrt u.p on inner wl over 1f out: btn over 1f out: sn wknd* **28/1**

0-43 8 8 **Chandrayaan**[309] 662 4-8-4 46 oh1 ..... (v) NataliaGemelova(3) 11 12
(John E Long) *wnt rt s and slowly away: a bhd: rdn and no rspnse over 2f out: lost tch wl over 1f out* **8/1**

1m 23.95s (-0.85) **Going Correction** -0.05s/f (Stan) — 8 Ran SP% **113.1**
Speed ratings (Par 101): **102,101,96,95,94 93,92,82**
toteswingers:1&2:£2.90, 1&3:£3.80, 2&3:£9.20 CSF £10.95 CT £58.62 TOTE £2.80: £1.10, £1.70, £2.80; EX 14.80 Trifecta £191.40 Pool: £507.06 - 1.96 winning units..
Owner John Duddy **Bred** Honeypuddle Stud **Trained** Upper Lambourn, Berks

FOCUS
The quicker of the two divisions by 0.73sec.

7924 TOTETRIFECTA H'CAP (DIV II) — 7f (P)
3:50 (3:50) (Class 6) (0-55,58) 3-Y-O+ — **£1,704** (£503; £251) **Stalls** Low

Form — RPR

-411 1 **Lucky Royale**[22] 7676 3-8-9 55 ..... RaulDaSilva(7) 8 66
(Jeremy Gask) *chsd ldng trio: rdn and effrt 2f out: 3rd and stl plenty to do 1f out: styd on wl to ld wl fnl 50yds* **7/2**[2]

0631 2 1 **Resplendent Alpha**[2] 7891 7-8-12 58 6ex ..... (p) RachealKneller(7) 4 66
(Alastair Lidderdale) *s.i.s: hld up bhd: stl last 2f out: hdwy over 1f out: styd on wl u.p ins fnl f: wnt 2nd nr fin: nt rch wnr* **11/2**[3]

0032 3 nk **Blueberry Fizz (IRE)**[2] 7899 3-8-0 46 ..... (v) NatashaEaton(7) 1 53
(John Ryan) *led: wnt clr over 2f out: rdn over 1f out: wknd u.p ins fnl f: hdd and lost 2 pls fnl 50yds* **7/2**[2]

0466 4 1 **Jonnie Skull (IRE)**[15] 7775 5-9-0 53 ..... (vt) KierenFallon 7 58
(Phil McEntee) *chsd ldr: 4 l down and rdn 2f out: plugged on u.p ins fnl f: no imp fnl 50yds* **10/3**[1]

0 5 1 ¼ **Rise To Glory (IRE)**[21] 7691 3-8-7 46 oh1 ..... (t) NeilChalmers 6 47
(Denis P Quinn, Ire) *s.i.s: in rr: rdn and racd awkwardly over 2f ut: hung lft and looked wl hld over 1f out: kpt on ins fnl f: nvr trbld ldrs* **16/1**

6000 6 1 ¼ **Grand Honour (IRE)**[15] 7768 5-8-7 46 oh1 ..... MichaelStainton 3 44
(Paul Howling) *hld up in midfield: rdn and effrt over 1f out: styd on ins fnl f: nvr trbld ldrs* **11/1**

0660 7 nk **Ain't Talkin'**[106] 6084 5-8-7 46 oh1 ..... (p) LukeMorris 9 43
(Michael Attwater) *sn rdn along in last trio: outpcd and wl hld 2f out: styd on ins fnl f: nvr trbld ldrs* **28/1**

306- 8 8 **Cheshire Lady (IRE)**[396] 7627 4-8-4 46 oh1 ..... AdamBeschizza(3) 2 22
(David Barron) *t.k.h: chsd ldrs: rdn and outpcd in 3rd 2f out: wknd and no ch fr over 1f out* **7/1**

00/0 9 2 ½ **Wee Buns**[228] 2162 6-8-11 50 ..... SamHitchcott 10 19
(Paul Burgoyne) *in tch in midfield: rdn wl over 2f out: wknd 2f out: wl btn over 1f out* **80/1**

1m 24.68s (-0.12) **Going Correction** -0.05s/f (Stan) — 9 Ran SP% **114.3**
Speed ratings (Par 101): **98,96,96,95,93 92,92,83,80**
toteswingers:1&2:£4.40, 1&3:£3.30, 2&3:£5.10 CSF £22.87 CT £71.62 TOTE £3.90: £1.40, £1.60, £2.50; EX 19.20 Trifecta £53.90 Pool: £1,138.69 - 15.63 winning units..
Owner Gracelands Stud Partnership **Bred** Gracelands Stud **Trained** Sutton Veny, Wilts

FOCUS
There was a good gallop on here, but the final time was slower than the first division.
T/Jkpt: £1,190.40 to a £1 stake. Pool:£20,871.77 - 21.00 winning tickets T/Plt: £36.60 to a £1 stake. Pool:£64,751.08 - 1,289.13 winning tickets T/Qpdt: £3.90 to a £1 stake. Pool:£7,111.79 - 1,338.06 winning tickets SP

7896 WOLVERHAMPTON (A.W) (L-H)
Friday, December 30

OFFICIAL GOING: Standard
Wind: Light behind Weather: Raining

7925 ENJOY THE PARTY PACK GROUP OFFER NURSERY — 5f 216y(P)
4:10 (4:13) (Class 6) (0-60,60) 2-Y-O — **£1,704** (£503; £251) **Stalls** Low

Form — RPR

000 1 **Chambles**[16] 7757 2-9-4 60 ..... (t) KieranO'Neill(3) 7 66
(Andrew Reid) *sn pushed along in rr: hdwy u.p over 1f out: edgd lft ins fnl f: styd on to ld nr fin* **7/2**[2]

250 2 ½ **Reve Du Jour (IRE)**[99] 6274 2-9-5 58 ..... ShaneKelly 4 63
(Alan McCabe) *sn led: rdn and hung rt over 1f out: hdd nr fin* **13/2**[3]

000 3 ½ **How Sweet It Is (IRE)**[67] 7056 2-9-7 60 ..... WilliamCarson 8 63
(James Bethell) *chsd ldr: rdn over 1f out: styd on* **12/1**

0600 4 1 ¾ **Dicky Mint**[92] 6489 2-9-3 56 ..... (t) PaddyAspell 9 54
(Michael Easterby) *chsd ldrs: rdn over 2f out: kpt on* **11/4**[1]

404 5 ¾ **Flaming Ferrari (IRE)**[18] 7736 2-9-4 57 ..... MartinLane 5 53
(Peter Chapple-Hyam) *chsd ldrs: rdn over 2f out: styd on same pce ins fnl f* **12/1**

6046 6 ½ **Sweet Ovation**[36] 7530 2-9-3 56 ..... SteveDrowne 1 50
(Mark Usher) *s.i.s: hld up: rdn and r.o ins fnl f: nvr nrr* **13/2**[3]

0040 7 5 **Chateau Lola**[14] 7780 2-8-6 45 ..... (v) AndrewMullen 10 24
(Derek Shaw) *mid-div: rdn over 2f out: wknd fnl f* **66/1**

5023 8 ½ **Ionwy**[69] 7038 2-9-6 59 ..... (p) FrankieMcDonald 2 37
(Derek Haydn Jones) *sn drvn along in rr: hdwy 4f out: rdn and wknd over 1f out* **14/1**

000 9 11 **Bonnie Blade**[14] 7783 2-8-6 50 ..... RyanPowell(5) 6 —
(James Unett) *s.i.s: pushed along in rr thrght: wknd over 2f out* **25/1**

1m 15.31s (0.31) **Going Correction** -0.10s/f (Stan) — 9 Ran SP% **102.9**
Speed ratings (Par 94): **93,92,91,89,88 87,81,80,65**
toteswingers:1&2:£42.20, 1&3:£6.80, 2&3:£24.10 CSF £21.16 CT £173.61 TOTE £3.40: £1.50, £2.70, £3.70; EX 32.20.
Owner A S Reid **Bred** A S Reid **Trained** Mill Hill, London NW7

FOCUS
A moderate nursery run at a fair gallop. The winner came down the centre in the straight and is progressing with racing.

NOTEBOOK
Chambles ◆, dropped in trip and easy in the market before the off, showed a good turn of foot and showed improved form in the first-time tongue-tie to win on this nursery debut when faring easily the best of those held up. She'll be as effective over 7f, and appeals as the type to win again this winter. (op 10-3 tchd 4-1)
Reve Du Jour(IRE) had the run of the race and turned in her best effort with the cheekpieces left off on this all-weather debut and first run since September. There's a similar race to be won with her on this surface.
How Sweet It Is(IRE) was fairly easy in the market but she ran creditably on this nursery and all-weather debut on only this second run since May. Her sister Sweet Cecily is a very useful sprinter and there may well be a bit more to come from this unexposed sort. (tchd 14-1)

The Form Book, Raceform Ltd, Compton, RG20 6NL

Dicky Mint, the only male in the race and with the blinkers left off for this drop in trip, attracted plenty of support and ran creditably on this first run since being gelded. He looks exposed but may be worth another chance returned to 7f. (op 7-2)

Flaming Ferrari(IRE) wasn't disgraced on this nursery debut but, although she isn't fully exposed and is in good hands, she'll have to improve to win a similar event from her current mark. (tchd 14-1)

7926 TOTEPOOL MOBILE TEXT TOTE TO 89660 H'CAP 5f 216y(P)

4:40 (4:42) (Class 4) (0-85,82) 3-Y-O+ **£4,204** (£1,251; £625; £312) **Stalls** Low

Form RPR

1202 **1** **Red Cape (FR)**[9] 7847 8-9-2 **77**....................(b) JamesSullivan 6 88
(Ruth Carr) *trckd ldrs: plld hrd: rdn to ld ins fnl f: r.o* **10/1**

1132 **2** *1 1/2* **One Way Or Another (AUS)**[4] 7876 8-8-12 **76**.......(b) KieranO'Neill(3) 2 82
(David Evans) *s.i.s: hld up: pushed along over 2f out: r.o wl ins fnl f: nt rch wnr* **12/1**

3331 **3** *shd* **Caldercruix (USA)**[11] 7819 4-9-1 **76** 6ex....................(v) SteveDrowne 7 82
(James Evans) *sn led: rdn over 1f out: hdd ins fnl f: styd on* **11/2**[1]

1405 **4** *shd* **Master Of Disguise**[9] 7846 5-9-3 **78**....................(t) WilliamCarson 9 84
(Brian Baugh) *chsd ldr: rdn over 1f out: styd on* **16/1**

4042 **5** *3/4* **Close To The Edge (IRE)**[9] 7846 3-9-5 **80**.................. MartinHarley 10 83
(Alan McCabe) *a.p: rdn over 1f out: styd on* **8/1**

0016 **6** *shd* **Dasho**[9] 7846 3-9-2 **82**.. LucyKBarry(5) 3 85
(Olivia Maylam) *trckd ldrs: plld hrd: rdn and ev ch 1f out: styd on same pce* **13/2**[3]

2001 **7** *1/2* **Tombi (USA)**[27] 7629 7-9-0 **75**.................................. FrannyNorton 1 76
(Ollie Pears) *s.i.s: hld up: plld hrd: hdwy over 1f out: nt rch ldrs* **12/1**

0133 **8** *nk* **Where's Reiley (USA)**[10] 7832 5-8-12 **80**..............(b) LeonnaMayor(7) 8 80
(Alastair Lidderdale) *hld up in tch: plld hrd: rdn over 1f out: nt trble ldrs* **12/1**

0013 **9** *hd* **Restless Bay (IRE)**[20] 7715 3-9-2 **77**....................(e) AdamKirby 13 77
(Reg Hollinshead) *s.i.s: hld up: rdn and r.o ins fnl f: nvr nrr* **7/1**

0423 **10** *3/4* **Bond Fastrac**[29] 7596 4-8-11 **75**.................................. DaleSwift(3) 12 72
(Geoffrey Oldroyd) *prom: rdn over 2f out: styd on same pce fnl f* **12/1**

6115 **11** *nk* **Titus Gent**[9] 7847 6-9-7 **82**.................................... MartinLane 5 78
(Jeremy Gask) *mid-div: rdn over 1f out: n.d* **25/1**

2201 **12** *2* **Dorback**[9] 7847 4-9-6 **81** 6ex.................................... BarryMcHugh 4 71
(Noel Wilson) *hld up: plld hrd: hdwy 2f out: rdn and hung rt over 1f out: no ex fnl f* **6/1**[2]

2002 **13** *2* **All Right Now**[51] 7339 4-9-1 **76**.............................. FrankieMcDonald 11 59
(Derek Haydn Jones) *sn pushed along in rr: lost tch fnl 2f* **25/1**

1m 14.44s (-0.56) **Going Correction** -0.10s/f (Stan) **13** Ran SP% **120.0**

Speed ratings (Par 105): **99,97,96,96,95 95,94,94,94,93 92,90,87**

toteswingers:1&2:£26.40, 1&3:£12.10, 2&3:£8.20 CSF £125.19 CT £730.79 TOTE £13.00: £4.60, £4.00, £1.40; EX 91.90.

Owner Middleham Park Racing LVI **Bred** Gilles And Mrs Forien **Trained** Huby, N Yorks

FOCUS

Mainly exposed sorts in a useful handicap. The gallop was just an ordinary one for a sprint and the winner raced centre-to-far-side in the straight.

Dorback Official explanation: vet said gelding finished distressed

7927 HAPPY NEW YEAR FROM WOLVERHAMPTON RACECOURSE CLAIMING STKS 7f 32y(P)

5:10 (5:10) (Class 6) 2-Y-O **£1,704** (£503; £251) **Stalls** High

Form RPR

5514 **1** **One More Roman (IRE)**[1] 7907 2-8-0 65................(bt) RyanPowell(5) 5 65
(J S Moore) *led over 6f out: rdn and hung rt fr over 1f out: styd on* **13/2**[3]

2004 **2** *nk* **Crowning Star (IRE)**[15] 7762 2-8-5 65.................. WilliamCarson 2 64
(J S Moore) *prom: hmpd sn after s: rdn over 1f out: r.o to go 2nd wl ins fnl f: nt quite rch wnr* **8/1**

2314 **3** *2* **Not Bad For A Boy (IRE)**[4] 7875 2-9-4 78.................. KieranO'Neill(3) 3 75
(Richard Hannon) *led: edgd rt and sn hdd: remained handy: chsd wnr 1/2-way: rdn over 1f out: hung rt and lost 2nd wl ins fnl f* **5/6**[1]

425 **4** *4* **Tiablo (IRE)**[62] 7174 2-8-1 66.................................. NicoleNordblad(7) 1 53
(David Simcock) *s.i.s: hmpd sn after s: hld up: racd keenly: effrt over 1f out: no ex fnl f* **3/1**[2]

6 **5** *3 3/4* **Jealous Hart**[18] 7736 2-8-4 0.................................... FrannyNorton 4 40
(Ollie Pears) *pushed along early: chsd wnr wl over 5f out tl 1/2-way: sn rdn: wknd wl over 1f out* **50/1**

0 **6** *30* **Danafisiak (IRE)**[11] 7821 2-9-7 0.............................. RussKennemore 6 —
(Frank Sheridan) *a in rr: rdn and wknd over 2f out* **125/1**

1m 29.54s (-0.06) **Going Correction** -0.10s/f (Stan) **6** Ran SP% **106.8**

Speed ratings (Par 94): **96,95,93,88,84 50**

toteswingers:1&2:£4.40, 1&3:£1.60, 2&3:£1.60 CSF £48.59 TOTE £13.10: £1.90, £7.50; EX 32.90.One More Roman was claimed by Miss Gay Kelleway for £6,000.

Owner Mrs Fitri Hay **Bred** Mrs Fitriani Hay **Trained** Upper Lambourn, Berks

FOCUS

A modest claimer run at just an ordinary gallop. The winner came down the centre. Straightforward form, with the third the best guide.

NOTEBOOK

One More Roman(IRE) hadn't been at his best at Kempton the previous evening but fared a good deal better returned to this trip after securing an easy lead. He didn't look entirely straightforward under pressure but he isn't fully exposed and may do a bit better over this trip in similar company. (op 7-1)

Crowning Star(IRE) had disappointed in a tongue-tie on his last two starts (and in blinkers last time) but he had no equipment on here and fared better in this ordinary event, despite leaving the impression that a stiffer test of stamina would have suited. It remains to be seen whether this is reproduced next time, though. (op 15-2 tchd 7-1 and 9-1)

Not Bad For A Boy(IRE), a fair sort, wasn't disgraced attempting to concede 16lb to the first two. A stronger gallop would have suited better and he should be able to pick up another small race on this surface. (tchd 10-11 and evens in places)

Tiablo(IRE),who failed to settle in this muddling event, was again below her best at this course. She may do better returned to Kempton (the scene of easily her best effort) but she doesn't look the most straightforward of individuals (pulls and hangs). (tchd 5-2)

Danafisiak(IRE) Official explanation: jockey said colt lost its action

7928 BET TOTEPOOL TEXT TOTE TO 89660 H'CAP 7f 32y(P)

5:40 (5:40) (Class 5) (0-75,79) 3-Y-O+ **£2,264** (£673; £336; £168) **Stalls** High

Form RPR

0222 **1** **Tislaam (IRE)**[15] 7767 4-9-4 **72**....................(p) MartinHarley 5 81
(Alan McCabe) *mde all: rdn ins fnl f: styd on* **11/2**[2]

1056 **2** *1 1/2* **Without Prejudice (USA)**[4] 7876 6-8-13 **67**.................. PaddyAspell 8 72
(Michael Easterby) *pushed along in rr early: hdwy over 5f out: chsd wnr 4f out: rdn over 2f out: styd on* **20/1**

0411 **3** *3/4* **Perfect Cracker**[9] 7842 3-9-11 **79** 6ex.............................. AdamKirby 7 82
(Clive Cox) *trckd ldrs: plld hrd: rdn over 1f out: styd on* **4/6**[1]

3000 **4** *1* **Viva Ronaldo (IRE)**[23] 7660 5-9-7 **75**.......................... TonyHamilton 10 75
(Richard Fahey) *hld up: rdn over 2f out: r.o ins fnl f: nrst fin* **10/1**[3]

0040 **5** *1/2* **Legal Legacy**[101] 6231 5-9-2 **70**.................................. AndrewMullen 2 69
(David C Griffiths) *s.i.s: hld up: hdwy over 1f out: r.o: nt trble ldrs* **66/1**

000 **6** *2* **Needwood Ridge**[28] 7605 4-8-13 **67**............................(bt) LiamKeniry 6 60
(Frank Sheridan) *hld up in tch: rdn over 2f out: styd on same appr fnl f* **25/1**

2410 **7** *nk* **Bahamian Lad**[20] 7716 6-9-0 **68**....................................(p) KellyHarrison 1 61
(Reg Hollinshead) *chsd wnr 3f: remained handy: rdn over 2f out: styd on same pce fr over 1f out* **16/1**

0050 **8** *1/2* **Avonrose**[20] 7715 4-9-3 **74**.. DaleSwift(3) 11 65
(Derek Shaw) *hld up in tch: rdn over 2f out: wknd fnl f* **16/1**

0145 **9** *4* **Khajaaly (IRE)**[46] 7417 4-9-5 **73**.................................. ShaneKelly 12 54
(Julia Feilden) *hld up: rdn over 1f out: a in rr* **12/1**

1242 **10** *hd* **Ryedane (IRE)**[20] 7715 9-8-11 **70**........................(b) AdamCarter(5) 4 50
(Tim Easterby) *hld up: plld hrd: rdn over 2f out: wknd wl over 1f out* **10/1**[3]

1m 28.36s (-1.24) **Going Correction** -0.10s/f (Stan) **10** Ran SP% **123.1**

Speed ratings (Par 103): **103,101,100,99,98 96,96,95,90,90**

CSF £113.46 CT £166.44 TOTE £5.20: £1.50, £2.80, £1.10; EX 127.50.

Owner Mrs Z Wentworth **Bred** Airlie Stud **Trained** Averham Park, Notts

FOCUS

A fair handicap but a muddling gallop saw several take a good hold early on and this race suited those right up with the pace. The winner raced centre-to-far-side in the straight.

Ryedane(IRE) Official explanation: jockey said gelding ran too freely

7929 MIRROR PUNTERS CLUB MEDIAN AUCTION MAIDEN STKS 1m 141y(P)

6:10 (6:10) (Class 6) 2-Y-O **£1,704** (£503; £251) **Stalls** Low

Form RPR

322 **1** **Final Delivery**[46] 7414 2-8-12 76.................................. DavidKenny(5) 2 74
(George Baker) *a.p: chsd ldr wl over 1f out: rdn to ld ins fnl f: edgd lft: styd on u.p* **4/11**[1]

05 **2** *1/2* **Foursquare Funtime**[34] 7559 2-9-3 0.......................... GrahamGibbons 6 72
(Reg Hollinshead) *set stdy pce tl qcknd over 2f out: rdn and edgd rt over 1f out: hdd and edgd lft ins fnl f: styd on* **6/1**[3]

04 **3** *3 3/4* **Abdul Malik**[10] 7835 2-9-3 0.. MartinLane 5 64
(David Simcock) *chsd ldr: rdn over 2f out: lost 2nd over 1f out: no ex ins fnl f* **5/1**[2]

00 **4** *14* **Aloysia**[46] 7414 2-8-12 0.. LiamKeniry 3 30
(Sylvester Kirk) *chsd ldrs: rdn 1/2-way: wknd over 2f out* **40/1**

1m 51.68s (1.18) **Going Correction** -0.10s/f (Stan) **4** Ran SP% **106.7**

Speed ratings (Par 94): **90,89,86,73**

CSF £2.89 TOTE £1.20; EX 2.50.

Owner M Khan X2 **Bred** Mallalieu Bloodstock Ltd **Trained** Whitsbury, Hants

FOCUS

An uncompetitive maiden run at a steady gallop. The winner raced centre-to-far-side in the straight. A slow time and not form to trust implicitly, but it makes a certain amount of sense.

NOTEBOOK

Final Delivery was well supported on this first start since being purchased by current connections for £14,000 but he didn't have to improve to get off the mark in workmanlike fashion. A stronger gallop would have suited better but he'll have to raise his game to follow up in a competitive handicap. (op 2-5)

Foursquare Funtime has improved with every start and posted his best effort, despite being allowed an easy time of it in front over this longer trip. His proximity to the winner won't have done his prospective handicap mark any favours but he should be able to pick up a small event. (op 5-1 tchd 13-2)

Abdul Malik ran to a similar level as on his previous start. He has a fair bit about him physically, will be suited by a stiffer test of stamina over this trip and will be one to keep an eye on in handicaps when a better gallop looks on the cards. (tchd 11-2)

Aloysia again had her limitations firmly exposed in this type of event. Low-grade handicaps will be the way forward with her but she'll have to show something more solid before she's a betting proposition. (op 33-1)

7930 DID BIG MONEY TOTEJACKPOT ROLLOVER TODAY H'CAP 1m 141y(P)

6:40 (6:41) (Class 6) (0-65,65) 3-Y-O+ **£1,701** ([illegible]) **Stalls** Low

Form RPR

3032 **1** **Rock Anthem (IRE)**[9] 7843 7-8-12 **59**.......................... KieranO'Neill(3) 10 69
(Mike Murphy) *a.p: chsd ldr over 2f out: rdn to ld over 1f out: styd on: edgd lft nr fin* **6/1**[3]

3010 **2** *1 1/4* **Nina Rose**[27] 7632 4-9-2 **60**.. AdamKirby 11 67
(Clive Cox) *led 7f out: rdn and hdd over 1f out: styd on same pce ins fnl f* **11/2**[2]

0063 **3** *nk* **Hydrant**[28] 7604 5-9-3 **61**.. AndrewMullen 5 67
(Peter Salmon) *led: hdd 7f out: chsd ldrs: rdn over 1f out: styd on* **8/1**

0564 **4** *1 1/4* **Striding Edge (IRE)**[9] 7851 5-8-8 **59**.................... NicoleNordblad(7) 7 62
(Hans Adielsson) *hld up: hdwy over 1f out: r.o: nt rch ldrs* **15/2**

341 **5** *nk* **Hierarch (IRE)**[9] 7843 4-8-8 **57**.................................... LauraPike(5) 8 60
(David Simcock) *hld up: hdwy over 1f out: sn rdn and hung lft: styd on* **4/1**[1]

0200 **6** *1 3/4* **Iron Green (FR)**[23] 7669 3-9-2 **62**........................(p) RichardKingscote 2 61
(Heather Main) *prom: rdn over 2f out: styd on same pce fnl f* **16/1**

3436 **7** *nk* **Transmit (IRE)**[21] 7695 4-9-1 **59**..............................(b) GrahamGibbons 9 57
(Tim Easterby) *hld up in tch: racd keenly: rdn over 1f out: wknd ins fnl f* **14/1**

3245 **8** *hd* **Chik's Dream**[94] 6438 4-8-9 **53**.............................. FrankieMcDonald 6 51
(Derek Haydn Jones) *hld up: rdn over 2f out: styd on ins fnl f: nvr nrr* **40/1**

4425 **9** *1 3/4* **Anjomarba (IRE)**[9] 7844 4-9-2 **60**..............................(p) HayleyTurner 3 54
(Conor Dore) *chsd ldrs: rdn over 2f out: wknd fnl f* **12/1**

3603 **10** *2* **Mr Chocolate Drop (IRE)**[20] 7711 7-9-4 **62**...........(t) TomMcLaughlin 4 51
(Mandy Rowland) *hld up: rdn over 2f out: nvr on terms* **20/1**

0416 **11** *1 1/4* **Justcallmehandsome**[18] 7734 9-9-0 **65**...............(be) JoshBaudains(7) 1 51
(Dominic Ffrench Davis) *s.i.s: hld up: rdn over 1f out: n.d* **10/1**

3-30 **12** *4* **Forbidden (IRE)**[9] 7851 8-8-13 **57**.........................(tp) PatrickMathers 12 34
(Ian McInnes) *hld up: rdn over 3f out: wknd over 2f out* **66/1**

1U00 **13** *3 1/2* **Regency Art (IRE)**[15] 7767 4-9-7 **65**...........................(b[1]) LiamKeniry 13 34
(Milton Bradley) *prom: chsd ldr over 6f out tl rdn over 2f out: wknd over 1f out* **20/1**

1m 49.49s (-1.01) **Going Correction** -0.10s/f (Stan)

WFA 3 from 4yo+ 2lb **13** Ran SP% **115.3**

Speed ratings (Par 101): **100,98,98,97,97 95,95,95,93,91 90,87,84**

CSF £35.88 CT £275.52 TOTE £5.70: £3.00, £2.00, £3.60; EX 39.00.

Owner Ronald Bright **Bred** Mervyn Stewkesbury **Trained** Westoning, Beds

FOCUS
A modest handicap run at an ordinary gallop and another race to suit the prominent-racers. The winner raced centre-to-far-side in the straight.

7931 PLAY LIFE CHANGING TOTESCOOP6 TOMORROW H'CAP 1m 4f 50y(P)
7:10 (7:10) (Class 6) (0-65,65) 3-Y-O **£1,704** (£503; £251) **Stalls** Low

Form RPR

6005 **1** **Illustrious Forest**[77] 6845 3-8-7 **51** oh1 FrannyNorton 2 69
(John Mackie) *mde all: rdn clr fr over 1f out: edgd rt: easily* **8/1**

0011 **2** *8* **Shirataki (IRE)**[10] 7836 3-8-10 **54** 6ex ChrisCatlin 1 59
(Peter Hiatt) *prom: rdn to chse wnr over 2f out: outpcd fr over 1f out* **11/4[2]**

1323 **3** *3 1/2* **Pinotage**[14] 7789 3-9-6 **64** TomEaves 6 64
(Peter Niven) *hld up: nt clr run over 2f out: hdwy over 1f out: nt trble ldrs* **5/1[3]**

2302 **4** *4* **McCool Bannanas**[14] 7788 3-9-7 **65** AdamKirby 3 58
(James Unett) *prom: rdn over 2f out: wknd over 1f out* **6/1**

1413 **5** *9* **Honourable Knight (IRE)**[9] 7839 3-9-3 **61** (be) DavidProbert 7 40
(Mark Usher) *prom: pushed along over 3f out: rdn over 2f out: hung lft and wknd over 1f out* **15/8[1]**

0426 **6** *hd* **Barachiel**[27] 7630 3-9-7 **65** WilliamCarson 4 43
(Ronald Harris) *chsd wnr 10f out tl rdn over 2f out: wknd over 1f out* **9/1**

303 **7** *11* **The Snorer**[15] 7766 3-9-4 **62** RussKennemore 8 23
(John Holt) *hld up: rdn 4f out: sn wknd: t.o* **33/1**

2m 38.78s (-2.32) **Going Correction** -0.10s/f (Stan) 7 Ran SP% **116.5**
Speed ratings (Par 98): **103,97,95,92,86 86,79**
toteswingers:1&2:£4.90, 1&3:£8.00, 2&3:£3.90 CSF £31.27 CT £123.71 TOTE £9.40: £3.20, £1.40; EX 51.90.
Owner Derbyshire Racing VII **Bred** Norman A Blyth **Trained** Church Broughton , Derbys

FOCUS
A modest handicap in which the steady gallop saw very few figure. The winner raced centre-to-far-side in the straight.
The Snorer Official explanation: jockey said gelding was never travelling
T/Plt: £196.00 to a £1 stake. Pool:£96,865.36 - 360.70 winning tickets T/Qpdt: £24.50 to a £1 stake Pool: £11,132.77 - 335.70 w. tckts CR

7932 - 7936a (Foreign Racing) - See RI

7918 LINGFIELD (L-H)
Saturday, December 31

OFFICIAL GOING: Standard
Wind: Fresh, half-behind. Weather: overcast, dry

7937 BET TOTEJACKPOT TEXT TOTE TO 89660 NURSERY 7f (P)
12:30 (12:32) (Class 6) (0-65,64) 2-Y-O **£1,704** (£503; £251) **Stalls** Low

Form RPR

000 **1** **My Scat Daddy (USA)**[89] 6588 2-8-2 **45** DavidProbert 12 54
(Brett Johnson) *chsd ldrs: rdn and ev ch ent fnl 2f: clr w ldr jst 1f out: led wl ins fnl f: r.o wl* **11/1**

326 **2** *1* **Majestic Zafeen**[195] 3201 2-9-7 **64** MartinHarley 7 70
(Alastair Lidderdale) *t.k.h: sn chsng ldr: led ent fnl 2f: rdn and clr w wnr jst over 1f out: hdd and no ex wl ins fnl f* **15/2**

0035 **3** *2* **Rooknrasbryripple**[19] 7735 2-8-13 **56** JamieGoldstein 6 57
(Ralph Smith) *hld up in tch towards rr: hdwy on outer to chse ldng pair jst over 2f out: styd on same pce u.p fnl f* **12/1**

062 **4** *1 3/4* **Moment In The Sun**[2] 7909 2-8-12 **55** WilliamCarson 8 51
(William Muir) *stdd s: hld up in tch towards rr: swtchd lft and effrt over 1f out: kpt on u.p fnl f: nvr trbld ldrs* **3/1[1]**

0004 **5** *nk* **Ice Loch**[38] 7514 2-8-8 **51** (b) LukeMorris 3 46
(Michael Blanshard) *in tch: rdn over 2f out: drvn and outpcd over 1f out: styd on same pce and no threat to ldrs fnl f* **6/1[3]**

6460 **6** *1 3/4* **Illustrious Lad (IRE)**[11] 7830 2-8-13 **56** HayleyTurner 10 47
(Jim Boyle) *stdd s: hld up in rr: stuck bhd a wall of horses jst over 2f out: hdwy on outer and rdn over 1f out: kpt on: nvr trbld ldrs* **7/1**

064 **7** *3/4* **Green Mountain (IRE)**[16] 7769 2-8-5 **51** (t) AdamBeschizza(3) 11 40
(Philip McBride) *s.i.s: niggled along in last trio: rdn and struggling over 2f out: wknd over 1f out* **25/1**

0664 **8** *shd* **Compton Target (IRE)**[13] 7808 2-8-13 **63** (t) NicoleNordblad(7) 4 52
(Hans Adielsson) *sn led: rdn and hdd ent fnl 2f: outpcd and btn over 1f out: wknd fnl f* **10/3[2]**

0340 **9** *1 3/4* **Liquid Sunshine**[38] 7514 2-8-5 **48** NickyMackay 1 32
(Sylvester Kirk) *in tch in midfield: nt clr run and shuffled bk to rr 2f out: rdn and effrt on inner over 1f out: nvr able to rcvr and n.d after* **14/1**

0000 **10** *1/2* **Awesome Rock (IRE)**[22] 7697 2-7-11 **45** RyanPowell(5) 5 28
(Louise Best) *t.k.h: hld up wl in tch: rdn and wknd jst over 2f out: bhd fnl f* **40/1**

0505 **11** *7* **Gadreel (IRE)**[155] 4485 2-8-11 **54** ChrisCatlin 2 19
(Anthony Middleton) *chsd ldrs: rdn and lost pl wl over 2f out: wl bhd fnl f* **40/1**

1m 24.96s (0.16) **Going Correction** -0.025s/f (Stan) 11 Ran SP% **118.0**
Speed ratings (Par 94): **98,96,94,92,92 90,89,89,87,86 78**
Tote Swingers:1&2:£20.50, 2&3:£12.60, 1&3:£24.50 CSF £89.92 CT £1026.98 TOTE £13.70: £3.70, £2.60, £6.20; EX 160.10 Trifecta £223.80 Part won. Pool 302.47 - 0.64 winning units..
Owner J Daniels **Bred** Fergus Galvin **Trained** Ashtead, Surrey

FOCUS
A moderate nursery in which the front pair were handy throughout. Fair form for the grade, and the winner probably has more to offer. The form has been pitched slightly positively.

NOTEBOOK
My Scat Daddy(USA) was making his nursery debut after showing nothing in three maidens, but didn't go unbacked here with David Probert a late replacement for the intended 7lb claimer. Always close to the pace, he showed a good attitude in a driving finish and his opening mark of 45 was obviously lenient. (op 16-1 tchd 18-1)
Majestic Zafeen ◆, ex-Mick Channon making her AW debut after 195 days off, arguably might have won with a recent outing under her belt and had she not been so keen early. This effort gives her new connections hope that the £13,000 they paid for her was money well spent. (tchd 13-2)
Rooknrasbryripple, another purchase from the Mick Channon stable (£1,800), showed nothing on her debut for the yard at Wolverhampton earlier this month, but ran much better here especially as she was trapped out wide throughout. (op 10-1 tchd 16-1)
Moment In The Sun seemed to stay the 1m well enough when runner-up at Kempton two days earlier, so the last thing she needed was to get messed about at the start over this shorter trip and find herself with ground to make up. Under the circumstances she did well to finish where she did. (op 10-3 tchd 7-2)
Ice Loch ran much better at Kempton last time and had been dropped another 2lb, but he was off the bridle passing the 3f pole and could only plug on. (op 8-1)
Compton Target(IRE) is now 7lb lower than when winning at Kempton in August and tried to make all, but proved to be a sitting duck. (op 9-2)
Liquid Sunshine Official explanation: jockey said filly was denied a clear run

7938 PLAY TOTESCOOP6 IN 1350 BETFRED SHOPS MEDIAN AUCTION MAIDEN STKS 7f (P)
1:05 (1:06) (Class 6) 2-Y-O **£1,704** (£503; £251) **Stalls** Low

Form RPR

4234 **1** **Safari Sunseeker (IRE)**[23] 7672 2-9-3 75 ShaneKelly 2 75+
(William Knight) *t.k.h: hld up wl in tch: wnt 2nd wl over 1f out: pushed along and qcknd to ld ins fnl f: sn in command: comf* **10/11[1]**

05 **2** *1/2* **Duke Of Clarence (IRE)**[11] 7835 2-9-0 0 KieranO'Neill(3) 5 72+
(Richard Hannon) *led at stdy gallop: rdn and qcknd 2f out: hdd ins fnl f: kpt on u.p but readily hld* **9/4[2]**

0 **3** *12* **Boris The Bold**[23] 7672 2-9-3 0 LukeMorris 7 41
(John Best) *t.k.h: chsd ldr tl rdn and unable qck 2f out: sn wknd and wl btn 1f out* **9/2[3]**

00 **4** *2 3/4* **Parque Atlantico**[11] 7835 2-9-3 0 DavidProbert 1 33
(Andrew Balding) *sn niggled along: chsd ldrs: rdn over 3f out: outpcd jst over 2f out: sn wl btn* **40/1**

630 **5** *1* **Godber (IRE)**[17] 7751 2-9-3 56 JamieGoldstein 3 31
(Ralph Smith) *t.k.h: hld up in tch in last pair: rdn and outpcd jst over 2f out: wknd 2f out and sn wl bhd* **40/1**

4 **6** *3* **Athletic**[17] 7758 2-9-3 0 WilliamCarson 4 23
(Andrew Reid) *rrd as stalls opened and v.s.a: sn rcvrd and in tch in midfield: hdwy and rdn to chse ldng pair over 2f out: hung bdly rt and wnt v wd bnd 2f out: lost pl and wl bhd after* **50/1**

7 *5* **Daphne Joy** 2-8-12 0 ChrisCatlin 6 5
(Peter Hedger) *hld up in tch in last pair: pushed along and struggling over 2f out: wknd qckly 2f out: t.o fnl f* **66/1**

1m 25.3s (0.50) **Going Correction** -0.025s/f (Stan) 7 Ran SP% **109.7**
Speed ratings (Par 94): **96,95,81,78,77 74,68**
Tote Swingers:1&2:£1.10, 2&3:£1.60, 1&3:£1.40 CSF £2.82 TOTE £1.90: £1.10, £1.60; EX 3.30.
Owner P Winkworth **Bred** D J Sweeney **Trained** Patching, W Sussex

FOCUS
As uncompetitive a maiden as 40-1 bar three would suggest and only the two market leaders counted. The winner and fourth are probably the best guides.

NOTEBOOK
Safari Sunseeker(IRE), in the frame in his first four starts and rated 75, didn't need to improve to win this. Ridden with plenty of confidence, the winning margin doesn't reflect his superiority and he should continue to pay his way in handicap company. (op 11-10 tchd 6-5)
Duke Of Clarence(IRE), unplaced when favourite for his first two starts, was ridden in contrasting fashion this time and tried to make all. He didn't look that happy on the home bend, but had every chance and just came up against a much superior rival on the day. He can now be handicapped. (op 15-8)
Boris The Bold, over 3l behind Safari Sunseeker on his Kempton debut earlier this month, was beaten much further by him this time and was made to look slow from over a furlong out. (op 11-2 tchd 4-1)
Parque Atlantico, beaten miles in his first two starts and thrashed again here, must be one of the more modest types in his yard.
Athletic looked a horrible ride on this second start, rearing badly as the stalls opened and hanging like a gate rounding the home bend. Official explanation: jockey said gelding reared as the stalls opened and was slowly away

7939 LINGFIELD PARK OWNERS CLUB (S) STKS 1m 4f (P)
1:40 (1:40) (Class 6) 3-Y-O+ **£1,704** (£503; £251) **Stalls** Low

Form RPR

0002 **1** **Irons On Fire (USA)**[14] 7800 3-8-13 65 (p) KierenFallon 4 70
(George Baker) *t.k.h: chsd ldr for 2f: wnt 2nd again 3f out: qcknd through on inner to ld over 2f out: sn clr: styd on wl* **2/1[1]**

2100 **2** *3 1/4* **Eagle Nebula**[72] 6976 7-9-8 69 IanMongan 2 69
(Brett Johnson) *hld up in tch: rdn and effrt to chse clr wnr wl over 1f out: kpt on but no imp* **3/1[2]**

4154 **3** *1 1/4* **Kames Park (IRE)**[5] 7878 9-9-1 67 CharlesEddery(7) 5 67
(Richard Guest) *stdd s: hld up in rr: rdn and effrt whn carried wd bnd 2f out: 3rd and kpt on fr 1f out: no threat to wnr* **7/2[3]**

6041 **4** *shd* **Rowan Ridge**[14] 7800 3-9-3 68 (b) StephenCraine 3 67
(Jim Boyle) *stdd s: hld up in tch: rdn and effrt whn swtchd lft wl over 1f out: hung lft jst over 1f out: kpt on but no threat to wnr* **4/1**

4243 **5** *3* **Dew Reward (IRE)**[12] 7818 3-9-3 56 AdamKirby 7 62
(Bill Turner) *led at stdy gallop: rdn and hdd over 2f out: edgd rt bnd and struggling bnd 2f out: wknd over 1f out* **20/1**

000- **6** *3/4* **Perfect Shot (IRE)**[30] 6808 5-9-1 79 (b[1]) RobertLButler(3) 1 57
(Jim Best) *stdd s: hld up in tch in last pair: swtchd rt 3f out: rdn and outpcd jst over 2f out: n.d fnl 2f* **16/1**

60/0 **7** *1 3/4* **Keep A Welcome**[29] 7600 8-9-1 34 SimonPearce(3) 6 54?
(Gerry Enright) *chsd ldr: rdn and lost pl wl over 2f out: wknd 2f out* **200/1**

2m 37.73s (4.73) **Going Correction** -0.025s/f (Stan)
WFA 3 from 5yo+ 5lb 7 Ran SP% **111.7**
Speed ratings (Par 101): **83,80,80,79,77 77,76**
Tote Swingers:1&2:£2.20, 2&3:£2.50, 1&3:£2.40 CSF £7.83 TOTE £2.30: £1.40, £3.00; EX 9.60.The winner was bought in for 5,800gns.
Owner George Baker & Partners **Bred** Woodford Thoroughbreds LLC **Trained** Whitsbury, Hants

FOCUS
A modest seller run at an ordinary pace.
Keep A Welcome Official explanation: jockey said gelding hung left

7940 BREATHE SPA AT LINGFIELD MARRIOTT H'CAP 5f (P)
2:15 (2:15) (Class 6) (0-65,65) 3-Y-O+ **£1,704** (£503; £251) **Stalls** High

Form RPR

3005 **1** **Royal Bajan (USA)**[30] 7594 3-9-6 **64** FrederikTylicki 7 76
(James Given) *mde all: rdn and clr over 1f out: styd on wl and in command fnl f* **5/2[1]**

4545 **2** *1 3/4* **Even Bolder**[14] 7804 8-9-7 **65** ShaneKelly 3 71
(Eric Wheeler) *hld up in tch in midfield: rdn and hdwy on inner over 1f out: chsd wnr and drvn ins fnl f: r.o but no imp* **7/1**

4506 **3** *1/2* **Welsh Inlet (IRE)**[24] 7649 3-9-2 **63** KieranO'Neill(3) 6 67
(John Bridger) *chsd ldrs: rdn and unable qck over 1f out: kpt on u.p ins fnl f* **17/2**

4455 **4** *1/2* **Dorothy's Dancing (IRE)**[19] 7737 3-9-0 **58** ow1 (p) AdamKirby 4 60
(Gary Moore) *t.k.h: hld up in last trio: rdn and hdwy over 1f out: styd on same pce fnl f* **6/1**

1564 **5** *1* **Vhujon (IRE)**[13] 7811 6-8-12 **56** LukeMorris 2 55
(Peter Grayson) *in tch in last pair: rdn and effrt 2f out: styd on fnl f: nvr trbld ldrs* **22/1**

2542 **6** *3/4* **Griffin Point (IRE)**[3] 7897 4-9-4 **62** (p) WilliamCarson 9 58
(William Muir) *in tch in midfield on outer: rdn 1/2-way: unable qck u.p wl over 1f out: no threat to wnr after* **9/2[2]**

3121 **7** *nk* **Wreningham**[9] 7854 6-9-1 **62** RyanClark(3) 5 57
(Pat Eddery) *chsd ldr: rdn and unable qck over 1f out: lost 2nd and wknd ins fnl f* **11/2**[3]
0560 **8** *3/4* **Sherjawy (IRE)**[24] 7649 7-9-4 **62** SamHitchcott 8 54
(Zoe Davison) *chsd ldrs: rdn and struggling whn short of room over 1f out: sn wknd* **20/1**
62-6 **9** *1 1/4* **Dells Breezer**[17] 7754 3-9-0 **58** IanMongan 1 46
(Pat Phelan) *a bhd: n.d* **20/1**
58.05 secs (-0.75) **Going Correction** -0.025s/f (Stan) **9** Ran SP% **113.3**
Speed ratings (Par 101): **105,102,101,100,99 97,97,96,94**
Tote Swingers:1&2:£4.10, 2&3:£14.00, 1&3:£8.20 CSF £19.24 CT £127.59 TOTE £2.90: £1.40, £2.80, £2.90; EX 22.00 Trifecta £246.90 Pool 450.43 - 1.35 winning units..
Owner Danethorpe Racing Partnership **Bred** West Wind Farm **Trained** Willoughton, Lincs
FOCUS
A modest sprint handicap.

7941 TOTEPOOL H'CAP 7f (P)
2:45 (2:45) (Class 4) (0-85,85) 3-Y-O+ **£4,204** (£1,251; £625; £312) **Stalls** Low

Form RPR
0002 **1** **Novellen Lad (IRE)**[45] 7439 6-9-7 **85** KierenFallon 6 94
(Willie Musson) *t.k.h: hld up in tch: rdn and hdwy over 1f out: str run u.p ins fnl f to ld last stride* **3/1**[2]
0066 **2** *shd* **Shifting Star (IRE)**[10] 7841 6-9-3 **81** (b) IanMongan 8 90
(John Bridger) *wore blinkers instead of declared hood: t.k.h: chsd ldrs: hdwy to ld and drvn 1f out: kpt on wl tl hdd last stride* **14/1**
5511 **3** *3/4* **Triple Charm**[38] 7519 3-8-12 **76** ShaneKelly 5 83
(Jeremy Noseda) *hld up in tch: hdwy on outer 3f out: hdwy u.p ent fnl f: pressed ldrs fnl 100yds: no ex* **11/4**[1]
0300 **4** *1 1/2* **Salient**[83] 6728 7-8-7 **71** oh1 LukeMorris 10 74
(Michael Attwater) *w ldr tl rdn to ld 2f out: drvn and hdd 1f out: no ex and btn fnl 100yds* **25/1**
0406 **5** *1* **Showboating (IRE)**[38] 7519 3-8-1 **72** (tp) NoraLooby(7) 4 72
(Alan McCabe) *stdd s: hld up in tch in rr: nt clr run over 1f out: rdn and effrt on inner ent fnl f: edgd lft and no prog ins fnl f* **25/1**
-302 **6** *nk* **Whaileyy (IRE)**[204] 2878 3-9-1 **82** AdamBeschizza(3) 2 81
(Marco Botti) *chsd ldrs: rdn and effrt wl over 1f out: stl pressing ldrs and drvn 1f out: no ex and sn btn: fdd fnl 100yds* **13/2**
5006 **7** *3/4* **Clear Praise (USA)**[23] 7675 4-9-3 **81** HayleyTurner 9 78
(Simon Dow) *taken down early: t.k.h: hld up in tch in rr: rdn and effrt on outer over 1f out: kpt on: nvr trbld ldrs* **15/2**
6065 **8** *2 1/4* **Taajub (IRE)**[23] 7675 4-9-5 **83** LiamKeniry 1 74
(Peter Crate) *in tch in midfield: nt clr run on inner 2f out: rdn and effrt over 1f out: styng on same pce and hld whn squeezed for room and hmpd ins fnl f: no ch and eased after* **7/2**[3]
4260 **9** *7* **Local Singer (IRE)**[23] 7675 3-9-2 **80** TomMcLaughlin 3 52
(Paul Howling) *led tl 2f out: lost pl qckly over 1f out: bhd fnl f* **40/1**
1m 24.56s (-0.24) **Going Correction** -0.025s/f (Stan) **9** Ran SP% **115.8**
Speed ratings (Par 105): **100,99,99,97,96 95,94,92,84**
Tote Swingers:1&2:£5.60, 2&3:£4.30, 1&3:£2.00 CSF £42.62 CT £128.12 TOTE £4.00: £1.40, £3.40, £1.50; EX 39.60 Trifecta £63.80 Pool 653.49 - 7.57 winning units..
Owner Johnson & Broughton **Bred** Mrs Chris Harrington **Trained** Newmarket, Suffolk
FOCUS
A decent handicap and a thrilling finish.

7942 DID BIG MONEY TOTEJACKPOT ROLLOVER H'CAP (DIV I) 6f (P)
3:15 (3:15) (Class 6) (0-65,65) 3-Y-O+ **£1,704** (£503; £251) **Stalls** Low

Form RPR
0006 **1** **Sulis Minerva (IRE)**[3] 7895 4-9-0 **65** RaulDaSilva(7) 3 75
(Jeremy Gask) *trckd ldrs: smooth hdwy on inner to join ldrs over 1f out: pushed ahd ent fnl f: in command fnl f: easily* **9/2**[1]
50-0 **2** *1 1/4* **Amosite**[106] 6119 5-9-3 **61** (p) FrederikTylicki 10 67
(J R Jenkins) *chsd ldrs: rdn to press ldrs 2f out: no ch w wnr but kpt on u.p fnl f to go 2nd towards fin* **11/2**[3]
6440 **3** *nk* **Paperetto**[17] 7754 3-8-13 **57** SteveDrowne 6 62
(Robert Mills) *in tch: rdn and unable qck over 1f out: no threat to wnr but kpt on u.p fnl f: wnt 2nd cl home* **5/1**[2]
0426 **4** *nk* **Dvinsky (USA)**[24] 7658 10-9-6 **64** (b) TomMcLaughlin 5 68
(Paul Howling) *t.k.h: w ldr: ev ch and rdn 2f out: led over 1f out: sn hdd and brushed aside by wnr: kpt on tl lost 2 pls towards fin* **16/1**
240 **5** *2* **Rightcar**[19] 7737 4-8-8 **52** LukeMorris 2 50
(Peter Grayson) *in tch in midfield: effrt u.p over 1f out: kpt on u.p fnl f but no threat to wnr* **16/1**
6505 **6** *hd* **Dickie Le Davoir**[18] 7744 7-9-2 **63** (b) RobertLButler(3) 4 60
(Richard Guest) *in tch in rr: rdn and hdwy over 1f out: styd on ins fnl f: nvr a threat to wnr* **11/1**
0000 **7** *1 1/2* **Mi Regalo**[3] 7895 3-9-2 **60** (be) AdamKirby 7 52
(Phil McEntee) *hld up in tch in last trio: nt clr run 2f out: effrt u.p over 1f out: no imp: n.d* **13/2**
0000 **8** *1* **Chjimes (IRE)**[30] 7594 7-9-4 **62** (b) HayleyTurner 9 51
(Conor Dore) *stdd and swtchd lft after s: t.k.h: hld up in rr: rdn and effrt over 1f out: no prog 1f out: wknd ins fnl f* **6/1**
0055 **9** *1* **Porthgwidden Beach (USA)**[9] 7854 3-8-7 **51** oh3 (t) ChrisCatlin 1 37
(Anthony Middleton) *led: rdn 2f out: hdd over 1f out: wknd fnl f* **33/1**
0030 **10** *3 1/4* **Custom House (IRE)**[31] 7588 3-9-3 **64** (b) NataliaGemelova(3) 8 39
(John E Long) *wnt bdly rt s and slowly away: in tch on outer: wd and lost pl 2f out: no ch after* **17/2**
0040 **11** *1* **Toms River Tess (IRE)**[192] 3292 3-9-1 **59** JamieGoldstein 11 31
(Zoe Davison) *in tch: rdn and losing pl whn wd bnd 2f out: bhd over 1f out* **50/1**
1m 11.82s (-0.08) **Going Correction** -0.025s/f (Stan) **11** Ran SP% **113.4**
Speed ratings (Par 101): **99,97,96,96,93 93,91,90,88,84 83**
Tote Tote Swingers:1&2:£5.80, 2&3:£4.90, 1&3:£4.00 CSF £27.76 CT £129.16 TOTE £4.10: £1.80, £2.30, £2.10; EX 34.50 Trifecta £202.20 Pool 833.77 - 3.05 winning units..
Owner Richard L Page **Bred** Kevin Blake **Trained** Sutton Veny, Wilts
FOCUS
A moderate sprint handicap, but as easy a winner of such a contest as you are likely to see.

7943 DID BIG MONEY TOTEJACKPOT ROLLOVER H'CAP (DIV II) 6f (P)
3:45 (3:45) (Class 6) (0-65,65) 3-Y-O+ **£1,704** (£503; £251) **Stalls** Low

Form RPR
0065 **1** **Efistorm**[3] 7895 10-9-0 **58** HayleyTurner 3 67
(Conor Dore) *chsd ldrs: rdn and clsd on ldng pair over 1f out: led ins fnl f: idling in front but a doing enough: pushed out* **4/1**[3]
3062 **2** *3/4* **Speak The Truth (IRE)**[31] 7587 5-8-13 **62** (p) NathanAlison(5) 8 69
(Jim Boyle) *racd off the pce: hdwy u.p over 1f out: chsd wnr ins fnl f: readily hld by wnr* **7/2**[2]
000 **3** *3/4* **Mister Green (FR)**[3] 7895 5-9-5 **63** (bt) StephenCraine 6 68
(David Flood) *stdd s: hld up in rr: gd hdwy u.p jst over 1f out: no imp wl ins fnl f* **12/1**
0022 **4** *hd* **Court Applause (IRE)**[10] 7845 3-9-5 **63** SteveDrowne 2 67
(William Muir) *stdd s: t.k.h: hld in rr: hdwy u.p over 1f out: chsd ldrs ins fnl f: no imp fnl f* **5/1**
0203 **5** *1/2* **Dingaan (IRE)**[13] 7811 8-8-11 **55** LukeMorris 4 57
(Peter Grayson) *towards rr: effrt u.p 2f out: styd on ins fnl f: unable to chal* **11/1**
0002 **6** *1* **Super Frank (IRE)**[17] 7760 8-8-8 **52** (b) SamHitchcott 9 51
(Zoe Davison) *sn clr w ldr: led 2f out: drvn ent fnl f: hdd ins fnl f: no ex and sn btn* **14/1**
0535 **7** *3/4* **Dualagi**[13] 7812 7-9-2 **60** LiamKeniry 10 57
(Martin Bosley) *chsd ldng pair: rdn wl over 1f out: drvn and no prog ent fnl f: wknd* **20/1**
0040 **8** *5* **Pharoh Jake**[13] 7807 3-8-4 **51** oh6 KieranO'Neill(3) 5 32
(John Bridger) *led and sn clr w rival: hdd 2f out and sn drvn: btn ent fnl f: fdd* **80/1**
0002 **9** *1 1/4* **Rapid Water**[13] 7811 5-9-2 **60** AdamKirby 11 37
(Gary Moore) *a in rr: rdn and no prog 2f out: wl bhd 1f out* **3/1**[1]
1m 11.83s (-0.07) **Going Correction** -0.025s/f (Stan) **9** Ran SP% **112.6**
Speed ratings (Par 101): **99,98,97,96,96 94,93,87,85**
Tote Swingers:1&2:£3.90, 2&3:£7.60, 1&3:£8.20 CSF £17.82 CT £151.04 TOTE £5.30: £2.20, £1.30, £2.70; EX 21.40 Trifecta £182.10 Pool 462.79 - 1.88 winning units..
Owner Sean J Murphy **Bred** E Duggan And D Churchman **Trained** Cowbit, Lincs
FOCUS
This was set up for the closers with Pharoh Jake and Super Frank taking each other on in front and doing too much. The winning time was 1/100th of a second slower than the first division.
Rapid Water Official explanation: jockey said gelding was never travelling
T/Plt: £126.10 to a 1 stake. Pool £61,896.93. 358.19 winning tickets T/Qpdt: £14.10 to a 1 stake. Pool £6,060.70. 316.78 winning tickets SP

INDEX TO MEETINGS FLAT 2011

† Abandoned
* All-Weather
(M) Mixed meeting

INDEX TO FLAT RACING

Horses are shown in alphabetical order; the trainer's name follows the name of the horse. The figures to the right are current master ratings for all-weather and turf; the all-weather rating is preceded by the letter 'a'.Underneath the horse's name is its age, colour and sex in abbreviated format e.g. 6 b g indicates the horse is six-years-old, bay in colour, and a gelding.The descriptive details are followed by the race numbers of the races in which it has taken part in chronological order; a superscript figure indicates its finishing position in that race (brackets indicate it was the winner of the race).

Aaim To Prosper (IRE) *Brian Meehan* a79 110
7 br g Val Royal(FR) —Bint Al Balad (IRE) (Ahonoora)
1601[5] ◆ 2438[4] 3066[8] 3647[2] 4469[6]

Aalsmeer *Karen George* a62 59
4 b m Invincible Spirit(IRE) —Flower Market (Cadeaux Genereux)
2555[9] 3216[5] 4272[6]

Aamaaq *A Al Raihe* a93 73
8 b g Danehill(USA) —Alabaq (USA) (Riverman (USA))
236[9]

Aaman (IRE) *Bernard Llewellyn* a81 73
5 gr g Dubai Destination(USA) —Amellnaa (IRE) (Sadler's Wells (USA))
2140[3]

Aanna Heneeih (IRE) *Ed Dunlop* a70 84
3 b g Desert Style(IRE) —Musica E Magia (IRE) (King's Theatre (IRE))
(905) ◆ 2216[3]

Aaraas *Kevin Prendergast* 94
2 b f Haafhd—Adaala (USA) (Sahm (USA))
3416a[4] 7185a[3]

Aaranyow (IRE) *Bryn Palling* 54
3 ch g Compton Place—Cutpurse Moll (Green Desert (USA))
1565[9] 3173[7] 3980[5] 4705[13] 6816[11]

Aather (IRE) *Alan Fleming* a66 73
6 b g Key Of Luck(USA) —Alkaffeyeh (IRE) (Sadler's Wells (USA))
621[6]

Aazif (IRE) *John Dunlop* 82
2 ch c Nayef(USA) —Ayun (USA) (Swain (IRE))
6160[5] ◆ (6726)

Abacist (IRE) *Ralph Beckett* a56 63
3 b g Desert Style(IRE) —Trishay (Petong)
593[6] 818[9] 905[4] 3173[3] 3512[8] (4271) 5539[11] 6434[9]

Abadejo *J R Jenkins* a63 62
3 b g Acclamation—Silvereine (FR) (Bering)
721[3] 1900[2] 2453[3] 3433[7] 6090[9] 7389[9] 7652[6]

Abandon (FR) *C Plisson* 38
3 b f King's Best(USA) —Abime (USA) (Woodman (USA))
852a[12]

Abaton *Vittorio Caruso* 104
5 b h Dansili—Guntakal (IRE) (Night Shift (USA))
6905a[7] 7311a[8]

Abbeyshrule (IRE) *Paul W Flynn* a30 51
3 gr g One Cool Cat(USA) —Grey Patience (IRE) (Common Grounds)
1663a[12]

Abbondanza (IRE) *C Boutin* a90 87
8 b g Cape Cross(IRE) —Ninth Wonder (USA) (Forty Niner (USA))
35[5] 196a[5] 481a[0]

Abbraccio *James Fanshawe* a75
3 b g Pivotal—Embraced (Pursuit Of Love)
1605[4] ◆

A B Celebration *John Bridger* a39 44
3 ch f Sleeping Indian—Silver Louie (IRE) (Titus Livius (FR))
1865[9] 2192[12] 2689[6] 3289[8] 3431[10] 3979[7] 4970[13] 5381[11] 6084[11] 6472[7]

Abdicate (IRE) *Richard Fahey* 79
3 b f Cape Cross(IRE) —Lady Salsa (IRE) (Gone West (USA))
[illegible] (2021) 3260[7] (4045) 4429[16] 5062[5] 5880[5] 6674[19]

Abdul Malik *David Simcock* a64
2 b c Bertolini(USA) —Muwasim (USA) (Meadowlake (USA))
7627[8] 7835[4] 7929[3]

Abeer (USA) *Ed Dunlop* a68 78
3 ch f Shamardal(USA) —Ekleel (IRE) (Danehill (USA))
1579[6] 2186[4] 2553[3] 2869[2] 3470[2]

Abercandy (IRE) *David Evans* a17 47
2 b f Clodovil(IRE) —Madam Waajib (IRE) (Waajib)
1290[7] 1827[4] 2523[6] (3955) 4907[11]

Aberdeen Park *David Evans* a40 60
9 gr m Environment Friend—Michelee (Merdon Melody)
8[RR]

Abergavenny *Brian Ellison* a64 92
4 b g Dubai Destination(USA) —Welsh Dawn (Zafonic (USA))
1098[4] 2107[8] 5685[7] ◆ 6690[13]

Abergeldie (USA) *Andrew Balding* a62 77
3 b f Street Cry(IRE) —Camlet (Green Desert (USA))
1607[5] 1986[3] 2550[5] (3803) 4313[6] 5328[6] 6062[7]

Abernethy (IRE) *Linda Perratt* a33 53
3 b g Hernando(FR) —Marsh Harrier (USA) (Woodman (USA))
1076[6] 1542[5] 2058[9] 3116[8] 3859[11] (4143) 4383[8] 4783[6] 5150[7] 5315[5] 5725[8] 6415[6] 7105[4] 7720[9]

Abhaath (USA) *Saeed Bin Suroor* a70 74
2 b g Hard Spun(USA) —Above Perfection (USA) (In Excess)
4087[10] 4815[4] 5727[11] 6132[2] 6972[2] 7205[3] 7358[6]

Abhainn (IRE) *Bryn Palling* a50 58
5 ch g Hawk Wing(USA) —Grannys Reluctance (IRE) (Anita's Prince)
70[11] 1633[5] 1905[10] 2555[7]

Abidhabidubai *John Quinn* 79
3 b f Dubai Destination(USA) —Madamoiselle Jones (Emperor Jones (USA))
1302[2] (2186) 2808[4] 3202[3] 3571[2] 3933[2] 4439[3] (4812) (5401) 6234[2]

Abigails Angel *Brett Johnson* a63 63
4 br m Olden Times—Make Ready (Beveled (USA))
225[2] 485[2] ◆ 555[5] 730[5] 862[3] 943[2] 1308[9] 3176[3] 3741[7] 3916[3] (5421) 6622[7] 7202[2] 7394[7] 7843[5]

Ability Girl *Chris Wall* a44 46
3 b f Domedriver(IRE) —Nocturnal Lady (Night Shift (USA))
360[5] 519[9] 811[8] 1078[5] 1331[10] 2172[6] 5352[12] 6033[9]

Ability N Delivery *Michael J Browne* a73 70
6 gr g Kyllachy—Tryptonic (FR) (Baryshnikov (AUS))
298[2] 4767a[6] 7567[4]

Abishena (IRE) *Mark Johnston* 94
2 ch f Pivotal—Massomah (USA) (Seeking The Gold (USA))
(6603) 7169[2]

Abjer (FR) *I Mohammed* a71 106
3 b c Singspiel(IRE) —Fine And Mellow (FR) (Lando (GER))
502a[10] 753a[10] 823a[4]

Able Master (IRE) *Jeremy Gask* a62 99
5 b g Elusive City(USA) —Foresta Verde (USA) (Green Forest (USA))
2954[16] 3982[10] 5852[14]

Able One (NZ) *J Moore* 123
9 b g Cape Cross(IRE) —Gardenia (NZ) (Danehill (USA))
1576a[13] (7731a)

Above All *William Haggas* a68 83
3 b g Nayef(USA) —Anyaas (IRE) (Green Desert (USA))
1843[3] 2472[2] 2891[3] 3557[2]

Above Average (IRE) *Anthony Freedman* 113
5 b g High Chaparral(IRE) —Crystal Valkyrie (IRE) (Danehill (USA))
6967a[11]

Above Limits (IRE) *David Simcock* a75 97
4 b m Exceed And Excel(AUS) —Cin Isa Luv (USA) (Private Account (USA))
1420a[10] 1848[6] 4644[2] ◆ 6906a[8]

Above Standard (IRE) *G P Kelly* 81
3 ch g Shamardal(USA) —Prealpina (IRE) (Indian Ridge)
1338[5] (3324) 3798[4] 4214[6] 5171[7] 7716[12]

Above The Stars *Richard Fahey* a76 77
3 b f Piccolo—Swindling (Bahamian Bounty)
1241[11] 4048[5] 4791[8] 5163[9] 5484[4] 6112[12] 6801[6] 7106[5] 7355[4] 7596[5] 7834[4]

A Boy Named Suzi *James Eustace* a87 93
3 b g Medecis—Classic Coral (USA) (Seattle Dancer (USA))
2764[2] (3469) 4966[2] (5641) ◆ 6103[2] 6294[3] 7017[2]

Abriachan *Noel Quinlan* a72 72
4 b g Celtic Swing—Cape Finisterre (IRE) (Cape Cross (IRE))
48[5] (268) 666[8] 820[8] 1557[4] 2382[3] 3735[3] 4866[7] (5014) 7517[10] 7715[6]

Absa Lutte (IRE) *Michael Mullineaux* a78 87
8 b m Darnay—Zenana (IRE) (Lucky Guest)
29[3] 125[3] 336[5] 403[3] 470[7] 646[9] 708[9] 833[6] 880[7] 946[4] 1279[3] 1371[3] 1656[5] (1899) 2286[6] 2609[8] 3166[2] 3579[3] 4195[4] 4310[8] 4780[5] 6177[7] 6283[4] (6932) 7428[4] 7512[8] 7594[8]

Absent Amy (IRE) *Willie Musson* 60
2 b f Redback—Twitcher's Delight (Polar Falcon (USA))
2997[4] 3865[13]

Abshir Zain (IRE) *Clive Brittain* a63 69
2 b c Green Desert(USA) —O Fourlunda (Halling (USA))
3182[15] 3795[4] 5886[5] 6484[8] 7081[3] 7337[4] 7576[4] 7875[2]

Absinthe (IRE) *Walter Swinburn* a84 96
5 b g King's Best(USA) —Triple Try (IRE) (Sadler's Wells (USA))
2604[7] 2909[10] 3592[3] 4253[2] 4959[2] 6803[2]

Absinthe Minded (USA) *D Wayne Lukas* a110 95
4 b m Quiet American(USA) —Rockford Peach (USA) (Great Above (USA))
6719a[10]

Absolute Bearing (IRE) *Tim Etherington* a37
2 b g Majestic Missile(IRE) —Garnock Academy (USA) (Royal Academy (USA))
7345[12]

Absolute Crackers (IRE) *Mrs John Harrington* 90
2 ch f Giant's Causeway(USA) —El Laoob (USA) (Red Ransom (USA))
6196a[2] ◆

Absolute Fun (IRE) *Tim Easterby* a27 60
2 b f Lawman(FR) —Jallaissine (IRE) (College Chapel)
5029[10] 5727[6] 6047[6] 6611[7]

Absolute Heretic (AUS) *Tom Tate* 94
5 b g Galileo(IRE) —Corniche Bay (AUS) (Flying Spur (AUS))
417a[7] ◆ 603a[6] 4410[18] 5271[12]

Absolutely (AUS) *Michael Kent* 116
4 bb f Redoute's Choice(AUS) —Catshaan (AUS) (Catrail (USA))
6886a[11]

Absolutely Me (IRE) *Dominic Ffrench Davis* 25
2 ch f Barathea(IRE) —Attymon Lill (IRE) (Marju (IRE))
7025[16]

Absolutely True *E Lellouche* 85
2 b f Westerner—Actrice Francaise (USA) (Dynaformer (USA))
5873a[5]

Absolute Music (USA) *Marco Botti* a60 99
4 bb m Consolidator(USA) —Allegro Lady (USA) (Souvenir Copy (USA))
986[5]

Absolute Princess *Scott Dixon* a74 55
3 b f Avonbridge—Park Ave Princess (IRE) (Titus Livius (FR))
714[6] (937) 1837[8] 2527[6] 3228[11] 7727[4] 7887[9]

Absolutly Yes (FR) *Y-M Porzier* 108
3 b c Country Reel(USA) —Semenova (FR) (Green Tune (USA))
(1965a) 2751a[10] 3653a[3] 4376a[8]

Abstrato (BRZ) *M F De Kock* a88 66
4 b g Major Storm(USA) —Faccao (BRZ) (Choctaw Ridge (USA))
238[14] 411a[10] 502a[12]

Abtaal (USA) *J-C Rouget* 109
2 b c Rock Hard Ten(USA) —Appealing Storm (USA) (Valid Appeal (USA))
4652a[2] (6660a)

Abtasaamah (USA) *Saeed Bin Suroor* a87 82
3 b f Distorted Humor(USA) —Fleet Lady (USA) (Avenue Of Flags (USA))
151a[3] 412a[5] 681a[7] 823a[8]

Abulharith *Ronald Harris* a59 68
5 b g Medicean—Limuru (Salse (USA))
24[4] 252[11] 630[7]

Abundantly *Hughie Morrison* a34 56
2 b f Sakhee(USA) —Composing (IRE) (Noverre (USA))
5537[6] 6000[8] 6977[5]

Abydos (GER) *J Hirschberger* 101
6 b h Monsun(GER) —Aiyana (GER) (Last Tycoon)
5497a[5]

Abzolutely (IRE) *David O'Meara* a37 69
3 ch f Chineur(FR) —Solo Symphony (IRE) (Fayruz)
3384[6] 3950[8]

Acacalia (GER) *C Sprengel* 101
3 b f Ransom O'War(USA) —Adorea (GER) (Dashing Blade)
7156a[2]

Academy (IRE) *Sir Michael Stoute* 77
3 br c Montjeu(IRE) —Rock The Casbah (FR) (Lavirco (GER))
6096[3]

Academy Blues (USA) *David Nicholls* a95 94
6 bb g Fusaichi Pegasus(USA) —Lover's Talk (CAN) (Vice Regent (CAN))
1109[10] 1467[3] 1603[16] 2115[2] 2398[5] 3190[3] 4361[4] 5502[2]

Acadius (GER) *J-P Carvalho* 103
3 ch c Lord Of England(GER) —Amouage (GER) (Tiger Hill (IRE))
2338a[3] 3334a[4]

Acapulco Bay *Dai Burchell* a51 10
7 b g Pursuit Of Love—Lapu-Lapu (Prince Sabo)
5379[10]

Accamelia *Chris Fairhurst* a65 60
5 br m Shinko Forest(IRE) —Bo' Babbity (Strong Gale)
798[6] 2238[7] 2464[9] 2765[4] 2989[6] 4078[7] 4362[8]

Accession (IRE) *Clive Cox* 91
2 b c Acclamation—Pivotal's Princess (IRE) (Pivotal)
[illegible] (6127) 7019[4]

Acclaben (IRE) *Alan Swinbank* 24
5 b g Acclamation—Jour De Grace (SWE) (Steve's Friend (USA))
5207[5]

Acclamatory *Stuart Williams* a60 59
3 b f Royal Applause—Degree (Warning)
208 [5] 1521[5] 1980[15] 2598[8] 3433[5] 4247[5] 5670[3] 6257[7]

Acclamazing (IRE) *Marco Botti* a90 105
3 b g Acclamation—Pearl Egg (IRE) (Mukaddamah (USA))
(254) ◆ (1079) ◆ (1322) 1844[2] 2934[2]

Accompanist *T G McCourt* a73 66
8 b g Pivotal—Abscond (USA) (Unbridled (USA))
286[2] 838[4] 849[6]

Accountforthegold (USA) *R Bouresly* a22 1
9 b g Successful Appeal(USA) —Accountess (USA) (Private Account (USA))
501a[14]

Accumulate *Bill Moore* a78 78
8 b g Second Empire(IRE) —Bee-Bee-Gee (IRE) (Lake Coniston (IRE))
539[2] 911[2] (965) (1470) 2285[8] 2459[2] 2888[13] 4719[9] 5389[4] 6306[8]

Accustomed *Sylvester Kirk* a67 66
2 ch f Motivator—Duty Paid (IRE) (Barathea (IRE))
3520[5] 3812[12] 4545[2] ◆ 5144[7] 5783[8] 6753[7] 7481[8]

Ace Master *Roy Bowring* a66 45
3 ch g Ballet Master(USA) —Ace Maite (Komaite (USA))
456[3] (550) 567[4] (868) 1503[4] 2163[4] 2524[7] 7462[5] 7610[5] 7728[8] (7885)

Ace Of Spies (IRE) *Conor Dore* a78 78
6 br g Machiavellian(USA) —Nadia (Nashwan (USA))
(17) 122[3] 148[4] 455[2] 572[5] 673[3] 1067[8] 1296[8] 1907[11] 2354[9] 2653[9] 3493[4] 3711[2] 4025[12] 4086[6] 4395[6] 4820[2] 5139[5] 5895[9] 6282[10] 7039[9] 7173[12] 7419[3] 7504[5] 7897[7]

Ace Of Valhalla *Sir Henry Cecil* a70 54
2 b c Authorized(IRE) —Trick Of Ace (USA) (Clever Trick (USA))
7109[7] 7494[2]

Acer Diamonds (IRE) *Julia Feilden* 64
2 b c Red Clubs(IRE) —Tree House (USA) (Woodman (USA))
2837[5] 3401[8] ◆

Ace Serve *Roger Varian* 64
3 b f King's Best(USA) —Match Point (Unfuwain (USA))
2026[9] 2871[4]

Aces Star (USA) *Fredrik Reuterskiold* a80 90
4 rg h Monarchos(USA) —Pray For Aces (USA) (Pulpit (USA))
2601a[DSQ] 5984a[8]

Achalas (IRE) *Heather Main* a84 84
3 b g Statue Of Liberty(USA) —Princess Of Iona (IRE) (Fasliyev (USA))
1609[4] ◆ (1997) 2228[3] 2677[5] (3233) 3479[2] 5149[8] 5971[2] 7022[3] 7677a[4]

Achinora *M G Mintchev* 86
3 b f Sleeping Indian—Via Borghese (USA) (Seattle Dancer (USA))
4839a[13]

Aciano (IRE) *Brian Meehan* a89 85
3 b g Kheleyf(USA) —Blue Crystal (IRE) (Lure (USA))
2229[8] (2675) 3285[6] 3840[5] 4506[2] 4914[6] 5056[7]

Acid Test (FR) *C Boutin* 68
4 b g Xaar—Beggars Belief (IRE) (Common Grounds)
1011a[0] 1033a[10]

Acina *F-X De Chevigny* 58
2 ch f Shirocco(GER) —Celebrate (IRE) (Generous (IRE))
6925a[9]

A Coeur Ouvert (FR) *H-A Pantall* 104
5 b h Dano-Mast—Lady Stapara (IRE) (Lead On Time (USA))
478a[4] 705a[10]

Acorous (FR) *Sprl Ittech* a57
3 b c Numerous(USA) —Acovia (Barathea (IRE))
520[8] 902a[0]

Acropolis (IRE) *Tony Carroll* a63 101
10 b g Sadler's Wells(USA) —Dedicated Lady (IRE) (Pennine Walk)
207 [5] 419[6] 588[3] 631[7] 911[6] (1050) 1218[5] 1959[5]

Across The Rhine (USA) *Tracey Collins* a98 111
5 ch g Cuvee(USA) —Seductive Smile (USA) (Silver Hawk (USA))
157a[3] 326a[8] (587a) 828a[7] 1118a[7] 1930a[2] 3109[10] (4116a) 5282[6] 5977a[3] 6561a[3] 6687[6]

Across The Sea (USA) *Geoffrey Harker* 62
4 rg g Giant's Causeway(USA) —Trust Your Heart (USA) (Relaunch (USA))
1211[9] 1556[6] 1798[9]

Action Chope (FR) *D Guillemin* a75 102
3 b f Muhaymin(USA) —Free Track (FR) (Solid Illusion (USA))
1207a[0]

Action Front (USA) *Amanda Perrett* a55 83
3 bb c Aptitude(USA) —Palisade (USA) (Gone West (USA))
(1840) 2819[10] 4473[10]

Actionmax (TUR) *B Dag* 98
6 ch m River Special(USA) —Harbinger (TUR) (Lockton)
[illegible]

Activate *Michael Bell* a86 101
4 b g Motivator—Princess Manila (CAN) (Manila (USA))
(2499) ◆ 3396[16] 4532[8] 5705[11] 6333[11]

Active Asset (IRE) *David C Griffiths* a62 53
9 ch g Sinndar(IRE) —Sacristy (Godswalk (USA))
79[5] 484[3] 1107[18]

Actodos (IRE) *Tony Newcombe* a72 86
7 ro g Act One—Really Gifted (IRE) (Cadeaux Genereux)
7244[5]

Act Of Love (IRE) *David Marnane* a76 83
3 b f Acclamation—Piaf (Pursuit Of Love)
6854a[6]

Actor (IRE) *Jeremy Noseda*
2 b c Montjeu(IRE) —Original (Caerleon (USA))
6954[10]

Act Your Shoe Size *Keith Dalgleish* 75
2 b f Librettist(USA) —Howards Heroine (IRE) (Danehill Dancer (IRE))
(2693) 3313[4] (4194) 4667[2] 5287[6] 6111[4] 6645[2] 6864[6]

Adaero Star *Karen George* 28
3 ch f Pastoral Pursuits—Ciccone (Singspiel (IRE))
4388[11] 4861[10] 5675[6] 6585[8]

Adaeze (IRE) *Jonathan Portman* 57
3 b f Footstepsinthesand—Ringmoor Down (Pivotal)
2689[8] 3091[4] 3465[9] 3998[2] 4227[5] 4950[11] 5346[2] 6479[13]

Adamantina *Vittorio Caruso* 103
3 b f Diktat—Royal Hawk (IRE) (Wolfhound (USA))
1738a[2] 2539a[5] 6370a[3]

Adam De Beaulieu (USA) *Ben Haslam* a70 61
4 b g Broken Vow(USA) —Gambling Champ (USA) (Fabulous Champ (USA))
1803[12] 3489[10] 4563[9] 7269[5]

Adam's Return (IRE) *W T Farrell* a50 76
5 b g Fath(USA) —Sally Anne (ITY) (Scenic)
7189a[11]

Adaria *David C Griffiths* a56 83
3 ch f Sleeping Indian—Isle Of Flame (Shirley Heights)
1393[6] (1648) 2073[6] 2615[3] 2935[7] 3757[7] 4202[7] 5056[12] 5735[9] 6382[6] 6764[5] 7024[11]

Addictive Dream (IRE) *Walter Swinburn* a89 107
4 ch g Kheleyf(USA) —Nottambula (IRE) (Thatching)
1680[2] 2099[4] (2620) 3410[4] 3846[5] 4776[5] 5060[17] 5927[3] 6332[11] 6522[2] 6706[15]

Addikt (IRE) *Michael Scudamore* a73 74
6 b h Diktat—Frond (Alzao (USA))
(944) ◆ (1756) 2567[2] 2843[8] 6005[9] 6669[11] 7346[11] 7647[8]

Add Lib *Matthew Salaman* a39 29
3 b f Librettist(USA) —Creme Caramel (USA) (Septieme Ciel (USA))
863[6] 1060[11] 1358[5] 2177[8] 2384[7]

Address Unknown *D K Weld* a92 106
4 b g Oasis Dream—Return (USA) (Sadler's Wells (USA))
(1705a) 3418a[4] 3695a[5]

Addwaitya *Laura Mongan* a84 84
6 br g Xaar—Three White Sox (Most Welcome)
81[2] (3352) 4097[5] 4423[13] 5198[5] 5692[2]

Adelais (IRE) *Ms Joanna Morgan* a14
2 b f Chineur(FR) —Edgeways (IRE) (Selkirk (USA))
7275a[14]

Adelina Patti *Walter Swinburn* 68
3 b f Leporello(IRE) —Camerlata (Common Grounds)
2223[4] 2673[4] 3202[6] 4244[6] 4699[2] 5137[2] 5673[6]

Adelindus *Walter Swinburn* a42 43
2 b f King's Best(USA) —Possessive Artiste (Shareef Dancer (USA))
6745[11] 7118[9]

Adeste *Sir Michael Stoute* 52
2 b f Dansili—Tu Eres Mi Amore (IRE) (Sadler's Wells (USA))
6984[6]

Adieu *Richard Hannon* a43
3 ch f Dr Fong(USA) —Blow Me A Kiss (Kris)
274[7] 434[5] 519[10]

Adilapour (IRE) *John M Oxx* 99
3 b c Azamour(IRE) —Adelfia (IRE) (Sinndar (IRE))
1259a[5] 2331a[8]

Adlington *Richard Fahey* 73
3 b g Dansili—Kiralik (Efisio)
1392[5] 1801[2] (2728) 2935[8] 3701[10] 4236[5] 5401[5]

Admirable Duchess *Dominic Ffrench Davis* a69 89
4 gr m Compton Place—Smart Hostess (Most Welcome)
1864[2] (2304) 3847[2] 4416[14] 5053[19]

Admirable Duque (IRE) *Dominic Ffrench Davis* a87 79
5 b g Selkirk(USA) —Stunning (USA) (Nureyev (USA))
68[3] 342[3] (849) 2156[8] 3120[7] 3533[8] 3817[10] 6023[11] 6976[7] 7264[4] 7570[4] 7661[7] (7738) 7900[5]

Admirable Spirit *Richard Hannon* a89 89
3 b f Invincible Spirit(IRE) —Demi Voix (Halling (USA))
2054[8] 2503[6] 2878[4] 3178[4] 3819[9] 4387[2] 5476[3] 5972[9] 6272[7] 7602[2]

Admiral Barry (IRE) *Eoin Griffin* a74 102
6 b g Kalanisi(IRE) —Kart Star (IRE) (Soviet Star (USA))
1808[5] 2534a[6] 3418a[6] 4398a[16] 7322a[16]

Admiral Of The Red (IRE) *A P O'Brien* 103
3 b c Galileo(IRE) —My Emma (Marju (IRE))
3418a[3] 5283[15]

Admirateur (FR) *M Pimbonnet* a69
3 b g Whipper(USA) —Allez Winner (IRE) (King Charlemagne (USA))
638a[5]

Admiration (AUS) *J Moore* 115
4 b c Encosta De Lago(AUS) —Provence (AUS) (Redoute's Choice (AUS))
7730a[7]

Adone (IRE) *Sir Michael Stoute* 69
3 br g Araafa(IRE) —Athene (IRE) (Rousillon (USA))
1774[5] 2427[3] 3002[6]

Adorable Choice (IRE) *Tom Dascombe* a73 76
3 bb f Choisir(AUS) —Burnin' Memories (USA) (Lit De Justice (USA))
1335[9] 2582[7] 2986[11] 3508[5] (5179) 5496[10] (6098) 6234[9] 6997[5]

Adorna (GER) *C Sprengel* 98
4 b m Tiger Hill(IRE) —Astilbe (GER) (Monsun (GER))
5980a[8]

Adoyen Spice *Mike Murphy* a70 51
4 ch m Doyen(IRE) —Ariadne (GER) (Kings Lake (USA))
(278) 687[5] 2204[6] 3739[8] 5042[7] 6789[10]

Adranian (IRE) *David C Griffiths* a72 62
2 gr g Dark Angel(IRE) —Make Me Blush (USA) (Blushing John (USA))
1095[9] 1673[4] 2120[3] 2283[6] 3584[5] 4194[10] 4922[7] 5899[7] (6280) 6487[4] 6699[8] (7196) 7490[2] (7539) 7686[2] 7725[5] 7881[7]

Ad Value (IRE) *Alan Swinbank* a48 60
3 b g Ad Valorem(USA) —Sopran Marida (IRE) (Darshaan)
1293[5] 5441[4] 5832[6] (6153) ◆ 6600[6] 7062[3] 7212[3]

Advanced *Kevin Ryan* a96 107
8 b g Night Shift(USA) —Wonderful World (GER) (Dashing Blade)
1111[5] 1885[13] 2116[2] 2495[2] 2706[4] 3109[17] 3578[9] 4314[17] 4494[10] 5272[4] 5852[8] 6145[3] (6347) 6987[7] 7295[7]

Adventure Seeker (FR) *A De Royer-Dupre* 112
3 ch f Bering—American Adventure (USA) (Miswaki (USA))
1922a[2] 3447a[4] 6909a[4]

Adventure Story *Peter Makin* a66 71
4 ch m Bold Edge—Birthday Venture (Soviet Star (USA))
1630[4] 2222[7] 3412[4] 3597[2] ◆ 4628[2] 5846[5] 6655[6] 7172[6]

Adverse (IRE) *Michael Bell* 51
2 b f Refuse To Bend(IRE) —Shadow Roll (IRE) (Mark Of Esteem (IRE))
5514[10]

Advertise *Joseph Tuite* a52 66
5 br g Passing Glance—Averami (Averti (IRE))
949[10] 1269[8] 1488[9] 1866[9] 2149[10] 3293[3] 3804[2] 4337[3] 4578[6] 4829[4] 5231[7] 5845[2] 6811[4]

Advertisement (USA) *Jeremy Noseda* a94 80
4 bb h Mr Greeley(USA) —Banner (USA) (A.P. Indy (USA))
(249) (385) 613[3] 1237[2]

Advisor (FR) *Michael Bell* 84
5 gr g Anabaa(USA) —Armilina (FR) (Linamix (FR))
1443[2] 1847[12] 2931[5] 4082[6] 5440[8]

Ad Vitam (IRE) *David C Griffiths* a64 62
3 ch g Ad Valorem(USA) —Love Sonnet (Singspiel (IRE))
5[2] 60[3] 192[4] 260[2] 296[4] (527) 686[4] 717[3] (817) 951[4] 1299[4] 1574[5] 1944[3] 2406[4] 2835[4] 3325[8] 3683[7] 5602[6] 6494[5] 6657[2] 6813[4] 7229[6] 7371[4] ◆ 7459[5] ◆

Aegean Destiny *John Mackie* a56 70
4 b m Beat Hollow—Starlist (Observatory (USA))
1324[8] 1658[5] 2091[4] 2952[9] 3581[5] 4204[2] 5107[8] (5791) 6029[2] 7264[5]

Aeneid *Declan Carroll* 73
6 b g Rainbow Quest(USA) —Grecian Slipper (Sadler's Wells (USA))
1692[6] 2219[6] 2458[7] 2952[4]

Aerial Acclaim (IRE) *Clive Cox* 89
3 b c Acclamation—Stratospheric (Slip Anchor)
3218[2] 3649[3] ◆ 4313[3] 4861[2] 5281[2] 6063[5]

Aerodynamic (IRE) *Michael Easterby* a81 92
4 b g Oratorio(IRE) —Willowbridge (IRE) (Entrepreneur)
1061[10] 1410[19] 1696[11] 2115[6] 2674[8] 3386[9] 4367[6] 5106[9] 6777[3] 7159[3] (7463) 7537[2] (7823)

Aesop's Fables (USA) *A Fabre* 96
2 b c Distorted Humor(USA) —Abhisheka (IRE) (Sadler's Wells (USA))
4036a[2] 5130a[5]

A'Faal *Clive Brittain* a34 32
3 ch f Dr Fong(USA) —Golubitsa (IRE) (Bluebird (USA))
1236[4] 4925[5]

Afaal (USA) *William Haggas* 79
2 b g Hard Spun(USA) —Alattrah (USA) (Shadeed (USA))
5447[9] (6768)

Affectionate *Mahmood Al Zarooni* 49
2 b f Distorted Humor(USA) —Loving Kindness (USA) (Seattle Slew (USA))
3270[8]

Affinity *James Given* a73 72
4 b m Sadler's Wells(USA) —Kalinka (IRE) (Soviet Star (USA))
278[11]

Afkar (IRE) *Clive Brittain* a88 85
3 b g Invincible Spirit(IRE) —Indienne (IRE) (Indian Ridge)
1315[2] 1606[2] 6069[7] 7023[11] 7168[13] 7354[3] 7532[13]

Aflaam (IRE) *Ronald Harris* a77 79
6 br g Dubai Destination(USA) —Arjuzah (IRE) (Ahonoora)
50[3] 247[7] (433) 562[8] 685[6] 761[3] 3804[9] 4158[10] 4578[3] 4822[3] 5178[14] 5611[10]

Afleet Again (USA) *Robert E Reid Jr* a118 96
4 rg h Afleet Alex(USA) —Lucky Again (USA) (Wild Again (USA))
(7300a)

Afnoon (USA) *John Dunlop* 72
2 b f Street Cry(IRE) —Tashawak (IRE) (Night Shift (USA))
5655[16] (6744)

African Art (USA) *P Schaerer* a71 89
5 ch g Johannesburg(USA) —Perovskia (USA) (Stravinsky (USA))
(629a)

African Cheetah *Reg Hollinshead* a83 72
5 ch h Pivotal—Miss Queen (USA) (Miswaki (USA))
(1083) 1390[13] 2301[13] 5608[3] 5968[9] 6290[5] 6773[10] 7036[8] 7237[10]

African Story *A Fabre* a94 110
4 ch g Pivotal—Blixen (USA) (Gone West (USA))
(830a) 2744a[4] 3654a[2] 5530a[3]

Afrikaans (IRE) *Mark Johnston* 66
3 b c Cape Cross(IRE) —Wajina (Rainbow Quest (USA))
3705[8] 4611[8] 6210[3] 6990[10]

Afsare *Luca Cumani* a91 114
4 b g Dubawi(IRE) —Jumaireyah (Fairy King (USA))
1528[6] 2439[5] 3403[2] 3775[4] 5776a[4]

After (IRE) *A P O'Brien* 96
2 b f Danehill Dancer(IRE) —Noahs Ark (IRE) (Charnwood Forest (IRE))
4131a[2] 4834a[9] 5217[5] 6389a[6]

After Timer (IRE) *Julie Camacho* 44
2 b f Kheleyf(USA) —Rustle In The Wind (Barathea (IRE))
4073[7] 4668[4] 5058[10] 5597[13] 6424[7] 6835[9]

Agadir Summer *David Simcock* a75 53
3 b f Cape Cross(IRE) —Easy To Love (USA) (Diesis)
4826[6] 6286[3] 7360[2]

Agapanthus (GER) *Barney Curley* a75 75
6 b g Tiger Hill(IRE) —Astilbe (GER) (Monsun (GER))
1156[6] 2170[4] 4612[7] 5340[9] 6037[4] 6811[10]

Agent Archie (USA) *William Haggas* a84 97
4 b g Smart Strike(CAN) —Dans La Ville (CHI) (Winning (USA))
441a[8] 628a[10] (3959) ◆ 5250[6] 5932[3]

Agent Secret (IRE) *F Rohaut* a87 113
5 b h Pyrus(USA) —Ron's Secret (Efisio)
920a[7] 1266a[3] 4223a[2] 5531a[5] 6321a[2] 6686a[2]

Age Of Reason (UAE) *Saeed Bin Suroor* a108 108
6 b g Halling(USA) —Time Changes (USA) (Danzig (USA))
329a[3] 603a[3] 826a[9] 5055[4]

Aggbag *Tony Carroll* a54 53
7 b g Fath(USA) —Emaura (Dominion)
229[6] 340[6] (382) 466[5] 575[5] 807[5] 950[8] 1625[4] (1763) 2171[5] 2386[7] 3096[2] 3280[3] 3475[7] 3943[10]

Agglestone Rock *Philip Kirby* a66 83
6 b g Josr Algarhoud(IRE) —Royalty (IRE) (Fairy King (USA))
3[3] (1215)

Agiaal (USA) *John Gosden* a73 86
3 b c Sakhee(USA) —Lahan (Unfuwain (USA))
1203[3] ◆ 1484[3] 1836[3] (2256) 3400[5]

Agilete *Lydia Pearce* a63 87
9 b g Piccolo—Ingerence (FR) (Akarad (FR))
5390[2] 5815[3] 7178[7]

Aglaja *Frank Sheridan* a47
2 b f Tiger Cafe(JPN) —Undovica (Primo Dominie)
4919[6] 5246[8] 5896[5] 7035[7]

Agonita (FR) *Mlle S Losch* a68
3 b f Vettori(IRE) —Agona (FR) (Wagon Master (FR))
288a[9]

Agony And Ecstasy *Ralph Beckett* a99 98
4 ch m Captain Rio—Agony Aunt (Formidable (USA))
(1104) 3527a[9]

Ahinga (FR) *X Nakkachdji*
2 gr f Chichicastenango(FR) —Annee De La Femme (IRE) (Common Grounds)
6925a[0]

Ahlaain (USA) *David Simcock* a97 97
3 b c Bernstein(USA) —Brocatelle (Green Desert (USA))
411a[4] 680a[2] 753a[2] 998a[7] 1341[5] 3068[9] 4313[5] 4965[4]

Ahlawy (IRE) *Frank Sheridan* a87 81
8 gr g Green Desert(USA) —On Call (Alleged (USA))
599[4] 877[6] (932) 1223[4] 1879[8] 2359[4] 4679[9] 5390[7] 5828[15] 6461[10] 6656[3] 7036[7] 7557[7] 7605[10] (7818) 7903[8]

Ahtoug *Mahmood Al Zarooni* a93 100
3 b c Byron—Cherokee Rose (IRE) (Dancing Brave (USA))
1545[2] (1852) 2928[9]

Ahwaak (USA) *Alastair Lidderdale* 40
7 b g Dynaformer(USA) —Saudia (USA) (Gone West (USA))
2219[7]

Ahzeemah (IRE) *Saeed Bin Suroor* a82 70
2 b g Dubawi(IRE) —Swiss Roll (IRE) (Entrepreneur)
5454[4] 6180[2] (6795) 7095[3]

Aiaam Al Wafa (IRE) *James Tate* a59 64
2 b f Authorized(IRE) —State Secret (Green Desert (USA))
6440[7] 6744[4] 7125[8] 7849[8]

Aigrette Garzette (IRE) *P Schiergen* 103
3 b f Peintre Celebre(USA) —Aigrette (USA) (Gone West (USA))
2337a[6] 3209a[4] 3651a[5] 4839a[3] 5749a[9] 6395a[8]

Aiken *John Gosden* 92
3 b c Selkirk(USA) —Las Flores (IRE) (Sadler's Wells (USA))
2930[7] ◆ (3377) ◆ (3988) ◆ (4316) ◆

Aikenite (USA) *Todd Pletcher* a116 93
4 bb h Yes It's True(USA) —Silverlado (USA) (Saint Ballado (CAN))
7302a[4]

Ailanthus *Henry Candy* 38
2 b f Trade Fair—The Abbess (Bishop Of Cashel)
5812[9] 6629[4]

Ailsa Craig (IRE) *Edwin Tuer* a66 83
5 b m Chevalier(IRE) —Sharplaw Destiny (IRE) (Petardia)
1970[5] ◆ 2545[6] 3051[2] 3275[12] (4901) 5593[5] 6155[4] 6708[13]

Aima D'Avril (GER) *P Schaerer* 45
3 b f Iron Mask(USA) —Alliance D'Avril (FR) (Dr Devious (IRE))
5307a[11]

Aimee Tricks *Ian Semple* a43 40
3 b f Librettist(USA) —Trick Of Ace (USA) (Clever Trick (USA))
713[5] 836[4] 2461[4] 3116[7]

Aim Higher *John Gosden* 70
2 ch c Exceed And Excel(AUS) —Enemy Action (USA) (Forty Niner (USA))
3552[5] 6768[7] 6992[4]

Ainebe Crocus (FR) *S Wattel* a75 75
10 ch g Dernier Empereur(USA) —Bright Crocus (USA) (Clev-Er-Tell (USA))
1013a[5]

Aine's Delight (IRE) *Andy Turnell* a61 58
5 b m King's Best(USA) —Gentle Thoughts (Darshaan)
346[3] 553[7] 943[6] 2638[5] 3176[2] 3690[3] 7603[8] 7805[9]

Ain't Talkin' *Michael Attwater* a40 28
5 ch g Zaha(CAN) —Royal Ivy (Mujtahid (USA))
662[11] 4699[6] 5422[6] 6084[9] 7924[7]

Airborne Again (IRE) *Richard Hannon* 84
2 gr g Acclamation—Bunditten (IRE) (Soviet Star (USA))
1835[3] (2023) 4094[11] 4536[10]

Aird Snout (USA) *David Simcock* a66
2 bb c Giant's Causeway(USA) —Gold Pattern (USA) (Slew O'Gold (USA))
7369[3] 7751[10]

Air Of Grace (IRE) *I Mohammed* a76 79
3 gr c Dalakhani(IRE) —Star On Stage (Sadler's Wells (USA))
502a[9] 753a[8]

Air Shot (FR) *C Ferland* a84 88
3 b c Rashbag—Balle De Golf (FR) (Homme De Loi (IRE))
882a[5]

Airspace (IRE) *M Halford* a74 92
5 bb g Kheleyf(USA) —Peace In The Park (IRE) (Ahonoora)
4135a[11] 4767a[12]

Air Traffic *Sir Henry Cecil* 82
3 b c Dansili—Emplane (USA) (Irish River (FR))
1338[2]

Aizavoski (IRE) *E Lellouche* 113
5 b h Monsun(GER) —Arlesienne (IRE) (Alzao (USA))
920a[5] (7733a)

Ajaafa *Michael Appleby* a57 68
3 b g Araafa(IRE) —Cloridja (Indian Ridge)
130[2] 263[9] 396[7] 875[7] 1078[7] 1359[8] 1980[9] 2172[9] 2598[6] 2827[6] 3619[5]

Ajaan *Sir Henry Cecil* 102
7 br h Machiavellian(USA) —Alakananda (Hernando (FR))
3157[3] 3875[14] 5705[4]

Ajara (IRE) *Mme L Braem* a77 77
5 b m Elusive City(USA) —My-Lorraine (IRE) (Mac's Imp (USA))
168[9] 815a[7]

Ajara Boy *Luke Dace* a16 33
4 ch g Avonbridge—Cultural Role (Night Shift (USA))
1993[8] 2202[5]

Ajdaad (USA) *Alan McCabe* a76 80
4 b g Horse Chestnut(SAF) —Hasene (FR) (Akarad (FR))
694[7] 835[5] 894[5] 2021[8] 2955[9] 3130[6] 3386[5] 3643[6] 4821[4] 5036[3] 6017[5] 6379[4] (6490) 6844[4] 7034[5] (7418) 7465[4] 7537[7] 7605[5] (7888)

Ajeeb (USA) *David Simcock* a83 72
3 b g Harlan's Holiday(USA) —Fair Settlement (USA) (Easy Goer (USA))
2306[2] 2847[7] 4208[3] 5837[4] (7179)

Ajjaadd (USA) *Ted Powell* a78 96
5 b g Elusive Quality(USA) —Millstream (USA) (Dayjur (USA))
910[3] ◆ 1140[3] 1864[4] 2304[3] (3174) (3847) 4742[4] (5278) (6224) 6522[7]

Ajla (IRE) *Richard Hannon* 36
3 b f Exceed And Excel(AUS) —Yukon Hope (USA) (Forty Niner (USA))
179[9]

Ajool (USA) *Zoe Davison* a58 72
4 ch m Aljabr(USA) —Tamgeed (USA) (Woodman (USA))
727[12]

Akarana (IRE) *Willie Musson* a51
4 b g Danehill Dancer(IRE) —Castle Quest (IRE) (Grand Lodge (USA))
4663[8] 5212[7] 5607[8]

Akarlina (FR) *N Clement* 108
5 gr m Martaline—Akaralda (FR) (Akarad (FR))
1266a[6] 1784a[8] 5075a[6] (6686a) 7193a[3]

Akawy (FR) *Mme A Blanchard* a49
3 ch g Malinas(GER) —Star Bahia (FR) (Starborough)
5463a[0]

Akeed Mofeed *John M Oxx* 114
2 b c Dubawi(IRE) —Wonder Why (GER) (Tiger Hill (IRE))
6391a[2]

Akhmatova *Gerard Butler* a98 82
4 b m Cape Cross(IRE) —Maganda (IRE) (Sadler's Wells (USA))
92a[7] 3208a[5]

Akinndi (IRE) *Evan Williams* 48
4 b g Intikhab(USA) —Akaliya (IRE) (Daylami (IRE))
2366[8]

Akmal *John Dunlop* 112
5 ch g Selkirk(USA) —Ayun (USA) (Swain (IRE))
1188[5] 1601[2] 2098[3] 2438[8] 3647[5] 5471[4]

Akrias (USA) *Luca Cumani* 44
3 b c Lemon Drop Kid(USA) —Prevail (USA) (Danzig (USA))
2068[9] 2469[11]

Aktia (IRE) *Luca Cumani* a82 95
4 b m Danehill Dancer(IRE) —La Gandilie (FR) (Highest Honor (FR))
2066[9] 2676[8] 4109[11] 6439[5]

Aktion Power (GER) *S Labate*
8 ch h Perugino(USA) —Alpha Sum (GER) (Surumu (GER))
372a[P]

Akton City (FR) *J-P Delaporte* a52 73
4 b g Sagacity(FR) —Tanea (FR) (Exit To Nowhere (USA))
(6959a)

Akula (IRE) *Mark H Tompkins* 63
4 ch g Soviet Star(USA) —Danielli (IRE) (Danehill (USA))
7107[6]

Al Aasifh (IRE) *Saeed Bin Suroor* 104
3 b g Invincible Spirit(IRE) —Urgele (FR) (Zafonic (USA))
4526[2] 5563[3] 6027[2] 6747[8]

Alabama Song (ITY) *R Menichetti* 71
3 b c Ad Valorem(USA) —Tenderlit (USA) (Lit De Justice (USA))
1431a[15]

Alabanda (IRE) *Tim Easterby* a39 75
2 b f Camacho—Alinda (IRE) (Revoque (IRE))
2148[5] 2580[6] 3123[2] 3780[4] (4285) 4867[5] 5847[5] 6222[10] 6599[7] 6864[3]

Alaghiraar (IRE) *Richard Ford* a69 84
7 b g Act One—Tarsheeh (USA) (Mr Prospector (USA))
2159[2] 7850[9]

Alainmaar (FR) *Roger Varian* 117
5 b g Johar(USA) —Lady Elgar (IRE) (Sadler's Wells (USA))
(1883)

Alakhan (IRE) *Ian Williams* a92 91
5 gr g Dalakhani(IRE) —Alte Kunst (IRE) (Royal Academy (USA))
(5879) ◆ 6290[12] 7168[8] ◆ 7523[2]

Al Amaan *Gary Moore* a78 72
6 b g Nayef(USA) —Siobhan (Generous (IRE))
32[3] 315[5]

Alamona (GER) *C Sprengel* 69
4 b m Sholokhov(IRE) —Ariana (GER) (Dashing Blade)
1033a[6]

Al Andaleeb (USA) *Saeed Bin Suroor* a71 47
2 b f Bernardini(USA) —Ajina (USA) (Strawberry Road (AUS))
5444^{12} *7124^3*

Al Andalyya (USA) *David Lanigan* 67
3 ch f Kingmambo(USA) —Kushnarenkovo (Sadler's Wells (USA))
1446^4 1972^7

Alanis (BEL) *Mme V Botte* a89
6 gr m Fabulous White(FR) —A La Une (BEL) (Sischa (BEL))
5195a^2

Alanza (IRE) *John M Oxx* 112
3 ch f Dubai Destination(USA) —Alasha (IRE) (Barathea (IRE))
(5228a) ◆ (5848) ◆ 6338^6

Al Aqabah (IRE) *Brian Gubby* a79 70
6 ch m Redback—Snow Eagle (IRE) (Polar Falcon (USA))
625^2 *(727)* *806^2* *1147^4* *2207^6* 2771^6 *6796^9* *(7097)* *7447^5* *7517^9* *7767^6*

Alareen (USA) *Saeed Bin Suroor* a62 64
3 b f Selkirk(USA) —Innuendo (IRE) (Caerleon (USA))
2849^4 3303^8

Alaskan Bullet (IRE) *Michael Bell* 88
2 b g Kodiac—Czars Princess (IRE) (Soviet Star (USA))
(5117) ◆ 5826^5

Alayir (IRE) *John M Oxx* a75 81
3 b g Azamour(IRE) —Alaya (IRE) (Ela-Mana-Mou)
1704a^2

Alazan (IRE) *Philip Hobbs* 92
5 ch g Dubai Destination(USA) —Marion Haste (IRE) (Ali-Royal (IRE))
3406^4 4464^3 5221^{11}

Alazeyab (USA) *A Al Raihe* a107 107
5 b h El Prado(IRE) —Itnab (Green Desert (USA))
414a^2 *582a^3* *755a^{12}* 825a^5

Albaasil (IRE) *Sir Michael Stoute* 106
3 b c Dansili—Wrong Key (IRE) (Key Of Luck (USA))
(2596) ◆ (3864) ◆ 4313^2

Albacocca *Sir Mark Prescott Bt* a61 60
4 gr m With Approval(CAN) —Ballymac Girl (Niniski (USA))
6798^3

Al Baidaa *Roger Varian* 61
2 b f Exceed And Excel(AUS) —Intrum Morshaan (IRE) (Darshaan)
7165^8

Albamara *Sir Mark Prescott Bt* a78 87
2 bb f Galileo(IRE) —Albanova (Alzao (USA))
5320^2 ◆ (5579) ◆ 6299^8

Albany Rose (IRE) *Rae Guest* a66 91
3 br f Noverre(USA) —Teide Lady (Nashwan (USA))
100^5 *422^2* 2375^3 2827^2 (3272) (3321) (3433) 4075^4 4498^2 6522^8

Albaqaa *P J O'Gorman* a103 106
6 ch g Medicean—Basbousate Nadia (Wolfhound (USA))
1614^2 3032^{22} 3411^6 (3825) (4537) 6339^{17} 6693^4

Albaraah (IRE) *F Head* 111
3 b f Oasis Dream—Coconut Show (Linamix (FR))
1553a^6 7090a^2

Albaraka *Sir Mark Prescott Bt* a81 92
3 gr f Selkirk(USA) —Alborada (Alzao (USA))
274^2 ◆ *(529)* 2839^9 4015^3 6395a^7

Albaspina (IRE) *Sir Mark Prescott Bt* 81
2 gr f Selkirk(USA) —Alabastrine (Green Desert (USA))
(5819)

Albeed *John Dunlop* 77
4 b m Tiger Hill(IRE) —Ayun (USA) (Swain (IRE))
1367^3 1700^8 [illegible] 4644^0

Albert Bridge *Ralph Beckett* 83
3 gr g Hernando(FR) —Alvarita (Selkirk (USA))
5556^4 (6130)

Albertus Pictor *Sir Mark Prescott Bt* a84
4 gr g Selkirk(USA) —Albanova (Alzao (USA))
67^2 *5866^6* *6121^6*

Alborz (IRE) *Mark Johnston* a61 65
2 b c Dubai Destination(USA) —Mount Elbrus (Barathea (IRE))
3534^5 4159^7 *4646^2* 5550^4 6154^6 *6443^5* 6807^4

Albret (IRE) *G Arizkorreta Elosegui* 49
2 gr c Clodovil(IRE) —Piccelina (Piccolo)
4843a^{10}

Al Burkaan (IRE) *Ed Dunlop* a76 83
3 br g Medicean—Lone Look (Danehill (USA))
2045^3 2392^4 (3508) *3924^4* (4281) ◆

Alcalde *John Berry* 94
5 b g Hernando(FR) —Alexandrine (IRE) (Nashwan (USA))
6333^8

Alcohuaz (CHI) *Lennart Reuterskiold Jr* a112 112
6 b g Merchant Of Venice(USA) —Giverny (CHI) (Hussonet (USA))
3531a^6 6563a^{13}

Alcopop (AUS) *Jake Stephens* 118
7 b g Jeune—Iota Of Luck (AUS) (Blevic (AUS))
6713a^9

Aldaado (IRE) *Paul Midgley* a37 78
5 b g Alhaarth(IRE) —Zobaida (IRE) (Green Desert (USA))
16^6

Al Dain (IRE) *Kevin Ryan* 21
2 b f Diamond Green(FR) —Mitchella (IRE) (Persian Bold)
6232^7

Aldedash (USA) *Sir Henry Cecil* a73 75
3 b g Aldebaran(USA) —Hawzah (Green Desert (USA))
1271^3 (1525) 2076^{11} 5049^6 *5641^6*

Alde Gott (FR) *D Prod'Homme* 59
8 gr g Medaaly—Sponte Sua (FR) (Spoleto (IRE))
843a^0

Aldermoor (USA) *Stuart Williams* a76 93
5 b g Tale Of The Cat(USA) —Notting Hill (BRZ) (Jules (USA))
1898^{12} 2398^9 *(5640)* *6051^9* *6665^6* *7767^8*

Aldgate (USA) *Mahmood Al Zarooni* a25 56
2 ch g Street Cry(IRE) —Adonesque (IRE) (Sadler's Wells (USA))
5013^{11} *6180^{11}*

Aldo *Alastair Lidderdale* a70 69
4 b h Lucky Owners(NZ) —Chaperone (Shaamit (IRE))
489^4 *1052^3* *1373^2* *1756^5* 5002^9 *6135^3*

Al Doha *Kevin Ryan* 53
2 ch f Iffraaj—Lobby Card (USA) (Saint Ballado (CAN))
3504^9 5486^4 6480^9

Aldwick Bay (IRE) *Richard Hannon* a79 86
3 b g Danehill Dancer(IRE) —Josie Doocey (IRE) (Sadler's Wells (USA))
2230^7 (2688) 3466^3 4253^4 4473^2 4957^6 6130^{10}

Alejandro (IRE) *Richard Fahey* 93
2 b g Dark Angel(IRE) —Carallia (IRE) (Common Grounds)
1199^2 (1515) 2007^5 2725^3 (3570) 4094^{14} (4575) 5849^{11} 6114^5

Aleksandar *Luca Cumani* 69
2 ch c Medicean—Alexander Celebre (IRE) (Peintre Celebre (USA))
5801^{12} 6483^5 7109^2

Alemaratiya *David Simcock* a33 50
3 b f Dalakhani(IRE) —Marannatha (IRE) (Pursuit Of Love)
1799^4 2432^3 2786^7

Alensgrove (IRE) *Paul Midgley* a30 63
3 ch f Byron—Unicamp (Royal Academy (USA))
1246^8 1749^2 2406^5 2781^5 3387^2 3571^3 4638^6 5034^4 6156^3 6450^8

Aleqa *Chris Wall* a61 79
4 b m Oasis Dream—Vanishing Point (USA) (Caller I.D. (USA))
1562^7 1990^5 2719^4 3555^4 (4681) 5119^6 *6051^6* 6759^8

Aleut *James Given* 70
2 b f Iceman—Gabacha (USA) (Woodman (USA))
5161^3 5819^2 6329^{10} 6866^4

Alexander Pope (IRE) *A P O'Brien* a98 108
3 b c Danehill Dancer(IRE) —Starship (IRE) (Galileo (IRE))
998a^6 (2331a) 3105^3

Alexandra Palace (IRE) *Mark Johnston* a47 51
2 b f Oratorio(IRE) —Alexandra S (IRE) (Sadler's Wells (USA))
4462^7 *5097^9* *5413^5* 6101^2

Alexs Rainbow (USA) *John Gallagher* a52 60
3 b f Silver Deputy(CAN) —Swirling Sky (USA) (Sky Classic (CAN))
729^8 1566^4 1986^6

Alfouzy *Roger Varian* a80 78
3 b c Red Ransom(USA) —Kartuzy (JPN) (Polish Precedent (USA))
1915^4 *3739^2* 4407^3 5064^8 *6005^5*

Alfraamsey *Sheena West* a58 75
3 b g Fraam—Evanesce (Lujain (USA))
655^8 ◆ *(834)* *964^7* *987^3* 1359^7 1494^{11} 1980^{13} 2805^4 *7640^7*

Alfred George *Richard Whitaker* 48
2 ch c Namid—Cosmic Song (Cosmonaut)
4606^5 5398^8

Alfred Hutchinson *Geoffrey Oldroyd* 74
3 ch g Monsieur Bond(IRE) —Chez Cherie (Wolfhound (USA))
5082^3 ◆ 5792^3

Al Freej (IRE) *Roger Varian* a71
2 b f Iffraaj—Why Now (Dansili)
7540^2 ◆

Alfresco *John Best* a79 81
7 b g Mtoto—Maureena (IRE) (Grand Lodge (USA))
557^6 *703^9* *867^9* (2557) 3427^4 4742^9 5972^6 *6796^8*

Al Furat (USA) *Ron Barr* a40 69
3 b g El Prado(IRE) —No Frills (IRE) (Darshaan)
1588^7 3976^2 5372^3 (5650) 6153^4 6838^6

Al Gillani (IRE) *Jim Boyle* a83 71
6 b g Monashee Mountain(USA) —Whisper Dawn (IRE) (Fasliyev (USA))
178^6 *470^5* *521^5* ◆ *612^5* *725^4* *867^8* *1044^4*

Algon (GER) *H Blume* a57
6 b h Invincible Spirit(IRE) —Augreta (GER) (Simply Great (FR))
617a^0

Algris *Sir Mark Prescott Bt* a38
3 gr g Domedriver(IRE) —Ballymac Girl (Niniski (USA))
477 *234^9*

Algurayn (IRE) *George Prodromou* a53 66
3 ch g Kheleyf(USA) —Majborah (IRE) (Entrepreneur)
1591^9 3089^7

Alhaban (IRE) *Ronald Harris* a101 76
5 gr g Verglas(IRE) —Anne Tudor (IRE) (Anabaa (USA))
99^3 ◆ *279^9* *438^{11}* *736^{10}* *1183^5* 5811^5 5970^6 6583^6 *6844^2* *7200^6* *7557^5*

Alhaque (USA) *David Flood* a58 54
5 ch g Galileo(IRE) —Safeen (USA) (Storm Cat (USA))
3170^7 3507^{10} 4024^9 4654^4 *6446^2* *6873^{10}* *7036^9*

Al Hazim (CAN) *J-L Pelletan* a72 104
3 b g Anabaa(USA) —Fantastic Women (USA) (Henbane (USA))
1206a^4

Alhira *David Simcock* a66 69
2 b f Royal Applause—Taghreed (IRE) (Zamindar (USA))
4961^2 ◆ *5691^4* 6030^8 *7140^4*

Alhudhud (USA) *Kevin Morgan* a46 35
5 b g Swain(IRE) —Wasnah (USA) (Nijinsky (CAN))
649^7 *819^{14}* 1993^6 2272^7

Aliante *Mark Johnston* a42 71
2 ch f Sir Percy—Alexandrine (IRE) (Nashwan (USA))
3826^{11} *4992^9* 5806^3 6275^9

Alianthus (GER) *J Hirschberger* 117
6 b h Hernando(FR) —Allure (GER) (Konigsstuhl (GER))
(1263a) (2657a) (3422a) (4138a) 5664a^2 (7048a)

Alice Rose (IRE) *Rae Guest* 68
2 ch f Manduro(GER) —Bold Assumption (Observatory (USA))
3308^2 3680^3 4232^2 4682^3 7081^4

Alice's Dancer (IRE) *William Muir* 81
2 br f Clodovil(IRE) —Islandagore (IRE) (Indian Ridge)
2302^5 3117^2 3547^6 (6222) 6413^5 7135^{11}

Alicudi (USA) *C Ferland* a64
4 b m Mr Greeley(USA) —Testy Trestle (USA) (Private Account (USA))
395a^0

Ali Hope (IRE) *Roger Charlton* 9
2 ch g Three Valleys(USA) —Alexander Duchess (IRE) (Desert Prince (IRE))
5382^{13} 5959^6 7109^{11}

Alioonagh (USA) *Peter Chapple-Hyam* a70 48
4 ch m Giant's Causeway(USA) —Alidiva (Chief Singer)
3457^7 4730^8 6033^{10}

Alis Aquilae (IRE) *Tim Etherington* a72 83
5 b g Captain Rio—Garnock Academy (USA) (Royal Academy (USA))
2491^4 ◆ 3582^8 4405^5 5732^8 *7201^2*

A Little Bit Dusty *Bill Turner* a71 70
3 ch g Needwood Blade—Dusty Dazzler (IRE) (Titus Livius (FR))
(366) *(519)* *609^3* *(717)*

Alive And Kicking *James Bethell* 73
3 b c Compton Place—Strawberry Dale (IRE) (Bering)
1459^8 1880^3 2479^2

Al Jaadl *William Jarvis* a70 69
4 b m Shamardal(USA) —Three Wishes (Sadler's Wells (USA))
52^2 *158^2*

Al Jabreiah *William Haggas* 68
2 b f Bertolini(USA) —Nihal (IRE) (Singspiel (IRE))
4961^9 (6973)

Aljamaaheer (IRE) *Roger Varian* 86
2 ch c Dubawi(IRE) —Kelly Nicole (IRE) (Rainbow Quest (USA))
(6935)

Al Janadeirya *David Lanigan* 72
3 b f Oasis Dream—Elegant Times (IRE) (Dansili)
1836^4

Al Jemailiya (IRE) *Kevin Ryan* a20 67
2 gr f Verglas(IRE) —Mrs Mason (IRE) (Turtle Island (IRE))
2409^3 2811^{10} 3336^2 4194^6 5645^8 *7763^{12}*

Aljosan *David Evans* 48
2 b f Compton Place—Little Caroline (IRE) (Great Commotion (USA))
1522^5 1691^9 2998^3 3631^5 3955^2 *4907^{12}*

Al Karlovyyh (IRE) *Clive Brittain* a33
2 b f Authorized(IRE) —Karlovy (Halling (USA))
7343^{14}

Al Kazeem *Roger Charlton* 115
3 b c Dubawi(IRE) —Kazeem (Darshaan)
1365^2 ◆ (2100) 5182^2 6161^2 7027^2

Alkazim (IRE) *David Wachman* a85 94
2 b c Holy Roman Emperor(IRE) —Tumbleweed Pearl (Aragon)
6170^2 6527^4

Al Khaleej (IRE) *David Simcock* a101 108
7 b g Sakhee(USA) —Mood Swings (IRE) (Shirley Heights)
3409^7 3862^9 ◆ 4554^5 5936^7 6521^{12}

[illegible] (USA) *William Mott* a84 111
5 b r Medaglia D'Oro(USA) —Maya (USA) (Capote (USA))
3888a^5 6203a^3

Al Khan (IRE) *Peter Chapple-Hyam* 93
2 b c Elnadim(USA) —Popolo (IRE) (Fasliyev (USA))
(3755) 5181^5 5926^5

Alkhana (IRE) *P Schiergen* 95
3 b f Dalakhani(IRE) —A Beautiful Mind (GER) (Winged Love (IRE))
2981a^8 3651a^3 4839a^7 7510a^0

Al Khawaneej *Ed Dunlop* a83 71
3 br c Arch(USA) —Fraulein (Acatenango (GER))
2218^{10} 2458^5 ◆ 2930^9 4336^9 *(5141)*

Alkhawarah (USA) *Mark Johnston* 60
3 b f Intidab(USA) —Futuh (USA) (Diesis)
1060^6 1459^{12} 2402^3 3114^5 3630^5

Alkimos (IRE) *Luca Cumani* 110
3 b c High Chaparral(IRE) —Bali Breeze (IRE) (Common Grounds)
1321^4 ◆ (1950) (2707) 3068^2

All Action (USA) *Sir Henry Cecil* a94 105
4 ch h Storm Cat(USA) —Wandesta (Nashwan (USA))
1402^6 ◆ *1760^2* 2884^2 (3844) 4410^{12}

Allanit (GER) *Barney Curley* a72 72
7 b g Tiger Hill(IRE) —Astilbe (GER) (Monsun (GER))
(555) *802^2* 2649^{10} 4253^{12} *7458^{14}* *7671^9*

All Annalena (IRE) *Lucy Wadham* 94
5 b m Dubai Destination(USA) —Alla Prima (IRE) (In The Wings)
4331^9 4788^{14} 6330^4 6989^5 7580a^{DSQ}

Alla Prossima *S Smrczek* a73 80
3 b f Sakhee(USA) —Alpe Fegg (FR) (Medicean)
7045a^6

Allashka (FR) *J-L Guillochon* 62
3 b f Touch Of The Blues(FR) —Alleged Star (USA) (Alleged (USA))
7016a^4

Allegorio (FR) *Mme J Bidgood* a43 58
3 b c One Cool Cat(USA) —Escouades (FR) (General Assembly (USA))
660a^9

Allegra Byron *Jonathan Portman* 38
2 ch f Byron—Colourflash (IRE) (College Chapel)
5779^6

Allegra Tak (ITY) *H Rogers* a50 85
5 b m Invincible Spirit(IRE) —No Tiktak (IRE) (Diktat)
6854a^{11}

Allegri (IRE) *Ann Duffield* a60 57
2 b c Key Of Luck(USA) —Bermuxa (FR) (Linamix (FR))
4073^9 4323^5 6048^7 *6487^7* *6695^5* *7421^3* *7742^7*

Allez Bailey (FR) *P Lacroix* a73 77
5 b g Orpen(USA) —Herba Buena (FR) (Fabulous Dancer (USA))
2867a^8

Allez Les Rouges (IRE) *Andrew Balding* a52
4 b g Saffron Walden(FR) —Louve Secrete (IRE) (Fasliyev (USA))
688^5

Allez Leulah (IRE) *Mark Johnston* 50
3 b f Cape Cross(IRE) —Kootenay (IRE) (Selkirk (USA))
1270^9 1858^8 2349^9

All For You (GER) *T Mundry* 55
2 b f Shirocco(GER) —All About Love (GER) (Winged Love (IRE))
6737a^9

All For You (IRE) *Jim Goldie* a68 72
5 b m High Chaparral(IRE) —Quatre Saisons (FR) (Homme De Loi (IRE))
3905^4 4380^6 (4784)

All Good News (IRE) *Lisa Williamson* a32
2 gr g Moss Vale(IRE) —Blanche Neige (USA) (Lit De Justice (USA))
5398^{12} *6308^{11}* *6539^{12}*

All Guns Firing (IRE) *Barry Leavy* a55 28
5 b g High Chaparral(IRE) —Lili Cup (FR) (Fabulous Dancer (USA))
3311^{12} *3951^6* *4868^5*

All Honesty *William Knight* a67 70
3 b f Medicean—Al Joudha (FR) (Green Desert (USA))
1607^6 2192^{10} 3292^6 (4244) 4544^6 5354^5 *5902^3* *6664^{10}*

Allied Powers (IRE) *Michael Bell* a70 115
6 b g Invincible Spirit(IRE) —Always Friendly (High Line)
1403^4 1851^2 2753a^3 3403^8 4037a^5 5284^5 5990a^8

All In A Paddy *Ed McMahon* a50 56
3 ch g With Approval(CAN) —Fervent Fan (IRE) (Soviet Lad (USA))
3226^{10} 4200^6 4929^2 5674^9 *6310^9* *7005^4*

All Moving Parts (USA) *Alan McCabe* a63 60
4 bb g Forest Camp(USA) —Smooth Player (USA) (Bertrando (USA))
135^{10} *203^8* *292^5* *425^7* *561^5*

All My Heart *Sir Mark Prescott Bt* a91 95
3 gr f Sadler's Wells(USA) —Alba Stella (Nashwan (USA))
3043^9 *3224^6* *3519^7* 4251^3 *(5599)* ◆ *(5714)* *(5897)* (6832) 7406a^0

All Night Blues (IRE) *Mlle Valerie Boussin* a51 36
5 ch g Night Shift(USA) —Tender Is Thenight (IRE) (Barathea (IRE))
42a^0

All Nighter (IRE) *Brian Meehan* a71 71
2 b g Bertolini(USA) —Symbol Of Peace (IRE) (Desert Sun)
2049^7 2510^8 6725^{13} *7358^3* *7752^3*

All Or Nothin (IRE) *John Quinn* 63
2 b g Majestic Missile(IRE) —Lady Peculiar (CAN) (Sunshine Forever (USA))
2936^5

All Right Now *Derek Haydn Jones* a84 64
[illegible] (USA) —Cookie Cutter (IRE) (Fasliyev (USA))
158^6 *893^9* *1496^2* *1814^2* *2178^{11}* *(2653)* 3348^7 *3924^2* 4792^8 *4921^2* *5717^{11}* 7050^8 7339^2 7926^{13}

All Shamar *W Hickst* 98
2 b c Shamardal(USA) —All Glory (Alzao (USA))
(7508a)

All That Jazz (JPN) *Katsuhiko Sumii* 97
3 b f Tanino Gimlet(JPN) —Diamond Pisa (JPN) (Sunday Silence (USA))
7410a^{15}

All That Rules *Sir Henry Cecil* a74
2 b c Galileo(IRE) —Alba Stella (Nashwan (USA))
7521^6

All The Aces (IRE) *Roger Varian* a113 104
6 b g Spartacus(IRE) —Lili Cup (FR) (Fabulous Dancer (USA))
3591^4 ◆ 5045^{10} 6301^3

Alltheclews *Lucinda Featherstone* a28 35
6 b g Zindabad(FR) —Burton Gold (Master Willie)
2813^{10} 4129^{12} 4396^8

All The Winds (GER) *Shaun Lycett* a83 83
6 ch g Samum(GER) —All Our Luck (GER) (Spectrum (IRE))
1402^8 *(7908)*

All Time *Sir Henry Cecil* 56
3 br f Dansili—Clepsydra (Sadler's Wells (USA))
1364^9

Allumeuse (USA) *Andrew Balding* a57 72
3 rg f Rockport Harbor(USA) —Atlantic Frost (USA) (Stormy Atlantic (USA))
1724^4 2528^4

Alluring Star *Michael Easterby* a50 73
3 b f Gentleman's Deal(IRE) —Alustar (Emarati (USA))
2163^7 (2350) (2986) 3854^7 (4435) ◆ 4854^9 5164^5 5731^{12} 6450^7 6867^8 7213^5

All Ways To Rome (FR) *H-A Pantall* a80 91
7 b g Slickly(FR) —Always On Time (Lead On Time (USA))
617a^8

Almaas (USA) *Saeed Bin Suroor* a82 83
2 ch c Hard Spun(USA) —Summer Dream Girl (USA) (Unbridled (USA))
5688^3 ◆ 6267^2

Almagest *John Gosden* 94
3 br g Galileo(IRE) —Arabesque (Zafonic (USA))
2231[2] 2648[4] (5327) 6068[6] 6497[4]

Almaguer *F-X Belvisi* a81 81
9 b g Spectrum(IRE) —Cerita (IRE) (Wolfhound (USA))
(372a) (533a) 1013a[3]

Almahaza (IRE) *Adrian Chamberlain* a87 56
7 b g Alzao(USA) —Morna's Moment (USA) (Timeless Moment (USA))
61[3] ◆ (504) (573) 870[2] (1467) 2000[11] 3045[3]

Al Mahmeyah *Richard Hannon* a76 76
2 b f Teofilo(IRE) —Aguilas Perla (IRE) (Indian Ridge)
3342[4] ◆ 3736[2] 4474[2] (5689)

Almail (USA) *Jamie Osborne* 103
5 b g Swain(IRE) —Khassah (Green Desert (USA))
5271[11] 5932[8]

Al Malek (FR) *Mario Hofer* a87
2 b c Anabaa(USA) —Rouge (FR) (Red Ransom (USA))
(7665a)

Al Mamzar (IRE) *David Simcock* 54
2 b c Teofilo(IRE) —Avila (Ajdal (USA))
6953[8]

Al Marmoom (USA) *A bin Huzaim* a81 58
5 b h Medaglia D'Oro(USA) —Lady Laika (USA) (Gone West (USA))
707a[2]

Almarmooq (USA) *John Gosden* a70 73
4 bb g Dynaformer(USA) —Tuscoga (USA) (Theatrical)
1212[3]

Almaty Express *John Weymes* a67 54
9 b g Almaty(IRE) —Express Girl (Sylvan Express)
(167) 511[7] 735[12] 933[10] 2162[2] 2803[9] (3714) 4000[5] 4518[12] 5244[9] (5603) 5895[11] 6602[11] 6841[10] 7567[8] 7844[3]

Al Mayasah (IRE) *David Simcock* 90
3 b f Shamardal(USA) —Mia Mambo (USA) (Affirmed (USA))
1894[7] 2432[2] 4093[4] (4559) 5354[2] 5657[7]

Almirah *Edward Creighton* 5
2 ch f Ishiguru(USA) —Brogue Lanterns (IRE) (Dr Devious (IRE))
3767[6] 3917[14] 6993[14]

Almond Branches *George Moore* 74
2 ch f Dutch Art—Queens Jubilee (Cayman Kai (IRE))
1199[3] 1515[2] 1797[4] (3504) 4343[8] 4558[5] 5591[P]

Almowj *George Jones* a34 39
8 b g Fasliyev(USA) —Tiriana (Common Grounds)
2569[5] 3716[9]

Almuder *Ed Dunlop* a60
2 b c Intikhab(USA) —Adraaj (USA) (Sahm (USA))
7369[6]

Almuftarris (USA) *Ed Dunlop* 75
2 b c Smart Strike(CAN) —Ranin (Unfuwain (USA))
3823[6] ◆ 6100[2] ◆

Al Muheer (IRE) *Ruth Carr* a106 99
6 b g Diktat—Dominion Rose (USA) (Spinning World (USA))
1094[20] 1406[11] 1885[25] 2495[12] 2783[6] ◆ 3169[5] 3541[8] 3924[5] ◆ 4314[12] (4503) 4810[6]

Almutaham (USA) *James Moffatt* 57
4 bb h Dynaformer(USA) —Forest Lady (USA) (Woodman (USA))
2733[8]

Alnair (IRE) *Declan Carroll* a59 64
2 b c Red Clubs(IRE) —Danccini (IRE) (Dancing Dissident (USA))
2504[7] 2992[5] 3398[4] 6293[13] 6645[8] 7294[14] 7692[2]

Alnashmy (FR) *David Marnane* a79 90
3 b c Shamardal(USA) —Legendary (FR) (Fabulous Dancer (USA))
4313[9]

Alnitak (USA) *Bent Olsen* 91
10 br g Nureyev(USA) —Very True (USA) (Proud Truth (USA))
4842a[11]

Alnoomaas (IRE) *Roger Varian* 26
2 b g Oasis Dream—Remarkable Story (Mark Of Esteem (IRE))
5051[7]

Aloneinthestreet (USA) *Mark Johnston* a73 44
3 b g Street Cry(IRE) —Crown Of Jewels (USA) (Half A Year (USA))
(379) 468[6] 738[2] 931[6] 1191[5] 1481[10]

Alo Pura *D Selvaratnam* a102 102
7 b m Anabaa(USA) —Rubies From Burma (USA) (Forty Niner (USA))
155a[3]

Aloysia *Sylvester Kirk* a43
2 b f Amadeus Wolf—Anthea (Tobougg (IRE))
6819[10] 7414[7] 7929[4]

Alpacco (IRE) *Sandie Kjaer Nortoft* a91 100
9 b g Desert King(IRE) —Albertville (GER) (Top Ville)
4842a[12]

Alpha (USA) *Kiaran McLaughlin* a108
2 b c Bernardini(USA) —Munnaya (USA) (Nijinsky (CAN))
7306a[11]

Alpha And Omega (IRE) *Patrick J Flynn* a54 65
3 b g Arakan(USA) —Dry Lightning (Shareef Dancer (USA))
6511a[8]

Alpha Delta Whisky *John Gallagher* a61 81
3 ch g Intikhab(USA) —Chispa (Imperial Frontier (USA))
818[3] 1130[2] 2151[6] 2611[2] (2881) 3269[4] 3985[3] 5278[9] 6246[12]

Alpha Tauri (USA) *Richard Guest* a84 46
5 b g Aldebaran(USA) —Seven Moons (JPN) (Sunday Silence (USA))
38[2] 105[7] (290) (856) 1014[3] 1462[2] 2095[19] 2494[12] 3222[10] 4434[7] 5034[9] 5789[15]

Alpina (FR) *J-V Toux* a59 58
5 gr m Pinmix(FR) —Very Very Nice (IRE) (Soviet Star (USA))
6959a[9]

Alqaahir (USA) *Paddy Butler* a74 66
9 b h Swain(IRE) —Crafty Example (USA) (Crafty Prospector (USA))
1172[4] 4088[6] 5836[12] 6486[12] 7006[12] 7092[9]

Alraased (USA) *John Dunlop* 74
2 bb c Exchange Rate(USA) —Alabaq (USA) (Riverman (USA))
7133[6] ◆

Al Raqi *Bryan Smart* 6
3 b g Beat Hollow—Merewood (USA) (Woodman (USA))
1496[9] 3684[8]

Alrasm (IRE) *E Charpy* a104 92
4 b g Acclamation—New Deal (Rainbow Quest (USA))
499a[12]

Al Rayanah *George Prodromou* a59 60
8 b m Almushtarak(IRE) —Desert Bloom (FR) (Last Tycoon)
69[7] 86[7] 340[7]

Al Rep (IRE) *D Camuffo* 105
3 ch g Trade Fair—Swizzle (Efisio)
(1431a)

Alsadaa (USA) *Laura Mongan* a91 87
8 b g Kingmambo(USA) —Aljawza (USA) (Riverman (USA))
2190[5] 3286[4] 3794[5]

Alsadeek (IRE) *Doug Watson* a110 55
5 b g Fasliyev(USA) —Khulan (USA) (Bahri (USA))
327a[14]

Al Saham *Saeed Bin Suroor* 88
2 b c Authorized(IRE) —Local Spirit (USA) (Lion Cavern (USA))
(6448) 6914[6]

Alsahil (USA) *Micky Hammond* a91 80
5 ch g Diesis—Tayibah (IRE) (Sadler's Wells (USA))
(5761) 6024[8] 6676[12]

Al Shababiya (IRE) *Alison Thorpe* a75 66
3 b m Dubawi(IRE) —Multaka (USA) (Gone West (USA))
7078[10] 7244[4]

Alshahbaa (IRE) *Ms Joanna Morgan* 78
4 b m Alhaarth(IRE) —Adaala (USA) (Sahm (USA))
923a[14]

Al Shaqab (IRE) *Kevin Ryan* a67 77
2 b g Amadeus Wolf—Common Rumpus (IRE) (Common Grounds)
(3707) 4502[4] 4984[4] 6111[8]

Alshazah *Rod Millman* a85 77
3 b g Haafhd—Mountain Law (USA) (Mountain Cat (USA))
2568[4] 3513[3] 4158[4] 4751[3] 5407[3] (6005) 6822[4] (7255) 7577[7]

Al Shemali *Mahmood Al Zarooni* a115 119
7 ch h Medicean—Bathilde (IRE) (Generous (IRE))
416a[4] 608a[6] 759a[10] 827a[6] 1001a[13] 5544[7] 6301[2] 7053[3]

Alshmemi (USA) *John Gosden* 78
2 bb c Bernardini(USA) —Capote's Crown (USA) (Capote (USA))
4762[12] 5447[4] ◆ 6059[3]

Alsindi (IRE) *Clive Brittain* 103
2 b f Acclamation—Needles And Pins (IRE) (Fasliyev (USA))
(5514) ◆ (6296) 6691[9]

Al's Memory (IRE) *David Evans* 76
2 b c Red Clubs(IRE) —Consensus (IRE) (Common Grounds)
3849[5] 4864[13] 5812[4] (6293) 6599[5] ◆ 6829[6] 7259[6]

Alspritza *Chris Wall* 38
3 b f Bahamian Bounty—Spritzeria (Bigstone (IRE))
1591[6] 2141[10] 2827[4] 4162[9]

Alston *David Arbuthnot* 32
3 ch g Cadeaux Genereux—Chetwynd (IRE) (Exit To Nowhere (USA))
3594[7]

Altair Star (IRE) *P Schiergen* 106
4 b h Kris Kin(USA) —Aglow (Spinning World (USA))
1128a[2] 1554a[4] 2749a[5] 5497a[3]

Altamir One *Mme B Valenti* a66
3 b c Act One—Princess D'Orange (FR) (Anabaa (USA))
7669a[8]

Altano (GER) *A Wohler* 108
5 b g Galileo(IRE) —Alanda (GER) (Lando (GER))
6200a[6] (7045a)

Alternative Choice (USA) *Nick Littmoden* a70 59
5 b g Grand Slam(USA) —Northern Fleet (USA) (Afleet (CAN))
244[6] 839[6] 4060[9] 5416[4] 6287[6] 6873[9] 7112[10]

Altnaharra *Jim Goldie* 53
2 b g Halling(USA) —Gargoyle Girl (Be My Chief (USA))
3899[6] 4140[6] 6187[6]

Altona (IRE) *Mick Channon* 69
2 b f Redback—Flawless (Warning)
6160[9] 6480[4] 6745[3] 7081[2]

Altos Reales *Michael Scudamore* a56 48
7 b m Mark Of Esteem(IRE) —Karsiyaka (IRE) (Kahyasi)
6613[13]

Alubari *Gordon Elliott* a73 74
4 b g Tiger Hill(IRE) —Why So Silent (Mill Reef (USA))
1325[6] 1994[2] 2170[3] 2830[8] 7556[3]

Alupka (IRE) *Richard Hannon* 40
2 b f Acclamation—Array Of Stars (IRE) (Barathea (IRE))
3463[6] 4552[14]

Alushta *Ed Dunlop* a58
2 b f Royal Applause—Degree (Warning)
7757[8]

Alvitude (USA) *Roger Charlton* 59
2 b g Aptitude(USA) —Alvernia (USA) (Alydar (USA))
4053[7]

Alwaaqi *John Dunlop* 74
2 b c Barathea(IRE) —Al Durrah (USA) (Darshaan)
5447[11] 6019[2]

Alwaary (USA) *John Gosden* a75 98
5 b g Dynaformer(USA) —Tabrir (IRE) (Unfuwain (USA))
3403[7] ◆ 5045[6]

Al Wajba (USA) *William Haggas* a65 44
2 ch f Ghostzapper(USA) —Crystal Symphony (USA) (Red Ransom (USA))
6525[5] 7125[4] ◆

Always A Sinner (USA) *William Knight* a62 46
2 ch c Jazil(USA) —Never A Saint (USA) (St Jovite (USA))
3986[12] 4390[8] 4906[6] 5634[9] 6443[11] 6937[8]

Always A Way *Mikael Magnusson*
3 ch f Danehill Dancer(IRE) —Waypoint (Cadeaux Genereux)
7250[11]

Always Dazzling *Ollie Pears* a67 66
4 ch m Cadeaux Genereux—Woodlass (USA) (Woodman (USA))
19[5] 231[2] 404[3]

Always De One *K F Clutterbuck* a53 49
4 b m Fruits Of Love(USA) —Yes Virginia (USA) (Roanoke (USA))
1[5] 749[5] 1233[5] 5666[6]

Always Dixie (IRE) *Andrew Crook* a57 57
4 b m Lucky Story(USA) —Jerre Jo Glanville (USA) (Skywalker (USA))
1305[12] 1556[8] 2492[8] 2618[8]

Always Eager *Mark Johnston* 62
2 b g With Approval(CAN) —Slew The Moon (ARG) (Kitwood (USA))
3779[6] 5269[5] 5697[11] 6372[7] 6829[5]

Always Ends Well (IRE) *Mark Johnston* 65
2 b f Tiger Hill(IRE) —Awwal Malika (USA) (Kingmambo (USA))
1165[5] 1455[2] 1632[4] 2148[7] 2630[3] 2886[10] 4069[6] 4538[5] 5577[2] 5844[2] 6399[7] 6864[11]

Always Et Toujours *Mark Johnston* a56 77
2 ch c Notnowcato—World's Heroine (IRE) (Spinning World (USA))
2234[3] 2617[4] 5565[5] (6102) 6599[3] 6972[12]

Always Gunner *Paul Midgley* a45 61
5 b g Mujahid(USA) —Westcourt Ruby (Petong)
7641[8]

Always In The Sky (FR) *T Larriviere* a44 73
5 b h Hawk Wing(USA) —Always On Time (Lead On Time (USA))
566a[9]

Always Like This (IRE) *Marco Botti* a72
3 br f Cape Cross(IRE) —Jazz Princess (IRE) (Bahhare (USA))
5633[2] 5946[4] 6796[11] 7448[13]

Always The Lady *Clive Cox* 84
3 ch f Halling(USA) —Hector's Girl (Hector Protector (USA))
1549[4] 1894[6] 5585[3] (6404) 6996[7] 7296[10]

Alyshakeys (DEN) *Wido Neuroth* a88 97
4 ch m Sendawar(IRE) —Alamea (IRE) (Ela-Mana-Mou)
4483a[9]

Al Zir (USA) *Saeed Bin Suroor* 111
4 b h Medaglia D'Oro(USA) —Bayou Plans (USA) (Bayou Hebert (USA))
2290[7] 2614[2]

Amadeus Denton (IRE) *Michael Dods* 84
2 b g Amadeus Wolf—Wood Sorrel (IRE) (Woodman (USA))
1691[2] (2093) 3022[3] 4079[5] (4500) 5922[7]

Amadeus Wolfe Tone (IRE) *Jamie Osborne* a54 79
2 b g Amadeus Wolf—Slieve (Selkirk (USA))
4864[5] 5269[6] (5841) (6484) 6829[4]

Amana (USA) *Mark Brisbourne* a59 76
7 b m Diesis—Ma-Arif (IRE) (Alzao (USA))
2259[6] (2991) 3300[9] (3546) 3760[6] 4747[7]

Amare *T Mundry* 99
4 b m Hernando(FR) —Amore (GER) (Lando (GER))
6739a[6]

Amarillo (IRE) *P Schiergen* 101
2 b c Holy Roman Emperor(IRE) —Alte Kunst (IRE) (Royal Academy (USA))
4372a[3] 5610a[6] 6901a[2]

Amaron *Andreas Lowe* 104
2 ch c Shamardal(USA) —Amandalini (Bertolini (USA))
(4372a) (5610a) 6901a[3]

Amaroni *John E Long* a19
3 b c Sulamani(IRE) —Fortunes Favourite (Barathea (IRE))
6473[12]

Amary (IRE) *John Harris* a87 68
4 b m Acclamation—Amistad (GER) (Winged Love (IRE))
(19) 128[7] 508[4] 1054[5] 1190[DSQ] 1373[6] 1499[4]

A Ma Yen (ITY) *Vittorio Caruso* 97
3 b f Doyen(IRE) —A Ma Guise (USA) (Silver Hawk (USA))
2539a[8]

Amaze *Brian Ellison* 62
3 ch g Pivotal—Dazzle (Gone West (USA))
2045[4] 2735[8]

Amazing Amoray (IRE) *David Barron* 87
3 b g Tagula(IRE) —Amistad (GER) (Winged Love (IRE))
(2151) 3052[7] 5434[7] 6113[12]

Amazing Beauty (GER) *M Figge* a92 99
4 ch m Bahamian Bounty—Amidala (GER) (Monsagem (USA))
1263a[8] 4373a[9] 6370a[7]

Amazing Beauty (IRE) *A P O'Brien* a88 102
3 b f Galileo(IRE) —Doula (USA) (Gone West (USA))
2004[5] 2968a[3] 4133a[9] 4589a[3] 5220[7] 6736a[3]

Amazing Blue Sky *Ruth Carr* a71 80
5 b g Barathea(IRE) —Azure Lake (USA) (Lac Ouimet (USA))
399[4] 551[5] 742[4] 1156[7] 2213[2] (2454) 2544[5] 3023[6] 3456[2] 3545[3] 3701[3] (4148) 4360[14] 4674[3] 4901[7] 5440[4] 5729[7] 6263[3] 6538[8] 6916[2] 7070[2] 7237[7] 7413[10]

Amazing King (IRE) *Philip Kirby* a68 84
7 b g King Charlemagne(USA) —Kraemer (USA) (Lyphard (USA))
(3453) 3660[2] 4059[3] 4577[2] 5273[4]

Amazingreyce *Owen Brennan* a45
6 gr m Rainbow High—Lightning Belle (Belfort (FR))
2359[7]

Amazing Star (IRE) *Declan Carroll* a73 85
6 b g Soviet Star(USA) —Sadika (IRE) (Bahhare (USA))
1696[3] ◆ 2995[2] 3169[3] 3740[6] 5059[2] 5205[8] 6290[10] 6658[12]

Amazing Storm (IRE) *Richard Hannon* 89
2 b c Clodovil(IRE) —Forest Storm (USA) (Woodman (USA))
3870[7] 4535[4] ◆ (4857) (5478) ◆ 5931[4] 6766[2]

Amazing Tiger (GER) *Peter Jardby* a87 64
5 b g Tiger Hill(IRE) —Allure (GER) (Konigsstuhl (GER))
5981a[7]

Amazing Win (IRE) *Mick Channon* a61 56
3 b f Marju(IRE) —Aqaba (Lake Coniston (IRE))
2960[10] 3289[4] 4963[5] 5346[5] 5793[8] 6179[4] 7084[9] 7538[8] 7755[2] 7848[10]

Amazombie (USA) *Bill Spawr* a121 108
5 b g Northern Afleet(USA) —Wilshe Amaze (USA) (In Excess)
(7302a)

Amazon Twilight *Brett Johnson* a73 65
3 b f Librettist(USA) —My Way (IRE) (Marju (IRE))
140[2] ◆ 3172[8]

Amba *Des Donovan* a66 18
5 ch m Hold That Tiger(USA) —Gal Gloria (PR) (Tralos (USA))
7411[3]

Ambala *Chris Wall* a73 61
3 b f Intikhab(USA) —Mighty Splash (Cape Cross (IRE))
1270[8] 1774[10] 2457[5] (5838) ◆ 6303[5]

Amber Heights *David Pinder* a65 59
3 b f Kyllachy—Jumairah Sun (IRE) (Scenic)
1759[8] 2174[6] 3090[5] 3818[6] 4244[9] 5511[8] 7488[2] 7652[2] 7812[6]

Amber Silk (IRE) *Charles Hills* a68 74
2 b f Lawman(FR) —Faraday Light (IRE) (Rainbow Quest (USA))
4471[2] 5583[5] 6440[4]

Ambitious Dragon (NZ) *A T Millard* 125
5 b g Pins(AUS) —Golden Gamble (NZ) (Oregon (USA))
(1742a) 7732a[4]

Ambitious Icarus *Richard Guest* a61
2 b g Striking Ambition—Nesting Box (Grand Lodge (USA))
7335[3] 7555[2] 7916[3]

Ambivalent (IRE) *Roger Varian* a69
2 b f Authorized(IRE) —Darrery (Darshaan)
(6180) 6623[8]

Ambrose Princess (IRE) *Michael Scudamore* a60 76
6 b m Chevalier(IRE) —Mark One (Mark Of Esteem (IRE))
4806[2]

Amelia May *John Gosden* 75
2 b f Dansili—Rebecca Sharp (Machiavellian (USA))
5444[9] 5806[10] 6168[4] 6757[8]

Amelia's Surprise *Michael Bell* a79 58
3 b f Ad Valorem(USA) —Salagama (IRE) (Alzao (USA))
(1084) (1579) 6505[2] 7024[10] 7141[4]

Amen (IRE) *A P O'Brien* a51 73
3 b c Galileo(IRE) —Kitza (IRE) (Danehill (USA))
1704a[6]

Amenable (IRE) *David Nicholls* a96 93
4 b g Bertolini(USA) —Graceful Air (IRE) (Danzero (AUS))
2116[8] 2620[11] 3395[13] 4369[11] 5434[2] ◆ 6113[23] (6917)

Amends (USA) *John Best* a66 63
4 b g Trippi(USA) —Day Of Atonement (USA) (Devil His Due (USA))
772[6] 814[7] 906[8]

Americain (USA) *A De Royer-Dupre* 127
6 b h Dynaformer(USA) —America (IRE) (Arazi (USA))
1231a[6] 1707a[6] 5304a[10] (7043a) 7218a[4] (7407a)

American Devil (FR) *J Van Handenhove* 111
2 b c American Post—Alcestes Selection (Selkirk (USA))
(4036a) 5770a[3] 6565a[5]

American Lover (FR) *John Wainwright* a49 63
4 b m American Post—Lovarisk (FR) (Take Risks (FR))
1328[5] 1710[8] 2402[4] 2781[2] 3355[3] 3934[7] 5469[4] 5649[5] 6156[4] 6816[6] 7211[3] 7781[6]

American Nizzy (FR) *Y De Nicolay* a86 100
4 b m American Post—Quietude (USA) (Woodman (USA))
92a[0]

American Saga (FR) *M Delzangles* a71
2 gr f American Post—Saga D'Or (FR) (Sagacity (FR))
7665a[5]

American Smooth *Jeremy Noseda* a58
4 b h Oasis Dream—Two Step (Mujtahid (USA))
(202)

American Spin *Luke Dace* a82 70
7 ch g Groom Dancer(USA) —Sea Vixen (Machiavellian (USA))
1839[7]

Ameriling (FR) *Mlle S-V Tarrou* 82
2 b f American Post—Krisling (FR) (Take Risks (FR))
7508a[8]

Amerthyst *Jo Crowley* a64 56
3 b f Doyen(IRE) —Seeking Utopia (Wolfhound (USA))
2885[11]

Amethyst Dawn (IRE) *Andrew Reid* a64 94
5 gr m Act One—A L'Aube (IRE) (Selkirk (USA))
1410[13] 1849[6] 2123[11] 2634[3] (3026) 3877[10] 4344[8] 4561[15] 5059[10] 5465[4] 6079[6] 7054[4] 7296[9] *7841[11]*

Ametrin (IRE) *J Hirschberger* 104
3 b c Tiger Hill(IRE) —Amarette (GER) (Monsun (GER))
3007a[2] 3672a[11]

Amfitryon *A Mykoniatis* a85
6 ch h Bertolini(USA) —Urban Dancer (IRE) (Generous (IRE))
5754a[5]

Amhran (IRE) *Brian Meehan* a75 73
3 b c Songandaprayer(USA) —Ra Hydee (USA) (Rahy (USA))
1568[5] *2306[4]* 2841[11] 3756[10] 4272[10]

Am I Blue *Mrs D Thomas* a32 33
5 b m Dubai Destination(USA) —Seal Indigo (IRE) (Glenstal (USA))
172[6] 407[5] 955[7] 2377[8]

Amica (SAF) *Gay Kelleway* a86 77
4 ch m Silvano(GER) —Light Fandango (SAF) (Cordoba I (USA))
92a[8] 412a[7] 681a[6] 753a[9]

Amical Risks (FR) *Ollie Pears* a62 65
7 bl g Take Risks(FR) —Miss High (FR) (Concorde Jr (USA))
252[4] 596[5] 1107[7] *1959[2]* 2259[3] *2656[6]* 3317[5] *3923[5]*

Amico Fritz (GER) *H-A Pantall* a80 114
5 b h Fasliyev(USA) —Arctic Appeal (IRE) (Ahonoora)
(1575a) 3154[6] 3863[16] 5528a[6] 7221a[10]

Amir Pasha (UAE) *Micky Hammond* a58 71
6 br g Halling(USA) —Clarinda (IRE) (Lomond (USA))
1039[10] 2454[4] 2830[2] 3301[4] 3456[4] 3858[4] 4129[2] (4198) 4499[5] 4747[2] 5650[5] 5723[2] 6029[6] 6155[5]

Amis Reunis *Richard Hannon* 78
2 b f Bahamian Bounty—Spring Clean (FR) (Danehill (USA))
2718[5] 2997[2] (3463) (4228) 4536[4] 5847[8] 6590[9]

Amistress *Eve Johnson Houghton* a35 80
3 b f Kalanisi(IRE) —Atwirl (Pivotal)
(1189) (1526) 2022[5] 3325[2] 3642[2] (3744) 4473[3] 4971[6] 5340[4] 6402[11] 6632[8]

Amitola (IRE) *David Barron* a94 96
4 ch m Choisir(AUS) —Emly Express (IRE) (High Estate)
2298[14] 3459[12] 5684[5] 6189[6] 6531[8] 7031[7] 7171[3] *(7439) 7660[2]*

Amno Dancer (IRE) *David Barron* a45 65
4 b g Namid—Special Dancer (Shareef Dancer (USA))
674[9] 1077[3] 1520[2] 2057[10] 2692[7]

Amongst Amigos (IRE) *Ian McInnes* a54 16
10 b g Imperial Ballet(IRE) —Red Lory (Bay Express)
3317[16] 3938[15]

Amoralist *Ed Dunlop* a74 77
2 b c Tobougg(IRE) —Ellablue (Bahamian Bounty)
4722[4] *5382[2]* 6400[2] *(6977)*

Amore Et Labore *Sylvester Kirk* a49 14
3 bg g Ivan Denisovich(IRE) —In The Highlands (Petong)
475 281[7] 456[11]

Amor Patrice *Les Hall* 28
3 b g Ransom O'War(USA) —Sweet Stormy (IRE) (Bluebird (USA))
2875[8]

Amosite *J R Jenkins* a72 63
5 b m Central Park(IRE) —Waterline Dancer (IRE) (Danehill Dancer (IRE))
6119[8] *7942[2]*

Amoure Medici *Noel Quinlan* a77 71
2 b g Medicean—Lifetime Romance (IRE) (Mozart (IRE))
3182[11] 4292[5] 4571[6] *(6487) 6699[2]* 6995[7] *7491[3]*

Amour Propre *Henry Candy* 114
5 ch g Paris House—Miss Prim (Case Law)
3874[2] ◆ 4468[2] (5524a)

Amoya (GER) *Philip McBride* a83 90
4 b m Royal Dragon(USA) —Arkona (GER) (Aspros (GER))
1950[10] 2855[4] 3555[6] 4066[5] (4393) 4807[7] 6069[8] *(6507)* 6996[13]

Amphora *Andrew Balding* 71
2 b f Oasis Dream—Carafe (Selkirk (USA))
4052[16] 5111[6] 6123[4]

Ampleforth *Mark Johnston* a67 79
3 ch g Pivotal—Anna Amalia (IRE) (In The Wings)
5212[3] ◆ *5598[3]* (6210) 6631[3] ◆ 7110[15] *7227[12]*

Amtaar *Ian Semple* a67 38
4 b m Nayef(USA) —Emerald Fire (Pivotal)
2399[8]

Amthal (IRE) *Clive Brittain* a65 73
2 b f Dalakhani(IRE) —Al Ihtithar (IRE) (Barathea (IRE))
6329[14] *(6819)* ◆ 7169[9]

Amtired *Brian Ellison* a65 58
5 gr g Beauchamp King—Rising Talisker (Primitive Rising (USA))
1386[6] 1542[8] 2218[9] 2734[8] 3110[5] *3496[3] 3952[2] 4179[2] 4651[3]* 5622[5]

Amun Ra (USA) *Jeremy Gask* a33 20
3 bb g E Dubai(USA) —Pocketbrook (USA) (Montbrook (USA))
4320[11]

Amwell Pinot *Alan Bailey* a96 91
3 ch g Dubawi(IRE) —Kartajana (Shernazar)
101[3] ◆ *177[2] 254[2] (750) 988[3]* 2471[8] 4335[6] 4550[12] *4993[9]* 5811[6] 7171[6]

Amy Dorrit *John Gosden* a67 77
2 b f Pivotal—Fascination Street (IRE) (Mujadil (USA))
6745[8] 6984[2] ◆ *7343[6]*

Anabedweyah (IRE) *Clive Brittain* a62 57
2 b f Authorized(IRE) —Al Kamah (USA) (Kingmambo (USA))
6934[9] *7599[4]*

Anaconda (FR) *Tom Dascombe* 71
2 b c Anabaa(USA) —Porretta (IRE) (Indian Ridge)
4652a[3] 5130a[7]

Anadolu (IRE) *Tracey Collins* 95
3 b f Statue Of Liberty(USA) —Afto (USA) (Relaunch (USA))
4135a[12] 5524a[8]

Ana Emarati (USA) *Ed Dunlop* a85 67
3 b c Forestry(USA) —Triple Edition (USA) (Lear Fan (USA))
523[3] 212 [2] (398) (1031) 1843[12]

Anak (IRE) *Jim Best* 46
5 b g Sinndar(IRE) —Akdara (IRE) (Sadler's Wells (USA))
597[6] 2758[3]

Anakindalika *John Ryan* 58
2 br f Footstepsinthesand—Sallysaysso (IRE) (Danehill Dancer (IRE))
2510[9] 3104[11]

Anam Allta (IRE) *D K Weld* 115
3 b f Invincible Spirit(IRE) —Kiltubber (IRE) (Sadler's Wells (USA))
5228a[2] ◆ (6561a)

Anam Chara (IRE) *Andrew Oliver* a94 94
5 gr m Soviet Star(USA) —Adelaide Pearl (USA) (Skip Away (USA))
2419 332a[14] 607a[9]

Ananda Kanda (USA) *Brian Ellison* a29 62
4 bb m Hero's Tribute(USA) —Roja (USA) (L'Enjoleur (CAN))
5149[5] 5723[9] 6157[7] *6546[9]* 7078[3]

Anathena *Reg Hollinshead* a30 52
3 gr f Act One—Goldeva (Makbul)
1853[10] 2281[5] 2673[11] 5917[7] *6494[13] 6653[9]*

Anatolian *Mahmood Al Zarooni* 103
3 ch c Pivotal—Poseidon's Bride (USA) (Seeking The Gold (USA))
2848[13] 3430[2] (4157) (5049) ◆ (6342) ◆

Anawin (FR) *F Chappet* a75 69
3 b f Meshaheer(USA) —Star Dancing (Danehill Dancer (IRE))
288a[0]

Anaxis (FR) *S Wattel* a101 103
4 ch h Muhtathir—Monadis (USA) (Miswaki (USA))
(840a)

Anaya *David Bourton* a67 70
4 b m Tobougg(IRE) —Nacho Venture (FR) (Rainbow Quest (USA))
529[7]

Ancient Cross *Michael Easterby* a73 107
7 b g Machiavellian(USA) —Magna Graecia (IRE) (Warning)
1240[3] (2028) 2317[7] 2890[3] ◆ (3357) 4534[8] 5180[6] 5927[4] 6147[14] 6706[14]

Ancient Greece *George Baker* a58 80
4 b g Pivotal—Classicism (USA) (A.P. Indy (USA))
1443[14] 2150[7] 2719[5] 4006[6] 4444[10] (5992) (6435)

Ancient Times (USA) *Philip Kirby* a75 49
4 bb g Smart Strike(CAN) —Histoire Sainte (FR) (Kendor (FR))
4198[5] 4951[8] 5166[7]

Anco Marzio *B Goudot* a32 85
5 b h American Post—Atlantic Blue (USA) (Nureyev (USA))
257a[10] 7534a[0]

Andalieb *David Simcock* a71 65
2 b c Zamindar(USA) —Sakhya (IRE) (Barathea (IRE))
5011[9] 5801[5] *7197[2] 7626[2]*

Anddante (IRE) *Tim Easterby* 74
3 b g Antonius Pius(USA) —Lady Digby (IRE) (Petorius)
1169[7] 1437[7] 1802[5] 2249[3] 2588[6]

Anderiego (IRE) *D K Weld* 00
3 b c Invincible Spirit(IRE) —Anna Frid (GER) (Big Shuffle (USA))
3440a[15]

Andiamo Via *Michael Smith* a66 62
4 b g Mujahid(USA) —Efizia (Efisio)
3684[6] 4282[4] 4813[2] 5314[9] 7063[8] *7648[5] (7857)*

Andorn (GER) *Philip Kirby* a70 74
7 b h Monsun(GER) —Anthyllis (GER) (Lycius (USA))
2183[3] 4129[7] 4562[10] *5692[4] 5947[6]*

Andrasta *Alan Berry* a45 55
6 b m Bertolini(USA) —Real Popcorn (IRE) (Jareer (USA))
3662[11] 3901[3] 4288[7] 4328[8] (4564) 4636[6] 5008[5] 5204[4] 5309[11] 5620[3] 5824[4] 7064[10]

Andrea Bellevica (IRE) *John Joseph Hanlon* 64
2 gr f Aussie Rules(USA) —Fire West (USA) (Academy Award (USA))
6772[9]

Andreino (IRE) *G Botti* a83 92
3 ch c Titus Livius(FR) —Piccelina (Piccolo)
5529a[9]

Andromeda Galaxy (FR) *E Lellouche* 109
3 b f Peintre Celebre(USA) —Arlesienne (IRE) (Alzao (USA))
2977a[5] 4036b[6] 7090a[3]

Aneedah (IRE) *John Gosden* 101
3 b f Invincible Spirit(IRE) —Fairy Of The Night (IRE) (Danehill (USA))
1404[13] 1602[2] ◆ 2298[10] 3365[2] 5827[7] 6531[5] 7298[16]

Angalia (IRE) *E Lellouche* 101
3 b f High Chaparral(IRE) —Azalee (IRE) (Peintre Celebre (USA))
4570a[0] 5958a[6] 7510a[6]

Angaric (IRE) *Bryan Smart* a63 67
8 ch g Pivotal—Grannys Reluctance (IRE) (Anita's Prince)
3025[6] 3856[8] 4503[7] 5437[5]

Angel Bright (IRE) *D K Weld* 79
2 b f Dark Angel(IRE) —Cover Girl (IRE) (Common Grounds)
6389a[10]

Angel Cake (IRE) *Phil McEntee* a52 54
2 b f Dark Angel(IRE) —Royal Jelly (King's Best (USA))
3182[12] 3865[11] 4276[7] 4841a[3] 5809[10] 6260[9] 7108[3] *7414[6] 7568[6] 7684[4] 7777[4] 7852[3]*

Angelena Ballerina (IRE) *Karen George* a68 70
4 ch m Indian Haven—Nom Francais (First Trump)
526[8] (800) (895) (1184) ◆ 1755[3] 2144[2] 3515[6] 4337[13] 4822[11]

Angelic Kitten (IRE) *Howard Johnson* 33
2 b f One Cool Cat(USA) —Termania (IRE) (Shirley Heights)
2587[6]

Angelic Note (IRE) *Brian Meehan* 52
2 b f Excellent Art—Evangeline (Sadler's Wells (USA))
6329[13] 7025[10]

Angelic Upstart (IRE) *Andrew Balding* a80 68
3 b g Singspiel(IRE) —Rada (IRE) (Danehill (USA))
177[3] 750[3] 1344[6] 2935[6]

Angel Instead (IRE) *Mrs K Burke* a38 14
6 b m Iron Mask(USA) —Amy G (IRE) (Common Grounds)
57[13]

Angel Kiss (IRE) *David O'Meara* 50
2 b f Dark Angel(IRE) —Sharplaw Destiny (IRE) (Petardia)
2318[7] 2587[3] 4002[12] 4983[4] 5555[12] 6532[11]

Angel Of Fashion (IRE) *Peter Charalambous* a43 62
4 b m Invincible Spirit(IRE) —Vanitycase (IRE) (Editor's Note (USA))
1989[8] *3517[10]* 4160[9] 4683[4] 5355[7]

Angel Of Harlem (FR) *H-A Pantall* a89 94
3 b f Holy Roman Emperor(IRE) —Music Express (FR) (Compton Place)
6809a[10]

Angel Of Hope (IRE) *Bryan Smart* a26 59
2 b f Dark Angel(IRE) —Amaniy (USA) (Dayjur (USA))
2430[9] 3125[3] 3483[3] 3932[6] 4406[7] 5147[4] 5399[10] *6612[6]*

Angel Of Rain (FR) *Robert Collet* a72 80
6 gr g Dalakhani(IRE) —Mystic Mile (IRE) (Sadler's Wells (USA))
219a[9]

Angelo Poliziano *Ann Duffield* a77 83
5 ch g Medicean—Helen Sharp (Pivotal)
1204[6] *1955[7]* (2126) 2832[2] 3087[5] 3832[12] 4174[3]

Angels Art (IRE) *G M Lyons* a68 76
2 b f Excellent Art—Danehill Kikin (IRE) (Danehill (USA))
7275a[6]

Angel's Pursuit (IRE) *Richard Hannon* a113 111
4 ch g Pastoral Pursuits—Midnight Angel (Machiavellian (USA))
700[6] 844[7] 986[3] 3548[3] 3862[8] 4092[8] 4526[5]

Angels Will Fall (IRE) *Charles Hills* 107
2 b f Acclamation—Coconut Squeak (Bahamian Bounty)
(1946) ◆ (4312) 5217[7] 5882[7] 6337[3]

Angel Warrior (IRE) *Ben Haslam* 59
2 b c Dark Angel(IRE) —Red Slipper (IRE) (Alzao (USA))
3035[8] 3755[8] 4192[6] 5287[12]

An Ghalanta (IRE) *J S Bolger* a88 95
2 b f Holy Roman Emperor(IRE) —Alamanta (IRE) (Ali-Royal (IRE))
2322a[4] 3884a[2] 5522a[3] 5950a[3]

Anginola (IRE) *Joseph Tuite* a68 63
2 b f Kodiac—Lady Montekin (Montekin)
3092[7] 4155[10] 5625[4] *6001[2] (6443)* 6806[3] *7205[4] 7569[4] 7582[4]*

Angle Of Attack (IRE) *Alan Brown* a64 37
6 b g Acclamation—Travel Spot Girl (Primo Dominie)
675 2828 [illegible]

Angolaner (GER) *X Nakkachdji* 100
4 b h Golan(IRE) —Anna Thea (IRE) (Turfkonig (GER))
4524a[8] 7733a[0]

Animal Kingdom (USA) *H Graham Motion* a126 106
3 ch c Leroidesanimaux(BRZ) —Dalicia (GER) (Acatenango (GER))
(1921a) 2328a[2] 2950a[6]

Animal Spirits (USA) *Albert M Stall Jr* 106
2 b c Arch(USA) —Pennant Champion (USA) (Mr Prospector (USA))
7301a[5]

Animate Bio (JPN) *Koji Maki* 108
4 ch m Zenno Rob Roy(JPN) —Regenbogen (JPN) (French Deputy (USA))
7410a[13]

Animator *Martin Hill* a59 35
6 b g Act One—Robsart (IRE) (Robellino (USA))
692[5] 944[4] 1567[8]

Aniseed (IRE) *William Haggas* 75
2 gr f Dalakhani(IRE) —Anna Karenina (USA) (Atticus (USA))
4552[7] 6526[6] ◆ 6933[4]

Anjaz (USA) *Saeed Bin Suroor* a80 88
2 b f Street Cry(IRE) —Playful Act (IRE) (Sadler's Wells (USA))
(5320) ◆ (5931)

Anjomarba (IRE) *Conor Dore* a69 75
4 b m Tillerman—Golden Charm (IRE) (Common Grounds)
165[5] 388[3] 1581[3] 1770[2] (2426) *3735[6]* 4246[2] (4711) 5018[4] 5442[5] 6044[8] *6491[4]* 6604[4] 6814[4] *7068[9]* 7349[7] 7579[9] 7591[4] 7695[4] 7820[2] 7844[5] 7930[9]

Ankhor Vat *J Van Handenhove* a62 65
6 b g Red Ransom(USA) —Airline (USA) (Woodman (USA))
533a[0]

Anmar (USA) *Ed Dunlop* a111 111
5 ch g Rahy(USA) —Ranin (Unfuwain (USA))
3403[6] 4095[3] 5252[4]

Anna (GER) *Peggy Bastiaens-Van Cauwenberg* 85
5 ch m Pentire—Albula (GER) (Dashing Blade)
6594a[7]

Annacaboe (IRE) *Martin Bosley* a49 44
4 b m Footstepsinthesand—Alexandria (IRE) (Irish River (FR))
3690[15] *4549[13]*

Anna Fontenail *Rod Millman* a64 58
3 gr f Proclamation(IRE) —Nina Fontenail (FR) (Kaldounevees (FR))
176[4] 520[7] 716[3] 898[8] 1997[10] 4888[7] 5380[4] 5845[11]

Annalika *Colin Teague* 26
3 b f King's Best(USA) —Anapola (GER) (Polish Precedent (USA))
2781[12] 3138[11] 3977[9] 4443[15]

Annaluna (IRE) *David Evans* 57
2 b f Whipper(USA) —Annaletta (Belmez (USA))
5537[7] 5841[6] 6400[6] 6825[8]

Anna Salai (USA) *Mahmood Al Zarooni* 110
4 b m Dubawi(IRE) —Anna Palariva (IRE) (Caerleon (USA))
1681[2] 3030[11] 4915[6]

Annelko *Andrew Haynes* a33 64
4 b g Sulamani(IRE) —Creeking (Persian Bold)
1454[3] 1631[3] (1833) 2246[3] (2856) ◆ 3960[7] 4630[5] 5379[9]

Anne Of Kiev (IRE) *Jeremy Gask* a101 107
6 b m Oasis Dream—Top Flight Queen (Mark Of Esteem (IRE))
(265) 700[2] (989) 1340[4] 1902[8] (2298) 3155[4] 3827[6] 4573[5] 5827[8] 6147[19] 6531[2] 6987[4]

Annes Rocket (IRE) *Jimmy Fox* a68 68
6 b h Fasliyev(USA) —Aguilas Perla (IRE) (Indian Ridge)
2560[8] 3293[11] *3720[3]* 3944[3] 4337[5] 4917[2] *5143[2]* 5667[5] *6051[4] 6488[2]* 6746[2] *6848[7]*

Annie Beach (IRE) *David Barron* 71
2 ch f Redback—Kiva (Indian Ridge)
5646[4] 6026[3] (6598)

Annie Walker (IRE) *David Nicholls* 68
2 b f Bertolini(USA) —Pantoufle (Bering)
4285[11] (4983) 6599[2] 6864[5]

Ann Of The Dance (USA) *Martin D Wolfson* a98 91
2 b f English Channel(USA) —Dans La Ville (CHI) (Winning (USA))
7281a[13]

Announce *A Fabre* 115
4 ch m Selkirk(USA) —Hachita (USA) (Gone West (USA))
(1784a) 2373a[2] 3008a[2] 4223a[4] (5306a) 6568a[2]

Anoint *William Haggas* 89
3 b g Pivotal—Pious (Bishop Of Cashel)
(1985) 2926[2] 4335[9] 5730[4]

Anomaly *Mahmood Al Zarooni* 82
2 ch c Pivotal—Anna Palariva (IRE) (Caerleon (USA))
6267[3] ◆ 7233[2]

Another Citizen (IRE) *Tim Easterby* 88
3 b g Byron—Royal Rival (IRE) (Marju (IRE))
1152[7] 1653[2] 2092[5] 2256[8] 3052[5] 3346[5] 3880[14] 4324[2] (4880) 5559[4] 6113[16] 7076[9]

Another For Joe *Ian Williams* 72
3 b g Lomitas—Anna Kalinka (GER) (Lion Cavern (USA))
1985[3] 3340[5] 5014[11]

Another Laugh *Alan King* a66 76
3 ch g Where Or When(IRE) —Jane Jubilee (IRE) (Mister Baileys)
2688[6] 3650[13]

Another Try (IRE) *Alan Jarvis* a88 88
6 b g Spinning World(USA) —Mad Annie (USA) (Anabaa (USA))
1110[7] 1603[6] 1771[6] (2557) 3535[2] 3880[9] *4909[2]* 5578[4] 6378[10]

Another Whisper (IRE) *Richard Hannon* a40 63
3 b f Montjeu(IRE) —Heavenly Whisper (IRE) (Halling (USA))
1836[8] 2689[4] 3430[8] 5845[5] *6253[10]*

Another Wise Kid (IRE) *Paul Midgley* 91
3 b g Whipper(USA) —Romancing (Dr Devious (IRE))
(1038) 1697[4] (1745) 2363[4] 3052[3] (3189) 3613[5] (6348) 6917[6]

Anrheg *David Brown* a51 56
3 b f Diktat—Dim Ots (Alhijaz)
3594[6] 4478[5] *5212[2] 5601[6]* 6578[3] 6746[4] *7229[8]*

Anshan Dreams *Adrian Maguire* a81 74
7 b g Anshan—Small Risk (Risk Me (FR))
7378a[3] 7544a[3]

Antara (GER) *Saeed Bin Suroor* 118
5 b m Platini(GER) —Auenpracht (GER) (General Assembly (USA))
(2678) 3822[9] 5753a[3]

Antarctic (IRE) *John Gosden* a77 75
3 ch g Alhaarth(IRE) —Holda (IRE) (Docksider (USA))
(2257) *2819[5]*

Anthemion (IRE) *Jean McGregor* a48 53
14 ch g Night Shift(USA) —New Sensitive (Wattlefield)
3903[9] 4379[13]

Anthology *C Von Der Recke* 81
5 b g Haafhd—Annapurna (IRE) (Brief Truce (USA))
69a[12]

Antigua Sunrise (IRE) *Richard Fahey* a58 88
5 b m Noverre(USA) —Staff Approved (Teenoso (USA))
1622[3] 2006[5] 2932[9] 3277[11] 4344[2] 5435[7] 6330[3] 6708[8] 7022[7] *7272[8]*

Antoella (IRE) *Philip Kirby* a42 47
4 gr m Antonius Pius(USA) —Bella Estella (GER) (Sternkoenig (IRE))
324[5] 7105[9]

Anton Chigurh *Tom Dascombe* 73
2 b c Oasis Dream—Barathiki (Barathea (IRE))
6025[3] ◆ 6673[7]

Anton Dolin (IRE) *John Dunlop* a88 87
3 ch g Danehill Dancer(IRE) —Ski For Gold (Shirley Heights)
1189[4] (1769) (2293) (2842) ◆ 3551[9] 4530[2] 5235[6] *6822[5]*

Antoniola (IRE) *Tim Easterby* 81
4 b g Antonius Pius(USA) —Balliamo (IRE) (Royal Academy (USA))
1109^{15} 1390^{10} 1859^{8} 2388^{6} 2589^{9}

Anudjawun (NZ) *Shaun Dwyer* 104
6 bl g Yamanin Vital(NZ) —Perceptible (NZ) (Personal Escort (USA))
6711a^{5} 7043a^{4} 7310a^{5}

Any Given Sunday (GER) *W Baltromei* a81 81
4 b m Royal Dragon(USA) —Arbarine (GER) (Aspros (GER))
831a^{8}

Aoife Alainn (IRE) *Tracey Collins* 111
4 ch m Dr Fong(USA) —Divine Secret (Hernando (FR))
3417a^{5} 4831a^{4} 5523a^{13} 6736a^{5}

Aomen (IRE) *James Fanshawe* 86
3 b g Shamardal(USA) —Kathy Caerleon (IRE) (Caerleon (USA))
(1568)

Apace (IRE) *Sir Michael Stoute* a71 91
3 b f Oasis Dream—Much Faster (IRE) (Fasliyev (USA))
2074^{2} (2505) 3181^{6} 3778^{4} 5278^{7}

Apache (IRE) *A P O'Brien* 108
3 b c Galileo(IRE) —Charroux (IRE) (Darshaan)
3069^{14} 5283^{3}

Apache Glory (USA) *Richard Hannon* a74 86
3 bb f Cherokee Run(USA) —Jumeirah Glory (USA) (Deputy Minister (CAN))
214^{6} ◆ 434^{3} (624) (890) 2022^{6} (2849) (3632) 4429^{17} 4914^{9}

Apache Kid (IRE) *Ian Williams* a69 66
4 b g Antonius Pius(USA) —She's The Tops (Shernazar)
7370^{4} 7528^{10}

Apache Ridge (IRE) *Keith Dalgleish* a70 82
5 ch g Indian Ridge—Seraphina (IRE) (Pips Pride)
(22) 230^{2} 388^{2} 538^{2} (746) 880^{9} 1037^{2} 1539^{8} 2543^{3} (2765) 3000^{2} 3359^{6} 4378^{9} 7253^{6} 7412^{10} 7565^{5}

Apache Warrior *George Moore* 66
4 b g Westerner—Aldevonie (Green Desert (USA))
1210^{6} 1909^{12} 2393^{12} 3088^{11}

Apapane (JPN) *Sakae Kunieda* 115
4 b m King Kamehameha(JPN) —Salty Bid (USA) (Salt Lake (USA))
7410a^{3} 7731a^{13}

Apartman (CZE) *George Charlton*
6 b g Scater(POL) —Apartma (CZE) (Dara Monarch)
4874a^{10}

Apassionforfashion *Bryan Smart* a30
3 b f Beat Hollow—Trinny (Rainbow Quest (USA))
4014^{7} 5443^{9} 7069^{4} 7714^{13}

Aphrodisia *Ian Williams* a81 86
7 b m Sakhee(USA) —Aegean Dream (IRE) (Royal Academy (USA))
272^{4} 369^{2} 723^{2}

Aphrodisiac (FR) *J-L Pelletan* a49 61
3 b g Timboroa—Land Bound (USA) (Boundary (USA))
638a^{0}

Apilado (GER) *Wido Neuroth* 69
3 ch c Singspiel(IRE) —Algoma (GER) (Monsun (GER))
1433a^{6}

A Pocketful Of Rye (IRE) *Paul Howling* a54 55
4 b m Acclamation—Rye (IRE) (Charnwood Forest (IRE))
129^{3} 204^{8} 312^{6} 485^{11} 662^{8} 7812^{3} 7923^{5}

Apollo D'Negro (IRE) *Clive Cox* a75 79
3 br g Fasliyev(USA) —Special One (Aragon)
(1131) (1483) 2025^{3} 2508^{6} 2878^{3} 3598^{6} 4353^{6} (5171) 6167^{6}

Apollo Star (GER) *F Holcak* 100
9 ch g Devil River Peek(USA) —Arwina (GER) (Windwurf (GER))
7048a^{4}

Apostle (IRE) *Michael Bell* 85
2 gr g Dark Angel(IRE) —Rosy Dudley (IRE) (Grand Lodge (USA))
1396^{9} 2033^{2} 2318^{2} (3552) 4536^{12} 5216^{7}

Apothecary *John Gosden* a70
2 br f Manduro(GER) —Sister Maria (USA) (Kingmambo (USA))
(7757)

Apparel (IRE) *Ed Dunlop* a57 71
3 b f Cape Cross(IRE) —Independence (Selkirk (USA))
1270^{6} 1568^{10} 2225^{6} (4510) 5107^{12}

Appeal (IRE) *Sir Mark Prescott Bt* a75 62
3 gr f Selkirk(USA) —Amenixa (FR) (Linamix (FR))
5999^{5} 6404^{5} 6804^{6} (7363) (7461) 7900^{2}

Appealing (IRE) *Marco Botti* a70
2 b f Bertolini(USA) —Radiant Energy (IRE) (Spectrum (IRE))
7757^{2}

Appel Au Maitre (FR) *Wido Neuroth* 109
7 ch h Starborough—Rotina (FR) (Crystal Glitters (USA))
1128a^{3}

Applaude *Jason Ward* a38 69
6 b g Royal Applause—Flossy (Efisio)
4442^{9} 4946^{6} 5349^{13} 5485^{11} 6235^{7} 7078^{6} 7426^{7}

Applaudere *Jamie Osborne* a42
2 b f Royal Applause—Let Alone (Warning)
7464^{8} 7634^{12} 7757^{9}

Appleby (GER) *S Smrczek* a88 96
3 b c Mamool(IRE) —Almudena (GER) (Law Society (USA))
3672a^{14}

Apple Dumpling *Stuart Williams* a48
3 b f Haafhd—Divina Mia (Dowsing (USA))
253^{4} 406^{5} 898^{9} 942^{5}

Applique *C Boutin* a65 87
4 ch m Halling(USA) —Needlecraft (IRE) (Mark Of Esteem (IRE))
7015a^{3}

Appointee (IRE) *John Gosden* 74
2 b f Exceed And Excel(AUS) —Anna Wi'Yaak (JPN) (Dubai Millennium)
3362^{3} 4961^{3} 5514^{5} (5854)

Appointment *Ralph Smith* a52 51
6 ch m Where Or When(IRE) —Shoshone (Be My Chief (USA))
2198^{8} 2820^{4} 3281^{6} 3769^{3}

Apprimus (IRE) *Marco Botti* a100 100
5 b g Trans Island—Athlumney Dancer (Shareef Dancer (USA))
1188^{4} 2098^{6} 2540a^{5} 3411^{8} (4294)

Appyjack *Tony Carroll* a66 54
3 b g Royal Applause—Petrikov (IRE) (In The Wings)
(142) 406^{10} 3226^{9} 3596^{8} 4827^{6} 5352^{3} 5642^{4} (5832) 6253^{3} (6659) 6923^{10} 7198^{6}

Apreslepetitbois *James Bethell* 49
3 b f Proclamation(IRE) —Scotland The Brave (Zilzal (USA))
2574^{4} 3111^{4}

April Belle *Tim McCarthy* a10
3 br f Diktat—Dodona (Lahib (USA))
791^{9} 1270^{12} 2175^{8} 6242^{10}

April Ciel *Andrew Haynes* 54
2 b g Septieme Ciel(USA) —By Definition (IRE) (Definite Article)
4339^{9} 4996^{7} 5375^{5}

April Fool *Ronald Harris* a78 87
7 ch g Pivotal—Palace Affair (Pursuit Of Love)
12^{3} (341) (483) (556) 665^{2} 703^{3} 1035^{4} 1356^{2} (1866) (1917) 2155^{2} 2300^{8} (2789) 4310^{15} 4910^{6} 5970^{5} 6616^{7}

April Leyf (IRE) *Mark Brisbourne* a34 12
2 b f Kheleyf(USA) —Maroussies Rock (Rock Of Gibraltar (IRE))
6322^{7} 6697^{12} 6977^{6}

Apriority (USA) *David Fawkes* a114
4 b h Grand Slam(USA) —Midway Squall (USA) (Storm Bird (CAN))
7302a^{6}

Apro Lunare (IRE) *Laura Grizzetti* a87 84
5 b h Orpen(USA) —My Filly (FR) (Last Tycoon)
661a^{7}

Apticanti (USA) *B W Hills* 61
3 b f Aptitude(USA) —Musicanti (USA) (Nijinsky (CAN))
1620^{4}

Apurna *John Harris* 35
6 ch m Rock Of Gibraltar(IRE) —Dance Lesson (In The Wings)
2530^{11} 3637^{6} 4164^{8}

Aqua Ardens (GER) *George Baker* a57
3 b g Nayef(USA) —Arduinna (GER) (Winged Love (IRE))
7249^{6} 7717^{2}

Aqua Aura (USA) *Saeed Bin Suroor* a80
3 b f Distorted Humor(USA) —Crystal Crossing (IRE) (Royal Academy (USA))
7250^{4} 7401^{2}

Aqua Lad *Mark Johnston* a25 56
3 b g Garrison Savannah(NZ) —Caysue (Cayman Kai (IRE))
5082^{12} 6605^{3} 6868^{9} 7099^{11} 7357^{9}

Aquamarine (JPN) *M Delzangles* 99
3 b f Deep Impact(JPN) —Angelita (GER) (Gay Mecene (USA))
7510a^{4}

Aquarian Spirit *Richard Fahey* 86
4 b g Fantastic Light(USA) —Notable Lady (IRE) (Victory Note (USA))
(1560) 1970^{3} 2674^{6} 6290^{16} 6533^{15}

Aquasulis (IRE) *David Evans* a72 67
2 ch f Titus Livius(FR) —Christoph's Girl (Efisio)
1049^{5} 1268^{3} 1434^{10} 1954^{2} 2889^{2} (2998) 3435^{2} 3700^{8} 3810^{3} 4085^{5} 4756^{2} (5245) 5562^{12} (5896) 6222^{7} (6284) 6590^{10} 6864^{12}

Aqua Vitae (IRE) *Tor Sturgis* a60 58
4 ch m Camacho—Baileys Cream (Mister Baileys)
210^{3}

Aquilifer (IRE) *Mrs K Burke* a79 56
3 b g Holy Roman Emperor(IRE) —Sassy Bird (USA) (Storm Bird (CAN))
(53) (227) (335) ◆ 594^{3} 1317^{10} 2383^{13} 4812^{6} 5828^{13} (7362) 7637^{8}

Aquilla (IRE) *Sir Henry Cecil* 65
2 b f Teofilo(IRE) —Dance Troupe (Rainbow Quest (USA))
7232^{4} ◆

Aquilonius (IRE) *J S Bolger* a82 66
2 b c Soviet Star(USA) —Via Verbano (IRE) (Caerleon (USA))
2329a^{9}

Arabian Falcon *A Kleinkorres* 93
2 ch c Dutch Art—Castilian Queen (USA) (Diesis)
1360^{8} 1835^{5} 2214^{4} 3388^{5} 7155a^{5}

Arabian Flight *John Bridger* a59 44
2 b f Exceed And Excel(AUS) —Emirates First (IRE) (In The Wings)
2153^{9} 4319^{4} 4720^{7} 5316^{8} 5737^{4} 7482^{4} 7597^{3} 7798^{3}

Arabian Heights *Sir Mark Prescott Bt* a78 89
3 gr g Araafa(IRE) —Makhsusah (IRE) (Darshaan)
2174^{5} ◆ 2650^{6} ◆ 2924^{4} ◆ 3747^{2} (3925) ◆ 4161^{2} ◆ 5177^{6} 5466^{3} 6755^{3}

Arabian Pearl (IRE) *Peter Chapple-Hyam* a70 83
5 b m Refuse To Bend(IRE) —Intercede (Pursuit Of Love)
2286^{8} 2917^{8}

Arabian Pride *Keith Dalgleish* a58 27
4 b g Cadeaux Genereux—Noble Peregrine (Lomond (USA))
1695^{12} 2046^{7}

Arabian Spirit *Richard Fahey* a96 97
6 b g Oasis Dream—Royal Flame (IRE) (Royal Academy (USA))
1410^{5} 2105^{2} 2679^{7} 3315^{3} 3825^{4} 4100^{4} 4561^{13} 6173^{4} 6672^{5} 7161^{7}

Arabian Star (IRE) *Andrew Balding* 92
3 b g Green Desert(USA) —Kassiopeia (IRE) (Galileo (IRE))
1593^{5} (1862) 2287^{5} 2711^{6} (3557) 4959^{3} 5892^{3} (6302)

Arabic *James Fanshawe* a64 60
2 b g Dubai Destination(USA) —Artifice (Green Desert (USA))
6064^{6} 6474^{6} 6792^{5}

Arab League (IRE) *Richard Price* 83
6 b g Dubai Destination(USA) —Johnny And Clyde (USA) (Sky Classic (CAN))
2183^{4} (2459) 2931^{6} 3428^{3} 3911^{5} 4719^{7}

Arachis Bow *Michael Easterby* 51
2 b f Byron—Bow Peep (IRE) (Shalford (IRE))
2248^{4} 2485^{7} 3050^{6} 4019^{8}

Arachnophobia (IRE) *Martin Bosley* a79 81
5 b g Redback—La Mata (IRE) (Danehill Dancer (IRE))
1296^{7} 2206^{7} 6433^{5}

Arakette (IRE) *Paul Burgoyne* a33 27
4 b m Arakan(USA) —Etiquette (Law Society (USA))
1750^{13} 2198^{9}

Arakova (IRE) *Matthew Salaman* a44 24
3 b f Araafa(IRE) —Blast (USA) (Roar (USA))
3724^{10} 4657^{7} 6176^{7}

Araneide (USA) *C Scandella* a75 53
3 b c Aragorn(IRE) —Carini (Vettori (IRE))
638a^{2}

Arashi *Lucinda Featherstone* a71 73
5 b g Fantastic Light(USA) —Arriving (Most Welcome)
1107^{8} 1658^{4} 2526^{4} 2846^{8} 3311^{2} 3538^{7} 4024^{2}

Arashone *John Weymes* 49
3 b f Araafa(IRE) —Shoshone (Be My Chief (USA))
1858^{7} 2236^{5}

Arbalo (IRE) *R Feligioni*
3 b c Motivator—No Quest (IRE) (Rainbow Quest (USA))
1126a^{3}

Arbeejay *Bill Turner* a9 18
2 b f Iceman—Diliza (Dilum (USA))
1757^{8} 2640^{7} 3288^{11} 3779^{11} 5374^{11} 5625^{9}

Arca (FR) *J Rossi* a49
6 b g Sagacity(FR) —Val Mass (FR) (Cariellor (FR))
832a^{0} 1013a^{0}

Archarcharch (USA) *William H Fires* a119
3 bb c Arch(USA) —Woodman's Dancer (USA) (Woodman (USA))
1921a^{15}

Archbishop (USA) *Brian Meehan* 86
2 b c Arch(USA) —Avaricity (USA) (Carson City (USA))
(4446) ◆ 5181^{6}

Archelao (IRE) *Marcus Tregoning* a76 43
3 br g Cape Cross(IRE) —Brindisi (Dr Fong (USA))
6750^{5} 7111^{7} 7440^{4} 7921^{2}

Archers Prize (IRE) *Ed McMahon* a66 63
2 b c Dark Angel(IRE) —Silver Arrow (USA) (Shadeed (USA))
4068^{5} 6092^{3} 6539^{3}

Archers Road (IRE) *David Barron* 99
4 b g Titus Livius(FR) —Somoushe (IRE) (Black Minnaloushe (USA))
1476^{12} 1809^{10} 2117^{10} 2727^{16}

Arch Fire (USA) *Sir Michael Stoute* 99
3 b c Arch(USA) —Quickfire (Dubai Millennium)
1338^{9} (2930) 3844^{3} 4426^{2} 5275^{7} 5700^{5}

Archie Rice (USA) *Tom Keddy* a80 79
5 b g Arch(USA) —Gold Bowl (USA) (Seeking The Gold (USA))
162^{2} 315^{3} 1651^{6} 2436^{10} (2923) 3244^{5} 5568^{12} 6005^{10} 7346^{6} 7522^{4} (7604) (7734) (7817)

Archilini *Brian Ellison* a45 18
6 b g Bertolini(USA) —Dizzy Knight (Distant Relative)
57^{4} 150^{7} 545^{8} 573^{4} 675^{6} 793^{7}

Archina (IRE) *Andrew Balding* a46
2 b f Arch(USA) —Cross Your Fingers (USA) (Woodman (USA))
7751^{9}

Arch Of Colours *Mahmood Al Zarooni* a64
2 b f Monsun(GER) —Sunray Superstar (Nashwan (USA))
4662^{6}

Arch Support (USA) *Gary Contessa* 102
3 bb f Arch(USA) —Two Ninety Jones (USA) (Sir Harry Lewis (USA))
6183a^{5}

Arch Villain (IRE) *Amanda Perrett* a67 63
2 b g Arch(USA) —Barzah (IRE) (Darshaan)
6795^{11} 6994^{4} 7329^{5}

Arch Walker (IRE) *John Weymes* 70
4 ch g Choisir(AUS) —Clunie (Inchinor)
(1612) 1861^{4} 2845^{4} 3359^{3} 4041^{2} 7065^{7}

Arco Felice (USA) *Keith Goldsworthy* a54
4 b h Giant's Causeway(USA) —Better Than Honour (USA) (Deputy Minister (CAN))
284^{4} 448^{4}

Arctic (IRE) *Tracey Collins* 106
4 gr h Shamardal(USA) —Shawanni (Shareef Dancer (USA))
3010^{15} 3441a^{5} 4836a^{3} 5979a^{6} 6388a^{21}

Arcticality (IRE) *Richard Fahey* a33 57
2 ch f Camacho—Storm Weave (IRE) (Polar Falcon (USA))
1414^{7} 1939^{2} (2362) 2889^{4} 3491^{5} 5555^{9}

Arctic Cat (IRE) *Geoffrey Harker* a32 62
3 b g Oratorio(IRE) —Ivy Queen (IRE) (Green Desert (USA))
1655^{5} 2675^{5} ◆ 3325^{3} 4878^{4} 6357^{10} 7557^{11}

Arctic Cosmos (USA) *John Gosden* a93 121
4 b h North Light(IRE) —Fifth Avenue Doll (USA) (Marquetry (USA))
6519^{2} 6910a^{4}

Arctic Feeling (IRE) *Richard Fahey* a85 102
3 ch g Camacho—Polar Lady (Polar Falcon (USA))
1687^{12} 2456^{3} 2714^{14} 2928^{5} 3820^{16} 4333^{10} 5054^{16} 5288^{5} 6145^{12} 6347^{8}

Arctic Lynx (IRE) *John Best* a86 82
4 b g One Cool Cat(USA) —Baldemara (FR) (Sanglamore (USA))
(264) ◆ 698^{5} 961^{3} 5012^{4} 5718^{6} 7171^{11} 7457^{9} 7675^{2} 7893^{2}

Arctic Maiden *Willie Musson* a58 71
3 br f Iceman—Eglantine (IRE) (Royal Academy (USA))
1958^{9} 2838^{8} 3413^{4} 4111^{7} 4827^{RR} (5178) ◆ (5352) 6923^{4}

Arctic Mirage *Michael Blanshard* a63 71
3 b g Iceman—Marysienka (Primo Dominie)
1131^{4} 1611^{6} 2582^{3} 3122^{5} 3432^{6} 3783^{2} 4271^{2} 4917^{5} 5423^{6} 5970^{9} 6434^{6}

Arctic Reach *Brendan Powell* a53 50
3 b g Phoenix Reach(IRE) —Arctic Queen (Linamix (FR))
1769^{10} 1999^{4} 2243^{3} 3220^{2} 4491^{3} 5566^{6}

Arctic Stryker *John Best* a42 69
2 b c Iceman—Khafayif (USA) (Swain (IRE))
4848^{7} 5424^{2} ◆ 6281^{7}

Arctic Wings (IRE) *Tony Carroll* a55 64
7 b g In The Wings—Arctic Hunt (IRE) (Bering)
2272^{5}

Ardlui (IRE) *Henry Candy* 96
3 b c Galileo(IRE) —Epping (Charnwood Forest (IRE))
1407^{6} ◆ (2114) ◆ 3291^{3} 5283^{4} 6333^{7}

Ardmay (IRE) *Kevin Ryan* 63
2 b g Strategic Prince—Right After Moyne (IRE) (Imperial Ballet (IRE))
5337^{7} 5786^{5} 6230^{6}

Area Fifty One *William Muir* a87 92
3 b c Green Desert(USA) —Secret History (USA) (Bahri (USA))
(300) 2819^{2} 3376^{5} 3650^{5} (4489) 4751^{2} 5266^{2} 6218^{2} (6632)

Areef (IRE) *Michael Bell* a51 68
3 b f Kheleyf(USA) —Sanpala (Sanglamore (USA))
1288^{5} 1790^{2} 1945^{5}

Areeg (IRE) *Alan Berry* a30 47
4 b m Doyen(IRE) —Total Aloof (Groom Dancer (USA))
144^{6} 185^{8} 1038^{10} 1715^{6} 2047^{9} 2498^{10}

Arganil (USA) *Kevin Ryan* a105 98
6 ch g Langfuhr(CAN) —Sherona (USA) (Mr Greeley (USA))
(293) 700^{12} 1166^{7} 1680^{6} 2116^{5} 2620^{8} 3395^{8} 3704^{10} 4195^{3} 4416^{11} 4516^{2} 5163^{5} 6112^{9} 7578^{11} 7793a^{12}

Argentine (IRE) *Ian Semple* a64 75
7 b g Fasliyev(USA) —Teller (ARG) (Southern Halo (USA))
1073^{12} 2632^{7} 2987^{9} 3662^{7} 4017^{2} 4504^{5} 4539^{4} 4881^{6} 6044^{9} 6696^{4} 6943^{2} 7854^{2}

Argocat (IRE) *Tom Tate* 84
3 b g Montjeu(IRE) —Spirit Of South (AUS) (Giant's Causeway (USA))
1365^{4} 1811^{5} 2108^{4} 4050^{3} 4941^{6}

Argun River (IRE) *R Gibson* a63 96
4 b h Oasis Dream—Apperella (Rainbow Quest (USA))
840a^{0}

Ariel Bender *Peter Grayson* a44 44
4 gr g Needwood Blade—Wandering Stranger (Petong)
132^{5} 224^{9} 311^{5} 386^{12}

Ariete Arrollador *G Arizkorreta Elosegui* a106 90
4 b h Kingsalsa(USA) —Proud Douna (FR) (Kaldoun (FR))
(831a) (7678a)

Ari Gold (IRE) *Tom Dascombe* a28 62
3 b g Motivator—Holy Nola (USA) (Silver Deputy (CAN))
1810^{7} 2419^{5} 3720^{11} 4284^{5}

Arisea (IRE) *James Moffatt* a51 41
8 b m Cape Cross(IRE) —Castelfranca (IRE) (Scenic)
6137^{7}

Aristeia *Richard Hannon* a76 83
3 b f Invincible Spirit(IRE) —Presto Vento (Air Express (IRE))
2963^{5} 3122^{2} 3635^{6} 4199^{2} (4973) 7457^{6} 7602^{5}

Aristote *P Van De Poele* a100 108
5 ch h Domedriver(IRE) —Abime (USA) (Woodman (USA))
7733a^{4}

Ariyfa (IRE) *Noel Quinlan* a76 75
3 br f Cape Cross(IRE) —Arameen (IRE) (Halling (USA))
(7822)

Arizona High *Andrew Crook* a63
3 ch g Phoenix Reach(IRE) —Floriana (Selkirk (USA))
713^{4} 801^{2} 2305^{2} 7858^{10}

Arizona Jewel *Sir Henry Cecil* 90
3 b f Dansili—Rainbow Lake (Rainbow Quest (USA))
(1549) ◆ 2004^{4} 3065^{9}

Arizona John (IRE) *John Mackie* a87 89
6 b g Rahy(USA) —Preseli (IRE) (Caerleon (USA))
948^{5} 1325^{4} 2006^{7} 2220^{6} 2708^{3} 3344^{6} 3758^{7} 6155^{9} 6676^{11}

Arizona Run (FR) *F Rossi* 111
3 b c Hurricane Run(IRE) —Arizona Sun (IRE) (Spinning World (USA))
7404a^{4}

Arkadia *Rod Millman*
2 b f Arkadian Hero(USA) —Ebony Anne (IRE) (Danetime (IRE))
5655^{17}

Arkaim *Pam Sly* a68 49
3 b g Oasis Dream—Habariya (IRE) (Perugino (USA))
2019^{8} 2511^{6} 2848^{11} 6032^{6} 6494^{2} (6698) 7788^{4} 7885^{2}

Arlequin *James Bethell* a86 108
4 b h Rock Of Gibraltar(IRE) —Fairy Dance (IRE) (Zafonic (USA))
371a^{0} 661a^{10} 1154^{4} (1387) 2002^{3} 2573^{10} (4410) 5185^{2} 6339^{20}

Arley Hall *Richard Fahey* 76
2 ch f Excellent Art—Gee Kel (IRE) (Danehill Dancer (IRE))
4002^{2} ◆ 4571^{2} 5029^{7}

Arlington (GER) *J Hirschberger* 77
3 b c Tertullian(USA) —Aline (GER) (Tiger Hill (IRE))
2979a^{7}

Armiger *William Muir* a45 66
2 b g Araafa(IRE) —Welsh Valley (USA) (Irish River (FR))
2143[4] 2767[4] 3505[6] 4704[8] 5385[8] 5998[10] 6695[10]

Armigerent (IRE) *G Collet* a57 57
7 b h In The Wings—Roses From Ridey (IRE) (Petorius)
706a[7]

Armoise *Marco Botti* a64 81
3 b f Sadler's Wells(USA) —Di Moi Oui (Warning)
1332[4] 5449[5] (6037) 6607[4]

Army Of Stars (IRE) *Michael Blake* a80 49
5 ch h Kyllachy—Land Army (IRE) (Desert Style (IRE))
17[2] (159) 290[3] 394[3] 446[4] 547[3] 763[9] 869[6] 1295[4] 1995[12] 2605[5] 3241[2] 4865[4] 5901[4] 6664[11] 7228[12]

Arnold Lane (IRE) *Mick Channon* 93
2 b c Footstepsinthesand—Capriole (Noverre (USA))
(2148) 2488[4] 5263[2] 6466[2] 6688[14]

Arondo (GER) *Patrick Martin* a50 53
8 ch g Areion(GER) —Arrancada (GER) (Riboprince (USA))
899[5]

Around The Clock (USA) *Amanda Perrett* a68 69
3 bb g Bernardini(USA) —Plenty Of Light (USA) (Colony Light (USA))
1620[6] 2068[8] 3018[2] 3460[7] (5420) 5897[3] 6729[9]

Around The Moon (IRE) *Robert Collet* a86 90
2 b c Danehill Dancer(IRE) —Moon Flower (IRE) (Sadler's Wells (USA))
4624a[7] 6184a[6]

Arowana (IRE) *Zoe Davison* a59
3 b f Kodiac—Bali Royal (King's Signet (USA))
208 [6] 380[9] 2720[U] 6251[5] 6929[9]

Arqaam *Doug Watson* a84 38
7 b h Machiavellian(USA) —Khams-Alhawas (IRE) (Marju (IRE))
328a[6] 608a[12]

Arrigo (GER) *J Hirschberger* 114
3 b c Shirocco(GER) —Aiyana (GER) (Last Tycoon)
2345a[2] (3007a) 3672a[18] 6907a[2]

Arrivaderci *Richard Guest* a64 66
3 b f Kyllachy—Arrivato (Efisio)
2498[4] 3075[2] 4110[7] 4680[2] 6353[2] 6634[4] 6929[6] 7341[7] 7419[7] 7641[11]

Arriva La Diva *Linda Perratt* 69
5 ch m Needwood Blade—Hillside Girl (IRE) (Tagula (IRE))
1856[3] 2062[3] 2694[12] 3662[2] (3901) 4504[3] 5313[8] 5719[11]

Arrivederla (IRE) *Mme J Bidgood* a86 86
5 b m Acclamation—Alwiyda (USA) (Trempolino (USA))
7256a[4]

Arrow Lake (FR) *Noel Quinlan* a46 60
2 b f Refuse To Bend(IRE) —Lake Nipigon (Selkirk (USA))
4205[8] 5393[9] 6117[5] 6662[5]

Arrowroot *Tim Easterby* 53
2 b g Sleeping Indian—Queen's Pudding (IRE) (Royal Applause)
2120[6] ◆ 2731[7] 3274[12] 4892[4] 5645[7] 6835[5] 7108[10]

Arrow Storm (USA) *Tom Dascombe* a73 53
3 bb g Sunday Break(JPN) —Sugars For Nanny (USA) (Brocco (USA))
1589[5] 1949[9] (2642) 3049[8]

Arry's Orse *Bryan Smart* a89 81
4 b g Exceed And Excel(AUS) —Georgianna (IRE) (Petardia)
557[7] 1438[4] 1695[7] 5434[8] 6350[4] 6917[17]

Arsaadi (IRE) *Ed Dunlop* a70 92
2 b f Dubawi(IRE) —Arsad (IRE) (Cape Cross (IRE))
3046[4] (3812) 4252[2] 5296a[10] 6596[5]

Art Dzeko *Tim Easterby* 61
2 b g Acclamation—Delitme (IRE) (Val Royal (FR))
1071[7] 2033[11] 2831[3]

Arte Del Calcio *David Elsworth* 52
2 b c Manduro(GER) —Movie Queen (Danehill (USA))
5447[14]

Arteus *George Margarson* a96 94
5 b g Fantastic Light(USA) —Enchanted (Magic Ring (IRE))
2470[16] 4556[15] 5516[10]

Artful Dawkins *Bent Olsen* 59
3 b g Compton Place—Winning Girl (Green Desert (USA))
4840a[2]

Artful Lady (IRE) *George Margarson* 38
2 br f Excellent Art—Fear And Greed (IRE) (Brief Truce (USA))
5323[13] 6030[11] 6579[6]

Art History (IRE) *Mark Johnston* a92 97
3 gr c Dalakhani(IRE) —What A Picture (FR) (Peintre Celebre (USA))
(191) ◆ (1168) (1344) 1723[5] 3069[13] 4473[5] 4777[7] 5177[5] 5693[2] 5888[6] (6277) (6528)

Arthur's Edge *Christopher Mason* a104 92
7 b g Diktat—Bright Edge (Danehill Dancer (IRE))
3410[14]

Artic Dancer (IRE) *Stuart Williams* 50
2 b f Ad Valorem(USA) —Positano Princess (Tobougg (IRE))
2854[2] 3554[2]

Artic Rose (IRE) *R Bouresly* a68 59
3 b f Antonius Pius(USA) —Positano Princess (Tobougg (IRE))
151a[10] 238[12]

Artisan *Brian Ellison* a65 70
3 ch g Medicean—Artisia (IRE) (Peintre Celebre (USA))
1759[9] 2723[7] 3232[4] 4089[7] 4674[2] 5311[10]

Artistic Jewel (IRE) *Ed McMahon* 98
2 ch f Excellent Art—Danish Gem (Danehill (USA))
(4386) 4999[5] ◆ 5826[3] (6466) (7135)

Artistic Thread (IRE) *Sir Mark Prescott Bt* a59 60
2 b g Barathea(IRE) —Jellett (IRE) (Green Desert (USA))
3349[6] 3609[10] 4159[5] ◆ 4907[5] 5342[7] 6937[2] 7035[3]

Artists Corner *Richard Fahey* a62 73
2 ch f Dutch Art—Justbetweenfriends (USA) (Diesis)
2093[2] 2485[4] 2889[9] 3631[2] (4808) 5246[3] 6284[6] 6652[5] 6835[2] 7196[6] 7353[7] 7505[4]

Artlana *Julie Camacho* a38 58
2 b f Dutch Art—Latanazul (Sakhee (USA))
5727[13] (7108) 7336[6] 7568[8]

Art Law (IRE) *Brian Meehan* a64 65
2 b g Kheleyf(USA) —Snippets (IRE) (Be My Guest (USA))
3425[6] 4080[3] 4798[3] 5446[8] 6599[6]

Art Of Dreams (FR) *L Riccardi* 93
2 b c Dutch Art—Giant Dream (Giant's Causeway (USA))
3212a[4]

Art Of Gold *Amy Weaver* a28 10
2 br f Excellent Art—Siena Gold (Key Of Luck (USA))
5688[9] 6776[12]

Art Scholar (IRE) *Michael Appleby* a84 83
4 b g Pyrus(USA) —Marigold (FR) (Marju (IRE))
341[7] 433[4] 719[10] 1045[7] 1357[6] 1987[9] 2600[3] ◆ (2824) ◆ (2900) 3559[3] (3641) (4004) ◆ 4553[5] 4818[5] 6068[5] (6976) 7272[4] 7699[4] 7908[3]

Art Show *Ed Dunlop* a64 59
2 b f Dutch Art—Regina (Green Desert (USA))
5117[5] 5689[5] 6654[3] 6919[3] 7597[9] 7830[4]

Art Thief *Michael Appleby* a61 54
3 b g Catcher In The Rye(IRE) —Eurolink Sundance (Night Shift (USA))
1682[6] 2311[7] 2599[5] 4162[10] 4847[5] 5321[3] (5739) 7495[2] 7528[5] 7723[7] 7903[7]

Aruna (USA) *H Graham Motion* a113 114
4 bb m Mr Greeley(USA) —Surya (USA) (Unbridled (USA))
7284a[5]

Asaid *Saeed Bin Suroor* a81 83
3 b g Singspiel(IRE) —Forum Floozie (NZ) (Danasinga (AUS))
4805[2] ◆ 5911[3] 6286[2] 6810[2]

Asanga (USA) *J E Hammond* a81 69
3 b c Smart Strike(CAN) —Surfside (USA) (Seattle Slew (USA))
980a[0]

Asatir (USA) *Saeed Bin Suroor* a89 79
2 b c Elusive Quality(USA) —Valid Warning (USA) (Valid Appeal (USA))
(4122) ◆ (7390)

Ascensive *Ralph Beckett* 30
3 ch f Pivotal—Tincture (Dr Fong (USA))
3824[10] 6804[11]

As De Trebol (USA) *M Delcher-Sanchez* a100 96
5 gr h Tapit(USA) —Adelphi (USA) (Danzig (USA))
606a[3] 756a[3] 997a[11] 2744a[6]

Asfurah's Image *Marco Botti* a57 65
3 br f Diktat—Asfurah (USA) (Dayjur (USA))
360[4]

Ashammar (FR) *Paul Webber* a70 69
6 b g King's Best(USA) —Asharna (IRE) (Darshaan)
6017[4] 6445[6] (7036) 7738[P] (Dead)

Ashbina *William Haggas* a70 69
2 b f Royal Applause—Crystal Power (USA) (Pleasant Colony (USA))
4474[5] 5299[3] 5541[3] 6281[2] 6921[9]

Ashbrittle *Ralph Beckett* 101
4 b g Rainbow Quest(USA) —Caesarea (GER) (Generous (IRE))
2499[5] 3013[10] 5705[6] 6690[9] 7406a[8]

Ash Cloud (IRE) *Tom Dascombe* a45 64
3 b f Hurricane Run(IRE) —Nasharaat (IRE) (Green Desert (USA))
1474[0] 1810[6] 2360[5] 3303[2]

Ashdown Lad *William Jarvis* a51
2 ch g Sir Percy—Antibes (IRE) (Grand Lodge (USA))
7835[7]

Asheerah *Kevin Prendergast* a79 99
3 b f Shamardal(USA) —Adaala (USA) (Sahm (USA))
2012a[10] 3444a[7] 4132a[9]

Ashes Star *Jonathan Portman* 28
2 b c Aussie Rules(USA) —Aptina (USA) (Aptitude (USA))
4384[8] 5564[13] 6178[9]

Ashgrove Nell (IRE) *Daniel Mark Loughnane* a63 60
3 b f Ad Valorem(USA) —Pennycairn (Last Tycoon)
4381[3] (6310) 6877[8] 7805[13] 7902[7]

Ashiri (IRE) *Sir Michael Stoute* 86
3 ch c Hurricane Run(IRE) —Gorband (USA) (Woodman (USA))
1338[6] 4157[4] 4617[2]

Ashkalara *Stuart Howe* a51 71
4 b m Footstepsinthesand—Asheyana (IRE) (Soviet Star (USA))
1868[6] 2872[7] 3632[10] 4949[2] (5538) 5962[8] 6888[6]

Ashkan *William Haggas* a31 55
2 b c Nayef(USA) —South Club Hill (Danehill (USA))
4276[13] 4525[6] 6344[5] 6667[9] 6937[14]

Ashpan Sam *John Spearing* 72
3 b c Firebreak—Sweet Patoopie (Indian Ridge)
3308[4] 3779[4] 4823[5] ◆ 5562[5] (6232) 7261[2]

Ashram (IRE) *Saeed Bin Suroor* a108 113
5 ch g Indian Haven—Tara's Girl (IRE) (Fayruz)
152a[5] 606a[11]

Ashva (USA) *Michael Dods* a80 95
3 b g Quiet American(USA) —Pondicherry (USA) (Sir Wimborne (USA))
(1027) 1384[4] 2030[5] 3067[12] 3830[5] 4467[12]

Ashwaat *Mark Johnston* 51
2 br c Authorized(IRE) —Asawer (IRE) (Darshaan)
6230[7] 6644[5]

Asifa (IRE) *Saeed Bin Suroor* a84 76
2 b c Green Desert(USA) —Agata (FR) (Poliglote)
5565[6] 6018[3] (6481) (7358)

Asiland (FR) *D Prod'Homme* a64 63
3 b f Lando(GER) —A Sinda (FR) (Sinndar (IRE))
480a[8]

Asiya (IRE) *Norman Cassidy* a86 91
5 b m Dilshaan—Alyska (IRE) (Owington)
5748a[2] 7544a[8]

Askar Tau (FR) *Marcus Tregoning* a106 113
6 b g Montjeu(IRE) —Autriche (IRE) (Acatenango (GER))
1188[3] (1601) 2072[6] 3066[5]

Askaud (IRE) *David Nicholls* a68 97
3 b f Iffraaj—Tarabaya (IRE) (Warning)
1837[2] ◆ 2188[7] 2634[7] 4325[5] ◆ (4429) 5483[12] 5730[12] (6330) 7296[5] 7584[6]

Ask Jack (USA) *Joseph G Murphy* a89 106
7 ch g Mt. Livermore(USA) —Moll (USA) (Criminal Type (USA))
3444a[4] 4418a[14] 4566a[12]

Ask The Moon (USA) *Martin D Wolfson* a119
6 b m Malibu Moon(USA) —Always Asking (USA) (Valid Appeal (USA))
7285a[6]

Aslana (IRE) *P Schiergen* 105
4 b m Rock Of Gibraltar(IRE) —Alte Kunst (IRE) (Royal Academy (USA))
1575a[4] 3531a[4] 5528a[5]

Asleep In Penn *Peter Niven* a10
3 ch g Cadeaux Genereux—Midnight Shift (IRE) (Night Shift (USA))
7822[9]

A Southside Boy (GER) *Jim Goldie* 42
3 b g Samum(GER) —Anthurium (GER) (Hector Protector (USA))
1542[7] 2730[2] 5152[4] 5489[6]

Asparella *Raymond York* a9
2 b f Equerry(USA) —Aspra (FR) (Green Tune (USA))
7118[14] 7598[8]

Aspasia De Mileto *C Laffon-Parias* 103
3 b f Hurricane Run(IRE) —Fabulous Speed (USA) (Silver Hawk (USA))
4036b[5]

Aspectoflove (IRE) *Saeed Bin Suroor* a103 111
5 b m Danetime(IRE) —Rose Vibert (Caerleon (USA))
(241) 607a[7]

Aspectus (IRE) *Jamie Osborne* a82 101
8 ch h Spectrum(IRE) —Anna Thea (IRE) (Turfkonig (GER))
1269[11] 1829[8] 2207[2] 3285[11] 4066[3] 4278[11] 5200[3] 5669[9] 6231[7] 6796[7]

Aspro Mavro (IRE) *Jim Best* a77 81
5 b g Spartacus(IRE) —Alexia Reveuse (IRE) (Dr Devious (IRE))
2150[8] 2769[3] 3434[RR] 3739[RR]

Asraab (IRE) *Saeed Bin Suroor* 95
4 b h Oasis Dream—Alexander Queen (IRE) (King's Best (USA))
1594[4] 6341[11]

Assizes *Mark Johnston* 84
2 gr c Teofilo(IRE) —Requesting (Rainbow Quest (USA))
(6993)

Astarix (FR) *E Danel* a63 95
6 gr h Sagamix(FR) —Abaya (GER) (Surumu (GER))
5095a[0]

Asterisk *John Berry* a57 66
4 b m Fantastic Light(USA) —Sydney Star (Machiavellian (USA))
184[10] 524[13]

Asterism *Sir Henry Cecil* a82 56
3 b f Motivator—Star Cluster (Observatory (USA))
2648[10] 3519[5] (6054)

Astonished Harry (GER) *Roy Hollinshead* a90 48
2 b g Dubai Destination(USA) —Aijala (FR) (Night Shift (USA))
4402[6] 4919[5] 5393[7] 6260[16]

Astragal *Andrew Balding* a23 60
3 b f Shamardal(USA) —Landinium (ITY) (Lando (GER))
6377[2] 6810[7] 7360[7] 7671[11]

Astra Hall *Ralph Beckett* a49
2 ch f Halling(USA) —Star Precision (Shavian)
7521[9]

Astraios (IRE) *Brian Meehan* a66 60
2 b c Oratorio(IRE) —Paper Moon (IRE) (Lake Coniston (IRE))
3590[8] 4201[9] 4748[7] 5343[11] 5634[11] 6471[2] 6763[3] 7735[3]

Astrakhan (TUR) *Z Temucin* 97
4 b h Sri Pekan(USA) —Primelta (Primo Dominie)
5777a[7]

Astrantia *Sir Henry Cecil* a68 65
3 b f Dansili—Ausherra (USA) (Diesis)
2648[7] 3224[5] 4279[5]

Astrodiva *Mark H Tompkins* a58 61
5 b m Where Or When(IRE) —Astromancer (USA) (Silver Hawk (USA))
277[9] 569[2] 3311[9]

Astrogold *Mark H Tompkins* 49
2 ch f Motivator—Mega (IRE) (Petardia)
7164[12]

Astroleo *Mark H Tompkins* a50 55
5 ch g Groom Dancer(USA) —Astrolove (IRE) (Bigstone (IRE))
39[3] 373[6] 1596[8] 2272[2] (2451) 2991[5] 3353[3] 3946[2]

Astrolibra *Mark H Tompkins* a33 58
7 b m Sakhee(USA) —Optimistic (Reprimand)
4164[4] 5519[4] 6613[7]

Astrology (IRE) *A P O'Brien* 108
2 b c Galileo(IRE) —Ask For The Moon (FR) (Dr Fong (USA))
5293a[3] 6692[3]

Astrology (USA) *Steven Asmussen* a117
3 b c A.P. Indy(USA) —Quiet Eclipse (USA) (Quiet American (USA))
2328a[3]

Astromagick *Mark H Tompkins* 77
3 b f Rainbow Quest(USA) —Astrocharm (IRE) (Charnwood Forest (IRE))
2065[7] 3325[5] 3770[2] 4190[2] (6104) ◆ 6707[6]

Astromoon *Mark H Tompkins* 55
4 b m Beat Hollow—Astromancer (USA) (Silver Hawk (USA))
2569[6] 2856[5] 3622[9] 5122[4] 5566[8]

Astronomy Domine *John Gosden* 58
2 b f Galileo(IRE) —Platonic (Zafonic (USA))
5029[9]

Astrophysical Jet *Ed McMahon* 114
4 b m Dubawi(IRE) —Common Knowledge (Rainbow Quest (USA))
1687[13] 3010[10] 3644[9] 6164[6] 6522[13]

Astroscarlet *Mark H Tompkins* a47 30
2 ch f Carnival Dancer—Astrolove (IRE) (Bigstone (IRE))
6018[9] 6458[15] 6795[10] 7432[2] 7708[3]

Astrovenus *Mark H Tompkins* a24 55
4 ch m Tobougg(IRE) —Astrolove (IRE) (Bigstone (IRE))
3352[5] 3769[2] 4732[6] 5628[5] 6798[8]

Astroverdi *Mark H Tompkins* 33
3 b g Green Desert(USA) —Nutmeg (IRE) (Lake Coniston (IRE))
2848[15] 3177[9] 3781[9] 4929[10]

Asulaman (GER) *Mario Hofer* a79 72
4 b g Sulamani(IRE) —Andrelhina (Tirol)
196a[4]

Atacama Sunrise *George Prodromou* a69 70
5 b m Desert Sun—Top Of The Morning (Keen)
90[5] 390[2] 553[4] 687[7] 897[6] 1063[9] 1233[9]

At A Premium (FR) *X Thomas-Demeaulte*
2 b c Dubai Destination(USA) —Lexington Dream (FR) (Peintre Celebre (USA))
7664a[4]

At First Sight (IRE) *Robert Hickmott* 117
4 ch h Galileo(IRE) —Healing Music (FR) (Bering)
7115a[2] 7218a[10]

Athaakeel (IRE) *Ronald Harris* a69 63
5 b m Almutawakel—Asaafeer (USA) (Dayjur (USA))
97[5] 231[3] 351[6] 487[7] 654[4] 746[3] 928[3] 1044[7] 1279[4] (2205) 2554[6] (3254) 3476[8] 4206[3] 4640[3] 4973[10] 5677[3] 6177[6] 6889[5] 7172[8] 7629[11] 7844[8]

Athenian (IRE) *Sir Mark Prescott Bt* a55
2 b f Acclamation—Ziria (IRE) (Danehill Dancer (IRE))
6252[9] 6612[3] 6946[8]

Athenian Garden (USA) *Richard Guest* a69 70
4 b m Royal Academy(USA) —Webee (USA) (Kingmambo (USA))
7745[5]

Athens (IRE) *A P O'Brien* 93
2 b c Dylan Thomas(IRE) —Rafina (USA) (Mr Prospector (USA))
5254[4] ◆ 6391a[3]

Athletic *Andrew Reid* a37
2 b g Doyen(IRE) —Gentle Irony (Mazilier (USA))
7758[4] 7938[6]

Athlumney Lass (IRE) *H Rogers* a68 35
2 br f Holy Roman Emperor(IRE) —Lady Gregory (IRE) (In The Wings)
7275a[8]

Athwaab *Noel Chance* a58 73
4 b m Cadeaux Genereux—Ahdaaf (USA) (Bahri (USA))
137[3] 197[6] 658[4] 812[4] 1336[7] (1523) 1787[2] (1938) 2193[5] 3579[6] 4046[3] 4395[3] 4895[6] 5658[3] 6815[9] 6932[9] 7512[11]

Atia *Jonathan Portman* a52 66
3 b f Royal Applause—Chrysalis (Soviet Star (USA))
1579[9] 1980[3] 2549[9] 3956[9] 4466[2] 5344[4] 5780[2] 6784[8] 6889[6]

Atila Sher Danon (GER) *W Hickst* a74 86
5 b h Sholokhov(IRE) —Art Of Easter (GER) (Dashing Blade)
5095a[4]

Atlantic Beach *Milton Bradley* a75 82
6 ch g Kyllachy—Amused (Prince Sabo)
1140[6] 1444[8] 1752[4] 1899[5] 2244[7] 2832[6] 3471[2] 3713[4] 5658[7] 7116[7] 7395[3] (7566) 7588[7] 7804[3] 7917[8]

Atlantic Brave *M Al Muhairi* a106 54
5 b h Piccolo—Princess Anabaa (FR) (Anabaa (USA))
152a[16] 604a[6]

Atlantic Cycle (IRE) *Milton Bradley* a72 75
4 ch m Stormy Atlantic(USA) —Cycle Of Life (USA) (Spinning World (USA))
3166[8] 3579[7] (4174) 4628[6] 5238[4] 6119[3] 7106[13] 7395[4] 7512[9] 7567[7] 7649[11]

Atlantico (SPA) *Y Durepaire* 51
6 b g Denver County(USA) —Astrid Phone (ARG) (Speakerphone (USA))
935a[6]

Atlantic Sport (USA) *Mick Channon* a105 106
6 b h Machiavellian(USA) —Shy Lady (FR) (Kaldoun (FR))
155a[7] 326a[5] 497a[4] 583a[4] 678a[4] 3109[13] 3626[2] 4092[6] 4314[5] 4534[9] 5060[15] 5699[5] 6209[2] 6521[8]

Atlantic Story (USA) *Michael Easterby* a104 79
9 bb g Stormy Atlantic(USA) —Story Book Girl (USA) (Siberian Express (USA))
429[4] 844[12]

Atlantic Swing (USA) *John M Oxx* a98 87
3 b f Stormy Atlantic(USA) —Turning Wheel (USA) (Seeking The Gold (USA))
7277a[3]

Atlantis Crossing (IRE) *Jim Boyle* a57 47
2 b g Elusive City(USA) —Back At De Front (IRE) (Cape Cross (IRE))
3408[5] 4455[5] 5812[11] 6937[7] 7081[10] (7251) 7358[7]

Atlantis Star *Mahmood Al Zarooni* a105 99
4 b h Cape Cross(IRE) —Ladeena (IRE) (Dubai Millennium)
326a[13] 605a[12] 827a[10] 5704[8] 6747[3] 7023[8]

Atlas Peak (IRE) *John G Carr* a71 65
6 b g Namid—My Delilah (IRE) (Last Tycoon)
6511a[13]

Atlas Shrugged (IRE) *Clive Cox* 69
3 bb g Red Ransom(USA) —Kalambara (IRE) (Bluebird (USA))
1139[6] 1407[11] 2253[9] 3002[3]

Atmanna *Clive Brittain* a48
2 br f Manduro(GER) —Samdaniya (Machiavellian (USA))
5689[8]

Atraaf (IRE) *Marcus Tregoning* a81
3 b c Intikhab(USA) —Kismah (Machiavellian (USA))
1234[P] (Dead)

Atromos (FR) *L Nyffels*
4 ch g Green Tune(USA) —Akhla (USA) (Nashwan (USA))
1011a[0]

Attenborough (USA) *Jeremy Noseda* 77
2 bb c Medaglia D'Oro(USA) —Julie's Prospect (USA) (Allen's Prospect (USA))
(4714) ◆

Attiki Oddo *P Monfort* a50 89
4 b g Footstepsinthesand—Chanteleau (USA) (A.P. Indy (USA))
5195a[8]

Attracted To You (IRE) *Richard Hannon* 88
3 b f Hurricane Run(IRE) —Haute Volta (FR) (Grape Tree Road)
1361[2]

Attraction Ticket *David Simcock* a61 58
2 b c Selkirk(USA) —Trick (IRE) (Shirley Heights)
6529[10] 7094[4]

Attrition *Andrew Reid* a64 50
4 b g Selkirk(USA) —Barsine (IRE) (Danehill (USA))
401[10] (545) 690[2] 743[2] 857[3] 1287[5] 2164[7]

Attwaal (IRE) *Roger Varian* 41
2 b g Teofilo(IRE) —Qasirah (IRE) (Machiavellian (USA))
7232[14]

Atyaab *Alan Swinbank* a73 72
4 b m Green Desert(USA) —Aspen Leaves (USA) (Woodman (USA))
2781[10] 4780[9] 5394[8] 6084[12]

Aubrietia *Edward Vaughan* 33
2 b f Dutch Art—Petong's Pet (Petong)
6300[10] 6758[7] 7056[8]

Auburn Lady *Alan Brown* 56
3 ch f Tobougg(IRE) —Carati (Selkirk (USA))
7781[8] 7912[7]

Audacious *Sir Michael Stoute* 87
3 b g Motivator—Flash Of Gold (Darshaan)
(1897) 2471[7] 4316[6] 4959[6]

Audemar (IRE) *Edward Vaughan* a97 92
5 ch g Exceed And Excel(AUS) —Bathe In Light (USA) (Sunshine Forever (USA))
180[5] 353[4] 438[2] 615[10] 3436[3] 4537[8] 5888[5] 6631[6]

Auden (USA) *Mahmood Al Zarooni* a92 79
3 b g Librettist(USA) —Moyesii (USA) (Diesis)
7204[3] 7328[11]

Auenwiese (GER) *S Cerulis* a56
7 b m Lando(GER) —Anatina (GER) (Big Shuffle (USA))
832a[6]

Auld Burns *Richard Hannon* 109
3 gr g Pastoral Pursuits—Crackle (Anshan)
(1339) 1548[3] 2191[4] 3068[10] 3405[6] (4022) 4788[2]

Aultcharn (FR) *Brian Meehan* a81 79
4 b g Kyllachy—Nuit Sans Fin (FR) (Lead On Time (USA))
2207[7] 2653[3] 2995[9]

A. U. Miner (USA) *Clark Hanna* a119
6 bb h Mineshaft(USA) —Clerical Etoile (ARG) (The Watcher (USA))
7300a[P]

Auntie Joy *Michael Easterby* a61 64
2 b f Pursuit Of Love—Aunt Hilda (Distant Relative)
1691[4] ◆ 2160[2] 2983[2] 3242[5] 3700[3] 4178[5]

Auntie Kathryn (IRE) *Stuart Williams* a48 44
2 b f Acclamation—Congress (IRE) (Dancing Brave (USA))
3463[9] 4155[13] 6018[10] 7342[2] 7432[11]

Aunty Mavis (IRE) *Ronald Harris* 28
2 ch f Sakhee(USA) —Sunlight (IRE) (Sinndar (IRE))
4205[13] 5325[9] 5802[8]

Aureate *Brian Forsey* a60 41
7 ch g Jade Robbery(USA) —Anne D'Autriche (IRE) (Rainbow Quest (USA))
596[7] 5916[10] 6182[9] 6287[4] 6613[3] 6873[6]

Aurens (IRE) *Michael Attwater* a62
2 b g One Cool Cat(USA) —Al Aqabah (IRE) (Redback)
7837[2]

Aurivorous *Anabel K Murphy* a30 58
3 ch f Reel Buddy(USA) —Vax Rapide (Sharpo)
1521[6] 2294[10] 2660[6] 5172[5] 5941[8]

Aurora Lights *Richard Fahey* a50
4 ch m Fantastic Light(USA) —Sweet Revival (Claude Monet (USA))
340[10] 574[2] 748[9] 969[7] 7639[10] 7805[10]

Aurora Sky (IRE) *Liam Corcoran* a79 77
5 gr m Hawk Wing(USA) —To The Skies (USA) (Sky Classic (CAN))
1772[5] 2156[5] 7328[12]

Aurorian (IRE) *Richard Hannon* a87 92
5 b g Fantastic Light(USA) —Aurelia (Rainbow Quest (USA))
1105[3] 1729[2] 2716[5] 4354[9]

Aussie Blue (IRE) *Richard Whitaker* a75 73
7 b g Bahamian Bounty—Luanshya (First Trump)
1150[12] 1460[7] 1621[6] 2985[12] 3462[8] 3936[8] 4076[3] 4679[10] 5248[2] 5740[2] 6098[8] (6544) 6878[9] 7146[12]

Aussie Dollar (IRE) *Andrew Balding* a68 58
3 b g Dansili—Spectacular Show (IRE) (Spectrum (IRE))
121[3]

Aussie Guest (IRE) *Mick Channon* 58
2 br g Aussie Rules(USA) —Scylla Cadeaux (IRE) (Cadeaux Genereux)
3793[7] 4264[7] 6123[10] 6628[3] 6817[14] 6937[15]

Australia Day (IRE) *Paul Webber* a98 103
8 gr g Key Of Luck(USA) —Atalina (FR) (Linamix (FR))
3013[12] 4778[10]

Autarch (USA) *Amanda Perrett* 71
2 ch g Gone West(USA) —Vargas Girl (USA) (Deputy Minister (CAN))
5891[13] 6953[4] 7109[4]

Authora (IRE) *Richard Hannon* a40 60
2 b f Authorized(IRE) —Danseuse Du Soir (IRE) (Thatching)
4614[11] 6127[4] 6291[7] 7051[17] 7432[10]

Authoritarian *Richard Hannon* a22 50
2 b f Authorized(IRE) —Favourita (Diktat)
6603[11] 7118[12]

Autobahn *Mahmood Al Zarooni* a54 75
3 b c Tiger Hill(IRE) —Ventura Highway (Machiavellian (USA))
2058[4] 2371[3]

Autocracy *Eric Alston* a69 63
4 b g Green Desert(USA) —Imperial Bailiwick (IRE) (Imperial Frontier (USA))
1861[5] 3662[15] 4017[8] 4461[5]

Auto Mac *Neville Bycroft* 72
3 b g Auction House(USA) —Charlottevalentina (IRE) (Perugino (USA))
1436[2] 1693[11] 2392[3] 3246[7] (3933) 5370[7] 6262[3] 6538[3] 6576[3] 7024[13] 7214[4]

Automotive *Julia Feilden* a63 53
3 b g Beat Hollow—Bina Ridge (Indian Ridge)
6668[6] 7754[2]

Autumn Blades (IRE) *Ruth Carr* a103 103
6 ch g Daggers Drawn(USA) —September Tide (IRE) (Thatching)
4774[10] 4993[13] 7352[13] 7565[2] 7726[2] 7776[5]

Autumn Fire *Andrew Balding* 60
2 b f Avonbridge—Brand (Shareef Dancer (USA))
7258[6]

Auvano (GER) *R Dzubasz* 108
7 b g Silvano(GER) —Auenfeuer (GER) (Big Shuffle (USA))
6595a[2] 7048a[5] 7409a[10]

Auzi (FR) *J Rossi* a70 67
8 b g Commands(AUS) —Time For Romance (IRE) (Cure The Blues (USA))
395a[8] 1142a[4] 5095a[0]

Available (IRE) *Richard Hannon* a52 72
2 b f Moss Vale(IRE) —Divert (IRE) (Averti (IRE))
6603[4] 6787[4]

Availed Speaker (IRE) *Richard Fahey* a65
2 ch g Iffraaj—Privileged Speech (USA) (General Assembly (USA))
7555[4] 7724[4] 7855[4]

Avalon Bay *Pat Eddery* a65 67
3 b g Avonbridge—Feeling Blue (Missed Flight)
(987) 1149[4] 1566[2] 1949[12] 2197[8] 3783[12] 4544[9] 4911[7] 5644[5] 5901[6] 7507[4] 7656[8] 7807[6]

Avanti (GER) *H J Groschel* 97
3 b c Malinas(GER) —Alphabetique (FR) (Zieten (USA))
2345a[5]

Avanti Albert (IRE) *A J Martin* a81 80
7 b g King Charlemagne(USA) —Albertville (GER) (Top Ville)
7378a[4] 7548a[8]

Avec Moi *Christine Dunnett* a53 51
4 b m Reset(AUS) —Pardon Moi (First Trump)
743[7] 1171[9] 1287[9] 1989[5] 2268[9] 2829[8] 3495[3] 4025[4] 4729[3] 6070[4] 6610[8]

Aventura (JPN) *Katsuhiko Sumii* 115
3 b f Jungle Pocket(JPN) —Admire Sunday (JPN) (Sunday Silence (USA))
7410a[2]

Avenue Express (IRE) *F-X De Chevigny* a69 46
3 b f Anabaa Blue—Passiflore (FR) (Sillery (USA))
288a[6]

Averroes (IRE) *Clive Cox* a88 107
4 ch h Galileo(IRE) —Shapely (USA) (Alleged (USA))
1102[6] 2071[2] 3156[3] (4778)

Avertis *Alastair Lidderdale* a67 84
6 b g Averti(IRE) —Double Stake (USA) (Kokand (USA))
4958[8] 6378[9] 6759[6] 7050[4] 7517[6] 7887[6]

Avertuoso *Bryan Smart* a43 75
7 b g Averti(IRE) —First Musical (First Trump)
2987[7] 4152[6] 4289[5] 4539[8] 5732[9] 6802[11] 7079[12] 7266[9]

Ave Sofia *John Holt* a40 52
2 b f Byron—Snoozy (Cadeaux Genereux)
2387[5] 2914[7] 4021[3] 4474[3] 4922[5] 5727[14] 6628[11]

Aviator (GER) *T Mundry* 103
3 b c Motivator—Amore (GER) (Lando (GER))
5308a[5] 6200a[5]

Avid Kale *Marco Botti* a79 75
3 gr g Keltos(FR) —Lake Diva (Docksider (USA))
1335[2] ◆

Avienus (AUS) *Mark C Webb* 117
6 b m Reset(AUS) —Genova (IRE) (Darshaan)
6713a[2] 7044a[13]

Aviso (GER) *David Evans* a76 75
8 b g Tertullian(USA) —Akasma (GER) (Windwurf (GER))
12[7] 341[5] 556[7] 806[8] 928[4] 1276[3] 1637[5] 2027[7] 2242[2] 2616[2] 3130[5] 3726[5] 4465[3] 4754[4] 5002[10] 6033[8] 6228[2] 6587[5] 6764[9] 6814[2] 6971[7] 7176[5] 7268[12] 7632[4] 7817[12]

Avison (IRE) *Richard Fahey* a58 68
3 b g Diamond Green(FR) —Actoris (USA) (Diesis)
6097[5] 7004[5] 7158[2]

Avon Blaise *Peter Hedger* a21 53
4 b m Avonbridge—Blaise Castle (USA) (Irish River (FR))
3980[6] 4826[5] 5386[7] 5916[14]

Avonbridge Lad *Alan Brown* 25
2 b g Avonbridge—All My Gold (GER) (Deploy)
6532[12] 6774[13] 7240[7]

Avoncharm *Mel Brittain* a14 53
3 b f Avonbridge—Be My Charm (Polish Precedent (USA))
5793[3] 6834[8] 7648[11] 7775[11]

Avoncreek *Brian Baugh* a51 55
7 b g Tipsy Creek(USA) —Avondale Girl (IRE) (Case Law)
752[4] 1248[4] 2162[6] 2990[4] 3943[2] (4563) 5309[9] 5677[4] 5881[8] 6694[8]

Avongrove *A Fabre* 105
3 b f Tiger Hill(IRE) —Vituisa (Bering)
2750a[4] 3447a[6]

Avon Lady *James Fanshawe* a96 96
4 b m Avonbridge—Delightful Rhythm (USA) (Diesis)
1610[7] 4509[2] ◆ 5016[6] 5702[5] 6219[2] (6770) 7128[4] 7516[12]

Avon Light *Milton Bradley* a41 55
3 ch g Avonbridge—Veronese (USA) (Bianconi (USA))
110[8] 253[5] 437[8] 558[8] 4431[10] 4950[3] 5540[9] 5674[5] 5864[7] (5996) 6610[15] 6889[4] 6999[8]

Avonlini *Brian Baugh* a59 55
5 b m Bertolini(USA) —Avondale Girl (IRE) (Case Law)
734[3] 912[3] 1247[7] (2161) 3714[2] 4230[5] 4564[12] 5244[11]

Avonmore Star *Richard Hannon* a75 95
3 b g Avonbridge—Pooka's Daughter (IRE) (Eagle Eyed (USA))
1322[2] ◆ 1725[9] 2508[7] 3535[6] 4333[19] 4779[6] 5972[8] 6467[12] 7138[4]

Avon Pearl *Henry Candy* 75
2 ch c Avonbridge—Warden Rose (Compton Place)
2584[6] 2962[2] (3511) 4536[8] 6166[8]

Avon Rising *Derek Shaw*
4 b g Avonbridge—Fairy Flight (IRE) (Fairy King (USA))
4863[9] 4923[7] 6251[9]

Avon River *Richard Hannon* a93 92
4 ch g Avonbridge—Night Kiss (FR) (Night Shift (USA))
99[10] (188) 525[8] 963[8] 1103[2] 1760[14] (1828) 2310[2] 2884[13] 3537[2] 3764[2] 4445[3] 4997[10] 5408[2] (6017) (6465) 6589[2] (6785)

Avonrose *Derek Shaw* a82 85
4 b m Avonbridge—Loveleaves (Polar Falcon (USA))
38[3] 160[3] 273[2] 405[3] 508[2] (736) 865[2] 1406[18] 1884[5] 2300[7] 2566[6] 6831[10] 7199[9] 7486[8] 7625[5] 7715[11] 7928[8]

Avon Supreme *Gay Kelleway* a61 57
3 ch f Avonbridge—Fredora (Inchinor)
3191[3] 4244[10] 4745[2] 6938[14] 7085[3] 7333[4] 7639[2] 7891[8]

Avontuur (FR) *Ruth Carr* a54 76
9 ch g Kabool—Ipoh (FR) (Funambule (USA))
577[10] 880[11] 1164[10] 2161[6] 2543[8]

Avonvalley *Peter Grayson* a64 75
4 b m Avonbridge—Piper's Ash (USA) (Royal Academy (USA))
84[4] 113[5] 276[7] 337[8] 537[11] 2424[8] 5175[2] ◆ 6238[4] 7230[3]

Avrilo *Malcolm Saunders* a58 75
5 ch m Piccolo—Arctic High (Polar Falcon (USA))
2959[6] 3687[8] 5265[6] 5658[8] 6119[12]

Await The Dawn (USA) *A P O'Brien* 125
4 b h Giant's Causeway(USA) —Valentine Band (USA) (Dixieland Band (USA))
(1821) ◆ (3153) 5183[3] 7305a[7]

Away My Love *R Pritchard-Gordon* a67
2 b f Gold Away(IRE) —Agapimou (IRE) (Spectrum (IRE))
7665a[7]

Awesome Belle (USA) *Stanley I Gold* a104
2 ch f Awesome Of Course(USA) —Bayou Plans (USA) (Bayou Hebert (USA))
7283a[12]

Awesome Pearl (USA) *Sir Mark Prescott Bt* a75 11
2 bb c Awesome Again(CAN) —Gottcha Last (USA) (Pleasant Tap (USA))
6774[11] (6945)

Awesome Rock (IRE) *Louise Best* a49 11
2 ch c Rock Of Gibraltar(IRE) —Dangerous Diva (IRE) (Royal Academy (USA))
5834[11] 6474[10] 6768[12] 7569[11] 7697[7] 7937[10]

Awjila *Ralph Beckett* 71
3 b f Oasis Dream—Asaawir (Royal Applause)
4102[3] ◆ (4796)

Awsaal *John Dunlop* 104
4 b h Nayef(USA) —Design Perfection (USA) (Diesis)
2071[13] 3156[9] (3829)

Awzaan *Mark Johnston* 114
4 br h Alhaarth(IRE) —Nufoos (Zafonic (USA))
2315[3] 2713[6] 3404[5] ◆ 3852[9]

Axiom *Ed Walker* a81 109
7 ch g Pivotal—Exhibitor (USA) (Royal Academy (USA))
1094[4] 1529[8] 3109[24] 4802[2] 5218[10] 5936[6] 6862[4] 7295[9]

Ayaarah (IRE) *Les Hall* a68 43
3 b f Cape Cross(IRE) —La Jwaab (Alhaarth (IRE))
5114[5]

Aydemirhan (TUR) *G Subasi* 70
4 b h Strike The Gold(USA) —Charmy (TUR) (Scenic)
5776a[9]

Aye Aye Digby (IRE) *Patrick Chamings* a88 91
6 b g Captain Rio—Jane Digby (IRE) (Magical Strike (USA))
1898[4] 2169[5] 3000[11] (3350) 3765[3] 4742[2] 5587[4] 6246[7] 6920[2] (7529)

Ayla's Emperor *Mick Channon* 54
2 b f Holy Roman Emperor(IRE) —Ayla (IRE) (Daylami (IRE))
7030[9] 7257[9]

Ay Tay Tate (IRE) *David C Griffiths* a72 69
5 b g Catcher In The Rye(IRE) —Vintage Belle (IRE) (Waajib)
319[3] 546[2] 644[3] 1107[12] 1291[8] 1386[4] 2618[4] (2988) 3074[2] ◆ 3317[3] 3848[4] 4367[3] 6990[6] 7237[6] 7458[3] 7647[6] 7689[2] 7772[4] 7914[9]

Ayun Tara (FR) *X Nakkachdji* a99 105
4 gr m Martaline—Annee De La Femme (IRE) (Common Grounds)
241[4] 497a[3] 604a[10]

Azamara Star *Derek Shaw*
2 ch f Three Valleys(USA) —Sunrise Girl (King's Signet (USA))
6620[11]

Azamata (IRE) *Kevin Prendergast* 85
2 b c Azamour(IRE) —Brave Madam (IRE) (Invincible Spirit (IRE))
6196a[3]

Azameera (IRE) *Clive Cox* 93
3 b f Azamour(IRE) —Claustra (FR) (Green Desert (USA))
2216[7] (2582) (3873) 5702[4] 6495[3]

Azarra (IRE) *R Mongil* 84
3 b f Green Tune(USA) —I C Cindy (USA) (Gallapiat (USA))
5307a[6]

Azimuth (USA) *Ann Duffield* a83 76
4 bb g Giant's Causeway(USA) —Zoe Montana (USA) (Seeking The Gold (USA))
1460[3] 1892[8] 3245[9] 3508[2]

Azmeel *John Gosden* 111
4 b h Azamour(IRE) —Best Side (IRE) (King's Best (USA))
242[10] 417a[11]

Azrael *Alan McCabe* 96
3 b g Makbul—Fontaine Lady (Millfontaine)
1384[3] 1674[2] 2110[3] 2847[8] 3774[15] 4550[11]

Azurinta (IRE) *Michael Bell* a56 54
3 b f Azamour(IRE) —Pinta (IRE) (Ahonoora)
1203[10] 1568[9] 1873[10] 5898[5] 6446[8] 7370[3] 7608[10]

Azygous *G P Kelly* a43 55
8 ch g Foxhound(USA) —Flag (Selkirk (USA))
537[6] 690[9]

Azzoom (IRE) *Clive Brittain* a53 71
3 br f Cadeaux Genereux—Prancing (Prince Sabo)
1853[12] 2200[11] 3630[6] 4322[12]

Azzurra Du Caprio (IRE) *Ben Haslam* 93
3 ch f Captain Rio—Dunbrody (FR) (Jeune Homme (USA))
(1650) 2122[3] 2468[9] (3384) 4779[4] 5852[12]

Baan (USA) *James Eustace* a66 61
8 ch g Diesis—Madaen (USA) (Nureyev (USA))
7113[6] (7441) 7564[8]

Baan Rim Pa (FR) *D Prod'Homme* a71 89
5 ch g Dyhim Diamond(IRE) —Tora Tune (FR) (Green Tune (USA))
1011a[10]

Babayigit (TUR) *A Gokce* a58
7 b h Royal Abjar(USA) —Prima Facie (Primo Dominie)
5754a[8]

Babich Bay (IRE) *Jo Hughes* a59 75
3 b g Captain Rio—Ibtihal (IRE) (Hamas (IRE))
2993[7] 3512[10] 3953[5] 4183[4] 5203[3] 5539[8] 5674[14] 6190[3] (6208) 6418[2] 6426[7]

Babycakes (IRE) *Michael Bell* a90 103
4 b m Marju(IRE) —Dark Rosaleen (IRE) (Darshaan)
2269[2] 2676[3] 3338[3] (5075a) 6362a[7] 7090a[0]

Baby Dottie *Pat Phelan* a77 76
4 ch m Dr Fong(USA) —Auntie Dot Com (Tagula (IRE))
1771[5] 2822[10] 5578[6]

Baby Driver *Tom Dascombe* a54 69
3 gr g Proclamation(IRE) —Renee (Wolfhound (USA))
1944[7] 2249[2] 2984[2] 3495[9] 4409[7] 4866[11] 5560[5] 6417[6] 6923[5] 7271[3] 7571[4] 7610[3]

Baby Judge (IRE) *Michael Chapman* a53 52
4 ch g Captain Rio—Darling Clementine (Lion Cavern (USA))
914[7] 1037[8] 3732[11]

Babylona (FR) *Philippe Le Geay* 43
4 b m Equerry(USA) —Branigann (FR) (Septieme Ciel (USA))
7015a[6] 7256a[0]

Baby Queen (IRE) *Brian Baugh* a40 80
5 b m Royal Applause—Kissing Time (Lugana Beach)
(2182) 2720[5] (3640) 3994[2] 4475[5]

Baby Strange *Derek Shaw* a90 98
7 gr g Superior Premium—The Manx Touch (IRE) (Petardia)
(970) 2099[15] 2456[4] 2717[10] 2954[11] 3379[5] 3841[8] 4104[2] 4346[5] 4531[20] 5278[3] 5758[7] 5879[2] 6326[4] 6672[17] 6862[19]

Bacarrita (FR) *L A Urbano-Grajales* a83 84
6 b m Marathon(USA) —Congostena (IRE) (Dr Devious (IRE))
3568a[6]

Baccarat (IRE) *Richard Fahey* a74
2 ch c Dutch Art—Zut Alors (IRE) (Pivotal)
7540[3] (7783)

Bacchelli *S Botti* 102
3 b c Mujahid(USA) —Bugia (GER) (Kendor (FR))
1920a[7]

Bachelor Knight (IRE) *Suzzanne France* a60 66
3 b g Bachelor Duke(USA) —Labetera (Lujain (USA))
187[4] 396[4] 964[5] 1494[6] 6266[13] 7213[9] 7412[8] 7565[7]

Bachelor's Dream *William Muir* 55
3 b f Bachelor Duke(USA) —Dyanita (Singspiel (IRE))
5429[3]

Back Burner (IRE) *Mrs John Harrington* a95 88
3 br g Big Bad Bob(IRE) —Marl (Lycius (USA))
3445a[7] 4566a[6] 5090a[6] 6513a[2]

Back For Tea (IRE) *K F Clutterbuck* a51 51
3 b g Redback—Jasmine Pearl (IRE) (King Of Kings (IRE))
966^{10} 1285^{3} 1500^{2} 1592^{2} 2307^{12} 2418^{3} 3363^{8} 7246^{13} 7557^{9} 7712^{7}

Back Hunting (USA) *A Renzoni* 95
4 b h Put It Back(USA) —Huntingland (USA) (Dove Hunt (USA))
6906a^{6} 7408a^{6}

Back In Black (NZ) *John Steffert* 112
6 bl g Storm Creek(USA) —Shutricia (NZ) (Grosvenor (NZ))
6967a^{6} 7115a^{6} 7310a^{8}

Back On Stage (FR) *Mlle S-V Tarrou* a49
3 b f Xaar—Back Row (In The Wings)
981a^{0}

Backstreet Fighter (IRE) *Gary Harrison* 78
3 b g Atraf—Saraparda (IRE) (Groom Dancer (USA))
4461^{7} 4970^{4} (5567)

Back To Paris (IRE) *Philip Kirby* a48 78
9 b g Lil's Boy(USA) —Alisco (IRE) (Shalford (IRE))
630^{U} 3600^{3} (3637) 3938^{3}

Backtrade (IRE) *Andrew Balding* a75 68
2 b g Holy Roman Emperor(IRE) —Braari (USA) (Gulch (USA))
1678^{4} 2880^{5} 4857^{3} 5385^{2}

Bada Bing *David Nicholls* a40 44
2 ch f Beat Hollow—Trustthunder (Selkirk (USA))
2430^{10} 4285^{10} 5464^{13} 6611^{3}

Baddam *Ian Williams* 79
9 b g Mujahid(USA) —Aude La Belle (FR) (Ela-Mana-Mou)
1788^{3} 3205^{8} 3794^{7}

Badea *Richard Fahey* 76
2 b g Cockney Rebel(IRE) —Gibraltar Bay (IRE) (Cape Cross (IRE))
2455^{4} 3123^{4} 3609^{2} 4714^{2}

Badeel (USA) *Saeed Bin Suroor* a86 102
3 b c El Prado(IRE) —Hasheema (IRE) (Darshaan)
(1903) 2191^{5}

Bad Sir Brian (IRE) *Nick Gifford* 33
6 b g Bach(IRE) —Ballyverane Pride (IRE) (Presenting)
1840^{8}

Baggsy (IRE) *Julia Feilden* a52 41
4 b m Statue Of Liberty(USA) —Nisibis (In The Wings)
419^{7}

Bahamian Ballet *Ed McMahon* a70 78
9 ch g Bahamian Bounty—Plie (Superlative)
2048^{9} 2667^{3}

Bahamian Jazz (IRE) *Robin Bastiman* 74
4 ch g Bahamian Bounty—Nandy's Cavern (Lion Cavern (USA))
1307^{5} 1911^{10} 2412^{10} 4110^{2} 4443^{11} 5121^{6} 5787^{12}

Bahamian Kid *George Foster* a76 67
6 b g Bahamian Bounty—Barachois Princess (USA) (Barachois (CAN))
1077^{11} 1520^{9} 1803^{9} 2670^{6} 4600^{12} 5787^{11}

Bahamian Lad *Reg Hollinshead* a73 82
6 b g Bahamian Bounty—Danehill Princess (IRE) (Danehill (USA))
316^{10} 577^{6} 708^{11} 2938^{13} 3339^{8} 3850^{10} 4516^{11} 4866^{3} 5881^{4} 7039^{2} 7265^{4} (7417) 7716^{8} 7928^{7}

Bahamian Music (IRE) *Richard Fahey* a86 87
4 b m Bahamian Bounty—Strings (Unfuwain (USA))
1325^{8} 1826^{3} 2282^{7} 2676^{7} (3164) 4553^{3}

Baharat (IRE) *Richard Guest* a79 77
3 b g Iffraaj—Gharam (USA) (Green Dancer (USA))
212^{5} 431^{2} (610) (931) 1051^{3} 1272^{3} 1652^{4} 1820^{8} 2092^{8} 2406^{9}

Bahati (IRE) *Jonathan Portman* a82 99
4 ch m Intikhab(USA) —Dawn Chorus (IRE) (Mukaddamah (USA))
1104^{10} 1884^{8} 2358^{4} 3407^{4} 4093^{7} 4429^{14}

Bahceli (IRE) *Richard Hannon* 100
3 gr g Mujadil(USA) —Miss Shaan (FR) (Darshaan)
(1690) 3067^{7} ◆ 4100^{13}

Baheeja *Roger Varian* 72
2 b f Dubawi(IRE) —Hasty Words (IRE) (Polish Patriot (USA))
5655^{7} 6934^{2}

Bahia Emerald (IRE) *Jeremy Noseda* 76
3 b f Bahamian Bounty—Emerald Peace (IRE) (Green Desert (USA))
1358^{4} (1672) 2180^{5} (2827) ◆ 3122^{4} 3555^{9}

Bahkov (IRE) *Eric Wheeler* a49 55
5 ch g Bahamian Bounty—Petrikov (IRE) (In The Wings)
1045^{9} 2155^{7} 2642^{8} 3293^{6} 3945^{7} 4389^{5} 4703^{7} 4974^{4} 5267^{2} 5612^{5}

Bahrain Storm (IRE) *Patrick J Flynn* a91 102
8 b g Bahhare(USA) —Dance Up A Storm (USA) (Storm Bird (CAN))
3420a^{7}

Bahri Beat (IRE) *John Norton* a33
3 b g Bahri(USA) —Optimal Quest (IRE) (Septieme Ciel (USA))
7352^{10} 7743^{7}

Bahri Sheen (IRE) *John Best* a68 67
3 b g Bahri(USA) —Kama's Wheel (Magic Ring (IRE))
1130^{4} 1236^{6}

Baiadera (GER) *T Potters* 91
4 ch m Tertullian(USA) —Belinga (GER) (Tannenkonig (IRE))
3654a^{11}

Bailadeira *Tim Etherington* a60 62
3 bb f Intikhab(USA) —Sainte Gig (FR) (Saint Cyrien (FR))
1302^{4} 1853^{11} 3126^{4} 3860^{5} 6839^{2} 7079^{2} 7245^{3} (7511) 7566^{2}

Baileys Agincourt *Mark Johnston* a60
3 ch g Beat Hollow—Numberonedance (USA) (Trempolino (USA))
319^{2} 420^{4} 643^{2} 789^{2} (1028) 7070^{8}

Baileys Dutch *Mark Johnston*
2 gr g Dutch Art—Southern Psychic (USA) (Alwasmi (USA))
7066^{6}

Baileys Etoile *M Figge* a76 76
3 ch f Bertolini(USA) —Kosmic View (USA) (Distant View (USA))
4896a^{9}

Baileys Over Ice *James Given* a27 63
2 b f Iceman—Exhibitor (USA) (Royal Academy (USA))
5398^{7} 6047^{3} 6458^{6} 6806^{4} 7223^{9}

Baileys Vert (FR) *W Walton* a72 61
3 b c Green Tune(USA) —Bahia Verde (FR) (Shining Steel)
370a^{10} 616a^{4}

Baisse *Sir Henry Cecil* a73 82
3 b f High Chaparral(IRE) —Best Side (IRE) (King's Best (USA))
1393^{4} (1915) 2287^{4} 5962^{3}

Bajan Bear *Michael Blanshard* 79
3 ch g Compton Place—Bajan Rose (Dashing Blade)
1400^{3} 1830^{4} 2180^{6} (2841) (3346) ◆ 4214^{7} 4550^{9} 5811^{9} 6167^{8} 6759^{9} 6997^{4}

Bajan Flash *David Nicholls* 73
4 gr g Bahamian Bounty—Molly Moon (IRE) (Primo Dominie)
1150^{4} 1394^{2} 1559^{2} 1714^{6} 2474^{7}

Bajan Hero *David Evans* a44 68
2 b g Haafhd—Maid To Dance (Pyramus (USA))
1827^{7} 2049^{12} 2283^{4} 2788^{2} 4462^{6} 5802^{7} 6489^{9}

Bajan Parkes *John Quinn* 72
8 bb g Zafonic(USA) —My Melody Parkes (Teenoso (USA))
2091^{7} (2575) 2952^{7}

Bajan Pride *Paul Midgley* a63 71
7 b g Selkirk(USA) —Spry (Suave Dancer (USA))
568^{5} 1164^{5} 1905^{7} 2149^{9} 2308^{4} ◆ 2589^{3} 2984^{4} 3306^{8} 3456^{12} 4183^{10} 4604^{8}

Bajan Tryst (USA) *Kevin Ryan* a103 105
5 bb g Speightstown(USA) —Garden Secrets (USA) (Time For A Change (USA))
2317^{12} 5086a^{3} 5927^{20} 6706^{11} (7149a) 7392^{12} 7721^{3}

Bakoura *John Dunlop* a69 81
3 b f Green Desert(USA) —Bunood (IRE) (Sadler's Wells (USA))
1358^{3} (2419) 3219^{4} (3549) ◆ 4202^{2} ◆ 4807^{5} 6062^{6} 7054^{3} 7542^{8}

Balady (IRE) *John Dunlop* 81
2 b f Zamindar(USA) —Faydah (USA) (Bahri (USA))
4061^{10} 5444^{2} 6329^{2} 7164^{4}

Balajo (FR) *Alison Batchelor* a94 94
5 ch g Kendor(FR) —Dareen (IRE) (Rahy (USA))
(195a) 4775^{9} 7430^{4}

Balance On Time (IRE) *Linda Perratt* 48
5 b m Imperial Ballet(IRE) —Balance The Books (Elmaamul (USA))
1803^{8} 2415^{4} 2809^{7} 3128^{7} 3657^{7} 3857^{10} 3902^{6}

Balandra *Luca Cumani* a71 79
3 gr f Medicean—Dali's Grey (Linamix (FR))
4529^{3} 5317^{6} 5877^{5} 6404^{2} 7204^{9} 7360^{5}

Balaton *Brian Meehan* 23
2 br f Singspiel(IRE) —Traverse City (USA) (Halo (USA))
6603^{16} 7030^{14}

Balaythous (FR) *Mlle B Renk* a89 107
5 ch g Bahhare(USA) —Silirisa (FR) (Sillery (USA))
6661a^{3} 7049a^{14}

Balbrown (FR) *A Savujev* 51
3 b c Refuse To Bend(IRE) —Style For Life (IRE) (Law Society (USA))
1965a^{7}

Balcarce Nov (ARG) *Tom Tate* a101 100
[illegible] Romanov(IRE) —Rosada Fitz (ARG) (Fitzcarraldo (ARG))
1385^{3} 1694^{14} 2284^{3} (2614) 2933^{10} 3542^{5}

Baldassarre (IRE) *Richard Fahey* a24
2 ch c Medicean—Cleide Da Silva (USA) (Monarchos (USA))
7368^{8}

Baldemar *Richard Fahey* a93 98
6 b g Namid—Keen Melody (USA) (Sharpen Up)
1197^{7} ◆ 1720^{19} 3028^{12} (3765) 3880^{7} 4609^{7} (5578) 6145^{18} 6331^{12} 6703^{18}

Balducci *Andrew Balding* a80 107
4 b g Dansili—Miss Meltemi (IRE) (Miswaki Tern (USA))
2031^{7} 3107^{9} 3409^{4} (4554)

Balesteem *Clifford Lines*
4 ch g Mark Of Esteem(IRE) —Ball Gown (Jalmood (USA))
5639^{11}

Balierus (GER) *M bin Shafya* a90 80
4 b h Singspiel(IRE) —Brighella (GER) (Lomitas)
608a^{8}

Ballade De La Mer *George Foster* a51 53
5 b m Ishiguru(USA) —Riviere Rouge (Forzando)
598^{11} 1519^{7} 2400^{4} 4785^{4} 5650^{11} 6876^{7}

Balladiene (IRE) *Jarlath P Fahey* a68 76
5 b m Noverre(USA) —Kinnego (IRE) (Sri Pekan (USA))
7189a^{12}

Ballagane (FR) *F Foresi* a60
3 ch f Ballingarry(IRE) —Lady Of Paris (FR) (Courtroom (FR))
288a^{8}

Ballarina *Eric Alston* a57 70
5 b m Compton Place—Miss Uluwatu (IRE) (Night Shift (USA))
(1034) 1213^{4} 1716^{3} 2832^{12} 4144^{2} 4881^{10} 5400^{8} 5719^{3} 6213^{10}

Ballesteros *Brian Meehan* 92
2 ch g Tomba—Flamenco Dancer (Mark Of Esteem (IRE))
1890^{3} 2455^{3} 3014^{14} 5681^{4} 5889^{2} (6292) (6590) (6827) ◆ 7019^{8}

Balletlou (IRE) *John Best* a30 79
4 b m Peintre Celebre(USA) —For Freedom (IRE) (King Of Kings (IRE))
3632^{11} 4083^{7} 5692^{11} 6894^{9}

Ballina Blue *Sheena West* a56
3 b g Phoenix Reach(IRE) —Katy-Q (IRE) (Taufan (USA))
3214^{6} 4023^{10} 6086^{6} 6823^{12}

Ballinargh Boy *Robert Wylie* a44 51
3 b g Royal Applause—Can Can Lady (Anshan)
2047^{3} 2396^{6} 3039^{9} 4041^{7} 5864^{10} 7426^{6} 7608^{6} 7902^{4}

Ballinargh Girl (IRE) *Robert Wylie* 82
3 b f Footstepsinthesand—Rack And Ruin (IRE) (King's Best (USA))
2986^{9} 3628^{5} 3853^{2} 4541^{2} 4792^{6} 5083^{11} 5683^{2} 6418^{3} 6778^{10}

Ballista (IRE) *Tom Dascombe* 94
3 b g Majestic Missile(IRE) —Ancient Secret (Warrshan (USA))
1241^{9} 1545^{7} 1852^{6} 2911^{3} 3181^{2} 3357^{11} 3820^{15} 4498^{7} 5706^{5} 6331^{9} 6723^{14} 7076^{3}

Ballodair (IRE) *Richard Fahey* a73 78
4 b g Antonius Pius(USA) —Vision Of Dreams (Efisio)
1998 4035

Ball Prince (IRE) *T Clout* 103
4 gr h Slickly(FR) —Queen's Ball (King's Theatre (IRE))
6783a^{2}

Ballroom Blitz *Richard Guest* 36
2 b f Ishiguru(USA) —Twilight Time (Aragon)
6425^{3}

Ballybacka Lady (IRE) *P A Fahy* a81 104
3 b f Hurricane Run(IRE) —Southern Queen (Anabaa (USA))
(1928a) 2334a^{12} 4132a^{11} 5745a^{6}

Ballyea (IRE) *Richard Hannon* 75
2 b f Acclamation—Petite Spectre (Spectrum (IRE))
3258^{3} ◆ (3547) 3800^{3} 4551^{10} 6058^{9}

Ballyheigue (IRE) *Brian Meehan* a68 67
2 b g High Chaparral(IRE) —Lypharden (IRE) (Lyphard's Special (USA))
3424^{10} 5899^{2} 6400^{5}

Balm *Patrick Morris* a68 64
2 b f Oasis Dream—Alovera (IRE) (King's Best (USA))
1946^{4} 2153^{4} 2661^{4} 3745^{3} 3993^{5} 4704^{6} 5316^{2} 6178^{3} (6540) 6843^{9} 7059^{13}

Balmont Mast (IRE) *Edward Lynam* a100 87
3 b g Balmont(USA) —Corn Futures (Nomination)
7012a^{3}

Balsha (USA) *Roy Arne Kvisla* a47 59
4 ch m Mr Greeley(USA) —Carefree Cheetah (USA) (Trempolino (USA))
5096a^{7} 5982a^{7}

Balthazaar's Gift (IRE) *Clive Cox* a56 115
8 b h Xaar—Thats Your Opinion (Last Tycoon)
2101^{7} 4412^{8} 5046^{7} 5510^{7} 5930^{4}

Baltic Bomber (IRE) *John Quinn* 61
2 b g Baltic King—Dieci Anno (IRE) (Classic Music (USA))
3050^{5} 3610^{4} 4365^{4} 4899^{5} 6045^{7} 6599^{4}

Baltic Fizz (IRE) *Mrs K Burke* a55 72
2 b f Baltic King—Holly Springs (Efisio)
3855^{2} (4319) 5562^{2} 6222^{8} 6699^{11} 7813a^{7}

Baltic Flyer (IRE) *Robert Eddery* a64 61
2 b f Baltic King—Negria (IRE) (Al Hareb (USA))
3257^{6} 3981^{3} 5337^{5} 6695^{8}

Baltic Light (USA) *Sir Henry Cecil* a79 65
3 ch f North Light(IRE) —Blush Damask (USA) (Green Dancer (USA))
1525^{2} ◆ (2175) ◆ 2819^{13} 7017^{15}

Baltimore Clipper (USA) *Paul Cole* a73 88
4 b g Mizzen Mast(USA) —Resounding Grace (USA) (Thunder Gulch (USA))
2686^{8} 2958^{6} 3593^{4} ◆ 4097^{4} (4341) 4806^{5} 5685^{4} ◆

[illegible] (IRE) *G P Kelly* a66 79
7 b g Night Shift(USA) —Itsibitsi (IRE) (Brief Truce (USA))
1017^{6} 1324^{12} 1909^{15} 2348^{6} 2800^{4} 4148^{7} 6494^{4} 7466^{6}

Baltimore Patriot (IRE) *Barry Brennan* a67 63
8 b g Tiger Hill(IRE) —Berenice (Groom Dancer (USA))
8^{6} 172^{2}

Balti's Sister (IRE) *Michael Easterby* a60 63
2 b f Tiger Hill(IRE) —Itsibitsi (IRE) (Brief Truce (USA))
2953^{4} 3342^{7} (3921) 4984^{5} 6345^{7} 6806^{16}

Balty Boys (IRE) *Charles Hills* 110
2 b c Cape Cross(IRE) —Chatham Islands (USA) (Elusive Quality (USA))
3823^{7} (4580) 5181^{9} 5479^{3} 6170^{4} 6688^{4}

Bambika *Jo Crowley* a54 56
3 ch f Kyllachy—True Precision (Presidium)
611^{5} 1020^{4} 3173^{5} 3724^{8} 5670^{2} 5996^{7} 6929^{7} 6981^{4}

Bambino (TUR) *B Dag* 32
4 ch m Perfect Storm(TUR) —Venuskizi (TUR) (Wolf (CHI))
5776a^{10}

Bana Wu *Andrew Balding* 105
2 ch f Shirocco(GER) —My Way (IRE) (Marju (IRE))
5445^{6} 6168^{2} 6691^{4}

Bancnuanaheireann (IRE) *J S Bolger* 88
4 b g Chevalier(IRE) —Alamanta (IRE) (Ali-Royal (IRE))
6736a^{11}

Bandanaman (IRE) *Alan Swinbank* a64 66
5 b g Danehill Dancer(IRE) —Band Of Angels (IRE) (Alzao (USA))
1556^{2} 1794^{5} 2433^{4} 3622^{4} 4602^{2} 5079^{3}

Bandidazo (USA) *A Fabre* 88
2 ch c Van Nistelrooy(USA) —Bailonguera (ARG) (Southern Halo (USA))
7155a^{4}

Band Of Thunder *Andrew Balding* 59
3 ch g Shirocco(GER) —Black Opal (Machiavellian (USA))
1728^{5} 2551^{11} 3214^{4} 4274^{4} 4510^{4} 5379^{7}

Bandstand *Bryan Smart* a84 78
5 b g Royal Applause—Incise (Dr Fong (USA))
(971) 1395^{10} ◆ 2497^{10} 3617^{2} 4362^{3} 4670^{9} 7586^{8}

Bang Tidy (IRE) *Brian Ellison* 60
2 b g Moss Vale(IRE) —Bound To Glitter (USA) (Boundary (USA))
3313^{6} 4347^{7} 4557^{9}

Banimpire (IRE) *J S Bolger* 114
3 br f Holy Roman Emperor(IRE) —My Renee (USA) (Kris S (USA))
924a^{3} (1259a) (2012a) 2334a^{5} (2968a) ◆ (3065) 4133a^{2} (4831a) 5219^{5} 6568a^{3} 6859^{7}

Bankable (IRE) *H J Brown* a115 118
7 b h Medicean—Dance To The Top (Sadler's Wells (USA))
155a^{4} ◆ 501a^{4} (755a) 1000a^{13}

Bank Bonus *Andrew Balding* 79
2 b g Motivator—Small Fortune (Anabaa (USA))
5447^{7} 6588^{3} ◆

Bank Guard (IRE) *Rod Collet* a76 85
6 ch g Peintre Celebre(USA) —Blue Cloud (IRE) (Nashwan (USA))
220a^{8}

Bank Merger (USA) *Saeed Bin Suroor* a113
4 ch h Consolidator(USA) —Lucrative (USA) (Seeking The Gold (USA))
606a^{10} 755a^{11}

Bank Of Burden (USA) *Niels Petersen* a76 101
4 ch g Hawk Wing(USA) —Wewantitall (Pivotal)
329a^{9} 585a^{12} 4842a^{2} (5984a)

Bank On Me *Philip McBride* 80
2 ch c Medicean—Red Garland (Selkirk (USA))
5013^{14} 6100^{8} (6956) 7167^{6}

Banksters Bonus (IRE) *Mrs John Harrington* 107
3 b g Big Bad Bob(IRE) —Heroine (Sadler's Wells (USA))
2331a^{10} 3695a^{3}

Banksy *Kevin Ryan* a70 57
2 ch c Dutch Art—Far Post (USA) (Defensive Play (USA))
1890^{4} 2173^{2} 3221^{2} 3707^{5} 6323^{9} 6597^{7}

Banna Boirche (IRE) *M Halford* a103 103
5 b g Lucky Owners(NZ) —Ziet D'Alsace (FR) (Zieten (USA))
414a^{7} 606a^{4} 756a^{5} 3445a^{13} 5361a^{5}

Banned (USA) *Thomas F Proctor* a69 115
3 b c Kitten's Joy(USA) —Cardinalli (USA) (Capote (USA))
5072a^{3}

Bannock (IRE) *Mark Johnston* a93 108
2 b c Bertolini(USA) —Laoub (USA) (Red Ransom (USA))
1673^{2} (1939) (2154) ◆ 2437^{2} 3064^{6} 3773^{3} 4495^{2} 6535^{13} (6705) 7012a^{6} 7220a^{6}

Baoli *Noel Chance* a65 66
4 b m Dansili—Thorntoun Piccolo (Groom Dancer (USA))
4713^{6} 5015^{13} 5406^{10} 6613^{14}

Bapak Chinta (USA) *Kevin Ryan* 106
2 rg c Speightstown(USA) —Suena Cay (USA) (Maria's Mon (USA))
(2042) (3064) ◆ 6688^{16}

Bapak Pintar *Kevin Ryan* 67
2 gr c Royal Applause—Victory Spirit (USA) (Alphabet Soup (USA))
3899^{3} 4606^{2} 5503^{3}

Baptist (USA) *Andrew Balding* 95
3 bb g Tapit(USA) —Twist A Lime (USA) (Copelan (USA))
2319^{10} 3067^{24} 3864^{3} ◆ 5081^{4} 5686^{12}

Baqaat (USA) *Ed Dunlop* a68 81
3 bb f Alhaarth(IRE) —Hachiyah (IRE) (Generous (IRE))
959^{2} (1481) 2184^{2} 4344^{5} 5020^{5} 5856^{9} 6401^{6}

[illegible] (IRE) [illegible]
2 b f Marju(IRE) —Ballyvarra (IRE) (Sadler's Wells (USA))
6925a^{0}

Baraan (FR) *J-C Rouget* a86 120
3 gr c Dalakhani(IRE) —Brusca (USA) (Grindstone (USA))
(902a) (1265a) 2751a^{3}

Baraaya (IRE) *William Haggas* a51 73
3 ch f Dalakhani(IRE) —Sayedati Eljamilah (USA) (Mr Prospector (USA))
6804^{9} 7446^{5}

Barachiel *Ronald Harris* a60 57
3 b c Pivotal—Coveted (Sinndar (IRE))
6473^{10} 6754^{4} 7536^{2} 7630^{6} 7931^{6}

Barack (IRE) *Francis Ennis* a91 107
5 b g Pyrus(USA) —Morna's Fan (FR) (Lear Fan (USA))
1930a^{5} 3444a^{9} 5361a^{2} 5746a^{7}

Baraconti (IRE) *Ruth Carr* a51 57
4 b g Barathea(IRE) —Continuous (IRE) (Darshaan)
14^{8}

Barakanda (IRE) *J Boisnard* a76 85
4 ch g Barathea(IRE) —Anda (Selkirk (USA))
5095a^{6}

Baralaka *Rose Dobbin* a91 95
4 ch g Barathea(IRE) —Shakalaka Baby (Nashwan (USA))
2932^{13}

Barateka (FR) *M Boutin*
5 ro g Barathea(IRE) —Snataka (FR) (Take Risks (FR))
617a^{0}

Barathea Dancer (IRE) *Roger Teal* a75 81
3 b f Barathea(IRE) —Showering (Danehill (USA))
1481^{2} 1894^{9} 2883^{2} 4009^{5} 5999^{2} 6256^{6}

Baratom (FR) *F-X De Chevigny* a64 83
5 ch g Beaudelaire(USA) —Belga Wood (USA) (Woodman (USA))
6959a^{2}

Barbayam *F Head* 99
2 gr f Stormy River(FR) —Senkaya (FR) (Valanour (IRE))
3567a^{3} 7219a^{2}

Barbecue Eddie (USA) *Doug Watson* a106 97
7 br g Stormy Atlantic(USA) —The Green Owl (USA) (Carson City (USA))
332a^{5} (606a) 755a^{9}

Barberton (USA) *Jeremy Noseda* 38
2 ch c Johannesburg(USA) —Mythical Echo (USA) (Stravinsky (USA))
5254^{16}

Barbican *Alan Bailey* a116 111
3 b g Hurricane Run(IRE) —The Faraway Tree (Suave Dancer (USA))
(693) ◆ (1113) ◆ 1548^{4} 1723^{2} 2507^{5} (4764) (5700) (6498) 7027^{3} (7584) ◆

Barbieri (IRE) *Jeremy Gask* a74 87
3 ch f Encosta De Lago(AUS) —Glenmara (USA) (Known Fact (USA))
1241^{13} 1758^{6} 7456^{11}

Barbirolli *William Stone* a53 52
9 b g Machiavellian(USA) —Blushing Barada (USA) (Blushing Groom (FR))
30^{9} 173^{4} 409^{3} 451^{5} 630^{4} (899) 1063^{6} 1310^{12} 1635^{3} 1987^{11} 2638^{6} 2759^{3} 3353^{2} 3946^{6} 4654^{2} 5357^{7} 6182^{8} 6356^{7}

Barclay Jelois (FR) *Robert Collet* 35
2 b c Marchand De Sable(USA) —Star Angels (FR) (Ski Chief (USA))
7664a^{0}

Bareback (IRE) *John Best* a70 53
2 b c Redback—Lady Lucia (IRE) (Royal Applause)
3746^{10} 6725^{12} 7225^{4} 7520^{10}

Barefoot Lady (IRE) *Richard Fahey* 110
3 b f Footstepsinthesand—Lady Angharad (IRE) (Tenby)
(1319) 1719^{5} 2004^{2} 3106^{3} 4533^{5} 5366a^{5} 5745a^{4}

Barentin (USA) *J-C Rouget* a92 107
3 b g Arch(USA) —Great Lady Slew (USA) (Seattle Slew (USA))
2136a^{4}

Bariolo (FR) *Noel Chance* a66 72
7 b g Priolo(USA) —La Bardane (FR) (Marignan (USA))
266^{4} 392^{5} 6503^{11} 7070^{7}

Barista (IRE) *Mick Channon* a66 85
3 b g Titus Livius(FR) —Cappuccino (IRE) (Mujadil (USA))
2319^{12} 2503^{5} 2834^{6} 2908^{6} 3231^{4} 3634^{2} 3854^{5} 4089^{5} 4338^{3} 4821^{5} 5401^{3} (5675) 5803^{3} 5821^{2} 6120^{4} 6433^{2} 6544^{7} 6840^{5} 7235^{4}

Barkston Ash *Eric Alston* 80
3 b g Kyllachy—Ae Kae Ae (USA) (King Of Kings (IRE))
1038^{6} 1437^{4} (1802) (1980) (2391) 2911^{5} (3598) 4048^{6} 5450^{10}

Barliffey (IRE) *Lucinda Russell* a73 75
6 b g Bahri(USA) —Kildare Lady (IRE) (Indian Ridge)
3453^{8} 3859^{9}

Barn Dance (FR) *Jonathan Portman* a73 72
2 b c Country Reel(USA) —Happy Clapper (Royal Applause)
6123^{8} 6763^{2} 7414^{3} (7684)

Barnet Fair *Richard Guest* a100 98
3 br g Iceman—Pavement Gates (Bishop Of Cashel)
20^{3} 302^{2} (465) 2074^{8} (2724) (3048) 3820^{7} 4333^{4} 5054^{5} 5288^{4} ◆ 5852^{5} 6217^{9}

Barney McGrew (IRE) *Michael Dods* a93 110
8 b g Mark Of Esteem(IRE) —Success Story (Sharrood (USA))
327a^{8} 500a^{3} 602a^{4} 1720^{20} 2028^{12} ◆ 2317^{11} 2706^{13} 3155^{16} 3627^{7} 4369^{13} 5852^{21} 6703^{3} ◆ 7018^{5}

Barney Rebel (IRE) *Charles Hills* 90
3 b c Holy Roman Emperor(IRE) —Opera Ridge (FR) (Indian Ridge)
(1480) 1723^{6} (2925) 3159^{3} 3825^{7} 4467^{13} 6574^{4}

Barnmore *Peter Hedger* a68 38
3 b g Royal Applause—Veronica Franco (Darshaan)
909^{4} ◆ 6789^{9}

Barnum (USA) *Michael Easterby* a71 59
3 b g Distorted Humor(USA) —Shady Reflection (USA) (Sultry Song (USA))
546^{7} 714^{4} 909^{3} 1475^{2} 1683^{13} 2835^{8} 3340^{6} 3854^{6} 4112^{10} (4403) 4751^{5} 5369^{8} 5791^{14} 6181^{5} 6236^{10} 6669^{7}

Barocci (JPN) *E Lellouche* 109
3 b c Deep Impact(JPN) —Bastet (IRE) (Giant's Causeway (USA))
1552a^{4} 2139a^{6} 2978a^{5} 4376a^{7} 6185a^{2}

Barodine *Ron Hodges* a66 54
8 ch g Barathea(IRE) —Granted (FR) (Cadeaux Genereux)
(81) (173) 252^{8} 418^{11} 588^{2} 808^{6} 6438^{9} 7121^{10}

Barolo Top (IRE) *Tom Dascombe* 79
2 b g Amadeus Wolf—Princess Mood (GER) (Muhtarram (USA))
2033^{5} (2831) 3012^{15} 3866^{10} 5487^{5} 6060^{4} 6829^{9}

Baron Davis (FR) *N Leenders* a76 64
4 b g Sevres Rose(IRE) —Zerelda (Exhibitioner)
831a^{4}

Baron De'L (IRE) *Edward P Harty* a78 97
8 ch g In The Wings—Lightstorm (IRE) (Darshaan)
4398a^{18}

Baroness (FR) *F Monnier* a92 96
4 b m Okawango(USA) —Danira (IRE) (Danehill (USA))
92a^{5} 7678a^{9}

Barongo (IRE) *U Suter* a80 97
6 ch g Distant Music(USA) —Blazing Soul (IRE) (Common Grounds)
534a^{6} 628a^{4}

Barons Spy (IRE) *Richard Price* a84 90
10 b g Danzero(AUS) —Princess Accord (USA) (D'Accord (USA))
1888^{18} (2903) 3784^{3} 3850^{6} (5262) (5339) 5972^{4} 6327^{6} 6920^{9}

Barosch (IRE) *Mario Hofer* 66
5 ch g Barathea(IRE) —Florida City (IRE) (Pennekamp (USA))
7314a^{2}

Barra Raider *Roger Fisher* a27 54
4 b g Avonbridge—Baileys Silver (USA) (Marlin (USA))
1731^{7} 1473^{8}

Barren Brook *Michael Easterby* 95
4 b g Beat Hollow—Carinthia (IRE) (Tirol)
1061^{8} 1410^{18} 1747^{8} 2112^{5} (2887) ◆ 3877^{3} ◆ (4528) 5185^{4} 5686^{3} 6672^{12}

Barreq (USA) *Mario Hofer* a79 67
4 b g Proud Citizen(USA) —The Wrong Face (USA) (Marlin (USA))
7314a^{4}

Barrow Island (IRE) *M Halford* a79 83
4 b g Chevalier(IRE) —Shelini (Robellino (USA))
1228a^{4}

Bartley *Bryan Smart* a67 76
2 ch g Monsieur Bond(IRE) —Annie Harvey (Fleetwood (IRE))
2731^{8} (2983) 3313^{5} 7021^{14} 7491^{7} 7686^{4}

Bartolomeu *Marco Botti* 69
2 b g Footstepsinthesand—Catch Us (FR) (Selkirk (USA))
3755^{4}

Barton Bounty *Peter Niven* a65 52
4 b g Bahamian Bounty—Tenebrae (IRE) (In The Wings)
730^{2} 749^{3} 895^{3} (969) ◆ 1273^{4} (1374) ◆ 1613^{8} 2589^{10} 2800^{8} 3086^{9} 3317^{14} 7178^{11} 7400^{9} (7571) 7698^{8} 7788^{5}

Barwick *Mark H Tompkins* a68 77
3 b g Beat Hollow—Tenpence (Bob Back (USA))
2008^{8} 6755^{5} 7453^{6}

Baryshnikov (USA) *Michael J Maker* a101 110
5 bb h Empire Maker(USA) —Ski Dancer (USA) (Baldski (USA))
7300a^{7}

Basantee *Tom Dascombe* a78 82
2 ch f Lucky Story(USA) —Soft Touch (IRE) (Petorius)
1744^{5} (2234) 2777a^{4} 3345^{2} 4372a^{4} (4717) 5234^{7} 6275^{5} (6826) 7259^{4}

Bashama *Clive Brittain* 58
3 ch f Dubai Destination(USA) —My Amalie (IRE) (Galileo (IRE))
3577^{7} 4963^{4}

Bashasha (USA) *Roger Varian* 68
3 bb f Kingmambo(USA) —Dessert (USA) (Storm Cat (USA))
2528^{5} 2960^{12}

Bashir Biyoum Zain (IRE) *Amy Weaver* a89 83
4 b g Green Desert(USA) —Alshamatry (USA) (Seeking The Gold (USA))
1854^{10} 2876^{9}

Bash On (IRE) *James Bethell*
3 b g High Chaparral(IRE) —Withorwithoutyou (IRE) (Danehill (USA))
5082^{13}

Basilica *Rod Millman* 78
3 ch g Zafeen(FR) —Thicket (Wolfhound (USA))
1361^{10}

Basle *Gay Kelleway* a64 79
4 b m Trade Fair—Gibaltarik (IRE) (Jareer (USA))
2303^{3} 3079^{2} 4064^{7} 4387^{13} 4741^{3} 4942^{6}

Basra (IRE) *Jo Crowley* a84 82
8 b g Soviet Star(USA) —Azra (IRE) (Danehill (USA))
174^{8} 562^{9}

Bassara (IRE) *Chris Wall* 64
2 b f Oasis Dream—Sauvage (FR) (Sri Pekan (USA))
6934^{7}

Bassett Road (IRE) *Willie Musson* a84 85
3 ch g Byron—Topiary (IRE) (Selkirk (USA))
(2255) 2619^{3} 3178^{8} 3536^{8} 5012^{11} 5451^{9} 6762^{11} 7097^{10} 7348^{7}

Batahola (USA) *A Fabre* a77 80
3 ch f Bluegrass Cat(USA) —Beauty Halo (ARG) (Southern Halo (USA))
901a^{5}

Batchelors Star (IRE) *W McCreery* a74 89
3 ch g Fath(USA) —Batchelor's Button (FR) (Kenmare (FR))
6733a^{6}

Batchworth Blaise *Eric Wheeler* a67 52
8 b g Little Jim—Batchworth Dancer (Ballacashtal (CAN))
387^{8} 589^{9} 1730^{5} 2386^{3} 4544^{5} 5653^{4} 7888^{5}

Bated Breath *Roger Charlton* 122
4 b h Dansili—Tantina (USA) (Distant View (USA))
1093^{10} (1891) (2370) 3154^{5} 3863^{2} 5253^{9} 5707^{2} 6908a^{2} 7730a^{8}

Bateleur *Mick Channon* a64 66
7 b g Fraam—Search Party (Rainbow Quest (USA))
1453^{3} 1627^{5} (1787) 1982^{5} 2142^{10} 2913^{4} 3020^{3} 3721^{9} 4057^{3} 4224^{7} 4631^{3} 4882^{4} 5139^{2} 5616^{11} 6238^{5} 6580^{2} 6765^{2} 6889^{2} (7086) 7224^{2} 7566^{9} 7811^{8}

Batgirl *John Berry* a56 81
4 ch m Mark Of Esteem(IRE) —Serriera (FR) (Highest Honor (FR))
(1570) (2270) 2674^{13} 3555^{3} 3825^{19} 4393^{3} 5516^{9} 6355^{11}

Bathwick Bear (IRE) *David Evans* a96 99
3 b g Kodiac—Bayleaf (Efisio)
883a^{3} 990^{6} 1322^{5} 1545^{3} 2054^{9} 2508^{5} 2934^{17} 3807^{2} 4333^{18} 4498^{4} 4644^{5} 5264^{9} 5805^{2} 6035^{2} 6224^{6} 6865^{6} 7018^{18}

Bathwick Freeze *David Evans* a44 52
3 b f Iceman—Society Rose (Saddlers' Hall (IRE))
53^{4} 142^{8} 406^{6}

Bathwick Man *David Pipe* a52 44
6 b g Mark Of Esteem(IRE) —Local Abbey (IRE) (Primo Dominie)
4974^{8}

Bathwick Scanno (IRE) *David Evans* a57 62
3 b g Aptitude(USA) —Hundred Year Flood (USA) (Giant's Causeway (USA))
47^{3} 234^{3} 469^{6}

Bathwick Street *David Evans* 59
2 ch g Compton Place—Bahawir Pour (USA) (Green Dancer (USA))
3076^{6} 5375^{6} 5536^{4} 6260^{4} 6460^{4}

Bathwick Xaara *Jonathan Portman* a29 73
4 br m Xaar—Anapola (GER) (Polish Precedent (USA))
1771^{11} 2610^{6} 3079^{8} 3217^{6} 4387^{11} (5513) 6408^{6} 7269^{9} 7691^{9}

Battery Power *Mark H Tompkins* a77 75
3 b f Royal Applause—Missouri (Charnwood Forest (IRE))
2764^{4} 3131^{2} 3989^{6} 4336^{5} 4932^{3} (6255) 6729^{8}

Battle Axe (FR) *Laura Mongan* a51
6 b m Cadoudal(FR) —Battle Quest (FR) (Noblequest (FR))
261^{2} 433^{8} 588^{5} 2820^{8} 3252^{4} 3743^{6}

Battle Honour *Sue Bradburne* a63 82
4 b g Mark Of Esteem(IRE) —Proserpine (Robellino (USA))
6078^{10}

Battle Of Britain *Giles Bravery* a68 84
3 b c Invincible Spirit(IRE) —Laramie (USA) (Gulch (USA))
1315^{5} 1611^{7} 2472^{4} (2853) 4457^{3} 5568^{2} 6241^{3} 6658^{9}

Battle Of Saratoga (IRE) *A P O'Brien* a80 92
2 b c Dylan Thomas(IRE) —Freedom (GER) (Second Empire (IRE))
5181^{13}

Battleoftrafalgar *Michael Attwater* a88 84
4 b g Galileo(IRE) —Pink Stone (FR) (Bigstone (IRE))
(1105) 1679^{10} 2499^{9} 7803^{9}

Battleoftheboyne (IRE) *Michael Mulvany* a70 83
2 b c Majestic Missile(IRE) —Khaytada (IRE) (Doyoun)
972a^{3} 6196a^{13}

Batya (IRE) *Tobias B P Coles* a62 71
4 b m Whipper(USA) —Runway Dancer (Dansili)
160^{6} 292^{8}

Bauer (IRE) *Luca Cumani* a47 110
8 gr g Halling(USA) —Dali's Grey (Linamix (FR))
4788^{10} (5705) 6711a^{6} 6967a^{3} 7310a^{4}

Bavarian Nordic (USA) *Richard Whitaker* a79 77
6 b g Barathea(IRE) —Dubai Diamond (Octagonal (NZ))
2892^{14} 3301^{6} 4294^{6} 5167^{3} 5405^{3} ◆ 5791^{12} 6419^{4} 7077^{5} 7689^{6}

Bavarian Princess (USA) *Mrs K Burke* a68 59
3 b f Invincible Spirit(IRE) —Lileagh (IRE) (Sadler's Wells (USA))
4370^{9} 6098^{16} 6541^{5} (7176) 7416^{3}

Bavarica *Julia Feilden* a71 79
9 b m Dansili—Blue Gentian (USA) (Known Fact (USA))
369^{3} 723^{8} 1183^{3} 1443^{7} 2159^{6} (2473) 2932^{11} 4613^{6} (5168) 5866^{8} 7032^{5}

Bawaardi (IRE) *Richard Fahey* a89 95
5 b g Acclamation—Global Trend (Bluebird (USA))
226^{7} 385^{2} 548^{5} 804^{2} (1382) 1594^{2} (2061) 2706^{10} 3397^{10} 4802^{9} 5032^{12} 5684^{3} ◆ 6335^{6} 7010a^{9} 7726^{4} (7876)

Bawdsey Bank *Ron Hodges* 41
5 b g Tipsy Creek(USA) —Busy (IRE) (In The Wings)
4706^{7} 6816^{12}

Bawinanga (USA) *J-C Rouget* a69 29
3 b f Dubawi(IRE) —River Bride (USA) (Kingmambo (USA))
258a^{5}

Bayan (IRE) *Brian Meehan* 64
2 b c Danehill Dancer(IRE) —Kindling (Dr Fong (USA))
6300^{6}

Baybshambles (IRE) *Ron Barr* 66
7 b g Compton Admiral—Payvashooz (Ballacashtal (CAN))
1204^{7} 1612^{4} 2126^{2} 2670^{2} 3087^{2} 3307^{5}

Bay Knight (IRE) *K J Condon* a87 104
5 b g Johannesburg(USA) —Sabeline (IRE) (Caerleon (USA))
1420a^{5} 3440a^{11} ◆ 4418a^{6} 4566a^{8} 5361a^{3} 6561a^{2} 6733a^{10}

Bayleyf (IRE) *John Best* a101 94
2 b c Kheleyf(USA) —Hi Katriona (IRE) (Second Empire (IRE))
1505^{2} ◆ 1886^{3} 3014^{7} (3761) (4536) 5715^{4}

Baylini *Jamie Osborne* a95 83
7 gr m Bertolini(USA) —Bay Of Plenty (FR) (Octagonal (NZ))
525^{3} 615^{5} 702^{6} 803^{5} 963^{2} (1103) 1269^{4} 1603^{10}

Bay Of Fires (IRE) *David O'Meara* 79
3 b f Iffraaj—No Tippling (IRE) (Unblest)
2466^{7} 2986^{5} 3318^{10} 3731^{2} 3975^{2} 4048^{10} 4610^{3} 5109^{8} 5559^{7} 6343^{11} 7073^{8}

Bay Shore (IRE) *J-C Rouget* 91
2 b f Kheleyf(USA) —Marillen (IRE) (Daylami (IRE))
3669a^{4} 4843a^{6}

Bay To Bay (USA) *Brian A Lynch* a103 112
4 b m Sligo Bay(IRE) —Bala (CAN) (With Approval (CAN))
6719a^{5}

Bay Willow (IRE) *Saeed Bin Suroor* a103 107
4 b g Singspiel(IRE) —Tree House (USA) (Woodman (USA))
328a^{7} 603a^{7} (677a) 824a^{3} 3625^{16} 4528^{9} 5250^{20} 6103^{8}

Bazguy *Garry Woodward* a38 69
6 ro g Josr Algarhoud(IRE) —Ewenny (Warrshan (USA))
402^{8} 798^{8} 874^{7} 6982^{11}

Beach Babe *Jonathan Portman* a73 66
3 b f Zafeen(FR) —Beechnut (IRE) (Mujadil (USA))
716^{8} (1053) (1566) 1958^{3} 2586^{4} 2964^{6} 3432^{8} 4888^{6} 5606^{4} 5860^{2} 6472^{9} 6872^{2} (7003)

Beach Candy (IRE) *Richard Hannon* 77
2 ch f Footstepsinthesand—Endure (IRE) (Green Desert (USA))
5323^{5} 5889^{7} (6406) (6921)

Beachfire *John Gosden* a76 111
4 ch g Indian Haven—Maine Lobster (USA) (Woodman (USA))
1479^{5} 1824^{2} 2289^{3} (3107) 3876^{4}

Beach Patrol (IRE) *Edward Creighton* a66 57
3 b g Antonius Pius(USA) —Slip Ashore (IRE) (Slip Anchor)
189^{7} 519^{7} 716^{9}

Beachwood Bay *Jo Hughes* a52 53
3 b g Tobougg(IRE) —The Terrier (Foxhound (USA))
4647^{4} 5206^{2} 5534^{9} (7911)

Beacon Hill (IRE) *J-P Carvalho* a77 80
3 b g Shamardal(USA) —Aleganza (IRE) (Lake Coniston (IRE))
2520a^{6}

Beacon Lady *Bill Turner* a29 49
2 ch f Haafhd—Oriental Lady (IRE) (King's Best (USA))
2651^{4} 5325^{4} 6471^{11}

Beacon Lodge (IRE) *Clive Cox* 115
6 b h Clodovil(IRE) —Royal House (FR) (Royal Academy (USA))
(1889) 2502^{5} 2980a^{3} 3404^{3} 4412^{3} 5046^{2} 5473^{3} 6129^{5}

Beaded (AUS) *Peter Snowden* 115
6 br m Lonhro(AUS) —Subtle (AUS) (Night Shift (USA))
3

Be A Devil *William Muir* a80 78
4 ch g Dubai Destination(USA) —Devil's Imp (IRE) (Cadeaux Genereux)
3740^{4} 4278^{8} 4910^{2} 5341^{4} 5717^{8} 6133^{9}

Beagle Boy (IRE) *A Wohler* a87 88
4 b h American Post—Heronetta (Halling (USA))
4373a^{11} 7256a^{6}

Be A Good Lady *Tony Coyle* a40 49
3 b f Goodricke—Lady Double U (Sheikh Albadou)
3049^{3} 4196^{10} 4647^{7}

Be Amazing (IRE) *David Lanigan* a69 28
3 b f Refuse To Bend(IRE) —Snow Peak (Arazi (USA))
1579^{3} 1869^{7} 2354^{11}

Beanstalk (IRE) *Richard Hannon* a12 6
2 ch c Titus Livius(FR) —Justice System (USA) (Criminal Type (USA))
5382^{12} 5937^{7}

Bea Persuasive *Shaun Harris* 30
2 b f Whipper(USA) —Thrasher (Hector Protector (USA))
4105^{7} 4512^{8} 4983^{7} 5597^{9} 6776^{11}

Bear Behind (IRE) *Tom Dascombe* 95
2 b c Kodiac—Gerobies Girl (USA) (Deposit Ticket (USA))
2423^{2} (2612) 3014^{5} 3589^{3} ◆ 4375a^{4} 4596a^{7} 5194a^{2} 5827^{6} 6535^{21}

Bea Remembered *Brian Meehan* 104
4 b m Doyen(IRE) —Leinster Mills (IRE) (Doyoun)
1884^{7} 2390^{4} (2676) 3107^{5} 4293^{6} 4915^{9} 5982a^{3} 6530^{3} 7296^{8}

Bearneen Boy (IRE) *Neil King* a36
8 b g Reprimand—Moyheez (IRE) (Naheez (USA))
688^{9}

Bearpath (USA) *Ian Wilkes* 112
5 b g Dynaformer(USA) —Song 'n Silk (USA) (Unbridled's Song (USA))
3888a^{6}

Beaten Up *William Haggas* 123
3 b g Beat Hollow—Frog (Akarad (FR))
(1415) (5888) (7027) ◆

Beating Harmony *Michael Appleby* a60 53
3 b g Beat Hollow—Heart's Harmony (Blushing Groom (FR))
270^{2} 366^{3} 527^{2} 668^{3} 817^{6} 967^{2} 1082^{7} 5843^{8} 6309^{12} 6545^{9} 7245^{9} 7419^{12} 7560^{3} 7656^{10} 7787^{8}

Beat Of The Blues *Alan McCabe* a79 40
3 b g Beat Hollow—Skies Are Blue (Unfuwain (USA))
4800^{3} 7446^{2} 7600^{5}

Beatrice Aurore (IRE) *John Dunlop* 112
3 b f Danehill Dancer(IRE) —Mondschein (Rainbow Quest (USA))
1113^{5} (1837) ◆ (2189) 2682^{6} (3671a) 4570a^{7} 5366a^{4} 7047a^{2}

Beat Route *Michael Attwater* a75 65
4 ch g Beat Hollow—Steppin Out (First Trump)
301^{2} 621^{5} 805^{8} 954^{3} 1174^{2} 3225^{3} 3739^{4} 4148^{6} 4660^{5} 5103^{2} 5580^{8} 6376^{10} 6789^{8} 7122^{4} 7346^{4} (7458) 7577^{5} 7661^{2} 7803^{6}

Beat The Bell *David Barron* a98 95
6 b g Beat All(USA) —Bella Beguine (Komaite (USA))
1166^{3} 1476^{2} ◆ 1809^{9} 2117^{3} ◆ 2317^{14} 2714^{13} 3160^{4} 3627^{6} 4556^{7} 5033^{19} 5680^{3} 5831^{15} 6112^{11}

Beat The Rush *Julie Camacho* 91
4 b g Tobougg(IRE) —Rush Hour (IRE) (Night Shift (USA))
1517^{3} 2888^{14} 3544^{9} 5729^{9}

Beat The Shower *Peter Niven* a46 83
5 b g Beat Hollow—Crimson Shower (Dowsing (USA))
1908^{4} 2364^{6} 3127^{4} 3851^{4} (4562) (4941) 5453^{2} 5759^{3} 6707^{4} 7102^{7}

Beat Up *Patrick Chamings* a67 26
5 b g Beat Hollow—Whitgift Rose (Polar Falcon (USA))
1867^{5} 2308^{13} 4869^{11}

Beau Amadeus (IRE) *Adrian McGuinness* a61 89
2 b c Amadeus Wolf—Degree Of Honor (FR) (Highest Honor (FR))
1699a^{8} 6196a^{6}

Beaubrav *Michael Madgwick* a99 74
5 b g Falbrav(IRE) —Wavy Up (IRE) (Brustolon)
(162) (392) 614^{2} (994) (1238) 1887^{11} 2649^{15} 3095^{11} 5135^{6} 5693^{9} 6592^{11} 7523^{7} 7802^{10}

Beau Bunny (IRE) *P D Deegan* a62 52
3 ch f Bahamian Bounty—Miswadah (IRE) (Machiavellian (USA))
973a^{3}

Beauchamp Best *Hans Adielsson* a39
2 ch f Compton Admiral—Bestemor (Selkirk (USA))
7398^{12} 7799^{5} 7889^{11}

Beauchamp Castle *Hans Adielsson* a60
2 b f Motivator—Ashford Castle (USA) (Bates Motel (USA))
7398^{9} 7799^{4} 7889^{7}

Beauchamp Orange *Hans Adielsson* a57
2 ch f Green Tune(USA) —Orange Sunset (IRE) (Roanoke (USA))
6440[8] 7197[5] 7396[6] 7763[8]

Beauchamp Viceroy *Gerard Butler* a110 84
7 ch g Compton Admiral—Compton Astoria (USA) (Lion Cavern (USA))
271[4] 700[8] 844[10]

Beauchamp Viking *Simon Burrough* a49 42
7 b g Compton Admiral—Beauchamp Jade (Kalaglow)
173[3] 277[10] 598[4]

Beauchamp Xerxes *Gerard Butler* a103 106
5 ch g Compton Admiral—Compton Astoria (USA) (Lion Cavern (USA))
2679[15] 3109[25] 3537[4]

Beauchamp Xiara *Hans Adielsson* a71 77
5 b m Compton Admiral—Beauchamp Buzz (High Top)
344[2] 529[4] 813[P] 2176[5] 2478[3] 2912[5] 3228[12] 4448[10] 5248[9] 5609[4] 5860[7] 6493[10] 6657[4] (6968) 7206[3] 7370[2] 7496[4]

Beauchamp Yeoman *Hans Adielsson* a41 41
4 b g Compton Admiral—One Way Street (Habitat)
850[8]

Beauchamp Yorker *Hans Adielsson* a66 79
4 ch g Compton Admiral—Compton Astoria (USA) (Lion Cavern (USA))
1564[5] 2105[11] 3740[11] 3987[7] 4268[7] 4910[9] 6797[10] 7176[9]

Beauchamp Zest *Hans Adielsson* a61 56
3 gr f Compton Admiral—Beauchamp Jade (Kalaglow)
811[6] 909[5] 1364[8] 2166[6] 3393[6] 5243[7]

Beauchamp Zorro *Henry Candy* 63
3 ch g Zamindar(USA) —Aquarelle (Kenmare (FR))
5449[7] 5960[4] 6754[2]

Beau Duke (IRE) *Andrew Balding* 74
2 b g Bachelor Duke(USA) —Xema (Danehill (USA))
4053[8] 4968[5] 5672[2]

Beau Fighter *Gary Moore* a79 80
6 b g Tobougg(IRE) —Belle De Jour (Exit To Nowhere (USA))
174[9] 266[6] 645[3] (859) (938) 1608[8] (1977) ◆

Beaufort Twelve *William Jarvis* 85
2 b c Hurricane Run(IRE) —Violette (Observatory (USA))
(7133)

Beaulieu (IRE) *E Libaud* 104
3 b c Motivator—Morning Sun (GER) (Law Society (USA))
2341a[4] 2979a[3]

Beaumaris (IRE) *Ann Duffield* a41 65
2 ch f Sir Percy—Red Spinel (Fantastic Light (USA))
(2797) 3345[3] 4194[11] 4512[10] 5246[7]

Beau Michael *Adrian McGuinness* a62 82
7 b g Medicean—Tender Moment (IRE) (Caerleon (USA))
1381a[13]

Beau Mistral (IRE) *Paul Green* a60 69
2 ch f Windsor Knot(IRE) —Carpet Lover (IRE) (Fayruz)
1095[7] 1414[2] 1806[7] 2523[3] 2612[2] 3237[3] 3375[4] 4787[5] (5174) 5922[6] 6293[4]

Beaumont Cooper *Anabel K Murphy*
2 b g Invincible Spirit(IRE) —Atlantide (USA) (Southern Halo (USA))
6274[9]

Beaumont's Party (IRE) *Andrew Balding* a71 100
4 b g High Chaparral(IRE) —Miss Champagne (FR) (Bering)
1530[3] 1684[12] (2282) (2378) 2681[4] 5275[2] 6163[5]

Beautiful Day *Kevin Ryan* a86 66
3 b g Piccolo—Evening (Mark Of Esteem (IRE))
179[5] 305[4] 611[4] 1020[2] 1246[6] 1465[2] (1813) 2294[4] 2736[5] 4527[5] 4786[5] 5274[U] 5373[4] 5895[8] 6010[illegible] 7004[8] 7388[2] (7727) (7782)

Beautiful Lando (FR) *Heather Main* a70 59
3 b g Lando(GER) —Beautiful Baroness (USA) (Fortunate Prospect (USA))
801[7] 888[4] 1047[3] (1176) 1768[4] 1869[3] 2838[5] 3172[9] 4908[4] 5529a[3] (5902) 6179[3] 6746[14] 7667a[5]

Beauty Flash (NZ) *A S Cruz* 119
6 ch g Golan(IRE) —Wychwood Rose (NZ) (Volksraad)
1000a[8] 1576a[4] 7731a[6]

Beauty Pageant (IRE) *Ed McMahon* 87
4 ch m Bahamian Bounty—My American Beauty (Wolfhound (USA))
(2365) 2987[4] 3579[2] (4628) ◆ 5679[3] (6350)

Beaver Patrol (IRE) *Eve Johnson Houghton* a109 87
9 ch g Tagula(IRE) —Erne Project (IRE) (Project Manager)
1530[4] 1832[6] 2169[2]

Becagand *D Prod'Homme*
4 b g Footstepsinthesand—Moher (ITY) (Zafonic (USA))
1033a[0]

Be Calm *Michael Easterby* a56 59
2 b f Gentleman's Deal(IRE) —Flower O'Cannie (IRE) (Mujadil (USA))
3274[4] 5786[7] 6110[U] 6291[5] 6667[3]

Becausewecan (USA) *Mark Johnston* a101 97
5 b g Giant's Causeway(USA) —Belle Sultane (USA) (Seattle Slew (USA))
1517[2] (1713) 2006[13] 3013[11] 3867[7] 4348[13] 5057[6] 5435[10] (5837) (6410) 6690[11]

Becebege (FR) *A Bonin* a41 77
2 ch f Layman(USA) —All Heart (FR) (Alhaarth (IRE))
(7449a)

Beckermet (IRE) *Ruth Carr* a93 91
9 b g Second Empire(IRE) —Razida (IRE) (Last Tycoon)
377[4] 673[5] 798[7] 928[5] 1612[2] 1911[3] (2412) 2609[3] 3025[3] 3348[2] 3657[3] 4145[2] 4378[2] 5006[2] 6081[9] (6426) 6778[9] (6869) (7076) 7171[2]

Beckfield Dancer *Stuart Williams* a50 39
3 b f Singspiel(IRE) —Saffwah (IRE) (King's Best (USA))
3689[6] 4241[4] 4826[8] 6253[6] 6622[9] 7122[8] 7394[9]

Beckfield Point *Stuart Williams*
2 b c Shirocco(GER) —Platinum Princess (Diktat)
5919[5]

Becksies *Paul Midgley* 46
2 b f Danbird(AUS) —Cut Back (Factual (USA))
1301[2] 5367[10] 5555[6]

Becquarey (FR) *A Trybuhl* a77
3 b c Soave(GER) —Top Warning (FR) (Piccolo)
980a[9]

Bedibyes *Richard Mitchell* a56 59
3 b f Sleeping Indian—Aunt Sadie (Pursuit Of Love)
212 [4] 655[7] 887[7] 1579[5] 2243[5] 3431[4] 3803[7] 6813[2] 7144[4]

Bedlam *Tim Easterby* 69
2 b f Auction House(USA) —Frantic (Fraam)
2936[3] ◆ 3274[7] 4002[7] 4943[5] 5287[9] 6260[2] 6911[11]

Bedloe's Island (IRE) *Neville Bycroft* a34 83
6 b g Statue Of Liberty(USA) —Scenaria (IRE) (Scenic)
2118[14] (2590) 2890[6] 3279[2] 4327[5] 4516[9]

Bedouin Bay *Alan McCabe* a85 82
4 b g Dubai Destination(USA) —Sahara Sonnet (USA) (Stravinsky (USA))
(515) 614[5] 849[3] 948[6] 1098[7] 1651[3] 3867[6] 4697[5]

Beechcraft Baron (IRE) *William Haggas* a78 66
3 b g Statue Of Liberty(USA) —Royale Figurine (IRE) (Dominion Royale)
1880[10] 2266[5] 2650[2] 3230[10] 3977[2] 4478[7] (5212) 6617[4]

Beechey's Beauty *Phil McEntee* 64
2 b g Camacho—Mix It Up (Linamix (FR))
1966[9] 2387[6] 2570[7] 3021[2] 3505[2] 4147[2] 4558[7] 4809[7] 7335[F]

Beech View (IRE) *Martin Bosley* a15 46
6 b m Desert Prince(IRE) —Karakapa (FR) (Subotica (FR))
819[12] 3353[5] 3946[9]

Beethoven (IRE) *Ahmed Kobeissi* a111 118
4 b h Oratorio(IRE) —Queen Titi (IRE) (Sadler's Wells (USA))
1000a[9]

Beetuna (IRE) *David Bourton* a78 82
6 b g Statue Of Liberty(USA) —High Atlas (Shirley Heights)
287[8] 405[8] 715[6] 897[8] 1058[7] 2996[3] 3251[4]

Be Fabulous (GER) *A Fabre* 111
4 b m Samum(GER) —Bandeira (GER) (Law Society (USA))
(6661a) (7049a)

Before Bruce *Brendan Powell* a11
4 b g Danbird(AUS) —Bisque (Inchinor)
7766[8]

Before The War (USA) *Jeremy Gask* a58 67
4 ch g El Corredor(USA) —Adrenalin Running (USA) (A.P. Indy (USA))
223[8] 409[6] 592[6]

Befortyfour *Richard Guest* a102 99
6 b g Kyllachy—Ivania (First Trump)
2028[11] 2317[13] 2489[2] 2727[8] 2890[11] 3846[9] 4104[5] 4346[13] 4556[11] 4791[9] 5434[12] 6177[11]

Beggers Belief *Eric Wheeler* a64 62
3 ch g Bertolini(USA) —Dropitlikeit's Hot (IRE) (Tagula (IRE))
1724[12] 3173[8] 4861[8] 6122[8] 6589[4] 6923[2] (7092) 7394[6] 7836[2] (7902)

Beginnings (USA) *Lydia Pearce* a75 86
3 b f Aptitude(USA) —Birthplace (USA) (King Of Kings (IRE))
7204 [4] 7806[6]

Behkabad (FR) *J-C Rouget* 125
4 bb h Cape Cross(IRE) —Behkara (IRE) (Kris)
2753a[2]

Behlul (IRE) *Gerard Butler* a59 61
2 rg c Verglas(IRE) —Queen's Quest (Rainbow Quest (USA))
3947[2] 4646[3] 5818[3]

Behma (FR) *Mme J Hendriks* 29
4 b m Kahyasi—Behnesa (IRE) (Suave Dancer (USA))
479a[8]

Be Kind *Karen George* a41 45
5 b m Generous(IRE) —Aquavita (Kalaglow)
4511[2]

Bel Cantor *Bill Ratcliffe* a88 84
8 b h Largesse—Palmstead Belle (IRE) (Wolfhound (USA))
13[2] 345[7] 402[3] 674[6]

Belenkaya (USA) *Mahmood Al Zarooni* a56
3 b f Giant's Causeway(USA) —Rings A Chime (USA) (Metfield (USA))
6137[6]

Belfast Boy (AUS) *Gordon Richards* 91
4 bb g Bel Esprit(AUS) —Fast Dolly (AUS) (Bureaucracy (NZ))
9029a[8]

Belgian Bill *George Baker* a106 104
3 b c Exceed And Excel(AUS) —Gay Romance (Singspiel (IRE))
(1384) 3064[7] ◆ 3802[3] 4467[8] 5230a[4] 5754a[2]

Bel Herve (FR) *J-M Capitte* a63
4 gr h Slickly(FR) —Zafonia (FR) (Zafonic (USA))
842a[4]

Belinsky (IRE) *Mark Campion* a68 75
4 b g Compton Place—Westwood (FR) (Anabaa (USA))
1907[7] 4291[5] 4793[6] 5338[3] 5732[4] 6261[7] 6609[6] 6940[3] 7123[2] 7419[10] 7587[P]

Bella Berti *Roger Ingram* a10
3 b f Bertolini(USA) —Dragon Star (Rudimentary (USA))
518[9]

Bellaboolou *David Pinder* a44 34
3 b f Compton Place—Al Corniche (IRE) (Bluebird (USA))
95[10] 214 [9] 600[10] 684[5] 1566[11] 1790[5] 1933[13]

Bella Montagna *John Quinn* a22 52
3 b f Dubai Destination(USA) —Hagwah (USA) (Dancing Brave (USA))
1648[3] 2185[10] 2785[2] 3976[9] 5380[6] 5898[9]

Bella Nemica *Edward Creighton* a32 28
3 b f Iceman—Bella Helena (Balidar)
2384[13] 4547[15] 4950[5] 5670[7] 6004[6]

Bella Noir *Mrs K Burke* a70 81
4 b m Kyllachy—Lady Broughton (IRE) (Grand Lodge (USA))
1279[7] 2398[4] 3112[3] 3620[3] (4127) 4448[4] 4807[3] ◆ 5164[4] 5702[8] 6330[15] 7033[6]

Bella Ophelia (IRE) *Hughie Morrison* a45
2 b f Baltic King—Banco Solo (Distant Relative)
7345[10] 7540[8]

Bella Ponte *John Gallagher* 45
2 b f Avonbridge—Michelle Shift (Night Shift (USA))
1136[6] 1765[6] 2241[4] 6222[14]

Bella Shara (FR) *D Windrif*
3 b f Super Celebre(FR) —Queen Shara (FR) (Welkin (CAN))
288a[0]

Bellaside (IRE) *E Leon Penate* 80
4 b m Le Vie Dei Colori—Brockton Saga (IRE) (Perugino (USA))
7386a[0]

Belle Bayardo (IRE) *Ronald Harris* a77 94
3 b g Le Vie Dei Colori—Heres The Plan (IRE) (Revoque (IRE))
1545[5] 2500[7] 4063[6] 4643[5] 4817[7] 5378[3] 5781[8] 5859[5] 6895[5] 7073[6] 7519[10]

Belle Boleyn *Chris Wall* a60 58
4 b m Tobougg(IRE) —Belle De Jour (Exit To Nowhere (USA))
1987[5] 2569[3] 2820[9] 5210[8] 5588[3] 6029[8]

Bellechance *Nigel Tinkler* a58 60
2 b f Acclamation—Silver Dip (Gulch (USA))
(2731) 3795[5] 4824[6] 5246[4] 5555[7]

Belle Masquee (IRE) *D Smaga* a90 104
4 b m Oratorio(IRE) —Secret Wells (USA) (Sadler's Wells (USA))
(91a) 1784a[6] 7404a[8]

Bellemere *Michael Easterby* 70
3 b f Ad Valorem(USA) —Five Lakes (USA) (Coronado's Quest (USA))
2074[18] 2391[10] 2736[6] 3087[8] 3702[10] 4288[11] 4607[6]

Belle Noverre (IRE) *Shaun Harley* a78 83
7 b m Noverre(USA) —Belle Etoile (FR) (Lead On Time (USA))
2807[2] (4501)

Belle Park *Karen George* a61 61
4 b m Hamairi(IRE) —Cape Siren (Warning)
893[6] 1273[12] 1755[6] 2385[4] 3926[3] 4444[4] (7006) 7208[10] 7537[11] 7741[9]

Belle Royale (IRE) *Mark Brisbourne* a61 112
3 b f Val Royal(FR) —Kahyasi Moll (IRE) (Brief Truce (USA))
(1326) 1820[6] 2189[6] 2833[2] 3873[2] 4093[5] 4790[9] (5272) (5730) (6325)

Belles Beau *Reg Hollinshead* a57
4 b m Fraam—Victory Flip (IRE) (Victory Note (USA))
88[4] 201[6]

Belle Trolette (FR) *J Van Handenhove* 53
2 b f Sulamani(IRE) —Makila (IRE) (Entrepreneur)
7449a[0]

Bellinda *Martin Bosley* a40
2 b f Aussie Rules(USA) —Bonnie Belle (Imperial Ballet (IRE))
6131[8] 7909[8]

Bellinissimo (IRE) *J-C Rouget* a95 91
5 b h Hawk Wing(USA) —Princess Electra (IRE) (Lake Coniston (IRE))
(257a)

Bellomi (IRE) *Ken Wingrove* a38 94
6 gr g Lemon Drop Kid(USA) —Reina Blanca (Darshaan)
445[7]

Bell's Ocean (USA) *John Ryan* a61 63
4 b m Proud Citizen(USA) —Golden Train (USA) (Slew O'Gold (USA))
2923[9] 3303[6] 3741[10] 4089[2] 4549[11] 4601[5] 4852[5] 5515[10] 5944[9] 6084[8] 6472[6]

Bells Of Berlin *Alan McCabe* 17
2 ch c Pivotal—Choirgirl (Unfuwain (USA))
5851[15] 6230[9] 6572[9]

Below Zero (IRE) *Mark Johnston* a101 103
4 b g Shamardal(USA) —Chilly Start (IRE) (Caerleon (USA))
(710) 830a[5] 2470[14] 2706[18] 3109[15] 3535[9] 3841[6] (4188) 4314[21] 4556[12] (5086a) 5272[2] 5474[3] (5746a) ◆ 5887[8] 6147[26] 6521[14] 7023[13]

Beltanus (GER) *T Potters* 83
7 ch h Tertullian(USA) —Brighella (GER) (Lomitas)
1263a[6]

Be My Spy *Peter Salmon* 31
3 b f Monsieur Bond(IRE) —Star Sign (Robellino (USA))
1910[9] 2786[9] 3206[10]

Benamy Boy *Neville Bycroft* 31
5 ch g First Trump—Carol Again (Kind Of Hush)
800[11] 1692[10]

Benandonner (USA) *Mike Murphy* a100 97
8 ch g Giant's Causeway(USA) —Cape Verdi (IRE) (Caerleon (USA))
271[5] 615[6] 846[4] (1014) 1172[2] 1529[5] (2105) 2679[12] 3645[11] 4100[2] 4993[5] 5712[9] 5940[10] 6496[4] 6541[4] 7168[18]

Benaojan (FR) *X Nakkachdji* a68 82
5 b m Alhaarth(IRE) —Agapimou (IRE) (Spectrum (IRE))
221a[7]

Benato The Great (IRE) *David Nicholls* a78 67
5 b g Acclamation—Teodora (IRE) (Fairy King (USA))
58[4] 1289[4]

Bencoolen (IRE) *D De Waele* a76 97
6 b g Daylami(IRE) —Jakarta (IRE) (Machiavellian (USA))
6[9] 195a[9] 257a[6] 372a[9] 566a[2] 903a[0] 1142a[7]

Ben Croy *Brian Meehan* a57 40
2 b g Nayef(USA) —Chrysalis (Soviet Star (USA))
6805[9] 7134[10] 7521[8]

Bendzoldan (IRE) *Thomas Cleary* a72 67
3 b f Refuse To Bend(IRE) —Zoldan (Deploy)
7740[5]

Beneath *Neil Mulholland* a74 83
4 b g Dansili—Neath (Rainbow Quest (USA))
1798[8] 2388[4] 2696[3] 3129[4] 3453[3] 3637[4] 3811[5] 4605[2] 5611[8] 6135[7] 6434[10] 6784[12]

Benefit Of Porter (IRE) *Patrick Sinnott* a69 78
7 b m Beneficial—Porter Tastes Nice (IRE) (Dry Dock)
5748a[5]

Bengaline *David Nicholls* a69 48
2 b c Bahamian Bounty—Indian Silk (IRE) (Dolphin Street (FR))
3229[14] 5104[5] 5596[2] 6045[5] 6673[12] 7335[2] 7555[9] 7642[6]

Bengal Tiger *Tony Carroll* a34 61
5 ch g Tagula(IRE) —Floriana (Selkirk (USA))
7557[10] 7651[14] 7831[11]

Benhego *Gary Moore* a87 76
6 ch g Act One—Sadaka (USA) (Kingmambo (USA))
209 [6] 486[2]

Benidorm *John Wainwright* a45 62
3 b g Bahamian Bounty—Famcred (Inchinor)
1203[8] 6578[6]

Benjamin (FR) *L A Urbano-Grajales* a90 90
6 b g Highest Honor(FR) —Mia's Baby (USA) (Rahy (USA))
(259a) 479a[3]

Bennelong *Richard Rowe* a76 66
5 b g Bahamian Bounty—Bundle Up (USA) (Miner's Mark (USA))
1570[3] 1875[6] 5300[2] 5740[10] (5994) 6468[9] (6871) 7203 [5] (7346) 7577[10] 7761[4]

Benny The Bear *Linda Perratt* 65
4 ch g Rambling Bear—Mitchelland (Namaqualand (USA))
4141[8] 4379[5] (4782) 4876[4] 5309[10] 5721[11] (6428) 6777[6]

Bentley *Brian Baugh* a77 62
7 b g Piccolo—April Lee (Superpower)
61[2] 148[3] 291[2] (400) 528[6] 744[7] 2159[7] 2401[11] 2653[7] 2985[2] 3306[2] 3643[5] 4579[6] 4821[6] 5208[6] 7556[11] 7720[10]

Benzanno (IRE) *Andrew Balding* 74
2 b g Refuse To Bend(IRE) —Crossanza (IRE) (Cape Cross (IRE))
3986[11] 4201[2] 4853[3] 5446[6] 6268[6]

Berberana (IRE) *Tim Easterby* a78 88
3 b f Acclamation—Barbera (GER) (Night Shift (USA))
1241[12] 1650[5] 2074[19] 2505[4] 2911[4] 3975[7] (4295) 4541[3] 5288[11] 5831[11] 6348[2] 6913[12]

Berbice (IRE) *Linda Perratt* a72 74
6 gr g Acclamation—Pearl Bright (FR) (Kaldoun (FR))
1073[10] 1712[6] 1861[3] 2353[7] 2633[8] 3128[2] 3657[11] 3856[5] 3902[2] 4141[3] 4362[5] 4503[2] 4539[7] 5053[7] 5314[13] 5722[7] 6081[8] 6426[5] 6779[5] 7100[3] (7268) (7591) 7696[4] 7715[10]

Berengar (IRE) *Brian Meehan* a74 63
2 b g Holy Roman Emperor(IRE) —Double Fantasy (GER) (Indian Ridge)
5480[6] 5861[3]

Bergo (GER) *Gary Moore* 112
8 b g Silvano(GER) —Bella Figura (USA) (Surumu (GER))
584a[9] 826a[2] 4469[5] 5284[3] 5884[4]

Bergonzi (IRE) *C Von Der Recke* a76 85
7 ch g Indian Ridge—Lady Windley (Baillamont (USA))
(843a) 1013a[7]

Berigny (FR) *E Lellouche* 83
3 b c Red Ransom(USA) —Beyond The Dream (USA) (Fusaichi Pegasus (USA))
1923a[9]

Berling (IRE) *John Dunlop* 102
4 gr h Montjeu(IRE) —Danaskaya (IRE) (Danehill (USA))
1887[6] 2716[2] 3411[4] (4677) (5271) ◆ 5921[4]

Berlusca (IRE) *William Jarvis* a67 66
2 b c Holy Roman Emperor(IRE) —Shemanikha (FR) (Sendawar (IRE))
2844[8] 3237[U] 4068[2] 4857[10] 5840[9] (6695) 7592[3] 7798[4]

Bermondsey Bob (IRE) *John Spearing* a14 25
5 b g Trans Island—Tread Softly (IRE) (Roi Danzig (USA))
1912[12] 2222[5] 2555[2] 2609[6] 2845[2] 3255[4] (3512) (3940) 4434[4] 4795[2] 4960[7] 5425[7] 5561[4] 6634[5] 6752[5]

Bernieres (IRE) *Mme Pia Brandt* 108
3 b f Montjeu(IRE) —Bounce (FR) (Trempolino (USA))
1922a[5] 2750a[8] 4036b[7] (5839a) 6555a[4]

Bernie The Bolt (IRE) *Andrew Balding* a50 102
5 br g Milan—Chaparral Lady (IRE) (Broken Hearted)
6690[22]

Bernisdale *George Moore* a55 65
3 ch f Bertolini(USA) —Carradale (Pursuit Of Love)
59[3] 379[3] 1413[3] (1877) (2565)

Bernix *Mark Campion* a68 58
9 gr g Linamix(FR) —Bernique (USA) (Affirmed (USA))
1373[10] 6235[15]

Bertbrand *Ian McInnes* a52 51
6 b g Bertolini(USA) —Mi Amor (IRE) (Alzao (USA))
57[6] 107[3] 289[4] 517[5] 545[5] 941[2] 1029[6] 1464[7] 7079[7] 7230[15] 7366[11] 7459[11] 7785[9]

Bertie Blu Boy *Paul Green* a72 63
3 b g Central Park(IRE) —Shaymee's Girl (Wizard King)
516[6] 579[4] 898[5] ◆ (1082) 1392[8] (1475) 1768[3] 2216[9] 2527[10] 5803[8] 5924[9] 6543[10] 7538[10] 7716[10] 7820[9]

Bertie Boo *Michael Appleby* a49 52
6 b g Where Or When(IRE) —Lucy Boo (Singspiel (IRE))
6877[7] 7270[6] 7581[14] 7740[10]

Bertie Dancing (IRE) *Nigel Tinkler* 38
2 b g Bertolini(USA) —Dancing Nelly (Shareef Dancer (USA))
1165[7] 1744[8] 3932[9] 4105[4] 4808[7]

Bertie's Best *F Doumen* a77 83
4 ch m King's Best(USA) —Just Wood (FR) (Highest Honor (FR))
(108a)

Bertie Southstreet *Paul Midgley* a63 76
8 bb g Bertolini(USA) —Salvezza (IRE) (Superpower)
2766[8] 3640[4] 4152[10] 4475[4] 4895[12] 5895[5]

Bertiewhittle *David Barron* a65 98
3 ch g Bahamian Bounty—Minette (Bishop Of Cashel)
1246[2] 1813[3] 2094[3] 2281[3] (2729) 2937[3] (3378) 4472[5] (5054) 6145[7]

Bertoliver *Stuart Williams* a85 92
7 b g Bertolini(USA) —Calcavella (Pursuit Of Love)
1476[13] 1680[10] 2069[4] 2714[11] 3427[6] 3778[9] (5923)

Bertorella (IRE) *Ralph Beckett* a11 44
2 b f Bertolini(USA) —Dictatrice (FR) (Anabaa (USA))
2153[12] 2374[9] 2901[7] 4069[P] 5325[7] 5637[8]

Bert The Alert *Gary Moore* a63
3 b g Proclamation(IRE) —Megalex (Karinga Bay)
7766[2] 7921[3]

Berwin (IRE) *Sylvester Kirk* a74
2 b f Lawman(FR) —Topiary (IRE) (Selkirk (USA))
5813[3] 6215[3]

Beseech (USA) *Julia Feilden* a49 14
4 rg m Maria's Mon(USA) —Concert Hall (USA) (Stravinsky (USA))
184[6] 507[4] 795[3] 911[4] 1181[7]

Besito (IRE) *William Jarvis* 79
2 b f Kodiac—Christmas Kiss (Taufan (USA))
2914[5] 4263 [2] (4961) 5847[7] 6146[DSQ] 7135[10]

Beso (IRE) *Luca Cumani* a68 68
3 ch f Medicean—Olivia Grace (Pivotal)
1393[5] 2643[7] 3260[8]

Best Be Careful (IRE) *Mark Usher* a57 75
3 b f Exceed And Excel(AUS) —Precautionary (Green Desert (USA))
(1776) 2294[8] 2660[3] 3433[3] 5115[2] 5265[3] (5615) 5914[5] (6456) 6801[9]

Best Dating (IRE) *S Wattel* 116
4 b g King's Best(USA) —Just Special (Cadeaux Genereux)
(5772a) 6556a[3]

Best Hello *P D Deegan* 103
3 b c Beat Hollow—Jumeela (Rainbow Quest (USA))
1927a[4] 2331a[4]

Best In Show *J W Hills* a54 53
2 b g Exceed And Excel(AUS) —Alashaan (Darshaan)
2901[8] 3746[9] 4339[5]

Best Known Secret (IRE) *Chris Bealby* a52 50
5 b m Captain Rio—Secret Justice (USA) (Lit De Justice (USA))
57[8] 690[10] 3241[7]

Best One *Ronald Harris* a63 60
7 ch g Best Of The Bests(IRE) —Nasaieb (IRE) (Fairy King (USA))
185[10] 276[10] 3721[8] 3939[7] 4272[7] 4487[6] 4882[6] 5617[4] 5678[2] 5996[6] 6175[7] 6398[4]

Bestowed *Tim Vaughan* a68 58
6 b g Kyllachy—Granted (FR) (Cadeaux Genereux)
181[7] 574[8]

Best Prospect (IRE) *Michael Dods* a87 83
9 b g Orpen(USA) —Bright Prospect (USA) (Miswaki (USA))
2059[12] 3399[11] 5440[9] 5757[10] 7237[12]

Best Terms *Richard Hannon* 114
2 b f Exceed And Excel(AUS) —Sharp Terms (Kris)
(1441) ◆ (2053) (3033) (5217) ◆ 6337[5]

Best Trip (IRE) *Richard Guest* a89 67
4 b g Whipper(USA) —Tereed Elhawa (Cadeaux Genereux)
(269) 725[3] 867[2] (946) (1197) 1476[5] 2497[9] 3222[2] 4909[10] 5831[18] 7832[9]

Bestwecan (IRE) *Mark Johnston* a76 76
3 b g King's Best(USA) —Datsdawayitis (USA) (Known Fact (USA))
762[3] (891) ◆ 1170[4] 1456[5]

Besty *David Nicholls* a76 81
4 ch g Compton Place—Petrovna (IRE) (Petardia)
58[3] 377[6] 673[7] 794[8] 4078[9] 4371[5] 5455[7] 5732[12] 6634[14]

Betcherev (IRE) *S Cerulis* a63 62
7 ch g Barathea(IRE) —Clare Bridge (USA) (Little Current (USA))
439a[0]

Betpak Dala *A Savujev* 103
2 ch c Shamardal(USA) —Quelle Amore (GER) (Monsun (GER))
6902a[5] 7405a[6]

Better Announce (IRE) *Ed Walker* 79
2 b c Invincible Spirit(IRE) —Doula (USA) (Gone West (USA))
(7134)

Betteras Bertie *Tony Coyle* a62 67
8 gr g Paris House—Suffolk Girl (Statoblest)
1814[10] (4367)

Better Be Blue (IRE) *Tony Carroll* a47 65
4 b m Big Bad Bob(IRE) —Ginger Lily (IRE) (Lucky Guest)
448[8] 771[11]

Better Be Mine (IRE) *John Dunlop* a50 52
2 br f Big Bad Bob(IRE) —Cara Fantasy (IRE) (Sadler's Wells (USA))
3813[10] 4245[7] 5299[12] 5945[3] ◆ (6460)

Better Be The One (AUS) *M Freedman* 115
5 b g More Than Ready(USA) —Common Smytzer (AUS) (Snippets (AUS))
996a[3] 2339a[9]

Better Self *David Evans* a71 64
3 b f With Approval(CAN) —Alter Ego (Alzao (USA))
27[5] (192) (270) 423[2] 576[3] 609[2] (770) 817[3] 886[3] 951[3] 1526[9] 1828[7] 2381[3]

Better Than Ever (AUS) *L Laxon* a102 102
5 b g French Deputy(USA) —Songfest (AUS) (Unbridled's Song (USA))
1000a[14]

Betty Brook (IRE) *Nick Littmoden* a58 47
2 b f Refuse To Bend(IRE) —Ikan (IRE) (Sri Pekan (USA))
7056[6] 7267[3] 7435[5]

Betty Fontaine (IRE) *Mick Channon* 93
2 b f Mujadil(USA) —Dance Fontaine (IRE) (Danehill Dancer (IRE))
(2241) 2476[4] (2902) (3435) 3821[7] 4312[4] 4999[9] 5849[19] 6518[14]

Between The Lines (IRE) *Sir Michael Stoute* 62
2 gr c Dalakhani(IRE) —Stage Struck (IRE) (Sadler's Wells (USA))
6954[7]

Between Us *Sir Mark Prescott Bt* a73
2 b f Galileo(IRE) —Confidante (USA) (Dayjur (USA))
7598[3] ◆

Bevis Marks (USA) *Mark Johnston* a12 48
2 b c Street Cry(IRE) —Blue Duster (USA) (Danzig (USA))
5688[11] 6059[10]

Bewilder *John Gosden* a70 64
2 b c Invincible Spirit(IRE) —Dubai Sunrise (USA) (Seeking The Gold (USA))
3132[15] 3954[4] 4912[5] 5324[9] 6053[2] 6623[11]

Bewitched (IRE) *Charles O'Brien* a81 113
4 gr m Dansili—Abbatiale (FR) (Kaldoun (FR))
(2533a) ◆ 3154[14] 5707[8] (5979a) 6566a[4] 6908a[7]

Beyeh (IRE) *Michael Appleby* a49 74
3 b f King's Best(USA) —Cradle Rock (IRE) (Desert Sun)
2184[4] 2791[7] 4727[5] 5020[8] 6311[10] 7727[5] 7839[6]

Beyond (IRE) *David Pipe* a81 87
4 ch g Galileo(IRE) —Run To Jane (IRE) (Doyoun)
(3593) 6690[7]

Beyond Conceit (IRE) *Tom Tate* 82
2 b c Galileo(IRE) —Baraka (IRE) (Danehill (USA))
4122[3] ◆ 4714[3] (6825)

Beyond Desire *Roger Varian* 106
4 b m Invincible Spirit(IRE) —Compradore (Mujtahid (USA))
1902[6] 2861a[4] 3644[2] 4468[4] 6164[4] 6563a[14]

Beyond Hubris (IRE) *Tom Tate* 26
2 ch g Rock Of Gibraltar(IRE) —Florista Gg (URU) (Gulpha Gorge (USA))
3382[11] 7060[11]

Bezique *M Gasparini* 101
3 gr f Cape Cross(IRE) —Batik (IRE) (Peintre Celebre (USA))
1738a[11]

B Fifty Two (IRE) *J W Hills* 107
2 br c Dark Angel(IRE) —Petite Maxine (Sharpo)
1360[10] (1628) (2109) 3012[6] 4055[6] 4596a[2] 5251[5] 6162[8] 6688[8]

Bianca De Medici *Hughie Morrison* a80 79
4 b m Medicean—Tremiere (FR) (Anabaa (USA))
1499[2] 1884[4] 2313[6] 3278[5] (4387) 6065[5] 7243[3] 7625[4] 7745[2]

Biancarosa (IRE) *Simon Dow* 84
4 b m Dalakhani(IRE) —Rosa Di Brema (ITY) (Lomitas)
5992[11]

Bianco Boy (USA) *John Best* a55
4 rg g Roman Ruler(USA) —Sterling Cat (USA) (Event Of The Year (USA))
653[3] 1043[11] 6940[12] 7524[13]

Biaraafa (IRE) *Michael Bell* a66 80
3 b f Araafa(IRE) —Bianca Nera (Salse (USA))
(1571) 2102[4] 2506[9] 4202[6] 5862[10]

Biba Diva (IRE) *Jeremy Noseda* 75
2 b f Danehill Dancer(IRE) —Mowaadah (IRE) (Alzao (USA))
5655[8] (6099) 6724[7]

Bibiana Bay *Gary Moore* a42 35
4 b m Leporello(IRE) —Polisonne (Polish Precedent (USA))
164[8] 299[7]

Bible Belt (IRE) *Mrs John Harrington* 114
3 br f Big Bad Bob(IRE) —Shine Silently (IRE) (Bering)
(5523a) 5976a[7] 6859[2] ◆

Bible Black (IRE) *G M Lyons* a99 93
2 br g Big Bad Bob(IRE) —Convent Girl (IRE) (Bishop Of Cashel)
972a[5] 5950a[6]

Bidable *Bryn Palling* a56 76
7 b m Auction House(USA) —Dubitable (Formidable (USA))
1658[7] (1755) 2719[9] 3514[5] 4158[8] 4701[3] 4949[5] 5376[3] 5808[6] 6435[2] 7538[6] 7698[7]

Bid For Gold *Jedd O'Keeffe* a36 63
7 b g Auction House(USA) —Gold And Blue (IRE) (Bluebird (USA))
(2990)

Bigalo's Laura B (IRE) *G P Kelly* 53
3 ch f Needwood Blade—Rash (Pursuit Of Love)
1303[9] 1967[8] 4560[15] 4897[9]

Bigalo's Princessa *Lawrence Mullaney* a32 19
3 b f Kyllachy—Emouna (Cadeaux Genereux)
183[9]

Bigalo's Vera B *Lawrence Mullaney* a51 32
3 b f Ishiguru(USA) —Maid For Running (Namaqualand (USA))
60[7] 146[2] 741[3] 868[7]

Big Audio (IRE) *Saeed Bin Suroor* 103
4 b g Oratorio(IRE) —Tarbela (IRE) (Grand Lodge (USA))
605a[5]

Big Bad Lily (IRE) *Augustine Leahy* a74 69
3 b f Big Bad Bob(IRE) —Ginger Lily (IRE) (Lucky Guest)
973a[10] 1663a[11]

Big Bay (USA) *Jane Chapple-Hyam* a87 61
5 b g Horse Chestnut(SAF) —Takipy (USA) (Persian Bold)
141[3] 279[10] (623) 908[10] 2301[14] 2999[11] 3521[6] 5014[15] 6948[10] 7651[9]

Big City Boy (IRE) *Phil McEntee* a26
3 b g Tamarisk(IRE) —Cuddles (IRE) (Taufan (USA))
693[6] 720[4]

Big Creek (IRE) *Jeremy Noseda* a84 98
4 b h Galileo(IRE) —Baranja (USA) (St Jovite (USA))
242[12] 332a[8] 605a[10] 991[11] 1883[5] 6249[8] 6528[8]

Big Drama (USA) *David Fawkes* a126
5 bb h Montbrook(USA) —Riveting Drama (USA) (Notebook (USA))
7302a[7]

Bigelow (AUS) *Clinton McDonald* 105
4 b g Al Maher(AUS) —Academy Angel (AUS) (Royal Academy (USA))
9029a[5]

Bigern *Michael Mullineaux* a9 12
4 b g Firebreak—Lady Boxer (Komaite (USA))
2219[10] 6609[12]

Big Hunter (FR) *E Kurdu* 106
4 ch h Green Tune(USA) —Ashley River (Ashkalani (IRE))
5530a[5] 7048a[7]

Big Johnny D (IRE) *John Dunlop* 76
2 ch c Alhaarth(IRE) —Bakiya (USA) (Trempolino (USA))
4762[3] 5697[8]

Big Noise *Dr Jon Scargill* a86 95
7 b h Lake Coniston(IRE) —Mitsubishi Video (IRE) (Doulab (USA))
1760[7] 2310[7] 3134[8] 4020[2] 4509[3] 6378[14] 7171[14]

Big Note (IRE) *Andrew Balding* 92
2 b c Amadeus Wolf—Double Vie (IRE) (Tagula (IRE))
(2907) ◆ 4575[3] (5492) 5849[21]

Big Occasion (IRE) *David Pipe* 94
4 b g Sadler's Wells(USA) —Asnieres (USA) (Spend A Buck (USA))
6171[9] 6690[25]

Big Slick (IRE) *Mel Brittain* a36 52
6 ch h Rossini(USA) —Why Worry Now (IRE) (College Chapel)
1213[8] ◆ 2412[6] 3024[6] 4517[7] 4876[6] 5008[9]

Big Sur *Tom Keddy* a64 61
5 ch g Selkirk(USA) —Bombazine (IRE) (Generous (IRE))
1582[2] 2567[4] 3130[13]

Big Talk *David Bridgwater* 38
4 b g Selkirk(USA) —Common Request (USA) (Lear Fan (USA))
114[11]

Big Tex (IRE) *W McCreery* a73 70
3 ch g Captain Rio—Bonne Mere (FR) (Stepneyev (IRE))
(973a) (Dead)

Big Time Charlie (IRE) *Richard Hannon* a59 46
2 b c Elusive City(USA) —Brennie (IRE) (Grand Lodge (USA))
4525[8] 4815[11] 5861[6] 6443[12] 7514[7] 7582[5] 7762[3]

Big Whitfield *Tracy Waggott* a51 57
5 b g Tobougg(IRE) —Natalie Jay (Ballacashtal (CAN))
2985[13] 3936[12]

Big Zaf *Paul Midgley* 32
3 b g Zafeen(FR) —Raasors Edge (Ajraas (USA))
1304[4] 1692[11]

Bijou Dan *George Moore* a49 67
10 ch g Bijou D'Inde—Cal Norma's Lady (IRE) (Lyphard's Special (USA))
3510[6] 4856[4] 5369[5] 7075[6]

Bikini Babe (IRE) *Mark Johnston* a106 106
4 b m Montjeu(IRE) —Zeiting (IRE) (Zieten (USA))
1100[9] 1416[3] 1705a[3] 2044[8] 2573[12] 4058[6] 4410[6] 4660[3]

Bilash *Reg Hollinshead* 72
4 gr h Choisir(AUS) —Goldeva (Makbul)
(1899) 2142[4] 2585[12] 3640[7] 4895[4] 5658[5] 5914[6]

Bilidn *Noel Quinlan* a57 78
3 b f Tiger Hill(IRE) —Brightest Star (Unfuwain (USA))
1807[6] 3624[7] 5303[6] 6093[10] 6773[7] ◆ 6978[9] 7831[9]

Bilko Pak (IRE) *Derek Shaw* a88 86
3 b g Barathea(IRE) —Vale View (FR) (Anabaa (USA))
10[3] 2910[3] 3238[2] 3731[3] 3972[2] 4431[2] 5419[7] 6179[9] 6505[9] 7488[7] 7566[11]

Billionaire Boy (IRE) *Patrick Morris* a47 51
4 b g Acclamation—Shalwell (IRE) (Shalford (IRE))
690[12] 857[11]

Billion Dollar Kid *Jo Davis* a72 77
6 br g Averti(IRE) —Fredora (Inchinor)
2557[7] 2995[4] 3815[9] 4255[3] 5511[2] 6022[6] 6924[4] 7130[8]

Billy Buttons *Andrew Balding* a79 90
3 gr g Act One—Dolce Thundera (USA) (Thunder Gulch (USA))
1409[10] 4157[2] 5140[2] 6248[2] ◆ 6749[14]

Billy Cadiz *Julie Camacho* a58 57
6 b g Zilzal(USA) —Faraway Moon (Distant Relative)
2691[4] 3326[7] 3903[2] 5788[4] 6262[9] 7063[6] 7351[2] 7781[3]

Billyford (IRE) *Liam Roche* a83 104
6 b g Lil's Boy(USA) —Alamanta (IRE) (Ali-Royal (IRE))
6513a[12] 7468a[8] (7792a)

Billyrayvalentine (CAN) *George Baker* a60 86
2 b c Elusive Quality(USA) —Sweet And Careless (USA) (Hennessy (USA))
2997[3] 3686[6] 4864[4] (6058) (6237) 7138[2]

Billy Red *J R Jenkins* a92 81
7 ch g Dr Fong(USA) —Liberty Bound (Primo Dominie)
87[5] 701[4] 961[5] 1371[5] 1506[5] 2069[7] 2167[2] 2447[3] 2903[5] 3482[4] 6119[2] 6815[3] 7487[4] 7602[8]

Billyruben *David Nicholls* a57 22
3 ch g Bertolini(USA) —River Crossing (Zafonic (USA))
2765[10]

Bin End *Barry Brennan* a64 68
5 b g King's Best(USA) —Overboard (IRE) (Rainbow Quest (USA))
1215[5] 1577[4] 2846[7] 3546[7] 6621[2] 7121[7]

Binglybonglyboo *Lawrence Mullaney* 62
5 b g Elmaamul(USA) —Sabotini (Prince Sabo)
2492[6]

Bint Alakaaber (IRE) *J R Jenkins* a60
3 b f Elusive City(USA) —Lady Of Pleasure (IRE) (Marju (IRE))
3494[3] 3747[6] 6251[6]

Bint Elnadim (IRE) *Derek Shaw* a54
3 b f Elnadim(USA) —Redrightreturning (Diktat)
6874[10] 6981[7] 7249[2] 7655[12] 7747[4] 7848[12] 7911[6]

Bint Mazyouna *Richard Guest* a64 66
3 ch f Cadeaux Genereux—Resistance Heroine (Dr Fong (USA))
3278[7] 4672[8] 5243[12]

Bint Nas (IRE) *Mick Channon* 61
3 b f Clodovil(IRE) —Molomo (Barathea (IRE))
1845[8] 2461[3] 2858[11]

Bint Susu (IRE) *Bryan Smart* a70
4 b m Singspiel(IRE) —Susu (Machiavellian (USA))
253[2]

Bio Logique (FR) *D Allard* 35
3 b f Apsis—Garantie Bio (FR) (Take Risks (FR))
852a[13]

Biondetti (USA) *Mahmood Al Zarooni* a98 105
3 b c Bernardini(USA) —Lyphard's Delta (USA) (Lyphard (USA))
4120a[2] 5252[10]

Birbone (FR) *S Seemar* a95 86
6 b g Sendawar(IRE) —Labour Of Love (USA) (Silver Deputy (CAN))
153a[12] 331a[9]

Bird Dog *Phil McEntee* a55
5 ch g Compton Place—Form At Last (Formidable (USA))
85[9] 347[6] 1813[9] 3173[10] 4187[8] 6238[8] 7071[9] 7691[7] (7747) 7854[7] 7911[3]

Birdie For Diki (GER) *R Rohne*
2 b c Kornado—Bestens (IRE) (Mull Of Kintyre (USA))
7312a[0]

Birdinthehand (FR) *D Rabhi* a56 73
5 b m Nayef(USA) —Bird In The Sky (CAN) (Sky Classic (CAN))
533a[8]

Birdolini *Alan King* a79 78
3 ch f Bertolini(USA) —Bird Over (Bold Edge)
3818[5] 4271[4] 5113[3] 6003[2] ◆ 6457[5] 7130[4] 7361[3]

Birdrun (USA) *William Mott* a115
5 ch h Birdstone(USA) —Run Like Martha (USA) (Jolie's Halo (USA))
7300a[2]

Birdwatcher (IRE) *Mark Johnston* a71 79
3 ch g Cadeaux Genereux—Dancing Feather (Suave Dancer (USA))
(930) (1300) ◆ 1872[P] 6136[7] 6451[4] (6577) 6891[8]

Birkside *Linda Perratt* a67 64
8 ch g Spinning World(USA) —Bright Hope (IRE) (Danehill (USA))
1538[4] 2059[8] 2636[4] 3129[10] 3453[5] 4173[10] 4499[7] 4785[6] 5405[9]

Birs *B Beaunez* a71
3 b g Compton Place—Four Penny Road (Josr Algarhoud (IRE))
7016a[0]

Birthday Lion (GER) *U Stoltefuss* a86 100
6 ch g Areion(GER) —Boucheron (GER) (Turfkonig (GER))
(6594a) 7221a[0]

Birthday Prince (GER) *Uwe Ostmann* 52
3 ch c Areion(GER) —Birthday Spectrum (GER) (Spectrum (IRE))
2520a[8]

Birthday Star (IRE) *Linda Jewell* a48 8
9 b g Desert King(IRE) —White Paper (IRE) (Marignan (USA))
1135[9]

Bishopbriggs (USA) *K F Clutterbuck* a70 46
6 ch g Victory Gallop(CAN) —Inny River (USA) (Seattle Slew (USA))
1190[6] 1368[8] 1995[14] 3241[9] 3720[8] 4183[9] 4651[10]

Bit A Craic *John Ryan* a43 45
2 ch f Avonbridge—Twenty Seven (IRE) (Efisio)
3302[5] 3718[3] 4662[11] 5099[10] 5605[5] 6950[15] 7108[9] 7708[6] 7725[7]

Bitaphon (IRE) *Deborah Sanderson* a69 64
2 br g Acclamation—Pitrizzia (Lando (GER))
2672[6] 3082[5] 4402[5] (5597) 6807[8] 7915[4]

Bitter Lemon *Kevin Ryan* a54 55
2 b f Indesatchel(IRE) —Citron (Reel Buddy (USA))
1957[7] 5590[5] 6092[8] 6540[4] 6821[9] 7059[5]

Bivouac (UAE) *Alan Swinbank* a83 65
7 b g Jade Robbery(USA) —Tentpole (USA) (Rainbow Quest (USA))
(7722) 7884[3]

Bizarrely (IRE) *Sir Mark Prescott Bt* a66 67
4 b g Antonius Pius(USA) —Diamond Field (USA) (Mr Prospector (USA))
390[7]

Bizertin (FR) *D Allard* a74 68
3 b c Great Pretender(IRE) —Dissidente (FR) (Double Bed (FR))
776a[7]

Blackamoor Zara *Bruce Hellier* 34
2 b f Haafhd—Sara Mana Mou (Medicean)
6539[11] 6837[7] 7210[5]

Black Annis Bower *Michael Easterby* 75
3 gr f Proclamation(IRE) —Bow Bridge (Bertolini (USA))
2122[8] 2363[6] 3360[3] 3832[6] 5371[3] 6076[10] 6801[2] 7073[5]

Black Arrow (IRE) *A Wohler* 105
2 b c Teofilo(IRE) —Fann (USA) (Diesis)
7325a[2]

Black Baccara *Phil McEntee* a74 68
4 b m Superior Premium—Areish (IRE) (Keen)
123[4] 138[2] 250[2] (337) 421[2] 487[2] 554[2] 696[3] 766[3] 812[2] 910[7] 1043[2] (1281) 1507[5] 1899[4] 2182[2] 2193[6] 6065[10] 6655[13] 6931[2] 7201[7] 7341[8] (7649) 7804[9] 7833[3] 7917[7]

Black Belt (IRE) *Tracey Collins* a76 76
3 b f Big Bad Bob(IRE) —Spanish Rainbow (IRE) (Rainbow Quest (USA))
1706a[2]

Blackburn *Clive Cox* a66 60
2 b g Elusive City(USA) —Cuppacocoa (Bertolini (USA))
4912[6] 5613[6] 5889[10] 6846[2]

Black Cadillac (IRE) *Andrew Balding* a35 66
3 bl g Kheleyf(USA) —Desert Design (Desert King (IRE))
1236[DSQ] (2141) 2662[4] 3271[5]

Black Caviar (AUS) *Peter G Moody* 133
5 br m Bel Esprit(AUS) —Helsinge (AUS) (Desert Sun)
( )

Black Coffee *Mark Brisbourne* a79 72
6 br g Vettori(IRE) —In The Woods (You And I (USA))
(115) (203) 541[5] (711) (772) ◆ 897[2] ◆ 1066[3] 1222[7] 3848[7] 4432[9] 4825[9] 5036[8] (5485) 6028[6] 6295[7] 7215[10] 7397[10] 7556[7]

Black Douglas *William Jarvis* a42
2 b g Kyllachy—Penmayne (Inchinor)
5863[8]

Blackdown Fair *Rod Millman* 78
2 b f Trade Fair—Shielaligh (Aragon)
2309[3] (2787) 3429[6]

Black Eagle (IRE) *A bin Huzaim* a104 107
5 b h Cape Cross(IRE) —Shimna (Mr Prospector (USA))
157a[12] 2391[3]

Black Feather *Alan McCabe* a57 11
3 br f Avonbridge—Fly South (Polar Falcon (USA))
909[6] 993[6] 1096[12]

Black Iceman *Lydia Pearce* a59 44
3 bl g Iceman—Slite (Mind Games)
2722[11] 3227[12] 4686[5] 5898[3] 6585[5] 7195[3] 7515[10]

Black Jacari (IRE) *Philip Kirby* a33 79
6 b g Black Sam Bellamy(IRE) —Amalia (IRE) (Danehill (USA))
7884[7]

Black Mambazo (IRE) *L Riccardi* 106
6 b h Statue Of Liberty(USA) —Rich Gift (Cadeaux Genereux)
7408a[10]

Black Minstrel (IRE) *Amanda Perrett* 66
2 b c Dylan Thomas(IRE) —Overlook (Generous (IRE))
4446[6]

Blackmore *Julia Feilden* a78 76
4 b g Rainbow Quest(USA) —Waki Music (USA) (Miswaki (USA))
(894) ◆ 1153[2] 2034[10] 6451[9] 6915[12] 7674[4] 7753[4] 7914[2]

Black N Brew (USA) *John C McConnell* a82 78
5 b g Milwaukee Brew(USA) —Natural Glow (USA) (Siphon (BRZ))
7548a[11] 7792a[3]

Black Pond (USA) *Mark Johnston* a71 76
3 b g Forestry(USA) —Golden Ballet (USA) (Moscow Ballet (USA))
579[2] 713[3] 993[3] 1311[4] 1593[2] 2058[5] 2664[6] 3366[8] 4287[4] 5042[3] 5372[7] 5784[10]

[illegible] Boy *[illegible]* a47 47
8 ch g Muhtarram(USA) —Full Stop (IRE) (Zieten (USA))
444[4]

Black Sheep (USA) *G Botti* a77 76
3 b g Anabaa(USA) —Royale (IRE) (Royal Academy (USA))
5463a[4]

Black Spirit (USA) *Clive Cox* 110
4 b g Black Minnaloushe(USA) —L'Extra Honor (USA) (Hero's Honor (USA))
1528[2] 2439[8] 3591[3] 4095[6] 5829[3] 6161[4]

Blackstone Vegas *Derek Shaw* a64 68
5 ch g Nayef(USA) —Waqood (USA) (Riverman (USA))
1063[3] (1253) 1473[2] 1586[2] ◆ 1761[2] 2034[2] 2459[5] 3205[4] 3738[7]

Black Tor Figarro (IRE) *Lawney Hill* a58 67
6 b g Rock Of Gibraltar(IRE) —Will Be Blue (IRE) (Darshaan)
33[2] 3047[9] 3951[P]

Blacky The Bull (USA) *Jeff Bonde* a90
2 bb c Flashy Bull(USA) —Image Of Honor (USA) (Honour And Glory (USA))
7280a[8]

Blade *Mark Brisbourne* a41 49
3 ch g Needwood Blade—Ellina (Robellino (USA))
2239[10]

Blade Pirate *John Ryan* a50 51
3 ch g Needwood Blade—CC Canova (Millkom)
5[4] 10[5] 1872[6] 2172[10] 2382[8] 2825[6]

Blades Lad *Richard Fahey* 74
2 ch g Haafhd—Blades Girl (Bertolini (USA))
5727[2] ◆ 6048[2] 6675[3]

Blaise Chorus (IRE) *Charles Hills* a87 93
3 br f Singspiel(IRE) —Blaise Castle (USA) (Irish River (FR))
339[2] ◆ 901a[3] 1807[2] 2682[11] 4208[5] 4790[8] (5317) 6325[7]

Blake Dean *Ben Haslam* 65
3 b g Halling(USA) —Antediluvian (Air Express (IRE))
2058[6] 7212[10]

Blakeshall Diamond *Frank Sheridan* a26 47
6 gr m Piccolo—Hi Hoh (IRE) (Fayruz)
691[9]

Blakey's Boy *Harry Dunlop* a42 85
4 b g Hawk Wing(USA) —Divine Grace (IRE) (Definite Article)
55[7]

Blanc De Chine (IRE) *Peter Makin* a70 73
2 gr f Dark Angel(IRE) —Nullarbor (Green Desert (USA))
3722[2] 4094[17] 4720[5] 5174[2] 6590[2] ◆ 6919[2] 7482[2] (7607)

Blanche Dubawi (IRE) *Noel Quinlan* a73 106
3 b f Dubawi(IRE) —Dixie Belle (Diktat)
2102[3] 2468[2] 3459[5] (4353) 5054[12] (5476) 5935[3] (6531)

Blank Czech (IRE) *Amanda Perrett* 80
2 b g Clodovil(IRE) —Shambodia (IRE) (Petardia)
1835[7] ◆ 4535[6] ◆ 4996[3] 5541[2] 5967[2]

Blanzac (FR) *T Lemer* a62
2 b c Early March—The Lucky Go Girl (GER) (Dr Devious (IRE))
7814a[6]

Blaugrana (IRE) *John Gosden* a60
2 ch f Exceed And Excel(AUS) —Acts Of Grace (USA) (Bahri (USA))
7757[5]

Blaze Brightly (IRE) *Mrs John Harrington* a84 102
4 b m Big Bad Bob(IRE) —Kristal's Paradise (IRE) (Bluebird (USA))
3527a[7] 4132a[6] 5523a[5] 6362a[9]

Blaze Of Thunder (IRE) *Alan Swinbank* 80
3 ch g Ad Valorem(USA) —Palatine Dancer (IRE) (Namid)
1152[9] 1697[7]

Blaze On By *John Bridger* a49 56
3 ch f Firebreak—Yanomami (USA) (Slew O'Gold (USA))
519[6] 591[4] 760[8] 2964[9]

Blazing Apostle (IRE) *Christine Dunnett* a48 43
3 ch f Redback—Salonika Sky (Pursuit Of Love)
916[7] 1060[10] 1933[8] 2186[9] 2598[4] 3431[8] 4929[7] 5670[9] 6070[9]

Blazing Buck *Tony Carroll* a47 58
5 ch g Fraam—Anapola (GER) (Polish Precedent (USA))
1310[13] (2400) 2873[9] 3281[9] 3492[3] (4274) 5566[5]

Blazing Desert *John Quinn* 79
7 b g Beat All(USA) —Kingsfold Blaze (Mazilier (USA))
2034[12] 2622[4] 3817[9]

Blazing Field *Clive Cox* 81
3 ch f Halling(USA) —Autumn Wealth (IRE) (Cadeaux Genereux)
1845[9] 3907[3] 4449[2] ◆ 5035[9] (6893)

Blazing Speed *James Fanshawe* 56
2 b g Dylan Thomas(IRE) —Leukippids (IRE) (Sadler's Wells (USA))
7083[12]

Blek (FR) *E Lellouche* 112
6 gr h Chichicastenango(FR) —Exande (FR) (Exit To Nowhere (USA))
1231a[7] 4524a[4]

Blessed Biata (USA) *William Haggas* a62 92
3 b f Mr Greeley(USA) —June Moon (IRE) (Sadler's Wells (USA))
3034[6] (3689) 4429[13]

Blessed Place *Dominic Ffrench Davis* a43 62
11 ch g Compton Place—Cathedra (So Blessed)
4272[9]

Blessing Belle (IRE) *Mme G Rarick* a52 63
5 ch m Traditionally(USA) —Kind Of Loving (Diesis)
706a[8]

Bless You *Henry Candy* a68 88
3 b f Bahamian Bounty—Follow Flanders (Pursuit Of Love)
1607[3] (2009) [illegible]

Blimey O'Riley (IRE) *Mark H Tompkins* 79
6 b g Kalanisi(IRE) —Kafayef (USA) (Secreto (USA))
6249[9] (6998) 7139[7]

Blind Stag (IRE) *David Thompson* a48 58
3 b g Majestic Missile(IRE) —Floralia (Auction Ring (USA))
1303[P] 1860[8] 2265[6] 2547[11] 3192[9]

Bling (FR) *C Ferland* a104 92
4 b h Kingsalsa(USA) —Bricoleuse (USA) (A.P. Indy (USA))
371a[6] 778a[2]

Bling King *F Vermeulen* 94
2 b c Haafhd—Bling Bling (IRE) (Indian Ridge)
1619[2] 2181[7] (2448) 2868[2] 3152[7] 4055[7] (4572) 4858[5] 5876[3] 6535[12] 7508a[9]

Blinka Me *Alex Hales* a54 65
4 b g Tiger Hill(IRE) —Easy To Love (USA) (Diesis)
1297[7]

Blink Of An Eye *Michael Bell* a77 49
3 ch g Compton Place—Wink (Salse (USA))
811[2] 1108[9] (4991) 6442[7] 6980[5]

Blissful Moment (USA) *Sir Michael Stoute* 105
4 br g Dynaformer(USA) —Arabian Spell (IRE) (Desert Prince (IRE))
1887[2] 3156[2] 5285[9] 5705[10]

Blizzard Blues (USA) *Jamie Osborne* 104
5 ch g Mr Greeley(USA) —Blush Damask (USA) (Green Dancer (USA))
2716[9] 3013[16]

Blockley (USA) *Ian Williams* a64 70
7 b g Johannesburg(USA) —Saintly Manner (USA) (St Jovite (USA))
252[7]

Blodwen Abbey *James Unett* a75 60
2 b f Firebreak—Miss Mirasol (Sheikh Albadou)
1957[2] ◆ 2254[5] 2907[5] 3849[3] (6131) 6843[2] (7140) 7364[5]

Blonde (IRE) *Richard Hannon* 58
2 ch f Pivotal—Sister Golden Hair (IRE) (Glint Of Gold)
6744[7] ◆

Blonde Maite *Roy Bowring* a12
5 ch g Ballet Master(USA) —Ace Maite (Komaite (USA))
1496[11] 5212[11] 6262[13]

Bloodson (FR) *X Thomas-Demeaulte* a96 96
3 b c Miesque's Son(USA) —Great Blood (FR) (Great Palm (USA))
883a[4]

Bloodsweatandtears *William Knight* a75 82
3 b g Barathea(IRE) —Celestial Princess (Observatory (USA))
2008[9] 3291[8] 4009[3] 4725[2] 5240[11] 6543[5] 6990[9]

Blowing A Hoolie (IRE) *Gay Kelleway* a40
3 b f Val Royal(FR) —Moly (Inchinor)
983[7] 3175[5]

Blown It (USA) *Keith Dalgleish* a43 74
5 bb g More Than Ready(USA) —Short Shadow (USA) (Out Of Place (USA))
1612[8] 2543[11] 3451[7] 3489[9] 4144[4] 4504[2] (4636) 4780[2] (4881) 4986[2] 5148[2] 5313[5] 5720[8] 6076[8] 6426[10] 7040[4] 7173[2] 7395[2] 7566[4]

Bluberry *Gary Moore* a54 4
3 b f Kyllachy—Stormy Monday (Cadeaux Genereux)
130[6] 263[6] 383[10]

Blu Constellation (ITY) *Vittorio Caruso* 119
3 b c Orpen(USA) —Stella Celtica (ITY) (Celtic Swing)
4121a[10] 7311a[2]

Blue Bajan (IRE) *David O'Meara* a98 116
9 b g Montjeu(IRE) —Gentle Thoughts (Darshaan)
1808[6] 2072[2] (2438) 3066[10] 4469[3] 5284[7] 5884[6]

Blue Belle Lady *Richard Fahey* 53
2 b f Orientor—Lafontaine Bleu (Piccolo)
3021[4] 3504[5] ◆

Bluebells Are Blue (IRE) *Eve Johnson Houghton* 55
2 b g Three Valleys(USA) —Blue Bamboo (Green Desert (USA))
1522[3] 1827[5]

Blueberry Fizz (IRE) *John Ryan* a53 28
3 b f Kheleyf(USA) —Miss Poppets (Polar Falcon (USA))
6353[5] 6626[9] 6939[7] 7084[13] 7524[3] 7581[12] 7663[9] 7768[3] 7899[2] 7924[3]

Blue Blue Sea *Y De Nicolay* 102
3 ch f Galileo(IRE) —Blue Blue Sky (IRE) (Anabaa (USA))
5695a[5] 6809a[4] 7509a[10]

Bluebok *Milton Bradley* a61 67
10 ch g Indian Ridge—Blue Sirocco (Bluebird (USA))
102[6] 123[2] 256[4] (464) 537[7] 735[7] 861[3] 1274[5]

Blue Bunting (USA) *Mahmood Al Zarooni* 120
3 rg f Dynaformer(USA) —Miarixa (FR) (Linamix (FR))
(1719) ◆ 2682[4] (4133a) (5219) 5928[6]

Blue Cannon (IRE) *Kevin Prendergast* a58 71
3 b g High Chaparral(IRE) —Blushing Barada (USA) (Blushing Groom (FR))
1663a[10]

Blue Charm *Ian McInnes* a56 68
7 b g Averti(IRE) —Exotic Forest (Dominion)
490[9] (2233) 2415[2] 2809[5] 3280[10] 3944[13] 4179[9] 6430[8]

Blue Cossack (IRE) *Mark Usher* a64 38
3 b g Ivan Denisovich(IRE) —Biasca (Erhaab (USA))
(47) 234[2] 469[2] 650[2] (731) 866[5] 2819[12] 2904[7] 4476[9] 5249[6] 6052[11] 6493[5] 6613[2] (6823) 7145[4] 7738[B]

Blue Cross Boy (USA) *Adrian McGuinness* a48 51
6 rg g Sunday Break(JPN) —Introducer (USA) (Cozzene (USA))
7740[8]

Blue [illegible] (IRE) *[illegible]* a85 101
4 b m Shamardal(USA) —Blueberry (USA) (Bertrando (USA))
(923a) 2967a[8] 3440a[23] 4767a[5] 6388a[13] 6733a[11]

Blue Dazzler (IRE) *Amanda Perrett* a41 72
3 b g Dalakhani(IRE) —Lady Ragazza (IRE) (Bering)
1951[9]

Blue Deer (IRE) *John Akehurst* a69 72
3 b g Bahamian Bounty—Jaywick (UAE) (Jade Robbery (USA))
1408[6] 2419[3] 2869[4] 4110[5] (5344) 5542[2] 5615[8] 5669[2] 5859[2] 6442[10] 6797[11] 7208[8] 7455[10] (7663) 7754[8]

Blue Destination *Philip McBride* 87
3 b g Dubai Destination(USA) —Bluebelle (Generous (IRE))
(1991) 2471[5] 4723[5] 5242[2]

Blue Ivy *Chris Fairhurst* a43 45
3 b f Blue Dakota(IRE) —Matilda Peace (Namaqualand (USA))
183[6] 396[5] 745[8]

Blue Jack *Tom Dascombe* a84 113
6 b g Cadeaux Genereux—Fairy Flight (IRE) (Fairy King (USA))
1809[7] 2028[10] 3155[21] 3626[6] 4573[7]

Blue Maisey *Peter Makin* a69 73
3 b f Monsieur Bond(IRE) —Blue Nile (IRE) (Bluebird (USA))
1986[11] 2821[6] 3432[2] (3688) 5179[4] 5992[7] 6888[2] 7235[6]

Blue Mamba *Reg Hollinshead* 56
4 b m Bollin Eric—Maradata (IRE) (Shardari)
1751[S]

Blue Mimosa (IRE) *Kevin Prendergast* 78
2 b f Holy Roman Emperor(IRE) —Mercury Blue (Montjeu (IRE))
6196a[9]

Blue Moon *Kevin Ryan* a101 83
4 gr m Trade Fair—Sunningdale (IRE) (Indian Ridge)
226[9] (348) 703[5] 925a[9] 4561[12] 5455[4] 6219[5] 6383[3] (6658) (6854a) 7277a[13] 7393[5] 7606[3] 7719[3]

Blue Noodles *John Wainwright* a59 69
5 b g Reset(AUS) —Gleam Of Light (IRE) (Danehill (USA))
1714[10] 2487[10] 4041[6] 4517[8] 4852[4] 5788[12] 6084[2] 6784[5] 7229[5]

Blue Nymph *John Quinn* a91 80
5 ch m Selkirk(USA) —Blue Icon (Peintre Celebre (USA))
68[4] 1305[6] 2526[7]

Blue Panis (FR) *F Chappet* a94 113
4 b h Panis(USA) —Rhapsody In Blue (FR) (Bering)
2980a[5] 3654a[8] 5664a[3] 6201a[4]

Blue Pencil *Paul Fitzsimons* 24
2 b g Ishiguru(USA) —Gold And Blue (IRE) (Bluebird (USA))
6825[7] 7232[16] 7685[7]

Blue Ridge Lane (IRE) *John C McConnell* a79 67
5 ch g Indian Ridge—Upperville (IRE) (Selkirk (USA))
925a[12] 1381a[6] 4398a[9] 7378a[8] 7548a[9]

Blue Ridges (IRE) *Geoffrey Harker* 50
2 b f Dubawi(IRE) —Line Ahead (IRE) (Sadler's Wells (USA))
2886[8] 3504[10] 4140[7] 6611[9]

Blue Roses (IRE) *H-A Pantall* a64
3 b f Oratorio(IRE) —Colour Coordinated (IRE) (Spectrum (IRE))
901a[10]

Blue Rum (IRE) *Alan Kirtley* a30 41
4 b g Pyrus(USA) —Secret Combe (IRE) (Mujadil (USA))
2247[9] 2670[8] 3027[9] 3248[6] 3569[9] 3972[10] 6343[6] 6602[9] 7063[11]

Blues Dream (FR) *E Danel*
2 ch f Touch Of The Blues(FR) —Miss Lena (Medicean)
7814a[10]

Blue Shoes (IRE) *Tim Easterby* 67
2 b f Kodiac—Alexander Capetown (IRE) (Fasliyev (USA))
1515[3] 1876[2] 2261[3] 2570[5] 4192[2] 4557[10] (5058) 5591[2] 5847[10] 6413[2] 6645[10] 7294[3]

Blues Jazz *Ian Semple* a69 87
5 b g Josr Algarhoud(IRE) —Belle Of The Blues (IRE) (Blues Traveller (IRE))
(2047) 2632[4] 3128[4] (3489) (3856) (4780) (4876) (5760) 6174[14] 6949[10]

Blue Soave (FR) *F Chappet* a100 112
3 ch g Soave(GER) —Rhapsody In Blue (FR) (Bering)
2978a[3] 5772a[4]

Blue Spartan (IRE) *Brian Meehan* a79 76
6 gr g Spartacus(IRE) —Bridelina (FR) (Linamix (FR))
948[3] 1443[4] 2055[9] 2512[8] 4249[2] 5110[3] 5893[9] 6402[6]

Blue Spinnaker (IRE) *Michael Easterby* a51 76
12 b g Bluebird(USA) —Suedoise (Kris)
1099[12] 1324[11] 3456[7] 5622[13] 5823[9]

Blue Surf *Amanda Perrett* 80
2 ch g Excellent Art—Wavy Up (IRE) (Brustolon)
4414[7] 4969[3] 5475[2]

Blue Tiger *Saeed Bin Suroor* 49
2 b g Pivotal—Poised (USA) (Rahy (USA))
4352[6] 5104[U] 6025[9]

Blue Tomato *Donal Nolan* a88 93
10 b g Orpen(USA) —Ocean Grove (IRE) (Fairy King (USA))
4539[11]

Blue Top *Tim Walford* 63
2 b g Millkom—Pompey Blue (Abou Zouz (USA))
5454[13] 6278[3] 6532[8] 6911[10]

Blue White Fire (IRE) *D K Weld* 95
2 b c Montjeu(IRE) —Desert Ease (IRE) (Green Desert (USA))
6391a[5]

Blu [illegible] (IRE) *[illegible] Suroor*
2 b c Teofilo(IRE) —Fafinta (IRE) (Indian Ridge)
7217a[4]

Bluster (FR) *Robert Collet* 109
5 b g Indian Rocket—Tell Me Why (FR) (Distant Relative)
1122a[4] 2138a[10] 2754a[8] 4739a[3] 5532a[0] 5985a[6] 6563a[11]

Boa *Reg Hollinshead* a76 70
6 b m Mtoto—Maradata (IRE) (Shardari)
(1398) (1750) 2091[8] 2436[9] 3509[4] 4024[3] 4463[3] 4626[3] 5609[2] (6182) 6666[5] 7556[2] 7570[7] 7738[3] 7878[6]

Boastful (IRE) *H-A Pantall* a81 88
3 gr f Clodovil(IRE) —Vanity (IRE) (Thatching)
775a[2] 981a[8]

Bobby Dazzler (IRE) *Jim Best* a59 30
3 b g Refuse To Bend(IRE) —Just My Hobby (Kris)
1189[10] 1588[5] 2195[3] 2722[5] 4654[9]

Bobbyow *Bryn Palling* a53 59
3 b g Bertolini(USA) —Brooklyn's Sky (Septieme Ciel (USA))
146[5] 322[5] 745[10] 2918[8] 3216[11] 3804[7]

Bobby's Doll *Terry Clement* a55 73
4 ch m Needwood Blade—Nine To Five (Imp Society (USA))
1331[3] 2710[3] 3090[4] 3556[2] (3678) ◆ 3957[6] 4967[4] (5139) 5517[3]

Bobering *Brian Baugh* a46 43
11 b g Bob's Return(IRE) —Ring The Rafters (Batshoof)
115[9] 771[7] 899[12]

Bob Le Beau (IRE) *Mrs John Harrington* a103 110
4 br g Big Bad Bob(IRE) —Shine Silently (IRE) (Bering)
1781a[2] 4035a[2] 4737a[3] 6514a[8]

Boblini *Mark Usher* a43
3 b f Bertolini(USA) —Boojum (Mujtahid (USA))
3747[7]

Bobs Pride (IRE) *D K Weld* a96 57
9 b g Marju(IRE) —Vyatka (Lion Cavern (USA))
3420a[12]

Bob Stock (IRE) *Willie Musson* a67 67
5 b g Dubai Destination(USA) —Red Rita (IRE) (Kefaah (USA))
674[11]

Boccalino (GER) *H-A Pantall* a95 98
3 b c Iron Mask(USA) —Bella Monica (GER) (Big Shuffle (USA))
883a[6] 2520a[5]

Bocciani (GER) *Brian Ellison* 73
6 b g Banyumanik(IRE) —Baila (Lando (GER))
1833[2] (5166)

Bodie *Pam Sly* a67 54
3 ch g Iceman—Saida Lenasera (FR) (Fasliyev (USA))
260[6] 406[2] 543[3] 716[5] 801[5] 1869[9] 2598[10] 7235[8]

Body Language (IRE) *Ann Duffield* a82 77
3 b f Beat Hollow—Banco Suivi (IRE) (Nashwan (USA))
1616[2] 2114[5] 2813[5] 3487[4] 4151[2] 4671[7] 5650[2] 6577[2] (7062) *7461[3] 7738[5]*

Boga (IRE) *Karen Tutty* a47 55
4 b m Invincible Spirit(IRE) —Miznapp (Pennekamp (USA))
1044[6] 1247[12] 1453[9] 1627[7] 1938[4] *2161[10]* 3247[4] 3662[9] (3732) 4564[10] 4600[13] 4987[6] 5502[8] 6158[8] 6602[12]

Bogart *Kevin Ryan* 107
2 ch c Bahamian Bounty—Lauren Louise (Tagula (IRE))
(2395) 4495[7] (5216) 5849[6] (6535) 7220a[8]

Bogey Hole (IRE) *Nikki Evans* a59 42
2 gr f Aussie Rules(USA) —Sticky Green (Lion Cavern (USA))
4648[4] 5596[6] 6280[5] 6763[4] *7177[4] 7569[12]*

Bogside Theatre (IRE) *David O'Meara* a32 75
7 b m Fruits Of Love(USA) —Royal Jubilee (IRE) (King's Theatre (IRE))
7102[4]

Bohemian Melody *Marco Botti* a100 108
4 b g Desert Sun—Chamonis (USA) (Affirmed (USA))
844[5] 5272[9] 5699[10] 6347[3] ◆ (6987) ◆

Bohemian Rhap (IRE) *B Grizzetti* 45
2 br c Footstepsinthesand—Kuaicoss (IRE) (Lujain (USA))
7311a[7]

Bohemian Rhapsody (IRE) *J W Hills* 71
2 b c Galileo(IRE) —Quiet Mouse (USA) (Quiet American (USA))
6160[7] 6726[5]

Boise (FR) *E Libaud* a92 94
4 b m Marchand De Sable(USA) —Yezidis (FR) (Ski Chief (USA))
92a[3]

Boisterous (USA) *Claude McGaughey III* 112
4 bb h Distorted Humor(USA) —Emanating (USA) (Cox's Ridge (USA))
3888a[3]

Bojangle (IRE) *Dominic Ffrench Davis* a45 48
2 b f Namid—Fine Detail (IRE) (Shirley Heights)
1290[4] 1957[4] 2160[5] 4390[7] 4913[7] 5343[8] 6293[11]

Bolanderi (USA) *Andy Turnell* a78 72
6 ch g Seeking The Gold(USA) —Lilium (Nashwan (USA))
4916[2] 5804[14]

Bold Adventure *Willie Musson* a67 65
7 ch g Arkadian Hero(USA) —Impatiente (USA) (Vaguely Noble)
67[3] 392[8] 560[11] 838[10] 1032[3] 1466[3] 1973[3] 7528[7]

Bold Ambition (IRE) *Ruth Carr*
3 ch f Bold Fact(USA) —Alethea Gee (Sure Blade (USA))
7250[10] 7424[13]

Bold Apache (IRE) *J J Lambe* a41 57
7 ch g Rock Of Gibraltar(IRE) —Velvet Moon (IRE) (Shaadi (USA))
5166[6]

Bold Argument (IRE) *Nerys Dutfield* a56 52
8 ch g Shinko Forest(IRE) —Ivory Bride (Domynsky)
2222[8] 4230[9] 4948[12] 5298[5] 5677[10]

Bold Bidder *Kevin Ryan* 88
3 b f Indesatchel(IRE) —Quiz Show (Primo Dominie)
1650[2] 1852[2] 2724[2] 3158[6] 3807[5] 4498[8] 5923[7] 6913[9]

Bold Bomber *Paul Green* a53 35
5 b g Kyllachy—Latina (IRE) (King's Theatre (IRE))
255[3] 363[9] (517) 575[4] 752[6] 933[9] 2547[7] *3234[7]*

Bold Cross (IRE) *Edward Bevan* a65 79
8 b g Cape Cross(IRE) —Machikane Akaiito (IRE) (Persian Bold)
2051[7] (2242) 2376[4] 2872[3] 3170[5] 3326[3] 4051[2] 4444[12] 4821[3] 5376[2] 5611[2] *5942[11]* 6402[9] 6583[8]

Bold Cuffs *Sir Mark Prescott Bt* a74
2 b c Dutch Art—Chambray (IRE) (Barathea (IRE))
7724[2] ◆ 7855[2]

Bold Deceiver *Phil McEntee* a37 14
3 b f Proclamation(IRE) —Naivety (Machiavellian (USA))
251[9]

Bold Diva *Tony Carroll* a66 36
6 ch m Bold Edge—Trina's Pet (Efisio)
485[5] 619[4] 793[3] 912[2] 1041[5] 1336[3] (1498) 1814[7] 3241[5] 3495[8]

Bold Identity (IRE) *Richard Phillips* 77
5 b g Tagula(IRE) —Identify (IRE) (Persian Bold)
2649[16]

Bold Indian (IRE) *Mike Sowersby* a58 57
7 b g Indian Danehill(IRE) —Desert Gift (Green Desert (USA))
1164[7] 3141[7] 3569[7] 4123[11] 4409[10] 5470[3] *6656[11]*

Boldinor *Martin Bosley* a68 63
8 b g Inchinor—Rambold (Rambo Dancer (CAN))
(947) 1171[4] 1581[9] 1912[6] 2222[6] 3350[3] 4025[10] 5138[3] *5603[7]*

Bold Marc (IRE) *Mrs K Burke* a60 81
9 b g Bold Fact(USA) —Zara's Birthday (IRE) (Waajib)
42a[4] 903a[4] 1373[4] 1614[3] (1857) 2046[6] (2815) 3629[4] (4051) 4278[10] 4656[12] 5549[6] 6017[3] 7015a[5] 7314a[0]

Boldogsag (FR) *P Bary* 105
2 ch f Layman(USA) —Belga Wood (USA) (Woodman (USA))
(6941a)

Bold Ring *Eric Wheeler* a71 64
5 ch m Bold Edge—Floppie Disk (Magic Ring (IRE))
98[4] 128[2] 231[4] 303[4] 792[5] 865[5] 2001[9] 2642[5] 3253[2] 3476[6] (3943) 4696[3] 4822[2] 5040[2] 7131[13] (7485) (7524) 7579[5] 7591[3] 7895[14]

Bold Silvano (SAF) *M F De Kock* a119 117
5 b h Silvano(GER) —Bold Saffron (SAF) (Al Mufti (USA))
(416a) ◆

Bold Thady Quill (IRE) *K J Condon* a64 85
4 ch g Tale Of The Cat(USA) —Jazzie (FR) (Zilzal (USA))
3445a[11]

Bold Trumpeter *Milton Bradley* a20
5 b g Zahran(IRE) —Stolen Owl (Bold Owl)
170[6] 253[11] 1250[6]

Bold Warning *Alex Hales* a50
7 b g Erhaab(USA) —Celandine (Warning)
11[8]

Bolero (GER) *Manfred Hofer* a75 96
3 b c Tertullian(USA) —Beautiful (GER) (Lando (GER))
980a[8]

Bolivia (GER) *Lucy Wadham* a90 90
5 ch m Monsun(GER) —Be My Lady (GER) (Be My Guest (USA))
6125[5] *7129[8]* 7296[16] *7584[3]*

Bollin Dolly *Tim Easterby* 86
8 ch m Bien Bien(USA) —Bollin Roberta (Bob's Return (IRE))
1388[7] 1622[7] 2150[3] 2403[2] 2906[4] 3632[6] 4083[3]

Bollin Felix *Tim Easterby* 93
7 br g Generous(IRE) —Bollin Magdalene (Teenoso (USA))
2285[10]

Bollin Freddie *Alan Lockwood* a53 69
7 ch g Golden Snake(USA) —Bollin Roberta (Bob's Return (IRE))
1324[14]

Bollin Greta *Tim Easterby* a47 90
6 bb m Mtoto—Bollin Zola (Alzao (USA))
(1901) 2262[9] 3344[3] 3828[3] 4719[3] ◆ 5035[3] 5759[2] 6151[2] 6988[4]

Bollin Harry *Tim Easterby* 49
3 br c Val Royal(FR) —Bollin Dolly (Bien Bien (USA))
1203[16]

Bollin Judith *Tim Easterby* a51 88
5 br m Bollin Eric—Bollin Nellie (Rock Hopper)
1798[3] (2060) (2888) 3851[5] 4348[7] (4890) 6115[8] 7102[5]

Bollin Mandy *Tim Easterby* 62
3 b f Bollin Eric—Bollin Annabel (King's Theatre (IRE))
2621[7] 3167[8] 3385[4] ◆ 3976[5] 4515[4] 5489[4] 5790[15] 6577[7]

Bollin Tommy *Tim Easterby* 65
2 ch g Carnival Dancer—Bollin Ann (Anshan)
4080[9] 5003[2] ◆ 5727[10]

Bollistick *Michael Mullineaux* a48
5 b g Bollin Eric—Slip Killick (Cosmonaut)
7536[5]

Bollywood Style *John Best* a66 65
6 b m Josr Algarhoud(IRE) —Dane Dancing (IRE) (Danehill (USA))
304[2] 435[9] 654[2] 719[6]

Bolodenka (IRE) *Richard Fahey* a78 81
9 b g Soviet Star(USA) —My-Lorraine (IRE) (Mac's Imp (USA))
(1538) *(1976)* 2301[10] 3576[3] 3934[4] 4404[5] (4897) (5151) 5485[10] *7034[7] 7425[4]*

Bolshoi Melody *Jeremy Gask* a38 51
2 b f Librettist(USA) —Bullion (Sabrehill (USA))
5323[10] 5812[7] 6291[11] *6821[11] 7143[8] 7541[7]*

Bolt (FR) *M Boutin* a70 66
3 b g Night Tango(GER) —Roannaise (FR) (Octagonal (NZ))
616a[3]

Bolton Hall (IRE) *Keith Goldsworthy* a34 50
9 b g Imperial Ballet(IRE) —Muneera (USA) (Green Dancer (USA))
286[7]

Bombay Mist *Richard Guest* a33 48
4 b m Rambling Bear—Paris Mist (Paris House)
453[9] 4650[9] 6765[8] 7230[12]

Bomber Jet *Nigel Tinkler* 82
2 b g Avonbridge—Strawberry Leaf (Unfuwain (USA))
3314[6] (3899) 4749[3] (5184)

Bon Allumage *Sir Henry Cecil* a76
2 b f Nayef(USA) —Brisk Breeze (GER) (Monsun (GER))
7118[5]

Bonamassa *Michael Attwater* a48
4 b g Sulamani(IRE) —Anastasia Venture (Lion Cavern (USA))
2608[7] 3281[11] 5642[11]

Bon Appetit *Micky Hammond* a57 44
3 gr f Exceed And Excel(AUS) —Welcome Band (Dixieland Band (USA))
2498[8] 3192[7] 4564[11]

Bondage (IRE) *Gordon Elliott* a67 93
4 b g Whipper(USA) —Shamah (Unfuwain (USA))
(3163) ◆

Bond Artist (IRE) *Geoffrey Oldroyd* 64
2 b f Excellent Art—Pitrizza (IRE) (Machiavellian (USA))
5464[6] ◆ 6047[U] 6985[8]

Bond Blade *Geoffrey Oldroyd* a68 65
3 ch g Needwood Blade—Bond Cat (IRE) (Raise A Grand (IRE))
4282[7] 5443[6] *(6615)* 7064[4] *7395[9] 7567[10] 7854[6]*

Bond City (IRE) *Geoffrey Oldroyd* a94 90
9 b g Trans Island—Where's Charlotte (Sure Blade (USA))
2112[11] 4349[6] 5488[9]

Bond Fastrac *Geoffrey Oldroyd* a81 80
4 b g Monsieur Bond(IRE) —Kanisfluh (Pivotal)
1695[5] 2095[5] 2938[19] 3880[8] 4145[4] 4793[5] *5736[4]* (5824) 6276[8] *6665[4]* 6779[2] *7596[3] 7926[10]*

Bondie *John Bridger* a20
3 ch g Monsieur Bond(IRE) —Mockingbird (Sharpo)
7207[7] 7327[9] 7766[9]

Bondi Mist (IRE) *Jonathan Portman* 38
2 gr f Aussie Rules(USA) —Akoya (IRE) (Anabaa (USA))
7025[14]

Bond Style *Bryan Smart* a62 31
2 ch c Monsieur Bond(IRE) —In Some Style (IRE) (Grand Lodge (USA))
4292[6] 7210[6] *7724[3]*

Bonfire *Andrew Balding* 114
2 b c Manduro(GER) —Night Frolic (Night Shift (USA))
(6463) 7192a[3]

Bonfire Knight *John Quinn* a71 97
4 b g Red Ransom(USA) —Attune (Singspiel (IRE))
(1098) 2002[13] 2509[4] 2909[11] 3315[10]

Bon Grain (FR) *M bin Shafya* a85 97
6 br g Muhtathir—Such Is Life (FR) (Akarad (FR))
242[9] *328a[14]* 581a[5] *679a[13]*

Bonne Idee (FR) *F Head* a81 84
2 b f Choisir(AUS) —Balsannda (USA) (Rahy (USA))
7326a[6]

Bonne Millie *Ollie Pears* 38
3 b f Compton Place—Bonne Etoile (Diesis)
2350[9] 2798[12]

Bonne Pioche (FR) *P Khozian* a54
3 b c Vespone(IRE) —Marietta (FR) (Bluebird (USA))
660a[5]

Bonnet De Douche (IRE) *Peter Chapple-Hyam* 58
2 ch f Modigliani(USA) —Isadora Duncan (IRE) (Sadler's Wells (USA))
7083[5]

Bonnie Acclamation (IRE) *Patrick J Flynn* a55 79
3 b g Acclamation—Lake Bonneville (USA) (Diesis)
(6139a) 6388a[25]

Bonnie Blade *James Unett* a44
2 b f Needwood Blade—Kyrhena (Desert Prince (IRE))
7142[8] 7396[9] 7783[9] 7925[9]

Bonnie Brae *David Elsworth* a59 103
4 b m Mujahid(USA) —Skara Brae (Inchinor)
2566[2] (2963) 3180[2] 3845[6] (4332) 6341[10] 6987[11] ◆ (7295)

Bonnie Charlie *David Nicholls* a76 98
5 ch g Intikhab(USA) —Scottish Exile (IRE) (Ashkalani (IRE))
2116[15] 2668[3] 4369[9] 6917[3]

Bonnie Prince Blue *Ian McInnes* a87 82
8 ch g Tipsy Creek(USA) —Heart So Blue (Dilum (USA))
(35) 376[2] 493[4] 651[10] 822[8] 960[3] (1044) 1180[3] (1289) 1471[5] 1906[4] 2205[5] 3083[4] 3711[4] 3953[3] 4897[4] 5502[6] 6208[11] 6414[2] 6426[6] 6777[10] 7268[11] 7419[11]

Bon Royale *Phil McEntee* a44
3 b f Val Royal(FR) —Bonella (IRE) (Eagle Eyed (USA))
7207[5] 7750[10]

Bon Spiel *Chris Gordon* a78 75
7 b g Singspiel(IRE) —L'Affaire Monique (Machiavellian (USA))
2991[4]

Bonzai Boy (IRE) *George Moore*
3 ch g Atraf—High Chart (Robellino (USA))
2621[11]

Boo *James Unett* a75 56
9 b g Namaqualand(USA) —Violet (IRE) (Mukaddamah (USA))
2159[11]

Boogie Dancer *Stuart Howe* a59 34
7 b m Tobougg(IRE) —Bolero (Rainbow Quest (USA))
862[5] 954[8] 2608[3] 3256[10] 4703[8]

Boogie Diva *George Margarson* 85
4 b m Tobougg(IRE) —Distant Diva (Distant Relative)
2111[9]

Boogie Shoes *Roger Varian* a75 100
3 b g Bertolini(USA) —Space Time (FR) (Bering)
(1727) 2711[3] ◆ 4467[6] (6273)

Boogie Star *J S Moore* a62 53
3 b c Tobougg(IRE) —Donyana (Mark Of Esteem (IRE))
5[3] 47[4]

Boogie Waltzer *Stuart Williams* a80 77
4 b m Tobougg(IRE) —Upping The Tempo (Dunbeath (USA))
1762[7] 2179[3] 3493[2] 4239[2] 4416[5] 5108[3] 5468[9] 5890[9] 6250[3] *6932[2]*

Bookiebasher Babe (IRE) *Michael Quinn* a49 69
6 b m Orpen(USA) —Jay Gee (IRE) (Second Set (IRE))
115[7] 354[5]

Bookiesindex Boy *J R Jenkins* a80 55
7 bb g Piccolo—United Passion (Emarati (USA))
294[3] (491) 794[10] 946[7] 1196[6] 2179[9] 3493[5] 3678[4] 3939[3] *4182[4]* 4740[5] 4930[6] 5846[8] 6616[8] 7356[7] 7420[4] 7649[3] 7896[8]

Bookiesindexdotnet *J R Jenkins* a72 58
2 b f Piccolo—United Passion (Emarati (USA))
7042[7] 7435[6] 4848[3] 5351[5] *(6620) 7452[2] 7642[2] 7905[3]*

Boom And Bust (IRE) *Marcus Tregoning* a69 103
4 b g Footstepsinthesand—Forest Call (Wolfhound (USA))
(1448) (2310) (2783) ◆ 3409[5] (4494)

Boomerang Bob (IRE) *J W Hills* a73 102
2 b g Aussie Rules(USA) —Cozzene's Pride (USA) (Cozzene (USA))
(1757) 2367[2] 3064[2] 3669a[2]

Boom 'n' Zoom (AUS) *Ken Keys* 106
6 bb g Dash For Cash(AUS) —Entice (AUS) (Last Tycoon)
7115a[4] 7310a[10]

Boom To Bust (IRE) *G M Lyons* a80 81
3 b g Big Bad Bob(IRE) —Forever Phoenix (Shareef Dancer (USA))
7189a[13]

Boots And Spurs *Mrs K Burke* a69
2 b g Oasis Dream—Arctic Char (Polar Falcon (USA))
7526[7] 7758[2]

Bop It *Bryan Smart* 85
2 b c Misu Bond(IRE) —Forever Bond (Danetime (IRE))
2033[6] 2485[8] (3274) (4538) 6535[19] 7138[5]

Bop Till Dawn (IRE) *Harry Dunlop* a13 41
3 b f Big Bad Bob(IRE) —Dawn's Sharp Shot (IRE) (Son Of Sharp Shot (IRE))
1580[10] 2790[10] *3494[7]*

Boragh Jamal (IRE) *Brian Meehan* a71 70
4 b m Namid—Danccini (IRE) (Dancing Dissident (USA))
725[2] 946[6] 3174[4] 3261[6] 3512[15]

Border Abby *Rae Guest* a41 62
3 ch f Selkirk(USA) —Perfect Solution (IRE) (Entrepreneur)
2394[3] 2964[2] *3227[5]* 3913[2] (4329) ◆ 4673[12] 5137[4] 5515[7]

Border Hill Jack *Robin Bastiman* 20
2 b g Danbird(AUS) —Edge Of Darkness (Vaigly Great)
7060[7]

Borderlescott *Robin Bastiman* a105 116
9 b g Compton Place—Jeewan (Touching Wood (USA))
1687[5] 2297[4] 3874[9]

Border Owl (IRE) *Peter Salmon* a70 73
6 b g Selkirk(USA) —Nightbird (IRE) (Night Shift (USA))
528[3] 1190[2] 1613[5] *(1978)*

Border Patrol *Roger Charlton* 106
5 b g Selkirk(USA) —Ffestiniog (IRE) (Efisio)
2961[3]

Border Revia (IRE) *Richard Fahey* 78
2 b g Celtic Swing—Maraami (Selkirk (USA))
5486[8] 5786[8] (6344)

Boris Grigoriev (IRE) *A P O'Brien* 97
2 bb g Excellent Art—Strategy (Machiavellian (USA))
4131a[3] 4413[8] 5522a[4] 5849[14]

Boris The Bold *John Best* a63
2 b c Librettist(USA) —Santiburi Girl (Casteddu)
7672[8] 7938[3]

Borley Ghost (FR) *John Quinn* 16
2 ro c Layman(USA) —Lovarisk (FR) (Take Risks (FR))
3611[9] 4192[11]

Born To Be Achamp (BRZ) *Geoffrey Harker* a48 62
5 ch g Redattore(BRZ) —Small High Plain (BRZ) (Spring Halo (ARG))
2955[8] 3620[13] 4634[7] 5404[9] *6490[8]*

Born To Sea (IRE) *John M Oxx* 104
2 b c Invincible Spirit(IRE) —Urban Sea (USA) (Miswaki (USA))
(5950a) ◆ 7185a[2]

Born To Shine (USA) *Alan Swinbank* 39
3 b g Suave(USA) —Sentimental Keep (USA) (Behrens (USA))
2785[4]

Born To Surprise *Michael Bell* 69
2 b c Exceed And Excel(AUS) —Dubai Surprise (IRE) (King's Best (USA))
6483[2] ◆

Borug (USA) *Saeed Bin Suroor* a90 92
3 b c Kingmambo(USA) —Marienbad (FR) (Darshaan)
411a[5] *753a[3]* 1478[2] 1895[4] 3108[8] 6342[4] 7053[5]

Bosambo *Alan Swinbank* a74 85
3 b g King's Best(USA) —Roseum (Lahib (USA))
559[2] (720) 845[8] ◆ 1437[2] (1653) 2096[4] 4335[11]

Bosco (GER) *C Von Der Recke* a59
5 b g City On A Hill(USA) —Bedford Set (GER) (Second Set (IRE))
42a[3]

Boss's Destination *Alan Swinbank* a76 85
4 b g Dubai Destination(USA) —Blushing Sunrise (USA) (Cox's Ridge (USA))
2810[3] ◆ 4382[5] 4879[4] (5453) 5759[6] 6115[9]

Bossy Kitty *Nigel Tinkler* 73
4 gr m Avonbridge—Between The Sticks (Pharly (FR))
1907[13] 2182[4] 2546[10] 2798[11] 3248[3] 3573[10] 3937[7] 4233[8] 5490[6]

Boston Blue *Tony Carroll* a41 88
4 b g Halling(USA) —City Of Gold (IRE) (Sadler's Wells (USA))
1517[12] 2034[8] 2512[5] 2892[9] *3738[10]* 4562[9] (5588) 5857[5] 6749[10]

Boston Court (IRE) *Brian Meehan* 56
3 b g Tomba—Chiffon (Polish Precedent (USA))
2231[8] 2637[12] 3077[3] *3393[11]*

Bosun Breese *David Barron* a61 82
6 b g Bahamian Bounty—Nellie Melba (Hurricane Sky (AUS))
1411[2] 1698[14] 2116[6] 2299[6] 2694[2] 3078[4] 3582[4] 3759[4] 4539[2] 5400[6] 5720[12] 6212[5]

Botanist *Tobias B P Coles* a74 79
4 b g Selkirk(USA) —Red Camellia (Polar Falcon (USA))
2178[9] 3592[8] 5547[5] *6254[6]* 6592[12] 7237[9]

Botham (USA) *Jim Goldie* a58 75
7 bb g Cryptoclearance(USA) —Oval (USA) (Kris S (USA))
1714[5] 2260[6] (3110) (3306) 3859[4] 4045[3] 4603[6] 5205[12] 5314[3] 5622[4] (6211) (6417)

Bothy *Brian Ellison* a81 83
5 ch g Pivotal—Villa Carlotta (Rainbow Quest (USA))
5435[6]

Boucher Garcon (IRE) *Declan Carroll* a37 44
3 b g Spartacus(IRE) —Valamander (IRE) (Val Royal (FR))
3949[4] 4863[5] 5469[7] *5865[8]* 7100[7] 7230[5]

Boudoir (IRE) *Richard Hannon* a66
2 gr f Clodovil(IRE) —Adultress (IRE) (Ela-Mana-Mou)
7526[5] 7838[3]

Bouggatti *William Jarvis* a71 72
3 b g Tobougg(IRE) —Western Sal (Salse (USA))
(1327) 2076[9] 2677[6] 4902[4] 5518[2] *5942[3]* 6577[4]

Boulba D'Alben (FR) *H-A Pantall* 64
2 b f Dark Angel(IRE) —Wixon (FR) (Fioravanti (USA))
7814a[7]

Bouncing Lily (FR) *C Boutin* a71 69
2 b f Trempolino(USA) —Golden Lily (FR) (Dolphin Street (FR))
6925a[2] 7312a[6]

Bouncy Bouncy (IRE) *Michael Bell* a51 72
4 ch m Chineur(FR) —Wunderbra (IRE) (Second Empire (IRE))
1213[5] 2182[6] (3261) 3597[3] (4189) 4541[7] 5484[7] 5997[2] 6802[3]

Boundaries *Tim Easterby* 85
3 b g Indesatchel(IRE) —On The Brink (Mind Games)
1241[3] 1650[4] 1825[3] 2319[11] 2505[7] 2911[6] 4855[7] 5559[2] 6762[6] 6917[5]

Boundless Applause *Ian Wood* a50 54
5 b m Royal Applause—Liberty Bound (Primo Dominie)
204 [7] 312[5] 619[8]

Boundless Spirit *David Nicholls* 88
3 b g Invincible Spirit(IRE) —Bye Bold Aileen (IRE) (Warning)
1241[15] 1391[9] 1745[6] 2180[12] 3040[3] (3860) 4359[4] 5274[6] 6265[7] 6537[7] 6801[13]

Bountiful Catch *Pam Sly* a50 54
2 ch c Bahamian Bounty—Saida Lenasera (FR) (Fasliyev (USA))
3954[10] 5565[10] 6483[6] *6821[10]* 7294[13] *7337[3] 7421[4] 7530[12]*

Bountiful Girl *Richard Fahey* 78
2 b f Bahamian Bounty—Cheeky Girl (College Chapel)
4285[2] (4853) 5478[4] 6077[2]

Bountiful Guest *Brian Baugh* a68 21
3 ch g Bahamian Bounty—Perfect Partner (Be My Chief (USA))
519[3] 717[2] ◆ *850[4] (916)* 2835[9] 4081[12] 4435[10] *4920[8]*

Bounty Box *Chris Wall* 107
5 b m Bahamian Bounty—Bible Box (IRE) (Bin Ajwaad (IRE))
1340[7] (1902)

Bounty Seeker (USA) *Mark Johnston* a72 73
2 b g A.P. Indy(USA) —Plenty Of Light (USA) (Colony Light (USA))
2355[4] 2584[4] 3152[16] 4496[15] *(4919)* ◆ *7095[9]*

Bourbon Bay (USA) *Neil Drysdale* a114 114
5 b g Sligo Bay(IRE) —Coral Necklace (USA) (Conquistador Cielo (USA))
1001a[11] 6203a[8]

Bourne *Luca Cumani* a78 98
5 gr g Linamix(FR) —L'Affaire Monique (Machiavellian (USA))
1402[4] ◆ (1892) 2716[11] 3625[2] 4528[7] 5883[3] 6569a[4]

Boushra *Sylvester Kirk* a53
3 ch f Redback—Esdaraat (Pivotal)
109[8] 383[11]

Bouzy *Simon Dow* a54 57
3 rg f Proclamation(IRE) —Ambonnay (Ashkalani (IRE))
655[5] 788[5]

Bovs Castle *Lucinda Featherstone*
2 gr f Proclamation(IRE) —Focosa (ITY) (In The Wings)
6329[15] 6603[17] 6985[11]

Bowdler's Magic *Mark Johnston* a92 97
4 b g Hernando(FR) —Slew The Moon (ARG) (Kitwood (USA))
994[3] 2071[6] 2285[4] 2932[4] 3163[6] 3625[3] 4423[6] 4775[5] 5250[15] 5878[3] (6103) 6690[17] 7102[6]

Bowmaker *Mark Johnston* a92 85
4 b g Dubawi(IRE) —Viola Da Braccio (IRE) (Vettori (IRE))
(557) 1240[10] 1541[4] 1898[2] 2390[11] 2876[8] 3339[9] 3659[4]

Bowmans Well (IRE) *Peter Purdy*
6 b m Cadeaux Genereux—Guignol (IRE) (Anita's Prince)
3090[11] *7411[7] 7606[7] 7903[11]*

Bow River Arch (USA) *Jeremy Noseda* a73 79
3 b f Arch(USA) —Bow River Gold (Rainbow Quest (USA))
214 [3] 1272[5] 1872[3] 2874[3] 3978[3] 6584[4] *7503[3]*

Bowsers Brave (USA) *Marcus Tregoning* a79 80
5 ch g Dixieland Band(USA) —Hazimah (USA) (Gone West (USA))
2436[11] *3042[3]* (5808) 6402[4] 6676[2] 6893[7]

Bow To No One (IRE) *Alan Jarvis* a89 93
5 b m Refuse To Bend(IRE) —Deadly Buzz (IRE) (Darshaan)
1847[7] 2931[7] 3828[2] 4423[4] 5221[6] (5759) 6499[7] 6690[15]

Boxer Shorts *Michael Mullineaux* a42 13
5 b g Puissance—Lady Boxer (Komaite (USA))
166[8] 652[11] 1875[9] 2352[11] 2593[15]

Boxing Day *Bent Olsen* 92
4 b h Galileo(IRE) —Special Oasis (Green Desert (USA))
4842a[5] 5984a[7]

Boy Blue *Peter Salmon* a58 75
6 b r Observatory(USA) —Rowan Flower (IRE) (Ashkalani (IRE))
528[5] 3245[10]

Boynagh Joy (IRE) *James Halpin* a95 100
6 b m Definite Article—Bramble Cottage (IRE) (Eurobus)
2325a[6] 3445a[4]

Boy The Bell *Ollie Pears* a78 76
4 b g Choisir(AUS) —Bella Beguine (Komaite (USA))
13[5] 169[11] 363[8] 1204[4] *(1815)* 2247[2] 2464[4] 2670[5] (3049) (3359) 3662[3] (4604) 6044[6] 6382[2] *6617[2]* 7055[4] 7214[6] 7352[4] 7646[3] 7857[7]

Boz *M Gasparini* a99 97
7 gr g Grand Lodge(USA) —Dali's Grey (Linamix (FR))
6569a[6]

Brabazon (IRE) *Emmet Michael Butterly* a69 70
8 b g In The Wings—Azure Lake (USA) (Lac Ouimet (USA))
33[9] (444) (560) (1297) ◆ *5692[7]*

Brackendale *John Weymes* a43 40
2 br g Three Valleys(USA) —Heather Mix (Linamix (FR))
3947[5] 4193[3] 4983[5] *7590[6]*

Bradbury (IRE) *James Bethell* a67 72
3 ch g Redback—Simonaventura (IRE) (Dr Devious (IRE))
480a[7] 638a[6] 1189[5] 1623[3] 2571[5] (3460) (3811) 4366[15] 5504[5] 6191[6]

Braddock (IRE) *Bill Turner* a73 70
8 b g Pivotal—Sedna (FR) (Bering)
181[4] 807[12]

Braehead (IRE) *David Evans* a73 52
3 b g Ivan Denisovich(IRE) —Poppy's Song (Owington)
182[4] 198[5] 333[3]

Brae Hill (IRE) *Richard Fahey* a74 104
5 b g Fath(USA) —Auriga (Belmez (USA))
1094[2] 1406[6] 1885[4] 2284[8] 3032[24] 3397[6] (3862) 4314[20] 5474[11] 5699[14]

Brailsford (IRE) *Mahmood Al Zarooni* 75
2 b c Dubawi(IRE) —Meynell (Sakhee (USA))
5851[5] ◆ 6447[7] 6805[6]

Bramalea *Hughie Morrison* a70 96
6 b m Whitmore's Conn(USA) —Aster (IRE) (Danehill (USA))
2686[3] 3204[5] 4470[8] (5545) 6269[8] 7297[19]

Bramshaw (USA) *Amanda Perrett* a86 90
4 rg g Langfuhr(CAN) —Milagra (USA) (Maria's Mon (USA))
1269[10]

Bramshill Lass *Amanda Perrett* 57
2 ch f Notnowcato—Disco Ball (Fantastic Light (USA))
6744[8]

Branderburgo (IRE) *L Riccardi* 109
4 b h High Chaparral(IRE) —Farhad (Red Ransom (USA))
2134a[5] 2982a[5] 7324a[9]

Brandy Alexander *Neil Mulholland* a59 59
3 b g Invincible Spirit(IRE) —Valhalla Moon (USA) (Sadler's Wells (USA))
520[6] 634[7] 2225[8]

Brandywell Boy (IRE) *Dominic Ffrench Davis* a73 81
8 b g Danetime(IRE) —Alexander Eliott (IRE) (Night Shift (USA))
133[5] 178[7] 2069[6] 2244[4] 2557[6] 2645[4] 2903[7] 3427[5] 4615[9] 4895[8] 5616[9] 5781[5] *6056[4] 6257[5]* 6479[8] 6794[8] 6931[5] 7123[6]

Brasileira *J-M Beguigne* 103
3 b f Dubai Destination(USA) —Shifting Sands (FR) (Hernando (FR))
5958a[2] 7580a[6]

Brasingaman Eric *George Moore* a51 68
4 b g Bollin Eric—Serene Pearl (IRE) (Night Shift (USA))
1324[4] 1615[12] 2830[3] (3574) ◆ 4366[9] (5167) 5595[9] 6279[2] 6838[3] (7107)

Brasingaman Espee *George Moore* 41
2 b c Silver Patriarch(IRE) —Serene Pearl (IRE) (Night Shift (USA))
2831[6] 3570[3] 5454[11]

Brave Battle *Ron Barr* a68 67
[illegible]
1176[7] 1334[5] 1482[3] 2356[7] 2588[5] 3661[2] 3931[7] 4041[5] 4638[11] (5437) 6190[7] 6343[12]

Brave Decision *Robert Cowell* a50 53
4 gr g With Approval(CAN) —Brave Vanessa (USA) (Private Account (USA))
225[4] 517[7] 773[4] 7787[4]

Brave Dream *Kevin Ryan* a76 76
3 b g Sleeping Indian—Aimee's Delight (Robellino (USA))
1214[7] 1802[11] 3347[9] 4067[3] (4511) 4680[4] 5338[8] 6634[2]

Brave Enough (USA) *Roger Curtis* a42 45
4 b g Yes It's True(USA) —Courageous (USA) (Kingmambo (USA))
1935[4] 2659[6] *7581[9] 7850[7]*

Braveheart Move (IRE) *Geoffrey Harker* a78 102
5 b g Cape Cross(IRE) —Token Gesture (IRE) (Alzao (USA))
4528[13] 5221[9] 6690[32] 7022[6]

Brave Kid (AUS) *J Size* 111
6 b g Elusive City(USA) —Gordon's (NZ) (Kaapstad (NZ))
1576a[12]

Bravely Fought (IRE) *Sabrina J Harty* a102 103
6 b g Indian Ridge—Amazing Tale (Shareef Dancer (USA))
328a[8] 503a[14] *585a[11] 1381a[10] 7544a[5] 7618a[5]*

Brave One (IRE) *David Nicholls* 32
2 b f Moss Vale(IRE) —Smart Pet (Petong)
6344[8] 6598[6] 7058[9]

Brave Prospector *Richard Fahey* a107 104
6 b h Oasis Dream—Simply Times (USA) (Dodge (USA))
46[2] (429) 700[4] 1093[3] 1340[13] 2284[10] 4042[7] 4534[23] 5474[12] 6147[23] *6541[8]*

Bravestofthebrave (USA) *John Gosden* a74 57
3 b g Elusive Quality(USA) —Victoria Cross (IRE) (Mark Of Esteem (IRE))
7111[3] *7401[3] 7712[2]*

Brave Tiger (IRE) *Hugo Palmer* a58 49
3 b g Shamardal(USA) —Designed (Zamindar (USA))
1193[4] 2155[11] 4657[3] *5214[13]*

Bravo Biloute (FR) *S Jesus* a66 75
3 b g Reste Tranquille(FR) —Like The Wind (Polish Precedent (USA))
7016a[5]

Bravo Bravo *Mick Channon* a63 61
4 b g Sadler's Wells(USA) —Top Table (Shirley Heights)
(1016)

Bravo Echo *Michael Attwater* a107 89
5 b g Oasis Dream—Bold Empress (USA) (Diesis)
(99) (271) 1406[15] 1885[15] 2470[15] 3290[11] 3796[2] 4556[14] 5043[13] *7433[5] 7516[9] 7801[7]*

Bravo King (IRE) *Richard Guest* a83 86
3 b g Sakhee(USA) —Ashbilya (USA) (Nureyev (USA))
1774[9] 2427[2] *(3747)* 5119[4] 5378[5] (5456) 5918[10] 6327[4] 7262[12] *7500[10] 7643[6] 7726[8] 7832[8]*

Brazilian Breeze (IRE) *Kevin Prendergast* a78 79
3 b f Invincible Spirit(IRE) —Brazilian Bride (IRE) (Pivotal)
6854a[8]

Brazilian Brush (IRE) *Milton Bradley* a60 32
6 ch g Captain Rio—Ejder (IRE) (Indian Ridge)
107[7] 167[5]

Bread Loft (FR) *Mme M Bollack-Badel* a81 85
3 ch c Touch Of The Blues(FR) —Jamouna (FR) (Trempolino (USA))
5529a[0]

Break Free (FR) *Y De Nicolay* 68
2 b c Zamindar(USA) —Summer Melody (USA) (War Chant (USA))
4652a[4] *7665a[0]*

Breakheart (IRE) *Michael Dods* a68 98
4 b g Sakhee(USA) —Exorcet (FR) (Selkirk (USA))
1092[17] 1387[4] 1684[3] 2573[7] 3032[20] 4058[7] 4415[17] 5686[8] 6078[12] 6989[18]

Breaking The Bank *William Muir* 72
2 ch c Medicean—Russian Dance (USA) (Nureyev (USA))
2687[6] 3408[2] 3986[8] 6165[5] 6970[4]

Breathless Kiss (USA) *Kevin Ryan* a99 101
4 b m Roman Ruler(USA) —Crusading Miss Cox (USA) (Crusader Sword (USA))
87[4] 265[7] (523) 700[10] (1166) 1476[8] ◆ 1687[7] 1809[12] 4468[6] 5253[12] 5467[5] 5827[9] 6147[15] 6706[13] *7012a[2]* 7392[8]

Breedj (IRE) *Clive Brittain* a68 92
3 b f Acclamation—Kildare Lady (IRE) (Indian Ridge)
1059[3] 1404[8] 1688[11] 2508[13] 3459[11] 4332[10] 5018[6] 6065[6]

Breezed Well (IRE) *James McAuley* a60 61
4 b g Pyrus(USA) —Full Traceability (IRE) (Ron's Victory (USA))
809[2] 977a[6] 3720[7]

Breeze On Bye *Brian Meehan* 34
2 b g Monsieur Bond(IRE) —Breezy Louise (Dilum (USA))
6890[8]

Breezolini *Richard Whitaker* a51 78
3 b f Bertolini(USA) —African Breeze (Atraf)
2363[7] 2763[3] 3052[6] 3461[3] 5164[6] 5370[4] 6094[5] 6450[4] 6840[11] 7074[9] *7141[9]*

Breezy Hawk (GER) *S Smrczek* 92
3 b f Hawk Wing(USA) —Be My Lady (GER) (Be My Guest (USA))
4839a[14]

Brehat *E Lellouche* 85
3 b c Motivator—Pelagic (Rainbow Quest (USA))
5132a[6]

Bremen *Paul W Flynn* a59 86
8 b g Sadler's Wells(USA) —Anka Germania (Malinowski (USA))
4398a[5]

Brendan's Gift *Brendan Powell*
3 b f Phoenix Reach(IRE) —Digyourheelsin (IRE) [illegible]
559[8]

Brenhines *David Simcock* 50
3 gr f Proclamation(IRE) —Silver Chime (Robellino (USA))
2427[5]

Brent Pelham *Tobias B P Coles* a49
4 b h Royal Applause—Little Firefly (IRE) (Danehill (USA))
1015[2] 1370[5] 2419[6]

Breton Star *David Simcock* a61 58
3 b g Medicean—Wannabe Grand (IRE) (Danehill (USA))
1442[4] ◆ 2152[8] *3175[3] 3393[2]*

Bretzele *J-P Roman* 49
3 b f Westerner—Fruhling Feuer (FR) (Green Tune (USA))
288a[0]

Brevity (USA) *Brian Meehan* 106
3 b f Street Cry(IRE) —Cut Short (USA) (Diesis)
5277[3] ◆ 5695a[8]

Brezza Di Mare (IRE) *Brian Meehan* a26 71
3 b g Rainbow Quest(USA) —Sea Picture (IRE) (Royal Academy (USA))
1751[2] 2613[9] 3770[P]

Briannsta (IRE) *John E Long* a58 41
9 b g Bluebird(USA) —Nacote (IRE) (Mtoto)
590[4] 1044[5] 1180[6] 4547[6]

Brian's Best *Bruce Hellier* a18
2 ch g Tobougg(IRE) —Approved Quality (IRE) (Persian Heights)
4012[9] *6352[7] 6540[12] 7514[11]*

Brian Sprout *John Weymes* a28 57
3 ch g Zafeen(FR) —Ducal Diva (Bahamian Bounty)
2252[9] 3143[2] 3272[9] 3785[6] 4146[8] 4607[3] 5719[10] *6943[5] 7366[5] 7429[2] 7676[8] 7785[6]*

Briary Mac *Peter Pritchard* a20 65
4 b m Royal Applause—Red May (IRE) (Persian Bold)
861[3] 730[8]

Brick Dust (IRE) *Luca Cumani* a74 73
3 b g Noverre(USA) —Reddening (Blushing Flame (USA))
2568[8] *2924[6]* 3324[2] 3781[5] 4478[4] *5687[7] 6307[3] 6981[2]*

Brickfielder (IRE) *Roger Charlton* 70
2 b c Jeremy(USA) —Graceful Air (IRE) (Danzero (AUS))
(4708) 5708[7] 6484[7]

Brick Red *Andrew Balding* a90 97
4 ch g Dubawi(IRE) —Duchcov (Caerleon (USA))
1406[19] 1684[10] 2441[4] 3032[25] 5940[6] ◆ 6339[13] ◆

Bricks And Porter (IRE) *Adrian McGuinness* a58 54
11 b g College Chapel—Camassina (IRE) (Taufan (USA))
387[5] 425[3]

Brick Tops *Ralph Beckett* 76
2 br f Danehill Dancer(IRE) —Rag Top (IRE) (Barathea (IRE))
(7293)

Bridgefield (USA) *Mahmood Al Zarooni* a100 105
3 ch c Speightstown(USA) —Treysta (USA) (Belong To Me (USA))
238[3] 502a[4] 753a[5] 3067[15] (3777) 4472[6] 5699[7]

Bridgehampton *Michael Bell* 47
2 b c Lando(GER) —Gaze (Galileo (IRE))
5851[12]

Bridge Of Gold (USA) *Mikael Magnusson* a109 112
5 b h Giant's Causeway(USA) —Lady Doc (USA) (Doc's Leader (USA))
705a[6] 1403[2]

Bridgetown (USA) *Todd Pletcher* 113
4 ch h Speightstown(USA) —Ellesmere (USA) (Tabasco Cat (USA))
3010[12]

Bridgets Call *Des Donovan* a7 19
2 b f Echo Of Light—Sforzando (Robellino (USA))
2854[5] 4961[11] *5637[9]*

Bridget The Fidget *Edward Creighton* a44 6
3 b f Avonbridge—Long Tall Sally (IRE) (Danehill Dancer (IRE))
189[11]

Bridge Valley *Jason Ward* a53 30
4 ch g Avonbridge—Go Between (Daggers Drawn (USA))
6536[9] *6844[7] 7371[8] 7561[4] 7911[7]*

Bridle Belle *Richard Fahey* 96
3 b f Dansili—River Belle (Lahib (USA))
1384[6] 1723[3] ◆ 2726[8] (4108) 4426[6] 5700[6] 6151[8]

Brief Chat (USA) *Amanda Perrett* a66 55
2 bb f Pleasant Tap(USA) —Sambac (USA) (Mr Prospector (USA))
6745[6] *7125[3]*

Brief Encounter (IRE) *Ibrahaim Al Malki* a105 103
5 br g Pyrus(USA) —Just One Look (Barathea (IRE))
605a[11]

Brigadoon *William Jarvis* a83 79
4 b g Compton Place—Briggsmaid (Elegant Air)
1398[8] *6507[3]* (6918) 7237[4] *7458[2] 7803[3] 7908[7]*

Brigantin (USA) *A Fabre* a65 114
4 ch h Cozzene(USA) —Banyu Dewi (GER) (Poliglote)
1707a[4] (2344a) 3066[3] 5304a[3] 5990a[7] 6562a[3] *7300a[8]*

Bright Abbey *Walter Swinburn* a73 57
3 ch g Halling(USA) —Bright Hope (IRE) (Danehill (USA))
2231[9] 2648[13] 3430[9] 4510[3] *(6052)* ◆

Bright Applause *Tracy Waggott* a57 65
3 b g Royal Applause—Sadaka (USA) (Kingmambo (USA))
3380[4] 3679[3] 4150[4] 4902[5] 5405[10] 5822[2] 6211[6] 6775[7] 7099[6]

Bright Eyed Girl (IRE) *Kate Walton* 15
2 b f King's Best(USA) —Bright Smile (IRE) (Caerleon (USA))
6449[9] 6866[10]

Bright Sparky (GER) *Michael Easterby* a59 40
8 ch g Dashing Blade—Braissim (Dancing Brave (USA))
451[2] (598) 631[2] 2830[6] 2952[14] 3086[11] 6600[8] *6873[8]*

Brillante Etoile (FR) *Y Durepaire* 99
2 b f American Post—Black Dalhia (FR) (Sanglamore (USA))
6941a[4]

Brilliant Barca *Mick Channon* a70 57
3 b g Imperial Dancer—Fading Away (Fraam)
591[2] (801) 1057[4] 1442[5] 1947[10] 2186[8]

Brilliant Crystal *Mrs K Burke* a13 37
2 b f Compton Place—Anatase (Danehill (USA))
4283[9] 4702[3] *6352[6]*

Brilliant Speed (USA) *Thomas Albertrani* a120 121
3 bb c Dynaformer(USA) —Speed Succeeds (USA) (Gone West (USA))
1921a[7] 2950a[3] 6716a[2] 7305a[3]

Brimstone Hill (IRE) *Charles Hills* a70 77
2 b c Royal Applause—Right As Rain (Rainbow Quest (USA))
1619[9] 2181[5] 2523[2] 3842[5] *4661[5]* 5280[6] 6484[5] 6757[P] (6986)

Bring It On Home *Brendan Powell* a48 31
7 b g Beat Hollow—Dernier Cri (Slip Anchor)
5209[5] 6486[11] *7574[3]*

Bring Sweets (IRE) *Brian Ellison* a59 56
4 b g Firebreak—Missperon (IRE) (Orpen (USA))
74 [1] 181[6] (507) 645[2] 2393[10] 2666[5] 3072[6] *3492[2]* 4173[9] *5210[4]*

Brinmore *William Knight* a56 72
3 ch f Kyllachy—Ringarooma (Erhaab (USA))
2192[5] ◆ 2689[2] 4163[11] *4849[5] 5639[9]*

Brio *Alan McCabe* a69 64
3 b g Araafa(IRE) —Salsa Brava (IRE) (Almutawakel)
1984[5] 2361[10] 2802[8] 3633[5] *4647[2] 5215[8] 5734[7]* 6223[4] (6767) *7352[6] 7420[2] 7646[7] 7726[6] 7744[8]*

Brisbane (IRE) *Dianne Sayer* 49
4 b g Kheleyf(USA) —Waroonga (IRE) (Brief Truce (USA))
1520[6] 2047[8] 4600[7] 4852[6] 5403[7] 5788[5]

Britney (FR) *Mario Hofer* 79
2 b f Kheleyf(USA) —Nappe Di Cardinale (IRE) (Distinctly North (USA))
7813a[3]

Broad Meaning *James McAuley* a92 100
5 b g Oasis Dream—Avoidance (USA) (Cryptoclearance (USA))
614[3] 835[DSQ] 1381a[12]

Broad Street (JPN) *Hideaki Fujiwara* 110
5 b m Agnes Tachyon(JPN) —Phila Street (USA) (Cozzene (USA))
7410a[10]

Brockfield *Mel Brittain* a73 70
5 ch g Falbrav(IRE) —Irish Light (USA) (Irish River (FR))
1324[2] 2388[7] 2887[17] 6211[2] 6453[5] 6916[3] 7215[8] 7237[2] (7506)

Brocklebank (IRE) *Kevin Ryan* 89
2 b g Diamond Green(FR) —La Stellina (IRE) (Marju (IRE))
1890[2] (2318) 3012[21] 4717[3]

Brockovich (IRE) *John Geoghegan* a45 49
5 b m Danetime(IRE) —Scant (FR) (Septieme Ciel (USA))
874[11]

Brockwell *Tom Dascombe* 72
2 b c Singspiel(IRE) —Noble Plum (IRE) (King's Best (USA))
6702[4] ◆ 7101[6]

Brocottes (FR) *N Clement* 105
2 b f Lando(GER) —Macotte (FR) (Nicolotte)
7405a[2]

Broctune Papa Gio *Keith Reveley* 72
4 b g Tobougg(IRE) —Fairlie (Halling (USA))
1216[8] 1803[3] 2353[4] 2593[10] (3142) 4123[5] (4441) (5652) 5788[9] 6452[7] 6777[7]

Brog Deas (IRE) *Patrick J Flynn* a53
2 b g Arakan(USA) —Whitegate Way (Greensmith)
7273a[12]

Broken Belle (IRE) *J W Hills* a32 25
3 gr f Clodovil(IRE) —Lady Express (IRE) (Soviet Star (USA))
2174[12]

Broken Dreams (USA) *Thomas F Proctor* a93 106
5 ch m Broken Vow(USA) —Our Dreamer (USA) (Storm Cat (USA))
7303a[13]

Broken Eagle (USA) *Mikael Magnusson* a29 37
3 b c Broken Vow(USA) —Tricky Bird (USA) (Storm Bird (CAN))
4617[9] 5816[12] 6475[8]

Bromhead (USA) *Kevin Morgan* a43 60
5 ch g Johannesburg(USA) —Caramel Queen (NZ) (Turbulent Dancer (USA))
409[8]

Bronterre *Richard Hannon* 115
2 b c Oasis Dream—Wondrous Story (USA) (Royal Academy (USA))
(3870) (5933) ◆ 6689[4]

Bronze Angel (IRE) *Marcus Tregoning* a80 85
2 b c Dark Angel(IRE) —Rihana (IRE) (Priolo (USA))
2291[4] 2687[3] 3424[3] 4496[4] 5133[2] (7889)

Bronze Beau *Linda Stubbs* a64 89
4 ch g Compton Place—Bella Cantata (Singspiel (IRE))
1140[13] 1698[7] (2250) 2590[5] 4239[5] 4886[2] ◆ 5679[4] 6036[3] 6703[20] 6913[5]

Bronze Cannon (USA) *H J Brown* a109 105
6 bb h Lemon Drop Kid(USA) —Victoria Cross (IRE) (Mark Of Esteem (IRE))
157a[8] (330a) 608a[7] 824a[10] 5711[2] 6910a[16]

Bronze Prince *John Gosden* a82 100
4 b h Oasis Dream—Sweet Pea (Persian Bold)
2020[5] 2706[3] ◆ 3032[15] 3825[9] (4314) 5474[5]

Brookley Lady (IRE) *Seamus G O'Donnell* a65 75
3 b f Kheleyf(USA) —Daylight Ahead (IRE) (Tenby)
1663a[5]

Brook Star (IRE) *Michael Dods* 56
3 b f Refuse To Bend(IRE) —Star Of Cayman (IRE) (Unfuwain (USA))
1799[2] 2432[4] 3037[4] 4044[4] (5489) 6153[9]

Broox (IRE) *E J O'Neill* 111
3 b c Xaar—Miss Brooks (Bishop Of Cashel)
1686[13] 3644[7] 4739a[9]

Brother Tiger *George Margarson* 40
2 b c Singspiel(IRE) —Three Secrets (IRE) (Danehill (USA))
6099[8]

Broughton Place *Willie Musson*
3 b f Compton Place—Classic Millennium (Midyan (USA))
7920[6]

Broughton Sands *Willie Musson*
3 b f Nayef(USA) —Pachanga (Inchinor)
7921[4]

Broughtons Bandit *Willie Musson* a43 44
4 b g Kyllachy—Broughton Bounty (Bahamian Bounty)
7859[4]

Broughtons Day *Willie Musson* a71 62
4 b g Mujahid(USA) —Rainy Day Song (Persian Bold)
268[2] (361) 367[7] 2381[4] 3361[7]

Broughtons Fawn *Willie Musson* a45
3 ch f Domedriver(IRE) —Cressida (Polish Precedent (USA))
130[7] 275[6] 368[6] 6358[7] 6872[4]

Broughtons Paradis (IRE) *Willie Musson* a70 79
5 b m Royal Applause—Amankila (IRE) (Revoque (IRE))
354[2] 449[2] 771[3] 862[4] (1063) 1372[2] 1956[3] (2372) 3003[3] 3467[3] (4275) 4962[2] 5761[6] 6922[3] 7272[6] 7556[5] 7761[6] 7903[2]

Broughtons Point *Willie Musson* a60 74
5 b m Falbrav(IRE) —Glowing Reference (Reference Point)
3095[3]

Broughtons Silk *Alistair Whillans* a46 49
6 b m Medicean—Soviet Cry (Soviet Star (USA))
3306[6] 3454[9] 4143[5] 4379[6] 4876[7] 5153[3] 5208[3] 5788[13] 6428[7]

Broughtons Swinger *Willie Musson* a67 74
4 b m Celtic Swing—Pachanga (Inchinor)
2649[13] (3256) (3466) 5015[4] 5568[3] 5893[4] 6790[9] 7363[9] 7603[7]

Brouhaha *Tom Dascombe* a87 87
7 b g Bahhare(USA) —Top Of The Morning (Keen)
326[6] 287[4] 528[2] 647[2] 877[3] 1443[12] 1855[11] 4716[3] 5266[4] 5580[2] (6028) ◆ 6263[5] 6922[8] 7272[2] 7699[6]

Brown Colt (IRE) *Mme I T Oakes-Cottin* a62 62
6 b g Statue Of Liberty(USA) —Olivia Jane (IRE) (Ela-Mana-Mou)
6593a[0]

Brown Eyed Lass *Laura Young* 15
2 br f Striking Ambition—Tullochrome (Foxhound (USA))
4702[5] 4947[7] 5375[10] 6579[8]

Browning Dream (GER) *Frau C Barsig* a83 73
4 b h Whipper(USA) —Birthday Night (USA) (Southern Halo (USA))
5195a[3]

Brown Panther *Tom Dascombe* a75 119
3 b c Shirocco(GER) —Treble Heights (IRE) (Unfuwain (USA))
1485[4] (1811) ◆ (2295) ◆ (3069) ◆ 3672a[5] 5045[2] 5928[2]

Brown Pete (IRE) *Richard Guest* a76 72
3 bb g Aussie Rules(USA) —Banba (IRE) (Docksider (USA))
7605[3] 7761[9] 7840[3] 7890[5]

Broxbourne (IRE) *Mark Johnston* 69
2 b f Refuse To Bend(IRE) —Rafting (IRE) (Darshaan)
(3242) 4508[4] 4943[7]

Brubeck (IRE) *Tom Dascombe* 71
2 b c Red Clubs(IRE) —Cheeky Weeky (Cadeaux Genereux)
4748[4] ◆

Brundon *Henry Candy* 56
2 ch f Refuse To Bend(IRE) —Anna Of Brunswick (Rainbow Quest (USA))
5537[8] 6168[9]

Brunelleschi *Patrick Gilligan* a56 86
8 ch g Bertolini(USA) —Petrovna (IRE) (Petardia)
683[9]

Brunello *Walter Swinburn* a56 44
3 b g Leporello(IRE) —Lydia Maria (Dancing Brave (USA))
2231[12] 3430[11] 4208[10]

Brunoy *J Rossi* a94 56
9 b g Spectrum(IRE) —Timing (FR) (Funambule (USA))
372a[0]

Brunston *Roger Charlton* a85 94
5 gr g High Chaparral(IRE) —Molly Mello (GER) (Big Shuffle (USA))
7803[7]

Brunston Keys *Tony Carroll* 17
3 ch f Hawk Wing(USA) —Molly Mello (GER) (Big Shuffle (USA))
4826[10] 6404[8]

Brunswick Vale (IRE) *Paul Midgley* 30
2 b f Moss Vale(IRE) —Brunswick (Warning)
5486[14] 6045[9] 6232[6]

Brushing *Mark H Tompkins* a97 106
5 ch m Medicean—Seasonal Blossom (IRE) (Fairy King (USA))
2029[5] 5219[6] 5711[6] 6269[5] 6859[8]

Brynfa Boy *Patrick Morris* a79 83
5 b g Namid—Funny Girl (IRE) (Darshaan)
2069[8] 3222[3] 3588[7] 3869[2] 4416[13] 4990[3] 5604[2] 6133[2] 6502[4] 6793[9] 7173[10]

Buaiteoir (FR) *Paul D'Arcy* a89 79
5 b g Mineshaft(USA) —Witching Hour (FR) (Fairy King (USA))
21[2] 48[2] (226) ◆ 348[4] ◆ 703[6] ◆ 908[2] 995[2] 1109[7] 1684[9] 3285[12]

Bubber (IRE) *Ollie Pears* a49 52
4 b m Westerner—Bubble N Squeak (IRE) (Catrail (USA))
4783[10] 5502[5]

Bubble Chic (FR) *G Botti* 121
3 b c Chichicastenango(FR) —Bubble Back (FR) (Grand Lodge (USA))
1923a[2] 2751a[2] 4038a[5] 6185a[4] (6693)

Bubbly Ballerina *Alan Bailey* a76 86
2 ch f Footstepsinthesand—Pain Perdu (IRE) (Waajib)
982[2] 2070[3] (2416) 3033[14] 3808[4] 5270[5] (5922) 6323[4] 7261[3] 7918[6]

Bubbly Bellini (IRE) *Adrian McGuinness* a66 65
4 b g Mull Of Kintyre(USA) —Gwapa (IRE) (Imperial Frontier (USA))
421[3] 432[3]

Bubbly Braveheart (IRE) *Pat Phelan* a67 70
4 b g Cape Cross(IRE) —Infinity (FR) (Bering)
(1308) 1486[7] 2608[2] 3256[3] 3760[9] 5580[6] 6622[6] 6794[10] 7097[13] 7805[3]

Buccaneer Bob (IRE) *G M Lyons* a84 83
3 br g Big Bad Bob(IRE) —Cosmic Speed Queen (USA) (On To Glory (USA))
7549a[8]

Bucked Off (SAF) *C Von Der Recke* a70 94
7 b g Casey Tibbs(IRE) —See Me Fly (SAF) (Caesour (USA))
441a[5] 534a[4] 629a[4]

Buckers Beauty (IRE) *Alan McCabe* a21 57
5 b m Viking Ruler(AUS) —Kingpin Delight (Emarati (USA))
969[11]

Buckie Massa *S Arthur* a79 80
7 ch g Best Of The Bests(IRE) —Up On Points (Royal Academy (USA))
5778a[4]

Buckland (IRE) *Brian Meehan* a80 84
3 b g Oratorio(IRE) —Dollar Bird (IRE) (Kris)
1843[6] 2926[6] 3557[8] 4011[6]

Buckley Boy *K F Clutterbuck* 14
2 b g Araafa(IRE) —Waseyla (IRE) (Sri Pekan (USA))
5011[16]

Buddy Holly *Robert Eddery* a73 84
6 b g Reel Buddy(USA) —Night Symphonie (Cloudings (IRE))
418[8] 1398[2] 1461[7] 2051[15] 3042[11] (3225) 3581[3] 3867[14] 4578[7] 6789[13] 7121[3] 7831[P]

Buddy Miracle *Andrew Balding* a67 72
3 ch f Reel Buddy(USA) —Sukuma (IRE) (Highest Honor (FR))
126[5]

Budley *Bill Turner* a55 67
3 b g Avonbridge—Icecap (Polar Falcon (USA))
2790[7] ◆ 3236[5] 3513[4]

Buena Vista (JPN) *Hiroyoshi Matsuda* a107 122
5 bb m Special Week(JPN) —Biwa Heidi (JPN) (Caerleon (USA))
1002a[8] (7563a) 7873a[7]

Buenos Aires (TUR) *S Karagoz* a90
4 ch h Unaccounted For(USA) —Angelica (TUR) (Spectrum (IRE))
5754a[4]

Buen Rumbero (USA) *Niels Petersen* a80
5 ch g City Zip(USA) —Knoosh (USA) (Storm Bird (CAN))
5981a[9]

Buffum (USA) *Saeed Bin Suroor* a99
3 b c Bernardini(USA) —Storm Beauty (USA) (Storm Cat (USA))
502a[5]

Bugaboo (IRE) *J E Hammond* 101
3 b f Dalakhani(IRE) —Babalu (IRE) (Doyoun)
7090a[9]

Bugie D'Amore *B Grizzetti* 103
2 b f Rail Link—Asmita (Efisio)
(6904a)

Bugler's Dream (USA) *Mahmood Al Zarooni* 72
3 bb g Medaglia D'Oro(USA) —Marquet Rent (USA) (Marquetry (USA))
2648[6]

Bugsy (FR) *Mme J Bidgood* 65
4 b m Numerous(USA) —Anna Deesse (FR) (Anabaa (USA))
6593a[0]

Bulldog Beasley (USA) *Brian Meehan* a58 44
2 b g Van Nistelrooy(USA) —Dixie Eyes Blazing (USA) (Gone West (USA))
6951[14] 7133[10] 7783[5]

Bullet Man (USA) *Paul Webber* a62 85
6 br g Mr Greeley(USA) —Silk Tapestry (USA) (Tank's Prospect (USA))
(1651) 4998[8]

Bullet Train *Sir Henry Cecil* 113
4 b h Sadler's Wells(USA) —Kind (IRE) (Danehill (USA))
1342[7] 6860[8]

Bull Five *Nick Littmoden* a68
4 b g Intikhab(USA) —Digamist Girl (IRE) (Digamist (USA))
1[4] 136[2] 309[2] 7609[4]

Bullring (FR) *Peter Niven* a58
5 ch g Green Tune(USA) —Capework (USA) (El Gran Senor (USA))
11[5] 570[5] 733[12]

Bulwark (IRE) *Ian Williams* a74 69
9 b g Montjeu(IRE) —Bulaxie (Bustino)
4562[6] 5079[15]

Bumbling Bertie *Andrew Balding* a32 45
3 b g Bertolini(USA) —Putuna (Generous (IRE))
1566[5] 2166[9] 2964[11]

Bu Naaji (IRE) *Roger Varian* a72 77
2 b c Kheleyf(USA) —Atamana (IRE) (Lahib (USA))
2584[10] (4205) ◆ (4913) 6102[4] 6599[8]

Bunacurry *Barry Murtagh* 47
6 b g Best Of The Bests(IRE) —Miss Doody (Gorytus (USA))
2045[8] 2347[7] 2984[6] 3658[7] 4673[10] 5651[10]

Bunce (IRE) *Richard Hannon* a86 83
3 b c Good Reward(USA) —Bold Desire (Cadeaux Genereux)
1023[2] 1688[5] 2199[9] 2619[5] 3179[5] 4006[5]

Bunkered Again *Jeremy Gask* a49 38
4 b m Footstepsinthesand—Cragreen (Green Desert (USA))
4970[12] 5810[5] 6591[5] 7260[6] 7834[6]

Buona Sarah (IRE) *Sheena West* a75 66
4 ch m Bertolini(USA) —Midnight Partner (IRE) (Marju (IRE))
381[12] (475) 687[8] 723[7]

Burano (IRE) *Brian Meehan* 89
2 ch c Dalakhani(IRE) —Kalimanta (IRE) (Lake Coniston (IRE))
3401[2] ◆ 4330[4] 5254[5] 5931[2]

Burdlaz (IRE) *Mahmood Al Zarooni* a103 99
6 ch h Indian Ridge—Babalu (IRE) (Doyoun)
153a[7] 328a[3] 498a[6] 677a[6]

Bureaucrat *Kate Walton* a71 65
9 b g Machiavellian(USA) —Lajna (Be My Guest (USA))
1713[5]

Burgundy (FR) *F Head* a77
3 b c Green Tune(USA) —Baleare (FR) (Saumarez)
777a[3]

Burj Alzain (IRE) *Gerard Butler* a107
3 b c Marju(IRE) —Bahareeya (USA) (Riverman (USA))
1234[3]

Burj Hatta (USA) *Saeed Bin Suroor* a77 87
3 bb g Kingmambo(USA) —Vadahilla (FR) (Danehill (USA))
2185[3] 2596[2] ◆ 3218[3] 3980[2] 4514[3] 5598[2]

Burj Nahar *Saeed Bin Suroor* 106
4 b h Shamardal(USA) —Melikah (IRE) (Lammtarra (USA))
(3406) 4354[8] 4788[12] 5853[8] 7297[18]

Burma Gold (IRE) *P Schiergen* 110
4 ch h Java Gold(USA) —Bougainvillea (GER) (Acatenango (GER))
2538a[4]

Burnbrake *Les Hall* a58 52
6 b g Mujahid(USA) —Duena (Grand Lodge (USA))
79[7] 301[4] 553[8] 2820[10] 3599[12] 5643[6] 6622[11]

Burnem Green *Derek Shaw* a42 27
3 b f Librettist(USA) —Lambeth Belle (USA) (Arazi (USA))
760[10] 834[9]

Burnham *Hughie Morrison* 63
2 b c Nayef(USA) —Salim Toto (Mtoto)
6462[8] ◆ 6726[9] 6994[8]

Burnhope *David Nicholls* a63
2 b g Choisir(AUS) —Isengard (USA) (Cobra King (USA))
7066[3] 7240[4]

Burning Stone (USA) *Gay Kelleway* a75 79
4 ch g Giant's Causeway(USA) —True Flare (USA) (Capote (USA))
1795[2] 2419[2] 3361[9] 4066[6] 4310[11] 5015[11] 5414[2] 6133[3] 6472[2] 6793[5] 7589[3] 7716[2] 7823[11]

Burning Thread (IRE) *Tim Etherington* a38 104
4 b g Captain Rio—Desert Rose (Green Desert (USA))
1518[7] 2489[7] (2727) 3155[25] 3644[10] 3874[13] 4776[10] 5927[19]

Burns Night *Geoffrey Harker* a77 80
5 ch g Selkirk(USA) —Night Frolic (Night Shift (USA))
1748[6] (2487) 3319[2] 4477[7] 5314[11] 5728[5] 6830[12] 7236[13]

Burn The Floor (IRE) *J S Bolger* 80
3 b f Indian Haven—Dance Time (IRE) (Sadler's Wells (USA))
924a[9]

Burnt Oak (UAE) *Chris Fairhurst* a60 51
9 b g Timber Country(USA) —Anaam (Caerleon (USA))
1215[6]

Burnwynd Boy *Ian Semple* a55 68
6 b g Tobougg(IRE) —Cadeau Speciale (Cadeaux Genereux)
2464[3] 2633[7] 3359[12] 3657[4] 4145[6] 4379[2] 4782[5] 5309[8] 5725[4] 5788[6] 6494[3] 6847[6]

Burnwynd Spirit (IRE) *Ian Semple* a51 48
2 b g Kodiac—Bluebird Spirit (Bluebird (USA))
3452[8] 3855[7] 4040[5] 5431[4] 6384[11] 6597[12] 6842[6] 7143[9] 7365[3] 7770[3]

Bursting Bubbles (IRE) *Ed Dunlop* a57
2 br f Big Bad Bob(IRE) —Ski For Gold (Shirley Heights)
6818[3] 7177[3] 7673[4]

Burst Of Applause (IRE) *Noel Quinlan* a57
3 b f Royal Applause—Lake Nipigon (Selkirk (USA))
3742[12]

Burst Of Stardust *Bryn Palling* 55
3 ch f Peintre Celebre(USA) —Ymlaen (IRE) (Desert Prince (IRE))
2223[6] 2848[9] 3803[8] 4466[7] 4827[13]

Burwaaz *Ed Dunlop* 110
2 b c Exceed And Excel(AUS) —Nidhaal (IRE) (Observatory (USA))
2181[2] (2563) 3064[4] ◆ 3776[2] 4413[2] 5251[3] 5882[2] 6688[15]

Burza *John Mackie* a63 67
5 ch m Bold Edge—Welcome Star (IRE) (Most Welcome)
2051[10] 2478[6] 2887[9] 3545[2] ◆ 4275[9] 5178[11]

Bu Samra (IRE) *Kevin Ryan* 2
2 b g Lawman(FR) —Distant Drama (USA) (Distant View (USA))
5202[7] 5618[11] 6045[12]

Bushman *David Simcock* a82 115
7 gr g Maria's Mon(USA) —Housa Dancer (FR) (Fabulous Dancer (USA))
331a[5] 586a[12]

Bushy Dell (IRE) *Julia Feilden* a73 91
6 br m King Charlemagne(USA) —Nisibis (In The Wings)
33[6]

Business Bay (USA) *Patrick Clinton* a64 64
4 bb g Salt Lake(USA) —Jeweled Lady (USA) (General Meeting (USA))
2991[13] 3705[6] 4164[9] 4945[8]

Busker (USA) *M bin Shafya* a79 78
3 ch c Street Cry(IRE) —Adonesque (IRE) (Sadler's Wells (USA))
411a[8]

Bussa *David Evans* a67 81
3 b g Iceman—Maid To Dance (Pyramus (USA))
988[6] 1214[6] 1697[6] 1949[3] (2226) 2357[2] 3340[8] 3629[3] 4022[3] 7734[8]

Bussell Along (IRE) *Pam Ford* a58 58
5 b m Mujadil(USA) —Waaedah (USA) (Halling (USA))
930[5] 1750[9] 2246[2] 2569[9] 2905[4] 3637[8] 4270[12] 4952[11] 5612[9]

Buster Brown (IRE) *James Given* 73
2 ch c Singspiel(IRE) —Gold Dodger (USA) (Slew O'Gold (USA))
3229[3] ◆ 6165[4] 6532[3] 6986[8]

Busy Bimbo (IRE) *Alan Berry* 60
2 b f Red Clubs(IRE) —Unfortunate (Komaite (USA))
2113[9] 2886[4] 3200[4] 4106[5] 4557[5] 5479[13] 6169[13] 6384[2] ◆ 6673[8] 7103[3]

But Beautiful (IRE) *Robert Mills* a71 74
4 ch m Pivotal—Sweet Firebird (IRE) (Sadler's Wells (USA))
(128) ◆ 303[2] (626) 889[4] 1569[3] 2051[4] 3172[4] 4185[5]

Bute Hall *Mark Johnston* a54
2 ch c Halling(USA) —Les Hurlants (IRE) (Barathea (IRE))
7398[6]

Bute Street *Ron Hodges* a65 64
6 b g Superior Premium—Hard To Follow (Dilum (USA))
172[8] 286[4] 407[2] 622[8] 6405[11] 7195[12]

Buthelezi (USA) *John Gosden* 105
3 bb g Dynaformer(USA) —Ntombi (USA) (Quiet American (USA))
(1723) 2507[2] 2707[3] 3775[3] 5045[4] 5928[7] 6498[6]

Butler (IRE) *Luca Cumani* a70 92
4 ch g Noverre(USA) —True Fantasy (USA) (Seeking The Gold (USA))
1603[12] (2124) 2649[4] 3544[2] 4360[2] 5435[8] 6528[3]

Buttonhole *Sir Michael Stoute* 64
3 b f Montjeu(IRE) —Red Camellia (Polar Falcon (USA))
1549[11]

Button Moon (IRE) *Ian Wood* a67 90
3 ch f Compton Place—Portelet (Night Shift (USA))
1317[4] (1591) 2054[7] 2520a[3] 2928[6] 4101[8] 4573[9] 5264[4] 5703[7] 6174[3] 6531[7]

Buxfizz (USA) *Robert Mills* a87 79
3 b g Elusive Quality(USA) —Argentina (USA) (Storm Cat (USA))
1550[8] 2230[5] 2607[3] 3231[8] 5547[9] 7204[10] 7601[3] 7661[10]

Buxted (IRE) *Robert Mills* a108 108
5 b g Dynaformer(USA) —Bintalreef (USA) (Diesis)
2072[5] 2438[6]

Buxton *Roger Ingram* a77 79
7 b g Auction House(USA) —Dam Certain (IRE) (Damister (USA))
96[7] 249[6] 367[2] 763[4] 1232[9] (1356) 1634[2] 1898[7] 2169[6] 3674[8] 4210[8] 4865[7] 5669[5] 6814[13] 7484[9] 7663[10] 7810[5] 7895[8]

Buy Back Bob (IRE) *A J Martin* a78 94
4 b g Big Bad Bob(IRE) —Abeyr (Unfuwain (USA))
6690[12]

Buzkashi (IRE) *Roger Varian* 73
2 b f Nayef(USA) —Min Alhawa (USA) (Riverman (USA))
4552[3] ◆ 5806[5] 6526[13]

Buzz Bird *David Barron* a72 41
4 b m Danbird(AUS) —Asharoute (USA) (Holy Bull (USA))
388 291[5] 572[4] 747[3] 895[9] 1468[3] 1814[8] 6430[12]

Buzz Law (IRE) *Mrs K Burke* a75 82
3 b g Fasliyev(USA) —Buzz Two (IRE) (Case Law) (1191) (1437) 1843[7] 3864[7] 4290[3] 4750[2] 5081[6] 6674[16] 7397[6]

Buzzword *Mahmood Al Zarooni* 113
4 b h Pivotal—Bustling (Danehill (USA))
413a[8]

Bygones For Coins (IRE) *Alan Berry* 50
3 ch f Danroad(AUS) —Reservation (IRE) (Common Grounds)
182[7] 1459[10] 2281[6] 2498[7] 2697[3] 2805[5] 3143[6] 3192[8] 3731[7] 3860[10] 4172[6] 5010[4] 5063[5] 5793[11] 6427[5] 6602[14]

By Implication *Patrick Morris* a51
3 br g Cacique(IRE) —Insinuate (USA) (Mr Prospector (USA))
4363[10] 4863[8] 6494[12]

By Invitation (USA) *Ralph Beckett* a69 62
2 b f Van Nistelrooy(USA) —Sahara Star (Green Desert (USA))
3736[3] ◆ 4430[4] 6612[4] 7838[2]

Byrama *Nigel Tinkler* 77
2 b f Byron—Aymara (Darshaan)
3932[3] ◆ (4358)

Byrd In Hand (IRE) *John Bridger* a65 70
4 b g Fasliyev(USA) —Military Tune (IRE) (Nashwan (USA))
1582[3] 2385[2] (2560) 2923[6] 3814[DSQ] 4154[9] 4444[5] 5040[8] 5509[2] 5653[5] 6816[5]

Byron Bay *Robert Johnson* a49 73
9 b g My Best Valentine—Candarela (Damister (USA))
507[11] 670[6] 796[3]

Byron Bear (IRE) *Paul Midgley* 58
3 b g Byron—Paulas Pride (Pivotal)
1074[5] 1495[3] ◆ 1945[12] 2465[2] 3142[4] (3706) 4128[4] 4676[3] 6049[6]

Byron Blue (IRE) *Jamie Osborne* 69
2 br c Dylan Thomas(IRE) —High Society (IRE) (Key Of Luck (USA))
4995[10] 5727[3] 6230[5] 6807[9]

Byronic Hero *Jedd O'Keeffe* 81
2 b g Byron—Starbeck (IRE) (Spectrum (IRE))
3273[4] 4073[2] 5216[17] 6673[5] (6912)

Byrons Beau (IRE) *Brett Johnson* a12
3 ch c Byron—Day Is Dawning (IRE) (Green Forest (USA))
313[7] 726[5]

Byrony (IRE) *Richard Hannon* a90 91
3 ch f Byron—Saphire (College Chapel)
1599[7] 2705[4] 2847[3] 3873[3] 4093[10] 5702[11] 6062[12] (6728) 6949[3] 7523[8]

Byton *Henry Candy* 63
2 b f Byron—Arculinge (Paris House)
5323[3]

Byword *A Fabre* 125
5 ch h Peintre Celebre(USA) —Binche (USA) (Woodman (USA))
1740a[2] 2343a[5] (2980a) (6558a) ◆ 7307a[8] 7732a[6]

Cabal *Andrew Crook* a51 83
4 br m Kyllachy—Secret Flame (Machiavellian (USA))
2674[12] 2906[6] 3581[8] 4612[12] 6049[7] 6871[8] 7462[4] 7537[6] 7714[7]

Cabimas *P Schiergen* 102
4 b g King's Best(USA) —Casanga (IRE) (Rainbow Quest (USA))
2538a[5]

Cabriac (FR) *G Nicot* a66 65
3 b c Miesque's Son(USA) —Calyx (FR) (Irish River (FR))
777a[0]

Cabuchon (GER) *Barney Curley* a53
4 b h Fantastic Light(USA) —Catella (GER) (Generous (IRE))
11[10] 301[11]

Cactus King *Louise Best* a61 47
8 b g Green Desert(USA) —Apache Star (Arazi (USA))
2386[9] 2816[13]

Cadeau For Maggi *H-A Pantall* a90 106
6 ch h Cadeaux Genereux—Maggi For Margaret (Shavian)
2754a[10] 7534a[0]

Cadeaux Fax *Gordon Elliott* a72 63
6 ch g Largesse—Facsimile (Superlative)
3905[3]

Cadeaux Pearl *Scott Dixon* a61 89
3 b g Acclamation—Anneliina (Cadeaux Genereux)
1688[6] 2067[3] 2505[6] 2770[3] 2890[14] (3975) 4498[9] 5033[20] 5852[20] 6350[7] 6703[13] 7356[12] 7602[7] (7917)

Cades Reef (IRE) *Andrew Balding* 72
2 gr g Dalakhani(IRE) —Just Special (Cadeaux Genereux)
4330[11] 5269[9] 5891[6] ◆

Cadgers Brig *Keith Dalgleish* a74 59
3 ch g Halling(USA) —Burghmuir (IRE) (Cadeaux Genereux)
191[6] 378[4] 634[5] 5152[3] 5489[3] 5790[14] 6701[3] 6870[13] (7608) 7720[3]

Cadmium Loch *Reg Hollinshead* a69 66
3 b g Needwood Blade—Vermilion Creek (Makbul)
1472[8] (1952) 2243[6] (2792) 3337[7] 3783[6] 4819[4] 5274[4] 5603[2] 5864[2] 6179[10] 6479[7]

Cadologis (FR) *J-M Capitte* a66
3 b g Numerous(USA) —Marie Eugenie (FR) (Zieten (USA))
660a[3]

Cadore (IRE) *Peter Chapple-Hyam* 78
3 b g Hurricane Run(IRE) —Mansiya (Vettori (IRE))
1593[4] 2052[5] 3340[4] 4576[2] 5925[7] 6918[12]

Caelis *Ralph Beckett* a80 83
3 b f Avonbridge—Shona (USA) (Lyphard (USA))
(663) 887[4] 1400[4] 1766[3] 2313[2] 2821[5] (3387) 3818[2] (4458) 5255[4] 5862[3] 7031[3]

Caesarion (GER) *H J Groschel* 86
3 b c Areion(GER) —Caesarina (Hernando (FR))
2520a[7]

Cafe Express (IRE) *Linda Perratt* 71
2 ch f Bertolini(USA) —Cafe Creme (IRE) (Catrail (USA))
(4377) 6146[8]

Cahala Dancer (IRE) *Roger Teal* a65 66
3 ch f Elnadim(USA) —Ranma (In The Wings)
3747[4] ◆ 4320[2] 4849[3] 5496[6] 5894[12] 6468[6]

Cairanne *Tom Keddy* a37 39
3 b f High Chaparral(IRE) —Celestial Choir (Celestial Storm (USA))
6591[6] 7084[10] 7354[7] 7610[12] 7750[3]

Cairncross (IRE) *Mark Johnston* 76
3 b f Cape Cross(IRE) —Sassenach (IRE) (Night Shift (USA))
4363[4] 5082[2] 5327[3] 5856[6] 6383[8] 6888[10] 7236[10]

Cai Shen (IRE) *Richard Hannon* 109
3 ch c Iffraaj—Collada (IRE) (Desert Prince (IRE)) (1365) ◆ 1689[2] 2507[3] 3067[2] 3777[3] 4494[7] 5275[11] (5829)

Caitania (IRE) *H-W Hiller* 91
2 gr f Aussie Rules(USA) —Celestia (Anabaa (USA))
5610a[4] 6737a[5]

Caitlin *Andrew Balding* 71
2 b f Dylan Thomas(IRE) —Kassiopeia (IRE) (Galileo (IRE))
7025[3]

Calabaza *Michael Attwater* a32 14
9 ch g Zaha(CAN) —Mo Stopher (Sharpo)
683[8] 1043[10] 2385[9]

Calaf *Richard Fahey* a53 87
3 b g Dubai Destination(USA) —Tarandot (IRE) (Singspiel (IRE))
1203[5] 1480[3] 1812[4] 2215[7] 2957[2] 3340[2] (3809) ◆ 4467[9] 5880[2] 6429[4]

Calahorra (FR) *C Baillet* 98
2 ch f Soave(GER) —Kendorya (FR) (Kendor (FR)) (5194a) 6042a[3] 6808a[6] 7220a[7]

Cala Santanyi *Gerard Butler* a76 82
3 b f Green Desert(USA) —Fantastic Santanyi (Fantastic Light (USA))
1605[2] 1853[3] 2875[2] 3405[10] 3873[8]

Calatagan (IRE) *Malcolm Jefferson* a35 74
12 ch g Danzig Connection(USA) —Calachuchi (Martinmas)
8[10]

[illegible] (FR) *B Dutruel* a65 100
7 b g Kendor(FR) —Pennegale (IRE) (Pennekamp (USA))
815a[2] 1122a[5]

Calculated Risk *Willie Musson* a61
2 ch g Motivator—Glen Rosie (IRE) (Mujtahid (USA))
5411[8] 6214[7] 6308[6] 6699[10]

Calculating (IRE) *Mark Usher* a83 69
7 b g Machiavellian(USA) —Zaheemah (USA) (El Prado (IRE))
68[5] 209[8] 314[4] 457[3] 549[2] 671[2] 872[2] 1030[4] 1291[2] (1817) 3095[12] 6666[11] 7070[5] 7244[2] 7506[3] 7674[6] 7753[8] 7914[6]

Caldercruix (USA) *James Evans* a82 96
4 ch g Rahy(USA) —Al Theraab (USA) (Roberto (USA))
2002[18] 3542[8] 5383[4] 6226[9] 6544[4] 6895[11] 7299[3] 7532[3] 7637[3] (7819) 7926[3]

Caldermud (IRE) *Olivia Maylam* a74 78
4 ch g Chineur(FR) —Dalal (Cadeaux Genereux)
867[10] 1196[10] 1581[7] 1995[10] 2412[2] 3512[13] 4187[3] 4651[8] 5040[4] 5789[13] 6071[2] (6746) 6938[8]

Caleb's Posse (USA) *Donnie K Von Hemel* a127
3 b c Posse(USA) —Abbey's Missy (USA) (Slewacide (USA))
(7304a)

Caledonia Lady *Jo Hughes* 105
2 b f Firebreak—Granuaile O'Malley (IRE) (Mark Of Esteem (IRE))
2580[5] 3033[3] ◆ 3821[8] 4883[3] 5217[4] 5882[3] (6114) 6518[3]

Caledonian Lad *Hughie Morrison* 50
2 ch g Pastoral Pursuits—Jasmick (IRE) (Definite Article)
4968[10]

Caledonian Spring (IRE) *Paul D'Arcy* 106
2 b c Amadeus Wolf—Mathuna (IRE) (Tagula (IRE))
1886[4] 2181[3] 3014[13] (4264) 5181[4] (5709)

Caledonia Prince *Jo Hughes* a57 52
3 b g Needwood Blade—Granuaile O'Malley (IRE) (Mark Of Esteem (IRE))
1969[8] 2583[5] 3690[12] (5602) 6192[7] 6411[5] 6816[8]

Caledonia Princess *Jo Hughes* a79 82
5 b m Kyllachy—Granuaile O'Malley (IRE) (Mark Of Esteem (IRE))
3687[4] 3996[7] 4387[6] 4988[4] 5173[2] 5467[10] 6283[7] 6537[8] (7173)

Calendar King *Mick Channon* a59 1
2 b g Three Valleys(USA) —Fanny's Fancy (Groom Dancer (USA))
2380[6] 2641[5] 5475[10]

Calico Bay (IRE) *Alan McCabe* a23 38
3 b g Whipper(USA) —Caribbean Escape (Pivotal)
6608[6] 6767[9] 7235[11]

California Dreams (SWI) *U Suter* a59 97
4 b m Footstepsinthesand—Copacabana (IRE) (Entrepreneur)
840a[0]

California English (IRE) *Marco Botti* a78 33
2 b g Oasis Dream—Muwali (USA) (Kingmambo (USA))
4762[13] 7493[2] (7751)

California Flag (USA) *Brian Koriner* a93 116
7 rg g Avenue Of Flags(USA) —Ultrafleet (USA) (Afleet (CAN))
7303a[12]

California Memory (USA) *A S Cruz* 122
5 gr g Highest Honor(FR) —Kalpita (USA) (Spinning World (USA))
1742a[2] 2340a[8] (7732a)

Calle Aneto (IRE) *Michael John Phillips* a43 73
5 ch g Lahib(USA) —Red Fanfare (First Trump)
6511a[12]

Callie's Angel *Bryn Palling* a44 64
3 b g Piccolo—Oriel Girl (Beveled (USA))
2550[10] 5538[10] 6437[7]

Calling Elvis (BRZ) *A De Royer-Dupre* a103 108
4 ch c Romarin(BRZ) —Calunga (USA) (Sea Of Secrets (USA))
411a[13] 680a[7] 823a[11]

Callisto Light *George Prodromou* a53 44
4 ch m Medicean—Luminda (IRE) (Danehill (USA))
5999[7] 7069[6]

Callisto Moon *Jo Hughes* a69 87
7 b g Mujahid(USA) —Nursling (IRE) (Kahyasi)
3725[3] 4097[12] 4463[4] 5273[6]

Call Of Duty (IRE) *Dianne Sayer* a52 75
6 br g Storming Home—Blushing Barada (USA) (Blushing Groom (FR))
1520[8] 1909[2] 2046[8] 2671[8] 4109[8] 4604[13] 5106[15] 5594[6] 6236[9] 6833[2] 7112[4]

Call The Law (IRE) *Pam Sly* a39 51
5 b m Acclamation—Savvy Shopper (USA) (Stravinsky (USA))
1818[6] 1989[10] 2247[7]

Call To Reason (IRE) *Jeremy Noseda* a85 92
4 ch m Pivotal—Venturi (Danehill Dancer (IRE))
1760[8] 6335[2] ◆ 7127[8] 7486[10]

Calm Bay (IRE) *H Rogers* a93 95
5 b g Medecis—Queen Sigi (IRE) (Fairy King (USA))
1420a[6] 2967a[4] 3441a[6] 6388a[24] 7012a[9]

Calormen *Alan Juckes* a46 59
3 b g Imperial Dancer—Queen Of Narnia (Hunting Lion (IRE))
2652[7]

Calrissian (GER) *Fredrik Reuterskiold* a96 109
7 ch g Efisio—Centaine (Royal Academy (USA))
3531a[2] 6594a[4]

Calusa Bay (IRE) *Pat Phelan* 29
2 b f Bertolini(USA) —Think (FR) (Marchand De Sable (USA))
2153[13] 2787[12] 3408[7]

Calvados Blues (FR) *Mahmood Al Zarooni* a109 117
5 ch h Lando(GER) —Persian Belle (Machiavellian (USA))
240[10] 413a[2] (603a) 757a[2] 1001a[3] 3153[6]

[illegible] (FR) *[illegible]* a83 79
4 b g Sabiango(GER) —La Bastoche (IRE) (Kaldoun (FR))
831a[0]

Calypso Cay *Mark Johnston* a64
3 b g Tiger Hill(IRE) —Tessa Reef (IRE) (Mark Of Esteem (IRE))
(7662) 7839[8]

Calypso Magic (IRE) *Linda Jewell* a86 92
3 gr g Aussie Rules(USA) —Calypso Dancer (FR) (Celtic Swing)
(1076) 1516[2] 3159[5] 4015[6] 7719[7]

Calzaghe (IRE) *Martin Hill* a70 75
7 ch g Galileo(IRE) —Novelette (Darshaan)
7850[11]

Camache Queen (IRE) *Denis Coakley* a73 86
3 b f Camacho—Alinda (IRE) (Revoque (IRE))
1141[3] 2102[8] 2986[3] 3782[6] 5811[3] (6467) 7262[8]

Camarade (FR) *J-C Rouget* 83
2 b c Footstepsinthesand—Celebre Fragance (FR) (Peintre Celebre (USA))
(4624a)

Camberley Two *Roger Charlton* 90
3 bg g Invincible Spirit(IRE) —Diamond Line (FR) (Linamix (FR))
1724[8] 2792[3] (3253) ◆ (3431) ◆ (3481) (4394) (4676) (4750) 6989[6]

Cambina (IRE) *Jeff Bonde* 113
3 ch f Hawk Wing(USA) —Await (IRE) (Peintre Celebre (USA))
7284a[8]

Camborne *John Gosden* a75
3 b g Doyen(IRE) —Dumnoni (Titus Livius (FR))
(7327)

Cambridge Duchess *Stuart Williams* a55
2 br f Singspiel(IRE) —Roseum (Lahib (USA))
6441[6]

Camelia Rose (FR) *J-C Rouget* 108
3 b f Oratorio(IRE) —Solaz (IRE) (Galileo (IRE))
1709a[4] 2342a[5] 4570a[5]

Camelot *A P O'Brien* 119
2 b c Montjeu(IRE) —Tarfah (USA) (Kingmambo (USA))
(7020)

Camera Shy (IRE) *Kevin Morgan* a61 23
7 ch g Pivotal—Shy Danceuse (FR) (Groom Dancer (USA))
728[3] 954[5] (1310) (2608) 3054[7] 4396[11] 7441[6]

Cameron Highland (IRE) *Roger Varian* 67
2 b c Galileo(IRE) —Landmark (USA) (Arch (USA))
7109[3]

Camerooney *Brian Ellison* a64 97
8 b g Sugarfoot—Enkindle (Relkino)
1092[20] 1410[8] 1828[3] 2105[3] 2495[10] 3315[12] 3397[9] 4601[2] 5888[15] 6173[10] 6302[9]

Camina *Michael Smith*
3 b f Bertolini(USA) —Efizia (Efisio)
5792[11] 6096[12] 7214[9]

Caminar (FR) *S Wattel* a86 91
3 gr g Cardoun(FR) —Bocarosa (IRE) (Linamix (FR))
(5463a)

Campanillas (IRE) *C Laffon-Parias* 110
3 b f Montjeu(IRE) —West Brooklyn (USA) (Gone West (USA))
2750a[3] 3447a[2] 5027a[8]

Campanologist (USA) *Saeed Bin Suroor* a102 117
6 b h Kingmambo(USA) —Ring Of Music (Sadler's Wells (USA))
1685[4] 2332a[2] 3153[5] 3775[5] 4492[10] 5776a[2] (6396a) (6907a) 7729a[5]

Campanology *Richard Hannon* 95
2 b c Royal Applause—Savannah Belle (Green Desert (USA))
2672[2] ◆ 3012[13] 3583[2] 4053[3] 5184[6] 5849[7] (6525)

Campas Bay (IRE) *M Halford* a39
3 b c Oratorio(IRE) —Love Of The Game (IRE) (Croco Rouge (IRE))
1704a[10] (Dead)

Camporosso *Mark Johnston* 78
3 b c Cape Cross(IRE) —Marine City (JPN) (Carnegie (IRE))
1203[11] 1407[13] 1542[2] 1840[P] (Dead)

Camps Bay (USA) *Conor Dore* a85 85
7 b g Cozzene(USA) —Seewillo (USA) (Pleasant Colony (USA))
24[2] 127[2] 216[2] 374[2] 384[2] 514[3] 570[3] 772[5] 805[3] 858[4] 1046[3] 1977[7] 2159[5] 2526[6] 2721[3] 3047[12] 4177[9] 4649[12]

Camp Victory (USA) *Mike Mitchell* a120 112
4 bb g Forest Camp(USA) —Victory Trick (CAN) (Clever Trick (USA))
7303a[7]

Camrock Star (IRE) *David Evans* a54 62
2 b f Rock Of Gibraltar(IRE) —Night Cam (IRE) (Night Shift (USA))
3547[9] 4245[6] 5047[9] 5690[6] 6487[9] (6763) 7222[5] 7414[5] 7763[9]

Canadian Danehill (IRE) *Robert Cowell* a63 64
9 b g Indian Danehill(IRE) —San Jovita (CAN) (St Jovite (USA))
1469[6] 1523[7] 2126[11] 2920[13] 3556[7] 6175[2] 6501[3] 6765[4] 6943[8] 7366[10] 7691[6] 7785[3]

Canalside *P Monfort* a67 72
5 ch m Nayef(USA) —Bayswater (Caerleon (USA))
832a[8]

Canashito *B W Hills* 53
3 b f Oasis Dream—Far Shores (USA) (Distant View (USA))
1155[7] 1607[12] 2311[3]

Canaveral *Brian Meehan* 94
3 bb g Cape Cross(IRE) —Tarneem (USA) (Zilzal (USA))
1445[5] (2146) (2664)

Can Can Dancer *Charles Smith* a33 51
6 b m Fantastic Light(USA) —Bitwa (USA) (Conquistador Cielo (USA))
2402[5] 2828[5] 3496[7] 4177[5] 4732[3] 5209[8] 5566[10] 7087[12]

Candler (IRE) *Y De Nicolay*
3 b c Oratorio(IRE) —Open Way (IRE) (Giant's Causeway (USA))
902a[0]

Can Do Les (IRE) *Keith Dalgleish* a56 57
2 b g Modigliani(USA) —Yulara (IRE) (Night Shift (USA))
2532a[6] 7196[4] 7423[3] 7568[3] 7684[6] 7763[4]

Candrea (USA) *Bob Baffert* a109
2 b f Trippi(USA) —Burn Brightly (USA) (American Chance (USA))
7283a[11]

Candycakes (IRE) *Michael Bell* 74
2 b f Cape Cross(IRE) —Charita (IRE) (Lycius (USA))
4804[4] 5444[5]

Cane Cat (IRE) *Tony Carroll* a65 60
4 bb m One Cool Cat(USA) —Seven Wonders (USA) (Rahy (USA))
70[6] 204[4] 386[6] 552[11] 749[8] (950) (2268) 2600[2] (2851) 3228[7] 4490[5] (4869) 5248[5] 5356[4] 6357[6] 7203[3]

Canford Cliffs (IRE) *Richard Hannon* 130
4 b h Tagula(IRE) —Mrs Marsh (Marju (IRE)) (2101) (3009) 4425[2]

Canna (IRE) *B W Hills* 82
3 b g High Chaparral(IRE) —Brave Madam (IRE) (Invincible Spirit (IRE))
1096[2] 1548[8] 1689[7] 3781[2]

Canning Vale *Julia Feilden* a56
2 ch f Araafa(IRE) —Elegant Beauty (Olden Times)
4646[4] 5299[14] 7909[3]

Cannon Bolt (IRE) *Robin Bastiman* a20 54
3 b g Chineur(FR) —Prime Time Girl (Primo Dominie)
1812[9] 2782[13] 3455[2] 3724[12] 4505[2] 4929[6] 5725[7] 6982[10]

Cantal *Sir Michael Stoute* a77 70
2 ch f Pivotal—Canda (USA) (Storm Cat (USA))
6168[7] (7124)

Cant Catch Cathy (IRE) *P Costes* a74 78
3 b f Catcher In The Rye(IRE) —Note To Cathy (USA) (Notebook (USA))
(288a)

Cantor *Giles Bravery* a55 50
3 b g Iceman—Choir Mistress (Chief Singer)
3183[9] 4065[7] 5321[4] 5832[5]

Cant Sell (IRE) *David Evans* 22
3 b g Trade Fair—Ejder (IRE) (Indian Ridge)
6589[8] 6750[6] 6804[14]

Capablanca (AUS) *D Baertschiger* a104 105
10 br g Scenic—Ahava (AUS) (Southern Appeal (USA))
2339a[8]

Capable Guest (IRE) *George Moore* a71 71
9 bb g Cape Cross(IRE) —Alexander Confranc (IRE) (Magical Wonder (USA))
118[10] (1491) 1798[7] 2496[5] 2666[3] 3507[3] 4562[8]

Capacity (IRE) *T G McCourt* a59 67
4 b g Cape Cross(IRE) —Carry On Katie (USA) (Fasliyev (USA))
283[10] 7741[10]

Capaill Liath (IRE) *Michael Bell* 94
3 gr g Iffraaj—Bethesda (Distant Relative)
3067[16] 3825[5] (4335) 5450[4] 6302[20]

Cape Blanco (IRE) *A P O'Brien* a118 124
4 ch h Galileo(IRE) —Laurel Delight (Presidium)
1002a[4] 1708a[4] 3009[6] (3888a) (5074a) (6548a)

Cape Classic (IRE) *William Haggas* a71 87
3 b c Cape Cross(IRE) —Politesse (USA) (Barathea (IRE))
1540[2] ◆ 3178[3] (4340) (4643) ◆ 6174[4] 6495[2]

Cape Crossing *Andrew Balding* 48
2 br f Cape Cross(IRE) —Dame Hester (IRE) (Diktat)
7165[11]

Cape Dollar (IRE) *Sir Michael Stoute* 106
3 b f Cape Cross(IRE) —Green Dollar (IRE) (Kingmambo (USA))
1404[7] 1719[12] 3034[4] 3648[3] 5366a[11]

Cape Joy (IRE) *Richard Hannon* a14
2 b f Cape Cross(IRE) —Perils Of Joy (IRE) (Rainbow Quest (USA))
7330[10]

Cape Kimberley *Tony Newcombe* a77 71
4 b g Arakan(USA) —Etoile Volant (USA) (Silver Hawk (USA))
641[6] 1171[7] (1730) 2376[3] 2870[11] 4025[11] 5143[5] (5539) 6434[5]

Cape Melody *George Baker* a78 78
5 b m Piccolo—Cape Charlotte (Mon Tresor)
(243) 792[2] 865[3] 1024[3] 1147[6] 4479[8] 5100[7] 5676[4] 6228[9]

Cape Moss (IRE) *Tom Dascombe* 74
2 b g Moss Vale(IRE) —Cape Sydney (IRE) (Cape Cross (IRE))
2504[6] 2902[2] 3583[5]

Cape Of Dance (IRE) *Mark Johnston* 69
3 b f Cape Cross(IRE) —Nesaah's Princess (Sinndar (IRE))
1392[10] 2808[5] 3303[3] 3681[4]

Cape Of Good Grace (IRE) *John M Oxx* 94
3 b f Cape Cross(IRE) —Daganya (IRE) (Danehill Dancer (IRE))
6736a[8]

Cape Of Storms *Roy Brotherton* a71 24
8 b g Cape Cross(IRE) —Lloc (Absalom)
13[8] 402[5] (641) 928[6] 1289[3] (1463) 7502[10] 7646[5] 7744[11]

Cape Princess *Michael Bell* a74 66
3 b f Cape Cross(IRE) —Karla June (Unfuwain (USA))
1364[5] 1692[5] 6054[6] 6507[6] 6894[6]

Cape Rainbow *Mark Usher* 76
2 b c Cape Cross(IRE) —Mambo Halo (USA) (Southern Halo (USA))
5891[3] 6464[5] 6994[10]

Cape Rambler *Henry Candy* a48 82
3 ch g Pastoral Pursuits—Cape Charlotte (Mon Tresor)
(4320) 5322[10] 6239[4] 6728[9]

Capercaillie (USA) *Clive Cox* a93 97
4 ch m Elusive Quality(USA) —Silent Eskimo (USA) (Eskimo (USA))
1067[2] ◆ 1366[7] 1902[4] 2298[5] 2861a[5] 3852[3] 5080[8] 5879[4]

Cape Rising (IRE) *Alan Swinbank* 79
4 b m Cape Cross(IRE) —Woodrising (Nomination)
2458[8] 4014[3] ◆ (4611)

Cape Royal *Milton Bradley* a68 87
11 b g Prince Sabo—Indigo (Primo Dominie)
80[9] 401[3] 443[5] 1140[9] 1476[3] 2118[7] 2585[6] 2645[8] 3078[7] 3847[9] 4615[8] 4895[9] 5326[10] 5846[2] 5997[6] 6436[3] 6580[5] (6802) 7106[7] 7567[9]

Cape Safari (IRE) *James Tate* a65 62
2 b f Cape Cross(IRE) —Finnmark (Halling (USA))
6934[8] 7599[3]

Cape Samba *Peter Chapple-Hyam* 51
2 b c Cape Cross(IRE) —Dancing Feather (Suave Dancer (USA))
4996[9]

Cape Savannah *David Simcock* a59
2 b c Cape Cross(IRE) —Lady High Havens (IRE) (Bluebird (USA))
7751[5]

Cape To Rio (IRE) *Richard Hannon* 102
3 b c Captain Rio—Misaayef (USA) (Swain (IRE))
1322[3] 2054[2] 2934[18] 4092[7] 4534[26] 6027[4]

Cape Vale (IRE) *David Nicholls* a91 93
6 b g Cape Cross(IRE) —Wolf Cleugh (IRE) (Last Tycoon)
2[5] 376[4] (1200) 1675[6] 2434[2] 2717[6] 3357[7]

Cape Velvet (IRE) *Mme J Bidgood* a80 81
7 b m Cape Cross(IRE) —Material Lady (IRE) (Barathea (IRE))
93a[7] 3568a[0]

Capitaine Courage (IRE) *F Doumen* a100 100
6 ch g Bering—Four Green (FR) (Green Tune (USA))
778a[4]

Capital Attraction (USA) *Sir Henry Cecil* a106 93
4 ch g Speightstown(USA) —Cecilia's Crown (USA) (Chief's Crown (USA))
1406[P] 2031[13] 3032[10] 3877[16] 4428[10]

Capone (IRE) *David Nicholls* a101 91
6 b g Daggers Drawn(USA) —Order Of The Day (USA) (Dayjur (USA))
4188[2] (4909) ◆ 5481[7] 5758[9] ◆ 6145[15] 6347[6] 6987[9] 7433[3] (7578)

Cappielow Park *William Jarvis* a73 71
2 b c Exceed And Excel(AUS) —Barakat (Bustino)
6935[3] 7367[2]

Capponi (IRE) *Mahmood Al Zarooni* a100 110
4 ch h Medicean—Nawaiet (USA) (Zilzal (USA))
827a[7]

Caprio (IRE) *Jim Boyle* a89 83
6 ch g Captain Rio—Disarm (IRE) (Bahamian Bounty)
(45) 1178[5] 1610[11] 2169[7]

Capriska *Willie Musson* a48
2 b f Bahri(USA) —Guignol (IRE) (Anita's Prince)
6308[7] 6818[6] 7038[6]

Captain Baldwin *David Evans* a43 26
2 b g Dubai Destination(USA) —Tripti (IRE) (Sesaro (USA))
1827[6] 5625[8] 5861[9] 6786[7]

Captain Bellamy (USA) *Hughie Morrison* a71 44
3 ch g Bellamy Road(USA) —Thesky'sthelimit (USA) (Northern Prospect (USA))
1312[7] 1502[2] (2239) 2842[11] (4181) 5145[4]

Captain Bertie (IRE) *Charles Hills* 96
3 ch g Captain Rio—Sadika (IRE) (Bahhare (USA))
1547[2] 1820[3] 3067[22] 3877[7] ◆ 5936[5] ◆ 6290[13] 7295[13]

Captain Bluebird (IRE) *Des Donovan* a61 61
4 gr g Captain Rio—Dolly Blue (IRE) (Pennekamp (USA))
14[11]

Captain Brown *Sir Mark Prescott Bt* 84
3 b g Lomitas—Nicola Bella (IRE) (Sadler's Wells (USA))
(2461) 2726[6] 4050[4]

Captain Bufalo (IRE) *J-M Capitte* a38
8 b g Spinning World(USA) —Double Opus (IRE) (Petorius)
481a[0]

Captain Cardington (IRE) *Mick Channon* a66 73
2 b g Strategic Prince—Alkaffeyeh (IRE) (Sadler's Wells (USA))
2882[10] (3534) 4496[7] 5233[9] 5931[10] 7259[2] 7414[4] 7752[7]

Captain Carey *Malcolm Saunders* a99 100
5 b g Fraam—Brigadiers Bird (IRE) (Mujadil (USA))
1366[3] 1680[3] 2890[4] 3410[6] (4135a)

Captain Cat (IRE) *Roger Charlton* 59
2 bb g Dylan Thomas(IRE) —Mother Of Pearl (IRE) (Sadler's Wells (USA))
6994[5]

Captain Chop (FR) *D Guillemin* a102 106
3 b c Indian Rocket—Hatane Chope (FR) (Sin Kiang (FR))
883a[2] 1206a[5] 7534a[10]

Captain Cool (IRE) *Richard Hannon* a62 66
4 ch g Captain Rio—Aiaie (Zafonic (USA))
(524) (631) 728[5]

Captain Dimitrios *David Evans* a73 74
3 b g Dubai Destination(USA) —Tripti (IRE) (Sesaro (USA))
140[4] 208[3] 364[2] 423[3] 476[2] 578[6] 620[3] 724[3] 787[2] 847[3] 929[3] 1056[4] 4199[9] 4431[6] 4885[3] 6223[6] 6305[6] 6343[9]

Captain Dunne (IRE) *Tim Easterby* a107 111
6 b g Captain Rio—Queen Bodicea (IRE) (Revoque (IRE))
1186[6] 1809[2] 2138a[2] (2714) 5253[7] 5467[4] 5827[5] 6563a[8]

Captain Imperial (IRE) *Robin Bastiman* a51 71
5 b g Captain Rio—Imperialist (IRE) (Imperial Frontier (USA))
363[13] 490[7] 800[10]

Captain James (IRE) *Emmanuel Hughes* 47
4 b g Captain Rio—Jay And-A (IRE) (Elbio)
6139a[11]

Captain John Nixon *Pat Eddery* a103 91
4 b h Beat Hollow—Leaping Flame (USA) (Trempolino (USA))
1102[5] 1855[5] (2224) (3522) 4532[P]

Captain Kendall (IRE) *David Evans* 59
2 b g Clodovil(IRE) —Queen's Lace (IRE) (King's Best (USA))
3686[5]

Captain Kolo (IRE) *Tim Easterby* 76
3 b g Captain Rio—Patsy Grimes (Beveled (USA))
1391[10] 2074[11] 2363[3] 2411[8] 3384[3] 3853[9] 4295[6] 4610[5] 5010[5] 5456[2] 5821[5] 6190[2] 6778[13]

Captain Loui (IRE) *Dai Burchell* a65 59
3 gr g Verglas(IRE) —Miss Corinne (Mark Of Esteem (IRE))
349[2] 364[4] 601[4] 724[5] 1056[3] 1295[5] 6409[6]

Captain Macarry (IRE) *Stuart Williams* a83 79
6 ch g Captain Rio—Grannys Reluctance (IRE) (Anita's Prince)
1245[13] 3620[11] 4656[15] 5106[10] (6453) 6634[8] 6759[7] 6949[4]

Captain Noble (IRE) *Peter Makin* a75 47
3 b c Captain Rio—Noble Nova (Fraam)
(1483) 5146[3]

Captain Oats (IRE) *Pam Ford* a54 57
8 b g Bahhare(USA) —Adarika (Kings Lake (USA))
3516[3] 4274[3] 4951[2]

Captain Obvious (IRE) *David Wachman* a97 82
2 b c Choisir(AUS) —Taqqara (IRE) (Spectrum (IRE))
5522a[5]

Captain Peachey *Alistair Whillans* 53
5 b g Pursuit Of Love—Dekelsmary (Komaite (USA))
3658[8] 4198[10] 4673[4] 5622[15] 6430[10]

Captain Ramius (IRE) *Kevin Ryan* a97 107
5 b g Kheleyf(USA) —Princess Mood (GER) (Muhtarram (USA))
613[5] 710[4] 848[9] 1228a[3] 1849[11] 3134[4] 3397[5] (4310) 4574[4] (4802) ◆

Captainrisk (IRE) *Christine Dunnett* a58 67
5 b g Captain Rio—Helderberg (USA) (Diesis)
2016[9] 2201[11] 2829[3] (3956) 4187[4] 5355[9]

Captain Royale (IRE) *Tracy Waggott* a61 83
6 ch g Captain Rio—Paix Royale (Royal Academy (USA))
1438[11] 2397[8] 2633[10] 3087[2] 3359[8] 6209[5] 6276[11] 6779[7] (7104)

Captain Scooby *Richard Guest* a83 86
5 b g Captain Rio—Scooby Dooby Do (Atraf)
1878[11] 1968[6] 2286[9] 2766[5] 3087[6] 3279[5] 3305[4] 4327[8] 4405[3] 5163[6] 5400[4] 5647[6] 6044[4] (6212) (6418) (6427) 7355[6] 7500[5] 7644[3] 7832[5]

Captain Sharpe *Bernard Llewellyn* a44 68
3 ch g Tobougg(IRE) —Helen Sharp (Pivotal)
951[6] 1137[4] 3214[2] 4273[8] 4642[5]

Captain Slow *Julie Camacho*
4 ch g Monsieur Bond(IRE) —Tayovullin (IRE) (Shalford (IRE))
1496[12]

Captivator *James Fanshawe* a77 97
4 gr m Motivator—Cashew (Sharrood (USA))
(284) (1388) ◆ 3338[2] (5303) 6066[3] 7296[11]

Captivity *Mahmood Al Zarooni* a76 51
2 b c Echo Of Light—Tee Cee (Lion Cavern (USA))
3314[10] 6448[7] 6697[2] 7205[11]

Caraboss *Sir Michael Stoute* 97
3 b f Cape Cross(IRE) —Fairy Godmother (Fairy King (USA))
1363[2] (2432) 4723[3]

Caracal *Gordon Elliott* a67 67
4 b g Dubai Destination(USA) —Desert Lynx (IRE) (Green Desert (USA))
7564[10]

Cara Carmela *Stuart Williams* a46 50
3 gr f Compton Place—Carmela Owen (Owington)
953[4] 1764[3] 2524[10] 6258[6] 6694[12] 7693[8] 7829[6]

Caracortado (USA) *Michael Machowsky* a115 116
4 ch g Cat Dreams(USA) —Mons Venus (CAN) (Maria's Mon (USA))
7303a[5]

Caramelita *J R Jenkins* a72 72
4 b m Deportivo—Apple Of My Eye (Fraam)
(62) 318[4] 487[3] 865[6] 1024[6] 1816[4] 4395[5] 4850[9] 6694[2] 6939[9] 7504[4] 7728[3]

Caranbola *Mel Brittain* a65 85
5 br m Lucky Story(USA) —Ladywell Blaise (IRE) (Turtle Island (IRE))
1878[3] 1968[7] 2668[2] 2938[8] 3506[4] 3880[13] 4152[2] ◆ 4288[2] (4405) 4516[10] (4900) 5760[4] 6094[3]

Cara's Delight (AUS) *Frederick Watson*
4 b f Fusaichi Pegasus(USA) —Carahill (AUS) (Danehill (USA))
7063[15]

Cara's Request (AUS) *David Nicholls* a55 89
6 gr g Urgent Request(IRE) —Carahill (AUS) (Danehill (USA))
1110[14] 2112[4] 2398[8] 2783[10] 4811[6] 5059[12] 6113[24] 6381[5] 6867[7]

Caravan Rolls On *Peter Chapple-Hyam* a84 93
3 b c Hernando(FR) —Grain Only (Machiavellian (USA))
262[7] 516[4] (591) ◆ (2152) 2407[4] (6136) (6497) ◆

Carbon Print (USA) *James Evans* a54 60
6 ch g Johannesburg(USA) —Caithness (USA) (Roberto (USA))
277[4] 444[5] 769[3] 3047[11]

Carcinetto (IRE) *David Evans* a71 98
9 b m Danetime(IRE) —Dolphin Stamp (IRE) (Dolphin Street (FR))
4387[10] 4865[5] 5496[9] 5653[3] ◆ 5862[5] 5924[6] 6138[2] 6285[7] 6355[3] 6877[3] 7146[5] 7418[6] 7465[6] 7604[6] 7816[10]

Cardi Crystal (IRE) *Ian Wood* a36 17
4 b m Fasliyev(USA) —Tinsel (Lion Cavern (USA))
5317[10] 6067[6]

Cardigan (IRE) *William Haggas* 86
2 ch f Barathea(IRE) —Precipitous (IRE) (Indian Ridge)
(6291) ◆

Cardi King *Ian Wood* a53 55
3 b g Fasliyev(USA) —Tinsel (Lion Cavern (USA))
5386[5] 6086[7] 6475[3] 7263[5] 7527[9]

Cardinal *Robert Cowell* a86 79
6 ch h Pivotal—Fictitious (Machiavellian (USA))
168[5] 651[12] 3000[8] 3179[7] 4188[3] 5451[5] 5890[7] 6762[4] 7456[7] 7596[8]

Cardinal Walter (IRE) *David Simcock* 59
2 bb c Cape Cross(IRE) —Sheer Spirit (IRE) (Caerleon (USA))
7209[4]

Cardrona *John Gosden* 65
3 b f Selkirk(USA) —Lady Links (Bahamian Bounty)
2836[7] ◆ 4157[6] 5001[6] 6450[10]

Career Quest *Bill Moore* a24
3 b f Proclamation(IRE) —Vocation (IRE) (Royal Academy (USA))
6700[6] 6874[9] 7249[10]

Carimo (IRE) *P Adda* a68 76
7 b h Fasliyev(USA) —Barnabas (ITY) (Slip Anchor)
93a[5]

Carinya (IRE) *Amy Weaver* a64 85
3 br f Iffraaj—Ma N'leme Biche (USA) (Key To The Kingdom (USA))
3177[3] ◆ 4065[6] 5007[4] 5630[10] 6437[2] (6888) (7236) ◆

Carlcol Girl *Christine Dunnett* a4 25
4 b m Where Or When(IRE) —Capstick (JPN) (Machiavellian (USA))
1993[10] 2600[8] 2824[7] 3559[6] 4927[9] 5667[9]

Carlitos Spirit (IRE) *Ian McInnes* a48 75
7 ch g Redback—Negria (IRE) (Al Hareb (USA))
1150[7] 1857[7] 2490[2] 2799[8] 3683[8] 4039[5] 4150[5] 4945[2] 5208[4] 5402[9] 5822[7] 7119[6]

Carlton House (USA) *Sir Michael Stoute* 121
3 b c Street Cry(IRE) —Talented (Bustino)
(2030) 2715[3] ◆ 3442a[4]

Carlton Mac *Simon Griffiths* a26 58
6 ch g Timeless Times(USA) —Julie's Gift (Presidium)
8[12] 324[11] 444[8] 596[9] 769[8] 939[8]

Carlton Scroop (FR) *Paddy Butler* a73 72
8 ch g Priolo(USA) —Elms Schooldays (Emarati (USA))
89[3] (232) (2721) 4088[3] 4846[3] 5168[6] 5815[4] 6622[10] 7441[8] 7573[4] 7816[4]

Carmela Maria *Mike Sowersby* a68 47
6 b m Medicean—Carmela Owen (Owington)
3574[12] 4129[11]

Carnaby Street (IRE) *Mahmood Al Zarooni* a98 107
4 b h Le Vie Dei Colori—Prodigal Daughter (Alhaarth (IRE))
152a[13] 326a[14]

Carnac (IRE) *Alan McCabe* a63 72
5 gr g Dalakhani(IRE) —Traou Mad (IRE) (Barathea (IRE))
16[2] 118[5] 184[4] (324) 373[2] 444[2] 645[4] 768[2] 838[3] 859[2] 4177[7] 4649[7] 4870[6] 6182[6] 6722[7] 7107[5] 7195[5] 7426[4] 7573[3] 7645[2] (7688) 7858[2] 7914[7]

Carnelian (IRE) *Ian Semple* 36
4 b g Singspiel(IRE) —Red Zinger (USA) (Red Ransom (USA))
5432[6] 6210[6] 6504[7]

Carnevalo (IRE) *F Rossi* a96 104
3 b c Slickly(FR) —Tounsi (FR) (Sendawar (IRE))
532a[4]

Carnival Dream *Hugh McWilliams* a52 57
6 b m Carnival Dancer—Reach The Wind (USA) (Relaunch (USA))
70[7] 229[5] 512[5] 690[5] 1803[11] 2809[2] 3139[4] 3317[8] 4361[8] 6134[7] 7399[13] 7740[7]

Carolingian (IRE) *William Knight* a58 55
2 b g Holy Roman Emperor(IRE) —Sliding Scale (Sadler's Wells (USA))
3282[9] 3954[8] 4205[7] 4907[7] 6937[6]

Caroun (IRE) *A De Royer-Dupre* 90
3 b c Montjeu(IRE) —Carlitta (USA) (Olympio (USA))
(5132a)

Carousel *Ralph Beckett* 73
3 b f Pivotal—Supereva (IRE) (Sadler's Wells (USA))
1480[2] (1910)

Carpentras *Dr Jon Scargill* a51 51
3 b f Val Royal(FR) —Molly Brown (Rudimentary (USA))
2174[8] 2848[7] 5449[11] 6033[7] 7437[10]

Carragold *Mel Brittain* a55 77
5 b g Diktat—Shadow Roll (IRE) (Mark Of Esteem (IRE))
1216[9] (4076) 4513[8] (4902) (5150) 5311[2] 5761[5] 6302[4] 7236[2] 7771[7]

Carr Hall (IRE) *Tony Carroll* a62 72
8 b g Rossini(USA) —Pidgeon Bay (IRE) (Perugino (USA))
30[10] 223[12] 390[5] (862) 944[3] 1107[10] 1308[6] 1750[7] 2616[3] 2991[9]

Carrick A Rede (IRE) *Clive Cox* a79 65
3 b g Footstepsinthesand—Intricate Design (Zafonic (USA))
(726) 1550[9]

Carrieann's Boy *Nigel Tinkler*
2 ch g Dubai Destination(USA) —Presentation (IRE) (Mujadil (USA))
2362[9]

Carrie's Magic *Alistair Whillans* a67 73
4 b m Kyllachy—Carrie Pooter (Tragic Role (USA))
1239[3] 1555[3] 1816[2] 2062[4] (2631) 3305[2] 3856[6] 5400[9] 5725[11] 6212[9] 6414[6] 7100[8] 7216[9] 7463[8]

Carrignavar (USA) *Ralph Beckett* 88
3 br f Tale Of The Cat(USA) —Wendy Vaala (USA) (Dayjur (USA))
2690[3] 3323[4] 4101[6]

Carrowbeg (IRE) *Mark Johnston* a73 73
3 b c Cape Cross(IRE) —Love And Affection (USA) (Exclusive Era (USA))
1027[4] 1415[3] 1704a[5] 2394[2] 3038[5] 3485[3] 3706[2]

Carrside Lady *Garry Woodward* a41 23
5 ch m Zaha(CAN) —Bolham Lady (Timeless Times (USA))
546[6] 873[6] 1399[6] 1567[11] 6096[8] 7069[3]

Carsington *Lucinda Featherstone* 40
7 ch m And Beyond(IRE) —Nutmeg Point (Nashwan (USA))
1496[10]

Carter *Ian Williams* a86 81
5 b g Reset(AUS) —Cameo Role (GER) (Acatenango (GER))
(114) (207) (252) 531[2] (597) 1855[7] 5685[12]

Carver County (IRE) *Mandy Rowland* a35 18
3 b g Desert Style(IRE) —Chaska (Reprimand)
1526[10]

Casa Bex *Philip McBride* 65
2 b c Auction House(USA) —Feather Game (Hernando (FR))
2109[4] 2510[11] 4159[2] 4760[5]

Casaca *J-M Osorio* 101
5 ch m Medicean—Priena (IRE) (Priolo (USA))
7386a[3]

Casa Ingrid (FR) *Y De Nicolay* a72 74
4 b m Singspiel(IRE) —Nigrita (GER) (Lichine (USA))
91a[7]

Casamento (IRE) *Mahmood Al Zarooni* 121
3 ch c Shamardal(USA) —Wedding Gift (FR) (Always Fair (USA))
1686[10] 2751a[9] (6185a) 6861[11]

Casela Park (IRE) *Jaclyn Tyrrell* a73 89
6 ch g Elnadim(USA) —Taormina (IRE) (Ela-Mana-Mou)
3445a[3] 7010a[14] 7793a[10]

Cashelgar (IRE) *Jeremy Noseda* 96
5 b g Anabaa(USA) —Tropical Barth (IRE) (Peintre Celebre (USA))
1781a[5] 5218[18]

Cash Injection *Karen George* a48 43
2 b c Halling(USA) —Cape Siren (Warning)
4087[7] 5375[7] 7494[8]

Cashmere Or Caviar (IRE) *B W Hills* 48
2 b f Tagula(IRE) —Sandystones (Selkirk (USA))
2767[10] 3257[11]

Cashpoint *Anthony Middleton* a89 88
6 b g Fantastic Light(USA) —Cashew (Sharrood (USA))
1402[5] ◆ 1887[5] 2686[7] 3277[5] 4253[7] 5103[3]
Casino Host (USA) *Chad C Brown* 111
3 bb c Dynaformer(USA) —Ensenada (USA) (Seeking The Gold (USA))
5072a[5] 6716a[6] 7572a[6]
Casino Night *Barry Murtagh* a52 76
6 ch m Night Shift(USA) —Come Fly With Me (Bluebird (USA))
1520[3] 1857[2] 2046[3] 2399[4] 2636[6] (3303) 3486[4] 4877[7] 5314[10] 5622[9]
Caspar Netscher *Alan McCabe* 114
2 b c Dutch Art—Bella Cantata (Singspiel (IRE))
(1966) 2476[2] 2712[4] 3014[3] 4055[2] 4495[3] (5251) (6162) 6688[5] 7301a[8]
Cassini Flight (USA) *Jeremy Noseda* a77
3 bb c Bernardini(USA) —Cassis (USA) (Red Ransom (USA))
(158)
Castalian Spring (IRE) *Robert Eddery* a40 47
2 b f Oasis Dream—Lady Lafitte (USA) (Stravinsky (USA))
6215[9] 6744[14] 7526[11] 7692[7] 7830[10]
Cast Away (IRE) *S Cannavo'* 99
3 b c Refuse To Bend(IRE) —Corgetta (Hernando (FR))
1431a[14]
Casternova *Hughie Morrison* 47
3 ch f Avonbridge—Casterossa (Rossini (USA))
1284[4] 1565[10] 1865[6]
Castle Bar Sling (USA) *T J O'Mara* a80 98
6 b g Diesis—Lady Of The Woods (USA) (Woodman (USA))
4566a[9] 7189a[5]
Castlebury (IRE) *Ruth Carr* a51 58
6 b g Spartacus(IRE) —La Vie En Rouge (IRE) (College Chapel)
490[5] 631[6] 899[3] 969[10] 1063[7]
Castlemorris King *Michael Attwater* a75 59
3 br c And Beyond(IRE) —Brookshield Baby (IRE) (Sadler's Wells (USA))
1769[5] 2715[12] (5898) (6701) ◆ 7413[5] 7638[2] 7839[4]
Castle Myth (USA) *Jim Best* a69 65
5 bb g Johannesburg(USA) —Castlemania (CAN) (Bold Ruckus (USA))
(103) 374[3] 4177[11]
Castles In The Air *Richard Fahey* a95 109
6 b g Oasis Dream—Dance Parade (USA) (Gone West (USA))
1094[13] 1242[4] 1885[23] 3109[18] 4314[7] 5474[13] 5887[4] 6147[20] 6706[20] 6862[3]
Castries (IRE) *A De Royer-Dupre* a69 79
4 b m Captain Rio—Without Shoes (FR) (Highest Honor (FR))
395a[0]
Casual Garcia *Mark Gillard* a56 59
6 gr g Hernando(FR) —Frosty Welcome (USA) (With Approval (CAN))
3353[8]
Casual Glimpse *Richard Hannon* 108
3 b c Compton Place—Glimpse (Night Shift (USA))
1341[4] 2338a[6] 2683[6] 3777[2] (4472) 5474[10] 5929[3] 6521[15] 7295[16]
Casual Mover (IRE) *John Best* a73 58
3 b c Diamond Green(FR) —Baileys On Line (Shareef Dancer (USA))
(434) 1344[7] 7842[6]
Catalinas Diamond (IRE) *Pat Murphy* a67 86
3 b f One Cool Cat(USA) —Diamondiferous (USA) (Danzig (USA))
1654[6] 2223[2] 3091[5] 3523[6] 4057[4] 4615[6] 5115[5] 5615[4] 5846[4] 6257[3] 6931[3] 7123[8] (7488)
Catallout (IRE) *Declan Carroll* a54 73
3 b f One Cool Cat(USA) —America Lontana (FR) (King's Theatre (IRE))
1155[11] 1459[7] 1693[9] 2350[2] 2986[6] 3661[4] 4638[2] 4987[2] (5725) 6228[6] 6450[6] 6860[12] 7100[8]
Catalyze *Andrew Balding* a59 91
3 b g Tumblebrutus(USA) —Clarita Dear (CHI) (Hussonet (USA))
2506[12] 3067[21] 3649[10] 4010[3] 4243[3] 4656[11] 6223[3]
Cataract *John Weymes* a46 48
2 ch f Avonbridge—Catspraddle (USA) (High Yield (USA))
2587[4] 2780[5] 3273[10] 4069[2] 5562[13] 6628[7] 6942[6] 7143[7]
Catawollow *Richard Guest* a39 52
4 b m Beat Hollow—Catalonia (IRE) (Catrail (USA))
3317[12] 3496[11] 4441[8] 5403[10] 6049[12]
Catbells (IRE) *Alan Bailey* a78 74
4 ch m Rakti—Moonbi Ridge (IRE) (Definite Article)
83[2] (201) 278[5] 475[3]
Catchanova (IRE) *Eve Johnson Houghton* a81 76
4 b g Catcher In The Rye(IRE) —Head For The Stars (IRE) (Head For Heights)
2144[6] 2560[2] (2816) 3071[4] 3468[2] 3815[11] 4338[4] (5101) (5383) 5835[7] (6586) 7098[5] 7227[8] 7362[5] 7447[7]
Catcher Of Dreams (IRE) *George Foster* a62 52
5 b g Catcher In The Rye(IRE) —No Islands (Lomond (USA))
1216[12] 2415[8] 2990[8]
Catching Zeds *Ian Williams* a65 58
4 b m Lucky Story(USA) —Perfect Poppy (Shareef Dancer (USA))
200[3] 425[5] 526[6] (897) 1052[8] 3814[7] (4846)
Catch Me A Dream (IRE) *Barry McGann* 54
3 b f Cape Cross(IRE) —Kindling (Dr Fong (USA))
5982a[8]
Catchword (FR) *M Mace* 52
2 b g Trempolino(USA) —Nan's Catch (FR) (Loup Solitaire (USA))
4624a[8]
Catchy Tune (IRE) *David Brown* 53
2 ch c Redback—Magic Melody (Petong)
3382[8] 3917[11] 4632[5] ◆

Categorical *Keith Reveley* a69 68
8 b g Diktat—Zibet (Kris)
6838[2]
Category Five (IRE) *A Klimscha Jr* 55
2 b c Hurricane Run(IRE) —Feather (USA) (Unbridled's Song (USA))
4624a[10]
Category Seven (USA) *Kenneth L Hargrave* 103
6 bb m Gulf Storm(USA) —Spectacular Lace (USA) (Jokester (USA))
6719a[12]
Caterina *Richard Hannon* 64
2 b f Medicean—Senta's Dream (Danehill (USA))
2254[8] 3865[6] 4263 [5]
Catfish (IRE) *Brian Meehan* 92
3 bb f One Cool Cat(USA) —Castellane (FR) (Danehill (USA))
1837[5] 2102[7] 2468[5] (2916) 3367[4] 3807[6] (4498)
Catfromtherock (IRE) *David Marnane* a74 61
2 b g One Cool Cat(USA) —Campbellite (Desert Prince (IRE))
7275a[2]
Catharos (FR) *Mali Droueche* 28
3 ch f Limnos(JPN) —Rossinante (FR) (Calling Collect (USA))
7016a[9]
Cathcart Castle *Mick Channon* a60 65
3 b g Imperial Dancer—Stephanie's Mind (Mind Games)
109[7] 1952[3] 2172[3] 2351[3] 2421[2] 2792[10] 3223[10] 3724[2] 3999[4] 4247[3] 4729[4] 5619[5] (6545) 6657[3] 6698[5] 6811[6] 7085[5] 7496[2]
Cathedral *Brian Meehan* 76
2 b c Invincible Spirit(IRE) —Capades Dancer (USA) (Gate Dancer (USA))
6165[3] ◆
Cathedral Spires *Howard Johnson* 86
3 b g Intikhab(USA) —Munakashah (IRE) (Machiavellian (USA))
(1942)
Catherine Laboure (IRE) *David Arbuthnot* a65
2 br f Kheleyf(USA) —Caro Mio (IRE) (Danehill Dancer (IRE))
3520[7]
Catherines Call (IRE) *Des Donovan* a81 75
4 b m Captain Rio—It's Academic (Royal Academy (USA))
(530) 666[2] 956[5] 1200[10]
Cat Hunter *Ronald Harris* a75 74
4 b m One Cool Cat(USA) —Eoz (IRE) (Sadler's Wells (USA))
55[2] (160) 307[5] 689[3] 2566[10] 3413[9] 4010[2] 4210[3] 4458[2] 4949[6] 5547[4] 5992[5]
Cat Island *Mark H Tompkins* 57
3 b f Bahamian Bounty—Dolls House (Dancing Spree (USA))
2827[8] 3485[7] 4929[13]
Cativo Cavallino *John E Long* a70 74
8 ch g Bertolini(USA) —Sea Isle (Selkirk (USA))
473[9] (1026) 1488[7] 2207[9] 3172[5] 4160[2] 4546[4] 5516[7] 6051[3] (6939) 7362[6] 7637[4]
Cat Junior (USA) *Niels Petersen* a116 116
6 b h Storm Cat(USA) —Luna Wells (IRE) (Sadler's Wells (USA))
501a[7] 756a[13]
Cat Nova (FR) *Y Barberot* a78 101
3 gr f Hurricane Cat(USA) —Las Americas (FR) (Linamix (FR))
7386a[7]
Cato Minor *Amanda Perrett* a50 57
2 b g Notnowcato—Violet (IRE) (Mukaddamah (USA))
4545[9] 4798[10] 5382[7] 6053[7] 6399[2]
Cat O' Nine Tails *Brian Rothwell* 82
4 b m Motivator—Purring (USA) (Mountain Cat (USA))
1847[6] 2262[7] 2512[7] 2888[6] 3115[7] 3730[3] 4382[2] 4635[5] 5340[6] 6095[9] (6229) 6707[11] 6916[7]
Cat Queen *Gay Kelleway* a54 58
2 b f One Cool Cat(USA) —Oatey (Master Willie)
3865[7] 4471[16] 4961[10] 5998[6] 6628[9] 7697[4] (7769)
Catramis *Geoffrey Oldroyd* 54
2 b g Misu Bond(IRE) —Bond Cat (IRE) (Raise A Grand (IRE))
4122[11] 5818[4] 6572[5]
Cattiva (FR) *Mme B Valenti* 19
2 b f Zieten(USA) —Byre Bird (USA) (Diesis)
7326a[8]
Caucus *John Gosden* 106
4 b g Cape Cross(IRE) —Maid To Perfection (Sadler's Wells (USA))
2438[5]
Caudillo (GER) *Dr A Bolte* 106
8 b h Acatenango(GER) —Corsita (Top Ville)
2540a[2] 6569a[2] 7045a[5]
Cause For Applause (IRE) *Ray Craggs* a52 29
5 b m Royal Applause—Polyandry (IRE) (Pennekamp (USA))
120[4] 408[7] 675[9] 3187[5]
Cavaleiro (IRE) *Marcus Tregoning* 93
2 ch c Sir Percy—Khibraat (Alhaarth (IRE))
3425[3] 4264[3] 4722[2] (5375) (6126)
Cavalry Guard (USA) *Tim McCarthy* a50 57
7 ch g Officer(USA) —Leeward City (USA) (Carson City (USA))
135[12] 225[5] 662[4] 719[2] 950[7] 1184[7] 2385[5] 7131[12] 7923[7]
Cavalryman *Saeed Bin Suroor* a114 119
5 b h Halling(USA) —Silversword (FR) (Highest Honor (FR))
2439[4] 3403[2] 4374a[10] 5092a[6] 7049a[5]
Cavitie *Frank Sheridan* a75 55
5 b g Teofilio(IRE) —Kirriemuir (Lochnager)
401[9] 571[6] 735[2] 880[3] 1248[3] 1471[3] (1581) (2165) 3045[10] 3713[2] 4206[2] (5734) 6133[11] 6502[9]
Cawdor (IRE) *Linda Stubbs* a63 76
5 b g Kyllachy—Dim Ots (Alhijaz)
1239[10] 2815[8] 3190[2] 3856[12] 4604[11] 5034[5] 7561[7]

Cayman (IRE) *C Von Der Recke* a72
4 b g Big Shuffle(USA) —Call Me Alice (IRE) (Alzao (USA))
442a[9] 629a[10]
Caymana Girl (IRE) *Micky Hammond* 18
2 ch f Indian Haven—Sally Green (IRE) (Common Grounds)
3855[6] 4192[10]
Cayman Fox *Linda Perratt* a57 77
6 ch m Cayman Kai(IRE) —Kalarram (Muhtarram (USA))
2987[10] 4327[10] 4504[10] 4541[8] 4881[9] 5436[8] 5719[8] 6265[2] 6386[2] 6454[4] 7100[2] 7266[5]
Cayman Islands *A Fabre* a84 100
3 b g Shirocco(GER) —Barbuda (Rainbow Quest (USA))
1551a[7]
Caymans (AUS) *Saeed Bin Suroor* a99 107
6 b g Secret Savings(USA) —Easy Out (AUS) (Anabaa (USA))
331a[3] 604a[5] 828a[11] 3409[6] 5055[5]
Cayuga *Sir Michael Stoute* 50
2 b c Montjeu(IRE) —Ithaca (USA) (Distant View (USA))
6300[9]
Cazals (IRE) *B Grizzetti* 111
3 b c Aussie Rules(USA) —Secrete Marina (IRE) (Mujadil (USA))
(1127a) 1920a[2]
Cease (USA) *Albert M Stall Jr* a112
4 b g War Chant(USA) —Limit (USA) (Cox's Ridge (USA))
7300a[5]
Cecile De Volanges *Tor Sturgis* a56
3 ch f Kheleyf(USA) —Fyvie (Grand Lodge (USA))
420[3]
Ceffyl Gwell *Richard Hannon* a85 76
3 b c Compton Place—Corinium (IRE) (Turtle Island (IRE))
(864) ◆ 1106[5] 1830[2] 2200[2] 2383[2] 5000[8] 5859[8]
Ceilidh House *Ralph Beckett* a101 103
4 ch m Selkirk(USA) —Villa Carlotta (Rainbow Quest (USA))
2994[3] 5934[6] 7296[3] 7584[2] 7802[6]
Cejac (FR) *J Rossi* a58 58
4 b h Sagacity(FR) —Bakrice (FR) (Housamix (FR))
831a[0]
Celani *Tim Walford* a72 72
3 b f Jelani(IRE) —Celandine (Warning)
1168[5] 1456[6] 2850[2] 4005[7] 4515[2]
Celebrissime (IRE) *F Head* a80 107
6 ch g Peintre Celebre(USA) —Ring Beaune (USA) (Bering)
5195a[5]
Celebrity *Richard Hannon* 84
3 b f Pivotal—Dance Solo (Sadler's Wells (USA))
1361[7] 1884[12]
Celebrity Choice (IRE) *B Dutruel* a75 82
4 b h Choisir(AUS) —Femme Celebre (IRE) (Peintre Celebre (USA))
1033a[4]
Celerina (IRE) *T Stack* a89 103
4 ch m Choisir(AUS) —Chantarella (IRE) (Royal Academy (USA))
2317[3] ◆ 3158[2] 4768a[6] 5524a[6]
Celestial Dawn *John Weymes* 59
2 b f Echo Of Light—Celestial Welcome (Most Welcome)
1797[7] 5058[5] 5398[6] 5817[2] 6186[4] 7059[17] 7103[4]
Celestial Flyer (IRE) *Tor Sturgis* a42 43
3 b g Balmont(USA) —Pearly Gates (IRE) (Night Shift (USA))
2384[4] 2598[5] 3227[8] 3724[9]
Celestial Girl *Hughie Morrison* a76 84
4 b m Dubai Destination(USA) —[illegible] (Unfuwain (USA))
2170[2] 2417[2] 3814[6] 4090[4] (5135) (5546) 6066[8]
Celestrial (IRE) *Bryan Smart* 25
2 gr g Verglas(IRE) —Blue Azure (USA) (American Chance (USA))
4012[7] 4323[7]
Celestyna *Sir Henry Cecil* a64 71
3 b f Observatory(USA) —Mysterix (IRE) (Linamix (FR))
2266[6] (3766) 4727[6] 6759[13]
Celine (SWE) *Roy Arne Kvisla*
2 b f Sleeping Indian—Robin Lane (Tenby)
5983a[12]
Celtic Celeb (IRE) *F Doumen* 115
4 ch h Peintre Celebre(USA) —Gaelic Bird (FR) (Gay Mecene (USA))
1266a[8] 1842a[6] ◆ 2753a[7] 5304a[12] 5990a[5] 6562a[9] 7049a[3]
Celtic Change (IRE) *Geoffrey Harker* a47 91
7 br g Celtic Swing—Changi (IRE) (Lear Fan (USA))
2217[12]
Celtic Commitment *Simon Dow* a70 68
5 gr g Mull Of Kintyre(USA) —Grey Again (Unfuwain (USA))
124[3] 381[11] 561[2] 656[6]
Celtic Conviction (CAN) *Michael J Doyle* 99
3 ch g Strut The Stage(USA) —All My Lovin' (USA) (Cat's Career (USA))
6910a[10]
Celtic Life (IRE) *Amy Weaver* a49 48
5 gr g Celtic Swing—Night Life (IRE) (Night Shift (USA))
69[12]
Celtic Ransom *Gary Moore* a60 62
4 b g Red Ransom(USA) —Welsh Valley (USA) (Irish River (FR))
203[10] 391[6] 727[13] 896[9]
Celtic Sixpence (IRE) *Noel Quinlan* a73 84
3 b f Celtic Swing—Penny Ha'Penny (Bishop Of Cashel)
2180[11] 3079[6] 3702[7] 4715[2] ◆ (5542) 5939[3] 6762[3] 7262[13]

Celtic Soprano (IRE) *P D Deegan* 98
6 b m Celtic Swing—Midnight Glimmer (IRE) (Dr Devious (IRE))
6736a[4]
Celtic Step *Peter Niven* a61 57
7 br g Selkirk(USA) —Inchiri (Sadler's Wells (USA))
1911[13] 2057[14] 3952[13] 4112[2] 4902[11] 5823[7] 6871[2] 7178[5] 7698[5]
Celtic Sultan (IRE) *Tom Tate* a94 95
7 b g Celtic Swing—Farjah (IRE) (Charnwood Forest (IRE))
1240[12] 4609[8] 5032[18] 5272[13] 5879[13] (6478) 7076[12]
Celtic Whisper *Jeremy Gask* a42
3 b f Bertolini(USA) —Celt Song (IRE) (Unfuwain (USA))
380[8] 663[6] 959[5] 1331[9]
Celtie Rod (IRE) *X Nakkachdji* a95 91
7 b g Dansili—Lady Golconda (FR) (Kendor (FR))
3568a[5] 7256a[10]
Cenon (IRE) *J-C Rouget* a80
3 b c Montjeu(IRE) —Krissante (USA) (Kris)
370a[3]
Census (IRE) *Richard Hannon* 118
3 b g Cacique(IRE) —Slieve (Selkirk (USA))
(2052) 3069[2] ◆ 3772[2] (5045) ◆ 5928[5]
Centeo (SPA) *L De Clerck* a78 60
6 b h Wagon Master(FR) —Red White And Blue (Zafonic (USA))
7314a[7]
Centre Stage *George Margarson* 42
3 b g Fasliyev(USA) —Purple Rain (IRE) (Celtic Swing)
2596[14]
Century Dancer *Tor Sturgis* a55 30
3 b f Trade Fair—Be Bop Aloha (Most Welcome)
(966) 1952[10] 2598[11] 3223[13] 6657[9]
Ceodora (GER) *P Monfort* a68 70
6 b m Efisio—Caerosa (Caerleon (USA))
7315a[5]
Cerejeira (IRE) *Eric Alston* a57 46
3 b f Exceed And Excel(AUS) —Camassina (IRE) (Taufan (USA))
6839[4] 7245[7] 7585[3] 7820[6]
Ceremonial Jade (UAE) *Marco Botti* a98 82
8 b g Jade Robbery(USA) —Talah (Danehill (USA))
4392[4] 5046[9] 7628[5]
Cerences (FR) *J-C Rouget* a75
3 b c Oratorio(IRE) —Pennegale (IRE) (Pennekamp (USA))
258a[3]
Certral *Brian Ellison* a59 82
3 b f Iffraaj—Craigmill (Slip Anchor)
(1137) 1904[3] (2466) 2615[4] (3363) 3845[4] 4344[3] ◆ 5220[9] 5702[9]
Cerveza *Mme Pia Brandt* a89 102
3 ch f Medicean—Kalindi (Efisio)
(841a) 2752a[5] 5695a[7]
Cesseras (IRE) *M Delzangles* 94
3 b f Cape Cross(IRE) —Lafleur (IRE) (Grand Lodge (USA))
5958a[9]
C'Est L'Amour (GER) *Frau E Mader* 85
4 b m Whipper(USA) —Centaine (Royal Academy (USA))
5980a[6]
Chabada (JPN) *Sir Henry Cecil* a77
3 b f Bago(FR) —Taygete (USA) (Miswaki (USA))
6054[3]
Chacha Heels (FR) *H-A Pantall* 46
2 b f Meshaheer(USA) —Just Fizzy (Efisio)
4843a[11]
Chachamaidee (IRE) *Sir Henry Cecil* 116
4 b m Footstepsinthesand—Canterbury Lace (USA) (Danehill (USA))
1718[3] (2315) 3030[2] (4497) ◆ 5848[3] 6338[2] 6687[2]
Cha Ching (IRE) [illegible]
2 b f Elnadim(USA) —Sudden Interest (FR) (Highest Honor (FR))
6819[5]
Chadford *Tim Walford* 60
3 b g Trade Fair—Quiz Time (Efisio)
1169[12] 1495[4] 1945[8] 3706[3] 4128[5] 5556[3] 5788[8]
Chadwell Spring (IRE) *Mike Sowersby* a68 55
5 b m Statue Of Liberty(USA) —Cresalin (Coquelin (USA))
2618[9]
Chain Lightning *Richard Hannon* 106
3 ch c Hurricane Run(IRE) —Sachet (USA) (Royal Academy (USA))
(1550) 3067[8] 3592[2] 4467[2] 5275[5] 5853[2]
Chain Of Events *Neil King* a76 80
4 ch g Nayef(USA) —Ermine (IRE) (Cadeaux Genereux)
(2021) 2436[2] 2769[2] 3366[7] 4280[6] 4763[3] 5281[3] 5482[15] 6592[10]
Chalice Welcome *Neil King* a88 74
8 b g Most Welcome—Blue Peru (IRE) (Perugino (USA))
614[11]
Chalk And Cheese (USA) *John Gosden* a75 66
2 ch g Rahy(USA) —Escoltada (ARG) (Political Ambition (USA))
4748[9] 5480[9] 6099[4] (6699)
Chalkie *Marjorie Fife*
3 gr g Generous(IRE) —Paris Flash (IRE) (Paris House)
3138[12]
Chalsa (FR) *P Khozian* a97 104
5 b h Kingsalsa(USA) —Karmichah (FR) (Nice Havrais (USA))
371a[3] 661a[2]
Chamberlain Bridge (USA) *W Bret Calhoun* 121
7 b g War Chant(USA) —Shes Got Class (USA) (Trempolino (USA))
9100a[4] 7303a[8]
Chambers (IRE) *Bruce Hellier* a26 62
5 b g Green Desert(USA) —Court Lane (USA) (Machiavellian (USA))
1558[8] 1909[16] 2354[10] 2494[10] 3657[6] 4078[3] ◆ 4378[4] 5083[14] 6609[11] 6999[11] 7696[9]

Chambles *Andrew Reid* a66 54
2 b f Shamardal(USA) —Pants (Pivotal)
6480[8] 6991[8] 7757[7] (7925) ◆

Chamir (FR) *J-M Capitte* a64 52
5 b g Charming Groom(FR) —Sheer Drop (FR) (Kenmare (FR))
(832a)

Champagne All Day *Simon Griffiths* a27 29
5 ch g Timeless Times(USA) —Miss Ceylon (Brief Truce (USA))
185[11] 321[5] 445[5] 547[5]

Champagne D'Oro (USA) *Eric J Guillot* a115
4 b m Medaglia D'Oro(USA) —Champagne Glow (USA) (Saratoga Six (USA))
7282a[6]

Champagne Katie *Bryan Smart* 24
2 ch f Medicean—Palace Affair (Pursuit Of Love)
7058[6]

Champagne Reefing (USA) *Jane Chapple-Hyam* a67
2 ch c Van Nistelrooy(USA) —Wewantitall (Pivotal)
7000[3]

Champagne Style (USA) *Richard Guest* a54 79
4 ch g Lion Heart(USA) —Statute (USA) (Verzy (CAN))
1092[19] 1696[9] ◆ 2115[3] 2301[12] 3275[6] 3641[4] 3659[6] 4537[15] 4958[11] 5608[7]

Champagne Valley *Sharon Watt* 49
2 ch f Three Valleys(USA) —Volitant (Ashkalani (IRE))
4002[9] 4675[2] 5819[5] 6611[14]

Champ Pegasus (USA) *Richard E Mandella* 119
5 b h Fusaichi Pegasus(USA) —Salt Champ (ARG) (Salt Lake (USA))
1001a[12]

Chandigarh (IRE) *Paul Fitzsimons* 76
2 b f Moss Vale(IRE) —Secret Justice (USA) (Lit De Justice (USA))
3200[5] (4229) 4824[7] 5263[4] (6021) 6196a[15]

Chandlery (IRE) *Richard Hannon* 110
2 b c Choisir(AUS) —Masai Queen (IRE) (Mujadil (USA))
(2687) 3012[11] 3861[2] (4424)

Chandrayaan *John E Long* a65 62
4 ch g Bertolini(USA) —Muffled (USA) (Mizaaya)
482[4] 662[3] 7923[8]

Change The Subject (USA) *David Simcock* a84 78
3 rg c Maria's Mon(USA) —Victory Lap (USA) (Touch Gold (USA))
1408[9] 1810[3] 2258[11] 5056[4] 5607[3] 5960[2] 7098[2] ◆ 7542[2] (7894)

Changing The Guard *Richard Fahey* a87 91
5 b g King's Best(USA) —Our Queen Of Kings (Arazi (USA))
1154[2] 1387[6] 1824[7] 4537[11] 4959[5] 5757[5] 6188[3] (6631)

Chankillo *Mark H Tompkins* a50 35
2 ch c Observatory(USA) —Seasonal Blossom (IRE) (Fairy King (USA))
7133[11] 7709[2]

Chantilly Dancer (IRE) *Michael Quinn* a29 49
5 b m Danehill Dancer(IRE) —Antiguan Jane (Shirley Heights)
1993[3] 2600[6] 3637[2] 4275[12] 5178[10] 6968[3] 7206[12] 7573[6] 7858[11]

Chantilly Jewel (USA) *Robert Cowell* a63 60
6 b m Century City(IRE) —Betty's Star (USA) (Pentelicus (USA))
224[4] (421) (664) 947[4] 1043[3]

Chapatti (IRE) *Stuart Williams* a21 42
3 b f High Chaparral(IRE) —Tropical Lass (IRE) (Ballad Rock)
5327[12] 6286[9]

Chapellerie (IRE) *Brian Meehan* a66 70
2 b f Acclamation—Castellane (FR) (Danehill (USA))
4614[7] 5047[2] 5480[4] 7593[4] 7889[5]

Chaperno (USA) *M bin Shafya* a77 93
4 br g More Than Ready(USA) —Timeless Forest (USA) (Forestry (USA))
536a[10]

Chapman (GER) *P Schiergen* 54
2 b c Big Shuffle(USA) —Cominales (IRE) (Primo Dominie)
7155a[9]

Chapter And Verse (IRE) *Mike Murphy* a106 94
5 gr g One Cool Cat(USA) —Beautiful Hill (IRE) (Danehill (USA))
1100[8] 1684[6] 3032[9] 4415[8] 4993[10] 5712[5] 6273[3] 6728[6] 7110[3] 7393[6]

Chapter Five *Keith Reveley* 66
4 b m Grape Tree Road—Northern Shadows (Rock Hopper)
1211[4] 1616[4] 3138[3] 4127[4] 4329[2] 6775[10]

Chapter Seven *Richard Fahey* 85
2 ch c Excellent Art—My First Romance (Danehill (USA))
2953[6] 3761[2] 5479[4] 6170[13]

Chaqueta *Chris Wall* a61 56
4 b m High Chaparral(IRE) —New Design (IRE) (Bluebird (USA))
301[8]

Chardonnay Star (IRE) *Colin Teague* a22 52
4 b m Bertolini(USA) —Coup De Coeur (IRE) (Kahyasi)
1439[11] 1813[7] 1906[7] 2047[2] 2415[7] 3191[7] 3857[5] 4437[3] 4600[14] 4987[10] 5649[6] 6839[7] 7246[12]

Chardonney Tcheque (FR) *T Satra* 102
3 bb c One Cool Cat(USA) —Genevale (FR) (Unfuwain (USA))
6905a[5]

Charismas Birthday (IRE) *Daniel Mark Loughnane* a30 56
3 b f Choisir(AUS) —Paradise Blue (IRE) (Bluebird (USA))
4379[7]

Charitable Act (FR) *William Muir* a76 88
2 b c Cadeaux Genereux—Acatama (USA) (Efisio)
3686[12] ◆ 4339[2] (4906) 5479[11] 6527[6] ◆ 7026[14]

Charity Fair *Ron Barr* a15 41
4 ch m Bahamian Bounty—Be Most Welcome (Most Welcome)
1248[11] 1497[8] 2809[9] 3974[7] 4438[5] 4601[10] 5549[7] 6264[8]

Charles Bear *Bruce Hellier* a53
4 br m Needwood Blade—Zamyatina (IRE) (Danehill Dancer (IRE))
224[8] 256[12]

Charles Camoin (IRE) *Sylvester Kirk* 95
3 b g Peintre Celebre(USA) —Birthday (IRE) (Singspiel (IRE))
2229[2] ◆ (2711) ◆ 3069[9] ◆

Charles Darwin (IRE) *Michael Blanshard* a70 70
8 ch g Tagula(IRE) —Seymour (IRE) (Eagle Eyed (USA))
306[7] 477[2] 589[11] 893[5] 933[6] 1041[10]

Charles De Mille *George Moore* 61
3 b g Tiger Hill(IRE) —Apple Town (Warning)
1151[6] 2394[5]

Charles Fosterkane *John Best* a81 53
3 br c Three Wonders(USA) —Retainage (USA) (Polish Numbers (USA))
4447[9] 4994[5] 5171[8] 5322[11] 6120[6] 6442[8] 6752[13] 6929[4]

Charles Parnell (IRE) *Simon Griffiths* a78 71
8 b g Elnadim(USA) —Titania (Fairy King (USA))
13[4] 150[4] 289[7] 544[8] 1815[7] 2238[2] 2412[12] 3972[9] 4196[9] 4893[10] 5490[10] 5787[3]

Charles The Great (IRE) *Andrew Balding* 102
2 b g Holy Roman Emperor(IRE) —Jojeema (Barathea (IRE))
1886[6] (2367) 3064[10] (4094) 4413[3]

Charleston Lady *Ralph Beckett* a99 99
3 b f Hurricane Run(IRE) —Dance Lively (USA) (Kingmambo (USA))
1722[2] 4099[6] 4915[8] 6530[4] (7129)

Charley's Mount (IRE) *Brian Meehan* 60
2 ch c Danehill Dancer(IRE) —Farthingale (IRE) (Nashwan (USA))
4996[6] 6170[14] 6768[14]

Charlie Cool *Ruth Carr* a75 101
8 ch h Rainbow Quest(USA) —Tigwa (Cadeaux Genereux)
1092[12] 1387[11] 1694[8] 2123[4] 2217[4] 2933[6] 3085[3] 3315[6] 3576[2] (3831) 4415[9] 4794[8] 5502[3] (5648) 6006[4] 6533[16] 7034[6] 7424[7]

Charlie Delta *John O'Shea* a67 61
8 b g Pennekamp(USA) —Papita (IRE) (Law Society (USA))
1730[13] 1828[8] 4487[3] 4882[8] 5204[5] 5540[6] 6304[9]

Charlie Fable (IRE) *Hughie Morrison* a43 64
3 b g Intikhab(USA) —Fiaba (Precocious)
3430[6] 3781[6] 4157[7] 4822[10] 6253[9]

Charlie's Boy *Tobias B P Coles*
5 gr g Mutamarkiz(IRE) —Lavender Della (IRE) (Shernazar)
448[7]

Charlie Smirke (USA) *Gary Moore* a83 73
5 b g Gulch(USA) —Two Altazano (USA) (Manzotti (USA))
82[2] 310[8] 885[5] 1868[5] 2207[4] (2381)

Charlie's Moment (USA) *Saeed Bin Suroor* a109
5 br g Indian Charlie(USA) —Moment Of Light (CAN) (Bold Revenue (CAN))
(678a) ◆ 999a[5]

Charlietoo *Pam Ford* a56 54
5 b g King Charlemagne(USA) —Ticcatoo (IRE) (Dolphin Street (FR))
(2162) 2233[2] 2555[3] 2655[4] 3475[12] 3714[11] 4487[8] 6494[11] 7112[11]

Charlize (FR) *F Doumen* 52
2 ch f Bedawin(FR) —Dauphine (SAF) (Rich Man's Gold (USA))
6925a[7]

Charlotte Point (USA) *J E Pease* a87 90
5 b m Distorted Humor(USA) —Skygusty (USA) (Skywalker (USA))
92a[0]

Charlotte Rosina *Roger Teal* 79
2 b f Choisir(AUS) —Intriguing Glimpse (Piccolo)
(2227) 3033[11] 5237[5] 6590[5]

Charmeur (USA) *Philip Hobbs* 81
4 b g War Chant(USA) —Arme Ancienne (Sillery (USA))
3466[5] 3911[7] 4465[6]

Charming River (FR) *Mlle V Dissaux* a59 59
5 b g Charming Groom(FR) —Crystal River (FR) (River River (FR))
832a[3]

Charming Woman (IRE) *Vittorio Caruso* 103
4 b m Invincible Spirit(IRE) —Sospel (Kendor (FR))
1432a[2] 1919a[3]

Charmouth Girl *John Mackie* a15 45
5 b m Makbul—Impish Jude (Imp Society (USA))
2621[10] 3218[7] 5212[10] 6135[9]

Chart *William Jarvis* a18 60
2 b c Dutch Art—Masandra (IRE) (Desert Prince (IRE))
6800[7] 7292[9] 7593[9]

Chasin' Rainbows *Sylvester Kirk* a55
3 b f Piccolo—Tamara (Marju (IRE))
7207[3] 7443[7] 7822[5]

Chasm (AUS) *Heath Conners* 117
7 ch g Umatilla(NZ) —Arabian Poppi (AUS) (Al Hareb (USA))
[8]

Chat De La Burg (USA) *John Best* a77 80
4 ch g Johannesburg(USA) —Catsuit (USA) (Sir Cat (USA))
442a[7] 534a[5] 629a[9] 822[10]

Chateau Galliard (IRE) *Terry Clement* a23
5 bb g Xaar—Chalosse (Doyoun)
56[8]

Chateau Lola *Derek Shaw* a39 29
2 b f Byron—Glensara (Petoski)
7165[12] 7293[13] 7396[10] 7541[9] 7694[4] 7780[7] 7925[7]

Chateau Zara *Derek Shaw* a52 62
4 b m Zaha(CAN) —Glensara (Petoski)
800[8] 893[7] 3241[10]

Chater Garden (IRE) *Alan Jarvis* a56 18
2 b g Kheleyf(USA) —Laraissa (Machiavellian (USA))
2194[6] 2523[8] 4823[10] 5385[6] 6817[8]

Chat Room *Mahmood Al Zarooni* 84
3 ch g Dubawi(IRE) —Contradictive (USA) (Kingmambo (USA))
1568[2]

Chatterati (USA) *Mahmood Al Zarooni* a68 65
2 b f Street Cry(IRE) —Melhor Ainda (USA) (Pulpit (USA))
4992[8] 5444[7] 6441[4] 7081[7]

Chatterer (IRE) *Marcus Tregoning* a65 79
3 b f Alhaarth(IRE) —Miss Bellbird (IRE) (Danehill (USA))
3043[10] (3392) 3771[3] 4584[3] 5804[3] 6412[2] 6729[3]

Chaud Lapin *Anthony Carson* a72
2 ch c Haafhd—Culture Queen (King's Best (USA))
6654[6] 7749[2] 7898[5]

Chaussini *James Toller* a76 81
4 b m Dubawi(IRE) —Miss Chaussini (IRE) (Rossini (USA))
1762[5] 2168[2] (2852) 3367[6] 4909[8] 5671[5] 6256[5] 6793[7]

Check The Label (USA) *H Graham Motion* a111 111
4 b m Stormin Fever(USA) —Don't Trick Her (USA) (Mazel Trick (USA))
5073a[10]

Cheddar George *Peter Chapple-Hyam* a68 73
5 ch g Pivotal—Grandalea (Grand Lodge (USA))
(5015) 6916[6]

Cheeky Wee Red *Richard Fahey* a47 48
3 ch f Pastoral Pursuits—Swynford Elegance (Charmer)
4863[3] 5433[4] 5865[6] 6213[3] 6386[10] 6646[7]

Cheerful Giver (IRE) *J S Bolger* a65 82
2 b c Bachelor Duke(USA) —Aoibhneas (USA) (Dehere (USA))
4131a[7] 4257a[5] 5293a[8] 7275a[4]

Cheers *Oliver Sherwood* a58 54
3 b f Haafhd—Ziggy Zaggy (Diktat)
966[2] 7001[8] 7462[7] (7923)

Cheers Buddy (IRE) *John Joseph Hanlon* a74 84
3 b g Acclamation—Victorian Dancer (IRE) (Groom Dancer (USA))
(1663a) 7150a[12] 7710[5]

Cheers For Thea (IRE) *Tim Easterby* a91 92
6 gr m Distant Music(USA) —Popiplu (USA) (Cozzene (USA))
1114[9] 1970[2] ◆ 2217[5] 2706[8] 2933[9] 3407[7] 3757[8]

Cheery Cat (USA) *John Balding* a67 43
7 bb g Catienus(USA) —Olinka (USA) (Wolfhound (USA))
97[6] 345[6] 874[9] 1612[9]

Cheetah *Christophe Clement* a103 107
4 b m Tiger Hill(IRE) —Kassiyra (IRE) (Kendor (FR))
5073a[9]

Chef *Andrew Balding* 105
3 b g Selkirk(USA) —Ego (Green Desert (USA))
1339[6] ◆ (2705) 3405[4] 4493[2]

Chegei Has (FR) *J-P Gallorini* 102
3 b f Kahyasi—Nasou (FR) (Kaldounevees (FR))
2750a[2] 3447a[7]

Cheherazad (IRE) *Paul Cole* a66 77
3 b f Elusive City(USA) —Hawksbill Special (IRE) (Taufan (USA))
1362[2] 1853[4] 3090[6] 3577[3] 3998[3] 5368[3] 5842[2] 6407[2] 7093[2] (7389)

Chelsea Mick *John Mackie* a75 72
2 b c Hawk Wing(USA) —Chelsey Jayne (IRE) (Galileo (IRE))
4714[5] 5393[2] 5919[2] (6663) 7786[3] 7875[6]

Chemin Faisant (FR) *R Chotard* a58 64
7 b g Dyhim Diamond(IRE) —Thunder Road (FR) (Nikos)
(7015a)

Chenim (IRE) *John Best* a36
3 b g Chineur(FR) —Kenema (IRE) (Petardia)
518[7]

Cheque Book *B W Hills* a81 72
3 b f Araafa(IRE) —Black Belt Shopper (IRE) (Desert Prince (IRE))
841a[4] 1773[6] 2102[13] 2883[9]

Cherchedi (IRE) *Alan Berry* 23
2 ch f Bachelor Duke(USA) —Flaunting (IRE) (Cadeaux Genereux)
5161[8] 5618[10] 5819[10] 6449[12] 7072[12]

Cherma (USA) *J-P Delaporte* a63 66
5 b m Cherokee Run(USA) —Dharma (USA) (Zilzal (USA))
617a[4]

Cherokee Queen (USA) *Martin D Wolfson* 108
6 bb m Cherokee Run(USA) —Virginia Bee (USA) (Virginia Rapids (USA))
6719a[8]

Cherrego (USA) *Bryn Palling* a40 32
3 ch f Borrego(USA) —My Cherie (USA) (Woodman (USA))
3218[8]

Cherry Collect (IRE) *S Botti* 106
2 b f Oratorio(IRE) —Holy Moon (IRE) (Hernando (FR))
6904a[2]

Cherry Linx (IRE) *Mme C Barande-Barbe* a100 69
6 gr h Linamix(FR) —Cherry Moon (USA) (Quiet American (USA))
778a[6]

Cherry Street *Andrew Balding* a70 88
2 b c Alhaarth(IRE) —Weqaar (USA) (Red Ransom (USA))
5142[3] 5937[2] (6572) ◆

Cherry Tree Hill (IRE) *Alan Swinbank* 20
3 b g Ivan Denisovich(IRE) —Ring Pink (USA) (Bering)
2591[6] 6804[15]

Cheshire Lady (IRE) *David Barron* a52 41
4 b m Marju(IRE) —Kiris World (Distant Relative)
7924[8]

Chester Aristocrat *Eric Alston* 44
2 ch g Sakhee(USA) —New Light (Generous (IRE))
1823[9] 2214[7]

Chester Deelyte (IRE) *Lisa Williamson* a25 57
3 b f Desert Style(IRE) —Bakewell Tart (IRE) (Tagula (IRE))
1217[4] 1294[5] 1764[5] (2918) 3192[4] 3724[6] 4124[3] 4786[6] 5274[5] 5388[U] 6238[6] 6999[4] 7366[12] (7459) (7785)

Chester'Slittlegem (IRE) *Ed de Giles* a66
2 b f Atraf—Ceylon Round (FR) (Royal Applause)
7784[4] (7898)

Chevanah (IRE) *Ann Duffield* 66
2 b f Chevalier(IRE) —Omanah (USA) (Kayrawan (USA))
(1876) 2404[8] 3700[9] 4538[4] 5645[6]

Cheveton *Richard Price* a106 105
7 ch g Most Welcome—Attribute (Warning)
2075[8] 2727[10] 3155[12] 3410[10] 3846[7] 5706[4] ◆ (6145) 6332[10] 6987[12] 7295[11]

Cheveyo (IRE) *Lisa Williamson* a54 51
5 br g Celtic Swing—La Catalane (IRE) (Marju (IRE))
102[2] 185[4] 256[2] 401[2] 537[8] 691[3] 857[5] 1217[5] 1287[7] 1464[2] 1544[6] 2162[10] 2655[7] 3027[12]

Cheviot (USA) *Reginald Roberts* a70 103
5 b g Rahy(USA) —Camlet (Green Desert (USA))
3440a[2] 4135a[2] 6388a[18] 6733a[3]

Cheviot Quest (IRE) *William Jarvis* a55 62
2 ch c Sir Percy—Cushat Law (IRE) (Montjeu (IRE))
4390[11] 4682[4] 5480[7] 6102[6] 6487[6]

Chevise (IRE) *Steve Woodman* a84 80
3 b f Holy Roman Emperor(IRE) —Lipica (IRE) (Night Shift (USA))
(333) (476) (620) (1145) 2690[5] 2878[5] 3283[4] 3985[4] 4387[3] 4994[3] 5412[5] 6003[4] 6256[3] ◆ 6728[12] 7486[3] 7660[5]

Cheworee *David Elsworth* 69
2 b f Milk It Mick—Jodrell Bank (IRE) (Observatory (USA))
3362[5] 3865[2] ◆

Cheyenne Red (IRE) *Michael Herrington* a50 75
5 br g Namid—Red Leggings (Shareef Dancer (USA))
1239[11] 1712[8] 2353[9] 3036[10] 3573[12] 4782[6] 5008[2] 5436[5] 5787[4] 6208[2] (6646) 7690[3] 7853[6]

Cheylesmore (IRE) *Stuart Williams* a72 78
3 b g Kodiac—Hemaca (Distinctly North (USA))
119[3] (228) 1983[8] 2368[6] 2838[11] 3347[8] 3621[3] (3674) 3729[3] 4244[4] (4695) 5136[3] 5602[5] 5992[9] (6814) 7842[2]

Chez Vrony *Dave Morris* a60 60
5 b g Lujain(USA) —Polish Abbey (Polish Precedent (USA))
61[5] 121[4] 553[11] 675[4] 4578[9] 4927[7] 5214[7] 7437[7] 7741[6]

Chiberta King *Andrew Balding* 111
5 b g King's Best(USA) —Glam Rock (Nashwan (USA))
1717[12] 2107[4] (3120) (3647) 4469[9] 5284[10] 6271[2] 6857[10]

Chica Loca (FR) *M Figge* 102
2 ch f American Post—Comete (FR) (Jeune Homme (USA))
4596a[3] 6808a[2] 7220a[4]

Chicamia *Michael Mullineaux* a34 55
7 b m Kyllachy—Inflation (Primo Dominie)
3657[9] 4701[6] 6049[8] 6610[2] 7524[11] 7740[6]

Chicarito *John Gallagher* a58 59
2 b g Striking Ambition—Mary Jane (Tina's Pet)
5613[9] 6292[6] 6579[5] 7059[6] 7452[3]

Chicaya (FR) *F Vermeulen* a57 74
7 b m Kaldounevees(FR) —Peaceful Paradise (Turtle Island (IRE))
325a[7]

Chichen Daawe *Brian Ellison* a54 56
5 b m Daawe(USA) —Chichen Itza (Shareef Dancer (USA))
451[9] 675[8]

Chickini (IRE) *Simon Waugh* 48
6 b m Rossini(USA) —Fast Chick (Henbit (USA))
2045[7] 2432[5]

Chico Del Sol (FR) *J Rossi* a84 83
6 b g Divine Light(JPN) —Lady Flasheart (FR) (Wolfhound (USA))
3568a[4]

Chiefdom Prince (IRE) *Sir Michael Stoute* 89
4 b h Dansili—Jouet (Reprimand)
(1459) ◆ 1888[7] 4188[4]

Chief Exec *Jeremy Gask* a79 55
9 br g Zafonic(USA) —Shot At Love (IRE) (Last Tycoon)
249[4] 473[3] (685) 897[5] 1026[3] 1868[9] 2900[3] 3426[3]

Chief Hawkeye (IRE) *J-V Toux* 65
2 b c Hawk Wing(USA) —Pacy's Ridge (IRE) (Indian Ridge)
4652a[5]

Chief Of Men *Denis Coakley* a72 71
3 b g Sleeping Indian—Hidden Meaning (Cadeaux Genereux)
(1580) 2229[11] 3871[5]

Chieftess (IRE) *A P O'Brien* 91
2 ch f Mr Greeley(USA) —Cherokee (USA) (Storm Cat (USA))
4833a[8]

Chignon (IRE) *Sir Henry Cecil* a50
2 b f Dalakhani(IRE) —Fringe (In The Wings)
7396[5] 7599[9]

Chik's Dream *Derek Haydn Jones* a26 57
4 ch g Dreams End—Chik's Secret (Nalchik (USA))
202[4] 873[7] 1655[4] 2530[9] 3515[5] 3912[6] 4645[3] 5428[2] 5964[4] 6438[5] 7930[8]

Child Bride *Paul Cole* a20 73
3 b f Invincible Spirit(IRE) —Cultured Pearl (IRE) (Lammtarra (USA))
7518[7]

Child Of Our Time (IRE) *Tracy Waggott* a20 72
4 b m Oratorio(IRE) —Shariyfa (FR) (Zayyani)
1245[11] 1440[7] 2399[10] 2807[4] 3317[6] 3938[8] 4329[8] 5791[5] 7061[4] 7077[P]

Chill (IRE) *Luca Cumani* 79
3 b c Diamond Green(FR) —Time To Relax (IRE) (Orpen (USA))
2646^5 3168^2

Chilled *Sir Michael Stoute* 98
3 b g Iceman—Irresistible (Cadeaux Genereux)
(2568) 3378^7 (3649)

Chilledtothebone *Linda Stubbs* a68 63
3 ch g Iceman—Spanish Craft (IRE) (Jareer (USA))
1074^6 *1482^4* 2588^2 3309^2 3619^4 4200^2 (4728) *5631^2* 7061^5

Chillianwallah *James Unett* a42
3 ch g Primo Valentino(IRE) —Spark Up (Lahib (USA))
1015^3 1984^{13} 4505^8 *5898^7* *7851^9*

Chillie Billie *Phil McEntee* a70 70
2 ch c Piccolo—Chilly Cracker (Largesse)
1316^3 1505^6 3132^6 3388^2 3879^7 *5863^2* *6281^4* *6492^7*

Chillie Peppar *George Prodromou* a49 51
3 b g Araafa(IRE) —Obsessive (USA) (Seeking The Gold (USA))
1132^3 *1472^{10}* 3049^4 3309^6 3958^7 4162^5 4511^6 4929^{11} 5120^7 *6004^5* *7443^4* *7525^8* *7676^{10}*

Chilli Green *John Akehurst* a88 86
4 b m Desert Sun—Jade Pet (Petong)
(279) *623^3* *2000^8* 2647^8 3121^3 3536^4 ◆ 4415^{10} *7660^3* *7841^{10}*

Chill Out Charley *Ronald Harris* 6
4 b g Cyrano De Bergerac—We're Joken (Statoblest)
3094^9 3480^{11}

Chilly Filly (IRE) *Brian Ellison* a69 97
5 b m Montjeu(IRE) —Chill Seeking (USA) (Theatrical)
2071^{12} 2716^{14} 3867^{11} 4477^3 5221^2 5878^7 6172^{10}

Chilpa (FR) *P Capelle* 67
4 b m Panis(USA) —O'Tango (FR) (Fijar Tango (FR))
1740a^{10}

Chil The Kite *Hughie Morrison* 87
2 b c Notnowcato—Copy-Cat (Lion Cavern (USA))
4995^6 (5475) ◆ 6268^2

Chilworth Lad *Mick Channon* 114
3 b g Diktat—Dowhatjen (Desert Style (IRE))
1322^7 (1725) 2683^3 3067^{19} (4096) 4472^4 5474^7 (6129) (6534)

Chilworth Lass (IRE) *Mick Channon* a57 57
3 b f Imperial Dancer—Inching (Inchinor)
2722^{12}

Chimpunk (USA) *Michael Wigham* a74
5 br g Orientate(USA) —Hurry Home (USA) (Lost Soldier (USA))
(593) ◆ *914^3* *1180^4*

Chinchon (IRE) *C Laffon-Parias* 116
6 b h Marju(IRE) —Jarama (IRE) (Hector Protector (USA))
1001a^5 2340a^5

Chinese Democracy (USA) *David Evans* a64 66
4 b m Proud Citizen(USA) —Double's Lass (USA) (Mr. Leader (USA))
56^3 *210^2* *255^2* *304^8* *477^6* *544^{10}* *763^8* 1831^4 2452^8 2555^5 3512^6 4025^9 4086^2 4270^3 4434^8 4917^6

Chinese Wall (IRE) *D Guillemin* 104
3 b f Aussie Rules(USA) —Ganar El Cielo (Ashkalani (IRE))
4739a^6 5985a^7

Chink Of Light *Andrew Balding* a83 97
4 ch g Dr Fong(USA) —Isle Of Flame (Shirley Heights)
1851^5 3157^{14} 4775^8 5482^{12}

Chip Leader (FR) *R Martens* a58 50
3 b f Night Tango(GER) —Claire (IRE) (Polish Precedent (USA))
288a^0

Chipofftheoldblock *Bruce Hellier* [illegible]
[illegible] Librettist(USA) —Bettys Pride (Lion Cavern (USA))
1220^6 *1813^{10}*

Chippy *John Holt* 20
3 b g Diktat—French Mannequin (IRE) (Key Of Luck (USA))
2565^4 3080^9

Chiswick Bey (IRE) *Richard Fahey* 95
3 b g Elusive City(USA) —Victoria Lodge (IRE) (Grand Lodge (USA))
1152^6 2003^2

Chjimes (IRE) *Conor Dore* a76 79
7 b g Fath(USA) —Radiance (IRE) (Thatching)
98^2 *178^5* *264^4* *336^6* *522^5* *(654)* *698^4* *786^5* *904^3* 6932^8 7172^{11} 7395^7 7594^{10} 7942^8

Chlodan *Ollie Pears* 50
4 b g Mark Of Esteem(IRE) —Latch Key Lady (USA) (Tejano (USA))
1654^5 2457^{13} *3469^6*

Choc'A'Moca (IRE) *Paul Midgley* 72
4 b g Camacho—Dear Catch (IRE) (Bluebird (USA))
1204^3 1493^3 2247^6 (2798) (2989) 3359^{14} 3880^{17} 5468^7 6266^4 6646^8 7065^5

Chocapix (IRE) *C Le Lay* a59 53
5 gr m Refuse To Bend(IRE) —Lina Bella (FR) (Linamix (FR))
1013a^{10}

Choccywoccydoodah *James Given* a64 34
2 b f Dr Fong(USA) —Galaxy Of Stars (Observatory (USA))
7293^{12} *7559^6* *(7784)*

Chock A Block (IRE) *Saeed Bin Suroor* a94 109
5 gr g Dalakhani(IRE) —Choc Ice (IRE) (Kahyasi)
2289^{11} 3396^{12} 4354^3 4778^5 5482^7 6333^9

Chocolat Chaud (IRE) *J W Hills* 59
2 b f Excellent Art—Thaidah (CAN) (Vice Regent (CAN))
4446^7 5029^8 6776^8

Chocolate Caramel (USA) *Richard Fahey* a77 72
9 b g Storm Creek(USA) —Sandhill (BRZ) (Baynoun)
596^4 *(769)* *838^8* 1153^5 1458^{10}

Chocolate Hills (FR) *G M Lyons* a89 75
2 b f Exceed And Excel(AUS) —Rawabi (Sadler's Wells (USA))
7012a^5 ◆

Chocolicious (SAF) *H J Brown* a95 105
4 b m Kahal—Candy Box (SAF) (Exclusive Patriot (USA))
151a^4 *412a^3* 823a^2

Choice Of Remark (IRE) *David Evans* a71 82
2 ch c Choisir(AUS) —Ellanova (Kyllachy)
1042^3 1185^2 1505^3 1806^4 (1913) 3429^5 3816^8 4512^9

Choir (IRE) *A P O'Brien* 92
2 b g Danehill Dancer(IRE) —Singing Diva (IRE) (Royal Academy (USA))
3439a^4

Choisan (IRE) *Tim Easterby* 81
2 b g Choisir(AUS) —Attanagh (IRE) (Darnay)
1383^4 1797^2 3878^3 4347^9 5548^2 6187^2 6447^2 6702^2 6983^4 (7101)

Choisirez (IRE) *David Evans* 55
2 b f Choisir(AUS) —Filimeala (IRE) (Pennekamp (USA))
1185^4 1628^5 2053^3 5577^6 5844^7 6399^{10}

Choisir Shadow (IRE) *B Grizzetti* 102
2 ch f Choisir(AUS) —Mujadil Shadow (IRE) (Mujadil (USA))
7220a^9

Chokidar (IRE) *David Nicholls* a80 77
3 b g Sleeping Indian—Lola Sapola (IRE) (Benny The Dip (USA))
2255^6 3594^4 4062^3 4370^{11} 4854^P 5030^2 5821^3 *6307^2* *6653^3* *(7249)* *7579^2* *(7625)*

Chokurei (IRE) *Clive Cox* a86 91
3 b f Bertolini(USA) —Catch Us (FR) (Selkirk (USA))
(1130) 2313^5 *(2821)* (3310) 3819^2 5016^4 5657^3 (6457)

Chombo (FR) *L A Urbano-Grajales* a90 69
5 b h Diktat—Atlantique (IRE) (Alzao (USA))
661a^4

Chookie Avon *Keith Dalgleish* a77 67
4 ch g Avonbridge—Lady Of Windsor (IRE) (Woods Of Windsor (USA))
4782^4 4987^5 ◆ 5309^6 5404^6 5725^3 (5789) 6428^2 6646^{10} *7146^6* *(7175)* *7268^3* *7767^4* *7857^2*

Chookie Hamilton *Keith Dalgleish* a88 88
7 ch g Compton Place—Lady Of Windsor (IRE) (Woods Of Windsor (USA))
1036^3 1713^6 2262^{10} 3115^6 4879^9 (5149) 5724^5 6151^7 6385^3 6838^4 7162^2

Chookie Royale *Keith Dalgleish* a86 82
3 ch g Monsieur Bond(IRE) —Lady Of Windsor (IRE) (Woods Of Windsor (USA))
3977^6 (4542) ◆ 5314^{14} 6381^4 6778^2 6869^2 *(6980)*

Chooseday (IRE) *Kevin Ryan* 83
2 b g Choisir(AUS) —Break Of Day (USA) (Favorite Trick (USA))
(4047) ◆ 4891^3 5708^4 6111^3 6827^5

Choose The Moment *Eve Johnson Houghton* 68
3 b f Choisir(AUS) —Enclave (USA) (Woodman (USA))
1949^{10} 2311^3 2869^6 3818^{12} 5626^3 6070^8 (6407) 6746^8

Chopouest (FR) *A Spanu* a98 101
4 b g Indian Rocket—Free Track (FR) (Solid Illusion (USA))
5532a^0

Chopsoave (FR) *Mme C Dufreche* 100
3 ch c Soave(GER) —Moon Serenade (Key Of Luck (USA))
1552a^9

Choral *Richard Hannon* a79 78
3 b f Oratorio(IRE) —Sierra (Dr Fong (USA))
(1047) 2917^4 3310^3 4550^{15} *5718^3* *6089^3* *7334^2* [illegible]

Choral Bee *Henry Candy* 41
2 b f Oratorio(IRE) —Chief Bee (Chief's Crown (USA))
6950^{14} 7233^9

Choral Festival *John Bridger* a77 75
5 b m Pivotal—Choirgirl (Unfuwain (USA))
2372^4 2759^4 (3003) 3467^2 3771^4 4613^2 (4825) 5110^2 5509^5 5968^5 6376^9 6592^4 *7130^5* *7347^6* *7458^5* *(7601)* 7759^5 7831^2

Chorister Girl *Richard Ford* a20 51
2 b f Acclamation—Hazelhurst (IRE) (Night Shift (USA))
2113^5 2430^6 4012^5 6627^8 *7697^6*

Chorister Sport (IRE) *William Jarvis* a71
2 br c Diamond Green(FR) —Spend A Rubble (USA) (Spend A Buck (USA))
4073^{11} *7435^2* *7837^6*

Chosen Character (IRE) *Tom Dascombe* 86
3 b g Choisir(AUS) —Out Of Thanks (IRE) (Sadler's Wells (USA))
1437^3 1904^2 (2215) (2477) 3378^3 3864^{12} 5081^5 5581^5 5920^{13} 6727^7 7050^3

Chosen Forever *Geoffrey Oldroyd* a86 79
6 b g Choisir(AUS) —Forever Bond (Danetime (IRE))
235^6 *405^9* 2115^7 *6658^8* 6990^4 *(7397)* *7558^5* *7877^2*

Chosen One (IRE) *Ruth Carr* a66 76
6 ch g Choisir(AUS) —Copious (IRE) (Generous (IRE))
970^8 1073^6 1411^{14} 1539^3 1907^5 3166^{13} 3582^7 3901^5 4144^7 4678^2 4900^9 5400^{10} 5719^{12} 6076^9 6427^6 6802^{15}

Chris's Ridge *Eric Alston* a76 45
4 gr g Indian Ridge—Dundel (IRE) (Machiavellian (USA))
5341^7 5924^{13} 6479^{16}

Chrissycross (IRE) *Roger Teal* a70 58
2 b f Cape Cross(IRE) —Penang (IRE) (Xaar)
3761^6 5424^4 *5834^4* 6581^5 *7223^5* *7432^3* *(7708)* ◆

Christian Love (ITY) *R Menichetti* 101
4 b h Tout Seul(IRE) —Nicol Love (ITY) (Nicolotte)
1554a^5

Christmas Aria (IRE) *Simon Dow* a73 68
3 b c Oratorio(IRE) —Christmas Cracker (FR) (Alhaarth (IRE))
179^2 *(295)* *764^3* *1106^3* *2200^7* 2581^3 3350^6

Christmas Carnival *Michael Easterby* a79 90
4 ch g Cadeaux Genereux—Ellebanna (Tina's Pet)
1223^5 3169^9 3620^{10} 4349^{20} 5059^{14} 5441^2 5728^{10} *7771^9* *7876^9*

Christmas Coming *Tony Carroll* a69 67
4 b g Cape Cross(IRE) —Aunty Rose (IRE) (Caerleon (USA))
350^4 *448^5* *722^2* *906^{10}* *1184^4* *1486^9* 1805a^3 2900^6 *3240^8*

Christmas Light *David O'Meara* 81
4 b m Zafeen(FR) —Arabian Dancer (Dansili)
2366^6 2808^{DSQ} 3386^7 ◆ 3572^2 ◆ 3757^4 4127^3 (4440) 5062^4 5485^8 6601^8 6918^7 7061^3

Christopher Chua (IRE) *Simon Dow* 34
2 gr g Clodovil(IRE) —Pearls Of Wisdom (Kyllachy)
3388^8 4240^4

Christophers Quest *Natalie Lloyd-Beavis* a36 54
6 b g Forzando—Kaprisky (IRE) (Red Sunset)
555^{11}

Chrysanthemum (IRE) *David Wachman* 104
3 b f Danehill Dancer(IRE) —Well Spoken (IRE) (Sadler's Wells (USA))
2334a^7 3417a^3 5976a^6

Ch'Tio Bilote (FR) *J-P Gallorini* 112
3 b c Ultimately Lucky(IRE) —Neicha (FR) (Neverneyev (USA))
1965a^3 2978a^2

Chunky Diamond (IRE) *Peter Chapple-Hyam* 100
2 b c Diamond Green(FR) —Balance The Books (Elmaamul (USA))
1360^5 1721^5 (3915) 4413^{13} (5701) 6518^6 7019^2

Church Music (IRE) *Michael Scudamore* 85
2 b c Amadeus Wolf—Cappella (IRE) (College Chapel)
(2886) ◆ 3773^7 4413^{10} 5286^8 6518^9

Churriana (IRE) *Mlle A Voraz* a87 89
6 gr m Anabaa(USA) —Souvenir Souvenir (Highest Honor (FR))
195a^4

Ciara Boo (IRE) *David Evans* a37 49
2 b f Red Clubs(IRE) —National Ballet (Shareef Dancer (USA))
982^4 1136^5 1435^2 2362^7 3955^5 *4178^4* 7108^5 *7342^{11}* *7568^9*

Ciboney Moon (FR) *Alex Fracas* a78 78
8 b g Bahamian Bounty—Lunevision (FR) (Solid Illusion (USA))
93a^4

Cilium (IRE) *Jeffrey Ian Mulhern* a80 93
5 b m War Chant(USA) —Venturi (Danehill Dancer (IRE))
1119a^2 2012a^8 2325a^8

Cill Rialaig *Hughie Morrison* a98 108
6 gr m Environment Friend—Pang Valley Girl (Rock Hopper)
4582^3 5285^{10} 5839a^3 6269^3 6859^6 *7129^3*

Cils Blancs (IRE) *Jane Chapple-Hyam* a10 53
5 b m Barathea(IRE) —Immortelle (Arazi (USA))
2820^{11} 3636^8

Cima De Pluie *B Grizzetti* 104
4 b g Singspiel(IRE) —Grey Way (USA) (Cozzene (USA))
(1554a) 2134a^4 2982a^9 6202a^6

Cinarosa (IRE) *Francis Ennis* a65 72
3 b f Kodiac—Inter Madera (IRE) (Toca Madera)
1663a^8

Cincinnati Kit *Stuart Williams* a53 58
2 b f Cape Cross(IRE) —Princess Georgina (Royal Applause)
5834^9 6480^5 *7583^5* *7830^8*

Cinderella [illegible] a40 12
4 ch m Zafeen(FR) —Flighty Dancer (Pivotal)
993^7 *1171^U* *1331^7* *1815^{10}* 3293^{12} *3713^9*

Cinderkamp *Edward Vaughan* a80 100
3 b c Kyllachy—Topkamp (Pennekamp (USA))
2199^7 (2736) (4048) 4333^3 5481^8 5935^9

Cinematique (IRE) *Laura Mongan* a18
3 b g King's Theatre(IRE) —Chantoue Royale (FR) (Cadoudal (FR))
3980^8 *4800^{12}*

Cinq Heavens (IRE) *Tom Dascombe* a50 47
3 b g Chevalier(IRE) —Prime Site (IRE) (Burslem)
426^6 *550^7*

Cinta *Marco Botti* a75 72
3 b f Monsun(GER) —Night Year (IRE) (Jareer (USA))
1251^2 1722^7 3133^5

Circle Of Angels *Ian Williams* a56 75
3 b f Royal Applause—City Of Angels (Woodman (USA))
2802^4 (3037) 3486^5 3904^6 6295^{11} 6756^7 6894^4 *7255^7* *7603^{10}*

Circuitous *Keith Dalgleish* a66 62
3 b g Fasliyev(USA) —Seren Devious (Dr Devious (IRE))
1900^4 2141^3 2611^6 *2818^{11}* 3272^8 5208^9 5490^{12} (5619) *5864^4* *6696^5* *6999^2* *7266^4* *7366^9* *7560^7* 7690^{10}

Circumvent *Paul Cole* a107 112
4 ch g Tobougg(IRE) —Seren Devious (Dr Devious (IRE))
3107^{10} 3645^{10} 4100^6 4410^9 4774^2 5275^6 (5940) 6339^6 6672^4 7029^6 *7391^2* *7802^{12}*

Circus Act *Mahmood Al Zarooni* 68
3 b c Cape Cross(IRE) —Carry On Katie (USA) (Fasliyev (USA))
1620^3 2203^3 2835^6

Circus Clown (IRE) *Jim Goldie* 66
6 b g Vettori(IRE) —Comic (IRE) (Be My Chief (USA))
(4785) 5166^2 5790^3

Circus Master *James Eustace* a36 37
3 b g Kyllachy—Alegria (Night Shift (USA))
2174^{14} 2825^4 *3175^7*

Circus Mondao (USA) *Mahmood Al Zarooni* a72 76
2 b g Hard Spun(USA) —Dominique's Show (USA) (Theatrical)
6462^3 ◆ *7094^3*

Circus Polka (USA) *Owen Brennan* a49
7 br g Stravinsky(USA) —Far Wiser (USA) (Private Terms (USA))
6135^8 *6494^{10}* *6871^6* 7077^{13} *7426^8*

Circus Star (USA) *Brian Meehan* a72 75
3 b g Borrego(USA) —Picadilly Circus (USA) (Fantastic Fellow (USA))
1572^2 2076^5 2874^{11} 3366^2 3919^8 4489^6 5014^{13} 6990^{18}

Cirrus Des Aigles (FR) *Mme C Barande-Barbe* a112 130
5 b g Even Top(IRE) —Taille De Guepe (FR) (Septieme Ciel (USA))
920a^2 1708a^3 2343a^2 (3008a) 3448a^2 (4223a) (5094a) (5531a) 6558a^2 (6861) 7732a^5

Citizen's Charter (USA) *Mahmood Al Zarooni* 76
2 b c Proud Citizen(USA) —Outsource (USA) (Storm Bird (CAN))
(3314) 3776^4 4760^3 5755^7

Citrus Star (USA) *Chris Wall* a105 107
4 b g Broken Vow(USA) —Twist A Lime (USA) (Copelan (USA))
1720^{21} 2679^8 4802^{11} 5474^{15} 5887^5 6341^6 *(7127)* ◆ *7433^4*

Cityar (FR) *John O'Shea* a42
7 b g Sagacity(FR) —Starry Dust (FR) (Zino)
222^5

Citybell (IRE) *Richard Fahey* a57 60
2 b f Elusive City(USA) —Bella Vie (IRE) (Sadler's Wells (USA))
4283^4 *4848^2* 5286^{10}

City Dazzler (IRE) *Richard Hannon* 64
2 b f Elusive City(USA) —Shady Nook (IRE) (Key Of Luck (USA))
4052^8 4545^3 5959^3 6196a^{11} 6950^{11}

City Leader (IRE) *Brian Meehan* 114
6 gr h Fasliyev(USA) —Kanmary (FR) (Kenmare (FR))
1600^5 (2290) 5094a^7 6519^7

City Legend *Alan McCabe* a71 80
3 b g Lucky Story(USA) —Urban Calm (Cadeaux Genereux)
(109) *140^3* *887^2* (1169) 1329^5 1653^5 1916^2 2147^2 2319^2 2564^8 2684^8 3649^{12} 3830^8 *6980^{11}* *7097^9* *7348^8* (7518) 7807^4

City Of The Kings (IRE) *Ollie Pears* a83 95
6 b g Cape Cross(IRE) —Prima Volta (Primo Dominie)
1410^{15} 2124^3 (3051) 5557^{13} 6672^{13}

Cityscape *Roger Charlton* 123
5 ch h Selkirk(USA) —Tantina (USA) (Distant View (USA))
1527^2 3009^3 5129a^8 (5977a) 6369a^2 (7193a) 7731a^2

City Stable (IRE) *Michael Wigham* a77 67
6 b g Machiavellian(USA) —Rainbow City (IRE) (Rainbow Quest (USA))
245^3 *261^4* *393^8* *742^5* *872^4*

City Style (USA) *Mahmood Al Zarooni* a103 105
5 ch g City Zip(USA) —Brattothecore (CAN) (Katahaula County (CAN))
236^8 *(326a)*

Claiomh Solais (IRE) *J S Bolger* 110
3 ch f Galileo(IRE) —Scribonia (IRE) (Danehill (USA))
1779a^5 2334a^4 3106^9 3417a^4 3527a^2 4132a^3 5228a^3

Clairvoyance (IRE) *H-A Pantall* a93 104
4 b m Shamardal(USA) —Crystal View (IRE) (Imperial Ballet (IRE))
[illegible] 7221a^0 7534a^0

Clanachy *George Foster* 28
5 b m Kyllachy—Antonia's Dream (Clantime)
5793^{10} 6386^{14}

Clapped *Edward Vaughan* a47 36
2 b g Royal Applause—Susun Kelapa (USA) (St Jovite (USA))
6300^{11} *6697^{11}* 7292^{15}

Clara De Lune (FR) *C Boutin* 43
2 b f Bleu D'Altair(FR) —Lidawar (FR) (Sendawar (IRE))
6925a^0

Clara Zetkin *J S Moore* 75
3 b f Elusive City(USA) —Pantita (Polish Precedent (USA))
1155^2 (1436) (2043) 2468^{11} 4353^8

Clare Glen (IRE) *Sarah Dawson* a89 93
5 b m Sakhee(USA) —Desert Grouse (USA) (Gulch (USA))
6514a^5

Clare Island Boy (IRE) *Richard Hannon* 82
2 ch c Strategic Prince—Tea Chest (IRE) (In The Wings)
3609^8 (4213) 4717^2 6031^2

Claremont (IRE) *Mahmood Al Zarooni* 113
5 b h Sadler's Wells(USA) —Mezzo Soprano (USA) (Darshaan)
154a^{11} 329a^5 (584a) 826a^{10} 5045^9

Claretintheblood (IRE) *Richard Fahey* a58 57
2 b c Elusive City(USA) —River Abouali (Bluebird (USA))
5398^{10} 6259^4 *6654^{10}* *7143^3* 7294^{12} *7452^9* *7692^6* *(7770)*

Clarion Call *Eve Johnson Houghton* a67 73
3 b g Beat Hollow—Fanfare (Deploy)
983^3 *1484^6* *1998^4* 3676^2 ◆ 4385^8 4845^3 5420^3 *5630^9*

Clarkson (IRE) *Jamie Osborne* a54 65
2 b g Jeremy(USA) —Gold Marie (IRE) (Green Desert (USA))
2644^7 2997^5 *3221^3* 3810^9 4226^3 4658^3 *7780^8*

Clasp *Doug Watson* a95 98
9 ch g Singspiel(IRE) —Embrace Me (Nashwan (USA))
157a^6 332a^{12} *585a^8*

Class Attraction (IRE) *Mme C Barande-Barbe* a69 72
7 b m Act One—She's All Class (USA) (Rahy (USA))
42a[5] 566a[7] 903a[5] 1142a[3]

Classical Air *John Dunlop* 23
3 b f Dubai Destination(USA) —Claxon (Caerleon (USA))
3550[6]

Classical Chloe *Richard Guest* 30
3 b f Sleeping Indian—Mana Pools (IRE) (Brief Truce (USA))
3191[6] 5598[11] 5792[13]

Classically (IRE) *Peter Hedger* a82 71
5 b g Indian Haven—Specifically (USA) (Sky Classic (CAN))
175[5] 381[5] (484) 963[3] 1443[13] 2021[4] 2436[8] 3042[5] 4763[4] 5178[13] 6005[4] 6254[2] 6507[9] 7513[7] 7651[12] 7831[8]

Classic Blade (IRE) *Doug Watson* a95 94
5 b h Daggers Drawn(USA) —Queen Bodicea (IRE) (Revoque (IRE))
239[5] 587a[7]

Classic Colori (IRE) *David O'Meara* a90 99
4 b g Le Vie Dei Colori—Beryl (Bering)
1824[6] ◆ 2509[6] 3542[4] 5593[3] 6302[2] 6496[5] 7029[8] 7391[8]

Classic Contours (USA) *Tracy Waggott* 70
5 b g Najran(USA) —What's Up Kittycat (USA) (Tabasco Cat (USA))
1039[6] 1617[5]

Classic Descent *Ruth Carr* a77 67
6 b g Auction House(USA) —Polish Descent (IRE) (Danehill (USA))
1077[8] 1150[2] 1373[5] 1613[3] 1857[4] 2348[9] 2815[2] (3088) 3462[4] 4143[4] 4852[11] 4946[7] 5441[5] 5721[10] 6098[4] 6453[9]

Classic Falcon (IRE) *William Haggas* a60 44
2 ch f Dubawi(IRE) —Livius Lady (IRE) (Titus Livius (FR))
5514[11] 6274[4] 6946[4]

Classic Punch (IRE) *David Elsworth* a109 108
8 b g Mozart(IRE) —Rum Cay (USA) (Our Native (USA))
2933[13] 3406[5] 4331[4] (4801) 5711[5] 6277[8] 7170[3]

Classic Vintage (USA) *Amanda Perrett* 100
5 b g El Prado(IRE) —Cellars Shiraz (USA) (Kissin Kris (USA))
2289[8] (2812) 3625[7] 4532[7] 4778[6] 5250[13] (5963) 7297[5]

Classic Voice (IRE) *Roy Brotherton* a74 71
3 b g Oratorio(IRE) —Pearly Brooks (Efisio)
1400[2] 1611[2] 1904[5] (2652) 3133[13] 4009[6] 4664[7]

Class Is Class (IRE) *Sir Michael Stoute* 118
5 b g Montjeu(IRE) —Hector's Girl (Hector Protector (USA))
2290[2] (3591) 4345[4] (4789)

Classlin *Jim Goldie* 52
4 b m Bertolini(USA) —Class Wan (Safawan)
2412[9] 3662[14] 3901[8] 4144[6] 4379[11] 4564[3] 4881[13] 5009[3] 5437[4] 6076[17] 6208[14]

Class Monitor *Mrs K Burke* a53 67
2 b f Indesatchel(IRE) —First Tarf (Primo Dominie)
(4147) 4502[5] 5591[3] 5896[7] 6628[2] 7275a[10] 7539[3] 7814a[2]

Classy Lass *Derek Shaw* a19
2 b f Trade Fair—Kythia (IRE) (Kahyasi)
7368[10] 7540[10] 7783[10] 7915[8]

Classy Strike (IRE) *Richard Hannon* 22
2 b c Oratorio(IRE) —Goldster (IRE) (Intikhab (USA))
3408[9] 4708[6]

Clavis (FR) *Mme J Bidgood* a82 89
3 b g Super Celebre(FR) —La Clef Des Songes (FR) (Sky Lawyer (FR))
882a[3]

Clean Bowled (IRE) *Alan McCabe* a62 56
2 b g Footstepsinthesand—Miznapp (Pennekamp (USA))
2767[14] 3282[5] 3780[9] 4907[3] 5413[4] 5783[7] 7875[5]

Clear Ice (IRE) *Gay Kelleway* a73 79
4 gr g Verglas(IRE) —Mynu Girl (IRE) (Charnwood Forest (IRE))
321[2] 538[3] 1029[2] 1287[6] 1501[2] 1907[2] 1968[2] 2048[8] (2238) 3307[3] 3617[3] 3711[5] 4041[4] 4395[2] (4659) (4742) 5053[18] 5173[4] 5578[2] ◆ 6036[7] 6815[7] 7893[11]

Clearing House *John Ryan* a66 59
6 ch g Zamindar(USA) —Easy Option (IRE) (Prince Sabo)
574[6] (722) 748[4] (906) 950[2] 969[6] 1184[2] 1333[5] 1486[10] 1570[5] 1995[9] 2386[2] 2642[3] 2922[4]

Clearly Silver (SAF) *M F De Kock* a93 100
5 b g Silvano(GER) —Clear Up (ZIM) (Goldkeeper (USA))
152a[3] 327a[9] 497a[6]

Clear Praise (USA) *Simon Dow* a90 80
4 b g Songandaprayer(USA) —Pretty Clear (USA) (Mr Prospector (USA))
134[3] (316) 651[4] 1197[3] 1720[16] 3765[4] ◆ 4239[4] 4765[9] 5578[8] 7675[6] 7941[7]

Clear Sailing *Noel Quinlan* a69 51
8 b g Selkirk(USA) —Welsh Autumn (Tenby)
835[9] 948[7] 1174[5] 1608[11]

Clear Spring (IRE) *John Spearing* a19 41
3 b c Chineur(FR) —Holly Springs (Efisio)
7260[7] 7585[9] 7750[6]

Clerical (USA) *Robert Cowell* a61 61
5 b g Yes It's True(USA) —Clerical Etoile (ARG) (The Watcher (USA))
3556[5] 3956[8] 4683[7] 5355[5] 6105[9] 6619[3] 7429[8] 7655[9]

Clever Omneya (USA) *J R Jenkins* a70 36
5 ch m Toccet(USA) —Clever Empress (Crafty Prospector (USA))
397[2] 4183[3] (4651)

Clianthus *Paul Cole* 22
2 b c Authorized(IRE) —Miss Queen (USA) (Miswaki (USA))
4968[12]

Cliffords Reprieve *Eric Wheeler* a66 55
3 b g Kheleyf(USA) —Bijan (IRE) (Mukaddamah (USA))
3433[6] 3999[5] 4224[5] 4684[4] 6398[9] 6619[2] 6943[3] 7366[2] 7511[2] 7649[4] (7829)

Clifton Bridge *Peter Grayson* a82 79
4 b g Avonbridge—Ambitious (Ardkinglass)
84[5] 215[6] 1309[7]

Climaxfortackle (IRE) *Derek Shaw* a71 71
3 b f Refuse To Bend(IRE) —Miss Asia Quest (Rainbow Quest (USA))
1472[4] 1952[4] 2163[2] ◆ 2818[4] 3079[4] 3470[3] 3635[3] 4359[5] 5121[4] (5392) 5856[2] 6093[9] 6383[10] 6830[3] 6990[8]

Clinical *Sir Mark Prescott Bt* a105 105
3 gr f Motivator—Doctor's Glory (USA) (Elmaamul (USA))
2678[3] 3106[12] 4915[7] (6394a) (7128) (7277a) 7516[3]

Clipthorne *Ollie Pears* 70
3 gr f Ivan Denisovich(IRE) —Dim Ofan (Petong)
1967[7]

Clockmaker (IRE) *Tim Easterby* a101 95
5 b g Danetime(IRE) —Lady Ingabelle (IRE) (Catrail (USA))
3877[17] 4325[2] ◆ 4609[12] 6326[10] 6672[15] (7074) 7295[17] (7628) 7801[3] ◆

Clodhopper (IRE) *Jamie Osborne* a31 39
2 bb f Clodovil(IRE) —Clochette (IRE) (Namaqualand (USA))
3257[12] 4225[4] 4648[6]

Clon Brulee (IRE) *David Barron* a39 66
2 ch g Modigliani(USA) —Cloneden (IRE) (Definite Article)
6448[4] 7101[4] 7367[7]

Clone Devil (IRE) *Alastair Lidderdale* a49
2 gr g Clodovil(IRE) —Mrs Willy Nilly (Timeless Times (USA))
2559[14] 3816[14] 4068[10] 4995[15] 5144[5] 5409[2] 5597[10] 6001[11]

Clonusker (IRE) *Linda Jewell* a32 40
3 b g Fasliyev(USA) —Tamburello (IRE) (Roi Danzig (USA))
437[9] 663[8] 953[6] 1137[5] 1933[14] 2305[7]

Close To The Edge (IRE) *Alan McCabe* a87 87
3 b f Iffraaj—Iktidar (Green Desert (USA))
36[2] 119[4] 182[2] 422[6] (1624) 1980[2] 2765[2] (3207) 3598[3] 4156[7] 4817[3] (5862) 6094[4] 6495[7] 7602[4] 7846[2] 7926[5]

Cloth Ears *Phil McEntee* a63 58
5 b m Fraam—Estimada (Mark Of Esteem (IRE))
1816[5] 2303[4] 3367[8] 4189[5] 5865[9] 5997[3] 6238[3] 6619[5] 6943[7] 7086[4] 7230[10]

Cloud Cuckooland (IRE) *James Given* 47
2 ch f Dr Fong(USA) —High Barn (Shirley Heights)
5161[6] 5819[9] 6278[5] 6911[9]

Cloudgazer (IRE) *Noel Meade* a77 79
3 b g Dalakhani(IRE) —City Zone (IRE) (Zafonic (USA))
7378a[5]

Cloud Illusions (USA) *Heather Main* a78 83
3 rg f Smarty Jones(USA) —Ilusoria (USA) (Maria's Mon (USA))
(2018) ◆ 2506[6] 3648[6] 3982[8] 5113[9] 7361[4] 7486[7] 7558[7]

Cloud Man (USA) *John Shirreffs* 106
3 ch c Thunder Gulch(USA) —Kaydara (USA) (Kris S (USA))
7572a[P]

Cloud Rock *Peter Chapple-Hyam* a75 91
3 b g Tiger Hill(IRE) —Tambourin (Halling (USA))
1688[7] 2684[5] 3634[11] 5119[2] (5516)

Cloud's End *Robert Cowell* a82 82
4 b m Dubawi(IRE) —Kangra Valley (Indian Ridge)
1762[2] 2122[10] 4101[3] 4556[13] 6094[7] 6491[10]

Clouds Of Glory *Ron Hodges*
2 b f Resplendent Glory(IRE) —Rosewings (In The Wings)
6252[10] 6892[8] 7196[10]

Cloudy Bay (USA) *John Flint* a77 78
4 b g Tiznow(USA) —Heart That Matters (USA) (Carson City (USA))
448[3] 842a[0] 1033a[3] 1278[3] 1538[2] 1879[6] 2708[8] 3051[5] 3716[2] 4385[10] 5389[10] 6656[8] 7203[9]

Cloudy Spirit *Reg Hollinshead* a62 58
6 gr m Silver Patriarch(IRE) —Miss Lacroix (Picea)
7053[6] 7630[3]

Cloudy Start *Jamie Osborne* a103 93
5 b g Oasis Dream—Set Fair (USA) (Alleged (USA))
2441[9] 2955[5] 3982[9] 4432[8] 4887[4] 5340[5] 6023[10] 6769[4] 7461[9] 7603[6] 7756[6]

Clowance *Roger Charlton* 116
6 b m Montjeu(IRE) —Freni (GER) (Sternkoenig (IRE))
2680[3]

Clowance Keys *Rod Millman* 29
2 b g High Chaparral(IRE) —Seasons Parks (Desert Prince (IRE))
3424[11]

Cluain Alainn (IRE) *Ian Williams* a78 70
5 b g Dalakhani(IRE) —Josh's Pearl (IRE) (Sadler's Wells (USA))
2259[5] 3978[8]

Cluain Dara (IRE) *Mark Johnston* a77 74
3 b f Hawk Wing(USA) —Act Of The Pace (IRE) (King's Theatre (IRE))
2871[6] 3214[3] (4180) 4677[5] 5966[9]

Cluain Meala (USA) *Susan Cooney*
2 b f Service Stripe(USA) —Honey's Sky (USA) (Sky Classic (CAN))
6205a[5]

Club Oceanic *Jeremy Noseda* a85 107
3 b g Cape Cross(IRE) —My Lass (Elmaamul (USA))
1175[3] (2188) (2877) ◆ 3774[10] (4331) 5185[3] (5853)

Clueless *Keith Dalgleish* a33 60
9 b g Royal Applause—Pure (Slip Anchor)
4602[9] 4785[2] 5167[6] 5651[9]

Clumber Place *Richard Guest* a64 80
5 ch m Compton Place—Inquirendo (USA) (Roberto (USA))
2398[2] 3026[4] 3113[2] 5255[14] 5551[5] 5970[8] 6869[4] 7076[5]

C'Mon You Irons (IRE) *Mark Hoad* a80 71
6 b g Orpen(USA) —Laissez Faire (IRE) (Tagula (IRE))
1770[4] 2879[2] 3412[9] 4795[6] 7529[11] 7834[7]

Cnocandancer (IRE) *T Stack* 88
4 ch m Danehill Dancer(IRE) —Dancing Diva (FR) (Sadler's Wells (USA))
5748a[18]

Coach Montana (IRE) *Jane Chapple-Hyam* a53 55
2 b g Proud Citizen(USA) —Market Day (Tobougg (IRE))
1360[9] 2395[7] 3282[6] 3780[11] 5342[8] (6101) 6937[9] 7223[4] 7432[4] 7763[7]

Coalburn *Gary Harrison* 38
3 ch g Captain Rio—Pusey Street Girl (Gildoran)
4461[6] 5377[5] 5780[7]

Coalport (USA) *Wayne Catalano* 103
2 ch c Kitten's Joy(USA) —Ballade's Girl (USA) (Saint Ballado (CAN))
7301a[11]

Coastal Passage *John Balding* a64
3 b g Ishiguru(USA) —Ellcon (IRE) (Royal Applause)
6615[2] 6874[2] 7245[5] 7420[10] 7648[13] 7911[8]

Coax *Patrick Holmes* a62 75
3 b g Red Ransom(USA) —True Glory (IRE) (In The Wings)
1031[4] (1749) 2188[5] 2550[4] 3124[2] 3337[5] 3508[7] 5725[10]

Cobbs Quay *John Gosden* 87
3 b g Danehill Dancer(IRE) —Rave Reviews (IRE) (Sadler's Wells (USA))
1542[3] 2258[5] 5482[14] 5938[7]

Cobo Bay *Linda Stubbs* a83 89
6 b g Primo Valentino(IRE) —Fisher Island (IRE) (Sri Pekan (USA))
31[4] 170[5] 282[3] 457[2] (742) 835[6] 1977[4] 2235[3] 2656[5] 3716[3] 4920[6] 6918[11]

Cochabamba (IRE) *Roger Teal* a98 100
3 ch f Hurricane Run(IRE) —Bolivia (USA) (Distant View (USA))
1404[6] 3648[5] 4497[12] 5277[8] 5481[6] 6272[3] 6531[9] 7392[4] 7578[8]

Cockney Class (USA) *Brian Meehan* a96 98
4 rg g Speightstown(USA) —Snappy Little Cat (USA) (Tactical Cat (USA))
991[5]

Cockney Dancer *Charles Hills* 83
2 ch f Cockney Rebel(IRE) —Roo (Rudimentary (USA))
(5323) ◆ 5849[15] 6296[9]

Cockney Fire *David Evans* 80
2 ch f Cockney Rebel(IRE) —Camp Fire (IRE) (Lahib (USA))
(1396) (1726) 4999[7] 5656[10] 6535[18] 7019[9]

Cockney Rhyme *Heather Main* a71 76
2 b f Cockney Rebel(IRE) —Regent's Park (Green Desert (USA))
6818[5] 6984[3] 7164[3] 7454[2]

Cockney Rocker *Jane Chapple-Hyam* a75 69
2 br c Cockney Rebel(IRE) —Fur Will Fly (Petong)
2318[3] ◆ 2767[8] 3349[3] 6064[5] (7653)

Cocktail Charlie *Tim Easterby* 97
3 b g Danbird(AUS) —Royal Punch (Royal Applause)
1241[5] 1711[2] 2934[2] 3820[6] 5288[10] 5758[15] 6347[7] 6865[4] 7018[13]

Cocktail Party (IRE) *James Unett* a56 54
5 b m Acclamation—Irish Moss (USA) (Irish River (FR))
362[7] 690[6] 752[5] 941[6] 1247[2]

Coco Demure (IRE) *A Candi* 90
3 b f Titus Livius(FR) —Alma Thomas (IRE) (Orpen (USA))
1738a[7]

Cocohatchee *Pat Phelan* 77
3 b c Avonbridge—Chilly Cracker (Largesse)
2646[9] 3122[3] 3798[5] 4238[2] 4459[5] 5892[12]

Coco Rouge (IRE) *Walter Swinburn* a73 67
3 ch f Shamardal(USA) —Coquette Rouge (IRE) (Croco Rouge (IRE))
1759[4] 2157[5]

Cocozza (USA) *John M Oxx* 103
3 b c Elusive Quality(USA) —Watership Crystal (IRE) (Sadler's Wells (USA))
4831a[5]

Coda Agency *Brendan Powell* a74 55
8 b g Agnes World(USA) —The Frog Lady (IRE) (Al Hareb (USA))
(131) 393[7] 1148[2] 1761[8] 3738[14] 5692[10] 6121[10]

Code Cracker *Sir Mark Prescott Bt* a59 65
2 b f Medicean—Confidential Lady (Singspiel (IRE))
4245[3] 4632[3] 4992[5]

Co Dependent (USA) *Jamie Osborne* a76 34
5 ch g Cozzene(USA) —Glowing Breeze (USA) (Southern Halo (USA))
199[3] (345) 820[6] 904[4] 985[3] 1314[2] 1562[14] 2426[9] 3019[7] 3713[3] 3953[8] 4182[9] 4990[4] 6056[2] ◆ 6491[7] 6793[8] 7349[5]

Code Six (IRE) *Bryan Smart* a65 60
2 gr f Kodiac—Grey Pursuit (IRE) (Pursuit Of Love)
6045[6] 6800[2] (7267)

Coedmor Boy *John Flint* a46 43
3 b g Leporello(IRE) —Denise Best (IRE) (Goldmark (USA))
2964[13]

Coeur De Perle (FR) *Y De Nicolay* a63
2 b f Touch Of The Blues(FR) —Romantic Pearl (FR) (Kahyasi)
7449a[0]

Coeus *Sir Mark Prescott Bt* a87 100
3 gr g Ishiguru(USA) —Lady Georgia (Arazi (USA))
1688[2] ◆ 1844[4] 3181[3] (3820)

Cogito Ergo Sum (ITY) *Frank Sheridan* a27
6 b g Dashing Blade—Sopran Danys (IRE) (Dancing Dissident (USA))
6286[8]

Coin Box *Mahmood Al Zarooni* a69 45
3 b f Dubai Destination(USA) —Small Change (IRE) (Danzig (USA))
2174[7] 2821[7]

Coin Of The Realm (IRE) *Gary Moore* a78 104
6 b g Galileo(IRE) —Common Knowledge (Rainbow Quest (USA))
1717[9] 2716[7] 3156[8]

Colamandis *Hugh McWilliams* a57 53
4 b m Lucky Story(USA) —Merry Mary (Magic Ring (IRE))
65[3] 345[8] 517[2] 734[12] 1216[13] 2352[4] 2548[8] 3142[6] 3905[8] 4813[7] 6266[15] 7411[6] 7462[9] 7696[10]

Colbyor *Richard Fahey* a68 68
2 ch g Orientor—College Maid (IRE) (College Chapel)
5398[9] 7072[2] 7267[2]

Cold Blow Den *Jim Boyle* 3
2 b c Piccolo—Den's-Joy (Archway (IRE))
4087[11] 4722[9]

Cold Case (FR) *F-X De Chevigny* a69 71
3 gr f Slickly(FR) —Miss Balines (FR) (Grape Tree Road)
7016a[7]

Cold Quest (USA) *Linda Perratt* a86 63
7 b g Seeking The Gold(USA) —Polaire (IRE) (Polish Patriot (USA))
1520[10] 2692[12] 3110[8] 3454[11] 4143[10] 4383[3] 4501[3] 4783[9] 5402[5] 5725[12]

Cold Secret *David Elsworth* a70 50
3 ch c Iceman—Dance Sequence (USA) (Mr Prospector (USA))
313[2] 559[7] 811[4] 1611[9] 2673[7]

Colebrooke *Mark Johnston* a69 71
3 b g Shamardal(USA) —Shimna (Mr Prospector (USA))
510[3] 657[2] 866[3] 1189[3] 1475[4]

Colima (IRE) *Ralph Beckett* 80
2 b f Authorized(IRE) —Coyote (Indian Ridge)
(7232) ◆

Colinca's Lad (IRE) *Peter Charalambous* a65 72
9 b g Lahib(USA) —Real Flame (Cyrano De Bergerac)
2268[3] 3130[7] (4165) (4385) (5110) 5328[9] 5356[2] 6241[4] 7203[2] 7528[2] 7805[4]

Collaborate (IRE) *Andrew Balding* a65
3 b g Librettist(USA) —Impassion (FR) (In The Wings)
4991[8] 6668[3]

Collateral Damage (IRE) *Tim Easterby* a92 98
8 b g Orpen(USA) —Jay Gee (IRE) (Second Set (IRE))
1240[7] 1694[15] 1849[8] 2123[12] 2495[3] 2783[7] 3169[4] 3315[7] 3620[6]

Collect Art (IRE) *Andrew Haynes* a72 93
4 b g Footstepsinthesand—Night Scent (IRE) (Scenic)
139[3] 248[8] 433[3] 633[4] (933) (1307) 1355[2] 1771[3] 1838[2] (2016) 2095[3] (2244) 2497[2] (2794) (2826) 2938[2] 3535[7] 3784[2] 3846[6] 3996[6]

Colliers Castle (IRE) *Lisa Williamson* a59 29
5 b m Karinga Bay—Aneeza (IRE) (Charnwood Forest (IRE))
4611[7] 5140[4] 5386[4] 6121[5] 6476[9]

Collingwood (IRE) *T M Walsh* a93 92
9 br g Machiavellian(USA) —Almaaseh (IRE) (Dancing Brave (USA))
3440a[3] 4135a[7] 4566a[10] 5746a[10] 7010a[4]

Colloquial *Henry Candy* a90 98
10 b g Classic Cliche(IRE) —Celia Brady (Last Tycoon)
1729[6] 2499[P] (3794) 6499[4]

Colombian (IRE) *John Gosden* 117
3 b c Azamour(IRE) —Clodora (FR) (Linamix (FR))
1409[3] (1810) ◆ 2751a[4] 4376a[3] ◆ 5128a[4] 5987a[4] 7053[2] (7313a)

Colonel Flay *Nerys Dutfield* a66 63
7 ch g Danehill Dancer(IRE) —Bobbie Dee (Blakeney)
6476[13]

Colonel Henry *Simon Dow* a46
4 br g Imperial Dancer—Spark Of Life (Rainbows For Life (CAN))
207[8]

Colonel Mak *David Barron* 106
4 br g Makbul—Colonel's Daughter (Colonel Collins (USA))
1111[10] 1720[9] 2727[13] 3155[10] 3440a[10] 4042[2] ◆ 4534[22] 5060[6] (5430) ◆ 6147[4] 6706[17]

Colonel Sherman (USA) *Philip Kirby* a65 54
6 bb h Mr Greeley(USA) —Spankin 'n Fannin (USA) (Lear Fan (USA))
897[11] 1372[4] 1956[5] 2462[11] 2820[3] 3225[5] (3923) 4868[2] 5249[3] 5651[5]

Colonel Whitmore (IRE) *E J O'Neill* 71
2 b g Zamindar(USA) —Welcome Band (Dixieland Band (USA))
7664a[0]

Colonial (IRE) *Saeed Bin Suroor* a110 112
4 b h Cape Cross(IRE) —Elizabeth Bay (USA) (Mr Prospector (USA))
156a[4] 415a[8] 682a[12] 4003[5] 4554[3] 5032[4] (5563) 6129[2] 6534[5]

Colonial Harry *Neil Mulholland*
4 b g Sir Harry Lewis(USA) —Shaadin (USA) (Sharpen Up)
7565[9]

Colonsay (USA) *Mahmood Al Zarooni* 59
2 b c Kingmambo(USA) —Danelagh (AUS) (Danehill (USA))
5447[10] 6019[6]

Colony (IRE) *M bin Shafya* a91 92
6 b h Statue Of Liberty(USA) —Funoon (IRE) (Kris)
153a[6]

Colorado Gold *Ed de Giles* a83 85
3 ch g Dubawi(IRE) —Yanka (USA) (Blushing John (USA))
2834[8] 3351[7] 4342[4] (5412) 6167[15] 6478[11]

Colorful Notion (IRE) *Marco Botti* a80 77
2 b f Danehill Dancer(IRE) —Red Yellow Blue (USA) (Sky Classic (CAN))
2302[4] 2606[3] (3342) ◆ 7445[2] ◆ 7799[3]

Colori D'Amore *Derek Shaw*
2 b f Le Vie Dei Colori—Muscida (USA) (Woodman (USA))
5117[9]

Colorus (IRE) *Bill Ratcliffe* a84 75
8 b g Night Shift(USA) —Duck Over (Warning)
294[7] 453[2] 506[4] 571[3] 658[5]

Colourbearer (IRE) *Milton Bradley* a79 68
4 ch g Pivotal—Centifolia (FR) (Kendor (FR))
1459[6] 1589[6] 1984[9] 2603[10] 2869[7] 3216[6] 4272[2] 4930[3] (5244) 5534[2] (5600) 5677[6] 5846[3] (6655) 7039[8] 7356[3]

Colourful Event (IRE) *David Arbuthnot* a56 56
2 b f Baltic King—Terra Nova (Polar Falcon (USA))
3639[6] 3984[5] (4629) 5409[7] 6053[6] 6280[8] 6807[12] 7035[6] 7205[10] 7530[9] 7592[6] 7742[8]

Colour Of Love (IRE) *W McCreery* a77 92
3 ch f Le Vie Dei Colori—Priceoflove (IRE) (Inchinor)
(7262)

Colour Scheme (IRE) *Brian Meehan* a91 93
4 ch h Peintre Celebre(USA) —Lipica (IRE) (Night Shift (USA))
1684[11] 2217[10] 5686[6] (6068) 6375[6] 7029[14]

Colour Vision (FR) *Mark Johnston* 113
3 gr g Rainbow Quest(USA) —Give Me Five (GER) (Monsun (GER))
1811[3] 2726[9] 3291[7] (3851) ◆ (4050) ◆ 4266[2] 5131a[4] 5659[8] 5921[5] (6575) 6690[3] ◆ 6857[3]

Colwyn (FR) *Annelies Mathis* a64 90
6 b g Marchand De Sable(USA) —Any Colour (Anshan)
257a[8]

Colzium *Mark H Tompkins* a33 42
3 b g Zafeen(FR) —Mild Deception (IRE) (Glow (USA))
2857[7] 3487[5] 4177[6] 5118[4]

Comadoir (IRE) *Jo Crowley* a71 76
5 ch g Medecis—Hymn Of The Dawn (USA) (Phone Trick (USA))
264[12] 470[8] 3261[8] 3940[2] 4828[4] 5995[4]

Combat Rock (IRE) *Jo Hughes*
2 ch g Insatiable(IRE) —Dashing Place (IRE) (Compton Place)
6768[15]

Combat Zone (IRE) *Mario Hofer* 96
5 b g Refuse To Bend(IRE) —Zeiting (IRE) (Zieten (USA))
4373a[3] 6339[18] 7048a[6]

Come And Go (UAE) *Ian McInnes* a8 86
5 b g Halling(USA) —Woven Silk (USA) (Danzig (USA))
1244[7] 2366[5] 3025[9] 3732[5] 4148[3] 4612[8] 5178[9] 6033[6] 6070[11] 7005[11]

Comedy Act *David O'Meara* a41 93
4 b g Motivator—Comic (IRE) (Be My Chief (USA))
1847[9] 2285[5] 3205[5] 4043[2] 4294[4] 4890[8] 5221[12] 5761[3] 6191[5] (6582) 6868[2] 7017[3]

Come Here Yew (IRE) *Declan Carroll* 84
3 ch g Refuse To Bend(IRE) —Red Zinger (USA) (Red Ransom (USA))
2457[6] 3543[6] ◆ 4370[4] 5056[13] 5594[2] 6079[2] 6457[10] 6674[9]

Come Hither *Michael Easterby* 54
2 b f Pastoral Pursuits—Stolen Glance (Mujahid (USA))
2113[12] 2387[4] 3314[15] 4194[9]

Come Il Vento (ITY) *A Cottu* 81
3 b c Gold Sphinx(USA) —Queen Joan (ITY) (Risk Me (FR))
1431a[9]

Come On Blue Chip (IRE) *Paul D'Arcy* a82 75
2 b g Holy Roman Emperor(IRE) —Rapid Action (USA) (Quest For Fame)
1721[3] 2033[7] 2953[5] 4857[12] 5446[9] 6132[5] (6489) (6667) 6957[7]

Come On Dave (IRE) *David Nicholls* 73
2 b g Red Clubs(IRE) —Desert Sprite (IRE) (Tagula (IRE))
3021[9] 3728[9] 4105[8] 5367[2] 6598[3]

Come On Eileen (IRE) *Richard Guest* a18 23
3 b f Diamond Green(FR) —Lady Taverner (Marju (IRE))
456[9] 550[6] 672[5] 871[4]

Come On Safari (IRE) *Joseph Tuite* a65 71
4 b g Antonius Pius(USA) —Calypso Dancer (FR) (Celtic Swing)
1026[5] 1562[13] 2027[2] 2376[9] (4089) 4444[3] 4604[7] 5002[13] 6587[6] 7146[7] 7455[13] 7843[7]

Come On The Irons (USA) *Ralph Smith* a59 68
3 ch c Birdstone(USA) —Spa (USA) (Strodes Creek (USA))
684[9] 887[11] 1022[11] 3742[3] (3945) 4746[2] 5168[2] (5302) 5628[6] 6052[9]

Come To Mind *Alan Berry* 46
2 b g Mind Games—Hillside Heather (IRE) (Tagula (IRE))
1791[7] 2261[7] 2542[7] 3082[9] 3539[3] 3855[5] 4572[7] 4808[5] 5310[4] 6293[14] 7157[5]

Comical *Mark Johnston* 79
2 b g Dubai Destination(USA) —Amusing Time (IRE) (Sadler's Wells (USA))
2318[5] 3186[3] (3954) ◆ 4311[6] 5287[10] 6031[8] 6345[9]

Commanche *Bryan Smart* 74
2 ch c Sleeping Indian—Happy Memories (IRE) (Thatching)
2542[5] 3314[4] 3755[3] (4171) 4496[12]

Commanche Raider (IRE) *Michael Dods* 80
4 b g Tale Of The Cat(USA) —Alsharq (IRE) (Machiavellian (USA))
1205[10] 3832[10] 4152[9] 4405[9] 4678[4] 5400[5] 5732[2] 6265[5] 6779[9]

Commander Veejay *Brian Rothwell* 49
3 ch g Piccolo—Poly Blue (IRE) (Thatching)
1303[7] 1494[8] 1945[4] 2465[7] 2786[3] 3116[5] 3460[3] 4151[4] 4403[5] 6229[3]

Commander Wish *Lucinda Featherstone* a50 62
8 ch g Arkadian Hero(USA) —Flighty Dancer (Pivotal)
363[11] 765[6] 950[12] 3931[2] ◆ 4371[9] 4547[4] 4893[3] 5083[8] 6501[6]

Commandingpresence (USA) *John Bridger* a56 75
5 bb m Thunder Gulch(USA) —Sehra (USA) (Silver Hawk (USA))
485[6] 619[7] 664[6] 812[3] 1043[9] 1182[3] 2193[3] 2720[4] (2755) 2920[3] 3685[8] 3768[3] 4086[3] 4387[8] 4547[2] 4828[6] 4960[5] 5426[2] (5658) (5997) 6119[11] 6815[6] 6974[12] 7512[10]

Command Marshal (FR) *Ed de Giles* a59 66
8 b g Commands(AUS) —Marsakara (IRE) (Turtle Island (IRE))
(2996) 3515[11] 3946[4] 4889[4] 5994[RR] 6437[3]

Commando Cat (FR) *L A Urbano-Grajales* a74
4 b g Munaafis(USA) —Coopina (FR) (Dear Doctor (FR))
842a[0]

Comma To The Top (USA) *Peter Miller* a119 102
3 b g Bwana Charlie(USA) —Maggies Storm (USA) (Stormy Atlantic (USA))
1921a[19]

Commend *Sir Michael Stoute* 64
2 ch c Pivotal—Reputable I (Medicean)
7080[4]

Commended *B W Hills* 86
3 b g Royal Applause—Granted (FR) (Cadeaux Genereux)
(1315) 1688[12]

Commerce *Gary Moore* a70 70
4 b m Trade Fair—Well Away (IRE) (Sadler's Wells (USA))
54[7] 1789[4] 2204[3] 2685[7] 3467[8] 3814[3] 4317[8] 5318[14] 5942[6] 6468[12] 7003[6] 7203[11]

Commercial (IRE) *Jamie Osborne* a62 28
3 br g Kodiac—Call Collect (IRE) (Houmayoun (FR))
2722[7]

Commissar *Mahmood Al Zarooni* 92
2 b c Soviet Star(USA) —Sari (Faustus (USA))
1360[3] ◆ (1721) ◆ 3012[22] 3861[6] 4964[4]

Commitment *Luca Cumani* 71
2 b g Motivator—Courting (Pursuit Of Love)
6529[4] ◆ 7082[4]

Common Touch (IRE) *Richard Fahey* 101
3 ch g Compton Place—Flying Finish (FR) (Priolo (USA))
1326[2] (2003) (2319) ◆ 3067[18] 4428[2]

Communicator *Michael Bell* 93
3 b g Motivator—Goodie Twosues (Fraam)
1096[6] 1445[2] (2076) 3069[4] ◆ 5283[17] 5700[15]

Community (USA) *Phil McEntee* a65
3 b f Proud Citizen(USA) —Rimini Road (USA) (Dynaformer (USA))
7354[4] 7585[U] 7662[5] (7856)

Compasivo Cat (ARG) *E Charpy* a101 77
7 b h Easing Along(USA) —La Tosquera (ARG) (Tempranero (CHI))
500a[9] 602a[10]

Compassion *Michael Bell* a48 73
3 b f Tiger Hill(IRE) —Windmill (Ezzoud (IRE))
1549[10] 2065[6] 2840[8] 3467[11] 5477[2] 6057[5] 6891[6]

Complex *David Evans* a50 56
2 b f Multiplex—Dockside Strike (Docksider (USA))
1583[5] 2160[4] 2630[5] 7035[11] 7423[5] 7590[3] (7821)

Complexion *Sir Michael Stoute* a87 86
3 b f Hurricane Run(IRE) —Ithaca (USA) (Distant View (USA))
2960[6] (4185) 4807[8] 6439[3]

Compliance Officer (USA) *Bruce R Brown* 119
5 bb g Officer(USA) —Purple Hills (USA) (Dynaformer (USA))
7307a[11]

Complicate *Andrew Reid* a38 46
3 b f Storming Home—Gentle Irony (Mazilier (USA))
966[7] 1869[8]

Compromis (IRE) *F Rossi* a64 80
4 gr h Verglas(IRE) —Compromise (FR) (Fasliyev (USA))
(842a)

Compton *Ralph Beckett* a60 92
2 ch g Compton Place—Look So (Efisio)
(3917) ◆ 4858[2] ◆ 5558[3] 6055[5]

Compton Air (USA) *Hans Adielsson* a59
2 b g Langfuhr(CAN) —Air Kiss (Red Ransom (USA))
4906[9] 6216[6] 7197[7]

Compton Ashdown *Hans Adielsson* a64
2 b g Proclamation(IRE) —Ashlinn (IRE) (Ashkalani (IRE))
6492[3] (7248)

Compton Bell *Hans Adielsson* a53 47
2 b g Shirocco(GER) —Bela-M (IRE) (Ela-Mana-Mou)
5142[6] 5899[10] 6400[10]

Compton Bird *Hans Adielsson* a62 34
2 b f Motivator—Noble Peregrine (Lomond (USA))
3736[10] 4052[14] 4548[7] 4992[6] 5316[7] (7432) 7514[2]

Compton Blue *Richard Hannon* a63 82
5 b g Compton Place—Blue Goddess (IRE) (Blues Traveller (IRE))
3815[3] 4215[6] 4310[12] 5200[5] 5586[5] 6227[2] 6727[2] 7228[9]

Compton Micky *Owen Brennan* a40 35
10 ch g Compton Place—Nunthorpe (Mystiko (USA))
793[9]

Compton Monarch *Hans Adielsson* a12 40
2 b g Red Ransom(USA) —Monaiya (Shareef Dancer (USA))
1757[7] 3870[11] 4947[6] 5316[10]

Compton Rainbow *Hans Adielsson* a62 60
2 b f Exceed And Excel(AUS) —Rainbow Goddess (Rainbow Quest (USA))
6441[11] 6620[4] 6892[6] 7222[3] 7342[6]

Compton Shuttle (IRE) *Hans Adielsson* a38
2 b f Shirocco(GER) —Shuheb (Nashwan (USA))
1957[8] 4992[10] 5410[8]

Comptonspirit *Brian Baugh* a29 83
7 ch m Compton Place—Croeso Cynnes (Most Welcome)
1067[11] 1444[10] 1562[6] 1968[5] ◆ 2585[3] 2766[6] 3582[2] 3995[2] 4231[3] (4678) (5265) 5914[8] 6913[16]

Compton Target (IRE) *Hans Adielsson* a72 68
2 b g Strategic Prince—Tarakana (USA) (Shahrastani (USA))
4054[9] 4548[6] 4947[2] (5385) 5913[3] 6399[11] 6921[10] 7364[6] 7752[6] 7808[4] 7937[8]

Comrade Bond *Mark H Tompkins* a61 75
3 ch g Monsieur Bond(IRE) —Eurolink Cafe (Grand Lodge (USA))
2583[10] 3942[2] 5121[2] 5644[8] 6940[2] (7084) 7213[2]

Comradeship (IRE) *R Bouresly* a95 82
4 ch h Dubawi(IRE) —Friendlier (Zafonic (USA))
157a[14] 239[14] 501a[10] 583a[9]

Con Artist (IRE) *Saeed Bin Suroor* a83 105
4 b h Invincible Spirit(IRE) —Hoodwink (IRE) (Selkirk (USA))
2105[12] (6375)

Concealed Identity (USA) *Edmond D Gaudet* a107
3 b g Smarty Jones(USA) —Richetta (USA) (Polish Numbers (USA))
2328a[10]

Conciliatory *Rae Guest* a93 98
4 gr m Medicean—Condoleezza (USA) (Cozzene (USA))
1681[5] 2994[10] 3436[7] (4656) 5096a[5] 6394a[4] 7128[7]

Concordia Notte (IRE) *Richard Guest* a50 56
2 b f Elusive City(USA) —Laylati (IRE) (Green Desert (USA))
2309[6] 2644[6] 4391[7] 4648[2] 4922[10] 5535[9]

Concrete Jungle (IRE) *Andrew Haynes* a44 62
3 b g Chineur(FR) —Finty (IRE) (Entrepreneur)
2790[11] 3324[6] 3513[6] 5165[3] 5394[10]

Condor (DEN) *Soren Jensen* 90
6 br g Kendor(FR) —Liberty (DEN) (Kris)
4842a[6]

Conducting *Gay Kelleway* a82 78
3 b g Oratorio(IRE) —Aiming (Highest Honor (FR))
990[4] 1725[12] 3178[10] 3739[5] 4685[2] 5631[4] 5828[6] 6181[3] 6799[5] 7137[2] 7453[3] 7779[3]

Cone Donkey (IRE) *Bryan Smart* a59 38
2 b f Medicean—Nan Scurry (FR) (Danehill (USA))
6259[9] 7248[2]

Conesuala *Alan Jarvis* a36
4 b m Zamindar(USA) —Fifth Avenue (Unfuwain (USA))
2258[13] 5639[4] 5999[10] 6589[9] 6767[11]

Confederation (USA) *S Seemar* a56 56
9 br g Dixie Union(USA) —Pure Speed (USA) (Gulch (USA))
536a[7]

Confessional *Tim Easterby* a92 105
4 b g Dubawi(IRE) —Golden Nun (Bishop Of Cashel)
1166[4] 1809[4] 2317[16] 2714[2] 3357[9] 3846[3] 4135a[9] 4531[2] ◆ 5060[9] 5927[2] 6332[2] 6522[4] 7018[10]

Confide In Me *Mark Hoad* a61 66
7 b g Medicean—Confidante (USA) (Dayjur (USA))
656[7] 7910[11]

Confidence (USA) *Luke Comer* a90 76
4 b g More Than Ready(USA) —Caramel Custard (USA) (Chief Honcho (USA))
6514a[6]

Confirmed *Marco Botti* a67 67
2 b g Authorized(IRE) —Vas Y Carla (USA) (Gone West (USA))
5727[7] ◆ 6300[5] 7494[3]

Confront *Sir Michael Stoute* a95 111
6 b g Nayef(USA) —[illegible] (USA) (Danzig (USA))
(2933) 3646[5] 4494[13] 7166[6]

Confucius Elite *Jim Boyle* a84 61
2 b g Bertolini(USA) —Cavernista (Lion Cavern (USA))
4352[5] 5410[2] ◆ (6352)

Confused Sphere (IRE) *Noel Wilson*
2 b g Kheleyf(USA) —Daymoon (USA) (Dayjur (USA))
6025[7] 6702[10] 7072[11]

Conjuror's Bluff *Richard Hannon* 66
3 b c Tiger Hill(IRE) —Portmeirion (Polish Precedent (USA))
2885[13] 3133[11] 3688[5] 4154[13]

Connishka *Alan Bailey* 46
2 gr f Verglas(IRE) —Profit Alert (IRE) (Alzao (USA))
6758[8] 6933[13]

Cono (IRE) *Colin Teague*
3 b g Librettist(USA) —Lilyfoot (IRE) (Sanglamore (USA))
2785[6]

Conowen *William Jarvis* 64
2 ch c Ishiguru(USA) —Velma Kelly (Vettori (IRE))
4823[11] 6099[6] 6525[4]

Cono Zur (FR) *Ruth Carr* 83
4 b g Anabaa(USA) —Alaskan Idol (USA) (Carson City (USA))
(1394) 1621[2] (1747) 2112[10] 2301[8] 2955[3] 3386[8] 3659[2] 4070[2] 4268[4] 4811[3] 5314[12] 5722[8] 6093[12] 6533[9] 6990[17]

Conry (IRE) *Patrick Morris* a79 88
5 ch g Captain Rio—Altizaf (Zafonic (USA))
149[2] 186[6] 6327[11] 6617[5] 6979[10] 7176[7]

Conservatorium (AUS) *Gary Kennewell* 106
4 ch g Royal Academy(USA) —Belong To Madam (AUS) (Belong To Me (USA))
9029a[4]

Consistant *Brian Baugh* a65 47
3 b g Reel Buddy(USA) —Compact Disc (IRE) (Royal Academy (USA))
1064[3] 2252[6] 2592[8] 4067[7] 4924[6] 5388[4] 5864[5]

Constant Contact *Andrew Balding* a102 100
4 b g Passing Glance—Floriana (Selkirk (USA))
1834[2] (2604) 3876[7] 4410[17] 6339[29]

Constant Craving *Clive Cox* 70
4 b m Pastoral Pursuits—Addicted To Love (Touching Wood (USA))
1772[8] 2213[14]

Continuity (IRE) *Ralph Beckett* a66 65
2 b f Amadeus Wolf—No Tippling (IRE) (Unblest)
3388[4] 3981[5] 4462[2] 5144[2] 6921[12]

Contredanse (IRE) *Luca Cumani* a73 112
4 bl m Danehill Dancer(IRE) —Ahdaab (USA) (Rahy (USA))
1718[7] 2373a[4] 4293[3] 5523a[10]

Control Chief *Ralph Beckett* a42 59
3 b g Medicean—Sahara Rose (Green Desert (USA))
1392[9] 2368[9] 3220[9] 4088[5] 4796[2] 5176[4] 5675[4]

Convention *Ed Dunlop* a77 76
3 b f Encosta De Lago(AUS) —Model Queen (USA) (Kingmambo (USA))
2840[7] 3385[6] 4014[4] 5391[3] ◆ 5964[2] 6255[5] (7033)

Conveyance (USA) *S Seemar* a114
4 gr h Indian Charlie(USA) —Emptythetill (USA) (Holy Bull (USA))
755a[2] 997a[8]

Convidada (IRE) *M Delcher-Sanchez* 87
4 b m Trans Island—Provacatrice (USA) (Irish River (FR))
5075a[10]

Convince (USA) *Kevin M Prendergast* a64 62
10 ch g Mt. Livermore(USA) —Conical (Zafonic (USA))
289[5] 545[4] 674[2] 1803[2] 2353[5] 2732[5]

Convitezza *Mike Sowersby* 34
5 b m Domedriver(IRE) —Condoleezza (USA) (Cozzene (USA))
4945[6] 5402[13] 6049[11] 7061[6] 7211[7]

Cooke's Bar (IRE) *Noel Lawlor* a31 23
4 b m Invincible Spirit(IRE) —St Clair Star (Sallust)
253[9]

Cookie Galore *John Harris* a45 48
4 ch m Monsieur Bond(IRE) —Ginger Cookie (Bold Edge)
1979[10] 2547[12]

Cookies (IRE) *E Botti* 80
3 b f Orpen(USA) —Embracing (Reference Point)
1738a[9]

Cookieshake *Nick Littmoden* a67 67
3 b g Cadeaux Genereux—Hawait Al Barr (Green Desert (USA))
4849[4] 5443[2] 5810[3] 6669[12] 7388[10]

Coolagad Wonder (IRE) *Neville Bycroft* a51 56
6 ch g Fath(USA) —Wonder Bell (IRE) (Magical Wonder (USA))
893[8]

Cool Baranca (GER) *Dianne Sayer* 75
5 b m Beat Hollow—Cool Storm (IRE) (Rainbow Quest (USA))
1440[6] 3129[11] 4605[11] 5107[10] 6833[5]

Cooldine Cat (IRE) *John Quinn* 49
2 b c Mujadil(USA) —Kathy Sun (IRE) (Intikhab (USA))
2387[8] 3273[9] 3728[4] 4105[3]

Cool Dude (FR) *Mme C Head-Maarek* a86 108
3 b c Lemon Drop Kid(USA) —Toupie (Intikhab (USA))
(1010a) 4376a[5]

Coolella (IRE) *John Weymes* a45 57
4 gr m Verglas(IRE) —Tianella (GER) (Acatenango (GER))
1625[11] 2260[11] 3110[3] 3454[8] 3732[8] 3857[7]

Cool Fantasy (IRE) *Paul D'Arcy* a48 9
2 b g One Cool Cat(USA) —Regal Fantasy (IRE) (King's Theatre (IRE))
3171[9] 6506[8] 7422[6]

Cool Hand Jake *Peter Makin* a81 53
5 b g Storming Home—Monawara (IRE) (Namaqualand (USA))
1198[5] 2816[4] 4158[7] 5101[3] 5835[9] 7208[3] 7447[6]

Cool Hand Luke (IRE) *Tom Dascombe* a71 68
2 br g Le Vie Dei Colori—Thelma Louise (IRE) (Desert Style (IRE))
4571[5] 4919[2] 5565[9]

Cool Ice *Ron Hodges*
2 b f Iceman—Kowthar (Mark Of Esteem (IRE))
5779[8] 6280[11]

Cool In The Shade *Paul Midgley* 76
3 b f Pastoral Pursuits—Captain Margaret (Royal Applause)
1155[9] 1941[3] 2350[3] 3191[2] 3630[3] 4288[4] 4563[7] 4942[2] 5010[2] (5469) 6076[3] (6454) (6801)

Cool Light *Alan Jarvis* a33 47
2 ch f Iceman—Living Daylights (IRE) (Night Shift (USA))
3258[7] 3779[8] 5382[8] 6458[9] 6973[6] 7432[9] 7582[7]

Cool Luke *Alan Swinbank* a62 42
3 b g Piccolo—Icy (Mind Games)
509[3] 717[4]

Cool Macavity (IRE) *B W Hills* a75 88
3 b g One Cool Cat(USA) —Cause Celebre (IRE) (Peintre Celebre (USA))
(811) 2477[3] 2908[5] (3650) 4467[15]

Cool Marble (IRE) *Y De Nicolay* a78 96
4 b h Oasis Dream—Nini Princesse (IRE) (Niniski (USA))
830a[4]

Coolminx (IRE) *Richard Fahey* a84 95
4 b m One Cool Cat(USA) —Greta D'Argent (IRE) (Great Commotion (USA))
736[7] 1205[4] 2620[6] 3113[3] 3880[16] (5006) 5255[9] (6113) 6854a[10]

Cool Rhythm *David O'Meara* a68 73
3 b g Iceman—With Music In Mind (Mind Games)
5793[2] 6353[3] 6834[3] 7073[3]

Cool Star (FR) *A Bonin* a92 100
6 ch h Starborough—Valverda (USA) (Irish River (FR))
778a[7]

Cool Water Oasis *Rae Guest* a69 61
3 b f Elnadim(USA) —Creek Dancer (Josr Algarhoud (IRE))
3956[6] 4705[15] 5172[2] 5355[3] 5946[2] 6105[2]

Cool Wave *B Grizzetti* 94
2 b f One Cool Cat(USA) —Onda Chiara (ITY) (Dane Friendly)
6904a[3] 7219a[5]

Cootehill Lass (IRE) *David Evans* a71 78
3 b f Ivan Denisovich(IRE) —Heat Alert (USA) (Valid Expectations (USA))
(1056) 1585[2] (2356) 3207[11] (4431) 5581[7] 5803[2] 6051[2] 6227[8] 6433[3] 7055[2] 7388[4] 7565[6]

Coplow *Richard Hannon* 80
2 ch f Manduro(GER) —Anna Oleanda (IRE) (Old Vic)
6128[3] ◆ 6526[11] 7164[2]

Copper Dock (IRE) *T G McCourt* a81 61
7 b g Docksider(USA) —Sundown (Polish Precedent (USA))
5086a[4] 5430[7] 7790a[7]

Copper Falls *Brendan Powell* a56 64
2 b f Trade Fair—Strat's Quest (Nicholas (USA))
1055[4] 1451[2] 1757[3] 3014[22] 3673[4] 4548[4] 5099[9] 7143[10] 7452[6] 7530[3] 7830[5]

Copperwood *Michael Blanshard* a77 68
6 ch g Bahamian Bounty—Sophielu (Rudimentary (USA))
82[5] 473[4] 763[3] (915) 1221[3] 1368[2] 1917[9] 2354[3] 2719[8] 5322[5] 5835[10] 6354[8] 7097[6]

Copp The Lot (USA) *David Nicholls* 61
2 rg g Exchange Rate(USA) —Argentum (USA) (Silver Deputy (CAN))
3755[15] 4365[4] 5367[9]

Cops And Robbers *Sir Michael Stoute* 91
3 ch g Pivotal—Threefold (USA) (Gulch (USA))
4279[2] ◆ (4805) ◆ 5710[6]

Coquet *Hughie Morrison* a78 95
2 b f Sir Percy—One So Marvellous (Nashwan (USA))
6000[4] (6697) ◆ (7169) ◆

Coracle *David Nicholls* a49 54
3 b g Fasliyev(USA) —Cora Pearl (IRE) (Montjeu (IRE))
1392[11] 1543[9] 1812[5] 2119[5] 2581[6]

Coral Moon (IRE) *Richard Fahey* a69
3 b f Dubai Destination(USA) —Flying Wanda (Alzao (USA))
101[4] 192[3] 750[6]

Coral Sands (IRE) *Alan Swinbank*
3 b g Footstepsinthesand—Daziyra (IRE) (Doyoun)
7886[7]

Coral Wave (IRE) *P J Prendergast* 105
2 b f Rock Of Gibraltar(IRE) —Common Knowledge (Rainbow Quest (USA))
(5974a) (6389a)

Cordillera *Luca Cumani* a56 56
3 ch f Araafa(IRE) —Alexander Celebre (IRE) (Peintre Celebre (USA))
3043[7] 3478[4]

Core Element (IRE) *S Buggy* a66 79
4 b m Consolidator(USA) —Millstream (USA) (Dayjur (USA))
5228a[13]

Coriante (FR) *Mme C Dufreche* a40 60
4 b m Indian Rocket—Camibas (FR) (Solicitor (FR))
108a[8]

Corlough Mountain *Paddy Butler* a37 46
7 ch g Inchinor—Two Step (Mujtahid (USA))
418[13] 450[8] 2451[6] 2685[12] 3480[3] 3946[8] 4579[7] 4700[3] 5421[7] 6968[9] 7574[7]

Cornakill (USA) *Kevin Prendergast* a89 92
4 b m Stormin Fever(USA) —It's Heidi's Dance (USA) (Green Dancer (USA))
1228a[7] 6513a[10]

Cornish Beau (IRE) *Mark H Tompkins* a69 76
4 ch g Pearl Of Love(IRE) —Marimar (IRE) (Grand Lodge (USA))
1461[11] 2055[3] 2952[13] 3533[5] 3817[8] 4204[3] 4697[7] 5357[9] 6303[4]

Cornish Quest *Mark H Tompkins* 67
3 ch g Needwood Blade—Persuasion (Batshoof)
3557[11] 4281[9] 4926[3] 5137[6] 6938[10]

Corn Maiden *Phil McEntee* 35
2 b f Refuse To Bend(IRE) —Namat (IRE) (Daylami (IRE))
6168[11]

Corn Rigs *Ed Dunlop* a37 28
2 b f Exceed And Excel(AUS) —Corndavon (USA) (Sheikh Albadou)
5111[12] 5689[9]

Cornus *Alan McCabe* a80 91
9 ch g Inchinor—Demerger (USA) (Distant View (USA))
3383[6] 3704[5] 4078[2] 4369[5] 4516[4] 4742[7] 5083[2] 5341[2] 5682[9] 5972[10] 6174[7] 6382[3] 6762[8] 7074[11]

Corporal Maddox *Jamie Osborne* 105
4 b g Royal Applause—Noble View (USA) (Distant View (USA))
1186[9] 1885[26] 2288[10] 2954[15] 3850[3] 4346[12] 4556[8] 4997[7] 5879[7] 6327[2] 6723[11]

Correct *Michael Bell* a69 64
2 b f Oasis Dream—Dusty Answer (Zafonic (USA))
2709[7] 3342[8] 3981[2] 4551[7] 5409[4] 5945[5] 6484[6]

Corrib (IRE) *Bryn Palling* a59 60
8 b m Lahib(USA) —Montana Miss (IRE) (Earl Of Barking (IRE))
69[3] 408[5] 635[4] 1374[3] 2900[2] 3094[2] (3515) 3912[4] 4317[6] 5178[7] 5611[3] 5912[11] 6888[3] 7263[8] 7571[7] 7698[3] 7892[6]

Corr Point (IRE) *Jamie Osborne* a77 74
4 b g Azamour(IRE) —Naazeq (Nashwan (USA))
1148[5] ◆ 1596[4] 3352[4] 3960[5] (4642) 4870[2] 6666[7]

Corsetry (USA) *Sir Henry Cecil* 68
2 b f Distorted Humor(USA) —Lingerie (Shirley Heights)
5807[3] 6329[6]

Corseurasien (FR) *W J Cargeeg* a62 74
6 b h Hamas(IRE) —La Corsasienne (FR) (Sky Lawyer (FR))
221a[9]

Corsican Boy *Roger Charlton* a77 77
3 gr g Tobougg(IRE) —Madiyla (Darshaan)
5568[6] 6124[10]

Corsicanrun (IRE) *Richard Fahey* 77
3 ch g Medicean—Castara Beach (IRE) (Danehill (USA))
1168[4] 2891[5] 3614[2] 3936[9] 4362[9]

Corvette *Michael Appleby* a68 62
3 b f Araafa(IRE) —Clipper (Salse (USA))
1270[5] 1683[12] 2196[8] 2850[3] 3467[5] 4072[10] 5321[2] 6052[3] 6622[4] 6891[5] 7121[6] 7327[4] 7885[4]

Cosimo de Medici *Hughie Morrison* a95 93
4 b g Medicean—Wish (Danehill (USA))
1729[5] (2190) 3205[10] 4097[6] 4423[5] (5448) (6171) ◆ 6690[16]

Cosmetic *Colin Teague*
6 ch m Where Or When(IRE) —Cosmology (USA) (Distant View (USA))
795[5]

Cosmic Halo *Richard Fahey* 66
2 ch f Halling(USA) —Cosmic Case (Casteddu)
4875[2]

Cosmic Moon *Richard Fahey* 72
3 b f Doyen(IRE) —Cosmic Case (Casteddu)
2256[3] 2695[6] 3632[5] 4367[7] 4784[6] 6116[10]

Cosmic Sun *Richard Fahey* a100 92
5 b g Helissio(FR) —Cosmic Case (Casteddu)
(614) (1102) ◆ 2107[10]

Cosmonaut (AUS) *Bart Cummings* 105
4 b g Starcraft(NZ) —Julez (AUS) (Zabeel (NZ))
7115a[12]

Cossack Prince *Laura Mongan* a64 26
6 b g Dubai Destination(USA) —Danemere (IRE) (Danehill (USA))
223[6] 1635[8] 3281[8]

Costa Del Fortune (IRE) *Richard Hannon* a80 78
2 ch f Heliostatic(IRE) —Midris (IRE) (Namid)
1996[2] 2563[2] 3520[3] 4581[7] (5197) 6623[4] 6829[7]

Cotes Du Rhone (IRE) *David Evans* a31 20
2 b g Catcher In The Rye(IRE) —La Vie En Rouge (IRE) (College Chapel)
1290[8] 1890[9] 5325[11] 7117[5]

Cotswold Village (AUS) *Adrian Chamberlain* a32 75
5 b m Hawk Wing(USA) —Scenic Bold Dancer (AUS) (Scenic)
3514[6] 4020[9] 4949[9] 5653[9]

Cottam Donny *Mel Brittain* 65
3 ch g Doyen(IRE) —Northern Bird (Interrex (CAN))
6097[3] 6674[8] 6918[6]

Cottam Stella *Mel Brittain* a38 54
3 br f Diktat—Flower Breeze (USA) (Rahy (USA))
3616[6] 4110[8] 4149[2] 4560[13] 4902[12] 6840[12] 7213[7] 7399[9]

Cottonfields (USA) *Heather Main* a68 57
5 rg g Maria's Mon(USA) —Known Romance (USA) (Known Fact (USA))
7810[10]

Cotton Grass *Mark H Tompkins* 64
3 b f Medicean—Astromancer (USA) (Silver Hawk (USA))
2068[7] (2858) 4044[3] 4175[3]

Cotton King *Tobias B P Coles* a84 78
4 b g Dubawi(IRE) —Spinning The Yarn (Barathea (IRE))
162[5] 190[4] (449) (596) 849[9] 5198[3] 5729[6] 5761[8]

Cotton Trader (USA) *John Gosden* a76
2 b c Hard Spun(USA) —Saytarra (USA) (Seeking The Gold (USA))
7398[3] 7521[3] 7664a[2]

Could It Be Magic *Bill Turner* a77 76
4 b g Dubai Destination(USA) —Lomapamar (Nashwan (USA))
82[3] 307[6] 557[3] 666[6] 915[3] 1221[2] 1634[3] 3473[3] 5345[3] 5675[2] 6586[7]

Councellor (FR) *Derek Shaw* a74 56
9 b g Gilded Time(USA) —Sudden Storm Bird (USA) (Storm Bird (CAN))
4993[12] 6220[9] 6541[7] 6797[9] 7034[8] 7243[6] 7425[5] 7455[9]

Counsel (IRE) *Sir Michael Stoute* 68
2 b c Dansili—Kitty O'Shea (Sadler's Wells (USA))
5801[6] 6588[5] 7082[5] ◆

Count Bertoni (IRE) *David O'Meara* a77 85
4 b g Bertolini(USA) —Queen Sceptre (IRE) (Fairy King (USA))
(854) 1110[9] (1460) 1621[4] 2887[3] 3276[5] 4004[4] 4901[5] 5383[7] (6355)

Count Ceprano (IRE) *Lydia Pearce* a57 74
7 b g Desert Prince(IRE) —Camerlata (Common Grounds)
2923[8] (4454) (4754) 5110[4] 7237[8] 7601[12] 7904[7]

Count Cougar (USA) *Simon Griffiths* a12 19
11 b g Sir Cat(USA) —Gold Script (USA) (Seeking The Gold (USA))
874[13]

Counterbid (IRE) *J Heloury* a68 70
5 b g Rainbow Quest(USA) —Brooklyn Gleam (FR) (Caerleon (USA))
220a[5] 903a[7] 1013a[0]

Counterglow (IRE) *Mahmood Al Zarooni* a86 86
2 b g Echo Of Light—Quintellina (Robellino (USA))
(4655) 5487[3] 6055[3]

Countermarch *Richard Hannon* a73 78
3 b f Selkirk(USA) —Day Of Reckoning (Daylami (IRE))
(850) 3180[5] 4056[4] 5113[8] 5962[6]

Counterparty *Alan King* 57
3 b f Nayef(USA) —Mistress Bankes (IRE) (Petardia)
4388[5] 5001[9]

Countess Comet (IRE) *Ralph Beckett* a84 84
4 b m Medicean—Countess Sybil (IRE) (Dr Devious (IRE))
1388[5] 1992[3] 2906[5] 3434[7] 5915[3] (6592)

Countess Ellen (IRE) *Gerard Butler* a67 62
3 b f Fasliyev(USA) —Princess Ellen (Tirol)
1768[5] 1958[6] 2478[5] 3432[4] 4011[7] 4458[7]

Countess Ferrama *William Haggas* 46
2 b f Authorized(IRE) —Madame Dubois (Legend Of France (USA))
6984[10]

Countess Salome (IRE) *Muredach Kelly* a42 63
4 gr m Noverre(USA) —Remiss (IRE) (Indian Ridge)
291[6] 599[5] 3910[10]

Counting House (IRE) *Jim Old* a68 56
8 ch g King's Best(USA) —Inforapenny (Deploy)
2034[9]

Count Paris (USA) *A bin Huzaim* a79 9
5 ch h Pivotal—Dearly (Rahy (USA))
536a[3]

Countrycraft *Sally Hall* a37 32
4 b g Pastoral Pursuits—Turn Back (Pivotal)
120[8] 7246[14]

Country Day (USA) *Steve Margolis* a100 117
5 b h Speightstown(USA) —Hidden Assets (USA) (Mt. Livermore (USA))
7303a[2]

Country Road (IRE) *Tony Carroll* a81 71
5 b g Montjeu(IRE) —Souffle (Zafonic (USA))
3240[6] (3743)

Countrystar (FR) *C Boutin* 67
2 b c Country Reel(USA) —Starlaire (FR) (Beaudelaire (USA))
7238a[5] 7666a[0] 7814a[0]

Country Waltz *Linda Perratt* a52 63
3 b f Pastoral Pursuits—Elegant Dance (Statoblest)
1543[7] 1802[7] 2265[12] 2631[6] 3661[7] 3860[9] 4146[7]

Countrywide Flame *John Quinn* a63 87
3 b g Haafhd—Third Party (Terimon)
1588[3] (1858) 2152[5] (2635) 4540[3] 5064[4] (6838)

Country Wolf *Michael Wigham* a48 41
2 br f Amadeus Wolf—Naharnook (Fantastic Light (USA))
3981[7] ◆ 4961[8]

County Hotel (IRE) *Barry Brennan* 54
4 b m Sulamani(IRE) —Seasons Parks (Desert Prince (IRE))
2689[5] 3119[4] 3916[7]

Coup De Grace (IRE) *Amanda Perrett* 50
2 b g Elusive City(USA) —No Way (IRE) (Rainbows For Life (CAN))
6127[8] 6455[7]

Coupe De Ville (IRE) *Richard Hannon* 104
2 b c Clodovil(IRE) —Fantastic Account (Fantastic Light (USA))
2687[2] (3182) ◆ (4091) (5234) ◆ 6170[5] (6527)

Coupland Lass (IRE) *Willie Musson* a62 59
3 b f Chineur(FR) —Negria (IRE) (Al Hareb (USA))
1985[6] 2723[4]

Courageous (IRE) *Kevin Ryan* 100
5 ch g Refuse To Bend(IRE) —Bella Bella (IRE) (Sri Pekan (USA))
1366[11] 2028[18] 2727[14] 3109[6] 3841[15] 4531[25] 5033[6] 5706[3] ◆ 6112[17] (6327) 6865[11]

Courageous Cat (USA) *William Mott* 120
5 b h Storm Cat(USA) —Tranquility Lake (USA) (Rahy (USA))
6204a[2] 7307a[13]

Courchevel (IRE) *Robert Collet* a81 99
4 b m Whipper(USA) —Choc Ice (IRE) (Kahyasi)
1125a[8]

Court Applause (IRE) *William Muir* a67 53
3 b g Royal Applause—Forever Blue (Spectrum (IRE))
1047[2] 1869[2] 2375[5] 3523[8] 7349[11] 7389[2] 7845[2] 7943[4]

Court Canibal *M Delzangles* 112
6 b h Montjeu(IRE) —Pas D'Heure (IRE) (Arazi (USA))
920a[9] 2749a[6]

Courtesy Call (IRE) *Mark Johnston* a64 64
2 br g Manduro(GER) —Three Wrens (IRE) (Second Empire (IRE))
4171[5] 4455[2] ◆ 4781[5] 6489[5] ◆ 6667[2] 6986[9] 7223[10]

Courtland Avenue (IRE) *Jonathan Portman* 71
2 b g Kodiac—Chingford (IRE) (Redback)
3229[5] 4229[4] 4947[5] (5779) 6524[15]

Courtland King (IRE) *David Evans* a70 76
2 b c Baltic King—Red Rabbit (Suave Dancer (USA))
1268[7] 1451[6] 1583[2] 1823[4] 2143[5] 2380[2] 2907[3] 3375[5] (4021) 4343[11] 4460[3] 5348[6] 5625[2] 6540[7] 6843[7] 6975[4]

Court Princess *Richard Price* a34 53
8 b m Mtoto—Fairfields Cone (Celtic Cone)
1473[11] 1833[3] 2377[4] 2733[4] 3281[7] 4274[8] 5267[8] 5379[4] 5612[7]

Court Vision (USA) *Dale Romans* a110 123
6 bb h Gulch(USA) —Weekend Storm (USA) (Storm Bird (CAN))
6204a[7] (7307a)

Court Wing (IRE) *Richard Price* a52 58
5 b m Hawk Wing(USA) —Nicely (IRE) (Bustino)
1297[6] 1973[5] 2526[5] 2873[7] 3095[8] 7631[11]

Coutances *M Delzangles* 103
3 b f Shamardal(USA) —Broadway Hit (Sadler's Wells (USA))
3671a[7]

Covert Decree *Clive Cox* a71 90
3 ch f Proclamation(IRE) —Armada Grove (Fleetwood (IRE))
529[2] (737) 3919[4] 4625[3] (5050) (5938)

Covert Desire *Mahmood Al Zarooni* a59 80
3 ch c Pivotal—Secret Flame (Machiavellian (USA))
2185[7] 2735[2] 6804[7]

Covington (IRE) *Ann Duffield* 38
2 b c Balmont(USA) —Pearl Creek (IRE) (Spinning World (USA))
6835[8]

Cozy Kitten (USA) *Wesley A Ward* 111
3 b g Kitten's Joy(USA) —Caterette (USA) (Cozzene (USA))
7572a[7]

Cozy Tiger (USA) *Willie Musson* a80 70
6 gr g Hold That Tiger(USA) —Cozelia (USA) (Cozzene (USA))
32[2] 1470[10]

C P Joe (IRE) *Paul Green* a73 68
3 br g One Cool Cat(USA) —Trinity Fair (Polish Precedent (USA))
1299[3] 2152[7] 2613[3] 3587[4] 4476[4] 6584[5] 7078[4] (7264) 7506[P] 7564[2] (7689) 7884[4]

Crabbies Bay *Lisa Williamson* 47
3 b f Indesatchel(IRE) —Multi-Sofft (Northern State (USA))
2151[10] 2781[3] 3227[9] 3913[6] 4505[10] 5352[14]

Crabbies Ginger *Lisa Williamson* 49
3 ch g Needwood Blade—Dazzling Quintet (Superlative)
1900[5] 2281[7] 2574[3] 3661[11]

Crabbies Gold (IRE) *Lisa Williamson* 53
3 ch g Sleeping Indian—Sharpe's Lady (Prince Des Coeurs (USA))
2094[7] 2673[8] 3039[12] 4081[6] 4888[4] 5352[13]

Crackentorp *Tim Easterby* a91 98
6 b g Generous(IRE) —Raspberry Sauce (Niniski (USA))
1154[5] 1713[3] 2071[11] (2932) 3625[17] 4360[13] (5250) 5705[9] 7297[7]

Crackerjack King (IRE) *S Botti* 112
3 gr c Shamardal(USA) —Claba Di San Jore (IRE) (Barathea (IRE))
(1920a) 2751a[15]

Cracking Lass (IRE) *Richard Fahey* 103
4 b m Whipper(USA) —Lady From Limerick (IRE) (Rainbows For Life (CAN))
(1112) 2044[2] 2316[6] 3356[7] 3875[17] 5220[2] 5850[4] 6149[4]

Crafty George (IRE) *Daniel Mark Loughnane* a29 43
6 ch g Rossini(USA) —Tidler (IRE) (Rainbows For Life (CAN))
114[10] 6876[11] 7495[7]

Crafty Roberto *Noel Quinlan* a76 76
3 ch g Intikhab(USA) —Mowazana (IRE) (Galileo (IRE))
262[2] 368[2] 1127a[4]

Cragganmore Creek *Dave Morris* a47 13
8 b g Tipsy Creek(USA) —Polish Abbey (Polish Precedent (USA))
117[6] 939[7] 2600[9] 4579[9] 5209[12] 7441[7] 7573[7] 7743[5]

Craicajack (IRE) *Edward Creighton* a62 45
4 ch g Avonbridge—Rash Gift (Cadeaux Genereux)
280[7] 390[9]

Craicattack (IRE) *Sharon Watt* a70 54
4 ch g Arakan(USA) —Jack-N-Jilly (IRE) (Anita's Prince)
37[7] 1498[8] 3489[11] 3638[4] 3903[5] 4443[14] 4600[15] 4852[13]

Cranworth Quest (IRE) *Tim Etherington* a16 56
3 b f Royal Applause—Seven Of Nine (IRE) (Alzao (USA))
3577[8] 4559[7] 5317[11] 7123[9]

Crassula *Terry Clement* a77 89
3 b f Cacique(IRE) —Neath (Rainbow Quest (USA))
1549[7] 2065[2] (3224) 3867[5] 5057[2] 6172[9]

Cravat *Mark Johnston* 92
2 b c Dubai Destination(USA) —Crinolette (IRE) (Sadler's Wells (USA))
(1744) 2007[6] 2488[2] 3064[14] 3810[4] 4502[2] 4984[2] 5184[15] 5478[3] (5876) (6766) 6914[7]

Crazy Bold (GER) *Tony Carroll* a52 51
8 ch g Erminius(GER) —Crazy Love (GER) (Presto)
207[3] 773[9] 1987[7] 3600[6] 4273[2] 4952[5]

Crazy Chris *John Flint* a83 83
6 b m Ishiguru(USA) —Ellopassoff (Librate)
2378[9] 4158[9] 4707[7]

Crazy Colours *Zoe Davison* a39
5 ch g Dalakhani(IRE) —Eternity Ring (Alzao (USA))
127[5] 355[10] 552[7]

Crazy In Love *Olivia Maylam* a52 54
3 ch f Bertolini(USA) —Fission (Efisio)
189[10] 558[11] 655[13] 1753[8] 1933[7] 2756[7] 3248[5] 3724[5]

Crazy Parachute *Gary Moore* a64 58
4 b g Bahamian Bounty—Shersha (IRE) (Priolo (USA))
432[6] 722[10] 810[6] 1045[12] 1633[9]

Crazy Too (IRE) *David Simcock* a65 66
2 b f Invincible Spirit(IRE) —Reform Act (USA) (Lemon Drop Kid (USA))
6030[10] 6758[5] 7194[3]

Creative Cause (USA) *Mike Harrington* a118
2 rg c Giant's Causeway(USA) —Dream Of Summer (USA) (Siberian Summer (USA))
7306a[3]

Credential *John Harris* a41 51
9 b g Dansili—Sabria (USA) (Miswaki (USA))
104[6] 451[6] 670[4] 796[11]

Credit Swap *Venetia Williams* a84 99
6 b g Diktat—Locharia (Wolfhound (USA))
5940[9] ◆ 6339[26]

Creekside *John M Oxx* a95 104
3 b g Dubai Destination(USA) —Khubza (Green Desert (USA))
3444a[10] 4259a[3] 5090a[5]

Creme Anglaise *Michael Bell* 97
3 b f Motivator—Reading Habit (USA) (Half A Year (USA))
1363[4] (1845) 3065[11] 4344[4] ◆ 5177[2] 6172[8]

Cresta (SWI) *Carmen Bocskai* 62
3 br f Blue Canari(FR) —Chapadinha (SWI) (Beldale Flutter (USA))
5307a[8]

Cresta Star *Richard Hannon* a72 71
2 b f Teofilo(IRE) —Fleet Hill (IRE) (Warrshan (USA))
2309[10] 5337[2] 6168[6] (6441) 7358[4]

Crew Cut (IRE) *Jeremy Gask* a80 77
3 gb g Acclamation—Carabine (USA) (Dehere (USA))
2094[11] 2710[2] 3465[5] 4156[5] 4615[7] (5176) 5914[2] 6442[3] 6895[3] 7428[10] 7595[2]

Crianza *Mrs J L Le Brocq* a49 56
5 ch m Polish Precedent(USA) —Red To Violet (Spectrum (IRE))
69[4] 382[3] 652[9] (1743a) 1805a[P]

Cried For You (IRE) *Tim Easterby* 58
2 b f Moss Vale(IRE) —Baywood (Emarati (USA))
4406[4]

Crimea (IRE) *David Nicholls* a67 93
5 b g Kheleyf(USA) —Russian Countess (USA) (Nureyev (USA))
5033[4] 5543[6] 6350[5]

Crimson Cloud *Richard Fahey* a85 76
3 ch f Kyllachy—Calamanco (Clantime)
1697[5] 2365[3] 2736[2] 3166[7] 3759[5] 4295[4] 4988[3] 7104[4] (7356) 7643[7]

Crimson Knight *Brian Meehan* 83
3 ch c Zafeen(FR) —Kaylianni (Kalanisi (IRE))
1408[10] 2097[7] 2813[3] (3364) 3772[6]

Crimson Knot (IRE) *Alan Berry* 79
3 b f Red Ransom(USA) —Green Minstrel (FR) (Green Tune (USA))
1711[3] 1825[5] 2411[4] 2724[3] 3807[4] 3975[3] 4295[3] 4610[2] 5268[9] 6112[10] 7073[7]

Crimson Monarch (USA) *Peter Hiatt* a44 75
7 b g Red Ransom(USA) —Tolltally Light (USA) (Majestic Light (USA))
104[5]

Crimson Queen *Roy Brotherton* a67 71
4 ch m Red Ransom(USA) —Rainbow Queen (Rainbow Quest (USA))
1523[10] 1766[4] 2555[8] 3714[12] 4230[4] (5019) (5175) 5326[7] 6479[15] 7201[3] 7395[13] 7649[8] 7896[6]

Crimson Sea (IRE) *Ben Haslam* 47
2 ch f Redback—Fantastic Cee (IRE) (Noverre (USA))
4406[6] 4899[11] 5555[4]

Crimson Sunrise (IRE) *D K Weld* 81
2 b f Holy Roman Emperor(IRE) —Zanida (IRE) (Mujadil (USA))
2777a[7]

Cri Na Mara (IRE) *Mark Michael McNiff* a57 32
3 b f Tagula(IRE) —Northweststar (IRE) (Revoque (IRE))
5433[6] 7460[6] (7693) 7785[4]

Crinan Classic *George Baker* a60 34
4 b g Fraam—Black And Amber (Weldnaas (USA))
684[4] 984[5] 1333[2] 1756[6] 4928[8] 5143[13]

Criostal (IRE) *J S Bolger* 98
2 b f Teofilo(IRE) —Crystal Ballet (USA) (Royal Academy (USA))
5525a[7]

Cristal Gem *Andrew Reid* a75 67
2 ch f Cadeaux Genereux—Desert Cristal (IRE) (Desert King (IRE))
2302[2] ◆ 6725[5] (6927) 7582[2] 7657[2]

Cristaliyev *Jim Boyle* a65 68
3 b g Fasliyev(USA) —Desert Cristal (IRE) (Desert King (IRE))
958[4] 1131[2] 1830[3] 2869[11] 6794[9] 7137[11] 7448[9] 7518[3]

Critical Moment (USA) *Charles Hills* 110
4 b h Aptitude(USA) —Rouwaki (USA) (Miswaki (USA))
1600[3] ◆ 1821[4] 4789[4] 5252[9] 6061[5]

Critical Point *Sir Mark Prescott Bt* a11
2 ch g Pivotal—Finlaggan (Be My Chief (USA))
7080[13] 7197[11] 7368[11] 7431[11]

Criticize (USA) *C Von Der Recke* a45 62
5 b g Mizzen Mast(USA) —Euphonize (USA) (Seattle Slew (USA))
935a[9]

Crius (IRE) *Richard Hannon* 110
2 b c Heliostatic(IRE) —Fearless Flyer (IRE) (Brave Act)
(3780) (4508) 5287[2] 5709[2] (6270)

Crocodile Bay (IRE) *Richard Guest* a65 62
8 b g Spectrum(IRE) —Shenkara (IRE) (Night Shift (USA))
292[6] 547[4] 568[4] 674[8] 730[6] 896[6] 1068[4] [illegible] 2029 3025 3658 4039[7] 4123[3] 4438[5] 4651[11] 5214[9] 5601[11] 5789[9] 6159[11] 6541[10]

Crocus Rose *Harry Dunlop* a88 88
5 gr m Royal Applause—Crodelle (IRE) (Formidable (USA))
1105[7] 1470[2] 2931[3] 3911[4] 4555[6] 5471[5] 7226[5]

Croeso Mawr *John Spearing* 61
5 ch m Bertolini(USA) —Croeso-I-Cymru (Welsh Captain)
1989[9] 4270[8] 4948[10] 5349[12] 6033[2] 6411[4] (6938)

Croftamie *Mark Johnston* 71
2 b f Selkirk(USA) —Embraced (Pursuit Of Love)
7232[3]

Croisultan (IRE) *Liam McAteer* a83 108
5 ch g Refuse To Bend(IRE) —Zoudie (Ezzoud (IRE))
1118a[4] 2323a[7] 3440a[12] 4978a[6] 5979a[3] 6147[7] 6733a[7]

Croix Madame (FR) *F Doumen* a83 90
4 b m Forestier(FR) —She Runs (FR) (Sheyrann)
900a[4]

Croix Rouge (USA) *Ralph Smith* a57 60
9 b g Chester House(USA) —Rougeur (USA) (Blushing Groom (FR))
4211[2] 5692[9] 6379[2] 6417[2] 6621[11] 7091[5] 7206[4] 7528[4] 7654[7]

Cronsa (GER) *S Botti* 101
4 b m Martino Alonso(IRE) —Croa (IRE) (Alzao (USA))
3213a[8]

Croquembouche (IRE) *Sir Michael Stoute* 76
2 b c Acclamation—Wedding Cake (IRE) (Groom Dancer (USA))
3954[2] ◆ (4402) 5280[3] 6031[7]

Cross Culture (IRE) *Andrew Balding* 80
3 b g Cape Cross(IRE) —Margay (IRE) (Marju (IRE))
3514[12] (4011) 4457[4]

Crossley *Geoffrey Oldroyd* 68
2 ch g Monsieur Bond(IRE) —Dispol Diamond (Sharpo)
4122[8] 6274[5] 6837[3]

Cross Of Lorraine (IRE) *Chris Grant* a38 72
8 b g Pivotal—My-Lorraine (IRE) (Mac's Imp (USA))
2803[11] 3305[6] 4328[4] (4672) (5009) 5552[3] 5824[9] 6778[3]

Cross The Boss (IRE) *Ben Haslam* a66 62
4 b g Cape Cross(IRE) —Lady Salsa (IRE) (Gone West (USA))
1558[5] 2057[3] 3088[13]

Crossword *Marco Botti* a64 68
3 b g Cape Cross(IRE) —Foxilla (IRE) (Foxhound (USA))
543[4] 716[4] (898) 1574[2]

Crowded House *B Cecil* a116 111
5 ch h Rainbow Quest(USA) —Wiener Wald (USA) (Woodman (USA))
416a[7] 756a[9] 997a[14]

Crown Choice *Walter Swinburn* a104 102
6 b g King's Best(USA) —Belle Allemande (CAN) (Royal Academy (USA))
1457[3] ◆ 1888[14] (2288) 3410[11] 3862[5] 4534[21] 5032[16]

Crown Counsel (IRE) *Mark Johnston* a82 98
3 b c Invincible Spirit(IRE) —Virgin Hawk (USA) (Silver Hawk (USA))
636[2] 776a[2] 980a[2] (1203) 1690[4] (1820) 2296[14] 2705[8] 3067[20] (3542) 3763[2] 4313[11] 5272[3] 5712[15] 5929[5] 6339[15] 6574[3] 6862[29] 7295[19]

Crown Dependency (IRE) *Richard Hannon* a98 99
2 b g Acclamation—Top Row (Observatory (USA))
(1835) ◆ 3064[3] ◆ 4413[4] 5216[14] 5715[5] 6162[7]

Crowning Star (IRE) *J S Moore* a74 75
2 b g Royal Applause—Dossier (Octagonal (NZ))
1095[3] ◆ 2148[4] 3014[20] (3746) 4226[2] 6699[9] 7358[8] 7762[4] 7927[2]

Crown Ridge (IRE) *Mick Channon* a61 66
3 b g Oratorio(IRE) —Don't Care (IRE) (Nordico (USA))
716[6] 1022[3] 1169[3] 1303[2] 1495[8] 1790[4] 4018[2] 4200[4] 4435[4] 4728[3] 5120[3] (5298)

Crucis Abbey (IRE) *James Unett* a70 62
3 b g Acclamation—Golden Ribes (USA) (Charismatic (USA))
1084[2] 1980[8] 2375[2] 3337[9] 3853[8] 4199[8] 5419[3] 5736[9] 6179[6]

Cruise Control *Richard Price* a54 54
5 b g Piccolo—Urban Dancer (IRE) (Generous (IRE))
4703[5] 4953[6] 5785[3]

Cruiser *William Muir* 92
3 b g Oasis Dream—Good Girl (IRE) (College Chapel)
1317[5] 1725[3] 2296[7] 2506[4] 3067[6] 3840[2] 4723[7] 5450[5] 5892[6] 6273[2] 6574[7]

Cruise Tothelimit (IRE) *Mark Brisbourne* a60 77
3 b g Le Vie Dei Colori—Kiva (Indian Ridge)
2043[5] 2505[3] 2694[11] 3166[10] 3239[3] 3379[8] (3914) (4195) 4643[2] 4880[5] 5378[4] 5918[7] 6212[8] 7106[12] 7395[6] 7566[10]

Crunched *Tim Pitt* a81 77
4 b g Dubai Destination(USA) —Amica (Averti (IRE))
1144[2] ◆ 1325[10] 7878[3]

Crusade (USA) *A P O'Brien* a103 114
2 bb c Mr Greeley(USA) —La Traviata (USA) (Johannesburg (USA))
5254[8] 6270[4] (6688) 7306a[6]

Crusch (IRE) *S Botti* 97
5 gr h Daylami(IRE) —Guest Harbour (IRE) (Be My Guest (USA))
6569a[7]

Cry Alot Boy *Kevin Morgan* a80 59
8 ch g Spinning World(USA) —Intellectuelle (Caerleon (USA))
1538[3] 3391[3] 4060[8] 4763[9]

Cry For The [illegible]
5 b g Street Cry(IRE) —Kafaf (USA) (Zilzal (USA))
3420a[2] 4398a[2]

Cry Fury *Roger Charlton* a86 101
3 b g Beat Hollow—Cantanta (Top Ville)
(1484) 2295[5] (4959) ◆ 5929[8] 6339[24]

Crying Lightening (IRE) *Peter Chapple-Hyam* a69 102
3 b f Holy Roman Emperor(IRE) —Auction Room (USA) (Chester House (USA))
151a[7] 412a[8] 680a[9] (823a) 1319[8] 5848[7] (6523)

Crying Wolf (USA) *Mahmood Al Zarooni*
2 bb c Street Cry(IRE) —Don't Tacha Me (USA) (A.P. Indy (USA))
5254[17]

Cry Of Liberty (IRE) *L Riccardi* 98
4 b m Statue Of Liberty(USA) —Martine Bellis (ITY) (Darshaan)
1432a[5]

Cryptic Choice (IRE) *Charles Hills* 73
2 b g Johannesburg(USA) —Royal Fupeg (USA) (Fusaichi Pegasus (USA))
4762[4] 5697[5] 5849[20]

Crystal Belle (IRE) *Patrick Martin* a84 79
3 b f Ivan Denisovich(IRE) —Crystal Springs (IRE) (Kahyasi)
1706a[3]

Crystal Bridge *Bill Moore* a25 22
4 b m Avonbridge—Heaven-Liegh-Grey (Grey Desire)
233[6] 538[8] 1274[6] 1905[12]

Crystal Capella *Sir Michael Stoute* a75 121
6 b m Cape Cross(IRE) —Crystal Star (Mark Of Esteem (IRE))
2501[4] (3775) 4533[4] 5219[4] 6859[4]

Crystal Celebre (IRE) *Henry Candy* a64 72
5 b g Peintre Celebre(USA) —Top Crystal (IRE) (Sadler's Wells (USA))
1443[9] ◆ 2235[4]

Crystal Child *Brian Rothwell* a40 33
3 b f Keltos(FR) —Aliuska (IRE) (Fijar Tango (FR))
7063[12] 7250[8]

Crystal Etoile *Sir Michael Stoute* a59 75
3 b f Dansili—Crystal Star (Mark Of Esteem (IRE))
1270[2] 2026[5] ◆ 4215[5] ◆ 5598[4] 6586[4] 7237[13]

Crystal Gal (IRE) *Lucy Wadham* 103
4 b m Galileo(IRE) —Park Crystal (IRE) (Danehill (USA))
1718[8] 2031[10] 2994[6] 3356[4] 3876[14] (4790) 6370a[4]

Crystal Gale (IRE) *William Knight* a70 64
4 gr m Verglas(IRE) —Mango Groove (IRE) (Unfuwain (USA))
83[3] 1582[5] 2091[3]

Crystal High *Marco Botti* 75
3 b f High Chaparral(IRE) —Park Crystal (IRE) (Danehill (USA))
2529[5] 3577[2] 4186[2]

Crystal Lily (AUS) *Mathew Ellerton & Simon Zahra* 112
4 b f Stratum(AUS) —Crystal Snip (AUS) (Snippets (AUS))
2

Crystallize *Andrew Haynes* a64 64
5 b g Bertolini(USA) —Adamas (IRE) (Fairy King (USA))
129[9] 211[2] 312[3] (386) 1177[5] (1283) 1357[10] 1730[9] 2027[9] 2426[8] 2920[16] 4246[5]

Crystallus (IRE) *Ann Duffield* a70 73
3 b f Diamond Green(FR) —Lominda (IRE) (Lomond (USA))
2365[2] 3360[8]

Crystal Morning (IRE) *Mrs John Harrington* a74 82
3 bb f Cape Cross(IRE) —Follow My Lead (Night Shift (USA))
7150a[8]

Crystal Sky (IRE) *Andrew Haynes* a65 63
3 b f Bachelor Duke(USA) —Fen Style (IRE) (Desert Style (IRE))
520[5] (634) 931[5] 1286[3] 1958[5] 5243[4] 5838[8] 6067[7] 7144[5]

C. S. Silk (USA) *Dale Romans* a105 115
5 bb m Medaglia D'Oro(USA) —Remember The Day (USA) (Settlement Day (USA))
6719a[7]

Ctappers *Mick Channon* a44 64
2 b g Imperial Dancer—Stride Home (Absalom)
5937[6] 6245[3] 6630[7] 7786[5]

Cubanita *Ralph Beckett* 81
2 ch f Selkirk(USA) —Caribana (Hernando (FR))
6463[2] ◆ (7233) ◆

Cuban Piece (IRE) *Tom Dascombe* a63 63
3 b g Azamour(IRE) —Naazeq (Nashwan (USA))
1189[8] 1442[6] 1872[4] 2571[6] 3301[5]

Cuban Quality (USA) *Tom Dascombe* a27 68
3 bb g Elusive Quality(USA) —Russian Lullaby (IRE) (Galileo (IRE))
2186[7] 2722[10]

Cuckney Bear *Ed McMahon* a45 75
3 ch g Bertolini(USA) —Inveraray (Selkirk (USA))
1812[6] 2185[8] 2650[9] (3485) (4381) 5407[7] 5925[10]

Cuckoo Rock (IRE) *Jonathan Portman* a54 66
4 b g Refuse To Bend(IRE) —Ringmoor Down (Pivotal)
3515[2] 4273[5] 5611[4] 6438[3]

Cuddly *Robert Cowell* a34 14
3 b f Royal Applause—Smooch (Inchinor)
380[7] 513[5]

Cufflink *Rae Guest* a49
2 b f Rail Link—Fred's Dream (Cadeaux Genereux)
7838[8]

Cullybackey (IRE) *John Harris* a41 52
6 ch m Golan(IRE) —Leitrim Lodge (IRE) (Classic Music (USA))
136[5] 382[9]

Cultural Desert *Ralph Beckett* 80
3 b g Footstepsinthesand—Border Minstral (IRE) (Sri Pekan (USA))
1108[8] 2392[7] 2885[6] (4337) 4725[3] 5495[7]

Cumberwell Cracker *Bill Turner*
3 b f Monsieur Bond(IRE) —Mimic (Royal Applause)
396[8]

Cumulus Nimbus *Richard Hannon* a104 104
4 ch h Muhtathir—Supreme Talent (Desert King (IRE))
1100[5] 1403[7] 1684[8] 2289[6]

Cunning Act *Jonathan Portman* a70 100
3 ch g Act One—Saffron Fox (Safawan)
1475[3] 1951[3] 2226[2] (2874) 3364[3] (4449) 5283[8] (5966) 6499[2]

Curl Cat (USA) *K J Condon* a71 73
5 b g Tale Of The Cat(USA) —Charade Queen (USA) (A.P. Indy (USA))
977a[10]

Curlew (IRE) *Chris Down* a70 60
5 b g Cape Cross(IRE) —Billbill (USA) (Storm Cat (USA))
4822[6] 5231[8] 7263[9]

Curly Come Home *Chris Wall* 46
2 b f Notnowcato—Cuyamaca (IRE) (Desert King (IRE))
6956[8] 7232[9]

Curragh Dancer (FR) *Paddy Butler* a1 34
8 ch g Grand Lodge(USA) —Native Twine (Be My Native (USA))
277[13]

Curren Chan (JPN) *Takayuki Yasuda* 120
4 gr m Kurofune(USA) —Spring Ticket (JPN) (Tony Bin)
7730a[5]

Curro Perote (FR) *L A Urbano-Grajales* a95 89
4 gr g Smadoun(FR) —First Choice (FR) (Exit To Nowhere (USA))
840a[2]

Curtain Patch (USA) *Bryan Smart* a37 59
2 rg f Macho Uno(USA) —Biogio's Kids (USA) (Lemon Drop Kid (USA))
3656[4] 4122[10] 4898[3] 5503[4] 6047[5] 6667[6] 6846[11]

Curtains *Simon Dow* a80 91
4 b m Dubawi(IRE) —Voile (IRE) (Barathea (IRE))
(961) 1720[23] 1902[11] 3351[3] 3845[9] 4416[17]

Curzon Line *Mahmood Al Zarooni* a78 75
2 b c Dubawi(IRE) —Polska (USA) (Danzig (USA))
5851[4] 6334[10] 6795[2] 7095[5]

Custard Cream Kid (IRE) *Richard Fahey* a51 55
5 b g Statue Of Liberty(USA) —Diniesque (Rainbow Quest (USA))
129[4] 204[11]

Custodian (IRE) *James M Barrett* a50 78
9 gr g Giant's Causeway(USA) —Desert Bluebell (Kalaglow)
7378a[13] 7544a[10]

Customer Base (USA) *Thomas F Proctor* a89 93
2 bb f Lemon Drop Kid(USA) —Little Cat Feet (USA) (Tale Of The Cat (USA))
7281a[11]

Custom House (IRE) *John E Long* a80 80
3 b g Tale Of The Cat(USA) —L'Acajou (CAN) (Gulch (USA))
1175[8] 1843[11] 1999[3] 2642[4] 4321[4] 4709[2] 5171[9] 6586[10] 6814[9] 7349[3] 7588[9] 7942[10]

Cut And Thrust (IRE) *Mark Wellings* a73 62
5 b g Haafhd—Ego (Green Desert (USA))
249[5] 394[4] 637[9] 820[9] 984[4] 2201[12] 6784[10] 7229[3] (7656)

Cuthbert (IRE) *William Jarvis* a74 75
4 ch g Bertolini(USA) —Tequise (IRE) (Victory Note (USA))
55[3] 249[3] 562[6] 2354[5] 3555[2] 4160[7] 5803[11] 6980[10]

Cut The Cackle (IRE) *Richard Guest* a79 71
5 b m Danetime(IRE) —Alexander Anapolis (IRE) (Spectrum (IRE))
4918[8] 5788[11] 6444[8] 6618[8] 6791[3] 7485[3] 7655[5]

Cwmni *Bryn Palling* a65 66
5 b m Auction House(USA) —Sontime (Son Pardo)
432[2] 589[7] 3512[7] 4270[7] 4705[5] 4918[10] 5540[8] 5843[9] 6309[7] 6609[15] 7696[3]

Cyber Star *James Fanshawe* a46 65
3 b f King's Best(USA) —Spectral Star (Unfuwain (USA))
1950[8] 5639[6] 6255[8] 6823[9]

Cycladelle (FR) *C Restout*
4 b m Passing Sale(FR) —Cyclades (FR) (Sicyos (USA))
1012a[0]

Cyflymder (IRE) *David C Griffiths* a79 93
5 b g Mujadil(USA) —Nashwan Star (IRE) (Nashwan (USA))
1109[6] 1382[13] 2280[5] 2671[7] 3093[3] 3341[5] 3806[5] 4176[4] 6990[12] 7418[8] 7455[7] 7648[2] 7748[3]

Cynthia Calhoun *Clive Cox* 56
2 b f Exceed And Excel(AUS) —The Jotter (Night Shift (USA))
6725[9]

Cyril The Squirrel *Karen George* a71 56
7 b g Cyrano De Bergerac—All Done (Northern State (USA))
(425)

Cyrus (IRE) *John C McConnell* a47 56
4 b m Reset(AUS) —Triple Wood (USA) (Woodman (USA))
6419[6]

Cyrus Sod *David Simcock* 60
2 b g Nayef(USA) —Tahirah (Green Desert (USA))
7083[6]

Daa'lman *Clive Brittain* a60 22
3 b f Dansili—Sauterne (Rainbow Quest (USA))
3594[10]

Daaweitza *Brian Ellison* a83 85
8 ch g Daawe(USA) —Chichen Itza (Shareef Dancer (USA))
2006[12] 2364[5] 3701[8] 4083[8] (4649) 4982[9] 6263[7] 6538[6] 7506[6]

Dabbers Ridge (IRE) *Ian McInnes* a72 83
9 b h Indian Ridge—Much Commended (Most Welcome)
881[5] 1164[3] 2046[2] 2413[4] 3275[15] 3831[6] 4150[6] 4679[11] 5414[10] 6235[14]

Dabbiton (GER) [illegible]
2 b c Soldier Hollow—Djidda (GER) (Lando (GER))
7325a[4]

Dabirsim (FR) *C Ferland* 120
2 b c Hat Trick(JPN) —Rumored (USA) (Royal Academy (USA))
(4596a) (5305a) (6565a) ◆

Da Capo (IRE) *Mme Pia Brandt* a82 91
5 b g Peintre Celebre(USA) —Specificity (USA) (Alleged (USA))
7733a[0]

Daddy Long Legs (USA) *A P O'Brien* a81 112
2 ch c Scat Daddy(USA) —Dreamy Maiden (USA) (Meadowlake (USA))
5926[4] (6336) 7306a[12]

Daddy Nose Best (USA) *Steven Asmussen* 106
2 b c Scat Daddy(USA) —Follow Your Bliss (USA) (Thunder Gulch (USA))
7301a[6]

Daddyow *Bryn Palling* a70 25
3 b g Indesatchel(IRE) —Generous Share (Cadeaux Genereux)
1580[2] 2723[3] 3717[5] 4385[11]

Daddy Warbucks (IRE) *David Nicholls* 69
2 b g Multiplex—Skerries (IRE) (Dr Fong (USA))
3826[7] 4171[2] 4535[16] 6110[8] (6835)

Dado Mush *Terry Clement* a29 42
8 b g Almushtarak(IRE) —Princess Of Spain (King Of Spain)
1468[7] 7775[7]

Dads Amigo *George Foster* 83
3 b g Bertolini(USA) —Pip's Way (IRE) (Pips Pride)
1214[3]

Dafeef *William Haggas* 112
4 b g Medicean—Almahab (USA) (Danzig (USA))
5282[5] 5930[2] 6858[15]

Daffyd *Roger Charlton* 62
2 b g Green Desert(USA) —Ffestiniog (IRE) (Efisio)
6991[6]

Daffydowndilly *Hughie Morrison* a75 73
3 b f Oasis Dream—Art Eyes (USA) (Halling (USA))
4437[4] 5387[3] ◆ 5640[4] 6156[11] 6591[3] 6971[2] 7447[4] (7748)

Dagda Mor (ITY) *S Botti* 113
4 b h Martino Alonso(IRE) —Bagnolese (ITY) (Cape Cross (IRE))
1919a[2] (6906a) 7408a[2]

Daggerman *Barry Leavy* a44 36
6 ch g Daggers Drawn(USA) —Another Mans Cause (FR) (Highest Honor (FR))
173[7] 451[10]

Daghash *Clive Brittain* 77
2 b c Tiger Hill(IRE) —Zibet (Kris)
5337[6] 5654[6] (6048) 6170[11] 6527[9] 6986[4]

Dahaam *David Simcock* a89 85
4 b g Red Ransom(USA) —Almansoora (USA) (Bahri (USA))
235[2] 1477[9] 1855[3] 2220[13] 2810[6] 3538[5]

Dahab Gold (IRE) *Jane Chapple-Hyam* a65
2 gr f Clodovil(IRE) —Desert Alchemy (IRE) (Green Desert (USA))
7583[3] 7784[5]

Dahindar (IRE) *Edward Lynam* a104 94
6 b g Invincible Spirit(IRE) —Daftara (IRE) (Caerleon (USA))
1228a[2]

Daily Double *Martin Bosley* a40 60
5 gr g Needwood Blade—Coffee To Go (Environment Friend)
70[10] 312[11]

Daily Dreams (FR) *R Rohne* 50
3 b f Auenadler(GER) —Daily Daylight (GER) (Waky Nao)
852a[8]

Daisyclipper *Ann Duffield* 65
3 b f Indesatchel(IRE) —My Daisychain (Hector Protector (USA))
1155[8] 1459[5] 2094[2] 2986[10]

Daisy Crazy *Gary Harrison*
4 b m Auction House(USA) —Silk Daisy (Barathea (IRE))
5960[7]

Dakar (GER) *Pat Phelan* 62
3 b c Cape Cross(IRE) —Darakshaana (IRE) (Barathea (IRE))
1480[5] 2648[15] 3183[6] *3518[11]*

Dakota Canyon (IRE) *Richard Fahey* 76
2 b g Rock Of Gibraltar(IRE) —Dakota Sioux (IRE) (College Chapel)
6768[9] (7052)

Dalacara *Clive Cox* a61 56
2 ch f Dalakhani(IRE) —Wild Clover (Lomitas)
4968[9] 5583[10] 6603[7] *7035[4]*

Dalarna (GER) *W Hickst* 102
3 b f Dashing Blade—Daily Mail (GER) (Konigsstuhl (GER))
2337a[2] 2981a[7] 4839a[8]

Dalarua (IRE) *S Wattel* 107
3 b f King's Best(USA) —Djenanne (FR) (Danzero (AUS))
2342a[8] 3671a[5] (4570a) 5366a[8] 6686a[7]

Daleel (IRE) *John Dunlop*
2 ch c Intikhab(USA) —Bahareeya (USA) (Riverman (USA))
6953[13]

Dalghar (FR) *Andrew Balding* a105 119
5 gr h Anabaa(USA) —Daltawa (IRE) (Miswaki (USA))
2005[6] ◆ 3154[12] 3863[11] 4412[6] 5070[7] ◆

Dalhaan (USA) *Luke Dace* a78 72
6 b g Fusaichi Pegasus(USA) —Khazayin (USA) (Bahri (USA))
209 [7] 486[6] 4687[6] *5318[13]*

Daliana *Michael Bell* a36 53
3 gr f Verglas(IRE) —Up And About (Barathea (IRE))
1146[8] 1480[6] 1873[9] 3958[9] 4929[4]

Daliance (IRE) *Tom Dascombe* 74
2 ch c Dalakhani(IRE) —Everlasting Love (Pursuit Of Love)
4624a[5]

Dalida (GER) *Markus Klug* 42
2 ch f Desert Prince(IRE) —Desimona (GER) (Monsun (GER))
6737a[10]

Dalkova *Sir Michael Stoute* a32
2 b f Galileo(IRE) —Dalasyla (IRE) (Marju (IRE))
5691[6]

Dal'Oro (FR) *Jean De Roualle* a52
4 b g Daliapour(IRE) —Golden Fortuna (Turtle Island (IRE))
842a[5]

Dalrymple (IRE) *Michael Madgwick* a44 53
5 ch g Daylami(IRE) —Dallaah (Green Desert (USA))
163[4] 245[5] 552[14]

Damascus Symphony *James Bethell* a21 70
3 b f Pastoral Pursuits—Syrian Queen (Slip Anchor)
1974[7] 2349[3] 3116[2] 4111[4] 4364[7] 5405[13] 5553[2] (6192) (6775) 7062[4]

Damask (IRE) *Kevin Ryan* 63
2 b f Red Clubs(IRE) —Goldthroat (IRE) (Zafonic (USA))
2467[8] 2914[4] 3812[13] 6222[5] 6911[8]

Dam Beautiful *Kevin Ryan* 92
2 b f Sleeping Indian—Nellie Melba (Hurricane Sky (AUS))
(3092) 3416a[5] 3884a[3]

Dam D'Augy (FR) *Mlle S-V Tarrou* a91 100
6 ch m Bernebeau(FR) —Cardamome (FR) (Cardoun (FR))
92a[10] 1122a[9] 4121a[6] 5985a[5]

Damika (IRE) *Richard Whitaker* a97 103
8 ch g Namid—Emly Express (IRE) (High Estate)
1242[6] 2075[6] 2284[6] 2706[11] 4325[8] 4609[5] 5278[2] ◆ 5508[5] 5852[17]

Danadana (IRE) *Luca Cumani* a73 90
3 b c Dubawi(IRE) —Zeeba (IRE) (Barathea (IRE))
(1492) ◆ 2471[2] 3069[5]

Danafisiak (IRE) *Frank Sheridan* a10
2 b c Stardan(IRE) —Afisiak (Efisio)
7821[9] 7927[6]

Dana's Present *George Baker* a18 59
2 ch g Osorio(GER) —Euro Empire (USA) (Bartok (IRE))
2448[5] 5111[13] *5410[9] 6489[12]*

Dan Buoy (FR) *Richard Guest* a40 75
8 b g Slip Anchor—Bramosia (Forzando)
1153[13] 1458[11] 2762[7] 6095[3] *6356[9]* 6575[4] 6915[11]

Dance And Dance (IRE) *Edward Vaughan* a91 116
5 b g Royal Applause—Caldy Dancer (IRE) (Soviet Star (USA))
1092[2] 1529[14] 2031[3] (2679) 3032[2] ◆ 4494[5] ◆ 4972[2] 6204a[6] 6721a[5]

Dance City (USA) *Todd Pletcher* a112
3 b c City Zip(USA) —Ballet Colony (USA) (Pleasant Colony (USA))
2328a[5]

Dance Company *William Knight* 74
2 b f Aussie Rules(USA) —Corps De Ballet (IRE) (Fasliyev (USA))
4052[3] ◆ 5048[5]

Dance For Georgie *Ben Haslam* 47
2 ch f Motivator—Chetwynd (IRE) (Exit To Nowhere (USA))
4232[5] 6259[6]

Dance For Julie (IRE) *Ben Haslam* a66 72
4 b m Redback—Dancing Steps (Zafonic (USA))
(1167) 4237[5] 5107[7] 6264[5]

Dance For Livvy (IRE) *Robin Dickin* a69 63
3 br f Kodiac—Dancing Steps (Zafonic (USA))
456[4] (1018) (1969) 7839[2]

Dance In The Dark (FR) *S Wattel* a61 80
3 b f Kendor(FR) —Khaylama (IRE) (Dr Devious (IRE))
7667a[6]

Danceintothelight *Micky Hammond* a60 71
4 gr g Dansili—Kali (Linamix (FR))
1039[7] 3023[7] 3507[6] 3730[4] 4366[12] 4982[2] 5369[2] 6157[3]

Dance Of The Ocean (AUS) *John P Thompson* 92
4 b f Danzero(AUS) —Dolphin Dance (AUS) (Dolphin Street (FR))
9029a[7]

Dancera (GER) *Mervyn Torrens* a79 49
7 b m Johan Cruyff—Dancin' Doll (Grand Lodge (USA))
1381a[14]

Dancerella *David Elsworth* 55
3 b f Norse Dancer(IRE) —Cinder's Prize (Sinndar (IRE))
2068[12] 3363[9]

Dance Secretary (IRE) *John M Oxx* 98
3 ch f Danehill Dancer(IRE) —Ball Chairman (USA) (Secretariat (USA))
1928a[3]

Dances With Words (IRE) *Rodney Farrant* a56 52
3 b g Mujadil(USA) —Lyric Dances (FR) (Sendawar (IRE))
53[6] 275[4] 335[6]

Dance Tempo *Hughie Morrison* 90
4 b g Dansili—Musical Twist (USA) (Woodman (USA))
(2156) ◆ 2812[8] 3867[10] 6249[12]

Dance The Rain *Bryan Smart* 78
2 b f Rock Of Gibraltar(IRE) —Antediluvian (Air Express (IRE))
(4525) 4964[3] 5931[5] 6986[11]

Dance The Star (USA) *Mme J Bidgood* a86 75
6 b g Dynaformer(USA) —Dance The Slew (USA) (Slew City Slew (USA))
533a[4]

Dance To Destiny *Phil McEntee* a57
3 ch f Carnival Dancer—Java Dawn (IRE) (Fleetwood (IRE))
121[6] 262[4]

Dance With Me (IRE) *Andrew Balding* 72
2 b g Danehill Dancer(IRE) —Perpetual Time (Sadler's Wells (USA))
6170[15] 6527[10]

Danceyourselfdizzy (IRE) *Phil McEntee* a58 66
3 b g Danehill Dancer(IRE) —Gamra (IRE) (Green Desert (USA))
987[5] 2024[2] *2196[5]* 2581[2] 2789[4] 3089[3] 3804[6] 4200[8] *5041[6] 5860[10]* 6067[4] *6446[14] 6659[5]*

Danchai *David Lanigan* 78
2 gr c Authorized(IRE) —Scarlet Empire (IRE) (Red Ransom (USA))
6953[2]

Dancheur (IRE) *Mrs K Burke* 67
2 ch f Chineur(FR) —Daneville (IRE) (Danetime (IRE))
(6800)

Dancing Again *Eric Wheeler* a34 41
5 ch m Reel Buddy(USA) —Batchworth Breeze (Beveled (USA))
28[6] 1041[8] 1627[6]

Dancing Belle *J R Jenkins* a29 46
6 b m Fasliyev(USA) —May Ball (Cadeaux Genereux)
354[7]

Dancing Cavalier (IRE) *Reg Hollinshead* a47 29
3 ch g Halling(USA) —El Tigress (GER) (Tiger Hill (IRE))
1300[7] 1769[13] *2166[11]* 3077[6]

Dancing Freddy (IRE) *Richard Guest* a81 86
4 b g Chineur(FR) —Majesty's Dancer (IRE) (Danehill Dancer (IRE))
122[5] 289[3] 345[2] (375) 696[7] 794[6] 1239[9] *1463[8] 1503[2]* 1796[3] 1907[14] 2397[6] 2913[3] 3040[2] 3711[10] 4272[3] (4539) 4900[7] 5148[3] 5720[13] 6044[7] (6276) 6762[7] 6917[2] 7355[3] 7428[9] 7643[4] 7746[5] 7917[8]

Dancing Gizmo *Alistair Whillans* 44
6 b g Where Or When(IRE) —Tactile (Groom Dancer (USA))
1076[4]

Dancinginmydreams (IRE) *U Suter* a69 76
2 b f Aussie Rules(USA) —Yasmin Satine (IRE) (Key Of Luck (USA))
7814a[0]

Dancing Lancer *Kate Walton* 11
2 b g Alhaarth(IRE) —Mafatin (IRE) (Sadler's Wells (USA))
7109[10] *7398[13]*

Dancing Maite *Roy Bowring* a83 80
6 ch g Ballet Master(USA) —Ace Maite (Komaite (USA))
1061[6] 1395[6] 2938[3] 6778[12] 7299[10] *7643[5]*

Dancing Poppy *Ben De Haan* a56 58
4 b m Kyllachy—Broughtons Motto (Mtoto)
69[8] 631[5] 771[5]

Dancing Primo *Mark Brisbourne* a41 78
5 b m Primo Valentino(IRE) —Tycoon's Last (Nalchik (USA))
1474[8] 1915[5] 2258[10] (2905) 3256[4] (3910) 4164[2] 4626[2] (4747) ◆ 4887[7] (6029) 6676[3]

Dancing Rain (IRE) *William Haggas* 118
3 ch f Danehill Dancer(IRE) —Rain Flower (IRE) (Indian Ridge)
(1364) 2050[2] (2682) 4133a[5] (4839a) (6859) 7410a[16]

Dancing Storm *Stuart Kittow* a56 68
8 b m Trans Island—Stormswell (Persian Bold)
1750[5] 2552[4] 3184[3] (3762) 5580[7]

Dancing Tara *David Evans* a2 59
3 b f Chevalier(IRE) —Prayer (IRE) (Rainbow Quest (USA))
850[10] 1056[5] *1293[6]* 1449[2] 1629[3] 1980[6] 2141[7]

Dancing Wave *Michael Chapman* a50 65
5 b m Baryshnikov(AUS) —Wavet (Pursuit Of Love)
318[6] 375[4]

Dancing Welcome *Milton Bradley* a73 60
5 b m Kyllachy—Highland Gait (Most Welcome)
97[2] 268[3] (351) 435[8] 522[4] 698[8] 1875[5] 2222[2] 2555[4] ◆ 2921[9] 3476[5] 3943[3] 4086[4] (4270) 4705[3] 4948[6] 5540[5] 5674[2] 5843[5] 6479[4] 6610[5]

Dandarrell *Julie Camacho* a61 59
4 b g Makbul—Dress Design (IRE) (Brief Truce (USA))
496[4] 1956[9] 2462[4] 2988[6] 3317[9] *6134[3] 6698[7]*

Danderek *Brian Meehan* a86 89
5 ch g Fantastic Light(USA) —Maureena (IRE) (Grand Lodge (USA))
405[5] 694[3] 1075[5] 1390[5] (1746) 2320[7] 3848[5] 4577[4] (6241) 7029[5]

Dandino *James Given* 117
4 br h Dansili—Generous Diana (Generous (IRE))
(1416) (1685) 2680[4] 4374a[7] 5284[9]

Dan Donnelly (IRE) *Jeremy Gask* a30 46
3 b g Antonius Pius(USA) —Lacinia (Groom Dancer (USA))
6251[8] 6591[4] *7093[9]*

Dandy (GER) *Andrew Balding* 83
2 b c Nayef(USA) —Diacada (GER) (Cadeaux Genereux)
4446[8] (6267)

Dandy Boy (ITY) *David Marnane* a102 112
5 b h Danetime(IRE) —Fleet Of Light (Spectrum (IRE))
(152a) *501a[12]*

Dandy's Hero (IRE) *David Nicholls* 54
2 b g One Cool Cat(USA) —Monsusu (IRE) (Montjeu (IRE))
3610[8] 4147[4] ◆

Dane Cottage *Brian Ellison* a56 68
4 ch m Beat Hollow—Lady Soleas (Be My Guest (USA))
69[5] 115[6] (3317) 4173[2] 4605[6] 5036[4] *5609[6]* 5723[4] 6600[3] *6873[11]*

Danedream (GER) *P Schiergen* 128
3 b f Lomitas—Danedrop (IRE) (Danehill (USA))
1920a[3] (2539a) 3447a[5] (4374a) (5773a) (6567a) 7563a[6]

Danehill Dante (IRE) *Richard Hannon* a80 82
3 ch g Danehill Dancer(IRE) —En Garde (USA) (Irish River (FR))
1408[3] ◆ *1759[2]* 2648[11] 3183[2] 4102[2] 4335[8] 5547[3] 5938[8] *6796[6]* 6997[3]

Danehill Intellect (IRE) *Harry Dunlop* a49 66
4 ch m Danehill Dancer(IRE) —Intellectuelle (Caerleon (USA))
737[3] 954[11]

Daneking *John Gosden* 80
2 b c Dylan Thomas(IRE) —Sadie Thompson (IRE) (King's Best (USA))
5013[7] (5937) 6829[3]

Daneside (IRE) *Gary Harrison* a64 77
4 b g Danehill Dancer(IRE) —Sidecar (IRE) (Spectrum (IRE))
3266[2] 3515[3] 4444[2] (4822) 4948[2] 5673[4] (5894) *6219[10]* 6830[8] 7050[7] 7110[12]

Danesman *David Evans* a33 66
6 ch g Danehill Dancer(IRE) —Gaily Grecian (IRE) (Ela-Mana-Mou)
6324[10]

Dangerous Illusion (IRE) *Michael Quinn* a57 49
3 bl f Statue Of Liberty(USA) —Miss Dangerous (Komaite (USA))
246[4] 380[6] 787[5] 1056[8] 1280[2] 1595[4] 3136[8] (4684) *(5388) 5941[2] 7760[8]*

Dangerous Midge (USA) *Brian Meehan* 121
5 b h Lion Heart(USA) —Adored Slew (USA) (Seattle Slew (USA))
1001a[14] 6161[7] 6671[6] 7170[7]

Dangerous To Know *Hughie Morrison* 43
2 b f Byron—Bogus Mix (IRE) (Linamix (FR))
5613[7] 6581[8]

Daniel Thomas (IRE) *Richard Guest* a65 71
9 b g Dansili—Last Look (Rainbow Quest (USA))
6309[2] 6698[6] 7003[10] 7246[7] 7442[2] 7640[3] 7848[4] 7904[3]

Dani's Girl (IRE) *Pat Phelan* a85 83
8 bb m Second Empire(IRE) —Quench The Lamp (IRE) (Glow (USA))
209 [11]

Danish Pastry *John Gosden* a47 49
3 b f Dansili—Foodbroker Fancy (IRE) (Halling (USA))
1480[4] *2306[9]*

Dank *Sir Michael Stoute* 84
2 b f Dansili—Masskana (IRE) (Darshaan)
6128[2]

Dannios *Ed Walker* a41 76
5 b g Tobougg(IRE) —Fleuve D'Or (IRE) (Last Tycoon)
(2828) *3475[9]* (4927) (5116) 5653[10] 6587[8]

Dansable (IRE) *Paul Cole* a32
2 b f Dansili—Sheepscot (USA) (Easy Goer (USA))
7520[11]

Dansette *Jim Boyle* a55 49
3 b f Dansili—Kalinka (IRE) (Soviet Star (USA))
1759[10] 2097[9] 3437[9] 4888[5]

Dan's Heir *Wilf Storey* a56 63
9 b g Dansili—Million Heiress (Auction Ring (USA))
1556[5] 2496[3]

Dansili Dancer *Clive Cox* a113 96
9 b g Dansili—Magic Slipper (Habitat)
991[2] 1887[7] 2812[6] 3625[9] 5932[7]

Dansili Dutch (IRE) *David Barron* a44 61
2 gr f Dutch Art—Joyful Leap (Dansili)
2542[6] 3201[5] 3656[6] (4892) 5431[3] 6186[8] *7592[9]*

Dansilver *Jim Best* a69 67
7 b g Dansili—Silver Gyre (IRE) (Silver Hawk (USA))
(216) (1025) 1181[3] ◆ *3391[5]*

Dan's Martha *Ben Haslam* a74 60
3 b f Tagula(IRE) —Piedmont (UAE) (Jade Robbery (USA))
2466[8] 3508[4] 5109[9] *6285[6]*

Dantari (IRE) *Evan Williams* a63 52
6 b g Alhaarth(IRE) —Daniysha (IRE) (Doyoun)
4952[6]

Danube Dancer (IRE) *J S Moore* a60 69
3 b f Balmont(USA) —Green Danube (USA) (Irish River (FR))
234[8]

Danum Dancer *Neville Bycroft* a68 59
7 ch g Allied Forces(USA) —Branston Dancer (Rudimentary (USA))
5552[4] 6602[5] 7079[11] 7216[15]

Danvilla *Paul Webber* a76 87
4 b m Dansili—Newtown Villa (Spectrum (IRE))
(2176) ◆ (2793) *3522[3]* 4097[2] (4806) 5448[5] 5878[8]

Danziger (IRE) *D K Weld* a83 79
2 b f Modigliani(USA) —Star On A Hill (IRE) (City On A Hill (USA))
1699a[2]

Danzig Fox *Michael Mullineaux* a57 45
6 b g Foxhound(USA) —Via Dolorosa (Chaddleworth (IRE))
2910[8] 3341[10] 4563[5] 4893[5] 5540[15]

Danzigs Grandchild (USA) *J S Moore* a74 76
3 b f Anabaa(USA) —Millie's Choice (IRE) (Taufan (USA))
51[3] 288a[3]

Danzoe (IRE) *Christine Dunnett* a78 73
4 br g Kheleyf(USA) —Fiaba (Precocious)
264[7] 522[3] 646[8] 2609[10] 3412[7] 3640[8] (3957) 4683[6] 5326[9] *5387[4] 5640[10]* 5890[4] 6119[5] 6479[12] 6802[14] 7512[4] 7588[4] 7649[5]

Daphne Joy *Peter Hedger*
2 ch f
7938[7]

Da Ponte *Walter Swinburn* a74 79
3 b g Librettist(USA) —Naharnook (Fantastic Light (USA))
1064[2] 2180[7] (3122) 3598[8] 4353[7] 6167[17]

Dapper's Dancer *David O'Meara*
2 b f Dapper—Party Princess (IRE) (Orpen (USA))
3504[11] *3708[10]* 4193[6]

Da'Quonde (IRE) *Bryan Smart* a56 42
3 br f Pivotal—Bobcat Greeley (USA) (Mr Greeley (USA))
3756[9] *7411[5] (7886)*

Daraa (IRE) *Clive Brittain* 72
2 b f Cape Cross(IRE) —Guarantia (Selkirk (USA))
(4726) 5698[6] 7135[RR]

Darabani (FR) *P Monfort* a95 101
6 b g Fantastic Light(USA) —Darakiyla (IRE) (Last Tycoon)
395a[0] 566a[0]

Darajaat (USA) *Marcus Tregoning* a84 99
3 bb f Elusive Quality(USA) —Misterah (Alhaarth (IRE))
1404[9] 2054[5] 4063[4] 5080[2] 6147[24] 6522[14]

Darcey *Amy Weaver* a80 77
5 ch m Noverre(USA) —Firozi (Forzando)
2597[7] 2876[10] 3361[12] 4066[9] 4394[4] (5677) (6065) 6261[5] 6759[10] *7040[3] 7416[5] 7595[6]*

Darcy May *Garry Woodward*
3 b f Danbird(AUS) —Oakwell Ace (Clantime)
7913[5]

Daredevil Dan *Tina Jackson* 74
5 b g Golden Snake(USA) —Tiempo (King Of Spain)
1908[11]

Dare I Ask *Bill Turner* a35
2 ch f Dutch Art—Dance Away (Pivotal)
6131[10] 6927[10]

Dare It And Smile (USA) *David Simcock* a65 59
3 bb f Bandini(USA) —Grin And Dare It (USA) (Exploit (USA))
(88) 217 [5]

Darej (USA) *William Haggas* a86 79
3 ch g Speightstown(USA) —Hi Lili (USA) (Silver Deputy (CAN))
1690[8]

Darenjan (IRE) *John Joseph Hanlon* 72
8 br g Alhaarth(IRE) —Darariyna (IRE) (Shirley Heights)
3420a[5]

Dar Es Salaam *Brian Ellison* 74
7 ch g King's Best(USA) —Place De L'Opera (Sadler's Wells (USA))
1243[11] 1798[2] ◆ 2091[2] 2262[8] 3828[13] 4142[8]

Dare To Bare (IRE) *Amanda Perrett* a82 74
3 b g Byron—Naked Poser (IRE) (Night Shift (USA))
1580[9] 1836[14] 2231[4] *3392[2]* 3770[4] 4755[6] *5318[2] 5630[2] 5942[2] (6089)* 6583[9] 6728[7]

Dare To Dance (IRE) *Jeremy Noseda* a81 111
3 b c Danehill Dancer(IRE) —Beneventa (Most Welcome)
1605[3] ◆ (4254) (5483) ◆ (6429)

Dare To Dream *Richard Hannon* 79
2 b f Exceed And Excel(AUS) —Secret History (USA) (Bahri (USA))
2254[2] 2811[5] 3812[3] (4581) 6340[4] 7169[10]

Darfour *Martin Hill* a52 9
7 b g Inchinor—Gai Bulga (Kris)
969[5] *1233*[12] 1750[12]

Daring Damsel (IRE) *Paul Cole* 59
2 b f Van Nistelrooy(USA) —Serengeti Day (USA) (Alleged (USA))
3609[4] 4201[4] 4969[10] 5343[4] 6275[3] 6760[11]

Daring Dream (GER) *Jim Goldie* a65 86
6 ch g Big Shuffle(USA) —Daring Action (Arazi (USA))
1696[4] 2115[5] 2413[2] (3112) (3358) 4325[9] 5059[15] 5455[5] 6079[10] 6148[8] 7161[5]

Daring Indian *Ian Williams* a78 79
3 ch g Zamindar(USA) —Anasazi (IRE) (Sadler's Wells (USA))
7179[4] *7601*[6] *(7806)*

Dariole (FR) *P Bary* 108
4 b m Highest Honor(FR) —Dzinigane (FR) (Exit To Nowhere (USA))
7090a[8]

Dariya (GER) *S Smrczek* 88
3 ch f Titus Livius(FR) —Dax Empress (IRE) (General Monash (USA))
6394a[7]

Darizi (FR) *J-C Rouget* a75 101
4 gr h Daylami(IRE) —Darakiyla (IRE) (Last Tycoon)
1011a[5]

Dark Ages (IRE) *Noel Quinlan* a57 70
2 bl f Dark Angel(IRE) —Prosaic Star (IRE) (Common Grounds)
1337[4] ◆ 1657[2] (2523) *3745*[5] 4079[4] 5438[3] *5833*[6] 6058[4] 6597[3] *6975*[3]

Dark Ambition (IRE) *William Haggas* a68 69
2 b c Dark Angel(IRE) —Date Mate (USA) (Thorn Dance (USA))
3610[10] 3878[9] 4240[2] 4913[4] *5409*[3] 5809[3] 6447[4]

Dark And Dangerous (IRE) *Peter Winkworth* a55 63
3 b g Cacique(IRE) —Gilah (IRE) (Saddlers' Hall (IRE))
2722[6] 3018[5] *3393*[10] (5784) 6240[3] 6891[4]

Dark Castle *Sylvester Kirk* a58
2 b c Dark Angel(IRE) —True Magic (Magic Ring (IRE))
7751[6]

Dark Celt (IRE) *Tim Pitt* 42
2 b g Lawman(FR) —Dark Raider (IRE) (Definite Article)
3382[9] 4675[5]

Dark Don (IRE) *Charles Hills* 73
2 b c Dark Angel(IRE) —Bint Al Hammour (IRE) (Grand Lodge (USA))
5254[14] 5801[4] 6344[2]

Dark Dune (IRE) *Tim Easterby* a83 74
3 b g Diamond Green(FR) —Panpipes (USA) (Woodman (USA))
1327[5] (1623) 2076[6] 2613[2] 3084[5] (3587) 4050[2] 5273[7] 6294[5] 6838[5] *7255*[4] *(7413)* ◆ *7699*[5]

Dark Falcon (IRE) *James Tate* a77
2 bb c Dark Angel(IRE) —Absolute Pleasure (Polar Falcon (USA))
5393[4] *7634*[2] *(7855)*

Dark Islander (IRE) *J S Moore* a61 94
8 b h Singspiel(IRE) —Lamanka Lass (USA) (Woodman (USA))
4554[6] *5319*[7]

Dark Isle *J W Hills* a72 75
3 b g Singspiel(IRE) —Peyto Princess (Bold Arrangement)
1236[3] 1565[2] 2094[5] 2802[3] *4799*[8] *5735*[6] *6120*[3]

Dark Lane *Tony Carroll* a81 83
5 b g Namid—Corps De Ballet (IRE) (Fasliyev (USA))
168[3] *316*[4] *577*[2] (1267) 1438[6] 1943[3] 2300[10] 2631[3] 3880[15] 4291[9] *(4990)* 5345[4] *5604*[4] 6433[6] 6920[13]

Dark Orchid *Peter Chapple-Hyam* 35
2 br f Shamardal(USA) —Misty Waters (IRE) (Caerleon (USA))
7233[10]

Dark Pegasus *Karen George* a28 47
3 b g Avonbridge—Miss Equinox (Presidium)
2790[17] 3173[4] 4320[9] 4950[9] *5644*[9] *6653*[10] *7202*[11]

Dark Promise *Roger Varian* a93 109
4 b m Shamardal(USA) —La Sky (IRE) (Law Society (USA))
(3407) ◆ 3703[4] 5704[3] (6297)

Dark Ranger *Tim Pitt* a79 80
5 br g Where Or When(IRE) —Dark Raider (IRE) (Definite Article)
1144[5] (2034) 2888[11] *3522*[7] 4635[2] 6171[2] ◆ 7139[3] *7753*[2]

Dark Ray (IRE) *L Riccardi* 91
2 b f Dark Angel(IRE) —Magiustrina (IRE) (Indian Ridge)
6904a[6]

Dark Ruler (IRE) *Alan Swinbank* 25
2 b g Dark Angel(IRE) —Gino Lady (IRE) (Perugino (USA))
6836[10]

Dark Spirit (IRE) *Alison Thorpe* a60 76
3 b f Whipper(USA) —Dark Raider (IRE) (Definite Article)
1146[4] *1474*[5] 2591[4] *3518*[6] 4403[2] (4633) ◆ 4887[2] *7244*[6]

Dark Stranger (USA) *John Gosden* 63
2 b c Stormy Atlantic(USA) —Vivacious Vivian (USA) (Distorted Humor (USA))
7233[6]

Darleas Gift (IRE) *Kevin Ryan* a35
2 b f Bertolini(USA) —Sastre (IRE) (Bluebird (USA))
6975[8] *7267*[6] *7353*[9]

Darley Sun (IRE) *Saeed Bin Suroor* a61 107
5 b h Tiger Hill(IRE) —Sagamartha (Rainbow Quest (USA))
1808[8] 6857[8]

Darling Grace *William Haggas* 66
2 b f Nayef(USA) —Lady Grace (IRE) (Orpen (USA))
5514[3] 6934[6]

Darling Lexi (IRE) *Richard Fahey* 67
2 b f Dylan Thomas(IRE) —My Girl Lisa (USA) (With Approval (CAN))
2630[4] 4232[9] 4748[6] 5342[4]

Darling Pearl (FR) *J-C Rouget* a78 91
4 b m Vespone(IRE) —Magic Motion (USA) (Green Dancer (USA))
3568a[2]

Darnathean *Paul D'Arcy* a75 67
2 b g Librettist(USA) —Meddle (Diktat)
1290[5] 1988[6] 2844[3] 4277[5] *5144*[3] ◆ *(5690)* 5876[4] 6573[6]

Darnell *P Schiergen* 85
3 ch c Dubai Destination(USA) —Dallaah (Green Desert (USA))
2520a[4]

Darrow (IRE) *William Knight* 68
2 b g Lawman(FR) —Azolla (Cadeaux Genereux)
4330[16] 4996[11] 5564[6]

Darsan (IRE) *Chris Wall* a67 53
3 ch f Iffraaj—Coolrain Lady (IRE) (Common Grounds)
5633[3] ◆ *6473*[7] 7063[5] *7418*[4]

Dart *John Mackie* a75 49
7 br m Diktat—Eilean Shona (Suave Dancer (USA))
3[5] *(286)* *514*[2] *671*[4] *838*[6] *1470*[8] *7415*[7] *7570*[9] *7850*[3]

D'Artagnan (SAF) *Gay Kelleway* a71 66
4 gr g Count Dubois—Russian Nature (SAF) (Russian Fox (USA))
21[5] 411a[11] *536a*[11]

Dartford (USA) *John Gosden* a61
2 ch c Giant's Causeway(USA) —Apple Of Kent (USA) (Kris S (USA))
7493[5]

Daruband *Alan McCabe* a77 74
3 ch g Singspiel(IRE) —Gagajulu (Al Hareb (USA))
2257[12] 2621[3] 3206[4] *6136*[U] *6978*[5] *7179*[5] *(7388)* *7532*[9] *7637*[11] *7727*[6]

Darwin Star *Dean Ivory* a62 66
3 gr f Aussie Rules(USA) —Fine Lady (Selkirk (USA))
7754[11] *7853*[8]

Dashing Eddie (IRE) *Kevin Ryan* a60 52
3 b c Dubawi(IRE) —Step Too Far (USA) (Cozzene (USA))
1945[7] 7085[4] *7270*[3] *(7560)* *7696*[2] *7781*[5]

Dasho *Olivia Maylam* a86 77
3 ch g Dubawi(IRE) —New Choice (IRE) (Barathea (IRE))
(110) *601*[2] *845*[2] ◆ *1313*[4] 1725[7] 2255[4] 2411[7] 5000[6] *(5419)* *5735*[2] 6467[15] 7171[19] *7439*[9] (7675) 7846[6] 7926[6]

Dashwood *Anthony Carson* a80 81
4 b h Pivotal—Most Charming (FR) (Darshaan)
(1336) *1497*[3] *(2001)* (2609) 2879[3] 4066[4] (4926) *5948*[4] *7847*[9]

Date With Destiny (IRE) *Richard Hannon* 94
3 b f George Washington(IRE) —Flawlessly (FR) (Rainbow Quest (USA))
1339[8] 1894[3] 2189[5] 6066[4]

Daunt (IRE) *Richard Hannon* 74
2 ch c Namid—Pearl Egg (IRE) (Mukaddamah (USA))
2844[4] 3388[6] 3917[3] 5237[2] 5840[3]

Dauntsey Park (IRE) *Tor Sturgis* a60 31
4 ch g Refuse To Bend(IRE) —Shauna's Honey (IRE) (Danehill (USA))
115[8] *299*[6] *748*[5] *1273*[9] 2900[11] *3280*[8]

Davana *Colin Teague* a57 42
5 b m Primo Valentino(IRE) —Bombay Sapphire (Be My Chief (USA))
324[6] *507*[5] *(569)* *796*[2] *1032*[9]

Daveron (GER) *H Graham Motion* 114
6 ch m Black Sam Bellamy(IRE) —Darwinia (GER) (Acatenango (GER))
6719a[3]

David Livingston (IRE) *A P O'Brien* 115
2 b c Galileo(IRE) —Mora Bai (IRE) (Indian Ridge)
5293a[4] 5951a[3] (6391a)

Davids Dilemma *Andrew Reid*
3 ch g Teofilio(IRE) —Prairie Oyster (Emperor Jones (USA))
5319[10]

Dawaraki (FR) *F Seguin*
7 b g Sendawar(IRE) —Kendoraki (FR) (Kendor (FR))
6959a[0]

Dawariya (IRE) *John M Oxx* a95 97
3 ch f Selkirk(USA) —Dawera (IRE) (Spinning World (USA))
6513a[7]

Dawn Auction (IRE) *Anthony Middleton* a25
4 b g Auction House(USA) —Isle Of Sodor (Cyrano De Bergerac)
878[9]

Dawn Eclipse (IRE) *T G McCourt* a80 101
6 b m Acclamation—Prima (Primo Dominie)
1533a[3] 2861a[9] 3527a[4] 4497[14] 5228a[4] 5979a[5] 6561a[4] 7298[15]

Dawn Gale (IRE) *Hughie Morrison* a37 78
3 b f Hurricane Run(IRE) —Latest Chapter (IRE) (Ahonoora)
1364[11] 2026[3] ◆ 2458[4] 4279[3] *5317*[9]

Dawn Glory *Roger Charlton* 13
2 b f Oasis Dream—Fairy Godmother (Fairy King (USA))
5299[13]

Dawn Lightning *Alan McCabe* a62 66
2 gr f Dark Angel(IRE) —River Crossing (Zafonic (USA))
1055[2] *(1235)* 1598[3] 3589[6] 3776[5]

Dawn Story *Hughie Morrison* a35
3 b f Lucky Story(USA) —Red Cloud (IRE) (Taufan (USA))
3519[8] *7327*[7]

Dawn Twister (GER) *J Hirschberger* 107
4 b h Monsun(GER) —Dawn Side (CAN) (Bold Forbes (USA))
4524a[6] 5092a[4] 6200a[3] 6710a[6] 7406a[9]

Dawson Creek (IRE) *Mark Hoad* a55 45
7 ch g Titus Livius(FR) —Particular Friend (Cadeaux Genereux)
79[6] *2771*[4] *8191*[0] 2202[P] 2420[4] 3017[7] 3480[9] 3945[8]

Dayatthespa (USA) *Chad C Brown* 100
2 ch f City Zip(USA) —M'Lady Doc (USA) (Doc's Leader (USA))
7281a[9]

Dayia (IRE) *Lydia Pearce* a97 97
7 b m Act One—Mashariк (IRE) (Caerleon (USA))
3157[4] 4266[9] 6690[30] 7322a[11] 7406a[10]

Daylami Dreams *John Harris* a60 72
7 gr g Daylami(IRE) —Kite Mark (Mark Of Esteem (IRE))
1901[4] 2183[5]

Day Of Victory (FR) *T Castanheira* 98
2 b f Victory Note(USA) —Day Of Dream (IRE) (Rainbows For Life (CAN))
6941a[6]

Days In May (IRE) *Edward Vaughan* a57 46
3 ch f More Than Ready(USA) —Maybe In May (USA) (Miswaki (USA))
5449[10] *6137*[5] 6608[4] *7387*[9] *7910*[10]

Days Of Summer (IRE) *Ralph Beckett* a78 80
3 b f Bachelor Duke(USA) —Pharaoh's Delight (Fairy King (USA))
2255[9] *6256*[9]

Daytime Dreamer (IRE) *Martin Todhunter* a57 73
7 b g Diktat—Tuppenny (Salse (USA))
3858[9] 4198[11] (4605) 5166[3] 6157[2] 6838[10] 7077[8]

Dazakhee *Jo Hughes* a71 71
4 ch m Sakhee(USA) —Ziya (IRE) (Lion Cavern (USA))
797[8] *1052*[7] *(1468)* 2057[2] 2454[10] 2815[7] 3510[9] *3952*[6] ◆ *5414*[6] *(5836)* *6182*[5] 6621[13] 6831[9] 6878[2] 7418[11] 7538[5] 7745[4]

Dazeen *David Flood* a79 84
4 b g Zafeen(FR) —Bond Finesse (IRE) (Danehill Dancer (IRE))
794[3] ◆ 1035[8] *1463*[7] (1795) (2301) 2674[2] 2814[8] 3169[2] 3506[5] (4107) 4656[13] *5835*[4] ◆ *6282*[3] ◆ 6520[10]

Dazinski *Mark H Tompkins* 98
5 ch g Sulamani(IRE) —Shuheb (Nashwan (USA))
1679[6] 2190[3] 2888[4] 3205[2] 3794[10] 4423[9] (5221) 6690[23]

Dazzled *James Fanshawe* a69 54
4 b m Starcraft(NZ) —Morning After (Emperor Jones (USA))
(360)

Dazzlin Bluebell (IRE) *Tim Easterby* 54
2 b f Strategic Prince—Sharamaine (IRE) (King Charlemagne (USA))
3273[7] 3609[11] 4851[3] 5161[5] 5786[10] 6293[5]

Dazzling Begum *Des Donovan* a59 61
6 b m Okawango(USA) —Dream On Me (Prince Sabo)
7202[9] *7357*[11] *7573*[5]

Dazzling Light (UAE) *Jim Goldie* a77 86
6 bb m Halling(USA) —Crown Of Light (Mtoto)
1517[4] 2071[10] 2285[6] 3127[3] 3828[5] 4344[7] 5035[6] 7102[3] *7378a*[2]

Dazzling Valentine *Alan Bailey* a80 78
3 b f Oratorio(IRE) —Bedazzling (IRE) (Darshaan)
(1251) 1392[4] 1593[6] 2018[6] 7237[3] *7461*[4] *7577*[9] *7823*[2]

Deacon Blue (FR) *C Boutin* a80 83
6 ch g Anabaa Blue—Kansas (Kahyasi)
395a[7]

Deacon Blues *James Fanshawe* 125
4 b g Compton Place—Persario (Bishop Of Cashel)
1888[2] ◆ (3155) (4092) ◆ (4836a) (6164) (6858)

Dead Cool *Hughie Morrison* a69 72
3 ch f Kyllachy—Dead Certain (Absalom)
1724[5] [illegible] *7173*[4] *7448*[7]

Deadly Silence (USA) *Dr Jon Scargill* a75 38
6 b g Diesis—Mill Guineas (USA) (Salse (USA))
2512[9]

Dealbata (IRE) *M Delzangles* 103
3 ch f Dubawi(IRE) —Save Me The Waltz (FR) (Halling (USA))
(7510a)

Dean Iarracht (IRE) *Tracy Waggott* a60 68
5 b g Danetime(IRE) —Sirdhana (Selkirk (USA))
1107[14] 1491[7] 1798[5] 2251[7] 2734[4] 2804[5] 3319[8] 3658[2] 4123[7] 5622[11] (6235) 6538[7] 6833[4] 7215[12]

Dean's Kitten (USA) *Michael J Maker* a115 119
4 ch h Kitten's Joy(USA) —Summer Theatre (USA) (Ide (USA))
5074a[3] 6548a[2] 7305a[9]

Dean Swift *Brian Meehan* a40 85
3 b c Dansili—Magical Romance (IRE) (Barathea (IRE))
4514[4] (4956) 5893[2] *6439*[13] 6922[12]

Dear Bela (ARG) *Saeed Bin Suroor* a62
5 b m Indygo Shiner(USA) —Dear Peggy (ARG) (Southern Halo (USA))
499a[13] *679a*[14]

Dearest (IRE) *John Joseph Murphy* a54 64
3 br f Arch(USA) —Fatwa (IRE) (Lahib (USA))
1706a[9]

Dearest Girl (IRE) *Charles O'Brien* a61 86
4 b m Galileo(IRE) —Shastri (USA) (Alleged (USA))
3420a[3] 5291a[7] *7378a*[9]

Dear Lavinia (USA) *J-C Rouget* 98
2 b f Grand Slam(USA) —Baroness Richter (IRE) (Montjeu (IRE))
4569a[3] 7281a[14]

Dear Maurice *Tobias B P Coles* a77 72
7 b g Indian Ridge—Shamaiel (IRE) (Lycius (USA))
3464[6] 5200[4] *7424*[5]

Deauville Flyer *Tim Easterby* 101
5 b g Dubai Destination(USA) —Reaf (In The Wings)
1412[6] 2071[4] 2499[4] ◆ 3396[3] 3875[4] 5221[3] 5705[7] 6333[14]

Deauville Post (FR) *Richard Hannon* a83 89
4 b g American Post—Loyola (FR) (Sicyos (USA))
(1046) 1517[11]

Debating Society (IRE) *Sir Michael Stoute* 76
2 b c Invincible Spirit(IRE) —Drama Class (IRE) (Caerleon (USA))
5239[4] ◆ 6064[2]

Debbie Doo *Anthony Carson* a47
3 b f Beat Hollow—Pleasing (Dr Fong (USA))
6668[5] *7739*[6]

De Bon Matin (FR) *Mme C Dufreche* a82 82
3 b c Charge D'Affaires—Learning Game (USA) (Carnegie (IRE))
882a[6]

Debussy (IRE) *Mahmood Al Zarooni* a110 122
5 bb h Diesis—Opera Comique (FR) (Singspiel (IRE))
758a[13] 1000a[15] 3031[7] 4315[4] (5921) 6247[7]

Decadence *Eric Alston* a20 56
3 b f Singspiel(IRE) —Penny Cross (Efisio)
1393[7] 1880[4] 2351[9] 3138[7] 3615[7] 4199[6] 4466[5]

Decana *Hughie Morrison* a67 49
3 ch f Doyen(IRE) —Sahara Belle (USA) (Sanglamore (USA))
2371[9] 3001[11] 4157[8] *5321*[5] ◆ *5838*[5] *6823*[2] ◆ *(7645)*

December *James Given* a61 60
5 b g Oasis Dream—Winter Solstice (Unfuwain (USA))
1466[7] 2669[2] 3086[13]

December Draw (IRE) *Mark Kavanagh* a105 117
5 br g Medecis—New York (IRE) (Danzero (AUS))
6886a[18]

Decency (IRE) *Harry Dunlop* a63 69
4 b m Celtic Swing—Siem Reap (USA) (El Gran Senor (USA))
56[6] *159*[2] *268*[4] *304*[5]

Decent Fella (IRE) *Andrew Balding* a73 102
5 b g Marju(IRE) —Mac Melody (IRE) (Entrepreneur)
(2020) ◆ 2300[4] 3109[4] 3645[8] 4428[5] (5936) 6521[11]

Deceptive *Roger Charlton* a77 65
3 b f Red Ransom(USA) —Fleeting Memory (Danehill (USA))
1751[3] 2225[4] 2874[7] *(6621)* *6789*[4] *7255*[9]

Dechiper (IRE) *Robert Johnson* a35 54
9 bb g Almutawakel—Safiya (USA) (Riverman (USA))
1617[4] 2060[4] 2433[7] (2733) 3316[9] 3450[10] 4671[5] 5549[3] 5790[9]

Decider (USA) *Ronald Harris* a69 61
8 ch g High Yield(USA) —Nikita Moon (USA) (Secret Hello (USA))
22[6] *(165)* *306*[3] *443*[8] *538*[4] *732*[3] *934*[3] *1274*[2] *1503*[3] (1627) 1955[3] 2603[2] 2913[5] 3216[2] 3471[4] 3721[11] 7897[9]

Decimate *Andrew Reid* 64
3 br g Teofilio(IRE) —Kirriemuir (Lochnager)
5346[6] 6034[3]

Decision By One *Tom Dascombe* a80
2 ch c Bahamian Bounty—Intellibet One (Compton Place)
6654[5] *7174*[2] *(7540)*

Decisive Moment (USA) *Juan D Arias* a109
3 bb c With Distinction(USA) —Lady Samira (USA) (Dehere (USA))
1921a[14]

Deck Walk (USA) *Roger Charlton* a54 80
3 rg f Mizzen Mast(USA) —Trekking (USA) (Gone West (USA))
2529[3] *3392*[7] (5001) 5938[10]

Decorum (USA) *F Vermeulen* a60 53
5 b g Dynaformer(USA) —Shy Greeting (ARG) (Shy Tom (USA))
832a[7]

D[illegible] *Roger Charlton* 56
2 b f Beat Hollow—Total Devotion (Desert Prince (IRE))
6463[7] 6985[6]

Deduction (IRE) *Nigel Tinkler* a23 58
2 b f Holy Roman Emperor(IRE) —Briery (IRE) (Salse (USA))
4427[8] 5047[7] 5347[4] 6058[6] 6628[10] *7882*[4]

Deejan (IRE) *Bryn Palling* a60 65
6 b m Oscar(IRE) —Boleree (IRE) (Mandalus)
3233[3] *457*[4]

Deem (IRE) *J Barton* a101 117
6 gr m Dalakhani(IRE) —Hijaz (IRE) (Sadler's Wells (USA))
2417 *608a*[2] 1001a[8]

Deep Applause *Michael Dods* 68
3 b g Royal Applause—Deep Deep Blue (Hernando (FR))
1189[9] 1801[4] 2252[3] 3039[8] 3318[11] 3706[5] 3977[8] 4284[2] 4505[7] (5165) 5401[4] 5823[2] 6192[3]

Deepsand (IRE) *Tim Easterby* 81
2 bb c Footstepsinthesand—Sinamay (USA) (Saint Ballado (CAN))
5104[2] (5486) (6111) 6670[3] 7021[4]

Deerslayer (USA) *Amy Weaver* a87 78
5 ch g Rahy(USA) —Al Theraab (USA) (Roberto (USA))
1284[2] 1568[8] (2168) 2719[10] 3351[4] (4741) *4990*[2] (5300) *(5604)* 5831[17] *(6351)* 6761[9] 6974[8] *7487*[6] *(7575)*

Defector (IRE) *Seamus Durack* a82 67
5 b g Fasliyev(USA) —Rich Dancer (Halling (USA))
577[9] 1912[2] 2280[8] 2610[5] 3512[14] *4206*[5] *4850*[4] *5101*[12] *6133*[8] *6655*[8] *6841*[3]

Defence Council (IRE) *Mel Brittain* a84 81
3 b g Kheleyf(USA) —Miss Gally (IRE) (Galileo (IRE))
1391[2] 1650[7] 2074[13] 3461[2] 3682[4] *7489*[2] *7644*[9] *7846*[10]

Defence Of Duress (IRE) *Tom Tate* 89
3 b g Motivator—Ultra Finesse (USA) (Rahy (USA))
2008[5] 2435[2] 3084[2] 3828[11] 6832[5] 7139[8]

Defer *Jeremy Noseda* a13
3 b f Kyllachy—Succumb (Pursuit Of Love)
43[5]

Deferto Delphi *Barry Murtagh* a15 51
4 ch g Mark Of Esteem(IRE) —Delphic Way (Warning)
1979^{8} 3041^{6} 3574^{6} 4903^{6} 5167^{10}

Definightly *Roger Charlton* 115
5 b g Diktat—Perfect Night (Danzig Connection (USA))
3154^{15} $5532a^{2}$ $5979a^{2}$ $7221a^{3}$ $7534a^{7}$

Defining Year (IRE) *M Halford* 106
3 b g Hawk Wing(USA) —Tajaathub (USA) (Aljabr (USA))
$1116a^{2}$ $4418a^{3}$

Defy The Odds *Sir Henry Cecil* 72
2 b f Galileo(IRE) —Fully Invested (USA) (Irish River (FR))
4552^{6} 5583^{3} ◆

Degas Art (IRE) *Lucinda Russell* 82
8 b g Danehill Dancer(IRE) —Answer (Warning)
3157^{7}

Deia Sunrise (IRE) *John Gosden* 78
2 gr g Clodovil(IRE) —Hedera (USA) (Woodman (USA))
5851^{6} (6447)

Deire Na Sli (IRE) *J S Bolger* a91 95
3 b f Aussie Rules(USA) —Malignia (IRE) (Pursuit Of Love)
$1116a^{3}$

Deity *Jeremy Noseda* 89
3 b f Danehill Dancer(IRE) —Golden Flyer (FR) (Machiavellian (USA))
(1343) 1837^{9} 2926^{3} 6383^{11} 7031^{5}

Delagoa Bay (IRE) *Sylvester Kirk* a56 47
3 b f Encosta De Lago(AUS) —Amory (GER) (Goofalik (USA))
406^{4} 1018^{3} 2379^{6} 2904^{4} 3393^{5} 3910^{6} 4181^{4}

Delamour *M Weiss* 80
3 ch f Dubai Destination(USA) —Feathers Flying (IRE) (Royal Applause)
$5307a^{5}$

Delaney's Dream *David Nicholls* 70
3 gr g Distant Music(USA) —Kilmovee (Inchinor)
1074^{4}

Delaware Dancer (IRE) *Jeremy Gask* a66 65
4 b m Danehill Dancer(IRE) —Labrusca (Grand Lodge (USA))
2845^{6} 3512^{5} 3869^{4} 4270^{2} 4709^{5}

Delegator *Saeed Bin Suroor* 117
5 b h Dansili—Indian Love Bird (Efisio)
(2005) 3863^{5} 4412^{9} 5707^{14}

Delft *Jeremy Noseda* a75
2 b f Dutch Art—Plucky (Kyllachy)
6820^{4} (7627) 7799^{2} ◆

Delia Mary *Jedd O'Keeffe* 45
2 gr f Avonbridge—Negligee (Night Shift (USA))
3201^{2} 3680^{6} 4073^{10}

Deliberation (IRE) *Kevin Ryan* a61 78
3 b g Antonius Pius(USA) —Pursuit Of Truth (USA) (Irish River (FR))
669^{9} 855^{8} 3857^{4} 4638^{8} (5203) (5433) (5859) 6190^{6} 7073^{2} 7172^{9} 7299^{2} 7504^{6} 7646^{10} 7840^{4}

Delictuelle (FR) *R Le Gal* a65 66
3 b f High Yield(USA) —Rince Deas (IRE) (Alzao (USA))
$288a^{7}$

Delight Of The Eye *Alastair Lidderdale* a50 44
3 br f Trade Fair—Rowan Flower (IRE) (Ashkalani (IRE))
3550^{5} 4180^{4}

Delira (IRE) *Jonathan Portman* a66 60
3 b f Namid—Singing Millie (Millfontaine)
1149^{2} 1483^{8} 1986^{10} 2553^{5} 3230^{5} (3597) 4486^{2} 5338^{11} 5671^{3} 6403^{3} 6752^{6}

Delishuss *Dominic Ffrench Davis* 40
2 gr f Aussie Rules(USA) —Effie (Royal Academy (USA))
6117^{13} 7257^{7}

Dellarte (FR) *L A Urbano-Grajales* a78 86
3 b g Della Francesca(USA) —Arletta (USA) (Quest For Fame)
$370a^{4}$

Dells Breezer *Pat Phelan* a59 60
3 ch g Kheleyf(USA) —Here To Me (Muhtarram (USA))
7754^{6} 7940^{9}

Delorain (IRE) *William Stone* a58 44
8 b g Kalanisi(IRE) —Lady Nasrana (FR) (Al Nasr (FR))
(118) (277) 407^{3} 549^{5} 955^{5} 4870^{4} 5209^{4} 6087^{2} 6476^{8} 6876^{3} 7087^{6} 7331^{7}

Democretes *Richard Hannon* a77 87
2 ch c Cadeaux Genereux—Petite Epaulette (Night Shift (USA))
1721^{7} (2510) 3866^{6} 4661^{2} (5708) 6166^{3}

Demoiselle Bond *Lydia Richards* a56 16
3 ch f Monsieur Bond(IRE) —Baytown Flyer (Whittingham (IRE))
721^{5} 863^{5} 1020^{6} 5995^{5} 6257^{8} (7096) 7348^{4} 7484^{10} 7754^{4}

Demo Jo *Geoffrey Harker* a28 45
5 gr m Auction House(USA) —Demolition Jo (Petong)
4442^{5}

Demokles (FR) *J-M Beguigne* 93
2 b c Anabaa Blue—Domus Orea (USA) (Gone West (USA))
$6184a^{5}$

Demolition *Noel Wilson* a86 99
7 ch g Starborough—Movie Star (IRE) (Barathea (IRE))
3876^{16} ◆ 4331^{3} 4801^{4} 5185^{7} (5757) 6277^{5} (6803) 7297^{21}

Demolition Blue (IRE) *Ben Haslam*
2 b f Diamond Green(FR) —Amoras (IRE) (Hamas (IRE))
5727^{12} 6047^{9} 6532^{14}

Denison Flyer *Lawrence Mullaney* a42 53
4 b g Tobougg(IRE) —Bollin Victoria (Jalmood (USA))
2237^{9} 2462^{6} (3185) 3712^{6} 4129^{10} 4814^{3} 4904^{5} 5651^{6}

Den Maschine *John Flint* a44 57
6 b g Sakhee(USA) —Flamingo Flower (USA) (Diesis)
5832^{7}

Denny Crane *Edward Lynam* a92 85
5 b g Red Ransom(USA) —Fleeting Rainbow (Rainbow Quest (USA))
$1381a^{5}$ $7549a^{2}$ $7618a^{4}$

Den's Gift (IRE) *Clive Cox* a96 86
7 rg g City On A Hill(USA) —Romanylei (IRE) (Blues Traveller (IRE))
623^{8} 995^{5} 1382^{2} 1898^{6} 3285^{9} 4310^{4} 5053^{11} 5687^{2} 6948^{9}

Denton (NZ) *Jeremy Gask* a93 91
8 b g Montjeu(IRE) —Melora (NZ) (Sir Tristram)
353^{5} 525^{11} 1097^{7} 1470^{3} 2512^{14} (3286) 3844^{12} 5221^{10}

Denton Dancer *James Eustace* a42 61
2 bb g Halling(USA) —Rapid Revalation (USA) (Bianconi (USA))
1863^{4} 3229^{15} 5812^{8} 6581^{4} 7222^{10}

Denton Ryal *Sheena West* a54 59
4 b m Trade Fair—My Valentina (Royal Academy (USA))
164^{7}

Deny *Sir Michael Stoute* a61 71
3 ch g Mr Greeley(USA) —Sulk (IRE) (Selkirk (USA))
2646^{6} 2957^{7} 3919^{3} 4338^{8}

Deorai (IRE) *Jo Crowley* a74 84
3 ch g Choisir(AUS) —Tropical Lake (IRE) (Lomond (USA))
1727^{4} 3044^{6}

Depden (IRE) *Richard Price* a6
3 ch g Captain Rio—Attribute (Warning)
88^{7} 233^{5}

Deraasa (USA) *Saeed Bin Suroor* a88 70
3 b f Bernardini(USA) —Saywaan (USA) (Fusaichi Pegasus (USA))
2848^{14} 4241^{2} 4989^{2} 6054^{4} (6614) 6822^{9}

Derbaas (USA) *A Al Raihe* a104 117
5 b h Seeking The Gold(USA) —Sultana (USA) (Storm Cat (USA))
(239) (586a) $1000a^{16}$

Derby Desire (IRE) *Des Donovan* a57 61
7 b m Swallow Flight(IRE) —Jaldi (IRE) (Nordico (USA))
173^{5} 1135^{4} 1353^{6} 1508^{6} 5116^{2} 5520^{3} 5667^{7} 5994^{5} 6657^{10}

Derby Kitten (USA) *Michael J Maker* a109 108
3 b c Kitten's Joy(USA) —Blush (USA) (Menifee (USA))
$1921a^{13}$ $5072a^{7}$

Derek The Diamond *J R Jenkins* a23
2 b c Araafa(IRE) —West One (Gone West (USA))
7080^{14} 7329^{10}

Derfenna Art (IRE) *Seamus Durack* a70 60
2 b c Excellent Art—Cordelia (Green Desert (USA))
4857^{7} 5384^{3} 5697^{9} 6753^{10}

Derison (USA) *P Monfort* a82 84
9 b g Miesque's Son(USA) —Devolli (Saumarez)
$325a^{6}$

Derivatives (IRE) *John Gosden* a72 70
2 b f Dansili—Favourable Terms (Selkirk (USA))
6776^{6} 7030^{5} 7344^{4} $7665a^{3}$ 7906^{3}

Dervis Aga (TUR) *S Mutlu* a111
6 b h Unaccounted For(USA) —Mesitas (GER) (Surumu (GER))
$5754a^{6}$

Dervisher (IRE) *Sir Henry Cecil* 73
3 b c Dansili—Whirly Bird (Nashwan (USA))
1415^{4} 2185^{6} 2848^{4} 3557^{12} 4394^{5}

Derwisch (IRE) *Andreas Lowe* 101
5 ch g Aeskulap(GER) —Distella (GER) (Big Shuffle (USA))
$1931a^{7}$ $3334a^{6}$

Descarado (NZ) *Gai Waterhouse* 123
5 b g High Chaparral(IRE) —Karamea Lady (NZ) (Lord Ballina (AUS))
(6713a)

Descaro (USA) *David O'Meara* a64 77
5 gr g Dr Fong(USA) —Miarixa (FR) (Linamix (FR))
(1153) 1458^{3} 2034^{4} 2622^{3} 2888^{5} 3851^{3} 4635^{3} 4941^{3} 5453^{4} 5759^{9} 6095^{11} (6915) 7075^{7}

Desert Auction (IRE) *Ian Semple* a80 73
4 b g Desert Style(IRE) —Double Gamble (Ela-Mana-Mou)
932^{5} 1103^{5} 2428^{6} 2642^{2} 2789^{8} 4782^{7} 5151^{5} 6208^{8} 6490^{3} 7269^{7} 7565^{4} 7851^{8}

Desert Blanc *P Bary* a101 109
3 b c Desert Style(IRE) —Lumiere Rouge (FR) (Indian Ridge)
$6185a^{3}$ $6558a^{8}$

Desert Chieftain *Luca Cumani* a57 66
3 b g Green Desert(USA) —Donna Anna (Be My Chief (USA))
2103^{11} 2479^{6} 2790^{14} 4081^{11} 4666^{3} 5178^{6} (6033) 6586^{11} 6764^{8}

Desert Creek (IRE) *David Nicholls* a87 97
5 ch g Refuse To Bend(IRE) —Flagship (Rainbow Quest (USA))
844^{11} 2075^{20} 4415^{15} 5006^{6} ◆ 6078^{11} 6113^{20}

Desert Dreamer (IRE) *David Evans* a85 88
10 b g Green Desert(USA) —Follow That Dream (Darshaan)
78^{6} 159^{4} 188^{4}

Desert Fairy *James Unett* a54 46
5 b m Tobougg(IRE) —Regal Fairy (IRE) (Desert King (IRE))
85^{5} 409^{11}

Desert Falls *Richard Whitaker* a66 69
5 b g Pyrus(USA) —Sally Traffic (River Falls)
673^{6} 1634^{6} 1906^{9} 4741^{4} 5138^{2} 6304^{5} 6542^{3} 6930^{7} 7001^{7}

Desert Gazelle (USA) *Saeed Bin Suroor* 91
2 ch f Smart Strike(CAN) —Code Book (USA) (Giant's Causeway (USA))
(3865) ◆ 4803^{4} 6296^{5} 6705^{7}

Desert Hunter (IRE) *Micky Hammond* a54 64
8 b g Desert Story(IRE) —She-Wolff (IRE) (Pips Pride)
1150^{8} 1461^{9} 2589^{2} 2985^{3} 3462^{2} 3683^{4} 4123^{4} 4674^{6} 5622^{14}

Desert Icon (IRE) *Alan McCabe* a78 78
5 b g Desert Style(IRE) —Gilded Vanity (IRE) (Indian Ridge)
98^{5} ◆ 269^{6} 336^{2} 435^{5} 1771^{9} 2016^{4} 2464^{8} 2806^{4} 3412^{2} 3869^{3} 4683^{5} (5037) 6056^{3} (6414) 6794^{5} 7068^{7} (7253) 7529^{6} 7629^{7} 7746^{3} 7883^{2}

Desert Kiss *Walter Swinburn* a92 95
6 b m Cape Cross(IRE) —Kiss And Don'Tell (USA) (Rahy (USA))
3406^{6} ◆ 4058^{4} 4429^{5} 5557^{15} 5940^{7}

Desert Law (IRE) *Andrew Balding* a76 109
3 b c Oasis Dream—Speed Cop (Cadeaux Genereux)
2508^{2} ◆ 2934^{19} 3820^{4} 4779^{2} (5264) ◆ 5935^{6} 6522^{10}

Desert Location *Michael Bell* a63 56
3 b f Dubai Destination(USA) —Film Script (Unfuwain (USA))
1299^{7}

Desert Nova (IRE) *Mark Campion* 49
9 ch g Desert King(IRE) —Assafiyah (IRE) (Kris)
4329^{5} 5470^{6}

Desert Phantom (USA) *David Simcock* 98
5 b g Arch(USA) —Junkinthetrunk (USA) (Top Account (USA))
1680^{5}

Desert Philosopher *Kevin Ryan* a80 76
2 b c Pastoral Pursuits—Tembladora (IRE) (Docksider (USA))
6579^{3} 6912^{2} (7174)

Desert Poppy (IRE) *Walter Swinburn* a78 105
4 b m Oasis Dream—Flanders (IRE) (Common Grounds)
1675^{7} 2690^{2} 3459^{2} (4101) 5080^{3} 5935^{2} 6520^{3}

Desert Red (IRE) *George Baker* 35
2 b f Green Desert(USA) —Penicuik (Hernando (FR))
7052^{7}

Desert Romance (IRE) *David O'Meara* a71 97
5 b g Green Desert(USA) —Springtime Romance (USA) (Kris S (USA))
(1490) 2002^{9} 2573^{3} 4100^{9} 4528^{12} 5059^{4} 5557^{7} 6339^{27} 6803^{8} 7110^{4}

Desert Sea (IRE) *David Arbuthnot* a96 100
8 b g Desert Sun—Sea Of Time (USA) (Gilded Time (USA))
1105^{4} ◆ 3013^{18} 3647^{8}

Desert Shine (IRE) *Michael Bell* a69 76
3 b f Green Desert(USA) —Star Express (Sadler's Wells (USA))
(751) 1837^{6}

Desert Spree *Jeremy Gask* a40 40
2 ch f Byron—Babaraja (Dancing Spree (USA))
6406^{9} 6820^{9}

Desert Strike *Alan McCabe* a86 78
5 b g Bertolini(USA) —Mary Jane (Tina's Pet)
13^{9} 178^{8} 294^{10} 357^{4} (443) 612^{8} (646) 708^{3} 767^{2} 861^{2} 946^{3} (1048) 1395^{12} 1562^{4} 1698^{9} 1907^{3} 2069^{2} 2250^{7} 2369^{7} 2491^{6} 2938^{14} 3078^{3} 3383^{5} 3588^{6} 3737^{2} 4152^{7} 7253^{10} 7535^{5} 4289^{3} 4371^{3} 4678^{3} 4765^{2}

Desert Vision *Michael Easterby* a94 84
7 b g Alhaarth(IRE) —Fragrant Oasis (USA) (Rahy (USA))
1490^{5} 1671^{4} 2112^{9} 2887^{15} 3701^{9} 4442^{3} (5622) (6461) 6676^{13} 7237^{11}

Designated Decoy (USA) *C Von Der Recke* a78 83
6 b g Danzig(USA) —Suitably Discreet (USA) (Mr Prospector (USA))
$628a^{8}$

Deslaya (IRE) *Linda Stubbs* a58 57
3 b f Green Desert(USA) —Behlaya (IRE) (Kahyasi)
3343^{8} ◆ 4657^{2} 5019^{4} 5388^{2} 6105^{5} 6626^{6} 7006^{3} 7740^{2} 7910^{8}

Despatch *Ralph Beckett* 47
2 b f Nayef(USA) —Time Saved (Green Desert (USA))
6985^{7}

Desperate Dan *Andrew Haynes* a79 81
10 b g Danzero(AUS) —Alzianah (Alzao (USA))
1274^{4} 1752^{10} 2585^{11}

Dessau (GER) *W Hickst* 95
2 b f Soldier Hollow—Desabina (GER) (Big Shuffle (USA))
$6737a^{2}$

Destined For Glory (IRE) *J Moore* a104 117
4 b g Azamour(IRE) —Tekindia (FR) (Indian Ridge)
$1742a^{12}$ $7731a^{12}$

Destiny Blue (IRE) *Jamie Osborne* a66 88
4 b g Danehill Dancer(IRE) —Arpege (IRE) (Sadler's Wells (USA))
1874^{6} (2597) ◆ 3276^{8} 3959^{2} 4477^{2} 4724^{5} 5593^{8} 6302^{16}

Destiny Of A Diva *Reg Hollinshead* a91 88
4 b m Denounce—Royal Fontaine (IRE) (Royal Academy (USA))
(23) 287^{7} (1658) 2486^{3} (2915) 3338^{7} 4432^{2} 6439^{4} 6631^{9} 7272^{3}

Destiny Of Dreams *Jo Crowley* a66 87
3 b f Dubai Destination(USA) —Valjarv (IRE) (Bluebird (USA))
1146^{3} 3259^{3} 3803^{2} (4713) 5407^{2} (5915) 6996^{11}

Destinys Dream (IRE) *Tracy Waggott* 91
6 b m Mull Of Kintyre(USA) —Dream Of Jenny (Caerleon (USA))
1387^{9} 1855^{10} 2006^{P}

Deutschland (USA) *W P Mullins* a82 99
8 b g Red Ransom(USA) —Rhine Valley (USA) (Danzig (USA))
3157^{8} $7322a^{13}$ $7544a^{7}$

Deva Le Deva (IRE) *Tom Dascombe* a54 62
3 b f Acclamation—Margaux Dancer (IRE) (Danehill Dancer (IRE))
2581^{9} 3083^{6}

Devastation *John Gosden* 89
3 b f Montjeu(IRE) —Attraction (Efisio)
2050^{5}

Devdas (IRE) *Clive Cox* a64 81
2 b c Dylan Thomas(IRE) —Drifting (IRE) (Sadler's Wells (USA))
3282^{3} 3870^{4} 4815^{2} (5446) 6268^{3} 6986^{3}

Dever Dream *William Haggas* a97 111
4 b m Medicean—Sharplaw Venture (Polar Falcon (USA))
1893^{5} ◆ 3030^{10} 3827^{2} 4497^{2} ◆ 5080^{4} 5848^{2} $6566a^{P}$

De Vesci (IRE) *J T Gorman* a20 48
3 b g Statue Of Liberty(USA) —Goldenfort Queen (IRE) (Distinctly North (USA))
$1704a^{7}$

Deveze (IRE) *Milton Bradley* a19 39
3 b f Kyllachy—La Caprice (USA) (Housebuster (USA))
1465^{6} 1933^{10} 2177^{7} 7565^{8} 7693^{2} 7785^{7}

Devilish Lips (GER) *Andreas Lowe* 102
4 b m Konigstiger(GER) —Djidda (GER) (Lando (GER))
$3897a^{4}$

Devil You Know (IRE) *Michael Easterby* a76 63
5 b g Elusive City(USA) —Certainly Brave (Indian Ridge)
1991^{1} 1274^{3} 2165^{4} 3036^{11} 7595^{7} 7629^{9}

Devlin *Richard Fahey* 63
2 b g Auction House(USA) —Dancing Loma (FR) (Danehill Dancer (IRE))
1071^{3} 2042^{4} 2346^{6} 4194^{8}

Devonelli (IRE) *M Halford* a79 74
3 b f Mujadil(USA) —Ann's Annie (IRE) (Alzao (USA))
$1663a^{2}$ $7792a^{7}$

Devoted (IRE) *Ralph Beckett* 84
3 gr f Dalakhani(IRE) —Wavertree Girl (IRE) (Marju (IRE))
1456^{3} 3233^{2} 4336^{2} 6328^{5} 6749^{13}

Devotion (IRE) *A P O'Brien* 92
2 b f Dylan Thomas(IRE) —Bright Bank (IRE) (Sadler's Wells (USA))
$5974a^{4}$ 6299^{6}

Dew Reward (IRE) *Bill Turner* a62 63
3 b g Aussie Rules(USA) —Shariyfa (FR) (Zayyani)
866^{6} 1137^{2} 1312^{5} 1623^{4} 2146^{5} 2305^{3} 2637^{10} (3175) (3916) 4153^{5} 4685^{3} 4868^{4} 5415^{2} 6004^{4} 7818^{3} 7939^{5}

De Zephyr (FR) *Robert Collet* a67 64
9 b h Zieten(USA) —Lyceta (Shirley Heights)
$481a^{6}$ $935a^{10}$

Dffra (IRE) *Clive Brittain* a46 61
3 b f Refuse To Bend(IRE) —Sonachan (IRE) (Darshaan)
1338^{10} 5598^{5} 6066^{10} 7084^{5}

Dhaamer (IRE) *John Gosden* a71 102
4 ch g Dubai Destination(USA) —Arjuzah (IRE) (Ahonoora)
2681^{3} 3203^{4} 4267^{7} (4788) 6163^{10} 6803^{7}

Dhampas *Jim Boyle* a45 49
3 b c Tobougg(IRE) —Darshay (FR) (Darshaan)
2760^{8} 3268^{8} 3690^{9} 5022^{5} 5566^{3} 6240^{5} 6823^{4} 7195^{8}

Dhaular Dhar (IRE) *Jim Goldie* a87 95
9 b h Indian Ridge—Pescara (IRE) (Common Grounds)
1240^{4} 1694^{4} 1885^{22} 2706^{16} 2909^{5} 3397^{4} 3825^{18} 4528^{2} 4788^{11} 5686^{10} 5888^{10} 6302^{17} 6708^{9} (6989) $7618a^{10}$ 7719^{4}

Dhhamaan (IRE) *Ruth Carr* a68 76
6 b g Dilshaan—Safe Care (IRE) (Caerleon (USA))
893^{10} (1911) 2354^{12} 2671^{2} 3024^{4} 3733^{10} 4141^{2} (4379) (4517) 5034^{2} 5455^{10} 5760^{13} 6354^{6} 6867^{11} 7175^{9}

Diable Des Aigles (FR) *J Lepenant* a52 53
5 b g Diableneyev(USA) —Lesoria (FR) (Lesotho (USA))
$93a^{0}$

Diableside (FR) *J-P Delaporte* a86 99
5 b g Diableneyev(USA) —Karnatika (FR) (Kendor (FR))
$481a^{9}$

Diablo Dancer *Tim Walford* 77
3 b f Zafeen(FR) —Faithful Beauty (IRE) (Last Tycoon)
1860^{2} ◆ 2094^{8} 3025^{11} 4854^{2} (5164) 5760^{8}

Diademas (USA) *Conor Dore* a69 70
6 bb g Grand Slam(USA) —Kona Kat (USA) (Mountain Cat (USA))
4475^{6} 4650^{8} 4930^{9}

Diala (IRE) *William Haggas* 85
2 b f Iffraaj—Quaich (Danehill (USA))
5445^{2} ◆ (6950)

Dialed In (USA) *Nicholas Zito* a120
3 bb c Mineshaft(USA) —Miss Doolittle (USA) (Storm Cat (USA))
$1921a^{8}$ $2328a^{4}$

Dialogue *Ollie Pears* a89 74
5 b g Singspiel(IRE) —Zonda (Fabulous Dancer (USA))
1558^{4} ◆ 3142^{5} 4513^{2} 5828^{3} (6541) 7492^{5}

Diamant Rouge (FR) *C Boutin*
2 b g Leadership—Jarama (IRE) (Hector Protector (USA))
$7664a^{8}$

Diamond Belle *Noel Quinlan* 68
2 b f Rock Of Gibraltar(IRE) —Dixie Belle (Diktat)
4155^{11} 5726^{2} 6725^{10}

Diamond Blue *Richard Whitaker* 73
3 ch f Namid—Petra Nova (First Trump)
(2493) 3189^{3} 4715^{4} 6044^{3}

Diamond Bob *Ed Dunlop* a45 66
3 b g Diamond Green(FR) —Songsheet (Dominion)
2257^{7} 2621^{8} 3131^{8} 5243^{10} 6122^{13}

Diamond Boy (FR) *F Doumen* a67 108
5 b h Mansonnien(FR) —Gold Or Silver (FR) (Glint Of Gold)
$4037a^{9}$

Diamond Charlie (IRE) *Simon Dow* a89 86
3 br g Diamond Green(FR) —Rosy Lydgate (Last Tycoon)
208^{2} ◆ 578^{7} 1322^{8} 3687^{2} (4238) 5543^{10} 6217^{4} (7833) ◆

Diamond City (IRE) *Deborah Sanderson* a25 44
3 b g Diamond Green(FR) —Easter Girl (Efisio)
1211[10] 4403[9] 4633[7]

Diamond Daisy (IRE) *Ann Duffield* a53 76
5 b m Elnadim(USA) —Charlotte's Dancer (Kris)
37[8]

Diamond Fay (IRE) *Richard Guest*
3 ch f Fayruz—Waroonga (IRE) (Brief Truce (USA))
5030[7]

Diamond Finesse (IRE) *Ed Dunlop* a51 74
2 b f Red Clubs(IRE) —Birthday Present (Cadeaux Genereux)
2153[2] ◆ 4427[10] 7838[7]

Diamond Fire (IRE) *Adrian McGuinness* a51 55
7 b g King Charlemagne(USA) —Diamond Sun (Primo Dominie)
3234[8]

Diamondhead (IRE) *Brian Meehan* 91
2 b c Kyllachy—Hammrah (Danehill (USA))
3288[3] ◆ (4098) 5251[7] 7026[12]

Diamond Johnny G (USA) *Edward Creighton* a69 87
4 b g Omega Code(USA) —My Dancin Girl (USA) (Sun War Dancer (USA))
1371[7] 1507[3] 1864[9] 2497[11] 2756[3] 3350[4] 3685[5] 3914[3] 4057[7] 4182[2] 4709[4] 4828[11] 6305[5]

Diamond Marks (IRE) *John Gallagher* 36
2 b g Diamond Green(FR) —Miss Megs (IRE) (Croco Rouge (IRE))
3595[7]

Diamond Rainbow (IRE) *Rodger Sweeney* a52 52
2 b g Diamond Green(FR) —Graze On Too (IRE) (Rainbow Quest (USA))
972a[8] 6406[6]

Diamond Run *J W Hills* a65 68
3 b f Hurricane Run(IRE) —Rubies From Burma (USA) (Forty Niner (USA))
1724[7] 4102[6] 4340[7] (4758) ◆ 4911[3] ◆ 5511[7] (6071) 6488[5] 7269[3] 7485[12]

Diamond Sunrise (IRE) *Noel Wilson* a54 54
3 b f Diamond Green(FR) —Sunrise (IRE) (Sri Pekan (USA))
88[3] 505[7] 3455[8] 4505[4] (6049) 6545[13]

Diamond Twister (USA) *Lisa Williamson* a72 71
5 b g Omega Code(USA) —King's Pact (USA) (Slewacide (USA))
223[7] 592[5] 697[3] 808[5] 2473[3] 2991[12] 3225[7] 7892[10]

Diamond Vine (IRE) *Ronald Harris* a62 79
3 b c Diamond Green(FR) —Glasnas Giant (Giant's Causeway (USA))
2074[14] 2564[4] 2916[8] 3723[6] 3869[7] 4271[5] 4819[2] 4885[2] 5542[7] 6223[5] 6403[2] 6752[9] 6895[10] 7349[6] 7504[7] 7587[5]

Diamond Vision (IRE) *Robert Mills* a56 80
3 b g Diamond Green(FR) —Tranquil Sky (Intikhab (USA))
(1572) 2052[7] 4665[8]

Diapason (IRE) *Tom Dascombe* a78 76
5 b m Mull Of Kintyre(USA) —Suaad (IRE) (Fools Holme (USA))
200[2] 446[3] 577[3] 1762[6] 2566[8] 4973[4] ◆ 5265[4] ◆ 5781[4] 6604[12] 7039[3] ◆ 7173[9] 7417[9]

Dibella (IRE) *Paul Nolan* 81
4 b m Observatory(USA) —Dibiya (IRE) (Caerleon (USA))
7322a[5]

Dice (IRE) *Chris Grant* a79 34
5 b g Kalanisi(IRE) —Rain Dancer (IRE) (Sadler's Wells (USA))
6780[11]

Dicey Vows (USA) *Alan Jarvis* 50
3 b g Broken Vow(USA) —Pretty Dicey (USA) (Cherokee Run (USA))
6459[12] 7111[5]

Dichoh *[illegible]* [illegible] 66
8 b g Diktat—Hoh Dancer (Indian Ridge)
248[2] 488[3] 626[3] 765[2] 885[4] 1730[11] 2382[6] 3096[5] 4544[7] 5319[9] 5836[3] (6624) 6784[6] 7455[6] 7663[3]

Dick Doughtywylie *John Gosden* 96
3 b g Oasis Dream—Sugar Mill (FR) (Polar Falcon (USA))
3824[3] 5585[2] (6324)

Dickens Rules (IRE) *Sylvester Kirk* a67 68
2 gr g Aussie Rules(USA) —Lisfannon (Bahamian Bounty)
3288[7] 3779[3] 4205[2] 4581[9] 6132[8] 6806[15] 7222[4] 7432[12]

Dickie Le Davoir *Richard Guest* a68 93
7 b g Kyllachy—Downeaster Alexa (USA) (Red Ryder (USA))
545[6] 734[9] 874[2] (912) (1029) (1239) (1395) 1878[9] 2118[10] (2299) 2434[3] 2954[12] 3140[5] 3704[12] 4042[11] 4126[8] 6761[5] 6913[14] 7262[6] 7356[6] 7502[5] 7595[8] 7744[5] ◆ 7942[6]

Dickie's Lad (IRE) *Kevin Ryan* a98 97
3 b g Diamond Green(FR) —Shadow Mountain (Selkirk (USA))
(1900) 3052[9] 5288[2] 6723[8] 7578[2] 7790a[2]

Dick Turpin (IRE) *Richard Hannon* 124
4 b h Arakan(USA) —Merrily (Sharrood (USA))
(1527) ◆ 2101[4] 2343a[9] (3843) 5129a[7] (6369a) 6860[5]

Dicky Mint *Michael Easterby* a55 68
2 ch g Osorio(GER) —Oh Bej Oh Bej (IRE) (Distinctly North (USA))
2007[8] 2387[2] 2936[6] 3948[3] 4343[7] 5184[8] 5755[6] 6154[9] 6489[8] 7925[4]

Dictate *Mark H Tompkins* a72 66
3 ch g Araafa(IRE) —Navajo Love Song (IRE) (Dancing Brave (USA))
2874[10] 3460[8]

Dictionary *William Haggas* a57 64
3 ch g Zamindar(USA) —She Is Zen (FR) (Zieten (USA))
2673[6] ◆ 3343[3] ◆ 3616[2] 4796[4] 5121[3] 5388[3] 5864[11] 6940[9]

Diddums *Alastair Lidderdale* a59 65
5 b g Royal Applause—Sahara Shade (USA) (Shadeed (USA))
821[4] 912[7] 950[5] 1283[2] 1357[4] 1486[2] 1604[6] 1770[5] 2027[3] 2245[3] (2420) 2452[3] 2561[5] 3256[8] 3475[6] 3477[8] 4211[4] 4322[6] 4656[10] 5002[4] 5040[10] 5298[4]

Dido Park (FR) *B Legros*
4 b h Northern Park(USA) —Miss Alida (FR) (Amthaal (USA))
6593a[0]

Diego (GER) *T Mundry* 86
3 b c High Chaparral(IRE) —Dea (GER) (Shareef Dancer (USA))
1433a[7]

Diescentric (USA) *Sir Henry Cecil* 97
4 b g Diesis—Hawzah (Green Desert (USA))
2002[20] 3203[3] 3592[6] 4537[6] (5059) ◆

Dies Solis *Jeremy Gask* a61 67
4 ch h Exceed And Excel(AUS) —Rose Of America (Brief Truce (USA))
2001[3] 2554[10] 3517[4] 3714[4] 4544[8]

Diglett (IRE) *P Riccioni* 87
5 b g One Cool Cat(USA) —Rich Gift (Cadeaux Genereux)
1919a[13]

Dijarvo *Tony Carroll* a66 97
2 b f Iceman—Thicket (Wolfhound (USA))
(1049) ◆ 1726[2] 2053[2] (2866a)

Dikta Melody (FR) *P Demercastel* a56 71
4 b m Diktat—Desert Melody (FR) (Green Desert (USA))
196a[6]

Dildar (IRE) *A De Royer-Dupre* 106
3 b g Red Ransom(USA) —Diamond Tango (FR) (Acatenango (GER))
1923a[4]

Dililah *Linda Stubbs* a55 46
3 b f Auction House(USA) —Jezadil (IRE) (Mujadil (USA))
1934[3] 2157[13] 2722[13] 5352[10] 6982[9] 7460[5] 7755[8]

Dilys Maud *Roger Ingram* a61 58
4 b m Auction House(USA) —Dam Certain (IRE) (Damister (USA))
164[2] 278[8] 553[9] 687[6] 809[7] 944[5] 1233[11] 1567[2]

Dimaire *Derek Haydn Jones* a60 60
4 b m Kheleyf(USA) —Dim Ots (Alhijaz)
637[8] 874[4] 1463[10] 3909[3] 4224[11] 6433[7] 6767[2] 7055[9] 7773[4]

Diman Waters (IRE) *Eric Alston* 86
4 br g Namid—Phantom Waters (Pharly (FR))
1675[5] ◆ 2118[6] 2590[7] 3339[3] 3880[6] 4291[6] 5465[5] 5760[11]

Dimashq *Paul Midgley* a33 54
9 b m Mtoto—Agwaas (IRE) (Rainbow Quest (USA))
1305[8] 1617[6] 2492[4] (3086) 3129[5] 3509[7] 4499[3] 4982[7] 5405[6] 6236[13] 6379[8]

Dimension *James Fanshawe* a99 102
3 b g Medicean—Palatial (Green Desert (USA))
(1759) ◆ 2506[5] 3649[6] ◆ 3864[2] 4472[2] 5852[6] 6217[2] (6495)

Dim Sum *J Moore* a98 120
7 b g Kyllachy—Heckle (In The Wings)
999a[7]

Dinaday (FR) *N Leenders*
5 ch m Daylami(IRE) —Udina (Unfuwain (USA))
93a[0]

Dine Out *Mark H Tompkins* 60
2 b f Piccolo—Sosumi (Be My Chief (USA))
2580[9] 3362[10] 3767[2] 6021[9] 6724[9] 7051[9]

Dingaan (IRE) *Peter Grayson* a86 86
8 b g Tagula(IRE) —Boughtbyphone (Warning)
96[8] 213[7] 521[11] 1995[13] 2922[11] 3714[8] 5143[10] 5244[4] ◆ 5603[5] 5943[6] 6304[8] 6791[2] 6982[7] [illegible]

Dingle Two (IRE) *David Evans* a10
2 br f Mujadil(USA) —Puerto Oro (IRE) (Entrepreneur)
5632[11]

Dinkum Diamond (IRE) *Henry Candy* 111
3 b c Aussie Rules(USA) —Moving Diamonds (Lomitas)
1340[3] 2054[3] 2928[2] (4063) 5467[3] 5827[2] 6164[3] 6520[9]

Dinner Date *Tom Keddy* a81 64
9 ch g Groom Dancer(USA) —Misleading Lady (Warning)
48[8] 206[7] 381[9]

Dinner's Out *J-C Rouget* a100 95
3 b f War Front(USA) —Spring Stroll (USA) (Skywalker (USA))
5958a[8]

Dinvar Diva *John Gosden* 67
2 gr f Dalakhani(IRE) —Musique Magique (IRE) (Mozart (IRE))
5807[4]

Diocese (USA) *Marco Botti* a50 21
3 b g Pulpit(USA) —Dalisay (IRE) (Sadler's Wells (USA))
850[6] 992[9] 1312[9]

Diodoros (FR) *C Laffon-Parias* a95 98
5 ch g High Chaparral(IRE) —Light Quest (USA) (Quest For Fame)
705a[5]

Diplomasi *Clive Brittain* a70 72
3 b g Iceman—Piper's Ash (USA) (Royal Academy (USA))
193[4] 1481[3] (1609) 2152[3] 2819[11] 4268[5] 4664[6] 5318[9] 6089[5] 6764[11] 7085[6] 7698[9]

Diplomatic (IRE) *Michael Squance* a68
6 b g Cape Cross(IRE) —Embassy (Cadeaux Genereux)
23[5] (437) 666[12] 1026[4] 1232[7] 1460[12] 1868[7] 4210[7] 4865[10] 5944[8]

Diptimat *Marco Botti* 90
3 b g Royal Applause—Desacara (Arctic Tern (USA))
2258[6] 2591[2] 3080[6] 3642[3]

Dirar (IRE) *Gordon Elliott* a99 111
6 b g King's Best(USA) —Dibiya (IRE) (Caerleon (USA))
667[3] ◆ 1808[14] 2534a[7]

Direct Answer (USA) *Sir Michael Stoute* a84 91
4 b g Dynaformer(USA) —Proud Fact (USA) (Known Fact (USA))
(5169) 5693[6] 6068[2] (7017)

Directa Princess (GER) *Andreas Lowe* 92
3 bb f Dubai Destination(USA) —Dawlah (Shirley Heights)
2981a[6]

Director General (USA) *Julie Camacho* a61 61
4 b g Bernstein(USA) —Champagne Royal (USA) (Jeblar (USA))
283[3] 712[10] 896[7]

Directorship *Patrick Chamings* 97
5 br g Diktat—Away To Me (Exit To Nowhere (USA))
1529[7] 2647[5] 3436[6] (3840) (5043) ◆ 6862[9] 7168[12]

Diriculous *Robert Mills* a93 73
7 b g Diktat—Sheila's Secret (IRE) (Bluebird (USA))
(87) 316[8] 1067[7] 3000[12] 3685[11] 4064[4] 4909[5] 5717[10]

Disa (FR) *D Sepulchre* a71
3 b f Victory Note(USA) —Messini (IRE) (Ballad Rock)
775a[7]

Discanti (IRE) *Tim Easterby* a58 94
6 ch g Distant Music(USA) —Gertie Laurie (Lomond (USA))
1200[2] 1457[5] (1878) 2116[12] 2890[12] 3627[14] 5033[17] 5852[18] 6347[12] 6913[15]

Discern *James Fanshawe* a46
2 b f Medicean—Discerning (Darshaan)
7344[10] 7493[9]

Disco Dancing *Sir Henry Cecil*
3 b f Singspiel(IRE) —Disco Ball (Fantastic Light (USA))
2360[6]

Disco Des *Chris Grant*
3 b g Desert Style(IRE) —Jubilee Treat (USA) (Seeking The Gold (USA))
2461[9]

Disco Doll *Patrick Chamings* a45 53
3 b f Diktat—Cookie Cutter (IRE) (Fasliyev (USA))
3747[9] 4657[4] 5540[12]

Disco Sensation *David Nicholls* a39 56
2 b f Dubai Destination(USA) —Discoed (Distinctly North (USA))
5104[6] 5464[10] 6048[10] 6611[4] 7569[10]

Discoteca *Andrew Balding* 93
3 b g Nayef(USA) —Blaenavon (Cadeaux Genereux)
(1139) 1689[4] 3069[16] 3774[16] (6922)

Discourse (USA) *Mahmood Al Zarooni* 113
2 bb f Street Cry(IRE) —Divine Dixie (USA) (Dixieland Band (USA))
(3362) (4803) ◆

Discoverer (IRE) *John Gosden* a78
2 b c Bernardini(USA) —Danuta (USA) (Sunday Silence (USA))
7889[2]

Discovery Bay *Roger Charlton* a27 83
3 b c Dansili—Rainbow's Edge (Rainbow Quest (USA))
1408[2] 2008[6] 4310[18] 4914[5] 5598[9] 6401[2]

Discression *Kevin Ryan* 84
2 b c Indesatchel(IRE) —Night Gypsy (Mind Games)
2936[2] ◆ 3878[2]

Dishy Guru *Michael Blanshard* a71 69
2 ch c Ishiguru(USA) —Pick A Nice Name (Polar Falcon (USA))
2181[9] 4912[4] (5411) 5913[6] 6484[4] 6921[11] [illegible]

Disluiquejelaime *C Ferland* a77 75
3 b f Elusive City(USA) —Domniga (IRE) (Be My Guest (USA))
981a[5]

Dispol Grand (IRE) *Paul Midgley* a63 72
5 b g Raise A Grand(IRE) —Hever Rosina (Efisio)
185[3] 401[8] 1247[6] 1716[4] 3027[8] 3247[5] (3307) 3662[12] (4289) 4328[2] 4986[4] 5457[2] 6265[4] 6427[3]

Dispol Kylie (IRE) *Kate Walton* a46 77
5 b m Kheleyf(USA) —Professional Mom (USA) (Spinning World (USA))
(1555) 2062[2] 2690[7] 3083[3] 3579[4] 4126[4] 4405[6]

Disposition *John Gosden* a79
2 ch f Selkirk(USA) —Far Shores (USA) (Distant View (USA))
7396[2]

Dissent (IRE) *Gerard Butler* a81 66
2 b c Dansili—Centifolia (FR) (Kendor (FR))
1886[5] (6787) 7445[3]

Distant Love (IRE) *Andrew Balding* 62
2 b f Halling(USA) —Conference (IRE) (Montjeu (IRE))
4471[7]

Distant Memories (IRE) *Tom Tate* 116
5 b g Falbrav(IRE) —Amathia (IRE) (Darshaan)
1821[2] 2439[7] (3204) 4492[7] 5494[6] 6247[4]

Distant Sun (USA) *Linda Perratt* a50 75
7 b g Distant View(USA) —The Great Flora (USA) (Unaccounted For (USA))
1712[11] 1856[13] 2632[9] 2694[4] 2989[3] ◆ 3036[9] 3451[10] 4378[6] 4780[7] 5719[2] 6076[14] 6266[5] (6386) 6694[10] 7100[9] 7216[7] 7265[9]

Distant Voyage *Michael Blanshard* a33 1
2 ch g Kyllachy—Nevada Princess (IRE) (Desert Prince (IRE))
3408[11] 4205[10] 5232[10]

Distant Waters *Alan Jarvis* a60 62
4 gr m Lomitas—Silent Waters (Polish Precedent (USA))
3636[9] 4322[7] (4755) 5832[2] 6082[3]

Di Stefano *David Nicholls* a72 80
4 b g Bahamian Bounty—Marisa (GER) (Desert Sun)
1205[8] 1878[13] 2263[4]

Distinctive Image (USA) *C Von Der Recke* a96 75
6 b g Mineshaft(USA) —Dock Leaf (USA) (Woodman (USA))
180[10] 436[7] 1011a[7]

Distingue Lovers (IRE) *G Collet* 98
4 b h High Chaparral(IRE) —Sunburst (Gone West (USA))
4524a[7]

Distinguish (IRE) *Mark Johnston* a46 67
3 ch f Refuse To Bend(IRE) —Colourful Cast (IRE) (Nashwan (USA))
543[6] 898[11]

Distorted Legacy (USA) *Angel Penna Jr* a101 114
4 ch m Distorted Humor(USA) —Bunting (USA) (Private Account (USA))
7284a[4]

District Attorney (IRE) *William Haggas* 64
2 b c Lawman(FR) —Mood Indigo (IRE) (Indian Ridge)
6951[12] 7134[7]

Disturbia (IRE) *J W Hills* a50 51
3 b f Dubai Destination(USA) —Eoz (IRE) (Sadler's Wells (USA))
1580[8] 1934[5] 2583[4] 2801[4] 3268[12] 3910[5] 4491[5] 4847[3] 5665[5] 6701[5] 6781[3] 7091[4] 7263[4]

Diumara *Neville Bycroft*
4 b m Presidium—Nishara (Nishapour (FR))
5368[8] 6264[14]

Diva Donkey (IRE) *Bryan Smart* a44
2 b f Acclamation—Lupulina (CAN) (Saratoga Six (USA))
7559[10] 7685[5]

Divertimenti (IRE) *Roy Bowring* a62 85
7 b g Green Desert(USA) —Ballet Shoes (IRE) (Ela-Mana-Mou)
293[6] 455[7] 708[10] 1048[6] 1200[9] 1656[9] 2491[5] ◆ 3179[8] 3640[2] 3880[10] 4518[7] 4793[11] 5083[13] 6266[7] (6479) 6609[4] 6802[10] 7057[7] 7566[5] 7844[11]

Diverting *William Jarvis* a64 92
3 b f Nayef(USA) —Tawny Way (Polar Falcon (USA))
260[3] 2307[3] 3467[9] (4730) (5356) (6062) (6574) 7168[4]

Divinatore *James Moffatt* a64 59
5 b g Sakhee(USA) —Divina Mia (Dowsing (USA))
6915[8]

Divine Call *William Haggas* a89 82
4 b g Pivotal—Pious (Bishop Of Cashel)
2398[10] (2822) 3825[6] 4310[7] 5451[10] 6478[7]

Divine Music (IRE) *P Van De Poele* a92 109
4 b m Gold Away(IRE) —Divine Island (FR) (Anabaa (USA))
5306a[4]

Divine Rule (IRE) *Laura Mongan* a68 58
3 br g Cacique(IRE) —Island Destiny (Kris)
1819[4] 2196[7] 2583[6] 3089[4] 6240[10] 7122[7] 7333[12] 7756[4] 7910[6]

Divine Success (IRE) *Richard Fahey* 56
2 b g Amadeus Wolf—Divine Pursuit (Kris)
3755[9] 4365[8] 4851[7] 6260[15]

Divinite Green (IRE) *Peter Chapple-Hyam* 72
3 b c Diamond Green(FR) —Divinite (USA) (Alleged (USA))
1572[4] 1991[4] 2677[10] 6037[5]

Divin Leon (FR) *M Boutin* a88 100
3 b c Divine Light(JPN) —Nera Zilzal (IRE) (Zilzal (USA))
5230a[6]

Divin Tremp *C Scandella* a62 67
7 ch g Trempolino(USA) —Divinite (USA) (Alleged (USA))
479a[4]

Dixie Gwalia *David Simcock* a47 60
3 b f Tobougg(IRE) —Dixieanna (Night Shift (USA))
4162[2] ◆ 4466[4] 4950[4] (6940)

Dixie Land Band *Bill T[illegible]* a29 40
3 b f Diktat—Spring Mood (FR) (Nashwan (USA))
2192[13] 3220[8] 3690[14] 5267[6] 5566[11]

Dixie's Dream (IRE) *Richard Hannon* 75
2 b c Hawk Wing(USA) —Hams (USA) (Dixie Union (USA))
1913[4] 3229[4] (3941) 4892[2] 6724[2]

Diyaraka (FR) *Michael Moroney* 100
4 gr m Clodovil(IRE) —Diamonaka (FR) (Akarad (FR))
6967a[12]

Djalalabad (FR) *Jeff Pearce* a56 53
7 b m King's Best(USA) —Daraydala (IRE) (Royal Academy (USA))
69[9]

Django (SWE) *Jessica Long* a75 96
8 b g Acatenango(GER) —Praeriens Drottning (SWE) (Elmaamul (USA))
4842a[4]

Djumama (IRE) *Andreas Lowe* 110
3 b f Aussie Rules(USA) —Western Sky (Barathea (IRE))
(2337a) 3209a[5] 4839a[2] 5749a[2] 6568a[5] 7047a[4]

Doberdan (USA) *Patrick Holmes* a58 24
6 b g Street Cry(IRE) —Sophonisbe (Wollow)
3187[7] 3622[12] 4944[7]

Doc Hay (USA) *Keith Dalgleish* a74 94
4 bb g Elusive Quality(USA) —Coherent (USA) (Danzig (USA))
1314[5] 1838[9] (2632) (2987) 3279[6] (3305) 3588[3] 4042[13] 4327[6] 5163[7] 5720[10] 6212[2] (6913) 7298[3]

Doc Hill *Michael Blanshard* a54 30
2 ch c Dr Fong(USA) —Cultural Role (Night Shift (USA))
2788[12] 4580[9] 4969[8] 6002[2] 6927[6] 7223[8]

Docofthebay (IRE) *David Nicholls* a109 101
7 ch g Docksider(USA) —Baize (Efisio)
844[2] 1094[6] 1720[3] 2075[4] 3109[5] 3862[6] 4534[17] 5032[3] 5474[9] 5887[9] 6672[10] 6862[22] 7295[2] (7392)

Docs Legacy (IRE) *Richard Fahey* a66 68
2 b g Ad Valorem(USA) —Lunamixa (GER) (Linamix (FR))
3505[7] 4047[5] 4436[10] 4943[3] 6345[8] (7035) (7157)

Doctor Banner *Mick Channon* a61 59
2 b g Compton Place—Icing (Polar Falcon (USA))
2837[7] 3288[9] 3722[8] 5197[8] *5634[3]* 5844[4] 6101[4] 6260[5] *6667[5]* 6760[3] 6937[12]
Doctor Crane (USA) *David Nicholls* a83 91
5 b g Doneraile Court(USA) —Sharons Song (USA) (Badger Land (USA))
1094[21] 4445[2] 4774[7] 6262[8]
Doctor Dalek (IRE) *Edward Creighton* a50 35
2 b c Elusive City(USA) —Aquiform (Cadeaux Genereux)
4384[12] *5211[8]* 6019[9] *6308[8]* 7231[10]
Doctor Hilary *Mark Hoad* a67 69
9 b g Mujahid(USA) —Agony Aunt (Formidable (USA))
2155[8] 2920[7] 3261[3] 3939[5] *4759[6]* 5038[3] 5540[3] 5843[2] 6746[10] *(7224)* *7588[6]* *7811[7]*
Doctor Parkes *Eric Alston* 102
5 b g Diktat—Lucky Parkes (Full Extent (USA))
(1438) (1809) 2317[2] 2727[4] 3874[12] 4776[8] 5927[13] 6706[18]
Doctor's Cave *Ken Cunningham-Brown* a22 61
9 b g Night Shift(USA) —Periquitum (Dilum (USA))
137[4]
Doctor Zhivago *Ian McInnes* a87 93
4 b g Shamardal(USA) —Balalaika (Sadler's Wells (USA))
1154[6] 1387[7] 1747[2] 2006[9] 2403[5] 3164[2] 3399[9] (4125) 5250[19] 5757[8] 6346[15]
Doesn't Care (IRE) *Richard Fahey* a42
3 gr c Shamardal(USA) —Senegal (IRE) (Grand Lodge (USA))
263[8]
Dohasa (IRE) *I Mohammed* a109 109
6 b g Bold Fact(USA) —Zara's Birthday (IRE) (Waajib)
155a[8] 327a[2] *414a[6]* *606a[5]* 754a[6]
Dollar Bill *Andrew Balding* 72
2 ch g Medicean—Jardin (Sinndar (IRE))
3401[12] 4213[8] 5196[3] 5967[8]
Dollar Deal *Luca Cumani* a63 58
3 b c Dubai Destination(USA) —Design Perfection (USA) (Diesis)
2511[7] 3167[5] *5816[5]* *6947[2]*
Dolly Bay *Julia Feilden* a50 43
3 ch f Kyllachy—Loblolly Bay (Halling (USA))
4925[4] 5626[6] 6591[7] 6940[11] *7511[3]* *7693[9]*
Dolly Colman (IRE) *Michael Blake* a52 53
3 bg f Diamond Green(FR) —Absolutely Cool (IRE) (Indian Ridge)
2825[3] 3958[5] 4248[6] 5134[2] 5665[3] *7333[2]* *7720[4]* *7836[6]*
Dolly Danca *Paul Midgley* 56
2 ch f Deportivo—Otylia (Wolfhound (USA))
1691[11] 2113[6] 2665[4] 6597[11] 6800[3] 7059[18]
Dolly Parton (IRE) *John Bridger* a61 76
3 b f Tagula(IRE) —Batool (USA) (Bahri (USA))
847[6] *913[3]* 1439[6] 1543[3] (1906) 2215[12] 2264[6] 3049[7] 5972[14] 6250[6] 6746[12] *7201[11]* *7437[11]*
Dolores Ortiz (IRE) *Dr Jeremy Naylor* 56
5 b m High Chaparral(IRE) —Ma N'Ieme Biche (USA) (Key To The Kingdom (USA))
6798[9]
Dolphin Rock *David Barron* a86 91
4 b g Mark Of Esteem(IRE) —Lark In The Park (IRE) (Grand Lodge (USA))
1879[4] 2301[2] 2814[2] 3085[2] 3585[4] 4561[3] 4794[4] 5557[2] 6302[11]
Domeside *C Delcher-Sanchez* 102
5 b h Domedriver(IRE) —Buck's Fizz (Kris)
7733a[7]
Domesky (AUS) *Michael Kent* 112
4 b g Domesday(AUS) —Miss Aryan (NZ) (Masterclass (USA))
6886a[16]
Dominant (IRE) *Roger Varian* 115
3 bl c Cacique(IRE) —Es Que (Inchinor)
1550[2] ◆ 2100[5] (3405) ◆ 4345[3]
Domination *C Byrnes* a82 86
4 b g Motivator—Soliza (IRE) (Intikhab (USA))
7322a[10]
Dominium (USA) *Jeremy Gask* a82 82
4 b g E Dubai(USA) —Sudenlylastsummer (USA) (Rinka Das (USA))
3737[6] (4509) ◆ 5043[6] 5811[7] *6477[3]* 6762[12] *7253[5]* *7439[3]*
Domino Rock (FR) *C Boutin* a90 91
3 b c Indian Rocket—Lady Domino (FR) (Second Empire (IRE))
532a[9] 1206a[6] *5529a[7]*
Domo Arigato (SWE) *Caroline Malmborg*
2 ch f Eishin Dunkirk(USA) —Persian Flight (Catrail (USA))
5983a[6]
Do More Business (IRE) *Pat Phelan* a63 56
4 b g Dubai Destination(USA) —Tokyo Song (USA) (Stravinsky (USA))
3517[10] *1232[8]* 1770[7] 2426[7] 2794[6] 3254[2] 3482[2] 3939[2] 4740[2] 5138[7] *7655[11]* *7892[8]*
Dom'Son (FR) *Y Fertillet* 65
3 b c Miesque's Son(USA) —Marie De Bourbon (FR) (Sicyos (USA))
370a[0]
Dom Tom (USA) *Mme C Head-Maarek* a77 83
3 b c Anabaa(USA) —Dedication (FR) (Highest Honor (FR))
1010a[9]
Don Bosco (FR) *D Smaga* 107
4 ch h Barathea(IRE) —Perfidie (IRE) (Monsun (GER))
7404a[5]
Don Carlino (POL) *S Bigus*
6 b g Don Corleone—Donna Grafia (POL) (Graf (USA))
259a[0]
Doncaster Rover (USA) *David Brown* a90 114
5 b h War Chant(USA) —Rebridled Dreams (USA) (Unbridled's Song (USA))
582a[7] 825a[4] 1093[8] 1340[11] 2502[3] 3394[2] 3852[4] 4412[5] 5046[5] (5282) 5510[6] 5707[11] 6534[4]
Doncosaque (IRE) *P J O'Gorman* a74 77
5 b g Xaar—Darabela (IRE) (Desert King (IRE))
4278[13] *5383[6]* ◆ *6220[6]* *(6793)* (6924)

Don Libre *Paul Cole* a72
2 b c Librettist(USA) —Darwinia (GER) (Acatenango (GER))
7240[3] *7422[2]*
Donnaconna (CAN) *Mark Johnston* 35
3 ch g Elusive Quality(USA) —Brandy Lake (CAN) (Meadowlake (USA))
1338[13] 1540[7] 2045[10] 2858[12]
Donna Elvira *Edwin Tuer* a39 78
4 b m Doyen(IRE) —Impatiente (USA) (Vaguely Noble)
1036[7] 1324[9] 1616[3] 2091[6] 2830[4] 3574[10] 5791[9] 6157[12] 7077[3] *7357[7]*
Donny Briggs *Tim Easterby* a66 66
6 b g Orpen(USA) —Passionate Pursuit (Pursuit Of Love)
1[3]
Donnywardsbird *Eric Alston* 5
3 b g Danbird(AUS) —Sweetly Sharp (IRE) (Daggers Drawn (USA))
2493[8] 3616[9] 5030[8]
Don Salluste (FR) *Mme M-C Naim* a77 75
3 b c Enrique—Wondernight (FR) (Shining Steel)
902a[4]
Don't Call Me (IRE) *David Nicholls* a70 101
4 ch g Haafhd—Just Call Me (NZ) (Blues Traveller (IRE))
3397[3] 4310[3] ◆ 4415[4] ◆ 4794[3] 5059[3] 5546[9] (6150)
Don't Call Me Tiny (IRE) *Don Cantillon* a34 37
3 b f Acclamation—Holly Rose (Charnwood Forest (IRE))
2650[8] 2852[4] 3173[6] 3742[7]
Don't Hurry Me (IRE) *J-C Rouget* a95 107
3 ch f Hurricane Run(IRE) —Beringold (Bering)
(1513a) 2342a[8] 3449a[2] 6686a[10] 7386a[8]
Dontpaytheferryman (USA) *Brian Ellison* a86 15
6 ch g Wiseman's Ferry(USA) —Expletive Deleted (USA) (Dr Blum (USA))
(63) *(104)* 1387[12] *7241[4]*
Dont Take Me Alive *Clive Cox* a58 67
2 b c Araafa(IRE) —Up At Dawn (Inchinor)
3986[10] *4906[8]* 5375[2] 6399[5]
Don't Tempt Me (IRE) *Sylvester Kirk*
2 b f Moss Vale(IRE) —Banutan (IRE) (Charnwood Forest (IRE))
2767[15] *6214[14]*
Dont Teutch (FR) *D Smaga* 97
2 b f Country Reel(USA) —Simonkikou (FR) (Panis (USA))
5305a[6] 6042a[5] 6808a[4] 7220a[3]
Doo Lang (USA) *J-C Rouget* a72 100
3 b f Pulpit(USA) —Wonder Woman (USA) (Storm Cat (USA))
1553a[7]
Doonard Prince (IRE) *Miss Elizabeth Doyle* a30 47
2 b c Footstepsinthesand—Fly Haia (IRE) (Flying Spur (AUS))
1699a[10]
Doquet (IRE) *B Grizzetti* 98
3 b c Aussie Rules(USA) —Imitation (GER) (Highest Honor (FR))
1431a[7] 1920a[5]
Dora's Gift *Hughie Morrison* a56 64
2 b f Cadeaux Genereux—Conquestadora (Hernando (FR))
7258[4] *7422[3]* *7777[6]*
Dora's Sister (IRE) *John Quinn* a39 57
2 b f Dark Angel(IRE) —Teodora (IRE) (Fairy King (USA))
1414[8] *6131[9]* 6866[3]
Dorback *Noel Wilson* a84 86
4 ch g Kyllachy—Pink Supreme (Night Shift (USA))
2099[6] ◆ 2954[14] 3796[5] 4859[10] 5339[2] 6703[17] 7076[7] *7332[2]* *7502[2]* ◆ *7675[10]* *(7847)* *7926[12]*
Dorcas Lane *Lucy Wadham* a87 107
3 ch f Norse Dancer(IRE) —Waqood (USA) (Riverman (USA))
(214) *468[2]* ◆ 1113[2] (1722) 3065[3] 3624[3] 4570a[3] 5366a[9]
Dorden *Noel Wilson*
4 gr m Paris House—Dolphin Dancer (Dolphin Street (FR))
1941[7]
Dordogne (IRE) *Mark Johnston* a109 104
3 bb c Singspiel(IRE) —Riberac (Efisio)
(1320) ◆ 1548[9] (1895) 3775[6] *(5754a)*
Doric Echo *Kevin M Prendergast* a32 75
5 b g Bertolini(USA) —Latour (Sri Pekan (USA))
670[7] *798[11]*
Doricemay (IRE) *Clive Cox* 76
3 b f Cape Cross(IRE) —Callanish (Inchinor)
1362[10] (2192) 2615[5] 3650[10] 4093[9] 6062[5] 6997[7]
Dorlion (IRE) *Mme J Bidgood*
2 b c Gold Away(IRE) —Farnesina (FR) (Anabaa (USA))
7665a[0]
Dormello (IRE) *P Bary* 108
3 b c Dansili—Field Of Hope (IRE) (Selkirk (USA))
6903a[6]
Dorothy's Dancing (IRE) *Gary Moore* a61 59
3 b f Acclamation—Segoria (IRE) (Shinko Forest (IRE))
(788) *(958)* *1193[3]* 1776[4] 5279[4] *7201[5]* *7737[5]* *7940[4]*
Dorothy's Dream (IRE) *John O'Shea* 18
3 b f Diamond Green(FR) —Penny Rye (IRE) (Pennekamp (USA))
1629[7] 2141[11] 2581[10] 3272[13]
Dorrit *Roger Charlton* a23
2 b f Dalakhani(IRE) —Pretty As Can Be (Giant's Causeway (USA))
7494[11] *7598[7]*
Dorry K (IRE) *David Barron* 64
2 b f Ad Valorem(USA) —Ashtaroute (USA) (Holy Bull (USA))
3583[4] 4632[4] 5464[9] 6275[4] 6807[7]
Dos Amigos (IRE) *Michael Dods* 65
2 b c Clodovil(IRE) —Ide Say (IRE) (Grand Lodge (USA))
7209[3]

Do The Bosanova (IRE) *J S Bolger* a71 88
3 ch f Galileo(IRE) —Sateen (Barathea (IRE))
6513a[14]
Dot's Delight *Mark Rimell* a53 51
7 b m Golden Snake(USA) —Hotel California (IRE) (Last Tycoon)
172[3] *598[6]* *1218[2]* *1473[5]* *1973[6]* 5267[5] 5916[5]
Dotty Darroch *Robin Bastiman* a30 57
3 b f Ad Valorem(USA) —Sensible Idea (Dr Fong (USA))
1074[3] 1303[4] 2396[5] (2805) 3860[8] 4638[4] 5506[5] 5719[7] 6261[4] *6618[7]*
Double Bass (USA) *Mahmood Al Zarooni* 53
2 bb c Bernardini(USA) —Dundrummin' (USA) (Gone West (USA))
4080[7] 6774[12]
Double Carpet (IRE) *Garry Woodward* a71 65
8 b g Lahib(USA) —Cupid Miss (Anita's Prince)
(34) *107[2]* *166[5]* *446[2]* *(666)* *820[3]* *949[7]* *1368[7]* *2653[10]* 6939[13] *7715[7]*
Double Cee *Richard Fahey* a18 64
2 ch g Haafhd—Razzle (IRE) (Green Desert (USA))
4080[4] 5503[6] 6110[5] *6846[10]*
Double Dealer *Mahmood Al Zarooni* a85 101
3 b c Dubawi(IRE) —Infiel (Luge)
1313[2] 1571[6] 5516[3] 5892[2] 7168[3] ◆
Double Dice *George Margarson*
3 rg f Verglas(IRE) —Fiddle-Dee-Dee (IRE) (Mujtahid (USA))
2825[8]
Double Duchess *Paul D'Arcy* a75
3 b f Val Royal(FR) —Ti Adora (IRE) (Montjeu (IRE))
(5) *142[P]* *227[6]* *(296)* *379[2]* *750[4]* *5630[12]* *6181[6]* *7068[10]* *7424[3]* 7773[3]
Double Fortune *Jamie Poulton* a66 53
4 b m Singspiel(IRE) —Four-Legged Friend (Aragon)
943[7] 1839[11] 2145[6] 2451[9]
Double Handful (GER) *Venetia Williams* 76
5 bl g Pentire—Durania (GER) (Surumu (GER))
2716[8] 3593[8] 4719[4] 5453[5] 6104[2] 6485[7] 6722[4] 6998[2]
Double Trouble *Marco Botti* a68 61
3 b f Royal Applause—Requiem (USA) (Royal Anthem (USA))
4478[3] *6137[2]* *7004[2]* *(7609)*
Dougie Boy *Bill Turner* a55 61
2 b g Trade Fair—Wavet (Pursuit Of Love)
1055[3] *1290[2]* 1988[4] *4646[5]*
Douze Points (IRE) *Pat Murphy* a83 94
5 b g Redback—Grade A Star (IRE) (Alzao (USA))
1410[4] 1885[18] 2217[9] 3445a[10] *3740[3]* 4566a[16] *5322[7]* 5879[14] *7098[10]* *7339[11]* *7589[8]* *7788[9]* *7911[10]*
Dove Cottage (IRE) *Stuart Kittow* a42 68
9 b g Great Commotion(USA) —Pooka (Dominion)
1631[2] 2377[3] 2659[3] 3599[13] 3978[6] 5612[2] 5916[2] *6503[7]*
Dovedon Angel *Gay Kelleway* a56 56
5 b m Winged Love(IRE) —Alexander Star (IRE) (Inzar (USA))
114[5]
Dovils Date *Rod Millman* 67
2 gr g Clodovil(IRE) —Lucky Date (IRE) (Halling (USA))
1835[6] 2584[8] 3171[2] 3780[5]
Dower Glen *Keith Dalgleish* a59 59
4 b m Camacho—Aimee's Delight (Robellino (USA))
1544[4] 1716[5] 1856[2] 2047[4] (2263) 2546[6] 2803[10] 3451[3] 3901[2] 4504[8] 4881[11] 5148[10] 6386[4] 6602[7]
Downhiller (IRE) *John Dunlop* a99 94
6 ch g Alhaarth(IRE) —Ski For Gold (Shirley Heights)
4266[8] 4806[4] 5448[2]
Downhill Skier (IRE) *Mark Brisbourne* a70 74
7 ch g Danehill Dancer(IRE) —Duchy Of Cornwall (USA) (The Minstrel (CAN))
14[4] *111[4]* *169[3]* *255[4]* *(362)* *512[8]* *(544)* *743[6]* *915[6]* 928[10] 3806[11] (4518) 4793[3] 5201[6] 5561[6] (5732) 5881[6] 6354[10] 6979[5] 7716[5] 7819[3] ◆
Downton Abbey (IRE) *Richard Hannon* a61 56
2 b f Dubai Destination(USA) —Morality (Elusive Quality (USA))
6215[6] 6588[6] *6928[7]*
Downtown Boy (IRE) *Ray Craggs* 58
3 br g Kheleyf(USA) —Uptown (IRE) (Be My Guest (USA))
1495[2] 1945[6] 3024[10] (4044) 4612[14] 6153[6]
Doynosaur *Mrs K Burke* 61
4 b m Doyen(IRE) —Daring Destiny (Daring March)
1211[5]
Doyouknowwhoiam *Bryan Smart* a59 57
2 ch g Monsieur Bond(IRE) —Tibesti (Machiavellian (USA))
3878[10] 4347[10] 4851[4] 5161[11] 6384[10] *7780[3]* *7915[7]*
Dozy (IRE) *Kevin Ryan* 98
2 ch f Exceed And Excel(AUS) —Star Profile (IRE) (Sadler's Wells (USA))
(1870) (2404) 3033[12]
Dozy Joe *Ian Wood* a91 84
3 b c Sleeping Indian—Surrey Down (USA) (Forest Wildcat (USA))
2199[2] 2934[11] 3820[11] *7578[12]*
Dragon Ball (FR) *J Van Handenhove* 74
2 b f Trempolino(USA) —Anamiglia (Anabaa (USA))
6925a[3] 7449a[4]
Dragonera *Ed Dunlop* a88 86
3 b f Doyen(IRE) —Time Will Show (FR) (Exit To Nowhere (USA))
(1958) ◆ 2232[8] (2891) (3681) *6822[6]*
Dragon Khan (IRE) *C Roche* 56
2 b c Dr Fong(USA) —Desert Magic (IRE) (Green Desert (USA))
2329a[7]
Dragon Pulse (IRE) *Mrs John Harrington* 117
2 ch c Kyllachy—Poetical (IRE) (Croco Rouge (IRE))
(5293a) 5951a[2]

Dragon Slayer (IRE) *John Harris* a56 74
9 ch g Night Shift(USA) —Arandora Star (USA) (Sagace (FR))
692[7] 1099[14] 1871[6] 2530[3] (2616) 2851[5] 3637[5] 4165[6]
Drakes Drum *Clive Cox* a73 72
3 b g Dansili—Perfect Echo (Lycius (USA))
5449[6] 5960[3] 6750[4] *7334[3]*
Dr Albert *Frank Sheridan* a57
2 b c Son And Heir(IRE) —Tyne Goddess (Warningford)
7718[9] *7821[7]* *7879[3]*
Draoicht (IRE) *John Joseph Murphy* 47
3 b f Namid—Flower Drum (FR) (Celtic Swing)
6411[10]
Drawback (IRE) *Barry Brennan* a59 53
8 b g Daggers Drawn(USA) —Sacred Heart (IRE) (Catrail (USA))
393[6] *809[9]* 2638[2] *3176[14]* *5416[3]* 5612[3] 6870[8] 7077[9]
Drawnfromthepast (IRE) *Jamie Osborne* a101 98
6 ch g Tagula(IRE) —Ball Cat (FR) (Cricket Ball (USA))
1720[24] 2099[10] 2525[10] (3996) 4644[4] 5033[14] *6351[3]* *6875[5]* *7575[3]*
Drawn Gold *Reg Hollinshead* a46 67
7 b g Daggers Drawn(USA) —Gold Belt (IRE) (Bellypha)
2224[10] 3599[6] 4082[5] 4341[7] 5566[2] 6029[10] *6503[8]*
Dr Darcey *Richard Hannon* a60 69
3 b g Dr Fong(USA) —Ballet (Sharrood (USA))
1769[2] 2225[5] 2904[2] 3599[3] 4242[6] 4974[2] 5236[8]
Dreamacha *Stuart Williams* a71 93
4 b m Oasis Dream—Machaera (Machiavellian (USA))
(113) 1555[2] 2016[7] 2566[4] (2720) (3078) 6594a[5] 7018[15]
Dream Achieved *B W Hills* a91 95
3 b g Oasis Dream—Achieve (Rainbow Quest (USA))
1321[3] *(1606)* 3067[29] 4794[14]
Dream Ahead (USA) *David Simcock* 129
3 b c Diktat—Land Of Dreams (Cadeaux Genereux)
3011[5] (3863) ◆ 4838a[7] (5707) (6566a)
Dream Catcher (FR) *David Pinder* a86 88
3 gr g Della Francesca(USA) —Gallopade (FR) (Kendor (FR))
609[4] *740[4]* *847[2]* 1391[5] 2216[8] (2363) 2619[4] 2910[2] *3737[12]* 4459[4] *5419[5]* *5948[10]* 6246[9] *6442[9]* 6895[12] 7265[11] 7519[5]
Dream Catcher (SWE) *Jonjo O'Neill* a67 64
8 b g Songline(SWE) —Queen Ida (SWE) (Diligo (FR))
3311[5] 4318[3] 4974[9] 5379[3] *7495[4]* *(7850)*
Dream Dream Dream (IRE) *Kevin M Prendergast* a3 58
4 b m Oasis Dream—Egoli (USA) (Seeking The Gold (USA))
1941[2] 2593[8] 4288[15] 4559[5] 5031[10]
Dream Eater (IRE) *Andrew Balding* a103 119
6 gr h Night Shift(USA) —Kapria (FR) (Simon Du Desert (FR))
1527[3] 1821[5] 5282[8] 5777a[4] 6521[13]
Dream Express (IRE) *Bill Turner* a51 53
6 b g Fasliyev(USA) —Lothlorien (USA) (Woodman (USA))
1557[10] 2543[10] 2989[7] 3732[6] 5008[8] 6889[13] *7518[8]*
Dreaming Of Rubies *Ben Haslam* 52
2 b f Oasis Dream—Rubies From Burma (USA) (Forty Niner (USA))
6045[2]
Dream Land (FR) *B Goudot* a79 79
5 b h Oasis Dream—Marie Vison (IRE) (Entrepreneur)
(93a)
Dream Lioness *Ben Haslam* 33
2 b f Acclamation—Dream Vision (USA) (Distant View (USA))
5590[7] *7000[7]*
Dream Lodge (IRE) *David Nicholls* a96 108
7 ch g Grand Lodge(USA) —Secret Dream (IRE) (Zafonic (USA))
1094[17] 1694[11] 2123[9] 3537[3] 5557[16] 6093[13]
Dream Number (IRE) *William Muir* a66 72
4 ch m Fath(USA) —Very Nice (Daylami (IRE))
(1024) 1281[3] *1581[8]* 3079[7] 3685[10] 5301[4] 6408[8]
Dream Of Fortune (IRE) *David Evans* a74 68
7 b g Danehill Dancer(IRE) —Tootling (IRE) (Pennine Walk)
94[4] *175[2]* *341[2]* *352[2]* *427[2]* *472[5]* *541[8]* *599[3]* *656[4]* 790[5] 2616[6] 2768[4] 3240[3] 3380[6] 3923[7] 4088[4] 4645[4] 4869[3] 5112[3] 5390[3] 5611[6] 5740[3] 5815[2] 6287[8] 6357[2] 6543[2] 6669[4] 7034[2] 7178[3] 7418[5] 7465[8]
Dream Of Wunders *James Given*
3 br f Cape Cross(IRE) —Wunders Dream (IRE) (Averti (IRE))
2185[14] 3355[4] 3684[9]
Dream Peace (IRE) *Robert Collet* a82 114
3 b f Dansili—Truly A Dream (IRE) (Darshaan)
3671a[3] 4570a[2] (5366a) 6909a[3]
Dream Pedlar (AUS) *Troy Blacker* 110
7 br g West Quest(CAN) —Unamah (AUS) (Top Avenger (AUS))
6886a[15] 7115a[9]
Dreams Of Dawn *Mick Channon* 76
3 b g Invincible Spirit(IRE) —Castilian Queen (USA) (Diesis)
2103[3] 3909[2] 4706[4]
Dreams Of Fire (USA) *Sir Michael Stoute* a79 64
2 b f Dynaformer(USA) —Angel In My Heart (FR) (Rainbow Quest (USA))
6744[6] ◆ *(7118)* ◆
Dreams Of Glory *Ron Hodges* a55 66
3 ch c Resplendent Glory(IRE) —Pip's Dream (Glint Of Gold)
(1294) 1764[8] 2549[5] 3272[3] (3724) (4227) (4486) 5279[2] 5615[5]
Dream Spinner *Dr Richard Newland* a68 76
4 b g Royal Applause—Dream Quest (Rainbow Quest (USA))
5112[5]

Dream The Blues (IRE) *Kevin Ryan* 70
3 b f Oasis Dream—Catch The Blues (IRE) (Bluebird (USA))
(6834)

Dream Tune *Clive Cox* 69
2 b c Oasis Dream—Play Bouzouki (Halling (USA))
6993[6] ◆

Dream Walker (FR) *Ian McInnes* 44
2 gr g Gold Away(IRE) —Minnie's Mystery (FR) (Highest Honor (FR))
3932[8] 4436[9] 4899[9]

Dreamweaving (IRE) *Nigel Tinkler* 49
3 b f Sleeping Indian—Wicked (Common Grounds)
2236[4] 2574[5] 3049[6] 4284[8]

Dream Whisperer *Dominic Ffrench Davis* 70
2 b f Piccolo—Sweet Whisper (Petong)
1055[5] 1785[2] 2880[3] 3092[8] 4557[8] 6524[5] 6919[6]

Dream Win *Brian Ellison* a79 79
5 b h Oasis Dream—Wince (Selkirk (USA))
2115[4] 2454[6] 3112[2]

Dreamwriter (USA) *Richard Hannon* 88
2 ch f Tale Of The Cat(USA) —Rebridled Dreams (USA) (Unbridled's Song (USA))
(5047) ◆ 5656[11] 7019[6]

Dreamy Gent (IRE) *Mrs John Harrington* a81 80
9 b g Trans Island—Calamity Kate (IRE) (Fairy King (USA))
1381a[2]

Dreamy Nights *Gary Harrison* 26
3 b f Statue Of Liberty(USA) —Hairy Night (IRE) (Night Shift (USA))
5429[8] 5842[4]

Dream Youn (FR) *J Van Handenhove* a82 85
6 b g Dream Well(FR) —Ghayouna (FR) (Doyoun)
219a[4] 439a[5]

Dresden (IRE) *Luca Cumani* 55
3 b g Diamond Green(FR) —So Precious (IRE) (Batshoof)
2068[10] 2511[8] 4163[5]

Dressed In Lace *Andrew Balding* a58 68
2 b f Dark Angel(IRE) —Pure Speculation (Salse (USA))
2309[14] 2641[4] 3287[2] 3849[4] 4955[5] 5316[4] (5840) 6166[5] 6921[2]

Dressing Room (USA) *Mark Johnston* 78
3 bb g Dixie Union(USA) —Green Room (USA) (Theatrical)
1076[3] 1272[2] 1445[3] 1692[4] 2146[2] 2891[4]

Dr Faustus (IRE) *Doug Watson* a97 97
6 gr g Sadler's Wells(USA) —Requesting (Rainbow Quest (USA))
153a[11] 328a[9] 535a[7] 827a[4]

Dr Finley (IRE) *Lydia Pearce* a70 74
4 ch g Dr Fong(USA) —Farrfesheena (USA) (Rahy (USA))
1016[4] 1956[7] 2856[2] 3281[3] 3712[4] (4396) 5628[2] 6095[2] 6780[7] 6915[3] 7415[5] 7674[5]

Drift And Dream *Chris Wall* 86
4 b m Exceed And Excel(AUS) —Sea Drift (FR) (Warning)
5278[8] 5831[7] ◆ 6348[5] 6761[3] ◆

Drill (USA) *Bob Baffert* a109
2 bb c Lawyer Ron(USA) —Cat Dancer (USA) (Storm Cat (USA))
7306a[10]

Dr Irv *Kate Walton* 61
2 ch g Dr Fong(USA) —Grateful (Generous (IRE))
2214[13] 4402[3] 4853[13] 5503[5] 6911[4]

Drive Home (USA) *Noel Wilson* a50 68
4 bb g Mr Greeley(USA) —Unique Pose (IRE) (Sadler's Wells (USA))
1038[7] 1803[7] 2412[14] 2692[5] (3128) 3454[10] (3903) 4379[9] 5721[5] 5924[11] 6488[6]

Drivemode *Dr Jon Scargill* a45 26
4 b g Domedriver(IRE) —Miss Prism (Niniski (USA))
4889[6] 5916[7] 7087[8]

Drizzi (IRE) *Phil McEntee* a70 72
10 b g Night Shift(USA) —Woopi Gold (IRE) (Last Tycoon)
[illegible]

Dr Livingstone (IRE) *Charles Egerton* a85 89
6 b g Dr Fong(USA) —Radhwa (FR) (Shining Steel)
1325[7] (4887) 5685[8] 6130[9] 6499[8] (7430) 7600[3]

Droit Au Reve (FR) *D De Watrigant*
2 b c Della Francesca(USA) —Zelenski (USA) (Woodman (USA))
7664a[6]

Droit Devant (FR) *S Morineau* a78 87
3 b f Bernebeau(FR) —Lettre A France (USA) (Lear Fan (USA))
7667a[7]

Drombeg Dawn (IRE) *A J McNamara* 91
5 b m Orpen(USA) —Dawn's Sharp Shot (IRE) (Son Of Sharp Shot (IRE))
(925a) 4418a[17] 4566a[14]

Drop The Hammer *David O'Meara* a22 67
5 b m Lucky Story(USA) —Paperweight (In The Wings)
1039[8] 1305[10] 1794[7] 2618[2] 3507[4] 4633[3]

Drosselmeyer (USA) *William Mott* a126 95
4 ch h Distorted Humor(USA) —Golden Ballet (USA) (Moscow Ballet (USA))
(7308a)

Dr Red Eye *David Nicholls* a85 75
3 ch g Dr Fong(USA) —Camp Fire (IRE) (Lahib (USA))
709[4] 855[2] 1514[6] 1812[2] 2186[2] 2406[2] 2957[4] 3485[4] 4081[2] 4560[8] 5151[3] 5828[7] 6116[2] (7068) 7339[7]

Drumadoon (IRE) *Liam Corcoran* a47 61
3 b c Hawk Wing(USA) —Lady Taufan (IRE) (Taufan (USA))
2293[2] ◆ 2637[3] 3268[5] 3770[3] 4745[5] 5421[3] 5993[3] 6621[10] 7515[9] 7639[8]

Drumfire (IRE) *Eoin Griffin* 94
7 b g Danehill Dancer(IRE) —Witch Of Fife (USA) (Lear Fan (USA))
4035a[7]

Drummer Boy *Peter Winkworth* a33 57
3 ch g Haafhd—Largo (IRE) (Selkirk (USA))
2196[9] 3220[12]

Drummers Drumming (USA) *Charlie Morlock* a54 46
5 b g Stroll(USA) —Afleet Summer (USA) (Afleet (CAN))
33[7]

Drummond *Clive Cox* 73
2 b g Zamindar(USA) —Alrisha (IRE) (Persian Bold)
3424[5] 4053[9] 5891[5]

Drummoyne (USA) *Mark Johnston* 67
2 ch g Street Cry(IRE) —Strike Hard (IRE) (Green Desert (USA))
1515[6] 1835[4] 4192[7] 4414[5] 5280[4] 5755[8]

Drumpellier (IRE) *Simon West* a1 62
4 ch m Rakti—Early Memory (USA) (Devil's Bag (USA))
5824[8] 6386[8] 6618[13] 7079[13] 7230[6]

Drunken Sailor (IRE) *Luca Cumani* a109 118
6 b g Tendulkar(USA) —Ronni Pancake (Mujadil (USA))
329a[4] 584a[4] 826a[6] (2098) 3153[3] (4492) 5471[3] 6886a[7] 7218a[12]

Dr Wintringham (IRE) *Karen George* a75 83
5 b m Monsieur Bond(IRE) —Shirley Collins (Robellino (USA))
949[6] 1269[7] 1448[2] 1789[2] 3514[3] 3801[3] 4445[4] 5836[7] (6583)

Dschahan (GER) *Mario Hofer* a90 98
3 b c Oasis Dream—Desca (GER) (Cadeaux Genereux)
(7667a)

Dualagi *Martin Bosley* a66 68
7 b m Royal Applause—Lady Melbourne (IRE) (Indian Ridge)
(231) 351[7] 487[5] (1630) 2313[9] 3020[5] 3995[5] 4711[3] 4973[5] 5561[10] 6444[5] 7488[3] 7812[5] 7943[7]

Dualite (IRE) *John Dunlop* 63
3 ch f Dubawi(IRE) —Morality (Elusive Quality (USA))
2192[7] 2963[4] 4743[5] 5626[5]

Duar Mapel (USA) *Brian Baugh* a60 49
5 b g Lemon Drop Kid(USA) —Pitchacurve (USA) (Defrere (USA))
117[5] 232[4] 645[5] 733[3] 839[5] 917[3] 1016[5] 1107[19] 2400[5] 3240[4] 3300[5] 3599[5] 3754[7]

Dubai Affair *Ronald Harris* a71 59
3 b f Dubawi(IRE) —Palace Affair (Pursuit Of Love)
1630[6] 3174[3] 3994[5] 4227[6] 5115[9]

Dubaianswer *Tony Coyle* a79 69
3 b f Dubawi(IRE) —Answered Prayer (Green Desert (USA))
(952) 1599[6] 2607[8] 3283[5] 4234[6] 7438[9] 7887[5]

Dubai Bay (FR) *Paul Midgley* a75 72
3 b f Zafeen(FR) —Yemen Desert (IRE) (Sadler's Wells (USA))
(6137) 6383[6]

Dubai Bounty *Gerard Butler* a84 87
4 ch m Dubai Destination(USA) —Mary Read (Bahamian Bounty)
1622[5] 6439[10] 7577[8] 7908[11]

Dubai Celebration *Jedd O'Keeffe* 83
3 b g Dubai Destination(USA) —Pretty Poppy (Song)
2096[3] 2477[5] 3318[6] 4362[4] 4670[7] 5404[4] 5731[7] 5925[9] 6634[12]

Dubai Destiny *Tim Easterby* 34
2 b g Dubai Destination(USA) —Ukraine (IRE) (Cape Cross (IRE))
3186[6] 4122[12] 6048[13]

Dubai Dynamo *Ruth Carr* a100 106
6 b g Kyllachy—Miss Mercy (IRE) (Law Society (USA))
799[6] 932[6] 1110[8] 1541[5] (1695) 2061[2] ◆ 2123[2] ◆ (2390) 2431[2] 3397[2] 3578[5] 4100[3] 4314[11] 4774[3] 5218[9] 5272[7] 5557[11] 6273[5] 6326[2] 6672[6] 6862[20]

Dubai Gem *Olivia Maylam* a59 54
5 b m Fantastic Light(USA) —Reflectance (Sadler's Wells (USA))
2401[4] 3110[2] 3709[4] 4666[12]

Dubai Glory *Sheena West* a60 84
3 b f Dubai Destination(USA) —Rosse (Kris)
801[4] 891[3] (1442) (1951) (2225) 2842[5] 3233[5] 3872[3] 4449[7] (4971) 6172[4] 6376[11] 6822[14]

Dubai Hills *Bryan Smart* a102 85
5 b g Dubai Destination(USA) —Hill Welcome (Most Welcome)
(9) (105) (149) 710[3] 846[7] 1094[3] 1406[16] 2390[10] 6326[9] 6672[14]

Dubai Legend *Noel Wilson* a22 77
5 ch m Cadeaux Genereux—Royal Future (IRE) (Royal Academy (USA))
107[8] 201[5]

Dubai Media (CAN) *Ed Dunlop* a95 97
4 b m Songandaprayer(USA) —Forty Gran (USA) (El Gran Senor (USA))
1902[5] 2298[2] 3827[8] 4531[13] 5080[9] 6272[8]

Dubai Miracle (USA) *Laura Young* a85 93
4 ch g Consolidator(USA) —East Cape (USA) (Mr Prospector (USA))
141[7] 405[7] 816[2] (876) 1443[11] 1530[10] 3215[6] 3912[8] 5379[11] 6087[11]

Dubai Prince (IRE) *Mahmood Al Zarooni* 114
3 b c Shamardal(USA) —Desert Frolic (IRE) (Persian Bold)
(6125) 6861[12]

Dubai Queen (USA) *Luca Cumani* a74 102
3 b f Kingmambo(USA) —Zomaradah (Deploy)
(1836) 2506[2] ◆ 3034[2] 3648[4] 5657[2] 6523[9]

Dubai Rythm *Michael Appleby* a32 15
2 br c Echo Of Light—Slave To The Rythm (IRE) (Hamas (IRE))
5202[6] 5536[9] 5896[8]

Dubai Sunshine (IRE) *Michael Bell* a54
2 b g Dubawi(IRE) —Star Express (Sadler's Wells (USA))
6795[9] 7367[5]

Dubara Reef (IRE) *Paul Green* a46 76
4 ch g Dubawi(IRE) —Mamara Reef (Salse (USA))
597[4] 838[11] 1305[4] 1914[5] 2259[2] 2526[2] 2888[15] 3851[9] 4635[4] 5369[7] 5804[5] 6157[9] 6870[11] 7077[2] 7264[6] 7570[12] 7850[6] 7914[8]

Dubar Way (IRE) *Kevin Ryan*
2 b f Dubawi(IRE) —Enlightened Way (FR) (Indian Ridge)
3921[7] 7736[7]

Dubawi Dancer *William Haggas* a38 84
3 ch f Dubawi(IRE) —Adees Dancer (Danehill Dancer (IRE))
(2599) ◆ 2964[12] (3958) ◆ (4236) (4751) ◆ 5614[2] 6046[2] 6497[7]

Dubawi Gold *Richard Hannon* a105 121
3 b c Dubawi(IRE) —Savannah Belle (Green Desert (USA))
(990) ◆ (1234) ◆ 1686[2] 2324a[2] 3011[6] 5046[4] (5473) 5988a[4] 6860[4] 7731a[4] ◆

Dubawi Heights *Simon Callaghan* 117
4 b m Dubawi(IRE) —Rosie's Posy (IRE) (Suave Dancer (USA))
5073a[2] 7284a[6]

Dubawi Island (FR) *Mahmood Al Zarooni*
2 b c Dubawi(IRE) —Housa Dancer (FR) (Fabulous Dancer (USA))
6463[14]

Dubawi Junior (IRE) *J-C Rouget* a87 91
4 b g Dubawi(IRE) —Lady Bex (IRE) (Sadler's Wells (USA))
6958a[2]

Dubawi Phantom *I Mohammed* a75 105
4 ch g Dubawi(IRE) —Anna Amalia (IRE) (In The Wings)
242[8] 328a[10] 587a[11]

Dubawi Sound *Roger Varian* 94
3 b c Dubawi(IRE) —Hannah's Music (Music Boy)
(1409) ◆ 6374[4] 7168[10] ◆

Dubawi Star *John M Oxx* a92 98
3 b g Dubawi(IRE) —Cloud Hill (Danehill (USA))
6514a[9]

Dubburg (USA) *Willie Musson* a68 73
6 ch g Johannesburg(USA) —Plaisir Des Yeux (FR) (Funambule (USA))
(223) 393[3]

Dubious Escapade (IRE) *Ann Duffield* 68
2 b f Dubawi(IRE) —Brief Escapade (IRE) (Brief Truce (USA))
3035[4] 5618[4] 6152[3] 6424[3] 6911[2] 7157[4]

Dubonny *Frank Sheridan* a38
4 b m Dubawi(IRE) —Ravishing (IRE) (Bigstone (IRE))
7717[9] 7822[8] 7876[10]

Ducal *Mike Murphy* a83 60
3 b g Iceman—Noble Lady (Primo Dominie)
2266[7] 2650[5] ◆ 2924[7] 5735[3] ◆ 6089[2] (6653) 6980[2] 7716[4]

Duchamp (FR) *O Pessi* 103
3 b c Vettori(IRE) —Durella (IRE) (Royal Academy (USA))
1431a[2]

Duchess Dora (IRE) *John Quinn* 107
4 b m Tagula(IRE) —Teodora (IRE) (Fairy King (USA))
1166[9] 2028[6] 2397[3] 2890[8] (3379) (4075) 4357[2] 4776[3] 5467[2] 5827[10]

Duchesse Satin (IRE) *Tim Easterby* 51
2 b f Barathea(IRE) —Carmona (Rainbow Quest (USA))
6048[12] 6344[7] 6984[7]

Duchess Of Foxland (IRE) *Mark L Fagan* a95 101
4 br m Medecis—Itsanothergirl (Reprimand)
1779a[9] 5361a[10] 5523a[7] 7277a[4]

Duchess Of Magenta (IRE) *Eve Johnson Houghton* a18 49
3 b f Bachelor Duke(USA) —Felin Gruvy (IRE) (Tagula (IRE))
1362[13] 1836[12] 2568[7] 3226[13] 3596[7]

Duck Feet (IRE) *S Botti* 103
2 bb c Aussie Rules(USA) —Benelux (Zafonic (USA))
(7217a)

Dudley *Jonathan Portman* a46 51
4 ch g Compton Place—Just A Glimmer (Bishop Of Cashel)
662[7]

Duel Au Pistolet (FR) *Y Fouin* a57 69
4 b h Maille Pistol(FR) —Planete Interdite (FR) (Tip Moss (FR))
221a[10]

Duff (IRE) *Edward Lynam* a106 113
8 b g Spinning World(USA) —Shining Prospect (Lycius (USA))
700[3] 844[4] 1397[4] 1889[4] 2533a[6] 4116a[6] 4978a[5] 5746a[12] 5930[5] 7010a[5] 7468a[4] 7793a[11]

Duke Liam (IRE) *David Nicholls* a63 35
2 b g Bachelor Duke(USA) —Petite Arvine (USA) (Gulch (USA))
6912[8] 7209[8] 7685[2] 7769[5]

Duke Of Aricabeau (IRE) *Michael Easterby* a46 63
2 ch g Modigliani(USA) —Essential Fear (IRE) (Pivotal)
2387[7] 4283[5] ◆ 4748[8] ◆ 5099[4] 5399[2]

Duke Of Burgundy (FR) *Jennie Candlish* 74
8 b g Danehill(USA) —Valley Of Gold (FR) (Shirley Heights)
2769[5] 3170[3] 6093[8]

Duke Of Clarence (IRE) *Richard Hannon* a72
2 gr c Verglas(IRE) —Special Lady (FR) (Kaldoun (FR))
7634[7] 7835[5] 7938[2]

Duke Of Firenze *Sir Michael Stoute* 81
2 ch c Pivotal—Nannina (Medicean)
4384[3] (5618)

Duke Of Florence (IRE) *Richard Hannon* a72 68
3 b g Medicean—Bonheur (IRE) (Royal Academy (USA))
95[2] 202[3]

Duke Of Rainford *Michael Herrington* a58 56
4 gr g Bahamian Bounty—Night Haven (Night Shift (USA))
(123) 256[11] 2547[8] 3247[6] 3937[6] 4197[7] (4328) 4650[4] 5019[2]

Duke Of Rutherford (USA) *P D Deegan* a76 76
3 ch g Stormy Atlantic(USA) —Metal Blues (USA) (Cure The Blues (USA))
7790a[10]

Dukes Art *James Toller* a90 90
5 b g Bachelor Duke(USA) —Creme Caramel (USA) (Septieme Ciel (USA))
1760[5] ◆ 2441[7] 3285[2] 3987[3] 5043[14] 5718[4] 6378[12]

Dulkashe (IRE) *Luca Cumani* a78 77
2 br f Pivotal—Saik (USA) (Riverman (USA))
5655[4] 6776[2] 7118[2]

Dullahan (USA) *Dale Romans* a115 104
2 ch c Even The Score(USA) —Mining My Own (USA) (Smart Strike (CAN))
7306a[4]

Dumbarton (IRE) *Sir Michael Stoute* 87
3 br c Danehill Dancer(IRE) —Scottish Stage (IRE) (Selkirk (USA))
(4388) 5049[10] 5888[16]

Dunaden (FR) *M Delzangles* a75 121
5 b h Nicobar—La Marlia (FR) (Kaldounevees (FR))
705a[3] (1707a) 2344a[2] 5304a[9] (6967a) (7218a) (7729a)

Dunaskin (IRE) *Richard Guest* a64 65
11 b g Bahhare(USA) —Mirwara (IRE) (Darshaan)
40[2] 103[2] 2235[5] 4366[16] 4649[10] 5209[6] 5643[9] 6613[6] (7912)

Dunboyne Express (IRE) *Kevin Prendergast* 114
3 b c Shamardal(USA) —Love Excelling (FR) (Polish Precedent (USA))
(1004a) 2324a[5] 3442a[5] 4259a[2] 4831a[2] 5128a[7] 5747a[4]

Duncan *John Gosden* 123
6 b g Dalakhani(IRE) —Dolores (Danehill (USA))
(2072) ◆ 3066[6] 5284[2] (5952a)

Duneen Dream (USA) *Nikki Evans* a64 64
6 ch g Hennessy(USA) —T N T Red (USA) (Explosive Red (CAN))
86[9] (408) 712[2] 944[2] (1454) 2245[4] 2663[3] 2905[5] 3235[12] 7003[11] 7571[11]

Dune Island *John Bridger* a49
3 b f Compton Admiral—Desert Island Disc (Turtle Island (IRE))
158[10] 1683[15] 1999[6] 2637[13]

Dunelight (IRE) *Clive Cox* a110 109
8 ch h Desert Sun—Badee'A (IRE) (Marju (IRE))
(844) 1397[6] 1948[5]

Dungannon *Andrew Balding* a77 103
4 b g Monsieur Bond(IRE) —May Light (Midyan (USA))
1888[8] 2288[6] (2954) 3841[7] (4776) 5927[9] 6147[16]

Dunhoy (IRE) *Stef Higgins* a80 87
3 ch c Goodricke—Belle Of The Blues (IRE) (Blues Traveller (IRE))
1983[7] 2607[9] (3133) 3797[3] 4447[8] 5056[9]

Dunmore Boy (IRE) *Richard Fahey* a68 65
3 ch g Iffraaj—Night Club (Mozart (IRE))
44[4] 845[9] 1079[3] 1323[6] 7504[10] 7728[7]

Dunn'o (IRE) *Clive Cox* a100 102
6 b g Cape Cross(IRE) —Indian Express (Indian Ridge)
1529[4] (2441) 3645[14] 4774[9] 5474[8]

Dunseverick (IRE) *Jo Hughes* a77 70
3 ch g Footstepsinthesand—Theatrale (USA) (Theatrical)
1315[8] 1606[5] 1985[4] 2383[3] ◆ 3133[7] 5101[4] 5213[5] 6089[7] 7341[9] 7504[9] 7754[4]

Du Plessis *Brian Ellison* a17 48
4 b g Kyllachy—Shrink (Mind Games)
1439[9] 1803[13] 2593[12]

Duplicity *Richard Guest* a83 95
4 b g Cadeaux Genereux—Artful (IRE) (Green Desert (USA))
2[7] 46[6] 470[9] 568[3] 633[6] 732[6] 1244[8] 1331[6] 1498[5] 1911[12] 5298[6] 5601[10]

Duquesa (IRE) *David Evans* a74 78
3 b f Intikhab(USA) —Love Of Silver (USA) (Arctic Tern (USA))
2963[2] 3228[4] 3337[2] 3413[5] 3689[7] 5670[3] 6104[?] 6181[2] 6435[5] (6756) 7017[13] 7255[6]

Durante Alighieri *Sir Henry Cecil* a80 79
3 b c Galileo(IRE) —Puce (Darshaan)
5327[8] (5964)

Durban Thunder (GER) *T Mundry* a95 119
5 ch h Samum(GER) —Donna Alicia (GER) (Highland Chieftain)
2749a[3] 3446a[2] (4599a) 6558a[11] 7732a[10]

Durer (FR) *J-C Rouget* a91 108
3 ch g Motivator—Dissertation (FR) (Sillery (USA))
(882a) 1551a[2]

Durgan *Linda Jewell* a63 63
5 b g Dansili—Peryllys (Warning)
947[5] 1581[6] 1813[8] 2420[11] 2561[4] 2921[5] 3768[5] 4445[5] 6310[7]

Durham Express (IRE) *Michael Dods* a40 74
4 b g Acclamation—Edwina (IRE) (Caerleon (USA))
673[8] 2464[12] 2543[14] 3359[13] 4362[7] 5554[9] 6426[8] 6646[9] 7064[8]

Durham Town (IRE) *Dean Ivory* a68 62
4 b g Arakan(USA) —Southern Spectrum (IRE) (Spectrum (IRE))
34[7] 205[5]

Duskill (FR) *P Chevillard* a70
3 b g Ski Chief(USA) —Dulcica (FR) (Katoleme (FR))
902a[8]

Dust Cloud (IRE) *Peter Winkworth* a56 54
3 gr g Verglas(IRE) —For Freedom (IRE) (King Of Kings (IRE))
6242[6] 6816[3] 6969[6]

Duster *Hughie Morrison* a90 94
4 b g Pastoral Pursuits—Spring Clean (FR) (Danehill (USA))
1603[18] (2995) 3645[5] 3802[2] 4415[5] 5940[12] 6273[4] 6862[25] 7168[9]

Dust On The Ground *Marco Botti* a64
2 ch f Dutch Art—Confetti (Groom Dancer (USA))
4662[5] 5097[5]

Dusty Bluebells (IRE) *J S Moore* a58 54
3 ch f Le Vie Dei Colori—Flying Ridge (IRE) (Indian Ridge)
1607[7] 2790[9] 4758[8] 5376[8] 5674[11] 6929[2] 7389[4] 7755[10] 7919[6]

Dusty Red *William Knight* 53
2 ch f Teofilo(IRE) —Dust Dancer (Suave Dancer (USA))
7030[10]

Dusty Spirit *Bill Turner* a78 68
4 b g Invincible Spirit(IRE) —Dusty Dazzler (IRE) (Titus Livius (FR))
1838[U] 2142[8] 2356[4] 2642[10]

Dutch Diamond *John Gosden* 68
2 ch f Dutch Art—Treasure Trove (USA) (The Minstrel (CAN))
6950[10] 7165[3]

Dutchessa *C Ferland* 71
2 b f Dutch Art—Nippy (FR) (Anabaa (USA))
7219a[7]

Dutch Heritage *Richard Fahey* 72
2 bb g Dutch Art—Starstone (Diktat)
2936[10] 3878[7] 4347[4] (4851) 6670[7]

Dutchman's Field *David Nicholls* a52 55
2 ch g Dutch Art—Yavari (IRE) (Alzao (USA))
3076[7] 3941[4] 5851[13] 6471[4] 6807[13] 7108[13] 7338[2] 7569[3] 7718[7]

Dutch Master *Andrew Balding* a67 73
2 ch g Dutch Art—Duena (Grand Lodge (USA))
6432[4] 6742[2] 7082[6] 7350[3]

Dutch Rose (IRE) *Ralph Beckett* 70
2 ch f Dutch Art—Eloquent Rose (IRE) (Elnadim (USA))
3686[2] ◆ 4339[13] 5613[5]

Dux Scholar *Sir Michael Stoute* 115
3 b c Oasis Dream—Alumni (Selkirk (USA))
3409[3] (4095) 5252[3] 5494[2] 6693[2] 7170[2]

Dvinsky (USA) *Paul Howling* a76 55
10 b g Stravinsky(USA) —Festive Season (USA) (Lypheor)
98[6] 143[2] 269[3] 351[4] 435[2] 612[11] (820) 985[2] 1314[3] 1634[5] 2001[10] 2205[2] 2452[6] 2756[9] 3464[3] 4206[9] 4910[8] 5387[9] 5640[3] ◆ 6752[8] 6931[6] 7349[8] 7529[4] 7588[2] 7658[6] 7942[4]

Dylan's Dream (IRE) *Tim Easterby* 53
2 b f Dark Angel(IRE) —Catherinofaragon (USA) (Chief's Crown (USA))
2214[11] 3274[11] 3680[5] 4943[10] 5555[3] 6627[12] 6835[3]

Dylans Verse (IRE) *Reg Hollinshead* a60 47
2 b g Dylan Thomas(IRE) —In My Dreams (IRE) (Sadler's Wells (USA))
7109[8] 7233[13] 7501[4] 7568[2]

Dynamic Blitz (AUS) *P F Yiu* a115 106
7 ch g Elusive Quality(USA) —Assertive Lass (AUS) (Zeditave (AUS))
(414a) 999a[8]

Dynamic Drive (IRE) *Walter Swinburn* a81 88
4 b g Motivator—Biriyani (IRE) (Danehill (USA))
1477[6] 1855[8] 2224[8] 2931[9] 3593[3] 4097[8] 4957[5] 5837[8] 7002[10]

Dynamic Duo (IRE) *Richard Hannon* a73 75
2 ch c Iffraaj—Collada (IRE) (Desert Prince (IRE))
5013[6] 5579[2] 5851[7] 6216[4]

Dynamic Idol (USA) *Mikael Magnusson* a78 70
4 bb g Dynaformer(USA) —El Nafis (USA) (Kingmambo (USA))
2055[7] 3715[3] 4237[6] 5389[12] 5866[3] 6121[8]

Dynamic Rhythm (USA) *David Thompson* a65 59
8 b g Kingmambo(USA) —Palme D'Or (IRE) (Sadler's Wells (USA))
244[4] 492[6] 3622[13]

Dynamic Saint (USA) *Doug Watson* a85 25
8 b g Sweetsouthernsaint(USA) —Le Nat (USA) (Dynaformer (USA))
535a[5] 707a[4]

Dynaslew (USA) *Seth Benzel* 108
5 bb m Dynaformer(USA) —Slew's Final Answer (USA) (Seattle Slew (USA))
7284a[11]

Dynastic *Sir Michael Stoute* a78 74
2 b c Dynaformer(USA) —Demure (Machiavellian (USA))
6059[6] 7094[2]

Dyna Waltz *Jonathan E Sheppard* a77 107
4 b m Dynaformer(USA) —Valentine Waltz (IRE) (Be My Guest (USA))
6909a[8]

Dysios (IRE) *Luca Cumani* a79 83
3 b g Invincible Spirit(IRE) —Hataana (USA) (Robellino (USA))
1495[6] (2197) ◆ (2421) 2838[7] 3629[2] 4724[3] 5240[8] 6674[5] ◆

Dzesmin (POL) *Richard Guest* a64 69
9 b g Professional(IRE) —Dzakarta (POL) (Aprizzo (IRE))
1908[10] 2892[15] 5791[2] 6155[12] 6775[5]

Eager To Bow (IRE) *Patrick Chamings* a70 71
5 b g Acclamation—Tullawadgeen (IRE) (Sinndar (IRE))
1177[3] 2201[3] 2605[7] 4546[5] 6664[6] 6971[5] 7485[4] 7579[4] 7895[2]

Eagle Cliff *J E Hammond* a52 77
4 ch g Dubai Destination(USA) —Alessandra (Generous (IRE))
842a[7]

Eagle Falls (AUS) *David Hayes* a109 118
6 br g Hussonet(USA) —Desina (AUS) (Desert King (IRE))
9

Eagle Nebula *Brett Johnson* a75 76
7 ch g Observatory(USA) —Tarocchi (USA) (Affirmed (USA))
223[2] 622[4] 1148[3] 1577[2] 2721[2] 3047[6] (3391) (4153) 5015[2] (5866) 6254[9] 6976[9] 7939[2]

Eagle Of Rome (IRE) *Nick Littmoden* 58
2 b g Holy Roman Emperor(IRE) —Adjalisa (IRE) (Darshaan)
2559[13] 2962[6] 3553[7] 5875[P]

Eagle Power (IRE) *James Fanshawe* 55
2 b g Teofilo(IRE) —Changeable (Dansili)
7082[8]

Eagle Rock (IRE) *Tom Tate* 82
3 b g High Chaparral(IRE) —Silk Fan (IRE) (Unfuwain (USA))
3684[2] 4370[5] 5007[3] (6349) 7017[5]

Eagle's Pass (IRE) *T J O'Mara* a96 95
9 b g Brave Act—Cd Super Targeting (IRE) (Polish Patriot (USA))
4398a[4]

Eagles Peak *Sir Michael Stoute* 91
3 b c Galileo(IRE) —High Praise (USA) (Quest For Fame)
(3824) ◆ 5185[15]

Earl Of Carrick (USA) *Mahmood Al Zarooni* 65
3 b c Selkirk(USA) —Without A Trace (IRE) (Darshaan)
3177[4]

Earl Of Fire (GER) *Alex Fracas* a87 109
6 ch g Areion(GER) —Evry (GER) (Torgos)
3422a[7] (7256a)

Earl Of Tinsdal (GER) *A Wohler* 115
3 b c Black Sam Bellamy(IRE) —Earthly Paradise (GER) (Dashing Blade)
(1739a) 2345a[4] 3672a[2] (5092a) 6396a[3]

Earlsalsa (GER) *C Von Der Recke* 106
7 bb g Kingsalsa(USA) —Earthly Paradise (GER) (Dashing Blade)
2538a[2] 6200a[4]

Earlsmedic *Stuart Williams* a78 80
6 ch g Dr Fong(USA) —Area Girl (Jareer (USA))
125[8] 455[8] 2116[16] 3351[6] 4434[3] (5387) 6974[3] 7832[2] ◆

Early Ambition *Andrew Haynes* a18
2 b f Striking Ambition—Priorite (IRE) (Kenmare (FR))
1049[6] 1563[5] 1954[6] 4947[U]

Early Applause *Charles Hills* 84
3 b g Royal Applause—Early Evening (Daylami (IRE))
1108[5] (2392) 2847[2] 4718[7] 6457[7] 6922[4]

Earnestly (JPN) *Shozo Sasaki* 124
6 b h Grass Wonder(USA) —Lettre D'Amour (JPN) (Tony Bin)
7873a[10]

Easter Diva (IRE) *Amanda Perrett* 60
2 b f Dansili—Easter Fairy (USA) (Fusaichi Pegasus (USA))
6745[5] ◆

Easterland (IRE) *F Chappet* a92 85
5 b g Starborough—Aerdee (FR) (Highest Honor (FR))
2867a[7]

Eastern Breeze (IRE) *Saeed Bin Suroor* 80
3 b f Red Ransom(USA) —Alsharq (IRE) (Machiavellian (USA))
2960[8] 3437[4] 4370[2] ◆ (5114) 5894[7]

Eastern Destiny *Richard Fahey* 67
2 rg f Dubai Destination(USA) —Night Haven (Night Shift (USA))
4552[11] (5104)

Eastern Gift *Gay Kelleway* a74 76
6 ch g Cadeaux Genereux—Dahshah (Mujtahid (USA))
93a[3] 488[8] 626[2] (765) (949) 1083[4] 1355[3] 1637[2] 1936[4] 2589[4] 2816[7] 3130[15] 3361[8] 4656[3] 5406[9] 5740[6] 6138[3] 6355[5] 6587[4] 7455[3] 7632[10] 7711[2] 7775[5]

Eastern Hills *Alan McCabe* a87 69
6 b g Dubai Destination(USA) —Rainbow Mountain (Rainbow Quest (USA))
367[5] 562[10] 640[4] 744[6] 854[8] 1463[3] 1814[3] (3496) 3741[5] 3952[3] (4182) ◆ 4900[7] (6617) (7243) 7339[6] 7771[P]

Eastern Magic *Reg Hollinshead* a59 71
4 b g Observatory(USA) —Inchtina (Inchinor)
2055[2] 2793[6] 2952[8] 4204[4] 5804[4] 7032[4]

Eastern Paramour (IRE) *Rod Millman* a62 85
6 b m Kris Kin(USA) —Hishi Lover (USA) (Pleasant Colony (USA))
4432[5] ◆ 5050[5] 6005[6]

Eastern Seel *Tim Easterby* 39
2 b g Dubai Destination(USA) —Maraseel (USA) (Machiavellian (USA))
4898[8] 5454[14] 5818[6]

Eastern Sun (IRE) *John Gosden* 93
2 b c Kodiac—Always Friendly (High Line)
(2837) ◆ 5276[3]

Eastlands Lad (IRE) *Micky Hammond* a61 46
2 bb c Strategic Prince—Uisce Tine (IRE) (Bluebird (USA))
4073[15] 6828[7] 7368[3]

East Meets West (IRE) *A P O'Brien* a95 95
2 b c Dansili—Minkova (IRE) (Sadler's Wells (USA))
5181[11]

Eastward Ho *Jason Ward* a67 63
3 ch g Resplendent Glory(IRE) —Mofeyda (IRE) (Mtoto)
2125[8] 2361[12] 3077[5] 6576[2] 6845[3] 7144[3] 7370[5] (7741) (7848)

Easydoesit (IRE) *Tony Carroll* a40 48
3 b g Iffraaj—Fawaayid (USA) (Vaguely Noble)
1933[5] 2599[3] 2858[6] 4654[3] 5118[2] 5321[7] 6585[3]

Easy Over (IRE) *Ed McMahon* 76
3 ch g Dr Fong(USA) —Desert Alchemy (IRE) (Green Desert (USA))
3053[2] (3575) 4550[7] ◆ 5820[7]

Easy Terms *Edwin Tuer* 91
4 b m Trade Fair—Effie (Royal Academy (USA))
1099[10] (1440) (2388) (3023) (3277) 6172[6]

Eavesdropper *Mahmood Al Zarooni* a109 91
4 br h Singspiel(IRE) —Echoes In Eternity (IRE) (Spinning World (USA))
608a[3] 758a[8]

Ebony Boom (IRE) *Gary Moore* a77 77
4 b g Boreal(GER) —Elegant As Well (IRE) (Sadler's Wells (USA))
4613[7]

Ebony Breeze (IRE) *Ian Semple* 25
3 b g One Cool Cat(USA) —Renada (Sinndar (IRE))
2461[7] 3037[7] 3304[6]

Ebony Clarets *Richard Fahey* 67
2 b f Kyllachy—Pachanga (Inchinor)
(1455) ◆ 3033[13] 4094[22] 5847[11]

Ebony Shades (IRE) *Muredach Kelly* 70
10 bl g Bob Back(USA) —Silks Princess (Prince Tenderfoot (USA))
596[8]

Ebony Song (USA) *Jo Crowley* a70 72
3 bb g Songandaprayer(USA) —Thiscatsforcaryl (USA) (Storm Cat (USA))
4435[2] 6089[6] 6924[11]

Ebraam (USA) *Ronald Harris* a105 82
8 b g Red Ransom(USA) —Futuh (USA) (Diesis)
316[3] 523[3] (651) 986[2] 1395[8] 1562[2] 2244[3] 2662[5] (3995) 4357[6] 4583[3] 5262[7]

Echo Dancer *Trevor Wall* a56 62
5 br g Danehill Dancer(IRE) —Entail (USA) (Riverman (USA))
712[6] 1373[8]

Echoes Of Joy *David Evans* 39
2 b g Echo Of Light—Lambadora (Suave Dancer (USA))
1890[6] 4330[20]

Echo Of Dream *Mahmood Al Zarooni* a52 39
2 br c Echo Of Light—Rahcak (IRE) (Generous (IRE))
5899[11] 6588[9]

Echo Of Dubai (IRE) *Clive Brittain* a44 46
2 b f Echo Of Light—Papabile (USA) (Chief's Crown (USA))
2718[9] 5596[7] 5899[12] 6628[4]

Echo Of Thunder (IRE) *David Lanigan* a42 58
2 b f Echo Of Light—Aquatic Warrior (USA) (Fantastic Light (USA))
5299[9] ◆ 5813[7]

Echo Ridge (IRE) *Ralph Beckett* a75 73
3 b f Oratorio(IRE) —Lochridge (Indian Ridge)
2025[4] 2772[3] 3310[5] 5100[9]

Echos Of Motivator *Ronald Harris* a75 75
3 ch c Motivator—Echo River (USA) (Irish River (FR))
564[4] 716[2] 891[2] 1300[4] 1526[2] 1951[2] 2360[4] 6756[8] 7630[2] 7779[2] 7839[5]

Eclair De Lune (GER) *Ronald McAnally* 110
5 b m Marchand De Sable(USA) —Elegante (GER) (Acatenango (GER))
5073a[6] 6719a[9]

Eclair Fastpass (AUS) *D Koh* 110
5 b g Fastnet Rock(AUS) —Hanover (AUS) (Marscay (AUS))
2339a[2]

Eclipseoftheheart *James Fanshawe* a85 76
3 b f Shamardal(USA) —Heart Stopping (USA) (Chester House (USA))
3577[5] ◆ 4254[4] 5021[2] (5633) (6256) ◆

Ecliptic (USA) *Mahmood Al Zarooni* 111
3 ch c Kingmambo(USA) —Indy Five Hundred (USA) (A.P. Indy (USA))
(6747) 7166[4]

Economic Crisis (IRE) *Alan Berry* a50 62
2 ch f Excellent Art—Try The Air (IRE) (Foxhound (USA))
1434[7] 1957[3] 2248[3] 2725[5] 2907[7] 3849[6] 4283[7] 4406[10] 5147[5] 5590[3] 5817[10] 6232[8]

Ecossaise *Mark Johnston* a76 79
3 ch f Selkirk(USA) —Diablerette (Green Desert (USA))
4023[4] 4370[6] 5317[3] 5915[2] 6412[3] 7033[8] 7360[4] 7661[9] 7856[2] 7913[3]

Edas *Thomas Cuthbert* a74 73
9 b g Celtic Swing—Eden (IRE) (Polish Precedent (USA))
2454[8] 3129[7] 4045[7] 4605[5] (4945) 5485[4] 6453[4] 6833[6]

Eddie Jock (IRE) *S Seemar* a92 92
7 ch g Almutawakel—Al Euro (FR) (Mujtahid (USA))
417a[9] 605a[6]

Eden's Drift *M Delzangles* 93
2 ch c Bachelor Duke(USA) —Ela Merici (FR) (Beaudelaire (USA))
6042a[7]

Edensor (IRE) *John Dunlop* 44
2 b g Bachelor Duke(USA) —Venetian Lullaby (USA) (Lear Fan (USA))
2687[8] 5579[7] 5802[10]

Ede'Sajolygoodfelo *Pat Phelan* a21
3 b g Exceed And Excel(AUS) —For Love (USA) (Sultry Song (USA))
684[8] 1047[5]

Ede's Dot Com (IRE) *Pat Phelan* a68 68
7 b g Trans Island—Kilkee Bay (IRE) (Case Law)
(304) (390) 565[7] 765[7] 1868[2] 2051[9] 2450[2] 3538[10] 5002[6] 5491[2] 7447[10]

Ede Sensation (SWE) *Patrick Wahl* 74
3 ch f Eishin Dunkirk(USA) —Maycy Star (SWE) (Malvernico (IRE))
6741a[5]

Edge Closer *David Arbuthnot* a111 106
7 b g Bold Edge—Blue Goddess (IRE) (Blues Traveller (IRE))
3410[8] 3841[13]

Edge End *Lisa Williamson* a50 61
7 ch g Bold Edge—Rag Time Belle (Raga Navarro (ITY))
229[9] 6621[3] 1875[8] 2247[10]

Edgewater (IRE) *John Akehurst* a84 88
4 b g Bahamian Bounty—Esteemed Lady (IRE) (Mark Of Esteem (IRE))
822[4] ◆ 949[5] 1269[2] (1530) 2310[6] 2647[12] 3466[2] 3844[7] 4537[10]

Edgeworth (IRE) *David Bridgwater* a77 76
5 b g Pyrus(USA) —Credibility (Komaite (USA))
(94) 1746 (247) 418[2] 565[4] (790) (885) 1450[3] 1772[4] 2378[4] 2769[4] 3256[2] 3546[4] 4825[5] 5110[5] 5653[7] 6295[8]

Edgware Road *Paul Rich* a70 65
3 ch g Selkirk(USA) —Bayswater (Caerleon (USA))
1409[13] (5206) 5624[6] 5821[4] 6777[9] 7216[8] 7610[2] 7698[2] 7904[2]

Edinburgh Knight (IRE) *Paul D'Arcy* a106 102
4 b g Selkirk(USA) —Pippas Song (Reference Point)
1888[3] 2075[16] (3395) ◆ 4534[11] 5060[14] 6145[16] (6862) (7516)

Edraaq *Brian Meehan* 56
2 b g Dubai Destination(USA) —Shatarah (Gulch (USA))
6463[9]

Eduardo *Jedd O'Keeffe* a60 54
3 b g Beat Hollow—Cuyamaca (IRE) (Desert King (IRE))
1169[6] 1526[6] 2166[8] 2652[5] 3039[6]

Educated Son *Ben De Haan* a65 61
3 br g Diktat—Spring Sunrise (Robellino (USA))
2586[7]

Eeny Mac (IRE) *Neville Bycroft* a47 59
4 ch g Redback—Sally Green (IRE) (Common Grounds)
1815[3] 2233[8] 3245[6] 3569[2] 3936[6] 4110[3] 5437[3] 5788[3] 6050[3] 6343[10]

Effervesce (IRE) *David Pipe* a47 81
4 ch m Galileo(IRE) —Royal Fizz (IRE) (Royal Academy (USA))
6583[10] 6922[10] 7272[9] 7506[5]

Efficient (NZ) *Robert Hickmott* 118
8 gr g Zabeel(NZ) —Refused The Dance (NZ) (Defensive Play (USA))
7044a[6]

Effigy *Henry Candy* a80 84
7 b g Efisio—Hymne D'Amour (USA) (Dixieland Band (USA))
1460[8] 1772[6] (2150) 2769[7] 3760[4] 4385[4] 4724[7] 5582[5] 5968[4] 6226[6] 6592[6]

Effort *A bin Huzaim* a90 89
5 ch g Dr Fong(USA) —Party Doll (Be My Guest (USA))
237[9] 754a[9]

Efidium *Suzzanne France* a54 37
13 b g Presidium—Efipetite (Efisio)
1557[7] 2530[10]

Efisio Princess *John E Long* a49 72
8 br m Efisio—Hardiprincess (Keen)
7341[12] 7744[14]

Efistorm *Conor Dore* a76 87
10 b g Efisio—Abundance (Cadeaux Genereux)
133[4] 215[2] 298[6] 430[5] 708[5] 766[4] 833[7] 1140[11] (1274) 1501[3] 2603[8] 2938[7] 3083[2] 3350[2] (3464) 3713[6] (4246) (4618) (5301) 5452[2] 6931[7] 7173[6] 7588[8] 7696[7] 7844[6] 7895[5] (7943)

Egotist (IRE) *A Fabre* a83 97
3 ch c Halling(USA) —Devil's Imp (IRE) (Cadeaux Genereux)
777a[8] 902a[6]

Egretta (IRE) *Hughie Morrison* 67
2 b f Motivator—Firecrest (IRE) (Darshaan)
5806[6]

Egyptian Cross *John Weymes* a16 41
2 ch g Firebreak—Lapadar (IRE) (Woodborough (USA))
1209[5] 1890[11] 3505[8] 3708[5] 3955[6]

Egyptian Lord *Peter Grayson* a42 57
8 ch g Bold Edge—Calypso Lady (IRE) (Priolo (USA))
15[6] 185[7] 1029[8] 3493[7] 4650[5] 6875[8]

Ehkam (USA) *Saeed Bin Suroor* a66
2 ch c Seeking The Gold(USA) —Ishtak (Nashwan (USA))
6697[3]

Eightfold *Richard Hannon* a66 70
2 b c Cadeaux Genereux—Nirvana (Marju (IRE))
3870[3] 4276[5] 5111[3] 5690[4] 6921[14]

Eightfold Path (USA) *P Bary* 102
4 b h Giant's Causeway(USA) —Divine Proportions (USA) (Kingmambo (USA))
3654a[7]

Eijaaz (IRE) *Geoffrey Harker* a40 67
10 b g Green Desert(USA) —Kismah (Machiavellian (USA))
1039[4] 1305[2] 1615[4] 1792[2] 2393[5] 2616[8] (3141) 3510[2] (3974) (4637) 6157[4] 6601[5] 6868[5] 7215[5]

Eila Wheeler *Robert Johnson* 45
4 b m Central Park(IRE) —Only So Far (Teenoso (USA))
5792[12] 6349[5] 6781[8] 7105[8]

Eilean Eeve *George Foster* a13 55
5 b m And Beyond(IRE) —Yeveed (IRE) (Wassl)
575[8] 1213[13] 1540[4] 2412[3] 2803[6] 3128[6] 3355[2] 4176[5] 5153[4] 5551[2] 5789[14] 6428[5] 7370[9] 7714[11]

Eilean Mor *Bryan Smart* a65 68
3 ch g Ishiguru(USA) —Cheviot Heights (Intikhab (USA))
295[2] 398[2] 454[3] (510) 1031[3] 1074[2] 1329[6] 1543[6]

Eire *M Nigge* a103 98
7 ch m Medicean—Mavourneen (USA) (Dynaformer (USA))
371a[0]

Eirnin (IRE) *A P O'Brien* 97
3 ch f Galileo(IRE) —Litani River (USA) (Irish River (FR))
2012a[9] 2682[8] 2968a[9] 4132a[5] 5228a[11]

Eishin Flash (JPN) *Hideaki Fujiwara* 124
4 bb h King's Best(USA) —Moonlady (GER) (Platini (GER))
7563a[8] 7873a[2]

Ejteyaaz *Richard Fahey* 86
4 b g Red Ransom(USA) —Camaret (IRE) (Danehill (USA))
1097[9] 2124[6] 2932[7] 3277[8] 3828[9] 4348[5] 4879[11] 5759[10] 6211[5] 6676[6]

Ekasin *Marco Botti* a78 91
3 b c Bertolini(USA) —Eye To Eye (Exit To Nowhere (USA))
171[2] (431) 1127a[2] 1920a[12]

Ekhraaj (USA) *Roger Varian*
3 b f El Prado(IRE) —Mostaqeleh (USA) (Rahy (USA))
5001[8]

Ektibaas *B W Hills* a71 92
3 ch c Haafhd—Aspen Leaves (USA) (Woodman (USA))
(1328) (1983) 2506[3] 3067[25] 3864[11]

Ektihaam (IRE) *Roger Varian* 98
2 b c Invincible Spirit(IRE) —Liscune (IRE) (King's Best (USA))
(4053) ◆ (5886) 6689[9]

El Abrego (GER) *A Wohler* a80 74
5 b g Samum(GER) —Emy Coasting (USA) (El Gran Senor (USA))
(7314a)

Ela Gonda Mou *Peter Charalambous* a56 74
4 ch m Where Or When(IRE) —Real Flame (Cyrano De Bergerac)
2848[5] 3244[6] 4265[4] 4681[2] 5113[6] 6242[2] 6530[6] *(7271) 7513[8]*

Ela Gorrie Mou *Peter Charalambous* a51 83
5 b m Mujahid(USA) —Real Flame (Cyrano De Bergerac)
1992[4] 2269[3] 2884[3] 3338[4]

Elammato (IRE) *Lisa Williamson* a25
2 b g Strategic Prince—Boadicea (Celtic Swing)
2831[5] *3947[6] 7177[9]*

Eland Ally *Tom Tate* 88
3 b g Striking Ambition—Dream Rose (IRE) (Anabaa (USA))
2074[4] (2710) 3384[2] ◆ 3628[2] 4610[6] 5831[2] 6703[15]

Elavssom (IRE) *Jo Hughes* 41
2 b g Moss Vale(IRE) —Noble Rocket (Reprimand)
5672[6]

Elbe *Sir Henry Cecil* 82
2 b f Dansili—Imroz (USA) (Nureyev (USA))
2467[6] (4002) 5039[5] 5656[9]

Elbow Beach *Dr Jon Scargill* a58 66
2 gr f Choisir(AUS) —Impulsive Decision (IRE) (Nomination)
3362[9] *5097[6]* 6117[4] 6742[10]

El Bulli (USA) *F Chappet* a74 63
4 b g Saint Liam(USA) —Out With The Old (USA) (Time For A Change (USA))
842a[2] 1012a[6]

Elby *Eve Johnson Houghton* 35
4 b g Compton Place—Shall We Run (Hotfoot I)
1751[7] 1984[11] 2427[7] 2921[14]

El Caballito (FR) *J Helouiry* a75 76
3 b g Super Celebre(FR) —Manadouna (FR) (Kaldounevees (FR))
7669a[6]

Eldaafer (USA) *Diane Alvarado* a111 106
6 bb g A.P. Indy(USA) —Habibti (USA) (Tabasco Cat (USA))
7300a[6]

El Decency (USA) *Richard Guest* a82 75
7 b g Seeking The Gold(USA) —Ashraakat (USA) (Danzig (USA))
18[5] 495[7] (547) 1109[13] 1671[7] 2095[6] *2653[8]* 3348[7] 4076[5] 4441[7] 4793[8] 5031[5] 5436[4] 6610[6] 6811[8] (6889) 7079[5] 7216[10] 7744[2]

El Diamante (FR) *Richard Hannon* 64
2 b f Royal Applause—Lumiere Rouge (FR) (Indian Ridge)
2880[4]

El Djebena (IRE) *Sir Mark Prescott Bt* a73 62
3 b g Invincible Spirit(IRE) —Sun Seasons (IRE) (Salse (USA))
(20) 2200[5] 2383[6] 5213[6] 5608[8] 6225[4] *6490[9]*

Eleanora Duse (IRE) *Sir Michael Stoute* a79 114
4 b m Azamour(IRE) —Drama Class (IRE) (Caerleon (USA))
1718[6] 3624[4] 4345[6] 5976a[5]

Electioneer (USA) *Michael Easterby* a69 80
4 b g Elusive Quality(USA) —Secret Charm (IRE) (Green Desert (USA))
165[6] (857) 1612[3] 2352[5] 4152[4] 4443[7] 5400[7] 5732[3] 6158[6] 6779[11]

Electra Star *William Haggas* a78 98
3 b f Shamardal(USA) —Ascot Cyclone (USA) (Rahy (USA))
2960[2] (3437) (4447) ◆ 4914[2] (5702) ◆ 6297[6] 6704[5]

Electrelane *Ralph Beckett* 90
2 ch f Dubawi(IRE) —Imperialistic (IRE) (Imperial Ballet (IRE))
(6432) 7508a[4]

Electric Blue Sky *Stuart Williams* a44
3 b g Intikhab(USA) —Northwick Girl (IRE) (Cape Cross (IRE))
437[7]

Electric Daydream (IRE) *J S Moore* a32 14
2 b f Elusive Quality(USA) —Paris Glory (USA) (Honour And Glory (USA))
5323[15] *6252[7] 6620[6] 7481[9]*

Electrician *John Gosden* 86
2 b g Echo Of Light—Primrose Lane (JPN) (Sunday Silence (USA))
5697[2] ◆ (6064) 6270[9]

Electrickery *Mark Johnston* a24 57
2 b f Excellent Art—Exultate Jubilate (USA) (With Approval (CAN))
3274[5] 3755[7] 4012[3] *4907[9] 5597[11]* 6154[8]

Electric Qatar *Tom Dascombe* 87
2 b c Pastoral Pursuits—Valandraud (IRE) (College Chapel)
3314[3] ◆ 3540[3] 4094[10] 5216[12]

Electric Waves (IRE) *Naif Alatawi* a87 105
3 ch f Exceed And Excel(AUS) —Radiant Energy (IRE) (Spectrum (IRE))
681a[3] 823a[7]

Electrolyser (IRE) *Clive Cox* a90 114
6 gr g Daylami(IRE) —Iviza (IRE) (Sadler's Wells (USA))
2072[8] 3647[3] 4469[13] 6661a[6] 7049a[7]

Elegant Dancer (IRE) *Paul Green* a34 53
4 ch m Choisir(AUS) —Sofistication (IRE) (Dayjur (USA))
169[8] 2546[11] 5008[6] 5803[10] 6159[10] 6609[10] *7415[8]*

Elegant Flight *Alan Jarvis* a68 61
2 ch f Deportivo—On The Wing (Pivotal)
2113[11] 3984[3] 4857[4] 5324[8] *5690[8]* 6222[13] 6627[6] *(6821) (7514)*

Elegant Muse *Walter Swinburn* a68 72
3 b f Fraam—Georgianna (IRE) (Petardia)
2313[13] 3688[8] 4270[6] *4911[5]* 5423[3] *5736[3] 6179[2] 6624[9]* 6938[9]

Elegant Star (IRE) *Dave Morris* a11
3 b f Where Or When(IRE) —So Elegant (IRE) (Bahhare (USA))
591[7] 1293[7] 1574[8]

Elfaaten (USA) *Marcus Tregoning* 69
3 bb c Forestry(USA) —Thaminah (USA) (Danzig (USA))
2231[5] 4611[4]

Elfine (IRE) *Rae Guest* a76 67
3 b f Invincible Spirit(IRE) —Donnelly's Hollow (IRE) (Docksider (USA))
1139[4] *1819[2]* 2232[9] 3228[10] *5415[4] 6004[3] 7388[6] 7427[5]*

El Gran Torino (IRE) *G M Lyons* 80
3 b g Ad Valorem(USA) —Silview (USA) (Saint Ballado (CAN))
1704a[9]

El Greco (IRE) *Sir Michael Stoute* 78
2 ch c Monsun(GER) —Olympienne (IRE) (Sadler's Wells (USA))
4213[2] ◆ 5891[4]

Elhamri *Conor Dore* a83 71
7 bb g Noverre(USA) —Seamstress (IRE) (Barathea (IRE))
29[4] 84[2] 134[8] 199[5] 243[2] (321) (455) 572[6] 1067[9] 1197[9] 1395[9] 1562[9] 1955[5] 2205[3] 2653[5] 2765[8] 3711[3] 4000[4] 4086[9] 4395[7] 4893[2] 4988[8] 5732[6] 5895[13] 7040[6] 7265[10] (7420) 7504[3] 7744[10] 7857[3]

Elijah Pepper (USA) *David Barron* a86 83
6 ch g Crafty Prospector(USA) —Dovie Dee (USA) (Housebuster (USA))
405[2] 541[4] 932[3] 1075[3] 1747[3] 1970[6] 2366[3] 3071[5] 3386[3] 4679[3] 5106[5] 5465[6] 5733[3] *(6543)* 7199[2] 7922[8] ◆

Elite *Mick Channon* a65 64
2 b f Invincible Spirit(IRE) —Garah (Ajdal (USA))
3132[7] 5889[4] *6492[4] 7491[4]*

Elite Land *Brian Ellison* a71 74
8 b g Namaqualand(USA) —Petite Elite (Anfield)
8[2]

Elite Syncopations *Andrew Haynes* a26 42
3 b f Haafhd—Sabalara (IRE) (Mujadil (USA))
916[6] 1053[9] 1865[8] 3724[16] 5137[7] 5670[5]

Elizabeth Coffee (IRE) *M Halford* a80 64
3 b f Byron—Queens Wharf (IRE) (Ela-Mana-Mou)
(7549a)

Eljowzah (IRE) *Clive Brittain* a65 47
3 b f Acclamation—Express Logic (Air Express (IRE))
959[3]

Elke's Friend's *W Hickst* 99
4 b m Starcraft(NZ) —Saphila (IRE) (Sadler's Wells (USA))
7678a[0]

Elkhart (IRE) *Mark Johnston* 97
2 b c Refuse To Bend(IRE) —Princess Taise (USA) (Cozzene (USA))
2831[4] 3401[3] (3609) 4424[5] 4964[2] 5487[4]

Elkmait *Clive Brittain* a60 80
3 b f Trade Fair—Rich Dancer (Halling (USA))
6272[9] *6477[10]* 7054[9]

Elk Trail (IRE) *Michael Mullineaux* a71 61
6 ch g Captain Rio—Panpipes (USA) (Woodman (USA))
5312[3] 6029[5] 7105[10]

Ellaal *Charles Hills* 83
2 b c Oasis Dream—Capistrano Day (USA) (Diesis)
6300[2] ◆ (6951)

El Lail (USA) *Mark Johnston* 83
2 ch f Haafhd—Dufoof (USA) (Kingmambo (USA))
6278[2] (6675)

Ellastina (IRE) *Richard Fahey* a44 62
2 b f Zafeen(FR) —Elle's Angel (IRE) (Tobougg (IRE))
5486[7] 6230[4] *6842[7]*

Ella Woodcock (IRE) *Eric Alston* a76 71
7 b g Daggers Drawn(USA) —Hollow Haze (USA) (Woodman (USA))
5402[7] 6211[10]

Ellemental *Mrs K Burke* 33
3 b f Elnadim(USA) —Double Top (IRE) (Thatching)
1108[10] 2045[9] 4514[9] 5165[9]

Ellemujie *Dean Ivory* a91 91
6 b g Mujahid(USA) —Jennelle (Nomination)
1138[3] 1684[5] 2066[8] 2884[10] (3366) 3844[5] 4553[2] 5483[6] 6068[4] 6163[13] 7022[9] *7328[3] 7651[3] 7908[5]*

Ellephil (IRE) *Bryn Palling* a27 3
3 b f Elusive City(USA) —Carna (IRE) (Anita's Prince)
4920[7] 5842[5] 6605[6]

Elle Shadow (IRE) *P Schiergen* 112
4 b m Shamardal(USA) —Elle Danzig (GER) (Roi Danzig (USA))
(3334a) 4599a[3] 5497a[4] 7047a[5] 7409a[9]

El Libertador (USA) *Eric Wheeler* a68 57
5 bb g Giant's Causeway(USA) —Istikbal (USA) (Kingmambo (USA))
111[3] 317[3] 489[5] 933[3] (1276) 2653[11] 2870[7] *3720[6]* 4444[6] 4829[8] *5143[8]* 5611[7] 5912[7] (6845) 7003[8] 7399[10] 7527[3] 7654[8]

Ellie Arter *Richard Hannon*
2 ch f Needwood Blade—Alula (In The Wings)
3257[14]

Ellie In The Pink (IRE) *Alan Jarvis* a69 84
3 ch f Johannesburg(USA) —Stravinia (USA) (Stravinsky (USA))
(1149) 1579[4] 1986[2] *2821[4]* 3782[4] (5040) (5511) (6167) 6997[2]

Ellielusive (IRE) *Mark Brisbourne* a22 46
4 b m Elusive City(USA) —Danzolin (Danzero (AUS))
1252[5] 1393[8] 1985[8] 2498[6] 2593[9] 3090[14] 4640[7] 5490[11] *5865[10]*

Ellies Girl (IRE) *Ronald Harris*
3 b f Clodovil(IRE) —Miss Toto (Mtoto)
1751[8] *1998[10]* 2639[9]

Ellies Image *Brian Baugh* a35 68
4 b m Lucky Story(USA) —Crown City (USA) (Coronado's Quest (USA))
1054[6] 1394[10] 2671[11] 3093[11] 4513[9] (5034) 5404[2] ◆ (5674) *6138[4]* 6450[5] 6939[10]

El Maachi *Jim Best* a68 71
3 b g Librettist(USA) —Tatanka (IRE) (Lear Fan (USA))
1812[3] 2197[3] 2792[2] 4321[5] 5121[5]

Elmaam *William Haggas* 85
3 ch f Nayef(USA) —Almahab (USA) (Danzig (USA))
1853[2] ◆ (2402) (3180) 4344[9]

El Mansour (USA) *Clive Cox* a84 83
3 ch c Rahy(USA) —La Vida Loca (IRE) (Caerleon (USA))
1485[3] 2052[4] *2819[3] (3519)*

El McGlynn (IRE) *John O'Shea* a62 72
2 b f Elnadim(USA) —Evelyn One (Alhaarth (IRE))
7898[3]

Elmfield Giant (USA) *Richard Fahey* a82 76
4 ch g Giant's Causeway(USA) —Princess Atoosa (USA) (Gone West (USA))
1243[8] 1671[5] 1874[5] 2454[9] 3319[7] *3739[3] 4660[2] 5103[6] 5716[3]*

Elmora *Sylvester Kirk* a51
2 ch f Elnadim(USA) —Ringarooma (Erhaab (USA))
6663[4]

El Muqbil (IRE) *Brian Meehan* 88
3 b g Medicean—Tariysha (IRE) (Daylami (IRE))
1361[9] 2503[4] 2847[4] (3980) 4553[4] 5049[4] 6346[5]

Elna Bright *Peter Crate* a99 92
6 b g Elnadim(USA) —Acicula (IRE) (Night Shift (USA))
99[6] 438[7] 615[9] 700[7] 844[8] 3796[11] 4616[3] 5043[11] (5703) 6341[13] 6723[6] *(7489) 7578[7]* 7801[9]

Elnawin *Richard Hannon* a106 113
5 b g Elnadim(USA) —Acicula (IRE) (Night Shift (USA))
1518[4] (1848) (2961)

Elodie *F Head* 88
3 b f Dansili—In Clover (Inchinor)
1597a[5]

Elpais (ITY) *G Botti* a76 76
4 ch g Altieri—Lady Caribe (FR) (Kendor (FR))
2867a[0]

El Pib D'Oro (IRE) *Mlle S-V Tarrou* a81 85
5 b h Oasis Dream—Trinity Joy (Vettori (IRE))
3568a[10]

Elraabeya (CAN) *Sir Michael Stoute* 73
3 ch f Seeking The Gold(USA) —Seattle Envoy (CAN) (Deputy Minister (CAN))
1343[5] 4072[4] (5241) 6124[5]

Elrasheed *John Dunlop* a82 81
3 b c Red Ransom(USA) —Ayun (USA) (Swain (IRE))
1321[6] 2648[8] 3872[4] (4336) 5035[7] 5710[3] 6499[6] *7002[8]*

Elshabakiya (IRE) *Clive Brittain* a99 100
3 b f Diktat—Amalie (IRE) (Fasliyev (USA))
990[2] 1319[7] 1719[10] 2298[4] 3106[10] 5935[7] 6523[2] 6687[5] *7392[5]*

Elsie's Orphan *Patrick Chamings* a78 76
4 br m Pastoral Pursuits—Elsie Plunkett (Mind Games)
1581[2] (3020) 3940[4] *(5100) 7097[8]*

Elsie Tanner (IRE) *David Nicholls*
2 b f One Cool Cat(USA) —Beechesville (IRE) (Night Shift (USA))
2665[6] 2797[5]

Elspeth's Boy (USA) *Philip Kirby* a85 82
4 bb g Tiznow(USA) —Miss Waki Club (USA) (Miswaki (USA))
4010[5] 5119[3] 5516[6] (7211) *7397[12]*

El Suacillo (IRE) *D Camuffo* 89
4 br h Invincible Spirit(IRE) —Max Almabrouka (USA) (Hennessy (USA))
1919a[7]

Eltheeb *George Moore* a75 87
4 gr g Red Ransom(USA) —Snowdrops (Gulch (USA))
1324[7] (3244) 3701[4] (3858) 4280[9] 4528[4] 5686[11]

El Torbellino (IRE) *David O'Meara* 91
3 b f Chineur(FR) —Deeday Bay (IRE) (Brave Act)
1384[7] 2008[4] 2891[2] 3809[3] 4103[4] (5020) 6330[10]

El Toreros (USA) *D K Weld* a62 67
3 b g El Prado(IRE) —Soul Reason (USA) (Seeking The Gold (USA))
6511a[5]

Eluding *Mahmood Al Zarooni* a78 76
2 b f Street Cry(IRE) —Without A Trace (IRE) (Darshaan)
6603[3] *7118[2] 7396[3]*

Elusive Award (USA) *Andrew Oliver* a84 90
4 b g Elusive Quality(USA) —Victoria Cross (IRE) (Mark Of Esteem (IRE))
3445a[14] 4566a[7] 7189a[2]

Elusive Bonus (IRE) *David O'Meara* 58
2 b f Elusive City(USA) —Over Rating (Desert King (IRE))
3273[8] 3504[8] 3610[7] 4899[4] (5590) 6043[11] 6597[4]

Elusive Diva (IRE) *Edward Creighton* a48 31
3 b f Elusive City(USA) —Wonders Gift (Dr Devious (IRE))
3433[4] 3766[7]

Elusive Express (IRE) *H Rogers* a68 58
3 b f Elusive City(USA) —Curie Express (IRE) (Fayruz)
973a[5]

Elusive Fame (USA) *Mark Johnston* a89 42
5 b g Elusive Quality(USA) —Advancing Star (USA) (Soviet Star (USA))
18[3] 105[6] 186[4] 377[2] ◆ 799[3] 869[5] 977a[9] 1292[3] 1538[5] *1978[2]* 2047[7]

Elusive Flame *David Elsworth* 87
2 b f Elusive City(USA) —Dimelight (Fantastic Light (USA))
2467[11] 4155[2] 4857[8] (5480) (5847) 6296[8]

Elusive Force (ITY) *P Riccioni* 42
5 b m Elusive City(USA) —Sopran Rahp (Primo Dominie)
1432a[13]

Elusive Hawk (IRE) *Barney Curley* a83 78
7 b g Noverre(USA) —Two Clubs (First Trump)
1444[9] 3555[11] 4020[8] 6939[3]

Elusive Island (USA) *Ann Duffield* 60
2 b g Elusive Quality(USA) —Quiet Word (USA) (Quiet American (USA))
4012[4] 4436[7] 5681[9]

Elusive Kate (USA) *John Gosden* a80 115
2 b f Elusive Quality(USA) —Gout De Terroir (USA) (Lemon Drop Kid (USA))
2709[4] ◆ *(3046)* (4569a) (5296a) (6564a) 7281a[8]

Elusive Love (IRE) *Mark Johnston* a61 52
3 b c Elusive City(USA) —Love Ridot (IRE) (Fruits Of Love (USA))
253[10] 653[2] 936[5] 1056[9]

Elusive Lucy (IRE) *Linda Jewell*
3 b f Elusive City(USA) —Glebe Garden (Soviet Star (USA))
2427[6]

Elusive Pimpernel (USA) *John Dunlop* 116
4 bb h Elusive Quality(USA) —Cara Fantasy (IRE) (Sadler's Wells (USA))
1342[3] 2439[6] 4095[5] 4789[2] 5493[3] 5829[5]

Elusive Prince *David Barron* a80 97
3 b g Storming Home—Ewenny (Warrshan (USA))
(1880) (2619) 2934[12] 3682[7] 4333[6] 5054[2] (5559) 6145[22] 6500[6]

Elusive Ridge (IRE) *H Rogers* a99 90
5 b g Elusive City(USA) —Woodwing (USA) (Indian Ridge)
4418a[15] *5090a[4] 6513a[4] 7549a[5] 7618a[3] (7793a)*

Elusive Storm (FR) *F Rohaut*
2 b f Elusive City(USA) —Queen Of Fairies (IRE) (Fairy King (USA))
7814a[3]

Elusive Sue (USA) *Richard Fahey* 78
4 bb m Elusive Quality(USA) —Show Me The Stage (USA) (Slew The Surgeon (USA))
1244[4] 2095[11] 2566[5] 3024[3] (3278) 3634[4] 4349[10] 4811[5]

Elusive Time (IRE) *Francisco Castro* 91
3 b g Elusive City(USA) —Brosna Time (IRE) (Danetime (IRE))
4483a[5]

Elusive Warrior (USA) *Alan McCabe* a75 46
8 b g Elusive Quality(USA) —Love To Fight (CAN) (Fit To Fight (USA))
9[4] 17[3] 122[4] 290[4] 495[4] 547[2] 568[2] 674[4] 858[6] 1292[6] 1979[3] ◆ 2237[5] 3495[5] 3953[2] 4183[2] 4651[2] 5600[3] 6617[3] 7068[2] 7243[5] 7648[6]

Elusivity (IRE) *Brian Meehan* a74 102
3 b g Elusive City(USA) —Tough Chic (IRE) (Indian Ridge)
(1611) 2064[2] 2582[2] 2834[2] 3346[2] ◆ 3649[2] 4062[4] 5054[4] (5451) ◆ 6500[2] ◆ 6987[2] ◆

El Vettorio (GER) *C Boutin* a66 70
8 gr g Vettori(IRE) —Erminora (GER) (Highest Honor (FR))
617a[3] 706a[5] *832a[4]*

El Viento (FR) *Richard Fahey* 98
3 ch g Compton Place—Blue Sirocco (Bluebird (USA))
1241[8] 2067[2] 2508[12] 3052[4] (3682) 4472[3] 4965[5] 6145[21] 6987[8]

Elvira Delight (IRE) *Jeremy Noseda* a75 65
3 b f Desert Style(IRE) —Entente Cordiale (IRE) (Ela-Mana-Mou)
(77) 543[2] ◆ 2184[5] 3688[4] 4744[6]

El Wasmi *Clive Brittain* 87
3 b c Oasis Dream—Wendylina (IRE) (In The Wings)
1568[3] 1810[9] 2511[3] (2838) 3797[2] 6457[8] 6708[16]

El'Wringo *Rod Millman* a43
7 b g Karinga Bay—Wishy (IRE) (Leading Counsel (USA))
539[6] 688[7]

Elyaadi *John Queally* a96 100
7 b m Singspiel(IRE) —Abyaan (IRE) (Ela-Mana-Mou)
[illegible] 6710a[7] [illegible]

Elzaam (AUS) *Roger Varian* 117
3 b c Redoute's Choice(AUS) —Mambo In Freeport (USA) (Kingmambo (USA))
1318[5] (2054) 3154[4] ◆ 3863[8] 5707[5] 6520[4]

El Zorrito (FR) *Mme M-L Oget*
3 b g Sevres Rose(IRE) —Alluring Mamselle (USA) (Sagace (FR))
5132a[0]

Email Exit (IRE) *C Plisson* a64 54
4 ch g Titus Livius(FR) —Christoph's Girl (Efisio)
220a[0] 842a[6] 1012a[2] 7315a[0]

Embassy Pearl (IRE) *Sir Mark Prescott Bt* a78
3 b f Invincible Spirit(IRE) —Embassy Belle (IRE) (Marju (IRE))
454[4] ◆ (1220) ◆

Embra (IRE) *Tim Etherington* a64 58
6 b g Monashee Mountain(USA) —Ivory Turner (Efisio)
4144[8] 4881[5]

Embsay Crag *Kate Walton* 87
5 b g Elmaamul(USA) —Wigman Lady (IRE) (Tenby)
1387[2] ◆ 2006[11] 2544[4] 2932[F] 4109[6] 4577[7] 6024[7] 6773[15]

Emeebee *Willie Musson* a73 71
5 b g Medicean—Broughtons Motto (Mtoto)
1867[7] 2915[3] 4253[U]

Emerald Commander (IRE) *Saeed Bin Suroor* 115
4 b h Pivotal—Brigitta (IRE) (Sadler's Wells (USA))
3422a[4] 4138a[2] (4368) 4972[7] 5473[4] 6061[3] 6298[5] 7323a[2]

Emerald Girl (IRE) *Richard Guest* a68 75
4 b m Chineur(FR) —Faypool (IRE) (Fayruz)
200[5] 334[4] 590[5] 687[9] 802[8] 5376[13] *5944[13]* 6764[12] *7006[7] 7091[8] 7119[10]* 7247[10]

Emerald Glade (IRE) *Milton Harris* 70
4 b m Azamour(IRE) —Woodland Glade (Mark Of Esteem (IRE))
1577[7]

Emerald Ring (IRE) *David Wachman* a90 90
3 ch f Johannesburg(USA) —Inkling (USA) (Seeking The Gold (USA))
1006a[13]

Emerald Royal *Edward Creighton* a49
3 b c Royal Applause—Bakhtawar (IRE) (Lomitas)
262[11] 655[14] 7096[13] 7429[6] 7575[8] 7656[13] 7676[6]

Emerald Smile (IRE) *J S Moore* a51 55
2 ch f King's Best(USA) —Starsazi (Observatory (USA))
2997[7] 4386[5] 4485[4] 5245[10] 5637[3] 6280[3] 7108[2] 7481[4]

Emeralds Spirit (IRE) *John Weymes* a50 67
4 b m Rock Of Gibraltar(IRE) —Spiritual Air (Royal Applause)
1909[8] 2260[8] 2487[8] 4383[6] 4513[4] 4876[2] 4987[3] 5455[3] 5721[4] 6159[6] (6430) 7068[8] 7399[7] 7820[7]

Emerald Wilderness (IRE) *Robert Cowell* a93 90
7 b g Green Desert(USA) —Simla Bibi (Indian Ridge)
3645[9] 3982[6] 4553[8] 5275[9] (5687) 5894[8] 6302[10] 6922[5] 7328[2] 7651[2] (7759)

Emerging Artist (FR) *Mark Johnston* a100 101
5 b g Dubai Destination(USA) —Picture Princess (Sadler's Wells (USA))
525[4] 1381a[8]

Emil (DEN) *Ole Larsen* a90 92
7 b g Cajun Cadet—Elysian Fields (IRE) (Marju (IRE))
4483a[7]

Emilio Largo *Sir Henry Cecil* 94
3 b g Cadeaux Genereux—Gloved Hand (Royal Applause)
1934[2] ◆ (2790) (3871) (4214) ◆

Emily Hall *Bryan Smart* 50
2 ch f Paris House—Raven (IRE) (Alzao (USA))
5618[9] 6045[10] 6344[4] (7059)

Emirate Isle *Brian Storey* 57
7 b g Cois Na Tine(IRE) —Emmajoun (Emarati (USA))
1039[11]

Emirates Art *David Simcock* a62 89
2 b f Excellent Art—Going To Work (IRE) (Night Shift (USA))
3746[3] ◆ (4184) (5039) 6296[6]

Emirates Champion *Saeed Bin Suroor* a110 98
5 b h Haafhd—Janaat (Kris)
(585a) (824a) 3591[6] 5754a[3]

Emiratesdotcom *Milton Bradley* a84 75
5 b g Pivotal—Teggiano (IRE) (Mujtahid (USA))
1730[7] 1838[3] 2201[2] (2554) 2870[6] 3217[2] 3512[4] 4434[2] (4640) 5262[5] 5616[5] (5895) (6177) 6974[11] 7457[5]

Emirates Dream (USA) *Saeed Bin Suroor* 103
4 b g Kingmambo(USA) —My Boston Gal (USA) (Boston Harbor (USA))
5218[12] 6080[8] 6955[5]

Emirates Jack (IRE) *George Baker* a52 45
2 b g Red Clubs(IRE) —Lady Windley (Baillamont (USA))
4339[10] 5834[7] 6581[6] 7051[12] 7342[9]

Emiyna (USA) *John M Oxx* a86 109
3 b f Maria's Mon(USA) —Ebaza (IRE) (Sinndar (IRE))
(1779a) ◆ 2334a[10] 4978a[2] 5745a[8] 5977a[5]

Emkanaat *Roger Varian* 79
3 b g Green Desert(USA) —Miss Anabaa (Anabaa (USA))
5346[3] (5810) 6239[5]

Emley Moor *Chris Fairhurst* a32 54
2 b f Misu Bond(IRE) —Royal Curtsy (Pivotal)
2430[7] 3314[11] 4002[10] 4808[3] 5597[4] 6260[17] 6599[11]

Emma Jean (IRE) *J S Moore* a42 59
2 b f Jeremy(USA) —Second Prayer (IRE) (Singspiel (IRE))
2374[5] 2788[4] 2998[2] 3584[4] 3816[5] 4225[2] 4704[3] 4756[5] 5374[4] 5535[4] 6001[7]

Emma Jean Boy *J S Moore* a50 53
2 b g Echo Of Light—Lucky Find (IRE) (Key Of Luck (USA))
4201[17] 4545[6] 4884[7] 5343[6] 7718[6]

Emman Bee (IRE) *John Gallagher* a62 62
2 gr f Dark Angel(IRE) —Two Sets To Love (IRE) (Cadeaux Genereux)
5564[10] 6000[7] 6581[3] 7051[5] 7223[3]

Emma's Gift (IRE) *Julia Feilden* a85 96
3 gr f Aussie Rules(USA) —Rose Of Mooncoin (IRE) (Brief Truce (USA))
1234[7] (1599) 2073[5] 3034[10] 3407[5] 4265[6] 5053[17] 6273[8] 6632[9] 7361[2] 7486[2] ◆ 7806[2] ◆

Emmeline Pankhurst (IRE) *Julia Feilden* a30 56
3 b f Marju(IRE) —Mango Groove (IRE) (Unfuwain (USA))
1579[10] 1933[8] 2293[5] 2583[8] 2875[7] 3251[5]

Emmrooz *D Selvaratnam* a102 103
6 b g Red Ransom(USA) —Nasmatt (Danehill (USA))
581a[6]

Emmuska *Richard Hannon* a81 76
2 b f Sir Percy—Tintac (Intikhab (USA))
4155[7] 4992[2] (5891) 6340[6] (7436) (7576)

Emper Holly (ARG) *M bin Shafya* a34 52
5 b m Emperor Jones(USA) —Miss Holly (ARG) (Numerous (USA))
241[10]

Emperor Of Rome (IRE) *Michael Dods* 75
3 b g Antonius Pius(USA) —Fire Flower (Sri Pekan (USA))
2058[3] 2461[2] (3138) 4050[5] 4674[5] 5064[9] 6916[10]

Emperors Pearl (IRE) *Charles Hills* a55 68
2 b f Holy Roman Emperor(IRE) —On The Nile (IRE) (Sadler's Wells (USA))
2709[8] 3780[3] 4087[5] 5052[8] 6946[7]

Emperor's Princess (FR) *J E Hammond* a68 62
3 b f Holy Roman Emperor(IRE) —Elanaaka (Lion Cavern (USA))
7667a[9]

Emperors Waltz (IRE) *Rae Guest* 55
2 b f Antonius Pius(USA) —Gavotte (Sadler's Wells (USA))
6018[6] 6771[11]

Emperor Vespasian *Andrew Balding* 83
2 b g Royal Applause—Flavian (Catrail (USA))
5697[10] 6464[3] 6992[6]

Empire Rose (ARG) *M F De Kock* a93 92
4 br f Sunray Spirit(USA) —Empire Lady (ARG) (Acceptable (USA))
151a[5] 412a[4] 681a[5]

Empire Storm (GER) *A Wohler* a103 108
4 b h Storming Home—Emy Coasting (USA) (El Gran Senor (USA))
4373a[2] 5497a[2] 6595a[5] 7048a[2]

Empirico (FR) *David Marnane* a86 80
5 b g Oasis Dream—Esprit Libre (Daylami (IRE))
4135a[4]

Empowering (IRE) *A P O'Brien* a84 104
3 b f Encosta De Lago(AUS) —Blue Cloud (IRE) (Nashwan (USA))
(1006a) 1719[15] 3417a[7] 4836a[2] 5524a[7] 5979a[4]

Empress Charlotte *Michael Bell* a68 72
3 b f Holy Roman Emperor(IRE) —Charlotte O Fraise (IRE) (Beat Hollow)
1472[2] 1986[12] 2821[2] 3688[2] 4011[5] (4727) 5666[2] 6311[6]

Empressive *William Muir* 52
2 b f Holy Roman Emperor(IRE) —Dodo (IRE) (Alzao (USA))
3270[11] 3639[4] 4225[3] 4702[4] 6237[10]

Empress Leizu (IRE) *Tony Carroll* a64 51
4 b m Chineur(FR) —Silk Point (IRE) (Barathea (IRE))
163[5] 555[4] 895[4] ◆ 1068[8] 2401[5] (4920) 5390[4] 5740[7] 6490[5] 6844[3] 7034[3]

Empress Royal *Michael Dods* 66
3 b f Royal Applause—Akhira (Emperor Jones (USA))
452[8] 1187[5] 2265[10] 2410[4]

Empyrean (USA) *Sir Mark Prescott Bt* a35
3 b f Aptitude(USA) —Eternity (Suave Dancer (USA))
4989[9] 5247[7] 7440[6] 7631[8] 7858[4]

Emrani (USA) *Donald McCain* a76 83
4 b g Rahy(USA) —Ebaza (IRE) (Sinndar (IRE))
1105[10] 1901[6] 3725[4]

Emsiyah (USA) *Saeed Bin Suroor* 53
3 bb f Bernardini(USA) —Menhoubah (USA) (Dixieland Band (USA))
2836[8] 3385[9]

Emulous *D K Weld* 120
4 b m Dansili—Aspiring Diva (USA) (Distant View (USA))
1118a[6] (2325a) (3527a) ◆ (5745a) ◆

Enak (ARG) *Saeed Bin Suroor* a110 110
5 b h Orpen(USA) —Enfeite (ARG) (Roy (USA))
157a[2] 330a[3] 581a[2] 829a[2] 4095[9] 4456[3] 6088[3] 6671[5]

Enchanted Dream *George Margarson* a57 52
3 b f Halling(USA) —Enchanted (Magic Ring (IRE))
5626[4] 7069[2] 7354[8]

Enchanted Evening (IRE) *D K Weld* a88 99
5 b m High Chaparral(IRE) —Glen Kate (Glenstal (USA))
924a[7] 1779a[7] 6362a[8] 7277a[11]

Enchanting Smile (FR) *David Nicholls* a2 70
4 b m Rakti—A Thousand Smiles (IRE) (Sadler's Wells (USA))
856[6]

Encircled *J R Jenkins* a86 92
7 b m In The Wings—Ring Of Esteem (Mark Of Esteem (IRE))
315[4] (384)

Encke (USA) *Mahmood Al Zarooni* 89
2 b c Kingmambo(USA) —Shawanda (IRE) (Sinndar (IRE))
5851[2] ◆ (6529) ◆

Encore Une Annee *Ralph Beckett* a78 82
3 b f Hernando(FR) —Eternelle (Green Desert (USA))
1807[8] 5235[3] 6294[7] 7136[8]

Encore Un Fois *George Baker* a70 78
3 br g Val Royal(FR) —Factice (USA) (Known Fact (USA))
4102[4] 4663[7] 5356[3] 5992[2] 6435[3] 6924[5] (7427) 7638[5] (7840) 7920[4]

Encore View *Nick Littmoden* a61
3 b f Oasis Dream—Aricia (IRE) (Nashwan (USA))
110[6] 1149[6] 1472[11] 2163[9] 2821[13]

Endangered Species *John Weymes*
2 ch g Lucky Story(USA) —Lucky Dip (Tirol)
4140[9] 5003[5] 6572[10]

Endaxi Mana Mou *Noel Quinlan* a68 44
3 bb f Araafa(IRE) —Lake Nyasa (IRE) (Lake Coniston (IRE))
379[4] 1176[8] 2527[9] 3710[5] 5631[8] 6310[5] 6545[11] 7119[4] 7246[5]

Endeavor *Dianne Sayer* 18
6 ch g Selkirk(USA) —Midnight Mambo (USA) (Kingmambo (USA))
1794[8]

Enderby Spirit (GR) *Bryan Smart* 99
5 gr g Invincible Spirit(IRE) —Arctic Ice (IRE) (Zafonic (USA))
(1675) 2075[11] 4042[4] 4428[11] 5060[18] 6987[22]

Endless Applause *Richard Whitaker* 59
2 b f Royal Applause—Petra Nova (First Trump)
4283[6] 5592[6] 6344[3] 6627[3]

End Of Dreams (USA) *Kevin Ryan* a44
2 ch f Horse Chestnut(SAF) —Folk Tale (USA) (Woodman (USA))
6441[12]

End Of May (IRE) *Rebecca Curtis* 16
2 b f Iffraaj—Lucky Bet (IRE) (Lucky Guest)
3287[9]

End Of The Affair (IRE) *V C Ward* a99 95
7 ch m Indian Ridge—Blend Of Pace (IRE) (Sadler's Wells (USA))
4398a[10] 6271[7]

End Or Beginning *Paul Cole* 87
3 b c Sadler's Wells(USA) —Smart 'n Noble (USA) (Smarten (USA))
2104[2] 2735[3] 3108[7] 3550[2]

Endowing (IRE) *Richard Hannon* 86
2 b c Danehill Dancer(IRE) —Brazilian Samba (IRE) (Sadler's Wells (USA))
4330[15] 5013[2] ◆ 5564[4]

Energia Carioca (BRZ) *E Martins* a88 64
4 br c Thignon Lafre(BRZ) —Bear Hunter (BRZ) (Infamous Deed (USA))
411a[12] 753a[7]

Energia Cintilante (BRZ) *E Martins* a67
4 b f Torrential(USA) —Key Largo (BRZ) (Roi Normand (USA))
151a[9]

Energia Colonial (BRZ) *Fabricio Borges* a104 64
4 bb g Giant Gentleman(USA) —Karla Dora (BRZ) (Nugget Point (IRE))
238[13] 680a[11] (5981a)

Energize (FR) *Sir Michael Stoute* 66
2 ch c Pivotal—Breathe (FR) (Ocean Of Wisdom (USA))
7232[5]

Energizer (GER) *J Hirschberger* 105
2 b c Monsun(GER) —Erytheis (USA) (Theatrical)
6901a[4] 7325a[5]

Enery (IRE) *Mahmood Al Zarooni* a72 67
2 b c Teofilo(IRE) —Annee Lumiere (IRE) (Giant's Causeway (USA))
5170[4] 5605[4] 6581[2] 6792[2] 7350[2]

En Ete *Bill Turner* 46
2 b f Three Valleys(USA) —Summer Lightning (IRE) (Tamure (IRE))
1396[P] 1726[4]

En Fuego *Geoffrey Harker* 78
4 b g Firebreak—Yanomami (USA) (Slew O'Gold (USA))
1747[7] 1942[5] 2398[7] 3508[8] 4125[3] 5311[8] 5589[3] 6264[4] 6536[4]

England Rules (IRE) *Jeremy Noseda* 83
3 b c Aussie Rules(USA) —Nymphs Echo (IRE) (Mujtahid (USA))
1338[4] (1774) 2925[8] 3959[5]

Englishgreek (IRE) *George Prodromou* a27
2 b g Desert Style(IRE) —Hot Dish (USA) (Stravinsky (USA))
7490[7] 7670[5]

English Summer *Mark Johnston* 97
4 b g Montjeu(IRE) —Hunt The Sun (Rainbow Quest (USA))
1412[5] 1729[3] 2071[8] (2285) 3396[19] 3625[12] 4354[6] 4778[8] 5878[5] 6333[6]

Engrossing *David Elsworth* a42 79
2 b c Tiger Hill(IRE) —Pan Galactic (USA) (Lear Fan (USA))
6267[4] ◆ 6954[4] 7454[9]

En Hiver *Ralph Beckett* a68 58
3 b f Royal Applause—Cotton House (IRE) (Mujadil (USA))
4991[5] 5567[6] 6473[5] 7093[4]

Enigma Code (UAE) *James McAuley* a75 62
6 b g Elusive Quality(USA) —Tempting Fate (IRE) (Persian Bold)
612[9] 820[2] 3713[5] 7790a[11]

Enjoying (IRE) *Richard Hannon* a60 62
2 b c Marju(IRE) —Jazzy Jan (IRE) (Royal Academy (USA))
3132[5] 3986[5] 4264[10] 5144[8] 5342[6] (5783) 6399[6] 6806[12] 7569[7]

Enjoyment *Alan McCabe* 10
4 b m Dansili—Have Fun (Indian Ridge)
3541[9]

Enjoy The Life *Mario Hofer* 71
2 b f Medicean—Accusation (IRE) (Barathea (IRE))
5873a[7]

Enjoy Today (USA) *Brian Meehan* a48 76
3 ch c Kingmambo(USA) —Queen's Logic (IRE) (Grand Lodge (USA))
1338[8]

Enlightening (IRE) *Richard Hannon* a69 73
3 b c Elusive City(USA) —Mono Star (IRE) (Soviet Star (USA))
2256[9] 3363[4]

Enlil (FR) *J Parize* 72
5 ch g Welkin(CAN) —Miss Kenbold (FR) (Star Maite (FR))
221a[0]

En Pointe *James Given* 23
3 b f Medicean—On Point (Kris)
2185[13] 3385[11]

Enreve (FR) *J-M Capitte* a72 76
5 b g Enrique—Oa Chereve (FR) (Kaldounevees (FR))
219a[0] 439a[0]

Enriching (USA) *Noel Quinlan* a73 58
3 ch c Lemon Drop Kid(USA) —Popozinha (USA) (Rahy (USA))
610[5] 726[3] 909[2] 2253[10] 3131[6] 3596[3] 3916[2] 5836[13] 6412[4]

Enroller (IRE) *William Muir* 81
6 b g Marju(IRE) —Walk On Quest (FR) (Rainbow Quest (USA))
5493[4] 5963[3] 7297[22]

Ensemble (FR) *F Head* a66 68
3 b f Iron Mask(USA) —Only Seule (USA) (Lyphard (USA))
775a[5]

Ensnare *Noel Quinlan* a69 71
6 b g Pivotal—Entrap (USA) (Phone Trick (USA))
82[8] 949[12] 1177[12] 1488[10] 1868[8] (3720) ◆ 7418[13]

Entangle *Arnfinn Lund* a82 99
5 b m Pivotal—Entwine (Primo Dominie)
4483a[4] 5982a[2] 6741a[2]

Enthrall (IRE) *Denis Coakley* a38 29
2 b f Holy Roman Emperor(IRE) —Intriguing (IRE) (Fasliyev (USA))
6117[12] 6474[13] 7344[11]

Enthusiastic *Luca Cumani* 69
3 b c Galileo(IRE) —Que Puntual (ARG) (Contested Bid (USA))
5911[4]

Enthusing (IRE) *David Elsworth* 85
3 b c Noverre(USA) —Catatonic (Zafonic (USA))
(2256)

Entifaadha *William Haggas* 107
2 b c Dansili—Model Queen (USA) (Kingmambo (USA))
(4330) (5181) 5926[3] 6527[5]

Entitled *Sir Michael Stoute* a81 95
4 ch m Pivotal—Noble One (Primo Dominie)
1884[9] (2938) 3459[4] 4346[11] 7031[2] ◆ 7295[18]

Entrance *Julia Feilden* a69 66
3 ch f Iceman—Enrapture (USA) (Lear Fan (USA))
77[5] 469[4] 540[5] 649[5] (2850) 3456[3] 4275[7] 4579[4] 5302[4] 5666[5] 7113[3] 7387[3] 7608[7] 7800[3] 7816[8]

Entrapment (AUS) *J Size* 122
5 b g Halo Homewrecker(USA) —Miabondialee (AUS) (Vettori (IRE))
7730a[2]

Epernay *Ian Williams* a78 78
4 b m Tiger Hill(IRE) —Riberac (Efisio)
(2348) 2548[2] (3413) 4215[2] 4275[2] 5593[13] 6383[5] 6888 [5] (7465) 7651[10]

Epic (IRE) *Mark Johnston* a77 89
4 b g Celtic Swing—Needwood Epic (Midyan (USA))
2932[14] 3544[8] 4008[7] 4555[8] 5078[10] (5609) 6037[P] (6419) 6676[7] 7017[9]

Epic Love (IRE) *P Bary* 113
3 b f Dansili—Leopard Hunt (USA) (Diesis)
(1709a) 2342a[2] 2977a[8] 5366a[2] 6568a[6]

Epic Storm (IRE) *Jeremy Noseda* a64 68
3 b c Montjeu(IRE) —Jaya (USA) (Ela-Mana-Mou)
3519[6] 4279[6]

Epoque (USA) *Sir Henry Cecil* 75
2 b f Empire Maker(USA) —Dock Leaf (USA) (Woodman (USA))
6168[3] ◆

Epsom Salts *Pat Phelan* a81 83
6 b g Josr Algarhoud(IRE) —Captive Heart (Conquistador Cielo (USA))
475[8] 718[3] ◆ 805[2] ◆ 1367[11] 3095[9] 4488[2] 5545[2] 5857[4] 6376[7] (6722) 6998[3] (7674)

Eqtiraab (IRE) *Tony Coyle* 61
3 b g Dalakhani(IRE) —Mayara (IRE) (Ashkalani (IRE))
5443[5] 6156[9] 6324[7] 6834[4] 7064[9] 7158[6]

Equation Of Time *David Flood* a49
2 gr c Proclamation(IRE) —Winter Ice (Wolfhound (USA))
7634[10]

Equine Science *Jane Chapple-Hyam* a61 31
4 b g Lucky Owners(NZ) —Miles (Selkirk (USA))
7805[6]

Equinity *Jeff Pearce* a63 52
5 b m Ishiguru(USA) —Notable Lady (IRE) (Victory Note (USA))
22[5]

Equiparada (ARG) *M F De Kock* 102
5 b m Editor's Note(USA) —Equity (ARG) (Equalize (USA))
154a[2] ◆

Equity Card (FR) *Mahmood Al Zarooni* a72 65
2 bb f Dubai Destination(USA) —Snow Ballerina (Sadler's Wells (USA))
4159[U] 4245[4] 4992[3] 6214[2] (6928)

Equuleus Pictor *John Spearing* a67 81
7 br g Piccolo—Vax Rapide (Sharpo)
1140[5] 1444[4] 2585[5] 3261[2] (3711) 3914[5] 4731[5] 5616[7] 5890[6] (6436) 7341[5] 7746[6] 7776[3]

Eraada *Mark Johnston* 72
2 ch f Medicean—Elfaslah (IRE) (Green Desert (USA))
2811[7] 4140[5] (4632) ◆

Eraadaat (IRE) *Ed Dunlop* 54
3 ch f Intikhab(USA) —Ta Rib (USA) (Mr Prospector (USA))
2529[6]

Eragons Dream (IRE) *P Bary* a77 84
4 b h Arakan(USA) —Embraceable (IRE) (Mull Of Kintyre (USA))
7256a[5]

Ereka (IRE) *John Best* a56 44
3 ch f Tau Ceti—Most-Saucy (Most Welcome)
383[3] ◆ 558[7] 1179[4] 1933[6] 2177[9] 3227[6] 4162[4] 5120[8] 6848[3] 7442[3] 7561[2] 7655[2] 7768[6]

Erfaan (USA) *Julie Camacho* a47 59
4 bb g Forest Camp(USA) —Look For Good (USA) (Unbridled's Song (USA))
2162[RR] 2593[11] 3719[9] 4442[8]

Ergo (FR) *James Moffatt* a67 55
7 b h Grand Lodge(USA) —Erhawah (Mark Of Esteem (IRE))
596[6] 6916[9] 7077[10]

Erin Court (JPN) *Kazuhide Sasada* 109
3 bb f Durandal(JPN) —Erin Bird (FR) (Bluebird (USA))
7410a[12]

Erinjay (IRE) *Emmet Michael Butterly* a78 66
5 b g Bachelor Duke(USA) —Quinella (Generous (IRE))
(31) 226[10] (561) (633) (837) 1250[3]

Ermyn Flyer *Pat Phelan* a56 59
2 b f Sakhee(USA) —Famcred (Inchinor)
1235[5] 3257[9] 4319[5] 5197[2] 5577[3] 6817[5] 7342[3]

Ermyn Lodge *Pat Phelan* a82 98
5 br g Singspiel(IRE) —Rosewood Belle (USA) (Woodman (USA))
1847[2] 3013[2] 4775[4] 6690[2]

Ermyntrude *Pat Phelan* a64 63
4 bb m Rock Of Gibraltar(IRE) —Ruthie (Pursuit Of Love)
387[3] (488) 727[8] 3176[8] 3741[3] 4090[5] 4454[2] 5582[3] 6486[9]

Ernest Speak (IRE) *Bill Turner* a49 45
2 b c Jeremy(USA) —Mijouter (IRE) (Coquelin (USA))
2901[9] 3171[6] 3718[4] 4194[12] 4867[6]

Errigal Lad *Garry Woodward* a60 64
6 ch g Bertolini(USA) —La Belle Vie (Indian King (USA))
13[10] 35[3] 150[3] 289[6] 375[5] 641[3] 793[10] 2162[7] 2609[2] 4025[7] 4434[9] 6940[8]

Erroll (SWE) *Patrick Wahl* a63 98
5 ch h King Charlemagne(USA) —Trisha (SWE) (Brief Truce (USA))
2601a[3]

Erycina (IRE) *Noel Wilson* a18 52
3 gr f Aussie Rules(USA) —Golden (FR) (Sanglamore (USA))
7357[10]

Escape Artist *John Bridger* a52 63
4 gr g Act One—Free At Last (Shirley Heights)
118[6] 252[3] 409[7] 2575[5] 3072[7] 3574[9] (4123) 4716[7] (4852) 5403[6] 5622[12] 6264[3] 7228[11] 7394[10]

Escape Route (USA) *S Seemar* a106 103
7 b g Elusive Quality(USA) —Away (USA) (Dixieland Band (USA))
152a[4] 999a[6]

Escape To Glory (USA) *Mikael Magnusson* a85 80
3 b c Bernstein(USA) —Escape To Victory (Salse (USA))
2306[3] 3173[2] 3594[2] (4210) ◆ 4994[4] 5412[3] 6003[3]

Escardo (GER) *David Bridgwater* a66 51
8 b g Silvano(GER) —Epik (GER) (Selkirk (USA))
173[6] 204[3] 346[5] 355[8] 552[9] 573[3] 807[10] 896[8] 968[5] 1253[8] 1374[5] 1625[6] 1763[4] 2233[7] 2450[4] 2600[5]

Escargot (GER) *Y Fertillet* a62 68
5 b g Pentire—Eshaya (GER) (Platini (GER))
42a[2] 220a[7] 832a[0]

Eseej (USA) *Peter Hiatt* a84 78
6 ch g Aljabr(USA) —Jinaan (USA) (Mr Prospector (USA))
104[3] (272) (399) (671)

Esentepe (IRE) *Richard Hannon* 93
2 b f Oratorio(IRE) —Mythie (FR) (Octagonal (NZ))
1726[3] 1981[3] 2309[2] 3152[4] 3424[2] 3761[3] 5464[2] (5807) 7169[3]

Eshaab (USA) *Ed Dunlop* 75
2 bb c Dynaformer(USA) —Jaish (USA) (Seeking The Gold (USA))
5891[7] 6462[4]

Eshoog (IRE) *Phil McEntee* a68 77
3 b f Kyllachy—Catherine Wheel (Primo Dominie)
2855[5] 3222[5] 3461[5] 4923[2] 5176[2] (5346) 5542[9] 5736[2] 6065[8] 6655[12] 6841[12] 7351[11] 7420[13]

Eshtibaak (IRE) *John Gosden* 90
3 b c Dalakhani(IRE) —Nanabanana (IRE) (Anabaa (USA))
1408[5] ◆ (6804) ◆

Eshtyaaq *David Evans* a74 73
4 b g Mark Of Esteem(IRE) —Fleet Hill (IRE) (Warrshan (USA))
11[3] 1443[10] 2224[3] 2793[4] 3817[2] 4348[2] 5273[2] 6171[12]

Esoterica (IRE) *Jim Goldie* 97
8 b g Bluebird(USA) —Mysterious Plans (IRE) (Last Tycoon)
1541[10]

Especially Red (IRE) *Lisa Williamson* 73
2 b f Red Clubs(IRE) —Midnight Special (IRE) (Danetime (IRE))
2992[7] 3767[4] (4250) 4824[P]

Espirita (FR) *E Lellouche* 107
3 b f Iffraaj—Belle Esprit (Warning)
1553a[4] 2137a[6] 2752a[7] 5028a[6] 5772a[8]

Espiritu (FR) *G Al Marri* a86 95
5 b g Dansili—Red Bravo (USA) (Red Ransom (USA))
330a[11] 676a[3] 829a[8]

Esprit Danseur *Jim Boyle* a66 61
2 b f Invincible Spirit(IRE) —Oulianovsk (IRE) (Peintre Celebre (USA))
4720[3] 5323[6] 5814[5] 6372[8]

Esprit De Midas *David Nicholls* a88 97
5 b g Namid—Spritzeria (Bigstone (IRE))
1111[11] 1467[5] 1715[2] 2717[13] (5162) 6113[3] 6331[7]

Espy *Ian McInnes* a73 59
6 b g Piccolo—Running Glimpse (IRE) (Runnett)
683[5] 928[2] 1247[3] 1612[12]

Es Que L[illegible] (IRE) *[illegible]* [illegible]
2 br c Clodovil(IRE) —Es Que (Inchinor)
1827[3] (2485) 2725[2] 3014[9] 3866[5] 4536[2] 5184[11] 5825[8] 6535[9]

Esquinade (FR) *A Bonin* a71 74
2 b f Archange D'Or(IRE) —Estafilade (FR) (Gold Away (IRE))
7449a[7]

Essex Boy *Richard Guest* 23
3 b g Spartacus(IRE) —Polar Rock (Polar Falcon (USA))
3206[8] 5386[U]

Essexvale (IRE) *Alan Berry* a57 66
2 b f Moss Vale(IRE) —Danccalli (IRE) (Traditionally (USA))
2606[8] 5232[2] 5424[6] 5945[4] 6695[13] 7724[5] 7778[6] 7916[5]

Estedaama (IRE) *Marcus Tregoning* 61
2 b f Marju(IRE) —Mohafazaat (IRE) (Sadler's Wells (USA))
4471[10] 5583[8]

Esteem Lord *Dean Ivory* a66 69
5 ch g Mark Of Esteem(IRE) —Milady Lillie (IRE) (Distinctly North (USA))
247[3] 390[3] 625[4] 790[6] 837[2]

Estee Will *John E Long*
4 ch m Mark Of Esteem(IRE) —Irja (Minshaanshu Amad (USA))
7894[8]

Estejo (GER) *R Rohne* 112
7 b h Johan Cruyff—Este (GER) (The Noble Player (USA))
1554a[2] (2134a)

Estimate (IRE) *Sir Michael Stoute* 61
2 b f Monsun(GER) —Ebaziya (IRE) (Darshaan)
5807[7]

Estiqbaal *Saeed Bin Suroor* 49
2 b f Oasis Dream—Manayer (IRE) (Sadler's Wells (USA))
6603[10]

Estithmaar (IRE) *Kevin Prendergast* 88
3 ch c Pivotal—Walayef (USA) (Danzig (USA))
3445a[8]

Estonia *Michael Squance* a82 74
4 b m Exceed And Excel(AUS) —Global Trend (Bluebird (USA))
80[2] ◆ 133[3] 646[3] (766) 910[5] 1196[3] 1309[4] 1864[8] 2603[9] 4207[2] 4416[4] 5412[4] 5914[9] 6351[5] 6932[7] 7106[10] (7201) (7428) 7594[7] 7833[5]

Estourah (IRE) *Saeed Bin Suroor* a91 87
3 b g Dalakhani(IRE) —Canouan (IRE) (Sadler's Wells (USA))
1692[8] 5716[2] 6248[3] 6631[4]

Estrela *Roger Charlton* 85
2 b f Authorized(IRE) —Wannabe Grand (IRE) (Danehill (USA))
6462[5] (7025) ◆

Etarre (IRE) *Gerard Butler* a68 67
3 br f Giant's Causeway(USA) —Speedy Sonata (USA) (Stravinsky (USA))
3133[4]

Etched (USA) *Mahmood Al Zarooni* a124
6 ch h Forestry(USA) —Unbridled Elaine (USA) (Unbridled's Song (USA))
758a[14]

Et Contretout (FR) *Mme C Dufreche* a68 64
8 gr g Nombre Premier—Anvers (FR) (Ganges (USA))
219a[0]

Eternal Heart (IRE) *Mark Johnston* 106
3 b c Alhaarth(IRE) —Lady In Pace (Burslem)
1151[3] (1542) (2228) ◆ (2726) 3108[3] 3875[5] 5271[7] 5471[2] 5883[11] 6498[4] 6857[6]

Eternal Instinct *Jim Goldie* 73
4 b m Exceed And Excel(AUS) —Glenhurich (IRE) (Sri Pekan (USA))
1618[9] 2046[10] 2399[6] ◆ 3162[5] 3387[3] (3662) 3900[3] 4145[8] 4881[7] 5148[11] 5719[9] 6076[11]

Eternal Ruler (IRE) *Alan Swinbank* 84
3 gr g Aussie Rules(USA) —Villafranca (IRE) (In The Wings)
1202[2]

Eternal Youth (IRE) *Ronald Harris* a68 60
3 ch g Intikhab(USA) —Endless Peace (IRE) (Russian Revival (USA))
208[7] 519[4] (787) 929[4] 1056[2] (1334) 1585[3] 3309[9] 3920[6] 4816[8] 5345[8] 5644[4]

Etheldreda (IRE) *Clive Cox* a54 51
3 b f Arch(USA) —Last Tango (IRE) (Lion Cavern (USA))
3043[8] 3550[4]

Ethics Girl (IRE) *John Berry* a89 87
5 b m Hernando(FR) —Palinisa (FR) (Night Shift (USA))
209[5] 342[2] 597[3] 894[2] 1030[7] 3987[4] 4537[12] 5057[8] 5729[3] 6155[3] 6485[4] 6749[5]

Etive (USA) *H-A Pantall* a94 105
3 b f Elusive Quality(USA) —Firth Of Lorne (IRE) (Danehill (USA))
532a[3] 1207a[4] 2137a[15] 3897a[5] 7534a[0]

Etoile Filante (IRE) *Jeremy Gask* a47
4 br m Key Of Luck(USA) —Callisto (IRE) (Darshaan)
33[5] 207[10]

Eton Fable (IRE) *Colin Teague* a64 83
6 b g Val Royal(FR) —Lina Story (Linamix (FR))
352[8] 474[4] 570[2] (670) 797[4] 939[4] 1072[3] 1243[12] 2091[11] 2462[10]

Eton Forever (IRE) *Roger Varian* a96 110
4 b g Oratorio(IRE) —True Joy (IRE) (Zilzal (USA))
(1092) ◆ 1600[4] 3032[5] 5929[2]

Eton Rifles (IRE) *Stuart Williams* 113
6 b g Pivotal—Maritsa (IRE) (Danehill (USA))
1094[5] 3394[4] (5474) 5699[3] 6147[2] (6733a) 7298[4] (7534a)

Etruscan (IRE) *Chris Gordon* a59 71
6 b g Selkirk(USA) —Maddelina (IRE) (Sadler's Wells (USA))
30[5] 299[4] 553[13]

Ettrick Mill *Milton Bradley* a37 45
5 ch g Selkirk(USA) —Milly-M (Cadeaux Genereux)
107[9]

[illegible] (IRE) *Richard Hannon* a90 98
3 b f Acclamation—Satin Rose (Lujain (USA))
1404[3] ◆ 1893[6] 3323[5] 4096[3] 4332[11]

Eupolis (FR) *D Rabhi*
3 b c Loup Solitaire(USA) —Eurybie (FR) (Kendor (FR))
638a[0]

Eureka (IRE) *Richard Hannon* 101
2 b c Kheleyf(USA) —Fancy Theory (USA) (Quest For Fame)
(2181) (3429) ◆ 4094[5] 4495[6] (5826)

Eur Elusive (IRE) *J C Hayden* a70 77
4 b m Elusive City(USA) —Europaea (IRE) (Tagula (IRE))
6388a[3]

Euroears (USA) *Bob Baffert* a121 70
7 ch h Langfuhr(CAN) —Unky And Ally (USA) (Heff (USA))
999a[2] 7302a[9]

European Dream (IRE) *Richard Guest* a72 88
8 br g Kalanisi(IRE) —Tereed Elhawa (Cadeaux Genereux)
180[12] 1517[5] 1713[7] (7161) 7558[12]

Euroquip Boy (IRE) *Michael Scudamore* a64 69
4 b g Antonius Pius(USA) —La Shalak (IRE) (Shalford (IRE))
1912[3] 2554[3] 2921[10] (3512) 3714[5] 4866[6] 5539[17]

Eurystheus (IRE) *Richard Hannon* 79
2 b c Acclamation—Dust Flicker (Suave Dancer (USA))
4535[10] ◆ 5697[4] (6588)

Euston Square *Alistair Whillans* a83 86
5 b g Oasis Dream—Krisia (Kris)
648[5] 1075[7] (1714) 2046[4] 2674[4] 3620[2] (4109) 5435[9] 6079[9] 6346[6] 6708[6]

Evaporation (FR) *C Laffon-Parias* a90 109
4 b m Red Ransom(USA) —Polygreen (FR) (Green Tune (USA))
2744a[3] 3654a[3] 4838a[6] 5772a[2] 6556a[8]

Evelith Regent (IRE) *John Davies* a31 47
8 b g Imperial Ballet(IRE) —No Avail (IRE) (Imperial Frontier (USA))
4441[9] 5405[7]

Evelyn May (IRE) *B W Hills* a81 80
5 b m Acclamation—Lady Eberspacher (IRE) (Royal Abjar (USA))
1140[7]

Evelyns Diamond *Paul Midgley* a34 35
3 b f Act One—Warning Belle (Warning)
5[5] 147[2] 456[7] 494[4] 1151[8] 1413[7]

Even Bolder *Eric Wheeler* a81 81
8 ch g Bold Edge—Level Pegging (IRE) (Common Grounds)
215[3] 701[6] 910[4] 1140[2] 1267[5] 1752[6] 2557[9] 3914[2] 4057[2] 4615[4] 5513[5] 5658[4] 6119[6] 6250[4] 6815[5] 6932[4] 7804[5] 7940[2]

Evening Dress *Mark Johnston* 59
3 ch f Medicean—Miss Hawai (FR) (Peintre Celebre (USA))
3387[7] 3632[12]

Evening In (IRE) *Tony Coyle* 49
3 b f Balmont(USA) —By Candlelight (IRE) (Roi Danzig (USA))
4197[8]

Evening Pinot *Simon Dow* a48 12
3 ch f Auction House(USA) —Lady Of Limerick (IRE) (Thatching)
6591[10] 7093[7] 7659[3]

Evens And Odds (IRE) *Kevin Ryan* a88 110
7 ch g Johannesburg(USA) —Coeur De La Mer (IRE) (Caerleon (USA))
327a[5] 497a[14] (1242) 1687[8] 2370[8] 3155[11] 4042[12] 4534[15] 5060[7] 6147[6] 6875[4] 7253[4]

Even Stevens *David Nicholls* a97 83
3 br g Ishiguru(USA) —Promised (IRE) (Petardia)
(4) 1064[4] (940) 1241[6] 4295[8] 4498[10] 4855[6] 5680[2] 5831[8] 6112[20] 7489[8] (7643)

Ever Cheerful *Andrew Haynes* a66 47
10 b g Atraf—Big Story (Cadeaux Genereux)
1381[6] 210[5] 5891[2]

Evergreen Forest (IRE) *Alastair Lidderdale* a73 73
3 ch g Haafhd—Inaaq (Lammtarra (USA))
1606[7] 2103[8] 2368[5] 5132a[3] 5141[6] 5784[3] (6475) 6789[5] 7075[10]

Everlong *Peter Chapple-Hyam* 89
2 b f Authorized(IRE) —Crooked Wood (USA) (Woodman (USA))
4804[2] ◆ 5565[4] 5885[6]

Ever Roses *Paul Midgley* a56 63
3 br f Pastoral Pursuits—Eljariha (Unfuwain (USA))
41[8] 322[6] 454[6] 741[4] 1323[3] 1465[3] 2249[8] 3192[2] 3248[11] 3950[6] (5010) 5433[5]

Ever The Optimist (IRE) *Stef Higgins* a61 59
3 b g Cape Cross(IRE) —Have Faith (IRE) (Machiavellian (USA))
52[4] ◆ 3232[7] 4340[5]

Evervescent (IRE) *J S Moore* 87
2 b g Elnadim(USA) —Purepleasureseeker (IRE) (Grand Lodge (USA))
1678[5] (2214) 2712[2] 3012[17] 4055[10] 4891[2] 6196a[8] 6535[4]

Everybody Out *Reg Hollinshead* a15
3 b g Striking Ambition—Nanna (IRE) (Danetime (IRE))
513[4] 669[8]

Everyday Dave (CAN) *Wesley A Ward* a89 96
2 b g Weather Warning(USA) —Numerieus (FR) (Numerous (USA))
3064[11]

Everyday Heroes (USA) *Saeed Bin Suroor* a104 104
5 b h Awesome Again(CAN) —Lucette (USA) (Dayjur (USA))
237[3] 602a[9] 754a[7] 825a[10]

Everymanforhimself (IRE) *Kevin Ryan* a94 96
7 b g Fasliyev(USA) —Luisa Demon (IRE) (Barathea (IRE))
105[3] (186) 438[10] 1695[2] 1854[6] 2288[11] 3395[2] 4042[8] 4531[14] 4609[10] 5684[8] 5920[8] 6542[6] (7339) 7439[5]

Evey P (IRE) *[illegible]* [illegible]
4 ch m Choisir(AUS) —Adelaide Pearl (USA) (Skip Away (USA))
380[5] 518[5] 664[5] ◆ 809[11] 1283[5] 1331[4] 1604[8] 1633[6]

Eviction (IRE) *Mandy Rowland* a67 56
4 b g Kheleyf(USA) —La Belle Katherine (USA) (Lyphard (USA))
345[9]

Evident Pride (USA) *Brett Johnson* a83 58
8 b g Chester House(USA) —Proud Fact (USA) (Known Fact (USA))
614[10] 813[3] 965[4] 1636[3] 2372[5] 2721[4]

Ewell Place (IRE) *Robert Mills* 96
2 br g Namid—Miss Gibraltar (Rock Of Gibraltar (IRE))
1598[4] 1835[2] (4710) 5216[3]

Ewenny Star *Bryn Palling* a26
2 b f Indesatchel(IRE) —My Bonus (Cyrano De Bergerac)
7258[11] 7889[12]

Exactness *K J Condon* a38 49
2 b f Strategic Prince—Elusive Kitty (USA) (Elusive Quality (USA))
972a[7]

Excaper (USA) *Ian Black* a93 110
2 rg c Exchange Rate(USA) —Ada Ruckus (CAN) (Bold Ruckus (USA))
7301a[2]

Excavator *Roger Charlton* a72 72
2 b g Bahamian Bounty—Digger Girl (USA) (Black Minnaloushe (USA))
1628[2] 2602[2] 3539[2] 5562[14]

Exceedance *Bryan Smart* a81 72
2 ch c Exceed And Excel(AUS) —Hill Welcome (Most Welcome)
2261[2] 6892[4] (7194)

Exceeded *Robert Johnson*
3 b f Exceed And Excel(AUS) —Wings Of Love (Groom Dancer (USA))
5793[12] 6343[15]

Exceedingly Bold *Jo Crowley* a74 84
4 b g Exceed And Excel(AUS) —Grey Pearl (Ali-Royal (IRE))
666[4] 806[7] 1488[6] 2870[12] 3735[7]

Exceedingly Good (IRE) *Roy Bowring* a64 59
5 ch m Exceed And Excel(AUS) —Ikan (IRE) (Sri Pekan (USA))
(793) 893[11] 1497[2] 1815[2] 1875[4] 2845[11] 3096[6] 3248[4] 3495[6] 3937[8] 4563[10]

Exceedingthestars *Michael Squance*
4 b m Exceed And Excel(AUS) —Starbeck (IRE) (Spectrum (IRE))
1065[11] 1358[7] 1591[11]

Excel Bolt *Bryan Smart* 101
3 ch c Exceed And Excel(AUS) —Dearest Daisy (Forzando)
1711[4] 7018[17]

Excelebration (IRE) *Marco Botti* 129
3 b c Exceed And Excel(AUS) —Sun Shower (IRE) (Indian Ridge)
1405[2] ◆ (2338a) 3011[3] (5046) ◆ (5988a) 6860[2]

Excelette (IRE) *Bryan Smart* 99
2 b f Exceed And Excel(AUS) —Madam Ninette (Mark Of Esteem (IRE))
1876[4] 3165[2] 3504[2] (3849) (4502) 4999[2] 5286[3] 6535[2] 7135[2]

Excellence (IRE) *Karen George* a41 24
3 b f Exceed And Excel(AUS) —Aphra Benn (IRE) (In The Wings)
1179[6] 1449[7] 1753[11] 2384[8] 7610[9]

Excellent Aim *George Margarson* a67 71
4 b g Exceed And Excel(AUS) —Snugfit Annie (Midyan (USA))
2270[3] 2829[10] 7245[2] (7460) 7587[3] 7896[2]

Excellent Guest *George Margarson* 102
4 b g Exceed And Excel(AUS) —Princess Speedfit (FR) (Desert Prince (IRE))
(1594) 1885[10] 3109[2] 3862[2] ◆ 4314[13]

Excellent Jem *George Margarson* 72
2 b c Exceed And Excel(AUS) —Polar Jem (Polar Falcon (USA))
6064[3] 6629[5] 7080[7]

Excellent News (IRE) *J W Hills* a63 59
2 ch f Excellent Art—Subito (Darshaan)
6603[14] 7030[7] 7344[6] 7653[6]

Excellent Show *Bryan Smart* a89 82
5 ch m Exceed And Excel(AUS) —Quiz Show (Primo Dominie)
168[8] (403) 521[6] 1279[8]

Excellent Vision *Milton Bradley* a61 54
4 b g Exceed And Excel(AUS) —Classic Vision (Classic Cliche (IRE))
1171[10] 1523[11] 2142[11] 2869[12] 3480[2] 3726[6] 3945[6] 4953[13] 5248[4] (5606) 5943[8] 6083[10] 6310[6] 6657[6] 7270[2] 7370[6] 7571[8] 7740[3] 7848[6]

Excello *Malcolm Saunders* a87 95
3 b f Exceed And Excel(AUS) —Muffled (USA) (Mizaaya)
3181[8]

Exceptionally (NZ) *Terry & Karina O'Sullivan* 113
5 bb m Ekraar(USA) —Sahayb (NZ) (Zabeel (NZ))
6711a[14]

Exchange *Andrew Haynes* a70 73
3 b g Kheleyf(USA) —Quantum Lady (Mujadil (USA))
873[5] 1176[5] (1323) (1578) (2024) 2453[4] 3318[12] (4338) 4550[10] 5041[3] 5835[6] 6794[12] 6944[3] 7057[14]

Exciting Life (IRE) *P Schiergen* 102
3 b c Titus Livius(FR) —Puerto Oro (IRE) (Entrepreneur)
(2520a) 3531a[8] 5985a[8] 6594a[2] 7311a[3]

Excuse Me *Kevin Ryan* a58
3 b g Diktat—After You (Pursuit Of Love)
937[6] 2125[9] 7739[4]

Excusez Moi (USA) *Ruth Carr* a58 90
9 b g Fusaichi Pegasus(USA) —Jiving (Generous (IRE))
321[6] 376[7] 1906[3] 2431[4] 2668[6]

Exemplary *Mark Johnston* a96 93
4 b g Sulamani(IRE) —Epitome (IRE) (Nashwan (USA))
(342) (486) 1030[6] 1412[3] 1679[8] 4423[3] 4775[10] 5221[15] 5705[14] 6988[2]

Exeptional Girl *Frank Sheridan*
5 b m Medicean—Crimson Rosella (Polar Falcon (USA))
7856[7]

Exhibition (IRE) *Francisco Castro* a97 96
6 b g Invincible Spirit(IRE) —Moonbi Ridge (IRE) (Definite Article)
4483a[2]

Exit Smiling *Paul Midgley* a69 91
9 ch g Dr Fong(USA) —Away To Me (Exit To Nowhere (USA))
548[6] 870[6] 1292[8]

Exning Halt *James Fanshawe* 54
2 b g Rail Link—Phi Phi (IRE) (Fasliyev (USA))
4159[8] 7109[6]

Exocet Missile (IRE) *Ann Duffield* a8
3 b g Majestic Missile(IRE) —Memphis Raines (IRE) (Revoque (IRE))
855[6]

Exodus *A P O'Brien* 94
3 b c Montjeu(IRE) —Spacecraft (USA) (Distant View (USA))
1004a[2] 1259a[6]

Exopuntia *Julia Feilden* a63 61
5 b m Sure Blade(USA) —Opuntia (Rousillon (USA))
19[4] 148[2] 181[8] 3130[3] 4185[6] 4278[3] 4927[5] 5014[16] 5515[11] 6938[2] 7711[7] 7885[6]

Ex Oriente (IRE) *John Gosden* a63 71
2 b g Azamour(IRE) —Little Whisper (IRE) (Be My Guest (USA))
3182[13] 3590[5] 4919[4] 6031[9]

Exotic Dream (FR) *Ronald Harris* a51 64
5 b m Fantastic Light(USA) —Elouallee (FR) (Anabaa (USA))
2159[U] 2436[12] 3311[6] 3391[4] 3712[7] 3923[6]

Expense Claim (IRE) *Andrew Balding* 70
2 b g Intikhab(USA) —Indolente (IRE) (Diesis)
4091[5] 4535[7] 6244[3]

Expensive Legacy *Tor Sturgis* a31 56
4 ch m Piccolo—American Rouge (IRE) (Grand Lodge (USA))
7639^{12}

Expensive Problem *Ralph Smith* a77 73
8 b g Medicean—Dance Steppe (Rambo Dancer (CAN))
82^{7}

Experience (IRE) *David Wachman* 99
2 b f Excellent Art—Kloonlara (IRE) (Green Desert (USA))
(3416a) $3884a^{4}$ $5522a^{2}$ $5950a^{4}$

Experimentalist *Hughie Morrison* a67 76
3 b g Monsieur Bond(IRE) —Floppie (FR) (Law Society (USA))
1683^{4} 2226^{3} 2768^{3} 3233^{4} 3587^{5}

Expert Fighter (USA) *Saeed Bin Suroor* 79
2 ch c Dubai Destination(USA) —Porto Roca (AUS) (Barathea (IRE))
6334^{7} (6812)

Expose *William Haggas* a76 94
3 ch g Compton Place—Show Off (Efisio)
2772^{2} (3136)

Extra (ITY) *L Riccardi* 64
3 b f Oasis Dream—Egesia (Kaldoun (FR))
$1738a^{10}$

Extra Steps (IRE) *Paul Cashman* a74 71
3 b f Footstepsinthesand—Extraordinary (IRE) (Swain (IRE))
$973a^{4}$ $1663a^{4}$

Extraterrestrial *Richard Fahey* a105 96
7 b g Mind Games—Expectation (IRE) (Night Shift (USA))
1110^{6} (2115) ◆ 2679^{6} 3315^{4} 3831^{2} 4325^{3} 5059^{6} 6150^{2} 6335^{4} 6672^{2} $7189a^{6}$

Eyedoro (USA) *Mark Johnston* a75 76
3 bb g Medaglia D'Oro(USA) —Critical Eye (USA) (Dynaformer (USA))
6349^{3} 6614^{2} 6810^{3} 7255^{10}

Eyeforglory *Suzzanne France* 29
5 b m Grape Tree Road—Blackburn Meadows (Flying Tyke)
6264^{7} 7061^{11} 7503^{12}

Eye For The Girls *Les Hall* 59
5 ch g Bertolini(USA) —Aunt Ruby (USA) (Rubiano (USA))
2920^{17}

Eyes On *Philip McBride* a59 64
3 b f Diktat—Almost Amber (USA) (Mt. Livermore (USA))
1400^{9} 1958^{10} 2827^{7}

Eyes On Me (IRE) *J E Hammond* a78 93
5 b m Celtic Swing—Golden (FR) (Sanglamore (USA))
$6958a^{7}$

Ezalli (IRE) *Edward Lynam* 101
4 b m Cape Cross(IRE) —Ezilla (IRE) (Darshaan)
$3444a^{2}$

Ezdeyaad (USA) *Ed Walker* a92 98
7 b g Lemon Drop Kid(USA) —August Storm (USA) (Storm Creek (USA))
438^{8} 615^{4} ◆ 1240^{11} 1529^{15} 2105^{6} (2428) 3542^{9} 3982^{7} 4997^{2} 5319^{3} 5734^{6}

Ezra Church (IRE) *David Barron* a80 78
4 br g Viking Ruler(AUS) —Redrightreturning (Diktat)
(454) 1245^{5} 1800^{2} 1942^{4} 7502^{8} (7658) 7876^{3}

Ezzles (USA) *Alan McCabe* a65 52
3 bb g Speightstown(USA) —Paris Glory (USA) (Honour And Glory (USA))
1040^{9} 1334^{2} 3321^{6} 3470^{9}

Fabled City (USA) *Clive Cox* a70 70
2 ch c Johannesburg(USA) —Fabulous Fairy (USA) (Alydar (USA))
6725^{8} 6992^{3} 7330^{3}

Fabreze *Peter Makin* a96 90
6 ch g Choisir(AUS) —Impulsive Decision (IRE) (Nomination)
3784^{7} 4765^{3} (5683) 6174^{8} ◆

Fabulouslyspirited *Ralph Beckett* a84 59
3 b f Selkirk(USA) —Fabulously Fast (USA) (Deputy Minister (CAN))
4340^{3} ◆ 5030^{3} (5999) 6996^{14} 7339^{14} 7486^{9}

Face East (USA) *Alan Berry* 42
3 b g Orientate(USA) —Yes Honey (USA) (Royal Academy (USA))
1860^{9} 2265^{13} 2697^{4} 3455^{7} 3661^{12} 4172^{5}

Face Reality (USA) *David Marnane* a92 95
3 ch f More Than Ready(USA) —Tivadare (FR) (Distant View (USA))
$1928a^{8}$ $5228a^{10}$ $7277a^{7}$ 7516^{10}

Face The Problem (IRE) *Charles Hills* 102
3 b g Johannesburg(USA) —Foofaraw (USA) (Cherokee Run (USA))
1186^{3} 1852^{5} 2724^{4} 3181^{7} 3820^{14} 4859^{4} ◆ 5180^{15} 7018^{3} ◆

Face Value *Brian Meehan* a70 60
3 b g Tobougg(IRE) —Zia (GER) (Grand Lodge (USA))
1481^{7} 2885^{8} 3325^{9}

Factor Three *Michael Appleby* a33 23
2 ro g Three Valleys(USA) —Desert Daisy (IRE) (Desert Prince (IRE))
3554^{5} 6652^{10}

Factory Time (IRE) *Mick Channon* a87 107
2 b c Baltic King—Mark One (Mark Of Esteem (IRE))
(1451) (2868) 4055^{3} 4495^{9} 5286^{7} 5849^{2} 6162^{5} 6689^{6}

Fadela Style (FR) *F Rossi* a89 106
4 b m Desert Style(IRE) —Tounsi (FR) (Sendawar (IRE))
$5075a^{5}$ $7404a^{2}$

Fadhaa (IRE) *Charles Hills* a82 90
3 b c Bahri(USA) —Weqaar (USA) (Red Ransom (USA))
(1298) ◆ 1811^{2} 3291^{6} 3774^{13} 4723^{2} 5483^{9} 6063^{2}

Failasoof (USA) *B W Hills* a84 57
3 bb c Dynaformer(USA) —Curriculum (USA) (Danzig (USA))
(909) ◆ 1365^{5}

Fair Attitude (IRE) *Robert Collet* a55 57
7 b g King's Theatre(IRE) —No Way (IRE) (Rainbows For Life (CAN))
$706a^{0}$

Fair Boss (IRE) *W Hickst* 111
3 ch c Mamool(IRE) —Fair Dream (GER) (Dashing Blade)
$6200a^{2}$ $7045a^{8}$

Fair Breeze *Richard Phillips* a57 27
4 b m Trade Fair—Soft Touch (IRE) (Petorius)
2922^{10} 3804^{8} 4705^{12} (5349) 5912^{14} 6486^{3} 6811^{7} 7006^{2} 7270^{5} 7805^{7}

Fair Bunny *Alan Brown* a54 57
4 b m Trade Fair—Coney Hills (Beverley Boy)
107^{6} 375^{11} 3573^{14} 4196^{3} 4987^{8} 5620^{2} 7064^{7} (7230) 7419^{13}

Fair Dinkum (IRE) *Jamie Osborne* a53
3 gr g Aussie Rules(USA) —Set Fair (USA) (Alleged (USA))
4180^{8} 4868^{3} 5415^{5} 5832^{11} 6446^{11}

Fairest Isle (IRE) *James Fanshawe* a57 40
3 b f Intikhab(USA) —Eilean Shona (Suave Dancer (USA))
1991^{8} 5607^{4} 6086^{3} ◆ 6621^{8} 6838^{9}

Fairhope (GER) *Barbara Sofsky* 73
9 bb g Protektor(GER) —Fairlight (GER) (Big Shuffle (USA))
$6594a^{10}$

Fairlie Dinkum *Bryan Smart* a62 78
3 b f Tobougg(IRE) —Fairlie (Halling (USA))
1251^{5} (2264) 2986^{2} 3278^{3} 7024^{17}

Fairling *Hughie Morrison* a27 69
3 ch f Halling(USA) —Fairy Story (IRE) (Persian Bold)
3689^{4} 4157^{11} 4617^{7} (5665) 6136^{6} 6756^{11}

Fair Passion *Derek Shaw* a83 52
4 b m Trade Fair—United Passion (Emarati (USA))
430^{8} 554^{7} 708^{12} 1048^{5} 1196^{2} ◆ 1309^{2} (1584) 1816^{3} (4988) 5484^{5}

Fair Value (IRE) *Simon Dow* a92 90
3 b f Compton Place—Intriguing Glimpse (Piccolo)
(1020) 1758^{3} 2158^{4} 5115^{10} (5627) (6217) 6272^{4}

Fairyhall *B Grizzetti* 92
3 b c Halling(USA) —Fairy Sensazione (Fairy King (USA))
$1920a^{10}$

Fairyinthewind (IRE) *Paul D'Arcy* a71 62
2 ch f Indian Haven—Blue Daze (Danzero (AUS))
2063^{3} 5323^{9} 6131^{6} 7223^{2} ◆ (7342)

Fairy Mist (IRE) *Brian Rothwell* a50 57
4 b g Oratorio(IRE) —Prealpina (IRE) (Indian Ridge)
2361^{5} 2802^{5} 3075^{5} 3683^{6} 4112^{4} 4442^{6} 4903^{7} 5178^{8} 5822^{5} (6050) 6310^{4} 7061^{9} 7246^{11}

Fairy Moss (IRE) *David Evans* 45
2 b f Amadeus Wolf—Frond (Alzao (USA))
1870^{3} 2563^{4} 3388^{7} 4708^{5} 7051^{16}

Fairy Pose *Amanda Perrett* 73
3 b f Azamour(IRE) —Plum Fairy (Sadler's Wells (USA))
2836^{6} 3907^{2} 4753^{8}

Fairys In A Storm (IRE) *Alan Lockwood* 37
4 gr m Choisir(AUS) —Fidra (IRE) (Vettori (IRE))
6049^{13}

Fairy Tales *John Bridger* a62 45
3 ch f Monsieur Bond(IRE) —True Magic (Magic Ring (IRE))
44^{3} 246^{2} 338^{7} 620^{2} 721^{4} 1149^{3} 1359^{6} 2025^{7} 3254^{5} 3476^{11} 4057^{6} 4247^{7} 4796^{7} 5381^{12} 6943^{9} 7224^{9}

Faith And Hope (IRE) *James Fanshawe* a52 65
3 ro f Barathea(IRE) —Santa Sophia (IRE) (Linamix (FR))
624^{5} 1974^{10} 2529^{4} 3633^{9} 5803^{6} 6653^{4} 6938^{12}

Faithful One (IRE) *F Doumen* a90 87
4 b m Dubawi(IRE) —Have Faith (IRE) (Machiavellian (USA))
$6783a^{9}$

Faithful Ruler (USA) *Ronald Harris* a84 90
7 bb g Elusive Quality(USA) —Fancy Ruler (USA) (Half A Year (USA))
(175) 427^{3} 447^{2} 599^{2} 790^{4} 1017^{3} 1448^{5} 1976^{2} (7412) 7518^{5} 7876^{4}

Faith Jicaro (IRE) *Nicky Vaughan* a68 76
4 b m One Cool Cat(USA) —Wings To Soar (USA) (Woodman (USA))
114^{4} 277^{6} 444^{6}

Fa'lz (IRE) *Saeed Bin Suroor* a77 80
2 b c Dansili—Carisolo (Dubai Millennium)
4726^{4} 5269^{2} ◆ 5861^{2} 6532^{2} 7133^{3}

Fajer Al Kuwait *George Prodromou* a51 19
3 b g Byron—Sweetypie (IRE) (Golan (IRE))
3089^{8}

Fakhuur *Clive Brittain* a83 56
3 b f Dansili—Halska (Unfuwain (USA))
6473^{2} 7250^{3} (7745) 7877^{11}

Falasteen (IRE) *Kevin Ryan* a79 100
4 ch g Titus Livius(FR) —Law Review (IRE) (Case Law)
651^{11} 970^{5} ◆ 1166^{2} 1395^{14} (1476) 1809^{6} 2028^{2} 2714^{9} 5180^{19} 5706^{13} 6332^{14}

Falcativ *I Mohammed* a86 86
6 b g Falbrav(IRE) —Frottola (Muhtarram (USA))
$756a^{11}$

Falcharge *S Sordi* 90
5 b h Falbrav(IRE) —Polar Charge (Polar Falcon (USA))
$220a^{0}$

Falcun *Micky Hammond* a30 65
4 b g Danehill Dancer(IRE) —Fanofadiga (IRE) (Alzao (USA))
1617^{2} ◆ 2462^{5} 3187^{2} 4326^{2} 4671^{3} 5651^{2}

Faldal *Michael Quinlan* a42 85
5 br m Falbrav(IRE) —Tidal (Bin Ajwaad (IRE))
272^{8}

Fallen For You *John Gosden* 111
2 b f Dansili—Fallen Star (Brief Truce (USA))
(4552) ◆ 5885^{2} 6299^{5}

Fallen Idol *John Gosden* a82 113
4 b h Pivotal—Fallen Star (Brief Truce (USA))
3591^{5} 4789^{5} (5275) 5829^{4} 6247^{2}

Fallible *Tony Carroll* 33
2 b c Piccolo—Fittonia (FR) (Ashkalani (IRE))
4823^{12} 5480^{14} 5889^{13}

Falls Of Lora (IRE) *Mahmood Al Zarooni* 99
2 b f Street Cry(IRE) —Firth Of Lorne (IRE) (Danehill (USA))
2187^{2} ◆ (2709) 3152^{8} 3866^{4} (5698) ◆ $6564a^{5}$

Falmouth Bay (USA) *Mark Johnston* a83 64
3 rg c Elusive Quality(USA) —Halo America (USA) (Waquoit (USA))
(368) 750^{2} 2096^{7} 2684^{11} 3081^{7} 3614^{4} 3959^{10}

Famagusta *Peter Charalambous* a46 47
4 b m Sakhee(USA) —Gitane (FR) (Grand Lodge (USA))
3224^{11} 4163^{6} 5140^{6} 7087^{3} 7527^{7} 7688^{3}

Fama Mac *Neville Bycroft* 63
4 b g Fraam—Umbrian Gold (IRE) (Perugino (USA))
1245^{10} 2388^{8} 3074^{9} 5470^{7} 7063^{7}

Fame And Glory *A P O'Brien* 125
5 b h Montjeu(IRE) —Gryada (Shirley Heights)
(1427a) (2534a) (3066) $5291a^{2}$ $5952a^{4}$ (6857)

Family One (FR) *Y Barberot* 111
2 b c Dubai Destination(USA) —Ascot Family (IRE) (Desert Style (IRE))
(3669a) (4375a) $5305a^{2}$ 6688^{10}

Famous Name *D K Weld* 123
6 b h Dansili—Fame At Last (USA) (Quest For Fame)
(1930a) $2332a^{3}$ (3371a) (4259a) $4599a^{2}$ $5747a^{3}$ $6558a^{4}$

Famous Poet (IRE) *Saeed Bin Suroor* 76
2 b c Exceed And Excel(AUS) —Asfurah (USA) (Dayjur (USA))
5855^{5} (6483)

Famous Warrior (IRE) *Doug Watson* a101 101
4 b g Alhaarth(IRE) —Oriental Fashion (IRE) (Marju (IRE))
240^{12} $497a^{5}$ ◆ (604a) $756a^{8}$

Famusa *Marco Botti* a101 101
4 b m Medicean—Step Danzer (IRE) (Desert Prince (IRE))
7296^{6} 7606^{2} ◆

Fancourt *William Muir* a22
3 b f Diktat—Santorini (USA) (Spinning World (USA))
7829^{7}

Fancy Diamond (GER) *J-M Capitte* a58 92
5 b m Ransom O'War(USA) —Francais (Mark Of Esteem (IRE))
$257a^{7}$

Fanditha (IRE) *Mick Channon* a93 98
5 ch m Danehill Dancer(IRE) —Splendid (IRE) (Mujtahid (USA))
(908) (963) 1104^{8} 1851^{4} 3356^{2} 4095^{7} 4293^{4} 4915^{11} $5075a^{11}$

Fanny May *Denis Coakley* a67 91
3 b f Nayef(USA) —Sweet Wilhelmina (Indian Ridge)
2839^{5} 4022^{2} 4429^{9} 5546^{2} 6822^{12}

Fanoos *John Gosden* 71
2 b f Dutch Art—Miss Otis (Danetime (IRE))
1657^{4} 6758^{4} 7056^{2}

Fanrouge (IRE) *Malcolm Saunders* a13 87
2 b f Red Clubs(IRE) —Silk Fan (IRE) (Unfuwain (USA))
1957^{9} 2374^{10} (2901) 3800^{2} (3993) (4226) 5701^{2} 6166^{10} 6518^{11}

Fantale *David Evans* a38
3 ch f Arakan(USA) —Question (USA) (Coronado's Quest (USA))
43^{6} 333^{4} 558^{12}

Fantasia *Jonathan E Sheppard* 112
5 b m Sadler's Wells(USA) —Blue Symphony (Darshaan)
$5073a^{4}$

Fantastic Smartie *David Evans* a62 60
2 b f Fantastic Spain(USA) —Smart Cassie (Allied Forces (USA))
5347^{2} 5863^{4} 6492^{8}

Fantastic Song (USA) *Chad C Brown* 99
2 b c Lemon Drop Kid(USA) —Fantastic Shirl (USA) (Fantastic Light (USA))
$7301a^{10}$

Fantastic Storm *Robin Bastiman* 45
4 b g Fantastic Light(USA) —Answered Prayer (Green Desert (USA))
2272^{6} 2618^{5} 3622^{10} 4499^{9} 5122^{5}

Fantastic Times *Mel Brittain* 32
5 b g Fantastic Light(USA) —Goodnight Kiss (Night Shift (USA))
6097^{6} 6349^{10}

Fantasy Explorer *John Quinn* a93 82
8 b g Compton Place—Zinzi (Song)
613^{9} 961^{9} 2069^{5} 2645^{2} 3383^{7} 3588^{5} 3847^{4} 4583^{2}

Fantasy Fighter (IRE) *John E Long* a79 54
6 b g Danetime(IRE) —Lady Montekin (Montekin)
105^{8} 336^{3} 521^{8} 577^{5} 867^{7} 1912^{11} 2920^{5} 3517^{5} 3956^{4} 4206^{8} 5736^{10} 5895^{4} 6282^{6} 6930^{4} 7488^{4}

Fantasy Fry *Tom Dascombe* a77 68
3 b g Avonbridge—Footlight Fantasy (USA) (Nureyev (USA))
228^{7} 494^{2} (672) (739) 1452^{4} 1745^{10} 2199^{11} 3493^{8} 7243^{11} 7425^{13} 7591^{8} 7820^{3}

Fantasy Gladiator *Robert Cowell* a93 89
5 b g Ishiguru(USA) —Fancier Bit (Lion Cavern (USA))
2111^{5} 2647^{6} 2909^{4} ◆ 3290^{6} 3797^{5} 4268^{2} 5240^{6} 5516^{2} 5712^{3} 6069^{6} 6273^{9} (7110) 7393^{9}

Fantasy Hero *Ronald Harris* a14 42
2 br c Notnowcato—Pearly River (Elegant Air)
4545^{7} 5142^{7}

Fantasy King *Charles O'Brien* a87 81
5 b g Acclamation—Fantasy Ridge (Indian Ridge)
$4398a^{19}$ (7544a)

Fantino *John Mackie* a78 76
5 b g Shinko Forest(IRE) —Illustre Inconnue (USA) (Septieme Ciel (USA))
2475^{6} 2892^{12} 4237^{7} 5650^{8} 6666^{3}

Fanunalter *Marco Botti* a111 118
5 b g Falbrav(IRE) —Step Danzer (IRE) (Desert Prince (IRE))
$503a^{2}$ $828a^{3}$ (2713) 3843^{2} 4972^{5} ◆ $6369a^{4}$

Faranadooney (USA) *Ms Joanna Morgan* a51 69
4 bb g Sahm(USA) —Sarina's Princess (USA) (Captain Bodgit (USA))
7357^{5}

Farang Kondiew *Declan Carroll* 80
2 ch c Selkirk(USA) —Passiflora (Night Shift (USA))
1691^{6} ◆ 2504^{3} (6075)

Farasha (FR) *M Boutin* a62 82
2 gr f Layman(USA) —Mixture (Linamix (FR))
$7814a^{0}$

Faraway *Ronald Harris* a70 65
2 b c Royal Applause—Somersault (Pivotal)
2143^{6} 2644^{5} 3016^{5} (3584) 3842^{4} 4069^{5} 4460^{7} 5625^{5} (6178) 6284^{4} 6471^{3} 6699^{7} 6972^{8} 7390^{5} (7694) 7881^{4} 7907^{2}

Fareedha (IRE) *John Dunlop* a63 67
2 b f Green Desert(USA) —Shahaamah (IRE) (Red Ransom (USA))
5480^{11} 6030^{4} 6820^{5}

Fareej (USA) *I Mohammed* a63 90
4 b h Kingmambo(USA) —Adonesque (IRE) (Sadler's Wells (USA))
$707a^{12}$

Fareer *Ed Dunlop* a100 112
5 ch g Bahamian Bounty—Songsheet (Dominion)
$332a^{16}$ $604a^{4}$ $682a^{3}$ $828a^{2}$ 1385^{5} 2031^{8} 3032^{8} 3843^{5} 4410^{10} 5218^{13}

Far Flung (IRE) *Jim Best* 62
4 b m Rakti—Fling (Pursuit Of Love)
3734^{2} 4165^{4}

Far From Old (IRE) *Michael Bell* a24 101
8 b g Vettori(IRE) —Jabali (FR) (Shirley Heights)
597^{5}

Farhaan (USA) *John Dunlop* 98
2 b c Jazil(USA) —Alshadiyah (USA) (Danzig (USA))
4054^{2} ◆ (5011) ◆ (5654) 6336^{5}

Farhan (FR) *C Lerner* a60 78
5 b g Okawango(USA) —Arolla (FR) (Shareef Dancer (USA))
$1142a^{9}$

Farhh *Saeed Bin Suroor* 107
3 b c Pivotal—Gonbarda (GER) (Lando (GER))
(7168) ◆

Farleaze *Brian Meehan* 73
2 b f Rail Link—Monkshill (Fraam)
3813^{9} 4552^{4} 6458^{5} 6950^{8}

Farleigh *Alex Hales* a52 74
5 b m Trans Island—Medway (IRE) (Shernazar)
418^{12} 631^{10} 1273^{13}

Farleigh House (USA) *Neil King* a82 34
7 b g Lear Fan(USA) —Verasina (USA) (Woodman (USA))
235^{9} 3366^{9}

Farlino (FR) *J-P Delaporte* a76 66
7 b h Trempolino(USA) —Far Mist (FR) (River Mist (USA))
$617a^{5}$ $935a^{0}$

Farlow (IRE) *Ralph Beckett* a66 94
3 ch g Exceed And Excel(AUS) —Emly Express (IRE) (High Estate)
(3075) (3785) 4078^{4} (4797) 5000^{2} 5852^{9}

Farmers Dream (IRE) *Richard Price* a53 60
4 b m Antonius Pius(USA) —Beucaire (IRE) (Entrepreneur)
169^{6} 382^{8} 5143^{4} 5539^{3} 5674^{6} 6309^{11} 7119^{9}

Farmers Glory *Neil King* a38 53
4 b g Mujahid(USA) —Action De Grace (USA) (Riverman (USA))
433^{7}

Farmers Hill *Mark Hoad* a44 44
3 ch g Dalakhani(IRE) —Wemyss Bight (Dancing Brave (USA))
3001^{13} 3781^{7} 4989^{6} 5916^{9} 7091^{6} 7333^{11} 7891^{7}

Farmer's Wife *Bernard Llewellyn* a57 31
3 b f Bertolini(USA) —Lady Mayor (Kris)
171^{7} 424^{5} 543^{5} 817^{5} 951^{7} 4645^{7} 4953^{14} 6767^{13}

Farmleigh House (IRE) *W J Martin* a81 48
4 ch g Medecis—Tabessa (USA) (Shahrastani (USA))
(7790a) ◆

Farraaj (IRE) *Roger Varian* 110
2 b c Dubai Destination(USA) —Pastorale (Nureyev (USA))
4446^{2} ◆ (5564) (6060) ◆ 6270^{2} $7301a^{3}$

Farrel (IRE) *B Grizzetti* 102
6 b g Fruits Of Love(USA) —Folcungi (IRE) (Mukaddamah (USA))
$1919a^{9}$

Far View (IRE) *George Baker* a69 51
4 b g Oasis Dream—Night Mirage (USA) (Silver Hawk (USA))
(683) 734^{7} 1041^{2} 1182^{9} 1581^{11} 1838^{12}

Farzan (IRE) *Tim Easterby* 59
2 b c Elusive City(USA) —Brosna Time (IRE) (Danetime (IRE))
4347^{11} 4853^{6} 5161^{9} 5755^{9} 6092^{4} 6293^{12} 6597^{9}

Fascinating (IRE) *Mark Johnston* a87 50
3 b c Cape Cross(IRE) —Something Exciting (Halling (USA))
2848^{10} 3267^{7} 6377^{5} ◆ 6756^{6} (6873) (7037) ◆ (7121) ◆

Fashion (GER) *A Wohler* 78
2 b f Anabaa(USA) —Felina (GER) (Acatenango (GER))
$5610a^{8}$

Fashionable Gal (IRE) *Neil King* a84 85
4 b m Galileo(IRE) —Fashion (Bin Ajwaad (IRE))
(687) 814^{2} (1183) ◆ 1388^{6} 3170^{2} (4090) 6330^{11} 6996^{2}

Fashion Icon (USA) *David O'Meara* a72 67
5 ch m Van Nistelrooy(USA) —Los Altos (USA) (Robin Des Pins (USA))
62^{3} 318^{7} 794^{7} 1034^{11} 1204^{2} 1411^{15} 1503^{5} 1555^{7}

Fashion's Flight (USA) *Brian Meehan* 71
2 bb f Dixie Union(USA) —General Jeanne (USA) (Honour And Glory (USA))
4804[5] 5445[4] 6205a[2]

Fasilight *Braem Horse Racing Sprl* a69 63
4 b m Fasliyev(USA) —Rajmata (IRE) (Prince Sabo)
6593a[6]

Fastada (IRE) *Jonathan Portman* a42 66
3 b f Holy Roman Emperor(IRE) —Mellow Park (IRE) (In The Wings)
1997[13] 3268[14] 3690[7] 4827[4] 4953[3] 5512[4] 6437[4] 6823[5] 6968[7]

Fast Connection (IRE) *F Poulsen* a57 51
3 b f Redback—Catch A Smile (USA) (Silver Hawk (USA))
852a[5]

Fast Draw *P Vovcenko* a66 56
3 b f Striking Ambition—Mosquera's Rock (IRE) (Rock Of Gibraltar (IRE))
5463a[9]

Fast Elaine (IRE) *Martin Bosley* a26 33
4 ch m Bahamian Bounty—Miss A Note (USA) (Miswaki (USA))
943[12] 1135[10]

Fast Finian (IRE) *M Halford* a73 76
2 gr c Clodovil(IRE) —Delphie Queen (IRE) (Desert Sun)
7273a[3]

Fast Freddie *Mrs A Corson* a76 55
7 b g Agnes World(USA) —Bella Chica (IRE) (Bigstone (IRE))
1804a[RR]

Fastidious *D K Weld* 74
2 b g Exceed And Excel(AUS) —Felicitous (King's Best (USA))
2329a[5]

Fastinthestraight (IRE) *Jim Boyle* a68 27
4 b g Catcher In The Rye(IRE) —La Colombari (ITY) (Lomond (USA))
86[8] (355) ◆ (466) ◆ 645[10] 2905[7] 3176[4] (4549) 5042[6]

Fastnet Storm (IRE) *David Barron* a95 96
5 br g Rock Of Gibraltar(IRE) —Dreams (Rainbow Quest (USA))
2604[14] 3203[6] 4109[2] 4537[16] 5593[7] 6346[13] 6708[10] 7877[10]

Fastnette (IRE) *Ian Wood* a48
4 b m Fasliyev(USA) —Nanette (Hernando (FR))
5633[5] 6307[8]

Fast On (IRE) *Ed McMahon* a66 65
2 gr c Verglas(IRE) —Dream State (IRE) (Machiavellian (USA))
2374[8] 2983[3] 3921[4] 4538[3] 5374[3] 6284[2] 6645[7]

Fast Or Free *William Haggas* 60
2 ch c Notnowcato—Ewenny (Warrshan (USA))
6951[6]

Fast Samurai (USA) *David Simcock* a32 54
3 ch c First Samurai(USA) —Lady Blockbuster (USA) (Silent Screen (USA))
850[9]

Fast Shot *Tim Easterby* a51 89
3 b g Fasliyev(USA) —Final Pursuit (Pursuit Of Love)
2265[3] ◆ (2592) 3126[3] 3347[3] (3731) (4234) 4817[2] 5370[2] 5621[4] 7074[3]

Fatal Bullet (USA) *Reade Baker* a110 111
6 b g Red Bullet(USA) —Sararegal (CAN) (Regal Classic (CAN))
6908a[10]

Fat Choy Oohlala *C H Yip* 112
4 b g Dr Fong(USA) —Macina (IRE) (Platini (GER))
7731a[11]

Father Martin (IRE) *Richard Phillips*
4 b g Xaar—Order Of The Day (USA) (Dayjur (USA))
[illegible]

Fathey (IRE) *Charles Smith* a46 62
5 ch g Fath(USA) —Christoph's Girl (Efisio)
185[5] 289[11] (1875) 2424[6] 2829[11] 4025[8] 4563[8] 5214[4] 5601[9] 6070[5] 7230[11]

Fathom Five (IRE) *David Nicholls* 95
7 b g Fath(USA) —Ambria (ITY) (Final Straw)
1809[13] 2714[5] 3160[8] 4104[4] 4416[3] 5033[11] 5543[4] 6332[16] 6865[12]

Fathsta (IRE) *David Simcock* a96 107
6 b g Fath(USA) —Kilbride Lass (IRE) (Lahib (USA))
1397[7] (1564) 1885[6] 2288[8] 3155[6] 3410[9] 3862[3] 4346[4] ◆ 4534[18] 5060[11] 5758[5] ◆ 5887[3] 6145[9]

Fat Kid (NZ) *H K Tan* 102
5 bg g Handsome Ransom(AUS) —Grace Jones (NZ) (Maroof (USA))
2340a[12]

Fattsota *Marco Botti* a90 101
3 b g Oasis Dream—Gift Of The Night (USA) (Slewpy (USA))
6277[3] 6803[13] 7719[8]

Fault *Alastair Lidderdale* a71 76
5 b g Bahamian Bounty—Trundley Wood (Wassl)
9[7] 2149[2] 2561[3] 2870[2] 3019[6] (3636) 4394[6] 4897[6] 5300[5] 6587[9] 6814[10] 6878[7] 7098[6] 7269[8] 7412[4] 7462[3] 7507[8] 7663[11] 7812[7]

Faustina (FR) *J E Hammond* 109
3 b f Antonius Pius(USA) —Party Bag (Cadeaux Genereux)
(6809a) 7221a[0]

Favorite Girl (GER) *Sir Henry Cecil* 61
3 b f Shirocco(GER) —Favorite (GER) (Montjeu (IRE))
2203[2] ◆ 3206[7] 4241[3]

Favourite Girl (IRE) *Tim Easterby* 99
5 b m Refuse To Bend(IRE) —Zuccini Wind (IRE) (Revoque (IRE))
1680[4] 2117[4] 2727[7] 3158[5] 3459[3] 4075[5] 4346[7] 5180[3] 5476[7] 5927[16] 6233[2] 6865[2] 7018[19] 7298[14]

Fawara *Ruth Carr* a23 33
3 b f Ishiguru(USA) —Yarrita (Tragic Role (USA))
741[8] 929[6] 1369[6] 1561[5] 2265[9] 2697[6] 3192[6]

Fawley Green *William Muir* a80 77
4 b g Shamardal(USA) —Wars (IRE) (Green Desert (USA))
961[12] 1267[8] 1592[3] 2149[6] 2206[4] ◆ 2452[5] 2756[2] 2920[4] 3464[5]

Fayre Bella *John Gallagher* a56 71
4 ch m Zafeen(FR) —Hollybell (Beveled (USA))
165[9] 6791[9] 7119[3] 7581[13] 7768[7]

Fayr Fall (IRE) *Tim Easterby* a71 73
2 b g Fayruz—Keshena Falls (IRE) (Desert Prince (IRE))
1434[4] 1691[3] (2160) 3700[10] 4343[5] 4809[2] 5431[2] 5755[2] 6154[3] 6699[6] 7021[11]

Fazza *Edwin Tuer* a74 82
4 ch g Sulamani(IRE) —Markievicz (IRE) (Doyoun)
1035[6] 1245[4] (1613) (1909) 2366[4] (2985) 3620[7] 4561[4] 5059[8] 5733[2] 6346[14] 6831[3]

Fearless Dream *John Gosden* 62
2 b f Oasis Dream—Fearless Spirit (USA) (Spinning World (USA))
5583[7]

Fearless Poet (IRE) *Bryan Smart* a57 36
3 b g Byron—Fear Not (IRE) (Alzao (USA))
6982[3] ◆ 7247[2] 7714[3] 7781[4]

Fear Nothing *Ian McInnes* a76 74
4 ch g Exceed And Excel(AUS) —Galatrix (Be My Guest (USA))
29[2] 178[12] 269[4] 298[8] 470[6] 1034[5] 1469[4] 1968[4] 2491[10] 2798[9] 6501[7] 6655[4] 7266[7]

Feather Falls (USA) *Mark Johnston* 62
3 ch f Henny Hughes(USA) —Merrill Gold (USA) (Gold Fever (USA))
4663[11]

Feathers And Bows (USA) *David Wachman* a74 75
2 b f Street Cry(IRE) —Dianehill (IRE) (Danehill (USA))
2777a[5]

February Sun *J-C Rouget* 111
3 b f Monsun(GER) —Flawly (Old Vic)
(5749a)

Feb Thirtyfirst *Sheena West* a36
2 ch c Shirocco(GER) —My Mariam (Salse (USA))
7454[10] 7650[7]

Fedemartina (ITY) *S Botti* 94
3 b f Martino Alonso(IRE) —Fedegarcia Gioffry (Last Tycoon)
3449a[13]

Federation *Roger Charlton* 86
3 b f Motivator—Flirtation (Pursuit Of Love)
1362[7] 3385[3] 4065[2] (4514) 5730[7]

Fedora (IRE) *Olivia Maylam* a66 65
5 b m Cape Cross(IRE) —Mahamuni (IRE) (Sadler's Wells (USA))
128[6] 248[6] 473[6] 687[4] 802[6] 1013a[9] 1374[6] 1625[5] 2420[7] 2828[2] 2921[7] 3943[4] 6070[3] 6105[7] (6626) 7131[3]

Feelin Foxy *James Given* a89 87
7 b m Foxhound(USA) —Charlie Girl (Puissance)
(29) 125[2] 293[4] 429[3] 523[6] 701[3] 1371[6]

Feeling (IRE) *Dai Burchell* a46 37
7 b g Sadler's Wells(USA) —La Pitie (USA) (Devil's Bag (USA))
4952[9]

Feeling Fresh (IRE) *Paul Green* a61 84
6 b h Xaar—Oh'Cecilia (IRE) (Scenic)
1296[6] 1878[4] (2543) 2938[17] 3169[7]

Feeling Good *Brian Ellison* 50
2 b c Shamardal(USA) —Lady Golan (IRE) (Golan (IRE))
5786[11]

Feeling Peckish (USA) *Michael Chapman* a43 16
7 ch g Point Given(USA) —Sunday Bazaar (USA) (Nureyev (USA))
1153[14]

Feelthedifference *Sir Henry Cecil* a64 72
2 b f Iceman—Miss McGuire (Averti (IRE))
5632[4] (6047) 6864[8]

Feel The [illegible] [illegible] 79
4 ch g Firebreak—Spindara (IRE) (Spinning World (USA))
1200[8] 1800[4] 2732[4] 3359[4] 4126[2] 4516[7]

Feet Of Fury *Ian Williams* a81 62
5 b m Deportivo—Fury Dance (USA) (Cryptoclearance (USA))
(37) (397)

Feisty Champion (IRE) *J W Hills* a69 65
2 b c Captain Rio—Deylviyna (IRE) (Doyoun)
6742[6] (7177)

Fellini (GER) *P Monfort* a88 95
4 b h Hernando(FR) —Fancy Lady (Cadeaux Genereux)
478a[3] 705a[6]

Fellisha (IRE) *Andrew Heffernan* a66 56
3 b f Officer(USA) —St Aye (USA) (Nureyev (USA))
1663a[7] 6926[2] 7121[2] 7178[2]

Femme D'Espere *Christopher Kellett*
5 b m Celts Espere—Drummer's Dream (IRE) (Drumalis)
4861[12] 5900[11] 6459[14]

Femme Royale *Robert Cowell* a26 12
3 b f Val Royal(FR) —Charmante Femme (Bin Ajwaad (IRE))
3949[5] 4320[12] 4925[6] 5352[16] 5670[8] 6071[12]

Fencing (USA) *John Gosden* 111
2 ch c Street Cry(IRE) —Latice (IRE) (Inchinor)
4330[3] ◆ (5044) ◆ 7020[3]

Fencing Master *H J Brown* a86 114
4 b h Oratorio(IRE) —Moonlight Dance (USA) (Alysheba (USA))
156a[13] 417a[14]

Fenella Fudge *James Given* a69 85
3 b f Rock Hard Ten(USA) —Rahcak (IRE) (Generous (IRE))
2466[2] 2850[6] 3586[4] (4437) 5109[4] 5551[3] 6089[4] 6450[13] 7213[4] 7484[3] 7587[4]

Fen Flyer *Chris Dwyer* 34
2 ch g Piccolo—Maraffi (IRE) (Halling (USA))
2594[5] 3132[14] 5638[4] 6101[6]

Fennell Bay (IRE) *Mahmood Al Zarooni* a30 72
2 b c Dubawi(IRE) —Woodrising (Nomination)
6216[11] (6630) 6957[6]

Fennica (USA) *John Gosden* a72 67
3 b f Empire Maker(USA) —Stellaria (USA) (Roberto (USA))
1549[8] 2849[7]

Ferdoos *Roger Varian* a86 118
4 b m Dansili—Blaze Of Colour (Rainbow Quest (USA))
(2501) ◆ 6859[10]

Ferdy (IRE) *Paul Green* a46 43
2 b c Antonius Pius(USA) —Trinity Fair (Polish Precedent (USA))
1823[8] 5486[12] 5681[16] 6627[14] 7252[9] 7780[4]

Ferneley (IRE) *B Cecil* a97 117
7 b h Ishiguru(USA) —Amber Tide (IRE) (Pursuit Of Love)
415a[7] 759a[11] 828a[12]

Ferney Boy *Chris Fairhurst* a45 57
5 b g Courteous—Jendorcet (Grey Ghost)
2575[6] 3187[4] 4129[6] (4903) 5405[4] 5791[3] 6503[6] 7077[6]

Ferro Sensation (GER) *J Pubben* 100
5 b g Paolini(GER) —Fit To Ski (Niniski (USA))
3531a[10]

Ferroviere *Ollie Pears*
3 b g Ferrule(IRE) —Fiore Di Bosco (IRE) (Charnwood Forest (IRE))
5082[8] 6096[10]

Ferruccio (IRE) *James Fanshawe* a81 77
3 br g Marju(IRE) —Unreal (Dansili)
1568[6] 2064[6] 2527[2] 3312[2] 3959[7] 4478[2] 5101[2] 5835[2] 6227[3] 6796[10] 6997[11]

Festival Dance *Ron Hodges* 65
3 b f Captain Rio—Temple Dancer (Magic Ring (IRE))
3091[9] 3465[3] 3998[5] 4628[4] 5534[3] 5917[5] 6403[7]

Festival Spirit *Mark Johnston*
2 ch g Notnowcato—Party Doll (Be My Guest (USA))
2953[16] 3553[9] 4292[9] 5342[9]

Fettuccine (IRE) *John Gallagher* a66 72
3 b f Invincible Spirit(IRE) —Capannacce (IRE) (Lahib (USA))
(253) 2838[12] 3390[8] 3818[10] 4973[12] 5419[9]

Feu De Glace (FR) *C Boutin* a64
2 ch c Bernebeau(FR) —Lettre A France (USA) (Lear Fan (USA))
7449a[0]

Feuergott (GER) *Ian Williams* a46 42
5 br g Eden Rock(GER) —Francisca (GER) (Lagunas)
4408[12] 4703[12] 4953[7]

Fever Tree *Peter Makin* a60 62
4 b m Trade Fair—Spielbound (Singspiel (IRE))
433[6]

Few Are Chosen (IRE) *Tracey Collins* 90
5 ch m Sulamani(IRE) —Much Commended (Most Welcome)
1119a[4]

Ffajir (IRE) *Clive Brittain* 68
3 b f Noverre(USA) —Very Nice (Daylami (IRE))
3324[5] 4388[2] 4861[3] 5356[5] 6450[12]

Fiammella (IRE) *A Bonin* 90
3 gr f Verglas(IRE) —Sovana (IRE) (Desert King (IRE))
7510a[9]

Fiancee (IRE) *Roy Brotherton* a51 53
5 b m Pivotal—Name Of Love (IRE) (Petardia)
107[4] 362[4] 517[9] 821[2] 912[5] 1248[10]

Fibs And Flannel *Tony Coyle* a46 79
4 ch g Tobougg(IRE) —Queens Jubilee (Cayman Kai (IRE))
1110[10] 1747[4] 2301[4] 2545[8] 3386[4] 3683[5] 5314[5] 5722[6] 6453[6] 7425[12] 7641[9]

Ficelle (IRE) *Mrs K Burke* a30
2 b f Chineur(FR) —Petite Boulangere (IRE) (Namid)
7353[6] 7506[5]

Fictional Account (IRE) *V C Ward* a90 106
6 ch m Stravinsky(USA) —Romantic Venture (IRE) (Indian Ridge)
1427a[3] 2534a[4] 3066[12] 4035a[3] (5291a) 5952a[6] 6271[4]

Fiction Or Fact (IRE) *Kevin Ryan* a68 79
2 ch g Dutch Art—Fable (Absalom)
1890[5] 2214[6] 2731[4] 3070[5] (6132) (6260) 6986[10]

Fiddlers Patriot (USA) *George Weaver* 105
5 ch g Proud Citizen(USA) —Thorette (USA) (Affirmed (USA))
6908a[5]

Fidler Bay *Henry Candy* 70
5 b g Falbrav(IRE) —Fiddle-Dee-Dee (IRE) (Mujtahid (USA))
3130[12] 4154[12]

Fiefs Dolois (FR) *A Bonin*
2 b g Royal Assault(USA) —Claire Des Fieffes (FR) (Adieu Au Roi (IRE))
7665a[0]

Field Day (IRE) *Brian Meehan* 109
4 br m Cape Cross(IRE) —Naval Affair (IRE) (Last Tycoon)
1718[4] 2029[7] 3030[6] 4533[6] 5523a[12]

Field Event (SAF) *S Al Harabi* a93 98
7 ch h Western Winter(USA) —Field Princess (SAF) (Northfields (USA))
828a[9]

Field Finner *David Nicholls* a12
3 ch f Goodricke—Princess Carranita (IRE) (Desert Sun)
7354[9] 7747[7]

Fieldgunner Kirkup (GER) *David Barron* 82
3 b g Acclamation—Fire Finch (Halling (USA))
2363[2] 2763[6] 3830[4] 5730[11] 6167[14] 6382[10] 7024[8] 7213[3]

Field Of Dream *Luca Cumani* 109
4 b g Oasis Dream—Field Of Hope (IRE) (Selkirk (USA))
1397[2] 2541a[4] 3404[7] 4972[10] 6027[3] 6416[3]

Field Of Miracles (IRE) *John Gosden* a84 110
3 b f Galileo(IRE) —Landmark (USA) (Arch (USA))
(1332) 1894[2] 3065[2] ◆ 4470[9] 5220[6]

Fiesta Becquerel (FR) *Mme E Siavy-Julien*
4 b m Sheyrann—Punky Party (FR) (Epervier Bleu)
1012a[0]

Fifteentwo *David Nicholls* 71
2 b g Piccolo—Turkish Delight (Prince Sabo)
2617[11] 3855[3] 4283[11] 5399[4] (6628)

Fifth Auntie *J R Jenkins* a17
4 ch m Nayef(USA) —Subtle One (IRE) (Polish Patriot (USA))
7250[9] 7717[10]

Fifth Estate *Jamie Osborne* a56
3 br g Needwood Blade—Passata (FR) (Polar Falcon (USA))
420[5]

Fifth In Line (IRE) *David Flood* a67
3 b f Kodiac—Surrender To Me (USA) (Royal Anthem (USA))
20[2] 66[3] (130) 275[5] (396) 724[4] 886[2] 1021[4] 1176[6] 1334[4] 2177[4] 3238[6]

Fifty Cents *Brendan Powell* a63 68
7 ch g Diesis—Solaia (USA) (Miswaki (USA))
2242[5] 2685[11] 2843[7] 5318[7] 5832[3] (6446) 6790[3] 7122[2] 7495[5] 7528[9]

Fifty Moore *Jedd O'Keeffe* 73
4 b g Selkirk(USA) —Franglais (GER) (Lion Cavern (USA))
1909[10] ◆ 2548[10] 2804[6] 3492[5]

Fiftynotout (IRE) *Alan Berry* a51 22
4 ch g Desert Prince(IRE) —Tasha's Dream (USA) (Woodman (USA))
1370[4] 3543[14] 3974[10]

Figaro *William Haggas* 88
3 ch g Medicean—Chorist (Pivotal)
3543[4] 4763[2] 5629[6] 6096[2] (6633)

Figaro Flyer (IRE) *Paul Howling* a61 64
8 b g Mozart(IRE) —Ellway Star (IRE) (Night Shift (USA))
(57) 276[6] 545[7] 1043[4] 2162[8] 7655[13]

Fighter Boy (IRE) *David Barron* a83 106
4 b g Rock Of Gibraltar(IRE) —In My Life (IRE) (Rainbow Quest (USA))
542[5] ◆

Fight For Freedom (IRE) *P Schiergen* 58
4 b g Hawk Wing(USA) —Freedom (GER) (Second Empire (IRE))
628a[16]

Fighting Brave (USA) *David Wachman* a98 102
4 br h Storm Cat(USA) —Get Lucky (USA) (Mr Prospector (USA))
157a[9] 330a[12] 1930a[3] 6513a[5]

Fight Or Flight *Brendan Powell* a51 32
4 b m Mark Of Esteem(IRE) —My Preference (Reference Point)
791[7] 905[8] 1354[5]

Figli Fanesi (IRE) *Vittorio Caruso* 108
3 b c Tiger Hill(IRE) —Fanofadiga (IRE) (Alzao (USA))
1920a[6] (6569a) 6907a[5]

File And Paint (IRE) *Lawrence Mullaney* a58 81
3 b f Chevalier(IRE) —Have A Heart (IRE) (Daggers Drawn (USA))
4127[2] 4439[2] 5062[5] 5255[17] 6533[10]

Filibuster *Chris Wall* 40
4 b g Tobougg(IRE) —Blinding Mission (IRE) (Marju (IRE))
1871[8] 2268[8]

Fille De Famille (FR) *R Chotard* a77 79
3 b f Miesque's Son(USA) —Saga (FR) (Nombre Premier)
901a[8]

Fillionaire *Mick Channon* 94
2 b f Kyllachy—Autumn Pearl (Orpen (USA))
(6725) ◆ 7028[3] ◆

Filozef (IRE) *C Ferland* [illegible]
3 ch c Footstepsinthesand—Aspen Falls (IRE) (Elnadim (USA))
(258a) 532a[6]

Filun *Anthony Middleton* a59 76
6 b g Montjeu(IRE) —Sispre (FR) (Master Willie)
574[7] 819[5] 899[7] ◆ 1253[2] 1310[2] (1635) (2202) (2417) 2793[3] 3533[2] 5580[9]

Fimias (IRE) *Geoffrey Harker* a68 65
3 bb g Aussie Rules(USA) —Miss Lacey (IRE) (Diktat)
1168[7] 1801[6] 3976[7] 4403[4] 4633[5]

Final Delivery *George Baker* a75 73
2 b g Three Valleys(USA) —Bowled Out (GER) (Dansili)
4708[4] 5393[3] 5899[3] 6837[2] 7414[2] (7929)

Final Drive (IRE) *John Ryan* a105 63
5 b g Viking Ruler(AUS) —Forest Delight (IRE) (Shinko Forest (IRE))
326a[3] 499a[4] 583a[7] 604a[8] 846[9]

Finale (USA) *Todd Pletcher* 104
2 bb c Scat Daddy(USA) —Twinkle (USA) (Lively One (USA))
[3] 7301a[7]

Finalist *Dean Ivory* a60 46
2 b f Avonbridge—High Finale (Sure Blade (USA))
2227[3] 2817[3] 3435[7] 6942[5] ◆ 7452[8] 7530[2] 7749[4]

Final Liberation (FR) *Sir Mark Prescott Bt* a90 82
3 b g Sinndar(IRE) —Hispalis (IRE) (Barathea (IRE))
2786[6] (3393) 3518[5] (4476) (4687) (5417) 6485[5]

Final Rhapsody *Willie Musson* a56 59
5 b m Royal Applause—Rivers Rhapsody (Dominion)
138[3] 276[3]

Final Salute *Bryan Smart* a68 59
5 b g Royal Applause—Wildwood Flower (Distant Relative)
150[8] (402) 743[5] 853[5] 1244[10] 2543[13]

Final Try *Paddy Butler* a49 41
4 ch g Baryshnikov(AUS) —Scotland Bay (Then Again)
1021[6] 1184[8] 1508[5] 2451[8] 2759[7]

Final Tune (IRE) *Mandy Rowland* a60 79
8 ch g Grand Lodge(USA) —Jackie's Opera (FR) (Indian Ridge)
749[6] 957[6] 1273[6] 1814[14] 3926[6] 4869[2] 7788[8] 7848[9]

Final Verse *Matthew Salaman* a81 73
8 b g Mark Of Esteem(IRE) —Tamassos (Dance In Time (CAN))
31[3] 282[4] 562[5] 5538[3] 5992[10] 6435[9]

Finbar *James Given* a77 72
2 b c Nayef(USA) —Baralinka (IRE) (Barathea (IRE))
2523[5] 2953[3] 5269[10] 6807[3] (7336) (7501)

Finch Flyer (IRE) *Gary Moore* a48 62
4 ch g Indian Ridge—Imelda (USA) (Manila (USA))
6968[5]

Findhornbay *Mark Johnston* a39 64
2 b f Ishiguru(USA) —Sweet Cando (IRE) (Royal Applause)
4436[12] 5618[3] 6152[4] 6573[11] 7051[4] 7251[8] 7337[6]

Finding Neverland (FR) *N Clement* 102
3 b f Green Desert(USA) —Francais (Mark Of Esteem (IRE))
1709a[5] 6809a[9]

Fine Altomis *Michael Dods* 54
2 b g Lomitas—Mi Anna (GER) (Lake Coniston (IRE))
4080[6] 5548[8] 6259[7]

Fine Finale *Jeremy Gask* a41
2 b c Lucky Story(USA) —Lamees (USA) (Lomond (USA))
6214[12] 6772[11] 7493[10] 7697[12]

Finefrenzyrolling (IRE) *Mrs K Burke* a55 68
3 ch f Refuse To Bend(IRE) —Oasis Star (IRE) (Desert King (IRE))
852a[2] 981a[0] 1220[2] 1986[13] 2782[2] 3207[4] 3638[2] 3729[2] 5100[8] 7388[5] 7658[3]

Fine Kingdom *Michael Dods* 57
2 b g King's Best(USA) —Eurolink Sundance (Night Shift (USA))
3186[4] 4122[5] 4853[9] 6260[18] 6774[8]

Finellas Fortune *George Moore* 61
6 b m Elmaamul(USA) —Fortune's Filly (Nomination)
2575[2] 3187[8] 3622[2] 4671[2] 5079[6]

Fine Painting (IRE) *Gary Moore* a72
2 ch f Iffraaj—Just One Look (Barathea (IRE))
5632[6] 6441[2] 6820[3] 6946[9]

Fine Resolve *Andrew Balding* a65 70
2 b g Refuse To Bend(IRE) —Papillon De Bronze (IRE) (Marju (IRE))
6462[13] 6928[8] 7257[3] 7752[5]

Fine Ruler (IRE) *Martin Bosley* a66 70
7 b g King's Best(USA) —Bint Alajwaad (IRE) (Fairy King (USA))
280[3] 555[3] ◆ 809[8] 957[10]

Fine Style (IRE) *Neil King* a56 66
3 ch g Pivotal—Hidden Hope (Daylami (IRE))
1027[5] (1574) 1858[3] 6785[7] 6936[4]

Fine The World *Mrs J L Le Brocq*
7 b m Agnes World(USA) —Fine Honor (FR) (Highest Honor (FR))
1743a[5]

Fine Threads *Charles Hills* 90
3 b f Barathea(IRE) —Pink Cristal (Dilum (USA))
(1947) 3260[3] ◆ 6124[2]

Fine Tolerance *Sam Davison* a62 57
5 b m Bertolini(USA) —Sashay (Bishop Of Cashel)
114[9] 277[7] 524[8] 899[6] 1218[6]

Finicius (USA) *Eoin Griffin* a96 103
7 b g Officer(USA) —Glorious Linda (FR) (Le Glorieux)
2533a[7] 5086a[11]

Finisteria (FR) *Mme C Barande-Barbe* 63
2 b f Kingsalsa(USA) —First Precedent (FR) (Polish Precedent (USA))
7326a[9] 7665a[0]

Finisterien (IRE) *J-V Toux* 81
2 b c Whipper(USA) —Foreplay (IRE) (Lujain (USA))
7238a[8] 7814a[0]

Finity Run (GER) *Mark Johnston* 59
2 b f Hurricane Run(IRE) —Finity (USA) (Diesis)
5029[11] 5464[8]

Finjaan *Doug Watson* a81 105
5 b h Royal Applause—Alhufoof (USA) (Dayjur (USA))
327a[13] 586a[7] 682a[10]

Finley Connolly (IRE) *Brian Meehan* a56 62
2 b g Cockney Rebel(IRE) —Impetious (Inchinor)
2017[6] 2817[7] 4857[11] 5634[5] 6757[2]

Finlodex *Murty McGrath*
4 ch g Pastoral Pursuits—Ela Aphrodite (Halling (USA))
7894[6]

Finnegans Rainbow *Michael Chapman* a39 38
9 ch g Spectrum(IRE) —Fairy Story (IRE) (Persian Bold)
5116[6]

Finn's Rainbow *John Weymes* a76 55
3 ch g Iffraaj—Aptina (USA) (Aptitude (USA))
(41) (119) 2391[9] 3114[6] 3621[9] 3731[6] 7675[12] 7776[10] 7883[4]

Fiorente (IRE) *Sir Michael Stoute* 111
3 br c Monsun(GER) —Desert Bloom (IRE) (Pilsudski (IRE))
1407[5] ◆ (2097) ◆ 3105[2] ◆ 4411[2]

Firdaws (USA) *Roger Varian* 98
2 b f Mr Greeley(USA) —Eswarah (Unfuwain (USA))
4995[2] ◆ (5655) 6299[3] ◆

Fire And Sparks *David Simcock* a71 22
2 b f Shamardal(USA) —Celtic Triumph (IRE) (Montjeu (IRE))
2718[8] 3736[5] (3981)

Fireback *Andrew Balding* a76 95
4 b g Firebreak—So Discreet (Tragic Role (USA))
1720[14] 2717[3] 3535[8] 3862[10] 4556[5] 5508[4] 5887[11]

Fireball Express *Brian Baugh*
3 ch g Firebreak—Ashfield (Zilzal (USA))
7845[9]

Firebeam *William Haggas* a64 109
3 b g Cadeaux Genereux—Firebelly (Nicolotte)
1108[2] ◆ 1496[3] (3173) (3830) 4779[3] (6027)

Fire Commander *Brian Baugh* a43
3 b g Firebreak—Spectrum Queen (IRE) (Spectrum (IRE))
7460[9] 7696[11]

Fire Crystal *Mick Channon* a53 58
3 b f High Chaparral(IRE) —Bint Alajwaad (IRE) (Fairy King (USA))
1566[6] (1790) 2119[7] 2243[4] 2465[8] 3226[3] 4284[13]

Fire Fighter (IRE) *Sir Mark Prescott Bt* a97 88
3 b g Tiger Hill(IRE) —Firecrest (IRE) (Darshaan)
2635[2] 3487[2] (3770) (4712) 5079[8] (6057) ◆ (6306) ◆ 6575[2]

Firefly *John Weymes* 59
2 b g Firebreak—Quick Flight (Polar Falcon (USA))
5548[10] 6230[8] 6532[7]

Fire In Babylon (IRE) *Michael Wigham* 52
3 b g Montjeu(IRE) —Three Owls (IRE) (Warning)
2311[6] 2852[6] 3053[7]

Fire King *Andrew Haynes* a61 72
5 b g Falbrav(IRE) —Dancing Fire (USA) (Dayjur (USA))
2242[3] 2420[2] 3142[7] (3677) 3944[11] 5136[2]

Fire Lily (IRE) *David Wachman* 109
2 b f Dansili—Beauty Is Truth (IRE) (Pivotal)
2322a[3] 3033[4] ◆ (4131a) ◆ 5217[2] ◆ 5525a[2] 6564a[2]

Fire N'Brimstone *Mouse Hamilton-Fairley* a50 35
3 b g Firebreak—Ellovamul (Elmaamul (USA))
760[9] 1500[3]

Fire Ship *Peter Winkworth* a56 79
2 b g Firebreak—Mays Dream (Josr Algarhoud (IRE))
2640[5] (3171) 4913[2] 5233[2] (6757)

Firestarter *David Elsworth* a76 81
2 b g Cockney Rebel(IRE) —Good Girl (IRE) (College Chapel)
4098[4] 4580[2] 4906[3] 5254[9] 5697[3] 6160[4] 6812[3]

First Avenue *Laura Mongan* a75 56
6 b g Montjeu(IRE) —Marciala (IRE) (Machiavellian (USA))
3411[10] 4253[11] 6445[2] 7908[4]

First Battalion (IRE) *Keith Dalgleish* 76
3 b g Sadler's Wells(USA) —Mubkera (IRE) (Nashwan (USA))
(1272) 2076[7] 5205[16]

First Bid *James Given* a46 67
2 b c Kyllachy—Toucantini (Inchinor)
1434[6] (2267) 3021[3] 4105[5] 4892[3] 6186[3] 7642[5] 7881[8]

First Blade *Roy Bowring* a73 58
5 ch g Needwood Blade—Antonias Melody (Rambo Dancer (CAN))
294[14] 402[4] 743[8] (2164) 2845[5]

First Blush (IRE) *H-A Pantall* 86
4 b m Pivotal—Zibilene (Rainbow Quest (USA))
6470a[9]

First Cat *Richard Hannon* a65 91
4 b g One Cool Cat(USA) —Zina La Belle (Mark Of Esteem (IRE))
1834[5] 2441[6] 2647[2] 3134[6] 3840[4] 4310[6] 4656[4] 4958[5] 5894[6]

First City *David Simcock* 112
5 b m Diktat—City Maiden (USA) (Carson City (USA))
1681[6] 2678[2] 3030[3] 3822[3] 4597a[4] 5704[5]

First Class *Rae Guest* a43 31
3 b g Oasis Dream—Break Point (Reference Point)
6591[8] 7111[9] 7354[6] 7676[4]

First Class Favour (IRE) *Tim Easterby* a52 83
3 b f Exceed And Excel(AUS) —Lamh Eile (IRE) (Lend A Hand)
1820[9] 2319[8] 2503[10] 2834[7] 3346[6] 3854[4] 4107[2] 4854[6] 5164[7] 5862[11] 6231[8] 6869[6] 7024[12] 7235[5]

First Fandango *Tim Vaughan* a75 85
4 b g Hernando(FR) —First Fantasy (Be My Chief (USA))
1470[7]

First Fast Now (IRE) *Nigel Tinkler* 67
2 b f Kheleyf(USA) —Montana Lady (IRE) (Be My Guest (USA))
1414[12] 1744[4] 2570[4] 3125[2] 3452[2] 3932[2] 4406[2] 4899[2] (5147)

First Glance *Michael Appleby* a42
2 br g Passing Glance—Lady Santana (IRE) (Doyoun)
7626[5]

First In Command (IRE) *Daniel Mark Loughnane* a74 75
6 b g Captain Rio—Queen Sigi (IRE) (Fairy King (USA))
1752[7] 5736[6] 6283[6] 7812[4] 7896[5]

Firstknight *Marco Botti* a80 66
3 b c Kyllachy—Wedding Party (Groom Dancer (USA))
1141[4] 1626[4] (2383) 3048[3] 3737[8]

First Mask (FR) *C Boutin*
3 b c Iron Mask(USA) —Drop Dead Gorgeous (IRE) (Bering)
660a[10]

First Of February (IRE) *Jim Boyle* 44
2 b f Amadeus Wolf—Thea Di Bisanzio (IRE) (Dr Fong (USA))
1846[9] 2153[14] 5854[8] 6628[8]

First Phase *Mel Brittain* 63
2 b f First Trump—Melandre (Lujain (USA))
4940[2] 5756[6] 6045[11] (6645) 7294[16]

First Point (GER) *Nicky Henderson*
8 b g Trempolino(USA) —First Smile (Surumu (GER))
2312[P]

First Post (IRE) *Derek Haydn Jones* a77 93
4 b g Celtic Swing—Consignia (IRE) (Definite Article)
877[8] 1138[5] 1603[3] 2066[6] 2647[3] 3542[2] (4268) 4794[5] (5240) 5686[13] 6163[4] 6339[25]

First Pressing *John Berry* 51
3 b f Bertolini(USA) —Lady Donatella (Last Tycoon)
2710[7] 4827[11] 5380[8]

First Rebellion *Tony Carroll* a46 52
2 ch g Cockney Rebel(IRE) —First Dawn (Dr Fong (USA))
1129[4] 1396[5] 1632[5] 2998[4] 4019[9] 5099[5] 5374[5] (5535) 5833[3] 6627[5] 7252[5]

First Rock (IRE) *Alan Swinbank* a72 66
5 b g Rock Of Gibraltar(IRE) —Sakkara (IRE) (Sadler's Wells (USA))
145[2] 563[4] 762[5] 1466[2] 1817[3] 6451[2] 6780[6] (7244) 7914[3]

First Service (IRE) *Michael Attwater* a68 60
5 ch g Intikhab(USA) —Princess Sceptre (Cadeaux Genereux)
280[9] 477[3] 906[11]

First Smash (GER) *Milton Harris* a60 64
6 b g Monsun(GER) —First Smile (Surumu (GER))
301[6]

First Swallow *David Brown* a68 66
6 ch g Bahamian Bounty—Promise Fulfilled (USA) (Bet Twice (USA))
116[3]

First Term *Malcolm Saunders* a16 59
4 b m Acclamation—School Days (Slip Anchor)
1054[7] 1220[8] 1289[5]

Fiscal *John Gosden* 71
2 b c Cape Cross(IRE) —Fibou (USA) (Seeking The Gold (USA))
3401[6] 3823[8]

Fish Called Peppa (IRE) *Peter Fahey*
4 b m Definite Article—Hernameismary (IRE) (Revoque (IRE))
7630[7]

Fisher *Richard Hannon* a66 45
2 b c Jeremy(USA) —Elfin Laughter (Alzao (USA))
5801[10] 6214[11] 7126[6] 7336[4]

Fishforcompliments *Richard Fahey* a82 88
7 b g Royal Applause—Flyfisher (USA) (Riverman (USA))
105[2] 285[4] 2095[13] 2497[6] 3275[11] 3805[8] 4310[5] 5760[6] 6081[2] (6381) 7150a[7] 7636[2] 7807[2]

Fistful Of Dollars (IRE) *Jamie Osborne* a68
2 b g Holy Roman Emperor(IRE) —Taking Liberties (IRE) (Royal Academy (USA))
7197[6] 7559[2] (7685)

Fists And Stones *Mick Channon* a55 76
3 b g Distant Music(USA) —Keeping The Faith (IRE) (Ajraas (USA))
1682[10] 2103[12] 5449[8] 6181[8] 6578[4] 6764[15]

Fityaan *B W Hills* a79 94
3 b g Haafhd—Welsh Diva (Selkirk (USA))
(1984) 2684[5] 3830[2] (4550) ◆

Fitz *Matthew Salaman* a67 65
5 b g Mind Games—Timoko (Dancing Spree (USA))
1045[6] 1625[3] 1995[4] 2560[5] 2843[3] 3293[2] 3741[2] 3804[3] 4322[5] 4948[3] (6411) 7314a[3] 7663[8] 7810[6]

Fitz Flyer (IRE) *Bryan Smart* a104 103
5 b g Acclamation—Starry Night (Sheikh Albadou)
1093[13] 1518[3] 2028[9] 2489[5] 2954[9] (3140) 3626[3] 3874[8] 4534[20] 4894[2] 5180[16]

Fitzwarren *Alan Brown* a31 49
10 b g Presidium—Coney Hills (Beverley Boy)
691[3] 408[13] 895[10] 4408[14] 6050[10] 7851[10]

Five Cents *A Al Raihe* a103 78
4 b h Exceed And Excel(AUS) —Native Nickel (IRE) (Be My Native (USA))
(707a)

Five Cool Kats (IRE) *Bill Turner* a46 14
3 b g One Cool Cat(USA) —Katavi (USA) (Stravinsky (USA))
43[7] 212[8] 905[7] 1022[9] 1753[14] 1953[6] 2384[5] 3226[5] 7768[12]

Fivefold (USA) *John Akehurst* a80 81
4 bb g Hennessy(USA) —Calming (USA) (Wild Again (USA))
(139) 213[2] 334[2] 483[6] 4010[9] 4210[12] 4910[10] 5836[8] 6258[5]

Five Gold Rings (IRE) *Seamus Durack* a46 45
5 ch m Captain Rio—Metisse (IRE) (Indian Ridge)
464[8] 575[10]

Five Hearts *Mark H Tompkins* 69
3 b f Bertolini(USA) —Light Hand (Star Appeal)
3246[8] 4163[7] 5120[4]

Five Star Junior (USA) *Linda Stubbs* a102 99
5 b g Five Star Day(USA) —Sir Harriett (USA) (Sir Harry Lewis (USA))
46[3] 265[2] (613) 700[9] 989[4] 1186[4] 1366[8] 1720[15] 3140[3] 3778[10] 4063[2] 4531[8] 4894[5] 5033[13] 5430[3] 5852[3] 7149a[3] 7392[7] 7578[9]

Five Two *Gavin Patrick Cromwell* a68 66
8 ch g Mark Of Esteem(IRE) —Queen's Gallery (USA) (Forty Niner (USA))
749[2]

Flag Officer *Saeed Bin Suroor* a87 101
3 b g Dubai Destination(USA) —Dusty Answer (Zafonic (USA))
2471[3] 2935[2]

Flag Of Glory *Peter Hiatt* a79 73
4 b g Trade Fair—Rainbow Sky (Rainbow Quest (USA))
908[8] 2999[8] 7130[11] 7397[7] 7458[13] 7564[13]

Flambard House (IRE) *Howard Johnson* 72
2 b g Camacho—Sixfields Flyer (IRE) (Desert Style (IRE))
1434[2] ◆ 2346[4] 3314[2] 3899[2] 4632[2]

Flambeau *Henry Candy* 113
4 b m Oasis Dream—Flavian (Catrail (USA))
(1397) ◆ 1893[2] 3404[10] 5848[6] 6523[8]

Flamborough Breeze *Edward Vaughan* a68 74
2 ro f Ad Valorem(USA) —Lothian Lass (IRE) (Daylami (IRE))
3865[8] 4614[2] 5424[5] 7464[3] 7672[2]

Flame Of Hestia (IRE) *James Fanshawe* 76
5 ch m Giant's Causeway(USA) —Ellen (IRE) (Machiavellian (USA))
3558[2] 4730[4] 5357[2] 6037[2]

Flameoftheforest (IRE) *Ed de Giles* a82 87
4 b g Danehill Dancer(IRE) —Coralita (IRE) (Night Shift (USA))
3081[8] 4020[7] 4670[4] ◆ 5201[2] 6022[2] 6378[4] (6779) 7262[4]

Flamestone *Andrew Price* a55 52
7 b g Piccolo—Renee (Wolfhound (USA))
2246[7]

Flaming Ferrari (IRE) *Peter Chapple-Hyam* a53 58
2 b f Authorized(IRE) —Spirit Of Pearl (IRE) (Invincible Spirit (IRE))
5514[4] 6474[7] 7736[4] 7925[5]

Flaming Nora *James Fanshawe* a56 60
3 b f Tobougg(IRE) —Morning After (Emperor Jones (USA))
3246[3] 4163[10] 5098[4] 5666[7] 6225[5]

Flamingo Fantasy (GER) *S Smrczek* 108
6 ch h Fantastic Light(USA) —Flamingo Road (GER) (Acatenango (GER))
2538a[3] 3446a[4] 4524a[3] 5990a[6] 6396a[5]

Flashbak (IRE) *Alan Bailey* 33
2 ch f Redback—Flashy Life (Averti (IRE))
3552[8] 4012[8]

Flashbang *Paul Cole* a82 76
3 ch f Dubawi(IRE) —Colourflash (IRE) (College Chapel)
1155[3] 1343[2] (1607) 2102[6] 2468[8] 3048[7] 4387[5] 4799[6] 6604[11] 7137[7]

Flash City (ITY) *Bryan Smart* a86 88
3 b g Elusive City(USA) —Furnish (Green Desert (USA))
1241[2] 1391[4] 5918[8] 6703[4] ◆ 7487[5]

Flash Crash *Robert Cowell* a57
2 b c Val Royal(FR) —Tessara (GER) (Big Shuffle (USA))
7751[7]

Flash Dance (IRE) *F Head* 106
5 ch m Zamindar(USA) —Resquilleuse (USA) (Dehere (USA))
1125a[7] 2343a[4] 3009[7] 4597a[8] 5129a[11] 6566a[7]

Flashman *Richard Fahey* a61 47
2 ch g Doyen(IRE) —Si Si Si (Lomitas)
6697[8] 7060[5] 7369[8]

Flashpoint (USA) *Wesley A Ward* a115
3 rg c Pomeroy(USA) —Two Punch Lil (USA) (Two Punch (USA))
2328a[14]

Flatford Mill *K F Clutterbuck*
2 b g Librettist(USA) —Loch Leven (Selkirk (USA))
1988[7] 5668[6]

Flat Out (USA) *Charles L Dickey* a125
5 b h Flatter(USA) —Cresta Lil (USA) (Cresta Rider (USA))
7308a[5]

Flaunter (USA) *Mahmood Al Zarooni* 70
3 bb f Dynaformer(USA) —Calista (Caerleon (USA))
2157[4]

Flavia Tatiana (IRE) *A P O'Brien* a83 75
3 b f Holy Roman Emperor(IRE) —Sanctify (IRE) (Sadler's Wells (USA))
7548a[6]

Flavius Victor (IRE) *Richard Hannon* a68 67
2 b c Holy Roman Emperor(IRE) —Teslemi (USA) (Ogygian (USA))
2584[9] 3237[2] 4815[5] 5385[5]

Flaxen Flare (IRE) *Andrew Balding* 80
2 ch g Windsor Knot(IRE) —Golden Angel (USA) (Slew O'Gold (USA))
6768[3] ◆ 7080[2]

Flaxen Lake *Milton Bradley* a63 61
4 b g Sampower Star—Cloudy Reef (Cragador)
102[9] 3471[6] 3721[5] (4230) 4547[3] 4893[4] 5540[4] 5617[7] 5677[2] 5996[3] 6304[4] 6479[2] 6626[5]

Fleeting Echo *Richard Hannon* a82 98
4 b m Beat Hollow—Sempre Sorriso (Fleetwood (IRE))
1681[7] 2099[14] 3365[4] 4101[10]

Fleeting Fashion *Michael Appleby* a33
2 b f Alhaarth(IRE) —Sempre Sorriso (Fleetwood (IRE))
7422[7] 7777[9]

Fleeting Moment (IRE) *Patrick Martin* a71 67
6 b g Oasis Dream—Snippets (IRE) (Be My Guest (USA))
6511a[2]

Fleeting Storm *Hughie Morrison* a57 54
3 b f Storming Home—Fleeting Moon (Fleetwood (IRE))
95[7] 420[2] 649[3] 1018[11] 3268[6] 4476[8]

Fleeting Tiger *John Dunlop* 57
3 b g Tiger Hill(IRE) —Fleeting Rainbow (Rainbow Quest (USA))
1683[8] 2225[3] 2874[5] 3690[4] 4248[5]

Fleetwood Daughter *Bernard Llewellyn* 35
9 b m Fleetwood(IRE) —Mezza Luna (Distant Relative)
4706[8] 5112[7]

Fleetwoodmaxi (USA) *Peter Makin* 59
4 bb g Afleet Alex(USA) —Swain's Gold (USA) (Swain (IRE))
4340[10] 4970[5] 6020[6]

Fleetwoodsands (IRE) *Milton Bradley* a74 62
4 b g Footstepsinthesand—Litchfield Hills (USA) (Relaunch (USA))
213[5] 556[4] 914[2] (1017) 1558[11] (3473) 4866[10] 5538[5] 6434[4] 6980[7] 7178[8] 7418[3] 7455[8] 7696[6] (7820)

Fleur De Cactus (IRE) *Sir Michael Stoute* 56
2 b f Montjeu(IRE) —Desert Beauty (IRE) (Green Desert (USA))
7164[10]

Fleur De General (FR) *R Roels*
2 b f Vicegeneral(GER) —Diamond Girl (GER) (Ali-Royal (IRE))
7312a[0]

Fleur De La Vie (IRE) *Ralph Beckett* a55 62
2 ch f Primary(USA) —Francophilia (Lomitas)
5537[4] 7343[11] 7650[5]

Fleur De'Lion (IRE) *Sylvester Kirk* a67 57
5 ch m Lion Heart(USA) —Viburnum (USA) (El Gran Senor (USA))
79[9] 114[8]

Fleur De Nuit (IRE) *J Bleahen* 90
6 b m Montjeu(IRE) —Green Castle (IRE) (Indian Ridge)
5748a[3]

Fleur Enchantee (FR) *P Van De Poele* a99 109
7 b m Marchand De Sable(USA) —Mademoiselle Fleur (FR) (River Mist (USA))
5306a[5] 6686a[9] 7090a[5] 7580a[7]

Fleurie Lover (IRE) *Richard Guest* a46 59
3 ch f Chineur(FR) —Carpet Lover (IRE) (Fayruz)
653[4] 863[4] 1155[6] 2264[7] 2592[2] 2782[4] 3207[7] 3347[6] 4564[9] 4672[3] 4929[12]

Flexible Flyer *Hughie Morrison* 56
2 b c Exceed And Excel(AUS) —Windermere Island (Cadeaux Genereux)
6751[5]

Flic Flac (IRE) *D K Weld* a92 87
3 ch f Bahamian Bounty—Polite Reply (IRE) (Be My Guest (USA))
6388a[23] 6854a[3] (7010a) 7149a[14]

Flight Connection *Clive Brittain* a41 35
2 b c Rail Link—Simacota (GER) (Acatenango (GER))
4330[12] 5382[9] 5688[7] 6760[12]

Flinty *Richard Hannon* 51
3 b c Cape Cross(IRE) —Favourita (Diktat)
1354[4] 1588[8]

Flipando (IRE) *David Barron* a106 102
10 b g Sri Pekan(USA) —Magic Touch (Fairy King (USA))
613[4] (848) 1111[15] (1457) 2075[14] 2284[9] 2717[9] 3109[20]

Flipping *Eric Alston* a64 84
4 br g Kheleyf(USA) —Felona (Caerleon (USA))
3276[16] 6290[6] 7161[3] ◆ 7339[13]

Flirty Gerty (IRE) *Tom Dascombe* a54 55
2 b f Diamond Green(FR) —Amorous Pursuits (Pursuit Of Love)
2983[10] 3273[11] 4021[2] 4756[3]

Floating Angel (USA) *John Best* a6 36
4 bb m Alke(USA) —Relic Notebook (USA) (Notebook (USA))
4948[14] 5943[10]

Floating Mountain *William Jarvis* 59
3 b f Sakhee(USA) —Engulfed (USA) (Gulch (USA))
6750[3]

Floating World (IRE) *A Fabre* a84 88
3 b f King's Best(USA) —Larrocha (IRE) (Sadler's Wells (USA))
7580a[0]

Flodden (USA) *Paul Cole* a57 75
3 ch g Henny Hughes(USA) —Dundrummin' (USA) (Gone West (USA))
1328[4] 1565[11]

Flo Motion (IRE) *J W Hills* 53
3 b f Sadler's Wells(USA) —Darling (Darshaan)
4279[14]

Flood Plain *John Gosden* 93
3 b f Orpen(USA) —Delta (Zafonic (USA))
1599[3] ◆ 2073[7]

Floor Show *Noel Wilson* 86
5 ch g Bahamian Bounty—Dancing Spirit (IRE) (Ahonoora)
1205[11] 1463[11]

Floral Beauty *Sir Michael Stoute* 83
3 b f Shamardal(USA) —Shell Garland (USA) (Sadler's Wells (USA))
1845[3] 2836[2] 4985[4] (5877)

Flora's Pride *Keith Reveley* 60
7 b m Alflora(IRE) —Pennys Pride (IRE) (Pips Pride)
1039[9] 3510[10] 7077[4]

Florence Craye *Bent Olsen*
2 b f Pastoral Pursuits—Darya (USA) (Gulch (USA))
4841a[4]

Florentino (JPN) *Mahmood Al Zarooni* 104
5 b h Swept Overboard(USA) —Must Be Loved (JPN) (Sunday Silence (USA))
239[12] 417a[10] 581a[8]

Flores Sea (USA) *Ruth Carr* a78 80
7 ch g Luhuk(USA) —Perceptive (USA) (Capote (USA))
291[9] 504[11] 675[7] 800[4]

Florestans Match *Ralph Beckett* a63 85
3 ch f Medicean—Fidelio's Miracle (USA) (Mountain Cat (USA))
(1155) 1844[5]

Floriade (IRE) *H-A Pantall* 54
3 b f Invincible Spirit(IRE) —Sharapova (IRE) (Elusive Quality (USA))
852a[4]

Florio Vincitore (IRE) *Edward Creighton* a77 54
4 b g High Chaparral(IRE) —Salome's Attack (Anabaa (USA))
190[6] (432) 727[2] 949[4] 1177[2] 1232[3] 3042[10] 3235[4] 6793[11] 6920[10]

Florry Knox (IRE) *Patrick J Flynn* a49 64
3 b g Captain Rio—Ciaras Diamond (IRE) (Dyhim Diamond (IRE))
6139a[7]

Flosse *Ed Walker* a56 55
2 ch f Three Valleys(USA) —Palisandra (USA) (Chief's Crown (USA))
1996[7] 2731[5] 3070[4] 3746[4] 4019[5] 5998[8] 6627[10]

Flotate (USA) *Gay Kelleway* a55 4
4 bb m Orientate(USA) —Flo Jo (USA) (Graustark)
4729[RR]

Flotation (USA) *Roy Brotherton* a37 74
4 b m Chapel Royal(USA) —Storm Dove (USA) (Storm Bird (CAN))
7418[12] 7556[10]

Flow Chart (IRE) *Peter Grayson* a72 67
4 b g Acclamation—Free Flow (Mujahid (USA))
57[9] 107[5] 150[6] 289[6] 654[6] 1815[6] 2655[3]

Flowers Of Spring (IRE) *Andrew Oliver* 105
4 bb m Celtic Swing—Albaiyda (IRE) (Brief Truce (USA))
5976a[4] (6362a)

Flowing Cape (IRE) *Reg Hollinshead* a94 93
6 b g Cape Cross(IRE) —Jet Lock (USA) (Crafty Prospector (USA))
1397[10] 1656[2] 2244[2] (2497) 3578[7] 3704[9] 4609[6] 5264[8] 5682[7] 6477[4] (6542) 6948[4] 7034[F]

Fluctuation (IRE) *Ian Williams* a58 49
3 b g Street Cry(IRE) —Rise And Fall (USA) (Quiet American (USA))
2103[14] 2596[6] 3177[8] 3710[2] 4743[4] 5803[7] 6618[5] 7071[2] 7371[3] 7463[3] 7655[4] 7695[9] 7911[2]

Flugelhorn (IRE) *Ed McMahon* 52
2 b c Elusive City(USA) —Prepare For War (IRE) (Marju (IRE))
3583[7] 5011[13] 5447[13]

Flurry Of Hands (IRE) *Ann Duffield* a22 58
2 b f Acclamation—Leopard Hunt (USA) (Diesis)
1414[10] 2430[4] 3070[2] 4194[5] ◆ (4667) 5550[7] 6667[10]

Fluvial (IRE) *Mark Johnston* a73 76
3 ch f Exceed And Excel(AUS) —Flamanda (Niniski (USA))
2643[6] 4845[5] 5391[8] 6135[2] 6311[3] 6511a[14] 7024[9]

Fly By Nelly *Mark Hoad* a63 62
5 b m Compton Place—Dancing Nelly (Shareef Dancer (USA))
135[8] 225[8] 2171[8] 3017[4] 3496[12]

Fly By White (IRE) *Barry Murtagh* a72 73
3 ch f Hawk Wing(USA) —Le Montrachet (Nashwan (USA))
2022[7] 2688[7] 3743[3] 4200[3] 5401[6]

Fly Down (USA) *Nicholas Zito* a124
4 ch h Mineshaft(USA) —Queen Randi (USA) (Fly So Free (USA))
1002a[13]

Flying Applause *Roy Bowring* a59 75
6 b g Royal Applause—Mrs Gray (Red Sunset)
400[8] 544[6] (734) 793[6] 895[6] 1276[4] 1649[3] 2161[3] 2487[6] (2610) (2845) 3643[8] 4517[9] 4793[12] 5034[3] 6261[11] 6479[3] 6777[2] 7057[4] 7424[9] 7571[2] 7788[7] 7912[2]

Flying Blue (AUS) *J Size* 118
5 br g Piccolo—Bright Blue (AUS) (Scenic)
7731a[14]

Flying Cherry (IRE) *Jo Crowley* a52 21
4 ch m Medecis—Fly With Wings (IRE) (In The Wings)
129[6] 863[3] 1331[5] 2921[15] 5843[7] 6084[4] 7005[7]

Flying Cross (IRE) *John Gosden* 113
4 b h Sadler's Wells(USA) —Ramruma (USA) (Diesis)
4524a[5]

Flying Eagle (POL) *Katerina Berthier*
4 ch h Jape(USA) —Flaming Girl (FR) (Alywar (USA))
4874a[9]

Flying Kitty *John Bridger* a41 52
2 b f One Cool Cat(USA) —Flying Millie (IRE) (Flying Spur (AUS))
2788[7] 3221[4] 3941[6] 4319[3] 5634[12]

Flying Phoenix *Gay Kelleway* a66 70
3 b f Phoenix Reach(IRE) —Rasmalai (Sadler's Wells (USA))
171[3] (516) (2463) 2850[8] 3363[2] 3918[3] 4490[4] 4713[5] 5631[7] 6067[5] (6223) 6490[7] 6767[3] 6936[5] 7055[5] 7211[4]

Flying Pickets (IRE) *Alan McCabe* a75 56
2 b g Piccolo—Burn (Selkirk (USA))
1165[6] 1383[8] 2409[5] 2784[3] 2797[2] (3137) 3491[2] 3973[4] 5597[2] 6053[10] 6652[4] 6846[9] (7423) (7725) 7849[6] 7881[6]

Flying Power *David Lanigan* a71 81
3 b g Dubai Destination(USA) —Rah Wa (USA) (Rahy (USA))
3952[8] 4367[5] 4755[2] (5340) 6023[6] 6592[2]

Flying Star (GER) *R Rohne* 64
2 b f Desert Prince(IRE) —Flying Wings (IRE) (Monsun (GER))
6737a[8]

Flying Tomato (FR) *T Lemer* a79 91
3 ch c Big Shuffle(USA) —Serena (IRE) (Rainbow Quest (USA))
5529a[0]

Flying Trader (USA) *Jane Chapple-Hyam* a72 69
2 rg c Mizzen Mast(USA) —Remediate (USA) (Miswaki (USA))
2817[4] 3401[9] 3986[3] 4714[4] 5013[9] 6102[5] 6757[4] 7436[3] (7786)

Flyjack (USA) *Lisa Williamson* a49 67
4 b g Johannesburg(USA) —Let Fly (USA) (Flying Paster (USA))
86[10] 173[8] 3041[10] 3733[8] 4128[9] 4783[12] 5860[8]

Flynn's Boy *Rae Guest* a77 84
3 ch g Tobougg(IRE) —Bukhoor (IRE) (Danehill (USA))
(509) (764) 1335[6] 2926[7] (4342) 4550[3] 5054[9] 5450[7]

Fly Tartare (FR) *T Larriviere* a86 87
4 b m Greengroom(FR) —Magic Tartare (FR) (Lesotho (USA))
92a[0]

Fly The Stars (GER) *W Hickst* a83 88
3 b c Lomitas—Fly To Win (IRE) (Ali-Royal (IRE))
1739a[7]

Focail Eile *John Ryan* a84 84
6 b g Noverre(USA) —Glittering Image (IRE) (Sadler's Wells (USA))
623[9] 881[8] 1867[8] 2915[8] 3130[11] (3741) 4143[2] 4278[12] (5722) 5894[2] 6796[2] 6830[5] 7234[4] 7299[5] 7922[7]

Focail Maith *John Ryan* a82 76
3 b g Oratorio(IRE) —Glittering Image (IRE) (Sadler's Wells (USA))
1051[4] 1313[6] 2064[11] 3133[3] 4060[2] 4142[2] 4665[5] 5004[3] 5892[7] (6799) 7236[3] 7601[7] 7734[3]

Focal *Sir Michael Stoute* 73
3 b f Pivotal—Coy (IRE) (Danehill (USA))
2529[2]

Fog Cutter (IRE) *James McAuley* a73
3 b g Mujadil(USA) —Park Approach (IRE) (Indian Ridge)
610[2] 811[5] 3717[3]

Fol Hollow (IRE) *David Nicholls* a58 103
6 b g Monashee Mountain(USA) —Constance Do (Risk Me (FR))
1166[17] 1715[4] 2727[5] 3778[6] (4197) 5204[2] 5831[20] 6112[2] 6913[8] 7116[8]

Folio (IRE) *Willie Musson* a72 63
11 b g Perugino(USA) —Bayleaf (Efisio)
174[10] 352[6] 621[7] 1233[10] 3690[13] 4730[9]

Folk Tune (IRE) *John Quinn* 78
8 b g Danehill(USA) —Musk Lime (USA) (Private Account (USA))
1156[5] 2492[3] 3510[3] 4856[6]

Follow The Dream *Karen George* a67 57
8 b m Double Trigger(IRE) —Aquavita (Kalaglow)
252[10] 560[14]

Follow The Flag (IRE) *Alan McCabe* a92 93
7 ch g Traditionally(USA) —Iktidar (Green Desert (USA))
(18) 186[2] 235[11] 548[4] 615[8] (703) 995[7] 1092[22] 3578[10] 4004[11] 4404[8] 4679[8] 4818[4] 5328[11] 6302[14] 6583[5] 6727[9] 7054[7] 7339[8] 7397[5] 7542[10] 7637[6] (7713) 7772[2] 7877[3]

Follow The Sun (IRE) *Peter Niven* a52 61
7 br g Tertullian(USA) —Sun Mate (IRE) (Miller's Mate)
3510[7] 3754[10] 4326[6] 4856[8] 6870[9]

Folly Bridge *Roger Charlton* 104
4 b m Avonbridge—Jalissa (Mister Baileys)
1889[6] (2470) 3703[6] 4332[5] 5080[11]

Folly Drove *Jonathan Portman* a67 65
3 b f Bahri(USA) —Zoena (Emarati (USA))
3259[6] 3818[7] 4270[5] 4707[3] 6468[11]

Fonnie (IRE) *Rae Guest* a51 56
3 ch f Barathea(IRE) —Top Row (Observatory (USA))
6668[4] 7271[6] 7723[5]

Font *Lawney Hill* 87
8 b g Sadler's Wells(USA) —River Saint (USA) (Irish River (FR))
3157[6] 4423[19]

Fonterutoli (IRE) *Roger Ingram* a77 73
4 gr g Verglas(IRE) —Goldendale (IRE) (Ali-Royal (IRE))
54[5] 124[6] 475[7] 647[10] 4317[13] 5281[8]

Fontley *Eve Johnson Houghton* 105
4 b m Sadler's Wells(USA) —Horatia (IRE) (Machiavellian (USA))
1884[3] 2558[5] 3030[9] 3703[2] 4132a[8] 4582[8] 5704[6] 6061[2]

Foolproof (IRE) *John Joseph Murphy* a84 84
3 ch c King's Best(USA) —Reasonably Devout (CAN) (St Jovite (USA))
2324a[8] (Dead)

Foolscap (IRE) *Jim Boyle* a15 1
2 ch c Choisir(AUS) —Notepad (King's Best (USA))
1268[8] 1786[6] 1954[5]

Fools Gold *Richard Guest* a32 43
6 b g Ishiguru(USA) —Sally Green (IRE) (Common Grounds)
122[7] 640[6] 950[14] 1497[9]

Fool Too Cool (IRE) *Niels Petersen*
2 b f One Cool Cat(USA) —Memory Motel (DEN) (Always Fair (USA))
5983a[10]

Foot Perfect (IRE) *David Marnane* a82 84
3 b f Footstepsinthesand—Lupine (IRE) (Lake Coniston (IRE))
6388a[22] 6854a[5] 7468a[6]

Foot Soldier (IRE) *A P O'Brien* 81
2 b c Danehill Dancer(IRE) —West Brooklyn (USA) (Gone West (USA))
2329a[4] ◆

Footstepsofspring (FR) *Willie Musson* a41 89
4 b g Footstepsinthesand—Moon West (USA) (Gone West (USA))
1177[13] 7641[10]

Foot Tapper *Chris Wall* 70
2 b c Invincible Spirit(IRE) —Jazz Princess (IRE) (Bahhare (USA))
6127[11] 6935[4] 7293[9]

Forbidden (IRE) *Ian McInnes* a65 68
8 ch g Singspiel(IRE) —Fragrant Oasis (USA) (Rahy (USA))
30[3] 7851[11] 7930[12]

Force Freeze (USA) *Peter R Walder* a120 105
6 bb g Forest Camp(USA) —Antifreeze (USA) (It's Freezing (USA))
155a[11] 414a[12] 755a[3] 999a[9] 7302a[2]

Forceful Appeal (USA) *Simon Dow* a81 82
3 bb c Successful Appeal(USA) —Kinetic Force (USA) (Holy Bull (USA))
980a[5] 7894[2]

Force Group (IRE) *Nick Littmoden* a70 78
7 b g Invincible Spirit(IRE) —Spicebird (IRE) (Ela-Mana-Mou)
266[7] 472[2] 695[2] 813[6] 897[9] 1577[6]

Force To Spend *Des Donovan* a54 50
4 b m Reset(AUS) —Mon Petit Diamant (Hector Protector (USA))
123[3] 250[5] 421[8] 7429[10] 7760[4] (7812) 7919[8]

Foreign King (USA) *Mike Hammond* a59 42
7 b g Kingmambo(USA) —Foreign Aid (USA) (Danzig (USA))
955[4] 3599[9]

Foreign Rhythm (IRE) *Ron Barr* 71
6 ch m Distant Music(USA) —Happy Talk (IRE) (Hamas (IRE))
(2062) 2365[6] 3805[6] 4126[10] 4288[6] 4942[4] 5309[7] 5442[3] 5647[4] 6159[7] 6266[9] 6778[11]

Foreign Tune *C Laffon-Parias* 79
2 b f Invincible Spirit(IRE) —Gwenseb (FR) (Green Tune (USA))
6808a[5]

Forest *Lydia Richards*
4 b g Josr Algarhoud(IRE) —Severance (USA) (Dispersal (USA))
420[7]

Forest Crown *Ralph Beckett* a98 99
4 b m Royal Applause—Wiener Wald (USA) (Woodman (USA))
241[5] 607a[4]

Forest Edge (IRE) *David Evans* a71 78
2 b g Amadeus Wolf—Compass Light (USA) (Lear Fan (USA))
4201[16] 4433[2] 5269[3] 5922[8] 6432[2] 6524[3] 6725[17] (7038) 7491[8]

Forest Row *Clive Cox* 78
2 b c Cockney Rebel(IRE) —Forest Fire (SWE) (Never So Bold)
2049[5] 6991[5]

Forever Janey *Paul Green* a50 37
2 b f Indesatchel(IRE) —Nee Lemon Left (Puissance)
7072[6] 7396[4] 7559[11] 7916[2]

Forever's Girl *Geoffrey Oldroyd* a85 79
5 b m Monsieur Bond(IRE) —Forever Bond (Danetime (IRE))
294[2] 403[6] (1279) 4288[8] 6044[5] (6537) 7356[4] 7847[4]

Forevertheoptimist (IRE) *Linda Stubbs* 97
2 gr g Verglas(IRE) —Hankering (IRE) (Missed Flight)
1209[3] (1673) 2056[4] 3064[7] (3589) 5286[9] 6518[7]

Forget Me Not Lane (IRE) *Kevin Ryan* 44
2 b g Holy Roman Emperor(IRE) —Mrs Arkada (FR) (Akarad (FR))
6673[9] 7293[14]

Forgive *Richard Hannon* 74
2 b f Pivotal—Amira (Efisio)
5655[9] 6329[7] (6934)

Forgiving Light *Andrew Oliver* 71
2 b c Echo Of Light—Redeem (IRE) (Doyoun)
2329a[6]

Forgotten (FR) *B Dutruel* a83 84
4 ch h Hernando(FR) —Only Alone (USA) (Rahy (USA))
900a[5]

Forgotten Hero (IRE) *Charles Hills* 81
2 bb c High Chaparral(IRE) —Sundown (Polish Precedent (USA))
6951[3]

Forjatt (IRE) *Roger Varian* 105
3 b g Iffraaj—Graceful Air (IRE) (Danzero (AUS))
1688[4] ◆ 2934[10] 3820[9] 4965[2] 5563[2]

Fork Handles *Mick Channon* 98
3 b f Doyen(IRE) —Natalie Jay (Ballacashtal (CAN))
1807[3] 2682[13] 3624[6] 4108[6]

Forks *Jane Chapple-Hyam* a75 68
4 ch g Fraam—Balinsky (IRE) (Skyliner)
4716[8] 5356[7] 5894[11] 6609[2] 6939[2] 7485[7] (7579) 7767[3]

For Life (IRE) *John E Long* a82 79
9 b g Bachir(IRE) —Zest (USA) (Zilzal (USA))
2719[11] 4246[3] 5038[4] 6794[2] 7485[11] 7636[5] 7919[5]

Formal Demand *Edward Vaughan* a79 75
3 b c Invincible Spirit(IRE) —Lady High Havens (IRE) (Bluebird (USA))
2151[2] (2650) 4255[6] 7024[5]

Formal Dining (USA) *Edward Vaughan* a60 63
3 b f Dynaformer(USA) —Zuppardo Ardo (USA) (Zuppardo's Prince (USA))
1363[11] 1845[10] 2157[12] 2637[4] 3220[3]

Formalite (FR) *T Larriviere* a76 68
4 b m Equerry(USA) —Expedition (FR) (Jabbar)
1033a[8]

Formidable Girl (USA) *Kevin Ryan* a55 59
3 bb f Roman Ruler(USA) —Gracility (USA) (Known Fact (USA))
1958[7] 2349[7] 3039[14] 3455[3] 4149[7] 6545[12]

Formidable Guest *Jamie Poulton* a66 60
7 b m Dilshaan—Fizzy Treat (Efisio)
3468[12] 4060[3] 4275[8] 4578[4] 7363[2] 7603[3] 7761[5]

Formulation (IRE) *Hughie Morrison* a79 78
4 b g Danehill Dancer(IRE) —Formal Approval (USA) (Kingmambo (USA))
1058[2] 1292[2] 2454[7]

Forrest Flyer (IRE) *Jim Goldie* 77
7 b g Daylami(IRE) —Gerante (USA) (Private Account (USA))
3115[4] (3660) 4382[4] 5724[9] 6082[4] 6707[7]

For Shia And Lula (IRE) *Daniel Mark Loughnane* a75 55
2 b c Majestic Missile(IRE) —Jack-N-Jilly (IRE) (Anita's Prince)
(6281) 7491[6]

Forster Street (IRE) *Tim Easterby* 55
2 b g Acclamation—Easy To Thrill (Soviet Star (USA))
2617[9] 3583[8] 4898[4]

Fort Bastion (IRE) *Richard Hannon* 106
2 b c Lawman(FR) —French Fern (IRE) (Royal Applause)
2455[2] ◆ 3152[2] 3861[5] 5181[2] 6565a[7]

Forte Dei Marmi *Roger L Attfield* a64 116
5 b g Selkirk(USA) —Frangy (Sadler's Wells (USA))
1342[6] 1821[3] ◆ 2290[5] 3591[10] 4410[8] ◆ 5544[3] 6204a[10]

Forthe Millionkiss (GER) *Uwe Ostmann* a24 101
7 b h Dashing Blade—Forever Nice (GER) (Greinton)
2657a[10]

Fortieth And Fifth (IRE) *Michael Bell* a71
2 b g Lemon Drop Kid(USA) —Maugusta (USA) (Saint Ballado (CAN))
7751[2] ◆

Fort Loudon (USA) *Stanley I Gold* a102
2 b c Awesome Of Course(USA) —Lottsa Talc (USA) (Talc (USA))
7306a[7]

Fortrose Academy (IRE) *Andrew Balding* a74 71
2 b c Iceman—Auspicious (Shirley Heights)
2214[3] (7345) 7765[5] 7875[7]

Fortunate Bid (IRE) *Linda Stubbs* a67 65
5 ch g Modigliani(USA) —Mystery Bid (Auction Ring (USA))
69[2] 283[4] 526[9] (619) 893[3] 957[7] (1633) 1911[7] (3719) 4604[2] 4918[2] 5143[7] 5902[6] 7463[4]

Fortunateencounter (FR) *John Gosden* a56 72
3 b f Muhtathir—Tashtiyana (IRE) (Doyoun)
952[6] 2850[9]

Fortunato (GER) *W Figge* a63
6 b h Monsun(GER) —Finora (GER) (Dashing Blade)
441a[6] 629a[15]

Fortune King (AUS) *W Baltromei* 37
6 b g El Moxie(USA) —Katysue (AUS) (Radiant Echo (AUS))
481a[10]

Fortunelini *Frank Sheridan* a48
6 b m Bertolini(USA) —River Of Fortune (IRE) (Lahib (USA))
3716[10] 7717[5] 7822[7]

Fortune Star (IRE) *Noel Wilson* 45
2 b g Soviet Star(USA) —Miss Tardy (JPN) (Lammtarra (USA))
2693[3] 3125[4] 3302[7] 4193[4] 4538[8] 7423[7]

Forty Proof (IRE) *Alan McCabe* a78 77
3 b g Invincible Spirit(IRE) —Cefira (USA) (Distant View (USA))
2199[8] 2508[10] 3975[5] 4486[5] 4960[8] 6403[4] 6752[3] 7575[4] 7629[4] 7746[10] 7776[9] 7893[10]

Forward Feline (IRE) *Bryn Palling* a73 54
5 b m One Cool Cat(USA) —Ymlaen (IRE) (Desert Prince (IRE))
367[6] 637[3] (1052) (1373) 2376[7] 4865[6] 5376[7] 5845[6] 6285[9] 6434[7] 7146[8] 7537[12]

For What (USA) *David Lanigan* a79 56
3 ch c Mingun(USA) —Cuanto Es (USA) (Exbourne (USA))
3650[14] 4489[5] 5103[5] 5630[4] 6311[7]

Forzarzi (IRE) *Hugh McWilliams* a52 54
7 b g Forzando—Zarzi (IRE) (Suave Dancer (USA))
1068[2] 1273[7] 1621[8] 2990[6] 3489[4] 3902[8]

Fossgate *James Bethell* a60 81
10 ch g Halling(USA) —Peryllys (Warning)
1617[8] 2393[2] (2462) (3054) (3581) 4173[5] (4612) 4901[4] 5761[4]

Fosters Cross (IRE) *Thomas Mullins* 83
9 b g Dr Massini(IRE) —Francie's Treble (Quayside)
(4398a)

Foster's Road *Mick Channon* a61 70
2 b g Imperial Dancer—Search Party (Rainbow Quest (USA))
4535[8] 5044[6] 5382[6] 5783[3] 6245[7] 6460[5] 6806[8] 7763[10]

Foundation Filly *F Doumen* a83 98
4 ch m Lando(GER) —Fureau (GER) (Ferdinand (USA))
1707a[9] 7580a[9]

Fountain Of Honour (IRE) *Noel Meade* a76 76
3 b f Sadler's Wells(USA) —Belle Of Honour (USA) (Honour And Glory (USA))
7792a[5]

Fouracres *Michael Appleby* a32
2 ch f Firebreak—Capponicus (IRE) (Woodborough (USA))
5514[12] 6180[9] 6308[12] 7231[11] 7421[8] 7725[6]

Four Better *Jamie Osborne* 72
2 b f Holy Roman Emperor(IRE) —Moonshadow (Diesis)
(6117) 6757[5] 7081[8]

Fourlanends *Noel Wilson* 30
4 ch g Dubawi(IRE) —Nova Cyngi (USA) (Kris S (USA))
2415[11] 3510[11]

Four Nations (USA) *Amanda Perrett* a62 89
3 ch g Langfuhr(CAN) —Kiswahili (Selkirk (USA))
(1683) ◆ 2842[2] 3551[5] 4426[4] 5035[2] ◆ 5710[2] 5966[4]

Four Poorer (IRE) *Jamie Osborne* 34
2 b f Oasis Dream—Venturi (Danehill Dancer (IRE))
4474[7] 4954[8] 5779[7] 7251[11]

Four Richer *Jamie Osborne* a71 42
2 b c Ishiguru(USA) —To The Woods (IRE) (Woodborough (USA))
3229[10] (3490)

Foursquare Funtime *Reg Hollinshead* a72
2 b g Common World(USA) —Farina (IRE) (Golan (IRE))
7197[8] 7559[5] 7929[2]

Four Steps Back *Mark Usher* a42
4 ch g Royal Academy(USA) —Runaway Queen (USA) (Runaway Groom (CAN))
6475[7] 6947[9] 7662[6]

Fourth Generation (IRE) *Alan Swinbank* a82 79
4 ch g Kris Kin(USA) —Merewood Lodge (IRE) (Grand Lodge (USA))
1651[4] 2282[5] 2544[9]

Fourth Of June (IRE) *Ed Dunlop* a61 74
2 b c Amadeus Wolf—Our Joia (Dansili)
6123[6] 6768[2] 7367[3]

Foxhaven *Patrick Chamings* a79 85
9 ch g Unfuwain(USA) —Dancing Mirage (IRE) (Machiavellian (USA))
3434[4] 4008[5] 4957[4] 6130[5] 6445[4] 7430[3]

Fox Hunt (IRE) *Mark Johnston* a101 118
4 ch g Dubawi(IRE) —Kiltubber (IRE) (Sadler's Wells (USA))
667[2] ◆ (900a) 1717[6] 2044[4] (2716) (3156) ◆ 3875[2] 4469[4] 5285[6] (6200a) 7218a[7]

Foxley (IRE) *Robin Bastiman* 68
3 ch f Indian Haven—Maidford (IRE) (Singspiel (IRE))
(1767) 2232[5] 3219[3] 3468[6] 4560[14] 6939[14]

Fox's Ambers (FR) *Richard Hannon* a33 36
2 ch f Shirocco(GER) —Magic Hill (FR) (Danehill Dancer (IRE))
4007[10] 4662[10] 5320[9] 5844[10] 6805[10]

Foxtrot Alpha (IRE) *Peter Winkworth* a68 74
5 b m Desert Prince(IRE) —Imelda (USA) (Manila (USA))
1995[3] 2605[2] 3019[2] (3250) 3735[9]

Foxtrot Golf (IRE) *Peter Winkworth* a68 38
3 b g Diamond Green(FR) —Tides (Bahamian Bounty)
228[3] 313[6] 594[2]

Foxtrot Hotel (IRE) *Peter Winkworth* a86 89
3 b g Majestic Missile(IRE) —Opalescent (IRE) (Polish Precedent (USA))
1724[2] (2311) ◆ 2763[4] 4353[3] 5322[3]

Foxtrot India (IRE) *Peter Winkworth* 83
2 b c Tagula(IRE) —Mayfair (Green Desert (USA))
(1678) 2154[4] 2437[6] 5492[3]

Foxtrot Romeo (IRE) *Bryan Smart* 102
2 b c Danehill Dancer(IRE) —Hawala (IRE) (Warning)
(5202) 5826[4] 6162[4]

Foxy Music *Eric Alston* a74 93
7 b g Foxhound(USA) —Primum Tempus (Primo Dominie)
2028[15] 2397[10] 3279[8] 3379[2] 4195[5] 5033[16] (5918) 6332[12] 7018[14]

Fragment (IRE) *R Pritchard-Gordon* 76
2 b f Iffraaj—Choice Pickings (IRE) (Among Men (USA))
7326a[2]

Fragonard *Sir Henry Cecil* 82
2 ch f Teofilo(IRE) —Delicieuse Lady (Trempolino (USA))
4061[2]

Frameit (IRE) *James Given* a65 64
4 b g Antonius Pius(USA) —Delisha (Salse (USA))
131[4] 277[2] (393) 486[5] 560[3] 718[6] 769[2] 2846[5] 3281[4] 4633[6]

Francesco Rules (USA) *David Fawkes* 81
2 bb g Roman Ruler(USA) —Critical Factor (USA) (Star De Naskra)
( )

Frances Stuart (IRE) *Andrew Balding* a76 83
4 b m King's Best(USA) —Higher Love (IRE) (Sadler's Wells (USA))
1884[14] 3740[5]

Francis Albert *Michael Mullineaux* a65 61
5 b g Mind Games—Via Dolorosa (Chaddleworth (IRE))
123[11] 256[5] 362[5] 691[7] 734[6] 892[3] 934[7] 1065[4] 1247[8] (1469) 1716[8] 1982[4] 2164[8] 3908[5] 4564[5] (4895) 5175[4] 5603[3] 5865[3] 6602[8] 6694[7] (6943) 7266[12] 7737[7]

Franciscan *Luca Cumani* a56 94
3 b g Medicean—Frangy (Sadler's Wells (USA))
(1392) ◆ 1949[5] 2389[4] (3558) (4084) 4966[3] 5938[2] (6607)

Franco Is My Name *Peter Hedger* a94 78
5 b g Namid—Veronica Franco (Darshaan)
180[3] 525[5] 702[5] 991[6] 2604[5] 3815[5] 4432[7]

Frankel *Sir Henry Cecil* 139
3 b c Galileo(IRE) —Kind (IRE) (Danehill (USA))
(1405) (1686) (3011) (4425) (6860)

Frankenstein (ITY) *B Grizzetti* 111
4 b g Dubawi(IRE) —Lifting (IRE) (Nordance (USA))
1918a[3] (2540a) 2982a[6]

Frankie Valley *J S Moore* 13
2 ch g Three Valleys(USA) —Breathing Space (USA) (Expelled (USA))
1563[6] 2425[5]

Frank Street *Eve Johnson Houghton* a59 72
5 ch g Fraam—Pudding Lane (IRE) (College Chapel)
489[P]

Frantic Storm (GER) *Frau J Mayer* 102
5 b h Nayef(USA) —Flamingo Road (GER) (Acatenango (GER))
7045a[7]

Frantz De Galais (FR) *J-M Lefebvre* a57 65
5 ch g Trempolino(USA) —Exceptionnel Lady (FR) (Vertical Speed (FR))
706a[3]

Frasers Hill *Roger Varian* 72
2 ch c Selkirk(USA) —Shemriyna (IRE) (King Of Kings (IRE))
7082[3]

Fratellino *Alan McCabe* a97 101
4 ch h Auction House(USA) —Vida (IRE) (Wolfhound (USA))
989[7] 1111[18] 1476[10] 1720[2]

Freckenham (IRE) *Michael Bell* a74 81
3 ch f Exceed And Excel(AUS) —Farrfesheena (USA) (Rahy (USA))
(1358) (1916) 2468[12] 3283[9]

Fred Archer (IRE) *David Marnane* a89 85
3 b g Iffraaj—Fairy Contessa (IRE) (Fairy King (USA))
5086a[13]

Freda's Rose (IRE) *Owen Brennan* a43 55
7 b m Rossini(USA) —African Scene (IRE) (Scenic)
(4946) 5470[8] 6049[10] 6262[4] 7270[8] 7424[12]

Freddie Bolt *Frederick Watson* 40
5 b h Diktat—Birjand (Green Desert (USA))
2591[7] 4408[6] 4904[7] 7061[7]

Freddie's Girl (USA) *Seamus Durack* a82 56
4 bb m More Than Ready(USA) —Carib Gal (USA) (Awesome Again (CAN))
215[5] 910[2] ◆ 1196[11] 2027[11] 3517[9]

Freddy Q (IRE) *Richard Hannon* a43 83
2 ch c Iffraaj—Barnabas (ITY) (Slip Anchor)
2817[9] 4087[2] 4446[4] 5196[2] (5967)

Frederick Engels *David Brown* 111
2 b c Iceman—Colonel's Daughter (Colonel Collins (USA))
2042[2] 2504[2] (2725) ◆ (3014) (3773) 4834a[6] 5305a[5]

Fredericktheqreat *Hughie Morrison* a67 59
2 b c Exceed And Excel(AUS) —Torgau (IRE) (Zieten (USA))
6481[9] 6993[8] 7369[4] 7569[2]

Frederick William *Peter Makin* a47 72
3 b g Tobougg(IRE) —Bisaat (USA) (Bahri (USA))
3002[2] 4154[11] 4627[3] 5420[5]

Fred Fenster (IRE) *Edward Lynam* a58 97
3 b g Fasliyev(USA) —Royal Bounty (IRE) (Generous (IRE))
7189a[4]

Fred Lalloupet *D Smaga* 108
4 b h Elusive City(USA) —Firm Friend (IRE) (Affirmed (USA))
815a[5] (1122a) 2138a[7] 2754a[9] 4121a[2] 5532a[4] 7221a[2] 7534a[2]

Fred Willetts (IRE) *David Evans* a97 94
3 b g Noverre(USA) —Intaglia (GER) (Lomitas)
(59) (106) (302) 845[8] 1202[5] 1384[2] 1725[6] 1820[2] 2296[9] 2705[6] (2908) 3378[6] 4333[12] 4574[9] 5450[8]

Free Agent *Richard Hannon* 112
5 b g Dr Fong(USA) —Film Script (Unfuwain (USA))
1188[2] 1601[3] 2072[7] 3204[7]

Free Art *Geoffrey Harker* a83 89
3 b g Iffraaj—Possessive Artiste (Shareef Dancer (USA))
2802[6] 3571[5] 3729[7] 4142[3] 5560[3] 6192[6]

Freedom (IRE) *A P O'Brien* a105 103
3 b c Hurricane Run(IRE) —Cute Cait (Atraf)
5744a[3] (6514a)

Freedom Flyer (IRE) *Brian Ellison* a68 57
3 b g Librettist(USA) —Sama (IRE) (Machiavellian (USA))
431[4] 579[5] 714[5] 1018[4] (1819) 1969[7]

Freedom Trail *Tim Fitzgerald* a54 60
3 b f Bertolini(USA) —Film Buff (Midyan (USA))
868[8] 5034[8] 5490[14] 5787[10] 7006[9]

Freeforaday (USA) *John Best* a93 103
4 ch h Freefourinternet(USA) —All My Yesterdays (USA) (Wild Again (USA))
440a[2] 627a[7] 844[9] 1406[24] 3109[9] 4993[8] 5936[14] 6219[11] 6948[7]

Free For All (IRE) *Sylvester Kirk* 94
4 br g Statue Of Liberty(USA) —Allegorica (IRE) (Alzao (USA))
(1898) 3109[12] 3535[3] ◆

Free House *Brian Meehan* 75
2 ch g Sir Percy—Coming Home (Vettori (IRE))
5011[7] 6059[5] 6630[4] 6911[5]

Freemusic (IRE) *L Riccardi* 97
7 b h Celtic Swing—Favignana (GER) (Grand Lodge (USA))
2134a[9]

Free Tussy (ARG) *Gary Moore* a79 72
7 b g Freelancer(USA) —Perlada (ARG) (Cipayo (ARG))
54[8] 272[6] 472[4] 565[2] 814[3] 1144[7] 2308[5] 2685[2] 3426[7] 6621[6]

Free Verse *Richard Hannon* 86
2 b f Danehill Dancer(IRE) —Fictitious (Machiavellian (USA))
(4155) 4999[11] 5584[3] (6864)

Free Winner (IRE) *B Grizzetti* 95
3 b c Oratorio(IRE) —Freedom (GER) (Second Empire (IRE))
1431a[5]

Free Zone *Bryan Smart* 87
2 b g Kyllachy—Aldora (Magic Ring (IRE))
2455[8] 3398[2] 4094[23] 5077[9] (5367) 5922[2] (6323) 6535[15] (7103)

Fremen (USA) *David Nicholls* a78 86
11 ch g Rahy(USA) —Northern Trick (USA) (Northern Dancer (CAN))
856[6] 1037[4] 1382[10] (1614) 1828[2] (2149) (2347) 2807[3] 3831[5] 4501[5] 6006[3] 6262[7]

Freminius (GER) *W Baltromei* a72 107
7 b h Erminius(GER) —Freixenet (GER) (Big Shuffle (USA))
2867a[2] 4373a[5] 5095a[2]

Fremont (IRE) *Richard Hannon* a82 84
4 b g Marju(IRE) —Snow Peak (Arazi (USA))
1094[9] 1529[10] 2604[8] 3797[9] 6220[4] 6439[7]

French Applause (IRE) *Mike Sowersby* 70
5 b g Royal Applause—A Ma Guise (USA) (Silver Hawk (USA))
4904[8] 5403[11]

French Art *Nigel Tinkler* a64 75
6 ch g Peintre Celebre(USA) —Orange Sunset (IRE) (Roanoke (USA))
148[7] 317[2] 489[7] 933[7] (1216) 1394[4] 2027[6] 2560[4] 3088[9] 3326[8]

French Emperor (IRE) *Edward Lynam* a53 98
2 b c Holy Roman Emperor(IRE) —Se La Vie (FR) (Highest Honor (FR))
972a[6] 2776a[3] 3439a[3]

French Express (IRE) *John C McConnell* a35 61
4 ch m Namid—She Legged It (IRE) (Cape Cross (IRE))
255[9]

French Fifteen (FR) *N Clement* 115
2 ch c Turtle Bowl(IRE) —Spring Morning (FR) (Ashkalani (IRE))
6660a[2] (7192a)

French Hollow *Tim Fitzgerald* a77 82
6 b g Beat Hollow—Campaspe (Dominion)
(89) (172) 286[6] 1215[3] 2262[5] 2696[9] (3828) (4043) (5273) ◆ 6171[6] 6707[3]

French Navy *Mahmood Al Zarooni* 113
3 b c Shamardal(USA) —First Fleet (USA) (Woodman (USA))
(5055) (5934) ◆ 6558a[9] 7027[6]

French Quebec (IRE) *K J Condon* 85
2 b f Excellent Art—Soul Mountain (IRE) (Rock Of Gibraltar (IRE))
2532a[5]

French Rules (FR) *H-A Pantall*
2 gr c Aussie Rules(USA) —Ouarzazate (IRE) (Enrique)
7449a[0]

French Seventyfive *Tim Walford* 53
4 b g Pursuit Of Love—Miss Tun (Komaite (USA))
3450[7]

Frequency *Keith Dalgleish* a86 78
4 br g Starcraft(NZ) —Soundwave (Prince Sabo)
213[4] (388) (404) 538[5] 665[3] 746[2] 786[3] (904) 985[7] 1044[2] (1180) (1439) 1800[3] 2016[3] 2280[9] 2633[2] 2806[9] 3162[4] (3657) 4503[9] 5371[11] 6081[13] 6779[4] (7172) 7265[6] (7416)

Fresa *Sir Mark Prescott Bt* a55 68
2 b f Selkirk(USA) —Flor Y Nata (USA) (Fusaichi Pegasus (USA))
3490[4] 3736[7] (4140) 4760[4]

Fresteem *Luke Dace* a39 33
2 b c Fraam—Grezie (Mark Of Esteem (IRE))
1835[8] 2641[9] 5382[14] 5809[11]

Friboy (FR) *K Borgel* a71 70
3 b c Bad As I Wanna Be(IRE) —Peutiot (FR) (Valanour (IRE))
638a[3]

Friday Night Lad (IRE) *Alan Swinbank* 46
4 b g Redback—Social Butterfly (USA) (Sir Ivor (USA))
1210[8] 1540[8] 1860[6] 6158[11] 6870[14]

Frill A Minute *Lynn Siddall* a35 25
7 b m Lake Coniston(IRE) —Superfrills (Superpower)
57[11] 512[10] 600[7] 752[10]

Frock (IRE) *Sylvester Kirk* a67
2 b f Excellent Art—Maimana (IRE) (Desert King (IRE))
7454[7] 7598[4]

Frog Hollow *Ralph Beckett* a90 88
2 gr g Intikhab(USA) —The Manx Touch (IRE) (Petardia)
4068[3] (4969) ◆ (6464) ◆ 7390[3]

Frognal (IRE) *Richard Guest* a65 83
5 b g Kheleyf(USA) —Shannon Dore (IRE) (Turtle Island (IRE))
1035[2] 1942[9] 2280[10] 2494[4] (2588) (2917) 3276[15] 3801[2] 4006[3] 4509[10] 5341[3] 5502[9] 6056[8] 6351[9] 6616[9] (6759) 6794[5] 7074[7] 7262[10] 7420[11] 7484[8] 7588[5] 7748[5] 7895[3]

Frolic Along (IRE) *J R Jenkins* a29 16
4 b m Medecis—High Glider (High Top)
1285[4] 4180[5] 5098[6]

Frolic's Revenge (USA) *Milton W Wolfson* a99
2 bb f Vindication(USA) —Stormy Frolic (USA) (Summer Squall (USA))
7283a[9]

Fromsong (IRE) *Dean Ivory* a76 69
13 b g Fayruz—Lindas Delight (Batshoof)
298[9]

Fromthestables Com (IRE) *J W Hills* a58 65
2 b c Strategic Prince—Kathy Tolfa (IRE) (Sri Pekan (USA))
1505[8] 1913[2] 2194[5] 2788[6] 3780[7]

Frontier Star (USA) *Fredrik Reuterskiold* a81
4 b g Canadian Frontier(USA) —Famous Colony (USA) (Pleasant Colony (USA))
5981a[8]

Frontline Girl (IRE) *Mrs K Burke* 82
5 b m Fath(USA) —Ellistown Lady (IRE) (Red Sunset)
1114[2] 2301[7] (2413) 3164[3] 3338[5] 4361[7] 6081[12] 6831[13]

Frontline Phantom (IRE) *Mrs K Burke* a42 77
4 b g Noverre(USA) —Daisy Hill (Indian Ridge)
(1099) (1671) (1874) 2810[4] 4004[8] 4784[5] 5036[5] 6225[3] 6379[5] (6589) 7178[10]

Front Rank (IRE) *Dianne Sayer* a52 46
11 b g Sadler's Wells(USA) —Alignment (IRE) (Alzao (USA))
1519[9]

Frosted Grape (IRE) *David Pipe* a57 64
5 b m Kheleyf(USA) —Two Shonas (IRE) (Persian Heights)
6476[7]

Frosty Friday *J R Jenkins* a63
3 b f Storming Home—Seasonal Blossom (IRE) (Fairy King (USA))
1974[3] 7739[2]

Frosty Reception *Michael Appleby* a56 19
3 b f Iceman—Toleration (Petong)
214[7] 559[5] 791[3] 1134[8] 1270[11] 4950[8] 5674[13] 6182[11]

Frosty Secret *Jane Chapple-Hyam* 66
2 b f Echo Of Light—Raze (Halling (USA))
6480[3] 7164[8]

Frosty Secret (USA) *M F De Kock* a105 96
7 br h Put It Back(USA) —Secret From Above (USA) (Great Above (USA))
414a[9] 501a[11] 606a[6]

Frozen Over *Stuart Kittow* a26 73
3 b g Iceman—Pearly River (Elegant Air)
1654[3] (2427) 2916[5] 3801[4] 6378[6] 6924[7] ◆ 7235[3]

Frozen Power (IRE) *Mahmood Al Zarooni* a106 106
4 b h Oasis Dream—Musical Treat (IRE) (Royal Academy (USA))
156a[7] 331a[8] 503a[11] 4972[11]

Fruehling (IRE) *Sir Michael Stoute* 95
3 b c Azamour(IRE) —Spring Symphony (IRE) (Darshaan)
4065[3] 4956[2] 6324[2]

Fu Fic Fas *Paul Fitzsimons* 61
2 b f Multiplex—Sarcita (Primo Dominie)
3779[7] 4245[5]

Fugitive Motel (IRE) *Richard Hannon* a70 66
2 b g Holy Roman Emperor(IRE) —Zing Ping (IRE) (Thatching)
2997[10] 3779[5] 4201[6] ◆ 5142[4]

Fugnina *Marco Botti* a84 89
3 b f Hurricane Run(IRE) —Step Danzer (IRE) (Desert Prince (IRE))
6027[7] 6770[4] 7361[5]

Fujin Dancer (FR) *Brian Ellison* a75 86
6 ch g Storming Home—Badaayer (USA) (Silver Hawk (USA))
(3456) 4360[9] 4603[3] 6303[3]

Fulani's (IRE) *Robert Cowell* a62 64
3 gr f Tobougg(IRE) —Tarkwa (Doyoun)
214[10]

Fulbright *Mark Johnston* 95
2 b c Exceed And Excel(AUS) —Lindfield Belle (IRE) (Fairy King (USA))
1966[3] (2261) ◆ (2712) 3012[16] 4131a[5] 6323[3] 6535[11] 7021[3]

Fulford *Mel Brittain* a65 56
6 ch g Elmaamul(USA) —Last Impression (Imp Society (USA))
1463[6] 4518[9] 5009[8] 5789[4] 6208[15]

Fulgur *Luca Cumani* 106
3 b c High Chaparral(IRE) —Selebela (Grand Lodge (USA))
1320[7] 2100[3] ◆ 3105[5] (3774) 4467[5] 5700[9]

Full Bloom *Gerard Butler* a80 76
3 ch f Camacho—Bint Alhabib (Nashwan (USA))
191[4] 344[5] 684[2] (3771) 4275[11] 4713[2] 5391[7] 5856[3] 6583[4] (7208) 7453[4] 7745[3]

Full Footage *Roger Charlton* 62
3 b f Lando(GER) —Widescreen (USA) (Distant View (USA))
1865[3] 2568[10] 3432[9]

Full Pelt (USA) *Tom Dascombe* a67 61
3 bb g Orientate(USA) —Class (USA) (Thunder Gulch (USA))
1436[5] 1693[6] *2174[9]* 4435[3] 4812[5] *5392[3]* *5739[8]*

Full Shilling (IRE) *John Spearing* a66 64
3 b f Intikhab(USA) —Full Cream (USA) (Hennessy (USA))
709[3] *971[4]* *1220[7]* 2993[3] 3230[3] 4321[6] (4950) 5344[2] 5677[8] 6479[10] *(6696)* 6940[5]

Full Speed (GER) *Alan Swinbank* a95 86
6 b g Sholokhov(IRE) —Flagny (FR) (Kaldoun (FR))
1154[9] 1713[9] 2124[8] 2544[8] 2892[5] 3858[2] 4360[3] (4555)

Full Steam *Ed Dunlop* a95 97
4 b m Oasis Dream—Western Appeal (USA) (Gone West (USA))
92a[0] 1883[6]

Full Stretch (USA) *Pat Eddery* a54
3 bb c Aptitude(USA) —Overwhelmed (USA) (Unbridled (USA))
2568[11] *5140[5]* *5816[7]* *6545[7]*

Full Support (IRE) *F Vermeulen* 76
2 b c Acclamation—My Love Thomas (IRE) (Cadeaux Genereux)
3915[6] (4557) 6431[3] *7666a[4]*

Full Toss *Jim Goldie* a80 65
5 b g Nayef(USA) —Spinning Top (Alzao (USA))
6079[12] 6429[5] 7161[9] *7397[4]* *7549a[4]*

Fully Armed (IRE) *Rae Guest* a26 41
3 ch f Indian Haven—Madame Marjou (IRE) (Marju (IRE))
1236[5] 1945[11] *2384[12]* 2598[3] 2829[14] 3309[7]

Fulney *James Eustace* 81
2 b f Dr Fong(USA) —Postage Stampe (Singspiel (IRE))
6603[2] ◆ 6950[3]

Fumino Imagine (JPN) *Masaru Honda* 111
5 b m Manhattan Cafe(JPN) —Shinko Imagine (USA) (Dixieland Band (USA))
7410a[8]

Fun Affair (USA) *John Gosden* a87 76
4 b m Distorted Humor(USA) —Caressing (USA) (Honour And Glory (USA))
1104[9] 1622[6]

Funatfuntasia *Michael J Browne* a67 87
7 b g Dansili—Guntakal (IRE) (Night Shift (USA))
6511a[11]

Funky Munky *Alistair Whillans* a36 56
6 b g Talaash(IRE) —Chilibang Bang (Chilibang)
1216[11] 5402[12] 5822[11] 6430[2] (7159)

Funny Crazy (FR) *J E Hammond* 62
2 gr f Chichicastenango(FR) —Folle Garde (FR) (Garde Royale)
3567a[5]

Funny Enough *George Baker* 65
3 b f Dansili—Good Enough (FR) (Mukaddamah (USA))
2026[8] 2960[13] 3689[5]

Funon (IRE) *F Head* 93
3 b g Cape Cross(IRE) —Baqah (IRE) (Bahhare (USA))
5230a[8]

Furiosa (IRE) *Edward Creighton* a25 41
3 b f Captain Rio—Proud Myth (IRE) (Mark Of Esteem (IRE))
2493[10]

Furner's Green (IRE) *A P O'Brien* 113
2 b c Dylan Thomas(IRE) —Lady Icarus (Rainbow Quest (USA))
5181[7] 5951a[4] 6391a[4]

Fury *William Haggas* 109
3 gb g Invincible Spirit(IRE) —Courting (Pursuit Of Love)
1686[5] 2440[2] 3777[5] 4096[4] 6955[7]

Furzanah *Luca Cumani* a50 63
2 b f Dubawi(IRE) —Latent Lover (IRE) (In The Wings)
6440[12] 6933[9]

[illegible] Thompson a38 45
5 b m Bertolini(USA) —Georgianna (IRE) (Petardia)
2990[11] 3451[8] 3733[11] 3972[11] 4636[7] 4986[12] 6386[7] 6454[5] 7065[9]

Future Generation (IRE) *G M Lyons* a80 109
3 b f Hurricane Run(IRE) —Posterity (IRE) (Indian Ridge)
3527a[10] 4116a[2] (4978a)

Future Impact (IRE) *Ed de Giles* a54 74
3 b g Kheleyf(USA) —Daring Imp (IRE) (Mac's Imp (USA))
973a[13] 4950[7] *5941[6]* *6696[9]* *6999[10]* *7429[11]*

Future Security (IRE) *Saeed Bin Suroor* 80
2 ch c Dalakhani(IRE) —Schust Madame (IRE) (Second Set (IRE))
6774[3] (7060)

Future Wonder (IRE) *Rae Guest* a48
2 b f Whipper(USA) —Savage (IRE) (Polish Patriot (USA))
5834[6] ◆

Futurism *Richard Hannon* a71 53
3 b c Bertolini(USA) —Pastel (Lion Cavern (USA))
(945) *1194[3]* 5653[11] *6254[8]* *6790[12]*

Futurista (USA) *F Head* 104
3 b f Awesome Again(CAN) —Raise A Beauty (USA) (Alydar (USA))
5028a[0] 5958a[3]

Fylarchos (FR) *C Laffon-Parias* 93
4 ch g Muhtathir—Alfreda (Unfuwain (USA))
195a[0]

Gabbiano *Jeremy Gask* a81
2 b g Zafeen(FR) —Hollybell (Beveled (USA))
7526[2] ◆ *(7749)*

Gabrial (IRE) *Richard Fahey* 89
2 b c Dark Angel(IRE) —Guajira (FR) (Mtoto)
(1823) ◆ (2488) ◆ 3012[20]

Gabrial's Bounty (IRE) *Mick Channon* a61 53
2 ch g Bahamian Bounty—Social Storm (USA) (Future Storm (USA))
6165[12] 6406[5] *6620[3]* 7051[8]

Gabrial's Gift (IRE) *David Simcock* a84 68
2 gr c Verglas(IRE) —Sahara Lady (IRE) (Lomitas)
4159[6] 4815[6] *(5382)* ◆ 6373[4]

Gabrial's Girl (IRE) *Ian Williams*
2 b f Whipper(USA) —Aldburgh (Bluebird (USA))
1823[11] *3708[9]*

Gabrial's Hope (FR) *Mark Johnston*
2 b c Teofilo(IRE) —Wedding Night (FR) (Valanour (IRE))
7709[7]

Gabrial's King (IRE) *Ian Williams* a46 8
2 b c Hurricane Run(IRE) —Danella (IRE) (Platini (GER))
7109[12] *7368[5]*

Gabrial's Layla (IRE) *Mark Johnston* a49 44
2 b f Dylan Thomas(IRE) —Marlene-D (Selkirk (USA))
6322[5] 6985[9] *7493[7]*

Gabrial's Princess (IRE) *Bryan Smart* a39 61
2 b f Royal Applause—Happy Go Lily (In The Wings)
3336[5] 4080[8] 5269[12] 5645[9] *7742[6]*

Gabrial's Star *Bryan Smart* 81
2 b c Hernando(FR) —Grain Only (Machiavellian (USA))
(6187)

Gabrial The Great (IRE) *Michael Bell* 62
2 b c Montjeu(IRE) —Bayourida (USA) (Slew O'Gold (USA))
6447[5]

Gabrial The King (USA) *Michael Bell* a62 89
2 b c Speightstown(USA) —Dynamous (USA) (Dynaformer (USA))
4365[3] (4639) ◆ *6055[6]*

Gabrial The Prince (IRE) *David Simcock* a46 35
2 b g Motivator—Set Fire (IRE) (Bertolini (USA))
6245[9] 7082[13] *7369 [12]*

Gabrielle Da Vinci *David Evans* a44
5 b m Erhaab(USA) —Gulshan (Batshoof)
85[4] *161[7]* *309[6]*

Gabriel's Lad (IRE) *Denis Coakley* a71 71
2 b g Dark Angel(IRE) —Catherine Wheel (Primo Dominie)
5812[2] *6539[2]* *7345[2]*

Gadobout Dancer *Declan Carroll* a37 60
4 b m Tobougg(IRE) —Delta Tempo (IRE) (Bluebird (USA))
1216[10] *3741[12]* 4143[6]

Gadreel (IRE) *Anthony Middleton* a46 54
2 b g Dark Angel(IRE) —Borsalino (USA) (Trempolino (USA))
2641[7] 3308[5] 4201[15] 4485[5] *7937[11]*

Gaelic Wizard (IRE) *Dominic Ffrench Davis* 50
3 b c Fasliyev(USA) —Fife (IRE) (Lomond (USA))
4970[8]

Gagarina (IRE) *J-C Rouget* 89
3 b f Galileo(IRE) —Guarded (Eagle Eyed (USA))
1597a[3]

Gagnant (IRE) *Mrs Prunella Dobbs* a64 70
5 b g Modigliani(USA) —Roraima (Top Ville)
6511a[6]

Gaily Game *J-C Rouget* 110
3 b c Montjeu(IRE) —Gaily Tiara (USA) (Caerleon (USA))
(5131a) 6555a[5]

Gaily Noble (IRE) *Andrew Haynes* a93 95
5 b g One Cool Cat(USA) —Dream Genie (Puissance)
1102[8] 1479[11] *2000[6]* 5451[8] *6948[13]*

Gala Casino Star (IRE) *Richard Fahey* a88 81
6 ch g Dr Fong(USA) —Àbir (Soviet Star (USA))
186[7] *385[8]* *572[7]* *977a[11]* 1099[3] 1461[3] (1859) 2413[5] 2887[5] (3170) 4477[4] 5465[12] 6263[6] *7130[7]*

Galandora *Dr Jeremy Naylor* a24 39
11 b m Bijou D'Inde—Jelabna (Jalmood (USA))
2140[10]

Galant De Giverny (FR) *C Diard* 30
4 gr g Blackdoun(FR) —Giverny (FR) (Marignan (USA))
842a[0]

Galantery (FR) [illegible]
3 b f Tobougg(IRE) —Anchorage (FR) (Slip Anchor)
4874a[3]

Galant Star (FR) *Gary Moore* a54 82
5 b m Galileo(IRE) —La Norvegienne (Darshaan)
314[3] *622[6]*

Gala Sakhee *B Grizzetti* 94
2 b f Sakhee(USA) —Tenuta Di Gala (IRE) (Nashwan (USA))
6904a[4]

Gala Spirit (IRE) *Peter Niven* a68 70
4 b m Invincible Spirit(IRE) —Luggala (IRE) (Kahyasi)
1196[9] *1581[10]* *2001[8]* 3027[16] 4371[10] *5943[4]* *6618[9]* *(6982)* *7268[4]*

Galatian *Rod Millman* 88
4 ch g Traditionally(USA) —Easy To Imagine (USA) (Cozzene (USA))
1140[14] 1656[3] ◆ (2111) 2470[7] 3801[5] 4958[4] 5451[4] 5970[7] *6467[7]* 7262[3]

Galaxie Sud (USA) *J-C Rouget* a93 96
3 b f El Prado(IRE) —Germance (USA) (Silver Hawk (USA))
(901a) 5958a[10]

Gale Green *Henry Candy* 74
4 b m Galileo(IRE) —Anna Of Brunswick (Rainbow Quest (USA))
2956[11] 3632[8] (6402) 6894[2]

Galiando *Jeremy Noseda* a89 97
3 b c Galileo(IRE) —Nando's Dream (Hernando (FR))
(2875) ◆ 3987[2] ◆ *4665[3]* (5328) 6302[22]

Galician *Mark Johnston* a79 72
2 gr f Redoute's Choice(AUS) —Gweneira (Machiavellian (USA))
7209[2] *7431[2]* *(7526)*

Galicuix *Luca Cumani* 42
3 ch f Galileo(IRE) —Clizia (IRE) (Machiavellian (USA))
1549[12] 2026[10]

Galikova (FR) *F Head* 121
3 b f Galileo(IRE) —Born Gold (USA) (Blushing Groom (FR))
(1922a) ◆ 2977a[2] (5128a) (5989a) 6567a[9]

Galilee Chapel (IRE) *David Elsworth* a66 62
2 b g Baltic King—Triple Zero (IRE) (Raise A Grand (IRE))
1939[5] 2731[6] 3273[5] 6021[3] *6487[2]* *(6662)*

Galileo Figaro (AUS) *Philip Kirby* a30
7 b g Galileo(IRE) —Overnight (GER) (Windwurf (GER))
6873[12]

Galileo's Choice (IRE) *D K Weld* 111
5 b g Galileo(IRE) —Sevi's Choice (USA) (Sir Ivor (USA))
(5744a)

Galiotto (IRE) *Gary Moore* a64 67
5 b g Galileo(IRE) —Welsh Motto (USA) (Mtoto)
524[4] *592[4]* *819[6]* 2451[5] (2638) 2991[7] 3690[8] 3946[3] *7331[3]* *(7574)*

Galivant (IRE) *J W Hills* a79 82
3 b f Galileo(IRE) —Valdara (Darshaan)
1332[2] 1894[4] 2551[2] ◆ (3214) 4036b[8] 4998[7] 5966[2] 6749[12]

Galixi (FR) *R Laplanche* a60 81
6 b m Bernebeau(FR) —Gaelika (IRE) (Pistolet Bleu (IRE))
566a[6]

Gallagher *Ruth Carr* a104 104
5 ch g Bahamian Bounty—Roo (Rudimentary (USA))
4609[14] 5060[19] 5703[10] 6145[14] 6341[9] 6703[19] 7074[13]

Gallahad (BRZ) *A De Royer-Dupre* a81 99
5 b h Hard Buck(BRZ) —Vexclusive Fly (BRZ) (Executioner (USA))
240[11] 417a[13] *608a[11]*

Gallant Eagle (IRE) *Ed de Giles* a85 81
4 ch g Hawk Wing(USA) —Generous Gesture (IRE) (Fasliyev (USA))
2178[3] 2649[11] 3354[5] 4479[2] 5106[7] *5948[3]* 6435[8] 6924[12] *7227[10]*

Gallantry *Paul Howling* a84 43
9 b g Green Desert(USA) —Gay Gallanta (USA) (Woodman (USA))
(206) *385[6]* *623[7]* *876[4]* *1021[3]* 1530[11] *2178[7]* *2642[6]* *2816[6]* 3130[14] 3558[7] *4666[9]* 6624[5] 7202[3] (7437) 7663[4] 7810[9]

Gallego *Richard Price* a49 70
9 br g Danzero(AUS) —Shafir (IRE) (Shaadi (USA))
3514[11] 3912[9] 4211[6] 4337[4] (5002) 5509[6] (5653) 6226[10] 6461[6] 6773[14] 6990[15] 7113[5]

Galleon *Sir Michael Stoute* 73
2 b c Galileo(IRE) —Tempting Prospect (Shirley Heights)
6059[8]

Gallery *William Haggas* 71
2 ch f Excellent Art—Starparty (USA) (Cozzene (USA))
4720[2] 5351[3] 6169[14]

Gallery's Platine (FR) *Carmen Bocskai* a82
4 ch m Gallery Of Zurich(IRE) —Couture Platine (FR) (Top Waltz (FR))
6958a[6]

Galletto (IRE) *Luca Cumani* 30
2 b g Azamour(IRE) —Galleta (Hernando (FR))
7232[15]

Gallic Star (IRE) *Mick Channon* 104
4 b m Galileo(IRE) —Oman Sea (USA) (Rahy (USA))
607a[10] 1677[6] 2994[8] 3107[6] 4470[7]

Gallipot *John Gosden* 70
2 b f Galileo(IRE) —Spinning Queen (Spinning World (USA))
7025[5]

Galloping Minister (IRE) *Tom Dascombe* a62 53
3 b g Ad Valorem(USA) —Gladstone Street (IRE) (Waajib)
1338[12] *4923[4]* 5206[4] *6700[4]* *7001[4]* *7507[13]*

Galloping Queen (IRE) *Sheena West* a57 86
[illegible] Refuse To Bend(IRE) —Rouge Noir (USA) (Saint Ballado (CAN))
1415[7] 1626[3] 2018[10] 2466[4] 2808[6] 3980[4] 4822[8] *5243[6]* 5614[7] *5815[5]* 6968[2]

Galma (FR) *Robert Collet* a72 81
8 b m Goldneyev(USA) —Clarstone (FR) (Bigstone (IRE))
7256a[P]

Galpin Junior (USA) *Ruth Carr* a77 79
5 ch g Hennessy(USA) —Reluctant Diva (Sadler's Wells (USA))
294[13] *404[4]* *506[3]* *767[3]* *857[8]* 1213[9] 1493[5] 3573[2] 3937[3] 4152[5] 4634[8]

Gambatte *Tony Carroll* 50
4 b m One Cool Cat(USA) —Dahshah (Mujtahid (USA))
1984[10] 2848[12] 3091[8] 4110[9] 4681[5]

Gamedor (FR) *Daniel O'Brien* a42 42
6 ch g Kendor(FR) —Garmeria (FR) (Kadrou (FR))
2473[8]

Game On Dude (USA) *Bob Baffert* a123
4 bb g Awesome Again(CAN) —Worldly Pleasure (USA) (Devil His Due (USA))
7308a[2]

Game Stalker (USA) *A Al Raihe* a75 79
5 br h Elusive Quality(USA) —Windsharp (USA) (Lear Fan (USA))
(536a)

Gamilati *Mahmood Al Zarooni* 108
2 b f Bernardini(USA) —Illustrious Miss (USA) (Kingmambo (USA))
2467[2] ◆ 3362[2] (3821) ◆ 5217[11]

Gammarth (FR) *H-A Pantall* a98 80
3 ch c Layman(USA) —Emouna Queen (IRE) (Indian Ridge)
(7669a)

Ganas (IRE) *Clive Cox* a91 89
3 b g Oasis Dream—Hollow Dynasty (USA) (Deputy Commander (USA))
4666[3] (5030) 5683[3] *6217[3]*

Gandalf *Amy Weaver* a73 73
9 b g Sadler's Wells(USA) —Enchant (Lion Cavern (USA))
244[2] *(622)* *1148[4]*

Gap Princess (IRE) *Geoffrey Harker* a81 97
7 b m Noverre(USA) —Safe Care (IRE) (Caerleon (USA))
1675[13] 2122[9] 2495[7] 3383[9] 4609[2] 5012[9] 5434[9] *5862[6]* 7074[8] *7456[5]* *7596[13]*

Garbah (IRE) *Clive Brittain* a64 76
3 b f Kodiac—Baraloti (IRE) (Barathea (IRE))
3689[2]

Gardes (IRE) *Zdena Havlickova* a60 62
6 b g Xaar—Golden Honor (IRE) (Hero's Honor (USA))
4874a[7]

Garde Slickly (FR) *Mlle Valerie Boussin* a91 99
3 b c Slickly(FR) —Royal Bride (FR) (Garde Royale)
5530a[8]

Garmerita (FR) *D Sepulchre* a88 96
7 b m Poliglote—Garmeritte (FR) (Garde Royale)
7386a[9]

Garrarufa (IRE) *Rod Millman* a50 60
2 ch c Chineur(FR) —Face The Storm (IRE) (Barathea (IRE))
1136[10] 4969[9] 5325[8] 5802[3] 6101[7] *6652[7]* *6667[11]*

Garstang *Bruce Hellier* a82 63
8 ch g Atraf—Approved Quality (IRE) (Persian Heights)
(133) *430[7]* *522[2]* *725[9]* *910[6]* *1371[2]* *1584[6]* 2694[6] 3027[11] *3222[7]* 3759[7] 5457[4] 6177[8] 6491[5] 7079[6] 7230[8] 7517[4] 7696[5]

Garter Knight *Pam Sly* a60 29
5 b g Mark Of Esteem(IRE) —Granted (FR) (Cadeaux Genereux)
7236[9]

Garth Mountain *David Evans* 65
4 b g Rock Of Gibraltar(IRE) —One Of The Family (Alzao (USA))
1212[6] 1692[9] 2140[5]

Garud (IRE) *Marco Botti* 86
3 b g High Chaparral(IRE) —Global Pearl (GER) (Acatenango (GER))
3543[2] ◆ 4254[3] (5021)

Garzoni *Sir Mark Prescott Bt* a47
2 ch f Medicean—Rainbow Queen (Rainbow Quest (USA))
6440[13]

Gaselee (USA) *Rae Guest* a75 94
5 b m Toccet(USA) —Vingt Et Une (FR) (Sadler's Wells (USA))
894[6] *1817[5]* 3157[9] *3738[11]* 6405[5] 6780[5] (7075) 7406a[0]

Gasquet (ITY) *Gianfranco Verricelli* a91
5 b h Denon(USA) —Minnelli (USA) (Manila (USA))
661a[8]

Gassin Golf *Sir Mark Prescott Bt* a78
2 b g Montjeu(IRE) —Miss Riviera Golf (Hernando (FR))
4798[2] *(5142)* *7095[6]*

Gatamalata (IRE) *Joseph G Murphy* 93
3 b f Spartacus(IRE) —Ardent Lady (Alhaarth (IRE))
1006a[9]

Gatepost (IRE) *Mick Channon* 105
2 br c Footstepsinthesand—Mandama (IRE) (Warning)
(1505) ◆ (2007) 3012[5] 4834a[7] 5305a[7] 6196a[16]

Gatewood *John Gosden* 89
3 b c Galileo(IRE) —Felicity (IRE) (Selkirk (USA))
3001[2] (3430) ◆ 4355[4]

Gathering (USA) *John Gosden* 84
2 b f Street Cry(IRE) —Seebe (USA) (Danzig (USA))
4061[4] (6168) ◆

Gaul Wood (IRE) *Tom Dascombe* a76
2 b c Amadeus Wolf—Emly Express (IRE) (High Estate)
4864[2]

Gawaarib (USA) *John Gosden* a74 56
[illegible](USA) —Beautifulballerina (USA) (Nureyev (USA))
983[4] *(1173)* 1811[8]

Gayego (USA) *Saeed Bin Suroor* a118
6 bb h Gilded Time(USA) —Devils Lake (USA) (Lost Code (USA))
501a[9]

Gay Gallivanter *Michael Quinn* a50 72
3 b f Iceman—Gallivant (Danehill (USA))
1133[4] 2018[8] 2916[7] 4185[9] *4758[9]* 5352[2] 6764[13] 6813[6] *7270[9]* *7387[6]* *7466[4]* *7639[13]* *7782[4]* 7920[3]

Gazamali (IRE) *Michael Scudamore* a48 55
4 b g Namid—Frond (Alzao (USA))
555[8] *798[13]* 3476[9]

Gazboolou *David Pinder* a72 72
7 b g Royal Applause—Warning Star (Warning)
2165[10] 2561[9] 3326[5] *3719[7]* 4444[8] 4822[9] *(5394)* *5836[5]* *6138[9]* *6784[2]* *7001[5]* 7228[3] 7400[5] 7524[2] 7663[7] 7810[7] 7843[4]

Geanie Mac (IRE) *Tim Pitt* a24
2 ch f Needwood Blade—Dixie Evans (Efisio)
5418[6]

Gearbox (IRE) *Liam Corcoran* a67 63
5 br g Tillerman—Persian Empress (IRE) (Persian Bold)
(85) *695[3]*

Geblah (IRE) *David Simcock* a38 62
3 b f Green Desert(USA) —Cedar Sea (IRE) (Persian Bold)
2463[2] 3467[10] 3679[4]

Gee Ceffyl Bach *Garry Woodward* a4 41
7 b m Josr Algarhoud(IRE) —Miletrian Cares (IRE) (Hamas (IRE))
3457[9] 3576[5]

Gee Dee Nen *Gary Moore* a95 69
8 b g Mister Baileys—Special Beat (Bustino)
1847[11]

Gee Major *Nicky Vaughan* a57 60
4 b g Reset(AUS) —Polly Golightly (Weldnaas (USA))
1625[7] 1905[11] 4705[8] 4948[11] *(6083)* *6310[8]* *6657[7]* *7092[3]* *7437[2]* *7640[10]*

Gekko (IRE) *Patrick Morris* a50 49
3 b g Iffraaj—Acidanthera (Alzao (USA))
383[4] *558[10]* *655[9]*

Geminus (IRE) *Jedd O'Keeffe* 58
3 b g Choisir(AUS) —Macca Luna (IRE) (Kahyasi)
1620[5] 2058[8] 3460[4] 4151[5] 4476[7] 5650[9]

Gemma's Delight (IRE) *James Unett* a66 67
4 gr m Clodovil(IRE) —Duckmore Bay (IRE) (Titus Livius (FR))
1054[3] 1464[9] 1766[2] 2280[4] 2671[4] 3234[4] (3341) 3806[2] 4503[5] 5414[5] 5924[4] 6355[10] 6664[7] 7001[10]

Gemo Lotus (IRE) *Mme Pia Brandt* a58 73
4 b h Alamshar(IRE) —Lily Beth (IRE) (Desert King (IRE))
1012a[3]

Gems *Peter Hiatt* a48 73
4 b m Haafhd—Megdale (IRE) (Waajib)
86[11] 204[9] 283[7] 524[5] 630[9] 749[9] (1135) 1567[6] 1987[14] 2145[2] 2451[2] (2759) 3086[2] 3311[8] 3946[P] (4626) 5107[3] 5504[2] 6023[9] 6469[8] 6893[6]

Gemstone (IRE) *A P O'Brien* 105
3 b f Galileo(IRE) —Kincob (USA) (Kingmambo (USA))
924a[2] 1928a[9] 2968a[5] 4133a[6] 4831a[6] 5523a[11]

General Duke's *Kevin Ryan* a65 62
4 ch g Starcraft(NZ) —Bellflower (IRE) (Indian Ridge)
774[4] 850[5] 1243[5] 1491[5]

General Eliott (IRE) *Barry Brennan* a74 99
6 b g Rock Of Gibraltar(IRE) —Marlene-D (Selkirk (USA))
(5095a)

General Perfect (USA) *Glenn R Thompson* a83 118
8 b g Perfect(USA) —General Tree (USA) (General Assembly (USA))
5074a[10]

General Sam (USA) *Richard Mitchell* a47
5 ch g Trippi(USA) —Milagro Blue (USA) (Cure The Blues (USA))
5231[12]

General Synod *Richard Hannon* a73 83
3 b g Invincible Spirit(IRE) —New Assembly (IRE) (Machiavellian (USA))
1409[2] 2100[7] 4617[6] 5635[10] 6020[3] 6457[12]

General Truce (AUS) *Ricky Maund* 108
4 b g Brief Truce(USA) —General Resolve (AUS) (General Nediym (AUS))
9029a[3]

General Tufto *Charles Smith* a76 81
6 b g Fantastic Light(USA) —Miss Pinkerton (Danehill (USA))
38[6] 287[9] 496[5] (568) 744[4] 799[4] 870[5] 1099[17] 1292[5] 1461[6] 1814[4] 2530[7] 3074[3] 3574[11] 6236[2] 6486[8] 6764[16] 6938[13] 7507[3] 7775[4]

Generalyse *Ben De Haan* 73
2 b c Cadeaux Genereux—Dance To The Blues (IRE) (Danehill Dancer (IRE))
5681[11] 6123[5] 6725[6] 7294[5]

Generous Genella *Julia Feilden* a45 54
3 b f Cape Cross(IRE) —Gombay Girl (USA) (Woodman (USA))
898[10] 1134[5] 1502[5] 2858[9] 3457[3]

Generous Pursuit *Phil McEntee*
3 b f Pursuit Of Love—Not So Generous (IRE) (Fayruz)
2511[9] 2825[7] 4065[10]

Genes Of A Dancer (AUS) *Adrian Chamberlain* a62 59
5 ch g Galileo(IRE) —Jugah's Dancer (AUS) (Jugah (USA))
3326[2] 3944[12] 4337[6] 5673[5] (5943) 6784[7] 7202[7]

Genius Beast (USA) *Mahmood Al Zarooni* 110
3 b c Kingmambo(USA) —Shawanda (IRE) (Sinndar (IRE))
(1548) 2136a[3] 3105[6] 5182[4] 5928[8]

Genius Step (IRE) *Mahmood Al Zarooni* 83
2 b c Dubawi(IRE) —Kathy College (IRE) (College Chapel)
2510[3] (6244)

Genki (IRE) *Roger Charlton* a53 117
7 ch g Shinko Forest(IRE) —Emma's Star (ITY) (Darshaan)
(1340) 2005[7] 3154[8] (3394) 3863[6] 4838a[4] 5707[4] 6520[5] 6858[8]

Gennie *Richard Hannon* a50 48
3 b f Diktat—Gennie Bond (Pivotal)
1146[6] 2223[7] 5567[9] 6084[7] 7084[12]

Gentle Lord *Tom Dascombe* 95
3 b c Ishiguru(USA) —Soft Touch (IRE) (Petorius)
1361[5] 5012[3] 5578[3] 6331[4] (6723)

Gentleman Duke (IRE) *A L T Moore* a73 89
3 b g Bachelor Duke(USA) —Housekeeping (Dansili)
5090a[13]

Gentleman Is Back (USA) *Ed de Giles* a81 47
3 bb g Johannesburg(USA) —Torros Straits (USA) (Boundary (USA))
4062[10] 4994[9] 5341[6] 6051[11] 6505[8]

Gentleman Jeff (USA) *Chris Grant* a75 72
7 ch g Mr Greeley(USA) —Wooing (USA) (Stage Door Johnny (USA))
6155[11]

Gentlemans Code (USA) *Wesley A Ward* a87 94
2 b g Proud Accolade(USA) —American Saint (USA) (Saint Ballado (CAN))
[2] (2423) 3014[4]

Gentle Sands *Clive Cox* 35
2 b f Multiplex—Asinara (GER) (Big Shuffle (USA))
6291[8] 6745[13]

Gentleshaw (FR) *J Van Handenhove* 72
2 b f Gentlewave(IRE) —Grenshaw (IRE) (Persian Heights)
7449a[2]

Gentoo (FR) *A Lyon* a96 115
7 b g Loup Solitaire(USA) —Ifni (FR) (Bering)
1231a[2] 5304a[13] 6562a[6] 7049a[10]

Genzy (FR) *J E Pease* 105
3 b c Gentlewave(IRE) —Zycia (IRE) (Bishop Of Cashel)
1551a[5] 2341a[2] 2979a[5]

Geordie Iris (IRE) *Wido Neuroth* a85 80
3 b f Elusive City(USA) —Tiger Desert (GER) (Desert King (IRE))
177[5] (297) (540) ◆ (657) 5982a[6]

Geordieland (FR) *Jamie Osborne* a96 121
10 gr h Johann Quatz(FR) —Aerdee (FR) (Highest Honor (FR))
3066[P] 4469[15]

George Adamson (IRE) *Alan Swinbank* a84 83
5 b g Where Or When(IRE) —Tactile (Groom Dancer (USA))
(1908) ◆ 2475[5] 4331[6] 4962[4] 5311[3] 6155[2] 6279[8] (7803)

George Baker (IRE) *George Baker* a63 86
4 b g Camacho—Petite Maxine (Sharpo)
387[7] 472[7] 957[2] 1730[2] (1905) (2027) 2354[7] (4066) (5341) 6174[17]

George Benjamin *David Nicholls* a75 86
4 b g Trade Fair—Unchain My Heart (Pursuit Of Love)
(1245) 1560[6] 1793[2] 3506[13] 4349[18] 4810[4]

Georgebernardshaw (IRE) *John Quinn* a93 105
6 b g Danehill Dancer(IRE) —Khamseh (Thatching)
271[6] 615[11] (803) 846[6] 1479[7] 1824[4] 2282[9] 3380[2] 3877[14] 4107[6] 4501[2] 5924[10] 6831[12]

George Fenton *Richard Guest* 29
2 ch g Piccolo—Mashmoum (Lycius (USA))
5147[6] 5367[11] 6912[7]

George Guru *Michael Attwater* a87
4 b g Ishiguru(USA) —Waraqa (USA) (Red Ransom (USA))
4991[6] 5633[4] 6085[5] 6473[3] (6796) ◆ 7227[2] ◆

Georgeoflancashire *Bruce Hellier* 16
3 ch g Sulamani(IRE) —Geegee Emmarr (Rakaposhi King)
2457[14]

George Thisby *Rod Millman* a59 73
5 b g Royal Applause—Warning Belle (Warning)
2354[8] 3426[6] 4179[3] 4337[2] 4640[2] ◆ (4917) 5231[2] 5539[5] (6228) 6468[13] 7057[8]

George Tilehurst *J S Moore* 26
2 ch g Needwood Blade—Batchworth Breeze (Beveled (USA))
4384[9] 4761[7] 5325[13]

George Woolf *Alan McCabe* a73 71
3 b g Iceman—Beading (Polish Precedent (USA))
260[5] (424) 686[2] 789[3] 1392[6] 1652[3]

Georgey Girl *Alan Swinbank* a69
3 b f Doyen(IRE) —Thrasher (Hector Protector (USA))
1027[3] 2058[10]

Georgian Silver *George Foster* a46 42
3 ch f Auction House(USA) —Proud Titania (IRE) (Fairy King (USA))
595[4] 1040[6] 1514[7] 3661[10] 6874[6] 7690[6]

Georgina Bailey (IRE) *Alan McCabe* a24 43
3 ch f Iffraaj—Baileys First (IRE) (Alzao (USA))
6137[10]

Geraldines Lass (IRE) *W McCreery* a77 81
3 ch f Titus Livius(FR) —Nullarbor (Green Desert (USA))
4767a[8]

Gereon (GER) *C Zschache* 103
3 b c Next Desert(IRE) —Golden Time (GER) (Surumu (GER))
2338a[2] 3007a[3] 3672a[10] 4374a[9] 5308a[4] 6201a[8]

Gerfalcon *Brian Meehan* 99
2 ch g Hawk Wing(USA) —Give A Whistle (IRE) (Mujadil (USA))
3793[2] (4339) 5216[3] (5558)

Germanico (IRE) *J-M Capitte* a69 74
3 b c Holy Roman Emperor(IRE) —Tartouche (Pursuit Of Love)
638a[4]

Geronimo Chief (IRE) *Ben Haslam* a63 50
3 b g Sleeping Indian—Portorosa (USA) (Irish River (FR))
1293[4] 3039[11] 3460[9]

Gertmegalush (IRE) *John Harris* a44 77
4 b g One Cool Cat(USA) —Aiming Upwards (Blushing Flame (USA))
1523[8] 1968[9] 2546[7] 2845[3] (3638) 4078[8] 4443[13] 5338[10] 6091[6] 7055[10]

Gertrude Bell *John Gosden* a76 111
4 ch m Sinndar(IRE) —Sugar Mill (FR) (Polar Falcon (USA))
(1677) (3624) 6859[3]

Gessabelle *Phil McEntee* a46 49
4 b m Largesse—Palmstead Belle (IRE) (Wolfhound (USA))
2720[8] 3090[9] 3494[6] 4006[7] 4711[5] 5231[9] 5860[11] 6071[11] 6653[8] 6874[5] 7069[8]

Getabuzz *Tim Easterby* 84
3 b g Beat Hollow—Ailincala (IRE) (Pursuit Of Love)
1151[5] 1415[8] 2677[3] (3487) ◆ 4084[4] (5064) 5710[4] 6191[2]

Getcarter *John Best* a83 91
5 b g Fasliyev(USA) —Pourquoi Pas (IRE) (Nordico (USA))
1103[3] ◆ 1771[8] 2155[4] 2794[2] 2910[4] 5383[8] 6303[6]

Get Happy (IRE) *Mme Pia Brandt* 92
2 ch f Zamindar(USA) —Happy At Last (In The Wings)
7508a[3]

Get Stormy (USA) *Thomas Bush* 120
5 b h Stormy Atlantic(USA) —Foolish Gal (USA) (Kiri's Clown (USA))
6721a[2] 7307a[12]

Get The Trip *Giles Bravery* a50 48
2 ch f Three Valleys(USA) —Amiata (Pennekamp (USA))
3092[9] 3673[5] 4848[4] 6131[5] 6919[4] 7421[12]

Ghaayer *C Von Der Recke* a52 26
5 ch g Nayef(USA) —Valthea (FR) (Antheus (USA))
5095a[9]

Ghalaa (IRE) *Mark Johnston* 65
2 bb f Nayef(USA) —Mouwadh (USA) (Nureyev (USA))
4402[2] 4898[5] 6047[2]

Ghar Shoop (IRE) *Clive Brittain* 58
3 b f Dubai Destination(USA) —Lunda (IRE) (Soviet Star (USA))
6530[7]

Ghost (IRE) *David Nicholls* 81
4 b g Invincible Spirit(IRE) —Alexander Phantom (IRE) (Soviet Star (USA))
1438[9] 1618[5] 1942[8] 2494[5] 4349[14] 4503[8] 4810[5] ◆ 5404[8] 6159[8]

Ghost Dancer *Milton Bradley* a54 62
7 ch g Danehill Dancer(IRE) —Reservation (IRE) (Common Grounds)
2161[4] ◆ 2756[8] 2921[3] 3234[5] 5603[6] 5677[7] 6609[8] 6889[3] 7524[10] 7656[6] 7768[5] 7899[8]

Ghost Protocol (IRE) *David Simcock* 90
2 b g Cockney Rebel(IRE) —Stroke Of Six (IRE) (Woodborough (USA))
4525[2] ◆ (5196) 6270[8]

Ghost Train (IRE) *Mark Johnston* a26 38
2 b g Holy Roman Emperor(IRE) —Adrastea (IRE) (Monsun (GER))
4433[5] 5596[5]

Ghostwing *James Evans* a97 92
4 gr g Kheleyf(USA) —Someone's Angel (USA) (Runaway Groom (CAN))
1476[14] 1888[6] 2169[4] 2995[11] 3536[10] 7438[11] 7660[12] 7917[2] ◆

Ghostwriting (USA) *John Gosden* a86 91
2 b c Ghostzapper(USA) —Miss Halory (USA) (Mr Prospector (USA))
(3472) ◆ 3861[7] (5825) 6268[8] 6788[4]

Ghozi (AUS) *John O'Hara* 110
6 b g Catbird(AUS) —Finito Fling (AUS) (Luskin Star (AUS))
2339a[4]

Ghufa (IRE) *Lydia Pearce* a73 77
7 b g Sakhee(USA) —Hawriyah (USA) (Dayjur (USA))
1372[3] (2696) 3434[6] 4687[2] 5866[2] 7200[9] 7556[9] 7761[7]

Giant Among Men (USA) *Richard Guest* a71 75
6 ch g Giant's Causeway(USA) —Dissemble (Ahonoora)
1245[14]

Giant Generation (GER) *G Martin* 68
7 b g Tertullian(USA) —Glen Royal (GER) (Mtoto)
196a[0] 325a[0] 7314a[0]

Giant Oak (USA) *Chris Block* a119 109
5 ch h Giant's Causeway(USA) —Crafty Oak (USA) (Crafty Prospector (USA))
7300a[3]

Giantrio (IRE) *A Althoffer* a76 80
3 ch c Shamardal(USA) —Apperella (Rainbow Quest (USA))
5463a[0]

Giant Ryan (USA) *Bisnath Parboo* a120
5 b h Freud(USA) —Kheyrah (USA) (Dayjur (USA))
7302a[8]

Giant Sandman (IRE) *Rune Haugen* a87 102
4 b h Footstepsinthesand—Sharamana (IRE) (Darshaan)
(4483a) 6687[7]

Giant Step (IRE) *David Wachman* 91
3 b c Giant's Causeway(USA) —Brown Eyes (Danehill (USA))
1927a[7]

Gibraltar Lass (USA) *Mike Murphy* a48 28
4 ch m Concerto(USA) —Mango Lassie (USA) (Montreal Red (USA))
5843[12]

Gibraltar Road *John Quinn* 38
2 b c Iffraaj—Kerry's Dream (Tobougg (IRE))
5726[6] 6425[6]

Gifted Dancer *Henry Candy* 71
2 b f Cadeaux Genereux—Puteri Sas (IRE) (Fasliyev (USA))
2559[10] 4052[5] 4823[2] 6222[2] ◆ 6742[4]

Gifted Girl (IRE) *Paul Cole* 90
2 b f Azamour(IRE) —Hoodwink (IRE) (Selkirk (USA))
3813[3] ◆ (4471) 7169[4]

Gifted Leader (USA) *Ian Williams* 92
6 b g Diesis—Zaghruta (USA) (Gone West (USA))
2006[8] 2512[2] 2888[8] (2931) 6690[19]

Gilded Age *Chris Gordon* a75 73
5 b g Cape Cross(IRE) —Sweet Folly (IRE) (Singspiel (IRE))
6023[5]

Gilderoy *Dominic Ffrench Davis* a53 51
4 b g Compton Place—Lola Sapola (IRE) (Benny The Dip (USA))
70[9] 167[3] 311[6] 517[6]

Gilly's Giant (IRE) *Patrick Morris*
2 b g Diamond Green(FR) —Sirindiya (IRE) (Night Shift (USA))
5596[8]

Gilt (USA) *Ed Dunlop* 47
3 rg f Bernardini(USA) —Sterling Pound (USA) (Seeking The Gold (USA))
2104[5] 3080[8] 3519[12] 5791[11]

Gimli's Rock (IRE) *Mrs John Harrington* a67 100
5 b g Rock Of Gibraltar(IRE) —Beltisaal (FR) (Belmez (USA))
925a[6]

Ginger Grey (IRE) *David O'Meara* a77 78
4 gr g Bertolini(USA) —Just In Love (FR) (Highest Honor (FR))
2494[8] 3348[3] 3612[2] 4051[6] 4404[7] 4897[3] 5828[10] 6262[5] 6767[4]

Ginger Jack *Geoffrey Harker* a88 98
4 ch g Refuse To Bend(IRE) —Coretta (IRE) (Caerleon (USA))
2061[9] 2390[8] 2783[8] 4404[3] 5593[10] 6346[7] 6533[4] 6989[17]

Ginger Ted (IRE) *Richard Guest* a35 96
4 ch g Fath(USA) —Estertide (IRE) (Tagula (IRE))
1695[6] 2116[11] (2397) 3000[4] ◆ (3028) 3395[6] 4042[14] 4346[3] ◆ 5033[7] 5180[13] 6145[24] 7018[9] ◆

Gino Vanilli (FR) *F Seguin* 63
7 b g Sagacity(FR) —Stamingala (IRE) (Alzao (USA))
6959a[4]

Gin Twist *Tom Dascombe* a68 68
2 b f Invincible Spirit(IRE) —Winding (USA) (Irish River (FR))
1823[6] 1946[7] 3165[4] 3745[2] 3993[2] 4212[4] 4548[3] 5737[5] 6946[5] 7251[4] (7541) 7765[7]

Ginzan *Malcolm Saunders* a52 67
3 b f Desert Style(IRE) —Zyzania (Zafonic (USA))
1217[2] 1589[3] 1813[4] 2549[2] 3216[4] 4924[4] 5377[3] 5615[2] (5917) 6403[5] 6802[7]

Giofra *A De Royer-Dupre* 107
3 b f Dansili—Gracefully (IRE) (Orpen (USA))
(7156a)

Gio Ponti (USA) *Christophe Clement* a127 123
6 b h Tale Of The Cat(USA) —Chipeta Springs (USA) (Alydar (USA))
1002a[5] 3888a[2] 5074a[2] (6721a) 7307a[4]

Giorgio's Dragon (IRE) *Richard Fahey* 59
2 b c Le Vie Dei Colori—Broadways Millie (IRE) (Imperial Ballet (IRE))
2033[10] 2617[5] 5618[7]

Girevole *A Fabre*
3 b g Tiger Hill(IRE) —Taranto (Machiavellian (USA))
5771a[7]

Gitano Hernando *H J Brown* a123 120
5 ch h Hernando(FR) —Gino's Spirits (Perugino (USA))
416a[5] 758a[3] 1002a[6] 1742a[8] (2340a)

Giu La Testa (IRE) *A Giorgi* 81
3 ch f Muhtathir—Deraasaat (Nashwan (USA))
2539a[6]

Giulietta Da Vinci *Steve Woodman* a63 63
4 b m Mujahid(USA) —Gennie Bond (Pivotal)
432[5] 561[4] 1633[2] 2420[8] 2921[11] 3253[8] 3943[9]

Giuly Forever (IRE) *S Botti* 88
2 b f Motivator—El Soprano (IRE) (Noverre (USA))
6904a[8]

Give Me Shelter (IRE) *Bernard Anthony Heffernan* a61 68
3 b g Araafa(IRE) —Genny Lim (IRE) (Barathea (IRE))
7175[10]

Give Or Take *Christine Dunnett*
3 ch g Where Or When(IRE) —Tata Naka (Nashwan (USA))
7766[10]

Give Your Verdict (USA) *Sir Michael Stoute* 93
4 b g Arch(USA) —Remediate (USA) (Miswaki (USA))
4100[11]

Glad Eye Gladys *David Nicholls* 66
2 b f Milk It Mick—Thunderous Days (Diktat)
3229[6] 3609[5] 4285[4] 4471[11] 5029[3]

Glad Panther *M Weiss* a59 92
5 b g Seattle Dancer(USA) —Glady Beauty (GER) (Big Shuffle (USA))
441a[7] 628a[17]

Glad Sky *J-L Pelletan* 106
5 b g Big Shuffle(USA) —Glady Sum (GER) (Surumu (GER))
1575a[6] 3654a[6] 6783a[0] 7193a[0] 7534a[0]

Glady Romana (GER) *W Baltromei* 103
4 b m Doyen(IRE) —Glady Sum (GER) (Surumu (GER))
3897a[6] (5980a) 7534a[0]

Gladys' Gal *Roger Varian* a91 96
3 b f Tobougg(IRE) —Charming Lotte (Nicolotte)
1607[4] (2924) (4235) ◆

Glaisdale *James Toller* a58
2 b f Hurricane Run(IRE) —Picacho (IRE) (Sinndar (IRE))
7329[6]

Glamorous Angel (IRE) *Alan Swinbank* 82
2 b g Dark Angel(IRE) —Glamorous Air (IRE) (Air Express (IRE))
5202[4] 5618[2] (6274) 6863[5]

Glamour Profession (IRE) *Mme J Hendriks* a67 69
4 ch m Captain Rio—Kriva (Reference Point)
7314a[5]

Glamstar (FR) *M Pimbonnet* 104
5 gr g Numerous(USA) —Dibenoise (FR) (Kendor (FR))
220a[0] 372a[0]

Glas Burn *Jonathan Portman* 89
3 b f Avonbridge—Dunya (Unfuwain (USA))
1059[2] 1404[12] 1902[7] 3323[6] 4101[4] 4779[9] 5476[4] 6094[10]

Glasgow Kid (GER) *J-C Rouget* a83 100
3 b g Ransom O'War(USA) —Ginza (GER) (Acatenango (GER))
(777a)

Glass Harmonium (IRE) *Michael Moroney* 121
5 gr h Verglas(IRE) —Spring Symphony (IRE) (Darshaan)
7044a[10] 7218a[22]

Glasshoughton *T Potters* a73 79
8 b g Dansili—Roseum (Lahib (USA))
2867a[4]

Glass Mountain (IRE) *James Fanshawe* a68 78
3 gr g Verglas(IRE) —Exotic Mix (FR) (Linamix (FR))
1605[9] 2094[4] 3093[5] 4160[6] 4908[5] 5381[10] (6764) (6969)

Glastonberry *Geoffrey Deacon* a65 34
3 gr f Piccolo—Elderberry (Bin Ajwaad (IRE))
5567[12] 5946[6] 6251[2] (6791) 7812[8]

Glaswegian *P Bary* 111
3 ch c Selkirk(USA) —Starfan (USA) (Lear Fan (USA))
(1552a) 2139a[8] 2751a[7] 4376a[2] 5128a[5]

Glaze *Hughie Morrison* 55
2 ch f Kyllachy—Raindrop (Primo Dominie)
6744[10] 6992[8]

Gleaming Spirit (IRE) *Peter Grayson* a55 30
7 b g Mujadil(USA) —Gleam (Green Desert (USA))
256[9] 1309[6]

Glee *Richard Hannon* 82
2 b f Bahamian Bounty—Syrian Queen (Slip Anchor)
1946[2] ◆ (2187) 4496[10] 5052[4] 5446[4] 5783[6] 6169[2] 6526[3]

Glencadam Gold (IRE) *Sir Henry Cecil* 101
3 b c Refuse To Bend(IRE) —Sandrella (IRE) (Darshaan)
1344[2] ◆ 1550[3] (2108) 3105[9] 3774[12] 7029[10]

Glencairn Star *Frederick Watson* a23 28
10 b g Selkirk(USA) —Bianca Nera (Salse (USA))
1037^{9} 1557^{11} 1803^{14} 1943^{5}

Glen Ellyn *Mark Johnston* 62
2 gr c Shamardal(USA) —Giorgia Rae (IRE) (Green Desert (USA))
6455^{4} 6912^{6} 7132^{4}

Glenlini *Jim Goldie* 57
5 b m Bertolini(USA) —Glenhurich (IRE) (Sri Pekan (USA))
4144^{5}

Glenluji *Jim Goldie* 68
6 b g Lujain(USA) —Glenhurich (IRE) (Sri Pekan (USA))
1520^{12} 1857^{6} 2401^{7} 3038^{4} 3454^{2} 3805^{3} 4039^{2} 4143^{3} 5721^{7}

Glen Moss (IRE) *Charles Hills* 83
2 b c Moss Vale(IRE) —Sail With The Wind (Saddlers' Hall (IRE))
4352^{2} 4748^{2} 6127^{2} 6579^{2}

Glenmuir (IRE) *John Quinn* a46 74
8 b g Josr Algarhoud(IRE) —Beryl (Bering)
3569^{3} 5106^{6} 5652^{2}

Glen Nevis (USA) *A Al Raihe* a98 90
7 br h Gulch(USA) —Beating The Buzz (IRE) (Bluebird (USA))
499a^{3} 679a^{10}

Glenridding *James Given* a77 92
7 b g Averti(IRE) —Appelone (Emperor Jones (USA))
1240^{13} 1849^{10} 2300^{6} 2495^{11} 2995^{6} 3506^{12} 4010^{4} 4243^{6} 4574^{5} (4865) (5455) 5879^{5} 6354^{7} (6979) 7175^{4} 7416^{4} 7625^{11}

Glen's Diamond *Richard Fahey* 107
3 b g Intikhab(USA) —Posta Vecchia (USA) (Rainbow Quest (USA))
(1516) ◆ (1850) 3105^{7}

Glens Wobbly *Jonathan Geake* a49
3 ch g Kier Park(IRE) —Wobbly (Atraf)
6085^{9} 6473^{13}

Glitter (IRE) *Richard Hannon* 28
2 gr g Verglas(IRE) —Call Me Crazy (IRE) (Key Of Luck (USA))
4968^{14} 5325^{10}

Global *Brian Ellison* a66 74
5 ch g Bahamian Bounty—Tuppenny Blue (Pennekamp (USA))
1107^{21} 1461^{8} (2260) ◆ 2474^{9} 2887^{10} 3386^{11} 5594^{10} 5722^{14} 6264^{6} 6546^{2} ◆ 7556^{8} 7722^{6}

Global City (IRE) *Saeed Bin Suroor* a105 95
5 b h Exceed And Excel(AUS) —Victory Peak (Shirley Heights)
678a^{2} 755a^{8} 3410^{7} 4534^{14} 5879^{10} 7392^{3}

Global Recovery (IRE) *J S Bolger* a61 64
4 b g El Corredor(USA) —Altarejos (IRE) (Vettori (IRE))
977a^{13}

Global Village (IRE) *Brian Ellison* a83 68
6 b g Dubai Destination(USA) —Zelding (IRE) (Warning)
141^{8} 279^{6} 666^{11} 1198^{7} 6138^{5} (6664) 7175^{3} (7646) (7744)

Gloomy Sunday (FR) *C Ferland* 99
2 b f Singspiel(IRE) —Fine And Mellow (FR) (Lando (GER))
6941a^{5}

Gloriam (USA) *David Simcock* a86 66
2 b c War Chant(USA) —Amandas Bandit (USA) (Royal Academy (USA))
4996^{5} (7142) 7390^{2}

Glorious Gift (IRE) *A Al Shamsi* a91 78
6 b h Elnadim(USA) —Queen Of Arabia (USA) (Wild Again (USA))
536a^{2}

Glorious Grey (IRE) *Ottavio Di Paolo* 106
4 b h Highest Honor(FR) —Southerncape (USA) (Dixieland Band (USA))
2540a^{4}

Glorious Sight (IRE) *Robert Collet* [illegible]
[illegible] Singspiel(IRE) —Zelding (IRE) (Warning)
1553a^{5} 2137a^{2} 2342a^{4} 2977a^{3} 3670a^{4} 4570a^{9} 6568a^{9}

Glor Na Mara (IRE) *J S Bolger* a84 113
3 b c Leroidesanimaux(BRZ) —Sister Angelina (USA) (Saint Ballado (CAN))
1116a^{6} 2533a^{3} 2967a^{5} 3440a^{24}

Gloucester *Michael Scudamore* a79 77
8 b g Montjeu(IRE) —Birdlip (USA) (Sanglamore (USA))
(531) 2156^{7} 2793^{5} 3533^{3}

Glyn Ceiriog *George Baker* 75
3 b f Hawk Wing(USA) —Ceiriog Valley (In The Wings)
1060^{4} ◆ 1950^{5} 2957^{3} 3467^{6} 4576^{3} 5925^{2} 6295^{3} 6888^{11}

Go *Micky Hammond* a56 57
3 b g Royal Applause—Kind Of Light (Primo Dominie)
1203^{15} 1945^{10} 2635^{7} 2786^{12} 4403^{8} 5507^{8}

Goal (IRE) *Richard Guest* a72 79
3 b g Mujadil(USA) —Classic Lin (FR) (Linamix (FR))
505^{4} 642^{2} 873^{4} (942) 1082^{4} 1819^{8} 1975^{3} (2236) 2729^{2} 2964^{4} (3235) 3485^{8} 3679^{2} 4005^{4} (4560) 4744^{2} 4854^{5} 7299^{15}

Goal Hanger *Tom Dascombe* a29 64
2 b f Exceed And Excel(AUS) —Mrs Gray (Red Sunset)
3200^{2} 3336^{3} 3718^{7} 5374^{9}

Go Amwell *J R Jenkins* a61 53
8 b g Kayf Tara—Daarat Alayaam (IRE) (Reference Point)
4396^{2} 5079^{11} 5379^{8}

Gobama *J W Hills* a89 98
4 br m Dr Fong(USA) —Chine (Inchinor)
1467^{6} 2000^{3} (2634) 3213a^{6} 3703^{5} 5657^{8} ◆ 6219^{7} 6741a^{4}

Gobi (FR) *J-M Capitte* a52
4 b g Prince Kirk(FR) —Gezabelle (FR) (Garde Royale)
1012a^{4}

Goboll *William Haggas* a88 80
3 gr c Invincible Spirit(IRE) —Exclusive Approval (USA) (With Approval (CAN))
3183^{3} (4989) 5880^{6} 6409^{3}

Godber (IRE) *Ralph Smith* a41 57
2 br g Imperial Dancer—Ambrix (IRE) (Xaar)
2854^{6} 3242^{3} 7751^{12} 7938^{5}

Goddess Of Light (IRE) *Daniel Mark Loughnane* a76 74
4 b m Chineur(FR) —Blues Over (IRE) (Sri Pekan (USA))
113^{2} 231^{7} 336^{8}

Go Dutch (IRE) *Roger Varian* 83
2 ch c Dutch Art—Paix Royale (Royal Academy (USA))
4507^{2} 5051^{3} (5991)

Gogeo (IRE) *Alan Swinbank* 87
4 b g Val Royal(FR) —Steal 'Em (Efisio)
1211^{3} ◆ (1386) ◆ 2220^{9} 4677^{4} 4998^{4} 5435^{5} 6151^{9}

Go Go Green (IRE) *Jim Goldie* a82 84
5 b g Acclamation—Preponderance (IRE) (Cyrano De Bergerac)
1073^{13} 1715^{5} 3160^{3} 3488^{6} 5108^{6} (5452) 6112^{16} 7104^{2}

Going Grey (IRE) *Richard Fahey* a64 50
2 b c Diamond Green(FR) —Incendio (Siberian Express (USA))
6837^{6} 7627^{2}

Go Jo Go (FR) *Robert Collet* 79
3 b g Gone West(USA) —Joint Aspiration (Pivotal)
5463a^{0}

Golan Heights (IRE) *Adrian McGuinness* a56 67
5 br g Golan(IRE) —Lady Abigail (IRE) (Royal Academy (USA))
252^{12} (771) 911^{5} 3240^{10}

Gold City (IRE) *Saeed Bin Suroor* 98
2 b c Pivotal—Storm Lily (USA) (Storm Cat (USA))
(4433) (4891) 5558^{2} 5826^{2} 6535^{6}

Gold Coin *J W Hills* a66 66
2 b f Rail Link—Rosa De Mi Corazon (USA) (Cozzene (USA))
3812^{10} 4390^{4} 5097^{3} 6021^{8} 6484^{13}

Golden Aria (IRE) *Richard Hannon* 81
4 b m Rakti—Yellow Trumpet (Petong)
1114^{6} 2232^{7} (2791)

Golden Arrow (IRE) *E Charpy* a104 97
8 b h Danehill(USA) —Cheal Rose (IRE) (Dr Devious (IRE))
583a^{6}

Golden Blaze *James Moffatt* 69
3 ch g Iceman—Astrolove (IRE) (Bigstone (IRE))
4043^{9} 4290^{11} 6116^{11}

Golden City (IRE) *Chris Wall* a64 74
3 b f Azamour(IRE) —Generous Lady (Generous (IRE))
1364^{6} ◆ 2218^{6} 2871^{3} ◆ 3989^{4} 5477^{8} 6136^{5}

Golden Compass *Giles Bravery* a70 61
3 ch f Sakhee(USA) —Northern Bows (Bertolini (USA))
1343^{8} 2384^{2} 3230^{2} (4162) 4511^{3} 5120^{2} (5644) 6444^{2} 6696^{3}

Golden Creek (USA) *Mrs K Burke* a76 65
3 b g Seeking The Gold(USA) —Oyster Bay (USA) (Saint Ballado (CAN))
(3710) 4665^{9} 5213^{2} 5602^{2} 6188^{5} 7034^{9} 7352^{9} 7424^{6} 7773^{2}

Golden Delicious *Hughie Morrison* 92
3 ch f Cadeaux Genereux—Playgirl (IRE) (Caerleon (USA))
1837^{11} 3632^{9} (3845) 4332^{2} 4790^{6} (5657) 6341^{5} 7031^{10}

Golden Desert (IRE) *Simon Dow* a101 107
7 b g Desert Prince(IRE) —Jules (IRE) (Danehill (USA))
236^{11} 327a^{12} 587a^{10} 1885^{27} 3155^{19} 4428^{4} ◆ 4531^{21} 5043^{7} 5936^{8} (6341) 6521^{16} 6862^{16} 7518^{2} 7636^{4}

Golden Destiny (IRE) *Peter Makin* a56 108
[illegible] Dutch (IRE) (Bluebird (USA))
2298^{15} 3874^{4} ◆ 4468^{11} 5467^{7} 6233^{5} 6522^{16}

Golden Eagle *A Savujev* 100
5 b h Montjeu(IRE) —Grain Of Gold (Mr Prospector (USA))
4121a^{7} 5528a^{7} 6594a^{6}

Golden Emperor (IRE) *Keith Dalgleish* a57 56
4 ro g Antonius Pius(USA) —Lily Shing Shang (Spectrum (IRE))
3709^{12}

Golden Future *Peter Niven* a48 69
8 b g Muhtarram(USA) —Nazca (Zilzal (USA))
2091^{10} 2462^{3} 2696^{2} 3086^{4} 3129^{3} (3509) 3574^{3} 4129^{3} 4562^{3} 5079^{16} 5504^{4}

Golden Halo (IRE) *David Marnane* 78
2 ch c Titus Livius(FR) —Golden Ora (ITY) (Nordance (USA))
7101^{2}

Golden Heliostatic (IRE) *G Fratini*
2 gr c Heliostatic(IRE) —Oiselina (FR) (Linamix (FR))
7217a^{8}

Golden Hinde *Ronald Harris* 82
3 b c Red Ransom(USA) —Treacle (USA) (Seeking The Gold (USA))
1344^{8} 1723^{7} 2506^{8} 3399^{12} 4613^{8} 5376^{14} 5539^{6} 5845^{3}

Golden Jubilee (USA) *Richard Hannon* 61
2 bb c Zavata(USA) —Love Play (USA) (Friendly Lover (USA))
6165^{9} 6463^{8} 6812^{7}

Golden Lilac (IRE) *A Fabre* 116
3 b f Galileo(IRE) —Grey Lilas (IRE) (Danehill (USA))
(1553a) (2137a) (2977a) 5128a^{3}

Golden Mystery (USA) *Juan Carlos Guerrero* a96
5 ch m Awesome Again(CAN) —Mysterious Angel (USA) (Saint Ballado (CAN))
7282a^{7}

Golden Prospect *Paul Fitzsimons* a68 66
7 b g Lujain(USA) —Petonellajill (Petong)
2051^{6}

Golden Shine *Alan Bailey* a64 83
3 b f Royal Applause—Branston Jewel (IRE) (Prince Sabo)
100^{7} 263^{5}

Golden Shoe (IRE) *J T Gorman* a81 81
3 br g Footstepsinthesand—Goldilocks (IRE) (Caerleon (USA))
7150a^{5}

Golden Slipper *Ed Dunlop* a57 73
3 b f Danehill Dancer(IRE) —Dancing Box (BRZ) (Royal Academy (USA))
1362^{11} 2457^{4} 3001^{3} 4931^{3} 6137^{4}

Golden Speed (SPA) *L A Urbano-Grajales* a83
3 ch f Delfos(IRE) —Manilia (FR) (Kris)
5463a^{6}

Golden Sword *M F De Kock* a111 114
5 b h High Chaparral(IRE) —Sitara (Salse (USA))
326a^{2} ◆ (499a) ◆ (608a) 1002a^{11}

Golden Taurus (IRE) *J W Hills* a76 78
3 b g Danehill Dancer(IRE) —Nadwah (USA) (Shadeed (USA))
(1219) 1697^{3} 2200^{9} 3122^{6} 3461^{7} 5171^{6} 5858^{7} 6181^{4} 6664^{9} 7057^{6}

Golden Tempest (IRE) *Walter Swinburn* a91 93
3 b f Clodovil(IRE) —Honey Storm (IRE) (Mujadil (USA))
2102^{12} 2468^{6} 3283^{3} 4156^{4} (5322) 6062^{2} 6495^{8}

Golden Tirol (GER) *Adam Wyrzyk* 97
5 bb h Is Tirol(IRE) —Goldglockchen (GER) (Big Shuffle (USA))
2657a^{8}

Golden Valley *Rod Millman* 70
2 ch f Three Valleys(USA) —Reaf (In The Wings)
3686^{7} (4232) 4803^{9} 6372^{5} 6524^{12}

Goldenveil (IRE) *Richard Fahey* a64 85
3 b f Iffraaj—Line Ahead (IRE) (Sadler's Wells (USA))
1113^{4} 4473^{11} 5466^{4} 6191^{8} 7160^{5} 7453^{8}

Golden Waters *Eve Johnson Houghton* a30 78
4 b m Dubai Destination(USA) —Faraway Waters (Pharly (FR))
2232^{3} 2824^{2} (3251) 3641^{5} 4490^{2} 5135^{7} (5666) 6172^{5} 6592^{5}

Golden Whip (GER) *W Hickst* 105
4 b m Seattle Dancer(USA) —Genevra (IRE) (Danehill (USA))
1575a^{5}

Gold Falcon (IRE) *David Simcock* a62
2 b c Iffraaj—Pretty Majestic (IRE) (Invincible Spirit (IRE))
7627^{3} 7837^{5}

Goldies Band *Phil McEntee* a3
2 ch f Sakhee(USA) —Panic Stations (Singspiel (IRE))
2640^{9}

Goldikova (IRE) *F Head* 126
6 b m Anabaa(USA) —Born Gold (USA) (Blushing Groom (FR))
(2343a) 3009^{2} (4597a) 5129a^{2} 6566a^{2} 7307a^{3}

Goldinova (USA) *Lennart Reuterskiold Jr*
2 bb f Touch Gold(USA) —Soiree Russe (USA) (Nureyev (USA))
5983a^{5}

Gold Lace (IRE) *P J Prendergast* 82
2 b f Invincible Spirit(IRE) —Brigitta (IRE) (Sadler's Wells (USA))
921a^{4} 2322a^{5} 2777a^{8}

Gold Mine *Andrew Balding* a81 79
3 b g Diktat—Memsahib (Alzao (USA))
(1751) 3538^{3} ◆ (4209) ◆

Goldoni (IRE) *Andrew Balding* 88
2 ch g Dylan Thomas(IRE) —Lasso (Indian Ridge)
2882^{5} 3152^{9} 4007^{2} ◆ (4496) ◆ 5234^{4} 5709^{7}

Gold Pearl (USA) *S Seemar* a87 86
3 br c Henny Hughes(USA) —Gold Pattern (USA) (Slew O'Gold (USA))
823a^{9}

[illegible] (IRE) *John Joseph Murphy* 100
3 ch f Selkirk(USA) —Thermal Spring (Zafonic (USA))
(5748a) 5850^{5}

Gold Rally (USA) *Mahmood Al Zarooni* 81
2 rg c Medaglia D'Oro(USA) —Beright (USA) (Gray Slewpy (USA))
(6828)

Goldream *Luca Cumani* a81 78
2 b c Oasis Dream—Clizia (IRE) (Machiavellian (USA))
4330^{6} 5447^{3} 6216^{2} 6774^{6} 7095^{7}

Gold Rules *Michael Easterby* a87 93
4 ch g Gold Away(IRE) —Raphaela (FR) (Octagonal (NZ))
2002^{16} 2314^{5} 2708^{6} 2932^{10} 3277^{10} 3701^{7} 4440^{2}

Gold Sceptre (FR) *Richard Hannon* 75
2 b g Gold Away(IRE) —Cap Serena (FR) (Highest Honor (FR))
3425^{7} 4054^{3} 4580^{4} 5967^{6}

Gold Sprinter (IRE) *B Grizzetti* 83
3 ch c Gold Sphinx(USA) —Laissez Faire (USA) (Talinum (USA))
1127a^{3}

Goldstorm *Brian Baugh* a48
3 ch f Storming Home—Antonia Bertolini (Bertolini (USA))
4923^{5} 5946^{8} 6653^{5}

Gold Story *Chris Gordon* a62 56
4 ch g Lucky Story(USA) —Incatinka (Inca Chief (USA))
14^{2} 150^{2} 289^{2} 375^{2} 506^{2} 1283^{3} 1979^{9} 3720^{5}

Goldtara (FR) *A Lyon* a70 86
3 ch f Gold Away(IRE) —Diatara (FR) (Sillery (USA))
1597a^{2}

Goldtiming (FR) *D Prod'Homme* a70 75
3 ch f Gold Away(IRE) —Timely Lady (FR) (Lead On Time (USA))
258a^{6}

Gold Tobougg *David Simcock* a60 64
3 b f Tobougg(IRE) —Maristax (Reprimand)
4163^{3} 5007^{6} 6981^{3} (7845)

Goldtrek (USA) *Roger Charlton* a62 83
4 b m Medallist(USA) —Traipse (USA) (Digression (USA))
1775^{3} ◆ 2220^{11} 2791^{5} (3533) 4971^{10} 5303^{5}

Goldzar (USA) *Randall Granger* a104 93
6 b g Cozar(USA) —Golden Asset (USA) (Gold Crest (USA))
9100a^{7}

Golestan Palace (IRE) *Ed Walker* a63 62
3 b c Galileo(IRE) —Danse Spectre (IRE) (Spectrum (IRE))
1728^{4} 2307^{5} 2904^{5} 3922^{2} 4248^{2} 5321^{9} 5651^{8} 6701^{2} 7037^{3}

Go Maggie Go (IRE) *Kevin Ryan* a69 28
3 b f Kheleyf(USA) —Born To Glamour (Ajdal (USA))
64^{2} 183^{2} 322^{3} 452^{2} (595) 788^{2} (847) (875)

Gomrath (IRE) *Mick Channon* a78 87
4 b g Lomitas—Diner De Lune (IRE) (Be My Guest (USA))
994^{8} 5057^{9}

Go Nani Go *Ed de Giles* a82 88
5 b g Kyllachy—Go Between (Daggers Drawn (USA))
701^{5} 1140^{4} 1698^{15} 2369^{11} 3322^{9} 3759^{2} (4475) 5238^{3} 5627^{2} 6250^{5} 6932^{3}

Gone By Sunrise *Richard Fahey* 45
2 b c Three Valleys(USA) —Quadrophenia (College Chapel)
1434^{8} 6425^{4} 7072^{7}

Gone Fighting (FR) *Y De Nicolay* a64 68
3 b f Iron Mask(USA) —Gone Fishing (IRE) (Cadeaux Genereux)
7667a^{0}

Gone To Ground *Jeremy Gask* a45 17
2 ch g Grape Tree Road—Chase The Fox (Foxhound (USA))
5863^{11} 6292^{7} 6768^{13} 7490^{4} 7626^{4}

Gonetrio (USA) *Rod Collet* a82 78
4 b h Gone West(USA) —Balletomaine (IRE) (Sadler's Wells (USA))
840a^{0} 5095a^{7}

Goninodaethat *Jim Goldie* 62
3 b g Proclamation(IRE) —Big Mystery (IRE) (Grand Lodge (USA))
3304^{4} 3857^{9} 4016^{5} 4852^{2} 4876^{3} ◆ 5725^{2} ◆ 6116^{5} 6430^{5} 7099^{4}

Good Again *Gerard Butler* a92 99
5 ch m Dubai Destination(USA) —Good Girl (IRE) (College Chapel)
141^{2} 353^{7} 525^{7}

Good Authority (IRE) *Karen George* a78 72
4 b g Chineur(FR) —Lady Alexander (IRE) (Night Shift (USA))
6177^{2} 6653^{2} (6981) ◆ 7227^{5} 7532^{5}

Good Ba Ba (USA) *C W Chang* 112
9 b g Lear Fan(USA) —Elle Meme (USA) (Zilzal (USA))
1576a^{14}

Good Boy Jackson *Kevin Ryan* a23 89
3 b g Firebreak—Fisher Island (IRE) (Sri Pekan (USA))
1074^{10} (1904) (2835) 3623^{7} 4473^{13} 5730^{3} 6079^{3} 6346^{12} 6708^{4}

Good Buy Dubai (USA) *Mark Hoad* a34 62
5 gr g Essence Of Dubai(USA) —Sofisticada (USA) (Northern Jove (CAN))
7805^{11}

Goodbye Cash (IRE) *Ralph Smith* a64 65
7 b m Danetime(IRE) —Jellybeen (IRE) (Petardia)
78^{4} 135^{3} 211^{4} 485^{7} 590^{2} 689^{7} 3280^{5} 3942^{5}

Good Bye My Friend (FR) *C Boutin* a98 83
5 b h Kendor(FR) —The Wise Lady (FR) (Ganges (USA))
481a^{8} 6959a^{0}

Good Clodora (IRE) *Brian Meehan* a58 62
2 b f Red Clubs(IRE) —Geht Schnell (Fairy King (USA))
1996^{5} 2467^{9} 6329^{12}

Good Faith *George Moore* 45
3 b g Sleeping Indian—Femme Femme (USA) (Lyphard (USA))
2392^{6} 3084^{6} 3734^{6} 4112^{9} 4985^{8}

Goodfellows Quest (IRE) *Ann Duffield* 31
2 ch c Intikhab(USA) —Poppys Footprint (IRE) (Titus Livius (FR))
4436^{11} 4714^{7}

Goodison Park *Tim McCarthy* a15 53
4 ch m Big Shuffle(USA) —Perfect Dream (Emperor Jones (USA))
6240^{11}

Good Karma (ITY) *S Botti* 100
3 b f Tobougg(IRE) —Greedy Slewpy (USA) (Slewpy (USA))
1738a^{3} 2539a^{2} 3449a^{5}

Good Luck Charm *Gary Moore* a69 39
2 b g Doyen(IRE) —Lucky Dice (Perugino (USA))
5855^{9} 6928^{4} 7142^{4} 7436^{8} 7653^{2} 7835^{6}

Goodlukin Lucy *Pat Eddery* a73 83
4 ch m Supreme Sound—Suka Ramai (Nashwan (USA))
531^{4} 742^{3} 2176^{8} 2552^{7} 3256^{6} 3533^{4} 3951^{4} ◆ 4204^{5} 4971^{11}

Goodmanyourself *Paul Midgley* a48 49
3 b g Dubawi(IRE) —Frazzled (USA) (Prized (USA))
1293^{3} 1969^{5} 2239^{4} 2786^{2} 3496^{5} 4403^{3} 6229^{4} 6536^{6} 7061^{8} 7211^{9}

Good Morning Star (IRE) *Mark Johnston* a48 72
2 bb f Shirocco(GER) —Hollow Ridge (Beat Hollow)
5537^{2} 6245^{4} 6529^{5} 6792^{7}

Goodness *Sir Michael Stoute* a64 74
3 ch g Cadeaux Genereux—Dayrose (Daylami (IRE))
1415^{10} 2306^{5} 3044^{7}

Good News (FR) *C Laffon-Parias* a74 83
3 b f Numerous(USA) —Great News (FR) (Bering)
775a^{4} 7667a^{0}

Good Star (FR) *B Dutruel* a59 67
5 ch m Bad As I Wanna Be(IRE) —Arctic Starry (FR) (Star Maite (FR))
196a^{0}

Good Time Sue (IRE) *Ms M Dowdall Blake* a91 93
7 b m Commander Collins(IRE) —Poppy Lewis (IRE) (Paris House)
2325a[7] 5523a[14]

Good Timin' *David Brown* a51 56
3 b g Royal Applause—Record Time (Clantime)
6615[6] 7086[7] 7245[4] 7460[3] 7693[3] 7853[10]

Goodwood Atlantis (IRE) *John Dunlop* 80
2 b c Elusive City(USA) —Kayak (Singspiel (IRE))
4213[9] (4968)

Goodwood Starlight (IRE) *Jim Best* a55 90
6 br g Mtoto—Starring (FR) (Ashkalani (IRE))
3538[9]

Goodwood Treasure *John Dunlop* a70 76
3 ch f Bahamian Bounty—Lalectra (King Charlemagne (USA))
2025[9] 3351[5] 4244[8] 5381[3] (6122) 6799[2]

Googlette (IRE) *Edward Vaughan* a93 85
3 b f Exceed And Excel(AUS) —Jayzdoll (IRE) (Stravinsky (USA))
3158[7] 4779[7] (7457)

Goon Piper *Tom Dascombe* a10 13
2 b g Oratorio(IRE) —Penelewey (Groom Dancer (USA))
4714[8] 5413[7] 6280[12]

Go On The Badger *James Toller* a52
3 b f Bachelor Duke(USA) —Swissmatic (Petong)
2174[13] 2924[11] 3926[12]

Gooseberry Bush *Peter Makin* a38 72
4 b m Tobougg(IRE) —Away To Me (Exit To Nowhere (USA))
4547[5] (4882) 5890[2] 6276[6]

Gooseberry Fool *Sir Mark Prescott Bt* a75 96
2 br f Danehill Dancer(IRE) —Last Second (IRE) (Alzao (USA))
3237[4] (3520) 4031a[3] 5296a[9]

Goose Green (IRE) *Ron Hodges* a64 69
7 b g Invincible Spirit(IRE) —Narbayda (IRE) (Kahyasi)
810[8] 1625[2] 2144[4] 2171[4] 2450[3] 2900[4] 3726[5]

Gorau Glas *Mark Brisbourne*
3 b f Blue Dakota(IRE) —Glesni (Key Of Luck (USA))
5877[7] 6324[9]

Gordon Lord Byron (IRE) *T Hogan* a93 76
3 b g Byron—Boa Estrela (IRE) (Intikhab (USA))
(7468a) 7790a[3]

Gordonsville *Jim Goldie* a89 89
8 b g Generous(IRE) —Kimba (USA) (Kris S (USA))
1517[10] 2262[3] 2888[9] 3163[5] 4043[5] 5685[3] 6171[3] 6988[7] 7102[2] 7544a[4]

Gordy Bee (USA) *Richard Guest* a70 56
5 b g More Than Ready(USA) —Honoria (USA) (Danzig (USA))
60[2] 291[3] 637[4] 712[3] 897[7] 1058[3] 1978[3] 2490[3] 2828[7] 7748[6]

Gorgeous Goblin (IRE) *David C Griffiths* a52 57
4 b m Lujain(USA) —Tama (IRE) (Indian Ridge)
65[6] 343[4] 691[8] 732[4] 892[2] 1246[4] 1287[3] 1464[4] 1589[7] 1672[4] 1941[4] 2094[6] 2365[5] 2710[4] 2910[9] 3049[5] 7690[2] ◆ 7747[2] 7845[8] 7886[2]

Gorgeous Sixty (FR) *Y Fouin* 94
3 b f Touch Of The Blues(FR) —Sixty Six (IRE) (Exit To Nowhere (USA))
2750a[5]

Gosbeck *Henry Candy* 90
3 ch f Dubawi(IRE) —Goslar (In The Wings)
2026[7] (2836) 3623[5] 4251[7] 5235[4] ◆ 6996[4]

Gosforth Park *Mel Brittain* a65 58
5 ch g Generous(IRE) —Love And Kisses (Salse (USA))
6775[6] (7357) 7426[10] 7689[4]

Gospel Choir *Sir Michael Stoute* 83
2 ch c Galileo(IRE) —Chorist (Pivotal)
5013[3] ◆

Gossamer Seed (IRE) *John Joseph Murphy* a94 96
3 ro f Choisir(AUS) —Light And Airy (Linamix (FR))
1006a[11] 5361a[7] 6733a[5] 7149a[7] 7277a[6]

Gothen Niece (IRE) *C P Donoghue* a39 40
7 b m Gothenberg(IRE) —Homestead Niece (USA) (Soviet Lad (USA))
6411[6]

Gothic Chick *Alan McCabe* a35 65
3 br f Araafa(IRE) —Entail (USA) (Riverman (USA))
964[9] 1082[8] 1524[6] 1980[7] (2424) 2918[9] 3482[6] 3630[9] 6696[11]

Gotlandia (FR) *M Delzangles* a76 109
4 b m Anabaa(USA) —Grenade (FR) (Bering)
1125a[6] 6783a[5]

Gottany O'S *Mick Channon* a83 92
3 b g Storming Home—Miletrian Cares (IRE) (Hamas (IRE))
520[4] 649[2] (836) (1304) 1811[6] 2295[4] 2711[8] (3376) 4251[5] (5235) 6046[5] (6328)

Gottcher *David Barron* a76 82
3 b g Fasliyev(USA) —Danalia (IRE) (Danehill (USA))
(1589) 2074[7] 2505[2] 2724[7] (3628) 3975[6] 4855[4] 5679[7] 6112[22] 6350[10] 6801[12] 7104[11]

Gouray Girl (IRE) *Walter Swinburn* a89 102
4 b m Redback—Brillano (FR) (Desert King (IRE))
1594[5] 1885[11] 2470[8] 3134[5] 4993[11] 5702[7] 6272[5] ◆ 6723[5] 7031[9]

Govenor Eliott (IRE) *Alan Lockwood* a45 39
6 ch g Rock Of Gibraltar(IRE) —Lac Dessert (USA) (Lac Ouimet (USA))
3569[12] 4408[13] 5368[6]

Govenor General (IRE) *Jeremy Noseda* a67 57
3 b c Araafa(IRE) —Requested Pleasure (IRE) (Rainbow Quest (USA))
335[4] 550[2] (760) 890[5]

Govinda (USA) *A Wohler* 103
4 bb h Pulpit(USA) —Garden In The Rain (FR) (Dolphin Street (FR))
3531a[11]

Gowanharry (IRE) *Michael Dods* 43
2 ch f Choisir(AUS) —Aahgowangowan (IRE) (Tagula (IRE))
5367[5] ◆

Gower Rules (IRE) *John Bridger* a66 67
3 gr g Aussie Rules(USA) —Holy Norma (Nashwan (USA))
339[5] 469[5] 650[5] 866[4] 1272[4] (1312) 1487[2] 1997[2] 2293[7] 2819[9] 3518[8] (3690) 3919[7] 4389[8] 4862[6] 4905[3] 5491[5] 5838[3] 6052[5]

Gower Sophia *Ronald Harris* a64 53
4 b m Captain Rio—Hollow Quaill (IRE) (Entrepreneur)
28[8] 65[4]

Gracchus (USA) *Noel Meade* a68 70
5 b g Black Minnaloushe(USA) —Montessa (USA) (Montbrook (USA))
977a[7]

Grace And Virtue (IRE) *S Donohoe* a60 59
4 b m Statue Of Liberty(USA) —One For Fun (Unfuwain (USA))
169[7] 408[9] 893[4]

Gracefield (USA) *Mahmood Al Zarooni* 86
3 b f Storm Cat(USA) —Illustrious Miss (USA) (Kingmambo (USA))
(2529) 2839[8] 3757[2] 4235[6]

Graceful Act *James Toller* a60 59
3 b f Royal Applause—Minnina (IRE) (In The Wings)
2723[9] 3437[6] 6086[8] 6799[6]

Graceful Descent (FR) *Jim Goldie* a74 84
6 b m Hawk Wing(USA) —Itab (USA) (Dayjur (USA))
3163[7] 4360[15] 6151[6] 7162[6]

Graceful Spirit *Des Donovan* a23 46
4 b m Reset(AUS) —Naemi (GER) (Tannenkonig (IRE))
983[8] 1399[5] 1767[5] 2268[4] 2561[6] 2828[4]

Grace Hall (USA) *Anthony Dutrow* a113
2 b f Empire Maker(USA) —Season's Greetings (IRE) (Ezzoud (IRE))
7283a[2]

Gracelightening *Bruce Hellier* a42 64
4 b m Reset(AUS) —Monica Geller (Komaite (USA))
516[5] 1978[6]

Gracie's Games *Richard Price* a56 65
5 b m Mind Games—Little Kenny (Warning)
1469[7] 2182[7] (2555) 2989[4] (3217) 3711[8] 4270[10] 4793[4] 5513[6] 5917[12] 6408[4] 6889[12]

Gracie's Gift (IRE) *Richard Guest* a59 70
9 b g Imperial Ballet(IRE) —Settle Petal (IRE) (Roi Danzig (USA))
2165[11] 2653[6] 3024[9] 4651[13] 5034[7] 5601[12] 6426[4] 6646[4] 7071[4] 7229[11] 7420[3] 7728[4]

Gracious Melange *Marco Botti* a84
4 b m Medicean—Goodness Gracious (IRE) (Green Desert (USA))
932[4] 1499[5]

Gradara *S Wattel* a80 102
4 b m Montjeu(IRE) —Gracefully (IRE) (Orpen (USA))
5839a[7] (6470a) 7049a[12]

Grafitti *Niels Petersen* a83 96
6 b m Dansili—Reading Habit (USA) (Half A Year (USA))
(5982a)

Grain Of Sand *Andrew Balding* a59 55
2 b g Dubai Destination(USA) —Grain Of Salt (Montjeu (IRE))
6481[7] 6928[5]

Gramercy (IRE) *Michael Bell* a82 106
4 b g Whipper(USA) —Topiary (IRE) (Selkirk (USA))
3155[5] 5699[2] ◆ 6035[4] 6520[7]

Grams And Ounces *Amy Weaver* a62 82
4 b g Royal Applause—Ashdown Princess (IRE) (King's Theatre (IRE))
1390[6] 1829[3] 2414[3] 3399[4]

Gran Canaria Queen *Ian Semple* 47
2 bb f Compton Place—Ex Mill Lady (Bishop Of Cashel)
5618[12] 6598[4] ◆

Grandad Bill (IRE) *Jim Goldie* a47 65
8 ch g Intikhab(USA) —Matikanehanafubuki (IRE) (Caerleon (USA))
3453[6] (4879) 5723[6] 6082[8]

Grandad Mac *Jane Chapple-Hyam* 64
3 b g Invincible Spirit(IRE) —No Rehearsal (FR) (Baillamont (USA))
4102[5] 4861[7] 5539[9] (6437)

Grand Adventure (USA) *Mark Frostad* 117
5 bb h Grand Slam(USA) —Val Marie (USA) (Coronado's Quest (USA))
9100a[2] 6204a[9] 6908a[4] 7303a[10]

Grand Akbar (FR) *Y-M Porzier* a73 82
4 b g Muhtathir—Grande Epoque (FR) (Valanour (IRE))
7733a[0]

Grand Art (IRE) *Frank Sheridan* a73 51
7 b g Raise A Grand(IRE) —Mulberry River (IRE) (Bluebird (USA))
3157[17] 6306[6] 6656[4]

Grand Diamond (IRE) *Jim Goldie* a68 74
7 b g Grand Lodge(USA) —Winona (IRE) (Alzao (USA))
1072[2] 2734[3] 2887[11] 4142[6] 5149[6] 5723[11] 6385[4]

Grand Duchy *M Al Muhairi* a67 79
3 b c Medicean—Pazzazz (IRE) (Green Desert (USA))
238[10] 823a[12]

Grand Duels (AUS) *Byron Cozamanis* 110
8 bb g Marechal(AUS) —Valentine's Gift (AUS) (Ifrad (USA))
[11]

Grande Amore (IRE) *Manfred Hofer* a79 79
3 b f Refuse To Bend(IRE) —Balting Lass (IRE) (Orpen (USA))
981a[6]

Grande Caiman (IRE) *Geoffrey Harker* a74 78
7 ch g Grand Lodge(USA) —Sweet Retreat (Indian Ridge)
392[6] (813) 2888[16]

Grande Illusion *J W Hills* a48 23
2 br g Singspiel(IRE) —Larousse (Unfuwain (USA))
5672[11] 6216[9]

Grandeur (IRE) *Jeremy Noseda* 85
2 gr c Verglas(IRE) —Misskinta (IRE) (Desert Sun)
4535[2] (5133)

Grand Gold *Seamus Durack* 76
2 b c Librettist(USA) —Night Symphonie (Cloudings (IRE))
1913[3] 2120[2] (2460) 3595[5] 6829[10]

Grand Hombre (USA) *R Bouresly* a79 69
11 br g Grand Slam(USA) —Santona (CHI) (Winning (USA))
331a[10]

Grand Honour (IRE) *Paul Howling* a57 41
5 gr g Verglas(IRE) —Rosy Dudley (IRE) (Grand Lodge (USA))
211[6] 421[4] 485[3] 662[6] 950[10] 7581[10] 7768[8] 7924[6]

Grandiloquent *Sir Michael Stoute* a75
2 b c Rail Link—High Praise (USA) (Quest For Fame)
6928[2]

Grand Liaison *John Berry* 26
2 b f Sir Percy—Dancinginthedark (IRE) (Fasliyev (USA))
6581[9] 6950[13]

Grand Lucius (FR) *D Windrif* a85 88
4 b g Baroud D'Honneur(FR) —Khayriya (FR) (Valanour (IRE))
831a[6]

Grandmas Dream *Richard Guest* a74 84
3 b f Kyllachy—Sabina (Prince Sabo)
(611) 875[3] 1141[6] 1521[7] 2881[2] 3174[2] 3389[2] 4721[2] 4988[5] 5301[3] 5452[3] (6056) 6442[5] (6815) 7039[7] 7116[5]

Grand Palace (IRE) *Derek Shaw* a40 39
8 b g Grand Lodge(USA) —Pocket Book (IRE) (Reference Point)
167[9] 250[8] 362[6] 443[9]

Grand Piano (IRE) *Andrew Balding* a73 69
4 b g Arakan(USA) —Stately Princess (Robellino (USA))
663[2] 863[2] 1730[6] (2605) 3473[7] 4997[3] 5836[11] 7448[10]

Grand Prix Boss (JPN) *Yoshito Yahagi* 119
3 b c Sakura Bakushin O(JPN) —Rosy Mist (JPN) (Sunday Silence (USA))
3011[8]

Grand Rapids (USA) *Mahmood Al Zarooni* 49
2 b c Bernardini(USA) —Cajun Cat (USA) (Storm Cat (USA))
3954[6] 4655[4]

Grandretour *J-C Rouget* a69 90
7 b g Grand Lodge(USA) —Entail (USA) (Riverman (USA))
843a[9]

Grand Sort *Tony Newcombe* a35 33
3 b g Raise A Grand(IRE) —Allsorts (USA) (Lemon Drop Kid (USA))
6085[11] 6804[12] 7327[6] 7740[9]

Grand Stitch (USA) *Declan Carroll* a78 64
5 b g Grand Slam(USA) —Lil Sister Stich (USA) (Seattle Bound (USA))
1035[14] 1411[10] 1698[13] 2609[12] 3027[14] 4144[3] 4518[8] 4820[7] 4986[11] 6655[11] 6802[8] 7266[3] 7737[3] 7897[6]

Grand Tard (FR) *Y-M Porzier* 105
5 b g Tot Ou Tard(IRE) —Strabit (Stradavinsky (IRE))
3008a[5]

Grand Theft Equine *Jim Boyle* a75
3 b g Piccolo—Red Storm (Dancing Spree (USA))
4800[5] 5816[2] 6377[8] 7204[7] 7327[3] 7662[2] 7806[5]

Grand Vent (IRE) *A Fabre* 112
3 b c Shirocco(GER) —Housa Dancer (FR) (Fabulous Dancer (USA))
(1551a) 2136a[2] 2751a[11]

Grand Vizier (IRE) *Conor Dore* a91 74
7 b g Desert Style(IRE) —Distant Decree (USA) (Distant View (USA))
45[5] 282[2] 433[5] 670[5] 837[4]

Granny Anne (IRE) *Paul D'Arcy* a63 53
3 ch f Redback—Krayyalei (IRE) (Krayyan)
53[7] 109[3] 187[3] (426) 510[4] 4431[9] 4920[3] 5014[10] 5213[3] 5631[5] 7113[9] 7441[11] 7507[6] 7655[6] 7910[13]

Granny McPhee *Alan Bailey* a74 87
5 b m Bahri(USA) —Allumette (Rainbow Quest (USA))
235[8] 515[3] (1826) 1855[4] 2282[8] 2634[4] 2906[7] (3380) 3848[3] 4577[5] 5716[8]

Granston (IRE) *James Bethell* a99 94
10 gr g Revoque(IRE) —Gracious Gretclo (Common Grounds)
(1325) 1879[3] 2812[2] 3625[5] 4280[5] 5078[8]

Graphic (IRE) *Richard Hannon* a97 85
2 ch c Excellent Art—Follow My Lead (Night Shift (USA))
2837[6] (3424) 5039[4] (6055) 6788[2] 7026[13]

Graser (IRE) *Marco Botti* a76 90
2 b f Motivator—Queen Padme (IRE) (Halling (USA))
6030[7] (6818) ◆ 7169[5]

Grassy (USA) *Christophe Clement* 113
5 rg h El Prado(IRE) —High Savannah (Rousillon (USA))
6548a[3]

Graycliffe (IRE) *Jennie Candlish* a57 60
5 gr g Val Royal(FR) —Popiplu (USA) (Cozzene (USA))
1253[6] 1959[6] 2237[4] 6613[11] 7036[4] 7195[9] 7495[6]

Grayfriars *J R Jenkins* a37 35
3 gr c Proclamation(IRE) —Hilltop (Absalom)
2266[8] 3465[10] 5176[6] 6251[7] 7245[11] 7525[9]

Graylyn Olivaa *Robert Eddery* a43 3
2 b g Cockney Rebel(IRE) —Gaelic Roulette (IRE) (Turtle Island (IRE))
7094[10] 7292[16] 7521[11]

Graylyn Valentino *Robin Dickin* a64
2 b g Primo Valentino(IRE) —Rhuby River (IRE) (Bahhare (USA))
7225[7] 7672[7] 7837[4]

Gray Pearl *Charles Hills* 109
2 gr f Excellent Art—Divine Grace (IRE) (Definite Article)
(5048) ◆ 6691[3]

Grazeon Again (IRE) *John Quinn* 67
3 b g Diamond Green(FR) —Saviolo (Rossini (USA))
1624[8] 2406[7] 3124[7] 4110[10]

Great Ability (IRE) *Stephen Michael Cox* a74 69
2 b g Great Exhibition(USA) —Final Contest (USA) (Grand Slam (USA))
5211[9]

Great Acclaim *James Fanshawe* a86 71
3 b g Acclamation—Pearl Bright (FR) (Kaldoun (FR))
(1654) 2646[7] 3346[7] (3737) ◆ 4909[4] 5718[2] 6477[P]

Great Attack (USA) *Wesley A Ward* 113
4 b h Greatness(USA) —Cat Attack (USA) (Storm Cat (USA))
9100a[3] 7303a[4]

Great Charm (IRE) *Eric Alston* a81 87
6 b g Orpen(USA) —Briery (IRE) (Salse (USA))
1067[6] 2299[11] 2806[10]

Greatest Dancer (IRE) *Jamie Osborne* a80 61
2 b f Iffraaj—Seasonal Style (IRE) (Generous (IRE))
1996[6] (2651) 3866[7] 5197[9] 5637[6]

Great Event (FR) *M Cheno* 100
4 b g Anabaa(USA) —Great News (FR) (Bering)
6321a[6]

Great Expectations *J R Jenkins* a60
3 b c Storming Home—Fresh Fruit Daily (Reprimand)
7585[5] (7913)

Great Heavens *John Gosden* 68
2 b f Galileo(IRE) —Magnificient Style (USA) (Silver Hawk (USA))
6329[5] ◆

Great Hot (BRZ) *A C Avila* a107 98
3 bb f Orientate(USA) —That's Hot (USA) (Seeking The Gold (USA))
7282a[11]

Great Mystery (IRE) *J W Hills* a55 55
2 b c Diamond Green(FR) —Molaaf (Shareef Dancer (USA))
2559[12] 2767[9] 5411[6] 6002[3] 6662[7] 6937[10]

Great Nicanor (IRE) *Ian Semple* a61
2 b g Bertolini(USA) —No More Maybes (IRE) (Swain (IRE))
5003[6] 7369[5] 7769[2]

Great Shot *Sylvester Kirk* a79 79
3 b g Marju(IRE) —Highland Shot (Selkirk (USA))
(993) 1754[3] 2477[4] 5242[4] 6124[6] 6797[4] ◆ 6997[8]

Great Show *Bernard Llewellyn*
4 ch m Choisir(AUS) —Maple Branch (USA) (Stravinsky (USA))
6767[12] 7264[13]

Great Surprise *Reg Hollinshead* a71 71
3 ch g Hernando(FR) —Moment (Nashwan (USA))
258a[0] 410a[5] 480a[3] 660a[2]

Grecian Goddess (IRE) *John Ryan* a57 69
3 b f Kris Kin(USA) —Grecian Air (FR) (King's Best (USA))
2018[11] 2418[6] 3709[10] 3925[6] 4190[4] 4449[9] 4510[6]

Greek Canyon (IRE) *G M Lyons* a56 85
2 br c Moss Vale(IRE) —Lazaretta (IRE) (Dalakhani (IRE))
1699a[5]

Greek Islands (IRE) *Ed de Giles* a75 78
3 b g Oasis Dream—Serisia (FR) (Exit To Nowhere (USA))
3594[5] 4281[8] 4799[2] 6227[9] 6796[4]

Greek Music *George Prodromou* 25
2 gr f Librettist(USA) —Silver Spell (Aragon)
5117[8] 5351[6]

Greek Secret *Paul Midgley* a62 63
8 b g Josr Algarhoud(IRE) —Mazurkanova (Song)
3556[4] 3931[10] 4443[4] 5175[7] 6261[2] 6304[6] 6618[6]

Greek War (IRE) *Mahmood Al Zarooni* 79
2 ch g Monsun(GER) —Gonfilia (GER) (Big Shuffle (USA))
4213[5] ◆ 5013[4] 6059[2]

Greeley House *Chris Wall* a30 57
3 b g Mr Greeley(USA) —Sauvage (FR) (Sri Pekan (USA))
1605[14] 6286[6] 6754[3]

Green Agenda *Derek Shaw* a61 81
5 b g Anabaa(USA) —Capistrano Day (USA) (Diesis)
4865[9] 4918[9] 5143[11] 5414[12]

Green Apple *Peter Makin* a74 42
3 b f Needwood Blade—Scarlett Ribbon (Most Welcome)
(513) 1141[8] 2199[3] 2818[6] 6895[15] 7141[10] 7332[7]

Green Army *Mick Channon* a25 46
4 b g Sulamani(IRE) —Dowhatjen (Desert Style (IRE))
354[8]

Greenbelt *George Moore* a61 56
10 b g Desert Prince(IRE) —Emerald (USA) (El Gran Senor (USA))
374[5]

Greenbelt Star *Mrs John Harrington* a76 78
5 ch g Generous(IRE) —Dusty Shoes (Shareef Dancer (USA))
3420a[11]

Green Beret (IRE) *A Al Raihe* a106 99
5 b g Fayruz—Grandel (Owington)
(582a) 755a[5] 825a[3]

Green Birdie (NZ) *C Fownes* a117 115
8 b g Catbird(AUS) —Mrs Squillionaire (AUS) (Last Tycoon)
999a[4] 2339a[7] 7730a[11]

Green China (FR) *S Wattel* a95 91
4 b m Green Tune(USA) —China Moon (USA) (Gone West (USA))
91a[2]

Green Coast (IRE) *Doug Watson* a115 95
8 b h Green Desert(USA) —Oriental Fashion (IRE) (Marju (IRE))
156a[6] 501a[6]

Green Dandy (IRE) *E J O'Neill* a83 102
4 b m Green Desert(USA) —Hawas (Mujtahid (USA))
1893[8] 4121a[9] 4739a[0] 7534a[6]

Green Destiny (IRE) *William Haggas* a65 121
4 b g Marju(IRE) —Mubkera (IRE) (Nashwan (USA))
(1684) 3107[7] (3876) ◆ 4494[16] (5252) (6161) 6861[6]

Green Earth (IRE) *Pat Phelan* a79 71
4 b g Cape Cross(IRE) —Inchyre (Shirley Heights)
473[8] 822[14] 985[9] 2920[8] (3944) 4317[5] 4656[2] 5547[6] 5858[4] 6586[6] *6931[11] 7346[14] 7522[9]* (7810)

Green Ensign (IRE) *Alan McCabe* a32 16
4 b g Traditionally(USA) —Green Green Grass (Green Desert (USA))
930[6] 1399[9] 2710[8]

Greenflash *Richard Hannon* a73 78
3 b f Green Desert(USA) —Empress Anna (IRE) (Imperial Ballet (IRE))
952[2] ◆ *(1179)* 1481[4] 2018[7] 2313[11] 2878[7] 4202[9]

Green Future (USA) *Amanda Perrett* a61 59
3 bb g Arch(USA) —Saturday's Child (USA) (Storm Cat (USA))
2469[8] 2930[8] 3267[6] 3960[4] 4974[5] 5566[4] *5947[4] 6087[4]* 6482[5] *6823[10]*

Greenhead High *David Nicholls* a66 59
3 b g Statue Of Liberty(USA) —Artistry (Night Shift (USA))
(126) 349[3] 476[3] 601[3] 659[5] 764[7] 890[3] 1149[8] 5731[14] 6802[9] 7065[2] 7216[11] 7420[5] 7641[2] 7728[2]

Green Howard *Robin Bastiman* 85
3 ch g Bahamian Bounty—Dash Of Lime (Bold Edge)
3756[3] 4282[2] (5368) ◆ 6231[12] (6840) (7213)

Green Legacy (USA) *Amanda Perrett* a56
2 ch c Discreet Cat(USA) —Mira Costa (USA) (Thunder Gulch (USA))
6795[13] 7634[11] 7751[8]

Green Lightning (IRE) *Mark Johnston* a76 90
4 b g Montjeu(IRE) —Angelic Song (CAN) (Halo (USA))
1325[9] 1908[7] 2364[3] 2892[7] 3758[4] 4465[4] 5149[7] 5504[9] *6182[3] 6287[5] (6503) 6621[5] 7002[11]*

Green Manalishi *Kevin Ryan* a102 88
10 b g Green Desert(USA) —Silca-Cisa (Hallgate)
2[6] 265[5] 613[6] 970[2] 1371[4] 1698[5] *1955[6]* 2250[5] 2938[18] 3028[9]

Green Moon (IRE) *Robert Hickmott* 114
4 b h Montjeu(IRE) —Green Noon (FR) (Green Tune (USA))
6886a[2]

Green Mountain (IRE) *Philip McBride* a42 45
2 b f Diamond Green(FR) —Mountain Dancer (IRE) (Rainbow Quest (USA))
6934[11] *7582[6] 7769[4] 7937[7]*

Green Park (IRE) *Declan Carroll* a99 97
8 b g Shinko Forest(IRE) —Danccini (IRE) (Dancing Dissident (USA))
1166[15] 1457[9] 1809[11] 2117[9] 2717[11] 3279[11] 3613[4] 4291[4] 4791[10] (5148) 5468[8] 5923[4] 6913[13]

Green Pastures (IRE) *Howard Johnson* 57
3 b g Diamond Green(FR) —Continuous (IRE) (Darshaan)
2350[10] 2571[12]

Green Pearl (IRE) *Ralph Beckett* a69 70
3 b g Green Desert(USA) —Kinnaird (IRE) (Dr Devious (IRE))
1446[7] 1626[7] 3363[6] *7455[14]*

Green Pride *G Martin* a62 67
8 b g Piccolo—Little Greenbird (Ardkinglass)
196a[10] 325a[8]

Greensward *Mike Murphy* a99 95
5 b g Green Desert(USA) —Frizzante (Efisio)
2020[7] 2470[11] *(5717)* (6326) 7023[5] *7628[11]*

Green Tango (FR) *P Van De Poele* a95 106
8 ch h Majorien—Miss Bonfosse (FR) (Hard Leaf (FR))
4524a[9] 7406a[6]

Green To Gold (IRE) *Don Cantillon* a64 68
6 gr g Daylami(IRE) —Alonsa (IRE) (Trempolino (USA))
6790[11] 7122[10] 7496[8]

Green Velvet *Peter Makin* a68 64
6 b m Iron Mask(USA) —Scarlett Ribbon (Most Welcome)
435[11]

Green Wadi *Gary Moore* a83 74
6 b g Dansili—Peryllys (Warning)
174[7] 4154[3] 4385[3] 4845[6] 5135[4] *(6789) (7130) 7577[6] 7759[6]*

Green Warrior *Richard Guest* a54 76
3 b g Invincible Spirit(IRE) —Starlit Sky (Galileo (IRE))
1494[5] 2375[8] 2918[2] 3192[5] 3573[11] (4172) 5457[7] 5939[2] 6265[9] 6801[11] *7746[14] 7896[11]*

Gregorian (IRE) *John Gosden* 86
2 b c Clodovil(IRE) —Three Days In May (Cadeaux Genereux)
5447[15] 6170[7] (6983)

Gremlin *Bernard Llewellyn* a78 65
7 b g Mujahid(USA) —Fairy Free (Rousillon (USA))
1050[3] 3799[4] 4488[4] *4870[3] 5417[5]*

Grenane (IRE) *Mrs A Malzard* a63 62
8 b g Princely Heir(IRE) —Another Rainbow (IRE) (Rainbows For Life (CAN))
1743a[3]

Grethel (IRE) *Alan Berry* a35 55
7 b m Fruits Of Love(USA) —Stay Sharpe (USA) (Sharpen Up)
2912[9] 3380[5] 3658[3] 4142[5] 4408[5] 4605[4] 6029[13] 6236[7]

Gretzky *Robert Alan Hennessy* 86
4 b g King's Best(USA) —Estabilizada (ARG) (Halo Sunshine (USA))
4398a[20]

Grey Boy (GER) *Tony Carroll* a70 62
10 gr g Medaaly—Grey Perri (Siberian Express (USA))
210[4] 652[2] 662[2] (730) 809[3] (896) 943[4] (1625) 1763[3] 1905[3] 2268[7]

Grey Command (USA) *Mel Brittain* a73 73
6 gr g Daylami(IRE) —Shmoose (IRE) (Caerleon (USA))
1617[3] 1881[4] 2393[6] *2654[7]* 3574[2] 4366[6] (4407) 4612[4] (4904) 5149[9]

Grey Danube (IRE) *D J Bunyan* a69 43
2 gr g Verglas(IRE) —Redrightreturning (Diktat)
6912[4]

Greyemkay *Richard Price* 52
3 gb g Fair Mix(IRE) —Magic Orb (Primo Dominie)
3218[10] 3781[10] 4706[5] 5344[8] 5965[6] 6398[5] 6889[16]

Greyfriarschorista *Brian Ellison* a94 107
4 ch g King's Best(USA) —Misty Heights (Fasliyev (USA))
271[7] 702[4] 1102[10] 1406[21] *1760[13]* 2123[10] 2814[7] *3285[13]* 4013[3] 4392[6] 4792[10] 5151[2] *(7589)* (7687) ◆ 7771[6]

Greyfriars Drummer *Mark Johnston* a85 87
3 ch c Where Or When(IRE) —Loveleaves (Polar Falcon (USA))
1298[4] 1484[2] (1620) 2295[9] 3069[7] 3829[4] 4426[11] 6046[7] 7022[8]

Grey Granite (IRE) *Warren Greatrex* a80 78
5 gr g Dalakhani(IRE) —Royal Ballerina (IRE) (Sadler's Wells (USA))
3738[13]

Greyhope *Lucinda Russell* 64
2 gr g Pastoral Pursuits—Espana (Hernando (FR))
5202[3] 6187[8]

Greylami (IRE) *Robert Mills* a101 98
6 gr g Daylami(IRE) —Silent Crystal (USA) (Diesis)
1684[14] 2289[5] 2884[6] *5693[3]* 6528[6]

Grey Mirage *Marco Botti* 61
2 b c Oasis Dream—Grey Way (USA) (Cozzene (USA))
6630[5] ◆ 7232[6]

Grey Panel (FR) *T Le Brocq*
3 gr g Largesse—Minnie's Mystery (FR) (Highest Honor (FR))
5778a[5]

Grey Seal (IRE) *James Fanshawe* 20
2 gr f Cape Cross(IRE) —Mundus Novus (USA) (Unbridled's Song (USA))
6758[9]

Grey Soldier (IRE) *Gordon Elliott* a98 98
6 gr g Galileo(IRE) —Crusch Alva (FR) (Unfuwain (USA))
1381a[4]

Griffin Point (IRE) *William Muir* a68 67
4 b m Tagula(IRE) —Lady Corduff (IRE) (Titus Livius (FR))
1655[6] 2155[5] 2845[7] 2921[12] 3464[7] 5377[2] (5678) 5965[4] *(6175)* 6580[3] 6802[5] *7201[6] 7512[2] 7567[5] 7804[4]* 7897[2] 7940[6]

Grippa *David Brown* 53
2 ch g Avonbridge—Easy Mover (IRE) (Bluebird (USA))
2387[10] 2672[5] 2953[14] *5597[8]* 5818[7] 6187[9]

Griraz (FR) *J-L Dubord* a81 100
6 gr g Nombre Premier—Niraz (FR) (Nikos)
705a[4] 7733a[10]

Gris D'Honneur (FR) *D De Watrigant* a92 92
4 gr h Baroud D'Honneur(FR)—Belle Lagune (Barathea (IRE))
1011a[8]

Grissom (IRE) *Tim Easterby* 97
5 b g Desert Prince(IRE) —Misty Peak (IRE) (Sri Pekan (USA))
1205[5] 1618[2] 2095[16] 2620[2] (2806) 3383[2] 3850[5] (4369) (5032) 5887[7] 6145[10] 6987[21]

Gritstone *Richard Fahey* a88 87
4 b g Dansili—Cape Trafalgar (IRE) (Cape Cross (IRE))
2909[8] ◆ 3406[7] 4901[6] 6028[7] *(6669) (7199) 7877[5]*

Grizzle *Mahmood Al Zarooni* a82 82
2 b c Shamardal(USA) —Pearl Grey (Gone West (USA))
4098[2] 4507[4] 5786[3] *6308[3]* ◆ 6829[2] *(7126)*

Groomed (IRE) *William Haggas* a66 89
3 b g Acclamation—Enamoured (Groom Dancer (USA))
(3614) 4355[7] (5242) 6063[4] 6325[8]

Gross Prophet *Alastair Lidderdale* a75 77
6 b g Lujain(USA) —Done And Dusted (IRE) (Up And At 'Em)
5568[9]

Group Therapy *David Barron* a72 112
6 ch g Choisir(AUS) —Licence To Thrill (Wolfhound (USA))
1687[11] 2297[5] 3010[14] 3874[5] 4468[3] 4768a[4] 5827[4] 6233[4]

Grudge *Conor Dore* a79 80
6 b g Timeless Times(USA) —Envy (IRE) (Paris House)
125[9] 197[2] 294[11] 430[6] 523[5] 1048[8] 1196[8] 1309[3] 1507[U] 1940[2] 2304[4] 2603[4] 2845[14] (3471) 4475[2] 5457[3] 6119[14] 7395[11] 7512[3] 7659[2] 7804[6] 7883[3]

Grumeti *Michael Bell* 89
3 b g Sakhee(USA) —Tetravella (IRE) (Groom Dancer (USA))
1683[3] ◆ (2253) (2885) 3650[3] 4355[2] 5968[3]

Grymeos (FR) *J Heloury* a69 81
4 b g Peintre Celebre(USA) —Obsidianne (FR) (Machiavellian (USA))
196a[7] 325a[9]

Guardi (IRE) *Mahmood Al Zarooni* 59
2 gr c Dalakhani(IRE) —Grizel (Lion Cavern (USA))
6447[6]

Guards Chapel *Gary Moore* a64 65
3 b g Motivator—Intaaj (IRE) (Machiavellian (USA))
1836[11] (2637) ◆ 5420[4] *6052[6] 7515[4] 7800[4]*

Guava *Richard Hannon* a69 68
2 b f Kyllachy—Spunger (Fraam)
3117[6] 4155[5] 4720[4] 4947[4] *5245[5]* 5625[6] (6627) *6821[2]* 6972[3] 7294[7] *7597[4] (7718)*

Gucci D'Oro (USA) *David Simcock* 54
2 bb c Medaglia D'Oro(USA)—Ninette (USA) (Alleged (USA))
5959[4] 7060[6]

Gud Day (IRE) *Ronald Harris* a23 72
3 gr g Aussie Rules(USA) —Queen Al Andalous (IRE) (King's Best (USA))
1210[4] 1971[5] (2583) (3077) 4154[10] 4489[8]

Guest Book (IRE) *Michael Scudamore* a70 95
4 b g Green Desert(USA) —Your Welcome (Darshaan)
1075[2] 1410[DSQ] 1529[2] 1603[5] 4415[2] 4537[5] 6803[14] *7558[9] 7699[8]*

Guga (IRE) *John Mackie* a69 69
5 b g Rock Of Gibraltar(IRE) —Attitre (FR) (Mtoto)
1190[5] 1993[9] (2530) 2851[8] 3974[3] 5349[11] 6236[11] 7113[11]

Guiana (GER) *J Hirschberger* 85
4 b m Tiger Hill(IRE) —Guadalupe (GER) (Monsun (GER))
5075a[9] 6395a[10]

Guided Missile (IRE) *Andrew Balding* a69 84
3 b f Night Shift(USA) —Exorcet (FR) (Selkirk (USA))
1483[9] (2553) ◆ 4101[5] 4387[12]

Guilded Warrior *Paddy Butler* a96 94
8 b g Mujahid(USA) —Pearly River (Elegant Air)
1138[4] 1832[3] 2428[4] 3436[8] (4006) 4310[10] 4603[11] 5198[10] 5858[6]

Guildenstern (IRE) *Alastair Lidderdale* a64 46
9 b g Danetime(IRE) —Lyphard Abu (IRE) (Lyphard's Special (USA))
70[3] 129[13] 229[4] 382[2] 517[3] 652[5] 752[3] (1045) 1177[9] 1486[11] 2206[6] 2642[7] 2816[9] 2922[7] 3235[9] 3480[5]

Guinea Seeker *Tim Easterby* a32 64
3 b g Mujadil(USA) —Nefeli (First Trump)
2391[3] 3318[3] 3616[4] 4146[9] 4638[13] 5063[4] 5619[11]

Guisho (IRE) *Brian Meehan* a51 76
3 b g Iffraaj—Jorghinia (FR) (Seattle Slew (USA))
2511[4] 3543[12] 3988[7] *6311[8]* 6605[4]

Gulf Of Alaska *Mahmood Al Zarooni* 71
2 b c Sinndar(IRE) —Vituisa (Bering)
4292[3] ◆ 5541[9]

Gulf Of Aqaba (USA) *Ian Williams* a61 60
5 bb g Mr Greeley(USA) —Ocean Jewel (USA) (Alleged (USA))
635[6] (733) 838[9]

Gulf Of Naples (IRE) *Mark Johnston* 96
3 gb c Dubawi(IRE) —Kapria (FR) (Simon Du Desert (FR))
4514[10] (4985) ◆ 5710[7] (6988) (7139)

Gulf Punch *Milton Harris* a37 57
4 b m Dubawi(IRE) —Fruit Punch (IRE) (Barathea (IRE))
1032[6]

Gulf Storm (IRE) *Bryan Smart* a52 57
2 b c Pivotal—Beyrouth (USA) (Alleged (USA))
5726[7] 6292[5] *7000[6]* 7231[6] *7916[4]*

Gullveig (JPN) *Katsuhiko Sumii* 98
3 bb f Deep Impact(JPN) —Air Groove (JPN) (Tony Bin)
7410a[14]

Gumnd (IRE) *Chris Grant* a82 86
4 b g Selkirk(USA) —Surval (IRE) (Sadler's Wells (USA))
2124[10] 2955[7] 4170[6] *4866[12]*

Gunalt Joy *Michael Easterby* a52 38
3 b f Blue Dakota(IRE) —Lawless Bridget (Alnasr Alwasheek)
146[6] 251[7] 595[5]

Gung Ho Jack *John Best* 82
2 b g Moss Vale(IRE) —Bijan (IRE) (Mukaddamah (USA))
3567a[7] (4276) 4858[6] (5584) 6670[13]

Gunner Lindley (IRE) *B W Hills* 99
4 ch g Medicean—Lasso (Indian Ridge)
[illegible]

Gunner Will (IRE) *George Baker* 80
2 b g Le Vie Dei Colori—Ros The Boss (IRE) (Danehill (USA))
3590[2] 4053[4] 5541[4] 6986[7]

Gunslinger (FR) *Michael Scudamore* a77 88
6 b g High Chaparral(IRE) —Gamine (IRE) (High Estate)
614[6] (697) 872[5] (962) 1156[3] *1470[5] 1761[7]* 2312[2] (2846) 4719[5] (6376) 7017[7]

Guru Girl *Mrs K Burke* 77
2 b f Ishiguru(USA) —Startori (Vettori (IRE))
1337[3] (1846) 2777a[6] 3435[4] (4558) 4787[2] 5701[7] 6670[17]

Gush (USA) *Mrs John Harrington* a70 76
2 b f Empire Maker(USA) —Enthused (USA) (Seeking The Gold (USA))
5950a[8]

Gusting *Mahmood Al Zarooni* 90
3 b g Tobougg(IRE) —Tempete (Dubai Millennium)
(2058) ◆ 2707[P]

Gusto *Richard Hannon* a96 101
2 b c Oasis Dream—Pickle (Piccolo)
4339[3] (4748) ◆ 5286[4] 5558[6] 6466[4] *(6625)* ◆ (7019)

Guto *Bill Ratcliffe* a74 64
8 b g Foxhound(USA) —Mujadilly (Mujadil (USA))
15[3] 401[5] 571[7]

Gwilym (GER) *Derek Haydn Jones* a76 78
8 b g Agnes World(USA) —Glady Rose (GER) (Surumu (GER))
134[5] 178[9] 336[4] 577[11] 708[7] 880[2] 1267[6] 1770[8] 2304[6] 2609[9] 3512[11]

Gypsie Queen (IRE) *Ms Joanna Morgan* a60 79
4 b m Xaar—Erstwhile (FR) (Desert Prince (IRE))
5748a[17]

Gypsy Ballad *Mahmood Al Zarooni* a66
2 b f Sinndar(IRE) —Summer Serenade (Sadler's Wells (USA))
3520[6]

Gypsy Boy (USA) *Jo Hughes* a38 64
4 bb g Dixie Union(USA) —Think Fast (USA) (Crafty Prospector (USA))
727[10] 3515[10] *3926[11]*

Gypsy Carnival *Ralph Beckett* 80
4 b m Trade Fair—Czarna Roza (Polish Precedent (USA))
2647[9]

Gypsy Rider *Bryn Palling* 58
2 b g Ishiguru(USA) —Spaniola (IRE) (Desert King (IRE))
2374[4] 2787[5] 3511[5] *4922[11]* 5374[6]

Gypsy Ring (CAN) *Paul M Buttigieg* a111 116
5 b g Where's The Ring(USA) —Gypsy Genna (USA) (Varick (USA))
6908a[3]

Gypsy Robin (USA) *Wesley A Ward* a96 93
2 bb f Daaher(CAN) —Feisty Princess (USA) (Indian Charlie (USA))
3033[7]

Gypsy Style *Kate Walton* 51
4 gr m Desert Style(IRE) —Gentle Gypsy (Junius (USA))
2548[12] 3024[12]

Gypsy's Warning (SAF) *H Graham Motion* 113
6 b m Mogok(USA) —Gypsy Queen (SAF) (Royal Chalice (SAF))
6719a[6]

Haadeej (USA) *C Boutin* a67 66
6 ch g Stravinsky(USA) —Tamgeed (USA) (Woodman (USA))
93a[0]

Haadeeth *Richard Fahey* a81 86
4 b g Oasis Dream—Musical Key (Key Of Luck (USA))
2299[12] 3028[13] 3704[8] 4141[11] 4780[3] 5083[9] 5647[7] 6076[12] *(6841) 7040[8] 7265[2] 7395[5] 7744[12]*

Haader (USA) *F Rohaut* a73
3 gr g First Samurai(USA) —Queen's Triomphe (USA) (Cure The Blues (USA))
370a[8]

Haaf A Sixpence *Ralph Beckett* a71
2 b g Haafhd—Melody Maker (Diktat)
7330[2] (7559)

Haafhd Decent (IRE) *Karen George* a47 38
3 ch f Haafhd—Idolize (Polish Precedent (USA))
2174[10] 3925[8] 4826[7]

Haafhd Handsome *Richard Hannon* a72 73
2 ch c Haafhd—Lines Of Beauty (USA) (Line In The Sand (USA))
4823[6] *5834[5]* 6743[3] 6956[3] *7650[2]*

Haafkry *Linda Stubbs* 70
2 b g Haafhd—Kryena (Kris)
2395[5] 2731[2] 3035[3] 3302[2] (3618)

Haajes *Paul Midgley* a96 94
7 ch g Indian Ridge—Imelda (USA) (Manila (USA))
1457[11] 1675[11] 2118[9] 2299[10] 2890[10] 3704[11] 4327[4] ◆ 4900[2] (5831) 6112[5] 6348[6] 6703[16] 6913[2] 7298[8]

Haamaat (IRE) *William Haggas* a75 65
3 b f Shamardal(USA) —Exultate Jubilate (USA) (With Approval (CAN))
6608[3] *(7411)*

Haatheq (USA) *A Al Raihe* a107 101
4 b h Seeking The Gold(USA) —Alshadiyah (USA) (Danzig (USA))
240[2] 417a[6] 503a[4] *(583a) 758a[11] 827a[2]*

Habalwatan (IRE) *A Al Raihe* a79 65
7 b h In The Wings—Mureefa (USA) (Bahri (USA))
535a[6] 707a[11]

Hab Reeh *Clive Brittain* a73
3 gr g Diktat—Asian Love (Petong)
1321[7] *1974[2] 2650[7]* 3133[12] 3462[9] *5902[10]*

Habsburg *Paul Fitzsimons* a53 54
3 b g Holy Roman Emperor(IRE) —Blue Indigo (FR) (Pistolet Bleu (IRE))
1759[13] 2103[10] 3675[5] 4705[14] 5349[10] *6845[7]*

Hachico *A Candi* 92
2 b c King's Best(USA) —Hamsaat (IRE) (Sadler's Wells (USA))
[illegible]

Hacienda (IRE) *Mark Johnston* a91 102
4 br g Kheleyf(USA) —Hartstown House (IRE) (Primo Dominie)
1240[2] 1529[6] 1694[10] 2217[8] 2679[16] 3032[18] 3797[7] 4404[2] 4509[4] 5240[5] 5465[7] (5920) 6173[2] 6290[3]

Hackett (IRE) *Michael Quinn* a64 57
3 b c Hawk Wing(USA) —Khudud (Green Desert (USA))
270[3] 519[2] 760[2] 1022[12] 2064[10] 2825[5] 6070[10] *6472[8]*

Hadaj *Clive Brittain* 84
2 b c Green Desert(USA) —My Amalie (IRE) (Galileo (IRE))
(3132) 3776[3]

Hada Men (USA) *Tina Jackson* a69 46
6 b g Dynaformer(USA) —Catchy (USA) (Storm Cat (USA))
2892[16] 3974[6] 4129[8] 5405[8] 5650[7] 5790[7]

Hadrians Rule (IRE) *Tim Easterby* 49
2 b g Holy Roman Emperor(IRE) —Farbenspiel (IRE) (Desert Prince (IRE))
2033[8] ◆

Hail Bold Chief (USA) *Alan Swinbank* a55 78
4 b g Dynaformer(USA) —Yanaseeni (USA) (Trempolino (USA))
1460[4] 2454[11] 3051[6] 4366[13] (5036) ◆ 5311[6] 6078[4]

Hail Holy Queen (IRE) *J E Hammond* a83 83
3 ch f Highest Honor(FR) —Gabare (FR) (Galileo (IRE))
7509a[0]

Hail Promenader (IRE) *Andrew Haynes* a81 89
5 b g Acclamation—Tribal Rite (Be My Native (USA))
1097[11] 1402[14] (1621) 1970[4] 2955[2] 3634[6] 4656[14] 5495[8]

Hailstone (USA) *Mark Casse* 110
4 b h City Zip(USA) —Weekend Storm (USA) (Storm Bird (CAN))
6203a[5]

Hail Tiberius *Tim Walford* 76
4 b g Iktibas—Untidy Daughter (Sabrehill (USA))
1107[3] 1491[2] 1798[4] 2213[10] 3054[4]

Haim (FR) *K Borgel* 88
3 b c Poliglote—Anamiglia (Anabaa (USA))
370a[0]
Hair Of The Dog *George Charlton* a43 44
7 b g Foxhound(USA) —Bebe De Cham (Tragic Role (USA))
2347[9] 2696[8] 3317[15] 4128[11]
Hairpin (USA) *Mahmood Al Zarooni* a56
3 bb f Bernardini(USA) —Daneleta (IRE) (Danehill (USA))
5999[6] 6404[9]
Hairstyle *Sir Michael Stoute* a54 83
3 b f Dansili—Quiff (Sadler's Wells (USA))
2026[2] 2840[5] 5317[5]
Haka Dancer (USA) *Philip Kirby* a52 49
8 b g War Chant(USA) —Safe Return (USA) (Mr Prospector (USA))
3187[3] 3599[10] 4814[2] 6600[10]
Hakkar (TUR) *B Dag* 107
4 b h Halling(USA) —Valleria (Sadler's Wells (USA))
5776a[6]
Hakuna Matata *Brian Ellison* a81 73
4 b g Dubai Destination(USA) —Green Song (FR) (Green Tune (USA))
1244[11] 2059[5] 2656[2] 3319[5] 3399[6]
Haldibari (IRE) *Shaun Lycett* a54 55
7 b g Kahyasi—Haladiya (IRE) (Darshaan)
1297[2] 4951[4]
Half A Billion (IRE) *Michael Dods* a66 72
2 b g Acclamation—Amankila (IRE) (Revoque (IRE))
3273[2] 4040[2] 4358[3] 4984[3] 5438[4] 5726[3] 6232[3] 6598[5] 7038[2]
Half A Crown (IRE) *Peter Salmon* a38 65
6 b g Compton Place—Penny Ha'Penny (Bishop Of Cashel)
2845[13] 3512[16] 4869[10] 5732[5] 6091[2] 6610[4] 7057[5] (7216) 7420[9]
Halfsin (IRE) *Marco Botti* a78 106
3 b g Haafhd—Firesteed (IRE) (Common Grounds)
(1151) (1652) (4103) 4764[2] 5700[11]
Half Truth (IRE) *H-A Pantall* a62 73
3 gr f Verglas(IRE) —Millennium Tale (FR) (Distant Relative)
841a[7]
Halicarnassus (IRE) *Mick Channon* a111 109
7 b h Cape Cross(IRE) —Launch Time (USA) (Relaunch (USA))
153a[2] 328a[4] 585a[2] 1403[6] 2289[4] 2573[4] 3156[5] (3625) 4410[11] 4492[5] 5285[20] 5776a[5] 6161[6]
Halifax (IRE) *Mark Johnston* a81 95
3 ch c Halling(USA) —Lady Zonda (Lion Cavern (USA))
(699) (2435) ◆ 3108[5] ◆ 4426[7] 4777[6] 5283[18] 6485[2]
Haljaferia (UAE) *David Elsworth* a82 84
5 ch g Halling(USA) —Melisendra (FR) (Highest Honor (FR))
2649[5] 2932[12]
Halla San *Richard Fahey* a91 102
9 b g Halling(USA) —St Radegund (Green Desert (USA))
1412[4] 1808[13] 2314[3] 3157[16]
Hallelujah *James Fanshawe* a83 74
3 b f Avonbridge—My Golly (Mozart (IRE))
(3283)
Halling Dancer *John Akehurst* a78 71
2 b c Halling(USA) —Ballet Ballon (USA) (Rahy (USA))
3229[2] 4007[6] (6474) 7095[8]
Halling Gal *Evan Williams* a49 32
5 b m Halling(USA) —Saik (USA) (Riverman (USA))
4949[10]
Hallings Comet *Andrew Balding* 79
2 ch c Halling(USA) —Landinium (ITY) (Lando (GER))
6993[2]
Halling's Quest *Hughie Morrison* a86 66
2 b c Halling(USA) —Capriolla (In The Wings)
6463[6] (7066)
Hallmark Star *Gerard Butler* a77 70
2 b g Nayef(USA) —Spring (Sadler's Wells (USA))
6771[6] ◆ 7177[2] 7454[3]
Hallstatt (IRE) *John Mackie* a71 76
5 ch g Halling(USA) —Last Resort (Lahib (USA))
531[3] 715[4] 839[3] 1156[2] 1586[4] 1901[2] 2459[3] 2846[2] 3828[6] 5273[5] 5685[11] 7036[2] 7413[8] 7570[8]
Hal Of A Lover *David O'Meara* a53 63
3 b g Halling(USA) —Latent Lover (IRE) (In The Wings)
1945[9] 2407[7] 2571[2] (2801) 3587[8] 3976[3] 4044[2] (4175) 5022[7] 5152[2] 5489[5] 7062[9] 7723[4] 7789[8]
Halsion Chancer *John Best* a86 81
7 b g Atraf—Lucky Dip (Tirol)
440a[6] 534a[2] 628a[14] 723[6] 908[7] 995[8]
Halyard (IRE) *Walter Swinburn* a74 76
4 b g Halling(USA) —Brindisi (Dr Fong (USA))
(2245) 3538[8] 5110[8] 6005[13] 6893[13]
Hamalka (IRE) *P Cluskey* a55 53
6 br m Alhaarth(IRE) —Night Owl (Night Shift (USA))
7145[5] 7549a[10]
Hamamba (USA) *Mme J Bidgood*
2 b f Black Mambo(USA) —Halo Of Truth (USA) (Nelson (USA))
7666a[10]
Haman (CAN) *Mahmood Al Zarooni* 68
3 bb c Street Cry(IRE) —Penny Perfect (CAN) (Alydeed (CAN))
4617[3]
Hamazing Destiny (USA) *D Wayne Lukas* a122
5 b h Salt Lake(USA) —Ms Proud Destiny (USA) (Artax (USA))
7302a[5]
Hamble *William Haggas* a69 83
2 b g Librettist(USA) —Time For Tea (IRE) (Imperial Frontier (USA))
2194[7] (4390) 5280[2] 5638[3]
Hambledon Hill *Paul Burgoyne* a58 75
5 ch g Selkirk(USA) —Dominica (Alhaarth (IRE))
1333[11]

Hambleton *Bryan Smart* a53 59
4 b g Monsieur Bond(IRE) —Only Yours (Aragon)
120[5] 289[10] 874[10] (2593) 2803[2] 3937[2] 4196[6] 5490[8] 6999[6]
Hamilton Hill *Tobias B P Coles* a51 56
4 b g Groom Dancer(USA) —Loriner's Lass (Saddlers' Hall (IRE))
649[6] 1568[12] 1774[11] 2271[9] 2654[5] (7087)
Hamis Al Bin (IRE) *Mark Johnston* 70
2 b g Acclamation—Paimpolaise (IRE) (Priolo (USA))
2291[8] 2936[9] 4571[4]
Hamish McGonagall *Tim Easterby* 117
6 b g Namid—Anatase (Danehill (USA))
1242[3] (1518) 2005[8] 2297[8] 2754a[4] 3441a[2] 3874[3] 5253[2] 5985a[3]
Hamlool (IRE) *Clive Brittain* a99 89
3 b c Red Ransom(USA) —Chelsea Rose (IRE) (Desert King (IRE))
1234[2] ◆ 1689[6]
Hammer *Geoffrey Harker* a48 32
6 b g Beat Hollow—Tranquil Moon (Deploy)
6287[9] 6613[8] 6870[6] 7077[7]
Hamoody (USA) *David Nicholls* 93
7 ch g Johannesburg(USA) —Northern Gulch (USA) (Gulch (USA))
1166[10] 1720[6] ◆ 2116[14] 2590[3] 2890[5] 3535[4] ◆
Hamza (IRE) *Kevin Ryan* 89
2 b g Amadeus Wolf—Lady Shanghai (IRE) (Alhaarth (IRE))
(1071) 2007[2] 2488[3] 3014[6] 4094[12] 4575[6] 5216[20]
Handassa *Kevin Prendergast* 104
3 br f Dubawi(IRE) —Starstone (Diktat)
1928a[4] 2334a[8] 6362a[6]
Handel's Messiah (IRE) *Michael Bell* a34 22
3 bg g Oratorio(IRE) —Silver Pursuit (Rainbow Quest (USA))
2306[12] 2596[12] 3393[7]
Handicraft (IRE) *Kevin Ryan* a48 44
3 ch f Halling(USA) —Luana (Shaadi (USA))
469[7] 731[8] 3733[5] 3902[9]
Handles For Forks (IRE) *Mick Channon* a70 76
3 b f Hawk Wing(USA) —Wood Sprite (Mister Baileys)
2591[5] 3224[4] 3907[4] 4449[5] 5122[2] 5477[5] 5784[2] 6095[4] 6584[3]
Hand Painted *Anthony Middleton* a77 78
5 b g Lend A Hand—Scarlett Holly (Red Sunset)
404[2] 985[5] 1444[3] 1838[4] 2870[8] 3713[8] 4741[2] 5037[4] 5425[3] 6022[7] 6479[11] 7057[17] 7412[9]
Handsome Falcon *Ollie Pears* a65 86
7 b g Kyllachy—Bonne Etoile (Diesis)
932[8] 1614[4] 1748[2] 1970[7] 2347[6] 3569[5]
Handsome Hawk (IRE) *Wido Neuroth* a75 91
5 b g Hawk Wing(USA) —She Is Zen (FR) (Zieten (USA))
5984a[9]
Handsome King *J R Jenkins* a67 60
4 ch g Lucky Story(USA) —Samar Qand (Selkirk (USA))
4163[9]
Handsome Maestro (IRE) *Robert Collet* a75 105
5 b h Dansili—Graceful Bering (USA) (Bering)
5195a[7] 5530a[7] 5988a[6]
Handsome Man (IRE) *Saeed Bin Suroor* 80
2 ch c Nayef(USA) —Danceabout (Shareef Dancer (USA))
6774[4] (7083)
Handsome Ransom *John Gosden* 69
2 b c Red Ransom(USA) —Maid For The Hills (Indian Ridge)
6100[5] ◆
Hannibal Hayes (USA) *Jeremy Noseda* 67
2 ch c Elusive Quality(USA) —Top Ten List (CAN) (Bold Executive (CAN))
3984[2]
Hanoverian Baron *Tony Newcombe* a60 100
6 b g Green Desert(USA) —Josh's Pearl (IRE) (Sadler's Wells (USA))
2071[7] 7297[4] 7523[10]
Hansen (USA) *Michael J Maker* a120
2 rg c Tapit(USA) —Stormy Sunday (USA) (Sir Cat (USA))
(7306a)
Hansinger (IRE) *Cathrine Erichsen* a72 96
6 b g Namid—Whistfilly (First Trump)
4483a[6]
Hansomis (IRE) *Bruce Mactaggart* 69
7 b m Titus Livius(FR) —Handsome Anna (IRE) (Bigstone (IRE))
2062[8] 2352[2] 2543[6] 2990[5] 3902[4] 4379[4]
Happy Dubai (IRE) *A Al Raihe* a99 111
4 ch h Indian Ridge—Gentle Wind (USA) (Gentlemen (ARG))
152a[8] (237) (327a) ◆ 500a[5] (754a) 996a[10] 2339a[10]
Happy Fleet *Natalie Lloyd-Beavis* a44 46
8 b m Beat All(USA) —Fleeting Affair (Hotfoot I)
1839[12] 2659[5] 6087[10]
Happy March (FR) *D Allard*
2 b g Early March—Luna De Miel (Shareef Dancer (USA))
7664a[9]
Happy Sun Percy *Jo Hughes* 63
2 ch c Sir Percy—Question (USA) (Coronado's Quest (USA))
6110[7] 6481[6] 6702[5]
Happy The Man (IRE) *John Norton* 38
4 b g Kyllachy—Jazan (IRE) (Danehill (USA))
575[11]
Happy Today (USA) *Brian Meehan* a41 102
3 b c Gone West(USA) —Shy Lady (FR) (Kaldoun (FR))
1320[2] 1686[6] 3068[15]
Happy Trails (AUS) *Paul Beshara* 112
4 ch g Good Journey(USA) —Madame Flurry (AUS) (Perugino (USA))
9029a[2]
Happy Valley (ARG) *M F De Kock* a68 105
5 gr g Alphabet Soup(USA) —Perfect Valley (BRZ) (Clackson (BRZ))
154a[9] 328a[12]

Harare *Karen Tutty* a54 66
10 b g Bahhare(USA) —Springs Eternal (Salse (USA))
2991[6] 3240[5] 3938[12] 4409[9] 4605[10] 4945[3] 5248[8] 5485[5] 5822[8] (6236) 6486[7] 6833[8] 7113[4] 7426[9]
Harbour Sands *James Given* 32
2 b c Bahamian Bounty—Sahara Silk (IRE) (Desert Style (IRE))
5104[8] 6152[8]
Harbour Watch (IRE) *Richard Hannon* 117
2 b c Acclamation—Gorband (USA) (Woodman (USA))
(2962) ◆ (3776) ◆ (4495) ◆
Hardanger (IRE) *Tim Fitzgerald* a37 31
6 b g Halling(USA) —Naughty Nell (Danehill Dancer (IRE))
114[7] 252[6] 451[8] 4177[8]
Hard Bargain (IRE) *Denis Coakley* a65 72
3 b g Refuse To Bend(IRE) —Super Gift (IRE) (Darshaan)
1774[8] 2841[9] 3259[7] 5243[11] 5838[9]
Hard Not To Like (CAN) *Gail Cox* 104
2 rg f Hard Spun(USA) —Like A Gem (CAN) (Tactical Cat (USA))
7281a[5]
Hard Road *Chris Wall* 10
2 b g Cape Cross(IRE) —Ivy League Star (IRE) (Sadler's Wells (USA))
7082[15] 7233[15]
Hard Rock City (USA) *Declan Carroll* a86 93
11 b g Danzig(USA) —All The Moves (USA) (A.P. Indy (USA))
12[5] 376[5] 2474[5] 3024[5] 4076[10]
Hardrock Diamond *Ian Semple* 51
3 b g Avonbridge—Clansinge (Clantime)
1038[11] 1246[10] 1459[9] 3860[3] 4146[2] 4505[4] 4786[3] 5206[3] 5433[7]
Hard Rok (IRE) *Richard Whitaker* 31
3 gr g Verglas(IRE) —Emerald Dancer (Groom Dancer (USA))
1910[10] 2802[12] 3304[5] 4876[9]
Hardy Plume *Denis Coakley* a33 44
2 ch g Manduro(GER) —Macleya (GER) (Winged Love (IRE))
6742[11] 7329[9] 7627[9]
Hareby (IRE) *Tim Easterby* 62
2 b g Strategic Prince—Red Beach (IRE) (Turtle Island (IRE))
4073[8] 6048[4] 6572[7] 6986[12]
Hareem Dancer *David Nicholls* a28 41
2 ch f Milk It Mick—Veils Of Salome (Arkadian Hero (USA))
4283[10] 4899[6] 5211[7]
Harlech Castle *Jim Boyle* a95 84
6 b g Royal Applause—Ffestiniog (IRE) (Efisio)
58[5] 213[6] 243[3] 321[3]
Harlequin Girl *Terry Clement* a32
3 ch f Where Or When(IRE) —Lauren Louise (Tagula (IRE))
7207[6] 7585[10]
Harlestone Times (IRE) *John Dunlop* 106
4 b g Olden Times—Harlestone Lady (Shaamit (IRE))
1477[3] (2289) 3396[15] 4532[6] 5285[11] 5883[5] 7297[14]
Harlestone Wood *John Dunlop* 61
2 b c Olden Times—Harlestone Lady (Shaamit (IRE))
7134[9]
Harmonie (IRE) *Noel Quinlan* 49
2 b f Teofilo(IRE) —Harmonist (USA) (Hennessy (USA))
6329[9]
Harmonious (USA) *John Shirreffs* a104 113
4 bb m Dynaformer(USA) —Jade Tree (USA) (Storm Cat (USA))
7284a[9]
Harmony Wold *Declan Carroll* a25 35
3 b f Ishiguru(USA) —Light Of Aragon (Aragon)
2710[9] 3075[14] 3324[8] 3857[6] 3950[5] 4288[14]
Harrier Hill (USA) *Mahmood Al Zarooni* a70 44
2 b c Bernardini(USA) —Inca (ARG) (Interprete (ARG))
4087[6] 4919[3]
Harrison George (IRE) *Richard Fahey* a73 113
6 b g Danetime(IRE) —Dry Lightning (Shareef Dancer (USA))
1094[19] 2031[16] 2933[8] 3645[13] 5218[7] 6150[4] 6339[12] 6672[11]
Harrison's Cave *A P O'Brien* a88 94
3 b c Galileo(IRE) —Sitara (Salse (USA))
7300a[9]
Harris Tweed *William Haggas* a106 118
4 b g Hernando(FR) —Frog (Akarad (FR))
1851[3] 3153[2] 4492[2] 5284[4] 5711[3]
Harris Tweed (NZ) *Murray Baker* 120
6 b g Montjeu(IRE) —Sally (NZ) (Prized (USA))
7043a[6]
Harry Buckle *Philip McBride* a68 62
2 ch c Byron—Native Ring (FR) (Bering)
5011[11] 6529[8] 7369[2]
Harry Hunt *Graeme McPherson* a83 68
4 b g Bertolini(USA) —Qasirah (IRE) (Machiavellian (USA))
(6504)
Harry Lime *Chris Dwyer* a62 62
3 b c Cape Cross(IRE) —Wiener Wald (USA) (Woodman (USA))
634[9] 992[5] 1211[7] 1487[6] 3018[4] 3742[4] 4164[7] (6067) 6253[4] 6799[10] 6923[9] 7085[9] 7333[9]
Harry Luck (IRE) *Henry Candy* a76 83
3 b g Red Ransom(USA) —Tara Gold (IRE) (Royal Academy (USA))
(1773) 2607[10] 2925[7] 3650[7] ◆ 4316[8]
Harrys *Michael Squance* a48
4 b g Desert Sun—Emerald Angel (IRE) (In The Wings)
309[4] 524[11] 569[4] 819[11] 1025[5] 1311[10] 1761[9] 2372[7]

Harrys Yer Man *Mark Brisbourne* a57
7 b g Nomadic Way(USA) —Barden Lady (Presidium)
6286[10] 6656[10] 7036[5] 7564[12] 7720[8]
Harry Tricker *Gary Moore* a67 91
7 b g Hernando(FR) —Katy Nowaitee (Komaite (USA))
1679[5] 3120[8] 3522[6]
Harry Trotter (IRE) *David Marnane* a77 77
2 b g Kodiac—Defined Feature (IRE) (Nabeel Dancer (USA))
7273a[5]
Harsh But Fair *Michael Easterby* a43 45
5 br g Sakhee(USA) —Royal Distant (USA) (Distant View (USA))
2733[5] 3185[10] 3622[6] 4637[4] 4856[11]
Hartforth *James Bethell* a53 62
3 ch g Haafhd—St Edith (IRE) (Desert King (IRE))
1437[5] 1877[3] 2613[6] 4151[6]
Harting Hill *Marcus Tregoning* a72 66
6 b g Mujahid(USA) —Mossy Rose (King Of Spain)
6411[2] 6938[4]
Hartside (GER) *Sir Michael Stoute* 60
2 b g Montjeu(IRE) —Helvellyn (USA) (Gone West (USA))
5239[7] 6100[9] 6400[12]
Harvard N Yale (USA) *Jeremy Noseda* a86 92
2 ch c Smart Strike(CAN) —Compete (USA) (El Prado (IRE))
4053[2] ◆ (5013) 6126[2] 7879[2]
Harvest Mist (IRE) *Michael Blanshard* a54 54
3 ch f Captain Rio—Thaw (Cadeaux Genereux)
4320[5] 5810[4] 6307[5] 6889[8] 7096[8] 7437[6] 7656[7] 7787[3]
Harvey's Hope *Keith Reveley* 79
5 b g Sinndar(IRE) —Ancara (Dancing Brave (USA))
1492[3] 2114[8] 3138[2] 3581[2] (4129) 4237[3] 5685[5] ◆ 6451[8]
Hassadin *Michael Blake* a49 54
5 ch g Reset(AUS) —Crocolat (Croco Rouge (IRE))
6876[4]
Hatch A Plan (IRE) *Mouse Hamilton-Fairley* a56 60
10 b g Vettori(IRE) —Fast Chick (Henbit (USA))
30[6] 81[3] 81[9]
Hathaway (IRE) *Mark Brisbourne* a57 59
4 ch m Redback—Finty (IRE) (Entrepreneur)
1273[5] 1763[2] 1905[4] 2401[6] 2912[12] 4112[3] 4612[5] 5107[5] 5349[9] 5860[4] 6309[3] 6494[7] 7466[8] 7604[9] 7787[7] 7851[2]
Hatha Zain (IRE) *Milton Bradley* a17 38
2 b g Bahamian Bounty—Arabian Dancer (Dansili)
5263[5] 5863[9] 6118[7]
Hatsumomo (IRE) *Tim Easterby* 10
2 b f Aussie Rules(USA) —Starry Night (Sheikh Albadou)
3610[11] 4232[12] 4668[9]
Hattan (IRE) *M Al Muhairi* a108 99
9 ch h Halling(USA) —Luana (Shaadi (USA))
240[8] 326a[11]
Hatta Stream (IRE) *Lydia Pearce* a85 75
5 b g Oasis Dream—Rubies From Burma (USA) (Forty Niner (USA))
2938[20] 3322[12] 6949[11] 7416[9] 7625[6] (7893)
Hatton Flight *Andrew Balding* a89 93
7 b g Kahyasi—Platonic (Zafonic (USA))
32[4] 359[5]
Haulit *Gary Moore* a55 48
5 b g Fraam—Amazing Bay (Mazilier (USA))
163[2] 280[12] 589[5] ◆ 809[4] 1184[6] 1625[10] 2385[3] 3480[4] 3944[8]
Havane Smoker *J-C Rouget* 112
3 ch c Dubawi(IRE) —Ballet Ballon (USA) (Rahy (USA))
1206a[2] 2139a[2] 3029[8] 4838a[13]
Havant *Sir Michael Stoute* 104
3 b f Halling(USA) —Louella (USA) (El Gran Senor (USA))
1719[6] ◆ 2682[10]
Haveahaarth (IRE) *Michael Quinlan* a61 39
4 b g Alhaarth(IRE) —Castelletto (Komaite (USA))
112[3] 135[7]
Have Another *Richard Hannon* a52
3 b g Noverre(USA) —Swift Baba (USA) (Deerhound (USA))
158[12] 262[9] 471[8]
Havelock (USA) *Darrin Miller* a110 120
4 b g Great Notion(USA) —Piconeach (NZ) (Spectacular Love (USA))
7303a[14]
Having A Ball *Jonathan Portman* a70 54
7 b g Mark Of Esteem(IRE) —All Smiles (Halling (USA))
48[7] 361[4] 483[2] 626[7] 949[9] 1333[12] 2816[11] 3266[6] 3741[11] 6971[4] 7228[2] 7656[3] 7910[4]
Havre De Grace (USA) *J Larry Jones* a125
4 b m Saint Liam(USA) —Easter Bunnette (USA) (Carson City (USA))
7308a[4]
Hawaafez *Marcus Tregoning* a78 104
3 b f Nayef(USA) —Merayaat (IRE) (Darshaan)
1168[2] 1622[2] 2108[2] 3108[6] (7136)
Hawaana (IRE) *Gay Kelleway* a87 90
6 b g Bahri(USA) —Congress (IRE) (Dancing Brave (USA))
667[5] 835[4] 963[4] 1097[4] 1477[8] 1829[5] 3042[8] (3386) (3760) 4697[3] 4962[3] ◆ 5281[4] 6069[4] 6302[13] 6631[5]
Hawaass (USA) *Ruth Carr* a55 98
6 b g Seeking The Gold(USA) —Sheroog (USA) (Shareef Dancer (USA))
548[7] 633[5] 796[4]
Hawaiian Freeze *Richard Ford* 39
2 b f Avonbridge—Autumn Affair (Lugana Beach)
2248[7] 2844[7] 3270[9] 3993[4]
Hawawi *David Lanigan* a72 71
3 b g Motivator—Abide (FR) (Pivotal)
3519[4]
Hawdyerwheesht *Mark Johnston* a76 80
3 b g Librettist(USA) —Rapsgate (IRE) (Mozart (IRE))
3159[8] 3659[7] 4287[3] 4540[4] 4879[10] 5723[5]

Hawfinch *John Gosden* a84 86
2 b f Kyllachy—Bukhoor (IRE) (Danehill (USA))
(2606) 3402[5] ◆ 4252[3] 4803[6]

Hawkeyethenoo (IRE) *Jim Goldie* a48 110
5 b g Hawk Wing(USA) —Stardance (USA) (Rahy (USA))
1720[4] (1885) 4314[16] 6147[10] 6521[4]

Hawkhill (IRE) *M Halford* 90
5 b g Hawk Wing(USA) —Crimphill (IRE) (Sadler's Wells (USA))
925a[8]

Hawkino (IRE) *Derek Shaw* a28 51
2 b g Hawk Wing(USA) —Halicardia (Halling (USA))
3823[13] 4276[10] 4864[11] 5343[7] 6937[13] 7117[6]

Hawk Island (IRE) *Chris Waller* a65 117
6 b g Hawk Wing(USA) —Crimphill (IRE) (Sadler's Wells (USA))
6886a[13] 7218a[18]

Hawk Moth (IRE) *John Spearing* a68 69
3 b g Hawk Wing(USA) —Sasimoto (USA) (Saratoga Six (USA))
1191[4] 1949[11] 2792[6] 3481[2] 4546[2] ◆ 4799[7] 5423[7] 5735[7]

Hawk Mountain (UAE) *John Quinn* 96
6 b g Halling(USA) —Friendly (USA) (Lear Fan (USA))
(2262) 2888[2] 4348[3] 4775[7] 5221[4] 5883[9]

Hawks Reef *Richard Fahey* 78
2 b g Bahamian Bounty—Karisal (IRE) (Persian Bold)
6836[6] 7293[2]

Hawridge King *Stuart Kittow* a65 80
9 b g Erhaab(USA) —Sadaka (USA) (Kingmambo (USA))
2224[5] 2846[3] 4463[6] 5236[4] 5966[8] (6469) 7139[5]

Hawridge Knight *Rod Millman* a38 52
3 ch g Peintre Celebre(USA) —Desiraka (Kris)
2586[8] 3226[6] 3910[3] 4491[4] 6482[4]

Hawridge Song *Rod Millman* 71
3 ch g Singspiel(IRE) —Clear Vision (Observatory (USA))
1984[6] 2848[3] 3430[3] 4236[4]

Hawridge Star (IRE) *Stuart Kittow* a42 81
9 b g Alzao(USA) —Serenity (Selkirk (USA))
2034[3]

Hayaku (USA) *Ralph Beckett* a48 78
3 b f Arch(USA) —Promptly (IRE) (Lead On Time (USA))
2511[2] 3632[3] 4956[4] 5962[5] 6459[2] (6750)

Haya Landa (FR) *Mme L Audon* a85 110
3 b f Lando(GER) —Haya Samma (IRE) (Pivotal)
2977a[4] 4570a[8] 5366a[3] 6568a[7] 7510a[2]

Hayek *Tim Easterby* a75 69
4 b g Royal Applause—Salagama (IRE) (Alzao (USA))
1649[5] 2593[3] (2803) 3489[2] ◆ 3805[7] 4141[5] 4513[3] 4604[5] 4945[7] 5309[5] 6081[6] 7057[2]

Haylaman (IRE) *Ed Dunlop* a90 93
3 b g Diamond Green(FR) —Schonbein (IRE) (Persian Heights)
1862[2] 2230[2] 3376[7] (4553) 5693[7] 6342[3]

Haymarket *Mahmood Al Zarooni* a53 72
2 b c Singspiel(IRE) —Quickstyx (Night Shift (USA))
4762[5] 6180[6] 6675[6]

Hayzoom *Peter Chapple-Hyam* 88
4 b h Anabaa(USA) —Green Swallow (FR) (Green Tune (USA))
2006[4] 2512[6] 6103[5] 6988[10]

Hazaz (IRE) *Clive Brittain* 98
2 b c Dubawi(IRE) —Treble Seven (USA) (Fusaichi Pegasus (USA))
3182[7] 3552[2] 6170[10] 6527[8] 7026[3] 7167[4]

Hazel Lavery (IRE) *Charles Hills* 89
2 b f Excellent Art—Reprise (Darshaan)
5444[3] (6128) ◆ 6526[2]

Hazelrigg (IRE) *Tim [illegible]* [illegible]
6 b g Namid—Emma's Star (ITY) (Darshaan)
2028[14] 2317[5] ◆ 2727[9] 3357[6] 3613[2] 5033[2] 5706[7] 6224[3] 6332[4] 7018[6]

Hazel Wand (IRE) *Kevin Prendergast* a46 65
2 b f Rail Link—Carina Ari (IRE) (Imperial Ballet (IRE))
7275a[9]

Haziyna (IRE) *John M Oxx* a80 103
3 b f Halling(USA) —Hazariya (IRE) (Xaar)
1706a[6] 3695a[2] 4589a[2] 5523a[15]

Hazzard County (USA) *David Simcock* a101 81
7 ch g Grand Slam(USA) —Sweet Lexy May (USA) (Danzig (USA))
99[2] ◆ (438) 846[8] 7127[5] ◆ 7393[10] 7719[9]

Headache *Brendan W Duke* a76 73
6 b g Cape Cross(IRE) —Romantic Myth (Mind Games)
9[6]

Headache (USA) *Michael J Maker* a114
5 rg g Tapit(USA) —Pamric (USA) (Woodman (USA))
7308a[12]

Headford View (IRE) *James Halpin* a69 98
7 b m Bold Fact(USA) —Headfort Rose (IRE) (Desert Style (IRE))
1779a[8] 2325a[4] 7793a[13]

Head Held High (USA) *E Libaud* a63 76
3 b c Bluegrass Cat(USA) —Princess Pietrina (USA) (Spectacular Bid (USA))
902a[10]

Heading To First *Paddy Butler* a52 73
4 b g Sulamani(IRE) —Bahirah (Ashkalani (IRE))
473[10] 621[10] 1233[7] 3176[12] 7437[8] 7640[14] 7892[7]

Headline News (IRE) *Rae Guest* 63
2 ch f Peintre Celebre(USA) —Donnelly's Hollow (IRE) (Docksider (USA))
6772[5] ◆

Headstight (IRE) *Paul Midgley* 56
2 b f Holy Roman Emperor(IRE) —Regal Star (Sadler's Wells (USA))
1165[8] 2113[7] 2248[6] 6043[4] 6384[3] 6836[4] 7058[3]

Head To Head (IRE) *Alan Brown* a61 39
7 gr g Mull Of Kintyre(USA) —Shoka (FR) (Kaldoun (FR))
57[10] 185[6] 256[7] 691[2] 821[6] 941[14] 1213[15]

Heardthefirsttime (IRE) *Barney Curley* a20 1
2 b g Tiger Hill(IRE) —Caona (USA) (Miswaki (USA))
6935[12] 7329[11] 7835[13]

Heart Attack (FR) *G Martin* a82 94
5 b h Double Heart(FR) —Indefinite (FR) (Definite Article)
257a[5]

Heart Beat (SAF) *A Al Raihe* a59 56
8 b g Jet Master(SAF) —Hear My Heart (NZ) (Personal Escort (USA))
536a[4]

Heart Felt *Roy Brotherton* a45 65
3 b f Beat Hollow—Name Of Love (IRE) (Petardia)
543[7] 817[7] 1018[12] 1566[9] 1985[10] 3724[15]

Heart Of Dixie (IRE) *Paul Cole* a53 55
3 b f Dubawi(IRE) —Sweet Home Alabama (IRE) (Desert Prince (IRE))
2836[9] 3224[9] 4072[9] 4666[5] 4827[3] 5243[5] 5665[4] 5832[12]

Heart Of Dubai (USA) *Micky Hammond* a69 61
6 b g Outofthebox(USA) —Diablo's Blend (USA) (Diablo (USA))
1153[6] 1491[6] (1794) 2496[8] 3185[3] 3754[2] 4602[4] 5166[4] 6095[12]

Hearts And Minds (IRE) *Jamie Osborne* a69 63
2 b g Clodovil(IRE) —Heart's Desire (IRE) (Royal Applause)
4205[9] 4545[4] 4884[3] 5343[2] 5597[12] 6489[6] ◆ (6846)

Hearts Of Fire *Ibrahaim Al Malki* a100 119
4 b h Firebreak—Alexander Ballet (Mind Games)
586a[4] 759a[5] 828a[5] 997a[9]

Heartsong (IRE) *John Gallagher* 65
2 b f Kheleyf(USA) —Semiquaver (IRE) (Mark Of Esteem (IRE))
4155[12] 4430[3] 5017[2]

Heatherbird *William Jarvis* a74 79
3 b f Shamardal(USA) —Bronwen (IRE) (King's Best (USA))
1343[4] 1853[7] 2615[7] 4448[2] ◆ 5169[6] 6063[3] 7130[9] (7440) 7831[10]

Heaven King (FR) *M Pimbonnet* a93 93
4 b g Kingsalsa(USA) —Heaven Giant (USA) (Giant's Causeway (USA))
6593a[5]

Heavenly Dawn *Sir Michael Stoute* 102
4 ch m Pivotal—Heavenly Ray (USA) (Rahy (USA))
3407[2] ◆ (4093) ◆ 4790[3] ◆ 5277[11]

Heavenly Games *Jeremy Gask* a38
4 b m Septieme Ciel(USA) —Holly Games (Mind Games)
5633[9] 6473[11] 7093[8]

Heavenly Music (IRE) *Sylvester Kirk* a60
3 b f Oratorio(IRE) —Treca (IRE) (Darshaan)
95[3] 2175[6] 4090[12] 4666[13]

Heavenly Pursuit *Jim Boyle* a54 54
3 b f Pastoral Pursuits—Stylish Clare (IRE) (Desert Style (IRE))
1284[6] 3476[4] 4162[12] 4759[7] 5996[9]

Heaven's Gift (GER) *S Smrczek* a59 92
3 ch f Green Tune(USA) —Hokulea (GER) (Lando (GER))
4839a[10]

Hecton Lad (USA) *John Best* a69 52
4 bb g Posse(USA) —Foxy Queen (USA) (Fit To Fight (USA))
466[3] 773[8] 944[9] (1604) 2268[11] (2385) 2560[6] 2816[3] ◆ 3568a[0] 7455[11] 7810[2]

Hector's Chance *Heather Main* a50 41
2 ch c Byron—Fleur A Lay (USA) (Mr Greeley (USA))
5861[7] 6994[11]

[illegible] (IRE) *[illegible]* a68 64
5 gr g Verglas(IRE) —Halicardia (Halling (USA))
26[5] 90[4] 428[9]

Hector The Brave (IRE) *John E Long* a49 46
4 b g Spartacus(IRE) —Unaria (Prince Tenderfoot (USA))
684[7] 1606[10] 2790[15] 4322[8] 5406[6] 5832[13]

Heddwyn (IRE) *Marcus Tregoning* a98 95
4 b g Bahri(USA) —Penny Rouge (IRE) (Pennekamp (USA))
2604[2] 3156[16]

Hedgerow (IRE) *Dianne Sayer* a32 53
4 b m Azamour(IRE) —Miss Childrey (IRE) (Dr Fong (USA))
69[10] 229[10] 5402[11] 6208[5] 6454[7]

Heeraat (IRE) *William Haggas* a86 88
2 b c Dark Angel(IRE) —Thawrah (IRE) (Green Desert (USA))
4098[3] (4675) ◆ 5715[6]

Heezararity *Stuart Kittow* 75
3 b g Librettist(USA) —Extremely Rare (IRE) (Mark Of Esteem (IRE))
2103[6] 2790[6] 3688[9] 6167[3] 6583[7] 7057[13] 7235[7]

Hefner (IRE) *Richard Hannon* 83
2 b c Tagula(IRE) —Classic Style (IRE) (Desert Style (IRE))
4722[5] 5447[5] 6994[2]

Heidikly (FR) *B De Montzey* a91 85
3 gr f Slickly(FR) —Hier Deja (FR) (Neverneyev (USA))
841a[3] 7667a[3]

Heidi's Delight (IRE) *Ann Duffield* a53 41
2 b f Red Clubs(IRE) —Alexander Confranc (IRE) (Magical Wonder (USA))
4106[9] 4668[5] 5174[7] 7000[5] 7251[3] 7592[4] (7742) ◆

Height Of Summer (IRE) *Chris Wall* a79 7
3 b f Alhaarth(IRE) —Summer Dreams (IRE) (Sadler's Wells (USA))
2596[13] 3001[14] 4800[4] (5318) 5938[11] 6822[13]

Heliodor (USA) *Mahmood Al Zarooni* a107 110
5 b g Scrimshaw(USA) —Playing Footsie (USA) (Valiant Nature (USA))
242[11] 498a[7] 677a[8]

Heliograph *Mahmood Al Zarooni* a52
3 br f Ishiguru(USA) —Photo Flash (IRE) (Bahamian Bounty)
1607[9]

Hellbender (IRE) *George Foster* a86 69
5 ch g Exceed And Excel(AUS) —Desert Rose (Green Desert (USA))
1712[4] 2352[3] 2633[5] 3128[5] 3657[10] 5008[3] 5437[2] 5725[9]

Helleborine *Mme C Head-Maarek* 112
3 b f Observatory(USA) —New Orchid (USA) (Quest For Fame)
1207a[2] 2137a[13] 6809a[7]

Hellenistic *Mahmood Al Zarooni*
2 ch f Street Cry(IRE) —Rahiyah (USA) (Rahy (USA))
4285[13]

Hello Dubai *David Simcock* a60
2 ch f Teofilo(IRE) —Bush Cat (USA) (Kingmambo (USA))
7118[7]

Hello Glory *David Simcock* 95
2 b f Zamindar(USA) —Affair Of State (IRE) (Tate Gallery (USA))
3865[5] ◆ (4263) 5217[3] ◆ 6337[6]

Hello Man (IRE) *S M Duffy* a65 75
8 b g Princely Heir(IRE) —Mignon (Midyan (USA))
6139a[12]

Hello Tomorrow (USA) *David Lanigan* a63 66
3 b f Forest Wildcat(USA) —Never Gone (USA) (Gone West (USA))
2583[9]

Helly (FR) *R Pritchard-Gordon* a76 73
4 ch m Numerous(USA) —Heritiere (AUS) (Anabaa (USA))
(1012a)

Helmet (AUS) *Peter Snowden* 121
3 ch c Exceed And Excel(AUS) —Accessories (Singspiel (IRE))
7044a[8]

Helpmeronda *Ian Williams* a46 61
5 b m Medicean—Lady Donatella (Last Tycoon)
575[7] 748[8] 819[8] 2237[10]

Hel's Angel (IRE) *Ann Duffield* a71 84
5 b m Pyrus(USA) —Any Dream (IRE) (Shernazar)
(1792) 2251[5] 3243[3] 3974[2] 4637[2]

Henry Allingham *Roger Varian* 74
2 ch g Three Valleys(USA) —Hoh Dancer (Indian Ridge)
7293[4]

Henry Bond *Shaun Harris* 12
3 ch g Monsieur Bond(IRE) —Decatur (Deploy)
4181[P]

Henry Chettle (IRE) *David O'Meara* 30
3 ch g Iffraaj—Nipitinthebud (USA) (Night Shift (USA))
3455[6]

Henry Clay *Mark Johnston* 79
2 b c Dubawi(IRE) —Congressional (IRE) (Grand Lodge (USA))
6970[2]

Henry George *Mark Johnston* 15
2 b g Zamindar(USA) —Melpomene (Peintre Celebre (USA))
6532[13]

Henry Holmes *Lydia Richards* a53
8 b g Josr Algarhoud(IRE) —Henrietta Holmes (IRE) (Persian Bold)
216 [3] 419[3] 6087[8] (6798) 7331[4] 7574[2]

Henry Morgan *Bryan Smart* 70
4 ch g Bahamian Bounty—Hill Welcome (Most Welcome)
1239[7] 1712[5] 6779[13] (7064)

Henrys Air *David Bridgwater* a65 57
3 b g Piccolo—Humble Gift (Cadeaux Genereux)
(2243) 2599[7] 3913[7] 4657[6] 4768[13] 5110[6] 6300[8]

Henry San (IRE) *Alan King* 58
4 ch g Exceed And Excel(AUS) —Esclava (USA) (Nureyev (USA))
7236[8]

Henrys Gift (IRE) *Michael Dods* 60
3 b g Titus Livius(FR) —Xania (Mujtahid (USA))
1693[8] 2392[11] 3116[3] 3487[6] 4381[4] 4878[3] 5315[2] 6116[6] 7159[5]

Henry's Hero *Chris Dwyer* 50
5 b g Mujahid(USA) —Primavera (Anshan)
6542[8] 6668[7] 6920[12] 7387[12]

Hepworth *John Gosden* 90
2 b f Singspiel(IRE) —Annalina (USA) (Cozzene (USA))
6985[2] ◆

Heraclius *J-M Beguigne* a82 77
3 b g Lemon Drop Kid(USA) —Hermance (Enrique)
7669a[4]

Herbaceous *Jeremy Noseda* a44
2 b f Medicean—Red Blossom (Green Desert (USA))
5814[8]

Here Comes Jeanie *Michael Madgwick* a55
2 b f Act One—Full English (Perugino (USA))
6118[10] 6812[9] 7435[6] 7749[7]

Herecomethegirls *Olivia Maylam* a58 46
5 b m Falbrav(IRE) —Always On My Mind (Distant Relative)
346[4] 862[12] 1959[8] 2820[2] 3496[9] 4317[12] 4549[5] 4945[11]

Hereditary *Linda Jewell* a47 9
9 ch g Hernando(FR) —Eversince (USA) (Foolish Pleasure (USA))
1135[8]

Hereford Boy *Dean Ivory* a79 74
7 ch g Tomba—Grown At Rowan (Gabitat)
348[5] 623[10] 949[8] 1198[3] 2178[12] 2822[7] 3217[3] 3412[5] 4160[5] 4349[3] ◆ 4910[4] 5835[11] 7208[6] 7362[2] 7637[2] 7823[7]

Here Now And Why (IRE) *Ian Semple* a65 64
4 br g Pastoral Pursuits—Why Now (Dansili)
4017[4] 4672[5] 5153[7] (5313) 5787[7] (7100) 7266[6] 7566[8]

Hereselle (IRE) *Michael Chapman* a64 32
3 b f Clodovil(IRE) —Special Dissident (Dancing Dissident (USA))
183[10] 396[2] 505[6] 672[4] 913[4] 936[7] 2918[6] 3247[11] 4607[7] 6615[8] 7691[10]

Here To Eternity (USA) *Peter Chapple-Hyam* a54 71
3 bb f Stormy Atlantic(USA) —Heat Of The Night (Lear Fan (USA))
(1133) 1986[4] ◆ 3292[7] 4926[5] 5803[12] 6258[8]

Here To Win (BRZ) *M F De Kock* a101 105
5 br m Roi Normand(USA) —Ascot Belle (BRZ) (Falcon Jet (BRZ))
239[2] ◆ 417a[8] 604a[3] 827a[5]

Hermes *Ralph Beckett* a46 76
3 b g Observatory(USA) —Parisette (Dansili)
546[4] 2930[11] 3764[4]

Herminella *William Muir* a71 60
3 b f Lucky Story(USA) —Herminoe (Rainbow Quest (USA))
2102[11] 2615[8] 3259[8] 3782[8] 5319[6] 5631[3] (6004) 6493[11]

Hernando's Boy *Keith Reveley* 46
10 b g Hernando(FR) —Leave At Dawn (Slip Anchor)
3974[5]

Hernando Torres *Michael Easterby* a53 69
3 b g Iffraaj—Espana (Hernando (FR))
(2119) 2675[2] 3358[3] 3809[6] 4177[10] 4560[6] 5064[5] 5372[2] 6674[18]

Herostatus *Mark Johnston* a94 77
4 ch g Dalakhani(IRE) —Desired (Rainbow Quest (USA))
2107[13] 2499[8] 3157[15] 3794[6] 4423[16]

Herrera (IRE) *Richard Fahey* a51 68
6 b m High Chaparral(IRE) —Silk (IRE) (Machiavellian (USA))
2734[6] 3319[9] 3906[5] 4366[7] 4674[7] (5470) 6082[2] 6235[8] 6780[12] 7573[8] 7850[8]

Herschel (IRE) *Gary Moore* a56 65
5 br g Dr Fong(USA) —Rafting (IRE) (Darshaan)
2308[9] 3479[6] 5857[7] 7818[5]

Her Smile (USA) *Todd Pletcher* a114 89
3 bb f Include(USA) —Hepburn (USA) (Capote (USA))
7282a[3]

Hertford Street *Peter Makin* a45 43
3 ch g Nayef(USA) —Monawara (IRE) (Namaqualand (USA))
1606[9] 1985[9] 2790[12] 3724[7] 4758[12] 5845[9] 6084[5] 6701[8]

He's A Humbug (IRE) *Paul Midgley* a63 68
7 b g Tagula(IRE) —Acidanthera (Alzao (USA))
3732[3] 4233[4] 4517[2] 4893[6] 5338[7] 5734[5] 5901[10]

He's Got Rhythm (IRE) *David Marnane* a87 91
6 b g Invincible Spirit(IRE) —Kathy Jet (USA) (Singspiel (IRE))
4566a[15] 7010a[12] 7468a[7] 7792a[2]

Hesindamood *Joanne Priest* a44
4 b g Mind Games—Vax Rapide (Sharpo)
253[6] 663[10] 1015[4] 2161[12]

Hesperides *Harry Dunlop* a62 20
2 ch f Halling(USA) —Nando's Dream (Hernando (FR))
5812[13] 6474[5] 6819[3] 7514[10]

He's So Cool (IRE) *Bill Turner* a54 87
2 b c One Cool Cat(USA) —Love Ridot (IRE) (Fruits Of Love (USA))
982[3] (1095) 1806[5] ◆ (2056) 2712[6] 3345[5] 3810[10] 4085[2] 4572[6]

Hestian (IRE) *T Stack* a103 91
2 b c Kodiac—Tides (Bahamian Bounty)
5216[19] 6518[11]

Hettie Hubble *David Thompson* 50
5 ch m Dr Fong(USA) —White Rabbit (Zilzal (USA))
1557[6] 1857[5] 2548[9] 2781[9]

Heureux (USA) *Jens Erik Lindstol* 93
6 b g [illegible](USA) —[illegible] West (USA) (Gone West (USA))
4483a[8]

Hexagonal (IRE) *Lee Smyth* a74 96
2 b c One Cool Cat(USA) —Dubai Diamond (Octagonal (NZ))
1699a[4] 2322a[8] 6114[2] 6518[16]

Heyaaraat (IRE) *Charles Hills* 53
2 b f Lawman(FR) —Lanzana (IRE) (Kalanisi (IRE))
7165[10]

Hey Fiddle Fiddle (IRE) *Charles Hills* a63 61
2 b f One Cool Cat(USA) —Crystal Valkyrie (IRE) (Danehill (USA))
5323[4] ◆ 6019[4] 7197[4] 7514[5] (7874)

Hey Mambo *Roger Ingram* a42 29
3 b f Bertolini(USA) —Upping The Tempo (Dunbeath (USA))
641[1] 338[6] 787[4] 886[5] 958[6] 1132[8]

Hey Up There (IRE) *Ruth Carr* 16
3 b f Ekraar(USA) —Lady White (IRE) (Barathea (IRE))
855[7] 1323[7] 2249[11] 2786[11]

Heyward Girl (IRE) *Robert Eddery* a71 82
2 ch f Bertolini(USA) —Rancho Cucamonga (IRE) (Raphane (USA))
1441[2] (5834) 6625[4] (7138)

Hezmah *John Gosden* 92
3 b f Oasis Dream—Bright Moll (Mind Games)
(1362) ◆ 1599[4] 3819[7] 4556[3] ◆ 5012[5] 5476[2]

Hibba (USA) *Mouse Hamilton-Fairley* a65 63
4 bb m Sahm(USA) —Nuzooa (USA) (A.P. Indy (USA))
79[10] 1635[9] 2145[5] 2377[10]

Hibiki (IRE) *Sarah Humphrey* 62
7 b g Montjeu(IRE) —White Queen (IRE) (Spectrum (IRE))
2224[9]

Hi Dancer *Ben Haslam* a55 70
8 b g Medicean—Sea Music (Inchinor)
8[7] 2622[5] 3086[10] 3754[9] 4326[11] 4856[10] 6600[2] 6870[3]

Hidden Destiny *Peter Makin* a72 41
4 ch g Bahamian Bounty—Cayetana's Raid (USA) (Rahy (USA))
2794[8] 3711[6] 4057[10]

Hidden Fire *David Elsworth* a74 80
4 b m Alhaarth(IRE) —Premier Prize (Selkirk (USA))
6330^{6} ◆ *6658^{7}* 72375

Hidden Glory *James Given* a91 87
4 b g Mujahid(USA) —Leominda (Lion Cavern (USA))
6^{5} 180^{9} (353) 525^{12} 702^{8} 991^{12} 3051^{3} 3277^{13} 3701^{2} 4045^{4} 4440^{5} 5593^{9} 6155^{10} 6538^{2} 6773^{3} (7237) 7523^{11} 7651^{11} 7877^{8}

Hidden Justice (IRE) *Amanda Perrett* a70 41
2 b g Lawman(FR) —Uncharted Haven (Turtle Island (IRE))
4054^{7} *7520^{8} (7758)*

Hidden Passion (USA) *Brian Meehan* a79 85
2 ch f Elusive Quality(USA) —To Be A Lover (USA) (The Minstrel (CAN))
2606^{P} 2811^{2} 3402^{8} (3722) *4757^{3}* 5270^{3} 5656^{8} 6535^{14} 7135^{4} *7483^{3}*

Hidden Universe (IRE) *D K Weld* 94
5 gr g Linamix(FR) —Hint Of Humour (USA) (Woodman (USA))
(7322a)

Hidden Valley *Andrew Balding* a74 77
3 b f Haafhd—Spurned (USA) (Robellino (USA))
1363^{5} 1722^{6} *2175^{2} 3469^{2}* 4056^{9} *5103^{4}* 5938^{5} (6891)

Hide The Evidence (IRE) *Niall Moran* a63 57
10 ch g Carroll House—Andarta (Ballymore)
448^{2}

Hiding In The Open (IRE) *Brian Meehan* a17
2 gr g Verglas(IRE) —La Caprice (USA) (Housebuster (USA))
2017^{8} 2214^{12} *3472^{7}* 3816^{12}

Hierarch (IRE) *David Simcock* a70 73
4 b g Dansili—Danse Classique (IRE) (Night Shift (USA))
96^{11} 174^{13} 522^{8} 719^{7} 4928^{4} 5667^{3} *6784^{3} 7537^{4} (7843) 7930^{5}*

High Avon *Dean Ivory* a49 56
3 b g Avonbridge—High Finale (Sure Blade (USA))
383^{6} 519^{8} 558^{9}

High Carol (IRE) *Andy Turnell* 28
9 ch g Presenting—Madam Chloe (Dalsaan)
5911^{11}

High Class Lady *Walter Swinburn* a37 65
3 b f Royal Applause—Lekka Ding (IRE) (Raise A Grand (IRE))
745^{11} 987^{6} 1953^{9} 5601^{13} 5995^{6}

Highdar (FR) *P Demercastel* a76 70
3 ch c Sinndar(IRE) —High Mecene (FR) (Highest Honor (FR))
902a^{7}

High Endeavour (IRE) *Robert Mills* 34
2 b f High Chaparral(IRE) —Green Tambourine (Green Desert (USA))
5299^{11}

Higher Ground (FR) *S-A Ghoumrassi* a69 69
4 b h Agnes Kamikaze(JPN) —Honorable Sister (FR) (Highest Honor (FR))
259a^{5}

Higher Spen Jess *Julie Camacho* a25
3 ch f Blue Dakota(IRE) —Enchanting Eve (Risk Me (FR))
253^{8} 600^{8} 1053^{10}

Higher Spen Rose *Julie Camacho*
3 b f Dubawi(IRE) —Balwarah (IRE) (Soviet Star (USA))
1210^{10}

Highest *John Gosden* a93 96
3 b f Dynaformer(USA) —Solaia (USA) (Miswaki (USA))
1364^{2} ◆ (1616) 2189^{2} ◆ 3065^{7} *7129^{7}* 7580a^{0}

Highest Red *Andrew Haynes*
2 ch c Byron—Honor Rouge (IRE) (Highest Honor (FR))
7142^{9}

High Fallutin (IRE) *Eve Johnson Houghton* a14 52
3 b f Ad Valorem(USA) —Top Brex (FR) (Top Ville)
1363^{10} 2613^{4} 2857^{6}

High Figurine (IRE) *William Haggas* 87
4 b m High Chaparral(IRE) —Royale Figurine (IRE) (Dominion Royale)
267a^{2} 705a^{0} 2676^{5} 3381^{3} (4008) ◆

High Five Prince (IRE) *Mark Usher* a8 44
2 br g Strategic Prince—Lady Georgina (Linamix (FR))
2644^{8} 3308^{10} 4201^{12} 4704^{5} *5099^{6}* 5625^{7} 6021^{5} 6807^{10}

High Five Society *Roy Bowring* a68 79
7 b g Compton Admiral—Sarah Madeline (Pelder (IRE))
711^{6} 897^{4} 2213^{13} (3089) (3576) 4070^{7} 5733^{9}

High Importance (USA) *A J Martin* a83 86
4 b g Arch(USA) —Music Lane (USA) (Miswaki (USA))
1381a^{3}

High Jinx (IRE) *James Fanshawe* 99
3 b c High Chaparral(IRE) —Leonara (GER) (Surumu (GER))
2258^{3} (2956) 5482^{3} ◆

High Kickin *Alan McCabe* a59 48
3 ch f Noverre(USA) —Grateful (Generous (IRE))
142^{7} 234^{7}

Highkingofireland *Mrs K Burke* 66
5 br g Danehill Dancer(IRE) —Lucky Date (IRE) (Halling (USA))
6830^{9} 7159^{10}

Highland Bridge *David Elsworth* a65 29
4 b g Avonbridge—Reciprocal (IRE) (Night Shift (USA))
394^{6}

Highland Cadett *Pam Ford* a59 56
4 ch g Putra Sandhurst(IRE) —Highland Rossie (Pablond)
6582^{5} 7107^{7}

Highland Castle *David Elsworth* 113
3 b g Halling(USA) —Reciprocal (IRE) (Night Shift (USA))
2648^{3} (3001) ◆ (3623) 4411^{5} 5284^{8} (5659) ◆ 6498^{2}

Highland Colori (IRE) *Tom Dascombe* a81 73
3 b g Le Vie Dei Colori—Emma's Star (ITY) (Darshaan)
2185^{9} 3543^{8} *(3949)* ◆ 4817^{5}

Highland Duke (IRE) *Clive Cox* 64
2 b c Dansili—House In Wood (FR) (Woodman (USA))
6160^{8}

Highland Glen *S Seemar* a79 86
5 b g Montjeu(IRE) —Daring Aim (Daylami (IRE))
240^{14}

Highland Harvest *Jamie Poulton* a80 71
7 b g Averti(IRE) —Bee One (IRE) (Catrail (USA))
55^{4} 249^{9} 763^{5} 1838^{10} 2167^{4} 3020^{4} 3255^{5} 3940^{8} *(4206)* 4659^{2} *(4850) 5412^{2}* 5669^{8} 5997^{4} 7675^{8} 7893^{6}

Highland Knight (IRE) *Andrew Balding* a96 102
4 b g Night Shift(USA) —Highland Shot (Selkirk (USA))
1092^{13} 1527^{5} *1760^{3}* 2679^{2} (3645) 4494^{8}

Highland Love *Jedd O'Keeffe* a62 64
6 b g Fruits Of Love(USA) —Diabaig (Precocious)
2213^{15} 2530^{4} 2804^{3} 3074^{6} 4111^{10} 4367^{4} 4902^{10} *6698^{10}*

Highland Park (IRE) *Michael Wigham* a53 80
4 ch g Pivotal—Highland Gift (IRE) (Generous (IRE))
930^{3} 2021^{10} 2512^{10} 3184^{12}

Highland Warrior *Paul Midgley* a62 78
12 b g Makbul—Highland Rowena (Royben)
1073^{9} (1968) 2263^{5} 3087^{7} 3305^{7} 3832^{11} 5148^{6}

Highlife Dancer *Mick Channon* a68 80
3 br g Imperial Dancer—Wrong Bride (Reprimand)
594^{4} 890^{4} 1170^{5} (1413) 3018^{7} 3596^{6} (3979) (4317) 4627^{2} (4845) 5135^{3} (5582) 5880^{7} 6248^{6} 6409^{9} 6674^{7} 6916^{4}

High Link (FR) *X Thomas-Demeaulte* a91 96
4 b g High Yield(USA) —Sante De Fer (FR) (Shining Steel)
830a^{3}

Highly Efficient *Thomas Mullins* 92
3 b g Dalakhani(IRE) —Ammo (IRE) (Sadler's Wells (USA))
7322a^{3}

Highly Likely (IRE) *John Dunlop* a16 50
2 b g Elnadim(USA) —Height Of Fantasy (IRE) (Shirley Heights)
3870^{9} 4330^{14} 5011^{12} *6053^{11}* 6757^{7}

Highly Regal (IRE) *Chris Gordon* a83 85
6 b g High Chaparral(IRE) —Regal Portrait (IRE) (Royal Academy (USA))
206 ^{9} 473^{2} 623^{6} 908^{6} 2562^{8} *7756^{9}*

High Miswaki (FR) *Jeremy Noseda*
2 b c High Chaparral(IRE) —Driving Miswaki (USA) (Miswaki (USA))
6059^{P}

High Office *Richard Fahey* a82 98
5 b g High Chaparral(IRE) —White House (Pursuit Of Love)
(1517) 2107^{7} 3163^{2} 3396^{8} 3875^{10} 5271^{8} 6151^{4}

High On A Hill (IRE) *Sylvester Kirk* a81 85
4 b g Val Royal(FR) —Blue Kestrel (IRE) (Bluebird (USA))
209 ^{2} 1367^{5} *1761^{3}* (2312) 2931^{13} 3428^{6} 3794^{8} 5050^{2} 6485^{6} (6749)

High On The Hog (IRE) *Paul Howling* a55 76
3 b c Clodovil(IRE) —Maraami (Selkirk (USA))
1481^{5} 2146^{4} 3259^{9} 4011^{2} ◆ (5423) 5669^{6} *7453^{9} 7601^{14} 7764^{8}*

High Ransom *Micky Hammond* a72 73
4 b m Red Ransom(USA) —Shortfall (Last Tycoon)
1215^{7} 7075^{5}

High Resolution *Linda Perratt* a53 87
4 ch g Haafhd—Individual Talents (USA) (Distant View (USA))
1541^{7} 1859^{2} 2217^{13} 2414^{7} 3276^{6} 3659^{5} 4380^{2} 4540^{6} 5205^{7} 5722^{13} 6079^{8}

High Rolling *Tim Easterby* 67
4 b g Fantastic Light(USA) —Roller Girl (Merdon Melody)
1245^{2} 1558^{3}

High Ruler (USA) *A P O'Brien* a104 104
3 b c Mr Greeley(USA) —Lady Carla (Caerleon (USA))
2324a^{4} *6514a^{2}*

High Samana *Ralph Beckett* a50 76
3 b g High Chaparral(IRE) —Kirkby Belle (Bay Express)
1399^{2} 1840^{5} 3080^{4} 3978^{4} 4753^{7} 5784^{6} 6377^{7}

High Speed (SWI) *H-A Pantall* a69 67
3 gr c Blue Canari(FR) —High Mare (FR) (Highest Honor (FR))
258a^{8} 370a^{0} 480a^{9}

High Spice (USA) *Robert Cowell* a84 84
4 b m Songandaprayer(USA) —Erin Moor (USA) (Holy Bull (USA))
3579^{8} 3847^{5} 4416^{16}

High Standing (USA) *William Haggas* a87 114
6 bb g High Yield(USA) —Nena Maka (Selkirk (USA))
1397^{5} 2502^{6} 2961^{2} 3155^{15} (3626) 4534^{27} 5510^{3} 6147^{12} 6534^{3}

High Table (IRE) *Tom Dascombe* a32 16
3 b g High Chaparral(IRE) —Inner Strength (FR) (Take Risks (FR))
1565^{12}

Hight Blue Sails (FR) *J-P Roman* a55 78
7 gr h Chichicastenango(FR) —Green Sails (IRE) (Slip Anchor)
533a^{10}

High Twelve (IRE) *Mahmood Al Zarooni* a106 110
4 b g Montjeu(IRE) —Much Faster (IRE) (Fasliyev (USA))
242^{4} (4267) 5185^{17}

High Ville (FR) *P Chevillard* a92 71
5 b m Highest Honor(FR) —Kadouville I (FR) (Kaldoun (FR))
92a^{4}

High Vintage (IRE) *Edmond Kent* 89
6 b m High Chaparral(IRE) —Vintage Escape (IRE) (Cyrano De Bergerac)
2968a^{8}

High Window (IRE) *G P Kelly* a47 25
11 b g King's Theatre(IRE) —Kayradja (IRE) (Last Tycoon)
4563^{11}

Hikkaduwa *John Holt*
2 br f Sakhee(USA) —Numanthia (IRE) (Barathea (IRE))
6950^{16}

Hikma (USA) *Saeed Bin Suroor* 47
2 b f Street Cry(IRE) —Innuendo (IRE) (Caerleon (USA))
6934^{10}

Hilali (IRE) *Gary Brown* a62 50
2 b g Sakhee(USA) —Mufradat (IRE) (Desert Prince (IRE))
6652^{2} 6994^{9}

Hilbre Court (USA) *Brian Baugh* a61 56
6 br g Doneraile Court(USA) —Glasgow's Gold (USA) (Seeking The Gold (USA))
6659^{4} 7005^{8} 7687^{2} 7775^{2} 7885^{5}

Hill Of Clare (IRE) *George Jones* a30 6
9 gr m Daylami(IRE) —Sarah-Clare (Reach)
340^{11} 407^{4} 695^{5} 769^{6} 1567^{F}

Hill Of Dreams (IRE) *Dean Ivory* a60
2 b f Indian Danehill(IRE) —Shaunas Vision (IRE) (Dolphin Street (FR))
7142^{6} 7634^{5} (7909)

Hills Of Dakota *David Barron* 82
3 b g Sleeping Indian—Pontressina (USA) (St Jovite (USA))
4514^{5} (5063) (6190)

Hilltop Artistry *J R Jenkins* a44 52
5 b g Polish Precedent(USA) —Hilltop (Absalom)
2560^{10} 2828^{9} 4928^{5} 6032^{9}

Hill Tribe *Richard Guest* a73 68
4 b m Tiger Hill(IRE) —Morning Queen (GER) (Konigsstuhl (GER))
(508) (747) 870^{3} 1167^{3} *1292^{7} 1587^{6}* 1909^{13} 2399^{12} 4394^{3} 4543^{3} 4783^{8} 4945^{5} 5205^{14} 5402^{10} *5740^{8} 6285^{3}* (6358) 6543^{9} 6669^{10}

Hillview Boy (IRE) *Jim Goldie* 99
7 bb g Bishop Of Cashel—Arandora Star (USA) (Sagace (FR))
5285^{16}

Himalayan Moon *Ian Wood* a51 56
4 gr m Tiger Hill(IRE) —Sita (IRE) (Indian Ridge)
1332^{7} 4208^{9} 4753^{4} *5209^{11} 5947^{11} 6356^{8} 6656^{9}* 6769^{8}

Himalya (IRE) *Roger Charlton* a106 114
5 b g Danehill Dancer(IRE) —Lady Miletrian (IRE) (Barathea (IRE))
1340^{12} 1885^{17} 2502^{7} 5282^{11} 6129^{7}

Hi Molly (FR) *D Guillemin* 105
2 b c Della Francesca(USA) —Bubbly Molly (FR) (Wagon Master (FR))
(3567a) 4596a^{6} 6042a^{6} 6808a^{3}

Hinchinbrook (AUS) *Peter G Moody* 115
4 b c Fastnet Rock(AUS) —Snippets' Lass (AUS) (Snippets (AUS))
6

Hindu Kush (IRE) *Robert Mills* a75 82
6 b g Sadler's Wells(USA) —Tambora (Darshaan)
384^{6} 795^{2} (1032)

Hi Note *Sheena West* a58 50
3 b f Acclamation—Top Tune (Victory Note (USA))
1018^{5} (3227) 3742^{6} 3958^{8} *5636^{3} 6926^{8}*

Hint Of Honey *Tony Newcombe* a33 51
5 ch m King Charlemagne(USA) —Jugendliebe (IRE) (Persian Bold)
4953^{2} 5349^{5} *7092^{5}*

Hint Of Mint *Andrew Balding* 74
2 b g Passing Glance—Juno Mint (Sula Bula)
4995^{14} 5375^{3} 6373^{2}

Hint Of Silver (IRE) *Andrew Haynes* 50
3 gr f Aussie Rules(USA) —Dream Genie (Puissance)
1873^{11} 2185^{12} 2639^{6} 3268^{11} 3910^{11}

Hinton Admiral *Keith Dalgleish* a85 82
7 b g Spectrum(IRE) —Shawanni (Shareef Dancer (USA))
134^{2} (334) (467) 648^{3} 804^{3} (960) 1245^{7} 1618^{4} 2464^{6} 2543^{4} (2766) 3036^{3} 3488^{3} 4013^{6} 4503^{6} 5151^{6} (6076) 6418^{5} 6875^{3} 7629^{2}

Hip Hip Hooray *Luke Dace* a75 71
5 ch m Monsieur Bond(IRE) —Birthday Belle (Lycius (USA))
(48) 206 ^{8} 483^{3} 666^{10} 1990^{7} 2354^{6} 2829^{2} (3468) 4429^{15} 4725^{4} 5281^{7} 5894^{9} *6544^{6}* 6924^{13} *7033^{9}*

Hip Hop *Brett Johnson* a12
2 b f Excellent Art—Whassup (FR) (Midyan (USA))
6441^{13} 7118^{13} 7330^{11}

Hippique *Jeremy Gask* a65 29
4 b m Bertolini(USA) —Elemental (Rudimentary (USA))
2313^{12} 2870^{9} 3341^{9}

Hippolyte (FR) *T Clout* 95
2 b g Gold Away(IRE) —Standout (FR) (Robellino (USA))
7508a^{2}

Hiruno D'Amour (JPN) *Mitsugu Kon* 125
4 b h Manhattan Cafe(JPN) —Share Elegance (JPN) (Lammtarra (USA))
5986a^{2} 6567a^{10} 7873a^{6}

Hiscano *Terry Clement*
3 ch c Paolini(GER) —Hollywood Love (GER) (Lomitas)
7921^{7}

His Grace (IRE) *Andrew Haynes* a58 71
3 gr g Proclamation(IRE) —Little Miss Gracie (Efisio)
1130^{3} 1302^{3} 1449^{6} 3122^{10} 3481^{3} 4729^{5} 4950^{2} 5038^{6} 5534^{3}

Hi Shinko *Mme G Rarick* a80 89
5 b g Shinko Forest(IRE) —Up Front (IRE) (Up And At 'Em)
3568a^{9}

Hi Spec (IRE) *Mandy Rowland* a57 49
8 b m Spectrum(IRE) —Queen Of Fibres (IRE) (Scenic)
229^{2} (312) 340^{9} 619^{9} 950^{11} 6310^{11} 6657^{5} 7119^{8} 7400^{4}

His Royal Highness (CAN) *Mikael Magnusson* a65
2 b c Awesome Again(CAN) —Royally Chosen (USA) (In Excess)
5697^{12} *6180^{3} 6795^{5}*

History Girl (IRE) *Sir Henry Cecil* a59 62
3 b f Hernando(FR) —City Of Gold (IRE) (Sadler's Wells (USA))
1285^{2} *1609^{8}* 2571^{8} *3175^{2}*

History Note (IRE) *John M Oxx* 108
3 b f Azamour(IRE) —Cadence (Cadeaux Genereux)
1006a^{3} ◆ 2334a^{6} 3527a^{5}

History Repeating *Mark Usher* a68 63
3 b f Singspiel(IRE) —Annapurna (IRE) (Brief Truce (USA))
4448^{5} (5614) 6402^{10} *7033^{3} 7255^{5} 7515^{3}* ◆ *7789^{6}*

Hitchens (IRE) *David Barron* a106 117
6 b g Acclamation—Royal Fizz (IRE) (Royal Academy (USA))
700^{5} 989^{5} 1093^{4} 2005^{4} (2323a) 3154^{11} 3863^{3} 5707^{9} 6908a^{6}

Hitches Dubai (BRZ) *Geoffrey Harker* 70
6 ch g A Good Reason(BRZ) —Orquidea Vermelha (BRZ) (Lucence (USA))
1940^{6} 2798^{10} 3937^{11} 5436^{6} 5787^{13} 6266^{14} 7100^{10}

Hi There (IRE) *J W Hills* a51 67
2 b g Dark Angel(IRE) —Ornellaia (IRE) (Mujadil (USA))
2787^{11} 3308^{3} 3761^{8} 4277^{4} 4913^{3} 5478^{8} *6663^{6}* 6973^{3}

Hitman Hatton *Lucinda Featherstone* a49 63
4 b g Pastoral Pursuits—Richenda (Mister Baileys)
1654^{2} *6307^{7}*

Hits Only Cash *Lydia Pearce* a47 64
9 b g Inchinor—Persian Blue (Persian Bold)
5860^{9}

Hits Only Jude (IRE) *Declan Carroll* a69 69
8 gr g Bold Fact(USA) —Grey Goddess (Godswalk (USA))
(1077) (1150) 1394^{6} *1462^{3}* 1874^{4} 2213^{9} 2320^{6} 2474^{3} 2548^{5} 2996^{2} (3859) 4039^{4} 4142^{9} 4701^{4} 4852^{10} 4946^{5} 5470^{9} 6098^{6} 6227^{4} 6430^{9} 7159^{9} 7352^{3} 7424^{4} 7713^{5} 7743^{2} 7901^{9}

Hit The Switch *Jennie Candlish* a72 69
5 b g Reset(AUS) —Scenic Venture (IRE) (Desert King (IRE))
1814^{6} 2237^{3} ◆ *(2656) 7070^{3} 7200^{5} (7415)*

Hoar Frost *Karen Tutty* a48 37
6 b m Fraam—Natalie Jay (Ballacashtal (CAN))
4602^{10}

Hobson *Eve Johnson Houghton* a70 79
6 b g Choisir(AUS) —Educating Rita (Emarati (USA))
1755^{9} 2789^{7} 2870^{5}

Hogmaneigh (IRE) *Mark Johnston* a106 77
8 b g Namid—Magical Peace (IRE) (Magical Wonder (USA))
2620^{9} 3569^{8}

Hoh Hoh Hoh *Richard Price* a83 75
9 ch g Piccolo—Nesting (Thatching)
1752^{8} 2142^{9} 2610^{10} 3216^{8} 3908^{8}

Hohrod *Ron Hodges* a13 40
5 ch g Tipsy Creek(USA) —Agara (Young Ern)
4701^{10}

Holberg (UAE) *Saeed Bin Suroor* a112 117
5 b h Halling(USA) —Sweet Willa (USA) (Assert)
2438^{3} 3066^{13}

Holcombe Boy *Noel Quinlan* a69
3 b g Intikhab(USA) —Lady Lindsay (IRE) (Danehill Dancer (IRE))
887^{10} 1611^{11}

Holden Eagle *Tony Newcombe* a62 63
6 b g Catcher In The Rye(IRE) —Bird Of Prey (IRE) (Last Tycoon)
488^{U} 862^{6} 1756^{8} 3799^{3} *5141^{3}* 5612^{8} *7206^{7} 7573^{2}*

Holdin Bullets (USA) *Wesley A Ward* a95
2 b g Ghostzapper(USA) —Holy Bubbette (USA) (Holy Bull (USA))
7280a^{3}

Hold On Tiger (IRE) *Nicky Richards* a54 56
4 b g Acclamation—Our Juliette (IRE) (Namid)
545^{9} 734^{11} 1077^{10} 2989^{8} 3489^{8} 4636^{8}

Hold The Bucks (USA) *Adrian Chamberlain* a48 63
5 b g Hold That Tiger(USA) —Buck's Lady (USA) (Alleged (USA))
6844^{6}

Holiday For Kitten (USA) *Wesley A Ward* a110 103
3 b f Kitten's Joy(USA) —Blue Holiday (USA) (Cure The Blues (USA))
3010^{13} 7303a^{9}

Holiday Reading (USA) *Brian Meehan* a72 77
2 b c Harlan's Holiday(USA) —County Fair (USA) (Mr Prospector (USA))
4213^{7} 5013^{8} (6018) *6699^{5}* 7021^{12}

Holiday Snap *Mary Hambro* a74 63
5 ch m American Post—High Summer (USA) (Nureyev (USA))
2605^{4} 3322^{5} 3512^{12} *5901^{2} 6877^{6}*

Hollie *Peter Makin* a57 58
3 ch f Bertolini(USA) —Musical Refrain (IRE) (Dancing Dissident (USA))
3465^{6} 3998^{6} *5946^{5} 7093^{6}* 7260^{3}

Hollinger (CAN) *Roger L Attfield* a101 106
4 rg g Black Minnaloushe(USA) —Dynamite Cocktail (USA) (Dynaformer (USA))
6204a^{8}

Hollins *Micky Hammond* 85
7 b g Lost Soldier(USA) —Cutting Reef (IRE) (Kris)
2034^{14} 2762^{2} 3205^{7} (4423) 6171^{10}

Hollow Jo *J R Jenkins* a72 36
11 b g Most Welcome—Sir Hollow (USA) (Sir Ivor (USA))
1989^{6}

Hollow Tree *Andrew Balding* a68 90
3 b g Beat Hollow—Hesperia (Slip Anchor)
1484^{4} 2228^{5} *3474^{4}* (3989) (4251)

Holly Martins *Hans Adielsson* a78
2 b g Rail Link—Pretty Girl (IRE) (Polish Precedent (USA))
6506^{5} 6792^{3} (7094)

Hollywood All Star (IRE) *William Muir* a46 37
2 b g Kheleyf(USA) —Camassina (IRE) (Taufan (USA))
2194^{9} 5991^{4} 6474^{11} 7035^{9} 7432^{8} 7673^{5}

Holtby (IRE) *Mel Brittain*
3 b g Millkom—Pompey Blue (Abou Zouz (USA))
4282^{P}

Holy Angel (IRE) *Tim Easterby* 58
2 b g Dark Angel(IRE) —Bakewell Tart (IRE) (Tagula (IRE))
5486^{9} 5726^{4} 6152^{5} 7059^{14}

Holy Empress (IRE) *Michael Bell* a44 34
2 b f Holy Roman Emperor(IRE) —Kahira (IRE) (King's Best (USA))
3816^{7} 4232^{8} 7626^{3}

Holyfield Warrior (IRE) *Michael Attwater* a57 48
7 b g Princely Heir(IRE) —Perugino Lady (IRE) (Perugino (USA))
204^{2} 312^{9} 552^{2} 652^{3} 807^{2} 899^{10} 1068^{2} 1233^{6} 7639^{5} 7910^{9}

Holy Roman (FR) *J Van Handenhove* a68 74
3 b c Holy Roman Emperor(IRE) —Alcestes Selection (Selkirk (USA))
980a^{0}

Holy Roman Warrior (IRE) *Richard Fahey* 78
2 br g Holy Roman Emperor(IRE) —Cedar Sea (IRE) (Persian Bold)
2395^{2} 3161^{4} (4292) 5287^{8} 6144^{6}

Holyrood *Tim Vaughan* a75 84
5 b g Falbrav(IRE) —White Palace (Shirley Heights)
103^{4}

Homajaefef (FR) *Mlle S-V Tarrou* a87 87
3 gr c Divine Light(JPN) —Via Roma (FR) (Kahyasi)
776a^{5}

Home *Brendan Powell* a65 56
6 b g Domedriver(IRE) —Swahili (IRE) (Kendor (FR))
127^{3} 301^{5} (450) 551^{4}

Homeboy (IRE) *Marcus Tregoning* a71 63
3 b g Camacho—Berenica (IRE) (College Chapel)
1176^{2} 1335^{8} 2363^{9} 3075^{4}

Homebrew (IRE) *M A Molloy* a66 56
6 br g Celtic Swing—Irish Ensign (SAF) (National Emblem (SAF))
5912^{2}

Homecoming Queen (IRE) *A P O'Brien* a76 104
2 b f Holy Roman Emperor(IRE) —Lagrion (USA) (Diesis)
1699a^{6} 2777a^{9} 6389a^{2} 7283a^{14}

Home Office *Mark Johnston* a82 79
3 b c Nayef(USA) —Humility (Polar Falcon (USA))
1361^{11} 2229^{5} 2477^{6} 2834^{9} 3168^{7} 3514^{13}

Home On A Wing (AUS) *Anthony Cummings* 105
5 b g Hawk Wing(USA) —Extra Terrestial (AUS) (Quest For Fame)
7310a^{11}

Homeric (IRE) *Ed Dunlop* 56
2 b c Montjeu(IRE) —Al Saqiya (USA) (Woodman (USA))
7232^{8}

Home Run (GER) *P Schiergen* a88 95
3 ch g Motivator—Hold Off (IRE) (Bering)
5463a^{2}

Homeward Strut *David O'Meara* 36
2 ch g Needwood Blade—Piccante (Wolfhound (USA))
2387^{9}

Homework *Richard Fahey* 24
2 b c Exceed And Excel(AUS) —Right Answer (Lujain (USA))
6836^{11}

Honest And True (IRE) [illegible]
4 b g Desert Prince(IRE) —Highly Respected (IRE) (High Estate)
3859^{8} 4143^{7} 4543^{7} 5860^{6} 6049^{4} 6414^{7} 6657^{8}

Honest Buck *Kate Walton* a34 58
4 ch g Chineur(FR) —Noble Penny (Pennekamp (USA))
1210^{3} 1710^{4} 2593^{6} 3903^{8} 5214^{8} 5789^{11} 7211^{10}

Honest Deal *Alan Swinbank* a75 80
3 b g Trade Fair—Sincerely (Singspiel (IRE))
873^{2} 1096^{4} 1415^{2} (1710) 2092^{3} 3400^{6} 3904^{5} 5560^{6}

Honest Strike (USA) *Daniel Mark Loughnane* a88 79
4 b g Smart Strike(CAN) —Honest Lady (USA) (Seattle Slew (USA))
6976^{12}

Honeymead (IRE) *Richard Fahey* 91
3 b f Pivotal—Camaret (IRE) (Danehill (USA))
2503^{3} 3159^{7} 5820^{2} 6148^{4}

Honey Of A Kitten (USA) *David Evans* a86 92
3 b g Kitten's Joy(USA) —Sweet Baby Jane (USA) (Kingmambo (USA))
3067^{23} 5090a^{11} 7877^{4}

Hong Kong Island (IRE) *Micky Hammond* 92
4 br g Alhaarth(IRE) —Three Owls (IRE) (Warning)
1099^{11} (1461) 1658^{2} (2475) 2544^{2} 3867^{4} 4280^{7} 4677^{2} 5078^{3} 5435^{2} 6277^{4}

Honimiere (IRE) *Roger L Attfield* a99 103
5 b m Fasliyev(USA) —Sugar (Hernando (FR))
3208a^{3}

Honkers Bonkers *Alan McCabe* a67 56
3 b g Val Royal(FR) —Amerissage (USA) (Rahy (USA))
10^{2} 130^{3} 183^{3} (494) (576) 672^{3}

Honour *Sir Michael Stoute* a60
2 b f Dansili—Virtuous (Exit To Nowhere (USA))
6215^{7}

Honourable Knight (IRE) *Mark Usher* a69 70
3 b c Celtic Swing—Deemeh (IRE) (Brief Truce (USA))
2838^{9} 3259^{11} 6468^{14} 6871^{7} 7122^{3} (7333) 7527^{4} (7720) 7839^{3} 7931^{5}

Honoured (IRE) *Nicky Henderson* a60 67
4 ch g Mark Of Esteem(IRE) —Traou Mad (IRE) (Barathea (IRE))
6486^{13} 7032^{8} 7441^{3} 7564^{5}

Honour System (IRE) *Saeed Bin Suroor* a100 102
4 ch g King's Best(USA) —Rawabi (Sadler's Wells (USA))
330a^{9} 679a^{5} (827a) 7170^{6}

Hoof It *Michael Easterby* 124
4 b g Monsieur Bond(IRE) —Forever Bond (Danetime (IRE))
(2075) ◆ 3155^{7} (4346) (4534) ◆ 5253^{6} 5707^{3} ◆

Hoofit (NZ) *H Graham Motion* a112 98
4 b g Mossman(AUS) —Chuckle (AUS) (Danehill (USA))
7303a^{11}

Hoofprintinthesnow *Amanda Perrett* a51 64
3 b g Footstepsinthesand—Spring Snowdrop (IRE) (Danehill Dancer (IRE))
1774^{7} 2371^{4} 3872^{5} 4190^{6} 5243^{8}

Hooligan Sean *Henry Candy* a63 77
4 ch g Ishiguru(USA) —Sheesha (USA) (Shadeed (USA))
7585^{2} 7750^{2}

Hoop *John Gosden*
2 ch f Dutch Art—Hooplah (Pivotal)
6215^{12}

Hooray *Sir Mark Prescott Bt* a113 117
3 b f Invincible Spirit(IRE) —Hypnotize (Machiavellian (USA))
1719^{8} (2683) 3154^{7} 5228a^{8} 5510^{4} 6858^{11}

Hoot (IRE) *A bin Huzaim* a82 81
3 b c Invincible Spirit(IRE) —Roslea Lady (IRE) (Alhaarth (IRE))
502a^{11}

Hootys Agogo *Declan Carroll* a51 54
3 ch g Kheleyf(USA) —Calgary (Pivotal)
1065^{3} ◆ 1217^{7} 1672^{6} 2524^{3} 2918^{3} 3143^{3} 3321^{5} 4124^{6} 4564^{8} 4786^{4} 5506^{4} 5864^{9} 6694^{9} 7460^{4} 7690^{8} 7845^{5}

Hoover *Jim Boyle* a73 43
3 b g Sleeping Indian—Spring Clean (FR) (Danehill (USA))
593^{3} (653) 864^{3} 2200^{6} 3122^{11} 3523^{2} 3853^{11} 4206^{3}

Hopeand *Mandy Rowland*
6 b m King's Theatre(IRE) —Land Of Glory (Supreme Leader)
6286^{11}

Hopefull Blue (IRE) *James Evans* a47
5 b m High Chaparral(IRE) —Misbelief (Shirley Heights)
407^{9}

Hope It Is (USA) *David Simcock* a62
3 b c Yes It's True(USA) —Nice Pic (USA) (Piccolino (USA))
95^{5} 300^{4}

Hope On Earth (FR) *Jens Erik Lindstol* 74
2 ch f Footstepsinthesand—Alyousufeya (IRE) (Kingmambo (USA))
5983a^{4}

Hope Point *Mark Usher* 46
3 b f Overbury(IRE) —East Rose (Keen)
2871^{9}

Hopeshedoes (USA) *Linda Jewell* a44 50
4 ch m Johannesburg(USA) —Flirting (USA) (Pleasant Colony (USA))
1815^{8}

Hopes Rebellion *Declan Carroll* 59
2 b g Royal Applause—Relativity (IRE) (Distant Relative)
2983^{13} 3452^{3} 3849^{7} 4079^{6}

Hopes Up *Ian Williams* a18
4 ch m Trade Fair—Nursling (IRE) (Kahyasi)
836^{6}

[illegible] a60 80
3 b f Country Reel(USA) —Madeleine's Blush (USA) (Rahy (USA))
1220^{4} 2782^{3} 3337^{3} 3806^{8} 4290^{9} 5924^{2} 6158^{2} 6840^{13} (7063)

Hopscotch *Michael Bell* a49 30
3 br f Pivotal—Bonnie Doon (IRE) (Grand Lodge (USA))
2392^{9} 3227^{10}

Horatio Carter *David O'Meara* a66 93
6 b g Bahamian Bounty—Jitterbug (IRE) (Marju (IRE))
2431^{9} 3038^{6} 3506^{9} 4141^{12} (5733) 6453^{3} 6831^{11} 6990^{13} 7425^{8} 7646^{6} 7857^{4}

Horseradish *Michael Bell* a76 109
4 b g Kyllachy—Lihou Island (Beveled (USA))
(1111) 1885^{5} 2075^{2} 2370^{5}

Horsewithnoname (IRE) *T G McCourt* a62 62
4 b g Daylami(IRE) —City Zone (IRE) (Zafonic (USA))
839^{4}

Horsley Warrior *Ed McMahon* a67 66
5 b g Alhaarth(IRE) —Polish Lake (Polish Precedent (USA))
449^{3} 733^{4} 1032^{5}

Hoseo (GER) *Frau E Mader* 50
3 b c Konigstiger(GER) —Hosea (GER) (Lagunas)
3672a^{17}

Host The Band *Tony Newcombe* a67 60
7 b m Bandmaster(USA) —Hosting (Thatching)
1271^{11} 2235^{2} 2871^{5}

Hot Blood (IRE) *A Fabre* 103
3 ch f Galileo(IRE) —Hold On (GER) (Surumu (GER))
7406a^{3} 7580a^{0}

Hotep (CAN) *Mark Frostad* a100 102
4 b h A.P. Indy(USA) —Eye Of The Sphynx (CAN) (Smart Strike (CAN))
6203a^{6}

Hotfoot *John Berry* a29 58
4 ch m Desert Sun—Heneseys Leg (Sure Blade (USA))
2268^{5} 2828^{8} 4454^{3} 5168^{8} 7092^{8}

Hotham *Noel Wilson* a61 101
8 b g Komaite(USA) —Malcesine (IRE) (Auction Ring (USA))
1111^{19} 1675^{8} 2117^{11} 2317^{17} 2620^{12} 3028^{8} 3339^{7} 3880^{2} ◆ 4075^{6} 4291^{2} (4516) 5683^{5} 5918^{9} 6112^{15} 6913^{3} 7356^{9} 7776^{4}

Hot Prospect *Roger Varian* 116
4 b g Motivator—Model Queen (USA) (Kingmambo (USA))
4095^{2} 4789^{3} 5494^{4} 6149^{3}

Hot Pursuits *Hughie Morrison* a75 86
4 br m Pastoral Pursuits—Perfect Partner (Be My Chief (USA))
1395^{3} 2298^{7}

Hot Rod Mamma (IRE) *Dianne Sayer* a42 96
4 ch m Traditionally(USA) —Try The Air (IRE) (Foxhound (USA))
1612^{11} 2352^{7} 2670^{9} 2803^{7} (3733) (4111) (4603) (5594) (5728) 6080^{11} 6672^{3} 7023^{12} 7234^{6}

Hot Sand (IRE) *Gerard O'Leary* a77 78
4 bb g Desert Style(IRE) —Veiled Threat (IRE) (Be My Guest (USA))
6511a^{4}

Hot Six (BRZ) *Fabricio Borges* a102 104
6 gr g Burooj—Babysix (USA) (With Approval (CAN))
157a^{4} 417a^{12} 758a^{12} 5984a^{3} 6710a^{4}

Hot Spark *John Akehurst* a90 89
4 b h Firebreak—On The Brink (Mind Games)
1610^{2} 3290^{10} 4509^{7} 5043^{10}

Hot Spice *John Dunlop* 88
3 b g Kodiac—Harlestone Lady (Shaamit (IRE))
2838^{6} (3545) ◆ 4367^{8} 5015^{5} (5804) 6607^{2} 7017^{12}

Hot Spot (FR) *S Cerulis* a72 82
7 b g Kahyasi—Hokey Pokey (FR) (Lead On Time (USA))
7314a^{6}

Hot Sugar (USA) *Kevin Ryan* 84
2 b g Lemon Drop Kid(USA) —Plaisir Des Yeux (FR) (Funambule (USA))
(3452) ◆ 5061^{2} 5886^{4} 6524^{9}

Hot Toddie *James Given* a9 32
3 b f Firebreak—Bebe De Cham (Tragic Role (USA))
2781^{8} 3385^{10}

Hot Tub *Christine Dunnett* a41
3 b g Iceman—Starminda (Zamindar (USA))
4163^{12} 7585^{6} 7750^{5}

House Limit (IRE) *Harry Dunlop* a57 47
2 br c Red Clubs(IRE) —Fritillary (Vettori (IRE))
2817^{5} 3308^{9} 4319^{6} 6817^{10} 7342^{4} 7635^{3}

House Of Mirrors (USA) *John Gosden*
3 b c Medaglia D'Oro(USA) —Thousand Thrills (USA) (Crafty Prospector (USA))
7921^{6}

House Of Rules *Julie Camacho* a24 55
4 b g Forzando—Bramble Bear (Beveled (USA))
291^{8} 574^{9}

Houston Dynimo (IRE) *Nicky Richards* a76 74
6 b g Rock Of Gibraltar(IRE) —Quiet Mouse (USA) (Quiet American (USA))
68^{6} 1243^{7} (1798) 2251^{2} 2636^{2} 3316^{5} 4360^{10}

How Sweet It Is (IRE) *James Bethell* a63 62
2 b f Kodiac—Yaqootah (USA) (Gone West (USA))
2070^{7} 2542^{8} 7056^{7} 7925^{3}

Howyadoingnotsobad (IRE) *Karen George* a62 56
3 b g Kodiac—Beau Petite (Kyllachy)
2141^{4} 4863^{4} 5346^{4} 5917^{10} (6176) 6655^{5} 7201^{4} 7567^{6}

Huangdi (FR) *M Boutin* a82 82
5 b g Slickly(FR) —Lady Nora (FR) (Warrshan (USA))
195a^{7}

Hubood *Clive Brittain* a52
3 b f Refuse To Bend(IRE) —Shuheb (Nashwan (USA))
[illegible]

Huff And Puff *Amanda Perrett* a81 85
4 b g Azamour(IRE) —Coyote (Indian Ridge)
(1450) ◆ 2686^{4} 2931^{12} 5266^{3} 5685^{2} 6103^{7} 6749^{7} 7120^{6}

Hugely Exciting *J S Moore* a87 76
3 b c Bahamian Bounty—Princess Louise (Efisio)
258a^{4} 370a^{0} 532a^{7} 616a^{6} 916^{2} 1329^{2} (1865) 2684^{9} 3815^{10} 5392^{6} 5735^{5} (6120) 6794^{3} 6944^{4}

Hujaylea (IRE) *M Halford* a87 110
9 b g Almutawakel—Red Eagle (IRE) (Eagle Eyed (USA))
152a^{2} 332a^{6} 415a^{3} 587a^{4} 682a^{7} 3444a^{8} 4116a^{3} 4418a^{7} 4978a^{4} 5746a^{2}

Hulcote Rose (IRE) *Sylvester Kirk* a97 74
4 b m Rock Of Gibraltar(IRE) —Siksikawa (Mark Of Esteem (IRE))
92a^{6}

Huma Bird *Mahmood Al Zarooni* 80
2 b f Invincible Spirit(IRE) —Persian Secret (FR) (Persian Heights)
2227^{6} (2718) 3014^{15} 5961^{4}

Humdrum *Richard Hannon* a93 101
3 b f Dr Fong(USA) —Spinning Top (Alzao (USA))
(2607) 3034^{5} 5277^{6} 5958a^{4}

Hume (NZ) *David Brideoake & David Feek* 102
8 b g Zabeel(NZ) —Lolette (Arazi (USA))
6967a^{9}

Humidor (IRE) *George Baker* a91 113
4 b g Camacho—Miss Indigo (Indian Ridge)
613^{7} 1166^{12} (1680) 2525^{5} 3644^{3} 4468^{5} (5827) 6906a^{5}

Humor Me Rene (USA) *George Baker* a70 78
4 bb m Kitten's Joy(USA) —Star Of Humor (USA) (Distorted Humor (USA))
808^{7} 879^{2} (2195) 3141^{3}

Humungosaur *Paul Cole* 95
2 b c Red Ransom(USA) —Fabulously Fast (USA) (Deputy Minister (CAN))
4352^{4} 4995^{4} 5365a^{3} 6572^{3} 6970^{3}

Humungous (IRE) *Charles Egerton* a70 87
8 ch g Giant's Causeway(USA) —Doula (USA) (Gone West (USA))
54^{6} 272^{5} 621^{8} 954^{7}

Hung Parliament (FR) *Tom Dascombe* a80 107
3 b g Numerous(USA) —Sensational Mover (USA) (Theatrical)
1552a^{11} 2139a^{13} 7023^{9} 7234^{5}

Hungry Island (USA) *Claude McGaughey III* 110
3 b f More Than Ready(USA) —Flying Passage (USA) (A.P. Indy (USA))
6183a^{4}

Hunt A Mistress (IRE) *Paul Cole* 55
2 ch f Teofilo(IRE) —Arctic Hunt (IRE) (Bering)
7025^{9}

Hunter Forward (AUS) *Luca Cumani* 81
5 ch m Galileo(IRE) —Ooh Gorgeous Me (USA) (Williamstown (USA))
(4448) ◆ (4716) 5440^{3} 6632^{2} 6996^{5}

Hunters' Glen (USA) *Doug Watson* a67 97
8 b h Bahri(USA) —Hedera (USA) (Woodman (USA))
707a^{3}

Hunter's Light (IRE) *Saeed Bin Suroor* a109 116
3 ch c Dubawi(IRE) —Portmanteau (Barathea (IRE))
(2469) 3068^{8} (4015) 4411^{3} 5182^{6} (6247) (7391)

Huntingfortreasure *Philip Kirby* 77
4 b g Pastoral Pursuits—Treasure Trove (USA) (The Minstrel (CAN))
5648^{7} 6295^{14} 6536^{8}

Hunting Gonk *James Given* a23 69
2 b c Amadeus Wolf—Para Siempre (Mujahid (USA))
6048^{8} 6644^{2} 7066^{4}

Hunting Tower *J J Lambe* a86 76
7 b g Sadler's Wells(USA) —Fictitious (Machiavellian (USA))
(6451) 7163^{4}

Hunting Tower (SAF) *M F De Kock* a107 105
9 ch g Fort Wood(USA) —Stirrup Cup (SAF) (Royal Chalice (SAF))
152a^{15} 242^{7} 417a^{4} (498a) 676a^{4} 824a^{6}

Hunza Dancer (IRE) *John Gosden* 92
3 b f Danehill Dancer(IRE) —Hawala (IRE) (Warning)
1060^{3} (1540) 2018^{3}

Hurakan (IRE) *George Baker* a79 76
5 gr g Daylami(IRE) —Gothic Dream (IRE) (Nashwan (USA))
2378^{7} 2872^{2} 3844^{6} 4385^{6} 6023^{7} 6592^{8}

Hurler And Farmer (IRE) *Richard Fahey* a77
2 b g Red Clubs(IRE) —Undercover Glamour (USA) (Kingmambo (USA))
7142^{3} (7422)

Hurlingham *Michael Easterby* a77 73
7 b g Halling(USA) —Society (IRE) (Barathea (IRE))
1491^{9} 2388^{12} 2804^{4} 3574^{5} 4173^{4} 4612^{2} 4902^{3} 6775^{4}

Hurricane Emerald (IRE) *Mark Johnston* 66
2 b g Hurricane Run(IRE) —Love Emerald (USA) (Mister Baileys)
3382^{3} 3823^{12} 4201^{5} 6460^{3} 6911^{14}

Hurricane Guest *George Margarson* 16
3 ch g Hurricane Run(IRE) —Figlette (Darshaan)
4279^{13}

Hurricane Havoc (IRE) *J S Bolger* a83 100
3 b f Hurricane Run(IRE) —Cheeky Madam (IRE) (Night Shift (USA))
1006a^{7} 1928a^{7} 4133a^{8} 5748a^{19} 6362a^{3}

Hurricane Higgins (IRE) *Mark Johnston* a90 105
3 b g Hurricane Run(IRE) —Mare Aux Fees (Kenmare (FR))
(95) ◆ 882a^{2} 1895^{2} 2341a^{7} 3105^{8} 3772^{4} 4411^{6}

Hurricane Hymnbook (USA) *Willie Musson* a76 62
6 b g Pulpit(USA) —April Squall (USA) (Summer Squall (USA))
6938^{11} (7387) 7601^{8} 7831^{4}

Hurricane In Dubai (IRE) *Denis Coakley* a76
2 ch g Hurricane Run(IRE) —In Dubai (USA) (Giant's Causeway (USA))
7521^{2}

Hurricane Lady (IRE) *Walter Swinburn* a70 85
3 b f Hurricane Run(IRE) —Yaria (IRE) (Danehill (USA))
1579^{2} 1986^{7} (2550) (3312) 3918^{2} 4807^{2} 5892^{11}

Hurricane Spear *Gary Moore* a40 41
3 ch g Hurricane Run(IRE) —Sarissa (USA) (Diesis)
1836^{15} 2307^{6} 3393^{9}

Hurricane Spirit (IRE) *Terry Clement* a83 81
7 b g Invincible Spirit(IRE) —Gale Warning (IRE) (Last Tycoon)
3045^{11} 3982^{5} 4616^{8} 4860^{4} 5894^{13} 6220^{8} 6797^{6} 7130^{3} (7513) 7601^{9} 7831^{7}

Hurricane Thomas (IRE) *Karen Tutty* a61 64
7 b g Celtic Swing—Viola Royale (IRE) (Royal Academy (USA))
2991^{11} 3637^{7} 3938^{13} 4408^{7} 4499^{8} 5178^{5} 5485^{7} 6235^{2} 6870^{15} 7032^{10} 7112^{9}

Hurriya *Saeed Bin Suroor* a47
2 b f Invincible Spirit(IRE) —Adonita (Singspiel (IRE))
6612^{5} 7058^{12}

Hurry Up George *Ralph Beckett* a83
2 b g Intikhab(USA) —Digamist Girl (IRE) (Digamist (USA))
7593^{2} (7906)

Hursley Hope (IRE) *David Elsworth* a45 55
3 b f Barathea(IRE) —Hendrina (IRE) (Daylami (IRE))
2019^{7} 2469^{9} 2840^{10} 7387^{10} 7750^{4}

Huwayit (IRE) *Clive Brittain* a72 14
3 ch f Dalakhani(IRE) —Matin De Tempete (FR) (Cardoun (FR))
5999^{3} 6459^{11} 6796^{5} 6997^{12} 7542^{11} 7839^{7}

Huygens *Denis Coakley* a98 99
4 b g Zafeen(FR) —Lindfield Belle (IRE) (Fairy King (USA))
1760^{4} (2509)

Huzzah (IRE) *Paul Howling* a66 91
6 b g Acclamation—Borders Belle (IRE) (Pursuit Of Love)
1603[7] 2310[5] 2876[3] 3290[5] 4215[4] 4921[5] 5495[6] 7532[7] 7637[10] 7857[11]

Hydrant *Peter Salmon* a81 81
5 b g Haafhd—Spring (Sadler's Wells (USA))
772[2] 1098[6] 1874[2] 3544[7] 3828[17] 4294[5] 5036[9] 6507[10] 7215[13] 7425[6] 7604[3] 7930[3]

Hygrove Gal *Bryan Smart* a31 68
3 b f Auction House(USA) —Vida (IRE) (Wolfhound (USA))
2736[4] 3143[9] 6454[3] 6889[7] 7100[12]

Hygrove Welshlady (IRE) *J W Hills* a74 73
3 b f Langfuhr(CAN) —Milwaukee (FR) (Desert King (IRE))
1767[4] 2175[4] 3267[8] 4686[3] 5302[3] 6037[3] 6493[2] (6585) 6775[3] 7255[2] 7458[7]

Hyperlink (IRE) *Mark Johnston* 76
2 b g Cape Cross(IRE) —Surf The Web (IRE) (Ela-Mana-Mou)
2181[10] 4535[9] 5536[2] 5875[2] 6187[5]

Hypnosis *Noel Wilson* a70 81
8 b m Mind Games—Salacious (Sallust)
62[4] 231[6] 696[2] 1555[6] 1796[5] (3579) 4504[7] 5720[9] 6265[3] 6537[6]

Hypnotic Gaze (IRE) *Andrew Haynes* a77 59
5 b g Chevalier(IRE) —Red Trance (IRE) (Soviet Star (USA))
3559[4]

Hysterical (USA) *A Fabre* a60
3 b f Distorted Humor(USA) —Tout Charmant (USA) (Slewvescent (USA))
775a[6]

I Am That (IRE) *Mme L Braem* a76 78
4 b g Statue Of Liberty(USA) —Victory Again (IRE) (Victory Note (USA))
3568a[0]

I B A Gee Gee *Tony Newcombe* a33
2 b c Proclamation(IRE) —Elvina (Mark Of Esteem (IRE))
6725[16] 7482[6] 7670[4]

Ibelieveinmiracles (IRE) *Paul A Roche* a66 64
4 b m Invincible Spirit(IRE) —Catfoot Lane (Batshoof)
1420a[9]

Iberian Rock *Ann Duffield* 53
2 b f Rock Of Gibraltar(IRE) —Karsiyaka (IRE) (Kahyasi)
4232[11] 5464[12] 6047[7] 6911[12]

Ibicenco (GER) *J Hirschberger* 113
3 b c Shirocco(GER) —Iberi (GER) (Rainbow Quest (USA))
2341a[3] 2979a[2] 3672a[8] 5771a[3] 6396a[2]

Ibiza Sunset (IRE) *Brendan Powell* a73 76
3 b g Chineur(FR) —Romanylei (IRE) (Blues Traveller (IRE))
2723[8] 3392[6] 4320[3] 4908[3] 5731[3] 6089[9] 6944[7] 7817[8]

I Bloody Do (FR) *Rod Collet* 79
3 b f Tiger Hill(IRE) —Trazando (Forzando)
7667a[0]

Ibrox (IRE) *Alan Brown* a37 73
6 b g Mujahid(USA) —Ling Lane (Slip Anchor)
7506[4] 7858[8]

Ibsaar *William Haggas* a79 80
3 gr g Red Ransom(USA) —Mosquera (GER) (Acatenango (GER))
907[4] 1313[3] 1727[7] 3044[5]

Ibtahaj *Saeed Bin Suroor* 71
2 b c Invincible Spirit(IRE) —Maroussies Wings (IRE) (In The Wings)
6447[3]

Ice Angel *Derek Shaw*
3 b f Iceman—Someone's Angel (USA) (Runaway Groom (CAN))
5[6] 110[12]

Iceblast *Michael Easterby* 86
3 b g Iceman—Medici Princess (Medicean)
1246[7] 1543[2] (1697) 2003[3] 2319[3] 2935[5] 3830[7] 4349[13] 4561[10] 5006[7] 5370[6] 5760[14] 6234[5]

Ice Box (USA) *Nicholas Zito* a117
4 ch h Pulpit(USA) —Spice Island (USA) (Tabasco Cat (USA))
7308a[8]

Icebuster *Rod Millman* a65 89
3 ch g Iceman—Radiate (Sadler's Wells (USA))
110[4] ◆ 2582[5] 3133[2] (3633) 4447[6] 4914[3] 5560[2] (5893) 6409[5]

Ice Cold Bex *Philip McBride* a58 73
3 ch g Iceman—Musica (Primo Dominie)
2472[3] 3133[9] 7137[8] 7427[2] 7600[6] 7840[2] 7890[4]

Ice Cool (FR) *W Hefter* 103
2 b c Lateral—Indianapolis (GER) (Tiger Hill (IRE))
6660a[3] 7192a[9]

Iced Opal *Michael Blanshard* a69 69
2 ch f Iceman—Marysienka (Primo Dominie)
2718[6] 4052[7] 4662[4] 5689[4] 6293[3]

Ice Girl *Michael Easterby* 54
3 b f Iceman—Descriptive (IRE) (Desert King (IRE))
2782[8] 3248[9]

Icelandic *Frank Sheridan* a89 93
9 b g Selkirk(USA) —Icicle (Polar Falcon (USA))
1067[3] 1467[7] 2000[13] 6209[4]

Ice Loch *Michael Blanshard* a52 56
2 gr c Avonbridge—Bountiful (Pivotal)
3288[10] 4007[9] 4708[3] 5409[9] 7035[10] 7196[8] 7514[4] 7937[5]

Ice Missile *Sylvester Kirk* 57
2 br f One Cool Cat(USA) —Exorcet (FR) (Selkirk (USA))
4052[6] 4427[12]

Ice Nelly (IRE) *Hughie Morrison* a68 71
3 b f Iceman—Dancing Nelly (Shareef Dancer (USA))
2197[4] 2550[3] ◆ 2964[3] (3912) 4584[4] 5428[7] 6799[4] (7112) 7413[9]

Iceni Girl *John Gosden* a74 92
2 b f Iceman—Mini Mosa (Indian Ridge)
1657[5] 2187[4] 2882[2] 3520[2] (4245) 5873a[4]

Ice On Fire *Philip McBride* a63
2 b f Iceman—Bluebelle (Generous (IRE))
7344[5]

Ice Road Trucker (IRE) *Jim Boyle* a58 40
4 ch g Bertolini(USA) —Bye Bold Aileen (IRE) (Warning)
30[2] (164) 299[3]

Ice Trooper *Linda Stubbs* a80 78
3 b g Iceman—Out Like Magic (Magic Ring (IRE))
2405[3] 3189[6] 3628[4] 4669[2] 5115[7] 6044[12] 6456[9] (6929) 7519[2] 7596[10]

Icon Dream (IRE) *David Simcock* 104
4 b g Sadler's Wells(USA) —Silver Skates (IRE) (Slip Anchor)
1416[2] 1808[7] 2289[7] 3396[7] 3875[6] 4532[2]

I Confess *Geoffrey Harker* a78 71
6 br g Fantastic Light(USA) —Vadsagreya (FR) (Linamix (FR))
96[2] (213) 334[6] 556[3] (590) 633[2] (761) (816) 956[6] 1021[2] 1250[2] (1295) (1805a) (2206) (2382) 3934[3] 4440[8] 4679[6] 7465[2] 7625[3] 7823[4]

Icy Blue *Richard Whitaker* 80
3 b g Iceman—Bridal Path (Groom Dancer (USA))
1108[11] 1624[9] 2834[3] 3318[2] 4560[2] (4813) (5109) 5621[6] 6830[2]

Icy River (FR) *P Monfort* a61 61
6 gr g Verglas(IRE) —River Sans Retour (FR) (Vacarme (USA))
843a[6]

Ida Inkley (IRE) *Jonathan Portman* 59
2 b f One Cool Cat(USA) —Tara Too (IRE) (Danetime (IRE))
1441[10] 1946[6] 2241[3] 2919[5]

Idarah (USA) *Paul Cashman* 86
8 gr g Aljabr(USA) —Fatina (Nashwan (USA))
3420a[6]

Ideal *David Wachman* a56 80
3 b f Galileo(IRE) —Tarfah (USA) (Kingmambo (USA))
5748a[10]

Idealism *Micky Hammond* 73
4 b g Motivator—Fickle (Danehill (USA))
1038[5] 1460[5] 2393[11] 2988[8] 3701[6] 4077[9] 6028[9] 6453[13]

Ideechic (FR) *D Allard* 94
2 b f Chichicastenango(FR) —Princess Petardia (IRE) (Petardia)
5130a[8]

Ideology *Mario Hofer* a98 99
5 b g Oasis Dream—Kid Gloves (In The Wings)
1011a[4] 6339[9] 7409a[12]

Idiom (IRE) *David Simcock* 82
3 ch f Iffraaj—Alexander Confranc (IRE) (Magical Wonder (USA))
1844[6] 2690[6] 3390[10]

Idler (IRE) *Mark Johnston* 77
2 b g Exceed And Excel(AUS) —Dilly Dally (AUS) (Rubiton (AUS))
1071[4] 6099[2] 6380[3] 6629[2] (7072)

Idol Deputy (FR) *Mark Usher* a60
5 gr g Silver Deputy(CAN) —Runaway Venus (USA) (Runaway Groom (CAN))
408[2] 552[3] 773[2] 969[4] 1374[4] 2308[15] 7466[2] 7571[3] 7741[3] (7787) 7892[2]

Idols Eye *Richard Hannon* a70 68
2 b f Red Ransom(USA) —Whoopsie (Unfuwain (USA))
4052[9] 4662[8] 5320[4] 5814[3] (6026) 7135[13]

I Dreamed A Dream *Dean Ivory* a24
3 b f Tobougg(IRE) —Janaah (In The Wings)
47[9] 297[6]

I Dream Of Genie *Peter Winkworth* 53
2 b f Desert Style(IRE) —April Lee (Superpower)
1932[5] 2556[6]

Idyllic Star (IRE) *J S Moore* a61 71
2 ch f Choisir(AUS) —Idolize (Polish Precedent (USA))
3812[5] ◆ 5320[5]

I Feel Fine *Alan Kirtley* a46 35
8 ch m Minster Son—Jendorcet (Grey Ghost)
1792[5]

Iffraam (IRE) *Michael Dods* 76
2 br c Iffraaj—Madamaa (IRE) (Alzao (USA))
2617[2] ◆ 7293[11]

If I Were A Boy (IRE) *Dominic Ffrench Davis* a80 83
4 b m Invincible Spirit(IRE) —Attymon Lill (IRE) (Marju (IRE))
2378[6] 2771[4] 3538[4] 4008[2] 5545[8] 6005[2] 6306[7] 7328[7]

If Paradise *Charles Coakley* a73 71
10 b g Compton Place—Sunley Stars (Sallust)
6139a[4]

If Per Chance (IRE) *M Halford* a84 96
6 b g Danetime(IRE) —Zafaraya (IRE) (Ashkalani (IRE))
7150a[4] 7618a[6] 7793a[4]

If What And Maybe *John Ryan* a62 63
3 ch g Needwood Blade—Pink Champagne (Cosmonaut)
3922[6] 4181[3] 4476[6] 4800[7] 5042[2] 5636[2] 6122[3] 6936[3] (7085) 7144[7] 7387[11] 7441[13]

If You Whisper (IRE) *Mike Murphy* a77 49
3 b g Iffraaj—Little Whisper (IRE) (Be My Guest (USA))
101[2] 5635[11] 6477[8] 7204[5] 7601[4] 7771[8] 7901[6]

Ignatieff (IRE) *Linda Stubbs* a57 84
4 b g Fasliyev(USA) —Genial Jenny (IRE) (Danehill (USA))
1073[8] 1539[11] 2048[5] 2304[5] 2667[6] 4988[7] 5552[6] 6655[10] 7086[11]

I Got Music *Keith Reveley* 49
4 gr m Silver Patriarch(IRE) —I Got Rhythm (Lycius (USA))
1153[7] 1458[7] 7075[8]

I Got You Babe (IRE) *Richard Guest* a66 65
3 gr f Clodovil(IRE) —Duck Over (Warning)
3207[2] 3489[3] ◆ 3571[4] 4518[11] 4729[2] 5009[2] 5244[3] 5506[3] 5859[3] 6190[8] 6208[4]

Igoyougo *Noel Wilson* 83
5 b g Millkom—Club Oasis (Forzando)
4678[7] 5148[13] 5720[4] 6537[2] 7106[4]

Iguacu *George Baker* a61 58
7 b g Desert Prince(IRE) —Gay Gallanta (USA) (Woodman (USA))
115[4] 409[4] 862[2] 943[9] 1987[10] 2451[3] (2685) 3256[7] 3637[10]

Iguazu Falls (USA) *M bin Shafya* a65 98
6 ch g Pivotal—Anna Palariva (IRE) (Caerleon (USA))
415a[4] 503a[8] 682a[6]

I Hate To Lose (USA) *Philip McBride* a57 62
3 b f Medaglia D'Oro(USA) —My Alibi (USA) (Sheikh Albadou)
1853[5] 2192[8] 2853[7] 4911[10] 5515[15]

Ihsas (USA) *Saeed Bin Suroor* a83 85
2 ch f Rahy(USA) —Express Way (ARG) (Ahmad (ARG))
(5813) ◆ 6466[3]

Ihtiraam (IRE) *Saeed Bin Suroor* 79
2 b f Teofilo(IRE) —Park Romance (IRE) (Dr Fong (USA))
(6758)

Il Battista *Alan McCabe* a90 68
3 b g Medicean—Peace (Sadler's Wells (USA))
106[2] 254[4] 468[5] 1202[8] 1384[9] 4234[8] 4527[4] 5338[5] 5718[9] 6133[12] (6616) 7500[3] 7727[2] (7771)

Ile De Re (FR) *Ian Williams* 99
5 gr g Linamix(FR) —Ile Mamou (IRE) (Ela-Mana-Mou)
3156[6] (4775) 5271[4] 5705[12] 6661a[7] 7297[U]

Il Grande Maurizio (IRE) *A Al Raihe* a96 102
7 b h King Charlemagne(USA) —Ciubanga (IRE) (Arazi (USA))
152a[10] 236[12] 501a[13]

Ilie Nastase (FR) *Conor Dore* a82 80
7 b g Royal Applause—Flying Diva (Chief Singer)
82[6] 188[3] 206[6] 308[3] 562[3] 685[7] 806[5] 938[5] 1198[4] 3130[10] 3468[3] 3636[3] 3677[4] 6355[8] 6624[5] 6871[5] 7003[7] 7122[6]

Ilissos (USA) *Jeremy Noseda* a67
3 b g Mineshaft(USA) —Ema Bovary (CHI) (Edgy Diplomat (USA))
339[3] 591[3] 731[2] 789[4] 1442[7] 2381[2]

Illandrane (IRE) *Ed Dunlop* a29 75
3 b f Cape Cross(IRE) —Lalindi (IRE) (Cadeaux Genereux)
1836[10] 4923[6]

Illaunglass (IRE) *Jeremy Noseda* a77 98
2 b f Red Clubs(IRE) —Esterlina (IRE) (Highest Honor (FR))
(2641) 3104[3] 3821[6] 4803[8]

Illawalla *Hugh McWilliams* 46
3 b g Indesatchel(IRE) —Adorable Cherub (USA) (Halo (USA))
1971[6] 2350[5] 5082[10] 5165[10] 7198[12] 7610[13]

I'll Be Good *Robert Johnson* 81
2 b c Red Clubs(IRE) —Willisa (Polar Falcon (USA))
3398[6] 3826[12] 4283[2] 4557[2] 5077[3] 5438[6] 5756[5] 5786[4] (6207) 6524[8] (6863) 7103[2]

I'Lldoit *Michael Scudamore* a60 16
4 br g Tamayaz(CAN) —Club Oasis (Forzando)
539[3] 797[3] 1582[10] 2237[11] 3235[8]

Illo (GER) *Bart Cummings* 109
5 b h Tertullian(USA) —Iora (GER) (Konigsstuhl (GER))
(1128a) 3334a[2] 7043a[3] 7218a[19]

Illuminative (USA) *Zoe Davison* a60 70
5 b g Point Given(USA) —Pretty Clear (USA) (Mr Prospector (USA))
361[7] 722[4] 809[6] 862[10] 2386[8] 2449[4] 2638[5] 3769[6]

Illusio (FR) *D Smaga* a69 70
4 b m Voix Du Nord(FR) —Celere (FR) (Kabool)
1033a[9]

Illustration (IRE) *Mark Johnston* a47 71
3 b c Pivotal—In Anticipation (IRE) (Sadler's Wells (USA))
5443[8] 5792[4] 6242[8] 6613[5] ◆ 6872[10] (7077)

Illustrious Forest *John Mackie* a49 59
3 ch c Shinko Forest(IRE) —Illustre Inconnue (USA) (Septieme Ciel (USA))
2119[6] 2677[8] 5912[12] 6845[5] (7931)

Illustrious Lad (IRE) *Jim Boyle* a66 21
2 ch g Bertolini(USA) —Squeak (Selkirk (USA))
1268[9] 2640[4] 3917[12] 4661[6] 7530[4] 7597[6] 7830[9] 7937[6]

Illustrious Prince (IRE) *Declan Carroll* a88 85
4 b g Acclamation—Sacred Love (IRE) (Barathea (IRE))
1205[7] 1695[4] 2398[3] 3028[10] 3880[12] 4107[3] 4349[5] 4670[6] 5083[5] 5760[2] (5924) 6081[7] 7076[6]

I Love Loup (FR) *M Boutin* a76 78
7 ch g Loup Solitaire(USA) —Kaldona (FR) (Kaldoun (FR))
395a[10] (1142a)

I Love Me *Andrew Balding* 108
3 b f Cape Cross(IRE) —Garanciere (FR) (Anabaa (USA))
1719[9] 2106[2] 3106[4]

Il Pazzo *Mike Murphy* 68
2 b c Multiplex—Nut (IRE) (Fasliyev (USA))
3429[7] 4201[10] 4815[3] ◆ 5697[7] 6921[8]

I'm A Celebrity *Marco Botti* a48 54
3 ch c Peintre Celebre(USA) —Zoom Lens (IRE) (Caerleon (USA))
878[5] 1311[9] 1950[11] 2571[7]

I'm A Doughnut *Tom Dascombe* a25 55
2 b g Piccolo—Fizzy Treat (Efisio)
4575[5] 5161[12] 6045[4] 6627[17] 7353[5]

I'm A Dreamer (IRE) *David Simcock* 115
4 b m Noverre(USA) —Summer Dreams (IRE) (Sadler's Wells (USA))
(1718) ◆ 3030[5] 3822[6] 6338[4] 6909a[2]

Imaginary Diva *George Margarson* a32 69
5 b m Lend A Hand—Distant Diva (Distant Relative)
1248[9] 1938[2] 2755[2] 3015[7] 3307[4] 3556[6] (3939) 4615[2] (4930) 5326[3] (5517) 6119[4] 6580[7]

Imaginary World (IRE) *Alan McCabe* a73 84
3 b f Exceed And Excel(AUS) —Plutonia (Sadler's Wells (USA))
254[7] 365[2] 540[4] 1327[6] 1768[2] 2018[2] 2229[4] 2615[2] 3310[4] 3586[3] 4093[2] 4265[5] 4429[3] 5056[3] 5255[5] 5684[6] (6093) 6383[7]

Imagine This *E J O'Neill* 41
2 b f Excellent Art—Creative Mind (IRE) (Danehill Dancer (IRE))
7813a[8]

Imagining (USA) *Claude McGaughey III* 115
3 ch c Giant's Causeway(USA) —Daydreaming (USA) (A.P. Indy (USA))
7572a[2]

Imasci *Manfred Hofer* a85 82
4 ch h Medicean—She's Classy (USA) (Boundary (USA))
1011a[6]

Imazagan (FR) *C Baillet* 86
2 ch f Muhaymin(USA) —Voliere (USA) (Arctic Tern (USA))
7813a[9]

Imbongi (SAF) *M F De Kock* a115 117
7 ch g Russian Revival(USA) —Garden Verse (SAF) (Foveros)
156a[2] 501a[3] 997a[13]

Imelda Mayhem *J S Moore* 82
2 ch f Byron—Halland Park Girl (IRE) (Primo Dominie)
2644[4] 2901[3] (3680) 4551[4] ◆ 5052[9] (5427) 5708[2] 6535[5] 7028[14]

Ime Not Bitter *Bill Moore* a45 10
3 b g Needwood Blade—Gymcrak Flyer (Aragon)
4715[6] 5248[11] 5606[12]

I'm Harry *Charles Hills* a69 71
2 b c Haafhd—First Approval (Royal Applause)
4996[8] 5384[10] 6308[4] 6753[5] 7157[3] 7494[6]

I'm Jake (NZ) *David Brideoake & David Feek* 102
6 ch g Pins(AUS) —Venetian Court (NZ) (Pompeii Court (USA))
6967a[8]

Imjin River (IRE) *Mark H Tompkins* a56 75
4 b g Namid—Lady Nasrana (FR) (Al Nasr (FR))
2645[11] 3179[11] 3617[4] 3956[3] 4206[10] 5138[5] 5387[8] 5640[11] 6939[P]

Immortal Verse (IRE) *Robert Collet* 123
3 b f Pivotal—Side Of Paradise (IRE) (Sadler's Wells (USA))
2137a[11] (2752a) (3106) (5129a) 6860[3]

Imogen Louise (IRE) *Richard Guest* a65 69
3 gr f Verglas(IRE) —Strina (IRE) (Indian Ridge)
179[7] (263) 349[5] 423[5] 7567[12] 7748[8]

Impassive *Ed McMahon* 76
2 ch f Choisir(AUS) —Frigid (Indian Ridge)
3092[2] (3639) 4094[18] 6827[6]

Impel (IRE) *Richard Hannon* a74 72
2 b c Excellent Art—Tencarola (IRE) (Night Shift (USA))
6244[7] 6725[3] 7126[4]

Imperator Augustus (IRE) *Patrick Holmes* a79 93
3 b g Holy Roman Emperor(IRE) —Coralita (IRE) (Night Shift (USA))
1880[6] 2256[10] 3124[4] (3621) 5722[2] ◆ (6382) ◆

Imperial Djay (IRE) *Ruth Carr* a66 99
6 b g Dilshaan—Slayjay (IRE) (Mujtahid (USA))
1109[4] 1560[3] (1696) (1854) 2495[8] 2706[7] 3134[10] 3315[8] (3397) 3862[13] 4049[5] 4314[10] ◆ 4802[14] 6148[11]

Imperial Elegance *Mick Channon* 32
2 b f Imperial Dancer—Canadian Capers (Ballacashtal (CAN))
6160[13]

Imperiale Noire (FR) *R Laplanche* a66 54
3 b f Avonbridge—Haabina (Erhaab (USA))
7667a[10]

Imperial Fong *Chris Dwyer* a56 54
3 b f Dr Fong(USA) —Chine (Inchinor)
212[3] 406[8] 760[5] 909[7] 1566[7] 3709[11] 4728[5] 5118[3] 5350[3] 5784[7] 6122[12] (6482) 6823[8] 7608[2]

Imperial Guest *George Margarson* 103
5 ch g Imperial Dancer—Princess Speedfit (FR) (Desert Prince (IRE))
(1888) 3155[13] 3841[5] 4314[8] ◆ 4802[5] 6035[3] 6521[7] 6862[6]

Imperial Order (IRE) *Richard Hannon* 73
2 b c Excellent Art—Sao Gabriel (IRE) (Persian Bold)
5254[7] 5851[8] 6267[7]

Imperial Pippin (USA) *John Gosden* 104
3 b f Empire Maker(USA) —Apple Of Kent (USA) (Kris S (USA))
(1363) ◆ 2189[3] 2839[2] 4099[4] 4915[5] 6269[2]

Imperial Rome (IRE) *David Wachman* a106 109
3 b c Holy Roman Emperor(IRE) —Ripalong (IRE) (Revoque (IRE))
2139a[7] 2533a[4]

Imperial Stargazer *Mick Channon* 68
2 gr g Imperial Dancer—Sky Light Dreams (Dreams To Reality (USA))
6165[11] 6462[7] 6726[7] 7259[7] 7763[14]

Imperial Unity (USA) *Sir Henry Cecil*
3 b c Empire Maker(USA) —Dokki (USA) (Northern Dancer (CAN))
3001[15]

Imperial Waltzer *George Moore* 55
3 gr g Imperial Dancer—Sky Light Dreams (Dreams To Reality (USA))
6153[8]

Imperial Weapon (IRE) *John Spearing* a14 30
2 ch f Majestic Missile(IRE) —Regal Lustre (Averti (IRE))
1441[12] 1791[6] 2919[4] 4702[6] 5099[7] 5833[8] 6540[13]

Impostor (GER) *W Figge* 97
3 b c Motivator—Indian Jewel (GER) (Local Suitor (USA))
2345a[6] 4599a[5]

Imprimis Tagula (IRE) *Alan Bailey* a89 83
7 b g Tagula(IRE) —Strelitzia (IRE) (Bluebird (USA))
2633[4] 2917[6] 3036[4] 3162[7] 5322[9] 5425[6]

Impulse Dancer *John Bridger*
3 b f Bertolini(USA) —Galatrix (Be My Guest (USA))
1682[11]

I'm So Glad *Mick Channon* 77
2 b f Clodovil(IRE) —Dilag (IRE) (Almutawakel)
4263 [3] (4823)

Im Spartacus *Ian Williams* a70 59
9 b g Namaqualand(USA) —Captivating (IRE) (Wolfhound (USA))
2654[2] 3072[4] 3712[2] 3951[3]

I'm Still The Man (IRE) *Bill Turner* a66 72
2 b c Acclamation—Kapera (FR) (Linamix (FR))
(2644) 3014[19] 3284[4] 3745[4] 5562[11] 7694[2] 7798[6]

I'm Super Too (IRE) *Alan Swinbank* a70 89
4 b g Fasliyev(USA) —Congress (IRE) (Dancing Brave (USA))
1292[4] 1859[5] 2388[13] 4361[3] (4543) 4877[3] (5205) (5314) 5722[9] 6290[7]

I'm Talking (IRE) *David Evans* 18
2 ch f Chineur(FR) —Dianella (IRE) (Gold Away (IRE))
1563[4] 2556[7] 4193[5]

Imvula (AUS) *M bin Shafya* a86 76
7 br g Rock Of Gibraltar(IRE) —African Rain (AUS) (Woodman (USA))
328a[13]

In A Jiffy (IRE) *David Barron* 41
2 b f Iffraaj—Beginners Luck (IRE) (Key Of Luck (USA))
2761[5] 3082[10] 4012[6] 4943[12] 5555[8]

In A Nutshell (IRE) *C Byrnes* a71 75
4 b g Xaar—Trilemma (Slip Anchor)
7002[4]

In Babylon (GER) *Ann Duffield* a63 47
3 b g Oasis Dream—Ice Dream (GER) (Mondrian (GER))
1108[12] 1483[3] 1869[5] 3729[4]

Inbaileysfootsteps (IRE) *E J O'Neill* 65
2 b f Footstepsinthesand—Miss Bali Dancer (IRE) (Mister Baileys)
7666a[0]

Inca Blue *Tim Easterby* a46 59
3 ch g Indian Haven—Gold And Blue (IRE) (Bluebird (USA))
1945[2] 2166[7] 2465[3] 3124[5] 4111[6] 4812[4] 5433[2] 5619[4] 5787[6]

Inca Chief *Ann Duffield* a30 54
3 b g Sleeping Indian—Queen Of Havana (USA) (King Of Kings (IRE))
1437[8] 1749[10]

Incendiary (IRE) *Hugo Palmer* a52
2 b c Excellent Art—Clytha (Mark Of Esteem (IRE))
7248[5]

Incendo *James Fanshawe* a91 92
5 ch g King's Best(USA) —Kindle (Selkirk (USA))
1651[2] 2066[2] 2884[5] 3580[2] 4555[5] 5837[2] 6528[5] 6989[3] 7328[8]

Inchando (FR) *Tony Carroll* a40 57
7 ch h Hernando(FR) —Nordican Inch (Inchinor)
466[8] 769[7]

Inches Away (FR) *S Wattel* 56
2 b f Gold Away(IRE) —Tchikala (Inchinor)
6925a[5] 7312a[2]

Inchina *Roger Charlton* 73
2 b f Montjeu(IRE) —Incheni (IRE) (Nashwan (USA))
7030[3] ◆

Inch Or Two *Des Donovan* a34 33
2 ch c Notnowcato—Amaryllis (IRE) (Sadler's Wells (USA))
5337[11] 6100[10] 6506[10]

Incitement *Ed Dunlop* 78
3 b g Motivator—Dardshi (IRE) (Darshaan)
2097[4]

Incomparable *David Nicholls* a80 81
6 ch g Compton Place—Indian Silk (IRE) (Dolphin Street (FR))
134[4] ◆ 199[2] 294[8] 430[2] 521[9] 708[4] 794[2] 1048[3] 1196[7] 1411[13] 1907[12] 5732[11] 6802[16] 7535[7] 7646[4] 7744[6]

Indared *Tracey Barfoot-Saunt*
7 ch g Daggers Drawn(USA) —Bogus John (CAN) (Blushing John (USA))
5960[8]

Inde Country *Nicky Vaughan* a59 53
3 b f Indesatchel(IRE) —Countrywide Girl (IRE) (Catrail (USA))
65[5] 183[4] 251[2] 452[4] 1294[6] 2524[6] 2990[10] (3920) 4636[9] 4930[8] 5215[4] 7230[2] 7737[13]

Indefinite Hope (ITY) *Frank Sheridan* a63 50
4 b m Ekraar(USA) —Ricredes (IRE) (Night Shift (USA))
201[4] 391[9] 1374[9] 1473[10] 4747[6] 4869[9] 4953[5] 5912[8] 6309[9]

Indego Blues *David Nicholls* 80
2 b g Indesatchel(IRE) —Yanomami (USA) (Slew O'Gold (USA))
4192[3] 5398[3] (6152)

Independent Girl (IRE) *Ms Joanna Morgan* a73 79
3 ch f Bachelor Duke(USA) —Miss Childrey (IRE) (Dr Fong (USA))
7189a[20]

Indepub *Kevin Ryan* 80
2 b g Indesatchel(IRE) —Champenoise (Forzando)
1797[5] 2120[9] (3035) 3700[2] 4536[9] 5184[10] 5645[2] 5825[5] (6599) 7021[9]

Indiana Guest (IRE) *George Margarson* 50
2 b g Indian Haven—Princess Speedfit (FR) (Desert Prince (IRE))
5480[13] 6099[5]

Indian Arrow *John Quinn* a66 43
3 b c Sleeping Indian—Hillside Girl (IRE) (Tagula (IRE))
7213[8] 7591[7] 7739[3]

Indian Art (IRE) *Richard Hannon* a81 84
5 b h Choisir(AUS) —Eastern Ember (Indian King (USA))
6467[5] ◆

Indian Ballad (IRE) *Ed McMahon* a76 91
3 b g Oratorio(IRE) —Cherokee Stream (IRE) (Indian Ridge)
1322[4] 1688[10] 2043[2] 2503[11] 3052[2] 3682[3] 4817[6] 5559[3]

Indian Blossom *Harry Dunlop* 54
2 b f Sakhee(USA) —Al Corniche (IRE) (Bluebird (USA))
6742[7]

Indian Breeze (GER) *J Hirschberger* 105
4 b m Monsun(GER) —Indian Jewel (GER) (Local Suitor (USA))
5749a[4]

Indian City (FR) *J-M Capitte* a72 61
7 ch g City On A Hill(USA) —Mary Linda (Grand Lodge (USA))
(220a)

Indian Days *James Given* a105 117
6 ch h Daylami(IRE) —Cap Coz (IRE) (Indian Ridge)
(1403) 1685[3] 2680[5] 3448a[5] 4492[9] (5776a)

Indian Dumaani *David Bridgwater* a46 50
4 gr m Indian Ridge—Mubadalah (USA) (Dumaani (USA))
5345[7] 5843[3] 6310[10] 6982[6]

Indian Emperor (IRE) *Peter Niven* a72 72
3 b g Araafa(IRE) —Soft (USA) (Lear Fan (USA))
2215[10] 2916[9] 4188[6] 5456[6] 5735[10] 6179[11] 7538[4] 7610[7] 7687[6] 7859[10]

Indian Ghyll (IRE) *Roger Teal* a68 67
5 ch h Indian Haven—Arzachena (FR) (Grand Lodge (USA))
223[5] ◆ 622[3] 808[3] 962[3] 1148[7]

Indian Giver *Hugh McWilliams* 66
3 b f Indesatchel(IRE) —Bint Baddi (FR) (Shareef Dancer (USA))
5006[3] 5164[9] 5821[7] 6415[7]

Indian Jack (IRE) *Alan Bailey* a91 95
3 ch g Indian Haven—Almaviva (IRE) (Grand Lodge (USA))
(1106) ◆ (1175) 1547[7] 2296[13] 5712[6] (6173) ◆ 6495[6] 7168[17]

Indian Lizzy *Paul Cole* a49 49
2 b f Tobougg(IRE) —Saristar (Starborough)
1590[4] 2194[4] 2362[4] 2998[10] 4390[6]

Indian Mist (IRE) *Roger Varian* a23 73
3 gr f Cape Cross(IRE) —Indian Belle (IRE) (Indian Ridge)
3437[5] 4356[7] 4826[3] 5598[8] (6754)

Indian Pipe Dream (IRE) *Aytach Sadik* a63 20
9 br g Indian Danehill(IRE) —Build A Dream (USA) (Runaway Groom (CAN))
639[4] 7244[7]

Indian Shuffle (IRE) *Jonathan Portman* a66 73
3 b g Sleeping Indian—Hufflepuff (IRE) (Desert King (IRE))
1187[2] (1449) 2155[3] 2881[4] (3271) 3995[6] 4486[4] 5000[9] 5781[10]

Indian St Jovite (IRE) *Seamus Fahey* a47 66
4 b g Indian Haven—Meritorious (USA) (St Jovite (USA))
545[12]

Indian Tinker *Robert Cowell* a55 81
2 b g Sleeping Indian—Breakfast Creek (Hallgate)
5117[7] 5351[2] (5889) 6625[5]

Indian Trail *David Nicholls* a74 91
11 ch g Indian Ridge—Take Heart (Electric)
1476[7] 1698[3] 2118[13] 2299[8] 2714[6] 3028[7] 5543[8] 5831[4] 6112[21] 6348[8] 6703[7]

Indian Valley (USA) *Hugo Palmer* a78 80
4 b m Cherokee Run(USA) —Shade Dance (USA) (Nureyev (USA))
2771[3] 3366[6] 4448[3] 4949[7] 5496[4] 6285[2] 6543[4] 7033[5]

Indian Violet (IRE) *Ralph Smith* a67 67
5 b g Indian Ridge—Violet Spring (IRE) (Exactly Sharp (USA))
162[6] 247[2] 565[3] 685[10] 765[8] 2171[3] 2385[8] 3944[2] 4322[3] 4699[4] 5667[2] 6358[9] [illegible] [illegible] [illegible] 7394[2]

Indian Wish (USA) *Tim McCarthy* a62 60
3 bb f Indian Charlie(USA) —Sister Girl (USA) (Conquistador Cielo (USA))
47[2] 234[10] 297[5] 1284[3] 1683[14] 2307[8] 3945[9] 4827[5] 5352[7] 7119[12]

Indieslad *Ann Duffield* a67 77
3 b g Indesatchel(IRE) —Sontime (Son Pardo)
1241[7] 2043[3] 2363[8] 3052[8] 4634[5] 5083[6] ◆ 5652[7] 6133[5] 7024[2]

Indigo Sands (IRE) *Alan Berry* 38
3 b g Tagula(IRE) —Bella Vie (IRE) (Sadler's Wells (USA))
3053[5] 3616[10] 3949[7] 4813[6] 5368[9] 6839[9]

Indivisible *Tim Easterby* 52
2 b f Indesatchel(IRE) —Milliscent (Primo Dominie)
6045[8] 6449[7]

Indochina *Ian Williams* a68 77
4 b g Sulamani(IRE) —Lane County (USA) (Rahy (USA))
836[2] 2892[10] 3352[9] 4747[3] 5122[3] 5784[9] 6229[5]

Indomito (GER) *A Wohler* a104 105
5 b h Areion(GER) —Insola (GER) (Royal Solo (IRE))
236[4] 497a[8] 755a[7] 825a[7] 4373a[7] 5777a[3] 6201a[7] 7323a[5]

Indran (FR) *B Dutruel* a64 70
6 b g Indian Rocket—Siran (FR) (R B Chesne)
935a[7]

Indus Valley (IRE) *Des Donovan* a70 76
4 ch g Indian Ridge—Gloriously Bright (USA) (Nureyev (USA))
7579[11] 7901[10]

Indycisive *Simon West* 42
3 b g Indesatchel(IRE) —Pearls (Mon Tresor)
2058[7] 2461[5] 2735[9] 5489[7]

Indyend *Tim Easterby* 47
2 b f Indesatchel(IRE) —Be Most Welcome (Most Welcome)
4606[4] 4899[10] 5367[7] 5646[7] 6043[8] 6611[10]

Inef (IRE) *Laura Mongan* a73 83
4 b m Nayef(USA) —Intimaa (IRE) (Caerleon (USA))
226[11] 1530[7] 2232[2] 2649[14] (3354) 3763[3]

Inestimable *M Al Muhairi* a93 100
6 b g Mark Of Esteem(IRE) —Tiyi (FR) (Fairy King (USA))
605a[8] 679a[8]

Inetrobil (IRE) *Kevin Ryan* 103
2 ch f Bertolini(USA) —Tigava (USA) (Machiavellian (USA))
(2587) ◆ 3104[2] 3821[4] 5217[6] 5656[4]

Inffiraaj (IRE) *Mick Channon* 64
2 b f Iffraaj—Incense (Unfuwain (USA))
6458[3] ◆ 6984[8]

Infidelite *A Fabre* a87 83
3 b f Diktat—Loyal Love (USA) (Danzig (USA))
852a[3]

Infinite Jest *J W Hills* a22 64
2 ch c Danehill Dancer(IRE) —Noelani (IRE) (Indian Ridge)
7134[8] 7330[7]

Influence (FR) *G Henrot* 87
2 b f Dansili—Moiava (FR) (Bering)
5130a[6]

Informed Award *John Gosden* 73
3 bb c Dansili—La Paz (Nashwan (USA))
1139[3] ◆ 1271[5] 2019[4] 2688[5] 3118[11] 3478[2]

Ingenti *Christopher Wilson* 60
3 ch f Blue Dakota(IRE) —Kungfu Kerry (Celtic Swing)
1880[12] 3616[8] 4282[10] 4986[8] 5469[2] (5620) 6840[16] 7079[10]

Ingleby Angel (IRE) *David O'Meara* a57 44
2 bb g Dark Angel(IRE) —Mistress Twister (Pivotal)
2234[2] 2780[6] 3274[6] 4809[6] 5817[7] 6611[11]

Ingleby Arch (USA) *David Barron* a91 76
8 b g Arch(USA) —Inca Dove (USA) (Mr Prospector (USA))
376[3] (493) 1289[2] 2633[3] 2806[5] 3359[7] 4145[3] 5554[6] 5647[2] 6426[2] 6778[5] 7502[7] (7726)

Ingleby Exceed (IRE) *David O'Meara* 80
3 ch f Exceed And Excel(AUS) —Mistress Twister (Pivotal)
2592[7] (3729) ◆ 4081[3] (4290) 4718[2] 5730[5] 5820[3]

Ingleby King (USA) *David O'Meara* a70 61
5 bb g Doneraile Court(USA) —Smart Lady Too (USA) (Clever Trick (USA))
122[2] ◆

Ingleby Lady *David O'Meara* 102
5 ch m Captain Rio—Petra Nova (First Trump)
5758[17]

Ingleby Spirit *Richard Fahey* a79 96
4 b g Avonbridge—Encore Du Cristal (USA) (Quiet American (USA))
(1154) 1479[9] 2002[6] 2573[8] 5185[13] 6163[11]

Ingleby Star (IRE) *Ian McInnes* a77 82
6 b g Fath(USA) —Rosy Scintilla (IRE) (Thatching)
116[4] 230[3] 511[4] (1213) 1411[12] 1856[8] 2048[2] 2491[2] 2832[3] 3488[2] 3759[3] 4152[3] 4504[9] 4539[6] 4900[5] 5313[3] (5468) (5720) ◆ 6212[7] 6913[7]

Inimitable Romanee (USA) *Amanda Perrett* a67 77
3 gr f Maria's Mon(USA) —Cellars Shiraz (USA) (Kissin Kris (USA))
7204 [6]

Initiator *Jeremy Noseda* 72
2 b c Motivator—Dawnus (IRE) (Night Shift (USA))
5011[4]

Inklet *Marco Botti* a76 78
3 b f Intikhab(USA) —Digamist Girl (IRE) (Digamist (USA))
1393[2] 2157[8] 3236[4] (5247)

Inler (IRE) *Brian Meehan* 110
4 br g Red Ransom(USA) —Wedding Gift (FR) (Always Fair (USA))
1340[5] 2005[13] 2502[4] 3404[8] 5563[5] 6747[6] (6955)

Inner Secret (USA) *Mahmood Al Zarooni* 80
3 b f Singspiel(IRE) —Mysterial (USA) (Alleged (USA))
[illegible] ◆

Inniscastle Boy *William Muir* a67 65
2 b c Sir Percy—Galapagar (USA) (Miswaki (USA))
3686[15] 3917[13] 4446[9] (6001) 6487[10] 7051[2] 7222[2] 7436[4]

Innocent Lady (NZ) *Graeme & Mark Sanders* 100
5 bb m Viking Ruler(AUS) —Startling Lady (NZ) (Gold And Ivory (USA))
7115a[10]

Innovator (GER) *Zuzana Kubovicova* 87
4 b h Refuse To Bend(IRE) —Intuition (GER) (Gold And Ivory (USA))
4599a[6]

Inorato (IRE) *F & L Camici* 101
3 b c Oratorio(IRE) —Intimaa (IRE) (Caerleon (USA))
7324a[8]

Inoubliable *A Fabre* 101
3 b c Singspiel(IRE) —Soft Pleasure (USA) (Diesis)
1965a[4]

Inpursuitoffreedom *Philip McBride* a76 74
4 b m Pastoral Pursuits—Quilt (Terimon)
889[5] 2021[7] 2816[5] 3130[8] 4506[3] 5014[2] 5516[5] 5828[4]

Inqadh (USA) *Saeed Bin Suroor* a65 46
2 b g Invasor(ARG) —Saywaan (USA) (Fusaichi Pegasus (USA))
5899[6] 6400[11]

Inquisitress *John Bridger* a54 57
7 b m Hernando(FR) —Caribbean Star (Soviet Star (USA))
163[6] 280[13] 355[4] 552[4] 652[7] (3017) 3253[6] 3677[7] 3943[5] 4154[8] 4544[4] 4699[3] 5136[4] 5422[2] 5667[8] 5995[3] 6083[7] 6811[11] 6971[8] 7131[7] 7387[8]

Insciaveghen (ITY) *Vittorio Caruso* 96
3 ch c Dr Fong(USA) —Coimbra (USA) (Trempolino (USA))
1431a[4]

Inside *Richard Fahey* 60
3 b f Iron Mask(USA) —Only Alone (USA) (Rahy (USA))
1169[11] 2349[4] 3039[4] 3455[10] 3621[4]

Inside Knowledge (USA) *Garry Woodward* a68 55
5 rg g Mizzen Mast(USA) —Kithira (Danehill (USA))
(33) 314[2] 514[6] 955[6] 6915[4]

Insidious *William Jarvis* a22 13
3 b c Sakhee(USA) —Inseparable (Insan (USA))
2924[10] 3743[5]

Insieme (IRE) *Paul Cashman* a68 71
3 b f Barathea(IRE) —Rasana (Royal Academy (USA))
(791) 7150a[14]

Insolenceofoffice (IRE) *Bruce Hellier* a83 74
3 b g Kodiac—Sharp Diversion (USA) (Diesis)
263[2] 578[4] 845[7] 864[6] 1214[8] 1745[7] 2074[15] 2250[8] 5924[12] 6283[10] 6840[7] (7065) 7216[5] 7349[9]

Inspector (TUR) *K Saglam* 83
7 b h Bin Ajwaad(IRE) —Pandora (GER) (Platini (GER))
5776a[8]

Inspirina (IRE) *Richard Ford* a75 87
7 b g Invincible Spirit(IRE) —La Stellina (IRE) (Marju (IRE))
1826[4] 2282[6] 2932[2]

Instance *Jeremy Noseda* a84 99
3 b f Invincible Spirit(IRE) —Hannda (IRE) (Dr Devious (IRE))
(2199) ◆ 2468[3] (3819) 4332[8]

Instructress *Robert Cowell* a58 73
3 b f Diktat—Two Step (Mujtahid (USA))
847[8] 929[5] 3136[9] 4684[5] 5517[4] 5941[3] 6176[5] 6501[12] 7429[9]

Instrumentalist (IRE) *John Best* a73
2 b c Amadeus Wolf—Kobalt Sea (FR) (Akarad (FR))
6795[4] ◆ (7634)

Intapeace (IRE) *Francis Ennis* a88 96
4 b m Intikhab(USA) —Magical Peace (IRE) (Magical Wonder (USA))
1779a[4]

Intarsia (GER) *A Fabre* 101
4 ch m Pentire—Iphianassa (GER) (Selkirk (USA))
5075a[3] 7386a[4] 7733a[6]

Integral (GER) *Stanislav Otruba* 93
7 b h Lando(GER) —Incenza (GER) (Local Suitor (USA))
7409a[14]

Integria *George Baker* a46 74
5 b g Intikhab(USA) —Alegria (Night Shift (USA))
802[10] 1333[14] 1582[11] (1933) (2171) 2268[2] 2449[3] 3266[7] 3326[4] 3477[6]

Integrity (IRE) *Jeremy Noseda* a81
2 b c Dark Angel(IRE) —Law Review (IRE) (Case Law)
(5410) ◆

Intense Pink *Chris Wall* 74
2 b f Pivotal—Clincher Club (Polish Patriot (USA))
6128[7] 6758[3] ◆

Interaction (ARG) *P Bary* a108 109
5 b h Easing Along(USA) —Inter Rails (ARG) (Ride The Rails (USA))
416a[3] ◆ 757a[7]

Interaction *John Gosden* 75
3 b f Oasis Dream—Indication (Sadler's Wells (USA))
4356[4] 4963[2]

Interakt *Joseph Tuite* a51 76
4 b m Rakti—Amelie Pouliche (FR) (Desert Prince (IRE))
727[11] 906[12] 1933[2] 2420[10] 2921[4] 3019[3] (3476) 4025[3] (4224) 4973[2] (5425) 5671[2] 6246[4]

Intercept (IRE) *John Gosden* a79 72
3 b g Iffraaj—Sharp Catch (IRE) (Common Grounds)
(6473) 7171[12] 7457[10]

Interchoice Star *Ray Peacock* a70 61
6 b g Josr Algarhoud(IRE) —Blakeshall Girl (Piccolo)
345[3] 402[2] (673) 853[4] 1463[5] 4850[5] 5616[6] 5881[3] 6282[5] 6841[4] 7039[6] 7216[2]

Interian (GER) *C Ferland* a77
5 b g Tertullian(USA) —Indian Night (GER) (Windwurf (GER))
195a[8] (395a)

Internationaldebut (IRE) *Paul Midgley* a89 108
6 b g High Chaparral(IRE) —Whisper Light (IRE) (Caerleon (USA))
1109[2] 1457[2] 1675[4] 2116[3] 2706[6] 4369[3] 4802[6] 5032[8] (5758) (5852) (6233) 6706[7]

Inthar (USA) *Saeed Bin Suroor* 56
2 ch c Medicean—Mont Etoile (IRE) (Montjeu (IRE))
7082[7]

In The Long Grass (IRE) *Jim Boyle* a46
3 b g Ivan Denisovich(IRE) —Dabtiyra (IRE) (Dr Devious (IRE))
4800[8] 4989[5] 5816[9] 6926[11] 7688[5]

Intiqaal (IRE) *Keith Dalgleish* 71
4 b g Tiger Hill(IRE) —Pride In Me (Indian Ridge)
1540[3] ◆ 2266[4] 2815[4] 3477[5] 4441[4]

Intolerance (FR) *A Fabre* a87 96
4 ch m Gold Away(IRE) —Moiava (FR) (Bering)
92a[9]

Into Mac *Neville Bycroft* 47
5 b g Shinko Forest(IRE) —Efipetite (Efisio)
873[DSQ] 1559[8] 2114[12] 2785[3] 3683[11]

Intomist (IRE) *Jim Boyle* a64 58
2 ch c Strategic Prince—Fast Temper (USA) (In The Wings)
2194[8] 3761[7] 4240[3] 6972[5] ◆ 7337[5] (7530) 7808[2]

Into The Light *Philip Kirby* a62 68
6 b g Fantastic Light(USA) —Boadicea's Chariot (Commanche Run)
2060[8] 4562[11] 5609[8]

Into The Wind *Rod Millman* 62
4 ch m Piccolo—In The Stocks (Reprimand)
3293[7] 4086[7] 4816[4] 5112[2] 5349[2] 5785[5] 6486[U] 6894[7]

Into Wain (USA) *Steve Gollings* a97 98
4 b g Eddington(USA) —Serene Nobility (USA) (His Majesty (USA))
667[4] 1105[6]

Intransigent *Andrew Balding* a84 58
2 b g Trans Island—Mara River (Efisio)
6743^{7} *(7359)*

Introvert (IRE) *Mahmood Al Zarooni* a87 97
3 b c Iffraaj—Isana (JPN) (Sunday Silence (USA))
238^{6} 411a^{3} (680a) *998a^{12}*

Intuition *Richard Hannon* a72 72
2 b c Multiplex—Shallow Ground (IRE) (Common Grounds)
6481^{2} 6828^{5} *(7225)*

Intyre Trail (IRE) *Peter Fahey* a70 67
6 b g Mull Of Kintyre(USA) —Desert Trail (IRE) (Desert Style (IRE))
(181) 495^{6}

Invasor Girl (USA) *William Haggas* a72 35
2 bb f Invasor(ARG) —Millenia (Unfuwain (USA))
5814^{2} 6532^{10}

Invent *Robert Eddery* a63 50
3 b g Dansili—Fantasize (Groom Dancer (USA))
2463^{4} 2858^{7} 3431^{11} 3958^{3} *4183^{12}* 4829^{6} 5015^{10}

Investissement *John Gosden* 105
5 b g Singspiel(IRE) —Underwater (USA) (Theatrical)
(1679) 3396^{18} 4532^{3} 5285^{3}

Investment World (IRE) *Mark Johnston* a63 42
3 b c Akbar(IRE) —Superb Investment (IRE) (Hatim (USA))
53^{2} (234) ◆ *1312^{4} 1502^{4}* 2613^{8} 3487^{10} 4190^{7}

Invigilator *Harry Dunlop* a56 43
3 b c Motivator—Midpoint (USA) (Point Given (USA))
(1331) 1952^{5} 2524^{8}

Invincibility (IRE) *Simon Dow* a81 73
4 b g Invincible Spirit(IRE) —Wonders Gift (Dr Devious (IRE))
726^{4}

Invincible Ash (IRE) *M Halford* a102 110
6 b m Invincible Spirit(IRE) —Fully Fashioned (IRE) (Brief Truce (USA))
155a^{5} 500a^{2} *582a^{5}* 754a^{3} 996a^{4} 2861a^{6} (3441a) 4768a^{3} 5524a^{5}

Invincible Beauty (IRE) *Seamus Durack* a42
2 b f Invincible Spirit(IRE) —Beautiful Note (USA) (Red Ransom (USA))
6252^{6}

Invincible Dream (IRE) *Robert Mills* a68 70
2 b g Invincible Spirit(IRE) —Justly Royal (USA) (Royal Academy (USA))
3288^{5} ◆ 3552^{4} *3921^{3} 5385^{7}* 6058^{5} 6237^{3}

Invincible Force (IRE) *Paul Green* a70 97
7 b g Invincible Spirit(IRE) —Highly Respected (IRE) (High Estate)
1854^{13} 2299^{13} 3169^{8} 3339^{5} 3541^{2} ◆ 3850^{9} 4046^{4} *4921^{4}* 5371^{6} (5400) 5682^{5} 6917^{10} *7199^{12}*

Invincible Hero (IRE) *Declan Carroll* a58 84
4 b g Invincible Spirit(IRE) —Bridelina (FR) (Linamix (FR))
1065^{9} (3096) *3952^{4}* (4783) (5828) 6173^{3}

Invincible Lad (IRE) *David Nicholls* a98 90
7 b g Invincible Spirit(IRE) —Lady Ellen (Horage)
1205^{3} 1618^{6} 2694^{10} 4416^{7} 5108^{9} 5679^{2} 6112^{18}

Invincible Ridge (IRE) *Richard Hannon* 96
3 b c Invincible Spirit(IRE) —Dani Ridge (IRE) (Indian Ridge)
1547^{8} 2003^{4} 4333^{13}

Invincible Soul (IRE) *Richard Hannon* 104
4 b g Invincible Spirit(IRE) —Licorne (Sadler's Wells (USA))
1529^{12} 2558^{3} 3032^{28} 3290^{13} 5563^{8} 5940^{13} 6496^{7}

Invincible Viking (IRE) *Y Barberot* a71 71
3 b c Invincible Spirit(IRE) —Lille Hammer (Sadler's Wells (USA))
2978a^{10} 5772a^{9}

Invisible Hunter (USA) *Saeed Bin Suroor* 64
2 ch c Rahy(USA) —Madeline P (USA) (Theatrical)
7080^{5}

Invisible Man *Saeed Bin Suroor* a97 111
5 ch g Elusive Quality(USA) —Eternal Reve (USA) (Diesis)
239^{4} 586a^{9} 828a^{8} 3032^{3} 4003^{2} 4554^{2} 5218^{15} 5777a^{2}

Inxile (IRE) *David Nicholls* a108 118
6 b g Fayruz—Grandel (Owington)
155a^{2} ◆ *414a^{5}* ◆ 602a^{7} 996a^{6} (1420a) (1533a) (2138a) 2754a^{3} (2967a) 3441a^{4} (4768a) 5253^{15}

Inya House *Nigel Tinkler* a54 52
2 b g Auction House(USA) —Inya Lake (Whittingham (IRE))
2318^{6} 3050^{4} 3314^{8} 4892^{6} 5486^{10} *5998^{2}* 6628^{6}

Ionwy *Derek Haydn Jones* a57 55
2 b f Piccolo—Dim Ots (Alhijaz)
3511^{7} *3981^{8}* 4883^{5} 5840^{11} *6695^{2} 7038^{3} 7925^{8}*

Ippi N Tombi (IRE) *Phil McEntee* a53 57
3 bb f Captain Rio—Xema (Danehill (USA))
347^{2} 693^{5} 716^{7} 2307^{7} 2858^{8} *3175^{6}* 4728^{4} 5352^{4} (5515) *5943^{3}* 6033^{4} *6545^{8}*

Ippios *Luca Cumani* 80
3 b c Cadeaux Genereux—Siena Gold (Key Of Luck (USA))
1724^{9} 2311^{2}

Irian (GER) *J Moore* 119
5 br g Tertullian(USA) —Iberi (GER) (Rainbow Quest (USA))
1742a^{4} 2340a^{3} 7732a^{2}

Irie Ute *Sylvester Kirk* a65 61
3 b g Sleeping Indian—Prends Ca (IRE) (Reprimand)
27^{4} 228^{2} 931^{4} 1022^{2} 2550^{P}

Irini (GER) *H J Groschel* 103
5 ch m Areion(GER) —Ircanda (GER) (Nebos (GER))
6739a^{5}

Irish Art (USA) *Carla Gaines* 111
3 b c Artie Schiller(USA) —Irish Linnet (USA) (Seattle Song (USA))
7572a^{9}

Irish Boy (IRE) *Paul Midgley* a54 70
3 b g Desert Millennium(IRE) —Shone Island (IRE) (Desert Sun)
(1306) 1561^{2} (1764) 2265^{7} (3126) ◆ 3702^{2} 4295^{5} 5719^{6} 6456^{2} ◆

Irish Cat (IRE) *N Clement* a90 98
4 b m One Cool Cat(USA) —Babacora (IRE) (Indian Ridge)
108a^{2}

Irish Flame (SAF) *M F De Kock* a116 116
5 b h Dynasty(SAF) —Clock The Rock (SAF) (Flaming Rock (IRE))
331a^{4} 503a^{7} ◆ *758a^{9}* 1001a^{7} 7166^{8} *(7347)*

Irish Gypsy (USA) *Bob Baffert* a112
5 b m Hennessy(USA) —Rayelle (USA) (Relaunch (USA))
7282a^{8}

Irish Heartbeat (IRE) *Richard Fahey* 102
6 b g Celtic Swing—She's All Class (USA) (Rahy (USA))
1094^{10} 2075^{9} 2927^{12} 4042^{9} 4346^{9} 5032^{2} 5180^{4}

Irish Jugger (USA) *Rod Millman* a76 58
4 ch g Johannesburg(USA) —Jinny's Gold (USA) (Gold Fever (USA))
203^{4} 418^{9} (645) (797) 1174^{6} (1466) 1817^{4} 2312^{9} *5866^{7} 6546^{6}* 7200^{4} 7689^{3}

Irish Kelt (IRE) *F-X Belvisi* a51 63
8 b h Indian Danehill(IRE) —My Simpaty (IRE) (Spectrum (IRE))
42a^{0}

Irish Law *John Balding*
3 b g Redoubtable(USA) —Largs (Sheikh Albadou)
6839^{8} *7245^{12} 7886^{8}*

Irish Song (FR) *A Couetil* 100
4 ch m Singspiel(IRE) —Irish Order (USA) (Irish River (FR))
6661a^{8}

Irishstone (IRE) *Gerard Butler* a75 52
2 b f Danehill Dancer(IRE) —Speak Softly To Me (USA) (Ogygian (USA))
6215^{2} 6603^{8}

Iron Age *M bin Shafya* 101
4 gr g Pivotal—Amenixa (FR) (Linamix (FR))
499a^{14}

Iron Condor *James Eustace* a85 75
4 b g Tobougg(IRE) —Coh Sho No (Old Vic)
209 ^{4} 5057^{5} (5357) *5837^{6}*

Iron Green (FR) *Heather Main* a68 68
3 b g Iron Mask(USA) —Love For Ever (FR) (Kaldoun (FR))
1299^{2} 1683^{5} 2583^{11} *5463a^{0} 5900^{2} 6181^{9} 7669a^{10} 7930^{6}*

Ironically (IRE) *David Lanigan* a61 66
2 b f Refuse To Bend(IRE) —Dutch Auction (USA) (Mr Greeley (USA))
4804^{6} *5393^{5} 5899^{8} 6443^{6}*

Iron Major (IRE) *Edward Lynam* a88 87
4 ch g Titus Livius(FR) —Bent Al Fala (IRE) (Green Desert (USA))
5746a^{8} *7010a^{11} 7793a^{5}*

Iron Out (USA) *Reg Hollinshead* a87 84
5 b g Straight Man(USA) —Fit Fighter (USA) (Fit To Fight (USA))
220a^{0} 479a^{5} *533a^{6} 617a^{7}* 706a^{2} *832a^{5}*

Iron Range (IRE) *Ed McMahon* 92
3 b c Clodovil(IRE) —Islandagore (IRE) (Indian Ridge)
6467^{8} ◆

Irons On Fire (USA) *George Baker* a75
3 ch g Tale Of The Cat(USA) —One And Twenty (USA) (Honour And Glory (USA))
3045^{13} 3740^{10} 4664^{9} 7200^{8} 7800^{2} (7939)

Ironstein (AUS) *Gerald Ryan* 111
6 br g Zabeel(NZ) —Gentle Genius (AUS) (Danehill (USA))
(7310a)

Iron Step *Nicky Vaughan* a94 88
3 gr g Dubawi(IRE) —Giorgia Rae (IRE) (Green Desert (USA))
(1655) (2064) 2675^{8} 4281^{12} 5014^{3} 5488^{5} *(5835)* (7054) *(7531)*

Irrational *Bryan Smart* 61
2 b f Kyllachy—Belladera (IRE) (Alzao (USA))
(4040) ◆ 6186^{6} 6573^{8}

Irrefutable (USA) *Bob Baffert* a117
5 rg h Unbridled's Song(USA) —Honestly Darling (USA) (Kingmambo (USA))
7304a^{9}

Iryklon (POL) *Vaclav Luka II* 106
5 b g Nowogrodek(POL) —Imma (POL) (Beaconsfield)
6905a^{6}

Isabellareine (GER) *Mervyn Torrens* a76 73
8 bl m Goofalik(USA) —Irma La Douce (GER) (Local Suitor (USA))
7378a^{7} 7544a^{9}

Isabella Romee (IRE) *Terry Clement* a50 57
5 gr m Bahri(USA) —Silver Clasp (IRE) (Linamix (FR))
450^{11}

Isatis *Sir Henry Cecil* a72
2 ch f Zamindar(USA) —Isis (USA) (Royal Academy (USA))
7344^{2} ◆

Isdaal *Kevin Morgan* a63 59
4 ch m Dubawi(IRE) —Faydah (USA) (Bahri (USA))
1540^{6} *2306^{10}* 3320^{5} 4394^{7} *7228^{6} 7604^{5} 7810^{3} 7904^{5}*

I See You *George Margarson* a65 56
2 ch f Sleeping Indian—Pikaboo (Pivotal)
5323^{8} 5514^{6} *7267^{4} (7452)*

Ishbelle *Ralph Beckett* 98
3 gr f Invincible Spirit(IRE) —Belle Reine (King Of Kings (IRE))
3819^{3} 4332^{4} 5080^{5} 5657^{10} 7031^{11}

Isheforreal (IRE) *Brian Ellison* 58
4 b g Starcraft(NZ) —Diamondiferous (USA) (Danzig (USA))
4282^{5} 4514^{6} 4816^{7} 5549^{5} 5721^{6} 6452^{4}

Ishetoo *Ollie Pears* a77 84
7 b g Ishiguru(USA) —Ticcatoo (IRE) (Dolphin Street (FR))
2590^{6} 2938^{10} 3188^{4} 3806^{3} 4517^{6} 5031^{7} *5895^{2} 6177^{4} 6491^{9}* 7106^{2}

Ishiadancer *Eric Alston* a78 93
6 b m Ishiguru(USA) —Abaklea (IRE) (Doyoun)
3459^{9} 4349^{12} 4574^{8} 5164^{3} 5551^{4} *5862^{8} 6354^{2} 6979^{8}*

Ishiamiracle *Phil McEntee* a69 59
2 ch f Ishiguru(USA) —Sukuma (IRE) (Highest Honor (FR))
3868^{6} 4427^{9} 6118^{6} *6819^{4}* 7051^{3} *7240^{2} 7336^{2} 7350^{4} 7725^{3} 7780^{2} 7855^{3} (7916)*

Ishikawa (IRE) *Alan King* a60 59
3 b g Chineur(FR) —Nautical Light (Slip Anchor)
1588^{2} ◆ *(2166)* ◆ 4317^{3} 4745^{3} 5380^{2}

Ishipink *Ron Hodges* a43 47
4 gr m Ishiguru(USA) —Christmas Rose (Absalom)
2164^{10} 2424^{2} 2755^{5} 2869^{10} 3307^{10} 3939^{6} 5617^{10}

Ishismart *Reg Hollinshead* a52 53
7 ch m Ishiguru(USA) —Smartie Lee (Dominion)
2569^{2} 3600^{5} 5267^{3}

Ishvana (IRE) *A P O'Brien* a79 93
2 b f Holy Roman Emperor(IRE) —Song Of The Sea (Bering)
4131a^{4} 7185a^{4}

Isingy Red (FR) *Jim Boyle* a75 74
3 ch g Chichicastenango(FR) —Loving Smile (FR) (Sillery (USA))
2383^{12} 2838^{10} (3337) 3854^{3} 4214^{4} 5171^{10} *6796^{3}* 7137^{4} *7334^{7} 7532^{11}*

Island Bird *Kate Walton* 31
2 b f Danbird(AUS) —Dispol Isle (IRE) (Trans Island)
2429^{3} 2797^{4}

Island Chief *Michael Easterby* a35 78
5 b g Reel Buddy(USA) —Fisher Island (IRE) (Sri Pekan (USA))
2671^{10} 4051^{5} 4601^{4} 4945^{10} 5402^{8} 5822^{3} 6235^{13} *6878^{10}*

Island Legend (IRE) *Milton Bradley* a89 64
5 b g Trans Island—Legand Of Tara (USA) (Gold Legend (USA))
298^{5} (430) (554) 708^{8} 1048^{2} (1196) 1584^{2} 1982^{3} 2645^{9} *3222^{6}* 7355^{5} 7487^{3} 7644^{5} 7832^{6}

Island Melody (IRE) *J S Moore* a67 69
2 b g Oratorio(IRE) —Pout (IRE) (Namid)
2788^{11} 3152^{12} 4390^{5} *(7809)*

Island Paradise (IRE) *Charles Hills* a83 91
2 b f Trans Island—Athlumney Dancer (Shareef Dancer (USA))
5097^{2} (5691) 7562a^{3}

Isle Of Ellis (IRE) *Ron Barr* a39 49
4 b g Statue Of Liberty(USA) —Fable (Absalom)
1439^{10} 1557^{5} 1943^{4} 2249^{5} 2593^{7} 3733^{9} 4564^{2} 4813^{5} 5490^{5} 6261^{14} 6602^{10}

Isle Of Pearl (IRE) *Y De Nicolay* a75 78
4 gr m Verglas(IRE) —Sahara Snow (Linamix (FR))
7256a^{0}

Islesman *Heather Main* a85 81
3 b g Oratorio(IRE) —Purple Vision (Rainbow Quest (USA))
27^{2} 1773^{2} 2229^{12} 3178^{9} *(3521)* 4268^{9} *6949^{5} 7227^{4} 7542^{7}*

Isn't He Perfect (USA) *Doodnauth Shivmangal* a104
3 b c Pleasantly Perfect(USA) —Reciclada (CHI) (Rictorious (USA))
2328a^{9} 2950a^{12}

Isobar (GER) *Luca Cumani* a86 81
5 b g Monsun(GER) —Ice Dream (GER) (Mondrian (GER))
4555^{7} 5078^{11} 6469^{3}

Isobella *Hughie Morrison* a55 50
2 b f Royal Applause—Gwyneth (Zafonic (USA))
6818^{9} 7257^{5} *7599^{6} 7763^{13}*

Isola Bella *Jonathan Portman* a26 43
2 ch f Sleeping Indian—Tetravella (IRE) (Groom Dancer (USA))
5672^{9} 6117^{9} *7177^{8}*

Isolate *Hughie Morrison* a68 86
3 gr f Verglas(IRE) —Nirvana (Marju (IRE))
2791^{2} 3260^{10} 4473^{9} *5716^{P}*

Isolde's Return *George Moore* 10
2 b f Avonbridge—Up And About (Barathea (IRE))
2113^{16} 2617^{12} 3200^{9} 6345^{11}

Isometric (USA) *Mahmood Al Zarooni* a68 54
3 b c Dubawi(IRE) —Mighty Isis (USA) (Pleasant Colony (USA))
4065^{9} *4663^{4}* 5169^{7}

Issabella Gem (IRE) *Clive Cox* 84
4 b m Marju(IRE) —Robin (Slip Anchor)
2220^{8} 2552^{11} 3817^{6} 4341^{6} 6469^{6}

Issacar (IRE) *A De Watrigant* a86 90
4 ch h Traditionally(USA) —Indolente (IRE) (Diesis)
840a^{5}

Istan Star (USA) *Julie Camacho* 53
2 b g Istan(USA) —Migygian (USA) (Ogygian (USA))
4122^{7} 5454^{9} 5818^{8} 6760^{2} ◆

Isthmus *Amanda Perrett* a75 71
2 b c Oasis Dream—Krisia (Kris)
6481^{3} *7126^{5} 7521^{4}*

Istiqdaam *Conor Dore* a69 81
6 b g Pivotal—Auspicious (Shirley Heights)
881^{7} 1276^{8} 3720^{2} ◆ (4025) 4176^{2} (4670) (5404) *6544^{8} 7595^{11} 7715^{12}*

Istishaara (USA) *John Dunlop* 84
3 b f Kingmambo(USA) —Itnab (Green Desert (USA))
2022^{3} ◆ 2791^{4} 3580^{4} 4287^{2}

Italian Ice *Bryan Smart* a37 16
2 b f Milk It Mick—Segretezza (IRE) (Perugino (USA))
7058^{10} *7540^{12} 7607^{4} 7882^{2}*

Italian Red (JPN) *Sei Ishizaka* 109
5 b m Neo Universe(JPN) —Bardonecchia (IRE) (Indian Ridge)
7410a^{9}

Italian Tom (IRE) *Ronald Harris* a78 83
4 b h Le Vie Dei Colori—Brave Cat (IRE) (Catrail (USA))
(357) 554^{3} 725^{6} 786^{4} 946^{5} (1314) 2179^{2} 2585^{4} 2794^{5} 3359^{5} (3869) 4546^{7} (5238) 5425^{5} 5972^{11} 6913^{6} 7457^{7} 7596^{6} 7746^{9}

Italo (USA) *Wesley A Ward* a85 98
2 b g With Distinction(USA) —Dance Forthe Green (USA) (West By West (USA))
3012^{23}

Itasip (IRE) *B Grizzetti* 90
3 b f Desert Style(IRE) —El Gran Love (USA) (El Gran Senor (USA))
1738a^{13} 2539a^{7}

Itathir (FR) *J-C Rouget* a61 82
4 ch g Muhtathir—Italienne (USA) (Distant View (USA))
220a^{4}

Ithoughtitwasover (IRE) *Mark Johnston* 99
3 b c Hurricane Run(IRE) —Green Castle (IRE) (Indian Ridge)
2813^{6} (3267) (4280) 4777^{2} 5185^{14} 5700^{12} 6333^{5} 6497^{2}

Itlaaq *Michael Easterby* a89 99
5 b g Alhaarth(IRE) —Hathrah (IRE) (Linamix (FR))
1154^{8} 1387^{5} 2002^{12} 2933^{7} 3829^{3} (4348) 5221^{5} 5883^{10} 6333^{15} 6528^{4} 7297^{17}

It's A Girl Thing (IRE) *George Baker* a67
2 ch f Hurricane Run(IRE) —Princess Magdalena (Pennekamp (USA))
6820^{7} 7454^{4} 7599^{5}

It's A Mans World *Kevin M Prendergast* a59 54
5 b g Kyllachy—Exhibitor (USA) (Royal Academy (USA))
504^{3} 793^{5} 2348^{8}

It's A Privilege *Ralph Beckett* a74 46
2 gr g Verglas(IRE) —No Rehearsal (FR) (Baillamont (USA))
5475^{9} *6474^{3} 6928^{3} 7454^{8}*

It's Dubai Dolly *Alastair Lidderdale* a61 73
5 ch m Dubai Destination(USA) —Betrothal (IRE) (Groom Dancer (USA))
79^{8} 278^{6} 553^{10} 2308^{14} 3003^{4} 3467^{12} 4953^{9} *7091^{3} 7654^{6} 7787^{6}*

It's My Time *David Simcock* 54
2 b f Green Desert(USA) —Soviet Terms (Soviet Star (USA))
7058^{4} ◆

Itsonlymakebelieve (IRE) *Ian Wood* 35
2 b f Amadeus Wolf—Alexander Ridge (IRE) (Indian Ridge)
3425^{8} 5133^{9} 5479^{12} 6170^{16} 6526^{16}

Itsthursdayalready *Mark Brisbourne* a62 62
4 b g Exceed And Excel(AUS) —Succinct (Hector Protector (USA))
14^{3} (107) 167^{4} 210 ^{6} 375^{6} 512^{3} 544^{4} 1247^{5} 1497^{4} (1818) 2238^{3} 2286^{7} 2555^{6} 3093^{6} 3234^{3} 3714^{6} 4187^{5} 4563^{3} 4918^{5} 5244^{8} 5603^{4} 5881^{13} 6138^{6}

It's Tricky (USA) *Kiaran McLaughlin* a119
3 b f Mineshaft(USA) —Catboat (USA) (Tale Of The Cat (USA))
7285a^{2}

Its You Again *Braem Horse Racing Sprl* a84 95
3 b g Avonbridge—Summer Lightning (IRE) (Tamure (IRE))
106^{6} (364) (724) 4739a^{0} 7534a^{0}

Ittasal *Saeed Bin Suroor* a77 77
2 b f Any Given Saturday(USA) —Journalist (IRE) (Night Shift (USA))
(4992) 5698^{3}

Ittirad (USA) *Roger Varian* 93
3 b g Dubai Destination(USA) —Noushkey (Polish Precedent (USA))
(1212) 2076^{2} ◆ 3108^{9} 4108^{3} 5482^{13}

Itum *Christine Dunnett* a57 29
4 ch g Bahamian Bounty—Petomi (Presidium)
6034^{5} *6251^{3} 7266^{11} 7511^{5} 7755^{5} 7853^{3}*

Itwasonlyakiss (IRE) *J W Hills* a54 78
4 b m Exceed And Excel(AUS) —Reem One (IRE) (Rainbow Quest (USA))
57^{7} 211 ^{3} 276^{8}

Iulus *John Quinn* 79
3 ch g Kheleyf(USA) —Miri (IRE) (Sillery (USA))
3246^{2} (4363) 5199^{6} 6155^{13}

Ivanov (IRE) *K F Clutterbuck* a63 63
3 ch g Beat Hollow—Indy's Princess (USA) (A.P. Indy (USA))
1018^{6} (1502) 2857^{3} 3599^{7} *(5209)* 5790^{5}

Ivan's A Star (IRE) *J S Moore* a64 64
3 b g Ivan Denisovich(IRE) —Try The Air (IRE) (Foxhound (USA))
51^{4}

Ivan The Terrible (IRE) *Richard Guest* a46 46
3 b g Ivan Denisovich(IRE) —Pussie Willow (IRE) (Catrail (USA))
6781^{7} *7401^{7} 7609^{5} 7902^{3}*

Ivan Vasilevich (IRE) *Jane Chapple-Hyam* a90 93
3 b c Ivan Denisovich(IRE) —Delisha (Salse (USA))
217 ^{2} (1593) 2230^{4} (2357) *(3044)* 3366^{4} 3809^{2} (4355) 5177^{7} 6325^{6} 6497^{10}

Iver Bridge Lad *John Ryan* a106 114
4 b h Avonbridge—Fittonia (FR) (Ashkalani (IRE))
497a^{10} 606a^{8} 678a^{3} 755a^{6} 825a^{2} *(986)* 1093^{2} (1186) 1340^{2} 1687^{10} 3010^{7} 6563a^{12} 6987^{17} (7221a) 7298^{11}

Ivestar (IRE) *Ben Haslam* a59 66
6 b g Fraam—Hazardous (Night Shift (USA))
362^{3} 2803^{4} 4600^{8} 5309^{2} 6208^{7} *6304^{2} 6999^{7}* 7216^{17}

Ivor's Princess *Rod Millman* 73
2 b f Atraf—Rosina May (IRE) (Danehill Dancer (IRE))
1981^{6} 2661^{2} 3270^{3} 4263 ^{6} 4913^{10} 5577^{5} 6484^{10} 6806^{11}

Ivory Bird *P Khozian* a72 73
3 b c Iceman—Stella Nova (FR) (Bering)
410a^{8}

Ivory Jazz *Richard Guest* a80 58
4 b g Dubai Destination(USA) —Slow Jazz (USA) (Chief's Crown (USA))
(1172) 1826^{10} 4070^{8} 4404^{10}

Ivory Lace *Steve Woodman* a71 74
10 b m Atraf—Miriam (Forzando)
304[3] 387[4] 477[7] 589[10] 2561[2] 3250[2] 3477[4] 3674[5] 4444[7] 4696[4] 4917[3] 5136[7]

Ivory Land (FR) *A De Royer-Dupre* 114
4 ch h Lando(GER) —Ivory Coast (FR) (Peintre Celebre (USA))
(1842a) 2753a[5] 5531a[6] 6903a[3] 7406a[0]

Ivory Silk *Jeremy Gask* a85 91
6 b m Diktat—Ivory's Joy (Tina's Pet)
134[7] 530[2] (689) (763) 1110[2] 1395[2] 1762[4] 2369[3] (3179) 3796[12] 4101[7] 5852[7] 6467[11] 6761[11] 7253[2] 7438[7] 7660[14] 7846[9] 7893[9]

Ivory Trilogy (IRE) *Tim Etherington* a25 35
3 b g Antonius Pius(USA) —Ivory Turner (Efisio)
2094[9] 3075[11] 4863[7] 5780[9]

Ivy And Gold *Alan Berry* a38 49
3 b g Bertolini(USA) —Free Spirit (IRE) (Caerleon (USA))
147[3] 1302[5] 3337[14] 3621[7] 4110[6] 4359[7] 4607[9] 5206[6] 5401[RR]

I Want Revenge (USA) *Richard Dutrow Jr* a115
5 br h Stephen Got Even(USA) —Meguial (ARG) (Roy (USA))
997a[10]

Izalia (FR) *F Rossi* 111
3 b f Iron Mask(USA) —Tarabela (FR) (Johann Quatz (FR))
1207a[10] 5532a[0]

Iztaccihuatl *Michael Scudamore* a46 30
3 br f Iceman—Three White Sox (Most Welcome)
2689[10] 3090[13] 4270[13] 4705[11] 5832[9] 6446[9] 7092[10]

Izzet *Ron Barr* 58
3 b g Cadeaux Genereux—Asbo (Abou Zouz (USA))
2598[2] 3309[3] 3619[3] 4560[11] 5165[5] 5652[6] 6050[4] 6840[6]

Izzi Top *John Gosden* 111
3 b f Pivotal—Zee Zee Top (Zafonic (USA))
1270[DSQ] 1722[3] (2050) 2682[3] (7090a)

Izzy The Ozzy (IRE) *David Barron* 85
3 b f Encosta De Lago(AUS) —Naziriya (FR) (Darshaan)
2151[5] (2394) 3904[2] 5062[3] ◆ 5730[15] 6383[9]

Jaaryah (IRE) *Roger Varian* a91 91
3 ch f Halling(USA) —Albahja (Sinndar (IRE))
1807[5]

Jaasoos (IRE) *D Selvaratnam* a100 107
7 ch g Noverre(USA) —Nymphs Echo (IRE) (Mujtahid (USA))
239[10] 583a[5]

Jaci Uzzi (IRE) *David Evans* a49 49
2 b f Aussie Rules(USA) —Ceannanas (IRE) (Magical Wonder (USA))
1786[4] 2362[6] 3631[6] 4193[2] 4512[6] 5246[5] 6101[5] 6760[4] 7108[4] 7423[6] 7568[4] 7821[8]

Jackaroo (IRE) *A P O'Brien* a106 99
3 b c Galileo(IRE) —Ardbrae Lady (Overbury (IRE))
1548[6] (5090a)

Jack Barker *Robin Bastiman* 32
2 b g Danbird(AUS) —Smiddy Hill (Factual (USA))
4557[11]

Jack Bell (IRE) *Alan Swinbank* 15
4 ch g Rock Of Gibraltar(IRE) —Slip Ashore (IRE) (Slip Anchor)
4363[9] 5432[5]

Jack Dawkins (USA) *David Nicholls* a71 74
6 b g Fantastic Light(USA) —Do The Mambo (USA) (Kingmambo (USA))
744[5] (858)

Jackday (IRE) *Tim Easterby* 73
6 b g Daylami(IRE) —Magic Lady (IRE) (Bigstone (IRE))
1243[13] 1881[6] (2622) 3127[6] 3730[7] 4082[7]

Jackie Kiely *Roy Brotherton* a61 60
10 ch g Vettori(IRE) —Fudge (Polar Falcon (USA))
104[4] (451) 645[7] 6613[12] 7426[11]

Jackie Love (IRE) *Olivia Maylam* a62 42
3 b f Tobougg(IRE) —Gutter Press (IRE) (Raise A Grand (IRE))
811[3] 959[4] 1132[4] 1369[4] 2381[5] 2821[8] 3227[4] 4089[3] 5041[4] 5787[5] 6120[5] 6472[5] 7131[11] 7268[6] 7388[8] 7655[3] (7768) 7899[9]

Jackies Solitaire *Roger Charlton* a58
3 ch f Generous(IRE) —Bond Solitaire (Atraf)
471[6]

Jack Jicaro *Nicky Vaughan* a42 19
5 b g Mind Games—Makeover (Priolo (USA))
23[6]

Jack Junior (USA) *C Boutin* a80 69
7 b g Songandaprayer(USA) —Ra Hydee (USA) (Rahy (USA))
221a[2] 372a[5] (935a)

Jack Luey *Lawrence Mullaney* a63 78
4 b g Danbird(AUS) —Icenaslice (IRE) (Fayruz)
2280[2] 2938[6]

Jack My Boy (IRE) *David Evans* a88 100
4 b g Tagula(IRE) —Bobanlyn (IRE) (Dance Of Life (USA))
848[8] 1093[11] 1564[4] 1720[22] 2706[17] 3704[4] 4188[5] 4556[10] 4886[3] 5451[6] 6174[2] ◆ 6467[3] 6761[4] 7262[2]

Jack Of Diamonds (IRE) *Roger Teal* a78 69
2 b g Red Clubs(IRE) —Sakkara Star (IRE) (Mozart (IRE))
5382[4] ◆ 6214[3] 6524[6] 7095[2] ◆

Jack O'Lantern *Ian Williams* a31 76
4 b g Shamardal(USA) —Bush Cat (USA) (Kingmambo (USA))
22[3] 307[8]

Jack Rackham *Bryan Smart* a88 73
7 ch g Kyllachy—Hill Welcome (Most Welcome)
(199) 651[2] (1067) 3383[4] 5012[13] 5831[19]

Jack Smudge *James Given* a88 88
3 br g One Cool Cat(USA) —Forever Fine (USA) (Sunshine Forever (USA))
1825[11] 2508[8] 2724[5] 3052[10] 3384[4] 5456[5] 5939[8] 6801[P]

Jackson (BRZ) *Richard Guest* a49 54
9 ch g Clackson(BRZ) —More Luck (BRZ) (Baynoun)
409[5] 466[9] 1153[8] 1458[9] 2400[3] 2762[8] 3492[4] 4198[8] 4396[6]

Jackson Bend (USA) *Nicholas Zito* a122 97
4 ch h Hear No Evil(USA) —Sexy Stockings (USA) (Tabasco Cat (USA))
7302a[3]

Jack's Revenge (IRE) *George Baker* a66 75
3 br g Footstepsinthesand—Spirit Of Age (IRE) (Indian Ridge)
(456) 567[2] (716) ◆ 1819[3] (2418) 2583[2] 3118[9] (6605) 6936[7]

Jack's Rocket *Richard Guest* a19 22
4 b g Beckett(IRE) —Aybeegirl (Mazilier (USA))
319[5] 509[6] 546[8] 3074[8] 4123[8]

Jack Who's He (IRE) *David Evans* 92
2 b g Red Clubs(IRE) —Annus Iucundus (IRE) (Desert King (IRE))
(1055) (1316) 3012[8] 3589[5] 4055[8] 4311[3] 4575[4] 5876[5] 6535[8] 7021[7]

Jacob Cats *Richard Hannon* 82
2 b c Dutch Art—Ballet (Sharrood (USA))
2049[8] (4912) ◆ 5479[8]

Jacobee *J Moore* a85 109
4 b g Mark Of Esteem(IRE) —Sweet Cando (IRE) (Royal Applause)
7732a[9]

Jacob McCandles *David Barron* 66
4 br g Trade Fair—Feather Circle (IRE) (Indian Ridge)
3705[7] 4611[5] 4985[5] 5761[9]

Jacobs Son *Robert Mills* a78 82
3 ch g Refuse To Bend(IRE) —Woodwin (IRE) (Woodman (USA))
699[2] (762) 1057[2] 2228[2] 4336[7] 5966[11]

Jacqueline Quest (IRE) *Ian Williams* 111
4 b m Rock Of Gibraltar(IRE) —Coquette Rouge (IRE) (Croco Rouge (IRE))
2358[3] 3030[RR] 4790[4] 5510[2] 5848[11] 7128[P]

Jade *Ollie Pears* 85
3 b f Cadeaux Genereux—Ashdown Princess (IRE) (King's Theatre (IRE))
1697[2] 2122[2] 2763[2] 2986[8] 3819[5] 4235[5] 4676[2] 5081[7] 6094[2]

Jaguar Mail (JPN) *Noriyuki Hori* 123
7 b h Jungle Pocket(JPN) —Haya Beni Komachi (JPN) (Sunday Silence (USA))
7563a[3] 7873a[11]

Jag War (FR) *H-A Pantall* a91 81
3 b c Meshaheer(USA) —Just Fizzy (Efisio)
(5529a) 7667a[4]

Jahanara (IRE) *Richard Hannon* a66 72
3 b f Exceed And Excel(AUS) —Silversword (FR) (Highest Honor (FR))
3259[10] 3633[8] (5172) 5671[4]

Jake Mo (USA) *Allen Milligan* a90
2 bb c Giacomo(USA) —Credit Approval (USA) (With Approval (CAN))
7280a[5]

Jake's Destiny (IRE) *George Baker* a82
2 b g Desert Style(IRE) —Skehana (IRE) (Mukaddamah (USA))
6281[3] (6842) 7483[2]

Jake The Snake (IRE) *Tony Carroll* a93 77
10 ch g Intikhab(USA) —Tilbrook (IRE) (Don't Forget Me)
45[2] 279[4] 467[2] 648[2] (804) 956[2] 1172[3] 2111[6] 3045[6]

Jakeys Girl *Pat Phelan* a45 47
4 b m Dubai Destination(USA) —Rosewood Belle (USA) (Woodman (USA))
207[11]

Jakkalberry (IRE) *Marco Botti* 122
5 b h Storming Home—Claba Di San Jore (IRE) (Barathea (IRE))
(1918a) 2982a[4] 6202a[2] 7729a[7]

Jakor (ITY) *M Marcialis* 104
5 b h Orpen(USA) —Jackie (ITY) (Horage)
1919a[12]

Jaldarshaan (IRE) *Colin Teague* a67 67
4 b m Fath(USA) —Jaldini (IRE) (Darshaan)
[illegible] 6158[4] 6358[4]

Jalil (USA) *Mahmood Al Zarooni* a97 87
7 br h Storm Cat(USA) —Tranquility Lake (USA) (Rahy (USA))
240[6] 330a[5] 608a[5] 679a[7]

Jamaica Grande *Terry Clement* a49 66
3 ch g Doyen(IRE) —Mary Sea (FR) (Selkirk (USA))
4162[13]

Jamaican Bolt (IRE) *Bryan Smart* a81 79
3 b g Pivotal—Chiming (IRE) (Danehill (USA))
(1465) 3832[3] 4855[5]

Jamarjo (IRE) *Steve Gollings* a62 41
4 b g Marju(IRE) —Athlumney Lady (Lycius (USA))
1570[8] 1818[3] 1979[2] 3496[6] 3709[8] 5788[10] (7654) (7789) 7903[5]

Jambo Bibi (IRE) *Bruce Hellier* a72 65
3 b f Iffraaj—Nouveau Riche (IRE) (Entrepreneur)
66[7] 344[4] 601[6] 1543[8] 1975[6]

Jambobo *William Knight*
2 b g Acclamation—Hovering (IRE) (In The Wings)
3870[10] 4330[19]

Jameel (USA) *Saeed Bin Suroor* a70 92
3 b g Monsun(GER) —Maids Causeway (IRE) (Giant's Causeway (USA))
5327[2] (6096) 6528[7] 6989[4]

Jameela Girl *Robert Cowell* a54 83
3 ch f Haafhd—Peach Sorbet (IRE) (Spectrum (IRE))
6348[10] 7356[10]

Jamesie (IRE) *David Marnane* a94 97
3 b g Kodiac—Pretty Woman (IRE) (Night Shift (USA))
1825[2] 4566a[2] 5746a[6] 7790a[6]

James Pollard (IRE) *Bernard Llewellyn* a68 71
6 ch g Indian Ridge—Manuetti (IRE) (Sadler's Wells (USA))
1107[5] 1750[6] 4273[4] (4674) (5428) 6461[5] 7816[6]

Jamesway (IRE) *Richard Fahey* a85 91
3 ch g Camacho—Charlene Lacy (IRE) (Pips Pride)
1241[4] 1852[3] 2714[7] ◆ 2934[9] 3357[4] 3778[7] 4498[5] 5268[3]

Jamhara *Clive Brittain* 58
2 b f Authorized(IRE) —Wimple (USA) (Kingmambo (USA))
6030[9] 6458[7]

Jamhoori *Clive Brittain* a30 80
3 b c Tiger Hill(IRE) —Tanasie (Cadeaux Genereux)
4060[5] 4385[2] 4456[2]

Jam Maker *J R Jenkins* a19 24
3 b f Diktat—Jawwala (USA) (Green Dancer (USA))
456[10] 4248[7]

Jamr *Saeed Bin Suroor* a94 30
3 br g Singspiel(IRE) —Never Enough (GER) (Monsun (GER))
4208[2] 4753[6] 5629[10]

Jane Lachatte (IRE) *Stuart Williams* a45 52
2 b f Doyen(IRE) —Simonda (Singspiel (IRE))
5812[5] ◆ 7672[10]

Jane's Legacy *Reg Hollinshead* a52 28
3 b f Needwood Blade—Victory Flip (IRE) (Victory Note (USA))
194[2] 516[3] 731[9] 1300[6] 1769[12] 2565[2] 2801[6] 3596[9]

Janet's Pearl (IRE) *Paul Midgley* a70 69
3 ch f Refuse To Bend(IRE) —Sassari (IRE) (Darshaan)
2728[2] 3363[3] (3679) 4685[4] 4728[2] (5589)

Janey Muddles (IRE) *J S Bolger* 102
2 b f Lawman(FR) —Slip Dance (IRE) (Celtic Swing)
6691[6]

Janicellaine (IRE) *B W Hills* 84
3 b f Beat Hollow—Danielli (IRE) (Danehill (USA))
2184[3]

Janood (IRE) *Saeed Bin Suroor* a95 100
3 b g Medicean—Alluring Park (IRE) (Green Desert (USA))
238[4] 680a[5] 1339[10] 5853[6] 6704[6] 7127[4]

Jan Smuts (IRE) *Wilf Storey* a27 40
3 b g Johannesburg(USA) —Choice House (USA) (Chester House (USA))
6750[P] 7214[7]

Jan Vermeer (IRE) *A P O'Brien* 118
4 b h Montjeu(IRE) —Shadow Song (IRE) (Pennekamp (USA))
2439[3] 3031[6] 3371a[2] 4259a[4]

Jardina (GER) *P Schiergen* 99
3 b f Shirocco(GER) —Juvena (GER) (Platini (GER))
2981a[9] 6394a[3]

Jaridh (USA) *Saeed Bin Suroor* a72 50
3 b g Bernardini(USA) —Mansfield Park (Green Desert (USA))
1947[11] 3642[7]

Jarrah *Saeed Bin Suroor* 53
2 b c Oasis Dream—Fraulein (Acatenango (GER))
6278[7] 6994[7]

Jarrow (IRE) *David Nicholls* a96 93
4 ch g Shamardal(USA) —Wolf Cleugh (IRE) (Last Tycoon)
1438[5] 2095[2] 2694[14] 3028[6] (4013) 4516[3] 5683[9] 6382[9]

Jasie Jac (IRE) *Robert Mills* a70 66
2 b c Namid—Dynah Mo Hum (IRE) (Key Of Luck (USA))
3424[6] 6018[4] 6474[2]

Jasmeno *Hughie Morrison* a76 77
4 b m Catcher In The Rye(IRE) —Jasmick (IRE) (Definite Article)
(6666) 6893[10] 7120[10] 7570[5]

Jasmin Rai *Des Donovan* a55 55
4 b m Doyen(IRE) —Ella's Wish (IRE) (Bluebird (USA))
3[4] 449[5] 645[9] 854[7] 1190[3] 1636[5] 2149[5] 2271[8]

Jawaab (IRE) *Richard Guest* a87 84
7 ch g King's Best(USA) —Canis Star (Wolfhound (USA))
(835) 5729[10] 5888[13] 7022[14] 7272[7] 7759[10] 7877[9]

Jawad (IRE) *Ms Joanna Morgan* a74 80
10 b g Kahyasi—Mystic Charm (Nashwan (USA))
3420a[9]

Jawhar (IRE) *William Haggas* 81
3 ch g Halling(USA) —Kawn (Cadeaux Genereux)
(5792)

Jawim *Malcolm Saunders* a50 48
2 br f Piccolo—Craic Sa Ceili (IRE) (Danehill Dancer (IRE))
1583[8] 2143[8] 3722[7] 5535[3] 6492[5] 6890[5]

Jawking *David Evans* a65 22
2 b g Compton Place—Just Down The Road (IRE) (Night Shift (USA))
(1101) 1806[9] 7875[8]

Jay Bee Blue *Tom Dascombe* 74
2 b c Kyllachy—Czarna Roza (Polish Precedent (USA))
5486[6] 6025[2] 6292[2] 6725[7] 6995[12]

Jay Jays Joy *Paul Midgley* a65 51
3 b g Diktat—Agrippina (Timeless Times (USA))
41[3] 550[3] (1293) 1975[2] 2236[2] 2652[2] 3077[4] 4409[11] 7424[10] 7711[9] 7885[3]

Jay Kay *Robert Wylie* 52
2 b g Librettist(USA) —Turn Back (Pivotal)
2983[6] 3583[6] 4040[3] 5399[5] 6413[3] 6627[11]

Jay Peas Jacko *Lucinda Featherstone* a67
2 b g Pastoral Pursuits—Anniversary Guest (IRE) (Desert King (IRE))
6983[16] 7142[7] 7539[2]

Jazacosta (USA) *Jo Crowley* a66 73
5 ch g Dixieland Band(USA) —Dance With Del (USA) (Sword Dance)
4322[P]

J Cunningham *Mark Usher* a41 40
2 b f Compton Place—Applauding (IRE) (Royal Applause)
1870[4] 2919[6] 4021[4] 4704[7] 5099[8] 5896[6] 6942[10] 7635[6] 7742[9]

Jealous Hart *Ollie Pears* a40
2 b f Pastoral Pursuits—Khaiyala (FR) (Kahyasi)
7736[6] 7927[5]

Jeannie Galloway (IRE) *Richard Fahey* 95
4 b m Bahamian Bounty—Housekeeper (IRE) (Common Grounds)
923a[6] 2495[9] 3278[4] 4235[4] 5032[6] ◆ 5255[3] ◆ 6113[2] ◆ (6189)

Jedi *A bin Huzaim* a96 105
5 ch g Pivotal—Threefold (USA) (Gulch (USA))
242[6] ◆ 329a[11] 498a[4] 677a[4]

Jedward (IRE) *Charles O'Brien* 81
4 ch m Namid—Input (Primo Dominie)
6388a[4]

Jeer (IRE) *Michael Easterby* a76 84
7 ch g Selkirk(USA) —Purring (USA) (Mountain Cat (USA))
531[5] 715[2] (1107) 2320[9] 3580[6] 4237[9] 7699[11]

Jeeran *Alastair Lidderdale* a56 71
3 b g Acclamation—Savvy Shopper (USA) (Stravinsky (USA))
1152[11] 2818[9] 3136[5] 3523[5] 4067[4] 6408[9] 6624[12]

Jeewana *Henry Candy*
3 b f Compton Place—Jeewan (Touching Wood (USA))
3465[11]

Jehanbux (USA) *Richard Hannon* 95
3 b c Giant's Causeway(USA) —Harlan Honey (USA) (Silver Hawk (USA))
(1834) 2471[4] 3069[10] 4777[8]

Jehannedarc (IRE) *A De Royer-Dupre* 98
3 b f Montjeu(IRE) —Lucky Rainbow (USA) (Rainbow Quest (USA))
1922a[4] 2750a[6] 7580a[5]

Jellicle (IRE) *John Gosden* a67 73
2 b f Successful Appeal(USA) —Catboat (USA) (Tale Of The Cat (USA))
6030[5] ◆ 6440[5] 6950[4] 7292[3]

Jelyvator *Alex Hales* a56 45
3 b g Motivator—Camcorder (Nashwan (USA))
731[4] 1018[7]

Jembatt (IRE) *Michael Mulvany* a80 94
4 ch g Captain Rio—Silly Imp (IRE) (Imperial Frontier (USA))
923a[10] 3445a[16] 4566a[5] 5746a[14] 7468a[13]

Jemimaville (IRE) *Giles Bravery* a50 65
4 b m Fasliyev(USA) —Sparkling Isle (Inchinor)
123[5] 138[11] 250[7] 482[2] 619[10] 3254[3] 3556[8] 4189[4] 5996[8] 6258[4] 6619[7] 7676[5]

Jenio Horse (IRE) *E Botti*
3 b g Hawk Wing(USA) —Temeko (IRE) (Soviet Star (USA))
1126a[5]

Jenndale *Chris Dwyer* 8
2 b g Common World(USA) —Jennelle (Nomination)
5011[17] 5410[10] 7540[11]

Jennerous Blue *Dean Ivory* a55 51
4 b m Generous(IRE) —Jennelle (Nomination)
5519[7] 6087[6] 6476[12] 7087[9]

Jennifer J *Mark H Tompkins* a51
2 ch f Motivator—Trew Class (Inchinor)
7634[8]

Jenny Potts *Chris Down* a71 74
7 b m Robellino(USA) —Fleeting Vision (IRE) (Vision (USA))
79[2] ◆ 162[4] 392[3]

Jenny Soba *Lucinda Featherstone* a50 61
8 b m Observatory(USA) —Majalis (Mujadil (USA))
1107[13] 3243[5] 3599[8]

Jenny's So Great (CAN) *Gregory De Gannes* a112 97
4 b m Greatness(USA) —Jenny's Search (USA) (Lost Soldier (USA))
6908a[11]

Jeranimo (USA) *Michael Pender* a109 119
5 b h Congaree(USA) —Jera (USA) (Jeblar (USA))
7307a[7]

Jeremiah (IRE) *Laura Young* a65 68
5 ch g Captain Rio—Miss Garuda (Persian Bold)
449[4] 1604[10] 2308[16]

Jeremy Sue *Derek Haydn Jones* a28
2 b f Amadeus Wolf—Dearest Daisy (Forzando)
6406[10] 6654[13] 7593[8] 7898[6]

Jericho (IRE) *Jamie Osborne* a62 61
2 br g Manduro(GER) —Jinsiyah (USA) (Housebuster (USA))
6180[10] 6771[10] 7177[6] 7444[11]

Jersey Girl (DEN) *Lennart Reuterskiold Jr*
2 b f Binary File(USA) —Dianella (GER) (Bin Ajwaad (IRE))
4841a[5]

Jersey Joe (IRE) *Brian Ellison* a43 22
4 br g Trans Island—Meigiu (IRE) (Catrail (USA))
284[5] 2461[6] 2669[5]

Jersey Town (USA) *Barclay Tagg* a119
5 ch h Speightstown(USA) —Jersey Girl (USA) (Belong To Me (USA))
7304a[6]

Jessica Wigmo *Tony Carroll* a58 50
8 b m Bahamian Bounty—Queen Of Shannon (IRE) (Nordico (USA))
211[9] 311[2] 482[6] 690[4] 821[7] 1043[8]

Jessie's Spirit (IRE) *Ann Duffield* 85
2 gr f Clodovil(IRE) —Alexander Anapolis (IRE) (Spectrum (IRE))
(4430) (5061) 5825[6] 6670[4]

Je Suis Unrockstar *David Nicholls* a70 56
3 b g Monsieur Bond(IRE) —Discoed (Distinctly North (USA))
4[3] 119[5] 198[2] 465[5] 659[4] 740[5] 847[7] 875[5] 3702[8] 4328[12] 5600[8] 6615[4]

Jet Away *Sir Henry Cecil* 116
4 b h Cape Cross(IRE) —Kalima (Kahyasi)
(1896) ◆ 2292[2] 3591[9] 6125[2] (6671) ◆ 7170[4]

Jet Express (SAF) *A Al Raihe* a109 71
9 b g Jet Master(SAF) —Outback Romance (SAF) (Sharp Romance (USA))
503a[13]

Jettie *David Evans* 36
2 ch f Needwood Blade—Danjet (IRE) (Danehill Dancer (IRE))
1049[7] 1628[6] 2153[11] 2998[8]

Jeu De Roseau (IRE) *Chris Grant* a57 75
7 b g Montjeu(IRE) —Roseau (Nashwan (USA))
2433[2] 3072[2] ◆ 3507[7] (4326) 5079[4] 6451[3]

Jeu De Vivre (IRE) *Mark Johnston* a57 87
3 b f Montjeu(IRE) —In My Life (IRE) (Rainbow Quest (USA))
1327[3] 1574[7] 1972[4] 2478[2] (2730) 3116[6] (3301) 3858[5] 4510[5] 4879[3] 5107[2] (5207) 5504[6] (6191) 6385[2] 7136[6]

Jewelled *Lady Herries* a68 82
5 b m Fantastic Light(USA) —Danemere (IRE) (Danehill (USA))
1269[6] 1789[3] (2144) 2597[2] (3436) 4616[4] ◆ 4931[2] 5586[3] 6302[19]

Jewelled Dagger (IRE) *Keith Dalgleish* a31 82
7 b g Daggers Drawn(USA) —Cappadoce (IRE) (General Monash (USA))
2260[4] 3399[10] (3906) 4142[4] (4382) (4499) 5035[12] 5724[12] 6601[3] 6868[6] 7002[12]

Jezza *Victor Dartnall* a79 59
5 br g Pentire—Lara (GER) (Sharpo)
68[2] 697[6] 872[3] 7461[5]

Jibaal (IRE) *Marco Botti* a78 76
3 b g Acclamation—Maid To Order (IRE) (Zafonic (USA))
1624[2] (2472) 2847[6] 3358[5] 5735[8] 6543[3] ◆ 6978[4]

Jibouti (IRE) *Clive Brittain* a59 20
3 b g Exceed And Excel(AUS) —Treble Seven (USA) (Fusaichi Pegasus (USA))
4989[7] 5381[0] 5561[12] 6071[10] 6939[12] 7352[7] 7538[3] 7571[9] 7848[3]

Jigajig *Kevin Ryan* a78 75
4 ch g Compton Place—Eau Rouge (Grand Lodge (USA))
168[7] 708[2] 1411[6] 1955[4] 2263[3] 2766[2] 3471[7]

Jiggalong *Mrs D Thomas* a55 52
5 ch m Mark Of Esteem(IRE) —Kalamansi (IRE) (Sadler's Wells (USA))
173[12] 408[11] 552[6] 911[10] 1625[9] 1833[5]

Jimmy Choux (NZ) *John Bary* 124
4 b c Thorn Park(AUS) —Cierzo (NZ) (Centaine (AUS))
7044a[2] 7731a[9]

Jimmy Ryan (IRE) *Tim McCarthy* a64 65
10 b g Orpen(USA) —Kaysama (FR) (Kenmare (FR))
80[4] 224[2] 812[6] 1182[2] 1581[5] (4207) 4759[2] 7201[10]

Jimmy Styles *Clive Cox* a105 111
7 ch g Inchinor—Inya Lake (Whittingham (IRE))
237[6] 602a[6] 848[3] (1093) 1340[8] 3154[9] 3863[14] 4092[3] 4534[12] 5927[6] 6522[9] 6858[10]

Jimmy The Lollipop (IRE) *Neil Mulholland* a67 72
2 b g Amadeus Wolf—Royal Consort (IRE) (Green Desert (USA))
1095[5] 1522[6] 2346[2] 3879[6] 4094[24] 4512[4] 4943[11] (5413) 6345[3] 6652[6] 7849[7]

Jimtown *Kevin Prendergast* a81 83
2 b g Avonbridge—Gorgeous Dancer (IRE) (Nordico (USA))
2532a[4]

Jingoism (USA) *Brian Ellison* a47
5 b g Empire Maker(USA) —Pert Lady (USA) (Cox's Ridge (USA))
61[6] 145[5]

Jinker Noble *Clive Cox* 80
2 b c Green Desert(USA) —Depressed (Most Welcome)
4857[15] (6579)

Jinto *David Elsworth* a64 70
4 ch g Halling(USA) —Sweet Willa (USA) (Assert)
1608[9] 2021[9] 2991[10] 4317[4] 4974[3] 5519[2] 5947[2] 6798[5]

Jivry *Henry Candy* 88
4 ch m Generous(IRE) —Jadidh (Touching Wood (USA))
3434[2] 4890[6] 5963[4]

Jiwen (CAN) *Roger Varian* 92
3 bb f Singspiel(IRE) —Love Medicine (USA) (Mining (USA))
2648[12] (4072) (4931) 6062[4] (6996)

J J Leary (IRE) *David Nicholls* 51
2 b g Amadeus Wolf—Nautical Design (USA) (Seeking The Gold (USA))
1383[9] 1673[6] 2214[10]

Jjs Pride (IRE) *Paul W Flynn* a47 66
2 b g One Cool Cat(USA) —Yaselda (Green Desert (USA))
2329a[8]

J J The Jet Plane (SAF) *M Houdalakis* a95 125
7 b g Jet Master(SAF) —Majestic Guest (SAF) (Northern Guest (USA))
582a[11] (825a) ◆ (996a)

Jkt Prince (IRE) *Daniel Mark Loughnane* a60 62
2 b g Strategic Prince—Hazardous (Night Shift (USA))
6842[5] 7038[4]

Joan D'Arc (IRE) *Noel Quinlan* a66 70
4 b m Invincible Spirit(IRE) —Prakara (IRE) (Indian Ridge)
4626[6] (5519) 5790[10] 6182[4] 6503[13] 6969[8]

Jobe (USA) *Kevin Ryan* a88 86
5 b g Johannesburg(USA) —Bello Cielo (USA) (Conquistador Cielo (USA))
1200[6] 1878[8] 2095[10] (2633) 2806[6] 5434[5] 5682[6] (7352) 7531[13] 7726[3]

Jobekani (IRE) *Lisa Williamson* a32 64
5 b g Tagula(IRE) —Lyca Ballerina (Marju (IRE))
3952[14]

Jo Boy *David Simcock* a64 17
4 b h Royal Applause—Bad Kitty (USA) (Mt. Livermore (USA))
437[5] 546[3]

Jo'Burg (USA) *David O'Meara* a75 96
7 b g Johannesburg(USA) —La Martina (Atraf)
2573[15] 3203[8] 4004[6] 4477[5] 5205[13] 5488[10] 6302[7] ◆ 6533[2] ◆ 6708[2] 6989[10]

Jocheski (IRE) *Tony Newcombe* a58 56
7 b g Mull Of Kintyre(USA) —Ludovica (Bustino)
2905[3] 3600[4]

Jodawes (USA) *John Best* a71 67
4 bb g Burning Roma(USA) —Venetian Peach (USA) (Desert Wine (USA))
206 [12] 565[6] 4249[5] 4754[3] 5318[4] 6032[2] 6468[8] 6621[3] 6789[12]

Jody Bear *Jonathan Portman* a47 45
3 b f Joe Bear(IRE) —Colins Lady (FR) (Colonel Collins (USA))
2192[9] 3226[11] 5912[5]

Joe Le Taxi (IRE) *Mark Johnston* a80 56
3 ch g Johannesburg(USA) —Attasliyah (IRE) (Marju (IRE))
(189) ◆ (322) 476[5] (659) (1019) 1313[5]

Joe M *Simon Dow* a43 36
2 ch g Araafa(IRE) —Ambonnay (Ashkalani (IRE))
2423[3] 2997[11] 4848[8] 6625[7] 7359[6] 7541[5] 7657[5]

Joe Packet *Jonathan Portman* a89 107
4 ch g Joe Bear(IRE) —Costa Packet (IRE) (Hussonet (USA))
700[11] 1111[16] 1888[13] (4859) 5264[2] 5927[14] 6129[3] 6521[5] 6706[19]

Joe Rocco (IRE) *Alan Swinbank* 39
3 br g Shirocco(GER) —Nenuphar (IRE) (Night Shift (USA))
1203[14] 1693[12] 2125[5] 5623[5] 6868[8]

Joe Strummer (IRE) *Michael Bell* a65 67
3 b g Librettist(USA) —Post Modern (USA) (Nureyev (USA))
1298[7] 1774[6] 3002[9] 3643[3] 4281[3] 4506[4] 5178[3] 6052[4] 7037[4]

Joey Hayes *Noel Quinlan* a56 48
2 b c Araafa(IRE) —Tanwir (Unfuwain (USA))
1095[8] 1235[3]

Johanna Fosie (IRE) *Mick Channon* 58
2 ch f Peintre Celebre(USA) —Yding (IRE) (Danehill (USA))
5537[5]

Johannes (IRE) *Richard Fahey* a90 105
8 b g Mozart(IRE) —Blue Sirocco (Bluebird (USA))
1111[12] 1720[8] ◆ 2028[7] 2317[10] 3395[3] 3841[10] 5060[13] 5180[12] 5758[4] 7149a[6]

Johannesgray (IRE) *Noel Wilson* a73 70
4 gr g Verglas(IRE) —Prepare For War (IRE) (Marju (IRE))
22[4] 3508[6] 3972[4] 5437[9] 5881[12] 6847[10]

Johansen *Kate Walton*
2 b g Primo Valentino(IRE) —Ryans Daughter (Night Shift (USA))
2542[10] 3021[10]

John Biscuit (IRE) *Andrew Balding* a87 84
3 ch g Hawk Wing(USA) —Princess Magdalena (Pennekamp (USA))
1175[4] 1547[6] 3825[14] 4447[3] 5199[3]

John Fitgerald (IRE) *Y Durepaire* a79
4 b h Bahri(USA) —Madaeh (USA) (Swain (IRE))
831a[2]

John Forbes *Brian Ellison* a66 78
9 b g High Estate—Mavourneen (USA) (Dynaformer (USA))
1977[6] 2320[4] ◆ (2952) (3316) 3935[3] 4423[14] 5149[4] 6115[5] 7772[5]

John Lightbody *Mark Johnston* 79
2 b g Teofilo(IRE) —Patacake Patacake (USA) (Bahri (USA))
(2882) 3861[11] 6077[5]

John Louis *Philip McBride* a70 68
3 ch g Bertolini(USA) —Native Ring (FR) (Bering)
3138[4] 4163[4] 4663[3]

Johnmanderville *Mme F Lauffer* a82 82
5 b g Kheleyf(USA) —Lady's Walk (IRE) (Charnwood Forest (IRE))
221a[0]

Johnno *J W Hills* a75 72
2 br c Excellent Art—Vert Val (USA) (Septieme Ciel (USA))
4264[6] 4995[11] 6951[5] (7197)

Johnny Castle *John Gosden* a79 103
3 b g Shamardal(USA) —Photogenic (Midyan (USA))
2216[2] (2673) (3178) ◆ 3649[11] 5830[3]

Johnny Cavagin *Richard Guest* a31 33
2 b g Superior Premium—Beyond The Rainbow (Mind Games)
1383[10] 1966[7] 7422[8]

Johnny Hancocks (IRE) *Linda Stubbs* a74 78
3 b g Kodiac—Taisho (IRE) (Namaqualand (USA))
100[4] 198[3] 356[3] 465[6] 632[4] 875[6] 1193[2] 1514[4] 1595[3] 1967[2] 2524[5] 3189[4] 3321[3] 3433[2] 3920[2]

Johnny Splash (IRE) *Roger Teal* a53 6
2 b g Dark Angel(IRE) —Ja Ganhou (Midyan (USA))
6118[9] 7345[9] 7526[10]

John Potts *Brian Baugh* a74 1
6 b g Josr Algarhoud(IRE) —Crown City (USA) (Coronado's Quest (USA))
(69) (283) 488[5] 635[2] (749) (881) 1066[4] 7465[10] 7816[2] ◆ 7901[5]

Johnson's Cat (IRE) *Richard Guest* a51 55
2 b g One Cool Cat(USA) —Takanewa (IRE) (Danetime (IRE))
3050[7] 3491[4] 3755[14] 5324[4] 5597[7] 6425[2] 6645[4]

Johnstown Lad (IRE) *Daniel Mark Loughnane* a86 80
7 b g Invincible Spirit(IRE) —Pretext (Polish Precedent (USA))
3160[7] 5616[10] 6408[5] 7039[4] 7819[8] 7846[7] 7893[7]

John The Glass *Mark Wellings* a45
4 b g Deportivo—Brendas Nightmare (Tina's Pet)
1053[8] 1277[8] 2565[6]

John Veale (USA) *Thomas McLaughlin* a77 74
5 b g Strong Hope(USA) —Soccory (USA) (Tricky Creek (USA))
381[7] 427[4] 949[11]

Joie De Deauville (FR) *M Figge* a78 85
3 ch f High Yield(USA) —River Sans Retour (FR) (Vacarme (USA))
981a[3]

Join Up *Mark Brisbourne* a65 58
5 b g Green Desert(USA) —Rise (Polar Falcon (USA))
26[4] 90[6] 361[5] (526) 712[8] 1052[9] 1486[4] 1763[6] 1905[6] 2268[6] 2561[10] 7538[9] (7740) 7848[7]

Jojo Bonita (FR) *L Polito* 80
3 b f Altieri—Red Rosie (USA) (Red Ransom (USA))
3449a[9]

Jolah *Clive Brittain* a64 75
3 b f Oasis Dream—Fanny's Fancy (Groom Dancer (USA))
2383[10] 3983[6] 7842[7]

Joli Colourful (IRE) *Tony Newcombe* a20 29
2 b c Tiger Hill(IRE) —Coloma (JPN) (Forty Niner (USA))
1136[7] 2788[13] 3708[4] 5374[10] 5535[6] 6021[U] 7432[13]

Jolly Ranch *Tony Newcombe* a65 69
5 gr m Compton Place—How Do I Know (Petong)
443[3] 812[7] (3721) 3999[2] 4224[10] 5175[5] (6398)

Joly Nelsa (FR) *M Cesandri* a66 77
6 b m Brier Creek(USA) —Joly Coeur (FR) (Mont Basile (FR))
219a[10] 439a[6]

Jo Mania (IRE) *J-M Capitte* a48
4 ch g Rock Of Gibraltar(IRE) —Tycoon's Drama (IRE) (Last Tycoon)
1012a[8]

Jonnie Skull (IRE) *Phil McEntee* a67 63
5 b g Pyrus(USA) —Sovereign Touch (IRE) (Pennine Walk)
743[3] 800[6] 809[5] 906[3] 1045[5] (1497) (1875) 1989[3] (2452) 2829[5] 3495[2] 3953[4] 4064[5] 5037[2] 5298[3] 5394[4] 6070[7] (6138) 6488[10] 6624[2] 6848[8] 7228[8] 7351[6] 7507[9] 7648[4] 7711[6] 7775[6] 7924[4]

Jonny Delta *Jim Goldie* 77
4 ch g Sulamani(IRE) —Send Me An Angel (IRE) (Lycius (USA))
1542[4] 2045[6] 2735[7] 4879[2] 5311[5] (5724) ◆ 6191[3] 6832[3]

Jonny Ebeneezer *David Flood* a62 66
12 b g Hurricane Sky(AUS) —Leap Of Faith (IRE) (Northiam (USA))
129[11] (210) 276[4] (311) 947[7] 1041[7] 1177[8] 1486[P]

Jonny Lesters Hair (IRE) *Tim Easterby* a71 88
6 b g Danetime(IRE) —Jupiter Inlet (IRE) (Jupiter Island)
1098[5] 1879[5] 2124[5] 2544[6] 3085[4] 3399[3] 4109[7] (4404) 4608[4] 5205[9] 5488[3] 6093[5] (6346) 6533[7]

Jonny Mudball *Tom Dascombe* a100 111
5 b g Oasis Dream—Waypoint (Cadeaux Genereux)
1687[3] 2138a[11]

Jordans Chrissy (IRE) *Tim Pitt* 21
3 gr f Iffraaj—Gentilesse (Generous (IRE))
5792[9]

Jordans Express *Noel Wilson*
3 b g Primo Valentino(IRE) —Staff Nurse (IRE) (Night Shift (USA))
2361[14]

Jordaura *Gay Kelleway* a82 92
5 br g Primo Valentino(IRE) —Christina's Dream (Spectrum (IRE))
279[7] 557[8] 1395[4] 2301[3] (2867a) 3348[5] 3473[2] 4310[9] 4990[5] (5390) 6226[3] (6401) 7050[6] 7877[6]

Josam (IRE) *Richard Hannon* a72
2 b c Montjeu(IRE) —Bella Miranda (Sinndar (IRE))
7627[4] ◆ 7809[2]

Joseph Henry *David Nicholls* a81 97
9 b g Mujadil(USA) —Iris May (Brief Truce (USA))
(1240) 1849[12] 2717[5] 4314[19] 4531[4] 5758[19] 6145[11]

Josephine Malines *John Flint* a51 51
7 b m Inchinor—Alrisha (IRE) (Persian Bold)
278[10] 355[5] 3910[8]

Josephines Baby (FR) *L A Urbano-Grajales* a89 76
4 b m Great Pretender(IRE) —Reine Josephine (FR) (Loup Solitaire (USA))
903a[3]

Joshua The First *Keith Dalgleish* 72
2 br c Kheleyf(USA) —Newkeylets (Diktat)
2042[3] 2395[4] 3035[2] 3274[2] 3656[2] 4012[2] 4140[2] 4632[7] 5161[4] 5645[4] 6144[3] 6644[3] 7157[2]

Joshua Tree (IRE) *Marco Botti* 118
4 b h Montjeu(IRE) —Madeira Mist (IRE) (Grand Lodge (USA))
5055[2] 5773a[3] 6910a[2]

Jossy Johnston (IRE) *Eric Alston* a47 61
3 ch g Captain Rio—Darzao (IRE) (Alzao (USA))
4084[6] 4576[5] 6981[9]

Journalistic (USA) *Marcus Tregoning* a58 79
2 b c Street Sense(USA) —Cajun Two Step (USA) (Tabasco Cat (USA))
3686[11] 5384[7] 5959[2] 6462[2]

Jovial (IRE) *Denis Coakley* a66 68
4 b g Sakhee(USA) —Baalbek (Barathea (IRE))
1608[7] 2312[11] 3225[4] 4847[2] 5406[2] 6005[7]

Joviality *John Gosden* 109
3 b f Cape Cross(IRE) —Night Frolic (Night Shift (USA))
1546[2] (2004) 3106[6] 3822[4] 5366a[7]

Joy And Fun (NZ) *D Cruz* 120
8 b g Cullen(AUS) —Gin Player (NZ) (Defensive Play (USA))
7730a[2]

Joyful Sound (IRE) *Andrew Haynes* 63
3 b g Acclamation—Eman's Joy (Lion Cavern (USA))
1865[7] 2790[5] 3138[5] 3913[3] 4435[7] 4686[4] 5134[6]

Joyful Spirit (IRE) *John Dunlop* 63
2 b f Invincible Spirit(IRE) —Pershaan (IRE) (Darshaan)
3812[11] 4552[12] 5299[8] 5809[5] ◆ 6753[2]

Joyously *Richard Guest* a69 78
3 ch f Needwood Blade—Lambadora (Suave Dancer (USA))
7610[10] 7775[10]

Joy To The World (IRE) *Paul Cole* a56
2 ch f Dylan Thomas(IRE) —Speciale (USA) (War Chant (USA))
6440[10]

J R Hartley *Bryan Smart* a81 40
3 b g Refuse To Bend(IRE) —Flyfisher (USA) (Riverman (USA))
546[5] (873) 2319[14] 4107[7] 4513[10] 5439[5] 6616[2] 7243[4] 7502[3]

Juarla (IRE) *Ronald Harris* a69 69
3 ch c Tagula(IRE) —Jersey Lillie (IRE) (Hector Protector (USA))
(64) 251[3] (452) ◆ 788[3] 868[3] 1294[3] (2163) 2396[2] 4227[4] 4486[8] 5344[6]

Jubilance (IRE) *Jeremy Noseda* a87 86
2 b c Oratorio(IRE) —Literacy (USA) (Diesis)
3686[8] (4201) ◆ 4508[2] (5638) ◆ 6170[8] 6952[3]

Judas Jo (FR) *Gay Kelleway* 69
2 ch f Muhtathir—Lovna (USA) (Tale Of The Cat (USA))
(1791) 3104[9] 3973[3] 4551[8] (5983a) 7135[9]

Judd Street *Eve Johnson Houghton* a83 103
9 b g Compton Place—Pudding Lane (IRE) (College Chapel)
1186[7] 1457[7] 2099[8] 2826[6] 3627[13] 6728[11] 7127[6] 7438[4] 7602[3] 7660[9]

Judgement *John Gosden* a70
3 ch f Medicean—Virtuosity (Pivotal)
791[4]

Judge 'n Jury *Ronald Harris* a85 104
7 ch g Pivotal—Cyclone Connie (Dr Devious (IRE))
1680[8] 2028[4] 2397[4] 4104[3] 4357[4] 4416[15] 4886[5] (5484) 5703[3] 6224[11] 6332[5] 7018[4]

Judgethemoment (USA) *Jane Chapple-Hyam* a59 71
6 br g Judge T C(USA) —Rachael Tennessee (USA) (Matsadoon (USA))
244[7] 4396[7]

Judicious *Geoffrey Harker* 85
4 ch g Pivotal—Virtuous (Exit To Nowhere (USA))
1212[4] ◆ 1692[7] (2800) ◆ 2988[3] (3572) (4432) 6024[3] 6989[13]

Jukebox Jury (IRE) *Mark Johnston* 120
5 gr h Montjeu(IRE) —Mare Aux Fees (Kenmare (FR))
(3403) 4492[3] (5304a) (5952a) 7218a[20]

Julienas (IRE) *Walter Swinburn* a99 105
4 b g Cape Cross(IRE) —Dora Carrington (IRE) (Sri Pekan (USA))
1529[3] 2441[3] (3032) 4972[8] 5494[10]

Julie's Love *Manfred Hofer* a84 104
3 ch f Ad Valorem(USA) —Skimmia (Mark Of Esteem (IRE))
2981a[2] 3651a[4] 5980a[5] 6394a[2] 6568a[8]

Juliet Capulet (IRE) *A P O'Brien* a85 94
3 b f Holy Roman Emperor(IRE) —Royal Ballerina (IRE) (Sadler's Wells (USA))
1006a[6] (Dead)

Julius Geezer (IRE) *Tom Dascombe* 94
3 b g Antonius Pius(USA) —Victoria's Secret (IRE) (Law Society (USA))
1545[4] 1852[8] 2684[7] 2908[7] 3682[2] 4779[10] 5706[11] 6327[7] 6913[17]

July Days (IRE) *Brian Baugh* a60 83
5 b m Exceed And Excel(AUS) —Tocade (IRE) (Kenmare (FR))
2814[10] 3805[11] 4949[11] 5394[5] 5740[11] 6488[4]

Jumeira Field (USA) *Robert Cowell* a73 61
3 bb c Arch(USA) —Chic Joy (USA) (A.P. Indy (USA))
1409[8] 2596[5] 4849[2] 5633[7]

Jumeirah Liberty *Zoe Davison* a55
3 ch g Proclamation(IRE) —Gleam Of Light (IRE) (Danehill (USA))
4991[7] 7662[4] 7894[4]

Jumeirah Palm Star *Richard Hannon* 66
2 b f Invincible Spirit(IRE) —Golden Flyer (FR) (Machiavellian (USA))
3201[7] 4002[5] 4614[8]

Jumooh *F Head* a67 77
4 b m Monsun(GER) —Eshaadeh (USA) (Storm Cat (USA))
108a[3]

June Thirteen (IRE) *Richard Hannon* 38
2 ch c Choisir(AUS) —Recast (IRE) (Traditionally (USA))
2998[12] 3631[4] 3816[15]

Jungle *B W Hills* 61
2 gr f Dark Angel(IRE) —Forest Prize (Charnwood Forest (IRE))
3257[7] ◆ 3779[10]

Jungle Bay *Jane Chapple-Hyam* a87 87
4 b h Oasis Dream—Dominica (Alhaarth (IRE))
99[11] 264[5] 394[2] 521[3] 725[8] 1977[8] 2816[2] 3361[10] (3806) 4255[2] 5195a[6] 5924[3] 6246[6] 6759[3] 7299[9]

Jungle Beat (IRE) *John Gosden* 83
2 ch c Galileo(IRE) —Flamingo Guitar (USA) (Storm Cat (USA))
(4054) ◆

Junior *David Pipe* a93 98
8 ch g Singspiel(IRE) —For More (FR) (Sanglamore (USA))
3013[9]

Junket *Dr Jon Scargill* a80 79
4 b m Medicean—Gallivant (Danehill (USA))
4255[5] ◆ 5100[3] 5383[11] 7299[6]

Junoob *Tom Dascombe* a99 90
3 ch g Haafhd—Faydah (USA) (Bahri (USA))
1409[12] 1836[5] (2760) ◆ 6068[3] 6497[11] (7446) (7600) 7802[2]

Juno The Muffinman (IRE) *Tom Dascombe* a75 73
2 b g Holy Roman Emperor(IRE) —Mackenzie's Friend (Selkirk (USA))
3076[4] 3472[2] 4068[6] 5899[3] 6825[4]

Jupiter Fidius *Kate Walton* 70
4 b g Haafhd—Kyda (USA) (Gulch (USA))
1244[9] 2348[5] 2494[6] 3088[2] 3306[3] 3612[8] 4852[3] 5150[2] 5594[3] 6028[3] 6452[9] 7099[10]

Jupiter Storm *Gary Moore* 87
2 ch c Galileo(IRE) —Exciting Times (FR) (Jeune Homme (USA))
6165[7] ◆ 6527[13] (6970)

Just Bond (IRE) *Geoffrey Oldroyd* a90 91
9 b g Namid—Give Warning (IRE) (Warning)
235[4] 932[2] 1560[2] (1970) 2783[2] 4561[9] 4794[10] 5929[9] 6533[3] 7110[7]

Justbookie Dot Com (IRE) *David Evans* a80 66
3 ch g Fath(USA) —Dream On Deya (IRE) (Dolphin Street (FR))
1031[5] 2383[9] 2926[14] 3238[5] 3920[3] 4640[4] 4758[3] 5274[3] 5539[12] (5864) (6179) 6354[3] 6505[4] 6830[7] 7348[2] 7417[3] 7531[12]
Justbookies Dotnet *Louise Best* a57 57
2 b g Kheleyf(USA) —Moly (Inchinor)
3686[16] 5812[6] 7526[8] 7692[4] 7830[6] 7837[3]
Just Breathe (IRE) *Chris Down* a62
2 b f Choisir(AUS) —Opium Creek (IRE) (Darshaan)
(7490)
Justcallmehandsome *Dominic Ffrench Davis* a72 67
9 ch g Handsome Ridge—Pearl Dawn (IRE) (Jareer (USA))
26[7] (90) 169[4] 428[4] 562[7] 685[9] 1052[12] 2165[7] 3235[5] (3475) 5414[9] 5740[9] 6543[6] 6878[6] 7400[2] 7538[7] 7589[4] (7632) 7734[6] 7930[11]
Just Dixie *John Weymes* a16 41
2 b f Avonbridge—Fly South (Polar Falcon (USA))
1165[9] 1301[5] 2234[5] 4500[4] 5245[9] 6043[13]
Just Fabulous *George Moore* 84
2 b f Sakhee(USA) —Tipsy Me (Selkirk (USA))
(4323) (5487) ◆
Just Five (IRE) *John Weymes* a81 79
5 b g Olmodavor(USA) —Wildsplash (USA) (Deputy Minister (CAN))
495[2] ◆ 1110[16] 1614[5] 2149[4] 3141[2] 3244[3] 3486[2] 4603[9] 5205[15] 6188[6] 6616[11] 7099[8] 7425[9] 7772[6] 7887[7]
Just For Leo (IRE) *David Evans* a59 68
3 b g Camacho—Coppelia (IRE) (Mac's Imp (USA))
66[2] 100[3] 183[12] 198[6] 349[4]
Just For Mary *Daniel Mark Loughnane* a68 85
7 b g Groom Dancer(USA) —Summer Dance (Sadler's Wells (USA))
(3908) 4272[5] 4882[2] 6388a[10]
Just Gillian *Peter Hiatt* a17
3 br f Bertolini(USA) —Comme Ca (Cyrano De Bergerac)
5247[6] 6377[9]
Justice Walk (IRE) *Paul Fitzsimons* 55
3 ch g Exceed And Excel(AUS) —True Joy (IRE) (Zilzal (USA))
1682[8] 2103[15] 5843[10]
Justineo *William Haggas* 105
2 b c Oasis Dream—Loulwa (IRE) (Montjeu (IRE))
2612[3] 3553[2] (4507) 5251[4] ◆ 5933[2] 6688[11]
Justine Time (IRE) *David Barron* a50 59
2 b f Kodiac—Sinn Time (IRE) (Key Of Luck (USA))
2113[10] 2693[4] 3021[5] 3728[3] 4105[2] ◆ 5005[2] ◆ 5399[6] 6043[7] 6229[8] 6597[8] 6695[6]
Just Like Heaven (IRE) *Tim Easterby* 69
2 b g Kodiac—Night Beauty (King Of Kings (IRE))
1797[6] 2570[3] 2983[12] 4809[3] ◆ 5058[2] 5398[5] 5726[5] 6232[2] 6827[9]
Just Lille (IRE) *Ann Duffield* a98 98
8 b m Mull Of Kintyre(USA) —Tamasriya (IRE) (Doyoun)
(2314) (6006) 7136[4]
Just Mossie *Bill Turner* a40 34
6 ch g Ishiguru(USA) —Marinsky (USA) (Diesis)
3240[7]
Just Observing *Neville Bycroft* a74 49
8 ch g Observatory(USA) —Just Speculation (IRE) (Ahonoora)
2473[7] 2666[6] 3072[10]
Justonefortheroad *Richard Fahey* a91 99
5 b g Domedriver(IRE) —Lavinia's Grace (USA) (Green Desert (USA))
1092[4] (1694) 2031[6] 7168[20] 7628[6] 7719[10]
Just On Fire (IRE) *Andrew Oliver* a75 64
3 ch g Barathea(IRE) —Cool Cousin (IRE) (Distant Relative)
(6511a)
Just Rob *Ian Williams* [illegible]
[illegible](USA) —Scapavia (FR) (Alzao (USA))
6410[4]
Just Sam (IRE) *Ron Barr* a61 79
6 b m Mull Of Kintyre(USA) —Strawberry Sands (Lugana Beach)
3387[9] 3569[6] 3856[11] 4563[2] 4672[4] 5437[7] 5732[7]
Just Say Please *Martin Bosley* a51
4 ch m Needwood Blade—Roonah Quay (IRE) (Soviet Lad (USA))
7904[8]
Just The Tonic *Marjorie Fife* a59 73
4 ch m Medicean—Goodwood Blizzard (Inchinor)
1244[5] 1558[12] 2799[5] 3245[3] 3805[5] 3936[2] 4141[7] 4670[11] 5488[4] (5721) 6450[2] 6533[14] 6869[U] 7141[6]
Just Timmy Marcus *Brian Baugh* a72 61
5 ch g Ishiguru(USA) —Grandads Dream (Never So Bold)
287[10] 428[3] 637[6] 933[8] 1052[10]
Just When *Andrew Balding* 54
2 b c Dalakhani(IRE) —Cape Grace (IRE) (Priolo (USA))
6954[8]
Just Zak *Owen Brennan* a51 33
6 b g Superior Premium—Goodbye Millie (Sayf El Arab (USA))
399[6] 1567[9]
Jutland *Mark Johnston* 104
4 b g Halling(USA) —Dramatique (Darshaan)
(1824) 2044[6] 2573[14] (2909) 3156[14] 3876[19] 4410[4] 4788[4] 5853[5] 6163[19] 6339[22]
Juvenal (IRE) *Richard Hannon* a75 78
2 b c Holy Roman Emperor(IRE) —Final Opinion (IRE) (King's Theatre (IRE))
4762[6] 5239[3] 5713[3] 6463[3]
Juwireya *Peter Hiatt* a63 69
4 b m Nayef(USA) —Katayeb (IRE) (Machiavellian (USA))
89[4] 223[10] 373[4] 596[3] 733[11]
Jwala *Robert Cowell* a77 74
2 b f Oasis Dream—Kangra Valley (Indian Ridge)
6758[6] 6946[2] 7135[8] 7526[3] (7736)
Kaafel (IRE) *Charles Hills* 78
2 b c Nayef(USA) —Tafaani (IRE) (Green Desert (USA))
6165[2] ◆ 6768[6]
Kadoodd (IRE) *Mick Channon* 78
3 b g Motivator—Briery (IRE) (Salse (USA))
1692[2] 2551[7] 3206[6] 3705[3]
Kadouchski (FR) *John Berry* a60 67
7 b g Ski Chief(USA) —Douchka (FR) (Fijar Tango (FR))
(955) ◆ 1148[6] 1839[9] 3047[3] 3281[2] (3769) 4712[2]
Kadyny *T Lerner* 98
2 b c Zamindar(USA) —Hoh My Darling (Dansili)
6184a[3] 6660a[7]
Kagera *B Grizzetti* 92
3 b f Halling(USA) —Baila Salsa (IRE) (Barathea (IRE))
1432a[11] 1738a[12]
Kagura (USA) *G Henrot* a97 100
3 b f Vindication(USA) —Miss Emma (IRE) (Key Of Luck (USA))
1122a[0] 2138a[9] 4739a[0]
Kahfre *Gary Moore* a76 55
4 ch g Peintre Celebre(USA) —Minerva (IRE) (Caerleon (USA))
131[3] (309) (718)
Kahraba (USA) *Saeed Bin Suroor* 81
3 bb f Unbridled's Song(USA) —Thunder Kitten (USA) (Storm Cat (USA))
5001[3] 5877[2] 6242[3] (7111)
Kahruman (USA) *William Haggas* 68
2 bb c Mr Greeley(USA) —Jaleela (USA) (Kingmambo (USA))
6805[4]
Kahsabelle (FR) *Venetia Williams* a65 71
6 b m Kahyasi—Lysabelle (FR) (Lesotho (USA))
5236[3] 5966[10]
Kai *Michael Bell* 32
2 b g Kyllachy—Belle Ile (USA) (Diesis)
5480[15] 6160[14]
Kaifi (IRE) *Clive Brittain* 36
3 b f Dansili—Easter Fairy (USA) (Fusaichi Pegasus (USA))
1588[6] 2598[9]
Kailani *Mahmood Al Zarooni* 79
2 b f Monsun(GER) —Kazzia (GER) (Zinaad)
(6933)
Kai Mook *Roger Ingram* a66 40
4 gb m Littletown Boy(USA) —Beenaboutabit (Komaite (USA))
55[6] 128[5] 477[4] 689[4] 1054[2] 1357[5] 1995[5] 2198[3] 2922[2] 6624[10] 7131[9] 7394[4] 7522[7] 7698[10] 7805[5] 7891[3]
Kaiser Wilhelm (IRE) *Paul Cole* 63
2 b c Hurricane Run(IRE) —Luana (Shaadi (USA))
5851[11] 6245[10]
Kajima *R Pritchard-Gordon* a102 97
4 b g Oasis Dream—Mambo Mistress (USA) (Kingmambo (USA))
2679[17] 3578[3] 4100[12] 4415[18] 4993[3] 5712[2] 7015a[2]
Kajsa Kavat (FR) *Mme Pia Brandt* a79 82
3 ch f Layman(USA) —Territorial (Selkirk (USA))
5463a[10]
Kakapuka *Anabel K Murphy* a86 81
4 br g Shinko Forest(IRE) —No Rehearsal (FR) (Baillamont (USA))
1395[13] 1968[10] (2719) ◆ 3348[4] 3634[8] (5948) 6378[15] 7227[6] 7531[14]
Kakatosi *Andrew Balding* a107 109
4 br g Pastoral Pursuits—Ladywell Blaise (IRE) (Turtle Island (IRE))
1889[2] 2315[2] 2502[8] 3404[9] 4049[2] 7433[8] 7801[5]
Kalabaya (IRE) *John M Oxx* 102
3 b f Sinndar(IRE) —Kalandara (IRE) (Rainbow Quest (USA))
4035a[4] ◆
Kalahaag (IRE) *David Nicholls* a51 84
3 ch f Iffraaj—[illegible] (IRE) (In The Wings)
1884[10] 2188[6] 2925[10] 3260[5] 4584[6] 5213[4] 5560[7] 5828[11] 6472[10] 7099[7] 7241[5] 7357[6] 7743[6]
Kalahari Desert (IRE) *Richard Whitaker* a35 58
4 b g Captain Rio—Sally Traffic (River Falls)
1501[5] 2249[10] 2985[11] 3248[8] 3573[3] 3937[5] 4636[3] 4881[8] 4986[7] 5373[5] 5620[4] 6208[13] 6343[5]
Kalahari Gold (IRE) *F Rohaut* a108 104
6 ch g Trans Island—Neat Shilling (IRE) (Bob Back (USA))
7221a[5]
Kala Kanta (IRE) *S Seemar* a75 64
5 gr h Verglas(IRE) —Rappide (IRE) (Fayruz)
707a[5]
Kalamkas (USA) *Jeremy Noseda* 61
3 bb f Kingmambo(USA) —Reach For The Moon (USA) (Pulpit (USA))
4388[3] 5001[7]
Kalann (IRE) *Sabrina J Harty* a69 86
4 b g Barathea(IRE) —Karkiyla (IRE) (Darshaan)
4398a[6]
Kalathir (FR) *R Schoof*
3 ch f Muhtathir—Kalatuna (FR) (Green Tune (USA))
7016a[0]
Kal Barg *D Selvaratnam* a101 89
5 b g Medicean—Persian Air (Persian Bold)
240[9] 499a[6] 605a[9] 824a[8]
Kaldera (IRE) *Bodil Hallencreutz* 48
3 ch g Kheleyf(USA) —St Finan's Bay (IRE) (Ashkalani (IRE))
4840a[3]
Kaldougold (BEL) *Andre Hermans* 31
4 b m Kaldounevees(FR) —Lions Gold (GER) (Java Gold (USA))
7315a[0]
Kaldoun Kingdom (IRE) *Richard Fahey* a47 111
6 b g King's Best(USA) —Bint Kaldoun (IRE) (Kaldoun (FR))
2075[15] 2317[15] 2727[3] ◆ 6147[18] 6209[3] 6706[2] 6987[10]
Kalendar Girl (IRE) *Willie Musson* a78 67
3 b f Motivator—Kalanda (Desert King (IRE))
952[7] 1984[4] 3312[3] 4060[6] 5179[3] 5838[RR] 7037[2]
Kalgoolie *Rae Guest* a51 43
3 b f Aussie Rules(USA) —Kilbride (Selkirk (USA))
2457[12] 3226[12] 3431[7]
Kalkan Bay *Jedd O'Keeffe* a72 71
3 b g Pastoral Pursuits—Gibraltar Bay (IRE) (Cape Cross (IRE))
1801[8] 2096[8] 2406[8] 3337[13]
Kalk Bay (IRE) *William Haggas* a94 89
4 b g Hawk Wing(USA) —Politesse (USA) (Barathea (IRE))
1092[14] 3109[14] 5936[9] 6862[26]
Kalleidoscope *Mick Channon* 74
3 ch f Pivotal—Brush Strokes (Cadeaux Genereux)
1516[6] 2092[9]
Kalokagathia (IRE) *Jo Crowley* a72
2 b c Kodiac—Seabound (Prince Sabo)
7330[5] 7672[3]
Kambis *Luca Cumani* a54 46
3 b g Tobougg(IRE) —Queen Tomyra (IRE) (Montjeu (IRE))
1974[6] 2469[10] 3518[7]
Kameruka *R Pritchard-Gordon* a96 90
5 ch m Auction House(USA) —Love Letters (Pursuit Of Love)
(5195a) 6783a[7] 7128[9]
Kames Park (IRE) *Richard Guest* a77 81
9 b g Desert Sun—Persian Sally (IRE) (Persian Bold)
190[3] 232[3] (1608) 2159[3] 2320[5] 2708[7] 3023[11] 3243[7] 4747[4] 5357[6] 5504[3] 5804[9] 6546[4] 6790[5] 7087[7] 7556[6] 7661[4] (7761) 7789[5] 7878[4] 7939[3]
Kaminski Kabs *Phil McEntee* a42
3 b f Pastoral Pursuits—Demi Tasse (Largesse)
892[5] 971[6] 1065[10] 1953[10]
Kammamuri (IRE) *Frank Sheridan* a68
6 b g Kalanisi(IRE) —Speedybird (IRE) (Danehill (USA))
247[5] 425[2] 854[6] 1373[3]
Kampai *John Akehurst* a36
3 b f Sakhee(USA) —Green Supreme (Primo Dominie)
5633[8] 6020[8]
Kanace *Noel Quinlan* a59 50
4 ch g Pastoral Pursuits—Pendulum (Pursuit Of Love)
70[2] 1604[2] 1911[9]
Kanaf (IRE) *Ed Dunlop* a88 101
4 b g Elnadim(USA) —Catcher Applause (Royal Applause)
1680[11] 2826[2] ◆ (3796) 4534[5] ◆ 5180[5] ◆ 5887[6] 6347[9]
Ka Nordik (FR) *N Leenders* a50 47
9 b m Myrakalu(FR) —Kissey (FR) (Red Paradise (IRE))
1013a[0]
Kansai Spirit (IRE) *John Gosden* a94 107
5 ch g Sinndar(IRE) —Daanat Nawal (Machiavellian (USA))
2071[3]
Kantata *James Toller* a12
3 b f Piccolo—Mory Kante (USA) (Icecapade (USA))
2924[U] 4186[6] 5639[10] 6981[8]
Kanzee Gold (SWE) *Henrik Engblom*
2 ch f Eishin Dunkirk(USA) —Ok Maite (Komaite (USA))
5983a[9]
Kapga De Cerisy (FR) *Mme L Audon* 62
3 ch g Kapgarde(FR) —Non Liquet (Kendor (FR))
5132a[7]
Kapitala (FR) *Andreas Lowe* a73 89
2 b f Hawk Wing(USA) —Key To Fortune (GER) (Big Shuffle (USA))
4375a[5] 6941a[8]
Kapitale (GER) *A Wohler* 109
3 b f Dubawi(IRE) —Kapitol (GER) (Winged Love (IRE))
3449a[11] 4839a[6] (6395a) 7047a[3]
[illegible] *[illegible]* a91 90
4 ch g Pivotal—Mauri Moon (Green Desert (USA))
1110[12] 1438[3] ◆ 1695[3] 2299[2] 2806[3] (4349) 4794[6] 5684[4] ◆ 6113[8] 7110[13]
Karam Albaari (IRE) *J R Jenkins* a73 106
3 b c King's Best(USA) —Lilakiya (IRE) (Dr Fong (USA))
5510[8] 5934[7] 6298[6] 7516[13]
Karasenir (IRE) *Philip Hobbs* a53
5 b g Sendawar(IRE) —Karasta (IRE) (Lake Coniston (IRE))
1028[4]
Kara's Orientation (USA) *Steven Chircop* a105 114
4 bb h Orientate(USA) —Crissy Aya (USA) (Saros)
6204a[11] 6910a[11]
Kara's Vision *Robert Cowell* 46
2 b f Kyllachy—Classic Vision (Classic Cliche (IRE))
4940[5] 5351[4] 5590[6]
Karate (IRE) *Hans Adielsson* a68 70
3 ch g Exceed And Excel(AUS) —La Belle Katherine (USA) (Lyphard (USA))
106[5] 358[5] 764[5] 887[8] 1020[3] 1400[7] 3523[4] 3783[8] (3924) 4547[8] 4911[2] 5143[9] 5381[4] 5902[2] 6122[5] 6488[7] 6847[5] 7131[8] 7848[5] (7910)
Karate Queen *Ron Barr* a25 47
6 b m King's Best(USA) —Black Belt Shopper (IRE) (Desert Prince (IRE))
1247[10] 1557[8] 2593[2]
Karatoya (IRE) *E Lellouche* a63 104
4 b h Tiger Hill(IRE) —Wajd (USA) (Northern Dancer (CAN))
1842a[7]
Kardo (GER) *W Baltromei* a83 82
4 b h Paolini(GER) —Kedah (GER) (Local Suitor (USA))
267a[5] 478a[6]
Karens Legacy (IRE) *Ian McInnes* a30 28
3 ch f Exceed And Excel(AUS) —Stardance (USA) (Rahy (USA))
2781[6] 7845[7]
Kargali (IRE) *Luke Comer* a56 105
6 gr h Invincible Spirit(IRE) —Karliyka (IRE) (Last Tycoon)
5086a[12]
Kargarann (IRE) *Seamus Durack* a46 49
4 b g Danehill Dancer(IRE) —Romancia (USA) (Woodman (USA))
2246[6]
Karistar (IRE) *Tom Keddy*
2 b f Montjeu(IRE) —Showcall (USA) (Kingmambo (USA))
6934[12]
Karma Chameleon *John Berry* a76 57
2 b g Haafhd—Mrs Snaffles (IRE) (Indian Danehill (IRE))
3070[6] 4171[4] 4390[9] 5645[3] 6260[12] 6424[5] 7444[2] (7763) (7849) (7915)
Karmarouge (IRE) *Brian Rothwell* 45
3 b f Croco Rouge(IRE) —Karmafair (IRE) (Always Fair (USA))
1151[7] 1413[4] 2239[8]
Karsabruni (FR) *H-A Pantall* 103
3 b f Speedmaster(GER) —Karsawina (GER) (Lando (GER))
1597a[4] (3651a) 4839a[11] 7090a[6] 7386a[10]
Kartica *P Demercastel* 106
4 b m Rainbow Quest(USA) —Cayman Sunset (IRE) (Night Shift (USA))
920a[8] 1784a[5] 5075a[4]
Karuga *Richard Hannon* 77
2 ch f Kyllachy—Bolshaya (Cadeaux Genereux)
1505[4] 1846[6] 2997[9] 4277[2] 4581[4] (5324) 6021[2] (6431)
Kasbah Bliss (FR) *F Doumen* a78 114
8 b g Kahyasi—Marital Bliss (FR) (Double Bed (FR))
757a[4] (1231a) 1707a[3] 3066[7] 4037a[10] 5304a[2] (6562a)
Kasla (USA) *Clive Brittain*
3 b f More Than Ready(USA) —Should Excell (USA) (Dixieland Band (USA))
4388[P]
Kassaab *Ian Semple* a64 64
3 br g Kyllachy—Aconite (Primo Dominie)
132[3] 335[7] (558) 745[2] 868[2] 1249[4] 1776[9] 3238[4] 3860[6] 5203[5] 5436[7] 6501[9]
Kassiodor (GER) *Barney Curley* a57
4 b g Tiger Hill(IRE) —Kitcat (GER) (Monsun (GER))
52[10] 202[2] 428[8] 684[6] 7202[8]
Kassyield (FR) *H Paysan* a85 84
3 b g High Yield(USA) —Kassande (FR) (Midyan (USA))
7677a[5]
Katerini (FR) *F Head* a92 92
3 b f Cacique(IRE) —Chanteleau (USA) (A.P. Indy (USA))
7509a[7]
Kate Skate *Gay Kelleway* a61 67
4 ch m Mark Of Esteem(IRE) —Saristar (Starborough)
113[4] 144[5] 1034[15] 1770[9] 2249[4] 2450[6] 2829[4] 3190[6] 3476[7] 3638[7]
Katherine Lee (IRE) *M Halford* a86 74
3 b f Azamour(IRE) —Lady Of Kildare (IRE) (Mujadil (USA))
(7150a) 7277a[10]
Katherine Parr *Peter Chapple-Hyam* a52
3 ch f Haafhd—Kristina (Kris)
171[6] 214[11] 456[8]
Kathindi (IRE) *Michael Chapman* a65 57
4 ch g Pearl Of Love(IRE) —Turfcare Flight (IRE) (Mujadil (USA))
1976[3] 3243[8] 3496[10] 5116[5] 7743[9]
Kathlatino *Micky Hammond* 73
4 b m Danbird(AUS) —Silver Rhythm (Silver Patriarch (IRE))
2548[7] 2988[9] 5107[6] 7078[8]
Kathleen Frances *Mark H Tompkins* 86
4 b m Sakhee(USA) —Trew Class (Inchinor)
2006[10] 2892[4] 3277[2] 3829[5] 4537[13] 5729[8] 7136[7]
Kath[illegible] *[illegible] Jonathan Geake* a55 82
11 b m Turtle Island(IRE) —Evaporate (Insan (USA))
466[2] 544[5] 1068[6] 1987[6] 3251[6] 4090[8] 4544[3] 5349[3] (5611) (5785) (5912)
Kathleensluckylad (IRE) *Kevin Ryan* a50 60
2 b c Antonius Pius(USA) —Jacobina (Magic Ring (IRE))
6532[5] 7292[11] 7540[5]
Kathmanblu (USA) *Kenneth McPeek* a107 107
3 b f Bluegrass Cat(USA) —Abba Gold (USA) (Devil's Bag (USA))
6183a[8] 6887a[8]
Kathryn Perry (IRE) *David Evans* 46
2 b f Amadeus Wolf—Misty Peak (IRE) (Sri Pekan (USA))
2787[15] 3117[5] 3408[6] 5535[8] 6627[16]
Katie's Ten (USA) *John W Sadler* 79
2 bb f Rock Hard Ten(USA) —Hawayil (USA) (Halling (USA))
7562a[6]
Katies Tuitor *J S Moore* a68 39
8 b g Kayf Tara—Penny Gold (IRE) (Millfontaine)
3817[11] 4273[10] 4870[5] (5947) 6087[3] 6476[5]
Katla (IRE) *J F Grogan* 106
3 b f Majestic Missile(IRE) —Bratislava (Dr Fong (USA))
1006a[8] 1533a[2] 3158[4] 6164[9] 6733a[14]
Katmai River (IRE) *Mark Usher* a71 69
4 b g Choisir(AUS) —Katavi (USA) (Stravinsky (USA))
26[10] 280[4] 488[4] 719[5] (893) (984) 1177[4] 1368[3] 1995[2] 2201[7] 2605[9] 4230[3] 4742[5] (5201) 5539[4] 7448[11] 7588[10] 7715[9] 7820[5]
Katmandoune (FR) *J Boisnard* 101
3 gr f Country Reel(USA) —Louvardie (FR) (Loup Solitaire (USA))
(5230a)
Katsya (FR) *J E Pease* a88 95
4 b m Sinndar(IRE) —Labyrinth (FR) (Exit To Nowhere (USA))
1784a[10]
Katy's Secret *William Jarvis* a36 73
4 b m Mind Games—Katy O'Hara (Komaite (USA))
2001[4] 2756[6] 3714[3] (4187) 4918[3] (5355) 5862[2] 6065[2] 6979[7] (7776)

Kaua'i Girl *Ann Duffield* 62
3 ch f Dubawi(IRE) —Sara Mana Mou (Medicean)
1557[9] 1906[8]

Kaulbach (GER) *Mme L Barreaud*
5 ch g Areion(GER) —Karthesia (Efisio)
93a[0]

Kavachi (IRE) *Gary Moore* a70 87
8 b g Cadeaux Genereux—Answered Prayer (Green Desert (USA))
1382[8] 1834[6] 2310[8] 3081[6] 3477[7] 4278[5] 4725[6] 5422[5] 5994[3] 6437[5]

Kavaloti (IRE) *Gary Moore* a78 50
7 b g Kahyasi—Just As Good (FR) (Kaldounevees (FR))
342[6] 1050[2] 1148[8] ◆ 1761[4] 3047[2] (3281) 3738[3] 3978[7]

Kavango (IRE) *M bin Shafya* a102 107
4 b h Cape Cross(IRE) —Wood Vine (USA) (Woodman (USA))
583a[2] 682a[2] 759a[9] 828a[4]

Kawssaj *Roger Varian* a86 85
3 b c Dubawi(IRE) —Ameerat (Mark Of Esteem (IRE))
2457[2] 3320[2] (4849) 5322[13]

Kayaan *Pam Sly* a67 70
4 br g Marju(IRE) —Raheefa (USA) (Riverman (USA))
1398[4] 2202[2] 2526[8] (3311) 6790[8]

Kaya Belle (GER) *Stanislav Otruba* 87
4 b m Lando(GER) —Kahina (GER) (Warning)
5980a[9]

Kayef (GER) *Michael Scudamore* 92
4 ch h Nayef(USA) —Kassna (IRE) (Ashkalani (IRE))
1412[9] 1847[4] 2499[2] 3157[10] 6832[6]

Kay Gee Be (IRE) *Richard Fahey* a96 98
7 b g Fasliyev(USA) —Pursuit Of Truth (USA) (Irish River (FR))
(1269) 1684[4] (2123) 2933[3] 3032[17] 3876[6] 4528[5] 5185[9] 5920[9] 6326[7] 6803[10] 7110[2]

Kaylee *Gary Moore* a54 52
2 b f Selkirk(USA) —Mrs Brown (Royal Applause)
4954[7] 5424[7] 6252[3] 6821[8] 6942[8]

Kaylena *Jeremy Noseda* 56
2 b f Teofilo(IRE) —Kootenay (IRE) (Selkirk (USA))
5655[10] ◆ 6726[10]

Kazbow (IRE) *Luca Cumani* a79 98
5 b g Rainbow Quest(USA) —Kasota (IRE) (Alzao (USA))
2107[12] 2888[12] (3344) 4890[2] 5878[2] 6690[33]

Kazuri (FR) *Mme J Hendriks* a34 17
4 b m Kahyasi—Zukhruf (Unfuwain (USA))
479a[9]

Kazzene (USA) *David Pipe* a80 89
4 b g Cozzene(USA) —Coconut Willamina (USA) (Pleasant Colony (USA))
2931[8] 3428[7]

Kecek (IRE) *M Guarnieri* a53
8 ch g Mark Of Esteem(IRE) —Charming Helene (Star Appeal (IRE))
617a[6]

Keene Dancer *Sir Michael Stoute* 64
2 ch f Danehill Dancer(IRE) —Kinnaird (IRE) (Dr Devious (IRE))
7165[5]

Keep A Welcome *Gerry Enright* a32
8 ch g Most Welcome—Celtic Chimes (Celtic Cone)
7600[7] 7939[7]

Keepax *Chris Wall* 74
2 b g Dubai Destination(USA) —Stellar Brilliant (USA) (Kris S (USA))
6123[9] (6742)

Keep Cool *Andreas Lowe* 100
4 b h Starcraft(NZ) —Kirov (Darshaan)
6202a[4] 6710a[5] 7409a[5]

Keep It Cool (IRE) *P F O'Donnell* a86 86
7 ch g Spinning World(USA) —Sudden Stir (USA) (Woodman (USA))
3445a[12]

Keep Swinging (IRE) *Tom Tate* 47
2 br c Oasis Dream—Whisper To Dream (USA) (Gone West (USA))
3186[5] 3755[11]

Kel Away (FR) *Mlle M Henry* a72 79
4 gr m Keltos(FR) —Flamaway (FR) (Gold Away (IRE))
219a[8] 371a[0]

Kelkene (FR) *C Diard* 88
2 b c Della Francesca(USA) —Louve Solitaire (FR) (Loup Solitaire (USA))
4624a[3]

Kellemoi De Pepita *R Dzubasz* 86
3 br f Hawk Wing(USA) —Golightly (USA) (Take Me Out (USA))
2337a[8] 2981a[10] 3651a[7]

Kellys Eye (IRE) *George Foster* 101
4 b g Noverre(USA) —Limit (IRE) (Barathea (IRE))
1111[9] 2620[7] 3134[12] 4802[12] 5434[10]

Kelpie Blitz (IRE) *Seamus Durack* a64 37
2 gr g Verglas(IRE) —Summer Spice (IRE) (Key Of Luck (USA))
3229[12] 6214[10] 6792[4]

Keltbray (IRE) *Robert Mills* a54
3 b g Galileo(IRE) —Mill Guineas (USA) (Salse (USA))
7712[5] ◆

Kendam (FR) *H-A Pantall* 105
2 b f Kendargent(FR) —Damdam Freeze (FR) (Indian Rocket)
4843a[5] 6042a[2] (6808a) 7192a[5]

Kenmay (IRE) *Brian Meehan* 57
2 b g Marju(IRE) —Queen Margrethe (Grand Lodge (USA))
6334[13] 6953[7]

Kenmour (FR) *F Rossi* a99 102
4 gr h Azamour(IRE) —Marie De Ken (FR) (Kendor (FR))
267a[6] (661a)

Kennessey (USA) *Christopher Speckert* a87 85
5 ch g Tapit(USA) —Gennessy (USA) (Hennessy (USA))
9100a[8]

Kenny Powers *Tom Dascombe* 94
2 b c Vital Equine(IRE) —Alexander Ballet (Mind Games)
3082[4] ◆ 3313[3] ◆ 3773[5]

Kensei (IRE) *David O'Meara* a77 86
4 ch g Peintre Celebre(USA) —Journey Of Hope (USA) (Slew O'Gold (USA))
1560[4] (2112) ◆ 3276[7] 3585[6] 4608[2] 5593[12]

Ken's Girl *Stuart Kittow* a64 85
7 ch m Ishiguru(USA) —There's Two (IRE) (Ashkalani (IRE))
(2769) 3632[2] 4429[12] 5328[5] 5968[6] 6330[5] 6996[10] 7236[4]

Kenswick *Pat Eddery* a56 61
4 b m Avonbridge—The Jotter (Night Shift (USA))
129[2] 229[8] 312[2] 467[5] 555[6] 652[4] 807[9] 950[9] 2149[3] (2921) 3280[7] 3944[15] 4270[4] 4549[10] 4705[2] 5539[15] 5843[4] 6609[13] 7581[11] 7843[3]

Kentish (USA) *Noel Quinlan* a73 53
4 bb g Storm Cat(USA) —Apple Of Kent (USA) (Kris S (USA))
253[3] ◆ 636[4] 993[5] (1195) 3514[10] 3763[7]

Kenton Street *Michael J Browne* a70 65
6 ch g Compton Place—Western Applause (Royal Applause)
139[2] 7764[9]

Kenyan Cat *Ed McMahon* a66 90
4 br m One Cool Cat(USA) —Nairobi (FR) (Anabaa (USA))
1658[3] 2204[2] (2912) ◆ (3848) 5062[2] 5888[4] 6330[2] 6996[3]

Kephas (IRE) *F Iovine* 79
3 b c Oratorio(IRE) —Secret Wells (USA) (Sadler's Wells (USA))
1920a[11]

Kepler's Law *Sir Mark Prescott Bt* a92 73
3 b g Galileo(IRE) —Tina Heights (Shirley Heights)
(2379) (2613) (5249) (5416) 6218[5]

Kerchak (USA) *William Jarvis* a81 81
4 b g Royal Academy(USA) —Traude (USA) (River Special (USA))
1443[8] 1935[3] 3184[9]

Kerrys Requiem (IRE) *Tim Pitt* a86 93
5 b m King's Best(USA) —Moonlight Wish (IRE) (Peintre Celebre (USA))
2122[7] 2806[8] 3386[2] 3757[5] 4349[9] 5106[3] 5314[8] 7299[14]

Kersivay *David J Evans* a76 73
5 b g Royal Applause—Lochmaddy (Selkirk (USA))
22[2] 56[7] 538[6] 746[7] 786[6] 880[8] 1034[2] 1213[11] (1804a)

Kettle River (USA) *Saeed Bin Suroor* a100
4 b h Congaree(USA) —La Grande Mamma (CAN) (Compadre (USA))
583a[11]

Key Addition (IRE) *William Muir* a58 68
2 br c Kheleyf(USA) —Adeptation (USA) (Exceller (USA))
4250[4] 4485[2] 4848[5] 5161[2] 5613[13] 5840[12] 6284[7] 6540[11] 6919[7]

Key Ambition *Bryan Smart* a47 79
2 ch g Auction House(USA) —Love Thing (Phountzi (USA))
4358[2] (4899) 5505[4] 6166[2] 6670[10] 6827[4] 7445[9]

Key Appointment *Tom Tate* 81
2 b c Pivotal—Appointed One (USA) (Danzig (USA))
6828[3] 7232[2]

Key Breeze *Kevin Ryan* a76 71
4 b g Exceed And Excel(AUS) —Cayman Sound (Turtle Island (IRE))
1714[4] 2046[9] 3112[5] (3938) 4540[8] 5205[5] 5622[3] 6355[2] 6669[3] 7214[2] (7548a) 7792a[6]

Key Decision (IRE) *Jo Davis* a28 58
7 br g Key Of Luck(USA) —Adalya (IRE) (Darshaan)
2804[8] 7787[10]

Keyed Up (FR) *F Doumen* 88
3 b f Key Of Luck(USA) —Tipsy Topsy (Ashkalani (IRE))
1597a[7]

Key Gold *Mark Johnston* 69
2 b f Cape Cross(IRE) —Key Academy (Royal Academy (USA))
6458[10] 6771[5]

Keyhole Kate *Tim Walford* 66
2 b f Kheleyf(USA) —Striking Pose (IRE) (Darshaan)
2430[3] 2983[17] 3680[8]

Key Impeller *Bill Turner* 41
3 b g Bertolini(USA) —Latch Key Lady (USA) (Tejano (USA))
4320[13] 4607[8]

Key News (IRE) *Patrick Martin* a66 36
6 br m Halling(USA) —Belle Argentine (FR) (Fijar Tango (FR))
7159[11]

Keys (IRE) *Roger Charlton* a84 100
4 b g Doyen(IRE) —Freni (GER) (Sternkoenig (IRE))
1998[2] 2813[4] 3519[2] (4097) (4266) 6690[18]

Keys Of Cyprus *David Nicholls* a26 91
9 ch g Deploy—Krisia (Kris)
1410[7] 1696[5] 2061[7] 2301[11] 3275[16] 3358[4] 5106[17] 5594[9] (6081) 6830[6] 7074[10]

Key To The Motion (IRE) *Paul Midgley* a17 49
3 b f Kheleyf(USA) —Rustle In The Wind (Barathea (IRE))
183[11]

Khajaaly (IRE) *Julia Feilden* a79 70
4 b g Kheleyf(USA) —Joyfullness (USA) (Dixieland Band (USA))
96[10] 692[2] 915[4] 2165[3] 3093[9] 3674[4] 4866[2] 5422[7] (6354) 6979[4] 7417[5] 7928[9]

Khaki (IRE) *David Evans* a56 30
3 b f Key Of Luck(USA) —Tithcar (Cadeaux Genereux)
634[6] 791[5] 4888[8] 6253[12] 6816[4] 7096[4] 7270[4] 7412[11]

Khalashan (FR) *Peter Niven* 54
5 gr g Sinndar(IRE) —Khalasha (FR) (Linamix (FR))
1328[6] 1492[4] 2219[9] 2575[F] (Dead)

Khaleeji *J W Hills* a76 62
3 b c Kyllachy—Fly In Style (Hernando (FR))
1335[12] 2158[5] 2772[5] 3783[11] 4281[10]

Khaleejiya (IRE) *James Toller* 70
2 b f Jeremy(USA) —Certainly Brave (Indian Ridge)
4726[3] 5117[3] 6449[2]

Khan (DEN) *Soren Jensen*
2 b g Binary File(USA) —Kutbeya (USA) (Diesis)
(4841a)

Khanbaligh (FR) *C Lerner* a76 71
2 b f Panis(USA) —Lady Time (FR) (Orpen (USA))
7814a[0]

Khandaq (USA) *Keith Dalgleish* a81 78
4 b g Gulch(USA) —Jadarah (USA) (Red Ransom (USA))
(1368) 1793[4] 2545[12] 3113[5] 4380[9]

Khanivorous *Jim Boyle* a83 59
4 b g Dubai Destination(USA) —Bright Edge (Danehill Dancer (IRE))
279[3] 495[3] 736[4]

Khan Of Khans (IRE) *Rebecca Curtis* 48
2 b c Hurricane Run(IRE) —Roman Love (IRE) (Perugino (USA))
5536[7] 5959[7]

Khaos (IRE) *P D Deegan* a81 78
2 b f Kodiac—Church Mice (IRE) (Petardia)
7012a[12]

Khawlah (IRE) *Saeed Bin Suroor* a111 91
3 b f Cape Cross(IRE) —Villarrica (USA) (Selkirk (USA))
(681a) ◆ (998a)

Khazium (IRE) *Pat Eddery* a71 69
2 br c Kheleyf(USA) —Hazium (IRE) (In The Wings)
2767[5] 3171[3] 3534[4] 5099[3] 5690[2] 6484[3]

Kheley (IRE) *Mark Brisbourne* a67 72
5 b m Kheleyf(USA) —Namesake (Nashwan (USA))
(102) 166[3] 185[2] 318[3] 363[6] 511[5] 664[4] 912[4] 941[3] 1029[4] 1287[8] 1464[3] 1818[2] 2162[3] 2655[5]

Kheskianto (IRE) *Michael Chapman* a52 53
5 b m Kheleyf(USA) —Gently (IRE) (Darshaan)
517[8] 1164[6] 1905[5] 2359[3] 2851[4] 3245[8] 3636[4] 3938[9] 4409[3] 4945[9] 6050[2] 6235[9]

Kheya (IRE) *George Moore* a28 64
3 b f Kheleyf(USA) —Monarchy (IRE) (Common Grounds)
119[6]

Khione *Luca Cumani* 49
2 b f Dalakhani(IRE) —Sularina (IRE) (Alhaarth (IRE))
5806[8]

Khor Sheed *Luca Cumani* 108
3 ch f Dubawi(IRE) —Princess Manila (CAN) (Manila (USA))
1317[3] 1902[2] (3323) 4497[9] (6370a)

Khubala (IRE) *Ed Dunlop* a41
2 b c Acclamation—Raghida (IRE) (Nordico (USA))
6787[5]

Khun John (IRE) *Willie Musson* a66 66
8 b g Marju(IRE) —Kathy Caerleon (IRE) (Caerleon (USA))
54[2] 7671[10] 7901[8]

Kialoskar (IRE) *T Lerner* a73 76
3 b f Refuse To Bend(IRE) —Romea (Muhtarram (USA))
7667a[0]

Kiama Bay (IRE) *John Quinn* a84 106
5 b g Fraam—La Panthere (USA) (Pine Bluff (USA))
(67) (1036) (3381) 4354[2] 5250[2] 5921[2] 7297[9]

Kian's Delight *Jedd O'Keeffe* a42 65
3 b g Whipper(USA) —Desert Royalty (IRE) (Alhaarth (IRE))
1812[7] 2635[3] 3487[9] (4366) 4903[5] (5372) 6279[9]

Kian's Joy *Jedd O'Keeffe* a22 22
2 b g Mind Games—Lunasa (IRE) (Don't Forget Me)
6774[10] 6912[10] 7240[6]

Kickahead (USA) *Ian Williams* a59 65
9 b g Danzig(USA) —Krissante (USA) (Kris)
6873[4] 7195[7]

Kickingthelilly *Rae Guest* a59
2 ch f Byron—Teller (ARG) (Southern Halo (USA))
7526[6] 7784[3]

Kid Charlemagne (IRE) *Warren Greatrex* 98
8 b g King Charlemagne(USA) —Albertville (GER) (Top Ville)
2289[9] 2931[11] 5629[4]

Kidibul (BEL) *J-C Blandiot* 57
5 b g Pyramus(USA) —Lettre Persanne (IRE) (Persian Bold)
6593a[0]

Kidlat *Alan Bailey* a88 87
6 b g Cape Cross(IRE) —Arruhan (IRE) (Mujtahid (USA))
(21) 54[3] (124) 359[3] 525[9] 694[2] (723) 877[7] 1183[2] 1671[6] 1824[3] 2604[12] 3164[9] 3844[11] 4432[3] 4660[6] 5608[9] 7199[4] 7328[5] 7397[11] 7492[6] 7557[3] 7734[5]

Kidnapped (AUS) *Saeed Bin Suroor* 114
5 bb g Viscount(AUS) —Youthful Presence (AUS) (Dehere (USA))
417a[5] 3625[15] 5659[6]

Kid Suitor (IRE) *Richard Hannon* 83
2 ch c Choisir(AUS) —Fancy Intense (Peintre Celebre (USA))
5239[2] ◆ (5536) 6268[4] ◆ 6826[2]

Kie (IRE) *Frank Sheridan* 55
3 b g Old Vic—Asura (GER) (Surumu (GER))
4476[2] 5022[8]

Kielder (IRE) *Braem Horse Racing Sprl* a56 73
4 ch g Shinko Forest(IRE) —Ctesiphon (USA) (Arch (USA))
7315a[7]

Kielty's Folly *Brian Baugh* a66 65
7 gr g Weet-A-Minute(IRE) —Three Sweeties (Cruise Missile)
14[6] 115[5] (204) 340[4] 555[2] 712[4] 896[4] 957[4] 1273[8] 3096[3] (3280) 3741[6] (3926) 4322[2] 4666[4]

Kieron's Rock (IRE) *Jedd O'Keeffe* 59
2 ch g Rock Of Gibraltar(IRE) —Princess Killeen (IRE) (Sinndar (IRE))
5786[9] 6048[6] 6598[8] 7051[15]

Kilburn *Alastair Lidderdale* a89 79
7 b g Grand Lodge(USA) —Lady Lahar (Fraam)
(82) 348[3] 438[3] 1138[7] 1269[9]

Kildare Sun (IRE) *John Mackie* a74 73
9 b g Desert Sun—Megan's Dream (IRE) (Fayruz)
282[6] 341[6]

Kilea (FR) *Y Barberot* a90 92
4 b m Della Francesca(USA) —Klee (FR) (Magwal (FR))
840a[0] 7404a[9]

Kilk *Tony Newcombe* a14 54
3 b f Striking Ambition—Bathwick Alice (Mark Of Esteem (IRE))
2243[11]

Kimbali (IRE) *Richard Fahey* 83
2 b g Clodovil(IRE) —Winnifred (Green Desert (USA))
3610[2] 4106[2] 5077[4] (5310) 5876[2] 6323[5] (6413)

Kimberley Downs (USA) *David Nicholls* a75 70
5 gr g Giant's Causeway(USA) —Fountain Lake (USA) (Vigors (USA))
195a[0] 259a[8] 533a[0]

Kindlelight Soleil (FR) *Nick Littmoden* 56
4 b g Anabaa(USA) —Fee Du Nord (Inchinor)
1897[5] 3167[10] 3324[7] 4060[12]

Kindlelight Sun (JPN) *Nick Littmoden* a80
5 br g King Kamehameha(JPN) —Nicer (IRE) (Pennine Walk)
359[4] 515[5]

Kinetica *Sir Mark Prescott Bt* a79 98
2 b f Stormy Atlantic(USA) —Kiswahili (Selkirk (USA))
3046[2] (3336) (4252) 4803[3] 5873a[3] 6389a[7]

Kingaroo (IRE) *Garry Woodward* a67 58
5 b g King Charlemagne(USA) —Lady Naomi (USA) (Distant View (USA))
63[5] 324[10] (551) 858[2] 938[2] (954) 1466[5] 1956[8] 4024[6] 4407[6] 4889[5] 6870[12] 7070[P] 7859[14] 7912[5]

Kingarrick *Eve Johnson Houghton* a77 77
3 ch g Selkirk(USA) —Rosacara (Green Desert (USA))
2229[10] 2841[4] 3312[6] 4255[4] 4665[4] 5407[6] 5893[5] 6465[3] 6799[7]

King Bertolini (IRE) *Alan Berry* a53 48
4 b h Bertolini(USA) —Bareilly (USA) (Lyphard (USA))
295[3] 509[5] 1857[11] 2260[10] 2593[4] 2803[12] 3191[8] 3805[9] 3857[3] 4542[5] 4600[10] 5153[6] 5789[12] 6208[6] 6414[5] 6602[13] 6834[9]

King Charles *A bin Huzaim* a78 79
7 b g King's Best(USA) —Charlecote (IRE) (Caerleon (USA))
535a[9]

King Cobra (IRE) *J W Hills* a53 50
3 ch c Bachelor Duke(USA) —Remedy (Pivotal)
142[10]

King Columbo (IRE) *Julia Feilden* a67 73
6 ch g King Charlemagne(USA) —Columbian Sand (IRE) (Salmon Leap (USA))
1730[10] 1866[5] 2685[9] 2843[6] 4179[6] 4928[3] 5231[4] 5667[4] 5994[2] 6357[11]

King Congie (USA) *Thomas Albertrani* a112 110
3 bb c Badge Of Silver(USA) —Wise Ending (USA) (End Sweep (USA))
2328a[7]

King Dancer (IRE) *S Woods* 116
5 ch g Danehill Dancer(IRE) —Uriah (GER) (Acatenango (GER))
1001a[9] 1742a[14]

King David (FR) *M Boutin* a95 99
3 b g Iffraaj—Azucar (IRE) (Desert Prince (IRE))
883a[5] 7669a[0]

King Des Aigles (FR) *Mme C Barande-Barbe* a65 66
4 b g Kingsalsa(USA) —Vipassana (Sadler's Wells (USA))
1033a[0]

Kingdom Of Munster (IRE) *Richard Fahey* a61 68
4 b g Danehill Dancer(IRE) —Kitty O'Shea (Sadler's Wells (USA))
839[7] 1324[10]

King Ferdinand *Andrew Balding* a88 95
3 b g Tobougg(IRE) —Spanish Gold (Vettori (IRE))
1682[3] (2281) 2763[5] (3523) 3737[5] 4353[2] 5054[17] 6500[4]

King Fingal (IRE) *John Quinn* 85
6 b g King's Best(USA) —Llia (Shirley Heights)
1746[7]

Kingfisher Blue (IRE) *Jamie Osborne* a54 53
3 b g Majestic Missile(IRE) —Queenfisher (Scottish Reel)
1193[5]

King Fong *John Ryan* a21 45
2 b g Dr Fong(USA) —Like A Virgin (IRE) (Iron Mask (USA))
1095[11] 5637[7] 5891[11] 6611[13] 7108[12]

King In Waiting (IRE) *David O'Meara* a63 67
8 b g Sadler's Wells(USA) —Ballerina (IRE) (Dancing Brave (USA))
549[6] 1153[10] (1556) 1881[5] 3316[3]

King Kenobi (IRE) *J S Moore* a62 61
2 gr g Aussie Rules(USA) —Intisab (Green Desert (USA))
3816[9] 4391[4] 4761[3] 5325[5] (5802) 6280[2] 6471[5] 7035[8] 7718[5]

King Kieren (IRE) *Linda Jewell* a63 50
6 ch g King's Best(USA) —Across The Ice (USA) (General Holme (USA))
563[3] 688[2] 992[6] 1582[7] 1833[6] 2638[3] 3047[13] 3769[7]

King Kurt (IRE) *Kevin Ryan* 90
3 b g Holy Roman Emperor(IRE) —Rutledge (IRE) (Entrepreneur)
1526[4] (2251) ◆ 2808[2] 3131[3] (3701) 4553[9] 5888[7] 6151[3]

King Laertis (IRE) *Ben Haslam* 28
2 br g Baltic King—Vltava (IRE) (Sri Pekan (USA))
2120[10] 2346[9] 2780[7]

Kinglami *Brian Gubby* a61 50
2 b c Kingsalsa(USA)—Red Japonica (Daylami (IRE))
4414[12] 5111[7] 7330[6]

Kinglet (USA) *Mahmood Al Zarooni* a99 90
2 bb c Kingmambo(USA)—Karen's Caper (USA) (War Chant (USA))
(4762) ◆ 5654[3] 6060[3] (6788)

King Lou (FR) *P Demercastel* a67 73
4 b g Kingsalsa(USA)—Loupy Glitters (FR) (Loup Solitaire (USA))
220a[2] 395a[0]

King Of Arnor *A Fabre* 112
3 b c Monsun(GER)—Luce (IRE) (Sadler's Wells (USA))
5987a[5]

King Of Connacht *Mark Wellings* a56 36
8 b g Polish Precedent(USA)—Lady Melbourne (IRE) (Indian Ridge)
203[11] 299[9] 425[6] 574[3] 635[5] 895[7] 1068[11] 1454[7] 1987[13] 6357[12]

King Of Dixie (USA) *William Knight* a106 112
7 ch g Kingmambo(USA)—Dixie Accent (USA) (Dixieland Band (USA))
1600[8] 3109[23] 3548[4] 3862[20] 4554[4] 5032[5] ◆ 5699[12] 6088[2]

King Of Dudes *Sir Henry Cecil* a72
2 b c Dansili—Leto (USA) (Diesis)
7398[2]

King Of Eden (IRE) *Eric Alston* 94
5 b g Royal Applause—Moonlight Paradise (USA) (Irish River (FR))
(1110) (1618) ◆ 2061[5] 2954[10] 3796[3] 4609[9] 5684[11] 5758[12] 6327[3] 7171[7]

King Of Forces *Nick Littmoden*
2 b g Halling(USA)—Group Force (IRE) (Montjeu (IRE))
3823[14]

King Of Jazz (IRE) *Richard Hannon* 104
3 b g Acclamation—Grand Slam Maria (FR) (Anabaa (USA))
(1108) 1546[4] 2296[2] 3862[15] 4096[2] 4472[7] 5054[13] 5699[8]

King Of Paradise (IRE) *Eric Alston*
2 b g Hurricane Run(IRE)—Silly Game (IRE) (Bigstone (IRE))
5269[14]

King Of Risk (FR) *P Le Ponner* 27
7 gr g Grey Risk(FR)—Argelido Pardo (FR) (Kadrou (FR))
7015a[9]

King Of Rome (IRE) *M F De Kock* a106 50
6 b g Montjeu(IRE)—Amizette (USA) (Forty Niner (USA))
156a[10] 240[5] 328a[5]

King Of Swords (IRE) *Nigel Tinkler* a54 69
7 b g Desert Prince(IRE)—Okey Dorey (IRE) (Lake Coniston (IRE))
1034[14] 1493[9] 1856[9] 2126[8] 2547[4] 2766[7] 3247[7] 3573[4] 3931[4] 4000[7] 4371[6] 4820[6] 5620[5]

King Of The Celts (IRE) *Tim Easterby* 83
3 b g Celtic Swing—Flamands (IRE) (Sadler's Wells (USA))
1203[4] 1692[3] (2669) 4108[2] 5593[6] 6046[3] 6328[8] 6674[15]

King Of The Titans (IRE) *Patrick Gilligan* a48 26
8 b g Titus Livius(FR)—She's The Tops (Shernazar)
347[4] 552[5] 652[8]

King Of Windsor (IRE) *Ralph Beckett* a83 95
4 b g Intikhab(USA)—Kismah (Machiavellian (USA))
5240[7] 6173[11] 7110[9] 7637[7] 7759[3]

King Of Wing (IRE) *Richard Hannon* a68 76
2 b c Hawk Wing(USA)—Miss Shivvy (IRE) (Montjeu (IRE))
3229[9] 3746[2] 4269[3] 4954[2] 5633[5] (6010)

King Olav (UAE) *Tony Carroll* a97 93
6 ch g Halling(USA)—Karamzin (USA) (Nureyev (USA))
180[2] 436[5] (667) 1102[13] 1238[2] 1479[12] 2604[13]

King Pin *Tracy Waggott* a65 66
6 b g Pivotal—Danehurst (Danehill (USA))
7424[2] 7711[4] 7885[8]

King Pulse (AUS) *Michael Moroney* 114
5 ch g Canny Lad(AUS)—Pleasure Ground (AUS) (Arena (AUS))
5

Kings Apollo *Tom Symonds* 19
2 b g King's Theatre(IRE)—Temple Dancer (Magic Ring (IRE))
7257[10]

King's Bastion (IRE) *Luke Comer* a76 78
7 b g Royal Applause—Aunty Mary (Common Grounds)
977a[2]

Kings Bayonet *Alan King* a80 85
4 ch g Needwood Blade—Retaliator (Rudimentary (USA))
1603[15] 2647[14] 2995[7] (3817) 4216[5] 4957[3] 5857[9]

Kings Canyon (FR) *S Kobayashi* a92 94
4 b h Kingsalsa(USA)—Always Pretty (FR) (El Prado (IRE))
6556a[11]

King's Caprice *Jimmy Fox* a66 78
10 ch g Pursuit Of Love—Palace Street (USA) (Secreto (USA))
34[8]

King's Ciel *George Baker* a28 68
2 ch g Septieme Ciel(USA)—King's Jewel (King's Signet (USA))
2962[4] 3425[4] 4229[3] 4704[4] 6890[11] 7763[11]

King's Colour *Brett Johnson* a85 88
6 b g King's Best(USA)—Red Garland (Selkirk (USA))
226[8] 5240[13] 5547[10] 5811[8] 6239[6] 7362[8] (7756)

Kingscombe (USA) *Pat Eddery* a54 49
2 rg c Mizzen Mast(USA)—Gombeen (USA) (Private Account (USA))
3986[13] 5536[6] 7593[6]

King's Counsel (IRE) *David O'Meara* a55 73
5 ch g Refuse To Bend(IRE)—Nesaah's Princess (Sinndar (IRE))
400[5] 1099[5] (1305) 1676[4] 2091[9] (2393) 3054[5] 3453[2] 3730[5] 3811[3] 4612[6]

Kingscroft (IRE) *Mark Johnston* a85 96
3 b g Antonius Pius(USA)—Handsome Anna (IRE) (Bigstone (IRE))
27[3] (233) (349) ◆ 578[3] (845) (1023) 1326[3] 1547[9] 1820[4] ◆ 2908[2] (3134) 3378[4] 3634[10] (4243) 4314[22] (4574) 4779[8] 5272[15] 5730[8] 5936[13] 6326[6]

Kingsdale Orion (IRE) *Brian Ellison* a58 85
7 bb g Intikhab(USA)—Jinsiyah (USA) (Housebuster (USA))
1908[9] 2320[8] 2544[10] 3938[6] ◆ 4407[5] 4879[7] 5167[4] 5723[13] 6656[6] 6876[10]

Kings Decree *Rod Millman* 67
2 gr g Proclamation(IRE)—Nina Fontenail (FR) (Kaldounevees (FR))
4995[7] 5375[4] 6099[7] 6524[11]

Kingsdesire (IRE) *Marco Botti* a79
2 b c King's Best(USA)—Lucky Clio (IRE) (Key Of Luck (USA))
(7673) ◆

Kingsdine (IRE) *Malcolm Saunders* a90 88
4 b g King's Best(USA)—Lunadine (FR) (Bering)
1138[6] 2111[2] 3045[2] 3802[6]

Kingsfort (USA) *Saeed Bin Suroor* 113
4 b h War Chant(USA)—Princess Kris (Kris)
239[3] 503a[5] 1740a[6]

Kings Fortune *Michael Bell* a52 28
3 b g Tobougg(IRE)—Polished Up (Polish Precedent (USA))
2306[11] 2723[10] 3183[10]

King's Future *John Akehurst* a60 41
2 b g King's Best(USA)—Las Beatas (Green Desert (USA))
3229[11] 3761[9] 6118[8] 6663[5] 6787[2] 7252[8] 7444[5] 7530[7]

Kings Gambit (SAF) *Tom Tate* 116
7 ch g Silvano(GER)—Lady Brompton (SAF) (Al Mufti (USA))
1201[2] (1528) 3153[7] 4410[7] 5252[8]

Kingsgate Choice (IRE) *John Best* a86 97
4 b h Choisir(AUS)—Kenema (IRE) (Petardia)
1888[11] 2099[11] 3222[4] 3687[3] 3796[6] 4531[22]

Kingsgate Native (IRE) *Sir Michael Stoute* 120
6 b g Mujadil(USA)—Native Force (IRE) (Indian Ridge)
2297[2] 3010[6] 3154[10] 3644[6] 4468[7] 5253[4] 5707[10]

King's Guest (IRE) *Sir Michael Stoute* a67
2 b f King's Best(USA)—Temple Street (IRE) (Machiavellian (USA))
5814[4]

King's Hall *A Wohler* 106
3 ch c Halling(USA)—Konigin Turf (GER) (Turfkonig (GER))
(7409a)

Kingshill Lad (IRE) *Terry Clement* a46
2 bb c Marju(IRE)—Brogan's Well (IRE) (Caerleon (USA))
7435[10] 7769[6]

Kings Maiden (IRE) *James Moffatt* a65 68
8 b m King's Theatre(IRE)—Maidenhair (IRE) (Darshaan)
1956[4]

Kings 'n Dreams *Dean Ivory* a70 79
4 b g Royal Applause—Last Dream (IRE) (Alzao (USA))
1267[4] 2610[8] 3000[7] 3348[9] (4233) (4793) 5588[7] 5948[9] 6467[10] 6980[6]

King's Revenge *Shaun Lycett* a64 48
8 br g Wizard King—Retaliator (Rudimentary (USA))
1458[4]

King's Road *Anabel K Murphy* 65
6 ch g King's Best(USA)—Saphire (College Chapel)
5168[4] 5804[8]

King's Rose (NZ) *Peter G Moody* 116
4 b f Redoute's Choice(AUS)—Nureyev's Girl (AUS) (Nureyev (USA))
7044a[7]

King's Star (IRE) *D Gambarota* 38
3 b g King's Best(USA)—Bareilly (USA) (Lyphard (USA))
(1126a)

Kingston Folly *Andrew Haynes* a55
4 gr g Septieme Ciel(USA)—Napapijri (FR) (Highest Honor (FR))
862[13]

Kingston Tiger *Michael Wigham* a58 80
3 b g Tiger Hill(IRE)—Gretna (Groom Dancer (USA))
5738[2] 7022[13]

King's Trail (JPN) *Takashi Kodama* a90 103
9 bb h Sunday Silence(USA)—Santa Fe Trail (JPN) (Northern Taste (CAN))
7802[9]

Kings Troop *Alan King* a70 89
5 ch g Bertolini(USA)—Glorious Colours (Spectrum (IRE))
1477[7] 2006[17] 5857[3] 6676[9] 6988[9]

King Supreme (IRE) *Richard Hannon* a72 78
6 b g King's Best(USA)—Oregon Trail (USA) (Gone West (USA))
622[7]

King's Wharf (IRE) *David Evans* a61
2 gr g Clodovil(IRE)—Global Tour (USA) (Tour D'Or (USA))
7650[P] 7783[4]

Kingswinford (IRE) *Brian Ellison* a78 88
5 b g Noverre(USA)—Berenica (IRE) (College Chapel)
1037[3] 1634[4] 1917[4] 2286[3] 2356[2] (2910) (3805) 6381[2] 6541[3] 7074[6] 7211[5] 7876[5]

King Top Gun (JPN) *Ippo Sameshima* 111
8 b h Mayano Top Gun(JPN)—Glittering Flower (JPN) (Maruzensky (JPN))
7563a[15] 7873a[13]

King Torus (IRE) *Richard Hannon* 114
3 b c Oratorio(IRE)—Dipterous (IRE) (Mujadil (USA))
5282[4] ◆ (5704) 6061[7] 6693[10] (7234)

King Vahe (IRE) *Alan Jarvis* a70
2 b g One Cool Cat(USA)—Tethkar (Machiavellian (USA))
7672[5] 7835[12]

King Zeal (IRE) *Barry Leavy* a67 86
7 b g King's Best(USA)—Manureva (USA) (Nureyev (USA))
1390[7] 2220[3] 2892[13] 3641[8] 5568[11] 6028[4] 6507[8]

Kinigi (IRE) *Ronald Harris* a75 79
5 gr m Verglas(IRE)—Kamalame (USA) (Souvenir Copy (USA))
2179[10] 2585[8] 3020[2] 3217[5] 3482[5] 4231[2] 4628[3] 5053[14] 5426[5] 6580[8] 6841[7]

Kinky Afro (IRE) *J S Moore* a94 100
4 b m Modigliani(USA)—Feet Of Flame (USA) (Theatrical)
241[6] 607a[8] 756a[14] 1104[4] 1718[11] 2325a[3] 3109[19] 3703[7] 6909a[11] 7128[10]

Kinloch Castle *Mark Johnston* a81 77
2 b c Echo Of Light—Sound Of Sleat (Primo Dominie)
6866[2] 7126[3] (7240)

Kinlochrannoch *Ben Haslam* a67 79
3 b f Kyllachy—Guermantes (Distant Relative)
2505[11] 2911[7] 3461[6] 4942[5] 5824[10] 6501[2] 7266[10]

Kin Super (FR) *F Leralle*
4 b m Super Celebre(FR)—Kinotcha (FR) (Jefferson)
1012a[0]

Kinyras (IRE) *Sir Michael Stoute* 95
3 ch g Peintre Celebre(USA)—Amathusia (Selkirk (USA))
(2371) 3291[2] (4473) 5283[14] 6497[3]

Kipchak (IRE) *Conor Dore* a72 72
6 bb g Soviet Star(USA)—Khawafi (Kris)
78[5] 334[5] 556[8] 644[2] (796) 854[2] 939[2] 1278[5] 1372[5] 1814[11] 2165[8] 2382[4] 2719[2] (2922) 3235[6] 3569[4] 4025[6] 4322[10] (4709) 5736[5] 5901[7] 6841[11] 7265[7] 7507[7] 7647[5] 7859[9] 7912[3]

Kirinda (IRE) *John M Oxx* a83 102
3 b f Tiger Hill(IRE)—Kerania (IRE) (Daylami (IRE))
4132a[2] ◆ 5976a[8]

Kirocco (FR) *F Doumen* 61
3 b f Shirocco(GER)—Killgra (IRE) (Grand Lodge (USA))
1597a[8]

Kirsty's Boy (IRE) *J P Broderick* a71 78
4 ch g Tagula(IRE)—Mayfair (Green Desert (USA))
2382[5]

Kirstys Lad *Michael Mullineaux* a19 59
9 b g Lake Coniston(IRE)—Killick (Slip Anchor)
7851[12] 7899[10]

Kirthill (IRE) *Luca Cumani* 104
3 b c Danehill Dancer(IRE)—Kirtle (Hector Protector (USA))
1408[8] (3177) ◆ 4103[2] 4801[5] 5483[2] 6163[9] (7029)

Kishanda *Gay Kelleway* a71 68
3 gr f Sleeping Indian—Kali (Linamix (FR))
121[2] 378[2] 937[3] 2550[8] 3002[4] 4154[2] 4389[7] 6785[6] 7068[5] 7241[2] 7774[3]

Kissable (IRE) *Kevin Prendergast* 110
3 b f Danehill Dancer(IRE)—Kitty O'Shea (Sadler's Wells (USA))
5744a[5] 6736a[2]

Kiss A Prince *Dean Ivory* a84 66
5 b g Fraam—Prancing (Prince Sabo)
[illegible] 5518[6] 5837[9] 6469[7] 7130[10] 7363[4] 7661[5] 7816[3] ◆

Kiss N Kick *Lucinda Featherstone* a41 34
5 b g And Beyond(IRE)—Silent Angel (Petong)
3716[7] 4203[4]

Kite Hunter (IRE) *C Boutin* a78 103
4 ch h Muhtathir—Miss Chryss (IRE) (Indian Ridge)
661a[0] 1263a[4] 7314a[9]

Kittens *William Muir* a46 56
2 b f Marju(IRE)—Purring (USA) (Mountain Cat (USA))
7030[8] 7369[10]

Kitty Fisher *Ron Hodges* a55
3 b f Kyllachy—Alzianah (Alzao (USA))
130[4] (251)

Kitty Wells *Luca Cumani* a85 89
4 b m Sadler's Wells(USA)—Kithanga (IRE) (Darshaan)
2220[2] ◆ 2812[7] 3593[9] 5035[4] 5685[13] 6749[11]

Kiwayu *Luca Cumani* a66 60
2 b c Medicean—Kibara (Sadler's Wells (USA))
5384[6] ◆ 5861[4] ◆ 6588[0] 6768[8]

Kiwi Bay *Michael Dods* a88 100
6 b g Mujahid(USA)—Bay Of Plenty (FR) (Octagonal (NZ))
1094[14] 1694[12] 2123[7] 2783[5] 3315[11] 3877[6] 4794[11] 5648[2] 6079[7] (6533) 6862[17] 7295[10]

Kiz Kulesi *Mahmood Al Zarooni* 81
2 ch c Street Cry(IRE)—Maiden Tower (Groom Dancer (USA))
(6953)

Kleitomachos (IRE) *Stuart Kittow* 79
3 b g Barathea(IRE)—Theben (GER) (Monsun (GER))
1774[3] ◆ 3001[6] 3430[4] 4084[2] 5235[2] ◆ 6294[4] 6891[7]

Klynch *Ruth Carr* a76 93
5 b g Kyllachy—Inchcoonan (Emperor Jones (USA))
853[2] 1307[8] 1558[6] (1861) (2353) (2464) 2633[9] (3162) 3395[4] 3704[2] 4369[10] 4531[7] 5032[17] 5434[3] 5682[10] 6113[17] 7076[14]

Knave Of Clubs (IRE) *Peter Makin* a56 77
2 b c Red Clubs(IRE)—Royal Bounty (IRE) (Generous (IRE))
6697[7] (7258)

Knight Express *Richard Fahey* 49
2 b c Bahamian Bounty—Broughtons Revival (Pivotal)
3274[8] 3826[9]

Knightfire (IRE) *Walter Swinburn* a78 53
4 b g Invincible Spirit(IRE)—The Castles (IRE) (Imperial Ballet (IRE))
1314[8] 2001[6] 2554[9] 3015[4]

Knightly Escapade *John Dunlop* a53 82
3 ch g Sakhee(USA)—Queen Of Iceni (Erhaab (USA))
1950[3] 4956[5] 5816[6] (6729)

Knight Valliant *Barry Murtagh* 37
8 bl g Dansili—Aristocratique (Cadeaux Genereux)
4602[8]

Knight Vision *David Nicholls* 71
2 b g Haafhd—Enford Princess (Pivotal)
2767[3] 3082[3]

Knocker Knowles (IRE) *David Evans* 81
2 b g Refuse To Bend(IRE)—Yomalo (IRE) (Woodborough (USA))
4639[3] (5347)

Knock Stars (IRE) *Patrick Martin* a89 98
3 b f Soviet Star(USA)—Knockatotaun (Spectrum (IRE))
1006a[14] 1420a[2] 1533a[5] 2861a[3] 3440a[26] 5086a[5] 5979a[8] 6733a[8] 7012a[8] 7149a[9] 7468a[10]

Knowe Head (NZ) *James Unett* a72 62
4 b g High Chaparral(IRE)—Royal Errant (NZ) (Royal Academy (USA))
3167[4] 4023[7] 4478[6] 5040[9] 5740[4] (6134) 6357[3] 7068[11] 7604[2] 7823[3] 7901[2]

Knowledgeable *Bryn Palling* a4 48
4 b g Reset(AUS)—Belle's Edge (Danehill Dancer (IRE))
7609[7]

Know No Fear *Alastair Lidderdale* a72 56
6 b g Primo Valentino(IRE)—Alustar (Emarati (USA))
26[6] 6238[7] 6488[3] 6609[3] 6847[2] 6877[4] (7001) 7269[2] 7418[2] 7455[4]

Knox Overstreet *Mick Channon* a60 57
3 b g Indesatchel(IRE)—Charlie Girl (Puissance)
335[5]

Knoydart (USA) *Amanda Perrett* a37 15
2 bb g Forest Wildcat(USA)—Chasenthebluesaway (USA) (Real Quiet (USA))
6019[11] 6539[8] 6725[14]

Koalition (IRE) *David O'Meara* a10 61
2 b g Kodiac—Arbitration (IRE) (Bigstone (IRE))
2485[6] ◆ 2983[5] 3382[6] 3973[2] 4512[5] 4983[2] 5555[10] 6599[9] 6912[5] 7059[9] 7242[13] 7852[4]

Kodiac King (IRE) *Kevin Ryan* 56
2 b c Kodiac—Prodigal Daughter (Alhaarth (IRE))
1199[5] 1515[5] 2485[12] 3505[9]

Kodicil (IRE) *Tim Walford* 71
3 b g Kodiac—Miss Caoimhe (IRE) (Barathea (IRE))
1327[4] 1972[2] 4904[3] (5507) 6295[5] 6577[3] (6916) 7215[7]

Kogershin (USA) *Jeremy Noseda* 60
2 ch f Giant's Causeway(USA)—Kokadrie (USA) (Coronado's Quest (USA))
6603[9] 7025[6]

Koha (USA) *Dean Ivory* a43 56
3 b f Medaglia D'Oro(USA)—Puzzled Look (USA) (Gulch (USA))
44[6] 2172[11] 2384[10] 7086[14] 7754[12]

Kohala (IRE) *David Barron* 99
2 gr f Kodiac—Annahala (IRE) (Ridgewood Ben)
2093[3] (2570) ◆ 3033[5] 3589[2] (4999) 5882[5]

Kokojo (IRE) *Brendan Powell* a66 56
3 ch f Majestic Missile(IRE)—Drawing Room (IRE) (Grand Lodge (USA))
518[6] 729[5] 3230[13] 3908[4] 4547[13] 4950[6]

Koko Loca (IRE) *Marco Botti* a75
2 br f Kodiac—Pure Folly (IRE) (Machiavellian (USA))
(6792) 7436[2]

Kolokol (IRE) *D Prod'Homme* a87 102
4 b g Statue Of Liberty(USA)—Hecterine (IRE) (Hector Protector (USA))
4135a[8] 6593a[4]

Konig Bernard (FR) *W Baltromei* a85 106
5 b h Touch Down(GER)—Kween (GER) (Surumu (GER))
195a[2] 371a[9] 2980a[8] 6783a[0] 7678a[0]

Konig Concorde (GER) *C Sprengel* a105 110
6 b g Big Shuffle(USA)—Kaiserin (GER) (Ile De Bourbon (USA))
1575a[3] 3531a[7] 5772a[6] 6783a[8] (7311a) 7678a[8]

Konigstreuer (GER) *S Smrczek* a64
3 ch c Tertullian(USA)—Konigsalpen (GER) (Second Set (IRE))
776a[9]

Konstantin (IRE) *Marcus Tregoning* a66 84
3 br g Balmont(USA)—Manuka Magic (IRE) (Key Of Luck (USA))
(1400) ◆ 1949[4] 2675[3] 3798[3] 4321[2] (5136) (5581) ◆

Koo And The Gang (IRE) *Brian Ellison* a83 84
4 b g Le Vie Dei Colori—Entertain (Royal Applause)
1099[18] 1463[4] (1814) (1979) ◆ 2653[2] (3188) 3840[3] 5059[5] 5648[4] 7339[9]

Koolgreycat (IRE) *Noel Wilson* 61
2 gr f One Cool Cat(USA)—Brooks Masquerade (Absalom)
3314[14] 3899[4] 4283[3] 5147[7] 5646[8]

Kool Henry (IRE) *David O'Meara* 87
2 br c One Cool Cat(USA)—Hurricane Lily (IRE) (Ali-Royal (IRE))
1619[7] 2261[4] 2485[2] ◆ 2907[2] (3398) 3879[2] 4343[2] 4558[3] 5592[2] 6114[4] 6535[22]

Kool Shuffle (GER) *Tom Tate* 57
3 ch g Big Shuffle(USA)—Kedah (GER) (Local Suitor (USA))
2673[9] 3246[6] 3684[5] 5031[8] 7112[3]

Korabushka *Jeremy Noseda* 81
3 b f Selkirk(USA) —Russian Dance (USA) (Nureyev (USA))
1271^{10} 2956^{4} (3550) 4251^{8} 4890^{7}

Koraleva Tectona (IRE) *Mark H Tompkins* a61 31
6 b m Fasliyev(USA) —Miss Teak (USA) (Woodman (USA))
206 ^{13} 397^{3} 2829^{13} 3202^{8} (Dead)

Korgon *J-L Guillochon* a88
3 b g Oratorio(IRE) —Lake Baino (Highest Honor (FR))
7677a^{2}

Korithi *Roger Charlton* a19 61
3 b f Oasis Dream—Zante (Zafonic (USA))
1605^{13} 6096^{4} 6459^{9} (Dead)

Korngold *John Dunlop* 79
3 b c Dansili—Eve (Rainbow Quest (USA))
2064^{8} 3118^{3} (4273) 5064^{3} ◆ 5938^{6}

Korovos (FR) *L A Urbano-Grajales* a70 78
6 b g Act One—Arikaria (IRE) (Sri Pekan (USA))
(439a)

Kortoba (USA) *Mme C Head-Maarek* 91
2 ch f Distorted Humor(USA) —La Sorbonne (ARG) (Southern Halo (USA))
3567a^{2}

Kourdo (FR) *J Parize* a73 77
3 b g Double Heart(FR) —Sea Launch (FR) (Neverneyev (USA))
410a^{3}

Ko Zin (IRE) *Yvonne Durant*
2 b f Chineur(FR) —Erinys (FR) (Kendor (FR))
5983a^{3}

Kozmina Bay *Jonathan Portman* 30
2 b f Notnowcato—Kozmina (IRE) (Sadler's Wells (USA))
3986^{14} 5537^{9}

Kreem *A Fabre* 107
3 b c Hurricane Run(IRE) —En Public (FR) (Rainbow Quest (USA))
(2979a) 4038a^{7}

Kristalette (IRE) *Walter Swinburn* a93 63
4 ch m Leporello(IRE) —Kristal Bridge (Kris)
2676^{9} *5693^{4}* ◆ 6249^{13}

Kristollini *William Muir* a59
3 b f Bertolini(USA) —Lady Kris (IRE) (Kris)
88^{2} 233^{4} 5603^{9} 6309^{5} (6848)

Krypton Factor *F Nass* a100 100
3 br g Kyllachy—Cool Question (Polar Falcon (USA))
238^{5} 411a^{2} *502a^{3}* 680a^{6} 823a^{3}

Ksaros (FR) *F Leralle* a59 70
8 b g Keos(USA) —Ksardane (FR) (Ksardar (FR))
1013a^{0}

Ksenia (ITY) *R Menichetti* 87
3 bb f Tejano Run(USA) —Essie's Link (USA) (Cherokee Colony (USA))
1738a^{8} 2539a^{9}

Kuala Limper (IRE) *David Elsworth* a90 94
3 b g Royal Applause—Mandolin (IRE) (Sabrehill (USA))
(43) (358) (468) 988^{2} (2847) 3067^{26}

Kuanyao (IRE) *Peter Makin* a76 97
5 b g American Post—Nullarbor (Green Desert (USA))
1888^{15} 3627^{15} 5043^{5} 5887^{10} 6723^{13}

Kublahara (IRE) *Martin Bosley* a54 57
3 b f Pulpit(USA) —Kisses For Me (IRE) (Sadler's Wells (USA))
3689^{7}

Kucharova (IRE) *Seamus Mullins* 61
3 b f Danehill Dancer(IRE) —Gates Of Eden (USA) (Kingmambo (USA))
7890^{3}

Kuda Huraa (IRE) *Paul Cole* 61
3 b g Montjeu(IRE) —Healing Music (FR) (Bering)
1407^{10}

Kula Kangri (IRE) *Rebecca Curtis* 6
2 b g Manduro(GER) —Camaret (IRE) (Danehill (USA))
4053^{11}

Kummel Excess (IRE) *George Baker* a75 76
4 ch m Exceed And Excel(AUS) —Ipanema Beach (Lion Cavern (USA))
264^{9} 455^{6} 641^{4}

Kune Kune *Marco Botti* a91 85
2 b f Sir Percy—Katy O'Hara (Komaite (USA))
3257^{4} 3865^{10} 4557^{3} (5077) 6146^{6} *(7445)*

Kung Hei Fat Choy (USA) *James Given* 65
2 b c Elusive Quality(USA) —Lady Succeed (JPN) (Brian's Time (USA))
5851^{10} 6448^{8} 6983^{10}

Kunooz (IRE) *Mahmood Al Zarooni* 86
2 b f Hard Spun(USA) —Aviacion (BRZ) (Know Heights (IRE))
(4061) 5698^{2}

Kurtiniadis (IRE) *S Kulak* 94
8 b h Mujahid(USA) —Fiddler's Moll (IRE) (Dr Devious (IRE))
5777a^{6}

Kuwait Moon *Alan McCabe* a39
2 br g Resplendent Glory(IRE) —Tapsalteerie (Tipsy Creek (USA))
7368^{6} 7626^{7}

Kuwait Star *Alan McCabe* a44
2 ch c Resplendent Glory(IRE) —Mofeyda (IRE) (Mtoto)
7367^{9} 7590^{5}

Kwik As Kwik *Robin Bastiman*
3 br g One Cool Cat(USA) —Nippy (FR) (Anabaa (USA))
5063^{6}

Kwik Lightening *Ben Haslam* a21 35
3 b g Avonbridge—Runs In The Family (Distant Relative)
1082^{6}

Kwik Time *Robin Bastiman* 46
3 b g Avonbridge—Never Away (Royal Applause)
3075^{6} 3661^{5} 4162^{11} 4930^{5}

Kyanight (IRE) *Clive Cox* 77
2 b f Kodiac—Blue Holly (IRE) (Blues Traveller (IRE))
(4720) 4999^{10} 6169^{10}

Kya One (FR) *Y De Nicolay* 107
3 b f One Cool Cat(USA) —Kya Gulch (USA) (Thunder Gulch (USA))
6321a^{3}

Kyleakin Lass *Ian Wood* a79 70
2 b f Kyllachy—Local Fancy (Bahamian Bounty)
3287^{4} 6449^{3} 7052^{2} *7451^{2} 7597^{5} (7905)*

Kyle Of Bute *Brian Baugh* a70 68
5 ch g Kyllachy—Blinding Mission (IRE) (Marju (IRE))
203^{2} 299^{8} 553^{2} 748^{2} 897^{3} 1052^{4} 2308^{6} 2567^{5} *3235^{2} 3475^{2}* 3938^{4} 4408^{2} 4716^{5} (5414) 6134^{4}

Kylesku (IRE) *Kevin Ryan* 75
2 b f Moss Vale(IRE) —Gisela (IRE) (King Charlemagne (USA))
(4365) 4999^{12} 5348^{8}

Kylin *Richard Hannon* 59
2 ch f Kyllachy—Descriptive (IRE) (Desert King (IRE))
6480^{7} 6751^{3} 7030^{15}

Kyllachy Dancer *John Quinn* 63
2 b f Kyllachy—Aunt Susan (Distant Relative)
3504^{4} ◆ 7293^{8}

Kyllachykov (IRE) *Robin Bastiman* 48
3 ch g Kyllachy—Dance On (Caerleon (USA))
4286^{7} 5368^{7} 5793^{6} 6602^{6} 6940^{6} 7084^{6}

Kyllachy Spirit *William Knight* a89 72
3 b g Kyllachy—Cartuccia (IRE) (Doyoun)
1998^{3} 3118^{10} *(5607) (5942) 6439^{12}*

Kyllachy Star *Richard Fahey* a98 102
5 b g Kyllachy—Jaljuli (Jalmood (USA))
925a^{3} 1092^{11} (1849) 2284^{7} 3032^{7} 3645^{15} 4418a^{16} 5272^{12} 5879^{8} 6326^{5}

Kyllachy Storm *Ron Hodges* a71 77
7 b g Kyllachy—Social Storm (USA) (Future Storm (USA))
1453^{6} 1937^{4} (2142) 2426^{3} (2662) 2959^{7} 3427^{7} 3995^{4} 4618^{7} 4795^{4} 5231^{6} 5539^{7} *6283^{9}* 6398^{7}

Kylladdie *Steve Gollings* a84 81
4 ch g Kyllachy—Chance For Romance (Entrepreneur)
1444 470^{4} 646^{5} (833) 946^{2} 1048^{4} 1584^{3} 1955^{2} (2179) 3222^{9} 3541^{3} 4291^{10}

Kyllasie *Richard Hannon* a64 65
2 b f Kyllachy—Tanasie (Cadeaux Genereux)
1101^{4} 1765^{4} 3463^{3} 4212^{3} *5409^{6}* 6480^{6} *7222^{8} 7481^{7}*

Kyncraighe (IRE) *Joseph Tuite* a59 72
3 b g Kyllachy—Brighella (Sadler's Wells (USA))
52^{8} 817^{4} 916^{5} 942^{3} 967^{4} 1303^{6} *7581^{4} 7768^{10}*

Kyrnollia (FR) *J Van Handenhove* a70 65
3 b f Timboroa—Kallistea (FR) (Sicyos (USA))
288a^{0}

Kyzer Chief *Ron Barr* 65
6 b g Rouvres(FR) —Payvashooz (Ballacashtal (CAN))
1034^{13} 1213^{10} (1796) 2126^{7} 2247^{5} 2667^{2}

Laafhd *Tony Newcombe* a26 32
3 ch f Haafhd—Lady In Colour (IRE) (Cadeaux Genereux)
1139^{10}

Laaheb *Roger Varian* a118 118
5 b g Cape Cross(IRE) —Maskunah (IRE) (Sadler's Wells (USA))
1001a^{4} 1685^{5} 3153^{4} 3775^{7} *7226^{3} 7584^{4}*

Laajooj (IRE) *Mahmood Al Zarooni* a78 108
3 b c Azamour(IRE) —Flanders (IRE) (Common Grounds)
(1408) 1850^{4} (2507) 3068^{6}

Laa Rayb (USA) *D Selvaratnam* a87 84
7 b g Storm Cat(USA) —Society Lady (USA) (Mr Prospector (USA))
152a^{11}

Laashak (USA) *Sir Michael Stoute* 78
3 b g Malibu Moon(USA) —Catch The Blue Hat (USA) (Storm Cat (USA))
1338^{3} ◆ 1897^{2} 2735^{6} 5242^{11}

Laatafreet (IRE) *Saeed Bin Suroor* a89 99
3 ch c Singspiel(IRE) —Cerulean Sky (IRE) (Darshaan)
(4023)

La Bacouetteuse (FR) *Iain Jardine* a28 68
6 b g Miesque's Son(USA) —Toryka (Vettori (IRE))
(4673) (5405) 6419^{3} 7105^{2}

La Bambagini *Olivia Maylam* a29
4 b m Reset(AUS) —Indian Flag (IRE) (Indian Ridge)
684^{10} 1173^{6}

Labarinto *Sir Michael Stoute* 104
3 b c Dansili—Tarocchi (USA) (Affirmed (USA))
1344^{4} 2100^{2} 3774^{3} ◆ (4467) 6163^{15}

La Bauloise (FR) *T Lemer* a64 68
2 b f Della Francesca(USA) —Coup De Colere (FR) (Pistolet Bleu (IRE))
4843a^{7}

La Belle Au Bois (IRE) *Nick Lampard* 48
5 b m Val Royal(FR) —Pomme Pomme (USA) (Dayjur (USA))
1767^{6} 2639^{7} 2871^{8} 3515^{4}

La Biriquina (USA) *T Doumen* a58 66
6 gr m Aljabr(USA) —Samut (IRE) (Danehill (USA))
7315a^{3}

La Bocca (USA) *Roger Charlton* a55 68
2 b f Latent Heat(USA) —Danzante (USA) (Danzig (USA))
5111^{4} *5632^{7}* 6118^{2}

Labore *Marco Botti* a86 79
3 b g Bertolini(USA) —Hoh Intrepid (IRE) (Namid)
2230^{8} 2572^{2} 3081^{3} 3557^{10} (4479) *5392^{2}*

Labrice *T Mundry* 100
3 b f Dubawi(IRE) —Laurella (Acatenango (GER))
3651a^{2} 4839a^{15}

Labroc (IRE) *William Haggas* a59 55
3 b g Marju(IRE) —Opera Comica (Dr Fong (USA))
1568^{11} 6097^{11} 6349^{6} 7212^{5} *7340^{3} 7515^{8}*

La Capriosa *David Nicholls* a79 78
5 ch m Kyllachy—La Caprice (USA) (Housebuster (USA))
133^{7} 294^{6} 430^{9} 491^{4} 794^{12} 7535^{8} 7746^{4} ◆

Lacateno *W Hickst* 106
4 b h Green Tune(USA) —Lacatena (GER) (Acatenango (GER))
4524a^{2} 6200a^{7} 6661a^{5} 7045a^{3}

Lacily (USA) *Mahmood Al Zarooni* 80
2 b f Elusive Quality(USA) —Lailani (Unfuwain (USA))
(6984) ◆

La Collina (IRE) *Kevin Prendergast* 114
2 ch f Strategic Prince—Starfish (IRE) (Galileo (IRE))
4031a^{2} ◆ (4834a) 5525a^{3}

La Columbina *Michael Scudamore* a60 49
6 ch m Carnival Dancer—Darshay (FR) (Darshaan)
771^{9}

La Confession *J W Hills* a28 54
2 b f Dylan Thomas(IRE) —Clinet (IRE) (Docksider (USA))
3813^{7} 4525^{7} *5813^{9}*

Laconicos (IRE) *William Stone* a62 68
9 ch g Foxhound(USA) —Thermopylae (Tenby)
1066^{5} 1233^{3} 2021^{2} 2308^{7} 2685^{4} *3176^{10}* 4060^{7} *4549^{2}* 5015^{3} *5739^{3}* 6235^{5} *6873^{7} 7206^{5} 7441^{2}* 7891^{5}

La Danse Champetre *Charles Smith* 19
3 ch f Pastoral Pursuits—Dancing Spirit (IRE) (Ahonoora)
5469^{10} *7710^{7}*

Laddove (ITY) *M Gasparini* 94
4 b h Colossus(IRE) —Luvinatese (IRE) (Fools Holme (USA))
7311a^{9}

La De Two (IRE) *Saeed Bin Suroor* a83 113
5 ch g Galileo(IRE) —Firecrest (IRE) (Darshaan)
413a^{7} 826a^{7} 3204^{6}

Ladies Are Forever *Geoffrey Oldroyd* 111
3 b f Monsieur Bond(IRE) —Forever Bond (Danetime (IRE))
1319^{5} 2005^{10} 2500^{4} 3158^{3} (3827) 6858^{14}

Ladies Best *James Given* a81 39
7 b g King's Best(USA) —Lady Of The Lake (Caerleon (USA))
3157^{12} 3730^{10}

Ladouce (FR) *Robert Collet* a52 70
5 b m Ski Chief(USA) —Veliana (FR) (Vettori (IRE))
196a^{9}

Ladram Bay (IRE) *Jonathan Portman*
2 b f Oratorio(IRE) —Ringmoor Down (Pivotal)
6480^{10} 6743^{10}

Lady Advocate (IRE) *Tim Easterby* 57
2 b f Lawman(FR) —Shalev (GER) (Java Gold (USA))
3186^{8} 3680^{7} 4512^{12} (5555) 7051^{10}

Lady Alba Rosa (JPN) *Kazuhide Sasada* 113
4 b m King Kamehameha(JPN) —One For Rose (CAN) (Tejano Run (USA))
7410a^{17}

Lady Amakhala *George Moore* 81
3 b f Val Royal(FR) —Isla Negra (IRE) (Last Tycoon)
2218^{2} (3084) 4108^{4} 5035^{8}

Lady Arabella (IRE) *Alastair Lidderdale* a61 29
2 b f Dark Angel(IRE) —Lady Fabiola (USA) (Open Forum (USA))
5812^{12} *6927^{4} 7345^{6} 7514^{3}* ◆

Lady Author *Richard Fahey* a39
2 b f Authorized(IRE) —Kelucia (IRE) (Grand Lodge (USA))
7367^{10} 7685^{6} 7777^{7}

Lady Barastar (IRE) *Walter Swinburn* a72 72
3 b f Barathea(IRE) —Stariya (IRE) (Soviet Star (USA))
1958^{4} 2583^{3} 3228^{9} 3771^{5} 4686^{2} 5302^{2} 5784^{4} *(6493)* 6756^{3} 7062^{6}

Lady Bayside *Malcolm Saunders* 72
3 ch f Ishiguru(USA) —Seldemosa (Selkirk (USA))
2790^{16} 3218^{4} 3513^{2} 4271^{3} (4706) 5376^{6}

Lady Bellatrix *Mark H Tompkins* a66 55
2 b f Singspiel(IRE) —Humility (Polar Falcon (USA))
3534^{6} *5142^{2}* 5698^{5}

Lady Bluesky *Alistair Whillans* 72
8 gr m Cloudings(IRE) —M N L Lady (Polar Falcon (USA))
2034^{5} ◆ 6385^{5} 6780^{3} 7163^{2}

Lady Bridget *Mark Gillard* a58 70
3 b f Hawk Wing(USA) —Change Partners (IRE) (Hernando (FR))
1151^{10} *1580^{5}* 2152^{9} 3289^{6} *3952^{7}* 4337^{12}

Lady Brookie *Peter Grayson* a45 78
3 br f Makbul—Miss Brookie (The West (USA))
100^{6} 198^{7} 7567^{11} 7812^{9}

Lady Burlesque (IRE) *Mick Channon* a42
2 ch f Sir Percy—Soubrette (USA) (Opening Verse (USA))
7494^{9}

Lady By Red (IRE) *Michael Dods* 50
3 ch f Redback—Antonia's Dream (Clantime)
4559^{3} 5030^{6} 6156^{6}

Lady Caprice *Ann Duffield* a50 57
2 b f Kyllachy—Lady Betambeau (IRE) (Grand Lodge (USA))
3082^{6} 3273^{6} 3504^{7} (3728) 4500^{5} 4808^{4} 5105^{3} *5245^{6}* 5535^{5}

Lady Chaparral *Michael Dods* 91
4 b m High Chaparral(IRE) —La Sylphide (Rudimentary (USA))
(1211) 1908^{2} 2220^{15} 3023^{2} 3828^{7} (4360) 5250^{12} 5435^{4} 7022^{12}

Lady Chloe *Philip Kirby* 84
3 b f Noverre(USA) —Iwunder (IRE) (King's Best (USA))
1440^{2} 2058^{2} (2591) 3641^{3} 4584^{2}

Lady Christie *Michael Blanshard* a35 33
4 b m Tobougg(IRE) —Atnab (USA) (Riverman (USA))
3011^{0} 407^{7}

Lady Cresta (IRE) *Ronald Harris* 34
2 b f Choisir(AUS) —Dancing Drop (Green Desert (USA))
1863^{5} *3491^{7}* 4629^{4} 5174^{9}

Lady Cricketer *Jane Chapple-Hyam* 44
2 b f Compton Place—Hickleton Lady (IRE) (Kala Shikari)
7292^{10}

Lady D'Argentelle (FR) *J Parize*
3 b f Konig Shuffle(GER) —Miss Kenbold (FR) (Star Maite (FR))
288a^{0}

Lady Deanie (IRE) *Bryn Palling* a50 59
3 ch f Noverre(USA) —Darling Deanie (IRE) (Sinndar (IRE))
1179^{5} 1958^{13} 7198^{11} 7463^{5}

Lady Del Sol *Marjorie Fife* 78
3 b f Monsieur Bond(IRE) —Villa Del Sol (Tagula (IRE))
1437^{6} 2391^{5} 2619^{8} 3347^{4} 3702^{9} 4145^{11} 4288^{3} 5442^{4} 5824^{5} 6261^{3} 6840^{15} 7064^{5} 7216^{13}

Lady Des Biches (FR) *J-V Toux* a55 67
4 b m Ski Chief(USA) —Lady Beauvallon (Coquelin (USA))
108a^{4}

Ladydolly *Roy Brotherton* a58 55
3 b f Kyllachy—Lady Pekan (Sri Pekan (USA))
64^{9} 251^{5} 452^{3} 669^{2} 1465^{5} 1764^{4} 2141^{2} 2549^{4} *5215^{2}* 5678^{10}

Lady Ellice *Phil McEntee* a49 28
3 b f Iceman—Optimise (IRE) (Danehill (USA))
126^{7} 389^{4} 558^{4} 729^{7} 834^{4} 967^{8} 5946^{7} 6874^{8} 7525^{7} 7714^{12}

Lady Elsie *Alan McCabe* a71 68
3 b f Singspiel(IRE) —Lady Hen (Efisio)
714^{2} 1311^{3} 3224^{2} 3781^{4} 5241^{3} 5512^{2} *7070^{9}*

Lady Excel (IRE) *Brian Rothwell* a61 62
5 b m Exceed And Excel(AUS) —Material Lady (IRE) (Barathea (IRE))
200^{4} 580^{4} 1857^{9} 2057^{7} 2260^{5} 2589^{5} 2800^{3} 3074^{7} 3457^{4} 3733^{4} 4128^{2} 4441^{5} 5622^{8} 6264^{13}

Lady Excellentia (IRE) *Ronald Harris* a15 57
3 gr f Exceed And Excel(AUS) —Cayman Sunrise (IRE) (Peintre Celebre (USA))
2375^{9} 2549^{7} 2918^{10} 3272^{7} 3724^{4} 4224^{3} 4466^{6} 4631^{5} 5176^{3} 5344^{5} 5780^{5} 6889^{15} 7260^{P}

Lady Fashion *P D Deegan* a98 83
3 b f Oasis Dream—Carinae (USA) (Nureyev (USA))
6854a^{U} 7010a^{7}

Lady Florence *David C Griffiths* a56 79
6 gr m Bollin Eric—Silver Fan (Lear Fan (USA))
1356^{3} 1878^{14} 2149^{7} 2566^{9} 2985^{7} 3326^{6} *3473^{5}* 3683^{9} 4233^{10} (4696) 4742^{8} 5053^{10}

Lady Freda *Alan Coogan* a26
5 ch m Best Of The Bests(IRE) —Super Sally (Superlative)
905^{9} 1015^{5} 1358^{6} 1633^{10} 2600^{11}

Lady Gabrielle (IRE) *David Elsworth* a56 77
3 b f Dansili—Zither (Zafonic (USA))
(3018) 3228^{2} (3919) 4448^{7} 4971^{4} 5518^{8} 6577^{8}

Lady Gadfly *Micky Hammond* 49
2 b f Three Valleys(USA) —Firozi (Forzando)
1691^{10} 2587^{7} 3505^{4} 4538^{7} 4983^{3} 6627^{13}

Lady Gar Gar *Geoffrey Oldroyd* a67 73
3 ch f Monsieur Bond(IRE) —Triple Tricks (IRE) (Royal Academy (USA))
(1329) 1653^{3} 2406^{3} 2835^{5} 3614^{6} 4560^{7} 5439^{3} 5821^{6} *7198^{5} 7591^{5} 7782^{7}*

Lady Gargoyle *Jim Goldie* 45
3 b f Lucky Story(USA) —Gargoyle Girl (Be My Chief (USA))
6210^{5} 7158^{4}

Lady Gibraltar *Alan Jarvis* a76 73
2 b f Rock Of Gibraltar(IRE) —Lady Adnil (IRE) (Stravinsky (USA))
2309^{7} 2811^{3} 3257^{2} 4824^{3} 5577^{7} 6075^{4} *7225^{2} 7451^{3} (7597)*

Lady Gorgeous *Mick Channon* 90
2 ch f Compton Place—Cayman Sunset (IRE) (Night Shift (USA))
3547^{2} (4052) ◆ 5217^{9} 6337^{7}

Lady Heartbeat *Michael Blanshard* a50 51
2 b f Avonbridge—Take Heart (Electric)
4269^{6} 4629^{3} 5232^{7} *7432^{6} 7569^{5} 7763^{5}*

Lady Hello (IRE) *Mick Channon* a36 47
2 b f Baltic King—Persian Light (IRE) (Persian Heights)
4106^{6} 4406^{9} *5418^{4}* 6043^{3}

Lady Intrigue (IRE) *Richard Fahey* 51
3 b f Hurricane Run(IRE) —Intriguing (IRE) (Fasliyev (USA))
3684^{7} 4363^{6} 5372^{4}

Lady Jameela *Mick Channon* 71
2 b f Acclamation—Shahmina (IRE) (Danehill (USA))
3257^{3} ◆ 3865^{4} 4225^{U} 4580^{3} 4961^{4} 5464^{7} 5779^{2} 6291^{3}

Lady Jane Grace (IRE) *David Evans* a11 10
2 b f Amadeus Wolf—Mascara (Mtoto)
3408^{10} 3686^{14} 7257^{11} *7735^{6}*

Lady Jourdain (IRE) *Mrs K Burke* a63 71
2 b f Chineur(FR) —Cladantom (IRE) (High Estate)
3728^{7} ◆ (4105) (4193) 4512^{2} *5246^{2} 5413^{6} 6001^{5}* (6925a) (7312a)

Lady Kashaan (IRE) *Alan Swinbank* 15
2 b f Manduro(GER) —Lady's Secret (IRE) (Alzao (USA))
6448^{13} 7058^{11}

Lady Kildare (IRE) *Jedd O'Keeffe* a62 73
3 br f Bachelor Duke(USA) —Teodora (IRE) (Fairy King (USA))
(1941) 2592^{9} 3630^{4} 4124^{9} (4669) (5371) 6044^{13} 6276^{3} *7040^{9}*

Ladykin (IRE) *Richard Fahey* a76 76
2 b f Holy Roman Emperor(IRE) —Engraving (Sadler's Wells (USA))
2504^{5} (3161) 3866^{3} *4867^{3}* 5755^{5} 6864^{4}

Lady Lam *Sylvester Kirk* a70 66
5 b m Slip Anchor—Tamara (Marju (IRE))
1353^{4} 1636^{6} *1756^{7}* 2202^{3} 2843^{5} 2991^{2}

Lady Layla *Bryan Smart* 79
2 b f Excellent Art—Tartouche (Pursuit Of Love)
4285^{3} (4875) (5755) ◆ 6826^{3}

Lady Libby Lamb *David C Griffiths*
3 bl f Statue Of Liberty(USA) —Lady Caroline Lamb (IRE) (Contract Law (USA))
7245^{10}

Lady Loch *Richard Fahey* 73
2 b f Dutch Art—Locharia (Wolfhound (USA))
4347^{3} ◆ 4961^{5}

Lady Lube Rye (IRE) *Noel Wilson* a21 46
4 b m Catcher In The Rye(IRE) —Lady Lucia (IRE) (Royal Applause)
1213^{12} 1493^{7} 3573^{9} 3937^{4} 4328^{6} 4563^{4} 5009^{5} 6343^{7} 6541^{9}

Lady Lyrath (IRE) *S M Duffy* a48 48
4 b m Whipper(USA) —Poly Dancer (Suave Dancer (USA))
7401^{6}

Lady Lyricist *Reg Hollinshead* a57
2 b f Librettist(USA) —Victory Flip (IRE) (Victory Note (USA))
7464^{7} 7627^{5} 7783^{11}

Lady Macduff (IRE) *Mark Johnston* 63
2 b f Iffraaj—Tamora (Dr Fong (USA))
6935^{5}

Lady Mandy *Richard Fahey* 50
2 b f Teofilo(IRE) —Bedara (Barathea (IRE))
6629^{3} 7058^{8} 7292^{14}

Lady Mango (IRE) *Ronald Harris* a60 48
3 ch f Bahamian Bounty—Opera (Forzando)
110^{9} 600^{6} 964^{6} 1589^{2} 1980^{10} 3223^{3} 3742^{10} 4911^{6}

Lady Meydan (FR) *F Rohaut* a93 104
3 b f American Post—Open Offer (Cadeaux Genereux)
6809a^{5} (7509a)

Lady Morganna (IRE) *Olivia Maylam* a59 62
3 b f Diamond Green(FR) —Lucky Flirt (USA) (Gulch (USA))
649^{4} 898^{7} 1134^{7} 3220^{4} 3926^{10} 7571^{13} 7756^{8}

Lady Nickandy (IRE) *Alan McCabe* a54 58
2 b f Kheleyf(USA) —Tanzie (IRE) (Soviet Star (USA))
2214^{8} 2523^{4} (2823) 4001^{3} 4892^{8} 5998^{5} 6284^{8} 6821^{7} 7635^{8} 7725^{4} 7742^{4} (7882)

Lady Norlela *Brian Rothwell* a27 65
5 b m Reset(AUS) —Lady Netbetsports (IRE) (In The Wings)
507^{9} 1039^{2} 1305^{9} 1491^{4} 2496^{4} 2622^{7} 3509^{3} 4077^{2} 4366^{4} (5107) 5791^{7} 6157^{11} 6775^{8}

Lady Ocarina *John Dunlop* 17
2 b f Piccolo—Queen Of Iceni (Erhaab (USA))
4804^{14}

Lady of Burgundy *Mark Usher* a77 74
5 b m Montjeu(IRE) —Helena's Paris (IRE) (Peintre Celebre (USA))
1220^{3} 1474^{7} (3907) 4887^{6} 5962^{7} 6410^{7} 6976^{3} 7570^{6}

Lady Of Edge *Keith Dalgleish* 33
2 b f Librettist(USA) —Lady Of Windsor (IRE) (Woods Of Windsor (USA))
1515^{7} 3123^{6}

Lady Of Killough *Stef Higgins*
3 b f Marju(IRE) —Twilight Patrol (Robellino (USA))
1500^{4}

Lady Of The Knight (IRE) *Hugh McWilliams* 49
3 b f Chevalier(IRE) —Temptation Island (IRE) (Spectrum (IRE))
600^{9} 1799^{3}

Lady On Top (IRE) *Nerys Dutfield* a54 52
3 b f Oratorio(IRE) —Ascot Lady (IRE) (Spinning World (USA))
1578^{3} 2172^{4} (2384) 2792^{15} 6253^{11}

Lady Orpen (FR) *Y Durepaire* 84
2 b f Orpen(USA) —Lady Morgane (IRE) (Medaaly)
4036a^{4} 4843a^{8}

Lady Pacha *Tim Pitt* a24 44
4 b m Dubai Destination(USA) —St Radegund (Green Desert (USA))
507^{7}

Lady Paris (IRE) *Bryan Smart* 95
3 b f Invincible Spirit(IRE) —[illegible] (IRE) ([illegible] Ridge)
3853^{10} 4324^{3} (4680) ◆ (5018) 5255^{7} 6189^{3} 7298^{13}

Lady Pastrana (IRE) *B P Galvin* a50 83
2 br f Key Of Luck(USA) —Caribbean Queen (IRE) (Celtic Swing)
5522a^{6}

Lady Percy (IRE) *Mark Usher* a41 57
2 b f Sir Percy—Genuinely (IRE) (Entrepreneur)
5232^{4} 5841^{3} 6818^{7}

Lady Platinum Club *Geoffrey Oldroyd* a66 69
3 ch f Monsieur Bond(IRE) —Bond Platinum Club (Pivotal)
971^{2} 1246^{3} 1494^{10} 3238^{3} 4110^{4} 4647^{5}

Lady Prodee *Bill Turner* a73
3 b f Proclamation(IRE) —Dee-Lady (Deploy)
198^{4} 465^{3}

Lady Rochford (IRE) *G M Lyons* 82
2 b f Invincible Spirit(IRE) —Sheezalady (Zafonic (USA))
5974a^{6}

Lady Rocket (FR) *C Boutin* 58
2 b f Indian Rocket—Lady Domino (FR) (Second Empire (IRE))
7238a^{7} 7666a^{0}

Lady Romanza (IRE) *Tim Easterby* 37
2 b f Holy Roman Emperor(IRE) —Sharakawa (IRE) (Darshaan)
5548^{9} 5819^{6} 6152^{7}

Lady Rosamunde *Marcus Tregoning* a70 78
3 gr f Maria's Mon(USA) —String Quartet (IRE) (Sadler's Wells (USA))
214^{2} 1151^{4} (1659)

Lady Rossetti *Marcus Tregoning* a54
4 ch m Reset(AUS) —Cottage Maid (Inchinor)
225^{3} 409^{9} 575^{6} 3280^{6}

Lady Royale *Geoffrey Oldroyd* 88
3 ch f Monsieur Bond(IRE) —Bond Royale (Piccolo)
2363^{10} 2832^{5} ◆ 3189^{2} (3702) (4610) ◆ 5288^{7} 6350^{6} 6703^{10}

Lady Royal Oak (IRE) *Olivia Maylam* a49 66
4 b m Exceed And Excel(AUS) —Enclave (USA) (Woodman (USA))
3640^{9} 6593a^{0} 7116^{10} 7201^{8} 7389^{11} 7659^{4} 7785^{8} 7854^{8}

Lady Rumba *John O'Shea* a29 45
3 b f Ishiguru(USA) —Costa Packet (IRE) (Hussonet (USA))
1629^{5} 2141^{6} 2710^{6} 3272^{10} 6176^{8}

Lady Sefton *James Given* a30
3 b f Oratorio(IRE) —Saxon Maid (Sadler's Wells (USA))
6086^{10}

Ladys First *Richard Fahey* 87
2 b f Dutch Art—Like A Dame (Danehill (USA))
(3878) ◆ 5270^{2} ◆ 5849^{5}

Ladyship *Sir Michael Stoute* 81
2 b f Oasis Dream—Peeress (Pivotal)
3865^{3} ◆ 5323^{2}

Lady Sledmere (IRE) *Paul Midgley* 76
3 b f Barathea(IRE) —Helena's Paris (IRE) (Peintre Celebre (USA))
4370^{3} ◆ 5082^{6} (5443) 6234^{8}

Lady Sylvia *Joseph Tuite* a63 29
2 ch f Haafhd—Abide (FR) (Pivotal)
6462^{10} 7454^{5}

Lady Titticaca *Ron Hodges* a15 16
3 br f Striking Ambition—Sunrise Girl (King's Signet (USA))
130^{9} 383^{9} 2720^{7}

Lady Tycoon *Mark Brisbourne* a55 37
2 b f Indesatchel(IRE) —Tycoon's Last (Nalchik (USA))
3718^{2} 4390^{10} 4884^{5} 5597^{14} 7368^{4}

Lady Valtas *Robert Eddery* 37
3 b f Val Royal(FR) —Phantasmagoria (Fraam)
3437^{10} 4065^{8} 4861^{11} 5643^{10} 6032^{10}

Lady Victory (IRE) *Mick Channon* a62 68
2 b f Kheleyf(USA) —Victoria Lodge (IRE) (Grand Lodge (USA))
2113^{14} (2302) 3700^{4} 4277^{6} 5052^{10} 5809^{4} 6487^{3}

Lady Vivien *George Foster* a51 56
5 b m Kyllachy—Elsie Plunkett (Mind Games)
2655^{6} 3471^{5}

Lady Wingshot (IRE) *J S Bolger* 99
2 b f Lawman(FR) —Nassma (IRE) (Sadler's Wells (USA))
5974a^{2} 6389a^{4}

La Estrella (USA) *Don Cantillon* a92 91
8 b g Theatrical—Princess Ellen (Tirol)
(374) (570) (639) (795) (1030) (2235) 3013^{5} 3420a^{8} 6249^{6} 6690^{26} (7241) 7753^{3} (7900)

Laeyos (GER) *Markus Klug*
2 b c Soldier Hollow—Laeya Star (GER) (Royal Dragon (USA))
7325a^{3}

Laffan (IRE) *Kevin Ryan* 63
2 b g Dark Angel(IRE) —Lady Corduff (IRE) (Titus Livius (FR))
2953^{8} 3398^{5} 4436^{4}

Laffraaj (IRE) *Pat Eddery* a59 52
3 br g Iffraaj—Have Fun (Indian Ridge)
699^{5} 1028^{3} 1311^{5} 1997^{9} 2637^{5} 3268^{7} 3922^{7} 4274^{11} 5210^{9} 5643^{5} 5898^{8} 6585^{2} 6968^{10}

La Folie (IRE) *E Lellouche* 95
3 b f Footstepsinthesand—Flames Last (IRE) (Montjeu (IRE))
7510a^{3}

La Fortunata *Mike Murphy* a74 92
4 b m Lucky Story(USA) —Phantasmagoria (Fraam)
1584^{8} 2714^{3} 3778^{5} ◆ 4416^{2} 5278^{6} 5543^{4} 6224^{15} (6272) 6723^{15}

Lagalp (GER) *P Schiergen* 103
4 b m Galileo(IRE) —La Dane (IRE) (Danehill (USA))
1931a^{6} 5093a^{10} 5749a^{7} 6395a^{3}

Lagan Lullaby *Neil Mulholland*
3 gr f Goodricke—Due To Me (Compton Place)
380^{11} 1449^{9}

[illegible] (IRE) *Peter Fahey* a54 76
4 br g Namid—My Potters (USA) (Irish River (FR))
504^{8} 798^{5}

La Haye *J-C Rouget* 81
2 b f Acclamation—Moonbaby (FR) (Le Balafre (FR))
(7813a)

L'Aiglon (USA) *Gennadi Dorochenkous*
3 b c Montjeu(IRE) —Look To The King (USA) (Kingmambo (USA))
5072a^{P}

Lajidaal (USA) *Gary Moore* 81
4 b g Dynaformer(USA) —Tayibah (IRE) (Sadler's Wells (USA))
1367^{13}

La Joie De Vivre (USA) *R Gibson* a65 74
3 b g During(USA) —Creme De La Creme (FR) (Vettori (IRE))
638a^{10}

Lake Chini (IRE) *Michael Easterby* a66 71
9 b g Raise A Grand(IRE) —Where's The Money (Lochnager)
512^{2} 928^{11} 1856^{11} 2987^{8} 7629^{13} 7695^{10}

Lake Drop (USA) *S Botti* 104
3 b c Lemon Drop Kid(USA) —Lake Charles (USA) (El Gran Senor (USA))
1920a^{9}

Lake George (IRE) *James M Barrett* a80 78
3 b g Alkaadhem—Ballyronan Girl (IRE) (Elbio)
6388a^{5}

Lakeman (IRE) *Brian Ellison* a70 68
5 b g Tillerman—Bishop's Lake (Lake Coniston (IRE))
12^{2} 148^{6} 3088^{12} 3358^{8} 3938^{14} 4637^{3} 4944^{2}

Lake Wanaka (IRE) *Ms Joanna Morgan* a49 54
3 b f Fasliyev(USA) —Poppys Footprint (IRE) (Titus Livius (FR))
973a^{14} 5865^{2} 5965^{2}

Lakota Ghost (USA) *Seamus Durack* a64 67
3 b g Rockport Harbor(USA) —Political Alert (USA) (Giant's Causeway (USA))
110^{7} 262^{5} 520^{9} ◆ 760^{4} 898^{2} 5942^{7} 6295^{4} 6926^{7} 7263^{3}

L'Albatros (FR) *Mme C Barande-Barbe* a44 50
6 b g Beaudelaire(USA) —Adolescente (FR) (Jeune Homme (USA))
832a^{0}

Lalla Rookh (AUS) *Leon Macdonald & Andrew Gluyas* 101
4 b f Street Cry(IRE) —Grand Manners (AUS) (Grand Lodge (USA))
7043a^{10}

Lamasaas (USA) *B W Hills* 80
3 b g Henny Hughes(USA) —Quick Feet (USA) (Dynaformer (USA))
(1693) 2729^{3} 3178^{7}

Lamasery (AUS) *David Vandyke* 112
5 br g Commands(AUS) —Verse (AUS) (Quest For Fame)
7407a^{4}

Lambrini Belle *Lisa Williamson*
5 ch m Bold Edge—Rag Time Belle (Raga Navarro (ITY))
2402^{7}

Lambrini Lace (IRE) *Lisa Williamson* a33 43
6 b m Namid—Feather 'n Lace (IRE) (Green Desert (USA))
2412^{5} 2632^{12} 4288^{13} 5437^{6} 5678^{8} 6427^{7}

L'Ami Louis (IRE) *Henry Candy* 87
3 b g Elusive City(USA) —Princess Electra (IRE) (Lake Coniston (IRE))
1315^{3} (1724) 2508^{3} 3841^{16}

Lamool (GER) *Mario Hofer* 106
4 b h Mamool(IRE) —Linara (GER) (Windwurf (GER))
1231a^{9} 1931a^{5} 2540a^{6}

La Mouche *E Lellouche* 102
3 b f Dubawi(IRE) —Summer Sea (Bahhare (USA))
1709a^{8} 7156a^{4}

Lana (IRE) *David Evans* a37 61
2 b f Amadeus Wolf—Carn Lady (IRE) (Woodman (USA))
2992^{3} 3984^{4} 6118^{4} 7555^{6}

Lana Mae *Jeremy Gask* a50
2 ch f Proclamation(IRE) —Saharan Song (IRE) (Singspiel (IRE))
6654^{11} 7174^{7} 7435^{9} 7592^{8} 7830^{7}

Lancaster Gate *Amanda Perrett* a74
2 b c Zamindar(USA) —Bayswater (Caerleon (USA))
7520^{9} (7835)

Lancelot (FR) *F Head* a95 112
4 b h Bahri(USA) —Lunata (IRE) (Marju (IRE))
581a^{4} 759a^{7} 5094a^{2} 6321a^{4}

Landaho *Hugh McWilliams* 40
2 b f Tobougg(IRE) —Ellovamul (Elmaamul (USA))
2346^{11} 4632^{8} 5003^{3} 5819^{8} 6413^{6}

Landaman (IRE) *Mark Johnston* 91
3 br g Cape Cross(IRE) —Mayoress (Machiavellian (USA))
5169^{2} 5556^{5} (6097) 6632^{7}

Landesherr (GER) *Steve Gollings* a63
4 b g Black Sam Bellamy(IRE) —Lutte Marie (GER) (Frontal)
954^{9}

Land Hawk (IRE) *Lydia Pearce* a64 67
5 br g Trans Island—Heike (Glenstal (USA))
7522^{3} 7810^{3}

Landown Littlerock *Reg Hollinshead* a57 66
2 b g Sakhee(USA) —Maraha (Lammtarra (USA))
4402^{4} 4853^{4} 6048^{3} 6806^{14} 7177^{5}

Landscape (FR) *J E Pease* 95
3 b c Lando(GER) —Universelle (USA) (Miswaki (USA))
5771a^{6}

Lanett Lady (IRE) *M Halford* 83
2 br f Teufelsberg(USA) —Smoken Rosa (USA) (Smoke Glacken (USA))
5950a^{5}

Langham Lily (USA) *Chris Wall* 47
2 b bf Badge Of Silver(USA) —Silver Frau (USA) (Silver Charm (USA))
6933^{12}

Langley *Pat Murphy* a85 93
4 b g Trempolino(USA) —Late Night (GER) (Groom Dancer (USA))
994^{4} 1105^{8} 1775^{7} 5102^{11} 5866^{4} 6306^{5} 6785^{2}

Lang Shining (IRE) *Jamie Osborne* a86 91
7 ch g Dr Fong(USA) —Dragnet (IRE) (Rainbow Quest (USA))
175^{3} 2359^{2} 3380^{3} 3537^{6} 3764^{3} 4211^{5} 4825^{4} 5110^{7} 5857^{10}

Langtoon Lass *Brian Storey* 43
3 b f Captain Rio—Mindanao (Most Welcome)
2361^{6} 3053^{8} 3756^{11} 4149^{6} 4505^{6} 5623^{7}

La Pampita (IRE) *William Knight* 64
2 b f Intikhab(USA) —Jacaranda Ridge (Indian Ridge)
6432^{3}

Lapao (GER) *W Himmel* a49 81
5 b g Daylami(IRE) —La Candela (GER) (Alzao (USA))
441a^{10}

La Passionata *Robert Mills* a39 29
2 ch f Proclamation(IRE) —Miss Madame (IRE) (Cape Cross (IRE))
5655^{14} 7598^{6} 7757^{10}

La Pernelle (IRE) *Y De Nicolay* a87 107
3 b f Beat Hollow—Luna Celtica (IRE) (Celtic Swing)
1709a^{2} 2342a^{6} 4570a^{4} 5366a^{10}

La Pomme D'Amour *A Fabre* 100
3 ch f Peintre Celebre(USA) —Winnebago (Kris)
4036b^{4} 5027a^{6}

Larga Charla (IRE) *G Botti*
2 b c Elusive City(USA) —Tinareena (IRE) (Barathea (IRE))
7449a^{0}

Largem *J R Jenkins* a61 28
5 b g Largesse—Jem's Law (Contract Law (USA))
645^{11} 728^{4} 1310^{4}

Larimar (IRE) *Amanda Perrett* a52
3 ch g Selkirk(USA) —Campbellite (Desert Prince (IRE))
95^{8} 300^{5}

Larkrise Star *Dean Ivory* a74 69
4 b m Where Or When(IRE) —Katy Ivory (IRE) (Night Shift (USA))
4579^{5} 5515^{2} (6032) (6472) 6924^{6} 7447^{2} ◆ 7671^{4}

L'Arlesienne *Sylvester Kirk* a44
2 ch f Dutch Art—Angry Bark (USA) (Woodman (USA))
7396^{8} 7599^{10} 7838^{10}

La Rogerais (FR) *T Doumen* a68 67
6 gr m Verglas(IRE) —La Legende (FR) (Desert Prince (IRE))
325a^{0}

La Romantique (IRE) *Marco Botti* a68 53
2 b f Acclamation—Cloonkeary (In The Wings)
6117^{7} 6506^{4} 6927^{2} 7444^{3} 7752^{4} 7821^{4}

La Route De Lisa (FR) *F Rohaut* a59
3 b f High Yield(USA) —Lisatine (FR) (Linamix (FR))
288a^{10}

Larwood (IRE) *Henry Candy* a43 68
2 gr g Aussie Rules(USA) —Ashbilya (USA) (Nureyev (USA))
4414^{10} 5077^{6} 5889^{5} ◆ 6293^{7} (6890) 7445^{7}

La Salida *David Barron* 66
2 b f Proclamation(IRE) —Anapola (GER) (Polish Precedent (USA))
(3302)

La Salvita (GER) *A Wohler* 103
3 ch f Big Shuffle(USA) —La Hermana (Hernando (FR))
2337a^{10}

Laser Blazer *Jeremy Gask* a55
3 b g Zafeen(FR) —Sashay (Bishop Of Cashel)
7249^{8} 7537^{8} 7698^{6} 7892^{5} ◆

Laser Bullet (JPN) *Kiyoshi Hagiwara* a82
3 b c Brian's Time(USA) —Complicata (JPN) (Mr Prospector (USA))
998a^{9}

Laser Ruby *Andrew Balding* a66 61
4 b m Compton Place—Lighted Way (Kris)
304^{6}

La Sonadora *John Spearing* a44 49
2 gr f Proclamation(IRE) —Evening Falls (Beveled (USA))
5347^{7} 6281^{6} 6742^{8} 7342^{10}

Lasse (GER) *C Ferland* a71 77
8 b g Hamond(GER) —Liberia (GER) (Pentathlon)
533a^{2} 843a^{0}

Last Act (IRE) *Mark Hoad* a44 34
3 gr f Act One—Laissez Faire (IRE) (Tagula (IRE))
2637^{8} 3432^{10} 5042^{9}

Last Bid *Tim Easterby* 96
2 b f Vital Equine(IRE) —Manderina (Mind Games)
1966^{2} ◆ 2485^{3} (3050) (3879) (4343) 4787^{6} 5286^{2} 5558^{5}

Last Crusade (IRE) *A P O'Brien* a76 95
3 gr c Galileo(IRE) —St Roch (IRE) (Danehill (USA))
2331a^{5} 3371a^{4}

Last Destination (IRE) *Nigel Tinkler* a51 72
3 b g Dubai Destination(USA) —Maimana (IRE) (Desert King (IRE))
1944^{6} 2406^{10} (4149) (4505) 4908^{8} 6116^{12} 6840^{9} 7024^{14}

Lastkingofscotland (IRE) *Conor Dore* a82 81
5 b g Danehill Dancer(IRE) —Arcade (Rousillon (USA))
(55) 249^{8} (307) 467^{4} 557^{4} 665^{4} (786) 961^{4} 1061^{5} 1296^{4} 1530^{12} 1990^{6} 2206^{2} 3172^{2} 3250^{4} 4089^{6} 4990^{7} 5318^{12} 6794^{13} 7146^{11} 7349^{2} 7485^{9} 7596^{4} 7716^{3} 7895^{10}

Lastofthemohicans (FR) *Paul Webber* a91 65
4 b g Galileo(IRE) —Peace Time (GER) (Surumu (GER))
4962^{9} 6375^{8}

L'Astre De Choisir (IRE) *[illegible]* [illegible]
3 ch g Choisir(AUS) —Starring (FR) (Ashkalani (IRE))
6354^{5} (6587) ◆ 6797^{3}

Lastroarofdtiger (USA) *Mrs K Burke* a59 54
5 b g Cherokee Run(USA) —Innocent Affair (IRE) (Night Shift (USA))
367^{8}

Lastroseofsummer (IRE) *Rae Guest* a72 79
5 ch m Haafhd—Broken Romance (IRE) (Ela-Mana-Mou)
(3599) (4488)

Last Sovereign *Ollie Pears* a84 88
7 b g Pivotal—Zayala (Royal Applause)
2431^{5} 2917^{2} 3506^{8} 4020^{4} 4349^{15} (5083) 5371^{4} 5879^{12} 6327^{10}

Last Storm *J-M Capitte* a73 75
7 b m Marju(IRE) —Trombe (FR) (Bering)
220a^{6} 395a^{9}

Last Supper *James Bethell*
2 b f Echo Of Light—Scotland The Brave (Zilzal (USA))
6449^{11}

Last Zak *Michael Easterby* a20 47
2 b g Lucky Story(USA) —Zakuska (Zafonic (USA))
5727^{8} 6180^{12} 6572^{6}

Las Verglas Star (IRE) *Richard Fahey* a69 96
3 gr g Verglas(IRE) —Magnificent Bell (IRE) (Octagonal (NZ))
(1074) 1214^{2} (3168) 3864^{5} 4467^{4} 5466^{2} 6080^{2}

La Taniere *Michael Easterby* a12 61
2 b g Misu Bond(IRE) —Medici Princess (Medicean)
2886^{5} 3237^{9} 3826^{8} 4047^{7} 4749^{4} 6293^{10}

Latansaa *Marcus Tregoning* a82 82
4 b g Indian Ridge—Sahool (Unfuwain (USA))
3521^{9} 4970^{7}

Late Debate (USA) *J S Bolger* a37 79
3 br c Successful Appeal(USA) —Saintly Hertfield (USA) (Saint Ballado (CAN))
973a^{8}

Latenfast *Michael Easterby* 44
2 b g Avonbridge—Eurolink Cafe (Grand Lodge (USA))
5919^{4} 6152^{10} 6675^{7} 6835^{6}

La Terrible (IRE) *F Vermeulen* a55 63
5 b m Fasliyev(USA) —Mondsee (Caerleon (USA))
832a0

Late Telegraph (IRE) *Sir Henry Cecil* a98 99
3 b c Montjeu(IRE) —Bywayofthestars (Danehill (USA))
(5585) 70534 73473 ◆

La Tropezienne (FR) *T Civel*
5 gr m Subotica(FR) —La Serenite (Dowsing (USA))
372a0

Latte *Linda Stubbs* a67 67
2 b g Multiplex—Coffee To Go (Environment Friend)
11855 14345 21943 24094 27842 33454 36565 45127 (5353) 58024 (6652) 68354

Lauberhorn *Eve Johnson Houghton* a75 75
4 b g Dubai Destination(USA) —Ski Run (Petoski)
24173 28566 36902 40247 (4746) 580410 62797 65822

Laughing (IRE) *Charles O'Brien* a78 104
3 b f Dansili—Comic (IRE) (Be My Chief (USA))
6909a7

Laughing Jack *Ed Dunlop* a80 80
3 b g Beat Hollow—Bronzewing (Beldale Flutter (USA))
(1271) 18955 32317 612411 66586 697611

Laughing Lashes (USA) *Mrs John Harrington* 113
3 gr f Mr Greeley(USA) —Adventure (USA) (Unbridled's Song (USA))
171917 2334a3 4133a4 ◆ 52198

Laugh Or Cry *Dean Ivory* a69 73
3 br g Firebreak—Turkish Delight (Prince Sabo)
3983 622810 66536

Launch On Line *Bill Turner* a72 52
2 b f Majestic Missile(IRE) —Savvy Shopper (USA) (Stravinsky (USA))
10422 14145 195710 71947 73597

Laura Land *Mark Brisbourne* a55 48
5 b m Lujain(USA) —Perdicula (IRE) (Persian Heights)
865 3242 40912 4502 (630) 7714 8594 10634 12537 19594 765412

Lauralu *Michael Blanshard* a42
3 ch f Shirocco(GER) —Suzuki (IRE) (Barathea (IRE))
2148 7374 13328

Laura's Bairn *J R Jenkins* a65 35
2 ch c Piccolo—Primula Bairn (Bairn (USA))
299712 322913 (4648) 569010

Laureate Conductor (USA) *Michael P De Paulo* a86 106
5 b h Bernstein(USA) —Lavender Baby (USA) (Rubiano (USA))
6203a4 6910a9

Laurel Lad (IRE) *Charles Hills* a17 64
2 b c Oratorio(IRE) —Laurel Delight (Presidium)
26877 32378 48575 55778 62607 666712

Lava Steps (USA) *Paul Midgley* a74 59
5 b g Giant's Causeway(USA) —Miznah (IRE) (Sadler's Wells (USA))
1035

La Vecchia Scuola (IRE) *Jim Goldie* a39 102
7 b m Mull Of Kintyre(USA) —Force Divine (FR) (L'Emigrant (USA))
180816 210711 339611 38757 47753 633313

Laverre (IRE) *Lucy Wadham* a37 76
4 b m Noverre(USA) —Ladood (Unfuwain (USA))
(1567) (1871) (2145) 255212 28464 40743 46265

La Verte Rue (USA) *Mrs A Malzard* a48 65
5 b m Johannesburg(USA) —Settling In (USA) (Green Desert (USA))
5778a3

Law Blade (FR) *H-A Pantall* a70 64
6 b g Dashing Blade—Lonia (GER) (Royal Academy (USA))
843a2

Lawn Jamil (USA) *Charles Hills* 74
2 b c Jazil(USA) —Khazayin (USA) (Bahri (USA))
56815 ◆ (6259)

Law Of The Range *Marco Botti* 107
4 b m Alhaarth(IRE) —Mountain Law (USA) (Mountain Cat (USA))
11144 (1884) (2927) (3703) 44973

Lawspeaker *Mahmood Al Zarooni* 108
4 b h Singspiel(IRE) —Forum Floozie (NZ) (Danasinga (AUS))
154a7 413a6 603aP

Law To Himself (IRE) *Alan Swinbank* 75
4 b g Rakti—Samhat Mtoto (Mtoto)
10997 14913 17143 22136 30388 41705 48112 51504 53144 ◆ 56227 653312 69182 (7215)

Layali Dubai (USA) *Saeed Bin Suroor* a67 53
2 b f Street Sense(USA) —Make My Heart Sing (USA) (King Of Kings (IRE))
64588 71186

Lay Claim (USA) *Alan McCabe* a79 80
4 bb h Seeking The Gold(USA) —Promptly (IRE) (Lead On Time (USA))
2875 (381) 5417

Layla Jamil (IRE) *Mick Channon* 81
3 b f Exceed And Excel(AUS) —Guana Bay (Cadeaux Genereux)
(1853) 250312 29375 38537 42023 43425 52685 (5551) 60946 637811 675914 70558

Layla's Boy *John Mackie* a56 77
4 ch g Sakhee(USA) —Gay Romance (Singspiel (IRE))
65039 66669 71956

Layla's Dancer *Tony Carroll* a78 83
4 b g Danehill Dancer(IRE) —Crumpetsfortea (IRE) (Henbit (USA))
943 2722 (474) 6972 7153 9653 12233 16763 17755 21952 23596 438910

Layla's Hero (IRE) *John Quinn* a93 97
4 b g One Cool Cat(USA) —Capua (USA) (Private Terms (USA))
111113 188528 221711 24954 33394 48103 (5554) 61136 633113

Layla's King *George Margarson* a70 65
3 b c Dubawi(IRE) —Top Jem (Damister (USA))
18105 22287 29575 33768 36812 75156

Layline (IRE) *Gay Kelleway* a97 92
4 b g King's Best(USA) —Belle Reine (King Of Kings (IRE))
91a3 (525) 7023 8033 9917 288411 30855 (3982) 49936 571216 5981a10 63026 780110

Layman Junior (FR) *D De Waele* a75 66
3 ch g Layman(USA) —Summer Rain (Cadeaux Genereux)
7016a2

Lay Time *Andrew Balding* 111
3 b f Galileo(IRE) —Time Saved (Green Desert (USA))
(4102) ◆ 45502 ◆ 52774 (6061)

La Zamora *David Barron* a84 91
5 b m Lujain(USA) —Love Quest (Pursuit Of Love)
451612 47914 ◆ 52558 568211 611314

Lazeez (USA) *Clive Brittain* a60 32
2 b f Green Desert(USA) —Ballet School (IRE) (Sadler's Wells (USA))
58136 652912

La Zona (IRE) *Wido Neuroth* a93 101
5 b m Singspiel(IRE) —Reine De Neige (Kris)
(5096a) 5981a4 (6741a)

Lazy Darren *Chris Grant* a79 70
7 b g Largesse—Palmstead Belle (IRE) (Wolfhound (USA))
707512

Leadenhall Lass (IRE) *Pat Phelan* a73 73
5 ch m Monsieur Bond(IRE) —Zest (USA) (Zilzal (USA))
(1147) 18988 40107 44583 53268 58905 64795 74484

Leader Of The Land (IRE) *David Lanigan* a57 91
4 ch g Halling(USA) —Cheerleader (Singspiel (IRE))
18924 24753 (3580)

Leading Star *Michael Madgwick* a31 25
2 b f Motivator—Movie Mogul (Sakhee (USA))
22277 32822 42458 73427 77528

League Champion (USA) *R Bouresly* a90 73
8 b g Rahy(USA) —Meiosis (USA) (Danzig (USA))
23714

Leahness (IRE) *Ken Wingrove* a46 42
4 br m Arakan(USA) —En Retard (IRE) (Petardia)
6908 124711

Leah's Angel (IRE) *Michael Mullineaux* 36
3 b f Oratorio(IRE) —First Bank (FR) (Anabaa (USA))
18108 221811 37344 41815

Lean Machine *Ronald Harris* a70 68
4 b h Exceed And Excel(AUS) —Al Corniche (IRE) (Bluebird (USA))
946 (391) 6353 9683 12784 21954 25653 30895 31767 39268

Lean On Pete (IRE) *David Lanigan* 29
2 b g Oasis Dream—Superfonic (FR) (Zafonic (USA))
646211 680511

Learco (FR) *Y Fertillet* a60 62
10 ch g Ashkalani(IRE) —Fly Me (FR) (Luthier)
42a0 221a6 706a0 832a10

Learn (IRE) *A P O'Brien* 111
2 b c Galileo(IRE) —Kentucky Warbler (IRE) (Spinning World (USA))
70204 7192a4

Leaves You Baby (IRE) *M Halford* a78 76
4 b m Pivotal—Royal Devotion (IRE) (Sadler's Wells (USA))
7378a10 7548a5

Leaving Alone (USA) *Edwin Tuer* a71 68
4 ch m Mr Greeley(USA) —Spankin' (USA) (A.P. Indy (USA))
10393 13055 15198 18812 24967 37546 43269

Le Bahamien (FR) *F Head* 94
2 ch c Kentucky Dynamite(USA) —La Bahamienne (IRE) (Fasliyev (USA))
6902a6

Le Big (GER) *U Stoltefuss* a94 104
7 b g Big Shuffle(USA) —La Luganese (IRE) (Surumu (GER))
3422a2 4138a4 5664a5 6201a9 7048a8 7311a6

Le Cagnard *Michael Bell* 67
2 b c Danehill Dancer(IRE) —Miss Provence (Hernando (FR))
453513 55796 60188 64606

Leceile (USA) *Noel Meade* a64 91
5 b m Forest Camp(USA) —Summerwood (USA) (Boston Harbor (USA))
4737a5

Le Chat D'Or *Michael Dods* 70
3 b g One Cool Cat(USA) —Oh So Well (IRE) (Sadler's Wells (USA))
19106 23925 31386 54033 68402

Lechevalier Choisi (IRE) *James Bernard McCabe* 106
3 b c Choisir(AUS) —Creekhaven (IRE) (Definite Article)
2967a6 3440a16 52823 66878

Lechlade Lass *Adrian Chamberlain* a53 50
3 b f Doyen(IRE) —Cotswold Dancer (AUS) (Carnegie (IRE))
35139 48269 511410 55678 60843 65854

Le Corvee (IRE) *Tony Carroll* a46 55
9 b g Rossini(USA) —Elupa (IRE) (Mtoto)
2778 5989 29058 46545

Le Danu (FR) *E Libaud*
2 b g Victory Note(USA) —Petite Chance (FR) (Le Balafre (FR))
7665a0

Ledgerwood *Adrian Chamberlain* a30 48
6 b g Royal Applause—Skies Are Blue (Unfuwain (USA))
4904 63010 89610 35159

Le Drakkar (AUS) *Saeed Bin Suroor* a108 113
6 gr g Anabaa(USA) —My Mo Rally (NZ) (Mi Preferido (USA))
157a7 331a7 503a3 586a3 759a4 997a6 66714

Leelu *David Arbuthnot* a71 66
5 b m Largesse—Strat's Quest (Nicholas (USA))
11475 18676 34137 39246 46962 51002 64342

Leenavesta (USA) *Richard Hannon* a68 69
2 b f Arch(USA) —Shoshaloza (USA) (Diesis)
21535 25595 30923 40853 46582 49553 69958 729410 74912

Lees Anthem *Colin Teague* a53 67
4 b g Mujahid(USA) —Lady Rock (Mistertopogigo (IRE))
14114 15234 196811 21265 26095 30272 34514 39014 45046 51758 63866

Le Francois (GER) *W Figge* 60
4 b h Sholokhov(IRE) —La Zarina (GER) (Cadeaux Genereux)
2657a9

Legal Eagle (IRE) *Paul Green* a77 85
6 b g Invincible Spirit(IRE) —Lupulina (CAN) (Saratoga Six (USA))
9327 13957 ◆ 18782 211812 26685 479211 56806 59182 63502 691714

Legal Legacy *David C Griffiths* 81
5 ch g Beat Hollow—Dans Delight (Machiavellian (USA))
10357 16968 190911 254510 (3348) 43497 510611 57284 623114 79285

Legendaire (USA) *Mlle H Van Zuylen* a74
3 gr c El Prado(IRE) —England's Legend (FR) (Lure (USA))
902a5

Le Home (FR) *S Wattel* a83 83
4 b g Anabaa(USA) —Desert Jewel (USA) (Caerleon (USA))
840a0

Leitrim King (IRE) *William Haggas* 60
2 b c High Chaparral(IRE) —Therry Girl (IRE) (Lahib (USA))
65299 71095

Leitzu (IRE) *Mick Channon* a48 68
4 b m Barathea(IRE) —Ann's Annie (IRE) (Alzao (USA))
11674 21453 25754 28307 32286 37268 42497 46667 50027

Lejaam *John Dunlop* 72
3 b c Dansili—Acts Of Grace (USA) (Bahri (USA))
28427 33646

Le King Beau (USA) *John Bridger* a71 59
2 b c Leroidesanimaux(BRZ) —Berine (IRE) (Bering)
65326 ◆ 68374 70674 71962 (7434) 75052 (7762) (7798) (7907)

Lelaps (USA) *Marco Botti* 80
2 ch c Mr Greeley(USA) —Rebecca Parisi (IRE) (Persian Heights)
68282 72335

Le Larron (IRE) *A De Royer-Dupre* 109
4 gr h High Chaparral(IRE) —Mare Aux Fees (Kenmare (FR))
1231a3 1707a7 2344a5

Lemon Drop Red (USA) *Ed Dunlop* a76 85
3 b g Lemon Drop Kid(USA) —Skipper's Mate (USA) (Skip Away (USA))
10227 15244 19722 24075 28744 (3479) (3715) 44072 53896 61213 (6412) 666612

Lemon Queen (IRE) *John Quinn* 55
5 ch m Desert Sun—Calendula (Be My Guest (USA))
15595 17957 24026 308810

Lemon Rock *Noel Quinlan* a39 76
2 b f Green Desert(USA) —Lady Links (Bahamian Bounty)
20632 ◆ 29146 39152 54796 61693 652614 79066

Lemon Twirl (USA) *John Mattine* 95
7 b m Lemon Drop Kid(USA) —Longing To Dance (USA) (Nureyev (USA))
(3208a)

Lend A Grand (IRE) *Jo Crowley* a59 39
7 br g Lend A Hand—Grand Madam (Grand Lodge (USA))
5903 11783 432211 679312

Lend A Light *Philip Hobbs* a51 55
5 b g Lend A Hand—No Candles Tonight (Star Appeal)
9504

Lennie Briscoe (IRE) *Martin Bosley* a51 60
5 b g Rock Of Gibraltar(IRE) —Tammany Hall (IRE) (Petorius)
3175 ◆ 55312 9579

Lennoxwood (IRE) *Mark Usher* a55 11
3 rg g Verglas(IRE) —Sigonella (IRE) (Priolo (USA))
2332 ◆ 6367 8185 9874 19527 553916 584311 60834 641114 70059 71312 75613 76557 77682 78995

Lenny Bee *Deborah Sanderson* a97 85
5 rg g Kyllachy—Smart Hostess (Most Welcome)
116611 503315 57036 617410 67625 69178 73552 74872 76444 78476

Leo Gali (IRE) *Vaclav Luka II* 102
4 b m Galileo(IRE) —Reprise (Darshaan)
7045a2

Leonid Glow *Michael Dods* a70 83
6 b m Hunting Lion(IRE) —On Till Morning (IRE) (Never So Bold)
190716 335911 42889

Leonverre (IRE) *David O'Meara*
3 b g Noverre(USA) —Queen Leonor (IRE) (Caerleon (USA))
37106

Leopardin (GER) *H J Groschel* 97
3 b f Areion(GER) —Lolli Pop (GER) (Cagliostro (GER))
2981a5 4839a9

Leqqaa (USA) *Mark Johnston* 97
2 b c Street Cry(IRE) —Guerre Et Paix (USA) (Soviet Star (USA))
(3076) 40912 50443 57093 69522

Le Reveur *Richard Guest* a53 60
9 b g Machiavellian(USA) —Brooklyn's Dance (FR) (Shirley Heights)
573910 63579 65425 687710 7352P 778712

Le Roi Mage (IRE) *T Lallie* a97 104
6 ch g City On A Hill(USA) —Lycius Girl (ITY) (Lycius (USA))
4223a6

Lesley's Choice *Paul Rich* a65 80
5 b g Lucky Story(USA) —Wathbat Mtoto (Mtoto)
107314 153910 20483 22632 25857 68759 711611 735211 75757 774413

Lesotho (IRE) *Noel Quinlan* 73
2 gr f Excellent Art—Limpopo (Green Desert (USA))
33422 ◆ (3855)

L'Espagna (FR) *T Trapenard* 85
2 b f Rock Of Gibraltar(IRE) —Luanda (IRE) (Bigstone (IRE))
4569a6

Les Troyens *A Fabre* a94 103
3 b c Librettist(USA) —Native Blue (Seeking The Gold (USA))
(776a) 1010a4

Les Verguettes (IRE) *Chris Wall* a72 55
3 b f Iffraaj—Mitsina (Fantastic Light (USA))
363 32837 35135 74112

Les Veys *E Libaud* a69 69
3 b c Green Desert(USA) —Rababah (USA) (Woodman (USA))
776a8

Lethal *Richard Price* a59 60
8 ch g Nashwan(USA) —Ipanema Beach (Lion Cavern (USA))
375 (363) 6966 9288 12486 13366 55407 59965 63047 66182 70713 74198 75619

Lethal Force (IRE) *Clive Cox* 105
2 gr c Dark Angel(IRE) —Land Army (IRE) (Desert Style (IRE))
18862 25593 30124 44244

Letham Cottage *David Evans* a37
2 b c Imperial Dancer—Fascinatin Rhythm (Fantastic Light (USA))
70949 725810 749312

Let It Rock (IRE) *Mrs K Burke* a61 52
4 b m Noverre(USA) —Green Life (Green Desert (USA))
108a6 831a0 6959a0 7315a0 74127 769511

Let Me Fight (IRE) *J Moore* 120
4 b g Hawk Wing(USA) —Riva Royale (Royal Applause)
1576a8

Le Toreador *Kevin Ryan* a94 94
6 ch g Piccolo—Peggy Spencer (Formidable (USA))
(701) 15394 16988 (2118) 23979 26947 (3279) 622414 63517 67032 748911 75752 78324 (7883)

Let's Dance (IRE) *Tom Dascombe* 67
3 b f Danehill Dancer(IRE) —Corrine (IRE) (Spectrum (IRE))
16553 22574

Let's Face Facts *Jim Goldie* a6 61
4 b m Lucky Story(USA) —Rhinefield Beauty (IRE) (Shalford (IRE))
24985 27814 33034 365810 467010 48778 51532 70999

Letsgoroundagain (IRE) *Charles Hills* 101
2 b c Redback—Starring (FR) (Ashkalani (IRE))
13604 ◆ 23953 31612 (3583) 40914 52168 58493 62705 (6914) 7405a7

Lets Move It *Derek Shaw* a61 40
4 b g Piccolo—Park Star (Gothenberg (IRE))
154 572 1667 2898 8572 9419 10297

Letty *A Klimscha Jr* 89
4 ch m Trade Fair—Love Is All (IRE) (Second Empire (IRE))
6783a0

Let Your Love Flow (IRE) *Sylvester Kirk* a67 67
2 b f Iffraaj—Miss Odlum (IRE) (Mtoto)
56052 6196a12 65063 69564 (7414) 77182 ◆ 78212 78493

Le Valentin (FR) *Y De Nicolay* a79 104
5 b g Slickly(FR) —Vallabelle (FR) (Valanour (IRE))
1122a10 4739a4 5532a3 5985a10 7534a9

Levantera (IRE) *Paul Howling* a59 75
3 ch f Hurricane Run(IRE) —Ellway Star (IRE) (Night Shift (USA))
19474 28429 32336 50495 56143 64387 73349

Leviathan *Tony Newcombe* a48 98
4 b h Dubawi(IRE) —Gipsy Moth (Efisio)
14067 20614 24412 29335 (3290) 36457 ◆ 431423 548311 616316

Levi Draper *James Fanshawe* 55
2 b g Rock Of Gibraltar(IRE) —Splice (Sharpo)
33088 41844

Le Vie Infinite (IRE) *R Brogi* 105
4 b h Le Vie Dei Colori—Looking Back (IRE) (Stravinsky (USA))
1919a6 (6905a) 7323a8

Levitate *Alan McCabe* a87 87
3 ch g Pivotal—Soar (Danzero (AUS))
22293 ◆ 28383 ◆ 35573 (4817) ◆ 50547 583011 61137 67617 75863 76757

Lewis De La Vis (FR) *D Windrif* a75 75
3 b g Ski Chief(USA) —Mummy's Kris (IRE) (Mummy's Game)
7669a7

Lewyn *Jeremy Gask* a84 72
4 b m Exceed And Excel(AUS) —Panoramic View (Polar Falcon (USA))
19733 (658) (861) 12747 72533 73328

Lexington Bay (IRE) *Richard Fahey* a72 92
3 b g High Chaparral(IRE) —Schust Madame (IRE) (Second Set (IRE))
16097 20763 (2695) 30844 57105 (6151) (6333) 710210

Lexington Pearl (USA) *Ralph Beckett* a79
2 ch f Elusive Quality(USA) —Lexington Girl (USA) (Storm Cat (USA))
(6820) ◆

Lexington Spirit (IRE) *Richard Fahey* 75
2 b f Iffraaj—Festivite (IRE) (Fasliyev (USA))
(2113) ◆ (2429) 301412

Lexi's Boy (IRE) *Kevin Ryan* a81 85
3 gr g Verglas(IRE) —Jazan (IRE) (Danehill (USA))
45 (406) ◆ (543) (1706a) 27267 33762 (3474)

Lexi's Hero (IRE) *Kevin Ryan* 108
3 b g Invincible Spirit(IRE) —Christel Flame (Darshaan)
1152[2] (1825) 2508[11] (2934) 3820[2] 4573[4] 5054[6] 5927[11] 6706[16]
Lexi's Prince (IRE) *Tom Dascombe* 71
2 gr c Clodovil(IRE) —Bent Al Fala (IRE) (Green Desert (USA))
1890[8] 2455[5] 2780[2] 3035[7]
Ley Hunter (USA) *A Fabre* 118
4 b h Kingmambo(USA) —Lailani (Unfuwain (USA))
1266a[2] 1708a[5] 2753a[4] 4037a[6] 5304a[11] (5990a) 6562a[3]
Leyte Gulf (USA) *Chris Bealby* a68 54
8 b g Cozzene(USA) —Gabacha (USA) (Woodman (USA))
514[5] 596[2] 733[2] 1080[5] 1586[3] 1956[6] 2846[6] *7564[7] 7850[4]*
L Frank Baum (IRE) *Gay Kelleway* a69 95
4 b g Sinndar(IRE) —Rainbow City (IRE) (Rainbow Quest (USA))
3157[5] 4266[7] 4423[10] *5102[8]* 5759[7] 6171[7] (6405) 6690[21] 6832[9]
L'Hermitage (IRE) *Brian Meehan* a71 79
3 b g Encosta De Lago(AUS) —Autumnal (IRE) (Indian Ridge)
1315[4] 1626[5] 2052[6] *(2305)* (2677) 3108[10] 4336[8] *6822[10] 6976[8]*
L'Hirondelle (IRE) *Michael Attwater* a92 83
7 b g Anabaa(USA) —Auratum (USA) (Carson City (USA))
438[9] 822[12] 2647[16] 2999[9] *3285[8]* 5240[9] *6355[6] 6797[5] 7362[7]*
L'Homme De Nuit (GER) *Jim Best* a73 26
7 b g Samum(GER) —La Bouche (GER) (In The Wings)
89[5] 955[3] 1839[13] *3047[8] 3712[8]* 4318[8]
Lhotse Sherpa *John Holt* a52
2 b c Byron—Soyalang (FR) (Alydeed (CAN))
7367[6] 7783[6]
Liang Kay (GER) *A De Royer-Dupre* 110
6 b h Dai Jin—Linton Bay (GER) (Funambule (USA))
7193a[5] 7409a[4]
Libano (IRE) *D K Weld* 90
5 b h Indian Ridge—Daniela Grassi (Bound For Honour (USA))
923a[7] 1930a[6] 3445a[15]
Liberal Lady *Ralph Smith* a64 61
3 b f Statue Of Liberty(USA) —Noble Story (Last Tycoon)
43[3] 305[3] (380) 3230[4] 3908[3] *4182[6] 7332[9] 7812[2]*
Liberate *Philip Hobbs* a88 84
8 ch g Lomitas—Eversince (USA) (Foolish Pleasure (USA))
4423[7]
Libertia *Tony Newcombe* 47
3 b f Statue Of Liberty(USA) —Imperia (GER) (Tertullian (USA))
834[10]
Libertino (IRE) *Tony Carroll* a65 60
4 ch g Bertolini(USA) —Villafranca (IRE) (In The Wings)
65[2] 166[2] 345[5] 485[14] 893[12] 1084[5] 1171[2] 1331[2] 1770[3] 1875[3] 2161[2] 2554[5]
Liberty Green (IRE) *Alan McCabe* a76 51
3 b f Statue Of Liberty(USA) —Green Green Grass (Green Desert (USA))
(100) 302[6] 578[5] 875[4] 940[4] 1391[13] 3785[8]
Liberty Island (IRE) *K J Condon* a81 80
6 b g Statue Of Liberty(USA) —Birthday (IRE) (Singspiel (IRE))
4767a[11]
Liberty Lady (IRE) *Des Donovan* a78 100
4 b m Statue Of Liberty(USA) —Crossed Wire (Lycius (USA))
651[6] 970[4] 1186[5] *1279[5]* (1507) (1864) 2489[3] 2967a[2] 3874[11] 4357[7] [illegible]
Liberty Ship *Mark Buckley* a66 77
6 b g Statue Of Liberty(USA) —Flag (Selkirk (USA))
2182[3] 2585[10] 3640[6] (4000) 4189[2] (4395) 4636[2] 4986[6] 5468[3] 5680[4]
Libranno *Richard Hannon* 117
3 b c Librettist(USA) —Annabelle Ja (FR) (Singspiel (IRE))
1341[2] 1602[4] 2370[3] (3404) 3863[4] 4412[4] 4838a[11] (5510) 6298[7] 6858[3] 7298[12]
Libre *Violet M Jordan* a45 56
11 b g Bahamian Bounty—Premier Blues (FR) (Law Society (USA))
283[6] 408[10] 773[13] 2824[6] 3094[6] 3515[8] *7741[8] 7891[10]*
Librettela *Alan Jarvis* a62 71
3 b g Librettist(USA) —Ella's Wish (IRE) (Bluebird (USA))
1774[12] *2174[11]* 2599[10] *(5042) 5636[U] 5838[4]* ◆ *(6253)* (6923)
Libretto (GER) *H-W Hiller* a70
5 b g Orpen(USA) —Lupita (GER) (Niniski (USA))
93a[2] 325a[3] (627a)
Libritish *Marco Botti* a79 71
3 b f Librettist(USA) —Tanwir (Unfuwain (USA))
(344) 1862[3] *4090[2]* 4530[5] *4905[5]*
Libys Dream (IRE) *Tom Dascombe* a85 51
3 b f Invincible Spirit(IRE) —Perilous Pursuit (USA) (Lemon Drop Kid (USA))
5030[4] 5469[5] *(5946) 6442[2] 6931[4]* ◆ *7141[7] (7595) (7715)*
Licence To Till (USA) *Mark Johnston* a97 92
4 b g War Chant(USA) —With A Wink (USA) (Clever Trick (USA))
846[12] 1477[11] 1887[8] 2509[3] 2681[7] 3203[5] 3844[9] 4253[6] 4528[3] 4801[2] 4901[2] 5275[3] 5546[8] 6124[3] ◆ 6302[8] *(6513a)* (6708)
Lidar (FR) *Alan King* 86
6 ch g Take Risks(FR) —Light Wave (FR) (Marignan (USA))
1840[4] 2219[3] 2956[2] 3593[7] 5911[2]
Lidari (FR) *J-C Rouget* 101
2 b c Acclamation—Laxlova (FR) (Linamix (FR))
5130a[3] 5770a[5] 6902a[3]
Liebesziel *Alan McCabe* a57 69
2 br g Pursuit Of Love—Pretty Miss (Averti (IRE))
1383[5] 1721[4] 1886[7] 2485[9] 2889[10] *5896[4] 6178[2]* 6384[8] *6540[5]*
Liesl (IRE) *Kevin Ryan* 53
2 b f Iffraaj—Thats Your Opinion (Last Tycoon)
1337[9] 4285[7] 5104[3]
Lieutenant Kojak *Peter Charalambous* a67 77
3 b g Iceman—Red Duchess (Halling (USA))
1315[6] 5449[4] 6061[6] *(6668)* 7137[9]
Life And Soul (IRE) *Amanda Perrett* a80 99
4 b g Azamour(IRE) —Way For Life (GER) (Platini (GER))
1717[3] ◆ 2716[4] 3156[15] 3411[3] 4778[3] 5250[11]
Lifetime (IRE) *Brian Ellison* a71 81
3 b g Shamardal(USA) —La Vita E Bella (IRE) (Definite Article)
4186[5] 4529[3] 5007[2] ◆ (5432) 5880[4] 6241[7] 6674[17] *7722[2]*
Lift The Gloom *Noel Lawlor* a62 69
5 gr g Verglas(IRE) —Leinster Mills (IRE) (Doyoun)
7740[4]
Light Blow (USA) *Sir Henry Cecil* 81
3 b f Kingmambo(USA) —Lingerie (Shirley Heights)
1915[2] 2639[5] 4805[4] 6046[6] (6584)
Light Burst (USA) *Mahmood Al Zarooni* 65
2 b c Hard Spun(USA) —Kew Garden (USA) (Seattle Slew (USA))
2221[4] 6483[4] 6768[10]
Lightening Force *Ian Patrick Browne* a45
4 b r h Fantastic Light(USA) —Eujane (IRE) (Alzao (USA))
245[4] 374[6] 1250[5]
Lightening Pearl (IRE) *G M Lyons* 111
2 b f Marju(IRE) —Jioconda (IRE) (Rossini (USA))
4833a[3] (5522a) ◆ (6337)
Lightening Sticks (IRE) *Richard Brabazon* a91 94
4 b g King's Best(USA) —Opera Comique (FR) (Singspiel (IRE))
(1228a) 4418a[10] 5361a[8]
Light From Mars *John Quinn* a105 106
6 gr g Fantastic Light(USA) —Hylandra (USA) (Bering)
1094[8] (1406) 2031[9] 2909[12] 3645[16] 6147[17] 6335[11]
Light Lustre (IRE) *A Peraino* 87
2 b f Rock Of Gibraltar(IRE) —Lunar Lustre (IRE) (Desert Prince (IRE))
3212a[7]
Lightning Cloud (IRE) *Kevin Ryan* a79 103
3 gr g Sleeping Indian—Spree (IRE) (Dansili)
(1288) (2147) 2729[4] (3798) (4020) 4310[2] ◆ (5830)
Lightning Spirit *Gary Moore* a59 52
3 b f Storming Home—Lucky Dice (Perugino (USA))
1362[9] 1865[5] 4320[7] *4758[7]* 5423[4] 6411[7] 6764[7] *6982[5] (7119)*
Light Of Equuleus (IRE) *T G McCourt* a28 24
2 b f Antonius Pius(USA) —Gentian Mist (IRE) (Bluebird (USA))
1699a[9]
Light Show *A Fabre* 51
3 b c Tiger Hill(IRE) —Bright Morning (Dubai Millennium)
5132a[0]
Lights Of Heaven (NZ) *Peter G Moody* 116
4 b f Zabeel(NZ) —I'm In Heaven (NZ) (Volksraad)
6713a[3]
Lights On Me *H-W Hiller* 70
2 ch f Kyllachy—Time Will Show (FR) (Exit To Nowhere (USA))
6737a[6]
Light The City (IRE) *Ruth Carr* a62 62
4 b g Fantastic Light(USA) —Marine City (JPN) (Carnegie (IRE))
184[8] 373[3] [illegible] (3510) *(3712)* 3906[6] 4366[10] 4903[3] 5210[3] 5651[4] 5791[4] 6236[15]
Light Well (IRE) *John Gosden* a82 82
3 b g Sadler's Wells(USA) —L'Ancresse (IRE) (Darshaan)
2956[5] *6504[2]* 6810[4]
Ligurian Sea *Walter Swinburn* 69
2 b f Medicean—Shamara (IRE) (Spectrum (IRE))
3547[3] 4614[9]
Likeable Lad *Ruth Carr* 12
3 ch g Redoubtable(USA) —Some Like It Hot (Ashkalani (IRE))
187[7] 296[6] 322[7]
Like A Boy *Bill Turner* a57 57
3 b c Medicean—Like A Dame (Danehill (USA))
1139[8] 2104[4] 2904[6] *3709[3]* 4888[3] *6545[10] 7333[10] 7714[5]* ◆ *7910[2]*
Like Clockwork *Mark H Tompkins* 45
2 b g Rail Link—Tenpence (Bob Back (USA))
3401[15] 3954[9] 6951[13]
Like For Like (IRE) *Ron Hodges* a66 42
5 ch m Kheleyf(USA) —Just Like Annie (IRE) (Mujadil (USA))
5617[9]
Like The Night *Marco Botti* a62
2 ch f Byron—Twitch Hill (Piccolo)
7607[2] 7784[2]
Lilbourne Lad (IRE) *Richard Hannon* 112
2 b c Acclamation—Sogno Verde (IRE) (Green Desert (USA))
(1383) 2109[2] (2776a) ◆ (3439a) 4834a[4] 5251[2] 5882[4] 6688[2]
Lil Ella (IRE) *Patrick Holmes* 80
4 b m Pearl Of Love(IRE) —Royal Jubilee (IRE) (King's Theatre (IRE))
4294[7] 5062[7] 5311[9] 6236[14]
Lileo (IRE) *Nikki Evans* 65
3 b g Galileo(IRE) —Jabali (FR) (Shirley Heights)
7536[7]
Lilli Palmer (IRE) *Mike Murphy* a62 62
4 ch m Bertolini(USA) —Little Whisper (IRE) (Be My Guest (USA))
490[2] 807[3] (1068) ◆ 1354[2] 1936[3] *2198[5] 3280[2]* 5040[11] *5606[7] 6083[11]*
Lily Again *Paul Cole* a80 98
3 ch f American Post—Sari (Faustus (USA))
1319[9] 1884[11]
Lilyannabanana *David Evans* a24 27
4 ch m Avonbridge—Bundle (Cadeaux Genereux)
580[5] 747[6] 1755[10] 2399[9]
Lily Eva *Des Donovan* a40 50
5 ch m Definite Article—Avanindra (Zamindar (USA))
5267[11]
Lilygloves *Mick Channon* a28 45
2 ch f Imperial Dancer—Queen Of Narnia (Hunting Lion (IRE))
982[7] 1301[4] 4430[6] *4756[7] 4907[10]*
Lily In Pink *Jonathan Portman* a77 82
3 b f Sakhee(USA) —In Luck (In The Wings)
4157[10] 4826[2] *5386[3]* (5782)
Lily Le Braz *Gary Harrison* 25
6 b m Montjeu(IRE) —Mar Blue (FR) (Marju (IRE))
5911[10]
Lily Of The Valley (FR) *J-C Rouget* 120
4 b m Galileo(IRE) —Pennegale (IRE) (Pennekamp (USA))
2373a[5] 3822[7] 5306a[3]
Lily Potts *Chris Down* a52 70
2 gr f Proclamation(IRE) —Jucinda (Midyan (USA))
6441[8] 7030[4] *7343[13]*
Lily's Angel (IRE) *Richard Fahey* 101
2 b f Dark Angel(IRE) —Noyelles (IRE) (Docksider (USA))
(1165) (1489) (1806) 2404[3] 3104[5] (3402) 4094[2] 4803[2] 5472[6]
Lily's Star (IRE) *H Rogers* a67 67
4 b m Chineur(FR) —Voodoo Lily (IRE) (Petardia)
977a[12]
Lily Wood *James Unett* a58 53
5 ch m Central Park(IRE) —Lady Castanea (Superlative)
167[2] 363[4] 912[9] 1248[2] 1763[7] *2161[7] 3241[4] 3720[9] 5603[11] 6176[9] 7844[9]*
Limpopo Tom (IRE) *Paul W Flynn* a74 60
4 ch g Saffron Walden(FR) —Sharpe (FR) (Dr Devious (IRE))
(7631)
L'Impressioniste (FR) *F Chappet* a64 79
7 ch g Peintre Celebre(USA) —La Panthere (USA) (Pine Bluff (USA))
1013a[4]
Lindenthaler (GER) *P Schiergen* 108
3 b c Azamour(IRE) —Lasira (GER) (Vettori (IRE))
(1433a) 2136a[5] 3672a[7] 5308a[2] 6185a[7] 6595a[3] 7324a[6]
Lindner (GER) *I Mohammed* a88 102
6 b g Golan(IRE) —Lindenblute (Surumu (GER))
328a[11] 608a[9]
Lindo Erro *John Mackie* a53
3 b f Camacho—Katie Savage (Emperor Jones (USA))
576[4] 770[4] 967[5] 1251[4] 1588[4] 2652[6]
Lindoro *Kevin M Prendergast* a66 70
6 b g Marju(IRE) —Floppie (FR) (Law Society (USA))
(798) 874[3] 1035[5] (1244) 2487[4] 2671[6] 3025[2] 4517[5] 5455[12] 6159[3] *7844[9]*
Lindsay's Dream *Zoe Davison* a61 53
5 b m Montjeu(IRE) —Lady Lindsay (IRE) (Danehill Dancer (IRE))
314[6]
Linenhall Lady (IRE) *M J Grassick* a55
2 ch f Indian Haven—Gentle Wind (USA) (Gentlemen (ARG))
7275a[12]
Line Of Duty (IRE) *Alan Swinbank* a72 94
4 b g Arakan(USA) —Zibaline (FR) (Linamix (FR))
1490[2] (2006) 3163[3] 5705[16] 6803[6]
Line of Sight (USA) *Mahmood Al Zarooni* 52
[illegible] —Lakefront (USA) (Deputy Minister (CAN))
3824[7] 4529[8]
Lingfield Bound (IRE) *John Best* a80 69
4 ch g Dubai Destination(USA) —Timewee (USA) (Romanov (IRE))
(174) 475[5] 647[4] 1046[7] 1746[9] 2213[11]
Linkable *Charles Hills* 74
2 b c Rail Link—Fashionable (Nashwan (USA))
6126[5] 6675[4]
Links Drive Lady *Mark Rimmer* a64 71
3 br f Striking Ambition—Miskina (Mark Of Esteem (IRE))
77[4] 729[6] 3390[7] 4244[2] 4822[5] 5040[5] 5624[2] 6022[4] 6228[3] 6604[3] 7024[6]
Linnens Star (IRE) *Ralph Beckett* a90 92
4 b g Traditionally(USA) —Capestar (IRE) (Cape Cross (IRE))
1092[15] 2020[8] 3290[7] 3634[7]
Lion Court (IRE) *John Stimpson* a62 74
3 ch g Iffraaj—Spanish Falls (Belmez (USA))
3037[3] 4163[2] *5103[8] 5602[4]* 6831[5] *7418[9]*
Lion King (FR) *N Clement* a83 79
3 b c Xaar—Lion's Bride (FR) (Highest Honor (FR))
7669a[3]
Lion Road (USA) *Alan King* 52
5 ch g Lion Heart(USA) —Elusive Road (USA) (Elusive Quality (USA))
1751[4] 2569[7] 3094[3]
Lionrock (FR) *Mahmood Al Zarooni* a60 55
2 ch c Shamardal(USA) —Genevale (FR) (Unfuwain (USA))
4213[10] *4798[4]*
Lion Sands *A bin Huzaim* a90 88
7 b g Montjeu(IRE) —Puce (Darshaan)
153a[9] 585a[7]
Lion Tamer (NZ) *Murray & Bjorn Baker* 126
4 b c Storming Home—Lioness (NZ) (Generous (IRE))
6713a[8] 7044a[14]
Lipfix (ITY) *V di Napoli* 91
3 b c St Paul House—Lucky Lips (IRE) (Emperor Jones (USA))
1919a[4]
Lipocco *Rod Collet* a93 108
7 br g Piccolo—Magical Dancer (IRE) (Magical Wonder (USA))
497a[12] 582a[6] 678a[10]
Lips Poison (GER) *Andreas Lowe* 104
3 ch f Mamool(IRE) —Lips Plane (IRE) (Ashkalani (IRE))
2520a[2] (3209a) 4138a[5]
Liquid Sunshine *Sylvester Kirk* a52 11
2 br f Baltic King—Sylvan (IRE) (Shinko Forest (IRE))
2919[7] *3921[6] 6819[7] 7251[10] 7434[3] 7444[4] 7514[8] 7937[9]*
Lisahane Bog *Peter Hedger* a79 63
4 b g Royal Applause—Veronica Franco (Darshaan)
96[6] 206[3] 310[3] 475[4] 565[5] 685[2] 949[13] 1608[2] 2051[14] *4660[9]* 5942[8] 6790[7] (7202) 7513[3] 7601[11] 7759[4]
Lisa's Strong (IRE) *L Polito* 96
4 b m Kalanisi(IRE) —Bauci (IRE) (Desert King (IRE))
6739a[11]
Lisbon Lion (IRE) *Martin Todhunter* a60 57
6 bg g Mull Of Kintyre(USA) —Ludovica (Bustino)
598[7] 4329[9] 4814[10]
Lisiere (IRE) *Richard Fahey* 72
2 b f Excellent Art—Sahara Sky (IRE) (Danehill (USA))
5756[2] 6673[4]
Lisselan Diva (IRE) *Mme J Bidgood* 108
5 b m Barathea(IRE) —Vintage Escape (IRE) (Cyrano De Bergerac)
(815a) 1122a[2] 1687[6] 2754a[14] (4739a) 5985a[12]
Lisselan Gardens (USA) *Mme J Bidgood* a70 79
8 b g Concern(USA) —Sambacarioca (USA) (Irish Tower (USA))
6593a[9]
Lisselan Hurricane (USA) *Y Marie-Nelly* a67 67
5 b g Dance Master(USA) —Sense Of Propriety (USA) (Seattle Song (USA))
(7315a)
Lisselan Missile (USA) *Mme J Bidgood*
3 b g Honor Glide(USA) —Cute Connie (USA) (Struggler)
777a[0]
Lisselan Muse (USA) *Mme J Bidgood* a72 77
7 b g Devil His Due(USA) —Musical Talent (USA) (Local Talent (USA))
(196a) 3568a[0]
Lisselan Pleasure (USA) *Bernard Llewellyn* a74 74
4 gr m Macho Uno(USA) —Cute Connie (USA) (Struggler)
7823[10]
Lisselan Prospect (USA) *Mme J Bidgood* a65 64
6 b g Suave Prospect(USA) —Right Again Rose (USA) (Royal And Regal (USA))
6959a[3]
Lisselan Rightcall (USA) *Mme J Bidgood* a65 65
7 b g World Stage(IRE) —Right Again Rose (USA) (Royal And Regal (USA))
6959a[0]
Lisselton Cross *Martin Bosley* a60 47
3 ch g Compton Place—Sweet Myrtle (USA) (Mutakddim (USA))
338[4] 958[3] 3721[7] *7693[5] 7829[2]*
Litenup (IRE) *Gay Kelleway* a59 26
5 b m Trans Island—Common Cause (Polish Patriot (USA))
164[4]
Lithaam (IRE) *Milton Bradley* a51 59
7 ch g Elnadim(USA) —Elhida (IRE) (Mujtahid (USA))
401[13] 464[5] 691[4] 812[10] 857[12] 861[6] 3015[5] 3216[3] 3721[10] 4487[7] 4930[4] 5534[6] 5678[7] 5865[5] [illegible]
Lithograph (USA) *Mahmood Al Zarooni* a49
2 b f Echo Of Light—Forum Floozie (NZ) (Danasinga (AUS))
6697[9] 6977[4]
Litotes *Michael Attwater* a57
3 b f Librettist(USA) —Royal Ivy (Mujtahid (USA))
126[8] 274[5] 2384[9] (3226) 4758[10] 4908[9] 5944[11] 7229[9]
Little Arrows (IRE) *K J Condon* a77 81
5 b g Danehill Dancer(IRE) —Lovers Walk (USA) (Diesis)
7549a[3] 7792a[8]
Little Black Book (IRE) *Gerard Butler* a87 85
3 ch g Shamardal(USA) —Extreme Beauty (USA) (Rahy (USA))
(1496) 1947[3] 2230[3] 2877[5] 4335[2] 4447[2] 5056[8] *5635[2] 6003[5]*
Little Book *Jim Goldie* a47 61
3 b f Librettist(USA) —Cal Norma's Lady (IRE) (Lyphard's Special (USA))
1312[11] 3039[5] 3431[6] 6428[3] 7159[6] *7399[5]*
Little Bridge (NZ) *C S Shum* 119
5 b g Faltaat(USA) —Golden Rose (NZ) (Gold Brose (AUS))
7730a[4]
Little China *William Muir* a75 45
2 b f Kyllachy—China Beads (Medicean)
4386[6] *(6492) 7364[4]*
Littlecote Lady *Mark Usher* a56 57
2 b f Byron—Barefooted Flyer (USA) (Fly So Free (USA))
2817[6] 3511[6] 4250[3] *4922[9] 5385[4] (5998) 6821[6] 7444[7] 7742[5]*
Little Cottonsocks *Clive Cox* 67
3 b f Sulamani(IRE) —Caytinga (Docksider (USA))
2960[11] 3689[3] 4356[5] 5049[7] 5915[8]
Little Curtsey *Hughie Morrison* a84 85
3 b f Royal Applause—Tychy (Suave Dancer (USA))
3283[8] 6167[2] *6477[2]* 7054[8]
Little Dutch Girl *Clive Cox* 73
2 ch f Dutch Art—Photographie (USA) (Trempolino (USA))
(5537)

Little Garcon (USA) *Marco Botti* a95 102
4 b g Bernstein(USA) —Demure (Machiavellian (USA))
848[11] 3410[U] *7721[6]*

Little Jazz *Paul D'Arcy* a70 73
3 b f Doyen(IRE) —Meddle (Diktat)
212[6] *434[4]* *663[3]* *898[3]* *1028[2]* *1293[2]* *(1588)* 2186[3] 2850[5] 3325[6] (4389) 4966[4] 6037[P] 6136[3] 6756[5] 7254[3] 7446[4]

Little Jimmy Odsox (IRE) *Tim Easterby* a83 81
3 b g Namid—September Tide (IRE) (Thatching)
(3343) (4124) ◆ 4669[3] 5554[2] *(6283)*

Little Luxury (IRE) *Denis W Cullen* a62 53
4 b m Tagula(IRE) —Erne Project (IRE) (Project Manager)
111[5] *428[7]* *446[5]*

Little Meadow (IRE) *Julia Feilden* a55 52
4 b m Antonius Pius(USA) —Cresalin (Coquelin (USA))
30[4] *207[12]* *504[6]* *796[8]*

Little Pandora *Lee James* a34 39
7 b m Komaite(USA) —Little Talitha (Lugana Beach)
318[5] *798[12]*

Little Perisher *Paul Howling* a57 54
4 b g Desert Sun—Sasperella (Observatory (USA))
725[7] *947[6]* *1276[10]* 1730[8] 1787[5] 2222[3] 2554[8] 4086[5] 4795[3] 5345[9] 5678[4] 5917[3] *6175[4]* *6696[2]* 7459[3] 7560[6] 7760[6] 7853[4]

Little Pete (IRE) *Ian McInnes* a83 45
6 ch g City On A Hill(USA) —Full Traceability (IRE) (Ron's Victory (USA))
1109[9] 1649[6] *2165[12]* 3024[11]

Littleportnbrandy (IRE) *Richard Guest* a50 68
3 ch f Camacho—Sharplaw Destiny (IRE) (Petardia)
275[3] *366[6]* *494[6]* *7610[11]* *7747[6]*

Littlepromisedland (IRE) *Richard Guest* a36 35
3 b f Titus Livius(FR) —Land Army (IRE) (Desert Style (IRE))
456[5] *642[3]* *942[7]* *967[7]* 3619[6] 4442[7] 4673[9] 5116[7] 5352[11] 5507[6] 6050[12]

Little Rainbow *Clive Cox* 68
2 ch f King's Best(USA) —Little Nymph (Emperor Fountain)
5048[4] 6524[16] 7056[3]

Little Red Minx (IRE) *Peter Chapple-Hyam* a60 49
2 b f Red Clubs(IRE) —Bid Dancer (Spectacular Bid (USA))
7082[10] *7520[7]* *7777[10]*

Little Richard (IRE) *Mark Wellings* a61 59
12 b g Alhaarth(IRE) —Intricacy (Formidable (USA))
223[11] *598[2]* *771[6]* *(819)* *911[3]* *1080[4]* *1310[8]*

Little Rocky *David Simcock* 91
3 b c Cadeaux Genereux—Tahirah (Green Desert (USA))
(2045) 3168[3] 4335[4] 5483[7]

Little Roxy (IRE) *Anna Newton-Smith* a16
6 b m Dilshaan—Brunswick (Warning)
222[6]

Little Storm (FR) *C Ferland* 103
3 b c Anabaa Blue—Domus Orea (USA) (Gone West (USA))
1551a[4]

Littlesuzie *Hans Adielsson* a68 61
2 b f Kyllachy—Golubitsa (IRE) (Bluebird (USA))
6892[5] *7194[2]* *7555[5]* *7830[2]*

Little Ted *David Evans* 51
2 b c Librettist(USA) —Mondello (IRE) (Tagula (IRE))
2556[4] 4391[5] ◆

Little Village (IRE) *John C McConnell* 53
5 b m Captain Rio—Rainbow Princess (IRE) (Spectrum (IRE))
6940[10]

Litura (IRE) *J-V Toux* 77
2 b f Whipper(USA) —Acciacatura (USA) (Stravinsky (USA))
7449a[6] *7666a[6]*

Livandar (FR) *P Van De Poele* a109 109
5 b g Fantastic Light(USA) —Luna Caerla (IRE) (Caerleon (USA))
(371a)

Liveandletdie (AUS) *Mark Kavanagh* 106
4 ch c Street Cry(IRE) —Janella (IRE) (Great Commotion (USA))
9029a[10]

Livia's Dream (IRE) *Ed Walker* 69
2 b f Teofilo(IRE) —Brindisi (Dr Fong (USA))
4525[3] 5299[5] 6458[13]

Living It Large (FR) *Ed de Giles* a91 95
4 ch g Bertolini(USA) —Dilag (IRE) (Almutawakel)
970[7] *1584[4]* (3687) (4239) 5278[4] 5703[8] 6224[12] (6703)

Lixirova (FR) *D Smaga* a84 100
4 gr m Slickly(FR) —Linorova (USA) (Trempolino (USA))
6958a[3]

Lizzie (IRE) *Tim Easterby* 74
3 b f Acclamation—Sky Galaxy (USA) (Sky Classic (CAN))
(4288) 4680[8] 5456[3] 6265[8] 6604[7] 7024[3]

Lizzie Drippin *Michael Easterby* a22 38
2 ch f Pursuit Of Love—Royal Starlet (Royal Applause)
5819[7] 6344[6] *6539[9]* 6675[8] 6835[7]

Lizzy's Dream *Robin Bastiman* a39
3 ch g Choisir(AUS) —Flyingit (USA) (Lear Fan (USA))
3494[4] *3949[3]* 5082[9]

Llanarmon Lad (IRE) *B W Hills* 86
2 b c Red Clubs(IRE) —Blue Crystal (IRE) (Lure (USA))
4414[2] 5254[3] ◆

Llewellyn *James Fanshawe* a53 73
3 b g Shamardal(USA) —Ffestiniog (IRE) (Efisio)
1606[8] 3183[8] 4186[3] *4910[7]* 5649[2] *6617[8]*

Local Diktator *Ronald Harris* a62 54
3 br c Diktat—Just Down The Road (IRE) (Night Shift (USA))
(10) *119[2]* *187[5]* *672[2]* *739[5]* *1064[4]* 1753[7] *1975[5]* *2177[3]* 2375[7] 2792[14] 3309[5] 3724[3] 4466[8]

Local Singer (IRE) *Paul Howling* a80 87
3 b g Elusive City(USA) —Alinga (IRE) (King's Theatre (IRE))
2199[4] ◆ 2646[2] 2926[4] ◆ 3649[4] 4342[2] *5322[6]* *7675[11]* *7941[9]*

Loch Fleet (IRE) *Gary Moore* a74 62
3 br g Celtic Swing—Share The Feeling (IRE) (Desert King (IRE))
(684) *988[5]* 1550[7] 3133[10] 5512[6] *5815[7]* *7522[11]* *7888[6]*

Lochiel *Ian Semple* a91 88
7 b g Mind Games—Summerhill Special (IRE) (Roi Danzig (USA))
5729[12] 6191[9] 7102[9]

Lochinver (USA) *Saeed Bin Suroor* a80 110
4 b h Kingmambo(USA) —Campsie Fells (UAE) (Indian Ridge)
332a[9] *501a[8]*

Lockantanks *Michael Appleby* a95 74
4 ch g Compton Place—Locharia (Wolfhound (USA))
96[5] *249[2]* *(310)* *623[2]* *703[4]* *877[4]* *908[4]* 1269[5] *1467[8]* 3341[2] 3805[4] 5101[5] 5538[2] 5828[5] 6544[2] 6658[2] 6830[4] ◆ 7199[5] 7447[3] (7532) 7628[2] (7841) (7922)

Lockhart (FR) *Mlle V Dissaux* a69 66
3 b c Muhtathir—Iza Bere (FR) (Shining Steel)
1010a[8]

Locum *Mark H Tompkins* a66 72
6 ch g Dr Fong(USA) —Exhibitor (USA) (Royal Academy (USA))
1573[2] 2824[5] 3184[6] 3960[3] 5520[2] *6873[3]* *7195[10]* *7357[2]* *7647[4]* *7859[8]*

Lodano (FR) *M Weiss*
6 gr g Verglas(IRE) —Maria Thai (FR) (Siam (USA))
440a[5] *627a[2]*

Loden *Luca Cumani* a82 79
4 b g Barathea(IRE) —Tentpole (USA) (Rainbow Quest (USA))
1775[2] ◆ 2224[7] *3286[2]*

Lofthouse *Alistair Whillans* a57 56
4 b g Hunting Lion(IRE) —Noble Destiny (Dancing Brave (USA))
7341[0] *748[10]*

Loganberry *Robert Cowell*
3 gr f Act One—Rowanberry (Bishop Of Cashel)
6067[9] *6490[10]*

Logans Legend (IRE) *Lawrence Mullaney* a68 67
3 b g Johannesburg(USA) —Almost Blue (USA) (Mr Greeley (USA))
1565[7] 2151[3] 3320[4] 6414[8] *7646[12]*

Logic Way (USA) *Ibrahaim Al Malki* a101 98
7 b g Freud(USA) —Just A Ginny (USA) (Go For Gin (USA))
585a[5] *677a[7]* 829a[11]

Loi (IRE) *J-M Beguigne* 106
2 b c Lawman(FR) —Lockup (IRE) (Inchinor)
(6902a)

Lois Lane *Ron Hodges* a54 34
3 br f Striking Ambition—Straight As A Die (Pyramus (USA))
380[4] *(518)* *745[12]* *1193[6]* 2720[9] 3216[9] *3920[4]* *7785[10]* *7899[11]*

Loki's Revenge *William Jarvis* a92 88
3 b c Kyllachy—Amira (Efisio)
4333[16] 4779[5] 5012[6] 5451[7] 5972[7] 6113[10] (6762)

Lolamar (ITY) *Marco Botti* a55 100
4 b m Martino Alonso(IRE) —Lodgetta (IRE) (Grand Lodge (USA))
(417a) 607a[6] 676a[5] *827a[11]*

Lolita Lebron (IRE) *Lawrence Mullaney* a68 67
2 b f Royal Applause—Alsharq (IRE) (Machiavellian (USA))
2187[5] 3816[4] (4512) ◆ 5287[7] 5645[5] *6132[3]* 6573[10] *7140[3]*

Lollina Paulina *Kevin Ryan* a73 66
2 b f Holy Roman Emperor(IRE) —Alexia Reveuse (IRE) (Dr Devious (IRE))
3610[9] 4430[2] *(6946)*

Lolly For Dolly (IRE) *T Stack* 115
4 b m Oratorio(IRE) —Heart Stopping (USA) (Chester House (USA))
(924a) (1118a) 1779a[2] 2325a[2] (3030) 5228a[9] 5745a[7]

Lollypop Lady *Linda Perratt*
2 b f Misu Bond(IRE) —Frabrofen (Mind Games)
3452[7]

Lombatina (FR) *F Head* 92
2 b f King's Best(USA) —Sahel (GER) (Monsun (GER))
5194a[5]

Lombok *Gary Moore* a80 74
5 b g Hernando(FR) —Miss Rinjani (Shirley Heights)
2562[5] 6466[9]

Lomirana (FR) *N Caullery* a70 58
5 ch g Lomitas—Morlane (IRE) (Entrepreneur)
42a[10] *903a[0]* *5095a[0]*

Londinieres *C Lerner* 36
3 b f Librettist(USA) —Mrs Ting (USA) (Lyphard (USA))
5463a[0]

London Avenue (IRE) *Dominic Ffrench Davis* a55 32
3 ch g Compton Place—Great Joy (IRE) (Grand Lodge (USA))
4203[5] 4461[4] *7093[5]* *7366[8]*

London Welsh *William Muir* 39
2 b f Cape Cross(IRE) —Croeso Cariad (Most Welcome)
7030[13]

Lone Foot Laddie (IRE) *Sylvester Kirk* 63
2 b g Red Clubs(IRE) —Alexander Phantom (IRE) (Soviet Star (USA))
4968[7] 5672[4]

Lone Star State (IRE) *Frank Sheridan* a60 32
2 b c Stardan(IRE) —Rachelsfriend (IRE) (Dolphin Street (FR))
1185[7] *7718[8]* *7821[5]*

Long Awaited (IRE) *Roger Varian* 88
3 b g Pivotal—Desertion (IRE) (Danehill (USA))
(3053) 3850[4] 4765[6] 5484[3]

Long Lashes (USA) *Saeed Bin Suroor* 106
4 b m Rock Hard Ten(USA) —Border Dispute (USA) (Boundary (USA))
607a[3]

Long Live Love (USA) *Mark Johnston* a51 13
3 bb g Forestry(USA) —Angela's Love (USA) (Not For Love (USA))
937[4] 3513[10] *5639[5]* 7085[10]

Long Lost Love *Mark Johnston* a61 74
2 b f Langfuhr(CAN) —Heat Of The Night (Lear Fan (USA))
4205[3] ◆ (4545) 4892[7] 5809[2] *6132[7]*

Lonsome Drive (FR) *Y De Nicolay* a81 84
4 b m Domedriver(IRE) —Lone Spirit (IRE) (El Gran Senor (USA))
5195a[4]

Look At Me (IRE) *A P O'Brien* 106
3 b f Danehill Dancer(IRE) —Queen Cleopatra (IRE) (Kingmambo (USA))
1779a[6] 2334a[15] 3065[4] 4132a[4] 5228a[12] 5523a[3] 5744a[2] 5976a[3] 6362a[4] 6561a[5]

Look At Me Now *Jim Boyle* a61 55
2 ch c Choisir(AUS) —Sweet Pickle (Piccolo)
4857[13] 5174[6] 5889[11] *7692[2]* *7874[4]*

Look Busy (IRE) *P J Prendergast* 106
6 b m Danetime(IRE) —Unfortunate (Komaite (USA))
1420a[8] 4135a[10]

Look For Love *Reg Hollinshead* a54 49
3 b g Pursuit Of Love—Look Here's May (Revoque (IRE))
1953[7] 2581[11] *4647[8]* 5349[7] 6049[2] *6358[10]* *6545[5]* 6605[5] *7006[5]* *7741[2]* *7787[5]* *7899[6]*

Look Here's Lady *Ed McMahon* a65 60
2 b f Kyllachy—Look Here's Carol (IRE) (Safawan)
2665[5] *3237[5]* 3755[10] 5555[2] (6043) 6597[2] *(7143)*

Looking On *Henry Candy* 82
3 b g Observatory(USA) —Dove Tree (FR) (Charnwood Forest (IRE))
5021[3] 5449[3] 5892[10] 6773[2]

Look Left *John Gosden* 87
3 ch g Observatory(USA) —Stage Left (Nashwan (USA))
(4529) 5235[7] 6063[6] 6674[3]

Look'N'Listen (IRE) *Alan Brown* a48 47
3 b f Fasliyev(USA) —Royal Lady (IRE) (Royal Academy (USA))
64[7] *183[8]* *281[6]*

Looks Like Rain *Michael Bell* 29
2 ch f Medicean—Hippogator (USA) (Dixieland Band (USA))
4061[11]

Looksmart *Richard Hannon* a59 73
3 b f Observatory(USA) —Dimakya (USA) (Dayjur (USA))
1022[8] 1524[2] 1986[9] *2821[10]*

Look Twice *Alex Hales* a53 61
3 b f Royal Applause—Exchanging Glances (Diktat)
43[4] *274[3]* *2163[11]* 2993[2] 3272[4] 4199[10] 6105[11]

Look Who's Kool *Ed McMahon* a78 73
3 b g Compton Place—Where's Carol (Anfield)
1650[6] 2158[7] 3384[7] 4197[5] 4895[5] 5615[7] *6351[6]* *6875[7]*

Looney Les (IRE) *Jo Hughes* a31 40
3 ch g Redback—Trivandrun (IRE) (Lend A Hand)
5212[4] *7247[11]*

Loonora (FR) *D De Watrigant* a85 102
5 b m Valanour(IRE) —Eleora (FR) (Highest Honor (FR))
5093a[9] 6470a[2]

Loose Quality (USA) *Chris Gordon* a57 58
3 b g Elusive Quality(USA) —Djebel Amour (USA) (Mt. Livermore (USA))
1672[3] 2180[8] *3223[4]* 3944[10] *4183[6]* *4759[4]*

Lopinot (IRE) *Martin Bosley* a68 24
8 br g Pursuit Of Love—La Suquet (Puissance)
248[4] *477[5]* *625[6]* *765[4]* *906[4]* 2922[9] *3280[9]* 3942[12]

Lopov (NZ) *Danny O'Brien* 96
4 b g Savabeel(AUS) —Prickle (NZ) (Pins (AUS))
6711a[11]

Lord Aeryn (IRE) *Richard Fahey* 95
4 b g Antonius Pius(USA) —White Paper (IRE) (Marignan (USA))
(1109) 1603[2] 2390[2] 3032[26] 3877[5] 4415[13] 5557[5] 6150[3]

Lord Ali McJones *S Smrczek* a67 71
2 b g Elusive City(USA) —Combloux (USA) (Southern Halo (USA))
1583[3] 1823[3] ◆ 2143[7] 2997[6] *3490[6]* 5297[4] 5324[10] 6043[9] *7666a[3]*

Lord Avon *Bill Turner* a85 96
3 ch g Avonbridge—Lady Filly (Atraf)
(929) *(1062)* (1452) 2032[7] (2911)

Lord Buffhead *Richard Guest* a42 57
2 br g Iceman—Royal Pardon (Royal Applause)
3490[5] 4040[6] 4358[8] (5005) ◆ 5399[8] 5591[4] *7770[5]* *7882[3]*

Lord Chaparral (IRE) *R Brogi* 117
4 b h High Chaparral(IRE) —Freccia D'Oro (GER) (Acatenango (GER))
1918a[2] 2134a[8] 6907a[3] 7324a[7]

Lord Cornwall (IRE) *Ed Walker* a48 13
3 b g Encosta De Lago(AUS) —Duchy Of Cornwall (USA) (The Minstrel (CAN))
383[12] *655[10]* *904[7]* *1082[10]*

Lord Deevert *Bill Turner* a67 49
6 br g Averti(IRE) —Dee-Lady (Deploy)
56[2] *210[9]* *346[6]* *574[4]* 4337[7]

Lord Emerson *Richard Fahey* a56 59
3 ch g Pursuit Of Love—Lady Emm (Emarati (USA))
3684[3] 4282[6] 5556[7] 6049[5] *6545[3]* 6775[12]

Lord Franklin *Eric Alston* 48
2 ch g Iceman—Zell (IRE) (Lend A Hand)
5269[13] 6025[5] 6702[7]

Lord Golan *Des Donovan*
3 b g Singspiel(IRE) —Lady Golan (IRE) (Golan (IRE))
6242[9]

Lord Howe (GER) *J-Y Artu* a75 76
4 b g Areion(GER) —Lady Anna (GER) (Acatenango (GER))
903a[0]

Lord Lansing (IRE) *Mrs K Burke* a73 71
4 b g Mull Of Kintyre(USA) —Miss Beverley (Beveled (USA))
(86) *247[4]* *425[4]* *842a[9]* *1012a[5]* 2388[3] 3054[6] 3545[8] 4125[6] 4601[7] 5036[6] *7387[2]* *7522[2]* 7671[3]

Lord Nandi *Sir Henry Cecil* a44
2 b c Oasis Dream—Pink Cristal (Dilum (USA))
7493[8]

Lord Of The Dance (IRE) *Mark Brisbourne* a77 76
5 ch g Indian Haven—Maine Lobster (USA) (Woodman (USA))
1917[5] 2270[2] 2494[3] 2910[7] 4821[7] 5733[4] 5924[7] *7176[3]*

Lordofthehouse (IRE) *William Haggas* 84
3 ch g Danehill Dancer(IRE) —Bordighera (USA) (Alysheba (USA))
4005[3] ◆ (4752) (5553) (6294) ◆

Lord Of The Reins (IRE) *P J O'Gorman* a75 75
7 b g Imperial Ballet(IRE) —Waroonga (IRE) (Brief Truce (USA))
29[7] *143[7]* *357[2]* *453[4]* *646[6]* *732[7]* *947[3]* *(1171)* *(1309)* 3737[10] 4210[10] (6238) 6522[15] 6932[6] 7106[3]

Lord Ofthe Shadows (IRE) *Richard Hannon* 101
2 ch c Kyllachy—Golden Shadow (IRE) (Selkirk (USA))
1136[2] ◆ (1268) 2367[2] 4496[3] ◆ 5234[2] 5654[4] 6464[2] (6952)

Lord Of The Stars (USA) *David Simcock* a91 103
3 bb g Speightstown(USA) —Charmant Forest (USA) (Forestry (USA))
238[7] (411a) 680a[3] 823a[5] 2683[2]

Lord Of The Storm *Bill Turner* a50 65
3 b g Avonbridge—Just Run (IRE) (Runnett)
4209[6] 4576[4] 6067[3] 6465[8] 6769[2] 7212[6] *7333[8]*

Lord Raglan (IRE) *Mrs K Burke* a48 85
4 b g Noverre(USA) —Raglan Rose (USA) (Giant's Causeway (USA))
1097[12] 1859[4] 2414[5] 3170[6] 3831[3] 4083[2]

Lord Sam (GER) *K Borgel* a68 71
5 ch g Samum(GER) —Lady From Lucca (Inchinor)
439a[8]

Lord Sandicliffe (IRE) *Mme J Hendriks* a61 75
6 ch g Spartacus(IRE) —Devious Miss (IRE) (Dr Devious (IRE))
617a[9]

Lordship (IRE) *Tony Carroll* a21 63
7 b g King's Best(USA) —Rahika Rose (Unfuwain (USA))
6228[11] *6626[12]*

Lord Shuffle (GER) *H Blume* a83
3 ch c Big Shuffle(USA) —Legata (GER) (Sternkoenig (IRE))
7669a[2]

Lord's Seat *Alan Berry* a50 49
4 b g Trade Fair—Clashfern (Smackover)
37[6] *184[11]* *341[8]*

Lord Sun *Peter Grayson* a30
3 ch g Bertolini(USA) —Read Federica (Fusaichi Pegasus (USA))
811[11] *1065[8]* *3494[5]*

Lord Theo *Nick Littmoden* a83 80
7 b g Averti(IRE) —Love You Too (Be My Chief (USA))
(83) *174[4]* *(352)* 3366[11] 4553[10] 5198[9] 5611[11] 6938[15]

Lord Wheathill *Lisa Williamson* 47
4 b g Tobougg(IRE) —Classic Quartet (Classic Cliche (IRE))
1987[17] 2830[10] *3951[9]*

Lord Zenith *Andrew Balding* a100 108
4 b g Zamindar(USA) —Lady Donatella (Last Tycoon)
1600[7] 4003[3] 4456[4] 6747[7]

Los Cristianos (FR) *A Couetil* 108
5 ch h Gold Away(IRE) —Perspective (FR) (Funambule (USA))
1231a[4] 1707a[8]

Los Nadis (GER) *Jim Goldie* 83
7 ch g Hernando(FR) —La Estrella (GER) (Desert King (IRE))
2696[6] 3127[5] (3450) 3730[2] 4562[7] 5724[3] 6707[5] (7102)

Lost City (IRE) *Richard Fahey* a71 29
2 b g Elusive City(USA) —Farthing (IRE) (Mujadil (USA))
921a[5] *7359[2]* *7736[3]*

Lost Highway (IRE) *Mark Johnston* 60
2 b f Danehill Dancer(IRE) —En Garde (USA) (Irish River (FR))
6526[17] 6772[6] 7101[8]

Lost In Paris (IRE) *Tim Easterby* a86 93
5 b g Elusive City(USA) —Brazilia (Forzando)
1698[10] 2118[3] 2497[3] (2694) 3379[3] 4357[12] 5033[10] 5831[9]

Lost In The Moment (IRE) *Saeed Bin Suroor* a101 115
4 b h Danehill Dancer(IRE) —Streetcar (IRE) (In The Wings)
(328a) *498a[8]* *824a[9]* 2909[2] 3107[2] ◆ 3876[3] ◆ 4469[2] 5285[7] 6519[4] 7218a[6]

Lost Soldier Three (IRE) *F-X Belvisi* a36 85
10 b g Barathea(IRE) —Donya (Mill Reef (USA))
479a[10]

Lotarespect *John Best* a35
2 b f Byron—Epineuse (Gorse)
7435[11] *7482[5]* *7762[5]*

Lothian Sky (IRE) *William Jarvis* 66
2 b c Authorized(IRE) —Golly Gosh (IRE) (Danehill (USA))
7134[5]

Lough Corrib (USA) *Alastair Lidderdale* a62 52
3 b g Tiznow(USA) —Desert Glow (IRE) (Machiavellian (USA))
424[6] 519[5] 770[3] 887[13] 1303[5] 1369[2] 1801[5] 5780[6] 5901[8] 6610[14] 6813[10] 7270[11]

Louie's Lad *John Bridger* a26 54
5 gr g Compton Place—Silver Louie (IRE) (Titus Livius (FR))
28[9] 280[10]

Louis Hull *George Foster* 68
2 b g Three Valleys(USA) —Zietunzeen (IRE) (Zieten (USA))
2460[7] 2731[2] 2953[9] 3618[4] 4019[7]

Louis The Pious *Kevin Ryan* 103
3 bb g Holy Roman Emperor(IRE) —Whole Grain (Polish Precedent (USA))
(1860) 2216[4] (2763) (3853) (4324) 5054[3] 5830[2] 6500[3]

Loukas (IRE) *Alan Swinbank* a72 77
2 b c Haafhd—Mount Street (IRE) (Pennekamp (USA))
4436[8] (4781)

Louphole *J R Jenkins* a65 58
9 ch g Loup Sauvage(USA) —Goodwood Lass (IRE) (Alzao (USA))
402[6] 719[3] 1045[2] 4759[5] 5355[6]

Louvakhova (USA) *J-C Rouget* a89 95
3 b f Maria's Mon(USA) —Louvain (IRE) (Sinndar (IRE))
841a[2]

Louve Rouge (FR) *C Boutin* 91
2 ch f Gold Away(IRE) —Loup The Loup (FR) (Loup Solitaire (USA))
2866a[4] 4375a[2] 6042a[8] 6808a[7]

Louvigny (FR) *C Lerner* 74
2 b c Lando(GER) —Queen Maeve (Selkirk (USA))
4624a[4] 7449a[3]

Lovage *Roger Charlton* 67
2 b f Exceed And Excel(AUS) —Name Of Love (IRE) (Petardia)
3547[10] ◆ 4155[4] 5854[4] 6724[5] ◆

Lovat Lane *Eve Johnson Houghton* a50 60
3 b f Avonbridge—Pudding Lane (IRE) (College Chapel)
142[6] 227[4] 426[4] 558[2] 787[3] 1149[7] 7525[3] 7652[4] 7829[3] 7886[4]

Love Club *Brian Baugh* 54
3 ch g Kheleyf(USA) —Avondale Girl (IRE) (Case Law)
2993[6] 3321[7] 3638[6] 3939[8]

Lovecraft (USA) *A Fabre* a69 32
4 b h Kingmambo(USA) —Loving Kindness (USA) (Seattle Slew (USA))
830a[7]

Loved By All (IRE) *Brian Meehan* 59
2 b f Elusive City(USA) —Bianca Cappello (IRE) (Glenstal (USA))
4804[13] 5170[3] 6168[10]

Love Delta (USA) *Kevin Ryan* a105 102
4 bb g Seeking The Gold(USA) —Delta Princess (USA) (A.P. Indy (USA))
2288[2] 2489[6] 2717[15] 3155[22] 3627[10] 7468a[14]

Loved To Bits *Peter Makin* a59 55
3 b f Storming Home—Agent Kensington (Mujahid (USA))
1980[12]

Love For Love *David O'Meara* a51 62
3 b f Pastoral Pursuits—Trundley Wood (Wassl)
1880[9] 2125[4] 2351[8] 2786[8] 3455[4] 4638[5] 5381[13]

Love Grows Wild (USA) *Michael Bell* 52
2 rg f Cozzene(USA) —Dierks Timber (USA) (Prime Timber (USA))
2309[13] 3257[10] 3761[11]

Love In The Park *Roy Brotherton* a62 64
6 b m Pivotal—Naughty Crown (USA) (Chief's Crown (USA))
30[7] 203[7] 749[4] 943[5] 2900[9] 4578[8] 4953[8] 7466[3] 7640[4] 7851[7]

Love In The West (IRE) *John Harris* a65 60
5 b m Fruits Of Love(USA) —Sandhill (IRE) (Danehill (USA))
323[5] 507[8] 695[4] 1374[10]

Love Island *Richard Whitaker* a65 65
2 b f Acclamation—Sally Traffic (River Falls)
5681[15] 6026[4] 7482[3]

Lovelace *Richard Fahey* a73 112
7 b h Royal Applause—Loveleaves (Polar Falcon (USA))
1093[5] 1397[8] 1889[5] 3862[16] 4494[19] 5218[17] 6148[9] 6542[4] 7352[5] 7492[3] 7565[3]

Lovely Lynn (IRE) *Declan Carroll* a34 28
3 ch f Compton Place—Dhairkana (IRE) (Soviet Star (USA))
3075[13] 3343[9] 3616[7] 5373[12] 6176[6] 6700[8]

Love Match *Marco Botti* a64 84
4 b m Danehill Dancer(IRE) —Name Of Love (IRE) (Petardia)
206[10] 530[4]

Love Nest *John Dunlop* a61 55
3 b c Compton Place—Encore My Love (Royal Applause)
2384[3] 3227[2] 3677[2] 4758[6] (5944) 6626[4] 7096[9] 7437[4] 7655[8]

Love Over Gold (FR) *Ralph Beckett* a77 87
4 ch m Peintre Celebre(USA) —Via Saleria (IRE) (Arazi (USA))
2791[3] 4344[10] 4962[5] 5303[3] 6470a[8]

Love Queen (IRE) *Mlle V Dissaux* a95 93
4 gr m Val Royal(FR) —Lone Spectre (Linamix (FR))
(92a)

Lovers Causeway (USA) *Mark Johnston* a97 84
4 b g Giant's Causeway(USA) —Heeremandi (IRE) (Royal Academy (USA))
(359) 436[2] 1102[9] (1855) 2006[15] 2071[15] 3381[4]

Lovers Peace (IRE) *Edmond Kent* a34 81
3 b f Oratorio(IRE) —Puck's Castle (Shirley Heights)
5748a[14]

Loves Theme (IRE) *Alan Bailey* a70 74
3 ch f Iffraaj—Bauci (IRE) (Desert King (IRE))
335[8] (422) 601[7] 724[6] 913[2] 1219[4] 1359[5] 1766[7] (2177) 2382[2] 2770[6] 3470[7] 3783[9] 7085[2] 7198[4]

Lovestoned (IRE) *G A Kingston* a47 61
5 b g Modigliani(USA) —Errachidia (IRE) (King Of Kings (IRE))
5617[6] 5965[5]

Love Tale *Mark Rimell* a56 64
2 ch f Lucky Story(USA) —Bold Love (Bold Edge)
3915[8] 4474[4] 5801[7] 6284[5] (7051) 7294[6]

Love You Louis *J R Jenkins* a79 80
5 b g Mark Of Esteem(IRE) —Maddie's A Jem (Emperor Jones (USA))
29[8] 2929[9]

Love Your Looks *Mike Murphy* a73 49
3 b f Iffraaj—Play Around (IRE) (Niniski (USA))
5241[4] 5639[3] 6459[6] 6816[2] (7144) 7453[2]

Loving Emma *John Weymes* 22
2 ch f Pursuit Of Love—Not So Generous (IRE) (Fayruz)
4512[11] 4808[9] 5802[9]

Loving Spirit *James Toller* 100
3 b g Azamour(IRE) —Lolla's Spirit (IRE) (Montjeu (IRE))
1686[9] 2440[5] 3068[14] 6273[7] 7166[5]

Loving Thought *Sir Henry Cecil* a67 70
3 b f Oasis Dream—Brazilian Style (Exit To Nowhere (USA))
2528[6] (3390) 4202[8] 4807[6] 5581[3] 6167[13]

Lowawatha *D Grilli* 89
3 b c Sleeping Indian—Redeem (IRE) (Doyoun)
1431a[10]

Low Budget (FR) *F Foresi* a47 61
8 gr g Kaldounevees(FR) —Spring Of Passion (FR) (Zieten (USA))
257a[9]

Lowenherz (GER) *J-P Perruchot* a94 99
7 b g Silvano(GER) —Lutte Marie (GER) (Frontal)
705a[0] 1142a[10] 5095a[10]

Low Pastures *Michael Easterby* a11 29
2 ch g Lucky Story(USA) —Ring Of Roses (Efisio)
3021[7] 3237[10] 3728[11]

Lowther *Alan Bailey* a108 107
6 b g Beat All(USA) —Ever So Lonely (Headin' Up)
6[3] 271[2] (542) (846) 1094[7] 1406[3] 1849[3] 1885[16] 2284[5] 3109[21] 4042[10] 4802[4] 5272[6] 5474[4] 5699[15]

Lowtherwood *Bryan Smart* 59
2 b c Green Desert(USA) —Imperial Bailiwick (IRE) (Imperial Frontier (USA))
3452[5] 4436[5] 5017[4]

Loxton Lad (IRE) *Roger Charlton* a55 59
2 b c Lawman(FR) —Scoring (Giant's Causeway (USA))
3868[5] 4339[7] 5337[4] 6053[5] 6757[6] 7108[6]

Loyaliste (FR) *Richard Hannon* a77 73
4 ch h Green Tune(USA) —Whitby (FR) (Gold Away (IRE))
1144[3] 1950[4] 4385[5] 4862[7] (5509) 5968[8] 6592[14]

Loyal Knight (IRE) *Paul Midgley* a75 39
6 ch g Choisir(AUS) —Always True (USA) (Geiger Counter (USA))
3569[10] 4367[15]

Loyal Master (IRE) *George Foster* 77
2 b g Modigliani(USA) —Santa Gertrudis (IRE) (Machiavellian (USA))
2460[4] (3070) ◆ 3595[3] 3866[9] (4943) 5550[3] 6144[5]

Loyal N Trusted *Michael Wigham* a68 50
3 b g Motivator—Baby Don't Cry (USA) (Street Cry (IRE))
158[4] 339[6] 634[2] 714[3] 5014[12] 5381[5] 6872[5] 7084[8]

Loyal Royal (IRE) *Milton Bradley* a71 57
8 b g King Charlemagne(USA) —Supportive (IRE) (Nashamaa)
98[3] 218[7] 351[11] 435[10] 683[2] 810[10] (1041) (1247) 1453[5] [illegible] 2170[11] [illegible] [illegible] 7172[4] 7519[3] 7819[4] ◆ 7893[8]

Loyalty *Derek Shaw* a104 60
4 b g Medicean—Ecoutila (USA) (Rahy (USA))
287[2] 541[3] (694) 1097[13] 3285[3] 3521[2] 3848[10] 5712[8] (6219) (6949) ◆ 7393[3] 7516[7] (7606) 7719[2] (7801)

Lo Zoccolo Duro (IRE) *B Grizzetti* 97
2 b c Acclamation—Sopran Lori (USA) (Irish River (FR))
6740a[6]

Luberon *P Schaerer* a78 101
8 b g Fantastic Light(USA) —Luxurious (USA) (Lyphard (USA))
843a[0]

Luca Brasi (FR) *Francisco Castro* a104 97
7 b g Singspiel(IRE) —Diamond Field (USA) (Mr Prospector (USA))
5981a[5]

Lucas Cranach (GER) *Anthony Freedman* 118
4 b h Mamool(IRE) —Lots Of Love (GER) (Java Gold (USA))
1842a[4] (3446a) 4374a[5] ◆ 6886a[5] 7218a[3]

Lucas Pitt *Michael Scudamore* a60 51
4 b g Kyllachy—Bardot (Efisio)
7121[5] 7264[8] 7527[11] 7654[9]

Lucayan Dancer *David Nicholls* a59 73
11 b g Zieten(USA) —Tittle Tattle (IRE) (Soviet Lad (USA))
854[4] 939[5] 1615[8] 3074[4] 3938[10] 3974[4] 4198[3] (4408) 4601[6] 5208[8]

Luce Polare (FR) *B Grizzetti* 31
2 b f Lawman(FR) —Contemporary (IRE) (Alzao (USA))
6904a[10]

Lucertola *Ralph Beckett* 48
2 b f Bahamian Bounty—Science Fiction (Starborough)
6950[9]

Lucidor (GER) *M Rulec* a37 100
8 b g Zafonic(USA) —La Felicita (Shareef Dancer (USA))
442a[8]

Lucifers Shadow (IRE) *Sylvester Kirk* 50
2 gr g Dark Angel(IRE) —Marianne's Dancer (IRE) (Bold Fact (USA))
2181[11] 2992[6] 3941[5]

Luckbealadytonight (IRE) *Mark Johnston* a54 24
3 b f Mr Greeley(USA) —Sumora (IRE) (Danehill (USA))
179[6] 422[3] 668[5] 1566[12] 2197[9]

Luck By Chance (IRE) *Richard Fahey* 51
3 b f Choisir(AUS) —Atlantic City (GER) (Medicus (GER))
3977[7]

Luck Of The Draw (IRE) *Sir Mark Prescott Bt* a80 66
4 b g Key Of Luck(USA) —Sarifa (IRE) (Kahyasi)
(1) (40) (79) 671[P]

Lucky Art (USA) *Conor Dore* a84 86
5 b g Johannesburg(USA) —Syrian Summer (USA) (Damascus (USA))
102[5] 401[7] 537[5] (941) (1204) 1287[2] 1968[8] (2667) (3087) 3367[7] 3832[5] 4195[2] 5679[8] 6351[4] 6875[2] (7116) 7356[11] 7487[7]

Lucky Cap *Paul Midgley* 22
3 ch g Sleeping Indian—Class Wan (Safawan)
1436[8] 1900[6]

Lucky Chappy (IRE) *H Graham Motion* 107
2 b c High Chaparral(IRE) —Germane (Distant Relative)
7301a[4]

Lucky Country (IRE) *Jeremy Gask* a32
3 b f Iffraaj—Lucky For Me (USA) (King Of Kings (IRE))
1589[9]

Lucky Dan (IRE) *Paul Green* a85 83
5 b g Danetime(IRE) —Katherine Gorge (USA) (Hansel (USA))
(168) 455[5] 4791[6] 5923[6] 6276[12] 7417[8] 7535[4] 7595[9] 7819[10]

Lucky Dance (BRZ) *Mark Rimmer* a80 96
9 b h Mutakddim(USA) —Linda Francesa (ARG) (Equalize (USA))
1098[9]

Lucky Dime *Noel Quinlan* a56
3 ch f Dubai Destination(USA) —Lucky Token (IRE) (Key Of Luck (USA))
4663[12] 5317[12] 6475[5] 7004[3] 7370[10] 7609[3] 7768[9] 7886[6]

Lucky Diva *Bill Turner* a59 57
4 ch m Lucky Story(USA) —Cosmic Countess (IRE) (Lahib (USA))
83[7] 115[2] 225[7] 346[10] 773[11] 2638[4] 2900[5] (3600) 4024[5] (4630) 5267[4] 5916[4] 7850[2]

Lucky Eighty Eight (AUS) *Mathew Ellerton & Simon Zahra* 108
6 b g Lucky Owners(NZ) —Bukhoor (AUS) (Jeune)
6711a[9]

Lucky Harry (FR) *Alex Fracas* a85 87
4 b g Equerry(USA) —Adulaire (FR) (Highest Honor (FR))
840a[8]

Lucky Henry *Clive Cox* 80
2 br c Lucky Story(USA) —Seldemosa (Selkirk (USA))
6123[3] (6629)

Lucky Last *Tim Easterby*
2 b f Lucky Story(USA) —Eboracum (IRE) (Alzao (USA))
3314[16]

Lucky Legs (IRE) *Charles Hills* a59 85
3 b f Danehill Dancer(IRE) —Singing Diva (IRE) (Royal Academy (USA))
1139[2] 1339[12] 2735[4] 3437[2] 4363[2] (4861) 5392[7] (6755) 7296[15]

Lucky Mark (IRE) *George Foster* 40
2 b g Moss Vale(IRE) —Vracca (Vettori (IRE))
1515[8] 2485[11]

Lucky Meadows (IRE) *Richard Hannon* a69 69
3 b f Noverre(USA) —Summerhill Parkes (Zafonic (USA))
[illegible] ([illegible]) [illegible] 6107[13] 6587[10] 6793[13]

Lucky Mellor *Barry Murtagh* a79 62
4 b g Lucky Story(USA) —Lady Natilda (First Trump)
316[9] 708[6] 794[9] 1140[12] 6056[7] 7355[13] 7535[12]

Lucky Money *Sir Mark Prescott Bt* a76 72
2 ch g Selkirk(USA) —Autumn Wealth (IRE) (Cadeaux Genereux)
3553[6] 4122[4] 4455[4] 4867[2] 5233[8] (5863)

Lucky Nine (IRE) *C Fownes* a81 121
4 b g Dubawi(IRE) —Birjand (Green Desert (USA))
1576a[2] (7730a)

Lucky Numbers (IRE) *Paul Green* a80 94
5 b g Key Of Luck(USA) —Pure Folly (IRE) (Machiavellian (USA))
(1205) 1849[5] 2117[8] 3379[9] 3627[11] 5006[5] 5163[2] 5683[6] 5923[2] ◆ 6865[5] 6913[10] 7074[12] 7262[7]

Lucky Royale *Jeremy Gask* a62
3 b f Lucky Story(USA) —Bella Bertolini (Bertolini (USA))
6874[4] (7429) (7676) ◆ (7924)

Lucky Tricks *Jeremy Gask* a29 21
3 ch f Lucky Story(USA) —Miss Madame (IRE) (Cape Cross (IRE))
3909[7] 5137[8] 6411[15] 7249[9]

Lucky Windmill *Alan Swinbank* 84
4 b g Lucky Story(USA) —Windmill Princess (Gorytus (USA))
1098[11] 2112[8] 4107[5] (4540) 5440[7] 6346[3] 7022[5]

Luctor Emergo (IRE) *Keith Dalgleish* a25 25
2 b g Amadeus Wolf—Batilde (IRE) (Victory Piper (USA))
6448[12] 7855[7]

Lucy In The Sky (FR) *N Leenders*
4 gr m Blackdoun(FR) —Lucia Nova (GER) (Surumu (GER))
842a[0]

Lucy Limelites *Roger Charlton* 78
3 b f Medicean—In The Limelight (IRE) (Sadler's Wells (USA))
1862[5] 2849[3] 4056[5] 4727[4]

Lui E La Luna *B Grizzetti* 104
2 b c Nayef(USA) —Luna D'Estate (Alzao (USA))
6740a[5] 7217a[2]

Lui Rei (ITY) *Robert Cowell* a102 104
5 b g Reinaldo(FR) —My Luigia (IRE) (High Estate)
2374 582a[8] 989[3] 1420a[3] 1720[11] 2117[5] ◆ 2288[5] 2717[4] ◆ 3155[9] 3410[5] 3846[11] 4534[25] 5927[17]

Luisant *J A Nash* a114 114
8 ch g Pivotal—La Legere (USA) (Lit De Justice (USA))
923a[3] 1118a[3] 1533a[9] 3444a[6] 5086a[6] 5746a[5] 6388a[12] 6561a[6] 6733a[12] 7010a[13] 7149a[5]

Luisa Tetrazzini (IRE) *Michael Attwater* a60 56
5 b m Hawk Wing(USA) —Break Of Day (USA) (Favorite Trick (USA))
2424[4] 4340[6] 4659[4] 5139[3]

Lujano *Ollie Pears* a64 67
6 b g Lujain(USA) —Latch Key Lady (USA) (Tejano (USA))
3142[2] 3926[9] 4076[4] 4852[7] 5601[2] 6098[12] (7351) 7507[2] 7648[7] 7885[7]

Lujeanie *Dean Ivory* a93 89
5 br g Lujain(USA) —Ivory's Joy (Tina's Pet)
87[3] 316[7] 2938[11] 3367[2] 3778[3] 4556[6] 5831[3] 6036[5] 6703[9] 7457[3] (7602) 7846[4]

Lujiana *Mel Brittain* a54 56
6 b m Lujain(USA) —Compact Disc (IRE) (Royal Academy (USA))
1464[6] 2655[8] 6213[9] 6454[6] 7071[12] 7691[3]

Lulla *Marcus Tregoning* 83
2 b f Oasis Dream—Dominica (Alhaarth (IRE))
2880[9] 4427[2] 5047[4]

Luna Negra (GER) *C Boutin* a79 86
3 b f Big Shuffle(USA) —Lindgren (GER) (Second Set (IRE))
4896a[8]

Lunar Deity *Eve Johnson Houghton* 87
2 b c Medicean—Luminda (IRE) (Danehill (USA))
3424[8] 3986[7] (4462) 5184[14]

Lunar Limelight *Peter Makin* a51 54
6 b g Royal Applause—Moon Magic (Polish Precedent (USA))
2820[7] 4549[4] 6698[11]

Lunar Phase (IRE) *Clive Cox* 78
3 b f Galileo(IRE) —Taraya (IRE) (Doyoun)
(1270) 2026[6] 2883[6] 3260[6] 4084[3] 5235[5] 6024[5]

Lunar Promise (IRE) *Ian Williams* a71 76
9 b g Mujadil(USA) —Lunadine (FR) (Bering)
(2820) (3074) ◆

Lunar River (FR) *David Pinder* a66 66
8 b m Muhtathir—Moon Gorge (Pursuit Of Love)
164[6] 346[7] (552) (652) 954[4] 1756[10] 2308[3] 2685[5] 3176[11] 3546[6] 4953[12] 6135[5] 6357[7] 6486[5] 6926[4]

Lunar Victory (USA) *John Gosden* a94 91
4 b h Speightstown(USA) —Lunar Colony (USA) (A.P. Indy (USA))
1102[3] ◆ 2066[5]

Luna Tune (FR) *D De Watrigant* a91 107
3 gr f Green Tune(USA) —Luna Negra (IRE) (Kaldoun (FR))
2342a[7] 7510a[8]

Luna Vale *Robert Eddery* a30 23
2 b f Dubai Destination(USA) —Fly Me To The Moon (GER) (Galileo (IRE))
7293[15] 7520[12] 7909[10]

Lupa Montana (USA) *Ralph Beckett* 63
3 ch f Giant's Causeway(USA) —Louve Royale (IRE) (Peintre Celebre (USA))
2960[7] 3980[3] 5169[8] 5838[7]

Lupin Pooter *David Barron* 66
2 b g Bertolini(USA) —Carrie Pooter (Tragic Role (USA))
(3125)

Lupo D'Oro (IRE) *John Best* a74 77
2 b g Amadeus Wolf—Vital Laser (USA) (Seeking The Gold (USA))
2214[5] 2602[3] 3014[23] 4079[2] 5348[3] 6058[2] 6252[2] 6673[2] 7359[3]

Lure of The Night (IRE) *Brian Rothwell* 60
4 b g Sadler's Wells(USA) —Moneefa (Darshaan)
1212[5] 1492[7] 2114[7] 2393[7] 2636[3] 2952[12] 3581[6] 3951[7]

Luscivious *Scott Dixon* a99 89
7 ch g Kyllachy—Lloc (Absalom)
2[4] 293[5] 429[6] 5148[7] 7644[7] 7917[6]

Lustre (FR) *Y De Nicolay* 104
3 b c American Post—Lunaska (FR) (Ashkalani (IRE))
1923a[6] 3653a[6] 6321a[8]

Lutfen Yavas (IRE) *Bernard Anthony Heffernan* a58
2 b g Chevalier(IRE) —Silver Harbour (USA) (Silver Hawk (USA))
6928[9]

Lutine Bell *Mike Murphy* a100 101
4 ch g Starcraft(NZ) —Satin Bell (Midyan (USA))
1111[4] 1885[21] 2288[4] 2954[6] 3627[2] 3841[2] 4428[9] 5887[2] 6341[12] 6706[8] 6862[21]

Lutine Charlie (IRE) *Ronald Harris* a79 73
4 b g Kheleyf(USA) —Silvery Halo (USA) (Silver Ghost (USA))
1755[7] 2027[12] 2870[4] 3266[3] 3512[17] (4544) 4865[8] 5300[3] 5836[6] 6472[3] 6793[6] (7332) 7484[2] 7529[7] 7807[5] 7834[5] 7919[3]

Luv U Forever *Jo Hughes* 93
2 b f Multiplex—Lady Suesanne (IRE) (Cape Cross (IRE))
2153[7] (2661) 3104[6] 3808[2] 4312[4] 4843a[2] 5270[4] 6042a[4] 6146[7] 6705[4] 7155a[10]

Luv U Noo *Brian Baugh* a48 68
4 b m Needwood Blade—Lady Suesanne (IRE) (Cape Cross (IRE))
1273[11] 2799[11] 3387[6] 3944[5] 5538[7] 5823[10] 6050[6] 7400[6] 7604[10] 7851[6]

Luv U Too *Jo Hughes* a61 80
3 b f Needwood Blade—Lady Suesanne (IRE) (Cape Cross (IRE))
2411[5] (3586) 3818[4] 4335[7] 5493[6] 6078[9] 6830[10] 7243[10]

Luxurious (IRE) *A P O'Brien* 96
3 b f Galileo(IRE) —Parvenue (FR) (Ezzoud (IRE))
2012a[4]

Lycidas (GER) *Tobias B P Coles* a75 72
2 b c Zamindar(USA) —La Felicita (Shareef Dancer (USA))
7257^{2} (7494)

Lyford Lad *George Moore* a54 22
4 ch g Bahamian Bounty—Carradale (Pursuit Of Love)
121^{5} 873^{10} 1212^{9}

Lynchpin *Ronald Harris* a55 46
3 b c Iceman—Danehurst (Danehill (USA))
52^{5} 109^{5} 227^{5} 426^{8} 655^{4} 886^{4} 966^{8}

Lynott (IRE) *Gerard Keane* a73 71
8 ch g Pivotal—Cassilis (IRE) (Persian Bold)
286^{3}

Lyrical Intent *Maurice Barnes* a63
5 ch g Imperial Dancer—Magical Flute (Piccolo)
4605^{13} 4868^{6}

Lyricist *Kevin Ryan* 1
2 b f Librettist(USA) —Tamzin (Hernando (FR))
1455^{8}

Lyric Of Light *Mahmood Al Zarooni* 113
2 b f Street Cry(IRE) —Suez (Green Desert (USA))
(5445) (5885) (6299) ◆

Lyric Poet (USA) *Anthony Carson* a84 74
4 bb g Distorted Humor(USA) —Baltic Nations (USA) (Seattle Slew (USA))
3959^{9} 4432^{6} 6773^{13} 7651^{7}

Lyric Street (IRE) *Luca Cumani* 102
3 b g Hurricane Run(IRE) —Elle Danzig (GER) (Roi Danzig (USA))
(2019) 3405^{5} ◆ 5283^{6} 6333^{10}

Lyrique (IRE) *A Fabre* a94 97
3 b f Iffraaj—Opera Comique (FR) (Singspiel (IRE))
5958a^{7} 7510a^{0}

Lyssio (GER) *Michael Attwater* a91 103
4 b g Motivator—Lysuna (GER) (Monsun (GER))
4373a^{4} 6710a^{7} 7802^{8}

Lytham (IRE) *Tony Carroll* a68 62
10 b g Spectrum(IRE) —Nousaiyra (IRE) (Be My Guest (USA))
21^{6} 203^{13} 553^{5} 728^{2} 802^{3} 1310^{9} 1582^{8} (1987) 2271^{6} 3225^{2} 3923^{4} 4153^{8}

Maal (IRE) *David Marnane* a80 83
8 b g Mozart(IRE) —Dalayil (IRE) (Sadler's Wells (USA))
7189a^{14}

Maali (IRE) *Clive Brittain* a101 100
3 b c Street Cry(IRE) —Agata (FR) (Poliglote)
1759^{3} 2185^{2} 2707^{2} 3068^{12} 5021^{4} 6339^{8} 6693^{8} 7166^{3} 7391^{4}

Maarek *David Peter Nagle* a61 99
4 b g Pivotal—Ruby Rocket (IRE) (Indian Rocket)
3440a^{6} 4135a^{5} 5086a^{8} 6145^{4} (6388a)

Maastricht (IRE) *Mark Johnston* 77
2 b g Tiger Hill(IRE) —Eurolink Raindance (IRE) (Alzao (USA))
2120^{4} 2460^{3} 3123^{5} 5197^{5} (5503) 5783^{2}

Mabaany *William Haggas* 88
2 b c Exceed And Excel(AUS) —Tarbiyah (Singspiel (IRE))
4352^{3} ◆ (5919) 6766^{3}

Mabait *David Simcock* a94 115
5 b h Kyllachy—Czarna Roza (Polish Precedent (USA))
156a^{11} 415a^{6} 586a^{10} 6747^{5} 7801^{8}

Mabel's Song *Henry Candy* 56
2 b f Sakhee(USA) —War Shanty (Warrshan (USA))
6744^{9}

Mabroor (USA) *Mark Johnston* a87 87
2 b c Hard Spun(USA) —Mayfield (USA) (Exploit (USA))
(1890) 2594^{4} (3284) 4496^{14} 5708^{6} 6670^{18}

Ma Browne (IRE) *Tony Coyle* 36
3 ch f Danehill Dancer(IRE) —Lac Dessert (USA) (Lac Ouimet (USA))
7608^{12}

Macao (IRE) *R Dzubasz* 91
2 b c Motivator—Missing Link (IRE) (Elusive Quality (USA))
6901a^{5}

Maccabees *Rod Millman* a55 71
2 b g Motivator—Takarna (IRE) (Mark Of Esteem (IRE))
2584^{7} 3425^{2} 3986^{2} 4968^{6} 5324^{5} 5967^{7} 6280^{6}

Macchiara *Rae Guest* 34
2 ch f Medicean—Castaway Queen (IRE) (Selkirk (USA))
6169^{12}

Maccool (IRE) *Barney Curley* a36
5 b g King's Best(USA) —Mellow Park (IRE) (In The Wings)
161^{8}

Macdillon *Stuart Kittow* a89 86
5 b g Acclamation—Dilys (Efisio)
2369^{4} (2929) 3588^{4} 4765^{5} 5484^{2} 5914^{3} 6467^{9} 7262^{5}

Macdonald Mor (IRE) *David Simcock* 76
2 b c Dansili—Imperial Beauty (USA) (Imperial Ballet (IRE))
2049^{14} 2291^{2} 3408^{4} 5959^{5}

Macedonian (NZ) *Peter G Moody* 109
6 b g Zabeel(NZ) —Society Walk (NZ) (Carnegie (IRE))
6711a^{7} 6886a^{8} 7310a^{9}

Mac Federal (IRE) *Sheena West* a61
9 b g In The Wings—Tocade (IRE) (Kenmare (FR))
1181^{2} 1761^{5}

Mac Gille Eoin *John Gallagher* a93 99
7 b h Bertolini(USA) —Peruvian Jade (Petong)
986^{4} 1197^{5} 1888^{10} 3179^{4} (3535) 4531^{10} 4859^{11} 5508^{2} 5935^{10} 6723^{4} 7127^{10} 7456^{2}

Machinate (USA) *Mark Brisbourne* a54 35
9 bb g Machiavellian(USA) —Dancing Sea (USA) (Storm Cat (USA))
1068^{10}

Machir Bay *Keith Dalgleish* a34 53
4 b g Auction House(USA) —Sabre Lady (Sabrehill (USA))
1216^{4} 1374^{8} 1710^{7} 2691^{6} 2809^{3} 3110^{4} 3905^{6} 4379^{12} 4783^{4} 5208^{2} 5403^{5} 5822^{6} 7400^{10}

Macie (IRE) *Derek Shaw* a27 52
4 b m Green Desert(USA) —Fatat Alarab (USA) (Capote (USA))
709^{6} 934^{9} 3234^{9} 3556^{9}

Mackintosh (IRE) *Patrick Morris* a60 32
5 ch g Kyllachy—Louhossoa (USA) (Trempolino (USA))
37^{4}

Mack's Sister *Dean Ivory* a71 60
4 ch m Pastoral Pursuits—Linda's Schoolgirl (IRE) (Grand Lodge (USA))
6752^{12} 7448^{6} (7588)

Mac Love *Roger Charlton* a101 105
10 b g Cape Cross(IRE) —My Lass (Elmaamul (USA))
156a^{12} 239^{6} 503a^{10} 605a^{7} 2713^{5} 4972^{9} 7166^{7} 7516^{4}

Macnas (USA) *James J Hartnett* a75 76
4 ch m Orientate(USA) —All My Lovin' (USA) (Cat's Career (USA))
1228a^{6}

Ma Coeur (FR) *M Delzangles* 95
4 b m Sholokhov(IRE) —Monbijou (GER) (Dashing Blade)
6470a^{6}

Mac Row (IRE) *J-C Rouget* 111
2 b c Le Vie Dei Colori—Kointreau (IRE) (Desert King (IRE))
4375a^{3} 5194a^{4} 5770a^{2} 6565a^{6}

Mac's Power (IRE) *James Fanshawe* a97 108
5 b g Exceed And Excel(AUS) —Easter Girl (Efisio)
2099^{2} 3155^{8} 3841^{3} 4534^{3} 5481^{4} 6147^{25} 6987^{5} ◆

Mac Tiernan (IRE) *Pat Murphy* a74 74
4 b g Minashki(IRE) —Softly Softly (IRE) (Lucky Guest)
977a^{4} 7097^{12} 7341^{11} 7591^{9} 7820^{10}

Macy Anne (IRE) *Robert Mills* a63
2 b f King's Best(USA) —Gilah (IRE) (Saddlers' Hall (IRE))
7673^{2}

Madam Blanche (IRE) *E J O'Neill* 78
2 ch f Iffraaj—Countess Majella (IRE) (Grand Lodge (USA))
7405a^{8}

Madam Bonny (IRE) *Jim Goldie* 20
2 b f Arcadio(GER) —Kashi Miss (USA) (Miswaki (USA))
4781^{6} 5398^{11} 6075^{8}

Madame Boot (FR) *Peter Makin* a64 59
4 b m Diktat—Esprit Libre (Daylami (IRE))
544^{3} (640) 1333^{4} 1604^{3} 2996^{6} 3516^{9} 4869^{8} 5912^{9}

Madame Excelerate *Mark Brisbourne* a77 74
4 b m Pursuit Of Love—Skovshoved (IRE) (Danetime (IRE))
1394^{9} 1766^{6} 2198^{4} 2399^{2} 2589^{12} 2912^{10} 3306^{4} 3912^{2} 4185^{2} 4394^{2} (4444)

Madame Feu *Henry Candy* 57
2 ch f Tumbleweed Ridge—Raffelina (USA) (Carson City (USA))
6455^{9} 6892^{7}

Madame Jane (IRE) *Ole Larsen*
2 b f Titus Livius(FR) —Mevlana (IRE) (Red Sunset)
4841a^{2}

Madame Kintyre *Rod Millman* 69
3 b f Trade Fair—Chorus (Bandmaster (USA))
1724^{11} 2223^{5} (2660) 3136^{3} 3635^{5} 5615^{6} 6119^{10} 6408^{2} ◆ 6604^{2} 6801^{8}

Madame St Clair (IRE) *Brian Meehan* 63
2 b f High Chaparral(IRE) —Numbers Game (Rainbow Quest (USA))
3258^{6} 4061^{8} 4552^{10}

Madam Isshe *Mandy Rowland* a62 60
4 b m Ishiguru(USA) —Lucky Dip (Tirol)
934^{10} 2222^{9} 3216^{12} 3721^{4} 4882^{3} 5326^{2} 5534^{4} 5678^{6} 6398^{3} 6889^{10} 7691^{4} 7853^{7} 7911^{9}

Madam Lilibet (IRE) *Sharon Watt* 91
2 b f Authorized(IRE) —Foxilla (IRE) (Foxhound (USA))
7210^{9}

Madamlily (IRE) *John Quinn* a71 72
5 b m Refuse To Bend(IRE) —Rainbow Dream (Rainbow Quest (USA))
(1039) 1243^{9} 2496^{2} 3316^{6} 4173^{3} 4719^{6}

Madam Macie (IRE) *David O'Meara* 93
4 ch m Bertolini(USA) —Dictatrice (FR) (Anabaa (USA))
5255^{11} 5702^{10} 6094^{8} 7076^{4}

Madam Markievicz (IRE) *Yvonne Durant* a67 68
3 gr f Aussie Rules(USA) —Fragrant (Cadeaux Genereux)
5982a^{5}

Madam Mayem *Tom Dascombe* a65 60
3 ro f Needwood Blade—Etienne Lady (IRE) (Imperial Frontier (USA))
(65) 254^{6}

Madam Tessa (IRE) *Bryn Palling* a51 62
3 br f Hawk Wing(USA) —Anita's Contessa (IRE) (Anita's Prince)
3218^{5} 4641^{4} 5429^{5} 6748^{6} 7264^{12} 7608^{3}

Madany (IRE) *Charles Hills* 92
3 b f Acclamation—Belle De Cadix (IRE) (Law Society (USA))
1317^{2} 1602^{5} 2934^{15} 6987^{20}

Madawi *Clive Brittain* a63 96
3 b c Oasis Dream—Lady In Waiting (Kylian (USA))
1339^{9} 1822^{5} 3067^{9} 3405^{11}

Madda's Force (ITY) *R Betti* 100
5 b m Blu Air Force(IRE) —Madda'sblueyes (Selkirk (USA))
1432a^{3} 1919a^{11}

Made In The Shade *Paul Midgley* 53
2 b f Ishiguru(USA) —Dispol Katie (Komaite (USA))
1071^{6} 1939^{3} 2346^{8} 7059^{12}

Madeira Man (IRE) *J A Nash* a82 82
3 gr g Verglas(IRE) —Lingering Melody (IRE) (Nordico (USA))
7468a^{11}

Mad For Fun (IRE) *Paul Midgley* 50
2 b f Ivan Denisovich(IRE) —Franny (Selkirk (USA))
1435^{4} 1966^{8} 2362^{3} 2784^{4} 3137^{2} 5342^{5}

Madgenta (IRE) *Richard Hannon* a74 64
2 br f Manduro(GER) —Ruby Affair (IRE) (Night Shift (USA))
6751^{2} 7052^{5} (7343)

Mad Ginger Alice *Olivia Maylam* a61
3 ch f Beat Hollow—Peryllys (Warning)
5778a^{6} 6668^{2} (7207) 7532^{14}

Madhal *Matthew Salaman* a56 55
5 b g First Trump—Jane Grey (Tragic Role (USA))
1933^{11}

Madhmoonah (IRE) *D K Weld* 92
2 b f Invincible Spirit(IRE) —Laywaan (USA) (Fantastic Light (USA))
6389a^{8}

Madhulika (FR) *R Mongil* a78 88
3 b f Marchand De Sable(USA) —Young Manila (USA) (Manila (USA))
5307a^{3}

Madison Square (USA) *Mark Johnston* a76 65
3 bb c More Than Ready(USA) —Star Of Broadway (USA) (Broad Brush (USA))
1415^{5} 1623^{5} 3913^{5} 4364^{2} 4491^{2} 4703^{9} (5103)

Madly In Love (FR) *J-L Gay* a81 97
3 gr f Slickly(FR) —Hourloupe (IRE) (Damister (USA))
841a^{5} 1207a^{7}

Mad Millie (IRE) *David O'Meara* a44 58
4 b m Pyrus(USA) —Tipsy Lady (Intikhab (USA))
3709^{6} 4196^{5}

Madonna Dell'Orto *Walter Swinburn* 78
4 b m Montjeu(IRE) —Sabria (USA) (Miswaki (USA))
3413^{6} 4790^{10}

Madrasa (IRE) *Keith Reveley* a63 71
3 b g High Chaparral(IRE) —Shir Dar (FR) (Lead On Time (USA))
1389^{2} 2218^{3} 2874^{9} 3642^{4} 4209^{4} 5553^{3} 6453^{10} 6775^{9} 7062^{8} 7212^{2}

Madushka (FR) *Y De Nicolay* a73 77
4 gr m Muhtathir—Kaldushka (FR) (Kaldounevees (FR))
91a^{5}

Mae Rose Cottage (IRE) *Hughie Morrison* 58
2 ch f Dylan Thomas(IRE) —Maskaya (IRE) (Machiavellian (USA))
3722^{5} 4386^{3}

Mafeking (UAE) *Mark Hoad* a98 84
7 b g Jade Robbery(USA) —Melisendra (FR) (Highest Honor (FR))
180^{6} 438^{4} 615^{3}

Mafeteng *John Dunlop* a58 68
3 b f Nayef(USA) —Marakabei (Hernando (FR))
2258^{8} 5585^{4} 6248^{7} 7236^{14} 7453^{7}

Mafra (IRE) *P Monfort* a80 80
5 b m Kalanisi(IRE) —Sovana (IRE) (Desert King (IRE))
219a^{7}

Mafroodh *John Dunlop*
3 ch c Pivotal—Khulood (USA) (Storm Cat (USA))
3177^{11}

Maggie Aron *Tim Vaughan* a51
5 gr m Generous(IRE) —Pems Gift (Environment Friend)
7536^{3} 7774^{6} 7894^{7}

Maggie Mey (IRE) *Paul Midgley* 79
3 b f Kodiac—Christmas Kiss (Taufan (USA))
2096^{6} 2391^{4} (2782) 3207^{5} 3586^{2} 4290^{2} 4750^{4} 5081^{3} 5370^{5} 6093^{15} 6831^{8} 7024^{15}

Maggie Neary (IRE) *C F Swan* a84 78
3 b f Hurricane Run(IRE) —Pleiade (FR) (Baryshnikov (AUS))
(7618a)

Maggie's Treasure (IRE) *John Gallagher* a55 72
3 gr g Clodovil(IRE) —Rectify (IRE) (Mujadil (USA))
764^{8} 964^{10} 2421^{4} 3920^{7}

Maggi Fong *H-A Pantall* a71 79
5 ch m Dr Fong(USA) —Maggi For Margaret (Shavian)
196a^{F}

Magical Flower *Mme G Rarick* a71 76
3 b f Oasis Dream—Fancy Rose (USA) (Joyeux Danseur (USA))
1609^{9} 2065^{3} 2688^{3} 3267^{3} 5463a^{8}

Magical Illusion *David Evans* a21 64
5 b m Tobougg(IRE) —Magical Gift (Groom Dancer (USA))
1276^{9}

Magical Macey (USA) *David Barron* a86 96
4 ch g Rossini(USA) —Spring's Glory (USA) (Honour And Glory (USA))
(1371) 1680^{7} 2118^{5} 2694^{5} 2890^{2} 4075^{7} 4516^{6} (5108) 5703^{12} (6112)

Magicalmysterytour (IRE) *Willie Musson* a87 99
8 b g Sadler's Wells(USA) —Jude (Darshaan)
1238^{4} 2931^{10} 3411^{2} 3867^{8} 4266^{6} 5221^{7} 5759^{5} 6893^{8} 7139^{9}

Magical Speedfit (IRE) *George Margarson* a77 81
6 ch g Bold Fact(USA) —Magical Peace (IRE) (Magical Wonder (USA))
1281^{2} 1507^{4} 1866^{4} 1937^{2} 2169^{3} (2422) 2826^{3} 3555^{8} 3914^{4} 4659^{5} 5173^{3} 5627^{4} 6815^{4}

Magical Star *Michael Wigham* a50 42
3 b f Arkadian Hero(USA) —Aastral Magic (Magic Ring (IRE))
189^{4} 834^{8} 966^{4} 1132^{5} 1280^{3} 1482^{5} 3226^{7} 3431^{5}

Magic Bounty *Tim Easterby* 63
2 ch g Bahamian Bounty—Magic Myth (IRE) (Revoque (IRE))
3382^{4} 3755^{6} 4557^{6} 5005^{5}

Magic Cat *Mrs K Burke* 91
5 b g One Cool Cat(USA) —Magic Music (IRE) (Magic Ring (IRE))
1110^{5} 2061^{11} 2300^{3} (2814) 3169^{6} 4325^{7} 6078^{8} 6150^{6} 7256a^{0}

Magic City (IRE) *Richard Hannon* 93
2 b g Elusive City(USA) —Annmarie's Magic (IRE) (Flying Spur (AUS))
(1360) ◆ 1598^{2} 2154^{2} ◆ 2437^{3} 3014^{17} 4334^{2} 5216^{13} 5825^{3} 6268^{5}

Magic Cross *Philip McBride* a74 57
3 b f Bertolini(USA) —T G's Girl (Selkirk (USA))
(1482) 2818^{3} 3136^{7} 5644^{2} (6090) 6502^{3}

Magic Destiny *Mrs K Burke* 69
2 b f Dubai Destination(USA) —Magic Music (IRE) (Magic Ring (IRE))
4047^{2} 4748^{3} 6110^{4}

Magic Echo *Rose Dobbin* a46 87
7 b m Wizard King—Sunday News'N'Echo (USA) (Trempolino (USA))
4344^{11} 5440^{6} 7713^{8}

Magic Eye (IRE) *Marco Botti* a100 104
6 b m Nayef(USA) —Much Commended (Most Welcome)
1263a^{2} 2657a^{6} 3897a^{3} 4497^{6} 5277^{12} 5848^{9}

Magic Haze *Sally Hall* a67 62
5 b g Makbul—Turn Back (Pivotal)
63^{2} (184) 323^{4} 859^{5} 3510^{5} 3951^{2} 4814^{9}

Magic Maid (GER) *Barney Curley* 28
3 b f Monsun(GER) —Madhya (USA) (Gone West (USA))
3675^{6}

Magic Millie (IRE) *David O'Meara* a58 61
4 bb m Marju(IRE) —Fille De La Terre (IRE) (Namaqualand (USA))
2388^{9} 2912^{3} 3319^{10} 4173^{7} 4438^{3} 4902^{9} 6235^{10} 6536^{5} 6769^{7} 7722^{3} 7859^{3}

Magic Minstrel *Andrew Balding* a62
3 b g Norse Dancer(IRE) —Lochsong (Song)
3925^{9} 6086^{2} 6947^{6}

Magic Moon (FR) *T Lerner* a95 96
5 b m Fly To The Stars—Queen Elodie (FR) (Cardoun (FR))
371a^{10}

Magic Of The Sea (IRE) *Marco Botti* a69 1
3 b f Refuse To Bend(IRE) —Mureefa (USA) (Bahri (USA))
228^{6} 358^{4} 729^{2}

Magic Rhythm *Mrs K Burke* 61
3 b f Librettist(USA) —Magic Music (IRE) (Magic Ring (IRE))
1672^{5} 2479^{4} 3167^{3} 3621^{5} 4081^{7} 4880^{3} 5731^{11} 6223^{8} 6343^{2}

Magic Secret *Jeremy Gask* 83
3 b g Trade Fair—Just Devine (IRE) (Montjeu (IRE))
(6839)

Magic Stella *Alan Jarvis* a70 78
3 b f Danbird(AUS) —Sasperella (Observatory (USA))
198^{8} 364^{5} 4067^{5} 4511^{8}

Magik Maggie *Chris Wall* a26 37
2 ch f Deportivo—Sasperella (Observatory (USA))
4720^{6} 5245^{8}

Magilini (IRE) *David Barron* a53
2 b f Bertolini(USA) —Magic Annemarie (IRE) (Dancing Dissident (USA))
7874^{2}

Magnini (IRE) *Kevin Ryan* 74
3 b g Exceed And Excel(AUS) —Sanpa Fan (ITY) (Sikeston (USA))
1241^{0}

Magnitude *Brian Baugh* a67 60
6 ch g Pivotal—Miswaki Belle (USA) (Miswaki (USA))
301^{9} 496^{3} 645^{6} 911^{7} (2569) 3094^{4} 3811^{7}

Mahab El Shamaal *David Simcock* a71 76
3 b c Motivator—Soliza (IRE) (Intikhab (USA))
3291^{9} 5714^{4} 6419^{8}

Mahadee (IRE) *Ed de Giles* a78 101
6 br g Cape Cross(IRE) —Rafiya (Halling (USA))
2927^{13} 3802^{7} 4616^{5} 4860^{8} 5969^{3} 6273^{11} 6727^{3} 7110^{8} 7518^{6}

Maharanee (USA) *Ann Duffield* a43 65
3 rg f Mr Greeley(USA) —Queen (IRE) (Sadler's Wells (USA))
1971^{4} 3577^{9} 4072^{8} 4673^{13} 5404^{10} 5864^{6} 6696^{8} 7420^{12}

Mahayogin (USA) *Sir Henry Cecil* 70
3 bb g Dixie Union(USA) —Shiva (JPN) (Hector Protector (USA))
5629^{7} 6096^{6}

Mahbooba (AUS) *M F De Kock* a108 108
4 b f Galileo(IRE) —Sogha (AUS) (Red Ransom (USA))
151a^{2} ◆ (412a) ◆ 681a^{2} 998a^{3} 5055^{3} 5494^{5} (6301) 6909a^{6}

Maher (USA) *David Simcock* a76 78
3 b g Medaglia D'Oro(USA) —Bourbon Blues (USA) (Seeking The Gold (USA))
191^{2} 634^{3} 3872^{7} 4510^{2} 4755^{3} 5266^{7} 5897^{2} 6504^{3} 6789^{7}

Mahfal (FR) *Brian Ellison* a62 55
3 b g Dalakhani(IRE) —Peace Talk (FR) (Sadler's Wells (USA))
5607^{5} 5900^{6} 6493^{8}

Mahkama (USA) *Saeed Bin Suroor* a81 83
2 b f Bernardini(USA) —Rahy Rose (USA) (Rahy (USA))
2811^{8} (3736) ◆ 4661^{4} 5584^{2} 5922^{5} 6573^{7}

Mahubo (SAF) *Tom Tate* a96 97
5 ch g National Emblem(SAF) —Garden Verse (SAF) (Foveros)
587a^{2} 682a^{11} 4049^{6}

Mahya Glaz *Y Fertillet* a64 44
3 ch f Gentlewave(IRE) —Mahyara (FR) (Lomitas)
480a^{4}

Maid In Heaven (IRE) *Walter Swinburn* a96 97
4 b m Clodovil(IRE) —Serious Delight (Lomond (USA))
1104^{3} 1681^{4} 1884^{6} 3407^{6}

Maid Of Meft *Linda Perratt* 69
4 b m Auction House(USA) —Lady Margaret (Sir Harry Lewis (USA))
1519^{4} 2060^{3} (2433) 2696^{4} 3316^{7} 4326^{7} 5723^{10} 6780^{13}

Maidstone Mealy (FR) *R Le Gal* a76 76
5 gr h Take Risks(FR) —Tekameli (FR) (Groom Dancer (USA))
219a^{5}

Maid To Master (IRE) *Mrs John Harrington* 75
2 ch f Danehill Dancer(IRE) —Starlight Dreams (USA) (Black Tie Affair)
4031a[6]
Maiguri (IRE) *C Baillet* 114
3 ch c Panis(USA) —Zanada (FR) (Sinndar (IRE))
1552a[8] 2139a[10] 2978a[8]
Maimonides *Ed Dunlop* a21
5 b g Galileo(IRE) —Windy Britain (Mark Of Esteem (IRE))
6254[13]
Main Attraction *Tobias B P Coles* a42 53
4 ch m Zamindar(USA) —Balleta (USA) (Lyphard (USA))
158[7] 313[8] 389[6]
Main Beach *Tobias B P Coles* a90 74
4 ch g Starcraft(NZ) —Ocean View (USA) (Gone West (USA))
1715 (2094) 5669[7] (6305) 6762[10] 7438[8] (7456) 7586[5] 7628[7]
Main Focus (USA) *John Gosden* a78 76
2 b c Mizzen Mast(USA) —Tsar's Pride (Sadler's Wells (USA))
1678[7] 2049[6] (2817) 6995[10] 7261[5] 7445[8]
Mainland (USA) *Robert Johnson* 75
5 b g Empire Maker(USA) —Imroz (USA) (Nureyev (USA))
1097[8] 1490[6] 2213[12] 3453[7] 4109[12] 4902[13] 7077[11]
Main Opinion (IRE) *Mick Channon* a34 37
3 b f Ivan Denisovich(IRE) —Mainstream Opinion (IRE) (Indian Ridge)
4991[10] 5241[5] 5429[6] 5842[3] 6696[7]
Main Sequence (USA) *David Lanigan* 92
2 ch c Aldebaran(USA) —Ikat (IRE) (Pivotal)
(6100) ◆ (6957) ◆
Maison Brillet (IRE) *Clive Drew* a75 76
4 b g Pyrus(USA) —Stormchaser (IRE) (Titus Livius (FR))
2526[13] 3225[6]
Maistro (IRE) *Luca Cumani* a71
2 b c Excellent Art—Kicking Bird (FR) (Darshaan)
6474[4] ◆ 7126[7]
Maita (GER) *F Vermeulen* a74 81
4 ch m Tertullian(USA) —Mavirca (GER) (Lavirco (GER))
481a[0]
Maitre 'D *Christopher Kellett* a23 15
4 b g Rakti—Giusina Mia (USA) (Diesis)
85[8] 204[12]
Majestical (IRE) *Peter Hedger* a48 48
9 b g Fayruz—Haraabah (USA) (Topsider (USA))
1743a[2] 6920[11] 7518[9] 7636[7] 7658[5]
Majestic Art *F Sanchez* a59 71
2 gr c Dutch Art—Blushing Queen (IRE) (Desert King (IRE))
4624a[9]
Majestic Bounty *Chris Fairhurst* 22
2 b f Bahamian Bounty—Princess Louise (Efisio)
5486[13]
Majestic Breeze (IRE) *Brian Ellison* a39 51
2 ch f Majestic Missile(IRE) —Sofistication (IRE) (Dayjur (USA))
4851[5] 5590[8] 6352[4] ◆
Majestic Bright *Luca Cumani* a68 55
4 ch m Pivotal—L'Affaire Monique (Machiavellian (USA))
1330[7] 1756[4] 2478[8]
Majestic Chap (IRE) *F Sanchez* 43
2 b f High Chaparral(IRE) —Amy G (IRE) (Common Grounds)
6925a[0]
Majestic City (USA) *Peter Miller* a113 80
2 ch c City Zip(USA) —It'Schemistrybaby (USA) (Meadowlake (USA))
7301a[13]
Majestic Dowsing (IRE) *Bent Olsen*
2 b c Majestic Missile(IRE) —Go Likecrazy (Dowsing (USA))
4041a[P]
Majestic Dream (IRE) *Walter Swinburn* a85 91
3 b g Exceed And Excel(AUS) —Tallassee (Indian Ridge)
1571[2] 2319[4] 2646[4] 3798[2] 4550[13] 5240[10] 6003[6] 6457[2] 6949[8]
Majestic Dubawi *Mick Channon* 101
3 b f Dubawi(IRE) —Tidal Chorus (Singspiel (IRE))
1318[6] 2334a[11] 2934[7] 3820[17] 4333[15]
Majestic Manannan (IRE) *David Nicholls*
2 bb g Majestic Missile(IRE) —Miraculous (IRE) (Marju (IRE))
3398[9] 5058[12]
Majestic Millie (IRE) *David O'Meara* a36 45
3 b f Majestic Missile(IRE) —Emerald High (IRE) (Danetime (IRE))
1040[4] 1306[3] 1561[7] 2493[6] 2805[2] 3950[4] 4172[4] 4607[4] 5490[9]
Majestic Myles (IRE) *Richard Fahey* a85 114
3 b g Majestic Missile(IRE) —Gala Style (IRE) (Elnadim (USA))
(2508) ◆ 2934[5] 3029[7] (3852) 4412[7] 5282[2] 6147[13] 6534[2]
Majestic Ridge (IRE) *David Evans* a61 55
3 ch g Majestic Missile(IRE) —Darling Clementine (Lion Cavern (USA))
655[2] 745[7] 847[10] 1359[3] 1776[5] 1980[14] 2141[8] 2396[11]
Majestic Rose *Mick Channon* a75 66
2 br f Imperial Dancer—Solmorin (Fraam)
(1192) 2404[7] 3152[14] 4228[3] 5584[5] 6166[4]
Majestic Zafeen *Alastair Lidderdale* a70 65
2 b f Zafeen(FR) —Arasong (Aragon)
2017[3] 2761[2] 3201[6] 7937[2] ◆
Majestueux (USA) *Mark Hoad* a62 73
4 ch g Royal Academy(USA) —Buck Aspen (USA) (Seeking The Gold (USA))
391[5] 728[7] 943[8] 1582[12] 6969[9] 7888[7]
Major Conquest (IRE) *J W Hills* a61 83
3 b g Librettist(USA) —Arabis (Arazi (USA))
1725[8] 2319[13] 2684[4] 3378[2] 3798[9] 4214[3] 4574[11] 6378[7] 6761[12] 6929[3]
Majordome (FR) *P Van De Poele* a51
4 b g Country Reel(USA) —Napeta (IRE) (Woodman (USA))
91a[9]
Major Domo (FR) *Harry Dunlop* a68 71
3 ch g Domedriver(IRE) —Raphaela (FR) (Octagonal (NZ))
1173[3] 1525[3] 3392[4] 3925[4] 4337[10] 5639[13]
Major Eradicator (USA) *Alastair Lidderdale* a49 54
4 b g Purge(USA) —Pontook (USA) (French Deputy (USA))
820[10] 1068[9] (2450) 2618[3] 3256[11] 3480[8]
Major Maximus *Mrs C Gilbert* a69 31
4 br g Domedriver(IRE) —Madame Maxine (USA) (Dayjur (USA))
(5778a)
Major Muscari (IRE) *Geoffrey Oldroyd* a81 80
3 ch g Exceed And Excel(AUS) —Muscari (Indian Ridge)
1650[3] 2505[10] 5831[13] 6348[11] 6979[11]
Major Victory (SAF) *Gay Kelleway* a86 73
4 b h Victory Moon(SAF) —Sintra (SAF) (National Assembly (CAN))
411a[9] 535a[8] 707a[8]
Majuro (IRE) *Richard Guest* a91 91
7 b g Danetime(IRE) —First Fling (IRE) (Last Tycoon)
(205) (427) ◆ 790[2] (1081) 1467[4] 1610[3] 1854[4] 2095[14] (2495) 2706[9] 2955[4] 4561[17] 4794[13] 5648[9] 5929[10]
Makadane *J-C Rouget* 92
4 ch m Danehill Dancer(IRE) —Makam (IRE) (Green Desert (USA))
6470a[7]
Makbullet *Michael Smith* 72
4 gr g Makbul—Gold Belt (IRE) (Bellypha)
5441[7] 6231[3] (6867) 7074[4]
Make A Dance (USA) *Charles Hills* a60 87
3 b f Empire Maker(USA) —Clog Dance (Pursuit Of Love)
1719[16] 7168[19]
Make A Fuss *Sylvester Kirk* a50
2 b f Proclamation(IRE) —Fustaan (IRE) (Royal Applause)
7345[8] 7583[7] 7909[9]
Make Me Smyle *Stuart Kittow*
2 b c Cockney Rebel(IRE) —Upstream (Prince Sabo)
7257[12]
Make Music For Me (USA) *Alexis Barba* a114 105
4 b h Bernstein(USA) —Miss Cheers (USA) (Carson City (USA))
997a[7]
Make My Dream *John Gallagher* a67 79
8 b g My Best Valentine—Sandkatoon (IRE) (Archway (IRE))
1562[11] 1864[7] (1982) 2585[9] 2903[4] 3389[3] 3768[4] 4272[8] 4795[5] 5561[5] 5616[8] 6580[11] 6802[6] 7086[2] 7488[8]
Make My Heart Sing (IRE) *A P O'Brien* 84
3 b f Sadler's Wells(USA) —Lyrical (Shirley Heights)
3065[10] 4589a[11] 5748a[16] 6736a[9]
Make My Mark (IRE) *John Gallagher* a30 51
3 b f Orpen(USA) —Annies Valentine (My Best Valentine)
1449[4] 2168[4] 2549[10]
Make Up *Noel Wilson* a60 56
2 b f Kyllachy—Christmas Tart (IRE) (Danetime (IRE))
3287[8] 3520[8] 4614[14] 4761[6] 5325[2] 5802[2] 6144[8] 7196[3] (7353) 7421[5] 7735[4]
Makheelah *Clive Brittain* 65
3 b f Dansili—Woodlass (USA) (Woodman (USA))
2596[7] 3633[3] 3757[6] 4185[8] 4696[5] 6033[3] 6811[9]
Making Eyes (IRE) *Hugo Palmer* a90 92
3 b f Dansili—Lady's View (USA) (Distant View (USA))
(2960) (3739) ◆ 5940[5] 6330[12] 7168[16]
Makyaal (IRE) *John Dunlop* a65 60
3 b c Nayef(USA) —Ros The Boss (IRE) (Danehill (USA))
4529[7] 4916[5] 5673[2] 6032[4] (6816) 7001[3]
Malacca Straits *B W Hills* a71 69
3 b f Cacique(IRE) —Stormy Channel (USA) (Storm Cat (USA))
1616[5]
Malagenia (IRE) *L Riccardi* 101
3 b f Whipper(USA) —Croanda (IRE) (Grand Lodge (USA))
1738a[6] 3213a[2] 6370a[2] 7047a[10]
Mal And Dave (IRE) *Mme Pia Brandt* a73 82
4 b g Redback—Louvolite (IRE) (Fayruz)
831a[7]
Malanos (IRE) *David Elsworth* a70 74
3 bb g Lord Of England(GER) —Majorata (GER) (Acatenango (GER))
2019[5] 2257[3] 2819[7] 3291[5] 3824[9] 5327[7] 5992[8] 6589[5]
Malariska (FR) *A Lyon* a78 74
4 b m My Risk(FR) —Mala Mala (FR) (Balleroy (USA))
1033a[5]
Malayan Mist (IRE) *D K Weld* 94
3 b f Dansili—Misty Heights (Fasliyev (USA))
6362a[5]
Malcheek (IRE) *Tim Easterby* a106 86
9 br g Lend A Hand—Russland (GER) (Surumu (GER))
844[3] 1541[3] 1854[8] 2495[6] 3028[4] 3506[11] 6381[8] 6867[6]
Malekat Jamal (IRE) *David Simcock* a63 59
2 b f Dutch Art—Haretha (IRE) (Alhaarth (IRE))
4552[13] 5097[4] 6214[8]
Malgoof (IRE) *Torben Christensen* 83
3 b c Kodiac—Mira (IRE) (Turtle Island (IRE))
4840a[DSQ]
Malice Or Mischief (IRE) *J S Moore* a80 81
3 ch g Intikhab(USA) —Unimpeachable (IRE) (Namaqualand (USA))
468[4] (609) (686) 770[2] (951) 1113[6] 1485[5] (1754) 3231[6] 3363[7] 4489[4] (4685) (5118) 5757[3]
Malicia (USA) *X Thomas-Demeaulte* a90 104
3 ch f Tapit(USA) —Malia (USA) (Regal Classic (CAN))
3671a[6] 4570a[6] 7156a[5]
Malih *Peter Makin* 64
2 b c Echo Of Light—Sultry Lass (USA) (Private Account (USA))
6165[13] 6743[6]
Maliha (IRE) *Kevin Ryan* 66
2 b f Amadeus Wolf—Folcara (IRE) (Brief Truce (USA))
3201[9] 5029[4] 5806[9] 6275[8]
Malikayah (IRE) *D Camuffo* 95
3 b f Fasliyev(USA) —Trombe (FR) (Bering)
1432a[7] 7408a[11]
Mallak (IRE) *Philip McBride* 52
2 b f Moss Vale(IRE) —Henrietta Mews (Compton Place)
5514[9]
Maloof *Roger Varian* a46 70
3 ch c Bahamian Bounty—Medway (IRE) (Shernazar)
3543[5] ◆ 4478[9] 6475[4] 6748[10]
Malpas Missile (IRE) *Tom Dascombe* a81 80
3 b f Elusive City(USA) —Second Prayer (IRE) (Singspiel (IRE))
2520a[9] 3168[5] 3549[8] 7348[5] 7767[5]
Maltease Ah *Andrew Reid* a67 66
2 br f Librettist(USA) —Manic (Polar Falcon (USA))
2380[4] 2641[3] 3050[3] 3700[5] 4386[4] 4662[9] 7056[10] 7267[7]
Malthouse (GER) *Mark Johnston* a85 106
3 b g Green Desert(USA) —Maltage (USA) (Affirmed (USA))
1010a[3] 1202[6] 1516[4] (2230) (2471) ◆ 2711[5] 3069[8] 3405[2] 3774[4] 4015[2] 5275[8] 5466[6] 6163[18]
Malvesi *Ann Duffield* a5 50
2 b c Iceman—Madam Valentine (Primo Valentino (IRE))
4365[9] 6836[8] 7108[7] 7338[4]
Mama Lulu (USA) *Michael Bell* 78
3 bb f Kingmambo(USA) —Kamarinskaya (USA) (Storm Cat (USA))
1843[5]
Mama Sox (IRE) *John C McConnell* 70
3 b f Bachelor Duke(USA) —Marghelan (FR) (Soviet Star (USA))
(7158)
Mamath (IRE) *R Brogi*
2 b c Le Vie Dei Colori—Mind And Life (IRE) (Monsun (GER))
7217a[3]
Mambia *J-C Rouget* 105
3 ch f Aldebaran(USA) —Algoa (FR) (Common Grounds)
1207a[9] 2137a[14]
Mambo Spirit (IRE) *Tony Newcombe* a86 82
7 b g Invincible Spirit(IRE) —Mambodorga (USA) (Kingmambo (USA))
4246[6] 5319[8] 6090[7] 6479[6] (7123) 7448[8] 7596[2] (7834)
Mambo Star (FR) *F Vermeulen* a70 87
4 ch g Okawango(USA) —Saskya's Dream (IRE) (Ashkalani (IRE))
267a[9]
Mamlook (IRE) *David Pipe* 102
7 br g Key Of Luck(USA) —Cradle Brief (IRE) (Brief Truce (USA))
1808[15]
Manaaber (USA) *B W Hills* 76
3 ch f Medicean—Needlecraft (IRE) (Mark Of Esteem (IRE))
2256[5] ◆ 2883[8]
Manager Mick (IRE) *John Norton* 41
3 b g Clodovil(IRE) —Nashua Song (IRE) (Kahyasi)
2565[5] 4125[8] 4611[9]
Manana Manana *Richard Guest* a17 63
5 b g Tobougg(IRE) —Midnight Allure (Aragon)
5787[14] 7245[8]
Manarola *Mahmood Al Zarooni* a34 54
3 b c Tiger Hill(IRE) —Porto Roca (AUS) (Barathea (IRE))
3519[9] 3781[8]
Manasha *John Dunlop* 40
3 b f Piccolo—Madurai (Chilibang)
3254[4] 3943[11] 5624[9]
Manassas (IRE) *Brian Meehan* 104
6 b g Cape Cross(IRE) —Monnavanna (IRE) (Machiavellian (USA))
1092[3] 1406[8] 1885[2] (3109) 3862[19] 4314[9] 4802[10] 5032[10] 5474[14]
Manbaa (USA) *John Dunlop* 42
2 b f Jazil(USA) —Itnab (Green Desert (USA))
4052[15] 6603[13]
Manchester (FR) *Niels Petersen* 95
3 ch c Domedriver(IRE) —Metaline (FR) (Dr Fong (USA))
680a[10]
Mancunian (IRE) *John Best* a25 61
3 b c Motivator—Winesong (IRE) (Giant's Causeway (USA))
2257[9] 4753[3] 5477[7]
Mandaean *A Fabre* 113
2 b c Manduro(GER) —Summertime Legacy (Darshaan)
(7405a)
Mandalay King (IRE) *Marjorie Fife* a49 82
6 b g King's Best(USA) —Mahamuni (IRE) (Sadler's Wells (USA))
1239[2] 1793[5] 1907[9] 2543[2] 3028[11] (3488) (3759) 4013[7] 5760[10] 6113[4] 7074[15]
Mandalay Prince *Willie Musson* a47 69
7 b g Tobougg(IRE) —Autumn Affair (Lugana Beach)
492[3] 768[P] 1466[6]
Mandarin Spirit (IRE) *Linda Perratt* a75 75
11 b g Primo Dominie—Lithe Spirit (IRE) (Dancing Dissident (USA))
1712[7] 2048[11] 2263[6] 2694[9] 3040[5] 4017[6] 4539[3]
Mandatori (IRE) *Nicky Vaughan* 59
3 b f Oratorio(IRE) —Mandaraka (FR) (Ashkalani (IRE))
1362[16] 2673[5] 3091[3] 3621[8]
Manderston *Mark Johnston* a53 55
2 b g Araafa(IRE) —Ballet Princess (Muhtarram (USA))
1290[6] 1913[5] 2121[3] 2362[5] 2854[4] 3554[4] 6101[3] 6611[6] 6763[5] 7117[3]
Mandhooma *Peter Hiatt* a65 74
5 b m Oasis Dream—Shatarah (Gulch (USA))
1357[2] (1634) ◆ 1917[6] 2201[8] 2452[4] 2799[3] (3019) 3477[2] 3674[2] 3940[3] 5136[5] (5669) 6091[7] 6814[6]
Mandianna (IRE) *Jo Crowley* a55 48
2 b f Manduro(GER) —Lock's Heath (CAN) (Topsider (USA))
6751[6] 7124[9]
Mandilion (USA) *A Fabre* a75
3 b c Forestry(USA) —Spun Silk (USA) (A.P. Indy (USA))
777a[4]
Mandurah (IRE) *David Nicholls* a70 77
7 b g Tagula(IRE) —Fearfully Grand (Grand Lodge (USA))
1073[11] 1239[5] (1411) 1796[4] 2126[9] 4371[8]
Mandy's Hero *Olivia Maylam* a74 55
3 b g Compton Place—Bandanna (Bandmaster (USA))
28[2] (132) (356) 465[4] 2074[17] 3628[7] 7746[11] 7832[10]
Maneki Neko (IRE) *Edwin Tuer* a75 79
9 b g Rudimentary(USA) —Ardbess (Balla Cove)
1908[3]
Mangham (IRE) *George Foster* a74 73
6 b g Montjeu(IRE) —Lovisa (USA) (Gone West (USA))
1714[7] 2348[3] 2692[10] 2988[4] 3658[11] (4170) 4543[6] 4783[2] 5150[6] 5721[P]
Mango Music *Richard Fahey* a73 84
8 ch m Distant Music(USA) —Eurolink Sundance (Night Shift (USA))
2497[4] 3160[6] 3459[7] 3900[2] 4541[4] 4609[4] ◆ 5442[2]
Manieree (IRE) *John M Oxx* 112
3 br f Medicean—Sheer Spirit (IRE) (Caerleon (USA))
1006a[4] (4132a) (5976a)
Manifestation *John Gosden* a83 96
3 b g Doyen(IRE) —Jadidh (Touching Wood (USA))
95[6] ◆ 339[4] ◆ (649) 1550[5] ◆ 3551[2] 4251[4] (5035) 5448[6]
Manighar (FR) *Luca Cumani* 118
5 gr g Linamix(FR) —Mintly Fresh (USA) (Rubiano (USA))
2072[3] 3066[4] 4469[8] 5304a[4] 6886a[4] 7218a[5] 7407a[2]
Manjakani *A Fabre* 97
3 b c Barathea(IRE) —Spring Oak (Mark Of Esteem (IRE))
5131a[5] 5771a[5]
Manjam (IRE) *Braem Horse Racing Sprl* 77
7 b h Almutawakel—Mubkera (IRE) (Nashwan (USA))
7314a[0]
Man Of Action (USA) *Saeed Bin Suroor* 107
4 ch g Elusive Quality(USA) —Dixie Melody (USA) (Dixieland Band (USA))
2284[11] 3645[6] 4494[6] (5929) 6339[19] ◆
Man Of God (IRE) *John Gosden* 82
3 b c Sadler's Wells(USA) —Jude (Darshaan)
2253[5] 3364[8] 4236[2] 4752[2] 5236[6] 6294[8] 6729[4]
Man Of Ice *Jane Chapple-Hyam* a64 50
2 br g Iceman—Never Enough (GER) (Monsun (GER))
6951[11] 7634[6]
Man Of Iron (USA) *Luca Cumani* a100 103
5 ch h Giant's Causeway(USA) —Better Than Honour (USA) (Deputy Minister (CAN))
153a[13] 329a[P]
Man Of My Word *Scott Dixon* a71 58
2 b g Milk It Mick—Promised (IRE) (Petardia)
2455[7] 2886[11] 3490[7] 5104[4] 5597[6] 5825[11] 6611[2] 6806[13] 7242[2] 7708[4] (7881)
Man Of Plenty *John Dunlop* 65
2 ch c Manduro(GER) —Credit-A-Plenty (Generous (IRE))
6059[9] 6954[6] ◆
Manomine *Clive Brittain* a66 64
2 b g Manduro(GER) —Fascinating Hill (FR) (Danehill (USA))
2109[6] 2448[6] 3152[15] 5446[7] 5634[4] 6031[5] 6972[4] 7336[5] 7763[2]
Manoori (IRE) *Chris Wall* a86 88
3 b f Dalakhani(IRE) —Kiris World (Distant Relative)
2074[6] (2611) (3985) ◆ 5146[4] 6272[6]
Manshoor (IRE) *Lucy Wadham* a66 70
6 gr g Linamix(FR) —Lady Wells (IRE) (Sadler's Wells (USA))
6287[3] 6546[8]
Mantatisi *James Fanshawe* a73 73
3 ch f Motivator—Magongo (Be My Chief (USA))
2313[8] 2675[4] 3557[7]
Mantoba *Brian Meehan* a99 106
3 b c Noverre(USA) —Coming Home (Vettori (IRE))
998a[14] 6955[4] 7404a[6] 7802[3]
Mantuana (IRE) *David O'Meara* a61 51
2 b f Kodiac—Al Shakoor (Barathea (IRE))
3452[4] 3707[2] 3932[5] 4406[8] 4940[6] 5399[11]
Manuka (USA) *D Smaga* 78
2 ch f Mr Greeley(USA) —Chaibia (IRE) (Peintre Celebre (USA))
7219a[8]
Many Welcomes *Brian Baugh* a53 66
6 ch m Young Ern—Croeso Cynnes (Most Welcome)
747[4] 2399[11] 2799[6] 3341[3]
Maoi Chinn Tire (IRE) *Jennie Candlish* a69 73
4 b g Mull Of Kintyre(USA) —Primrose And Rose (Primo Dominie)
2251[3] 2762[6] 3544[3] 5249[4] 5609[7]

Map Of Heaven *William Haggas* a56 73
3 b f Pivotal—Superstar Leo (IRE) (College Chapel)
2643[9] 3390[9] 4067[2] 4559[2] 5423[2] (5842)

Mappin Time (IRE) *Tim Easterby* a78 90
3 b g Orientate(USA) —Different Story (USA) (Stravinsky (USA))
1852[4] 2724[6] 2934[16] 3682[5] 4324[6] 4791[3] (5268) 6113[25]

Maqaasid *John Gosden* 111
3 b f Green Desert(USA) —Eshaadeh (USA) (Storm Cat (USA))
1319[3] 1719[3] 2137a[8] 3822[8] 4497[5] 6687[3]

Maqaraat (IRE) *Charles Hills* 102
3 gr c Dalakhani(IRE) —Raghida (IRE) (Nordico (USA))
1321[2] ◆ 1850[2] 2469[2] (3167) 6339[30]

Ma Quillet *Henry Candy* a50 72
3 gr f Tumbleweed Ridge—Raffelina (USA) (Carson City (USA))
2223[3] ◆ (2993) 3390[3]

Mar Adentro (FR) *R Chotard* a89 113
5 b g Marju(IRE) —Guermantes (Distant Relative)
996a[9] 2138a[5] 2754a[5] 3010[9] 4739a[2] 5985a[2] 6563a[4] 7221a[8]

Maradini (FR) *A De Royer-Dupre* 101
2 b c Galileo(IRE) —Marque Royale (Royal Academy (USA))
6660a[4]

Marafong *Brian Baugh* a45 65
4 ch g Dr Fong(USA) —Marakabei (Hernando (FR))
6295[13] *7004[9]*

Maraheb *John Dunlop* 105
3 b c Redoute's Choice(AUS) —Hureya (USA) (Woodman (USA))
(3183) 3871[2] (4718) ◆

Marah Music *Peter Makin* a45 65
2 b c Royal Applause—Marah (Machiavellian (USA))
4384[4] 6123[7] 6956[9] *7530[8]*

Marajaa (IRE) *Willie Musson* a85 101
9 b g Green Desert(USA) —Ghyraan (IRE) (Cadeaux Genereux)
1092[10] 1406[14] 2310[3] ◆ 3134[3] 3825[16] 4415[14] 5043[8] *5687[4]* 6728[3] *7531[4]* *(7807)*

Marasia (FR) *Mme M-C Naim* a84 84
2 gr f Country Reel(USA) —Premiraza (FR) (Nombre Premier)
7813a[4]

Maratib (USA) *David Lanigan* a53 59
3 b g Street Cry(IRE) —Colcon (USA) (Pleasant Colony (USA))
1683[16]

Marble Game (FR) *E Libaud*
2 b f Orpen(USA) —Julia's Dance (IRE) (Alhaarth (IRE))
7813a[5]

Marchand D'Or (FR) *M Delzangles* a56 114
8 gr g Marchand De Sable(USA) —Fedora (FR) (Kendor (FR))
2754a[7] 3654a[4] 4838a[3] (5532a) 6566a[6] 7221a[0]

Marching Home *Walter Swinburn* a77
4 ch g Leporello(IRE) —Marchetta (Mujadil (USA))
206 [2] ◆ *483[4]*

Marching On (IRE) *Kevin Ryan* 77
2 b c Rock Of Gibraltar(IRE) —Miss Delila (USA) (Malibu Moon (USA))
3123[3] 3826[4] 4323[4] 5727[5] 6274[3] 6702[6]

Marching Orders (IRE) *Natalie Lloyd-Beavis* a39 56
4 b g Rock Of Gibraltar(IRE) —Phantom Rain (Rainbow Quest (USA))
7574[4]

Marching Time *Doug Watson* a25 96
5 b g Sadler's Wells(USA) —Marching West (USA) (Gone West (USA))
605a[3]

March On Beetroot *Robert Cowell* a79 100
3 b g Cape Cross(IRE) —Parisian Elegance (Zilzal (USA))
2106[6] 2500[2] ◆

Marcret (ITY) *S Botti* 109
4 b h Martino Alonso(IRE) —Love Secret (USA) (Secreto (USA))
6905a[3] 7323a[3]

Marcus Antonius *Jim Boyle* a72 71
4 b g Mark Of Esteem(IRE) —Star Of The Course (USA) (Theatrical)
1153[3] 1282[4] 1839[4] 2856[7] 3978[2] 4396[5] (6240) *6798[2]* 6988[11]

Marcus Augustus (IRE) *Richard Hannon* 74
2 b g Holy Roman Emperor(IRE) —Lulua (USA) (Bahri (USA))
2023[2] ◆ 2644[2] 3064[15] 4655[3] 6018[2] 6293[6]

Mardood *Chris Grant* 39
6 b g Oasis Dream—Gaelic Swan (IRE) (Nashwan (USA))
3622[8]

Marford Missile (IRE) *Tom Dascombe* 84
2 b g Majestic Missile(IRE) —Khawafi (Kris)
(1209) 1489[3] 1806[2]

Margo Channing *Micky Hammond* 57
2 ch f Three Valleys(USA) —Charlotte Vale (Pivotal)
3201[4] 3826[U] 4122[6] 4606[3] 6260[6] 6911[3]

Margot De Medici (FR) *Micky Hammond* 25
3 b f Medicean—Ratukidul (FR) (Danehill (USA))
2125[6] 2394[U]

Margot Did (IRE) *Michael Bell* 118
3 b f Exceed And Excel(AUS) —Special Dancer (Shareef Dancer (USA))
1602[3] 2032[4] (2928) (3158) 3644[4] (5253) 6563a[15]

Margravine (USA) *A Fabre* 106
3 ch f King's Best(USA) —Arlette (IRE) (King Of Kings (IRE))
1709a[6] 3671a[4] 4570a[0]

Marhaba Malyoon (IRE) *David Simcock* 76
3 b g Tiger Hill(IRE) —Mamonta (Fantastic Light (USA))
1895[6] 2715[13]

Marhoona (USA) *John Dunlop* 65
2 b f Elusive Quality(USA) —Elrehaan (Sadler's Wells (USA))
4804[9] 5445[9]

Maria Anna (IRE) *Ann Duffield* 34
2 b f Amadeus Wolf—Corryvreckan (IRE) (Night Shift (USA))
1876[5] 2113[13] 3302[8] 3728[10]

Mariachi Man *Tim Easterby* 102
3 b g Haafhd—Popocatepetl (FR) (Nashwan (USA))
1202[4] 2296[4] 2935[4] (3159) 4313[8]

Maria Grazie (IRE) *Mlle C Cardenne* a83 79
3 ch f Haafhd—Olonella (Selkirk (USA))
5463a[7] *7667a[8]*

Maria Letizia *John Gosden* 52
2 b f Galileo(IRE) —Napoleon's Sister (IRE) (Alzao (USA))
4804[10]

Maria Medecis (IRE) *Ann Duffield* a49 60
2 b f Medecis—Aweigh (Polar Falcon (USA))
1744[6] 2120[5] 3878[8] 4343[10] *4922[6]* *5245[4]* 6043[10] *6540[9]*

Maria Montez *J W Hills* a59
2 b f Piccolo—Easy Feeling (IRE) (Night Shift (USA))
7540[7] *7798[5]*

Mariannes *John Dunlop* a39
2 br f Piccolo—Madurai (Chilibang)
7431[8] *7672[12]* *7837[8]*

Maria Royal (IRE) *A De Royer-Dupre* 112
4 b m Montjeu(IRE) —Notable (Zafonic (USA))
5773a[4] 6562a[7] 7049a[11]

Maricopa *Mahmood Al Zarooni* 67
3 b c Dubawi(IRE) —Surprise Visitor (IRE) (Be My Guest (USA))
2068[6] 2735[5] 3135[5] 3676[5]

Marie Cuddy (IRE) *Karen George* a2 42
4 b m Galileo(IRE) —Corrine (IRE) (Spectrum (IRE))
1755[11]

Marie Rose *Brian Meehan* a64 68
3 b f Sadler's Wells(USA) —Langoustine (AUS) (Danehill (USA))
1845[6] 2458[10] 3118[7] 3688[3] 4081[5] 4435[6] 4916[4] *5243[9]* *6669[8]*

Marie's Fantasy *Zoe Davison* a54 58
2 b f Whipper(USA) —My American Beauty (Wolfhound (USA))
1337[5] 1590[2] 2248[5] *6652[8]* *7670[3]* *7830[3]*

Marina Ballerina *Roy Bowring* a57 44
3 bb f Ballet Master(USA) —Marinaite (Komaite (USA))
2529[8] 4559[6] 5021[5] *7247[3]* *7426[3]* *7608[5]* *7723[2]* *7859[7]*

Marina's Ocean *Roy Bowring* a17 47
7 b m Beat All(USA) —Ocean Song (Savahra Sound)
7246[8] *7775[9]* *7858[7]* *7912[4]*

Marine Boy (IRE) *Tom Dascombe* a88 87
5 b g One Cool Cat(USA) —Bahamamia (Vettori (IRE))
1849[7]

Marine Commando *Richard Fahey* 101
3 b g Pastoral Pursuits—Carollan (IRE) (Marju (IRE))
1602[7] 2500[8] 2934[20] 3807[3] 5288[6] 5852[2] ◆ (6332) 7018[16]

Mariner's Dream (IRE) *C W J Farrell* 48
3 b f Mujadil(USA) —Beenablaw (IRE) (Alzao (USA))
642[7]

Mariners Lodge (USA) *Mark Johnston* a69 91
3 ch c Distorted Humor(USA) —Sanibel Island (USA) (Capote (USA))
1409[7] 1624[6] (4380) 4625[2] 5568[7] 5968[2]

Marino Prince (FR) *Joanne Foster* a57 59
6 b g Dr Fong(USA) —Hula Queen (USA) (Irish River (FR))
114[3] *1374[2]* 1615[11] *2237[7]* (2401) 3139[5] 4112[6] 4329[6] ◆ *4869[4]* 4944[6] 7112[7]

Marinous (FR) *F Head* a104 119
5 b h Numerous(USA) —Marende (FR) (Panoramic)
757a[6] 1001a[10] 1707a[5] 2344a[3] 4037a[0] 5304a[7] 5531a[3] 6903a[7]

Mariol (FR) *Robert Collet* a94 110
8 b g Munir—La Bastoche (IRE) (Kaldoun (FR))
327a[7] *606a[9]* 825a[12] 5532a[0] 7221a[0] 7534a[0]

Mariposa (IRE) *Sir Michael Stoute* 66
2 b f Oasis Dream—Mary Stuart (IRE) (Nashwan (USA))
6168[8]

Maristar (USA) *Gerard Butler* a106 20
4 b m Giant's Causeway(USA) —Jewel Princess (USA) (Key To The Mint (USA))
(1499)

Mariyah *Michael Blanshard* a22 31
3 gr f Kyllachy—Molly Moon (IRE) (Primo Dominie)
1082[9] *1312[10]*

Mariyca (IRE) *Ole Larsen* a90 73
5 gr m Daylami(IRE) —Masakala (IRE) (Cadeaux Genereux)
4842a[10] 5982a[4]

Marju King (IRE) *Stuart Kittow* a60 73
5 b g Marju(IRE) —Blue Reema (IRE) (Bluebird (USA))
1750[2] 2312[6] 3003[2] 4008[6]

Marjury Daw (IRE) *James Given* a83 90
5 b m Marju(IRE) —The Stick (Singspiel (IRE))
1826[8] 2217[16] 2545[9] 2999[2] 3275[9] 3641[6] 4070[3] 4561[6] 4877[4] *5391[4]* 5728[3]

Markab *Henry Candy* a107 121
8 b g Green Desert(USA) —Hawafiz (Nashwan (USA))
2005[9] 2297[11] 4092[2] 4838a[10] 5935[4]

Mark Anthony (IRE) *Shaun Harris* a58 79
4 b g Antonius Pius(USA) —Zuniga's Date (USA) (Diesis)
522[10] *673[9]* *870[7]* 1715[3] 1906[2] 2356[5] 4513[7] 4897[8] 5034[6] *5603[12]* 5881[5] 6208[3] 6343[3] 6646[2] 6869[7] 6939[5]

Markazzi *Sir Michael Stoute* 98
4 b g Dansili—Bandanna (Bandmaster (USA))
2884[4] 3825[3] (4794) 5218[5] 6339[5] ◆

Marketing Mix (CAN) *Thomas F Proctor* a99 111
3 bb f Medaglia D'Oro(USA) —Instant Thought (USA) (Kris S (USA))
6887a[2]

Market Maker (IRE) *Tim Easterby* a25 61
3 ch g Trade Fair—Papier Mache (IRE) (Desert Prince (IRE))
1526[8] 1969[4] *2239[6]* 2801[2] 4151[3] 4904[4]

Market Puzzle (IRE) *Mark Brisbourne* a56 65
4 ch g Bahamian Bounty—Trempjane (Lujain (USA))
943[3] *1308[7]* *1374[7]* 1567[5] 1871[3] 2271[4] 2900[7] 3637[3] 4111[5] ◆ 4165[3] 4645[6] 4889[2] 5178[2] (5520) ◆ 5808[7] (6295) 6833[3] 7113[7] 7263[10]

Markington *Peter Bowen* a74 83
8 b g Medicean—Nemesia (Mill Reef (USA))
1458[12] 3935[2] 4463[7]

Markmanship (FR) *Mme V Deiss* a44 64
6 b g Mark Of Esteem(IRE) —Miss Dish (IRE) (Marju (IRE))
832a[2]

Marksbury *Mark Brisbourne* a66 27
4 b m Mark Of Esteem(IRE) —Penelewey (Groom Dancer (USA))
273[5] *7632[12]*

Marksmanship (IRE) *A P O'Brien* 110
3 b c Galileo(IRE) —Maroochydore (IRE) (Danehill (USA))
3068[7] 4038a[6] 4737a[2]

Marlos Moment *Mark Michael McNiff* a49 43
5 b g Where Or When(IRE) —Tender Moment (IRE) (Caerleon (USA))
7720[4] *7858[12]*

Marlow (GER) *Mario Hofer* a81 76
5 b g Lomitas—Manon (Alzao (USA))
219a[3]

Marmaduke *John Bridger* 44
3 ch g Bertolini(USA) —Lihou Island (Beveled (USA))
4321[11] *4911[11]*

Marmalade Moon *Robert Cowell* a48
2 ch f Shamardal(USA) —Frascati (Emarati (USA))
6946[11] *7194[4]*

Marmooq *Michael Attwater* a69 62
8 ch g Cadeaux Genereux—Portelet (Night Shift (USA))
174[11] *299[5]* *5531[4]*

Marny (GER) *H Blume* a89 91
6 b m Dashing Blade—Magic Dawn (IRE) (Caerleon (USA))
92a[0]

Maroni (IRE) *F Rohaut* a89 86
6 b g Oasis Dream—Miss Chryss (IRE) (Indian Ridge)
195a[10] *371a[4]* *661a[3]*

Maroon Machine (IRE) *E J O'Neill* a96 101
4 ch g Muhtathir—Mediaeval (FR) (Medaaly)
1011a[0]

Maroosh *Brian Meehan* a75 75
2 br c Kyllachy—Madamoiselle Jones (Emperor Jones (USA))
2291[6] 2559[8] 3511[3] (4760) 5478[6] 6372[4] *6623[5]* 6995[5]

Marquis Du Nonan (FR) *G Collet* 71
2 b c Apsis—Marquise Fador (FR) (Northern Crystal)
7449a[8]

Marron Flore *Alastair Lidderdale* a38 27
8 ch m Compton Place—Flore Fair (Polar Falcon (USA))
573[6] *752[8]*

Marshall Art *John Quinn* a42
2 b c Lawman(FR) —Portrait Of A Lady (IRE) (Peintre Celebre (USA))
7494[10] *7709[6]*

Marshal Plat Club *Alan Bailey* a51
4 b m Monsieur Bond(IRE) —Bond May Day (Among Men (USA))
511[9]

Marshmallow *Chris Wall* a50 58
3 b f Tiger Hill(IRE) —Gooseberry Pie (Green Desert (USA))
5327[9] 6324[5] *7004[6]* 7212[11]

Marsh's Gift *Colin Teague* a32 50
4 b g Tamayaz(CAN) —Maureen Ann (Elmaamul (USA))
1498[9]

Marsh Warbler *Brian Ellison* a83 82
4 ch g Barathea(IRE) —Echo River (USA) (Irish River (FR))
(7070)

Martha's Way *Michael Easterby* 51
2 b f Tiger Hill(IRE) —Pilgrim's Way (USA) (Gone West (USA))
4285[8] 4853[7] 5104[7]

Martin Chuzzlewit (IRE) *Sir Michael Stoute* 93
2 ch c Galileo(IRE) —Alta Anna (FR) (Anabaa (USA))
4053[5] (4722) 5709[5]

Martine's Spirit (IRE) *William Haggas* a77 75
3 b f Invincible Spirit(IRE) —Mayenne (USA) (Nureyev (USA))
6459[8] 6804[3] *7179[2]* *7360[3]* *(7630)*

Marvada (IRE) *K J Condon* a79 102
3 b f Elusive City(USA) —Theory Of Law (Generous (IRE))
5361a[4] 5523a[6] 5848[4] 6523[3]

Marvelloso *E J O'Neill* a59
3 b g Tobougg(IRE) —Qudrah (IRE) (Darshaan)
777a[10]

Marvellous City (IRE) *Mandy Rowland* a43
3 b c Captain Rio—Existence (Zafonic (USA))
295[5] *873[8]* *1065[5]* *1589[11]*

Marvellous Value (IRE) *Michael Dods* a84 100
6 b g Danetime(IRE) —Despondent (IRE) (Broken Hearted)
455[3] 1200[4] 1618[3] (2434) 3395[12] 4369[4] (5682) 6145[2] 6987[18]

Marvo *Mark H Tompkins* a78 86
7 b g Bahamian Bounty—Mega (IRE) (Petardia)
348[8] *799[7]* 3361[5] 3620[9] 4045[5] 4170[2] 5728[6] *7600[2]* *7710[2]*

Mary Fildes (IRE) *J S Moore* 99
2 b f Chineur(FR) —Scarlet Empress (Second Empire (IRE))
(4225) 4999[3] 5656[6] 6146[3] 6691[7] 7028[5]

Mary Frith *Peter Winkworth* a45
2 b f Acclamation—Cutpurse Moll (Green Desert (USA))
6946[10]

Marygold *John Akehurst* a42 80
2 b f Cockney Rebel(IRE) —Contrary Mary (Mujadil (USA))
1441[6] *1757[4]* 2187[3] 2559[7] (3249) 3842[6] 4824[2] 5197[3] (5913) 6524[4]

Mary Helen *Mark Brisbourne* a64 55
4 b m Dandoun—Hotel California (IRE) (Last Tycoon)
408[3] *598[5]* *631[9]* *773[7]* *899[4]* *1063[5]* *1253[3]*

Maryolini *Tom Keddy* a59 65
6 b m Bertolini(USA) —Mary Jane (Tina's Pet)
2167[5] *2603[5]* (3247) 3685[3] 4025[5]

Mary's Pet *John Akehurst* a68 65
4 b m Where Or When(IRE) —Contrary Mary (Mujadil (USA))
98[10] *143[11]* *268[9]* *654[3]* *(792)* *1024[5]* 3322[11] 3765[8] 4255[8] (5540) 5917[6] 6889[17] *7349[10]* 7579[12] 7767[13]

Marzante (USA) *Roger Charlton* a70 79
3 rg g Maria's Mon(USA) —Danzante (USA) (Danzig (USA))
1773[4] *2607[11]*

Masai Moon *Rod Millman* a93 94
7 b g Lujain(USA) —Easy To Imagine (USA) (Cozzene (USA))
1467[2] 2020[4] 2441[11] 2995[10] 3634[3]

Masamah (IRE) *Kevin Ryan* a97 118
5 gr g Exceed And Excel(AUS) —Bethesda (Distant Relative)
1809[3] (2317) 2714[8] (3874) (4468) 5253[8] 5707[15] 6164[2] 6563a[10]

Masaraat (FR) *John Dunlop* a84 91
3 b f Alhaarth(IRE) —Kahalah (IRE) (Darshaan)
1727[6] (2184) 3260[2] ◆ 4316[2] 5283[11] 6172[11]

Masaya *Clive Brittain* 97
3 b f Dansili—Anbella (FR) (Common Grounds)
1317[6] 2106[3] 3323[3] 3822[10] 6035[5] 7295[21]

Mascarpone (GER) *M Weiss* a97 83
7 b h Monsun(GER) —Mamourina (IRE) (Barathea (IRE))
(441a) 628a[9]

Mashaaref *Roger Varian* a73 93
3 b g Cape Cross(IRE) —Etizaaz (USA) (Diesis)
1605[6] (2185) 2925[4] 3844[2] 5888[2] 6325[2]

Mashatu *James Fanshawe* a75 79
4 b g Pivotal—Wannabe Grand (IRE) (Danehill (USA))
1569[2] 1990[2] *2822[4]* 4278[9]

Mashdood (USA) *Peter Hiatt* a70 82
5 b g Sinndar(IRE) —Rahayeb (Arazi (USA))
8[4] *118[2]* ◆ *(244)* *393[2]*

Mashoor (FR) *A Fabre* 112
4 b h Monsun(GER) —Gontcharova (IRE) (Zafonic (USA))
1231a[5] 1707a[2] 2344a[0]

Mashoora (IRE) *J-C Rouget* 105
2 ch f Barathea(IRE) —Lovely Blossom (FR) (Spinning World (USA))
5296a[2] 6941a[2]

Masie Grey *David Elsworth*
3 ch f Compton Place—Night Kiss (FR) (Night Shift (USA))
179[8] *559[9]* *818[8]*

Masivo Man (IRE) *Chris Dwyer* a50 49
2 br g Titus Livius(FR) —Maddie's Pearl (IRE) (Clodovil (IRE))
1590[6] *1954[7]* 2267[4] 2595[2] 2823[3] *5316[9]* 6043[14] 6237[4] *6540[8]* *6942[4]*

Masked Dance (IRE) *David Nicholls* a75 96
4 gr g Captain Rio—Brooks Masquerade (Absalom)
58[6] *310[7]* *455[4]* (1035) (2398) 3134[7] 3397[8] (4325) 4802[13] 5218[16] 5557[14] 6148[5] 7295[12] *7586[10]*

Masked Marvel *John Gosden* 124
3 b c Montjeu(IRE) —Waldmark (GER) (Mark Of Esteem (IRE))
1548[5] (2191) 2715[8] (3772) (5928) 6567a[16]

Maslak (IRE) *Peter Hiatt* a81 76
7 b g In The Wings—Jeed (IRE) (Mujtahid (USA))
392[7] *531[6]* *938[4]* *1046[2]* 1243[4] 2055[8] 4366[8] 4613[3] 4903[4] 5491[4] 5804[13] 6157[5] 6870[4] *7195[4]* 7357[3] 7645[4] 7818[2]

Mason Hindmarsh *Karen McLintock* 72
4 ch g Dr Fong(USA) —Sierra Virgen (USA) (Stack (USA))
1036[6] 2262[4] 3507[2] 3828[12] 4382[6] (4671) 5369[4] 5724[6] 6279[3] 7102[8]

Mass Rally (IRE) *Michael Dods* a96 104
4 b g Kheleyf(USA) —Reunion (IRE) (Be My Guest (USA))
2031[18] 2927[8] 3397[11] 5032[9] 5758[6] ◆ 6145[5] 6331[2] ◆ 6987[3] ◆ 7295[6]

Massyaf (IRE) *Mlle A Imaz-Ceca*
3 b c One Cool Cat(USA) —Vanitycase (IRE) (Editor's Note (USA))
660a[11]

Masta Plasta (IRE) *David Nicholls* a97 108
8 b g Mujadil(USA) —Silver Arrow (USA) (Shadeed (USA))
2371[13] *582a[12]* 1518[6] 2117[6] 2714[15] 4894[6]

Masteeat (USA) *Olivia Maylam* a44 43
4 ch m Delaware Township(USA) —White Hot Cat (USA) (Tactical Cat (USA))
283[11] *382[7]*

Master At Arms *Daniel Mark Loughnane* a73 58
8 ch g Grand Lodge(USA) —L'Ideale (USA) (Alysheba (USA))
89[2] *314[5]*

Master Bond *Bryan Smart* 79
2 b g Misu Bond(IRE) —Bond Royale (Piccolo)
1744[7] 5486[2] ◆ 6673[6] (6836) 7294[2]

Master Chipper *Michael Dods*
2 ch g Medicean—Spiralling (Pivotal)
6259[10]

Master Jack *Bill Turner* 50
3 b g Avonbridge—Inch By Inch (Inchinor)
6020[4] 6608[8]
Master Kid (DEN) *Bent Olsen* 94
6 b h Academy Award(IRE) —Stolga (FR) (Baillamont (USA))
4842a[7]
Master Leon *Bryan Smart* a79 65
4 b g Monsieur Bond(IRE) —Bollin Rita (Rambo Dancer (CAN))
(122) 2057[13] 2487[3] 2985[8] 3657[12] (4039) 4441[2] 5403[8] 6979[6] 7339[10] 7589[7] 7887[10]
Master Mylo (IRE) *Dean Ivory* a82 89
4 ch g Bertolini(USA) —Sheboygan (IRE) (Grand Lodge (USA))
1610[8] 2111[4] 2647[15] 2917[3] (3361) (3815) 5718[8] 6173[8]
Master Nimbus *John Quinn* a53 70
11 b g Cloudings(IRE) —Miss Charlie (Pharly (FR))
4366[14] 4903[8] 5650[4]
Master Of Ages (IRE) *Mark Johnston* 81
2 b g Exceed And Excel(AUS) —Historian (IRE) (Pennekamp (USA))
2346[7] 2612[4] 3016[4] (7081)
Master Of Arts (USA) *Mark Johnston* a78 98
6 bb g Swain(IRE) —Grazia (Sharpo)
4774[6] 5185[8] 5557[17] 6163[3] 6335[3] ◆
Master Of Dance (IRE) *Keith Dalgleish* a77 76
4 ch h Noverre(USA) —Shambodia (IRE) (Petardia)
1741[2] 2825 433[2] 489[2] ◆ 625[7] 727[6] 1164[8] 1295[2] 3088[5] 3612[7] 4866[8] 5314[2] (5549) 6211[7] (6452) 6664[4] 6979[3] 7211[2] 7625[9]
Master Of Disguise *Brian Baugh* a81 101
5 b g Kyllachy—St James's Antigua (IRE) (Law Society (USA))
6351[2] (6875) 7116[4] 7253[9] 7846[5] 7926[4]
Master Of Hounds (USA) *A P O'Brien* a115 115
3 b c Kingmambo(USA) —Silk And Scarlet (Sadler's Wells (USA))
998a[2] 1921a[5] 2950a[10]
Master Of Song *Roy Bowring* a68 54
4 ch g Ballet Master(USA) —Ocean Song (Savahra Sound)
2828[3] 3496[2] 3709[2] 5214[3] 6049[9] (6613) 7604[4] 7789[7]
Masterofthérolls (IRE) *A Fabre* a81 103
3 b c Refuse To Bend(IRE) —Miss Sally (IRE) (Danetime (IRE))
980a[4]
Master O'Reilly (NZ) *Judy Mawer* 116
9 bb g O'Reilly(NZ) —Without Remorse (NZ) (Bakharoff (USA))
6711a[15]
Master Rooney (IRE) *Bryan Smart* 94
5 bb g Cape Cross(IRE) —Wimple (USA) (Kingmambo (USA))
2118[8] 2434[9] 3279[7] (3613) 4075[8] 5033[3] 5706[2] 6332[6] 6865[8]
Masters Blazing *John Ryan* a68
2 ch c Iceman—Loquacity (Diktat)
7634[9] 7751[3] 7835[9]
Masters Club *John Ryan* a64 63
2 b g Red Clubs(IRE) —Waaedah (USA) (Halling (USA))
2998[9] 3132[12] 4391[2] 4761[9] 5353[6] 5998[12] (7481) (7568) 7763[6]
Mastership (IRE) *John Quinn* a80 91
7 ch g Best Of The Bests(IRE) —Shady Point (IRE) (Unfuwain (USA))
997 ◆ 285[6] 447[5] 1110[3] 1793[7] 2347[5]
Mataajir (USA) *Derek Shaw* a59 39
3 b g Redoute's Choice(AUS) —Hamasah (USA) (Irish River (FR))
7249[7] 7401[8] (7714) (7899) ◆
Mataaleb *Lydia Pearce* 98
4 b h Dalakhani(IRE) —Elfaslah (IRE) (Green Desert (USA))
2071[16] 5482[10] 5963[5]
Mata Hari Blue *John Holt* a67 76
5 ch m Monsieur Bond(IRE) —Feeling Blue (Missed Flight)
491[8] 571[4] 734[2] (874) 947[2] 1307[4] 3079[3] 3307[6] 3711[9] 4025[2] (4434) 4960[4] 5338[9] 5890[3] (6250) 6779[3]
Mata Keranjang (USA) *Paul Cole* 98
4 bb g More Than Ready(USA) —Love Sick (USA) (Salt Lake (USA))
1092[21] 1594[8]
Matavia Bay (IRE) *Alan Jarvis* a68 65
3 b g Bahamian Bounty—Rosewater (GER) (Winged Love (IRE))
1392[2] 2196[3] 2527[8] 4908[7] 6752[7] 7055[7]
Match Point (FR) *Niels Petersen* 86
5 gr m Verglas(IRE) —Danira (IRE) (Danehill (USA))
5096a[3] 6741a[3]
Materialism *Mark Johnston* a71 77
3 b c Librettist(USA) —Crinolette (IRE) (Sadler's Wells (USA))
(212) 2264[3] 2564[5] 3024[7] (3571)
Mater Mater *Andrew Reid* a64 37
4 gr m Silver Patriarch(IRE) —Emily-Mou (IRE) (Cadeaux Genereux)
5519[10] 6037[7]
Mathurino (FR) *H Billot* a45 25
4 b g Trempolino(USA) —La Mathurine (FR) (Le Glorieux)
91a[10]
Matilda May *Colin Teague*
4 b m Leporello(IRE) —Seems So Easy (USA) (Palmister (USA))
2807[6]
Matilda's Waltz *Ralph Beckett* a58 72
3 ch f Medicean—Australian Dreams (Magic Ring (IRE))
1620[2] 2891[6] 7334[8]
Matjar (IRE) *Joseph Quinn* a72 72
8 ch g Grand Lodge(USA) —Tajawuz (Kris)
3361[11]
Matsunosuke *Ronald Harris* a110 94
9 b g Magic Ring(IRE) —Lon Isa (Grey Desire)
137[2]

Mattamia (IRE) *Rod Millman* 87
5 b g Makbul—Lady Dominatrix (IRE) (Danehill Dancer (IRE))
1680[9]
Matterofact (IRE) *Malcolm Saunders* a49 79
8 b m Bold Fact(USA) —Willow Dale (IRE) (Danehill (USA))
1752[2] 1816[6] 2304[8] 2959[9]
Mattoral *Peter Makin* a74 77
3 b c High Chaparral(IRE) —Angry Bark (USA) (Woodman (USA))
1727[5] 2076[8] 2842[6] 3650[6] 4215[3] 4724[6] 5407[5]
Matula (IRE) *Ralph Beckett* 86
3 ch f Halling(USA) —Quaich (Danehill (USA))
2839[7] 3356[9] 4093[11]
Maundy Money *David Marnane* a98 98
8 b g King's Best(USA) —Royal Gift (Cadeaux Genereux)
1228a[9] 1849[14] 7010a[10] 7189a[18] 7468a[9]
Mauritino (GER) *Jonjo O'Neill* a79 80
7 b g Dashing Blade—Miss Page (Gorytus (USA))
(2051) 2649[2] 4825[8] 6254[4]
Maven *Tim Easterby* a75 55
3 b f Doyen(IRE) —Bollin Jeannie (Royal Applause)
5556[6] 6156[5] 6834[5] 7213[10] (7610) ◆ (7698) (7816)
Maverik *Michael Dods* a81 81
3 ch g Iceman—Nouvelle Lune (Fantastic Light (USA))
(1214) ◆ 2096[2] 2729[5] 3178[6] 3346[9] 4234[4] 5370[3] 6282[7] (6505)
Ma Victoryan (FR) *C Baillet*
2 b f Kheleyf(USA) —Victorian Dancer (IRE) (Groom Dancer (USA))
7814a[4]
Mavi Kumsal (TUR) *A Isgoren* a52
4 b h Bin Ajwaad(IRE) —Mavi Sema (TUR) (Sun Music (IRE))
5754a[7]
Mawaakef (IRE) *J R Jenkins* a88 101
3 b g Azamour(IRE) —Al Euro (FR) (Mujtahid (USA))
1259a[7] 5830[12] 7523[6]
Mawaqeet (USA) *Sir Michael Stoute* 77
2 b g Dynaformer(USA) —Lady Ilsley (USA) (Trempolino (USA))
5891[12] 6828[4] 7134[3] ◆
Mawingo (GER) *J Hirschberger* 112
3 b c Tertullian(USA) —Montfleur (Sadler's Wells (USA))
1739a[3] (2345a) 3672a[4] 7324a[5]
Mawjoodah *Brian Ellison* a76 71
3 ch f Cadeaux Genereux—Isis (USA) (Royal Academy (USA))
1611[5] 2018[5] 2821[3] 3390[5] 4518[5] (4923) 5554[10] 5735[4] 6094[12] 6665[3] 7529[10] 7629[6]
Maxamillion Bounty *Michael Dods* 70
3 ch g Bahamian Bounty—Never Say Deya (Dansili)
1246[11] 1693[2] 2361[3] 3037[2] 3706[8]
Maxi Chop (FR) *A De Watrigant* a76 100
3 b g Muhaymin(USA) —Scotch Mockery (FR) (Persifleur (USA))
5131a[6]
Maxi Moo (IRE) *Ollie Pears* a12 49
4 b g Atraf—Kealbra Lady (Petong)
1911[6] ◆ 2057[6] 3317[7] 4814[5] 5210[6]
Maxios *J E Pease* 104
3 b c Monsun(GER) —Moonlight's Box (USA) (Nureyev (USA))
1265a[5] 1923a[8]
Maxiyow (IRE) *Bryn Palling* 28
3 b f Royal Applause—Fudge (Polar Falcon (USA))
2172[12] 2243[9]
Max My Boy (IRE) *Ollie Pears* 51
4 ch g Refuse To Bend(IRE) —Lucky Fountain (IRE) (Lafontaine (USA))
6781[4]
Mayan Flight (IRE) *Tony Carroll* a53 54
3 b g Hawk Wing(USA) —Balimaya (IRE) (Barathea (IRE))
1969[3] 2239[7] 2801[3] 4077[8] 4403[6] 5064[6] 5738[3] 5898[4] 6701[6] 7836[3]
Maybach *Lars Bexell* a88 87
10 gr h Machiavellian(USA) —Capote Line (USA) (Capote (USA))
5981a[6]
Maybe (IRE) *A P O'Brien* 114
2 b f Galileo(IRE) —Sumora (IRE) (Danehill (USA))
(3152) ◆ (4031a) (4833a) (5525a) ◆
Maybeagrey *Tim Easterby* a71 58
2 b f Shamardal(USA) —Grey Again (Unfuwain (USA))
6702[9] 6985[5] 7210[3] (7569) (7697)
Maybe I Wont *Lucinda Featherstone* a43 74
6 b g Kyllachy—Surprise Surprise (Robellino (USA))
2459[10] 2708[5] 3533[9] (4889) 5545[7] 5808[5] 6669[9] 6918[13]
Maybeme *Neville Bycroft* a39 67
5 b m Lujain(USA) —Malvadilla (IRE) (Doyoun)
11[7] 4125[4] 4903[2] (5504) 6029[7] 6235[3] 6676[10] 6838[8]
May Be Some Time *Stuart Kittow* a42 73
3 ch g Iceman—Let Alone (Warning)
2064[3] ◆ (2586) 2835[7] 3466[7] 5242[10] 5942[10] 6468[3] (7137)
May Burnett (IRE) *Brian Rothwell* 50
3 b f Oratorio(IRE) —Ghost Tree (IRE) (Caerleon (USA))
1096[13] 1495[10] 2350[6] 3615[4] 3976[6] 4005[8] 4284[6] 4515[6] 5589[6]
May Contain Nuts *Brendan Powell* a68 80
3 b g Auction House(USA) —Sweet Coincidence (Mujahid (USA))
1139[8] 1271[9] 1484[8] 2152[2] 2857[2] 3989[2] (4974) 5599[7] (6095) 6707[12] 7120[8]
Mayday (FR) *F Rossi* a74 48
3 b c Xaar—Miss Maybach (FR) (Monsun (GER))
370a[5]

Maydream *Jimmy Fox* a61 64
4 b m Sea Freedom—Maedance (Groom Dancer (USA))
466[6] 768[P] 819[3] (1181) ◆ 3047[5] 3516[4] (5612) (5916) 6476[3]
Mayfair Lad *A Al Raihe* a86 84
3 ch c Bertolini(USA) —Flower Market (Cadeaux Genereux)
411a[6] 502a[8]
Mayfair's Future *J R Jenkins* a57 57
6 b g High Estate—Riva La Belle (Ron's Victory (USA))
355[2] 466[12] 1635[6] 1993[5]
Mayo Lad (IRE) *Richard Hannon* 64
2 b c Holy Roman Emperor(IRE) —Mrs Marsh (Marju (IRE))
5447[8] 5855[7] 6463[10]
Mayoman (IRE) *Declan Carroll* a64 88
6 b g Namid—America Lontana (FR) (King's Theatre (IRE))
2397[5] ◆ 2890[16] 3832[4] 4126[3] 4792[5] 5108[5] (5679) 5918[6] 6112[4]
May's Boy *Mark Usher* a83 79
3 gr c Proclamation(IRE) —Sweet Portia (IRE) (Pennekamp (USA))
140[7] (275) (423) 1106[2] 1335[4] 2147[6] (2646) 2926[9] 3649[7] 5201[9] 6003[9] 6457[14]
Mayson *Richard Fahey* a100 105
3 b c Invincible Spirit(IRE) —Mayleaf (Pivotal)
5060[3] ◆ 6147[21] 6522[3] ◆ 7012a[4] 7298[2]
Maywood *Mahmood Al Zarooni* a77 100
3 b c Cape Cross(IRE) —Murrieta (Docksider (USA))
(2506) ◆
Maz *Alan Bailey* a51 68
3 ch f Needwood Blade—Lady Mytton (Lake Coniston (IRE))
4728[6] 4925[3] 5317[7] 6116[4] 6831[2] 6971[6] 7112[6] 7816[9]
Mazagee (FR) *David Lanigan* a90 89
3 b f Muhtathir—Zafonia (FR) (Zafonic (USA))
4752[3] 5389[5] (6121) 6306[2] 6749[2] 6988[6]
Mazamorra (USA) *Marco Botti* a87 82
4 bb m Orientate(USA) —Mumbo Jumbo (USA) (Kingmambo (USA))
2269[7] 2822[6] 3757[3] 4066[8] 5608[4] 6949[6] 7362[3] 7465[5] (7637) 7922[4]
Maze (IRE) *Tony Carroll* a83 91
6 ch g Dr Fong(USA) —Aryadne (Rainbow Quest (USA))
206[11] 556[2] (1178) 1488[2] 1937[3] 2597[6] 3000[5] (3427) 4416[12] 5262[6] (5914) 6467[2] 6762[9] 6920[8]
Mazeydd *Roger Varian* 81
2 b c Motivator—Jathaabeh (Nashwan (USA))
5454[8] (6334) ◆
Mazij *Peter Hiatt* a25 58
3 b f Haafhd—Salim Toto (Mtoto)
4826[4] 5598[6] 6122[10] (6936) 7241[3] (7496) (7556) (7772)
Mazovian (USA) *Michael Chapman* a68 71
3 b g E Dubai(USA) —Polish Style (USA) (Danzig (USA))
513[2] 669[3] (741) 940[3] 1219[2] 1674[3] 1745[8] 2180[9] 2592[3] 2916[2] 3230[11] 3731[5] 4062[6] (4199) 4518[6] 4819[5] 6456[10] 7057[9] 7504[8] 7646[8] 7857[5] 7887[3]
Mazzore (IRE) *M Gasparini*
3 b c Diamond Green(FR) —Viola D'Amore (IRE) (Celtic Swing)
1126a[2]
Mcbirney (USA) *Paul D'Arcy* a76 88
4 b g Danehill Dancer(IRE) —Dear Girl (IRE) (Fairy King (USA))
295[4] 454[9] 636[3] (1372) ◆ (2213) 2544[3] ◆ 3399[5] 4280[2] 5250[7] 5482[11] 6173[6] 6632[6] 6976[10]
McCarren Park (USA) *Dominick A Schettino*
2 ch f Posse(USA) —History (USA) (Coronado's Quest (USA))
6205a[4]
McCartney (GER) *S Seemar* a73 108
6 b g In The Wings—Messina (GER) (Dashing Blade)
152a[9]
Mcconnell (USA) *Gary Moore* a85 70
6 ch g Petionville(USA) —Warsaw Girl (IRE) (Polish Precedent (USA))
(38) 3740[12] 4215[11] 5319[5] 6017[7] 6433[4] 7098[8] (7424) 7710[4]
McCool Bannanas *James Unett* a70
3 b g Firebreak—Dances With Angels (IRE) (Mukaddamah (USA))
916[4] 1053[4] 1277[2] 1974[4] 5740[12] 6181[11] 7198[2] 7400[3] 7538[11] 7788[2] 7931[4]
Mcvicar *Mick Channon* a66 75
2 b c Tobougg(IRE) —Aries (GER) (Big Shuffle (USA))
3590[10] 3816[2] 4073[6] 5144[4] ◆ 5342[3] 5550[2] (5875) 6345[6] 6753[6]
Meandmyshadow *Alan Brown* a21 77
3 ch f Tobougg(IRE) —Queen Jean (Pivotal)
1187[6] (1323) 1802[6] (1967) 2524[4] 2798[13] 3360[6] 3931[3] 4638[3] 4897[2] 5502[7] 5619[3] 6159[2] (6343) (6604) 6869[5] 7073[4]
Meandre (FR) *A Fabre* 123
3 gr c Slickly(FR) —Penne (FR) (Sevres Rose (IRE))
(2341a) (4038a) 5987a[2] 6567a[6]
Meanwhile (IRE) *William Knight* a60 58
2 b f Haafhd—Interim Payment (USA) (Red Ransom (USA))
2787[9] (3718) 4581[5] 5233[5] 6667[4] 6937[4]
Measuring Time *Richard Hannon* 105
3 b c Dubai Destination(USA) —Inchberry (Barathea (IRE))
1339[2] 1548[2] 1895[3] 3405[8] 4411[9] 5544[2] 5934[3]
Mebsuta (IRE) *Kevin Ryan* 58
2 b f Amadeus Wolf—Zinstar (IRE) (Sinndar (IRE))
1414[6] 1791[4] 2983[9]
Mecca's Team *Michael Dods* a29 71
3 ch f Ishiguru(USA) —Clancassie (Clantime)
454[7] 1038[2] 1813[6] 2493[3] (3143) 4124[2] ◆

Mecox Bay (IRE) *Michael Appleby* a63 80
4 b g Noverre(USA) —Birdsong (IRE) (Dolphin Street (FR))
1443[15] 2312[12] 7078[7] 7254[5] 7340[2] 7570[10] 7645[5] 7688[4]
Medaille D'Or *Roger Varian* a74 80
3 ch f With Approval(CAN) —Crockadore (USA) (Nijinsky (CAN))
(260) ◆ 3131[5] 3615[2] (4249) 5303[4] 6241[5]
Medal Of Valour (JPN) *Mark Johnston* a48 72
3 b c Medaglia D'Oro(USA) —Tres Tres Joli (USA) (Gone West (USA))
6324[8] (6578) ◆ 7130[12]
Medam *Shaun Harris* a40 51
2 b f Medicean—Mamounia (IRE) (Green Desert (USA))
2651[3] ◆ 5786[15] 6612[7] 6935[9] 7293[10] 7421[7]
Medea (IRE) *Sir Michael Stoute* a74
2 ch f Danehill Dancer(IRE) —Scoop Of Gold (USA) (Giant's Causeway (USA))
5813[2]
Media Hype *Luca Cumani* a64 76
4 b h Tiger Hill(IRE) —Hyperspectra (Rainbow Quest (USA))
1605[10] 1985[7] 2596[9] (3559)
Media Jury *John Wainwright* 61
4 b g Lucky Owners(NZ) —Landofheartsdesire (IRE) (Up And At 'Em)
2547[5] 2798[4] 3143[8] 3616[3] (3937) 4405[4] 4820[9] 4900[10] 5620[9]
Media Stars *Robert Johnson* a65 64
6 gr g Green Desert(USA) —Starine (FR) (Mendocino (USA))
1615[2] 2057[5] 2462[12] 2734[2] (3139) 3319[11] 3620[5] 4123[12] 4329[4] 4673[5] 5402[3] 5822[13] 6833[9]
Medibah (FR) *S Wattel* a63 51
2 b f After Market(USA) —Al Ribh (USA) (A.P. Indy (USA))
7312a[5]
Medicean Man *Jeremy Gask* a108 113
5 ch g Medicean—Kalindi (Efisio)
848[2] 1111[8] 2075[7] 2954[3] 3410[2] (3846) (4357) 4776[2] 5827[3] 6164[8] 6858[13]
Medicinal Compound *Kevin Ryan* 93
4 b g Dr Fong(USA) —Liska's Dance (USA) (Riverman (USA))
1092[18] 6080[9]
Medici Time *Tim Easterby* 95
6 gr g Medicean—Pendulum (Pursuit Of Love)
1205[2] 1675[10] 2620[4] (2890) (3367) 3846[4] 4346[16] 5706[9] 6224[9] 7018[12]
Medieval Bishop (IRE) *David Elsworth* 77
2 b g Bachelor Duke(USA) —On The Backfoot (IRE) (Bob Back (USA))
2983[4] ◆ 3618[5] 4073[4] (6743)
Mediterranean Sea (IRE) *J R Jenkins* a74 64
5 b m Medecis—High Glider (High Top)
104[2] 323[2] 457[5] 2176[4] 4649[4] 5141[2] 5947[8] 6621[7] (7340) (7647)
Medlaur *James Given* a34
2 ch f Medicean—Laurena (GER) (Acatenango (GER))
7777[8]
Meeriss (IRE) *D Selvaratnam* a103 101
6 b g Dubai Destination(USA) —Bless The Bride (IRE) (Darshaan)
153a[8] (535a) 677a[2]
Meetings Man (IRE) *Micky Hammond* 86
4 gr g Footstepsinthesand—Missella (IRE) (Danehill (USA))
2320[2] ◆ 2932[3] 3344[8] 4360[4] 5149[2] 5724[2]
Meet Joe Black (IRE) *David Evans* a49 36
2 bb g Red Clubs(IRE) —Pascali (Compton Place)
6252[8] 6455[5] 6630[8] 7225[8] 7421[11] 7697[5] 7821[3]
Meeznah (USA) *David Lanigan* 115
4 b m Dynaformer(USA) —String Quartet (IRE) (Sadler's Wells (USA))
2501[3] 4099[2] (4470) 5045[7] (5850) 6859[5] 7300a[P]
Megalala (IRE) *John Bridger* a82 79
10 b g Petardia—Avionne (Derrylin)
2685[6] 2843[2] (3252) 3760[7] 4059[5] (4700) (5198) 5491[3] 5545[3] 5971[7] 7032[7] (7203) 7346[9] 7513[6] (7671) 7908[9]
Mega Watt (IRE) *Dai Burchell* 63
6 b g Acclamation—Kilshanny (Groom Dancer (USA))
3215[5]
Meglio Ancora *Alastair Lidderdale* 79
4 ch g Best Of The Bests(IRE) —May Fox (Zilzal (USA))
1443[3] 2156[6] 2769[9] 3546[8] 3916[4] 4153[6] 4869[13]
Mehdi (IRE) *Brian Meehan* 99
2 b c Holy Roman Emperor(IRE) —College Fund Girl (IRE) (Kahyasi)
2584[3] ◆ 3182[2] 4264[2] (4606) 4858[3] (5479) 5849[10] 6170[3] 6527[3] 7026[7]
Meia Noite *Chris Wall* a67 64
4 b m Tobougg(IRE) —Executive Lady (Night Shift (USA))
2201[4] 2869[8] 3719[2] 4187[6] 6694[3] 7265[8] 7844[2]
Mekong Melody (IRE) *Roger L Attfield* a79 108
6 b m Cape Cross(IRE) —Nini Princesse (IRE) (Niniski (USA))
6909a[9]
Melancholy Hill (IRE) *Alan King* a53 50
3 b f Marju(IRE) —Vyatka (Lion Cavern (USA))
1329[7] 3744[4] 6446[10]
Melanistic *Ian Williams*
4 b m Pastoral Pursuits—Cosmology (USA) (Distant View (USA))
4388[12]
Melbury *Michael Squance* a54
3 b f Diktat—Lovely Lyca (Night Shift (USA))
383[7] 655[3] 1524[8] 1953[8]
Melodie D'Amour (IRE) *M Halford* a74 74
4 b m Hawk Wing(USA) —Darkling (IRE) (Grand Lodge (USA))
7548a[4]
Melodize *David O'Meara* a37 65
3 ch f Iceman—Rhapsodize (Halling (USA))
(1561) 1745[11] 2265[8] 3628[6] 4124[4] (4607)

Melodrama (IRE) *David Lanigan* a44 53
2 b f Oratorio(IRE) —Lila (Zafonic (USA))
4804[11] *6928[10]* 7165[9]

Melody Belle (IRE) *Tobias B P Coles* a27 49
3 gr f Verglas(IRE) —Reside (IRE) (Montjeu (IRE))
4112[12] *5388[7]*

Meloneras *Rod Millman* a66 70
2 b f Kyllachy—Overcome (Belmez (USA))
1360[12] 1827[2] 2580[3] 3092[11] 4155[6] 4462[4] 4702[2] *5833[2] 6252[4]*

Melting Pot *Hugo Palmer* a49 60
2 ch g Camacho—Thaw (Cadeaux Genereux)
2291[9] *3746[11]* 4159[3] 4581[6]

Memorabilia *Mark Johnston* a79 81
3 b g Dansili—Sentimental Value (USA) (Diesis)
(25) (217) (365) 2925[11] 3460[2]

Memory (IRE) *Richard Hannon* 111
3 b f Danehill Dancer(IRE) —Nausicaa (USA) (Diesis)
1719[18] 3106[7] 3822[11] 4497[RR]

Memory Cloth *Brian Ellison* 106
4 b g Cape Cross(IRE) —Gossamer (Sadler's Wells (USA))
6150[9] 6335[10]

Memory Lane *Sir Mark Prescott Bt* a69 83
3 b f With Approval(CAN) —Miss Prism (Niniski (USA))
2293[4] 2857[4] (3734) (3976) 4449[3] 6376[5] 6707[10]

Memphis Man *David Evans* a62 77
8 b g Bertolini(USA) —Something Blue (Petong)
13[7] 111[9] 218[6] 276[2] 363[5] 421[5] 512[6] 664[7] 734[4] 1287[10] (1770) 1912[5] 1989[4] (2222) 2633[6] 2794[7] 3412[3] 3685[7] 3805[10] 4187[7] 4618[3] 5345[6] 5513[2] 5677[5] 5881[2] 6261[9] 6694[4] 7224[3] (7371) 7420[7] 6752[10] 6920[6] 7459[8] 7529[8]

Memphis Tennessee (IRE) *A P O'Brien* a81 119
3 b c Hurricane Run(IRE) —Hit The Sky (IRE) (Cozzene (USA))
1927a[2] 2715[4] 3442a[3]

Menadati (USA) *Peter Hiatt* a68 78
3 b g More Than Ready(USA) —Ramatuelle (CHI) (Jeune Homme (USA))
2582[9] 6435[4] ◆ 6727[10] ◆ 7137[6] *7334[6]*

Mendip (USA) *Saeed Bin Suroor* a117 112
4 bb h Harlan's Holiday(USA) —Well Spring (USA) (Coronado's Quest (USA))
(156a) (756a) 1000a[6]

Men Don't Cry (IRE) *Ed Dunlop* a57 29
2 b g Street Cry(IRE) —Naissance Royale (IRE) (Giant's Causeway (USA))
5013[13] *5384[8]* 5801[13]

Menelas *J Rossi* a70 80
4 b h Refuse To Bend(IRE) —Blanche (FR) (Loup Solitaire (USA))
830a[6]

Menelik (IRE) *Tom Dascombe* 66
2 b g Oasis Dream—Chica Roca (USA) (Woodman (USA))
3823[9] 4414[8] 6983[13] ◆

Menestrol (FR) *D Prod'Homme* a76 93
9 ch h Dyhim Diamond(IRE) —Magaletta (FR) (Galetto (FR))
5095a[0]

Meneur (FR) *Gary Moore* a48 71
9 gr g Septieme Ciel(USA) —Mamamia (FR) (Linamix (FR))
560[12]

Menha *John Gallagher* a58 69
3 ch f Dubawi(IRE) —Tessara (GER) (Big Shuffle (USA))
7063[9] *7249[4] 7484[7]*

Meniska (FR) *C Laffon-Parias* 78
2 b f Invincible Spirit(IRE) —Royal Liverpool (USA) (Gulch (USA))
(7238a)

Mention (IRE) *Brian Meehan* 76
2 b f Acclamation—Somaggia (IRE) (Desert King (IRE))
2718[4] (3257) 4094[13] 4551[5] 5052[6] 7028[11]

Meora (FR) *P Demercastel* a65 64
5 b m Choisir(AUS) —Dubai Victory (IRE) (Victory Note (USA))
93a[9]

Merals Choice *Jim Boyle* a54
4 b m Night Shift(USA) —Mena (Blakeney)
225[9] 432[6] 552[13]

Mercers Row *Noel Wilson* 66
4 b g Bahamian Bounty—Invincible (Slip Anchor)
5373[6] *7897[5]*

Merchant Of Dubai *Jim Goldie* a103 105
6 b g Dubai Destination(USA) —Chameleon (Green Desert (USA))
2044[5] 2573[13] 3876[9] 5705[8] 6163[17] 7297[3]

Merchant Of Medici *William Muir* a91 84
4 b g Medicean—Regal Rose (Danehill (USA))
1061[9] 1406[10] *(1760)* 2310[4] 2679[10] *3045[4] 3521[3]* 3825[10] 4765[4] 5012[8] *5712[14] 6219[9] 6658[3]*

Merito *Kevin Ryan* 62
3 b g Exceed And Excel(AUS) —First Approval (Royal Applause)
2802[11] 3575[7] 3977[5] 5649[4] 6940[14]

Merlot (SWE) *Henrik Engblom*
2 b f Mandrake El Mago(CHI) —Adventurous Girl (Danzero (AUS))
5983a[13]

Merrion Tiger (IRE) *George Foster* a59 14
6 ch g Choisir(AUS) —Akita (IRE) (Foxhound (USA))
2696[10] *3712[5]* 4173[11] *5209[3]*

Merrjanah *John Wainwright* a60 65
3 b f Diktat—Aberdovey (Mister Baileys)
1060[5] 1766[5] 2266[3] 3180[6] *3470[5]* 7057[11] *7507[11] 7610[6] 7817[3] 7902[2]*

Merrymadcap (IRE) *Matthew Salaman* a79 74
9 b g Lujain(USA) —Carina Clare (Slip Anchor)
26[11]

Merton Lady *John Flint* a68 38
3 b f Beat Hollow—Tesary (Danehill (USA))
(1999) 2849[8] *3715[4] 4209[5] 5389[13] 7034[P]*

Merv (IRE) *Henry Candy* 59
2 b g Royal Applause—Shauna's Honey (IRE) (Danehill (USA))
2767[11] 3424[7] 4954[5] 6455[6] (Dead)

Mesariya (IRE) *John M Oxx* 94
3 ch f Sinndar(IRE) —Masakala (IRE) (Cadeaux Genereux)
2012a[6] 2968a[7]

Meshfi *Clive Brittain* 51
3 b g Tiger Hill(IRE) —Aegean Sea (USA) (Gulch (USA))
3824[8] 4370[10] 4805[8] 5519[9]

Metal Dealer (IRE) *George Foster* 40
2 b g Amadeus Wolf—Trebbia (IRE) (Soviet Star (USA))
1876[6] 2120[7] 2570[8] *3708[8]*

Metalmark (IRE) *Mahmood Al Zarooni* 46
2 b c Dansili—Butterfly Blue (IRE) (Sadler's Wells (USA))
4762[10]

Methaaly (IRE) *Michael Mullineaux* a85 76
8 b g Red Ransom(USA) —Santorini (USA) (Spinning World (USA))
87[2] 168[4] 316[6] 651[7] 736[9] 1382[7] *1584[7]* 2095[17] 2280[3] 2610[3] *6665[10] 7173[5]* 7265[3] 7416[7] 7519[4] 7595[10]

Methaen (USA) *Ed Dunlop* a54 60
2 ch c Smart Strike(CAN) —Ekleel (IRE) (Danehill (USA))
3755[12] *4798[7]* 5564[9] *6443[9] 6846[6]*

Methayel (IRE) *Clive Brittain* a69 76
3 br f Araafa(IRE) —First Breeze (USA) (Woodman (USA))
2568[5] 3218[6] 4199[7] 6604[5] (6813) (6971) *7334[4]*

Metropolitan Miss (IRE) *Mick Channon* a75 92
3 b f Bertolini(USA) —City Maiden (USA) (Carson City (USA))
(1146) 1599[2] 1837[3] 2189[7] 5730[9] 6062[3] ◆ (6383) 6770[5]

Metropolitan Chief *Paul Burgoyne* a58 52
7 b g Compton Place—Miss Up N Go (Gorytus (USA))
138[4] (250) 363[2] 485[13] 696[5] 734[8] 912[8] 1248[5] 1453[2] 1787[3] ◆ 7459[4]

Mexican Jay (USA) *Bryan Smart* a67 43
5 b m Elusive Quality(USA) —Mistle Song (Nashwan (USA))
373[9] 644[4] 797[7]

Mexican Wave *Michael Bell* a9 25
2 b c Rock Of Gibraltar(IRE) —La Belga (ARG) (Roy (USA))
4201[14] 4525[9] *5861[10]*

Mey Blossom *Richard Whitaker* a68 85
6 ch m Captain Rio—Petra Nova (First Trump)
1698[12] 2122[6] 2832[7] 3579[9] 5108[11] 6094[9] 6276[10] 6537[9] 7106[6] *7172[2] 7265[5]*

Meydan Style (USA) *Bruce Hellier* a56 36
5 b g Essence Of Dubai(USA) —Polish Ruby (USA) (Polish Pro (USA))
115[10] 229[3] 340[3] 575[9] 793[2] 933[2] 1498[2] 1818[4] 1979[6] 2809[8] (3234) 3720[12] 4604[12] 5901[9] 6138[7] 6494[8] 7006[6] 7463[6] 7695[8]

Mezmaar *Charles Hills* 92
2 b c Teofilo(IRE) —Bay Tree (IRE) (Daylami (IRE))
(2455) 3012[10] (6221)

Mezyaad (USA) *Roger Varian* 82
3 b g Tiger Hill(IRE) —Zayn Zen (Singspiel (IRE))
(1399) 1903[2] 6328[6]

Mezzotint (IRE) *Marco Botti* a85 79
2 b c Diamond Green(FR) —Aquatint (Dansili)
6935[2] *(7593) (7765)*

Miabeach (FR) *C Boutin* 77
2 gr f Dr Fong(USA) —Mamamia (FR) (Linamix (FR))
4569a[8]

Miakora *Michael Quinn* a46 46
3 ch f Compton Place—Hickleton Lady (IRE) (Kala Shikari)
1020[5] 1591[4] 5176[5] 5780[4] *6251[4]* 6765[6] 7086[13] *7389[5] 7511[6] 7652[7]*

Mia Madonna *Brian Meehan* a66 71
3 b f Motivator—Musique Magique (IRE) (Mozart (IRE))
1915[3] 2253[7] 3907[5] *5630[6]* 5915[6]

Miami Deco (CAN) *Brian A Lynch* 101
4 bb h Limehouse(USA) —Miami Dreams (USA) (Secret Hello (USA))
6910a[15]

Miami Gator (IRE) *Mrs K Burke* a85 89
4 ch g Titus Livius(FR) —Lovere (St Jovite (USA))
226[3] ◆ *405[4] 831a[5]* 1033a[7] 2545[4] (3276) 3877[8] (4445) 6150[11]

Mia's Boy *Chris Dwyer* a106 111
7 b g Pivotal—Bint Zamayem (IRE) (Rainbow Quest (USA))
3548[2] 5032[11] 5563[6] 5929[7] 6341[2] 6862[7] (7023) *7393[4] (7719)*

Miblish *Clive Brittain* 79
2 b c Teofilo(IRE) —Triton Dance (IRE) (Hector Protector (USA))
(6165) 6527[12]

Mica Mika (IRE) *Richard Fahey* 90
3 ch g Needwood Blade—Happy Talk (IRE) (Hamas (IRE))
1304[2] 2008[2] 2287[2] 2726[2] 3069[12] 3774[11] 4473[6] 6155[7]

Michael's Nook *David Barron* a65 64
4 b g Intikhab(USA) —Mysterious Plans (IRE) (Last Tycoon)
2922[8] 4337[8] (6610) *(6847) 7268[2] 7462[2] 7728[5]*

Michelle (IRE) *Paddy Butler* a48 24
5 b m Marju(IRE) —Bel Sole (ITY) (Spectrum (IRE))
3253[13] 3678[6]

Michevious Spirit (IRE) *David Thompson* 36
4 gr m Dalakhani(IRE) —Roseanna (FR) (Anabaa (USA))
1305[11] 1519[10]

Mick Bora (FR) *Mme E Siavy-Julien*
4 b m Voix Du Nord(FR) —Mick Monika (FR) (Cyborg (FR))
842a[0]

Mickdaam (IRE) *Richard Fahey* 85
2 b c Dubawi(IRE) —Ribot's Guest (IRE) (Be My Guest (USA))
3823[3] ◆ 4535[11] (6702)

Mick's Dancer *Richard Phillips* a71 50
6 b g Pivotal—La Piaf (FR) (Fabulous Dancer (USA))
3434[8] 4158[11] *5318[6]* ◆ *6005[8] 6873[2]*

Mick Slates (IRE) *Declan Carroll* a52 45
2 b g Moss Vale(IRE) —Sonic Night (IRE) (Night Shift (USA))
1165[10] 2983[8] 3611[7] 5367[12] 6806[7] *(7242)*

Micky Mac (IRE) *Colin Teague* a64 69
7 b g Lend A Hand—Gazette It Tonight (Merdon Melody)
1899[6] 2464[10] 3027[10] 3901[7] 4443[8] 6261[12]

Micky P *Stuart Williams* a72 68
4 gr g Dr Fong(USA) —Carmela Owen (Owington)
2179[5] ◆ *3045[9]* 3536[9] *4206[7]* 5803[5] *(6257)*

Micky's Bird *Richard Guest* a24 48
4 ch m Needwood Blade—Silver Peak (FR) (Sillery (USA))
4180[9]

Micqus (IRE) *Andrew Balding* 33
2 b g High Chaparral(IRE) —My Potters (USA) (Irish River (FR))
6994[12] 7233[14]

Microlight *John E Long* a58 50
3 b g Sleeping Indian—Skytrial (USA) (Sky Classic (CAN))
760[11] 987[7] 1178[6] 2384[11] 3227[7] 4162[7] 4657[5] 4930[7] (5670) *7442[5] (7760)*

Midas Medusa (FR) *Richard Hannon* 70
2 b f Elusive City(USA) —Bonne Mere (FR) (Stepneyev (IRE))
2063[4] 2580[2] 3270[2] 3865[12] 5184[13] 6222[9]

Midas Moment *William Muir* a77 76
3 b f Danehill Dancer(IRE) —Special Moment (IRE) (Sadler's Wells (USA))
1659[2] 4931[4] *5391[6] (6181)* 6583[12]

Midas Touch (TUR) *S Tasbek* 93
4 b h Unaccounted For(USA) —Flicker Of Hope (IRE) (Baillamont (USA))
5777a[5]

Midday *Sir Henry Cecil* 124
5 b m Oasis Dream—Midsummer (Kingmambo (USA))
(2029) 2680[2] 3417a[2] (4533) 5183[2] 6861[4] 7305a[6]

Middlemarch (IRE) *Jim Goldie* a64 65
11 ch g Grand Lodge(USA) —Blanche Dubois (Nashwan (USA))
4605[14] 5207[6]

Middleton Flyer (IRE) *David Evans* 74
2 ch f Titus Livius(FR) —Autumn Star (IRE) (Mujadil (USA))
1136[9] 1268[5] 1434[3] (1786) 2154[5] 3375[3] 3700[7] 3810[7] 4572[2] 5270[7] 5324[3] 5840[2] 6222[3] 6323[7] 6827[7] 7261[6]

Midget *Declan Carroll* a34 61
4 b m Invincible Spirit(IRE) —Sharp Mode (USA) (Diesis)
1716[9] 3027[17]

Mid Mon Lady (IRE) *H Rogers* a98 99
6 br m Danetime(IRE) —Shining Desert (IRE) (Green Desert (USA))
924a[8] 1781a[3] 2012a[3] 2332a[4] 3371a[3] 4418a[4] 5976a[11] *6514a[4] 7618a[9]*

Midnight Bahia (IRE) *Dean Ivory* 27
2 b f Refuse To Bend(IRE) —Midnight Partner (IRE) (Marju (IRE))
2882[9] *3282[11]*

Midnight Caller *John Gosden* 89
3 br f Dansili—Midnight Air (USA) (Green Dancer (USA))
1807[9] 6172[7]

Midnight Diva *Christopher Kellett*
2 ch f Deportivo—Star Cast (IRE) (In The Wings)
6352[8] 7174[8]

Midnight Dynamo *Jim Goldie* 77
4 b m Lujain(USA) —Miss Hermione (Bahamian Bounty)
(2498) 3036[5] 3856[4] 4013[8] (4504) 4541[6] 5148[8] 5720[7] 6076[7]

Midnight Feast *Peter Winkworth* a86 82
3 b g Ishiguru(USA) —Prince's Feather (IRE) (Cadeaux Genereux)
2924[3] (3465) 4156[6] 4797[2] 5171[5] *6478[8]*

Midnight Interlude (USA) *Bob Baffert* a116 112
3 b c War Chant(USA) —Midnight Kiss (NZ) (Groom Dancer (USA))
1921a[16] 2328a[13]

Midnight Martini (AUS) *Mark Kavanagh* 107
4 b f Street Cry(IRE) —Benvenuta (NZ) (Zabeel (NZ))
6711a[4]

Midnight Martini *Tim Easterby* 98
4 b m Night Shift(USA) —Shaken And Stirred (Cadeaux Genereux)
1166[8] 2075[5] 2298[6] 4346[19] 4609[3] 5180[10] 5758[10]

Midnight Moon *Saeed Bin Suroor* 73
3 b g Singspiel(IRE) —Carisolo (Dubai Millennium)
4279[4] 4956[3]

Midnight Oil *Luca Cumani* 101
3 b g Motivator—One So Marvellous (Nashwan (USA))
2258[9] 2648[5] ◆ (3080) 4108[9] (5057) 5482[6] ◆ 5932[2] 6497[5]

Midnight Rider (IRE) *Chris Wall* a70 79
3 b g Red Ransom(USA) —Foreplay (IRE) (Lujain (USA))
593[2] 818[4] 3785[3] (4731) 6036[4] *6442[6]*

Midnight Sequel *Michael Blake* 25
2 b f Midnight Legend—Silver Sequel (Silver Patriarch (IRE))
5375[9] *7751[14]*

Midnight Show (IRE) *G M Lyons* 43
3 b g Refuse To Bend(IRE) —Sheboygan (IRE) (Grand Lodge (USA))
1704a[8]

Midnight Strider (IRE) *Joseph Tuite* a69 16
5 br g Golan(IRE) —Danish Gem (Danehill (USA))
(112) 170[4] 814[6] 876[2] 968[4] 1250[4] 6355[9]

Midnight Tiger *George Prodromou* 13
3 b g Advise(FR) —Midnight Pebbles (Pebble Powder)
5408[4] 6067[8]

Midnight Trader (IRE) *David Flood* a66 65
3 b g Iffraaj—Nilassiba (Daylami (IRE))
611[2] ◆ *892[4] 1176[4] 1869[6]* 3093[4] 3312[5] 3979[5] ◆ 4249[6] 4730[5] *6179[7] 7388[9]*

Midnight Tryst *Ann Duffield* 55
2 ch f Cockney Rebel(IRE) —Shaken And Stirred (Cadeaux Genereux)
6912[3]

Midnight Waltz *Sir Mark Prescott Bt* a69
3 b f Rainbow Quest(USA) —Silver Rhapsody (USA) (Silver Hawk (USA))
5317[8] 5607[2] ◆ *6286[5] 7244[3] 7503[8]*

Midnite Motivation *Derek Shaw*
2 b f Motivator—Tamise (USA) (Time For A Change (USA))
7673[6]

Midsummer Fair (USA) *Mahmood Al Zarooni* 92
3 b c Medaglia D'Oro(USA) —Vanity Flair (CAN) (Affirmed (USA))
(1338) 2139a[14] 2707[4] 4718[6] 5730[13]

Midsummer Sun *Sir Henry Cecil* 100
3 b c Monsun(GER) —Midsummer (Kingmambo (USA))
1321[5] (2218) 3068[13] (5880) 6803[11]

Miereveldt *Shaun Harris* a60 53
4 b g Red Ransom(USA) —Mythic (Zafonic (USA))
16[4] 5210[2] 5485[6] *5599[4]* 6451[10] 6775[11] *7743[3] 7859[11] 7920[5]*

Mighty Ambition (USA) *Mahmood Al Zarooni* 81
2 b c Street Cry(IRE) —New Morning (IRE) (Sadler's Wells (USA))
(6160) ◆

Mighty Aphrodite *Olivia Maylam* a56 63
4 b m Observatory(USA) —Sahara Rose (Green Desert (USA))
466[10] 652[10]

Mighty Clarets (IRE) *Richard Fahey* a80 71
4 br g Whipper(USA) —Collected (IRE) (Taufan (USA))
94[2] (235) 436[6] 723[3] 5106[14] 6028[5] 6225[2] 6916[11] *7465[3] 7557[2] 7887[4]*

Mighty High (FR) *J Moore* 122
5 b g Peintre Celebre(USA) —Bernimixa (FR) (Linamix (FR))
1742a[3] 6713a[4] 6886a[17] 7729a[8]

Mighty Mambo *George Margarson* a73 74
4 b g Fantastic Light(USA) —Mambo's Melody (Kingmambo (USA))
2526[9] 3311[4] *4177[2] 4649[3]* 4700[2] 6775[2]

Mighty Motive *John Mackie* a62
2 ch c Motivator—Mitraillette (USA) (Miswaki (USA))
7783[3]

Mighty Mouse (GER) *P Vovcenko* 101
3 b g King's Best(USA) —Megaperls (GER) (Zinaad)
7313a[3]

Mighty Whitey (IRE) *Noel C Kelly* a56 62
5 b g Sesaro(USA) —Deeco Valley (IRE) (Satco (FR))
6211[3] 6417[4] 7105[6] *7340[4] 7357[8]*

Mijhaar *Roger Varian* 111
3 b c Shirocco(GER) —Jathaabeh (Nashwan (USA))
(2258) ◆ 3105[4] ◆ 3774[2] ◆

Mikeys Sister *Tony Carroll* a18
6 b m Dancing Maestro(USA) —Debbie's Darling (Baron Blakeney)
6504[9] 7036[10]

Mikhail Glinka (IRE) *H J Brown* a100 112
4 b h Galileo(IRE) —Lady Karr (Mark Of Esteem (IRE))
154a[5] 413a[5] 603a[2] 826a[4] 6061[4] 6910a[14]

Mikos (FR) *Robert Collet* 66
11 b g Sicyos(USA) —Sex Pistol (FR) (Pistolet Bleu (IRE))
481a[2] 935a[8]

Milago (GER) *W Kujath* 101
4 b h Monsun(GER) —Montserrat (GER) (Zilzal (USA))
7406a[7]

Mildoura (FR) *Laura Mongan* a93 93
6 b m Sendawar(IRE) —Miliana (IRE) (Polar Falcon (USA))
2958[3] 3428[2]

Miles Gloriosus (USA) *R Menichetti* a108 108
8 b h Repriced(USA) —Treasure Coast (CAN) (Foolish Pleasure (USA))
2541a[P]

Miles Of Sunshine *Ron Hodges* a57 58
6 b g Thowra(FR) —Rainbow Nation (Rainbow Quest (USA))
688[6] 762[6] 992[8] 1181[5] 1473[3] 1586[7] 2140[2] 2377[5] 2659[4] 2873[4] *3923[9]* 4274[6]

Military Bowl (USA) *F Rohaut* a86 109
3 b c Mr Greeley(USA) —Turtle Bow (FR) (Turtle Island (IRE))
(7404a)

Military Call *Alistair Whillans* a36 66
4 b g Royal Applause—Trump Street (First Trump)
2260[9] 2692[8] 3112[4] (4383) 4783[5] 5721[2] 6538[5] *6872[9]* 7099[3]

Milk Maid (IRE) *Bill Turner* a9 40
3 b f Millkom—La Fija (USA) (Dixieland Band (USA))
787[6] 2305[8]

Millden *Milton Bradley* a51 67
4 b g Compton Place—Pretty Poppy (Song)
1912[9] 2142[12] 2921[16] *3241[8]* 3942[11]

Millennium Star (IRE) *Sir Henry Cecil* a55 60
3 gr f High Chaparral(IRE) —Diamonaka (FR) (Akarad (FR))
4611[6] *5816[4]* 6804[10]

Millers Crossing *Michael Squance* 61
5 b g Tobougg(IRE) —Tweed Mill (Selkirk (USA))
4177^{13} 4928^{9}

Millers Dhustone *Pam Ford* 14
5 ch m Sly—Whistler's Gem (Blow The Whistle)
4706^{9} 5607^{10} 5900^{10}

Mille Secrets (FR) *A Bonin*
2 b f Lost World(IRE) —Ma Priorite (GER) (Great Lakes)
7666a^{0}

Millet (FR) *G Botti* 92
3 ch c Panis(USA) —Magnific Fitz (ARG) (Fitzcarraldo (ARG))
4896a^{2}

Millibar (IRE) *Nick Littmoden* a70 83
2 b f Manduro(GER) —Iktidar (Green Desert (USA))
2467^{12} 2880^{7} 3092^{6} 6284^{3} 6742^{3} 7028^{9} 7464^{4} 7593^{5} 7889^{4}

Millies Folly *Paul Midgley* 68
3 ch f Araafa(IRE) —Basemah (FR) (Lemon Drop Kid (USA))
1749^{5} 2252^{5}

Million Faces *Rae Guest* 65
2 ch f Exceed And Excel(AUS) —Millyant (Primo Dominie)
5889^{8} ◆ 6406^{3}

Mill Mick *John Mackie* a64 71
4 b g Karinga Bay—Step On Degas (Superpower)
2257^{5} 2621^{4} 3377^{4} 4083^{5} 5376^{10} 6028^{2} 6669^{5} 7004^{4} 7200^{7}

Millyluvstobougie *Clive Cox* a81 80
3 b f Tobougg(IRE) —Milly's Lass (Mind Games)
1452^{3} 2074^{9} 2505^{8} 2881^{5} 3283^{2} (3630) 4387^{4} 5000^{5} 5476^{5} 6442^{4} (7039)

Millymonkin *Michael Easterby* 63
2 b f Gentleman's Deal(IRE) —Royal Distant (USA) (Distant View (USA))
6776^{5} 6985^{3}

Milnagavie *Richard Hannon* a92 86
4 ch m Tobougg(IRE) —Abyaan (IRE) (Ela-Mana-Mou)
(1935) 2224^{4} 2958^{9} (4660) 7136^{5} 7347^{7}

Milton Hill *Dominic Ffrench Davis* 53
4 ch g Compton Admiral—Stay With Me Baby (Nicholas Bill)
2231^{11} 3080^{11} 3743^{4} 4703^{4} 6600^{P}

Milton Of Campsie *Richard Guest* a57 78
6 ch m Medicean—La Caprice (USA) (Housebuster (USA))
2590^{8} 3759^{6} 4942^{7} 6213^{7} 6604^{9} 6764^{14} 6847^{8} 7216^{19}

Milwr *Chris Dwyer* a44 31
2 b g Rail Link—Pilcomayo (IRE) (Rahy (USA))
2017^{7} 3472^{6} 3816^{13} 5343^{5} 5634^{8} 6001^{6} 6471^{7} 6763^{6} 6942^{7}

Milyas (FR) *C Laffon-Parias* 85
2 ch g Muhtathir—Miss Clem's (FR) (Barathea (IRE))
7449a^{9}

Miming *Hughie Morrison* a15
3 b f Royal Applause—A Thousand Smiles (IRE) (Sadler's Wells (USA))
1020^{7} 1465^{7} 2419^{7}

Minal *Richard Hannon* a44 96
2 ch c Compton Place—Night Kiss (FR) (Night Shift (USA))
1757^{5} 2559^{2} ◆ 3288^{2} 3429^{3} (4087) 4424^{6}

Minaret (IRE) *Mahmood Al Zarooni* 55
3 b f Cape Cross(IRE) —Dubai Opera (USA) (Dubai Millennium)
3119^{3}

Mina's Boy *Ed Dunlop* a50 69
3 bb g Sinndar(IRE) —Kozmina (IRE) (Sadler's Wells (USA))
1311^{8} 1572^{6} 1950^{12} 2613^{5} (4151) ◆ (4732) (5566) 6451^{6}

Minaudiere (IRE) *Remy Nerbonne*
2 b f Whipper(USA) —Be My Lover (Pursuit Of Love)
7666a^{0}

Mince *Roger Charlton* 89
2 ch f Medicean—Strut (Danehill Dancer (IRE))
4580^{8} (6123) ◆ (6573) ◆ 6827^{2} ◆

Minder *Jonathan Portman* a55 63
5 b g Mind Games—Exotic Forest (Dominion)
524^{2} 769^{4} 1310^{3} 1631^{5} 5916^{6}

Mind The Monarch *Roger Teal* a56 58
4 b m Mind Games—Enford Princess (Pivotal)
98^{9} 276^{9} 357^{6}

Minerva (FR) *Mme M Bollack-Badel* a63 75
3 b f Muhtathir—Karlinight (IRE) (Night Shift (USA))
981a^{0}

Minety Lass *Adrian Chamberlain* 84
3 br f Needwood Blade—Mary Jane (Tina's Pet)
3320^{3} 3783^{4} (4828) 5587^{6} (6403)

Ming Meng (IRE) *Michael Bell* 84
4 gr m Intikhab(USA) —Petula (Petong)
1109^{5} 2855^{3}

Mingun Bell (USA) *Ed de Giles* a92 86
4 b g Mingun(USA) —Miss Tippins (USA) (Squadron Leader (USA))
1621^{3} 2301^{5} 2771^{8} 4066^{2} 5083^{3} 5425^{2} (6239) 7171^{15}

Mini Bon Bon *David O'Meara* a58 60
3 ch f Kyllachy—Dahshah (Mujtahid (USA))
41^{7} (146) 338^{2} 788^{4} 2365^{8} 3360^{7} 4527^{6} 4942^{8}

Minidress *Mahmood Al Zarooni* 95
2 br f Street Cry(IRE) —Short Skirt (Diktat)
(4804) ◆ 6296^{4}

Mini's Destination *John Holt* a52 69
3 b f Dubai Destination(USA) —Heather Mix (Linamix (FR))
398^{4} 456^{6} 600^{4} 751^{5} 1288^{4} 1557^{2} 1933^{3} (2351) 2792^{3} (2964) 3457^{2} 4060^{10} 4949^{4} 5231^{3} 6748^{9}

Ministry *John Best* a71 56
3 b c Iceman—Choirgirl (Unfuwain (USA))
1997^{4} 2637^{11} 3518^{3} 4317^{7} 5141^{4} 5321^{6} (6087) 6356^{2}

Minkie Moon (IRE) *Amanda Perrett* 57
3 b g Danehill Dancer(IRE) —Minkova (IRE) (Sadler's Wells (USA))
1840^{7} 2203^{4} 2458^{12} 3268^{9}

Minne Wa Wa *David Brown* 51
2 b f Bahamian Bounty—Crimson Dancer (Groom Dancer (USA))
2811^{9} 4365^{6} 6458^{14}

Minnie Diva (IRE) *Kevin Ryan* a50 70
2 b f Multiplex—Looker (Barathea (IRE))
6329^{4} 7777^{5}

Minnie Mambo (USA) *Michael Bell* 44
3 ch f Kingmambo(USA) —Winds Of March (IRE) (Sadler's Wells (USA))
4279^{11} 6349^{8}

Minortransgression (USA) *Paul Rich* a74 59
4 ch g Yes It's True(USA) —Casting Pearls (USA) (Fusaichi Pegasus (USA))
63^{4} 320^{6} 3253^{11} 4089^{8} 4210^{11} 4651^{4} 5248^{7} 5832^{4} 6236^{8} (7247) (7507) (7711) 7887^{2}

Minsky Mine (IRE) *Michael Appleby* a76 76
4 b g Montjeu(IRE) —Summer Trysting (USA) (Alleged (USA))
284^{3} 539^{5} 4077^{4} 4818^{6} (5518) 5808^{2} 6401^{3} 6546^{3}

Minstrel Lad *Des Donovan*
3 ch g Where Or When(IRE) —Teal Flower (Pivotal)
2650^{12}

Mint Imperial (IRE) *Amy Weaver* a25 26
3 b g Diamond Green(FR) —Imperialist (IRE) (Imperial Frontier (USA))
1203^{13} 1591^{10}

Minty Jones *Michael Mullineaux* a23
2 b c Primo Valentino(IRE) —Reveur (Rossini (USA))
6842^{9} 7197^{10}

Mirabile Visu *Heather Main* a40 66
3 b f Diktat—Parting Gift (Cadeaux Genereux)
5859^{7} 5972^{12} 6434^{13} 6930^{8} 7811^{9}

Miracle Maid *Clive Cox* 71
2 b f Selkirk(USA) —Miracle (Ezzoud (IRE))
7025^{4} ◆

Miracle Play (IRE) *David Evans* a64 66
3 ch f Singspiel(IRE) —Avila (Ajdal (USA))
4023^{8} 4388^{9} 4617^{5} (5243) 5380^{3} 5582^{4} 6136^{4} 6601^{4} 6701^{4} 7037^{9}

Miranda's Girl (IRE) *Thomas Cleary* a88 83
6 b m Titus Livius(FR) —Ela Tina (IRE) (Ela-Mana-Mou)
6854a^{9} 7277a^{12}

Mirandola (FR) *Y De Nicolay* 103
2 ch f Anabaa Blue—Connaissance (IRE) (Choisir (AUS))
7405a^{4}

Mi Regalo *Phil McEntee* a75 64
3 b g Cadeaux Genereux—Lloc (Absalom)
302^{7} 624^{6} 6815^{8} 7352^{12} 7519^{7} 7649^{9} 7754^{7} 7895^{11} 7942^{7}

Mir Hy (USA) *Clive Brittain*
3 b c Rahy(USA) —Plenty Of Grace (USA) (Roberto (USA))
1620^{8} 2360^{7}

Miriam's Song *Stuart Kittow* a66 58
2 br f Royal Applause—Miriam (Forzando)
5681^{12} 7056^{4} (7435)

Mirror Ball *Peter Chapple-Hyam* 72
2 b f Notnowcato—Disco Lights (Spectrum (IRE))
6480^{2}

Mirrored *Tim Easterby* a86 94
5 b g Dansili—Reflections (Sadler's Wells (USA))
(1097) 2573^{5} 2909^{7} 3877^{11} 4410^{14} 4528^{6} 4788^{5} 5250^{16} 5593^{2} 5888^{11} 6080^{3} 6429^{2} 6803^{5}

Mirror Lake *Amanda Perrett* a91 111
4 b m Dubai Destination(USA) —Reflections (Sadler's Wells (USA))
1718^{5} 2994^{4} 4582^{2} 5220^{5} 6247^{3} (7296)

Mirza *Rae Guest* a68 99
4 b g Oasis Dream—Millyant (Primo Dominie)
2927^{10} 4314^{18} (4792) 5430^{2} 6145^{6} 7221a^{9}

Misaro (GER) *Ronald Harris* a79 77
10 b g Acambaro(GER) —Misniniski (Niniski (USA))
98^{7} 224^{3} 343^{2} 435^{7} 511^{6} 683^{3} 735^{13} 1041^{4} 1180^{2} 1336^{4} 1453^{10} 1752^{9} 2162^{4}

Misdemeanour (IRE) *Richard Hannon* a87
2 b f Azamour(IRE) —Miss Takeortwo (IRE) (Danehill Dancer (IRE))
(6000) (6623)

Misedargent (FR) *C Boutin* 63
2 gr f Kendargent(FR) —Miss Sindbad (FR) (Peintre Celebre (USA))
6808a^{8} 7155a^{11} 7814a^{5}

Misefi *Martin Bosley* a49 25
3 b f Nayef(USA) —Simonida (IRE) (Royal Academy (USA))
3232^{6} 4023^{6} 5042^{8}

Mi Senor (GER) *A Wohler* 90
3 b c Azamour(IRE) —Mi Anna (GER) (Lake Coniston (IRE))
3672a^{12}

Misere *Kevin Ryan* a65
3 b f Val Royal(FR) —Card Games (First Trump)
600^{5} 751^{6} 855^{3} 1472^{9} 1953^{2} 2163^{6} 7648^{12} 7820^{8} 7902^{8}

Miserere Mei (IRE) *Richard Guest* a62 17
2 b f Moss Vale(IRE) —Flying Clouds (Batshoof)
2953^{13} 3200^{8} (4756) 5385^{3} 5690^{5} 6001^{9} 7353^{8} 7423^{4} 7742^{2}

Mishhar (IRE) *Clive Brittain* a59
2 b f Authorized(IRE) —Jakarta (IRE) (Machiavellian (USA))
7344^{8}

Mishrif (USA) *J R Jenkins* a85 84
5 bb g Arch(USA) —Peppy Priscilla (USA) (Latin American (USA))
2178^{6} 2822^{8} 2999^{6} 3514^{9} 4910^{3} (6051) 6478^{6} 7199^{6}

Miskin Diamond (IRE) *Bryn Palling* a15 53
3 b f Diamond Green(FR) —Spring To Light (USA) (Blushing Groom (FR))
1952^{11} 2586^{3} 2904^{8} 3214^{5} (4953) 5380^{7} 5642^{10} 6438^{8}

Misk Khitaam (USA) *John Dunlop* 78
3 b g Distorted Humor(USA) —Tashawak (IRE) (Night Shift (USA))
1315^{7} 2230^{6} 2664^{4} 4009^{4}

Misplaced Fortune *Nigel Tinkler* a46 96
6 b m Compton Place—Tide Of Fortune (Soviet Star (USA))
2122^{4} 4369^{7} 5255^{12} 5683^{4} (6094) 6531^{10} 7031^{4}

Misred Melissa (IRE) *John Gallagher* 44
2 b f Red Clubs(IRE) —Almasa (Faustus (USA))
2901^{6} 3270^{10} 3767^{5}

Misrepresent (USA) *John Gosden* 72
3 ch f Distorted Humor(USA) —Halory Leigh (USA) (Halory Hunter (USA))
1362^{3} ◆ 1873^{5} 2960^{9} (3355)

Miss Aix *Michael Bell* 85
3 b f Selkirk(USA) —Miss Provence (Hernando (FR))
1210^{2} ◆ 1549^{3} (2735) 4429^{7} 5020^{3} 5962^{2} 6241^{2} 6996^{6} 7510a^{0}

Miss Astragal (IRE) *Richard Hannon* a72 73
2 b f Oratorio(IRE) —Mansiya (Vettori (IRE))
1846^{8} 3547^{4} 3813^{4} 4427^{5} 5475^{4} 7125^{2} 7344^{3} 7598^{2} 7909^{4}

Miss Azeza *David Simcock* 84
2 b f Dutch Art—Miss Respect (Mark Of Esteem (IRE))
(4883) 5656^{7} ◆

Miss Beat (IRE) *Declan Carroll* a63 52
5 b m Beat Hollow—Bolas (Unfuwain (USA))
2366^{7} 6990^{14} 7200^{3} 7604^{7} 7689^{7} 7851^{5}

Miss Blakeney *Marcus Tregoning* a63
2 b f Sir Percy—Misplace (IRE) (Green Desert (USA))
7125^{6} 7343^{7}

Miss Blink *Robin Bastiman* 79
4 ch m Compton Place—Tawny Way (Polar Falcon (USA))
1077^{6} (1615) (2271) 3301^{3} 3726^{3} 4440^{6} (5406) (6263)

Miss Bloom *Garry Woodward* a24
2 ch f Byron—Demolition Molly (Rudimentary (USA))
4068^{11} 7784^{7}

Miss Boom Boom *Chris Dwyer*
2 ch f Reel Buddy(USA) —Princess Ling (IRE) (Tagula (IRE))
7056^{11}

Miss Boops (IRE) *Zoe Davison* a54 72
3 b f Johannesburg(USA) —Sky Bird (IRE) (Galileo (IRE))
907^{5} 1335^{11} 1837^{7} 1999^{7} 2964^{10}

Miss Bootylishes *Paul Burgoyne* a79 82
6 b m Mujahid(USA) —Moxby (Efisio)
160^{5} 394^{7} 508^{3} 1978^{4} 2198^{6} 2999^{3} 3413^{2} 3514^{2} (3804) 4158^{3} 4255^{7} 4949^{3} 5328^{4} (5496) 5962^{9} 6330^{14} 6727^{11}

Miss Bounty *Jim Boyle* a58 68
6 ch m Bahamian Bounty—Maniere D'Amour (FR) (Baillamont (USA))
248^{7} 555^{10} 722^{5} (809) 862^{9} 957^{11} 1508^{2} 1636^{2} (1936) 2308^{2} 2562^{4} 3533^{6} 3760^{3} 4242^{3} 4454^{5} 6926^{10} 7121^{4} 7394^{5} 7528^{3}

Miss Cap Estel *Andrew Balding* 70
2 b f Hernando(FR) —Miss Cap Ferrat (Darshaan)
5655^{5} ◆ 6329^{11} 6950^{6}

Miss Carmie (FR) *Mlle S-V Tarrou* 81
2 b f Excellent Art—Moortown (IRE) (Grand Lodge (USA))
7813a^{6}

Miss Chamanda (IRE) *David Evans* a78 68
5 ch m Choisir(AUS) —Smandar (USA) (Sahm (USA))
4618^{9} 5627^{3} 6065^{11}

Miss Chicane *Walter Swinburn* a65 78
3 b f Refuse To Bend(IRE) —Sharp Terms (Kris)
1251^{6} (2232) 2791^{8} 3650^{12} 3919^{9} 4448^{9} 5014 6227 6740 7033

Miss Conduct *John Spearing* 64
2 b f Overbury(IRE) —Risky Valentine (Risk Me (FR))
2787^{3} 3249^{2} 4073^{5} 5324^{7} 6524^{17}

Miss Coral (GER) *H-W Hiller* 61
2 ch f Big Shuffle(USA) —Multi Task (USA) (Stravinsky (USA))
4372a^{7} 6737a^{7}

Miss Crissy (IRE) *M Delzangles* 108
3 gr f Verglas(IRE) —Seracina (Nashwan (USA))
4036b^{3} 5093a^{2} 5771a^{4} 6557a^{2} 6903a^{4}

Miss Diagnosis (IRE) *Ralph Beckett* 95
3 b f Medicean—Changeable (Dansili)
2050^{8} (3260) ◆ 4429^{11} 5483^{4} ◆

Miss Dutee *Richard Hannon* a30 68
3 b f Dubawi(IRE) —Tee Cee (Lion Cavern (USA))
1483^{11} 1764^{6} (2172) 2553^{4} 2792^{9} 3818^{8} 4973^{11} 5669^{4} 6434^{11}

Miss Dylan (IRE) *J S Bolger* 90
2 b f Dylan Thomas(IRE) —Marette (IRE) (Soviet Star (USA))
4031a^{5} ◆

Miss Elegance *Brian Meehan* 69
3 b f Mind Games—Mania (IRE) (Danehill (USA))
(3909) (4466)

Miss Ella Jade *Richard Whitaker* a47 41
2 b f Danbird(AUS) —Keen Melody (USA) (Sharpen Up)
5077^{8} 5487^{6} 7422^{5} 7708^{5}

Miss Elliemay (IRE) *John O'Shea*
2 ch f Elnadim(USA) —Woodstamp (IRE) (Woodborough (USA))
6992^{9}

Miss Emily (IRE) *George Moore* 34
3 b f Camacho—Northumbrian Belle (IRE) (Distinctly North (USA))
2498^{9} 2802^{10} 3138^{9} 3679^{5}

Miss Excel *Edward Creighton* a20 56
4 b m Exceed And Excel(AUS) —Shaiybara (IRE) (Kahyasi)
2419^{4} 2760^{4} 3478^{5} 4713^{4} 4953^{4} 5210^{5}

Miss Exhibitionist *James Eustace* a78 76
3 b f Trade Fair—Miss McGuire (Averti (IRE))
2383^{7} 2883^{3} 3717^{2} 4584^{5} 6311^{4}

Miss Eze *Paul Cashman* a83 85
5 b m Danehill Dancer(IRE) —Miss Corniche (Hernando (FR))
923a^{12}

Miss Fantastick (IRE) *M McDonagh* a1 29
4 b m Fantastic Light(USA) —Nadayem (USA) (Gulch (USA))
6139a^{8}

Miss Ferney *Alan Kirtley* a66 69
7 ch m Cayman Kai(IRE) —Jendorcet (Grey Ghost)
4074^{4} 4367^{11} 5107^{9} 5369^{6} (5651) 5791^{6} (6157) 6287^{7} (6385) 6666^{8}

Miss Fifty (IRE) *U Suter* 103
3 b f Whipper(USA) —Annatto (USA) (Mister Baileys)
1207a^{3}

Miss Firefly *Ron Hodges* a65 63
6 b m Compton Place—Popocatepetl (FR) (Nashwan (USA))
1043^{5} 1248^{8} 1469^{2} 1938^{3} 2167^{3} 2554^{2} 2756^{4} 3217^{4} 3464^{2} 4230^{2} 4487^{5} 5038^{2} 5394^{11}

Miss Firefox *Nicky Vaughan* a53 59
3 ch f Haafhd—Hayden Grace (In The Wings)
368^{3} 1566^{3} 2243^{7} 4927^{10} 6816^{13}

Miss Granger *Ronald Harris* a46 38
2 ch f Needwood Blade—Sweet Coincidence (Mujahid (USA))
5375^{8} 5841^{9} 6662^{6}

Misshollygolightly *Brian Baugh* 37
3 b f Kheleyf(USA) —Crown City (USA) (Coronado's Quest (USA))
2479^{5} 2802^{14} 3091^{11} 4715^{5} 4819^{6}

Missile Attack (IRE) *Ian Semple* a60 54
3 b g Majestic Missile(IRE) —Aquatint (Dansili)
3075^{7} 3616^{5} 4542^{7} 4924^{2} ◆ 6386^{3} ◆ 6700^{5} 6874^{3}

Missionaire (USA) *Tony Carroll* a72 87
4 bb g El Corredor(USA) —Fapindy (USA) (A.P. Indy (USA))
1102^{14} 1477^{12} 6376^{12} 6789^{11} 7202^{5}

Mission Approved (USA) *Naipaul Chatterpaul* 115
7 b h With Approval(CAN) —Fortunate Find (USA) (Fortunate Prospect (USA))
3888a^{4} 5074a^{7} 6548a^{4} 7563a^{14}

Mission Impossible *Tracy Waggott* a28 64
6 gr g Kyllachy—Eastern Lyric (Petong)
1464^{10} 1815^{9} 2412^{7} 2546^{3} 3027^{3} 3248^{7} 4328^{5} (5552) (5787) 5824^{2} 6208^{12} 6778^{6} 7100^{5} 7216^{4}

Miss Keller (IRE) *Roger L Attfield* 114
5 b m Montjeu(IRE) —Ingozi (Warning)
(6909a)

Miss Kessie *Paul Midgley*
5 b m Where Or When(IRE) —Ladies Day (Robellino (USA))
4180^{7} 4514^{11}

Miss Lago (IRE) *E Lellouche* 110
3 ch f Encosta De Lago(AUS) —Athyka (USA) (Secretariat (USA))
5131a^{2} 5771a^{2} 6555a^{2} 7049a^{2}

Miss Lahar *Mick Channon* 100
2 b f Clodovil(IRE) —Brigadiers Bird (IRE) (Mujadil (USA))
2153^{3} 2661^{3} 3917^{5} 4312^{3} (4702) 4999^{4} 5882^{9} 6146^{5} 6518^{2} 6705^{2} 7019^{3} 7135^{5}

Miss Liberty (FR) *Mme Pia Brandt* a97 104
3 b f Statue Of Liberty(USA) —Miss America (FR) (Spinning World (USA))
2137a^{10} 5028a^{5}

Miss Match (ARG) *Neil Drysdale* a111 95
6 bb m Indygo Shiner(USA) —Miss Simpatia (ARG) (Southern Halo (USA))
7285a^{9}

Miss Mediator (USA) *Richard Hannon* a63 75
3 ch f Consolidator(USA) —Gender Dance (USA) (Miesque's Son (USA))
1704^{3} 2100^{4} 2040^{6} 2000^{3}

Miss Medici (IRE) *Des Donovan* a43 17
2 b f Medecis—Noble Nova (Fraam)
2651^{5} 3708^{3} 4178^{2} 4391^{8} 5211^{6}

Miss Miracle *Jonjo O'Neill* a63 82
4 gr m Motivator—Miracle (Ezzoud (IRE))
2190^{6}

Miss Moneypenni *Nick Littmoden* a52 64
3 ch f Monsieur Bond(IRE) —Dazzling Daisy (Shareef Dancer (USA))
10^{4} 142^{9}

Miss Muga *Edward Creighton* 62
2 b f Imperial Dancer—Blakeshall Rose (Tobougg (IRE))
1563^{3} 1786^{2} (2121) (2425) 2712^{8} 2998^{5} 4085^{7}

Miss Mysterious (FR) *Kate Walton* 52
3 b f Dubai Destination(USA) —Torrealta (In The Wings)
6781^{2} 7212^{4}

Miss Netta (USA) *Kiaran McLaughlin* a98
2 bb f Street Sense(USA) —Dyna Peak (USA) (Dynaformer (USA))
7283a^{6}

Miss Noble *Stuart Williams* 26
2 b f Exceed And Excel(AUS) —Dorothea Brooke (IRE) (Dancing Brave (USA))
1441^{13}

Miss Polly Plum *Chris Dwyer* a52 75
4 b m Doyen(IRE) —Mrs Plum (Emarati (USA))
250^{12} 1357^{7} (1989) 2238^{5} 2720^{2} (2920) (3389) 3759^{8} 4392^{3} 4731^{4} 5173^{5} 5484^{6} 6065^{9}

Missprint *Brian Baugh* a51
4 b m Ishiguru(USA) —Miss Up N Go (Gorytus (USA))
1053^{5} 1277^{6} 3475^{11}

Miss Pronounce *Linda Perratt* 39
3 b f Denounce—Miss Pigalle (Good Times (ITY))
5206^{5} 5432^{7} 5793^{5} 6208^{16} 7158^{5}

Miss Purity Pinker (IRE) *David Evans* a52 60
2 b f One Cool Cat(USA) —Consultant Stylist (IRE) (Desert Style (IRE))
4269^{2} 4864^{12} 6291^{10} 6695^{9}

Miss Rosie *Mark Johnston* a71 66
2 b f Librettist(USA) —Hunter's Fortune (USA) (Charismatic (USA))
1791^{3} (3932) 5099^{2}

Miss Sabiango (FR) *J-Y Artu* 55
2 b f Sabiango(GER) —Logonna (FR) (Lost World (IRE))
6925a[0]

Miss T *James Given* 46
3 br f Bertolini(USA) —Chalosse (Doyoun)
2166[12]

Miss Tenacious *Ron Hodges* 38
4 b m Refuse To Bend(IRE) —Very Speed (USA) (Silver Hawk (USA))
1374[11] 1625[8]

Miss Toldyaso (IRE) *Michael Quinlan* a56 54
3 b f Barathea(IRE) —Toldya (Beveled (USA))
64[5] 183[7]

Miss Tonic (FR) *C Boutin* a73 67
7 b m Priolo(USA) —Tonic Stream (FR) (Bering)
439a[2]

Miss Topsy Turvy (IRE) *John Dunlop* 81
3 br f Mr Greeley(USA) —Cara Fantasy (IRE) (Sadler's Wells (USA))
1364[7] (2022) ◆ 2850[7] 3467[4] 4074[2] (4515) 6749[4] 7136[3]

Miss Villefranche *Michael Bell* a66 61
3 b f Danehill Dancer(IRE) —Miss Corniche (Hernando (FR))
1958[12] 3487[8] 4185[4] 5515[4] 7096[2] (7270) (7399) 7537[5] ◆

Miss Wendy *Mark H Tompkins* a52 58
4 b m Where Or When(IRE) —Grove Dancer (Reprimand)
592[8] 796[7] 3243[6] 3574[4]

Miss Whippy *Paul Howling* a54 55
4 b m Whipper(USA) —Glorious (Nashwan (USA))
2473[6] 2856[3] 3559[2] 3960[6] 4732[2] 5519[8] 6600[11] 7206[13]

Miss Work Of Art *Richard Fahey* a85 102
2 ch f Dutch Art—Lacework (Pivotal)
(1042) (1598) ◆ (2070) 3821[9] 4413[9] 5216[2] 6146[2] 6337[4]

Mister Angry (IRE) *Mark Johnston* a92 94
4 b g Cape Cross(IRE) —Yaya (USA) (Rahy (USA))
1477[13] 1887[9] 2289[10] 2812[5] 3381[5] 3762[6] 4555[3] (5102) 5448[10] 5759[11] 6485[8] 7017[11]

Mister Ben Vereen *Eve Johnson Houghton* a61 67
3 b g Compton Place—La Fanciulla (Robellino (USA))
1624[10] 2243[2] 2853[6] 3633[6] 3675[2] 3783[5] 4486[7] 4743[2] 4911[9] 5675[3] 6609[14]

Mister Bit (IRE) *John Best* a70 70
4 b g Tobougg(IRE) —Santiburi Girl (Casteddu)
8141[0] (1508) 6622[8] 6969[10]

Mister Bob (GER) *James Bethell* 21
2 ch c Black Sam Bellamy(IRE) —Mosquera (GER) (Acatenango (GER))
4525[10]

Mister Carter (IRE) *T Stack* a72 90
4 b g Antonius Pius(USA) —Kotdiji (Mtoto)
7618a[12]

Mister Fantastic *Dai Burchell* a56 53
5 ch g Green Tune(USA) —Lomapamar (Nashwan (USA))
1454[5] 1828[6] 2872[5] 5611[5] (6084) 6411[8] 7370[8]

Mister Fasliyev (IRE) *E Charpy* a92 87
9 b g Fasliyev(USA) —Carisheba (USA) (Alysheba (USA))
153a[14]

Mister Frosty (IRE) *George Prodromou* a63 62
5 gr g Verglas(IRE) —La Chinampina (FR) (Darshaan)
(161) 266[3] 645[8] 2923[5] 3353[7] 6845[6] 7087[4] 7527[5]

Mister Green (FR) *David Flood* a75 83
5 b g Green Desert(USA) —Summertime Legacy (Darshaan)
175[7] 307[3] 400[6] (489) (565) 614[8] 703[10] 867[5] 991[13] 1103[7] 1355[4] 2304[9] 7208[9] 7362[4] 7522[6] 7671[12] 7759[8] 7895[12] 7943[3]

Mister Hughie (IRE) *Tim Easterby* 108
4 b h Elusive City(USA) —Bonne Mere (FR) (Stepneyev (IRE))
1687[14] 2075[13] 3155[24] 3874[6] 4346[18] 4526[7]

Mister Iceman (FR) *D Smaga* a100 108
3 b c Iceman—Parma (IRE) (Grand Lodge (USA))
1552a[5]

Mister Mackenzie *John Best* a67 64
2 br c Kodiac—Dazzling View (USA) (Distant View (USA))
5411[3] 6118[3] 6751[4]

Mister Manannan (IRE) *David Nicholls* 110
4 b g Desert Style(IRE) —Cover Girl (IRE) (Common Grounds)
237[5] ◆ 500a[6] 754a[8] 2456[5] ◆ 3846[8] 4776[9] (5805) 6233[3]

Mister Music *Richard Hannon* 90
2 b c Singspiel(IRE) —Sierra (Dr Fong (USA))
3401[7] ◆ (3986) ◆ 4508[3] 5044[4] 5654[2] (6373) 6914[8]

Mister Musicmaster *Rod Millman* 88
2 b g Amadeus Wolf—Misty Eyed (IRE) (Paris House)
2049[11] 2880[8] 3722[4] (4212) (4749) 5184[3] 5558[9] 6166[9]

Mister New York (USA) *Noel Chance* a93 46
6 b g Forest Wildcat(USA) —Shebane (USA) (Alysheba (USA))
436[3] ◆ 702[9]

Mister Par Coeur (FR) *D Allard* a66 76
3 b g Shaanmer(IRE) —Beautiful May (FR) (Kaldoun (FR))
5529a[8]

Mister Segway (IRE) *Robert Collet* a74 74
3 b c Dansili—Aplysia (USA) (Storm Cat (USA))
480a[6] 5529a[6]

Mister Tancred *David Nicholls* 21
2 b g Indesatchel(IRE) —Tancred Miss (Presidium)
2121[6] 2693[5]

Mister Thatcher (IRE) *Mrs Annette McMahon-Reidy* a68 21
7 ch g Tagula(IRE) —Thatching Craft (IRE) (Alzao (USA))
6580[12] 6958a[0]

Mistoffelees *Luca Cumani* a64 81
5 b g Tiger Hill(IRE) —Auenlust (GER) (Surumu (GER))
1390[14] 2810[7]

Mistress Of Rome *Michael Dods* 66
2 b f Holy Roman Emperor(IRE) —Fairy Dance (IRE) (Zafonic (USA))
4073[U] 4875[3] 5819[3] 6075[2] (6425) 6806[5]

Mistress Quick *Ben De Haan* a36 50
3 ch f Sulamani(IRE) —Bold Byzantium (Bold Arrangement)
952[8] 2311[5] 3090[7] 3724[11]

Mistress Shy *Robin Dickin* a28 30
4 b m Zafeen(FR) —Nicholas Mistress (Beveled (USA))
937[7] 1173[7] 1567[7] 1763[8] 2420[9] 3726[7]

Misty Conquest (IRE) *Tom Dascombe* 96
2 b f Mujadil(USA) —Polish Belle (Polish Precedent (USA))
1441[5] 1673[3] (2017) (2476) 3402[3] 4036a[5] 5656[2] 6146[4] 7135[7]

Misty Eyes *Geoffrey Harker*
2 b f Byron—Wax Eloquent (Zaha (CAN))
6630[9]

Misty For Me (IRE) *A P O'Brien* 119
3 b f Galileo(IRE) —Butterfly Cove (USA) (Storm Cat (USA))
1719[11] (2334a) 2682[5] (3417a) 5745a[3] 7284a[3]

Misty Isles *Heather Main* 77
3 b f High Chaparral(IRE) —Meshhed (USA) (Gulch (USA))
2836[3] (3478) 3988[6] 4473[8] 5962[4] 6402[3] 6755[7] 7136[10]

Misty Morn *Alan Brown* a54 64
3 ch f Cadeaux Genereux—Dolce Piccata (Piccolo)
66[4] 251[4] (1040) 1306[6] 1514[3] 2592[6]

Mi Sun Donk *Brett Johnson* a50 36
3 gr g Proclamation(IRE) —Days Of Grace (Wolfhound (USA))
64[6] 338[5] 558[6] 4657[10] 5865[4] 6619[8]

Mitch Rapp (USA) *Harry Dunlop* 60
2 b g Yankee Gentleman(USA) —Foolish Party (USA) (Party Manners (USA))
3870[6] 5254[12] 5891[10]

Mitchum *David Barron* a84 82
2 b c Elnadim(USA) —Maid To Matter (Pivotal)
(1290) 2488[5] 3012[19] 6111[5]

Mitie Mouse *Mike Murphy* a73 77
2 b c Exceed And Excel(AUS) —Mimi Mouse (Diktat)
(2602) 3014[24] 4558[2] 5348[7] 5701[9]

Mitsui (IRE) *H Blume*
4 b h Soviet Star(USA) —Moonchild (GER) (Acatenango (GER))
325a[0]

Mixed Emotions (IRE) *Richard Hannon* 71
3 b f Exceed And Excel(AUS) —L-Way First (IRE) (Vision (USA))
1358[2] 2151[8] 2223[8] 3465[7] 4321[7] 5542[6]

Mixed Intention (IRE) *F Vermeulen* a99 110
3 b f Elusive City(USA) —Chiosina (IRE) (Danehill Dancer (IRE))
(532a) 1553a[2] 2137a[7] 2752a[2] 5028a[2] (5695a)

Mixora (USA) *Sir Henry Cecil* a65 58
2 rg f Mizzen Mast(USA) —Ixora (USA) (Dynaformer (USA))
5814[6] 6933[10]

Miyakejima (FR) *E Libaud* 38
3 b f Dubai Destination(USA) —Shangai Princess (IRE) (Indian Ridge)
852a[10]

Mizbah *Saeed Bin Suroor* 79
2 b g Dubai Destination(USA) —Candice (IRE) (Caerleon (USA))
1721[6] 2460[2] 2953[2] (3349) 5446[3] 6031[3] 6957[3]

Mizwaaj (IRE) *Saeed Bin Suroor* 82
2 b c Invincible Spirit(IRE) —My Dubai (IRE) (Dubai Millennium)
5254[6] 5886[2] 6525[3]

M J Woodward *Paul Green* a58 50
2 b c Needwood Blade—Canina (Foxhound (USA))
3165[7] 3583[9] 4047[9] 5005[4] 6597[5] ◆ 7143[2] 7251[2] 7541[4] 7592[5] (7778) 7881[5]

Mnarani (IRE) *Emmet Michael Butterly* a59 44
4 b g Oasis Dream—Finity (USA) (Diesis)
(2386) 7005[10]

Moannaa *Roger Varian* a79
3 b g Pivotal—Belle Argentine (FR) (Fijar Tango (FR))
6085[4]

Moataz (USA) *Mark Johnston* 40
2 ch g Elusive Quality(USA) —Ramatuelle (CHI) (Jeune Homme (USA))
6579[7] 6768[11] 7052[8]

Mobaasher (USA) *Rod Millman* 80
8 ch g Rahy(USA) —Balistroika (USA) (Nijinsky (CAN))
5966[6] 6485[9]

Mobus Wan (FR) *Shaun Harley* a27
8 b g Le Triton(USA) —Brustanette (FR) (Brustolon)
7092[6]

Mocca Mare *Manfred Hofer* a62
2 b f Motivator—Marias Magic (Mtoto)
7666a[0]

Mockingbird (FR) *D Sepulchre* a79 86
4 ch g Green Tune(USA) —Museum Piece (Rainbow Quest (USA))
840a[10]

Model Pupil *Charles Hills* 79
2 b c Sindar(IRE) —Modesta (IRE) (Sadler's Wells (USA))
6160[3] ◆

Moderator *Gary Moore* a74
2 b g Motivator—Alessandra (Generous (IRE))
(7672) ◆

Modern History (IRE) *A Fabre* 107
3 b c Shamardal(USA) —Fatefully (USA) (Private Account (USA))
2139a[12] 2978a[7]

Modeyra *Saeed Bin Suroor* 110
4 br m Shamardal(USA) —Zahrat Dubai (Unfuwain (USA))
5277[2] ◆ 6066[2] 6557a[3] 7047a[7]

Modun (IRE) *Saeed Bin Suroor* a113 110
4 br g King's Best(USA) —Olympienne (IRE) (Sadler's Wells (USA))
(1402) ◆ 3156[13] 3876[2] ◆ 4410[2] 5285[4] (5711) 7218a[23]

Moe Green (IRE) *Francisco Castro* 97
4 b g Xaar—Scripture (IRE) (Sadler's Wells (USA))
2601a[P]

Mofarij *D Selvaratnam* a96 82
7 ch g Bering—Pastorale (Nureyev (USA))
2371[0]

Mogadishio (FR) *A Couetil* a90 94
4 b h American Post—Nebraska I (FR) (Octagonal (NZ))
840a[0]

Moghaayer *James Moffatt* 78
6 b g Sinndar(IRE) —Guest Of Anchor (Slip Anchor)
6832[10]

Mogok Ruby *Brett Johnson* a58 30
7 gr g Bertolini(USA) —Days Of Grace (Wolfhound (USA))
143[4] 269[6] 1357[9] 1633[8]

Mohanad (IRE) *Sheena West* a71 65
5 b g Invincible Spirit(IRE) —Irish Design (IRE) (Alhaarth (IRE))
718[2] (1148) 1839[2] 4216[3] (4318) 4844[2] 5857[2] 6171[5]

Mohawk Ridge *Michael Dods* a65 75
5 b g Storming Home—Ipsa Loquitur (Unfuwain (USA))
2393[3] 2952[6] 4671[4] (5369) 6115[3] 6451[7] 7075[2]

Mohedian Lady (IRE) *Luca Cumani* 108
3 b f Hurricane Run(IRE) —Amathia (IRE) (Darshaan)
2050[7] (5177) 5748a[6] (6269) ◆ 7027[4]

Moheebb (IRE) *Ruth Carr* a72 90
7 b g Machiavellian(USA) —Rockerlong (Deploy)
2347[4] 2545[3] 2887[8] 3275[3] (3620) 3987[5] 4603[7] 5059[7] 6290[4] 6544[5] 6989[15] 7178[4]

Moidore *Roger Charlton* 82
2 b c Galileo(IRE) —Flash Of Gold (Darshaan)
6165[10] 6772[3] ◆ (7109)

Moiqen (IRE) *Doug Watson* a53 42
6 b g Red Ransom(USA) —Za Aamah (USA) (Mr Prospector (USA))
154a[13]

Mojave (IRE) *Mahmood Al Zarooni* 96
2 b c Dubawi(IRE) —Desert Frolic (IRE) (Persian Bold)
6334[9] (6772) ◆ (7167) ◆

Mojave Moon *M bin Shafya* a92 99
5 br g Singspiel(IRE) —Moon Cactus (Kris)
153a[5] 329a[10] 584a[7]

Mojeerr *Alan McCabe* a55 58
5 b g Royal Applause—Princess Miletrian (IRE) (Danehill (USA))
16[7] 145[3] 184[7] 324[3] 450[10] 507[2] 639[5] 795[4] 879[4]

Mojita (IRE) *K J Condon* a76 82
3 b f Montjeu(IRE) —Hatalan (Mark Of Esteem (IRE))
5748a[8] 7378a[6]

Mojolika *Tim Easterby* a65 81
3 ch g Motivator—Kalandika (Diesis)
1456[4] 2152[6] (2571) 3474[3] (3935) 4941[7] 5453[6]

Mokalif *Michael Bell* a24 72
3 b g Halling(USA) —Velvet Waters (Unfuwain (USA))
1934[4] 2637[2] (2857) 3364[5] 3599[2] 4318[7]

Mokbil (IRE) *Roger Varian* a56 69
2 b g Dansili—Chatifa (IRE) (Titus Livius (FR))
6768[5] 7126[8]

Molamento (IRE) *Gary Moore* a60 70
2 b f Elusive City(USA) —Satin Cape (IRE) (Cape Cross (IRE))
5245[2] 5834[8] (6118)

Molannarch *Keith Reveley* 45
5 b m Old Vic—La Femme En Rouge (Slip Anchor)
1212[10] 1559[7] 1799[7] 2575[7] 3185[6] 3622[11]

Molesden Glen (IRE) *Simon Waugh* a67 30
5 b g Spartacus(IRE) —Sea Glen (IRE) (Glenstal (USA))
5791[13]

Molesne Bay (FR) *D Allard* 73
4 b g Panis(USA) —Amour Parfait (IRE) (Spinning World (USA))
6958a[0]

Molly Jones *Derek Haydn Jones* a61 70
2 b f Three Valleys(USA) —And Toto Too (Averti (IRE))
2374[11] 3270[4] 3707[3] (4085) 4460[2] 5427[5] 6222[6] 6843[6]

Molly Malone (FR) *M Delzangles* 100
3 b f Lomitas—Moonlight Melody (GER) (Law Society (USA))
7580a[2]

Mollyow (IRE) *Bryn Palling* a24 59
3 ch f Iceman—Corryvreckan (IRE) (Night Shift (USA))
2155[10]

Momaris *Roger Varian* a54 66
3 b g Dubai Destination(USA) —Anaamil (IRE) (Darshaan)
2257[6] 2930[6] 4208[11]

Mombasa (GER) *P Schiergen* 97
4 b m Black Sam Bellamy(IRE) —Murnau (IRE) (Rudimentary (USA))
6395a[9]

Moment In The Sun *William Muir* a57 51
2 ch f Dubai Destination(USA) —Special Moment (IRE) (Sadler's Wells (USA))
3680[4] 4232[6] 4954[6] 5605[3] 5844[8] 6817[6] 7909[2] 7937[4]

Moment In Time (IRE) *David Simcock* 69
2 b f Tiger Hill(IRE) —Horatia (IRE) (Machiavellian (USA))
5807[8] 6933[5]

Moment Juste *John Gosden* a83 84
3 b f Pivotal—Place De L'Opera (Sadler's Wells (USA))
1332[3] 3224[3] 5389[2] ◆ 6054[5] 6988[3]

Moment Of Clarity *Shaun Harris* a49 46
9 b g Lujain(USA) —Kicka (Shirley Heights)
466[11] 730[3] 895[5] 1068[5] 1253[4] 1871[4] 1993[7] 2233[4] 2600[7]

Moment Of Time *Andrew Balding* 95
3 b f Rainbow Quest(USA) —Not Before Time (IRE) (Polish Precedent (USA))
1549[5] ◆ 1950[2] 2839[3] 5911[6] 7136[2]

Mo Mhuirnin (IRE) *Richard Fahey* a93 88
5 b m Danetime(IRE) —Cotton Grace (IRE) (Case Law)
2[9] 125[10] 923a[9] 1541[9]

Momkinzain (USA) *Mick Channon* a73 84
4 b g Rahy(USA) —Fait Accompli (USA) (Louis Quatorze (USA))
(563) 1367[6] (1729) 2224[6] 3157[11] 4097[7]

Monadreen Dancer *Daniel Mark Loughnane* a61 49
3 b f Kheleyf(USA) —Volitant (Ashkalani (IRE))
110[3] 335[9] 4271[8] 7716[11]

Monahullan Prince *Gerard Keane* a62 72
10 b g Pyramus(USA) —Classic Artiste (USA) (Arctic Tern (USA))
7631[6]

Monami (GER) *A Wohler* 100
2 ch f Sholokhov(IRE) —Monbijou (GER) (Dashing Blade)
(6737a)

Monashee Rock (IRE) *Matthew Salaman* a59 68
6 b m Monashee Mountain(USA) —Polar Rock (Polar Falcon (USA))
4918[7] 5414[7] 5944[6] (6309) 6610[11]

Monblue *B Grizzetti* 103
4 b m Monsun(GER) —Salonblue (IRE) (Bluebird (USA))
3213a[3]

Mon Brav *Brian Ellison* a76 95
4 b g Sampower Star—Danehill Princess (IRE) (Danehill (USA))
1073[4] (1539) (2116) 2317[9] 2954[2] 3357[8] 3841[18] 5180[11] 5852[10] 6113[5] 7076[10]

Mon Cadeaux *Andrew Balding* 104
4 b g Cadeaux Genereux—Ushindi (IRE) (Montjeu (IRE))
1885[14] 2284[2] 2927[9] 3410F 3852[2] 4534[19] 5272[5] ◆ 5563[7] 6747[2]

Moncofar (IRE) *J-C Rouget* a78 87
3 b c Refuse To Bend(IRE) —Moonbaby (FR) (Le Balafre (FR))
5529a[4]

Monday Night (SWI) *H-A Pantall* a66
2 b f Feliciano(SWI) —Mescalina (IRE) (Brief Truce (USA))
7665a[8]

Mondovino (FR) *M Boutin* a78 85
8 b h Black Minnaloushe(USA) —Divinite (USA) (Alleged (USA))
259a[3] 439a[10] 479a[2]

Monel *Jim Goldie* 66
3 ch g Cadeaux Genereux—Kelucia (IRE) (Grand Lodge (USA))
1074[8] 1494[7] (2396) (3661) 4145[9] 4880[4] 5439[4] 6116[8] 6426[9]

Monessa (IRE) *Edward Creighton* a9 60
2 ch f Le Vie Dei Colori—Nasaria (IRE) (Starborough)
2380[7] 3249[6] 3767[3] 4708[2] 5170[6] 6053[13]

Money Bridge *Derek Shaw* a23
4 ch g Doyen(IRE) —Crochet (IRE) (Mark Of Esteem (IRE))
1974[8]

Money Money Money *Rod Millman* a74 83
5 b m Generous(IRE) —Shi Shi (Alnasr Alwasheek)
117[3] 277[5] (350) 592[3] 733[7] 1080[2] (1218) 1586[6] 2145[4] (2659) (3047) 3738[5] (3978) 4463[2] 4719[2]

Money Never Sleeps *John Gosden* 82
2 b c Kyllachy—Shine Like A Star (Fantastic Light (USA))
4098[5] 5480[2] 5855[4] 6292[3] (6751)

Money Note *Tobias B P Coles* a35 69
3 b f Librettist(USA) —Janaat (Kris)
5624[7] 6071[7] 6358[8] 6701[9]

Money Trader (IRE) *J T Gorman* a81 88
4 br h Trade Fair—Honey For Money (IRE) (Alzao (USA))
925a[5] 3440a[25] 7189a[10] 7792a[10]

Mongoose Alert (IRE) *Jim Best* a88
9 b g Oscar(IRE) —Before (IRE) (Ore)
235[3] 474[2] 656[2]

Monicalew *Walter Swinburn* a63 75
3 ch f Refuse To Bend(IRE) —White House (Pursuit Of Love)
1364[10] 2018[4] 2349[6] (3726) 4099[7]

Monique Bisou (FR) *Y Fertillet* a61 70
5 b m Kahyasi—Monique Tartine (Clantime)
533a[7] 843a[4]

Monitor Closely (IRE) *Michael Bell* 110
5 b h Oasis Dream—Independence (Selkirk (USA))
1201[3] 1685[6]

Mon Julien (USA) *J-C Rouget* 71
3 b g Street Cry(IRE) —Moonavvara (IRE) (Sadler's Wells (USA))
616a[2]

Monkton Vale (IRE) *Noel Wilson* a70 81
4 b g Catcher In The Rye(IRE) —Byproxy (IRE) (Mujtahid (USA))
1098[10] 1608[12] 2059[3] 2486[4] 2892[11] 3509[5] 3905[7] 5721[8] 6264[9]

Mon Mon (IRE) *Brian Storey* a29
4 b m Refuse To Bend(IRE) —Adaja (Cadeaux Genereux)
445[6]

Monnoyer *David Nicholls* a78 78
2 ch g Dutch Art—Ellebanna (Tina's Pet)
(1583) ◆ 2007[4] 2594[2] 3014[18] 4334[6] 6535[16]

Monopoli *Ralph Beckett* 66
2 ch f Cadeaux Genereux—Jump Ship (Night Shift (USA))
5655[11] 6805[3]

Monopolize *Sir Henry Cecil* a57 84
3 b c Oasis Dream—Modesta (IRE) (Sadler's Wells (USA))
2231[3] 2930[4] 3364[4] 4805[3] 5911[7] 6633[2]

Mon Petit Bijou *Lydia Pearce* a19
3 b f Sulamani(IRE) —Mon Petit Diamant (Hector Protector (USA))
7111[11] 7440[7] 7557[12]

Mons Calpe (IRE) *Paul Cole* a77 76
5 b g Rock Of Gibraltar(IRE) —Taking Liberties (IRE) (Royal Academy (USA))
1325[5] (1775) 2156[4] 2793[9] 3533[11] 4389[11] 6592[3] (6790)

Monserrat (FR) *P Demercastel* a72 95
5 b g Celtic Swing—Mabalane (IRE) (Danehill (USA))
42a[0] 220a[10]

Monsieur Broughton *Willie Musson* a41 59
3 ch g Monsieur Bond(IRE) —Rainy Day Song (Persian Bold)
4388[7] 5449[9] 5900[8] 7698[11]

Monsieur Chevalier (IRE) *Richard Hannon* a106 117
4 b h Chevalier(IRE) —Blue Holly (IRE) (Blues Traveller (IRE))
2370[4] 3010[11] 3154[2] 3863[15] 5481[5] (5935)

Monsieur Harvey *Bryan Smart* a51 52
5 ch g Monsieur Bond(IRE) —Annie Harvey (Fleetwood (IRE))
363[3] 537[4] 735[6] 857[6]

Monsieur Jamie *J R Jenkins* a89 70
3 b c Monsieur Bond(IRE) —Primula Bairn (Bairn (USA))
476[6] (740) 940[U] 6217[6] (7355) ◆ 7643[2]

Monsieur Joe (IRE) *Walter Swinburn* a86 107
4 b g Choisir(AUS) —Pascali (Compton Place)
237[2] 500a[4] 678a[8] 754a[2] 996a[12] 1848[3] 2370[7] 5805[4] 6522[11]

Monsieur Kiss Kiss *Annelies Mathis* 59
5 b g Monsieur Bond(IRE) —Known Class (USA) (Known Fact (USA))
259a[0]

Monsieur Pontaven *Robin Bastiman* a61 57
4 b g Avonbridge—Take Heart (Electric)
1468[8] 2415[5] 3142[8] 4379[3] 4876[8] 5490[4] 5789[3] 6159[5] (7561) 7714[10]

Monster Munchie (JPN) *William Knight* a74 63
3 b f Deep Impact(JPN) —Muncie (IRE) (Sadler's Wells (USA))
471[3] 699[3] (1252) 2463[3] 5266[6] (6135) 6669[6] 7263[6]

Montaff *Mick Channon* a79 110
5 b g Montjeu(IRE) —Meshhed (USA) (Gulch (USA))
329a[7] 584a[6] 1102[11] (1412) 1808[10] 2316[3] 2438[2] 3396[2] 4469[12] 5285[19] 7297[11]

Mont Agel *Michael Bell* 102
4 b g Danehill Dancer(IRE) —Miss Riviera Golf (Hernando (FR))
2031[2] 3032[21] 3862[17] 4494[15] 5218[11]

Montaser (IRE) *David Simcock* 80
2 b c Rail Link—For Example (USA) (Northern Baby (CAN))
(4884) ◆ 6144[2]

Monte Alto (IRE) *A Al Raihe* a101 89
7 b g Danehill Dancer(IRE) —Peruvian Witch (IRE) (Perugino (USA))
154a[10] 242[13] 330a[6] 498a[3] 585a[6] 824a[5]

Monte Cassino (IRE) *Bryan Smart* a57 48
6 ch g Choisir(AUS) —Saucy Maid (IRE) (Sure Blade (USA))
5793[4] 6386[11] 7366[7] (7728) 7911[5]

Montecatini (IRE) *M Weiss* a65
7 b h Galileo(IRE) —Spring Easy (IRE) (Alzao (USA))
534a[8]

Montefeltro *Mahmood Al Zarooni* 81
3 ch c Medicean—Bustling (Danehill (USA))
6097[3] 6804[2]

Montego Breeze *Derek Shaw* a42 56
5 b m Tipsy Creek(USA) —Mofeyda (IRE) (Mtoto)
7[6] 19[6]

Montegonian (USA) *Marcus Tregoning* a76 41
3 gr g Maria's Mon(USA) —Nadeszhda (Nashwan (USA))
1408[14] 1605[5] 1759[5] ◆ 2819[8] 4489[7] 6797[8] 7070[4] 7346[12] 7522[12]

Monte Major (IRE) *Derek Shaw* a68 42
10 b g Docksider(USA) —Danalia (IRE) (Danehill (USA))
97[10] 511[8]

Monte Mayor One *Jim Goldie* a62 66
4 b m Lujain(USA) —Alvarinho Lady (Royal Applause)
4539[10] 4780[8] 5309[12] (5719) 6076[13] 6213[8] 6386[13] 6646[6]

Monteriggioni (IRE) *John Geoghegan* a79 102
9 b g Blue Ocean(USA) —Jibabit (IRE) (Waajib)
7618a[8]

Monterosso *Mahmood Al Zarooni* a118 116
4 b h Dubawi(IRE) —Porto Roca (AUS) (Barathea (IRE))
(757a) 1002a[3]

Montgomery (NZ) *Colin & Cindy Alderson* 101
6 b g Montjeu(IRE) —All Zalute (NZ) (Zabeel (NZ))
7310a[7]

Monthly Medal *Wilf Storey* a68 77
8 b g Danehill Dancer(IRE) —Sovereign Abbey (IRE) (Royal Academy (USA))
4897[7] 5549[4] 6006[5] 6777[8] 7099[2] 7216[16]

Montmarin (FR) *Mlle V Dissaux* a54 61
9 b g Dansili—Monacita (FR) (Bering)
832a[9]

Montmorency (IRE) *S Seemar* a99 94
5 ch h Pivotal—Clear Spring (USA) (Irish River (FR))
327a[6] 497a[2] 587a[12] 825a[11]

Montnamix (FR) *J-Y Artu* a66 70
6 gr g Linamix(FR) —Our Highness (FR) (Highest Honor (FR))
1142a[8]

Montparnasse (IRE) *Mark Johnston* 71
4 b g Montjeu(IRE) —Capades Dancer (USA) (Gate Dancer (USA))
1412[2] 1679[9] 2071[14] 2888[7] 3344[7] 4577[3]

Montpazier (FR) *W Walton* 53
7 b g Noblequest(FR) —Les Taillades (FR) (Satin Wood)
6959a[8]

Montpellier (IRE) *A Al Raihe* a107 91
8 br g Montjeu(IRE) —Ring Of Esteem (Mark Of Esteem (IRE))
155a[12]

Mont Ras (IRE) *David O'Meara* 92
4 ch g Indian Ridge—Khayrat (IRE) (Polar Falcon (USA))
(2252) (2474) (3169) 3877[4]

Monty Fay (IRE) *Derek Haydn Jones* a64 52
2 bb g Iffraaj—Blast (USA) (Roar (USA))
3237[7] 3921[2] 4462[5] 6132[11] 6539[7] 7252[3] 7541[3] 7770[4]

Monumental Man *James Unett* a65 63
2 b g Vital Equine(IRE) —Spark Up (Lahib (USA))
1396[8] 2160[3] 2283[5] 6539[6] 6654[8] 7251[7]

Mon Visage *Chris Wall* a73 76
3 ch f Ishiguru(USA) —Pikaboo (Pivotal)
4202[5] 4799[3] 5542[3] ◆

Monymusk *David Elsworth* 70
2 b g Norse Dancer(IRE) —Bee One (IRE) (Catrail (USA))
3915[7] 4330[5]

Monzon (USA) *Ignacio Correas IV* a102 97
3 bb g Thunder Gulch(USA) —Shadow Of Mine (USA) (Belong To Me (USA))
2950a[9]

Moodhill *Charles Hills* 78
2 b c Dansili—Almurooj (Zafonic (USA))
7134[2]

Mood Music *Mario Hofer* a100 108
7 b g Kyllachy—Something Blue (Petong)
5528a[8]

Moody Dancer *William Muir* a63 47
2 b f Cape Cross(IRE) —Bluebelle Dancer (IRE) (Danehill Dancer (IRE))
5655[13] 6169[11] 7124[6]

Moody Tunes *Tom Dascombe* a60 85
8 b g Merdon Melody—Lady-Love (Pursuit Of Love)
935a[2] 2347[3] 2413[3] (2807) (2984) 3585[8] 3848[8] 4603[2] 5485[2] 5920[6] 7032[9] 7236[11] 7816[7]

Moonbalej *Wilf Storey* a61 57
4 ch g Motivator—Glam Rock (Nashwan (USA))
6833[13] 7061[12]

Moone's My Name *Ralph Beckett* 85
3 gr f Intikhab(USA) —The Manx Touch (IRE) (Petardia)
1591[2] (2103) 2790[3] (3594) (4202) ◆ 6062[11] 7054[2]

Moonlark *John Holt* a42 35
3 b f Kodiac—Sophie'Jo (Agnes World (USA))
5567[11] 5999[8] 6608[9] 7561[8]

Moonlight Blaze *Chris Fairhurst* a49 59
4 b g Barathea(IRE) —Moonlight (IRE) (Night Shift (USA))
1039[12]

Moonlight Cloud *F Head* a94 122
3 b f Invincible Spirit(IRE) —Ventura (IRE) (Spectrum (IRE))
(1207a) 1719[7] 2744a[2] (3654a) (4838a) 6858[5] ◆

Moonlight Fantasy (IRE) *Lucinda Featherstone* a40 54
8 b g Night Shift(USA) —County Girl (IRE) (Prince Rupert (FR))
2271[3] 2851[P] 3176[9] 4133[6] 4540[6] [illegible]

Moonlight Mystery *Chris Wall* a54 73
3 ch f Pivotal—Mauri Moon (Green Desert (USA))
1606[6] 2821[9] 5788[2] (6777)

Moon Lightning (IRE) *Tina Jackson* a43 68
5 b g Desert Prince(IRE) —Moon Tango (IRE) (Last Tycoon)
290[6] 400[7] 547[6] 800[7] 1979[7] 2233[6] 3733[12] 4443[9]

Moonlight Rhapsody (IRE) *B W Hills* a64 73
3 b f Danehill Dancer(IRE) —Moon Flower (IRE) (Sadler's Wells (USA))
(420) 1170[3] 1659[3] 3325[4] 3615[5]

Moonlight Serenade *Simon Earle* a54 54
4 b m Mind Games—Rasseem (IRE) (Fasliyev (USA))
1045[14] 2642[9]

Moonlit Garden (IRE) *D K Weld* a79 98
3 b f Exceed And Excel(AUS) —Fingal Nights (IRE) (Night Shift (USA))
4767a[13] 7012a[13]

Moon Over Water (IRE) *Roger Varian* a64 64
3 b f Galileo(IRE) —Velvet Moon (IRE) (Shaadi (USA))
6137[3] 6804[4] 7250[7] 7856[4]

Moon Pearl (USA) *Ralph Beckett* 98
2 bb g Johannesburg(USA) —Moonavvara (IRE) (Sadler's Wells (USA))
(3793) 5181[8] 5849[4] 6692[7]

Moonreach (IRE) *James J Hartnett* a96 93
4 b g Chineur(FR) —Ribbon Glade (UAE) (Zafonic (USA))
923a[5] 1533a[6] 3109[11] 3440a[14]

Moon Rock *D Menard* a81 88
7 b g Anabaa Blue—Moonlight Melody (GER) (Law Society (USA))
843a[0]

Moonsail *Mahmood Al Zarooni* 77
3 b f Monsun(GER) —Kazzia (GER) (Zinaad)
3385[5] 5062[8]

Moonscape *Sir Michael Stoute* a79 82
3 ch g Pivotal—Moon Goddess (Rainbow Quest (USA))
6085[3] 6578[2]

Moonship *Sir Michael Stoute* 53
2 b c Halling(USA) —Soviet Moon (IRE) (Sadler's Wells (USA))
6267[9]

Moon Trip *Mark Johnston* a66 80
2 b g Cape Cross(IRE) —Fading Light (King's Best (USA))
2033[9] 2395[8] 3472[4] 4194[4] (5343) 5446[11] 5931[9]

Moonville (IRE) *Richard Fahey* 77
2 gr c Clodovil(IRE) —Moone Cross (IRE) (Cape Cross (IRE))
1797[3] (2283)

Moonwalk In Paris (FR) *J-C Rouget* a100 92
3 b g Oratorio(IRE) —Shining Glory (Singspiel (IRE))
777a[2] (980a)

Moonyr (FR) *F Head* 97
3 b c Hernando(FR) —Mydarshaan (Darshaan)
1551a[8]

Moorhouse Girl *George Foster* a40 70
4 b m Makbul—Record Time (Clantime)
1813[5]

Moorhouse Lad *Bryan Smart* a93 105
8 b g Bertolini(USA) —Record Time (Clantime)
1366[9] 1809[8] 5543[2] 6164[10]

Moorland Boy *Jamie Osborne* a58 61
3 gr g Proclamation(IRE) —Superlove (IRE) (Hector Protector (USA))
142[3] 260[4]

Moorside Magic *Richard Fahey* 17
2 b f Dubai Destination(USA) —Parsonagehotelyork (IRE) (Danehill (USA))
7209[10]

Morache Music *Peter Makin* 108
3 b g Sleeping Indian—Enchanted Princess (Royal Applause)
3649[8] (4779) 5532a[5] 6733a[9]

Moral Issue *Ian McInnes* a73 74
3 b g Ishiguru(USA) —Morale (Bluebird (USA))
1436[4] 1880[2] 2574[2] 3111[2] 3461[4] (3977) 5109[7] 5760[16] 6231[6] 6634[11] 6867[10] 7695[2]

Moran Gra (USA) *Ms Joanna Morgan* a71 107
4 ch g Rahy(USA) —Super Supreme (IND) (Zafonic (USA))
923a[15] (3445a) 4418a[13] 4978a[3]

Morant Bay (IRE) *Sir Henry Cecil* 70
2 b f Montjeu(IRE) —Quad's Melody (IRE) (Spinning World (USA))
7233[4]

Morar *Laura Mongan* a81 81
5 b m Kalanisi(IRE) —Moidart (Electric)
209[12] 3184[7] 4216[2] (4844) 7120[13]

More Bottle (IRE) *Tom Tate* a23 46
2 b f Barathea(IRE) —More Respect (IRE) (Spectrum (IRE))
3200[6] 5818[5] 6448[10] 7242[9]

More For Less *Owen Brennan* a20 49
4 b g Danbird(AUS) —Patricia Philomena (IRE) (Prince Of Birds (USA))
7004[8] 7195[11]

More Is To Come (USA) *Ralph Beckett* a49 40
2 b f War Front(USA) —Ava's Crown (USA) (Don't Say Halo (USA))
2606[6] 3547[12] 5854[7]

Morermaloke *Ian McInnes* a69 68
3 ch g Bahamian Bounty—Rainbow End (Botanic (USA))
43[2] (246) 356[5] 1187[4] 1323[5] 4124[8] 4680[6] 4895[7] 5274[7] 6261[13] 6655[3] 7123[7] 7266[8] 7737[12] 7911[4]

Moresweets 'n Lace *Gary Moore* a73 74
4 b m Zafeen(FR) —Another Secret (Efisio)
214[5] 313[5] 647[3] 945[2] (1233) ◆ 1587[3] 2051[2] (2204)

Mores Wells *M Delzangles* a103 114
7 b h Sadler's Wells(USA) —Endorsement (Warning)
778a[5] 4037a[7] 5045[5] 5984a[2] 6910a[8]

More Than A Lot (IRE) *M Halford* a63 65
3 ch f Mr Greeley(USA) —Jellett (IRE) (Green Desert (USA))
973a[6] (Dead)

More Than Enough (IRE) *Richard Fahey* a64
3 b g Danehill Dancer(IRE) —Showbiz (IRE) (Sadler's Wells (USA))
234[11] 469[8]

More Than Love (USA) *John Terranova II* 100
2 ch f More Than Ready(USA) —I'm In Love (USA) (Zafonic (USA))
(7562a)

More Than Many (USA) *Richard Fahey* 71
5 bb h More Than Ready(USA) —Slewnami (AUS) (Seattle Slew (USA))
1909[9] 2388[10]

More Than Real (USA) *Todd Pletcher* 112
3 ch f More Than Ready(USA) —Miss Seffens (USA) (Dehere (USA))
3106[11] 6183a[3] 6887a[7]

More Than Words (IRE) *Richard Hannon* a78
2 b f Lawman(FR) —Gilded (IRE) (Redback)
6820[2] ◆ 7359[4]

Morethanyouknow (IRE) *John Spearing*
2 b f Aragorn(IRE) —Parade Scene (USA) (Parade Ground (USA))
7038[P]

Moretta Blanche *Ralph Beckett* a79 85
4 br m Dansili—Cotton House (IRE) (Mujadil (USA))
1854[14] 3045[7] 3536[6] 3845[8] 5043[4] 5322[4]

Morgana *Brendan Powell* a29
3 b f Norse Dancer(IRE) —En Vacances (IRE) (Old Vic)
2175[7] 6459[13]

Morgan Drive (IRE) *M Gasparini* a108 101
6 b h Namid—Morning Prancer (Caerleon (USA))
7408a[8]

Moriarty (IRE) *Richard Hannon* 104
3 b c Clodovil(IRE) —Justice System (USA) (Criminal Type (USA))
1320[3] 2331a[2] 3068[11] 4411[8] 4764[3] 6163[14]

Mormoran *Chris Dwyer* a40 22
2 b f Proclamation(IRE) —Split Briefs (IRE) (Mull Of Kintyre (USA))
3182[14] 5320[10] 5637[2] 6002[7] 6280[7] 6763[8]

Morna's Glory *Ron Hodges* a15
2 b f Resplendent Glory(IRE) —Tipsy Cake (Tipsy Creek (USA))
7197[9]

Morning Air (IRE) *Ann Duffield* 50
3 b f Refuse To Bend(IRE) —Dawn Air (USA) (Diesis)
3206[9] 3684[4] 4072[7] 4673[11] 6050[11] 6600[9]

Morning Chief (IRE) *Clive Cox* a75 73
4 b h Noverre(USA) —Convenience (IRE) (Ela-Mana-Mou)
1144[8] 1450[4] 2051[3] 2454[5] 3042[7] 5002[12]

Morning Glory (FR) *Y De Nicolay* a71 39
4 b m Kaldounevees(FR) —Kerry Rose (FR) (Tel Quel (FR))
5095a[0] 7256a[0]

Morning Muse (IRE) *Peter Winkworth* a49 51
2 b f Amadeus Wolf—Am I (USA) (Thunder Gulch (USA))
4954[4] 5323[7] 5689[7] 6002[6] 6817[13]

Morning Time (IRE) *Lucinda Russell* a80 63
5 b g Hawk Wing(USA) —Desert Trail (IRE) (Desert Style (IRE))
3319[6] 3858[7] 4499[4] 4785[3]

Mororless *Zoe Davison* a64 47
4 b m Exceed And Excel(AUS) —Final Pursuit (Pursuit Of Love)
45[6] 211[5] 312[10] 386[10]

Morrow *Mahmood Al Zarooni* 69
2 ch f Pivotal—Morning Pride (IRE) (Machiavellian (USA))
6934[3]

Mortitia *Brian Meehan* 95
3 b f Dansili—Simianna (Bluegrass Prince (IRE))
1404[5] 1902[9] 2358[5] 3034[14]

Mosaicist (IRE) *James Fanshawe* a89 90
3 gr f Aussie Rules(USA) —Sovereign Grace (IRE) (Standaan (FR))
(2266) (2818) ◆ 3459[6] 5146[5] 6762[2] ◆

Mosa Mine *Bryn Palling* a56 55
4 b m Exceed And Excel(AUS) —Baldemosa (FR) (Lead On Time (USA))
132[6] 337[5] 518[4] 664[9] 7366[3] 7737[4]

Moscow Eight (IRE) *E J O'Neill* a81 88
5 b g Elusive City(USA) —Hurricane Lily (IRE) (Ali-Royal (IRE))
6593a[2]

Moscow Oznick *Des Donovan* a70 67
6 br g Auction House(USA) —Cozette (IRE) (Danehill Dancer (IRE))
7805[14] 7903[10]

Moshaagib (USA) *John Gosden* 76
2 bb c Dynaformer(USA) —Ensenada (USA) (Seeking The Gold (USA))
7083[2]

Mosqueras Romance *Marco Botti* a101 107
5 br m Rock Of Gibraltar(IRE) —Mosquera (GER) (Acatenango (GER))
1104[7] 5980a[2] 7128[3] 7277a[9]

Mossbrae *Roger Varian* 71
2 ch g Selkirk(USA) —Frosty Welcome (USA) (With Approval (CAN))
7083[3]

Most Improved (IRE) *Brian Meehan* 116
2 b c Lawman(FR) —Tonnara (IRE) (Linamix (FR))
4762[2] ◆ (5447) ◆ 6689[3]

Motafarred (IRE) *Micky Hammond* a72 72
9 ch g Machiavellian(USA) —Thurayya (Nashwan (USA))
4076[2] 4603[10] 4679[4] 5504[8] 6098[15]

Motarjm (USA) *Lydia Pearce* a61 65
7 br g Elusive Quality(USA) —Agama (USA) (Nureyev (USA))
1310[5] 2820[5] 3353[4] 5357[10] 5416[2] 5739[7]

Motheeba (USA) *Ed Dunlop* a41 87
2 b f Mustanfar(USA) —Ishraak (USA) (Sahm (USA))
5320[8] 5807[11]

Mother Jones *Bryan Smart* a72 76
3 b f Sleeping Indian—Bella Chica (IRE) (Bigstone (IRE))
1060[2] 1436[3] 1880[8] (3191) 3900[5]

Motirani *Lydia Pearce* a71 71
4 br g Motivator—Maharani (USA) (Red Ransom (USA))
1297[3] 1596[2] 2496[9] 5692[8] 6104[6] 7107[9] 7858[5]

Motivado *Sir Mark Prescott Bt* a81 105
3 b c Motivator—Tamise (USA) (Time For A Change (USA))
(2389) 2695[2] 4108[5] 5283[13] (5710) 6333[4] ◆

Motrice *Sir Mark Prescott Bt* a64 112
4 gr m Motivator—Entente Cordiale (USA) (Affirmed (USA))
3066[9] 4470[3] (5471) 5884[3] 6857[9]

Mottley Crewe *Richard Guest* a88 70
4 b g Mujahid(USA) —Ticcatoo (IRE) (Dolphin Street (FR))
(743) 1067[5] 1584[5] 2543[12] 3471[3] 4393[5] 6133[4] 6305[2] 6646[5] 6793[10] (7079) 7356[2] (7502) ◆ 7586[4] 7644[2]

Motty's Gift *Walter Swinburn* a57 58
4 ch g Lucky Story(USA) —Oatcake (Selkirk (USA))
1177[10] 1486[8] 1993[12]

Mouchez *Dean Ivory* a50 31
4 b g Needwood Blade—Mouchez Le Nez (IRE) (Cyrano De Bergerac)
86[12] 6656[12]

Mount Abora (IRE) *Charles O'Brien* a73 69
4 br m Rock Of Gibraltar(IRE) —Ragtime Blues (IRE) (Grand Lodge (USA))
977a[5] 7548a[13]

Mountain Cat (IRE) *Mrs K Burke* a84 84
7 b g Red Ransom(USA) —Timewee (USA) (Romanov (IRE))
666[7] ◆ 949[3] ◆ (1222) 2115[8] 2887[14]

Mountain Coral (IRE) *F Oakes* a88 88
7 b g Jammaal—Coral Windsor (IRE) (Woods Of Windsor (USA))
1228a^5 7150a^6 7790a^4

Mountain Hiker (IRE) *Jeremy Noseda* 99
4 b g Azamour(IRE) —Sagamartha (Rainbow Quest (USA))
2509^7 2888^3 3794^2 4266^4 5659^5

Mountain Mama (IRE) *C W J Farrell* a7 56
4 b m Mujadil(USA) —Beenablaw (IRE) (Alzao (USA))
6139a^2

Mountain Myst *William Muir* a53 54
3 b g Val Royal(FR) —Brecon (Unfuwain (USA))
77^3 ◆ 171^8 564^5 2307^9 3268^{10} 3587^7 3922^4 5022^3 5566^9 6057^4 6356^5 6823^6

Mountainofstrength *Tony Coyle*
2 b c Iceman—Dream Again (Medicean)
6506^{11}

Mountain Onyx (SWE) *Tina Langstrom*
2 br f Melmac(SWE) —Crystal Rosie (Ardkinglass)
5983a^{11}

Mountain Range (IRE) *John Dunlop* a92 94
3 b g High Chaparral(IRE) —Tuscany Lady (IRE) (Danetime (IRE))
1947^2 2688^4 (4253) 5049^2 5482^9 6130^6 (7328) 7523^4

Mountain Rose (GER) *Mario Hofer* 88
4 b m Tiger Hill(IRE) —Montfleur (Sadler's Wells (USA))
2678^6 3213a^9

Mount Athos (IRE) *David Wachman* a102 108
4 b g Montjeu(IRE) —Ionian Sea (Slip Anchor)
(1381a) 1808^4 ◆ 3625^4 ◆ 4737a^4 5285^8 6690^4

Mount Berry (FR) *D Sepulchre* a81 78
4 gr h Okawango(USA) —Kalberry (FR) (Kaldounevees (FR))
3568a^3

Mount Crystal (IRE) *Charles Hills* a72 67
3 b f Montjeu(IRE) —State Crystal (IRE) (High Estate)
4641^3 ◆ 6810^6 (7503)

Mount Helicon *T Hogan* 106
6 b g Montjeu(IRE) —Model Queen (USA) (Kingmambo (USA))
1119a^5

Mount Hollow *Reg Hollinshead* a82 79
6 b g Beat Hollow—Lady Lindsay (IRE) (Danehill Dancer (IRE))
169^2 428^2 637^7 915^5 2354^4 3348^6 3806^4 4233^2 4793^{10} (5338) (6091) 6283^3 6491^2 6895^2 (7500) 7595^5

Mount Mayday (IRE) *Stuart Williams*
2 b c Rock Of Gibraltar(IRE) —Fille De Joie (IRE) (Royal Academy (USA))
5170^9

Mount McLeod (IRE) *Alan McCabe* a58 56
2 b f Holy Roman Emperor(IRE) —Northern Gulch (USA) (Gulch (USA))
1946^8 2374^7 2661^6 5998^7 6627^2 6942^3 7143^4 7252^2 7337^2 7421^2 7530^5 7541^2 7916^{RR}

Mountrath *Gary Moore* a73 75
4 b g Dubai Destination(USA) —Eurolink Sundance (Night Shift (USA))
248^{10} 1756^2 (2354) 2560^3 2887^{18} 3285^{10} 6254^{12} 6728^{13} (7228) 7447^{11} 7579^8 7764^2

Mount St Mistress *George Baker* 51
2 ch f Zamindar(USA) —Capannina (Grand Lodge (USA))
3870^8 4698^5 5541^7 6101^9

Mourasana *C Lerner* 99
3 b f Shirocco(GER) —Mamoura (IRE) (Lomond (USA))
2750a^9 4036b^2 5027a^7 7580a^0

Mourayan (IRE) *Robert Hickmott* 119
5 b h Alhaarth(IRE) —Mouramara (IRE) (Kahyasi)
7407a^3

Mousie *Alan McCabe* a47 63
2 b f Auction House(USA) —Goes A Treat (IRE) (Common Grounds)
1049^4 1290^3 (1590) 1806^8 2425^2 2797^3 6975^6 7067^5

Moustache (IRE) *Richard Hannon* 94
2 b c Mujadil(USA) —Spree (IRE) (Dansili)
2837^2 ◆ 3511^4 (4414) ◆ 5216^{10} 5701^8 6431^2

Move In Time *Bryan Smart* 106
3 ch c Monsieur Bond(IRE) —Tibesti (Machiavellian (USA))
1122a^3 2032^2 (2405) 2928^3 3441a^3 4768a^2 5524a^4 (6522) ◆

Moyenne Corniche *Brian Ellison* a101 110
6 ch g Selkirk(USA) —Miss Corniche (Hernando (FR))
1112^2 1679^2 2044^3 3396^5 3876^{10} (5285) 6711a^3 7218a^{15}

Moynahan (USA) *Paul Cole* a81 96
6 ch g Johannesburg(USA) —Lakab (USA) (Manila (USA))
1834^3 2441^8 2884^9 3436^2 3802^4 4537^4 4958^{10} 5328^7 6727^5 6948^8 7492^7

Mozayada (USA) *Mel Brittain* a80 53
7 ch m Street Cry(IRE) —Fatina (Nashwan (USA))
1245^6 1499^3 1909^{17} 2399^5 2653^4

Mr Brock (SAF) *M F De Kock* a119 114
8 b g Fort Wood(USA) —Cape Badger (SAF) (Badger Land (USA))
156a^5 330a^2 608a^4 757a^3 824a^2

Mr Chocolate Drop (IRE) *Mandy Rowland* a68 65
7 b g Danetime(IRE) —Forest Blade (IRE) (Charnwood Forest (IRE))
169^5 (317) 626^6 881^2 (1190) 1613^7 1905^2 2809^4 3643^4 4889^3 5349^8 5414^3 5902^7 6544^3 6938^6 7418^7 7711^3 7930^{10}

Mr Churchill (IRE) *Mahmood Al Zarooni* 72
2 b c Invincible Spirit(IRE) —Mayoress (Machiavellian (USA))
5801^8 6300^4 6726^3

Mr. Commons (USA) *John Shirreffs* a110 118
3 b c Artie Schiller(USA) —Joustabout (USA) (Apalachee (USA))
2328a^8 7307a^5

Mr. Crazy Boy (ARG) *M F De Kock* a86 97
5 br g Numerous(USA) —Crazy Fitz (ARG) (Fitzcarraldo (ARG))
157a^{10} 329a^{12} 585a^{10}

Mr Crystal (FR) *Micky Hammond* a41 75
7 ch g Trempolino(USA) —Iyrbila (FR) (Lashkari)
5759^8 6279^4 6915^7

Mr David (USA) *Jamie Osborne* 99
4 b g Sky Mesa(USA) —Dancewiththebride (USA) (Belong To Me (USA))
3032^{23} 3862^4 4494^{18} 4802^3 5272^{14} 5699^6 6341^{14} 6862^{13}

Mr Dob (USA) *Mlle C Brunaud* a66 81
6 b g Dynaformer(USA) —Dorcinea (USA) (Nureyev (USA))
395a^0

Mr Dream Maker (IRE) *Ian Williams* 63
3 b g Araafa(IRE) —Paola Maria (Daylami (IRE))
2582^4 3642^6 4281^{11}

Mr Emirati (USA) *Bryan Smart* a76 52
4 ch g Mr Greeley(USA) —Kathy K D (USA) (Saint Ballado (CAN))
400^3 495^5 637^{10} 869^3 1083^5 1394^{11} 1520^7 1911^8 2589^6 2804^9 3454^7 4128^7 4442^4

Mr Fickle (IRE) *Gary Moore* a41
2 b g Jeremy(USA) —Mamara Reef (Salse (USA))
7126^{10}

Mr Fong *David Simcock* a61 72
2 ch g Dr Fong(USA) —Selkirk Sky (Selkirk (USA))
6697^4 ◆ 6956^5

Mr Funshine *Derek Shaw* a63 62
6 b g Namid—Sunrise Girl (King's Signet (USA))
123^9 250^{10} 311^3 691^6 735^9 1041^6

Mr Gruff (USA) *Ronald W Ellis* 112
7 br g Mr Greeley(USA) —Ruff (USA) (Clever Trick (USA))
996a^{16}

Mr Harmoosh (IRE) *Sheena West* a71 79
4 b g Noverre(USA) —Polish Affair (IRE) (Polish Patriot (USA))
2769^{11}

Mr Hendrix *Brett Johnson* a60 49
2 b g Librettist(USA) —Sprinkle (Selkirk (USA))
3221^5 4007^{12} 4710^4 5316^5 6620^5 (6942) 7452^{11} 7905^5

Mr Hichens *Karen George* a90 87
6 b g Makbul—Lake Melody (Sizzling Melody)
542^4 799^5 3740^7 4268^3 4860^7

Mr Khan *Linda Perratt* 51
3 ch g Rambling Bear—Frabrofen (Mind Games)
1074^9 1494^9

Mr Knightley (IRE) *Jim Boyle* a81 71
2 b c Strategic Prince—Emma's Surprise (Tobougg (IRE))
2787^8 3349^4 3868^3 4496^8 4913^{12} 5233^7 (5637) 6623^3 (6786) (7365) 7670^2 7798^2 7918^4

Mr Macattack *Tom Dascombe* a86 85
6 b g Machiavellian(USA) —Aunty Rose (IRE) (Caerleon (USA))
99^5 ◆ 285^8 736^8 956^4 1061^2 1244^2 1854^7 2020^6

Mr Mackintosh *Anthony Middleton*
3 b g Bertolini(USA) —Caleta (Hernando (FR))
726^6

Mr Majeika (IRE) *Richard Hannon* a85 89
2 b c Oasis Dream—Before The Storm (Sadler's Wells (USA))
1515^4 (1827) 3284^3 4757^2 5592^5 6221^3

Mr Mallo *Richard Ford* a10
2 b g Bertolini(USA) —Londonnet (IRE) (Catrail (USA))
2234^6

Mr Maximas *Bryn Palling* a60 50
4 ch g Auction House(USA) —Cashiki (IRE) (Case Law)
86^3 347^3 (773) 896^2 1273^2 1582^6 4549^7 4948^{13}

Mr Maynard *Sir Michael Stoute* a76 72
2 ch c Notnowcato—Crystal Cavern (USA) (Be My Guest (USA))
4213^6 (5384) ◆ 6995^9

Mr Medici (IRE) *L Ho* a101 121
6 b h Medicean—Way For Life (GER) (Platini (GER))
1742a^9 7729a^{12}

Mr Mo Jo *Lawrence Mullaney* 69
3 b g Danbird(AUS) —Nampara Bay (Emarati (USA))
(1514) 2611^5 3189^5 3702^3 4124^5 5373^9 5719^{13}

Mr Muddle *Sheena West* 35
4 gr g Imperial Dancer—Spatham Rose (Environment Friend)
1619

Mr Mystere *Chris Wall* a12 18
3 b g Dubai Destination(USA) —Vanishing Point (USA) (Caller I.D. (USA))
6307^9 6591^9

Mr Optimistic *Richard Fahey* a79 89
3 b g Kyllachy—Noble Desert (FR) (Green Desert (USA))
(198) 356^2 (1391) 2074^5 ◆ (2411) 2890^{15} 4333^9 5054^{11} 6112^{14}

Mr Opulence *Henry Candy* 56
2 ch g Generous(IRE) —Miss Opulence (IRE) (Kylian (USA))
6463^{12} 6951^9

Mr Perceptive (IRE) *Richard Hannon* 82
3 b g Iffraaj—Astuti (IRE) (Waajib)
1983^6 2877^8 3312^4 3650^2 3988^4 4489^2 5242^8

Mr Plod *Andrew Reid* a62 52
6 ch g Silver Patriarch(IRE) —Emily-Mou (IRE) (Cadeaux Genereux)
(514) 733^{10} 3715^5 4389^{12} 5588^6 7254^2

Mr Pyramus *Jonathan Portman* a49
3 b g Act One—Eiszeit (GER) (Java Gold (USA))
1998^6

Mr Rainbow *Alan Swinbank* a98 95
5 ch g Efisio—Blossom (Warning)
2123^5 2927^5 ◆ 3188^5 4325^6 4794^7 5465^2 6148^3

Mr Red Clubs (IRE) *Tim Pitt* a76 70
2 b g Red Clubs(IRE) —Queen Cobra (IRE) (Indian Rocket)
(7275a) (7590) (7735) (7875)

Mrs Awkward *Mark Brisbourne*
2 b f Primo Valentino(IRE) —Musical Chimes (Josr Algarhoud (IRE))
6977^7 7197^{12} 7367^{11}

Mrs Boss *Rod Millman* a72 78
4 b m Makbul—Chorus (Bandmaster (USA))
792^4 928^7 7484^{12}

Mrs Cash (IRE) *Sylvester Kirk* a51
2 b f Holy Roman Emperor(IRE) —Ring Of Fire (USA) (Nureyev (USA))
7435^8 ◆ 7749^8

Mrs Dee Bee (IRE) *Charles Hills* a85 79
3 b f Barathea(IRE) —Daqtora (Dr Devious (IRE))
3232^F (4478) 5496^2 (6285) 6996^8

Mrs E *Michael Easterby* a42 43
4 b m Doyen(IRE) —Fille De Bucheron (USA) (Woodman (USA))
1277^5 1803^5

Mrs Greeley *Eve Johnson Houghton* 82
3 b f Mr Greeley(USA) —Swain's Gold (USA) (Swain (IRE))
2792^5 ◆ 3292^2 3782^7 4340^2 (4925) (5676) 6167^{10} 7050^9

Mrs Huffey *Henry Candy* 70
2 b f Acclamation—Passing Hour (USA) (Red Ransom (USA))
7292^4 ◆

Mr Skipiton (IRE) *Brian McMath* a63 55
6 b g Statue Of Liberty(USA) —Salty Air (IRE) (Singspiel (IRE))
218^4 5244^5 6105^3 6765^3

Mrs Medley *Garry Woodward* a15 21
5 b m Rambling Bear—Animal Cracker (Primo Dominie)
2593^{13} 3616^{11} 4189^6 4650^6 6034^6 7069^7 7747^8

Mrs Mogg *Tom Dascombe* a69 67
4 b m Green Desert(USA) —Maybe Forever (Zafonic (USA))
113^6 397^6 689^6

Mrs Mop (IRE) *Richard Hannon* a55 53
2 b f Amadeus Wolf—Look Who's Dancing (Observatory (USA))
1143^3 1441^8 1786^3

Mrs Neat (IRE) *Sylvester Kirk* a69 71
3 b f Refuse To Bend(IRE) —Cambara (Dancing Brave (USA))
25^3 142^2 194^5 424^2 (564) 866^2 1057^3 4056^6 4579^2 5050^3 5630^5 6052^7 6493^3 6888^4

Mr Snoozy *Tim Walford* 22
2 b g Pursuit Of Love—Hard To Follow (Dilum (USA))
4292^8

Mr Spiggott (IRE) *Mick Channon* 83
2 b g Intikhab(USA) —Green Green Grass (Green Desert (USA))
5117^4 (5786) (6829)

Mr Splendid (FR) *G Doleuze* a68
2 gr c Zieten(USA) —Salina Sea (FR) (Baryshnikov (AUS))
7665a^{10}

Mr Udagawa *Bernard Llewellyn* a70 72
5 b g Bahamian Bounty—Untold Riches (USA) (Red Ransom (USA))
1530^9 1829^9 2144^3 2685^3 3293^{10} 3804^5 4337^{11} (4701) (5845) 6435^6 7057^{18}

Mr Willis *Terry Clement* a96 89
5 b g Desert Sun—Santiburi Girl (Casteddu)
1100^6 1717^7 2066^{11} 4962^8 7127^{11} 7628^3 7801^6

Mr Wolf *John Quinn* a77 83
10 b g Wolfhound(USA) —Madam Millie (Milford)
1793^9 2250^6 2766^4 3704^7 4078^6 4371^2 ◆ 4678^6 5371^5 6091^5 6276^7

Muaamara *Mick Channon* 80
2 ch f Bahamian Bounty—Mamma Morton (IRE) (Elnadim (USA))
(7132)

Muarrab *Ed Dunlop* 66
2 b c Oasis Dream—Licence To Thrill (Wolfhound (USA))
4414^6 ◆

Mubaarez *F Vermeulen* a85 86
3 b c Green Desert(USA) —Straight Lass (IRE) (Machiavellian (USA))
7669a^5

Mubaraza (IRE) *John Dunlop* 84
2 ch c Dalakhani(IRE) —Mokaraba (Unfuwain (USA))
4330^7 ◆ 5013^5 6954^2 ◆

Mubtadi *David Simcock* 90
3 b c Dr Fong(USA) —Noble Peregrine (Lomond (USA))
1690^5 2296^{12} 2705^2 3067^{13} 3864^9 4550^6 5970^4

Much Acclaimed (IRE) *J Morrison* 88
4 b g Sulamani(IRE) —Much Commended (Most Welcome)
4398a^8

Mucho Macho Man (USA) *Kathy Ritvo* a119
3 b c Macho Uno(USA) —Ponche De Leona (USA) (Ponche (CAN))
1921a^3 2328a^6 2950a^7

Muckle Bahoochie (IRE) *G M Lyons* a78 71
2 b f Moss Vale(IRE) —Multiple (IRE) (Mull Of Kintyre (USA))
2322a^6 3416a^6

Mucky Molly *Olivia Maylam* a44 62
3 ch f Bahamian Bounty—Indian Flag (IRE) (Indian Ridge)
3747^{10} 4203^2 4796^3 5540^2 5787^2 5996^2 6694^{13} 7216^{12} 7269^6 7525^4 7690^9

Mudhish (IRE) *Clive Brittain* a72 69
6 b g Lujain(USA) —Silver Satire (Dr Fong (USA))
1978^5 3130^9 3555^5 4160^8

Mufarrh (IRE) *A Al Raihe* a117 93
4 b g Marju(IRE) —What A Picture (FR) (Peintre Celebre (USA))
583a^3 (679a) 758a^7 997a^2

Mufasa Rules (USA) *Sylvester Kirk* a10 37
3 ch g Tale Of The Cat(USA) —Royal Shyness (Royal Academy (USA))
6020^7 6608^7 7492^8

Muffin McLeay (IRE) *David Barron* 88
3 b g Hawk Wing(USA) —Youngus (USA) (Atticus (USA))
1108^7 1910^4 2361^4 (3304) 5205^2

Muffraaj *David Simcock* a46 86
3 b c Iffraaj—Heckle (In The Wings)
2281^2 (2772) 3181^5 3853^3 4333^{17} 5268^2 6246^{11}

Muftarres (IRE) *Paul Midgley* a67 74
6 b g Green Desert(USA) —Ghazal (USA) (Gone West (USA))
1558^2 1857^3 2487^2 2799^7 3636^5 (4513) 4604^6 5031^4 5455^9 6228^4 6583^3 6990^7 7175^5

Mugazala (IRE) *Ed Dunlop* 74
2 ch f Sakhee(USA) —Nasij (USA) (Elusive Quality (USA))
4804^3

Muhamee (IRE) *Saeed Bin Suroor* a57
2 ch c Proud Citizen(USA) —Santolina (USA) (Boundary (USA))
6928^6 7398^{11}

Muhandis (IRE) *Nick Littmoden* a70 79
3 b g Muhtathir—Ahdaaf (USA) (Bahri (USA))
1203^2 1516^5 (1934) 2389^6 3081^5 7137^{10} 7519^9

Muhta Speed (FR) *A Lyon* 45
2 b g Muhtathir—Love In Paradise (Dalakhani (IRE))
7449a^0

Mujaadel (USA) *David Nicholls* a88 86
6 ch g Street Cry(IRE) —Quiet Rumour (USA) (Alleged (USA))
1244^3 (1793) 1909^3 2061^{12} 2783^9 3506^{10} 3877^{12} 4561^2 5059^{16} 5684^7 6381^9 6533^8 7076^{13}

Mujaazef *A Al Raihe* a104 96
4 b g Dubawi(IRE) —Khubza (Green Desert (USA))
501a^5

Mujady Star (IRE) *Kevin M Prendergast* a33 61
3 b g Mujadil(USA) —Ruwy (Soviet Star (USA))
6659^8 7246^9 7787^{11}

Mujahope *Colin Teague* a42 41
6 b g Mujahid(USA) —Speak (Barathea (IRE))
1468^{11} 1818^5 2233^9 3662^{10} 3972^7 4443^{10} 6158^{10}

Mujarah (IRE) *John Dunlop* 58
3 b f Marju(IRE) —Tanaghum (Darshaan)
3118^6 6729^{10}

Mujood *Eve Johnson Houghton* a60 101
8 b g Mujahid(USA) —Waqood (USA) (Riverman (USA))
1406^{17} 1564^6 1834^7 2876^6 3801^6 4656^8 4997^9 5815^6

Mujrayaat (IRE) *Roger Varian* a80 94
3 b g Invincible Spirit(IRE) —Ellen (IRE) (Machiavellian (USA))
(3543) 4404^4 (6069)

Mulan (GER) *Elisabeth Gautier* 105
4 b g Marju(IRE) —Morning Light (GER) (Law Society (USA))
4842a^9 5984a^6

Mulaqen *Marcus Tregoning* a83 87
3 ch g Haafhd—Burqa (Nashwan (USA))
(1998) 2726^5 4316^3

Mulberry Brite *Karen George* 36
3 b f Librettist(USA) —Thea (USA) (Marju (IRE))
4388^{10}

Muller (ARG) *S Al Harabi* a96 98
8 br g El Compinche(ARG) —Martina Girl (ARG) (Mat-Boy (ARG))
826a^{11}

Mullglen *Tim Easterby* 81
5 b g Mull Of Kintyre(USA) —However (IRE) (Hector Protector (USA))
1698^6 ◆ 1907^{10} 2694^8 2987^2 3832^9 4145^7

Mullins Way (USA) *Jo Hughes* 90
3 ch g Mr Greeley(USA) —Aljawza (USA) (Riverman (USA))
(4439) 6148^{10} 6533^{13} 6949^{14}

Mull Of Killough (IRE) *Richard Fahey* a101 100
5 b g Mull Of Kintyre(USA) —Sun Shower (IRE) (Indian Ridge)
6335^8 7168^5 ◆ 7393^2 ◆ 7523^3 7719^5

Multi Bene *Tom Dascombe* a64
2 b g Multiplex—Attlongglast (Groom Dancer (USA))
6842^3

Multi Blessing *Alan Jarvis* a77 58
2 b c Multiplex—Bahamian Belle (Bahamian Bounty)
1143^4 1932^4 (2380) 6178^8 6786^8 7365^2 7490^6 7635^4

Multilateral (USA) *Amanda Perrett* a53 49
2 rg g Mizzen Mast(USA) —Single Market (USA) (Dynaformer (USA))
5801^9 6216^7

Mumtaz Begum *John E Long* a45 32
6 ch m Kyllachy—Indian Gift (Cadeaux Genereux)
1021^5 1233^{13}

Munaa's Dream *Mrs K Burke* a18 35
3 b f Oasis Dream—Munaawashat (IRE) (Marju (IRE))
2361^{13} 5212^6 5368^5 6609^9 6978^{11}

Munaaseb *Ed Dunlop* a88 60
3 ch g Zafeen(FR) —Miss Prim (Case Law)
(1236) ◆ 2199^5 4909^6 6003^7 6467^{14}

Munaawer (USA) *James Bethell* a64 78
4 ch g Mr Greeley(USA) —Tap Dance (USA) (Pleasant Tap (USA))
2388^2 2800^2 3572^4 4148^4 6182^7 7003^5

Munaawib *David C Griffiths* a20 65
3 b c Haafhd—Mouwadh (USA) (Nureyev (USA))
2691^5 3478^3 5598^{10} 6279^5 6633^4

Munaddam (USA) *E Charpy* a107 97
9 ch g Aljabr(USA) —Etizaaz (USA) (Diesis)
152a^6 332a^{10} 415a^5 587a^9 682a^4

Munbaher (IRE) *Mark Johnston* 84
3 b c King's Best(USA) —Muwajaha (Night Shift (USA))
1151^2 1492^2

Mundana (IRE) *Luca Cumani* 95
3 b f King's Best(USA) —Mail Express (IRE) (Cape Cross (IRE))
2192^{2} ◆ (3289) ◆ (5354) (6496)

Mundesley *Tom Dascombe* a40
3 b g Bahamian Bounty—Ocean Ballad (Bering)
1277^{7} 1484^{9} 2551^{13}

Mungo Park *Mark Johnston* a82 84
3 b g Selkirk(USA) —Key Academy (Royal Academy (USA))
3781^{3} (4014) 4449^{6} 4941^{8} *5714^{3}* 6988^{15}

Munich (IRE) *Barry Brennan* a71 58
7 b g Noverre(USA) —Mayara (IRE) (Ashkalani (IRE))
30^{11} 317^{9} 5994^{7}

Munsarim (IRE) *Keith Dalgleish* a85 86
4 b g Shamardal(USA) —Etizaaz (USA) (Diesis)
1490^{3} 1859^{3} (2734) 3275^{10} (3659) 4415^{12} 5648^{5} 6708^{14} *7199^{3} 7397^{3} 7542^{4}*

Munsef *Ian Williams* a87 112
9 b g Zafonic(USA) —Mazaya (IRE) (Sadler's Wells (USA))
(24) 232^{2}

Muntasib (USA) *Marcus Tregoning* a86 87
3 ch g Mr Greeley(USA) —Halo River (USA) (Irish River (FR))
1175^{5} 2607^{6} 3840^{6} 4355^{3} 5049^{9} 5892^{4} 6574^{5}

Muntasir (IRE) *Saeed Bin Suroor* a71 71
2 b c Distorted Humor(USA) —Mansfield Park (Green Desert (USA))
5384^{4} ◆ 6100^{4}

Muqalad (IRE) *Bryan Smart* a58 75
4 b g Indian Ridge—Tutu Much (IRE) (Sadler's Wells (USA))
255^{8} 375^{3} 545^{3} 674^{7} 798^{4} 912^{10} 1029^{3} 1247^{4} 1464^{8}

Muqtarrib (IRE) *Brian Meehan* 81
3 b c Medicean—Anna Karenina (USA) (Atticus (USA))
2019^{3} 2956^{8} 3623^{6} 4529^{2} 5169^{5} 5894^{5} 6459^{4} 6916^{8}

Murano (IRE) *B De Montzey* 100
2 b c Whipper(USA) —Ask For Love (IRE) (Montjeu (IRE))
3669a^{5} 7220a^{5}

Murbeh (IRE) *Brian Meehan* 101
3 b g Elusive City(USA) —My Funny Valentine (IRE) (Mukaddamah (USA))
1602^{6} 2500^{6} 2911^{2} 3820^{3} 6347^{U}

Murcielago (GER) *M Keller* a85 93
4 ch g Areion(GER) —My Angel (GER) (Luigi (GER))
1263a^{5} 1575a^{7} 3531a^{9}

Murmur (IRE) *Sir Henry Cecil*
2 b f Marju(IRE) —Siphon Melody (USA) (Siphon (BRZ))
5854^{9}

Muroona (IRE) *Mark Johnston* 64
3 b f Invincible Spirit(IRE) —Knight's Place (IRE) (Hamas (IRE))
1984^{7} 2479^{3} 2869^{3} 3387^{4}

Murura (IRE) *Kevin Ryan* a77 95
4 b g Green Desert(USA) —Victoria Regia (IRE) (Lomond (USA))
(3778) 4357^{5} ◆ (6174) 6388a^{2}

Musaalem (USA) *Doug Watson* a85 87
7 gr g Aljabr(USA) —Atyab (USA) (Mr Prospector (USA))
602a^{8} 825a^{6}

Musashi (IRE) *Laura Mongan* a65 63
6 ch g Hawk Wing(USA) —Soubrette (USA) (Opening Verse (USA))
1135^{2} *1582^{4}* 1636^{4} 2759^{5} 4445^{6} 5667^{6} 6722^{11} *7091^{7} 7206^{6}*

Musawama (IRE) *John Gosden* a83 77
3 b g Azamour(IRE) —Chater (Alhaarth (IRE))
(992) ◆ *(1194)* 1478^{4} 2228^{6}

Musharakaat (IRE) *Ed Dunlop* a77 92
3 b f Iffraaj—Gift Of Spring (USA) (Gilded Time (USA))
1320^{6} 1807^{4} 3065^{8} 4420^{6} [illegible]

Mush Mir (IRE) *Jim Boyle* a98 94
4 b g Key Of Luck(USA) —Mawaheb (IRE) (Nashwan (USA))
266^{5} (457) (492) (549) 1030^{2} 1416^{4}

Mushroom *Roger Charlton* a31
3 b f Domedriver(IRE) —Spout (Salse (USA))
171^{10} 360^{7}

Mushy Peas (IRE) *David Evans* a58 57
4 b g Bahri(USA) —Unintentional (Dr Devious (IRE))
98^{8} 362^{12} 432^{4} 1247^{9} 1357^{8}

Musical Bridge *Lisa Williamson* a62 76
5 b g Night Shift(USA) —Carrie Pooter (Tragic Role (USA))
1523^{2} 1856^{6} (2913) 3640^{5} (3768) 3994^{3}

Musical Contest (SWE) *Kerstin Helander*
2 b f Songline(SWE) —Bongo Quest (IRE) (Be My Guest (USA))
5983a^{2}

Musical Flight *Charles Hills* 68
3 b c Hurricane Run(IRE) —Chaminade (USA) (Danzig (USA))
1271^{8} 6324^{3}

Musical Leap *Shaun Harris* a35 43
3 b g Superior Premium—Musical Fair (Piccolo)
4647^{9} 5021^{P} 5649^{8} 5996^{10} 6940^{13} 7230^{4} *7245^{6}*

Musically *Mick Channon* a54 70
2 b f Singspiel(IRE) —Pelagia (IRE) (Lycius (USA))
3258^{4} *3981^{6}* 4471^{14} 4913^{5}

Musical Romance (USA) *William Kaplan* a119 92
4 bb m Concorde's Tune(USA) —Candlelightdinner (USA) (Slew Gin Fizz (USA))
(7282a)

Musical Script (USA) *Mouse Hamilton-Fairley* a74 66
8 b g Stravinsky(USA) —Cyrillic (USA) (Irish River (FR))
34^{2} 96^{9} 139^{6}

Musical Strike *Shaun Harris* a51 35
2 b g Striking Ambition—Musical Fair (Piccolo)
1939^{7} 2523^{7} 6890^{10} *7267^{5} 7364^{7} 7530^{10}*

Musical Valley *Tom Dascombe* a70 74
2 ch g Three Valleys(USA) —Musical Horizon (USA) (Distant View (USA))
1791^{8} 2570^{6} 2901^{2} (3539) 3810^{6} ◆ 4069^{7} 4572^{3} 4809^{4} 5348^{2} 5562^{9} 6323^{8} *6540^{2} 6975^{9}* 7231^{7}

Music City (IRE) *Mark Johnston* 81
4 ch g Dalakhani(IRE) —Mia Mambo (USA) (Affirmed (USA))
1390^{12} 2544^{11} 3580^{7}

Music Festival (USA) *Jim Goldie* a64 73
4 b h Storm Cat(USA) —Musical Chimes (USA) (In Excess)
(1649) 2095^{7} 2732^{3} 3113^{4} 3657^{2} 4141^{6} 4380^{5} 4782^{2} 4877^{2} 5722^{5} 6098^{9} 6381^{3} 6869^{8} *7695^{5} 7716^{9}*

Music Girl *Michael Blanshard* 40
2 b f Oratorio(IRE) —Gwen John (USA) (Peintre Celebre (USA))
2767^{13} 4430^{7} 4884^{4} 5343^{9}

Music In The Rain (IRE) *J S Bolger* 88
3 b g Invincible Spirit(IRE) —Greek Symphony (IRE) (Mozart (IRE))
5746a^{16}

Music Lover *John Panvert* a57 58
4 b g Piccolo—Ligne D'Amour (Pursuit Of Love)
280^{11} 388^{5}

Music On D Waters (IRE) *Peter Casey* a42 62
3 br f Byron—Tarafiya (USA) (Trempolino (USA))
1663a^{9}

Music Show (IRE) *Mick Channon* 119
4 b m Noverre(USA) —Dreamboat (USA) (Mr Prospector (USA))
1527^{4} 2029^{4} 3030^{7} 5753a^{4} 6338^{5}

Musigny (USA) *Sally Hall* a31 47
5 bb g Forest Wildcat(USA) —Water Rights (USA) (Kris S (USA))
6262^{11}

Musir (AUS) *M F De Kock* a122 120
5 b h Redoute's Choice(AUS) —Dizzy De Lago (AUS) (Encosta De Lago (AUS))
501a^{2} ◆ *758a^{2} 1002a^{7}* 1576a^{3} 5046^{3} (5777a)

Musk (SAF) *S Gouvaze* 51
5 b h Spectrum(IRE) —Scent Of Pine (SAF) (Badger Land (USA))
903a^{0}

Muskat Princesse (FR) *Mario Hofer*
2 b f Lord Of England(GER) —Muskatwolke (GER) (Acatenango (GER))
6925a^{0}

Muskatsturm (GER) *Shaun Harley* a2 87
12 b g Lecroix(GER) —Myrthe (GER) (Konigsstuhl (GER))
6868^{3}

Musketier (GER) *Roger L Attfield* 115
9 rg h Acatenango(GER) —Myth And Reality (Linamix (FR))
6910a^{6}

Musleh (USA) *E Charpy* a66 42
5 b g Forestry(USA) —Lucifer's Stone (USA) (Horse Chestnut (SAF))
536a^{9}

Musnad (USA) *Brian Ellison* 84
3 ch g Mr Greeley(USA) —Jadarah (USA) (Red Ransom (USA))
1985^{5} 2511^{5} 3377^{5} 5469^{6} 6098^{7} ◆ 6674^{2} ◆

Mustafeed (USA) *Keith Dalgleish* a51
3 bb g Distorted Humor(USA) —Word Of Mouth (USA) (Saint Ballado (CAN))
6834^{10} *7179^{6} 7249^{5} 7755^{7} 7854^{10}*

Mustajed *Rod Millman* a66 70
10 b g Alhaarth(IRE) —Jasarah (IRE) (Green Desert (USA))
1107^{17} 1833^{4} 2308^{10} (2843) *3240^{2}* 3754^{8} 4579^{3} 5588^{2} 6029^{9} 6461^{4} *6656^{5} 7254^{7} 7441^{12} 7564^{11}*

Mut'Ab (USA) *Edward Creighton* a76 48
6 b g Alhaarth(IRE) —Mistle Song (Nashwan (USA))
1355^{5}

Mutabayen (USA) *M Ramadan* a36 48
6 br h Doneraile Court(USA) —La Frou Frou (IRE) (Night Shift (USA))
536a^{8}

Mutadarrej (IRE) *Mrs Y Dunleavy* a60 66
7 ch g Fantastic Light(USA) —Najayeb (USA) (Silver Hawk (USA))
7631^{5}

Mutahadee (IRE) *T Stack* a89 106
3 b c Encosta De Lago(AUS) —Mosaique Bleue (Shirley Heights)
4831a^{3} 5744a^{4}

Mutajaaser (USA) *Kevin Morgan* a69 11
6 b g War Chant(USA) —Hazimah (USA) (Gone West (USA))
475^{9} 647^{9} 802^{5} 1273^{3} 1373^{7}

Mutajare (IRE) *Mark Johnston* a89 86
3 b g Cadeaux Genereux—Bona Dea (IRE) (Danehill (USA))
1152^{10} 1688^{8} 2092^{2} 2503^{9} 3159^{6} 4335^{10} 5056^{2} 5892^{5} *(6439)*

Mutamaleq (IRE) *Ian McInnes* a69 74
4 b g Refuse To Bend(IRE) —Chaturanga (Night Shift (USA))
684^{3} 878^{3} 1190^{4} 2487^{7} *3234^{P}*

Mutarjim (USA) *Saeed Bin Suroor* a49
2 bb c Dynaformer(USA) —Thunder Kitten (USA) (Storm Cat (USA))
7398^{8}

Mutasadder (USA) *Roger Varian* 73
2 b c Distorted Humor(USA) —Dessert (USA) (Storm Cat (USA))
6993^{4}

Mutayaser *Sir Michael Stoute* a52 81
3 b g Shamardal(USA) —Borgia (GER) (Acatenango (GER))
2188^{3} 2764^{6}

Mutheeb (USA) *M Al Muhairi* a114 105
6 b h Danzig(USA) —Magicalmysterykate (USA) (Woodman (USA))
155a^{9} 414a^{3} ◆ 602a^{5} 754a^{10}

Mutiska (IRE) *J C Hayden* a69 71
4 ch m Muhtarram(USA) —Biasca (Erhaab (USA))
7544a^{6}

Mutual Force (USA) *A Al Raihe* a86 77
3 b c Arch(USA) —Freeroll (USA) (Touch Gold (USA))
411a^{14}

Mutual Regard (IRE) *Sir Mark Prescott Bt* a60
2 b g Hernando(FR) —Hidden Charm (IRE) (Big Shuffle (USA))
6697^{5} 6977^{3} 7240^{5}

Mutual Trust *A Fabre* 119
3 b c Cacique(IRE) —Posteritas (USA) (Lear Fan (USA))
(2978a) (3670a) 5129a^{10}

Muwalla *Chris Grant* a82 77
4 b g Bahri(USA) —Easy Sunshine (IRE) (Sadler's Wells (USA))
3545^{4} (4024) 4366^{5} 4747^{5} 5441^{6} 7215^{11}

Muzdaan (IRE) *Roger Varian* 60
2 ch f Exceed And Excel(AUS) —Belle Genius (USA) (Beau Genius (CAN))
7164^{9}

Muzdahi (USA) *John Dunlop* 86
3 bb g Smarty Jones(USA) —Reem Al Barari (USA) (Storm Cat (USA))
2068^{4} (2841) 3649^{9}

Muzey's Princess *Michael Mullineaux*
5 b m Grape Tree Road—Premier Princess (Hard Fought)
6504^{8}

Muzo (USA) *Chris Dwyer* a82 74
5 b g Gone West(USA) —Bowl Of Emeralds (USA) (A.P. Indy (USA))
(127) (314) 486^{3} 849^{2} 1105^{5} 1847^{10} 2312^{4}

My Arch *Ollie Pears* 93
9 b g Silver Patriarch(IRE) —My Desire (Grey Desire)
1412^{8} 1847^{8} 2499^{7} (3205) 3396^{9} 4423^{12} 5448^{4} 6171^{8} 6690^{14}

Myasun (FR) *C Baillet* a101 103
4 ch g Panis(USA) —Spain (FR) (Bering)
3654a^{5} 7534a^{5} *7678a^{5}*

My Best Bet *Derek Shaw* a85 82
5 ch m Best Of The Bests(IRE) —Cibenze (Owington)
6256^{8} 7332^{5} 7531^{10}

My Best Man *Tony Carroll* a54 23
5 b g Forzando—Victoria Sioux (Ron's Victory (USA))
138^{5} 250^{4} 312^{7} 421^{9} 6398^{8} 6610^{13} *7389^{6} 7511^{4} 7525^{2} 7676^{7} 7747^{3}*

My Body Is A Cage (IRE) *Peter Chapple-Hyam* 72
2 ch f Strategic Prince—Moonlight Wish (IRE) (Peintre Celebre (USA))
4726^{2}

Myboyalfie (USA) *J R Jenkins* a59 72
4 b g Johannesburg(USA) —Scotchbonnetpepper (USA) (El Gran Senor (USA))
2596^{8} *3739^{6}* 5015^{8} 5518^{7} 5845^{4} (6434)

My Boy Davis (IRE) *J-P Perruchot* a68 84
4 b g Whipper(USA) —Aldovea (Nashwan (USA))
479a^{6}

My Boy Ginger *Rod Millman* 55
2 ch c Byron—Lady Chef (Double Trigger (IRE))
3779^{9} 5841^{7} 6432^{5}

My Cherie Amour *Richard Guest*
3 b f Pastoral Pursuits—Beleza (IRE) (Revoque (IRE))
5607^{11} 6096^{11}

My Delirium *Ralph Beckett* 83
3 b f Haafhd—Clare Hills (IRE) (Orpen (USA))
2102^{15} 2926^{13}

My Destination (IRE) *Mahmood Al Zarooni* 80
2 b c Dubai Destination(USA) —Gossamer (Sadler's Wells (USA))
6400^{7} [illegible]

My Elliemay *David Evans* 58
3 b f Oratorio(IRE) —Virginia Reel (King's Best (USA))
1525^{4} 2550^{11}

My Flame *J R Jenkins* a52 57
6 b g Cool Jazz—Suselja (IRE) (Mon Tresor)
1486^{5} 1911^{11} 3942^{4} *5944^{5} 6083^{9} 7119^{7}*

Myfourthboy *Alan Berry*
4 b g Grape Tree Road—Firedancer (Nashwan (USA))
7913^{6}

My Freedom (IRE) *Saeed Bin Suroor* 97
3 b g Invincible Spirit(IRE) —Priere (Machiavellian (USA))
3400^{2} 3825^{2} ◆ 4313^{7} 5450^{2} ◆ 6335^{5}

My Gacho (IRE) *David Nicholls* a88 89
9 b g Shinko Forest(IRE) —Floralia (Auction Ring (USA))
1109^{8} (1748) 2300^{11} 3071^{6} 3506^{3} 4537^{9} 5760^{18} 5920^{2} 6113^{19} 7074^{14}

My Gi Gi (USA) *Brian Koriner* a102 93
2 b f E Dubai(USA) —Relish The Thought (IRE) (Sadler's Wells (USA))
7281a^{12}

My Girl Anna (IRE) *Muredach Kelly* a76 83
4 b m Orpen(USA) —Kooyong (IRE) (College Chapel)
7149a^{13} 7468a^{12}

My Guardian Angel *Mark H Tompkins* 64
2 b g Araafa(IRE) —Angels Guard You (Bahamian Bounty)
3132^{10} 3553^{8} 3954^{3}

My Heart's On Fire (IRE) *Tom Dascombe* a78 75
3 b f Beat Hollow—Rafting (IRE) (Darshaan)
2551^{5} 4985^{2} *(5386)* 6294^{6}

My Indy (ARG) *M bin Shafya* a102
7 br h Indygo Shiner(USA) —My Light (ARG) (Southern Halo (USA))
156a^{9} 416a^{6} 604a^{9}

My Jeanie (IRE) *Jimmy Fox* a23 48
7 ch m King Charlemagne(USA) —Home Comforts (Most Welcome)
3096^{4} 3636^{11} 4928^{6} 5653^{6} *7581^{7}*

Myjestic Melody (IRE) *Noel Wilson* a32 56
3 b f Majestic Missile(IRE) —Bucaramanga (IRE) (Distinctly North (USA))
3207^{9} 4146^{4} 4786^{2} 5010^{3} 5506^{6} *6874^{7}*

My Juju (FR) *B De Montzey*
4 gr m Blackdoun(FR) —Mary The Second (IRE) (Marju (IRE))
5195a^{0}

My Kingdom (IRE) *Ian Williams* a68 98
5 b g King's Best(USA) —Nebraas (Green Desert (USA))
1849^{4} 2706^{20} 3395^{9} ◆ 3704^{3} 4574^{10} 5043^{2} 5272^{11} 6327^{9} 6762^{13} 7050^{10} *7542^{9}*

My Lady Picolla *Dr Jon Scargill* a16
2 ch f Piccolo—Glider (IRE) (Silver Kite (USA))
6927^{9} 7330^{8} 7481^{10}

My Learned Friend (IRE) *Andrew Balding* a74 82
7 b g Marju(IRE) —Stately Princess (Robellino (USA))
2719^{6} 3674^{6} 4066^{10} 4546^{3} 6378^{2} *7579^{3}*

My Liberty *Chris Dwyer* a23
2 b f Librettist(USA) —Debby (USA) (Woodman (USA))
5813^{10}

My Lord *Ronald Harris* a81 71
3 br g Ishiguru(USA) —Lady Smith (Greensmith)
576^{2} 724^{2} 845^{10} (913) 1178^{2} 1334^{3} 6767^{7} 7055^{6} *7332^{6} 7629^{12}*

My Love Fajer (IRE) *Alan McCabe* a71 66
3 ch g Exceed And Excel(AUS) —Karenaragon (Aragon)
1065^{2} 1595^{6} 2524^{9} 3075^{8} 3307^{7} *3523^{3}* 4067^{8} *4207^{6}* 4527^{2} 4820^{8} *(4924)* 5019^{5} *5244^{10} 5941^{7}* 6386^{12}

My Lucky Liz (IRE) *David Simcock* 85
2 b f Exceed And Excel(AUS) —Areyaam (USA) (Elusive Quality (USA))
1846^{4} 2153^{6} (3016) 3435^{3} 3842^{3} 4551^{3} (5270) 5933^{6}

My Mandy (IRE) *Ronald Harris* a59 69
4 b m Xaar—Ikan (IRE) (Sri Pekan (USA))
653^{6}

My Mate Jake (IRE) *James Given* a65 74
3 ch g Captain Rio—Jam (IRE) (Arazi (USA))
(1277) 2527^{4} 3002^{8} 3340^{7} 4854^{11} *6181^{7}* (6833) 7112^{DSQ} 7215^{14}

My Mate Les (IRE) *John Best* a49 52
3 b g High Chaparral(IRE) —Precedence (IRE) (Polish Precedent (USA))
3675^{4} 4827^{10} *5832^{10} 6844^{5}*

My Mate Mal *William Stone* a74 75
7 b g Daawe(USA) —Kandymal (IRE) (Prince Of Birds (USA))
117^{2} 252^{9} 418^{6} 551^{3} 939^{3}

My Mate Max *Reg Hollinshead* a70 82
6 b g Fraam—Victory Flip (IRE) (Victory Note (USA))
1914^{2} 3095^{10} 3507^{11}

My Meteor *Tony Newcombe* a59 65
4 b g Bahamian Bounty—Emerald Peace (IRE) (Green Desert (USA))
912^{12} 3721^{2} (3999) 4230^{6} (4487) 5917^{2} 6398^{2} 6802^{13}

My Miss Aurelia (USA) *Steven Asmussen* a120
2 b f Smart Strike(CAN) —My Miss Storm Cat (USA) (Sea Of Secrets (USA))
(7283a)

Mymumsaysimthebest *Gary Moore* a96 86
6 b g Reel Buddy(USA) —Night Gypsy (Mind Games)
818^{6} 1444^{2} ◆ (1838) 2369^{6} 2557^{3} *(3222) (3517)* 4531^{17}

My Name Is Bert *Lucinda Featherstone* a61 57
5 b g Bertolini(USA) —Argostoli (Marju (IRE))
3719^{8} 4987^{4} 5547^{7} *5902^{8}*

My Name Is Sam *Ronald Harris* a44 18
2 b c Green Desert(USA) —Caught You Looking (Observatory (USA))
5613^{11} *6620^{8} 7593^{7}*

My New Angel (IRE) *Paul Green* a40 37
2 gr f Dark Angel(IRE) —Mynu Girl (IRE) (Charnwood Forest (IRE))
4283^{8} 4748^{10} 5367^{8} 5817^{12} *7697^{9} 7915^{5}*

My One Weakness (IRE) *Brian Ellison* a61 60
4 ch g Bertolini(USA) —Lucina (Machiavellian (USA))
1077^{9}

My Own Way Home *Des Donovan* a63 65
3 b f Danbird(AUS) —Wenden Belle (IRE) (Brave Act)
2852^{3} 3343^{2} (3756) 4234^{7} 5119^{7} *5640^{6}* 6604^{10}

My Pearl (IRE) *Kevin Ryan* 55
2 b g Sleeping Indian—My-Lorraine (IRE) (Mac's Imp (USA))
4377^{4} 5161^{7} 5681^{6} 6293^{9}

My Piccadill *Stuart Kittow* 33
3 b f Piccolo—Dilys (Efisio)
4340^{11} 5346^{P}

Myplacelater *David Elsworth* a102 111
4 ch m Where Or When(IRE) —Star Welcome (Most Welcome)
2029^{8} 3775^{8} 4293^{2} 4789^{6} 5093a^{8} *5711^{4}* 6301^{5}

My Propeller (IRE) *Peter Chapple-Hyam* 100
2 b f Holy Roman Emperor(IRE) —Incise (Dr Fong (USA))
2467^{7} (3201) ◆ 3821^{10} (5286) 5882^{8} 6518^{10}

My Queenie (IRE) *Richard Hannon* 96
2 b f Nayef(USA) —Margay (IRE) (Marju (IRE))
4061^{5} 4427^{3} 4969^{2} 5472^{5} (5806) 6128^{4} 7028^{8}

My Ruby (IRE) *Jim Best* 65
3 b f Oasis Dream—Dreams Come True (FR) (Zafonic (USA))
1853^{6} 2192^{6} 3432^{14} 4321^{10}

My Scat Daddy (USA) *Brett Johnson* a54 41
2 b g Scat Daddy(USA) —Will Be A Bates (USA) (Bates Motel (USA))
3282^{10} 4087^{8} 6588^{10} *(7937)*

My Scotsgrey (NZ) *Shaune Ritchie* 93
6 gr g Golan(IRE) —My Chameleon (NZ) (Grosvenor (NZ))
6711a^{12}

My Sharona *Sylvester Kirk* a73 71
2 br f Dark Angel(IRE) —Tanda Tula (IRE) (Alhaarth (IRE))
2787[4] 3257[5] 4184[2] (4682) 5233[3] *5945*[2]

My Single Malt (IRE) *Tom Tate* 83
3 b g Danehill Dancer(IRE) —Slip Dance (IRE) (Celtic Swing)
1152[3] 2043[4] 2319[6] 3578[6] 4854[3] 5621[2] 5820[5]

My Sister *Mark Usher* a54 67
4 b m Royal Applause—Mysistra (FR) (Machiavellian (USA))
90[3] *278*[9] 4322[4] 4949[8] 5538[4] 5912[6] 6438[4]

My Solitaire (IRE) *Clive Cox* 71
2 b f Clodovil(IRE) —Bint Kaldoun (IRE) (Kaldoun (FR))
1337[6] 2580[4] (3117) 3842[7] 4913[8] 6196a[14] 6921[6]

My Son Max *Richard Hannon* a85 86
3 b g Avonbridge—Pendulum (Pursuit Of Love)
1916[5] 2147[3] (2937) 3798[8] 5056[5] *5717*[9] 6728[4]

Mystake (IRE) *David Nicholls*
2 ch g Strategic Prince—Without Words (Lion Cavern (USA))
2362[8]

My St Clair (IRE) *C Byrnes* a65 67
6 b m Xaar—Joy St Clair (IRE) (Try My Best (USA))
7003[12]

Mysterious Man (IRE) *Andrew Balding* 79
2 b c Manduro(GER) —Edabiya (IRE) (Rainbow Quest (USA))
6126[4] ◆ 6771[4]

Mystery Cool (IRE) *Stuart Williams* a51 87
2 b f One Cool Cat(USA) —Lost Icon (IRE) (Intikhab (USA))
2823[2] 3171[7] *3746*[6]

Mystery Star (IRE) *Mark H Tompkins* a102 104
6 ch g Kris Kin(USA) —Mystery Hill (USA) (Danehill (USA))
1808[3] 3396[13] 4532[5] 5659[7] 6690[31]

Mystica (IRE) *Dominic Ffrench Davis* a61 61
3 b f Noverre(USA) —Mystery Play (IRE) (Sadler's Wells (USA))
4270[11] 4640[6] 5138[8]

Mystical Power (FR) *D Windrif* a63
2 ch f Tomorrows Cat(USA) —Miss Maguilove (FR) (Dyhim Diamond (IRE))
7666a[5]

Mystical Storm (TUR) *H Caliskan* 97
4 b m Unaccounted For(USA) —Nagme (TUR) (Lockton)
5753a[6]

Mystic Dream *B W Hills* a85 79
3 b f Oasis Dream—Tarot Card (Fasliyev (USA))
(775a) 1599[5] 2073[8] 3819[11]

Mystic Edge *Michael Bell* a63 77
3 ch f Needwood Blade—Magic Flo (Magic Ring (IRE))
2166[3] 2849[2] (3742) (4009) 4584[9] 5518[5] 7137[12]

Mystic Halo *Frank Sheridan* a52
8 ch m Medicean—Aglow (Spinning World (USA))
7717[3]

Mystic Joy (IRE) *N Leenders* a83 79
4 gr g Shamardal(USA) —Mystic Mile (IRE) (Sadler's Wells (USA))
840a[7]

Mystified (IRE) *Alan Berry* a59 25
8 b g Raise A Grand(IRE) —Sunrise (IRE) (Sri Pekan (USA))
172[5] *560*[9] *1473*[9] 6379[7]

My Sweet Baby (USA) *F Nass* a78 102
5 b m Minardi(USA) —Gmaasha (IRE) (Kris)
241[11]

My Tendresse (FR) *P Demercastel* 44
2 b f Stormy River(FR) —My Fantasy (IRE) (Desert King (IRE))
6925a[10] 7312a[8]

Mythical Blue (IRE) *Peter Grayson* a46 83
5 b g Acclamation—Proud Myth (IRE) (Mark Of Esteem (IRE))
464[9] *691*[10]

My Valley (IRE) *Pat Phelan* a70 76
9 b m Saddlers' Hall(IRE) —Marble Sound (IRE) (Be My Native (USA))
(301) *486*[7] *955*[2] (1282) 1839[3] 3352[2] 4697[4] 5198[6]

My Vindication (USA) *Richard Hannon* a77 78
3 bb g Vindication(USA) —Classy Mirage (USA) (Storm Bird (CAN))
1446[2] *1609*[2] *3044*[9] 3514[8] 4081[4] 4447[10] 4825[10] *5630*[7] 6586[14]

My Xaar In Blue (SWI) *P Vovcenko*
5 b g Xaar—My Lucky Star (FR) (Caerleon (USA))
629a[14]

Naabegha *Ed de Giles* 97
4 ch g Muhtathir—Hawafiz (Nashwan (USA))
5684[9] 6326[3] 6862[14]

Naafetha (IRE) *George Foster* 59
3 b f Alhaarth(IRE) —Doctrine (Barathea (IRE))
4542[4] ◆ 5443[3] 5792[10] 6777[12]

Naaset *John Dunlop* a81
4 b h Pivotal—Hathrah (IRE) (Linamix (FR))
1606[3]

Nabah *Clive Brittain* a74 93
3 b f Motivator—Kiss And Fly (IRE) (Priolo (USA))
1096[7] 1722[5] 2358[2] 2678[7] 4356[2]

Nacho Libre *Michael Easterby* a65 72
6 b g Kyllachy—Expectation (IRE) (Night Shift (USA))
367[9] *674*[10] *915*[9] *7504*[11] *7728*[9]

Nachos (FR) *R Chotard* a67 67
7 b g Anabaa Blue—Starlaire (FR) (Beaudelaire (USA))
2867a[10]

Nachtschwarmer (GER) *Frau Marion Rotering*
7 ch g Platini(GER) —Nava Jogini (FR) (Noblequest (FR))
629a[11] *903a*[0]

Nadeaud (FR) *D Guillemin* 97
2 gr f Soave(GER) —Halix (FR) (Tropular)
5365a[7] 7155a[3]

Nadeen (IRE) *Michael Smith* a86 89
4 b g Bahamian Bounty—Janayen (USA) (Zafonic (USA))
(1073) 1539[5] 1878[5] 2434[8] 2890[13] 3279[10] 4327[9] 5108[4] 5554[7] 6537[11] *7356*[8] *7646*[9]

Nadia's Place *Nigel Tinkler* 31
2 b f Compton Place—Basbousate Nadia (Wolfhound (USA))
3201[10] 3680[9] 4232[7] 4668[6] 5105[6] 5555[11]

Nafa (IRE) *Michael Mullineaux* a62 58
3 br f Shamardal(USA) —Champs Elysees (USA) (Distant Relative)
3091[6] 3577[11] 3909[4] 4466[3] (4786) 5274[8] *5941*[5] *6501*[5] *7853*[2]

Nagham (IRE) *Kevin Ryan* 90
2 b f Camacho—Happy Talk (IRE) (Hamas (IRE))
(2580) 3022[2] 4094[3]

Nahab *David Lanigan* a91 74
4 b m Selkirk(USA) —State Secret (Green Desert (USA))
(1587) ◆ *(1867)* 2269[6] *3521*[5] *3740*[2] 4253[8] *5687*[5]

Naheell *George Prodromou* a67 34
5 ch h Lomitas—Seyooll (IRE) (Danehill (USA))
247[8] *496*[2] *644*[7] *917*[4] *7122*[5] *7363*[5] *7496*[7]

Nahrain *Roger Varian* 116
3 ch f Selkirk(USA) —Bahr (Generous (IRE))
(2157) ◆ (2833) (3648) ◆ (6568a) 7284a[2]

Naidoo (GER) *Frau Marion Rotering* a72 71
9 b g Goofalik(USA) —Nirvana (USA) (Green Dancer (USA))
903a[6]

Najoum (USA) *Saeed Bin Suroor* a85 75
3 b f Giant's Causeway(USA) —Divine Dixie (USA) (Dixieland Band (USA))
151a[8]

Najraan *Clive Brittain* 50
3 b f Cadeaux Genereux—Madam Ninette (Mark Of Esteem (IRE))
3135[7] 6608[5]

Nakaling (FR) *E Danel* a65 61
8 ch h Calling Collect(USA) —Nakama (IRE) (General Holme (USA))
935a[4]

Nakayama Festa (JPN) *Yoshitaka Ninomiya* 129
5 b h Stay Gold(JPN) —Dear Wink (JPN) (Tight Spot (USA))
5986a[4] 6567a[11]

Nakayama Knight (JPN) *Yoshitaka Ninomiya* 110
3 ch c Stay Gold(JPN) —Fiji Girl (JPN) (Cacoethes (USA))
5987a[6] 6558a[10]

Nakhutha (FR) *Mahmood Al Zarooni* 52
3 b c Dalakhani(IRE) —Alharir (USA) (Zafonic (USA))
5960[5] 6242[7]

Naledi *Richard Price* a53 51
7 b g Indian Ridge—Red Carnation (IRE) (Polar Falcon (USA))
346[9] *574*[5] *675*[5] *896*[3] *1253*[5] 2851[2] 3311[3] 3600[2] 3910[7]

Namecheck (GER) *Mahmood Al Zarooni* 107
4 ch h Shamardal(USA) —Nadia (Nashwan (USA))
1684[16] 2927[6] (4100) 4494[11]

Nameitwhatyoulike *Michael Easterby* 78
2 b g Trade Fair—Emma Peel (Emarati (USA))
1619[8] 1691[13] 2007[9] 2665[3] (2889) 3700[11] 4943[2] 5825[9] 6111[2] 6670[11]

Namibian (IRE) *Mark Johnston* 115
3 b c Cape Cross(IRE) —Disco Volante (Sadler's Wells (USA))
1339[4] 1689[5] 2191[2] 2507[4] 2726[3] (3108) (4411) 5182[5]

Namir (IRE) *James Evans* a65 63
9 b g Namid—Danalia (IRE) (Danehill (USA))
169[9] *512*[7] 6436[8] *7224*[8] *7371*[2] *7737*[11]

Namwahjobo (IRE) *Jim Goldie* 88
3 b c Namid—Notley Park (Wolfhound (USA))
(2574) (3114) ◆ 3346[4] 4324[4] 5054[14] 6113[9] ◆ 7171[16]

Nanard De Pail (FR) *B Beaunez*
3 b g Great Pretender(IRE) —Peremption (FR) (Villez (USA))
5132a[0]

Nani Jani *Bruce Hellier*
2 ch f Halling(USA) —Bettys Pride (Lion Cavern (USA))
6131[11]

Nannerl (IRE) *Kevin Ryan* a49 46
2 b f Amadeus Wolf—Orpendonna (IRE) (Orpen (USA))
1049[3] 1301[3] 3125[5] *3708*[7]

Nanni Pepi (ITY) *M Innocenti*
3 b c Coral Reef(ITY) —Villa Sinius (ITY) (Sesin)
1126a[9]

Nanton (USA) *Jim Goldie* a104 109
9 rg g Spinning World(USA) —Grab The Green (USA) (Cozzene (USA))
1112[5] 1717[5] 2107[9] (2573) 3876[13] 5285[14] 5883[2] 6339[4] 6519[3] 7029[13]

Nant Saeson (IRE) *Richard Hannon* 74
2 b c Elusive City(USA) —Lady Power (IRE) (Almutawakel)
3590[4] 4213[3] 4995[5] 5937[4]

Napa Starr (FR) *Eoin Griffin* a84 93
7 b g Marchand De Sable(USA) —Jade D'Eau (IRE) (Lion Cavern (USA))
6513a[11] *7793a*[8]

Napoleons Mistress (IRE) *Nicky Henderson* a34 40
4 ch m Peintre Celebre(USA) —State Crystal (IRE) (High Estate)
1474[9]

Napoleon's Muse (IRE) *Ralph Beckett* a75 58
2 b f Peintre Celebre(USA) —Art Work (Zafonic (USA))
5583[9] *(6215)*

Napoletano (ITY) *Robert Johnson* a49 52
5 b g Kyllachy—Nationality (Nashwan (USA))
2060[9]

Naqshabban (USA) *Luca Cumani* 111
3 b g Street Cry(IRE) —Reem Three (Mark Of Esteem (IRE))
(1546) ◆ 2507[6] 5185[6] 6163[2] 7029[3]

Nareion (GER) *W Baltromei* a79 99
5 b h Areion(GER) —Ninigretta (GER) (Dashing Blade)
257a[4] 1575a[10] *6958a*[10]

Narla *Sir Henry Cecil* a54
2 b f Nayef(USA) —Polygueza (FR) (Be My Guest (USA))
7343[9]

Naromdia (FR) *J Boisnard* a92 96
3 ch f High Yield(USA) —Renegade Run (FR) (In The Wings)
5230a[9]

Naseem Alyasmeen (IRE) *Mick Channon* a66 67
2 bl f Clodovil(IRE) —Phillippa (IRE) (Galileo (IRE))
1981[4] 2430[2] *4992*[4] 5503[2] 5818[2]

Naseem Sea (IRE) *P D Deegan* a88 93
2 b f Bahri(USA) —Laqataat (IRE) (Alhaarth (IRE))
(1699a) 2777a[3] 3416a[3] 3884a[5]

Nasharra (IRE) *Kevin Ryan* 92
3 ch g Iffraaj—There With Me (USA) (Distant View (USA))
1326[5] 3820[18] 4353[5] 5559[5] 5820[6]

Nasri *David Nicholls* 104
5 b g Kyllachy—Triple Sharp (Selkirk (USA))
1111[7] (1541) 1885[3] 3155[14] 3862[7] 4534[4] ◆ (6209) 6521[6]

Nassau Storm *William Knight* a66 48
2 b c Bahamian Bounty—Got To Go (Shareef Dancer (USA))
2837[9] *7330*[4]

Nathaniel (IRE) *John Gosden* 126
3 b c Galileo(IRE) —Magnificient Style (USA) (Silver Hawk (USA))
(1389) 1822[2] (3105) ◆ (4315) 6861[5]

National Hero (IRE) *Mark Johnston*
2 ch c Exceed And Excel(AUS) —Miss Marvellous (USA) (Diesis)
7626[8] *7855*[8]

National Hope (IRE) *George Baker* a70 71
3 b f Exceed And Excel(AUS) —Zandaka (FR) (Doyoun)
(305) *764*[4] 2147[7] 3918[5] 4707[6] (5624) *6617*[6] 7137[5]

Nationalism *John Gosden* 111
4 b g Pivotal—Las Flores (IRE) (Sadler's Wells (USA))
2713[4] (3409) 5252[6] 5934[5]

National Pride (USA) *Mahmood Al Zarooni* a102
6 ch g Macho Uno(USA) —Corporate Vision (USA) (Corporate Report (USA))
583a[12]

Native Colony *Roger Varian* 80
3 b g St Jovite(USA) —Self Esteem (Suave Dancer (USA))
1271[6] 1568[13] 2231[10] 3960[2] ◆ (5122) *5599*[6] 6584[2] 6891[3]

Native Hedgerow (IRE) *Peter Hedger* 46
2 ch c With Approval(CAN) —Cherrycombe-Row (Classic Cliche (IRE))
2049[15] 2787[10]

Native Khan (FR) *Ed Dunlop* 118
3 gr c Azamour(IRE) —Viva Maria (FR) (Kendor (FR))
(1341) 1686[3] 2715[5] 3442a[7]

Native Picture (IRE) *Richard Hannon* 74
3 br f Kodiac—Native Force (IRE) (Indian Ridge)
(1359) 2025[8]

Native Ruler *Sir Henry Cecil* 117
5 b h Cape Cross(IRE) —Love Divine (Diesis)
1685[2] 2072[4]

Natural High (IRE) *D K Weld* 91
6 b g Sadler's Wells(USA) —Cool Clarity (IRE) (Indian Ridge)
4398a[7]

Naturalmente (IRE) *Kevin Ryan* a40 41
2 b f Captain Rio—Blusienka (IRE) (Blues Traveller (IRE))
6047[8] *6820*[8] 7058[7]

Naughtical *J W Hills* a59 23
2 ch f Haafhd—Mid Ocean (Sakhee (USA))
6919[8] *7174*[4] *7540*[4]

Nausycaa (IRE) *Mlle S-V Tarrou* a78 75
3 b f Noverre(USA) —Glace Magique (IRE) (King's Best (USA))
775a[3]

Nautika Danon (GER) *W Hickst* 98
3 bb f Kallisto(GER) —Nagoya (GER) (Goofalik (USA))
6395a[5]

Navaho Spirit *Terry Clement* a66
2 ch g Sleeping Indian—Sefemm (Alhaarth (IRE))
5834[3]

Navajo Charm *Alan Jarvis* a59 40
2 b f Authorized(IRE) —Navajo Love Song (IRE) (Dancing Brave (USA))
4996[13] *5814*[7] 6991[11]

Navajo Chief *Alan Jarvis* a92 113
4 b g King's Best(USA) —Navajo Rainbow (Rainbow Quest (USA))
236[14] 332a[2] 587a[5] (682a) 828a[6] (5218) 5704[9] 6129[6] 6693[6] *7802*[7]

Navarasa (FR) *A Lamotte D'Argy* 93
3 b f Martillo(GER) —Night Symphony (GER) (Big Shuffle (USA))
(852a)

Navarra Queen *P Schiergen* 105
3 b f Singspiel(IRE) —Navona (GER) (Leone (GER))
(3449a) 4839a[4] 5308a[3] 6739a[8]

Nave (USA) *Mark Johnston* a92 95
4 b g Pulpit(USA) —Lakabi (USA) (Nureyev (USA))
1325[3] 1517[8] 1676[2] 2107[5] 2289[2] 3396[17] 3829[10] 4890[10] 5482[4] 5705[13] 6249[5]

Navigation Track *David Simcock* a58 67
3 b g King's Best(USA) —Tegwen (USA) (Nijinsky (CAN))
1407[12] 2813[8] (4888) ◆

Nawaashi *Mark Johnston* 83
3 b f Green Desert(USA) —Shatarah (Gulch (USA))
1202[3] 1916[3] 2319[9] 2729[7] 3278[6]

Nawwaar (USA) *John Dunlop* 85
2 ch c Distorted Humor(USA) —Mostaqeleh (USA) (Rahy (USA))
3793[3] (4535) ◆ 7026[8]

Nayarra (IRE) *Mick Channon* 108
2 b f Cape Cross(IRE) —Massarra (Danehill (USA))
1765[2] 2227[2] 2718[2] 3402[9] 5077[2] 5472[4] 5933[3] 6296[3] (6740a)

Nayef Flyer *Richard Fahey* 56
2 ch c Nayef(USA) —Abunai (Pivotal)
3035[6] 4140[8] 4781[4] 6260[8]

Nayessence *Michael Easterby* a65 57
5 ch g Nayef(USA) —Fragrant Oasis (USA) (Rahy (USA))
1617[9]

Nayfashion *Karin Suter-Weber* 93
3 b f Nayef(USA) —Curfew (Marju (IRE))
(5307a)

Nay Secret *Jim Goldie* 46
3 b g Nayef(USA) —Nouveau Cheval (Picea)
2635[6] 3301[7] 3487[7]

Na Zdorovie *Charles Hills* a75 85
2 b f Cockney Rebel(IRE) —Vino Veritas (USA) (Chief's Crown (USA))
3812[2] ◆ *4662*[2] (5269) 5885[7] 7169[6]

Nazreef *Hughie Morrison* a106 92
4 b g Zafeen(FR) —Roofer (IRE) (Barathea (IRE))
1406[5] 2105[10] 2441[5] 3290[4] 3840[7] 6124[9] 6429[6] (6727) 7110[5] *7393*[8]

Nearly A Gift (IRE) *Tim Easterby* 84
2 b f Tagula(IRE) —Chaukao (IRE) (Inchinor)
1823[5] ◆ 2630[2] 2907[6] (3200) 4551[2] 5184[9] 5708[8] 6323[10] 6670[15] 6864[9]

Neatico (GER) *P Schiergen* 107
4 b h Medicean—Nicola Bella (IRE) (Sadler's Wells (USA))
2657a[3] 3422a[6] 4373a[6] 5664a[7] 6201a[6] 7048a[3] 7409a[2]

Neat Sweep (IRE) *Alan McCabe* a68 20
3 b f Tiger Hill(IRE) —Flagship (Rainbow Quest (USA))
952[4] 1399[7] 2392[10] *7068*[13] *7557*[8]

Nebbia Di Latte (ITY) *M Massimi Jr* 88
4 b m Colossus(IRE) —Oropa (IRE) (Indian Ridge)
1432a[8]

Nebukadnezar (GER) *P L Giannotti* 111
4 ch h Lomitas—Nova (GER) (Winged Love (IRE))
2540a[3]

Nebula Storm (IRE) *John M Oxx* 107
4 b h Galileo(IRE) —Epping (Charnwood Forest (IRE))
1427a[2] 2534a[5] 3418a[7]

Ned Causer *Reg Hollinshead* a54
2 b g Phoenix Reach(IRE) —Cocorica (IRE) (Croco Rouge (IRE))
5246[6] *6280*[9] *6652*[11]

Ned Ludd (IRE) *Jonathan Portman* a67 64
8 b g Montjeu(IRE) —Zanella (IRE) (Nordico (USA))
563[2] 1839[10] 4951[5] 6722[3]

Neebras (IRE) *Mahmood Al Zarooni* 116
3 b c Oasis Dream—Crossmolina (IRE) (Halling (USA))
1317[8] (2110) 2440[3] 3011[4] 3670a[6] (4493) (Dead)

Needwood Park *Ray Craggs* a12 59
3 br g Needwood Blade—Waterpark (Namaqualand (USA))
3756[5] 4542[6] 4813[3] 5619[10] 6158[7] *6618*[10]

Needwood Ridge *Frank Sheridan* a76 51
4 ch g Needwood Blade—Aspen Ridge (IRE) (Namid)
(713) *881*[3] *1083*[2] *1222*[5] 1917[8] 2378[8] 4701[7] *(4866)* *6354*[9] *6979*[2] *7175*[7] *7417*[7] 7605[9] 7928[6]

Needwood Rose *David Nicholls* 28
2 ch f Needwood Blade—Sharoura (Inchinor)
4105[6] 4808[6] 5105[7]

Needy McCredie *James Turner* 69
5 ch m Needwood Blade—Vocation (IRE) (Royal Academy (USA))
2353[2] (2546) 2989[2] (3617) 3856[3] 4288[5] 6779[12]

Negin *Ed Dunlop* 68
2 b f Selkirk(USA) —Snow Goose (Polar Falcon (USA))
4471[5]

Negotiate *Andrew Oliver* 99
3 b f Red Ransom(USA) —Poised (USA) (Rahy (USA))
4589a[4] 6362a[10]

Negotiation (IRE) *Michael Quinn* a77 78
5 b g Refuse To Bend(IRE) —Dona Royale (IRE) (Darshaan)
279[5] *381*[4] *647*[7] *790*[7] 2021[5] 2597[5] 2887[2] 3361[6] 3959[3] 4730[6] 4845[4] 5356[RR] *6445*[8] 6969[11]

Negramaro (IRE) *M Boutin* a58 61
6 b g Orpen(USA) —Pinky Mouse (IRE) (Machiavellian (USA))
832a[0]

Nehaam *John Gosden* 113
5 b g Nayef(USA) —Charm The Stars (Roi Danzig (USA))
2438[7] (4354) 5285[12] 5705[2] 6271[3] 6857[4]

Nehro (USA) *Steven Asmussen* a120
3 b c Mineshaft(USA) —The Administrator (USA) (Afleet (CAN))
1921a[2] *2950a*[4]

Neige D'Antan *Sir Mark Prescott Bt* a48
2 gr f Aussie Rules(USA) —Ninotchka (USA) (Nijinsky (CAN))
7626[6] *7783*[7] *7838*[9]

Neighbourhood (USA) *James Evans* a49 49
3 bb g Street Cry(IRE) —Miznah (IRE) (Sadler's Wells (USA))
520[11] *878*[8] *1018*[10] *1487*[4] *3922*[5] 5566[7] *6087*[9]

Neil's Pride *Richard Fahey* 56
2 b f Dubai Destination(USA) —Collette's Choice (Royal Applause)
1939[6] 2430[5] ◆ 3022[6] 4194[3] ◆

Nektarus (FR) *J Rossi* a78
3 b c Layman(USA) —Valmacey (FR) (Housamix (FR))
776a[6] 980a[0]
Nella Sofia *James Given* a27 31
3 bl f Diktat—Night Symphonie (Cloudings (IRE))
6097[9] 6781[9] 7503[9] 7688[6]
Nellie Ellis (IRE) *George Baker* a62 65
3 ch f Compton Place—Tamora (Dr Fong (USA))
2524[11]
Nellie Pickersgill *Tim Easterby* 53
2 b f Royal Applause—Branston Gem (So Factual (USA))
1165[3] 1619[6] 2113[4] 2387[11] 6232[9] 7231[12]
Nelson's Bay *Brian Meehan* 81
2 b g Needwood Blade—In Good Faith (USA) (Dynaformer (USA))
5051[5] (6230)
Nelson's Bounty *Paul D'Arcy* a86 94
4 b g Bahamian Bounty—Santisima Trinidad (IRE) (Definite Article)
(1603) ◆ 2105[4] 3797[10] 4100[10] 5712[12] 6069[2] 6302[21] 7110[11]
Nemo Spirit (IRE) *Tom Dascombe* a97 85
6 gr g Daylami(IRE) —La Bayadere (Sadler's Wells (USA))
1215[2] 1367[7] 2034[17]
Nemushka *Richard Fahey* 83
2 ch f Sakhee(USA) —Dame De Noche (Lion Cavern (USA))
(3656) (5645) 6340[2]
Nennella (GER) *S Smrczek* a65
4 b m Golan(IRE) —Nonette (Marju (IRE))
842a[10]
Nephrite *A P O'Brien* 108
2 ch c Pivotal—Cape Merino (Clantime)
(7185a) ◆
Neptune Equester *Brian Ellison* 74
8 b g Sovereign Water(FR) —All Things Nice (Sweet Monday)
2219[8] 2458[13] (3622) 4856[5] 4941[2]
Nereid (USA) *John Shirreffs* 108
3 bb f Rock Hard Ten(USA) —Dowry (USA) (Belong To Me (USA))
6887a[3]
Nero Emperor (IRE) *T Stack* a95 69
2 b c Holy Roman Emperor(IRE) —Blue Iris (Petong)
7273a[7] ◆
Nesnaas (USA) *Alastair Lidderdale* a24 48
10 ch g Gulch(USA) —Sedrah (USA) (Dixieland Band (USA))
3311[10] 5947[12] 7091[10] 7892[11]
Nesno (USA) *Chris Grant* a60 60
8 ch g Royal Academy(USA) —Cognac Lady (USA) (Olympio (USA))
6006[6]
Nessia (IRE) *Y Fertillet* 59
3 b f Aragorn(IRE) —Seattle's Wood (USA) (Woodman (USA))
288a[0]
Netley Marsh *Richard Hannon* a60 70
2 ch g Haafhd—Ha'Penny Beacon (Erhaab (USA))
2602[5] (2788) ◆ 3595[6]
Nettis *George Prodromou* a26 55
3 ch g Monsieur Bond(IRE) —Stream (Unfuwain (USA))
2524[12] 2993[5] 3958[11] 4431[8]
Net Whizz (USA) *Jeremy Noseda* 62
2 bb c Mr Greeley(USA) —Reboot (USA) (Rubiano (USA))
3823[10]
Neumark (GER) *Sir Henry Cecil* a79 89
3 b f High Chaparral(IRE) —Notre Dame (GER) (Acatenango (GER))
3043[2] (4241) 5020[4] 6248[5]
Neutrafa (IRE) *John Mackie* 86
3 ch f Araafa(IRE) —Neutrina (IRE) (Hector Protector (USA))
5082[5] (5556) 6062[10] 6383[2] ◆ (7160)
Nevada (GER) *P Schiergen* 86
2 b f Dubai Destination(USA) —Norwegian Pride (FR) (Diktat)
6737a[4]
Nevada Desert (IRE) *Richard Whitaker* a62 67
11 b g Desert King(IRE) —Kayanga (Green Desert (USA))
504[4] 675[2] (748) 837[3] 1814[12] 2401[8] 3088[4] 3306[9]
Nevaeh *Pat Eddery* a62
2 b f Firebreak—Mitsuki (Puissance)
7345[7] 7838[4]
Never Can Tell (IRE) *Jamie Osborne* a85 98
4 b m Montjeu(IRE) —Shaanara (IRE) (Darshaan)
1470[4] 1788[2] (2906) 3851[2] (5878) (6690)
Never Forget (FR) *E Lellouche* 107
4 b m Westerner—Topira (FR) (Pistolet Bleu (IRE))
2501[8] 4099[5] 4788[13] 6470a[10] 7090a[0]
Never In (IRE) *Alan Berry* 49
2 b f Elusive City(USA) —Priceoflove (IRE) (Inchinor)
3273[12] 3618[6] 4040[4] 4358[5] 5058[9] 5505[3] 5786[13] 6026[5] 6186[10] 6425[5]
Never Never Land *John Gosden* a73 66
3 b g Elusive City(USA) —Absolve (USA) (Diesis)
1335[10] 2383[11] 2841[8] 3347[5]
Never Perfect (IRE) *Tom Tate* 74
2 b g Galileo(IRE) —Dapprima (GER) (Shareef Dancer (USA))
5548[4] (6644) 6986[6]
Never Retreat (USA) *Chris Block* a93 118
6 bb m Smart Strike(CAN) —Lisieux (USA) (Steady Growth (CAN))
5073a[7] (6719a)
Never Satisfied *Charles Hills* 65
2 ch g Haafhd—Pirouetting (Pivotal)
4995[8] 5564[7] 6483[7]
Newbury Street *Patrick Holmes* a65 69
4 b g Namid—Cautious Joe (First Trump)
1906[5] 2464[5] 2588[3] 3088[6] 3902[3] (4600)
Newby Lodge (IRE) *Alan Bailey* a66 59
3 b f Intikhab(USA) —Titans Clash (IRE) (Grand Lodge (USA))
1991[5] 2621[5] 3268[13] 3596[2] 3958[6] 4732[4] (5134) 5421[5] (5636) 5642[5] 6621[9]
Newcastle (FR) *C Baillet* a85 90
3 ch f High Yield(USA) —Cruelle (USA) (Irish River (FR))
6809a[8]
New Code *Gary Moore* a83 84
4 ch g Reset(AUS) —Illeana (GER) (Lomitas)
(1443) 2686[5] 3762[3] 4008[3] 5050[7]
New Decade *Mark Johnston* a69 61
2 ch g Pivotal—Irresistible (Cadeaux Genereux)
3082[7] 3302[3] (3947) 5550[5] 6806[10] 7259[3] 7336[7]
New Deerfield *Henry Candy* 115
3 b c Choisir(AUS) —Verbal Intrigue (USA) (Dahar (USA))
(2106) ◆ 3029[2]
New Delight (FR) *S Morineau*
2 b c Lugny(FR) —Green House (FR) (Houston (FR))
7664a[0]
New Den *Jim Boyle* a61 55
4 ch g Piccolo—Den's-Joy (Archway (IRE))
85[2] 161[3] 222[2] 350[5] 1050[U]
New Guinea *H Albloushi* a83 90
8 b g Fantastic Light(USA) —Isle Of Spice (USA) (Diesis)
329a[13] 608a[13]
New Hampshire (USA) *John Gosden* a94 84
3 b c Elusive Quality(USA) —Downtown Blues (USA) (Seattle Song (USA))
1606[11] 2648[2] (3135) 6989[12] 7204[2] 7523[5]
New Jape (POL) *Pavlina Bastova*
6 ch g Jape(USA) —Niderlandia (POL) (Saragan)
4874a[6]
Newlands Princess (IRE) *Ollie Pears* a68 74
3 b f Titus Livius(FR) —Equity Princess (Warning)
5392[5] 5924[8]
New Latin (IRE) *Frank Sheridan* a74 76
3 b g Iffraaj—Babacora (IRE) (Indian Ridge)
(378) 739[2] 1578[2] 2581[4]
New Leyf (IRE) *Ed Walker* a94 93
5 bb g Kheleyf(USA) —Society Fair (FR) (Always Fair (USA))
613[11] (822) 1109[3] 1771[2] 2061[6] 3000[6] (3383) 3796[14] 4556[4] 4859[8] 6478[5] 6974[5] 7457[2] 7531[3]
New Magic (IRE) *Dermot Anthony McLoughlin* a86 93
4 b m Statue Of Liberty(USA) —Magic Mushroom (Pivotal)
4418a[9] 7189a[8]
Newnton Lodge *Roger Charlton* 83
2 b c Rail Link—Widescreen (USA) (Distant View (USA))
(5239) ◆ 6766[6]
New Planet (IRE) *John Quinn* 105
3 ch g Majestic Missile(IRE) —Xena (IRE) (Mull Of Kintyre (USA))
2297[12] 2934[6] 3820[10] 4526[3]
Newport Arch *John Quinn* a63 67
3 b c Pastoral Pursuits—Mashmoum (Lycius (USA))
5731[10] 6452[15] 7159[8] 7859[2]
New River (IRE) *Richard Hannon* 76
3 b f Montjeu(IRE) —Quiet Waters (USA) (Quiet American (USA))
2836[5] ◆ 3135[3] 4385[9] 4763[8]
New Romantic *Julie Camacho* a52 52
2 b f Singspiel(IRE) —Kalinova (IRE) (Red Ransom (USA))
4047[6] 4875[5] 5596[4] 6628[5] 6846[4] 7242[11]
New Rose Wood (AUS) *D Koh* 100
6 b m Love A Dane(AUS) —Western Explorer (AUS) (Is It True (USA))
2340a[11]
Newsdad (USA) *William Mott* a110 104
3 bb c Arch(USA) —Storm Tracer (USA) (Pulpit (USA))
5072a[6]
News Desk *John Gosden* a52
2 b f Cape Cross(IRE) —La Presse (USA) (Gone West (USA))
7599[8] 7889[8]
News Show *David Simcock* 66
2 b f Sinndar(IRE) —Yemen Desert (IRE) (Sadler's Wells (USA))
5937[5] 6934[4]
Newzflash *Ollie Pears* 46
3 ch g Lucky Story(USA) —Lark In The Park (IRE) (Grand Lodge (USA))
1495[9] 2351[7] 2786[10]
Next Cry (USA) *Richard Hannon* a72 66
2 ch c Street Cry(IRE) —Storm Alert (USA) (Storm Cat (USA))
4054[8] 4857[9] 5384[5] 5668[4] 6245[6] 6757[3] (7223) 7653[4]
Next Edition (IRE) *Howard Johnson* 88
3 b g Antonius Pius(USA) —Starfish (IRE) (Galileo (IRE))
2572[3] 3399[8] 3904[3] 4608[6]
Next Holy (IRE) *P Schiergen* 94
3 b f Holy Roman Emperor(IRE) —Night Petticoat (GER) (Petoski)
4839a[12]
Next Move (IRE) *A bin Huzaim* a62 82
4 b h Tiger Hill(IRE) —Cinnamon Rose (USA) (Trempolino (USA))
707a[6]
Neytiri *Linda Stubbs* a56 47
3 ch f Sleeping Indian—Science Fiction (Starborough)
275[2] 494[3] 834[3] 966[5] 1439[4] 2047[6] 2249[6]
Nezami (IRE) *John Akehurst* a82 89
6 b g Elnadim(USA) —Stands To Reason (USA) (Gulch (USA))
956[7] 1898[3] 2428[5] 2876[7] 3536[2] 4006[4] 4997[6] 5201[4] 5640[5] 6056[6] 6478[9]
Nezhenka *Mark Johnston* a94 95
4 b m With Approval(CAN) —Ninotchka (USA) (Nijinsky (CAN))
6832[7] 7017[8] 7699[7]
Nha Trang (IRE) *Michael Appleby* a42 47
4 b g Indian Danehill(IRE) —Baileys On Line (Shareef Dancer (USA))
937[8] 1212[8] 4985[9] 7247[8] 7647[7] 7741[5] 7859[6]
Nially Noo *Derek Shaw* a73 33
3 b g Oasis Dream—Millyant (Primo Dominie)
5633[12] 6027[8] (7245) 7428[3] 7512[7]
Nibani (IRE) *Alastair Lidderdale* a79 84
4 ch g Dalakhani(IRE) —Dance Of The Sea (IRE) (Sinndar (IRE))
1271[2] 1826[6] 2958[5] ◆ 3593[6] 5837[7] 6410[9] 6658[10] 6785[3] 7130[2] 7178[P] 7601[10] 7774[2] 7831[3] (7920)
Nicea (GER) *P Schiergen* a94 106
4 b m Lando(GER) —Nicolaia (GER) (Alkalde (GER))
2749a[7] 5749a[3] 6395a[4]
Nice Danon *A Wohler* 101
3 gr c Sakhee(USA) —Miss Universe (IRE) (Warning)
1433a[3] 2338a[11] 4138a[6]
Nice Land (GER) *Frau P Bastiaens-Vancauwenberg* 56
7 b m Lando(GER) —Nice Wind (GER) (Windwurf (GER))
7314a[0]
Niceofyoutotellme *Ralph Beckett* 74
2 b c Hernando(FR) —Swain's Gold (USA) (Swain (IRE))
3780[2] 4535[12]
Niceonemyson *Christopher Wilson* 13
2 b g Misu Bond(IRE) —Kungfu Kerry (Celtic Swing)
7072[10] 7209[12]
Nice Style (IRE) *Jeremy Gask* a101 91
6 b g Desert Style(IRE) —Great Idea (IRE) (Lion Cavern (USA))
(180) ◆ 991[8] 2002[11] 3411[5] 4553[7] 6339[10] 6989[9] 7391[5] 7523[9]
Nicholascopernicus (IRE) *Ed Walker* a60
2 ch c Medicean—Ascendancy (Sadler's Wells (USA))
7225[6] 7435[7] 7627[6]
Nicholas Pocock (IRE) *Ian McInnes* a67 66
5 b g King's Best(USA) —Sea Picture (IRE) (Royal Academy (USA))
21[4] 61[7] 3245[4] 4233[6] 4920[2] 5502[4] 5740[5] 6134[5] 6417[7] 6430[3] 7003[9]
Nickel Silver *Bryan Smart* a99 88
6 gr g Choisir(AUS) —Negligee (Night Shift (USA))
2[8] 125[6]
Nicky Nutjob (GER) *John O'Shea* a21 54
5 b g Fasliyev(USA) —Natalie Too (USA) (Irish River (FR))
6309[10]
Nic Nok *Harry Dunlop* a21 10
2 b c Iceman—Past 'N' Present (Cadeaux Genereux)
2837[10] 4205[12]
Nicola's Dream *Richard Fahey* a57 73
3 b f Alhaarth(IRE) —She's Classy (USA) (Boundary (USA))
2264[2] ◆ 2675[6] 3038[2] ◆ 3400[4] 4077[5] 4290[5] 5150[3] 6192[4] 6799[9] 7198[10] 7604[12]
Nideeb *Clive Brittain* a112 108
4 ch h Exceed And Excel(AUS) —Mantesera (IRE) (In The Wings)
(991)
Nifty Shiftin *David Elsworth* a67 64
2 ro g Norse Dancer(IRE) —Reciprocal (IRE) (Night Shift (USA))
2817[10] 3132[12] 3780[8] (4277) 4907[2]
Night Affair *David Arbuthnot* a61 82
5 b m Bold Edge—Twilight Mistress (Bin Ajwaad (IRE))
1864[10] 2244[6] 3222[8] 3588[2]
Night And Dance (IRE) *Clive Cox* a83 79
3 b f Danehill Dancer(IRE) —Evensong (GER) (Waky Nao)
2068[3] ◆ 5877[6] (7401)
Night Angel (IRE) *Rod Millman* a51 71
2 gr f Dark Angel(IRE) —Dangle (IRE) (Desert Style (IRE))
1042[6] 1505[5] 1870[2] 2448[2] 2992[4] 3842[9] 4460[5] 4892[5] 5374[2] 5613[2] 5840[7] 6406[4] 6695[11]
Night Carnation *Andrew Balding* a61 113
3 ch f Sleeping Indian—Rimba (USA) (Dayjur (USA))
(1545) ◆ (2032) 2928[4] (3644) 6164[5] 6858[6]
Nightdance Victor (GER) *P Schiergen* a64 82
4 b g Pentire—Nightdance Forest (IRE) (Charnwood Forest (IRE))
5095a[8] 7256a[7]
Night Flash (GER) *James Given* a75 52
2 b c Oratorio(IRE) —Night Woman (GER) (Monsun (GER))
2460[8] 6259[8] 6644[4] (7222) (7444) ◆ 7653[5]
Nightjar (USA) *Kevin Ryan* a100 89
6 b g Smoke Glacken(USA) —Night Risk (USA) (Wild Again (USA))
6[2]
Night Lily (IRE) *Paul D'Arcy* a100 88
5 b m Night Shift(USA) —Kedross (IRE) (King Of Kings (IRE))
438[6] (615) 1104[2] ◆ 1406[9] 2269[3] 2647[11] 3632[7] (4070) 4537[2] 4656[5] 4993[7] 5712[7] 6302[18] 7128[8] 7277a[2] 7391[9] 7606[5] 7801[2]
Night Magic (GER) *W Figge* 114
5 br m Sholokhov(IRE) —Night Woman (GER) (Monsun (GER))
1931a[4] (2749a) 4374a[4] 5773a[2]
Night Of Dubai (IRE) *Mario Hofer* 101
3 b f Lord Of England(GER) —Night Woman (GER) (Monsun (GER))
2981a[3] 4839a[5] 7047a[8]
Night Orbit *Julia Feilden* a61 64
7 b g Observatory(USA) —Dansara (Dancing Brave (USA))
8[3] 1458[2] 2034[6] 2856[4] 3205[9]
Night Reveller (IRE) *Michael Chapman* a31 26
8 b m Night Shift(USA) —Tir-An-Oir (IRE) (Law Society (USA))
7743[8]
Night Serenade (IRE) *H-A Pantall* 102
4 b m Golan(IRE) —Night Teeny (Platini (GER))
7386a[6] 7733a[8]
Night Sky *Peter Makin* a61 68
4 b m Starcraft(NZ) —War Shanty (Warrshan (USA))
2027[4] 4337[9]
Night Trade (IRE) *Ronald Harris* a82 86
4 b m Trade Fair—Compton Girl (Compton Place)
1109[11] 1296[3] 1382[12] 1793[10] 2566[3] 3036[2] 3737[11] 4291[7] (4634) (4816) 5587[3] 5972[2] 6246[3] 6974[6] 7262[11] 7456[3] 7502[9] 7847[3]
Night Witch (IRE) *Edward Creighton* a69 64
3 b f Kheleyf(USA) —Nasaria (IRE) (Starborough)
177[4] 379[5] 3002[12] 3354[7] 3432[5] 3953[6] 4829[7] 5213[8]
Nimiety *Mark Johnston* 76
2 b f Stormy Atlantic(USA) —Nadeszhda (Nashwan (USA))
1981[5] (2430) 5052[3] 5708[3] 6340[3]
Nimohe (FR) *J Heloury* 95
2 ch f Excellent Art—Time Tulip (USA) (Gilded Time (USA))
5296a[6] 5873a[6] 7219a[6]
Nimue (USA) *Paul Cole* a50 88
4 bb m Speightstown(USA) —Flag Support (USA) (Personal Flag (USA))
(1061) 2298[12]
Nina Rose *Clive Cox* a65 56
4 ro m Pastoral Pursuits—Magnolia (Petong)
3814[8] 5912[4] 6624[3] 7203[7] (7400) 7632[8] 7930[2]
Nine Before Ten (IRE) *John Balding* a72 79
3 ch f Captain Rio—Sagaing (Machiavellian (USA))
1275[3] 1521[4] 2391[2] (5038) 5268[7] 5647[5] 6456[12] 6615[7]
Nine Carrot Gold *George Charlton*
4 ch g Denounce—Edged With Gold (Bold Edge)
6156[13]
Ninfea (IRE) *Sylvester Kirk* a72 72
3 b f Le Vie Dei Colori—Attymon Lill (IRE) (Marju (IRE))
4056[7] 4584[8] 5179[6] 5496[7] 5845[10] 6624[4] 6811[2] (7122) 7461[7] (7603)
Nini Ok (IRE) *John Joseph Murphy* a79 71
2 b f Acclamation—Charmed Forest (IRE) (Shinko Forest (IRE))
(7451)
Ninita *Mark Rimmer* a73 68
3 b f Storming Home—Danceatdusk (Desert Prince (IRE))
845[6] ◆ 1113[8] 1571[5] 2018[12]
Ninth House (USA) *Ruth Carr* a66 70
9 b h Chester House(USA) —Ninette (USA) (Alleged (USA))
292[9] 544[7] 895[8] 2260[12] 2548[11] 2809[12]
Ninth Parallel (USA) *Ann Duffield* 54
3 bb g Mr Greeley(USA) —Nemea (USA) (The Minstrel (CAN))
1710[3] 2786[4]
Nip And Tuck *William Jarvis* a62
2 b c Green Desert(USA) —Coveted (Sinndar (IRE))
7889[6]
Nippy Nikki *John Norton* a52 43
3 b f Needwood Blade—Spielbound (Singspiel (IRE))
4284[11] 7113[12] 7774[5]
Niran (IRE) *Ruth Carr* a89 50
4 b g Captain Rio—Valley Lights (IRE) (Dance Of Life (USA))
1200[11] 1462[4]
Niwot (AUS) *Michael, Wayne & John Hawkes* 114
7 b g Galileo(IRE) —Too Darn Hot (NZ) (Noble Bijou (USA))
6886a[12] 7218a[8]
Noah Jameel *Tony Newcombe* a63 58
9 ch g Mark Of Esteem(IRE) —Subtle One (IRE) (Polish Patriot (USA))
391[4] (553) 630[3] 1308[3] 2140[9]
Nobbys Girl *Ronald Harris* a26 14
6 b m Double Trigger(IRE) —Mini Mandy (Petoski)
1750[11] 1973[7] 2873[10]
Nobel Winner (FR) *J-M Beguigne* 104
3 b c Grand Slam(USA) —Banyu Dewi (GER) (Poliglote)
1965a[2] 2751a[12] 3653a[5] 6783a[0]
Noble Attitude *Richard Guest* a51 35
5 b m Best Of The Bests(IRE) —Charming Lotte (Nicolotte)
19[3] 120[2] 490[3] 675[3] 802[11] 1468[6] 2260[7] 2401[9]
Noble Citizen (USA) *David Simcock* a89 99
6 b h Proud Citizen(USA) —Serene Nobility (USA) (His Majesty (USA))
1594[6] 1885[9] ◆ 2706[14] 3109[16] (3841) 4314[3] 5887[13] 6862[18]
Noble Defender *Stuart Kittow* 60
3 ch g Haafhd—Aquamarine (Shardari)
2371[6] 2930[14] 5350[4] 5916[8] 6585[6]
Noble Edge *Lee James* a41 57
8 ch g Bold Edge—Noble Soul (Sayf El Arab (USA))
879[5]
Noble Heir (SAF) *H J Brown* 82
6 gr m Kahal—Irish Honour (SAF) (Kilconnel (USA))
237[12] 500a[8]
Noble Jack (IRE) *Muredach Kelly* a73 74
5 b g Elusive City(USA) —Begine (IRE) (Germany (USA))
977a[8] 3912[7]
Noble Mission *Sir Henry Cecil* 73
2 b c Galileo(IRE) —Kind (IRE) (Danehill (USA))
7082[2]
Noble Prince (GER) *Paul Nolan* 35
7 b g Montjeu(IRE) —Noble Pearl (GER) (Dashing Blade)
6736a[13]
Noble Silk *Lucy Wadham* 78
2 gr g Sir Percy—Tussah (Daylami (IRE))
3878[5] ◆

Noble Storm (USA) *Ed McMahon* a112 114
5 b h Yankee Gentleman(USA) —Changed Tune (USA) (Tunerup (USA))
(1366) ◆ 1848[2] (2456) 4468[9]

Noble Thought (IRE) *William Haggas* 41
2 b c Rock Of Gibraltar(IRE) —Apache Dream (IRE) (Indian Ridge)
7133[9]

Nobunaga *Venetia Williams* 81
6 ch g Beat Hollow—Absolute Precision (USA) (Irish River (FR))
3366[3] 4083[6] 4555[2] 5057[4] 5857[8]

No Complaining (IRE) *Barney Curley* a72 38
4 b m Alhaarth(IRE) —Rambler (Selkirk (USA))
26[2] (163) (299) 580[2]

No Compromise *Hughie Morrison* a80 73
2 b f Avonbridge—Highly Liquid (Entrepreneur)
6440[3] 6743[2] 7165[4] (7350)

Nocturnal Affair (SAF) *David Marnane* a104 111
5 b g Victory Moon(SAF) —Aretha (SAF) (Centenary (USA))
236[7] 497a[9] (5927) 6706[5] (7012a) ◆

Nocturnal Knight *J J Lambe* a59 42
8 b g Diktat—Foreign Mistress (Darshaan)
3622[5]

No Dominion (IRE) *James Given* 59
2 b c Dylan Thomas(IRE) —Boast (Most Welcome)
6278[6] 6805[5]

Noels Princess *David O'Meara* 40
4 rg m Piccolo—Rum Lass (Distant Relative)
1941[8] 2710[5] 3343[6] 3931[5] 4328[9] 4672[7]

No Explaining (IRE) *Roger L Attfield* 101
4 b m Azamour(IRE) —Claustra (FR) (Green Desert (USA))
3208a[2]

Noguchi (IRE) *Jeremy Noseda* a87 85
6 ch g Pivotal—Tuscania (USA) (Woodman (USA))
6989[8] 7328[4]

No Heretic *Paul Cole* 88
3 b c Galileo(IRE) —Intrigued (Darshaan)
2097[2] ◆ (2360)

No Hubris (USA) *Roger Varian* 99
4 b g Proud Citizen(USA) —Innateness (USA) (Flying Paster (USA))
1564[2] 2470[3] 3578[11] 5879[11]

Noimead Draiochta (IRE) *David Nicholls* a63 74
3 ch c Captain Rio—Chennai (IRE) (Mozart (IRE))
6343[13]

Noisy Silence (IRE) *A Manuel* a100 85
7 b h Giant's Causeway(USA) —Golightly (USA) (Take Me Out (USA))
330a[13] 535a[2]

Nolan (FR) *C Baillet* a66
3 bl g Indian Rocket—Slyders (IRE) (Hector Protector (USA))
777a[0]

No Larking (IRE) *Henry Candy* a36 73
3 b g Refuse To Bend(IRE) —Dawn Chorus (IRE) (Mukaddamah (USA))
1446[9] 1768[6] 3804[4] 4244[5] 4763[5] 5137[3] (5422) 5992[6] 7057[3] 7425[11]

Nolecce *Richard Guest* a73 70
4 ch g Reset(AUS) —Ghassanah (Pas De Seul)
640[3] 744[3] (943) 1150[6] 1573[3] 2413[8] 2486[2] 3042[2] 3311[11] 4367[10] 4902[6] 4946[2] 5441[3] 6211[9] 6785[5] 6990[2] 7817[10]

No Legs (IRE) *David Evans*
2 b f Camacho—Charlene Lacy (IRE) (Pips Pride)
1199[8] 1301[6]

Nolhac (FR) *Y Fertillet* a70 73
7 b h Smadoun(FR) —One Way (FR) (Exit To Nowhere (USA))
566a[5]

Nollaig Shona (IRE) *George Prodromou* a66 60
4 b m Statue Of Liberty(USA) —Lucy In The Sky (IRE) (Lycius (USA))
143[10] 318[2] 794[11] 1171[5]

No Mean Trick (USA) *Paul Midgley* a70 70
5 b g Grand Slam(USA) —Ruby's Reception (USA) (Rubiano (USA))
2490[7] 2765[9] 3931[8] 4182[5] (4650) ◆ 5019[6] (7594) 7897[3]

Nomoreblondes *Paul Midgley* a66 79
7 ch m Ishiguru(USA) —Statuette (Statoblest)
1204[9] 1555[9] (1940) 2590[2] 3579[5] (3832) 4046[2] 4291[3] 5679[9] 6044[11] 6350[8] 6537[5] 7106[15]

No More Games *Kevin Ryan* a53 57
2 b g Mind Games—Straight And True (Lake Coniston (IRE))
4147[5] 4899[7] 5105[5] 5817[11] 6043[2] 6487[11] 6817[7] 7852[P]

No More Shoes (IRE) *Brendan Powell* a15 42
2 b g Strategic Prince—Jus'Chillin' (IRE) (Elbio)
2563[5] 2902[6] 6165[15] 6942[11]

Nonaynever *Jeremy Noseda* a72 44
3 ch g Nayef(USA) —Qirmazi (USA) (Riverman (USA))
7111[6] 7440[5]

Non Dom (IRE) *Hughie Morrison* a58 65
5 br g Hawk Wing(USA) —Kafayef (USA) (Secreto (USA))
1367[9]

Noneedtofret *Bill Moore*
3 b f Needwood Blade—Theatre Lady (IRE) (King's Theatre (IRE))
5607[12]

None Shall Sleep (IRE) *Paul Cole* a72 87
3 b g Invincible Spirit(IRE) —Moonbi Ridge (IRE) (Definite Article)
1361[6]

Nonsuch Way (IRE) *F Vermeulen* a93 110
3 gr f Verglas(IRE) —Lucky Lune (FR) (Priolo (USA))
2342a[3]

Noodles Blue Boy *Ollie Pears* a65 92
5 b g Makbul—Dee Dee Girl (IRE) (Primo Dominie)
1166[16] 2434[5] 2662[3] 3140[2] 3357[2] 3613[3] 4075[2] 4416[8] 5033[18] 6703[12] 6917[12] 7355[10]

Noor Zabeel (USA) *Mick Channon* a87 88
2 b c Elusive Quality(USA) —Brave The Storm (USA) (Storm Cat (USA))
1678[3] (2033) 5709[6] 6055[2] 6527[14]

No Plan B (IRE) *Noel Quinlan* a50 14
2 b f Le Vie Dei Colori—Heres The Plan (IRE) (Revoque (IRE))
5269[11] 5899[9] 6506[9] 7342[5]

No Poppy (IRE) *Tim Easterby* 85
3 b f Chineur(FR) —Capetown Girl (Danzero (AUS))
1825[7] 2255[8] (2581) 2986[4] 3278[2] 3782[2] 4235[2] 4718[5] 5255[13] 5820[4] 6383[4] 6576[4] 7076[8]

No Quarter (IRE) *Tracy Waggott* 69
4 b g Refuse To Bend(IRE) —Moonlight Wish (IRE) (Peintre Celebre (USA))
1037[7] 1439[8] (1558) 2057[9] 2494[9] 3024[2] 3508[3] 4362[6] 4517[4] 5455[8] (6158) 6381[10]

Norcroft *Christine Dunnett* a55 51
9 b g Fasliyev(USA) —Norcroft Joy (Rock Hopper)
145 129[5] 204[10] 312[4] 386[9] 800[3] 1177[11] 1498[4] 1570[7] (4183) 4651[6] 5116[4] 5601[4] 6071[3] 6228[7] 6939[6] 7269[4] 7351[3] 7442[7] 7581[3] 7656[5]

Norcroft Jem *George Margarson* 23
4 br m Red Ransom(USA) —Polar Jem (Polar Falcon (USA))
2596[11]

Nordic Light (USA) *Mrs A Malzard* a47 39
7 bb g Belong To Me(USA) —Midriff (USA) (Naevus (USA))
5917[9] 6176[2] 6501[11]

Nordic Quest (IRE) *Gerard Butler* a66 49
2 b c Montjeu(IRE) —Nordtanzerin (GER) (Danehill Dancer (IRE))
7082[11] 7494[4]

Nordic Sky (USA) *William Haggas* 92
3 b c Arch(USA) —Magic Of Love (Magic Ring (IRE))
(4370) (5056) ◆

Nordic Spruce (USA) *Sir Henry Cecil* 85
3 b f Dynaformer(USA) —Nyramba (Night Shift (USA))
1546[3] 2319[7] 3873[6]

No Refraction (IRE) *Mark Usher* a37 32
3 b f Refuse To Bend(IRE) —Sunblush (UAE) (Timber Country (USA))
1607[11] 2243[8] 2586[9] 6404[7]

Norfolk Sky *Chris Wall* 42
2 ch f Haafhd—Cayman Sound (Turtle Island (IRE))
4961[12] 5564[12] 6588[8]

Norlander *Ralph Beckett* a64
2 b f Royal Applause—Arrivato (Efisio)
7435[4]

Norman Asbjornson (USA) *Christopher W Grove* a107
3 b c Real Quiet(USA) —Merryland Missy (USA) (Citidancer (USA))
2328a[11]

Normandy Maid *Richard Fahey* 73
3 b f American Post—Arculinge (Paris House)
1624[4] 2391[7] 3114[4] 3613[6] 4880[7]

Norman Orpen (IRE) *Jane Chapple-Hyam* a100 97
4 b g Orpen(USA) —Lady Naomi (USA) (Distant View (USA))
542[2] 846[5] 1092[5] 1826[7] (2647) 3436[5] (3877) 4794[12] 5185[5]

Norman The Great *Alan King* a74 77
7 b g Night Shift(USA) —Encore Du Cristal (USA) (Quiet American (USA))
2378[3] 3095[6] 4389[6]

Norse Blues *Sylvester Kirk* a92 91
3 ch g Norse Dancer(IRE) —Indiana Blues (Indian Ridge)
1361[4] 1725[5] 2100[8] (2684) 3067[28] 4472[9] 5936[12] 6374[7] 6500[9] 6948[2] 7227[9]

Norse Dame *David Elsworth* a69 72
4 b m Halling(USA) —Rosewater (GER) (Winged Love (IRE))
278[7] 539[4]

Norse Gold *David Elsworth* a79 82
2 ch c Norse Dancer(IRE) —Rainbow End (Botanic (USA))
(2194) 2712[7] 3284[2] 5280[8] 6464[4]

Norse Wing *Ralph Beckett* 64
3 ch f Norse Dancer(IRE) —Angel Wing (Barathea (IRE))
1774[4] 2849[6] 3537[5] 4338[7]

North Central (USA) *Jim Goldie* 76
4 bb g Forest Camp(USA) —Brittan Lee (USA) (Forty Niner (USA))
1712[9] 2048[6] 2412[4] (2670) 2803[5] 3341[5] 3733[2] 3903[4] 4378[5] 4634[2] 5371[2] 5720[14] 6081[11] 6382[7]

Norther Bay (FR) *Eoin Griffin* a41 33
8 b g Alamo Bay(USA) —Northern Mixa (Linamix (FR))
7548a[14]

Northern Acres *Sue Bradburne* 75
5 b g Mtoto—Bunting (Shaadi (USA))
5311[12]

Northern Bolt *Ian McInnes* a55 81
6 b g Cadeaux Genereux—Shafir (IRE) (Shaadi (USA))
1239[8] 1861[6] 2238[6] 2352[6] 3359[10] (4196) 4793[9] 5162[3] (5204) 5468[4] 5554[4] 6414[3] 6426[3] 6778[8]

Northern Dare (IRE) *Richard Fahey* a82 78
7 b g Fath(USA) —Farmers Swing (IRE) (River Falls)
87[6] (215) 298[7] 658[2] 665[5] 786[2] 1073[5] 2280[6] 2491[9] 3040[4] 3488[5] 4145[5]

Northern Dream (FR) *F Chappet* 35
4 b g Anabaa(USA) —Northern Mixa (Linamix (FR))
7015a[8]

Northern Fling *Jim Goldie* a17 91
7 b g Mujadil(USA) —Donna Anna (Be My Chief (USA))
1075[4] 1695[8] 2112[2] 2398[6] 2783[12] 3276[10] 3659[3] 5006[4] 6533[11] 7299[7]

Northern Flyer (GER) *John Quinn* a71 70
5 b g Hawk Wing(USA) —Nachtigall (GER) (Danehill (USA))
(692) 897[10] 1150[9] 1558[10] 2487[9] 3454[4] 3859[5] 4670[3] 5031[2] ◆ 5404[3] 6133[7] 6847[9]

Northern Genes (AUS) *Michael Appleby* a48 48
5 b g Refuse To Bend(IRE) —Cotswold Dancer (AUS) (Carnegie (IRE))
5540[10] 5674[12] 6542[7] 6844[8] 7822[6]

Northern Glory *W Figge* a107 111
8 b g Rainbow Quest(USA) —Northern Goddess (Night Shift (USA))
(442a) 628a[13]

Northern Jewel (IRE) *Richard Fahey* 60
2 b f Nayef(USA) —Tekindia (FR) (Indian Ridge)
5454[10] 6047[4] 6702[8]

Northern Outlook *Andrew Balding* a71 53
2 b c Selkirk(USA) —Casual Glance (Sinndar (IRE))
6953[9] 7520[4]

Northern Passion (CAN) *Mark Casse* a100 103
2 ch f First Samurai(USA) —A Touch Of Glory (CAN) (Golden Gear (USA))
7283a[7]

Northern Rocked (IRE) *D K Weld* a79 101
5 b g Refuse To Bend(IRE) —Gifts Galore (IRE) (Darshaan)
4566a[4] 5746a[3] 6733a[4]

Northern Spy (USA) *Simon Dow* a69 68
7 b g War Chant(USA) —Sunray Superstar (Nashwan (USA))
2308[8] 2843[4] (3293) 7817[2]

Northern Territory (IRE) *Jim Boyle* a57 57
2 b c Choisir(AUS) —Krasivaya (IRE) (Soviet Star (USA))
4087[9] 4798[5] 5541[6] 6443[10] 6937[5]

Northgate (IRE) *Joseph G Murphy* a102 105
6 b g Mujadil(USA) —Arcevia (IRE) (Archway (IRE))
3445a[2] 5090a[2] 5744a[6] 6514a[7]

Northgate Lodge (USA) *Mel Brittain* a42 45
6 ch g Hold That Tiger(USA) —Sabaah Elfull (Kris)
6050[5] 6839[5] 7400[7]

North Shadow *Alan Brown* a60 56
4 ch g Motivator—Matoaka (USA) (A.P. Indy (USA))
6453[12] 6868[10]

Northside Prince (IRE) *Alan Swinbank* a75 97
5 b g Desert Prince(IRE) —Spartan Girl (IRE) (Ela-Mana-Mou)
1387[3] ◆ 2002[10] 5078[2] 5482[8] 6080[5] 6803[3]

North Star Boy (IRE) *Richard Hannon* 96
2 b c Acclamation—Isla Azul (IRE) (Machiavellian (USA))
1678[2] (1886) 3012[7] 3773[4] 4055[4] 4858[4] 5849[9] 6535[20]

Northumberland *Owen Brennan* a47 38
5 b g Bertolini(USA) —Cal Norma's Lady (IRE) (Lyphard's Special (USA))
16[9] 120[3] 319[4] 398[5] 6050[7] 7078[12] 7271[4] 7503[7]

Norton Girl *Tracy Waggott* a56 67
3 b f Diktat—Opening Ceremony (USA) (Quest For Fame)
2493[7] 3387[11] 4183[8] 5165[7] 7071[10] 7714[9]

No Rules *Mark H Tompkins* a24 58
6 b g Fraam—Golden Daring (IRE) (Night Shift (USA))
6722[10] 7120[12]

Norville (IRE) *David Evans* a95 104
4 b h Elusive City(USA) —Saraposa (IRE) (Ahonoora)
97[3] 143[5] 268[5] 351[5] (435) (521) 612[4] (698) 961[2] (1656) (1771) 1854[2] 2284[4] 2954[8] (3410) 3626[4] 3852[7] 4049[4] 4836a[4] 5430[6] 7392[11] 7578[6]

Norwood Lane *Peter Hedger* a41
2 b c Kyllachy—Lay A Whisper (Night Shift (USA))
7889[9]

Notabadlad *Simon Dow* a30 64
4 br g Denounce—Lady Jo (Phountzi (USA))
1897[3] 3519[11] 4208[12] 4829[9] 5406[3]

Notable Graduate (IRE) *D K Weld* 105
3 b g Galileo(IRE) —Market Slide (USA) (Gulch (USA))
3442a[8]

Not Bad For A Boy (IRE) *Richard Hannon* a76 70
2 b c Elusive City(USA) —Reign Of Fire (IRE) (Perugino (USA))
2844[6] 4080[2] 4384[2] 4969[7] 6866[5] 7358[2] 7653[3] (7799) 7875[4] 7927[3]

Not For Sale (GER) *T Mundry* 105
4 ch m Monsun(GER) —North America (GER) (Pivotal)
5749a[8] 6739a[3] 7047a[6] 7409a[7]

Nothing To Hide (IRE) *Dominic Ffrench Davis* a73 78
3 ch g Barathea(IRE) —Fine Detail (IRE) (Shirley Heights)
95[4] 6005[12] 6402[8] 6756[9]

Notia (IRE) *D Prod'Homme* a67 79
6 b m Numerous(USA) —Tritonia (GR) (Saddlers' Hall (IRE))
220a[0] 372a[0]

Notify *Patrick Chamings* a48 32
3 b f Nayef(USA) —Whitgift Rose (Polar Falcon (USA))
2192[11] 3742[11] 4745[6]

No Time For Tears (IRE) *Lucinda Featherstone* a54 59
4 br m Celtic Swing—Galitizine (USA) (Riverman (USA))
762[4] 992[7] 1310[11] (2526) 4074[5] 5079[10] 6306[11] 6503[12]

No Time To Cry *Ann Duffield* a28 57
2 b f Josr Algarhoud(IRE) —Autumn Bloom (IRE) (Fantastic Light (USA))
6837[5] 7101[5] 7398[10]

No Time To Lose *Jamie Osborne* 71
2 b g Authorized(IRE) —Ballymore Celebre (IRE) (Peintre Celebre (USA))
5239[9] 6400[3] 6825[5]

Not My Choice (IRE) *David C Griffiths* a76 84
6 ch g Choisir(AUS) —Northgate Raver (Absalom)
1110[11] 1793[3] 2165[9] 2286[2] (2494) 3071[8] 3506[7] 3852[8] 4126[9] 5341[5] 5760[17] 6093[14] 6583[13] 6759[12] 7106[8] 7243[8] 7428[11]

Notnowstanley *J S Moore* a30 42
2 ch g Notnowcato—Denice (Night Shift (USA))
5111[10] 5637[5] 7108[8] 7338[3] 7718[10]

No Trimmings (IRE) *Gerard Keane* a76 79
5 ch m Medecis—Cheviot Indian (IRE) (Indian Ridge)
283[9] 6854a[7] 7792a[12]

Not So Bright (USA) *Des Donovan* a61 59
3 bb g Sky Mesa(USA) —Melrose Morning (USA) (Shadeed (USA))
109[2] 194[3] 406[3] 564[3] 650[3] 891[4] 987[2] 1134[2] 1400[5] 1592[4] 2722[8] 2853[8] 3253[5]

Not Til Monday (IRE) *J R Jenkins* a70 78
5 b g Spartacus(IRE) —Halomix (Linamix (FR))
1282[3] (1596) (2183) 3157[13] 7236[7]

Nounou *Joanne Foster* a63 60
10 b g Starborough—Watheeqah (USA) (Topsider (USA))
5209[13]

Nouriya *Sir Michael Stoute* a76 104
4 b m Danehill Dancer(IRE) —Majestic Sakeena (IRE) (King's Best (USA))
1528[4] 2029[6] 4492[8] 6066[6]

Novabridge *Neil Mulholland* a68 71
3 ch g Avonbridge—Petrovna (IRE) (Petardia)
(1280) (1595) 1753[5] 2447[6] 2662[6] 2827[3] 3321[4] 3908[6] 5172[3] 5576[5] 7566[3] 7737[2] 7844[4]

Nova Hawk *Rod Collet* 110
3 b f Hawk Wing(USA) —Reveuse De Jour (IRE) (Sadler's Wells (USA))
1719[4] 2137a[4] 3106[2] 4597a[7] 6809a[3] 7193a[7]

Novalist *Robin Bastiman* a59 69
3 ch g Avonbridge—Malelane (IRE) (Prince Sabo)
1561[6] 1967[5] 2410[3] (3192) 4359[3] 4650[2] (5215) 5824[3] 7100[13]

Nova Med (IRE) *Y Fertillet* a75 88
4 b h Whipper(USA) —Prima Volta (Primo Dominie)
842a[8] 1012a[7]

Novastasia (IRE) *Dean Ivory* a49 46
5 b m Noverre(USA) —Pink Sovietstaia (FR) (Soviet Star (USA))
311[4] 386[4] 485[8] 662[5] 793[4] 1468[4] 1604[7]

Nova Step *F Rohaut* a103 103
3 ch f Dubawi(IRE) —Light Step (USA) (Nureyev (USA))
1207a[6] 2137a[12] 5028a[10] 5772a[7] 7678a[4]

Nova Valorem (IRE) *F Rohaut* a84
3 ch c Ad Valorem(USA) —Utr (USA) (Mr Prospector (USA))
5529a[5]

Novay Essjay (IRE) *Alan Juckes* a71 71
4 ch g Noverre(USA) —Arabian Hideway (IRE) (Desert Prince (IRE))
427[9] 854[10] 914[6] 1052[11] (1248) 1818[9]

Nova Zarga (IRE) *S Labate* a64 60
3 b f Dubawi(IRE) —Hurricane Irene (IRE) (Green Desert (USA))
288a[5]

Novel Dancer *Lydia Richards* a63 76
3 b g Dansili—Fictitious (Machiavellian (USA))
2097[10] 2664[2] 3267[5] 3919[5] 4338[6] 4755[5] 7202[6] 7441[5]

Novellen Lad (IRE) *Willie Musson* a92 98
6 b g Noverre(USA) —Lady Ellen (Horage)
1720[17] (2099) 3627[8] 4531[18] 4859[3] 5278[10] 5852[19] 6723[10] 7439[2] (7941)

Noverre To Go (IRE) *Ronald Harris* a103 106
5 ch g Noverre(USA) —Ukraine Venture (Slip Anchor)
1366[10] 1809[5] ◆ 2620[13] 3627[9] 4531[15] (5345) 6331[8] 6723[18]

Noverton *James Eustace* a53 68
3 b f Noverre(USA) —Quintrell (Royal Applause)
2790[8] 3289[2] ◆ 4186[4] 4849[6] 5354[7] 6814[14]

Novestar (IRE) *Michael Appleby* a45 68
6 ch g Noverre(USA) —Star Of Cayman (IRE) (Unfuwain (USA))
63[7] 203[9] 324[8]

Novillero *Jimmy Fox* a50 31
4 b h Noverre(USA) —Fairy Story (IRE) (Persian Bold)
129[10] 229[7] 552[10] 773[10] 1308[8] 2685[8]

Novirak (IRE) *James Fanshawe* a48 79
3 gr g Noverre(USA) —Manchaca (FR) (Highest Honor (FR))
5140[7] 5607[7] (6242)

Now *Rod Millman* a52 58
5 br m Where Or When(IRE) —Tup Tim (Emperor Jones (USA))
944[6] 7528[6] 7654[10]

Now My Sun *Mrs K Burke* 70
2 ch g Notnowcato—Sienna Sunset (IRE) (Spectrum (IRE))
(4080) 5181[10]

Now What *Jonathan Portman* a69 71
4 ch m Where Or When(IRE) —Vallauris (Faustus (USA))
1608[4] 2176[6] 2552[2] 2873[6] 4341[4] 4626[4] 5236[9] 6476[6] 6769[5]

Nuba (IRE) *Luke Dace* a54 58
3 b f Exceed And Excel(AUS) —Little Doll (Gulch (USA))
4254[5] 4861[5] 6032[8] 6545[6] 7037[6]

Nubar Boy *David Evans* a75 76
4 ch g Compton Place—Out Like Magic (Magic Ring (IRE))
97[4] 249[10] 306[5] 435[6] 522[6] 612[3] 698[10] 1730[4] (2155) 2222[4] 2609[7]

Nubian Gem (IRE) *John Best* a47 36
3 b f Desert Style(IRE) —True Love (Robellino (USA))
360[6] 4478[10] 4849[7] 5352[9] 5944[10] 7084[14]

Nude (IRE) *Sylvester Kirk* a30 59
2 b f Redback—Flower Bowl (IRE) (Noverre (USA))
2309[11] 2901[4] 3117[7] 3639[5] 3993[3] 4629[2] 4922[8] 5353[4] 5637[4] 6101[8] 6620[7]

Nufoudh (IRE) *Tracy Waggott* 75
7 b g Key Of Luck(USA) —Limpopo (Green Desert (USA))
2494[11] 2671[5] 3732[2] 3806[6] 4503[3] 6382[8]

Nuit De Glace (FR) *Mlle Valerie Boussin* a73 95
7 gr m Verglas(IRE) —La Frandiere (FR) (Kaldoun (FR))
4739a[0] 5532a[7]

Nuit Polaire (IRE) *J-C Rouget* a91
3 b f Kheleyf(USA) —Night Teeny (Platini (GER))
(981a)

Number One Guy *Philip Kirby* a49 54
4 br g Rock Of Gibraltar(IRE) —Dubious (Darshaan)
6872[6] 7099[12] 7370[11]

Numbers Talk (IRE) *X Thomas-Demeaulte* a92 92
3 b c Kingsalsa(USA) —Combloux (USA) (Southern Halo (USA))
1010a[2]

Number Theory *John Holt* 82
3 b g Halling(USA) —Numanthia (IRE) (Barathea (IRE))
1392[3] 1904[4] 2835[2] 3377[2] (4083) 5064[2] 5568[5] 6749[6]

Numeral (IRE) *Richard Hannon* a91 79
3 b g Holy Roman Emperor(IRE) —Savieres (IRE) (Sadler's Wells (USA))
3232[U] 3575[4] (4203) 4797[3] 5856[8] (6442) (7348) ◆ 7531[2] (7660)

Numerologie (FR) *Mme M Bollack-Badel* a96 98
5 b m Numerous(USA) —Operam (Kris)
5075a[8]

Numide (FR) *Rod Millman* a99 78
8 b g Highest Honor(FR) —Numidie (FR) (Baillamont (USA))
5971[8] 6469[5]

Nurai *Paul D'Arcy* a55 62
4 b m Danehill Dancer(IRE) —Lady High Havens (IRE) (Bluebird (USA))
292[7] 1993[2] 2271[RR]

Nutshell *Harry Dunlop* a65 64
3 b f Dubai Destination(USA) —Cashew (Sharrood (USA))
2307[2] (2722) 3518[4] 4389[3] 5519[5] 6122[6] 6926[3] 7363[7]

Nuzool (IRE) *John Dunlop* 73
3 b c Red Ransom(USA) —Eternity Ring (Alzao (USA))
1338[11] 1751[5] 2219[4]

Nymfia (IRE) *C Laffon-Parias* a75 51
3 b f Invincible Spirit(IRE) —Aguinaga (IRE) (Machiavellian (USA))
852a[6]

Oakbrook *Ann Duffield* 2
2 b g Indesatchel(IRE) —Statuette (Statoblest)
5174[10] 5681[17]

Oakdown *Alan King* 19
3 ch g Selkirk(USA) —Miss Katmandu (IRE) (Rainbow Quest (USA))
2723[11] 3080[10]

Oak Leaves *Nikki Evans* a56 57
4 b m Mark Of Esteem(IRE) —Exotic Forest (Dominion)
85[3] 409[10] 598[8] 773[6] 2659[2] 3516[2] 3910[4] 4703[10] 4952[8] 5612[6]

Oaksana (SWE) *Bo Neuman*
2 b f Heart Of Oak(USA) —Talaila (IRE) (Turtle Island (IRE))
5983a[7]

Oakwell (IRE) *Sally Hall* 35
3 b g Antonius Pius(USA) —Cindy's Star (IRE) (Dancing Dissident (USA))
4018[5]

Oakwood Princess (IRE) *W McCreery* a41 68
3 b f Antonius Pius(USA) —Lucky Oakwood (USA) (Elmaamul (USA))
1663a[14]

Oasis Dancer *Ralph Beckett* a103 108
4 bg g Oasis Dream—Good Enough (FR) (Mukaddamah (USA))
332a[7] 604a[7] 678a[7] 1885[24] 2706[19] 6747[4] 7433[2] (7721) ◆

Oasis Knight (IRE) *Nicky Henderson* 101
5 b g Oasis Dream—Generous Lady (Generous (IRE))
2316[8]

Oasis Memory (IRE) *John Gosden* a57
3 b f Dalakhani(IRE) —Political Parody (USA) (Doonesbury (USA))
3043[6] 3519[10]

Oasis Storm *Michael Dods* a77 84
3 b g Oasis Dream—Mouriyana (IRE) (Akarad (FR))
1168[6] 1652[2] 2435[4] 3376[10] 4109[9] 4432[10] 6234[7] 6978[10]

Obama Rule (IRE) *Ms Joanna Morgan* 102
4 b m Danehill Dancer(IRE) —Mennetou (IRE) (Entrepreneur)
2325a[5] 3417a[6] 4132a[10] 4566a[13] 5523a[4] 5976a[9]

Obara D'Avril (FR) *Simon West* a17 54
9 gr m April Night(FR) —Baraka De Thaix II (FR) (Olmeto)
3074[5] 4123[2] 4198[2] (4409) 4499[10] 6236[5] 6613[10] 7078[11]

Obiter Dicta *Henry Candy* 70
3 b f Diktat—Phoebe Woodstock (IRE) (Grand Lodge (USA))
1459[3] ◆ 2102[9] 3122[7] 3803[4] 4970[2] 5539[10] 6591[2] 6814[11]

Obligada (IRE) *Kevin Prendergast* a94 94
3 ch f Beat Hollow—Oblique (IRE) (Giant's Causeway (USA))
7010a[3] 7277a[14]

Obliteright (IRE) *William Knight* a74 57
2 ch g Bertolini(USA) —Doctrine (Barathea (IRE))
4545[5] 4906[2] 6795[3] 7431[4]

Obsequious (AUS) *Peter Snowden* 108
4 br f Lonhro(AUS) —Sycophant (AUS) (Commands (AUS))
9029a[9]

Obsession (IRE) *Jeremy Noseda* a80 81
3 b g Marju(IRE) —Athlumney Lady (Lycius (USA))
176[2] (520) 1843[4] 2064[4] 2368[8] 6773[4] 6976[2]

Obsidienne (FR) *C Gourdain* 68
2 b f Slickly(FR) —Hap (GER) (Loup Solitaire (USA))
7666a[7]

Ocarito (GER) *Elliott Cooper* a50
10 b g Auenadler(GER) —Okkasion (Konigsstuhl (GER))
340[5] 3496[13]

Ocean Bay *John Ryan* a86 97
3 b g Dubai Destination(USA) —Aldora (Magic Ring (IRE))
7166[9] (7443) 7606[6]

Ocean Bluff (IRE) *Mike Sowersby* a35 56
3 bb f Dalakhani(IRE) —Karaliyfa (IRE) (Kahyasi)
(4944)

Ocean Countess (IRE) *Tony Carroll* a58 79
5 b m Storming Home—Pennycairn (Last Tycoon)
26[8] 278[2] ◆ 391[8] 712[5] 957[5] 1936[5] 3251[7] 3944[4] (4699) 4948[8] 5422[3] 6586[12] 7442[4] 7581[6]

Ocean Legend (IRE) *Tony Carroll* a89 89
6 b g Night Shift(USA) —Rose Of Mooncoin (IRE) (Brief Truce (USA))
99[4] 226[2] ◆ 385[3] (557) 822[3] 908[5] 1103[8] 2300[12] 3383[3] 3784[5] 4310[17] 4860[6] 5322[8] 5828[14] 6979[9] (7517)

Ocean Myth *William Haggas* 70
2 b f Acclamation—Mystery Ocean (Dr Fong (USA))
3270[6] (3611) 4069[4] 4558[4] 4955[2] 5562[10]

Ocean Of Peace (FR) *Martin Bosley* a62 62
8 b g Volochine(IRE) —Sumatra (IRE) (Mukaddamah (USA))
164[5] (354) 466[4] 1308[2] (1582) 2051[5] 2616[4] 2663[5] 3176[5] 7202[10] 7394[F]

Ocean Rosie (IRE) *Tony Carroll* a59 63
4 b m One Cool Cat(USA) —Rose Of Mooncoin (IRE) (Brief Truce (USA))
816[6] 1220[5] 1333[10] 2271[5] 2820[13] 3253[12] 3942[7] 5421[8]

Ocean's Dream Day (IRE) *John Ryan* a59 51
3 b g Dubawi(IRE) —Dream Day (FR) (Spectrum (IRE))
191[5] 339[7] 471[7] 942[4] 1134[6] 1487[7] 1872[5] 5118[5] 5416[5] 5636[6]

Ocean Tempest *John Ryan* a78 76
2 gr c Act One—Ipsa Loquitur (Unfuwain (USA))
3401[13] 4390[2] 7167[7] (7454) 7576[3] 7786[2]

Ocean Transit (IRE) *Richard Price* a74 86
6 b m Trans Island—Wings Awarded (Shareef Dancer (USA))
2499[3] 2888[10] 6832[11]

Ocean Treasure (IRE) *Edward Vaughan* a39
4 ch m Barathea(IRE) —Coeur De La Mer (IRE) (Caerleon (USA))
1998[8]

Ocean War *Mahmood Al Zarooni* 108
3 gr g Dalakhani(IRE) —Atlantic Destiny (IRE) (Royal Academy (USA))
(1321) (1689) 2715[11]

Oceanway (USA) *Mark Johnston* a83 101
3 b f Street Cry(IRE) —Sea Gift (USA) (A.P. Indy (USA))
990[5] 1884[13] 2256[7] 2634[5] (3338) (3592) 4267[2] 4467[10] 5090a[14] 5483[15] 5940[4] 6163[6] ◆ (6704) 7029[7] 7297[13]

Ochilview Warrior (IRE) *Robin Bastiman* a29 47
4 b h Trans Island—Lonely Brook (USA) (El Gran Senor (USA))
800[9] 937[5] 1413[6]

Oculist *Jamie Osborne* a61 67
3 b g Dr Fong(USA) —Eyes Wide Open (Fraam)
2760[5] 3001[10] 3392[5] 3922[8] 4642[2] ◆ 5477[6] 5947[10]

Odd Ball (IRE) *Lisa Williamson* a59 34
4 b g Redback—Luceball (IRE) (Bluebird (USA))
(1217) 1544[7] 2164[9] 7911[11]

Oddsmaker (IRE) *Maurice Barnes* a42 71
10 b g Barathea(IRE) —Archipova (IRE) (Ela-Mana-Mou)
1036[8] (1519) 2544[7] 3129[9] 4499[6] 4982[3] 5166[5] 5405[12]

Oddysey (IRE) *Michael Dods* 67
2 b f Acclamation—Darling Smile (IRE) (Darshaan)
3342[3] 4232[3] 5058[4] 5817[6]

Odin (IRE) *David Elsworth* a79 79
3 b c Norse Dancer(IRE) —Dimelight (Fantastic Light (USA))
(140) ◆ 1485[7]

Odin's Raven (IRE) *Brian Ellison* a72 80
6 ro g Dalakhani(IRE) —Oriane (Nashwan (USA))
(11) 117[4] (2892) 3127[2] 4382[3]

Oekaki (FR) *Y Barberot* a75 101
4 b m Martillo(GER) —Pyu (GER) (Surumu (GER))
5093a[5] 5839a[6] 6321a[7]

Oetzi *Alan Jarvis* a63 73
3 ch g Iceman—Mad Annie (USA) (Anabaa (USA))
2119[3] 2841[5] (3783) 4447[4] ◆ 5835[5] 6227[5] ◆ 6748[2]

Oeuvre D'Art (IRE) *B Grizzetti* 100
3 b f Marju(IRE) —Midefix (ITY) (Night Shift (USA))
1738a[5] 2539a[3] 3449a[3] 6739a[9] 7047a[9]

Off Chance *Tim Easterby* 104
5 b m Olden Times—La Notte (Factual (USA))
1385[2] 1681[3] 2031[5] 3703[3] 4368[3] 4790[2] 5277[5] 5848[10] 6297[4]

Officer In Command (USA) *J S Moore* a85 77
5 bb h Officer(USA) —Luv To Stay N Chat (USA) (Candi's Gold (USA))
221a[4] 395a[6] 566a[8] 617a[0] 885[2] 968[6]

Officer Lily (USA) *John Best* a51 49
4 bb m Officer(USA) —Anagalia (USA) (Cherokee Colony (USA))
722[8] 809[9] 862[8] 1582[13] 2271[7] 2760[6]

O'Gorman *Kevin Ryan* 86
2 b g Sleeping Indian—Harryana (Efisio)
3755[5] (4283) ◆ 4787[3] 5505[2]

Ohceecee *Jason Ward*
2 b g One Cool Cat(USA) —Serramanna (Grand Lodge (USA))
2953[17]

Oh Landino (GER) *Jim Goldie* 46
6 b g Lando(GER) —Oh La Belle (GER) (Dashing Blade)
1519[2] 2400[6] 2733[7]

Oh My Days (IRE) *Clive Cox* a63 53
3 ch g Bahamian Bounty—Princess Speedfit (FR) (Desert Prince (IRE))
818[2] 971[3]

Oh So Kool *Stuart Williams* a73 69
3 b g Bertolini(USA) —Pretty Kool (Inchinor)
(182) 2074[16] 2881[6] 3178[10]

Oh So Saucy *Chris Wall* a60 82
7 b m Imperial Ballet(IRE) —Almasi (IRE) (Petorius)
1569[5] 2545[13] 4278[6] 5014[5] 5496[5] 6990[5]

Oh So Spicy *Chris Wall* 78
4 ch m Pastoral Pursuits—Almasi (IRE) (Petorius)
1570[2] 2270[5] 2845[9] (4729) 5561[2] 6065[3] (6752)

Ohwhatalady (IRE) *Noel Quinlan* a42 46
3 b f Invincible Spirit(IRE) —Silly Goose (IRE) (Sadler's Wells (USA))
6096[9] 7085[8] 7466[10]

Oh What's Occuring *Terry Clement* a34
3 b f Spartacus(IRE) —Liferaft (Kahyasi)
109[10] 296[5]

Oil Strike *Peter Winkworth* a98 93
4 b g Lucky Story(USA) —Willisa (Polar Falcon (USA))
2099[7] 2826[4] 3796[4] 4609[13] 5278[5] 5811[2] 6467[4]

Okalydokely (IRE) *Andrew Crook* a51 65
7 b g Shinko Forest(IRE) —Delirious Tantrum (IRE) (Taufan (USA))
652[12]

Ok Annie (IRE) *Patrick Martin* a60 71
2 b f Amadeus Wolf—Joint Destiny (IRE) (Desert Prince (IRE))
7275a[5]

Ok Coral (FR) *K Borgel* 103
4 bl h Timboroa—Coraloune (FR) (Valanour (IRE))
267a[8] 7733a[5]

O'Kelly Hammer (IRE) *A Fabre* a69 82
3 b c Intikhab(USA) —Aladiyna (IRE) (Indian Danehill (IRE))
1965a[6]

Oken Bruce Lee (JPN) *Hidetaka Otonashi* 124
6 ch h Jungle Pocket(JPN) —Silver Joy (CAN) (Silver Deputy (CAN))
7563a[10]

Okimono *Mahmood Al Zarooni* 77
2 b c Invincible Spirit(IRE) —Ivory Gala (FR) (Galileo (IRE))
6244[2]

Old Boy Ted *Mark H Tompkins* 53
3 b g Tobougg(IRE) —Grove Dancer (Reprimand)
6701[10] 7212[9]

Old English (IRE) *Noel Wilson* a70 71
3 b g Marju(IRE) —Princess Mood (GER) (Muhtarram (USA))
509[4] 610[3] (887) 973a[11] 1176[9] 3934[2] ◆ 4176[6] 4506[6] 4812[2] 5314[15] 5721[P] 5821[8] 7424[P]

Older Than Time (AUS) *Gai Waterhouse* 106
5 b m Don Eduardo(NZ) —Up The Hill (AUS) (Danehill (USA))
7218a[17]

Old Firm *Ian Semple* a49 25
5 ch g Compton Place—Miriam (Forzando)
2631[8] 2809[11]

Old Hundred (IRE) *James Fanshawe* a87 93
4 b g Tiger Hill(IRE) —Bordighera (USA) (Alysheba (USA))
(1676) ◆ 2512[13] 3344[2] 4348[10] 5448[12] (5883)

Oldjoesaid *Kevin Ryan* a77 94
7 b g Royal Applause—Border Minstral (IRE) (Sri Pekan (USA))
1073[3] 1539[2] (1698) 2117[7] 2714[10] 3160[2] 3379[4] 3613[7] 4369[8] 4531[11] 4791[7] 5108[2] 5679[5] 5831[12] 6112[18] 6917[13] 7116[9] 7332[4] 7500[4] 7644[6] 7834[3]

Oldmeldrum (IRE) *Peter Salmon* 59
3 gr f Verglas(IRE) —Nassma (IRE) (Sadler's Wells (USA))
1038[9] 1749[11] 2835[3] 3545[7] 4084[5] 4441[3] 5315[U]

Old Navy *John Gosden* 69
3 b c Shirocco(GER) —So Admirable (Suave Dancer (USA))
4805[6] ◆

Oldrik (GER) *Philip Hobbs* 84
8 b g Tannenkonig(IRE) —Onestep (GER) (Konigsstuhl (GER))
6410[2]

Olimamu (IRE) *Lydia Pearce* a57 54
4 b m Barathea(IRE) —La Galeisa (IRE) (Warning)
136[3] 983[6] 1252[4] 3311[7] 3946[5] 4164[6] 4549[3] 4869[5] 5520[4] 5994[4] 7640[11]

Oliver's Gold *Amanda Perrett* a61 66
3 b g Danehill Dancer(IRE) —Gemini Gold (IRE) (King's Best (USA))
1769[8] 2293[6] 2722[4] 3226[2] 3431[3] 3742[2]

Olivino (GER) *Bernard Llewellyn* a49 40
10 ch g Second Set(IRE) —Osdemona (GER) (Solarstern (FR))
173[9] 419[4] 1833[7]

Ollianna (IRE) *Tom Dascombe* 41
3 b f Majestic Missile(IRE) —Aspired (IRE) (Mark Of Esteem (IRE))
1795[6] 2151[9] 2493[9]

Ollon (USA) *Richard Fahey* a63 76
3 bb g Mr Greeley(USA) —Town Branch (USA) (Cape Town (USA))
(1944) 2389[3] 2764[3] 3758[3] 4367[14] 5004[5] 5622[10] 7003[4]

Ollywood *Tony Carroll* a50 35
3 b g Needwood Blade—Angel Maid (Forzando)
2103[13] 2311[8] 3431[9] 3717[6] 4284[12] 4827[12]

Olney Lass *Lydia Pearce* a53 67
4 b m Lucky Story(USA) —Zalebe (Bahamian Bounty)
201[3] 450[7] 773[3] 969[3] 1308[4] (3942) 4444[11] 5298[2] (5667) (5995) 6814[8]

Olympic Ceremony *Tracy Waggott* a63 38
4 br g Kyllachy—Opening Ceremony (USA) (Quest For Fame)
3732[10] 4017[10]

Olympic Dream *Michael Herrington* a60 79
5 b g Kyllachy—Opening Ceremony (USA) (Quest For Fame)
37[2] 255[5] 504[5] 798[3] 1498[10]

Olympic Win (NZ) *Robert Smerdon* 104
6 b g Montjeu(IRE) —Tennessee Moon (Darshaan)
7115a[5]

Olynard (IRE) *Michael Mullineaux* a73 97
5 b g Exceed And Excel(AUS) —Reddening (Blushing Flame (USA))
2099[17] 2525[7] 2717[12] 3000[10] 3383[8] 3796[13] 4369[14] 4990[6] 5452[5] 5604[5] 7897[10]

O Ma Lad (IRE) *Sylvester Kirk* a82 83
3 ch g Redback—Raydaniya (IRE) (In The Wings)
2371[8] 2591[3] (4800) 5804[2]

Omkara *E Borromeo* 94
3 b f Zamindar(USA) —Orange Walk (IRE) (Alzao (USA))
3449a[6] 6370a[6]

Omnipotent (IRE) *Richard Hannon* a55 63
3 b c Tagula(IRE) —Bobbydazzle (Rock Hopper)
4320[4] 5538[6] 5942[9] 6052[8]

On Alert *Seamus Durack* a27
3 b g Deploy—Morina (USA) (Lyphard (USA))
5911[12] 6286[7] 6504[6]

Onceaponatime (IRE) *Michael Squance* a89 73
6 b g Invincible Spirit(IRE) —Lake Nyasa (IRE) (Lake Coniston (IRE))
58[2] ◆ 168[2] 199[7] 377[3] 904[5] 985[8] 1171[3] 1314[3] 1995[11] 2179[3]

Once More Dubai (USA) *Saeed Bin Suroor* a112 104
6 br h E Dubai(USA) —Go Again Girl (USA) (Broad Brush (USA))
242[2] 498a[5]

Once Upon A Cat (IRE) *Mrs K Burke* a66 65
7 b m Tale Of The Cat(USA) —Whatdidyoucallme (USA) (Darshaan)
1142a[0]

Ondeafears (IRE) *Stuart Howe* a41 71
4 b m Chineur(FR) —Irma La Douce (IRE) (Elbio)
1984[8] 2689[3]

Onebytheknows *Richard Hannon* a67 66
2 b c Royal Applause—Garmoucheh (USA) (Silver Hawk (USA))
3917[10] 4339[11] 4906[3] ◆ 5409[5] 6630[3] 6807[11]

One Clever Cat (IRE) *T Clout* a87 109
5 b m One Cool Cat(USA) —Burn Baby Burn (IRE) (King's Theatre (IRE))
1784a[4] 2373a[3] 3008a[4] 4120a[4] 4597a[5] (6321a) 6556a[4]

One Cool Breeze (IRE) *Ralph Beckett* a14
2 b f One Cool Cat(USA) —Breezit (USA) (Stravinsky (USA))
6786[9]

One Cool Chick *John Bridger* a64 52
3 b f Iceman—Barrantes (Distant Relative)
1724[10] 2025[6] 2294[9] 2792[16] 3292[4] 3818[11] 4086[8] 4759[3] 5542[8] (6258) 6746[5] 7348[3] 7488[6] 7588[12]

One Cool Dancer (IRE) *John Gallagher* 11
2 br f One Cool Cat(USA) —Dancing Duchess (IRE) (Danehill Dancer (IRE))
5337[8]

One Cool Poppy (IRE) *Mrs A Malzard* a47 57
4 b m One Cool Cat(USA) —Elusive Kitty (USA) (Elusive Quality (USA))
5778a[7]

Oneeightofamile (IRE) *John E Kiely* 83
6 b g Catcher In The Rye(IRE) —Punta Gorda (IRE) (Roi Danzig (USA))
3420a[4] 4398a[11]

One Hit Wonder *Jonathan Portman* a56 74
4 b g Whipper(USA) —Swiftly (Cadeaux Genereux)
2051[13] 2376[5] 2771[2] 3266[4] (3814) (4154) 4825[3] 5568[10] 6017[6]

Oneiric *Ralph Beckett* a63 78
3 gr f Act One—Ecstasy (Pursuit Of Love)
1767[3] 2371[2] 2871[2] 3872[2] 5098[2] 6405[7]

One Kool Dude *Richard Fahey* a72 73
2 ch g Iceman—Hiraeth (Petong)
972a[2] 1165[2] 1383[3] 1876[3] 2318[4] 3082[2] 3618[3] 4343[9] 5646[2] 6075[5] 6800[5]

Oneladyowner *David Brown* a64 92
3 b c Auction House(USA) —Inya Lake (Whittingham (IRE))
940[2] (1141) 1825[4] 2363[5] (5000) (5508) 5972[3] 6174[11] 6500[8]

One London (IRE) *Paul Cole* 43
4 b g Bertolini(USA) —Mellow Park (IRE) (In The Wings)
1271[13]

One Lucky Lady *Charles Hills* a76 79
3 b f Lucky Story(USA) —One For Philip (Blushing Flame (USA))
2877[7] 3919[6] 4862[4] (5266) 5782[4] 6328[4] 6893[3]

One More Roman (IRE) *J S Moore* a65 26
2 b c Holy Roman Emperor(IRE) —Satulagi (USA) (Officer (USA))
2787[13] 7038[5] 7464[5] (7635) 7907[4] (7927)

One New Cat (IRE) *Ed Dunlop* 52
2 br c One Cool Cat(USA) —Iris May (Brief Truce (USA))
2181[6] 2617[8] 3554[3]

Oneniteinheaven (IRE) *Ann Duffield* 61
2 ch f Choisir(AUS) —Westlife (IRE) (Mind Games)
1455[5] 1791[2] 2093[6] 5399[9] 6043[15]

Oneofapear (IRE) *Alan Swinbank* a57 93
5 b g Pyrus(USA) —Whitegate Way (Greensmith)
1097[2] 2124[7] 2814[9] 4608[5]

One Of Three (IRE) *Michael Mulvany* a57 74
5 b m Tamarisk(IRE) —Call Me Vicki (IRE) (Bigstone (IRE))
6388a[19]

One Of Twins *Michael Easterby* a58 60
3 b g Gentleman's Deal(IRE) —Miss Twiddles (IRE) (Desert King (IRE))
1495[5] 1945[3] 2166[5] 2809[6] (4638) 5248[3] 6179[12] 6545[2] 7005[6]

One Oi *David Arbuthnot* a66
6 b g Bertolini(USA) —Bogus Penny (IRE) (Pennekamp (USA))
48[3] 310[5] 727[5] 1333[3]

One Pursuit (IRE) *David Nicholls* a71 84
3 br g Pastoral Pursuits—Karinski (USA) (Palace Music (USA))
431[3] (546) (738) 2527[5] 3038[3] ◆ (4364)

Onertother *Joseph Tuite* 20
2 b g Nomadic Way(USA) —Ceilidh Band (Celtic Swing)
6993[11]

One Scoop Or Two *Reg Hollinshead* a85 89
5 b g Needwood Blade—Rebel County (IRE) (Maelstrom Lake)
1390^{3} ◆ 1826^{5} 2282^{2} 2814^{5} 2887^{4} 3275^{2} 3848^{9} 4574^{2} (5684) 5879^{3} 5920^{7} 6326^{8}

One Spirit (IRE) *F Dunne* 98
3 b f Invincible Spirit(IRE) —Recite (JPN) (Forty Niner (USA))
3444a^{3} 5523a^{8} 5977a^{4}

One Way Or Another (AUS) *David Evans* a87 88
8 b g Carnegie(IRE) —True Blonde (AUS) (Naturalism (NZ))
226^{5} ◆ 2095^{8} 3275^{4} 4215^{7} 6174^{13} 6895^{9} 7243^{9} 7412^{2} (7565) (7636) 7695^{3} 7876^{2} 7926^{2} ◆

Ongoodform (IRE) *Paul D'Arcy* a85 82
4 b h Invincible Spirit(IRE) —Elfin Queen (IRE) (Fairy King (USA))
385^{7} 651^{9} 867^{3} 1488^{5} 1990^{3} 2016^{2} 3172^{7} 4064^{3} (5119) 5948^{2} 6478^{4} 6949^{13}

On Her Way *Luca Cumani* a87 91
4 ch m Medicean—Singed (Zamindar (USA))
3585^{2} 5686^{2} 6708^{12}

Oniz Tiptoes (IRE) *John Wainwright* 29
10 ch g Russian Revival(USA) —Edionda (IRE) (Magical Strike (USA))
3072^{9}

On Khee *Hughie Morrison* a77 87
4 b m Sakhee(USA) —Star Precision (Shavian)
2055^{10} 2552^{5} 3228^{3} 3815^{7} (4613) 4971^{9} 5328^{2}

Only A Game (IRE) *Ian McInnes* a64 67
6 b g Foxhound(USA) —Compendium (Puissance)
167^{10} 421^{10}

Only A Round (IRE) *Micky Hammond* 37
2 b g Tagula(IRE) —Scepter'd Isle (Shirley Heights)
4073^{12} 4853^{12} 6274^{6}

Onlyfoalsandhorses (IRE) *J S Moore* a56 52
3 b f Chineur(FR) —Scarletta (USA) (Red Ransom (USA))
(967) 1472^{6} 1958^{11} 2196^{11} 2825^{2} 3175^{8} 3958^{10}

Only Orsenfoolsies *Micky Hammond* 57
2 b g Trade Fair—Desert Gold (IRE) (Desert Prince (IRE))
2318^{9} 2476^{5} 2780^{8} 3728^{6} 3948^{7} 7072^{4}

Only Ten Per Cent (IRE) *J R Jenkins* a59 43
3 b g Kheleyf(USA) —Cory Everson (IRE) (Brief Truce (USA))
7714^{2} 7886^{3}

Only You Maggie (IRE) *Gary Harrison* 73
4 b m Atraf—First Kiss (GER) (Night Shift (USA))
2996^{7} 3266^{5} 4158^{5} (4645) 4707^{2} 5002^{2} 5614^{6} 5915^{5} 6894^{5} 7112^{8}

On Terms (USA) *Simon Dow* a81 84
5 b m Aptitude(USA) —Silver Yen (USA) (Silver Hawk (USA))
209^{9} 1509^{3} 1677^{8} (2758)

On The Cusp (IRE) *Richard Guest* a78 74
4 b g Footstepsinthesand—Roman Love (IRE) (Perugino (USA))
61^{4} 340^{2} (490) 807^{13} 1068^{7} 1468^{2} 2057^{11} 2237^{2} 2415^{3} (2809) 3306^{5} (4179) 4543^{8} 5150^{5} 5721^{12} 6971^{3} 7068^{4} (7263) 7425^{7} 7687^{3} (7773) (7887)

On The Dark Side (IRE) *Kevin Ryan* 95
2 b f Kheleyf(USA) —Red Fuschia (Polish Precedent (USA))
(2248) 2712^{3} ◆ 3033^{9} 4094^{9} 4413^{5} 4999^{6} 5558^{7} 5882^{10} 6670^{16}

On The Feather *Rod Millman* a70 76
5 br m Josr Algarhoud(IRE) —Fotheringhay (Loup Sauvage (USA))
1608^{3} 2176^{2} 2923^{2} 3215^{2} (3872) 4465^{2} 4971^{8} 5340^{7} 5804^{6} 6592^{9}

On The High Tops (IRE) *Ruth Carr* a43 84
3 b g Kheleyf(USA) —Diplomats Daughter (Unfuwain (USA))
(1241) 2505^{5} 4295^{7} 5268^{4} 5559^{6} 5923^{8} 6350^{9} 7355^{12} 7535^{11}

On The Hoof *Michael Easterby* 76
2 ch g Monsieur Bond(IRE) —Smart Hostess (Most Welcome)
3274^{10} 3755^{13} 4192^{8} 4347^{5} 5058^{3} 5184^{4} 5755^{4} 6670^{14}

On The Lash (IRE) *Alan Swinbank*
3 b g Whipper(USA) —Try To Catch Me (USA) (Shareef Dancer (USA))
1812^{11}

Onwards'N'Upwards *Christine Dunnett* a22
3 b g Diktat—Lunar Goddess (Royal Applause)
7662^{7}

On Wings Of Love (IRE) *John Gallagher* a51 66
3 ch f Hawk Wing(USA) —Grenouillere (USA) (Alysheba (USA))
801^{8} 966^{6}

Onyx Of Arabia (IRE) *Brian Meehan* a76 77
4 br h Avonbridge—Fiamma Royale (IRE) (Fumo Di Londra (IRE))
1892^{2} 2213^{5} 2656^{4} 2958^{8} 3184^{P}

Ooi Long *Mark Rimmer* 40
2 b g Echo Of Light—Danceatdusk (Desert Prince (IRE))
2109^{7} 3401^{14} 3954^{11} 6099^{9} 7242^{14}

Oojooba *Roger Varian* 85
2 b f Monsun(GER) —Ameerat (Mark Of Esteem (IRE))
(6329) ◆ 7169^{7}

Oondiri (IRE) *Tim Easterby* 67
4 b m Trans Island—Nullarbor (Green Desert (USA))
1411^{16} 1555^{4} 2365^{4}

Oops Caroline (IRE) *David O'Meara* 56
2 ch f Strategic Prince—Annette Vallon (IRE) (Efisio)
6776^{7} 6984^{9}

Oor Jock (IRE) *Tracey Collins* 98
3 ch c Shamardal(USA) —Katdogawn (Bahhare (USA))
2500^{5} 2967a^{3} 3852^{10} 4836a^{8} 5288^{3}

Oosisit *Ruth Carr* a51 30
3 b f Iffraaj—Presentation (IRE) (Mujadil (USA))
5469^{9} 5793^{9} 6353^{6} 6765^{9}

Opening Nite (IRE) *Denis W Cullen* a76 75
4 b g Azamour(IRE) —Night Club (Mozart (IRE))
(977a)

Openly *James Fanshawe* 66
2 b f Singspiel(IRE) —Grand Opening (IRE) (Desert King (IRE))
6984^{5}

Open Water (FR) *Andrew Balding* 83
2 b c Orpen(USA) —So Stream (ITY) (Elmaamul (USA))
(6059) ◆ 6957^{2}

Opera Box *Marcus Tregoning* 59
3 b f Singspiel(IRE) —Annex (Anabaa (USA))
2257^{8}

Opera Buff *Sylvester Kirk* 77
2 b c Oratorio(IRE) —Opera Glass (Barathea (IRE))
2962^{5} 4054^{4} 4535^{3} 5234^{6} 6995^{4} 7258^{2}

Opera Dancer *Sylvester Kirk* a75 77
3 ch f Norse Dancer(IRE) —Optaria (Song)
1626^{6} 2102^{14} 2821^{12}

Opera Flute (IRE) *Richard Hannon* 78
2 b c Amadeus Wolf—Southern Queen (Anabaa (USA))
6725^{2} 6951^{4} 7132^{3}

Opera Gal (IRE) *Andrew Balding* a77 104
4 b m Galileo(IRE) —Opera Glass (Barathea (IRE))
1479^{4} 2676^{2} 2909^{3} 3356^{5} 4099^{3} 4915^{2} (5493) 5934^{4} 6247^{6}

Opera Prince *Simon Earle* a70 83
6 b g Kyllachy—Optaria (Song)
1046^{5} 1174^{3} 7671^{2} 7789^{9}

Operateur (IRE) *Ben Haslam* a64 67
3 b g Oratorio(IRE) —Kassariya (IRE) (Be My Guest (USA))
1300^{5} 1858^{4} 2571^{3} 4904^{6} 6503^{10}

Operation Tracer *Michael Bell* 68
2 ch g Rock Of Gibraltar(IRE) —Quite Elusive (USA) (Elusive Quality (USA))
3986^{9} 5475^{5} 6048^{5}

Opera Vert (FR) *D Sepulchre* 102
3 b c Green Tune(USA) —Caramba Kelly (IRE) (Mtoto)
5131a^{3}

Operettist *Richard Hannon* a56 75
2 b f Singspiel(IRE) —Demi Voix (Halling (USA))
6440^{9} (6745)

Opinion (IRE) *Sir Michael Stoute* 61
2 b c Oasis Dream—Kiltubber (IRE) (Sadler's Wells (USA))
6064^{7} 6953^{6}

Opinion Poll (IRE) *Mahmood Al Zarooni* 120
5 b h Halling(USA) —Ahead (Shirley Heights)
329a^{2} 584a^{2} 826a^{3} 2344a^{4} 3066^{2} ◆ (4469) (5284) 5884^{2} 6857^{2}

Oppenort (IRE) *M Delzangles* 101
3 b c Aussie Rules(USA) —Odessa (IRE) (Sadler's Wells (USA))
1551a^{6}

Optimizer (USA) *D Wayne Lukas* a111 109
2 b c English Channel(USA) —Indy Pick (USA) (A.P. Indy (USA))
7306a^{8}

Optimum Rose (IRE) *David O'Meara* 28
2 b f Chineur(FR) —Finty (IRE) (Entrepreneur)
2617^{7}

Opus Dei *David Nicholls* a72 76
4 b g Oasis Dream—Grail (USA) (Quest For Fame)
3856^{2} 4517^{10}

Opus Maximus (IRE) *Conor Dore* a83 94
6 ch g Titus Livius(FR) —Law Review (IRE) (Case Law)
31^{2} 1164^{4} 2910^{6} 3275^{14} (3569) 3972^{3} 4361^{5} (4601) 4897^{5} 5390^{6} 6098^{2} (6433) 6831^{4} (7034) 7412^{6} 7492^{2} 7589^{2} (7605) 7734^{2} 7759^{2} 7831^{6} (7877)

Oracle (IRE) *A P O'Brien* 114
3 b c Danehill Dancer(IRE) —Zibilene (Rainbow Quest (USA))
2324a^{3} 3029^{4} 3863^{13}

Oranais (IRE) *E Lellouche* 102
4 gr h Dalakhani(IRE) —Odessa (IRE) (Sadler's Wells (USA))
4524a^{10}

Orange Ace *Paul Cole* a77 66
3 b c Medicean—Promenade Again (USA) (Wild Again (USA))
1384^{8} 1862^{4} 5635^{8} 6063^{7} 6262^{2} 6465^{6} 6605^{2}

Oratorian (IRE) *Sylvester Kirk* a66
2 b g Oratorio(IRE) —Raindancing (IRE) (Tirol)
7454^{6} 7673^{3} 7809^{3}

Oratory (IRE) *Geoffrey Harker* a82 99
5 b g Danehill Dancer(IRE) —Gentle Night (Zafonic (USA))
1240^{8} 3397^{12} 4794^{15} 5465^{3} 6631^{7} 6989^{19}

Oratouch (IRE) *Marco Botti* a63
3 b f Oratorio(IRE) —Ravish (Efisio)
234^{5} 366^{2}

Oratrix (IRE) *Denis Coakley* a51 9
2 b f Oratorio(IRE) —Divine Secret (Hernando (FR))
5814^{9} 6214^{13} 6474^{8} 6760^{8}

Orbital Orchid *Nick Williams* a56 60
6 b m Mujahid(USA) —Carati (Selkirk (USA))
2377^{2} 2873^{3} 4630^{3} 5379^{6}

Orbit The Moon (IRE) *Michael Dods* 86
3 b c Oratorio(IRE) —Catch The Moon (IRE) (Peintre Celebre (USA))
1693^{10} 1971^{2} ◆ (2361) 2834^{4}

Orchard Supreme *Ralph Smith* a93 82
8 ch g Titus Livius(FR) —Bogus Penny (IRE) (Pennekamp (USA))
50^{2} 588^{4} 656^{5} 1195^{3}

Orchestra Leader (USA) *David Wachman* 87
2 b c Van Nistelrooy(USA) —Magic Of Life (USA) (Seattle Slew (USA))
4257a^{6}

Orchid Street (USA) *Ann Duffield* a44 78
3 bb f Street Cry(IRE) —Ella Eria (FR) (Bluebird (USA))
1825^{9} 2619^{7} (3309) 3629^{5}

Orchid Wing *Tobias B P Coles* a68 67
4 ch g Avonbridge—First Ace (First Trump)
298^{11} 388^{4}

Orcus (FR) *C Ferland* 99
2 b c Russian Blue(IRE) —Perfidie (IRE) (Monsun (GER))
5365a^{2}

Ordensritter (GER) *H Steinmetz* a87 97
3 ch c Samum(GER) —Dramraire Mist (Darshaan)
3007a^{7} 3672a^{16}

Ordenstreuer (IRE) *H-W Hiller* a95 99
5 b h Nayef(USA) —Dramraire Mist (Darshaan)
1011a^{0} 1554a^{7}

Orders From Rome (IRE) *Eve Johnson Houghton* 90
2 b g Holy Roman Emperor(IRE) —Fatat Alarab (USA) (Capote (USA))
2291^{7} 2880^{2} ◆ 4094^{6} ◆ 4580^{5} 5479^{5} 6170^{12}

Ordnance Row *Roger Varian* 107
8 b g Mark Of Esteem(IRE) —Language Of Love (Rock City)
3290^{12} 3877^{18}

Orfevre (JPN) *Yasutoshi Ikee* 128
3 ch c Stay Gold(JPN) —Oriental Art (JPN) (Mejiro McQueen (JPN))
(7873a)

Oriental Cavalier *Mark Buckley* a76 83
5 ch g Ishiguru(USA) —Gurleigh (IRE) (Pivotal)
1390^{2} 1855^{6} 2282^{2} (2708) 3544^{6} 4004^{5} 4577^{6} 5568^{13}

Oriental Fox (GER) *Carmen Bocskai* 104
3 ch c Lomitas—Oriental Pearl (GER) (Big Shuffle (USA))
7045a^{4}

Oriental Girl *Jonathan Geake* a62 77
6 b m Dr Fong(USA) —Zacchera (Zamindar (USA))
2378^{5} 2872^{6} 3426^{2} 4154^{4} 4916^{7} 5614^{4} 5915^{4} 6401^{4} 6894^{3}

Orientalist *Eve Johnson Houghton* a83 89
3 ch g Haafhd—Oriental Queen (GER) (Big Shuffle (USA))
1326^{4} 1725^{10} 2296^{8} 2607^{5} 3231^{4} 3650^{9} 3988^{5} 4860^{5} ◆ (5547) 5892^{8} 6374^{5} 6576^{5} 6997^{9}

Oriental Scot *William Jarvis* a74 96
4 ch g Selkirk(USA) —Robe Chinoise (Robellino (USA))
1092^{7} ◆ 1694^{9} 2681^{10} 3585^{5} 4070^{4} 4561^{14} 5012^{12} (6290) 7168^{11}

Orife (IRE) *Stephane Chevalier* a98 99
4 b h Marchand De Sable(USA) —Entente Cordiale (IRE) (Ela-Mana-Mou)
602a^{3} 678a^{5} 825a^{8}

Orinocco *John Ryan*
2 b c Shirocco(GER) —Norcroft Joy (Rock Hopper)
7167^{8}

Ornella Vanoni *B Grizzetti*
3 b f Oasis Dream—Supercharger (Zamindar (USA))
1126a^{8}

Ornithologist (USA) *David O'Meara* 68
3 b g Elusive Quality(USA) —On A Lark (USA) (The Prime Minister (USA))
6349^{7} 6804^{5} 7063^{4} ◆

Oroveso (BRZ) *Fabricio Borges* a102 98
5 gr h Fahim—Voile D'Or (BRZ) (Effervescing (USA))
240^{13} 499a^{11} 5981a^{2}

Orpen'Arry (IRE) *Andrew Haynes* 78
3 b g Orpen(USA) —Closing Time (IRE) (Topanoora)
4340^{9} 4706^{2} ◆ (4970) 5392^{8} 6167^{18}

Orpen Bid (IRE) *Michael Mullineaux* a34 51
6 b m Orpen(USA) —Glorious Bid (IRE) (Horage)
1063^{8} 2654^{4} 3581^{4} 3910^{9} 4951^{9} 6295^{9} 7426^{14} 7903^{9}

Orpenindeed (IRE) *Frank Sheridan* a93 87
8 bb g Orpen(USA) —Indian Goddess (IRE) (Indian Ridge)
(230) 445^{2} 914^{5} 1471^{2} (1557) 2179^{7} (2286) 4921^{7} 5734^{3}

Orpen's Art (IRE) *R Houthoofd* a77 72
6 b g Invincible Spirit(IRE) —Bells Of Ireland (UAE) (Machiavellian (USA))
6593a^{10}

Orpens Peach (IRE) *Seamus Fahey* a76 64
4 b m Orpen(USA) —Shes A Peach (IRE) (Bahhare (USA))
(229) 250^{3} 730^{4} 748^{7} 7141^{5} (7695) 7792a^{4}

Orpen Wide (IRE) *Michael Chapman* a45 68
9 b g Orpen(USA) —Melba (IRE) (Namaqualand (USA))
181^{10} 6236^{12}

Orpsie Boy (IRE) *Ruth Carr* a94 96
8 b g Orpen(USA) —Nordicolini (IRE) (Nordico (USA))
2299^{5} ◆ 2938^{15} (3506) (3784) 4369^{15} 5032^{7} 5758^{8} 5879^{9} 6347^{11} 6761^{6} 7074^{5}

Orrell Post *Richard Fahey* 39
2 b f Kyllachy—Dame Blanche (IRE) (Be My Guest (USA))
3092^{10} 3398^{8}

Orsino (GER) *R Rohne* 99
4 b h Mamool(IRE) —Orosole (GER) (Platini (GER))
6569a^{3} 7045a^{9}

Orsippus (USA) *Michael Smith* a78 73
5 bb g Sunday Break(JPN) —Mirror Dancing (USA) (Caveat (USA))
2433^{3} (6707) 7139^{6}

Ortac Rock (IRE) *Richard Hannon* 90
2 b c Aussie Rules(USA) —Fashion Guide (IRE) (Bluebird (USA))
(5697) (6166) ◆ 7021^{2}

Ortea *David Evans* 78
2 b c Vital Equine(IRE) —Artistic (IRE) (Noverre (USA))
1209^{4} (1522) ◆ 2154^{6} 2868^{4} 5216^{16} 6345^{10}

Orthodox Lad *John Best* a68 77
3 ch g Monsieur Bond(IRE) —Ashantiana (Ashkalani (IRE))
2216^{6} 2841^{3} 3346^{3} 4011^{3} 4473^{4} 5242^{3} 5938^{9} (6748)

Orwellian *Brian Meehan* a65 64
2 b g Bahamian Bounty—Trinny (Rainbow Quest (USA))
3308^{6} 4815^{8} ◆ 5337^{3} 6443^{4} 6667^{8} 7849^{4}

Oscan (USA) *Mahmood Al Zarooni* a75 82
2 b c Street Cry(IRE) —Moyesii (USA) (Diesis)
(5801) 6126^{7} 6699^{4} ◆ (6972)

Oscar Close (IRE) *George Baker* 64
6 br g Oscar(IRE) —Upham Close (Oats)
6722^{5}

Osgood *Mick Channon* a76 83
4 b g Danehill Dancer(IRE) —Sabreon (Caerleon (USA))
2486^{5} 2915^{5} (3215) 3244^{7} 3848^{2} 4109^{5} 4537^{14} 5059^{13} 5495^{2} 5733^{8} 6079^{11} 6188^{4} 6435^{7} 6543^{7} 6869^{10} 7236^{12}

Osgoodisgood *Stuart Williams* a42 37
3 ch g Compton Place—Protectorate (Hector Protector (USA))
579^{6} 909^{8} 5644^{7} 6105^{10} 6610^{7}

Osiris Way *Patrick Chamings* a83 94
9 ch g Indian Ridge—Heady (Rousillon (USA))
2069^{3} 2645^{3} 2959^{4} 3687^{6} 4583^{5} 5627^{6} 7116^{2} 7575^{5}

Osirixamix (IRE) *A J Martin* 74
8 b g Desert Prince(IRE) —Osirixa (FR) (Linamix (FR))
925a^{11}

Oskari *Mike Sowersby* a70 31
6 b g Lear Spear(USA) —Cedar Jeneva (Muhtarram (USA))
3141^{6}

Ossie Ardiles (IRE) *Michael Appleby* a57 30
3 gr g Aussie Rules(USA) —Look Who's Dancing (Observatory (USA))
2206^{8} 3167^{11} 3716^{5} 4431^{7} 4666^{11} 4920^{4}

Ostentation *Roger Teal* a75 70
4 ch g Dubawi(IRE) —Oshiponga (Barathea (IRE))
7713^{3} 7884^{5}

Osteopathic Remedy (IRE) *Michael Dods* a87 103
7 ch g Inchinor—Dolce Vita (IRE) (Ela-Mana-Mou)
1111^{17} 1457^{4} 1694^{5} 2031^{17} 2706^{12} 2933^{15} 3397^{14} (4561) 5557^{4} 6150^{7} 6672^{7}

Ostrea (FR) *Y Barberot* a80 98
2 b c Early March—Mia's Baby (USA) (Rahy (USA))
6184a^{4}

Ottavino (IRE) *Nigel Tinkler* 12
2 b g Piccolo—Indian's Feather (IRE) (Indian Ridge)
5726^{10} 6448^{14}

Otto The Great *Walter Swinburn* a41 87
2 b g Holy Roman Emperor(IRE) —Vayavaig (Damister (USA))
1757^{6} 2143^{2} (4384) 6162^{9} 6766^{4}

Ouilly (IRE) *J-C Rouget* a74
3 b c Danehill Dancer(IRE) —Luna Wells (IRE) (Sadler's Wells (USA))
1010a^{5}

Our Boy Barrington (IRE) *David Nicholls* 81
4 b g Catcher In The Rye(IRE) —Daily Double (FR) (Unfuwain (USA))
1909^{18} 2761^{9} 3936^{5} ◆ 4176^{3} 4670^{5}

Our Boy Billy *Robert Cowell* a24 39
2 b g Piccolo—Overwing (IRE) (Fasliyev (USA))
2640^{8} 3552^{7} 3984^{8} 6021^{7} 6540^{10}

Our Boy Jack (IRE) *Richard Fahey* 69
2 b g Camacho—Jina (IRE) (Petardia)
1095^{12} 3611^{4} 4106^{4} ◆ 4572^{4} (4809) 5184^{7} 6670^{6}

Our Cool Cat (IRE) *Gary Moore* 79
2 b c One Cool Cat(USA) —Beautiful Dancer (IRE) (Danehill Dancer (IRE))
3249^{5} 3816^{10} 4485^{3} 6058^{3} (6524)

Our Freedom *David Lanigan* a3
3 b f New Freedom(BRZ) —Ortigueira (BRZ) (Yagli (USA))
5607^{9}

Our Gal *Noel Quinlan* a63 94
3 b f Kyllachy—Moxby (Efisio)
1873^{2} 3183^{7} (4186) 5016^{8} 5702^{3} 6374^{3} 7510a^{7}

Our Giant (AUS) *M F De Kock* a104 102
8 ch g Giant's Causeway(USA) —Macrosa (NZ) (Mcginty (NZ))
(155a) 414a^{4} 586a^{8} 756a^{7}

Our Ivor *Michael Appleby* a53 49
2 gr c Cape Town(IRE) —Caprice (Mystiko (USA))
7232^{10} 7501^{3} 7709^{4}

Our Joe Mac (IRE) *Richard Fahey* 105
4 b g Celtic Swing—Vade Retro (IRE) (Desert Sun)
925a^{13} 1094^{11} 1694^{13} 2217^{3} 3203^{2} ◆ 4410^{3} (5185) 6163^{8}

Our Jonathan *Kevin Ryan* a103 117
4 b g Invincible Spirit(IRE) —Sheik'n Swing (Celtic Swing)
1111^{3} 2075^{3} (2284) 2927^{2} 3109^{8} ◆ 3852^{5} 4314^{6} 5060^{2} ◆ (6147) 7298^{10}

Our Kes (IRE) *Michael Squance* a63 67
9 gr m Revoque(IRE) —Gracious Gretclo (Common Grounds)
86^{4} 207^{2} 524^{3} 598^{3} 771^{8} 899^{8} 1310^{10}

Our Merv (IRE) *Terry Clement* 68
2 b c Elnadim(USA) —Chiloe Wigeon (IRE) (Docksider (USA))
6127^{3}

Our Monica (IRE) *Ann Duffield* a33 38
2 b f Acclamation—Szabo (IRE) (Anabaa (USA))
3718^{8} 4358^{7} 5245^{7} 6597^{6} 7252^{11}

Our Phylli Vera (IRE) *Harry Dunlop* a41 50
2 b f Motivator—With Colour (Rainbow Quest (USA))
5097^{10} 5841^{5} 6524^{10}

Our Piccadilly (IRE) *Stuart Kittow* a83 82
6 b m Piccolo—Dilys (Efisio)
3179^{3} ◆ 3685^{2} 4057^{9} 4387^{9} 5345^{5}

Our Play (IRE) *Lydia Richards* a64 66
3 b g Oratorio(IRE) —Red Shoe (Selkirk (USA))
3183^{5} 6947^{4} 7346^{7} 7515^{7}

Our Princess Ellie (USA) *Derek Shaw* a46 36
3 ch f Borrego(USA) —Dear Abigail (USA) (Dehere (USA))
4991^{9} 5247^{9} 5793^{7} 7389^{7} 7485^{8} 7693^{6} 7845^{6} 7910^{5}

Ours (IRE) *John Harris* a95 83
8 b g Mark Of Esteem(IRE) —Ellebanna (Tina's Pet)
(12) 18[2] 816[3] 1061[7] ◆ 1621[5] 2474[2] 2545[5] 2887[6] 3275[7] 3576[4] 4150[2] 4404[9] 5594[7] 6231[9] 6831[7] 7424[8]

Out Do *Luca Cumani* 79
2 ch c Exceed And Excel(AUS) —Ludynosa (USA) (Cadeaux Genereux)
4347[8] 5051[2]

Outdoor Pegasus *P F Yiu* a83 115
4 ch g Dubawi(IRE) —Kelang (Kris)
7731a[10]

Outland (IRE) *J R Jenkins* a34 69
5 br g Indian Haven—Sensuality (IRE) (Idris (IRE))
1750[4] 2526[3] 3184[2] 3516[6] 4164[3] 4952[3] 5519[3]

Outlaw Torn (IRE) *Alan McCabe* a59 43
2 ch g Iffraaj—Touch And Love (IRE) (Green Desert (USA))
1095[10] 1522[7] 4864[10] (6002) 6489[4] 6817[9]

Out Of Nothing *Kevin M Prendergast* a61 90
8 br m Perryston View—Loves To Dare (IRE) (Desert King (IRE))
2315[5] 3026[6] 3358[7]

Out Of The Storm *Simon Dow* a65 65
3 b f Elmhurst Boy—Night Storm (Night Shift (USA))
887[12] 1022[5] 1790[3] 2197[10] 3251[2] 3742[5] 3945[5] (4745) 5135[5] 5666[3] 6472[4] 6923[11]

Outpost (IRE) *Alan Bailey* a78 60
3 ch c Giant's Causeway(USA) —Southern Migration (USA) (Kingmambo (USA))
3594[9] 4388[6] 5212[5] (5598) 6078[13]

Outsmart *Mahmood Al Zarooni* a90 81
3 b c Exceed And Excel(AUS) —Ribh (Zafonic (USA))
2266[2] 2924[2] (3513)

Out The Ordinary *Stal Pink Panther* a64 62
8 b g Whittingham(IRE) —Special One (Aragon)
6593a[8]

Ovambo Queen (GER) *Dr A Bolte* 109
4 bb m Kalatos(GER) —Oxalaguna (GER) (Lagunas)
3334a[3] (4842a) 6395a[2]

Overdose *Jozef Roszival* 119
6 b h Starborough—Our Poppet (IRE) (Warning)
2297[7] 3010[4] (7408a)

Overpowered *Paul Cole* 92
2 b c Choisir(AUS) —Tafiya (Bahri (USA))
2033[4] ◆ (3082) (3866) ◆ (Dead)

Overrule (USA) *Brian Ellison* a51 90
7 b g Diesis—Her Own Way (USA) (Danzig (USA))
1154[11] 1517[14] 2059[9] 3344[5] 4294[2] 5050[6] 5757[6] 6676[14] 7722[5]

Overturn (IRE) *Donald McCain* a94 110
7 b g Barathea(IRE) —Kristal Bridge (Kris)
(1808) 3396[6] 4469[7]

Overturned *E J O'Neill* a83 83
3 b f Cape Cross(IRE) —Upend (Main Reef)
7156a[11]

Overwhelm *Andrew Reid* a73 73
3 ch f Bahamian Bounty—Depressed (Most Welcome)
632[3] 875[2] 1145[U] 1391[7] 2383[8] 2818[5] 3239[6] 7172[10] 7395[12]

Ownwan (USA) *Saeed Bin Suroor*
3 b f Kingmambo(USA) —Helena Molony (IRE) (Sadler's Wells (USA))
2930[13]

Oxbow (IRE) *Mahmood Al Zarooni* 17
2 b g Shirocco(GER) —Maeander (FR) (Nashwan (USA))
7060[8]

Oxford Charley (USA) *Mikael Magnusson* 81
2 b c Lemon Drop Kid(USA) —La Sarto (USA) (Cormorant (USA))
(6462) 7026[10]

Oxford Gold (IRE) *Edward Vaughan* a32 39
4 b g High Chaparral(IRE) —Charmed Forest (IRE) (Shinko Forest (IRE))
7246[6] 7639[9]

Ozeta (FR) *E Lellouche* 107
3 gr f Martaline—Ozehy (USA) (Rahy (USA))
2750a[7]

Ozzia (GER) *Y Fertillet* a52
7 b m Zinaad—Oxalaguna (GER) (Lagunas)
533a[5]

Pab Special (IRE) *Brett Johnson* a60 64
8 b g City On A Hill(USA) —Tinos Island (IRE) (Alzao (USA))
390[4] 765[5] 950[13] 969[8]

Pabusar *Ralph Beckett* 109
3 b g Oasis Dream—Autumn Pearl (Orpen (USA))
2054[6] 2928[7] 4333[2] 5054[15] 5805[3] 6500[7]

Pacey Outswinger (IRE) *John C McConnell* a41 53
4 b m Intikhab(USA) —Dusky Virgin (Missed Flight)
6430[4] 7159[2]

Pacha (GER) *Mario Hofer* 64
2 b g Big Shuffle(USA) —Pasaquina (GER) (Acatenango (GER))
6901a[7]

Pacha Des Galas (FR) *F Cheyer* a36 40
8 b g Lord Of Men—Sarema (FR) (Primo Dominie)
479a[0]

Pachattack (USA) *Gerard Butler* a112 108
5 ch m Pulpit(USA) —El Laoob (USA) (Red Ransom (USA))
991[3] 1718[9] 5073a[8] 7285a[3]

Pacific Heights (IRE) *Tim Pitt* a61 82
2 b c Galileo(IRE) —Song To Remember (USA) (Storm Cat (USA))
7292[2]

Pacific Islands (IRE) *Mahmood Al Zarooni* 56
2 ch c Teofilo(IRE) —Tropical Lady (IRE) (Sri Pekan (USA))
2510[10]

Pacific Reach *Brendan Powell* a58
3 b c Phoenix Reach(IRE) —Pearl's Girl (King's Best (USA))
5247[5] 5911[13] 7207[4] 7756[7]

Pacific Trader *William Haggas* a57 15
2 b c Haafhd—Tiger Tango (USA) (Johannesburg (USA))
5726[8] 6474[12] 6927[5]

Pacifique (IRE) *A De Royer-Dupre* 109
3 b f Montjeu(IRE) —Platonic (Zafonic (USA))
5027a[2] (5771a) 6555a[3]

Packing Winner (NZ) *L Ho* 117
9 b g Zabeel(NZ) —Musical Note (AUS) (Marscay (AUS))
1742a[10]

Pack Of Cards (IRE) *Terry Clement* a50 5
2 b g Red Clubs(IRE) —Truly A Gift (IRE) (Arazi (USA))
3553[10] 5688[10] 6100[12] 7481[5] 7650[6]

Paco Belle (IRE) *Andrew Crook* a66 65
3 b f Whipper(USA) —Raindancing (IRE) (Tirol)
(51) 193[2] 227[3] 686[3] 951[2] 2349[5] 2466[6] 3141[4] 3460[6]

Paddyfrommenlo (IRE) *J W Hills* a72
2 ch c Hurricane Run(IRE) —Dolce Dovo (Medicean)
7520[3]

Paddy O'Reilly (NZ) *Robert Smerdon* 107
6 b g O'Reilly(NZ) —Star Of Amarissa (USA) (Assert)
7043a[7] 7310a[3]

Pagan Steps (IRE) *Stephen Michael Cox* a34 55
4 b m Footstepsinthesand—Pagan Game (IRE) (Montjeu (IRE))
6139a[6] 6659[7]

Pagan Warrior (IRE) *Clive Cox* 58
3 b g Sadler's Wells(USA) —Brigid (USA) (Irish River (FR))
1315[10] 2875[6] 3594[11] 6411[9]

Pagera (FR) *Y Fouin* 100
3 ch f Gentlewave(IRE) —Panthesilea (FR) (Kendor (FR))
1513a[4] 2342a[11] 3447a[8]

Pain Perdu (FR) *W Figge* 115
4 b g Vespone(IRE) —Coastline (Night Shift (USA))
7409a[6]

Painted Black (ITY) *G Botti*
3 b c High Chaparral(IRE) —Welsh Poppy (Sharpo)
902a[0]

Painted Tail (IRE) *Alan Swinbank* a72 73
4 b m Mark Of Esteem(IRE) —Bronwen (IRE) (King's Best (USA))
4514[7] 5082[7] 5443[4] 5900[3] (6357) 6601[2]

Paint The Town Red *Richard Guest* a63 38
6 b g Mujahid(USA) —Onefortheditch (USA) (With Approval (CAN))
598[10] 630[8] 1586[5] 1993[4] 2235[6] 2608[4] 3185[9]

Pakal (GER) *Mario Hofer* 112
2 b c Lord Of England(GER) —Perima (GER) (Kornado)
5610a[2] 7192a[2]

Paker (IRE) *W Olkowski* 69
2 b c Kodiac—Storm Lady (IRE) (Alhaarth (IRE))
7155a[6]

Palace Moon *William Knight* 114
6 b g Fantastic Light(USA) —Palace Street (USA) (Secreto (USA))
2315[4] 3154[16] 3404[11] 4526[4] 5699[13]

Paladin (IRE) *Mahmood Al Zarooni* a65 72
2 b g Dubawi(IRE) —Palwina (FR) (Unfuwain (USA))
3401[5] 4330[10] 5688[5] 6334[14]

Palagonia *Mark Johnston* a65 53
3 b c Exceed And Excel(AUS) —Sicily (USA) (Kris S (USA))
3167[7] 3377[6] 3706[7]

Palais Glide *Richard Hannon* a77 83
3 gr f Proclamation(IRE) —Careful Dancer (Gorytus (USA))
(179) 465[2] 864[2] 1521[2] 1758[4] (2180) 2564[3] 4156[3] 5000[4] 7489[9]

Palavicini (USA) *John Dunlop* 111
5 b h Giant's Causeway(USA) —Cara Fantasy (IRE) (Sadler's Wells (USA))
4003[4]

Palawi (IRE) *John Quinn* a64 82
4 ch g Dubawi(IRE) —Palwina (FR) (Unfuwain (USA))
11[2] 5857[6]

Palazzo Bianco *John Gosden* a94 88
3 b c Shirocco(GER) —White Palace (Shirley Heights)
4279[10] 4617[4] 4989[4] (5685) ◆ 6328[3] 6832[4] 7120[2] ◆

Palea (GER) *S Jesus* a70 62
5 b m Red Ransom(USA) —Palanca (Inchinor)
706a[4]

Pale Orchid (IRE) *David Evans* a75 75
2 b f Invincible Spirit(IRE) —Chelsea Rose (IRE) (Desert King (IRE))
7736[2] 7906[2]

Palermo (GER) *Cathrine Erichsen* 97
5 b h Kalatos(GER) —Palma (GER) (Goofalik (USA))
5984a[5]

Palindromic (IRE) *Jeremy Gask* a61 51
3 ch g Chineur(FR) —Compton Girl (Compton Place)
1294[2]

Palio Square (USA) *Ralph Beckett* a91 76
4 br g Harlan's Holiday(USA) —Teewee's Hope (CAN) (Defrere (USA))
628a[18] 1030[5]

Pallasator *Sir Mark Prescott Bt* a66
2 b g Motivator—Ela Athena (Ezzoud (IRE))
7634[4]

Pallodio (IRE) *J E Hammond* a110 113
6 br h Medecis—Bent Al Fala (IRE) (Green Desert (USA))
330a[8] 585a[9] 829a[10]

Palm Court *A Al Raihe* a81 79
6 b g Green Desert(USA) —Amenixa (FR) (Linamix (FR))
535a[11]

Palm Pilot (IRE) *Ed Dunlop* a81 91
3 b f Oasis Dream—Off Message (IRE) (In The Wings)
(27) (177) (1051) 1894[8] 2839[4] 4015[5]

Palmyra (IRE) *David Simcock* a52
2 ch f Haafhd—Tasjeel (USA) (Aljabr (USA))
7909[6]

Palomar (USA) *Brian Ellison* a81 96
9 bb g Chester House(USA) —Ball Gown (USA) (Silver Hawk (USA))
2316[7] 3013[7] 3243[4] 6171[11] 6690[27]

Paloma's Prince (IRE) *Jim Boyle* 73
2 ch c Nayef(USA) —Ma Paloma (FR) (Highest Honor (FR))
4722[8] 5579[3] 6953[3]

Palus San Marco (IRE) *Peter Chapple-Hyam* 57
2 b c Holy Roman Emperor(IRE) —Kylemore (IRE) (Sadler's Wells (USA))
3401[11]

Pam (IRE) *Robert Collet* a78 83
3 b c Whipper(USA) —Graten (IRE) (Zieten (USA))
1010a[6]

Pandorea *Henry Candy* 79
3 b f Diktat—Puya (Kris)
3310[6] 3918[6]

Pandorica *Clive Cox* 79
3 b f Indesatchel(IRE) —Hope Chest (Kris)
1949[7] 2885[4] (3118) 4083[4] 6248[4] 6729[7]

Pandoro De Lago (IRE) *Richard Fahey* 76
3 ch f Encosta De Lago(AUS) —Fig Tree Drive (USA) (Miswaki (USA))
(1799) 2253[11] 3486[3] 4540[9]

Panettone (IRE) *Roger Varian* a46 64
2 b f Montjeu(IRE) —Tea Break (Daylami (IRE))
5320[7] 6933[8] 7431[7]

Pani Ash *Pat Phelan* 18
3 b f Cadeaux Genereux—Puteri Sas (IRE) (Fasliyev (USA))
3980[7] 4956[6] 5636[7]

Panipro (FR) *F Lemercier* a62 74
3 b g Panis(USA) —Kermaria (IRE) (Spectrum (IRE))
7669a[9]

Panoptic *Sir Henry Cecil* 81
3 b f Dubawi(IRE) —Pan Galactic (USA) (Lear Fan (USA))
2192[3] 2673[2] (3577)

Pan River (TUR) *R Tetik* 117
6 b h Red Bishop(USA) —Wanganui River (Unfuwain (USA))
2343a[7]

Pantella (IRE) *Kevin Ryan* 69
3 b f Fasliyev(USA) —Double Fantasy (GER) (Indian Ridge)
1941[6] 2697[5] 3075[3] 3360[4] (3616)

Pants On Fire (USA) *Kelly Breen* a118
3 bb c Jump Start(USA) —Cabo De Noche (USA) (Cape Town (USA))
1921a[9]

Panzanella *John Gosden* 64
2 b f Dansili—Zenda (Zamindar (USA))
7293[5]

Paoletta (USA) *Mahmood Al Zarooni* 89
3 bb f Medaglia D'Oro(USA) —Val Gardena (CHI) (Roy (USA))
2157[2] ◆ 2528[2] 6404[4]

Papageno *J R Jenkins* a59 50
4 b g Piccolo—Fresh Fruit Daily (Reprimand)
224[7] 537[9] 941[8] 6943[10]

Papal Power (IRE) *J W Hills* a21
2 b c Holy Roman Emperor(IRE) —Summerhill Parkes (Zafonic (USA))
3221[6] 6525[7] 6751[11]

Paparazzi (SWI) *Karin Suter-Weber*
7 ch g Arazi(USA) —Pocahonta (GER) (Dashing Blade)
620a[7]

Paperback (IRE) *J-V Toux* a53 65
3 b f Catcher In The Rye(IRE) —Irinatinvidio (Rudimentary (USA))
852a[11]

Paperchain *A Fabre* a81 100
3 ch f Dubawi(IRE) —Papabile (USA) (Chief's Crown (USA))
7509a[4]

Paper Dreams (IRE) *Kevin Ryan* a59 67
3 b f Green Desert(USA) —Pickwick Papers (Singspiel (IRE))
(1975) 3207[10] (3972) 4647[6] 5109[5] 6305[3]

Paperetto *Robert Mills* a62 68
3 b g Selkirk(USA) —Song Of Hope (Chief Singer)
1836[7] 2368[10] 2792[7] 3230[9] 4758[4] 5040[6] 5300[4] 7524[4] 7754[9] 7942[3]

Paphos *Stuart Williams* a71 23
4 b g Oasis Dream—Tychy (Suave Dancer (USA))
2001[5] 3172[10] 3517[2] (3735) 4066[12] 4725[7] 4910[5] 6090[4] 6543[8]

Pappas Fc *Milton Bradley*
4 ch g Zafeen(FR) —Mammas F-C (IRE) (Case Law)
1331[11] 1449[8]

Paradise Place *Robert Cowell* a58 64
3 ch f Compton Place—Passiflora (Night Shift (USA))
(1078) ◆ 1595[2] 1764[2] 2453[2] 2827[5] 3957[4] 4238[4] 4695[3]

Paradise Sea (USA) *Mikael Magnusson* a36
2 b f Stormy Atlantic(USA) —Paradise River (USA) (Irish River (FR))
7118[10]

Paradise Spectre *Mrs K Burke* a64 81
4 b g Firebreak—Amber's Bluff (Mind Games)
1221[7] 1520[5] 4604[9] 4782[3] (5121) (5561) 6091[4] (6634)

Paraggi *M Delzangles* 82
2 ch c Iffraaj—Topkamp (Pennekamp (USA))
7508a[10]

Paragraph *Paul Fitzsimons* 36
4 b g Lucky Story(USA) —Barossa (IRE) (Barathea (IRE))
4846[4]

Paragua (GER) *A Wohler* 95
3 b f Nayef(USA) —Prada (GER) (Lagunas)
2981a[4] 3651a[6]

Paraisa *A Wohler* 91
2 b f Red Ransom(USA) —Praia (GER) (Big Shuffle (USA))
6737a[3]

Paramour *David O'Meara* 91
4 b g Selkirk(USA) —Embraced (Pursuit Of Love)
4514[2] ◆ (5082) 5483[5] 5969[5] 6302[12]

Paramythi (IRE) *Luca Cumani* 67
2 ch c Peintre Celebre(USA) —The Spirit Of Pace (IRE) (In The Wings)
7134[4]

Paraphernalia (IRE) *David Wachman* 96
4 bb m Dalakhani(IRE) —Vassiana (FR) (Anabaa (USA))
924a[5] 1118a[9]

Parc Aux Boules *John C McConnell* a67 74
10 gr g Royal Applause—Aristocratique (Cadeaux Genereux)
6939[4]

Parc De Launay *Tom Tate* 91
2 ch g Monsieur Bond(IRE) —Franglais (GER) (Lion Cavern (USA))
(2387) (3313) 4495[10] 5216[15] 6670[5] 7138[3]

Parc Des Princes (USA) *Nicky Richards* a76 73
5 bb g Ten Most Wanted(USA) —Miss Orah (Unfuwain (USA))
2091[5] 2696[7] 3453[4] 3660[4]

Par Cinq (FR) *P Demercastel* a76 88
3 b c High Chaparral(IRE) —Princesse Jasmine (FR) (Gold Away (IRE))
370a[2]

Parhelion *Derek Haydn Jones* a82 85
4 b g Fantastic Light(USA) —Shamaiel (IRE) (Lycius (USA))
266[2] 392[2] 597[2] (872) 1030[3] 1367[4] 1847[3] 2512[12] 3344[10] 3911[3] 4464[7] 6410[8] 6893[14]

Parigino (FR) *F Chappet* a73 87
3 b g Panis(USA) —Loretta Gianni (FR) (Classic Account (USA))
370a[6] (616a)

Paris Blue (FR) *J-L Pelletan* 88
2 b c Anabaa(USA) —Diamond Laly (Observatory (USA))
(7326a)

Parish Hall (IRE) *J S Bolger* 118
2 b c Teofilo(IRE) —Halla Siamsa (IRE) (Montjeu (IRE))
4257a[2] ◆ 4834a[8] 5293a[2] (6689)

Parisian Dream *Tim Pitt* a50 55
7 b g Sakhee(USA) —Boojum (Mujtahid (USA))
6938[16]

Parisian Princess (IRE) *George Baker* a75 51
2 b f Teofilo(IRE) —Night Sphere (IRE) (Night Shift (USA))
4087[4] 4662[3] ◆ 6000[2] 6995[11]

Parisian Pyramid (IRE) *Kevin Ryan* 104
5 gr g Verglas(IRE) —Sharadja (IRE) (Doyoun)
1111[14] 1885[8] 2288[3] 5060[4] ◆ 5758[2] 6145[20] 6521[9] 6706[5] 6987[14] 7295[15]

Paris To Peking (ITY) *S Botti* 100
3 b f Intikhab(USA) —Khanstan (IRE) (Barathea (IRE))
7311a[10]

Park Ballet (IRE) *Jonathan Portman* 68
3 b f Fasliyev(USA) —Abbey Park (USA) (Known Fact (USA))
1141[7]

Parkers Mill (IRE) *T Stack* 87
3 b g High Chaparral(IRE) —Celtic Wing (Midyan (USA))
2331a[9]

Park Ranger (IRE) *C Roche* a68 95
5 b g High Chaparral(IRE) —Ivowen (USA) (Theatrical)
5090a[12]

Park's Prodigy *David Thompson* a14 68
7 b g Desert Prince(IRE) —Up And About (Barathea (IRE))
3450[6] 3754[5] 4856[15]

Parle Toujours (FR) *H-A Pantall* a79 78
5 gr m Slickly(FR) —Pistolera (GER) (Monsun (GER))
439a[3]

Parley (USA) *Mahmood Al Zarooni* a72 78
2 bb f Street Cry(IRE) —Tout Charmant (USA) (Slewvescent (USA))
3520[4] 4061[3]

Parlour Games *Mahmood Al Zarooni* a103 104
3 ch c Monsun(GER) —Petrushka (IRE) (Unfuwain (USA))
(1485) 2108[3] 3650[4] 4316[4] (4777) (5283) 5700[7] 7226[2]

Parque Atlantico *Andrew Balding* a33 1
2 bb g Piccolo—Silken Dalliance (Rambo Dancer (CAN))
3779[12] 7835[11] 7938[4]

Participation *Laura Young* a64 58
8 b g Dansili—Andaleeb (USA) (Lyphard (USA))
(7573)

Partly Pickled *David Nicholls*
3 b g Piccolo—Queen's College (IRE) (College Chapel)
2650[11] 3594[12] 4647[13]

Partner (IRE) *David Marnane* a92 96
5 b g Indian Ridge—Oregon Trail (USA) (Gone West (USA))
1420a[4] 2323a[6] 4767a[9] 5086a[7]

Party Doctor *Tom Dascombe* a71 101
4 ch g Dr Fong(USA) —Wedding Party (Groom Dancer (USA))
2031[14]

Party Line *Mark Johnston* 62
2 b f Montjeu(IRE) —Party (IRE) (Cadeaux Genereux)
4002[13] 5548[5] 6526[18]

Party Palace *Stuart Howe* a27 53
7 b m Auction House(USA) —Lady-Love (Pursuit Of Love)
955[8]

Parvana (IRE) *William Haggas* 88
3 b f Galileo(IRE) —Lucina (Machiavellian (USA))
1845[4] 3267[2] (4074) 4473[7] 6269[6]

Parvati (FR) *Mlle V Dissaux* 41
4 b g Equerry(USA) —Donastia (FR) (Green Tune (USA))
7015a[7]

Pasalsa (FR) *Carmen Bocskai* a77 93
3 b f Kingsalsa(USA) —Pasupata (IRE) (Barathea (IRE))
5307a[2]

Pascalina *John Akehurst* a54 54
4 b m Tobougg(IRE) —Persistent Memory (USA) (Red Ransom (USA))
163[7] 355[7] 524[6]

Pas De Trois (JPN) *Ippo Sameshima* 119
4 b h Swept Overboard(USA) —Grand Pas De Deux (JPN) (Fuji Kiseki (JPN))
7730a[14]

Pas Perdus *M Delzangles* a97 96
3 b c Footstepsinthesand—Pas D'Heure (IRE) (Arazi (USA))
6783a[0] *7678a[0]*

Passaggio (ITY) *A Cascio* 100
3 b c Exceed And Excel(AUS) —Copious (IRE) (Generous (IRE))
1431a[8] 7323a[6]

Passei (FR) *Mlle V Dissaux* a77 81
3 b f Panis(USA) —Plaintarra (SWI) (Dashing Blade)
841a[6]

Passenger (FR) *Mme Pia Brandt* a62
3 b g Ivan Denisovich(IRE) —Passing Lady (FR) (Anabaa (USA))
777a[9]

Passing Chop (FR) *C Boutin* 83
4 b g Panis(USA) —Lycee (IRE) (Entrepreneur)
267a[7]

Passing Moment *Brian Baugh* a42 44
3 b f Fraam—Passing Fancy (Grand Lodge (USA))
971[7] 1155[10] *1370[3]* 2396[7] 2993[4] *3470[8]* 3942[9]

Passing Stranger (IRE) *Jeremy Noseda* 72
3 b f Dixie Union(USA) —Square Pants (USA) (King Of Kings (IRE))
3465[2] (5626) ◆

Passionada *Ollie Pears* 72
2 bb f Avonbridge—Lark In The Park (IRE) (Grand Lodge (USA))
4668[2] ◆ (6092) 6670[12]

Passion For Gold (USA) *Saeed Bin Suroor* 115
4 b h Medaglia D'Oro(USA) —C'est L'Amour (USA) (Thunder Gulch (USA))
1896[3] (2292) 3153[9] 6161[8]

Passion Play *William Knight* a64 21
3 gr f Act One—Addicted To Love (Touching Wood (USA))
5098[3] (6086) 6546[5] 7264[7]

Pass Muster *Ollie Pears* 92
4 b g Theatrical—Morning Pride (IRE) (Machiavellian (USA))
1387[10] (2403) 3203[10] 4528[10] 5078[4] 5888[9] 6346[2] 6708[7]

Pastoral Jet *Richard Rowe* a51 31
3 bb c Pastoral Pursuits—Genteel (IRE) (Titus Livius (FR))
3173[9] 3594[8] *4849[8] 5633[10] 7442[8] 7768[4]*

Pastoral Player *Hughie Morrison* 114
4 b g Pastoral Pursuits—Copy-Cat (Lion Cavern (USA))
(1720) ◆ 3155[3] 3644[8] 4092[5] 4534[6] ◆ 5474[6] 5699[4] 6147[5] ◆ (6521)

Pastorius (GER) *Mario Hofer* 100
2 b c Soldier Hollow—Princess Li (GER) (Monsun (GER))
(7325a)

Pastures New *Des Donovan* a39
3 ch g Proclamation(IRE) —Gal Gloria (PR) (Tralos (USA))
7609[6] 7921[8]

Patavium (IRE) *Edwin Tuer* a55 81
8 b g Titus Livius(FR) —Arcevia (IRE) (Archway (IRE))
1243[3] 1651[5] 2251[4] (3129) 3758[5] 4360[5] (4982)

Patavium Prince (IRE) *Jo Crowley* a67 78
8 ch g Titus Livius(FR) —Hoyland Common (IRE) (Common Grounds)
589[3] (810) 3674[3] 5669[3] *7895[9]*

Patch Patch *Derek Shaw* a62 72
4 b g Avonbridge—Sandgate Cygnet (Fleetwood (IRE))
1796[2] 1940[4] 3040[6] 3972[6] 4197[2] *4988[6]* 5326[4] *5600[6] 6258[3] 6444[9]* 6802[17]

Pateese (FR) *Philip Hobbs* 80
6 b g Priolo(USA) —Flyer (FR) (Highest Honor (FR))
6405[2]

Path Finder (FR) *Reg Hollinshead* a60 37
2 ch g Medecis—Desirous Of Peace (Forzando)
3718[5] 4201[13] *6663[3]*

Pathfork (USA) *Mrs John Harrington* 119
3 b c Distorted Humor(USA) —Visions Of Clarity (IRE) (Sadler's Wells (USA))
1686[7]

Patricias Pride *Lucinda Featherstone* a37 24
4 ch g Silver Patriarch(IRE) —Anniversary Guest (IRE) (Desert King (IRE))
2813[12] *3717[8]* 4023[9]

Patrickswell (IRE) *Marcus Callaghan* a77 84
7 gr g Iron Mask(USA) —Gladstone Street (IRE) (Waajib)
1228a[8] 4135a[13] 4767a[7]

Patriotic (IRE) *Chris Dwyer* a73 52
3 b g Pivotal—Pescara (IRE) (Common Grounds)
2596[10] 3111[5] *(3709)* 4281[13] 4730[7] *7727[3] 7842[5]*

Pat's Legacy (USA) *Jo Hughes* a59 95
5 ch g Yankee Gentleman(USA) —Sugars For Nanny (USA) (Brocco (USA))
(3514) 3802[5] 4616[2] (5495) (5586) 6150[8]

Pattern Mark *Ollie Pears* a61 64
5 b g Mark Of Esteem(IRE) —Latch Key Lady (USA) (Tejano (USA))
1871[7] 2530[6] (3317) 4128[10] 4673[3]

Paulaya (GER) *P Schiergen* 90
3 ch f Peintre Celebre(USA) —Pacific Blue (GER) (Bluebird (USA))
7580a[0]

Paulinho (ARG) *H J Brown* a87 98
4 br c Equal Stripes(ARG) —Paula Sexy (ARG) (Ride The Rails (USA))
502a[7] 753a[6] 823a[6]

Pausanias *Richard Hannon* a99 109
3 b c Kyllachy—The Strand (Gone West (USA))
(1318) ◆ 2440[4] 3404[2]

Pavement Games *Richard Guest* a54 54
4 b m Mind Games—Pavement Gates (Bishop Of Cashel)
941[10] 2655[9] 6427[4] 6765[7] 7086[10]

Pavershooz *Noel Wilson* a91 95
6 b g Bahamian Bounty—Stormswept (USA) (Storm Bird (CAN))
1539[9] 2118[11] 2590[9] 3832[2] 4327[2] ◆ 4792[9] 5680[8]

Pavers Star *Noel Wilson* 26
2 ch g Pastoral Pursuits—Pride Of Kinloch (Dr Devious (IRE))
6026[6] 6274[8] 6702[11] 7072[8]

Pawprints (IRE) *William Haggas* 69
2 ch f Footstepsinthesand—Samphire Red (IRE) (Sri Pekan (USA))
5854[6] 6743[4]

Pax Soprana (IRE) *Braem Horse Racing Sprl* a70 73
5 b m Namid—Sportsticketing (IRE) (Spectrum (IRE))
6593a[3]

Peace Corps *Jim Boyle* a80 79
5 ch g Medicean—Tromond (Lomond (USA))
245[2] (308)

Peaceful Means (IRE) *Michael Appleby* a54 65
8 b m Witness Box(USA) —Princess Satco (IRE) (Satco (FR))
369[5] 526[11] 1987[8] 5178[4] 5519[6] *5739[5] 6656[7] 6876[9]*

Peaceful Soul (USA) *David Lanigan* a22 65
4 b m Dynaformer(USA) —Serenity Jane (USA) (Affirmed (USA))
1631[6] *1956[10]*

Peace Keeper (FR) *U Suter* a68 80
5 b g Namid—Desirous Of Peace (Forzando)
(42a) 629a[8]

Peace Seeker *Anthony Carson* a79 46
3 b g Oasis Dream—Mina (Selkirk (USA))
5021[7] 5567[10] *6700[7] 7656[2] (7755)* ◆ *(7811) (7896)* ◆

Peachez *Alastair Lidderdale* a58 76
3 ch f Observatory(USA) —Streccia (Old Vic)
801[3] 945[5] 1298[6] 2305[4] 3228[5] 3910[2] (4248) (4491) 6756[2] 6893[9] 7236[6]

Peadar Miguel *Noel Quinlan* a76 51
4 b g Danroad(AUS) —La Corujera (Case Law)
139[5] 488[6] (562) 685[3] 806[4] 1398[6] 1649[7]

Peahen *G M Lyons* a96 99
3 b f Ishiguru(USA) —Ulysses Daughter (IRE) (College Chapel)
2861a[2] 3527a[6] 5746a[4] 6388a[14] *7149a[10]*

Peak Storm *John Gallagher* 70
2 b g Sleeping Indian—Jitterbug (IRE) (Marju (IRE))
2868[5] 6768[4] 7080[6]

Pearl Argyle (FR) *J Boisnard* a80 66
4 gr m Oasis Dream—Alcadia (USA) (Holy Bull (USA))
108a[5]

Pearl Blue (IRE) *Chris Wall* 88
3 b f Exceed And Excel(AUS) —Sanfrancullinan (IRE) (Bluebird (USA))
1591[3] (3230) ◆ 4199[3] (5279) ◆ 6327[5]

Pearl Catcher (IRE) *Tim Easterby* a49 53
2 b g Catcher In The Rye(IRE) —Midnight Pearl (USA) (Woodman (USA))
3242[4] *3947[4]* 4323[6] 4943[8] 5645[10]

Pearl Charm (USA) *Richard Hannon* a68 83
2 ch c Distorted Humor(USA) —Charmed Gift (USA) (A.P. Indy (USA))
(3382) ◆ 4311[5] *5715[7]* 5931[8] 6957[10]

Pearl Diva (IRE) *Peter Chapple-Hyam* 93
2 b f Acclamation—Lassie's Gold (USA) (Seeking The Gold (USA))
2914[3] 3402[2] (3767)

Pearl Frost *Ralph Beckett* a41 40
2 gr g Verglas(IRE) —Eternelle (Green Desert (USA))
7292[13] *7758[3]*

Pearl Ice *Sir Mark Prescott Bt* a88 75
3 b c Iffraaj—Jezebel (Owington)
6862[14]

Pearl In The Sand (IRE) *G M Lyons* 94
2 b f Footstepsinthesand—Champagne Toni (IRE) (Second Empire (IRE))
5950a[2]

Pearl Mix (IRE) *Ralph Beckett* a94 97
2 gr c Oratorio(IRE) —Rosamixa (FR) (Linamix (FR))
2817[2] ◆ *(3282)* 3861[4]

Pearl Mountain (IRE) *Lydia Pearce* a51 58
4 b m Pearl Of Love(IRE) —Latest Chapter (IRE) (Ahonoora)
1173[5] 1572[8] *1998[5]* 2733[3]

Pearl Of Romance (IRE) *W McCreery* a52
2 b f Refuse To Bend(IRE) —Dissitation (IRE) (Spectrum (IRE))
7273a[14]

Pearl Opera *Denis Coakley* a62 50
3 b f Librettist(USA) —Letsimpress (IRE) (General Monash (USA))
1607[8] 2196[4] 3742[9] *4758[5]* ◆ *5041[2] (5381)* 6813[8] *7228[10]*

Pearl Rebel *Stuart Williams* a66
2 b c Cockney Rebel(IRE) —Lilli Marlane (Sri Pekan (USA))
(7837)

Pearl Secret *David Barron* 86
2 ch c Compton Place—Our Little Secret (IRE) (Rossini (USA))
(6673) ◆

Pearls From Sydney *Paul Cole* 28
2 b f Librettist(USA) —Cultured Pearl (IRE) (Lammtarra (USA))
5655[15]

Pearl Storm (IRE) *William Haggas* 67
3 b g Balmont(USA) —Brewing Storm (IRE) (King Charlemagne (USA))
1880[11] 2141[9]

Pearl War (USA) *William Haggas* a56 75
2 b f War Front(USA) —B W Chargit (USA) (Meadowlake (USA))
5444[4] ◆ *7124[8]*

Pearly King (USA) *M Al Muhairi* a88 88
8 br g Kingmambo(USA) —Mother Of Pearl (IRE) (Sadler's Wells (USA))
535a[12]

Pearly Wey *Ian McInnes* a52 81
8 b g Lujain(USA) —Dunkellin (USA) (Irish River (FR))
1204[10] 1411[17] 1612[7] 1861[7] 4078[5] 4443[3] 4564[4] 5083[10] *5244[13]* 6071[4] 6105[6] *6657[11]*

Peas And Carrots (DEN) *Lennart Reuterskiold Jr* a98 98
8 b g Final Appearance(IRE) —Dominet Hope (Primo Dominie)
2601a[7] 4842a[2] *5981a[3]*

Pea Shooter *Kevin Ryan* a77 98
2 b g Piccolo—Sparkling Eyes (Lujain (USA))
1383[2] ◆ *1699a[3]* 4748[5] (5756) ◆

Peccato Di Gola *B Grizzetti* 90
2 ch c Three Valleys(USA) —Pursuit Of Charge (Pursuit Of Love)
3212a[6]

Pedasus (USA) *Ronald Harris* a69 66
5 b g Fusaichi Pegasus(USA) —Butterfly Cove (USA) (Storm Cat (USA))
30[12] 161[5] 222[7]

Peering *Nick Littmoden* a16
2 b g Beat Hollow—Ennobling (Mark Of Esteem (IRE))
2160[8] 2556[8] *5834[12]*

Pegasus Again (USA) *Robert Mills* a88 79
6 b g Fusaichi Pegasus(USA) —Chit Chatter (USA) (Lost Soldier (USA))
141[6] 348[7] 623[4] 703[11] 2000[9] 3285[4] 4158[2] *5319[2]*

Pegasus Prince (USA) *Keith Reveley* a72 51
7 b g Fusaichi Pegasus(USA) —Avian Eden (USA) (Storm Bird (CAN))
1153[9]

Peg Peg *Nerys Dutfield* 42
2 ch f Arkadian Hero(USA) —Lady Eberspacher (IRE) (Royal Abjar (USA))
4339[6] 4912[8]

Peinted Song (USA) *A De Royer-Dupre* a100 103
4 gr m Unbridled's Song(USA) —Peinture Rose (USA) (Storm Cat (USA))
5075a[2]

Peintre D'Argent (IRE) *William Knight* a69 85
5 ch m Peintre Celebre(USA) —Petite-D-Argent (Noalto)
(2055) 2262[2] 4555[4]

Peintre Du Roi (USA) *Natalie Lloyd-Beavis* a49
7 ch g El Prado(IRE) —Peinture Bleue (USA) (Alydar (USA))
216 [5] 407[6]

Peintre Modern (FR) *L Nyffels* a66 53
8 ch g Peintre Celebre(USA) —Spring Haven (USA) (Lear Fan (USA))
832a[0]

Peinture Abstraite *A De Royer-Dupre* 108
3 b f Holy Roman Emperor(IRE) —Peinture Bleue (USA) (Alydar (USA))
2752a[3] 3671a[2] 5958a[0]

Peinture Texane (FR) *M Boutin* a67 73
5 b m Peintre Celebre(USA) —Texalina (FR) (Kaldoun (FR))
93a[6] 395a[5] 1142a[0] 7256a[9]

Peira *Jane Chapple-Hyam* a67 72
3 b f Intikhab(USA) —Anqood (IRE) (Elmaamul (USA))
1997[3] 2613[7] 2885[12] 3558[4] (4686) 4932[2] 5420 [U] 5782[5] *6255[6]* 6888 [7]

Pekan Star *Roger Varian* 97
4 b g Montjeu(IRE) —Delicieuse Lady (Trempolino (USA))
(2002) 3876[15] 4801[6] 7297[10]

Pelham Crescent (IRE) *Bryn Palling* a83 83
8 ch g Giant's Causeway(USA) —Sweet Times (Riverman (USA))
2351[0] 436[4] 614[9] 835[2] (1829) 2156[2] 2810[5] 3762[4] 3911[2] 4464[6] 4887[5] 5266[5] 6893[11] *7002[7]* 7461[6] 7738[4] 7878[5]

Pelican Rock (IRE) *Tom Dascombe* a50 28
2 b g Amadeus Wolf—Darby Shaw (IRE) (Kris)
5681[14] *6180[7]* 6912[14]

Peligroso (FR) *Saeed Bin Suroor* a94 107
5 ch h Trempolino(USA) —Pitpit (IRE) (Rudimentary (USA))
2425 413a[3]

Pelmanism *Brian Ellison* a83 86
4 b g Piccolo—Card Games (First Trump)
165[2] (306) 435[3] 612[6] (725) (867) ◆ 1239[13] 1712[2] 1861[2] (2352) 2543[9] (3025) 3506[2] ◆ 4349[4] 4792[2] (5680) ◆ 6865[9]

Pelusa (JPN) *Kazuo Fujisawa* 122
4 ch h Zenno Rob Roy(JPN) —Argentine Star (ARG) (Candy Stripes (USA))
7563a[16]

Pembrey *Mahmood Al Zarooni* 84
2 b c Teofilo(IRE) —Miss Penton (Primo Dominie)
4080[10] (6954)

Penang Cinta *David Evans* a62 77
8 b g Halling(USA) —Penang Pearl (FR) (Bering)
266[8] 1454[4] (2170) 2246[4] 3252[2] 3479[3] 4465[5] 5580[5] *6306[9]* (6811) 6969[4]

Penangdouble O One *Ralph Beckett* a79 75
4 ch g Starcraft(NZ) —Penang Pearl (FR) (Bering)
1908[6] 2393[4] 3095[4] *3738[2]* 5035[11] *5692[5]* 6469[2] 6893[12]

Penang Pacific *Alan McCabe* 56
3 ch g Sakhee(USA) —Pulau Pinang (IRE) (Dolphin Street (FR))
1096[8] 1910[8] 2591[11]

Penang Pegasus *David O'Meara* 36
2 ch g Zamindar(USA) —Pulau Pinang (IRE) (Dolphin Street (FR))
6828[8]

Penang Princess *Chris Gordon* a85 85
5 gr m Act One—Pulau Pinang (IRE) (Dolphin Street (FR))
3184[5]

Pen Bal Crag (IRE) *Richard Fahey* 74
2 b c Exceed And Excel(AUS) —Rosse (Kris)
2387[3] 2886[3] (3273) 4094[20] 4538[6] 6111[7] 6921[13]

Penbryn (USA) *Nick Littmoden* a68 27
4 b g Pivotal—Brocatelle (Green Desert (USA))
234 477[9] 712[9] 7632[9] 7891[2]

Pencarrow *Mahmood Al Zarooni* a76 26
3 b f Green Desert(USA) —Al Hasnaa (Zafonic (USA))
2643[2]

Penchesco (IRE) *Amanda Perrett* a63 83
6 b g Orpen(USA) —Francesca (IRE) (Perugino (USA))
3426[5] 4211[3] 5582[6] 5893[6] 6402[7]

Penderyn *Charles Smith* a22 57
4 b m Sakhee(USA) —Brecon (Unfuwain (USA))
1592[6] 4370[8] 5470[4] *7247[9]*

Pendle Lady (IRE) *Mark Brisbourne* a35 65
2 b f Chineur(FR) —Rose Of Battle (Averti (IRE))
1414[11] (2761) 3700[6] 3810[8] *7252[10]*

Pendragon (USA) *Brian Ellison* a80 95
8 ch g Rahy(USA) —Turning Wheel (USA) (Seeking The Gold (USA))
1694[6] ◆ 2573[6] 3032[4] 3645[4] 5218[8] 6339[31] *7492[4]*

Pengula (IRE) *Robert Johnson*
4 b m Tagula(IRE) —Pride Of Pendle (Grey Desire)
1211[11] 1614[6]

Penitent *William Haggas* a98 116
5 b g Kyllachy—Pious (Bishop Of Cashel)
1100[4] 1948[3] 3444a[5] 5252[5] 6125[3] (6416)

Pennfield Pirate *Hughie Morrison* a65 69
4 ch g Bahamian Bounty—Sefemm (Alhaarth (IRE))
3814[2] *4177[3] 5141[5]* 5611[12] 6437[8]

Penny's Pearl (IRE) *David Evans* a87 89
3 b f Royal Applause—Pearl Venture (Salse (USA))
1361[8] 1602[8] 2158[6] *3048[8]* 3598[4] ◆ 3853[12] 4048[7] 4156[7] 4643[6] 5265[5] 5561[9] 6223[7] *(6502) 6841[5] 7116[6]*

Penrod Ballantyne (IRE) *Mike Hammond* a62 58
4 ch g Indian Ridge—Silvia Diletta (Mark Of Esteem (IRE))
(14) 181[9] 504[7] 712[11]

Pentameter *Amanda Perrett* 39
2 br c Dansili—Tuning (Rainbow Quest (USA))
7233[11]

Penthesilea Eile (USA) *Brendan W Duke* a70 81
5 ch m Rahy(USA) —Damask Rose (IRE) (Dr Devious (IRE))
3418a[5]

Penton Hook *Barry Murtagh* a82 60
5 gr g Lucky Owners(NZ) —Cosmic Star (Siberian Express (USA))
4601[11] 5441[9]

Peponi *Peter Makin* a81 81
5 ch h Kris Kin(USA) —Polmara (IRE) (Polish Precedent (USA))
5894[4] *6658[11] 7098[3] 7532[2] 7637[5] 7822[2]*

Peppercorn Rent (IRE) *John Davies* a45 53
3 b f Fasliyev(USA) —Skehana (IRE) (Mukaddamah (USA))
1074[7] 2984[5] 3732[7] 5652[8] 6158[9] 6261[15]

Pepper Lane *David O'Meara* a58 107
4 ch m Exceed And Excel(AUS) —Maid To Matter (Pivotal)
(2122) ◆ 2620[10] 3459[10] (4126) (4609) (5060) ◆ 6147[22] 6347[10]

Peppertree Lane (IRE) *Peter Bowen* 16
8 ch g Peintre Celebre(USA) —Salonrolle (IRE) (Tirol)
1188[6]

Perception (IRE) *Alan King* a79 71
5 b m Hawk Wing(USA) —Princesse Darsha (GER) (Darshaan)
5102[10] 5692[6] 6722[12]

Perchance *Sir Henry Cecil* a47 15
2 gr f Oasis Dream—La Persiana (Daylami (IRE))
5323[14] *6441[10]*

Percival Provost *Ralph Beckett* a44
2 br f Key Of Luck(USA) —Fluttering Rose (Compton Place)
7345[11]

Percy Jackson *Denis Coakley* 93
2 b c Sir Percy—Fly In Style (Hernando (FR))
(2143) 2868[3] (3595) 4372a[2] 5610a[7]

Percythepinto (IRE) *George Baker* a61 44
2 b g Tiger Hill(IRE) —Tullawadgeen (IRE) (Sinndar (IRE))
2510[12] *2602[4]* 3229[8] *6443[8]* 6937[11] *7242[3] (7338) 7342[12]*

Perennial *Charles Hills* 101
2 ch c Motivator—Arum Lily (USA) (Woodman (USA))
(5851) 6692[2] ◆

Perez (IRE) *Wilf Storey* a66 49
9 b g Mujadil(USA) —Kahla (Green Desert (USA))
1556[7] 3187[6]

Perfect Act *Andrew Balding* a91 69
6 b m Act One—Markova's Dance (Mark Of Esteem (IRE))
46[5] 265[6] 613[8] 960[2] 7529[5] 7586[9] 7834[2]

Perfect Blossom *Kevin Ryan* 96
4 b m One Cool Cat(USA) —Perfect Peach (Lycius (USA))
2714[12] 3778[8] 4357[11]

Perfect Ch'l (IRE) *Ian Wood* a74 74
4 b m Choisir(AUS) —Agouti (Pennekamp (USA))
(303) 394[U] 689[8] (865) 1147[3] 1330[5] 1866[2] 2313[3] 2822[9] 3045[8]

Perfect Cracker *Clive Cox* a91 76
3 ch g Dubai Destination(USA) —Perfect Story (IRE) (Desert Story (IRE))
1682[5] 3766[3] 4914[8] 7585[4] (7750) (7842) 7928[3]

Perfect Day (IRE) *Paul Cole* a54 29
2 b f Holy Roman Emperor(IRE) —Yesterday (IRE) (Sadler's Wells (USA))
1870[6] 6215[8] 6441[7] 6821[5] ◆ 7051[14] 7242[10]

Perfect Deal *Michael Easterby*
4 b g Gentleman's Deal(IRE) —Better Still (IRE) (Glenstal (USA))
8787[10] 2114[10]

Perfect Delight *Clive Cox* 75
2 b f Dubai Destination(USA) —Perfect Spirit (IRE) (Invincible Spirit (IRE))
3812[6] 4471[3] 5029[2] 5807[2] 6170[9] 6526[8]

Perfect Example (IRE) *Peter Chapple-Hyam* 33
2 b f Cape Cross(IRE) —Shining Debut (IRE) (In The Wings)
7080[11]

Perfect Gratitude (USA) *Ed Dunlop* a57 64
2 b c More Than Ready(USA) —Lenatareese (USA) (Broad Brush (USA))
3954[5] 4798[6] 5239[5] 5688[6] 6132[12]

Perfect Honour (IRE) *Des Donovan* a47 55
5 ch m Exceed And Excel(AUS) —Porcelana (IRE) (Highest Honor (FR))
5540[13] 5996[4] 7459[6] 7897[8]

Perfect Mission *Andrew Balding* a74 79
3 b g Bertolini(USA) —Sharp Secret (IRE) (College Chapel)
1725[2] 2215[11] 3324[4] 3798[7] 7443[2] (7739)

Perfect Officer (USA) *Michael V Pino* 114
5 b g Officer(USA) —Perfect Tradition (USA) (Perfect Vision (USA))
7303a[3]

Perfecto Tiempo (IRE) *Ronald Harris* a44 52
2 b c Le Vie Dei Colori—Majolica (Lujain (USA))
1522[4] 2160[6] 5613[12] 7541[10]

Perfect Paradise *John Gosden* a50 65
2 b f Giant's Causeway(USA) —Because (IRE) (Sadler's Wells (USA))
4002[6] 4992[7] 5583[6] 6449[10]

Perfect Pastime *Walter Swinburn* a71 85
3 ch g Pastoral Pursuits—Puritanical (IRE) (Desert King (IRE))
1187[3] (2294) 2770[4] 3048[5] 3765[2] 4459[2] 4994[6] 5587[2] 6467[6] 6917[4]

Perfect Pecs (AUS) *Rick Hore-Lacy* 105
4 b c Anabaa(USA) —Sahara Flight (NZ) (Towkay (AUS))
6967a[5]

Perfect Pins (NZ) *D Dragon* 109
6 b g Pins(AUS) —La Cent (NZ) (Centaine (AUS))
2339a[3]

Perfect Point (IRE) *Walter Swinburn* a82 70
4 b g Cape Cross(IRE) —Alessia (GER) (Warning)
(1488) ◆ 2178[10]

Perfect Rapture *Clive Cox* 51
3 b f Halling(USA) —Island Rapture (Royal Applause)
3430[10] 3907[7]

Perfect Shirl (USA) *Roger L Attfield* a95 116
4 b m Perfect Soul(IRE) —Lady Shirl (USA) (That's A Nice (USA))
(7284a)

Perfect Shot (IRE) *Jim Best* 94
5 b g High Chaparral(IRE) —Zoom Lens (IRE) (Caerleon (USA))
7939[6]

Perfect Silence *Clive Cox* a83 94
6 b m Dansili—Perfect Echo (Lycius (USA))
2470[5] ◆ 2927[4] 3845[3] 4332[3] 5255[6] 5657[6] 6523[5] 6862[5] 7031[8] 7295[8]

Perfect Son *C Zeitz* 45
4 ch h Sabiango(GER) —Pacific Blue (GER) (Bluebird (USA))
7409a[13]

Perfect Step (IRE) *Roger Varian* 70
2 b f Iffraaj—Spiritual Air (Royal Applause)
4614[5] ◆

Perfect Tribute *Clive Cox* 108
3 b f Dubawi(IRE) —Perfect Spirit (IRE) (Invincible Spirit (IRE))
1404[11] (1602) (1893) ◆ 2752a[6] 4497[13] 5046[8] 6520[8] 6858[9]

Perfect Union (IRE) *N Clement* a76 82
4 b h Alhaarth(IRE) —Debbie's Next (USA) (Arctic Tern (USA))
842a[3]

Perfect Vision *Charlie Longsdon* a68 71
4 b m Starcraft(NZ) —Auspicious (Shirley Heights)
9546 2176[3] 2459[7] 7671[8] 7850[5]

Performing Pocket (USA) *George Baker* a75 80
2 ch c Proud Citizen(USA) —Holy Fashion (USA) (Holy Bull (USA))
4912[3] ◆ 5632[3] 6126[6]

Pergamon (IRE) *Claire Dyson* a39 51
5 b g Dalakhani(IRE) —Pinaflore (FR) (Formidable (USA))
1443[16] 3600[8] 4274[9]

Pergola (NZ) *Colin & Cindy Alderson* 92
7 ch g Pentire—Gondolin (NZ) (Zabeel (NZ))
7043a[9]

Perilously (USA) *Jeremy Noseda* a71 55
3 ch f Mr Greeley(USA) —Shin Feign (USA) (El Prado (IRE))
2157[7] 5317[4] 6377[4] 6790[4] 7255[3] 7413[6]

Periphery (USA) *Mahmood Al Zarooni* 83
2 b c Elusive Quality(USA) —Punctilious (Danehill (USA))
6951[2]

Periwinkle Way *Sylvester Kirk* 45
2 b f Acclamation—Millsini (Rossini (USA))
4052[10] 4386[7] 5047[8]

Perks (IRE) *Jessica Long* a92 90
6 b g Selkirk(USA) —Green Charter (Green Desert (USA))
2601a[5] 5981a[11]

Perlachy *Ronald Harris* a72 72
7 b g Kyllachy—Perfect Dream (Emperor Jones (USA))
58[8] 199[4] 269[7] 3721[12] 5640[8] 5895[12] 6488[8] 6694[5] (7266) (7567) 7649[2]

Perla Du Ma (IRE) *Tobias B P Coles* a70 39
2 ch c Shamardal(USA) —Genoa (Zafonic (USA))
7275a[3] 7855[5]

Perle D'Amour (IRE) *Martin Bosley* a40 7
4 b m Pearl Of Love(IRE) —Bella Vie (IRE) (Sadler's Wells (USA))
136[4] 350[6]

Permesso *G Pucciatti* 108
6 b h Sakhee(USA) —Persian Filly (IRE) (Persian Bold)
1918a[4]

Perpetually (IRE) *Mark Johnston* a94 92
5 b g Singspiel(IRE) —Set In Motion (USA) (Mr Prospector (USA))
1717[11] 2475[2] 2884[15] 3344[11]

Persian Herald *William Muir* a77 81
3 gr g Proclamation(IRE) —Persian Fortune (Forzando)
1106[4] 1773[5] 2188[4] 2664[7] 3118[2] 3809[5] 4905[6] 5407[8] 5968[7] 6465[2] 7160[2]

Persian Peril *Alan Swinbank* a75 90
7 br g Erhaab(USA) —Brush Away (Ahonoora)
1291[7] 1977[3] 2656[3] (4142) (4173) 4440[3] 5205[3] 5729[2] 6024[2] 6989[11]

Persidha *Gay Kelleway* a51 69
2 b f Sir Percy—Azizam (Singspiel (IRE))
5410[3] 6030[3] 6449[4] 6970[5] 7196[7]

Persiste Et Signe (FR) *Stephane Chevalier* a100 101
4 b g With Approval(CAN) —Mahima (FR) (Linamix (FR))
499a[7] 679a[6] 827a[9]

Personal Touch *Richard Fahey* 75
2 ch g Pivotal—Validate (Alhaarth (IRE))
5202[2] 5756[4] 6207[2] (7210)

Personified (GER) *Mme J Bidgood* a77 98
4 b m Doyen(IRE) —Proudeyes (GER) (Dashing Blade)
815a[4] 1122a[8] 2744a[8] 7534a[3]

Pertemps Networks *Michael Easterby* a82 81
7 b g Golden Snake(USA) —Society Girl (Shavian)
1036[5] 2364[7] 3023[10] 3715[2] (6546) 6676[4] 7162[4] 7699[3]

Pertuis (IRE) *Harry Dunlop* a81 80
5 gr g Verglas(IRE) —Lady Killeen (IRE) (Marju (IRE))
(54) 381[6] 475[2] 1402[15] 1829[6] 3042[9]

Pestagua (IRE) *X Thomas-Demeaulte* 97
2 b f Lawman(FR) —Pop Alliance (IRE) (Entrepreneur)
4569a[2] 5296a[8]

Petaluma *Mick Channon* 71
2 b f Teofilo(IRE) —Poppo's Song (CAN) (Polish Navy (USA))
3813[5]

Petara Bay (IRE) *Robert Mills* 111
7 b g Peintre Celebre(USA) —Magnificient Style (USA) (Silver Hawk (USA))
1679[4] 3396[4] (4532)

Pete *Barry Murtagh* 53
8 b g Overbury(IRE) —Fen Terrier (Emarati (USA))
1212[7]

Petella *George Moore* 74
5 b m Tamure(IRE) —Miss Petronella (Petoski)
1519[6] (1881) 2060[2] 2622[2] 3316[4] (5079) 6095[8] 6707[9] 6915[6]

Peter Anders *Mark Johnston* 75
2 b c Pivotal—Astorg (USA) (Lear Fan (USA))
6448[5] 7052[3] ◆ 7210[2]

Peter Island (FR) *John Gallagher* a78 88
8 b g Dansili—Catania (USA) (Aloma's Ruler (USA))
1656[8] 1937[6] 2422[5] 3517[3] 3940[7]

Peteron *Colin Teague* 17
3 b g Danbird(AUS) —Lady Rock (Mistertopogigo (IRE))
4282[11] 5649[7] 6156[12]

Peter's Gift (IRE) *Kevin Ryan* a76 66
5 b m Catcher In The Rye(IRE) —Eastern Blue (IRE) (Be My Guest (USA))
9[5]

Peters Pleasure *Robert Cowell* a17
2 ch f Medicean—Swynford Pleasure (Reprimand)
6030[13] 6539[10] 7526[12]

Peter Spring (FR) *N Madamet* a66 71
7 b g Numerous(USA) —Danaide (FR) (Polish Precedent (USA))
7256a[2]

Peters Pursuit (IRE) *Richard Fahey* a33 59
2 ch g Bertolini(USA) —Xarzee (IRE) (Xaar)
1823[7] 2504[8] 3314[7] 4277[7] 4943[4] 5597[5]

Peter Tchaikovsky *Ian McInnes* a62 62
5 b g Dansili—Abbatiale (FR) (Kaldoun (FR))
2809[10] 3235[10] 3475[5] 3733[7] 5394[2] 6488[9] 6848[9] 7229[7]

Petit Chevalier (FR) *W Baltromei* 100
3 b c High Chaparral(IRE) —Pivoline (FR) (Pivotal)
7313a[4]

Petito (IRE) *Mark Gillard* 43
8 b g Imperial Ballet(IRE) —Fallacy (Selkirk (USA))
2793[10] 3480[6] 3943[8]

Petomic (IRE) *Richard Guest* a64 71
6 ch g Dubai Destination(USA) —Petomi (Presidium)
38[7] 428[6] (574) 692[3] 944[10] 1083[3] ◆ 1398[3] 1569[6] 3386[6] (3486) 4045[2] 4170[3] 4540[7] 4784[7] 4901[8] 5248[6] 5470[2] 5728[7] 6211[8] 6764[10] 6871[4] 7068[12] 7788[6]

Petrocelli *Wilf Storey* a49 62
4 b g Piccolo—Sarcita (Primo Dominie)
1216[7] 1615[9]

Petrol *Luca Cumani* 41
2 ch c Danehill Dancer(IRE) —Pongee (Barathea (IRE))
6935[11] 7133[8]

Petrosian *Lisa Williamson* a24 67
7 b g Sakhee(USA) —Arabis (Arazi (USA))
3041[9]

Petsas Pleasure *Ollie Pears* a59 69
5 b g Observatory(USA) —Swynford Pleasure (Reprimand)
2271[2] (2589) 3139[2] 3683[3] 4380[4] 5622[2] 6098[5] 6461[2] 6764[3] 7112[2]

Pettochside *Stuart Williams* a49
2 b g Refuse To Bend(IRE) —Clear Impression (IRE) (Danehill (USA))
7749[6]

Pevensey (IRE) *David Barron* a94 85
9 b g Danehill(USA) —Champaka (IRE) (Caerleon (USA))
2220[12] 2892[6]

Phair Winter *Alan Brown* a40 54
3 b f Sleeping Indian—Tuppenny Blue (Pennekamp (USA))
2465[5] 3039[2] ◆ 3246[5] 3706[6] 4284[10] 5165[8] 5789[5]

Pha Mai Blue *Jim Boyle* a73 61
6 b g Acclamation—Queen Of Silk (IRE) (Brief Truce (USA))
1397 317[11] 432[9]

Phantom Ranch *Mark H Tompkins* 21
2 b g Act One—Highbrook (USA) (Alphabatim (USA))
6953[11]

Pharoh Jake *John Bridger* a36 27
3 ch g Piccolo—Rose Amber (Double Trigger (IRE))
132[7] 863[7] 1504[4] 7807[7] 7943[8]

Phase Shift *William Muir* a68 62
3 b f Iceman—Silent Waters (Polish Precedent (USA))
3228[13] 3744[3] 4071[2]

Phenomena *Jeremy Gask* a43
2 b c Galileo(IRE) —Something Exciting (Halling (USA))
7751[11]

Philharmonic Hall *Richard Fahey* a50 68
3 b g Victory Note(USA) —Lambast (Relkino)
1038[3] 1329[3] 1611[10] 2119[4] 2252[2] 3318[5] 4018[3] 4364[3] 4902[2] 5311[7] 6192[5] 7779[5]

Philipstown *Richard Hannon* a69 71
2 ch g Notnowcato—Tahara (IRE) (Caerleon (USA))
4201[8] 4507[3] 5133[7] 6214[4] 6724[4]

Phlorian *Ian Patrick Browne* a35 40
5 b g Falbrav(IRE) —Ravishing (IRE) (Bigstone (IRE))
2790[13] 3320[8] 3716[8] 4544[11]

Phluke *Eve Johnson Houghton* a56 70
10 b g Most Welcome—Phlirty (Pharly (FR))
2171[2] 2420[3] (3477) 3677[3] 4444[15] 5201[5] 5845[8] (6538) 7203[10] 7522[13]

Phoenician Blaze *Tim Etherington* a38 50
2 b f Phoenix Reach(IRE) —Chelsea (USA) (Miswaki (USA))
4285[12] 5029[12] 6836[5] 7059[16] 7242[8] 7414[8]

Phoenix City (USA) *Michael Bell* a72 86
3 rg f El Prado(IRE) —Warsaw Girl (IRE) (Polish Precedent (USA))
1568[16] 4663[2] (4963)

Phoenix Clubs (IRE) *Paul Midgley* 66
2 b f Red Clubs(IRE) —Hollow Haze (USA) (Woodman (USA))
1939[4] 2430[8] 2886[6] 3639[3] 4406[3] (5399) 6222[11] 6384[4]

Phoenix Fantasy (IRE) *Jonathan Portman* a57 44
3 b g Phoenix Reach(IRE) —Ideal Figure (Zafonic (USA))
983[5] 1312[12] 1769[11] 2305[5]

Phoenix Flame *Alan McCabe* a61 59
3 ch f Phoenix Reach(IRE) —Generosia (Generous (IRE))
3633[4] 4435[8] 5179[9] 5823[3] 6235[6] 6415[3] 7037[10] 7712[4] 7859[5]

Phoenix Flight (IRE) *James Evans* a92 93
6 b g Hawk Wing(USA) —Firecrest (IRE) (Darshaan)
(209) 849[7] 1105[9] 3013[3] 3522[8] 4775[6] 6690[24]

Phoenix Order *Alan McCabe* 24
2 b g Phoenix Reach(IRE) —Pearl's Girl (King's Best (USA))
4402[8] 4646[6]

Phonic (IRE) *John Dunlop* a69 70
4 ch g Green Tune(USA) —Superfonic (FR) (Zafonic (USA))
2051[8] 2793[11] 3366[10] 6622[2] ◆ 7120[5] 7415[4] 7766[4]

Photo Opportunity *D K Weld* 88
4 b g Zamindar(USA) —Fame At Last (USA) (Quest For Fame)
925a[10]

Piano *John Gosden* a85 99
4 b m Azamour(IRE) —Humouresque (Pivotal)
1390[4] ◆ (1992) 2994[5] 3356[3] 4915[4] 6066[5]

Piave (IRE) *Peter Chapple-Hyam* a63 69
3 b c Oratorio(IRE) —Peace In The Park (IRE) (Ahonoora)
(1559) 2253[6] 2695[5] 3325[7] 6311[5] 6923[7]

Piazza San Pietro *Andrew Haynes* a59 98
5 ch g Compton Place—Rainbow Spectrum (FR) (Spectrum (IRE))
1476[4] 1864[5] (1937) 2717[8] 3140[4] (3627) 3841[14] 3996[5] 5758[18]

Picabo (IRE) *Lucy Wadham* a72 82
3 b f Elusive City(USA) —Gi La High (Rich Charlie)
2916[6] 3322[8] (4967) 5265[2] ◆ 5831[6] ◆ 6174[15] 6665[8]

Picalily *Sylvester Kirk* a48
2 b f Piccolo—Kaylianni (Kalanisi (IRE))
5632[9]

Picanina (FR) *H Julliot* 8
9 b m Abary(GER) —Azegno (FR) (Cupids Dew)
843a[0]

Picansort *Peter Crate* a76 71
4 b g Piccolo—Running Glimpse (IRE) (Runnett)
133[2] (178) 521[7] 698[9] 2645[10] 2929[8] 3517[7] 4210[9] 5326[5] 7804[2] ◆

Picante (IRE) *C Boutin* 80
2 b f Bertolini(USA) —Undertone (IRE) (Noverre (USA))
7155a[7]

Piccadilly Filly (IRE) *Edward Creighton* a93 107
4 ch m Exceed And Excel(AUS) —Tortue (IRE) (Turtle Island (IRE))
996a[15] 2138a[6] 2754a[13] 3827[5] 4063[3] 4739a[5] 5253[14] 6164[7]

Piccarello *Mark H Tompkins* a44 71
3 b g Piccolo—Latina (IRE) (King's Theatre (IRE))
3002[13] 3363[5] 3571[6] 4431[5] 5041[5] 6767[5] 6936[6]

Piccola Stella (FR) *Alex Fracas*
3 gr f Touch Of The Blues(FR) —Princess Palm (FR) (Great Palm (USA))
7016a[0]

Piccolete *Richard Hannon* a31 54
3 b f Piccolo—Blue Goddess (IRE) (Blues Traveller (IRE))
1724[6] ◆ 2792[13] 5674[10] 6070[6] 6813[7]

Piccolo Express *Brian Baugh* a67 60
5 b g Piccolo—Ashfield (Zilzal (USA))
(70) (255) 544[2] ◆ 637[5] 933[4] 3241[6] 4517[3] 4918[6] 5901[3] 6138[10]

Piccoluck *Amy Weaver* a62 68
3 b g Piccolo—Zephrina (Zafonic (USA))
1249[3] 1494[2] 1802[3] 2186[5] 3470[4] 4025[14] 4247[2] (4840a) 5624[8] 6266[12] 6794[11] 7084[11]

Piceno (IRE) *Scott Dixon* a81 79
3 b g Camacho—Ascoli (Skyliner)
1202[7] 4325[11] 4561[8] 5106[4] (5213) 5465[9] 5730[6] 6867[3] 7339[3] 7771[4]

Pick A Little *Ron Hodges* a68 84
3 b g Piccolo—Little Caroline (IRE) (Great Commotion (USA))
(1585) 2024[3] (2453) (2757) (3269) 3996[4] 5262[8]

Picking Apples (FR) *Mlle C Cardenne* 80
2 b c Oasis Dream—Gontcharova (IRE) (Zafonic (USA))
7664a[0]

Pickled Pelican (IRE) *William Haggas* a67 94
2 b g Dylan Thomas(IRE) —Starship (IRE) (Galileo (IRE))
1988[2] 2448[4] 4864[3] (5565) (6031)

Pickled Pumpkin *Olivia Maylam* a53 30
3 ch g Compton Place—Woodbury (Woodborough (USA))
28[5] 246[5] 380[3] 595[3] 1764[7] 2163[12] 2424[9] 2993[10] 3950[3] 4650[7]

Pick Well (FR) *Mme L Audon* a54 70
5 b g Dream Well(FR) —Pic Saint Loup (FR) (Kaid Pous (FR))
1142a[0]

Picot De Say *Bernard Llewellyn* a40 64
9 b g Largesse—Facsimile (Superlative)
3799[2] 4274[7] 5379[5]

Picture Dealer *Gary Moore* 52
2 b g Royal Applause—Tychy (Suave Dancer (USA))
6991[9]

Picture Editor *Sir Henry Cecil* 102
3 b c Dansili—Shirley Valentine (Shirley Heights)
1405[5] 2191[3] 3069[11] 5544[4] 5932[4]

Pictures (IRE) *Ron Barr* a56 58
4 b m Le Vie Dei Colori—So Glam So Hip (IRE) (Spectrum (IRE))
207[13] 354[4] 524[14] 624[6] 807[11] 943[10] 3317[10] 3658[4] 4123[9] 4441[6] 4673[8] 4945[12]

Picura *William Muir* 54
2 ch f King's Best(USA) —Picolette (Piccolo)
3270[7] 3673[3] 4430[8] 5297[3] 6237[8] 6628[13]

Piddie's Power *Ed McMahon* a81 79
4 ch m Starcraft(NZ) —Telori (Muhtarram (USA))
2566[7] 2938[16] 3541[5] 4020[6] 4793[2] 4973[3] 5616[4] 6502[2] 7040[2]

Piece By Piece *Tim Easterby* 86
2 ch c Byron—Queen Jean (Pivotal)
(2120) 3313[2] (3973)

Pie Poudre *Roy Brotherton* a63 55
4 ch g Zafeen(FR) —Eglantine (IRE) (Royal Academy (USA))
26[3] 283[5] 526[3] 895[2] (1273) 3475[3] 3926[5] 4705[16] 5040[7] 5414[11]

Pierre D'Or (IRE) *J T Gorman* a60 83
2 ch c Rock Of Gibraltar(IRE) —Gilded Edge (Cadeaux Genereux)
5950a[7]

Piers Gaveston (IRE) *George Baker* 67
2 b g Amadeus Wolf—Dancing Tempo (Vettori (IRE))
3870[5] 4698[4] 6019[3]

Pigeon Catcher (IRE) *Mme Pia Brandt* 65
2 ch c Dutch Art—Jakarta Jade (IRE) (Royal Abjar (USA))
7664a[3]

Pilgrim Dancer (IRE) *Tony Coyle* a66 67
4 b g Danehill Dancer(IRE) —Pilgrim's Way (USA) (Gone West (USA))
96[4] (169) 304[4] 544[9] 3235[11] 3475[10] 3719[6] 3806[9] 4383[7] 4605[12] 4869[12] 7899[3]

Pilgrims Rest (IRE) *Richard Hannon* a33 74
2 ch c Rock Of Gibraltar(IRE) —Holly Blue (Bluebird (USA))
6059[7] 6462[6] 6726[4] 6945[4]

Pill Boy *Dai Burchell* a11
3 b g Auction House(USA) —Tymeera (Timeless Times (USA))
7389[10] 7717[11]

Pillows Dreams (FR) *A Spanu* a62 56
3 ch g Martillo(GER) —Patin Couffin (Polar Falcon (USA))
616a[5]

Pim Pam (IRE) *C Ferland* a83 89
4 gr m Verglas(IRE) —Pacy's Ridge (IRE) (Indian Ridge)
481a[4] (1033a)

Pimpernel (IRE) *Mahmood Al Zarooni* 110
2 b f Invincible Spirit(IRE) —Anna Pallida (Sadler's Wells (USA))
(3388) 4001[2] (5052) 5656[3] (6340) 6691[2] (7028) ◆

Pinball (IRE) *Lisa Williamson* a56 60
5 b m Namid—Luceball (IRE) (Bluebird (USA))
57[3] 102[3] 185[9] 3248[10] 3714[U] 3908[2] 3999[7] (4272) 4820[3] 5175[6]

Pinch Of Posh (IRE) *Paul Cole* a45 74
3 gr f Pivotal—Limpopo (Green Desert (USA))
1362[8] 1607[10] (3091) 3630[7] (4807)

Pinch Pie (USA) *Anthony Dutrow* a109 99
3 b f Victory Gallop(CAN) —Romp And Stomp (USA) (Olympio (USA))
6183a[7]

Pindrop *Walter Swinburn* a22 57
2 ch f Exceed And Excel(AUS) —Why So Silent (Mill Reef (USA))
3270[5] ◆ 3736[11]

Pineapple Pete (IRE) *Alan McCabe* a62 65
3 b g Compton Place—Dilag (IRE) (Almutawakel)
100[2] 132[2] 246[3] 611[6] 669[6] 745[3] 847[4] 936[6] 958[5] (1187) 1306[7] 1595[5] 1745[4] 2180[4] 2524[2] 2611[4] 2845[8] 3635[4]

Pinewood Polly *Shaun Harris* a8
4 b m Lujain(USA) —Polmara (IRE) (Polish Precedent (USA))
229[11] 490[10] 796[12] 856[7] 1065[12]

Pinielde (FR) *C Boutin* a78 83
3 b f High Yield(USA) —Pimpinella (FR) (Highest Honor (FR))
288a[0]

Pink Belini *Alan McCabe* a47 36
2 ch f Phoenix Reach(IRE) —Pink Supreme (Night Shift (USA))
7080[9] 7396[7] 7583[10] 7915[9]

Pink Delight (IRE) *J S Moore* a36
2 ch f Rock Of Gibraltar(IRE) —Turkana Girl (Hernando (FR))
7835[10]

Pink Diva (IRE) *Tom Tate* 77
3 ch f Giant's Causeway(USA) —Saoire (Pivotal)
2076[10] 2849[5]

Pinker Pinker (AUS) *Greg Eurell* 118
4 b f Reset(AUS) —Miss Marion (AUS) (Success Express (USA))
(7044a)

Pink Evie *Gay Kelleway* a38
2 ch f Dutch Art—Cressida (Polish Precedent (USA))
7784[6]

Pink Gin (FR) *J-M Beguigne* 108
4 b h Kouroun(FR) —Pink Cloud (FR) (Octagonal (NZ))
1125a[4] 2744a[5]

Pinkisthecolour (IRE) *Kevin Prendergast* a53 74
2 b f Red Clubs(IRE) —Delicia (IRE) (Rainbow Quest (USA))
921a[3]

Pink Sapphire (IRE) *Richard Hannon* 79
2 ch f Danehill Dancer(IRE) —In Safe Hands (IRE) (Intikhab (USA))
2504[4] (3287) 3821[11] 4252[7] 4749[5]

Pink Sari *Peter Makin* a39
3 br f Kyllachy—Heart Of India (IRE) (Try My Best (USA))
513[3] 642[6]

Pink Symphony *David Wachman* a93 106
4 b m Montjeu(IRE) —Blue Symphony (Darshaan)
1100[3] 1677[3] 2501[5] 2994[7] (4589a) 6736a[7]

Pinotage *Peter Niven* a67 62
3 br g Danbird(AUS) —Keen Melody (USA) (Sharpen Up)
1413[2] 1944[5] (2786) 3572[3] 4112[7] 5243[3] (6926) 7003[3] 7144[2] 7789[3] 7931[3]

Pinseeker (IRE) *Peter Winkworth* a28 66
2 b g Oratorio(IRE) —Estivau (USA) (Lear Fan (USA))
4205[11] 4906[11] 6245[2]

Pinsplitter (USA) *Alan McCabe* a58 62
4 ch g Giant's Causeway(USA) —Lahinch (IRE) (Danehill Dancer (IRE))
94[5] 203[12] 419[2] 560[2] 1107[11] 1461[5] 1596[5] 2091[12] 3951[5] 4612[9]

Pintrada *James Bethell* 81
3 b g Tiger Hill(IRE) —Ballymore Celebre (IRE) (Peintre Celebre (USA))
1203[7] 1415[6] 1944[4] (2407) (3131) 3623[4] 4530[4]

Pint Size *Gay Kelleway* a84 76
2 b g Misu Bond(IRE) —Floral Spark (Forzando)
1890[10] 2362[2] 2693[2] (2784) (3491) 3948[2] (4178) 4661[3] 5896[2] 6540[3] 6786[6]

Pintura *David Simcock* a54 105
4 ch g Efisio—Picolette (Piccolo)
1092[9] 1406[2] 1849[2] 2031[4] 3032[12] 3876[12] 4494[3] 5218[3] 6339[11]

Pipers Piping (IRE) *Alastair Lidderdale* a76 67
5 b g Noverre(USA) —Monarchy (IRE) (Common Grounds)
178[3] 264[8] 522[7] 806[6] 904[2] 2179[6] 2605[6] 3130[16] 3468[10] 7131[4] ◆ 7268[5] 7463[2] (7537) 7579[6] 7658[4] 7764[6] 7888[2]

Piper's Song (IRE) *Linda Perratt* a67 57
8 gr g Distant Music(USA) —Dane's Lane (IRE) (Danehill (USA))
4673[2] ◆ (5208) 6430[6]

Pipette *Andrew Balding* a100 102
4 b m Pivotal—Amaryllis (IRE) (Sadler's Wells (USA))
2501[6] 2994[9] 4267[4] 4778[9]

Pippa's Gift *William Muir* a73 57
3 b c Royal Applause—Pippa's Dancer (IRE) (Desert Style (IRE))
140[6] 2180[13] 2818[10] 3048[2] 3271[4] 3983[4] 4715[7] 4850[7] 5279[6] 5387[10] 6305[4]

Pippas Prodigy (IRE) *Edward Creighton* a11
3 b f Ivan Denisovich(IRE) —Thara'A (IRE) (Desert Prince (IRE))
791[8] 1139[11] 1580[11]

Pippbrook Ministar *Jim Boyle* a67 65
4 br m Pastoral Pursuits—Chiaro (Safawan)
303[3] 487[6] 1045[10]

Piquante *Nigel Tinkler* a73 75
5 b m Selkirk(USA) —China (Royal Academy (USA))
128[3] (200) 530[3]

Piranha (IRE) *Ed Dunlop* a80 77
2 b f Exceed And Excel(AUS) —Mosaique Beauty (IRE) (Sadler's Wells (USA))
2709[5] (3221) (3745) 4551[6] 4999[8] 5708[5] 5961[3] 6625[6] 7445[10]

Pirate Coast *Tim Easterby* 73
4 ch g Bahamian Bounty—Highland Gait (Most Welcome)
1696[6] ◆ 2474[4] 2887[13]

Pirateer (IRE) *A P O'Brien* 104
3 b c Danehill Dancer(IRE) —Wannabe (Shirley Heights)
(3444a) ◆

Pires *A J Martin* a99 98
7 br g Generous(IRE) —Kaydee Queen (IRE) (Bob's Return (IRE))
1381a[11] 4418a[5] 5090a[3] 6339[16]

Pirika (IRE) *A Fabre* 106
3 b f Monsun(GER) —Paita (Intikhab (USA))
1513a[2] 1922a[6] 7090a[7]

Piri Wango (IRE) *G M Lyons* a82
2 ch g Choisir(AUS) —Zoldan (Deploy)
(7273a) ◆

Pisa No Varon (JPN) *S Kobayashi* 48
5 b g Manhattan Cafe(JPN) —Aldie Mill (USA) (Miswaki (USA))
6593a[0]

Piscean (USA) *Tom Keddy* a104 92
6 bb g Stravinsky(USA) —Navasha (USA) (Woodman (USA))
46[4] 429[2] 848[5] 5706[10] 6723[19] 7018[11] 7578[10] 7721[2]

Pisco Sour (USA) *Hughie Morrison* a76 113
3 bb c Lemon Drop Kid(USA) —Lynnwood Chase (USA) (Horse Chestnut (SAF))
2030[3] 2715[9] (3068) (4376a)

Piste *Tina Jackson* a68 65
5 b m Falbrav(IRE) —Arctic Char (Polar Falcon (USA))
2238[10] 2588[9] 2670[4] 2990[9] 3972[8] 4328[7] 4636[4] 4986[10] 5373[7]

Pitkin *Michael Easterby* a65 67
3 b g Proclamation(IRE) —Princess Oberon (IRE) (Fairy King (USA))
1494[4] ◆ 1802[2] 2216[10] 4527[3] 5009[4] 7566[7] 7896[4]

Pitti Sing *Richard Fahey* 47
2 b f Refuse To Bend(IRE) —Murielle (Diktat)
3899[5] 4474[6] 5003[4]

Pittodrie Star (IRE) *Andrew Balding* a85 83
4 ch g Choisir(AUS) —Jupiter Inlet (IRE) (Jupiter Island)
131[2] 209[10] 2220[4] 2762[3] 3851[6] (4719) 5448[9] 5685[9] 6130[7] 6893[2] 7577[3]

Pitt Rivers *Mick Channon* 74
2 br g Vital Equine(IRE) —Silca Boo (Efisio)
1360[6] 1632[2] 2023[3] 3810[5] 5398[4] 5668[5] 6092[5] (6186)

Pius Parker (IRE) *John Gallagher* a59 72
2 b g Antonius Pius(USA) —Parker's Cove (USA) (Woodman (USA))
1632[3] 2148[9] 2448[7] 2953[10] 6221[5] 6817[4] 6972[9]

Piverina (IRE) *Julie Camacho* a46 56
6 b m Pivotal—Alassio (USA) (Gulch (USA))
450[4]

Pivoina (IRE) *G Henrot* a82 86
4 b m Marchand De Sable(USA) —Golden Wings (USA) (Devil's Bag (USA))
840a[0]

Pivotal Prospect *Tracy Waggott* 18
3 b f Nayef(USA) —Buon Amici (Pivotal)
6156[10]

Pivotal Rock (IRE) *T Stack* a76 56
4 b g Pivotal—Kitza (IRE) (Danehill (USA))
7548a[3] ◆

Pivot Bridge *Charles Hills* a60 75
3 ch c Pivotal—Specifically (USA) (Sky Classic (CAN))
1191[2] 1949[8] 3124[3] 3614[3] 4716[2] 5560[8] 6402[2]

Pivotman *Amanda Perrett* 101
3 ch g Pivotal—Grandalea (Grand Lodge (USA))
3291[11] 4426[3] 4777[10] 5283[16] 5971[6] (6409) 7029[2]

Pizzarra *James Given* a57 61
3 b f Shamardal(USA) —Pizzicato (Statoblest)
44[5] 2265[2] 2697[8] 3860[7]

Pizzetti (IRE) *Sir Mark Prescott Bt* a61 50
3 b g Singspiel(IRE) —Mazuna (IRE) (Cape Cross (IRE))
52[9] 262[8] 378[3] 2239[3] 2571[10] 5302[5] 5628[7] 6482[3] 6823[3] 7062[7]

Place And Chips *Tom Dascombe* a55 49
3 ch g Compton Place—Our Sheila (Bahamian Bounty)
64[4] 251[6]

Place In My Heart *George Baker* 84
2 ch f Compton Place—Lonely Heart (Midyan (USA))
2374[2] (5351) 6535[7]

Placere (IRE) *Richard Brabazon* a64 64
3 ch f Noverre(USA) —Puppet Play (IRE) (Broken Hearted)
7250[6]

Place That Face *Hughie Morrison* a66
2 b f Compton Place—Notjustaprettyface (USA) (Red Ransom (USA))
7583[6] 7749[3]

Place The Duchess *Alastair Lidderdale* a52 26
5 b m Compton Place—Barrantes (Distant Relative)
746[6] 941[7] 1247[13] 2424[7]

Plaisterer *Chris Wall* a58 96
6 b m Best Of The Bests(IRE) —Lumiere D'Espoir (FR) (Saumarez)
(2220) 2716[10] 3356[6] 4099[8]

Planet I T (IRE) *Mark Usher* a82 82
2 b g Majestic Missile(IRE) —Zara Whetei (IRE) (Lomond (USA))
5211[5] 5834[2] (6252) 6827[3] ◆ 7261[4]

Planetoid (IRE) *David Lanigan* a92 92
3 b g Galileo(IRE) —Palmeraie (USA) (Lear Fan (USA))
1445[6] ◆ 1810[4] ◆ 2469[5] ◆ (4664) ◆ (4966) 5641[4]

Planet Waves (IRE) *Clive Brittain* a80 81
3 b c Red Ransom(USA) —Rock Salt (Selkirk (USA))
1175[6] 1478[3] 1811[7] 2925[6] 3557[6] 4020[5]

Planteur (IRE) *E Lellouche* 124
4 b h Danehill Dancer(IRE) —Plante Rare (IRE) (Giant's Causeway (USA))
(1266a) (1708a) ◆ 3031[4] 5129a[5] 5988a[8]

Plastiki *Sir Michael Stoute* 57
2 b g Oasis Dream—Dayrose (Daylami (IRE))
6064[8]

Platinum (IRE) *Rebecca Curtis* a94 95
4 b g Azamour(IRE) —Dazzling Park (IRE) (Warning)
5963[7]

Plato (JPN) *Sir Henry Cecil* a85 92
4 ch h Bago(FR) —Taygete (USA) (Miswaki (USA))
2285[2] 3120[2] 3794[3] 4890[5] 5221[8] 5878[6]

Plattsburgh (USA) *Mark Johnston* a82 84
3 bb g Bernardini(USA) —Saranac Lake (USA) (Smart Strike (CAN))
1327[7] 1609[5] (3676) 3905[9] (4237) 4464[2] 4697[6] 6155[8] 6822[8] 7908[10]

Playa Blanca (FR) *Robert Collet* a67 47
4 ch m Forestier(FR) —Lattaquie (FR) (Fast Topaze (USA))
1012a[0]

Playful Girl (IRE) *Tim Easterby* 53
3 b f Byron—Feminine Touch (IRE) (Sadler's Wells (USA))
1495[7] 1858[5] 2571[9] 2786[5] (4112) 4381[5] 5107[11] 5507[3] 5823[11]

Playing God (AUS) *Neville Parnham* 118
4 br g Blackfriars(AUS) —Dolly Will Do (AUS) (Rubiton (AUS))
6713a[6] 7044a[11]

Play Music *Mick Channon* a57
3 gr f Proclamation(IRE) —Zacchera (Zamindar (USA))
1298[5]

Play Street *Jonathan Portman* a40
2 ch f Tobougg(IRE) —Zoena (Emarati (USA))
7909[7]

Play The Blues (IRE) *Mark Allen* a34 71
4 gr m Refuse To Bend(IRE) —Paldouna (IRE) (Kaldoun (FR))
878[6] 1133[2] 1814[13] 2426[2] 2870[10] 3412[11]

Play Up Pompey *John Bridger* a52 32
9 b g Dansili—Search For Love (FR) (Groom Dancer (USA))
164[9] 524[7]

Plead The Fifth (USA) *Brian Meehan* a38
2 b g Quiet American(USA) —Patnjohn (USA) (Known Fact (USA))
6471[10] 6763[7]

Pleasant Day (IRE) *Richard Fahey* a87 98
4 b g Noverre(USA) —Sunblush (UAE) (Timber Country (USA))
1092[16] 1879[2] 2002[17] 2681[8] (3085) 3876[17] 4494[14] 4788[9] 5593[4] 6080[6] 6862[10]

Pleasant Prince (USA) *Wesley A Ward* a115
4 ch h Indy King(USA) —Archduchess (USA) (Pleasant Tap (USA))
7300a[4]

Plenilune (IRE) *Mel Brittain* a52 29
6 b g Fantastic Light(USA) —Kathleen's Dream (USA) (Last Tycoon)
1468[9] 1498[6] 1615[13] 2656[7]

Plimsoll Line (USA) *Michael Bell* 71
3 ch c Pivotal—Showlady (USA) (Theatrical)
1408[11] 2258[4] 2621[12]

Plug In Baby *Nick Mitchell* a43 46
3 b f Xaar—Medinaceli (IRE) (Grand Lodge (USA))
6438[6]

Plum Bay *David Elsworth* 59
2 ch f Nayef(USA) —Pelican Key (IRE) (Mujadil (USA))
3362[7] 4061[9] 4330[17]

Plume *Roger Teal* a43 86
4 b m Pastoral Pursuits—Polar Storm (IRE) (Law Society (USA))
2690[8] 3536[7] 4509[9] 5100[10] 5890[11]

Plum Pretty (USA) *Bob Baffert* a121
3 b f Medaglia D'Oro(USA) —Liszy (USA) (A.P. Indy (USA))
7285a[5]

Plum Sugar (IRE) *P J Prendergast* a86 88
4 b m Footstepsinthesand—Bush Baby (Zamindar (USA))
1705a[4] 5090a[7] 5748a[4]

Plush *Shaun Lycett* a88 70
8 ch g Medicean—Glorious (Nashwan (USA))
427[8] 694[6] 968[2] 1081[2] 1586[8] 2359[5] 2567[6]

Plushenko (IRE) *L Riccardi* 94
3 b c Nayef(USA) —Vertigine Bianca (Sadler's Wells (USA))
1920a[8] 6202a[5]

Plutarque (FR) *H-A Pantall* a73 71
4 ch g Sinndar(IRE) —Peony Girl (FR) (Phantom Breeze)
259a[6]

Plym *Richard Hannon* a59 69
2 ch f Notnowcato—River Fantasy (USA) (Irish River (FR))
2309[8] 2787[7] 3425[5] ◆ (5233) 6753[8] 7205[6]

Plymouth Rock (IRE) *Jeremy Noseda* a89 99
5 b g Sadler's Wells(USA) —Zarawa (IRE) (Kahyasi)
1102[7] 1808[9] 3013[15] (Dead)

Pobs Trophy *Richard Guest* a14 54
4 b g Umistim—Admonish (Warning)
3712[9] 4198[6]

Pocket A Pound (IRE) *S Botti* 102
3 b f Azamour(IRE) —Rinass (IRE) (Indian Ridge)
3449a[4]

Pocket's Pick (IRE) *Jim Best* a73 65
5 ch g Exceed And Excel(AUS) —Swizzle (Efisio)
3556[3] 4189[7] 4740[3] 5139[6] 5426[4] 5997[7]

Pocket Too *Matthew Salaman* a66 2
8 b g Fleetwood(IRE) —Pocket Venus (IRE) (King's Theatre (IRE))
33[8] 1473[4] 1959[10]

Podgies Boy (IRE) *Richard Fahey* a77 69
3 b g Statue Of Liberty(USA) —Lake Victoria (IRE) (Lake Coniston (IRE))
7439[7] 7771[5] 7922[6]

Poeme Du Berlais (FR) *D Prod'Homme* 78
3 gr g Great Pretender(IRE) —Boheme Du Berlais (FR) (Simon Du Desert (FR))
(7016a)

Poesmulligan (IRE) *Linda Jewell* a49
5 ch g Pierre—Jamis (IRE) (Be My Guest (USA))
485[4] 662[9] 807[7] 1044[8]

Poet *Clive Cox* a48 118
6 b h Pivotal—Hyabella (Shirley Heights)
1403[3] 2439[2] 2753a[6] 3153[8] 5094a[4] (6149) 7409a[3]

Poetically *Joseph Tuite* a63 44
3 b g Balmont(USA) —Presently (Cadeaux Genereux)
855[5] 1249[5] 1369[3] 1566[8] 1933[12]

Poetic Dancer *Clive Cox* 89
2 ch f Byron—Crozon (Peintre Celebre (USA))
1441[3] (2309) ◆ 3795[3] 4496[6] 5847[2] (6995)

Poetic Lord *Richard Hannon* 85
2 b c Byron—Jumairah Sun (IRE) (Scenic)
2882[6] 3534[3] ◆ 4722[7] (5809) (6724) 6957[4]

Poetic Power (IRE) *David Elsworth* a59 00
2 b g Dylan Thomas(IRE) —Chalice Wells (Sadler's Wells (USA))
6630[6] 7233[3] 7369[7]

Poetry Writer *Michael Blanshard* a68 45
2 ch g Byron—Away To Me (Exit To Nowhere (USA))
5841[8] 6214[9] 7329[4]

Poet's Place (USA) *David Barron* a99 108
6 b g Mutakddim(USA) —Legion Of Merit (USA) (Danzig (USA))
1340[9]

Poet's Voice *Saeed Bin Suroor* a100 123
4 b h Dubawi(IRE) —Bright Tiara (USA) (Chief's Crown (USA))
759a[2] 1002a[14] 5473[7] 6298[3] 6860[6]

Poincon De France (IRE) *P Monfort* a70 77
7 b g Peintre Celebre(USA) —Poughkeepsie (IRE) (Sadler's Wells (USA))
439a[0] 705a[0]

Point At Issue (IRE) *David Nicholls* a59 55
2 b g One Cool Cat(USA) —Atishoo (IRE) (Revoque (IRE))
4192[9] 5486[5] 5726[11] 6912[11] 7337[7] 7421[6] (7505) 7684[2]

Point Blank (GER) *Mario Hofer* 105
3 bb c Royal Dragon(USA) —Princess Li (GER) (Monsun (GER))
2338a[5] (4373a) 5664a[6] 6201a[3] 6905a[2]

Point Du Jour (FR) *Ian Wood* a79 80
3 bb g Indian Rocket—Alaiz (Catrail (USA))
3133[14] 3468[7] 4281[5] (4908) ◆ 5635[3] 5835[3] 6254[11] 6505[7]

Point Made (IRE) *Ed McMahon* 76
2 b c Aussie Rules(USA) —Princess Clara (Dr Fong (USA))
5480[16] (6025) 6724[3]

Point North (IRE) *Jeremy Noseda* a96 86
4 b g Danehill Dancer(IRE) —Briolette (IRE) (Sadler's Wells (USA))
(2000) 2604[3] 3032[14] 4267[11] 6290[11] 7023[6]

Poisson D'Or *Rae Guest* 65
2 b f Cape Cross(IRE) —Lille Hammer (Sadler's Wells (USA))
4968[3] ◆

Poker Face (SWI) *U Suter* a71 77
4 b g Barathea(IRE) —Palmotia (FR) (Mtoto)
2867a[9]

Poker Hospital *George Baker* a66 76
2 b f Rock Of Gibraltar(IRE) —Empress Anna (IRE) (Imperial Ballet (IRE))
2962[8] 3463[4] 4823[3] 6099[3] 6921[3] 7225[3] 7539[4]

Pokfulham (IRE) *Jim Goldie* a51 71
5 b g Mull Of Kintyre(USA) —Marjinal (Marju (IRE))
(2636) 2892[3] 3115[2] 4173[8] 5723[3] 6115[7] 6419[2] 7163[3]

Polar Annie *Malcolm Saunders* a42 84
6 b m Fraam—Willisa (Polar Falcon (USA))
1444[11] 1755[5] 2027[8] (2870) 3549[6] (3801) 4387[7] (4707) 6747[9]

Polar Auroras *Tony Carroll* a66 59
3 b f Iceman—Noor El Houdah (IRE) (Fayruz)
2550[12] 2993[8] 4321[3] 6587[7] 6978[8] 7208[4] 7610[4] 7754[3]

Polarena (FR) *X Betron* 102
3 b f Policy Maker(IRE) —Arena (FR) (Marchand De Sable (USA))
6686a[6] 7386a[0]

Polar Explorer (IRE) *Niall Madden* 64
5 b g Pivotal—Polenta (IRE) (Sunday Silence (USA))
6139a[9]

Polarity *James Bethell* a37
5 b m Hamas(IRE) —Snowy Mantle (Siberian Express (USA))
643[5] 930[4]

Polar Kite (IRE) *Richard Fahey* 95
3 b g Marju(IRE) —Irina (IRE) (Polar Falcon (USA))
(1202) 2296[6] ◆ 3067[17] (5081) 5730[14]

Polemica (IRE) *Frank Sheridan* a72 21
5 b m Rock Of Gibraltar(IRE) —Lady Scarlett (Woodman (USA))
70[8] (537) (575) 746[4] 880[5] 933[5] (1054) 1279[2] 2165[5] 2356[9] 4865[2] 5604[3] (5901) 6354[11] 7596[12] 7819[6]

Polemique (IRE) *F Head* 93
3 b f Poliglote—Pony Girl (IRE) (Darshaan)
1922a[8] 2977a[9] 5129a[12]

Police Force (USA) *Mahmood Al Zarooni* 77
2 b c Street Sense(USA) —Land Of Dreams (Cadeaux Genereux)
3823[11] 4264[4] 5480[3] 6292[4]
Polish Steps (IRE) *Michael Mullineaux* a32 47
4 b m Footstepsinthesand—Polish Spring (IRE) (Polish Precedent (USA))
256[13]
Polish Sunset *Amy Weaver* a58 38
3 b g Noverre(USA) —Firozi (Forzando)
2266[9] 3223[6] 3636[10] 3958[12]
Polish World (USA) *Paul Midgley* a43 92
7 b g Danzig(USA) —Welcometotheworld (USA) (Woodman (USA))
1942[7] 2431[3] 3188[2] 3612[3] (3936) 5059[11] (5465) 6273[10] 7023[10]
Politbureau *Michael Easterby* a55 65
4 b g Red Ransom(USA) —Tereshkova (USA) (Mr Prospector (USA))
850[7] 1035[15] 1324[13] 1615[16] 4111[3] 4409[4] 4904[2] 5405[2] 5739[6] 6613[9]
Polly Adler *Alastair Lidderdale*
4 b m Fantastic Light(USA) —Urania (Most Welcome)
3224[12] 4445[7] 5816[10]
Polly Holder (IRE) *Paul D'Arcy* a63 67
3 b f Peintre Celebre(USA) —Love Emerald (USA) (Mister Baileys)
25[6] 51[5] 234[4] 260[7] 424[7] 527[3] 731[3] 1300[2] (1354) 1574[3] 1769[7] 5209[2]
Polly McGinty *Nicky Vaughan* a45 35
3 ch f Avonbridge—Polly Golightly (Weldnaas (USA))
1362[14] 1985[11] 6137[9] 6659[9]
Polly's Instinct *Peter Hiatt* a9
6 br m Killer Instinct—Polly Tino (Neltino)
31[5] 222[8]
Polly's Mark (IRE) *Clive Cox* 110
5 b m Mark Of Esteem(IRE) —Kotdiji (Mtoto)
1677[2] 2098[2] 2968a[4] 3624[5] 4470[4] 5220[3] 5850[3] 6857[7]
Polperro (USA) *John Gosden* 91
3 b c Kingmambo(USA) —Sand Springs (USA) (Dynaformer (USA))
1568[4] 2596[3] 2930[2] 4023[2] (4617) 5177[3]
Poltergeist (IRE) *William Haggas* 73
4 b g Invincible Spirit(IRE) —Bayalika (IRE) (Selkirk (USA))
2310[10]
Polydamos *Harry Dunlop* a48 73
2 b g Nayef(USA) —Spotlight (Dr Fong (USA))
2882[3] 3152[9] 7329[8]
Polygon (USA) *John Gosden* 104
3 b f Dynaformer(USA) —Polaire (IRE) (Polish Patriot (USA))
(2840) ◆ 4582[4] 5027a[3] 5839a[10]
Polytechnicien (USA) *A Fabre* a109 115
5 ch h Royal Academy(USA) —Golden Party (USA) (Seeking The Gold (USA))
(778a) (920a) 1342[2] 1740a[5] 4120a[3] 7193a[6]
Pomarine (USA) *Amanda Perrett* 62
2 b f Aptitude(USA) —Diese (USA) (Diesis)
7165[6]
Pomeroys Pistol (USA) *Amy Tarrant* a113
3 b f Pomeroy(USA) —Prettyatthetable (USA) (Point Given (USA))
7282a[4]
Pompeyano (IRE) *Saeed Bin Suroor* a71 110
6 b g Rainbow Quest(USA) —Lady Lodger (Be My Guest (USA))
154a[3] 584a[5]
Poncho *Sir Mark Prescott Bt* a23
2 b f Cape Cross(IRE) —Pixie Ring (Pivotal)
6215[11] 6758[11] 6820[11]
Pond Cottage (IRE) *Ms Joanna Morgan* 74
4 b g Kalanisi(IRE) —Attitude Of Blue (USA) (Distant View (USA))
7322a[9]
Ponderosa (FR) *J Bertran De Balanda* 69
4 b m Sevres Rose(IRE) —Check'n Raise (FR) (Art Sebal (USA))
842a[0]
Pond Life (IRE) *Amy Weaver* a47 59
2 b c Teofilo(IRE) —Water Feature (Dansili)
2817[8] 3408[3] 3917[7] 5343[3]
Pont Des Arts (FR) *A Schaerer* a96 106
7 b h Kingsalsa(USA) —Magic Arts (IRE) (Fairy King (USA))
441a[2] 628a[2] 920a[6]
Ponte Di Rosa *Michael Appleby* a44 64
3 b f Avonbridge—Ridgewood Ruby (IRE) (Indian Ridge)
1683[17] 1949[13] 7822[4]
Pontenuovo (FR) *Roger Charlton* 109
3 ch f Green Tune(USA) —Porlezza (FR) (Sicyos (USA))
1404[4] ◆
Ponte Vespucci (FR) *Y De Nicolay* 99
2 b f Anabaa(USA) —Porlezza (FR) (Sicyos (USA))
2866a[2] 4596a[4] 5296a[4]
Ponting (IRE) *Paul Midgley* a59 71
5 gr g Clodovil(IRE) —Polar Lady (Polar Falcon (USA))
150[5] 375[9] 493[6] 545[11]
Pontius Pilate (IRE) *Bryan Smart* 43
2 b g Holy Roman Emperor(IRE) —Shining Creek (CAN) (Bering)
1071[8] 2617[10] 5727[9] 6599[10]
Ponty Acclaim (IRE) *Tim Easterby* 104
2 b f Acclamation—Leopard Creek (Weldnaas (USA))
(1414) 2007[3] 2725[4] (3022) 4094[7] 5216[6] (5592) 6114[6] (6518)
Poole Harbour (IRE) *Richard Hannon* 85
2 b c Elusive City(USA) —Free Lance (IRE) (Grand Lodge (USA))
2049[2] 3793[5]
Pool Of Knowledge (FR) *D De Waele* a79 82
5 gr g Ocean Of Wisdom(USA) —Princess Mix (FR) (Linamix (FR))
219a[0] 439a[9] 533a[9] 903a[0]
Poontoon (IRE) *Richard Fahey* a50
2 gr c Clodovil(IRE) —Tahtheeb (IRE) (Muhtarram (USA))
7540[9] 7783[8]
Poor Prince *Chris Gordon* a65 68
4 b g Royal Applause—Kahira (IRE) (King's Best (USA))
1995[6] 2922[6] 6486[14]
Poosie Nansie (IRE) *George Foster* 27
4 b m Tobougg(IRE) —French Quartet (IRE) (Lycius (USA))
1210[12] 1799[8] 2114[11] 2461[8]
Pope Potter *Richard Guest* 14
3 b g Needwood Blade—Surrealist (ITY) (Night Shift (USA))
2673[13] 2785[5] 6153[10]
Poplin *Luca Cumani* a77 103
3 ch f Medicean—Pongee (Barathea (IRE))
1344[5] 2189[4] 2839[6] 5880[3] 6530[2] 7156a[8]
Poppanan (USA) *Simon Dow* a75 87
5 b g Mr Greeley(USA) —Tiny Decision (USA) (Ogygian (USA))
822[11] 2095[4] 2645[7] 3000[P] (Dead)
Poppet's Joy *Reg Hollinshead* a48 52
3 b f Bertolini(USA) —Our Poppet (IRE) (Warning)
3320[9] 4203[3] 6223[2] 6767[10] 6981[6] 7371[11] 7459[9]
Poppet's Treasure *R Pritchard-Gordon* a84 104
4 b m Dansili—Our Poppet (IRE) (Warning)
2754a[11] 5532a[0]
Poppy *Richard Hannon* a66 64
3 b f Monsieur Bond(IRE) —Niggle (Night Shift (USA))
4991[2] 5624[5] 6456[3] 6700[2] (7093) 7484[5] 7588[3] ◆
Poppy Golightly *Declan Carroll* a60 67
4 ch m Compton Place—Popocatepetl (FR) (Nashwan (USA))
128[4] (280) 555[7] 625[5] 862[7] 5822[12] 6310[3] 6659[3] 7851[3]
Poppy Gregg *Dr Jeremy Naylor* a54 45
6 b m Tamure(IRE) —Opalette (Sharrood (USA))
3281[5] 4488[5] 4951[7]
Poppy Seed *Richard Hannon* 97
4 br m Bold Edge—Opopmil (IRE) (Pips Pride)
1902[3] 2298[9] (2690) 4063[5] 4357[9] 4894[3] 5703[11]
Poppy Socks *Roy Brotherton*
3 b f Superior Premium—Hard To Follow (Dilum (USA))
6307[10]
Poppy's Rocket (IRE) *Marjorie Fife* a54 47
3 b f Iffraaj—Seven Wonders (USA) (Rahy (USA))
182[3] 396[6] 1967[3] 2365[7] 2782[6] 3247[10] 4196[7] 4638[12]
Popular *Sir Henry Cecil* a79
2 b f Oasis Dream—Midsummer (Kingmambo (USA))
7118[4] ◆
Popular Choice *Nick Littmoden* 20
2 ch c Medicean—Stella Marine (FR) (Anabaa (USA))
5479[14]
Porcini *Philip McBride* a56
2 b f Azamour(IRE) —Portal (Hernando (FR))
5691[5] 6506[6]
Porgy *David Simcock* a87 96
6 b g Dansili—Light Ballet (Sadler's Wells (USA))
(32) 209 [3] 849[4] 1412[7] 1892[5] 2285[7] (2686) 2812[4] (3243) 3625[10] 3867[3] 4464[5] 5250[9] 5757[4] 6445[3]
Porthgwidden Beach (USA) *Anthony Middleton* a58 57
3 b f Street Cry(IRE) —Suaviter (USA) (Roar (USA))
595[2] 2660[4] 3223[5] 3635[2] 3785[5] 3914[6] 4547[14] 4657[8] 5215[3] (5941) 6304[10] 6618[11] 6943[4] 7224[10] 7459[10] 7690[5] 7854[5] 7942[9]
Port Hill *Mark Brisbourne* a59 50
4 ch g Deportivo—Hill Farm Dancer (Gunner B)
252[2] 409[2] 644[5] 820[8]
Port Hollow *Charles Hills* a85 74
3 b f Beat Hollow—Maritima (Darshaan)
(4663) 6256[2] ◆
Portovino (FR) *E J O'Neill* a80 59
2 b c Cape Cross(IRE) —Portella (GER) (Protektor (GER))
7326a[5]
Portrait Painter (USA) *Rebecca Curtis* 59
3 ch g Giant's Causeway(USA) —Rhineland (USA) (Mr Prospector (USA))
3135[6]
Port Ronan (USA) *John Wainwright* a18 62
5 rg h Cozzene(USA) —Amber Token (USA) (Hennessy (USA))
2798[5] 3247[2] (3931) (4371) 4678[F]
Portrush Storm *Ray Peacock* a38 43
6 ch m Observatory(USA) —Overcast (IRE) (Caerleon (USA))
7885[12]
Port Star *John Mackie* 19
2 b g Deportivo—Welcome Star (IRE) (Most Welcome)
2672[8]
Pose (IRE) *Roger Ingram* a78 72
4 b m Acclamation—Lyca Ballerina (Marju (IRE))
125[7] 725[10] 3914[7] 4387[14] 4828[2] 5238[5] 6408[3] 6746[6] 7173[8] 7485[5] 7764[7]
Poseidon Grey (IRE) *Walter Swinburn* a79 17
2 gr g Kheleyf(USA) —Elitista (FR) (Linamix (FR))
5632[2] ◆ 5889[14] 6787[3]
Posh Cracker (USA) *G M Lyons* a80 80
3 br f Johannesburg(USA) —Holly's Kid (USA) (Pulpit (USA))
6854a[12]
Position *Sir Mark Prescott Bt* a86 38
2 b g Medicean—Poise (IRE) (Rainbow Quest (USA))
3282[8] (4646) ◆ 5550[6] 6623[2] ◆
Positivity *Bryan Smart* a75 64
5 ch m Monsieur Bond(IRE) —Pretty Pollyanna (General Assembly (USA))
19[2] 291[4] 397[4] 504[2] (675) 870[4] 1814[9] (2237) 2799[4] (3245) (3952)
Possibly *Peter Chapple-Hyam* 59
2 b f Exceed And Excel(AUS) —One Of The Family (Alzao (USA))
3362[11] 3761[5] 4250[2]
Postman *Bryan Smart* a76 71
5 b g Dr Fong(USA) —Mail The Desert (IRE) (Desert Prince (IRE))
287[11] 640[2] 744[2] (870) 1058[6] (1292) 5106[12] 5733[10]
Postscript (IRE) *Ian Williams* a76 75
3 ch g Pivotal—Persian Secret (FR) (Persian Heights)
6324[4] 6830[13] 7416[8]
Postsprofit (IRE) *Mme A-M Verschueren* a71 62
7 b g Marju(IRE) —Housekeeper (IRE) (Common Grounds)
7315a[9]
Potemkin (USA) *David Evans* a36 59
6 bb g Van Nistelrooy(USA) —Bolshoia (USA) (Moscow Ballet (USA))
85[6]
Potentiale (IRE) *J W Hills* a76 80
7 ch g Singspiel(IRE) —No Frills (IRE) (Darshaan)
1144[4] 1450[2] 1834[4] 2436[5] 2958[4] 3533[12] 3760[2] 4660[4] 5509[4] 5582[7] 6461[3] 6789[2] 7036[3] 7458[11] 7756[2]
Pour Moi (IRE) *A Fabre* 123
3 b c Montjeu(IRE) —Gwynn (IRE) (Darshaan)
1265a[3] (1923a) (2715)
Poussette (FR) *F Rossi* a91
4 b m Green Desert(USA) —Berceau (USA) (Alleged (USA))
661a[5]
Pouvoir Absolu *E Lellouche* 116
6 b h Sadler's Wells(USA) —Pine Chip (USA) (Nureyev (USA))
1708a[7] 6661a[2]
Powder Keg *Mark Johnston* 59
3 b c Redoute's Choice(AUS) —Primrose Lane (JPN) (Sunday Silence (USA))
2673[12] 3053[3] 3675[3]
Power *A P O'Brien* 118
2 b c Oasis Dream—Frappe (IRE) (Inchinor)
(2322a) (3012) 4834a[2] (5951a) 6689[2]
Powerball (IRE) *Lisa Williamson*
3 b f Redback—Luceball (IRE) (Bluebird (USA))
7093[11] 7460[10]
Power Broker *Sean Thornton* a16 51
8 b g Mark Of Esteem(IRE) —Galatrix (Be My Guest (USA))
408[12]
Power Force (SAF) *Tom Tate* 82
5 b g Jet Master(SAF) —Opposition (SAF) (Al Mufti (USA))
1382[5] ◆ 2301[9]
Powerful Pierre *Ian McInnes* a68 75
4 ch g Compton Place—Alzianah (Alzao (USA))
625[8] (928) 1239[6] 1558[7] 1748[3] 2487[5] 2799[2] 3071[3] 3245[5] 3612[4] 3880[5] (4078) 4349[17] 5083[7] 5465[11] 5760[12]
Powerful Presence (IRE) *David O'Meara* a87 86
5 ch g Refuse To Bend(IRE) —Miss A Note (USA) (Miswaki (USA))
7[2] (61) ◆ (120) ◆ 181[2] (2671) ◆ (3629) ◆ 4349[2] 4561[5] 5383[5] 6290[9] 6708[11] 7074[2] 7243[2] 7339[4]
Powerful Ruler (NZ) *B Dean* 107
6 b g Viking Ruler(AUS) —Capsimation (NZ) (Kaapstad (NZ))
2339a[5]
Powerful Wind (IRE) *Ronald Harris* a76 86
2 ch c Titus Livius(FR) —Queen Of Fools (IRE) (Xaar)
1360[13] 1583[6] (2173) 2437[5] 3745[6] (3800) 4228[2] 4413[12] (4460) 5237[3] (5348) 6114[8]
Power Punch (IRE) *B W Hills* 81
3 b c Medicean—Peneia (USA) (Nureyev (USA))
1971[3] (2802) 3378[8]
Poyle Judy *Ralph Beckett* a73 79
3 b f Iceman—Poyle Jenny (Piccolo)
2313[10] 3390[6] 3782[5] 4448[8] (4949) (5376) 5856[DSQ] (6576)
Poyle Punch *Ralph Beckett* a82 80
3 ch g Sleeping Indian—Poyle Amber (Sharrood (USA))
1179[3] 1580[3] (2174) 3178[5] (6944)
Poyle Todream *Ralph Beckett* a22 52
3 b c Oasis Dream—Lost In Lucca (Inchinor)
1606[12] 2103[16] 4706[6] 5540[11] 6084[10]
Pozyc (FR) *W P Mullins* a80 84
5 b g Polish Summer—Zycia (IRE) (Bishop Of Cashel)
7322a[2]
Pragmatist *Rod Millman* a64 67
7 b m Piccolo—Shi Shi (Alnasr Alwasheek)
143[6] 303[5]
Praha (IRE) *J-C Sarais* 41
5 b m Marchand De Sable(USA) —Sue Generoos (IRE) (Spectrum (IRE))
706a[10]
Prairie Star (FR) *E Lellouche* 112
3 b c Peintre Celebre(USA) —Prairie Runner (IRE) (Arazi (USA))
1265a[2] (2136a) 2751a[6]
Prairie Stella (GER) *M Weiss* 18
3 ch f Black Sam Bellamy(IRE) —Prairie Scilla (GER) (Dashing Blade)
5307a[13]
Prakasa (FR) *Markus Klug* 101
4 b m Areion(GER) —Pepples Beach (GER) (Lomitas)
6370a[5]
Pralin (FR) *Mme L Audon* 75
8 b g Thames(FR) —Pralyse (FR) (Highest Honor (FR))
439a[0]
Prana (USA) *Jeremy Gask* a30 39
3 b f Proud Citizen(USA) —Javana (USA) (Sandpit (BRZ))
4102[7] 4970[10] 5633[11] 6411[12]
Pravda Street *Brian Ellison* a79 93
6 ch g Soviet Star(USA) —Sari (Faustus (USA))
(2732) (3113) 3276[13] 4314[4] 5852[13] 6542[2]
Praxios *Luca Cumani* a71 69
3 b g Val Royal(FR) —Forest Fire (SWE) (Never So Bold)
1298[3] ◆ 1947[8]
Praxiteles (IRE) *Rebecca Curtis* a91 87
7 b g Sadler's Wells(USA) —Hellenic (Darshaan)
3277[7] (3725) (3911) 4398a[15] 4998[9]
Pray From Heaven (IRE) *Sandor Kovacs* 69
3 b f Shirocco(GER) —Power Girl (GER) (Dashing Blade)
1597a[9]
Prebends Bridge *Howard Johnson*
2 b g Antonius Pius(USA) —Golden Topaz (IRE) (Almutawakel)
2784[7]
Pre Catalan *Ed Dunlop* a55
2 b f Oasis Dream—Place De L'Opera (Sadler's Wells (USA))
6215[10] 6440[11] 7082[14] 7697[10]
Precedence (NZ) *Bart Cummings* 120
6 b g Zabeel(NZ) —Kowtow (USA) (Shadeed (USA))
6886a[10] 7218a[11]
Precious Dream (USA) *David Wachman* 75
2 ch f Mr Greeley(USA) —Lady Carla (Caerleon (USA))
2532a[3]
Precious Little *David Nicholls* 13
2 b f Milk It Mick—Capital Lass (Forzando)
3611[8] 3932[10] 5105[8]
Precision Break (USA) *David Simcock* a98 103
6 b g Silver Deputy(CAN) —Miss Kitty Cat (USA) (Tabasco Cat (USA))
5271[9] 5883[7] 6271[6] 7226[4] 7584[5]
Precocious Kid (IRE) *Chris Wall* a64
3 b g Whipper(USA) —Valley Lights (IRE) (Dance Of Life (USA))
953[2] ◆ 1288[3] 3710[4]
Premature *Dean Ivory* 33
2 ch f Needwood Blade—Ivory's Joy (Tina's Pet)
2153[10]
Premier Choice *Tim Easterby* 72
2 b g Exceed And Excel(AUS) —Simply Times (USA) (Dodge (USA))
3082[8] 4436[2] 5254[13] 5618[8] 6836[7]
Premier League *Julia Feilden* a68 46
4 b g Firebreak—Lizzie Simmonds (IRE) (Common Grounds)
545[2] 690[3] 798[2] 853[6] 1453[7] (2655) 3261[7] 3711[7] 4182[3] 5600[4] 6258[7]
Premier Violon (IRE) *Mlle C Cardenne* a65 77
8 gr g Highest Honor(FR) —Page Bleue (Sadler's Wells (USA))
843a[8] 1013a[0]
Premio Loco (USA) *Chris Wall* a108 121
7 ch g Prized(USA) —Crazee Mental (Magic Ring (IRE))
997a[4] 2101[3] 2713[7] 4972[6] 5473[5] (5930) 6298[2] 6693[7]
Premium Coffee *Joseph Tuite* a36 77
3 b g Superior Premium—Coffee Ice (Primo Dominie)
2926[8] 4156[10] 5718[10] 6056[9]
Prepared *Mahmood Al Zarooni* 72
2 ch c More Than Ready(USA) —Mannington (AUS) (Danehill (USA))
4330[9] 5454[3]
Presburg (IRE) *Joseph Tuite* a76 76
2 b g Balmont(USA) —Eschasse (USA) (Zilzal (USA))
4968[2] 5855[2] (6506)
Present Danger *Tom Dascombe* a86 86
3 b f Cadeaux Genereux—Lighthouse (Warning)
4670[2] ◆ 5164[2] 6062[8] 7054[6] (7334) 7509a[6]
Present Day *Clive Cox* 58
2 gr f Cadeaux Genereux—Crackle (Anshan)
6745[4]
Present Laughter *Ron Hodges*
3 b f Cadeaux Genereux—Darmagi (IRE) (Desert King (IRE))
3090[12] 3689[8]
Present Story *Gary Harrison* a63 60
4 b m Lucky Story(USA) —Aziz Presenting (IRE) (Charnwood Forest (IRE))
3042[12] 4154[7] 4448[6] 4645[2] 4916[6] 5428[4] 5673[10] 5912[10]
President Lincoln (USA) *A P O'Brien* a78 83
3 b c First Samurai(USA) —Preach (USA) (Mr Prospector (USA))
1706a[7]
Presque Perdre *George Moore* 53
7 ch g Desert Prince(IRE) —Kindle (Selkirk (USA))
6988[18]
Press Baron *J W Hills* a77 77
2 ch c King's Best(USA) —Esteraad (IRE) (Cadeaux Genereux)
7133[4] (7368)
Pressbuttonb *Giles Bravery*
4 b g Lomitas—Gena Ivor (USA) (Sir Ivor (USA))
3173[11]
Press Office (USA) *Mahmood Al Zarooni* a81 69
3 bb c Street Cry(IRE) —Call Her (USA) (Caller I.D. (USA))
2469[6] 6085[2] 6473[6]
Press The Button (GER) *Jim Boyle* a102 61
8 b g Dansili—Play Around (IRE) (Niniski (USA))
2716[13]
Press To Reset *Bill Turner* a17 10
4 b g Reset(AUS) —Lady De Londres (Mtoto)
2638[7]
Pressure Drop (IRE) *Jo Hughes* 68
2 b f Desert Style(IRE) —Easy Going (Hamas (IRE))
(2992) 3435[5] 3993[7]
Presumably (IRE) *Robert Collet* a75
4 b m Soviet Star(USA) —Presumed (USA) (Dynaformer (USA))
1011a[3]
Presvis *Luca Cumani* a113 123
7 b g Sakhee(USA) —Forest Fire (SWE) (Never So Bold)
(331a) 759a[3] (1000a) 1576a[6] 2340a[10]

Pretty Diamond (IRE) *Mark Johnston* a59 75
3 ch f Hurricane Run(IRE) —Cheal Rose (IRE) (Dr Devious (IRE))
(1170) 1442[2] 1623[2] 2407[2] 4515[5] 5307a[7]

Pretty Pebble (IRE) *Brian Meehan* 72
2 b f Cape Cross(IRE) —Diamond Light (USA) (Fantastic Light (USA))
5299[6] ◆ 6030[6] (6480) 7169[11]

Priceless Art (IRE) *Alan Swinbank* a78
6 b g Anabaa(USA) —My Ballerina (USA) (Sir Ivor (USA))
7503[2] (7774) 7900[4]

Priceless Jewel *Roger Charlton* 78
2 b f Selkirk(USA) —My Branch (Distant Relative)
6751[7] (6992)

Price Of Retrieval *Peter Chapple-Hyam* a38 46
4 b g Red Ransom(USA) —Rise (Polar Falcon (USA))
1605[12] 3543[13] 4023[5] *5642[8]*

Prices Lane *Michael Easterby* 54
4 b m Gentleman's Deal(IRE) —Prime Property (IRE) (Tirol)
2802[7] 3167[9] 3577[10] 4150[7] *4651[7]* 4987[9]

Prickles *Derek Shaw* a54 54
6 ch m Karinga Bay—Squeaky (Infantry)
114[2] 252[5] 6029[12] *6287[11] 6356[3] 6876[5]* 7087[5]

Pride And Joy (IRE) *Jamie Osborne* a82 88
2 b c Dark Angel(IRE) —Fey Rouge (IRE) (Fayruz)
2017[2] 2559[4] 3012[18] (3673) 4496[5] *(4867)* (5280) 5931[6] 6372[3]

Pride Of Mine *J R Jenkins* a41 35
8 b m Kayf Tara—Triple Zee (USA) (Zilzal (USA))
448[6] 643[4] 4805[9]

Prideus (IRE) *Brian Storey* 87
7 gr g Atticus(USA) —Pride Of Baino (USA) (Secretariat (USA))
3316[10]

Priest Field (IRE) *Pam Ford* a46 58
7 ch g Daggers Drawn(USA) —Masakira (IRE) (Royal Academy (USA))
6287[10]

Priestley's Reward (IRE) *Mrs K Burke* a67 65
2 b g Whipper(USA) —Prima Figlia (IRE) (Inchinor)
2056[3] 2455[9] 3186[7] 4667[2] ◆ 6260[10] 6807[6] *7035[2] (7117)*

Prigsnov Dancer (IRE) *Owen Brennan* a10 43
6 ch g Namid—Brave Dance (IRE) (Kris)
401[12]

Primaeval *James Fanshawe* a107 96
5 ch g Pivotal—Langoustine (AUS) (Danehill (USA))
2020[3] 2470[13] 3797[4] 4802[7] *(4993) 5712[4]* 6496[2] 6862[2] *(7433)*

Prim By Night *Richard Fahey* a30
2 b f Byron—Miss Prim (Case Law)
7555[8] 7724[6]

Prime Circle *Alan Brown* a58 69
5 b g Green Desert(USA) —First Of Many (Darshaan)
2589[11] 2799[10] 3088[6] 3317[13] *5214[6] 5944[7]* 6264[11] *(6494) 6659[2] 7006[11]*

Prime Cut (USA) *Neil J Howard* a106
3 b c Bernstein(USA) —Life Happened (USA) (Stravinsky (USA))
2950a[11]

Prime Defender *Charles Hills* a104 116
7 ch h Bertolini(USA) —Arian Da (Superlative)
1093[7] 1340[6] 1720[10] 2005[11] 3155[20] 3626[5] (4526) 5264[5] 6858[7] 7298[9]

Prime Exhibit *Richard Fahey* a106 96
6 b g Selkirk(USA) —First Exhibit (Machiavellian (USA))
846[3] ◆ 1094[12] 1406[20] 5218[4] 5684[2] ◆ 6145[8] 6672[9] 7295[5]

Prime Mover *Ed Dunlop* a71 74
3 ch g Motivator—Dream Quest (Rainbow Quest (USA))
993[4] 1328[3] *1759[7]* 2885[10] 4148[5] 4916[8]

Prime Preacher (USA) *X Thomas-Demeaulte* a70 56
3 b g Pulpit(USA) —Flashy Attraction (USA) (Fappiano (USA))
5529a[0]

Primera Rossa *J S Moore* a45 35
5 ch m Needwood Blade—Meandering Rose (USA) (Irish River (FR))
207[9] 419[5] 1473[7] 1635[5] 2140[8]

Primera Vista *Mario Hofer* a72 100
5 b g Haafhd—Colorvista (Shirley Heights)
6783a[3]

Prime Spirit (IRE) *X Thomas-Demeaulte* a92 89
5 b g Invincible Spirit(IRE) —Turtulla (IRE) (Night Shift (USA))
(6958a)

Primevere (IRE) *Roger Charlton* a87 107
3 ch f Singspiel(IRE) —Tree Peony (Woodman (USA))
1722[4] ◆ 2073[4] 3648[2] 4265[2] (4915) 5523a[9]

Primo De Vida (IRE) *Jim Boyle* a78 68
4 b g Trade Fair—Rampage (Pivotal)
249[11] 313[3] (389) 521[2] 612[12] 1562[8] 1838[6] 2609[4] 2903[10] *3517[8]*

Primo Lady *Gay Kelleway* a76 91
3 br f Lucky Story(USA) —Lady Natilda (First Trump)
1688[13] 2102[5] 2615[6] 3549[2] 4235[3] 5016[7] 5581[9] *6256[10]*

Primo Muscovado *Michael Mullineaux* a13
3 b c Primo Valentino(IRE) —Sugar Cube Treat (Lugana Beach)
6700[9]

Primo Paco (FR) *M Boutin* 56
2 ch g Soave(GER) —Miss Margaux (FR) (Script Ohio (USA))
7312a[9]

Primo Way *Donal Nolan* a76 48
10 b g Primo Dominie—Waypoint (Cadeaux Genereux)
1714[11]

Prince Alzain (USA) *Gerard Butler* a89 77
2 b c Street Sense(USA) —Monaassabaat (USA) (Zilzal (USA))
6216[3] 6588[4] *(7493) (7879)*

Prince Apollo *Gerard Butler* a77 80
6 b g Dansili—Mooring (Zafonic (USA))
(814) 1075[6] (1353) 1746[3] 2124[4] 2810[2] *3286[6]* 3701[11]

Prince Ayoob *John Best*
3 b g Noverre(USA) —Santiburi Girl (Casteddu)
5169[9]

Prince Bishop (IRE) *Saeed Bin Suroor* a112 118
4 ch g Dubawi(IRE) —North East Bay (USA) (Prospect Bay (CAN))
758a[5] 1002a[10] 5494[8] 5921[6] *(7226)*

Prince Blue *John E Long* a56 57
4 b g Doyen(IRE) —Dixie D'Oats (Alhijaz)
688[3] 819[4] 1025[3] 2820[6] 3047[10] (4847) *5642[3] 6622[5] 7121[9] 7603[5]* 7892[4]

Prince Chaparral (IRE) *Patrick J Flynn* a92 92
5 b g High Chaparral(IRE) —Eilanden (IRE) (Akarad (FR))
6513a[3] 7322a[15]

Prince Charlemagne (IRE) *Dr Jeremy Naylor* a74 48
8 br g King Charlemagne(USA) —Ciubanga (IRE) (Arazi (USA))
272[7] 457[6] 622[2] 768[3] 838[5] 1181[6] 2140[6] 4974[7] *6087[7]*

Prince Freddie *Philip Kirby* 74
3 b g Red Ransom(USA) —Pitcroy (Unfuwain (USA))
1170[2] 1456[2] 2076[12] 3364[9]

Prince Gabrial (IRE) *David Nicholls* 33
2 b g Moss Vale(IRE) —Baileys Cream (Mister Baileys)
2907[9]

Prince Golan (IRE) *Richard Price* a54 66
7 b g Golan(IRE) —Mohican Princess (Shirley Heights)
526[7] 692[6] 711[5] 5994[6] *7912[6]*

Prince James *Michael Easterby* a76 58
4 b g Danroad(AUS) —Lawless Bridget (Alnasr Alwasheek)
136[6] ◆ *144[7] 403[6] 673[10] 833[8] 934[11]* 1034[7] 6266[2] *(7040) (7395)* 7535[10]

Princely Sum (IRE) *Sir Michael Stoute* 68
2 b c Refuse To Bend(IRE) —Green Dollar (IRE) (Kingmambo (USA))
6983[5]

Prince Namid *Jonathen de Giles* a70 43
9 b g Namid—Fen Princess (IRE) (Trojan Fen)
1045[4] 2155[9]

Prince Of Burma (IRE) *Jeremy Gask* a82 83
3 b c Mujadil(USA) —Spinning Ruby (Pivotal)
2215[2] ◆ *2607[7]* 3557[5] 7171[8] ◆ *7439[4]* ◆ *7660[7] 7841[7]*

Prince Of Dance *Tom Tate* a76 100
5 b g Danehill Dancer(IRE) —Princess Ellen (Tirol)
846[10] 1094[16] 1410[6] 2390[9] 2814[4] 3315[2] 5059[17]

Prince Of Fashion (IRE) *John Geoghegan* a75 73
4 b g Desert Prince(IRE) —Fully Fashioned (IRE) (Brief Truce (USA))
7548a[2] ◆

Prince Of Johanne (IRE) *Tom Tate* a42 101
5 gr g Johannesburg(USA) —Paiute Princess (FR) (Darshaan)
(1390) (1879) 2573[2] 4410[5] 5853[4] (6339)

Prince Of Orange (IRE) *Mahmood Al Zarooni* 77
2 b c Shamardal(USA) —Cox Orange (USA) (Trempolino (USA))
6267[5] ◆

Prince Of Passion (CAN) *Derek Shaw* a63 66
3 ch g Roman Ruler(USA) —Rare Passion (CAN) (Out Of Place (USA))
1084[4] 1693[3] 2264[8] 2675[7] 3318[4] 3729[6] 4149[4] 4431[3] *4994[7] 5381[2]* ◆ 6033[4] *6181[10]* (6609) *6847[4]* 7057[10] *7208[7]*

Princeofperfection *Bruce Hellier* a7
2 b g Tobougg(IRE) —Princess Perfect (IRE) (Danehill Dancer (IRE))
7590[7]

Prince Of Sorrento *John Akehurst* a76 77
4 ch g Doyen(IRE) —Princess Galadriel (Magic Ring (IRE))
2207[5] (2771) 2999[4] ◆ 3468[9] 3825[17] 5002[14] 5495[5] 5894[10]

Prince Of Thebes (IRE) *Michael Attwater* a79 73
10 b g Desert Prince(IRE) —Persian Walk (FR) (Persian Bold)
310[6] 806[9] 1026[2] 1333[6] 1637[4] 2561[11] 3468[8] 3677[5] 4444[13] 4754[6] *5042[4] 5643[4]* 6358[5] 6811[3] 6969[3] 7387[4] 7522[5] 7640[2] (7892)

Prince Of Vasa (IRE) *Michael Smith* a62 81
4 b g Kheleyf(USA) —Suzy Street (IRE) (Dancing Dissident (USA))
1438[8] 1618[7] 1943[2] 2494[7] 2631[2] 3036[7] 3359[9] 4016[3] 5162[6] 6261[6] 7079[4] 7216[14] *7355[8] 7500[7] 7641[3]* 7857[6]

Prince Rhyddarch *Michael Dods* a18 63
6 b g Josr Algarhoud(IRE) —Nova Zembla (Young Ern)
1216[3] 2401[3] 2548[4] (2804) 3041[5] 5405[5]

Prince Samos (IRE) *Clive Mulhall* a28 76
9 b g Mujadil(USA) —Sabaniya (FR) (Lashkari)
675[11]

Prince Shaun (IRE) *Richard Guest* a107 86
6 b g Acclamation—Style Parade (USA) (Diesis)
236[10] 415a[10] *756a[10]* 4428[14] 5887[15]

Prince Siegfried (FR) *Saeed Bin Suroor* a89 116
5 b g Royal Applause—Intrum Morshaan (IRE) (Darshaan)
2290[6] 3591[8] (4456) (5494) 6247[5]

Princess Alessia *Terry Clement* a56 60
2 b f Byron—Break Of Dawn (USA) (Mt. Livermore (USA))
2880[10] 3388[3] *4548[5]* 6590[8] *7452[4]*

Princess Banu *Mick Channon* a60 80
2 b f Oasis Dream—Paradise Isle (Bahamian Bounty)
1199[4] (1337) 2070[8] 2429[2] 2712[5] 3458[2] 4094[25] 4551[11] 5427[4] *5833[7]* 5913[4] 6058[8] *6695[4]* 7059[3] 7231[3]

Princess Caetani (IRE) *Mark Johnston* 64
2 b f Dylan Thomas(IRE) —Caladira (IRE) (Darshaan)
5454[7] 5807[6] 6526[10]

Princess Dayna *Tom Dascombe* a72 60
3 b f Green Desert(USA) —Pilcomayo (IRE) (Rahy (USA))
66[5] (183) 452[6] 5215[7] 5600[7] (6999) (7071) 7268[8] 7629[5] 7876[7] 7919[2]

Princesse Fleur *Michael Scudamore* 59
3 b f Grape Tree Road—Princesse Grec (FR) (Grand Tresor (FR))
2528[8] 2871[7] 3587[6] 4274[2]

Princesse Gaelle *Marco Botti* a72
3 b f Osorio(GER) —Gaelic Queen (IRE) (Fairy King (USA))
3043[11] 3469[3] 3925[3] ◆ *4664[3] 6311[12]*

Princess Gail *Mark Brisbourne* a62 54
3 b f Ad Valorem(USA) —First Musical (First Trump)
(281) 426[5] 1082[5] 1472[5] 1952[6] 2351[6] *3226[4]* (3913) 4284[7] 4627[4] 5515[6] *5898[6] 6545[4] (6657)* 7005[2] 7198[3] 7399[6] 7610[8]

Princess Icicle *Jo Crowley* a75
3 b f Iceman—Sarabah (IRE) (Ela-Mana-Mou)
4663[10] (5639) 7208[2]

Princess Kaiulani (IRE) *William Muir* a49
2 b f Royal Applause—Scottish Exile (IRE) (Ashkalani (IRE))
6654[7] 7038[7] 7194[5] 7539[5] 7657[4] 7809[5]

Princess Lexi (IRE) *William Knight* a62 75
4 ch m Rock Of Gibraltar(IRE) —Etaaq (IRE) (Sadler's Wells (USA))
26[12] 201[2] 354[3] 598[12] (1355) (1637) 2232[10] 2912[11] (3202) 3338[6] *7228[4]* ◆ *7524[7] 7904[4]*

Princess Maya *Jo Crowley* a60 66
2 b f Royal Applause—Secret Blend (Pivotal)
6165[6] 6745[7] *7225[5] 7838[6]*

Princess Neenee (IRE) *Paul Green* 17
4 b m King's Best(USA) —Precedence (IRE) (Polish Precedent (USA))
4123[10]

Princess Of Orange *Rae Guest* a63 81
2 ch f Dutch Art—Radiate (Sadler's Wells (USA))
4614[6] *5411[2]* (5812) 6146[9]

Princess Of Rock *Richard Hannon* 22
2 ch f Rock Of Gibraltar(IRE) —Principessa (Machiavellian (USA))
5048[7]

Princess Palmer *Hugo Palmer* a49 49
2 b f Iceman—Tapas En Bal (FR) (Mille Balles (FR))
2227[5] 5854[5] *6281[5] 6842[10]*

Princess Runner *Des Donovan* a39
4 b m Doyen(IRE) —Stop Press (USA) (Sharpen Up)
6947[7] 7254[6] 7528[8]

Princess Severus (IRE) *Mrs John Harrington* a88 92
3 b f Barathea(IRE) —Wildsplash (USA) (Deputy Minister (CAN))
924a[6] *6854a[13] 7792a[14]*

Princess Sinead (IRE) *Mrs John Harrington* 104
2 bb f Jeremy(USA) —Princess Atoosa (USA) (Gone West (USA))
2777a[2] 5525a[5] 6389a[3]

Princess Spirit *Edward Creighton*
2 b f Invincible Spirit(IRE) —Habariya (IRE) (Perugino (USA))
6954[11]

Princess Tamina (IRE) *Mark Brisbourne* a48 12
2 bb f Strategic Prince—Taffeta And Tulle (IRE) (Lend A Hand)
2504[10] 5337[12] *7559[9] 7697[8]*

Princess Theophane (IRE) *Liam McAteer* a51 23
3 b f Holy Roman Emperor(IRE) —Eadaoin (USA) (King Of Kings (IRE))
973a[7]

Princess Vati (FR) *S Wattel* a65
2 ch f Vatori(FR) —Reine De Vati (FR) (Take Risks (FR))
7665a[9]

Princess Willow *John E Long* a52 60
3 b f Phoenix Reach(IRE) —Highland Hannah (IRE) (Persian Heights)
4320[8] *4991[3]* 5810[2] *6784[9] 7096[7]*

Princess Zahra (IRE) *S Demiral* 94
4 b m Oratorio(IRE) —Dablana (IRE) (Dr Fong (USA))
5753a[8]

Prince Titus (IRE) *Linda Stubbs* a33 60
3 b g Titus Livius(FR) —Lovere (St Jovite (USA))
182[6] 1860[4] 2396[14]

Princeton Girl *Tim Easterby* a28
3 br f Compton Place—Halland Park Girl (IRE) (Primo Dominie)
669[7] 1038[12]

Prince Valentine *Gary Moore* a56 53
10 b g My Best Valentine—Affaire De Coeur (Imperial Fling (USA))
2171[7] 3253[10]

Prince Verde (FR) *P Demercastel* a80 84
3 b g Vatori(FR) —Alba Verde (FR) (Midyan (USA))
410a[2]

Principal Role (USA) *Sir Henry Cecil* 114
4 b m Empire Maker(USA) —Interim (Sadler's Wells (USA))
2290[3] (3356) 4533[3] 5494[7] (6066) (6530) 7296[2]

Print (IRE) *Mlle M Henry* a75 54
5 b g Exceed And Excel(AUS) —Hariya (IRE) (Shernazar)
5195a[9]

Printmaker (IRE) *G M Lyons* a82 89
3 b g Shamardal(USA) —Marie Laurencin (Peintre Celebre (USA))
5090a[9]

Prinzde Glas (IRE) *E Danel* 100
4 gr g Verglas(IRE) —Bellacoola (GER) (Lomitas)
4739a[0]

Priomhbhean (IRE) *J S Bolger* a96 96
4 ch m Galileo(IRE) —Tropical Lake (IRE) (Lomond (USA))
3695a[8]

Priority Buy (IRE) *James McAuley* a61
4 br g Marju(IRE) —Lady Singspiel (IRE) (Singspiel (IRE))
816[5]

Priors Gold *Gordon Elliott* a84 76
4 ch g Sakhee(USA) —Complimentary Pass (Danehill (USA))
(7536) 7570[2] 7818[4]

Private Equity (IRE) *William Jarvis* a63 57
5 b m Haafhd—Profit Alert (IRE) (Alzao (USA))
223[4] 444[3] 622[5] 1310[6] 1959[3]

Private Eye (FR) *E Libaud* a85 103
3 b f American Post—Rose Of Tralee (FR) (Kendor (FR))
5230a[7] 5958a[5] 7156a[3] 7510a[3]

Private Jet (FR) *H-A Pantall* 104
3 gr c Aussie Rules(USA) —Norwegian Princess (IRE) (Fairy King (USA))
1552a[7] 6556a[10]

Private Joke *Terry Clement* a73 63
4 b g Oasis Dream—Wink (Salse (USA))
1460[6] 3361[14] *3952[9]* 5422[8]

Private Olley *Harry Dunlop* a70 42
4 ch g Exceed And Excel(AUS) —My Daisychain (Hector Protector (USA))
2605[11] 3216[10] 4086[11] *4759[8]*

Private Riviera *C Boutin* 94
2 gr f Stormy River(FR) —Private Dancer (FR) (Green Tune (USA))
5130a[4] 5365a[4] 5770a[7]

Private Story (USA) *Tim Vaughan* 100
4 b g Yes It's True(USA) —Said Privately (USA) (Private Account (USA))
3013[13]

Prizefighting (USA) *Mahmood Al Zarooni* a109 105
4 ch h Smart Strike(CAN) —Allencat (USA) (Storm Cat (USA))
153a[3] 328a[2] 585a[3] 677a[3] 824a[4]

Prize Point *Jim Boyle* a73 67
5 ch g Bahamian Bounty—Golden Symbol (Wolfhound (USA))
143[9] 178[2] 264[10] (336) 612[10]

Proceed Bee (USA) *Scott Becker* a105 107
5 b g Bernstein(USA) —Procession (USA) (Private Terms (USA))
5074a[8]

Procrastination *A Fabre* a84 106
3 b f Pivotal—Dilly Dally (AUS) (Rubiton (AUS))
5028a[7] 6809a[2]

Prodigality *Ronald Harris* a66
3 ch g Pivotal—Lady Bountiful (Spectrum (IRE))
(7717) 7842[4]

Producer *Richard Hannon* 97
2 ch c Dutch Art—River Saint (USA) (Irish River (FR))
4053[6] (4455) ◆ (5577) ◆ (6372) 7026[4]

Professor John (IRE) *Ian Wood* a70 63
4 b g Haafhd—Dancing Flower (IRE) (Compton Place)
124[2] 352[3] 381[8] 621[4] 728[6] 1454[6] 1871[2] 2308[11] 2851[7] 3637[9] 3945[2] 4242[8] 4746[3] 5135[2] (5642) 6005[11]

Professor Tim (IRE) *Patrick Morris* 27
2 gr g Verglas(IRE) —Cool Chron (Polar Falcon (USA))
3452[6] *3707[6]* 4377[7] 5535[10]

Profile Star (IRE) *David Barron* a79 78
2 b g Kodiac—Fingal Nights (IRE) (Night Shift (USA))
1071[5] 1383[6] (1691) 2007[10] 3879[4] 4094[19] 7103[6] *(7364) 7918[2]*

Profit's Reality (IRE) *Michael Attwater* a75 80
9 br g Key Of Luck(USA) —Teacher Preacher (IRE) (Taufan (USA))
374[4] 697[4] 808[4] 962[4] 1046[8] (1956) 2526[14]

Profligate (IRE) *William Jarvis* a71 68
4 b m Soviet Star(USA) —Profit Alert (IRE) (Alzao (USA))
45[4] 303[6]

Profondo Rosso (IRE) *Sir Michael Stoute* a62 84
3 b g Red Ransom(USA) —Desert Beauty (IRE) (Green Desert (USA))
1903[5] 2877[3] 3231[3]

Prohibit *Robert Cowell* a107 121
6 b g Oasis Dream—Well Warned (Warning)
414a[8] (500a) 754a[4] 996a[5] 1687[9] 2138a[4] 2297[3] 2754a[2] (3010) 5253[3] (5985a) 6563a[7]

Prohibition (IRE) *Alastair Lidderdale* a64 79
5 b g Danehill Dancer(IRE) —Crumpetsfortea (IRE) (Henbit (USA))
248[11] 361[3] 489[3] 727[14] 1353[5] 4215[9] 4948[9] 5002[15]

Promenadia *Roger Charlton* 79
3 b f Beat Hollow—Esplanade (Danehill (USA))
1565[5] 2368[7]

Promised Wings (GER) *Chris Gordon* a27 44
4 ch g Monsun(GER) —Panagia (USA) (Diesis)
271[9] 6121[9]

Prompter *Michael Bell* 109
4 b g Motivator—Penny Cross (Efisio)
1112[3] 2681[11] 3156[7] 4354[7] 5250[3]

Pronounce *Michael Appleby* a29
3 b g Denounce—Ivy Bridge (IRE) (Namid)
4370[12] *5598[7] 5900[9] 6845[11] 7354[10]*

Proof (IRE) *Mahmood Al Zarooni* 66
3 b g Monsun(GER) —Foolish Act (IRE) (Sadler's Wells (USA))
3001[7] 3430[7]

Proper Charlie *William Knight* 69
3 b g Cadeaux Genereux—Ring Of Love (Magic Ring (IRE))
1984[3] 2391[6] 2875[5] 3536[5] 4709[3]

Prophet In A Dream *Paddy Butler* a73 73
3 b g Fath(USA) —Princess Dariyba (IRE) (Victory Note (USA))
1983^{4} 2383^{4} 2841^{7} 3337^{12} 3638^{3} 4247^{4} 4744^{5} 5172^{6} 5423^{5} 6813^{12} 6929^{11}
Proponent (IRE) *Roger Charlton* a91 106
7 b g Peintre Celebre(USA) —Pont Audemer (USA) (Chief's Crown (USA))
1406^{4} 1684^{2} 3032^{19} 4494^{2} 6339^{3}
Propriano (FR) *M Boutin* a69 66
3 b c Panis(USA) —Paola (FR) (Fabulous Dancer (USA))
$660a^{8}$
Prorisks (FR) *C Boutin* a63 71
5 gr g Take Risks(FR) —Prostar (FR) (Procida (USA))
$2867a^{0}$ $6959a^{6}$
Prospective (USA) *Mark Casse* a99
3 bb c Malibu Moon(USA) —Spirited Away (USA) (Awesome Again (CAN))
$7306a^{13}$
Prospectorous (IRE) *J P Dempsey* a91 80
7 b g Monashee Mountain(USA) —Nocturne In March (IRE) (Dolphin Street (FR))
$4398a^{13}$
Prospect Wells (FR) *Howard Johnson* 107
6 b g Sadler's Wells(USA) —Brooklyn's Dance (FR) (Shirley Heights)
2316^{4} 3396^{10}
Protanto (IRE) *David Lanigan* a79 66
2 b g Lawman(FR) —Incoming Call (USA) (Red Ransom (USA))
4330^{8} 6064^{4} 7126^{2}
Protaras (USA) *Sir Henry Cecil* 86
4 bb g Lemon Drop Kid(USA) —Seven Moons (JPN) (Sunday Silence (USA))
5057^{3} (5629) 5963^{2} 6333^{12}
Protect *Sir Michael Stoute* 75
2 b f Nayef(USA) —Top Romance (IRE) (Entrepreneur)
3182^{5} 4061^{6} 5806^{2} 6933^{3}
Protractor (IRE) *B W Hills* a68 76
3 b c Galileo(IRE) —Comeraincomeshine (IRE) (Night Shift (USA))
(888) 2064^{5} 3740^{9} 4751^{4}
Proud Chieftain *Clifford Lines* a92 88
3 b g Sleeping Indian—Skimra (Hernando (FR))
2924^{5} 3361^{3} (4060) (4763) (7204) 7391^{7}
Proud Pearl (USA) *Brian Meehan* a65 72
2 b f Proud Citizen(USA) —Pacific Spell (USA) (Langfuhr (CAN))
2811^{4} ◆ 3362^{6} 6440^{6} 6950^{7}
Proud Times (USA) *Alan Swinbank* a91 90
5 b g Proud Citizen(USA) —Laura's Pistolette (USA) (Big Pistol (USA))
1470^{6}
Provost *Michael Easterby* a66 57
7 ch g Danehill Dancer(IRE) —Dixielake (IRE) (Lake Coniston (IRE))
526^{5} 712^{7}
Proximity *Sir Michael Stoute* 52
2 b f Nayef(USA) —Contiguous (USA) (Danzig (USA))
7164^{11}
Prussian Officer (AUS) *Steve Richards* 98
6 b g King Of Prussia(AUS) —Let's Remember (AUS) (Almaarad)
$6711a^{10}$
Psalm Twentythree *Ian Semple* 25
5 b g Josr Algarhoud(IRE) —Cadeau Speciale (Cadeaux Genereux)
2807^{5}
Psi (USA) *Gary Moore* 87
6 b g Hernando(FR) —Visions Of Clarity (IRE) (Sadler's Wells (USA))
2190^{7}
Psireve (FR) *J-M Capitte* 98
3 gr f Ansis—[illegible] (FR) [illegible] (FR))
$7156a^{6}$ $7510a^{10}$
Psychic Ability (USA) *Saeed Bin Suroor* a101 105
4 br g Kingmambo(USA) —Speed Of Thought (USA) (Broad Brush (USA))
$330a^{7}$ (581a) $829a^{5}$
Psychic's Dream *Marco Botti* a74 83
3 b f Oasis Dream—Psychic (IRE) (Alhaarth (IRE))
1607^{2} 2643^{4} (3079) 3819^{10} 4797^{4} 5018^{2} 6974^{4} 7457^{8}
Ptolemaic *Bryan Smart* 94
2 b c Excellent Art—Pompey Girl (Rainbow Quest (USA))
3302^{4} 3826^{10} (6380) 6914^{2}
Ptolomeos *Sean Regan* a43 60
8 b g Kayf Tara—Lucy Tufty (Vin St Benet)
4112^{8} 5405^{11} 5823^{12} 7113^{8} 7885^{10}
Public Image *Jamie Poulton* a49 29
5 b m Bahamian Bounty—Shouting The Odds (IRE) (Victory Note (USA))
50^{8} 631^{12} 761^{4} 2756^{10}
Pucon *Roger Teal* a68
2 b f Kyllachy—The Fugative (Nicholas (USA))
7359^{5} 7583^{2} 7837^{7}
Puddington Bear *Bill Moore* a20
7 b g Riverhead(USA) —Fly-Girl (Clantime)
232^{5} 542^{6}
Puff (IRE) *Ralph Beckett* a80 109
4 b m Camacho—Kelsey Rose (Most Welcome)
(3365) 3827^{4}
Pugnacious (IRE) *Mahmood Al Zarooni* 51
2 b c Street Cry(IRE) —Dignify (IRE) (Rainbow Quest (USA))
3182^{10}
Pull The Pin (IRE) *Lydia Pearce* a32
2 b c Kheleyf(USA) —Inscribed (IRE) (Fasliyev (USA))
7627^{10}
Pullyourfingerout (IRE) *Brendan Powell* a55 75
4 b g Indian Haven—Sandomierz (IRE) (Nordico (USA))
(4204) 4862^{5}

Pulsatilla *Bryan Smart* a55 65
3 b f Monsieur Bond(IRE) —Resemblance (State Diplomacy (USA))
4286^{3} 7063^{3} 7354^{2} 7711^{5} 7913^{2}
Pulverize (USA) *Sir Michael Stoute* a81 83
2 ch c Pulpit(USA) —Critical Eye (USA) (Dynaformer (USA))
4996^{2} 5688^{2}
Pumboo (FR) *Brian Ellison* 35
8 gr g Dadarissime(FR) —Contessina (FR) (Mistigri)
5007^{7}
Pumuki (FR) *P Chatelain* 63
7 b g Poliglote—Nakiya (FR) (Kendor (FR))
(706a)
Punchie *Tim Easterby*
2 b f Lucky Story(USA) —Royal Punch (Royal Applause)
1455^{11} 2121^{5}
Punching *Conor Dore* a84 65
7 b g Kyllachy—Candescent (Machiavellian (USA))
35^{2} (58) 343^{6} (376) 493^{2} 961^{11} 1197^{8} 4988^{9} 5732^{13} 6491^{11} 6665^{9} 6930^{6} 7086^{3} (7341) 7535^{9} 7893^{4}
Punita (USA) *Mahmood Al Zarooni* a78
2 ch f Distorted Humor(USA) —Indy Five Hundred (USA) (A.P. Indy (USA))
(5814) ◆
Punta Lara Lady (IRE) *Paul Green* 37
2 b f Desert Style(IRE) —Minehostess (IRE) (Shernazar)
3165^{6} 3336^{7}
Pure Champion (IRE) *A S Cruz* a102 117
4 b h Footstepsinthesand—Castara Beach (IRE) (Danehill (USA))
$7732a^{7}$
Pure Gossip (USA) *Philip M Serpe* a90 107
2 ch f Pure Prize(USA) —Dixieland Achiever (USA) (Dixieland Band (USA))
$7281a^{7}$
Purification (IRE) *John Gosden* 92
3 b g Hurricane Run(IRE) —Ceanothus (IRE) (Bluebird (USA))
(1445) 3069^{15}
Purkab *Jim Goldie* 60
3 ch g Intikhab(USA) —Pure Misk (Rainbow Quest (USA))
2264^{5} 2465^{4} 3116^{4} 3905^{5} 4175^{4} 4381^{2} 4878^{5} 5315^{4} 6415^{4}
Purley Queen (IRE) *Sylvester Kirk* a62 32
2 b f Piccolo—Queenie (Indian Ridge)
3997^{4} 5632^{10} 5863^{3} 6524^{13} 7514^{6}
Puro (CZE) *M Weiss* 53
9 ch g Rainbows For Life(CAN) —Pulnoc (CZE) (Shy Groom (USA))
$629a^{5}$
Purple Affair (IRE) *J S Moore* a62 56
2 rg g Clodovil(IRE) —Akariyda (IRE) (Salse (USA))
2687^{5} 3171^{5} 3746^{5} 4085^{4} 4907^{6}
Purple Angel *Jonathan Portman* 33
2 b f Dark Angel(IRE) —Cocabana (Captain Rio)
1765^{7} 2241^{5} 2901^{10} 4021^{6}
Purple 'n Gold (IRE) *George Baker* a76 54
2 b c Strategic Prince—Golden Dew (IRE) (Montjeu (IRE))
6118^{5} (6654) 7140^{2} 7501^{2}
Pursestrings *Laura Mongan* a55 38
4 b m Red Ransom(USA) —New Assembly (IRE) (Machiavellian (USA))
2204^{7} 2451^{7}
Pursuing *Nigel Tinkler* a58 53
3 b f Rainbow Quest(USA) —Kineta (USA) (Miswaki (USA))
5792^{7} 6253^{7} 6536^{3} ◆ 6845^{2} 7085^{7} 7741^{7}
Push Me (IRE) *Jamie Poulton* a56 79
4 gr m Verglas(IRE) —Gilda Lilly (USA) (War Chant (USA))
2561^{8} (4255) 4468^{4} [illegible]
Pussycat Dream *Ed McMahon* 78
2 b f Oasis Dream—The Cat's Whiskers (NZ) (Tale Of The Cat (USA))
(4474)
Putin (IRE) *Phil McEntee* a62 68
3 b g Fasliyev(USA) —Consignia (IRE) (Definite Article)
2025^{10} 2375^{6} 3230^{7} 3412^{8} 3688^{12} 4089^{4} 4179^{5} 4758^{2} (5143) 5606^{9} 5902^{5} 6179^{8} 6816^{7} (7246) 7351^{9} 7687^{4} 7782^{6} 7890^{6} 7923^{6}
Putthebabiesdown (USA) *Kenneth McPeek* a107 90
2 b f Closing Argument(USA) —Turtle Beach (USA) (Out Of Place (USA))
$7283a^{8}$
Puttingonthestyle (IRE) *Richard Hannon* a73 82
3 b c Desert Style(IRE) —Auriga (Belmez (USA))
1947^{5} 2368^{2} 2875^{3} 3232^{2} 3871^{6}
Puttore (IRE) *Kevin Prendergast* a80 98
3 b f High Chaparral(IRE) —Ugo Fire (IRE) (Bluebird (USA))
$6362a^{11}$ $6561a^{7}$
Putyball (USA) *X Nakkachdji* a85 99
3 ch f Silver Deputy(CAN) —Ball Gown (USA) (Silver Hawk (USA))
$1709a^{7}$
Puy D'Arnac (FR) *George Moore* a76 77
8 b g Acteur Francais(USA) —Chaumeil (FR) (Mad Captain)
1039^{5} 2364^{4} 3115^{3} 3730^{6} 4562^{5} (5790) 6115^{6} 6780^{2}
Pyjoma *Julia Feilden* a42 26
4 ch m Rainbow Quest(USA) —In Luck (In The Wings)
1332^{5} 2956^{13} 3712^{10} 4396^{10}
Pyman's Theory (IRE) *Tom Dascombe* 97
2 ch f Exceed And Excel(AUS) —Gazebo (Cadeaux Genereux)
1455^{3} (1657) ◆ 2070^{5} (2437) 3064^{9} $3669a^{3}$ 4094^{8} 4413^{11} $6042a^{9}$ 6518^{15}
Pyrenean *James Given* a59 38
3 b f Mull Of Kintyre(USA) —Gabacha (USA) (Woodman (USA))
109^{12} 270^{4}

Pyrenean Music (IRE) *David Wachman* a77 77
2 b c Oratorio(IRE) —Andorra (Cadeaux Genereux)
$7273a^{2}$
Pyrrha *Chris Wall* 109
5 b m Pyrus(USA) —Demeter (USA) (Diesis)
1893^{3} $2744a^{7}$ 4497^{P}
Pytheas (USA) *Michael Attwater* a71 71
4 b g Seeking The Gold(USA) —Neptune's Bride (USA) (Bering)
55^{5} 139^{4} 307^{7} 472^{6} 1867^{9} 2242^{6} 2452^{7} 2560^{7} 2922^{3} 3477^{3} 3719^{4} 3944^{14} 6071^{5} (6488) 6696^{6} 6848^{4} 7268^{7} 7579^{13}
Qaadira (USA) *John Gosden* 64
2 b f Mr Greeley(USA) —Makderah (IRE) (Danehill (USA))
7080^{3}
Qadar (IRE) *Alan McCabe* a79 74
9 b g Xaar—Iktidar (Green Desert (USA))
(612) 698^{3} 961^{6} 1368^{6} 1695^{11} 1866^{3} 2557^{8}
Qahriman *Luca Cumani* a94 89
3 b c Tiger Hill(IRE) —Jumaireyah (Fairy King (USA))
2930^{5} ◆ 4023^{3} (4641) 5641^{2} ◆ 6410^{3}
Qalahari (IRE) *Michael Quinlan* a83 87
5 b m Bahri(USA) —Daqtora (Dr Devious (IRE))
141^{5}
Qannaas (USA) *Charles Hills* 82
2 bb c Hard Spun(USA) —Windsong (USA) (Unbridled (USA))
6481^{4} ◆ 7133^{2}
Qaraaba *Seamus Durack* a54 81
4 b m Shamardal(USA) —Mokaraba (Unfuwain (USA))
2232^{6} (2649) 6330^{7}
Qaraqum (USA) *Denis Coakley* a61 62
4 bb m Vindication(USA) —Code Of Ethics (USA) (Honour And Glory (USA))
4549^{9} 5944^{3} 6411^{3} 6746^{9} 7096^{6} 7437^{5}
Qeethaara (USA) *Mark Brisbourne* a64 74
7 gr m Aljabr(USA) —Aghsaan (USA) (Wild Again (USA))
2282^{10} 2906^{8} (3326) (3457) 4051^{3} 4127^{7} 4701^{8} 5200^{7} 5653^{8} 6878^{5} 7146^{9} 7632^{13}
Qenaa *Mark Johnston* a81 79
3 b f Royal Applause—In The Woods (You And I (USA))
1565^{3} 2103^{4} (2392) 2883^{7} 3361^{2} 3815^{12} 4268^{6} (4910)
Quadra Hop (IRE) *Bryn Palling* a58 58
3 ch g Compton Place—Yding (IRE) (Danehill (USA))
146^{3} 338^{3} 452^{7} 1753^{4} 1980^{11} 2549^{3} 2918^{7} 3272^{12} 7230^{14} 7371^{10}
Quadrant (IRE) *Brian Meehan* 83
3 br g Shamardal(USA) —Quite Elusive (USA) (Elusive Quality (USA))
1409^{4} ◆ 2103^{DSQ} 2506^{10} 5556^{2} (5960) 6457^{13} 7054^{5}
Quadrifolio *Paul Green* a45 49
5 b g Key Of Luck(USA) —Berkeley Note (IRE) (Victory Note (USA))
169^{10} 375^{10}
Quaestor (IRE) *Andrew Crook* a63 45
4 b g Antonius Pius(USA) —Lucky Oakwood (USA) (Elmaamul (USA))
1307^{10} 1612^{10} 2233^{11} 2851^{6} 3185^{5} 3509^{6} 3906^{4} 4198^{7} 4612^{13} 7075^{11} 7426^{13}
Quahadi (IRE) *Chris Gordon* a41
5 b g Montjeu(IRE) —Kicking Bird (FR) (Darshaan)
129^{8} 280^{5} 311^{8} 386^{11}
Quails Hollow (IRE) *William Haggas* a71 80
3 b g Beat Hollow—Bloemfontain (IRE) (Cape Cross (IRE))
2469^{4} 3377^{3} 4180^{2} (5312) 5938^{3} 6328^{2}
Quaintly (USA) *David Wachman* a59 87
3 b f Giant's Causeway(USA) —Measure (USA) (Seeking The Gold (USA))
$5740a^{12}$
Quality Art (USA) *Gary Moore* a95 92
3 b g Elusive Quality(USA) —Katherine Seymour (Green Desert (USA))
(28) 1452^{2} (1758) (2158) ◆ 3181^{4} 4498^{11} 5288^{12} 6217^{8}
Quality Guitar (BRZ) *E Martins* 64
5 b h Principe Taio(BRZ) —La Guita (BRZ) (New Ghadeer (BRZ))
$413a^{9}$
Quambona (FR) *Ecurie'T Heyveld* 67
7 b m Kingsalsa(USA) —Natsylda (FR) (Fabulous Dancer (USA))
$7315a^{6}$
Quanah Parker (IRE) *Neil King* a76 86
5 b g Namid—Uncertain Affair (IRE) (Darshaan)
1892^{7} 2213^{3} (2414) (3319) 4109^{3} 4901^{3}
Quantum Of Solange (USA) *R Menichetti* 76
2 b f Shakespeare(USA) —Bolaro (USA) (Sandpit (BRZ))
$6904a^{7}$
Quaroma *Peter Hedger* a81 76
6 ch m Pivotal—Quiz Time (Efisio)
1197^{6} 1762^{3} 4909^{9}
Quarrel (USA) *William Haggas* a91 79
4 rg g Maria's Mon(USA) —Gender Dance (USA) (Miesque's Son (USA))
5053^{3} 6759^{2} 6980^{8}
Quartier Latin (ARG) *Doug Watson* a97 89
5 br h Orpen(USA) —Queen's Bench (ARG) (Southern Halo (USA))
239^{8}
Quartz (FR) *F Rohaut* a101 92
3 ch f Muhtathir—Queseraisjesanstoi (FR) (Rainbow Quest (USA))
$258a^{9}$
Quasi Congaree (GER) *Ian Wood* a85 95
5 ch g Congaree(USA) —Queens Wild (USA) (Spectacular Bid (USA))
2095^{18} 2369^{5} 3737^{4} 4064^{2} 4531^{24} (4765) ◆ 5012^{2} 5508^{6} 6331^{16} 6723^{7} 7439^{11} 7602^{6}
Quatre Tours (FR) *F Rossi* a81
5 b g Key Of Luck(USA) —Heaven Honor (FR) (Highest Honor (FR))
(219a)

Qubuh (IRE) *Linda Stubbs* a72 76
3 b g Invincible Spirit(IRE) —Chica Roca (USA) (Woodman (USA))
6116^{9} 6840^{4} (7349) 7819^{7}
Quebrador (GER) *Gay Kelleway*
3 gr g Captain Rio—Questina (GER) (Sternkoenig (IRE))
2650^{13}
Queen Grace (IRE) *Michael J Browne* a73 67
4 b m Choisir(AUS) —Petitesse (Petong)
2720^{3} 5965^{3} (6700)
Queenie Keen (IRE) *M Halford* a85 87
4 b m Refuse To Bend(IRE) —Calamander (IRE) (Alzao (USA))
$3440a^{18}$ $6388a^{9}$ $6854a^{4}$ $7010a^{6}$ $7468a^{5}$
Queenie's Star (IRE) *Michael Attwater* a56 44
4 b m Arakan(USA) —Starway To Heaven (ITY) (Nordance (USA))
129^{7} 204^{6} 382^{5} (807) 957^{8} 2386^{5} 2900^{8} 3176^{6} 4317^{11} 4549^{8} 5606^{3} 5943^{2} 6083^{6} 7119^{5} (7466) 7571^{6}
Queen Menantie (FR) *J Boisnard* a86 98
3 b f Kingsalsa(USA) —Heleniade (FR) (Entrepreneur)
$2342a^{12}$
Queen Myrine (IRE) *Richard Hannon* 24
3 b f Oratorio(IRE) —Slewvera (USA) (Seattle Slew (USA))
1362^{15}
Queen Of Cash (IRE) *Hughie Morrison* a89 88
3 b f Ad Valorem(USA) —Warrior Wings (Indian Ridge)
1131^{3} 2200^{4} (2643) 3549^{4} (3782) (4665) 5255^{15} 5920^{4} 7227^{7} 7486^{5}
Queen Of Epirus *George Baker* 57
3 ch f Kirkwall—Andromache (Hector Protector (USA))
2689^{3} 3119^{2}
Queen Of Heaven (USA) *Peter Makin* a26
3 bb f Mr Greeley(USA) —Be My Queen (IRE) (Sadler's Wells (USA))
7652^{5}
Queenofnerverland (IRE) *T Doumen* a54 62
5 ch m Kheleyf(USA) —Election Special (Chief Singer)
$93a^{0}$
Queen Of Silence (FR) *N Leenders* a73 73
4 b m Rosen Kavalier(JPN) —Queen Of Sin (FR) (Quai Voltaire (USA))
$91a^{4}$
Queen Of The Hop *J S Moore* a55 55
2 br f Cockney Rebel(IRE) —Korolieva (IRE) (Xaar)
1049^{2} 1129^{2} 1435^{3} 3070^{3} 3955^{3} 4761^{5} 4907^{8} 5325^{6} 5844^{9} 6524^{18}
Queen O'The Desert (IRE) *Andrew Balding* a68 69
3 b f Green Desert(USA) —Al Dhahab (USA) (Seeking The Gold (USA))
659^{2} (721)
Queen Ranavola (USA) *John Best* a32 50
4 bb m Medaglia D'Oro(USA) —Hour Regal Lady (USA) (Crafty Prospector (USA))
555^{12}
Queen's Choice (IRE) *Anabel K Murphy* a38 56
3 b f Choisir(AUS) —Queen Of Fibres (IRE) (Scenic)
3090^{8} 3594^{3} 4149^{5} 5803^{13} 7096^{10} 7270^{10}
Queenscliff (IRE) *David Wachman* a55
2 b f Danehill Dancer(IRE) —Bonheur (IRE) (Royal Academy (USA))
$7273a^{11}$
Queen's Estate (GER) *Mark Johnston* 51
2 b c Hurricane Run(IRE) —Questabelle (Rainbow Quest (USA))
6774^{7} 7060^{4}
Queen's Princess *John Wainwright* 16
[illegible] (AUS) —Queen's Lodge (IRE) (Grand Lodge (USA))
5030^{9} 5469^{11} 5649^{9}
Queens Revenge *Tim Easterby* 94
2 b f Multiplex—Retaliator (Rudimentary (USA))
(1199) 2404^{4} 3402^{10}
Queens Sandridge (IRE) *Alan Bailey* a77 70
2 b g Zamindar(USA) —Cabriole (Dansili)
3915^{9} 4507^{7} (4864) 5446^{10} 5809^{6} 6111^{9} 6788^{6}
Queen's Silk *Brett Johnson* a24 65
3 b f Barathea(IRE) —Queen Of Africa (USA) (Peintre Celebre (USA))
4617^{8} 5639^{8}
Queen's Star *Andrew Balding* 46
2 ch f With Approval(CAN) —Memsahib (Alzao (USA))
7257^{6}
Queens Troop *Dean Ivory* a43 45
3 ch f Iceman—Ivory's Joy (Tina's Pet)
1343^{7} 2177^{10} 7755^{6}
Querari (GER) *A Wohler* 121
5 bb h Oasis Dream—Quetena (GER) (Acatenango (GER))
$1263a^{7}$
Querido (GER) *Paddy Butler* a75 57
7 b g Acatenango(GER) —Quest Of Fire (FR) (Rainbow Quest (USA))
287^{6} 341^{4} 4660^{8} 5103^{9} 5836^{9} 6624^{11} 7005^{5} 7437^{3} 7639^{6} 7805^{8} 7888^{3}
Quernstone (USA) *Mahmood Al Zarooni*
2 b g Smart Strike(CAN) —Sluice (USA) (Seeking The Gold (USA))
7094^{12}
Querry Boy (FR) *H-A Pantall* a95 91
4 b g Equerry(USA) —Goldy Honor (FR) (Highest Honor (FR))
$195a^{5}$ $371a^{8}$
Quesada (IRE) *W Hickst* 101
3 b f Peintre Celebre(USA) —Queen Of Fire (Dr Fong (USA))
$3209a^{9}$ $6394a^{10}$
Quest For Peace (IRE) *Luca Cumani* 116
3 b c Galileo(IRE) —Play Misty For Me (IRE) (Danehill Dancer (IRE))
(3695a) (6519) ◆ $6910a^{5}$

Quest For Silver *Jeremy Gask* 22
3 b f Red Ransom(USA) —Silver Quest (Rainbow Quest (USA))
3091^{12}

Quest For Success (IRE) *Richard Fahey* a82 107
6 b g Noverre(USA) —Divine Pursuit (Kris)
1111^{6} (3160) (4042) 4534^{13} 5060^{5}

Questi Amori (IRE) *M Guarnieri* 96
4 gr h Choisir(AUS) —Light And Airy (Linamix (FR))
1919a^{14} 7408a^{4}

Questing *John Gosden* a97 100
2 b f Hard Spun(USA) —Chercheuse (USA) (Seeking The Gold (USA))
(3258) ◆ 5472^{3} 6296^{2} *7283a^{5}*

Question D'Or (FR) *Robert Collet* a70 81
5 b g Kendor(FR) —Charming Quest (USA) (Quest For Fame)
1142a^{6}

Questioning (IRE) *John Gosden* a80 112
3 b c Elusive Quality(USA) —Am I (USA) (Thunder Gulch (USA))
1339^{3} ◆ 1923a^{5} 3405^{3} 4493^{7} 5704^{2} ◆ 6339^{14} 6693^{3}

Questionnaire (IRE) *Nicky Vaughan* a30 80
3 b f Iffraaj—Kobalt Sea (FR) (Akarad (FR))
(2869) (3412) 4378^{8} *6665^{12}* 6895^{16}

Question Times *Peter Chapple-Hyam* a78 93
3 b f Shamardal(USA) —Forever Times (So Factual (USA))
2281^{4} 6034^{2} *(6353)*

Quest Of Paradise (FR) *Mlle S-V Tarrou* 72
3 ch f Captain Rio—Poker Chip (Bluebird (USA))
981a^{0}

Questor (FR) *M Boutin* a56 67
2 b g High Cotton(USA) —Equestria (USA) (Red Ransom (USA))
7238a^{6}

Quick Bite (IRE) *Hugo Palmer* a71 82
2 b f Redback—Park Haven (IRE) (Marju (IRE))
1996^{4} 2641^{2} 3282^{2} (5003) ◆ (5550) 6196a^{7} 7021^{5}

Quick Enough (USA) *Doug O'Neill* a109 113
7 br g High Brite(USA) —Donna B. Quick (USA) (Moscow Ballet (USA))
996a^{8}

Quick Single (USA) *Phil McEntee* a54 66
5 bb g Doneraile Court(USA) —Summer Strike (USA) (Smart Strike (CAN))
218^{5} 243^{5} 334^{7} 386^{5} 575^{3}

Quick Val (ARG) *H J Brown* a83 96
4 b f Val Royal(FR) —Que Llamarada (ARG) (Fumador (ARG))
151a^{6} 412a^{6} 681a^{4}

Quick Wit *Saeed Bin Suroor* a111 104
4 b h Oasis Dream—Roo (Rudimentary (USA))
415a^{2} *583a^{8}*

Quiet Appeal (IRE) *Mark Johnston* a52 52
2 b f Cape Cross(IRE) —Rise And Fall (USA) (Quiet American (USA))
3200^{3} 4073^{14} 4427^{11} 6260^{11} 6645^{9} *7242^{7} 7915^{2}*

Quiet Julia (FR) *G Pannier*
4 b m My Risk(FR) —Doctor Julia (FR) (Diamond Prospect (USA))
5095a^{0}

Quilmes (IRE) *C Lerner*
2 b g Hurricane Run(IRE) —Back To My Roots (USA) (Fusaichi Pegasus (USA))
7664a^{5}

Quinindo (GER) *A Wohler* a75 93
3 b c Monsun(GER) —Quebrada (IRE) (Devil's Bag (USA))
1433a^{5} 2338a^{10}

Quinmaster (USA) *M Halford* a102 72
9 gr g Linamix(FR) —Sherkiya (IRE) (Goldneyev (USA))
5086a^{9} 6388a^{11} *7010a^{8} 7149a^{8}*

Quinsman *J S Moore* a81 76
5 b g Singspiel(IRE) —Penny Cross (Efisio)
474^{3} 1016^{6} 1367^{10} 2526^{12} 3799^{7} *(4870)* 4974^{10} *(7254)* 7738^{2} *7753^{7}*

Quissisana (IRE) *S Ribarszki* 97
4 b m Antonius Pius(USA) —Lanark Belle (Selkirk (USA))
6370a^{8}

Quite A Catch (IRE) *Jonathan Portman* a51 73
3 b g Camacho—Dear Catch (IRE) (Bluebird (USA))
1137^{3} 2964^{5} (4200) (5673) 7137^{3} *7857^{12}*

Quite A Thing *Sir Mark Prescott Bt* a86 86
2 ch f Dutch Art—Amazed (Clantime)
(2919) ◆ 3570^{2} *(4757)* ◆ 5263^{3} 5592^{4} *6625^{2}* 6863^{2} *(7067) 7491^{5} 7918^{3}*

Quite Sparky *David O'Meara* 90
4 b g Lucky Story(USA) —Imperialistic (IRE) (Imperial Ballet (IRE))
1910^{3} (2366) 2937^{4} (3275) 3877^{13} 4325^{13} 5757^{9}

Quixote *Clive Brittain* a62 50
2 ch g Singspiel(IRE) —Rainbow Queen (FR) (Spectrum (IRE))
4762^{9} 5565^{11} 6572^{4} *7342^{8} 7569^{6} 7697^{2} 7849^{2}*

Quiza Quiza Quiza *L Riccardi* 112
5 b m Golden Snake(USA) —Quiz Chow (ITY) (Pelder (IRE))
2134a^{3} 3213a^{7} (7047a)

Quiz Mistress *Gerard Butler* a82 84
3 ch f Doyen(IRE) —Seren Quest (Rainbow Quest (USA))
2695^{7} *3474^{2}* 3959^{6} *5389^{7} 5714^{2}* 6172^{2} ◆ 6607^{3} *7129^{10} 7753^{6}*

Quizzed *Edward Vaughan* a74 75
2 b f Oratorio(IRE) —Tree Peony (Woodman (USA))
5445^{8} *6506^{2}* 6956^{2} *(7650)*

Quo Vadis River (FR) *P Cottier* a64
7 b g Trempolino(USA) —Madoudal (FR) (Cadoudal (FR))
259a^{7}

Qushchi *William Jarvis* a83 102
3 bb f Encosta De Lago(AUS) —La Persiana (Daylami (IRE))
1319^{10} 1903^{3} 2295^{3} 3108^{11} (4530) 5482^{2} (6172) *7129^{9}*

Raahin (IRE) *Sir Michael Stoute* a80 81
3 b c Oasis Dream—Sparkle Of Stones (FR) (Sadler's Wells (USA))
3135^{2} *4989^{3}* 6242^{5}

Raajih *Keith Dalgleish* 77
3 gr c Dalakhani(IRE) —Thakafaat (IRE) (Unfuwain (USA))
1211^{2} 4985^{6}

Raasekha *B W Hills* 87
3 b f Pivotal—Tahrir (IRE) (Linamix (FR))
3177^{5} (4356)

Rabbit Fighter (IRE) *Jo Hughes* a54 45
7 ch g Observatory(USA) —Furnish (Green Desert (USA))
5143^{12}

Racemate *S Wattel* 100
3 b f Hurricane Run(IRE) —Relight's Best (Grand Lodge (USA))
(7580a)

Race To Dubai (USA) *Saeed Bin Suroor* 45
3 b c Storm Cat(USA) —Delicatessa (USA) (Dare And Go (USA))
5327^{13}

Rachael's Ruby *Roger Teal* a37 33
4 b m Joe Bear(IRE) —Fajjoura (IRE) (Fairy King (USA))
1605^{11} 1998^{9} 3119^{5}

Racy *Kevin Ryan* a85 100
4 b g Medicean—Soar (Danzero (AUS))
2028^{3} ◆ 2727^{6} ◆ 3357^{5} 3841^{4} 4346^{10} 4531^{6} 5180^{2} 6332^{3} 6706^{3} 7018^{7}

Rada Angel (IRE) *Mme M Bollack-Badel* a102 98
4 b m Le Vie Dei Colori—Red Letter (Sri Pekan (USA))
92a^{2}

Radetsky March (IRE) *Mark Bradstock* 35
8 b g Taipan(IRE) —Jane Jones (IRE) (Beau Sher)
5659^{9}

Radharcnafarraige (IRE) *J S Bolger* 103
3 b f Distorted Humor(USA) —Extraterrestral (USA) (Storm Bird (CAN))
1006a^{12} 1928a^{6} (2861a) 4836a^{6}

Radiator Rooney (IRE) *Patrick Morris* a58 58
8 br g Elnadim(USA) —Queen Of The May (IRE) (Nicolotte)
80^{3} 167^{6} (218) 306^{2} 345^{4} 683^{4} 1034^{10} 1638^{4} 1787^{6} *2161^{5}* 2424^{3} 2755^{6} 6619^{6} 6791^{6} 6982^{2}

Radio Gaga *Ed McMahon* 86
2 b f Multiplex—Gagajulu (Al Hareb (USA))
(5681) 6670^{2} 7135^{3}

Radiomarelli (USA) *Ralph Beckett* 89
2 b g Van Nistelrooy(USA) —Sniffles (USA) (Dove Hunt (USA))
2291^{5} 3132^{2} (3686) ◆ 4334^{3}

Raesunbridledfaith (USA) *Craig A Lewis* 69
2 bb f After Market(USA) —Unbridled Hope (USA) (Unbridled (USA))
7562a^{7}

Rafaaf (IRE) *Robert Eddery* a55 78
3 b g Royal Applause—Sciunfona (IRE) (Danehill (USA))
368^{4} 1317^{7} 1865^{2} 3465^{8} *3523^{7}* 4511^{5} 4765^{8} 5423^{8} (5890) 6801^{3}

Rafaella *Harry Dunlop* a57 68
2 b f Holy Roman Emperor(IRE) —Cliche (IRE) (Diktat)
2787^{2} 3257^{8} 5232^{5} 6743^{8} *7117^{4} 7481^{2} 7590^{2} 7735^{2}*

Rafeej *Mark Johnston* 89
2 b c Iffraaj—Muffled (USA) (Mizaaya)
(6892) (7261) ◆

Rafella (IRE) *Michael Scudamore* a76 67
3 br f Iffraaj—Cappella (IRE) (College Chapel)
1579^{11} 2383^{14} 4799^{4} 5581^{8} 6586^{13} *6944^{11}*

Raffaello (AUS) *Patrick F Ryan* 113
7 b h Encosta De Lago(AUS) —Sweet Delight (AUS) (Rancho Ruler (AUS))
7310a^{12}

Raffinn *Sylvester Kirk* a62
2 b g Sakhee(USA) —Blue Mistral (IRE) (Spinning World (USA))
3746^{7} 6214^{6} 6539^{5}

Raganeyev (FR) *X Nakkachdji* a67 78
10 b g Neverneyev(USA) —Raganaf (FR) (Raga Navarro (ITY))
372a^{8} 481a^{7} *617a^{10}*

Ragda *Marco Botti* a38 46
3 b f Invincible Spirit(IRE) —Junior Council (IRE) (Sadler's Wells (USA))
2151^{7} *7717^{8} 7894^{5}*

Raghdaan *Peter Hiatt* a55 55
4 ch g Haafhd—Inaaq (Lammtarra (USA))
12^{4} 120^{7} 204^{5} 346^{12} 552^{12} 796^{9} 5002^{3} 5376^{5} 5785^{4} 5912^{13} *6446^{6}* 7247^{7} 7399^{12} 7503^{4} 7743^{4} 7859^{13}

Ragsah (IRE) *Saeed Bin Suroor* a86 98
3 ch f Shamardal(USA) —Colorado Dancer (Shareef Dancer (USA))
5277^{9} 6297^{9} 6770^{6}

Rahystrada (USA) *Byron G Hughes* 116
7 ch g Rahy(USA) —Ministrada (USA) (Deputy Minister (CAN))
5074a^{5} 6910a^{12}

Raihana (AUS) *M F De Kock* a113 113
5 b m Elusive Quality(USA) —Esubooh (AUS) (Sunday Silence (USA))
332a^{3} (503a) ◆ 586a^{2} ◆ 1000a^{11} 5277^{10}

Raimond Ridge (IRE) *Derek Shaw* a74 78
5 bb g Namid—Jinsiyah (USA) (Housebuster (USA))
165^{7} 421^{6} 443^{10} 821^{3} 912^{6} 1043^{7}

Rainbow Chorus *Paul Cole* a35 49
2 b c Royal Applause—Seren Devious (Dr Devious (IRE))
4384^{6} 4857^{14} 5133^{8} 5844^{6} *6053^{9}*

Rainbow Dahlia (JPN) *Yoshitaka Ninomiya* 107
4 ch m Brian's Time(USA) —Arome (JPN) (Northern Taste (CAN))
7410a^{5}

Rainbow Gold *Mark Johnston* 63
2 ch c Selkirk(USA) —Diablerette (Green Desert (USA))
5475^{7}

Rainbow Riches (IRE) *Roger Curtis* a47
2 b f Princely Heir(IRE) —Another Rainbow (IRE) (Rainbows For Life (CAN))
7583^{9} 7906^{5}

Rainbow Springs *John Gosden* 105
3 b f Selkirk(USA) —Pearl Dance (USA) (Nureyev (USA))
1393^{3} 1845^{2} 2840^{4} (3119) 4293^{5}

Rainbows Reach *Gay Kelleway* a46 46
3 b f Phoenix Reach(IRE) —Rainbows Guest (IRE) (Indian Lodge (IRE))
23^{3} 194^{6} 801^{6} 2349^{8} 2801^{5}

Rain Dance *Richard Hannon* a42 57
2 b f Green Desert(USA) —Dance Solo (Sadler's Wells (USA))
3258^{5} 4263^{7} 5232^{8} *6001^{10}*

Rain Delayed (IRE) *Michael Dods* a99 112
5 b g Oasis Dream—Forever Phoenix (Shareef Dancer (USA))
237^{15} 500a^{11} *678a^{9}* 1093^{9} 1366^{2} 1687^{2} 2005^{12} 3394^{8} 3874^{7} 4468^{8} 5180^{14} 5467^{8} 5927^{21} 6332^{13}

Raine's Cross *Peter Winkworth* a35 95
4 b g Cape Cross(IRE) —Branston Jewel (IRE) (Prince Sabo)
271^{8} 525^{13}

Rainfall (IRE) *Saeed Bin Suroor* 116
4 b m Oasis Dream—Molomo (Barathea (IRE))
2558^{6} 5704^{4} 6523^{6}

Rainforest Magic (IRE) *D K Weld* 87
4 b g Montjeu(IRE) —Top Lady (IRE) (Shirley Heights)
6690^{5} (Dead)

Rain Mac *John Gosden* a52 100
3 b c Beat Hollow—Quenched (Dansili)
2008^{3} 3774^{8} (5078) 5700^{10}

Rainsborough *Peter Hedger* a61 47
4 b g Trans Island—Greeba (Fairy King (USA))
135^{6} 485^{12} 619^{3} 906^{9} 957^{3} 1333^{7} 1486^{3} 1604^{4} 2201^{10} 3677^{8} 4666^{10} 6589^{6} 7091^{2} ◆ 7203^{6}

Rainy Champion (USA) *Gerard Butler* a61 72
3 b g Giant's Causeway(USA) —Olaya (USA) (Theatrical)
1076^{2} 1386^{2} 2203^{5} *3715^{8}*

Rainy Night *Reg Hollinshead* a76 73
5 b g Kyllachy—Rainy Day Song (Persian Bold)
880^{6} 1239^{15} *1471^{4}* 2356^{3} 2610^{7} 2794^{4} 3322^{10} 3573^{5} *3713^{7}* (4893) *5244^{2}* 5561^{11} *5895^{7} 6502^{7}* 6634^{7} 6802^{12} 7065^{6}

Raise All In (IRE) *Ian McInnes* a64 47
5 b m Exceed And Excel(AUS) —Inforapenny (Deploy)
2828^{6} 3943^{7}

Raise The Rafters (IRE) *Pat Murphy* a42 76
6 ch g Monashee Mountain(USA) —Zolube (IRE) (Titus Livius (FR))
7455^{12} 7648^{10}

Rajamand (FR) *Gary Moore* a50 82
5 gr g Linamix(FR) —Ridafa (IRE) (Darshaan)
7713^{7}

Rajastani (IRE) *S Wattel* a97 103
2 b f Zamindar(USA) —Rocky Mistress (Rock Of Gibraltar (IRE))
5873a^{2} 6941a^{3}

Rajeh (IRE) *John Spearing* 92
8 b g Key Of Luck(USA) —Saramacca (IRE) (Kahyasi)
1729^{4} 3344^{9} 4280^{3} 4890^{4} 6485^{10}

Rajik (IRE) *C F Swan* 111
6 b g Kalanisi(IRE) —Ridaiyma (IRE) (Kahyasi)
1601^{P} (Dead)

Raj Love Royale (FR) *J Phelippon* a49 53
6 b m Cardoun(FR) —Skoopie (FR) (Jeune Homme (USA))
7315a^{8}

Rajnagan (IRE) *Paul Webber* 70
7 ch g Muhtarram(USA) —Rajnagara (IRE) (Darshaan)
1750^{3} (4578) 5015^{7}

Rajsaman (FR) *F Head* a110 120
4 gr h Linamix(FR) —Rose Quartz (Lammtarra (USA))
758a^{6} 1000a^{10} (1740a) 2343a^{3} 4425^{4} 5988a^{3} (6556a) 7731a^{7}

Ra Junior (USA) *Paul Midgley* a86 82
5 b g Rahy(USA) —Fantasia Girl (IRE) (Caerleon (USA))
1077^{4} 1613^{9} 2260^{2} ◆ (2692) 2985^{4} ◆ 3462^{6} 4170^{4} 4603^{8} 5151^{4} 6227^{7} 6262^{6}

Rakaan (IRE) *Jamie Osborne* a101 106
4 ch g Bahamian Bounty—Petite Spectre (Spectrum (IRE))
326a^{4} (497a) 606a^{12} 3109^{22}

Rakasa *Mahmood Al Zarooni* 100
2 b f Redoute's Choice(AUS) —Danse Arabe (IRE) (Seeking The Gold (USA))
(4427) 5472^{2} 6296^{P}

Raktiman (IRE) *Tom Dascombe* a75 74
4 ch g Rakti—Wish List (IRE) (Mujadil (USA))
1914^{4} 2312^{7} 2830^{5} 3817^{5} 4204^{6} 4974^{11} *(5389) 5866^{5}* 6405^{6} *7002^{2}* ◆

Raleigh Quay (IRE) *Micky Hammond* 81
4 b g Bachelor Duke(USA) —Speedbird (USA) (Sky Classic (CAN))
1035^{13} 1244^{6} 1460^{9} 1793^{8} 2474^{6} 3859^{7} 4784^{4} 5729^{11}

Ralphy Boy (IRE) *David Nicholls* 88
2 b g Acclamation—Silcasue (Selkirk (USA))
(2665) (3540) 5061^{4}

Ramble On (FR) *G Botti* a95 103
4 ch h Tobougg(IRE) —Street Money (IRE) (Mark Of Esteem (IRE))
6958a^{5}

Rambling Dancer (IRE) *Mrs Valerie Keatley* a81 76
7 b g Imperial Ballet(IRE) —Wayfarer's Inn (IRE) (Lucky Guest)
7150a^{11} 7792a^{9}

Rambo Will *J R Jenkins* a76 73
3 b g Danbird(AUS) —Opera Belle (Dr Fong (USA))
126^{4} 380^{2} (818) (1193) 1483^{5} 3136^{4} 3985^{5} (4247) 4819^{3} *7746^{2}*

Ramona Chase *Michael Attwater* a83 91
6 b g High Chaparral(IRE) —Audacieuse (Rainbow Quest (USA))
1102^{4} 1479^{3} 2066^{7} 2681^{6} 2716^{6} 3538^{2} 3762^{2} 4008^{4} 4724^{2} 5275^{4} 5546^{3} (5968) 6375^{4}

Ramora (USA) *Olivia Maylam* a66 77
5 b m Monsun(GER) —Madame Cerito (USA) (Diesis)
16^{5} 301^{3} 843a^{7}

Ramvaswani (IRE) *Neil King* a41 41
8 b g Spectrum(IRE) —Caesarea (GER) (Generous (IRE))
118^{7}

Rangefinder *Andrew Crook* a87 96
7 gr g Linamix(FR) —Risen Raven (USA) (Risen Star (USA))
1412^{10} 3730^{9}

Rannoch Moor *Marcus Tregoning* a48 43
4 b g Hernando(FR) —Stormy Weather (Nashwan (USA))
2526^{10} 3072^{11}

Rano Pano (USA) *Brian Ellison* a55 53
2 b f Proud Citizen(USA) —Princess Aries (USA) (Royal Anthem (USA))
2404^{9} *3490^{3} 5211^{4}* ◆ *5597^{3}* 6144^{7}

Ransom Hope *L Riccardi* 108
6 b h Red Ransom(USA) —Field Of Hope (IRE) (Selkirk (USA))
1125a^{9} 2541a^{5} 6369a^{7} 7323a^{7}

Ransom Note *Charles Hills* 118
4 b h Red Ransom(USA) —Zacheta (Polish Precedent (USA))
(1342) 2343a^{8} 3009^{5} 4345^{2} 5094a^{5} (6298) 6861^{8} 7732a^{8}

Rapacious *Mark Rimmer* a27
3 b g Distant Music(USA) —Really Ravenous (Bijou D'Inde)
591^{8} 836^{5} 1028^{6}

Raphael Santi (IRE) *A P O'Brien* 86
2 b c Excellent Art—Jamrah (IRE) (Danehill (USA))
2776a^{4} 6196a^{10}

Rapid Heat Lad (IRE) *Reg Hollinshead* a66 62
2 b c Aussie Rules(USA) —Alwiyda (USA) (Trempolino (USA))
4047^{4} 5269^{8} 5681^{8} *6487^{8} 7569^{8} 7718^{3}*

Rapid Request (AUS) *David Nicholls*
5 gr g Urgent Request(IRE) —Carahill (AUS) (Danehill (USA))
873^{U}

Rapid Water *Gary Moore* a75 85
5 b g Anabaa(USA) —Lochsong (Song)
168^{10} 264^{11} 666^{5} 2605^{3} 2816^{8} 7485^{10} 7587^{7} 7811^{2} 7943^{9}

Rappel *J E Hammond* a68 89
5 b m Royal Applause—Parisian Elegance (Zilzal (USA))
4739a^{0}

Rapport (USA) *Ronny Werner* a104 104
4 bb m Songandaprayer(USA) —Irene's Talkin (USA) (At The Threshold (USA))
7303a^{6}

Rapturous Applause *Micky Hammond* 62
3 b g Royal Applause—Rapturous (Zafonic (USA))
1169^{13} 1944^{2} 2119^{12} 3729^{5} 4284^{4} 4560^{12} 4852^{8} 5623^{2} 6153^{5} 6577^{5}

Raqeeb (USA) *Ruth Carr* a38 82
4 b g Seeking The Gold(USA) —Sayedah (IRE) (Darshaan)
1460^{11}

Rare Bet *John Panvert* 7
5 b m Bertolini(USA) —Rare Old Times (IRE) (Inzar (USA))
3908^{7} 4310^{20}

Rare Coincidence *Alan Berry* a58 58
10 ch g Atraf—Green Seed (IRE) (Lead On Time (USA))
244^{3} 768^{8} 1218^{4} 3450^{8} 4602^{7} 5167^{7}

Rare Ruby (IRE) *Jennie Candlish* 82
7 b m Dilshaan—Ruby Setting (Gorytus (USA))
(1914) 2183^{2} 3344^{12} 4082^{3} 4719^{8} 5685^{10}

Rare Symphony (IRE) *Philip Hobbs* a76 89
4 br m Pastoral Pursuits—Rubileo (Galileo (IRE))
3407^{8}

Rasam Aldaar *Michael Wigham* a70 71
3 b g Sakhee(USA) —Recherchee (Rainbow Quest (USA))
983^{2} 1173^{2} 2076^{13} 4280^{10} 5491^{6} *5714^{5} 6052^{12}*

Rasaman (IRE) *Jim Goldie* a86 96
7 b g Namid—Rasana (Royal Academy (USA))
4327^{3} ◆ 5033^{9} 5434^{4} 6113^{20} 6703^{6} 6865^{10}

Rasheed *John Gosden* a77 68
3 b g Oasis Dream—Alexandrine (IRE) (Nashwan (USA))
1392^{12} 2229^{7} 3361^{13} 6797^{7} *7453^{5} (7839)*

Rashflower (FR) *M Roussel* 59
2 b f Rashbag—Fleur Du Bonheur (FR) (Vaguely Pleasant (FR))
6925a^{4}

Rash Judgement *Stuart Kittow* 97
6 b g Mark Of Esteem(IRE) —Let Alone (Warning)
1093^{12} 1242^{5} 2116^{10} 3395^{10} 3850^{7} 4327^{7} 5163^{8} 5434^{11} 6246^{2} 7171^{17}

Raslan *David Pipe* 67
8 b g Lomitas—Rosia (IRE) (Mr Prospector (USA))
4097^{10} 4423^{17}

Rasmy *Marcus Tregoning* 108
4 b g Red Ransom(USA) —Shadow Dancing (Unfuwain (USA))
3591^{7} 4492^{6} 5829^{8} 6671^{2}

Raspberry Fizz *Eve Johnson Houghton* a50 52
2 b f Red Ransom(USA) —Dubai Spirit (USA) (Mt. Livermore (USA))
1441[7] 2309[12] 2602[6] 4824[4] 5144[9] 5634[10] 5844[3] 6806[6] 7259[5] 7423[2] 7684[3]

Rasputin (IRE) *Michael Dods* 69
2 b c Marju(IRE) —Raspberry Beret (IRE) (Danehill Dancer (IRE))
3656[3] 4140[3] 4781[3]

Rassam (IRE) *Saeed Bin Suroor* a91
2 bb c Dansili—Vantive (USA) (Mr Prospector (USA))
(7330)

Rasselas (IRE) *David Nicholls* a75 88
4 b g Danehill Dancer(IRE) —Regal Darcey (IRE) (Darshaan)
6[8] 279[8] 2431[6] 2783[11] 3358[6] 4349[11] 6079[13]

Rastaban *William Haggas* 92
3 b g Diktat—Guilty Secret (IRE) (Kris)
1516[3] 2100[4] 3650[8] 3988[2] (4287) (4957) ◆ 6410[5]

Rasteau (IRE) *Tom Keddy* a53 34
3 b g Barathea(IRE) —Mistra (IRE) (Rainbow Quest (USA))
2196[10] 2586[6] 3922[9] 4932[4] 6459[7] 7004[7] 7327[5] 7496[3] 7608[9] 7800[7]

Rather Cool *John Bridger* a54 61
3 b f Iceman—Kowthar (Mark Of Esteem (IRE))
2792[12] 3431[13] 3916[5] (4579) 4827[7] 5134[5] 5321[8] 5630[13] 6589[7] 6823[11]

Rath Maeve *Alan McCabe* a59 29
3 b f Auction House(USA) —Westmead Tango (Pursuit Of Love)
296[3] 510[2] 550[5]

Rational Act (IRE) *Tim Easterby* a49 57
3 b g Antonius Pius(USA) —Givemethemoonlight (Woodborough (USA))
1169[5] 1524[5] 1749[4] 2163[8] 2252[8]

Rattan (USA) *W P Mullins* a92 87
6 ch g Royal Anthem(USA) —Rouwaki (USA) (Miswaki (USA))
3013[6] 4398a[12]

Rattlesnake Bridge (USA) *Kiaran McLaughlin* a119
3 rg c Tapit(USA) —Prall Street (USA) (Cherokee Run (USA))
7308a[9]

Rattleyurjewellery *David Brown* a32 31
3 b f Royal Applause—You Make Me Real (USA) (Give Me Strength (USA))
1078[6] 2351[10] 2765[5] 3387[12] 4025[13] 4289[6]

Raucous Behaviour (USA) *George Prodromou* a88 78
3 b g Street Cry(IRE) —Caffe Latte (IRE) (Seattle Dancer (USA))
2008[11] 2435[5] (6445) (7272) 7699[2] 7908[6]

Rava (IRE) *X Nakkachdji* a60 81
6 b m Nayef(USA) —Lucky Date (IRE) (Halling (USA))
395a[0]

Ravanchi *Frank Sheridan* a15
7 br m Indian Danehill(IRE) —Ravishing (IRE) (Bigstone (IRE))
7856[5]

Rave (IRE) *J W Hills* a56 109
3 b c Oratorio(IRE) —Almaaseh (IRE) (Dancing Brave (USA))
1759[12] 2068[2] ◆ (2511) 3159[2] ◆ (3797) ◆ (4313)

Ravindra *Sir Henry Cecil* 47
3 b g Red Ransom(USA) —Young And Daring (USA) (Woodman (USA))
2019[9]

Ravi River (IRE) *Brian Ellison* a70 84
7 ch g Barathea(IRE) —Echo River (USA) (Irish River (FR))
286[5] 1077[2] 1216[2] (1520) 1909[4] (2320) 3277[3] 3828[8] 5722[10] 6656[2] 6868[4] 7557[4]

Rawaafed (IRE) *Brian Meehan* 84
2 bb c Invasor(ARG) —Holly's Kid (USA) (Pulpit (USA))
5051[4] ◆ 5851[3]

Rawaaj *Donald McCain* a61 66
5 ro g Linamix(FR) —Inaaq (Lammtarra (USA))
3622[3] 4951[6]

Rawaki (IRE) *Andrew Balding* a84
3 b g Phoenix Reach(IRE) —Averami (Averti (IRE))
(3236)

Ray Diamond *Michael Madgwick* a31 52
6 ch g Medicean—Musical Twist (USA) (Woodman (USA))
5642[7]

Raymbek Batyr (IRE) *Jeremy Noseda* 71
3 b c Danehill Dancer(IRE) —Park Romance (IRE) (Dr Fong (USA))
2673[3]

Raynell *Noel Quinlan* a42 17
3 b g Araafa(IRE) —Milly-M (Cadeaux Genereux)
4279[12] 4800[10] 5386[6] 5898[10]

Rayo (CZE) *M Weiss* a70
6 br h Rainbows For Life(CAN) —Radiace (CZE) (Sharp End)
534a[3] 629a[2]

Ray Of Joy *J R Jenkins* a91 85
5 b m Tobougg(IRE) —Once Removed (Distant Relative)
125[4] 316[5] 651[7] (1762) 2122[4] 2690[4] 3351[2] 5018[5]

Rayvin Black *Mark H Tompkins* 76
2 b c Halling(USA) —Optimistic (Reprimand)
3182[4] (4159)

Razorbill (USA) *Charles Hills* 71
2 b c Speightstown(USA) —High Walden (USA) (El Gran Senor (USA))
6983[6] ◆

Reachforthebucks *Rae Guest* a83 42
3 ch g Phoenix Reach(IRE) —Miles (Selkirk (USA))
(567) ◆ (642) (668) ◆ 7531[9] 7841[9]

Reach For The Sky (IRE) *Alan Berry* a60 56
4 b m Elusive City(USA) —Zara Whetei (IRE) (Lomond (USA))
2631[7]

Reaching (IRE) *A P O'Brien* a45
2 b f Dansili—Maryinsky (IRE) (Sadler's Wells (USA))
7273a[13]

Reach Out *Brendan Powell* a56 40
3 ch g Phoenix Reach(IRE) —Cocorica (IRE) (Croco Rouge (IRE))
297[4] 731[6] 1018[8]

Reach The Stars (IRE) *D K Weld* 72
4 b m Galileo(IRE) —Claxton's Slew (USA) (Seattle Slew (USA))
5748a[20]

Reachtothestars (USA) *Noel Quinlan* a69 64
3 b c Silver Train(USA) —Gabrieles Princess (USA) (Our Emblem (USA))
140[5] 422[4] 668[4] 739[4] 964[2] 1482[2] 1776[7] 2177[6] 2918[5] 3470[6]

Readily Apparent *Brendan Powell*
3 b f Doyen(IRE) —Donna Vita (Vettori (IRE))
2551[14] 3224[13]

Ready When You Are (IRE) *Ralph Beckett* a60 74
3 b f Royal Applause—Grizel (Lion Cavern (USA))
7260[5] 7443[6]

Reai (IRE) *Richard Fahey* a49
4 gr g Verglas(IRE) —Sheen Falls (IRE) (Prince Rupert (FR))
431[5]

Real Diamond *Ollie Pears* a52 62
5 b m Bertolini(USA) —Miss Fit (IRE) (Hamas (IRE))
1307[11] 2238[9] 2990[7] 3248[12] 3732[4] 4196[8]

Realisation (USA) *Mark Johnston* a88 89
4 b g Alhaarth(IRE) —Live Your Dreams (USA) (Mt. Livermore (USA))
353[3] 515[2] 614[4] 994[5]

Realisatrice (FR) *Mme M Bollack-Badel* a93 99
3 b f Numerous(USA) —Riziere (FR) (Groom Dancer (USA))
(4896a) 5028a[9] 7509a[9]

Reality Show (IRE) *Brian Ellison* a88 88
4 b g Cape Cross(IRE) —Really (IRE) (Entrepreneur)
(5738)

Really Lovely (IRE) *Jeremy Noseda* a70 74
2 b f Galileo(IRE) —Simply Perfect (Danehill (USA))
4552[8] 5464[3] 6278[4] 6753[3] 7436[6] (7777)

Realt Na Mara (IRE) *Hughie Morrison* a60 81
8 bb g Tagula(IRE) —Dwingeloo (IRE) (Dancing Dissident (USA))
122[6] 493[5] 743[9] 1382[11] 1866[7] 2237[8] 2685[10] 3293[8] 4183[7] 5539[14]

Reasons Unknown (IRE) *G M Lyons* a63 67
3 ch c Camacho—Locorotondo (IRE) (Broken Hearted)
1706a[5]

Reason To Believe (IRE) *Ben Haslam* a66 68
3 ch g Spartacus(IRE) —Lady Fabiola (USA) (Open Forum (USA))
1169[9] 2119[9] 3485[6] 4329[3] 5004[4] (5788)

Re Barolo (IRE) *A bin Huzaim* a112 99
8 b h Cape Cross(IRE) —Dalaiya (USA) (Irish River (FR))
154a[12]

Rebecca Rolfe *M Gasparini* 103
5 b m Pivotal—Matoaka (USA) (A.P. Indy (USA))
237[8] 500a[10] 1432a[4] 1919a[5] 6906a[2] 7408a[12]

Rebecca Romero *Denis Coakley* a71 73
4 b m Exceed And Excel(AUS) —Cloud Dancer (Bishop Of Cashel)
(1182) 1627[2] 2603[3] 3261[4] (4057) (4615) 5658[2] 6932[5]

Rebel Dancer (FR) *Ian Williams* 75
6 b g Dark Moondancer—Poupee d'Ancyre (FR) (Brinkmanship (USA))
2312[8] 2459[4] 7022[11]

Rebel Duke (IRE) *Ollie Pears* a103 98
7 ch g Namid—Edwina (IRE) (Caerleon (USA))
6351[P]

Rebellious Guest *George Margarson* 99
2 b c Cockney Rebel(IRE) —Marisa (GER) (Desert Sun)
(2767) 3012[12] (4858) ◆ 6688[13]

Rebel Soldier (IRE) *David Hayes* a87 116
4 ch g Danehill Dancer(IRE) —En Garde (USA) (Irish River (FR))
6967a[P]

Rebel Song (IRE) *Mahmood Al Zarooni* a81 78
2 b c Refuse To Bend(IRE) —Dubai Opera (USA) (Dubai Millennium)
6230[3] 6805[2] ◆ (7398)

Recalcitrant *Simon Dow* a71 72
8 b g Josr Algarhoud(IRE) —Lady Isabell (Rambo Dancer (CAN))
2923[4] 3354[3] 3760[5] 4249[4] 4822[4] 5406[5] 6586[5] 6969[7]

Recital (FR) *A P O'Brien* 118
3 b c Montjeu(IRE) —Dibenoise (FR) (Kendor (FR))
1259a[3] (1927a) 2715[6] 5747a[6]

Reckoning (IRE) *Jeremy Noseda* 92
2 b f Danehill Dancer(IRE) —Great Hope (IRE) (Halling (USA))
(6985)

Record Breaker (IRE) *Mark Johnston* a89 91
7 b g In The Wings—Overruled (IRE) (Last Tycoon)
32[5] 180[11] 436[8] 849[5] (1156) 1291[4] 1517[13] 1713[4] 2320[12] 3127[7] 3911[8] 4407[7] 5311[11] 5599[2] 6121[2] (6379) (7002)

Recway Striker *Des Donovan* a40 38
2 b g Auction House(USA) —Persistent Memory (USA) (Red Ransom (USA))
4919[7] 5337[10] 5536[8] 6101[11]

Redact (IRE) *Richard Hannon* a81 109
2 b c Strategic Prince—Rainbow Java (IRE) (Fairy King (USA))
(2640) (3868) 4094[4] 5558[8] 6162[2]

Red Aggressor (IRE) *Clive Brittain* a74 91
2 b c Red Clubs(IRE) —Snap Crackle Pop (IRE) (Statoblest)
1721[8] 2148[2] 2767[2] 3012[9] (5605) 5933[4] 6692[8] 7019[5]

Redair (IRE) *David Evans* a80 80
2 b f Redback—Alexander Goldmine (Dansili)
(982) 1095[2] 1806[3] 2070[9] 3808[3] 4551[9] 5270[6] 5427[2] 6221[4] 6431[4] 6786[2] 6863[4]

Red Alex *James Given* 6
2 b c Nayef(USA) —Expedience (USA) (With Approval (CAN))
2983[14]

Red All Over (IRE) *Alan Berry*
2 gr f Dark Angel(IRE) —Rubies And Pearls (USA) (Chief's Crown (USA))
6025[10]

Red Alpha (IRE) *Jeremy Noseda* a78 81
2 b c Red Clubs(IRE) —Anthyllis (IRE) (Night Shift (USA))
2173[3] ◆ 2640[3] (3779) 6699[3] 6986[2]

Red Anthem *Gerard Butler* a76 88
4 bb g Singspiel(IRE) —Russian Rose (IRE) (Soviet Lad (USA))
5888[12] 6690[20] 6976[6]

Red Army Blues (IRE) *G M Lyons* a73 73
3 b g Soviet Star(USA) —Liscoa (IRE) (Foxhound (USA))
973a[2] ◆

Red Art (IRE) *Charles Hills* 94
2 b c Excellent Art—All Began (IRE) (Fasliyev (USA))
2023[6] 2409[2] (2997) (3375) 4575[2] 5216[5] 7026[5]

Red Bay *Jane Chapple-Hyam* a76 59
2 b c Haafhd—Red Zinnia (Pivotal)
6300[7] 6890[3] 7293[7] 7526[4] (7808)

Red Cadeaux *Ed Dunlop* a108 119
5 ch g Cadeaux Genereux—Artisia (IRE) (Peintre Celebre (USA))
1102[2] ◆ 1808[12] (2044) 3204[4] (3418a) 4469[10] 5304a[5] 5952a[3] 7218a[2] 7729a[3]

Red Cape (FR) *Ruth Carr* a84 89
8 b g Cape Cross(IRE) —Muirfield (FR) (Crystal Glitters (USA))
1205[9] 1438[7] 1878[10] 2095[15] 2497[5] 2620[3] 3028[2] 3359[2] 3541[7] 3880[4] 4013[4] (4327) 4609[11] 5108[8] 5683[12] 6502[5] 7040[5] 7253[8] (7535) 7594[2] 7644[8] 7847[2] (7926)

Red Chaparral (GER) *W Baltromei* a67 78
3 b g High Chaparral(IRE) —Ruby Hill (GER) (Tiger Hill (IRE))
7016a[8]

Redclue (IRE) *Marco Botti* a53
2 br g Red Clubs(IRE) —Stratospheric (Slip Anchor)
7821[6]

Red Copper *Michael Bell* a60 42
3 b f Cape Cross(IRE) —Red Conquest (Lycius (USA))
624[10] 888[2] 1328[7] 2838[13]

Red Courtier *Paul Cole* a91 83
4 b g Red Ransom(USA) —Lady In Waiting (Kylian (USA))
1402[7] 2006[16] 2686[2] 2931[4] (3738) 4348[8] 5102[2] 5417[3]

Red Current *Michael Scudamore* a67 60
7 b m Soviet Star(USA) —Fleet Amour (USA) (Afleet (CAN))
4703[3] (5267) (5628) 6240[6] 6876[2] 7331[5] 7631[2]

Red Czar (IRE) *Alan McCabe* 43
2 b c Red Clubs(IRE) —La Grande Zoa (IRE) (Fantastic Light (USA))
2882[8]

Red Dagger (IRE) *Richard Price* a44 58
5 b g Daggers Drawn(USA) —Dash Of Red (Red Sunset)
2815[5]

Red Davis (JPN) *Hidetaka Otonashi* 120
3 b g Agnes Tachyon(JPN) —Dixie Jazz (JPN) (Tony Bin)
7873a[9]

Red Dubawi (IRE) *A De Royer-Dupre* 107
3 ch c Dubawi(IRE) —Maredsous (FR) (Homme De Loi (IRE))
5128a[8] 7193a[8]

Red Duke (USA) *John Quinn* 111
2 ch c Hard Spun(USA) —Saudia (USA) (Gone West (USA))
2476[3] ◆ (3186) ◆ (3861) 4424[3] 5926[2] 6689[8]

Redemptor *J-C Rouget* a106 106
3 gr c Elusive City(USA) —Restless Rixa (FR) (Linamix (FR))
532a[5] (883a) 1206a[3]

Redesignation (IRE) *J-C Sarais* a80 98
6 b g Key Of Luck(USA) —Disregard That (IRE) (Don't Forget Me)
478a[5] 705a[0]

Red Eyes *Brian Meehan* a83 89
3 b c Beat Hollow—Kardelle (Kalaglow)
3001[8] (4065)

Red Eye Special (NZ) *Anthony Cummings* 106
5 b g Yamanin Vital(NZ) —Flight All Nite (NZ) (Personal Escort (USA))
6967a[10]

Red Fama *Neville Bycroft* a65 83
7 ch g Fraam—Carol Again (Kind Of Hush)
(2544) 3344[4] ◆ 3828[10] 4407[4] (5440) 5729[4] 6024[6] 6832[8]

Red Flash (IRE) *David Bridgwater* a53 52
4 b g Red Ransom(USA) —Mar Blue (FR) (Marju (IRE))
3096[9] 4444[9] 4917[4] 7787[2] 7891[4]

Redford (IRE) *David Nicholls* a106 117
6 b g Bahri(USA) —Ida Lupino (IRE) (Statoblest)
1242[2] 1889[3] 3404[6]

Red Gulch *Ed Walker* a108 104
4 b g Kyllachy—Enrapture (USA) (Lear Fan (USA))
2020[2] 2470[2] 3134[2] 3862[14] (4415) 4993[2] (5712) 6339[21] (6783a)

Red Halo (IRE) *Sir Michael Stoute* 58
2 gr f Galileo(IRE) —St Roch (IRE) (Danehill (USA))
6985[4]

Red Hearts (IRE) *Julia Feilden* a27 71
2 b f Red Clubs(IRE) —Red Trance (IRE) (Soviet Star (USA))
1441[11] (1632) 2070[6] 2594[3] 2902[4] 3595[4] 4391[3] 4756[9] 5353[2] (5625)

Red Hermes (IRE) *Mark H Tompkins* a47
2 ch f Windsor Knot(IRE) —Imposition (UAE) (Be My Guest (USA))
7350[5] 7635[5] 7769[3]

Redhotdoc *Bill Moore* a66 66
7 ch m Dr Fong(USA) —Gecko Rouge (Rousillon (USA))
1252[3] 1474[3] 2219[5] 2815[9] 7564[6]

Red Hot Penny (IRE) *Brian Meehan* 13
2 b g Kheleyf(USA) —Zawariq (IRE) (Marju (IRE))
3472[9] 3816[11] 4682[5]

Red Hot Secret *Jeremy Gask* 46
2 ch f Three Valleys(USA) —Princess Miletrian (IRE) (Danehill (USA))
7210[4]

Red Inca *Brian Meehan* 79
3 ch g Pivotal—Magicalmysterykate (USA) (Woodman (USA))
1409[9] 1836[9] 2226[4] (5281) ◆ 5925[6] ◆ 6409[7]

Red Jade *Richard Fahey* a67 93
6 ch g Dubai Destination(USA) —Red Slippers (USA) (Nureyev (USA))
5761[2] 6676[5] 7017[6]

Red Jazz (USA) *B W Hills* a110 122
4 b h Johannesburg(USA) —Now That's Jazz (USA) (Sword Dance)
997a[3] 2101[5] 3843[4] 4412[2]

Red Kestrel (USA) *Kevin Ryan* a73 89
6 ch g Swain(IRE) —The Caretaker (Caerleon (USA))
965[2] (1072) 1325[2] 1651[7] (3127) 3593[2] 4266[3] 5448[11] 6499[9]

Red Kingdom (IRE) *Dianne Sayer* 42
7 b g Red Ransom(USA) —Eucalyptus Hill (USA) (Peaks And Valleys (USA))
7105[7]

Red Lago (IRE) *Charles Hills* a70 68
3 b g Encosta De Lago(AUS) —Speciale (USA) (War Chant (USA))
777a[7] 1408[7] ◆ 5585[5] 6097[2]

Red Lancer *Jonathen de Giles* a50 86
10 ch g Deploy—Miss Bussell (Sabrehill (USA))
7527[6]

Red Larkspur (IRE) *Roger Teal* a76 83
2 b f Red Clubs(IRE) —Holda (IRE) (Docksider (USA))
1441[9] (1996) 3402[6] 4312[7]

Red Lite (IRE) *Wilf Storey* a41 64
3 b f Red Ransom(USA) —Cloudy Bay (GER) (Zilzal (USA))
1986[14] 2550[6] 3002[11] 5623[6] 5823[13] 7212[7]

Red Lover *Ed Dunlop* a71 83
3 b c Azamour(IRE) —Love Me Tender (Green Desert (USA))
7249[3] 7401[4]

Red Marksman *James Evans* a35 10
3 b g Red Ransom(USA) —Kissogram (Caerleon (USA))
6085[10] 6804[13]

Red Marling (IRE) *Charles Hills* a73 73
3 b c Danehill Dancer(IRE) —Marling (IRE) (Lomond (USA))
1611[3] 2147[4] 3633[2] 4271[6] 4706[3] 6617[7]

Red Mercury (IRE) *Alan King* a58 70
3 ch g Majestic Missile(IRE) —Fey Rouge (IRE) (Fayruz)
1947[9] 2368[11] 6461[9]

Red Mischief (IRE) *Harry Dunlop* a68 70
2 b f Red Clubs(IRE) —Mujadilly (Mujadil (USA))
1996[3] 2302[3] 2644[3] 3171[4] (4019) 5324[11]

Redoutable (IRE) *Kevin Prendergast* 95
2 b f Invincible Spirit(IRE) —Rebelline (IRE) (Robellino (USA))
4833a[7]

Red Quartet (IRE) *Robert Eddery* 81
2 b c Red Clubs(IRE) —Nans Lady (IRE) (Mozart (IRE))
4276[5] 4857[6] (5424) (6670) 6995[2]

Red Rani *Reg Hollinshead* a16 1
6 ch m Whittingham(IRE) —Crystal Magic (Mazilier (USA))
113[7]

Red Rhythm *Micky Hammond* a62 55
4 ch g Starcraft(NZ) —Araguaia (IRE) (Zafonic (USA))
2670[10]

Red River Boy *Chris Fairhurst* a44 58
6 ch g Bahamian Bounty—Riviere Rouge (Forzando)
2247[8] 3972[5] 4443[5] 4518[10] 4793[7] 5373[10]

Red Riverman *William Haggas* 80
3 b g Haafhd—Mocca (IRE) (Sri Pekan (USA))
2568[6] 2852[2] 4062[7]

Red Roar (IRE) *Alan Berry* a11 75
4 ch m Chineur(FR) —Unfortunate (Komaite (USA))
1968[3] ◆ 2062[6] 2286[5] 2694[3] 2832[10] 3166[6] 3541[6] (4152) 4405[2] (4942) 5400[3] 5918[11] 6189[4] 6779[6] 7341[13]

Red Samantha (IRE) *Alan Berry* 37
2 b f Ivan Denisovich(IRE) —Charming Vista (Josr Algarhoud (IRE))
1455[9] 3022[7] 3375[6] 3584[7] 3708[6]

Red Scintilla *Nigel Tinkler* 75
4 b m Doyen(IRE) —Red To Violet (Spectrum (IRE))
1909[14] 2366[11] 3387[5] 3903[7] 4600[4] 4672[6] 5008[4] 5652[3] 6450[11] 7065[3] 7351[U]

Red Senor (IRE) *B W Hills* 69
2 b c Red Clubs(IRE) —Belsay (Belmez (USA))
3288[8] 3686[4] ◆ 4462[3]

Red Seventy *Richard Hannon* 99
2 b c Sakhee(USA) —Dimakya (USA) (Dayjur (USA))
(3288) ◆ (3795) ◆ 4424[7] 6270[6] 6952[4]

Red Shadow *Alan Brown* 58
2 b f Royal Applause—Just A Glimmer (Bishop Of Cashel)
1199[7] 1414[4] 2113[2] 2886[9] 3611[2] 4106[7] 4558[8] 4899[3] 5590[2] 6863[3] 7059[8] 7231[5]

Red Shimmer (IRE) *Jo Hughes* 40
2 b g Red Clubs(IRE) —Subtle Shimmer (Danehill Dancer (IRE))
6075[7] 6483[8] 6828[10]

Redskin Dancer (IRE) *John M Oxx* 87
3 b f Namid—Red Affair (IRE) (Generous (IRE))
1006a[10]

Red Skipper (IRE) *Noel Wilson* a31 60
6 ch g Captain Rio—Speed To Lead (IRE) (Darshaan)
1099[19] 3129[12] 5723[14]

Red Socks (IRE) *Gay Kelleway* a68 62
2 b g Red Clubs(IRE) —Ball Cat (FR) (Cricket Ball (USA))
1522[8] *1757[2]* 1863[2] *2173[4]* *2380[3]* 2780[3] 3308[7] *7267[8]* *7451[4]* *7694[5]*

Red Somerset (USA) *Mike Murphy* a97 68
8 b g Red Ransom(USA) —Bielska (USA) (Deposit Ticket (USA))
447[3] *615[12]* *1103[4]* *2000[12]* 3130[4] 3426[8] 5014[9] *(5319)* *5687[9]* *6219[4]* *6948[6]*

Red Storm Rising *Kevin Morgan* a59 60
4 b g Red Ransom(USA) —Showery (Rainbow Quest (USA))
83[4]

Red Tyke (IRE) *John Quinn* a38 51
2 b g Red Clubs(IRE) —Teutonic (IRE) (Revoque (IRE))
1165[4] 2093[4] 2485[13] 5005[6] (6424) *7242[4]*

Red Valerian Two (IRE) *Paul Midgley* a52 41
4 ch g Hawk Wing(USA) —La Turque (IRE) (Diesis)
1[6]

Redvers (IRE) *Ralph Beckett* a87 94
3 br g Ishiguru(USA) —Cradle Brief (IRE) (Brief Truce (USA))
1459[2] (2479) *3048[6]* (3723) *(3983)* 4498[6] 5972[13] 6174[12] *6477[5]* 7023[3]

Red Willow *John E Long* a63 55
5 ch m Noverre(USA) —Chelsea Blue (ITY) (Barathea (IRE))
391[3] *687[3]* ◆

Redwood *Charles Hills* 118
5 b h High Chaparral(IRE) —Arum Lily (USA) (Woodman (USA))
1001a[2] 3775[2] 4492[4] 6910a[7] 7729a[11]

Red Yarn *Gary Moore* a69 78
4 b m Lucky Story(USA) —Aunt Ruby (USA) (Rubiano (USA))
1898[9] 2428[2] 3079[5] 3549[5] 3918[7] 4546[6] 5231[11] *6285[4]* 6969[5]

Red Zeus (IRE) *Jo Davis* a63 56
3 ch g Titus Livius(FR) —Cheviot Indian (IRE) (Indian Ridge)
(1132) 1659[4] 2789[5] *3235[13]* 3688[10] *6784[11]*

Reel Bluff *Noel Wilson* 53
5 b g Reel Buddy(USA) —Amber's Bluff (Mind Games)
2492[7]

Reel Buddy Star *George Moore* 96
6 ch g Reel Buddy(USA) —So Discreet (Tragic Role (USA))
1695[10] 1942[2] 2390[5] 2783[3] 3358[2] (3578)

Reem (AUS) *M F De Kock* a104 103
4 ch f Galileo(IRE) —Al Afreet (AUS) (Danehill (USA))
(151a) *412a[2]* 607a[2] *(753a)* *998a[8]* 4802[8] 5277[13] 6297[8]

Reemeya (USA) *Mark Johnston*
2 b f Bernardini(USA) —City Sister (USA) (Carson City (USA))
2983[16] *3520[9]* 4875[6]

Reem Star *Kevin Ryan* a83 83
3 b f Green Tune(USA) —Arlecchina (GER) (Mtoto)
2022[4] ◆ *4664[2]* *4905[4]* 6729[2] *7002[3]* *7577[2]*

Ree's Rascal (IRE) *Jim Boyle* a86 84
3 gr g Verglas(IRE) —Night Scent (IRE) (Scenic)
1335[5] (1949) 2229[6] 3231[2] 4010[6] 4860[2] *6478[2]* *6948[5]* *7439[6]*

Refik (FR) *M Cesandri* 98
8 b g Hawker's News(IRE) —Joly Coeur (FR) (Mont Basile (FR))
219a[0] (479a) 705a[2]

Reflect (IRE) *Richard Hannon* 93
3 b c Hurricane Run(IRE) —Raphimix (FR) (Linamix (FR))
1407[3] (1728) 2295[2] 3069[18] 3623[3] 4473[12]

Refractor (IRE) *James Fanshawe* a74 17
3 ch g Refuse To Bend(IRE) —Fancy Intense (Peintre Celebre (USA))
7111[10] *7327[2]* *(7766)*

Refreshestheparts (USA) *George Baker* a51 44
2 ch f Proud Citizen(USA) —St Francis Wood (USA) (Irish River (FR))
4052[11] *5863[7]* *6441[9]*

Refusal *Andrew Reid* 55
3 b g Teofilo(IRE) —Frankie Fair (IRE) (Red Sunset)
1271[12] 1728[3] 4685[6] 5179[8]

Refuse To Davis (IRE) *N Leenders* a62 68
4 b g Whipper(USA) —Beautiful Note (USA) (Red Ransom (USA))
1012a[9]

Refusetosurrender (IRE) *Richard Fahey* a56 7
3 b f Refuse To Bend(IRE) —Redstone Dancer (IRE) (Namid)
88[6] *344[6]* *593[5]* 6428[9] *6999[3]* *7071[7]*

Regal Acclaim (IRE) *Tim Easterby* 52
2 b g Acclamation—Certain Charm (USA) (Thunder Gulch (USA))
2120[8] 2617[6] 3878[11] (5817) ◆ 6424[2]

Regal Approval *Hughie Morrison* a83 82
3 br g Royal Applause—Enthralled (Zafonic (USA))
1688[9] 2255[3] 2770[5] 4459[6] *5717[2]* *6478[2]*

Regal Betty (USA) *John W Sadler* a96 88
2 b f Congrats(USA) —Singsingasong (USA) (Sultry Song (USA))
7562a[5]

Regal Bullet (IRE) *Dean Ivory* a58 56
3 b g Majestic Missile(IRE) —Royal Dream (Ardkinglass)
1483[4] 2294[7] 3272[5] 4162[8]

Regal Entrance *Jeremy Noseda*
2 b c Royal Applause—Umniya (IRE) (Bluebird (USA))
1360[P] (Dead)

Regal Gold *Richard Hannon* a60 66
2 b c Exceed And Excel(AUS) —Regal Asset (USA) (Regal Classic (CAN))
4762[11] 5541[8] 6455[8] *(6817)* (6937)

Regal Heiress *Sir Michael Stoute* 80
3 b f Pivotal—Regal Rose (Danehill (USA))
2157[3] ◆ 4356[3] 4963[3]

Regal Kiss *Mark Johnston* a61 76
3 ch f King's Best(USA) —Really Polish (USA) (Polish Numbers (USA))
2232[4] 3572[5] 5020[7] 5925[8] *6507[11]* *6799[8]*

Regal Lady *David Brown* a62 41
2 b f Captain Rio—Alvarinho Lady (Royal Applause)
5737[2] *6352[3]* *6492[2]* *6843[3]* 7059[15] 7103[5] *7490[8]* *7607[3]* *7692[5]* *7882[5]*

Regally Ready (USA) *Steven Asmussen* 122
4 ch g More Than Ready(USA) —Kivi (USA) (King Of Kings (IRE))
(6908a) (7303a)

Regal Parade *David Nicholls* a97 121
7 ch g Pivotal—Model Queen (USA) (Kingmambo (USA))
1118a[5] 2005[2] 2502[2] 3394[3] 3863[9] 4092[4] 5282[7] 6147[11]

Regal Park (IRE) *Marco Botti* a80 92
4 b g Montjeu(IRE) —Classic Park (Robellino (USA))
2285[9] 2931[2] *3522[5]* 4280[3] 4890[3] 5448[3] 6690[8]

Regal Rave (USA) *Peter Hedger* a68 42
4 b g Wild Event(USA) —Golden Crown (USA) (Defensive Play (USA))
727[3] 1058[8] *1333[13]* 1637[3] 2144[7] 2420[5] 3017[3] 3468[5] 4829[5] 5611[9] *6083[12]* 6811[5] *7206[8]* *7640[6]* *7805[2]* 7892[3]

Regal Realm *Jeremy Noseda* 106
2 b f Medicean—Regal Riband (Fantastic Light (USA))
(2467) 4312[2] (5472) 5885[4] 6691[8]

Regal Rocket (IRE) *John Weymes* a40 45
3 b f Majestic Missile(IRE) —Frenzy (Zafonic (USA))
595[10] *834[11]*

Regal Salute *Jeremy Noseda* 89
3 b f Medicean—Regency Rose (Danehill (USA))
1568[7] 3437[3] (4158) ◆ 5199[4]

Regarde Moi *S Botti* 106
3 b g King's Best(USA) —Life At Night (IRE) (Night Shift (USA))
1431a[12] 7323a[4]

Regency Art (IRE) *Milton Bradley* a47 76
4 b g Titus Livius(FR) —Honey Storm (IRE) (Mujadil (USA))
5371[10] (7055) *7517[U]* *7625[10]* *7767[11]* *7930[13]*

Regeneration (IRE) *Michael Bell* a86 85
5 b g Chevalier(IRE) —Cappuchino (IRE) (Roi Danzig (USA))
6477[6] 7076[11] *7438[10]* *7625[8]*

Regent's Secret (USA) *Jim Goldie* a85 66
11 br g Cryptoclearance(USA) —Misty Regent (CAN) (Vice Regent (CAN))
3858[8] 5207[4]

Regent Street (IRE) *A P O'Brien* a93 107
3 ch c Galileo(IRE) —Hanami (Hernando (FR))
1259a[2] 1927a[3] 3108[4] 5182[7]

Reggie Perrin *Pat Phelan* a60 58
3 ch g Storming Home—Tecktal (FR) (Pivotal)
3392[8] *3747[8]* 4320[10] 5421[2] *6122[4]* *6446[2]* *6926[5]*

Regimental (IRE) *Ann Duffield* 82
3 b g Refuse To Bend(IRE) —Red Fox (IRE) (Spectrum (IRE))
1392[7] 1801[7] (2834) (3124) (3462) 4325[12] 5648[6]

Regina Ejina (FR) *M Delzangles* a89 100
2 b f Muhtathir—Ejina (FR) (Highest Honor (FR))
5770a[4] 6660a[6]

Reginald Claude *Mark Usher* a73 75
3 b g Monsieur Bond(IRE) —Miller's Melody (Chief Singer)
44[2] *228[4]* *358[2]* *578[8]* 2772[4] 3122[9] 4199[4] 4511[9]

Regional Counsel *Alex Hales* a70 40
7 b g Medicean—Regency Rose (Danehill (USA))
2051[12]

Regy From Sedgy *Frederick Watson*
4 ch h Beckett(IRE) —Deekazz (IRE) (Definite Article)
3138[13]

Regythelion *Frederick Watson*
5 b g Hunting Lion(IRE) —Deekazz (IRE) (Definite Article)
3138[10]

Rei D'Oro (USA) *David Simcock* a69
2 bb c Seeking The Gold(USA) —Grand Marq (USA) (King Of Kings (IRE))
6697[10] *7835[3]*

Reignier *Mrs K Burke* a82 98
4 b g Kheleyf(USA) —Komena (Komaite (USA))
815a[8] 1122a[0] 3862[11] (4049) 4314[15] 5032[14] 5699[11] *6958a[9]*

Reillys Daughter *J S Moore* a70 67
3 b f Diktat—Compose (Anabaa (USA))
2528[7] 2840[9] *4209[3]* *5145[3]* 5784[8] 6482[2] 6582[3]

Reina Sofia *David Bridgwater* a52 58
2 b f Dutch Art—Fairmont (IRE) (Kingmambo (USA))
1396[4] 1657[3] 1846[6] 2563[3] *3491[3]* 4430[5] *4756[6]* 5353[3] *6280[10]*

Reine Du Froid (IRE) *Ben Haslam* 47
2 b f Baltic King—Meranie Girl (IRE) (Mujadil (USA))
4853[8] 5310[3] 5726[9]

Reine Heureuse (GER) *Uwe Ostmann* 102
4 b m Big Shuffle(USA) —Reine Galante (IRE) (Danehill (USA))
2657a[11] 6394a[6] 7534a[8]

Reine Liberte (GER) *Uwe Ostmann*
2 b f Big Shuffle(USA) —Reine Galante (IRE) (Danehill (USA))
6737a[U]

Reine Vite (GER) *Uwe Ostmann* 97
3 b f Big Shuffle(USA) —Reine Galante (IRE) (Danehill (USA))
2337a[3] 3209a[8] 3897a[8] 7509a[0]

Rek (POL) *Lenka Horakova*
5 ch h Hondo Mondo(IRE) —Radustka (IRE) (Priolo (USA))
4874a[8]

Rekindled Interest (AUS) *Jim Conlan* 120
4 b g Redoute's Choice(AUS) —Rekindled Affair (IRE) (Rainbow Quest (USA))
7044a[3]

Relative Strength (IRE) *Jennie Candlish* a76 77
6 ch g Kris Kin(USA) —Monalee Lass (IRE) (Mujtahid (USA))
162[8] *418[4]* *(879)* 1107[4] *(1577)* 1792[3] 3507[8] 3974[8] 4637[6]

Release The Funds (IRE) *David Nicholls* 26
2 ch g Kheleyf(USA) —Indian Imp (Indian Ridge)
6912[13] 7210[8]

Relentless Harry (IRE) *George Baker* a75 67
2 gr c Excellent Art—Les Alizes (IRE) (Cadeaux Genereux)
(5737) 6590[4] ◆

Reliable Man *A De Royer-Dupre* 123
3 gr c Dalakhani(IRE) —On Fair Stage (IRE) (Sadler's Wells (USA))
(2751a) 4038a[3] (5987a) 6567a[15]

Reluctant Heroine (USA) *Mark Johnston* 47
3 bb f Medaglia D'Oro(USA) —Dazed (IRE) (Danehill (USA))
5429[4] 5877[8] 6404[10]

Remember Alexander *Mrs John Harrington* 105
2 b f Teofilo(IRE) —Nausicaa (USA) (Diesis)
(4257a) 4833a[5] 6389a[5]

Remember Rocky *Steve Gollings* a41 58
2 ch c Haafhd—Flower Market (Cadeaux Genereux)
3490[8] 4068[8] 5337[9] (5844) 6760[5] *7223[6]*

Remix (IRE) *J W Hills* a68 51
2 b f Oratorio(IRE) —Miss Lopez (IRE) (Key Of Luck (USA))
4155[9] *6131[4]* *6654[2]* *6927[3]* *7464[2]* *7783[2]*

Remotelinx (IRE) *J W Hills* a61 90
3 ch g Choisir(AUS) —La Tintoretta (IRE) (Desert Prince (IRE))
1322[6] 1688[3] 2067[4] 2508[9] 4353[4] 4643[3] 4797[5] 5430[8] *6003[8]* 6920[4]

Renaione (IRE) *E Botti* a69 100
5 ch h Storming Home—Renilde (FR) (Bigstone (IRE))
(221a) 479a[7]

Rendelsham (FR) *J-P Gallorini* 79
8 b g Take Risks(FR) —Eloura (FR) (Top Ville)
935a[5]

Renege The Joker *Sean Regan* a35 41
8 b g Alflora(IRE) —Bunty (Presidium)
1993[11] 5822[10]

Renegotiate *Andrew Balding* a20 65
2 ch g Trade Fair—L'Extra Honor (USA) (Hero's Honor (USA))
5382[11] 6529[6] 6812[4]

Renesmee (IRE) *Peter Grayson* a38
3 ch f Bachelor Duke(USA) —Rose Of Battle (Averti (IRE))
64[8] *189[9]* *1217[6]* *1589[10]* *4863[6]*

Renn *Peter Grayson*
3 b f Iceman—Ladywell Blaise (IRE) (Turtle Island (IRE))
110[11]

Renoir's Lady *Simon Dow* 61
3 b f Peintre Celebre(USA) —Marie De Blois (IRE) (Barathea (IRE))
2648[14] 3437[7] 4584[11]

Rent Free *Nigel Tinkler* 83
2 b g Striking Ambition—Concentration (IRE) (Mind Games)
1691[5] (2409) 3014[21] 3879[3] 4343[3] (4787) (5505) 6670[20]

Repeater *Sir Mark Prescott Bt* a68 95
2 b g Montjeu(IRE) —Time Over (Mark Of Esteem (IRE))
3076[3] *3472[3]* (4007) 5931[7] 6154[2] (6345) ◆ 6606[2] 7167[2]

Replicator *Patrick Gilligan* a53 57
6 b g Mujahid(USA) —Valldemosa (Music Boy)
(138) *276[5]* *664[8]* 2920[11] 3412[12] *5603[10]* *6791[5]* 7230[7] *7429[5]* *7676[2]*

Reply (IRE) *A P O'Brien* 111
2 b c Oasis Dream—Cap Coz (IRE) (Indian Ridge)
(2329a) ◆ 4834a[5] 5251[6] (5849) 6688[3]

Reposer (IRE) *Noel Quinlan* a86 80
3 br g Kheleyf(USA) —Tragic Point (IRE) (Tragic Role (USA))
2215[3] 2684[2] 3796[15] 4472[14] *(4994)* *5717[7]* *6949[12]* *7531[11]* *7660[13]* *7846[8]*

Represent (IRE) *Mick Channon* a68 72
2 b f Exceed And Excel(AUS) —Craigmill (Slip Anchor)
1846[3] ◆ 2254[6] *2606[4]* 5565[7] 5854[2] 6207[3] 6935[8] *7205[8]*

Representation (USA) *Mahmood Al Zarooni* 73
2 ch c Street Cry(IRE) —Portrayal (USA) (Saint Ballado (CAN))
5668[3]

Requinto (IRE) *David Wachman* 110
2 b c Dansili—Damson (IRE) (Entrepreneur)
2776a[5] (3884a) (4413) 5253[13] (5882) 6563a[6]

Requisite *Ian Wood* a85 82
6 ch m Pivotal—Chicarica (USA) (The Minstrel (CAN))
3549[9] *4210[5]* *5100[6]* 5451[3] *(5718)* *5948[5]* *6256[7]* *7097[3]* 7298[6] *7438[3]* *7531[5]* *(7586)* 7675[3] 7833[6] 7846[3]

Rerouted (USA) *B W Hills* 108
3 ch c Stormy Atlantic(USA) —Rouwaki (USA) (Miswaki (USA))
1318[2] 1686[8] 3011[9] 3852[11]

Resentful Angel *Pat Eddery* a95 94
6 b m Danehill Dancer(IRE) —Leaping Flame (USA) (Trempolino (USA))
525[6] ◆ *702[2]* ◆ *1100[2]* 1677[7] *2604[10]* 3844[4] 4344[6] 4818[2]

Reset City *David Pipe* 70
5 ch m Reset(AUS) —City Of Angels (Woodman (USA))
4024[4] 4341[10]

Reset To Fit *Eric Alston* 63
4 b g Reset(AUS) —Miss Fit (IRE) (Hamas (IRE))
1803[10] 2593[5] 2845[10] 3543[10] (4077) 4716[9] 5349[6] 5823[4] 6295[10]

Residence And Spa (IRE) *Tim Easterby* 73
3 b g Dubai Destination(USA) —Toffee Nosed (Selkirk (USA))
1559[3] 1972[5] 2407[3] 3460[5] 3734[3] 4364[6]

Residency (IRE) *Bryan Smart* a67 65
5 b g Danetime(IRE) —Muckross Park (Nomination)
(15) *144[3]* *491[9]* *641[2]* *732[2]* *857[10]* 1213[14] *1463[9]*

Resplendent Ace (IRE) *Karen Tutty* a72 49
7 b g Trans Island—Persian Polly (Persian Bold)
4649[6] *5249[7]* *(6356)* *6666[4]* *7002[6]* *7070[6]* *7415[2]* *7564[4]*

Resplendent Alpha *Alastair Lidderdale* a65 57
7 ch g Best Of The Bests(IRE) —Sunley Scent (Wolfhound (USA))
56[4] *7437[9]* *7663[6]* *7775[3]* *(7891)* *7924[2]*

Resplendent Light *Bernard Llewellyn* a73 84
6 b g Fantastic Light(USA) —Bright Halo (IRE) (Bigstone (IRE))
813[2] *1046[4]* 1829[7] *2159[8]* (3799) 4059[6] 4674[4] 4982[8] (5112) 5545[4] 6437[6]

Response (AUS) *Mathew Ellerton & Simon Zahra* 114
5 b m Charge Forward(AUS) —Live It Up (AUS) (Match Winner (FR))
4

Responsive *Hughie Morrison* a53 91
2 b f Dutch Art—Xtrasensory (Royal Applause)
2641[6] (3270) 3842[2] 5656[5] 5847[3] 6340[5]

Restaurateur (IRE) *Andrew Balding* a77 66
2 b c Excellent Art—Velvet Appeal (IRE) (Petorius)
7134[6] *7368[2]* *(7521)*

Restiadargent (FR) *H-A Pantall* 112
2 b f Kendargent(FR) —Restia (FR) (Montjeu (IRE))
4569a[4] (6042a) (7220a)

Restless Bay (IRE) *Reg Hollinshead* a83 84
3 br g Elusive City(USA) —Argus Gal (IRE) (Alzao (USA))
208[4] *302[4]* *(538)* *578[2]* *(632)* *740[2]* *847[5]* *940[5]* 1059[4] 1391[6] 2180[3] 2611[3] 2916[4] 3078[5] 3269[2] 3598[2] 3996[2] 4234[5] 4610[4] 4817[U] 5262[2] 5680[7] 6174[9] 6456[11] 6491[8] (7596) 7715[3] 7926[9]

Resurge (IRE) *Stuart Kittow* a92 107
6 b g Danehill Dancer(IRE) —Resurgence (Polar Falcon (USA))
1479[2] 2002[7] (2681) 3107[12] 4410[15] 4788[6] 5544[5] 6163[7] 7029[9] 7297[12]

Resuscitator (USA) *Heather Main* a82 69
4 b g Bernstein(USA) —Lac Du Printemps (USA) (Meadowlake (USA))
(248) *(428)* *(528)* *1760[12]* *2000[7]*

Retainer (IRE) *Richard Hannon* 102
3 gr g Acclamation—Felicita (IRE) (Catrail (USA))
(1059) 3548[5] 4092[10] 5935[8] 6920[3]

Retreat Content (IRE) *Linda Perratt* a67 73
3 b g Dubai Destination(USA) —Sharp Point (IRE) (Royal Academy (USA))
1475[5] 2449[2] (3116) 3905[2] 4364[5] 4543[2] 4784[8] 7160[4] *7604[11]*

Retrieve (AUS) *Saeed Bin Suroor* 120
4 b c Rahy(USA) —Hold To Ransom (USA) (Red Ransom (USA))
6693[5] 7170[5]

Retromania (IRE) *John Best* a56 28
2 b g Moss Vale(IRE) —Vade Retro (IRE) (Desert Sun)
6927[7] 7080[12] *7094[5]*

Reveal The Light *Garry Woodward* a44 44
4 b m Fantastic Light(USA) —Paper Chase (FR) (Machiavellian (USA))
1998[7] 2257[10] 2591[8] 4185[7]

Reve De Nuit (USA) *Alan McCabe* a100 95
5 ch g Giant's Causeway(USA) —My Dream Castles (USA) (Woodman (USA))
(6) *353[8]*

Reve D'Essor (JPN) *Hiroyoshi Matsuda* 110
3 gr f Agnes Tachyon(JPN) —Reve D'Oscar (FR) (Highest Honor (FR))
7410a[11]

Reve Du Jour (IRE) *Alan McCabe* a63 60
2 b f Iffraaj—Melaaya (USA) (Aljabr (USA))
2709[6] 3092[5] 3553[5] 4365[2] 5077[5] 6274[7] *7925[2]*

Revelator (IRE) *Alan McCabe* a55 74
4 b g One Cool Cat(USA) —Capades Band (FR) (Chimes Band (USA))
38[4] *268[7]*

Reventon *B Grizzetti* 92
3 b c Galileo(IRE) —Frottola (Muhtarram (USA))
6569a[8]

Revered Citizen (USA) *Sir Michael Stoute* 77
2 b c Proud Citizen(USA) —Well Revered (USA) (Red Ransom (USA))
5011[2]

Reverence *Eric Alston* a103 108
10 ch g Mark Of Esteem(IRE) —Imperial Bailiwick (IRE) (Imperial Frontier (USA))
4776[7] 5467[6]

Reverend Green (IRE) *Chris Down* a81
5 b g Tagula(IRE) —Red Letter (Sri Pekan (USA))
6439[9] *7098[4]* ◆

Revitalise *Kevin Ryan* 55
2 b g Vital Equine(IRE) —Tancred Arms (Clantime)
2630[6] 2983[11] 3302[6] 5343[12] 6260[14]

Revolutionary *Alison Thorpe* a63 62
3 b g Thunder Gulch(USA) —Magic Spin (USA) (Lord Avie (USA))
176[5] *262[6]* *424[4]* *2239[2]* 2379[4] *2722[3]* 3268[4] *3393[8]* *3923[3]* *4181[2]* 4476[5] *5415[3]* 7340[7]

Revolverheld (GER) *G Martin* a83
5 b h Kingsalsa(USA) —Rosonora (GER) (Highest Honor (FR))
371a[0] 481a[0] (566a)

Revolving World (IRE) *Lee James* a45 21
8 b g Spinning World(USA) —Mannakea (USA) (Fairy King (USA))
450[5] ◆ 4112[11] 5209[7] 5650[10]

Rewarded *James Toller* 83
2 b c Motivator—Granted (FR) (Cadeaux Genereux)
6160[2] (7080)

Rewilding *Mahmood Al Zarooni* 130
4 b h Tiger Hill(IRE) —Darara (Top Ville)
(1001a) (3031) 4315[F] (Dead)

Rex Imperator *Roger Charlton* 95
2 b g Royal Applause—Elidore (Danetime (IRE))
3917[2] ◆ (5017) 5492[2] 5849[13] 6518[5] ◆

Rex Romanorum (IRE) *Patrick Holmes* 56
3 b g Holy Roman Emperor(IRE) —Willowbridge (IRE) (Entrepreneur)
7111[4]

Reyal (ITY) *S Botti* 102
3 b f Altieri—Cape Grey (IRE) (Cape Cross (IRE))
3449a[10]

Reynaldothewizard (USA) *S Seemar* a105 96
5 b h Speightstown(USA) —Holiday Runner (USA) (Meadowlake (USA))
326a[9] 606a[2]

Rezwaan *Murty McGrath* a82 83
4 b g Alhaarth(IRE) —Nasij (USA) (Elusive Quality (USA))
(625) (802) ◆ 1269[3] 1603[11] 5948[12] 6796[12] 7098[9] 7362[9] 7532[12] 7671[6] 7904[6]

Rhagori *Ralph Beckett* a71 71
2 b f Exceed And Excel(AUS) —Cresta Gold (Halling (USA))
5655[3] ◆ 6455[2] (7125)

Rhal (IRE) *Bryan Smart* a71 75
3 ch f Rahy(USA) —Queen Of Stars (USA) (Green Desert (USA))
41[2] 187[2] 281[5] 729[3] (964) 1078[2] ◆ 1249[2] 1745[2] 2062[7] 3702[4] 4942[3] (6265) 6537[12]

Rhenania (IRE) *M Nigge* a89 89
4 ch m Shamardal(USA) —Cois Cuain (IRE) (Night Shift (USA))
840a[3]

Rhianna Brianna (IRE) *Michael Easterby* 56
2 ch f Bertolini(USA) —Jewell In The Sky (IRE) (Sinndar (IRE))
2113[3] 2460[6] 3165[8] 4147[7] 4940[4] 6384[9]

Rhyme Royal *James Given* a55 24
2 b f Byron—Burton Ash (Diktat)
7210[7] 7464[6] 7777[3]

Rhythm Of Light *Tom Dascombe* 106
3 b f Beat Hollow—Luminda (IRE) (Danehill (USA))
1384[5] (2102) 2503[2] ◆ (3034) 4497[10] 5028a[3] 5753a[2]

Rhythm Stick *John Berry* a76 87
4 b g Whipper(USA) —Forever Loved (Deploy)
(190) (6023)

Rhyton (IRE) *Donald McCain* a61 67
4 b g Rainbow Quest(USA) —Sea Picture (IRE) (Royal Academy (USA))
3712[3] 4633[2]

Rich And Reckless *Tobias B P Coles* a63 56
4 b m Starcraft(NZ) —Krynica (USA) (Danzig (USA))
214[12] 360[3] 579[3] 747[5] 1770[6] 2201[9] 2447[4]

Richard's Kid (USA) *S Seemar* a122 106
6 br h Lemon Drop Kid(USA) —Tough Broad (USA) (Broad Brush (USA))
758a[10] 1002a[12]

Richbelle (USA) *George Weaver*
2 bb f With Distinction(USA) —Misty Springs (USA) (Wild Again (USA))
6205a[3]

Rich Boy *Laura Mongan* a68 62
4 ch g Bahamian Bounty—West Humble (Pharly (FR))
78[3] 3017[2] 3477[9]

Rich Coast *P Bary* 94
3 b c King's Best(USA) —Costa Rica (IRE) (Sadler's Wells (USA))
7313a[8]

Rich Harvest (USA) *Ray Peacock* a6 46
6 bb g High Yield(USA) —Mangano (USA) (Quiet American (USA))
517[11] 793[12] 4705[10] 5678[3] 5917[8]

Richhill Lady *F Chappet* a74 80
7 gr m Mark Of Esteem(IRE) —Mix Me Up (FR) (Linamix (FR))
325a[4] (481a) 617a[2]

Richo *Shaun Harris* a55 62
5 ch g Bertolini(USA) —Noble Water (FR) (Noblequest (FR))
3110[6] 3317[11] 3496[8] 4329[7] 4654[8] 5944[12]

Rich Tapestry (IRE) *D K Weld* a82 105
3 b c Holy Roman Emperor(IRE) —Genuine Charm (IRE) (Sadler's Wells (USA))
1259a[4] 1927a[6]

Rich Unicorn (AUS) *J Size* 115
5 br g Danehill Dancer(IRE) —Onwards (AUS) (Zeditave (AUS))
7730a[6]

Riczar *Tom Dascombe* a63 42
3 b f Intikhab(USA) —Tharwa (IRE) (Last Tycoon)
3543[15] 4282[9] 5432[3] 5943[11] 6262[10] 6767[6] 7246[4] (7354) 7711[8] 7782[5]

Ride The Wind *Chris Wall* a69 61
3 b f Cozzene(USA) —Wind Surf (USA) (Lil's Lad (USA))
1565[8] 2853[2] 3688[6] 4275[4] 5243[2] 6134[8] 7522[10]

Ridge City (IRE) *P Khozian* a92 96
4 gr h Elusive City(USA) —Absolutely Cool (IRE) (Indian Ridge)
257a[3]

Ridgeway Hawk *Mark Usher* a58 36
3 ch g Monsieur Bond(IRE) —Barefooted Flyer (USA) (Fly So Free (USA))
41[5] 322[2] (505) ◆ 550[4] (745) 936[2] 7728[11] 7844[12]

Ridgeway Sapphire *Mark Usher* a24 54
4 b m Zafeen(FR) —Barefooted Flyer (USA) (Fly So Free (USA))
2238[8] 2554[7] 3721[3] 4224[8] 4631[4] 4828[8] (5138) 5617[5] 5677[9]

Riding The River (USA) *David Cotey* a94 111
4 b g Wiseman's Ferry(USA) —Glow Ruby Go (USA) (Rubiano (USA))
6204a[5] 6908a[9]

Ridley Didley (IRE) *Noel Wilson* a68 75
6 b g Tagula(IRE) —Dioscorea (IRE) (Pharly (FR))
(144) 294[12] 453[3] 732[8] 1034[4] 1501[4] 1940[3] (2247) 2667[5] 3027[15] (3451) 4174[5] 4289[4] 6076[16] 6875[6] 7106[14]

Rien Ne Vas Plus (IRE) *Sir Michael Stoute* a76 67
3 b f Oasis Dream—Sought Out (IRE) (Rainbow Quest (USA))
1549[9] 4753[2] 6057[2] 6504[4]

Rievaulx World *Kevin Ryan* a77 87
5 b g Compton Place—Adhaaba (USA) (Dayjur (USA))
197[4] 343[3] 453[5]

Riflessione *Ronald Harris* a77 69
5 ch g Captain Rio—Hilites (IRE) (Desert King (IRE))
29[6] 178[10] 298[3] 430[3] 646[7] 833[5] 3995[7] 4224[6] 4547[7] 4828[10] 5244[7] 5534[5] 5846[6] (6501) (6618) 6752[4] 7173[7] 7535[3] 7744[3] 7819[11]

Riggins (IRE) *Ed Walker* a109 111
7 b g Cape Cross(IRE) —Rentless (Zafonic (USA))
326a[12] 3107[8] 4494[12] 5185[10] 5473[6] 6339[28] 6672[8] (7393) 7516[5]

Rightcar *Peter Grayson* a57 11
4 b g Bertolini(USA) —Loblolly Bay (Halling (USA))
167[7] (256) 421[7] 482[3] 690[7] 821[8] 1043[6] 1469[5] 2164[5] 2921[13] 4207[4] (5865) 6176[3] 7266[2] 7366[4] 7737[10] 7942[5]

Rightcar Dominic *Peter Grayson* a45
6 b g Kyllachy—Vallauris (Faustus (USA))
28[4] 166[4] 250[9] 2161[8] 4207[7]

Right Credentials *Bruce Hellier* a5
3 b f Diktat—Approved Quality (IRE) (Persian Heights)
1217[8] 2493[11] 2781[11] 3487[11] 4018[6]

Right Divine (IRE) *Brian Meehan* 84
2 gr g Verglas(IRE) —Yellow Trumpet (Petong)
3382[5] 4213[12] (6532) 7026[11]

Right One (FR) *Christophe Clement* a97 115
5 b g Anabaa(USA) —Riziere (FR) (Groom Dancer (USA))
6204a[3] 6908a[8]

Right Regal (IRE) *Marco Botti* 80
2 b g King's Best(USA) —Royal Esteem (Mark Of Esteem (IRE))
3182[3] ◆ 3823[4] 5855[8] 6983[8]

Right Result (IRE) *John Quinn* a88 78
2 b g Acclamation—Mist And Stone (IRE) (Xaar)
2221[2] 2617[3] 2886[2] 3610[3] 4094[21] 6274[2] (6539)

Right Step *Alan Jarvis* a100 104
4 b g Xaar—Maid To Dance (Pyramus (USA))
2002[2] 2681[2] 3107[4] 3829[9] 5250[18] 6375[7] 7029[U]

Right Stuff (FR) *Gary Moore* a94 40
8 bb g Dansili—Specificity (USA) (Alleged (USA))
1105[2] 2931[14] (7753)

Right To Dream (IRE) *Brian Meehan* 92
2 b c Oasis Dream—Granny Kelly (USA) (Irish River (FR))
2291[3] 2584[2] (3408) 4495[8]

Rigid *Tony Carroll* a54 52
4 ch g Refuse To Bend(IRE) —Supersonic (Shirley Heights)
86[6] 382[4] 517[4] 4681[6] 4829[3] 5643[8] 5944[4] 6310[2] 6494[6]

Rigolleto (IRE) *Mick Channon* a52 94
3 b g Ad Valorem(USA) —Jallaissine (IRE) (College Chapel)
1361[3] 2296[17] 2705[5] 2908[3] 3067[27] 3830[3] [illegible] ◆ 5043[12] 5830[9] 6290[8] 6948[11]

Rileys Crane *Christine Dunnett* a43 58
4 b g Reset(AUS) —Persian Blue (Persian Bold)
912[13] 1989[7] 2268[10] (2829) 3956[10] 6071[8] 6626[10] 6791[10] 7442[10] 7655[10]

Rileyskeepingfaith *Mahmood Al Zarooni* a108 114
5 b g Hunting Lion(IRE) —Keeping The Faith (IRE) (Ajraas (USA))
327a[4] 602a[2] 755a[4] (828a) 997a[12]

Rimth *Paul Cole* 106
3 b f Oasis Dream—Dorelia (IRE) (Efisio)
(1404) 2137a[9] 4497[4] ◆ 5080[10] 5848[8] 6687[4]

Ring Of Fire *John Spearing* a49
4 b g Firebreak—Sweet Patoopie (Indian Ridge)
355[9] 575[12]

Ringstead Bay (FR) *Ralph Beckett* a64 55
3 b g Intikhab(USA) —Praia Grande (GER) (Lagunas)
1408[13] 1836[13] 2226[6] 3002[7] 3479[5] 3715[7]

Rinko (FR) *C Boutin*
2 b f Oratorio(IRE) —Belle D'Argent (USA) (Silver Hawk (USA))
7449a[0]

Rio Caribe (IRE) *David Thompson* 69
4 b g Captain Rio—Kadja Chenee (Spectrum (IRE))
7503[11]

Rio Cobolo (IRE) *David Nicholls* a80 81
5 b g Captain Rio—Sofistication (IRE) (Dayjur (USA))
(869) 1110[4] 1382[9] 1696[2] 1942[3] 2431[7] 3339[6] 4792[3] 5455[13] 5682[2] 6081[3] 6869[11]

Rio De La Plata (USA) *Saeed Bin Suroor* 119
6 ch h Rahy(USA) —Express Way (ARG) (Ahmad (ARG))
2713[3] 3009[4] 4425[3] 5988a[2] 6556a[2] 7324a[2]

Rio Grande *Ann Duffield* a78 73
2 b g Invincible Spirit(IRE) —Pharma West (USA) (Gone West (USA))
2007[7] ◆ 2510[6] 5756[3] 7000[2] (7626) 7725[2]

Rio Park (IRE) *Bryan Smart* 65
3 b g Oratorio(IRE) —Janette Parkes (Pursuit Of Love)
1710[2] 2125[3] 2458[9] 3306[7] 3614[5]

Rio Prince *John Bridger* a32 53
4 b g Carnival Dancer—Princess Louise (Efisio)
1840[9] 2372[6] 2562[7] 2793[8] 3256[9] 3872[6] 4153[7] 4318[6]

Rio Royale (IRE) *Amanda Perrett* a70 68
5 b g Captain Rio—Lady Nasrana (FR) (Al Nasr (FR))
(97) 351[2] 698[2] 1232[6] 1838[8] 3020[7] 4547[9] 4850[6] 5513[8] 6090[5] 6746[3] (7131) ◆ 7485[2]

Rio Sands *Richard Whitaker* a46 63
6 b g Captain Rio—Sally Traffic (River Falls)
752[9] 2205[6] 2352[10] 2798[8] 3247[8] 3931[6] 5373[8] 6266[11] 6501[8]

Rio's Girl *Tony Coyle* a59 64
4 b m Captain Rio—African Breeze (Atraf)
735[5] ◆ 934[8] 1034[6] 1493[4] (1716) 2126[10] 2798[7] 3027[4] 4443[6] 4600[2] 5457[5] 6261[10] 6580[10] 7420[6] 7646[11] 7728[10]

Rio's Rosanna (IRE) *Richard Whitaker* a82 84
4 b m Captain Rio—Ling Lane (Slip Anchor)
1496[7] 2114[2] (2478) 2906[3] 4608[3] 6346[4] 6918[3] 7022[2] 7272[5]

Rio Tinto *Giles Bravery* a74 74
4 b g Cape Cross(IRE) —Hint Of Silver (USA) (Alysheba (USA))
1569[7] 2822[11] 3361[4] 4249[8] (4666) 5318[8]

Riot Of Colour *Ralph Beckett* a76 81
2 b f Excellent Art—Riotous Applause (Royal Applause)
5689[2] ◆ 6291[2]

Riot Police (USA) *David Simcock* a75 75
3 bb c Street Cry(IRE) —Lords Guest (USA) (Lord At War (ARG))
23[2] 193[3] 471[2] 699[4] 817[2]

Ripristini (IRE) *Patrick Holmes* a62 12
3 gr c Aussie Rules(USA) —Oiseau Grise (FR) (Linamix (FR))
7063[14] 7609[2]

Riptide *Michael Scudamore* 79
5 b g Val Royal(FR) —Glittering Image (IRE) (Sadler's Wells (USA))
(3095) 3935[5] 4562[2] 5079[5] 5759[4] 6780[9] 6915[2]

Riqa *F Head* 102
3 b f Dubawi(IRE) —Thamarat (Anabaa (USA))
7156a[9]

Riquita (IRE) *C Lerner* a76 79
3 b f High Chaparral(IRE) —Yxenery (IRE) (Sillery (USA))
7016a[3]

Rise To Glory (IRE) *Denis P Quinn* 1
3 ch c King's Best(USA) —Lady At War (Warning)
7691[11] 7924[5]

Rishikesh *Michael Bell* 72
3 b g Cape Cross(IRE) —Maycocks Bay (Muhtarram (USA))
2218[8] 3080[3]

Rising Kheleyf (IRE) *John Harris* a52 72
5 ch g Kheleyf(USA) —Rising Spirits (Cure The Blues (USA))
3643[7] 4076[6] 4409[8]

Rising Wind (IRE) *Kevin Prendergast* 93
3 b f Shirocco(GER) —Right Key (IRE) (Key Of Luck (USA))
3695a[9] 5291a[5] 5748a[15] 7322a[6]

Risk Assessed (IRE) *Mahmood Al Zarooni* 84
3 b c Shamardal(USA) —Love In The Mist (USA) (Silver Hawk (USA))
3824[4]

Risky Art *Michael Easterby* 85
2 ch f Dutch Art—Loblolly Bay (Halling (USA))
(2346) 3022[5] 4343[4] ◆ (5287) 6144[4] 7028[10]

Risky Business (AUS) *S Burridge* 115
7 br g Danehill Dancer(IRE) —Sky Watch (AUS) (Star Watch (AUS))
2340a[6]

Rite Of Passage *D K Weld* 122
7 ch g Giant's Causeway(USA) —Dahlia's Krissy (USA) (Kris S (USA))
2534a[3]

Ritorno (SWI) *M Weiss*
7 b g Desert Track—Moonshine Of Jester (SWI) (Wootton Rivers (USA))
629a[13]

Ritsi *Marjorie Fife* a56 52
8 b g Marju(IRE) —Anna Comnena (IRE) (Shareef Dancer (USA))
2654[6] 3300[2] 3754[11] 4198[4] 4856[16] 5166[9] 6419[5] 7078[13] 7145[7]

Ritual (IRE) *Jeremy Noseda* a91 93
4 b g Cape Cross(IRE) —Silver Queen (Arazi (USA))
(3588) ◆ 3841[19] 5180[8]

Rivabella (FR) *S Bietolini* 101
3 bl f Iron Mask(USA) —Royale Highnest (FR) (Highest Honor (FR))
3449a[8]

Rivas Rhapsody (IRE) *Ian Wood* a76 66
3 b f Hawk Wing(USA) —Riva Royale (Royal Applause)
(7260) (7587) ◆ (7767) ◆

River Ardeche *Tracy Waggott* a71 77
6 b g Elnadim(USA) —Overcome (Belmez (USA))
2159[9] 2492[5] 4177[12] 6309[6] (7710)

River Blade *Mark Brisbourne* 46
3 b g Needwood Blade—River Ensign (River God (USA))
1413[8]

River Bounty *Alan Jarvis* a55 53
6 b m Bahamian Bounty—Artistic Merit (Alhaarth (IRE))
1336[8] 5037[3] 6257[6] 6791[11]

Riverdale (IRE) *Nigel Tinkler* 80
3 ch g Choisir(AUS) —Hollow Haze (USA) (Woodman (USA))
1391[3] ◆ 3985[6] 5456[4] 5760[9] 6167[7]

River Dragon (IRE) *Tony Coyle* a71 70
6 b g Sadler's Wells(USA) —Diarshana (GER) (Darshaan)
11[4] 1211[6] 4985[7] 5595[4] 5790[6] (6780) 6915[5] (7163) 7914[4]

River Falcon *Jim Goldie* a93 85
11 b g Pivotal—Pearly River (Elegant Air)
1200[7] (1907) 2116[9] 2938[4] 3162[2] 3880[3] 5682[4] 6113[22] 7171[18]

River Jetez (SAF) *M F De Kock* 117
8 b m Jet Master(SAF) —Stormsvlei (SAF) (Prince Florimund (SAF))
241[3] ◆ (607a) 1000a[2] 1742a[6] 2340a[2] 3822[5] 5073a[3]

River Nova *Alan Berry* a44 50
2 b f Avonbridge—Assistacat (IRE) (Lend A Hand)
1846[10] 2173[6] 2556[3] 3463[5] 3631[3] 4756[4] 5325[3] 5634[13] 6002[5] 7338[5]

River Prospector (IRE) *P Khozian* a64
3 ch c Sinndar(IRE) —Angelina Carolina (IRE) (Kris)
638a[8]

River Speed (GER) *V Chaloupka*
7 b g Lecroix(GER) —Royal Palm (GER) (Surumu (GER))
4874a[4]

River Taff *Roger Ingram* a54
4 b g Auction House(USA) —Lady Ploy (Deploy)
688[4]

Rivertime (ITY) *R Menichetti* 96
2 b c Tout Seul(IRE) —Lady Susy (IRE) (Danetime (IRE))
3212a[8]

River Valley *Gary Moore* 48
2 b g Three Valleys(USA) —Amica (Averti (IRE))
4250[5] 4761[8]

Riviera Poet (IRE) *D K Weld* 106
2 b g Footstepsinthesand—Dance Clear (IRE) (Marju (IRE))
5293a[5]

Riviera Stars *Michael Bell* 72
3 b g Galileo(IRE) —Miss Riviera Golf (Hernando (FR))
5327[6] 5911[8] 6810[5] 7107[2]

Rivington *Richard Fahey* a44 18
2 b c Oasis Dream—Kiralik (Efisio)
2617[13] 6983[15] 7194[6] 7421[10]

Rizella (FR) *Mme C Head-Maarek* a74 85
3 b f Iron Mask(USA) —Rizierella (FR) (Bering)
981a[9]

Rjeef (IRE) *David Simcock* a93 94
4 b h Red Ransom(USA) —Sun Chaser (IRE) (King's Best (USA))
99[12]

Road To Glory *Hanne Bechmann*
2 b c Kyllachy—Danalova (Groom Dancer (USA))
4841a[6]

Roanstar *Andrew Balding* a66 77
4 gr g Act One—Dolce Thundera (USA) (Thunder Gulch (USA))
1173[4] 1608[13] 2055[5]

Roayh (USA) *Saeed Bin Suroor* a99 103
3 ch g Speightstown(USA) —Most Remarkable (USA) (Marquetry (USA))
411a[7] 4764[4] 6339[23] 6704[7] 7168[2]

Robber Stone *Mick Channon* a51 57
3 gr g Proclamation(IRE) —Amiata (Pennekamp (USA))
1953[5] 2350[8] 2421[5]

Robbmaa (FR) *Tony Carroll* a30 43
6 bl g Cape Cross(IRE) —Native Twine (Be My Native (USA))
3094[7] 3516[11]

Robby Bobby *Laura Mongan* a68 68
6 ch g Selkirk(USA) —Dancing Mirage (IRE) (Machiavellian (USA))
1577[3] 1839[8] (2562) 3003[9] 3225[8] 4242[4] 4847[8] 7121[6] 7331[8] 7654[11]

Robemaker *John Gosden* a72 98
3 b c Oasis Dream—Regal Velvet (Halling (USA))
1496[6] 1759[6] 2467[3] [illegible] ◆ [illegible] (4101) 5450[9] 5940[2] 6290[2] 7168[6]

Robert Le Diable (FR) *D Prod'Homme* 96
2 ch c Dutch Art—Red Begonia (Pivotal)
2866a[3]

Roberto Pegasus (USA) *Pat Phelan* 83
5 bb g Fusaichi Pegasus(USA) —Louju (USA) (Silver Hawk (USA))
(3184) 3794[4] 4806[7] 6499[5] 6893[4]

Robert The Painter (IRE) *Richard Fahey* 89
3 b g Whipper(USA) —Lidanna (Nicholas (USA))
1825[8] 2684[10] 3830[6] 4810[2] ◆ 5465[8] 6093[4] 6704[8]

Robin Du Nord (FR) *J-P Gauvin* a92 94
4 b h Voix Du Nord(FR) —La Romagne (FR) (Art Francais (USA))
830a[2]

Robin Hoods Bay *Edward Vaughan* a93 83
3 b g Motivator—Bijou A Moi (Rainbow Quest (USA))
(2196) 3118[4] 3919[2] (6218) 6822[2] ◆

Rocco Breeze (IRE) *Philip McBride* a42 44
2 b c Shirocco(GER) —Crossbreeze (USA) (Red Ransom (USA))
2510[13] 3132[9] 4433[4] 5634[7]

Rochdale *A Al Raihe* a101 101
8 ch g Bertolini(USA) —Owdbetts (IRE) (High Estate)
153a[10] 240[4] 326a[6] 499a[8] 679a[11]

Roche Ambeau (FR) *E Lellouche* 103
4 gr m Chichicastenango(FR) —Exande (FR) (Exit To Nowhere (USA))
1784a[9] 5075a[7] 7580a[3]

Roche Des Vents *Richard Hannon* a79 79
3 b c Bahamian Bounty—Tokyo Rose (Agnes World (USA))
(665)

Rock Ace (IRE) *Deborah Sanderson* a64 79
3 gr f Verglas(IRE) —Break Of Day (USA) (Favorite Trick (USA))
2092[7] 2564[5] 3346[8]

Rock A Doodle Doo (IRE) *William Jarvis* a80 105
4 b h Oratorio(IRE) —Nousaiyra (IRE) (Be My Guest (USA))
1477[2] ◆ (1887) ◆ 3156[4] ◆ 3875[9] 4778[7]

Rock An Run (IRE) *D Prod'Homme* a71 78
3 b f Hurricane Run(IRE) —Rock Chick (Halling (USA))
981a[10]

Rock Anthem (IRE) *Mike Murphy* a75 83
7 ch g Rock Of Gibraltar(IRE) —Regal Portrait (IRE) (Royal Academy (USA))
3740[8] 4215[10] 4656[9] 5101[6] 6226[5] 6727[8] 6924[3] 7098[7] 7632[3] 7843[2] (7930)

Rockatella (IRE) *W Hefter* 107
4 b m Rock Of Gibraltar(IRE) —Patrimony (Cadeaux Genereux)
1432a[6] 2657a[5] (3213a) 3897a[2] 4497[8] 5753a[10] 7193a[0]

Rock Band *Richard Hannon* 45
2 b c Rock Of Gibraltar(IRE) —Decision Maid (USA) (Diesis)
6462[9]

Rock Canyon (IRE) *Robert Mills* a56 72
2 b g Rock Of Gibraltar(IRE) —Tuesday Morning (Sadler's Wells (USA))
1988[3] 2882[4] 3472[5] 5197[6] 5809[9] 7808[5] 7907[3]

Rock Critic (IRE) *D K Weld* a103 104
6 b g Pivotal—Diamond Trim (IRE) (Highest Honor (FR))
(4566a)

Rocker *Gary Moore* a64 80
7 b g Rock Of Gibraltar(IRE) —Jessica's Dream (IRE) (Desert Style (IRE))
961[7] 1140[8] 1507[2] 1638[2] 1864[6] (2167) 2447[5] 2929[6] 3389[4]

Rockerfellow *J W Hills* 67
3 b c Shirocco(GER) —Mazaya (IRE) (Sadler's Wells (USA))
3232[5] 3543[7] 4254[6] 4908[10] 6748[11]

Rocket Man (AUS) *Patrick Shaw* a126 127
6 b g Viscount(AUS) —Macrosa (NZ) (Mcginty (NZ))
(999a) (2339a) 7730a[12]

Rocket Rob (IRE) *Willie Musson* a76 95
5 b g Danetime(IRE) —Queen Of Fibres (IRE) (Scenic)
613[12] 1166[14] 1720[18] 2299[4] ◆ 2525[3] 2890[9] 4765[10] 5033[8] ◆ 5831[5] 6327[8] 6761[8] 7171[13] 7428[6]

Rocket Twentyone (CAN) *W T Howard* a100
2 bb f Indian Charlie(USA) —Symphonic Lady (USA) (Blare Of Trumpets (USA))
7283a[13]

Rockfella *Denis Coakley* a59 83
5 ch g Rock Of Gibraltar(IRE) —Afreeta (USA) (Afleet (CAN))
(1509) 2686[6] 3817[3] (4998) 6103[9]

Rockhorse (IRE) *B Grizzetti* 114
6 ch g Rock Of Gibraltar(IRE) —Maelalong (IRE) (Maelstrom Lake)
2541a[3]

Rockinante (FR) *Richard Hannon* 105
2 ch c Rock Of Gibraltar(IRE) —Nantes (GER) (Night Shift (USA))
(3401) ◆ 4424[2] (5130a) 5365a[5] 6336[4] (6692)

Rock Jock (IRE) *Tracey Collins* a96 107
4 b g Rock Of Gibraltar(IRE) —Perfect Touch (USA) (Miswaki (USA))
155a[10] 327a[3] 582a[4] 754a[5] 825a[9] 1533a[8] 3440a[4] (4573) 5532a[10] 5979a[7]

Rock Magic (IRE) *John Joseph Murphy* a32 28
2 b f Rock Of Gibraltar(IRE) —Magic Sister (Cadeaux Genereux)
7454[11]

Rockme Cockney *Jeremy Gask* a75 72
2 ch f Cockney Rebel(IRE) —Rock Lily (Rock Of Gibraltar (IRE))
2606[2] 3201[8] 4853[2] 5393[6] 6819[9] 7248[4]

Rock My Soul (IRE) *A Fabre* 109
5 b m Clodovil(IRE) —Rondinay (FR) (Cadeaux Genereux)
1784a[3] 2373a[6] 5093a[5] 6321a[5] 7090a[10]

Rock My World (IRE) *Roger Varian* a75 75
4 b m Rock Of Gibraltar(IRE) —Arctic Hunt (IRE) (Bering)
2220[14] 2552[9]

Rock 'N' Roller (FR) *Gary Moore* a74 44
7 bb g Sagacity(FR) —Diamond Dance (FR) (Dancehall (USA))
216 [4]

Rock N Roll Ransom *Mahmood Al Zarooni* a100 103
4 b g Red Ransom(USA) —Zee Zee Top (Zafonic (USA))
(153a)

Rock 'N' Royal *Richard Fahey* 78
4 b g Royal Applause—Grande Terre (IRE) (Grand Lodge (USA))
1245[8] 1748[5] 2366[10]

Rock Of Monet *David Simcock* a50 60
2 b c Kyllachy—Level Pegging (IRE) (Common Grounds)
3793[6] 4276[11] 4947[3] 5690[7]

Rock Of Nassau (FR) *X Nakkachdji* 96
5 ch g Rock Of Gibraltar(IRE) —Solosole (USA) (Gulch (USA))
754a[11] 6593a[0] 6958a[0] 7256a[0]

Rock On Candy *Sylvester Kirk* a56 68
2 b f Excellent Art—Rock Candy (IRE) (Rock Of Gibraltar (IRE))
3547[5] 4471[11] 6048[11] 7444[6] 7569[9]

Rock Peak (IRE) *Bernard Llewellyn* a67 58
6 b g Dalakhani(IRE) —Convenience (IRE) (Ela-Mana-Mou)
3516[10] 3799[8] 4274[10] 4642[4] (4951) 7264[3]

Rock Relief (IRE) *David Thompson* a56 66
5 gr g Daylami(IRE) —Sheer Bliss (IRE) (Sadler's Wells (USA))
7536[6]

Rock Song *Amanda Perrett* 70
2 b c Rock Of Gibraltar(IRE) —Jackie's Opera (FR) (Indian Ridge)
4996[14] 6725[4]

Rock Supreme (IRE) *Michael Dods* 80
2 b c Rock Of Gibraltar(IRE) —Love And Affection (USA) (Exclusive Era (USA))
3186[2] (3826) 5181[12] 6527[15]

Rocktherunway (IRE) *Michael Dods* 76
2 ch g Nayef(USA) —Femme Fatale (Fairy King (USA))
4323[2] 5454[5] 6187[4] 6911[6]

Rock The Stars (IRE) *J W Hills* a46 82
4 ch g Rock Of Gibraltar(IRE) —Crimphill (IRE) (Sadler's Wells (USA))
1402[11] 1829[4] (2436) 2884[7] 3277[6] (4211) 4724[4] 5275[10] 6465[4] 7022[15]

Rockview Diamond (IRE) *John C McConnell* a79 82
2 b c Diamond Green(FR) —Touchy Feelings (IRE) (Ashkalani (IRE))
972a[4] 6196a[18]

Rockweiller *Steve Gollings* a25 73
4 b h Rock Of Gibraltar(IRE) —Ballerina Suprema (IRE) (Sadler's Wells (USA))
3545[9] 4148[2] 4716[4] 5178[12] 5791[8] (7113)

Rock With You *Pat Phelan* a68 65
4 b m Rock Of Gibraltar(IRE) —Karsiyaka (IRE) (Kahyasi)
1353[7] 1866[8] 2816[12] 3546[2] 3817[7]

Rocky Elsom (USA) *David Arbuthnot* 84
4 b g Rock Of Gibraltar(IRE) —Bowstring (IRE) (Sadler's Wells (USA))
7894[3]

Rocky Rainbow (ITY) *Vaclav Luka II*
3 b c Rainbows For Life(CAN) —Rose Of Millkom (Millkom)
4874a[2]

Rocky Rebel *Ralph Beckett* a75 76
3 b g Norse Dancer(IRE) —Gulchina (USA) (Gulch (USA))
4215[8] 5140[3] 5816[3] 6748[5]

Rocky Reef *Andrew Balding* a65 62
2 b c Danbird(AUS) —Leah's Pride (Atraf)
5384[9] 6127[7] 6662[2] ◆ 7358[5]

Roderic O'Connor (IRE) *A P O'Brien* 119
3 b c Galileo(IRE) —Secret Garden (IRE) (Danehill (USA))
1686[11] (2324a) 2751a[8] 3442a[6] 5747a[5]

Rode Two Destiny (IRE) *Peter Makin* 64
2 b f Dark Angel(IRE) —Dear Catch (IRE) (Bluebird (USA))
5779[3] 6890[6]

Rodrigo De Freitas (IRE) *Jim Boyle* a62 67
4 b g Captain Rio—Brazilian Sun (IRE) (Barathea (IRE))
2372[3] 3003[8] 3533[7] 3814[5] 4059[2] 4242[5] 4454[4] 6789[6] 7122[9] 7387[5] 7603[2] 7761[8]

Rodrigo De Torres *Mrs K Burke* 107
4 ch g Bahamian Bounty—Leonica (Lion Cavern (USA))
1533a[11] 3440a[19] 5282[10] 5563[4] 6027[6] 6145[23]

Roedean (IRE) *Richard Hannon* a73 77
2 b f Oratorio(IRE) —Exotic Mix (FR) (Linamix (FR))
2153[8] 2467[4] 3046[3] 4277[3] 4760[2] 5537[3] 6169[5] 6526[9]

Roe Valley (IRE) *Linda Jewell* a63 36
4 ch g Arakan(USA) —Waaedah (USA) (Halling (USA))
420[6] 649[10] 945[3] 2051[11] 2560[9] 3176[13]

Rogalt (IRE) *R Houthoofd* a68 76
5 b g Rock Of Gibraltar(IRE) —Rills (USA) (Clever Trick (USA))
6593a[0] 7315a[0]

Roger Sez (IRE) *Tim Easterby* 106
2 b f Red Clubs(IRE) —Stately Princess (Robellino (USA))
2113[15] (2780) ◆ (4079) (4551) 5216[9] 5558[4] 5847[4] (6146) 6705[5]

Rogue Reporter (IRE) *Luca Cumani* 65
2 b c Sir Percy—Princess Nala (IRE) (In The Wings)
5011[10] 6019[5] 6771[7]

Rohlindi *Jeremy Gask* a37 68
3 b f Red Ransom(USA) —Rohita (IRE) (Waajib)
1629[2] ◆ 3577[6] 4970[6] 7173[13]

Roicead (USA) *Brendan W Duke* 107
4 b g Giant's Causeway(USA) —Coachella (Danehill (USA))
3440a[5] (4767a) 5524a[3]

Roi Dana (FR) *R Ducasteele* a66 31
6 b g Dananeyev(FR) —Reine De Lutece (FR) (Synefos (USA))
7315a[10]

Roi Du Boeuf (IRE) *David Simcock* a61 63
3 b g Hurricane Run(IRE) —Princess Killeen (IRE) (Sinndar (IRE))
25[5] (194) 297[3]

Roilos (IRE) *Michael Wigham* a69
5 b h Bahri(USA) —Raiska (IRE) (Grand Lodge (USA))
315[2]

Rojo Boy *David Elsworth* a68 78
3 gr c Red Ransom(USA) —Way To The Stars (Dansili)
191[3] 520[2] 1339[11] 2068[5] 2841[13] 4281[7] 4829[2] 5381[7] 6468[5]

Roker Park (IRE) *David O'Meara* 95
6 b g Choisir(AUS) —Joyful (IRE) (Green Desert (USA))
2116[13] (2668) ◆ 3395[7] (3850) 4042[3] 4346[8] 5218[14]

Rolling Home (GER) *P Schaerer* a87 67
7 b h Dashing Blade—Roma Libera (GER) (Pharly (FR))
(534a) 628a[15]

Rollin 'n Tumblin *Michael Attwater* a34
7 ch g Zaha(CAN) —Steppin Out (First Trump)
962[6] 1148[10]

Roll Of Thunder *John Quinn* 54
2 b g Antonius Pius(USA) —Ischia (Lion Cavern (USA))
3314[12] 5618[6] 6448[9] 7051[11]

Roman Dancer (IRE) *John Gallagher* a69 77
3 b g Antonius Pius(USA) —Dancing Duchess (IRE) (Danehill Dancer (IRE))
1141[2] 1545[6] 2199[6] 2757[2] 3598[9] 4156[9] 4695[2] 5341[8] 5895[10] 6223[9]

Roman Eagle (IRE) *Roger Varian* 94
3 b g Holy Roman Emperor(IRE) —Qhazeenah (Marju (IRE))
3864[6] ◆ 4718[4] 6375[5]

Roman Flame *Michael Quinn* a75 64
3 ch f Bertolini(USA) —Dakhla Oasis (IRE) (Night Shift (USA))
360[2] 624[3] 888[3] 1400[8] 1572[3] 3018[6] 3742[8] 5630[14] 6122[2] 7271[5] 7427[3] 7638[4] 7800[6]

Roman Locket (IRE) *Andrew Oliver* a61 55
2 b f Holy Roman Emperor(IRE) —Oumaldaaya (USA) (Nureyev (USA))
7275a[7]

Roman Myst (IRE) *Sylvester Kirk* a57 7
2 b g Holy Roman Emperor(IRE) —Mystiara (IRE) (Orpen (USA))
5337[13] 6180[4] 6474[9]

Roman Province (IRE) *Roger Teal* a52 69
2 b f Holy Roman Emperor(IRE) —Crimphill (IRE) (Sadler's Wells (USA))
4245[2] 4662[7] 5855[6] 6268[7] 6792[8]

Roman Ruler (IRE) *Chris Fairhurst* a59 66
3 gr g Antonius Pius(USA) —Way Of Truth (Muhtarram (USA))
1494[3] 1802[10] 1880[5] 3661[9] 4443[12] (5248) 5731[13]

Roman Seal (IRE) *Tom Dascombe* a75 57
2 b f Holy Roman Emperor(IRE) —Gilded Vanity (IRE) (Indian Ridge)
3342[6] 5047[5] (5632)

Roman Senate (IRE) *Martin Bosley* 51
2 b c Holy Roman Emperor(IRE) —Indian Fun (Poliglote)
4269[7] 5613[8] 6018[5] 6972[11]

Roman Soldier (IRE) *Jeremy Noseda* 109
2 b g Holy Roman Emperor(IRE) —Fermion (IRE) (Sadler's Wells (USA))
1678[6] (2584) 3012[2] 3773[2]

Roman Strait *Michael Blanshard* a73 74
3 b c Refuse To Bend(IRE) —Oman Sea (USA) (Rahy (USA))
228[5] 335[2] 1749[6] 2025[2] 2564[2] 3207[3] 3347[2] 4062[5] 4511[7] 4799[9] 6282[2] 6930[2] 7173[3] 7417[6] 7893[5]

Romantic (IRE) *Sir Henry Cecil* a27 70
2 b c Holy Roman Emperor(IRE) —Welsh Love (Ela-Mana-Mou)
4798[9] 5564[5] 7083[10]

Romantic Girl (IRE) *Alan Juckes* a22 38
3 b f Byron—Urmia (Persian Bold)
3596[5] 5022[6] 5916[13]

Romantic Man (GER) *Traugott Stauffer* 68
8 b h Big Shuffle(USA) —Romanze (GER) (Surumu (GER))
440a[8]

Romantic Queen *George Baker* a70 24
5 b m Medicean—Bandit Queen (Desert Prince (IRE))
746[5] 766[5] 861[5]

Romantic Wish *Robert Mills* a75 93
3 b f Hawk Wing(USA) —Jules (IRE) (Danehill (USA))
764[2] 1446[3] 2643[3] (3818) 4062[2] 4958[2] 5657[4] 6239[2] 7031[6]

Romany Spirit (IRE) *Jim Boyle* a59 56
2 b f Invincible Spirit(IRE) —Attachment (USA) (Trempolino (USA))
4720[8] 5111[9] 5564[8] 5998[3] 6821[12]

Romeo Montague *Ed Dunlop* a71 89
3 b g Montjeu(IRE) —Issa (Pursuit Of Love)
(1299) ◆ 1951[8] 2293[3] 2677[2] 2957[6] 4237[2] (4697) 5283[7] 5971[3] 6375[2] 7017[4]

Romeo's On Fire (IRE) *G M Lyons* a77 86
7 b g Danehill(USA) —Fighting Countess (USA) (Ringside (USA))
7150a[10]

Romin Robin (USA) *David Kassen* 106
5 bb m Pure Precision(USA) —Italian Slew (USA) (Ocala Slew (USA))
5073a[11]

Rondeau (GR) *Patrick Chamings* a89 89
6 ch g Harmonic Way—Areti (GR) (Wadood (USA))
(1232) 1488[3] 2719[3] 3536[3] (4010) 4656[6] 5322[2] 6378[3] 7171[4]

Roninski (IRE) *Bryan Smart* a86 91
3 b c Cadeaux Genereux—Ruby Affair (IRE) (Night Shift (USA))
1027[2] (1370) 2092[6] (3854) 4290[4] (4810) (5370) 5830[10] 7531[8] 7628[4]

Ronnie Howe *Roy Bowring* a39 31
7 b g Hunting Lion(IRE) —Arasong (Aragon)
735[11] 800[5] 941[13] 1464[11] 1501[6] 1818[7] 1875[7] 2237[12] 7230[13] 7690[7]

Roodee Queen *Milton Bradley* a73 83
3 b f Kyllachy—Hilites (IRE) (Desert King (IRE))
1219[3] (1369) 1802[9] 2177[2] 2592[5] (2756) (3470) (4067) (4231) (4459) 4817[4] 5476[6] 5862[9] 7847[8]

Roodle *Eve Johnson Houghton* a79 89
4 b m Xaar—Roodeye (Inchinor)
1103[6] 1603[17] (2855) 5354[6] 5702[12]

Rooknrasbryripple *Ralph Smith* a66 66
2 b f Piccolo—Here To Me (Muhtarram (USA))
1441[14] 1932[2] 2194[2] 2416[2] 2640[2] 2889[5] (3021) 3584[6] 5577[4] 5840[8] 6166[6] 6489[10] 6627[9] 6821[3] 7735[5] 7937[3]

Room For A View *Marcus Tregoning* a66 57
4 b m Observatory(USA) —Annex (Anabaa (USA))
1333[8] 1608[6]

Roose Blox (IRE) *Roger Fisher* a38 70
4 b g Captain Rio—Kakatiya (IRE) (Barathea (IRE))
878[7] 965[5]

Rory Anna (IRE) *John J Walsh* 82
5 b m Viking Ruler(AUS) —Montana Miss (IRE) (Earl Of Barking (IRE))
925a[4]

Rory Boy (USA) *Graeme McPherson* a35 63
6 b g Aldebaran(USA) —Purr Pleasure (USA) (El Gran Senor (USA))
6504[5]

Rosa Bonheur (USA) *E Lellouche* a100 100
3 b f Mr Greeley(USA) —Rolly Polly (IRE) (Mukaddamah (USA))
5695a[2] 7678a[6]

Rosa Eglanteria *B Grizzetti* 107
2 b f Nayef(USA) —Rose Shift (IRE) (Night Shift (USA))
6740a[2]

Rosairlie (IRE) *Harry Dunlop* a69 71
3 ch f Halling(USA) —Mrs Mason (IRE) (Turtle Island (IRE))
3289[5] 3912[5] 5964[5] 6465[5] 6944[13] 7195[2] 7331[6]

Rosa Luxemburg *Bryan Smart*
3 ch f Needwood Blade—Colonel's Daughter (Colonel Collins (USA))
7747[9] 7856[6]

Rosa Midnight (USA) *Michael Bell* a61 57
3 b f Lemon Drop Kid(USA) —Christmas Player (USA) (Theatrical)
1526[5] 1997[11] 4686[6]

Rosanabad (FR) *J-C Rouget* 109
3 ch c Selkirk(USA) —Rosawa (FR) (Linamix (FR))
1552a[2]

Rosbay (IRE) *Tim Easterby* 85
7 b g Desert Prince(IRE) —Dark Rosaleen (IRE) (Darshaan)
1099[4] 1909[5] ◆ (2059) 2414[6] 2734[5] 3051[4] 3319[4] 3848[6] 4173[6] 4612[10] 5106[8] 5594[8]

Rosbertini *Linda Perratt* 62
5 ch g Bertolini(USA) —Rose Of America (Brief Truce (USA))
1714[8] 1857[10] 2057[8] 2631[5] 3110[7] 3454[5] 3658[9] 3857[8] 3902[5] 4143[9] 4379[10]

Rosco Flyer (IRE) *Roger Teal* a82 81
5 b g Val Royal(FR) —Palace Soy (IRE) (Tagula (IRE))
1402[13] 2021[3] 2769[6] 4059[4] 4660[7] 5102[6] 5942[5] 6790[2] 7203 [4] 7346[5] 7603[4]

Rose Aurora *Marcus Tregoning* a58 53
4 gr m Pastoral Pursuits—Khaladja (IRE) (Akarad (FR))
1135[6] 5785[2] 6236[4] 6476[4] 6876[12] (7528) 7761[10]

Rose Bed (IRE) *Michael Quinlan* a48 48
4 ch m Namid—Daqtora (Dr Devious (IRE))
57[12] 120[6]

Rosebel (FR) *Y Fouin* 45
3 bl g Dano-Mast—Eclat De Rose (FR) (Scribe (IRE))
5132a[8]

Rose Blossom *Richard Fahey* 109
4 b m Pastoral Pursuits—Lamarita (Emarati (USA))
2005[14] 2297[6] 3010[17] 3827[3] 4573[2] (5080) 5528a[4] 6531[3]

Rose Bonheur *Kevin Prendergast* a97 107
3 b f Danehill Dancer(IRE) —Red Feather (IRE) (Marju (IRE))
2334a[9] 3527a[3] 5228a[6] 5979a[9] 6520[2] 7277a[5]

Rose Bush (IRE) *Marco Botti* a48
3 b f Pivotal—Centifolia (FR) (Kendor (FR))
624[7]

Rosedale *James Toller* a54 76
4 b m Pastoral Pursuits—Wyoming (Inchinor)
2269[5] 2999[5] ◆ 4093[8] 5113[4] 5992[4] 6586[3] ◆ 6924[8]

Rose Danon (GER) *P Schiergen* 100
3 b c Sholokhov(IRE) —Rose Hedge (GER) (Highest Honor (FR))
2338a[8] 3422a[5]

Rose Kingdom (JPN) *Kojiro Hashiguchi* 124
4 bb h King Kamehameha(JPN) —Rosebud (JPN) (Sunday Silence (USA))
7563a[9] 7873a[12]

Rosenblatt (GER) *John Spearing* a54 22
9 b g Dashing Blade—Roseraie (GER) (Nebos (GER))
173[2] 4273[11] 7461[8]

Rosendhal (IRE) *M Narduzzi* 103
4 ch h Indian Ridge—Kathy College (IRE) (College Chapel)
1919a[8] 7408a[3]

Rose Of Sarratt (IRE) *Rae Guest* a61 74
3 b f Sadler's Wells(USA) —Sweet Gypsy Rose (IRE) (Darshaan)
3224[7] 4014[5] 4805[7] 5134[4] 5915[7] 6240[2] (7212)

Rose Season *Roger Varian* 57
2 b f Cape Cross(IRE) —Endorsement (Warning)
7233[7]

Rose The One (FR) *J-M Beguigne* a76
3 b f Meshaheer(USA) —Restless Mixa (IRE) (Linamix (FR))
981a[7]

Rose Willow (USA) *John Gosden* a70 32
3 b f Artie Schiller(USA) —Divi (Bustino)
1572[9] 2175[3]

Rosewin (IRE) *Ollie Pears* a71 89
5 b m Hawkeye(IRE) —African Scene (IRE) (Scenic)
1676[7] 2034[16] (2496) 3316[2] (3730) 4348[9] 5273[3] ◆ 6171[14]

Rosewood Lad *J S Moore* a78 63
4 ch g Needwood Blade—Meandering Rose (USA) (Irish River (FR))
161[2] (407) 492[2] 718[5] (838) 1016[2] 3205[6] 3522[4] 4488[3] 5102[4] 5417[2] 6722[8] 7120[7] 7753[5]

Rosie Raymond *Charles Smith* a23 46
6 b m Kris Kin(USA) —Iota (Niniski (USA))
2114[6] 2669[4] 4396[3] 5790[13]

Rosie's Lady (IRE) *David O'Meara* a9 52
2 b f Elusive City(USA) —Blushing Libra (Perugino (USA))
3201[3] 3609[7] 4171[3] 4943[9] 6611[8]

Rosina Grey *S Seemar* a78 85
3 gr f Proclamation(IRE) —Rosina May (IRE) (Danehill Dancer (IRE))
680a[4] 823a[10]

Rosselli (IRE) *Mrs K Burke* a55
2 b c Iffraaj—Special Ellie (FR) (Celtic Swing)
7398[4]

Rossetti *James Fanshawe* a84 83
3 gr g Dansili—Snowdrops (Gulch (USA))
(1335) 1916[4] 7171[20] 7531[7] 7841[8]

Rosslyn Castle *Roger Charlton* 76
2 ch c Selkirk(USA) —Margarula (IRE) (Doyoun)
6059[4] ◆
Rostrum (FR) *A Fabre* a102 110
4 b h Shamardal(USA) —En Public (FR) (Rainbow Quest (USA))
1125a[2] 1740a[9]
Rosy Dawn *Mark Hoad* a55 54
6 ch m Bertolini(USA) —Blushing Sunrise (USA) (Cox's Ridge (USA))
334 207 7 4667 4754[2] 5406[4] 5993[6] *6621[12] 7092[12]*
Rothesay Chancer *Jim Goldie* 83
3 ch g Monsieur Bond(IRE) —Rhinefield Beauty (IRE) (Shalford (IRE))
1514[2] (2265) (2697) 3126[2] (3360) 3853[6] 4791[2] 5054[8] 5720[3] ◆ 6112[6] 7104[8]
Roubiliac (USA) *Paul Webber* 57
4 ch h Rahy(USA) —Super Tassa (IRE) (Lahib (USA))
3001[9]
Rouge Emery (FR) *J Clais* a68 69
5 b m Bonnet Rouge(FR) —Natashwan (Shining Steel)
843a[10] 1013a[0]
Rougemont (IRE) *Richard Hannon* 86
2 b c Montjeu(IRE) —Spritza (IRE) (Spectrum (IRE))
(3823) ◆ 5044[5] (6606) 7167[3]
Rougette *Charles Hills* 84
3 b f Red Ransom(USA) —Never A Doubt (Night Shift (USA))
1362[4] ◆ 2103[2] ◆ (2689) 3034[8] 5255[16] 7296[17]
Rough Rock (IRE) *Chris Dwyer* a54 81
6 ch g Rock Of Gibraltar(IRE) —Amitie Fatale (IRE) (Night Shift (USA))
1109[12] 1506[4] 1990[4] 2270[4] 2597[3] 3130[2] 3179[6] (3555) (4160) 4393[4] 4765[7] 5119[5] 5516[4] 5760[5] 6069[5] 6378[8] 6759[4] 7299[13]
Rough Sketch (USA) *Ian Williams* a45 61
6 b g Peintre Celebre(USA) —Drama Club (IRE) (Sadler's Wells (USA))
115[11] 346[8] 630[6] 768[6]
Rougini (IRE) *Mrs K Burke* a71 67
2 ch f Bertolini(USA) —Stravinskaya (USA) (Stravinsky (USA))
1946[3] 2542[4] 3504[3] 3639[2] 4557[7] 5105[2] (5646) 6590[6] *(6975)*
Round Turn (IRE) *Ed McMahon* a70 55
3 b g Oratorio(IRE) —Half-Hitch (USA) (Diesis)
564[2] 7315 (1022)
Round Won (USA) *William Knight* a92 74
4 ch g Two Punch(USA) —Indy Go Go (USA) (A.P. Indy (USA))
381[2] (647) 803[2] 1102[12] 5328[12] *6948[14]*
Rova (FR) *P Demercastel*
3 ch f Vatori(FR) —Royal Lights (FR) (Royal Academy (USA))
5463a[0]
Rovos (FR) *S Wattel* a83 76
3 b c Johannesburg(USA) —Royal Liverpool (USA) (Gulch (USA))
(638a) 5529a[2]
Rowan Lodge (IRE) *Ollie Pears* a53 70
9 ch g Indian Lodge(IRE) —Tirol Hope (IRE) (Tirol)
(1164) 1658[6] 2490[4] 2800[7] 3938[2] 4409[5] 4946[9] 6236[3]
Rowan Ridge *Jim Boyle* a72 68
3 ch g Compton Place—Lemon Tree (USA) (Zilzal (USA))
2371[11] 2760[7] 3690[5] 4248[3] 4686[7] 5993[2] *6052[2] 6253[2] (6622) 6790[6] 7363[8] 7600[4] (7800) 7939[4]*
Rowan Spirit (IRE) *Mark Brisbourne* a83 76
3 gr g Captain Rio—Secret Justice (USA) (Lit De Justice (USA))
2180[10] *2818[8]* 3337[10] 3806[7] 4271[7] (4715) 5109[2] *5419[6] 5735[11]* 6840[8] (7073) *7341[2] 7500[8]*
Rowan Sun *Eve Johnson Houghton* 17
2 ch g Haafhd—Rowan Flower (IRE) (Ashkalani (IRE))
5672[10]
Rowan Tiger *Jim Boyle* a80 81
5 b g Tiger Hill(IRE) —Lemon Tree (USA) (Zilzal (USA))
1156[4] 2793[2] 3277[9] 4724[8] 5545[5] 6023[3] *6976[4]*
Rowayton *Muredach Kelly* a86 82
5 gr m Lujain(USA) —Bandanna (Bandmaster (USA))
6261[8]
Rowe Park *Linda Jewell* a108 106
8 b g Dancing Spree(USA) —Magic Legs (Reprimand)
989[10] 1848[5] 2288[13] 5543[11] 6522[12]
Roxy Flyer (IRE) *Amanda Perrett* a99 106
4 b m Rock Of Gibraltar(IRE) —Dyna Flyer (USA) (Marquetry (USA))
1677[4] 2292[4] 4470[6] 5271[10] 5659[2] 6269[4] *7129[2]*
Roxy Spirit (IRE) *Michael Mullineaux* a21
4 ch m Cape Town(IRE) —Preston Music (Accordion)
836[7] 1586[9]
Royaaty (IRE) *M bin Shafya* a93 104
5 b h Singspiel(IRE) —Whisper To Dream (USA) (Gone West (USA))
585a[4] 826a[8]
Royal Academician (USA) *Gary Moore* 73
2 b c Mr Greeley(USA) —Alta Moda (Sadler's Wells (USA))
3590[7] ◆ 4007[5] ◆ 4655[2] 5280[7] 6972[6]
Royal Acclamation (IRE) *Michael Scudamore* a62 58
6 b g Acclamation—Lady Abigail (IRE) (Royal Academy (USA))
312[8] (482) 619[2] 664[2] 874[8] 1182[5] ◆ *1336[9] 6138[11] 6659[11]* 7131[10] 7760[3] 7923[2]
Royal Alcor (IRE) *Alastair Lidderdale* a70 55
4 b g Chevalier(IRE) —Arundhati (IRE) (Royal Academy (USA))
5629[9] *6086[11]* 6589[3] *(7370) (7495) 7661[8] 7817[11]* ◆ *7903[6]*

Royal And Ancient (IRE) *David Thompson* a63 66
4 b g Danehill Dancer(IRE) —Champaka (IRE) (Caerleon (USA))
2433[5]
Royal Approval (ITY) *Maria Rita Salvioni* 91
2 b c Tout Seul(IRE) —Diche (USA) (With Approval (CAN))
6740a[7] 7217a[5]
Royal Award *Ian Wood* a77 82
2 b f Cadeaux Genereux—Red Sovereign (Danzig Connection (USA))
3287[6] 3915[4] *(4848)* (5961) 6518[13]
Royal Bajan (USA) *James Given* a73 74
3 rg g Speightstown(USA) —Crown You (USA) (Two Punch (USA))
(1065) 1294[4] 1980[5] (2524) *(3239)* 3628[3] 3975[4] 4234[9] 4855[3] 5939[7] 6456[7] *7594[5] (7940)*
Royal Bench (IRE) *Robert Collet* 119
4 b h Whipper(USA) —Hit The Sky (IRE) (Cozzene (USA))
1000a[4] 1576a[11] 2340a[9] 5129a[4] 5988a[5] 6556a[6]
Royal Bengali (USA) *A bin Huzaim* a79 101
4 b h Tiger Hill(IRE) —Joharra (USA) (Kris S (USA))
584a[8]
Royal Blade (IRE) *Alan Berry* a62 71
4 ch g Needwood Blade—Royal Dream (Ardkinglass)
1666 3435 362[13] 1439[7] 1716[7] 1856[4] 2353[8] 2632[5] 3049[2] 3248[2] 3662[4] 4000[2] (4145) 4289[2] (4378) 4780[4] 4881[2] 5371[9] 5720[11] 5881[10] 6213[4] 6343[4] 6414[9] 7065[10] 7728[12]
Royal Blue Star (IRE) *Mrs John Harrington* a69 95
3 b f Dalakhani(IRE) —Etizaan (IRE) (Unfuwain (USA))
4418a[2] 5228a[7] 5361a[9]
Royal Blush *Paul Cole* 74
2 b f Royal Applause—Applaud (USA) (Rahy (USA))
1337[2] ◆ (2063) 4496[13] 5052[7] 5324[6] 5847[12] 6237[7]
Royal Bonnie (USA) *George Weaver* 96
2 b f Yankee Gentleman(USA) —Royal Muskoka (USA) (Theatrical)
7281a[10]
Royal Bonsai *John Quinn* a61 66
3 b g Val Royal(FR) —Bonsai (IRE) (Woodman (USA))
1559[6] 2407[6] 4111[2] 4612[3] 5623[4] 6153[2] 6600[4] *7495[3]*
Royal Box *Dai Burchell* a65 67
4 b g Royal Applause—Diamond Lodge (Grand Lodge (USA))
3519 3637 (3216) 3512[3] *(4918)* 5539[2] (5881) 6436[5] *7817[6]*
Royal Composer (IRE) *Tim Easterby* 55
8 b g Mozart(IRE) —Susun Kelapa (USA) (St Jovite (USA))
2616[5] 2800[5] 3938[11] 4409[6] 4903[9]
Royal Cyclone (IRE) *M Boutin* a47 69
8 b g Royal Academy(USA) —Gulf Cyclone (USA) (Sheikh Albadou)
832a[0]
Royal Deal *Michael Easterby* 56
4 b g Gentleman's Deal(IRE) —Royal Distant (USA) (Distant View (USA))
2457[10] 2802[9] 3167[6] 3936[10] 4673[7] 4944[4]
Royal Defence (IRE) *Michael Quinn* a51 69
5 b g Refuse To Bend(IRE) —Alessia (GER) (Warning)
885[6] 1398[5] 2021[6] 2569[4] 2856[8] 3184[8] (3480) 3945[3] 4165[5] 4847[4] (5993) 6769[3]
Royal Delta (USA) *William Mott* a123
3 bb f Empire Maker(USA) —Delta Princess (USA) (A.P. Indy (USA))
(7285a)
Royal Destination (IRE) *F Nass* a102 109
6 b g Dubai Destination(USA) —Royale (IRE) (Royal Academy (USA))
499a[5] 679a[9]
Royal Diamond (IRE) *Jonjo O'Neill* a101 92
5 b g King's Best(USA) —Irresistible Jewel (IRE) (Danehill (USA))
3580[5] 4097[3] 4423[8]
Royal Dignitary (USA) *David Nicholls* a83 80
11 br g Saint Ballado(CAN) —Star Actress (USA) (Star De Naskra (USA))
1037[6] *(1462)*
Royal Dutch *Denis Coakley* a56
2 ch c Nayef(USA) —Shersha (IRE) (Priolo (USA))
7431[6]
Royale Again (FR) *P Monfort* a58 64
6 b m Fasliyev(USA) —Royale Figurine (IRE) (Dominion Royale)
706a[0]
Royale Celebre (FR) *Mlle C Rozais* a49 53
3 ch f Super Celebre(FR) —Louve De Siberie (FR) (Vettori (IRE))
901a[9]
Royal Entourage *Philip Kirby* a75 85
6 b g Royal Applause—Trempkate (USA) (Trempolino (USA))
7413[4]
Royal Envoy (IRE) *Paul Howling* a51 86
8 b g Royal Applause—Seven Notes (Zafonic (USA))
386[2] 807[4] 950[3] 7656[4] 7899[7]
Royale Ransom *Clive Cox* a63 50
2 b f Red Ransom(USA) —Prayer (IRE) (Rainbow Quest (USA))
6215[5] 6744[13] *6946[3] 7444[10]*
Royal Etiquette (IRE) *Lawney Hill* a72 70
4 b g Royal Applause—Alpine Gold (IRE) (Montjeu (IRE))
2771[5] 3466[4]
Royal Gig *Tim Etherington*
2 br f Val Royal(FR) —Sainte Gig (FR) (Saint Cyrien (FR))
7431[12]

Royal Holiday (IRE) *Brian Ellison* a62 51
4 ch g Captain Rio—Sunny Slope (Mujtahid (USA))
570[4] 670[3]
Royal Hush *Kevin Ryan* 73
3 b f Royal Applause—Sablonne (USA) (Silver Hawk (USA))
1648[2] (2691) 3586[5] 4439[5]
Royal Intruder *Richard Guest* a73 89
6 b g Royal Applause—Surprise Visitor (IRE) (Be My Guest (USA))
7189a[19] *7517[7] 7529[2] 7596[11] 7726[7]*
Royal Island (IRE) *Michael Quinlan* a60 86
9 b g Trans Island—Royal House (FR) (Royal Academy (USA))
7[3]
Royal Jet *Colin Teague* a98 74
9 b g Royal Applause—Red Bouquet (Reference Point)
4637[7]
Royal Liaison *Michael Bell* 72
3 b f Ad Valorem(USA) —Royal Mistress (Fasliyev (USA))
1860[3] 3292[5] 5442[6]
Royal Majestic *Mick Channon* a70 72
2 b f Tobougg(IRE) —Golden Symbol (Wolfhound (USA))
3336[4] 3779[2] 4201[7] *(4907)* 5478[7] (6275) 6864[10]
Royal Opera *Brian Ellison* a10 78
3 b g Acclamation—Desert Gold (IRE) (Desert Prince (IRE))
845[12] 1446[10] 1754[5] 2646[10] 3259[2] 3798[10] 4338[5] 4916[3] (5408) 6017[2] (6225) 6601[7]
Royal Patriot (IRE) *Paul Green* a47 56
4 b g King's Best(USA) —Lady Ragazza (IRE) (Bering)
1297[4] 5405[14]
Royal Peculiar *Sir Henry Cecil* a85 82
3 b c Galileo(IRE) —Distinctive Look (IRE) (Danehill (USA))
3824[5] ◆ *(4208)*
Royal Pepper *C Boutin* a71 84
6 b g Royal Applause—Royal Cat (Royal Academy (USA))
259a[10] 372a[7]
Royal Playmate *Keith Reveley*
3 ch f Beauchamp King—Playful Lady (Theatrical Charmer)
3355[5]
Royal Premier (IRE) *Tom Keddy* a37 65
8 b g King's Theatre(IRE) —Mystic Shadow (IRE) (Mtoto)
2272[3] 2526[11] 3086[7] 3559[5] (3960) 4366[11] 4732[5] 6240[8] *6476[11]* 7087[10]
Royal Premium *Bruce Hellier* a42 46
5 b h Superior Premium—Royal Shepley (Royal Applause)
3142[9] 3662[16] 4564[6] 4600[16] 5490[3] 5789[6] *6878[8] 7589[9]*
Royal Prospector *Richard Hannon* a74 48
2 b c Fantastic View(USA) —Royal Flame (IRE) (Royal Academy (USA))
6127[10] 7133[7] *7329[2] 7521[5] 7808[6]*
Royal Purse *Claes Bjorling* 57
2 b f Indesatchel(IRE) —Royal Future (IRE) (Royal Academy (USA))
1522[2] 1863[3] 2121[2] 5983a[8]
Royal Reason *Joseph Tuite* a54 62
3 b f Motivator—Elizabethan Age (FR) (King's Best (USA))
1189[6] 2842[10] *3220[6]* 5585[6] 6240[7] 6585[7]
Royal Red *Ralph Beckett* 76
2 b f Holy Roman Emperor(IRE) —Vermilliann (IRE) (Mujadil (USA))
2580[8] 3092[4] 3463[2] 4386[2] 5348[5] 5701[4]
Royal Reverie *Walter Swinburn* a69 78
3 b g Royal Applause—Christina's Dream (Spectrum (IRE))
1869[4] (2368) 2838[14] 3462[7] 4158[6] 5407[9]
Royal Revival *Saeed Bin Suroor* 106
4 gr h King's Best(USA) —Holy Nola (USA) (Silver Deputy (CAN))
332a[11] 503a[12] 829a[6] 6277[7]
Royal Reyah *Stuart Kittow* 75
2 b c Royal Applause—Dilys (Efisio)
2788[3] ◆ (5613) 6724[6] (7294)
Royal Rock *Chris Wall* a89 117
7 b g Sakhee(USA) —Vanishing Point (USA) (Caller I.D. (USA))
1093[6] 1891[3] 3154[13] 4092[9] 5481[3] (6035) (6520) 6858[4]
Royal Selection (IRE) *Karen George* a59 59
3 ch f Choisir(AUS) —Rustic Princess (IRE) (Daggers Drawn (USA))
4340[4] 4796[6] *6981[5]* ◆ *7207[2] (7525)*
Royal Sharp *G Botti*
2 b c Royal Applause—Triple Sharp (Selkirk (USA))
7449a[0]
Royal Straight *Linda Perratt* a66 76
6 ch g Halling(USA) —High Straits (Bering)
1072[4] 1520[4] 2059[6] 3859[3] 4142[7] 4380[3] 4543[5] 5015[9] 5311[4] 5723[8] 6082[7] 6417[8] *7003[2]* (7099)
Royal Swain (IRE) *Alan Swinbank* a52 86
5 b g Val Royal(FR) —Targhyb (IRE) (Unfuwain (USA))
1036[2] 1713[2] 2071[5] 5761[7] 6191[4] 7017[14] *7713[2] 7772[3]*
Royal Trix *Marcus Tregoning* 68
2 b f Royal Applause—Apple Town (Warning)
3722[6] 5613[3] ◆ 6092[2] 6573[5]
Royal Trooper (IRE) *James Given* a75 91
5 b g Hawk Wing(USA) —Strawberry Roan (IRE) (Sadler's Wells (USA))
3023[8] (3758) 4043[4] 4890[9] 5250[17] 5435[3] 5729[5] 6333[2] 6988[14]
Roy's Legacy *Shaun Harris* a67 59
2 b c Phoenix Reach(IRE) —Chocolada (Namid)
2542[9] 2983[15] 3314[13] *3708[2] 3948[6]* 4668[3] 5005[3] 5147[3] *(5316) (5833)* 6058[10] *6843[8]* 7231[8] 7294[11]
Roy The Boy (USA) *Jane Chapple-Hyam* 78
3 b g Pomeroy(USA) —Mrs. M (USA) (Mecke (USA))
2852[5] 3177[2] 4065[5] 5056[6] 6167[16]

Ruban (IRE) *Mahmood Al Zarooni* 69
2 ch c Dubawi(IRE) —Piece Unique (Barathea (IRE))
7083[4]
Rubber Duck (GER) *S Smrczek* 102
3 bb c Big Shuffle(USA) —Ripley (GER) (Platini (GER))
1433a[2]
Rubenstar (IRE) *Patrick Morris* a79 53
8 b g Soviet Star(USA) —Ansariya (USA) (Shahrastani (USA))
(56) (111) 213 3 307[4] (394) 736[6] 1178[4] 1295[3] 2206[3] 6616[10]
Rubi Dia *Kevin M Prendergast* a73 69
4 ch g Hernando(FR) —Oblique (IRE) (Giant's Causeway (USA))
2320[10] 2734[9] 3041[2] 3509[2] 5035[13] 5440[5] 6279[6] *7884[6]*
Rubina (IRE) *John M Oxx* 101
2 b f Invincible Spirit(IRE) —Riyafa (IRE) (Kahyasi)
4833a[4] 5525a[4] 5974a[3]
Rub Of The Relic (IRE) *Paul Midgley* a62 67
6 b g Chevalier(IRE) —Bayletta (IRE) (Woodborough (USA))
1557[3] *1814[5]* 2308[12] 2548[3] 2988[2] 3129[6] 3456[5] 3938[5] 4408[3] 4601[3] 4946[4] 4982[6] 5470[5]
Ruby Brook *Ralph Beckett* a72
3 b g Sakhee(USA) —Highbrook (USA) (Alphabatim (USA))
(262)
Ruby Night (IRE) *Michael Bell* 79
2 b g Red Clubs(IRE) —Stop Out (Rudimentary (USA))
4276[3] (4668) 5478[5]
Ruby's Day *E J O'Neill* 96
2 ch f Vital Equine(IRE) —Isabella's Best (IRE) (King's Best (USA))
3033[6] 4596a[5] 4843a[3] 5365a[6]
Rudegirl (IRE) *Conor Dore* a22 75
3 b f Trade Fair—Madam's View (IRE) (Entrepreneur)
1578[4] 1976[4]
Rudolph Schmidt (IRE) *A Mykoniatis* a79 82
5 ch m Catcher In The Rye(IRE) —Enaya (Caerleon (USA))
5753a[9]
Rue Du Soleil (USA) *R Menichetti* 77
3 ch c Forestry(USA) —Essence (USA) (Gulch (USA))
1431a[11]
Rue Soleil *John Weymes* a29 23
7 ch m Zaha(CAN) —Maria Cappuccini (Siberian Express (USA))
2415[10] 2989[10] 3489[12]
Rugell (ARG) *Derek Shaw* a90 91
6 b h Interprete(ARG) —Realize (ARG) (Confidental Talk (USA))
6[10] 180[13] 436[10] 835[8]
Rugged Cross *Henry Candy* 93
2 b c Cape Cross(IRE) —Lunda (IRE) (Soviet Star (USA))
4054[5] ◆ (5254)
Rugosa *Charles Hills* 66
2 b f Oasis Dream—Zathonia (Zafonic (USA))
7292[6]
Ruhar (IRE) *W McCreery* a47
2 b g Refuse To Bend(IRE) —Freezing Love (USA) (Danzig (USA))
7275a[11]
Ruler On Ice (USA) *Kelly Breen* a123
3 ch g Roman Ruler(USA) —Champagne Glow (USA) (Saratoga Six (USA))
(2950a) 7308a[3]
Rulership (JPN) *Katsuhiko Sumii* 123
4 b h King Kamehameha(JPN) —Air Groove (JPN) (Tony Bin)
1001a[6] 7873a[4]
Ruler's Honour (IRE) *Tim Etherington* a59 64
4 b g Antonius Pius(USA) —Naughty Reputation (IRE) (Shalford (IRE))
3075[10] 3247[12] 4328[11] 5008[7] 6156[7] *7571[12]*
Rulesn'regulations *Matthew Salaman* a94 102
5 b g Forzando—Al Awaalah (Mukaddamah (USA))
848[7] 1885[19] 2470[12] 4415[7] 4428[7] 5043[15] 5264[7] 5879[6] *(6477)* 6862[27] *7628[9]*
Rumble Of Thunder (IRE) *Kate Walton* a83 87
5 b g Fath(USA) —Honey Storm (IRE) (Mujadil (USA))
5593[11]
Rum Chocolate (GER) *C Ferland* a73 86
5 gr m Sholokhov(IRE) —Rose Hedge (GER) (Highest Honor (FR))
259a[4] 395a[3]
Rumh (GER) *Saeed Bin Suroor* a90 103
3 ch f Monsun(GER) —Royal Dubai (GER) (Dashing Blade)
2050[3] (2839) ◆ 3065[6] 4133a[7] 5219[7] 5928[9]
Rum King (USA) *S Donohoe* a86 79
4 bb g Montbrook(USA) —Cut Class Leanne (USA) (Cutlass (USA))
867[6] 1444[12] 1506[2] 1656[7] 5301[5] *5734[6]*
Runaway *Ms K Stenefeldt* 100
9 b h King's Best(USA) —Anasazi (IRE) (Sadler's Wells (USA))
2601a[10]
Runaway Tiger (IRE) *Paul D'Arcy* a61 33
3 b g Tiger Hill(IRE) —Last Rhapsody (IRE) (Kris)
176[6] (643) 1819[5] 2858[10] 3233[9]
Run Directa (GER) *D Moser* 74
4 ch h Dr Fong(USA) —Rill (Unfuwain (USA))
1575a[9]
Run For The Hills *Roger Charlton* a80 104
5 b g Oasis Dream—Maid For The Hills (Indian Ridge)
1366[5]
Running Deer (IRE) *Sir Henry Cecil* 69
2 b f Hurricane Run(IRE) —Sweet Sioux (Halling (USA))
6048[9] 6458[4] 6984[4]
Running Mate (IRE) *Jo Crowley* a59 63
4 b g Acclamation—It Takes Two (IRE) (Alzao (USA))
375[7] 556[9] (821) 1336[2] 2920[2] 3999[3] *6444[6]*

Running Reef (IRE) *Tracy Waggott* 41
2 b g Hurricane Run(IRE) —Half-Hitch (USA) (Diesis)
6983[12]

Running Water *Hugh McWilliams* a40 49
3 ch f Blue Dakota(IRE) —Floral Spark (Forzando)
595[6] 745[9] 1040[8] 1323[4] 1967[6] 2547[9] 2805[3] 3143[4] 3484[4] 3702[6] 3901[6] 4359[6] 5009[6] 5388[8] 6175[8] 7460[8] 7693[4] 7845[4]

Run Of The Day *Eve Johnson Houghton* 47
2 b f Three Valleys(USA) —Shall We Run (Hotfoot I)
6581[7] 6742[9]

Run On Ruby (FR) *David Lanigan* a75 62
3 bb f Muhtathir—Zigrala (FR) (Linamix (FR))
1609[3] 1951[11]

Run Rabbit Run *Roger Varian* 77
3 b g Hurricane Run(IRE) —Triple Gold (IRE) (Goldmark (USA))
2097[5] 2551[4] 3206[5]

Run Richard Run *Bryan Smart* 9
2 ch c Nayef(USA) —Milly Of The Vally (Caerleon (USA))
6278[8] 7233[16]

Run The Show (FR) *H-A Pantall* a74 77
3 bl c Dano-Mast—Money Bag (FR) (Badayoun)
370a[8]

Runtil Bere (FR) *Mme Pia Brandt* a67 75
6 ch g Until Sundown(USA) —Rue De Bellechasse (USA) (Geri (USA))
843a[3]

Rural Pursuits *Christine Dunnett* a54 48
3 b f Pastoral Pursuits—Mabrookah (Deploy)
1060[9] 1592[5] 2599[9] 4929[8] 5120[9]

Ruscello (IRE) *Sir Michael Stoute* 70
2 b c Cape Cross(IRE) —Sea Picture (IRE) (Royal Academy (USA))
5051[6] 6772[2]

Rushing Dasher (GER) *Natalie Friberg* a75 60
9 ch g Dashing Blade—Roma Libera (GER) (Pharly (FR))
(440a) 627a[4]

Ruskins View (IRE) *Alan Berry* 19
2 b f Clodovil(IRE) —Soft (USA) (Lear Fan (USA))
2346[10] 3021[8] 3728[8]

Rusoom *Marcus Tregoning* 72
3 b f Dalakhani(IRE) —Itqaan (USA) (Danzig (USA))
2840[6]

Russell (FR) *E Libaud* a70 67
3 b g Vettori(IRE) —Coffee Bean (FR) (Highest Honor (FR))
777a[6]

Russelliana *Sir Michael Stoute* 104
2 ch f Medicean—Rosacara (Green Desert (USA))
(2914) 3821[2] 4312[6]

Russian Affair *Roger Varian* a60 73
3 b c Haafhd—Russian Rhapsody (Cosmonaut)
5114[2] 5567[4] 6435[10] 6750[2] 7054[11]

Russian Bay (IRE) *John Joseph Hanlon* 5
5 b g Soviet Star(USA) —Echo Island (IRE) (Turtle Island (IRE))
7710[6]

Russian Brigadier *Mel Brittain* a34 46
4 b g Xaar—Brigadiers Bird (IRE) (Mujadil (USA))
1497[7] 1906[6] 2415[9] 5009[7]

Russian Bullet *Jamie Osborne* a61 42
2 b g Royal Applause—Gandini (Night Shift (USA))
3388[9] 3746[8] 3921[5] 4460[6] 4648[5] 4955[6] 5316[3] 5535[7] (7692) 7770[2] (7830)

Russian Davis (IRE) *P Monfort* a80 74
4 b g Mull Of Kintyre(USA) —Sunny Isles Beauty (USA) (Tale Of The Cat (USA))
5095a[5]

Russian George (IRE) *Steve Gollings* a84 89
5 ch g Sendawar(IRE) —Mannsara (IRE) (Royal Academy (USA))
835[3] 948[4] 1676[5] 7908[8]

Russian Ice *Dean Ivory* a76 64
3 ch f Iceman—Dark Eyed Lady (IRE) (Exhibitioner)
1579[8] 1986[5] 2599[6] (3223) 3481[4] (4911) 6089[8] 6944[2] ◆ (7448) 7842[3]

Russian King (GER) *R Rohne* a76 94
5 ch g Tertullian(USA) —Russian Rumba (GER) (Alkalde (GER))
441a[11] 1554a[6] 2134a[6]

Russian Rave *Jonathan Portman* a78 87
5 ch m Danehill Dancer(IRE) —Russian Ruby (FR) (Vettori (IRE))
1330[2] 2313[7] (2566) 3121[2] 3845[5] 4101[2] 5016[5] 5354[3] 5657[5] 6378[5]

Russian Rocker *Stuart Kittow* 72
2 b c Acclamation—Russian Ruby (FR) (Vettori (IRE))
5232[3] ◆

Russian Spirit *Roger Varian* a63 102
5 b m Falbrav(IRE) —Russian Rhapsody (Cosmonaut)
2298[16] 2961[4]

Russian Storm *Pat Phelan* a45 28
3 b f Hurricane Run(IRE) —Yesteryear (Green Desert (USA))
6085[8] 6377[6] 6754[0] 6929[8] 7388[7] 7640[8]

Russian Tango (GER) *A Wohler* 114
4 ch h Tertullian(USA) —Russian Samba (IRE) (Laroche (GER))
1128a[4] 2749a[2] 3446a[7] 4599a[4] (6595a) 7324a[4]

Russian Winter *Tim Etherington* a55 41
3 b g Tobougg(IRE) —Karminskey Park (Sabrehill (USA))
3053[6] 3343[7] 3931[9] 4207[8] 7443[5] 7561[5]

Rusticano (FR) *Gabriele Miliani*
3 ch g Tobougg(IRE) —Royalcombe (IRE) (Royal Academy (USA))
1126a[10]

Rustic Deacon *Willie Musson* a81 82
4 ch g Pastoral Pursuits—Anne-Lise (Inchinor)
(30) (2999) ◆ 4107[8] 4860[3] 6219[3] 6773[12]

Rustic Gold *Richard Ford* a64 47
7 ch g Tobougg(IRE) —Suave Shot (Suave Dancer (USA))
3300[8]

Rusty Rocket (IRE) *Paul Green* a57 73
2 ch c Majestic Missile(IRE) —Sweet Compliance (Safawan)
4283[12] 5174[3] 5367[3] (6154) 6699[12]

Rutland Boy *Ed Dunlop* a75 81
3 ch g Bertolini(USA) —Israar (Machiavellian (USA))
2008[7] 2877[4] ◆ 3291[10] 3959[4] ◆

Rutterkin (USA) *Alan Berry* a74 71
3 rg c Maria's Mon(USA) —Chilukki Cat (USA) (Storm Cat (USA))
2008[12] 2411[6] 2832[11] 3347[10] 3950[2] 4146[5] 4715[3] (5274) 5506[2] 5859[6] 6382[4] 6841[9]

R Woody *Dean Ivory* a79 98
4 ch g Ishiguru(USA) —Yarrita (Tragic Role (USA))
2099[16] 3410[3] 3841[9] 4346[14] 6224[5] 6987[19] 7127[12]

Ryan (IRE) *J Hanacek* 103
8 b h Generous(IRE) —Raysiza (IRE) (Alzao (USA))
6569a[9]

Ryan Style (IRE) *Lisa Williamson* a82 87
5 b g Desert Style(IRE) —Westlife (IRE) (Mind Games)
2832[8] 3367[3] (3541) 3880[11] 4239[DSQ] 4792[4] 5682[3] 5703[4] 6036[6] 6113[15]

Ryedale Dancer (IRE) *Tim Easterby* 71
3 ch f Refuse To Bend(IRE) —Saik (USA) (Riverman (USA))
1880[7] 2351[2] 2782[10] 3455[9] (3619) (4284) 4560[4] 5109[3] 5731[9] 6234[6] 6450[9]

Ryedale Lass *Joseph Tuite* 51
3 b f Val Royal(FR) —First Dawn (Dr Fong (USA))
5327[10]

Ryedane (IRE) *Tim Easterby* a78 78
9 b g Danetime(IRE) —Miss Valediction (IRE) (Petardia)
1035[12] 1239[14] 1382[6] 1793[6] 2250[4] 2491[7] ◆ 2798[2] 3279[12] 3617[6] 4152[8] 4405[8] 4518[4] 5031[6] (5309) 5647[8] 5881[11] 6266[6] 7064[6] (7265) 7416[2] 7595[4] 7715[2] 7928[10]

Rye House (IRE) *Sir Michael Stoute* 59
2 b c Dansili—Threefold (USA) (Gulch (USA))
6267[10] 7083[11]

Rylee Mooch *Richard Guest* a66 77
3 gr g Choisir(AUS) —Negligee (Night Shift (USA))
41[4] (338) 505[2] 632[2] 2410[2] 2826[7] 3136[2] 3360[2] (4359) 4669[4] 5053[5] 5468[5] 5923[3] 6112[3] 6212[10] 7746[8] 7917[3]

Rysbrack (USA) *Paul Webber* 79
5 ch g Selkirk(USA) —Super Tassa (IRE) (Lahib (USA))
4805[5] 5327[4]

Rysckly (FR) *Y De Nicolay* 104
4 gr h Slickly(FR) —Rylara Des Brosses (FR) (Rapid Man (USA))
1125a[5]

Rythmic *Mahmood Al Zarooni* a55 80
2 ch f Dubai Destination(USA) —Northern Melody (IRE) (Singspiel (IRE))
4552[2] ◆ (5029) 6275[6] 6623[10]

Ryton Runner (IRE) *John Gosden* a81 76
3 b g Sadler's Wells(USA) —Love For Ever (IRE) (Darshaan)
1096[5] 4763[7] 5641[3] 7002[5]

Saaboog *David Lanigan* a53 69
2 b f Teofilo(IRE) —Saabiq (USA) (Grand Slam (USA))
7164[7] ◆ 7431[5]

Saamidd *Saeed Bin Suroor* 114
3 b c Street Cry(IRE) —Aryaamm (IRE) (Galileo (IRE))
1686[12]

Sabhan (IRE) *Geoffrey Harker* 63
2 b c Marju(IRE) —Sister Sylvia (Fantastic Light (USA))
4436[6] 5786[12] 6259[3] 6937[3]

Sabianca (FR) *Chantal Zollet* 37
3 ch f Sabiango(GER) —Ombre De Cotte (FR) (Brier Creek (USA))
5307a[10]

Sable (IRE) *Adrian McGuinness* a24 61
5 ch m Choisir(AUS) —Fable (Absalom)
6139a[5]

Sabore *Richard Fahey* 43
2 br f Orientor—Annie Gee (Primo Valentino (IRE))
4675[4]

Saborido (USA) *Amanda Perrett* a76 86
5 gr g Dixie Union(USA) —Alexine (ARG) (Runaway Groom (CAN))
1443[5] (1788) 2190[2]

Sabotage (UAE) *Saeed Bin Suroor* a99 108
5 b g Halling(USA) —Cunas (USA) (Irish River (FR))
498a[2] 826a[5] 3403[5] 3875[11] 4532[10] 5271[5] 5659[4]

Sabot D'Or *Roger Ingram* a43 52
3 ch g Auction House(USA) —Perecapa (IRE) (Archway (IRE))
4547[11] 5115[12] 5381[9] 5665[6]

Sabratah *H-A Pantall* 97
3 b f Oasis Dream—Marika (Marju (IRE))
2138a[8]

Sabratha (IRE) *Linda Perratt* a49 74
3 b f Hawk Wing(USA) —Aitch (IRE) (Alhaarth (IRE))
1543[5] 1801[3] 2215[4] 2729[6] 3124[6] 3485[5] (4141) (4176) 5722[11] 7213[11]

Sabusa (IRE) *Alan McCabe* a61 67
2 b g Kheleyf(USA) —Black Tribal (IRE) (Mukaddamah (USA))
1042[5] 1101[3] 1316[4] 1619[3] 2148[8] 3609[9] 3948[5] 5077[7] 5413[8] 5802[5] 6043[12] 6274[10] 6628[12]

Sabys Gem (IRE) *Michael Wigham* 49
3 b g Diamond Green(FR) —Dust Flicker (Suave Dancer (USA))
5115[11] 6580[13]

Sacco D'Oro *Michael Mullineaux* a57 45
5 b m Rainbow High—Speedy Native (IRE) (Be My Native (USA))
451[4] 771[2] 2912[8] 3086[12]

Sacho (GER) *C Von Der Recke* 56
13 b g Dashing Blade—She's His Guest (IRE) (Be My Guest (USA))
440a[3] 627a[3]

Sacidevi (IRE) *F Trappolini* 75
3 b f Intikhab(USA) —Silver Sash (GER) (Mark Of Esteem (IRE))
1738a[15]

Sacred Kingdom (AUS) *P F Yiu* 125
8 b g Encosta De Lago(AUS) —Courtroom Sweetie (AUS) (Zeditave (AUS))
2339a[6] 7730a[10]

Sacred Shield *Sir Henry Cecil* a64 87
3 b f Beat Hollow—Quandary (USA) (Blushing Groom (FR))
(1474) 2022[2] 2688[2] 3260[4] (4056) 4723[4] 5303[2]

Sacred Sound (IRE) *Mick Channon* a62 64
3 b c Oratorio(IRE) —Affaire Royale (IRE) (Royal Academy (USA))
1407[9] 2813[7] 4208[7]

Sacrosanctus *David Nicholls* a86 91
3 ch g Sakhee(USA) —Catalonia (IRE) (Catrail (USA))
4[4] (208) (578) 1241[10] 1391[11] 2074[10] 2619[2] 2916[3] 3506[6] (4062) 4550[5] (5012) 5830[9]

Sadafiya *Ed Dunlop* a87 86
3 b f Oasis Dream—Nidhaal (IRE) (Observatory (USA))
1079[2] 3323[7] 4333[8] 5146[2] 6217[7]

Saddlers Bend (IRE) *George Baker* a77 88
5 b m Refuse To Bend(IRE) —Sudden Interest (FR) (Highest Honor (FR))
111[2] 626[4] 747[2] (1330) (1789) (2313) (2358) 2678[8]

Saddler's Rock (IRE) *John M Oxx* 122
3 b c Sadler's Wells(USA) —Grecian Bride (IRE) (Groom Dancer (USA))
5291a[3] (5884) ◆

Sadeek *Martin Bosley* a62 68
7 ch g Kyllachy—Miss Mercy (IRE) (Law Society (USA))
135[5] ◆ 387[6] 727[7]

Sadeek's Song (USA) *Mahmood Al Zarooni* a65 107
3 ch c Kingmambo(USA) —New Morning (IRE) (Sadler's Wells (USA))
6085[7] (6459) 6704[3] (7053)

Sadler's Risk (IRE) *Mark Johnston* 104
3 b g Sadler's Wells(USA) —Riskaverse (USA) (Dynaformer (USA))
(1057) ◆ 1339[7] 1822[4] 4426[8] 5271[6]

Sadma *Saeed Bin Suroor* 56
2 gr c Street Cry(IRE) —Blue Dress (USA) (Danzig (USA))
6529[11]

Sadyra (FR) *Y Fertillet* a62 62
5 b m Gold Away(IRE) —Scalotta (GER) (Winged Love (IRE))
42a[7]

Safari Guide *Dai Burchell* a66 59
5 b g Primo Valentino(IRE) —Sabalara (IRE) (Mujadil (USA))
2252[7] 2692[6] 4224[9] 4701[9] 5376[12] 5538[8]

Safari Mischief *Peter Winkworth* a73 84
8 b g Primo Valentino(IRE) —Night Gypsy (Mind Games)
3737[7] 4659[3] 4960[6]

Safari Storm (USA) *Brian Meehan* a60 77
2 b c Dubawi(IRE) —Londolozi (USA) (Forest Wildcat (USA))
1268[4] 1619[4] (3984) 4536[3] 5237[4] 5584[6] 6921[7] 7445[5] 7597[7]

Safari Sunbeam *Peter Pritchard* a39 13
3 br g Primo Valentino(IRE) —Bathwick Finesse (IRE) (Namid)
5415[6] 5898[11]

Safari Sunseeker (IRE) *William Knight* a75 54
2 b g Tagula(IRE) —Mooching Along (IRE) (Mujahid (USA))
6890[4] 7142[2] 7431[3] 7672[4] (7938)

Safari Team (IRE) *Pat Phelan* a81 29
3 b g Pleasantly Perfect(USA) —Perfectly Clear (USA) (Woodman (USA))
2607[4] 3044[8] 4724[10] (5815) 6944[6]

Safarjal (IRE) *Charles Hills* 75
2 b f Marju(IRE) —Wijdan (USA) (Mr Prospector (USA))
5655[6] ◆ 6950[2]

Safe Haven (IRE) *Derek Shaw* a42 53
3 gr f Indian Haven—Tiger's Gene (GER) (Perugino (USA))
3958[13]

Safe House (IRE) *Mahmood Al Zarooni* 73
2 ch f Exceed And Excel(AUS) —Last Resort (Lahib (USA))
6950[5]

Saffa Hill (IRE) *Tim Easterby* 77
2 b g Tiger Hill(IRE) —Saffa Garden (IRE) (King's Best (USA))
3609[6] 3826[3] 4292[2] 5454[6]

Saffron Park *John Best* 49
2 ch c Compton Place—Beacon Silver (Belmez (USA))
2559[9]

Safwaan *Willie Musson* a54 70
4 b g Selkirk(USA) —Kawn (Cadeaux Genereux)
135[11] 490[8]

Saga D'Oree (FR) *Mlle Valerie Boussin* a67
3 b f Sagacity(FR) —Scarborough (FR) (Starborough)
7677a[6]

Saga Dream (FR) *F Lemercier* 113
5 gr g Sagacity(FR) —Manixa (FR) (Manninamix)
4223a[3] 6558a[5] 6903a[5]

Sagaway (FR) *S-A Ghoumrassi* a39 73
3 b g Sagamix(FR) —Great Way (FR) (Great Palm (USA))
480a[10]

Saggiatore *William Muir* a82 82
4 b m Galileo(IRE) —Madame Dubois (Legend Of France (USA))
2512[11] 3095[5] 3738[9]

Sagramor *Hughie Morrison* a92 102
3 ch c Pastoral Pursuits—Jasmick (IRE) (Definite Article)
1983[2] (2296) (3067) 4494[17] 6339[32]

Sagredo (USA) *Jonjo O'Neill* a76 80
7 b g Diesis—Eternity (Suave Dancer (USA))
2436[6] 2872[4] 5340[3]

Sagunt (GER) *Jo Davis* a71 72
8 ch g Tertullian(USA) —Suva (GER) (Arazi (USA))
308[4]

Sahafh (USA) *Saeed Bin Suroor* a71 72
3 bb f Rock Hard Ten(USA) —Fireman's Ball (USA) (Hennessy (USA))
1626[2] 2466[3] 2883[10] 4807[9]

Sahara Kingdom (IRE) *Saeed Bin Suroor* a107 97
4 gr g Cozzene(USA) —Rose Indien (FR) (Crystal Glitters (USA))
236[6] 503a[6] ◆ 679a[2] 5704[7] 6088[4]

Sahara Sun (CHI) *Luca Cumani* 109
4 b c Milt's Overture(USA) —Dalaika (CHI) (Hussonet (USA))
5829[6] 6713a[7] 7115a[8] 7310a[6]

Saharia (IRE) *Michael Attwater* a86 86
4 b g Oratorio(IRE) —Inchiri (Sadler's Wells (USA))
168[6] 2910[5] 3612[6] 3936[7] 4816[2] 5412[6] 6051[7] 6354[4] (6844) 7146[3] 7605[4] 7823[5]

Sahpresa (USA) *Rod Collet* 121
6 b m Sahm(USA) —Sorpresa (USA) (Pleasant Tap (USA))
(2744a) 3822[2] 4597a[2] 5129a[3] (6338) 7731a[8]

Sahrati *Michael Blake* a68 93
7 ch g In The Wings—Shimna (Mr Prospector (USA))
667[6]

Saigon *James Toller* a106 109
2 b c Royal Applause—Luanshya (First Trump)
(3553) (4055) 4495[5] 5715[3] ◆ 6162[3] 6688[6] 7026[2]

Saigon Kitty (IRE) *John Best* a54 52
4 b m One Cool Cat(USA) —Miss Asia Quest (Rainbow Quest (USA))
261[3] 390[8]

Sail Home *Julia Feilden* a70 72
4 b m Mizzen Mast(USA) —Bristol Channel (Generous (IRE))
1[2] (145) 399[3] 1099[13] (1993) 2478[7] 3558[6] 4090[10] 4649[9] 5588[5] 6486[2] 7112[5] 7527[2] 7713[4]

Sailing North (USA) *Ronald Harris* a65 56
3 b g Mizzen Mast(USA) —Silver Star (Zafonic (USA))
126[2] 389[2] 741[6] 1449[3] 1753[12] 2356[8] 2549[8] 3272[11] 3747[5]

Sailor's Chant (USA) *Mark Johnston* 41
3 b c Medaglia D'Oro(USA) —Western Dreamer (USA) (Gone West (USA))
5449[12] 6324[6]

Sainglend *Paul Rich* a40 64
6 b g Galileo(IRE) —Verbal Intrigue (USA) (Dahar (USA))
7087[2]

Saint Boniface *Peter Makin* a24
2 ch g Bahamian Bounty—Nursling (IRE) (Kahyasi)
7736[5]

Saint By Day (IRE) *M Halford* a75 71
5 b g Marju(IRE) —Spring To Light (USA) (Blushing Groom (FR))
6511a[3] 7548a[10]

Saint Desir *E Lellouche* 103
3 b c Barathea(IRE) —Dirigeante (FR) (Lead On Time (USA))
1923a[7] 2751a[16]

Saint Emilion (JPN) *Masaaki Koga* 105
4 bb m Zenno Rob Roy(JPN) —Moteck (FR) (Last Tycoon)
7410a[18]

Saint Helena (IRE) *Harry Dunlop* a73 85
3 b f Holy Roman Emperor(IRE) —Tafseer (IRE) (Grand Lodge (USA))
726[2] (878) (1401) 1894[5] 2791[6] (4464) 5693[10]

Saint Hilary *William Muir* 48
2 b f Authorized(IRE) —Bright Halo (IRE) (Bigstone (IRE))
7025[11]

Saint Irene *Michael Blanshard* a63 63
2 ch f Halling(USA) —Santorini (USA) (Spinning World (USA))
3812[8] 4798[8] 5097[8] 6132[4] 6489[7]

Saint Pellerin (GER) *J-C Rouget* 105
2 b c Konigstiger(GER) —Salontasche (GER) (Dashing Blade)
(5365a) 6184a[2] 7192a[7]

Saint Pierre (USA) *Luca Cumani* a91 89
4 b h Speightstown(USA) —Drina (USA) (Regal And Royal (USA))
1406[22] 2390[7] 3578[8] 4509[6] 5043[9] 6220[3]

Saint Thomas (IRE) *John Mackie* a81 78
4 b g Alhaarth(IRE) —Aguilas Perla (IRE) (Indian Ridge)
1223[2] 1746[4] 2403[4] 3023[4] 3641[7] 5504[7] 6155[6] 6601[10] 7200[10]

Sairaam (IRE) *Charles Smith* a58 73
5 b m Marju(IRE) —Sayedati Eljamilah (USA) (Mr Prospector (USA))
1649[2] 1990[8] 2354[2] 2855[2] 3387[10] 4513[5] 4681[3] 5031[9] 5338[2] 5803[4] 6228[5] 6626[3]

Sajjhaa *Saeed Bin Suroor* 115
4 b m King's Best(USA) —Anaamil (IRE) (Darshaan)
2029[2] 3030[4] (4293) 4789[7]

Sajwah (IRE) *Charles Hills* 100
2 b f Exceed And Excel(AUS) —Tahrir (IRE) (Linamix (FR))
(1981) ◆ 3104[7] 3821[5] (5656) 6337[P] (Dead)

Sakheart *V Luka Jr* a68 100
5 b m Sakhee(USA) —Tanwir (Unfuwain (USA))
3213a[5]

Sakhee's Pearl *Jo Crowley* a84 80
5 gr m Sakhee(USA) —Grey Pearl (Ali-Royal (IRE))
822[6] ◆ 1610[6] 2822[3] 3549[7] 5383[3] 6256[4] 7097[5] 7513[4] (7831)

Saktoon (USA) *Clive Brittain* a26 57
3 b f El Prado(IRE) —Galore (USA) (Gulch (USA))
1362[12] 3756[4] 4796[5] *5606[11]* *6816[9]*

Salaaheb (IRE) *Alastair Lidderdale* a34 47
2 b f Tiger Hill(IRE) —Sayedati Eljamilah (USA) (Mr Prospector (USA))
6603[12] *7267[9]* *7414[9]*

Salacia (IRE) *Mahmood Al Zarooni* 86
2 b f Echo Of Light—Neptune's Bride (USA) (Bering)
6933[6] 7165[2]

Salair Haut (IRE) *M Delzangles* 95
2 b c Dalakhani(IRE) —Coxpippin (IRE) (Silver Hawk (USA))
7192a[11]

Salary Drive (USA) *Edward Plesa Jr* a87 100
3 bb f Mizzen Mast(USA) —Sporty Card (USA) (On To Glory (USA))
6183a[6]

Salcedo *M Delcher-Sanchez* a67
4 b h Dansili—Kindle (Selkirk (USA))
903a[2]

Saldenaera (GER) *Werner Glanz* 91
4 bb m Areion(GER) —Saldengeste (IRE) (Be My Guest (USA))
6594a[9]

Saleem (IRE) *Mark Johnston* a44
3 b f Oratorio(IRE) —Littlepacepaddocks (IRE) (Accordion)
7503[5]

Salerosa (IRE) *Ann Duffield* a84 73
6 b m Monashee Mountain(USA) —Sainte Gig (FR) (Saint Cyrien (FR))
1245[12] 1800[6] 2399[7] 3036[6] *3473[6]* *7352[2]* *7710[3]* *7857[9]*

Salesiano *Peter Makin* a58 52
3 b c Exceed And Excel(AUS) —Rose Moon (Montjeu (IRE))
559[6] *1149[9]* 2172[7] 2549[11] 4827[8] 5421[4] 5993[8]

Salford Art (IRE) *David Elsworth* 97
2 ch f Sir Percy—Millay (Polish Precedent (USA))
4155[3] ◆ (4614) 5052[2] ◆ 5446[5] ◆ 6299[4] ◆ 6914[5]

Salford Prince (IRE) *David Elsworth*
3 b g Invincible Spirit(IRE) —Bring Plenty (USA) (Southern Halo (USA))
6754[6]

Salient *Michael Attwater* a84 83
7 b g Fasliyev(USA) —Savannah Belle (Green Desert (USA))
394[5] *473[7]* *1232[4]* *1868[3]* 2771[7] (3266) (3763) 4150[3] 4725[5] 4958[9] 5547[8] 5894[3] 6378[13] 6728[10] *7941[4]* ◆

Salik Tag (USA) *David Nicholls* a53 71
3 ch g Hennessy(USA) —Clever Empress (Crafty Prospector (USA))
4286[8] *4647[3]* 5063[3] 5619[2] (6156)

Sallen (IRE) *S Wattel* a89 100
3 b f Oratorio(IRE) —Mackenzie's Friend (Selkirk (USA))
7580a[10]

Sally Anne *John Harris* 28
3 b f Samraan(USA) —Desert Bloom (FR) (Last Tycoon)
2195[5] 2871[10] 4071[4] 5021[6] 5350[5] 5589[5] 6229[6]

Sally Friday (IRE) *Peter Winkworth* a78 75
3 b f Footstepsinthesand—Salee (IRE) (Caerleon (USA))
2875[4] 3354[2] 4056[3] *4800[2]* *5386[2]* *6086[9]*

Sally Pepper (USA) *James Given* 58
2 bb f Rock Hard Ten(USA) —La Sila (USA) (Danzig (USA))
4875[4] 6458[11] 6984[11]

Sally's Swansong *Eric Alston* a57 51
5 b m Mind Games—Sister Sal (Bairn (USA))
233[3] *401[6]* *(735)* *934[6]*

Salona (GER) *J-P Carvalho* 97
3 ch f Lord Of England(GER) —Selana (GER) (Lomitas)
2337a[7] 3209a[7] 5028a[8] 6739a[10]

Salontanzerin (GER) *H-A Pantall* a90 90
6 b m Black Sam Bellamy(IRE) —Salontasche (GER) (Dashing Blade)
478a[2] 705a[0]

Salontyre (GER) *Bernard Llewellyn* a61 72
5 b g Pentire—Salonrolle (IRE) (Tirol)
1847[5] 2873[2] 4463[5] 4941[4] 6405[4]

Saloomy *David Simcock* 59
2 ch c Shamardal(USA) —Oystermouth (Averti (IRE))
6951[7]

Saloon (USA) *Jane Chapple-Hyam* a61 77
7 b g Sadler's Wells(USA) —Fire The Groom (USA) (Blushing Groom (FR))
2159[10] 2830[9] 4165[2] 4601[8] 5112[4] *5739[2]* *6287[2]* *6493[7]* *7527[10]*

Salorina (USA) *D Smaga* a76
3 b f A.P. Indy(USA) —Chaibia (IRE) (Peintre Celebre (USA))
532a[10]

Saltas (GER) *P Schiergen* 110
3 b c Lomitas—Salde (GER) (Alkalde (GER))
1739a[2] 3007a[4] 3672a[3] 5092a[2] 6396a[4] 6710a[3]

Salto (IRE) *F Head* 114
3 b c Pivotal—Danzigaway (USA) (Danehill (USA))
1552a[6] 2139a[9] 3654a[10] 5530a[4]

Salure *B Grizzetti* 113
2 ch c Sakhee(USA) —Davie's Lure (USA) (Lure (USA))
3212a[2] 6565a[3]

Salut (GER) *P Schiergen* 101
3 b c Lomitas—Saldentigerin (GER) (Tiger Hill (IRE))
1739a[4]

Salutary *Nigel Tinkler* 27
2 b g Kyllachy—Leonica (Lion Cavern (USA))
4292[7]

Salute Him (IRE) *A J Martin* a92 88
8 b g Mull Of Kintyre(USA) —Living Legend (ITY) (Archway (IRE))
5285[18]

Salut L'Africain (FR) *Robert Collet* a95 106
6 b h Ski Chief(USA) —Mamana (IRE) (Highest Honor (FR))
815a[3]

Salut Thomas (FR) *M Boutin* a88 59
9 ch h Adnaan(IRE) —Salut Bebs (FR) (Kendor (FR))
7315a[2]

Salvationist *John Dunlop* a42 64
3 b g Invincible Spirit(IRE) —Salvia (Pivotal)
1769[4] 3431[2] 3944[7] 4744[4] 5422[4]

Salybia Bay *Andy Turnell* a48 70
5 b m Fraam—Down The Valley (Kampala)
5642[6] 5916[12]

Samanda (IRE) *Luca Cumani* a58 28
3 b c Ad Valorem(USA) —Presently Blessed (IRE) (Inchinor)
3766[6] *6086[4]* *6475[9]* 6781[11]

Samardal (FR) *A Wohler* a78 95
4 b h Shamardal(USA) —Samando (FR) (Hernando (FR))
2657a[7]

Samarinda (USA) *P J O'Gorman* a94 78
8 ch g Rahy(USA) —Munnaya (USA) (Nijinsky (CAN))
188[2] *385[4]* *623[5]* *804[4]* 6469[10]

Samarkand (IRE) *Sir Mark Prescott Bt* a94 76
3 b g Sadler's Wells(USA) —Romantic Venture (IRE) (Indian Ridge)
2435[3] *(2819)* ◆ 3084[7] *6822[3]*

Samasana (IRE) *Ian Wood* a52 49
2 b f Redback—Singitta (Singspiel (IRE))
1505[9] 1870[5] 2953[11] 3424[9] 4557[12] 5133[5] *6001[4]* *6216[8]* 6812[5] 7051[13] *7242[5]* *7852[2]*

Samba King *Mahmood Al Zarooni* 78
2 b g Dubai Destination(USA) —Dance Of Leaves (Sadler's Wells (USA))
6245[5] 6825[3]

Samba Night (IRE) *Ed McMahon* a62 70
2 b g Dark Angel(IRE) —Brazilia (Forzando)
3707[4] 4377[2] 5347[3] *6352[2]* 6919[5]

Same As Gold (FR) *D De Waele* a71 76
7 b g Goldneyev(USA) —Same To You (FR) (Mujtahid (USA))
42a[8] 1142a[5]

Samedi *Mark Johnston* a50
2 b f Any Given Saturday(USA) —Hush Money (CHI) (Hussonet (USA))
7094[7]

Samitar *Mick Channon* 109
2 b f Rock Of Gibraltar(IRE) —Aileen's Gift (IRE) (Rainbow Quest (USA))
2467[3] (3104) 5479[2] 5885[3] 6299[2] (6526)

Samizdat (FR) *Dianne Sayer* 36
8 b g Soviet Star(USA) —Secret Account (FR) (Bering)
3300[7] 4602[11]

Sammie Fallon (IRE) *Andrew Haynes* 16
2 ch f Intikhab(USA) —Ishimagic (Ishiguru (USA))
4995[13] 5537[10]

Samminder (IRE) *Peter Chapple-Hyam* 94
2 b c Red Ransom(USA) —Gimasha (Cadeaux Genereux)
(1988) 6221[2] 6688[12]

Sammy Alexander *David Simcock* a76 73
3 b g Storming Home—Sweet Angeline (Deploy)
(49) *890[2]* 1593[3] 3172[3] 4160[4] *4908[6]*

Sam Nombulist *Richard Whitaker* 86
3 ch g Sleeping Indian—Owdbetts (IRE) (High Estate)
1710[6] 2256[6] 4877[6] 5731[5] 6081[4] 7076[2] (7299)

Sam Sharp (USA) *Ian Williams* a81 93
5 bb g Johannesburg(USA) —Caffe (USA) (Mr Prospector (USA))
(2217) 2909[9] 4267[6] 4788[8] 5940[11] *7339[5]* ◆

Samsons Son *Alan King* a84 93
7 b g Primo Valentino(IRE) —Santiburi Girl (Casteddu)
(3434) 4998[5] (6249) 7297[20]

Sams Spirit *Ian Semple* a15 13
5 br g Diktat—Winning Girl (Green Desert (USA))
2415[12]

Samuel Pickwick (IRE) *Sir Michael Stoute* a88 61
2 b c Holy Roman Emperor(IRE) —Save The Table (USA) (Tale Of The Cat (USA))
5239[6] *5713[2]* *(6308)* *6788[3]*

Samurai Sword *Mahmood Al Zarooni* 101
3 b c Motivator—Japanese Whisper (UAE) (Machiavellian (USA))
1550[4] (1843) 7166[2] ◆

Samysilver (USA) *Gianluca Bietolini* 103
3 bb c Indian Charlie(USA) —Hidden Ransom (USA) (Silver Ghost (USA))
1431a[6] 7408a[7]

Sanad (IRE) *Brian Meehan* 70
2 b c Red Clubs(IRE) —Knockatotaun (Spectrum (IRE))
3382[10] (4068) 5184[16] 5708[9]

San Antonio *Pam Sly* a77 81
11 b g Efisio—Winnebago (Kris)
(292) *361[2]* *400[2]* *640[5]* *2816[14]* *7068[6]* *7425[10]* *7687[5]*

San Cassiano (IRE) *Ruth Carr* a75 93
4 b g Bertolini(USA) —Celtic Silhouette (FR) (Celtic Swing)
1240[9] 1410[17] 1849[9] 2105[9] 2674[3] 2783[4] 3399[2] 3542[3] 3829[8] 4267[9] (4608) (4818)

Sancho Panza *Julia Feilden* a52 72
4 b g Zafeen(FR) —Malvadilla (IRE) (Doyoun)
1107[2] ◆ (1994) 2320[3] 2952[3] 4687[4] 5198[4] 5545[6] 6722[6] 7107[3]

Sanctum *Dr Jon Scargill* a25 53
5 b m Medicean—Auspicious (Shirley Heights)
1987[15] 2824[3] 3252[3] 4275[13]

Sandagiyr (FR) *A De Royer-Dupre* 108
3 b c Dr Fong(USA) —Sanariya (IRE) (Darshaan)
2751a[14] 4120a[7] 6556a[7]

Sandbanks *Sylvester Kirk* a35 1
2 ch f Three Valleys(USA) —Esdaraat (Pivotal)
5323[16] *6352[5]* *6620[9]* *6818[8]* *7432[7]*

Sandbanks Sizzler (IRE) *Ralph Beckett* 93
3 ch g Soviet Star(USA) —Isticanna (USA) (Far North (CAN))
2469[3] ◆ (6377)

Sandbetweenourtoes (IRE) *Brian Meehan* 73
2 b g Footstepsinthesand—Callanish (Inchinor)
2510[4] 2953[12]

San Deng *Micky Hammond* a68 53
9 gr g Averti(IRE) —Miss Mirror (Magic Mirror)
3510[4]

Sandfrankskipsgo *Brett Johnson* a24 80
2 ch g Piccolo—Alhufoof (USA) (Dayjur (USA))
4580[7] 5889[6] (6919) *7445[11]*

Sandinnar (FR) *J Boisnard* a54 72
4 b m Sinndar(IRE) —Ariel (IRE) (Caerleon (USA))
1012a[0]

Sandor *Peter Makin* a90 100
5 ch g Fantastic Light(USA) —Crystal Star (Mark Of Esteem (IRE))
1684[17]

Sand Owl *Peter Chapple-Hyam* a79 80
3 b f Dubawi(IRE) —Midnight Allure (Aragon)
(1060) 1571[4] 2102[10] *3048[4]* *6217[5]* 6913[4] *7456[8]*

Sandpipers Dream *Tim Walford* 38
3 b g Desert Style(IRE) —Maarees (Groom Dancer (USA))
1858[9]

Sandra Mia (FR) *F-X De Chevigny* a66 66
2 b f Enrique—Sandra Maria (FR) (Homme De Loi (IRE))
7666a[9]

Sand Repeal (IRE) *Julia Feilden* a58 61
9 b g Revoque(IRE) —Columbian Sand (IRE) (Salmon Leap (USA))
3754[12] 4613[9]

Sandrino (GER) *J-P Carvalho* 94
3 b c Lord Of England(GER) —Secret Of Salome (IRE) (Vision (USA))
2345a[7]

Sand Skier *Hans Adielsson* a81 97
4 b g Shamardal(USA) —Dubai Surprise (IRE) (King's Best (USA))
1011a[2] 1479[13] 1684[7] 2002[19] 2681[9] 3120[5] 3533[10] 6303[2] *6507[4]* *7002[9]* *7346[2]* *7413[2]* ◆ *7513[5]* 7661[3] 7803[2] 7900[7]

Sandslash (IRE) *Marco Botti* 105
3 b f Holy Roman Emperor(IRE) —Slap Shot (IRE) (Lycius (USA))
(1432a) 6531[4] ◆

Sandslide *M Trybuhl* 89
6 b m King's Best(USA) —Shifting Sands (FR) (Hernando (FR))
5839a[8]

Sands Of Dee (USA) *David Nicholls* a54 78
4 b g Dixieland Band(USA) —Diamond Bracelet (USA) (Metfield (USA))
2632[3] (3040) 3484[2] 4197[3] 4900[4] 5148[9] 7104[10] *7341[6]* *7641[6]*

Sandtail (IRE) *J W Hills* a58 49
3 gr f Verglas(IRE) —Goldthroat (IRE) (Zafonic (USA))
1953[4] 2599[8] *3227[11]*

Sand Tiger (IRE) *Richard Fahey* a80 93
5 ch g Indian Ridge—Anayid (A.P. Indy (USA))
427[7]

Sandusky *Mahmood Al Zarooni* a74 96
3 b c Tiger Hill(IRE) —Red Carnation (IRE) (Polar Falcon (USA))
(1311) ◆ 2076[4] (6248)

Sandwith *George Foster* a61 70
8 ch g Perryston View—Bodfari Times (Clantime)
1204[5] 1712[10] 1856[5] 2632[10] 3451[6] 4144[9] 4174[4] 4539[5] 4986[5] 5148[12] 5436[2] 5620[7] 7100[4] *7366[6]* *7691[2]* *(7853)*

Sandy Lonnen *Colin Teague* 49
3 b g Tobougg(IRE) —Legend Of Aragon (Aragon)
6781[10] 6833[12] 7017[13]

Sandy's Charm (FR) *F Rohaut* 113
3 b f Footstepsinthesand—First Charm (FR) (Anabaa (USA))
(5028a) 5530a[2] 6568a[4]

Sangar *Ollie Pears* 76
3 ch f Haafhd—Preference (Efisio)
3039[3] 3615[3] (4005) 4515[3] (5560) 5925[4] 6674[12]

Sangaree (USA) *Saeed Bin Suroor* a109
6 ch h Awesome Again(CAN) —Mari's Sheba (USA) (Mari's Book (USA))
414a[11] *604a[2]* *756a[6]*

Sangrail *William Muir* a41
2 b f Singspiel(IRE) —Wars (IRE) (Green Desert (USA))
6131[7]

Sanjii Danon (GER) *W Hickst* 100
5 b h Big Shuffle(USA) —Serpina (IRE) (Grand Lodge (USA))
1263a[3] 3422a[3] 4138a[7]

San Jose City (IRE) *Muredach Kelly* a24 71
6 b g Clodovil(IRE) —Allspice (Alzao (USA))
6304[11]

San Mambo *Marco Botti* a73 66
2 b c Singspiel(IRE) —Mambo Mistress (USA) (Kingmambo (USA))
6956[6] *7398[5]* *7650[4]*

Sannibel *Kevin Morgan* a69 60
3 ch f Needwood Blade—Socialise (Groom Dancer (USA))
3091[2] *4863[2]* 5377[4]

Sano Di Pietro *A De Royer-Dupre* 103
3 b c Dalakhani(IRE) —Special Delivery (IRE) (Danehill (USA))
2979a[4] 5230a[2]

Sanrivale (FR) *D Rabhi* 104
3 b f Enrique—Sagienne (FR) (Galetto (FR))
5027a[4]

Sansili *Peter Bowen* a64 63
4 gr g Dansili—Salinova (FR) (Linamix (FR))
3911[6] 5784[5]

Sans Loi (IRE) *Alan McCabe* 85
2 b c Lawman(FR) —Lady Elysees (USA) (Royal Academy (USA))
(2844) 3064[13] (3458) 3773[6] 6524[7]

Santa Biatra (FR) *A Couetil* a87 100
5 b m Highest Honor(FR) —Albiatra (USA) (Dixieland Band (USA))
5093a[7] 6470a[3]

Santadelacruze *Gary Moore* a68 9
2 b c Pastoral Pursuits—Jupiters Princess (Jupiter Island)
6725[15] *7520[6]* *7835[8]*

Sant'Alberto (ITY) *F Brogi* 98
3 b c Colossus(IRE) —Adya (FR) (Sillery (USA))
5230a[5]

Santarini (IRE) *Richard Hannon* 63
2 b f Lawman(FR) —Lapland (FR) (Linamix (FR))
4471[17] 7165[7]

Santefisio *Peter Makin* a92 94
5 b g Efisio—Impulsive Decision (IRE) (Nomination)
1610[4] ◆ 2020[9] 2647[7] 2995[8] 4616[7] 4958[3] *(6220)* *6948[3]* *7438[6]* *7841[5]*

Santera (IRE) *John Flint* a48 43
7 br m Gold Away(IRE) —Sainte Gig (FR) (Saint Cyrien (FR))
733[5]

Santino (GER) *J-P Carvalho* 107
4 b h Rock Of Gibraltar(IRE) —Selana (GER) (Lomitas)
2657a[4]

Santiva (USA) *Eddie Kenneally* a116 106
3 b c Giant's Causeway(USA) —Slide (USA) (Smarten (USA))
1921a[6] *2950a[8]*

Santo Padre (IRE) *David Marnane* a98 109
7 b g Elnadim(USA) —Tshusick (Dancing Brave (USA))
1533a[4] 2323a[3] 2456[2] 4768a[7]

Saorocain (IRE) *Patrick Morris* a36 3
5 b m Kheleyf(USA) —Compradore (Mujtahid (USA))
185[12]

Sapelli (NZ) *J Size* 113
6 ch g Flying Spur(AUS) —Ishkala (NZ) (Zabeel (NZ))
1742a[7]

Saphira (GER) *A Wohler*
2 b f Choisir(AUS) —Suenna (GER) (Lando (GER))
7813a[2]

Saphira's Fire (IRE) *William Muir* a93 106
6 b m Cape Cross(IRE) —All Our Hope (USA) (Gulch (USA))
1100[7] 1718[10]

Saphir Bere (FR) *Carmen Bocskai* a95 94
5 b h Nicobar—Leginit (USA) (Dehere (USA))
442a[3] *628a[6]*

Sapphire (FR) *Mario Hofer* a96 94
4 b g Meshaheer(USA) —Summer Dance (FR) (Machiavellian (USA))
6906a[7]

Sapphire (IRE) *D K Weld* 113
3 b f Medicean—Polished Gem (IRE) (Danehill (USA))
5976a[2] (6736a)

Sapphire Girl *Richard Fahey* a40 63
3 ch f Compton Place—Centre Court (Second Set (IRE))
130[5] *189[8]*

Sapphire Pendant (IRE) *David Wachman* 100
3 b f Danehill Dancer(IRE) —Butterfly Blue (IRE) (Sadler's Wells (USA))
1928a[2] ◆ 2331a[6] 5361a[11] 6362a[12]

Sapphire Seeker *Des Donovan* 39
2 br c Sakhee(USA) —Symphonia (IRE) (Zafonic (USA))
5480[12]

Saptapadi (IRE) *Brian Ellison* a106 113
5 ch g Indian Ridge—Olympienne (IRE) (Sadler's Wells (USA))
2044[7] 3876[5] ◆ 4345[5] ◆ 5285[5] 6711a[8] 6886a[14] 7218a[16] 7407a[5]

Saracenian *Jiri Janda*
4 ch h Samum(GER) —Soljanka (GER) (Halling (USA))
4874a[5]

Sarafina (FR) *A De Royer-Dupre* 125
4 b m Refuse To Bend(IRE) —Sanariya (IRE) (Darshaan)
1708a[2] (2373a) (3448a) (5986a) 6567a[7] 7305a[4]

Sarah Berry *Chris Dwyer* a49 53
2 b f First Trump—Dolly Coughdrop (IRE) (Titus Livius (FR))
6758[10] 7132[5] *7329[7]* *7530[11]*

Sarah Lynx (IRE) *J E Hammond* 120
4 b m Montjeu(IRE) —Steel Princess (IRE) (Danehill (USA))
(5093a) 5989a[4] (6910a) 7563a[12] 7729a[13]

Sarah's Art (IRE) *Gary Harrison* a81 79
8 gr g City On A Hill(USA) —Treasure Bleue (IRE) (Treasure Kay)
285[7] 2369[9] 2903[6] 5053[16] *6177[10]* *6283[8]* *6502[8]* *6794[4]* *7039[5]* *7172[3]* *7341[10]* 7529[3] 7629[8]

Sarando *Paul Webber* a65 58
6 b g Hernando(FR) —Dansara (Dancing Brave (USA))
6998[6]

Sarangoo *Malcolm Saunders* a69 71
3 b f Piccolo—Craic Sa Ceili (IRE) (Danehill Dancer (IRE))
1472[7] 2553[2] 2869[5] 3272[2] 3723[2] (3998) 4227[2] 4486[3] 4973[9] 6434[3] ◆ *6664[5]* *7455[5]* *7537[10]* *7591[6]*

Saratoga Black (IRE) *B Grizzetti* 113
4 b h Pyrus(USA) —Mary Martins (IRE) (Orpen (USA))
2982a[3]

Saratoga Slew (IRE) *Charles Hills* 64
2 b f Footstepsinthesand—Life Rely (USA) (Maria's Mon (USA))
4804[7] 5565[8] 6329[8]

Sardanapalus *Kevin Ryan* 76
2 b g Byron—Crinkle (IRE) (Distant Relative)
(4012) ◆ 5251[9] 6413[4]

Sareeah (IRE) *Clive Brittain* a59
2 b f Cadeaux Genereux—Jules (IRE) (Danehill (USA))
7672^{6} ◆

Saronsla Belle (FR) *L Edon* a74 78
4 b m Cardoun(FR) —Northern Honor (FR) (Northern Crystal)
$91a^{6}$

Sarrsar *Saeed Bin Suroor* a103 109
4 b g Shamardal(USA) —Bahr (Generous (IRE))
2123^{6} 2573^{11} 2933^{2} 3876^{18} (4774) 6150^{12} 7234^{2}

Sartingo (IRE) *Alan Swinbank* 75
4 b g Encosta De Lago(AUS) —Alicia (IRE) (Darshaan)
1559^{4} 1910^{5} 2393^{8} (3905) 4367^{9} 4784^{2} 5485^{3} 6263^{10}

Sarwin (USA) *Muredach Kelly* a71 75
8 gr g Holy Bull(USA) —Olive The Twist (USA) (Theatrical)
292^{10}

Sasheen *Jeremy Gask* a72 74
4 b m Zafeen(FR) —Sashay (Bishop Of Cashel)
34^{3} 160^{2} 248^{5} (1333) 1867^{3} 2242^{4} 2816^{10} (3426) 4154^{6} 5002^{5} 5782^{6} 6586^{2} 6888^{9} 7208^{5} 7532^{10} 7895^{13}

Saskia's Dream *Jane Chapple-Hyam* a79 82
3 b f Oasis Dream—Swynford Pleasure (Reprimand)
1873^{3} 2185^{5} 2582^{6} 3782^{3} (4321) 4994^{2} 5450^{3} 6173^{5} ◆ 6457^{11}

Saslong *Mark Johnston* a44
2 b c Zamindar(USA) —Cosmodrome (USA) (Bahri (USA))
7709^{3}

Sassanian (IRE) *Nikki Evans* a60 62
4 b g Clodovil(IRE) —Persian Sally (IRE) (Persian Bold)
7195^{13}

Satanic Beat (IRE) *Jedd O'Keeffe* 81
2 br g Dark Angel(IRE) —Slow Jazz (USA) (Chief's Crown (USA))
3398^{3} (4347) 5184^{5} 5755^{3} 6573^{4} 7021^{8}

Satans Quick Chick (USA) *Eric R Reed* a104
5 b m Sky Mesa(USA) —Dancing Devlette (USA) (Devil's Bag (USA))
$7285a^{8}$

Satcat (FR) *R Martin Sanchez*
3 b f Hurricane Cat(USA) —Satie (IRE) (Fasliyev (USA))
$5958a^{0}$

Satchmo Bay (FR) *C Boutin* a84 77
10 b g Alamo Bay(USA) —Royale Aube (FR) (Garde Royale)
$2867a^{0}$

Satin Love (USA) *Mark Johnston* a82 91
3 ch g Mineshaft(USA) —French Satin (USA) (French Deputy (USA))
864^{5} 1152^{4} 1825^{13} 2200^{8} 2619^{6} 3131^{9} 3701^{5}

Satu Mare (FR) *Mario Hofer* 83
3 ch f Namid—Smiling Eyes (Mark Of Esteem (IRE))
$1122a^{0}$

Saturn Way (GR) *Patrick Chamings* a74 80
5 b g Bachelor Duke(USA) —Senseansensibility (USA) (Capote (USA))
(1995) 3093^{12} 4866^{4} 5511^{4} 7448^{5}

Satwa Ballerina *Mark Rimmer* a52 48
3 b f Barathea(IRE) —Ballerina Rosa (FR) (Anabaa (USA))
2306^{8} 2836^{10} 3224^{10} 4928^{7} 7581^{8}

Satwa Dream (IRE) *Ed Dunlop* a83 86
4 b g Key Of Luck(USA) —Whisper To Dream (USA) (Gone West (USA))
2403^{6} 2760^{2} 3164^{7} 3925^{2} 4479^{3} 5014^{14} (5816) 6346^{11}

Satwa Gold (USA) *Seamus Durack* a86 88
5 ch h Rahy(USA) —No More Ironing (USA) (Slew O'Gold (USA))
486^{4} 718^{4} 894^{3} 1367^{12}

Satwa Laird *Ed Dunlop* a85 93
5 b g Johannesburg(USA) —Policy Setter (USA) (Deputy Minister (CAN))
1603^{14} 2217^{7} 2674^{7} 3815^{4} 4926^{2} 5383^{13} 5969^{4} 6727^{4}

Satwa Moon (USA) *Ed Dunlop* a85 92
5 ch h Horse Chestnut(SAF) —Double Schott (USA) (Demons Begone (USA))
1402^{3} 2006^{6}

Satwa Pearl *Ed Dunlop* a88 89
5 ch m Rock Of Gibraltar(IRE) —Uruk (Efisio)
(1011a) 1992^{2} 5608^{2} ◆ (5962) 7296^{7} 7391^{6}

Satwa Prince (FR) *Jean De Roualle* a85 97
8 b g Munir—Toryka (Vettori (IRE))
$566a^{0}$

Satwa Rose (FR) *Jean De Roualle* a60 77
5 b m Elusive City(USA) —Porza (FR) (Septieme Ciel (USA))
(903a)

Satwa Royal *Ed Dunlop* a71
4 b g Royal Applause—Dance For Fun (Anabaa (USA))
(52)

Satwa Sunrise (FR) *Ed Dunlop* a55 64
4 b m Meshaheer(USA) —Suvretta Queen (IRE) (Polish Precedent (USA))
1845^{7} 2157^{9} 2457^{8} 3353^{6} 4713^{3} 6285^{P} 6872^{3}

Saucy Brown (IRE) *David Nicholls* a67 92
5 b g Fasliyev(USA) —Danseuse Du Bois (USA) (Woodman (USA))
(1715) 2620^{5} 3162^{3} (3484) (3880) 4531^{5} 5163^{4}

Saucy Buck (IRE) *Ralph Smith* a69 76
3 b g Mujadil(USA) —Phantom Ring (Magic Ring (IRE))
601^{5} 887^{6} 1019^{3} 1483^{7} 3765^{6} 3983^{5} 5644^{3} 5859^{4} 6090^{6} 6944^{10} 7484^{6}

Saucy Cat (IRE) *Murty McGrath* a50 52
2 br f One Cool Cat(USA) —Most-Saucy (Most Welcome)
5117^{6} 6795^{6} 7125^{10}

Saudi Summer (KSA) *S Seemar* a70 37
4 ch g Dr Fong(USA) —High Summer (USA) (Nureyev (USA))
$536a^{5}$

Savanna Days (IRE) *Mick Channon* 74
2 ch f Danehill Dancer(IRE) —Dominante (GER) (Monsun (GER))
2811^{6} 3812^{4} 5583^{2} 6187^{3}

Savannah Blue (GER) *Markus Klug* 88
3 b f Lando(GER) —Sonia (GER) (Robellino (USA))
$6394a^{11}$

Savaronola (USA) *Barney Curley* a69 45
6 ch g Pulpit(USA) —Running Debate (USA) (Open Forum (USA))
40^{3} 5406^{7} 6446^{7}

Save The Bees *Declan Carroll* 76
3 b g Royal Applause—Rock Concert (Bishop Of Cashel)
2457^{7} (3039) 3485^{2} 3854^{2} 4290^{7} 4560^{5} 5731^{2} 6234^{4} 6674^{13}

Save The Day *A Schaerer* a52 59
5 b m Dr Fong(USA) —Modelliste (Machiavellian (USA))
$629a^{6}$

Savinien *David Evans* a42
3 br g Needwood Blade—Lady Roxanne (Cyrano De Bergerac)
663^{7} 818^{7} 1236^{7} 1524^{7}

Saviour Sand (IRE) *Olivia Maylam* a66 57
7 b g Desert Sun—Teacher Preacher (IRE) (Taufan (USA))
352^{7} 472^{3} 885^{3} 1608^{10} 1756^{11} 6872^{8} 7203^{8}

Sawahill *Clive Brittain* a45 53
3 b f Diktat—Youm Jadeed (IRE) (Sadler's Wells (USA))
3575^{5} 7585^{8} 7805^{12}

Saxby (IRE) *Alan Lockwood* a70 67
4 ch g Pastoral Pursuits—Madam Waajib (IRE) (Waajib)
2249^{12} 3569^{11} 3938^{16} 5490^{15}

Saxonette *Linda Perratt* a61 70
3 b f Piccolo—Solmorin (Fraam)
1514^{5} 1802^{4} 2396^{8} (2410) 2697^{7} 3126^{6} 3860^{2} 4359^{2} 4541^{5} 4669^{5} 4880^{6} 5313^{9} 5719^{4} 6076^{15} 6190^{5}

Say A Novena (USA) *Edward Plesa Jr* a103
2 b f Songandaprayer(USA) —Rabiadella (USA) (Dynaformer (USA))
$7283a^{10}$

Say A Prayer *Tim Easterby* 49
3 b f Indesatchel(IRE) —Golden Nun (Bishop Of Cashel)
1749^{7} 2396^{12}

Saytara (IRE) *Saeed Bin Suroor* 79
2 b f Nayef(USA) —Celtic Silhouette (FR) (Celtic Swing)
5806^{4} (6776)

Scalo *A Wohler* 121
4 b h Lando(GER) —Sky Dancing (IRE) (Exit To Nowhere (USA))
(1931a) $2982a^{2}$ $4374a^{2}$ ◆

Scamperdale *Brian Baugh* a100 88
9 br g Compton Place—Miss Up N Go (Gorytus (USA))
180^{7} 353^{2} (436) 525^{2} 803^{6} 994^{7} 3544^{4} 4004^{3} 4818^{3} 5568^{8} 5693^{5} 6445^{7} 7036^{6} 7430^{2} 7651^{13}

Scarab (IRE) *Tim Walford* a18 76
6 br g Machiavellian(USA) —Russian Society (Darshaan)
1099^{15} 1859^{7} 2259^{7} 3831^{4} 4111^{8} 4649^{8}

Scarabocio *Peter Chapple-Hyam* 65
2 b c Shamardal(USA) —My Sara (Mujahid (USA))
7292^{8}

Scarborough Lily *Edward Vaughan* a68 58
3 b f Dansili—Queen Isabella (El Prado (IRE))
52^{7} 1958^{8} 2307^{10} 3227^{3} 3958^{4} 4827^{2} 4927^{2} (5601) 7001^{2} 7351^{4} 7507^{5}

Scarlet Belle *Marcus Tregoning* a58 69
2 ch f Sir Percy—Nicola Bella (IRE) (Sadler's Wells (USA))
6744^{2} 7124^{7}

Scarlet Prince *Gary Moore* a54 24
2 b c Sir Percy—Trump Street (First Trump)
4535^{14} 4968^{11} 6471^{6} 6760^{9}

Scarlet Ridge *Dean Ivory* a32
4 ch m Tumbleweed Ridge—Kayartis (Kaytu)
3094^{8}

Scarlet Rocks (IRE) *George Baker* a76 84
3 b f Chineur(FR) —Alexander Duchess (IRE) (Desert Prince (IRE))
1758^{5} 1852^{7} 2158^{3} 2453^{5} 2770^{2} 3582^{3} 3785^{4} 4231^{4} 4618^{5} 5115^{4} 5268^{6} 5578^{7} 6283^{2} 6491^{6} (6920) 7457^{4} 7512^{6} 7804^{7} 7919^{4} ◆

Scarlet Warrior (AUT) *G Martin*
3 b g Akhisar(USA) —Silky Scarlet (AUT) (Idle Warrior)
$370a^{0}$ $480a^{0}$ $638a^{0}$

Scarlet Whispers *Pam Sly* 76
2 b f Sir Percy—Hieroglyph (Green Desert (USA))
4002^{4} 5029^{5} 5464^{4} 6275^{2}

Scary Movie (IRE) *Emmet Michael Butterly* a78 62
6 b g Daggers Drawn(USA) —Grinning (IRE) (Bellypha)
(50) 174^{3} 310^{4} 561^{3} (656) $977a^{3}$ 5687^{8} 7671^{5} 7734^{7}

Sceal Nua (IRE) *John M Oxx* a75 87
3 b f Iffraaj—Always Mine (Daylami (IRE))
$5748a^{9}$

Sceilin (IRE) *John Mackie* a52 66
7 b m Lil's Boy(USA) —Sharifa (IRE) (Cryptoclearance (USA))
369^{4}

Scented *Ian Semple* a69 69
3 b f Medicean—Red Garland (Selkirk (USA))
2466^{5} 2808^{7} 3124^{8} 3303^{7} 3858^{10}

Schism *Henry Candy* 80
3 ch f Shirocco(GER) —Alla Prima (IRE) (In The Wings)
2065^{5} (2871) 3551^{8} 4449^{4} 5236^{2} 5966^{5} 6891^{2}

Schmooze (IRE) *Linda Perratt* a45 59
2 b f One Cool Cat(USA) —If Dubai (USA) (Stephen Got Even (USA))
1996^{8} 2587^{5} (2854) 4194^{7} 4667^{4} 6186^{9}

Schoolboy Champ *Mark Brisbourne* a65 69
4 ch g Trade Fair—Aswhatilldois (IRE) (Blues Traveller (IRE))
1469^{3} 2048^{10} 2286^{10} 2547^{3} 2990^{3} 3166^{5} 3582^{6} 3956^{7} (4362) 4604^{4} 4866^{9} 5153^{5} 5404^{7} 5881^{7} 6430^{11} 7216^{6} ◆

School Fees *Henry Candy* 72
2 b f Royal Applause—Cankara (IRE) (Daggers Drawn (USA))
3287^{3} ◆ 3915^{3} ◆ 4710^{2} 5562^{3}

School For Scandal (IRE) *Mark Johnston* a84 80
3 b g Pivotal—Sensation (Soviet Star (USA))
540^{2} 693^{2} (774) 907^{2} 1051^{2} 1168^{3} 1485^{2}

Schoolmaster *Giles Bravery* a51
3 b g Motivator—Londonnetdotcom (IRE) (Night Shift (USA))
7354^{5}

Schutzenjunker (GER) *P Schaerer* a78 106
6 b h Lord Of Men—Schutzenliebe (GER) (Alkalde (GER))
$442a^{2}$ $628a^{5}$ $778a^{9}$

Sciampin *Marco Botti* 78
3 b g Invincible Spirit(IRE) —Gracious (Grand Lodge (USA))
1897^{4} 2218^{4} 2956^{12} 3558^{3} 4005^{2} (4916) 6538^{4}

Scintillating (IRE) *Ray Peacock* a41 17
4 b m Cape Cross(IRE) —Announcing Peace (Danehill (USA))
517^{10} 1468^{12} 1567^{10} 2569^{10} 4183^{11} 4822^{12} 5038^{5}

Scoglio *Frank Sheridan* a63 62
3 b g Monsieur Bond(IRE) —Ex Mill Lady (Bishop Of Cashel)
745^{5} 916^{3} 1053^{2} 1277^{4} 4750^{3} 5179^{7} 5606^{10} 6179^{5} 6659^{6} 7247^{6}

Scommettitrice (IRE) *Ronald Harris* a61 65
3 b f Le Vie Dei Colori—Hard To Lay (IRE) (Dolphin Street (FR))
109^{4} 189^{5} 558^{5} 834^{2} 964^{4} 1078^{3} 1753^{6} 2163^{5} 2375^{4} 2993^{9} 3226^{8}

Scorn (USA) *Richard Hannon* a72 84
4 b m Seeking The Gold(USA) —Sulk (IRE) (Selkirk (USA))
1353^{3} 1587^{4} 3636^{6} 4270^{9}

Scotsbrook Cloud *David Evans* 48
6 gr g Cloudings(IRE) —Angie Marinie (Sabrehill (USA))
4753^{5}

Scottish Glen *Patrick Chamings* a77 65
5 ch g Kyllachy—Dance For Fun (Anabaa (USA))
2822^{12} 3468^{11} 4210^{2} 5201^{8} 7417^{3} 7767^{7}

Scottish Lake *Jedd O'Keeffe* 69
3 b g Bertolini(USA) —Diabaig (Precocious)
3575^{3} 4290^{6} 4854^{4} 5403^{2} 6116^{3} 6452^{5} 6775^{13}

Scottish Star *James Eustace* a77 57
3 gr g Kirkwall—Child Star (FR) (Bellypha)
(471)

Scouting For Girls *Jim Boyle* 52
2 b g Sleeping Indian—Concubine (IRE) (Danehill (USA))
3408^{8} 4007^{8} 4446^{10}

Scrapper Smith (IRE) *Alistair Whillans* a65 96
5 b g Choisir(AUS) —Lady Ounavarra (IRE) (Simply Great (FR))
3275^{5} 4107^{4} (5593) (6080) 7161^{2} 7297^{6}

Screaming Brave *Sheena West* a55 65
5 br g Hunting Lion(IRE) —Hana Dee (Cadeaux Genereux)
355^{3} ◆

Screenprint *Michael Bell* 72
3 ch g Shamardal(USA) —Painted Moon (USA) (Gone West (USA))
1949^{2} 2728^{3} 3674^{9}

Scribe (IRE) *David Evans* a65 77
3 b c Montjeu(IRE) —Crafty Example (USA) (Crafty Prospector (USA))
7630^{4}

Script *Alan Berry*
2 b f Firebreak—Signs And Wonders (Danehill (USA))
6152^{9} 6598^{9}

Scriptwriter (IRE) *Howard Johnson* 112
9 b g Sadler's Wells(USA) —Dayanata (Shirley Heights)
2314^{6}

Scrooby Doo *David Nicholls* a67 67
2 b f Kheleyf(USA) —Scrooby Baby (Mind Games)
3490^{2} 3947^{3} 4427^{7} 5211^{2} 5596^{3} 5847^{6} (6612) 7067^{3}

Scruffy Skip (IRE) *Christine Dunnett* a57 64
6 b g Diktat—Capoeira (USA) (Nureyev (USA))
255^{6} 317^{7} 4651^{14} 5214^{12} 5515^{14} 5601^{8} 7071^{6} 7247^{4} 7524^{12} 7656^{12}

Scrupul (IRE) *Luca Cumani* 77
2 b c Dylan Thomas(IRE) —Pearl Quest (Rainbow Quest (USA))
5697^{13} 6675^{2} 7209^{6}

Sea Anemone *Andrew Balding* a52
2 b f Phoenix Reach(IRE) —Seaflower Reef (IRE) (Robellino (USA))
7118^{11} 7657^{3} 7909^{5}

Sea Change (IRE) *Jim Goldie* a88 67
4 b g Danehill Dancer(IRE) —Ibtikar (USA) (Private Account (USA))
5221^{12} 6171^{13}

Sea Cliff (IRE) *Andrew Crook* a59 36
7 b g Golan(IRE) —Prosaic Star (IRE) (Common Grounds)
551^{2} 859^{6}

Sea Crest *Mel Brittain* a30 65
5 b m Xaar—Talah (Danehill (USA))
1204^{8} 2798^{6} 3025^{7} 3937^{10}

Seadream *Mark Usher* a40 52
3 b g Bertolini(USA) —Last Dream (IRE) (Alzao (USA))
53^{5} 187^{6} 406^{7} 564^{6} 745^{6} 964^{8}

Sea Fever (IRE) *Luca Cumani* 50
2 b c Footstepsinthesand—Love And Laughter (IRE) (Theatrical)
7080^{8} ◆

Sea Flower (IRE) *Tim Easterby* 71
3 b f Acclamation—Rebel Clan (IRE) (Tagula (IRE))
1745^{5}

Sea Fret *Hughie Morrison* 27
2 b f Nayef(USA) —Shifting Mist (Night Shift (USA))
6726^{11} 7025^{15}

Sea Fury (IRE) *Suzy Smith* a14
4 b m Hawk Wing(USA) —Scruple (IRE) (Catrail (USA))
649^{9}

Seal Cove (USA) *Claude McGaughey III* 100
3 rg c Strong Hope(USA) —Meghan's Joy (USA) (A.P. Indy (USA))
$6716a^{7}$

Sea Lord (IRE) *Mahmood Al Zarooni* a100 116
4 b h Cape Cross(IRE) —First Fleet (USA) (Woodman (USA))
$156a^{8}$ $331a^{6}$ $682a^{9}$

Seal Rock *Henry Candy* 102
3 b g Ishiguru(USA) —Satin Doll (Diktat)
(1688) (2067) 2934^{8} 4333^{11} 4965^{8} 6723^{2} 6987^{6}

Sea Moon *Sir Michael Stoute* 126
3 b c Beat Hollow—Eva Luna (USA) (Alleged (USA))
(2935) (5182) ◆ 5928^{3} $7305a^{2}$

Seamster *Richard Ford* a61 52
4 ch g Pivotal—Needles And Pins (IRE) (Fasliyev (USA))
3250^{5} 3952^{10} 7416^{11} 7632^{6} (7781)

Seamus Shindig *Henry Candy* a59 86
9 b g Aragon—Sheesha (USA) (Shadeed (USA))
1444^{5} 1771^{4} 2095^{12} 2879^{4} 4434^{5} 4960^{2} 5513^{3} (5781) 6250^{2} 6895^{14}

Seanie (IRE) *David Marnane* a94 90
2 b g Kodiac—Cakestown Lady (IRE) (Petorius)
(6196a) ◆ $7185a^{6}$

Sean Og Coulston (IRE) *John J Coleman* a80 96
7 b g Raphane(USA) —Classic Silk (IRE) (Classic Secret (USA))
$3440a^{22}$ $4566a^{3}$

Sea Odyssey (IRE) *Charles Hills* a78 85
2 gr c Dark Angel(IRE) —Time To Dream (Gone West (USA))
1136^{3} ◆ 1823^{2} 2148^{6} 4079^{3} (4548) (4658) 5701^{3} 5849^{17} 6323^{2}

Sea Of Galilee *Henry Candy* 90
4 b m Galileo(IRE) —Mesange Royale (FR) (Garde Royale)
1622^{4} 3411^{11} 6632^{3} 7017^{10}

Sea Of Heartbreak (IRE) *Roger Charlton* a68 111
4 b m Rock Of Gibraltar(IRE) —Top Forty (Rainbow Quest (USA))
1718^{2} ◆ 2290^{4} 2994^{2} (4582) 6161^{3} (6557a) $6909a^{5}$

Sea Of Light (IRE) *Roger Charlton* 15
2 b f Diamond Green(FR) —Saviolo (Rossini (USA))
2606^{9} 2787^{14}

Sea Of Love (IRE) *Ronald Harris* a28
3 b f Dubawi(IRE) —Alta Gracia (IRE) (Danehill Dancer (IRE))
64^{10}

Sea Poet *John Bridger* a42 56
2 b g Byron—Beejay (Piccolo)
1129^{5} 1451^{4} 1932^{6} 2556^{2} 2854^{3} 2998^{6} 5998^{9} 6237^{9} 6724^{10} 6942^{9}

Search And Rescue (USA) *J W Hills* a59 32
2 bb c Seeking The Best(IRE) —Pattern Step (USA) (Nureyev (USA))
6180^{8} 6506^{7} 6956^{12}

Searing Heat (USA) *Sir Henry Cecil* 63
3 bb c Empire Maker(USA) —Valentine Band (USA) (Dixieland Band (USA))
2097^{8} 2956^{14}

Sea Rover (IRE) *Mel Brittain* a73 56
7 b h Jade Robbery(USA) —Talah (Danehill (USA))
1612^{13} 1907^{15}

Sea Salt *Ron Barr* a59 74
8 b g Titus Livius(FR) —Carati (Selkirk (USA))
1558^{13} 1907^{6} 2464^{7} 2765^{7} 3190^{4} 3662^{5} 4000^{3} 4233^{3} 4443^{2} 4600^{9} (5008) 5313^{7} 5647^{3} 6265^{6} 6779^{8}

Seaside Escape (USA) *Brian Meehan* 75
2 b f Bernardini(USA) —Promenade Girl (USA) (Carson City (USA))
5444^{8} 6168^{5}

Seaside Retreat (USA) *Mark Casse* a107 104
8 b g King Cugat(USA) —Shes Like Rio (USA) (Boundary (USA))
$6203a^{7}$

Seaside Sizzler *Ralph Beckett* a85 94
4 ch g Rahy(USA) —Via Borghese (USA) (Seattle Dancer (USA))
(1174) (1761) 2512^{4} 3522^{2} 4423^{2} 5221^{14} (6485)

Sea Soldier (IRE) *Andrew Balding* 87
3 b g Red Ransom(USA) —Placement (Kris)
2790^{2} (3320) 4965^{3} 5830^{8}

Season Spirit *James Given* a46 54
2 ch c Shirocco(GER) —Shadow Dancing (Unfuwain (USA))
4996^{12} 5891^{9} 6334^{12} 6825^{6} 7336^{3}

Sea The Flames (IRE) *Marcus Tregoning* a59 62
3 b g Chineur(FR) —Flames (Blushing Flame (USA))
3268^{2} 3989^{5} 4491^{7} 5022^{2} 5379^{2} 6087^{5}

Sea Tobougie *Mark Usher* a47 48
4 ch m Tobougg(IRE) —Mary Sea (FR) (Selkirk (USA))
172^{7} 391^{7} 652^{6} 722^{7}

Sea Trial (FR) *Mme C Head-Maarek* 92
2 b c Panis(USA) —Sea Life (FR) (Anabaa (USA))
$5194a^{3}$ $7155a^{2}$

Seattle Drive (IRE) *David Elsworth* a75 95
3 b c Motivator—Seattle Ribbon (USA) (Seattle Dancer (USA))
2847^{5} 3864^{8} ◆ 4313^{4} 4718^{3} 6080^{4}

Seattle Sounder (IRE) *Ann Duffield* a62 50
2 b g Choisir(AUS) —Bea's Ruby (IRE) (Fairy King (USA))
6448[6] 6836[9] 7248[3]

Seawood *Roy Bowring* a53
5 b g Needwood Blade—Ocean Song (Savahra Sound)
3324[9] 4180[6] 7241[6] 7645[3] 7858[6]

Second Encore *J S Moore* a70 72
3 b f Royal Applause—Empress Jain (Lujain (USA))
929[2] 1062[3]

Second Reef *Thomas Cuthbert* a64 58
9 b g Second Empire(IRE) —Vax Lady (Millfontaine)
2692[4] 3128[9] 4039[6] 4601[9] 4946[3] 5823[14]

Secoya *Ralph Beckett* a60 52
3 b f Sleeping Indian—Nazca (Zilzal (USA))
4090[6]

Secrecy *Saeed Bin Suroor* a111 116
5 b g King's Best(USA) —Wink (Salse (USA))
(4003) 4373a[8] 4972[4] 6416[2] 6955[2] (7166)

Secret Admirer (AUS) *Grahame Begg* 119
4 ch f Dubawi(IRE) —Secret Illusion (AUS) (Secret Savings (USA))
7044a[5]

Secretary Of State (IRE) *A P O'Brien* 97
2 b c Danehill Dancer(IRE) —Akuna Bay (USA) (Mr Prospector (USA))
2532a[2]

Secret Asset (IRE) *Jane Chapple-Hyam* a106 115
6 gr g Clodovil(IRE) —Skerray (Soviet Star (USA))
848[6] 989[9] 1186[2] 1366[4] 1687[15] 2525[9] 3627[4] 4075[9] (4416) 4534[7] (5180) 6563a[2] 7221a[4] 7392[6]

Secret Circle (USA) *Bob Baffert* a112
2 b c Eddington(USA) —Ragtime Hope (USA) (Dixieland Band (USA))
(7280a)

Secret City (IRE) *Robin Bastiman* 69
5 b g City On A Hill(USA) —Secret Combe (IRE) (Mujadil (USA))
1612[5] 2352[8] 2803[14] 3856[7] 4893[9] (5490) (6266) 6779[14] 7064[3]

Secret Edge *Alan King* a73 74
3 b g Tobougg(IRE) —Burton Ash (Diktat)
2885[9] 3551[6] 4336[6] 5145[2] ◆ (5477) 6057[3]

Secret Era *William Muir* a64 65
4 b m Cape Cross(IRE) —Secret History (USA) (Bahri (USA))
3167[2] 5429[7] (5900) 6507[13]

Secret Hero *Adrian McGuinness* a59 60
5 b g Cadeaux Genereux—Valiantly (Anabaa (USA))
6511a[9]

Secret Lake *George Margarson* 48
3 ch f Dubawi(IRE) —Three Secrets (IRE) (Danehill (USA))
2168[3]

Secret Lodge *Garry Woodward*
3 ch f Needwood Blade—Obsessive Secret (IRE) (Grand Lodge (USA))
4813[9] 6097[10]

Secret Love (IRE) *Mikael Magnusson* a83 89
3 gr f Dalakhani(IRE) —Sacred Love (IRE) (Barathea (IRE))
2050[6] 3034[11] 5635[9]

Secret Major (FR) *M Weiss* a41
7 bl h Majorien—Agincourt (FR) (Kaldoun (FR))
534a[7]

Secret Millionaire (IRE) *Patrick Morris* a93 97
4 b g Kyllachy—Mithl Al Hawa (Salse (USA))
2028[5] 2317[6] 2525[6] 2727[12] 3847[7] 4644[3] 4767a[4] 5706[6] ◆ (6036) 6348[7]

Secret Queen *Martin Hill* a73 73
4 b m Zafeen(FR) —Gold Queen (Grand Lodge (USA))
694[8] 1024[2] 1232[5] 1562[5] 2027[10] 2903[8] 3283[6]

Secret Tune *Shaun Lycett* 57
7 b g Generous(IRE) —Sing For Fame (USA) (Quest For Fame)
4998[6] 6171[4]

Secret Tycoon (IRE) *Patrick Morris* a39 67
3 gr g Aussie Rules(USA) —River Grand (IRE) (Grand Lodge (USA))
653[5] 741[7]

Secret Venue *Jedd O'Keeffe* a32 73
5 ch g Where Or When(IRE) —Sheila's Secret (IRE) (Bluebird (USA))
1698[4] 1899[8]

Secret Witness *Ronald Harris* a105 105
5 ch g Pivotal—It's A Secret (Polish Precedent (USA))
1888[16] 2099[3] 2717[7] 3394[7] 3627[3] 3841[12] 4531[12] 4859[6] (5033) 5264[6] 5430[5] 5927[10] 6332[7] ◆ 6522[6] 6987[15] 7018[2] 7298[7] 7392[2] 7578[5] 7721[5]

Secundus (GER) *M Nigge* a71 75
6 b g Daliapour(IRE) —Sly (GER) (Monsun (GER))
1013a[6]

Sedaine *Ralph Beckett* 71
3 b f Librettist(USA) —Spry (Suave Dancer (USA))
1873[4] 2960[5]

Sedgwick *Shaun Harris* a82 80
9 b g Nashwan(USA) —Imperial Bailiwick (IRE) (Imperial Frontier (USA))
1150[5]

Seduisant (GER) *Frau M Weber* 83
3 ch f Paolini(GER) —Solita (GER) (Lomitas)
5980a[10]

See Clearly *Tim Easterby* 78
2 b f Bertolini(USA) —True Vision (IRE) (Pulpit (USA))
1691[7] 2542[3] 2886[7] 3273[3] 3504[6] (4106) 4558[6] (4984) 5825[12] 6154[4] 6573[2] 6864[2]

See Emily Play (IRE) *John Gosden* 64
2 b f Galileo(IRE) —Tree Tops (Grand Lodge (USA))
5445[11] 6776[4]

Seeharn (IRE) *Kevin Prendergast* 107
3 b f Pivotal—Nebraas (Green Desert (USA))
1006a[5] 1779a[3] 2334a[13] 4116a[5] 6733a[2] 7509a[2]

Seeker (USA) *Steven Asmussen* a95
2 bb c Hard Spun(USA) —Classic Olympio (USA) (Olympio (USA))
7280a[4]

Seeking Magic *Clive Cox* a73 88
3 b g Haafhd—Atnab (USA) (Riverman (USA))
1176[3] 5000[3] ◆ 5279[3] 5781[2] (6895)

Seeking Rio *Ron Hodges* a47 32
4 b m Captain Rio—True Seeker (Lujain (USA))
256[3] 421[12] 464[7] 732[5] 1180[5] 1453[7]

Seek The Fair Land *Jim Boyle* a96 85
5 b g Noverre(USA) —Duchcov (Caerleon (USA))
99[9] 1594[3] 1898[5] 2300[5] 2876[4] 3179[2] 3765[5] 4392[5] 4531[9] 5012[10] 6761[10] 7127[2] (7438) 7628[8]

Seelo (USA) *John Gosden* a91 99
3 b c Dynaformer(USA) —Seebe (USA) (Danzig (USA))
2052[2] (2764) 3044[3] 3774[7] 4777[5] 5700[4]

Seemples (IRE) *Richard Hannon* a54 53
2 b g Moss Vale(IRE) —Ink Pot (USA) (Green Dancer (USA))
4996[15] 5475[8] 7481[3] 7568[7]

See That Girl *Martin Bosley* a49 44
5 b m Hawk Wing(USA) —Hampton Lucy (IRE) (Anabaa (USA))
70[12]

See The Smile (USA) *Jim Boyle* a74 56
3 b c Arch(USA) —Tink So (USA) (Meadowlake (USA))
878[2] 1076[5] 3131[4] 4664[5] 5389[11] 5838[6]

See The Storm *Patrick Morris* a52 57
3 bb g Statue Of Liberty(USA) —Khafayif (USA) (Swain (IRE))
28[7] 1465[4] 2351[4] (2598) 3142[3] 3455[5] 3643[2] 3958[2] 4364[4] 4929[9] 6050[8] 6428[6]

See Vermont *Robin Bastiman* 54
3 b g Kyllachy—Orange Lily (Royal Applause)
295[6] 2479[8] 3053[4] 4124[7] 4684[3] 5620[5] 6602[3] 7086[6]

See You Smile (IRE) *Liam McAteer* a51 80
4 b m Camacho—Celebrated Smile (IRE) (Cadeaux Genereux)
4882[9]

Sehnsucht (IRE) *Alan McCabe* 74
2 b c Amadeus Wolf—Kirk Wynd (Selkirk (USA))
3132[3] 3590[3] 3861[10]

Sehrezad (IRE) *Andreas Lowe* 119
6 b h Titus Livius(FR) —Trebles (IRE) (Kenmare (FR))
1740a[3] 2657a[2]

Seismos (IRE) *A Wohler* 103
3 ch c Dalakhani(IRE) —Sasuela (GER) (Dashing Blade)
6396a[6] 6710a[2]

Selbaar *Chris Dwyer* a60 52
2 b c Medicean—Puzzle Book (USA) (Distant View (USA))
2594[6] 3552[6] 4276[12] (4922) 5316[6] 5998[11] 6284[9]

Seldom (IRE) *Mel Brittain* a71 70
5 b g Sesaro(USA) —Daisy Dancer (IRE) (Distinctly North (USA))
1613[4] 1748[7] 2413[6] 3683[2] 3936[3] (4150) 4543[4] 5106[2] 5314[6] 5488[11] 6098[11] 6452[2]

Select Committee *John Quinn* 81
6 b g Fayruz—Demolition Jo (Petong)
1411[8] 1698[2] 1899[7] 2250[3] 2590[4] 2938[5] 4405[7] 4900[6] 5468[6] (6044) 6276[4] 6348[4] 6537[4]

Selective Spirit *John Weymes* 54
2 ch f Exceed And Excel(AUS) —Our Sheila (Bahamian Bounty)
2485[5] ◆

Selena (FR) *M Boutin* a64 83
4 b m Kendor(FR) —Seranda (IRE) (Petoski)
2867a[6]

Self Centred *Charles Hills* 85
2 ch f Medicean—Ego (Green Desert (USA))
2467[5] ◆ 3152[3] ◆ 3813[2] 4285[5] 5287[3] (6322) 7028[7]

Self Employed *Garry Woodward* 74
4 b g Sakhee(USA) —Twilight Sonnet (Exit To Nowhere (USA))
2361[2]

Self Preservation (USA) *B Cecil* a104 91
2 ch f Lion Heart(USA) —Saintly Speaking (USA) (Dahar (USA))
7283a[4]

Selinda *Mick Channon* a50 56
2 b f Piccolo—Evanesce (Lujain (USA))
1628[4] 1954[3] 2267[2] (2595) 2998[7] (3554) 3842[8] 4226[4] 4658[4]

Selkis (GER) *J Hirschberger* 97
3 ch f Monsun(GER) —Schwarzach (GER) (Grand Lodge (USA))
(2981a) 4839a[16]

Selkiss Eria (FR) *C Diard* 47
3 b f Muhtathir—Kassaboum (FR) (Double Bed (FR))
852a[9]

Semayyel (IRE) *Clive Brittain* 95
2 b f Green Desert(USA) —Lii Najma (Medicean)
4155[8] (5444) 5885[5] 6299[7] 6705[6] 7028[2]

Semester *A Fabre* 102
3 ch f Monsun(GER) —Favourable Terms (Selkirk (USA))
5027a[5]

Semi Detached (IRE) *James Unett* a59 37
8 b g Distant Music(USA) —Relankina (IRE) (Broken Hearted)
2616[7]

Semina (GER) *S Smrczek* 104
4 ch m Mamool(IRE) —Second Game (GER) (Second Set (IRE))
6394a[5]

Semmsu (IRE) *Luca Cumani* 83
3 b g Refuse To Bend(IRE) —Summer Queen (Robellino (USA))
2469[12] 2848[8] 3766[2] 4970[3] (6020) 6457[6]

Semos (FR) *D E Ferraris* 106
4 ch g American Post—Semire (FR) (Mizoram (USA))
1742a[13]

Senate *Saeed Bin Suroor* a45 108
4 ch g Pivotal—Sauterne (Rainbow Quest (USA))
417a[3]

Senate Majority *Tim Easterby* a64 74
4 ch g Avonbridge—Benjarong (Sharpo)
1411[3] 1544[2] 2126[4] 2353[3] (3166) 4539[9] 4895[10] 5720[6] 6076[4] 6537[13] 7104[12]

Sendali (FR) *Chris Grant* 66
7 b g Daliapour(IRE) —Lady Senk (FR) (Pink (FR))
1794[3] (3754) 4602[5]

Sendarose (IRE) *Tim Easterby* 31
3 b g Sendawar(IRE) —Tonalgee Rose (IRE) (Woodborough (USA))
4813[8] 5556[8] 5792[8] 7212[12]

Seneschal *Adrian Chamberlain* a64 46
10 br g Polar Falcon(USA) —Broughton Singer (IRE) (Common Grounds)
3784[8] 4268[8] 4997[8] 6051[10] 6488[11] 6752[2] (6931) 7131[6] 7488[9]

Sennockian Storm (USA) *Mark Johnston* a77 77
4 b m Storm Cat(USA) —Winning Season (USA) (Lemon Drop Kid (USA))
1058[5] 1859[6] 2490[6] 3088[7] 3457[10] (3946) 4204[7] (5210) 5389[8]

Sennybridge *J W Hills* a60 45
4 ch m Avonbridge—Friend For Life (Lahib (USA))
83[6] 203[5]

Senor Sassi (USA) *J S Moore* a46 48
3 bb c Johannesburg(USA) —County Fair (USA) (Mr Prospector (USA))
47[8]

Senor Tibor (USA) *Edward Creighton* a43 50
3 b g Tale Of The Cat(USA) —Pastel Colour (USA) (Distant View (USA))
1132[7] 1369[5] 1999[5] 2418[5] 2721[5] 4654[6]

Senor Tommie (IRE) *Seamus Fahey* a56 35
5 b g Statue Of Liberty(USA) —La Luna (USA) (Lyphard (USA))
752[2] 773[5] 7698[4]

Sensational Love (IRE) *Keith Dalgleish* a41 68
3 bb f Cadeaux Genereux—Szabo (IRE) (Anabaa (USA))
1776[6] 2294[11] 3230[8] 5153[9] 5620[10] 6176[10]

Sense Of Pride *John Gosden* 87
4 b m Sadler's Wells(USA) —Bonash (Rainbow Quest (USA))
2649[3] 3758[2] 4280[8]

Sense Of Purpose (IRE) *D K Weld* 108
4 ch m Galileo(IRE) —Super Gift (IRE) (Darshaan)
1427a[5] 2968a[2] (4035a) (4737a) 5850[7]

Sentimento (ISR) *Werner Glanz* a75 75
8 b g Surako(GER) —Summer Wind (GER) (Platini (GER))
442a[4] 629a[3]

Sentosa *Michael Blanshard* a69 74
4 b m Dansili—Katrina (IRE) (Ela-Mana-Mou)
2562[6] 2872[8]

Sentry Duty (FR) *Nicky Henderson* 106
9 b g Kahyasi—Standing Around (FR) (Garde Royale)
1808[17] 3647[6] 4532[8] 6690[6]

Senza Rete (IRE) *M Gasparini* 99
3 b f Barathea(IRE) —Lyrical Dance (USA) (Lear Fan (USA))
1738a[4] 2539a[4] 3449a[7]

Separate Ways (IRE) *David Marnane* a89 104
6 b g Chevalier(IRE) —Choralli (Inchinor)
239[11] 503a[9] 679a[12] 1930a[4] 4418a[8] (Dead)

September Draw (USA) *Richard Hannon* a53 64
3 bb f Southern Image(USA) —Stacey's Relic (USA) (Houston (USA))
1146[5] 1442[3] 1951[10] 2637[6] 2768[5] 3253[7]

Septime Severe (FR) *M Delzangles* 96
3 b c Chichicastenango(FR) —Highness Royale (FR) (Garde Royale)
5230a[10]

Sequence (IRE) *Sir Michael Stoute* 47
2 b f Selkirk(USA) —Sinntara (IRE) (Lashkari)
7233[8]

Sequoia *B W Hills* 76
2 b c Shamardal(USA) —Atnab (USA) (Riverman (USA))
3793[4] 4414[4]

Serafina (GER) *W Hickst* 84
3 b f Dubai Destination(USA) —Soljanka (GER) (Halling (USA))
2981a[11]

Seraphiel *Chris Down* 57
2 b c Royal Applause—Angel Sprints (Piccolo)
6123[11] 6463[13] 6992[7]

Serenader *David O'Meara* 49
4 ch g Singspiel(IRE) —Temora (IRE) (Ela-Mana-Mou)
1211[8] 1386[5] 2114[9] 2618[7]

Serena's Pride *Alan Jarvis* a59 95
3 b f Danbird(AUS) —Wachiwi (IRE) (Namid)
1825[10] 2255[7] 2646[8] (3322) 3682[6] 5268[8] 6974[10] 7456[9] 7767[10]

Serenata Mia *Michael Smith* 19
4 b m Mark Of Esteem(IRE) —Cartuccia (IRE) (Doyoun)
1076[7] 2249[9]

Serendipity Blue *John Weymes* 9
2 b f Cadeaux Genereux—Sister Bluebird (Bluebird (USA))
5786[14]

Serene Oasis (IRE) *Mick Channon* a70 72
2 gr f Oratorio(IRE) —Princess Serena (USA) (Unbridled's Song (USA))
5047[3] 5475[3] 5691[3] 6110[3] 6380[2] 6743[5] (6866) 7028[12]

Serenity Star *Mahmood Al Zarooni* a60 94
3 b f Monsun(GER) —Nalani (IRE) (Sadler's Wells (USA))
2639[4] 3224[8]

Sergeant Ablett (IRE) *James Given* 94
3 b c Danehill Dancer(IRE) —Dolydille (IRE) (Dolphin Street (FR))
1344[3] 1723[4] 2711[7] 3405[7] 3623[8] 4335[3] 5177[4] 5880[8] 6704[4]

Sergeant Pink (IRE) *Dianne Sayer* a57 63
5 b g Fasliyev(USA) —Ring Pink (USA) (Bering)
3129[8] 3300[4] 4602[6] 5166[8] 7105[5]

Sergeant Suzie *Michael Dods* a55 71
3 ch f Dr Fong(USA) —Pie High (Salse (USA))
913[5] 1214[4] 1802[8]

Sergeant Troy (IRE) *Roger Charlton* 77
3 gr g Aussie Rules(USA) —Et Dona Ferentes (Green Desert (USA))
1446[6] (1768) 2256[4] 3815[6] 4479[5] 5376[4]

Serial Sinner (IRE) *Paul Cole* a63 67
3 b f High Chaparral(IRE) —Putout (Dowsing (USA))
1270[3] ◆ 1605[8] 1873[7] 2553[7] 2841[12] 4244[7] 4911[8] 7561[6] 7652[3] 7768[11]

Serious Choice (IRE) *Philip Hobbs* a59 48
6 b g Choisir(AUS) —Printaniere (USA) (Sovereign Dancer (USA))
4253[10] 4579[8]

Serious Drinking (USA) *Walter Swinburn* a69 66
5 b m Successful Appeal(USA) —Cup Match (USA) (Kingmambo (USA))
248[3] ◆ 428[5] 625[3] 727[9] 1052[2] 1756[9] 3235[3]

Serious Impact (USA) *F Vermeulen* a84 89
6 b g Empire Maker(USA) —Diese (USA) (Diesis)
259a[2]

Serious Matters (IRE) *Walter Swinburn* a56 50
4 b g Invincible Spirit(IRE) —Quaeramus Seria (IRE) (Catrail (USA))
362[9]

Serious Spender (IRE) *Ralph Beckett* 68
2 b g Amadeus Wolf—Meanya (IRE) (Revoque (IRE))
1268[2] (Dead)

Serjeant Buzfuz *Richard Fahey* 60
2 b g Halling(USA) —Anastasia Storm (Mozart (IRE))
6675[5]

Sermons Mount (USA) *Paul Howling* a80 80
5 bb g Vicar(USA) —Ginny Auxier (USA) (Racing Star (USA))
1562[12] 2142[7] 2422[3] 3020[8] 4618[8] (4960) 5301[2] 5616[2] 5781[9] 6895[7] 7097[2] 7517[3] 7767[9] 7893[3]

Seta *Luca Cumani* 111
4 ch m Pivotal—Bombazine (IRE) (Generous (IRE))
(1681) 3030[8] 4915[3] 5848[5] 6297[2] 7090a[4]

Setareh (GER) *P Olsanik* 97
6 b h Areion(GER) —Sety's Spirit (USA) (Seattle Song (USA))
6201a[10]

Set Em Up Mo *Michael Attwater* a49
5 b m Reset(AUS) —Mo Stopher (Sharpo)
309[5] 563[5]

Set Me Free (IRE) *Luca Cumani* a83 68
3 b g Noverre(USA) —Lonesome Me (FR) (Zafonic (USA))
2174[2] ◆ (2785) 4161[4] 5383[2]

Settebellezze (FR) *J Rossi* a75 73
4 b h Muhtathir—Similitudine (FR) (Brief Truce (USA))
91a[8]

Setter's Princess *Ron Hodges* a67 62
5 ch m Generous(IRE) —Setter Country (Town And Country)
(409) 592[2] ◆ 733[6]

Set The Trend *Andrew Balding* a100 116
5 bb g Reset(AUS) —Masrora (USA) (Woodman (USA))
1385[4] (2558) 4138a[3] 5473[2] 6556a[9]

Set To Go *Tor Sturgis* a51 61
4 b g Reset(AUS) —Golubitsa (IRE) (Bluebird (USA))
418[14] 807[8] 1357[3] 1933[4] 2921[8] 3241[3] 3943[6]

Set To Music (IRE) *Michael Bell* a71 110
3 b f Danehill Dancer(IRE) —Zarabaya (IRE) (Doyoun)
1251[3] (2957) (3642) (4477) (5220) ◆ 5850[2]

Seven Stars *Mike Sowersby* 44
6 b g Dubai Destination(USA) —Galette (Caerleon (USA))
4129[5]

Seven Summits (IRE) *Barney Curley* a87 94
4 b g Danehill Dancer(IRE) —Mandavilla (IRE) (Sadler's Wells (USA))
3406[9] 3867[9]

Seventh Sky (GER) *P Schiergen* 104
4 b g King's Best(USA) —Sacarina (Old Vic)
3446a[6] 5092a[5]

Seven Veils (IRE) *Sir Mark Prescott Bt* a49 33
2 b f Danehill Dancer(IRE) —Ahdaab (USA) (Rahy (USA))
5384[12] 6180[5] 6400[13]

Seven Year Itch (IRE) *James Bethell* 55
2 b f Lawman(FR) —Stella Del Mattino (USA) (Golden Gear (USA))
1136[8] (1301) 3700[12]

Seville (GER) *A P O'Brien* 121
3 b c Galileo(IRE) —Silverskaya (USA) (Silver Hawk (USA))
2030[2] 2715[10] 3442a[2] 4038a[2] 5182[3] 5928[4]

Sevivon *J W Hills*
4 ch m Dubai Destination(USA) —Circle Of Light (Anshan)
945[7] 1050[4]

Sgt Schultz (IRE) *J S Moore* a95 73
8 b g In The Wings—Ann's Annie (IRE) (Alzao (USA))
175[4] 308[2]

Shabak Hom (IRE) *David Simcock* a57 81
4 b g Exceed And Excel(AUS) —Shbakni (USA) (Mr Prospector (USA))
1829[2] 2046[5] 2915[2] 3354[4] (4465) 5509[3] 6773[8] 7214[5]

Shabi *A Di Dio* 91
5 ch h Indian Ridge—Sagar Pride (IRE) (Jareer (USA))
7408a[9]

Shabora (IRE) *Roger Varian* a80 65
2 b f Cape Cross(IRE) —Wardat Allayl (IRE) (Mtoto)
6603[6] 7124[5] (7396)

Shackleford (USA) *Dale Romans* a121
3 ch c Forestry(USA) —Oatsee (USA) (Unbridled (USA))
1921a[4] (2328a) 2950a[5] 7304a[2]

Shada (IRE) *Sir Michael Stoute* 71
2 ch f Galileo(IRE) —Banquise (IRE) (Last Tycoon)
5445[3]

Shaded Edge *David Arbuthnot* a77 73
7 b g Bold Edge—Twilight Mistress (Bin Ajwaad (IRE))
135[2] ◆ *390[6] 722[3] 1045[11]* 1866[6]

Shades Of Grey *Clive Cox* a70 75
4 gr m Dr Fong(USA) —Twosixtythreewest (FR) (Kris)
805[4] 1174[4] 2552[8] 5782[2] (7032) *7346[8]*

Shadow Catcher *Michael Dods* 84
3 ch g Haafhd—Unchain My Heart (Pursuit Of Love)
(1302) 2216[5] (2527) 3168[4] 4081[8] (5004) 6674[6]

Shadow Of The Sun *Joseph Tuite* a63 68
3 b f Red Ransom(USA) —Hill Welcome (Most Welcome)
5626[2] ◆ *5946[3]* 6580[4] *6700[3]*

Shadows Lengthen *Michael Easterby* a96 80
5 b g Dansili—Bay Shade (USA) (Sharpen Up)
6989[16]

Shadowtime *Tracy Waggott* a73 88
6 b g Singspiel(IRE) —Massomah (USA) (Seeking The Gold (USA))
1410[12] 1747[6] 1970[8] 2545[11] 3188[3] (3612) 3934[6] 4349[8] 5594[5] 6093[7]

Shafgaan *Clive Brittain* a70 93
3 gr c Oasis Dream—Night Haven (Night Shift (USA))
1317[9] 1820[7] 2503[8] 2926[11] 4062[8]

Shahighyield (FR) *P Khozian* a69
3 b f High Yield(USA) —Shahrazad (FR) (Bering)
480a[2]

Shahwardi (FR) *A De Royer-Dupre* 103
5 b g Lando(GER) —Shamdara (IRE) (Dr Devious (IRE))
2044[9] 7406a[0]

Shahzan (IRE) *Roger Varian* 64
3 br c Dansili—Femme Fatale (Fairy King (USA))
2103[7]

Shakalaka (IRE) *Th Von Ballmoos* a82 88
5 b g Montjeu(IRE) —Sweet Times (Riverman (USA))
442a[6]

Shakespearean (IRE) *Saeed Bin Suroor* 118
4 b h Shamardal(USA) —Paimpolaise (IRE) (Priolo (USA))
759a[12] 2502[9] 3404[12]

Shakespeares Excel *Derek Shaw* a52 51
4 b g Exceed And Excel(AUS) —Catch The Wind (Bahamian Bounty)
669[4] 971[8] 1065[6] 1287[4] 1464[5] 2164[6] 4189[3] 4395[4] *4650[3]*

Shalambar (IRE) *Tony Carroll* a67 52
5 gr g Dalakhani(IRE) —Shalama (IRE) (Kahyasi)
1775[6] *6254[10] 6790[10] (7206) 7331[2]*

Shalamiyr (FR) *Edward Creighton* 14
6 gr g Linamix(FR) —Shamanara (IRE) (Danehill (USA))
1285[5]

Shaleek *Roger Varian* 79
2 ch f Pivotal—Dorrati (USA) (Dubai Millennium)
6030[2] ◆ 6758[2]

Shalloon (IRE) *Mark Johnston* 89
3 b c Cape Cross(IRE) —Sun Silk (USA) (Gone West (USA))
3304[3] (3684) 5199[2] 5557[12] (6063) 6328[7]

Shallow Bay *David Pipe* a91 92
4 b g Shamardal(USA) —Yawl (Rainbow Quest (USA))
1772[2] ◆ 2066[3] 2884[12] 3203[9] 6124[8]

Shaloo Diamond *Richard Whitaker* 58
6 b g Captain Rio—Alacrity (Alzao (USA))
3023[12]

Shamaal Nibras (USA) *Ed Dunlop* a80 78
2 b c First Samurai(USA) —Sashay Away (USA) (Farma Way (USA))
2687[4] *(3237)* 4760[6] 6031[4] *6623[7]*

Shamacam *Sir Michael Stoute* a69 84
3 ch c Shamardal(USA) —Dynacam (USA) (Dynaformer (USA))
1605[7] 2648[9] ◆ 3080[2] 3551[3] 4253[3]

Shamahan *Gary Moore* 81
2 b c Shamardal(USA) —Hanella (IRE) (Galileo (IRE))
4710[3] (5111) ◆

Shamakat *Rae Guest* 58
2 ch f Shamardal(USA) —Katina (USA) (Danzig (USA))
5889[9] 6800[6]

Shamalgan (FR) *A Savujev* 116
4 ch h Footstepsinthesand—Genevale (FR) (Unfuwain (USA))
1740a[7] 2343a[6] 4120a[6] (5664a) 6369a[5]

Shamali *William Haggas* a103 110
6 ch g Selkirk(USA) —Shamaiel (IRE) (Lycius (USA))
(1100) 1528[3] 1883[2] 3107[11]

Shamal Sally (USA) *Zuzana Kubovicova* 96
4 rg m E Dubai(USA) —Screaming Shamal (USA) (Tabasco Cat (USA))
6739a[7] 7047a[11]

Shamandar (FR) *William Haggas* 97
4 ch m Exceed And Excel(AUS) —Sensational Mover (USA) (Theatrical)
1885[7] 3030[12] 3862[18] 4049[3] 4428[12]

Shamanova (IRE) *A De Royer-Dupre* 109
4 b m Danehill Dancer(IRE) —Shamadara (IRE) (Kahyasi)
1784a[2] 4037a[3] 5093a[3] 5990a[3] 6557a[4] 7049a[6]

Shamar (FR) *A De Royer-Dupre* 95
3 b c Dr Fong(USA) —Shamalana (IRE) (Sinndar (IRE))
2341a[6]

Shamardal Phantom (IRE) *David Simcock* a69 77
4 b m Shamardal(USA) —Ripalong (IRE) (Revoque (IRE))
284[2] (448) 1992[6] 2204[4] (2663) 3413[8]

Shamardanse (IRE) *S Wattel* a93 100
3 b f Shamardal(USA) —Danse Bretonne (FR) (Exit To Nowhere (USA))
6321a[9] 6568a[10]

Shamardeliah (IRE) *James Tate* a68 28
2 b f Shamardal(USA) —Sunsetter (USA) (Diesis)
3132[11] *6308[5]* ◆ *7757[3]*

Shamdarley (IRE) *Michael Dods* 90
3 b g Shamardal(USA) —Siphon Melody (USA) (Siphon (BRZ))
1108[6] (2092) 2705[3] 3159[4] (3904) 5049[8] 6302[5] (6674)

Shame On You (IRE) *Charles Hills* 70
2 ch f Shamardal(USA) —Woodlass (USA) (Woodman (USA))
7293[3]

Shamir *Jo Crowley* a96 81
4 b g Dubai Destination(USA) —Lake Nyasa (IRE) (Lake Coniston (IRE))
702[7] 991[10] 1760[6] (3285) 3840[8] 4958[6] *5712[11] 7127[9]*

Shamo Hill Theatre *Colin Teague* 35
4 b g Millkom—Hannalou (FR) (Shareef Dancer (USA))
3128[8]

Shamrocked (IRE) *Mick Channon* 84
2 b g Rock Of Gibraltar(IRE) —Hallowed Park (IRE) (Barathea (IRE))
(3425) ◆ 4091[3] 6077[4] 6336[6]

Shamrocker (NZ) *Danny O'Brien* 116
4 b f O'Reilly(NZ) —Bohemian Blues (NZ) (Blues Traveller (IRE))
7044a[12] 7218a[21]

Shanaco (FR) *Mlle Valerie Boussin* a70 70
4 b h Ski Chief(USA) —Hollyhead (FR) (Green Tune (USA))
831a[0]

Shanjia (GER) *Mario Hofer* 59
2 b f Soldier Hollow—Shivara (GER) (Monsun (GER))
7666a[2]

Shankardeh (IRE) *M Delzangles* 112
3 b f Azamour(IRE) —Shalamantika (IRE) (Nashwan (USA))
3447a[3] 4470[2] ◆ (6555a) 7049a[3]

Shannons Brook *Brett Johnson* a45
3 ch f Bertolini(USA) —Sprinkle (Selkirk (USA))
5300[6] *6473[9]*

Shannon Spree *Richard Hannon* a72 65
2 b f Royal Applause—Some Diva (Dr Fong (USA))
3287[7] 4052[13] 4552[9] 5233[4] *(5634)* 5844[5] *7205[2] 7436[5]*

Shantaram *John Gosden* 81
2 b c Galileo(IRE) —All's Forgotten (USA) (Darshaan)
5891[2] ◆

Shaqira *Marcus Tregoning* 73
3 bb f Redoute's Choice(AUS) —Hammiya (IRE) (Darshaan)
4072[5] 4641[2] 5629[5] 6096[5]

Sharaayeen *Charles Hills* a91 104
4 br g Singspiel(IRE) —Corinium (IRE) (Turtle Island (IRE))
1717[2] ◆ 3156[10] 3625[8] 4532[11] 5250[5] 5853[3]

Sharakti (IRE) *Alan McCabe* a17 81
4 b g Rakti—Easter Parade (Entrepreneur)
1099[6] 1324[6] (1573) 1671[2] 2124[2] 2403[3] 2674[14] 2887[16] 4109[10] 4477[8]

Shared Account (USA) *H Graham Motion* a56 113
5 b m Pleasantly Perfect(USA) —Silk N' Sapphire (USA) (Smart Strike (CAN))
7284a[7]

Shared Moment (IRE) *John Gallagher* a66 65
5 ch m Tagula(IRE) —Good Thought (IRE) (Mukaddamah (USA))
78[2] (135) 273[3] (387) 562[2] 765[3] 889[2] 1183[4] 7764[4]

Share Option *Tony Carroll* a51 55
9 b g Polish Precedent(USA) —Quota (Rainbow Quest (USA))
173[10] 771[10]

Shareta (IRE) *A De Royer-Dupre* 120
3 b f Sinndar(IRE) —Shawara (IRE) (Barathea (IRE))
2977a[7] (4036b) (5027a) 5989a[3] 6567a[2] 7563a[7]

Sharisse (IRE) *W T Farrell* 93
5 ch m Noverre(USA) —Hayworth (IRE) (Night Shift (USA))
5746a[15]

Shark In The Sea *Brian Meehan* a67 52
2 b c Sakhee(USA) —Wassendale (Erhaab (USA))
4201[11] 4968[13] *5382[5]* 5783[9]

Sharnberry *Ed Dunlop* 105
3 b f Shamardal(USA) —Wimple (USA) (Kingmambo (USA))
1404[2] 2137a[5] 3527a[8] 4497[11] 5080[7] 6523[4]

Sharp And Chic *Richard Ford* a39 11
4 b m Needwood Blade—Moreover (IRE) (Caerleon (USA))
4602[12]

Sharp Bullet (IRE) *Bruce Hellier* a59 65
5 b g Royal Applause—Anna Frid (GER) (Big Shuffle (USA))
1544[3] 1716[2] 2048[7] 2546[2] 2632[2] 2987[3] 3166[4] 3488[4] 4017[5] 4328[3] 4986[3] 5313[6] 5719[5] *6175[3]* 6213[2] 6454[2] (6602) *6791[4]*

Sharpened Edge *Christopher Mason* a51 85
5 b m Exceed And Excel(AUS) —Beveled Edge (Beveled (USA))
(2645) 2929[4] 4583[6] 6246[10]

Sharp Relief (IRE) *Hughie Morrison* a73 79
3 b f Galileo(IRE) —Jinskys Gift (IRE) (Cadeaux Genereux)
1363[9] 2551[10] *4208[8]* (5022) (5623) 6151[5] 6729[5] *7129[11]*

Sharp Shoes *Ann Duffield* a73 75
4 br g Needwood Blade—Mary Jane (Tina's Pet)
144[2] 294[4] 491[5] (732) 746[8] 1073[7] 1411[9] (1856) (2048) 3305[8] 3832[8] 4197[6] 4881[4] 5313[2] 5552[5] 6427[2] 6655[7] 7395[8] 7594[9] 7853[5]

Sharp Sovereign (USA) *Ian McInnes* a53 75
5 b g Cactus Ridge(USA) —Queen Of Humor (USA) (Distorted Humor (USA))
1099[16] 1461[10] 2059[7] 2388[5] 2804[2] 3054[3] 3660[3] 4043[6] 4366[2] ◆ 4540[2] 5207[3] 5724[11] 6295[2] 6918[8] *7413[7]*

Shatter (IRE) *William Haggas* 59
2 b f Mr Greeley(USA) —Watership Crystal (IRE) (Sadler's Wells (USA))
6935[6] 7209[9]

Shaunas Spirit (IRE) *Dean Ivory* a58 44
3 b f Antonius Pius(USA) —Shaunas Vision (IRE) (Dolphin Street (FR))
360[8] 959[6] 1270[10] 1980[4] *3223[14] 5944[2] 6083[2] 7581[2] 7640[5] 7910[3]*

Shavansky *Rod Millman* a88 101
7 b g Rock Of Gibraltar(IRE) —Limelighting (USA) (Alleged (USA))
1479[6] 2002[5] 2509[2] 2884[8] 3290[3] (3802) 4428[6] 5557[3] 5940[8] 6339[7] 6803[4] 7029[11]

Shawkantango *Derek Shaw* a74 66
4 b g Piccolo—Kitty Kitty Cancan (Warrshan (USA))
(185) (401) (571) 696[4] 985[10] 1213[6] *(1503)* 2547[2] 3078[2] *3493[9] 7594[11] 7746[12] 7896[3]*

Shaws Diamond (USA) *Derek Shaw* a65 65
5 ch m Ecton Park(USA) —Dear Abigail (USA) (Dehere (USA))
2016[8] *2165[6]* ◆ *2386[6]* 3202[7] *6626[7] 6848[2]* 6940[4] *7096[3] 7270[7]*

Shayla *Alan Swinbank* a52 74
4 ch m Pastoral Pursuits—Honours Even (Highest Honor (FR))
(3902) 6098[10] 6450[3] 6867[9]

She Ain't A Saint *Jane Chapple-Hyam* a87 72
3 b f Dansili—Flamingo Sky (USA) (Silver Hawk (USA))
(274) ◆ *(907)* 1550[6] 1843[10] 3825[13] 4479[4] *5322[12] 5948[8] 7542[6] 7759[7]*

She Deals *Paul Midgley* a9 12
3 b f Gentleman's Deal(IRE) —Baymist (Mind Games)
4559[9]

Sheedal (IRE) *Linda Perratt* 47
3 b f Danroad(AUS) —Absolute Glee (USA) (Kenmare (FR))
3903[6] 4142[11] 4383[4] 4505[11] 4783[11]

Sheer Courage (IRE) *H J Brown* a50 96
3 b c Invincible Spirit(IRE) —Mood Swings (IRE) (Shirley Heights)
238[11]

Sheer Vanity (USA) *Ed McMahon* 69
2 b f Dixie Union(USA) —I'm Right (USA) (Rahy (USA))
6026[2] ◆ 6406[2] ◆ 6892[2]

Sheikh The Reins (IRE) *John Best* a75 79
2 b c Iffraaj—Wychwood Wanderer (IRE) (Barathea (IRE))
5480[10] 6525[2] 6991[3] *(7329)*

Sheila's Bond *John Flint* a64 65
4 ch m Monsieur Bond(IRE) —Loreto Rose (Lahib (USA))
162[3] (245) 514[4] 768[F]

Sheila's Buddy *J S Moore* a64 70
2 ch g Reel Buddy(USA) —Loreto Rose (Lahib (USA))
2017[5] 3016[2] 3242[2] 3866[8] 4698[2] 5170[5] *5413[2]* 5991[3] (6399) 6524[14] *7336[8]*

Sheila's Castle *Sean Regan* a66 65
7 b m Karinga Bay—Candarela (Damister (USA))
1994[3] 6600[7]

Sheila's Star (IRE) *J S Moore* a66 66
3 b f Hurricane Run(IRE) —Yaselda (Green Desert (USA))
192[2] 297[2] (480a)

She Is Great (IRE) *B Grizzetti* 101
4 b m Dalakhani(IRE) —She Bat (Batshoof)
6739a[4] 7047a[12]

Sheitan *F Brogi* 70
6 b g Dalakhani(IRE) —Biosphere (Pharly (FR))
372a[0]

Shek O Lad *Alan Jarvis* a35 26
2 b g Librettist(USA) —Lady Pahia (IRE) (Pivotal)
5011[15] *5688[8]* 6110[11]

Shelagh (IRE) *Jo Crowley* a73
3 b f Aussie Rules(USA) —Viburnum (USA) (El Gran Senor (USA))
811[9] (953) (7484) 7579[7] 7764[5]

Shelovestobouggie *Marco Botti* a68 71
3 b f Tobougg(IRE) —Bowled Out (GER) (Dansili)
1270[4] *1580[6]* 3312[7] 4163[8] *(6878) 7198[9] 7589[6]*

Shemoli *D Selvaratnam* a83 49
5 ch g Singspiel(IRE) —Felawnah (USA) (Mr Prospector (USA))
707a[9]

Sheniyan (IRE) *A De Royer-Dupre* 92
3 b c Sadler's Wells(USA) —Shemaya (IRE) (Darshaan)
5131a[7]

Shere Khan *Richard Hannon* a85 71
2 b g Royal Applause—Tokyo Rose (Agnes World (USA))
1932[3] ◆ 2148[3] 2907[4] *(4661) 5638[2]* 6166[7] *6625[3]*

Sheringarry (FR) *Mme C Dufreche* 74
5 ch h Ballingarry(IRE) —Shereda (IRE) (Indian Ridge)
903a[0]

Sherjawy (IRE) *Zoe Davison* a73 75
7 b g Diktat—Arruhan (IRE) (Mujtahid (USA))
29[5] 269[2] (298) 470[3] 554[4] 725[5] 867[4] (910) 985[6] 1309[5] 1506[3] 1638[3] 1937[5] 2193[2] 2422[4] 5640[9] 6282[8] 7512[5] 7587[6] 7649[7] 7940[8]

Sherky (FR) *Robert Collet* a59 65
2 b c Country Reel(USA) —Conciliante (FR) (Highest Honor (FR))
7312a[7]

Sherman McCoy *Rod Millman* a86 95
5 ch g Reset(AUS) —Naomi Wildman (USA) (Kingmambo (USA))
849[8] 994[6] 1729[7] 2190[4] (3428) 5448[8] 6749[8]

Shernando *Mark Johnston* a84 96
4 b g Hernando(FR) —Shimmering Sea (Slip Anchor)
1901[5] 3023[9] 3811[2] ◆ (4059) 4216[6] (4577) (5435) 5705[15] 5883[6]

She's A Character *Richard Fahey* a85 87
4 b m Invincible Spirit(IRE) —Cavernista (Lion Cavern (USA))
170[2] 772[4] (1114) 2217[6] 2634[2] 3026[2] 3763[5] 4794[9] 6078[7] 6330[13]

Shesastar *David Barron* 89
3 b f Bahamian Bounty—Celestial Welcome (Most Welcome)
1745[3] 2468[4] (3347) 4234[3] (5255) ◆ 5830[7]

She's Cool Too (IRE) *Bill Turner* a36 47
2 b f Multiplex—Mary's Way (GR) (Night Shift (USA))
1563[2] *1954[4]* 2267[3] 2425[3]

She's Flawless (USA) *Brian Meehan* a51 49
2 b f Smart Strike(CAN) —Diva (USA) (A.P. Indy (USA))
2254[7] 2709[9] *6000[9]* 6322[4] *6846[3] 7222[9]*

She's Got The Luck (IRE) *Richard Fahey* 76
3 b f Montjeu(IRE) —Fiamma (IRE) (Irish River (FR))
2257[2] 3206[3] 3681[3] 4363[5] (4878) 5925[5] 6674[4]

Shesha Bear *Jonathan Portman* a65 81
6 b m Tobougg(IRE) —Sunny Davis (USA) (Alydar (USA))
1635[4] ◆ 2055[6] 3003[7] 3516[8] (4242) (5580) ◆ (5857) 6376[2]

She Spirit Di Su (IRE) *Peter Chapple-Hyam* 78
2 b f Invincible Spirit(IRE) —She Bat (Batshoof)
5048[3] 5564[2]

She's Reel Dusty *Bill Turner* a38 5
2 ch f Reel Buddy(USA) —Dusty Dazzler (IRE) (Titus Livius (FR))
1101[5] 1786[5]

Shes Rosie *John O'Shea* a60 73
3 b f Trade Fair—Wintzig (Piccolo)
1753[2] (2375) 2553[6] 3269[3] 3630[2] 4486[9]

Shestheman *David Lanigan* 78
2 b f Manduro(GER) —Clear Vision (Observatory (USA))
6933[2] ◆

She's Untouchable *Gary Harrison* a52 46
4 b m Hawk Wing(USA) —Zambezi (USA) (Rahy (USA))
4705[6] 4953[10] 5376[15]

Shetan *M Weiss*
5 ch h Desert Prince(IRE) —Seven Notes (Zafonic (USA))
440a[7] 627a[6]

Shevington *Richard Fahey* a65 75
2 b g Choisir(AUS) —Miss Dixie (Bertolini (USA))
1209[2] ◆ 5849[18] ◆ 6380[4] *6842[4]*

Shewalksinbeauty (IRE) *Richard Hannon* a73 77
3 b f Byron—Election Special (Chief Singer)
1754[2] 2229[9] *3044[4]* 4056[11]

Shewan (AUS) *Robert Smerdon* 109
5 bb g Blevic(AUS) —Aberdeen Rose (NZ) (Clay Hero (AUS))
(6711a) 7043a[5]

She Wolf *Michael Bell* 24
3 ch f Medicean—Coyote (Indian Ridge)
1568[15] *4989[8]*

Shieldmaiden (USA) *Mark Johnston* a83 71
3 ch f Smart Strike(CAN) —Code Book (USA) (Giant's Causeway (USA))
2639[3] *3043[5] 7250[2] 7440[2] 7486[11] (7712) 7806[3]*

Shifting Gold (IRE) *Kevin Ryan* a73 67
5 b g Night Shift(USA) —Gold Bust (Nashwan (USA))
(3) 671[3] 1817[2] 2952[2] 3316[8] *(3951)* 4941[5] *7914[5]*

Shifting Star (IRE) *John Bridger* a91 98
6 ch g Night Shift(USA) —Ahshado (Bin Ajwaad (IRE))
1197[2] 1395[5] 1854[11] 2876[5] 3784[6] 4369[6] 4967[6] 5781[3] *(6282)* (6761) ◆ 6974[7] *7456[10] 7586[6] 7841[6]* 7941[2] ◆

Shihab (IRE) *Saeed Bin Suroor* a71
2 b c Dubawi(IRE) —Baya (USA) (Nureyev (USA))
(7369)

Shikra *Eugene Stanford* a11
3 b f Tiger Hill(IRE) —Snow Goose (Polar Falcon (USA))
751[7] 4963[6] *5317[13]*

Shimmei Fuji (JPN) *Takayuki Yasuda* a99 104
4 b m Fuji Kiseki(JPN) —Lady Muse (JPN) (Timber Country (USA))
7410a[7]

Shimmering Moment (USA) *James J Hartnett* a105 105
4 ch m Afleet Alex(USA) —Vassar (USA) (Royal Academy (USA))
242[14] 417a[2] 581a[7]

Shimmering Surf (IRE) *Peter Winkworth* a76 106
4 b m Danehill Dancer(IRE) —Sun On The Sea (IRE) (Bering)
2501[7] 3647[7] 4582[5] 5493[5]

Shimraan (FR) *A De Royer-Dupre* 119
4 b g Rainbow Quest(USA) —Shemriyna (IRE) (King Of Kings (IRE))
4095[4] 5094a[6] 6558a[3]

Shim Sham (IRE) *Brian Meehan* 84
3 ch f Danehill Dancer(IRE) —Pirie (USA) (Green Dancer (USA))
1317[11] 2102[16]

Shining Glory (GER) *W Hickst* 92
4 b m Konigstiger(GER) —Shoah (GER) (Acatenango (GER))
5980a[4]

Shining Grace *Bryn Palling* a6 36
2 gr f Proclamation(IRE) —Shining Oasis (IRE) (Mujtahid (USA))
4462[8] 6890[7] *7368[9]*

Ship's Biscuit *Sir Michael Stoute* a71 106
4 b m Tiger Hill(IRE) —Threefold (USA) (Gulch (USA))
2098[4] 3647[4] 4470[10]

Shirataki (IRE) *Peter Hiatt* a57 42
3 b g Cape Cross(IRE) —Noodle Soup (USA) (Alphabet Soup (USA))
2392[12] 2621[9] 3018[8] *7527[8] (7640) (7836) 7931[2]*

Shirley Blake (IRE) *Paul Cashman* a77 95
4 b m Acclamation—Longa (Blakeney)
7189a[7]

Shirls Son Sam *Chris Fairhurst* 58
3 b g Rambling Bear—Shirl (Shirley Heights)
3575[8] 4363[8] 5007[5] 5372[6] 5651[3] 6153[3] 6870[5]

Shirocco Junior *F Rohaut* a73 82
3 b c Shirocco(GER) —Ma Paloma (FR) (Highest Honor (FR))
370a[7]

Shirocco Star *Hughie Morrison* 76
2 b f Shirocco(GER) —Spectral Star (Unfuwain (USA))
6458[2] ◆ (7030) ◆

Shirocco Vice (IRE) *Richard Fahey* a36 40
3 b f Shirocco(GER) —Viscaria (IRE) (Barathea (IRE))
47[6]

Shivsingh *Mick Channon* 67
2 b g Montjeu(IRE) —Vistaria (USA) (Distant View (USA))
5044[7] 5579[5] 5937[3] 6399[9]

Shkspeare Shaliyah (USA) *Doodnauth Shivmangal* 99
2 b c Shakespeare(USA) —Tricky Mistress (USA) (Clever Trick (USA))
7301a[9]

Sholaan (IRE) *William Haggas* a71 87
2 b c Invincible Spirit(IRE) —Jazz Up (Cadeaux Genereux)
5384[2] ◆ 5875[4] 6448[2]

Shomberg *Mark H Tompkins* 62
2 b g Bahamian Bounty—Qilin (IRE) (Second Set (IRE))
3483[2] 6244[6] 7080[10]

Shooting Gallery *Mahmood Al Zarooni* 86
3 b c Shamardal(USA) —Sallanches (USA) (Gone West (USA))
2471[6]

Shooting Line (IRE) *Walter Swinburn* a86 88
3 b c Motivator—Juno Marlowe (IRE) (Danehill (USA))
(3232) ◆ *5635[5]* 6063[8] 6755[4]

Shootoff (NZ) *Graeme Rogerson* 117
4 b g Duelled(AUS) —Athenri (NZ) (Zabeel (NZ))
6886a[9] 7310a[2]

Shoot The Pot (IRE) *John Mackie* a63 61
4 b g Intikhab(USA) —Kerasana (IRE) (Kahyasi)
944[11] 5178[15]

Shopping Oasis *Mark Johnston* 64
3 b g Oasis Dream—Shopping For Love (USA) (Not For Love (USA))
1693[13] 3543[9] 6459[5]

Shopton Lane (USA) *Doug Watson* a79
7 b g Quiet American(USA) —Lightfoot Lane (USA) (Phone Trick (USA))
707a[7]

Short Supply (USA) *Tim Walford* a63 61
5 b m Point Given(USA) —Introducing (USA) (Deputy Minister (CAN))
(39) 492[4] 1466[4] 4856[3] 5369[3] 5790[12] 6870[10] *7340[5]*

Short Takes (USA) *John Gosden* a55 66
3 ch g Lemon Drop Kid(USA) —Gabriellina Giof (Ashkalani (IRE))
1203[12] 1445[7] *1997[5]*

Shoshoni (GER) *A Kleinkorres* 72
4 rg h Noroit(GER) —Sweet Dreams (GER) (Sternkoenig (IRE))
7409a[11]

Shoshoni Wind *Kevin Ryan* 98
3 b f Sleeping Indian—Cadeau Speciale (Cadeaux Genereux)
(1711) 2032[5] 2298[13] (3807) 4776[4] 5827[11]

Shostakovich (IRE) *Sylvester Kirk* a80 73
3 b g Fasliyev(USA) —Hi Katriona (IRE) (Second Empire (IRE))
4[2] 106[3] 1359[2] (1830) 2147[5] 2757[5] 3122[8] *(3238)* 4057[5] 4238[5] 5561[8] 5890[8] *6177[9] 6505[6]* 6793[2] (6930) ◆

Shot In The Dark (IRE) *Andrew Balding* a58 67
2 ch g Dr Fong(USA) —Highland Shot (Selkirk (USA))
5564[11] 5841[2] *7422[4]*

Shotley Mac *Neville Bycroft* 85
7 ch g Abou Zouz(USA) —Julie's Gift (Presidium)
5594[12] (6231) 6452[10] 6868[7]

Shotley Music *Neville Bycroft* 64
2 b g Amadeus Wolf—Silca Key (Inchinor)
4323[3] 5254[15]

Shouda (IRE) *Barney Curley* a68 58
5 b g Tiger Hill(IRE) —Sommernacht (GER) (Monsun (GER))
145[4] 1218[3] (2600) ◆ *(6287)*

Shoulder Arms *John Weymes*
3 ch g Compton Place—Petite Epaulette (Night Shift (USA))
4286[10] 4813[10]

Shout For Joy (IRE) *Richard Hannon* a38 65
2 b f Acclamation—Joyful Tears (IRE) (Barathea (IRE))
1785[5] 4319[2] 4954[3] 5613[4] *7452[10] 7635[7]*

Showboating (IRE) *Alan McCabe* a83 79
3 b g Shamardal(USA) —Sadinga (IRE) (Sadler's Wells (USA))
4511[2] 4680[9] (4819) *5419[2] 5717[6] 6177[3] 6491[3]* 6801[7] 7024[4] *7439[8] 7519[6] 7941[5]*

Showcause (AUS) *Frank Ritchie* 104
6 ch g Giant's Causeway(USA) —Showella (NZ) (Lord Ballina (AUS))
6967a[4]

Show Flower *Mick Channon* a70 76
2 b f Shamardal(USA) —Baldemosa (FR) (Lead On Time (USA))
2709[2] 4252[6] 4614[3] 4883[2] 5445[7] *5689[3]*

Showmepower (IRE) *John Dunlop* 46
2 ch g Choisir(AUS) —Spanish Rainbow (IRE) (Rainbow Quest (USA))
3917[9] 4339[12] 4912[7]

Show Of Faith (IRE) *Ed McMahon* 33
2 b f Acclamation—Khalkissa (USA) (Diesis)
4106[8] 5590[9]

Show Rainbow *Mick Channon* a74 96
3 b f Haafhd—Rainbow Sky (Rainbow Quest (USA))
1319[4] ◆ 1719[14] 2298[3] (2500) 3827[9]

Showsinger *Richard Fahey* a21
2 b f Singspiel(IRE) —Very Agreeable (Pursuit Of Love)
7855[6]

Shranaski (FR) *A Sagot* a61
6 b g Ski Chief(USA) —Shrana (FR) (Saint Cyrien (FR))
93a[8]

Shrapnel (AUS) *Mark Kavanagh* 117
4 br c Charge Forward(AUS) —Fragmentation (AUS) (Snippets (AUS))
(9029a)

Shredding (IRE) *Edward Vaughan* a37 53
2 b g Tiger Hill(IRE) —In The Ribbons (In The Wings)
6244[5] ◆ 6956[11] *7454[12] 7708[2]*

Shropshire (IRE) *Charles Hills* 97
3 gr g Shamardal(USA) —Shawanni (Shareef Dancer (USA))
1405[3] 2003[6] 4472[10] 5180[17] 5852[4] ◆

Shubaat *Roger Varian* a87 88
4 ch g Monsun(GER) —Zaynaat (Unfuwain (USA))
6130[3] ◆

Shuhra (IRE) *William Haggas* a75 75
3 b f Marju(IRE) —Wijdan (USA) (Mr Prospector (USA))
3043[3] 4072[3] *5098[5]* 5877[3] 6459[3] 7111[2]

Shuja (USA) *Saeed Bin Suroor* 76
2 b c Street Sense(USA) —Seba (Alzao (USA))
6983[2]

Shukal (ITY) *S Botti*
2 b c Big Shuffle(USA) —Kalabash (IRE) (Caerleon (USA))
7217a[6]

Shumoos (USA) *Brian Meehan* a106 106
2 ch f Distorted Humor(USA) —Wile Cat (USA) (Storm Cat (USA))
(2504) ◆ 3033[2] 3821[3] 5217[10] *(5715)* 6337[8] *7280a[2]*

Shumy Forever (ITY) *G Marras*
3 ch c Lomitas—Sarazade (Saumarez)
1126a[4]

Shunkawakhan (IRE) *Linda Perratt* a44 58
8 b g Indian Danehill(IRE) —Special Park (USA) (Trempolino (USA))
1077[12] 1803[4] (2415) 2692[2] 3128[3] 3454[3] 3657[8] 3903[3] 4143[8] 4783[7] 5153[10] 5725[5] 6428[8] *6698[8] 7006[4] 7399[8]*

Shutterbug *Stuart Williams* a59 48
3 ch f Dubai Destination(USA) —Nikolenka (IRE) (Indian Ridge)
64[3] 189[3] (383)

Shutupandrive *Mark Usher* a46 42
3 b f Forest Wildcat(USA) —Sharp Contrast (USA) (Diesis)
146[7] 338[9] 620[5]

Shy *Rod Millman* a45 73
6 ch m Erhaab(USA) —Shi Shi (Alnasr Alwasheek)
1291[6] 1631[4] 2552[3] 2991[8] 4273[7] (4952) 5236[5] 6023[8] 6438[2]

Shy Glance (USA) *Iain Jardine* a76 69
9 b g Red Ransom(USA) —Royal Shyness (Royal Academy (USA))
4605[7] 5208[10]

Siberian Belle (IRE) *Richard Fahey* a42 50
2 b f Red Clubs(IRE) —Miss Sharapova (IRE) (Almutawakel)
3736[9] 4192[5] 5681[7] 6424[6] 7051[7]

Sichuan Success (AUS) *J Size* 117
5 b g Fastnet Rock(AUS) —Coureuse (AUS) (Tierce (AUS))
7731a[5]

Sicyos De Juilley (FR) *J-L Guillochon* a69
10 ch g Sicyos(USA) —La Salviata (FR) (Houston (FR))
1013a[2]

Sid *Zoe Davison* a21
3 ch g Needwood Blade—Easter Moon (FR) (Easter Sun)
7525[6] 7750[7] 7829[8]

Side Glance *Andrew Balding* 119
4 br g Passing Glance—Averami (Averti (IRE))
1397[3] (1600) (1948) 3843[3] (4972) 6204a[4] 6860[7]

Sidney Girl *R Gibson* a84 83
4 b m Azamour(IRE) —Littleton Arwen (USA) (Bahri (USA))
840a[0]

Sidney's Candy (USA) *Todd Pletcher* a123 123
4 ch h Candy Ride(ARG) —Fair Exchange (USA) (Storm Cat (USA))
6721a[3] 7307a[6]

Sienna Blue *Malcolm Saunders* a68 58
3 ch f Doyen(IRE) —Lady Butler (IRE) (Puissance)
1053[7] 1277[3] 1474[10] (1953) 2550[9] 2963[3] 3803[3] 5674[3] *6490[6]*

Siete Vidas (IRE) *M Delzangles* a93 98
3 gr f Dalakhani(IRE) —Too Marvelous (FR) (Dansili)
4570a[10]

Sight Winner (NZ) *J Size* 117
8 b g Faltaat(USA) —Kinjinette (NZ) (Kinjite (NZ))
1576a[7]

Signifer (IRE) *Mick Channon* 87
2 br c Titus Livius(FR) —Extravagance (IRE) (King's Best (USA))
1360[2] (1785) 2154[3] 2322a[7] 3064[5] 3375[2] 4094[15] 4536[7] 4787[4] (5237) 5348[4] 5592[3] 5922[3] 6114[7] 6518[8] 6827[8] 7261[7]

Significant Move *Stuart Kittow* a65 87
4 b g Motivator—Strike Lightly (Rainbow Quest (USA))
1402[9] 2066[4] 2649[6] 3434[3] ◆ (5568) 5971[5] 6249[10]

Signora Frasi (IRE) *Tony Newcombe* a67 65
6 b m Indian Ridge—Sheba (IRE) (Lycius (USA))
489[P] 810[2] 1448[3] *3280[4] 3926[4]* 4656[7] *5318[10]* 5912[3] 6938[3] *(7522) 7671[7]*

Signorella *M Delzangles* 90
3 b f Pivotal—Signorina Cattiva (USA) (El Gran Senor (USA))
7313a[9]

Signore Momento (IRE) *Amy Weaver* 85
5 b g Captain Rio—Gitchee Gumee Rose (IRE) (Paris House)
5760[15] 6467[13] 6778[14] 7299[12]

Signorotto (FR) *J Rossi* a76
3 b c Enrique—Signorinella (FR) (Kendor (FR))
777a[5] 980a[7]

Signor Sassi *Roger Varian* 78
2 b c Acclamation—Fairy Contessa (IRE) (Fairy King (USA))
4276[2] 5111[2] 5786[2]

Signor Verdi *Brian Meehan* a75 94
4 b g Green Tune(USA) —Calling Card (Bering)
1406[12] 2105[13] 2647[10] 2955[6] 4962[7] 6465[7] *6785[4]*

Signs In The Sand *Saeed Bin Suroor* a97 90
3 b c Cape Cross(IRE) —Gonfilia (GER) (Big Shuffle (USA))
238[8]

Sigurwana (USA) *William Haggas* a67
2 bb f Arch(USA) —Nyarhini (Fantastic Light (USA))
7344[9] 7757[4]

Sikeeb (IRE) *Clive Brittain* 105
3 b g Alhaarth(IRE) —Erstwhile (FR) (Desert Prince (IRE))
(1361) 1690[2] 2296[10] 3029[6]

Silaah *David Nicholls* a106 97
7 b g Mind Games—Ocean Grove (IRE) (Fairy King (USA))
(2) (46) 582a[2] 678a[6] 755a[10] 989[2] 1476[9] 1720[7] ◆ 2117[2] 3357[12] 4346[17] 4573[6] 5180[7] *7392[10]*

Silas Marner (FR) *J-C Rouget* a60 102
4 b h Muhtathir—Street Kendra (FR) (Kendor (FR))
830a[8]

Silca Conegliano (IRE) *Mick Channon* a67 71
3 b f Alhaarth(IRE) —Sarah Stokes (IRE) (Brief Truce (USA))
1753[9] 2141[5] *2384[6]* 2549[6] 3272[6] 3724[14] 3998[4] (4657) 5138[4] *5388[5]*

Silca Meydan *Richard Price* a56 44
5 b g Diktat—Golden Silca (Inchinor)
340[8] 451[11] 675[12] 752[7]

Silence Is Easy *William Muir* a61 55
2 b f Cape Cross(IRE) —African Queen (IRE) (Cadeaux Genereux)
7025[7] *7344[7]*

Silenceofthewind (USA) *Mrs K Burke* a85 87
4 b g Eddington(USA) —Betty's Solutions (USA) (Eltish (USA))
4561[16] 5455[2] *5687[3]* 6148[6]

Silent Ambition *Mark Brisbourne* 22
2 b f Striking Ambition—Hi Rock (Hard Fought)
6322[6]

Silent Applause *Dr Jon Scargill* a63 73
8 b g Royal Applause—Billie Blue (Ballad Rock)
2312[10] 3479[7] 4024[10] 5015[6] 6968[4]

Silent Energy (IRE) *Ronald Harris* a60 54
2 b c Le Vie Dei Colori—Ghada (USA) (Belong To Me (USA))
7258[7] *7367[4] 7650[8] 7849[5]*

Silent Fright (USA) *Paul Cole* 59
3 b f Yes It's True(USA) —Val Marie (USA) (Coronado's Quest (USA))
1629[4]

Silent Fury (IRE) *Rae Guest* a13
3 ch f Kheleyf(USA) —Fifth Edition (Rock Hopper)
434[7]

Silent Land *Noel Quinlan*
3 b f Cape Cross(IRE) —Cheerleader (Singspiel (IRE))
1126a[6]

Silent Laughter *Jonathan Portman* 45
2 b f Shamardal(USA) —Tease (IRE) (Green Desert (USA))
4614[12] 6991[10]

Silent Lucidity (IRE) *Peter Niven* a59 61
7 ch g Ashkalani(IRE) —Mimansa (USA) (El Gran Senor (USA))
8[5] 118[4] 324[4] 373[5] 2666[4] 2952[15] 3450[11] 4326[3] 4856[14] 5790[11]

Silent Mistress *J R Jenkins* a28 36
2 b f Fraam—Once Removed (Distant Relative)
5812[10] *6820[10]*

Silent Moment (USA) *Saeed Bin Suroor* 65
2 ch f Giant's Causeway(USA) —Mari's Sheba (USA) (Mari's Book (USA))
6953[5]

Silent Ninja *Hughie Morrison* a66 54
3 b f Montjeu(IRE) —Farfala (FR) (Linamix (FR))
4208[6] 5001[5] *6054[9] 6799[12]*

Silent Oasis *Brendan Powell* a72 74
5 b m Oasis Dream—Silence Is Golden (Danehill Dancer (IRE))
814[4] (1058) 1530[6] 2232[11] 2915[6] 4707[5] 5428[5] 5808[3] 6894[8]

Silent Wisper (CAN) *Michael Keogh* a47 70
4 ch m Wando(CAN) —Silent Course (CAN) (Trajectory (USA))
3208a[6]

Silenzio *Richard Hannon* a84 83
3 b c Cadeaux Genereux—All Quiet (Piccolo)
1843[8] 2841[6] 3798[6] 4243[2] 4618[6] (6022) (6246) *7456[4] 7586[2] 7675[9]*

Silk Bounty *James Given* a62 70
3 b g Bahamian Bounty—Sahara Silk (IRE) (Desert Style (IRE))
183[5]

Silkee Supreme *Richard Hannon* 70
2 b c Primo Valentino(IRE) —Sodelk (Interrex (CAN))
4229[2]

Silken Aunt *Kevin McAuliffe* a56 30
4 b m Barathea(IRE) —Aunt Susan (Distant Relative)
939[6]

Silken Satinwood (IRE) *Ann Duffield* 21
2 b f Refuse To Bend(IRE) —Reine De Neige (Kris)
6866[9]

Silken Thoughts *John Berry* a46 82
3 b f Tobougg(IRE) —The Jotter (Night Shift (USA))
1624[5] 2550[7] 3390[4] 3988[3] (4584) 5049[2] (5407)

Silke Top *William Jarvis* a68 73
2 b f Librettist(USA) —Zaza Top (GER) (Lomitas)
3865[9] 4614[4] 5514[2] *6131[2]*

Silk Hall (UAE) *J J Lambe* a87 86
6 b g Halling(USA) —Velour (Mtoto)
(3420a) 4398a[17]

Silk Lingerie *Mandy Rowland* a61
3 ch f Dr Fong(USA) —Personal Love (USA) (Diesis)
737[2] 945[6] 3236[8] 6181[12] 6845[10]

Silky Bleu *Terry Clement* a49
2 b f Elnadim(USA) —Tattling (Warning)
7583[8]

Silky Lady (IRE) *Jonathan Geake* 61
4 b m Barathea(IRE) —Promising Lady (Thunder Gulch (USA))
2377[12] *2820[12]*

Silly Billy (IRE) *Sylvester Kirk* a76 65
3 b g Noverre(USA) —Rock Dove (IRE) (Danehill (USA))
423[4] (601) 750[5] 845[3] (886) 1335[7] 2024[4] 3259[12] 3537[7] *3983[7] 4799[5]* 5419[10] 5901[5] 6746[7] 7176[6] 7463[9] 7754[10]

Silly Dancer (IRE) *Adrian McGuinness* a56 70
8 b m King Charlemagne(USA) —Silly Imp (IRE) (Imperial Frontier (USA))
7006[10] 7033[7]

Silly Gilly (IRE) *Ron Barr* a40 69
7 b m Mull Of Kintyre(USA) —Richly Deserved (IRE) (Kings Lake (USA))
1911[2] 2348[2] 3025[8] 3202[2] 3806[10] 4127[6] 4409[2] 4604[3] 4946[8] (5402) 5733[5] 6453[8]

Silvaner (GER) *P Schiergen* 103
3 bb c Lomitas—Suisun (GER) (Monsun (GER))
1433a[4] 2345a[3] 3672a[9] 5092a[3] 5773a[5] (6710a)

Silvanus (IRE) *Paul Midgley* a81 71
6 b g Danehill Dancer(IRE) —Mala Mala (IRE) (Brief Truce (USA))
1034[9] (1544) 2182[5] 2491[8] 2766[3] 3573[7] 4371[7] 4678[5] 5373[2] 6276[2] 6537[10]

Silvas Romana (IRE) *Mark Brisbourne* a55 73
2 b f Holy Roman Emperor(IRE) —Triple Wood (USA) (Woodman (USA))
1957[6] 2283[3] *2651[2]* 3336[6] (3810) 4572[5] (4704) 5197[7] 5562[6] 5840[5] 6293[2] 6645[5] 7294[8]

Silvee *John Bridger* a62 62
4 gr m Avonbridge—Silver Louie (IRE) (Titus Livius (FR))
34[4] 3293[4] 3685[6] 3869[5] 4010[8] 4458[6] (4795) 4973[8] 5037[5] 5513[7] *6257[4] 6444[3] 6626[2] 7485[13]* 7811[5] 7895[7]

Silver Alliance *Walter Swinburn* a78 72
3 gr g Proclamation(IRE) —Aimee Vibert (Zilzal (USA))
2199[10] 2818[7] 3674[7] 4866[5] 5179[5] 5992[3] *(6311)* 6773[9] *6978[7]*

Silver Arrow (ITY) *Maria Rita Salvioni* 109
6 b g Silver Wizard(USA) —Eros Love (ITY) (Love The Groom (USA))
2982a[8] 7323a[10]

Silver Blaze *Alan Swinbank* 75
2 ch g Haafhd—Antigua (Selkirk (USA))
5548[7] 6260[2] 6774[3]

Silver Blossom (IRE) *Andrew Balding* a74 58
3 b f Galileo(IRE) —Lovely Blossom (FR) (Spinning World (USA))
6804[8] *7179[3] 7630[5]*

Silver Bullitt *Mark Johnston* a71 81
3 gr g Proclamation(IRE) —Eurolinka (IRE) (Tirol)
2371[12] (2848) 4914[10] *7759[9]*

Silverglas (IRE) *William Knight* a80 74
5 gr g Verglas(IRE) —Yellow Trumpet (Petong)
1772[9] 2436[4] *3042[6]* 3762[5] 4724[9] *5318[11]*

Silver Green (FR) *F Rohaut* a88
4 gr g Slickly(FR) —Love Green (FR) (Green Tune (USA))
840a[4]

Silver Grey (IRE) *Roger Ingram* a82 109
4 gr m Chineur(FR) —Operissimo (Singspiel (IRE))
702[10] 991[9] 1201[4] 3356[11] 3844[10] 4253[5] (4724) 4915[10] 6375[3] 6922[11] 7296[14]

Silver Guest *Ralph Smith* a84 73
6 br g Lujain(USA) —Ajig Dancer (Niniski (USA))
(78) 334[3] 472[9]

Silverheels (IRE) *Paul Cole* 102
2 gr c Verglas(IRE) —Vasilia (Dansili)
(1136) ◆ 3064[8] 3540[2] 3861[3] 4495[4] 5276[2] 6535[3] 7220a[10]

Silver Lace (IRE) *Chris Wall* 38
2 bg f Clodovil(IRE) —Rockahoolababy (IRE) (Kalanisi (IRE))
7292[12]

Silver Lime (USA) *Roger Charlton* 80
2 b c Mizzen Mast(USA) —Red Dot (USA) (Diesis)
4446[5] ◆ (5959)

Silver Linnet (IRE) *Noel Quinlan* a67 72
4 gr m Acclamation—Nadeema (FR) (Linamix (FR))
80[7] 165[3] 224[6] 362[8] 857[7]

Silver Marizah (IRE) *Gary Moore* a72 53
2 b f Manduro(GER) —Maharani (USA) (Red Ransom (USA))
5813[4] 6169[9] *6795[8] 7757[6]*

Silvermine Bay (IRE) *Pat Eddery* a40 41
4 gr m Act One—Quittance (USA) (Riverman (USA))
3799[5]

Silver Mountain (FR) *J-C Rouget* 81
5 gr g Linamix(FR) —Peace Talk (FR) (Sadler's Wells (USA))
219a[0]

Silver Native (IRE) *Mike Murphy* a18
2 b g Elusive City(USA) —Love Of Silver (USA) (Arctic Tern (USA))
4384[11] 7094[11] 7369[13] 7915[10]

Silver Northern (FR) *D Chenu* 93
2 b c Voix Du Nord(FR) —Silver Diane (FR) (Silver Rainbow)
5365a[8]

Silver Ocean (USA) *Riccardo Santini* a103 105
3 bb g Silver Train(USA) —Endless Sea (CAN) (Mt. Livermore (USA))
532a[2] 2541a[6] 6201a[2] 6369a[6]

Silver Point (FR) *Bryn Palling* a98 90
8 bb g Commands(AUS) —Silver Fame (USA) (Quest For Fame)
2884[14]

Silver Pond (FR) *F Head* 121
4 gr h Act One—Silver Fame (USA) (Quest For Fame)
920a[3] ◆ 1266a[4] 1708a[6] (2753a) 3448a[3] 5531a[2] 6567a[8] 7729a[3] ◆

Silver Rime (FR) *Linda Perratt* 94
6 gr g Verglas(IRE) —Severina (Darshaan)
1541[6] 2061[3] 2434[7] ◆ 3315[9] 4325[4] 5053[4] 5684[10] 6078[3] 6148[7] 7161[8]

Silver Samba *Andrew Balding* 57
2 gr f Dalakhani(IRE) —Fancy Dance (Rainbow Quest (USA))
5444[10] 6588[7]

Silver Shine (IRE) *Bent Olsen* a39 48
3 gr g Verglas(IRE) —Dream Time (Rainbow Quest (USA))
4840a[4]

Silver Show (IRE) *Mick Channon* a66 64
3 b f Noverre(USA) —Incense (Unfuwain (USA))
1958[2] 2196[6] 2418[2] 2853[4]

Silverside (USA) *F Sanchez* a106 111
5 b h Pleasantly Perfect(USA) —Lyrical Ghost (USA) (Silver Ghost (USA))
416a[9] 586a[6] 828a[10] 1125a[3] 1740a[8] 4483a[3] (5528a) 6858[16]

Silver Six *Mick Channon* a40 49
2 gr g Aussie Rules(USA) —Bahara (Barathea (IRE))
5410[7] 5672[8] 6018[7] 7108[11]

Silvers Spirit *Keith Reveley* 42
5 b m Makbul—Shadows Of Silver (Carwhite)
1210[7] 1492[6] 1799[5] 3187[RR]

Silver's Wish (FR) *T Larriviere* a61 59
8 bl g Lyphard's Wish(FR) —Poussilver (FR) (Kaid Pous (FR))
533a[3]

Silver Tiger *Chris Wall* 39
3 gb c Tiger Hill(IRE) —Moon Empress (FR) (Rainbow Quest (USA))
1096[11] 2394[6] 5352[15]

Silver Tigress *George Moore* 61
3 gr f Tiger Hill(IRE) —Cinnamon Tree (IRE) (Barathea (IRE))
1858[2] 2635[4] 3301[2] 3487[3] 4175[2] (5152) 5372[5] 6082[5] 7062[10]

Silver Timber (USA) *Chad C Brown* 119
8 gr g Prime Timber(USA) —River Princess (CAN) (Alwuhush (USA))
9100a[6]

Silver Turn *Jeremy Gask* a76 73
3 ch f Shamardal(USA) —Mambo Mistress (USA) (Kingmambo (USA))
(36) 254[5] 1214[9] 3731[4] 4618[2] 6929[10] 7332[3] 7629[10]

Silver Valny (FR) *Mlle M-L Mortier* a90 113
5 ch g Vertical Speed(FR) —Mendoreva (FR) (Mendocino (USA))
219a[2] 705a[9] 5990a[4] 6562a[5] 7049a[9] 7406a[2] 7733a[9]

Silverware (USA) *Richard Hannon* a76 83
3 bb g Eurosilver(USA) —Playing Footsie (USA) (Valiant Nature (USA))
1139[5] 1446[8] (1626) 2646[3] 4214[5] (5171) 5581[4] 6167[5] 6727[12]

Silver Wind *Alan McCabe* a72 84
6 b g Ishiguru(USA) —My Bonus (Cyrano De Bergerac)
58[7] 321[4] 445[3] 467[3] 683[7] 763[6] 893[2] 1267[3] 1523[5] (1562) 1656[6] 1917[3] (2095) 2369[10] 2557[10] 3000[9] 3322[4] 3796[10] 4349[16] 4618[4] 5012[7] 5345[2] 6022[5] 6174[5] (6694) 6841[6] (7462) 7591[2] 7715[4] 7819[2] 7895[4]

Silvery Moon (IRE) *Tim Easterby* 90
4 gr g Verglas(IRE) —Starry Night (Sheikh Albadou)
1746[5] 4004[10] (4811) ◆ 5557[8] (6078) ◆

Simayill *Clive Brittain* a85 83
3 b f Oasis Dream—Triennial (IRE) (Giant's Causeway (USA))
7171[5] (7361) 7841[4]

Simba (FR) *C Lerner* 103
3 gr c Anabaa Blue—Saiga (FR) (Baryshnikov (AUS))
6783a[10] 7313a[2]

Simbad (FR) *Hanne Bechmann* 69
7 b g Danehill(USA) —Napoli (Baillamont (USA))
7256a[3]

Simenon (IRE) *Andrew Balding* 103
4 b g Marju(IRE) —Epistoliere (IRE) (Alzao (USA))
1679[3] 2316[5] 3396[14]

Simla Sunset (IRE) *P J Prendergast* a87 98
5 b m One Cool Cat(USA) —Simla Bibi (Indian Ridge)
5746a[17] 6388a[6] 6733a[13]

Simmard (USA) *Roger L Attfield* a93 110
6 ch h Dixieland Band(USA) —Dibs (USA) (Spectacular Bid (USA))
6203a[2] 6910a[13]

Simon De Montfort (IRE) *Mahmood Al Zarooni* a97 112
4 b h King's Best(USA) —Noble Rose (IRE) (Caerleon (USA))
(242) 757a[10] 4789[U] 5494[3] 5711[7]

Simone Martini (IRE) *Milton Harris* a59 69
6 b g Montjeu(IRE) —Bona Dea (IRE) (Danehill (USA))
1466[8]

Simonside *Brian Ellison* a70 81
8 b g Shahrastani(USA) —Only So Far (Teenoso (USA))
1817[6] 2034[15] 2459[6] (3115) 3593[5] 4348[4] 4879[6] 5724[9] 6095[6]

Simple Jim (FR) *David O'Meara* a65 70
7 b g Jimble(FR) —Stop The Wedding (USA) (Stop The Music (USA))
1107[16] 1491[8] 2575[3] 3574[8] ◆ 4366[3] ◆ 4562[4] 4856[2] 5079[2] 5595[5] 5790[4] 6157[8] 6356[4] 6838[7] 7107[4] 7645[6]

Simple Mind (GER) *Y Fertillet* 54
6 gr g Protektor(GER) —Silver Magic (GER) (Indian Forest (USA))
221a[0] 706a[0] 832a[0]

Simple Rhythm *John Ryan* a65 70
5 b m Piccolo—Easy Beat (IRE) (Orpen (USA))
589[8] 664[3] 734[5] 874[5] 941[4] 1182[7] 1267[7] 2016[5] 2193[4] 2426[4] 2547[6] 2879[6] 3714[7] 4000[6] (4547) 4600[3] 4828[5] 5426[3] 5517[2] 6105[8] 7086[12] 7691[8] 7728[13]

Simply *Eve Johnson Houghton* 48
2 b f Nayef(USA) —Polish Lake (Polish Precedent (USA))
7025[12]

Simpson Millar *Noel Wilson* 46
2 b g Librettist(USA) —Scented Garden (Zamindar (USA))
3050[8] 4358[6] 5058[11] 6912[9]

Simpulse *Norma Twomey* a8 47
3 b f Noverre(USA) —Miss Kitty (Monsieur Cat (USA))
3548[6] 3909[5] 4486[6] 4828[12] 6747[10]

Sim Sala Bim *Stuart Williams* a63 80
3 rg c Act One—Francia (Legend Of France (USA))
713[2] (3002) 3340[3]

Sina (GER) *H-A Pantall* a68 92
6 b m Trans Island—Soiree De Vienne (IRE) (Marju (IRE))
42a[0] 220a[9] 372a[10]

Sinadinou *David Nicholls* a43 73
3 b g Dubai Destination(USA) —Beverley Bell (Bertolini (USA))
855[4] 1038[4] 1246[5] (2249) 2588[7]

Sinai (IRE) *Geoffrey Harker* 71
2 b f Moss Vale(IRE) —Ten Commandments (IRE) (Key Of Luck (USA))
2936[7] (3505) (5431) 6186[5] 6645[6]

Sinatramania *Tracy Waggott* 63
4 b g Dansili—Come Fly With Me (Bluebird (USA))
2057[4] (2548) 2988[5] 3319[3] 4128[6] 4440[9] 5403[4] 5488[6] 5823[8] 6264[2] 6536[2]

Sinbad The Sailor *George Baker* a79 60
6 b g Cape Cross(IRE) —Sinead (USA) (Irish River (FR))
4844[3]

Sincero (AUS) *Stephen Farley* 119
4 b g Umatilla(NZ) —Yours As Always (AUS) (Prego (IRE))
6713a[5] 7044a[9]

Sinchiroka (FR) *Ralph Smith* a54 49
5 b g Della Francesca(USA) —Great Care (USA) (El Gran Senor (USA))
4991[4] 5639[7]

Sindaco (GER) *W Hickst* 101
3 b c Sakhee(USA) —Sly (GER) (Monsun (GER))
3007a[6] 7409a[8]

Sinfonico (IRE) *Richard Hannon* a91 94
3 b g Iffraaj—Zinstar (IRE) (Sinndar (IRE))
1754[4] (2200) 2607[2] (2926) 4472[12] 5712[10] 6335[7] 7393[7]

Sing Alana Sing *Bill Turner* a44 40
3 b f Singspiel(IRE) —Choralist (Danehill (USA))
953[5] 1056[6] 1132[6] 1769[9] 2307[4] 2652[4] 3596[4]

Singalat *James Given* a77 77
2 b g Singspiel(IRE) —Crocolat (Croco Rouge (IRE))
2023[5] 2355[3] 3152[11] (4436) 5039[3] 6102[7] 7483[4] 7576[5] 7752[2]

Singapore Fairy (FR) *Robert Collet* a71 75
4 b m Sagacity(FR) —Madame Est Sortie (FR) (Longleat (USA))
267a[4]

Singapore Sling (FR) *A Bonin* 68
2 ch g Muhtathir—Spinning Secretary (USA) (Spinning World (USA))
7238a[3]

Singeur (IRE) *Robin Bastiman* a97 102
4 b g Chineur(FR) —Singitta (Singspiel (IRE))
(2117) (2489) 3073[2] 3395[5] 3841[11] 4346[15] 5758[13] 6347[2] 6706[9] 6865[3] 7018[8]

Single Girl (IRE) *Jonathan Portman* 53
2 ch f Singspiel(IRE) —Bumble (Rainbow Quest (USA))
2187[6] 2788[10] 4698[3] 5343[10]

Single Lady *Emmet Michael Butterly* a58 45
4 b m Beat Hollow—Breathing Space (USA) (Expelled (USA))
(5643) 5739[4]

Singmeasong *J W Hills* 32
2 ch f Singspiel(IRE) —Largo (IRE) (Selkirk (USA))
4804[12] 5672[7]

Singn On Themoon (USA) *Gary Contessa*
2 ch f Malibu Moon(USA) —Listen To My Song (USA) (Unbridled's Song (USA))
(6205a)

Sing Softly (USA) *A P O'Brien* a59 103
3 ch f Hennessy(USA) —Misty Hour (USA) (Miswaki (USA))
(1116a) 1319[2] 2323a[4] 2861a[8]

Singspiel Spirit *Clive Brittain* a25 47
2 ch g Singspiel(IRE) —Aberavon (Cadeaux Genereux)
2594[7] 4698[7] 6100[11] 6611[5] 7780[9]

Sing Sweetly *Gerard Butler* a89 87
4 b m Singspiel(IRE) —Sweetness Herself (Unfuwain (USA))
1388[8] 2604[9] 3042[4] 3632[4]

Singzak *Michael Easterby* a78 78
3 ch g Singspiel(IRE) —Zakuska (Zafonic (USA))
1693[5] ◆ 2125[7] 2392[8] 4367[2] ◆ 4752[4] 6182[2] 6503[2] (6601) 7062[2]

Sinndarina (FR) *P Demercastel* 99
4 b m Sinndar(IRE) —Ana Marie (FR) (Anabaa (USA))
5839a[9] 6470a[5] 7090a[0]

Sinnerman (GER) *J Hirschberger* 106
3 b c Tiger Hill(IRE) —Sommernacht (GER) (Monsun (GER))
5308a[7]

Sinntani (IRE) *John M Oxx* a72 93
3 b c Dalakhani(IRE) —Sinntara (IRE) (Lashkari)
6513a[13]

Sionan (IRE) *A P O'Brien* a59 71
3 b f Danehill Dancer(IRE) —Sacrosanct (IRE) (Sadler's Wells (USA))
6511a[7]

Sion Hill (IRE) *John Harris* a51 64
10 b g Desert Prince(IRE) —Mobilia (Last Tycoon)
14[10] 675[13]

Sioux City Sue *Jim Boyle* a26 12
5 b m Noverre(USA) —Sartigila (Efisio)
6947[8] 7360[6] 7574[8]

Siouxies Dream *Michael Appleby* a61
2 b f Zafeen(FR) —Lady De Londres (Mtoto)
7505[3] 7582[3] 7684[5]

Siouxperhero (IRE) *William Muir* a67 70
2 b g Sleeping Indian—Tintern (Diktat)
3171[8] 3534[2] 4201[3] 4525[4] 5133[6] 5809[7] 6132[10] 6443[3] 6812[2] 6973[2] 7205[9]

Sioux Rising (IRE) *Richard Fahey* a101 100
5 b m Danetime(IRE) —Arvika (FR) (Baillamont (USA))
265[3] 651[3] 710[2] 923a[8] 1541[2] 1854[5] (3459) 3827[7] 4332[6] 5080[6] 5255[2] 6145[19] 6706[4] 6854a[2]

Sir Bedivere (IRE) *Brian Meehan* 69
2 b c Dansili—Miss Ivanhoe (IRE) (Selkirk (USA))
6160[6] ◆ 6994[6]

Sir Boss (IRE) *Michael Mullineaux* a89 92
6 b g Tagula(IRE) —Good Thought (IRE) (Mukaddamah (USA))
8[9] 418[3] (621) (728) (805) 948[2] ◆ (1223) ◆ 1855[2] 2285[3] 2932[8] 7347[5] 7699[10]

Sir Bruno (FR) *Bryn Palling* a81 82
4 ch g Hernando(FR) —Moon Tree (FR) (Groom Dancer (USA))
1564[3] 1917[2] 2300[9] 3634[9] 4921[8]

Sircozy (IRE) *Gary Moore* a73 77
5 b g Celtic Swing—Furnish (Green Desert (USA))
1509[5] 7032[2] 7661[6]

Sirdave *Peter Hiatt* a53 69
5 ch g Where Or When(IRE) —Charming Tina (IRE) (Indian Ridge)
63[6] 309[3] 569[3] 688[8]

Sir Dolois (FR) *A Bonin* a60 66
5 b g Marchand De Sable(USA) —Dakarna (IRE) (Top Ville)
93a[10]

Sir Dylan *Ronald Harris* a62
2 b g Dylan Thomas(IRE) —Monteleone (IRE) (Montjeu (IRE))
7369[9] 7559[4]

Sir Elmo (IRE) *Declan Carroll* 53
2 ch c Redback—Sirene (Mystiko (USA))
2983[7] 3382[7] 3618[7] 5817[9] 6260[13]

Sirens *Phil McEntee* a56 62
3 ch f Bertolini(USA) —Natural Grace (Zamindar (USA))
2827[9] 3949[6]

Siren's Song (IRE) *Mrs John Harrington* 103
3 b f Azamour(IRE) —Lurina (IRE) (Lure (USA))
2682[7] 3405[9] 4589a[10] 5976a[10]

Sir Francis Drake *Mahmood Al Zarooni* 80
3 ch g Pivotal—Cape Verdi (IRE) (Caerleon (USA))
2125[2] 2621[2] 3001[5]

Sir Fredlot (IRE) *Peter Winkworth* 79
2 b g Choisir(AUS) —Wurfklinge (GER) (Acatenango (GER))
4339[4] 4857[2] ◆ 5812[3]

Sirgarfieldsobers (IRE) *Declan Carroll* a26 89
5 b g Montjeu(IRE) —Funsie (FR) (Saumarez)
2364[2] 2708[10] 3023[3] 3828[15] 4109[4] 4784[3] 5036[11] 5608[10] 6028[8] 6263[8] 6916[13] 7075[9] 7215[15] 7858[9]

Sir Geoffrey (IRE) *Scott Dixon* a92 84
5 b g Captain Rio—Disarm (IRE) (Bahamian Bounty)
2[3] 293[3] 523[2] 701[2] 970[3] 1200[3] 1476[11] 1878[12] 5680[9] 5831[16] 7489[3] 7602[9] 7846[11]

Sir George (IRE) *Ollie Pears* a73 93
6 b g Mujadil(USA) —Torrmana (IRE) (Ela-Mana-Mou)
1092[8] 1410[10] 2112[3] 2495[5] 2814[6] 3521[10] 4070[6] 4679[2] 5488[8] 6093[6] 6533[6]

Sir Gerry (USA) *Doug Watson* a108 115
6 ch h Carson City(USA) —Incredulous (FR) (Indian Ridge)
152a[7] 327a[10] 497a[11] 678a[12]

Sir Glanton (IRE) *Amanda Perrett* a82 90
2 ch g Choisir(AUS) —Ctesiphon (USA) (Arch (USA))
(2559) 3429[2] 3861[9] 4496[11] 6055[4]

Sir Graham Wade (IRE) *Mark Johnston* 82
2 gr c Dalakhani(IRE) —Needwood Epic (Midyan (USA))
6400[4] ◆ 6572[2] ◆

Sir Haydn *J R Jenkins* a56 35
11 ch g Definite Article—Snowscape (Niniski (USA))
103[3] 670[2] 797[5] (939) 1135[5] 1308[5]

Sir Henry (DEN) *Soren Jensen* 80
4 b h Academy Award(IRE) —Lady Clementine (DEN) (Richard Of York)
4842a[8]

Sir Ike (IRE) *Michael Appleby* a61 61
6 b g Xaar—Iktidar (Green Desert (USA))
3944[9] 4076[9] 4948[15] 7632[11] 7923[3]

Sirious Oss *Michael Easterby* 61
2 b g Sir Percy—Groom Landing (PR) (Runaway Groom (CAN))
6774[5] 6983[14]

Sirius Prospect (USA) *Dean Ivory* a79 115
3 bb g Gone West(USA) —Stella Blue (FR) (Anabaa (USA))
1175[7] 3178[2] ◆ (4156) ◆ 4333[14] (5887) (6500) ◆ (6706) ◆ (7298) ◆

Sirius Superstar *Andrew Balding* 80
3 b c Galileo(IRE) —Brightest (Rainbow Quest (USA))
1407[8] 1728[2] 2551[9] 3550[3]

Sirjosh *Des Donovan* a66 60
5 b g Josr Algarhoud(IRE) —Special Gesture (IRE) (Brief Truce (USA))
9[8] 526[12] 648[4] 984[6] 1633[4] 2149[8]

Sir Lando *Wido Neuroth* 112
4 b h Lando(GER) —Burqa (Nashwan (USA))
1931a[2] 2601a[2] 3446a[3] 4374a[6] 5984a[4]

Sir Loin *Paul Burgoyne* a41 2
10 ch g Compton Place—Charnwood Queen (Cadeaux Genereux)
123[10] 443[11] 861[7]

Sir Louis *Richard Fahey* a74 66
4 b g Compton Place—Heuston Station (IRE) (Fairy King (USA))
(13) (150) 377[7] 7500[9] 7746[13]

Sir Lunchalott *J S Moore* a68 71
3 b g Pastoral Pursuits—Jasmine Breeze (Saddlers' Hall (IRE))
192[5] 366[5]

Sir Mike *Amanda Perrett* 16
2 ch g Haafhd—Tara Moon (Pivotal)
5479[15]

Sir Mozart (IRE) *Barney Curley* a50 77
8 b g Mozart(IRE) —Lady Silver Hawk (USA) (Silver Hawk (USA))
4393[2] 4509[5] 5341[9] 6069[9] 6583[11] 7097[10] 7448[12]

Sir Nod *Julie Camacho* a80 83
9 b g Tagula(IRE) —Nordan Raider (Domynsky)
577[8] (880) 1205[6] 1907[8] 2286[4] 4233[7] 5400[2] 5881[9] 6282[4] 6665[11] 7172[7] 7265[12]

Sir Oscar (GER) *T Potters* 106
4 b h Mark Of Esteem(IRE) —Sintenis (GER) (Polish Precedent (USA))
2980a[6] 4120a[5] 5664a[4]

Sir Randolf (IRE) *Sylvester Kirk* a67 64
3 br g Statue Of Liberty(USA) —Pardoned (IRE) (Mujadil (USA))
227[2] 365[5] 931[8] 1191[3] 2527[7] 3220[5] 3979[4] 4491[8] 5349[4] 5636[4] 5832[8] 6253[8] 6446[5] 7092[4] 7333[3] 7496[5] 7836[4]

Sir Reginald *Richard Fahey* 101
3 b g Compton Place—Clincher Club (Polish Patriot (USA))
(1317)

Sir Royal (USA) *Brendan Powell* a77 83
6 b g Diesis—Only Royale (IRE) (Caerleon (USA))
723[4] 805[6]

Sir Trevor (IRE) *Tom Dascombe* 77
2 b g Refuse To Bend(IRE) —Joyfullness (USA) (Dixieland Band (USA))
5269[4] ◆ 5875[3] (6278)

Sirvino *David Barron* 104
6 b g Vettori(IRE) —Zenita (IRE) (Zieten (USA))
1479[10] 2002[15] 2573[9] (3411) 3625[13] 4532[4] 5285[15] 5493[2] 6301[4]

Sir William Orpen *Pat Phelan* a60 66
4 b g Orpen(USA) —Ashover Amber (Green Desert (USA))
247[6] 350[3] 592[7] 957[13]

Sir Windsorlot (IRE) *John Quinn* 65
2 b g Windsor Knot(IRE) —Hever Rosina (Efisio)
4899[8] 5646[3] 7072[3]

Si Sealy (IRE) *David Evans* a47 32
2 b g Lawman(FR) —Sharpville (USA) (Diesis)
1235[4] 1505[7] 2889[11]

Sister Andrea *James Fanshawe* a45 71
3 ch f Dr Fong(USA) —White Rabbit (Zilzal (USA))
3717[7] 4800[9] 5169[3] 5804[11] 6067[2]

Sister Guru *Peter Hedger* a42 72
2 b f Ishiguru(USA) —Ulysses Daughter (IRE) (College Chapel)
1192[4] 3046[6] 3547[11] 4212[2] 6237[2] 6590[7]

Sister June (IRE) *Edward Creighton*
3 b f Tiger Hill(IRE) —Littleton Arwen (USA) (Bahri (USA))
4950[10]

Sister Red (IRE) *Richard Hannon* 82
3 b f Diamond Green(FR) —Red Fuschia (Polish Precedent (USA))
1725[11] 3260[9]

Sister Sioux (IRE) *Robin Bastiman* a22 45
3 b f Antonius Pius(USA) —Blue Sioux (Indian Ridge)
966[9] 5214[11] 5822[4] 6153[7] 7426[12]

Sistine *Nicky Henderson* a62 62
3 b f Dubai Destination(USA) —Fickle (Danehill (USA))
2529[9] 3385[7] 4363[3] 4878[6] 7264[2] 7723[3]

Sisyphe (FR) *P Demercastel* 97
2 b c Slickly(FR) —European Style (FR) (Ezzoud (IRE))
4624a[6] 7508a[6]

Sit Tight *Chris Wall* a83 72
3 gr g Act One—Tease (IRE) (Green Desert (USA))
1991[7] 2551[12] 4529[5] 5247[4] (5630) (6254)

Situation Vacant *Mark Johnston* 26
4 b g Alhaarth(IRE) —Hampton Lucy (IRE) (Anabaa (USA))
1210[11] 1910[7]

Six Diamonds *Paddy Butler* a75 77
4 b m Exceed And Excel(AUS) —Daltak (Night Shift (USA))
133[8] 318[8] 477[10]

Six Of Clubs *Bill Turner* a60 48
5 ch g Bertolini(USA) —Windmill Princess (Gorytus (USA))
39[2] 118[3] 560[7] (768) 1032[2] (1473) 1973[4]

Six Of Hearts *Cecil Ross* a100 109
7 b g Pivotal—Additive (USA) (Devil's Bag (USA))
923a[11] 2533a[5] (3440a) 4116a[7] 4836a[7] 5746a[11] 7149a[11]

Six Silver Lane *Ms Joanna Morgan* a81 78
3 gr g Aussie Rules(USA) —Aurelia (Rainbow Quest (USA))
7150a^{3} ◆

Sixty Roses (IRE) *John Dunlop* 70
3 b f Barathea(IRE) —Pershaan (IRE) (Darshaan)
1134^{3} 1951^{6} 3002^{5} 4275^{3} 5107^{4}

Six Wives *David Nicholls* a84 78
4 b m Kingsalsa(USA) —Regina (Green Desert (USA))
(318) 491^{3} 646^{2} (708) 1024^{4} 1196^{5} 1411^{5} 1555^{5} 1838^{5} (2193) (2585) 2913^{2} 6665^{7} 7355^{9} 7428^{5} (7746)

Sixx *Richard Hannon* 89
2 b c Royal Applause—Teramo (IRE) (Cadeaux Genereux)
(2221) 2437^{4} 2868^{6} 3795^{2} 5933^{5}

Sizzle (FR) *Tom Dascombe* a54 37
3 b f Muhtathir—Lizzysue (USA) (Prospect Bay (CAN))
1252^{2} 1597a^{10} 2258^{12} 3202^{9}

Skadar Lake *D Guillemin* 86
2 ch f Footstepsinthesand—Ganar El Cielo (Ashkalani (IRE))
4843a^{9}

Skallet (FR) *S Wattel* a95 107
3 b f Muhaymin(USA) —Siran (FR) (R B Chesne)
1513a^{3} (5958a) 6686a^{3} 7386a^{2}

Skarabeus (USA) *G Wroblewski* 99
4 b g War Chant(USA) —Caffe Latte (IRE) (Seattle Dancer (USA))
6686a^{8}

Skeleton (IRE) *David Evans* a61 57
3 b f Tobougg(IRE) —Atamana (IRE) (Lahib (USA))
194^{4} 260^{9}

Sketchy Evidence (USA) *John Best* a71
3 ch c Officer(USA) —Drawing A Blank (USA) (El Prado (IRE))
7389^{3} (7652)

Skia (FR) *C Laffon-Parias* 102
4 b m Motivator—Light Quest (USA) (Quest For Fame)
(7386a)

Skilful *John Gosden* a94 112
3 ch c Selkirk(USA) —Prowess (IRE) (Peintre Celebre (USA))
(2306) ◆ 5730^{2} (6335) ◆ 7023^{2}

Skins Game *J-C Rouget* 111
5 b h Diktat—Mouriyana (IRE) (Akarad (FR))
(1125a) 1740a^{4} 5094a^{3} 7193a^{4}

Skip Along *John Gosden* 88
3 ch f Galileo(IRE) —Peony (Lion Cavern (USA))
1549^{2} ◆ (2065)

Skipping Stones (IRE) *Robert Collet* a63 70
3 b c Whipper(USA) —Halesia (USA) (Chief's Crown (USA))
638a^{9}

Skirmish *Mark Johnston* 53
2 b c Teofilo(IRE) —Jessica's Dream (IRE) (Desert Style (IRE))
6983^{9}

Skiryades (FR) *C Boutin*
4 ch m Ski Chief(USA) —Dryades (FR) (Baryshnikov (AUS))
1033a^{0}

Sky Blazer (USA) *Barclay Tagg* 103
3 b g Sky Mesa(USA) —Highland Hope (USA) (Unaccounted For (USA))
6716a^{5}

Skyblue *Tobias B P Coles* a33 29
2 b f Royal Applause—Fiina (Most Welcome)
6030^{14} 6758^{12} 6935^{10} 7248^{6} 7435^{12}

Sky Crossing *James Given* a75 56
2 b c Cape Cross(IRE) —Sky Wonder (Observatory (USA))
7209^{5} 7593^{3} (7724)

Sky Crystal (GER) *John Gosden* a76 47
3 ch f Galileo(IRE) —[illegible] (IRE) (Kingmambo (USA))
6404^{6} (7360)

Sky Diamond (IRE) *John Mackie* a72 72
3 b g Diamond Green(FR) —Jewell In The Sky (IRE) (Sinndar (IRE))
49^{3} 260^{8} 3002^{10} 3619^{2} 4284^{9} (5041) 5401^{2} (5631) 5836^{2} 6120^{2} 6490^{4} 6794^{7} 6944^{5} 7235^{9} 7388^{3} 7605^{6} 7901^{7}

Skye But N Ben *Alan McCabe* a37 53
7 b g Auction House(USA) —Island Colony (USA) (Pleasant Colony (USA))
6876^{8}

Skyeron *Mark Brisbourne* 41
2 b f Byron—Song Of Skye (Warning)
4571^{7} 4883^{6} 5270^{8}

Sky Falcon (USA) *Mark Johnston* 80
3 ch g Smarty Jones(USA) —Silent Eskimo (USA) (Eskimo (USA))
1903^{4} 2695^{3} 3084^{3}

Skyfire *Ed de Giles* a48 83
4 ch g Storm Cat(USA) —Sunray Superstar (Nashwan (USA))
703^{12} 799^{8} 2999^{7} 3514^{7} 4278^{4} 5014^{6} 5828^{2} 6586^{9}

Sky High Diver (IRE) *Alan Swinbank* a75 54
3 b f Celtic Swing—Limit (IRE) (Barathea (IRE))
6097^{8} (6781) (7426) ◆ (7723) (7779)

Sky Lazer (ITY) *S Botti* 107
5 b h Dr Devious(IRE) —Defeat Bay (USA) (El Gran Senor (USA))
6905a^{8}

Skylla *Derek Shaw* a60 93
4 b m Kyllachy—Day Star (Dayjur (USA))
1476^{6} 2028^{13} 2525^{11} 6351^{10} 6932^{10} 7395^{10} 7535^{6} 7649^{10} 7844^{10}

Sky Skipper (IRE) *G Doleuze* a64 77
4 ch h Golan(IRE) —Sky Gift (USA) (Stravinsky (USA))
6959a^{5}

Skystream (IRE) *Ian Semple* a49 56
3 bb f Captain Rio—Nuit Des Temps (Sadler's Wells (USA))
6415^{8} 6653^{7} 7144^{6} 7845^{3}

Skysurfers *Saeed Bin Suroor* a118 116
5 b h E Dubai(USA) —Fortune (IRE) (Night Shift (USA))
(501a) ◆ (997a)

Skyteam (FR) *M Boutin* a88 94
7 b g Anabaa(USA) —Spenderella (FR) (Common Grounds)
(6593a)

Skyway (IRE) *Takashi Kodama* a71 91
4 ch m Trans Island—Zilayah (USA) (Zilzal (USA))
2678^{5} 6066^{9}

Slade (IRE) *Andrew Heffernan* a76 82
4 b g Orpen(USA) —Slightly Shady (IRE) (Dr Devious (IRE))
7548a^{12}

Slade Power (IRE) *Edward Lynam* a83 78
2 b c Dutch Art—Girl Power (IRE) (Key Of Luck (USA))
2329a^{2}

Slatey Hen (IRE) *Richard Guest* a64 60
3 b f Acclamation—Silver Arrow (USA) (Shadeed (USA))
(66) 263^{4} 364^{6} 620^{4} 4149^{8} 5120^{6} 5540^{16} 5670^{6} 5787^{8} 5941^{4} 7676^{3} 7760^{7}

Sleek Gold *Brian Meehan* a66 77
3 b f Dansili—Ya Hajar (Lycius (USA))
1836^{6} 3043^{4} (3615) 5020^{9}

Sleep Dance *Eve Johnson Houghton* a59 52
3 b f Sleeping Indian—Crofters Ceilidh (Scottish Reel)
5780^{3} 6020^{5} (6251)

Sleeping Brave *Jim Boyle* a56 53
3 b g Sleeping Indian—Concubine (IRE) (Danehill (USA))
887^{3} ◆ 966^{3} 1354^{3} 1566^{13} 2172^{8} 2197^{7} 2722^{9}

Sleepy Blue Ocean *John Balding* a85 76
5 b g Oasis Dream—Esteemed Lady (IRE) (Mark Of Esteem (IRE))
165^{4} (294) 491^{6} 571^{2} 794^{5} 2610^{4} 3166^{3} (3493) 4371^{4} 4900^{3} 5468^{2} 5918^{3} 6112^{8} 7104^{7} 7341^{4} 7500^{2} (7644)

Sleepy Lucy *Richard Guest* a49
2 b f Multiplex—Millie The Filly (Erhaab (USA))
7210^{10} 7898^{4}

Sleigh Bells *Mark H Tompkins* 12
2 b f Three Valleys(USA) —Dolls House (Dancing Spree (USA))
3554^{6}

Sleights Boy (IRE) *Ian McInnes* 58
3 b g Kyllachy—Fanny Bay (IRE) (Key Of Luck (USA))
1331^{8} 1749^{9} 1967^{4} 2396^{13} 2918^{4} 3247^{9} 3573^{6} 3937^{9} 4162^{6} 4638^{9} 4680^{5} 5203^{4} (5506) 5824^{6}

Slenningford *Ollie Pears* a55 63
2 b f Vital Equine(IRE) —Dim Ofan (Petong)
2248^{2} 3022^{4} 3314^{5} 6132^{9} 6597^{10}

Slewtoo *Marco Botti* a68
2 b f Three Valleys(USA) —Red Slew (Red Ransom (USA))
(7838) ◆

Slight Advantage (IRE) *Clive Cox* a8 89
3 b f Peintre Celebre(USA) —Kournikova (SAF) (Sportsworld (USA))
1951^{4} 2842^{3} 3291^{4} 4251^{2} (5236) ◆ 5878^{4} ◆ 6410^{6}

Sligo All Star *Thomas McLaughlin* a51 42
6 b m Kyllachy—Top Spot (Cadeaux Genereux)
408^{6} 425^{8} 944^{7} 968^{7}

Slikback Jack (IRE) *David Nicholls* a83 76
4 ch g Dr Fong(USA) —Duelling (Diesis)
105^{4} 205^{4} 816^{4} 1037^{5} 1195^{2}

Slim Shadey *J S Moore* 96
3 br g Val Royal(FR) —Vino Veritas (USA) (Chief's Crown (USA))
1686^{4} 2324a^{7} 3068^{16} 3777^{4} 4493^{8} 4764^{5} 6273^{6}

Slip *Tim Vaughan* a49 72
6 b g Fraam—Niggle (Night Shift (USA))
6613^{4}

Slip Sliding Away (IRE) [illegible] [illegible]
4 b g Whipper(USA) —Sandy Lady (IRE) (Desert King (IRE))
2288^{9} 3000^{P}

Slipstick (IRE) *J-M Capitte* a60 88
2 gr f Slickly(FR) —Jillian (USA) (Royal Academy (USA))
7326a^{3}

Sloop Johnb *Conor Dore* a79 76
5 b g Bahamian Bounty—Soundwave (Prince Sabo)
(84) (197) (343) 491^{7} 506^{5} 1048^{9} 3087^{9}

Slow Pace (USA) *F Head* 114
3 b g Distorted Humor(USA) —Slow Down (USA) (Seattle Slew (USA))
2978a^{4} 3653a^{4} 4376a^{4} 5128a^{2} 6185a^{6}

Slugger O'Toole *Stuart Williams* a80 75
6 br g Intikhab(USA) —Haddeyah (USA) (Dayjur (USA))
1898^{10} 2369^{8} 2719^{7} 2917^{5} 3250^{6}

Sluggsy Morant *Henry Candy* 86
3 b g Monsieur Bond(IRE) —Breezy Louise (Dilum (USA))
(2025) ◆ 2564^{7} 3269^{5} 4156^{2} 4550^{4} 5171^{4} (5587) 6174^{6} 6974^{9}

Slumber *Charles Hills* 114
3 b c Cacique(IRE) —Sound Asleep (USA) (Woodman (USA))
(1478) 1822^{3} 3068^{3} ◆ 4411^{7} 5934^{2} (7170) 7572a^{4}

Slumbering Sioux *Harry Dunlop* a61 64
3 b f Sleeping Indian—Mi Amor (IRE) (Alzao (USA))
1022^{4} 2196^{12} 4317^{9} 5673^{9} 6434^{12}

Smacker (IRE) *Hughie Morrison* a58 60
2 ch g Redback—Sweet'n Sassy (IRE) (Grand Lodge (USA))
6127^{9} 6800^{4} 7353^{2}

Smaeldadi (FR) *Robert Collet*
3 ch g Muhtathir—Veliana (FR) (Vettori (IRE))
777a^{0}

Small Frida (FR) *Mme Pia Brandt* a75 76
2 ch f Gold Away(IRE) —Becky Moss (USA) (Red Ransom (USA))
7238a^{2} 7665a^{2}

Smalljohn *Bryan Smart* a81 78
5 ch g Needwood Blade—My Bonus (Cyrano De Bergerac)
(285) 572^{3} 736^{2} 1035^{3} 1245^{9} 2431^{10} 6980^{9} 7416^{6} 7625^{7} 7857^{10}

Small Steps (IRE) *Ed McMahon* a50 51
2 b f Acclamation—Last Tango (IRE) (Lion Cavern (USA))
4002^{8} 4864^{7} 5681^{10} 6222^{4} 7780^{6}

Smart Affair *Rod Millman* 42
2 b f Trade Fair—Che Chic (IRE) (Daggers Drawn (USA))
5323^{12} 5807^{9} 6019^{7}

Smartcity (USA) *Andrew Oliver* a78 104
3 ch c Smarty Jones(USA) —Gossamer (USA) (Seattle Slew (USA))
(1704a) ◆ 2331a^{3}

Smart George (IRE) *Paul W Flynn* a61 54
3 b g Kalanisi(IRE) —Yazmin (IRE) (Green Desert (USA))
1053^{6} ◆ 1683^{10} 7145^{3}

Smarties Party *Clive Mulhall* a66 54
8 b m Tamure(IRE) —Maries Party (The Parson)
407^{8} 1881^{9}

Smart Performance *Alan Jarvis* a17 48
3 b g Acclamation—Green Eyes (IRE) (Green Desert (USA))
1578^{5} 5041^{7}

Smart Step *Mark Johnston* a43 71
3 b f Montjeu(IRE) —Miss Pinkerton (Danehill (USA))
1189^{7} 1972^{6} 3039^{7} 3475^{8} 4018^{4} 4505^{9} 5372^{8} 5507^{5} (5823) 6122^{11} (6415) (6830) 7235^{10}

Smart Violetta (IRE) *Ann Duffield* a44 70
3 b f Smart Strike(CAN) —Dubai Diamond (Octagonal (NZ))
1858^{6} 2571^{11} 3716^{6} (4018) 4403^{7} 4878^{2} ◆ (5315) 5507^{2} (5822) 6211^{4}

Smarty Sam (USA) *Paul Midgley* a59 69
4 ch g Smarty Jones(USA) —Ascot Starre (CAN) (Ascot Knight (CAN))
1857^{8} 4125^{9} 4945^{13} 5390^{5} 5738^{4} 5943^{7} 6135^{4} 6309^{8}

Smarty Socks (IRE) *David O'Meara* a80 108
7 ch g Elnadim(USA) —Unicamp (Royal Academy (USA))
1092^{6} 1410^{11} 1694^{7} (2706) 3109^{7} 3876^{11} 4428^{3} 5218^{2} ◆ (5699) 6521^{2} 7023^{7}

Smerc (TUR) *S Coskun* 90
4 b h Ocean Crest(USA) —Knees To Knees (IRE) (Tagula (IRE))
5776a^{7}

Smirfy's Silver *Deborah Sanderson* a31 75
7 b g Desert Prince(IRE) —Goodwood Blizzard (Inchinor)
3139^{6} 4730^{2} 5356^{6} 6263^{9} 6773^{6}

Smoky Cloud (IRE) *Amy Weaver* a70 81
4 ch g Refuse To Bend(IRE) —Pirie (USA) (Green Dancer (USA))
7438^{12} 7602^{10} 7767^{12} 7893^{12}

Smooth Operator (GER) *Mario Hofer* 111
5 b g Big Shuffle(USA) —Salzgitter (Salse (USA))
1575a^{8} 3531a^{3} 4121a^{3} 4838a^{8} 5528a^{2} 6906a^{3} 7311a^{5}

Snaafy (USA) *M Al Muhairi* a114 117
7 b h Kingmambo(USA) —Nafisah (IRE) (Lahib (USA))
157a^{11} 586a^{11} 756a^{4}

Snaefell (IRE) *M Halford* a82 113
7 gr g Danehill Dancer(IRE) —Sovereign Grace (IRE) (Standaan (FR))
1420a^{7} 1533a^{7} 2323a^{5} 3440a^{9} 4116a^{8} 4566a^{11} 6388a^{8}

Snape Maltings (IRE) *H-A Pantall* 96
4 b g Sadler's Wells(USA) —Hanami (Hernando (FR))
1231a^{8}

[illegible] 64
5 b g Arazi(USA) —Shally's Magic (AUS) (Shalford (IRE))
10

Snapshott (IRE) *Ronald Harris* a31 13
3 b g Kodiac—Groovy (Shareef Dancer (USA))
1566^{14}

Snare *Ann Duffield* 37
4 b m Domedriver(IRE) —Catch (USA) (Blushing Groom (FR))
4014^{6} 4363^{7} 4611^{10}

Sneak A Peek (ITY) *S Botti* 115
3 b c Doyen(IRE) —Occhi Di Giada (GER) (Shantou (USA))
1920a^{4} (6202a) 6907a^{6}

Snooky *Henry Candy* 71
2 b c Exceed And Excel(AUS) —Quintrell (Royal Applause)
3870^{2} 4815^{9} 6300^{3}

Snoqualmie Boy *David Nicholls* a97 72
8 b g Montjeu(IRE) —Seattle Ribbon (USA) (Seattle Dancer (USA))
5594^{11} 6263^{12} 6601^{9}

Snoqualmie Star *David Elsworth* a92 93
4 ch m Galileo(IRE) —Seattle Ribbon (USA) (Seattle Dancer (USA))
1477^{10} 2066^{10} 3203^{11}

Snow Bay *David Nicholls* a90 103
5 ch g Bahamian Bounty—Goodwood Blizzard (Inchinor)
18^{4} 196a^{0} 481a^{5} (617a) (1075) (1410) 1694^{2} 2123^{3} 2390^{3} 3877^{2} 4100^{5} 4774^{8} 5557^{9} 6150^{10} 6672^{16}

Snow Dancer (IRE) *Hugh McWilliams* a86 87
7 b m Desert Style(IRE) —Bella Vie (IRE) (Sadler's Wells (USA))
235^{5} (541) 694^{5} 1098^{2} (1622) 1824^{5} 2676^{4} 3356^{8} 3703^{8} 4528^{8} 5078^{9} 5686^{7} 5888^{8} 6330^{8} 7199^{7} 7397^{2} 7558^{4} 7606^{4} 7877^{7}

Snowed In (IRE) *J S Moore* a73 73
2 gr g Dark Angel(IRE) —Spinning Gold (Spinning World (USA))
982^{5} (1143) 2109^{5} 2889^{3} 3595^{2} 3866^{12} (5246) 5783^{5} 6399^{4} (6471) 7117^{2} 7449a^{10} (7582)

Snow Fairy (IRE) *Ed Dunlop* a83 125
4 b m Intikhab(USA) —Woodland Dream (IRE) (Charnwood Forest (IRE))
3646^{4} 4533^{2} 5747a^{2} ◆ 6567a^{3} 6861^{3} ◆ (7410a)

Snowflake Dancer (IRE) *J S Bolger* a72 87
2 b g Dylan Thomas(IRE) —Snowy Day In La (IRE) (Sadler's Wells (USA))
(972a) 2776a^{2}

Snow Hill *Chris Wall* 86
3 gr g Halling(USA) —Swift Dispersal (Shareef Dancer (USA))
2458^{6} 2956^{10} (4190) 4862^{2} (6024)

Snow Magic (IRE) *James Fanshawe* a87 74
4 gr m Marju(IRE) —Santa Sophia (IRE) (Linamix (FR))
1114^{8} 1992^{5} 3026^{5} (3740) ◆ 6948^{12}

Snowmaster (USA) *Saeed Bin Suroor* a104
5 ch h Maria's Mon(USA) —Snowflake (IRE) (Caerleon (USA))
499a^{9}

Snow Ridge *Andrew Haynes* a65 56
3 b g Iceman—Confetti (Groom Dancer (USA))
1131^{5} 1483^{10} 2186^{6} 3709^{5}

Snow Runner (ARG) *Vanja Sandrup* a91 89
8 ch h Lode(USA) —Snow Pac (URU) (Snow Satyr (ARG))
778a^{10}

Snow Trooper *Dean Ivory* a68 76
3 ch g Iceman—Snow Shoes (Sri Pekan (USA))
668^{2} 931^{7} 2196^{2} (3259) ◆ 4281^{4} 6167^{4}

Snowy Peak *Jeremy Noseda* a69 52
3 ch f Pivotal—Snow Princess (IRE) (Ela-Mana-Mou)
262^{3} 624^{2} 898^{6} 4745^{4} (5391) ◆

Snuggle Up (IRE) *W McCreery* a46 55
3 b f High Chaparral(IRE) —Lovers Nest (Groom Dancer (USA))
7264^{10}

Soap Wars *Hugo Palmer* a95 94
6 b g Acclamation—Gooseberry Pie (Green Desert (USA))
(2369) 2557^{4} 3796^{7} 4416^{9} 5262^{3} 6036^{2} 6348^{9} 6761^{2}

So Bazaar (IRE) *Alan Swinbank* 70
4 b g Xaar—Nature Girl (USA) (Green Dancer (USA))
1035^{10} 2059^{4} 2474^{8} 2988^{7} 4045^{6} 4438^{4} 4612^{11} 4852^{9}

Sobea Star (IRE) *Pam Sly* 52
3 ch f Soviet Star(USA) —Nordic Cloud (IRE) (Lure (USA))
1151^{9} 1415^{11} 2621^{P}

Soccerjackpot (USA) *Paul Midgley* a100 78
7 b g Mizzen Mast(USA) —Rahbaby (USA) (Rahy (USA))
2768^{2} 5648^{3} 6262^{P}

So Cheeky *Richard Hannon* a54
2 ch f Fantastic View(USA) —Fallujah (Dr Fong (USA))
7124^{10} 7493^{6} 7889^{10}

So Choosy *Jeremy Gask* a29 55
3 b f Choisir(AUS) —Roxy (Rock City)
4340^{8} 5040^{12}

Social Forum (IRE) *David Elsworth* a76 75
3 b g Invincible Spirit(IRE) —Social Upheaval (USA) (Twilight Agenda (USA))
179^{3} (559) 5635^{7} 6081^{5} 6944^{12}

Social Rhythm *Alistair Whillans* a62 74
7 b m Beat All(USA) —Highly Sociable (Puissance)
3113^{6} 3859^{10} 4141^{10} 4670^{12} 5164^{8} 5721^{3} ◆ 6453^{11} 6878^{3} 7399^{11}

Society Rock (IRE) *James Fanshawe* 119
4 b h Rock Of Gibraltar(IRE) —High Society (IRE) (Key Of Luck (USA))
1340^{10} 1891^{2} (3154) 4838a^{2} 5707^{6} 6858^{12} 7730a^{13}

Society's Chairman (CAN) *Roger L Attfield* a103 114
8 b h Not Impossible(IRE) —Athena's Smile (CAN) (Olympio (USA))
6721a^{7}

Sofast (FR) *F Head* 113
2 ch c Rock Of Gibraltar(IRE) —Beautifix (GER) (Bering)
(4652a) 5305a^{4} (5770a) 6565a^{2}

Sofias Number One (USA) *Roy Bowring* a71 43
3 bb g Silver Deputy(CAN) —Storidawn (USA) (Hennessy (USA))
126^{3} ◆ 305^{2} 437^{3} 559^{4} (871) 951^{5} (1500) 2581^{8} 6777^{11} 7057^{12} 7425^{2} 7537^{9} 7647^{9}

Softly Killing Me *Brian Forsey* a42 56
6 b m Umistim—Slims Lady (Theatrical Charmer)
30^{14} 225^{6} 382^{6}

Softsong (FR) *C Laffon-Parias* 92
3 b g Singspiel(IRE) —Soft Gold (USA) (Gulch (USA))
5132a^{10}

Sohar *James Toller* 75
3 b f Iceman—Desert Joy (Daylami (IRE))
3135^{4} 3824^{6} 5001^{4}

Sohcahtoa (IRE) *Robert Mills* a74 92
5 b g Val Royal(FR) —Stroke Of Six (IRE) (Woodborough (USA))
1603^{9} ◆ 2649^{9} 3354^{6} 5893^{11} 6254^{5} 6722^{2} 6998^{4} 7139^{2}

Soho Rocks *James Toller* 66
2 b f Rock Of Gibraltar(IRE) —Millisecond (Royal Applause)
4961^{6} 5479^{9} 6169^{7} 6526^{12}

Soho Star *Gerard Butler* a50
3 ch f Smarty Jones(USA) —Performing Arts (The Minstrel (CAN))
6137^{8}

Sohraab *Hughie Morrison* a77 97
7 b g Erhaab(USA) —Riverine (Risk Me (FR))
1366^{6} 1888^{17} 2099^{9} 2714^{4} ◆ (2959) 3410^{12} 3846^{2} 4357^{8} 4776^{6} 5543^{3} 6224^{13}

Soir De Lune (IRE) *B Grizzetti* 83
3 bb f Invincible Spirit(IRE) —Martines (FR) (Linamix (FR))
1432a^{10}

Soir D'Ete (FR) *J-P Delaporte* 65
2 ch f Anabaa Blue—Shy Mail (ARG) (Shy Tom (USA))
7449a[5]

So Is She (IRE) *Alan Bailey* a70 72
3 b f Kheleyf(USA) —River Beau (IRE) (Galileo (IRE))
59[2] (147) 739[3] 1828[5] 1999[2] 2236[3] 3309[4] 3710[3] 5014[4] 5248[10] 5606[8] 5631[6] 6358[3] 6698[9] 6968[6] 7246[2] 7333[5]

Solange (IRE) *Tim Easterby*
2 ch f Van Nistelrooy(USA) —Bank On Her (USA) (Rahy (USA))
7058[13]

Solapur (GER) *Karin Suter-Weber* a54 87
6 ch h Ekraar(USA) —Shina (GER) (Lomitas)
441a[9] 628a[12]

Solar Deity (IRE) *Marco Botti* a85
2 b c Exceed And Excel(AUS) —Dawn Raid (IRE) (Docksider (USA))
(7431)

Solarea (FR) *T Clout* a69 75
4 b m Prince Kirk(FR) —Elessar (FR) (Kendor (FR))
2867a[0]

Solaria (FR) *Mlle V Dissaux* a74 76
5 b m Numerous(USA) —Soierie (FR) (Bering)
935a[3]

Solar Midnight (USA) *P Bary* 98
3 b f Lemon Drop Kid(USA) —Witching Hour (FR) (Fairy King (USA))
5695a[3]

Solar Sky *Sir Henry Cecil* 105
3 ch c Galileo(IRE) —La Sky (IRE) (Law Society (USA))
1407[2] ◆ (2219) 3108[2] ◆ 3772[5] 6498[3]

Solar Spirit (IRE) *Tracy Waggott* a76 87
6 b g Invincible Spirit(IRE) —Misaayef (USA) (Swain (IRE))
1110[13] 1438[2] 1618[8] 1854[12] 2028[17] 2497[8] 3275[8] 4013[5] 4126[6] (4361) 4821[2] 5205[6] 5314[7] 5722[4] 6093[2] 6346[10]

Solar View (IRE) *Sir Mark Prescott Bt* a38 14
2 ch g Galileo(IRE) —Ellen (IRE) (Machiavellian (USA))
6216[10] 6308[10] 6828[9]

Soldat (USA) *Kiaran McLaughlin* a117 111
3 bb c War Front(USA) —Le Relais (USA) (Coronado's Quest (USA))
1921a[11]

Soldiers Point *Jane Chapple-Hyam* a33 56
3 b g Indesatchel(IRE) —Wondrous Maid (GER) (Mondrian (GER))
2166[10] 2586[5] 3220[7] 3431[12]

Sole Bay *David Elsworth* a51
3 ch f Compton Place—Barboukh (Night Shift (USA))
313[9] 624[4] 953[3]

Sole Danser (IRE) *B W Hills* 75
3 b g Dansili—Plymsole (USA) (Diesis)
3111[3] 4286[4]

Solemia (IRE) *C Laffon-Parias* 112
3 b f Poliglote—Brooklyn's Dance (FR) (Shirley Heights)
5839a[2] 6903a[2]

Solemn *Milton Bradley* a81 92
6 b g Pivotal—Pious (Bishop Of Cashel)
1166[13] 1864[3] (2069) (2525) 2959[2] 3357[10] 3846[10] 5703[5] 6224[10] 6703[8]

Solemn Oath (USA) *Edward Vaughan* 59
2 b c Elusive Quality(USA) —Bathsheba (USA) (Dehere (USA))
6951[8] ◆

Solent Ridge (IRE) *G M Lyons* a89 85
6 b g Namid—Carrozzina (Vettori (IRE))
7468a[3]

Sole Power *Edward Lynam* a101 120
4 b g Kyllachy—Demerger (USA) (Distant View (USA))
996a[14] 1687[3] (2297) 3010[8] 4768a[5] 5524a[2] 5707[12] 6563a[3] ◆ 7730a[9]

Solfilia *Hughie Morrison* a44 77
2 ch f Teofilo(IRE) —Suntory (IRE) (Royal Applause)
2606[7] 2962[7] 3547[8] (4069)

Solicitor *Mark Johnston* a85 91
4 ch g Halling(USA) —Tolzey (USA) (Rahy (USA))
2403[8] 3286[3] 4004[7] 4360[6] 5198[8] 5857[11] 6916[5]

Solid Air *Edward Lynam* a56 76
6 gr g Linamix(FR) —Humouresque (Pivotal)
7792a[13]

Solidaro (GER) *J Hirschberger* 104
4 b g Monsun(GER) —Saderlina (IRE) (Sadler's Wells (USA))
3446a[8] 4374a[8]

Solid Choice (AUS) *M F De Kock* a105 101
5 b g Redoute's Choice(AUS) —Venetian Pride (USA) (Gone West (USA))
(236) ◆ 415a[11] 606a[7] 679a[3]

Solis *Micky Hammond* a42 52
5 b g Josr Algarhoud(IRE) —Passiflora (Night Shift (USA))
2985[9] 4408[9] 5079[14]

Solo Choice *Ian McInnes* a49 68
5 b g Needwood Blade—Top Of The Class (IRE) (Rudimentary (USA))
324[9] 450[9]

So Long Malpic (FR) *T Lemer* a102 99
4 b m Fairly Ransom(USA) —Poussiere D'Or (FR) (Marchand De Sable (USA))
5985a[4] 7678a[2]

Solo Performer (IRE) *H Rogers* a92 85
6 ch g Distant Music(USA) —Royal Pagent (IRE) (Balinger)
7322a[12] 7618a[11]

Solo Whisper (IRE) *Adrian McGuinness* a52 59
3 b g Whipper(USA) —Mijouter (IRE) (Coquelin (USA))
973a[12]

Somali Lemonade (USA) *Michael Matz* 105
2 b f Lemon Drop Kid(USA) —Chic Corine (USA) (Nureyev (USA))
7281a[6]

Somasach (USA) *J S Bolger* 93
2 b f Johannesburg(USA) —Easy Now (USA) (Danzig (USA))
3033[10] 3416a[2] 4031a[4]

Somemothersdohavem *John Ryan* 31
2 ch g Avonbridge—Show Off (Efisio)
5353[5]

Something (IRE) *P Monfort* a84 99
9 b g Trans Island—Persian Polly (Persian Bold)
196a[3] (325a) 1122a[0] 3568a[0]

Somewhere Else *Alan Berry* a5 14
4 b m Firebreak—Royal Future (IRE) (Royal Academy (USA))
2593[14]

Sommerabend *U Stoltefuss* 114
4 b h Shamardal(USA) —Sommernacht (GER) (Monsun (GER))
5772a[3] (6201a) 7193a[2]

Sommernachtstraum (GER) *W Hickst* 102
3 ch c Shirocco(GER) —Salonblue (IRE) (Bluebird (USA))
3672a[13]

Sommersturm (GER) *Barney Curley* a48 103
7 b g Tiger Hill(IRE) —Sommernacht (GER) (Monsun (GER))
1181[4] 3047[7] 7639[11]

Sonara (IRE) *Howard Johnson* 73
7 b g Peintre Celebre(USA) —Fay (IRE) (Polish Precedent (USA))
3730[8]

Sondeduro *Jamie Osborne* 73
2 br c Manduro(GER) —Madame Cerito (USA) (Diesis)
4213[4] ◆

Sondray *Jo Crowley* a24 35
3 b f Diktat—Hoh Dancer (Indian Ridge)
7111[8] 7585[7] 7921[5]

Son Du Silence (IRE) *J S Moore* 89
2 b c Elusive City(USA) —Fez (Mujtahid (USA))
2997[8] (3229) 3868[2] 5061[3] (5438) 5961[2] 6114[3] 7019[7]

Songbird Blues *Mark Usher* a52 46
2 b f Beat All(USA) —Billie Holiday (Fairy King (USA))
4213[11] 4864[8] 5384[11] 6695[7] 6846[7] 7251[5] 7592[2] 7780[5]

Songburst *Richard Hannon* a84 76
3 b c Singspiel(IRE) —Krynica (USA) (Danzig (USA))
437[6] (6085) 6592[13] 6797[2] 6997[6] (7227) 7651[8] 7806[4]

Songjiang *John Gosden* a79
3 b c Tiger Hill(IRE) —Showery (Rainbow Quest (USA))
(339) (650) 1485[6]

Song Of Joy (IRE) *Paul D'Arcy* a55
2 b f Oratorio(IRE) —Wondrous Joy (Machiavellian (USA))
2914[9] 7125[9] 7343[10]

Song Of Parkes *Eric Alston* 77
4 b m Fantastic Light(USA) —My Melody Parkes (Teenoso (USA))
1555[8] 2589[7] 3341[7] (4443) 5338[6] (6261)

Song Of Praise *Michael Blanshard* a56 63
5 b m Compton Place—Greensand (Green Desert (USA))
138[8]

Song Of The Siren *Andrew Balding* a60 81
3 ch f With Approval(CAN) —Sulitelma (USA) (The Minstrel (CAN))
3390[2] 3845[10] 4994[8] 5676[2]

Song Of Victory (GER) *M Weiss* a64 64
7 b g Silvano(GER) —Song Of Hope (GER) (Monsun (GER))
442a[5]

Songsmith *Lucy Wadham* a47 79
3 b g Librettist(USA) —Venus Rising (Observatory (USA))
1580[7] 3118[8] 3557[9] 4281[6] (4743) 5040[3] 5581[6] 5803[9]

Song To The Moon (IRE) *Jim Boyle* a77 82
4 b m Oratorio(IRE) —Jojeema (Barathea (IRE))
160[4] 273[4] 1114[5] (1592) 1877[2] (2449) (2768) (3537) 3763[6] 4457[6]

Sonik (FR) *J Heloury* a73
2 b g Irish Wells(FR) —Salvia (FR) (Septieme Ciel (USA))
7665a[6]

Sonko (IRE) *Tim Pitt* a73 67
2 b f Red Clubs(IRE) —Baltic Belle (IRE) (Redback)
1185[6] 2261[6] 2889[8] 3728[2] (3948) 4343[6] (5105) 5310[2] 5922[4] 6590[3] 7445[6] (7670) 7905[2]

Sonning Rose (IRE) *Mick Channon* 92
3 b f Hawk Wing(USA) —Shinkoh Rose (FR) (Warning)
1893[7] 2296[15] 2684[3] 3034[7] 3819[8] 4093[6] 4332[9] 4965[7] 5581[2] 5920[11] 6167[12] 6495[9]

Sonny G (IRE) *John Best* a63 57
4 ch h Desert Sun—Broughton Zest (Colonel Collins (USA))
387[2] 432[10] 727[4] 810[5] 1184[5] 1633[7] 4322[13] 4544[12] 6847[11] 7768[13]

Sonny Red (IRE) *David Nicholls* 99
7 b g Redback—Magic Melody (Petong)
2075[18] 2434[4] 2717[14] 3083[5] 3832[7] 4016[2] 4291[8] 5083[12] 5732[10] 6076[5] 6414[4] 7065[4]

Son Of May *Jo Hughes* a49 48
2 b g Royal Applause—Second Of May (Lion Cavern (USA))
4365[10] 6110[9] 6334[11] 7242[12] 7742[3]

Son Of Sophie *Christopher Kellett* a32 41
9 b g Band On The Run—Fair Enchantress (Enchantment I)
3600[7] 4952[7] 5209[9]

Son Of The Cat (USA) *Brian Gubby* a101 106
5 b g Tale Of The Cat(USA) —Dixieland Gal (USA) (Dixieland Band (USA))
(1237) 1888[9] 2099[5] 2370[6] (4531) 5481[2] 5935[5] 6147[3] 6706[12]

Sonoran Sands (IRE) *Peter Chapple-Hyam* a92 92
3 b g Footstepsinthesand—Atishoo (IRE) (Revoque (IRE))
238[9] 502a[6] 680a[8] 753a[4] 988[4] 1234[4] 1547[5] 2003[5] 3521[4] 4103[3] (4962) 5483[8]

Sonsie Lass *Keith Dalgleish* a65 46
2 b f Refuse To Bend(IRE) —Rapsgate (IRE) (Mozart (IRE))
3314[9] 4377[6] 5017[5] 6178[6] 6975[2] 7143[6] (7252) (7421) 7541[6] 7686[3]

Son Vida (IRE) *Mark Johnston* a79
3 b c Titus Livius(FR) —Sombreffe (Polish Precedent (USA))
(121)

Soon (IRE) *A P O'Brien* 98
2 b f Galileo(IRE) —Classic Park (Robellino (USA))
4833a[6] 5525a[8] 5974a[5]

Soopacal (IRE) *Michael Herrington* a75 51
6 b g Captain Rio—Fiddes (IRE) (Alzao (USA))
125[5] (506) 794[4] 1048[7] 2632[8] 7355[7] 7504[2] 7646[2]

Sooraah *William Haggas* a104 103
4 b m Dubawi(IRE) —Al Persian (IRE) (Persian Bold)
1541[11] 1884[2] 3032[13] 3645[3] (4265) 4494[4] ◆ 5929[4] 6297[7] 7128[2]

Sophar *Jason Ward* a11 40
2 b g Sakhee(USA) —Blades Baby (Bertolini (USA))
2563[6] 2784[6] 3137[3] 3491[6] 4983[6]

Sophie's Beau (USA) *Michael Chapman* a41 65
4 b g Stormy Atlantic(USA) —Lady Buttercup (USA) (Meadowlake (USA))
14[9] 376[6] 1289[6] 2356[6] 2588[8] 4816[4] 5339[3] 6618[12] 7055[11] 7646[13]

Sopran Nad (ITY) *Frank Sheridan* a63 57
7 b h Masad(IRE) —Sopran Newar (Warning)
69[6] 2162[5] 4179[4] (4705) 4948[4] (5214) 5394[6] 5843[6] 7001[6] 7560[5] 7648[9]

Soprano (GER) *Jim Goldie* 67
9 b g Sendawar(IRE) —Spirit Lake (GER) (Surumu (GER))
3450[2] (4602) (4856) 5453[3] 6115[4] 7105[3]

Sopran Prince (IRE) *M Mercalli* 99
5 b h Desert Prince(IRE) —Foolish Heart (IRE) (Fools Holme (USA))
371a[0] 1918a[5]

Sory *Tina Jackson* 58
4 b g Sakhee(USA) —Rule Britannia (Night Shift (USA))
6781[6] 7078[5]

Sos Brillante (CHI) *Terry Clement* a80 81
6 b m Dance Brightly(CAN) —Strike Out (CHI) (Mashaallah (USA))
6088[6] 7171[10] 7298[5] 7438[5] ◆ 7516[11]

So Stylish (USA) *A P O'Brien* 84
3 b f Johannesburg(USA) —Tacha (USA) (Mr Prospector (USA))
5086a[14]

So Surreal (IRE) *Gary Moore* a70 67
4 b m Avonbridge—Secret Circle (Magic Ring (IRE))
78[7]

Sotka *Mme G Rarick* 95
2 b f Dutch Art—Demerger (USA) (Distant View (USA))
2866a[5]

Sottovoce *Simon Dow* a69 33
3 b f Oratorio(IRE) —In A Silent Way (IRE) (Desert Prince (IRE))
52[6] 600[2] 1481[8] 6401[7] 6813[13] 7890[7]

Soul Heaven *James McAuley* a76 77
4 b g Oratorio(IRE) —Pilgrim Spirit (USA) (Saint Ballado (CAN))
614[12] 814[9]

Sound Advice *Keith Dalgleish* 87
2 b c Echo Of Light—Flylowflylong (IRE) (Danetime (IRE))
(3123) 3861[8] 4311[4] 5234[3] 6077[3]

Sound Amigo (IRE) *Ollie Pears* a83 82
3 b g Iceman—Holly Hayes (IRE) (Alzao (USA))
(709) (1249) ◆ (2216) 2926[12] 4680[3] (5735) 6658[4]

Soundbyte *John Gallagher* a71 74
6 b g Beat All(USA) —Gloaming (Celtic Swing)
79[3] 392[4] 808[8] 1750[10] 3479[4] 3738[6] (4703) 5236[7] 5692[3] 6376[6] 7254[4] 7363[6]

Sounds Of Thunder *Gordon Elliott* a65 69
4 b m Tobougg(IRE) —Distant Music (Darshaan)
7570[11]

Sour Mash (IRE) *Ed Dunlop* 95
4 b g Danehill Dancer(IRE) —Landmark (USA) (Arch (USA))
2509[5] 4801[9] (6124)

Souslecieldeparis (USA) *Y Barberot* 62
2 gr f Pulpit(USA) —Si Je N'Avais Plus (IRE) (Kaldoun (FR))
(7666a) (7814a)

Souter Point (USA) *Tony Carroll* a72 82
5 bb g Giant's Causeway(USA) —Wires Crossed (USA) (Caller I.D. (USA))
3428[9] 4216[4] 4423[15]

South African Gold (USA) *James Eustace* a67 68
4 ch h Johannesburg(USA) —Coesse Gold (USA) (Seeking The Gold (USA))
97[7] 654[5] (4683) 5355[4] 6119[13] 6634[13]

South Cape *Gary Moore* a94 94
8 b g Cape Cross(IRE) —Aunt Ruby (USA) (Rubiano (USA))
1406[13] 2217[15] 3290[9] 3797[8] 4537[6] 4958[7] 5328[8] 5969[7]

Southern Breeze *Sylvester Kirk* a43
4 b g Dansili—Michelle Ma Belle (IRE) (Shareef Dancer (USA))
1933[15]

Southern Speed (AUS) *Leon Macdonald & Andrew Gluyas* 115
4 bb f Southern Image(USA) —Golden Eagle (NZ) (Zabeel (NZ))
(6886a)

South Kenter (USA) *Heather Main* a14
2 ch c Silver Deputy(CAN) —Crystal Downs (USA) (Alleged (USA))
5863[10]

Southwark Newshawk *Christine Dunnett* a51 32
4 ch m Piccolo—Be Bop Aloha (Most Welcome)
36[4] 256[10] 311[7] 482[7] 719[9]

Sovento (GER) *Shaun Harley* a68 65
7 ch g Kornado—Second Game (GER) (Second Set (IRE))
(7639) 7654[2]

Sovereign Debt (IRE) *Michael Bell* 87
2 br c Dark Angel(IRE) —Kelsey Rose (Most Welcome)
2510[7] (2953) (3842) 4334[4] 6527[11]

Sovereign Secure (IRE) *Peter McCreery* a64 65
4 ch m Kyllachy—Affaire Royale (IRE) (Royal Academy (USA))
7460[7]

Sovereign Spirit (IRE) *Chris Gordon* a33 30
9 b g Desert Prince(IRE) —Sheer Spirit (IRE) (Caerleon (USA))
8[8] 419[8]

Sovereign Street *Ann Duffield* 64
3 ch f Compton Place—Mint Royale (IRE) (Cadeaux Genereux)
2782[5] 3347[7]

Sovereignty (JPN) *Dean Ivory* a64 50
9 b g King's Best(USA) —Calando (USA) (Storm Cat (USA))
205[3] 361[6] 489[6]

Sovereign Waters *Eve Johnson Houghton* 52
2 ch f Haafhd—Faraway Waters (Pharly (FR))
2788[5] 3258[10] 3997[2] 5342[10]

Sovietica Zurda (FR) *K Borgel*
5 b m Montjeu(IRE) —Fruhling Feuer (FR) (Green Tune (USA))
259a[0]

Soviet Spring (IRE) *Andrew Balding* a65 66
3 b g Soviet Star(USA) —Spring Will Come (IRE) (Desert Prince (IRE))
77[2] 109[6]

Sowaylm *Saeed Bin Suroor* a85 95
4 b h Tobougg(IRE) —Ameerat (Mark Of Esteem (IRE))
2679[18] 3203[12]

Soweto Star (IRE) *John Best* a62 82
3 ch g Johannesburg(USA) —Lady Of Talent (USA) (Siphon (BRZ))
1141[5] (1446) 1843[9] 6477[9] 6727[13]

So Wise (USA) *Keith Dalgleish* a89 68
3 b g Elusive Quality(USA) —Intercontinental (Danehill (USA))
3001[12] 4542[3] 5030[5] 5402[2] (5740) 6877[5] (6978) (7178) 7558[10]

So You Think (NZ) *A P O'Brien* a119 129
5 b h High Chaparral(IRE) —Triassic (NZ) (Tights (USA))
(1781a) ◆ (2332a) 3031[2] (3646) (5747a) 6567a[4] 6861[2] 7308a[6]

Spacecraft (IRE) *Christopher Kellett* a55 44
4 b g Starcraft(NZ) —Brazilian Samba (IRE) (Sadler's Wells (USA))
16[8] 1190[7] 2569[8] 2900[10] 4183[5] 5214[2] 5601[3] 7247[5] 7714[6] (7775)

Space Raider (AUS) *B W Hills* 69
2 ch g Starcraft(NZ) —Lacandona (USA) (Septieme Ciel (USA))
2049[9] 2355[6] 3076[2]

Space Station *Simon Dow* a91 94
5 b g Anabaa(USA) —Spacecraft (USA) (Distant View (USA))
822[7] ◆ 1061[4] 1760[11] 2470[6] 2679[11] (3536) 4428[8] 5043[3] 5936[11] 6341[8]

Space War *Michael Easterby* a67 97
4 b g Elusive City(USA) —Princess Luna (GER) (Grand Lodge (USA))
1541[8] 1694[3] 2123[8] 2706[5] 3542[6] 3877[9] 4528[11] 5185[16] 5757[2] 6080[7] 6708[5] ◆ 6989[2]

Spade *Tim Pitt* a56 71
3 bl f Halling(USA) —Digger Girl (USA) (Black Minnaloushe (USA))
2018[9] 2850[4] 3259[4] 3979[3] 4275[10] 6748[7] 6939[11] 7427[4] 7836[5]

Spahi (FR) *David O'Meara* a60 64
5 b g Dubai Destination(USA) —Lusitanie (IRE) (Barathea (IRE))
1468[10] 2462[2] 3317[4] 3510[8] 4129[4] 4814[4] 4856[12] 5079[13] 5167[5] 5788[7] 7246[3] 7426[2] 7647[3] (7859)

Spamix (IRE) *F Brogi* 80
5 gr h Linamix(FR) —Spa (Sadler's Wells (USA))
439a[0]

Spanish Acclaim *Ruth Carr* a63 76
4 b g Acclamation—Spanish Gold (Vettori (IRE))
3784[9] 4239[3] 4742[10] 4960[9] 5262[9] 6266[10]

Spanish Bounty *Jonathan Portman* a87 91
6 b g Bahamian Bounty—Spanish Gold (Vettori (IRE))
(1444) 2099[18] 2789[3] 5339[5] 6467[16]

Spanish Duke (IRE) *John Dunlop* a83 110
4 b g Big Bad Bob(IRE) —Spanish Lady (IRE) (Bering)
(1479) ◆ 2290[8] 3107[14] 4410[13] ◆ 5544[6]

Spanish Fork (IRE) *Mick Channon* 70
2 br g Trans Island—Wings Awarded (Shareef Dancer (USA))
6165[8] 6481[5] 6726[6] 6812[8]

Spanish Plume *Reg Hollinshead* a81 80
3 b g Ishiguru(USA) —Miss Up N Go (Gorytus (USA))
3717[4] 3925[7] 4529[4] 4902[7] 5350[2] (5925) ◆ 6325[5] 6674[11] 6978[3] ◆ (7453)

Spanish Pride (IRE) *John Dunlop* 75
3 b f Night Shift(USA) —Spanish Lady (IRE) (Bering)
2883[5] 3676[6] 6457[4] ◆ 6748[8]

Spanish Wedding *Marco Botti* a72 72
2 ch c Hernando(FR) —I Do (Selkirk (USA))
3986[6] 4722[6] 7835[2]

Spares And Repairs *Reg Hollinshead* a37 51
8 b g Robellino(USA) —Lady Blackfoot (Prince Tenderfoot (USA))
346[11] 408[7] 507[10]

Sparking *David Barron* a63 69
4 ch m Exceed And Excel(AUS) —Twilight Time (Aragon)
113[3] 511[3] (892) 2164[3] 3027[7] 4017[7] (5436) 6213[6]

Sparkling Portrait *Richard Fahey* a80 75
2 b c Excellent Art—Time Crystal (IRE) (Sadler's Wells (USA))
7101[3] 7493[3] (7709)

Sparkling Power (IRE) *A T Millard* 118
4 gr h Acclamation—Fritta Mista (IRE) (Linamix (FR))
1576a[5]

Sparkling Smile (IRE) *David Lanigan* a99 93
4 bb m Cape Cross(IRE) —Starlight Smile (USA) (Green Dancer (USA))
1887[10] 2676[6]

Spartan King (IRE) *Ian Williams* a53 61
3 ch g King's Best(USA) —Thermopylae (Tenby)
3337[8] 4081[10] 4435[5] 4927[8] 7037[7] 7789[4] 7903[3]

Spartan Spirit (IRE) *Hughie Morrison* a54 56
3 b g Invincible Spirit(IRE) —Kylemore (IRE) (Sadler's Wells (USA))
1047[4] 1496[4] 1769[3]

Spartic *Alan McCabe* a75 69
3 gr g Needwood Blade—Celtic Spa (IRE) (Celtic Swing)
358[3] 764[6] 907[3] 4680[7] 5213[7]

Spartilla *James Given* a58
2 b c Teofilo(IRE) —Wunders Dream (IRE) (Averti (IRE))
7350[6] 7568[5] 7718[4] (7852)

Spa's Dancer (IRE) *J W Hills* a87 87
4 b g Danehill Dancer(IRE) —Spa (Sadler's Wells (USA))
1296[5] 2178[4] 2822[5] 2995[3] 3276[9] 4331[7] (4725) 5240[3] 6173[7] 6728[8] 6949[9]

Spate River *Jonjo O'Neill* a85 82
6 b g Zaha(CAN) —Rion River (IRE) (Taufan (USA))
3286[5]

Spavento (IRE) *Eric Alston* a61 69
5 gr m Verglas(IRE) —Lanasara (Generous (IRE))
1440[4] 1714[2] (2057) 2399[3] 2887[7] 2912[4] 3457[6] (3658) 4051[4] 4127[5] 4877[5] 5594[4] 5721[9] 6831[6] 7159[7]

Speakers Corner *Barney Curley* a10
5 b g Dalakhani(IRE) —Abbey Strand (USA) (Shadeed (USA))
762[7]

Speak The Truth (IRE) *Jim Boyle* a69 68
5 br g Statue Of Liberty(USA) —Brave Truth (IRE) (Brief Truce (USA))
80[5] 218[3] 351[3] 435[4] 521[4] 698[6] (1043) 1314[6] 1581[4] 4850[8] 5858[3] 6793[3] 7097[7] 7485[6] 7587[2] 7943[2]

Spechenka (AUS) *Ben Ahrens* 104
6 bb g Danachenka(AUS) —Special Class (NZ) (Conquistarose (USA))
6967a[7] 7310a[14]

Special Boy (IRE) *Saeed Bin Suroor* 58
2 b g Invincible Spirit(IRE) —Ezilla (IRE) (Darshaan)
1890[7] 2882[7] 5841[4]

Special Endeavour (IRE) *William Muir* a58 62
3 b g Sleeping Indian—Hollow Quaill (IRE) (Entrepreneur)
3268[15] 3945[4] 4654[7] 4846[2] 5380[5] 5512[5]

Specific (IRE) *Mahmood Al Zarooni* 69
2 b f Dubawi(IRE) —Miss Particular (IRE) (Sadler's Wells (USA))
4552[5] ◆ 5583[4] 6776[10]

Specific Gravity (FR) *Sir Henry Cecil* 104
3 b g Dansili—Colza (USA) (Alleged (USA))
1020[1] 1540[7] 3008[1] 4467[illegible] 5466[illegible]

Spectacle *Sir Michael Stoute* 64
3 gr f Dalakhani(IRE) —Soviet Moon (IRE) (Sadler's Wells (USA))
2065[4]

Spectacle Du Mars (FR) *X Nakkachdji* a86 108
4 b g Martillo(GER) —Spectacular Groove (USA) (Trempolino (USA))
4121a[8] 5985a[9] 6563a[9] 7221a[6]

Spectait *Jonjo O'Neill* a95 86
9 b g Spectrum(IRE) —Shanghai Girl (Distant Relative)
3436[9] 4070[5] 4616[6] 5240[4] 6124[7] 7628[12]

Speculante (FR) *M Massimi Jr* 82
3 ch f Panis(USA) —Spectacular Groove (USA) (Trempolino (USA))
1738a[14]

Speed Awareness *Mark Usher* a22
3 b g Avonbridge—Over The Limit (IRE) (Diktat)
126[9] 454[8]

Speed Dancer *James Eustace* 46
3 b g Norse Dancer(IRE) —Speed Of Sound (Zafonic (USA))
1572[7] 1991[6] 2648[16]

Speed Dating *John Quinn* a93 90
5 ch g Pivotal—Courting (Pursuit Of Love)
1154[7] 1387[8] 1826[9] 2475[P]

Speed Dream (IRE) *Daniel Mark Loughnane* a48 79
7 ch g Pivotal—Copper Creek (Habitat)
4378[7]

Speedfit Girl (IRE) *George Margarson* 75
3 b f Kodiac—Staylily (IRE) (Grand Lodge (USA))
1571[7]

Speed Gene (IRE) *Martin Bosley* a24 43
3 b f Mujadil(USA) —Tallahassee Spirit (THA) (Presidential (USA))
130[8]

Speedi Mouse *Philip McBride* 60
2 b f Alhaarth(IRE) —Meredith (Medicean)
(4391) 4761[2]

Speeding *J W Hills* 51
2 b c Selkirk(USA) —Zooming (IRE) (Indian Ridge)
2455[10]

Speed Oway *D Cros*
5 ch g Namid—Hushed (Cape Cross (IRE))
935a[0]

Speedyfix *Christine Dunnett* a71 50
4 b g Chineur(FR) —Zonnebeke (Orpen (USA))
5355[8]

Speedy Joe *Bryan Smart* a61
3 b c Tobougg(IRE) —Bonny Ruan (So Factual (USA))
20[4] 936[4] 1062[4]

Speedy Senorita (IRE) *James Moffatt* a45 66
6 b m Fayruz—Sinora Wood (IRE) (Shinko Forest (IRE))
2546[8] 3027[13] 4986[9] 5313[10]

Speedy Yaki (IRE) *Daniel Mark Loughnane* 46
2 b c Refuse To Bend(IRE) —Love In The Mist (USA) (Silver Hawk (USA))
2329a[10] 6406[8]

Speightowns Kid (USA) *Matthew Salaman* a78 67
3 rg g Speightstown(USA) —Seize The Wind (USA) (Maria's Mon (USA))
1589[4] 2265[4] (2603) 2818[2] ◆ 2881[3] 3389[5] 4583[7] 4988[2] 5419[8]

Speightscity (USA) *Gary Contessa* a102 80
2 ch r Speightstown(USA) —My American Girl (USA) (Quiet American (USA))
7306a[9]

Spellmaker *Tony Newcombe* a51
2 b c Kheleyf(USA) —Midnight Spell (Night Shift (USA))
7749[5]

Spensley (IRE) *James Fanshawe* a97 82
5 ch g Dr Fong(USA) —Genoa (Zafonic (USA))
1887[12] 2708[9] 3817[4] ◆ 5340[2] (5693) 7226[6] 7347[4]

Speranza (FR) *J-P Roman* a45 75
5 b m Daliapour(IRE) —Fiama Bella (FR) (Hero's Honor (USA))
259a[9] 439a[0]

Spes Nostra *David Barron* 77
3 b g Ad Valorem(USA) —Millagros (IRE) (Pennekamp (USA))
2361[8] (3111) 4141[9] 4550[14] 5621[5] 6263[4] 6674[14] 7215[9] (7901)

Spey Song (IRE) *James Bethell* a65 77
3 b f Singspiel(IRE) —All Embracing (IRE) (Night Shift (USA))
5877[4] 6263[11] 6756[4] 7458[8]

Sphinx (FR) *Edwin Tuer* a59 79
13 b g Snurge—Egyptale (Crystal Glitters (USA))
5759[12] 6115[2] (7162)

Spice Bar *Declan Carroll* a60 63
7 b g Barathea(IRE) —Scottish Spice (Selkirk (USA))
4703[2] ◆ (5595) 5790[2] 6780[4] 7631[4] 7850[10]

Spice Fair *Mark Usher* a92 86
4 ch g Trade Fair—Focosa (ITY) (In The Wings)
(1839) 2562[2] 2958[7] 3738[8] (4216) 4998[2] 5971[4] 6499[3] 6749[3] (7120)

Spice Run *Stef Higgins* a26 29
8 b g Zafonic(USA) —Palatial (Green Desert (USA))
1198[8]

Spic 'n Span *Ronald Harris* a71 59
6 b g Piccolo—Sally Slade (Dowsing (USA))
(116) 197[5] 453[8] 934[12] 1182[4] (1287) (1501) 1787[7] 3015[3] 3493[3] 3678[3] 4057[8] 4182[7] 4487[2] (4631) 4882[5] 5175[3] 5600[5] 5678[5] 6398[6]

Spidello (FR) *Mme E Siavy-Julien* a67 73
6 b g Vertical Speed(FR) —Star Of Russia (FR) (Soviet Star (USA))
219a[0]

Spidermania (FR) *Robert Collet* 81
2 ch c Gentlewave(IRE) —Sudden Storm Bird (USA) (Storm Bird (CAN))
7449a[0]

Spiders Of Spring (IRE) *Richard Fahey* a38 54
2 b g Redback—March Star (IRE) (Mac's Imp (USA))
(1435) 2121[4] 7491[9] 7657[6]

Spiders Star *Simon West* 72
8 br m Cayman Kai(IRE) —Kiss In The Dark (Starry Night (USA))
2496[6] (3072) ◆ 3507[5] 3754[3] 3935[4] 6095[7] 6915[10]

Spiekeroog *David O'Meara* a22 76
5 ch g Lomitas—Special (Polar Falcon (USA))
3828[4] 4348[6] 5035[5] 5685[6] ◆ 6707[8] 6988[13]

Spifer (IRE) *Luca Cumani* a84 98
3 gr c Motivator—Zarawa (IRE) (Kahyasi)
(2104) 3044[2] 3867[2] ◆ 5700[2]

Spin (IRE) *A P O'Brien* 100
3 ch f Galileo(IRE) —Pieds De Plume (FR) (Seattle Slew (USA))
2012a[2] 4589a[7] 5220[4] 5850[6] 6269[7]

Spin Again (IRE) *Mark Wellings* a77 69
6 b g Intikhab(USA) —Queen Of The May (IRE) (Nicolotte)
199[10] 336[7] (477) 637[2] 763[7] 915[2] 1221[4] 2016[10] 7416[10] 7625[12] 7819[12]

Spinatrix *Michael Dods* 87
3 b f Diktat—Shrink (Mind Games)
1672[2] 1941[5] 2986[7] (4110) ◆ (4146) 4518[2] 4880[2] (5442) 5554[3] 6189[2] 6913[11]

Spin A Wish *Richard Whitaker* a53 49
3 b f Captain Rio—Be My Wish (Be My Chief (USA))
1945[13] 2350[7] 2782[12] 3933[3] 4987[11] 6428[4] 6694[6] 7424[11]

Spin Cast *Walter Swinburn* a75 21
3 b g Marju(IRE) —Some Diva (Dr Fong (USA))
6505[3] 6980[4]

Spin Cycle (IRE) *S Seemar* a105 113
5 b h Exceed And Excel(AUS) —Spinamix (Spinning World (USA))
500a[7] 996a[11]

Spinning Bailiwick *Gary Moore* a83 75
5 b m Spinning World(USA) —Zietunzeen (IRE) (Zieten (USA))
128[8] (273) (487) 689[2] 792[3] 1054[4] 1330[6]

Spinning Ridge (IRE) *Ronald Harris* a75 76
6 ch g Spinning World(USA) —Summer Style (IRE) (Indian Ridge)
111[7] 317[4] 512[4] 674[13] (719) ◆ 906[5] (957) 1276[5] 1486[6] 1604[5] 1995[7] 3017[8] 3741[9] 3926[2] 4869[7] 5042[8] 5376[9] 5606[2] (5843) 6434[8] 6664[3] 7175[8] (7455) 7538[2] 7605[2] 7823[8]

Spinning Spirit (IRE) *Milton Bradley* a63 67
4 b g Invincible Spirit(IRE) —Vencera (FR) (Green Tune (USA))
1171[8] 1730[14] 3217[7]

Spinning Waters *Dai Burchell* a44 57
5 b g Vettori(IRE) —Secret Waters (Pharly (FR))
2140[4] (2377) (2873) 6476[10]

Spinning Wings (IRE) *T Hogan* 90
5 ch m Spinning World(USA) —Wings To Soar (USA) (Woodman (USA))
3420a[13] 7378a[14]

Spinning Yarn *A Renzoni* 93
4 b m Pivotal—Subtle Charm (Machiavellian (USA))
1432a[12]

Spirit Danon (IRE) *P Schiergen* 94
2 b c Whipper(USA) —Cheyenne Spirit (Indian Ridge)
5610a[5] 6901a[6]

Spirit Na Heireann (IRE) *Richard Fahey* 64
2 ch f Dubawi(IRE) —Lady Angharad (IRE) (Tenby)
4471[8] 5464[5] 6187[7]

Spirit Of Adjisa (IRE) *Tim Vaughan* a84 52
7 br g Invincible Spirit(IRE) —Adjisa (IRE) (Doyoun)
4423[18]

Spirit Of A Nation (IRE) *James Moffatt* a89 81
6 b g Invincible Spirit(IRE) —Fabulous Pet (Somethingfabulous (USA))
2414[4] 3164[5] 3399[7] (4082) 4348[12] 4879[8] 5440[2] 6151[10]

Spirit Of Coniston *Paul Midgley* a66 67
8 b g Lake Coniston(IRE) —Kigema (IRE) (Case Law)
453[6] 1034[3] 1213[2] (1464) 1796[6] 1856[10] 2247[3] 2667[7] 3451[5] 4636[5] 5009[9] (5373) 5600[2] 6386[5] 6802[2] 7079[8]

Spirit Of Cuba (IRE) *Kevin Prendergast* a77 92
3 b f Invincible Spirit(IRE) —Hecuba (Hector Protector (USA))
5090a[10]

Spirit Of Dixie *Noel Wilson* a58 46
4 ch m Kheleyf(USA) —Decatur (Deploy)
37[9] 167[11] 6848[10] 7065[8] 7211[6] 7351[8]

Spirit Of Gondree (IRE) *John Dunlop* 69
3 b c Invincible Spirit(IRE) —Kristal's Paradise (IRE) (Bluebird (USA))
5242[6] ◆ 5893[8] 6468[4]

Spirit Of Grace *Alan McCabe* a64 70
3 b f Invincible Spirit(IRE) —Scottish Heights (IRE) (Selkirk (USA))
110[2] 214[4] 529[3] 751[4] 1579[7] (1986) 2215[8] 2782[9] 3783[3] 4210[13]

Spirit Of Love (IRE) *Michael Wigham* a65
4 b g Pearl Of Love(IRE) —Sesleria (IRE) (Mark Of Esteem (IRE))
291[7] 504[10] 807[6] 896[5] 1233[2] 2385[6] 2600[10] 2828[10]

Spirit Of Music (FR) *D Considerant* 40
8 ch g Music Palace(GER) —Cabin Hunter (IRE) (Huntingdale (IRE))
7314a[10]

Spirit Of Oakdale (IRE) *Walter Swinburn* a65 67
3 b g Acclamation—Nichodoula (Doulab (USA))
558[3] 760[6] (1472) 2197[5] 2792[11] 3783[10] (5120) 5624[4] 6814[7]

Spirit Of Sharjah (IRE) *Julia Feilden* a111 105
6 b g Invincible Spirit(IRE) —Rathbawn Realm (Doulah (USA))
844[6] 1397[9] 1948[6] 2031[11] 2288[7] 2679[5] 3134[11] 7516[8] 7801[4]

Spirit Of The King (FR) *S-A Ghoumrassi* a63 56
5 b g Kingsalsa(USA) —Lavayssiere (FR) (Sicyos (USA))
220a[3] 479a[0] 566a[10] 706a[6]

Spirit Of The Law (IRE) *Ed Dunlop* a70 74
2 b c Lawman(FR) —Passion Bleue (In The Wings)
3282[7] 4068[9] 4864[9] (5342) (6053) 6345[2] ◆

Spirit Of Xaar (IRE) *David Marnane* a82 88
5 b g Xaar—Jet Cat (IRE) (Catrail (USA))
3445a[9] 5746a[13]

Spiritonthemount (USA) *Peter Hiatt* a57 54
6 bb g Pulpit(USA) —Stirling Bridge (USA) (Prized (USA))
838[7] 1032[4] 1297[5] 1473[6] 1794[6] (2140) 2377[7]

Spirit Quartz (IRE) *D Grilli* 105
3 b c Invincible Spirit(IRE) —Crystal Gaze (IRE) (Rainbow Quest (USA))
(1919a)

Spiritual Art *Luke Dace* a79 73
5 b m Invincible Spirit(IRE) —Oatey (Master Willie)
1838[7] 2204[5] 2824[4] 7057[15]

Spiritual Star (IRE) *Andrew Balding* 106
2 b c Soviet Star(USA) —Million Spirits (IRE) (Invincible Spirit (IRE))
2837[3] (6300) ◆ 6689[7]

Spirituoso (FR) *E Lellouche* 66
4 ch g Bering—Appassionata (FR) (Jeune Homme (USA))
1033a[0]

Spitfire *J R Jenkins* a73 92
6 b g Mujahid(USA) —Fresh Fruit Daily (Reprimand)
3179[9] 4064[6] 5371[8] 6022[3] 7341[3] ◆ 7502[4] 7744[4]

Splash Point (USA) *Mahmood Al Zarooni* a104 111
3 b c Street Cry(IRE) —Dianehill (IRE) (Danehill (USA))
238[2] (502a) 998a[10] 3029[5]

Splendido (FR) *F Rossi* 110
3 ro f Slickly(FR) —Allegrete (FR) (Johann Quatz (FR))
5695a[4] 7386a[5]

Splice (USA) *Jeremy Noseda* a56
3 b c Dixie Union(USA) —Tawaaded (IRE) (Nashwan (USA))
6473[8]

Split Second (IRE) *Mick Channon* 76
2 b f Moss Vale(IRE) —Twenty Questions (Kyllachy)
2374[6] 2919[2] 3165[5]

Split Trois (FR) *Y De Nicolay* 110
3 b f Dubawi(IRE) —Auenpearl (GER) (Zafonic (USA))
2138a[3] 2754a[12] 4121a[5] 4838a[9] 5532a[9] 7221a[0]

Spoken Words *Hugh McWilliams* 57
2 b f Fruits Of Love(USA) —Jerre Jo Glanville (USA) (Skywalker (USA))
2214[9] 2672[7] 3483[4] 4525[5] 4809[5] 5817[8] 6260[3]

Spoke To Carlo *Eve Johnson Houghton* 80
2 b c Halling(USA) —Red Shareef (Marju (IRE))
5133[3] ◆ 5565[3] 6126[3]

Spontaneity (IRE) *Bryan Smart* a57 51
3 b f Holy Roman Emperor(IRE) —Blue Iris (Petong)
518[2] 632[5] 741[2] 1306[4] 1561[4] 2265[11]

Spoof Master (IRE) *Jeff Pearce* a62 61
7 b g Invincible Spirit(IRE) —Talbiya (IRE) (Mujtahid (USA))
123[6]

Sports Casual *Mrs Y Dunleavy* a66 53
8 br m Singspiel(IRE) —Black Fighter (USA) (Secretariat (USA))
6511a[10] 7632[5]

Sports Section *Mahmood Al Zarooni* 79
2 b c Any Given Saturday(USA) —Headline (Machiavellian (USA))
3823[2] ◆ 4535[5] (Dead)

Sposalizio (IRE) *Colin Teague* 53
4 ch g Dr Fong(USA) —Wedding Cake (IRE) (Groom Dancer (USA))
7774[7]

Spread Boy (IRE) *Alan Berry* a41 64
4 b g Tagula(IRE) —Marinka (Pivotal)
171[9] 1795[5] 2415[6] 2692[9] 3902[7] 4039[3] 4383[5] 4601[12] 5208[7] 5312[4] 5589[4] 5823[6] 6050[9] 6417[3] 6833[7] 7158[3] 7781[7]

Spring Bouquet (IRE) *Mick Channon* a61 63
3 b f King's Best(USA) —Marasem (Cadeaux Genereux)
1060[8] 1299[9]

Spring Buck (IRE) *Paul Cole* a51 41
6 b g Acclamation—Torosay Spring (First Trump)
5212[12] 5633[6] 6090[8] 6411[11] 6610[9] 6746[11] 7229[12]

Spring Daisy (IRE) *Tom Dascombe* a51 39
2 b f Bertolini(USA) —Charlotti Carlotti (IRE) (Celtic Swing)
1451[5] 2640[6] 2907[8] 3948[4] 4178[3] 4808[8] 5418[3] 6178[7]

Spring Hawk (IRE) *T G McCourt* a69 69
5 ch m Hawk Wing(USA) —Spring Easy (IRE) (Alzao (USA))
7002[13]

Springheel Jake *Ann Duffield* a75 64
2 b g Lawman(FR) —Rye (IRE) (Charnwood Forest (IRE))
6532[4] 6836[3] 7052[4] (7337)

Springinmystep (IRE) *Michael Dods* 80
2 b c Footstepsinthesand—Joyful (IRE) (Green Desert (USA))
2542[2] ◆ 3014[8] ◆ (3610) 4334[5] 5286[6] 5701[5] 6670[8]

Spring Jim *James Fanshawe* a88 87
10 b g First Trump—Spring Sixpence (Dowsing (USA))
359[2] 2314[4]

Springleaf (IRE) *Richard Fahey* 43
2 ch f Redback—Bayleaf (Efisio)
1455[4] ◆ 1673[5]

Spring Leap *Robert Cowell* a50
4 b g Kyllachy—Roses Of Spring (Shareef Dancer (USA))
132[4] 537[10] 821[9]

Spring Of Fame (USA) *Saeed Bin Suroor* a111 96
5 b h Grand Slam(USA) —Bloomy (USA) (Polish Numbers (USA))
(240) 416a[2] 827a[3] 4095[8] 5544[8] 6088[5]

Spring Secret *Bryn Palling* a70 79
5 b g Reset(AUS) —Miss Brooks (Bishop Of Cashel)
742[2] 858[5] 3215[4] 5428[3] 5804[7] 6401[5] 6773[5] 7200[11] 7264[11]

Spring Stock *Brendan Powell* 61
4 b m Tobougg(IRE) —April Stock (Beveled (USA))
3003[11] 4273[9]

Springtime Melody (FR) *David Bourton* 52
3 ch g Black Sam Bellamy(IRE) —Poisson D'Avril (FR) (Nikos)
2104[6] 2551[8] 2813[9] 3268[17]

Sprint Car (FR) *J-P Delaporte* a64 65
7 b h Sleeping Car(FR) —Lady Yasmine (FR) (Quiludi (FR))
617a[0]

Spruzzo *Chris Fairhurst* a15 63
5 b g Emperor Fountain—Ryewater Dream (Touching Wood (USA))
1032[8] (1458) 1881[3] 2762[4] 3072[5] 4602[3] 5079[9] 5595[2] 6095[10] 6575[3] 6915[9]

Spume (IRE) *John Balding* a43 25
7 b g Alhaarth(IRE) —Sea Spray (IRE) (Royal Academy (USA))
800[12]

Spunky *Luca Cumani* a62 62
2 b c Invincible Spirit(IRE) —Passe Passe (USA) (Lear Fan (USA))
3917[6] 4384[7] 4710[5] 5634[2] 6443[2] 6806[2]

Spyder *Jane Chapple-Hyam* a40 79
3 b g Resplendent Glory(IRE) —Collect (Vettori (IRE))
2295[8] 2885[3] 3233[7] 3739[9] 4236[6] 5004[2] 5518[3] 6248[8] 7236[5]

Spying *Ann Duffield* a86 87
4 ch g Observatory(USA) —Mint Royale (IRE) (Cadeaux Genereux)
1410[9] 1747[9] (3190) 3576[6]

Spykes Bay (USA) *Mrs K Burke* a73
2 ch c Speightstown(USA) —She's A Rich Girl (USA) (Affirmed (USA))
(7000) ◆

Squad *Simon Dow* a73 65
5 ch g Choisir(AUS) —Widescreen (USA) (Distant View (USA))
79[4] 223[3] (418) 1107[15] 1761[6] 2473[5] 3003[6] 4613[4] 5198[7] 5612[4] 6476[2] 6798[4] 7441[3] (7564) 7674[3]

Square Of Gold (FR) *Milton Bradley* 37
5 ch g Gold Away(IRE) —All Square (FR) (Holst (USA))
7565[10]

Squires Gate (IRE) *Charles Hills* a69 79
3 b g Namid—Roselyn (Efisio)
2255[5] 3737[9] 4750[5] 5370[8] 6929[5]

Srimenanti *Brian Rothwell* 62
3 b f Diktat—Lady Netbetsports (IRE) (In The Wings)
3385[8] 4072[11] 4514[8] 5372[9] 5623[3] 6192[2] 6870[7] 7062[11] 7608[11]

Srinagar Girl *Sir Henry Cecil* a77
2 b f Shamardal(USA) —Adees Dancer (Danehill Dancer (IRE))
7124[2]

Sri Putra *Roger Varian* 118
5 b h Oasis Dream—Wendylina (IRE) (In The Wings)
1896[2] 3031[3] 3646[3] 6161[5] 6693[9] 6861[7]

Srucahan (IRE) *P D Deegan* a80 82
2 b g Kheleyf(USA) —Giveupyeraulsins (IRE) (Mark Of Esteem (IRE))
7012a[11] 7273a[10]

Ssafa *J W Hills* a66 76
3 b f Motivator—Orange Sunset (IRE) (Roanoke (USA))
1146[2] 2960[4] ◆ 3815[2] 4356[6] 5101[8]

Stabilized (FR) *P Bary* 101
3 b c Cacique(IRE) —Estabilizada (ARG) (Halo Sunshine (USA))
5230a[3]

Stacelita (FR) *Chad C Brown* 121
5 b m Monsun(GER) —Soignee (GER) (Dashing Blade)
3008a[3] (5073a) 7284a[10]

Stadium Of Light (IRE) *James Given* a76 71
4 b g Fantastic Light(USA) —Treble Seven (USA) (Fusaichi Pegasus (USA))
3[2] 190[5] 320[3] 549[3] 639[2] 808[2] 894[4] 4879[12] 5369[9] 5738[5]

Staff Sergeant *Jim Goldie* a76 87
4 b g Dubawi(IRE) —Miss Particular (IRE) (Sadler's Wells (USA))
2414[2] 2932[5] 3164[6] 3829[7] 4561[7] 5205[4] 5488[2] 6078[5] 6148[2] 6533[5]

Stage Attraction (IRE) *Andrew Balding* 90
3 b g Royal Applause—Mona Em (IRE) (Catrail (USA))
1565[6] 2568[3] (3218) (3987) ◆ 4313[10] 7168[14]

Stagecoach Danman (IRE) *Mark Johnston* a65 90
3 b g Montjeu(IRE) —Gothic Dream (IRE) (Nashwan (USA))
300[2] 471[4] 2458[3] 2874[2] ◆ (3206) 3580[3] 4251[6] 5078[6] 6333[16] 7022[10]

Stag Hill (IRE) *Sylvester Kirk* a61 42
2 ch g Redback—Counting Blessings (Compton Place)
2788[14] 3761[10] 6662[4] 7035[5] 7223[7] 7432[5] 7697[3] 7763[3] 7875[3]

Stags Leap (IRE) *Alistair Whillans* a85 82
4 b g Refuse To Bend(IRE) —Swingsky (IRE) (Indian Ridge)
3164[8] 3659[8] 4142[10] 4879[5] 5207[2] 5723[7] 6379[6]

Stalking Shadow (USA) *S Seemar* a86 83
6 b h Storm Cat(USA) —Strategic Maneuver (USA) (Cryptoclearance (USA))
535a[3]

Stamp Duty (IRE) *Suzzanne France* a60 70
3 b g Ad Valorem(USA) —Lothian Lass (IRE) (Daylami (IRE))
845[11] 1214[5] 2215[6] 2765[3] 3036[8] 3711[13] 4199[5] 4854[12] 6343[8] 7057[16] 7560[2] 7885[11]

Stand Beside Me (IRE) *Sylvester Kirk* a58
4 b g Footstepsinthesand—Alegranza (IRE) (Lake Coniston (IRE))
389[3] 593[4] 709[5]

Stand Guard *Noel Quinlan* a88 70
7 b g Danehill(USA) —Protectress (Hector Protector (USA))
170[3] 447[4] 647[8] (968) 1577[5] (2159) (4088) (4868) 5757[7] 6254[3] 6666[10] 7413[3]

Stand My Ground (IRE) *Mme Pia Brandt* a92 108
4 b g Cape Cross(IRE) —Perfect Hedge (Unfuwain (USA))
6783a[6]

Standout *Richard Hannon* a77 80
3 b c Oratorio(IRE) —Muwali (USA) (Kingmambo (USA))
931[2] 1189[2] 1951[7] 2253[3] 2664[3] 3233[3] 3650[11]

Standpoint *Reg Hollinshead* a89 87
5 b g Oasis Dream—Waki Music (USA) (Miswaki (USA))
405[6] 736[3] 1061[3] 1603[4] 2105[5] 2301[6] 2674[5] 3641[2] 4004[2] 4477[6] 5568[4] 6093[3] 6658[5] (7492) 7558[2] 7771[2]

Stand To Reason (IRE) *Mikael Magnusson* a83 87
3 ch c Danehill Dancer(IRE) —Ho Hi The Moon (IRE) (Be My Guest (USA))
2306[6] ◆ (2723) 3815[8] (4215)

Stanley Rigby *Richard Fahey* a78 55
5 b g Dr Fong(USA) —Crystal (IRE) (Danehill (USA))
(16) (117) (323) (496) (644) 858[3] 7272[10] 7713[6]

Stans Deelyte *Lisa Williamson* a55 53
2 ch f Primo Valentino(IRE) —Wot A Liberty (Piccolo)
1583[9] 1823[10] 2504[9] 3993[6] 4500[2] 5245[3] 5297[2] 6237[6]

Stansonnit *Alan Swinbank* a81 63
3 b g Shirocco(GER) —Twilight Sonnet (Exit To Nowhere (USA))
1113[7] 4108[8] 4439[4] 7776[8] 7887[8]

Stanwell *H Edward Haynes*
3 ch g Kier Park(IRE) —Magical Dancer (IRE) (Magical Wonder (USA))
7807[8]

Staraco (FR) *C Boutin* a79 86
7 ch h Loup Solitaire(USA) —Linorova (USA) (Trempolino (USA))
325a[10]

Star Addition *Eric Alston* a62 62
5 ch g Medicean—Star Cast (IRE) (In The Wings)
1099[20] 1394[7] 1615[3] 2348[4] 2815[3] 2851[3] 3545[5] 3629[6] 4128[3] 4902[8] 5860[5] 6264[10] 6659[F]

Star Alliance (IRE) *John Dunlop* 65
3 ch g Dalakhani(IRE) —Kalagold (IRE) (Magical Strike (USA))
1399[4] 1840[6] 2218[7] 2874[8]

Star Billing (USA) *John Shirreffs* 114
3 b f Dynaformer(USA) —Topliner (USA) (Thunder Gulch (USA))
6887a[6]

Starboard *John Gosden* 92
2 b c Zamindar(USA) —Summer Shower (Sadler's Wells (USA))
5697[6] (7209) ◆

Starbound (IRE) *William Haggas* a77 69
3 ch f Captain Rio—Glinting Desert (IRE) (Desert Prince (IRE))
2174[4] 3236[2] (3675) 4727[3] 5731[6] 6634[9]

Starbust (IRE) *Jim Best* 35
3 b c Elnadim(USA) —Common Bond (IRE) (Common Grounds)
1504[3]

Star City (IRE) *Michael Dods* 75
2 b g Elusive City(USA) —Teacher Preacher (IRE) (Taufan (USA))
3618[2] 4377[3] 5398[2] 6110[6]

Starclass *Walter Swinburn* a87 82
4 b m Starcraft(NZ) —Classic Millennium (Midyan (USA))
1279[6] 2428[3] 2822[2] 3285[7]

Star Commander *Mark H Tompkins* a80 80
3 b g Desert Style(IRE) —Barakat (Bustino)
1683[2] 1991[3] 3206[2] 3705[4] (5140) 5716[7]

Star Crowned (USA) *R Bouresly* a111 110
8 b h Kingmambo(USA) —Fashion Star (USA) (Chief's Crown (USA))
237[16] 582a[9] 678a[11]

Star Danser *Tom Keddy* a48
3 b c Dansili—Violette (Observatory (USA))
347[5] 693[4] (Dead)

Star Date (IRE) *Gerard Butler* 69
2 b g Galileo(IRE) —Play Misty For Me (IRE) (Danehill Dancer (IRE))
6772[4] ◆ 7101[7]

Stardust Dancer *Paul Green* a37 45
4 b g Ziggy's Dancer(USA) —Veni Vici (IRE) (Namaqualand (USA))
253[7] 634[8] 1615[14] 3732[9] 4128[8]

Star Dust Melody (FR) *N Caullery* 90
3 b f Chichicastenango(FR) —Dark Beauty (Singspiel (IRE))
4739a[0]

Star Empire (SAF) *M F De Kock* a99 110
5 b g Second Empire(IRE) —Lady Maroof (NZ) (Maroof (USA))
240[3] ◆ (413a) 584a[3] 677a[5]

Starfly (IRE) *Jeremy Noseda* 75
2 b f Invincible Spirit(IRE) —Mythologie (FR) (Bering)
1846[5] (2153) 2367[5]

Starformer (USA) *Mme C Head-Maarek* 105
3 b f Dynaformer(USA) —Etoile Montante (USA) (Miswaki (USA))
1709a[3]

Stargazing (IRE) *Marco Botti* a70 56
5 b m Galileo(IRE) —Autumnal (IRE) (Indian Ridge)
(346) (580) 711[2] 1052[5] 1222[2] 2176[7] 5391[2] 7178[6]

Stargazy *Alastair Lidderdale* a45 58
7 b g Observatory(USA) —Romantic Myth (Mind Games)
1283[6]

Star In Flight *Brian Meehan* a77 86
4 b g Mtoto—Star Entry (In The Wings)
3267[4] (3781) 4354[4] 5057[7] 5693[8] 6632[5]

Starkat *George Margarson* a80 96
5 b m Diktat—Star Of Normandie (USA) (Gulch (USA))
3356[10] 4801[10] 5281[5] 5518[4] 7296[12]

Stark Danon (FR) *W Hickst* 105
3 b c Marchand De Sable(USA) —Sue Generoos (IRE) (Spectrum (IRE))
2338a[4] 5532a[6] 7311a[4]

Star Kingdom (IRE) *Robert Mills* a51 65
2 b g Marju(IRE) —Appetina (Perugino (USA))
5111[5] 5384[13] 6127[5] 7597[8]

Starlight Walk *Roger Charlton* 83
3 b f Galileo(IRE) —Tempting Prospect (Shirley Heights)
1840[3] 2360[2] 3364[2] 3907[6]

Star Links (USA) *S Donohoe* a88 89
5 b g Bernstein(USA) —Startarette (USA) (Dixieland Band (USA))
(170) (405) 877[5] 5746a[9] 7189a[15] 7542[3]

Star Of Bombay (FR) *Richard Hannon* 57
2 b f Zamindar(USA) —Brilliantly (FR) (Priolo (USA))
4471[13] 5444[11]

Staros (IRE) *E Lellouche* 109
3 b c Aussie Rules(USA) —Stylish (Anshan)
1265a[4] 1965a[5] 3653a[7] 6185a[5] 6686a[4] 7313a[5]

Star Rebel *George Margarson* a49 56
3 b g Doyen(IRE) —Star Of Normandie (USA) (Gulch (USA))
2371[10] 2956[7] 6923[6] 7503[6]

Star Rover (IRE) *David Evans* a95 102
4 ch g Camacho—Charlene Lacy (IRE) (Pips Pride)
429[5] 613[2] 848[4] 989[8] 1186[8] 1675[2] 1888[12] 2075[12] 2525[8] 2954[4] 3379[6] 3850[2] 4346[6] 4573[3] (4644) 4894[4] 5264[3] 5430[9] 5508[8] 6347[5] 6723[3] 6987[16] 7127[13] 7489[7] 7628[10] 7847[7]

Starry Mount *Andrew Haynes* a57 76
4 ch g Observatory(USA) —Lady Lindsay (IRE) (Danehill Dancer (IRE))
163[8] 524[12]

Starscope *John Gosden* 87
2 ch f Selkirk(USA) —Moon Goddess (Rainbow Quest (USA))
(7164) ◆

Star Seed (FR) *J-C Rouget* 84
2 b f Layman(USA) —Nefouda (FR) (Neverneyev (USA))
4843a[4]

Starship Flare (USA) *Kristin Mulhall* 98
2 ch f Stevie Wonderboy(USA) —Go To The Ink (USA) (Crafty Prospector (USA))
7562a[2]

Stars In Your Eyes *John Gosden* a72
3 b f Galileo(IRE) —Apache Star (Arazi (USA))
7250[5] 7440[3]

Starstuded (IRE) *William Haggas* a61 52
3 b f Galileo(IRE) —Miss Demure (Shy Groom (USA))
6578[5] 7198[7]

Star Surprise *Michael Bell* a92 93
3 ch c Dubawi(IRE) —Dubai Surprise (IRE) (King's Best (USA))
1547[3] 2296[16] 2925[3] 3774[6] 4723[8]

Start Right *Luca Cumani* a76 108
4 b g Footstepsinthesand—Time Crystal (IRE) (Sadler's Wells (USA))
332a[4] 2679[3] ◆ 3032[6] 3645[2]

Star Twilight *Derek Shaw* a62 67
4 b m King's Best(USA) —Star Express (Sadler's Wells (USA))
3640[3] 3957[3] 4207[3] 4731[3] 4967[5] 6119[7] 6501[4] 6765[5] 7086[5]

Starwatch *John Bridger* a69 90
4 b g Observatory(USA) —Trinity Reef (Bustino)
134[6] 306[4] 625[10] 2179[8] 2879[5] 3468[4] 3741[4] (4322) (4546) (4860) (5200) 5495[3] (5969)

Star Witness (AUS) *Danny O'Brien* 122
4 ch c Starcraft(NZ) —Leone Chiara (AUS) (Lion Hunter (AUS))
[7] 3010[2] 3154[3] 3863[10]

State General (IRE) *Tony Carroll* a58 61
5 b g Statue Of Liberty(USA) —Nisibis (In The Wings)
34[6] 280[6] 819[13] 899[11] 969[9]

Stately Victor (USA) *Michael J Maker* a118 110
4 b h Ghostzapper(USA) —Collect The Cash (USA) (Dynaformer (USA))
7305a[5]

Statementofintent (IRE) *Brian Meehan* 30
2 b c Tagula(IRE) —Key Girl (IRE) (Key Of Luck (USA))
6019[10] 6663[U]

State Of Mind *Paul Cole* a72 79
3 b c Zamindar(USA) —Pulpeuse (IRE) (Pursuit Of Love)
1152[5]

State Of Play (USA) *H Graham Motion* 110
2 bb c War Front(USA) —Valeta (USA) (Procida (USA))
7301a[12]

State Opera *Mark Johnston* 89
3 b g Shamardal(USA) —Strings (Unfuwain (USA))
1339[14] 2100[6] 3551[4] 3828[16] 4777[9]

Stateos (IRE) *Sir Henry Cecil* a69 77
2 b c Acclamation—Mary Arnold (IRE) (Hernando (FR))
3182[6] 4205[4] 5142[5] (5541) 6345[4] 6623[9]

State Senator (USA) *Sir Mark Prescott Bt* a66 73
3 bb g Mr Greeley(USA) —Summer Night (Nashwan (USA))
6353[4] 6608[2] 6978[6]

Stature (IRE) *Andrew Balding* 71
2 b g Montjeu(IRE) —Pescia (IRE) (Darshaan)
5654[5] ◆ 6334[8]

Status (IRE) *M Guarnieri* a71
6 b g Pivotal—Hidalguia (IRE) (Barathea (IRE))
566a[3]

Status Symbol (IRE) *Anthony Carson* a105 98
6 ch g Polish Precedent(USA) —Desired (Rainbow Quest (USA))
2292[5] 3406[8] 3867[12] (5482) 6333[3] 7297[16] 7802[13]

St Augustine (IRE) *John Best* a93 89
3 b g Holy Roman Emperor(IRE) —Najiya (Nashwan (USA))
2255[2] (2878) ◆ 3820[5] 4472[11] (5146)

Stay Alive (IRE) *B Grizzetti* 105
3 br f Iffraaj—Pursuit Of Life (Pursuit Of Love)
(1738a)

Stay Cool (FR) *D Smaga* a63 70
5 b h One Cool Cat(USA) —A La Longue (GER) (Mtoto)
6959a[7]

Stay On Track (IRE) *Garry Woodward* a15 14
4 b g Refuse To Bend(IRE) —Blue Lightning (Machiavellian (USA))
5601[14] 6659[10] 7214[8]

Stay Thirsty (USA) *Todd Pletcher* a122
3 bb c Bernardini(USA) —Marozia (USA) (Storm Bird (CAN))
1921a[12] 2950a[2] 7308a[11]

St Barths *Brian Meehan* 105
2 b c Cadeaux Genereux—Ile Deserte (Green Desert (USA))
2049[4] (2355) ◆ 3012[3]

Steady Gaze *Richard Rowe* a61 52
6 b g Zamindar(USA) —Krisia (Kris)
(3353) 3600[9] 5993[4] (6476) 6876[6] 6998[7]

Steady The Buffs *Hugo Palmer* a60 68
2 b f Piccolo—Artistry (Night Shift (USA))
1337[7] 1785[3] (1932) 2154[7] 2902[5] 6178[4] 6786[4] 7051[5]

Steed *Tim Vaughan* a99 84
4 b g Mujahid(USA) —Crinkle (IRE) (Distant Relative)
(291) (446) (495) (572) 925a[14] 1240[6] 1410[16] 5006[8] 5272[8] 5516[8] 5920[12] 6231[10] 6759[11] (7057) 7127[3] 7516[6] 7719[6]

Steel City Boy (IRE) *Garry Woodward* a65 65
8 b g Bold Fact(USA) —Balgren (IRE) (Ballad Rock)
15[7] 98[11] 337[3] 464[2] 537[3] (691) 735[4] 812[5] 934[4] 1463[2] (1912) 2238[4] 2610[2] 3322[7] 3711[11] 3956[2] 4187[2] 4233[5] 5561[3] 6035[6] 6479[9] 6580[9] 6802[4] 6943[11] 7641[12] (7690) 7854[4]

Steelcut *David Evans* a78 83
7 b g Iron Mask(USA) —Apple Sauce (Prince Sabo)
443[4] (767) 880[4] 1204[11] (1471) 1752[5] (1955) (2280) 2938[12] 2959[5] 3427[2] 3784[4] 3869[6] 4644[6] 5616[12] 6056[5] 6502[10] 7116[3] 7596[9] (7897)

Steele Tango (USA) *Roger Teal* a78 113
6 ch h Okawango(USA) —Waltzing Around (IRE) (Ela-Mana-Mou)
(157a) 331a[2] 759a[6] (829a) 1342[4] 2292[3]

Steel Rain *Nikki Evans* a48 63
3 b g Striking Ambition—Concentration (IRE) (Mind Games)
88[5] 189[6] (2549) (5965)

Steel Stockholder *Mel Brittain* a74 71
5 b g Mark Of Esteem(IRE) —Pompey Blue (Abou Zouz (USA))
5728[9] 5760[7] ◆ 6231[11] 6777[13]

Steely *Jim Best* a63 27
3 b g Librettist(USA) —No Comebacks (Last Tycoon)
2924[9] 3392[3] 5140[F] 5816[11] 6255[9] 6756[10]

Stef And Stelio *David Pipe* a71 45
4 ch g Bertolini(USA) —Cashmere (Barathea (IRE))
387[9] 3515[12]

Stefanki (IRE) *George Baker* a89 84
4 b g Danehill Dancer(IRE) —Ghana (IRE) (Lahib (USA))
651[5] 822[2] 2206[5] 2789[2] 4415[RR]

Stella Marris *Christopher Wilson* 45
4 br m Danroad(AUS) —Riyoom (USA) (Vaguely Noble)
1559[9] 2781[7] 3756[8] 4288[12] 5443[7] 6839[6]

Stella Point (IRE) *Mick Channon* 96
3 b f Pivotal—Venturi (Danehill Dancer (IRE))
1363[3] ◆ 2050[4] 2840[2] (3385) 4015[4] 5695a[6]

Stellar Express (IRE) *Michael Appleby* a65 80
2 b f Royal Applause—Aitch (IRE) (Alhaarth (IRE))
2767[6] 3117[3] 3584[2] (4571) 4867[4] 5876[7] 6489[3] (6806) 6986[13] 7167[5]

Stellarina (IRE) *William Knight* a42 54
5 b m Night Shift(USA) —Accelerating (USA) (Lear Fan (USA))
488[7] 719[8]

Stencive *William Haggas* 80
2 b c Dansili—Madeira Mist (IRE) (Grand Lodge (USA))
6994[3]

Stentorian (IRE) *Mark Johnston* 96
3 ch c Street Cry(IRE) —Nomistakeaboutit (CAN) (Affirmed (USA))
1234[8] 2108[5] 3405[12] 4103[7] 4489[3] 5893[7] 6409[2] 6601[6] 7139[4]

Step And Fetch (IRE) *Ann Duffield* a63
3 b f Redback—Alexander Icequeen (IRE) (Soviet Star (USA))
751[3] 1084[6]

Stephanie's Kitten (USA) *Wayne Catalano* a111 111
2 b f Kitten's Joy(USA) —Unfold The Rose (USA) (Catienus (USA))
(7281a)

Stepharlie *Bryan Smart* a59 51
2 ch f Dutch Art—Lady Agnes (Singspiel (IRE))
5618[5] 6075[6] 6654[4] 6912[12] 7251[6] 7444[9]

Stephen's Green (USA) *James M Ryan* a87 94
4 ch g North Light(IRE) —Grand Natalie Rose (USA) (Grand Slam (USA))
1705a[2] 5090a[8]

Step It Up (IRE) *Jim Boyle* a83 77
7 ch g Daggers Drawn(USA) —Leitrim Lodge (IRE) (Classic Music (USA))
133[6] 337[6] 522[9] 658[6] 766[6] 812[9]

Stepper Point *William Muir* 105
2 b c Kyllachy—Sacre Coeur (Compton Place)
1360[11] ◆ 2455[6] 2992[2] 3610[5] 4212[5] (4955) ◆ (5562) (7155a)

Steps (IRE) *Roger Varian* a84 97
3 br c Verglas(IRE) —Killinallan (Vettori (IRE))
1825[12] (2564) (3181) ◆ 3820[13] 6332[15] 6723[16] (7018)

Stepturn *Sir Michael Stoute* 52
2 b g Invincible Spirit(IRE) —Gay Gallanta (USA) (Woodman (USA))
3686[9] 5017[3]

Stern Dancer (FR) *F Foresi* 56
5 b h Sternkoenig(IRE) —Trance Dancer (Mtoto)
439a[0]

Stetson *Alan Swinbank* a53 63
5 b g Groom Dancer(USA) —Mindomica (Dominion)
836[3] 1542[6]

Stevie Gee (IRE) *Ian Williams* a80 82
7 b g Invincible Spirit(IRE) —Margaree Mary (CAN) (Seeking The Gold (USA))
820[5] 1017[4] 1267[2] 1562[3] 2095[9] 2369[2] 2557[5] 3179[10] 3322[2] 4369[12] 5578[5] (6133) 6920[7] 7412[3] 7636[6] 7658[2] 7776[2] 7876[8] (7919)

Stevie Thunder *Ian Williams* a81 99
6 ch g Storming Home—Social Storm (USA) (Future Storm (USA))
4004[9] (4506) (5557) 6339[2] ◆ 6955[3]

Stickleback *Harry Dunlop* a44 35
2 ch f Manduro(GER) —The Stick (Singspiel (IRE))
5672[5] 6117[11] 7343[12]

St Ignatius *Michael Appleby* a58 58
4 b g Ishiguru(USA) —Branston Berry (IRE) (Mukaddamah (USA))
362[11] 445[4] 575[2] 662[10] 800[2] 854[3] 906[7] 1307[7] (1357) 2171[6] 2233[3] 2655[2] 3019[5] 3496[4] 3942[10] 4651[5] 7714[4] 7899[4]

Stilettoesinthemud (IRE) *James Given* a51 63
3 ch f Footstepsinthesand—The Stick (Singspiel (IRE))
1795^{3} 2252^{4} 2498^{2} 3207^{6} 3621^{6} 3977^{4} 4638^{7} (5649) 5864^{8} 6456^{6} 6604^{8} 6847^{7}

Still I'm A Star (IRE) *Ed Dunlop* 67
2 b f Lawman(FR) —Aminata (Glenstal (USA))
6933^{7}

Stillington *Mel Brittain* 50
5 ch h Exit To Nowhere(USA) —First Harmony (First Trump)
5792^{6} 6096^{7} 6349^{9}

Still Point (IRE) *Noel Meade* 83
4 b g Invincible Spirit(IRE) —Galletina (IRE) (Persian Heights)
3440a^{21}

Stipulate *Sir Henry Cecil* 94
2 b c Dansili—Indication (Sadler's Wells (USA))
(4815) 5709^{4} 6914^{3}

Stirling Bridge *William Jarvis* a79 59
3 b g Kyllachy—Seine Bleue (FR) (Grand Lodge (USA))
(44) 302^{3} 2216^{11} 3521^{7}

Stirling Grove (AUS) *Richard Jolly* 113
4 b g Mossman(AUS) —Kalamata (AUS) (Desert Prince (IRE))
9029a^{6}

St Moritz (IRE) *David Nicholls* a95 112
5 b g Medicean—Statua (IRE) (Statoblest)
(1201) (1385) 1600^{2} (2031) 2713^{2} 4368^{2}

St Nicholas Abbey (IRE) *A P O'Brien* 124
4 b h Montjeu(IRE) —Leaping Water (Sure Blade (USA))
1119a^{3} (1851) (2680) 4315^{3} 5986a^{3} 6567a^{5} (7305a)

Stolt (IRE) *Linda Stubbs* a84 93
7 b g Tagula(IRE) —Cabcharge Princess (IRE) (Rambo Dancer (CAN))
15^{5}

Stoneacre Gareth (IRE) *K F Clutterbuck* a70 62
7 b g Grand Lodge(USA) —Tidal Reach (USA) (Kris S (USA))
(662) ◆ (752) 810^{4} 1995^{8}

Stoneacre Joe Joe *Peter Grayson* a31
3 b g Proclamation(IRE) —It's So Easy (Shaadi (USA))
246^{6} 380^{10} 518^{8} 892^{6} 5941^{9} 7693^{7} 7829^{9}

Stoneacre Wigan *Peter Grayson* a20
2 b c Byron—Milliegait (Tobougg (IRE))
5863^{12} 7194^{8}

Stonecrabstomorrow (IRE) *Michael Attwater* a67 70
8 b g Fasliyev(USA) —Tordasia (IRE) (Dr Devious (IRE))
821^{5} 874^{6} 1497^{5} 2382^{7} 2426^{5} 2756^{5} (3015) (3255) 3482^{3} 3765^{7} 3940^{5} 4740^{4} 4960^{3} 5138^{6} (5426) (5858) 6246^{5} 6814^{3} 6931^{9} 7097^{4}

Stonefield Flyer *Keith Dalgleish* 100
2 b c Kheleyf(USA) —Majestic Diva (IRE) (Royal Applause)
1071^{2} 1489^{2} (1797) 3014^{2} ◆ (4001) 4413^{7} 6518^{4}

Stonehaugh (IRE) *Howard Johnson* 74
8 b g King Charlemagne(USA) —Canary Bird (IRE) (Catrail (USA))
1438^{10} 2732^{7}

Stone Of Folca *John Best* 102
3 b g Kodiac—Soyalang (FR) (Alydeed (CAN))
(1504) 2297^{9} 3010^{16} 4468^{10} 4739a^{10} 5543^{9} 5805^{5}

Stoppers (IRE) *Robert Mills* a61 43
4 gr g Verglas(IRE) —Sharadja (IRE) (Doyoun)
313^{4} 556^{5} 802^{9} 968^{8} 7658^{7}

Stopshoppingmaria (USA) *Todd Pletcher* a105 109
2 bb f More Than Ready(USA) —Skybox (USA) (Spend A Buck (USA))
7281a^{2}

Storm Bell (USA) *Mahmood Al Zarooni* a57 59
2 bb c More Than Ready(USA) —Mari's Thunder (USA) (Thunder Gulch (USA))
2844^{5} 3282^{4} 4507^{6} 4907^{4}

Storm Blue (IRE) *Ollie Pears* 41
3 b g Bluegrass Cat(USA) —Simadartha (USA) (Gone West (USA))
2361^{7}

Storm Breaker (IRE) *J J Lambe* a53 54
9 b g Sadler's Wells(USA) —Well Bought (IRE) (Auction Ring (USA))
5167^{8}

Stormbringer (MOR) *P Bary* a79 82
3 b c Layman(USA) —Lemon Queen (USA) (Lemon Drop Kid (USA))
5463a^{0}

Stormburst (IRE) *Adrian Chamberlain* a51 40
7 b m Mujadil(USA) —Isca (Caerleon (USA))
230^{4} 363^{10}

Storm Fairy *Mrs K Burke* 51
2 b f Auction House(USA) —Proud Titania (IRE) (Fairy King (USA))
1434^{9} 3584^{3} 4171^{7} 4749^{7} 6021^{6} 7196^{9}

Storm Hawk (IRE) *Pat Eddery* a78 67
4 b g Hawk Wing(USA) —Stormy Larissa (IRE) (Royal Applause)
(911) 1148^{9} (1586) 1956^{2} 2312^{5} 3095^{7} 3738^{4} 4348^{11} 5102^{7} 5389^{9} 5947^{5} 6306^{10} 6503^{5} 7564^{9} (7858) (7914)

Storming Bernard (USA) *Alan Bailey* a92 96
2 bb g Stormy Atlantic(USA) —Anguilla (USA) (Seattle Slew (USA))
3917^{4} 4330^{2} 4571^{3} 5254^{2} 5478^{2} (5668) (6077) 6270^{7} 6788^{5} (7483)

Storming Honor (SPA) *L A Urbano-Grajales* a92 82
3 b f Storming Home—Leventina (IRE) (Anabaa (USA))
7509a^{8}

Stormin Gordon (IRE) *Michael Appleby* 21
2 b f Tagula(IRE) —Karashino (IRE) (Shinko Forest (IRE))
1455^{6} 1981^{7}

Storming Redd *James Eustace* a32 59
4 gr g Storming Home—Bogus Mix (IRE) (Linamix (FR))
5520^{6} 5993^{7}

Storming Spirit *B Goudot* a75 78
7 b g In The Wings—Aptostar (USA) (Fappiano (USA))
219a^{6}

Storm King *George Margarson* 62
2 b c Shamardal(USA) —Tarandot (IRE) (Singspiel (IRE))
6771^{9} 7082^{9}

Storm Runner (IRE) *George Margarson* a61 58
3 b g Rakti—Saibhreas (IRE) (Last Tycoon)
1655^{2} 3133^{8} 3558^{5} 4244^{11} 4699^{5} 4829^{10} 7084^{3} 7246^{10} 7524^{5} (7581) (7655) (7890)

Storm Tide *Rae Guest* a72 63
3 b f Tobougg(IRE) —Tide Of Love (Pursuit Of Love)
437^{4} 693^{3} (729) 1611^{8} 1986^{8}

Storm Ultralight (ARG) *Mahmood Al Zarooni* a112 79
5 b h Bernstein(USA) —Ultrasexy (ARG) (Equalize (USA))
156a^{14}

Stormy Morning *Pat Eddery* a71 69
5 ch g Nayef(USA) —Sokoa (USA) (Peintre Celebre (USA))
1282^{2} 1839^{5} 1914^{3} 2873^{8} 3725^{5} 4396^{9} 5916^{3} 6240^{4} 6870^{2} 7032^{3}

Stormy Whatever (FR) *James Given* 74
2 gr c Stormy River(FR) —Evening Serenade (IRE) (Night Shift (USA))
3505^{3} (4192) ◆ 4984^{6} 6154^{7} 6645^{3} 7238a^{4} 7326a^{4}

St Oswald *David O'Meara* a71 67
3 b g Royal Applause—Susun Kelapa (USA) (St Jovite (USA))
1753^{3} 2197^{6} 4854^{7} 5439^{2} 5731^{4} 6234^{3} 6777^{4} 7419^{2} (7648) 7782^{2}

Straboe (USA) *Stuart Williams* a74 65
5 b g Green Desert(USA) —Staff Nurse (USA) (Arch (USA))
165^{8} 298^{10} 443^{2} (511) (696) 833^{2} (934) 1856^{7} 3015^{6} 4475^{3} 4895^{11} (5173) 5658^{6} (6580)

Strada Facendo (USA) *Luca Cumani* 74
2 ch c Street Cry(IRE) —What A Treasure (IRE) (Cadeaux Genereux)
3823^{5} ◆ 4815^{7} 6983^{3}

Stradivinsky (USA) *Richard Dutrow Jr* a80 111
8 b g Stravinsky(USA) —Lubicon (CAN) (Apalachee (USA))
996a^{13}

Strait Of Zanzibar (USA) *K J Condon* 104
2 b g Arch(USA) —Royal Opportunity (USA) (Kingmambo (USA))
4257a^{4} 5293a^{6} 5951a^{6} 7026^{6}

Strandfield Lady (IRE) *H Rogers* a81 92
6 ch m Pairumani Star(IRE) —Stylish Chic (IRE) (Arazi (USA))
5748a^{13} (7378a) 7549a^{6}

Strategic Action (IRE) *Linda Jewell* a51
2 ch c Strategic Prince—Ruby Cairo (IRE) (Nashwan (USA))
6919^{9} 7431^{9} 7672^{9}

Strategic Bid *David Simcock* a50 70
3 b c Selkirk(USA) —Eminencia (Sadler's Wells (USA))
1409^{5} ◆ 3824^{11} 7401^{5}

Strategic Game (IRE) *S Botti* 102
2 b c Choisir(AUS) —Minodora (IRE) (Marju (IRE))
3212a^{3}

Strategic Mount *Paul Cole* a63 93
8 b g Montjeu(IRE) —Danlu (USA) (Danzig (USA))
3867^{13} 5281^{6}

Strategic Mover (USA) *Paddy Butler* a61 77
6 ch g Grand Slam(USA) —Efficient Frontier (USA) (Mt. Livermore (USA))
211^{7} 363^{12}

Stratford Hill (USA) *Todd Pletcher* 115
4 ch h A.P. Indy(USA) —Harmony Lodge (USA) (Hennessy (USA))
(9100a)

Strathnaver *Ed Dunlop* a74 67
2 b f Oasis Dream—River Belle (Lahib (USA))
6603^{5} ◆ 7124^{4} (7598)

Stratton Banker (IRE) *Stuart Williams* a87 75
4 b g One Cool Cat(USA) —Birthday (IRE) (Singspiel (IRE))
(125) 2118^{15} 5108^{10} 6815^{2}

Straversjoy *Reg Hollinshead* a72 66
4 b m Kayf Tara—Stravsea (Handsome Sailor)
67^{4} (369) 515^{4} 715^{5} 1855^{9} 2259^{4} 2530^{5} 2912^{2} 3811^{6} 4649^{5} 5249^{5} 7789^{2} 7903^{4}

Stravsambition *Reg Hollinshead* a61 50
3 b f Striking Ambition—Stravsea (Handsome Sailor)
1084^{3} 1589^{8} 1853^{9} 2163^{3} 2993^{11} 4067^{6} 4647^{11} 5344^{9}

Strawberrydaiquiri *Brian Meehan* 117
5 gr m Dansili—Strawberry Morn (CAN) (Travelling Victor (CAN))
607a^{5} 1000a^{7} 5277^{7} 6338^{3} 6909a^{10}

Street Angel (IRE) *Alan Bailey* a61 45
2 b f Kodiac—Perfectionist (In The Wings)
2580^{10} 2914^{8} 3472^{8} 4277^{8} 6424^{4} 7125^{7} 7444^{8} 7490^{5}

Street Cred (IRE) *Paul Burgoyne*
3 gr f Kheleyf(USA) —Kamadara (IRE) (Kahyasi)
1578^{6} 1790^{6}

Street Crime *Ron Hodges* a52 65
6 b g Tagula(IRE) —Brandon Princess (Waajib)
526^{10} 749^{11} 761^{2} 957^{12} 1184^{3} 1273^{10} 1497^{6}

Street Devil (USA) *Jo Hughes* a76 41
6 gr g Street Cry(IRE) —Math (USA) (Devil's Bag (USA))
2401^{10} 2413^{7} 4649^{11}

Street Lair (USA) *J-C Rouget* a90 96
4 ch g Street Cry(IRE) —Hideaway Heroine (IRE) (Hernando (FR))
195a^{6} 661a^{0}

Street Legal *Alan McCabe* a76 60
6 b g Alhaarth(IRE) —Musician (Shirley Heights)
3456^{13} 3951^{8} 4237^{8}

Street Power (USA) *Jeremy Gask* a96 87
6 bb g Street Cry(IRE) —Javana (USA) (Sandpit (BRZ))
385^{5} 956^{3} 1610^{12}

Street Secret (USA) *Roger Varian* a77 86
3 b f Street Cry(IRE) —Always Awesome (USA) (Awesome Again (CAN))
1873^{8} (2639) (3538) ◆ 5020^{2} 5716^{5} 6631^{8}

Streets Of War (USA) *Geoffrey Harker* a78 68
4 bb g Street Cry(IRE) —Saint Boom (USA) (Saint Ballado (CAN))
1243^{14} 2388^{14}

Street Talk *A bin Huzaim* a67 49
7 b h Machiavellian(USA) —Helen Street (Troy)
536a^{6}

Street Warrior (IRE) *James Evans* a26 55
8 b g Royal Applause—Anne Bonny (Ajdal (USA))
2608^{6} 3281^{10}

Strength And Stay (IRE) *Eve Johnson Houghton* 63
3 b g Motivator—Queen's Cape (King's Best (USA))
1407^{14} 3080^{7} 3989^{3} 4449^{8} 5477^{4}

Strewth (IRE) *John Best* a76 67
3 ch c Encosta De Lago(AUS) —Alpine Park (IRE) (Barathea (IRE))
520^{3} ◆ 1139^{7} 1409^{11} 2253^{8} (3518) 4316^{9} 6584^{6} 7120^{11}

Strictly Mine *Jonathan Portman* 54
2 ch f Piccolo—My Dancer (IRE) (Alhaarth (IRE))
2309^{15} 3258^{8} 5672^{3} 6760^{7}

Strictly Pink (IRE) *Alan Bailey* a78 83
3 b f Kodiac—Church Mice (IRE) (Petardia)
(600) 845^{4} (1152) 1319^{11} 2298^{8} 2763^{7} 2908^{4} 3114^{3} 3598^{7} 3853^{4} 4062^{9} 5354^{4} 5862^{7} 6081^{14} 7024^{7} 7348^{6} 7519^{8}

Strictly Private *Brian Meehan* 52
2 ch c Rahy(USA) —Al Theraab (USA) (Roberto (USA))
6951^{10}

Strictly Rhythm *Mme G Rarick* a82 82
3 b f Hawk Wing(USA) —Esteemed Lady (IRE) (Mark Of Esteem (IRE))
901a^{2}

Strictly Silver (IRE) *Alan Bailey* a75 86
2 gr c Dalakhani(IRE) —Miss Chaussini (IRE) (Rossini (USA))
5254^{11} 5565^{2} 5688^{4} (6110) (7021)

Strident Force *Sir Michael Stoute* 78
2 b g Refuse To Bend(IRE) —Takawiri (IRE) (Danehill (USA))
4264^{5} 5668^{2} 6334^{3}

Striding Edge (IRE) *Hans Adielsson* a74 81
5 bb g Rock Of Gibraltar(IRE) —For Criquette (IRE) (Barathea (IRE))
1198^{6} 1868^{4} 2207^{3} 2567^{3} 2923^{3} 3256^{5} 3546^{9} 5101^{11} 5318^{5} 5608^{6} 7851^{4} 7930^{4}

Strike Action *David Wachman* 70
2 b f Pivotal—Princess Manila (CAN) (Manila (USA))
6389a^{9}

Strike A Deal (IRE) *Chris Wall* 74
4 b m Chineur(FR) —Bishop's Lake (Lake Coniston (IRE))
1569^{4} 2548^{6} 3952^{11} 4927^{3} 5515^{5} 6610^{3}

Strike Force *Clifford Lines* a79 77
7 b g Dansili—Miswaki Belle (USA) (Miswaki (USA))
124^{7} 1222^{4} 1621^{7} (2308) 2473^{2} 3244^{2} 3456^{11} 4444^{14} 6507^{7} 6669^{2} 7032^{6} 7397^{8} 7577^{4} 7601^{5} 7761^{2} 7817^{4} ◆ 7901^{3}

Strike Impact (USA) *Patrick J Dupuy* a95 109
7 b g Smart Strike(CAN) —Foret Noire (USA) (Time For A Change (USA))
9100a^{5}

Strikemaster (IRE) *Lee James* a48 71
5 b g Xaar—Mas A Fuera (IRE) (Alzao (USA))
3072^{3} 3450^{3} 3754^{4} 4326^{5} 4814^{6} 5595^{3} (6600) (7105) 7415^{6}

Striker Torres (IRE) *Geoffrey Oldroyd* a76 78
5 ch g Danehill Dancer(IRE) —Silver Skates (IRE) (Slip Anchor)
149^{3} 285^{2} 446^{6} 736^{5} 869^{4} 1222^{6} 2213^{8} (3071) 3612^{5} 3936^{11} 4670^{8} 5404^{5} 5488^{7} 6616^{5} 7176^{2}

Strike Up The Band *David Nicholls* a52 94
8 b g Cyrano De Bergerac—Green Supreme (Primo Dominie)
2118^{2} 2397^{7} 2714^{16} 4174^{2} (4791) 5180^{18} 5543^{7} 6332^{8} 6703^{14}

Striking Eyes *Roger Charlton* a46
3 b f Striking Ambition—Tullochrome (Foxhound (USA))
126^{6} 263^{7}

Striking Priorite *Tim Fitzgerald* a69
3 b g Striking Ambition—Priorite (IRE) (Kenmare (FR))
6133^{10} 6453^{14} 7098^{11}

Striking Spirit *Tim Easterby* 105
6 b g Oasis Dream—Aspiring Diva (USA) (Distant View (USA))
1366^{12} ◆ 1518^{5} 1888^{5} 2727^{15} 3109^{3} ◆ 3862^{12} 4314^{14} ◆ 5060^{10} 5758^{14} 6341^{4} 6862^{12}

Striking The Wind (USA) *Mark Johnston* a72 76
3 bb c Mr Greeley(USA) —Cherokee (USA) (Storm Cat (USA))
454^{2} 873^{3} 1328^{2} 1496^{5} 2802^{2} 3304^{2}

Striking Veil (USA) *Sir Michael Stoute* 52
3 b f Smart Strike(CAN) —Yashmak (USA) (Danzig (USA))
2019^{6}

Striking Willow *Rod Millman* a42 11
3 b g Striking Ambition—Willows World (Agnes World (USA))
721^{6} 7755^{9} 7829^{4}

Strobe *Lucy Normile* a76 53
7 ch g Fantastic Light(USA) —Sadaka (USA) (Kingmambo (USA))
4382^{8} 5790^{16}

Stromboli (CZE) *Cestmir Olehla*
3 b f Enjoy Plan(USA) —Sweet Answer (Peintre Celebre (USA))
(4874a)

Stronger (FR) *N Clement* 73
2 bl f Early March—Ballade Viennoise (FR) (Cricket Ball (USA))
7814a^{9}

Strong Knight *Tim Walford* a63 56
4 ch g Observatory(USA) —Erudite (Generous (IRE))
1390^{11} 1746^{8} 3024^{8} 4077^{6} 4716^{6} 5106^{16} 5402^{4} 5823^{5} 7078^{2} 7357^{4}

Strong Man *Michael Easterby* a63 71
3 b g Gentleman's Deal(IRE) —Strong Hand (First Trump)
4923^{3} ◆ 5368^{2} ◆ 6156^{2} 6417^{5} 6869^{3}

Strong Suit (USA) *Richard Hannon* 126
3 ch c Rahy(USA) —Helwa (USA) (Silver Hawk (USA))
1405^{6} (3029) 3670a^{3} (4412) (6687) ◆ 7307a^{10}

Strong Vigilance (IRE) *Michael Bell* a81 79
4 ch g Mr Greeley(USA) —Zabadani (Zafonic (USA))
352^{4} (635) (1066) 1826^{11} 3641^{9} 5608^{11} 7465^{11} 7601^{13}

Strophic *Giles Bravery* a69 3
4 b g Singspiel(IRE) —Katina (USA) (Danzig (USA))
634^{4} 806^{3}

Strut In Style (IRE) *W McCreery* a23 61
3 b f Rakti—Seadas (USA) (Maria's Mon (USA))
7263^{11}

Stubbs Art (IRE) *A Al Raihe* a85 78
6 ch g Hawk Wing(USA) —Rich Dancer (Halling (USA))
707a^{10}

Stunning In Purple (IRE) *Andrew Haynes* a62 68
3 b f Kheleyf(USA) —Thank One's Stars (Alzao (USA))
1359^{4} 1776^{8}

Stunning View (IRE) *D K Weld* 104
4 ch h Shamardal(USA) —Sabaah (USA) (Nureyev (USA))
2533a^{8} 3032^{11} (4418a) 5361a^{6}

Sturmwolke (IRE) *M Figge* 43
2 b f Big Shuffle(USA) —Sylvette (USA) (Silver Hawk (USA))
7326a^{7}

Style And Panache (IRE) *David Evans* a74 82
3 b f Trans Island—El Corazon (IRE) (Mujadil (USA))
1391^{12} 2074^{12} 2158^{2} 2611^{9} (2770) 2959^{8} 3687^{7} 4048^{8} 5115^{6} 5627^{5} 5831^{14} 6537^{3} 6752^{11} 6801^{5} (7106)

Style De Lois (FR) *M Boutin* 86
4 gr g Blackdoun(FR) —Ziama (FR) (Jeune Homme (USA))
1033a^{2}

Style D'Or (FR) *Robert Collet* a59 59
3 gr g Smadoun(FR) —Valorys (FR) (Valanour (IRE))
660a^{4}

Style Majic (USA) *Michael F Brassil* a32 45
3 bb f Mizzen Mast(USA) —Wezzo (USA) (Bering)
6139a^{3}

Style Margi (IRE) *Ed de Giles* a71 42
3 b f Desert Style(IRE) —Margi (FR) (General Holme (USA))
3630^{8} 4973^{13} 5387^{5} 5995^{7} 6617^{9}

Style Show (USA) *Mme C Head-Maarek* 74
3 b f Red Ransom(USA) —Style Setter (USA) (Manila (USA))
1597a^{6}

Styleyf *David Brown*
2 b f Kheleyf(USA) —In Some Style (IRE) (Grand Lodge (USA))
2574^{6} 3075^{15} 4647^{12}

Stylistickhill (IRE) *David Nicholls* a66 54
3 gr f Desert Style(IRE) —Anemone (Arkadian Hero (USA))
2650^{4} 3246^{4} 4282^{8} 6618^{4} 7071^{5} (7198) 7537^{3} 7632^{2}

Sublim Star (FR) *Mlle M Henry*
4 b m Subliminal(FR) —Garden Star (FR) (Dr Devious (IRE))
5095a^{0}

Submariner (USA) *A bin Huzaim* a102 98
5 ch g Singspiel(IRE) —Neptune's Bride (USA) (Bering)
535a^{4}

Submission *Luca Cumani* a78 95
3 b f Beat Hollow—Idealistic (IRE) (Unfuwain (USA))
1837^{4} ◆ (2615) (3757) 4790^{7} 5702^{6}

Subramaniam *James Given* a57 65
3 ch g Medicean—Blithe (Pivotal)
1312^{6} 1526^{3} 1972^{8} 2239^{9} 3976^{8} 4236^{3} 4560^{10} 6845^{8}

Subtle Embrace (IRE) *Harry Dunlop* a40 64
2 b f Acclamation—Subtle Affair (IRE) (Barathea (IRE))
3981^{9} 4269^{4} (4947) 5840^{10}

Subtle Knife *Giles Bravery* a66 10
2 ch f Needwood Blade—Northern Bows (Bertolini (USA))
6612^{2} 7135^{12}

Suddenly Susan (IRE) *David Nicholls* a73 65
3 b f Acclamation—Westerly Gale (USA) (Gone West (USA))
1155^{5} 1624^{7} 2119^{11} 2650^{3} 2845^{12} 3489^{7} (4647) 5215^{5} 5824^{11} 6615^{3} 7079^{3} 7419^{5} 7567^{3} (7641) 7744^{9}

Sudden Wish (IRE) *Jim Best* a42 29
2 b f Jeremy(USA) —Fun Time (Fraam)
3463^{7} 3780^{10} 4848^{6}

Sud Pacifique (IRE) *Jeremy Noseda* 106
3 b g Montjeu(IRE) —Anestasia (IRE) (Anabaa (USA))
(1096) (2008) 3069^{6} 4058^{3} (5466)

Sue's Dream *Alan Jarvis* 13
3 ch f Monsieur Bond(IRE) —Sonneteer (IRE) (Victory Note (USA))
1334^{6}

Suffolini *William Stone* a38 27
3 b f Bertolini(USA) —Hotel California (IRE) (Last Tycoon)
5626^{7} 6034^{7} 6475^{6} 7333^{13} 7892^{9}

Suffolk Punch (IRE) *Andrew Balding* a85 87
4 ch g Barathea(IRE) —Lamanka Lass (USA) (Woodman (USA))
2111^{3} 2937^{2} 3339^{2} 4310^{13} 4574^{7}

Sugar Apple *James Given* 53
3 b f Tiger Hill(IRE) —Spring (Sadler's Wells (USA))
3138^{8} 3705^{5}

Sugar Beet *Ronald Harris* a92 87
3 b f Beat Hollow—Satin Bell (Midyan (USA))
364^{3} 740^{3} 847^{9} 1062^{2} (1521) 2505^{9} 3269^{6} 3785^{7} 3994^{4} 5378^{2} 5542^{5} (5939) 6917^{16} (7487) 7586^{7} (7832)

Sugarformyhoney (IRE) *Richard Hannon* a85 76
2 ch f Dutch Art—Sweetsformysweet (USA) (Forest Wildcat (USA))
4384^{5} (5097) 5698^{4}

Sugar Hiccup (IRE) *Clive Cox* 78
3 b f Refuse To Bend(IRE) —Raysiza (IRE) (Alzao (USA))
1950^{7} 2885^{7} 4056^{2} 4971^{2} (5350) 6130^{2}

Sugar Loaf *William Muir* a63 28
2 b f Singspiel(IRE) —Annapurna (IRE) (Brief Truce (USA))
5048^{6} 7125^{5} 7343^{8}

Sugarpine (IRE) *Richard Fahey* 61
2 b f Oratorio(IRE) —Maria Luisa (IRE) (King's Best (USA))
5269^{7} 5819^{4} 6110^{10} 6807^{5}

Sughera (IRE) *A J Martin* a51 56
4 b m Alhaarth(IRE) —Gold Bar (IRE) (Barathea (IRE))
7631^{3}

Suhailah *Michael Attwater* a58 32
5 ch m Sulamani(IRE) —Vrennan (Suave Dancer (USA))
207^{4} 278^{3} 524^{9} (592) 728^{8} 1025^{4} 1135^{7} 4242^{7} 5141^{7} 6621^{4} 6926^{9} 7206^{2}

Suhaili *Roger Varian* 93
3 b g Shirocco(GER) —Mezzogiorno (Unfuwain (USA))
1407^{7} (2458) ◆ 5710^{9} (7022)

Suhayl Star (IRE) *Paul Burgoyne* a45 64
7 b g Trans Island—Miss Odlum (IRE) (Mtoto)
166^{9} 210^{7} 2161^{11} 7760^{5} 7923^{4}

Suited And Booted (IRE) *Jane Chapple-Hyam* a94 100
4 ch h Tagula(IRE) —Carpet Lady (IRE) (Night Shift (USA))
1406^{23} 1529^{13} 2927^{11} 3290^{8} 3982^{3} 4415^{16} 4993^{4} 5483^{14} 6219^{6}

Suits Me *David Barron* a106 104
8 ch g Bertolini(USA) —Fancier Bit (Lion Cavern (USA))
271^{3} 542^{3} (702) 846^{11} 991^{4} 1410^{2} 2002^{4} 2390^{6} (3203) 4058^{2} 4267^{10} 6277^{2} 7391^{3} 7802^{5}

Sujet Bellagio *Brian Meehan* a78
2 b g Acclamation—Markova's Dance (Mark Of Esteem (IRE))
7559^{3} 7751^{4} 7889^{2}

Sukhothai (USA) *James Fanshawe* a64 54
3 rg f Maria's Mon(USA) —Succession (Groom Dancer (USA))
1312^{3} 1574^{6} 2166^{2} 2722^{2} 3393^{4}

Sula Two *Ron Hodges* a71 79
4 b m Sulamani(IRE) —There's Two (IRE) (Ashkalani (IRE))
1367^{8} 1729^{9} 4613^{5} 5050^{4} 5389^{3} 6405^{8}

Sulis Minerva (IRE) *Jeremy Gask* a61 73
4 b m Arakan(USA) —Lacinia (Groom Dancer (USA))
3756^{7} (4461) 4886^{6} 5890^{12} 6436^{7} 7804^{8} 7895^{6} (7942)

Sulle Orme (FR) *C Ferland* a108 105
3 gr g Chichicastenango(FR) —Santa Lady (FR) (Double Bed (FR))
$6783a^{4}$ $7678a^{3}$

Sulliman *George Margarson* a52 52
4 b g Sulamani(IRE) —Norcroft Joy (Rock Hopper)
2956^{9} 3469^{5} 4396^{4} 4732^{7}

Sultana Belle (IRE) *Lee Smyth* 39
3 b f Black Sam Bellamy(IRE) —Sultana (GER) (Law Society (USA))
6430^{7} 7159^{4}

Sumani (FR) *Simon Dow* a48 66
5 b g Della Francesca(USA) —Sumatra (IRE) (Mukaddamah (USA))
6121^{7} 7346^{10}

Sumaro (GER) *W Hickst* a91 82
4 b h Big Shuffle(USA) —Sarir (GER) (Platini (GER))
$6594a^{8}$ $6958a^{4}$

Sumay Buoy (IRE) *Jean McGregor* 41
4 b g Fasliyev(USA) —Mourir D'Aimer (USA) (Trempolino (USA))
1716^{6} 2263^{7} 2546^{5} 2632^{13}

Sumbe (USA) *Michael Wigham* a69 62
5 bb g Giant's Causeway(USA) —Sumoto (Mtoto)
1221^{8} 1656^{4} 2111^{7} 3235^{7} 4066^{7} 4828^{9} 6938^{7} 7848^{8}

Summathisnthat *Des Donovan* a55 62
2 b f Auction House(USA) —Summertime Parkes (Silver Patriarch (IRE))
1396^{3} 1765^{5} 2173^{5} 2467^{10}

Summer Affair (IRE) *Ben Case* a57 31
6 b g Alhaarth(IRE) —Late Summer (USA) (Gone West (USA))
3047^{4} 3923^{8} 4274^{12}

Summerandlightning (IRE) *Mark Usher* a55 45
5 gr m Great Palm(USA) —Young Love (FR) (Jeune Homme (USA))
791^{6} 952^{9} 2689^{7} 3311^{13}

Summer Dancer (IRE) *Paul Midgley* a76 86
7 br g Fasliyev(USA) —Summer Style (IRE) (Indian Ridge)
1382^{3} 1695^{9} 1942^{5} 2938^{9} 3071^{7} 3704^{6} 4310^{14} 5717^{3} 5948^{6} 6231^{5} 6381^{6} 6980^{3} 7176^{8}

Summer Games *R Bouresly* a92 78
6 b m Storming Home—Shawanni (Shareef Dancer (USA))
241^{8}

Summer Glow (IRE) *John Joseph Murphy* a61 52
3 ch f Exceed And Excel(AUS) —In The Ribbons (In The Wings)
(7091)

Summerinthecity (IRE) *Ed de Giles* a77 98
4 ch g Indian Ridge—Miss Assertive (Zafonic (USA))
2099^{13} 5852^{15} 6331^{10} (6974) 7295^{20} 7489^{6}

Summer Lane (IRE) *Richard Fahey* a48 55
2 b f Chevalier(IRE) —Greta D'Argent (IRE) (Great Commotion (USA))
3932^{4} ◆ 4358^{4} 4864^{6} 5817^{5}

Summerlea (IRE) *Patrick Holmes* a65 69
5 ch g Alhaarth(IRE) —Verbania (IRE) (In The Wings)
2666^{2}

Summer Soiree (USA) *H Graham Motion* a114 114
3 b f War Front(USA) —Mazel Tov (USA) (Mazel Trick (USA))
$6887a^{5}$

Sum Of The Parts (USA) *Thomas Amoss* a91
2 bb c Speightstown(USA) —Enjoy The Moment (USA) (Slew's Royalty (USA))
$7280a^{6}$

Sum Satisfaction *Dominic Ffrench Davis* a59 63
3 ch g Araafa(IRE) —Dina Line (USA) (Diesis)
1271^{7} 1819^{6} 2225^{7} 2874^{6} 3268^{3} 3922^{3} 4491^{6}

Sunayana (IRE) *R Mongil* a77 81
3 b f Shamardal(USA) —Shangri La (IRE) (Sadler's Wells (USA))
$5307a^{12}$

Sunblest *Lisa Williamson*
5 b m Medicean—Invincible (Slip Anchor)
850^{11}

Sunburnt *E J O'Neill* 80
2 b f Haafhd—Singed (Zamindar (USA))
$3567a^{4}$

Sun Central (IRE) *William Haggas* 59
2 ch c Galileo(IRE) —Bordighera (USA) (Alysheba (USA))
7083^{7} ◆

Sunday Bess (JPN) *Tom Dascombe* a81 80
3 b f Deep Impact(JPN) —Lhiz (CHI) (Hussonet (USA))
1364^{4} 1807^{7} 2219^{2} 3065^{12} 4014^{2} 4971^{3} 6136^{2} 6633^{3}

Sunday Nectar (IRE) *X Thomas-Demeaulte* a86 103
3 b f Footstepsinthesand—Pop Alliance (IRE) (Entrepreneur)
$2752a^{4}$ $5028a^{0}$

Sunday Times *Peter Chapple-Hyam* 110
2 b f Holy Roman Emperor(IRE) —Forever Times (So Factual (USA))
4427^{4} (4954) ◆ 5217^{7} 6337^{2} ◆ 6691^{5}

Sun Disc (IRE) *D T Hughes* a62 71
4 b m Noverre(USA) —Jungle Jewel (IRE) (Mull Of Kintyre (USA))
$7549a^{9}$

Sundream (GER) *A Wohler* 97
3 b c Lomitas—Salista (GER) (Heraldiste (USA))
$3007a^{8}$ $5308a^{6}$

Sunley Pride *Mick Channon* 76
2 ch c Three Valleys(USA) —Sunley Scent (Wolfhound (USA))
6244^{4} 6529^{2} 7258^{5}

Sunley Surprise *David Elsworth* a26
3 b g Domedriver(IRE) —Sunley Scent (Wolfhound (USA))
5201^{2} 817^{8}

Sunley Valentine *Mick Channon* a63 63
2 b f Kyllachy—Sunley Gift (Cadeaux Genereux)
4087^{3} 4471^{9} 5174^{5} 5690^{3} 5817^{3} 6002^{4} 6284^{P} (Dead)

Sunnandaeg *Jeremy Gask* 80
4 ch g Haafhd—Come Away With Me (IRE) (Machiavellian (USA))
2369^{12}

Sunny Bank *Andrew Balding* 37
2 b c Notnowcato—Sweet Mandolin (Soviet Star (USA))
7258^{8}

Sunnybridge Boy (IRE) *Richard Fahey* 82
2 br g Strategic Prince—Reem One (IRE) (Rainbow Quest (USA))
3382^{2}

Sunny Future (IRE) *Malcolm Saunders* a26 78
5 b g Masterful(USA) —Be Magic (Persian Bold)
1450^{5} 2224^{2} 3428^{5} 3725^{2} 4341^{9} 4974^{6} 6749^{9}

Sunny Game *Michael Bell* 100
4 b g Montjeu(IRE) —Sundrenched (IRE) (Desert King (IRE))
(1477)

Sunny King (IRE) *J Moore* a118 118
8 b g Desert Sun—Princess Mood (GER) (Muhtarram (USA))
$999a^{3}$ $1576a^{9}$

Sunnyside Tom (IRE) *Richard Fahey* a84 92
7 b g Danetime(IRE) —So Kind (Kind Of Hush)
1747^{5} 2300^{2} 3276^{11} 3620^{4} 4361^{2} 4603^{4} (5502) 6006^{2}

Sunny Side Up (IRE) *Richard Fahey* a66 59
2 b f Refuse To Bend(IRE) —Feeling Wonderful (IRE) (Fruits Of Love (USA))
2761^{3} 4073^{3} 4347^{6} 4943^{6} (7592) 7881^{2} ◆

Sunny Spells *Stuart Williams* a70 64
6 b g Zamindar(USA) —Bright Spells (Salse (USA))
838^{2} 1153^{15} 1291^{5}

Sun Of Jamaica *Mario Hofer* 92
2 b f Cape Cross(IRE) —Juno Marlowe (IRE) (Danehill (USA))
$4372a^{6}$ $5610a^{3}$ $6904a^{5}$

Sunpass *John Gosden* 59
2 ch c Pivotal—Tebee (Selkirk (USA))
7232^{7}

Sun Queen (USA) *A P O'Brien* a81 79
3 ch f Storm Cat(USA) —Fountain Of Peace (USA) (Kris S (USA))
$2861a^{11}$

Sunraider (IRE) *B W Hills* 101
4 b g Namid—Doctrine (Barathea (IRE))
1885^{20} 2706^{15}

Sunrise Dance *Alan Jarvis* a72 79
2 ch f Monsieur Bond(IRE) —Wachiwi (IRE) (Namid)
2254^{4} 2718^{3} 3878^{4} 4427^{6} 5184^{2} 6323^{6} 6620^{2} 7445^{4} 7765^{4}

Sunrise Lyric (IRE) *Paul Cole* a64 68
4 b m Rock Of Gibraltar(IRE) —Dawn Air (USA) (Diesis)
128^{9} 1604^{9} 1905^{9} 2155^{6} 2789^{9} 3293^{9} 4246^{4}

Sunrise Safari (IRE) *Richard Fahey* a73 89
8 b g Mozart(IRE) —Lady Scarlett (Woodman (USA))
1878^{6} 2434^{6} 3071^{2} 4013^{2} 4574^{6} 5162^{5} 5760^{3} 6113^{18} 6920^{5} 7171^{9} 7299^{11}

Sunset Beauty (IRE) *J S Bolger* a89 86
4 b m Whipper(USA) —Gaisce (IRE) (Bluebird (USA))
(7010a) $7277a^{8}$ $7793a^{9}$

Sunset Boulevard (IRE) *Paddy Butler* a63 52
8 b g Montjeu(IRE) —Lucy In The Sky (IRE) (Lycius (USA))
164^{3} 299^{2} 553^{3} 1508^{4} 2759^{6} (3176) 3480^{10} 4869^{6} 5042^{5} 5815^{8} 6926^{6} ◆ 7206^{11} 7441^{9} 7891^{6}

Sunset Cafe (AUS) *Leon Corstens* 99
5 ch g Bianconi(USA) —Cafe Del Mar (AUS) (Encosta De Lago (AUS))
$7115a^{7}$

Sunset Kitty (USA) *Mike Murphy* a88 90
4 bb m Gone West(USA) —Honorable Cat (USA) (Honor Grades (USA))
865^{4} 1147^{2} 1330^{3} (2207) (2674) 3180^{3} 3840^{9} 7841^{3} ◆

Sunset Place *Jonathan Geake* a68 71
4 ch g Compton Place—Manhattan Sunset (USA) (El Gran Senor (USA))
317^{8} 762^{2} 954^{2} 1025^{2} 1509^{4} (1631) 1839^{6} 2312^{3}

Sunshine Always (IRE) *Michael Attwater* a78 76
5 gr g Verglas(IRE) —Easy Sunshine (IRE) (Sadler's Wells (USA))
685^{4} 949^{2} 1198^{2} 1610^{10} 2207^{8} 3172^{6} 4210^{4} 4243^{4} 5053^{15} 5201^{7} 5511^{3} 5858^{5} 5970^{3}

Sunshine Buddy *Rod Millman* a45 56
4 b m Reel Buddy(USA) —Bullion (Sabrehill (USA))
6698^{12} 6947^{5} 7466^{9}

Sunshine Lemon (USA) *A Lyakhov* 37
7 b h Lemon Drop Kid(USA) —Awesome Strike (USA) (Theatrical)
$6595a^{7}$

Suntil Bere (FR) *P Monfort* 71
5 b h Until Sundown(USA) —Caroldean (USA) (Dixieland Band (USA))
$439a^{4}$

Suntracer (USA) *Chris Block* 103
3 ch c Kitten's Joy(USA) —Taxable Deduction (USA) (Prized (USA))
$5072a^{8}$

Suntrap *William Knight* a78 62
4 ch g Desert Sun—Regal Gallery (IRE) (Royal Academy (USA))
54^{4} 475^{10} 697^{5} 813^{5}

Sunwise (USA) *William Haggas* a84 93
5 b g Arch(USA) —Turning Wheel (USA) (Seeking The Gold (USA))
2314^{2} 3013^{8} 3794^{9} 6499^{10}

Suomi *James Fanshawe* a63 33
3 b g Librettist(USA) —Mycenae (Inchinor)
1580^{4} 2568^{9}

Supaheart *Hughie Morrison* 61
2 b f Lion Heart(USA) —Supamova (USA) (Seattle Slew (USA))
6745^{9} 7030^{6}

Supa Seeker (USA) *Tony Carroll* a63 82
5 bb g Petionville(USA) —Supamova (USA) (Seattle Slew (USA))
2150^{6} 2996^{4} 4154^{5} 4755^{4} 5606^{6} 6135^{6} 6486^{6}

Supastarqueen (USA) *Brian Baugh*
3 bb f El Corredor(USA) —Supamova (USA) (Seattle Slew (USA))
7739^{5}

Supatov (USA) *Hughie Morrison* a55 48
4 bb m Johannesburg(USA) —Supamova (USA) (Seattle Slew (USA))
354^{6} 7731^{2}

Supercharged (IRE) *G M Lyons* a77 83
3 b f Iffraaj—Glympse (IRE) (Spectrum (IRE))
3949^{2} (4863) 5419^{4} 6177^{5} 6665^{5} $7792a^{11}$

Superciliary *Ralph Beckett* a71 19
2 b g Dansili—Supereva (IRE) (Sadler's Wells (USA))
6993^{12} 7520^{5}

Super Collider *Michael Jarvis* a68 79
4 b g Montjeu(IRE) —Astorg (USA) (Lear Fan (USA))
(136)

Superduper *Mrs A Malzard* a46 88
6 b m Erhaab(USA) —I'm Magic (First Trump)
$1805a^{2}$ $5778a^{2}$

Super Duplex *Pat Phelan* a70 71
4 b g Footstepsinthesand—Penelope Tree (IRE) (Desert Prince (IRE))
1530^{5} 2436^{3} 2649^{12} 3685^{4} 4457^{2} 5200^{6} 6376^{4} 6592^{7} 7228^{7} 7587^{8}

Super Du Wal (FR) *S Jesus* 59
2 b c Subotica(FR) —Walzer Koenigin (FR) (Prince Mab (FR))
$7312a^{3}$

Super Espresso (USA) *Todd Pletcher* a112 18
4 bb m Medaglia D'Oro(USA) —Amizette (USA) (Forty Niner (USA))
$7285a^{7}$

Super Frank (IRE) *Zoe Davison* a70 65
8 b g Cape Cross(IRE) —Lady Joshua (IRE) (Royal Academy (USA))
143^{3} 357^{3} 556^{6} 904^{6} 5387^{11} 6090^{10} 6444^{11} 7224^{7} 7524^{8} 7676^{11} 7760^{2} 7943^{6}

Superinjunction *Brian Meehan* a55 58
2 ch f Van Nistelrooy(USA) —Wait It Out (USA) (Swain (IRE))
3362^{8} 3736^{6} 4155^{14} 6053^{12} 6753^{9} 6972^{13}

Superior Edge *Christopher Mason* a53 80
4 b m Exceed And Excel(AUS) —Beveled Edge (Beveled (USA))
2903^{9} 4707^{8} 5616^{13} 6408^{7} 6436^{6} 6895^{13}

Superius (IRE) *Emma Lavelle* a57 99
6 b g High Chaparral(IRE) —Zing Ping (IRE) (Thatching)
656^{3} 813^{7}

Superplex *John Quinn* a59 72
2 b c Multiplex—Hillside Girl (IRE) (Tagula (IRE))
1619^{5} 1744^{2} 1966^{5} 2665^{2} 3050^{2} 3505^{5} 4500^{3} 5367^{6} 7778^{3}

Super Satin (NZ) *C Fownes* 115
6 b g Danehill Dancer(IRE) —Mantles Princess (Rock City)
$7729a^{9}$

Super Say (IRE) *Andrew Oliver* a99 98
5 ch g Intikhab(USA) —Again Royale (IRE) (Royal Academy (USA))
3032^{27} $6513a^{8}$

Superstition (FR) *Markus Klug* 111
5 b m Kutub(IRE) —Secada (GER) (Saint Andrews (FR))
$329a^{6}$ $829a^{4}$ $4374a^{3}$ $5776a^{3}$

Supreme Luxury (IRE) *Kevin Ryan* 77
2 b f Iffraaj—Stay Hernanda (Hernando (FR))
6329^{3} ◆ 6776^{9}

Supreme Quest *Roger Charlton* 78
2 ch f Exceed And Excel(AUS) —Spanish Quest (Rainbow Quest (USA))
1441^{4} 1981^{2} 2309^{4}

Supreme Rock *Jim Boyle* a58 58
2 br c Rock Of Gibraltar(IRE) —Izadore (IRE) (In The Wings)
6792^{6} 7083^{8}

Supreme Seductress (IRE) *Charles Hills* 63
3 b f Montjeu(IRE) —Private Seductress (USA) (Private Account (USA))
1363^{8} 2065^{8} 6459^{10} 7158^{7}

Supreme Spirit (IRE) *George Margarson* a83 78
4 b m Invincible Spirit(IRE) —Asseverate (USA) (Trempolino (USA))
1411^{7} 1831^{3} 2633^{11} 6065^{7} (6408) 6779^{10} (7141) 7243^{7} 7486^{6}

Supreme Vendor (IRE) *Stuart Coltherd* a76 60
5 ch g Fath(USA) —Dispol Jazz (Alhijaz)
1615^{7} 2462^{9} 2636^{7}

Sure Fire (GER) *Barney Curley* a66 39
6 b g Monsun(GER) —Suivez (FR) (Fioravanti (USA))
1253^{9} 6240^{9}

Surely This Time (IRE) *Kevin Ryan* 68
3 b g Exceed And Excel(AUS) —Heart Of Svetlana (IRE) (Linamix (FR))
1745^{9} 2410^{5} 2611^{8} 5063^{2} 5469^{3} (5793) 6456^{4} 7079^{9}

Sure Route *Richard Hannon* a77 97
3 b f Ishiguru(USA) —Shore Light (USA) (Gulch (USA))
1362^{5} (1605) 2102^{2} 2883^{4} 3845^{7} 5113^{2} (5892) (6374)

Surfer (USA) *Mahmood Al Zarooni* a98 81
2 ch c Distorted Humor(USA) —Surf Club (USA) (Ocean Crest (USA))
3826^{2} 4446^{3} 5564^{3} 6230^{2} 6957^{5}

Surfrider (IRE) *S Wattel* a99 112
3 b c Dansili—Ecoutila (USA) (Rahy (USA))
(1206a) $2139a^{11}$ $6566a^{3}$ $7678a^{10}$

Surprise (IRE) *Mark Rimmer* a61 63
3 b f Anabaa Blue—Wicken Wonder (IRE) (Distant Relative)
529^{5} 655^{6} 760^{3} 942^{6} 1134^{4} 1574^{4} 1969^{2} ◆ 2418^{4} 2858^{2} 3393^{3} 4164^{5} 4248^{4}

Surrey Dream (IRE) *Roger Teal* 44
2 b c Oasis Dream—Trois Graces (USA) (Alysheba (USA))
6165^{14} 6751^{10}

Surrey Spirit *Harry Dunlop* 42
2 b f Invincible Spirit(IRE) —Anse Victorin (USA) (Mt. Livermore (USA))
5347^{6} 5889^{12} 6620^{10}

Surrey Star (IRE) *James Cassidy* a100 108
3 b c Dubawi(IRE) —Turning Light (GER) (Fantastic Light (USA))
$7572a^{10}$

Surrey Storm *Roger Teal* 67
2 b f Montjeu(IRE) —Dont Dili Dali (Dansili)
5299^{4} 6117^{3} 6373^{3} 6726^{8}

Survey (GER) *Mario Hofer* 100
2 ch f Big Shuffle(USA) —Shadow Queen (GER) (Lando (GER))
$7219a^{4}$

Surwaki (USA) *Robert Cowell* a52 79
9 b g Miswaki(USA) —Quinella (Generous (IRE))
2922^{5} 5943^{9}

Susan Stroman *Ed Dunlop* a83 76
3 b f Monsun(GER) —Twyla Tharp (IRE) (Sadler's Wells (USA))
3228^{8} (3922) ◆ 4190^{3} (5145) ◆ 5714^{6} 7120^{3}

Suspender Belt *John Best* a57
3 b f Kodiac—Broughton Zest (Colonel Collins (USA))
305^{5}

Susukino (FR) *S Kobayashi* 68
2 gr f Great Journey(JPN) —Sapporo (FR) (Smadoun (FR))
$2866a^{7}$

Suttonia (IRE) *Noel Chance* a46 38
5 b m Namid—Sassania (IRE) (Persian Bold)
70^{5} 204^{13} 386^{8}

Sutton Veny (IRE) *Jeremy Gask* a96 94
5 gr m Acclamation—Carabine (USA) (Dehere (USA))
2299[3] 2959[3] 4416[6] 5053[9] 5703[2] 6224[4] 6723[9] 7489[4] 7675[4]

Suzhou *Denis Coakley* a69 47
4 b m Tiger Hill(IRE) —Tora Bora (Grand Lodge (USA))
2201[5] 2869[9] 5836[14]

Suzi's A Class Act *James Eustace* a73 73
3 gr f Act One—Latour (Sri Pekan (USA))
2469[7] 3001[4] 4279[9] 5242[9] 5641[8] 6037[6] 6306[3] 7415[3] 7570[3]

Suzy Alexander *David Simcock* a64 69
4 b m Red Ransom(USA) —Fiveofive (IRE) (Fairy King (USA))
1330[4] 1831[2] 2303[2] 3597[4] 4711[2] (5780) 6065[4]

Swampfire (IRE) *John M Oxx* a93 98
3 b g Anabaa(USA) —Moonfire (Sadler's Wells (USA))
2331a[7] 6736a[10]

Swaninstockwell (IRE) *Pat Phelan* a54 66
3 b g Footstepsinthesand—Dans Delight (Machiavellian (USA))
2368[4] 2885[2] 3118[5] 3979[6] 4389[4] 6923[8] 7603[9]

Swans A Swimming (IRE) *Stal Garbo* a65 65
5 b h Mujadil(USA) —Danestar (Danehill (USA))
6959a[0] 7315a[4]

Swansea Jack *Stuart Williams* a70 70
4 ch g Singspiel(IRE) —Welsh Diva (Selkirk (USA))
1763[5] 2270[8] 2920[9] (6070) (6444) 6624[8] 6939[8]

Swan Song *Andrew Balding* 75
2 br f Green Desert(USA) —Lochsong (Song)
6991[2]

Sway Away (USA) *Jeff Bonde* a111
3 b c Afleet Alex(USA) —Seattle Shimmer (USA) (Seattle Slew (USA))
2328a[12]

Swedish Rhapsody (IRE) *John Joseph Murphy* a53 51
3 b f Choisir(AUS) —Baltic Rhapsody (Polish Precedent (USA))
6407[3] 7093[3]

Swedish Sailor *Mahmood Al Zarooni* 84
2 b c Monsun(GER) —Epitome (IRE) (Nashwan (USA))
(7082) ◆

Sweet Avon *Matthew Salaman* a62 65
4 gr m Avonbridge—Sweet Whisper (Petong)
351[8] 545[13]

Sweet Cat (USA) *Todd Pletcher* a74 106
2 bb f Kitten's Joy(USA) —Claire's Smile (USA) (Carson City (USA))
7281a[3]

Sweet Cecily (IRE) *Richard Hannon* 97
3 b f Kodiac—Yaqootah (USA) (Gone West (USA))
1319[6] 2054[4] 2500[3]

Sweet Cheeks (IRE) *Linda Perratt* 69
3 b f Kheleyf(USA) —Sunset Darling (IRE) (Distant Music (USA))
3114[P]

Sweet Child O'Mine *Richard Guest* a94 89
4 b m Singspiel(IRE) —Vendors Mistake (IRE) (Danehill (USA))
(548) 1154[10] 4429[8] 4959[4] (5488) 5969[6]

Sweet Chilli (IRE) *David Barron* 86
2 b f Intikhab(USA) —Ofayrah (USA) (Gilded Time (USA))
1414[3] (1619) 2070[4] 3104[8] 4094[16]

Sweet Ducky (USA) *H J Brown* a113
3 br c Pulpit(USA) —Storm's Darling (USA) (Storm Boot (USA))
998a[13]

Sweetest Of Peas (IRE) *Kevin Ryan* a35 54
4 b m Sadler's Wells(USA) —Sweet Gypsy Rose (IRE) (Darshaan)
40[4] 118[9]

Sweet Fairnando *Tim Easterby* 54
2 b f Hernando(FR) —Fairnilee (Selkirk (USA))
4002[11] 4898[6] 5464[11]

Sweet Grace *David Brown* a65
2 b f Echo Of Light—Sydney Star (Machiavellian (USA))
7060[9] 7685[4] 7777[2] 7915[6]

Sweetie Time *Michael Bell* 99
3 b f Invincible Spirit(IRE) —Blessing (Dubai Millennium)
3034[9] 3323[2] 3819[6] 6809a[6] 7509a[5]

Sweet Lavender (IRE) *Saeed Bin Suroor* a77 20
3 b f Dalakhani(IRE) —Dievotchkina (IRE) (Bluebird (USA))
5317[2] 6054[2] 6614[3] 7136[11]

Sweet Liberta (IRE) *Andrew Balding* 51
2 b f Cape Cross(IRE) —Hendrina (IRE) (Daylami (IRE))
5479[10]

Sweet Lightning *Michael Dods* a104 114
6 b g Fantastic Light(USA) —Sweetness Herself (Unfuwain (USA))
326a[7] 499a[2] 679a[4] 824a[7] (1094)

Sweet Mirasol (IRE) *Mandy Rowland* a54 54
4 b m Celtic Swing—Sallwa (IRE) (Entrepreneur)
167[8] 1276[7] 1612[6] 2162[9] 3096[8]

Sweetnessandlight *Jason Ward* a67 58
2 b f Aussie Rules(USA) —Taschlynn (IRE) (Second Empire (IRE))
6612[8] 7058[2] 7540[6] (7780) 7915[3] ◆

Sweet Ophelia *George Baker* 67
2 b f Shamardal(USA) —Showery (Rainbow Quest (USA))
6744[3]

Sweet Origin *Marco Botti* a96 88
4 ch g Osorio(GER) —Sweet Ludy (IRE) (Be My Guest (USA))
(539) (715) (948) 1717[10] 2604[4] 3203[7] ◆ 3592[5]

Sweet Ovation *Mark Usher* a57 56
2 b f Royal Applause—Sweetest Revenge (IRE) (Daggers Drawn (USA))
1946[5] 2227[4] 3287[5] 4019[6] 4460[4] 4955[4] (5374) 5840[6] 6627[7] 7252[4] 7530[6] 7925[6]

Sweet Possession (USA) *Pat Eddery* a62 41
5 b m Belong To Me(USA) —Bingo Meeting (USA) (General Meeting (USA))
14[7] 163[9] 355[6] 451[7] 1474[2] 1587[2] 1905[8] 2198[2] 2829[3] 3234[6] 3387[8] 3741[8] 4701[5]

Sweet Sanette (SAF) *A T Millard* 114
6 b m Jallad(USA) —Scented Samantha (SAF) (National Assembly (CAN))
3010[3]

Sweetscot (IRE) *Amy Weaver* a56 54
2 b f Selkirk(USA) —So Sweet (IRE) (Cape Cross (IRE))
6117[6] 6819[6]

Sweet Secret *Jeremy Gask* a76 74
4 ch m Singspiel(IRE) —Ballymore Celebre (IRE) (Peintre Celebre (USA))
2999[10] 3771[2] 4275[6] 4825[6] 5808[4] 6226[2] 6468[7] 7146[2] (7447) 7637[12] 7823[6] ◆

Sweet Seville (FR) *Terry Clement* a48 39
7 b m Agnes World(USA) —Hispalis (IRE) (Barathea (IRE))
11[6] 118[8] 5588[7] 7087[11]

Sweet Venture (FR) *M Weiss* 102
9 gr h Verglas(IRE) —Bitter Sweet (FR) (Esprit Du Nord (USA))
440a[4] 627a[5]

Sweet Whip (IRE) *K Borgel* a63 80
3 b f Whipper(USA) —Sierva (GER) (Darshaan)
258a[10]

Sweet World *Bernard Llewellyn* a64 69
7 b g Agnes World(USA) —Douce Maison (IRE) (Fools Holme (USA))
4273[3] 4645[5] 4952[2] (6438) 7263[7]

Swendab (IRE) *John O'Shea* a40 84
3 b g Trans Island—Lavish Spirit (USA) (Southern Halo (USA))
(1753) 2582[8] 3271[3] 3723[4] (4527) (5115) (5378) 6500[5]

Swift Alhaarth (IRE) *Mark Johnston* a79 100
3 b g Alhaarth(IRE) —Simla Bibi (Indian Ridge)
(2287) 2726[4] 3376[4] 3623[2] 3774[18] 4467[3] 4777[3] 5700[3] (5932) 6325[4]

Swift Bird (IRE) *Noel Quinlan* a70 76
3 b f Acclamation—She Legged It (IRE) (Cape Cross (IRE))
663[4] 791[2] 952[3] 3577[4] 3766[4] 4727[2] (5429) 6409[8] 6997[10]

Swift Blade (IRE) *Lady Herries* a68 75
3 ch g Exceed And Excel(AUS) —Gold Strike (IRE) (Rainbow Quest (USA))
1484[5] 1951[5] 2293[8] 4578[2] 5407[4] 5856[5] 6748[3] 6924[9]

Swift Breeze *William Haggas* a75 70
3 b f Exceed And Excel(AUS) —Mellow Jazz (Lycius (USA))
5100[5] 5676[3] 6285[8] 7141[2] 7334[5]

Swift Cat *John Best* a60 62
2 b c One Cool Cat(USA) —Hunzy (IRE) (Desert King (IRE))
4906[7] 5541[5] 6725[11] 7222[6]

Swift Chap *Rod Millman* a76 82
5 b g Diktat—Regent's Folly (IRE) (Touching Wood (USA))
1530[8] 2376[8] 2915[4]

Swift Encounter (IRE) *Ann Duffield* 70
2 bb g Antonius Pius(USA) —Eucalyptus Hill (USA) (Peaks And Valleys (USA))
4122[9] (4898)

Swift Gift *Ed Dunlop* a94 105
6 b g Cadeaux Genereux—Got To Go (Shareef Dancer (USA))
4774[5] 5699[9]

Swiftly Done (IRE) *Declan Carroll* a73 92
4 b g Whipper(USA) —Ziffany (Taufan (USA))
1099[9] 1460[2] 1714[9] 2985[10] (4278) (4877) 5722[3] 6078[2] 7161[6]

Swift Winged *Hughie Morrison* a39
2 b f Motivator—Swift Spring (FR) (Bluebird (USA))
6928[11] 7177[7]

Swilly Ferry (USA) *Charles Hills* a82 108
4 b g Wiseman's Ferry(USA) —Keepers Hill (IRE) (Danehill (USA))
1720[13] 2075[19] 3155[17] 3627[5] ◆ 4346[20] 4859[7] 5508[3] 5758[20] 7018[20]

Swimsuit *Michael Jarvis* a71 69
3 b f Sleeping Indian—Love Quest (Pursuit Of Love)
49[4] 254[3]

Swindy *Paul Cole* a87 84
3 b g Hurricane Run(IRE) —Red Passion (USA) (Seeking The Gold (USA))
1194[2] 3774[14] 4009[2] ◆ 4355[5] 4905[2] ◆ 5235[0]

Swing Alone (IRE) *Gay Kelleway* a72 98
2 b c Celtic Swing—Groupetime (USA) (Gilded Time (USA))
3152[5] 4390[3] 4722[3] (5899) 6692[6] 7192a[10]

Swing Danceur (FR) *Mme C Dufreche* a58 80
4 b h Charge D'Affaires—Little Swing (FR) (Celtic Swing)
900a[6]

Swing Door (IRE) *Robert Eddery* 50
3 ch f Pivotal—Passageway (USA) (Gold Fever (USA))
2103[9] 3289[7] 4179[10] 4544[10]

Swinger *David Nicholls* a20 63
3 ch g Singspiel(IRE) —Helen Bradley (IRE) (Indian Ridge)
4286[5] 5212[8]

Swinging Sixties (FR) *L Guilloux*
7 gr m Kaldounevees(FR) —Six Bells (FR) (Slip Anchor)
93a[0]

Swinging Sixties (IRE) *D Selvaratnam* a99 99
6 b g Singspiel(IRE) —Velvet Lady (Nashwan (USA))
236[13]

Swing It *Richard Hannon* 80
2 b c Bahamian Bounty—Haiyfoona (Zafonic (USA))
4276[9] 6123[2]

Swingkeel (IRE) *John Dunlop* a96 104
6 ch g Singspiel(IRE) —Anniversary (Salse (USA))
1808[11] 2499[6] (3157) 4469[11]

Swingland *Paul Cole* 80
2 b f Pivotal—Farfala (FR) (Linamix (FR))
4471[4] (5583)

Swish Dish (CAN) *Micky Hammond* a21 73
4 bb m El Corredor(USA) —Amelia Saratoga (JPN) (Dehere (USA))
1167[5] 2478[9] 3303[5] 3953[9]

Swiss Cross *Gerard Butler* a91 101
4 b g Cape Cross(IRE) —Swiss Lake (USA) (Indian Ridge)
1594[7] 1854[3] (2169) (2717) ◆ 3155[18] 4357[10]

Swiss Diva *David Elsworth* a94 116
5 b m Pivotal—Swiss Lake (USA) (Indian Ridge)
3010[18] 5253[10]

Swiss Dream *David Elsworth* a85 105
3 b f Oasis Dream—Swiss Lake (USA) (Indian Ridge)
1758[2] 2074[3] (2468) 2934[4] 3820[8] (4333) 4739a[8] (5481) 5927[18] 6272[2]

Swiss Franc *David Elsworth* a105 101
6 b g Mr Greeley(USA) —Swiss Lake (USA) (Indian Ridge)
2028[8] 2317[19] (4104) 4357[3] 4739a[7] 5180[9] 5887[14]

Swiss Spirit *David Elsworth* 92
2 b c Invincible Spirit(IRE) —Swiss Lake (USA) (Indian Ridge)
2510[2] ◆ (2936) 6162[6] 6705[3]

Switch (USA) *John W Sadler* a116 103
4 b m Quiet American(USA) —Antoniette (USA) (Nicholas (USA))
7282a[2]

Switchback *Sir Michael Stoute* a76 83
3 b g Medicean—Hooplah (Pivotal)
3177[7] 3575[2] 4161[6] 4665[2] 5635[4] (6234)

Switched Off *Ian Williams* 79
6 b g Catcher In The Rye(IRE) —Button Hole Flower (IRE) (Fairy King (USA))
6988[5]

Switcher (IRE) *Tom Dascombe* 100
2 b f Whipper(USA) —Bahamamia (Vettori (IRE))
(2254) 3104[4] 5296a[3] 5885[8]

Switzerland (IRE) *Mark Johnston* 71
2 b c Shamardal(USA) —Sahra Alsalam (USA) (Gone West (USA))
6525[6] 6991[4]

Swooper (AUS) *Darryl Dodson* 89
7 b m Black Hawk—Killorelin Belle (AUS) (Final Card (AUS))
7043a[8]

Swooping Hawk (IRE) *Sylvester Kirk* a50 58
4 b g Hawk Wing(USA) —Lolita's Gold (USA) (Royal Academy (USA))
5607[6] 6084[6]

Swop (IRE) *Luca Cumani* a103 96
8 b g Shinko Forest(IRE) —Changing Partners (Rainbow Quest (USA))
587a[2] 682a[5] 5032[13]

Swords *Ray Peacock* a45 40
9 b g Vettori(IRE) —Pomorie (IRE) (Be My Guest (USA))
373[7] 450[6] 631[4] 768[7] 911[8] 1080[6] 3799[6] 4847[7] 5209[10] 5267[10] 5739[9] 6029[11] 7496[6]

Swordsman (GER) *Chris Gordon* a81 74
9 b g Acatenango(GER) —Saiga (Windwurf (GER))
1282[5] 2758[4] 3352[7] 3769[4]

Syann (IRE) *David Marnane* a85 96
4 gr m Daylami(IRE) —Hedera (USA) (Woodman (USA))
5748a[11] 6513a[9]

Sygnature *Alan Swinbank* 68
2 b g Authorized(IRE) —Perfect Story (IRE) (Desert Story (IRE))
4140[4] 4714[6] 5058[8] 5727[4]

Sylas Ings *Pat Phelan* a71 77
3 b g Kyllachy—Ashlinn (IRE) (Ashkalani (IRE))
1947[12] 2841[10] 4011[8] 4321[9] 7096[12]

Sylphlike (IRE) *H-A Pantall* a56 45
3 b f Footstepsinthesand—Sylflore (FR) (Marignan (USA))
852a[7]

Sylvan Song (USA) *A Fabre* a78 95
2 b f Street Cry(IRE) —Forest Heiress (USA) (Forest Wildcat (USA))
4569a[5] 5296a[7]

Sylvestris (IRE) *Ralph Beckett* a77 92
3 b f Arch(USA) —Woodmaven (USA) (Woodman (USA))
1234[6] (1565) 2073[2] 3873[7] 4790[5] 6088[7]

Symbol Of Arch (USA) *Arnfinn Lund*
4 bb m Arch(USA) —Kicken High (USA) (High Yield (USA))
5096a[4]

Symphonic Dancer (USA) *Brian Baugh* a73 25
4 ch m Smart Strike(CAN) —Summer Exhibition (USA) (Royal Academy (USA))
636[6] 751[2] 850[2] 1017[5] 4479[7] 4865[3] ◆ 5391[9] 5900[4] 6285[5] 6546[7]

Symphony Of Space *Dai Burchell*
2 b f Primo Valentino(IRE) —Flying Lion (Hunting Lion (IRE))
4021[7]

Symphony Star (IRE) *Paul D'Arcy* 64
2 b f Amadeus Wolf—Bezant (IRE) (Zamindar (USA))
4804[8] 5479[7] 6169[8] 6526[15]

Symphony Time (IRE) *Brian Meehan* a72 71
2 b f Cape Cross(IRE) —Gems Of Araby (Zafonic (USA))
4232[4] 4853[11] 5418[2] 6169[4] 6818[2]

Syncopated Lady (IRE) *David O'Meara* a34 56
3 b f Acclamation—Perugino Lodge (IRE) (Perugino (USA))
2465[6] 4005[9] 4284[3] 4505[3] 5165[2] 5822[9] 6358[6]

Synfonica *Richard Hannon* a54 32
2 b f Iceman—Aegean Blue (Warning)
6117[10] 6819[8] 7599[7]

Syrian *S M Duffy* a89 82
4 b g Hawk Wing(USA) —Lady Lahar (Fraam)
824 205[2] (282) (447) (599) 1102[15] 1849[13] 7618a[14]

Sysmo (FR) *J-M Beguigne* 83
2 b c My Risk(FR) —La Soculente (FR) (Cape Cross (IRE))
4624a[2]

Szabo's Destiny *James Given* a71 74
3 b g Dubai Destination(USA) —Odette (Pursuit Of Love)
25[7] 1300[3] (1456) (1872) 2695[4] 3364[7] 3989[7] 6577[9]

Szerelem (FR) *F-X De Chevigny* a72 69
6 b g Canyon Creek(IRE) —Semire (FR) (Mizoram (USA))
372a[2] 566a[4]

Taajub (IRE) *Peter Crate* a86 91
4 b g Exceed And Excel(AUS) —Purple Tiger (IRE) (Rainbow Quest (USA))
1848[4] 2317[18] 3627[12] 4104[6] 7393[11] 7531[6] 7675[5] 7941[8]

Taameer *D K Weld* 103
5 b g Beat Hollow—Vayavaig (Damister (USA))
5291a[4] 5977a[6]

Taaresh (IRE) *Kevin Morgan* a88 81
6 b g Sakhee(USA) —Tanaghum (Darshaan)
(315) 436[9] 803[4] 7908[12]

Tabaret *Richard Whitaker* a71 95
8 ch g Bertolini(USA) —Luanshya (First Trump)
1166[6] 1457[8] 1675[9] 2028[16] 2299[14] 4075[10] 5452[4] 5683[11] 6044[10] 6655[2]

Tabiet *Linda Perratt* 61
4 ch m Danroad(AUS) —Frabrofen (Mind Games)
2062[9] 2632[11] 2694[13]

Table Forty Six (IRE) *K J Condon* a53 78
5 b m Refuse To Bend(IRE) —Tashreefat (IRE) (Danehill (USA))
7378a[12]

Table Mountain (IRE) *Robert Alan Hennessy* 98
4 b g Milan—Shirley Blue (IRE) (Shirley Heights)
4398a[3]

Tac De Boistron (FR) *A Lyon* 112
4 b g Take Risks(FR) —Pondiki (FR) (Sicyos (USA))
5990a[2] 6661a[4] 7049a[4] (7406a)

Tacma (IRE) *R Menichetti* 91
2 b f Baltic King—Prime Time Girl (Primo Dominie)
6904a[9]

Tactfully (IRE) *Mahmood Al Zarooni* 84
2 b f Discreet Cat(USA) —Kydd Gloves (USA) (Dubai Millennium)
(6458) ◆ 7169[8]

Tactic *David Hayes* 119
5 b g Sadler's Wells(USA) —Tanaghum (Darshaan)
7310a[13]

Tactician *Michael Bell* 113
4 b g Motivator—Tempting Prospect (Shirley Heights)
2107[2] (3875) 5285[2] 5884[7]

Tadabeer *Ian Williams* a72 77
3 b g Green Desert(USA) —Perfect Plum (IRE) (Darshaan)
3183[4] 5792[2] 6210[2] 7532[4] (7921)

Tadalavil *Linda Perratt* a76 74
6 gr g Clodovil(IRE) —Blandish (USA) (Wild Again (USA))
3305[5] 3488[7] 3856[10] 4145[10] 5053[2] 5554[5] 5720[5] 6076[6] 6208[10] 6646[3] 6778[4] 7104[6]

Tadmir (USA) *Saeed Bin Suroor* 53
2 bb c Bernardini(USA) —Owsley (USA) (Harlan (USA))
6805[7]

Tafaneen (USA) *Roger Varian* a71 58
3 bb f Dynaformer(USA) —Cozzy Corner (USA) (Cozzene (USA))
2218[5] 6054[8] 6798[6]

Tafawuk (USA) *Roger Varian* 61
2 b g Nayef(USA) —Yaqeen (Green Desert (USA))
6100[6] ◆

Taffe *James Given* a82 79
2 b c Byron—Blorenge (Prince Sabo)
5646[6] 6152[2] (6455) 6843[5] 7765[3] (7918)

Tagansky *Simon Dow* a70 64
3 b g Barathea(IRE) —Tenable (Polish Precedent (USA))
176[3] 434[2] (579) 1683[9] 1949[6] 3002[14] 4744[3] 5137[5] 5856[7] 6255[7] 6944[8]

Tagar Bere (FR) *M Pimbonnet* a86 104
4 ch h High Yield(USA) —Arrondie (FR) (Inchinor)
3568a[7] 6686a[5] 7404a[7]

Tagena (IRE) *Richard Price* 47
3 ch f Tagula(IRE) —Lamzena (IRE) (Fairy King (USA))
7111[12] 7560[8] 7740[11]

Tagula Night (IRE) *Walter Swinburn* a90 93
5 ch g Tagula(IRE) —Carpet Lady (IRE) (Night Shift (USA))
2525[2] 2954[7] 3796[8] 4556[9] 4859[12] 5508[9] (5972) 6331[3] 6723[12]

Tahaamah *Saeed Bin Suroor* a89 91
3 ch c King's Best(USA) —Russian Snows (IRE) (Sadler's Wells (USA))
(3340) 4103[6] 4723[6] 6249[2] 6439[2]

Tahini (GER) *J Hirschberger* 106
3 ch c Medicean—Tucana (GER) (Acatenango (GER))
3672a[6]

Tahitian Princess (IRE) *Ann Duffield* a36 59
3 b f One Cool Cat(USA) —Akarita (IRE) (Akarad (FR))
1299[8] 1952[9] 2047[5] 2396[4] 2990[2] ◆ 3489[5] (4041) 4196[4] 4876[5] 5203[2] 5490[7] 5619[8] 6208[9]

Tahnee Mara (IRE) *Kevin Ryan* 73
2 b f Sleeping Indian—Totally Yours (IRE) (Desert Sun)
3342[5] 3849[2] 4557[4] 6449[5]

Tai Chi (GER) *W Baltromei* 109
2 b c High Chaparral(IRE) —Taita (GER) (Big Shuffle (USA))
(6901a) 7405a[3]

Taikoo *Hughie Morrison* a83 91
6 b g Dr Fong(USA) —So True (So Blessed)
342[5] (1291) (6115) 6832[2]

Tajaaweed (USA) *Daniel Peitz* 115
6 b h Dynaformer(USA) —Uforia (USA) (Zilzal (USA))
5074a^6 6721a^6

Tajneed (IRE) *David Nicholls* a83 111
8 b g Alhaarth(IRE) —Indian Express (Indian Ridge)
1093^{14} 2075^{10} 2717^2 3440a^8 4042^5 4346^2 4534^{10} 5060^8 6147^9 6347^4 6706^{10}

Tajriba (IRE) *Saeed Bin Suroor* a71
2 b f Teofilo(IRE) —Caumshinaun (IRE) (Indian Ridge)
7343^2

Takajan (IRE) *Mark Brisbourne* a75 48
4 b g Barathea(IRE) —Takaliya (IRE) (Darshaan)
133^7 199^6 (377) 403^4 673^4 853^7 880^{10} 3341^{11} *3711^{12}* 4189^8 4893^8 5736^{12} 5895^6 6841^8 7351^7 7419^6 7641^{13} 7728^6

Takapour (IRE) *M Halford* a100 56
3 b c Shamardal(USA) —Takaliya (IRE) (Darshaan)
1704a^4

Takealookatmenow (IRE) *David Nicholls* 67
2 b f Moss Vale(IRE) —Batool (USA) (Bahri (USA))
5590^{10} 6075^3 6291^4 6836^2 (7058)

Take A Mile (IRE) *Seamus Mullins* a48 59
9 ch g Inchinor—Bu Hagab (IRE) (Royal Academy (USA))
560^8

Take A Note *Patrick Chamings* a65
2 b c Singspiel(IRE) —Ela Paparouna (Vettori (IRE))
6945^3 7526^9

Take A Spin *Paul Cole* a62 62
3 ch c Bahamian Bounty—Regal Run (USA) (Deputy Minister (CAN))
1311^7 1484^7 2371^5 3077^2 4071^3 *6122^7*

Take Charge Indy (USA) *Patrick Byrne* a107
2 bb c A.P. Indy(USA) —Take Charge Lady (USA) (Dehere (USA))
7306a^5

Take Cover *George Margarson* a86
4 b g Singspiel(IRE) —Enchanted (Magic Ring (IRE))
(7069) (7419) (7504) ◆

Takeitfromalady (IRE) *Ralph Beckett* 75
2 b g Intikhab(USA) —Pinheiros (IRE) (Rock Of Gibraltar (IRE))
3997^3 4455^3 4968^4 5342^2 6807^2 (7259)

Take It To The Max *Richard Fahey* 100
4 b g Bahamian Bounty—Up And About (Barathea (IRE))
(2046) 2545^2 3276^3 (4958) 5686^4 (6079) (7189a)

Take Root *Reg Hollinshead* a63 68
3 b g Indesatchel(IRE) —Lamarita (Emarati (USA))
1065^7 1217^3 2032^8 2493^2 3126^5 *3239^5* 3635^9

Take Ten *Mahmood Al Zarooni* a101 91
4 b g Bahamian Bounty—See You Later (Emarati (USA))
2288^{12}

Take Two *John O'Shea* 60
2 b c Act One—Lac Marmot (FR) (Marju (IRE))
6991^7 7257^4

Take Your Partner *Kevin Ryan* a84 54
3 b c Piccolo—Takes Two To Tango (Groom Dancer (USA))
(669) (936) (1064) (1275) 2363^{11} 3384^5

Takhreej (IRE) *Keith Dalgleish* a67 41
3 b c Marju(IRE) —Tomoohat (USA) (Danzig (USA))
2723^4 5082^{11} 5432^4

Takitwo *Peter Cundell* a51 65
8 b g Delta Dancer—Tiama (IRE) (Last Tycoon)
45^7 129^{12}

Talamahana *Andrew Haynes* a21 61
6 b m Kyllachy—Bahawir Pour (USA) (Green Dancer (USA))
1453^{11} 1630^2 1831^5 2142^5 2424^4 2921^2 3476^2 3678^2 3721^6 4231^5 4547^{12} 4973^7 *5244^{12}* 5674^{16}

Talayeb *Marcus Tregoning* a72 76
6 bb g Nayef(USA) —Paper Chase (FR) (Machiavellian (USA))
174^5

Talbot Green *William Muir* 65
3 b g Green Desert(USA) —One Of The Family (Alzao (USA))
2097^{11} 2648^{17} 3080^5 4190^5 4974^{12}

Taleia (GER) *A Wohler* 93
3 b f Dashing Blade—Tintina (USA) (General Assembly (USA))
2337a^5 3209a^6

Talelook Bareliere (FR) *Mme C Dufreche*
4 b m Mowgli(SPA) —River Lady (SPA) (Rage Hard (USA))
91a^0

Talenti (IRE) *P J McKenna* a75 75
8 b g Sadler's Wells(USA) —Sumoto (Mtoto)
127^4 7544a^2

Talent Scout (IRE) *Tim Walford* a62 74
5 b g Exceed And Excel(AUS) —Taalluf (USA) (Hansel (USA))
26^9 1493^8 *3719^3* (4442) (5403) ◆ 5828^{16} 6452^8 6830^{11}

Tales Of Grimm (USA) *Sir Michael Stoute* 88
2 b c Distorted Humor(USA) —Stupendous Miss (USA) (Dynaformer (USA))
(4995)

Talgado *F Neuberg* 101
4 ch h Lomitas—Haiyfoona (Zafonic (USA))
4037a^0 5990a^9

Talkative Guest (IRE) *George Margarson* 59
3 b f Oratorio(IRE) —Pedicure (Atticus (USA))
1060^7 *1251^8* 2172^5 2853^5 4248^8 4822^7 5352^6 5670^4 6071^6 6767^8

Talkin Italian *Ian Williams* a46
3 b f Medicean—Easy Sunshine (IRE) (Sadler's Wells (USA))
95^9 262^{10} 642^4 967^9 7400^{11} 7631^{10}

Talk Of Saafend (IRE) *Dianne Sayer* a31 68
6 b m Barathea(IRE) —Sopran Marida (IRE) (Darshaan)
1440^3 *1959^9* 3086^3 3300^3 4605^3 4982^5 7113^{10}

Talk Of The Nation (USA) *J-C Rouget* a74 74
3 gr c Empire Maker(USA) —Moon Queen (IRE) (Sadler's Wells (USA))
660a^7

Talk Of The North *Hugo Palmer* 70
2 b f Haafhd—Ammo (IRE) (Sadler's Wells (USA))
5548^3 6117^2 6448^3

Tallahasse (IRE) *Alan Swinbank* 89
3 b f Acclamation—Designer Chic (Red Ransom (USA))
1404^{10} 1902^{10} 4101^9 4516^8

Tallevu (IRE) *Tom Dascombe* 73
2 ch g Stormy River(FR) —Pascarina (FR) (Exit To Nowhere (USA))
5011^8 5579^4 6334^4 6957^{12}

Tallula (IRE) *Micky Hammond* a32 18
2 b f Tagula(IRE) —Talara (IRE) (Dansili)
1455^7 4073^{13} *7367^8*

Tallulah Mai *Matthew Salaman* a57
4 b m Kayf Tara—Al Awaalah (Mukaddamah (USA))
5947^7

Tally Ho (FR) *A Fabre* a94 93
4 b g Street Cry(IRE) —Bashful (IRE) (Brief Truce (USA))
1011a^9

Talwar (IRE) *Jeremy Noseda* 107
2 b c Acclamation—Moore's Melody (IRE) (Marju (IRE))
2953^7 (3590) (4311) (5276) ◆ 5951a^9 6527^7 7020^5

Talya's Storm *Jeremy Gask* a56 38
2 b c Milk It Mick—Absolutely Soaked (IRE) (Alhaarth (IRE))
5174^8 *5410^5* 6025^6 *7000^4 7252^6 7514^9*

Tamagin (USA) *Lydia Pearce* a109 75
8 b g Stravinsky(USA) —Luia (USA) (Forty Niner (USA))
1891^5 3841^{17} 4063^7 4609^{16} 5339^4

Tamam Namoose (IRE) *P D Deegan* 62
2 b g Exceed And Excel(AUS) —Journey's End (IRE) (In The Wings)
6196a^{17}

Tamanaco (IRE) *Tim Walford* 81
4 b g Catcher In The Rye(IRE) —Right After Moyne (IRE) (Imperial Ballet (IRE))
5686^9

Tamara Bay *William Haggas* a61 59
3 b f Selkirk(USA) —Tamalain (USA) (Royal Academy (USA))
3177^6 4065^4 *4663^5 5630^{11} 6253^5*

Tamareen (IRE) *Richard Fahey* a82 78
3 b g Bahamian Bounty—Damjanich (IRE) (Mull Of Kintyre (USA))
1335^3 ◆ 1916^6 *2383^5* 3555^7 4195^7 5274^2 5621^7 5918^4 *6283^5 (7716)*

Tamarind Hall (USA) *Jeremiah C Englehart* a110
4 ch m Graeme Hall(USA) —Turner's Hall (USA) (Forest Wildcat (USA))
7282a^{10}

Tamarix Boy (IRE) *M Marcialis*
3 bb c High Chaparral(IRE) —July Girl (Rousillon (USA))
1126a^7

Tamarrud *Saeed Bin Suroor* a76
2 b c Authorized(IRE) —Miss Hepburn (USA) (Gone West (USA))
(4798)

Tamasou (IRE) *Ed McMahon* a80 78
6 b g Tamarisk(IRE) —Soubresaut (IRE) (Danehill (USA))
1368^4 2165^2 (3093) *3924^3* 4503^4 5455^6

Tameen *John Dunlop* 99
3 b f Shirocco(GER) —Najah (IRE) (Nashwan (USA))
3180^4 4056^{10} (5062) ◆ 5483^{13} (5971) 6249^{11} 7296^4 ◆ 7580a^0

Tamima (USA) *Brian Meehan* 67
2 b f Dubai Destination(USA) —Zifaaf (USA) (Silver Hawk (USA))
4052^{12} 5299^7 5854^3

Tamino (IRE) *Mark Brisbourne* a62 43
8 b g Mozart(IRE) —Stop Out (Rudimentary (USA))
1498^3 1815^4

Tam Lin *M bin Shafya* a58 89
8 b g Selkirk(USA) —La Nuit Rose (FR) (Rainbow Quest (USA))
157a^{13} 331a^{13} 757a^9

Tanaami (USA) *Saeed Bin Suroor* 86
3 b f Elusive Quality(USA) —Ridaa (USA) (Seattle Slew (USA))
(5449) 6062^9 6457^3 6996^9

Tanaos (FR) *F Foresi* a67
5 b g Indian Rocket—Relire (FR) (Fabulous Dancer (USA))
706a^0

Tanassuq (USA) *John Dunlop* 65
3 b f Rahy(USA) —Wasnah (USA) (Nijinsky (CAN))
1343^6 2231^7

Tanby (AUS) *Robert Hickmott* 111
5 b g Galileo(IRE) —Dane Belltar (AUS) (Danewin (AUS))
6711a^2 6967a^2 (7115a)

Tancred Spirit *Paul Midgley* a50 51
3 b f Mind Games—Tancred Times (Clantime)
452^5 868^4 1040^2 1306^2 1561^3 2697^2 3143^5 3860^4 4172^2 4607^2 *5215^6* 5368^4 *7854^3*

Tanda (USA) *Mike Mitchell* a112 109
4 b m Sweetsouthernsaint(USA) —Docs Stormy Girl (USA) (Dr Caton (USA))
7282a^9

Tandakayou (FR) *J Boisnard*
2 gr c Kahyasi—Baryskaya (FR) (Baryshnikov (AUS))
7664a^0

Tanfeeth *Ed Dunlop* 101
3 ch c Singspiel(IRE) —Nasij (USA) (Elusive Quality (USA))
1408^4 ◆ 1810^2 (2231) 2711^4 (3867) 4426^5 5700^{14}

Tanforan *Brian Baugh* a40 69
9 b g Mujahid(USA) —Florentynna Bay (Aragon)
1058^4 2376^6 2815^6 3636^2 3944^6 (4948) 5402^6 5673^8 6452^{12}

Tangaspeed (FR) *R Laplanche* a97 93
6 b m Vertical Speed(FR) —Fitanga (FR) (Fijar Tango (FR))
371a^5

Tangerine Trees *Bryan Smart* a73 116
6 b g Mind Games—Easy To Imagine (USA) (Cozzene (USA))
(1687) 2297^{10} 3010^{19} (5467) (6563a)

Tango Master *Mouse Hamilton-Fairley* a46
4 ch g Doyen(IRE) —Silver Purse (Interrex (CAN))
649^8

Tango Sky (IRE) *Ralph Beckett* a76 74
2 b g Namid—Sky Galaxy (USA) (Sky Classic (CAN))
1136^4 3511^2 7292^5 *(7482)*

Tangtastic (IRE) *Edward Creighton* a50 46
2 b f Elusive City(USA) —Infozoid (IRE) (Barathea (IRE))
2380^5 2718^7 *3237^6 6001^8 6053^8* 7231^2 *7452^7 7592^{10}*

Tanjung Agas (IRE) *Roger Varian* 73
3 b g Montjeu(IRE) —Najmati (Green Desert (USA))
2379^2 (3268) 4242^2

Tanmawy (IRE) *Ed Dunlop* a80 76
3 bb g Alhaarth(IRE) —Roseanna (FR) (Anabaa (USA))
2258^7 *2723^6 3469^4* 4249^3 *5247^3 5639^2 (6307)* 6759^5

Tantalized *Andrew Balding* 11
2 b f Authorized(IRE) —Tarabela (CHI) (Hussonet (USA))
5851^{14}

Tantamount *Roger Charlton* 49
2 b c Observatory(USA) —Cantanta (Top Ville)
6828^6 7232^{12}

Tantrum (IRE) *Richard Hannon*
2 b f Jeremy(USA) —Astuti (IRE) (Waajib)
7025^{17}

Tap Dance Way (IRE) *Patrick Chamings* a73 75
4 b m Azamour(IRE) —Dance Lively (USA) (Kingmambo (USA))
1789^5 2376^2 2663^4 4707^4 5376^{11} 6587^2 6924^{10}

Tapis Libre *Michael Easterby* a68 73
3 b g Librettist(USA) —Stella Manuela (FR) (Galileo (IRE))
1524^3 (1801) 2008^{10} 3318^8 4005^5 4440^4 5064^7 5925^3 *6507^5* 6990^{16} 7215^2

Tapizar (USA) *Steven Asmussen* a114
3 b c Tapit(USA) —Winning Call (USA) (Deputy Minister (CAN))
7304a^5

Tappanappa (IRE) *Andrew Balding* a76 85
4 b g High Chaparral(IRE) —Itsibitsi (IRE) (Brief Truce (USA))
1311^2 ◆ 2458^2 3428^4

Taqaat (USA) *Tim McCarthy* a77 85
3 b c Forestry(USA) —Alrayihah (IRE) (Nashwan (USA))
(1971) 2389^2 *3521^8* 5056^{11} 6239^7 7054^{10}

Taqleed (IRE) *John Gosden* 108
4 bb g Shamardal(USA) —Thakafaat (IRE) (Unfuwain (USA))
2002^8 3156^{12} 4331^5 4801^7 (5686) (6163) (Dead)

Tarantella Lady *George Moore* 73
3 b f Noverre(USA) —Shortfall (Last Tycoon)
1203^9 1653^4 2349^2 2677^7 6155^{14}

Tara Tartan (IRE) *Michael Mulvany* a45 42
5 ch g Daggers Drawn(USA) —Running Tycoon (IRE) (Last Tycoon)
6139a^{10}

Tar Heel Mom (USA) *Stanley M Hough* a114 103
6 bb m Flatter(USA) —Perpetual Light (USA) (Sunny's Halo (CAN))
7282a^{12}

Tariq Too *David Simcock* a63 92
4 ch g Kyllachy—Tatora (Selkirk (USA))
1832^2 (2300) 3134^9 4509^8 (5970)

Tarjeyh (IRE) *Marcus Tregoning* 68
3 b c Medicean—Navajo Rainbow (Rainbow Quest (USA))
4388^4 4970^{11}

Tarkand (FR) *W Walton*
3 b c Green Tune(USA) —Shemrana (USA) (Woodman (USA))
370a^0

Tarkeeba (IRE) *Roger Varian* a77 74
3 ch f Halling(USA) —Zarara (USA) (Manila (USA))
1363^7 2836^4 *3519^3 6306^4*

Tarkheena Prince (USA) *C Von Der Recke* a80 104
6 b g Aldebaran(USA) —Tarkheena (USA) (Alleged (USA))
628a^3 7045a^{10}

Tarkoor *Peter Chapple-Hyam* 3
2 b c Cape Cross(IRE) —Bakhoor (IRE) (Royal Applause)
6300^{12} 6953^{12}

Tarooq (USA) *Richard Fahey* a92 78
5 b g War Chant(USA) —Rose Of Zollern (IRE) (Seattle Dancer (USA))
1394^3 *(2178)* ◆ *5608^5 (6797)* ◆ *6949^2 (7542) 7841^2*

Taro Tywod (IRE) *Ann Duffield* 68
2 br f Footstepsinthesand—Run To Jane (IRE) (Doyoun)
4285^6 (5726)

Tarpon *J C Napoli* a80 80
7 gr h Vettori(IRE) —Tadorne (FR) (Inchinor)
395a^4

Tarquin (IRE) *Linda Stubbs* 61
2 b g Excellent Art—Umlani (IRE) (Great Commotion (USA))
6232^4

Tarrsille (IRE) *G M Lyons* a86 89
5 b g Dansili—Tara Gold (IRE) (Royal Academy (USA))
7150a^2 7793a^3

Tartampion (IRE) *Robert Collet* a78 66
3 b c Cape Cross(IRE) —Zeiting (IRE) (Zieten (USA))
258a^2

Tartan Gigha (IRE) *Mark Johnston* a105 107
6 b g Green Desert(USA) —High Standard (Kris)
778a^3 846^2 1094^{18} 1479^8 1684^{15} 2679^{14} 2933^{12} 3315^{13} 4603^5 5205^{11} 6346^9 (6773) 6989^7

Tartan Gunna *Mark Johnston* a92 96
5 b g Anabaa(USA) —Embraced (Pursuit Of Love)
1410^{14} 1892^6 2282^4 2909^6 3085^6 3620^8 4818^7 6263^2 7022^4

Tartan Jura *Mark Johnston* 78
3 b c Green Desert(USA) —On A Soapbox (USA) (Mi Cielo (USA))
1096^9 1389^3 2360^3

Tartan Trip *Andrew Balding* a89 89
4 b g Selkirk(USA) —Marajuana (Robellino (USA))
1603^8 *2000^2* 2217^2 2933^{14} 3840^{10}

Tartiflette *Ed McMahon* 78
2 b f Dr Fong(USA) —Bright Moll (Mind Games)
6751^8 (7292)

Tarwiyna (IRE) *James McAuley* a57 54
4 ch m Medicean—Tarwila (IRE) (In The Wings)
813^4

Tasfeya *John Akehurst* a83 83
3 b g Haafhd—Nufoos (Zafonic (USA))
1175^2 1571^3 1983^5 2477^2 2833^4 3538^6 6374^6 6755^2 *7204^8*

Tasheba *David Pipe* a91 27
6 ch g Dubai Destination(USA) —Tatanka (IRE) (Lear Fan (USA))
6690^{28}

Tasheyaat *B W Hills* a65 83
3 b f Sakhee(USA) —Almurooj (Zafonic (USA))
992^3 ◆ 1364^3 (2026)

Tasman Tiger *Kate Walton* 55
4 b m Danbird(AUS) —Laylee (Deploy)
1648^4 2257^{11} 2669^3 3086^5 3906^3 4814^7

Tasmeem (IRE) *David Nicholls* a83 83
4 gr g Acclamation—Park Approach (IRE) (Indian Ridge)
446^7 (577) 1067^4 2299^9 2497^7 3028^3 3279^9 3617^5

Tastahil (IRE) *Charles Hills* a94 116
7 ch g Singspiel(IRE) —Luana (Shaadi (USA))
1808^2 3066^P 4469^{14} 5884^5

Taste The Victory (USA) *Alan Swinbank* 74
4 b g Victory Gallop(CAN) —Tastetheteardrops (USA) (What Luck (USA))
1492^5 1800^7 6295^{12}

Taste The Wine (IRE) *Bernard Llewellyn* a67 68
5 gr g Verglas(IRE) —Azia (IRE) (Desert Story (IRE))
172^4 418^5 1107^9 4952^{10} 5168^3 5588^8 (6486) 7263^2 *7817^7*

Tatoosh (IRE) *Niels Petersen* 70
5 br m Xaar—Dictatrice (FR) (Anabaa (USA))
5096a^2

Taurus Twins *Richard Price* a64 90
5 b g Deportivo—Intellibet One (Compton Place)
970^6 (1140) 1539^6 1771^{10} 2250^2 2645^6 (2832) 2929^2 3367^5 3687^5 3847^8 5831^{21} 6224^2 ◆ 6350^3 6703^{11} 6865^7

Taverners Jubilee *Patrick Morris* a37 34
3 b g Sleeping Indian—Page (Elmaamul (USA))
595^7 741^5 868^5 1040^7

Tawaagg *W P Mullins* a58 82
7 b g Kyllachy—Ascendancy (Sadler's Wells (USA))
7322a^4

Tawaasul *William Haggas* 72
2 b f Haafhd—Muwakleh (Machiavellian (USA))
6992^2

Tawseef (IRE) *Roy Brotherton* a35 59
3 b g Monsun(GER) —Sahool (Unfuwain (USA))
3218^9 4157^{12} 4861^6 6813^3 *7144^8 7463^7 7902^6*

Tawzeea (IRE) *Michael Dods* a64 75
6 ch g Cadeaux Genereux—Kismah (Machiavellian (USA))
641^5

Tax Break *David Barron* a84 80
4 b g Motivator—Mystic Lure (Green Desert (USA))
(636) 2545^7 *4921^9 5383^{10} 5717^4 6051^8*

Tax Free (IRE) *David Nicholls* a89 110
9 b g Tagula(IRE) —Grandel (Owington)
1242^7 2317^8 ◆ 2489^4 (3073) 3874^{10} 4534^2 5060^{16} 5467^9 5927^8 6145^{13}

Taxonomist (USA) *A Fabre* a79 57
3 ch c Seeking The Gold(USA) —Munnaya (USA) (Nijinsky (CAN))
776a^3 980a^{10}

Tayacoba (CAN) *Martin Todhunter* 69
4 bb g Smart Strike(CAN) —Bienandanza (USA) (Bien Bien (USA))
2059^{11} 2388^{11} 3023^{13} 5650^6 6419^7

Tayarat (IRE) *Michael Chapman* a72 47
6 b g Noverre(USA) —Sincere (IRE) (Bahhare (USA))
1036^9 1881^8 6235^{11}

Tazahum (USA) *Sir Michael Stoute* a86 116
3 b c Redoute's Choice(AUS) —Huja (IRE) (Alzao (USA))
(1547) (2440) 3068^5 4493^4 5252^2 6298^4

Tazeez (USA) *John Gosden* a103 120
7 bb g Silver Hawk(USA) —Soiree Russe (USA) (Nureyev (USA))
1000a^{12} 3591^2 4345^7

Tazweed (IRE) *Roger Varian* a56
2 b g Dubawi(IRE) —Albahja (Sinndar (IRE))
6795^{12} 7094^6 7521^{10}

Tea And Sympathy *John Holt*
3 b f Avonbridge—Merch Rhyd-Y-Grug (Sabrehill (USA))
3596^P

Teacher (IRE) *William Haggas* 37
2 ch g Danehill Dancer(IRE) —Lac Dessert (USA) (Lac Ouimet (USA))
6160^{15} 6481^8 6951^{15}

Tea Cup *Richard Hannon* 52
2 b f Danehill Dancer(IRE) —Quiet Storm (IRE) (Desert Prince (IRE))
1337^8 4614^{10}

Teaks North (USA) *Justin Sallusto* a103 121
4 bb g Northern Afleet(USA) —Teaksberry Road (USA) (High Honors (USA))
7305a[8]

Tealing *Richard Guest* a68 5
4 ch g Ishiguru(USA) —Renaissance Lady (IRE) (Imp Society (USA))
547[7]

Tearsforjoy (USA) *Richard Hannon* 39
2 b f Street Cry(IRE) —Nasheej (USA) (Swain (IRE))
7025[13]

Teazel *Dominic Ffrench Davis* a12 52
3 ch f Barathea(IRE) —Cream Tease (Pursuit Of Love)
4320[6] 4948[16] 6626[11] 6811[13] 7092[11]

Tech Exceed (GER) *A Wohler* 103
4 b m Exceed And Excel(AUS) —Technik (GER) (Nebos (GER))
5749a[5] 6394a[8]

Technokrat (IRE) *W Hickst* a91
3 b c Oratorio(IRE) —Tech Engine (GER) (Enrique)
(7677a)

Tecktal (FR) *Pat Phelan* a46 35
8 ch m Pivotal—Wenge (USA) (Housebuster (USA))
418[7] 560[6] 819[7] 3946[7]

Tectonic (IRE) *Chris Dwyer* a49 52
2 b c Dylan Thomas(IRE) —Pine Chip (USA) (Nureyev (USA))
5239[10] 5875[5] 6993[9] 7483[5]

Ted Dolly (IRE) *Ms Joanna Morgan* a75 85
7 b g Bob's Return(IRE) —Little Pearl (IRE) (Bigstone (IRE))
7189a[3]

Ted's Brother (IRE) *Richard Guest* a41 82
3 b g Fath(USA) —Estertide (IRE) (Tagula (IRE))
2163[10] (3318) ◆ 3621[2] (5031) (5439) 6079[4] 6867[4] (7024)

Tedsmore Dame *James Unett* a76 27
3 b f Indesatchel(IRE) —Dayville (USA) (Dayjur (USA))
3310[7] 3854[8] 4921[3] 5392[4]

Ted Spread *Mark H Tompkins* 110
4 b g Beat Hollow—Highbrook (USA) (Alphabatim (USA))
3204[2] 4037a[4] 5285[17] 5531a[4] 6519[6]

Teen Ager (FR) *Paul Burgoyne* a66 65
7 b g Invincible Spirit(IRE) —Tarwiya (IRE) (Dominion)
810[9] 950[6] 1045[13] 1177[7] (1486) 2201[6] 7442[6]

Tegan (IRE) *Richard Hannon* a72 75
3 b f Cape Cross(IRE) —Principessa (Machiavellian (USA))
158[9] 274[6] 624[7] 1022[10] 2307[11] 2583[7] 3726[2] (4625) (4827) (5321) 5665[2] 6255[10] (6894) 7458[6] 7638[6]

Teide Peak (IRE) *Mark Johnston* 71
2 b c Cape Cross(IRE) —Teide Lady (Nashwan (USA))
6630[2] 6954[5] 7233[12]

Teixidor (ITY) *Ottavio Di Paolo*
2 ch c St Paul House—Rosetta Stone (ITY) (Tisserand (ITY))
7217a[7]

Telescopic *James Frost* 50
4 b m Galileo(IRE) —Orlena (USA) (Gone West (USA))
2246[5]

Tell Dad *Richard Hannon* 104
2 b g Intikhab(USA) —Don't Tell Mum (IRE) (Dansili)
1316[2] ◆ 1721[2] 2109[3] 3064[12] 4536[5] (5591) 6060[2] (6170) 6527[2] (7026)

Tell Halaf *Noel Quinlan* a66 78
4 b g Oasis Dream—Topkamp (Pennekamp (USA))
3234[2] 3714[9]

Tellovoi (IRE) *L Polito* 101
3 b c Indian Haven—Khoonara (IRE) (Green Desert (USA))
1431a[13]

Tell The Wind (IRE) *Kevin Prendergast* a91 94
3 b f Mujadil(USA) —Fantastic Account (Fantastic Light (USA))
1116a[5] 2323a[8] 5086a[10] 7468a[2] 7793a[6]

Telluride *J E Hammond* a89 109
5 b h Montjeu(IRE) —Bayourida (USA) (Slew O'Gold (USA))
154a[4] 413a[4] ◆ 603a[5]

Telstar (GER) *A Kleinkorres*
2 b c Speedmaster(GER) —Thiara (GER) (Kornado)
(7664a)

Telwaar *Peter Chapple-Hyam* 100
2 ch c Haafhd—Hawafiah (Anabaa (USA))
2355[5] (2672) 3152[6] 4055[5] 5044[2]

Temida (IRE) *M G Mintchev* 106
3 b f Oratorio(IRE) —Interim Payment (USA) (Red Ransom (USA))
3209a[3] 6395a[6] (6739a)

Tempest Fugit (IRE) *John Gosden* 58
2 b f High Chaparral(IRE) —Diary (IRE) (Green Desert (USA))
6933[11]

Temps Au Temps (IRE) *M Delzangles* 108
3 b c Invincible Spirit(IRE) —Noahs Ark (IRE) (Charnwood Forest (IRE))
1552a[10] 2139a[4] 3670a[P]

Temps Perdus (IRE) *M Cheno* a86 81
5 b g Fasliyev(USA) —Silence (IRE) (Alzao (USA))
778a[8]

Tenacestream (CAN) *John Best* a82 55
4 b g Grand Slam(USA) —Heart Lake (CAN) (Unbridled (USA))
470[2]

Tenancy (IRE) *Shaun Harris* a61 66
7 b g Rock Of Gibraltar(IRE) —Brush Strokes (Cadeaux Genereux)
857[9] 1213[3] 1818[8] 2126[12] 2547[10] (3495) 4328[10] 4651[9] 5437[8] 5789[8] 5824[7] 6213[5] 6618[3] 6791[7] 7071[11]

Tenavon *William Knight* a61 65
3 b f Avonbridge—Tender (IRE) (Zieten (USA))
5241[2] 5567[7] 6307[4] 6407[4] 6940[7]

Tenbridge *Derek Haydn Jones* a66 10
2 b f Avonbridge—Tenebrae (IRE) (In The Wings)
4639[5] 5613[10] 6131[3] 6842[2] 7898[2]

Tenby Lady (USA) *Sir Mark Prescott Bt* a69 96
3 b f Anabaa(USA) —Bluebird Day (IRE) (Sadler's Wells (USA))
2253[4] ◆ 2664[5] 4090[7] (4344) (4490) (4723) 5546[5] 6066[7]

Tenderly Place *William Knight* 57
2 ch f Compton Place—Tender (IRE) (Zieten (USA))
7056[5]

Ten Down *Michael Quinn* a60 73
6 b g Royal Applause—Upstream (Prince Sabo)
80[6] 224[5] 337[9]

Tenessee *Peter Makin* a86 67
4 b h Nayef(USA) —Shukran (Hamas (IRE))
3434[9] 4097[11] 5716[4] 6254[7] 6592[15]

Tenhoo *Eric Alston* a59 80
5 b g Reset(AUS) —Bella Bambina (Turtle Island (IRE))
1107[6] 1461[2] (1617) (2091) (2259) 2892[2]

Ten On Ten *Charles Hills* 54
2 b c Cape Cross(IRE) —Kid Gloves (In The Wings)
5447[12]

Tenth Star (IRE) *A P O'Brien* 104
2 b c Dansili—Alpha Lupi (IRE) (Rahy (USA))
2329a[3] 4257a[3] 6336[2]

Ten To The Dozen *David Thompson* a55 50
8 b g Royal Applause—Almost Amber (USA) (Mt. Livermore (USA))
5652[9] 6452[6] 6833[14]

Teolane (IRE) *J S Bolger* 101
2 ch f Teofilo(IRE) —Masnada (IRE) (Erins Isle)
(2532a) ◆ (2777a) 3104[12] 4833a[9] 5525a[6]

Tepmokea (IRE) *Richard Fahey* a71 101
5 ch g Noverre(USA) —Eroica (GER) (Highest Honor (FR))
(2071) 3876[8] 5932[6] 7297[15]

Tequilla Heights (BRZ) *E Martins* a86 93
5 b h Know Heights(IRE) —Informal Dress (BRZ) (Clackson (BRZ))
331a[11]

Tequillo (FR) *J Bertin* a50 18
6 b h Enrique—Tequila Rose (FR) (Pancho Villa (USA))
7015a[10]

Terdaad (IRE) *Saeed Bin Suroor* a88 97
3 ch g Shamardal(USA) —Akrmina (Zafonic (USA))
(4914) ◆

Terenzium (IRE) *Micky Hammond* a52 60
9 br g Cape Cross(IRE) —Tatanka (ITY) (Luge)
1153[4] 1458[6] 1881[7] 2636[5] 3041[4] (3300) 3906[2] 4785[5] 5167[2] 5595[8]

Teriyaki (IRE) *Daniel Mark Loughnane* a45 70
3 b g Fath(USA) —Joy St Clair (IRE) (Try My Best (USA))
973a[9] 1753[10]

Termagant (IRE) *Kevin Prendergast* 98
4 b m Powerscourt—Rock Salt (Selkirk (USA))
924a[4] 1781a[4] 2325a[9]

Terre Du Vent (FR) *Y De Nicolay* a90 109
5 b m Kutub(IRE) —Phlizz (FR) (Kaldoun (FR))
(4524a) 5304a[6] 5839a[5] 6562a[8] 7406a[4]

Terrific Challenge (USA) *S Seemar* a108 104
9 ch h Royal Academy(USA) —Clever Empress (Crafty Prospector (USA))
237[7] 414a[10]

Terrys Flutter *Mark Allen* a16 60
3 ch f Noverre(USA) —Still As Sweet (IRE) (Fairy King (USA))
1044[9] 1812[10]

Tertio Bloom (SWE) *Fredrik Reutersklold* a105 105
6 ch g Tertullian(USA) —Yankee Bloom (USA) (El Gran Senor (USA))
2601a[6] 4121a[4]

Tertullus (FR) *Rune Haugen* a48 105
8 b h Monsun(GER) —Tryphosa (IRE) (Be My Guest (USA))
(2601a)

Testosterone (IRE) *P Bary* 116
3 b f Dansili—Epopee (IRE) (Sadler's Wells (USA))
(1597a) (2750a) (3447a) ◆ 5989a[2] 6567a[13]

Tetbury Lass *Adrian Chamberlain* a42 70
3 b f Hernando(FR) —Scenic Bold Dancer (AUS) (Scenic)
5114[3] 5999[9] 6404[3]

Teth *Mahmood Al Zarooni* 54
2 br f Dansili—Beta (Selkirk (USA))
4386[8] 5514[7]

Teutonic Knight (IRE) *Ian Williams* a19 46
4 ch g Daggers Drawn(USA) —Azyaa (Kris)
4861[9] 5114[4] 5247[8]

Tevez *Des Donovan* a86 96
6 b g Sakhee(USA) —Sosumi (Be My Chief (USA))
186[5] 1017[2] 1245[3] (1610) 2000[4] 2178[2] ◆ 2470[4] 3285[5] (3634) 3877[15] 4310[16]

Tewin Wood *Alan Bailey* a81 81
4 ch g Zaha(CAN) —Green Run (USA) (Green Dancer (USA))
666[9] (806) 908[3] 1110[15] 1296[2] (1569) 1832[4] 2020[10] 2597[4] 3805[2] 5383[12] 5687[6] 6079[5] 6583[2] 6990[3] 7110[6] 7299[4]

Texan Dream (IRE) *Mlle V Dissaux* a75 75
6 b h Oasis Dream—Texalina (FR) (Kaldoun (FR))
325a[0]

Thackeray *Chris Fairhurst* a53 49
4 b g Fasliyev(USA) —Chinon (IRE) (Entrepreneur)
6097[7] 6781[5] 7271[2]

Thai Haku (IRE) *M Delzangles* 103
4 b m Oasis Dream—Coconut Show (Linamix (FR))
241[2] 586a[5] 3654a[9] 4499[7]

Thalia Grace *Les Hall* a52 62
4 ch m Zafeen(FR) —Days Of Grace (Wolfhound (USA))
2920[15] 3597[5] 6791[8] 7429[4]

Thane Of Cawdor (IRE) *Tom Tate* 50
2 b g Danehill Dancer(IRE) —Holy Nola (USA) (Silver Deputy (CAN))
6805[8] 7233[17]

Thank You Joy *J R Jenkins* a58 64
3 b f Iceman—Once Removed (Distant Relative)
60[6] 3432[7] 4435[9] (5380) 6823[7] 7723[6]

Thatcherite (IRE) *Tony Coyle* a74 74
3 gr g Verglas(IRE) —Damiana (IRE) (Thatching)
1693[4] ◆ 3977[3] (4286) 4811[4] 5441[8] (5731) 6231[13] 6505[5] 7213[6]

That'll Do Nicely (IRE) *Nicky Richards* a35 81
8 b g Bahhare(USA) —Return Again (IRE) (Top Ville)
1390[8] 2734[7]

Thats A Fret (IRE) *Liam McAteer* a75 95
5 b g Choisir(AUS) —Reality Check (IRE) (Sri Pekan (USA))
923a[13] 3440a[U] (4886) 6112[13] 6388a[16] 7790a[5]

That's Dangerous *Roger Charlton* a66 81
2 ch c Three Valleys(USA) —St Edith (IRE) (Desert King (IRE))
1143[2] ◆ 1785[4] (3631) 4019[2] 4913[9] 5931[3] (6268) 6957[9]

Thatstheone *Bill Moore* a31 51
3 b f Needwood Blade—Danifah (IRE) (Perugino (USA))
7005[12] 7253[11]

Thawabel (IRE) *Marcus Tregoning* 50
2 b f Nayef(USA) —Shohrah (IRE) (Giant's Causeway (USA))
6745[10]

The Absent Mare *Robin Dickin* a64 46
3 gr f Fair Mix(IRE) —Precious Lucy (FR) (Kadrou (FR))
731[7] 930[2] 1018[2] 1299[6] 1769[6] 2166[4] 2379[5] 5642[2] 5898[2] (7145) (7331)

Theatrical Award (NOR) *Michael Taylor* a91 95
6 b m Academy Award(IRE) —Theatre Antique (USA) (Theatrical)
2601a[4] 5984a[11]

The Auctioneer (IRE) *Willie Musson* a61 42
3 ch g Medicean—Passe Passe (USA) (Lear Fan (USA))
7085[11]

The Bay Bandit *S Donohoe* a56 44
4 b g Highest Honor(FR) —Pescara (IRE) (Common Grounds)
5267[9]

The Bells O Peover *Mark Johnston* a77 95
3 b g Selkirk(USA) —Bay Tree (IRE) (Daylami (IRE))
902a[3] 1096[3] 1339[13] 2253[2] (2551) 3069[17] 4108[7] 4426[9] 5283[19] 5580[3] (6046) (6279) 6376[3] 6497[8]

The Betchworth Kid *Alan King* a83 104
6 b g Tobougg(IRE) —Runelia (Runnett)
(1188) 1601[4] 3066[11] 3875[13] 6528[9] 7297[8]

The Big Haerth (IRE) *David Evans* a75 76
5 b h Elusive City(USA) —Calypso Run (Lycius (USA))
159[3] 914[4] (1021) 1232[2] 1867[4] 2207[10] 3093[2] 3341[8] 3805[12]

The Black Lady (GER) *W Baltromei* 75
4 b m Big Shuffle(USA) —The Green (FR) (Greinton)
196a[0]

The Blind Side (IRE) *Michael Appleby* 10
3 b g Oratorio(IRE) —Grand Comity (IRE) (Grand Lodge (USA))
1056[7] 1302[6] 2149[11] 3309[8]

The Blue Banana (IRE) *Brian Meehan* 80
2 b g Red Clubs(IRE) —Rinneen (IRE) (Bien Bien (USA))
3182[8] 3755[2] (4269) 4749[2] 5280[5] 5825[2] 6724[8] 6986[5]

The Blue Dog (IRE) *Michael Wigham* a67 67
4 b m High Chaparral(IRE) —Jules (IRE) (Danehill (USA))
(588) 687[2] 839[2] 917[2] 1167[2] 1324[5] 1992[7] 2023[7] 3100[4] 1075[5]

The Boomingbittern *Edward Creighton*
2 b f Three Valleys(USA) —The Lady Mandarin (Groom Dancer (USA))
3547[13] 4545[10] 5170[8]

The Buska (IRE) *Declan Carroll* 73
3 ch g Haafhd—Play That Tune (Zilzal (USA))
3320[7] 3543[11] 4286[2] 5179[2] ◆ 5731[8] 6840[14]

The Calling Curlew *Henry Candy* a72 74
3 b g Soviet Star(USA) —The Lady Mandarin (Groom Dancer (USA))
3430[5] 4157[9] 4800[6] 5420 [2] 6023[4] 6729[6]

The Caped Crusader (IRE) *Ollie Pears* 84
4 b g Cape Cross(IRE) —Phariseek (IRE) (Rainbow Quest (USA))
1908[5] 2213[4] 3054[2] 4082[2] 4677[3]

The Cash Generator (IRE) *Ralph Smith* 71
3 b c Peintre Celebre(USA) —Majestic Launch (Lear Fan (USA))
2097[6]

The Catenian (IRE) *Eoin Doyle* a48 31
3 b g Hawk Wing(USA) —Belleclaire (IRE) (Bigstone (IRE))
7333[6] 7639[4]

The Cayterers *Tony Carroll* a96 86
9 b g Cayman Kai(IRE) —Silky Smooth (IRE) (Thatching)
180[4] 353[6] 1443[6] 2150[4] 5328[3]

The Cheka (IRE) *Eve Johnson Houghton* a104 113
5 b g Xaar—Veiled Beauty (USA) (Royal Academy (USA))
1118a[2] 1948[2] (2502) 3404[4] 4116a[4] 5046[6] 5510[4] 5930[3] 6521[3]

The Chester Giant *Patrick Morris* 35
4 b m Royal Applause—Serengeti Bride (USA) (Lion Cavern (USA))
1063[10] 2202[4] 2450[5] 3041[8]

The Clan Macdonald *David Barron* 83
2 b f Intikhab(USA) —Song Of Passion (IRE) (Orpen (USA))
(2630) 3402[7]

The Composer *Michael Blanshard* a45 50
9 b g Royal Applause—Superspring (Superlative)
2873[5] 3599[11] 4630[4]

The Confessor *Henry Candy* a96 97
4 b g Piccolo—Twilight Mistress (Bin Ajwaad (IRE))
2927[3] ◆ 3440a[7] 4314[2] ◆ 5936[3] 6862[11] 7295[3]

The Confessor (ITY) *L Riccardi* 102
3 ch c Footstepsinthesand—Scintillosa (Compton Place)
1431a[3]

Thecornishcockney *John Ryan* a60 82
2 bl g Cockney Rebel(IRE) —Glittering Image (IRE) (Sadler's Wells (USA))
2510[U] 3954[7] 4205[5] 4798[LFT] 5234[5] 6100[7] 6952[5]

Thecornishcowboy *John Ryan* a61 52
2 b c Haafhd—Oriental Dance (Fantastic Light (USA))
6064[9] 6300[8] 6663[2] 6956[7] 7140[5]

The Coulbeck Kid *Des Donovan* a38 40
2 b g Tobougg(IRE) —Billiard (Kirkwall)
1129[6] 1590[5] 2234[4] 2595[3] 3491[8]

The Dancing Lord *Bill Turner* a69 75
2 br g Imperial Dancer—Miss Brookie (The West (USA))
1042[4] (1129) 1316[5] 2367[6] (2556) 2902[3] 3728[5] 6786[3] 6975[5] 7196[5] 7353[3] 7490[3] 7635[2]

The Desert Saint *B Dutruel* a69 76
5 b g Dubai Destination(USA) —Maria Theresa (Primo Dominie)
7314a[8]

The Drunken Dr (IRE) *Niall Moran* a63 61
3 ch g Dr Fong(USA) —Evening Promise (Aragon)
(7195) 7608[4] 7631[7]

The Ducking Stool *Julia Feilden* a42 50
4 ch m Where Or When(IRE) —Dance Sequel (Selkirk (USA))
4578[4] 5168[7] 7581[5] 7695[7]

The Dukes Arch (USA) *Peter Fahey* a61 60
4 bb m Arch(USA) —Navarene (USA) (Known Fact (USA))
184[3] 507[6]

The Factor (USA) *Bob Baffert* a129
3 rg c War Front(USA) —Greyciousness (USA) (Miswaki (USA))
7304a[8]

The Fiery Cross *Ian Semple* a36 61
4 b g Acclamation—Miriam (Forzando)
2631[4] 3111[6] 3857[2] 5436[3] 5865[7]

The Fifth Member (IRE) *Jim Boyle* a96 95
7 b g Bishop Of Cashel—Palace Soy (IRE) (Tagula (IRE))
925a[7]

Thefillyfromsutton *Pat Phelan* 44
2 b f Ad Valorem(USA) —For Love (USA) (Sultry Song (USA))
2187[7] 2425[4] 2998[11]

The Flying Cholita (IRE) *Eve Johnson Houghton* a10 40
3 bb f Bold Fact(USA) —Secret Harbour (IRE) (Eagle Eyed (USA))
4970[9] 5346[7] 5999[11]

The Fonz *Sir Michael Stoute* a74 98
5 b g Oasis Dream—Crystal Cavern (USA) (Be My Guest (USA))
1717[4] 2071[9] 3625[6] 4267[8] 5250[10]

The Fox Tully (IRE) *Gerard Keane* a62 65
6 b g Monashee Mountain(USA) —Then Came Bronson (IRE) (Up And At 'Em)
7604[8]

The Fugue *John Gosden* 90
2 br f Dansili—Twyla Tharp (IRE) (Sadler's Wells (USA))
(7165) ◆

The Fun Crusher *Tim Easterby* 81
3 ch g Halling(USA) —South Rock (Rock City)
(1692)

The Galloping Shoe *Alistair Whillans* a83 89
6 b g Observatory(USA) —My Way (IRE) (Marju (IRE))
1000[3] 1100[4] 2000[8] 2716[12] 3163[4] 3585[9] 4043[8] 4380[7] 4540[5] 5724[8] 7215[4]

The Games Gone (IRE) *David Evans* a18 32
2 ch f Iffraaj—Ejder (IRE) (Indian Ridge)
5323[11] 6291[9] 6751[9] 7421[9] 7697[11]

The Gillie *Richard Fahey* a53 55
4 b g Pivotal—Red Tiara (USA) (Mr Prospector (USA))
774[3] 971[5] 1520[11] 1615[15]

The Giving Tree (IRE) *Sylvester Kirk* 75
2 b f Rock Of Gibraltar(IRE) —Starry Messenger (Galileo (IRE))
3813[8] 5807[5] 6322[2] (6807)

The Graig *John Holt* a59 58
7 b g Josr Algarhoud(IRE) —Souadah (USA) (General Holme (USA))
69[11]

The Guru Of Gloom (IRE) *William Muir* a87 78
3 b g Dubai Destination(USA) —Gabriella (Cape Cross (IRE))
1338[7] ◆ 1682[7] 2103[5] ◆ (3246) 4020[3] (4799) 5718[5] (6003)

The Happy Hammer (IRE) *Eugene Stanford* a76 64
5 b g Acclamation—Emma's Star (ITY) (Darshaan)
(96) 307[2] (473) 763[2] 995[4] 2111[8] 7532[6] 7716[6]

The Holyman (IRE) *Jo Crowley* a76 67
3 ch c Footstepsinthesand—Sunset (IRE) (Polish Precedent (USA))
1446[5] 4385[7] 5835[8] 6799[3] ◆ 7637[9]

The Ice Factor *Gordon Elliott* a51 31
3 b g Iceman—Kiruna (Northern Park (USA))
7688[2]

The Jailer *John O'Shea* a60 67
8 b m Mujahid(USA) —Once Removed (Distant Relative)
(1638) (1831) 2167[6] 3464[4] 4628[5] 4882[7] 5204[3] 5534[8] 5965[7] 6304[3] 7224[4] 7690[4]

The Joe McArdle (GER) *Alex Fracas* a75 94
6 b h Sharp Prod(USA) —The Bastienne (FR) (Baylis)
42a[6] 903a[9]

Theladyinquestion *Andrew Balding* 86
4 b m Dubawi(IRE) —Whazzat (Daylami (IRE))
(5016) 5657[11] 6523[7]

The Living Room (FR) *Stephane Chevalier* a103 103
4 b m Gold Away(IRE) —Leave of Absence (FR) (Exit To Nowhere (USA))
497a[13]

The Lock Master (IRE) *Michael Appleby* a85 79
4 b g Key Of Luck(USA) —Pitrizza (IRE) (Machiavellian (USA))
9[2] (148) (287) 541[6] 548[2] 723[5] 799[2] 1098[8] 1874[7] 1977[2] 2475[4] 3003[5] 3811[4] 4326[8] 7558[11] 7699[9] 7884[2]

The Lord *Bill Turner* a28 70
11 b g Averti(IRE) —Lady Longmead (Crimson Beau)
343[7] 401[11] 511[10]

The Magic Of Rio *John Balding* a50 66
5 b m Captain Rio—Good Health (Magic Ring (IRE))
102[7] 512[11] 941[12] 7691[5]

The Mellor Fella *Richard Fahey* 87
3 b g Compton Place—Grande Terre (IRE) (Grand Lodge (USA))
(2096) 3168[6] 3904[4]

The Midshipmaid *Lucinda Featherstone* a42 41
4 b m Zafeen(FR) —Ebba (Elmaamul (USA))
4077[7]

The Mighty Lohan (IRE) *Amy Weaver* a25 31
2 ch c Refuse To Bend(IRE) —Anda (Selkirk (USA))
3552[9] 4330[13] 5382[10] 6101[10]

The Mighty Mod (USA) *Michael Chapman* a39 50
4 b g Gone West(USA) —Michelle's Monarch (USA) (Wavering Monarch (USA))
1973[8] 6575[5] 7503[10]

The Mongoose *Sir Michael Stoute* 77
3 b g Montjeu(IRE) —Angara (Alzao (USA))
5327[5] 6377[3] 6755[6]

The Name Is Don (IRE) *Mark Gillard* a72 65
2 b g One Cool Cat(USA) —Waroonga (IRE) (Brief Truce (USA))
2788[8] 3288[6] 3868[4] 4823[9] 5625[3] 6252[5] 6695[12] 6890[9] 7242[6] (7464) (7657)

The Name Is Frank *Mark Gillard* a63 72
6 b g Lujain(USA) —Zaragossa (Paris House)
1787[4] 2142[6] 2789[6] 3293[5] 3720[10] 4224[2] 4487[4] 4828[7] (5616) 5914[7] 6258[2] 6444[7] 7123[4] 7462[6]

The New Black (IRE) *Gay Kelleway* 62
2 gr f Oratorio(IRE) —Zarawa (IRE) (Kahyasi)
2788[9] 3249[3] (3816) 7081[9]

The Nifty Duchess *Tim Easterby* 42
3 ch f Firebreak—Nifty Alice (First Trump)
1246[9] 1540[5] 1860[7] 2350[4] 3039[13] 3615[6]

The Nifty Fox *Tim Easterby* a87 94
7 b g Foxhound(USA) —Nifty Alice (First Trump)
1539[7] 2118[4] 2397[2] 2727[11] 3160[5] 3379[11] 4195[6] 4516[5] 5163[3] 5680[5] 6112[7] 6212[3] 6917[9]

The Nile *John Gosden* 84
2 ch c Three Valleys(USA) —Delta (Zafonic (USA))
4995[3]

The Noble Ord *Sylvester Kirk* 72
2 b c Indesatchel(IRE) —Four Legs Good (IRE) (Be My Guest (USA))
4269[5] (5232) 5584[4]

Theocritus (USA) *Claes Bjorling* a82 83
6 b g Theatrical—Candace In Aspen (USA) (Woodman (USA))
2601a[8] 5984a[10]

Theo Danon (GER) *P Schiergen* 109
3 ch c Lord Of England(GER) —Ticinella (GER) (Hernando (FR))
3007a[5] 3672a[15] (5308a) 6558a[6]

The Oil Magnate *Michael Dods* a77 78
6 ch g Dr Fong(USA) —Bob's Princess (Bob's Return (IRE))
320[4] 639[3] 1036[4] 3115[5] 3858[11] 5036[7] (6082) 6451[5] 6780[8] 7162[3]

Theology *Jeremy Noseda* 110
4 b g Galileo(IRE) —Biographie (Mtoto)
1601[6] 2316[2] 3875[16] 5271[3] 5883[8] 6271[5] 7027[7]

The Only Key *Jane Chapple-Hyam* a94 91
5 b m Key Of Luck(USA) —Sierra Virgen (USA) (Stack (USA))
1892[3] 2220[10] (2884) 3592[4] 4788[3] 6124[4] 7296[13]

Theorique (FR) *M Boutin* a58 48
8 b g Highest Honor(FR) —Theorie (FR) (Anabaa (USA))
706a[9]

The Osteopath (IRE) *Michael Dods* 98
8 ch g Danehill Dancer(IRE) —Miss Margate (IRE) (Don't Forget Me)
2061[8] 2347[2] 2984[3] 4125[2] 4361[6] 4811[7] 5549[2] (6831) 6990[11] 7161[4] 7339[12]

The Paddyman (IRE) *William Haggas* 105
3 b c Giant's Causeway(USA) —Winds Of Time (IRE) (Danehill (USA))
1318[4] 1850[5] 2338a[7]

The Penny Horse (IRE) *J S Moore* 83
2 bl g One Cool Cat(USA) —Nell Peters (IRE) (Singspiel (IRE))
(1185) 3014[10] 3589[4] 4228[4] 6535[17]

The Pier (IRE) *Joseph G Murphy* a92 86
5 ch g Alhaarth(IRE) —Cois Cuain (IRE) (Night Shift (USA))
7378a[11]

The Ploughman *John Bridger* a28 20
2 gr g Tillerman—Kilmovee (Inchinor)
4912[9] 6216[12] 6462[14]

The Quarterjack *Ron Hodges*
2 b g Haafhd—Caressed (Medicean)
6281[8]

The Reaper (IRE) *G M Lyons* a103 100
3 b g Footstepsinthesand—Lady Gregory (IRE) (In The Wings)
4333[7] 4767a[2] 5086a[2] 7012a[7] 7149a[2]

The Rectifier (USA) *Jim Boyle* 112
4 bb h Langfuhr(CAN) —Western Vision (USA) (Gone West (USA))
1385[6] 1948[4] 2558[2] 3409[2] 4972[3] 6061[8]

Theresnoneedfordat (IRE) *Lydia Pearce* 70
2 b c Holy Roman Emperor(IRE) —Manuscript (Machiavellian (USA))
4823[4] 5424[3] ◆ 6743[9]

There's No Rules *Richard Guest*
2 br g Authorized(IRE) —Excellent (Grand Lodge (USA))
7350[7]

The Right Time *Tony Carroll* a42 53
3 b f Val Royal(FR) —Esligier (IRE) (Sabrehill (USA))
4388[8] 4861[4] 5567[13] 6446[12] 6845[9] 7400[8]

The Rising (IRE) *Ed McMahon* a69 74
2 b c Pivotal—Jewel In The Sand (IRE) (Bluebird (USA))
3165[3] 3915[5] 4436[3] 5174[4] 5562[7] (6045) 6843[4]

The Rising (TUR) *S Aydogdi* 95
7 b m Strike The Gold(USA) —Free Trade (TUR) (Shareef Dancer (USA))
5753a[7]

The Scorching Wind (IRE) *Stuart Williams* a98 53
5 b g Fasliyev(USA) —Rose Of Mooncoin (IRE) (Brief Truce (USA))
265[8] 613[10] 822[9] 963[7] 1760[9] 3685[9]

Thescottishsoldier *Alistair Whillans* 49
4 ch g Observatory(USA) —Twenty Seven (IRE) (Efisio)
1519[5]

These Dreams *Richard Guest* a52 53
3 b f Sleeping Indian—White Turf (GER) (Tiger Hill (IRE))
322[4] 659[3] 745[4] 936[3] 2062[5] 2265[5] 2396[10] 3027[6] 3192[3] 3494[2] 3702[5] 4172[3] 4395[8] 5215[9] 6176[4]

The Shrew *John Gosden* a100 102
3 b f Dansili—Whazzat (Daylami (IRE))
(1313) 1719[13] 6297[3] 7128[6] 7516[2] 7678a[0]

The Snorer *John Holt* a52 37
3 b g Diktat—La Chesneraie (Groom Dancer (USA))
1304[3] 2114[13] 7766[3] 7931[7]

The Strig *Stuart Williams* a71 79
4 b g Mujahid(USA) —Pretty Kool (Inchinor)
1444[14] 2929[5] 3179[12] 6238[2] 6580[6] (6765) 7106[16] 7201[9] (7512)

The Tatling (IRE) *Milton Bradley* a71 75
14 bb g Perugino(USA) —Aunty Eileen (Ahonoora)
80[8] 443[5] 735[3] 857[4] 934[2] 1248[7] 1453[4] 1627[3] 2164[2] 2755[4] 3015[2] (3556) 3940[6] 4631[2] 4820[4] 5846[7] 5997[5] (7737)

The Thrill Is Gone *Mick Channon* a73 98
3 ch f Bahamian Bounty—Licence To Thrill (Wolfhound (USA))
2032[3] ◆ 2405[2] 2928[8] 4498[3] 5288[8] 5706[12]

The Tichborne (IRE) *Roger Teal* a85 94
3 b g Shinko Forest(IRE) —Brunswick (Warning)
(101) ◆ 1773[3] 2506[7] 3067[3] 4472[13]

The Tiger *Ed Dunlop* a57
3 b g Tiger Hill(IRE) —Rafiya (Halling (USA))
1311[6]

The Tooth Fairy (IRE) *Michael Mulvany* a86 93
5 b g Statue Of Liberty(USA) —Fairy Lore (IRE) (Fairy King (USA))
923a[4] 5746a[18]

Theturnofthesun (IRE) *John Gosden* 79
2 ch c Galileo(IRE) —Something Mon (USA) (Maria's Mon (USA))
6334[6] 6726[2]

The Verminator (AUS) *Chris Waller* 112
5 b g Jeune—Fraar Side (AUS) (Fraar (USA))
7218a[13]

The Wee Chief (IRE) *Jimmy Fox* a73 77
5 ch g King Charlemagne(USA) —La Belle Clare (IRE) (Paris House)
985[4] 1444[7] 1771[7] 2001[2] 2645[5] 2929[3] 3322[6]

The Which Doctor *Richard Guest* a91 92
6 b g Medicean—Oomph (Shareef Dancer (USA))
525[10] 615[7] 790[3] 1081[4] (1278) 1560[5] 1792[4] 1908[8] 4679[5] 4921[6] 5383[9] 5948[11] 6093[17] 6797[12] (7098) 7202[4] 7447[9] 7532[8] 7605[8] 7756[5]

The Wicked Lord *Stuart Kittow* a60 62
2 ch c Byron—Sable 'n Silk (Prince Sabo)
3229[7] 3984[6] 5232[6] 5998[4] 6489[11] 6890[2]

The Winged Assasin (USA) *Shaun Lycett* a74 69
5 b g Fusaichi Pegasus(USA) —Gran Dama (USA) (Rahy (USA))
190[2] 315[6] 711[3] 1066[2] 1874[3] 7556[4] 7900[3]

Thewinnatakesitall *Noel Wilson* a56 48
4 ch m King's Best(USA) —Powder Puff (IRE) (Sadler's Wells (USA))
690[11]

Thewinningmachine *Richard Fahey* 70
2 b f Kheleyf(USA) —Spinning Reel (Spinning World (USA))
4276[4] 4940[3] 5480[5] 6154[5] 6921[4]

The Wonder Land (FR) *J-P Perruchot* a53 75
7 b m Lord Of Men—Tel Reema (FR) (Tel Quel (FR))
221a[0]

The Wonga Coup (IRE) *Pat Phelan* a52 62
4 b g Northern Afleet(USA) —Quichesterbahn (USA) (Broad Brush (USA))
162[7] 361[8] 1233[8] 2170[5] 3253[9] 3476[10]

They All Laughed *Marjorie Fife* a15 61
8 ch g Zafonic(USA) —Royal Future (IRE) (Royal Academy (USA))
1032[7] 1556[3] 1794[2] 2060[10] 3185[7] 4856[9] 4944[3] 5650[3] 6600[5] 7077[12] 7645[P]

The Young Master *Neil Mulholland* a38
2 b g Echo Of Light—Fine Frenzy (IRE) (Great Commotion (USA))
7559[12] 7751[13]

Theyskens' Theory (USA) *Claude McGaughey III* a93 112
3 b f Bernardini(USA) —Heat Lightning (USA) (Summer Squall (USA))
(2073) 3106[8] (5277) 6183a[2] 6719a[11]

Theza Bere (FR) *P Monfort* a75 70
4 gr m High Yield(USA) —Miss Fine (FR) (Kaldoun (FR))
831a[3]

Thimaar (USA) *John Gosden* 99
3 bb g Dynaformer(USA) —Jinaan (USA) (Mr Prospector (USA))
1365[3] ◆ 3824[2] (4279) 5182[8] 5700[13] (6499)

Think *Clive Mulhall* a52 51
4 ch g Sulamani(IRE) —Natalie Jay (Ballacashtal (CAN))
4813[4] 5792[5] 7063[10] 7571[5] 7712[6]

Thinking *Tim Easterby* a51 76
4 b g Makbul—Concentration (IRE) (Mind Games)
1911[5] 2233[5] 2671[3] (2799) 3245[2] (3454) 3859[2] (5106) 5722[12]

Thinking Robins (IRE) *Ottavio Di Paolo* 97
8 b h Plumbird—Rose Jasmine (ITY) (Sikeston (USA))
1919a[10]

Think Its All Over (USA) *Julie Camacho* a78 80
4 b g Tiznow(USA) —A P Petal (USA) (A.P. Indy (USA))
1243[10] 2459[8] 2952[11] 3545[6] (4177) 4649[2] 5149[3] (5723) 6191[7]

Thin Red Line (IRE) *Michael Dods* a79 100
5 b g Red Ransom(USA) —Albaiyda (IRE) (Brief Truce (USA))
1824[8] 2604[6] 3381[2] 4360[7] 5035[10]

Third Half *Tom Dascombe* a75
2 b g Haafhd—Treble Heights (IRE) (Unfuwain (USA))
7066[2] (7367)

Third Set (IRE) *I Mohammed* a100 91
8 b g Royal Applause—Khamseh (Thatching)
239[9] 331a[12]

Thirkleby (IRE) *David Barron* 70
2 ch g Haafhd—Madame Boulangere (Royal Applause)
3161[6] 3826[5] 4853[5]

Thirsty Bear *Rebecca Curtis* 70
2 ch g Zamindar(USA) —Coolberry (USA) (Rahy (USA))
3132[4] 3722[3] 4995[9] 5427[3] 5840[4]

Thirteen Shivers *Michael Easterby* a74 94
3 b g Iceman—Thirteen Tricks (USA) (Grand Slam (USA))
1275[2] 1624[3] (2074) 2411[3] (3052) 4048[3] 4295[2] 4855[2] 5288[9] 6148[12] 6331[14]

This Is Us (IRE) *Eric Alston*
3 ch f Kheleyf(USA) —Mannsara (IRE) (Royal Academy (USA))
1436[7] 2094[12]

This Ones For Eddy *John Balding* a70 59
6 b g Kyllachy—Skirt Around (Deploy)
9[3] 292[4] 589[4] 906[6] 1989[2] 2670[3] ◆ (3241) 3719[5] (3953) 5902[9] 7175[6] 7268[10] 7648[8] 7748[2] 7820[4]

Thistle Bird *Roger Charlton* a56 101
3 b f Selkirk(USA) —Dolma (FR) (Marchand De Sable (USA))
1606[4] (2528) 3873[4] (5113) 5940[3] 6530[5]

Thomas Chippendale (IRE) *Sir Henry Cecil* 88
2 b c Dansili—All My Loving (IRE) (Sadler's Wells (USA))
5254[10] (6771) ◆

Thoroughly Red (IRE) *Linda Stubbs* a36 67
6 b g King's Best(USA) —Red Liason (IRE) (Selkirk (USA))
5652[5] 6081[10] 6453[7] 6877[9]

Thorpe Bay *Mark Rimmer* a63 62
2 b g Piccolo—My Valentina (Royal Academy (USA))
1129[3] 1396[7] 3553[4] 4085[6] 4922[4] 5535[2] 5833[4] 6695[3] 6846[8] 7353[4] 7642[4] 7770[6]

Thoughtsofstardom *Phil McEntee* a62 64
8 b g Mind Games—Alustar (Emarati (USA))
102[8] 165[10] 464[4] 537[2] 691[5] 812[8] 941[5] 1041[3] 1182[6] 1283[4] 1523[9] 7676[9] 7853[9]

Thought Worthy (USA) *John Gosden* 77
2 b c Dynaformer(USA) —Vignette (USA) (Diesis) (6774)

Three Am Tour (IRE) *Richard Hannon* a85 81
2 b f Strategic Prince—Murani (IRE) (Marju (IRE))
(5861) ◆ 6196a[4] 7095[4]

Three Bards (IRE) *Mark Johnston* 38
2 b c Dubawi(IRE) —Polish Affair (IRE) (Polish Patriot (USA))
7082[12]

Three Darlings (IRE) *David Nicholls* 68
2 gr f Elusive City(USA) —Tibouchina (IRE) (Daylami (IRE))
6702[3]

Three Gems (IRE) *E J O'Neill* 99
2 b f Jeremy(USA) —Neutrina (IRE) (Hector Protector (USA))
5296a[5]

Three Opera Divas *Mark Johnston* a63
3 b f Librettist(USA) —Tab's Gift (Bijou D'Inde)
456[2] 567[3]

Three Scoops *Dominic Ffrench Davis* a53 55
3 ch f Captain Rio—Sambarina (IRE) (Victory Note (USA))
109[9] 142[4] 834[5] 967[3] 1753[13] 1952[8] 4647[10] 4917[7] 5540[14] 6122[9]

Three Sugars (AUS) *Jeremy Noseda* a66 23
2 b f Starcraft(NZ) —Hoh Dear (IRE) (Sri Pekan (USA))
(5596) 6222[12]

Three Tenors *Gary Harrison* a41 36
2 ch c Three Valleys(USA) —First Musical (First Trump)
5170[7] 5393[8] 5802[6] 6471[8] 7258[9]

Three Way Stretch (IRE) *J T Gorman* 84
5 b g Intikhab(USA) —Chapka (IRE) (Green Desert (USA))
923a[2] 6388a[17]

Three White Socks (IRE) *Brian Ellison* a75 40
4 b g Whipper(USA) —Halesia (USA) (Chief's Crown (USA))
1210[9] 1519[3] (1973) ◆ (2654)

Threshing Days (IRE) *M Delzangles* a72 86
3 b f Oasis Dream—Amiarma (IRE) (Unfuwain (USA))
901a[7]

Throne *Richard Hannon* 33
2 b f Royal Applause—Pretty Poppy (Song)
6603[15] 7056[9]

Thrust Control (IRE) *Tracy Waggott* a88 88
4 ch g Fath(USA) —Anazah (USA) (Diesis)
377[5] 493[3] (744) 822[13] (1037) 1696[10] (1943) 2620[14] 2954[13] 3704[13] 4810[7] 5455[14] 5647[9] 5733[6] 6098[13] 6452[14] 6869[9]

Thsaam (FR) *Mlle S-V Tarrou* a67 75
4 ch m Refuse To Bend(IRE) —King's Folly (FR) (King's Best (USA))
5095a[3]

Thubiaan (USA) *William Haggas* 95
3 b c Dynaformer(USA) —Barzah (IRE) (Darshaan)
1840[2] 2813[2] (3705) 4777[4] 5283[9] 6103[4]

Thumbs Up (NZ) *C Fownes* 120
7 b g Shinko King(IRE) —Regelle (NZ) (Exploding Prospect (USA))
1576a[10] 7729a[2]

Thunda *Eve Johnson Houghton* a32 68
3 b f Stormy Atlantic(USA) —Lobby Card (USA) (Saint Ballado (CAN))
2790[4] 3324[3] 3723[5] 5136[6] 5624[3] 5836[10]

Thunderball *David Nicholls* a92 99
5 ch g Haafhd—Trustthunder (Selkirk (USA))
105[5] 175[6] 572[2] (648) 822[5] (956) 1610[4] 1854[9] (3045) (3704) 4531[19] 5032[15] 5887[12] 6862[23] 7433[6] 7578[4]

Thunder Bullet *Andrew Crook*
2 b c Auction House(USA) —Fresh Look (IRE) (Alzao (USA))
3505[10]

Thunder Gulf *Mrs K Burke* a52 39
3 b g Royal Applause—Statua (IRE) (Statoblest)
5120[5]

Thundering Home *George Baker* a67 65
4 gr g Storming Home—Citrine Spirit (IRE) (Soviet Star (USA))
399[5] 692[4] 814[5] 954[10] 1046[5] 1233[4] 1508[3] 1987[12] 3923[2] ◆ (4164) 4952[4] 6240[12] 7720[2] ◆ (7903)

Thunderstruck *David Nicholls* a91 49
6 b g Bertolini(USA) —Trustthunder (Selkirk (USA))
6[7] 180[8] 235[7] 541[2] 694[4] 877[2] 1098[12] 5036[10] 6918[10] 7558[6]

Thunderway (IRE) *Michael Dods* a40 29
3 b f Doyen(IRE) —Thunderbaby (USA) (Thunder Gulch (USA))
366[4] 643[3] 1413[5]

Thymesthree (IRE) *Chris Wall* a61 51
3 ch f Galileo(IRE) —Chervil (Dansili)
344[3] 529[6] 2858[5] 3690[10]

Tiablo (IRE) *David Simcock* a67
2 br f Red Clubs(IRE) —Canary Bird (IRE) (Catrail (USA))
6539[4] ◆ 6819[2] 7174[5] 7927[4]

Tibaldi (FR) *Mme C Head-Maarek* 93
2 b f Motivator—Treasure Queen (USA) (Kingmambo (USA))
4569a[7] 7219a[3]

Tiberina (IRE) *R Le Gal* a48 61
6 b m Hawk Wing(USA) —Perugina (FR) (Highest Honor (FR))
7256a[8]

Tiberius Claudius (IRE) *George Margarson* 74
3 b g Clodovil(IRE) —Final Favour (IRE) (Unblest)
1108[4] 1654[4] 3465[4] 4160[3] 4695[4] 6034[4] 6407[5]

Tibo Tibo (FR) *J-M Capitte* a73 79
3 gr c Vatori(FR) —Noa Sajani (FR) (Sagamix (FR))
410a[4]

Tickled Pink (IRE) *Sir Henry Cecil* 81
2 gr f Invincible Spirit(IRE) —Cassandra Go (IRE) (Indian Ridge)
2914[2] 4052[2]

Tick Tock Lover *Jo Crowley* a81 83
3 gr c Tikkanen(USA) —Ivory's Promise (Pursuit Of Love)
3871[4] 4253[9] 4665[6]

Tidal Run *Mick Channon* 70
3 b f Hurricane Run(IRE) —Tidie France (USA) (Cape Town (USA))
1751[6] (2349) 2637[7] (2904) 3587[3] 4476[3]

Tidal's Baby *Noel Quinlan* a68 73
2 b g Dutch Art—Tidal (Bin Ajwaad (IRE))
2017[4] 2559[11] 3761[4] 4184[3] 4682[2] 5170[2] 5991[2] 6786[5]

Tidal Star *Michael Quinlan* a72 70
3 b g Kyllachy—Tidal (Bin Ajwaad (IRE))
365[4]

Tidal Way (IRE) *Mick Channon* 81
2 gr c Red Clubs(IRE) —Taatof (IRE) (Lahib (USA))
2837[4] 3349[2] 3609[3] 4007[4] 4884[2] (5454) 6606[3]

Tiddliwinks *Kevin Ryan* a107 114
5 b g Piccolo—Card Games (First Trump)
1720[12] 2005[3] 2323a[2] 2967a[7] 4534[24] (4894) 5253[11] 5707[16]

Tidentime (USA) *Mick Channon* a82 87
2 bb c Speightstown(USA) —Casting Call (USA) (Dynaformer (USA))
(5051) (5713) 6170[6]

Tidespring (IRE) *H-A Pantall* 97
3 b f Monsun(GER) —Sweet Stream (ITY) (Shantou (USA))
7580a[8]

Tidy Affair (IRE) *Richard Hannon* a76 83
2 b c Amadeus Wolf—Pride Of My Heart (Lion Cavern (USA))
3288[4] ◆ 3686[3] ◆ 4414[3] ◆ 4996[10] (5855) 6372[2] 7390[4]

Tierceville (IRE) *E Libaud* a82 71
3 b f Oratorio(IRE) —Miss Sacha (IRE) (Last Tycoon)
901a[6]

Tifernati *Gary Moore* a35 94
7 b g Dansili—Pain Perdu (IRE) (Waajib)
308[5]

Tifongo (FR) *H-A Pantall* 107
2 b c Dr Fong(USA) —Tishkara (FR) (Xaar)
6660a[5] 6902a[4] 7405a[5]

Tiger Best (FR) *P Monfort*
2 b c Hold That Tiger(USA) —Art Fair (FR) (Fairy King (USA))
7664a[10]

Tigerbill *Nicky Vaughan* a60
3 ch g Hold That Tiger(USA) —Regal Asset (USA) (Regal Classic (CAN))
2151^{12} 3236^{6} 4478^{8} 5214^{5} 5900^{7} 6309^{4} 6698^{3}

Tiger Cub *Roger Charlton* a56 74
2 b f Dr Fong(USA) —Clouded Leopard (USA) (Danehill (USA))
3812^{9} 5320^{6} 5806^{7} 6460^{2} (6753)

Tiger Dream *Chris Down* a79 79
6 b g Oasis Dream—Grey Way (USA) (Cozzene (USA))
82^{9} 341^{9} 472^{8}

Tiger Goddess (IRE) *Bodil Hallencreutz* a71 80
5 gr m Verglas(IRE) —Googoosh (IRE) (Danehill (USA))
5096a^{9}

Tiger Hawk (USA) *Kevin M Prendergast* a69 35
4 b g Tale Of The Cat(USA) —Aura Of Glory (CAN) (Halo (USA))
573^{5} 796^{10} 854^{9} 1164^{9}

Tigerino (IRE) *Chris Fairhurst* a58 48
3 b g Tiger Hill(IRE) —Golden Shadow (IRE) (Selkirk (USA))
1969^{6} 2571^{4} 4814^{8} 5489^{2} 5790^{8} (6876) 7062^{5} 7145^{2}

Tiger Reigns *Michael Dods* 105
5 b g Tiger Hill(IRE) —Showery (Rainbow Quest (USA))
332a^{15} 605a^{4} 1154^{3} 1684^{18} 2933^{11} 3315^{5} 4331^{2} 4801^{8} 5185^{11} 6150^{5}

Tiger Royale *Michael Mullineaux* a44 22
3 b f Tiger Hill(IRE) —Arian Da (Superlative)
4559^{8} 7717^{7}

Tiger's Pride *Rod Millman* 56
3 b g Tiger Hill(IRE) —Riyma (IRE) (Dr Fong (USA))
4617^{10}

Tigers Tale (IRE) *Roger Teal* a62 66
2 b g Tiger Hill(IRE) —Vayenga (FR) (Highest Honor (FR))
3590^{6} 4007^{7} ◆ 4311^{7} 5233^{6} 5634^{6} 5967^{3} 6372^{6} 6817^{3}

Tiger Tess *Jonathan Portman* a51 58
3 b f Tiger Hill(IRE) —Vitesse (IRE) (Royal Academy (USA))
1474^{4} 2175^{5} 3437^{8} 4153^{3} 4703^{6}

Tigertoo (IRE) *Stuart Williams* a59 40
2 ch g Heliostatic(IRE) —Brightling (IRE) (Gorse)
5801^{11} 6267^{11} 6697^{6}

Tiger Webb *Michael Easterby* a79 86
3 b g Hurricane Run(IRE) —Wonderful Desert (Green Desert (USA))
1445^{4} (2203) 2877^{6} 5546^{4} (7214)

Tiger Would *David Elsworth* 4
2 b g Tiger Hill(IRE) —Ciboure (Norwick (USA))
6805^{12} 7134^{11}

Tight Lipped (IRE) *David Brown* 79
2 gr g Dark Angel(IRE) —Kayoko (IRE) (Shalford (IRE))
1744^{3} 2214^{2} 3161^{3} 3810^{2} 4194^{2} 4969^{4} 5287^{11} 5876^{6}

Tigresa (IRE) *Mark Johnston* 39
2 b f Tiger Hill(IRE) —Carakiysa (IRE) (Docksider (USA))
7257^{8}

Tigron (USA) *Mme C Barande-Barbe* a89 83
10 ch h Lion Cavern(USA) —Tidy Tune (USA) (The Minstrel (CAN))
481a^{3} 2867a^{3}

Tijori (IRE) *Richard Hannon* a74 74
3 b g Kyllachy—Polish Belle (Polish Precedent (USA))
(171) (594) 1727^{3} 1947^{6} 2819^{6} 3642^{5}

Tijuca (IRE) *Ed de Giles*
2 b f Captain Rio—Some Forest (IRE) (Charnwood Forest (IRE))
6291^{12}

[illegible] (IRE) *[illegible]* 63
3 ch g Kheleyf(USA) —Amravati (IRE) (Project Manager)
1683^{11} 2677^{9}

Till Dawn (IRE) *Tony Carroll* a59 60
3 br f Kheleyf(USA) —Tilbrook (IRE) (Don't Forget Me)
4684^{2} 4924^{3} 5615^{3} 6105^{4} 6444^{4} 6889^{14} 6943^{6} 7230^{9}

Tilliemint (IRE) *Tim Easterby* 69
3 b f Acclamation—Phantom Act (USA) (Theatrical)
1459^{4} 2498^{3} 2736^{3}

Tillietudlem (FR) *Jim Goldie* a35 74
5 gr g Kutub(IRE) —Queenhood (FR) (Linamix (FR))
2952^{10} (3507) 4326^{4} 4671^{6} 5079^{7} 6095^{5}

Tillys Tale *Paul Midgley* a77 77
4 ch m Lucky Story(USA) —Otylia (Wolfhound (USA))
1698^{11} (1816) 2126^{3} 3166^{12} 3379^{7} 3493^{6} 5918^{5} 6212^{11} 7104^{5} 7355^{11}

Tilos Gem (IRE) *Brian Ellison* a82 68
5 ch g Trans Island—Alpine Flair (IRE) (Tirol)
1324^{15} 7645^{7}

Tilsworth Glenboy *J R Jenkins* a70 75
4 b g Doyen(IRE) —Chara (Deploy)
647^{5} ◆ 1144^{6} 1867^{2} 2490^{5} 4666^{2} 5101^{9} 5969^{2}

Timber Treasure (USA) *Paul Green* a63 64
7 bb g Forest Wildcat(USA) —Lady Ilsley (USA) (Trempolino (USA))
748^{6} 3166^{11} 3341^{4} 4051^{7}

Time For A Tiger *Henry Candy*
2 b f Tiger Hill(IRE) —Last Slipper (Tobougg (IRE))
6745^{12}

Time For Gold (FR) *P Monfort* a85 85
6 ch g Gold Away(IRE) —Time For Romance (IRE) (Cure The Blues (USA))
196a^{0}

Timeless Call (IRE) *Reginald Roberts* a89 93
3 b f Sakhee(USA) —Pourquoi Pas (IRE) (Nordico (USA))
2861a^{10} 7012a^{10}

Timeless Elegance (IRE) *Howard Johnson* 80
4 b m Invincible Spirit(IRE) —Tidy Wager (IRE) (Catrail (USA))
1239^{4} 2494^{2} 3279^{4} (3900) 4126^{7}

Timeline *Mahmood Al Zarooni* 98
3 b c Elusive Quality(USA) —Last Second (IRE) (Alzao (USA))
2258^{2} (2648) ◆

Time Medicean *Tony Carroll* a70 85
5 gr g Medicean—Ribbons And Bows (IRE) (Dr Devious (IRE))
1493^{2} 2464^{11} 3166^{9} (3573) (5053) 5451^{2} 5972^{5} 6917^{7} 7660^{11}

Timepiece *Sir Henry Cecil* a80 116
4 b m Zamindar(USA) —Clepsydra (Sadler's Wells (USA))
2029^{3} 2678^{4} (2994) (3822) 4597a^{3} 5306a^{2} 6338^{8}

Time Prisoner (USA) *A Fabre* 109
4 gr h Elusive Quality(USA) —Zelanda (IRE) (Night Shift (USA))
815a^{6} (4121a) 5532a^{8}

Time Square (FR) *Tony Carroll* a75 81
4 b g Westerner—Sainte Parfaite (FR) (Septieme Ciel (USA))
384^{5} 621^{2} 805^{7} 1243^{2} 6130^{11} 6439^{11} 6988^{17} 7254^{8} 7458^{10}

Times Up *John Dunlop* 116
5 b g Olden Times—Princess Genista (Ile De Bourbon (USA))
1112^{4} (1717) (2316) 4037a^{2} 5045^{3} (6271) ◆ 6857^{5}

Timeteam (IRE) *K F Clutterbuck* a71 80
5 b g Danetime(IRE) —Ceannanas (IRE) (Magical Wonder (USA))
50^{5} 351^{RR} 5924^{5} 6257^{2} 6664^{8} 6793^{RR} 7332^{RR}

Time To Excel *Michael Dods* 51
2 ch g Exceed And Excel(AUS) —Treacle (USA) (Seeking The Gold (USA))
4047^{8} 4851^{8} 5486^{11}

Time To Play *Gary Brown* a52 65
6 b g Best Of The Bests(IRE) —Primavera (Anshan)
7466^{5} 7654^{5}

Time To Work (IRE) *Andrew Balding* 90
3 b g Hurricane Run(IRE) —Viscoumtess Brave (IRE) (Law Society (USA))
1811^{4} 2287^{3} 3376^{6} 4316^{5} 4998^{3} 5966^{7} 6249^{4}

Time Travel *James McAuley* a69 63
6 b g Fantastic Light(USA) —Nellie Nolan (USA) (Storm Cat (USA))
(839) 3715^{6}

Timocracy *Andrew Haynes* a71 74
6 br g Cape Cross(IRE) —Tithcar (Cadeaux Genereux)
1454^{2} ◆ (1636) 1936^{2} 2245^{2} 3139^{3} 3912^{3} 5135^{8}

Timolin (GER) *P Monfort* a73 62
4 ch h Tertullian(USA) —Tempelsonne (GER) (Acatenango (GER))
831a^{9}

Timos (GER) *T Doumen* 113
6 ch h Sholokhov(IRE) —Triclaria (GER) (Surumu (GER))
(478a) 705a^{8} 920a^{4} 1266a^{5}

Timpanist (USA) *Simon Dow* a62 70
4 b m Roman Ruler(USA) —Jazz Drummer (USA) (Dixieland Band (USA))
158^{3} 437^{2} 689^{5} 905^{5} 1133^{3} 1766^{8} 2605^{10} 4711^{4} 5201^{3} 5674^{8} 5858^{2} 5995^{2} ◆ 6814^{5} 7579^{14} 7658^{8}

Tinaar (USA) *F Nass* a99 103
5 b m Giant's Causeway(USA) —Seattle Tac (USA) (Seattle Slew (USA))
607a^{11}

Tinaheely (IRE) *Jonathan Portman* a64 7[illegible]
3 ch [illegible] (USA) —Tertia (IRE) (Polish Patriot (USA))
952^{5} 1682^{2} 2821^{11} 3219^{2} 3633^{11} 3803^{5} 5676^{6}

Tinas Exhibition (IRE) *Seamus Fahey* a58 62
4 ch m Great Exhibition(USA) —El Tina (Unfuwain (USA))
733^{9} 768^{5} 7631^{9}

Tina's Spirit (IRE) *Clive Cox* a72 79
2 gr f Invincible Spirit(IRE) —Dundel (IRE) (Machiavellian (USA))
2023^{4} ◆ 2606^{5} 4052^{4} 4536^{6} 5324^{2} 5562^{4} 6169^{6} 6526^{4} 6995^{6} 7343^{3} (7599)

Tindaro (FR) *Paul Webber* a85 92
4 gr g Kingsalsa(USA) —Star's Mixa (FR) (Linamix (FR))
2066^{12} 6439^{6}

Tingo In The Tale (IRE) *David Arbuthnot* 78
2 b g Oratorio(IRE) —Sunlit Skies (Selkirk (USA))
3780^{6} (4698) 5446^{2} 6957^{11}

Ting Ting (USA) *Jim Boyle* a53 61
4 b m Empire Maker(USA) —My Sweet Heart (USA) (You And I (USA))
175^{8}

Tin Horse (IRE) *D Guillemin* 117
3 gr c Sakhee(USA) —Joyeuse Entree (Kendor (FR))
1552a^{3} (2139a) 2751a^{5} 5129a^{6} 5988a^{7}

Tinkerbell Will *John E Long* a56 54
4 ch m Where Or When(IRE) —Highland Hannah (IRE) (Persian Heights)
663^{9} 905^{6} 1133^{5} 1604^{11} 2385^{7} 3253^{3} ◆ (4928) 5515^{9} 7119^{2} 7394^{8} 7640^{9}

Tinkertown (IRE) *Roger Varian* a102 102
3 gr c Verglas(IRE) —Kelly Nicole (IRE) (Rainbow Quest (USA))
(988) 1234^{5} 1850^{3} 2110^{2} 3067^{11} 4467^{7} 5466^{7} 6955^{6}

Tin Pan Alley *Mahmood Al Zarooni* 55
3 b c Singspiel(IRE) —Tazmeen (Darshaan)
2231^{6}

Tinseltown *Brian Rothwell* a41 52
5 b g Sadler's Wells(USA) —Peony (Lion Cavern (USA))
114^{6} 184^{5} 1216^{5}

Tinshu (IRE) *Derek Haydn Jones* a95 91
5 ch m Fantastic Light(USA) —Ring Of Esteem (Mark Of Esteem (IRE))
1402^{12} 1772^{3} 2105^{8} 2604^{11} 3592^{10} (4058) 4267^{3} 4788^{7} 6163^{12} 6302^{15} 6922^{7} 7328^{10} (7523) (7802)

Tintalle (FR) *Mlle C Brunaud* a39
4 b m Bahhare(USA) —True Vision (USA) (Lear Fan (USA))
1012a^{10}

Tiny Temper (IRE) *Richard Fahey* a47 73
3 b f Montjeu(IRE) —Lady Storm (IRE) (Mujadil (USA))
3705^{2} 4529^{6} 4985^{3} 5804^{12} 6577^{6} 7458^{12}

Tiny Tittle (IRE) *Deborah Sanderson*
2 b f Balmont(USA) —Rumuz (IRE) (Marju (IRE))
3021^{11}

Tinzapeas *Mick Channon* 72
2 b f Imperial Dancer—Noble Destiny (Dancing Brave (USA))
6117^{8} 6322^{3} 6742^{5} (7056)

Tinzo (IRE) *Alan Berry* 35
3 b g Auction House(USA) —Costa Verde (King Of Spain)
3191^{5} 3661^{13} 4146^{3} 4786^{7} 5203^{6} 5619^{RR} 6343^{14} 6428^{10}

Tioman Legend *Roger Charlton* 86
2 b g Kyllachy—Elegant Times (IRE) (Dansili)
1360^{7} (1863) 2367^{4}

Tioman Pearl *Roger Varian* 69
2 b c Royal Applause—Mazarine Blue (Bellypha)
6629^{6} 7052^{6} 7292^{7}

Tipsy Girl *Denis Coakley* 84
3 b f Haafhd—Disco Lights (Spectrum (IRE))
2926^{10} ◆ 3873^{5} 5240^{12}

Tip Toe (FR) *F Doumen* 107
4 b h Footstepsinthesand—Midnight Queen (GER) (Platini (GER))
7404a^{3} 7733a^{2}

Tip Top Gorgeous (IRE) *David O'Meara* 78
2 b f Red Clubs(IRE) —Amber's Bluff (Mind Games)
2404^{5} 2570^{2} 3104^{13} 4122^{2} 4347^{2} (5161) 5438^{2} 5967^{5} 6670^{9}

Tiradito (USA) *Michael Attwater* a88 81
4 bb g Tale Of The Cat(USA) —Saratoga Sugar (USA) (Gone West (USA))
285^{3} (1296) 2000^{5} 3045^{5} 5717^{5} 6220^{7} 6478^{10} 7199^{8} 7518^{4} 7636^{3}

Tirion (USA) *M Delcher-Sanchez* a81
3 b c Royal Academy(USA) —Domenica's Dream (USA) (Woodman (USA))
902a^{2}

Tislaam (IRE) *Alan McCabe* a77 72
4 gr g With Approval(CAN) —Lady Angola (USA) (Lord At War (ARG))
178^{4} 264^{6} 430^{4} (470) 612^{7} 956^{8} 1239^{12} 3517^{6} 4206^{6} 4909^{3} 5053^{8} 5387^{2} 5640^{2} 6091^{3} 6276^{5} 6634^{3} 7106^{9} 7448^{2} 7517^{2} 7767^{2} (7928)

Tis Rock 'N' Roll (USA) *David Lanigan* a59
2 bb c Rock Of Gibraltar(IRE) —Tis Me (USA) (Notebook (USA))
7083^{14} 7369 ^{11} 7521^{7}

Titan Diamond (IRE) *Mark Usher* a59 50
3 b g Diamond Green(FR) —Ditton Dancer (Danehill Dancer (IRE))
53^{3} 142^{5} 281^{2} 426^{2} ◆ (655) ◆ 760^{7} 887^{5} 1472^{3} 1953^{3} 2177^{5} 2421^{3} 2792^{8} 3223^{9} 3942^{8} 5143^{6} 5381^{8} 5902^{4} 6609^{5} 6982^{8} 7442^{9} 7524^{9}

Titan Triumph *William Knight* a87 76
7 b g Zamindar(USA) —Triple Green (Green Desert (USA))
(348) 615^{2} 703^{7} 995^{6} 1460^{10} 2000^{10} 7199^{11} 7439^{10} 7660^{4} 7922^{2} ◆

Titch The Witch *David C Griffiths*
3 br f Ferrule(IRE) —Lets Get It On (IRE) (Perugino (USA))
[illegible]

Titurel (GER) *Manfred Hofer* a104 108
6 ch h Dr Fong(USA) —Tucana (GER) (Acatenango (GER))
1128a^{7}

Titus Bolt (IRE) *Jim Boyle* a55 57
2 b g Titus Livius(FR) —Megan's Bay (Muhtarram (USA))
6019^{8} 6795^{7} 7132^{6}

Titus Gent *Jeremy Gask* a86 77
6 ch g Tumbleweed Ridge—Genteel (IRE) (Titus Livius (FR))
2903^{2} (3685) 4064^{8} 4742^{3} 5781^{6} (6491) (6665) 7847^{5} 7926^{11}

Titus Star (IRE) *J S Moore* a74 74
2 ch g Titus Livius(FR) —The Oldladysays No (IRE) (Perugino (USA))
3816^{3} 4969^{6} (5672) (7752) 7786^{4}

Tivers Song (USA) *John Harris* a57 56
7 gr g Buddha(USA) —Rousing (USA) (Alydar (USA))
16^{3} 184^{2} 324^{7} 450^{3}

Tiza (SAF) *F Rossi* a91 107
9 b g Goldkeeper(USA) —Mamushka (SAF) (Elliodor (FR))
1122a^{7}

Tiz Now Tiz Then (USA) *S Seemar* a82 81
6 b g Tiznow(USA) —Trepidation (USA) (Seeking The Gold (USA))
535a^{10}

Tlaad (USA) *Clive Brittain* 78
3 b c Kingmambo(USA) —Cloud Castle (In The Wings)
1850^{6}

Tmaam (USA) *Mark Johnston* 99
3 bb c Dynaformer(USA) —Thread (USA) (Topsider (USA))
2691^{2} 2930^{3} (5911) 6342^{2}

Tobago Bay *Gary Moore* a52 66
6 b g Tobougg(IRE) —Perfect Dream (Emperor Jones (USA))
560^{5} 2377^{11} 7145^{6}

Toballa *Clifford Lines* a49 51
6 b m Tobougg(IRE) —Ball Gown (Jalmood (USA))
2386^{4} 4090^{10} 4730^{3} 5357^{5} 5643^{3} 6083^{8}

Tobar Na Gaoise (IRE) *J S Bolger* 99
3 b c Whipper(USA) —Starchy (Cadeaux Genereux)
7189a^{9}

Tobayornottobay *Bruce Hellier* a25
5 b m Tobougg(IRE) —Rose Bay (Shareef Dancer (USA))
85^{7} 319^{6}

Tobernea (IRE) *Mark Johnston* a43 83
4 b g Indian Ridge—Act Of The Pace (IRE) (King's Theatre (IRE))
1994^{4} 2459^{9} 3072^{8} 3851^{8} 4326^{10} 4844^{4}

Tobetall *Malcolm Jefferson*
4 b m Tobougg(IRE) —Our Ethel (Be My Chief (USA))
1974^{9} 2432^{6}

Tobey (IRE) *W Baltromei* a61
3 b c Xaar—Toamasina (FR) (Marju (IRE))
410a^{7}

Tobrata *Mel Brittain* a66 61
5 ch g Tobougg(IRE) —Sabrata (IRE) (Zino)
1649^{4} 1909^{7} 2401^{2} 4111^{9} 7068^{3} 7589^{5} 7647^{2}

Toby Tyler *Paul Midgley* a70 85
5 b g Best Of The Bests(IRE) —Pain Perdu (IRE) (Waajib)
37^{3} (289) 402^{7} 743^{4} 853^{3} 1368^{5} (1712) 2543^{5} 3025^{4} (3036) 3856^{9} (4291) 5083^{4} 5434^{6} (5647) 6382^{5} (6778)

Toccata Jem (FR) *D Sepulchre* a44
4 b m Dubawi(IRE) —Real Secret (IRE) (Danehill (USA))
108a^{7} 6959a^{0}

Toffee Nose *Ron Barr* 41
4 b g Ishiguru(USA) —The Synergist (Botanic (USA))
1795^{8} 2591^{10} 3191^{4} 4286^{9} 4437^{6} 5490^{13}

Toffee Tart *J W Hills* 73
2 b f Dutch Art—Toffee Vodka (IRE) (Danehill Dancer (IRE))
1846^{2} 2241^{2} 2580^{7} 3104^{10} (4824) 5847^{9} 6524^{2}

Toga Tiger (IRE) *Jeremy Gask* a59 82
4 b g Antonius Pius(USA) —Minerwa (GER) (Protektor (GER))
7484^{11}

Together (IRE) *A P O'Brien* 114
3 b f Galileo(IRE) —Shadow Song (IRE) (Pennekamp (USA))
1339^{5} 1719^{2} 2334a^{2} 3106^{5} 5745a^{2} 6338^{7} 6719a^{2} (6887a)

Toggle *Mrs A Corson* a51 66
7 b g Tobougg(IRE) —Niggle (Night Shift (USA))
5778a^{8}

Togiak (IRE) *David Pipe* a90 98
4 b g Azamour(IRE) —Hawksbill Special (IRE) (Taufan (USA))
6125^{4} 6672^{18} 7029^{15}

To Honor And Serve (USA) *William Mott* a123
3 b c Bernardini(USA) —Pilfer (USA) (Deputy Minister (CAN))
7308a^{7}

Toi Et Moi (IRE) *P Bary* 106
4 b m Galileo(IRE) —Di Moi Oui (Warning)
1784a^{7} 2982a^{7} 5093a^{4} 5839a^{4} 6739a^{2} 7386a^{0}

Tokyo Brown (USA) *Heather Main* a40 21
2 b c Marquetry(USA) —Miasma (USA) (Lear Fan (USA))
5861^{8} 6462^{12}

Tombellini (IRE) *David Nicholls* a8 64
4 ch g Tomba—La Scala (USA) (Theatrical)
873^{9} 1398^{7} (1803) 1911^{4} 2057^{12} 2732^{6} 4196^{2} 4634^{6} 4987^{7} 6158^{5} 7064^{11}

Tombi (USA) *Ollie Pears* a73 98
7 b g Johannesburg(USA) —Tune In To The Cat (USA) (Tunerup (USA))
1457^{10} 2075^{17} 2890^{7} ◆ 3395^{11} 4792^{7} 5162^{2} 6351^{8} 7253^{7} (7629) 7926^{7}

Tominator *Reg Hollinshead* a95 105
4 gr g Generous(IRE) —[illegible]
267a^{3} 371a^{2} 478a^{7} 661a^{9} 840a^{9} 994^{2} 1238^{3} 2107^{6} 2812^{3} (3396) 3875^{8} ◆ 5271^{2} ◆ 5705^{5} 5883^{4}

Tomintoul Star *Ruth Carr* a64 42
5 gr m Dansili—Lixian (Linamix (FR))
181^{3} 292^{3} 397^{5} 580^{3} 1216^{6} 1468^{5} 1979^{4} 2237^{6}

Tommy Tiger *Stuart Williams* 52
3 b g Tiger Hill(IRE) —Special Green (FR) (Sadler's Wells (USA))
2119^{13} 2858^{3} 3268^{16} 5022^{9} 5636^{5}

Tomodachi (IRE) *Marco Botti* a12 47
4 b m Arakan(USA) —Ivory Bride (Domynsky)
3091^{10} 5100^{11}

Tom Sawyer *Julie Camacho* a88 88
3 b g Dansili—Cayman Sunset (IRE) (Night Shift (USA))
1019^{2} 1152^{8} 4048^{9} 4324^{5} 6801^{10} 7173^{11}

Toms River Tess (IRE) *Zoe Davison* a70 78
3 b f Kodiac—Sonorous (IRE) (Ashkalani (IRE))
302^{5} 476^{4} 864^{4} 1023^{3} 2200^{10} 2643^{10} 2757^{4} 3292^{8} 7942^{11}

Tom Wade (IRE) *John Harris* a64 61
4 b g Rakti—Plutonia (Sadler's Wells (USA))
4024^{8}

Tones (IRE) *Richard Hannon* a82 79
2 bb c Strategic Prince—Social Honour (IRE) (Entrepreneur)
3016^{3} 3673^{2} 4007^{3} (4240) (7491) 7576^{2}

Tongalooma *James Moffatt* a56 75
5 ch m Shinko Forest(IRE) —Schatzi (Chilibang)
1493^{10} 2412^{11} 4197^{4} 4881^{3} (4986) 5148^{4} 6076^{2} (6213) 6418^{4} 7104^{9}

Tonnerre (IRE) *Sir Michael Stoute* a89 74
3 gr c Dalakhani(IRE) —Rainbow City (IRE) (Rainbow Quest (USA))
5911^{5} (6286)

Tony Hollis *Rod Millman* a62 65
3 b g Antonius Pius(USA) —Seasons Parks (Desert Prince (IRE))
263^{3} 335^{3} 871^{2} 1022^{6} 1132^{2} 4431^{4}

Too Ambitious *Reg Hollinshead* a32
2 b f Striking Ambition—Ticcatoo (IRE) (Dolphin Street (FR))
7555^{7}

Toolain (IRE) *Roger Varian* a79 108
3 br g Diktat—Qasirah (IRE) (Machiavellian (USA))
1320^{5} 1844^{3} 2296^{5} 3645^{12} 6027^{5}

Too Late Jones (USA) *Richard Guest* a63
4 b g Smarty Jones(USA) —Bells Are Ringing (USA) (Sadler's Wells (USA))
7717^{6} 7913^{4}

Tooley Woods (IRE) *Tony Carroll*
2 b f Cape Cross(IRE) —Kondakova (IRE) (Soviet Star (USA))
2254^{9}

Too Many Questions (IRE) *David Evans* a66 68
3 ch g Whywhywhy(USA) —Global Tour (USA) (Tour D'Or (USA))
110^{5} 3093^{10} 3633^{10} 4230^{7} 4461^{3} 4924^{5} 5274^{9} 5388^{9} (6105) 6403^{6} 6634^{15} 7649^{12}

Too Nice Name (FR) *X Nakkachdji* a101 102
4 bl g Kingsalsa(USA) —Namona (IRE) (Halling (USA))
152a^{12} 327a^{11} 583a^{10}

Toothache *Garry Woodward* 35
3 gr f Proclamation(IRE) —Zilkha (Petong)
2673^{10}

Tootie Flutie *Richard Whitaker* a26 41
3 b f Piccolo—Birthday Venture (Soviet Star (USA))
1812^{8} 2361^{11} 4559^{4} 5619^{9} 6262^{12}

Toots Forest (USA) *Lisa Williamson*
5 bb m Teton Forest(USA) —Eastern Diva (USA) (Eastern Echo (USA))
3111^{7}

Top Achiever (IRE) *Bill Moore* a43
10 ch g Intikhab(USA) —Nancy Maloney (IRE) (Persian Bold)
1959^{7}

To Pack *Daniel Mark Loughnane* 23
4 b g Ishiguru(USA) —Red Cloud (IRE) (Taufan (USA))
3909^{8}

Topanga Canyon *Andrew Balding* 61
2 b g Nayef(USA) —Classical Dancer (Dr Fong (USA))
4264^{11} 5013^{10} 6245^{8}

Topaze Star *George Margarson* 59
4 br m Fantastic Light(USA) —Star Of Normandie (USA) (Gulch (USA))
4730^{10} 4889^{7}

Top Billing *John Gosden* 53
2 bg c Monsun(GER) —La Gandilie (FR) (Highest Honor (FR))
6954^{9}

Top Care (USA) *Mark Johnston* a82 79
3 bb g Bernstein(USA) —Secret Dream (IRE) (Zafonic (USA))
2833^{6} 3376^{9}

Topclas (FR) *M bin Shafya* a90 104
5 b h Kutub(IRE) —Noble Presence (FR) (Fasliyev (USA))
154a^{6} 329a^{8} 603a^{4} 757a^{5}

Topcoat (IRE) *Mark Johnston* a54 53
2 b c Exceed And Excel(AUS) —Janaat (Kris)
1199^{6} 1988^{5} 2672^{4} 3035^{5} 6846^{5}

Top Cop *Andrew Balding* 95
2 b c Acclamation—Speed Cop (Cadeaux Genereux)
4912^{2} ◆ (5263) ◆ 5849^{8}

Topcroft *Derek Shaw* a75 49
5 b g Mujahid(USA) —Starminda (Zamindar (USA))
290^{2} ◆ 483^{5}

Top Design *Karen George* 41
3 b g Zafeen(FR) —Dress Design (IRE) (Brief Truce (USA))
3513^{8}

Top Diktat *Sir Michael Stoute* a74 86
3 b g Diktat—Top Romance (IRE) (Entrepreneur)
2174^{3} 2924^{8} 3959^{8} (4163) 5240^{2} 6069^{3} (6997)

Topeka (IRE) *Robert Collet* 104
2 b f Whipper(USA) —Sovana (IRE) (Desert King (IRE))
(7219a)

Topflight Princess *Jeremy Gask* a74
2 b f Cockney Rebel(IRE) —Topflightcoolracer (Lujain (USA))
7345^{3} (7583) 7808^{3}

Top Frock (IRE) *Clive Cox* 70
2 b f Acclamation—Silk Dress (IRE) (Gulch (USA))
6463^{11} 7164^{5}

Top Level (IRE) *Mrs A Corson* a55 9
8 b m Fasliyev(USA) —Aiming Upwards (Blushing Flame (USA))
1743a^{4}

Top Offer *Roger Charlton* 92
2 b c Dansili—Zante (Zafonic (USA))
(4996) ◆

Topolski (IRE) *David Arbuthnot* a90 94
5 b g Peintre Celebre(USA) —Witching Hour (IRE) (Alzao (USA))
6528^{10}

Top Surprize (USA) *Naipaul Chatterpaul* 103
3 b r Pure Prize(USA) —Well At The Top (IRE) (Sadler's Wells (USA))
6716a^{4}

Toptempo *Mark H Tompkins* 86
2 ch f Halling(USA) —Topatoo (Bahamian Bounty)
5445^{5} ◆ 6914^{4}

Toraidhe (IRE) *J S Bolger* a97 98
5 br g High Chaparral(IRE) —Ramona (Desert King (IRE))
925a^{2} 1381a^{7} 3445a^{6} 4418a^{12}

Tornadodancer (IRE) *T G McCourt* a90 84
8 b g Princely Heir(IRE) —Purty Dancer (IRE) (Foxhound (USA))
3440a^{17} 4135a^{6} 6388a^{20} 7149a^{12} 7790a^{8}

Tornado Force (IRE) *Jeremy Noseda* a91 63
3 ch g Shamardal(USA) —Pharma West (USA) (Gone West (USA))
471^{5} (714) 931^{3} 2226^{5} 6978^{2} (7661) (7878)

Torran Sound *James Eustace* a49 60
4 b g Tobougg(IRE) —Velvet Waters (Unfuwain (USA))
277^{12} 560^{9} 1458^{8} (2272) 2526^{15} 6104^{5}

Torres Del Paine *Jimmy Fox* a69
4 b h Compton Place—Noble Story (Last Tycoon)
5640^{7} 6090^{2} 6841^{P} 7588^{11}

Torronto (FR) *P Monfort* a74 76
8 b g Commands(AUS) —Tamaziya (IRE) (Law Society (USA))
395a^{2} 566a^{0} 903a^{10}

Torteval (IRE) *David Evans* a49 43
3 b c Camacho—Hidden Agenda (FR) (Machiavellian (USA))
189^{2} 281^{3}

Tortilla (IRE) *Des Donovan* a55 60
3 ch f Choisir(AUS) —Alifandango (IRE) (Alzao (USA))
1865^{4} 2306^{7} 2529^{7} 3230^{6} 3636^{6} 4086^{10} 7370^{7} 7608^{8} 7639^{7} 7902^{5}

Tortoni (IRE) *Kevin Ryan* a75 77
2 b g Teofilo(IRE) —Nipping (IRE) (Night Shift (USA))
2033^{3} ◆ 2283^{2} 2672^{3} 4538^{2} 4749^{6} 6945^{2} 7197^{3}

Torun City *Richard Fahey* 65
3 b c Sulamani(IRE) —Polish Sprite (Danzig Connection (USA))
2457^{9} 3037^{5} 3976^{4} 4440^{7}

Tosen Jordan (JPN) *Yasutoshi Ikee* 126
5 b h Jungle Pocket(JPN) —Every Whisper (JPN) (Northern Taste (CAN))
7563a^{2} 7873a^{5}

Toshi (USA) *Jim Goldie* a57 53
9 b g Kingmambo(USA) —Majestic Role (FR) (Theatrical)
4499^{2}

Toss A Coin (IRE) *Roger Teal*
2 b g Antonius Pius(USA) —Irish Verse (IRE) (Indian Ridge)
7758^{5} 7907^{5}

Toss The Dice (IRE) *A De Royer-Dupre* a82 87
3 b c Medicean—Seltitude (IRE) (Fairy King (USA))
980a^{3}

Total Command *Sir Michael Stoute* 104
4 b g Sadler's Wells(USA) —Wince (Selkirk (USA))
1416^{5} 3875^{15} 5853^{7}

Total Excitement (IRE) *Thomas Cooper* a68 71
9 b g Michelozzo(USA) —Oak Court (IRE) (Bustineto)
7548a^{7}

Total Gallery (IRE) *Henry Candy* a95 107
5 br h Namid—Diary (IRE) (Green Desert (USA))
2754a^{6} 7221a^{7} 7392^{9}

Totally Ours *William Muir* a89 97
4 br m Singspiel(IRE) —Totally Yours (IRE) (Desert Sun)
1104^{6} 1677^{5} 2031^{15} 2679^{13} 3026^{3} 3592^{9} 4429^{10} 5113^{7} (5608) 6708^{15} 6996^{15} 7328^{6} 7542^{5}

Totally Trusted *David Nicholls* a62 60
3 b f Oasis Dream—Trustthunder (Selkirk (USA))
2185^{11} 2528^{9} 4282^{3} 4854^{8} 5598^{12} 6616^{3} 7069^{5} 7351^{10} 7748^{7}

Totheendoftheearth (IRE) *Sylvester Kirk* 83
3 b f Hurricane Run(IRE) —Lightwood Lady (IRE) (Anabaa (USA))
2528^{3} 2960^{3} 3289^{3} (3918) 4429^{2} 6457^{9} 6996^{12}

To The Glory (JPN) *Yasutoshi Ikee* 124
4 b h King Kamehameha(JPN) —To The Victory (JPN) (Sunday Silence (USA))
7563a^{11} 7873a^{3}

To The Sea (USA) *Mark Johnston* a58
2 ch f Giant's Causeway(USA) —Oceans Apart (Desert Prince (IRE))
7494^{5} 7685^{3}

To The Spring *William Haggas* a66 74
3 b f Medicean—Humouresque (Pivotal)
1343^{3} 1873^{6} 2691^{3} 3633^{7} 4560^{3} 5082^{4} 5391^{5}

Totom Chief *Gay Kelleway* a72 11
2 ch c Sleeping Indian—Serotina (IRE) (Mtoto)
7232^{17} 7650^{3}

Toto Skyllachy *Ollie Pears* a84 87
6 b g Kyllachy—Little Tramp (Trempolino (USA))
(2545) 3276^{14} (3934) 4404^{6} 5648^{8}

Toucan Tango (IRE) *Michael Quinn* a54 62
3 b g Mujadil(USA) —Walk On Quest (FR) (Rainbow Quest (USA))
2586^{2} 2858^{4} 3518^{12} 7037^{5} 7779^{4}

Touch Gold (IRE) *Sir Henry Cecil* 77
2 b c Oasis Dream—Seek Easy (USA) (Seeking The Gold (USA))
6334^{5} 7060^{3} ◆

Touching Kings (FR) *X Nakkachdji* a83 87
6 gr g Kutub(IRE) —Touchee D'Amour (GER) (Neshad (USA))
1142a^{2}

Touching The Stars *Mick Channon* 59
3 b g Singspiel(IRE) —Moonmaiden (Selkirk (USA))
5327^{11} 5585^{7}

Touch Of Hawk (FR) *Wido Neuroth* a94 105
5 bl g Hawk Wing(USA) —Touch Of Class (GER) (Be My Guest (USA))
1128a^{8} 2601a^{F}

Touch Of Roc *C Lerner* a87 96
3 b c Shirocco(GER) —Touch Of Class (GER) (Be My Guest (USA))
980a^{6}

Touch The Sky (FR) *M Nigge*
2 ch f Touch Of The Blues(FR) —Fleur Charmante (FR) (Beaudelaire (USA))
6925a^{0}

Touch Tone *Michael Dods* a82 83
4 b m Selkirk(USA) —Payphone (Anabaa (USA))
3620^{12} 4141^{4} 4670^{13}

Toufan Express *Adrian McGuinness* a86 90
9 ch g Fraam—Clan Scotia (Clantime)
3440a^{13} 6388a^{7} 7189a^{17} 7793a^{2}

Tough As Nails (IRE) *Michael Mulvany* 111
2 gr c Dark Angel(IRE) —Soreze (IRE) (Gallic League)
921a^{2} 2322a^{2} ◆ 3439a^{2} 4834a^{3} 5951a^{5} 6196a^{5} 6688^{9}

Tough Customer *Gary Brown* a19
3 b g Lucky Story(USA) —Fontaine House (Pyramus (USA))
246^{7}

Tourist *Ian Williams* a84 57
6 b g Oasis Dream—West Devon (USA) (Gone West (USA))
35^{4} 199^{9} 577^{7} 915^{8} 1014^{2} 1221^{6} 1394^{8} 3412^{10} 3942^{3} 4705^{4} 4948^{5} 5674^{4} (6794) 7176^{4} 7500^{6} 7716^{7} (7895)

Tournedos (IRE) *Ruth Carr* a75 67
9 b g Rossini(USA) —Don't Care (IRE) (Nordico (USA))
1544^{5} 1856^{12} 2247^{4} (2547) 2632^{6} 2798^{3} 2987^{5} 3662^{6} 4017^{9} 5309^{3}

Tourtiere *George Moore* 71
3 b g Act One—Kindle (Selkirk (USA))
2621^{6} 3037^{6} 4611^{3} 5553^{4}

Tous Les Deux *Dr Jeremy Naylor* a54 70
8 b g Efisio—Caerosa (Caerleon (USA))
163^{3} 280^{8} 555^{9} 809^{10} 7640^{13}

Touz Price (FR) *J-M Lefebvre* a81 103
3 b c Priolo(USA) —Touz De Saint Cyr (FR) (Saint Cyrien (FR))
1551a^{3} 2979a^{6}

Towbee *Michael Easterby* 63
2 b g Doyen(IRE) —Bow Bridge (Bertolini (USA))
4433^{3} 4851^{2} 5367^{4} 5817^{4}

Tower *Chris Grant* a63 64
4 b g Nayef(USA) —Palatial (Green Desert (USA))
244^{5} 393^{4} 2060^{5}

Towneley Arms (IRE) *Ollie Pears* 44
4 b g Pyrus(USA) —Grangeclare Lily (UAE) (Green Desert (USA))
7712^{8}

Towy Boy (IRE) *Ian Wood* a74 56
6 b g King Charlemagne(USA) —Solar Flare (IRE) (Danehill (USA))
1838^{11} 3261^{5} 3735^{10} 4207^{5} 4850^{3} 5387^{6} 5895^{3} 6655^{9} 6930^{5} 7488^{5} 7629^{3} (7844)

Toxeas (FR) *J Heloury* a76 83
4 b h One Cool Cat(USA) —Arikaria (IRE) (Sri Pekan (USA))
6958a^{0}

Toymaker *Rae Guest* 64
4 b g Starcraft(NZ) —Eurolink Raindance (IRE) (Alzao (USA))
1950^{9}

Trachonitis (IRE) *J R Jenkins* a83 75
7 b g Dansili—Hasina (IRE) (King's Theatre (IRE))
399^{2} 621^{9} 938^{3} 1509^{2} 1977^{5} 2562^{3}

Trade Centre *Milton Bradley* a72 56
6 b g Dubai Destination(USA) —Khubza (Green Desert (USA))
111^{6} 218^{2} 255^{7} 306^{6} 432^{7} 4224^{4} 4705^{7} 5617^{2} 5674^{7} 6609^{7}

Trader Jack *Roger Charlton* 84
2 b c Trade Fair—Azeema (IRE) (Averti (IRE))
6993^{3} (7257) ◆

Trade Secret *Mel Brittain* a78 81
4 b g Trade Fair—Kastaway (Distant Relative)
6044^{2} 6212^{4} 7356^{5} 7502^{6} 7595^{3}

Trade Storm *David Simcock* a97 103
3 b c Trade Fair—Frisson (Slip Anchor)
(1674) 2106^{4} 3067^{5} 3645^{P} 4493^{6} 4965^{6} 5830^{4} 7802^{4}

Trading *Tim Easterby* a42 68
3 b g Piccolo—Babcary (Bertolini (USA))
868^{6} 1040^{3} (1303) (1494) 2119^{10} 2264^{4}

Traditional Chic (IRE) *L Riccardi* 95
3 ch c Ad Valorem(USA) —Minimal Chic (IRE) (King's Best (USA))
6906a^{4} 7408a^{5}

Traffic Sister (USA) *J S Moore* a74 91
3 bb f More Than Ready(USA) —Street Scene (IRE) (Zafonic (USA))
(1873) 3034^{12} 5177^{8}

Trail Blaze (IRE) *Kevin Ryan* 80
2 b c Tagula(IRE) —Kingpin Delight (Emarati (USA))
4080^{5} 4781^{2} 5454^{2} 6110^{2}

Trailblazer (JPN) *Yasutoshi Ikee* 122
4 b h Zenno Rob Roy(JPN) —Lirio (USA) (Forty Niner (USA))
7563a^{4} 7729a^{6}

Trajano (USA) *M Delzangles* a92 102
6 b h Elusive Quality(USA) —Fly To The Moon (USA) (Blushing Groom (FR))
2980a^{7}

Transcend (JPN) *Takayuki Yasuda* a119 91
5 b h Wild Rush(USA) —Cinema Scope (JPN) (Tony Bin)
1002a^{2}

Trans City (IRE) *J A Nash* a74 83
3 ch g Trans Island—Where's Charlotte (Sure Blade (USA))
1663a^{3} 7618a^{13}

Transeggselence *Gary Harrison* 55
4 b m Trans Island—Breakfast Bay (IRE) (Charnwood Forest (IRE))
3043^{12} 3726^{8} 5540^{17} 5674^{15}

Transfer *Richard Price* a58 74
6 br g Trans Island—Sankaty Light (USA) (Summer Squall (USA))
1987^{3} 2530^{2} (2830) (3094) 3546^{3} 5588^{4} 6029^{3} 6773^{11} 7264^{9} 7441^{10}

Transfixed (IRE) *David Evans* a79 80
4 b m Trans Island—Rectify (IRE) (Mujadil (USA))
70^{4} (129)

Transformer (IRE) *William Jarvis* a70 57
5 b g Trans Island—Lady At War (Warning)
174^{2} (266) 384^{3}

Transmission (USA) *C Plisson* 70
4 b g Mingun(USA) —Enthused (USA) (Seeking The Gold (USA))
6593a^{0}

Transmit (IRE) *Tim Easterby* a65 73
4 ch g Trans Island—Apple Brandy (USA) (Cox's Ridge (USA))
1558^{9} 6452^{13} 6777^{5} 7216^{3} 7419^{4} 7648^{3} 7695^{6} 7930^{7}

Trans Sonic *David O'Meara* a43 80
8 ch g Trans Island—Sankaty Light (USA) (Summer Squall (USA))
6^{4} 186^{3} (320) 548^{3} (799) 1035^{9} 1382^{4} 1909^{6} 2320^{11} 7776^{7}

Traphalgar (IRE) *David Evans* a83 88
6 br g Cape Cross(IRE) —Conquestadora (Hernando (FR))
24^{3} 50^{6}

Trappe Shot (USA) *Kiaran McLaughlin* a123
4 ch h Tapit(USA) —Shopping (USA) (Private Account (USA))
7304a^{4}

Traveller's Tales *Richard Hannon* a65 74
2 b f Cape Cross(IRE) —Lost In Wonder (USA) (Galileo (IRE))
3362^{4} 6215^{4} 6745^{2} 7081^{6}

Travelling *J W Hills* a71 70
2 b f Dubai Destination(USA) —Attune (Singspiel (IRE))
4061^{7} 5011^{5} (5393) 6340^{8} 6753^{4}

Travis County (IRE) *Brian Ellison* 76
2 b c Jeremy(USA) —Manchaca (FR) (Highest Honor (FR))
2056^{2} (2617) 3429^{4} ◆ 4536^{11} 5825^{10}

Treacle Tart *James Ewart* a74 73
6 ch m Fleetwood(IRE) —Loriner's Lass (Saddlers' Hall (IRE))
(68) 342^{4} 484^{2} 3184^{10} 4687^{5} 5357^{4} 5628^{3} 7461^{10}

Treadwell (IRE) *Jamie Osborne* a87 105
4 b h Footstepsinthesand—Lady Wells (IRE) (Sadler's Wells (USA))
7433^{7} 7721^{4}

Treason Trial *Andrew Crook* a46 29
10 b g Peintre Celebre(USA) —Pampabella (IRE) (High Estate)
1153^{12}

Treasure Act *Patrick Chamings* a61 31
3 ch f Act One—Benjarong (Sharpo)
4800^{11} 6085^{6} 6754^{5} 7096^{11}

Treasure Beach *A P O'Brien* 122
3 b c Galileo(IRE) —Honorine (IRE) (Mark Of Esteem (IRE))
(1822) 2715^{2} (3442a) 4038a^{4} (5072a) 6567a^{14} 6910a^{3}

Treasure Way *Patrick Chamings* a71 72
4 ch m Galileo(IRE) —Gold Mark (Mark Of Esteem (IRE))
(1766) 4458^{5} 5100^{4} 5496^{8} 6051^{5}

Treasury Devil (USA) *John Gosden* a103 103
3 b c Bernardini(USA) —Crystal Music (USA) (Nureyev (USA))
1547^{4} 1689^{3} 6671^{3} 7347^{2}

Trebetherick (IRE) *J E Hammond* a99 82
3 gr g Verglas(IRE) —Kathy Sun (IRE) (Intikhab (USA))
4896a^{5}

Treble Jig (USA) *Sir Michael Stoute* 85
4 b h Gone West(USA) —Light Jig (Danehill (USA))
1529^{11} 2002^{14} 3411^{9}

Trecase *Tony Carroll* a58 54
4 b g Zafeen(FR) —Pewter Lass (Dowsing (USA))
1987^{16} 2608^{5} 3003^{10} 3926^{7} 4317^{2} 4754^{5} 5357^{8} 5943^{5}

Trend (IRE) *Michael Bell* a15 64
3 b g Marju(IRE) —Fashion (Bin Ajwaad (IRE))
3220^{10}

Trending (IRE) *Jeremy Gask* a46 49
2 bg g Dark Angel(IRE) —Call Later (USA) (Gone West (USA))
4485^{6} 5411^{5} 6025^{4} 6817^{12}

Trend Line (IRE) *Peter Chapple-Hyam* a78 77
3 b f Holy Roman Emperor(IRE) —Dabiliya (Vayrann)
158^{5} 1363^{6} 1845^{5} 3466^{6} 4090^{3} 4584^{7} 5496^{3} 6226^{8} 7638^{3} 7803^{4}

Tresabella *Michael Appleby* a7 2
2 b f Firebreak—Bella Tutrice (IRE) (Woodborough (USA))
4061^{12} 5806^{11} 7066^{5}

Tres Borrachos (USA) *Martin F Jones* a115 84
6 b g Ecton Park(USA) —Pete's Fancy (CAN) (Peteski (CAN))
7304a^{3}

Tres Coronas (IRE) *David Barron* a86 92
4 b g Key Of Luck(USA) —Almansa (IRE) (Dr Devious (IRE))
1097^{6} 1517^{9} 1826^{2} 2681^{5} 3164^{4} (3399) 5686^{5} 6429^{3} 6803^{12}

Tres Froide (FR) *Nigel Tinkler* a59 63
6 ch m Bering—Charmgoer (USA) (Nureyev (USA))
86^{2} 283^{2} 526^{4}

Tres Rock Danon (FR) *W Hickst* 113
5 b h Rock Of Gibraltar(IRE) —Tres Ravi (GER) (Monsun (GER))
(2538a) 4037a^{8} 5304a^{8} 6562a^{2} 7049a^{8}

Tribal Myth (IRE) *Kevin Ryan* 76
4 b g Johannesburg(USA) —Shadow Play (USA) (Theatrical)
1150^{3} (1324) 2059^{10} (2486) 3023^{5} 3244^{4} 5828^{12} 6093^{11}

Tribouley *Dean Ivory* a53
3 ch f Bahamian Bounty—Serriera (FR) (Highest Honor (FR))
7443^{3} 7750^{8}

Tricksofthetrade (IRE) *Alan Swinbank* a58 72
5 b g Mull Of Kintyre(USA) —Soden (IRE) (Mujadil (USA))
2114^{3} 6349^{4} 6614^{4} 7075^{4}

Tricky Situation *David Brown* a20 69
5 b m Mark Of Esteem(IRE) —Trick Of Ace (USA) (Clever Trick (USA))
4077^{3} ◆ 4367^{13}

Tricky Trev (USA) *Jo Davis* a62 52
5 ch g Toccet(USA) —Lady Houston (USA) (Houston (USA))
3690^{16}

Triggerlo *Mick Channon* a51 70
2 ch g Piccolo—Elegant Hawk (Generous (IRE))
1095^{6} 1185^{3} 1396^{2} 1691^{12} 2901^{5} 3249^{4} 3539^{4} 3955^{4} (5297) 5701^{6} 6021^{4} 6237^{5} 6384^{6} 7059^{2} 7143^{5}

Trille Divine *Mme C De La Soudiere-Niault* 70
3 b f Marchand De Sable(USA) —Brilliantly (FR) (Priolo (USA))
7667a^{0}

Trinniberg (USA) *Bisnath Parboo* a108 40
2 bb c Teuflesberg(USA) —Bella Dorato (USA) (Goldminers Gold (CAN))
7280a[7]

Trioomph *James Given* a30 59
2 b f Three Valleys(USA) —Oomph (Shareef Dancer (USA))
5486[3] 6092[6] 6449[6] 6864[7] *7248[7]*

Triple Aspect (IRE) *William Haggas* 114
5 b h Danetime(IRE) —Wicken Wonder (IRE) (Distant Relative)
996a[7] 2005[5] 2370[2] 3644[5]

Triple Charm *Jeremy Noseda* a82 76
3 ch f Pivotal—Triple Joy (Most Welcome)
5567[5] *5900[5]* (6591) ◆ *(7519)* *7941[3]*

Triple Dream *Milton Bradley* a80 80
6 ch g Vision Of Night—Triple Joy (Most Welcome)
1752[3] 1982[2] 2126[6] *2603[7]* 2832[9] (3994) 4272[4] 4615[5] 4895[2] 5238[2] 5781[11] 5890[10] 6436[2] 6895[6] *7428[2]* *7594[4]* *(7804)* 7917[4]

Triple Eight (IRE) *Philip Kirby* a93 94
3 b g Royal Applause—Hidden Charm (IRE) (Big Shuffle (USA))
1116a[4] 3445a[17] 6188[2] 6582[4] 7160[3] *7397[9]* *7625[2]* *7823[9]*

Triple Point (IRE) *J-M Plasschaert* a41
9 b g Perugino(USA) —Quench The Lamp (IRE) (Glow (USA))
484[4]

Triple Salchow *Alastair Lidderdale* a54
2 b f Needwood Blade—Icky Woo (Mark Of Esteem (IRE))
7345[5]

Trip Switch *George Prodromou* a66 58
5 b g Reset(AUS) —Caribbean Star (Soviet Star (USA))
(7442) *7663[2]* *(7851)* *(7904)*

Trip The Light *Richard Fahey* a92 91
6 b g Fantastic Light(USA) —Jumaireyah (Fairy King (USA))
2932[6] 3829[6] 4294[3] 4360[11] 4957[2] 5078[5] 5482[5] 6024[4] (6676) (6868)

Trisha's Boy (IRE) *Simon Dow* a29 49
2 ch g Exceed And Excel(AUS) —Golden Anthem (USA) (Lion Cavern (USA))
4384[10] 5111[8] *5411[7]*

Triskaidekaphobia *Wilf Storey* a62 54
8 b g Bertolini(USA) —Seren Teg (Timeless Times (USA))
337[4] *735[10]* *(812)* *934[5]* *1182[8]* 1523[6] *2164[4]* 3678[5] 5620[8] 6602[2] 7100[6]

Triumphus *Paul Fitzsimons* 28
7 b g Lear Spear(USA) —Sarcita (Primo Dominie)
2768[6]

Triveni (FR) *Mme M Bollack-Badel* 104
3 b f Lando(GER) —Teresa Balbi (Master Willie)
2342a[10] 2750a[10] 7156a[10]

Triviality (IRE) *Jamie Osborne* a69 58
3 b g Majestic Missile(IRE) —In Denial (IRE) (Maelstrom Lake)
1813[2] ◆ 2493[4] *(3494)*

Trois Rois (FR) *I Mohammed* a102 109
6 b h Hernando(FR) —Trevise (FR) (Anabaa (USA))
154a[8] *330a[4]* *416a[8]* 581a[3] 759a[8] *827a[8]*

Trois Vallees (USA) *Mahmood Al Zarooni* a84 69
2 bb c Elusive Quality(USA) —Chamrousse (USA) (Peaks And Valleys (USA))
5447[6] *(6216)*

Trojan Gift (USA) *Julie Camacho* a67 62
4 bb g War Chant(USA) —Extry (USA) (Broad Brush (USA))
769[5] *1291[3]* *1973[2]* 2400[8] *(3492)* 4326[12] 4856[13] *5599[5]*

Trojan Nights (USA) *William Haggas* a76 96
3 ch g Street Cry(IRE) —Dabaweyaa (Shareef Dancer (USA))
1836[2] (2125) 2711[2] ◆ 4103[5] 4553[6] 6173[9]

Trojan Rocket (IRE) *George Prodromou* a73 55
9 b g Elusive City(USA) —Tagula Bay (IRE) (Tagula (IRE))
1236[2] 3343[5] 3956[5] *4758[11]* *5864[3]* *(6304)* *6841[2]* *(7269)* *7448[3]* *7715[8]* 7819[5]

Trojan Touch (USA) *Chris Dwyer* a49 46
3 ch g Eddington(USA) —Lady Sky Racer (USA) (Skywalker (USA))
942[2] *1082[2]* *1502[3]* *2239[5]* 2599[4] 2857[5]

Tro Nesa (IRE) *Ann Duffield* a70 78
3 b f Chineur(FR) —Monsusu (IRE) (Montjeu (IRE))
1079[4] 1521[3] 2096[5] 2411[2] 3114[2] 3484[3] 3900[4] 4016[4] 5682[8] *6502[6]* 7055[3] *7419[9]* *7696[8]*

Troopingthecolour *Steve Gollings* a92 95
5 b g Nayef(USA) —Hyperspectra (Rainbow Quest (USA))
(1250) *(3042)* (3764) 4267[5] 5250[4]

Tropenfeuer (FR) *James Moffatt* a73 58
4 b m Banyumanik(IRE) —Tropensonne (GER) (Konigsstuhl (GER))
1491[11]

Tropical Bachelor (IRE) *Richard Ford* a52 77
5 b g Bachelor Duke(USA) —Tropical Coral (IRE) (Pennekamp (USA))
3456[8] 4082[4] 4341[3] 4982[4] 6157[6]

Tropical Beat *John Gosden* a68 93
3 b g Beat Hollow—Tropical Heights (FR) (Shirley Heights)
945[4] (1210) 1843[2] 2188[2] 3067[10] ◆ 3864[4] 4467[14]

Tropical Duke (IRE) *Ron Barr* a62 65
5 ch g Bachelor Duke(USA) —Tropical Dance (USA) (Thorn Dance (USA))
1615[6] 2589[8] 3086[6] 3456[10] 3683[10] 3938[7] 4408[4] 4605[8] 5485[9] 6235[4] 6833[11]

Tropical Paradise (IRE) *Peter Winkworth* a92 111
5 gr m Verglas(IRE) —Ladylishandra (IRE) (Mujadil (USA))
1893[4] 2558[4] 4497[15]

Tropical Treat *Ralph Beckett* 108
4 b m Bahamian Bounty—Notjustaprettyface (USA) (Red Ransom (USA))
3073[4] 4573[8]

Trouble Mountain (USA) *G P Kelly* a24 68
14 br g Mt. Livermore(USA) —Trouble Free (USA) (Nodouble (USA))
859[7]

Troubletimestwo (FR) *Tony Carroll* a60 40
5 gr g Linamix(FR) —Time Of Trouble (FR) (Warning)
2377[9]

Trovajoli (ITY) *F & L Camici* 101
4 b h Fisich—Pub In The Park (IRE) (Eagle Eyed (USA))
1918a[6]

Trovare (USA) *Amanda Perrett* 91
4 b g Smart Strike(CAN) —Abita (USA) (Dynaformer (USA))
1477[4] 2107[3] 2512[3] 3428[8] 4423[11] 4806[3] 5448[7] 7139[10]

Trove (IRE) *John Gosden* a55
2 b g Rock Of Gibraltar(IRE) —Cache Creek (IRE) (Marju (IRE))
7494[7]

True Bond *Geoffrey Oldroyd* a36 62
2 ch f Monsieur Bond(IRE) —Splicing (Sharpo)
3611[5] 4668[8] (4940) 5399[7] 7294[17] *7541[8]*

True Prince (USA) *Amanda Perrett* a54 50
2 ch c Yes It's True(USA) —Whenthedoveflies (USA) (Dove Hunt (USA))
4535[15] 4995[12] *5410[4]* *6001[3]* 6972[7] *7222[7]*

True Red (IRE) *Nikki Evans* a49 64
4 ch m Redback—Red Trance (IRE) (Soviet Star (USA))
123[8] *250[11]* *669[5]* *798[10]* *941[11]*

True Satire *Jane Chapple-Hyam* a57 57
3 b f Oasis Dream—Native Justice (USA) (Alleged (USA))
7063[2] *7411[4]* *7717[4]*

True To Form (IRE) *Ronald Harris* a94 77
4 b g Rock Of Gibraltar(IRE) —Truly Yours (IRE) (Barathea (IRE))
1772[7] 2793[7] *3739[7]* 5340[8] *(6872)* 7061[2] *(7557)* *(7651)* *7803[8]*

Truism *Amanda Perrett* 96
5 b g Daylami(IRE) —Real Trust (USA) (Danzig (USA))
2310[9] (2876) 4415[3] 4537[3] 5936[10] 6496[6]

Truly Genius (IRE) *C P Donoghue* a87 84
3 ch g Iffraaj—Truly Genuine (IRE) (Hernando (FR))
3440a[20] *7150a[9]*

Truly Magic *Liam Corcoran* a35 61
4 ch m Traditionally(USA) —Truly Bewitched (USA) (Affirmed (USA))
631[8]

Truly Magnificent (USA) *Brendan W Duke* a57
4 b m Elusive Quality(USA) —Magnificent Honour (USA) (A.P. Indy (USA))
11[9]

Trumpet Major (IRE) *Richard Hannon* 114
2 b c Arakan(USA) —Ashford Cross (Cape Cross (IRE))
2049[3] (2291) 3012[14] 4311[2] (4964) 5276[4] (5926) 6689[5]

Trumpet Voluntary (IRE) *Richard Fahey* 77
2 b c Red Clubs(IRE) —Woodmaven (USA) (Woodman (USA))
(5398) ◆ 6111[6]

Trumpington Street (IRE) *John Gosden* a95 75
3 ch c Noverre(USA) —Landela (Alhaarth (IRE))
1210[5] *2723[2]* *3236[3]* *(3717)* 4290[10] 4763[6] *(5635)* ◆ *6220[2]*

Trumpstoo (USA) *Richard Fahey* a52 63
5 b g Perfect Soul(IRE) —Cozzy Love (USA) (Cozzene (USA))
630[5]

Trust Fund Babe (IRE) *Tim Easterby* 58
2 b f Captain Rio—Perfect Order (USA) (Red Ransom (USA))
3610[6] 4106[3] 5161[10] 5590[4] 6092[7] 6232[5]

Trusting (IRE) *Eve Johnson Houghton* a59 58
2 b f Red Clubs(IRE) —Tertia (IRE) (Polish Patriot (USA))
5232[9] 5779[4] 6406[7] *6817[2]* *7205[5]*

Trust Me Boy *John E Long* a45 48
3 gr g Avonbridge—Eastern Lyric (Petong)
811[10] 1284[5] 3766[5] 4162[3] ◆ 4929[3] 5515[13] 6813[11] *7091[11]* *7387[13]*

Tryst *J E Hammond* a94 97
6 gr g Highest Honor(FR) —Courting (Pursuit Of Love)
661a[6] 7015a[4]

Try The Chance *Mick Channon* 97
3 b g Majestic Missile(IRE) —Danetime Out (IRE) (Danetime (IRE))
3649[5] ◆ 4550[8] 4914[7] (5621) (5820)

Tsar Bomba (USA) *David Barron* a68 65
4 bb g Red Bullet(USA) —Larry's Blackhoney (USA) (Hennessy (USA))
(453) *571[5]* *1503[6]*

Tsarina Louise *James Given* a30 24
3 b f Red Ransom(USA) —Imperial Bailiwick (IRE) (Imperial Frontier (USA))
1179[7] 2710[10]

Tsar Paul (IRE) *J A Nash* a73 78
6 b g Xaar—Jelba (Pursuit Of Love)
4767a[10]

Tt's Dream *Alastair Lidderdale* a37 60
4 gr g Imperial Dancer—On Cloud Nine (Cloudings (IRE))
765[9] *943[11]* 1987[4] 2600[4] 2905[6] 3480[7]

Tuaoi (USA) *Mlle A Voraz* a91 91
6 ch h Rahy(USA) —Turning Wheel (USA) (Seeking The Gold (USA))
257a[2] *6958a[8]*

Tubby Isaacs *Dean Ivory* a81 83
7 b g Cyrano De Bergerac—Opuntia (Rousillon (USA))
2179[12] 2369[13] 3412[6] *3735[2]* 4066[11] *4910[11]*

Tudora (AUT) *S Bigus* a57
6 b m Don Corleone—Turbulencja (POL) (Who Knows)
221a[5] *372a[6]* *566a[0]*

Tudor Empire (IRE) *John Gosden* 73
2 ch c Exceed And Excel(AUS) —Lady Catherine (Bering)
3132[8] 3401[4] 3986[4] 4292[3] 4913[6] 5446[12] 6031[6] 6399[3] 6806[9]

Tudor Prince (IRE) *Tony Carroll* a63 75
7 bb g Cape Cross(IRE) —Savona (IRE) (Cyrano De Bergerac)
48[6] *268[6]* *589[2]* *810[7]* *1177[6]* *3720[4]* *5394[3]* 6071[9] *6784[4]* *7229[4]*

Tuibama (IRE) *Ben Haslam* a54 54
2 ch g Bertolini(USA) —Supportive (IRE) (Nashamaa)
3125[6] 3932[7] *4648[3]*

Tukitinyasok (IRE) *Clive Mulhall* a69 87
4 b g Fath(USA) —Mevlana (IRE) (Red Sunset)
249[7] *562[4]* *881[6]* *1373[9]* 3831[7] 4349[19] 4501[4] 5733[7]

Tullamore (NZ) *Gai Waterhouse* 114
5 b g Savabeel(AUS) —Trocair (AUS) (Flying Spur (AUS))
6886a[3] 7043a[2] 7218a[14]

Tullius (IRE) *Peter Winkworth* a79 99
3 ch g Le Vie Dei Colori—Whipped Queen (USA) (Kingmambo (USA))
(2229) 2925[2] 3774[9] 5081[2] 5730[10] 6574[2]

Tumbleowtashoes *John Ryan*
2 ch g Tumbleweed Ridge—Darling Belinda (Silver Wizard (USA))
2267[5] 2854[7]

Tumooh (IRE) *Saeed Bin Suroor* a75
2 b f Authorized(IRE) —Sulaalah (IRE) (Darshaan)
(7344) ◆

Tundridge *Sylvester Kirk* a51 10
2 b g Authorized(IRE) —Salanka (IRE) (Persian Heights)
6993[13] *7398[7]*

Tunduce (IRE) *Noel Quinlan* a35
3 b f Tiger Hill(IRE) —Sun On The Sea (IRE) (Bering)
5816[8] 6229[7]

Tunza The Lion *Bruce Hellier* a29
4 b g Trade Fair—Bella Helena (Balidar)
7460[11] *7511[7]* *7693[11]*

Turallure (USA) *Charles Lopresti* 123
4 rg h Wando(CAN) —Personal Allure (USA) (Wekiva Springs (USA))
(6204a) 7307a[2]

Turati *E Botti* 88
5 b h Lomitas—Torrigiana (Celtic Swing)
7323a[9]

Turbotin (FR) *J-P Gallorini* 63
3 gr g Passing Sale(FR) —Turbotiere (FR) (Turgeon (USA))
5132a[5]

Turbulent Descent (USA) *Mike Puype* a119
3 b f Congrats(USA) —Roger's Sue (USA) (Forestry (USA))
7282a[5]

Turbulent Priest *Zoe Davison* a49
3 b c Storming Home—Hymn Book (IRE) (Darshaan)
6085[12] *7327[8]* *7766[6]*

Turf Time *David Nicholls* a55 52
4 b g Zafeen(FR) —Next Time (IRE) (Danetime (IRE))
453[7]

Turf Trivia *George Moore* 43
4 gr g Alhaarth(IRE) —Exclusive Approval (USA) (With Approval (CAN))
3185[8]

Turia (GER) *Uwe Ostmann* 79
3 b f Call Me Big(GER) —Tokara (GER) (Turfkonig (GER))
2337a[9]

Turjuman (USA) *Alan Bailey* a71 77
6 ch g Swain(IRE) —Hachiyah (IRE) (Generous (IRE))
[illegible] 2436[7] 3184[4] (3516) 4216[7] *5103[7]* *5609[5]* *6182[10]* 6503[3] 7564[3] 7720[7] 7817[5]

Turned To Gold (IRE) *Alan Jarvis* 71
2 ch g Teofilo(IRE) —Silver Bracelet (Machiavellian (USA))
6448[11] 6993[5]

Turn The Page *Alan McCabe*
2 b g Lucky Story(USA) —Maid For Running (Namaqualand (USA))
2318[10] 2953[15]

Turn The Tide *Mike Hammond* a66 82
3 b f Footstepsinthesand—Syrian Dancer (IRE) (Groom Dancer (USA))
2468[10] 2581[5] 3638[5] *3920[5]*

Tuscan Blue *Richard Hannon*
3 ch c Medicean—Belle Et Deluree (USA) (The Minstrel (CAN))
2790[18]

Tuscan Gold *Sir Mark Prescott Bt* a91 89
4 ch g Medicean—Louella (USA) (El Gran Senor (USA))
5221[U] 5966[3] 6690[29]

Tuscania *Sir Michael Stoute* a79 96
3 b f King's Best(USA) —Contiguous (USA) (Danzig (USA))
3819[4] 4472[8] 5016[3] 5450[6] 6495[4] 7168[15]

Tuscan King *Bernard Llewellyn* a69 64
4 ch g Medicean—Castaway Queen (IRE) (Selkirk (USA))
21[3] *685[5]* *810[3]* *906[2]* *1045[8]* 1448[4] 1730[12] 4701[2] 4948[7] 5428[6] 5845[7] 5994[8] 6411[13]

Tuscany Red *Richard Guest* a38 13
3 ch g Ad Valorem(USA) —Tuscany Gal (USA) (Gilded Time (USA))
713[6] *1027[6]* *3710[7]* 4403[10]

Tushuk Tash (USA) *Mick Channon* 67
2 bb g Arch(USA) —Illuminise (IRE) (Grand Lodge (USA))
5536[5] 5891[8] 6400[8] 6572[8] 6911[13]

Tuxedo *Peter Hiatt* a79 43
6 ch g Cadeaux Genereux—Serengeti Bride (USA) (Lion Cavern (USA))
141[4] *206[4]* *310[2]* *473[5]* *666[13]* *908[9]* 4255[10] 4479[6] *5101[10]* *5318[3]* 6227[10]

Tweedle Dee *Noel Quinlan* 61
2 b f Araafa(IRE) —Sismique (Warning)
4159[4] (4761)

Tweedledrum *Tom Symonds* a68 83
4 b m Beat Hollow—Tweed Mill (Selkirk (USA))
(983) (2552) ◆ 2906[2] 3277[4] 6988[16]

Tweedy (IRE) *Edward Lynam* a98 94
4 b m Oasis Dream—Shining Prospect (Lycius (USA))
2298[11] 2861a[7]

Tweet Lady *Rod Millman* a70 64
2 b f Royal Applause—Fuschia (Averti (IRE))
3046[5] *3718[6]* 4639[2] *(5144)* *(5945)*

Twelve Strings (IRE) *Luca Cumani* a61 72
2 b g Iffraaj—Favoritely (USA) (Favorite Trick (USA))
5410[6] *5863[5]* *6308[9]* (6911)

Twennyshortkid *Paul Midgley* a56 55
3 b g Sleeping Indian—Brandish (Warning)
1038[6] 1303[3] 1749[8] 2396[9] 2782[7] 3039[10] (3455) 4149[3] 4638[10] *5601[5]* *7420[8]* *7714[8]* *7781[2]*

Twenty One Choice (IRE) *Ed de Giles* 45
2 ch c Choisir(AUS) —Midnight Lace (Tomba)
5681[13] 6160[12] 6973[5]

Twenty Ten (FR) *P Khozian* a76 76
3 b c Poliglote—Distale (USA) (Trempolino (USA))
258a[7] *(660a)*

Twice Bitten *James Toller* a88 75
3 ch g Beat Hollow—Duena (Grand Lodge (USA))
1690[7] 2925[9] 3557[4] 4060[4] *(4905)* *5641[5]* 6104[4]

Twice Over *Sir Henry Cecil* a125 127
6 bb h Observatory(USA) —Double Crossed (Caerleon (USA))
(758a) *1002a[9]* 2101[6] 3031[5] (4345) (5183) 6861[10]

Twice Red *Derek Shaw* a77 29
3 b g Intikhab(USA) —Red Shareef (Marju (IRE))
(855) *3239[4]* 3853[13] *7744[7]* *7857[8]*

Twice The Appeal (USA) *Jeff Bonde* a113
3 bb c Successful Appeal(USA) —Double Boarded (USA) (Cormorant (USA))
1921a[10]

Twilight Allure *Kevin Ryan* a67 32
2 b f Shamardal(USA) —Midnight Allure (Aragon)
7058[5] *(7555)* ◆ *7778[4]* *7905[6]*

Twilight Express (IRE) *Emma Lavelle* a37 25
3 b f Golan(IRE) —Starlight Express (FR) (Air Express (IRE))
212[7] *591[5]* *891[5]* *1312[8]* 2243[10]

Twin Ivan (IRE) *Howard Johnson* 64
2 b g Ivan Denisovich(IRE) —Twin Logic (USA) (Diesis)
2460[5] 3274[9]

Twinkled *Michael Bell* a73 60
3 ch g Bahamian Bounty—Panic Stations (Singspiel (IRE))
1082[3] *(1869)* 6228[8] *6664[2]* ◆ 6971[10]

Twin Prince (IRE) *E Leenders* a63 56
6 b g Desert Prince(IRE) —Twin Island (IRE) (Standaan (FR))
42a[9] *903a[8]*

Twin Shadow (IRE) *James Fanshawe* a60 50
2 ch f Dubawi(IRE) —Its On The Air (IRE) (King's Theatre (IRE))
6441[5] 6935[7]

Twin Soul (IRE) *Andrew Balding* a98 95
3 br f Singspiel(IRE) —Kirk Wynd (Selkirk (USA))
217[4] ◆ *(469)* *(789)* *(866)* 4971[5] 6172[3] 6498[5] *7129[4]*

Twinspired (USA) *Michael J Maker* a113 102
3 rg c Harlan's Holiday(USA) —Historical Drive (USA) (El Prado (IRE))
1921a[17]

Twisted *Michael Easterby* a70 59
5 ch g Selkirk(USA) —Winding (USA) (Irish River (FR))
1052[6] 1613[6] 2985[6] 4112[5] 4408[8] *5606[5]* *5860[3]* 6493[6] 6871[3] 7034[10]

Twisted Wings (IRE) *Tim Easterby* a37
3 ch f Camacho—Westlife (IRE) (Mind Games)
182[5]

Two Bridges *Gary Moore* 56
2 ch f Avonbridge—Go Between (Daggers Drawn (USA))
3463[8] 3941[3] 4229[5] 5374[8]

Two Bucks More *Bill Turner* a11 10
3 b g Proclamation(IRE) —Zarzi (IRE) (Suave Dancer (USA))
3950[7] 5780[8]

Two Certainties *Stuart Williams* a70 70
4 ch g Zamindar(USA) —Ipsa Loquitur (Unfuwain (USA))
(3130) 3814[4] 4278[7] 4506[5] *6005[3]* 6226[4]

Two Cities (IRE) *David Wachman* a65
2 b c Excellent Art—Rock Dove (IRE) (Danehill (USA))
7273a[9]

Two Feet Of Snow (IRE) *Ian McInnes* a70 72
3 b f Holy Roman Emperor(IRE) —Current Affairs (Selkirk (USA))
422[5] *538[7]* *834[6]* *967[6]* *1078[8]*

Two For Tea (NZ) *Gai Waterhouse* 102
5 ch g Drama Critic(USA) —Sing (NZ) (Blanco (USA))
6711a[13] 7115a[11]

Two Kisses (IRE) *Brendan Powell* a66 58
4 b m Spartacus(IRE) —Flight Sequence (Polar Falcon (USA))
3546[5]

Two Sugars *John Akehurst*
3 b c Val Royal(FR) —Princess Galadriel (Magic Ring (IRE))
158[13]

Two Tone *Garry Woodward* a30 28
5 bb g Diktat—Fireburst (Spectrum (IRE))
300[7] *492[7]* *1173[8]*

Two Turtle Doves (IRE) *Michael Mullineaux* a67 69
5 b m Night Shift(USA) —Purple Rain (IRE) (Celtic Swing)
1307[6] 1712[3] 2016[6] 2353[6] 2803[3] 3307[2] 3662[8] 4600[6] 5309[4] (5534) (5846) 6436[4] 7104[3] *7349[4]* *7596[7]* *7896[9]*

Tybalt (USA) *Mahmood Al Zarooni* a102 106
7 b h Storm Cat(USA) —Tuzla (FR) (Panoramic)
236^{3}

Tycoon's Garden (FR) *E Lellouche* 96
2 b c Ski Chief(USA) —Queen's Garden (USA) (Kingmambo (USA))
7508a^{7}

Tyfos *Brian Baugh* a74 94
6 b g Bertolini(USA) —Warminghamsharpish (Nalchik (USA))
1395^{11} 2832^{4} 3322^{3} 3541^{4} (4064) (4583) 4967^{2} 5703^{9} 6331^{15}

Tymismoni (IRE) *Michael Attwater* a59 56
3 ch f Choisir(AUS) —Berenice (ITY) (Marouble)
383^{2} 655^{11} 1481^{9} 2172^{2} 2920^{14} 3223^{11} 6626^{8} 6813^{9}

Typography *William Muir* a72 65
2 br g Byron—Bold Byzantium (Bold Arrangement)
6992^{5} 7329^{3}

Tyrannosaurus Rex (IRE) *David O'Meara* a49 72
7 b g Bold Fact(USA) —Dungeon Princess (IRE) (Danehill (USA))
123^{7} 138^{7} 256^{8} 464^{3} 735^{8} 1213^{7} 1493^{6} 2546^{4} 5019^{3} 5373^{11}

Tyre Giant Dot Com *Geoffrey Oldroyd* a51 74
2 b g Misu Bond(IRE) —Villa Del Sol (Tagula (IRE))
1095^{4} 2318^{8} 3161^{5} 4105^{9} 4808^{2} 6178^{5} 6652^{9} 6975^{7}

Tyrrells Wood (IRE) *Ian Williams* a88 85
6 b g Sinndar(IRE) —Diner De Lune (IRE) (Be My Guest (USA))
3013^{17}

U A E Storm (USA) *David Simcock* a78 68
3 b c Bluegrass Cat(USA) —Skygusty (USA) (Skywalker (USA))
2808^{3} 3676^{4}

Ubenkor (IRE) *Michael Herrington* a73 56
6 b g Diktat—Lucky Dancer (FR) (Groom Dancer (USA))
148^{5} 292^{2} 400^{4} 674^{3} 854^{5} 1803^{6} 2543^{7} 3495^{4} 3953^{7} 4563^{6} 4852^{12}

Ubi Ace *Tim Walford* 86
5 b g First Trump—Faithful Beauty (IRE) (Last Tycoon)
(1243) 1517^{6} 2006^{2} 2708^{4} 3544^{5}

Uccellina (FR) *A Fabre* 81
2 b f Great Journey(JPN) —Up To Date (FR) (Valanour (IRE))
2866a^{5}

Udabaa (IRE) *Marcus Tregoning* a80 97
4 bb g Alhaarth(IRE) —Addaya (IRE) (Persian Bold)
1402^{2} 1887^{3} (2810) 3406^{3} 4058^{5} 6277^{6}

Uddy Mac *Neville Bycroft* a29 57
4 ch m Reel Buddy(USA) —Befriend (USA) (Allied Forces (USA))
798^{9} 874^{12} 1439^{2} 2249^{7} 2588^{10} 4518^{3} 5652^{4} 6091^{8} 6266^{8} 6602^{4} 6834^{6}

Ugalla *Jane Chapple-Hyam* a65 79
4 ch m Where Or When(IRE) —Baddi Heights (FR) (Shirley Heights)
3758^{6} 4341^{5} 4687^{3} 5102^{5} 6104^{3}

Ugo (USA) *Heather Main* a75 74
3 b g Street Cry(IRE) —Min Elreeh (USA) (Danzig (USA))
1271^{4} 1620^{7} 2152^{4} 2842^{8} (3325) 4664^{4} 4905^{7} 6507^{12} 6756^{12}

Uighur (FR) *A Fabre* a68 79
3 gr g Verglas(IRE) —Up To Date (FR) (Valanour (IRE))
1010a^{7}

Ujadil Bere (FR) *M Pimbonnet* a76 77
3 b c High Yield(USA) —Shadeed Vallee (USA) (Shadeed (USA))
(370a)

Uklanie (FR) *F Chappet* a78 85
3 b f Dalakhani(IRE) —Comete (FR) (Jeune Homme (USA))
981a^{2}

Ukrainian (IRE) *Mark Johnston* 58
2 b g Teofilo(IRE) —Livadiya (IRE) (Shernazar)
6259^{5} 6527^{16} 7083^{9}

Uldiko (FR) *Mme C Barande-Barbe* a93 96
3 b g Enrique—Nakamti (FR) (Lahint (USA))
532a^{8}

Ulivate (IRE) *M Pimbonnet* a69 85
3 b f Poliglote—Be Prepared (USA) (Broad Brush (USA))
288a^{2}

Ulla *Chris Wall* a68 56
3 ch f Singspiel(IRE) —Shining Vale (USA) (Twilight Agenda (USA))
2458^{15} 4279^{8} 4805^{10} (5860) 6622^{3} 7016a^{0}

Ullswater (IRE) *Mark Johnston* a79 79
3 b c Singspiel(IRE) —Uluwatu (IRE) (Unfuwain (USA))
5205^{10} 5582^{2} 5716^{6} 6218^{3} 6918^{9}

Ultimate *Brian Ellison* a94 89
5 b g Anabaa(USA) —Nirvana (Marju (IRE))
5465^{10} (6155)

Ultimate Best *Michael Mullineaux* a53
3 gr f King's Best(USA) —Success Story (Sharrood (USA))
6086^{5} ◆ 6475^{2} 6947^{3} 7340^{8} 7515^{5}

Ultimate Eagle (USA) *Michael Pender* 117
3 bb c Mizzen Mast(USA) —Letithappencaptain (USA) (Captain Bodgit (USA))
(7572a)

Ultimate Quest (IRE) *Michael Chapman* a75 75
6 ch g Rainbow Quest(USA) —Crepe Ginger (IRE) (Sadler's Wells (USA))
1153^{11} 1458^{5} 1794^{4}

Ultra Blend (USA) *Art Sherman* a111 102
5 b m Richly Blended(USA) —Ankha (USA) (Desert Classic (USA))
7285a^{4}

Ultra Cool (IRE) *Adrian McGuinness* a86 86
4 b m One Cool Cat(USA) —Non Ultra (USA) (Peintre Celebre (USA))
7618a^{2}

Ultrasonic (USA) *Sir Michael Stoute* 90
2 b f Mizzen Mast(USA) —Quickfire (Dubai Millennium)
(6030) ◆ 7028^{4}

Ultra Steps (IRE) *Adrian McGuinness* a59 32
2 b f Footstepsinthesand—Non Ultra (USA) (Peintre Celebre (USA))
7273a^{8}

Umayyad (IRE) *John Gosden* 23
2 b c Montjeu(IRE) —Janoubi (Dansili)
6953^{10}

Umbonga *Neville Bycroft*
3 b f Dr Fong(USA) —Adventuress (Singspiel (IRE))
5589^{7}

Umph (IRE) *David Evans* a65 63
2 b g Kodiac—Baraloti (IRE) (Barathea (IRE))
982^{6} 1101^{2} 1235^{2} 1383^{7} 1691^{14} 2374^{3} 2889^{6} 3021^{6} 4884^{6}

Umseyat (USA) *John Gosden* 86
3 bb f Arch(USA) —Tabrir (IRE) (Unfuwain (USA))
3809^{4} 4335^{5} 5020^{6} 6330^{9}

Umverti *Joanne Foster* 81
6 b m Averti(IRE) —Umbrian Gold (IRE) (Perugino (USA))
2932^{15}

Unaccompanied (IRE) *D K Weld* 104
4 b m Danehill Dancer(IRE) —Legend Has It (IRE) (Sadler's Wells (USA))
(1119a)

Un Air De Danse (FR) *S Wattel* 82
3 ch g Green Tune(USA) —Danse Quatz (FR) (Johann Quatz (FR))
7016a^{6}

Un Amor (FR) *D De Waele* a68 85
10 b h Septieme Ciel(USA) —Ballade Viennoise (FR) (Cricket Ball (USA))
935a^{0}

Una Pelota (IRE) *Tom Dascombe* a71 80
5 b g Refuse To Bend(IRE) —Sombreffe (Polish Precedent (USA))
203^{3} 427^{5} (712) 748^{3} 876^{3}

Una Vita Pius (IRE) *Patrick Gilligan* a46
3 b f Antonius Pius(USA) —Avit (IRE) (General Monash (USA))
28^{3} 383^{5} 595^{8} 2918^{11} 7693^{10} 7829^{5}

Unbeatable *William Knight* a24 44
3 b f Beat Hollow—Koniya (IRE) (Doyoun)
2157^{11} 3119^{6} 4641^{5} 5267^{7} 5898^{12}

Unbreak My Heart (IRE) *Richard Guest* a84 93
6 ch g Bahamian Bounty—Golden Heart (Salse (USA))
18^{6} 112^{2} (261) 320^{5} 475^{11} 685^{8} ◆ 806^{10} 4150^{8} 5149^{10} 5538^{9}

Uncle Bryn *John Quinn* 69
3 b g Royal Applause—Happy Omen (Warning)
1693^{7} 2650^{10} 5619^{6} 6415^{2} 6840^{10}

Uncle Dermot (IRE) *Brendan Powell* a70 71
3 b g Arakan(USA) —Cappadoce (IRE) (General Monash (USA))
720^{2} 905^{2} 1179^{2} 1481^{6} 2064^{7} 2885^{5} (3432) 4011^{4} 4447^{7} 6167^{11} 6586^{8} 6799^{11} 7235^{2} 7425^{14}

Uncle Fred *Patrick Chamings* a85 85
6 b g Royal Applause—Karla June (Unfuwain (USA))
(1138) 1530^{2} 2178^{8} 2769^{8} 3987^{6} (4616) 5586^{4} 6439^{8} 6949^{7}

Uncle Keef (IRE) *Brendan Powell* a69 67
5 b g Sadler's Wells(USA) —Love For Ever (IRE) (Darshaan)
3352^{8} 4274^{5} 5079^{12} 6405^{9}

Uncle Mo (USA) *Todd Pletcher* a127
3 b c Indian Charlie(USA) —Playa Maya (USA) (Arch (USA))
7308a^{10}

Uncle Roger (IRE) *Eve Johnson Houghton* 70
2 b g Camacho—Felin Gruvy (IRE) (Tagula (IRE))
3941^{2} 4229^{U} (4485) 5913^{5} 6484^{9} 6972^{10}

Uncle Timmy *John Quinn* a61 60
2 b g Multiplex—Park's Girl (Averti (IRE))
3611^{6} 4147^{6} 4851^{6} 5555^{5} 6043^{6} (6597) 7059^{4} (7231) ◆ 7364^{3}

Uncut Stone (IRE) *Peter Niven* a68 74
3 b g Awesome Again(CAN) —Suitably Discreet (USA) (Mr Prospector (USA))
7536^{4} 7689^{5} 7858^{3}

Under Fire (IRE) *Tony Carroll* a32 60
8 b g Lear Spear(USA) —Kahyasi Moll (IRE) (Brief Truce (USA))
4549^{12} 4953^{11} 5421^{6} 5785^{6} 7091^{9} 7394^{11}

Under Review (IRE) *Michael J Browne* a67 61
5 b g Danetime(IRE) —Coloma (JPN) (Forty Niner (USA))
(143) 6139a^{13}

Understory (USA) *Tim McCarthy* a79 79
4 b h Forestry(USA) —Sha Tha (USA) (Mr Prospector (USA))
647^{6} 963^{5} (1144) 2150^{5} 2649^{8} 2915^{7} 4825^{2} 5893^{10} 6241^{6} 7130^{6} 7513^{2} 7831^{5}

Underwritten *Andrew Balding* 47
2 b g Authorized(IRE) —Grain Of Gold (Mr Prospector (USA))
6956^{10} 7232^{13}

Undeux Croixnoire (FR) *C Baillet*
3 b g Muhaymin(USA) —Chande Sisi (FR) (Neverneyev (USA))
5529a^{0}

Undulant Way *Amanda Perrett* a76 83
3 b f Hurricane Run(IRE) —Arietta's Way (IRE) (Darshaan)
1947^{7} 2904^{3} (3467) 3744^{2} 4341^{2} 4971^{7} 5782^{3} 6121^{4}

Unescorted (IRE) *M J Grassick* a55 45
2 b f Holy Roman Emperor(IRE) —Eadaoin (USA) (King Of Kings (IRE))
7275a^{13}

Unex Canaletto *Paul Cole* 47
2 b g Motivator—Logic (Slip Anchor)
6993^{10}

Unex El Greco *John Gosden* 95
3 b g Holy Roman Emperor(IRE) —Friendlier (Zafonic (USA))
1234^{U} 4802^{15}

Unex Goya (IRE) *Michael Smith* a61 71
3 b g Medicean—Arabica (USA) (Red Ransom (USA))
610^{4} (2825) 3318^{9} 4125^{5} 4637^{5} 6264^{12}

Unex Michelangelo (IRE) *John Gosden* 93
2 b c Dansili—Chenchikova (IRE) (Sadler's Wells (USA))
4996^{4} (5727) 7508a^{5}

Unex Monet *Michael Bell* 24
3 b g Oratorio(IRE) —Lady Adnil (IRE) (Stravinsky (USA))
3177^{10}

Unex Picasso *William Haggas* 70
3 b g Galileo(IRE) —Ruff Shod (USA) (Storm Boot (USA))
2114^{4} 2930^{10}

Unex Renoir *John Gosden* a85 88
3 b c Nayef(USA) —Simacota (GER) (Acatenango (GER))
2097^{3} 2551^{6} 2956^{3} 3376^{3} 4208^{4} 6130^{4} 6822^{7}

Unforgiving (IRE) *Alan McCabe* 37
2 bb f Red Clubs(IRE) —Adjtiya (IRE) (Green Desert (USA))
1657^{6} 2355^{7} 2784^{5}

Un Hinged (IRE) *John J Coleman* a83 87
11 b g Danetime(IRE) —Classic Silk (IRE) (Classic Secret (USA))
7549a^{7}

Union Island (IRE) *Brian Ellison* a68 84
5 b g Rock Of Gibraltar(IRE) —Daftiyna (IRE) (Darshaan)
2220^{7} 3276^{12} 4043^{3} ◆ 4360^{8} (4635)

Union Rags (USA) *Michael Matz* a120 115
2 b c Dixie Union(USA) —Tempo (USA) (Gone West (USA))
7306a^{2}

Union Zak *Rod Millman* 35
7 b g Tobougg(IRE) —Seagreen (IRE) (Green Desert (USA))
2813^{11}

United Sport (FR) *P Chevillard* 45
3 b c Iron Mask(USA) —Linamixa (FR) (Lord Of Men)
902a^{0}

Unity (IRE) *David Wachman* 99
4 b m Sadler's Wells(USA) —Moments Of Joy (Darshaan)
1427a^{4} 3695a^{4} 4589a^{5}

Universal (IRE) *Mahmood Al Zarooni* 70
2 ch c Dubawi(IRE) —Winesong (IRE) (Giant's Causeway (USA))
2181^{4} 2584^{5} 3182^{9}

Universal Law (FR) *E Danel* a71
3 gr c Proclamation(IRE) —Grace Bankes (Efisio)
7669a^{0}

Universal Truth (IRE) *D K Weld* 69
6 b g Galileo(IRE) —Mistress Thames (Sharpo)
2534a^{8}

Un Jour (FR) *Mlle Valerie Boussin* 98
3 b f Kahyasi—Happy Town (FR) (Anabaa (USA))
7313a^{7} 7510a^{0}

Unknown Rebel (IRE) *Kevin Ryan* a60 86
3 b g Night Shift(USA) —Crystalline Stream (FR) (Polish Precedent (USA))
1327^{2} 1683^{7} (1972) (3038) 3462^{5} 3858^{3} (4576) (5311) 5724^{7}

Unleashed (IRE) *Charlie Mann* a44 79
6 br g Storming Home—Uriah (GER) (Acatenango (GER))
3013^{P}

Unlimited *Tony Carroll* a86 71
9 b g Bold Edge—Cabcharge Blue (Midyan (USA))
48^{4} 269^{5} (445) 625^{9} 633^{3} 856^{3} (914) 1014^{4} (1221) 1804a^{2} 2995^{5} 3250^{3} 3716^{4} 4544^{2} (4921) 5734^{2} 6541^{6}

Un Monde (SPA) *Mlle A Imaz-Ceca* a56
3 b c Baptize(USA) —Tymoon (FR) (Titus Livius (FR))
660a^{6}

Unnefer (FR) *P Bary* 108
6 b h Danehill Dancer(IRE) —Mimalia (USA) (Silver Hawk (USA))
2980a^{4} 5530a^{6}

Until The Man (IRE) *Jim Best* a62 71
4 b g Tillerman—Canoe Cove (IRE) (Grand Lodge (USA))
4088^{7} 4322^{14}

Untold Melody *Kevin Ryan* 61
2 b f Oratorio(IRE) —Different Story (USA) (Stravinsky (USA))
5786^{6} 6045^{3} 6598^{2}

Unusual Suspect (USA) *Michael Kent* a108 116
7 bb h Unusual Heat(USA) —Penpont (NZ) (Crested Wave (USA))
6886a^{6} 7218a^{9}

Unwrapit (USA) *Bryan Smart* a63 64
3 b f Tapit(USA) —Miss Thermal Tech (USA) (Distinctive Pro (USA))
368^{5} 509^{2} 600^{3} 738^{3} 1169^{10} 1400^{5} 2351^{5} (3248) 3489^{6} 3661^{8} 4288^{10} 5433^{3} 6190^{4} 7001^{9} 7641^{5} 7748^{4} 7782^{3}

Up (IRE) *A P O'Brien* a87 105
2 b f Galileo(IRE) —Halland Park Lass (IRE) (Spectrum (IRE))
7281a^{4}

Up And Coming (IRE) *J E Pease* a92 92
7 b g Compton Place—Uplifting (Magic Ring (IRE))
(3568a)

Upark Flyer *Patrick Morris* a53 63
3 br f Piccolo—Autumn Affair (Lugana Beach)
333^{5}

Upcountry *Charles Hills* 88
3 b g Oasis Dream—Five Fields (USA) (Chester House (USA))
5449^{2} ◆ 6020^{2} (6608)

Uphold *Gay Kelleway* a91 93
4 b g Oasis Dream—Allegro Viva (USA) (Distant View (USA))
1278^{2} 1828^{4} (2359) (2958) 3411^{7} 3982^{2} 4331^{8} 5435^{11} 6445^{5} (6656) 7241^{8} 7651^{6}

Uppercut *Stuart Kittow* 88
3 ch g Needwood Blade—Uplifting (Magic Ring (IRE))
1565^{4} 1984^{2} 2568^{2} 3543^{3} 4342^{3} 4914^{4} ◆ 5586^{2} 6167^{9} (7050)

Upper Lambourn (IRE) *Jamie Osborne* a73 63
3 b c Exceed And Excel(AUS) —In The Fashion (IRE) (In The Wings)
518^{3} ◆ (3950) ◆ 4721^{3} 5419^{11} 7746^{7}

Upperline (USA) *Michael Stidham* a111 111
4 b m Maria's Mon(USA) —Snowflake (IRE) (Caerleon (USA))
5073a^{5}

Uprise *Sir Michael Stoute* 73
2 b g Pivotal—Soar (Danzero (AUS))
4330^{18} 5801^{3} 6463^{4}

Upset *Richard Ford* 37
4 ch g Reset(AUS) —Carreamia (Weldnaas (USA))
427^{10}

Upside Down Cake *J E Hammond* a66
3 b f Encosta De Lago(AUS) —Saralea (FR) (Sillery (USA))
7667a^{2}

Up Ten Down Two (IRE) *Michael Easterby* a32 48
2 b g Hurricane Run(IRE) —Darabela (IRE) (Desert King (IRE))
4402^{7} 4853^{10} 5454^{12} 6667^{7}

Upton Crystal *Michael Easterby* a14 36
3 b f Gentleman's Deal(IRE) —Crystal Seas (Zamindar (USA))
4286^{6} 5212^{9}

Uptown Guy (USA) *William Haggas* a67 86
3 bb g Speightstown(USA) —Affordability (USA) (Unbridled (USA))
1611^{4} ◆ (3219) 3871^{3} 4281^{2} (4854) 5199^{5}

Urban Kode (IRE) *Ollie Pears* a65 68
3 b g Kodiac—Urbanize (USA) (Chester House (USA))
25^{2} (193) 217^{3} 365^{3} 424^{3} 527^{4} 540^{3} 2527^{3} 2635^{5} 2964^{7} 3089^{2} 3514^{4} (3596) 3916^{6} (4071) 4153^{2} 4812^{3}

Urban Space *John Flint* a78 84
5 ch g Sulamani(IRE) —Rasmalai (Sadler's Wells (USA))
1061^{11} 1977^{9} 2156^{3} 2454^{3} 2769^{10} 3434^{10} (4862) 5110^{6} 5761^{10}

Uriah Heep (FR) *Sir Michael Stoute* 75
2 b c Danehill Dancer(IRE) —Canasita (Zafonic (USA))
7133^{5}

Urlanie (FR) *Mme A-E Gareau* 25
3 b f Turbo Jet(FR) —Melanie Du Chenet (FR) (Nikos)
7016a^{10}

Ursula (IRE) *Mrs K Burke* a86 86
5 b m Namid—Fritta Mista (IRE) (Linamix (FR))
1109^{14} 2116^{4} ◆ 2806^{2} 3162^{6} 4392^{2} 4791^{5} 5554^{8} 6113^{11} 6189^{5}

Ursus *Christopher Wilson* a52 63
6 ch g Rambling Bear—Adar Jane (Ardar)
2670^{7}

Usain Colt *Richard Hannon* 86
2 b c Royal Applause—Bright Vision (Indian Ridge)
4580^{6} (6991)

Usbeke (GER) *J-P Carvalho* a92 105
5 b g Big Shuffle(USA) —Ustimona (GER) (Mondrian (GER))
5530a^{9} 6201a^{4}

Usquaebach *Pat Phelan* a62
4 b m Trade Fair—Mashmoum (Lycius (USA))
391^{10}

Utley (USA) *John Gosden* a81 108
3 b c Smart Strike(CAN) —No Matter What (USA) (Nureyev (USA))
998a^{11} 1318^{3} 2106^{5} 2683^{4} 3029^{9}

Utopia Jem (FR) *D Sepulchre* a76 85
3 b f Okawango(USA) —Odienne Jem (FR) (Cadeaux Genereux)
901a^{4}

Va Bene (FR) *J-M Capitte* a66
3 b f Iron Mask(USA) —Nigrita (GER) (Lichine (USA))
288a^{4}

Vadamar (FR) *A De Royer-Dupre* 119
3 b c Dalakhani(IRE) —Vadawina (IRE) (Unfuwain (USA))
1923a^{3} 2715^{7} 5987a^{3} (6903a) 7729a^{10}

Vagabond King *Edward Creighton* a18
2 b c Ishiguru(USA) —Feabhas (IRE) (Spectrum (IRE))
7094^{13} 7431^{10} 7481^{11}

Vagabond Shoes (IRE) *Y Durepaire* 113
4 ch h Beat Hollow—Atiza (IRE) (Singspiel (IRE))
2980a^{2} (4120a) 5777a^{8} 6558a^{7}

Vaiara (FR) *P Lacroix* 25
2 b f Go Between(FR) —Cayras Fair (FR) (Always Fair (USA))
7312a^{10}

Vain Boteli (GER) *Richard Ford* 3
5 b g Bertolini(USA) —Vanity Fair (Nashwan (USA))
2618^{10}

Vainglory (USA) *David Simcock* a94 99
7 ch h Swain(IRE) —Infinite Spirit (USA) (Maria's Mon (USA))
1684^{19} 2679^{4} 2933^{4} 3290^{2} 3542^{7} 4494^{9} 5218^{6} 5929^{6} 6496^{3} (6672) 7029^{12}

Valandraud (FR) *Y Fertillet* a47
10 ch g Nashamaa—Lady Albizzia (FR) (Riverquest (FR))
42a^{0}

Valantino Oyster (IRE) *Tracy Waggott* a62 69
4 b g Pearl Of Love(IRE) —Mishor (Slip Anchor)
373^{8} 1305^{3} 1556^{4} 2462^{7} (2618) 2804^{7} 4633^{4} 6229^{2} 6379^{3} 6601^{11} (7061)

Valdan (IRE) *David Evans* a59 71
7 b g Val Royal(FR) —Danedrop (IRE) (Danehill (USA))
1017^{7} 1243^{6} 1491^{10} 1713^{8} 1798^{6} 2060^{6} 2400^{2} 2696^{5} 3041^{7} 3185^{4} 3507^{9} 3828^{14} 4602^{U} 5595^{7} 5723^{12} 6157^{13} 6873^{5} 7426^{5} (7527) 7654^{4} 7817^{13}

Valdaw *Joseph Tuite* a55 53
3 b g Val Royal(FR) —Delight Of Dawn (Never So Bold)
811[7] 1053[3] 1997[12] 2964[8] 3690[11] 4200[5]

Val De Majorque (FR) *D Sepulchre* a90
3 b c Poliglote—Valdemossa (FR) (Highest Honor (FR))
7677a[3]

Valdemar *Alan Brown* a44 50
5 ch g Tobougg(IRE) —Stealthy Times (Timeless Times (USA))
102[4] 250[6] 482[8]

Val De Saone (FR) *J-C Rouget* 85
3 b c Hurricane Run(IRE) —Celebre Fragance (FR) (Peintre Celebre (USA))
5132a[2]

Valencha *Hughie Morrison* a76 96
4 ch m Domedriver(IRE) —Riverine (Risk Me (FR))
2313[4] 2876[2] (3121) 3845[2] 4429[4] 5702[2] 5970[2] (6378) 6862[24] (7031) 7295[14]

Valensole (FR) *P Lacroix* 57
2 b f Della Francesca(USA) —Truffle (IRE) (Ezzoud (IRE))
7312a[4]

Valentine's Gift *Neville Bycroft* 57
3 b g Presidium—Efipetite (Efisio)
2802[13] 3756[6] 4437[5] 5165[6] 5619[7] 6536[7] 7061[10]

Valentino Swing (IRE) *Michael Appleby* a56 49
8 ch g Titus Livius(FR) —Farmers Swing (IRE) (River Falls)
97[12] 210[8] 304[7] 386[3] 619[6] 664[10] 1912[10] 2554[4] 3617[9] 5208[5] 5539[13] 7517[8] 7843[6]

Vale Of Lingfield (IRE) *John Best* a70
2 b c Moss Vale(IRE) —Celtic Guest (IRE) (Be My Guest (USA))
7435[3]

Valeo Si Vales (IRE) *Jamie Osborne* a66 64
3 b g Oratorio(IRE) —Eurostorm (USA) (Storm Bird (CAN))
1749[3] 3432[12] 3913[4] 4743[3] 5143[3] 5388[6] 6090[3] 6848[6] 7123[3]

Valerie Anne (IRE) *Mme J Bidgood* 58
2 b f Oratorio(IRE) —Victoria Page (FR) (Anabaa (USA))
3567a[6]

Valerius Maximus *M Boutin* a78 83
3 b g Spartacus(IRE) —Capriolla (In The Wings)
5529a[10] 7669a[0]

Valery Borzov (IRE) *Richard Fahey* a94 98
7 b g Iron Mask(USA) —Fay's Song (IRE) (Fayruz)
3279[3] 4531[3] (5434) 5758[16] 6145[17] (6331) 6987[13] 7295[4]

Valiant Arthur *Michael Dods* 21
2 b g Avonbridge—Never Say Deya (Dansili)
4668[7]

Valiant Blue (IRE) *Nicky Vaughan* a42
2 b c Moss Vale(IRE) —Tiltili (IRE) (Spectrum (IRE))
6025[8] 6842[8]

Valiant Girl *Roger Charlton* 64
2 b f Lemon Drop Kid(USA) —Victoria Cross (IRE) (Mark Of Esteem (IRE))
6529[7] ◆

Valiant Knight (FR) *Richard Hannon* 87
4 ch h Night Shift(USA) —Pilgrim Of Grace (FR) (Bering)
1097[10]

Valiant Runner *Jeremy Noseda* a56 62
2 b f Haafhd—Valjarv (IRE) (Bluebird (USA))
4276[8] 4614[13] 5445[10] 6053[4] ◆ 6443[7]

Valid Reason *Dean Ivory* a87 87
4 b g Observatory(USA) —Real Trust (USA) (Danzig (USA))
5888[3] 6249[3] 6707[2]

Valid Sum (USA) *Mahmood Al Zarooni* a100 85
5 b h Street Cry(IRE) —Pay Bird (USA) (Storm Bird (CAN))
[illegible]

Validus *Luca Cumani* a95 89
2 b c Zamindar(USA) —Victoire Finale (Peintre Celebre (USA))
5011[3] (5688) ◆ 6692[5]

Valiyr (IRE) *A De Royer-Dupre* 109
3 b c Alhaarth(IRE) —Valima (FR) (Linamix (FR))
3653a[2] 4376a[6]

Valkov *Tony Carroll* a62 44
4 b m Val Royal(FR) —Petrikov (IRE) (In The Wings)
626[5] 814[8] 1333[9] 3096[7] 3952[12] 4317[10]

Valle (USA) *M Delcher-Sanchez*
3 b c E Dubai(USA) —Azelna (FR) (Tropular)
7678a[0]

Valley Ace *John Quinn* 43
2 b c Three Valleys(USA) —First Ace (First Trump)
2485[10] 2889[7] 3137[4]

Valley Of Hope *Richard Fahey* 59
2 gr g Three Valleys(USA) —Zaragossa (Paris House)
1966[6] 2261[5] 4192[4] ◆ 4984[7] 5438[5] 6043[5] 6384[5]

Valley Of Stars (IRE) *Edward Creighton* 52
2 b c Three Valleys(USA) —Graffiti Girl (IRE) (Sadler's Wells (USA))
2837[8] 3349[5] 4433[6]

Valley Queen *Mark Usher* 69
2 b f Three Valleys(USA) —Queen Of Havana (USA) (King Of Kings (IRE))
7164[6] ◆

Valley Tiger *Richard Fahey* a64 62
3 b g Tiger Hill(IRE) —Nantyglo (Mark Of Esteem (IRE))
1299[5] 1609[6] 2119[8] 2652[3] 3223[2] 3709[7] 4244[3] 4705[9] 5165[4] 5507[7] 6357[5] 6701[7] 6845[4] (7005) 7698[12] 7810[8]

Valmina *Tony Carroll* a73 64
4 b g Val Royal(FR) —Minnina (IRE) (In The Wings)
403[2] ◆ 577[4] 820[7] 984[2] 1314[7] 1755[2] 1917[7] 2270[7] 2610[9] 3093[7] 3735[8] 4322[9] (4759) 4850[2] 5387[7] (5736) 5917[4]

Val Mondo (GER) *Uwe Ostmann* 106
4 b h Lando(GER) —Valleria (GER) (Big Shuffle (USA))
1931a[3] 2749a[4] 3446a[5] 5497a[7]

Val O'Hara (IRE) *Peter Winkworth* a81 68
3 ch f Ad Valorem(USA) —Lady Scarlett (Woodman (USA))
(3043) 4355[6] 5641[7] 6822[11]

Valoro (FR) *N Leenders* a89 89
4 b g Kahyasi—Valverda (USA) (Irish River (FR))
900a[2]

Valugny (FR) *F Sanchez* a70 68
4 b h Lugny(FR) —Vahana (FR) (Sicyos (USA))
325a[0] 831a[10]

Vamoose *Kevin Ryan* 33
2 b g Vital Equine(IRE) —Golden Dagger (IRE) (Daggers Drawn (USA))
6774[9] 7060[10]

Van Der Art *Alan Jarvis* 83
2 ch f Dutch Art—Chase The Lady (USA) (Atticus (USA))
2919[3] ◆ 3680[2] 5117[2] ◆ 5681[3] (6449) 6995[3]

Van Doesburg (IRE) *Jonathan Portman* 55
3 gr g Westerner—Winter Daydream (IRE) (Soviet Star (USA))
6923[12]

Van Go Go *David Nicholls* a67 66
2 b f Dutch Art—Baldovina (Tale Of The Cat (USA))
1192[2] (1434) (1563) 1806[6] (1954) 2404[6] 3879[5] 4079[7] 4558[9]

Vanguard Dream *Richard Hannon* a96 102
3 b c Oasis Dream—Garmoucheh (USA) (Silver Hawk (USA))
990[3] 1405[4] 1844[7] 2683[4] 3067[14] 4493[5]

Vanilla Rum *John Mackie* a75 80
4 b g Reset(AUS) —Snoozy (Cadeaux Genereux)
285[5] 528[4] 1221[5] 2112[7] 2674[9] 3495[7] 4076[7] 5414[8] 6134[6] 6493[9] 6698[2] 7788[3]

Vaniloquio (IRE) *N Clement* a85 101
2 b c Acclamation—Trinity Joy (Vettori (IRE))
5130a[2] 5770a[6] 7220a[2]

Vanity Woman *Vittorio Caruso* 88
2 b f Nayef(USA) —Sospel (Kendor (FR))
3212a[5]

Vanjura (GER) *R Dzubasz* 115
4 ch m Areion(GER) —Venia Legendi (GER) (Zinaad)
2541a[2] (3897a) 4597a[6] (5753a) 6369a[3] (7323a)

Van Rooney (USA) *T Stack* a90 82
2 ch c Van Nistelrooy(USA) —Royal Shyness (Royal Academy (USA))
6308[2]

Vantaa (IRE) *Richard Fahey* a38 44
3 ch g Shamardal(USA) —Indian Express (Indian Ridge)
454[5]

Vantage Point (FR) *Mlle C Cardenne* a88 90
8 ch g Zafonic(USA) —Victory Cry (IRE) (Caerleon (USA))
3568a[8]

Varlak *K F Clutterbuck* a61 38
3 b g Val Royal(FR) —Kokila (Indian Danehill (IRE))
564[7] 716[10] 898[4] 1018[9] 1526[7] 4060[11] 4510[7] 5214[10]

Varnish *Richard Hannon* 76
2 ch f Choisir(AUS) —Bronze Star (Mark Of Esteem (IRE))
6160[10] 7030[2] ◆

Vasco Bere (FR) *F Head* 103
2 b c Hold That Tiger(USA) —Poet's Studio (USA) (Bertrando (USA))
7192a[8]

Vasily *Robert Eddery* 83
3 b c Sadler's Wells(USA) —Red Bloom (Selkirk (USA))
5911[9] 6242[4] (6810)

Vassaria (IRE) *Michael Dods* 79
2 b f Rock Of Gibraltar(IRE) —Vassiana (FR) (Anabaa (USA))
2254[3] 2709[3] (3483) 4252[5] 5847[13] 7021[10]

Vault (IRE) *A P O'Brien* a84 100
2 b c Danehill Dancer(IRE) —Simadartha (USA) (Gone West (USA))
3439a[5] 5293a[7] 5951a[8] 7185a[5]

Vauville (IRE) *Y De Nicolay* a78 89
3 b f Invincible Spirit(IRE) —Vadorga (Grand Lodge (USA))
981a[0] 4896a[3]

Vedelago (IRE) *L Polito* 109
2 b c Red Clubs(IRE) —Queen Shy (Marju (IRE)) (3212a) 6740a[3]

Vehement *Andy Turnell* a52
5 b m Refuse To Bend(IRE) —Velvet Lady (Nashwan (USA))
7856[3]

Veiled *Nicky Henderson* a83 98
5 b m Sadler's Wells(USA) —Evasive Quality (FR) (Highest Honor (FR))
(2512) ◆ (3013) 6690[10]

Veiled Applause *John Quinn* a74 87
8 b g Royal Applause—Scarlet Veil (Tyrnavos)
1097[3] 1671[3] 2006[14] 2403[7] 2892[8] 3277[12] 4237[4] 5036[2] 5200[2] 6078[6] 6346[8] 6676[8] 6918[4]

Veloce (IRE) *Ralph Beckett* a44 67
3 b g Hurricane Run(IRE) —Kiftsgate Rose (FR) (Nashwan (USA))
1399[3] 1872[2] 2228[4] ◆ 3587[2] 5477[3] 6798[7]

Velvet Band *Richard Whitaker* a62 35
4 gr m Verglas(IRE) —Applaud (USA) (Rahy (USA))
508[5] 839[9] 2237[13] 2348[7] 3025[10]

Velvet Star (IRE) *Paul Cole* 52
2 b f Galileo(IRE) —Velvet Moon (IRE) (Shaadi (USA))
5807[10] 6458[12] 7030[11]

Vena Amoris (USA) *Mahmood Al Zarooni* 5
2 b f Dixie Union(USA) —Love Locket (USA) (Thunder Gulch (USA))
6985[10]

Venegazzu (IRE) *Peter Chapple-Hyam* 70
2 br c Dubawi(IRE) —Vintage Tipple (IRE) (Entrepreneur)
5851[9] 6529[3]

Venetian View (IRE) *Gary Moore* a86 82
2 b g Amadeus Wolf—Twilight Tango (Groom Dancer (USA))
3686[10] ◆ 5133[4] 5889[3] ◆ (6214) 6484[2] (7095)

Venetien (FR) *M Delzangles* a97 63
3 b c Iron Mask(USA) —Vassia (USA) (Machiavellian (USA))
4896a[7]

Veneto (FR) *B De Montzey* a85 113
2 ch c Panis(USA) —Milanaise (FR) (Marignan (USA))
6565a[4] 7192a[6]

Venir Rouge *Matthew Salaman* a70 76
7 ch g Dancing Spree(USA) —Al Awaalah (Mukaddamah (USA))
3546[10] 5050[8] 6503[4]

Venise Jelois (FR) *Robert Collet* a75 96
3 b f Marchand De Sable(USA) —Star Angels (FR) (Ski Chief (USA))
1513a[5] 1922a[7] 5027a[9] 5839a[11]

Venomous *Leonard Powell* a91 115
3 b c Red Ransom(USA) —Snake Dancer (IRE) (Golden Snake (USA))
2139a[3] 2978a[6] 3670a[5] 5772a[5] 7572a[5]

Vent D'Avril *D Prod'Homme* 74
3 b f Xaar—Vent D'Avall (Observatory (USA))
258a[0]

Ventiane (GER) *H-W Hiller* 68
3 b f Konigstiger(GER) —Venia Legendi (GER) (Zinaad)
981a[0]

Ventura Cove (IRE) *Richard Fahey* a68 83
4 ch g Bahamian Bounty—Baby Bunting (Wolfhound (USA))
1200[5] 7039[10] 7456[6] 7579[10]

Ventura Sands (IRE) *Richard Fahey* 77
3 b g Footstepsinthesand—Beautiful Noise (Piccolo)
1169[8] (1543) 2092[4] 2833[5] 3337[6] 3706[4] (4081) 4560[9] 5560[4] (6116)

Ventura Spirit *Richard Fahey* 71
2 b g Royal Applause—Jalissa (Mister Baileys)
2936[4] 3826[6] 4898[2] ◆ 5287[5] (5818) 6911[7]

Ventus D'Or *Derek Shaw* 43
2 b c Shirocco(GER) —Perle D'Or (IRE) (Entrepreneur)
3686[13] 4339[8] 4823[8] 7569[13] 7725[8]

Venutius *Ed McMahon* a88 95
4 b g Doyen(IRE) —Boadicea's Chariot (Commanche Run)
2217[14] 2814[3] 3825[11] 4794[2] 5920[5] 6290[15] 7110[14]

Veradis *Clive Cox* 48
3 b f Hawk Wing(USA) —Victoire Finale (Peintre Celebre (USA))
2639[8] 4753[9]

Vera's Moscou (IRE) *Mlle V Dissaux* a67 75
5 b g Kheleyf(USA) —Inching (Inchinor)
221a[8]

Verbeeck *Alan McCabe* 81
2 b c Dutch Art—Tesary (Danehill (USA))
1628[3] 2355[2] (2880) 4502[3] 5061[5] 6670[19] 7021[13]

Verdant *Sir Michael Stoute* a82 108
4 b h Singspiel(IRE) —Orford Ness (Selkirk (USA))
1403[5] 1883[3] 3403[4] 4532[8]

Verde-Mar (BRZ) *E Martins* a106 90
4 b c Gilded Time(USA) —Jolie Marcia (BRZ) (Spend A Buck (USA))
155a[6] 582a[10] 756a[12]

Verge (IRE) *Edward Vaughan* 32
2 b f Acclamation—Marliana (IRE) (Mtoto)
2049[10]

Verglacial (IRE) *C Lerner* a93 100
4 gr h Verglas(IRE) —Apostrophe (IRE) (Barathea (IRE))
7193a[9]

Vergrigio (IRE) *Brian Meehan* a65 65
4 gr g Verglas(IRE) —Roystonea (Polish Precedent (USA))
3590[9] 4054[6] 4545[8] 6443[13] 6611[12] 6812[6] 6977[2]

Verinco *Bryan Smart* a70 103
5 b g Bahamian Bounty—Dark Eyed Lady (IRE) (Exhibitioner)
294[9] 1073[2] (2491) 2585[2] 2727[2] 3073[3] 3357[3] 4416[10] (5163) 5758[3] ◆ 5927[7] (6865)

Veri One (FR) *T Larriviere* a64 67
3 b f Iron Mask(USA) —Veri Star (FR) (Verglas (IRE))
258a[0]

Verluga (IRE) *Tim Easterby* a61 63
4 gr g Verglas(IRE) —Caviare (Cadeaux Genereux)
115[3] 346[2] 1077[7] 1394[5] 1615[10] 4408[10] 4604[10] 5167[9] 6236[6] 6461[7]

Vermeyen *Ann Duffield* a51
2 b g Dutch Art—Madame Maxine (USA) (Dayjur (USA))
7627[7]

Verona Bay (FR) *Julia Feilden* 19
2 b c Della Francesca(USA) —Verone (USA) (Dixie Union (USA))
5013[12]

Veroon (IRE) *James Given* a89 86
5 b g Noverre(USA) —Waroonga (IRE) (Brief Truce (USA))
38[5] 124[4] 287[3] 381[3] 475[6] 772[3] (877) 995[3] (2955) 3276[4] 3825[12] 4415[11] 5059[9] (6948) 7227[3] 7558[8] 7651[5] 7922[5]

Verrazano *Kevin Ryan* a66 68
3 b f Statue Of Liberty(USA) —Ailsa (Bishop Of Cashel)
505[3] 729[4] 1031[2] 1169[2] 1329[4]

Versaki (IRE) *J Clais* a42 71
5 gr g Verglas(IRE) —Mythie (FR) (Octagonal (NZ))
5195a[10] 6959a[10]

Verse Of Love *David Evans* 74
2 b g Byron—Lovellian (Machiavellian (USA))
2221[3] 2510[5] 2936[8] 4913[11] 5801[2] 6102[2]

Vertana (IRE) *H-A Pantall* a89 103
4 b m Sinndar(IRE) —Verzasca (IRE) (Sadler's Wells (USA))
5749a[6] 6470a[4] 7090a[0] 7386a[0]

Vertibes *Marcus Tregoning* a58
3 gr g Verglas(IRE) —Antibes (IRE) (Grand Lodge (USA))
7662[3] 7766[5]

Vertueux (FR) *Tony Carroll* a60 65
6 gr g Verglas(IRE) —Shahrazad (FR) (Bering)
223[9] 393[5] 768[4] 1080[3] 2377[6] 4318[2] 4697[2] 6721[3]

Vertumnus *Nick Littmoden* a56 56
4 ch g Pastoral Pursuits—Bombalarina (IRE) (Barathea (IRE))
138[6] 256[6] 421[11] 464[6] (690) 912[11] 1570[9] 1815[5] 2161[9]

Verus Delicia (IRE) *Patrick Morris* 56
2 b f Chineur(FR) —Ribbon Glade (UAE) (Zafonic (USA))
5147[2] 5779[5] 6598[7] 7059[11] 7231[4]

Very First Blade *Mark Brisbourne* a57 47
2 b g Needwood Blade—Dispol Verity (Averti (IRE))
2160[7] 2556[5] (3708) 4021[5] 4391[6] 4922[3] 5374[7]

Very Good Day (FR) *Mick Channon* 102
4 b g Sinndar(IRE) —Picture Princess (Sadler's Wells (USA))
1679[7] 3156[11] 3625[11] 4266[5] 4806[6]

Very Well Red *Peter Hiatt* a63 80
8 b m First Trump—Little Scarlett (Mazilier (USA))
7[5] 135[4] (225) (340) 553[6] 573[2] 722[6] (889) 1114[3] 1388[4] 2198[7] 2663[2] 2912[6] 3413[3] 3760[8] 5002[8] 5666[4] 6098[14] 6888 [8] 7538[12] 7775[8] 7910[7]

Vesuve (IRE) *Saeed Bin Suroor* a110 115
5 b h Green Tune(USA) —Verveine (USA) (Lear Fan (USA))
2713[8] 3591[11] (5544) 6149[2]

Veter (FR) *N Clement* 98
3 ch c Green Tune(USA) —Equity (FR) (Anabaa (USA))
2751a[13]

Vetvey (IRE) *Mark Johnston* a66 85
3 b g Fasliyev(USA) —Vert Val (USA) (Septieme Ciel (USA))
1169[4] (1495) 1543[4] 1663a[13] (1945) (2406)

Veuveveuvevoom *Gerry Enright* a35 33
3 gr f Superior Premium—Gran Clicquot (Gran Alba (USA))
338[8] 788[6] 1280[4] 3350[5] 3464[8]

Vexillum (IRE) *Mick Channon* 62
2 br c Mujadil(USA) —Common Cause (Polish Patriot (USA))
6160[11] 6455[3] 6772[8] 6983[7] 7294[15]

Vexor (USA) *John C Kimmel* a110
2 ch c Wildcat Heir(USA) —Real Clever Trick (USA) (Yes It's True (USA))
7280a[9]

Vezere (USA) *Simon Dow* a66 69
4 b m Point Given(USA) —Helstra (USA) (Nureyev (USA))
30[13] 135[9] 317[10] 1508[7] 2561[7] 2921[6] 3253[4] 3636[13] 3677[6]

Vezzali (USA) *Mahmood Al Zarooni* 75
2 bb f Medaglia D'Oro(USA) —Dirty Rush (USA) (Wild Rush (USA))
4002[3]

Vhujon (IRE) *Peter Grayson* a83 84
6 b g Mujadil(USA) —Livius Lady (IRE) (Titus Livius (FR))
45[3] (137) 243[4] 357[5] 646[10] 833[9] 915[10] 1276[6] 2001[7] 2603[6] 2920[10] 3714[10] 6175[5] (6619) (6784) 7123[5] 7566[6] 7811[4] 7940[5]

Via Archimede (USA) *Lucinda Russell* 56
6 ch g Hussonet(USA) —Azarina (IRE) (Kenmare (FR))
3450[9]

Via Del Corso *Paul W Flynn* a61 61
3 ch f Kyllachy—Burmese Princess (USA) (King Of Kings (IRE))
1706a[4]

Vianello (IRE) *D Rabhi* a85 99
4 b g Rimrod(USA) —Silview (USA) (Saint Ballado (CAN))
196a[8] 325a[5] 481a[0] 2867a[5] 7534a[4]

Vibration *Hughie Morrison* a16 38
3 ch g Cadeaux Genereux—Vivianna (Indian Ridge)
1496[8] 2257[13] 2458[14] 3233[8] 4179[8]

Vicgernic *Gary Moore* a46
2 b g Indesatchel(IRE) —Maysie (IRE) (Imperial Ballet (IRE))
7132[7] 7590[4] 7735[7]

Vickers Vimy *Ralph Beckett* a57
2 b f Montjeu(IRE) —First Bloom (USA) (Fusaichi Pegasus (USA))
7598[5]

Vicona (IRE) *Paul Cole* 71
3 b f Exceed And Excel(AUS) —Avezia (FR) (Night Shift (USA))
1362[6] (1629) 2025[5] 2294[2] 2660[5] 3136[6] 3635[8]

Victoire De Lyphar (IRE) *David Nicholls* 112
4 b g Bertolini(USA) —Victory Peak (Shirley Heights)
1891[4] 3155[23] 4534[16]

Victoire Pisa (JPN) *Katsuhiko Sumii* a120 124
4 bb h Neo Universe(JPN) —Whitewater Affair (Machiavellian (USA))
(1002a) 7563a[13] 7873a[8]

Victoria Lagrange (FR) *C Lerner* 54
2 b f Slickly(FR) —Princesse Lagrange (FR) (Lord Of Men)
6925a[6] 7312a[0]

Victorian Bounty *Tony Newcombe* a88 89
6 b g Bahamian Bounty—Baby Bunting (Wolfhound (USA))
1140[10] (1506) 2244[5] 3000[2] 3850[8] (4392) 4859[5] 5683[7] 7832[7]

Victorian Number (FR) *E J O'Neill* a84 92
3 ch g Numerous(USA) —Malaisia (FR) (Anabaa (USA))
882a[4] 1739a[6]

Victorious Venture (FR) *E Leenders*
2 ch g Vespone(IRE) —J'Attends Vincent (Inchinor)
7664a[7]

Victor's Cry (USA) *Eoin Harty* 118
6 bb h Street Cry(IRE) —Short Time (USA) (Clever Trick (USA))
1000a[5]

Vieira Da Silva (IRE) *Mick Channon* a48 38
2 ch f Van Nistelrooy(USA) —Terri's Charmer (USA) (Silver Charm (USA))
1414[9] 1957[5] 2241[6] 3955[7]

Viewing *Tony Newcombe* a68 81
4 b m Kingsalsa(USA) —Exhibitor (USA) (Royal Academy (USA))
1114[7] 1388[3] 1622[8] 2251[6] 2492[2] 3054[8] 3391[2] 3743[2] 4088[2]

Vigano (IRE) *Jaclyn Tyrrell* a37 64
6 b g Noverre(USA) —Perugia (IRE) (Perugino (USA))
7229[10]

Vigee Le Brun (USA) *M Delzangles* 96
3 b f Pulpit(USA) —Vatrouchka (USA) (Kingmambo (USA))
7156a[7]

Viguria (FR) *M Boutin* 85
4 ch h Green Tune(USA) —Blue Card (FR) (Trempolino (USA))
267a[10]

Viking Dancer *Ruth Carr* a50 48
4 b g Danehill Dancer(IRE) —Blue Siren (Bluebird (USA))
720[3] 1488[8] 1755[8] 5404[11] 5789[10] 6159[9]

Viking Rose (IRE) *James Eustace* a60 69
3 ch f Norse Dancer(IRE) —Rosy Outlook (USA) (Trempolino (USA))
1270[7] 1997[8] 3018[3] 3709[9] 4185[3] 4928[2] (5137) 5515[3] 6098[3] (6450) 6764[6]

Viking Storm *Harry Dunlop* a82 82
3 b g Hurricane Run(IRE) —Danehill's Dream (IRE) (Danehill (USA))
992[2] (1285) 2052[3] 2295[6] 3551[7] 4209[2] 5837[3] 6130[8]

Viking Warrior (IRE) *Michael Dods* 73
4 ch g Halling(USA) —Powder Paint (Mark Of Esteem (IRE))
1150[11] 1612[U] 2352[9] 2588[4] (3024) 3733[3] 4379[8] (6159) 6867[2]

Villa Molitor (FR) *F Rohaut* a99 105
5 b m Muhtathir—Sizal (FR) (Sicyos (USA))
195a[3] 371a[7]

Villa Reigns *John Weymes* a55 49
2 gr g Clodovil(IRE) —Moon Empress (FR) (Rainbow Quest (USA))
3483[5] 4171[6] 4632[6] 6627[15] 6866[8] 7072[5] 7592[7] 7874[3]

Villa Royale *Harry Dunlop* a65 70
2 b f Val Royal(FR) —Villa Carlotta (Rainbow Quest (USA))
6771[8] 7258[3] 7634[3]

Villeneuve *William Muir* a77 83
2 ch f Zamindar(USA) —Emilion (Fantastic Light (USA))
4883[4] (5418) 6296[7] 7135[6]

Vimiero (USA) *Walter Swinburn* a85 85
4 bb g Dynaformer(USA) —Merrymaker (ARG) (Rainbow Corner)
2848[2] 3844[8] 4962[6] 5495[4] 5893[12] 6507[2] 6922[2] 6976[5]

Vinces *Tim McCarthy* a60 65
7 gr g Lomitas—Vadinaxa (FR) (Linamix (FR))
30[8] 83[5] 247[9] 944[8] 1135[3] 1310[7] 1635[2] 2451[4] 2759[2] 5406[8] 5993[5] 6811[12] 7206[10] 7891[9]

Vinnie Jones *John Gosden* a73 75
2 ch g Piccolo—Fen Guest (Woodborough (USA))
1583[7] 3553[3] 5011[6] (5409) 6102[3]

Vinniespride (IRE) *Mark Michael McNiff* 60
4 b g Waky Nao—L'Accolade (IRE) (Seattle Dancer (USA))
5432[2] 6210[4]

Vintage (IRE) *John Akehurst* a85 66
7 b g Danetime(IRE) —Katherine Gorge (USA) (Hansel (USA))
265[4] 316[2] 961[8]

Vintage Grape (IRE) *Eric Alston* 50
3 b f Exceed And Excel(AUS) —Begin The Beguine (IRE) (Peintre Celebre (USA))
1459[11] 1860[5] 2805[6] 3143[7] 3661[6] 4017[3] 4607[5] 5344[7]

Vintage Quest *Dai Burchell* a49 45
9 b m Diktat—Sadly Sober (IRE) (Roi Danzig (USA))
362[10]

Viola Da Gamba (IRE) *William Knight* 74
2 b f Alhaarth(IRE) —Addaya (IRE) (Persian Bold)
3812[7] 4471[6] 5299[2]

Viola D'Amour (IRE) *Tom Dascombe* 79
2 b f Teofilo(IRE) —Dame's Violet (IRE) (Groom Dancer (USA))
(2811) 4372a[5]

Violent Velocity (IRE) *John Quinn* a75 80
8 b g Namid—Lear's Crown (USA) (Lear Fan (USA))
1035[11] 1613[2] 1748[4] 2260[3] (2490) 2692[3] 2887[12] 3462[3] 3936[4] 4679[7] 5728[2] 6231[2] (6990) 7146[4]

Violet's Gift (IRE) *James Fanshawe* a44 58
3 b f Cadeaux Genereux—Violet Ballerina (IRE) (Namid)
4663[9] 5649[3] 6834[7] 7084[4] 7462[8]

Virgil Earp *Noel Meade* 65
4 b g Fasliyev(USA) —Karakorum (IRE) (Fairy King (USA))
3420a[10]

Virginia Gallica (IRE) *J W Hills* a69 54
2 b f Galileo(IRE) —Papering (IRE) (Shaadi (USA))
7025[8] 7343[4]

Viscount Nelson (USA) *A P O'Brien* 117
4 b h Giant's Causeway(USA) —Imagine (IRE) (Sadler's Wells (USA))
1528[5] 5744a[7]

Viscount Rossini *Steve Gollings* a39 50
9 bb g Rossini(USA) —Spain (Polar Falcon (USA))
39[5]

Viscount Vert (IRE) *Andrew Balding* a65 69
2 br g Kheleyf(USA) —Viscountess Brave (IRE) (Law Society (USA))
2787[6] 4906[5] 5475[6]

Visions Of Johanna (USA) *Richard Guest* a73 80
6 b g Johannesburg(USA) —Belle Turquoise (FR) (Tel Quel (FR))
50[4] 206[5] 352[5] (472) (695) 805[8] 879[3] 1390[9] 1756[3] 2213[7] (2492) 2762[5] 2952[5] (3240) 3456[6] 3581[7] 4198[9] 4408[11] 5520[5] 6157[10] 6486[4] 6833[10] 6968[8] 7241[7]

Vital Gold *William Haggas* 88
2 b c Vital Equine(IRE) —Golden Nun (Bishop Of Cashel)
3552[3] (4073) 5039[2] 5487[2] 6535[10]

Vitalicious *Ed McMahon* a56 51
2 ch f Vital Equine(IRE) —Its Another Gift (Primo Dominie)
4406[5] 5058[7] 5418[5] 6540[6] 6821[4]

Vita Lika *Brian Meehan* 83
3 b f Dansili—Bayalika (IRE) (Selkirk (USA))
4807[4] ◆ 5429[2] (6303) 6674[10] 7136[9]

Vital Spirit (FR) *E J O'Neill* 78
2 b c Vital Equine(IRE) —Reel Twister (Reel Buddy (USA))
5194a[6]

Vital Wave (IRE) *E J O'Neill* 87
2 b g Vital Equine(IRE) —Ocean Sands (IRE) (Desert Prince (IRE))
4036a[6] 7155a[8]

Vita Nova (IRE) *Sir Henry Cecil* a74 119
4 b m Galileo(IRE) —Treca (IRE) (Darshaan)
(2066) ◆ 2501[2] ◆ 3624[2] 5219[2] ◆ 6859[9]

Vite (IRE) *Bryan Smart* 53
2 b c Acclamation—Assafiyah (IRE) (Kris)
6532[9] 7209[7]

Vitobello *Bryn Palling*
4 b g Auction House(USA) —Perecapa (IRE) (Archway (IRE))
3267[9]

Vito Volterra (IRE) *Michael Smith* a71 88
4 b g Antonius Pius(USA) —River Abouali (Bluebird (USA))
744[8] (1800) 2366[2] 2732[2] 3276[2] (3315) 3397[13] 4325[10] 4561[11] 6290[14]

Vitruvian Man *Sophie Leech* a72 91
5 b g Montjeu(IRE) —Portrait Of A Lady (IRE) (Peintre Celebre (USA))
3240[9]

Vittachi *Alistair Whillans* a70 66
4 b g Bertolini(USA) —Miss Lorilaw (FR) (Homme De Loi (IRE))
1107[20] 2400[7] 5403[9] 5791[10] 6082[6] (6870) (7078) 7461[2]

Vitznau (IRE) *Alastair Lidderdale* a77 105
7 b g Val Royal(FR) —Neat Dish (CAN) (Stalwart (USA))
587a[14] 2614[3] 2927[7] 3410[13] 3982[11] 4310[19] 5718[7] 5969[8] 6219[8] 7199[10] 7412[5] 7575[6] 7771[3] 7816[5] 7896[7]

Vivacious Vivienne (IRE) *Donal Kinsella* a81 104
5 b m Dubai Destination(USA) —Epistoliere (IRE) (Alzao (USA))
2012a[5] 2534a[2] 4589a[6]

Viva Colonia (IRE) *David O'Meara* 70
6 ch g Traditionally(USA) —Ansariya (USA) (Shahrastani (USA))
1676[6] 2034[13]

Viva Diva *David Lanigan* a74 71
3 ch f Hurricane Run(IRE) —Vas Y Carla (USA) (Gone West (USA))
4072[6] 4611[2] 5629[8] 6255[3] 6666[6] 7200[2] 7346[13]

Vivaldi (IRE) *J J Lambe* 72
6 b g Montjeu(IRE) —Parvenue (FR) (Ezzoud (IRE))
7162[5]

Viva Pataca *J Moore* a84 116
9 bb g Marju(IRE) —Comic (IRE) (Be My Chief (USA))
1742a[5]

Vivarini *John O'Shea* a52
7 b g Hernando(FR) —Venetian Red (USA) (Blushing Groom (FR))
222[4]

Viva Ronaldo (IRE) *Richard Fahey* a76 93
5 b g Xaar—Papaha (FR) (Green Desert (USA))
99[8] 2668[4] (3339) 4100[8] 4574[3] 5272[10] 5920[9] 7660[10] ◆ 7928[4]

Viva Vettori *David Elsworth* a105 93
7 ch h Vettori(IRE) —Cruinn A Bhord (Inchinor)
1684[13] 2105[7] 2647[4] 3081[2] 3825[8] 4415[5] 5483[3] 5888[14] 6302[3] 6708[3] 7168[7]

Viviani (IRE) *Amanda Perrett* a68 67
4 ch g Galileo(IRE) —Bintalreef (USA) (Diesis)
3599[4] 3978[5] 4630[2] 4951[3]

Vivid Blue *William Haggas* 78
2 ch f Haafhd—Vivianna (Indian Ridge)
7132[2]

Vivre La Secret *Bill Turner* a37 37
3 b f Ishiguru(USA) —Vivre Sa Vie (Nashwan (USA))
1629[6] 7636[8] 7888[4]

Vivre Libre *E Lellouche* a89 93
4 b g Sadler's Wells(USA) —Vallee Enchantee (IRE) (Peintre Celebre (USA))
900a[3]

Vizean (IRE) *John Mackie* a50 75
3 b f Medicean—Viz (IRE) (Darshaan)
1985[2] 3090[2] 3756[2] 4542[2] 4925[2] 6381[7] 6834[2] 7141[8]

Vizir Bere (FR) *D Prod'Homme* 107
2 b c Hurricane Cat(USA) —Olga Bere (FR) (Broadway Flyer (USA))
4036a[3] (6184a)

Vladimir (IRE) *M Delcher-Sanchez* 108
2 ch c Kheleyf(USA) —Catch The Sea (IRE) (Barathea (IRE))
(4843a) 5305a[3]

Vocational (USA) *Mark Johnston* a104 95
2 b f Exceed And Excel(AUS) —Carry On Katie (USA) (Fasliyev (USA))
(1765) ◆ 2070[2] 2404[2] 3033[8] (3808) 4413[6] 5286[5] 5715[2] 5882[6]

Vociferous (USA) *Mark Johnston* a78 61
2 bb f Street Cry(IRE) —Sander Camillo (USA) (Dixie Union (USA))
3490[9] 4047[3] 4285[9] 4922[2] ◆ 5144[6] 5967[4] 6487[5] (6611) 6760[10] 7436[9]

Vogarth *Michael Chapman* a41 39
7 ch g Arkadian Hero(USA) —Skara Brae (Inchinor)
12[6] 290[5] 1979[5] 3089[6] 4651[12] 5601[7] 7885[9]

Voila Ici (IRE) *Vittorio Caruso* 114
6 gr h Daylami(IRE) —Far Hope (Barathea (IRE))
1554a[3] 2134a[2] (2982a) 6202a[3] 6907a[4] 7324a[3]

Vola E Va *B Grizzetti* 103
2 b c Oratorio(IRE) —Veronica Franco (ITY) (Lomitas)
6740a[4]

Volcanic Ash (USA) *Mark Johnston* a76 62
3 b c Elusive Quality(USA) —Make Known (USA) (Mt. Livermore (USA))
(60)

Volcanic Dust (IRE) *Milton Bradley* a87 82
3 b f Ivan Denisovich(IRE) —Top Of The Form (IRE) (Masterclass (USA))
1630[3] 2660[2] 3239[2] (3635) 4238[3] (4721) 5000[7] 7833[4] ◆

Volcanic Lady (IRE) *David Simcock* a33 39
3 b f Invincible Spirit(IRE) —Starlight Smile (USA) (Green Dancer (USA))
406[9]

Volcanico (IRE) *F Rodriguez Puertas* a100 93
3 b c Refuse To Bend(IRE) —Zayana (IRE) (Darshaan)
7678a[7]

Volito *Anabel K Murphy* a62 73
5 ch g Bertolini(USA) —Vax Rapide (Sharpo)
1912[3] 2422[2] 2447[2] (2879) 3617[7] 4434[6] 5587[5] 6634[6] 6930[3] 7172[5]

Vollon (IRE) *M Delzangles* 46
3 b c Dansili—Vallee Enchantee (IRE) (Peintre Celebre (USA))
5132a[9]

Voodoo Prince *Ed Dunlop* a91 92
3 b g Kingmambo(USA) —Ouija Board (Cape Cross (IRE))
1409[6] (2457) 2925[5] 3585[3] 7558[3]

Voodoo Queen *Marco Botti* 9
3 br f Diktat—Monte Mayor Lady (IRE) (Brief Truce (USA))
1984[12] 3236[7] 4200[7]

Voodoo Rhythm (USA) *Brian Meehan* a72 72
2 b g Proud Citizen(USA) —Enchanted Kiss (USA) (Afternoon Deelites (USA))
3401[10] 4007[11] 4507[5] 5899[5] 6345[5] ◆ 6623[6] 6757[9] 6812[10]

Vulcanite (IRE) *Ralph Beckett* a74 106
4 b g Dubawi(IRE) —Daraliya (IRE) (Kahyasi)
3204[3] ◆ 3875[12] 5285[13] 7027[5]

Vuvuzela (SWI) *H Speck* 44
3 b f Konigstiger(GER) —Viscaya (GER) (Peintre Celebre (USA))
5307a[9]

Waabel *Richard Guest* a84 78
4 bb g Green Desert(USA) —Najah (IRE) (Nashwan (USA))
(134) 264[3] (522) 698[7] 961[10] 6761[13] 6974[13] 7487[8] 7529[9] 7644[10] 7726[5] 7857[13]

Waafid (USA) *Marcus Tregoning* 76
2 b c Hard Spun(USA) —Hazimah (USA) (Gone West (USA))
6267[6] ◆

Waahej *Peter Hiatt* a81 72
5 b g Haafhd—Madam Ninette (Mark Of Esteem (IRE))
802[4] 1066[6] 1222[3] 1608[5] 2996[5] 3515[7] 4177[4] 4389[2] 4862[3] (5491) 6029[4] 6789[3] 6918[5] (7200) 7346[3] 7506[2]

Wadha (IRE) *Saeed Bin Suroor* a69 72
3 b f Cape Cross(IRE) —Cashel Queen (USA) (Kingmambo (USA))
5567[2] 5999[4] 6473[4] 6839[3] 7141[3]

Wading (IRE) *A P O'Brien* a100 115
2 b f Montjeu(IRE) —Cherry Hinton (Green Desert (USA))
(6691) ◆

Waffle (IRE) *David Barron* a82 113
5 ch g Kheleyf(USA) —Saphire (College Chapel)
1111[2] ◆ 1518[2] 2317[4] 3155[2] 3394[5] 5060[12] 5927[12] 6147[8] 6332[9]

Wafiyah (GER) *W Baltromei* 89
2 b f Lord Of England(GER) —Wailangi (GER) (Banyumanik (IRE))
6941a[7]

Wahylah (IRE) *Clive Brittain* 80
2 b f Shamardal(USA) —Neshla (Singspiel (IRE))
4263[4] 4803[5] (6169) 6526[7]

Waikato (NZ) *L Laxon* 117
8 b g Pins(AUS) —Skywalker Wilkes (USA) (Skywalker (USA))
2340a[3]

Waitress (USA) *H-A Pantall* 101
3 b f Kingmambo(USA) —Do The Honours (IRE) (Highest Honor (FR))
7509a[3]

Wajir (FR) *Saeed Bin Suroor* 111
5 b h Danehill Dancer(IRE) —War Game (FR) (Caerleon (USA))
(154a)

Wake Up Call *Chris Wall* a78 100
5 b m Noverre(USA) —Up And About (Barathea (IRE))
3365[3] 4332[7] 5016[2] 5936[2] 6297[5]

Wake Up Sioux (IRE) *David C Griffiths* a54 57
2 b f Sleeping Indian—Dubious (Darshaan)
2709[10] 3200[7] 3398[7] 5211[3] 5737[6] (6384) 7059[7]

Wakidoun (FR) *D Allard* a74 72
2 b c Sandwaki(USA) —Ballidoun (FR) (Smadoun (FR))
2866a[8]

Waking Warrior *Kevin Ryan* a79 89
3 b g Sleeping Indian—Scented Garden (Zamindar (USA))
2032[6] ◆ 2934[13] 3378[5] 5852[11] 6224[7] 6917[11]

Waldjagd *A Wohler* 101
4 ch m Observatory(USA) —Wurftaube (GER) (Acatenango (GER))
3213a[4] 5980a[7]

Waldpark (GER) *A Wohler* 115
3 b c Dubawi(IRE) —Wurftaube (GER) (Acatenango (GER))
(3672a) 5128a[6] 5773a[6]

Waldsee (GER) *Jo Davis* 55
6 b g Xaar—Wurftaube (GER) (Acatenango (GER))
2905[2] 5916[11]

Waldstein *Andrew Haynes*
2 b g Royal Applause—Sabalara (IRE) (Mujadil (USA))
7080[15]

Waldvogel (IRE) *Nicky Richards* a102 100
7 ch g Polish Precedent(USA) —Wurftaube (GER) (Acatenango (GER))
3829[2] 4778[4] 5250[8] 5932[5] 6803[9]

Walero (GER) *Uwe Ostmann* 109
5 br h Big Shuffle(USA) —Waterbor (GER) (Lagunas)
1575a[2] (3531a) 5664a[8] 6594a[3]

Walkure (JPN) *Masaru Sayama* 105
7 bl m Stay Gold(JPN) —Kyoei Theory (JPN) (Generous (IRE))
7410a[6]

Walleyd (IRE) *Linda Perratt* 56
4 b g Cape Cross(IRE) —Najmat Jumairah (USA) (Mr Prospector (USA))
1710[5] 2045[5] 2401[13] 2692[11] 3454[6] 3903[P]

Wallis *Luca Cumani* a90 95
4 b m King's Best(USA) —Frangy (Sadler's Wells (USA))
(2269) 3407[3] 4235[7]

Wall Street (NZ) *Jeff Lynds* 122
7 b g Montjeu(IRE) —Villa Wanda (Grand Lodge (USA))
7044a[4]

Waltz Darling (IRE) *Richard Fahey* 91
3 b g Iffraaj—Aljafliyah (Halling (USA))
1322[9] 2705[7] 2935[3] 3774[17] 4530[3] 5283[12] 6046[4]

Waltzing Cat (USA) *Sir Mark Prescott Bt* a69 54
3 ch f More Than Ready(USA) —Hopeful Sign (Warning)
5630[3] 5838[2] ◆ 6255[4] 7255[8]

Walvis Bay (IRE) *Tom Tate* a87 91
4 gr g Footstepsinthesand—Limpopo (Green Desert (USA))
1878[7] 3028[5] 5108[7] 5679[6] 6212[12]

Walzertraum (USA) *Fredrik Reuterskiold* a105 97
6 b h Rahy(USA) —Walzerkoenigin (USA) (Kingmambo (USA))
2601a[9]

Wanchai Whisper *Michael Wigham* a71 71
4 b m Bahamian Bounty—Tiger Waltz (Pivotal)
97[9] 215[4] 337[2] 658[3] 861[4] 1034[8] 1411[11] 1938[5] 2720[6]

Wandering Lad *Declan Carroll* a61 61
3 b g Needwood Blade—Park's Girl (Averti (IRE))
2493[5] 3075[12] 3360[5] 3933[4] 4437[2] 5394[7] 6159[12] 6999[5] 7371[5] 7641[4] 7737[6] 7854[11] 7896[10]

Wannabe King *David Lanigan* 104
5 b g King's Best(USA) —Wannabe Grand (IRE) (Danehill (USA))
(1529) 2031[12] 2679[9] 4100[14] 4774[4] 5557[6] 6335[9]

War Artist (AUS) *Markus Klug* a119 116
8 b g Orpen(USA) —Royal Solitaire (AUS) (Brocco (USA))
2371[1] (602a) 996a[2] 3010[5] 3863[7] 5985a[11] 6520[6]

Warbond *Michael Madgwick* a60 51
3 ch g Monsieur Bond(IRE) —Pick A Nice Name (Polar Falcon (USA))
1581[1] 663[5] 887[9] 2550[13] 3432[11] 4827[9] 6083[5] 6813[5] 7092[7] 7640[12] 7910[2]

Warcrown (IRE) *Richard Fahey* 66
2 b c Azamour(IRE) —Alikhlas (Lahib (USA))
4414[11] 5548[6]

Warden Bond *William Stone* a59 51
3 ch g Monsieur Bond(IRE) —Warden Rose (Compton Place)
2064[9] 2598[7] 3223[12] 3636[12] 4111[11] 4927[4] 5352[5] 5515[8] 6032[3] 6357[4] 7092[2] 7394[3] 7639[3]

War Is War (IRE) *E J O'Neill* a99 96
3 b c Galileo(IRE) —Walkamia (FR) (Linamix (FR))
2341a[5] 7313a[6]

Warlu Way *John Dunlop* 99
4 b h Sakhee(USA) —Conspiracy (Rudimentary (USA))
1402[10] (1772) 2220[5] ◆ 2958[2] (3544) ◆ 4354[5] 5250[14] 6528[2]

Warm Breeze *Roger Varian* 88
3 b f Oasis Dream—Persian Jasmine (Dynaformer (USA))
5476[8]

Warm Hands *A Fabre* 100
3 b f Oasis Dream—Kid Gloves (In The Wings)
5028a[4]

Warm Memories *Simon Dow* a36 71
4 b g Dansili—Summer Breeze (Rainbow Quest (USA))
389[5] 1604[12]

War Monger (USA) *Doug Watson* a82 101
7 b h War Chant(USA) —Carnival Delight (USA) (Half A Year (USA))
157a[5] 239[7] (605a) 676a[6] 829a[7]

Warneford *Brian Meehan* a71 77
3 b g Dansili—Maramba (Rainbow Quest (USA))
2104[3] 4279[7] 5242[5] 5837[5] 6255[2] (6769)

Warne's Way (IRE) *Brendan Powell* 78
8 ch g Spinning World(USA) —Kafayef (USA) (Secreto (USA))
(1367) 2034[7] 3120[6] 3352[3] 6405[3] 6998[5]

War Of The Roses (IRE) *Roy Brotherton* a69 65
8 b g Singspiel(IRE) —Calvia Rose (Sharpo)
162[9] 797[6] (917) (1080) 7738[P]

War Pact (USA) *J-C Rouget* a100 100
3 b g War Front(USA) —Tempo West (USA) (Rahy (USA))
(410a)

War Poet *David O'Meara* 93
4 b g Singspiel(IRE) —Summer Sonnet (Baillamont (USA))
1212[2] ◆ 1386[3] 1910[2] ◆ (2364) 2708[2] 3625[14] 5078[7] (5729)

Warrant *Jane Chapple-Hyam* a64 53
3 b g Tobougg(IRE) —Witness (Efisio)
300[3] 469[3] 1997[7] 3131[7] 3518[10]

Warrior Nation (FR) *Adrian Chamberlain* a46 46
5 br g Statue Of Liberty(USA) —Tadawul (USA) (Diesis)
284[6] 382[10] 733[8] 1567[3] 2140[7] 2996[8] 3094[5] 5785[7] 7574[6]

Warrior Song (IRE) *P D Deegan* a74 63
3 b g A. P. Warrior(USA) —Amizette (USA) (Forty Niner (USA))
1704a[3] ◆

Warsaw (IRE) *M F De Kock* a103 105
6 ch h Danehill Dancer(IRE) —For Evva Silca (Piccolo)
152a[14] 236[5] (415a) 587a[6] 682a[8]

War Shandar (FR) *F Vermeulen* a70 27
3 b c Dalakhani(IRE) —Fasliyeva (FR) (Fasliyev (USA))
902a[9]

War Singer (USA) *J-C Rouget* a93 92
4 b g War Chant(USA) —Sister Marilyn (USA) (Saint Ballado (CAN))
(267a)

Wasabi's House (IRE) *John M Oxx* a73
2 br f Dark Angel(IRE) —Pent House (IRE) (Titus Livius (FR))
7273a[4] ◆

Wasara *Amy Weaver* a65 64
4 b m Marju(IRE) —Triennial (IRE) (Giant's Causeway (USA))
301[7] 384[4] 728[9]

Waseem Faris (IRE) *Mick Channon* a83 83
2 b c Exceed And Excel(AUS) —Kissing Time (Lugana Beach)
(3997) 4757[4] 5886[3] 6464[6] 7765[2] ◆ 7918[5]

Waspy *Ed Dunlop* a40 43
2 ch f King's Best(USA) —Gib (IRE) (Rock Of Gibraltar (IRE))
4471[15] 4906[10] 5813[8]

Wassiljew (IRE) *A Schaerer* a84 101
7 b g Zinaad—Wassiliki (IRE) (Night Shift (USA))
441a[3] 628a[7]

Wasted Tears (USA) *Bart B Evans* a102 114
6 bb m Najran(USA) —Wishes And Roses (USA) (Greinton)
6719a[4]

Watanee *Clive Brittain* 44
2 ch f Shamardal(USA) —Fascinating Rhythm (Slip Anchor)
5655[12] 6449[8]

Watar (IRE) *F Head* a86 112
6 b h Marju(IRE) —Ombrie (Zafonic (USA))
1842a[3] (4037a)

Watch Amigo (IRE) *Walter Swinburn* a75 92
5 b g Royal Applause—Miss Red Ink (USA) (Red Ransom (USA))
1760[10] 2470[9] (3081) 3797[6] 5811[4] 6239[3] 6727[6]

Watch Chain (IRE) *Alan McCabe* a70 72
4 b g Traditionally(USA) —Dangle (IRE) (Desert Style (IRE))
1570[4] (1990) 2270[6] 2765[6] 3555[10] 4683[2] 4820[5] 5031[3] 5338[12] 5736[11] 6479[14] 6616[4] 7352[8] 7507[14]

Watchmaker *Tor Sturgis* a66 62
8 b g Bering—Watchkeeper (IRE) (Rudimentary (USA))
203[6] 427[6] 749[10]

Watch Me Go (USA) *Kathleen O'Connell* a112 53
3 bb c West Acre(USA) —Sabbath Song (CAN) (Deputy Minister (CAN))
1921a[18]

Watch The Birdie (IRE) *Kevin Prendergast* a65 69
3 b f Kodiac—Silk Point (IRE) (Barathea (IRE))
1706a[8]

Waterborne *Roger Charlton* a62 66
3 b g Diktat—Waterfall One (Nashwan (USA))
1487[3] 1997[6] 2842[4]

Waterbury Girl *Bryn Palling* a11 41
3 ch f Needwood Blade—Spaniola (IRE) (Desert King (IRE))
1449[5] 1900[3] 3090[10] 3803[6] 6816[10] 6999[9] 7260[8]

Waterclock (IRE) *Roger Charlton* 83
2 ch g Notnowcato—Waterfall One (Nashwan (USA))
(6994)

Watercourse (IRE) *Nigel Tinkler* a58 91
3 b c Hurricane Run(IRE) —Water Feature (Dansili)
1759[11] 2185[4] 2764[5] (3585) 4426[10]

Watered Silk *Marcus Tregoning* a73 84
3 gr g Encosta De Lago(AUS) —Tussah (Daylami (IRE))
1312[2] ◆ (1487) 2225[2] ◆ 2677[4] 3518[2] 4336[3] (4627) (4932) 5710[8] 6497[9]

Waterford Star (IRE) *Mark Johnston* a48 45
3 b g Oratorio(IRE) —Robin (Slip Anchor)
1566[10] 1819[7]

Waterloo Dock *Michael Quinn* a73 6
6 b g Hunting Lion(IRE) —Scenic Air (Hadeer)
(98) 264[2] 521[10] 698[11] 1044[3] 2205[4] 4206[11] 7919[7]

Waterloo Girl *Michael Blanshard* a23 18
2 b f Rail Link—Elise (Fantastic Light (USA))
3258[9] 4232[10] 4756[8]

Waterloo Sunrise (IRE) *S M Duffy* a63 67
6 b g Craigsteel—Waterloo Sunset (Deep Run)
7399[3] 7848[2]

Watheeq (USA) *Roger Varian* a65 64
2 b g Street Cry(IRE) —Mehthaaf (USA) (Nureyev (USA))
5239[8] 6772[7] 7493[4]

Watneya *William Haggas* a76 85
3 b f Dubawi(IRE) —Quickstyx (Night Shift (USA))
2200[3] (2883) 3407[9] 4093[3] 4550[16]

Watts Up Son *Declan Carroll* a36 77
3 b g Diktat—Local Fancy (Bahamian Bounty)
1241[14] 1391[8] 1758[7] 2391[8] 3337[4] 3783[7] 4081[9] 4854[10] 5109[6] 5373[3] 5552[2] (5821) 6158[3] 6867[5] (7235)

Waveband *David Barron* a101 98
4 ch m Exceed And Excel(AUS) —Licence To Thrill (Wolfhound (USA))
2[2] 293[2] (700) 989[6]

Wavering (IRE) *A Fabre* 112
3 b f Refuse To Bend(IRE) —Summertime Legacy (Darshaan)
1922a[3] (2342a) 2977a[6] 5366a[6] 5989a[6]

Wavertree Warrior (IRE) *Nick Littmoden* a67 57
9 br g Indian Lodge(IRE) —Karamana (Habitat)
(26) 248[9]

Waybuloo (IRE) *Gay Kelleway*
2 b f Balmont(USA) —By Candlelight (IRE) (Roi Danzig (USA))
1055[7] 1455[10]

Way Chief (FR) *Richard Fahey* a45 62
3 bb g Xaar—Green Way (FR) (Green Tune (USA))
5315[3] 6311[11]

Waydownsouth (IRE) *Patrick J Flynn* a99 105
4 b g Chevalier(IRE) —Ruffit (IRE) (Revoque (IRE))
1119a[6] 3107[3] 4418a[11] 5291a[6] 5952a[5] 6513a[6] 7322a[8]

Wayne Manor (IRE) *Ralph Beckett* 59
2 br c Cape Cross(IRE) —Inchmahome (Galileo (IRE))
4762[8] 5536[3] 6772[10]

Way Of Love (FR) *Kevin Ryan* 32
2 ch c Gold Away(IRE) —Love Affair (FR) (Arctic Tern (USA))
2460[10]

Way Too Hot *Clive Cox* a83 88
2 br f King's Best(USA) —Street Fire (IRE) (Street Cry (IRE))
3258[2] ◆ (4662) 7028[6]

Wayward Glance *Michael Bell* 89
3 b g Sadler's Wells(USA) —Daring Aim (Daylami (IRE))
1407[4] 2295[10] 2956[6] 4336[4] (4753) 5283[5] 6294[2] 6988[12]

Weaam (IRE) *Marcus Tregoning* 57
2 b c Shamardal(USA) —Merayaat (IRE) (Darshaan)
6267[8] ◆

Wealth Whispers (IRE) *Paul D'Arcy* a48 45
3 b f Hawk Wing(USA) —Esperentos (IRE) (Spectrum (IRE))
4929[5]

Wealthy (IRE) *Saeed Bin Suroor* a93 112
4 b g Refuse To Bend(IRE) —Enrich (USA) (Dynaformer (USA))
330a[10] 608a[9] 4095[10] 5829[7]

Weapon Of Choice (IRE) *David Simcock* 93
3 b c Iffraaj—Tullawadgeen (IRE) (Sinndar (IRE))
1478[5] 1820[5] 2296[11] 2833[3] (3400) 3864[13] (5199) 5920[3] ◆ 6325[3] 6704[2]

Webbow (IRE) *Mark Campion* a84 104
9 b g Dr Devious(IRE) —Ower (IRE) (Lomond (USA))
6[6] 2706[2] 3578[2] (4428) 5474[2] 6521[10]

Wedding Dance (FR) *P Demercastel*
3 b f Chichicastenango(FR) —Wana Doo (USA) (Grand Slam (USA))
901a[0]

Wednesdays Boy (IRE) *Peter Niven* a35 61
8 b g Alhaarth(IRE) —Sheen Falls (IRE) (Prince Rupert (FR))
730[7]

Wee Buns *Paul Burgoyne* a69 59
6 b g Piccolo—Gigetta (IRE) (Brief Truce (USA))
2162[12] 7924[9]

Weemissfrankie (USA) *Peter Eurton* a110
2 ch f Sunriver(USA) —Starinthemeadow (USA) (Meadowlake (USA))
7283a[3]

Weet A Surprise *James Unett* a86 67
6 b m Bertolini(USA) —Ticcatoo (IRE) (Dolphin Street (FR))
84[3] 231[5] 403[8]

Weetentherty *Linda Perratt* a45 61
4 b g Bertolini(USA) —Binaa (IRE) (Marju (IRE))
3306[10] 3662[13] (3857) 4041[3] 4378[3] 4600[5] 4672[2] 4780[6] 7371[7]

Weetfromthechaff *Maurice Barnes* a62 54
6 gr g Weet-A-Minute(IRE) —Weet Ees Girl (IRE) (Common Grounds)
1305[7] 1615[5] 3317[P] 4601[14]

Wee Ziggy *Michael Mullineaux* a59 45
8 b g Ziggy's Dancer(USA) —Midnight Arrow (Robellino (USA))
444[7] 631[11]

We Have A Dream *William Muir* a90 95
6 bb g Oasis Dream—Final Shot (Dalsaan)
1197[4] 1675[12] 2826[5] (3000) (3351) 3535[5] 4042[6] 4531[23] 4859[2] 5852[16] 6331[6] 6723[17] 6974[2] 7127[7]

Welcome Approach *John Weymes* a67 62
8 b g Most Welcome—Lucky Thing (Green Desert (USA))
(166) (512) 928[9] 1307[3] (1453) 1627[4] 1912[7] 3617[8] 3999[6] 4600[11] 4634[3] 5244[6] 5371[7] 5603[8] (5617) 5736[8] 6889[11] 7844[7]

Welcome Gift *Mahmood Al Zarooni* 89
2 b c Pivotal—Gonbarda (GER) (Lando (GER))
5447[2] ◆ (6245)

Welease Bwian (IRE) *Stuart Williams* a56 39
2 b g Kheleyf(USA) —Urbanize (USA) (Chester House (USA))
3349[7] 3984[7] 6019[12] 6942[2] ◆

We'll Deal Again *Michael Easterby* a65 77
4 b g Gentleman's Deal(IRE) —Emma Amour (Emarati (USA))
401[4] 511[2] 709[2] 833[4] 1029[5] 1307[2] (1493) 1907[4] 2464[2] 3027[5] 3573[8] (4820)

Wellington Fair *Tor Sturgis* a59 80
4 br g Trade Fair—Milly's Lass (Mind Games)
947[9]

Wellmarked (IRE) *P G Fahey* a61 60
4 b g Choisir(AUS) —Radiance (IRE) (Thatching)
7641[7]

Well Sharp *Michael Dods* 98
3 b c Selkirk(USA) —Saphila (IRE) (Sadler's Wells (USA))
1113[3] 1690[6] (2572) 3069[3] ◆ 3774[5] 4411[10] 5700[8] 6497[6]

Wells Lyrical (IRE) *Bryan Smart* 84
6 b g Sadler's Wells(USA) —Lyrical (Shirley Heights)
1517[7] 2262[6] (2762) 3205[3] 3851[7]

Well Wishes *Bryan Smart* a39 43
2 ch f Piccolo—Muja Farewell (Mujtahid (USA))
2460[9] 3855[4] 4377[5] 5005[7] 7694[3]

Welsh Bard (IRE) *Sir Mark Prescott Bt* a56
2 ch g Dylan Thomas(IRE) —Delphinium (IRE) (Dr Massini (IRE))
7126[9] 7330[9] 7559[7]

Welsh Dancer *Ronald Harris* a54 79
3 b c Dubawi(IRE) —Rosie's Posy (IRE) (Suave Dancer (USA))
4281[14] 4666[8] 5141[8] 6889[9] 7260[2] 7460[2] 7560[4] 7785[5] 7886[5]

Welsh Dresser (IRE) *Peter Grayson* a45 48
3 b f King's Best(USA) —Welsh Motto (USA) (Mtoto)
66[6] 109[11] 383[8] 655[12] 834[7] 964[11] 1137[6] 1585[4] 2305[9]

Welsh Inlet (IRE) *John Bridger* a66 72
3 br f Kheleyf(USA) —Ervedya (IRE) (Doyoun)
179[4] 333[2] 356[4] 611[3] 958[2] 1145[2] 1504[2] 1776[2] ◆ 2294[5] 2757[3] 2878[8] 3255[3] (3482) 4459[3] 4615[3] 5115[8] 5542[4] 5939[5] 7428[7] 7649[6] 7940[3]

Welsh Nayber *Amanda Perrett* 64
2 ch g Nayef(USA) —Aberdovey (Mister Baileys)
4053[10] 4698[6] 4968[8] 5783[4] 6399[8] (6760)

Welsh Royale *William Muir* a60 59
2 b g Royal Applause—Brecon (Unfuwain (USA))
4068[7] 4639[4] 5632[8] 6489[2] 7252[7]

Went The Day Well (USA) *Ed McMahon* 85
2 b c Proud Citizen(USA) —Tiz Maie's Day (CAN) (Tiznow (USA))
6334[2] ◆ 6771[2] ◆

Weood (IRE) *Clive Brittain* a34 54
2 b f Dubawi(IRE) —Fawaayid (USA) (Vaguely Noble)
2811[11] 3402[11] 6673[11] 7653[7]

West Brit (IRE) *Ed Dunlop* 89
3 b g High Chaparral(IRE) —Aldburgh (Bluebird (USA))
2458[11] 3232[3] 4254[2] (5007) 6409[4]

West Coast Dream *Roy Brotherton* a68 92
4 b g Oasis Dream—Californie (IRE) (Rainbow Quest (USA))
5508[7] 6224[8] 6331[5] 7262[9]

West End Lad *Roy Bowring* a85 84
8 b g Tomba—Cliburnel News (IRE) (Horage)
541[9] 1201[5] 2674[11] 3081[4] 3275[13] 3934[5] (4821) 5728[6] (6227) 6632[4] 7050[5] 7234[3] (7743)

Western Approaches *Nicky Henderson* a31
4 b m Westerner—Bayariyka (IRE) (Slip Anchor)
7766[7]

Western Aristocrat (USA) *Jeremy Noseda* a109 114
3 bb c Mr Greeley(USA) —Aristocratic Lady (USA) (Kris S (USA))
(2503) ◆ 3029[3] ◆ 4493[3] 5252[7] (6088) (6716a) 7572a[3]

Western Choice (USA) *A Fabre* 101
3 b c Gone West(USA) —Choice Spirit (USA) (Danzig (USA))
4896a[4]

Western Hope (IRE) *Simon Dow* a37 20
4 b m High Chaparral(IRE) —All Our Hope (USA) (Gulch (USA))
161[6] 300[6] 1300[8]

Western Memory (USA) *Lennart Reuterskiold Jr* a54
4 b m Dehere(USA) —Dakkari (USA) (Affirmed (USA))
5096a[6]

Western Mystic (GER) *W Hickst* 104
4 b m Doyen(IRE) —Waleska (GER) (Valanour (IRE))
7678a[0]

Western Pearl *William Knight* a97 98
4 b m High Chaparral(IRE) —Pulau Pinang (IRE) (Dolphin Street (FR))
2098[5] 3120[3] 3875[3] ◆ 4582[6] 6736a[12] 7129[5] 7406a[5] 7580a[3]

Western Prize *Ralph Beckett* a76 84
3 b c High Chaparral(IRE) —Spot Prize (USA) (Seattle Dancer (USA))
(176) ◆ 2819[4] (3551) 5283[10]

Western Symbol (NZ) *Gai Waterhouse* 104
5 b g High Chaparral(IRE) —Blue Symbol (NZ) (Bluebird (USA))
7115a[3]

Wester Ross (IRE) *James Eustace* a64 60
7 b g Fruits Of Love(USA) —Diabaig (Precocious)
33[3] 1596[3]

Westhaven (IRE) *David Elsworth* a71 60
3 b g Alhaarth(IRE) —Dashiba (Dashing Blade)
110[10] 339[8] 591[6] 1487[5] (2307) 2379[3] (3220) 3518[9]

West Leake (IRE) *Paul Burgoyne* a74 66
5 b g Acclamation—Kilshanny (Groom Dancer (USA))
97[8] (211) 367[3] (485) (637) 820[4] 984[3] (1177) 1488[4] (1868) 2207[11] 7517[5]

West Leake Diman (IRE) *Charles Hills* 106
2 b c Namid—Roselyn (Efisio)
(3165) (4334) 5216[18] 5849[12] 6688[7] 7019[10]

West Leake Hare (IRE) *Charles Hills* 81
2 b c Choisir(AUS) —March Hare (Groom Dancer (USA))
2844[2] (3308) 4496[2] 5184[12] 5825[4] 6573[9]

West Leake Melody *Patrick Morris* a54 50
3 b g Royal Applause—Rada's Daughter (Robellino (USA))
(187) 296[2] 1293[8]

Westlin' Winds (IRE) *Brian Ellison* a71 67
5 b g Montjeu(IRE) —Uliana (USA) (Darshaan)
2060[7] 2393[9] 2733[2] 3450[4]

Westport *Robin Bastiman* a29 59
8 b g Xaar—Connemara (IRE) (Mujadil (USA))
289[12] 490[6] 675[10] 793[8]

West Side (IRE) *Jeremy Noseda* a59 58
3 b g Oratorio(IRE) —Castelletto (Komaite (USA))
1591[5] 2151[4] 3343[4] ◆ 4911[4] 5394[9]

Westtower Boy (IRE) *Edward Lynam* a85 86
5 ch g Hawk Wing(USA) —Shoooz (IRE) (Soviet Star (USA))
7618a[7]

Westward Hope (USA) *J W Hills* a53
2 bb c Mr Greeley(USA) —Morning Cry (USA) (Danzig (USA))
7559[8]

West Wing (FR) *F-X Belvisi* a78 70
6 ch g Hawk Wing(USA) —Wing And Wing (Singspiel (IRE))
372a[3] 533a[0] 843a[5] (1013a)

Westwiththenight (IRE) *William Haggas* 75
2 b f Cape Cross(IRE) —Hidden Hope (Daylami (IRE))
6128[5] 7025[2]

West With The Wind *Evan Williams* a81 72
6 b g Fasliyev(USA) —Midnight Angel (GER) (Acatenango (GER))
(4463) 4642[3]

Westwood *Derek Haydn Jones* a87 77
6 ch g Captain Rio—Consignia (IRE) (Definite Article)
1067[10] 3784[10]

Weybridge Light *Martin Bosley* a70 67
6 b g Fantastic Light(USA) —Nuryana (Nureyev (USA))
911[9]

Whaileyy (IRE) *Marco Botti* 86
3 b g Holy Roman Emperor(IRE) —Alshoowg (USA) (Riverman (USA))
1983[3] 2503[7] 2878[2] 7941[6] ◆

Whale Capture (JPN) *Kiyotaka Tanaka* 110
3 gr f Kurofune(USA) —Global Peace (JPN) (Sunday Silence (USA))
7410a[4]

Whaston (IRE) *Pauline Robson* a54 49
6 b g Hawk Wing(USA) —Sharafanya (IRE) (Zafonic (USA))
1077[5]

What About Me (IRE) *Brian Nolan* 89
4 bb m Bertolini(USA) —Marefonic (Zafonic (USA))
923a[16] 1420a[11]

What About Now *J W Hills* a65 65
3 b f Encosta De Lago(AUS) —Mini Driver (Danehill (USA))
1759[14] 2157[10] 2581[7] 3220[11] 3690[6] 4153[4] (4654) 5134[3] 5512[3] 6004[2] 6445[9] 6769[9] 6936[2]

What About You (IRE) *Richard Fahey* a90 89
3 b g Statue Of Liberty(USA) —Why Now (Dansili)
2508[4] ◆ 2934[14] 3820[12] 4333[5] 7149a[4] 7489[10] 7578[3] 7833[2]

What A Charm (IRE) *John M Oxx* 105
4 b m Key Of Luck(USA) —Atalina (FR) (Linamix (FR))
6736a[6] 7322a[7]

What Katie Did (IRE) *Milton Bradley* a60 61
6 b g Invincible Spirit(IRE) —Chatterberry (Aragon)
166[10] 337[7] 482[5] 2162[11] 3476[3] 3939[4] 4230[8] 4487[9] 5617[8] 5678[9]

Whats For Pudding (IRE) *Declan Carroll* a55 60
3 ch f Kheleyf(USA) —Margaret's Dream (IRE) (Muhtarram (USA))
2782[11] 3202[4] 3457[8] 4146[6] 4816[3] (4987) (5153) 5789[7] 6159[4] 6415[5] 6847[3] 7006[8] 7268[9] 7459[7]

What's For Tea *Paddy Butler* a18 53
6 b m Beat All(USA) —Come To Tea (IRE) (Be My Guest (USA))
7119[11]

Whatsofunny (IRE) *Roger Varian* a57
2 ch f Rock Of Gibraltar(IRE) —Celtic Heroine (IRE) (Hernando (FR))
6818[4]

What's The Point *Walter Swinburn* 54
3 ch g Bertolini(USA) —Point Of Balance (IRE) (Pivotal)
2371[7] 2930[12]

What's Up (IRE) *Jim Boyle* 71
2 b f Dylan Thomas(IRE) —Ridotto (Salse (USA))
3257[13] (5170) 6128[6]

What's Up Doc (IRE) *Lawney Hill* a70 79
10 b g Dr Massini(IRE) —Surprise Treat (IRE) (Shalford (IRE))
50[7] 341[3] 526[2] 711[4] 881[4]

Whats Your Story *Murty McGrath* a32
3 b g Bertolini(USA) —Legal Belle (Superpower)
7093[10] 7525[5] 7750[9]

Whatuthink (IRE) *Oliver McKiernan* 68
9 ch g Presenting—Glen's Encore (IRE) (Orchestra)
7322a[14]

Whatyoucallit (IRE) *David Lanigan* a43 61
2 ch c Kheleyf(USA) —Tarbela (IRE) (Grand Lodge (USA))
4068[4] 4365[7] 6654[9]

Whatyouwoodwishfor (USA) *Richard Guest* a54 60
5 ch g Forestry(USA) —Wishful Splendor (USA) (Smart Strike (CAN))
98[12] 2047[10] 2412[8]

Wheatfield (IRE) *Thomas McGivern* a7 50
7 b m Invincible Spirit(IRE) —Crimphill (IRE) (Sadler's Wells (USA))
5534[7] 5617[3] 6610[12]

Whenever *Richard Phillips* a70 71
7 ch g Medicean—Alessandra (Generous (IRE))
(5379) 5947[3] 6722[9]

Wheredreamsare *Frau J Mayer* 101
4 b h Monsun(GER) —Wakytara (GER) (Danehill (USA))
2749a[8] 4373a[10] 5497a[6] 6569a[5]

Where's Reiley (USA) *Alastair Lidderdale* a88 73
5 bb g Doneraile Court(USA) —Plateau (USA) (Seeking The Gold (USA))
294[5] ◆ 491[2] ◆ 673[2] (794) (853) 7500[11] (7659) 7807[3] 7832[3] 7926[8]

Where's Susie *Michael Madgwick* a82 76
6 ch m Where Or When(IRE) —Linda's Schoolgirl (IRE) (Grand Lodge (USA))
278[4] 621[3] (808) 962[2] 1775[4] 2552[10] 3434[5] 4389[9] 5102[3] (5692) 6405[10] 7120[4] (7577) 7803[5] 7908[2]

Whey Sauce (JPN) *Peter Chapple-Hyam* a84 90
3 gr f Kurofune(USA) —Histoire (JPN) (Sunday Silence (USA))
2004[3] 2596[4] (7250) 7802[11]

While You Wait (IRE) *J S Bolger* 75
2 b c Whipper(USA) —Azra (IRE) (Danehill (USA))
7185a[7]

Whimsical (IRE) *Richard Hannon* a85 81
2 b f Strategic Prince—Sweet Namibia (IRE) (Namid)
5047[6] 5655[2] 5849[16] (6440) 7028[13]

Whinging Willie (IRE) *Gary Moore* a61 73
2 b g Cape Cross(IRE) —Pacific Grove (Persian Bold)
2880[6] ◆ 3424[4] 3878[6] 4496[9] 5197[4] 6372[9] 7205[7] 7436[7]

Whip And Win (FR) *Robert Collet* 103
3 b f Whipper(USA) —Queensalsa (FR) (Kingsalsa (USA))
1207a[5] 1553a[3] 7509a[0]

Whipcrackaway (IRE) *Peter Hedger* a56 63
2 b g Whipper(USA) —Former Drama (USA) (Dynaformer (USA))
6483[3] 6927[8] 7809[4]

Whip It In (IRE) *Paul Midgley* 37
2 b f Whipper(USA) —Viami (IRE) (Daylami (IRE))
6152[6] 6673[10] 7072[9]

Whiplash Willie *Andrew Balding* a82 110
3 ch c Phoenix Reach(IRE) —Santa Isobel (Nashwan (USA))
1727[2] 2295[7] (3291) (4426) 5283[2]

Whipless (IRE) *J S Bolger* a90 93
3 b c Whipper(USA) —Kimola (IRE) (King's Theatre (IRE))
1004a[3] 1533a[10] 3440a[27]

Whipperoo (IRE) *Patrick Morris* a22 39
3 b f Whipper(USA) —Amaroo (FR) (Midyan (USA))
1303[8] 2989[9]

Whipperway (IRE) *Sheena West* a56 71
4 b m Whipper(USA) —Prince's Passion (Brief Truce (USA))
560[13]

Whipphound *Mark Brisbourne* a73 73
3 b g Whipper(USA) —Golden Symbol (Wolfhound (USA))
1825[6] 2215[9] 2834[5] 3598[5] 3853[5] 4048[4] 4511[4] 4643[4] 7595[12]

Whip Rule (IRE) *J S Bolger* a95 98
2 b c Whipper(USA) —Danemarque (AUS) (Danehill (USA))
(921a) 5951a[7] 6692[4]

Whirly Dancer *Lennart Reuterskiold Jr* a74 89
4 b m Danehill Dancer(IRE) —Whirly Bird (Nashwan (USA))
5096a[8]

Whiskey Junction *Michael Quinn* a76 80
7 b g Bold Edge—Victoria Mill (Free State)
178[11] 298[4] 554[6] 2609[11] 3255[2] 3307[9] (3713) 3957[2] 4233[9] 4731[2] 4967[3] 5425[4] 5781[7] 6119[9] 6793[4]

Whisky Bravo *David Brown* a76 69
2 b g Byron—Dress Design (IRE) (Brief Truce (USA))
1966[4] ◆ 2346[5] 2780[4] 4851[9] (5211) 5913[2] 6186[7] 6573[3] ◆ 6921[5] 7294[4] ◆ (7642) (7686) 7881[3]

Whispered *Sir Michael Stoute* a71 79
3 b f Medicean—Whispering Blues (IRE) (Sadler's Wells (USA))
2639[2] 4072[2] 5001[2] 5629[2] 6054[7]

Whispered Times (USA) *Tracy Waggott* a41 80
4 bb g More Than Ready(USA) —Lightning Show (USA) (Storm Cat (USA))
1800[5] 2431[8] 2806[7] 3190[5] 3657[5] 3733[6] 6231[4] (6262) 6453[2]

Whispering Gallery *Saeed Bin Suroor* a115 115
5 b g Daylami(IRE) —Echoes In Eternity (IRE) (Spinning World (USA))
(329a) (826a)

Whispering Spirit (IRE) *Ann Duffield* a85 66
5 b m Catcher In The Rye(IRE) —Celtic Guest (IRE) (Be My Guest (USA))
1610[9] 2634[6] 3038[9] 3473[4] (3716) 4920[5] 5789[2] 6133[6] 6490[2] 7099[5]

Whispering Warrior (IRE) *Jeremy Noseda* a56
2 b c Oasis Dream—Varenka (IRE) (Fasliyev (USA))
7906[4]

Whistledownwind *David Nicholls* a106 84
6 b g Danehill Dancer(IRE) —Mountain Ash (Dominion)
4609[15] 5465[13] 6093[16]

Whistle On By *Charles Hills* a77 85
3 b c Piccolo—Glory Oatway (IRE) (Desert Prince (IRE))
776a[4] 993[2] 1774[2] (3231) 3825[15] 4665[7] 5892[9]

Whitby Jet (IRE) *Edward Vaughan* a64 82
3 b g Mujadil(USA) —Anazah (USA) (Diesis)
1952[2] 2197[2] (2465) 2853[3] 3979[2] (4744) 5014[7] 5547[2] 5856[4]

Whitcombe Spirit *Jamie Poulton* a35 52
6 b g Diktat—L'Evangile (Danehill (USA))
3184[11] 3769[5] 4318[5] 4712[3]

White Burgundy (IRE) *C Boutin* 48
2 ch f Gold Away(IRE) —Johanie Cara (FR) (Johann Quatz (FR))
7449a[0]

Whitechapel *Andrew Balding* a75 76
4 gr g Oasis Dream—Barathiki (Barathea (IRE))
4255[9] 5053[13] 5653[2] 5828[8] 6477[7] (7764)

Whitecrest *John Spearing* a66 76
3 ch f Ishiguru(USA) —Risky Valentine (Risk Me (FR))
1483[6] 1776[3] 2294[3] 2611[7] 3321[2] 3785[2] 3994[6] 4461[2] 5115[3] (5377) 5939[4] (6119) 6456[5] 6801[4] 6895[4] 7040[7]

White Curtain (USA) *D Sepulchre*
3 ch c Mingun(USA) —Chimes Of Freedom (USA) (Private Account (USA))
777a[0] 902a[0]

White Deer (USA) *Geoffrey Harker* a60 68
7 b g Stravinsky(USA) —Brookshield Baby (IRE) (Sadler's Wells (USA))
391[2] 749[7] 1164[2] 1613[10] (2666) 3243[2] 4438[2] 5595[6] 6493[4] 7075[3]

White Diamond *Malcolm Jefferson* 77
4 b m Bertolini(USA) —Diamond White (Robellino (USA))
1097[5] 1388[2] 1879[7] 2454[2] 3386[10] 6916[12] 7215[6]

White Flight *Jonathan Portman* 53
2 gr f Doyen(IRE) —Reason To Dance (Damister (USA))
6744[12] 7030[12]

White Frost (IRE) *Charles Hills* 100
3 gr c Verglas(IRE) —Moivouloirtoi (USA) (Bering)
(4282) ◆ (4965) ◆ (5450) ◆ 5830[6] 6341[3] 6862[8]

White Fusion *Howard Johnson* 59
3 gr g Oratorio(IRE) —Divine Grace (IRE) (Definite Article)
1415[9] 2119[2] 3318[7] 3734[5]

White Ledger (IRE) *Ray Peacock* a47 50
12 ch g Ali-Royal(IRE) —Boranwood (IRE) (Exhibitioner)
375[8]

White Shift (IRE) *Paul Howling* a71 84
5 b m Night Shift(USA) —Ivy Queen (IRE) (Green Desert (USA))
97[11] 143[8] 268[8] 487[4] 683[6] 1171[6] 1336[5] 7656[11] 7811[6]

White Spirit (IRE) *Marco Botti* a65 22
2 b f Invincible Spirit(IRE) —Foofaraw (USA) (Cherokee Run (USA))
3092[12] 3736[4] 3981[4] 5737[3] 5833[5] 7231[9]

Whitley Bay (USA) *John Best* a48 46
4 b g Lion Heart(USA) —Sea Witch (USA) (Sea Hero (USA))
277[11] 588[6]

Whitstable Native *John Best* a51 65
3 b g Bertolini(USA) —Break Of Dawn (USA) (Mt. Livermore (USA))
4247[6] 4828[3] 5172[4] 5917[11] 6610[10]

Whoatealthepius (IRE) *Dean Ivory* a70 79
3 b f Antonius Pius(USA) —Affirmed Crown (USA) (Affirmed (USA))
1837[10] 2468[7] 2881[7] 3292[3] 3635[7] 5326[6] 5644[6] 5939[6] 6746[13] 7086[8] 7488[10] 7755[4] 7854[9]

Whodathought (IRE) *Paul Rich* a74 78
3 b c Choisir(AUS) —Consultant Stylist (IRE) (Desert Style (IRE))
49[2] 468[3] 1272[6] 2550[2] 2838[15] 3432[3] 3688[11] 4338[2] 4908[2] (5231) 6755[8] 6944[9] 7447[8] 7557[6] 7817[9]

Whodunit (UAE) *Peter Hiatt* a68 66
7 b g Mark Of Esteem(IRE) —Mystery Play (IRE) (Sadler's Wells (USA))
7202[U] 7387[7] 7522[8] 7654[3] (7805)

Who Loves Ya Baby *Peter Charalambous* a56 37
3 b g Sulamani(IRE) —Aberlady Bay (IRE) (Selkirk (USA))
1315[9] 1991[9] 2068[13] 7515[2] 7800[5]

Who's Shirl *Chris Fairhurst* a80 89
5 b m Shinko Forest(IRE) —Shirl (Shirley Heights)
1696[7] ◆ 2299[7] 2434[10] 3459[8] 4126[5] 5683[8] 5862[4] 6355[4]

Whozthecat (IRE) *Declan Carroll* a96 95
4 b g One Cool Cat(USA) —Intaglia (GER) (Lomitas)
1166[5] 1675[3] ◆ 2116[7] 2525[4] 2954[5] 3379[10] 3778[2] 4075[3] 4556[2] 5033[12] 5758[11] 6331[11] 6703[5] 6917[15] 7489[5] 7643[3]

Why (IRE) *A P O'Brien* 98
3 b f Galileo(IRE) —Rumplestiltskin (IRE) (Danehill (USA))
2012a[7] 2682[12] 2968a[6] 3695a[7] 4035a[5] 4589a[9]

Why So Serious *Peter Salmon* a52 51
5 ch g Falbrav(IRE) —Marrakech (IRE) (Barathea (IRE))
774[2] 1028[5] 1617[7] 1871[5] 2034[11] 2622[6] 3828[18] 4870[7] 5312[2] 5599[3] 7211[8]

Wicked Daze (IRE) *Linda Perratt* a92 87
8 ch g Generous(IRE) —Thrilling Day (Groom Dancer (USA))
3127[8] 3277[14] 3858[6] 4043[7] 4382[7] 4499[11]

Wicked Streak (IRE) *Micky Hammond* 52
6 b g Peintre Celebre(USA) —Peruvian Witch (IRE) (Perugino (USA))
1795[4] 2361[9] 2457[11]

Wicked Wench *Jo Hughes* a73 52
2 b f Kyllachy—Effervescent (Efisio)
6744[11] 7067[2] (7335) 7642[3] 7778[2] 7905[4]

Wicked Wilma (IRE) *Alan Berry* a44 79
7 b m Tagula(IRE) —Wicked (Common Grounds)
1796[7] 2048[4] 2280[7] 2667[4] 2987[6] 3087[4] 3451[2] 3582[5] (4017) (4144) (4541) 5148[5] 5313[4] (5457) 5720[2] 5923[5] 6212[6] 6348[3]

Widow Flower (IRE) *Michael Bell* 41
2 b f Moss Vale(IRE) —Satin Rose (Lujain (USA))
5011[14]

Widyaan (IRE) *John Gosden* a73
2 b c Lawman(FR) —Lady Livius (IRE) (Titus Livius (FR))
7520[2]

Wiener Walzer (GER) *J Hirschberger* 117
5 b h Dynaformer(USA) —Walzerkoenigin (USA) (Kingmambo (USA))
1266a[7] 1842a[5] 2753a[8] 6595a[4]

Wiggy Smith *Henry Candy* a60 84
12 ch g Master Willie—Monsoon (Royal Palace)
2150[2] 2649[7] 3366[5] 4432[4] 5546[6] 5893[3] 6631[2] 6922[6]

Wigmore Hall (IRE) *Michael Bell* 118
4 b g High Chaparral(IRE) —Love And Laughter (IRE) (Theatrical)
(759a) 1000a[3] 1742a[11] 2340a[7] 5074a[4] (6203a) 6861[9]

Wigram's Turn (USA) *Michael Easterby* a78 88
6 ch g Hussonet(USA) —Stacey's Relic (USA) (Houston (USA))
149[4] 367[10] 674[5] 4513[6] 4634[4] ◆ 4918[4] ◆ 7399[2] 7632[7] (7696)

Wilburn (USA) *Steven Asmussen* a122
3 b c Bernardini(USA) —Moonlight Sonata (USA) (Carson City (USA))
7304a[7]

Wildcat Wizard (USA) *David Nicholls* a103 99
5 b g Forest Wildcat(USA) —Tip the Scale (USA) (Valiant Nature (USA))
848[10] 1111[20] 1457[6] 1720[5] ◆

Wild Coco (GER) *Sir Henry Cecil* 114
3 ch f Shirocco(GER) —Wild Side (GER) (Sternkoenig (IRE))
2019[2] ◆ (2813) ◆ (4099) ◆ 4470[5] ◆ 5220[8]

Wild Desert (FR) *Charlie Longsdon* a88 83
6 bb g Desert Prince(IRE) —Sallivera (IRE) (Sillery (USA))
1901[3] 2758[2] 3095[2] 6485[3] 6988[8] 7120[9] 7397[13] (7570) 7674[2]

Wild Geese (IRE) *Jonathan Portman* a61 69
4 br g Cape Cross(IRE) —Intrepidity (Sadler's Wells (USA))
222[3] 350[2] 560[4]

Wild Hysteria (IRE) *Tom Tate* a37 61
3 gr g Verglas(IRE) —White Wisteria (Ahonoora)
1561[8] 1967[9] 2406[6]

Wild Sauce *Bryan Smart* a54 65
2 b f Exceed And Excel(AUS) —Salsa Brava (IRE) (Almutawakel)
2346[3] 7555[3]

Wild Silk *Sir Michael Stoute* 64
2 b f Dansili—So Silk (Rainbow Quest (USA))
5299[10] 6934[5]

Wild Wind (GER) *A P O'Brien* 110
3 b f Danehill Dancer(IRE) —Woman Secret (IRE) (Sadler's Wells (USA))
1006a[2] 2137a[3] 2334a[14] 4132a[7] 5228a[5] (5361a) 5523a[2] 5745a[5] 5977a[2]

Wilfred Pickles (IRE) *Jo Crowley* a89 81
5 ch g Cadeaux Genereux—Living Daylights (IRE) (Night Shift (USA))
226[4] (347) 703[2] (995) 1898[11] 3982[4] 7438[2] 7660[8] 7922[3]

Wilkinson (USA) *Neil J Howard* a107 109
3 bb c Lemon Drop Kid(USA) —Tasha's Delight (USA) (Afternoon Deelites (USA))
6716a[3]

Willbeme *Neville Bycroft* 60
3 b f Kyllachy—Befriend (USA) (Allied Forces (USA))
(2781)

Willcox Inn (USA) *Michael Stidham* a108 117
3 bb c Harlan's Holiday(USA) —De Aar (USA) (Gone West (USA))
5072a[4] 7572a[8]

William Haigh (IRE) *Alan Swinbank* a91 58
3 b g Refuse To Bend(IRE) —Ivowen (USA) (Theatrical)
(1974) ◆ 4380[8] 5004[6] 5602[3] 6116[7] (7425) (7558) (7699)

William Morgan (IRE) *Mike Hammond* a65 81
4 ch g Arakan(USA) —Dry Lightning (Shareef Dancer (USA))
17[4] 7720[11] 7848[11]

William's Way *Ian Wood* a77 61
9 b g Fraam—Silk Daisy (Barathea (IRE))
(373) 418[10] 549[4] 1016[3] 2159[4] 3738[12] 5102[9] 5947[9] 6356[6] 7574[5]

William Van Gogh *Michael Easterby* a73 82
4 b g Dansili—Flower Girl (Pharly (FR))
835[7] 965[6] 1372[6] 3475[4]

William Wainwright (IRE) *Ann Duffield* a53 49
3 b g Elnadim(USA) —Supportive (IRE) (Nashamaa)
41[6] 281[4] 426[3] 642[5] 856[4] 964[3] 1078[4] 1439[5] 1940[5] 2047[11]

Willibr (IRE) *P Costes* a75 72
2 b c Layman(USA) —Kate Winslet (USA) (Signal Tap (USA))
7665a[4]

Willies Diamond (IRE) *Michael Wigham*
2 ch f Modigliani(USA) —Billie Bailey (USA) (Mister Baileys)
2595[4] 2823[4]

Willies Wonder (IRE) *Charles Hills* 61
2 b c Moss Vale(IRE) —Red Letter (Sri Pekan (USA))
5480[8]

Willie Wag Tail (USA) *Ed Walker* a64 82
2 b c Theatrical—Night Risk (USA) (Wild Again (USA))
6216[5] (6837)

Willing Foe (USA) *Saeed Bin Suroor* a62 106
4 bb g Dynaformer(USA) —Thunder Kitten (USA) (Storm Cat (USA))
7029[4] 7297[2]

Will Of Dream (FR) *F-X De Chevigny* a68 53
3 gr g High Yield(USA) —Sur Sa Mine (FR) (Sevres Rose (IRE))
410a[6]

Willow Beauty *J R Jenkins* a51 53
2 br f Val Royal(FR) —Opera Belle (Dr Fong (USA))
4961[7] 5514[8] 6030[12] 6820[6] 7770[7]

Willow Dancer (IRE) *Walter Swinburn* a86 88
7 ch g Danehill Dancer(IRE) —Willowbridge (IRE) (Entrepreneur)
(1198) 1603[13] 2178[5] 2647[13] (3172) 3521[11] (4679) 5328[10] 5712[13] 6220[5] 6728[5] 7110[10]

Willow's Wish *George Moore* a26 45
3 b f Intikhab(USA) —Movie Star (IRE) (Barathea (IRE))
60[5] 456[12] 6780[10] 7212[8] 7340[6]

Willow The Rose *J R Jenkins* a39
4 b m Zamindar(USA) —Lilac Lady (Weld)
1332[6]

Willow Weep For Me (FR) *J-M Lefebvre* a58 66
8 ch g Cadeaux Genereux—Rosereine (USA) (Slew O'Gold (USA))
1013a[8]

Willy McBay *George Moore* 14
2 b g Multiplex—Meandering Rose (USA) (Irish River (FR))
6825[9] 7209[11] 7422[9]

Wiltshire Life (IRE) *Jeremy Gask* a61
2 b f Camacho—Miss Indigo (Indian Ridge)
6946[6] 7345[3] 7583[4]

Wily Fox *James Eustace* a63 83
4 ch g Observatory(USA) —Kamkova (USA) (Northern Dancer (CAN))
516[2] (688) 962[5] 1353[2] 1935[2] 2473[4] 5015[12] 5580[4] 6023[2] 6469[4]

Winchester (USA) *Christophe Clement* a105 115
6 b h Theatrical—Rum Charger (IRE) (Spectrum (IRE))
6548a[5]

Windjammer *Lawrence Mullaney* a63 56
7 b g Kyllachy—Absolve (USA) (Diesis)
3573[13] 5373[13]

Wind Of Tea *A Vetault* a50
7 b g Barathea(IRE) —Ante Futura (FR) (Suave Dancer (USA))
843a[0]

Windpfeil (IRE) *Brendan Powell* a57 29
5 bl g Indian Ridge—Flying Kiss (IRE) (Sadler's Wells (USA))
4703[11]

Wind Shuffle (GER) *Richard Fahey* 59
8 b g Big Shuffle(USA) —Wiesensturmerin (GER) (Lagunas)
3086[8] 3658[5]

Windsor Knights *Alastair Lidderdale* a64
3 b g Dubai Destination(USA) —Betrothal (IRE) (Groom Dancer (USA))
60[4] 234[6] 7037[8] 7333[7]

Windsor Palace (IRE) *A P O'Brien* a81 81
6 b h Danehill Dancer(IRE) —Simaat (USA) (Mr Prospector (USA))
1781a[6] 2332a[5] 5183[5]

Wine 'n Dine *Bernard Llewellyn* a35 76
6 b g Rainbow Quest(USA) —Seasonal Splendour (IRE) (Prince Rupert (FR))
5417[4]

Win For Sure (GER) *X Nakkachdji* a113 111
6 b g Stravinsky(USA) —Win For Us (GER) (Surumu (GER))
156a[3] (332a) 758a[4]

Winged Diva (IRE) *Andrew Balding* a56 38
3 b f Hawk Wing(USA) —Opera Glass (Barathea (IRE))
3513[7] 3925[5]

Winged Farasi *Joanne Foster* a58 58
7 b g Desert Style(IRE) —Clara Vale (IRE) (In The Wings)
4605[9]

Winged Valkyrie (IRE) *Charles Hills* a72 70
3 ch f Hawk Wing(USA) —Crystal Valkyrie (IRE) (Danehill (USA))
1853[8] 2427[4] 3259[5] 6311[9] (7538)

Wing N Prayer (IRE) *John Wainwright* a48 48
4 b m Xaar—Jazmeer (Sabrehill (USA))
1710[9] 2401[12] 2666[7] 3141[5] 3660[5] 5469[8] 6049[3] 6156[8] 6494[9] 7822[3]

Wings Of Apollo (IRE) *Mrs K Burke* a60 48
3 b g Librettist(USA) —Niobe (Pivotal)
4370[7] 5116[3] 6358[2]

Winker Watson *Mick Channon* 104
6 ch h Piccolo—Bonica (Rousillon (USA))
3394[6] 3863[12] 4526[6] 4836a[5]

Winner's Wish *Jeremy Noseda* a74 74
2 b f Clodovil(IRE) —Alla Prima (IRE) (In The Wings)
5444[6] 6000[3] (6400) 6957[8]

Winnie Dixie (USA) *Paul Cole* a74 70
3 bb f Dixie Union(USA) —Icy Demeanor (USA) (Allen's Prospect (USA))
2615[9]

Winniepeg *Clive Cox* a59 51
3 b f Bertolini(USA) —Court Lane (USA) (Machiavellian (USA))
(863) 1149[5] 1521[8] 2553[8] 3230[12] 6604[6]

Winning Draw (IRE) *Paul Midgley* a59 62
3 b f Redback—Desert Flair (Desert Style (IRE))
146[4] 396[3] 505[5] 1439[3] 1975[4] 2592[4] 3207[8] 3661[3] 4564[7] 5162[4] 5490[2] 5787[9] 6615[5] 7064[2] 7216[18]

Winning Impact (IRE) *J G Coogan* a75 80
4 br g Pyrus(USA) —Quizzical Lady (Mind Games)
3445a[5] ◆ 7189a[16] 7790a[9]

Winning Show *Chris Gordon* a68 51
7 b g Muhtarram(USA) —Rose Show (Belmez (USA))
1582[9] 4318[4] 5168[5] 5628[4]

Winning Spark (USA) *Gary Moore* a80 81
4 b g Theatrical—Spark Sept (FR) (Septieme Ciel (USA))
6376[8] (6947) 7458[4] 7601[2]

Winter Dream (IRE) *Robert Collet* 110
7 gr g Act One—Settler (Darshaan)
7406a[0]

Winter Dress *Roger Teal* a66 64
2 ch f Haafhd—Ermine (IRE) (Cadeaux Genereux)
5097[7] 6000[5] 6463[5] 7343[5]

Winter Hill *Tom Dascombe* 69
2 b f Three Valleys(USA) —White Turf (GER) (Tiger Hill (IRE))
2309[5] ◆ 2630[7] (4406) 5052[5]

Winter Memories (USA) *James J Toner* 115
3 rg f El Prado(IRE) —Memories Of Silver (USA) (Silver Hawk (USA))
(6183a) 6887a[4]

Winter's Night (IRE) *Clive Cox* 101
3 b f Night Shift(USA) —Woodland Glade (Mark Of Esteem (IRE))
(1844) 2296[3] 3034[3] 4265[3]

Winterwind (IRE) *Carmen Bocskai* a89 73
6 b h Orpen(USA) —Brickey Beech (IRE) (Precocious)
441a[4] (628a)

Win Variation (JPN) *Masahiro Matsunaga* 122
3 b c Heart's Cry(JPN) —Super Ballerina (CAN) (Storm Bird (CAN))
7563a[5]

Wiqaaya (IRE) *Ed Dunlop* a81 87
3 gr f Red Ransom(USA) —Masaader (USA) (Wild Again (USA))
(1015) 2926[5] 3310[2] 4161[3] 5635[6] 7227[11]

Wise Boy (GER) *W Baltromei* a65 79
4 b g Banyumanik(IRE) —Wahieda (GER) (Sternkoenig (IRE))
196a[2] 325a[2] 831a[0] 6593a[7]

Wisecraic *J S Moore* a67 78
4 ch g Kheleyf(USA) —Belle Genius (USA) (Beau Genius (CAN))
2937[6] 3436[10] 4997[4] 5319[4] 5828[9] 6401[8] 7756[3] 7920[2]

Wise Dan (USA) *Charles Lopresti* a129 117
4 ch g Wiseman's Ferry(USA) —Lisa Danielle (USA) (Wolf Power (SAF))
6721a[4]

Wise Lord *Andrew Haynes* 16
2 b g Yawmi—Timberlake (Bluegrass Prince (IRE))
5325[12]

Wiseman's Diamond (USA) *Paul Midgley* a51 73
6 b m Wiseman's Ferry(USA) —Aswhatilldois (IRE) (Blues Traveller (IRE))
1150[10] 1440[5] 2530[8] 3088[3] 3457[5] (3683) 4076[8] 4442[2] (5441) 6226[7] 6452[11]

Wise Venture (IRE) *Alan Jarvis* 85
2 b g Kheleyf(USA) —Chia Laguna (IRE) (Ela-Mana-Mou)
(2049) (2594) ◆ 4055[9] 5251[8] 6766[5] 7026[9]

Wish Again (IRE) *David Nicholls* 59
2 b g Moss Vale(IRE) —Wildwish (IRE) (Alhaarth (IRE))
3050[9] 4147[3] 5105[4] 6186[2] 6627[4] 7059[10]

Wishbone (IRE) *Jo Hughes* a52 77
4 b m Danehill Dancer(IRE) —Intricate Design (Zafonic (USA))
7428[12] 7819[9] ◆

Wishformore (IRE) *J S Moore* a67 68
4 b m Chevalier(IRE) —Terra Nova (Polar Falcon (USA))
56[5] 1370[2] (2198) (2561) 3017[5] 3549[3] 3918[4] 4490[3] 5002[11] 5673[7] 5836[4] 6624[7] 7034[4] 7399[4]

Witchry *Tony Newcombe* a65 70
9 gr g Green Desert(USA) —Indian Skimmer (USA) (Storm Bird (CAN))
1730[3] 2142[3] 2794[3] 2903[3] 3512[9] (4086) 5053[6] 5338[4] 5513[4] 7425[3]

With Hindsight (IRE) *Clive Cox* a74 79
3 ch g Ad Valorem(USA) —Lady From Limerick (IRE) (Rainbows For Life (CAN))
1108[3] 1682[4] 4457[5] 4845[2] 5242[7] 6402[5] (7004)

With Interest *A Al Raihe* a96 80
8 b h Selkirk(USA) —With Fascination (USA) (Dayjur (USA))
535a[13]

Without Equal *David Thompson* a47 61
5 ch m Tobougg(IRE) —Sans Egale (FR) (Lashkari)
2462[8] (3041) 3300[6] 3974[9] 5107[13] 5650[12] 7078[9]

Without Prejudice (USA) *Michael Easterby* a71 85
6 ch g Johannesburg(USA) —Awesome Strike (USA) (Theatrical)
2115[9] 2347[8] 2674[10] 3038[7] 3617[10] 4670[14] 5455[11] (5803) 7146[10] 7715[5] 7876[6] 7928[2]

Witnessed *Mahmood Al Zarooni* 80
2 b f Authorized(IRE) —Magic Mission (Machiavellian (USA))
(5464)

Witty Buck *Alan McCabe* 23
2 b g Multiplex—Divine Love (IRE) (Barathea (IRE))
1268[6] 1691[15] 2355[8]

Wizz Kid (IRE) *Robert Collet* 115
3 b f Whipper(USA) —Lidanski (IRE) (Soviet Star (USA))
1207a[8] (2754a) 5253[5] ◆ 6563a[5] 6858[2]

Wodian (IRE) *David Lanigan* a54 47
3 ch f Smarty Jones(USA) —Madame Anne Peters (Selkirk (USA))
2829[7] 3223[8] 4927[6] 5643[7] 6446[13]

Wogan's Sister *Paul Midgley* a65 72
6 b m Lahib(USA) —Dublivia (Midyan (USA))
104[7]

Wolds Agent *Tim Easterby* 52
3 b g Monsieur Bond(IRE) —Off Camera (Efisio)
1329[8] 1906[10]

Wolfgang (IRE) *Richard Hannon* a57 89
2 b c Amadeus Wolf—Eleuthere (USA) (Elusive Quality (USA))
1583[4] (2374) 3014[16] (3345) 3866[2] 4581[2] 5287[4] 5825[7] 7021[6]

Wolf Heart (IRE) *Saeed Bin Suroor* a76
3 b c Dalakhani(IRE) —Lisieux Orchid (IRE) (Sadler's Wells (USA))
6286[4]

Wolf Slayer *Tom Dascombe* a68 72
3 b f Diktat—Bolsena (USA) (Red Ransom (USA))
1452[5] 1916[7] 3337[11] 3983[2] 4896a[6] 5274[10] 5736[7] 6266[3] 6634[10]

Wolf Spirit (IRE) *Kevin Ryan* 75
2 b g Amadeus Wolf—Nasharaat (IRE) (Green Desert (USA))
2831[2] ◆ 3583[3] 4414[9] 5690[9] 6484[12]

Wolkenburg (GER) *P Schiergen* 101
3 b f Big Shuffle(USA) —Winterthur (GER) (Alkalde (GER))
2337a[4] 3209a[2] 3897a[7] 5980a[3]

Wom *Pam Sly* a36 63
3 b g Tiger Hill(IRE) —Vayavaig (Damister (USA))
3133[6] 3676[3] 5507[4] 6052[10] 7113[2]

Wonder Lawn (SAF) *M F De Kock* a100 104
8 b g Fort Wood(USA) —Velvet Green (BRZ) (Roy (USA))
153a[4] 499a[10] (676a) 829a[3]

Wonder Of Wonders (USA) *A P O'Brien* 113
3 b f Kingmambo(USA) —All Too Beautiful (IRE) (Sadler's Wells (USA))
(1807) ◆ 2682[2] 4133a[3] 5219[3] 5989a[5]

Wong Again *J W Hills* a58 46
3 b f Araafa(IRE) —Susi Wong (IRE) (Selkirk (USA))
1436[6] 3223[7] 3747[3] 4893[7]

Woodbourne (CAN) *Robert Tiller* 109
7 bb g Danzig(USA) —Checker Hall (USA) (Seeking The Gold (USA))
6204a[12]

Woodcote Place *Patrick Chamings* a92 94
8 b g Lujain(USA) —Giant Nipper (Nashwan (USA))
3436[4] 4006[2] (4997) 5936[4] 6341[7] 6862[28]

Wooden King (IRE) *Malcolm Saunders* a79 83
6 b g Danetime(IRE) —Olympic Rock (IRE) (Ballad Rock)
1444[6] (1752) 2142[2] 2304[2] (2447) 2929[7] 3427[3] 3847[3] 3995[3] 4886[4] 5262[4] 5616[3] 5914[4] 6665[2] 6895[8] 7428[8] 7535[2] 7594[6]

Wood Fair *Mrs K Burke* a57 61
4 b m Trade Fair—To The Woods (IRE) (Woodborough (USA))
1587[5] 1987[2] 2213[LFT] 2478[RR]

Wood Fairy *Richard Fahey* a70 69
5 b m Haafhd—Woodbeck (Terimon)
3041[3] 3574[7] (4128) 7033[2] 7418[10]

Wood Nymph (IRE) *Tim Easterby* 50
2 b f Acclamation—Forest Call (Wolfhound (USA))
5646[5] 6291[6]

Woodsley House (IRE) *Mark Rimmer* a49 75
9 b g Orpen(USA) —Flame And Shadow (IRE) (Turtle Island (IRE))
138[9] 204[14]

Woodstock City (FR) *R Chotard* 102
3 b g Sagacity(FR) —Yippee (IRE) (Orpen (USA))
2978a[9]

Woolamaloo *Tim Easterby* 42
3 b f Doyen(IRE) —Eboracum (IRE) (Alzao (USA))
1799[6] 2394[4] 2591[9]

Woolfall Sovereign (IRE) *George Margarson* a84 74
5 b g Noverre(USA) —Mandragore (USA) (Slew O'Gold (USA))
(367) 557[5] 915[7] 7175[2] 7417[2] (7846)

Woolfall Treasure *Gary Moore* a68 103
6 gr g Daylami(IRE) —Treasure Trove (USA) (The Minstrel (CAN))
3875[18] 4532[9] 4775[2] 5659[3] 6103[3] 7226[7]

Woolston Ferry (IRE) *David Pinder* a72 61
5 b g Fath(USA) —Cathy Garcia (IRE) (Be My Guest (USA))
(2201) 2605[8] 3093[8] 3735[4] 4210[6] 4666[6] 5414[4] 5942[4] 6468[10] 6877[2] 7228[5] 7455[2] 7764[3]

Woop Woop (IRE) *Ian Williams* a81 70
3 b f Oratorio(IRE) —Nihonpillow Mirai (IRE) (Zamindar (USA))
51[2] 1950[6] 2368[3] 3202[5] 3467[7] 3771[6] 4664[8] (5415) 5897[4] 6923[3] (7394) (7515) (7638) 7761[3] 7878[2]

Wootton Bassett *Richard Fahey* 120
3 b c Iffraaj—Balladonia (Primo Dominie)
2139a[5] 3011[7] 4838a[5] 5707[13]

Wordiness *Barry Brennan* a66 71
3 br c Dansili—Verbose (USA) (Storm Bird (CAN))
2848[5] 3320[6] 4157[5] 4825[7] 5630[8] 6461[8] 6969[2]

Wordismybond *Peter Makin* a38 68
2 b c Monsieur Bond(IRE) —La Gessa (Largesse)
5834[10] 6127[6] (6581) 7294[9]

Word Of Warning *Martin Todhunter* 59
7 gr g War Chant(USA) —Frosty Welcome (USA) (With Approval (CAN))
2733[6] 3185[2] 3622[7] 4856[7]

Word Power *Sir Henry Cecil* a82 79
3 b f Oasis Dream—Novellara (Sadler's Wells (USA))
3385[2] 4157[3] (4826) 6218[4]

Words Come Easy *Philip McBride* a63
2 ch f Byron—Aliena (IRE) (Grand Lodge (USA))
6680[6] 7174[3] 7220[5]

Words Of Wisdom (IRE) *Edward Lynam* a69 85
3 b g Diamond Green(FR) —Muscida (USA) (Woodman (USA))
1663a[6]

Word To The Wise (IRE) *Michael Smith*
3 b g Catcher In The Rye(IRE) —Pick A Witch (USA) (Fortunate Prospect (USA))
1151[11]

Workforce *Sir Michael Stoute* 130
4 b h King's Best(USA) —Soviet Moon (IRE) (Sadler's Wells (USA))
(2439) ◆ 3646[2] 4315[2] 6567a[12]

Work Shy *Tom Dascombe* a63
3 b f Striking Ambition—Angel's Camp (USA) (Honour And Glory (USA))
(6874)

World Cup (USA) *Michael P De Paulo* 91
4 b m Pleasantly Perfect(USA) —World Event (USA) (Quiet American (USA))
3208a[4]

World Domination (USA) *Sir Henry Cecil* 101
3 b c Empire Maker(USA) —Reams Of Verse (USA) (Nureyev (USA))
(1407) ◆ 2030[4] 3105[10]

World Heritage *Robert Eddery* 107
5 b g Kahyasi—Imbabala (Zafonic (USA))
1342[5] 1883[4] 3107[13] 4100[7] 4801[3] 5185[12] 5483[10]

World Ruler *David Marnane* a85 79
6 b g Dansili—Revealing (Halling (USA))
7150a[13]

World Star (GER) *W Hickst* 89
3 ch c Sholokhov(IRE) —Wonderful Dreams (GER) (Dashing Blade)
1739a[5]

Worth *Brian Meehan* a78 69
2 b f Indesatchel(IRE) —Woore Lass (IRE) (Persian Bold)
1451[3] 1765[3] 2641[8] 4019[4] 4704[2] (5099) 5562[8] 6058[7] (6843) 7364[2]

Worthadd (IRE) *Vittorio Caruso* 123
4 b h Dubawi(IRE) —Wigman (USA) (Rahy (USA))
2101[2] (2541a) 5129a[9] 6566a[5]

Worth A King'S *Dianne Sayer* a93 58
5 b g Red Ransom(USA) —Top Romance (IRE) (Entrepreneur)
4360[16] 4601[13]

Worthington (IRE) *Richard Fahey* 84
2 b f Kodiac—Idle Fancy (Mujtahid (USA))
(2542) ◆ 3014[11] 3402[4] 4252[4] 5216[11]

Wotatomboy *Richard Whitaker* a53 53
5 ch m Captain Rio—Keen Melody (USA) (Sharpen Up)
674[12] 793[11] 856[2] 1498[7] 1633[3] 2233[10] 2799[9] 2989[5] 3247[3] 3573[15] 4696[6] (4740) 5139[4] 6501[10] 6931[8] 7071[8] 7351[5] 7484[4]

Woy Woy (IRE) *Johan Reuterskiold* 62
7 ch g City On A Hill(USA) —Best Niece (Vaigly Great)
5984a[12]

Wrapped Up *Heather Main* a52 43
2 b f Clodovil(IRE) —Parting Gift (Cadeaux Genereux)
2767[12] 3736[8] 5896[3] 6817[11] 7452[5] 7666a[8]

Wreaths Of Empire (IRE) *Richard Hannon* 64
2 b c Dalakhani(IRE) —Eyrecourt (IRE) (Efisio)
6400[9] 6993[7]

Wrecking Crew (IRE) *Rod Millman* a63 62
7 b g Invincible Spirit(IRE) —Rushing (Deploy)
207[6] 451[3] ◆ 631[3] 819[2] 899[2] 969[2] (1959) 2372[2] 2991[3] 3516[5] 5198[11] 5609[3] 6486[10] 7113[13]

Wrekin Sunset *Mrs K Burke* 87
3 ch f Doyen(IRE) —Sienna Sunset (IRE) (Spectrum (IRE))
(1393) 2073[3] 3034[13] 4293[7] 4788[15]

Wreningham *Pat Eddery* a69 66
6 br g Diktat—Slave To The Rythm (IRE) (Hamas (IRE))
1982[6] 2585[13] 3307[8] 3957[5] 4182[8] 4395[9] 4930[2] 6619[4] 7086[9] 7429[3] (7691) ◆ 7785[2] (7854) 7940[7]

Wrote (IRE) *A P O'Brien* 115
2 b c High Chaparral(IRE) —Desert Classic (Green Desert (USA))
6336[3] (7301a)

Wrotham Heath *Sir Henry Cecil* 92
2 b c Dansili—Native Justice (USA) (Alleged (USA))
4762[7] (6805) ◆

Wyeth *Gary Moore* a63 67
7 ch g Grand Lodge(USA) —Bordighera (USA) (Alysheba (USA))
(419)

Wye Valley *Amanda Perrett* a69 62
2 b f Three Valleys(USA) —Welsh Autumn (Tenby)
5813[5] ◆ 6744[5]

Wyndham Wave *Rod Millman* 70
2 gr g Dr Fong(USA) —Atlantic Light (Linamix (FR))
4815[10] (5337) 6484[11]

Xclaim *Clive Cox* 69
3 ch g Proclamation(IRE) —Tahara (IRE) (Caerleon (USA))
1408[12] 5511[6]

Xenophon *Brendan Powell* a42 49
3 b g Phoenix Reach(IRE) —Comtesse Noire (CAN) (Woodman (USA))
2305[6] 2637[9] 3175[4] 5022[4]

Xilerator (IRE) *David Nicholls* a72 105
4 b g Arakan(USA) —Grandel (Owington)
2112[6] (2431) 3397[7] 5557[10] (6148)

Xinbama (IRE) *J W Hills* a68 70
2 b c Baltic King—Persian Empress (IRE) (Persian Bold)
1396[6] 1691[8] 2143[3] 2661[5] (3700) 4019[3] 4581[3] 5197[10] 5809[8] 6132[6]

Xin Xu Lin (BRZ) *Mahmood Al Zarooni* a110 118
4 b c Wondertross(USA) —Barbiera (BRZ) (Pleasant Variety (USA))
998a[5]

Xpres Maite *Roy Bowring* a77 65
8 b g Komaite(USA) —Antonias Melody (Rambo Dancer (CAN))
3245[7] 4945[4] 6226[11] 6452[3] 6764[4] 7465[7] 7722[4] (7884)

X Rated *Alan McCabe* a71 24
3 b g Dubai Destination(USA) —Miss Satamixa (FR) (Linamix (FR))
850[3] 937[2] 1096[10] 1288[2]

Xtension (IRE) *J Moore* 121
4 br h Xaar—Great Joy (IRE) (Grand Lodge (USA))
(1576a) 7731a[3]

Xyzzy *Linda Stubbs* a70 54
2 b f Royal Applause—Out Like Magic (Magic Ring (IRE))
1192[3] 1590[3] (1957)

Yaa Salam *Mahmood Al Zarooni* 80
2 ch c Any Given Saturday(USA) —Alizes (NZ) (Rory's Jester (AUS))
6100[3] 6588[2] ◆ 6954[3]

Yaa Wayl (IRE) *Saeed Bin Suroor* 115
4 b g Whipper(USA) —Lidanna (Nicholas (USA))
415a[9] 587a[13] (3548) 5282[9] 6129[4]

Ya Boy Sir (IRE) *Ian Semple* a52 63
4 ch g Alhaarth(IRE) —Champs Elysees (USA) (Distant Relative)
1204[12] 1307[9] 1544[8] 2412[13] 2803[13] 3451[9] 4041[8] 4504[4] 4881[12] 5153[8] 5725[6] 6386[9] 7100[11]

Ya Hafed *Sheena West* a64 76
3 ch g Haafhd—Rule Britannia (Night Shift (USA))
171[4] (319) 650[4] (1134) 1286[2]

Yahafedh Alaih *Clive Brittain* a67 72
3 ch c Haafhd—Farhana (Fayruz)
992[4] 1341[6] 2389[5] 4161[5] 4321[8] 4683[3] 4926[4] 5355[2] 5703[13]

Yahrab (IRE) *Declan Carroll* a106 83
6 gr g Dalakhani(IRE) —Loire Valley (IRE) (Sadler's Wells (USA))
1215[4] 1470[9] 1746[6] 2366[9] 2917[7] 3071[9]

Yair Hill (IRE) *John Dunlop* 93
3 b g Selkirk(USA) —Conspiracy (Rudimentary (USA))
(1284) 1725[4] 2319[5] 2878[6] 3634[5] 5171[3] (5811) 6495[5] (7171)

Yakama (IRE) *Christine Dunnett* a61 59
6 b g Indian Danehill(IRE) —Working Progress (IRE) (Marju (IRE))
211[8] 317[6] 485[9] 589[6] 722[9] 2829[6] 3942[6] 4179[7] 4681[4] 6032[5] 6764[2] (7229) 7524[6] 7663[5] 7843[8]

Yalding Dancer *John Best* a42
2 b f Zafeen(FR) —Daughters World (Agnes World (USA))
7672[11]

Yalumba (FR) *Mme Pia Brandt* 48
2 b f Epalo(GER) —Salamina (SWI) (Turtle Island (IRE))
6925a[8]

Yammos (IRE) *Mick Channon* a63 69
2 b g Sir Percy—Carenage (IRE) (Alzao (USA))
2181[8] 2448[3] 2962[3] 3152[13] 3866[11] 4512[3] 4761[4] (5325) 5413[3] 6053[3] 6471[9] 6760[6]

Yanabeeaa (USA) *Sir Michael Stoute* a79
2 rg f Street Cry(IRE) —Queen (IRE) (Sadler's Wells (USA))
6440[2]

Yanbu (USA) *Tobias B P Coles* a39 62
6 b m Swain(IRE) —Dufoof (USA) (Kingmambo (USA))
2452[2] 3019[4] 3735[5] 4278[2] 7463[10]

Yang Tse Kiang (FR) *R Chotard* a74 104
2 gr g Kahyasi—Mikalia (FR) (Kaldoun (FR))
6902a[2]

Yankee Storm *Tom Keddy* a80 65
6 b g Yankee Gentleman(USA) —Yes Virginia (USA) (Roanoke (USA))
96[3] 367[4] 612[2] 766[2] 833[3] (985) 1196[4] 1523[3]

Yarooh (USA) *Clive Brittain* a72 77
3 b f Medaglia D'Oro(USA) —Country Maiden (USA) (Forest Camp (USA))
1404[14]

Yarra Valley *Willie Musson* 35
2 b f Aussie Rules(USA) —Frambroise (Diesis)
4823[7]

Yaseer (IRE) *Marcus Tregoning* a86 108
3 b g Dansili—Tadris (USA) (Red Ransom (USA))
1341[3] ◆ 2030[6] 4411[4] 5045[8] 6519[5]

Yashila (IRE) *J S Moore* a61 71
3 b f Indian Haven—Tara's Girl (IRE) (Fayruz)
1682[9] 7260[4] 7389[8] (7585)

Yasir (USA) *Saeed Bin Suroor* a93 81
3 b c Dynaformer(USA) —Khazayin (USA) (Bahri (USA))
5169[4] 5629[3] ◆ 6349[2] (6822)

Yasmeena (USA) *Charles Hills* 73
3 ch f Mr Greeley(USA) —La Cucaracha (Piccolo)
2294[6] 3271[2] 3723[3] 4227[3] 5279[5] 6456[8]

Yasoodd *D Selvaratnam* a87 101
8 br g Inchinor—Needwood Epic (Midyan (USA))
332a[13]

Yearbook *Tim Easterby* 57
2 b f Byron—Dayville (USA) (Dayjur (USA))
1791[5] 2093[5] 2587[2] 2761[4] 5399[3] 5817[13] 6222[15] 6384[7]

Yeeoow (IRE) *Mrs K Burke* a65 74
2 b c Holy Roman Emperor(IRE) —Taraya (IRE) (Doyoun)
5202[5] 6492[6] 6673[3] 6892[3] 7273a[6]

Yellow Dandy (IRE) *Liam McAteer* 83
3 b f Kheleyf(USA) —Groves Preneur (IRE) (Entrepreneur)
(4885) 5430[4] 6388a[15]

Yellow Fairy (FR) *B Leclere* 31
5 gr m Nombre Premier—Quitate (FR) (Reprimand)
903a[0]

Yellow Printer *Mark Gillard* a60 33
5 b g Royal Applause—Robsart (IRE) (Robellino (USA))
5231[10] 5408[3] 6083[3] 6608[4] 7006[3] 7006[5] 7571[10] 7741[4]

Yellow Ridge (IRE) *Luke Comer* a32 48
8 ch g On The Ridge(IRE) —Jonathan's Rose (IRE) (Law Society (USA))
4385[12]

Yellow Rosebud (IRE) *D K Weld* 105
2 b f Jeremy(USA) —Nebraas (Green Desert (USA))
4833a[2] 6564a[4]

Yemeni Princess (IRE) *Brendan Powell* a69 81
5 b m Bahri(USA) —Celtic Ballet (Celtic Swing)
4097[9]

Yensi *George Baker* a71 82
4 b m Doyen(IRE) —Sifat (Marju (IRE))
4090[9] (4829) (6226) ◆ 6355[7]

Yeomanoftheguard *Richard Fahey* a63 65
2 b g Librettist(USA) —Red Blooded Woman (USA) (Red Ransom (USA))
3274[3] 6662[3]

Yeomanry *Ian Williams* a49 38
6 b g High Chaparral(IRE) —Charming Life (NZ) (Sir Tristram)
8[11] 2272[4] 2659[7]

Yer Woman (IRE) *Richard Hannon* a92 92
4 b m Kyllachy—Genny Lim (IRE) (Barathea (IRE))
1104[5] 1888[4] 2099[12] 3796[9] 4531[16] 4859[9] 5657[9]

Yes Chef *Rod Millman* a86 81
4 ch g Best Of The Bests(IRE) —Lady Chef (Double Trigger (IRE))
(313) 666[3] ◆ 1138[2] 1832[5] 2378[2] (2872) 3585[7] 4464[4] 4887[3] (5716) 6249[7] 6922[9]

Yes It's The Boy (USA) *Ed Walker* a56 64
2 b c Yes It's True(USA) —Storminthegarden (USA) (Stormy Atlantic (USA))
5861[5] 6579[4] 7094[8]

Yes We Can *Jeremy Gask* a64 67
4 b m Alhaarth(IRE) —Windermere Island (Cadeaux Genereux)
1630[5] 2426[6] 2920[12] 3719[10]

Yield Bogey (USA) *Patrick J Kelly* a64 104
7 b g Langfuhr(CAN) —Upper Noosh (USA) (Red Ransom (USA))
6908a[12]

Yirga *A Al Raihe* a99 99
5 b h Cape Cross(IRE) —Auratum (USA) (Carson City (USA))
236[2] 326a[10] 497a[7] 605a[2] 676a[2] 757a[8] 829a[9]

Ykikamoocow *Geoffrey Harker* 74
5 b m Cape Town(IRE) —Pigeon (Casteddu)
(2399)

Ymir *Michael Attwater* a61 58
5 b g Zaha(CAN) —Anastasia Venture (Lion Cavern (USA))
(589) 719[4] 1045[3]

Yo Credo (IRE) *Irene J Monaghan* a46 41
2 b f Elusive City(USA) —Baltic Beach (IRE) (Polish Precedent (USA))
972a[9] 1699a[7]

Yojimbo (IRE) *Mick Channon* a75 88
3 gr g Aussie Rules(USA) —Mythie (FR) (Octagonal (NZ))
1203[6] (1682) 2506[11] 3400[3] 4290[8] 4447[5] 5056[10] (5856) 6374[2] 6728[2] 7050[2]

Yojojo (IRE) *Gay Kelleway* 54
2 ch f Windsor Knot(IRE) —Belle Of The Blues (IRE) (Blues Traveller (IRE))
7293[6]

Yorgunnabelucky (USA) *Mark Johnston* 101
5 b h Giant's Causeway(USA) —Helsinki (Machiavellian (USA))
1717[8] (2107) 2716[15] 3013[14]

Yorketa *Michael Dods* a51 51
3 br f Needwood Blade—Mykeyta (Key Of Luck (USA))
494[5] 871[3]

York Glory (USA) *Kevin Ryan* a82 106
3 rg c Five Star Day(USA) —Minicolony (USA) (Pleasant Colony (USA))
559[3] ◆ 721[2] ◆ (1812) 2180[2] (3461) 4048[2] 4234[2] (4855) (5288) 5927[5]

Yorksters Prince (IRE) *Tony Coyle* a62 74
4 b g Beat Hollow—Odalisque (IRE) (Machiavellian (USA))
7[7] 408[4] 524[10] 552[8] 796[6] 899[9] 4125[7] (4438) 4673[6] 4944[5] 5589[2] (6264) (6536) 7214[3]

Yosha (IRE) *P Demercastel* a76 74
3 ch f Peintre Celebre(USA) —Double Platinum (Seeking The Gold (USA))
480a[5] 5463a[3]

Yossi (IRE) *Richard Guest* a63 71
7 b g Montjeu(IRE) —Raindancing (IRE) (Tirol)
63[3] 184[9] 320[2] 507[3] 796[5] 938[6] 1063[2] ◆ 1081[3] 4367[12] 4944[8] 5210[7] 5357[3] 5642[9] 6235[12] 7720[6] 7859[12] 7878[7]

Youcouldbelucky (USA) *Mark Johnston* 50
2 bb g El Corredor(USA) —Knock Twice (USA) (Two Punch (USA))
4264[9] 6447[8] 7109[9]

Yougoigo *Marjorie Fife* 39
3 b c Elnadim(USA) —Club Oasis (Forzando)
2094[10] 2479[7] 3075[9]

You Got The Love *Jeremy Gask* a45 29
2 ch f Hawk Wing(USA) —Precedence (IRE) (Polish Precedent (USA))
5111[11] 6654[12] 7344[12] 7481[6]

Youhavecontrol (IRE) *Michael Dods* 79
3 b g Hawk Wing(USA) —Chameleon (Green Desert (USA))
(1246) 2215[5] 3400[7] 4362[2] 4676[4] 5621[3] 6778[7] 7024[16]

Youm Mutamiez (USA) *P D Deegan* a84 78
4 br h Seeking The Gold(USA) —Shy Lady (FR) (Kaldoun (FR))
1118a[8]

Young Dottie *Pat Phelan* a85 72
5 b m Desert Sun—Auntie Dot Com (Tagula (IRE))
279[2] 703[8] 3763[4] 4243[5] 5113[5] 6587[3] 7328[8] (7486) 7660[6]

Young Dr Jekyll *Henry Candy* 38
3 b g Dr Fong(USA) —Jubilee Dawn (Mark Of Esteem (IRE))
5639[12] 5960[6]

Young Freddie (IRE) *Bryan Smart* 47
2 gr g Clodovil(IRE) —Quecha (IRE) (Indian Ridge)
6983[11]

Young Jackie *George Margarson* a47 42
3 b f Doyen(IRE) —Just Warning (Warning)
878[4] 1572[5]

Young Lou *Robin Dickin* a27
2 b f Kadastrof(FR) —Wanna Shout (Missed Flight)
7493[13]

Young Prince (IRE) *Robert Mills* a79 31
2 b g Strategic Prince—Aspasias Tizzy (USA) (Tiznow (USA))
4352[7] 5382[3] 6214[5] (7205) 7434[2] 7762[2]

Young Simon *George Margarson* a63 63
4 ch g Piccolo—Fragrant Cloud (Zilzal (USA))
(276) 362[2] 512[9] 947[8] 1041[9] 1989[11] 3254[6] 7224[6] 7371[6] 7459[2] 7656[9] 7755[3] 7897[4]

Young Tiger (FR) *F Rohaut* a99 108
10 b g Tiger Hill(IRE) —Youngolina (IRE) (Trempolino (USA))
(705a)

You'relikemefrank *John Balding* a79 61
5 ch g Bahamian Bounty—Proudfoot (IRE) (Shareef Dancer (USA))
(80) ◆ 523[4]

Your Gifted (IRE) *Patrick Morris* a69 94
4 b m Trans Island—Dame Laura (IRE) (Royal Academy (USA))
15[2] 62[2] 116[2] (224) 443[7] 554[5] 646[4] 2546[9] 2755[3] (3027) 3216[7] 3305[3] (3582) 3768[2] 3847[6] (4046) 4135a[3] 4583[4] 4767a[3] 5033[5] (5543) 5706[8]

Yourgolftravel Com *David Pipe* a62 68
6 b g Fasliyev(USA) —Hiddnah (USA) (Affirmed (USA))
1635[7] 2144[5] 2420[6] 3017[6]

Yourinthewill (USA) *Daniel Mark Loughnane* a74 67
3 ch g Aragorn(IRE) —Lenarue (USA) (Gone West (USA))
4273[6] 4888[2] 5964[3] 6311[2] 6872[7] (7788) 7901[4]

Yours *Kevin Ryan* a45 54
3 b f Piccolo—Uno (Efisio)
434[6] 520[10] 1040[5] 1306[5] 2396[3] 7641[14]

Yours Ever *Sir Mark Prescott Bt* a68 74
2 b f Dansili—Love Everlasting (Pursuit Of Love)
6441[3] 6776[3] 7709[5]

Your Special Day (USA) *James Cassidy* 92
2 bb f Kafwain(USA) —Young Ladies Day (USA) (General Meeting (USA))
7562a[4]

Your Word *Clive Cox* 32
2 b f Monsieur Bond(IRE) —Only Yours (Aragon)
6950[12]

You've Been Mowed *Richard Price* a64 87
5 ch m Ishiguru(USA) —Sandblaster (Most Welcome)
1755[4] 2027[5] (2376) 2870[3] 3215[3] (3643) 3952[5] (4457) 5101[7] 5546[7] (6188) 6878[4] 7178[9]

Ypres *Jason Ward* a58 42
2 b g Byron—Esligier (IRE) (Sabrehill (USA))
6866[7] 7142[5] 7368[7] 7778[5]

Yun (FR) *C Baillet*
2 b f Panis(USA) —Slyders (IRE) (Hector Protector (USA))
7814a[8]

Yungaburra (IRE) *David C Griffiths* a64 63
7 b g Fath(USA) —Nordic Living (IRE) (Nordico (USA))
880[12] 1034[12] 1471[6] 5787[15] 6138[8] 6694[11] 6848[5] 6982[4] 7224[5] (7366) 7429[7] 7567[2] 7737[8] 7844[13]

Yurituni *Eve Johnson Houghton* a77 83
4 b m Bahamian Bounty—Vax Star (Petong)
1562[10] 1899[3] (2303) 2491[3] ◆ 2662[2] 3078[6] 3996[3] 4742[6] 5018[3] (5671) 6094[11]

Zaahya (IRE) *John Dunlop* 65
2 ch f Shamardal(USA) —Najah (IRE) (Nashwan (USA))
3547[7] 5029[6]

Zabarajad (IRE) *John M Oxx* a100 108
3 b g Invincible Spirit(IRE) —Zalaiyma (FR) (Rainbow Quest (USA))
2324a[6] 7793a[7]

Zabeel Park (USA) *Saeed Bin Suroor* a62 91
3 ch f Medicean—Musical Treat (IRE) (Royal Academy (USA))
7138[6]

Zacinto *Sir Michael Stoute* 118
5 b h Dansili—Ithaca (USA) (Distant View (USA))
1600[6]

Zack Hall (FR) *M Delzangles* 117
4 b h Muhtathir—Halawa (IRE) (Dancing Brave (USA))
1842a[2] 3448a[4] 5074a[9]

Zack Yield (FR) *A Lamotte D'Argy* 97
3 ch g High Yield(USA) —Zafarana (FR) (Shernazar)
5463a[0]

Zacynthus (IRE) *Alan McCabe* a33 91
3 ch c Iffraaj—Ziria (IRE) (Danehill Dancer (IRE))
3134[13] 3864[10] 7023[4] 7393[12]

Zaeem *Mahmood Al Zarooni* 79
2 b c Echo Of Light—Across (ARG) (Roy (USA))
5855[3] 6771[3] 7060[2]

Zafaraan *Peter Chapple-Hyam* a34 67
3 b f Royal Applause—Sakhya (IRE) (Barathea (IRE))
1767[2] 2157[6] 2643[8] 3251[3]

Zafarana *Ed Dunlop* a92 76
3 b f Tiger Hill(IRE) —Miss Meltemi (IRE) (Miswaki Tern (USA))
1549[6] ◆ 2026[4] 2551[3] ◆ (5098) 5963[6] 7129[6]

Zafeen's Pearl *Dean Ivory* a82 74
4 ch m Zafeen(FR) —Deep Sea Pearl (Dr Fong (USA))
90[2] 488[2] 889[3] 5014[8] 6070[2] 6468[2] (6877) (7146) 7299[8] 7486[4]

Zafeen Speed *M Al Muhairi* a108 93
4 ch g Zafeen(FR) —Dakhla Oasis (IRE) (Night Shift (USA))
756a[2] 997a[5]

Zaffy (IRE) *Tim Easterby* 57
2 b f Iffraaj—Silkie Smooth (IRE) (Barathea (IRE))
2113[8] 3611[3]

Zafisio (IRE) *Jo Hughes* 91
5 b g Efisio—Goldthroat (IRE) (Zafonic (USA))
5183[4] 5494[9] 6149[5]

Zafonic Star *Ian Williams* a60 48
2 b g Cockney Rebel(IRE) —Enthralled (Zafonic (USA))
5347[5] 5863[6] 7174[6]

Zafranagar (IRE) *Tony Carroll* a73 72
6 b g Cape Cross(IRE) —Zafaraniya (IRE) (Doyoun)
161[4] (222) 392[9] 1099[2] 1461[4] 2055[4] (2567) 7363[3] 7734[4]

Zagalinis Speech *J R Jenkins* 48
3 b f Bertolini(USA) —Zagala (Polar Falcon (USA))
1591[8] 1900[7] 3091[7]

Zagarock *Bryn Palling* a49 56
4 b m Rock Of Gibraltar(IRE) —Zagaleta (Sri Pekan (USA))
477[8] 862[11] 1567[4] 1750[8] (2246) 2905[9] 3516[7] 3726[4] 7466[7]

Zaheeb *Dave Morris* a64 65
3 b g Haafhd—Gay Music (FR) (Gay Mecene (USA))
1568[14] 2068[11] 2599[2] ◆ 3432[13] 4005[6] 4685[5] (4929) 5515[12] 6032[7] 6938[5] 7507[12] (7754) 7890[2]

Zahraan (IRE) *Marcus Tregoning* a80 74
3 b c Elusive City(USA) —Rihana (IRE) (Priolo (USA))
5247[2]

Zaina (IRE) *Gerard Butler* a67
2 b f Shirocco(GER) —Ruacana Falls (USA) (Storm Bird (CAN))
7599[2] ◆

Zain Al Boldan *Mick Channon* 105
3 b f Poliglote—Carla (FR) (Cardoun (FR))
(1286) (1894) 2682[9] 3065[5] 3772[3] 4582[7]

Zain Point (IRE) *Gerard Butler* a65 59
2 ch c Barathea(IRE) —Niobe (Pivotal)
3917[8] 4548[2] 5411[4] 6866[6] 7081[5]

Zain Princess (IRE) *Gerard Butler* 54
2 b f Hawk Wing(USA) —Cosenza (Bahri (USA))
2309[9] 2709[11]

Zain Shamardal (IRE) *Brian Meehan* a94 94
3 b c Shamardal(USA) —Novelina (IRE) (Fusaichi Pegasus (USA))
1690[3] (2068) 2877[2] ◆ 3406[2]

Zakatal *Philip Hobbs* 85
5 gr g Kalanisi(IRE) —Zankara (FR) (Linamix (FR))
1367[2] 4806[8]

Zakon (IRE) *Denis Coakley* a78 79
3 b g Ivan Denisovich(IRE) —Franny (Selkirk (USA))
1298[2] 1991[2] 2760[3]

Zakreet *Kevin Ryan* 86
2 ch c Cadeaux Genereux—Chili Dip (Alhaarth (IRE))
4675[3] 5058[6] (5548) (6144) ◆ 6829[8]

Zalano *Derek Haydn Jones* a66 62
3 b g Zafeen(FR) —Alvarinho Lady (Royal Applause)
636[5] 3983[3] 4640[5] 4885[4] 5843[13]

Zamarelle *Roger Charlton* a56 62
2 b f Zamindar(USA) —Kardelle (Kalaglow)
4205[6] 4969[5] 6000[6]

Zambuka (FR) *Pat Murphy* a35 68
4 gr m Zieten(USA) —Mercalle (FR) (Kaldoun (FR))
504[9]

Zamina (IRE) *George Baker* a81 81
3 b f Hawk Wing(USA) —Termania (IRE) (Shirley Heights)
1251[7] (1524) 1683[6] 2146[3] 2838[4] (3228) 4056[8] 4316[7] 5249[2] (5512) 5938[4] 6666[2] 6893[5] 7446[3] 7900[6]

Zaminast *D K Weld* 109
3 b f Zamindar(USA) —Fame At Last (USA) (Quest For Fame)
1928a[5] 6362a[2] ◆

Zamind (FR) *X Thomas-Demeaulte* a88 94
4 b g Country Reel(USA) —Zamilia (IRE) (Zamindar (USA))
840a[6]

Zamindowa *B Grizzetti* 52
3 b f Zamindar(USA) —Sadowa (GER) (Lomitas)
3449a[12]

Zammy *Charles Hills* a64 65
2 ch g Zamindar(USA) —Barbs Pink Diamond (USA) (Johannesburg (USA))
2049[13] 2559[6] 5919[3] 6280[4] 6652[3]

Zanoubiatta (USA) *Ed Dunlop* a36 32
3 bb f Cherokee Run(USA) —Zanoubia (USA) (Our Emblem (USA))
1146[7] 1591[7] 2151[11]

Zantano (GER) *Uwe Ostmann* 91
3 b g Big Shuffle(USA) —Zanana (Zafonic (USA))
2338a[9]

Zantenda *F Head* 105
2 b f Zamindar(USA) —Tender Morn (USA) (Dayjur (USA))
(5873a) 6564a[3] ◆

Zanughan (IRE) *John M Oxx* a103 105
3 b c Azamour(IRE) —Zanara (IRE) (Kahyasi)
1927a[5] 6514a[3]

Zanzamar (SAF) *M F De Kock* a111
4 b h Fort Wood(USA) —Zanakiya (FR) (Doyoun)
(238) 502a[2] 998a[4]

Zapatero (GER) *X Nakkachdji* a79 83
3 b c Konigstiger(GER) —Zypern (GER) (Acatenango (GER))
5463a[5]

Zaphira (GER) *S Smrczek* a69 76
4 ch m Big Shuffle(USA) —Zarissa (GER) (Acatenango (GER))
6394a[9]

Zaplamation (IRE) *John Quinn* a40 76
6 b g Acclamation—Zapatista (Rainbow Quest (USA))
1099[8] 1324[3] 1746[2] 2059[2] 2486[6] 2800[6] 3456[9] 5622[6] 6295[6]

Zaralabad (IRE) *C F Swan* a86 95
7 b g Fantastic Light(USA) —Zarannda (IRE) (Last Tycoon)
1381a[9] 4398a[14]

Zarambar (IRE) *R Laplanche* a82 82
3 b g Zamindar(USA) —Praline Rouge (USA) (Red Ransom (USA))
5132a[4]

Zarazar *Tim Vaughan* 69
3 b g Statue Of Liberty(USA) —Babaraja (Dancing Spree (USA))
7901[P]

Zarebiya (IRE) *John M Oxx* 102
4 b m Galileo(IRE) —Zarlana (IRE) (Darshaan)
4589a[8]

Zareena *David Evans* a34
3 b f Needwood Blade—Samadilla (IRE) (Mujadil (USA))
344[7]

Zarius *Chris Wall* a67 51
4 br g Zamindar(USA) —Slave To The Rythm (IRE) (Hamas (IRE))
(7) 181[5] (674) 869[2] 3495[10] 6616[6] 7507[10]

Zarosa (IRE) *John Berry* a35
2 b f Barathea(IRE) —Shantalla Peak (IRE) (Darshaan)
6956[13] 7493[11]

Zartina (IRE) *Sylvester Kirk* a45 36
3 b f Antonius Pius(USA) —Miss Assertive (Zafonic (USA))
3289[9] 3724[13] 4657[9] 5352[8] 6357[8]

Zaungast (IRE) *W Hickst* 103
7 b h Alkalde(GER) —Zauberwelt (Polar Falcon (USA))
1128a[6] 3334a[5] 4373a[12]

Zavier (FR) *Mahmood Al Zarooni* 51
2 b c Shamardal(USA) —Zarkiyna (FR) (Sendawar (IRE))
4264[8] 4898[7]

Zazou (GER) *W Hickst* 119
4 b h Shamardal(USA) —Zaza Top (GER) (Lomitas)
1128a[5] 2134a[7] (5497a) 6595a[6] (7324a) 7732a[3]

Zebrano *Emma Lavelle* a91 88
5 br g Storming Home—Ambience Lady (Batshoof)
(141) 438[5] 1410[3] (1832) ◆ 2124[9] 2441[10] 6989[14] 7651[4]

Zed Candy (FR) *Richard Ford* a64 58
8 b g Medicean—Intrum Morshaan (IRE) (Darshaan)
(8) 394 2654[3]

Zeeman *Nicky Vaughan*
2 b g Reel Buddy(USA) —Anita In Wales (IRE) (Anita's Prince)
1055[6]

Zeetaan (FR) *P Khozian* a71
3 ch c No Danzig(USA) —Highest Spring (FR) (Hero's Honor (USA))
638a[7]

Zee Zee Dan (IRE) *Noel Quinlan* a33 54
3 b g Danroad(AUS) —Bella Boy Zee (IRE) (Anita's Prince)
3135[8] 3575[6] 3909[6] 4547[10] 4819[7] 6444[10] 7084[7] 7787[9]

Zeffirelli *Michael Quinn* a65 48
6 ch g Tomba—Risky Valentine (Risk Me (FR))
111[8] 280[2] 485[10] 809[12]

Zefooha (FR) *Tim Walford* a68 67
7 ch m Lomitas—Bezzaaf (Machiavellian (USA))
89[6] (3187) 3450[5] 4129[9] (4814) 5651[7] 7107[8]

Zeitoper *Mahmood Al Zarooni* 106
4 br h Singspiel(IRE) —Kazzia (GER) (Zinaad)
2423 5829[2]

Ze King *Chris Wall* 49
2 b g Manduro(GER) —Top Flight Queen (Mark Of Esteem (IRE))
7083[13] 7232[11]

Zelenia *Peter Winkworth* a45
3 b f Compton Place—Allegedly (IRE) (Alhaarth (IRE))
158[8] 274[4] 624[9]

Zelkova (FR) *M Delzangles* a77 77
3 ch f Johannesburg(USA) —Chalouchi (USA) (Mt. Livermore (USA))
981a[4]

Zelos Diktator *Gary Moore* a58 63
5 br g Diktat—Chanterelle (IRE) (Indian Ridge)
277[3] 4847[6] 5643[2] 6446[4] 6968[11] 7206[9]

Zelos Dream (IRE) *Bill Turner* a62 64
4 ch m Redback—Endless Peace (IRE) (Russian Revival (USA))
432[11] 857[13]

Zenaat *Sir Michael Stoute* a71
2 b f Galileo(IRE) —Janet (Emperor Jones (USA))
5320[3]

Zenarinda *Mark H Tompkins* a63 71
4 b m Zamindar(USA) —Tenpence (Bob Back (USA))
2912[7] 3170[4] 4180[3] 7215[3] 7458[9] 7712[3] 7774[4]

Zenella *Ann Duffield* a91 94
3 b f Kyllachy—West One (Gone West (USA))
3852[6] 4428[13] 5255[10] 6080[10] 6574[6]

Zen In Love (FR) *Mme J Bidgood*
2 b g Zieten(USA) —Kristina (SWI) (Konigsstuhl (GER))
7814a[0]

Zennor *Tom Dascombe* a58 92
4 b m Doyen(IRE) —Salanka (IRE) (Persian Heights)
1974[5] 2402[2] (2808) 3129[2] 4360[12] 5198[2] 5724[4] 5921[3] 6470a[11]

Zenone (IRE) *Laura Grizzetti* 102
7 b g Orpen(USA) —Luna D'Estate (Alzao (USA))
6905a[4]

Zenside (IRE) *Mlle A Voraz* a26 71
5 b m Diktat—Zenith (Shirley Heights)
7315a[0]

Zerashan (IRE) *M Halford* 101
4 b g Azamour(IRE) —Zarannda (IRE) (Last Tycoon)
3418a[2] 3695a[6] 4035a[6]

Zero Money (IRE) *Roger Charlton* a77 108
5 ch g Bachelor Duke(USA) —Dawn Chorus (IRE) (Mukaddamah (USA))
1885[12] 2470[10] 3578[4] 4369[2] (4556) ◆ (5706) ◆ 5927[15] 6522[5]

Zeruth (IRE) *Ann Duffield* a47 56
5 b g Oasis Dream—Dawn Air (USA) (Diesis)
2803[8]

Zibimix (IRE) *X Nakkachdji* a97 110
7 gr g Linamix(FR) —Izibi (FR) (Saint Cyrien (FR))
240[7]

Ziefhd *Paul Cole* a86 78
2 b f Haafhd—Zietory (Zieten (USA))
5048[2] ◆ (5299) 5691[2] 6340[7]

Zieto (FR) *J-M Capitte* a75 78
7 b g Zieten(USA) —La Perla (GER) (Dashing Blade)
221a[3] 372a[4]

Zigato *John Gosden* a85 98
4 b g Azamour(IRE) —Maycocks Bay (Muhtarram (USA))
1477[5] (1847) 3013[4]

Zigazag (IRE) *David Evans* a30 63
2 b g Refuse To Bend(IRE) —Most Charming (FR) (Darshaan)
2023[7] 2395[6] 3076[5] 3816[6] 4069[3] 4581[8] 6973[4] 7251[9]

Ziking (FR) *A Schaerer* a85 80
6 gr h Kingsalsa(USA) —Zizoune (FR) (Kadrou (FR))
628a[11]

Zillione Beauty (FR) *Mme P Butel* a82 99
5 ch m Ocean Of Wisdom(USA) —State Of Mind (FR) (Priolo (USA))
3008a[6] 7580a[0]

Zimbabwe (GER) *P Marion* a60 66
6 b g Lord Of Men—Zimbala (GER) (Local Suitor (USA))
439a[7]

Zim Ho *John Akehurst* a47
5 b h Zilzal(USA) —Robanna (Robellino (USA))
210[10] 386[7] 619[5] 662[12]

Zimira (IRE) *Ed Dunlop* a69
2 b f Invincible Spirit(IRE) —Zibilene (Rainbow Quest (USA))
(7520)

Zinabaa (FR) *M Mace* 113
6 gr g Anabaa Blue—Zigrala (FR) (Linamix (FR))
4223a^{5} (5530a) 6556a^{5} 7193a^{10}

Zingana *Eve Johnson Houghton* 76
2 b f Zamindar(USA) —Change Partners (IRE) (Hernando (FR))
(3813) 4803^{7} 6275^{7}

Zing Wing *Paul Cole* a77 77
3 ch f Hawk Wing(USA) —Zietory (Zieten (USA))
3121^{4} 3818^{3} 4202^{4} 4584^{10}

Zip Lock (IRE) *Olivia Maylam* a84 58
5 b g Invincible Spirit(IRE) —Buckle (IRE) (Common Grounds)
3045^{12} *3737^{3}* 4291^{11} *4909^{7}* *5948^{7}* *6282^{9}*

Zip Top (IRE) *J S Bolger* 111
2 b c Smart Strike(CAN) —Zofzig (USA) (Danzig (USA))
4131a^{6} 6270^{3} 7020^{2}

Ziraun *Clive Brittain* 91
3 b f Cadeaux Genereux—Eternal Beauty (USA) (Zafonic (USA))
1155^{4} 5567^{3} (6034) 6531^{6}

Ziyarid (IRE) *A De Royer-Dupre* 114
3 b g Desert Style(IRE) —Zayanida (IRE) (King's Best (USA))
(3653a) 5072a^{2}

Zobenigo (IRE) *L Polito* 98
4 b m Orpen(USA) —Doregan (IRE) (Bahhare (USA))
1432a^{9}

Zoffany (IRE) *A P O'Brien* 120
3 b c Dansili—Tyranny (Machiavellian (USA))
2533a^{2} 3011^{2} 3670a^{2} 4838a^{12} 6721a^{8} 7307a^{9}

Zohan (IRE) *Peter Grayson* a27
3 b g Diamond Green(FR) —Catfoot Lane (Batshoof)
146^{8} *251^{8}* *338^{10}* *426^{7}* *595^{9}* 2549^{12}

Zomerlust *John Quinn* a83 93
9 b g Josr Algarhoud(IRE) —Passiflora (Night Shift (USA))
1240^{5} 2061^{10} (3083) (4016) 4997^{5} 6113^{13}
6541^{2}

Zoom In *Lee James* 49
3 b g Indesatchel(IRE) —Korolieva (IRE) (Xaar)
2465^{9} 7063^{13}

Zoowraa *Mahmood Al Zarooni* a95 102
3 b f Azamour(IRE) —Beraysim (Lion Cavern (USA))
2137a^{16} 6770^{2} *7128^{5}*

Zoriana *Christine Dunnett*
3 ch f Halling(USA) —Olindera (GER) (Lomitas)
339^{9} *717^{5}* 6223^{10} 6608^{10} *7388^{11}*

Zorrita (IRE) *Carmen Bocskai* 82
3 ch f Captain Rio—Lady Stalker (Primo Dominie)
5307a^{4}

Zowaina *Roger Varian* a52
2 b f Manduro(GER) —Zaynaat (Unfuwain (USA))
7118^{8}

Zowington *Stuart Williams* a54 75
9 gr g Zafonic(USA) —Carmela Owen (Owington)
1444^{13} 2016^{11} 2304^{7} 3020^{6} 5053^{12}

Zuider Zee (GER) *John Gosden* a81 108
4 b g Sakhee(USA) —Zephyrine (IRE) (Highest Honor (FR))
1887^{4} 2716^{3} ◆ 3120^{4} 4778^{2} 5705^{3} 6103^{6}
(7297) 7733a^{3}

Zulu Principle *John Joseph Hanlon* a69 57
4 b g Tiger Hill(IRE) —Tu Eres Mi Amore (IRE) (Sadler's Wells (USA))
6769^{6}

Zumbi (IRE) *Sir Michael Stoute* 102
2 b c Dubawi(IRE) —Star Studded (Cadeaux Genereux)
(4352) 5181^{3}

Zuzu Angel (IRE) *William Knight* a63 69
2 gr f Clodovil(IRE) —Zither (Zafonic (USA))
[illegible] 3117^{4} 3813^{6} 4824^{5} *5409^{8}*

Leading Turf Flat Trainers 2011

(30th March - 5th November 2011)

NAME	WINS-RUNS		2nd	3rd	4th	WIN £	TOTAL £	£1 STAKE
Richard Hannon	159-1109	14%	158	123	130	£2,114,304	£3,485,327	-59.93
A P O'Brien	16-81	20%	10	10	10	£1,408,506	£2,894,457	+6.42
Sir Henry Cecil	51-249	20%	37	29	32	£2,084,319	£2,730,438	-58.67
John Gosden	76-452	17%	59	71	53	£1,769,799	£2,442,259	-41.45
Mahm'd Al Zarooni	73-346	21%	46	43	38	£1,444,072	£1,829,899	+154.38
Richard Fahey	118-983	12%	109	91	116	£889,061	£1,516,925	-250.14
Sir Michael Stoute	47-330	14%	55	44	36	£555,181	£1,501,267	-121.43
Mark Johnston	125-1050	12%	114	108	93	£804,054	£1,365,628	-244.45
Kevin Ryan	88-604	15%	74	58	48	£884,799	£1,198,285	-5.09
William Haggas	69-357	19%	60	49	34	£814,920	£1,167,428	-62.19
Mick Channon	79-682	12%	78	95	77	£576,213	£1,037,688	-131.08
Andrew Balding	54-427	13%	54	47	43	£584,739	£915,584	-30.59
Tim Easterby	80-860	9%	85	94	92	£456,688	£849,414	-113.14
Saeed Bin Suroor	43-320	13%	48	37	32	£419,046	£824,714	-100.31
A Fabre	1-3	33%	1	1	0	£709,625	£749,733	+2.00
Mme C B-Barbe	1-1	100%	0	0	0	£737,230	£737,230	+12.00
David Simcock	30-258	12%	29	30	32	£527,397	£737,227	-72.21
Roger Charlton	41-201	20%	28	19	25	£280,752	£705,629	+31.86
Brian Meehan	53-455	12%	40	38	45	£339,698	£693,814	-90.24
Roger Varian	48-234	21%	33	22	29	£373,949	£680,728	+67.54
Luca Cumani	43-274	16%	43	30	20	£351,466	£661,670	-70.68
James Fanshawe	18-131	14%	26	12	12	£556,997	£630,392	+104.00
Ed Dunlop	27-262	10%	32	27	32	£150,276	£570,770	-119.01
David Nicholls	61-727	8%	61	65	53	£302,012	£565,745	-193.05
Michael Bell	35-253	14%	30	26	21	£358,330	£547,719	-67.58
Marco Botti	19-129	15%	19	16	18	£207,369	£542,514	-12.00
B W Hills	41-302	14%	43	36	25	£228,273	£539,153	-79.38
Hughie Morrison	36-238	15%	22	21	22	£426,656	£534,729	+27.30
Clive Cox	37-311	12%	28	48	34	£252,897	£501,284	-71.63
David O'Meara	40-368	11%	43	43	43	£282,569	£455,066	-127.33
John Dunlop	44-289	15%	29	26	37	£313,853	£433,927	-18.01
Tom Dascombe	30-318	9%	34	30	32	£178,210	£398,359	-86.34
David Barron	35-317	11%	36	35	36	£187,301	£394,082	-84.88
Charles Hills	15-132	11%	19	17	14	£153,549	£375,249	-23.20
Bryan Smart	43-321	13%	32	32	35	£212,736	£364,263	+25.18
Jeremy Noseda	38-175	22%	15	20	19	£223,727	£349,175	+6.76
David Elsworth	22-163	13%	16	20	15	£238,585	£347,530	+16.54
Michael Easterby	31-357	9%	29	32	34	£228,789	£315,411	-64.00
Robert Collet	1-4	25%	1	1	0	£141,925	£310,678	+5.00
Brian Ellison	30-257	12%	24	17	27	£229,166	£309,477	-45.29
J S Bolger	2-11	18%	1	1	1	£236,541	£301,051	+14.00
Henry Candy	23-206	11%	30	25	24	£132,128	£296,433	-57.03
Michael Dods	36-378	10%	45	45	37	£182,396	£292,852	-135.16
Jim Goldie	35-353	10%	35	35	47	£174,353	£289,726	-65.13
Ralph Beckett	37-278	13%	36	35	33	£124,065	£261,300	-77.04
Sir Mark Prescott	26-121	21%	14	20	13	£190,899	£261,128	-18.16
Alan McCabe	21-302	7%	28	35	23	£174,580	£260,582	-105.11
Alan Bailey	17-138	12%	9	14	22	£193,746	£247,515	-26.40
Chris Wall	17-161	11%	9	19	11	£158,170	£245,440	-45.67
Tom Tate	14-117	12%	13	12	6	£196,676	£244,731	-1.94

Leading Turf Flat Jockeys 2011

(30th March - 5th November 2011)

NAME	WIN-RIDES		2nd	3rd	4th	WIN £	TOTAL £	£1 STAKE
Paul Hanagan	142-986	14%	142	111	101	£818,651	£1,435,862	-281.87
Silv. De Sousa	127-816	16%	113	86	77	£664,431	£1,108,923	-121.63
Kieren Fallon	114-709	16%	84	86	66	£938,214	£1,755,060	-107.51
Richard Hughes	108-619	17%	90	72	60	£1,701,036	£2,566,848	+8.18
Jamie Spencer	82-500	16%	58	64	49	£1,023,722	£1,700,340	-65.74
Ryan Moore	80-451	18%	69	47	52	£992,673	£2,539,101	-143.33
William Buick	78-495	16%	59	61	53	£1,767,211	£2,409,187	-57.33
Tom Queally	75-569	13%	53	46	55	£1,815,648	£2,481,508	-149.04
Frankie Dettori	68-342	20%	52	37	36	£1,671,431	£2,209,779	+5.20
Tom Eaves	65-722	9%	70	68	76	£263,481	£447,785	-178.11
Robert Winston	62-484	13%	43	65	47	£344,194	£506,598	+43.04
Phillip Makin	60-550	11%	49	51	46	£556,757	£744,229	-180.27
Neil Callan	57-528	11%	62	66	60	£494,746	£901,643	-118.45
P J McDonald	53-499	11%	54	47	59	£178,863	£278,253	-81.65
Frederik Tylicki	51-483	11%	46	47	67	£255,535	£372,112	-40.13
Dane O'Neill	51-476	11%	64	65	57	£249,115	£503,428	-136.56
Jimmy Fortune	50-465	11%	56	40	44	£546,480	£894,813	-55.96
David Allan	49-488	10%	52	61	54	£281,027	£530,942	-126.39
Richard Hills	49-337	15%	53	43	37	£298,693	£812,358	-143.79
Jim Crowley	48-455	11%	44	46	50	£366,039	£615,294	-109.85
Graham Gibbons	48-439	11%	55	51	34	£243,337	£406,741	-30.99
Hayley Turner	48-303	16%	26	32	34	£684,257	£803,870	+19.19
Cathy Gannon	46-513	9%	67	61	53	£139,305	£292,887	-192.01
Ted Durcan	46-376	12%	32	42	40	£336,518	£534,722	-59.44
Adam Kirby	46-371	12%	38	45	33	£278,621	£512,146	+0.33
Joe Fanning	46-308	15%	28	29	32	£262,560	£376,660	+34.11
Seb Sanders	42-366	11%	47	44	41	£211,387	£376,785	-107.04
Eddie Ahern	42-364	12%	38	46	29	£497,928	£699,494	-67.80
Daniel Tudhope	42-358	12%	40	42	42	£286,812	£463,847	-47.25
David Probert	41-359	11%	34	30	42	£308,356	£473,317	-79.01
Martin Dwyer	40-376	11%	34	34	38	£282,261	£486,995	-95.72
Kieran O'Neill	40-303	13%	32	38	40	£131,560	£225,097	+0.63
Pat Dobbs	39-268	15%	30	26	35	£221,039	£319,603	-20.34
James Sullivan	38-500	8%	47	39	44	£175,948	£259,883	-178.79
Harry Bentley	37-298	12%	36	33	34	£180,984	£259,924	+12.10
James Doyle	37-295	13%	23	28	32	£115,078	£169,353	+23.63
Martin Harley	36-301	12%	38	38	33	£106,121	£192,049	-53.04
Steve Drowne	34-333	10%	37	26	37	£235,270	£558,778	-38.28
Fergus Sweeney	33-354	9%	39	41	28	£133,864	£195,359	+123.79
George Baker	33-312	11%	33	29	35	£268,986	£488,017	+15.44
Rich'd Kingscote	33-287	11%	32	30	27	£187,439	£278,944	-51.97
Luke Morris	32-507	6%	54	65	56	£152,551	£335,163	-280.80
Adrian Nicholls	32-328	10%	30	33	29	£160,223	£285,884	-73.40
Lee Newman	32-282	11%	25	21	30	£118,169	£178,883	-47.38
Ian Mongan	32-274	12%	34	32	28	£507,868	£703,479	-43.43
Sean Levey	31-265	12%	40	24	20	£106,564	£164,929	-18.22
Duran Fentiman	30-373	8%	38	25	32	£92,728	£184,477	-14.75
Martin Lane	30-360	8%	30	41	34	£121,884	£228,508	-90.10
Franny Norton	30-305	10%	36	31	31	£209,968	£335,407	+11.39
Darryll Holland	30-297	10%	19	26	38	£309,995	£442,661	-85.92

Leading Flat Owners 2011

(30th March - 5th November 2011)

NAME	WINS-RUNS		2nd	3rd	4th	WIN £	TOTAL £
K Abdulla	56-289	19%	39	35	31	£2,296,306	£3,444,757
Godolphin	116-666	17%	94	80	70	£1,863,118	£2,654,613
Hamdan Al Maktoum	86-575	15%	83	67	63	£506,355	£1,101,389
Dr Marwan Koukash	52-406	13%	42	39	33	£612,657	£913,400
D Smith, Mrs J Magnier, M Tabor	5-20	25%	2	4	1	£341,166	£874,961
Mrs J Magnier, M Tabor & D Smith	2-11	18%	0	1	2	£743,651	£828,439
Lady Rothschild	12-41	29%	4	4	8	£741,357	£804,425
Sheikh Hamdan Bin Moh'med	61-425	14%	53	36	40	£476,022	£780,234
Jean-Claude-Alain Dupouy	1-1	100%	0	0	0	£737,230	£737,230
M Tabor, D Smith & Mrs J Magnier	7-34	21%	6	3	6	£305,482	£733,952
Andrew Tinkler	25-217	12%	28	29	18	£317,791	£659,498
Smith/Magnier/Tabor/Tan/Yahaya	1-3	33%	2	0	0	£226,840	£592,420
B E Nielsen	8-41	20%	4	4	5	£370,608	£426,191
Khalifa Dasmal	3-23	13%	0	2	1	£391,687	£408,887
The Queen	13-86	15%	13	10	6	£160,989	£390,763
Mrs J Wood	15-116	13%	17	17	12	£212,223	£363,161
M J & L A Taylor	3-7	43%	1	0	1	£330,811	£340,443
H R H Princess Haya Of Jordan	17-115	15%	16	20	14	£172,117	£323,161
Mrs Angie Bailey	10-54	19%	5	2	1	£282,368	£308,846
Heffer Syndicate, Tabor & Smith	2-3	67%	1	0	0	£241,273	£305,773
Cheveley Park Stud	24-167	14%	21	27	24	£132,322	£301,043
Coupe de Ville Partnership	4-6	67%	1	0	0	£290,649	£297,533
Pearl Bloodstock Ltd	10-65	15%	4	3	11	£201,345	£288,123
Jaber Abdullah	19-176	11%	25	25	22	£107,098	£283,955
N & O Dhandsa & J & Z Webster	4-21	19%	5	3	1	£204,617	£278,367
J & P Hopper & Michelle Morris	4-5	80%	1	0	0	£260,795	£263,300
Anamoine Limited	0-7		2	1	1	£0	£256,468
Saleh Al Homaizi & Imad Al Sagar	7-39	18%	6	3	6	£209,576	£251,749
R C Strauss	1-2	50%	0	1	0	£141,925	£249,525
Mrs J S Bolger	2-6	33%	0	0	0	£236,541	£244,880
Simon Gibson	3-12	25%	1	0	1	£230,315	£237,230
Sh'kh Sultan Bin Khalifa Al Nahyan	14-71	20%	7	11	8	£88,928	£226,964
J C Smith	12-123	10%	14	14	16	£130,702	£220,924
Manfredini, Tabor, Smith & Magnier	0-1		1	0	0	£0	£215,000
Mrs John Magnier	1-3	33%	0	0	1	£207,294	£212,664
John Manley	5-12	42%	1	1	2	£156,955	£208,963
Dasmal, Rix, Barr, Morley, Penney	1-4	25%	0	2	0	£170,310	£208,538
T Redman And P Philipps	3-6	50%	0	1	2	£195,805	£202,678
Normandie Stud Ltd	7-31	23%	7	2	4	£124,992	£199,195
Saeed Manana	12-179	7%	15	17	10	£107,270	£193,043
Iraj Parvizi	3-27	11%	4	5	1	£62,186	£181,661
George Strawbridge	13-54	24%	4	5	9	£114,632	£181,475
Owen Promotions Limited	3-9	33%	4	0	0	£50,191	£178,629
Lordship Stud	8-36	22%	6	5	3	£94,859	£168,668
P A Byrne	3-17	18%	3	2	1	£148,341	£164,993
H R H Sultan Ahmad Shah	11-42	26%	4	6	3	£61,891	£163,458
Mrs H Steel	7-69	10%	7	6	10	£71,082	£162,965
John Stocker	6-32	19%	4	4	2	£137,569	£162,767
A D Spence	9-98	9%	9	17	13	£66,452	£161,658
Charles Wentworth	6-37	16%	4	6	2	£130,831	£159,683

Leading All-Weather Flat Jockeys

(7th Nov 2010 - 29th March 2011)

NAME	WIN-RIDES		2nd	3rd	4th	WIN £	TOTAL £	£1 STAKE
Luke Morris	53-459	12%	56	57	53	£116,821	£177,915	+53.02
George Baker	47-277	17%	43	26	27	£106,236	£145,881	-17.13
Adam Kirby	39-235	17%	23	30	34	£99,201	£144,235	-1.13
Graham Gibbons	37-233	16%	27	33	28	£104,038	£137,891	-26.11
James Doyle	34-224	15%	41	25	29	£71,968	£109,570	+81.79
Dane O'Neill	33-259	13%	33	34	35	£68,115	£126,518	-124.66
Hayley Turner	33-247	13%	45	26	28	£64,595	£101,388	-65.58
Cathy Gannon	31-307	10%	35	37	44	£67,174	£102,953	-4.78
Joe Fanning	31-188	16%	38	17	25	£81,283	£120,340	+5.71
Jimmy Quinn	30-262	11%	27	34	41	£77,289	£108,097	-70.61
Shane Kelly	29-194	15%	34	21	24	£59,065	£95,705	-6.20
Phillip Makin	29-148	20%	16	21	24	£70,337	£90,871	-3.20
Neil Callan	28-109	26%	17	15	6	£74,543	£94,576	+61.02
Eddie Ahern	24-167	14%	21	25	20	£48,314	£76,438	-29.32
Tom Eaves	22-211	10%	26	29	24	£46,248	£74,453	-34.13
David Probert	22-185	12%	18	19	29	£46,050	£68,572	-54.50
Ian Mongan	22-168	13%	17	25	16	£47,819	£80,295	+61.82
Barry McHugh	22-121	18%	12	10	16	£43,135	£55,412	+11.06
Chris Catlin	21-303	7%	32	30	35	£62,874	£101,669	-195.23
Jamie Spencer	21-135	16%	24	25	16	£57,485	£88,271	-39.63
Rich'd Kingscote	21-134	16%	13	21	17	£40,038	£55,089	+6.79
Andrea Atzeni	20-137	15%	14	24	18	£35,304	£57,348	-68.47
Kieren Fox	19-200	10%	30	22	24	£43,234	£70,387	-90.28
Stevie Donohoe	19-130	15%	16	13	10	£44,437	£58,757	+6.41
William Carson	18-168	11%	17	12	17	£33,678	£51,435	-43.42
Fergus Sweeney	18-160	11%	17	15	27	£39,128	£55,722	-55.28
Steve Drowne	18-155	12%	12	12	15	£60,380	£86,601	-31.89
Jack Mitchell	18-84	21%	7	10	9	£40,718	£50,459	+7.44
Greg Fairley	17-97	18%	14	13	10	£43,279	£60,628	-31.02
Franny Norton	16-152	11%	24	19	14	£37,721	£59,927	-29.30
Jim Crowley	16-125	13%	13	15	16	£40,499	£60,694	-32.94
Billy Cray	15-90	17%	12	4	11	£27,733	£36,993	+34.24
Martin Lane	14-137	10%	14	21	12	£26,603	£42,775	-60.89
Ryan Clark	14-83	17%	6	13	10	£28,264	£35,065	+21.85
Matthew Davies	14-69	20%	7	6	12	£23,251	£32,921	-4.52
Liam Keniry	13-138	9%	14	16	16	£21,964	£34,612	-43.25
J-P Guillambert	13-110	12%	19	14	10	£40,650	£55,439	-29.50
Matt Cosham	13-102	13%	9	23	17	£23,695	£34,887	-49.90
Kirsty Milczarek	12-110	11%	9	11	14	£38,850	£49,213	-23.50
Liam Jones	12-91	13%	11	13	7	£34,769	£48,538	-5.75
Robert Havlin	12-83	14%	10	5	13	£22,222	£31,179	+27.16
Andr'w Heffernan	11-152	7%	19	24	12	£24,388	£40,867	-81.21
Robert Winston	11-121	9%	17	18	12	£21,472	£38,684	-66.75
Adam Carter	11-49	22%	8	7	3	£22,961	£29,982	+15.87
Nicky Mackay	10-96	10%	15	10	10	£19,696	£31,281	-17.46
Kieren Fallon	10-40	25%	7	7	2	£32,896	£58,301	-0.75
James Sullivan	9-149	6%	20	22	23	£25,135	£48,449	-58.25

Leading All-Weather Trainers

(7th Nov 2010 - 29th March 2011)

NAME	WINS-RUNS		2nd	3rd	4th	WIN £	TOTAL £	£1 STAKE
Mark Johnston	33-156	21%	27	24	17	£87,006	£124,480	-34.23
David Nicholls	29-168	17%	30	16	24	£76,142	£123,047	+26.99
Richard Fahey	32-200	16%	22	25	23	£73,043	£106,096	+20.91
Kevin Ryan	32-145	22%	26	17	16	£78,903	£104,777	+20.01
David Evans	29-272	11%	36	45	35	£62,734	£100,210	-96.12
Richard Hannon	21-107	20%	21	15	8	£62,497	£90,281	-8.50
Alan Bailey	19-98	19%	14	21	7	£61,796	£88,449	+10.35
Alan McCabe	21-231	9%	38	33	34	£50,460	£87,022	-51.40
David Barron	14-53	26%	6	12	5	£66,328	£80,556	+30.10
Jane Ch-Hyam	19-142	13%	18	24	18	£53,196	£78,715	-44.59
Clive Brittain	3-9	33%	3	1	2	£54,536	£70,692	+2.58
Jeremy Gask	11-73	15%	8	9	5	£47,207	£66,498	-8.70
Marco Botti	15-75	20%	12	8	11	£44,519	£66,303	-17.84
Ronald Harris	23-217	11%	22	36	29	£40,293	£65,754	-6.98
Bryan Smart	22-119	18%	19	20	12	£46,779	£64,378	+20.25
Tony Carroll	19-182	10%	26	18	20	£35,111	£57,465	-40.60
Conor Dore	18-138	13%	21	19	17	£32,865	£51,929	-55.38
Julia Feilden	9-61	15%	6	6	9	£44,290	£49,899	+23.75
Jim Boyle	19-130	15%	12	19	11	£32,692	£49,394	-46.94
Gerard Butler	6-29	21%	5	3	4	£29,585	£48,626	+18.25
Andrew Balding	14-67	21%	8	8	16	£37,258	£48,512	-3.00
Mark Brisbourne	21-110	19%	15	15	15	£35,405	£46,993	+11.38
Brian Ellison	14-92	15%	21	19	13	£25,963	£46,408	-35.50
James Given	8-124	6%	12	18	17	£26,586	£42,722	-43.83
Gary Moore	15-111	14%	13	12	10	£28,644	£42,368	-47.22
Luca Cumani	4-18	22%	5	3	0	£29,786	£41,427	+1.13
Sylvester Kirk	13-96	14%	17	8	11	£28,822	£41,361	-13.82
David Simcock	11-66	17%	13	8	5	£28,523	£41,023	-2.15
Clive Cox	5-24	21%	3	3	3	£26,903	£40,808	-0.45
Richard Guest	12-117	10%	18	20	15	£24,611	£40,455	-44.25
J R Jenkins	12-103	12%	17	13	13	£24,830	£40,341	-25.01
Brian Baugh	14-87	16%	14	12	11	£26,600	£39,736	-1.50
Ian Williams	18-72	25%	10	6	8	£31,420	£39,146	+52.46
John Ryan	9-36	25%	1	3	6	£36,636	£38,598	+21.33
Jeremy Noseda	13-45	29%	8	7	2	£29,876	£37,360	+7.22
J S Moore	13-77	17%	20	10	8	£21,104	£35,017	+2.35
Paul D'Arcy	6-42	14%	7	6	7	£24,021	£33,919	-6.38
Simon Dow	8-55	15%	11	7	4	£21,450	£30,699	-17.15
Tom Dascombe	13-57	23%	5	12	4	£22,965	£30,359	+2.29
Reg Hollinshead	7-68	10%	9	6	11	£18,995	£30,187	-38.50
Bill Turner	12-58	21%	9	10	5	£22,005	£30,030	+25.30
Stuart Williams	12-68	18%	8	3	10	£24,244	£29,682	-19.67
Derek Shaw	9-127	7%	9	12	13	£20,560	£29,520	+24.50
George Baker	15-66	23%	9	1	10	£24,206	£29,093	+2.92
Robert Cowell	7-52	13%	5	2	11	£19,806	£27,345	+4.69
Hughie Morrison	5-38	13%	13	4	2	£12,977	£26,912	-26.66
John Best	8-84	10%	7	8	6	£17,785	£25,453	-7.25
Mark Usher	10-87	11%	14	6	11	£15,593	£24,750	-37.88

Racing Post top rated 2011

(Best performance figures recorded between 1st January and 31st December 2011)

Frankel	139
Black Caviar (AUS)	133
Cirrus Des Aigles (FR)	130
Canford Cliffs (IRE)	130
Rewilding	130
So You Think (NZ)	129
Excelebration (IRE)	129
Dream Ahead (USA)	129
Wise Dan (USA)	129
The Factor (USA)	129
Workforce	128
Danedream (GER)	128
Americain (USA)	127
Rocket Man (AUS)	127
Hay List (AUS)	127
Caleb s Posse (USA)	127
Uncle Mo (USA)	127
Sepoy (AUS)	127
Twice Over	126
Goldikova (IRE)	126
Whobegotyou (AUS)	126
Tosen Jordan (JPN)	126
Smiling Tiger (USA)	126
Nathaniel (IRE)	126
Strong Suit (USA)	126
Drosselmeyer (USA)	126
Sea Moon	126
Animal Kingdom (USA)	126
Orfevre (JPN)	126
Big Drama (USA)	125
J J The Jet Plane (SAF)	125
Await The Dawn (USA)	125
Flat Out (USA)	125
Deacon Blues	125
Shocking (AUS)	125
Snow Fairy (IRE)	125
Behkabad (FR)	125
Tizway (USA)	125
Acclamation (USA)	125
Sarafina (FR)	125
Hiruno D Amour (JPN)	125
Havre De Grace (USA)	125
Twirling Candy (USA)	125
Ambitious Dragon (NZ)	125
Sacred Kingdom (AUS)	124
Oken Bruce Lee (JPN)	124
More Joyous (NZ)	124
Earnestly (JPN)	124
St Nicholas Abbey (IRE)	124
Hoof It	124
Planteur (IRE)	124
Rose Kingdom (JPN)	124
Victoire Pisa (JPN)	124
Jimmy Choux (NZ)	124
To The Glory (JPN)	124
Masked Marvel	124
Atlantic Jewel (AUS)	124
Able One (NZ)	123
Presvis	123
Famous Name	123
Court Vision (USA)	123
Mufhasa (NZ)	123
Smart Falcon (JPN)	123
Midday	123
Cityscape	123
Jaguar Mail (JPN)	123
Heart Of Dreams (AUS)	123
Love Conquers All (AUS)	123
Dick Turpin (IRE)	123
Descarado (NZ)	123
Reliable Man	123
Eishin Apollon (USA)	123
Game On Dude (USA)	123
Rulership (JPN)	123
Worthadd (IRE)	123
Trappe Shot (USA)	123
Immortal Verse (IRE)	123
Dark Shadow (JPN)	123
Meandre (FR)	123
Pour Moi (IRE)	123
To Honor And Serve (USA)	123
Turallure (USA)	123
Ruler On Ice (USA)	123
Beaten Up	123
Royal Delta (USA)	123
Coil (USA)	123
Danleigh (AUS)	122
Hold It Harvey (AUS)	122
Dao Dao (AUS)	122
Mighty High (FR)	122
Buena Vista (JPN)	122
Cape Blanco (IRE)	122
Fifth Petal (JPN)	122
California Memory (USA)	122
Byword	122
Jackson Bend (USA)	122
Bated Breath	122
Awesome Maria (USA)	122

Raceform median times 2011

ASCOT

5f	1m 1.2
5f 110y	1m 07.8
6f	1m 14.4
6f 110y	1m 20.8
7f	1m 27.2
1m Str	1m 40.6
1m Rnd	1m 40.7
1m 2f	2m 7.0
1m 4f	2m 32.5
2m	3m 29.0
2m 4f	4m 24.8
2m 5f 159y	4m 49.4

AYR

5f	59.4s
6f	1m 12.4
7f 50y	1m 33.4
1m	1m 43.8
1m 1f 20y	1m 57.5
1m 2f	2m 12.0
1m 5f 13y	2m 54.0
1m 7f	3m 20.4
2m 1f 105y	4m 0.5

BATH

5f 11y	1m 2.5
5f 161y	1m 11.2
1m 5y	1m 40.8
1m 2f 46y	2m 11.0
1m 3f 144y	2m 30.6
1m 5f 22y	2m 52.0
2m 1f 34y	3m 51.9

BEVERLEY

5f	1m 3.5
7f 100y	1m 33.8
1m 100y	1m 47.6
1m 1f 207y	2m 7.0
1m 4f 16y	2m 39.8
2m 35y	3m 39.8

BRIGHTON

5f 59y	1m 2.3
5f 213y	1m 10.2
6f 209y	1m 23.1
7f 214y	1m 36.0
1m 1f 209y	2m 3.6
1m 3f 196y	2m 32.7

CARLISLE

5f	1m 0.8
5f 193y	1m 13.7
6f 192y	1m 27.1
7f 200y	1m 40.0
1m 1f 61y	1m 57.6
1m 3f 107y	2m 23.1
1m 6f 32y	3m 7.5
2m 1f 52y	3m 53.0

CATTERICK

5f	59.8s
5f 212y	1m 13.6
7f	1m 27.0
1m 3f 214y	2m 38.9
1m 5f 175y	3m 3.6
1m 7f 177y	3m 32.0

CHEPSTOW

5f 16y	59.3s
6f 16y	1m 12.0
7f 16y	1m 23.2
1m 14y	1m 36.2
1m 2f 36y	2m 10.6
1m 4f 23y	2m 39.0
2m 49y	3m 38.9
2m 2f	4m 3.6

CHESTER

5f 16y	1m 1.0
6f 18y	1m 13.8
7f 2y	1m 26.5
7f 122y	1m 33.8
1m 2f 75y	2m 11.2
1m 3f 79y	2m 24.8
1m 4f 66y	2m 38.5
1m 5f 89y	2m 52.8
1m 7f 195y	3m 28.0
2m 2f 147y	4m 4.8

DONCASTER

5f	1m 0.5
5f 140y	1m 8.8
6f	1m 13.6
6f 110y	1m 19.9
7f	1m 26.3
1m Str	1m 39.3
1m Rnd	1m 39.7
1m 2f 60y	2m 9.4
1m 4f	2m 34.9
1m 6f 132y	3m 7.4
2m 110y	3m 40.4
2m 2f	3m 55.0

EPSOM

5f	55.7s
6f	1m 9.4
7f	1m 23.3
1m 114y	1m 46.1
1m 2f 18y	2m 9.7
1m 4f 10y	2m 38.9

FFOS LAS

5f	58.3s
6f	1m 10.0
1m	1m 41.0
1m 2f	2m 9.4
1m 4f	2m 37.4
1m 6f	3m 3.8
2m	3m 30.0

FOLKESTONE

5f	1m
6f	1m 12.7
7f	1m 27.3
1m 1f 149y	2m 4.9
1m 4f	2m 40.9
1m 7f 92y	3m 29.7
2m 93y	3m 37.2

GOODWOOD

5f	58.4s
6f	1m 12.2
7f	1m 26.9
1m	1m 39.9
1m 1f	1m 56.3
1m 1f 192y	2m 8.0
1m 3f	2m 26.5
1m 4f	2m 38.4
1m 6f	3m 3.6
2m	3m 29.0
2m 5f	4m 31.0

HAMILTON

5f 4y	1m
6f 5y	1m 12.2
1m 65y	1m 48.4
1m 1f 36y	1m 59.7
1m 3f 16y	2m 25.6
1m 4f 17y	2m 38.6
1m 5f 9y	2m 53.9

HAYDOCK

5f (inner)	1m 0.8
5f (outer)	1m 0.8
6f (inner)	1m 13.8
6f (outer)	1m 13.8
7f 30y	1m 32.7
1m 30y	1m 44.7
1m 2f 120y	2m 16.7
1m 3f 200y	2m 34.0
1m 6f	3m 1.2
2m 45y	3m 36.0

KEMPTON AW

5f	1m 0.5
6f	1m 13.1
7f	1m 26.0
1m	1m 39.8
1m 1f	1m 55.8
1m 2f	2m 8.0
1m 3f	2m 21.9
1m 4f	2m 34.5
2m	3m 30.1

LEICESTER

5f 2y	1m
5f 218y	1m 13.0
7f 9y	1m 26.2
1m 60y	1m 45.1
1m 1f 218y	2m 7.9
1m 3f 183y	2m 33.9

LINGFIELD TURF

5f	58.2s
6f	1m 11.2
7f	1m 23.3
7f 140y	1m 32.3
1m 1f	1m 56.6
1m 2f	2m 10.5
1m 3f 106y	2m 31.5
1m 6f	3m 10.0
2m	3m 34.8

LINGFIELD AW

5f	58.8s
6f	1m 11.9
7f	1m 24.8
1m	1m 38.2
1m 2f	2m 6.6
1m 4f	2m 33.0
1m 5f	2m 46.0
2m	3m 25.7

MUSSELBURGH

5f	1m 0.4
7f 30y	1m 29.0
1m	1m 41.2
1m 1f	1m 53.9
1m 4f	2m 39.7
1m 4f 100y	2m 42.0
1m 5f	2m 52.0
1m 6f	3m 5.3
2m	3m 33.5

NEWBURY

5f 34y	1m 1.4
6f 8y	1m 13.0
6f 110y	1m 19.3
7f	1m 25.7
1m	1m 39.7
1m 1f	1m 55.5
1m 2f 6y	2m 8.8
1m 3f 5y	2m 21.2
1m 4f 5y	2m 35.5
1m 5f 61y	2m 52.0
2m	3m 32.0

NEWCASTLE

5f	1m 1.1
6f	1m 14.6
7f	1m 27.8
1m Rnd	1m 45.3
1m 3y Str	1m 43.4
1m 1f 9y	1m 58.1
1m 2f 32y	2m 11.9
1m 4f 93y	2m 45.6
1m 6f 97y	3m 11.3
2m 19y	3m 39.4

NEWMARKET ROWLEY

5f 59.1s
6f 1m 12.2
7f 1m 25.4
1m 1m 38.6
1m 1f 1m 51.7
1m 2f 2m 5.8
1m 4f 2m 32.0
1m 6f 2m 57.0
2m 3m 30.5
2m 2f 3m 56.8

NEWMARKET JULY

5f 59.1s
6f 1m 12.5
7f 1m 25.7
1m 1m 40.0
1m 2f 2m 5.5
1m 4f 2m 32.9
1m5f 2m 44.0
1m 6f 175y...................3m 8.4
2m 24y.........................3m 27.0

NOTTINGHAM

5f 13y..........................1m 1.0
6f 15y..........................1m 14.9
1m 54y.........................1m 45.6
1m 1f 213y...................2m 10.7
1m 6f 15y.....................3m 7.3
2m 9y...........................3m 30.3

PONTEFRACT

5f 1m 3.3
6f 1m 16.9
1m 4y...........................1m 45.9
1m 2f 6y.......................2m 13.7
1m 4f 8y.......................2m 40.8
2m 1f 22y.....................3m 44.6
2m 1f 216y...................3m 56.2
2m 5f 122y...................4m 51.0

REDCAR

5f 58.6s
6f 1m 11.8
7f 1m 24.5
1m 1m 38.0
1m 1f 1m 53.0
1m 2f 2m 7.1
1m 3f 2m 21.7
1m 6f 19y.....................3m 4.7
2m 4y...........................3m 31.4

RIPON

5f 1m 0.7
6f 1m 13.0
1m 1m 41.4
1m 1f 1m 54.7
1m 1f 170y...................2m 5.4
1m 4f 10y.....................2m 36.7
2m 3m 31.8

SALISBURY

5f 1m 1.0
6f 1m 14.8
6f 212y.........................1m 28.6
1m 1m 43.5
1m 1f 198y...................2m 9.9
1m 4f 2m 38.0
1m 6f 21y.....................3m 7.4

SANDOWN

5f 6y............................1m 1.6
7f 16y..........................1m 29.5
1m 14y.........................1m 43.3
1m 1f 1m 55.7
1m 2f 7y.......................2m 10.5
1m 6f 3m 4.5
2m 78y.........................3m 38.7

SOUTHWELL AW

5f 59.7s
6f 1m 16.5
7f 1m 30.3
1m 1m 43.7
1m 3f 2m 28.0
1m 4f 2m 41.0
1m 6f 3m 8.3
2m 3m 45.5

THIRSK

5f 59.6s
6f 1m 12.7
7f 1m 27.2
1m 1m 40.1
1m 4f 2m 36.2
2m 3m 28.3

WARWICK

5f 59.6s
5f 110y........................1m 5.9
6f 1m 11.8
7f 26y..........................1m 24.6
1m 22y.........................1m 41.0
1m 2f 188y...................2m 21.1
1m 4f 134y...................2m 44.6
1m 6f 213y...................3m 19.0
2m 39y.........................3m 33.8

WINDSOR

5f 10y..........................1m 0.3
6f 1m 13.0
1m 67y.........................1m 44.7
1m 2f 7y.......................2m 8.7
1m 3f 135y...................2m 29.5

WOLVERHAMPTON AW

5f 20y..........................1m 2.3
5f 216y........................1m 15.0
7f 32y..........................1m 29.6
1m 141y.......................1m 50.5
1m 1f 103y...................2m 1.7
1m 4f 50y.....................2m 41.1
1m 5f 194y...................3m 6.0
2m 119y.......................3m 41.8

YARMOUTH

5f 43y..........................1m 2.7
6f 3y............................1m 14.4
7f 3y............................1m 26.6
1m 3y...........................1m 40.6
1m 2f 21y.....................2m 10.5
1m 3f 101y...................2m 28.7
1m 6f 17y.....................3m 7.6
2m 3m 32.4

YORK

5f 59.3s
5f 89y..........................1m 4.1
6f 1m 11.9
7f 1m 25.3
1m 1m 38.8
1m 208y.......................1m 52.0
1m 2f 88y.....................2m 12.5
1m 4f 2m 33.2
1m 6f 3m 0.2
2m 88y.........................3m 34.5
2m 2f 3m 58.2

Raceform Flat record times

ASCOT

Distance	Time	Age	Weight	Going	Horse	Date
5f	59.17 sec	2	8-12	Gd To Firm	Maqaasid	Jun 16 2010
5f	57.44 sec	6	9-1	Gd To Firm	Miss Andretti (AUS)	Jun 19 2007
6f	1m 12.46	2	9-1	Gd To Firm	Henrythenavigator(USA)	Jun 19 2007
6f	1m 12.27	2	8-11	Gd To Firm	LaddiesPoker Two (IRE)	Jun 19 2010
7f	1m 26.76	2	7-12	Gd To Firm	Relative Order	Aug 11 2007
7f	1m 24.94	3	8-12	Gd To Firm	Rainfall (IRE)	Jun 16 2010
1m (R)	1m 39.55	2	8-12	Good	Joshua Tree (IRE)	Sep 26 2009
1m (R)	1m 38.32	3	9-0	Gd To Firm	Ghanaati (USA)	Jun 19 2009
1m (S)	1m 37.16	4	8-9	Gd To Firm	Invisible Man	Jun 16 2010
1m 2f	2m 2.52	5	9-3	Good	Cirrus Des Aigles(FR)	Oct 15 2011
1m 4f	2m 26.78	4	9-7	Good	Harbinger	Jul 24 2010
2m	3m 24.13	3	9-1	Gd To Firm	Holberg (UAE)	Sept 16 2009
2m 4f	4m 16.92	6	9-2	Gd To Firm	Rite Of Passage	Jun 17 2010
2m 5f 159y	4m 47.90	7	9-2	Gd To Firm	Bergo (GER)	Jun 19 2010

AYR

Distance	Time	Age	Weight	Going	Horse	Date
5f	56.9 secs	2	8-11	Good	Boogie Street	Sep 18 2003
5f	55.68 secs	3	8-11	Gd to Firm	Look Busy (IRE)	Jun 21 2008
6f	69.7 secs	2	7-10	Good	Sir Bert	Sep 17 1969
6f	68.37 secs	5	8-6	Gd to Firm	Maison Dieu	Jun 21 2008
7f	1m 25.7	2	9-0	Gd to Firm	Jazeel	Sep 16 1993
7f	1m 24.9	5	7-11	Firm	Sir Arthur Hobbs	Jun 19 1992
7f 50y	1m 28.9	2	9-0	Good	Tafaahum (USA)	Sep 19 2003
7f 50y	1m 28.2	4	9-2	Gd to Firm	Flur Na H Alba	Jun 21 2003
1m	1m 39.2	2	9-0	Gd to Firm	Kribensis	Sep 17 1986
1m	1m 36.0	4	7-13	Firm	Sufi	Sep 16 1959
1m 1f 20y	1m 50.3	4	9-3	Good	Retirement	Sep 19 2003
1m 2f	2m 4.0	4	9-9	Gd to Firm	Endless Hall	Jly 17 2000
1m 2f192y	2m 13.3	4	9-0	Gd to Firm	Azzaam	Sep 18 1991
1m 5f 13y	2m 45.8	4	9-7	Gd to Firm	Eden s Close	Sep 18 1993
1m 7f	3m 13.1	3	9-4	Good	Romany Rye	Sep 19 1991
2m 1f105y	3m 45.0	4	6-13	Good	Curry	Sep 16 1955

BATH

Distance	Time	Age	Weight	Going	Horse	Date
5f 11y	59.50 secs	2	9-2	Firm	Amour Propre	Jly 24 2008
5f 11y	58.75 secs	3	8-12	Firm	Enticing (IRE)	May 1 2007
5f 161y	68.70 secs	2	8-12	Firm	Qalahari (IRE)	Jly 24 2008
5f 161y	68.1 secs	6	9-0	Firm	Madraco	May 22 1989
1m 5y	1m 39.7	2	8-9	Firm	Casual Look	Sep 16 2002
1m 5y	1m 37.2	5	8-12	Gd to Firm	Adobe	Jun 17 2000
1m 5y	1m 37.2	3	8-7	Firm	Alasha (IRE)	Aug 18 2002
1m 2f 46y	2m 5.8	3	9-0	Gd to Firm	Connoisseur Bay(USA)	May 29 1998
1m 3f144y	2m 25.74	3	9-0	Hard	Top Of The Charts	Sep 8 2005
1m 5f 22y	2m 47.2	4	10-0	Firm	Flown	Aug 13 1991
2m 1f 34y	3m 43.4	6	7-9	Firm	Yaheska (IRE)	Jun 14 2003

BEVERLEY

Distance	Time	Age	Weight	Going	Horse	Date
5f	61.0 secs	2	8-2	Gd to Firm	Addo (IRE)	Jly 17 2001
5f	60.1 secs	4	9-5	Firm	Pic Up Sticks	Apr 16 2003
7f 100y	1m 31.1	2	9-7	Gd to Firm	Champagne Prince	Aug 10 1995
7f 100y	1m 31.1	2	9-0	Firm	Majal (IRE)	Jly 30 1991
7f 100y	1m 29.5	3	7-8	Firm	Who s Tef	Jly 30 1991
1m 100y	1m 43.3	2	9-0	Firm	Arden	Sep 24 1986
1m 100y	1m 42.2	3	8-4	Firm	Legal Case	Jun 14 1989
1m 1f 207y	2m 1.00	3	9-7	Gd to Firm	Eastern Aria (UAE)	Aug 29 2009
1m 3f 216y	2m 30.8	3	8-1	Hard	Coinage	Jun 18 1986
1m 4f 16y	2m 34.88	6	10-0	Firm	WeeCharlieCastle(IRE)	Aug 30 2009
2m 35y	3m 29.5	4	9-2	Gd to Firm	Rushen Raider	Aug 14 1996

BRIGHTON

Distance	Time	Age	Weight	Going	Horse	Date
5f 59y	60.1 secs	2	9-0	Firm	Bid for Blue	May 6 1993
5f 59y	59.3 secs	3	8-9	Firm	Play Hever Golf	May 26 1993
5f 213y	68.1 secs	2	8-9	Firm	Song Mist (IRE)	Jly 16 1996
5f 213y	67.3 secs	3	8-9	Firm	Third Party	Jun 3 1997
5f 213y	67.3 secs	5	9-1	Gd to Firm	Blundell Lane	May 4 2000
6f 209y	1m 19.9	2	8-11	Hard	Rain Burst	Sep 15 1988
6f 209y	1m 19.4	4	9-3	Gd to Firm	Sawaki	Sep 3 1991
7f 214y	1m 32.8	2	9-7	Firm	Asian Pete	Oct 3 1989
7f 214y	1m 30.5	5	8-11	Firm	Mystic Ridge	May 27 1999
1m 1f 209y	2m 4.7	2	9-0	Gd to Soft	Esteemed Master	Nov 2 2001
1m 1f 209y	1m 57.2	3	9-0	Firm	Get The Message	Apr 30 1984
1m 3f 196y	2m 25.8	4	8-2	Firm	New Zealand	Jly 4 1985

CARLISLE

Distance	Time	Age	Weight	Going	Horse	Date
5f	60.1 secs	2	8-5	Firm	La Tortuga	Aug 2 1999
5f	58.8 secs	3	9-8	Gd to Firm	Esatto	Aug 21 2002
5f 193y	1m 12.45	2	9-6	Gd to Firm	Musical Guest (IRE)	Sep 11 2005
5f 193y	1m 10.83	4	9-0	Gd to Firm	Bo McGinty (IRE)	Sep 11 2005
6f 192y	1m 24.3	3	8-9	Gd to Firm	Marjurita (IRE)	Aug 21 2002
6f 206y	1m 26.5	2	9-4	Hard	Sense of Priority	Sep 10 1991
6f 206y	1m 25.3	4	9-1	Firm	Move With Edes	Jly 6 1996
7f 200y	1m 37.34	5	9-7	Gd to Firm	Hula Ballew	Aug 17 2005
7f 214y	1m 44.6	2	8-8	Firm	Blue Garter	Sep 9 1980
7f 214y	1m 37.3	5	7-12	Hard	Thatched (IRE)	Aug 21 1995
1m 1f 61y	1m 53.8	3	9-0	Firm	Little Jimbob	Jun 14 2004
1m 3f 107y	2m 22.25	5	9-6	Gd to Firm	Overrule (USA)	Jun 24 2009
1m 4f	2m 28.8	3	8-5	Firm	Desert Frolic (IRE)	Jun 27 1996
1m 6f 32y	3m 2.2	6	8-10	Firm	Explosive Speed	May 26 1994
2m 1f 52y	3m 46.2	3	7-10	Gd to Firm	Warring Kingdom	Aug 25 1999

CATTERICK

Distance	Time	Age	Weight	Going	Horse	Date
5f	57.6 secs	2	9-0	Firm	H Harrison	Oct 8 2002
5f	57.1 secs	4	8-7	Fast	Kabcast	Jly 7 1989
5f 212y	1m 11.4	2	9-4	Firm	Captain Nick	Jly 11 1978
5f 212y	69.8 secs	9	8-13	Gd to Firm	Sharp Hat	May 30 2003
7f	1m 24.1	2	8-11	Firm	Lindas Fantasy	Sep 18 1982
7f	1m 22.5	6	8-7	Firm	Differential (USA)	May 31 2003
1m 3f 214y	2m 30.5	3	8-8	Gd to Firm	Rahaf	May 30 2003
1m 5f 175y	2m 54.8	3	8-5	Firm	Geryon	May 31 1984
1m 7f 177y	3m 20.8	4	7-11	Firm	Bean Boy	Jly 8 1982

CHEPSTOW

Distance	Time	Age	Weight	Going	Horse	Date
5f 16y	57.6 secs	2	8-11	Firm	Micro Love	Jly 8 1986
5f 16y	56.8 secs	3	8-4	Firm	Torbay Express	Sep 15 1979
6f 16y	69.4 secs	2	9-0	Fast	Royal Fifi	Sep 9 1989
6f 16y	68.1 secs	3	9-7	Firm	America Calling (USA)	Sep 18 2001
7f 16y	1m 20.8	2	9-0	Gd to Firm	Royal Amaretto (IRE)	Sep 12 1996
7f 16y	1m 19.3	3	9-0	Firm	Taranaki	Sep 18 2001
1m 14y	1m 33.1	2	8-11	Gd to Firm	Ski Academy (IRE)	Aug 28 1995
1m 14y	1m 31.6	3	8-13	Firm	Stoli (IRE)	Sep 18 2001
1m 2f 36y	2m 4.1	5	8-9	Hard	Leonidas	Jly 5 1983
1m 2f 36y	2m 4.1	5	7-8	Gd to Firm	It s Varadan	Sep 9 1989
1m 2f 36y	2m 4.1	3	8-5	Gd to Firm	Ela Athena	Jly 23 1999
1m 4f 23y	2m 31.0	3	8-9	Gd to Firm	Spritsail	Jly 13 1989
1m 4f 23y	2m 31.0	7	9-6	Hard	Maintop	Aug 27 1984
2m 49y	3m 27.7	4	9-0	Gd to Firm	Wizzard Artist	Jly 1 1989
2m 2f	3m 56.4	5	8-7	Gd to Firm	Laffah	Jly 8 2000

CHESTER

Distance	Time	Age	Weight	Going	Horse	Date
5f 16y	59.94 secs	2	9-2	Gd to Firm	Leiba Leiba	Jun 26 2010
5f 16y	59.2 secs	3	10-0	Firm	Althrey Don	Jly 10 1964
6f 18y	1m 12.8	2	8-10	Gd to Firm	Flying Express	Aug 31 2002
6f 18y	1m 12.7	3	8-3	Gd to Firm	Play Hever Golf	May 4 1993
6f 18y	1m 12.7	6	9-2	Good	Stack Rock	Jun 23 1993
7f 2y	1m 25.2	2	9-0	Gd to Firm	Due Respect (IRE)	Sep 25 2002
7f 2y	1m 23.75	5	8-13	Gd to Firm	Three Graces (GER)	Jly 9 2005
7f 122y	1m 32.2	2	9-0	Gd to Firm	Big Bad Bob (IRE)	Sep 25 2002
7f 122y	1m 30.91	3	8-12	Gd to Firm	Cupid's Glory	Aug 18 2005
1m 2f 75y	2m 7.15	3	8-8	Gd to Firm	Stotsfold	May 7 2002
1m 3f 79y	2m 22.17	3	8-12	Gd to Firm	Perfect Truth (IRE)	May 6 2009
1m 4f 66y	2m 33.7	3	8-10	Gd to Firm	Fight Your Corner	May 7 2002
1m 5f 89y	2m 45.4	5	8-11	Firm	Rakaposhi King	May 7 1987
1m 7f 195y	3m 20.3	4	9-0	Gd to Firm	Grand Fromage (IRE)	Jly 13 2002
2m 2f 147y	3m 58.89	7	9-2	Gd to Firm	Greenwich Meantime	May 9 2007

DONCASTER

Distance	Time	Age	Weight	Going	Horse	Date
5f	58.1 secs	2	8-11	Gd to Firm	Sand Vixen	Sep 11 2009
5f	57.2 secs	6	9-12	Gd to Firm	Celtic Mill	Sep 9 2004
5f 140y	67.2 secs	2	9-0	Gd to Firm	Cartography (IRE)	Jun 29 2003
5f 140y	65.6 secs	9	9-10	Good	Halmahera (IRE)	Sep 8 2004
6f	69.6 secs	2	8-11	Good	Caesar Beware (IRE)	Sep 8 2004
6f	69.56 secs	3	8-10	Gd to Firm	Proclaim	May 30 2009
6f 110y	1m 17.22	2	8-3	Gd to Firm	Swilly Ferry (USA)	Sep 10 2009
7f	1m 22.6	2	9-1	Good	Librettist (USA)	Sep 8 2004
7f	1m 21.6	3	8-10	Gd to Firm	Pastoral Pursuits	Sep 9 2004
1m	1m 36.5	2	8-6	Gd to Firm	Singhalese	Sep 9 2004
1m (R)	1m 35.4	2	8-10	Good	Playful Act (IRE)	Sep 9 2004
1m	1m 35.52	4	8-9	Gd to Firm	Dream Lodge	Jly 24 2008
1m (R)	1m 34.46	4	8-12	Gd to Firm	Staying On (IRE)	Apr 18 2009
1m 2f 60y	2m 13.4	2	8-8	Good	Yard Bird	Nov 6 1981
1m 2f 60y	2m 4.81	4	8-13	Gd to Firm	Red Gala	Sep 12 2007

Distance	Time	Age	Weight	Going	Horse	Date
1m 4f	2m 27.48	3	8-4	Gd to Firm	Swift Alhaarth (IRE)	Sep 10 2011
1m 6f 132y	3m 0.44	3	9-0	Gd to Firm	Masked Marvel	Sep 10 2011
2m 2f	3m 48.41	4	9-4	Gd to Firm	Septimus (IRE)	Sep 14 2007

EPSOM

Distance	Time	Age	Weight	Going	Horse	Date
5f	55.0 secs	2	8-9	Gd to Firm	Prince Aslia	Jun 9 1995
5f	53.6 secs	4	9-5	Firm	Indigenous	Jun 2 1960
6f	67.8 secs	2	8-11	Gd to Firm	Showbrook	Jun 5 1991
6f	67.21 secs	5	9-13	Gd to Firm	Mac Gille Eoin	Jul 2 2009
7f	1m 21.3	2	8-9	Gd to Firm	Red Peony	Jly 29 2004
7f	1m 20.1	4	8-7	Firm	Capistrano	Jun 7 1972
1m 114y	1m 42.8	2	8-5	Gd to Firm	Nightstalker	Aug 30 1988
1m 114y	1m 40.7	3	8-6	Gd to Firm	Sylva Honda	Jun 5 1991
1m 2f 18y	2m 3.5	5	7-13	Good	Crossbow	Jun 7 1967
1m 4f 10y	2m 31.33	3	9-0	Gd to Firm	Workforce	Jun 5 2010

FFOS LAS

Distance	Time	Age	Weight	Going	Horse	Date
5f	57.06	2	9-3	Gd To Firm	Mr Majeika (IRE)	May 5 2011
5f	56.35	5	8-8	Good	Haajes	Sep 12 2009
6f	69.93	2	9-0	Gd To Firm	Lunair Deity	Jul 28 2011
6f	67.80	8	8-4	Gd To Firm	The Jailer	May 5 2011
1m	1m 40.61	2	9-0	Gd To Firm	Sharaayeen	Sep 13 2009
1m	1m 37.12	5	9-0	Gd To Firm	Zebrano	May 5 2011
1m 2f	2m 4.85	8	8-12	Gd To Firm	Pelham Crescent (IRE)	May 5 2011
1m 4f	2m 32.61	5	9-8	Gd To Firm	Lady Of Burgundy	Jly 11 2011
1m 6f	2m 58.61	4	9-7	Gd To Firm	Lady Eclair	Jly 12 2010
2m	3m 29.86	4	9-7	Good	Black Or Red (IRE)	Jly 21 2009

FOLKESTONE

Distance	Time	Age	Weight	Going	Horse	Date
5f	58.4 secs	2	9-2	Gd to Firm	Pivotal	Nov 6 1995
5f	58.18 secs	4	8-8	Gd to Firm	Black Baccara	Apr 12 2011
6f	1m 10.8	2	8-9	Good	Boomerang Blade	Jly 16 1998
6f	69.38 secs	4	9-8	Gd to Firm	Munaddam (USA)	Sep 18 2006
6f 189y	1m 23.7	2	8-11	Good	Hen Harrier	Jly 3 1996
6f 189y	1m 21.4	3	8-9	Firm	Cielamour (USA)	Aug 9 1988
7f	1m 25.01	2	9-0	Gd to Firm	Dona Alba (IRE)	Sep 2 2007
7f	1m 23.76	3	8-11	Gd to Firm	Welsh Cake	Sep 18 2006
1m 1f 149y	1m 59.7	3	8-6	Gd to Firm	Dizzy	Jly 23 1991
1m 4f	2m 33.2	4	8-8	Hard	Snow Blizzard	Jun 30 1992
1m 7f 92y	3m 23.1	3	9-11	Firm	Mata Askari	Sep 12 1991
2m 93y	3m 34.9	3	8-12	Gd to Firm	Candle Smoke (USA)	Aug 20 1996

GOODWOOD

Distance	Time	Age	Weight	Going	Horse	Date
5f	57.5 secs	2	8-12	Gd to Firm	Poets Cove	Aug 3 1990
5f	56.0 secs	5	9-0	Gd to Firm	Rudi s Pet	Jly 27 1999
6f	69.8 secs	2	8-11	Gd to Firm	Bachir (IRE)	Jly 28 1999
6f	69.10 secs	6	9-10	Gd to Firm	Tamagin (USA)	Sep 12 2009
7f	1m 24.9	2	8-11	Gd to Firm	Ekraar	Jly 29 1999
7f	1m 23.8	3	8-7	Firm	Brief Glimpse (IRE)	Jly 25 1995
1m	1m 37.21	2	9-0	Good	Caldra (IRE)	Sep 9 2006
1m 1f	1m 56.27	2	9-3	Gd to Firm	Dordogne (IRE)	Sep 22 2010
1m	1m 35.6	3	8-13	Gd to Firm	Aljabr (USA)	Jly 28 1999
1m 1f	1m 52.8	3	9-6	Good	Vena (IRE)	Jly 27 1995
1m 1f 192y	2m 2.81	3	9-3	Gd to Firm	Road To Love (IRE)	Aug 3 2006
1m 3f	2m 23.0	3	8-8	Gd to Firm	Asian Heights	May 22 2001
1m 4f	2m 31.5	3	8-10	Firm	Presenting	Jly 25 1995
1m 6f	2m 58.05	4	9-6	Gd to Firm	Eastern Aria	Jly 29 2010
2m	3m 21.55	5	9-10	Gd to Firm	Yeats (IRE)	Aug 3 2006
2m 4f	4m 11.7	3	7-10	Firm	Lucky Moon	Aug 2 1990

GREAT LEIGHS (A.W)

Distance	Time	Age	Weight	Going	Horse	Date
5f	60.36	2	8-12	Standard	Rublevka Star (USA)	Oct 23 2008
5f	59.34	6	9-0	Standard	Almaty Express	May 28 2008
6f	1m 13.13	2	8-9	Standard	Calahonda	Nov 15 2008
6f	1m 11.52	6	9-1	Standard	Nota Bene	May 29 2008
1m	1m 39.24	2	9-0	Standard	Shampagne	Sep 27 2008
1m	1m 37.16	3	8-8	Standard	Roaring Forte (IRE)	Sep 27 2008
1m 2f	2m 5.02	4	8-12	Standard	Mutajarred	May 28 2008
1m 5f 66y	2m 48.87	5	9-7	Standard	Red Gala	Sep 27 2008
1m 6f	3m 0.73	3	9-7	Standard	Detonator	Sep 14 2008
2m	3m 28.69	4	9-1	Standard	Whaxaar (IRE)	Apr 30 2008

HAMILTON

Distance	Time	Age	Weight	Going	Horse	Date
5f 4y	57.95 secs	2	8-8	Gd to Firm	Rose Blossom	May 29 2009
5f 4y	57.95 secs	2	8-8	Gd to Firm	Rose Blossom	May 29 2009
6f 5y	1m 10.0	2	8-12	Gd to Firm	Break The Code	Aug 24 1999
6f 5y	69.3 secs	4	8-7	Firm	Marcus Game	Jly 11 1974
1m 65y	1m 45.8	2	8-11	Firm	Hopeful Subject	Sep 24 1973
1m 65y	1m 42.7	6	7-7	Firm	Cranley	Sep 25 1972
1m 1f 36y	1m 53.6	5	9-6	Gd to Firm	Regent's Secret	Aug 10 2005
1m 3f 16y	2m 19.32	3	9-0	Gd to Firm	Captain Webb	May 16 2008
1m 4f 17y	2m 30.52	5	9-10	Gd to Firm	Record Breaker (IRE)	Jun 10 2009
1m 5f 9y	2m 45.1	6	9-6	Firm	Mentalasanythin	Jun 14 1995

HAYDOCK

Distance	Time	Age	Weight	Going	Horse	Date
5f	59.2 secs	2	9-4	Firm	Money For Nothing	Aug 21 1964
5f	57.15 secs	3	8-11	Gd to firm	Fleeting Spirit (IRE)	May 24 2008
6f	1m 10.9	4	9-9	Gd to Firm	Wolfhound (USA)	Sep 4 1993
6f	69.9 secs	4	9-0	Gd to Firm	Iktamal (USA)	Sep 7 1996
7f 30y	1m 29.4	2	9-0	Gd to Firm	Apprehension	Sep 7 1996
7f 30y	1m 26.8	3	8-7	Gd to Firm	Lady Zonda	Sep 28 2002
1m 30y	1m 40.6	2	8-12	Gd to Firm	Besiege	Sep 7 1996
1m 30y	1m 40.07	3	8-2	Gd to Firm	Sagramor	May 21 2011
1m2f 95y	2m 9.95	3	8-8	Good	Jukebox Jury (IRE)	Aug 8 2009
1m 2f 120y	2m 22.2	2	8-11	Soft	Persian Haze	Oct 9 1994
1m 2f 120y	2m 8.5	3	8-7	Gd to Firm	Fahal (USA)	Aug 5 1995
1m 3f 200y	2m 26.4	5	8-2	Firm	New Member	Jly 4 1970
1m 6f	2m 58.46	3	8-10	Gd to Firm	Meshtri (IRE)	Sep 27 2008
2m 45y	3m 27.0	4	8-13	Firm	Prince of Peace	May 26 1984
2m 1f 130y	3m 55.0	3	8-12	Good	Crystal Spirit	Sep 8 1990

KEMPTON (A.W)

Distance	Time	Age	Weight	Going	Horse	Date
5f	60.29 sec	2	9-1	Standard	Inflight (IRE)	Aug 23 2006
5f	59.77 sec	5	8-7	Standard	Harry Up	Dec 10 2006
6f	1m 11.91	2	9-0	Standard	Elnawin	Sep 6 2008
6f	1m 11.11	4	9-4	Standard	Edge Closer	May 29 2008
7f	1m 25.93	2	9-0	Standard	Boscobel	Nov 22 2006
7f	1m 23.29	5	8-11	Standard	Primaeval	Nov 16 2011
1m	1m 35.73	3	8-9	Standard	Western Aristocrat(USA)	Sep15 2011
1m 2f	2m 3.77	6	8-13	Standard	Kandidate	Mar 29 2008
1m 3f	2m 16.98	5	9-6	Standard	Irish Flame (SAF)	Nov 10 2011
1m 4f	2m 29.33	4	9-3	Standard	Prince Bishop (IRE)	Nov 2 2010
2m	3m 24.70	4	10-1	Standard	Spice Fair	Oct 27 2011

LEICESTER

Distance	Time	Age	Weight	Going	Horse	Date
5f 2y	58.4 secs	2	9-0	Firm	Cutting Blade	Jun 9 1986
5f 2y	59.85 secs	5	9-5	Gd to Firm	The Jobber (IRE)	Sep 18 2006
5f 218y	1m 10.1	2	9-0	Firm	Thordis (IRE)	Oct 24 1995
5f 218y	69.12 secs	6	8-12	Gd to Firm	Peter Island (FR)	Apr 25 2009
7f 9y	1m 22.60	2	9-0	Gd to Firm	Marie De Medici (USA)	Oct 6 2009
7f 9y	1m 20.8	3	8-7	Firm	Flower Bowl	Jun 9 1986
1m 60y	1m 44.05	2	8-11	Gd to Firm	Congressional (IRE)	Sep 6 2005
1m 60y	1m 41.89	5	9-7	Gd to Firm	Vainglory	Jun 18 2009
1m 1f 218y	2m 5.3	2	9-1	Gd to Firm	Windsor Castle	Oct 14 1996
1m 1f 218y	2m 2.4	3	8-11	Firm	Effigy	Nov 4 1985
1m 1f 218y	2m 2.4	4	9-6	Gd to Firm	Lady Angharad (IRE)	Jun 18 2000
1m 3f 183y	2m 27.1	5	8-12	Gd to Firm	Murghem (IRE)	Jun 18 2000

LINGFIELD (TURF)

Distance	Time	Age	Weight	Going	Horse	Date
5f	57.07 secs	2	9-0	Gd to Firm	Quite A Thing	Jul 11 2011
5f	56.2 secs	3	9-1	Gd to Firm	Eveningperformance	Jly 25 1994
6f	68.36 secs	2	8-12	Gd to Firm	Folly Bridge	Sept 8 2009
6f	68.2 secs	6	9-10	Firm	Al Amead	Jly 2 1986
7f	1m 21.3	2	7-6	Firm	Mandav	Oct 3 1980
7f	1m 20.05	3	8-5	Gd to Firm	Perfect Tribute	May 7 2011
7f 140y	1m 28.7	2	9-3	Gd to Firm	Al Muheer	Aug 4 2007
7f 140y	1m 26.7	3	8-6	Fast	Hiaam	Nov 7 1978
1m 1f	1m 52.4	4	9-2	Gd to Firm	Quandary (USA)	Jly 15 1995
1m 2f	2m 4.6	3	9-3	Firm	Usran	Jly 15 1989
1m 3f 106y	2m 23.9	3	8-5	Firm	Night-Shirt	Jly 14 1990
1m 6f	2m 59.1	5	9-5	Firm	Ibn Bey	Jly 1 1989
2m	3m 23.7	3	9-5	Gd to Firm	Lauries Crusader	Aug 13 1988

LINGFIELD (A.W)

Distance	Time	Age	Weight	Going	Horse	Date
5f	58.46 secs	2	8-2	Standard	Ruby Tallulah	Aug 12 2008
5f	57.26 secs	8	8-12	Standard	Magic Glade	Feb 24 2007
6f	1m 10.75	2	9-4	Standard	Global City (IRE)	Oct 15 2008
6f	69.61	6	9-0	Standard	Excusez Moi (USA)	Feb 23 2008
6f	69.61	4	9-5	Standard	Jaconet (USA)	Sept 4 2009
7f	1m 23.68	2	8-4	Standard	Young Dottie	Oct 21 2008
7f	1m 22.19	4	8-7	Standard	Red Spell	Nov 19 2005
1m	1m 36.5	2	9-5	Standard	San Pier Niceto	Nov 30 1989
1m	1m 34.77	4	9-3	Standard	Baharah (USA)	Oct 30 2008
1m 2f	2m 1.79	5	9-0	Standard	Cusoon	Feb 24 2007
1m 4f	2m 28.10	3	8-10	Standard	Falcativ	Oct 27 2008
1m 5f	2m 42.47	3	9-2	Standard	Raffaas	July 3 2007
2m	3m 20.0	3	9-0	Standard	Yenoora	Aug 8 1992

MUSSELBURGH

Distance	Time	Age	Weight	Going	Horse	Date
5f	57.7 secs	2	8-2	Firm	Arasong	May 16 1994
5f	57.3 secs	3	8-12	Firm	Corunna	Jun 3 2000
7f 30y	1m 27.46	2	8-8	Good	DurhamReflection(IRE)	Sept 14 2009
7f 30y	1m 26.3	3	9-5	Firm	Waltzing Wizard	Aug 22 2002
1m	1m 40.3	2	8-12	Gd to Firm	Succession	Sep 26 2004
1m	1m 36.83	3	9-5	Gd to Firm	Ginger Jack	Jul 13 2010
1m 1f	1m 50.42	8	8-11	Gd to Firm	Dhaular Dhar	Sept 3 2010
1m 4f	2m 33.7	3	9-11	Firm	Alexandrine	Jun 26 2000
1m4f 100y	2m 36.80	3	8-3	Gd to Firm	Harris Tweed	Jun 5 2010
1m 5f	2m 47.51	6	9-11	Gd to Firm	Dimashq	Jly 31 2008
1m 6f	2m 59.2	3	9-7	Firm	Forum Chris	Jly 3 2000
2m	3m 26.6	5	9-6	Gd to Firm	Jack Dawson (IRE)	Jun 1 2002

NEWBURY

Distance	Time	Age	Weight	Going	Horse	Date
5f 34y	59.1 secs	2	8-6	Gd to Firm	Superstar Leo	Jly 22 2000
5f 34y	59.2 secs	3	9-5	Gd to Firm	The Trader (IRE)	Aug 18 2001
6f 8y	1m 11.07	2	8-4	Gd to Firm	Bahati (IRE)	May 30 2009
6f 8y	69.42 secs	3	8-11	Gd to Firm	Nota Bene	May 13 2005
7f	1m 23.0	2	8-11	Gd to Firm	Haafhd	Aug 15 2003
7f	1m 21.5	3	8-4	Gd to Firm	Three Points	Jly 21 2000
1m	1m 37.5	2	9-1	Gd to firm	Winged Cupid (IRE)	Sep 16 2005
1m	1m 33.59	6	9-0	Firm	Rakti	May 14 2005
1m 1f	1m 49.6	3	8-0	Gd to Firm	Holtye	May 21 1995
1m 2f 6y	2m 1.2	3	8-7	Gd to Firm	Wall Street (USA)	Jly 20 1996
1m 3f 5y	2m 16.5	3	8-9	Gd to Firm	Grandera (IRE)	Sep 22 2001
1m 4f 5y	2m 28.26	4	9-7	Gd to Firm	Azamour (IRE)	Jul 23 2005
1m 5f 61y	2m 44.9	5	10-0	Gd to Firm	Mystic Hill	Jly 20 1996
2m	3m 25.4	8	9-12	Gd to Firm	Moonlight Quest	Jly 19 1996

NEWCASTLE

Distance	Time	Age	Weight	Going	Horse	Date
5f	58.8 secs	2	9-0	Firm	Atlantic Viking (IRE)	Jun 4 1997
5f	58.0 secs	4	9-2	Firm	Princess Oberon	Jly 23 1994
6f	1m 11.98	2	9-3	Good	Pearl Arch (IRE)	Sep 6 2010
6f	1m 10.58	4	9-9	Gd to Firm	Jonny Mudball	Jun 26 2010
7f	1m 24.2	2	9-0	Gd to Firm	Iscan (IRE)	Aug 31 1998
7f	1m 23.3	4	9-2	Gd to Firm	Quiet Venture	Aug 31 1998
1m	1m 38.9	2	9-0	Gd to Firm	Stowaway	Oct 2 1996
1m	1m 38.9	3	8-12	Firm	Jacamar	Jly 22 1989
1m 3y	1m 37.1	2	8-3	Gd to Firm	Hoh Steamer (IRE)	Aug 31 1998
1m 3y	1m 37.3	3	8-8	Gd to Firm	Its Magic	May 27 1999
1m 1f 9y	2m 3.2	2	8-13	Soft	Response	Oct 30 1993
1m 1f 9y	1m 52.3	3	6-3	Good	Ferniehurst	Jun 23 1936
1m 2f 32y	2m 6.5	4	8-9	Fast	Missionary Ridge	Jly 29 1990
1m 4f 93y	2m 37.3	5	8-12	Firm	Retender	Jun 25 1994
1m 6f 97y	3m 6.4	3	9-6	Gd to Firm	One Off	Aug 6 2003
2m 19y	3m 24.3	4	8-10	Good	Far Cry (IRE)	Jun 26 1999

NEWMARKET (ROWLEY)

Distance	Time	Age	Weight	Going	Horse	Date
5f	[illegible]	2	[illegible]	Gd to Firm	Valiant Romeo	Oct 3 2002
5f	56.8 secs	6	9-2	Gd to Firm	Lochsong	Apr 30 1994
6f	69.56 secs	2	8-12	Gd to Firm	Bushranger (IRE)	Oct 3 2008
6f	69.56 secs	2	8-12	Gd to Firm	Bushranger (IRE)	Oct 3 2008
7f	1m 22.39	2	8-12	Gd to Firm	Ashram (IRE)	Sep 21 2004
7f	1m 22.2	4	9-5	Gd to Firm	Perfolia	Oct 17 1991
1m	1m 35.7	2	9-0	Gd to Firm	Forward Move (IRE)	Sep 21 2004
1m	1m 34.07	4	9-0	Gd to Firm	Eagle Mountain	Oct 3 2008
1m 1f	1m 47.2	4	9-5	Firm	Beauchamp Pilot	Oct 5 2002
1m 2f	2m 4.6	2	9-4	Good	Highland Chieftain	Nov 2 1985
1m 2f	2m 0.13	3	8-12	Good	New Approach (IRE)	Oct 18 2008
1m 4f	2m 27.1	5	8-12	Gd to Firm	Eastern Breeze	Oct 3 2003
1m 6f	2m 51.59	3	8-7	Good	Art Eyes (USA)	Sep 29 2005
2m	3m 18.64	5	9-6	Gd to Firm	Times Up	Sep 22 2011
2m 2f	3m 47.5	3	7-12	Hard	Whiteway	Oct 15 1947

NEWMARKET (JULY)

Distance	Time	Age	Weight	Going	Horse	Date
5f	58.5 secs	2	8-10	Good	Seductress	Jly 10 1990
5f	56.09 secs	6	9-11	Good	Borderlescott	Aug 22 2008
6f	1m 10.35	2	8-11	Good	Elnawin	Aug 22 2008
6f	69.5 secs	3	8-13	Gd to Firm	Stravinsky (USA)	Jly 8 1999
7f	1m 23.96	2	8-12	Good	Discourse (USA)	Aug 6 2011
7f	1m 22.18	3	9-0	Gd to Firm	Codemaster	May 14 2011
1m	1m 37.47	2	8-13	Good	Whippers Love (IRE)	Aug 28 2009
1m	1m 35.5	3	8-6	Gd to Firm	Lovers Knot	Jly 8 1998
1m 110y	1m 44.1	3	8-11	Good	Golden Snake	Apr 15 1999
1m 2f	2m 0.9	4	9-3	Gd to Firm	Elhayq (IRE)	May 1 1999
1m 4f	2m 26.07	3	8-9	Gd to Firm	Mohedian Lady (IRE)	Sep 22 2011
1m 6f 175y	3m 4.2	3	8-5	Good	Arrive	Jly 11 2001
2m 24y	3m 20.2	7	9-10	Good	Yorkshire	Jly 11 2001

NOTTINGHAM

Distance	Time	Age	Weight	Going	Horse	Date
5f 13y	57.9 secs	2	8-9	Firm	Hoh Magic	May 13 1994
5f 13y	57.6 secs	6	9-2	Gd to firm	Catch The Cat (IRE)	May 14 2005
6f 15y	1m 11.4	2	811	Firm	Jameelapi	Aug 8 1983
6f 15y	1m 10.0	4	9-2	Firm	Ajanac	Aug 8 1988
1m75y	1m 45.23	2	9-0	Gd to Firm	Tactfully	Sep 28 2011
1m 75y	1m 42.25	5	9-1	Gd To Firm	Rio De La Plata	Jun 2 2010
1m 1f 213y	2m 5.6	2	9-0	Firm	Al Salite	Oct 28 1985
1m 1f 213y	2m 2.3	2	9-0	Firm	Ayaabi	Jly 21 1984
1m 2f 50y	2m 09.54	4	9-12	Gd To Firm	Geneva Geyser	Jly 3 2010
1m 6f 15y	2m 57.8	3	8-10	Firm	Buster Jo	Oct 1 1985
2m 9y	3m 24.0	5	7-7	Firm	Fet	Oct 5 2036
2m 2f 18y	3m 55.1	9	9-10	Gd to Firm	Pearl Run	May 1 1990

PONTEFRACT

Distance	Time	Age	Weight	Going	Horse	Date
5f	61.1 secs	2	9-0	Firm	Golden Bounty	Sep 20 2001
5f	60.8 secs	4	8-9	Firm	Blue Maeve	Sep 29 2004
6f	1m 14.0	2	9-3	Firm	Fawzi	Sep 6 1983
6f	1m 12.6	3	7-13	Firm	Merry One	Aug 29 1970
1m 4y	1m 42.8	2	9-13	Firm	Star Spray	Sep 6 1983
1m 4y	1m 42.8	2	9-0	Firm	Alasil (USA)	Sep 26 2002
1m 4y	1m 40.6	4	9-10	Gd to Firm	Island Light	Apr 13 2002
1m 2f 6y	2m 10.1	2	9-0	Firm	Shanty Star	Oct 7 2002
1m 2f 6y	2m 8.2	4	7-8	Hard	Happy Hector	Jly 9 1979
1m 2f 6y	2m 8.2	3	7-13	Hard	Tom Noddy	Aug 21 1972
1m 4f 8y	2m 33.72	3	8-7	Firm	Ajaan	Aug 8 2007
2m 1f 22y	3m 40.67	4	8-7	Gd to Firm	Paradise Flight	June 6 2005
2m 1f 216y	3m 51.1	3	8-8	Firm	Kudz	Sep 9 1986
2m 5f 122y	4m 47.8	4	8-4	Firm	Physical	May 14 1984

REDCAR

Distance	Time	Age	Weight	Going	Horse	Date
5f	56.9 secs	2	9-0	Firm	Mister Joel	Oct 24 1995
5f	56.01 secs	10	9-3	Firm	Henry Hall	Sep 20 2006
6f	68.8 secs	2	8-3	Gd to Firm	Obe Gold	Oct 2 2004
6f	68.6 secs	3	9-2	Gd to Firm	Sizzling Saga	Jun 21 1991
7f	1m 21.28	2	9-3	Firm	Karoo Blue	Sep 20 2006
7f	1m 21.0	3	9-1	Firm	Empty Quarter	Oct 3 1995
1m	1m 34.37	2	9-0	Firm	Mastership	Sep 20 2006
1m	1m 32.42	4	10-0	Firm	Nanton	Sep 20 2006
1m 1f	1m 52.4	2	9-0	Firm	Spear (IRE)	Sep 13 2004
1m 1f	1m 48.5	5	8-12	Firm	Mellottie	Jly 25 1990
1m 2f	2m 10.1	2	8-11	Good	Adding	Nov 10 1989
1m 2f	2m 1.4	5	9-2	Firm	Eradicate	May 28 1990
1m 3f	2m 17.2	3	8-9	Firm	Photo Call	Aug 7 1990
1m 5f 135y	2m 54.7	6	9-10	Firm	Brodessa	Jun 20 1992
1m 6f 19y	2m 59.81	4	9-1	Gd to Firm	Esprit De Corps	Sep 11 2006
2m 4y	3m 24.9	3	9-3	Gd to Firm	Subsonic	Oct 8 1991
2m 3f	4m 10.1	5	7-4	Gd to Firm	Seldom In	Aug 9 1991

RIPON

Distance	Time	Age	Weight	Going	Horse	Date
5f	57.8 secs	2	8-8	Firm	Super Rocky	Jly 5 1991
5f	57.6 secs	5	8-5	Good	Broadstairs Beauty	May 21 1995
6f	1m 10.4	2	9-2	Good	Cumbrian Venture	Aug 17 2002
6f	69.8 secs	4	9-8	Gd to Firm	Tadeo	Aug 16 1997
6f	69.8 secs	5	7-10	Firm	Quoit	Jly 23 1966
1m	1m 39.79	2	8-6	Good	Top Jaro (FR)	Sep 24 2005
1m	1m 36.62	4	8-11	Gd to Firm	Granston (IRE)	Aug 29 2005
1m 1f 170y	1m 59.12	5	8-9	Gd to Firm	Wahoo Sam (USA)	Aug 30 2005
1m 2f	2m 2.6	3	9-4	Firm	Swift Sword	Jly 20 1990
1m 4f 10y	2m 31.40	4	8-8	Gd to Firm	Dandino	Apr 16 2011
2m	3m 27.07	5	9-12	Gd to Firm	Greenwich Meantime	Aug 30 2005

SALISBURY

Distance	Time	Age	Weight	Going	Horse	Date
5f	59.3 secs	2	9-0	Gd to Firm	Ajigolo	May 12 2005
5f	59.3 secs	2	9-0	Gd to Firm	Ajigolo	May 12 2005
6f	1m 12.1	2	8-0	Gd to Firm	Parisian Lady (IRE)	Jun 10 1997
6f	1m 11.09	3	9-0	Firm	L'Ami Louis (IRE)	May 1 2011
6f 212y	1m 25.9	2	9-0	Firm	More Royal (USA)	Jun 29 1995
6f 212y	1m 24.9	3	9-7	Firm	High Summer (USA)	Sep 5 1996
1m	1m 40.4	2	8-13	Firm	Choir Master (USA)	Sep 17 2002
1m	1m 38.29	3	8-7	Gd to Firm	Layman (USA)	Aug 11 2005
1m 1f 198y	2m 4.81	3	8-5	Gd to Firm	Primevere (IRE)	Aug 10 2011
1m 4f	2m 31.6	3	9-5	Gd to Firm	Arrive	Jun 27 2001
1m 6f 15y	2m 59.4	3	8-6	Gd to Firm	Tabareeh	Sep 2 1999

SANDOWN

Distance	Time	Age	Weight	Going	Horse	Date
5f 6y	59.4 secs	2	9-3	Firm	Times Time	Jly 22 1982
5f 6y	58.8 secs	6	8-9	Gd to Firm	Palacegate Touch	Sep 17 1996
7f 16y	1m 26.56	2	9-0	Gd to Firm	Raven's Pass (USA)	Sep 1 2007

7f 16y	1m 26.3	3	9-0	Firm	Mawsuff	Jun 14 1983
1m 14y	1m 41.1	2	8-11	Fast	Reference Point	Sep 23 1986
1m 14y	1m 39.0	3	8-8	Firm	Linda s Fantasy	Aug 19 1983
1m 1f	1m 54.6	2	8-8	Gd to Firm	French Pretender	Sep 20 1988
1m 1f	1m 52.4	7	9-3	Gd to Firm	Bourgainville	Aug 11 2005
1m 2f 7y	2m 2.1	4	8-11	Firm	Kalaglow	May 31 1982
1m 3f 91y	2m 21.6	4	8-3	Fast	Aylesfield	Jly 7 1984
1m 6f	2m 56.9	4	8-7	Gd to Firm	Lady Rosanna	Jly 19 1989
2m 78y	3m 29.86	4	9-0	Gd to Firm	King Of Wands	Jul 3 2010

SOUTHWELL (TURF)

Distance	Time	Age	Weight	Going	Horse	Date
6f	1m 15.03	2	9-3	Good	Trepa	Sep 6 2006
6f	1m 13.48	4	8-10	Good	Paris Bell	Sep 6 2006
7f	1m 27.56	2	9-7	Good	Hart Of Gold	Sep 6 2006
7f	1m 25.95	3	9-0	Good	Aeroplane	Sep 6 2006
1m 2f	2m 7.470	3	8-11	Good	Desert Authority(USA)	Sep 6 2006
1m 3f	2m 20.13	4	9-12	Good	Sanchi	Sep 6 2006
1m 4f	2m 34.4	5	9-3	Gd to Firm	Corn Lily	Aug 10 1991
2m	3m 34.1	5	9-1	Gd to Firm	Triplicate	Sep 20 1991

SOUTHWELL (A.W)

Distance	Time	Age	Weight	Going	Horse	Date
5f	58.89 secs	2	8-6	Standard	Egyptian Lord	Dec 15 2005
5f	57.14 secs	5	9-5	Standard	Godfrey Street	Jan 24 2008
6f	1m 14.00	2	8-5	Standard	Panalo	Nov 8 1989
6f	1m 13.50	4	10-02	Standard	Saladan Knight	Dec 30 1989
7f	1m 27.10	2	8-2	Standard	Mystic Crystal	Nov 20 1990
7f	1m 26.80	5	8-4	Standard	Amenable	Dec 13 1990
1m	1m 38.00	2	8-9	Standard	Alpha Rascal	Nov 13 1990
1m	1m 38.00	2	8-10	Standard	Andrew s First	Dec 30 1989
1m	1m 37.25	3	8-6	Standard	Valira	Nov 3 1990
1m 3f	2m 21.50	4	9-7	Standard	Tempering	Dec 5 1990
1m 4f	2m 33.90	4	9-12	Standard	Fast Chick	Nov 8 1989
1m 6f	3m 1.60	3	7-8	Standard	Erevnon	Dec 29 1990
2m	3m 37.60	9	8-12	Standard	Old Hubert	Dec 5 1990

THIRSK

Distance	Time	Age	Weight	Going	Horse	Date
5f	57.2 secs	2	9-7	Gd to Firm	Proud Boast	Aug 5 2000
5f	56.9 secs	5	9-6	Firm	Charlie Parkes	April 11 2003
6f	69.2 secs	2	9-6	Gd to Firm	Westcourt Magic	Aug 25 1995
6f	68.8 secs	6	9-4	Firm	Johayro	Jly 23 1999
7f	1m 23.7	2	8-9	Firm	Courting	Jly 23 1999
7f	1m 22.8	4	8-5	Firm	Silver Haze	May 21 1988
1m	1m 37.9	2	9-0	Firm	Sunday Symphony	Sep 4 2004
1m	1m 34.8	4	8-13	Firm	Yearsley	May 5 1990
1m 4f	2m 29.9	5	9-12	Firm	Gallery God	Jun 4 2001
2m	3m 22.3	3	8-11	Firm	Tomaschek	Jly 17 1981

WARWICK

Distance	Time	Age	Weight	Going	Horse	Date
5f	57.95 secs	2	8-9	Gd to Firm	Amour Propre	Jun 26 2008
5f	57.7 secs	4	9-6	Gd to Firm	Little Edward	Jly 7 2002
5f 110y	63.6 secs	5	8-6	Gd to Firm	Dizzy In The Head	Jun 27 2004
6f	1m 11.22	2	9-3	Gd to Firm	Hurricane Hymnbook	Sep 15 2007
6f	69.44	5	8-12	Gd to Firm	Peter Island	Jun 26 2008
7f 26y	1m 22.9	2	9-0	Firm	Country Rambler(USA)	Jun 20 2004
7f 26y	1m 20.7	4	8-8	Good	Etlaala	Apr 17 2006
1m 22y	1m 37.1	3	8-11	Firm	Orinocovsky (IRE)	Jun 26 2002
1m 2f 188y	2m 14.98	4	8-12	Gd to Firm	Ronaldsay	Jun 16 2008
1m 4f 134y	2m 39.5	3	8-13	Gd to Firm	Maimana (IRE)	Jun 22 2002
1m 6f 135y	3m 7.5	3	9-7	Gd to Firm	Burma Baby (USA)	Jly 2 1999
2m 39y	3m 27.9	3	8-1	Firm	Decoy	Jun 26 2002

WINDSOR

Distance	Time	Age	Weight	Going	Horse	Date
5f 10y	58.69 secs	2	9-0	Gd to Firm	Charles the Great (IRE)	May 23 2011
5f 10y	58.08 secs	5	8-13	Gd to Firm	Taurus Twins	Apr 4 2011
6f	1m 10.5	2	9-5	Gd to Firm	Cubism (USA)	Aug 17 1998
6f	68.69 secs	4	9-0	Gd to Firm	Bated Breath	May 23 2011
1m 67y	1m 42.46	2	8-9	Gd to Firm	Tiger Cub	Oct 11 2011
1m 67y	1m 40.19	4	9-4	Good	Nationalism	Jun 25 2011
1m 2f 7y	2m 3.0	2	9-1	Firm	Moomba Masquerade	May 19 1990
1m2f 7y	2m 2.44	4	9-0	Gd to Firm	Campanologist (USA)	Aug 29 2009
1m 3f 135y	2m 21.5	3	9-2	Firm	Double Florin	May 19 1980

WOLVERHAMPTON (A.W.)

Distance	Time	Age	Weight	Going	Horse	Date
5f 20y	61.13 sec	2	8-8	Std to Fast	Yungaburra (IRE)	Nov 8 2006
5f 20y	60.22 sec	5	9-3	Standard	Deerslayer (USA)	Aug 30 2011
5f 216y	1m 12.61	2	9-0	Std to Fast	Prime Defender	Nov 8 2006
5f 216y	1m 13.32	5	8-12	Standard	Desert Opal	Sep 17 2005
7f 32y	1m 27.70	2	9-5	Standard	Billy Dane	Aug 14 2006
7f 32y	1m 26.65	4	8-12	Std to Fast	Capucci	Sept 30 2009
1m 141y	1m 48.08	2	8-9	Std to Fast	Worldly	Aug 30 2006
1m 141y	1m 46.48	3	8-9	Standard	Gitano Hernando	Sept 17 2009
1m 1f 103y	2m 0.76	2	9-0	Standard	Mr Excel (IRE)	Nov 14 2005
1m 1f 103y	1m 57.34	4	8-13	Standard	Bahar Shumaal (IRE)	Aug 31 2006
1m 4f 50y	2m 35.71	3	9-2	Std to Fast	Steppe Dancer (IRE)	Aug 30 2006
1m 5f 194y	2m 59.85	6	9-12	Std to Fast	Valance (IRE)	Aug 30 2006
2m 119y	3m 35.85	5	8-11	Std to Fast	Market Watcher (USA)	Nov 21 2006

YARMOUTH

Distance	Time	Age	Weight	Going	Horse	Date
5f 43y	60.4 secs	2	8-6	Gd to Firm	Ebba	Jly 26 1999
5f 43y	59.8 secs	4	8-13	Gd to Firm	Roxanne Mill	Aug 25 2002
6f 3y	1m 10.4	2	9-0	Fast	Lanchester	Aug 15 1988
6f 3y	69.9 secs	4	8-9	Firm	Malhub (USA)	Jun 13 2002
7f 3y	1m 22.2	2	9-0	Gd to Firm	Warrshan	Sep 14 1988
7f 3y	1m 22.12	4	9-4	Gd to Firm	Glenbuck (IRE)	Apr 26 2007
1m 3y	1m 36.3	2	8-2	Gd to Firm	Outrun	Sep 15 1988
1m 3y	1m 33.9	3	8-8	Firm	Bonne Etoile	Jun 27 1995
1m 1f	1m 53.01	3	8-13	Gd to Firm	Dubawi Dancer	Jul 12 2011
1m 2f 21y	2m 2.83	3	8-8	Firm	Reunite (IRE)	Jul 18 2006
1m 3f 101y	2m 23.1	3	8-9	Firm	Rahil	Jly 1 1993
1m 6f 17y	2m 57.8	3	8-2	Gd to Firm	Barakat	Jly 24 1990
2m	3m 26.7	4	8-2	Gd to Firm	Alhesn (USA)	Jly 26 1999
2m 2f 51y	3m 56.8	4	9-10	Firm	Provence	Sep 19 1991

YORK

Distance	Time	Age	Weight	Going	Horse	Date
5f	57.3 secs	2	7-8	Gd to Firm	Lyric Fantasy	Aug 20 1992
5f	56.1 secs	3	9-3	Gd to Firm	Dayjur	Aug 23 1990
5f 89y	63.81 secs	2	9-3	Gd to Firm	El Viento (FR)	Sep 5 2010
5f 89y	62.31 secs	6	9-5	Gd to Firm	Barney McGrew (IRE)	Aug 18 2009
6f	69.28 secs	2	8-12	Gd to Firm	Showcasing	Aug 19 2009
6f	68.58 secs	7	9-4	Firm	Cape Of Good Hope	Jun 16 2005
7f	1m 22.45	2	9-0	Gd to Firm	ElusivePimpernel(USA)	Aug 18 2009
7f	1m 21.85	4	8-11	Good	Chachamaidee (IRE)	May 20 2011
1m	1m 39.20	2	8-1	Gd to Firm	Missoula (IRE)	Aug 31 2005
1m	1m 36.24	3	9-2	Gd to Firm	Capponi	Jul 10 2010
1m 208y	1m 46.76	5	9-8	Gd to Firm	Echo Of Light	Sep 5 2007
1m 2f 88y	2m 5.29	3	8-11	Gd to Firm	Sea The Stars (IRE)	Aug 18 2009
1m 4f	2m 26.28	6	8-9	Firm	Bandari (IRE)	Jun 18 2005
1m 6f	2m 54.96	4	9-0	Gd to Firm	Tactic	May 22 2010
1m 7f 195y	3m 18.4	3	8-0	Gd to Firm	Dam Busters	Aug 16 1988
2m 88y	3m 30.63	4	9-1	Gd to Firm	Askar Tau (FR)	Aug 19 2009

Raceform Flat speed figures 2011

(Best time performances achieved 1st January - 31st December 2011 (min rating 110, 2-y-o 105)

THREE YEAR-OLDS AND UPWARDS - Turf

Aaim To Prosper 110 (16½f,San,G,Jly 2)
Addictive Dream 113 (5f,Asc,G,Oct 1)
Admiral Of The Red 111 (14f,Cur,YS,Jun 25)
African Story 111 (8f,Dea,VS,Aug 28)
Agent Secret 112 (10f,Lon,G,Apr 10)
Akarlina 112 (10f,Lon,G,Apr 10)
Alainmaar 110 (12f,Asc,GF,May 7)
Albaasil 112 (8f,Nmk,GF,Jly 9)
Alexander Pope 111 (10f,Cur,G,May 22)
Allied Powers 112 (12f,Cha,S,Jun 5)
Americain 112 (15f,Dea,G,Aug 21)
Amour Propre 113 (5f,Cur,G,Aug 28)
Aneedah 119 (6f,Asc,GF,Apr 27)
Aoife Alainn 111 (10f,Cur,G,Aug 7)
Apache 112 (12f,Leo,GF,May 29)
Asheerah 114 (8f,Cur,G,Jun 26)
Asiya 111 (12f,Leo,G,Sep 3)
Ask Jack 115 (8f,Cur,G,Jun 26)
Await The Dawn 116 (10½f,Chs,GF,May 5)

Banimpire 116 (12f,Asc,G,Oct 15)
Baraan 113 (10½f,Cha,S,Jun 5)
Barack 112 (8f,Cur,G,Jun 26)
Barefoot Lady 110 (8f,Leo,G,Sep 3)
Barocci 110 (8f,Cha,GS,Jun 12)
Bated Breath 114 (6f,Hay,GF,Sep 3)
Be Fabulous 117 (15½f,Lon,G,Oct 23)
Beachfire 111 (10f,Asc,GS,Jun 17)
Beacon Lodge 112 (8f,Goo,GS,Aug 27)
Beaulieu 112 (12f,Cha,GS,Jun 12)
Beaumont s Party 115 (10½f,Chs,G,May 21)
Behkabad 114 (12f,Cha,S,Jun 5)
Berling 111 (13½f,Chs,GF,Aug 20)
Bertiewhittle 111 (6f,Nmk,G,Aug 13)
Best Dating 113 (7f,Lon,VS,Sep 4)
Best Hello 112 (10f,Leo,G,May 8)
Bewitched 111 (6f,Cur,S,Sep 11)
Beyond Desire 111 (5f,Nby,G,Sep 17)
Bible Belt 118 (12f,Asc,G,Oct 15)
Big Hunter 110 (8f,Dea,VS,Aug 28)
Black Spirit 112 (10f,San,G,Apr 23)
Blue Bajan 110 (14f,Yor,GF,May 13)
Blue Bunting 114 (8f,Nmk,GF,May 1)
Blue Soave 112 (8f,Cha,GS,Jun 12)
Bob Le Beau 111 (10f,Cur,GF,Jun 3)
Boogie Shoes 115 (10f,Eps,GF,Jun 4)
Boom And Bust 111 (8f,Goo,GF,Jly 29)
Borderlescott 115 (5f,Hay,GF,May 21)
Bounty Box 112 (6f,Not,GF,May 7)
Bowdler s Magic 110 (14f,Yar,G,Sep 15)
Brigantin 113 (15f,Dea,G,Aug 21)
Brown Panther 112 (13f,Nby,G,Aug 13)
Brushing 115 (12f,Asc,G,Oct 15)
Bubble Chic 114 (10½f,Cha,S,Jun 5)
Byword 115 (9f,Lon,G,May 22)

Campanologist 112 (10½f,Cur,G,May 22)
Canford Cliffs 115 (8f,Asc,G,Jun 14)
Cape Of Good Grace110(10f,Cur,GY,Jun 25)
Captain Dunne 112 (5f,Lon,G,May 15)
Captain John Nixon 110 (14f,Sal,GF,May 19)
Carlton House 116 (12f,Eps,GF,Jun 4)
Cavalryman 115 (15½f,Lon,G,Oct 23)
Census 113 (13f,Nby,G,Aug 13)
Ch Tio Bilote 113 (8f,Cha,GS,Jun 12)
Charles Camoin 116 (10f,Eps,GF,Jun 4)
Chiberta King 119 (16f,Nmk,GF,Sep 22)
Chrysanthemum 111 (8f,Cur,G,May 22)
Cill Rialaig 116 (12f,Asc,G,Oct 15)
Circumvent 110 (9f,Nmk,GF,Sep 24)
Cirrus Des Aigles 121 (9f,Lon,G,May 22)
Cityscape 112 (8f,Asc,G,Jun 14)
Claiomh Solais 114 (8f,Cur,G,May 22)
Class Is Class 110 (10f,San,G,Jly 1)
Cocozza 110 (10f,Cur,G,Aug 7)
Colombian 112 (10½f,Cha,S,Jun 5)
Confessional 112 (5f,Asc,G,Oct 1)
Cracking Lass 110 (12f,Ham,G,May 13)
Creekside 112 (8f,Cur,G,Jun 26)
Crimea 110 (5f,Don,G,Aug 13)
Critical Moment 110 (10½f,Chs,GF,May 5)
Crystal Capella 117 (12f,Asc,G,Oct 15)
Crystal Gal 110 (8f,Hay,G,Aug 6)

Dance And Dance 112 (8f,Sal,GF,Aug 11)
Dancing Rain 120 (12f,Asc,G,Oct 15)
Dandino 114 (12f,Rip,GF,Apr 16)
Danedream 122 (12f,Lon,G,Oct 2)
Deacon Blues 115 (5f,Nby,G,Sep 17)
Deauville Flyer 110 (16f,Ncs,GS,Jun 25)
Debussy 112 (12f,Chs,G,Sep 10)
Definightly 112 (6f,Dea,VS,Aug 28)
Desert Law 111 (6f,Bat,GF,Aug 20)
Dever Dream 112 (6f,Yor,G,Jly 8)
DickDoughtywylie110 (10½f,Chs,GS,Sep 24)
Dick Turpin 110 (8f,San,G,Apr 23)
Dinkum Diamond 112 (5f,Nby,G,Sep 17)
Distant Memories 114 (12f,Pon,G,Jun 19)
Doncaster Rover 111 (7f,Yor,G,Aug 20)
Dream Ahead 117 (7f,Lon,G,Oct 2)
Drunken Sailor 111 (13f,Nby,GF,May 14)
Dubawi Gold 113 (8f,Goo,GS,Aug 27)
Duchess Dora 111 (5f,Bev,GS,Aug 27)
Dunaden 112 (15f,Dea,G,Aug 21)
Dunboyne Express 114 (10f,Cur,G,Aug 7)
Duncan 113 (14f,Cur,YS,Sep 10)
Dux Scholar 112 (10f,Wdr,GS,Aug 27)

Electrolyser 114 (15½f,Lon,G,Oct 23)
Elusive Pimpernel 110 (9f,Nmk,GF,Apr 14)
Elzaam 110 (6f,Hay,GF,Sep 3)
Emerald Commander 110 (8f,Sal,GF,Aug 11)
Emiyna 112 (8f,Leo,G,Aug 11)
Emulous 115 (8f,Leo,G,Sep 3)
End Of The Affair 114 (16f,Nmk,GF,Sep 22)
Eton Rifles 111 (6f,Cur,S,Oct 9)
Evaporation 112 (7f,Lon,VS,Sep 4)
Evens And Odds 110 (6f,Thi,G,Apr 9)
Excelebration 113 (8f,Lon,VS,Sep 11)
Ezalli 116 (8f,Cur,G,Jun 26)

Fallen Idol 114 (10f,Goo,S,Sep 21)
Famous Name 113 (9f,Leo,S,Jly 21)
Fanunalter 110 (8f,Sal,GF,Aug 11)
Fast Shot 110 (6f,Don,G,Jly 21)
Fictional Account 118 (16f,Nmk,GF,Sep 22)
Flag Officer 114 (10½f,Yor,G,Jun 11)
Flambeau 111 (7f,Lei,GF,Apr 16)
Flash Dance 116 (9f,Lon,G,May 22)
Fleur De Nuit 110 (12f,Leo,G,Sep 3)
Forever Glory 111 (10f,Cur,GY,Jun 25)
Forte Dei Marmi 112 (10½f,Chs,GF,May 5)
Fourth Generation 111 (10½f,Chs,G,May 21)
Fox Hunt 110 (12f,Ham,G,May 13)
Frankel 118 (8f,Nmk,GF,Apr 30)
Freedom 113 (10f,Cur,GY,Jun 25)
French Navy 111 (10f,Goo,GS,Sep 10)
Future Generation 113 (8f,Leo,G,Aug 11)

Galikova 114 (12f,Lon,G,Oct 2)
Galileo s Choice 111 (10f,Leo,G,Sep 3)
Genki 113 (6f,Hay,GF,Sep 3)
Gentoo 111 (15½f,Lon,G,Oct 23)
Genzy 112 (12f,Cha,GS,Jun 12)
Gertrude Bell 117 (12f,Asc,G,Oct 15)
Glaswegian 110 (10½f,Cha,S,Jun 5)
Glorious Sight 112 (8f,Cha,G,Jly 3)
Golden Lilac 110 (10½f,Cha,GS,Jun 12)
Goldikova 122 (9f,Lon,G,May 22)
Goldplated 112 (12f,Leo,G,Sep 3)
Gradara 110 (15½f,Lon,G,Oct 23)
Grand Vent 110 (10f,Lon,G,Apr 24)
Green Destiny 116 (10f,Asc,G,Oct 15)
Group Therapy 114 (5f,Hay,GF,May 21)

Hamish McGonagall 115 (5f,Yor,GS,Aug 19)
Handassa 111 (8f,Cur,G,May 22)
Harbour Watch 110 (6f,Goo,GF,Jly 29)
Harris Tweed 113 (12f,Asc,S,Jun 18)
Havane Smoker 110 (8f,Lon,G,May 15)
Hawkeyethenoo 112 (7f,Asc,GF,May 7)
Hazelrigg 111 (5f,Don,G,Aug 13)
Heavenly Dawn 111 (8f,Nby,G,Jly 16)
High Standing 110 (6f,Hay,GF,Jly 2)
Highland Castle 110 (12f,Hay,GF,Jly 2)
Highland Knight 111 (8f,San,G,Jly 2)
Hiruno D Amour 114 (12f,Lon,G,Oct 2)
History Note 114 (8f,Cur,G,May 22)
Hoof It 114 (6f,Hay,GF,Sep 3)
Horseradish 112 (6f,Don,G,Apr 3)
Hujaylea 114 (8f,Cur,G,Jun 26)
Hunter s Light 116 (10f,Goo,S,Sep 21)

I Love Me 112 (7f,Nmk,GF,May 14)
I m A Dreamer 113 (9f,Nmk,GF,May 1)
Ibicenco 114 (15f,Lon,VS,Sep 4)
Immortal Verse 114 (8f,Dea,GS,Aug 15)
Indian Days 110 (12f,Nby,GF,Apr 16)
Inspirina 110 (10½f,Chs,G,May 21)
Invincible Ash 110 (5f,Cur,G,Jun 26)
Inxile 113 (5f,Lon,G,May 15)
Ivory Land 111 (12f,Cha,S,Jun 5)

Jet Away 111 (10½f,Yor,G,Oct 7)
Jeu De Vivre 110 (13f,Ham,S,Sep 18)
Jimmy Styles 111 (6f,Don,G,Apr 2)
Jukebox Jury 115 (15f,Dea,G,Aug 21)
Julienas 111 (8f,Asc,G,Jun 15)
Kasbah Bliss 113 (15f,Dea,G,Aug 21)
Khor Sheed 111 (6f,Not,GF,May 7)
Kiama Bay 110 (12f,Chs,G,Sep 10)
Kings Gambit 113 (10f,San,G,Apr 23)
Kingsgate Native 117 (5f,Hay,GF,May 21)
Kreem 114 (12f,Cha,GS,Jun 12)

Laaheb 111 (12f,Asc,S,Jun 18)
Ladies Are Forever 113 (6f,Yor,G,Jly 8)
Laughing Lashes 115 (8f,Cur,G,May 22)
Le Valentin 111 (6f,Dea,VS,Aug 28)
Ley Hunter 113 (10f,Lon,G,Apr 10)
Libranno 118 (6f,Asc,GF,Apr 27)
Lolly For Dolly 113 (7f,Cur,HY,Apr 3)
Look At Me 110 (10f,Leo,G,Sep 3)
Luisant 114 (8f,Cur,G,Jun 26)

Madany 116 (6f,Asc,GF,Apr 27)
Majestic Myles 110 (7f,Yor,G,Aug 20)
Malthouse 112 (10f,Eps,GF,Jun 4)
Manieree 112 (10f,Cur,Y,Sep 11)
Manighar 113 (15f,Dea,G,Aug 21)
Manjakani 111 (15f,Lon,VS,Sep 4)
Maqaasid 112 (8f,Nmk,GF,May 1)
Mar Adentro 112 (5f,Lon,G,May 15)
Marchand D Or 113 (6f,Dea,VS,Aug 28)
Margot Did 118 (6f,Asc,GF,Apr 27)
Maria Royal 110 (15½f,Lon,G,Oct 23)
Marine Commando 111 (6f,Asc,GF,Apr 27)
Marinous 112 (15f,Dea,G,Aug 21)
Markazzi 110 (9f,Nmk,GF,Sep 24)
Masamah 113 (5f,Nby,G,Sep 17)
Masaya 110 (7f,Nmk,GF,May 14)
Masked Marvel 111 (12f,Eps,GF,Jun 4)
Master Rooney 110 (5f,Don,G,Aug 13)
Mayson 113 (5f,Asc,G,Oct 1)
Meandre 117 (12f,Lon,G,Oct 2)
Meeznah 116 (12f,Asc,G,Oct 15)
Memphis Tennessee 115 (12f,Eps,GF,Jun 4)
Midday 117 (10f,Asc,G,Oct 15)
Mirror Lake 110 (10f,Goo,S,Sep 21)
Miss Crissy 112 (15f,Lon,VS,Sep 4)
Miss Lago 116 (15½f,Lon,G,Oct 23)
Misty For Me 117 (8f,Cur,G,May 22)
Modun 110 (10½f,Yor,G,Jly 9)
Mohedian Lady 110 (12f,Nmk,GF,Sep 22)
Monsieur Chevalier 110 (6f,Goo,GS,Sep 10)
Montaff 112 (16f,Ncs,GS,Jun 25)
Moonlight Cloud 117 (6½f,Dea,S,Aug 7)
Moran Gra 110 (8f,Leo,G,Aug 11)
Mosaicist 112 (6f,Yar,GF,May 20)
Motrice 110 (14f,Goo,GF,Jly 28)
Move In Time 114 (5f,Asc,G,Oct 1)
Moyenne Corniche 110 (12f,Ham,G,May 13)
Murbeh 115 (6f,Asc,GF,Apr 27)
Mutahadee 112 (10f,Cur,G,Aug 7)
Mutual Trust 114 (8f,Cha,GS,Jun 12)

Nakayama Festa 112 (12f,Lon,G,Oct 2)
Nanton 111 (9f,Nmk,GF,Sep 24)
Nathaniel 117 (10f,Asc,G,Oct 15)
Native Khan 115 (12f,Eps,GF,Jun 4)
Native Ruler 110 (14f,Yor,GF,May 13)
Neebras 113 (8f,Nmk,GF,May 14)
Nehaam 119 (16f,Nmk,GF,Sep 22)
New Deerfield 115 (7f,Nmk,GF,May 14)
Night Carnation 113 (5f,San,GF,Jly 2)
Noble Storm 111 (5f,Hay,GF,May 27)
Nocturnal Affair 111 (6f,Don,GF,Sep 10)

One Scoop Or Two 112(10½f,Chs,G,May 21)
One Spirit 115 (8f,Cur,G,Jun 26)
Opinion Poll 111 (18f,Don,G,Sep 9)
Oracle 110 (8f,Cur,GF,May 21)
Oriental Cavalier 112 (10½f,Chs,G,May 21)
Our Jonathan 111 (6f,Ayr,S,Sep 17)
Outsmart 111 (6f,Yar,GF,May 20)
Overdose 112 (5f,Hay,GF,May 21)
Overturn 110 (19f,Chs,GF,May 4)

Pacifique 115 (15f,Lon,VS,Sep 4)
Pekan Star 112 (10½f,Yor,G,May 11)
Penitent 115 (8f,Cur,G,Jun 26)
Pepper Lane 110 (6f,Rip,GS,Aug 13)
Perfect Tribute 120 (6f,Asc,GF,Apr 27)
Petara Bay 110 (16f,Ncs,GS,Jun 25)
Piccadilly Filly 111 (5f,Lon,G,May 15)
Pintura 110 (8f,Goo,GF,Jly 29)
Pirateer 117 (8f,Cur,G,Jun 26)
Planteur 115 (10f,Lon,G,Apr 10)
Plum Sugar 110 (12f,Leo,G,Sep 3)
Poet 113 (10f,San,GS,May 26)
Poet s Voice 110 (8f,Nmk,GF,Sep 23)
Polly s Mark 110 (12f,Goo,GF,Apr 30)
Polytechnicien 111 (9f,Nmk,GF,Apr 14)
Pour Moi 117 (12f,Eps,GF,Jun 4)
Prairie Star 111 (11f,Lon,G,May 15)
Precision Break 115 (16f,Nmk,GF,Sep 22)
Premio Loco 111 (8f,Nmk,GF,Sep 23)
Primevere 110 (10f,Sal,GF,Aug 10)
Prince Of Johanne 113 (9f,Nmk,GF,Sep 24)
Prince Siegfried 113 (10f,Wdr,GS,Aug 27)
Prohibit 117 (5f,Hay,GF,May 21)
Proponent 111 (9f,Nmk,GF,Sep 24)

Rajsaman 121 (9f,Lon,G,May 22)
Ransom Note 114 (8f,Nmk,GF,Sep 23)
Recital 116 (10f,Leo,G,May 8)
Red Cadeaux 117 (14f,Cur,YS,Jun 25)
Red Gulch 110 (8f,Goo,G,Jly 26)
Regent Street 113 (10f,Leo,G,May 8)
Reliable Man 115 (10½f,Cha,S,Jun 5)
Rewilding 116 (10f,Asc,G,Jun 15)
Rich Tapestry 111 (10f,Leo,GF,Apr 10)
Right Step 111 (10½f,Yor,G,May 11)
Rio De La Plata 111 (8f,Lon,VS,Sep 11)
Roderic O Connor 112 (8f,Cur,GF,May 21)
Rose Blossom 113 (5f,Hay,GF,May 21)
Rose Bonheur 110 (8f,Cur,G,May 22)
Royal Bench 110 (8f,Dea,GS,Aug 15)
Royal Rock 112 (6f,Asc,G,Oct 15)

Saddler s Rock 113 (18f,Don,G,Sep 9)
Saga Dream 111 (10f,Lon,G,Oct 1)
Sahpresa 113 (8f,Dea,G,Jly 31)
Salto 111 (8f,Dea,VS,Aug 28)
Sandy s Charm 112 (8f,Dea,VS,Aug 28)
Sano Di Pietro 112 (12f,Cha,GS,Jun 12)
Sarafina 117 (12f,Lon,G,Oct 2)
Sea Moon 116 (10½f,Yor,G,Jun 11)
Secrecy 110 (8f,Sal,GF,Aug 11)
Secret Asset 112 (5f,Lon,G,Oct 2)
Secret Witness 112 (5f,Don,G,Aug 13)
Seeharn 110 (6f,Cur,S,Oct 9)
Set The Trend 112 (8f,Goo,GS,Aug 27)
Seta 111 (8f,Goo,GF,Apr 30)
Seville 113 (12f,Cur,G,Jun 26)
Shamalgan 110 (9f,Lon,G,May 22)
Shamali 111 (10f,San,G,Apr 23)
Shamanova 114 (15½f,Lon,G,Oct 23)
Shankardeh 116 (15½f,Lon,G,Oct 23)
Shareta 118 (12f,Lon,G,Oct 2)
Shimraan 113 (10f,Lon,G,Oct 1)
Side Glance 113 (8f,Sal,GF,Aug 11)
Silver Pond 117 (12f,Lon,G,Oct 2)
Silver Valny 113 (15½f,Lon,G,Oct 23)
Sirius Prospect 113 (6f,Don,S,Nov 5)
Slow Pace 110 (8f,Cha,GS,Jun 12)
Snow Fairy 119 (10f,Asc,G,Oct 15)
So You Think 119 (10f,Asc,G,Oct 15)
Society Rock 112 (6½f,Dea,S,Aug 7)
Sole Power 119 (5f,Hay,GF,May 21)
Sommerabend 111 (7f,Lon,VS,Sep 4)
Split Trois 112 (5f,Lon,G,May 15)
Sri Putra 114 (10f,Asc,G,Oct 15)
St Nicholas Abbey 118 (12f,Lon,G,Oct 2)
Star Witness 111 (5f,Asc,G,Jun 14)
Steele Tango 110 (9f,Nmk,GF,Apr 14)
Stevie Thunder 111 (9f,Nmk,GF,Sep 24)
Stone Of Folca 111 (5f,Hay,GF,May 21)
Strong Suit 115 (7f,Nmk,G,Oct 8)
Sweet Sanette 110 (5f,Asc,G,Jun 14)
Swingkeel 110 (22f,Asc,S,Jun 18)

Tac De Boistron 116 (15½f,Lon,G,Oct 23)
Takar 110 (7f,Leo,Y,Nov 6)
Tanfeeth 114 (10f,Eps,GF,Jun 4)
Tangerine Trees 113 (5f,Lon,G,Oct 2)
Tartan Gunna 111 (10½f,Chs,G,May 21)
Tazahum 111 (9f,Yor,GS,Aug 19)
Ted Spread 113 (12f,Pon,G,Jun 19)
Terminal Velocity 110 (10f,Cur,GF,Jun 3)
Terre Du Vent 112 (15f,Dea,G,Aug 21)
Testosterone 111 (12f,Lon,G,Oct 2)
The Betchworth Kid 110 (14f,Not,F,Apr 6)
The Cheka 112 (7f,Cur,HY,Apr 3)
The Rectifier 111 (8f,Sal,GF,Aug 11)
Theo Danon 110 (10f,Lon,G,Oct 1)
Theology 115 (16f,Nmk,GF,Sep 22)
Theyskens Theory 110 (8f,San,S,Aug 20)
Thistle Bird 110 (8f,Wdr,GF,Aug 15)
Timepiece 111 (8f,Dea,G,Jly 31)
Times Up 120 (16f,Nmk,GF,Sep 22)
Timos 112 (10f,Lon,G,Apr 10)
Tin Horse 112 (8f,Lon,G,May 15)
Together 116 (8f,Cur,G,May 22)
Tominator 113 (16f,Ncs,GS,Jun 25)
Touz Price 111 (12f,Cha,GS,Jun 12)
Treasure Beach 116 (12f,Eps,GF,Jun 4)
Tres Rock Danon 113 (15½f,Lon,G,Oct 23)
Trojan Nights 115 (10f,Eps,GF,Jun 4)
Twice Over 111 (10f,Asc,G,Oct 15)
Twirl 111 (7f,Leo,Y,Nov 6)

Unnefer 110 (8f,Cha,GS,Jun 12)

Vadamar 113 (12f,Eps,GF,Jun 4)
Vagabond Shoes 112 (8f,Cha,GS,Jun 12)
Venomous 112 (8f,Cha,G,Jly 3)
Viscount Nelson 114 (10f,Cur,GF,Jun 3)
Vita Nova 114 (12f,Asc,G,Oct 15)
Vulcanite 113 (12f,Pon,G,Jun 19)

Waffle 111 (6f,Don,G,Apr 3)
Western Aristocrat 110 (7f,Asc,G,Jun 15)
Wiener Walzer 110 (10f,Lon,G,Apr 10)
Wigmore Hall 112 (10f,Asc,G,Oct 15)
Wild Coco 113 (12f,Hay,GS,Jun 8)
Wild Wind 110 (8f,Leo,G,Sep 3)
Wizz Kid 113 (5f,Yor,GS,Aug 19)
Wonder Of Wonders 111 (12f,Cur,Y,Jly 17)
Wootton Bassett 110 (6½f,Dea,S,Aug 7)
Workforce 114 (10f,San,GS,May 26)
Worthadd 112 (8f,Nby,GF,May 14)

Your Gifted 110 (5f,Don,G,Aug 13)

Zaminast 110 (10f,Leo,Y,Oct 30)
Zennor 110 (12f,Chs,G,Sep 10)
Zerashan 111 (14f,Cur,YS,Jun 25)
Zero Money 111 (5f,Asc,G,Oct 1)
Zinabaa 113 (8f,Dea,VS,Aug 28)
Zoffany 114 (8f,Asc,G,Jun 14)

THREE YEAR-OLDS AND UPWARDS - Sand

Abtasaamah 110 (7f,Mey,SD,Jan 13)
Accumulate 111 (14f,Wol,SD,Apr 19)
Agony And Ecstasy 110 (8f,Kem,SD,Apr 2)
Al Shemali 110 (9½f,Mey,SD,Feb 3)
Alakhan 110 (10f,Lin,SD,Nov 23)
Alazeyab 110 (6f,Mey,SD,Feb 3)
Alpha Tauri 111 (7f,Sth,SD,Mar 15)
As De Trebol 116 (8f,Mey,SD,Mar 3)
Audemar 111 (8f,Lin,SD,Feb 5)
Averroes 112 (11f,Kem,SD,Apr 2)

Bankable 112 (6f,Mey,SD,Mar 3)
Banna Boirche 113 (8f,Mey,SD,Mar 3)
Barbecue Eddie 111 (7f,Mey,SD,Feb 18)
Barbican 117 (12f,Kem,SD,Nov 30)
Bay Willow 111 (11f,Mey,SD,Feb 24)
Benandonner 111 (7f,Wol,SD,Mar 28)
Big Bay 110 (8f,Kem,SD,Feb 20)
Bold Silvano 113 (9½f,Mey,SD,Feb 3)
Bravo Echo 114 (8f,Kem,SD,Jan 23)
Bronze Cannon 113 (10f,Mey,SD,Jan 27)
Burj Alzain 113 (8f,Lin,SD,Apr 9)

Capone 114 (6f,Lin,SD,Nov 29)
Captain John Nixon 112 (11f,Kem,SD,Apr 2)
Ceilidh House 113 (12f,Kem,SD,Nov 30)
Charleston Lady 110 (13f,Lin,SD,Oct 27)
Circumvent 113 (10f,Lin,SD,Nov 12)
Clear Praise 111 (6f,Kem,SD,Jan 27)
Clinical 110 (8f,Lin,SD,Oct 27)
Cockney Class 110 (10f,Lin,SD,Mar 26)
Conveyance 110 (6f,Mey,SD,Mar 3)
Cosmic Sun 118 (11f,Kem,SD,Apr 2)
Crimson Cloud 110 (5f,Sth,SD,Nov 10)
Crocus Rose 110 (14f,Wol,SD,Apr 19)
Crowded House 110 (8f,Mey,SD,Mar 3)
Curtains 112 (6f,Lin,SD,Mar 25)

Danderek 110 (9½f,Wol,SD,Feb 25)
Dansili Dancer 115 (10f,Lin,SD,Mar 26)
Decider 113 (5f,Lin,SD,Jan 14)
Deerslayer 111 (5f,Lin,SD,Nov 29)
Desert Strike 111 (5f,Wol,SD,Feb 7)
Dickie s Lad 113 (6f,Lin,SD,Nov 29)
Dubai Hills 112 (7f,Sth,SD,Jan 2)
Dubawi Gold 115 (8f,Lin,SD,Apr 9)
Dunelight 110 (7f,Wol,SD,Mar 12)
Dynamic Blitz 113 (6f,Mey,SD,Feb 3)

Edgeworth 114 (10f,Lin,SD,Mar 7)
Edinburgh Knight 112 (8f,Kem,SD,Nov 23)
Elhamri 110 (6f,Sth,SD,Jan 27)
Elshabakiya 110 (7f,Lin,SD,Mar 26)
Emirates Champion 111(11f,Mey,SD,Feb 17)
Enak 113 (8f,Kem,SD,Sep 15)
Everymanforhimself 112 (8f,Sth,SD,Nov 9)

Faithful Ruler 111 (10f,Lin,SD,Mar 7)
Famous Warrior 111 (8f,Mey,SD,Mar 3)
Final Liberation 112 (12f,Lin,SD,Jun 25)
Follow The Flag 110 (8f,Lin,SD,Feb 26)
Force Freeze 110 (6f,Mey,SD,Mar 3)
Franco Is My Name 110 (10f,Lin,SD,Mar 26)
Fred Willetts 110 (6f,Kem,SD,Jan 26)

Gitano Hernando 110 (10f,Mey,SD,Mar 3)
Golden Sword 112 (9½f,Mey,SD,Feb 10)

Haatheq 110 (8f,Mey,SD,Feb 17)
Hamlool 114 (8f,Lin,SD,Apr 9)
Hazzard County 112 (8f,Lin,SD,Feb 5)
Honour System 111 (9½f,Mey,SD,Mar 10)
Hunter s Light 114 (10f,Lin,SD,Nov 12)

Interaction 110 (9½f,Mey,SD,Feb 3)
Inxile 110 (6f,Mey,SD,Jan 13)
Irish Flame 113 (11f,Kem,SD,Nov 10)

Jalil 111 (10f,Mey,SD,Jan 27)
Junoob 110 (10f,Lin,SD,Dec 2)

Khawlah 112 (9½f,Mey,SD,Feb 24)
Kidlat 110 (9½f,Wol,SD,Feb 25)
Kilburn 111 (8f,Lin,SD,Feb 5)
King Of Dixie 117 (8f,Kem,SD,Sep 15)
Koo And The Gang 111 (8f,Sth,SD,May 4)

Laaheb 112 (12f,Kem,SD,Nov 2)
Le Toreador 110 (5f,Lin,SD,Nov 29)
Little Black Book 112 (8f,Sth,SD,Apr 20)
Lord Theo 111 (10f,Lin,SD,Jan 29)
Lost In The Moment 111(11f,Mey,SD,Jan 27)
Lovers Causeway 110 (12f,Lin,SD,Feb 5)
Lowther 113 (8f,Kem,SD,Jan 23)
Loyalty 114 (9½f,Wol,SD,Feb 25)
Lunar Victory 114 (11f,Kem,SD,Apr 2)

Maali 111 (10f,Lin,SD,Nov 12)
Mac Love 110 (8f,Kem,SD,Nov 23)
Mahbooba 113 (8f,Mey,SD,Feb 3)
Majuro 113 (10f,Lin,SD,Mar 7)
Mantoba 110 (10f,Lin,SD,Dec 17)
Maristar 110 (8f,Sth,SD,Apr 20)
Megalala 112 (10f,Kem,SD,Dec 8)
Mendip 117 (8f,Mey,SD,Mar 3)
Merchant Of Medici 110 (8f,Kem,SD,May 2)
Modun 112 (12f,Kem,SD,Sep 3)
Monte Alto 110 (10f,Mey,SD,Jan 27)
Moresweets n Lace 110 (10f,Lin,SD,Apr 9)
Mr Brock 112 (10f,Mey,SD,Jan 27)
Mr Maximas 110 (9½f,Wol,SD,Mar 4)
Mufarrh 111 (9½f,Mey,SD,Feb 24)
Musir 113 (8f,Mey,SD,Feb 10)

New Leyf 111 (7f,Kem,SD,Mar 10)
Nice Style 110 (10f,Lin,SD,Nov 12)
Nideeb 117 (10f,Lin,SD,Mar 26)
Norville 111 (6f,Lin,SD,Feb 26)

Oasis Dancer 111 (7f,Kem,SD,Nov 16)
Our Giant 112 (8f,Mey,SD,Mar 3)

Pachattack 112 (10f,Lin,SD,Mar 26)
Parlour Games 112 (12f,Kem,SD,Nov 2)
Pelmanism 112 (5f,Lin,SD,Jan 14)
Penitent 110 (10f,Kem,SD,Apr 2)
Pink Symphony 112 (10f,Kem,SD,Apr 2)
Precision Break 110 (12f,Kem,SD,Nov 2)
Primaeval 113 (7f,Kem,SD,Nov 16)
Prince Bishop 115 (12f,Kem,SD,Nov 2)
Prince Shaun 110 (8f,Mey,SD,Mar 3)
Prizefighting 110 (11f,Mey,SD,Jan 27)
Psychic Ability 110 (10f,Mey,SD,Jan 27)

Ramona Chase 114 (11f,Kem,SD,Apr 2)
Record Breaker 110 (14f,Wol,SD,Oct 21)
Red Cadeaux 117 (11f,Kem,SD,Apr 2)
Red Gulch 111 (8f,Kem,SD,Sep 3)
Reem 112 (7f,Mey,SD,Jan 13)
Resentful Angel 112 (10f,Kem,SD,Apr 2)
Resuscitator 110 (9f,Wol,SD,Feb 12)
Riggins 110 (8f,Lin,SD,Nov 12)

Sahara Kingdom 113 (8f,Kem,SD,Sep 15)
Sangaree 113 (8f,Mey,SD,Mar 3)
Scamperdale 111 (12f,Lin,SD,Feb 5)
Secret Witness 110 (6f,Lin,SD,Nov 29)
Shamali 114 (10f,Kem,SD,Apr 2)
Silaah 110 (6f,Kem,SD,Jan 5)
Skysurfers 115 (8f,Mey,SD,Feb 10)
Snaafy 115 (8f,Mey,SD,Mar 3)
Sonoran Sands 111 (8f,Lin,SD,Apr 9)
Spring Of Fame 111 (9½f,Mey,SD,Feb 3)
Star Links 110 (9f,Wol,SD,Feb 3)
Steelcut 112 (5f,Wol,SD,Mar 4)
Stefanki 110 (7f,Kem,SD,Mar 10)
Storm Hawk 110 (16f,Sth,SD,Dec 29)
Straboe 110 (5f,Wol,SD,Feb 7)
Suits Me 112 (8f,Kem,SD,Jan 23)
Sweet Child O Mine 112 (8f,Sth,SD,Feb 15)
Sweet Lightning 110 (9½f,Mey,SD,Feb 10)

The Shrew 111 (8f,Kem,SD,Nov 23)
The Which Doctor 113 (10f,Lin,SD,Mar 7)
Thunderball 110 (6f,Lin,SD,Nov 29)
Tinshu 111 (10f,Lin,SD,Nov 23)
Trade Storm 110 (10f,Lin,SD,Dec 17)
Treasury Devil 110 (11f,Kem,SD,Nov 10)
Trois Rois 111 (10f,Mey,SD,Jan 27)
True To Form 111 (9½f,Wol,SD,Nov 26)
Twice Over 113 (10f,Mey,SD,Mar 3)

Unlimited 110 (7f,Wol,SD,Mar 19)

Western Aristocrat 119 (8f,Kem,SD,Sep 15)
What About You 112 (6f,Lin,SD,Nov 29)
William Haigh 110 (9½f,Wol,SD,Nov 26)

Yes Chef 110 (11f,Kem,SD,Sep 3)

Zafeen Speed 116 (8f,Mey,SD,Mar 3)
Zanzamar 111 (7f,Mey,SD,Jan 20)

TWO YEAR-OLDS - Turf

Akeed Mofeed 109 (7f,Leo,G,Sep 3)
Aloof 105 (7f,Leo,G,Sep 3)
Alsindi 105 (6f,Yar,S,Aug 28)
American Devil 105 (7f,Lon,G,Oct 2)
Angels Will Fall 105 (6f,Nmk,GF,Sep 24)

Balty Boys 107 (6f,Nmk,G,Oct 8)
Bannock 107 (6f,Goo,GF,Jly 29)
Betpak Dala 105 (10f,Sai,HY,Nov 12)
Bogart 107 (6f,Red,GF,Oct 1)
Brocottes 108 (10f,Sai,HY,Nov 12)
Bronterre 107 (7f,Nmk,G,Oct 8)
Burwaaz 109 (5f,Don,G,Sep 9)

Caledonia Lady 109 (5f,Don,G,Sep 9)
Caspar Netscher 107 (6f,Nmk,G,Oct 8)
Charles The Great 105 (5f,Goo,G,Jly 26)
Coral Wave 107 (7f,Cur,HY,Sep 25)
Coupe De Ville 106 (7f,Nmk,GF,Oct 1)
Crius 105 (7f,Nmk,GF,Sep 22)
Crown Dependency 105 (5f,Goo,G,Jly 26)
Crusade 109 (6f,Nmk,G,Oct 8)

Dabirsim 108 (6f,Dea,G,Aug 21)
Daddy Long Legs 106 (8f,Nmk,GF,Sep 24)
Daliyan 107 (8f,Leo,Y,Oct 30)
David Livingston 107 (7f,Cur,YS,Sep 10)
Discourse 107 (7f,Nmk,G,Aug 6)
Dragon Pulse 108 (7f,Cur,YS,Sep 10)

Excelette 105 (6f,Red,GF,Oct 1)
Expert Fighter 105 (8f,Bri,GF,Oct 13)

Fatcatinthehat 111 (8f,Leo,Y,Oct 30)
Fire Lily 105 (6f,Cur,YS,Jly 17)
Frederick Engels 108 (5f,Mus,GF,Jun 4)
Furner s Green 106 (7f,Cur,YS,Sep 10)

Gabrial s Star 105 (8f,Ham,S,Sep 18)
Gatepost 106 (6f,Asc,G,Jun 14)
Golden Hill 109 (8f,Leo,Y,Oct 30)
Gray Pearl 106 (7f,Nmk,G,Oct 8)

Handazan 107 (8f,Leo,Y,Oct 30)
Harbour Watch 110 (6f,Goo,GF,Jly 29)
Harvard N Yale 105 (8f,Nmk,G,Aug 12)
Hello Glory 106 (6f,Asc,GS,Jly 22)
Homecoming Queen 106 (7f,Cur,HY,Sep 25)

I Have A Dream 111 (8f,Leo,Y,Oct 30)
Indego Blues 106 (6f,Cat,G,Sep 17)

King s Warrant 107 (8f,Leo,Y,Oct 30)
Kohala 105 (5f,Don,G,Sep 9)

Lady Gorgeous 107 (6f,Nby,GF,Jly 15)
Lethal Force 106 (6f,Asc,G,Jun 14)
Letsgoroundagain 105 (8f,Pon,G,Oct 17)
Lightening Pearl 108 (6f,Nmk,GF,Sep 24)
Lilbourne Lad 108 (5f,Don,G,Sep 9)
Lyric Of Light 108 (8f,Nmk,GF,Sep 23)

Mac Row 105 (7f,Lon,VS,Sep 4)
Magic City 105 (5f,Nby,GF,Apr 15)
Mandaean 110 (10f,Sai,HY,Nov 12)
Maybe 105 (7f,Cur,G,Aug 28)
Mirandola 107 (10f,Sai,HY,Nov 12)
Miss Lahar 106 (5f,Asc,G,Oct 1)
Miss Work Of Art 105 (5f,Asc,GF,Apr 27)
Most Improved 108 (7f,Nmk,G,Oct 8)

Nemushka 106 (7f,Nmk,GF,Sep 24)
Nephrite 106 (7f,Leo,Y,Oct 30)

Oh So Lucy 105 (7f,Leo,G,Sep 3)

Parish Hall 109 (7f,Nmk,G,Oct 8)
Parisian Pyramid 107 (6f,Goo,GF,May 21)
Pimpernel 108 (7f,Nmk,GF,Sep 24)
Ponty Acclaim 108 (5f,Asc,G,Oct 1)
Poplin 107 (10f,Nmk,GF,Oct 1)
Power 109 (6f,Asc,G,Jun 14)
Princess Sinead 106 (7f,Cur,HY,Sep 25)

Rafeej 109 (5f,Ffo,HY,Nov 4)
Red Duke 105 (7f,Nmk,GF,Jly 9)
Regulation 108 (8f,Leo,Y,Oct 30)
Reply 107 (6f,Nmk,G,Oct 8)
Requinto 110 (5f,Don,G,Sep 9)
Roman Soldier 108 (6f,Asc,G,Jun 14)

Saigon 107 (6f,Nmk,G,Oct 8)
Salure 106 (7f,Lon,G,Oct 2)
Samitar 107 (8f,Nmk,GF,Sep 23)
See Clearly 107 (5f,Rip,GS,Jly 16)
Silver Sycamore 109 (7f,Leo,G,Sep 3)
Sofast 106 (7f,Lon,VS,Sep 4)
St Barths 106 (6f,Asc,G,Jun 14)
Sunday Times 107 (6f,Nmk,GF,Sep 24)

Tai Chi 107 (10f,Sai,HY,Nov 12)
Takar 110 (7f,Leo,Y,Nov 6)
Tell Dad 107 (7f,Nby,GF,Oct 22)
Thomasgainsborough 112 (8f,Leo,Y,Oct 30)
Tickled Pink 105 (6f,Nby,GF,Jly 15)
Tifongo 107 (10f,Sai,HY,Nov 12)
Tough As Nails 105 (5f,Cur,S,Mar 20)
Trumpet Major 107 (7f,Nmk,G,Oct 8)
Twirl 111 (7f,Leo,Y,Nov 6)

Veneto 105 (7f,Lon,G,Oct 2)

Wading 109 (7f,Nmk,G,Oct 8)

West Leake Diman 105 (6f,Nmk,G,Oct 8)

TWO YEAR-OLDS - Sand

Colorful Notion 105 (6f,Kem,SD,Nov 17)

Decision By One 106 (6f,Wol,SD,Nov 25)

Halling s Quest 109 (8f,Sth,SD,Oct 24)

Jwala 106 (5f,Wol,SD,Dec 12)

Kune Kune 107 (6f,Kem,SD,Nov 17)

Shumoos 108 (6f,Kem,SD,Sep 3)

Vocational 107 (6f,Kem,SD,Sep 3)